THE OXFORD CLASSICAL DICTIONARY

THE OXFORD CLASSICAL DICTIONARY

THIRD EDITION
REVISED

Edited by Simon Hornblower
and Antony Spawforth

OXFORD
UNIVERSITY PRESS

OXFORD

UNIVERSITY PRESS

Great Clarendon Street, Oxford OX2 6DP

Oxford University Press is a department of the University of Oxford.
It furthers the University's objective of excellence in research, scholarship,
and education by publishing worldwide in

Oxford New York

Auckland Bangkok Buenos Aires Cape Town Chennai
Dar es Salaam Delhi Hong Kong Istanbul Karachi Kolkata
Kuala Lumpur Madrid Melbourne Mexico City Mumbai Nairobi
São Paulo Shanghai Taipei Tokyo Toronto

Oxford is a registered trade mark of Oxford University Press
in the UK and in certain other countries

Published in the United States
by Oxford University Press Inc., New York

© Oxford University Press 1949, 1970, 1996, 2003

Database right Oxford University Press (maker)

First edition published 1949
Second edition published 1970
Third edition published 1996
Revised third edition published 2003

British Library Cataloguing in Publication Data

Data available

Library of Congress Cataloging in Publication Data

Data available

ISBN 0–19–860641–9

3 5 7 9 10 8 6 4 2

Typeset by Selwood Systems, Midsomer Norton
Printed by
Giunti Industrie Grafiche
Prato, Italy

CONTENTS

PREFACE

1. *The usefulness of the* Oxford Classical Dictionary

As an authoritative one-volume guide to all aspects of the ancient world, *OCD* has no competitor in any language. At one and the same time it offers, across the whole range of the study of the ancient world, both information presented in a form accessible to non-specialists and factual material and bibliographies detailed and specific enough to be valuable to the professional reader. No other single-volume work of reference remotely approaches *OCD* in the sheer quality of factual detail contained, and all our informal enquiries at the outset of this project showed that scholars and non-specialists alike turn to *OCD* for quick but authoritative and well-documented answers to concrete questions about the ancient world.

2. *The need for a new edition*

The second edition, published in 1970 but conceived and written in the mid- to late 1960s, had come to seem very dated by the early 1990s. The intervening quarter-century had seen an explosion of scholarship, much of it important and innovative, in all areas covered. The individual bibliographies, which were so valuable a feature of *OCD2*, instantly betray the date of the material prefaced to them (and this of course will be no less true of the present edition). But the problem went deeper than that. The second edition itself contained much that was relatively lightly revised and carried over much material scarcely altered from the first edition of 1949. For instance, Greek religion and Greek economic life looked not much different in 1970 from the way they had looked in 1949, and it was obvious in 1990 that a complete overhaul was needed of these areas. Then there were the areas scarcely represented in the old editions because as fields of study they hardly existed at the time, notably the history of women, and topics (such as the near east) neglected because classical antiquity was conceived then in narrower terms than now (more on both these points below). Overall, that a new and up-to-date edition was called for in the 1990s is, we hope, uncontroversial.

3. *The third edition*

The new and largely rewritten edition gathers 6,250 contributions written by an international team of 364 scholars between 1991 and 1994. Five guiding principles have shaped its form and content:

Specificity Because so much of *OCD*'s value rests with its factual coverage, part of our task was simply to organize the updating or replacement of the existing material in the dictionary, and to fill in gaps in the coverage of *OCD2 on its own terms*. Every 1970 entry has been looked at by an expert or by ourselves; the very few retained unchanged are mostly extremely short entries (one important exception is H. T. Wade-Gery's article on 'Thucydides', an established classic from the 1949 edition, reprinted here, as in the second edition, but with a new section on work since 1970). By the same token, we have been very reluctant to cut back on factual material or to jettison whole entries altogether (except—rarely—where their usefulness now seems doubtful, as with the old entries for individual Greek pot-painters, here suppressed).

A less traditional OCD *but with the same title* As to definition and scope, we had no doubt that the centrality of Greece and Rome should be retained in the new edition and for this reason we have kept the old title. But our feeling was that in earlier editions a certain top-heaviness in favour of the purely literary aspects of those cultures was detectable and needed correcting.

Preface

First, we have tried to give a voice to the increasingly interdisciplinary character of classical studies. Thus we reject the sharp distinction made in the Preface to the second edition between 'classical' and 'archaeological'. In keeping with modern trends in our discipline, we have tried to integrate archaeological and non-archaeological methods and evidence. But, rather than seeking to single out archaeology alone, we have preferred to emphasize the whole range of disciplines informing classical studies these days: hence, for instance, the new entries on 'anthropology and the classics', 'literary theory and classical studies', and 'Marxism and classical antiquity'.

Secondly, we have sought to give more space to previously underrepresented areas—not least the history of women, along with the whole area of ancient sexuality (sufficiently inchoate as late as the mid-1960s for the entry on 'homosexuality' in this edition to be a new departure). We have also aimed to enhance the amount of coverage given to regions and cultures beyond the core areas of Greece and Italy. Whereas treatment of Rome's provinces (especially the western ones) has always been fairly thorough, the near-eastern world with which the Greeks (and Romans) interacted so fruitfully had—we felt—been given less than its due in previous editions. With the help of our three expert advisors on respectively women, the near east, and the Jews (for their names see p. xv) we have sought to remedy these weaknesses.

More thematic entries It was our firm belief that a new *OCD* should, subject to the retention of the specificity insisted on already, be much more *thematic* than its predecessors. Our enquiries stressed the needs of general readers looking for synoptic and accessible treatment of large topics still immediately relevant to the late twentieth century. Such readers, especially North American ones accustomed to thematically presented works of reference, ought to be catered for better than in the second edition. From the list of 'new entries' annexed to this Preface (p. xi below) it will be seen at a glance how far we have gone in this direction (for example, apart from ones already mentioned, 'disease', 'ecology', 'economy', 'imperialism', 'literacy', 'motherhood', and 'technology'). As a result, the new *OCD* has a flavour quite different from its predecessors.

Accessibility An important element in the philosophy governing this edition has been accessibility. Thus in the new edition, untranslated Greek and Latin has been kept to a minimum and plain English has been preferred to the 'mandarin' which sometimes characterized earlier editions. Generally, contributors were asked to express themselves in a manner intelligible to non-specialists. In order to save space and achieve a less cluttered-looking text, we have, to indicate cross-references, used asterisks in front of words rather than q.v. Two specific issues raised by this general philosophy of accessibility need flagging here.

First, there is a close connection between our desire for accessibility and the spelling of ancient (especially Greek) names. We were convinced that the more familiar form, which is usually the Latin one, should be preferred (for example, Aeschylus not Aiskhylos, Corinth not Korinth). The Graeco-Roman world, like the biblical, still remains a part of the common anglophone heritage. In a work of reference aimed at a general (as well as a specialist) readership, familiar spellings long domesticated in the English language should not, therefore, be jettisoned for the esoteric (any more than editors of biblical companions refer their users to the New Testament books of 'Markos', 'Timotheos', etc.). In preferring to be helpful, we do not claim to have been absolutely consistent, and have therefore included cross-references in doubtful cases (thus under 'Kronos' there is an entry 'see CRONUS').

Secondly, we have departed from the traditional form in which *OCD* lists Roman proper names of the republican and imperial periods (up to about AD 275). Instead of doing so by cognomen, we list by nomen—the logical and professional practice followed by standard works of reference such as Pauly-Wissowa's *Real-Encyclopädie*. In this way we have got rid of the absurd anomaly whereby, for instance, brothers from the *gens* Aemilia appeared under different letters of the alphabet (Lepidus; Paullus). For further details readers are directed to the Note to Readers (p. lv, below).

One innovation in 1970 has been dropped in this edition: the index of names etc. not featured as headwords in the dictionary (this was not an index in the conventional sense but a long alphabetical list of cross-references of the form 'Incense, *see* SACRIFICE; PRAYER'). Enquiries and our own experience suggested that this tool was, however useful in theory, not much used in practice; some of those to whom we asked for comment were actually unaware that it existed. Instead we have included (in this respect reverting to the practice of the first edition of 1949) a large number of 'signpost' cross-references in the body of the dictionary—the natural and time-saving place for them. Thus under 'malaria' you will find 'See DISEASE' and under 'Ulysses' you will find 'See ODYSSEUS'. We have also included plenty of thematic signposts such as 'demography See POPULATION' or 'representation, representative government See DEMES; FEDERAL STATES'. One reason for the old index has in any case been removed by our adoption of a more systematic and professional principle of ordering Roman names: some of the old index entries were evidently designed to lessen the confusion caused by operating a double system of nomen / cognomen. Many names in the old index now have new full-length entries of their own in the dictionary itself, such as Cytinium, Eucratides, Hippodamia, Scyros, Torone, and Xanthus (the Lycian city).

An international OCD We were concerned not to make the new *OCD* too parochially British— a criticism levelled by implication at the first edition and which the second edition did little to offset. This is not just internationalism for its own sake: the aim of all concerned has been to secure the best experts on the topics covered, wherever in the world they happen to be. So, in Greek religion alone, the distinguished team of contributors for *OCD3* is drawn from Belgium, Canada, France, Germany, Israel, the Netherlands, Great Britain, the United States, and Switzerland.

4. Format

In order to achieve the improved coverage on the lines outlined above, the new edition is some 30 per cent bigger than its predecessor. It retains the same basic format as the second edition— that is, a single alphabetically arranged volume, laid out in two columns, and without illustrations or maps. We were happy with this restriction, not least because to depart from it would make the book unwieldy and very expensive.

5. Acknowledgements

As editors we took on direct responsibility for revising about half the dictionary (the areas of Greek and Roman history, Greek law, historiography, art, and archaeology). For the other half, we relied on the help of a team of expert advisors (for a list see p. xv). If the new edition is judged a success, it is in no small part their doing, and we wish to put on record our heartfelt thanks to them, not least for the occasions on which individual advisors went well beyond the call of duty in giving us help. In particular, we acknowledge with deep gratitude the work of E. Badian, who, in and beyond his role as area advisor, spent a week in England during May 1994 correcting the numerous errors arising from our reorganization of the listing of Roman proper names (see above).

We acknowledge extra help from a number of individuals, some of them contributors, some not: Gisa Bielfeldt (for translation of some German entries which arrived at a late stage) and, for advice and comments on particular problems: Peter Jones, Lisa Kallet-Marx, Fergus Millar, Robin Osborne, and Bill Parry. The staff of the Hellenic and Roman Societies Library, London, deserve special thanks for their invariable helpfulness. Fred Williams generously helped with the proofs.

At the Press, both academic editors wish to record their appreciation of the unswerving support, good sense, and hard work of Pam Coote, the in-house editor of the Reference Division, and the prompt and good-humoured efficiency of her assistant Wendy Tuckey. Copy-editing was mainly done by Julian Ward, to whom we pay tribute for his splendid efforts on this vast task during the academic year 1994–5. We are grateful to Alysoun Owen for her cheerful and effective day-to-day guidance of the project during the production stage. Antony Spawforth would like to thank Newcastle upon Tyne University for a term's leave at a critical stage and the Institute for Advanced Study at Princeton, where he corrected proofs in ideal surroundings.

Although this Preface is not the place for mutual self-congratulation, it may as well be recorded (since not all academic collaborations end so happily) that the harmonious working relationship of the two academic editors—forged in Athens between 1979 and 1989, when both had lectured to courses for schoolteachers at the British School—was only strengthened by the years of collaboration over *OCD*; and that mutual respect grew as the *OCD* job grew—or rather, as its true and terrible size became apparent.

The postscript to the ninth (1940) edition of Liddell and Scott's *Greek–English Lexicon* ends with the moving words: 'the monument of unselfish industry is at last complete'. This edition of *OCD* was not so long in gestation as LSJ[9], and we hesitate—and not just from modesty—to claim all the altruism implicit in that 'unselfish'. Nevertheless, the pressures of university life are now in the direction of selfish productivity at the level of pure research. It is therefore profoundly encouraging that our contributors and area advisors were willing to make time and effort available for a collective (but we hope also creative) work of synthesis like this new edition of *OCD*, and to provide us and above all the book's users with work of such extraordinarily high quality. We hope and believe that *OCD3* is not merely an authoritative summing-up of classical scholarship, broadly defined, as it was in 1991–4 (no small achievement if true); but that the entries, particularly but by no means only the thematic ones, are stimulating and original enough to make a difference to the way their various subjects are viewed in the future.

SIMON HORNBLOWER
ANTONY SPAWFORTH
1996

PREFACE TO REVISED EDITION

In this revised edition, many small slips have been corrected (and one new definition entry added, on 'epinician poetry'). Most of these corrections are due to the vigilance and wide classical knowledge of Mr J. W. Roberts, who picked them up when preparing the *Concise Oxford Dictionary to the Classical World*. We thank him warmly for this help.

We are aware that the brief statements of the affiliations of the 1996 contributors are no longer up to date in that many of the contributors have now moved on to other jobs, but we have not tried to up-date these details (as we did feel confident about doing for the much shorter list of area advisors). We have however added to the main list of contributors a number of daggers indicating 'deceased', and we record here our sorrow at the deaths of these collaborators and our appreciation for what they did for *OCD3*. It is invidious to single out individuals but we would like specifically to mention in this category the names of Nicholas Hammond, one of the editors of the second edition and happily also a distinguished and authoritative contributor to the third, who died in 2001 in his 94th year, and of Don Fowler, our area co-advisor in Latin Literature, who died in 1999 at the tragically young age of 46. His input as both advisor and contributor greatly enhanced the quality of *OCD3*.

SIMON HORNBLOWER
ANTONY SPAWFORTH
July 2002

LIST OF NEW ENTRIES

List of New Entries

List of New Entries

AREA ADVISORS

PROFESSOR ERNST BADIAN
Formerly John Moors Cabot Professor of
History, Harvard University, USA
Roman Republican prosopography

PROFESSOR ANTHONY BIRLEY
Professor of Ancient History, Heinrich-Heine-
University, Düsseldorf, Germany
Roman Imperial prosopography

PROFESSOR ANNA MORPURGO DAVIES
Fellow of Somerville College and Professor of
Comparative Philology, University of Oxford,
UK
linguistics

PROFESSOR PATRICIA EASTERLING
Regius Professor of Greek Emerita, University
of Cambridge, UK
Greek literature

†DR DON FOWLER
Formerly Fellow and Tutor at Jesus College and
University Lecturer in Classical Languages and
Literature, University of Oxford, UK
Latin literature

DR PETA FOWLER
Lecturer in Classics at St Anne's College,
University of Oxford
Latin literature

DR MARTIN GOODMAN
Reader in Jewish Studies, University of Oxford,
UK
Jewish studies

PROFESSOR TONY HONORÉ
Fellow of All Souls College, and former Regius
Professor of Civil Law, University of Oxford, UK
Roman law

PROFESSOR SIMON HORNBLOWER
Professor of Classics and Ancient History,
University College London, UK
*Greek and Roman history, historiography, historical
individuals, institutions, topography, archaeology,
and art*

DR EMILY KEARNS
Lecturer in Classics at St Hilda's College,
University of Oxford, UK
Greek myth and religion

DR HELEN KING
Wellcome Research Fellow and Lecturer,
Department of Classics, University of Reading,
UK
women's studies

PROFESSOR AMÉLIE KUHRT
Professor of Ancient History, University College
London, UK
Near Eastern studies

PROFESSOR GEOFFREY LLOYD
Master of Darwin College and Professor of
Ancient Philosophy and Science, University of
Cambridge, UK
maths and science

PROFESSOR JOHN MATTHEWS
Professor of Roman History in the Departments
of Classics and History, Yale University, USA
late antiquity and Christianity

PROFESSOR MARTHA NUSSBAUM
Department of Law and Ethics, University of
Chicago, USA
philosophy

DR JOHN PENNEY
Fellow of Wolfson College and University
Lecturer in Classical Philology, University of
Oxford, UK
linguistics

DR SIMON PRICE
Fellow and Tutor in Ancient History at Lady
Margaret Hall, and University Lecturer in
Ancient History, University of Oxford, UK
Roman religion

PROFESSOR ANTONY SPAWFORTH
Professor of Ancient History, University of
Newcastle upon Tyne, UK
*Greek and Roman history, historiography, historical
individuals, institutions, topography, archaeology,
and art*

INDEX TO INITIALS OF CONTRIBUTORS

Note: Text entries are signed with the initials listed.

CONTRIBUTORS TO THE THIRD EDITION

F.R.A.   Francisco R. Adrados, Professor of Greek Philology, Complutense University, Madrid, Spain

G.A.   Graham Anderson, Professor of Classics, University of Kent at Canterbury, UK

J.A.   Julia Annas, Professor of Philosophy, University of Arizona, USA

J.K.A.   John Kinloch Anderson, Emeritus Professor of Classical Archaeology, University of California at Berkeley, USA

K.W.A.   Karim W. Arafat, Lecturer in Classical Archaeology, King's College London, UK

M.M.A.   Michel Mervyn Austin, Senior Lecturer in Ancient History, University of St Andrews, UK

W.G.A.   William Geoffrey Arnott, Emeritus Professor of Greek Language and Literature, University of Leeds, UK

W.S.A.   W. Sidney Allen, Emeritus Professor of Comparative Philology, University of Cambridge, UK

A.B.B.   Albert Brian Bosworth, Professor of Classics and Ancient History, University of Western Australia, Australia

A.D.B.   Andrew D. Barker, Professor of Classics, University of Otago, New Zealand

A.L.B.   Andrew L. Brown, London, UK

A.R.Bi.   Anthony R. Birley, Area Advisor in Roman Imperial prosopography

C.P.B.   †C. P. Bammel, Reader in Early Church History, University of Cambridge, UK

D.C.B.   David C. Braund, Professor, Department of Classics and Ancient History, University of Exeter, UK

E.B.   Ernst Badian, Area Advisor in Roman Republican prosopography

E.H.B   Edward Henry Bispham, Temporary Lecturer, University of Edinburgh, UK

E.L.B.   Ewen Lyall Bowie, Praelector in Classics, Corpus Christi College and Reader in Classical Languages and Literature, University of Oxford, UK

E.N.B.   Eugene N. Borza, Emeritus Professor of Ancient History, Pennsylvania State University, USA

G.P.B.   Graham Paul Burton, Lecturer in History, University of Manchester, UK

J.Be.   John Bennet, Associate Professor of Classics, University of Wisconsin-Madison, USA

J.Br.   John Briscoe, Reader in Latin, University of Manchester, UK

J.Bu.   John Buckler, Professor of Greek History, University of Illinois, USA

J.N.B.   Jan N. Bremmer, Professor of History of Religion, University of Groningen, Netherlands

K.B.   Kai Brodersen, Institute for Ancient History, University of Munich, Germany

K.R.B.   Keith R. Bradley, Professor of Classics, University of Victoria, Canada

L.B.   Liliane Bodson, Professor, Department of Classics, University of Liège, Belgium

M.B.   Mary Beard, Lecturer, Faculty of Classics and Fellow of Newnham College, University of Cambridge, UK

M.J.B.   Martin J. Brooke, Head of Classics, Sherborne School, Dorset, UK

P.B.   Pierre Briant, Professor of Ancient History, University of Toulouse le Mirail, France

P.G.M.B.   Peter George McCarthy Brown, Fellow and Tutor in Classics, Trinity College and Lecturer in Classical Language and Literature, University of Oxford, UK

R.B.   Robert Browning, Emeritus Professor of Classics, University of London, UK

R.L.B.   Roger L. Beck, Professor, University of Toronto, Canada

S.Bo.   Susanne Bobzien, Fellow and Praelector in Philosophy, The Queen's College, University of Oxford, UK

S.J.B.B.   Samuel James Beeching Barnish, Lecturer, Royal Holloway and Bedford New College, University of London, UK

S.M.B.   Susanna Morton Braund, Professor of Latin, Royal Holloway and Bedford New College, University of London, UK

T.C.B.   T. Corey Brennan, Assistant Professor, Departments of Greek and Latin, Bryn Mawr College, Philadelphia, USA

T.R.B.   Todd Richard Breyfogle, Doctorial Candidate, The Committee on Social Thought, University of Chicago, USA

A.D.E.C.   Alan Douglas Edward Cameron, Anthon Professor of Latin, Columbia University, New York, USA

Contributors to the Third Edition

A.M.C.	Averil M. Cameron, Warden, Keble College, University of Oxford, UK	
A.S.E.C.	A. Simon Esmonde Cleary, Senior Lecturer, Department of Ancient History and Archaeology, University of Birmingham, UK	
B.M.C.	Brian M. Caven, formerly Tutor, Faculty of Arts, Birkbeck College, University of London, UK	
C.C.	Christopher Carey, Professor of Classics, Royal Holloway and Bedford New College, University of London, UK	
E.C.	Edward Courtney, Gildersleeve Professor of Classics, University of Virginia, USA	
E.G.C.	Edith Gillian Clark, Senior Lecturer in Classics, University of Liverpool, UK	
G.B.C.	Gian Biagio Conte, Professor of Latin Literature, University of Pisa, Italy	
G.L.C.	George Law Cawkwell, Emeritus Fellow, University College, University of Oxford, UK	
H.W.C.	Hector William Catling, formerly Director, British School at Athens, Greece	
J.C.	†John Chadwick, Emeritus Reader, University of Cambridge, UK	
J.B.C.	John Brian Campbell, Senior Lecturer, Department of Ancient History, The Queen's University of Belfast, UK	
J.C.N.C.	Jonathan C. N. Coulston, Lecturer in Classical Archaeology, School of Greek, Latin and Ancient History, University of St Andrews, UK	
J.McK.C.	John McKesson Camp II, Professor, American School of Classical Studies, Director, Agora Excavations, Athens, Greece	
K.C.	Kevin Clinton, Professor, Department of Classics, Cornell University, USA	
M.Ci.	Mario Citroni, Professor of Latin Literature, University of Florence, Italy	
M.Co.	Michael Coffey, Emeritus Reader and Honorary Research Fellow, University College London, UK	
M.A.R.C.	Malcolm Andrew Richard Colledge, Professor of Classics, Queen Mary and Westfield College, University of London, UK	
M.H.C.	Michael H. Crawford, Professor of Ancient History, University College London, UK	
P.A.C.	Paul Anthony Cartledge, Fellow of Clare College and Reader in Greek History, University of Cambridge, UK	
R.G.C.	Robert G. Coleman, Professor of Comparative Philology, University of Cambridge, UK	
R.W.V.C.	Richard William Vyvyan Catling, Assistant Editor, *Lexicon of Greek Personal Names*, Oxford, UK	
T.J.Co.	Tim J. Cornell, Professor of Ancient	

	History, University of Manchester, UK
W.E.H.C.	Walter Eric Harold Cockle, Research Fellow in Greek and Latin Papyrology, University College London, UK
A.D.	Andrew Drummond, Lecturer in Classics, University of Nottingham, UK
A.C.D.	A. C. Dionisotti, Lecturer, Department of Classics, King's College London, UK
A.C.de la M.	†Albinia C. de la Mare, Professor of Palaeography, King's College London, UK
A.M.Da.	Anna Morpurgo Davies, Area Advisor in linguistics
B.C.D.	†B. C. Dietrich, Professor, Department of Classics, University of Wales, Aberystwyth, UK
C. de S.	Carlo de Simone, Professor of Comparative Linguistics, University of Tübingen, Germany
G.D.	Glenys Davies, Senior Lecturer in Classical Archaeology, University of Edinburgh, UK
H.D.	Hazel Dodge, Lecturer in Roman Archaeology, Trinity College Dublin, Ireland
J.D.	Janet DeLaine, Lecturer in Archaeology, University of Reading, UK
J.F.Dr.	John Frederick Drinkwater, Reader in Roman Provincial History, Department of Classics, University of Nottingham, UK
J.K.D.	John Kenyon Davies, Professor of Ancient History and Classical Archaeology, University of Liverpool, UK
J.M.D.	John Myles Dillon, Regius Professor of Greek, Trinity College Dublin, Ireland
K.D.	Ken Dowden, Senior Lecturer in Classics, University of Birmingham, UK
K.J.D.	Kenneth James Dover, Chancellor of St Andrews University, UK
K.M.D.D.	Katherine M. D. Dunbabin, Professor, Department of Classics, McMaster University, Ontario, Canada
O.T.P.K.D.	Oliver T. P. K. Dickinson, Senior Lecturer, Department of Classics and Ancient History, University of Durham, UK
P. de S.	Philip de Souza, Lecturer in Classical Studies, St Mary's University College, University of Surrey, UK
P.S.D.	Peter Sidney Derow, Hody Fellow and Tutor in Ancient History, Wadham College, University of Oxford, UK
R.P.D.	Raymond Peter Davis, Senior Lecturer in Ancient History, The Queen's University of Belfast, UK
S.Di.	Suzanne Dixon, Reader in Classics and

Ancient History, The University of
Queensland, Australia

S.M.D. Stephanie Mary Dalley, Shillito Fellow
of the Oriental Institute, Oxford and
Senior Research Fellow at Somerville
College, University of Oxford, UK

A.W.E. Andrew W. Erskine, College Lecturer,
Department of Classics, University
College Dublin, Ireland

D.F.E. Donald F. Easton, freelance
archaeologist, London, UK

J.C.E. Jonathan C. Edmondson, Associate
Professor, Department of History, York
University, Toronto, Canada

M.J.E. Mark Julian Edwards, Tutor in
Theology, Christ Church, University of
Oxford, UK

P.E.E. Patricia E. Easterling, Area Advisor in
Greek literature

R.M.E. R. M. Errington, Professor of Ancient
History, Philipps University, Marburg,
Germany

B.W.F. Bruce W. Frier, Professor of Classics and
Roman Law, H. K. Ransom Professor of
Law, University of Michigan, Ann Arbor,
USA

D.C.F. Denis C. Feeney, Professor of Classics,
University of Wisconsin, Madison,
USA

D.J.F. David John Furley, Emeritus Professor
of Classics, Princeton University, USA

D.P.F. †Don P. Fowler, Area Advisor in Latin
literature

E.F. Elaine Fantham, Giger Professor of
Latin, Princeton University, USA

L.F. Lin Foxhall, Lecturer, School of
Archaeological Studies, University of
Leicester, UK

M.F. Massimo Fusillo, Associate Professor of
Literary Theory, Department of Studies
on Modern Civilization, Messina, Italy

N.R.E.F. Nick R. E. Fisher, Senior Lecturer,
School of History and Archaeology,
University of Wales, Cardiff, UK

P.G.F. Peta G. Fowler, Area Advisor in Latin
literature

P.M.F. Peter Marshall Fraser, *Lexicon of Greek
Personal Names*, Oxford and formerly
Fellow of All Souls College and Reader
in Hellenistic History, University of
Oxford, UK

A.H.G. Alan H. Griffiths, Senior Lecturer,
Department of Greek and Latin,
University College London, UK

A.T.G. Anthony T. Grafton, Dodge Professor of
History, Princeton University, USA

C.G. Christopher John Gill, Reader in Ancient
Thought, University of Exeter, UK

D.W.J.G. David William John Gill, Lecturer in

Ancient History, University of Wales
Swansea, UK

E.J.G. Emily J. Gowers, Honorary Research
Fellow, University College London, UK

F.G. Fritz Graf, Professor of Classical
Philology and Religions of the Ancient
Mediterranean, University of Basel,
Switzerland

H.G.-T. Hero Granger-Taylor, specialist in
archaeological textiles, formerly
Department of Medieval and Later
Antiquities, The British Museum,
London, UK

I.C.G. Ian C. Glover, Reader in Southeast
African Archaeology, University
College London, UK

J.Gr. Jasper Griffin, Professor of Classical
Literature, University of Oxford, UK

J.P.A.G. †John P. A. Gould, Emeritus Professor
of Greek, University of Bristol, UK

J.R.G. J. Richard Green, Professor of Classical
Archaeology, University of Sydney,
Australia

K.T.G. Kevin T. Greene, Senior Lecturer in
Archaeology, University of Newcastle
upon Tyne, UK

M.G. Mark Golden, Professor of Classics,
University of Winnipeg, Canada

M.Ga. Michael Gagarin, Professor of Classics,
University of Texas at Austin, USA

M.D.G. Martin David Goodman, Area Advisor
in Jewish studies

M.T.G. Miriam T. Griffin, Tutorial Fellow in
Ancient History, Somerville College,
Lecturer in Ancient History, Trinity
College, and Lecturer in Ancient
History, University of Oxford, UK

R.L.G. Richard L. Gordon, Senior Fellow,
School of European Studies, University
of East Anglia, Norwich, UK

R.P.H.G. Roger P. H. Green, Professor, University
of Glasgow, UK

R.S.J.G. Robert S. J. Garland, Roy D. and
Margaret B. Wooster Professor of the
Classics, Colgate University, New York,
USA

V.R.G. Virginia Randolph Grace, lately
American School of Classical Studies,
Athens, Greece

A.H. Albert Henrichs, Eliot Professor of
Greek Literature, Harvard University,
USA

B.H. Bruno Helly, Research Director,
Fernand Courby Institute, Lyon, France

C.A.H. Carl A. Huffman, Associate Professor of
Classics, DePauw University,
Indianapolis, USA

D.M.H. David M. Halperin, Professor of
Literature, Massachusetts Institute of
Technology, Cambridge, USA

E.D.H. E. David Hunt, Lecturer in Classics and

Contributors to the Third Edition

Ancient History, University of Durham, UK

F.L.H.   Frank L. Holt, Associate Professor of History, University of Houston, Texas, USA

F.S.H.   F. Stephen Halliwell, Professor of Greek, University of St Andrews, UK

G.He.   Gabriel Herman, Senior Lecturer in Ancient History, Hebrew University, Jerusalem, Israel

H.M.H.   Harry Morrison Hine, Scotstarvit Professor of Humanity, University of St Andrews, UK

J.D.H.   Jill Diana Harries, Senior Lecturer in Ancient History, University of St Andrews, UK

J.D.Ha.   J. David Hawkins, Professor of Ancient Anatolian Languages, School of Oriental and African Studies, University of London, UK

J.F.H.   John F. Healey, Reader in Semitic Studies, University of Manchester, UK

L.A.H.-S.   Leofranc Adrian Holford-Strevens, copy-editor, Oxford University Press, Oxford, UK

M.H.H.   Mogens Herman Hansen, Director, Copenhagen Polis Centre, Copenhagen, Denmark

M.M.H.   Madeleine Mary Henry, Associate Professor, Classical Studies Program, Iowa State University, USA

N.H.   Neil Hopkinson, Fellow of Trinity College, University of Cambridge, UK

N.G.L.H.   †Nicholas Geoffrey Lemprière Hammond, Honorary Fellow, Clare College, University of Cambridge, UK

P.H.   Paul Halstead, Senior Lecturer, Department of Archaeology and Prehistory, University of Sheffield, UK

P.E.H.   Phillip Edward Harding, Associate Professor of Classics, University of British Columbia, Canada

P.J.H.   Peter John Heather, Lecturer in Early Medieval History, University College London, UK

P.R.H.   Philip Russell Hardie, University Lecturer in Classics and Fellow of New Hall, University of Cambridge, UK

R.Ha.   Robert Halleux, Director, Centre for the History of Science and Techniques, University of Liège, Belgium

R.L.Hu.   Richard L. Hunter, Fellow of Pembroke College and Lecturer in Classics, University of Cambridge, UK

S.H.   Simon Hornblower, General Editor and Area Advisor in Greek and Roman historiography, historical individuals, institutions, topography, archaeology, and art

S.E.H.   Stephen E. Hinds, Associate Professor of Classics, University of Washington, Seattle, USA

S.J.Ha.   Stephen J. Harrison, Fellow and Tutor in Classics, Corpus Christi College and Lecturer in Classical Languages and Literature, University of Oxford, UK

S.J.Ho.   Stephen J. Hodkinson, Lecturer in Ancient History, University of Manchester, UK

T.Hon.   Tony Honoré, Area Advisor in Roman law

V.L.H.   Victoria Lynn Harper, Assistant Professor of Philosophy, St Olaf College, Minnesota, USA

B.I.   Brad Inwood, Professor of Classics, University of Toronto, Canada

S.J.I.   Stephen J. Instone, Honorary Research Fellow, Department of Greek and Latin, University College London and Lecturer in Classics, St Mary's University College, University of Surrey, UK

A.W.J.   Alan William Johnston, Reader in Classical Archaeology, University College London, UK

D.E.L.J.   David E. L. Johnston, Fellow of Christ's College and Regius Professor of Civil Law, University of Cambridge, UK

H.D.J.   H. D. Jocelyn, Hulme Professor of Latin, Victoria University of Manchester, UK

J.E.J.   John Ellis Jones, Senior Lecturer in Classical Studies, University of Wales, Bangor, UK

J.H.J.   Jay H. Jasanoff, Jacob Gould Schurman Professor of Linguistics, Cornell University, USA

M.J.   Madeleine Jost, Professor of Greek History, University of Paris, France

M.H.J.   Michael H. Jameson, Emeritus Professor of Classics, Stanford University, USA

A.T.L.K.   Amélie Kuhrt, Area Advisor in Near Eastern Studies

C.F.K.   Christoph F. Konrad, Assistant Professor, Texas A & M University, USA

C.H.K.   Charles H. Kahn, Professor of Philosophy, University of Pennsylvania, USA

C.M.K.   Christopher M. Kelly, Fellow of Corpus Christi College, University of Cambridge, UK

D.K.   David Konstan, Professor of Classics and Comparative Literature, Brown University, USA

E.Ke.   Emily Kearns, Area Advisor in Greek myth and religion

E.Kr.   Eveline Krummen, Assistant at the Classical Philology Seminar, University of Zürich, Switzerland

H.K.	Helen King, Area Advisor in women's studies		Académie des Inscriptions et Belles-lettres, Paris, France
I.G.K.	Ian Gray Kidd, Emeritus Professor of Greek, University of St Andrews, UK	R.J.L.	Roger J. Ling, Professor of Classical Art and Archaeology, University of Manchester, UK
J.N.D.K.	†John Norman Davidson Kelly, formerly Principal of St Edmund Hall and Honorary Fellow of Queen's College and St Edmund Hall, University of Oxford, UK	R.O.A.M.L.	R. O. A. M. Lyne, Fellow and Tutor in Classics, Balliol College and Reader in Classical Languages and Literature, University of Oxford, UK
R.A.K.	Robert A. Kaster, Professor, Department of Classics, University of Chicago, USA	S.D.L.	Stephen D. Lambert, Fellow, Center for Hellenic Studies, Washington DC, USA
S.J.K.	Simon J. Keay, Senior Lecturer, Department of Archaeology, University of Southampton, UK	W.L.	W. Liebeschuetz, Emeritus Professor, Nottingham University, UK
W.K.	Wolfram Kinzig, Lecturer in Church History, University of Heidelberg, Germany and Fellow of King's College, University of Cambridge, UK	A.Mot.	André Motte, Professor, University of Liège, Belgium
		B.C.McG.	Brian C. McGing, Senior Lecturer and Fellow, Trinity College Dublin, Ireland
W.R.K.	Wilbur R. Knorr, Professor, Program in the History of Science, Stanford University, USA	C.A.M.	Catherine A. Morgan, Lecturer in Classics, Royal Holloway and Bedford New College, University of London, UK
		C.A.Ma.	Charles Anthony Martindale, Professor of Latin, University of Bristol, UK
A.L.	Andrew Louth, Professor of Cultural History, Goldsmiths' College, University of London, UK	C.B.M.	Christopher B. Mee, Charles W. Jones Senior Lecturer in Classical Archaeology, University of Liverpool, UK
A.B.L.	Alan Brian Lloyd, Professor of Classics and Ancient History, University of Wales, Swansea, UK		
A.D.E.L.	Andrew Dominic Edwards Lewis, Senior Lecturer in Laws, University College London, UK	D.J.Ma.	David J. Mattingly, Reader in Roman Archaeology, University of Leicester, UK
		D.M.M.	Douglas Maurice MacDowell, Professor of Greek, University of Glasgow, UK
A.J.W.L.	Andrew J. W. Laird, Lecturer, Department of Classics and Ancient History, University of Warwick, UK	E.M.	Elaine Matthews, Editor, *Lexicon of Greek Personal Names*, Oxford, UK
A.W.L.	Andrew William Lintott, Fellow and Tutor in Ancient History, Worcester College and Reader in Ancient History, University of Oxford, UK	G.W.M.	Glenn W. Most, Professor of Classics, University of Heidelberg, Germany
		H.Ma.	Herwig Maehler, Professor of Papyrology, University College London, UK
B.M.L.	Barbara M. Levick, Fellow and Tutor, St Hilda's College and Lecturer in Ancient History, University of Oxford, UK	H.C.M.	H. Craig Melchert, Charles S. Smith Distinguished Professor, Department of Linguistics, University of North Carolina at Chapel Hill, USA
D.G.L.	D. G. Lateiner, John R. Wright Professor of Greek, Ohio Wesleyan University, USA	I.M.	Irad Malkin, Associate Professor of Ancient Greek History, Tel Aviv University, Israel
D.R.L.	David R. Langslow, University Lecturer in Latin Philology and Linguistics, Wolfson College, University of Oxford, UK	I.Mo.	Ian Morris, Professor of Classics and History, Stanford University, USA
		J.D.M.	Jon D. Mikalson, Professor of Classics, University of Virginia, USA
G.E.R.L.	Sir Geoffrey Lloyd, Area Advisor in Maths and Science	J.F.Ma.	John F. Matthews, Area Advisor in late antiquity and Christianity
G.Ll.-M.	Glenys Lloyd-Morgan, archaeological small finds specialist, UK	J.F.Mo.	John F. Moreland, Lecturer, Department of Archaeology and Prehistory, University of Sheffield, UK
J.L.	Jerzy Linderski, Paddison Professor of Latin, University of North Carolina at Chapel Hill, USA	J.L.Mo.	John L. Moles, Reader in Classics, University of Durham, UK
J.F.La.	John F. Lazenby, Professor of Ancient History, University of Newcastle upon Tyne, UK	J.R.M.	Jennifer R. March, Honorary Fellow, University College London, UK
K.L.	H. Kathryn Lomas, Research Fellow, University of Newcastle upon Tyne, UK	J.R.Mo.	John R. Morgan, Lecturer in Classics, University of Wales Swansea, UK
M.Lej.	Michel Lejeune, Member of the	J.V.M.	J. V. Muir, Senior Lecturer, Department of Classics, King's College London, UK

Contributors to the Third Edition

K.M.	Klaus Meister, Professor of Ancient History, Institute for Historical Science, Berlin Technology University, Germany	D.O'M.	Dominic J. O'Meara, Professor of Ancient Philosophy and Metaphysics, University of Fribourg, Switzerland
M.J.M.	Martin J. Millett, Reader in Roman Archaeology, University of Durham, UK	J.M.O'B.	John Maxwell O'Brien, Professor of History, Queens College of the City University of New York, USA
O.Ma.	†Olivier Masson, Emeritus Professor, University of Paris, France	M.O.	Manfred Oppermann, Institute for the Science of Antiquity, Martin-Luther-University Halle, Germany
O.Mu.	Oswyn Murray, Fellow of Balliol College and Lecturer in Ancient History, University of Oxford, UK	R.G.O.	Robin G. Osborne, Fellow and Tutor of Corpus Christi College and Professor of Ancient History, University of Oxford, UK
P.MacC.	Proinsias Mac Cana, Senior Professor, School of Celtic Studies, Dublin, Ireland		
P.C.M.	Paul C. Millett, Fellow of Downing College and Lecturer in Ancient History, Faculty of Classics, University of Cambridge, UK	A.J.P.	A. J. Parker, Senior Lecturer in Archaeology, University of Bristol, UK
		A.W.P.	A. W. Price, Lecturer in Philosophy, Birkbeck College London, UK
P.K.M.	Peter Kenneth Marshall, Professor of Classics, Amherst College, Massachusetts, USA	C.B.R.P.	C. B. R. Pelling, Fellow and Praelector in Classics, University College and Lecturer in Classical Languages and Literature, University of Oxford, UK
R.Ma.	Robert Maltby, Senior Lecturer, University of Leeds, UK	C.R.P.	C. Robert Phillips III, Professor of Classics and Ancient History, Lehigh University, USA
R.G.M.	Robert G. Morkot, Teaching Assistant, Department of History, University College London, UK		
R.H.M.	Ronald Haithwaite Martin, Emeritus Professor of Classics, University of Leeds, UK	D.S.P.	David S. Potter, Associate Professor, Department of Classical Studies, University of Michigan, USA
S.M.	Stephen Mitchell, Professor of Classics, University of Wales Swansea, UK	D.T.P.	Daniel Thomas Potts, Edwin Cuthbert Hall Professor of Middle Eastern Archaeology, University of Sydney, Australia
V.A.M.	Valerie A. Maxfield, Reader in Roman Archaeology, University of Exeter, UK		
W.M.M.	William M. Murray, Associate Professor of Ancient History, University of South Florida at Tampa, USA	H.N.P.	Holt N. Parker, Associate Professor, University of Cincinnati, Ohio, USA
		H.W.Pl.	Henri Willy Pleket, Emeritus Professor of Ancient History and Greek and Latin Epigraphy, University of Leiden, Netherlands
A.N.	Alexander Nehamas, Edmund N. Carpenter Professor in the Humanities, Princeton University, USA	J.G.F.P.	Jonathan G. F. Powell, Professor of Latin, University of Newcastle upon Tyne, UK
A.M.N.	Alanna M. Nobbs, Associate Professor of Ancient History, MacQuarie University, Australia	J.H.W.P.	John Penney, Area Advisor in Linguistics
		J.J.P.	Jeremy James Paterson, Senior Lecturer in Ancient History, University of Newcastle upon Tyne, UK
B.N.	†Barry Nicholas, formerly Principal of Brasenose College, University of Oxford, UK	J.J.Po.	J. J. Pollitt, Sterling Professor of Classical Art and Archaeology, Yale University, USA
D.P.N.	Damien P. Nelis, Lecturer in Greek and Latin, Department of Classics, University of Durham, UK	J.R.P.	John Robert Patterson, University Lecturer in Classics, University of Cambridge, UK
J.A.N.	J. A. North, Professor, Department of History, University College London, UK		
L.F.N.	Lucia F. Nixon, College Lecturer in Archaeology, Magdalen College, University of Oxford, UK	L.P.E.P.	L. P. E. Parker, Fellow and Tutor, St Hugh's College, University of Oxford, UK
M.C.N.	Martha C. Nussbaum, Area Advisor in philosophy	N.P.	Nicholas Purcell, Fellow and Tutor in Ancient History, St John's College and Lecturer in Ancient History, University of Oxford, UK
V.N.	Vivian Nutton, Professor of the History of Medicine, University College London, UK		
		P.P.	Paola Pinotti, Associate Professor, Department of Classics, University of Bologna, Italy
D.O.	Dirk Obbink, Lecturer in Papyrology and Greek Literature, University of Oxford, UK	P.J.P.	P. J. Parsons, Regius Professor of Greek, University of Oxford, UK

R.C.T.P.   Robert Christopher Towneley Parker, Wykeham Professor of Ancient History, University of Oxford, UK

T.W.P.   T. W. Potter, Deputy Keeper, Department of Prehistoric and Romano-British Antiquities, The British Museum, London, UK

S.G.P.   †Simon Geoffrey Pembroke, formerly Department of Classics, Royal Holloway and Bedford New College, University of London, UK

S.R.F.P.   Simon R. F. Price, Area Advisor in Roman religion

V.P.-D.   Vinciane Pirenne-Delforge, Head of Research, National Foundation for Scientific Research, University of Liège, Belgium

A.R.   Amy Richlin, Professor of Classics, University of Southern California, USA

A.F.R.   Alan Ferguson Rodger, Lord Rodger of Earlsferry, PC QC, Lord Advocate, Scotland, UK

B.L.R.   Barney L. Rickenbacker, consultant, alcoholism and addictions, North Carolina, USA

C.R.   Charlotte Roueché, Reader in Classical and Byzantine Greek, King's College London, UK

C.C.R.   Christopher C. Rowland, Dean Ireland's Professor of the Exegesis of Holy Scripture, University of Oxford, UK

C.J.R.   Christopher J. Rowe, Professor of Greek, University of Durham, UK

D.A.R.   Donald Andrew Frank Moore Russell, formerly Fellow of St John's and Professor of Classical Literature, University of Oxford, UK

D.H.R.   Deborah H. Roberts, Associate Professor of Classics, Haverford College, Pennsylvania, USA

D.W.R.   Dominic W. Rathbone, Reader in Ancient History, King's College London, UK

D.W.R.R.   David William Robertson Ridgway, Reader in Classics, University of Edinburgh, UK

E.E.R.   Ellen E. Rice, Fellow of Wolfson College, University of Oxford, UK

H.R.   Helmut Rix, Emeritus Professor, Albert-Ludwigs-University, Freiburg, Germany

J.R.   James Roy, Senior Lecturer, University of Nottingham, UK

J.B.R.   James Boykin Rives, Assistant Professor, Classics and History, Columbia University in the City of New York, USA

J.M.R.   Joyce Maire Reynolds, Honorary Fellow, Newnham College, University of Cambridge, UK

J.M.Ri.   John M. Riddle, Professor of History, North Carolina State University, USA

J.S.R.   Jeffrey Stuart Rusten, Professor, Department of Classics, Cornell University, USA

J.S.Ri.   John Stuart Richardson, Professor of Classics, University of Edinburgh, UK

J.W.R.   John William Rich, Senior Lecturer in Classics, University of Nottingham, UK

K.R.   Kurt Raaflaub, Professor of Classics and History, Brown University, Rhode Island and Co-Director, Center for Hellenic Studies, Washington DC, USA

M.D.R.   Michael D. Reeve, Kennedy Professor of Latin, University of Cambridge, UK

N.J.R.   Nicholas J. Richardson, Fellow and Tutor, Merton College and Lecturer in Classical Languages and Literature, University of Oxford, UK

N.K.R.   N. K. Rutter, Senior Lecturer, University of Edinburgh, UK

O.R.   Oliver Rackham, Fellow of Corpus Christi College, University of Cambridge, UK

P.R.   Philip Rousseau, Associate Professor of History, University of Auckland, New Zealand

P.J.R.   P. J. Rhodes, Professor of Ancient History, University of Durham, UK

R.B.R.   R. B. Rutherford, Tutor in Greek and Latin Literature, Christ Church and Lecturer in Classical Languages and Literature, University of Oxford, UK

R.H.R.   R. H. Robins, Emeritus Professor of General Linguistics in the University of London, UK

T.R.   Tessa Rajak, Reader in Classics, University of Reading, UK

A.Sch.   Albert Schachter, Hiram Mills Professor of Classics, McGill University, Montreal, Canada

A.Schi.   Alessandro Schiesaro, Assistant Professor of Classics, Princeton University, USA

A.Sh.   Andrew Sherratt, Ashmolean Museum, Oxford, UK

A.Sm.   Andrew Smith, Professor of Classics, University College Dublin, Ireland

A.D.S.   Anne D. R. Sheppard, Senior Lecturer in Classics, Royal Holloway and Bedford New College, University of London, UK

A.F.S.   Andrew F. Stewart, Professor of Greek and Roman Art, University of California at Berkeley, USA

A.H.S.   Alan Herbert Sommerstein, Professor of Greek, University of Nottingham, UK

A.J.S.S.   Antony J. S. Spawforth, General Editor and Area Advisor in Greek and Roman historiography, historical individuals, institutions, topography, archaeology, and art

A.M.S.   Anthony M. Snodgrass, Laurence

Contributors to the Third Edition

Professor of Classical Archaeology, University of Cambridge, UK

C.S.-I. Christiane Sourvinou-Inwood, Reader in Classics, University of Reading, UK

D.G.J.S. D. Graham J. Shipley, Lecturer in Ancient History, University of Leicester, UK

D.N.S. David N. Sedley, Reader in Ancient Philosophy, University of Cambridge, UK

D.R.S. Danuta R. Shanzer, Professor of Classics, Cornell University, USA

G.S. Gisela Striker, George Martin Lane Professor of Philosophy and of The Classics, Harvard University, USA

H.So. Heikki Solin, Professor of Latin, University of Helsinki, Finland

H.S.-W. †Heleen Sancisi-Weerdenburg, Professor of Ancient History, University of Utrecht, Netherlands

H.P.S. Hans Peter Syndikus, formerly Director, Gymnasium Wilheim, Germany

J.Sca. John Scarborough, Professor, History of Pharmacy and Medicine, and Classics and Ancient History, School of Pharmacy and Department of Classics, University of Wisconsin, USA

J.Sch. John Scheid, Director of Studies, École Pratique des Hautes Études, Sorbonne, Paris, France

J.B.S. John B. Salmon, Senior Lecturer, University of Nottingham, UK

J.-F.S. Jean-François Salles, Director, School of Eastern Mediterranean Studies, Lyon, France

J.H.D.S. J. H. D. Scourfield, Associate Professor, Department of Classics, University of The Witwatersrand, Johannesburg, South Africa

J.R.S. J. Robert Sallares, Research Associate, University of Manchester Institute of Science and Technology, UK

K.S.S. Kenneth S. Sacks, Professor of History and Dean of the College, Brown University, USA

M.Sch. M. Schofield, Reader in Ancient Philosophy, University of Cambridge, USA

M.B.S. Marilyn B. Skinner, Professor of Classics, University of Arizona, USA

M.M.S. Maria Michela Sassi, Researcher, Senior High School, Pisa, Italy

M.S.Si. Michael S. Silk, Professor of Greek Language and Literature, King's College London, UK

M.S.Sp. M. Stephen Spurr, Head of Classics, Eton College, Windsor, UK

R.A.S.S. Richard A. S. Seaford, Professor of Greek Literature, University of Exeter, UK

R.B.E.S. Rowland B. E. Smith, Lecturer in Ancient History, University of Newcastle upon Tyne, UK

R.J.S. Robin J. Seager, Reader in Classics and Ancient History, University of Liverpool, UK

R.R.K.S. Richard R. K. Sorabji, Director, Institute of Classical Studies, and Professor of Ancient Philosophy, King's College London, UK

R.W.S. Robert William Sharples, Professor of Classics, University College London, UK

S.Sh. Susan Sherratt, Ashmolean Museum, Oxford, UK

S.S.-W. Susan Mary Sherwin-White, Senior Child Psychotherapist, Child and Family Consultation Centre, London, UK

T.J.S. Trevor J. Saunders, Professor of Greek, University of Newcastle upon Tyne, UK

C.C.W.T. Christopher C. W. Taylor, Fellow and Tutor in Philosophy, Corpus Christi College and Lecturer in Philosophy, University of Oxford, UK

C.J.T. Christopher J. Tuplin, Senior Lecturer, Department of Classics and Ancient History, University of Liverpool, UK

D.J.T. Dorothy J. Thompson, Lecturer, Girton College, University of Cambridge, UK

G.J.T. G. J. Toomer, Associate, Department of the History of Science, Harvard University, USA

J.C.T. Jeremy C. Trevett, Intercollegiate Lecturer in Ancient History, University of Oxford, UK

J.D.T. J. David Thomas, Emeritus Professor of Papyrology, University of Durham, UK

M.B.T. Michael Burney Trapp, Lecturer, Department of Classics, King's College London, UK

R.T. Rosalind Thomas, Lecturer in Ancient History, Royal Holloway and Bedford New College, University of London, UK

R.Th. Romila Thapar, Emeritus Professor, Jawaharlal Nehru University, New Delhi, India

R.A.T. Richard Allan Tomlinson, formerly Professor of Ancient History and Archaeology, University of Birmingham, UK

R.S.O.T. R. S. O. Tomlin, University Lecturer in Late-Roman History, University of Oxford, UK

S.C.T. Stephen C. Todd, Lecturer in Classics, University of Keele, UK

S.M.T. Susan M. Treggiari, Anne T. and Robert M. Bass Professor in the School of Humanities and Sciences, Stanford University, USA

J.U.	Jürgen Untermann, formerly Institute for Linguistics, University of Köln, Germany
H.v.S.	Heinrich von Staden, Professor of Classics and Comparative Literature, Yale University, USA
H.S.V.	H. S. Versnel, Professor of Ancient History, University of Leiden, Netherlands
M.V.	Michael Vickers, Senior Assistant Keeper, Department of Antiquities, Ashmolean Museum, Oxford, UK
J.T.V.	J. T. Vallance, Head of Classics, Sydney Grammar School, New South Wales, Australia
A.J.W.	A. J. Woodman, Professor of Latin, University of Durham, UK
A.M.W.	Anna M. Wilson, Department of Classics, University of Birmingham, UK
B.R.W.-P.	Bryan R. Ward-Perkins, Fellow of Trinity College and Lecturer in Modern History, University of Oxford, UK
D.W.	David Whitehead, Professor of Classics, The Queen's University of Belfast, UK
F.W.	Frederick John Williams, Professor of Greek, The Queen's University of Belfast, UK
I.N.W.	Ian N. Wood, Senior Lecturer, School of History, University of Leeds, UK
J.Wi.	Josef Wiesehöfer, Institute for the Science of Antiquity, Kiel University, Germany
J.E.W.	Jeffrey E. Wills, Assistant Professor of Classics, University of Wisconsin, USA
J.J.W.	John Joseph Wilkes, Yates Professor of Greek and Roman Archaeology, University College London, UK
J.P.W.	John Peter Wild, Reader in Archaeology, University of Manchester, UK
L.C.W.	Lindsay Cameron Watson, Senior Lecturer, Department of Classics, University of Sydney, Australia
L.M.W.	L. Michael Whitby, Professor, Department of Classics and Ancient History, University of Warwick, UK
M.W.	Michael Winterbottom, Corpus Professor of Latin, University of Oxford, UK
M.Wil.	Margaret Williamson, Senior Lecturer in Classical Studies, St Mary's University College, University of Surrey, UK
M.L.W.	Martin Litchfield West, Senior Research Fellow, All Souls College, University of Oxford, UK
M.M.W.	M. M. Willcock, Emeritus Professor of Latin, University College London, UK
N.G.W.	Nigel Guy Wilson, Fellow and Tutor in Classics, Lincoln College and Lecturer in Classical Languages and Literature, University of Oxford, UK
P.W.	Patricia Anne Watson, Senior Lecturer, Department of Classics, University of Sydney, Australia
P.J.W.	Peter James Wilson, Research Fellow, University of Warwick, UK
R.B.B.W.	Robert B. B. Wardy, Lecturer, University of Cambridge, UK
R.J.A.W.	Roger J. A. Wilson, Professor of Archaeology, University of Nottingham, UK
S.E.C.W.	Susan E. C. Walker, Deputy Keeper, Department of Greek and Roman Antiquities, The British Museum, London, UK
S.R.W.	Stephanie Roberta West, Senior Research Fellow, Hertford College, University of Oxford, UK
T.E.J.W.	†Thomas E. J. Wiedemann, Professor, Department of Classical and Archaeological Studies, University of Nottingham, UK
B.Z.	Bernhard Zimmermann, Professor, Seminar for Classical Philology, Heinrich-Heine-University Düsseldorf, Germany
R.Z.	Reinhard Zimmermann, Professor of Private Law, Roman Law and Comparative Legal History, University of Regensburg, Germany

CONTRIBUTORS TO THE PREVIOUS EDITIONS

A.A.	Antony Andrewes
A.E.A.	Alan E. Astin
J.K.A.	John Kinloch Anderson
J.W.H.A.	John Williams Hey Atkins
R.G.A.	Roland Gregory Austin
W.B.A.	William Blair Anderson
W.G.A.	William Geoffrey Arnott
A.B.	Adolf Berger
A.R.B.	Andrew Robert Burn
C.B.	Cyril Bailey
C.M.B.	Cecil Maurice Bowra
C.W.B.	Carl W. Blegen
D.J.B.	David John Blackman
D.M.B.	Donald Michael Bailey
E.A.B.	Eric Arthur Barber
E.B.	E. Badian
E.L.B.	Ewen Lyall Bowie
E.P.B.	E. Phillips Barker
F.A.G.B.	Frederick Arthur George Beck
G.E.B.	George Ewart Bean
G.L.B.	Godfrey Louis Barber

Contributors to the Previous Editions

H.B.	Herbert Bloch		L.E.	Ludwig Edelstein
H.E.B.	Harold Edgeworth Butler		P.J.E.	Petrus Johannes Enk
J.B.	John Boardman		S.E.	Sam Eitrem
J.P.B.	John Percy Vyvian Dacre Balsdon		V.E.	Victor Ehrenberg
O.B.	Olwen Phillis Frances Brogan		W.M.E.	Walter Manoel Edwards
P.R.L.B.	Peter Robert Lamont Brown			
R.B.	Robert Browning		B.F.	Benjamin Farrington
R.J.B.	Robert Johnson Bonner		C.F.	Charles Favez
S.B.	Sylvia Benton		C.J.F.	Christian James Fordyce
T.A.B.	Thomas Allan Brady		D.J.F.	David John Furley
T.R.S.B.	Thomas Robert Shannon Broughton		E.S.F.	Edward Seymour Forster
W.B.	William Beare		G.B.A.F.	Geoffrey Bernard Abbott Fletcher
W.Br.	William Barr		G.C.F.	Guy Cromwell Field
			J.E.F.	Joseph Eddy Fontenrose
A.D.E.C.	Alan Douglas Edward Cameron		K. von F.	Kurt von Fritz
A.H.C.	Allan Hartley Coxon		M.I.F.	M. I. Finley
A.M.C.	Averil Millicent Cameron		P.B.R.F.	Peter Barr Reid Forbes
D.J.C.	Donald John Campbell		P.M.F.	Peter Marshall Fraser
F.C.	Ferdinando Castagnoli		R.N.F.	Richard Nelson Frye
G.E.F.C.	Guy Edward Farquhar Chilver		S.S.F.	Sheppard S. Frere
G.H.C.	George Henry Chase		T.F.	Theodore Fyfe
G.L.C.	George Law Cawkwell		W.G.F.	William George Forrest
H.C.	Henry Chadwick		W.H.C.F.	William Hugh Clifford Frend
H.Cn.	Harry Caplan			
H.J.C.	Henry Joel Cadbury		A.J.G.	Alexander John Graham
I.M.C.	Ian McIntyre Campbell		A.W.G.	Arnold Wycombe Gomme
J.C.	John Chadwick		E.W.G.	Eric William Gray
J.H.C.	Johan Harm Croon		F.R.D.G.	Francis Richard David Goodyear
J.M.C.	John Manuel Cook		G.G.	Giuseppe Giangrande
J.M.R.C.	James Maxwell Ross Cormack		G.T.G.	Guy Thompson Griffith
M.A.R.C.	Malcolm Andrew Richard Colledge		J.G.	John Glucker
M.C.	Max Cary		K.G.	Kenneth Grayston
M.Co.	Michael Coffey		R.J.G.	Robert John Getty
M.P.C.	Martin Percival Charlesworth		S.G.	Stephen Gaselee
P.B.C.	Philip B. Corbett		S.L.G.	Stanley Lawrence Greenslade
R.C.C.	Roger Clifford Carrington		V.R.G.	Virginia Randolph Grace
R.P.C.	Robert Pierce Casey		W.C.G.	William Chase Greene
S.C.	Stanley Casson		W.K.C.G.	William Keith Chambers Guthrie
T.J.C.	Theodore John Cadoux			
W.M.C.	William Moir Calder		A.H.-W.	Alun Hudson-Williams
			B.R.H.	Brian Rodgerson Hartley
A.E.M.D.	Anna Elbina Morpurgo Davies		C.G.H.	Colin Graham Hardie
A.M.D.	Arnold Mackay Duff		C.P.H.	Caroline Penrose Hammond
D.R.D.	David Reginald Dicks		F.M.H.	Friedrich M. Heichelheim
E.R.D.	Erik Robertson Dodds		F.R.H.	F. R. Hodson
H.R.E.D.	Hilda Roderick Ellis Davidson		G.H.	Gilbert Highet
J.D.D.	John Dewar Denniston		G.M.A.H.	George M. A. Hanfmann
J.D.-G.	J. Duchesne-Guillemin		J.H.	Jacques Heurgon
J.F.D.	John Frederic Dobson		M.H.	Mason Hammond
J.W.D.	John Wight Duff		M.E.H.	Margaret E. Hubbard
K.J.D.	Kenneth James Dover		M.I.H.	M. Isobel Henderson
L.D.	Ludwig Deubner		M.S.F.H.	Martin Sinclair Frankland Hood
M.S.D.	Margaret Stephana Drower		N.G.L.H.	Nicholas Geoffrey Lemprière
O.A.W.D.	Oswald Ashton Wentworth Dilke			Hammond
O.D.	Oliver Davies		R.H.	Reginald Hackforth
R.P.D.-J.	Richard Phare Duncan-Jones		R.J.H.	Robert J. Hopper
S.D.	Sterling Dow		R.L.H.	Robert Leslie Howland
T.J.D.	Thomas James Dunbabin		R.M.H.	Robert Mitchell Henry
			T.H.	Thomas Little Heath
C.F.E.	Charles Farwell Edson		T.J.H.	Theodore Johannes Haarhoff
C.W.J.E.	Charles William John Eliot		A.H.M.J.	Arnold Hugh Martin Jones
D.E.E.	David Edward Eichholz		G.D.B.J.	Geraint Dyfed Barri Jones

L.H.J.	Lilian Hamilton Jeffery
R.L.J.	Robert Leoline James
A.K.	A. Ker
E.J.K.	Edward John Kenney
F.G.K.	Frederic George Kenyon
H.D.F.K.	Humphrey Davy Findlay Kitto
J.J.K.	John J. Keaney
J.N.D.K.	John Norman Davidson Kelly
M.K.	Martha Kneale
W.F.J.K.	William Francis Jackson Knight
A.W.L.	Andrew William Lintott
D.W.L.	Donald William Lucas
H.S.L.	Herbert Strainge Long
I.M.L.	Iain Malcolm Lonie
J.A.O.L.	Jakob Aall Ottesen Larsen
J.F.L.	John Francis Lockwood
L.B.L.	Lillian B. Lawler
M.L.	Mabel L. Lang
R.G.C.L.	Robert Graham Cochrane Levens
W.A.L.	William Allison Laidlaw
W.K.L.	Walter Kirkpatrick Lacey
A.M.	Arnaldo Momigliano
A.H.McD.	Alexander Hugh McDonald
B.M.M.	Bruce Manning Metzger
D.J.M.	Derek John Mosley
D.M.M.	Douglas Maurice MacDowell
E.C.M.	Edgar Cardew Marchant
E.H.M.	Ellis Hovell Minns
E.I.M.	Earl Ingram McQueen
E.W.M.	Eric William Marsden
F.G.B.M.	Fergus Graham Burtholme Millar
G.E.M.	George E. Mylonas
H.M.	Harold Mattingly
J.A.M.	James Alan Montgomery
J.C.M.	John C. Mann
J.F.M.	James Frederick Mountford
J.G.M.	Joseph Grafton Milne
J.G.McQ.	James Galloway Macqueen
J.L.M.	John Linton Myres
L.A.M.	Ludwig Alfred Moritz
M.F.M.	Malcolm F. McGregor
P.K.M.	Peter Kenneth Marshall
P.M.	Paul Maas
R.M.	Russell Meiggs
R.A.B.M.	Roger Aubrey Baskerville Mynors
T.B.M.	Terence Bruce Mitford
W.S.M.	William Stuart Maguinness
A.K.N.	Awadh Kishore Narain
B.N.	Barry Nicholas
J.N.	John North
M.P.N.	Nils Martin Persson Nilsson
O.N.	Otto E. Neugebauer
P.S.N.	Peter Scott Noble
A.O.	André Oltramare
G.E.L.O.	Gwilym Ellis Lane Owen
R.M.O.	Robert Maxwell Ogilvie
S.G.O.	Sidney George Owen
A.J.D.P.	Alexander James Dow Porteous
A.L.P.	Arthur Leslie Peck
A.S.P.	Arthur Stanley Pease
A.W.P.-C.	Arthur Wallace Pickard-Cambridge
B.E.P.	Ben Edwin Perry
F.N.P.	Frederick Norman Pryce
G.M.P.	George Mackay Paul
H.M.D.P.	Henry Michael Denne Parker
H.W.P.	Herbert William Parke
J.R.T.P.	John Richard Thornhill Pollard
J.W.P.	John William Pirie
L.P.	Lionel Pearson
L.R.P.	Leonard Robert Palmer
M.P.	Maurice Platnauer
R.A.P.	Roger Ambrose Pack
T.G.E.P.	Thomas George Eyre Powell
W.K.P.	W. Kendrick Pritchett
A.L.F.R.	A. L. F. Rivet
B.R.R.	Brinley Roderick Rees
C.H.R.	Colin Henderson Roberts
C.J.R.	Christopher J. Rowe
C.M.R.	Charles Martin Robertson
D.A.R.	Donald Andrew Frank Moore Russell
D.R.-M.	David Randall-MacIver
D.W.R.R.	David William Robertson Ridgway
E.S.G.R.	E. Stanley G. Robinson
F.J.E.R.	Frederick James Edward Raby
F.N.R.	Fred Norris Robinson
G.C.R.	George Chatterton Richards
G.M.A.R.	Gisela M.A. Richter
G.W.R.	Geoffrey Walter Richardson
H.J.R.	Herbert Jennings Rose
H.W.R.	H. W. Richmond
I.A.R.	Ian Archibald Richmond
J.M.R.	Joyce Maire Reynolds
L.D.R.	Leighton Durham Reynolds
N.R.	Noel Robertson
R.R.	Richard George Frederick Robinson
R.M.R.	Robert Mantle Rattenbury
T.T.B.R.	Timothy Thomas Bennett Ryder
T.T.R.	Tamara Talbot Rice
W.D.R.	William David Ross
A.N.S.-W.	A. N. Sherwin-White
A.S.	Alexander Souter
B.A.S.	Brian Allison Sparkes
C.S.	Charles Joseph Singer
C.E.S.	Courtenay Edward Stevens
C.G.S.	Chester G. Starr
C.H.V.S.	Carol Humphrey Vivian Sutherland
D.E.S.	Donald Emrys Strong
E.M.S.	Edith Mary Smallwood
E.S.S.	Eastland Stuart Staveley
E.T.S.	Edward Togo Salmon
F.A.W.S.	Franz A. W. Schehl
F.H.S.	Francis Henry Sandbach
G.H.S.	George Hope Stevenson
H.S.	Henri Seyrig
H.H.S.	Howard Hayes Scullard
J.S.	Jerry Stannard
Jas. S.	James Stevenson

Contributors to the Previous Editions

J.H.S.	John Hedley Simon	A.W.	Abraham Wasserstein
J.P.S.	John Patrick Sullivan	A.G.W.	Arthur Geoffrey Woodhead
M.S.	Margaret Elspeth Milne Smith	A.M.W.	Arthur Maurice Woodward
M.S.S.	Martin Stirling Smith	B.H.W.	Brian Herbert Warmington
O.J.L.S.	Oswald John Louis Szmerenyi	D.E.W.	Donald Ernest Wilson Wormell
O.S.	Otto Skutsch	E.H.W.	Eric Herbert Warmington
P.S.	Peter Salway	E.J.W.	Edward James Wood
R.S.	Ronald Syme	F.A.W.	Frederick Adam Wright
T.A.S.	Thomas Alan Sinclair	F.R.W.	Francis Redding Walton
W.H.S.	Walter Haywood Shewring	F.W.W.	Frank William Walbank
		G.C.W.	George Clement Whittick
C.A.T.	Constantine A. Trypanis	G.R.W.	George Ronald Watson
D.B.T.	Dorothy Burr Thompson	G.W.W.	Gordon Willis Williams
E.A.T.	Edward Arthur Thompson	H.D.W.	Henry Dickinson Westlake
G.B.T.	Gavin B. Townend	H.T.W.-G.	Henry Theodore Wade-Gery
G.J.T.	G. J. Toomer	J.W.	Joshua Whatmough
H.A.T.	Homer Armstrong Thompson	J.B.W.-P.	John Bryan Ward-Perkins
J.M.C.T.	Jocelyn M. C. Toynbee	J.J.W.	John Joseph Wilkes
J.T.	Jonathan Tate	K.D.W.	Kenneth Douglas White
L.R.T.	Lily Ross Taylor	M.W.	Michael Winterbottom
M.N.T.	Marcus Niebuhr Tod	M.L.W.	Martin Litchfield West
P.T.	Piero Treves	N.G.W.	Nigel Guy Wilson
S.J.T.	S. J. Tester	R.E.W.	Richard Ernest Wycherley
W.T.	William Telfer	R.P.W.-L.	Reginald Pepys Winnington-Ingram
W.W.T.	William Woodthorpe Tarn	S.W.	Sheila White
		T.B.L.W.	Thomas Bertram Lonsdale Webster
P.N.U.	Percy Neville Ure	T.E.W.	Thomas Erskine Wright
		T.J.P.W.	Thomas Joseph Patrick Williams
A.W. van B.	Albert William van Buren	W.G.W.	William Gillan Waddell
J.J. van N.	John James van Nostrand	W.S.W.	William Smith Watt

ABBREVIATIONS USED IN THE PRESENT WORK

A. GENERAL

abr.	abridged/abridgement	Fr.	French	NS	new series
adesp.	adespota	fr.	fragment	NT	New Testament
Akkad.	Akkadian	ft.	foot/feet	OE	Old English
app.	appendix	g.	gram/s	Ol.	Olympiad
app. crit.	apparatus criticus	Ger.	German	ON	Old Norse
Aeol.	Aeolic	Gk.	Greek	OP	Old Persian
art.	article	ha.	hectare/s	orig.	original (e.g. Ger./Fr.
Att.	Attic	Hebr.	Hebrew		orig. [edn.])
b.	born	HS	sesterces	OT	Old Testament
Bab.	Babylonian	hyp.	hypothesis	oz.	ounce/s
beg.	at/nr. beginning	*i.a.*	*inter alia*	p.a.	per annum
bibliog.	bibliography	ibid.	ibidem, in the same work	PIE	Proto-Indo-European
bk.	book	IE	Indo-European	pl.	plate
c.	*circa*	imp.	impression	plur.	plural
cent.	century	in.	inch/es	pref.	preface
cm.	centimetre/s	introd.	introduction	*Proc.*	*Proceedings*
comm.	commentary	Ion.	Ionic	prol.	prologue
corr.	corrected	It.	Italian	ps.-	pseudo-
d.	died	kg.	kilogram/s	pt.	part
Diss.	Dissertation	km.	kilometre/s	ref.	reference
Dor.	Doric	lb.	pound/s	repr.	reprint, reprinted
end	at/nr. end	l., ll.	line, lines	rev.	revised/by
ed.	editor, edited by	lit.	literally	sel.	selected
ed. maior/minor	major/minor	lt.	litre/s	ser.	series
	edition of critical text	L.	Linnaeus	sing.	singular
edn.	edition	Lat.	Latin	Skt.	Sanskrit
Einzelschr.	Einzelschrift	m.	metre/s	Sp.	Spanish
El.	Elamite	masc.	masculine	str.	strophe
Eng.	English	mi.	mile/s	Suppl.	Supplement
esp.	especially	ml.	millilitre/s	T	*testimonium* (i.e. piece of
Etr.	Etruscan	mod.	modern		ancient evidence about
exhib. cat.	exhibition catalogue	Mt.	Mount		an author)
fem.	feminine	n., nn.	note, notes	trans.	translation, translated by
f., ff.	and following	n.d.	no date	v., vv.	verse, verses
fig.	figure	neut.	neuter	Ven.	Venetic
fl.	floruit	no.	number		

B. AUTHORS AND BOOKS

Note: [--] names of authors or works in square brackets indicate false or doubtful attributions
A small number above the line indicates the number of an edition

A&A	*Antike und Abendland*	A²S	Inscription of Artaxerxes II at
AA	see Syme, *AA*		Susa
AAA	*Athens Annals of Archaeology*	*Abh.* followed by	*Abhandlungen*
AAHG	*Anzeiger für Altertumswissenschaft*	name of	
AAWM	*Abhandlungen der Akademie der*	Academy or	
	Wissenschaften in Mainz,	Society	
	geistes-und	*Abh. sächs. Ges. Wiss.*	*Abhandlungen der sächsischen*
	sozialwissenschaftliche Klasse		*Gesellschaft der Wissenschaften*
A²H	Inscription of Artaxerxes II at	*Abh. zu Gesch. d.*	*Abhandlungen zur Geschichte der*
	Hamadan	*Math.*	*mathematischen Wissenschaften*

Authors and Books

App.
  Pun.   *Λιβυκή*
  Sam.   *Σαυνιτική*
  Syr.   *Συριακή*
App. Verg.   *Appendix Vergiliana*
Apsines, *Rhet.*   Apsines, *Ars rhetorica*
Apth. *Prog.*   Aphthonius, *Progymnasmata*
Apul.   Apuleius
  Apol.   *Apologia*
  Asclep.   *Asclepius*
  De deo Soc.   *De deo Socratico*
  De dog. Plat.   *De dogmate Platonis*
  Flor.   *Florida*
  Met.   *Metamorphoses*
Ap. Rhod.   Apollonius Rhodius
  Argon.   *Argonautica*
Ar.   Aristophanes
  Ach.   *Acharnenses*
  Av.   *Aves*
  Eccl.   *Ecclesiazusae*
  Eq.   *Equites*
  Lys.   *Lysistrata*
  Nub.   *Nubes*
  Plut.   *Plutus*
  Ran.   *Ranae*
  Thesm.   *Thesmophoriazusae*
  Vesp.   *Vespae*
Aratus, *Phaen.*   Aratus, *Phaenomena*
  Progn.   *Prognostica*
Ar. Byz.   Aristophanes Byzantinus
Arch. Ael.   *Archaeologia Aeliana* (Newcastle-upon-Tyne)
Arch. Anz.   *Archäologischer Anzeiger in Jahrbuch des [kaiserlichen] deutschen archäologischen Instituts (JDAI)*
Arch. Class.   *Archaeologia Classica*
Ἀρχ. Ἐφ   *Ἀρχαιολογικὴ Ἐφημερίς*
Archil.   Archilochus
Archim. *Method*   Archimedes, *Method of Mechanical Theorems*
Arch. Journ.   *Archaeological Journal*
Arch. Laz.   *Archeologia Laziale*
Arch. Pap.   *Archiv für Papyrusforschung*
Arch. Rep.   *Archaeological Reports* published by the Hellenic Society
Arist.   Aristotle
  An. post.   *Analytica posteriora*
  An. pr.   *Analytica priora*
  [Ath. Pol.]   *Ἀθηναίων πολιτεία*
  Cael.   *De caelo*
  Cat.   *Categoriae*
  [Col.]   *De coloribus*
  De an.   *De anima*
  [De audib.]   *De audibilibus*
  De motu an.   *De motu animalium*
  Div. somn.   *De divinatione per somnia*
  Eth. Eud.   *Ethica Eudemia*
  Eth. Nic.   *Ethica Nicomachea*
  Gen. an.   *De generatione animalium*
  Gen. corr.   *De generatione et corruptione*
  Hist. an.   *Historia animalium*

  IA   *De incessu animalium*
  Int.   *De interpretatione*
  [Lin. Ins.]   *De lineis insecabilibus*
  [Mag. mor.]   *Magna moralia*
  [Mech.]   *Mechanica*
  Mem.   *De memoria*
  Metaph.   *Metaphysica*
  Mete.   *Meteorologica*
  [Mir. ausc.]   see *Mir. ausc.* under M
  [Mund.]   *De mundo*
  [Oec.]   *Oeconomica*
  Part. an.   *De partibus animalium*
  Parv. nat.   *Parva naturalia*
  Ph.   *Physica*
  [Phgn.]   *Physiognomonica*
  Poet.   *Poetica*
  Pol.   *Politica*
  [Pr.]   *Problemata*
  Resp.   *De respiratione*
  Rh.   *Rhetorica*
  [Rh. Al.]   *Rhetorica ad Alexandrum*
  Sens.   *De sensu*
  Soph. el.   *Sophistici elenchi*
  Top.   *Topica*
  [Xen.]   *De Xenophane*
Aristid. *Or.*   Aristides, *Orationes*
Aristid. Quint.   Aristides Quintilianus
Aristox.   Aristoxenus
  Fr. hist.   *Fragmenta historica*
  Harm.   *Harmonica*
  Rhythm.   *Rhythmica*
Arn.   Arnobius
  Adv. nat.   *Adversus nationes*
Arnim (von)   see *SVF*
Arr.   Arrian
  Anab.   *Anabasis*
  Cyn.   *Cynegeticus*
  Epict. diss.   *Epicteti dissertationes*
  Parth.   *Parthica*
  Peripl. M. Eux.   *Periplus Maris Euxini*
  Tact.   *Tactica*
Artem.   Artemidorus Daldianus
ARV   J. D. Beazley, *Attic Red-Figure Vase-Painters*, 2nd edn. (1963)
ARV Add   T. Carpenter, T. Mannack, and M. Mendonça, *Beazley Addenda*, 2nd edn. (1990)
ARV Para   J. D. Beazley, *Paralipomena Additions to Attic Black-Figure Vase-Painters and to Attic Red-Figure Vase-Painters* (1971)
ARW   *Archiv für Religionswissenschaft*
ASAA   *Annuario della Scuola archeologica di Atene e delle Missioni italiane in Oriente*
ASAE   *Annales du service des antiquités de l'Égypte*
Asc.   Asconius
  Corn.   Commentary on Cicero, *Pro Corneleo de maiestate*
  Mil.   Commentary on Cicero, *Pro Milone*

Authors and Books

Asc.	
Pis.	Commentary on Cicero, *In Pisonem*
Verr.	Commentary on Cicero, *In Verrem*
Asc. . . . C	Asconius, ed. A. C. Clark (OCT, 1907)
ASNP	*Annali della Scuola Normale Superiore di Pisa, Classe di Lettere e Filosofia*
ASSR	*Archives des sciences sociales de religion*
Astin, *Scipio*	A. E. Astin, *Scipio Aemilianus* (1967)
Ath.	Athenaeus
Athenaeum	*Athenaeum* (Pavia). NS (1923–)
Athenagoras, *Leg.*	Athenagoras, *Legatio pro Christianis*
pro Christ.	= Πρεσβεία περὶ Χριστιανῶν
Ath. pol.	*Athenaion politeia* (Aristotelian); see also Xen. for 'Old Oligarch' i.e. Ps.-Xen. *Ath. Pol.*
ATL	B. D. Meritt, H. T. Wade-Gery, and M. F. McGregor, *The Athenian Tribute Lists 1–4* (1939–53)
Auct. ad Her.	*Auctor ad Herennium*
August.	Augustine
Ad Rom.	*Expositio of Epist. ad Romanos*
C. acad.	*Contra academicos*
Conf.	*Confessions*
De civ. D.	*De civitate Dei*
Div. quaest.	*De diversis quaestionibus*
In Evang. Iohan.	*Tractatus in Evangelium Iohannis*
Ep.	*Epistulae*
Retract.	*Retractationes*
Serm.	*Sermones*
Aul. Gell.	see Gell.
Aur. Vict. *Caes.*	Aurelius Victor, *Caesares*
[Aur. Vict.] *De vir. ill.*	[Aurelius Victor], *De viris illustribus*
Auson.	Ausonius (see Green)
Cent. nupt.	*Cento nuptialis*
Grat. act.	*Gratiarum actio*
Mos.	*Mosella*
Ordo nob. urb.	*Ordo nobilium urbium*
Prof. Burd.	*Commemoratio professorum Burdigalensium*
Technop.	*Technopaegnion*
Austin	M. M. Austin, *The Hellenistic World from Alexander to the Roman Conquest* (1981)
Austin, *CGFP*	C. Austin, *Comicorum Graecorum fragmenta in papyris reperta* (1973)
BaBesch.	*Bulletin antieke Beschavung*
Bacchyl.	Bacchylides (ed. B. Snell and H. Maehler, 1970)
B Act.	*Bellum Actiacum*: see *B Aegypt.*
Badian, *Stud. Gr. Rom. Hist.*	E. Badian, *Studies in Greek and Roman History* (1964)

B Aegypt.	*Carmen de Bello Aegyptiaco sive Actiaco* (papyrus fragment)
Baehr.	E. Baehrens
FPR	*Fragmenta Poetarum Romanorum* (1866)
PLM	see *PLM* Vollmer/Morel
B Afr.	*Bellum Africum*
Bagnall and Derow	R. S. Bagnall and P. Derow, *Greek Historical Documents: The Hellenistic Period* (1981)
B Alex.	*Bellum Alexandrinum*
Basil. *De virg.*	Basilius, *De virginitate*
BASP	*Bulletin of the American Society of Papyrologists*
Bauman, *WPAR*	R. A. Bauman, *Women and Politics in Ancient Rome* (1992)
BCH	*Bulletin de Correspondance Hellénique*
BÉ	*Bulletin épigraphique*, pub. in *Revue des études grecques*
Beazley, *ABV*	J. D. Beazley, *Attic Black-figure Vase Painters* (1956)
ARV²	*Attic Red-figure Vase Painters*, 2nd edn. (1963)
Paralipomena	*Paralipomena: Additions to ABV and ARV²* (1971)
Beazley *Addenda*	T. H. Carpenter, *Beazley Addenda: Additional References to ABV, ARV² and Paralipomena*, 2nd edn. (1989)
BÉFEO	*Bulletin: École française d'Extrême Orient*
Beitr.	*Beitrag, Beiträge*
Beloch	K. J. Beloch
Gr. Gesch.	*Griechische Geschichte*, 2nd edn. (1912–27)
Röm. Gesch.	*Römische Geschichte bis zum Beginn der punischen Kriege* (1926)
Bengtson, *Strategie*	H. Bengtson, *Die Strategie in der hellenistischen Zeit*, Munchener Beiträge zur Papyrusforschung und Rechtsgeschichte 26 (1937), 32 (1944), 36 (1952)
Röm. Gesch.	*Grundriss der römischen Geschichte* (1967)
Bérard, *Bibl. topogr.*	J. Bérard, *Bibliographie topographique des principales cités grecques de l'Italie méridionale et de la Sicile dans l'antiquité* (1941)
Berl. Abh.	*Abhandlungen der preuß. Akademie d. Wissenschaften zu Berlin* (1786–1907; 1908–)
Bernabé, *PEG*	A. Bernabé, *Poetae Epici Graeci 1* (1988)
Ber. Sächs. Ges. Wiss.	*Berichte über die Verhandlungen der [Kgl.] sächsischen Gesellschaft der Wissenschaften zu Leipzig* (1848)

Berve, *Alexanderreich* — H. Berve, *Das Alexanderreich aus prosopographischer Grundlage* (1927)

BGU — *Berliner Griechische Urkunden (Ägyptische Urkunden aus den Kgl. Museen zu Berlin)*

BHisp. — *Bellum Hispaniense*

Bibl. Éc. Franc. — *Bibliothèque des Écoles françaises d' Athénes et de Rome* (1877–)

BICS — *Bulletin of the Institute of Classical Studies*, London

Bidez–Cumont — J. Bidez and F. Cumont, *Les Mages hellénisés*, 2 vols. (1938)

Bieber, *Sculpt. Hellenist. Age* — M. Bieber, *Sculpture of the Hellenistic Age*, 2nd edn. (1961)

BIFAO — *Bulletin de l'Institut français d' Archéologie Orientale* (Cairo)

BiOr — *Bibliotheca Orientalis*

BJ — *Bonner Jahrbücher*

BKT — *Berliner Klassikertexte, herausgegeben von der Generalverwaltung der Kgl. Museen zu Berlin* (1904–)

Blass, *Att. Ber.* — F. Blass, *Die Attische Beredsamkeit*, 2nd edn. (1887–98)

BM — British Museum

BMB — *Bulletin du Musée de Beyrouth*

BMC — British Museum Catalogue

BM Coins, Rom. Emp. — *British Museum Catalogue of Coins of the Roman Empire* (1923–)

BN — *Beiträge zur Namenforschung*, Heidelberg

Boll. d'Arte — *Bollettino d'arte*

Boll. Fil. Class. — *Bollettino di filologia classica* (1894–1929); NS (1930–)

Bonner Jahrb. — *Bonner Jahrbücher* (1895–)

Bosworth, *HCA* — A. B. Bosworth, *Historical Commentary on Arrian's History of Alexander* 1: *Commentary on Books i–iii* (1980); 2: *Commentary on Books iv–v* (1995)

Bouché-Leclerq, *Hist. div.* — A. Bouché-Leclerq, *Histoire de la divination dans l'antiquité*, 4 vols. (1879–82)

Bowersock, *AGW* — G. W. Bowersock, *Augustus and the Greek World* (1965)

B. phil. Woch. — *Berliner philologische Wochenschrift* (1881–1920)

Bremer — F. P. Bremer, *Iurisprudentiae antehadrianae quae supersunt*: 1 (1896); 2/1 (1898); 2/2 (1901)

Bresl. phil. Abh. — *Breslauer philologische Abhandlungen*

BRGK — *Bericht der römisch-germanischen Kommission des deutschen archäologischen Instituts*

Briant, *HEA* — P. Briant, *De Cyrus à Alexandre: l'Histoire de l'empire achéménide* (forthcoming) [published title: *Histoire de l'empire perse* (1996)]

Briscoe, *Comm. 31–33*; *Comm. 34–37* — J. Briscoe, *A Commentary on Livy Books xxxi–xxxiii* (1973); *A Commentary on Livy Books xxxiv–xxxvii* (1981)

Brommer, *Vasenlisten* — F. Brommer, *Vasenlisten zur griechischen Heldensage* (2nd edn. 1960; 3rd edn. 1973)

Broughton, *MRR* — T. R. S. Broughton, *The Magistrates of the Roman Republic* (1951–2); Suppl. (1986: supersedes Suppl. 1960)

Bruns, *Font.* — C. G. Bruns, *Fontes iuris Romani antiqui*, 7th edn. (1919)

Brunt, *RIT* — P. A. Brunt, *Roman Imperial Themes* (1990)

BSA — *Annual of the British School at Athens* (1895–)

BTCGI — G. Nenci and G. Vallet (eds), *Bibliografia topografica della colonizzazione greca in Italia e nelle isole tirreniche*

Büchner, *FPL* — see Morel–Büchner, *FPL*

Budé — Collection des Univ. de France, publiée sous le patronage de l'Assoc. Guillaume Budé

Buecheler, *Carm. Epigr.* — F. Buecheler, *Carmina Latina Epigraphica*, 2 vols. with Suppl. by E. Lommatzsch (1894–1930)

Bull. Com. Arch. — *Bullettino ella Commissione archeologica comunale in Roma*

Bull. Ist. Dir. Rom. — *Bullettino del Istituto di diritto romano*

Bull. Rylands Libr. — *Bulletin of John Rylands Library*

Burkert, *GR* — W. Burkert, trans. J. Raffan, *Greek Religion* (1985)

Burkert, *HN* — W. Burkert, trans. P. Bing, *Homo Necans* (1983)

Burnet, *EGP* — J. Burnet, *Early Greek Philosophy*, 4th edn. (1930)

Bursian — C. Bursian, *Geographie von Griechenland* 2 (1872)

Jahresb. — Bursian's *Jahresberichte über die Fortschritte der Altertumswissenschaft* (1873–)

Busolt, *Gr. Gesch.* — G. Busolt, *Griechische Geschichte*, 4 vols., vols. 1 and 2 in 2nd edn. (1893–1904)

Byz. Forsch. — *Byzantinische Forschungen*

Byz. und Neugr. Jahrb. — *Byzantinisch-neugriechische Jahrbücher*

Byz. Zeitschr. — *Byzantinische Zeitschrift*

C&M — *Classica et Mediaevalia*

Cabrol–Leclerq, *Dict. d'arch. chrétienne* — F. Cabrol and H. Leclerq (eds.), *Dictionnaire d'archéologie chrétienne et de liturgie*, 15 vols. (1907–53)

Authors and Books

Caes.	Caesar	Celsus, *Med.*	Celsus, *De medicina*
B Afr.	*Bellum Africum*	Censorinus, *DN*	Censorinus, *De die natali*
B Civ.	*Bellum Civile*	*CGF*	G. Kaibel, *Comicorum Graecorum*
B Gall.	*Bellum Gallicum*		*Fragmenta* (1899)
CAF	T. Kock, *Comicorum Atticorum*	Chalcid. *In Tim.*	Chalcidius, *In Platonis*
	Fragmenta (1880–8)		*Timaeum*
CAH	*Cambridge Ancient History*, 2nd	Charisius, *Gramm.*	Charisius, *Ars grammatica*
	edn. (1961– ; 1st edn. 1923–	*CHCL*	*Cambridge History of Classical*
	39)		*Literature*, 1: *Greek Literature*,
Cahiers de la DAFI	*Cahiers de la délégation française en*		ed. P. E. Easterling and B. M.
	Iran		W. Knox (1985); 2: *Latin*
Callim.	Callimachus		*Literature*, ed. E. J. Kenney and
Aet.	*Aetia*		W. V. Clausen (1982)
Epigr.	*Epigrammata*	*Chiron*	*Chiron: Mitteilungen der*
Hymn 1	*Hymn to Zeus*		*Kommission für alte Geschichte*
„ 2	„ „ *Apollo*		*und Epigraphik des deutschen*
„ 3	„ „ *Artemis*		*archäologischen Instituts*
„ 4	„ „ *Delos*	*CHJ*	*Cambridge Historical Journal*
„ 5	„ „ *Athena*	Christ–Schmid–	W. von Christ, *Geschichte d.*
„ 6	„ „ *Demeter*	Stählin	*griechischen Literatur*, rev. W.
Ia.	*Iambics*		Schmid and O. Stählin, vol.
Calp. *Ecl.*	Calpurnius Siculus, *Eclogues*		2/1⁶. See also 2/2⁶ Schmid–
Carm. arv.	*Carmen arvale*		Stählin
Carm. epigr.	*Carmina epigraphica* ('pars	*Chron. d'É*	*Chroniques d'Égypte*
	posterior' of *Anthologia*	*Chron. Marcell.*	Marcellinus, *Chronicon*
	Latina)	*Chron. min.*	*Chronica minora*
Carm. pop.	*Carmina popularia* in Diehl's	*Chron. Pasch.*	*Chronicon Paschale*
	*Anth. Lyr. Graec.*2, pp. 192–	*CIA*	*Corpus Inscriptionum Atticarum*
	208		(1825–)
Carm. Sal.	*Carmen Saliare*	Cic.	Cicero (Marcus Tullius)
Cary, *Geographic*	M. Cary, *The Geographic*	*Acad.*	*Academicae quaestiones*
Background	*Background of Greek and Roman*	*Acad. post.*	*Academica posteriora*
	History (1949)		(= Plasberg, Bk. 4)
Cary–	M. Cary and E. H. Warmington,	*Acad. Pr.*	*Academica Priora* (= Plasberg,
Warmington,	*The Ancient Explorers* (1929;		Bk. 1)
Explorers	Penguin/Pelican, 1963)	*Ad Brut.*	*Epistulae ad Brutum*
Cass. Dio	Cassius Dio	*Amic.*	*De amicitia*
Cassiod.	Cassiodorus	*Arch.*	*Pro Archia*
Inst.	*Institutiones*	*Att.*	*Epistulae ad Atticum*
Var.	*Variae*	*Balb.*	*Pro Balbo*
Castagnoli, *Stud.*	F. Castagnoli (ed.), *Studi di*	*Brut.*	*Brutus* or *De Claris Oratoribus*
urb.	*urbanistica antica* (1966)	*Caecin.*	*Pro Caecina*
Cat. Lit. Pap.	H. J. M. Milne, *Catalogue of the*	*Cael.*	*Pro Caelio*
	Literary Papyri in the British	*Cat.*	*In Catilinam*
	Museum (1927)	*Clu.*	*Pro Cluentio*
Cato, *Agr.*	Cato, *De agricultura* or *De re*	*Corn.*	*Pro Cornelio de maiestate*
	rustica		(fragmentary)
Orig.	*Origines*	*De imp. Cn. Pomp.*	see *Leg. Man.*
Catull.	Catullus	*Deiot.*	*Pro rege Deiotaro*
Caven, *Punic Wars*	B. Caven, *The Punic Wars* (1988)	*De or.*	*De oratore*
CCAG	*Catalogus Codicum Astrologorum*	*Div.*	*De divinatione*
	Graecorum, ed. F. Cumont and	*Div. Caec.*	*Divinatio in Caecilium*
	others 9 vols.	*Dom.*	*De domo sua*
CCGS	*Corpus Christianorum, series*	*Fam.*	*Epistulae ad familiares*
	Graeca (1977–)	*Fat.*	*De fato*
CCSL	*Corpus Christianorum, series*	*Fin.*	*De finibus*
	Latina (1953–)	*Flac.*	*Pro Flacco*
CÉFR	*Collections de l'École française de*	*Font.*	*Pro Fonteio*
	Rome (1976–)	*Har. resp.*	*De haruspicum responso*
CEG	P. A. Hansen, *Carmina*	*Inv. rhet.*	*De inventione rhetorica*
	Epigraphica Graeca, 2 vols.	*Leg.*	*De legibus*
	(1983–9)	*Leg. agr.*	*De lege agraria*

Cic.
  Leg. Man.   *Pro lege Manilia* or *De imperio Cn.*
     Pompeii
  Lig.   *Pro Ligario*
  Luc.   *Lucullus* or *Academica*
     posteriora
  Marcell.   *Pro Marcello*
  Mil.   *Pro Milone*
  Mur.   *Pro Murena*
  Nat. D.   *De natura deorum*
  Off.   *De officiis*
  Orat.   *Orator ad M. Brutum*
  Part. or.   *Partitiones oratoriae*
  Phil.   *Orationes Philippicae*
  Pis.   *In Pisonem*
  Planc.   *Pro Plancio*
  Prov. cons.   *De provinciis consularibus*
  Q Fr.   *Epistulae ad Quintum fratrem*
  Q Rosc.   *Pro Roscio comoedo*
  Quinct.   *Pro Quinctio*
  Rab. Post.   *Pro Rabirio Postumo*
  Red. pop.   *Post reditum ad populum*
  Red. sen.   *Post reditum in senatu*
  Rep.   *De republica*
  Rosc. Am.   *Pro Sexto Roscio Amerino*
  Scaur.   *Pro Scauro*
  Sen.   *De senectute*
  Sest.   *Pro Sestio*
  Somn.   *Somnium Scipionis*
  Sull.   *Pro Sulla*
  Tog. cand.   *Oratio in senatu in toga candida*
     (fragmentary)
  Top.   *Topica*
  Tusc.   *Tusculanae disputationes*
  Verr.   *In Verrem*
Cicero, *Comment.*   Cicero (Quintus),
  pet.   *Commentariolum petitionis*
Cichorius, *Röm.*   C. Cichorius, *Römische Studien*
  Stud.   (1922; repr. 1961) (cited by
     chapter and section)
CIE   *Corpus Inscriptionum Etruscarum*
     (1893–   )
CIJ   *Corpus Inscriptionum Iudaicarum*,
     ed. J.-B. Frey (1936–52)
CIL   *Corpus Inscriptionum Latinarum*
     (1863–   )
CISem.   *Corpus Inscriptionum Semiticarum*
     (1881–   )
CJ   *Classical Journal*
Cl. Ant.   *Classical Antiquity*
Claud.   Claudianus
  Cons. Hon. Cons.   *De consulatu Honorii De*
  Stil.   *consulatu Stilichonis*
CLE   F. Bücheler and E. Lommatzsch
     (eds.), *Carmina Latina*
     Epigraphica (1895–1926)
Clem. Al.   Clemens Alexandrinus
  Protr.   *Protrepticus*
  Strom.   *Stromateis*
Clinton, *Iconography*   K. Clinton, *Myth and Cult: The*
     Iconography of the Eleusinian
     Mysteries (1992)

Sacred Officials   *The Sacred Officials of the*
     Eleusinian Mysteries (1974)
CMG   *Corpus Medicorum Graecorum*
     (1908–   )
CML   *Corpus Medicorum Latinorum*
     (1915–   )
Coarelli, *Roma*   F. Coarelli, *Guida archeologica*
     Laterza: Roma, 6th edn.
     (1989)
Cod.   Codex
Codd. Lat. Ant.   E. A. Lowe, *Codices Latini*
  (Lowe)   *Antiquiores* (1934–66); Suppl.
     (1971); 2nd edn. of vol. 1
     (1972)
Cod. Iust.   *Codex Iustinianus*
Cod. Theod.   *Codex Theodosianus*
Coll. Alex.   see Powell
Collingwood–   R. G. Collingwood and J. N. L.
  Myres, *Roman*   Myres, *Roman Britain and the*
  Britain   *English Settlements*, 2nd edn.
     (1937; repr. 1963)
Collingwood–   R. G. Collingwood, R. P. Wright,
  Wright, *RIB*   and others, *The Roman In-*
     scriptions of Britain (1965–   )
Columella, *Rust.*   Columella, *De re rustica*
Comm. in Arist.   *Commentaria in Aristotelem Graeca*
  Graeca
Conon, *Narr.*   Conon Mythographus,
     Διηγήσεις
Const.   *Constitutio*
Conway, *Ital. Dial.*   R. S. Conway, *Italic Dialects*
     (1897)
Cook, *Zeus*   A. B. Cook, *Zeus: A Study in*
     Ancient Religion, vol. 1 (1914),
     2 (1925), 3 (1940)
Cornutus, *Theol.*   Cornutus (L. Annaeus),
  Graec.   Ἐπιδρομὴ τῶν κατὰ τὴν
     Ἑλληνικὴν Θεολογίαν
     παραδεδομένων
Corp. poes. ep. Graec.   *Corpusculum poesis epicae Graecae*
  lud.   *ludibundae* 1: *Parodia et*
     Archestratus, P. Brandt (1888);
     2: *Syllographi Graeci*, C.
     Wachsmuth (1885)
C Phil.   *Classical Philology*
Courtney, *FLP*   E. Courtney, *The Fragmentary*
     Latin Poets (1993)
CPL   *Corpus Poetarum Latinorum*
     (1894–1920)
CQ   *Classical Quarterly*
CR   *Classical Review*
CR Acad. Inscr.   *Comptes rendus de l'Académie des*
     Inscriptions et Belles-lettres
Cramer, *Anecd. Par.*   see *Anecd. Par.*
CRF   see Ribbeck
CronASA   *Cronache di archeologia e di storia*
     dell'arte
Cron. Erc.   *Bolletino del Centro*
     internazionale per lo studio dei
     papyri ercolanesi
CSEL   *Corpus Scriptorum Ecclesiasti-*
     corum Latinorum (1866 ff.)

Authors and Books

Cul.	*Culex* (see APPENDIX VERGILIANA)	*DFA*[3]	A. W. Pickard-Cambridge, rev. J. Gould and D. M. Lewis, *Dramatic Festivals of Athens*, 3rd edn. (1988)
Cumont, *Rel. or.*	F. Cumont, *Les Religions orientales dans le paganisme romain*, 4th edn. (1929)		
Curt.	Q. Curtius Rufus	*DHA*	*Dialogues d'histoire ancienne*
CVA	*Corpus Vasorum Antiquorum* (1925–)	*Dial. di Arch.*	*Dialoghi di archeologia*
		Dict. Sci. Biogr.	*Dictionary of Scientific Biography*, ed. C. Gillespie (1970–80)
Cyril. *Adv. Iul.*	Cyrillus, *Adversus Iulianum*		
Dam. *Isid.*	Damascius, *Vita Isidori*	*Dict. Spir.*	*Dictionnaire de spiritualité ascétique et mystique* (1933)
Dar.–Sag.	C. Daremberg and E. Saglio, *Dictionnaire des antiquités grecques et romaines d'après les textes et les monuments* (1877–1919)	*Did. Iul.*	Didius Iulianus, see SHA
		Diehl. *Anth. Lyr. Graec.*	E. Diehl, *Anthologia Lyrica Graeca* (1925; 2nd edn. 1942; 3rd edn. 1949–52)
Davies, *APF*	J. K. Davies, *Athenian Propertied Families 600–300 BC* (1971)	*Poet. Rom. vet.*	*Poetarum Romanorum veterum reliquiae* (1911)
Davies, *EGF*	M. Davies, *Epicorum Graecorum Fragmenta* (1988)	Diels, *Dox. Graec.*	H. Diels, *Doxographi Graeci* (1879)
PMGF	*Poetarum Melicorum Graecorum Fragmenta* (1991)	Diels–Kranz, *Vorsokr.*	see DK
DB	Inscription of Darius I at Bisutun	*Dig.*	*Digesta*
		Din.	Dinarchus
DCB	*Dictionary of Christian Biography and Literature*, ed. H. Wace and W. C. Piercy (1911)	Dio Cass.	Dio Cassius
		Dio Chrys.	Dio Chrysostomus
		Or.	*Orationes*
DCPP	*Dictionnaire de la civilisation phénicienne et punique* (1992)	Diocl. Magn.	Diocles of Magnesia
		Dio Cocc.	Dio Cocceianus; see Dio Chrys.
		Diod. Sic.	Diodorus Siculus
Déchelette, *Manuel*	J. Déchelette, *Manuel d'archéologie préhistorique, celtique et gallo-romaine* (1908–14)	Diogenian.	Diogenianus Paroemiographus
		Diog. Laert.	Diogenes Laertius
		Diom.	Diomedes Grammaticus
De Com.	see Anon. *De Com.*	Dion. Calliphon.	Dionysius Calliphontis filius
Def. tab. Audollent	A. Audollent, *Defixionum Tabellae* (1904)	Dion. Hal.	Dionysius Halicarnassensis
		Ant. Rom.	*Antiquitates Romanae*
Def. tab. Wünsch	R. Wünsch, *Defixionum Tabellae* (= IG 3/3) (1897)	*Comp.*	*De compositione verborum*
		De imit.	*De imitatione*
Degrasi, *ILLRP*	see *ILLRP*	*Dem.*	*De Demosthene*
Délos	*Explorations archéologiques de Délos* (1909–)	*Isoc.*	*De Isocrate*
		Lys.	*De Lysia*
		Pomp.	*Epistula ad Pompeium*
Dem.	Demosthenes	*Rhet.*	*Ars rhetorica*
De cor.	*De corona*	*Thuc.*	*De Thucydide*
Epit.	*Epitaphius*	*Vett. cens.*	*De veterum censura*
Lept.	*Against Leptines*	Dion. Thrax	Dionysius Thrax
Meid.	*Against Meidias*	Dionys. Per.	Dionysius Periegeta
Demetr. *Eloc.*	Demetrius [Phalereus] , *De Elocutione* = Περὶ ἑρμηνείας	*Diss. Pan.*	*Dissertationes Pannonicae* (1932–)
Demiańczuk, *Supp. Com.*	J. Demiańczuk, *Supplementum Comicum* (1912)	Dittenberg. *Syll.*[3]	see *Syll.*[3]
		Diz. Epigr.	see Ruggiero
Democr.	Democritus	DK	H. Diels and W. Kranz, *Fragmente der Vorsokratiker*, 6th edn. (1952)
De Sanctis, *Stor. Rom.*	G. De Sanctis, *Storia dei Romani*, vols. 1–2² (1959–60), 3² (1967–8), 4/1² (1969), 4/2–3 (1953–64)		
		Donat.	Aelius Donatus
		Vit. Verg.	*Vita Vergilii*
Dessau, *ILS*	H. Dessau, *Inscriptiones Latinae Selectae* (1892–1916)	*DOP*	*Dumbarton Oaks Papers*
		Dox. Graec.	see Diels
Deubner, *Attische Feste*	L. Deubner, *Attische Feste* (1932)	*D Serv.*	see *Serv. Dan.*
		DTC	*Dictionnaire de Théologie Catholique*, ed. A. Vacant, E. Mangenot and E. Amann, 15 vols. (1903–50)
Develin, *AO*	R. Develin, *Athenian Officials 684–321 BC* (1989)		
De vir. ill.	*De viris illustribus* (auctor ignotus)		

Duff, *Minor Lat. Poets* — J. W. and A. M. Duff, *Minor Latin Poets* (Loeb, 1935; repr. 1968, 1982)

Dumézil, *ARR* — G. Dumézil, *Archaic Roman Religion* (1987; Fr. orig. 1974)

Dunbabin, *Western Greeks* — T. J. Dunbabin, *The Western Greeks* (1948)

EA — *Epigraphica Anatolica*

EAA — *Enciclopedia dell'arte antica* (1958–)

Edmonds, *FAC* — J. M. Edmonds, *Fragments of Attic Comedy* 3 vols. (1957–61)

EEC — *Encyclopaedia of the Early Church*, 2 vols. (1992)

EGF — G. Kinkel, *Epicorum Graecorum Fragmenta* (1877): in part superseded by Bernabé, *PEG*

EJ — V. Ehrenberg and A. H. M. Jones, *Documents Illustrating the Reigns of Augustus and Tiberius*, 2nd edn. (1976)

Enc. Brit. — *Encyclopaedia Britannica*

Enc. Ir. — *Enciclopedia Iranica*, ed. E. Yar-Shater (1985–)

Enc. Virg. — *Enciclopedia Virgiliana*, 5 vols. (1984–90)

Enn. *Ann.* — Ennius, *Annales*

Entretiens Hardt — Fondation Hardt, *Essais sur l'antiquité classique* (1952–)

Ep. — *Epistula*

Eph. Epigr. — *Ephemeris Epigraphica, Corporis Inscriptionum Latinarum Supplementum* (1872–)

Epicharm. — Epicharmus

Epicurus — Epicurus

  Ep. — *Epistulae*

  Ep. Hdt. — *Epistula ad Herodotum*

  Ep. Men. — *Epistula ad Menoeceum*

  Ep. Pyth. — *Epistula ad Pythoclem*

  Sent. Vat. — *Vatican Sayings*, = *Gnomologium Vaticanum*

  RS — *Ratae sententiae*

Epigr. Gr. — G. Kaibel, *Epigrammata Graeca ex lapidibus conlecta* (1878)

Epiph. Adv. haeres. — Epiphanius, *Adversus haereses*

Epit. — *Epitome*

Epit. de Caes. — *Epitome de Caesaribus* (in Teubner Aur. Vict. *Caes.*, ed. F. Pichlmayer (1911), 133–76)

Epit. Oxyrh. — *Epitome Oxyrhynchica* of Livy

EPRO — *Études préliminaires aux religions orientales dans l'empire romain*

Eratosth. — Eratosthenes

  [*Cat.*] — [Καταστερισμοί]

ERE — see Hastings

Ἔργον — Τὸ Ἔργον τῆς Ἀρχαιολογικῆς Ἑταιρείας

Ét. de Pap. — *Études de papyrologie* (1932–74)

Etym. Magn. — *Etymologicum Magnum*

Euc. — Euclid

Eudem. — Eudemus

Eunap. — Eunapius

  VS — *Vitae sophistarum*

Eup. — Eupolis

Eur. — Euripides

  Alc. — *Alcestis*

  Andr. — *Andromache*

  Bacch. — *Bacchae*

  Beller. — *Bellerophon*

  Cyc. — *Cyclops*

  El. — *Electra*

  Hec. — *Hecuba*

  Hel. — *Helena*

  Heracl. — *Heraclidae*

  HF — *Hercules furens*

  Hipp. — *Hippolytus*

  Hyps. — *Hypsipyle*

  IA — *Iphigenia Aulidensis*

  IT — *Iphigenia Taurica*

  Med. — *Medea*

  Or. — *Orestes*

  Phoen. — *Phoenissae*

  Rhes. — *Rhesus*

  Sthen. — *Stheneboea*

  Supp. — *Supplices*

  Tro. — *Troades*

Euseb. — Eusebius

  Chron. — *Chronica*

  Hist. eccl. — *Historia ecclesiastica*

  Praep. evang. — *Praeparatio evangelica*

  Vit. Const. — *Vita Constantini*

Eust. — Eustathius

  Il. — *Ad Iliadem*

  Od. — *Ad Odysseam*

  Prooem. ad Pind. — *Eustathii prooemium commentariorum Pindaricorum*, ed. F. W. Schneidewin (1837)

Eutocius, *In Arch. circ. dim.* — Eutocius, *In Archimedis circuli dimensionem*

Eutr. — Eutropius

EW — *East and West*

FAC — see Edmonds

Farnell, *Cults* — L. R. Farnell, *The Cults of the Greek States* (1896–1909)

  Hero-Cults — *Greek Hero-Cults and Ideas of Immortality* (1921)

FCG — see Meineke

FCGM — see Olivieri

FD — *Fouilles de Delphes*

Festus, *Gloss. Lat.* — W. M. Lindsay's second edn. of Festus in his *Glossaria Latina*, vol. 4

FGrH — F. Jacoby, *Fragmente der griechischen Historiker* (1923–)

FHG — C. Müller, *Fragmenta Historicorum Graecorum* (1841–70)

FIRA — see Riccobono, *FIRA*

Authors and Books

Firm. Mat. Firmicus Maternus
   Err. prof. rel.   *De errore profanarum religionum*
Fittschen and   K. Fittschen and P. Zanker,
   Zanker   *Katalog der römischen Porträts in den capitolinischen Museen* (1983–)
Fleck J. Suppl. *Fleckeisens Jahrbücher für klassische Philologie*, Suppl. 24 (1898) = *Neue Jahrbücher f. d. klassische Altertum*
Flor. L. Annaeus Florus
FLP see Courtney, *FLP*
FOR *Forma Orbis Romanae. Carte archéologique de la Gaule romaine*, ed. A. Blanchet (1931–)
Forbes, *Stud. Anc.*   R. J. Forbes, *Studies in Ancient Technology*, 9 vols. (1957–64); 2nd edn., 9 vols. (1964–72)
Fornara C. W. Fornara (ed.), *Archaic Times to the End of the Peloponnesian War*, 2nd edn.: *Translated Documents of Greece and Rome* 1 (1983)
FPG F. W. A. Mullach, *Fragmenta Philosophorum Graecorum* (1860–81)
FPL see Morel–Büchner, *FPL*
FPR see Baehr.
Frank, *Econ. Survey* T. Frank (ed.) *An Economic Survey of Ancient Rome*, 5 vols. (1933–40)
Fraser, *Ptol. Alex.* P. M. Fraser, *Ptolemaic Alexandria*, 3 vols. (1972)
Frere, *Britannia* S. S. Frere, *Britannia* (1967; 3rd edn., extensively revised, 1987)
Friedländer, *Rom.* L. Friedländer, *Darstellung aus der Sittengeschichte Roms*[9–10] (1921–3), rev. G. Wissowa[6]; *Roman Life and Manners under the Early Empire*, Eng. trans. from 7th edn. (1908–13)
Frontin. Frontinus
   Aq.   *De aquae ductu urbis Romae*
   Str.   *Strategemata*
Fronto, *Ep.* Fronto, *Epistulae*
Fulg. Fulgentius
   Myth.   *Mitologiae tres libri*
Funaioli, *Gramm.* H. Funaioli, *Grammaticae Romanae fragmenta* (1907), vol. 1 alone published.
FUR *Forma Urbis Romae*, ed. G. Corettoni and others (1960)

G&R *Greece and Rome*, NS (1954/5–)
Gabba–Vallet, E. Gabba and G. Vallet (eds.),
   Sicilia antica   *La Sicilia antica*, 2 vols. in 5 (1980)

GAC R. Hope Simpson and O. Dickinson, *Gazetteer of Aegean Civilisation in the Bronze Age* 1: *The Mainland and Islands* (1979)
Gai. Inst. Gaius, *Institutiones*
Gal. Galen
   De loc. aff.   *De locis affectis*
   Libr. Propr.   Περὶ τῶν ἰδίων βιβλίων
   Nat. Fac.   Περὶ φυσικῶν δυνάμεων
GB *Grazer Beiträge: Zeitschrift für klassische Altertumswissenschaft*
GCS *Die griechischen christlichen Schriftsteller der ersten Jahrhunderte* (1897–)
GDI H. Collitz and others, *Sammlung der griechischen Dialektinschriften* (1884–1915)
Gell. Aulus Gellius
   NA   *Noctes Atticae*
German. Germanicus
   Arat.   *Aratea*
Gesch. *Geschichte*
GGM C. Müller, *Geographici Graeci Minores* (1855–61)
GJ *Geographical Journal*
Gjerstad, *Early* E. Gjerstad, *Early Rome*, 6 vols.
   Rome   (1953–73)
Gloss. Lat. see Lindsay
Glotz, *Hist. grecque* G. Glotz, R. Cohen, and P. Roussel, *Histoire grecque* vols. 1–4/1 (1925–38)
GLP see Page, *GLP*
Gnomon *Gnomon, Kritische Zeitschrift für d. gesamte klassische Altertumswiss.*
Gomperz T. Gomperz, *Griechische Denker* (1896); Eng. trans. ('Greek Thinkers'), vols. 1–4 (1901–12)
Gorg. Gorgias
   Hel.   *Helena*
   Pal.   *Palamedes*
Gött. Anz. *Göttingischer gelehrte Anzeigen*
Gött. Nachr. *Nachrichten von der Gesellschaft der Wissenschaften zu Göttingen*
Gow–Page, *GP* A. S. F. Gow and D. L. Page, *The Greek Anthology: Garland of Philip and some Contemporary Epigrams*, 2 vols. (1968)
Gow–Page, *HE* A. S. F. Gow and D. L. Page, *The Greek Anthology: Hellenistic Epigrams*, 2 vols. (1965)
Graf, *Eleusis* F. Graf, *Eleusis und die orphische Dichtung: Athens in vorhellenistischer Zeit* (1974)
Gramm. Lat. see Keil
Gramm. Rom. Frag. see Funaioli; Mazzarino
GRBS *Greek, Roman and Byzantine Studies*
Green R. P. H. Green, *The Works of Ausonius* (1991)

Greenidge, Clay, Gray, *Sources* — A. H. J. Greenidge, A. M. Clay, and E. W. Gray, *Sources for Roman History, 133–70 BC* (1960; 2nd edn., corrected and supplemented, 1986)

Gregory of Tours *Hist.* — Gregory of Tours *Historiae*

Glor. mart. — *Gloria martyrorum*

Grenier, *Manuel* — A. Grenier, *Manuel d'archéologie gallo-romaine* (1931–4); = vol. of Déchelette's *Manuel d'archéologie préhistorique*

Gruen, *LGRR* — E. S. Gruen, *The Last Generation of the Roman Republic* (1974)

Guthrie, *Hist. Gk. Phil.* — W. K. C. Guthrie, *History of Greek Philosophy* (1965–81)

GVI — W. Peek, *Griechische Vers-Inschriften* 1: *Grab-Epigramme* (1955)

Hainsworth, *Iliad* comm. — B. Hainsworth, *The Iliad: A Commentary* 3: *Books 9–12* (1993)

Hainsworth, *Odyssey* comm. — A. Heubeck, S. West, and J. B. Hainsworth, *A Commentary on Homer's Odyssey* 1: *Introduction and Books 1–8* (1988)

Halm, *Rhet. Lat. Min.* — K. Halm, *Rhetores Latini Minores* (1863)

HAMA — O. Neugebauer, *A History of Ancient Mathematical Astronomy*, 3 vols. (1975)

Hammond, *Epirus* — N. G. L. Hammond, *Epirus* (1967)

Hist. G. — *History of Greece* (2nd edn. 1967; 3rd edn. 1986)

Hansen, *Attalids* — C. V. Hansen, *The Attalids of Pergamum* (1947)

Harding — P. Harding, *From the End of the Peloponnesian War to the Battle of Ipsus: Translated Documents of Greece and Rome* 2 (1985)

Harp. — Harpocration

Harv. Stud. — *Harvard Studies in Classical Philology*

Harv. Theol. Rev. — *Harvard Theological Review*

Hastings, *ERE* — J. Hastings, *Encyclopaedia of Religion and Ethics*, 12 vols. (1908–21); index vol. (1926)

HCT — A. W. Gomme, A. Andrewes, and K. J. Dover, *A Historical Commentary on Thucydides*, 5 vols. (1945–81)

Hdn. — Herodianus

Hdt. — Herodotus

Head, *Hist. Num.* — B. V. Head, *Historia Numorum*, 2nd edn. (1911)

Heath, *Hist. of Greek Maths.* — T. L. Heath, *History of Greek Mathematics*, 2 vols. (1921)

Heckel, *Marshals* — W. Heckel, *The Marshals of Alexander's Empire* (1992)

Heitsch, *Griech. Dichterfr.* — E. Heitsch (ed.), *Die griechischen Dichterfragmente der römischen Kaiserzeit* 1, *Abh. der Akad. der Wissenschaften in Göttingen, phil.-hist. Kl.* 3. Folge, 49 (1961; ²1963), 58 (1964)

Heliod. *Aeth.* — Heliodorus, *Aethiopica*

Hell. Oxy. — *Hellenica Oxyrhynchia*

Heph. — Hephaestion

Heraclid. Pont. — Heraclides Ponticus

Hercher, *Epistolog. Graec.* — R. Hercher, *Epistolographi Graeci* (1873)

Hermes — *Hermes, Zeitschrift für klassische Philologie*

Hermog. — Hermogenes

Id. — Περὶ ἰδεῶν

Inv. — Περὶ εὑρέσεως

Prog. — Προγυμνάσματα

Herod. — Herodas

Heron, *Pneum.* — Heron, *Pneumatica*

Herzog–Schmidt — R. Herzog and P. Schmidt, *Handbuch der lateinischen Literatur der Antike* (1989–)

Hes. — Hesiod

Cat. — *Catalogus mulierum*

Op. — *Opera et Dies*

[Sc.] — *Scutum*

Theog. — *Theogonia*

Hesp. — *Hesperia: Journal of the American School of Classical Studies at Athens*

Hieron. — Hieronymus, see Jerome

Hignett, *Hist. Athen. Const.* — C. Hignett, *A History of the Athenian Constitution* (1952)

Himer. *Ecl.* — Himerius, *Eclogae*

Or. — *Orationes*

Hippoc. — Hippocrates

Acut. — *De diaeta in morbis acutis*

Aer. — *De aera, aquis, locis*

Art. — *De articulis*

[Ep.] — *Epistulae*

Epid. — *Epidemiae*

Morb. — Περὶ νούσων (On Diseases)

Morb. sacr. — *De morbo sacro*

Mul. — *De mulierum affectibus*

Nat. mul. — *De natura muliebri*

Nat. puer. — Περὶ φύσιος παιδίου (On the Nature of the Child)

Off. — *De officina medici*

Virg. — *De virginibus morbis*

VM — *De vetere medicina*

Hippol. — Hippolytus

Haer. — *Refutatio omnium haeresium*

Hist. — *Historia*

Hist. Aug. — *Historia Augusta* (see SHA)

HLL — see Herzog–Schmidt; see also Schanz–Hosius

HM — *History of Macedonia* 1, ed. N. G. L. Hammond (1972); 2, ed. N. G. L. Hammond and G. T. Griffith (1979); 3, ed. N. G. L. Hammond and F. W. Walbank (1988)

Authors and Books

Hom.	Homer	IK	Inschriften griechischer Städte aus
Il.	Iliad		Kleinasien (1972–)
Od.	Odyssey	ILabraunda	J. Crampa (ed.), Labraunda
Hom. Hymn Dem.	Homeric Hymn to Demeter		Swedish Excavations and
Homil. Clement.	Clementine Homilies		Researches 3 (1 and 2): The
Honoré 1962	A. M. Honoré, Gaius: A Biography		Greek Inscriptions (1969 and
	(1962)		1972)
Honoré 1981	T. Honoré, Emperors and Lawyers	ILAlg.	Inscriptions latines de l'Algérie 1,
	(1981; 2nd edn. 1994)		ed. S. Gsell (1922); 2, ed. H.-G.
Hor.	Horace		Pflaum (1957)
Ars P.	Ars poetica	Il.	Iliad
Carm.	Carmina or Odes	I. l. de Gaule	Inscriptions latines des trois
Carm. saec.	Carmen saeculare		Gaules, ed. P. Wuilleumier
Epist.	Epistulae		(1963)
Epod.	Epodi	ILLRP	Inscriptiones Latinae Liberae Rei
Sat.	Satirae or Sermones		Republicae, ed. A. Degrassi,
Hornblower,	S. Hornblower, Commentary on		vol. 1^2 (1965), 2 (1963)
Comm. on Thuc.	Thucydides 1: Books 1–3 (1991);	ILN	Illustrated London News
	2: Books 4–5.24 (1996)	ILS	see Dessau
HR	History of Religions	IMagn.	O. Kern (ed.), Die Inschriften
HRRel.	see under Peter		von Magnesia am Maeander
Hsch.	Hesychius		(1900)
Hyde, Greek	W. Hyde, Ancient Greek Mariners	IMU	Italia medioevale e umanistica
Mariners	(1947)	IMylasa	W. Blümel, Die Inschriften von
Hyg.	Hyginus		Mylasa (2 vols., 1987–8)
Fab.	Fabulae.	Indo-Germ. Forsch.	Indogermanische Forschungen
Poet. astr.	Poetica astronomica	Ind. Stoic. Herc.	J. Traversa, Index Stoicorum
Hymn. Hom. Ap.	Hymnus Homericus ad Apollinem		Herculanensis (1952)
Bacch.	„ „ „ Bacchum	Inscr. Ital.	Inscriptiones Italiae (1931/2–)
Cer.	„ „ „ Cererem	Inst. Iust.	Institutiones Iustiniani
Mart.	„ „ „ Martem	IPE	Inscriptiones orae septentrionalis
Merc.	„ „ „ Mercurium		Ponti Euxini (1885)
Pan.	„ „ „ Panem	IrAnt	Iranica Antiqua
Ven.	„ „ „ Venerem	Iron Age in S. Britain	S. S. Frere (ed.), Problems of the
Hymn. Mag.	Hymni Magici		Iron Age in Southern Britain
Hymn. Orph.	Hymni Orphici	Isae.	Isaeus
Hyp.	Hyperides	ISestos	J. Krauss, Die Inschriften von Sestos
Lyc.	For Lycophron		und der Thrakischen Chersones
			(1980)
Iambl.	Iamblichus	Isid.	Isidorus
Myst.	De mysteriis	De vir. ill.	De viris illustribus
VP	Vita Pythagorae	Etym.	Etymologiae
IBR	D. and F. R. Ridgway (eds.),	Isoc.	Isocrates
	Italy before the Romans	Bus.	Busiris
	(1979)	Antid.	Antidosis
Ibyc.	Ibycus	C. soph.	Contra sophistas
IC	M. Guarducci (ed.) Inscriptiones	Panath.	Panathenaicus
	Creticae, 4 vols. (1935–50)	Paneg.	Panegyricus
ICS	Illinois Classical Studies	Ist. Mitt.	Istanbuler Mitteilungen
IDélos	F. Dürrbach (ed.), Inscriptions de	It. Alex.	Itinerarium Alexandri
	Délos (1923–37)	It. Ant.	Itineraria Antonini Augusti
IDidyma	A. Rehm, Die Inschriften. Milet 3	IVO	Inschriften von Olympia, ed. W.
	(1914)		Dittenberger and K. Purgold
IE	Indo-European		(1896)
IEJ	Israel Exploration Journal		
IG	Inscriptiones Graecae (1873–)	JACT	Joint Association of Classical
IGBulg.	G. Mihailov, Inscriptiones		Teachers
	Graecae in Bulgaria repertae	Jahrb.	see [Neue] Jahrb.
	(1958–70)	Jahrb. f. cl. Phil.	Jahrbücher für classische Philologie,
IGRom.	Inscriptiones Graecae ad res	Suppl.	Supplementband
	Romanas pertinentes	Jahresb.	see Bursian
	(1906–)	JCS	Journal of Classical Studies

JDAI — *Jahrbuch des [kaiserlich] deutschen archäologischen Instituts* (1886–) (contains *Archäologischer Anzeiger*)

Jeffery, *LSAG* — L. Jeffery, *Local Scripts of Archaic Greece,* 2nd edn., rev. A. Johnston (1990)

JEg. Arch. — *Journal of Egyptian Archaeology*

Jer. — Jerome

  Ab Abr. — *Ab Abraham*, the chronological reckoning from the first year of Abraham followed in Jerome's translation and enlargement of Eusebius' Chronicle

  Adv. Iovinian. — *Adversus Iovinianum*

  Chron. — *Chronica = Ab Abr.*

  De script. eccles. proleg. — *De scriptoribus ecclesiasticis prolegomena*

  De vir. ill. — *De viris illustribus*

  Ep. — *Epistulae*

JHS — *Journal of Hellenic Studies*

JJP — *Journal of Juristic Papyrology*

JNES — *Journal of Near Eastern Studies*

JÖAI — *Jahreshefte des österreichischen archäologischen Instituts in Wien*

JÖB — *Jahrbuch des österreichischen Byzantinistik* (1951–)

Jones, *Cities E. Rom.* — A. H. M. Jones, *The Cities of the*

  Prov. — *Eastern Roman Provinces* (1937; 2nd edn. 1971)

  Later Rom. Emp. — *The Later Roman Empire 284–602* (1964)

Jord. Get. — Jordanes, *Getica*

Joseph — Josephus

  AJ — *Antiquitates Judaicae*

  Ap. — *Contra Apionem*

  BJ — *Bellum Judaicum*

  Vit. — *Vita*

Journ. Bib. Lit. — *Journal of Biblical Literature*

Journ. Hist. Bio. — *Journal of the History of Biology*

Journ. Hist. Med. — *Journal of the History of Medicine and Allied Sciences*

Journ. Phil. — *Journal of Philology* (1868–1920); index (1923)

Journ. Sav. — *Journal des savants,* NS (1903–)

JRA — *Journal of Roman Archaeology*

JRGZM — *Jahrbuch des römisch-germanischen Zentralmuseums*

JRS — *Journal of Roman Studies*

JSGU — *Jahrbuch der schweizerischen Gesellschaft für Ur- und Frühgeschichte*

JTS — *Journal of Theological Studies*

Julian. — Julianus imperator

  Apophth. — *Apophthegmata*

  Ep. — *Epistulae* (ps.-Julian. = *Ep.* wrongly attributed to Julian)

  Mis. — *Misopogon*

  Or. — *Orationes*

Just. *Epit.* — Justinus, *Epitome* (of Trogus)

Justin, *Apol.* — Justin Martyr, *Apologia*

Juv. — Juvenal

JWI — *Journal of the Warburg and Courtauld Institute*

κ — κατά

KA — see Kassel–Austin

Kaibel — see *CGF* and *Epigr. Gr.*

Kassel–Austin, *PCG* — R. Kassel and C. Austin, *Poetae Comici Graeci*, vol. 1 (1983), 2 (1991)

Kaster, *Guardians* — R. A. Kaster, *Guardians of Language: The Grammarian and Society in Late Antiquity* (1988)

Kearns, *Heroes of Attica* — E. Kearns, *The Heroes of Attica, BICS* Suppl. 57 (1989)

Keil, *Gramm. Lat.* — H. Keil, *Grammatici Latini*, 8 vols. (1855–1923; repr. 1961)

Kern — O. Kern

  Orph. frag. — *Orphica Fragmenta* (1922)

  Rel. d. Griech. — *Die Religion der Griechen*, 3 vols. (1926–38)

Kirk–Raven–Schofield, *Presocratic Philosophers* — G. S. Kirk, J. E. Raven, and M. Schofield, *The Presocratic Philosophers*, 2nd edn. (1983)

Klass. phil. Stud. — *Klassische philologische Studien,* ed. E. Bickel and C. Jensen

Klio — *Klio, Beiträge zur alten Geschichte*

Klotz, *Scaen. Rom. Frag.* — A. Klotz (ed.), *Scaenicorum Romanorum Fragmenta* (1953)

Kl. Pauly — *Der kleine Pauly* (1964–75)

Kl. Schr. — *Kleine Schriften* (of various authors)

Körte, *Men. Rel.* — A. Körte, *Menandri Reliquiae*

Kroll, *Rhet.* — W. Kroll, *Rhetorik* (1937): written as article for *RE*, but published separately

Kron, *Phylenheroen* — U. Kron, *Die zehn attischen Phylenheroen: MDAI(A)* Suppl. 5 (1976)

Kühn — K. G. Kühn, *Medicorum Graecorum Opera*

Kunkel 1967 — W. Kunkel, *Herkunft und soziale Stellung der römischen Juristen,* 2nd edn. (1967)

Lactant. — Lactantius

  De mort. pers. — *De mortibus persecutorum*

  Div. inst. — *Divinae institutiones*

LACTOR — London Association of Classical Teachers Original Records

Lambrechts, *Sénat* — P. Lambrechts, *La Composition du Sénat romain 117–192* (1936)

Latte, *RR* — K. Latte, *Römische Religionsgeschichte* (1960)

Laur. — Laurentian Library

LCM — *Liverpool Classical Monthly*

LdÄ — W. Helck, E. Otto, and W. Westendorf (eds.), *Lexicon der Ägyptologie* (1975–86)

Authors and Books

LEC — Les Études classiques

Leipz. Stud. — Leipziger Studien zur klassischen Philosophie (1878–95)

Lenel, Pal. — O. Lenel, Palingenesia Iuris Civilis, 2 vols. (1889)

Lex. — Lexicon

Lexikon der historischen Stätten — S. Lauffer (ed.), Lexikon der historischen Stätten von den Anfängen bis zur Gegenwart (1989)

Lex. Mess. — Lexicon Messanense

LGPN 1 — P. M. Fraser and E. Matthews (eds.), A Lexicon of Greek Personal Names 1 (1987)

LGPN 2 — M. Osborne and S. Byrne (eds.), A Lexicon of Greek Personal Names 2 (1994)

LH Citadels — S. Iakovidis, Late Helladic Citadels on Mainland Greece (1983)

Lib. — Libanius

Lib. colon. — Libri coloniarum

Liebs 1987 — D. Liebs, Die Jurisprudenz im spätantiken Italien (1987)

LIMC — Lexicon Iconographicum Mythologiae Classicae (1981–)

Lindsay, Gloss. Lat. — W. M. Lindsay, Glossaria Latina (1930)

Lind. Temp. Chron. — C. Blinkenberg, Die lindische Tempelchronik (1915)

Lintott, Violence — A. W. Lintott, Violence in Republican Rome (1968)

Lippold, Griech. Plastik — G. Lippold, Die griechische Plastik (Handbuch der Archäologie, 1950): in part superseded by J. Floren, Die griechische Plastik 1 (1987)

Liv. Andron. Od. — Livius Andronicus, Odyssia

Livy, Epit. — Livy, Epitomae
Per. — Periochae

Lobeck, Aglaoph. — C. A. Lobeck, Aglaophamus (1829)

Loeb — Loeb Classical Library

[Longinus], Subl. — [Longinus], Περὶ ὕψους

LP — E. Lobel and D. L. Page, Poetarum Lesbiorum Fragmenta (1955)

LSAG — See Jeffery, LSAG

LSAM — F. Sokolowski, Lois sacrées de l'Asie Mineure (1955)

LSCG — F. Sokolowski, Lois sacrées des cités grecques (1969)

LSJ — Liddell and Scott, Greek–English Lexicon, 9th edn., rev. H. Stuart Jones (1925–40); Suppl. by E. A. Barber and others (1968)

LSS — F. Sokolowski, Lois sacrées des cités grecques: Supplément (1962)

Luc. — Lucan

Lucian
Alex. — Alexander
Anach. — Anacharsis
Cal. — Calumniae non temere credendum
Catapl. — Cataplus
Demon. — Demonax
De mort. Peregr. — De morte peregrini
Dial. D. — Dialogi deorum
Dial. meret. — Dialogi meretricii
Dial. mort. — Dialogi mortuorum
Her. — Herodotus
Hermot. — Hermotimus
Hist. conscr. — Quomodo historia conscribenda sit
Ind. — Adversus indoctum
Iupp. trag. — Iuppiter tragoedus
Luct. — De luctu
Macr. — Macrobii
Nigr. — Nigrinus
Philops. — Philopseudes
Pseudol. — Pseudologista
Salt. — De saltatione
Somn. — Somnium
Symp. — Symposium
Syr. D. — De Syria dea
Trag. — Tragoedopodagra
Ver. hist. — Verae historiae, 1, 2
Vit. auct. — Vitarum auctio

Lucil. — Lucilius

Lucr. — Lucretius

Lugli, Fontes — G. Lugli, Fontes ad Topographiam Veteris Urbis Romanae Pertinentes, vols. 1–4 (1953–62) 8, 6/2 (1969)

LXX — Septuagint

Lycoph. — Lycophron
Alex. — Alexandra

Lycurg. — Lycurgus
Leoc. — Against Leocrates

Lydus, Mens. — Lydus, De mensibus
Mag. — De magistratibus

Lys. — Lysias

MAAR — Memoirs of the American Academy in Rome

Macrob. — Macrobius
In Somn. — Commentarius ex Cicerone in Somnium Scipionis
Sat. — Saturnalia

Magie, Rom. Rule Asia Min. — D. Magie, Roman Rule in Asia Minor

Malcovati, ORF — H. Malcovati, Oratorum Romanorum Fragmenta (2nd edn. 1955; 4th edn. 1967)

MAMA — Monumenta Asiae Minoris Antiquae (1928–)

Manitius — M. Manitius, Gesch. der lat. Lit. des Mittelalters (1911–23)

Marcellin. — Marcellinus

Marm. Par. — Marmor Parium (IG 12 (5), 444)

Marquardt	J. Marquardt	Men. Rhet.	Menander Rhetor
Privatleben	*Privatleben der Römer*, 2nd edn. besorgt von A. Mau, 2 vols. (1886). These together make up vol. 7 of *Handbuch der römischen Altertümer*, by J. Marquardt and T. Mommsen	Mette	H. J. Mette, *Urkunden dramatischer Aufführungen in Griechenland*, Texte und Kommentare no. 8 (1977)
		Meyer, *Forschungen*	Meyer (ed.), *Forschungen zur alten Geschichte* (1892–9)
		MGH	*Monumenta Germaniae Historica*, 15 vols. (1877–1919; repr. 1961)
Staatsverw.	*Römische Staatsverwaltung*, 2nd edn. (1881–5)		
Marshall, *Asconius Comm.*	B. A. Marshall, *A Historical Commentary on Asconius* (1985)	*AA*	*Auctores Antiquissimi*
		Ep.	Epistulae
		MGR	*Miscellanea greca e romana*
Mart.	Martial	*MH*	*Museum Helveticum*
Spect.	*Spectacula*	Michel	C. Michel, *Recueil d'inscriptions grecques* (1900–27)
Mart. Cap.	Martianus Capella		
Marx	F. Marx, *C. Lucilii Carminum Reliquiae* (1904–5)	*Michell, Econom. Anc. Gr.*	H. Michell, *The Economics of Ancient Greece*, 2nd edn., (1957)
Mattingly–Sydenham, *RIC*	H. Mattingly, E. A. Sydenham, and others *Roman Imperial Coinage* (1923–67); rev. edn. of vol. 1 only, C.H.V. Sutherland and R.A.G. Carson (1984)	*MIFAO*	*Mémoires de l'Institut français d'archéologie orientale*
		Migne, *PG*	Migne, *Patrologiae Cursus, series Graeca*
		PL	*Patrologiae Cursus, series Latina*
M. Aur. *Med.*	Marcus Aurelius, *Meditations*		
Mazard	J. Mazard, *Corpus Nummorum Numidiae Mauretaniaeque* (1955)	Milet.	T. Wiegand (ed.), *Melet: Ergebnisse der Ausgrabungen und Untersuchungen seit dem Jahre 1899* (1966–)
Mazzarino, *Gramm. Rom. Frag.*	A. Mazzarino, *Grammaticae Romanae Fragmenta Aetatis Caesarianae*, 2nd edn. (1955)	Millar, *ERW*	F. Millar, *The Emperor in the Roman World* (1977; 2nd edn. 1992)
MD	*Materiali e Discussioni*	Min. Fel.	Minucius Felix
MDAI	*Mitteilungen des deutschen archäologischen Instituts (A): Athenische Abteilung (1876–) (B): Baghdadische Abteilung (I): Istanbulische Abteilung (K): Kairoische Abteilung (R): Römische Abteilung (1886–)*	*Oct.*	*Octavius*
		Mir. ausc.	*De mirabilibus auscultationibus* (auctor ignotus)
		Mitteis, *Chr.*	L. Mitteis and U. Wilcken, *Grundzüge und Chrestomathie der Papyruskunde* (1912)
		ML	R. Meiggs and D. Lewis, *A Selection of Greek Historical Inscriptions to the End of the Fifth Century BC*, rev. edn. (1988)
MÉFRA	*Mélanges d'archéologie et d'histoire de l'École française de Rome*		
Meiggs, *AE*	R. Meiggs, *The Athenian Empire* (1972)	*MME*	W. MacDonald and G. Rapp, *The Minnesota Messenia Expedition* (1972)
Meineke, *FCG*	A. Meineke, *Fragmenta Comicorum Graecorum* (1839–57)	*MMR*	see Broughton, *MMR*
		Mnemos.	*Mnemosyne* (1852–)
Mél. Masp.	*Mélanges Maspéro* (1934–7)	*MNIR*	*Mededelingen van het Nederlandsch historisch Instituut te Rome*
Mel. *Steph.*	Meleager, *Stephanus*		
Mem. dei Lincei	*Memorie: Atti della Academia Nazionale dei Lincei, Classe di scienze morali, storiche e filogiche*	Momigliano, *Secondo contributo*	A. Momigliano, *Secondo contributo alla storia degli studi classici* (1960)
		Terzo contributo	*Terzo contributo alla storia degli studi classici* (1966)
Men.	Menander	*Quarto contributo*	*Quarto contributo alla storia degli studi classici* (1969)
Dys.	*Dyskolos*		
Epit.	*Epitrepontes*	*Quinto contributo*	*Quinto contributo alla storia degli studi classici* (1975)
Her.	*Hērōs*		
Pk.	*Perikeiromenē*	*Sesto contributo*	*Sesto contributo alla storia degli studi classici* (1980)
Sam.	*Samia*		

Authors and Books

Mommsen   T. Mommsen
  Ges. Schr.   *Gesammelte Schriften*, 8 vols. (1905–13)
  Röm. Forsch.   *Römische Forschungen*, 2 vols. (1 in 2nd edn.) (1864–79)
  Röm. Staatsr.   *Römisches Staatsrecht*, vols. 1³, 2³ (1887), (1888)
  Röm. Strafr.   *Römisches Strafrecht* (1899); *Stellenregister*, ed. J. Malitz (1982)
Mommsen–Marquardt, *Manuel*   *Manuel des antiquités romaines* (1887–1907): a Fr. trans. of Mommsen's *Römisches Staatsrecht*
Mon. Anc.   *Monumentum Ancyranum*
Mon. Ant.   *Monumenti Antichi pubblicati per cura della Reale Accademia dei Lincei*
Mon. Piot   *Monuments Piot*
Morel–Büchner, *FPL*   *Fragmenta Poetarum Latinorum epicorum et lyricorum praeter Ennium et Lucilium*, 1st edn., ed. W. Morel (1927); 2nd edn., ed. C. Büchner (1982)
Mosch. Ep. Bion.   Moschus, *Epitaphios Bionis*
MRR   see Broughton
Münzer, *Röm. Adelsparteien*   F. Münzer, *Römische Adelsparteien und Adelsfamilien* (1920)
Musa Tragica   B. Gauly, L. Käppel, and others (eds.), *Musa Tragica: Die griechische Tragödie von Thespis bis Ezechiel* (1991)
Mus. Belge   *Musée Belge*
Muson.   Musonius Rufus
MW   M. McCrum and A. G. Woodhead, *Select Documents of the Principates of the Flavian Emperors* (1961)
M–W   R. Merkelbach and M. L. West, *Fragmenta Hesiodea* (1967)
Myth. Vat.   *Mythographi Vaticani*, ed. Bode (1834)

Nachr. Ges. d. Wiss. Gött.   see *Gött. Nachr.*
Naev. fr. com.   Naevius, *fragmenta comoediarum*
Nash, *Pict. Dict. Rome*   E. Nash, *Pictorial Dictionary of Ancient Rome* (1961–2; 2nd edn. 1989)
Nauck   see *TGF*
Nauck/Snell   see *TGF*
Nemes.   Nemesianus
  Cyn.   *Cynegetica*
  Ecl.   *Eclogae*
Nep.   Nepos
  Att.   *Atticus*
  Epam.   *Epaminondas*
  Milt.   *Miltiades*
  Timoth.   *Timotheus*
[Neue] Jahrb.   (1) *[Neue] Jahrbücher für Philologie und Pädagogik* (1826–97)
[Neue] Jahrb.   (2) *Neue Jahrbücher für d. klassische Altertum* (1898–1925)
   (3) *Neue Jahrbücher für Wissenschaft und Jugendbildung*, (1925–36)
   ((1), (2), and (3) form a continuous series)
Nic.   Nicander
  Alex.   *Alexipharmaca*
  Ther.   *Theriaca*
Nic. Dam.   Nicolaus Damascenus
Nicolet, *OE*   C. Nicolet, *L'Ordre équestre* (1974)
Nilsson, *Feste*   M. P. Nilsson, *Griechische Feste v. religiöser Bedeutung m. Ausschluss d. attischen* (1906)
  GGR   *Geschichte der griechischen Religion*, vol. 1² (1955), 1³ (1967), 2² (1961)
  MMR   *The Minoan-Mycenaean Religion and its Survival in Greek Religion*, 2nd edn. (1950)
Non.   Nonius
Nonnus, *Dion.*   Nonnus, *Dionysiaca*
Norden, *Ant. Kunstpr.*   E. Norden, *Die antike Kunstprosa, vom 6. Jahrh. v. Chr. bis in d. Zeit d. Renaissance* (1898, repr. with supplements 1909; 3rd edn. 1915)
Not. Dign. [*occ.*] [*or.*]   *Notitia dignitatum in partibus occidentis/orientis*
Not. Scav.   *Notizie degli scavi di antichità* (1876–)
Nov.   *Novellae*
Nov. Theod   *Novellae Theodosianae*
NPNF   *Nicene and Post-Nicene Fathers*
Num. Chron.   *Numismatic Chronicle* (1861–)
Numen.   Numenius
NZ   *Numismatische Zeitschrift*
*OCD*¹   M. Cary and others (eds.), *The Oxford Classical Dictionary*, 1st edn. (1949)
*OCD*²   N. G. L. Hammond and H. H. Scullard (eds.), *The Oxford Classical Dictionary*, 2nd edn. (1970)
OCT   Oxford Classical Texts
Od.   *Odyssey*
ODB   *Oxford Dictionary of Byzantium* (1991)
ODCC   *Oxford Dictionary of the Christian Church*, ed. F. L. Cross and E. Livingstone, 2nd edn. (1974)
OGI   *Orientis Graeci Inscriptiones Selectae*
Ogilvie, *Comm. Livy 1–5*   R. M. Ogilvie, *Commentary on Livy, Books 1–5* (1965)
OJA   *Oxford Journal of Archaeology*
'Old Oligarch'   see Xen. for *Ath. Pol.* attributed to Xenophon (see entry OLD OLIGARCH)

xliv

Oliver | J. Oliver, *Greek Constitutions of Early Roman Emperors* (1989)

Olivieri, *FCGM* | A. Olivieri, *Frammenti della commedia greca e del mimo nella Sicilia e nella Magna Grecia*, 2nd edn. (1946–7)

OMS | see Robert, *OMS*

Op. Arch. | *Opuscula Archaeologica* (1935–52)

Op. Ath. | *Opuscula Atheniensia* (1953–   )

Or. | *Oratio*

ORF and *ORF*⁴ | see Malcovati, *ORF*

Origen, *C. Cels.* | Origen, *Contra Celsum*

Oros. | Orosius

Orph. | Orphica

   frs. | see Kern

   Lith. | *Lithica*

Ostwald, *Popular Sovereignty* | M. Ostwald, *From Popular Sovereignty to the Sovereignty of Law* (1986)

Ov. | Ovid

   Am. | *Amores*

   Ars am. | *Ars amatoria*

   Fast. | *Fasti*

   Hal. | *Halieuticon liber*

   Her. | *Heroides*

   Ib. | *Ibis*

   Medic. | *Medicamina faciei*

   Met. | *Metamorphoses*

   Pont. | *Epistulae ex Ponto*

   Rem. am. | *Remedia amoris*

   Tr. | *Tristia*

Overbeck | J. Overbeck, *Die antiken Schriftquellen zur Geschichte d. bildenden Künste bei den Griechen* (1868)

P&P | *Past and Present*

π | περί

PA | J. Kirchner, *Prosopographia Attica* (1901–3)

PACA | *Proceedings of the African Classical Associations*

ΠΑΕ | *Πρακτικά τῆς ἐν Ἀθήναις Ἀρχαιολογικῆς Ἐταιρείας*

Page, *FGE* | D. L. Page, *Further Greek Epigrams* (1981)

   GLP | *Greek Literary Papyri* (Loeb, 1942)

   PMG | *Poetae Melici Graeci* (1962)

   SLG | *Supplementum lyricis graecis* (1974)

P Amh. | *Amherst Papyri* (1900–1)

Pan. Lat. | *XII Panegyrici Latini*

P Antin | The *Antinoe Papyrus* of Theocritus

P Antinoop. | *Antinoopolis Papyri* (1950–67)

Parker, *ARH* | R. Parker, *Athenian Religion: A History* (1996)

   Miasma | *Miasma: Pollution and Purification in Early Greek Religion* (1983)

Parker, *Roman Legions* | H. M. D. Parker, *The Roman Legions*, 2nd edn. (1958)

Parod. Epic. Gr. Rel. | *Parodorum Epicorum Graecorum reliquiae*, vol. 1 of *Corpusculum Poesis Epicae Graecae Ludibundae*, P. Brandt and C. Wachsmuth (1888)

Paroemiogr. | *Corpus Paroemiographorum Graecorum*, ed. E. L. Leutsch and P. G. Schneidewin (1839)

Parth. | Parthenius

   Amat. narr. | *Narrationum amatoriarum libellus* (Ἐρωτικὰ παθήματα)

Paul. Fest. | see Festus, *Gloss. Lat.*

Paulus, *Sent.* | Iulius Paulus, *Sententiae*

Paus. | Pausanias

PB | P. Poralla and A. S. Bradford, *A Prosopography of Lacedaemonians from the Earliest Times to the Death of Alexander the Great*, 2nd edn. (1985; Ger. orig. 1913)

PBA | *Proceedings of the British Academy*

P Berol. | Berlin Papyri

PBrem. | *Die Bremer Papyri*, ed. U. Wilcken (1936; repr. 1970)

PBrux. | *Papyri bruxellenses graeci* 1: *Papyrus du nome Prosopite, Nos. 1–21*, by G. Nachtergael (1984); 2: *No. 22*, by M. Huys (1991). For *PBrux.* 7616 see C. Préaux and M. Hombert, *Recherches sur le recensement dans l'Égypte romaine*, *Papyrologica Lugduno-Batava* 5 (1952)

PBSR | *Papers of the British School at Rome*

P. Cairo Zeno | C. C. Edgar, *Zenon Papyri*, 4 vols. (1925–31)

PCG | see Kassel–Austin

PCharite | *Das Aurelia Charite Archiv*, ed. K. Worp (1980)

PCIA | *Popoli e civiltà dell'Italia antica* 4 vols. (1974–89)

PColon. | *Kölner Papyri* (1976–   )

PCPS | *Proceedings of the Cambridge Philological Society*

PDiog. | *Les Archives de Marcus Lucretius Diogenes et textes apparentés*, ed. P. Schubert (1990)

PDura | *The Excavations at Dura-Europos conducted by Yale University and the French Academy of Inscriptions and Letters* Final Report 5 pt. 1: *The Parchments and Papyri*, ed. C. B. Welles and others (1959)

Pearson, *Lost Histories of Alexander* | L. Pearson, *The Lost Histories of Alexander the Great* (1960)

PECS | R. Stillwell and others, *Princeton Encyclopedia of Classical Sites* (1976)

P Elph. | *Elephantine Papyri* (1907)

Authors and Books

Peripl. M. Rubr. — *Periplus Maris Rubri*

Pers. — Persius

Peter, *HRRel.* — H. Peter, *Historicorum Romanorum Reliquiae*, vol. 1² (1914), 2 (1906)

Petron. — Petronius

  Sat. — *Satyrica*

Pf. — R. Pfeiffer

PF — Persepolis Fortification Texts: R. T. Hallock, *Persepolis Fortification Tablets* (1969)

PFlor — *Papiri greco-egizii, papiri fiorentini*, ed. D. Comparetti and G. Vitelli (1906–15; repr. 1962)

P Fouad — P. Jouguet and others, *Les Papyrus Fouad I* (1939)

PFT — see *PF*

Pfuhl — E. Pfuhl, *Malerei u. Zeichnung d. Griechen*, 3 vols. (1923)

PG — see Migne

PGen. — *Les Papyrus de Genève* (1896–1990)

P Ghōran — P. Jouguet, *BCH* 1906, 103 ff.

P Giess. — *Griechische Papyri im Museum des oberhessischen Geschichtsvereins zu Giessen* (1910–12)

PGM — K. Preisendanz and others (eds.), *Papyri Graecae Magicae: Die griechischen Zauberpapyri*, 2 vols., 2nd edn. (1973–4)

PHal. — *Dikaiomata*, ed. by the Graeca Halensis (1913)

Ph. Bel. — Philon, *Belopoeica*

PHeid. — *Veröffentlichungen aus der Heidelberger Papyrussammlung* (1956–90)

PHerc. — *Papyri Herculanenses*; see *Catalogo dei papyri ercolanesi* (1979) and M. Capasso, *Manuale di papirologia ercolanese* (1991)

Pherec. — Pherecydes

PHerm. Landl. — *Zwei Landlisten aus dem Hermupolites*, ed. P. Sijpesteijn and K. Worp (1978)

P Hib. — *Hibeh Papyri* (1906–55)

Philo — Philo Judaeus

  CW — Edition of Philo Judaeus by L. Cohn and P. Wendland (1896–1916)

  In Flacc. — *In Flaccum*

  Leg. — *Legatio ad Gaium*

Philoch. — Philochorus

Philol. — *Philologus*

Philol. Suppl. — *Philologus*, Supplement

Philostr. — Philostratus

  Her. — *Heroicus*

  Imag. — *Imagines*

  V A — *Vita Apollonii*

  V S — *Vitae sophistarum*

Phil. Unters. — *Philologische Untersuchungen*

Phil. Wochenschr. — *Philologische Wochenschrift*

Phld. — Philodemus

Phlegon, *Mir.* — Phlegon, *Miracula*

PHolm. — *Papyrus Graecus Holmiensis*, ed. O. Lagercrantz (1913)

Phot. — Photius

  Bibl. — *Bibliotheca*

P Iand. — *Papyri Iandanae* (1912–38)

Pickard-Cambridge–Webster, *Dithyramb²* — A. W. Pickard-Cambridge, *Dithyramb, Tragedy and Comedy*, 2nd edn. rev. T. B. L. Webster (1962)

Pind. — Pindar (ed. B. Snell and H. Maehler, 1987–8)

  Isthm. — *Isthmian Odes*

  Nem. — *Nemean „*

  Ol. — *Olympian „*

  Pyth. — *Pythian „*

  Pae. — *Paeanes*

PIR — *Prosopographia Imperii Romani Saeculi I, II, III*, 1st edn. by E. Klebs and H. Dessau (1897–8); 2nd edn. by E. Groag, A. Stein, and others (1933–)

P-K, GL — A. Philippson and E. Kirsten, *Die griechischen Landschaften 1–4* (1950–9)

PL — see Migne

Pl. — Plato

  Alc. — *Alcibiades*

  Ap. — *Apologia*

  [Ax.] — *Axiochus*

  Chrm. — *Charmides*

  Cra. — *Cratylus*

  Cri. — *Crito*

  Criti. — *Critias*

  Epin. — *Epinomis*

  Euthphr. — *Euthyphro*

  Grg. — *Gorgias*

  [Hipparch.] — *Hipparchus*

  Hp. mai. — *Hippias maior*

  Hp. mi. — *Hippias Minor*

  La. or *Lach.* — *Laches*

  Leg. — *Leges*

  Menex. — *Menexenus*

  Phd. — *Phaedo*

  Phdr. — *Phaedrus*

  Phlb. — *Philebus*

  Plt. — *Politicus*

  Prm. — *Parmenides*

  Prt. — *Protagoras*

  Resp. — *Respublica*

  Symp. — *Symposium*

  Soph. — *Sophista*

  Tht. — *Theaetetus*

  Ti. — *Timaeus*

Platner–Ashby — S. B. Platner and T. Ashby, *A Topographical Dictionary of Ancient Rome* (1929)

Plato Com. — Plato Comicus

Platon. — Platonius

  Diff. com. — *De differentia comoediarum*

Plaut.	Plautus	De fac.	De facie in orbe lunae
Amph.	Amphitruo	De fort. Rom.	De fortuna Romanorum
Asin.	Asinaria	De frat. amor.	De fraterno amore
Bacch.	Bacchides	De garr.	De garrulitate
Capt.	Captivi	De gen.	De genio Socratis
Cas.	Casina	De glor. Ath.	De gloria Atheniensium
Cist.	Cistellaria	De Is. et Os.	De Iside et Osiride
Curc.	Curculio	De lat. viv.	De latenter vivendo
Men.	Menaechmi	De mul. vir.	De mulierum virtutibus
Merc.	Mercator	[De mus]	De musica
Mil.	Miles gloriosus	De prof. virt.	De profectu in virtute
Mostell.	Mostellaria	De Pyth, or.	De Pythiae oraculis
Poen.	Poenulus	De sera	De sera numinis vindicta
Pseud.	Pseudolus	De soll. an.	De sollertia animalium
Rud.	Rudens	De superst.	De superstitione
Stich.	Stichus	De tranq. anim.	De tranquillitate animi
Trin.	Trinummus	Prae. ger. reip.	Praecepta gerendae reipublicae
PLeid.	Papyri Graeci Musei Antiquarii Lugduni-Batavi, ed. C. Leemans (1843–85)	Quaest. conv.	Quaestiones convivales
		Quaest. Graec.	„ Graecae
		Quaest. Plat.	„ Platonicae
PLG	T. Bergk, Poetae Lyrici Graeci (1882; repr. 1914–15)	Quaest. Rom.	„ Romanae
		Quomodo adul.	Quomodo adulescens poetas audire debeat
PLille	Papyrus grecs (Institut papyrologique de l'Université de Lille, 1907–12)	Vit.	Vitae Parallelae
		Aem.	Aemilius Paulus
Plin.	Pliny (the Elder)	Ages.	Agesilaus
HN	Naturalis historia	Alc.	Alcibiades
Plin.	Pliny (the Younger)	Alex.	Alexander
Ep.	Epistulae	Ant.	Antonius
Pan.	Panegyricus	Arat.	Aratus
Tra.	Epistulae ad Traianum	Arist.	Aristides
P Lips.	Griechische Urkunden der Papyrussammlung zu Leipzig, ed. L. Mitteis (1906)	Artax.	Artaxerxes
		Brut.	Brutus
		Caes.	Caesar
PLM	Poetae Latini Minores ed. Vollmer,	Cam.	Camillus
Vollmer / Morel	1 (1909) emendavit Morel³ (1935)	Cat. Mai., Min.	Cato Maior, Minor
		C. Gracch.	Gaius Gracchus
PLond. Lit.	Catalogue of the Literary Papyri in the British Museum, ed. H. Milne (1927)	Cic.	Cicero
		Cim.	Cimon
		Cleom.	Cleomenes
P London	Greek Papyri in the British Museum (1893–)	Crass.	Crassus
		Dem.	Demosthenes
Plotinus, Enn.	Plotinus, Enneades	Demetr.	Demetrius
PLRE	Prosopography of the Later Roman Empire 1, ed. A. H. M. Jones and others (1970); 2 and 3, ed. J. R. Martindale (1980–92)	Eum.	Eumenes
		Flam.	Flamininus
		Galb.	Galba
		Luc.	Lucullus
P Lund.	Papyri Lundenses (1934/5–1946/7)	Lyc.	Lycurgus
Plut.	Plutarch	Lys.	Lysander
Mor.	Moralia	Mar.	Marius
Adv. Col.	Adversus Coloten	Marc.	Marcellus
Amat.	Amatorius	Nic.	Nicias
Am. narr.	Amatoriae narrationes	Num.	Numa
An seni	An seni respublica gerenda sit	Pel.	Pelopidas
Comm. not.	De communibus notitiis adversus Stoicos	Per.	Pericles
		Phil.	Philopoemen
Comp. Ar. et Men.	Comparatio Aristophanis et Menandri	Phoc.	Phocion
		Pomp.	Pompeius
Conv. sept. sap.	Convivium septem sapientium	Pyrrh.	Pyrrhus
De Alex. fort.	De fortuna Alexandri	Rom.	Romulus
De def. or.	De defectu oraculorum	Sert.	Sertorius
De exil.	De exilio	Sol.	Solon

Authors and Books

Sull.	Sulla
Them.	Themistocles
Thes.	Theseus
Ti. Gracch.	Tiberius Gracchus
Tim.	Timoleon
[Plut.] Cons. ad	[Plutarch], Consolatio ad
Apoll.	Apollonium
Vit. Hom.	Vita Homeri
X orat.	Vitae decem oratorum
PMG	see Page, PMG
PMGF	See Davies, PMGF
PMich.	Michigan Papyri (1931–)
P Milan.	Papiri Milanesi (1928–67)
PMonac.	Byzantinische Papyri in der Papyrussammlung der K. Hof- und Staatsbibliothek zu München, 2nd edn. D. Hagedorn (1986)
PO	Patrologia Orientalis (1904–)
Poet. Rom. Vet.	see Diehl
Poll.	Pollux
Onom.	Onomasticon
Polyaenus, Strat.	Polyaenus, Strategemata
Polyb.	Polybius
Pompon.	Pomponius
Porph	Porphyry
Abst.	De abstinentia
De antr. nymph.	De antro nympharum
Plot.	Vita Plotini
P Osl.	Papyri Osloenses (1925–36)
Pow.	see Powell, Coll. Alex.
Powell and Barber, New Chapters	J. U. Powell and E. A. Barber, New Chapters in the History of Greek Literature (1921); Second Series (1929); Third Series, J. U. Powell alone (1933)
Powell, Coll. Alex.	J. U. Powell, Collectanea Alexandrina (1925)
POxy.	Oxyrhynchus Papyri (1898–)
PP	La parola del passato (1946–)
PPF	H. Diels, Poetarum Philosophorum Graecorum Fragmenta (1901)
praef.	praefatio
Pratin. Lyr.	Pratinas, Fragmenta lyrica
Preisendanz	see PGM
Preller–Robert	L. Preller, Griechische Mythologie, 4th edn., rev. C. Robert (1894)
Prisc. Inst.	Priscian, Institutio de arte grammatica
Pritchett, GSW	W. K. Pritchett, The Greek State at War 5 vols. (1971–91)
Proc. Brit. Acad.	Proceedings of the British Academy (1903–)
Procl.	Proclus
Hypotyp.	Hypotyposis
In R.	In Platonis Rempublicam commentarii
In Ti.	In Platonis Timaeum commentarii
Procop.	Procopius
Aed.	De aedificiis
Goth.	De bello Gothico
Vand.	De bello Vandalico

Proc. Prehist. Soc.	Proceedings of the Prehistoric Society
Progr.	Programm
Prop.	Propertius
Prudent	Prudentius
Cath.	Cathemerina
C. Symm.	Contra Symmachum
Perist.	Peristephanon
P Ryl.	Catalogue of the Greek Papyri in the John Rylands Library at Manchester (1911–52)
PSAS	Proceedings of the Society of Antiquaries, Scotland
PSI	Papiri Greci e Latini, Pubblicazioni della Società italiana per la ricerca dei papiri greci e latini in Egitto (1912–)
PSorbonn.	Papyrus de la Sorbonne 1, nos. 1–68, ed. H. Cadell (1966)
PStras.	Griechische Papyrus der Kaiserlichen Universitäts- und Landesbibliothek zu Strassburg (1912–)
P Teb.	Tebtunis Papyri (1902–76)
Ptol.	Ptolemaeus mathematicus
Alm.	Almagest
Geog.	Geographia
Harm.	Harmonica
Tetr.	Tetrabiblos
P Vat. II	Il Papiro Vaticano Greco II, ed. M. Norsa and G. Vitelli (1931)
PVindob.	Papyrus Vindobonensis
PVS	Proceedings of the Vergil Society
PYale	J. F. Oates, A. E. Samuel, C. B. Welles (eds.), Yale Papyri in the Beinecke Rare Book and Manuscript Library (1967)
Quad. Ist. Top. Roma	Quaderni dell'Istituto di Topografia antica della Università de Roma
QAL	Quaderni di archeologia della Libia
Quint.	Quintilian
Ep. ad Tryph.	Epistula ad Tryphonem (introductory to the following)
Inst.	Institutio oratoria
Quint. Smyrn.	Quintus Smyrnaeus
RAC	Reallexikon für Antike und Christentum, Stuttgart (1941–)
Radke, Götter	G. Radke, Die Götter Altitaliens (1960; 2nd edn. 1979)
Entwicklung	Zur Entwicklung der Gottesvorstellung und der Gottesverehrung in Rom (1987)
Radt	see TrGF
Rav. Cosm.	Cosmographia Anonymi Ravennatis
RC	C. B. Welles, Royal Correspondence in the Hellenistic Period (1934)

RCHM	Royal Commission on Historic Monuments	Riv. d. Arch. Crist.	Rivista di archeologia cristiana
RD	see *RHDFÉ*	Riv. Fil.	Rivista di filologia
RDAC	*Report of the Department of Antiquities of Cyprus*	Riv. ital. per le sc. giur.	Rivista italiana per le scienze giuridiche
RDGE	R. E. Sherk, *Roman Documents from the Greek East* (1969)	RK	see Wissowa
		RLAC	see *RAC*
RE	A. Pauly, G. Wissowa, and W. Kroll, *Real-Encyclopädie d. klassischen Altertumswissenschaft* (1893–)	RLÖ	*Der römische Limes in Österreich* (1900–)
		RN	*Revue numismatique*
Reallexikon der Assyriologie	*Reallexikon der Assyriologie* (1932–)	Robert, *OMS*	L. Robert, *Opera Minora Selecta*, 7 vols. (1969–90)
Rend. 1st. Lomb.	*Rendiconti d. R. Istituto Lombardo di scienze e lettere*	Robin	L. Robin, *La Pensée grecque et l'origine de l'esprit scientifique*, 2nd edn. (1932); Eng. trans. *Greek Thought*
Rend. Linc.	*Rendiconti della reale accademia dei Lincei*, 6th ser. (1892–1924); 7th ser. (1925–)	Rohde, *Psyche*	E. Rohde, *Psyche*, trans. W. Hillis (1925)
Rend. Pont.	*Rendiconti della pontificia accademia romana di archeologia*	*Griech. Roman*	*Der griechische Roman u. s. Vorläufer*, 3rd edn. (1914)
Rer. nat. scr. Graec. min.	O. Keller, *Rerum naturalium scriptores Graeci minores* (1877)	röm.	*römisch*
		Röm. Forsch.	see Mommsen
Rev. Arch.	*Revue archéologique*	Röm. Gesch.	see Beloch
Rev. Bibl.	*Revue biblique*	Röm. Mitt.	see *MDAI(R)*
Rev. Ét. Anc.	*Revue des études anciennes*	Roscher, *Lex.*	W. H. Roscher, *Ausführliches Lexikon d. griechischen u. römischen Mythologie* (1884–)
Rev. Ét. Grec.	*Revue des études grecques*		
Rev. Ét. Lat.	*Revue des études latines*		
Rev. Hist.	*Revue historique*		
Rev. Hist. Rel.	*Revue de l'histoire des religions*	Rose, *Handb. Gk. Myth.*	H. J. Rose, *Handbook of Greek Mythology*, 6th edn. (1958)
Rev. Phil.	*Revue de philologie* NS (1877–)		
RG	see *Mon. Anc.*	Rostovtzeff	M. Rostovtzeff
RGVV	Religionsgeschichtliche Versuche und Vorarbeiten, ed. A. Dieterich, R. Wünsch, L. Malten, O. Weinreich, L. Deubner (1903–)	*Hellenistic World*	*The Social and Economic History of the Hellenistic World*, 3 vols., 2nd edn. (1953)
		Roman Empire[2]	*The Social and Economic History of the Roman Empire*, 2nd edn. (1957)
RHDFÉ	*Revue historique de droit français et étranger*	RPAA	see *Rend. Pont.*
Rhet.	see Spengel	RRC	M. H. Crawford, *Roman Republican Coinage* (1974)
Rhet. Her.	*Rhetorica ad Herennium*		
Rhet. Lat. Min.	see Halm	RSA	*Rivista storica dell'antichità*
Rh. Mus.	*Rheinisches Museum für Philologie* (1827–), NS (1842–)	Ruggiero, *Diz. Epigr.*	E. de Ruggiero, *Dizionario epigrafico di antichità romana* (1886–)
Rhodes, *CAAP*	P. J. Rhodes, *A Commentary on the Aristotelian Athenaion Politeia* (1981; new edn. 1993)	Rumpf., *Malerei u. Zeichn.*	A. Rumpf, *Malerei und Zeichnung* (1953)
Thuc. 2 comm.	(ed.), *Thucydides: History II* (1988)	Rut. Namat.	Rutilius Namatianus, *De reditu*
RIB	see Collingwood–Wright	RVV	*Religionsgeschichtliche Versuche und Vorarbeiten*
Ribbeck, *CRF*	O. Ribbeck, *Comicorum Romanorum Fragmenta*		
TRF	*Tragicorum Romanorum Fragmenta* [both in *Scaenicae Romanorum Poesis Fragmenta*[3], 1897–8][2] (1962)	Sachs–Hunger	A. Sachs and H. Hunger, *Astronomical Diaries and Related Texts from Babylonia 2* (1989)
RIC	see Mattingly–Sydenham, *RIC*	Sall.	Sallust
Riccobono, *FIRA*	S. Riccobono, *Fontes Iuris Romani Antelustiniani* (1941)	[*Ad Caes. sen.*]	*Epistulae ad Caesarem senem*
Richardson, *Topog. Dict. Ancient Rome*	L. Richardson, *A New Topographical Dictionary of Ancient Rome* (1992)	Cat.	*Bellum Catilinae* or *De Catilinae coniuratione*
		Hist.	*Historiae*
		Iug.	*Bellum Iugurthinum*
RIDA	*Revue Internationale des Droits de l'Antiquité*	Satyr.	Satyrus Historicus
		Vit. Eur.	*Vita Euripidis*

Authors and Books

SB	F. Preisigke and others, *Sammel-buch griechischen Urkunden aus Ägypten* (1915–)	*SEG*	*Supplementum epigraphicum Graecum* (1923–)
SC	Sources chrétiennes	Semon.	Semonides
SC	*Senatus consultum*	Sen.	Seneca (the Elder)
SCE	*Swedish Cyprus Expedition* (1934–72)	Con. ex.	*Controversiarum excerpta*
		Controv.	*Controversiae*
SCI	*Scripta Classica Israelica*	Suas.	*Suasoriae*
Schanz–Hosius	M. Schanz, *Geschichte d. römischen Literatur*, rev. 1⁴ (1927) and 2⁴ (1935) by C. Hosius; 3³ (1922), Hosius and Krüger; 4/1² (1914) and 4/2 (1920), Schanz, Hosius, and Krüger; retitled *Handbuch der lateinischen Literatur der Antike* from 1989 (see *HLL*)	Sen.	Seneca (the Younger)
		Apocol.	*Apocolocyntosis*
		Ben.	*De beneficiis*
		Clem.	*De clementia*
		Constant.	*De constantia sapientis*
		Dial.	*Dialogi*
		Ep.	*Epistulae*
		Epigr.	*Epigrammata super exilio*
		Helv.	*Ad Helviam*
		Med.	*Medea*
Schmid–Stählin	W. Schmid and O. Stählin, *Geschichte d. griechischen Literatur*, vol. 1/1 (1929), 1/2 (1934), 1/3 (1940), 1/4 (1946), 1/5 (1948). See also Christ–Schmid–Stählin	Prov.	*De providentia*
		Q Nat.	*Quaestiones naturales*
		Tranq.	*De tranquillitate animi*
		Serv.	Servius
		Praef.	*Praefatio*
		Serv. Dan.	*Scholia Danielis* (Pierre Daniel, first publisher in 1600 of supplements to Servius' commentary on Virgil)
Schmitt, *SdA*	H. H. Schmitt (ed.), *Die Staatsverträge des Altertums 3: Die Verträge der griechisch-römischen Welt von 338 bis 200 v. Chr.* (1969)		
schol.	scholiast or scholia	Sext. Emp.	Sextus Empiricus
Schol. Bern.	*Scholia Bernensia ad Vergilii bucolica et georgica*, ed. Hagen (1867)	Math.	*Adversus mathematicos*
		Pyr.	Πυρρώνειοι ὑποτυπώσεις
		SHA	Scriptores Historiae Augustae
Schol. Bob.	*Scholia Bobiensia*	Ael.	*Aelius*
Schol. Cruq.	*Scholia Cruquiana*	Alex. Sev.	*Alexander Severus*
Schol. Dan.	see *Serv. Dan.*	Ant. Pius	*Antoninus Pius*
Schol. Flor. Callim.	*Scholia Florentina in Callimachum*	Aurel.	*Aurelian*
		Avid. Cass.	*Avidius Cassius*
Schroeder, *Nov. Com. Fragm.*	O. Schroeder, *Novae Comoediae fragmenta in papyris reperta exceptis Menandreis* (1915)	Clod.	*Clodius*
		Comm.	*Commodus*
		Did. Iul.	*Didius Iulianus*
Schürer, *History*	F. Schürer, *History of the Jewish People in the Age of Jesus Christ*, rev. and ed. G. Vermes, F. Millar, and M. Goodman (1973–87)	Hadr.	*Hadrian*
		Heliogab.	*Heliogabalus*
		M. Ant.	*Marcus Aurelius Antoninus (Caracalla)*
Scol. Anon.	*Scolia Anonyma* in Diehl's *Anth. Lyr. Graec.* 2, pp. 181–92	Marc.	*Marcus*
		Max.	*Maximinus*
Scol. Att.	*Scolia Attica* in Diehl's *Anth. Lyr. Graec.* 2, pp. 181–9	Pert.	*Pertinax*
		Pesc. Nig.	*Pescennius Niger*
		Prob.	*Probus*
Scullard, *Rom. Pol.*	H. H. Scullard, *Roman Politics 220–150 BC* (1951; 2nd edn. 1973)	Sev.	*Severus*
		Tyr. Trig.	*Tyranni Triginta*
		Verus	*Lucius Verus*
Etr. Cities	*The Etruscan Cities and Rome* (1967)	Shackleton Bailey, *Anth. Lat.*	D. R. Shackleton Bailey, *Anthologia Latina 1: Carmina in codicibus scripta* (1982)
Sc. J. Theol.	see *Stud. Theol.*		
Scymn.	Scymnus	*CLA*	D. R. Shackleton Bailey (ed.), *Cicero's Letters to Atticus*, 7 vols. (1965–70)
SdA	*Die Staatsverträge des Altertums 2²: Die Verträge der griechisch-römischen Welt von 700 bis 338 v. Chr.*, ed. H. Bengtson (1975); 3: *Die Verträge der griechisch-römischen Welt von 338 bis 200 v. Chr.*, ed. H. H. Schmidt (1969)	Sherk, *Augustus*	R. E. Sherk, *Rome and the Greek East to the Death of Augustus*, Translated Documents of Greece and Rome 4 (1984)

1

Sherk, *Hadrian* — *The Roman Empire: Augustus to Hadrian*, Translated Documents of Greece and Rome 6 (1988)

Sid. Apoll. — Sidonius Apollinaris
  Carm. — *Carmina*
  Epist. — *Epistulae*
SIFC — see *Stud. Ital.*
SIG — see *Syll.*³
Sil. — Silius Italicus
  Pun. — *Punica*
Simon. — Simonides
Simpl. — Simplicius
  in Cael. — *in Aristotelis de Caelo Commentarii*
  in Phys. — *in Aristotelis de Physica Commentarii*
Sitz. followed by name of Academy or Society — *Sitzungsberichte*
Sitz. Wien — *Sitzungsberichte der Akad. der Wissenschaften in Wien*
SLG — See Page
Smallwood, *Docs.* . . . *Nerva* — E. M. Smallwood, *Documents illustrating the Principates of Nerva, Trajan and Hadrian* (1966)
  Docs. . . . *Gaius* — *Documents illustrating the Principates of Gaius, Claudius and Nero* (1967)
SMSR — *Studi e materiali di storia delle religioni*
Snell–Maehler — see Bacchyl. and Pind.
Snell / Mannicht / Radt — see TrGF
SNG — *Sylloge Numorum [sic] Graecorum*
SÖAW — *Sitzungsberichte. Österreichische Akademie der Wissenschaften in Wien, phil.-hist. Kl.* (1848–)
Socrates, *Hist. eccl.* — Socrates, *Historia ecclesiastica*
Solin. — Solinus
Soph. — Sophocles
  Aj. — *Ajax*
  Ant. — *Antigone*
  El. — *Electra*
  OC — *Oedipus Coloneus*
  OT — *Oedipus Tyrannus*
  Phil. — *Philoctetes*
  Trach. — *Trachiniae*
Sor. *Gyn.* — Soranus, *Gynaeceia*
Sozom. — Sozomen
  Hist. eccl. — *Historia ecclesiastica*
SPCK — Society for Promoting Christian Knowledge
Spengel–Hammer — C. Hammer, *Rhetores graeci ex recognitione Leonardi Spengel* (1894): 2nd edn. of vol. 1/2 of Spengel, *Rhet.*
Spengel, *Rhet.* — L. Spengel, *Rhetores Graeci*, 3 vols.: 1/1 (1885), 2 (1854), 3 (1856)
SSR — see *SMSR*

Stadiasmus = *Periplus* — *Stadiasmus Maris Magni* (in GGM 1. 427)
Stat. — Statius
  Achil. — *Achilleis*
  Silv. — *Silvae*
  Theb. — *Thebais*
Steinby, *Lexicon* — E. M. Steinby (ed.), *Lexicon Topographicum Urbis Romae* 1 (A–C) (1993)
Steph. Byz. — Stephanus Byzantius or Byzantinus
StIr — *Studia Iranica*
Stith Thompson — Stith Thompson, *Motif-Index of Folk-Literature*, 6 vols. in Indiana University Studies, 96–7, 100–1, 105–6, 108, 110–12; also published as FF Communication 106–9, 116–17 (1932–6)
Stob. — Stobaeus
  Ecl. — Ἐκλογαί
  Flor. — Ἀνθολόγιον
StPhoen — Collection *Studia Phoenicia*
Strack, *Reichsprägung* — P. L. Strack, *Untersuchungen zur römischen Reichsprägung des zweiten Jahrhunderts* (1931)
Stud. Doc. Hist. Iur. — *Studia et Documenta Historiae et Iuris*
Stud. Etr. — *Studi Etruschi*
Stud. Gesch. Kult. Alt. — *Studien zur Geschichte und Kultur des Altertums*
Stud. Ital. — *Studi italiani di filologia classica*
Stud. Theol. — *Studia Theologica*
Studi stor. — *Studi storici per l'antichità classica*
Suda — Greek Lexicon formerly known as *Suidas*
Suet. — Suetonius
  Aug. — *Divus Augustus*
  Calig. — *Gaius Caligula*
  Claud. — *Divus Claudius*
  Dom. — *Domitianus*
  Galb. — *Galba*
  Gram. — *De grammaticis*
  Iul. — *Divus Iulius*
  Ner. — *Nero*
  Poet. — *De Poetis*
  Rel. Reiff. — *Reliquiae*, ed. Reifferscheid
  Rhet. — *De rhetoribus*
  Tib. — *Tiberius*
  Tit. — *Divus Titus*
  Vesp. — *Divus Vespasianus*
  Vit. — *Vitellius*
  Vita Hor. — *Vita Horatii*
  Vita Luc. — *Vita Lucani*
Sumner, *Orators* — G. V. Sumner, *The Orators in Cicero's* Brutus (1973)
Supp. Aesch. — H. J. Mette, *Supplementum Aeschyleum* (1939)
Supp. Com. — see Demiańczuk
Suppl. Hell. — H. Lloyd-Jones and P. Parsons (eds.), *Supplementum Hellenisticum*, Texte und Kommentare no. 11 (1983)

Authors and Books

Suppl. Mag. — R. W. Daniel and F. Maltomini (eds.), *Supplementum Magicum*, Papyrologica Coloniensia 16/1–2, 2 vols. (1989–91)

Susemihl, *Gesch. gr. Lit. Alex.* — F. Susemihl, *Geschichte d. griechischen Literatur in d. Alexandriner-Zeit* (1891–2; repr. 1965)

SVF — H. von Arnim, *Stoicorum Veterum Fragmenta* (1903–)

Sydenham, *CRR* — E. A. Sydenham, *The Coinage of the Roman Republic* (1952)

*Syll.*³ — W. Dittenberger, *Sylloge Inscriptionum Graecarum*, 3rd edn. (1915–24)

Syll. Graec. — see *Corp. poes. ep. Graec. lud.*

Symb. — *Symbolum*

Symb. Osl. — *Symbolae Osloenses*

Symb. Philol. Danielsson — *Symbolae Philologicae O. A. Danielsson octogenario dicatae* (1932)

Syme — R. Syme
  AA — *The Augustan Aristocracy* (1986)
  Rom. Rev. — *The Roman Revolution* (1939)
  RP — *Roman Papers*, 7 vols. (1979–91)
  RR — see Syme, *Rom. Rev.*
  Tacitus — *Tacitus*, 2 vols. (1958)

Symmachus — Symmachus
  Ep. — *Epistulae*
  Relat. — *Relationes*

Tab. Agn. — *Tabula Agnoniensis*

TAPhS — *Transactions of the American Philosophical Society*

Tac. — Tacitus
  Agr. — *Agricola*
  Ann. — *Annales*
  Dial. — *Dialogus de oratoribus*
  Germ. — *Germania*
  Hist. — *Historiae*

TAM — E. Kalinka and others, *Tituli Asiae Minoris* (1901–)

TAPA — *Transactions of the American Philological Association*

Tarn, *Alexander* — W. W. Tarn, *Alexander the Great* (1948; repr. 1979)

Tatianus, *Ad Gr.* — Tatianus, *Oratio ad Graecos*

Taylor, *Voting Districts* — L. R. Taylor, *The Voting Districts of the Roman Republic* (1960)

Ter. — Terence
  Ad. — *Adelphoe*
  An. — *Andria*
  Eun. — *Eunuchus*
  Haut. — *H(e)autontimorumenos*
  Hec. — *Hecyra*
  Phorm. — *Phormio*

Tert. — Tertullian
  Ad nat. — *Ad nationes*
  Adv. Valent. — *Adversus Valentinianos*

  Apol. — *Apologeticus*
  De anim. — *De testimonio animae*
  De bapt. — *De baptismo*
  De monog. — *De monogamia*
  De praescr. haeret. — *De praescriptione haereticorum*
  De spect. — *De spectaculis*

Teubner — Bibliotheca Scriptorum Graecorum et Romanorum Teubneriana (1849–)

Teuffel–Kroll — W. S. Teuffel, *Geschichte der römischen Literatur*⁶, eds. W. Kroll and F. Skutsch (1910–26, vol. 2 7th edn. 1920)

Texts and Transmission — L. Reynolds (ed.), *Texts and Transmission: A Survey of the Latin Classics* (1983)

TGF — A. Nauck, *Tragicorum Graecorum Fragmenta*, 2nd edn. (1889); Suppl. by B. Snell (1964)

Them. Or. — Themistius, *Orationes*

Theoc. — Theocritus
  Epigr. — *Epigrammata*
  Id. — *Idylls*

Theoph. *Ad Autol.* — Theophilus, *Ad Autolycum*

Theophr. — Theophrastus
  Caus. pl. — *De causis plantarum*
  Char. — *Characteres*
  Hist. pl. — *Historia plantarum*
  Phys. op. — *Physicorum opiniones*
  Sens. — *De sensibus*

Theopomp. — Theopompus Historicus

Thgn. — Theognis

Thomson, *Hist. Anc. Geog.* — J. O. Thomson, *A History of Ancient Geography* (1948)

Thuc. — Thucydides

Tib. — Tibullus

Timoth. — Timotheus
  Pers. — *Persae*

TIR — *Tabula Imperii Romani*

TLG — *Thesaurus Linguae Graecae*

TLL — *Thesaurus Linguae Latinae* (1900–)

Tod — M. N. Tod, *Greek Historical Inscriptions* vol. 1² (1946), 2 (1948)

Trag. Adesp. — *Tragica Adespota* in Nauck's *Tragicorum Graecorum Fragmenta* (*TGF*), pp. 837–958

TRF — see Ribbeck

TrGF — B. Snell, R. Kannicht, S. Radt (eds.) *Tragicorum Graecorum Fragmenta*, 4 vols. (1971–85), vol. 1² (1986)

trib. — *tribunus*

trib. pot. — *tribunicia potestas*

Tyrrell and Purser — R. Y. Tyrrell and L. C. Purser (eds.), *The Correspondence of M. Tullius Cicero*, 7 vols. (1886–1904 and later edns.)

Tzetz. — Tzetzes
  Chil. — *Historiarum variarum Chiliades*

Ueberweg–Flashar	F. Ueberweg, *Grundriss der Geschichte der Philosophie*, rev. edn.: vol. 3, *Altere Akademie, Aristoteles-Peripatos*, ed. H. Flashar (1983); vol. 4, *Die hellenistische Philosophie*, ed. H. Flashar (1994)	Wegner, *Herrscherbild.* (1939)	M. Wegner, *Die Herrscherbildnisse in antoninischer Zeit* (1939)
		Herrscherbild (1956)	(ed.) *Das römische Herrscherbild* (1956–)
		Westd. Zeit.	*Westdeutsche Zeitschrift für Geschichte und Kunst*
Ueberweg–Praechter, *Grundriss*	F. Ueberweg, *Grundriss der Geschichte der Philosophie*, pt. 1: *Das Altertum*; 12th edn. by K. Praechter (1926)	West, *GLP*	M. L. West, *Greek Lyric Poetry* (1993)
		GM	*Greek Metre* (1982)
Ulp.	Ulpianus	*IE²*	*Iambi et Elegi*, 2nd edn. (1989–92)
UPZ	U. Wilcken, *Urkunden der Ptolemäerzeit* 1 (1922–7), 2 (1957)	Wieacker, *RRG*	F. Wieacker, *Römische Rechtsgeschichte* 1–2 (1988–)
		Wien. Stud.	*Wiener Studien*
		Wilamowitz	U. von Wilamowitz-Moellendorff
Val. Max.	Valerius Maximus	*Hell. Dicht.*	*Hellenistische Dichtung in der Zeit des Kallimachos* (1924)
Varro, *Ling.*	Varro, *De lingua Latina*		
Rust.	*De re rustica*	Wilcken, *Chr.*	see Mitteis, *Chr.*
Sat. Men.	*Saturae Menippeae*	Wilhelm, *Urkunden*	A. Wilhelm, *Urkunden dramatischer Aufführungen in Athen* (1906)
Vatin.	Vatinius		
VCH	*Victoria County History*		
Veg. Mil.	Vegetius, *De re militari*	Winter, *KB*	F. Winter, *Kunstgeschichte in Bildern* (1935 ff.)
Vell. Pat.	Velleius Paterculus		
Ventris–Chadwick, *Docs.*	M. Ventris and J. Chadwick, *Documents in Mycenaean Greece*, 2nd edn. (1973)	Wissowa, *RK*	G. Wissowa, *Religion und Kultus d. Römer*, 2nd edn. (1912)
		Ges. Abh.	*Gesammelte Abhandlungen zur römischen Religions- und Stadtgeschichte* (1904)
Verg.	Virgil		
Aen	*Aeneid*		
Catal.	*Catalepton*	*WJA*	*Würzburger Jahrbücher für die Altertumswissenschaft*, NS (1975–)
Ecl.	*Eclogues*		
G.	*Georgics*		
Vett. Val.	Vettius Valens	Xen.	Xenophon
Vig. Chr.	*Vigiliae Christianae*	*Ages.*	*Agesilaus*
Vit. Aesch.	*Vita Aeschyli* (OCT of Aeschylus)	*An.*	*Anabasis*
		Ap.	*Apologia Socratis*
Vit. Eurip.	*Vita Euripidis* (OCT of Euripides)	*[Ath. pol.]*	*[Respublica Atheniensium*; see entry OLD OLIGARCH]
Vitr.	Vitruvius	*Cyn.*	*Cynegeticus*
De arch.	*De architectura*	*Cyr.*	*Cyropaedia*
Vopiscus, *Cyn.*	Vopiscus, *Cynegetica*	*Eq.*	*De equitandi ratione*
Vorsokr.	see Diels–Kranz	*Eq. mag.*	*De equitum magistro*
		Hell.	*Hellenica*
W	see West, *GLP* and *IE²*	*Hier.*	*Hiero*
Walbank, *HCP*	F. W. Walbank, *A Historical Commentary on Polybius*, 3 vols. (1957–79)	*Lac.*	*Respublica Lacedaemoniorum*
		Mem.	*Memorabilia*
		Oec.	*Oeconomicus*
Philip V	*Philip V of Macedon* (1940)	*Symp.*	*Symposium*
Walz	C. Walz, *Rhetores Graeci*, 9 vols. (1832–6)	*Vect.*	*De vectigalibus*
		XPf	Inscription of Xerxes I at Persepolis (so-called 'Harem Inscription')
Warde Fowler, *Rel. Exper.*	W. Warde Fowler, *The Religious Experience of the Roman People* (1911)	*XPh*	Inscription of Xerxes I at Persepolis (so-called 'Daiva Inscription')
Warmington, *Indian Commerce*	E. H. Warmington, *The Commerce between the Roman Empire and India* (1928)		
Watson 1974	A. Watson, *Law Making in the Later Republic* (1974)	*YClS*	*Yale Classical Studies*
WdF	*Wege der Forschung*	*ZÄS*	*Zeitschrift für ägyptische Sprache und Altertumskunde*
Webster, *Later Greek Comedy*	T. B. L. Webster, *Studies in Later Greek Comedy* (1953; 2nd edn. 1970)	Zeller, *Phil. d. Gr.*	E. Zeller, *Die Philosophie d. Griechen*, 6th edn. (1920)

Authors and Books

Zeller, *Gesch. d. gr. Phil.*	*Grundriss d. Geschichte d. griechischen Philosophie,* 13th edn. (1928)	Zonar.	Zonaras
		Zos.	Zosimus
Plato, etc.	*Plato and the Older Academy,* Eng. trans. (1888)	ZPDV	*Zeitschrift des deutschen Palästina-Vereins*
Zen.	Zenobius	ZPE	*Zeitschrift für Papyrologie und Epigraphik*
Z. für die öst. Gym.	*Zeitschrift für die österreichischen Gymnasien*	ZRG	*Zeitschrift der Savigny-Stiftung für Rechtsgeschichte, romanistische Abteilung*
Ziolkowski, *Temples*	A. Ziolkowski, *The Temples of Mid-Republican Rome and their Historical Context* (1993)	ZRGG	*Zeitschrift für Religions- und Geistesgeschichte*

NOTE TO READERS

Entries are ordered in letter-by-letter alphabetical order up to the first punctuation in the headword.

PERSONS

Strict homonyms are differentiated by number, and (1) indicates the earliest bearer of the name. Thus **Pericles** (1) is the famous fifth-century BC Athenian statesman, and **Pericles** (2) is a later figure, a Lycian ruler of the fourth century BC. Mythical characters are listed before historical, see for instance **Perseus** (1), (2) and (3).

Roman persons of the republican and imperial periods are listed by their *nomen*, i.e. family name, rather than be their *cognomen*, i.e. third or other additional name (see entry NAMES, PERSONAL, ROMAN for a detailed explanation), and are thus located where a reader would most logically look for such entries. For example the famous man we call Caesar had three names (the *tria nomina*): Gaius Iulius Caesar. The first is the *praenomen*, the second the *nomen* (indicating family or *gens*), and the third the *cognomen*; and he appears under the headword **Iulius**. However there are two individuals called Gaius Iulius Caesar in the Dictionary. Thus we have **Iulius Caesar** (1), **Gaius** and **Iulius Caesar** (2), **Gaius**. The famous man happens to be the earlier of the two, so he is listed as **Iulius Caesar** (1), **Gaius**, see paragraph above. Under Caesar the reader will find a cross-reference: **Caesar** See IULIUS CAESAR (1), c. Note that the Roman *praenomen* Gaius is conventionally abbreviated C. (not G.) and similarly Gnaeus is abbreviated Cn. (not Gn.). Thus Marius, C. (and C. Marius) but Gaius Marius; and Gellius, Cn. (and Cn. Gellius) but Gnaeus Gellius. The shorter form is regularly used in cross-referencing, so in the course of the entry **annals** there is a cross-reference to Cn. *Gellius. The relevant headword however is **Gellius, Gnaeus**.

Within a *gens* like that of the Cornelii, the sequence is alphabetical; thus the two (female) entries are **Cornelia** (1) and (2), then comes a Cornelius with no *cognomen*, namely **Cornelius, Gaius**. (If there were a **Cornelius, Lucius** he would come next, and a **Cornelius, Aulus** would precede Gaius.) Then comes the first of the Cornelii with *cognomen*, **Cornelius Anullinus, Publius**. Within a large family group like the Cornelii Scipiones we arrange as follows: we begin with those four Cornelii with the single and simple *cognomen* Scipio (two men with the *praenomen* Lucius, then two with Publius, i.e. arranged alphabetically by *praenomen* i.e. **Cornelius Scipio** (1), **Lucius**, etc.) Where the individual has an additional *cognomen*, the alphabetical principle again determines order, so **Cornelius Scipio Asiagenes, Lucius** immediately precedes **Cornelius Scipio Barbatus, Lucius**. Similarly when *cognomina* proliferate even further, so **Cornelius Scipio Nasica Corculum, Publius** precedes **Cornelius Scipio Nasica Serapio, Publius**.

A slight departure from these principles is to list predominantly literary figures, and emperors, in the form in which they are most usually known: excepting nicknames (Caligula and Caracalla), **Decius** and **Elagabalus**. So readers will find literary figures under the *cognomen*, such as **Catullus, Gaius Valerius**, rather than under Valerius. Emperors are listed by the component of their (often long) name which is most familiar, such as **Nero (Claudius Caesar)** rather than Claudius Caesar, Nero.

Cross-references are indicated by an asterisk, or (where the precise form of the headword differs significantly from the flagged word in the text) by the use of 'see' and 'see also' followed by the headword to which the reader is being referred in small capitals. So, under **geocentricity** we have: '. . . earlier atomists (see ATOMISM) . . .'.

The contributor initials used at the end of entries, and contributor affiliations, are given on pages xvii–xxvii. For some entries there are two or three sets of initials. Where divided by semicolons these relate to contributors to previous editions of *OCD* and these are given in chronological order with initials for the third edition given last. Initials divided by commas indicate, for the third edition, that one or more contributors collaborated on an entry.

abacus (ἄβαξ, ἀβάκιον), a counting-board, the usual aid to reckoning in antiquity. The Egyptians, Greeks, and Romans alike used a board with vertical columns, on which (working from right to left) units, tens, hundreds, or (where money was in question) e.g. ⅛ obols, ¼ obols, ½ obols, obols, drachmae, sums of 10, 100, 1,000 drachmae, and talents were inscribed. When an addition sum was done, the totals of the columns were carried to the left, as in our ordinary addition. The numbers might be marked in writing or by pebbles, counters, or pegs.

W. D. R.; M. V.

Abaris, legendary devotee of *Apollo from the far north, a shamanistic missionary and saviour-figure like *Aristeas whom *Pindar (fr. 270 Snell–Maehler) associated with the time of *Croesus—perhaps in connection with the king's miraculous rescue from the pyre and translation to the *Hyperboreans. Herodotus, ending his discussion of the latter (4. 36), tantalizes by refusing to say more than that 'he carried the arrow around the whole world while fasting' (cf. the mission of *Triptolemus, and *Demeter's search for Persephone). The arrow was a token of Apolline authority, and may have been a cure for disease; later traditions have him present it to *Pythagoras (1), and *Heraclides (1) Ponticus described him flying on it like a witch's broomstick.

A. Lesky, *A History of Greek Literature* 158 f.; M. L. West, *The Orphic Poems* (1983), 54.   A. H. G.

Abdera, a flourishing Greek city east of the Nestus river on the coast of *Thrace (Diod. Sic. 13. 72. 2). It was traditionally founded as a colony of *Clazomenae in 654 BC, a date for which 7th-cent. Greek pottery affords some support. It was reoccupied by colonists from *Teos (among them *Anacreon) in the second half of the 6th cent. (Hdt. 1. 168; Pind. *Paean* 2); its site was near Bulustra, a corruption of the name it bore in the Middle Ages, Polystylon. Like *Aenus, Abdera owed its wealth (it was the third richest city in the *Delian League, with a contribution of 15 talents) to its corn production (see the coins), and to the fact that it was a port for the trade of inland Thrace and especially of the Odrysian rulers. Abdera was a resting-place for the army of Xerxes in 480 BC when it was marching to invade Greece (Hdt. 7. 120). In 431 BC Abdera, under Nymphodorus, an Athenian *proxenos (Thuc. 2. 29. 1), was the protagonist in an attempt to unite Thrace and Macedonia with Athens. Nymphodorus arranged an alliance between Athens and his brother-in-law, the Odrysian ruler, *Sitalces. Abdera was subjected to the rule of *Philip (1) II and remained in the hands of the successive masters of Macedonia. Under the Romans it was a '*free city' (Plin. *HN* 4. 42). The coin type of Abdera reached perfection c.450–425 BC. Though 'Abderites' was a by-word for stupidity (Cic. *Att.* 4. 17.

3, 7. 7. 4), Abdera boasted among its citizens *Democritus and *Protagoras. Extensive excavations continue. See DIOMEDES (1)

S. Casson, *Macedonia, Thrace and Illyria* (1926); M. Feyel, *BCH* 1942–3, 176 (bibliog.); D. K. Samsares, *Historical Geography of East Macedonia in Antiquity* (1976, in Greek); J. M. F. May, *The Coinage of Abdera* (1966); C. Koukouli-Chrysanthaki, *Archaeological Researches in Ancient Abdera* (1985, in Greek); *AEMΘ* 1987, 1988; A. J. Graham, *JHS* 1992 44ff.

J. M. R. C.; N. G. L. H.

abortion was controversial in antiquity. Doctors taking the Hippocratic Oath (see HIPPOCRATES (2)) swore not to administer abortifacients, but other Hippocratic texts suggest that prostitutes (see PROSTITUTION, SECULAR) often employed abortion. A *Lysias fragment suggests that abortion was a crime in Athens against the husband, if his wife was pregnant when he died, since his unborn child could have claimed the estate. Greek temple inscriptions show that abortion made a woman impure for 40 days (see POLLUTION).

The Stoics (see STOICISM) believed that the foetus resembled a plant and only became an animal at birth when it started breathing. This attitude made abortion acceptable. Roman jurisprudence maintained that the foetus was not autonomous from the mother's body. There is no evidence for laws against abortion during the Roman republic. It was common during the early Roman empire (e.g. Ov. *Am.* 2. 14), and was practised for many reasons, e.g. for family limitation, in case of *adultery, or because of a desire to maintain physical beauty. *Soranus (*Gynaecology* 1. 59–65, Eng. trans. 1956) distinguished deliberate from spontaneous abortion, and abortion from *contraception. He accepted abortion if the woman's life was in danger. *Galen and *Dioscorides (2) mention many plant products used, either orally or by vaginal suppository, to provoke abortions (see PHARMACOLOGY). Some plants, e.g. aristolochia and squirting cucumber, can indeed have such effects. Mechanical methods were also used.

The emperors *Severus and *Caracalla towards AD 211 introduced the first definite ban on abortion in Rome as a crime against the rights of parents, and punished it with temporary exile. The spread of *Christianity changed attitudes. The *Teachings of the Apostles*, the first Christian document to mention abortion, condemned it, as did the *Letter of Barnabas*, *Tertullian, and many later writers. Christians regarded abortion, once the foetus was fully formed (40 days after conception), as murder of a living being.

E. Nardi, *Procurato aborto nel mondo greco-romano* (1971).   J. R. S.

Abydos was the best harbour on the Asiatic side of the *Hellespont. In the *Iliad* (2. 836) an ally of Troy and then a Thracian settlement, it was colonized c.700 BC by Milesians (see COLONIZATION, GREEK; MILETUS). From 514 it was under Persian control and served in 480 as the Asiatic bridgehead from which *Xerxes crossed into Europe (Hdt 7. 34, 43 ff.). Thereafter it was successively part of the *Athenian empire until it revolted in 411 (Thuc. 8. 61–2), a Spartan ally until 394, and under Persian rule again until freed by *Alexander (3) the Great in 334. It put up heroic resistance when besieged by *Philip (3) V of Macedon in 200 (Polyb. 16. 29–34). In Roman times and in late antiquity it was an important customs-station (*OGI* 521). There are no significant archaeological remains at the site, but its coinage, including early electrum issues, is important.

Bean, *PECS*, 5; Magie, *Rom. Rule Asia Min.* 752 ff., 1012 ff.; G. Hirschfeld, *RE* 1. 129–30. S. M.

Academy, public *gymnasium at Athens, sacred to the hero Academus, north-west of the Dipylon gate. It gave its name to the school founded there by *Plato (1) in the early 4th cent. and maintained by an unbroken line of successors until the 1st cent. BC. The school's private property was never there, but, at least during the 4th cent., at Plato's nearby house.

The Early Academy is the phase of doctrinal Platonism under Plato himself (d. 347) and his successors *Speusippus, *Xenocrates (1), *Polemon (2), and Crates.

The 'New Academy' is the phase, from *c.*269 to the early or mid-1st cent. BC (its further subdivision, Sext. Emp. *Pyr.* 1. 220, is a later imposition), in which the school, initially under *Arcesilaus (1), interpreted true Platonism as scepticism. Dialectical criticism of doctrines, usually Stoic, was orchestrated to demonstrate *akatalēpsia*, the impossibility of knowledge, resulting in *epochē*, suspension of judgement. *Carneades, its most influential head (mid 2nd cent.), was a systematic critic of all doctrines. His successors disagreed about his true intentions: *Clitomachus (scholarch *c.*128–*c.*110) regarded his arguments as still promoting *epochē*, but *Metrodorus (3) of Stratonicea and *Philon (3) of Larissa (possibly the last scholarch, *c.*110–*c.*79) considered their intent doctrinal, albeit fallibilist, with the 'convincing' (*pithanon*) an adequate basis for both action and philosophical judgement. *Cicero's main philosophical works reflect his allegiance to the Philonian Academy.

In 87 BC, when the Academics were refugees from Athens, Philon was openly challenged by his disciple *Antiochus (11) of Ascalon, whose 'Old Academy' claimed to return to the doctrines of the 'ancients', meaning especially Plato and *Aristotle. Thereafter the Academy as an institution disintegrated (whether Antiochus ever became scholarch is uncertain), although the title 'Academic' lived on (cf. *Plutarch).

H. Cherniss, *The Riddle of the Early Academy* (1945); J. Glucker, *Antiochus and the Late Academy* (1978); T. Dorandi (ed.), *Filodemo, 'Storia dei filosofi: Platone e l'Academia'* (1991); M. Ostwald and J. P. Lynch, *CAH* 6² (1994), ch. 12a. D. N. S.

Acamas, son of *Theseus and brother of *Demophon (1). Unknown to the *Iliad*, the brothers are certainly present at Troy in the *Iliu Persis* (fr. 4 Davies), and free their grandmother *Aethra from her servitude there. They share other adventures in the later mythological tradition; when young, they are sent to Euboea for safety, and on their return from Troy both are connected with the seizure of the *Palladium and involuntary homicide. The usual distinguishing feature of Acamas is his interest in distant places, and as the leader of colonizing settlements he is the heroic prototype for Athenian interests in *Cyprus and the *Chersonesus (1). Acamas was one of the tribal *eponymoi* of Athens.

Kron, *Phylenheroen* 141–70, 269–75, and *LIMC* 1. 435–46. E. Ke.

Acanthus (mod. Ierissos) was a colony of *Andros (Thuc. 4. 84) near the narrowest point of the Akte prong of *Chalcidice and thus close to the canal dug in 480 BC on the orders of *Xerxes I of Persia (Hdt. 7. 22; Thuc. 4. 109); at this time it was an important Persian base. It remained loyal to Athens for much of the 5th cent. (paying a normal tribute of 3 talents in the *Delian League), until 424 when it was famously seduced by the rhetoric of the Spartan *Brasidas (Thuc. 4.85–7 for the speech, a *tour de force*), though Thuc. also drily notes (4. 88) that the Acanthians were concerned for their grape-vintage which Brasidas had threatened to destroy. Thuc. 4. 124. 1 (separate mention of Acanthians and Chalcidians in Brasidas' army) implies that like *Torone, Acanthus was not at this time a member of the Chalcidic League (see CHALCIDICE). In the Peace of *Nicias (1) Acanthus was 'autonomous but tribute-paying'. In the 380s Acanthus appears in outright opposition to the Chalcidic League (Xen. *Hell.* 5. 2. 11 ff., cf. Tod 111 for Acanthian independence in the 390s). It was taken by *Philip (1) II of Macedon in 350 and sacked by the Romans in 200 BC (Livy 31. 45. 16; not AD 200, as Miller). Finds from excavations on the site (including a 4th-cent. BC necropolis) can be seen in the museums at Polygiros and Thessalonike.

Thuc. 4. 84 ff.; M. Zahrnt, *Olynth und die Chalkidier* (1971) 146–150 and in *Lexikon der historischen Stätten* 89; S. G. Miller, *PECS* 23; Hornblower, *Comm. on Thuc.* For the canal, B. Isserlin and others, *BSA* 1994, 277–184. S. H.

Acarnan, eponym of *Acarnania. He was the son, with Amphoterus, of Callirhoë (the daughter of Acheloüs) and *Alcmaeon (1) (who had settled in the *Achelous floodplain to escape the *Erinyes). Later, when Alcmaeon was murdered by the sons of *Phegeus, Callirhoë begged *Zeus to age her sons prematurely so they might avenge their father's murder. Their vengeance exacted, Acarnan and Amphoterus gathered settlers and inhabited Acarnania (Thuc. 2. 102; Apollod. 3. 91–3; Strab. 10. 2. 6).

W. M. M.

Acarnania, a district of NW Greece, bounded by the *Ionian Sea, the gulf of Ambracia, and the *Acheloüs river. The district is divided into three main regions: (1) a rugged coast with small bays and small alluvial plains, (2) a mountainous interior range that parallels the coast from north-west to south-east, and (3) small plains between the mountains and the Acheloüs river to the east. Although Neolithic, early Helladic, and late Helladic remains have been located near Astacus (at Agios Nikolaos, Platygiali, Grabes, and Chrisovitsa), evidence for widespread prehistoric settlement is lacking. Homer seems ignorant of the region except as a part of the shadowy 'mainland' inside *Ithaca, although names like Melite and Marathus may point to *Phoenician seafarers using this coast for shelter on their westward voyages. Significant Greek influence began during the 7th cent. BC when *Corinth settled Anactorium, Sollium and Leucas and when (soon thereafter?) *Cephallenia settled Astacus. *Thucydides (2) mentions settlements at Alyzeia, Astacus, Coronta, Limnaea, Medion, *Oeniadae, Palaerus, Phytia (Phoetiae), and Stratus, some of which were surely fortified *poleis* (Oeniadae, Stratus, Astacus, Palaerus). At Stratus, the Acarnanians formed a loose confederacy (*koinon*), which primarily represented the concerns of the inland cities, and thus did not always constitute the unified will of the entire *ethnos* (see ETHNICITY). Because of its strategic position along the western sailing route to Italy, the district was involved in many wars: in the 5th cent. Athens helped expel the Corinthians from their Acarnanian colonies and successfully blocked Peloponnesian interference in the region (429–26); in the 4th cent. the Acarnanians capitulated to the Spartan king *Agesilaus (in 390 or 389) and they remained Spartan allies until 375 when they joined the *Second Athenian Confederacy. Acarnanians supported Boeotia in its triumph over Sparta and fought with Athens against *Philip (1) II at *Chaeronea. Subsequently they became dependants of Macedonia. In 314, at the instance of *Cassander, the Acarnanian communities near the Aetolian border agreed to concentrate into larger cities (the largest being Stratus). Frequent frontier disputes with the Aetolians led to the partition of Acarnania between Aetolia and Epirus (c.252–50). After the fall of the Epirote monarchy, the Epirote section recovered their independence (c.230), reorganized their league, and acquired from Epirus the island of *Leucas which became their new capital. They sided with *Philip (3) V of Macedon against the Romans (200), and as a result, Leucas was separated from the koinon; Thyrreion (with its strong pro-Roman faction) became the new capital. Although retaining their confederacy until 31–29 BC, the region suffered severely in the intervening years, first from *piracy, and then from the Roman civil wars. The cities thereafter became dependants of *Nicopolis (3).

Oberhummer, *Akarnanien* (1887); P–K *GL* 2. 368–417; J. A. O. Larsen, *Greek Federal States* (1968), 89–95; W. M. Murray, *Coastal Sites of Western Akarnania* (Diss. 1982); D. Domingo-Foraste, *A History of Northern Coastal Akarnania to 167 BC* (Diss. 1988).   W. M. M.

Acastus, in mythology, son of Pelias (see NELEUS); he took part in the Argonautic expedition and the Calydonian boar-hunt (see ARGONAUTS; MELEAGER (1)). When *Peleus took refuge with him, Acastus' wife (variously named) loved him, and being repulsed, accused him to her husband of improper advances. Acastus, therefore, stole Peleus' wonderful sword and left him alone on Mt. *Pelion, where he was rescued by Chiron (see CENTAURS). Afterwards Peleus took *Iolcus, putting to death Acastus' wife and, by some accounts, Acastus himself (Apollod. 3. 164–7, 173; schol. Ap. Rhod. 1. 224; cf. Paus. 3. 18. 16).   H. J. R.

Acca Larentia, obscure Roman goddess with a festival on 23 December (*Larentalia or Larentinalia). One tradition (Valerius Antias fr. 1 Peter) makes her a prostitute, contemporary with *Romulus, who left her property to the Roman people; another (Licinius Macer fr. 1 Peter) makes her wife of *Faustulus and hence adopted mother of Romulus. Cato (fr. 16 Peter) initially made the connection of she-wolf (*lupa*) with prostitute (*meretrix*); thus the courtesan name Faula is linked with Faustulus (*RE* 6.2090–1). The long quantity of the first syllable in Larentia (Auson. *Technop.* 8. 9 Peiper; p. 179 Green) suggests a connection with *Larunda and not Lar (short *a*), but this is not decisive, and the Lar as family ancestor would be appropriate (see LARES); cf. Ogilvie on Livy 1.4.7. Plutarch implausibly assigned her an April festival (*Quaest. Rom.* 35 with Rose's notes); cf. E. Tabeling, *Mater Larum* (1932), 57–8; Latte, *RR* 92.

Inscr. Ital. 13. 2. 543–4; *LIMC* 1. 10–11; J. Scheid, *Romulus et ses frères* (1990), 18–24, 590–2.   C. R. P.

accents, Greek See PRONUNCIATION, GREEK, § (D).

Accius, Lucius (170–*c*.86 BC), stage poet and literary scholar of municipal freedman birth. His family's lands were at Pisaurum in Umbria. He attached himself in Rome to D. *Iunius Brutus Callaicus (consul 138). Although of conservative political views, he believed that literary talent demanded in its context more respect than nobility of birth (cf. the anecdote about C. *Iulius Caesar Strabo Vopiscus at Val. Max. 3. 7. 11). He had a touchy

sense of his own importance, always avenging insults (*Rhet. Her.* 1. 24). Contemporaries were amused by the outsize statues of himself he had placed in the temple of the Muses (Plin. *HN* 34. 19).

Over 40 tragic titles and not one unmistakably comic title are transmitted. (*Achilles, Aegisthus, Agamemnonidae, Alcestis, Alcmeo, Alphesiboea, Amphitruo, Andromeda, Antenoridae, Antigona, Armorum iudicium, Astyanax, Athamas, Atreus, Bacchae, Chrysippus, Clytemestra, Deiphobus, Diomedes, Epigoni, Epinausimache, Erigona, Eriphyla, Eurysaces, Hecuba, Hellenes, Medea, Melanippus, Meleager, Minotaurus, Myrmidones, Neoptolemus, Nyctegresia, Oenomaus, Pelopidae, Persidae, Philocteta, Phinidae, Phoenissae, Prometheus, Stasiastae vel Tropaeum Liberi, Telephus, Tereus, Thebais, Troades*). A relatively large number concerned the Trojan cycle of legends. The earliest, probably the *Atreus*, was performed in 140 (Cic. *Brut.* 229). The year 104 saw the première of the *Tereus*. The *Brutus* dramatized the tyrannical deeds of the second Tarquin (L. *Tarquinius Superbus). It could have glanced at the ambitions of the *Gracchi. The *Aeneadae vel Decius* centred on the defeat of the Gallo-Etrusco-Samnite alliance at *Sentinum in 295. It must have given prominence to the non-Italian origin of the Romans; possibly in conscious criticism of the demands being formulated by the Italian allies (*socii) in the last part of the 2nd cent.

A lengthy hexameter poem, the *Annales*, found Greek origins for Roman religious festivals. The trochaic septenarii of the *Pragmatica* had something to do with the theatre. In the case of the *Parerga* and the *Praxidica* neither the style nor the range of content is clear. The *Didascalica* ran to at least nine books and comprehended among other things the history of both the Athenian and the Roman theatre. Accius cast his discourse here in a mixture of prose and diverse poetical metres. Later researchers demonstrated his dates for the activities of *Livius Andronicus to be too low (Cic., *Brut.* 72) and disputed his judgement that the *Gemini lenones, Condalium, Anus bis compressa, Boeotia, Agroecus* and *Commorientes* then attributed to Plautus were spurious (Gell. *NA* 3. 3). Various attempts by him to make the Latin orthographical system reflect more closely the actual *pronunciation of the language were not taken up. His desire to kill off the practice of giving Greek names Latin terminations (Varro, *Ling.* 10. 70) had more influence. Varro admired his learning sufficiently to dedicate to him his *De ambiguitate litterarum*. More respect for old Roman tradition was shown by his composition in *Saturnian verses of an *elogium* for his patron Brutus (*schol. Bob. Cic.* p. 179). Somewhat out of character with his dignified public mien seems a work of obscure content but clearly frivolous form cited by *Gellius and *Diomedes (3), the *Sotadica*. *Pliny the Younger put him among the Latin erotic poets (*Ep.* 5. 6).

The grandeur of Accius' tragic style caused some contemporaries to laugh (Pompon. *Hor. Serm.* 1. 10. 53). *Cicero, however, who was proud to have known him personally, admired his plays almost as highly as he did those of *Pacuvius and cited extensive passages in his rhetorical and philosophical dialogues. Performances are known of the *Eurysaces, Clytemestra, Tereus,* and *Brutus* on the mid 1st-cent. BC stage. The likes of *Columella and the younger Seneca (see L. ANNAEUS SENECA (2)) continued to read him. In late antiquity *Nonius Marcellus had access to at least 30 of his scripts, and a writer on old Latin metre could cite four at first hand (*Priscianus, ed. Keil, *Gramm. Lat.* 3 418 ff.).

FRAGMENTS E. H. Warmington, *Remains of Old Latin*, 2 (1936), 326 ff. (with trans.); dramatic frs.: *TRF* 157 ff.; non-dramatic frs.: Courtney, *FLP* 56 ff. DISCUSSIONS F. Marx, *RE* 1 (1893), 142 ff.; R. degli Innocenti Pierini, *Studi su Accio* (1980).   H. D. J.

acclamation vocal expressions of approval and good wishes in ritual form were an important part of Roman life, both private (e.g. at weddings) and public (for actors and the presiding magistrate at public performances, and above all at a *triumph). The title of *imperator was based on the soldiers' acclamation. A magistrate leaving for his province was escorted by crowds shouting ritual acclamations, and his return was received in a corresponding way. (See PROVINCIA §2.) Under the empire, these rituals were magnified, but confined to the emperor and approved members of his family. They were also ritually greeted at public appearances, especially at games and on their birthdays. By the 4th cent. AD such greetings had been made mandatory for certain high officials (*Cod. Theod.* 1. 6. 6, 6. 9. 2). By the late republic, rhythmical shouting at games, sometimes organized, expressed approval or disapproval of politicians. Cicero takes it very seriously, as expressions of public opinion (which of course counted only in the city of Rome), and P. *Clodius Pulcher organized such shouting at *contiones to simulate public opinion. Under the empire, such acclamations, especially at games, became the only expression of public opinion and they could rarely be suppressed. They were normally combined with ritual greetings of the emperor to express approval or disapproval of prominent persons and demand rewards or punishments for them. Ritualized acclamations spread to *recitations and *declamations and claques could be collected and even paid for this. Nero formed a large claque for his performances, importing the Alexandrian tradition of musical accompaniment to their chants.

In the senate ritual shouts of greeting and approval for the emperor appear very early. They were used to attract the emperor's notice by demanding punishment of 'traitors' (see MAIESTAS), and at the death of a hated emperor would demand (probably with more spontaneity) his *damnatio memoriae and punishment for his creatures (see e.g. Tac. *Hist.* 1. 72. 3; Suet. *Dom.* 23. 1). On Trajan's accession the acclamations welcoming him were first recorded on published documents (Pliny, *Pan.* 75. 2) and that practice spread. By this time acclamations also greeted (e.g.) the announcement of the names of designated consuls (ibid. 95. 2). But senate procedure was not basically affected. As the *Historia Augusta frequently attests (showing at least what was taken for granted), recorded acclamations increased in length and frequency. By the 4th cent., discussion and traditional procedure had lapsed and they provided an appearance of senatorial expression of opinion. The development was naturally imitated at the local level and ultimately reached the Church.

RE 1 'acclamation'; A. Alföldi, *MDAI(R)* 1934, 79 ff.; A. Cameron, *Circus Factions* (1976), esp. ch. 9; R. J. A. Talbert, *The Senate of Imperial Rome* (1984), 297 ff.; C. Roueché, *JRS* 1984, 181 ff.   E. B.

accountability, accounts See EUTHYNA.

Acestes (Αἰγέστης, Αἴγεστος), character in mythology, founder and king of *Segesta (Egesta) in Sicily and of Trojan descent (cf. Dion. Hal. *Ant. Rom.* 1. 52.1–4; *Schol. Dan. Aen.* 1. 550; schol. on Lycophron *Alex.* 952). In Virgil's *Aeneid* he is the son of a Trojan mother and the Sicilian river-god Crimisus, and entertains *Aeneas and his men in Sicily; Virgil in fact makes Segesta a foundation of Aeneas and not of Acestes (*Aen.* 5. 36–41, 708 ff.).

G. Manganaro, *Enc. virg.* 'Aceste'.   S. J. Ha.

Achaea Region on the NE of the Peloponnese, between the Corinthian Gulf and the Chelmos and Panachaikon mountains. Historically a federation of small territories (Paus. 7).

Achaea was settled from the palaeolithic period. During the late bronze age, numerous graves plus settlements (e.g. Aegira and Katarraktis) and the fortification of Teichos Dymaion indicate extensive activity (see AHHIYAWA). Geometric settlement has been found along the coast (including an 8th.-cent. temple at Aegira) and inland (the Pharae valley). Achaeans may have joined the Ionian migration; Achaean colonies include *Sybaris (720 BC), *Croton (708), *Metapontum, *Caulonia (all in Italy) and *Scione (in *Chalcidice). See COLONIZATION, GREEK.

According to Herodotus (1. 145), Achaea was divided into 12 *merides* each containing seven or eight *dēmoi* (cf. Polyb. 2. 41. 7). These comprise Pellene (the seat of games noted by Pindar), Helice, Bura, Aegira, Aegae, *Aegium, Rhypes, *Patrae, Pharae, Olenus, *Dyme, and Tritaea. The regional shrine of *Poseidon Heliconius was situated at Helice until the city was destroyed (along with Bura) by an earthquake in 373. Fourth-cent. foundations include Cerynia and Leontium.

There is scant evidence for the region's early political organization, although some form of federation may have existed by the 5th cent. In 468 Cerynia admitted refugees from the Argive sack of Mycenae. Achaea remained neutral in the Persian Wars and the extent of her involvement in the *Peloponnesian War is unclear. According to Thucydides (1. 115, 4. 21), the Achaeans may have allied with the Athenians in the early 450s only to be 'given up' 30 years later. Pellene acted independently in warring with *Sicyon during the 7th/6th cent., and joining the *Peloponnesian League. In 417 Sparta intervened in the Achaean cities to ensure more favourable government, and in 367 oligarchs are recorded as treating with *Epaminondas after the Theban alliance's expedition against Achaea. Achaeans were among the 10,000 who fought with *Cyrus (2). The region retained a reputation for justice and political stability, supplying arbitrators, for example between Thebes and Sparta in 371. See ARBITRATION, GREEK.

See ACHAEAN CONFEDERACY for Achaea's Hellenistic history. It fell under Roman rule in 146 BC; from 27 BC it was in the province of *Achaia. Dyme and Patrae became Roman colonies.

W. Alzinger, *Klio* 1985, 394–426; 1986, 6–62, 309–7; A. Papadopoulos, *Mycenaean Achaea* (1979); J. K. Anderson *BSA* 1954, 72–92; A. D. Rizakis, *Paysages d'Achaie* 1 (1992); A. Rizakis (ed.), *Achaia und Elis in der Antike* (1991).   C. A. M.

Achaea Phthiotis See PHTHIOTIS.

Achaean Confederacy, federal organization developed by the twelve Achaean cities (see ACHAEA) united in the cult of Zeus Hamarios. First mentioned in 453 BC as Athenian allies, Achaea's independence was guaranteed in 446 (*Thirty Years Peace). In the Peloponnesian War neutrality proved impossible and Achaea fell into Sparta's sphere of influence. Common citizenship existed by 389, when it had already been extended to non-Achaean Calydon. In the 4th cent. coins were issued. Polybius (2. 41. 4–6) claimed the 'democratic' constitution of his own time for the early confederacy, but since in 367 the ruling class was exiled and democracy installed (Xen. *Hell.* 7. 1. 43) this cannot be accurate, unless the two sources mean different things by 'democracy'. The confederacy was dissolved sometime before its revival in 281/280. It then exploited the political vacuum in Greece after the collapse of the empire of *Demetrius (4) Poliorcetes, soon expanded beyond Achaea, and under the leadership of *Aratus (2) of Sicyon developed a locally expansionist anti-Macedonian policy in the 240s and 230s. The admission of Arcadian cities, especially *Megalopolis (235), provoked Spartan hostility and led to reconciliation with Macedonia in 224. In the 'Cleomenic War' (see CLEOMENES (2) III), Achaea joined *Antigonus (3) Doson's Hellenic League which defeated Sparta at Sellasia (222).

The confederacy also received Macedonian aid against Aetolia (see AETOLIAN CONFEDERACY), *Messene and *Elis ('*Social Wars (2)': 219–217) and subsequently remained loyal to Macedonia during the First Macedonian War (215–205). Only under severe military pressure did Achaea join Rome against Macedonia in 198 and it benefited from the Roman peace after 196, eventually receiving the unusual distinction of a treaty of alliance (perhaps 191). During this period the Achaean Confederacy under the influence and leadership of *Philopoemen, Aristaenus, and Diophanes expanded to absorb the whole Peloponnese including the old enemies Sparta, Elis, and Messene; it supported Rome against *Antiochus (3) III and *Perseus (2) but internal pressures resulting from the sudden expansion led also to severe political tension with Rome and the internment of 1,000 leading Achaeans (including *Polybius (1)) in Italy after 167. Despite the dominance of *Callicrates (2) internal tensions continued to provoke Rome and culminated in the 'Achaean War' (146/5), which with the destruction of Corinth and partial dismemberment of the confederacy effectively ended Achaean political independence.

Polybius reports that in his time (2nd cent. BC) the whole Peloponnese, united within the Achaean Confederacy, used the same laws, weights and measures, and coinage, elected common officers and had a common council and judges (2. 37. 10–11). The annually elected leader was a *stratēgos* (before 255 two), re-electable only every second year, alongside whom stood a hipparch (cavalry commander), a secretary and 10 *dāmiourgoi*. Council membership was probably restricted to those over 30; its size is unknown, but it doubtless represented all member-cities. The council probably met together with a popular assembly consisting of all men of military age (*ekklēsia*) four times a year (*synodoi*); only in special sessions of both bodies (*synclētoi*), which met as required, could questions of war, alliance, or (in the 2nd cent.) communications from the Roman senate be treated.

J. A. O. Larsen, *Greek Federal States* (1968); Walbank, *Polybius*, esp. vol. 3. 406 f. (the assemblies); R. M. Errington, *Philopoemen* (1969).

R. M. E.

Achaean Confederacy (Roman) Permitted to reform after 146 BC, at first on a local basis only, the confederacy survived until at least the mid-3rd cent. AD, chiefly as a vehicle (from *c.* AD 50) for a federal *ruler-cult based at Corinth. For some of the 1st cent. AD, in temporary union with other regional confederacies (Boeotian, Euboean, etc.), it formed early-imperial *Achaia's nearest equivalent to a provincial *concilium.

T. Schwertfeger, *Das Achaiische Bund von 146 BC bis 27 v. Chr.* (1974); A. Spawforth, *Hesp.* 1994 and 1995.

A. J. S. S.

Achaemenid art The official sculpture of the Persian empire was made in a distinctive style which owed much to Mesopotamian forerunners, and like them tended to the glorification of the ruler. It used to be thought that the style arose from the presence of particular groups of foreign craftsmen, notably Ionian Greeks, but it is becoming increasingly apparent that the Median, Persian, Babylonian, Sardian, Egyptian, and Ionian artisans who worked on the great palace complexes subordinated any indigenous traits to an international style devised to articulate the ideology of Achaemenid kings.

Only a few sculptured reliefs are preserved from *Pasargadae, the city of *Cyrus (1). *Darius I is shown triumphant over a prostrate usurper in the *Bisutun relief, while *Ahuramazda hovers above. A colossal statue of Darius in Egyptian granite

found at *Susa presents many problems: was it (and its lost pair) originally made for an Egyptian setting, or were they commissioned for Darius' Susan palace? The tombs of Darius and his successors at *Naqš-i Rustam show a royal personage on a platform borne by personifications of the lands of the empire. The façades of the *Apadana at Persepolis showed the king granting an audience to an official, ranks of tribute bearers and courtiers, and lions attacking bulls. The theme of royal victory occurs in reliefs representing struggles between royal heroes and mythical beasts, motifs which are frequently repeated on seal-stones. Achaemenid tapestries no longer survive, and only a little gold and silver plate and jewellery, decorated with stylized goats or winged horned griffins, is extant.

E. F. Schmidt, *Persepolis*, 1–3 (1953–70); R. Ghirshman, *Persia from the Origins to Alexander the Great* (1964); *Cahiers de la DAFI* 4 (1974) (on the Darius statue at Susa); M. C. Root, *The King and Kingship in Achaemenid Art* (1979); E. Porada, *Cambridge History of Iran* 2 (1985), 793–827; P. Calmeyer, *Enc. Ir.* 2/6 (1990), 569–80.

M. V.

Achaemenids The term, as used by Herodotus (1. 125), refers to one of the three clans (*phrētrē*) of the Pasargadae tribe to which the Persian kings belonged; its eponymous ancestor was supposedly Achaemenes (Hdt. 7. 11). The statement corresponds in part to *Darius I's account at *Bisutun, where he links himself explicitly to Achaemenes (OP: Haxāmaniš): 'For this reason we are called Achaemenids. From long ago we have been noble. From long ago we have been kings' (DB 1. 2–3). But this is the official version promulgated by Darius after his brutal seizure of power. This also led him to erect inscriptions in *Cyrus (1)'s name at *Pasargadae describing the founder of the empire as an Achaemenid: they served to hide the fact that Darius himself had no genealogical claim to the throne in 522 BC. Probably around this time a foundation legend about Achaemenes was created and put into circulation; he is said to have been abandoned as a small child and brought up by an eagle (Ael. *NA* 12, 21). Throughout Persian history, the term Achaemenid had two quite distinct meanings: (1) the extensive circle of clan members, part of the Pasargadae tribe; (2) politically and dynastically, it describes only the fictional line of ancestors created by Darius and his descendants. When speaking of the Achaemenid dynasty and empire, the term is used in the second sense. Darius I's descendants (the royal line), down to, and including, *Darius III, effectively retained exclusive access to the kingship, and no 'outsider' was ever able to seize royal power. See PERSIA.

Briant, *HEA*, ch. 3.

P. B.

Achaeus (1), eponym of the Achaeans; in mythology, son of *Poseidon (Dion. Hal. *Ant. Rom.* 1. 17. 3), *Zeus (Serv. on *Aen.* 1. 242), *Xuthus (Apollod. 1. 50), or *Haemon (schol. *Il.* 2. 681).

Achaeus (2), of Eretria, Athenian tragic poet, to be distinguished from Achaeus of Syracuse, who may be the Achaeus who won a *Lenaean victory *c.*356. According to the *Suda* the Eretrian was born in 484–480 BC, wrote 44 or 30 or 24 plays, the first produced between 447 and 444, and won one victory. Being unmentioned at Ar. *Ran.* 73–87, he was probably dead by 405. Of 20 known titles at least eight are satyric, and the philosopher *Menedemus (1) thought his satyr-plays second only to those of *Aeschylus (Diog. Laert. 2. 133). Critics placed him in a *canon of five great tragedians, and *Didymus (1) seems to have written a commentary on him. *Euripides is said to have adapted a maxim from him (fr. 6, cf. Eur. fr. 895), and he is quoted three times by *Aristophanes (1) (*Vesp.* 1081, *Pax* 356, *Ran.* 184). *Athenaeus (1)

Achaeus

(10. 451c) describes him as polished in style but liable to become obscure and enigmatical.

TrGF 1² 115–28; *Musa Tragica* 80–9, 277–80; D. F. Sutton, *The Greek Satyr Play* (1980), 69–73.   A. L. B.

Achaeus (3) (d. 213 BC), viceroy for *Antiochus (3) III of Seleucid Asia Minor and his kinsman (maternal uncle), probably the grandson of the Seleucid official Achaeus the Elder. In 223/2 he recovered Seleucid possessions in Anatolia from *Pergamum; exploiting Antiochus' involvement in the east (Molon's revolt and war against *Ptolemy (1) IV), he proclaimed himself king (220). His soldiers refused to fight Antiochus, but he maintained power until the king was free to quell his rebellion. After a two-year siege in Sardis, he was captured and duly executed as a traitor.

Polyb. bks. 4–8. H. H. Schmitt, *Untersuchungen zur Geschichte Antiochus' der Grossen und seiner Zeit* (1964), 30 f., 138 f., 181 f.; E. Will, *Histoire politique du monde hellénistique* 2 (1982), 15 f.; S. M. Sherwin-White and A. Kuhrt, *From Samarkhand to Sardis* (1993), 125, 188 f.
G. T. G.; S. S.-W.

Achaia (correct spelling: J. Oliver, *The Civic Tradition and Roman Athens* (1983) 152 note 6), official name for the Roman province of *Greece, commemorating Rome's defeat of the *Achaean Confederacy in 146 BC (Paus. 7. 16. 20). After its initial and temporary formation by Caesar (46 BC), Augustus re-established it as a separate province (27 BC); joined to *Moesia in AD 15, it was detached in 44, 'freed' by Nero in 66, and definitively reconstituted by Vespasian c.70. Its early boundaries were unstable, including *Epirus and perhaps *Thessaly (by c.150 the former was a separate province, the latter part of *Macedonia). A public province, it was normally governed by junior (praetorian) proconsuls, upgraded under Constantine I to *consulares*. Although the procurator from Augustus on resided at *Corinth, the proconsuls were itinerant (e.g. Philostr. *VA* 8. 23), with residences attested at *Olympia (Paus. 5. 15. 2) and on *Aegina (L. Robert, *Hellenica* 1948, 5–34). Achaia at first excluded an important group of *free cities, notably Athens, Sparta, Elis, and Delphi; from Constantine I these were absorbed into the proconsul's routine jurisdiction. See CORRECTOR.

E. Groag, *Die römischen Reichsbeamten von Achaia bis auf Diokletian* (1939), and *Die Reichsbeamten von Achaia in spätrömischer Zeit* (1946); *LIMC* 1/1 (1981) 11 (personification in art).   A. J. S. S.

Acharnae, the largest Attic *deme. (The figure of 3,000 hoplites at Thuc. 2. 20. 4, cf. 21. 3, may be too high; 1,200 is likelier and a possible emendation; another is that πολῖται should be read for ὁπλῖται, 'citizens' not 'hoplites'). It lay around Menidi in the NW corner of the Attic plain, near the pass from the Thriasian plain along which *Archidamus II and the Spartans marched in 431 BC. It is possible that Acharnae was divided into two demes for some purposes, making the total of known demes 140 not 139; but this is disputed. Although famous as charcoal-burners in Aristophanes (*Ach.*), the Acharnians lived primarily by growing corn and cultivating vines and olives. They were also famously brave (Pind. *Nem.* 2. 16) and had, appropriately, a sanctuary to *Ares: the temple was moved to the Athenian Agora in the Roman period.

S. Dow, *TAPA* 1961, 66 ff.; J. Traill, *Demos and Trittys* (1986), 142 ff.; D. Whitehead, *Demes of Attica* (1986), 396 ff., and *Phoenix* 1987, 442 f.; Rhodes, *Thuc. 2 comm.* (1988), 276.   C. W. J. E.; S. H.

Achates, character in mythology, faithful lieutenant of *Aeneas in the *Aeneid*; a late source ascribes to him the killing of *Protesilaus (Eust. *Il.* 2. 701).

T. Weber, *Fidus Achates* (1988).   S. J. Ha.

Acheloüs, the longest of all Greek rivers, rising in central *Epirus and debouching, after a course of 240 km. (150 mi.; mostly through mountainous gorges), into the NW corner of the Corinthian Gulf. Its lower reaches were affected by heavy alluviation (Hdt. 2. 10. 3; Thuc. 2. 102. 3) and constituted the frequently disputed frontier between *Acarnania and *Aetolia. Acheloüs was personified early as a water- and *river-god (the son of *Oceanus and *Tethys), from whom all seas, rivers and springs derived (Hom. *Il.* 21. 194–7; Hes. *Theog.* 337–40). For his mythology and widespread depiction in art, see H. P. Isler, *LIMC* 1/1 (1981) 12–36.   W. M. M.

Acheron, a river of Thesprotia in southern *Epirus which breaks through an impenetrable gorge into the Acherusian plain where a lake (named Acherusia) lay in ancient times. The river empties into the Ionian Sea at the ancient Glycys Limen (or 'sweet harbour'). Homer (*Od.* 10. 513) describes the Acheron as a river of *Hades into which the Cocytus and Pyriphlegethon streams flow, the place where Odysseus consulted the spirits of the Underworld (*Od.* 11). Herodotus (5. 92. 7) mentions a death oracle (*nekyomanteion*) by the banks of the river where one called forth dead spirits for consultation. Remains of such an oracle have been excavated near Mesopotamo (see EPHYRA).

R. Bell, *Place Names in Classical Mythology* (1989), 4–5; S. I. Dakaris, *The Antiquity of Epirus* (n.d.), 3–7; P–K *GL* 2. 101–4.   W. M. M.

Achilles (Ἀχιλλεύς), son of *Peleus and *Thetis; greatest of the Greek heroes in the Trojan War; central character of *Homer's *Iliad*.

His name may be of Mycenaean Greek origin, meaning 'a grief to the army'. If so, the destructive Wrath of Achilles, which forms the subject of the *Iliad*, must have been central to his mythical existence from the first. He was the recipient of *hero-cults in various places, but these no doubt result from his prominence in the epic, and do nothing to explain his origins.

In Homer he is king of Phthia, or 'Hellas and Phthia', in southern Thessaly (see PHTHIOTIS), and his people are the Myrmidons. As described at *Il.* 2. 681–5 the size of his kingdom, and of his contingent in the Trojan expedition (50 ships), is not outstanding. But in terms of martial prowess, which is the measure of excellence for a Homeric hero, Achilles' status as 'best of the Achaeans' is unquestioned. We are reminded of his absolute supremacy throughout the poem, even during those long stretches for which he is absent from the battlefield.

His *character is complex. In many ways he carries the savage ethical code of the Homeric hero to its ultimate and terrifying conclusion. When *Agamemnon steals his concubine *Briseis in *Il.* 1, his anger at the insult to his personal honour is natural and approved by gods and men; but he carries this anger beyond any normal limit when he refuses an offer of immense compensation in *Il.* 9. Again, when he finally re-enters the war (*Il.* 19) after the death of his friend *Patroclus, his ruthless massacre of Trojans, culminating in the killing of *Hector (*Il.* 22), expresses a 'heroic' desire for revenge; but this too is taken beyond normal bounds by his contemptuous maltreatment of Hector's dead body (*Il.* 22. 395–404, 24. 14–22).

But what makes Achilles remarkable is the way in which his extreme expression of the 'heroic code' is combined with a unique degree of insight and self-knowledge. Unlike Hector, for instance, Achilles knows well that he is soon to die. In his great speech at *Il.* 9. 308–429 he calls the entire code into question, saying that he would rather live quietly at home than pursue glory in the Trojan War; but it is his 'heroic' rage against Agamemnon that has brought him to this point. In his encounter with Lycaon at *Il.* 21. 34–135, his sense of common mortality (the fact that Patroclus has died and Achilles himself will die) is a reason, not for sparing his suppliant, but for killing him in cold blood. Finally at *Il.* 24, when *Priam begs him to release Hector's body, it is human feeling, as well as the gods' command, that makes him yield (507–70); but even then he accepts a ransom, and his anger still threatens to break out afresh (568–70, 584–6).

Later writers seldom treated the subject-matter of the *Iliad* (though *Aeschylus did so, portraying Achilles and Patroclus as lovers: fr. 134a). But they did provide many further details of Achilles' career, often derived from cyclic epics (see EPIC CYCLE) such as the *Cypria* and *Aethiopis*. As a boy he was brought up by the wise *Centaur Chiron on Mt. *Pelion. Later his mother Thetis, knowing that he would be killed if he joined the expedition to Troy, hid him at the court of King Lycomedes on *Scyros, disguised as a girl (this episode is treated in the unfinished *Achilleis* of *Statius). There he fell in love with the king's daughter Deidamia, who bore him a son, *Neoptolemus (1), *Odysseus discovered his identity by trickery and he joined the Greek army at *Aulis, where he was involved in the story of *Iphigenia (see *Euripides' *Iphigenia at Aulis*). On the way to Troy he wounded *Telephus (1). His exploits at Troy included the ambush and killing of Priam's son *Troilus, a story linked with that of his love for Priam's daughter *Polyxena. After the events of the *Iliad* he killed two allies of the Trojans: the *Amazon queen *Penthesilea, with whom he is also said to have fallen in love, and the Ethiopian king *Memnon (1). Finally he was himself killed by *Paris and *Apollo (as predicted at *Il.* 22. 358–60). The fight over his body, and his funeral, are described in a dubious passage of the *Odyssey* (24. 36–94). His famous arms (described at *Il.* 18. 478–613) were then given to Odysseus (see *Sophocles' *Ajax*). After the fall of Troy his ghost demanded the sacrifice of Polyxena (see Euripides' *Hecuba*). A curious story, going back to *Ibycus (fr. 10 Page), is that in *Elysium he married *Medea (see also Paus. 3. 19. 13 for Achilles and *Helen on the White Island). Several of these episodes, including the ambush of Troilus and the killing of Penthesilea, were popular with vase-painters.

A late addition is the familiar motif of Achilles' heel: Thetis sought to make the infant Achilles invulnerable by dipping him in the *Styx, but omitted to dip the heel by which she held him, and it was there that he received his death-wound. This is alluded to by *Hyginus (3) (107) and *Statius (*Achil.* 1. 134, 269), but we have no full account until *Servius and '*Lactantius Placidus'.

A. Kossatz-Deissmann, *LIMC* 1 (1981), 37–200, 'Achilleus'; S. L. Schein, *The Mortal Hero* (1984). Cult: Farnell, *Hero-Cults* 409; H. Hommel, *Der Gott Achilleus* (1980); G. Hedreen, *Hesp.* 1991, 313–30; esp. on the cult in the *Black Sea area. A. L. B.

Achilles Tatius (1), Greek novelist (see NOVEL, GREEK) from *Alexandria (1), author of 'The Story of Leucippe and Cleitophon' (Tὰ κατὰ Λευκίππην καὶ Κλειτοφῶντα) in eight books. Shown by papyri to be circulating by the late 2nd cent. AD, it can hardly antedate AD 150. Of three other works ascribed to Achilles by the *Suda two are lost (an *Etymology* and a *Miscellaneous History of Many Great and Illustrious Men*), and the ascription of that partly preserved, *On the Sphere*, is debated. The *Suda's* story that later he became a Christian, and even a bishop, is probably false. Achilles varies patterns common to the genre: the enamoured couple elope and survive shipwreck, attacks by pirates and brig-

ands and complicated adventures in Egypt; they are eventually re-united in Ephesus after Leucippe has passed a chastity-test (cf. *Heliodorus (4)). The story is presented as Cleitophon's autobiographic narrative, told to the writer in a temple grove at Sidon (cf. *Longus). Unusually (but again cf. Longus) he succumbs (once) to the advances of a suitor, the married Ephesian Melite. Melodramatic effects include false deaths (three times Leucippe 'dies' and comes to life) and Achilles shares Heliodorus' and *Philostratus' fondness for learned digressions, some remote from his theme (e.g. on the phoenix, 3. 25, and the *elephant, 4. 4.), others making important if oblique contributions, like the *ekphrasis* of the painting of *Europa (1. 1) and the debate on the respective attractions of homosexual and heterosexual love (2. 35–8). His diction atticizes (see ASIANISM AND ATTICISM), though not consistently; his short, asyndetic sentences, sometimes of equal length and similar rhythm (*isokola*) class him with *Gorgias (1), 'Asianic' orators, and contemporaries like *Polemon (4), Longus, and *Aelian while a sophistic background is reflected in his characters' readiness to declaim. Ancient and modern critics alike have found him hard to evaluate. Some see his strained effects as humorous parody, but his attention to emotions and character-development is commended as realistic, and he handles sex explicitly enough to attract charges of *pornography. *Photius (*Bibl.* cod. 87, cf. *Anth. Pal.* 9. 203) praised Achilles' style but condemned his licentiousness; most moderns, uncertain how to evaluate him, prefer Longus and Heliodorus.

EDITIO PRINCEPS Heidelberg 1601; preceded by Latin translations (Della Croce, 1544 (partial), 1554 (complete).

STANDARD EDNS. E. Vilborg (1955); J. P. Garnaud (Budé, 1991).

COMMENTARIES F. Jacobs (1821); E. Vilborg (1962); Y. Yatromanolakis (1990).

ENGLISH TRANSLATIONS The best is by J. J. Winkler in B. P. Reardon (ed.), *Collected Ancient Greek Novels* (1989). Of numerous translations into modern languages since 1546, many are listed in S. Gaselee (Loeb, 1917), p. xvi: note esp. K. Plepelits (1980) (German, long introd. and comm.).

LEXICON J. N. O'Sullivan (1980).

CRITICISM Rohde, *Griech. Roman*, 498 ff.; W. Schmid, *RE* 1 (1894), 245–7, 'Achilleus Tatios' 1; Christ–Schmid–Stählin, 2/2[6], 1046 ff.; A. Lesky, *A History of Greek Literature* (1966), 865–6; E. L. Bowie, *CHCL* 1 (1985), 692–4 (= paperback 1/4 (1989), 132–4); H. Sexauer, *Der Sprachgebrauch des ... A. Tatius* (Diss. Heidelberg, 1899); H. Rommel, *Die naturwissenschaftlich-paradoxographischen Exkurse bei Philostratos, Heliodoros und Achilleus Tatios* (1923); T. Hägg, *Narrative Technique in Ancient Greek Romances* (1971), and *The Novel in Antiquity* (1983); G. Anderson, *Eros Sophistes* (1982), 23–32, and *Ancient Fiction* (1984); M. Laplace, *Recherches sur le roman d'Achille Tatius* (Thèse d'état dactyl. Paris-X, 1988); S. Bartsch, *Decoding the Ancient Novel* (1989). E. L. B.

Achilles Tatius (2) (probably 3rd cent. AD), author of a Greek commentary on *Aratus (1), the only surviving part of his work Περὶ σφαίρας.

Ed. E. Maass, *Commentariorum in Aratum Reliquiae* (1898), 25.

Achilleus See AURELIUS ACHILLEUS.

Acilii Glabriones, family. See generally M. Dondin–Payre, *Exercice du pouvoir et continuité gentilice: Les Acilii Glabriones* (1993).

Acilius (*RE* 4), **Gaius,** Roman senator and historian, who interpreted for *Carneades, *Diogenes (3), and *Critolaus in the senate in 155 BC, wrote a history of Rome, in Greek, from early Italian times to his own age, certainly to 184 BC (Dion. Hal. *Ant. Rom.* 3. 67. 5); it appeared *c*.142 (Livy, *Per.* 53: reading C. *Acilius*). His senatorial tradition is seen in the anecdote of P. *Cornelius Scipio Africanus and *Hannibal (Livy 35. 14. 5). His work was reproduced in Latin by a Claudius, probably *Claudius Quadrigarius, who would then have incorporated it in his annalistic form.

Peter, *HRRel.* 1² (1914), cxxi, 49; *FGrH* 3. C 881 ff.; E. Badian, in T. Dorey (ed.), *Latin Historians* (1966), 6 f.   A. H. McD.

Acilius Attianus, Publius, from Italica, fellow townsman of *Hadrian, whose guardian he became in AD 85 (SHA *Hadr.* 1. 4, where *Caelium* is a scribal error). Nothing more is known of his career before 117, when as *praefectus praetorio* at *Trajan's death he helped to ensure Hadrian's position: returning rapidly to Rome he arranged the execution of four ex-consuls (118) who had allegedly plotted against Hadrian. But he was soon (at latest 119) replaced and made a senator.

SHA *Hadr.*; Cass. Dio 69. *PIR²* A 45; A. Caballos Rufino, *Los senadores hispanorromanos* 1 (1990), 31 ff.   A. R. Bi.

Acilius (*RE* 35) **Glabrio** (1), **Manius,** a *novus homo*, was tribune of the plebs 201 BC when he supported peace with Carthage on the terms agreed with *Scipio Africanus. Praetor 196, he suppressed a slave revolt in Etruria. He was consul 191, defeating *Antiochus (3) III at Thermopylae and beginning operations against the Aetolians. In a famous scene he made it clear to the latter that *deditio* (see DEDITICII) to Rome precluded negotiations about terms. He was assisted by *Philip (3) V, whom he ordered to desist from the siege of Lamia (2), but allowed to appropriate territory in northern Greece. He embarked on the siege of *Naupactus, but was persuaded by *Flamininus to grant the Aetolians a truce to allow them to send ambassadors to Rome. He triumphed in 190 and in 189 stood for the censorship; accused of embezzlement during his command in Greece, he abandoned his candidacy. As consul he had carried the *lex Acilia de intercalando* (Acilian law on intercalation), necessitated by the fact that the Roman *calendar had become four months ahead of the seasons.

Walbank, *Philip V*, 202–9, and *Polybius* 3, see index; Briscoe, *Comm.* 31–33, *Comm.* 34–37, see indexes. On the *lex de intercalando* see V. M. Warrior in *Latomus* 1992.   J. Br.

Acilius (*RE* 37) **Glabrio** (2), **Manius,** grandson of (1), son-in-law of a Scaevola (probably Q. *Mucius Scaevola (1)), as tribune 122 BC passed a *repetundae* law providing for *equites as jurors and making procedure more severe (Cic. 1 *Verr.* 51 f.). He died soon after. The law, almost certainly part of C. *Sempronius Gracchus' programme, seems to be the *lex repetundarum* preserved on fragmentary bronze tablets.

FIRA 7, trans. E. G. Hardy, *Roman Laws and Charters* (1912), 1; E. Badian, *AJPhil.* 1954, 374 ff., and 1975, 67 ff.   E. B.

Acilius (*RE* 38) **Glabrio** (3), **Manius,** son of (2), as *praetor repetundarum* (70 BC) presided over *Verres' trial. Consul 67, he fought ineffectually against *Mithradates VI until superseded by *Pompey. 'Lazy and negligent' (Cic. *Brut.* 239), but well connected, he was a *pontifex and possibly *censor 64 (Broughton, *MRR* 3. 3).   E. B.

Acilius (*RE* 40; Suppl. 1) **Glabrio** (4), **Manius,** patrician and member of *Domitian's *consilium* (council of advisers); as consul in AD 91 he had to fight in the arena at Domitian's Alban estate (see ALBA LONGA) and was exiled. The cause is uncertain; Dio alleges jealousy of his prowess. His execution in 95 for plotting revolution contributed to Domitian's assassination the following year. The *catacomb to which his name is attached may belong to the end of the 2nd cent.

Suet. *Dom.* 10. 2; Cass. Dio 67. 14. 3. P. Styger, *Die römischen Katakomben*

(1933), 100 ff.; Cabrol–Leclerq, *Dict. d'arch. chrétienne* 6. 1259; K. Friedmann, *Atene e Roma* 1931, 69 ff.; B. Jones, *The Emperor Domitian* (1992), see index.   A. M.; B. M. L.

acoustics While sound and hearing were of marginal interest to most Presocratic philosophers, Pythagoreans became fascinated by observed correspondences of pitch-relations to ratios between lengths of string or pipe. They succeeded in showing that these correspondences held more generally, contriving 'demonstrations' with various other sound sources (see especially DK 18. 12, 13: the 'experiments' attributed to *Pythagoras (1) himself are insecurely attested). The resulting hypothesis that pitch itself is a quantitative variable prompted wider enquiries, beginning in the 4th cent., into the physical nature of sound, its causes, transmission, and attributes, and the processes involved in hearing.

The last issue was tackled mainly by biologists and medical writers: harmonics provided the usual context for the others. *Archytas' essay (fr. 1) is the direct ancestor of most later discussions. Sound, he says, is always caused by an impact (later writers specify the immediate cause as an impact on the air). It moves through the air like a missile until it strikes the ear: more vigorous movements constitute louder and higher-pitched sounds. Probably in *Plato (1), certainly in *Aristotle and after, what travels is not a 'missile' but an impulse in a stationary medium, variously conceived: as a succession of collisions between adjacent portions of air (e.g. ps.-Arist. *Pr.* 11. 6), or as a progressive 'tensing' or compression of the medium (Ptol. *Harm.* 1. 3), or by Stoics (see STOICISM) on the analogy with expanding circular ripples in water, but spreading 'spherically', in three dimensions (Diog. Laert. 7. 158). Aristotle's analysis, unlike Archytas', allowed for distinctions between the determinants of pitch (speed of transmission) and of volume (mass of air moved), each depending on relations between quantifiable features of the agent (esp. *De an.* 419ᵇ–421ᵃ, *Gen. an.* 786ᵇ–788ᵇ; cf. Pl. *Ti.* 67a–c). The correlation of pitch with speed (though Aristotle denies their strict identity) remained orthodox as late as *Boethius, despite difficulties (e.g. Arist. *Sens.* 448ᵃ⁻ᵇ, Theophr. fr. 89) and alternative hypotheses, correlating pitch with degrees of aerial tension (Ptol. *Harm.* 1. 3) or with the rapidity of successions of impacts on the air (Euc. *Secto canonis.* 149. 18–20). The causation of apparently continuous sounds by successions of discrete impacts is discussed at ps.-Arist. *De audibilibus* 803ᵇ–804ᵃ, later by *Heraclides (1) Ponticus (Porph. *On Ptolemy's Harmonics* 30. 1 ff.). The former passage is designed to explain the phenomenon of concord, another topic provoking much debate. Early treatments are Plato *Ti.* 79ᶜ–80ᵇ, Arist. *Sens.* 447ᵃ⁻ᵇ, and the proem to Euc. *Secto canonis*: most later discussions are elaborations of these (there are traces of still earlier investigations at DK 47 A 17).

Despite *Theophrastus' criticisms (fr. 89) of quantitative theories of pitch, later harmonic theorists drew freely on Platonic and *Peripatetic views to justify their treatment of intervals as numerical ratios, to explain many properties of instruments (e.g. Nicom. *Ench.* 4), especially the monochord and related 'scientific' devices (carefully discussed by *Ptolemy (4)), sometimes (as in *Theon (2) and *Aristides Quintilianus) to account for 'musical' attributes of the *soul and the universe. Practical applications were found: *Vitruvius discusses theatre design in the light of Stoic acoustics, explaining how hollow vessels, suitably pitched and placed, can improve an auditorium's resonance (*De arch.* 5. 3–5). Investigations of sound's pitch and transmission, and certain properties of sounding bodies, sometimes approached the scientific, though observations and experiments were never adequate to adjudicate conclusively between rival views. Discussions of other acoustic phenomena are usually uncoordinated and speculative (as in *Pr.* bk. 11): the fullest and most influential treatise, *De audibilibus*, is mainly a systematization of common sense, guided by the principle that a sound's qualities reflect those of its causes.

W. Burkert, *Lore and Science in Ancient Pythagoreanism* (1972; Ger. orig. 1962); H. Gottschalk, *Hermes* 1968; A. C. Bowen, *Ancient Philosophy* 1982; A. Barker, *Greek Musical Writings* 2 (1989). A. D. B.

Acquarossa, a plateau 6 km. (3½ mi.) north of Viterbo, is the site of a small and anonymous *Etruscan centre in the territory of *Caere. Excavation (1966–78) of its component areas—including the monumental complex in zone F, variously defined as a 'palace', a '*regia*', or a 'sacred area' (with a temple)—has combined with contemporary work at *Poggio Civitate to focus attention on early Etruscan building techniques, domestic and public architecture, town planning and non-funerary religious practice. Like Poggio Civitate, Acquarossa has yielded copious architectural *terracottas. The most important category, previously unknown or unrecognized, is that of the *orientalizing cut-out acroteria used on two-slope roofs between *c.*650/600 and *c.*575. They have no Greek models or counterparts, and clearly follow schemes derived from the strong indigenous tradition of exuberantly decorated roof-tops documented by the impasto hut-urns used as cinerary receptacles (but representing real huts) in Etruria and Latium between the 10th and 8th centuries.

C. E. Östenberg, *Case etrusche di Acquarossa* (1975); *Case e palazzi d'Etruria*, exhib. cat. (Siena 1985); *Architettura etrusca nel Viterbese*, exhib. cat. (Viterbo, 1986). The definitive report on the Acquarossa excavations by the Swedish Institute, Rome, appears in the fascicules of its *Skrifter/Acta*, 4th series (1981–): the cut-out acroteria are treated by E. Rystedt, *Acquarossa* 4 (1983). D. W. W. R.

Acrae (near mod. Palazzolo Acreide), founded by *Syracuse in 663 BC (Thuc. 6. 5. 3), stands on a hill protected by steep cliffs, commanding the westward route from the Syracusan plain. It enjoyed local self-government, but its fortunes were throughout its history linked with those of its metropolis. A late Archaic temple is known on the acropolis, but other known monuments are Hellenistic: a theatre, perhaps built under *Hieron (2) II, a *bouleutērion*, and a paved artery linking this with the agora. The series of extramural rock-cut reliefs in honour of *Cybele is unique. Also of note is a Hellenistic inscription found near Acrae, variously interpreted as oracular or as part of an epic poem. Acrae declined under the empire, but extensive *catacombs reveal it as still inhabited in the 4th and 5th cent. AD.

PECS 26–7; Gabba–Vallet, *Sicilia antica* 1. 497–507; L. Bernabò Brea, *Akrai* (1956), and *Il tempio di Afrodite di Akrai* (1986). Inscription: *SEG* 31. 821–2; cf. *ZPE* 50 (1983), 1–6; 60 (1985), 78–9; 63 (1986), 47–51. A. G. W.; R. J. A. W.

Acraephnium (mod. Karditza), city in NE *Boeotia, located above a small bay of Lake *Copais; perhaps the Homeric Arne. Fortifications and cemeteries have been excavated, the latter revealing splendid examples of early painted pottery. It entered the Boeotian Confederacy in 447 BC, and by 395 BC joined with *Copae and *Chaeronea to form one unit. It provided the Thebans with shelter after *Alexander (3) the Great destroyed their city in 335 BC (see THEBES (1)). In the wake of anti-Roman sentiment in 196 BC, Appius Claudius attacked the city. A long inscription details the benefactions of Epaminondas, a local magnate (mid-1st cent. AD), including repair of the Copais-dike

protecting the civic land from flood. The *Ptoion was in Acraephnium's territory.

J. Oliver, *GRBS* 1971, 221 ff.; Y. Garlan, *BCH* 1974, 95 ff.; J. Fossey, *Topography and Population of Ancient Boeotia* (1988). J. Bu.

Acragas (Lat. Agrigentum, mod. Agrigento) was founded *c.*580 BC by the Geloans in Sican territory in central southern Sicily. One of the most substantial Hellenic cities in size and affluence, it occupied a large bowl of land, rising to a lofty acropolis on the north and protected on the other by a ridge. Its early acquisition of power was owed to the tyrant *Phalaris. In 480 *Theron was the ally of *Gelon in his victory at *Himera. After expelling Thrasydaeus, Theron's son, Acragas had a limited democratic government, in which *Empedocles, its most famous citizen, took part in his generation. Acragantine 6th- and 5th-cent. prosperity is attested by a remarkable series of temples, the remains of which are among the most impressive of any Greek city, and by its extensive, wealthy necropoleis. Sacked by the Carthaginians in 406, Acragas revived to some extent under *Timoleon and Phintias (286–280 BC), but suffered much in the Punic Wars. By the late republic, to which period a temple, a *bouleutērion* and a gymnasium belong, it was again wealthy, and under Augustus it was one of the Sicilian cities favoured with a grant of *ius Latii. In the post-Roman period its inhabited area contracted to the old acropolis, where the heart of the modern city (which covers only a fraction of the area of its ancient counterpart) still lies.

Ancient descriptions: Pind. *Pyth.* 12 beg.; Polyb. 9. 27; Strab. 6. 2. 5. Modern works: *PECS* 23–6; *BTCGI* 1984, 66–128; Gabba–Vallet, *Sicilia antica*, 1. 485–95; J. A. de Waele, *Acragas Graeca: Die historische Topographie des griechischen Akragas auf Sizilien* 1 (1971); *Veder Greco: Le necropoli di Agrigento* (1988); L. Braccesi and E. de Miro (eds.), *Agrigento e la Sicilia greca* (1992); R. J. A. Wilson, *ANRW* 2. 11. 1 (1988) 177–85, and *Sicily under the Roman Empire* (1990) *passim*. A. G. W.; R. J. A. W.

Acrisius, in mythology, son of Abas, king of *Argos (2), and his wife Aglaïa, father of *Danaë and brother of *Proetus. After Abas' death the two brothers quarrelled; in their warfare they invented the shield. Proetus, defeated, left the country, returned with troops furnished by his father-in-law Iobates, and agreed to leave Argos to Acrisius, himself taking *Tiryns; both were fortified by the *Cyclopes. See schol. Eur. *Or.* 965. See PERSEUS (1).

J. J. Maffre, *LIMC* 1/1 (1981) 449 ff. H. J. R.

acropolis See ATHENS, TOPOGRAPHY; THEBES (1), *prehistoric*; and cf. CORINTH.

acrostic (Gk. ἀκροστιχίς, ἀκροστίχιον), a word or phrase formed from the initial letters of a number of consecutive lines of verse. Acrostics may occur by chance (Eust. *Il.* 24. 1; Gell. *NA* 14. 6. 4; Hilberg, *Wien. Stud.* (1899) 264–305, (1900) 317–18): whether they are accepted as significant will depend on their consonance with other aspects of the texts in which they occur. There are two broad types: proper names (especially the author's name as a kind of signature or *sphragis) and other words and phrases. Examples of the first type include *Nicander, *Ther.* 345–53 and *Alex.* 266–74 (inept or corrupt: cf. Lobel *CQ* 1928, 114), *Q. Ennius fecit* in a work of *Ennius (Cic. *Div.* 2. 111: *Epicharmus*? cf. Diog. Laert. 8. 78), and *Italicus . . . scripsit* at the beginning and end of the *Ilias Latina. The second type is rarer: perhaps the most famous example is the Hellenistic watchword λεπτή, 'fine', at *Aratus (1) *Phaen.* 783–7 (J.-M. Jacques, *Rev. Ét. Anc.* 1960, 48–61; compare perhaps (?) the equivalent section in Virgil's *Georgics*, 1. 428–33, with alternate lines beginning MA VA PU, for Publius Vergilius Maro backwards, E. Brown, *Numeri Vergilianae* (1963)), but note also MARS at *Aen.* 7. 601–4 (D. P. Fowler, *CQ* 1983, 298). Acrostics both draw attention to the written text and highlight the meaning of the word picked out; the effect is a complex one involving both form and content. They were particularly at home in prophetic literature and other religious or magical texts (Diels, *Sibyllinische Blätter* (1890), 33), but are found in many mainstream authors. See also PATTERN POETRY.

> H. Diels, *Sibyllinische Blätter* (1890), 25–37; I. Hilberg, *Wien. Stud.* 1899, 264–305; 1900, 317–18; Graf, *RE* 1, 'Akrostichis'; Pease on Cic. *Div.* 2. 111; E. Vogt, *AA* 1966, 80–97, with further literature; E. Courtney, *Philol.* 1990, 3–13.   D. P. F., P. G. F.

acta means 'the things that have been done' and has two specialized, overlapping senses in Roman history; one is a gazette, the other is official acts, especially of an emperor.

The *Acta diurna* were a gazette, whose publication dates from before 59 BC (a 2nd-cent. BC example of these is quoted by Renaissance antiquarians but its authenticity has been doubted); from the late republic onwards it recorded not only official events and ceremonies, but lawsuits and public speeches, and was read both at Rome and in the provinces (Asc. 30–1 C; Tac. *Ann.* 16. 22). The *Acta senatus* (or *Commentarii senatus*) constituted the official record of proceedings in the senate, first published in 59 BC (Suet. *Iul.* 20). Under the Principate a senator was selected by the emperor to be responsible for the record (Tac. *Ann.* 5. 4). The proceedings were available to senators but *Augustus forbade their wider publication (Suet. *Aug.* 36). Tacitus used, or depended on, authorities who used both the *Acta senatus* (e.g. *Ann.* 15. 74) and the *Acta diurna* (*Ann.* 3. 3.).

The exact definition of *acta* meaning enactments was not easy. The term was eventually held to cover the 'constitutions of emperors' (i.e. *edicta*, *decreta*, and *rescripta*, etc., see CONSTITUTIONS). Under the Roman republic magistrates took an oath, on entering office, to respect the laws of the state. The first recorded use of an oath to observe *acta* was that taken by all the magistrates to observe the *acta* of *Caesar in 45 BC (App. *BCiv.* 2. 106). When his *acta* were ratified by the senate after his murder (Cic. *Phil.* 1. 16 ff.), the looseness of the term gave scope for confusion and corruption. Oaths were taken to observe the *acta* of Augustus in 29 and in 24 BC. (Cass. Dio 51. 20, 53. 28). In order to equate the emperor's enactments with other sources of law, magistrates, emperors included (Cass. Dio. 60. 10), took the oath to observe the *acta* of previous emperors, except those whose *acta*, directly after their death, were explicitly rescinded (*rescissio actorum*) or at least excluded from the oath (Plin. *Ep.* 10. 58), though the wise enactments of even bad emperors might survive their death (Gai. *Inst.* 1. 33; *Dig.* 48. 3. 2). However, the relation of the *acta* of the living emperor to those of his predecessors raised problems. At first moderate emperors, such as *Tiberius and *Claudius, sought to restrict the oath to the *acta* of Divus Augustus, excluding their own *acta* (Suet. *Tib.* 67; Tac. *Ann.* 1. 72; Cass. Dio 60. 10), but with the increase of autocracy, the oath came to include the *acta* of reigning emperors.

> Mommsen, *Röm. Staatsr.* 2³. 906 ff., 3/2. 1015 ff.; A. W. Lintott, *PBSR* 1986.   J. P. B.; A. W. L.

Actaeon, in mythology son of *Aristaeus and Autonoë, daughter of *Cadmus, and a great huntsman. Ovid gives the most familiar version of his death (*Met.* 3. 138 ff.): one day on Mt. Cithaeron he came inadvertently upon *Artemis bathing, whereupon the offended goddess turned him into a stag and he was torn apart by his own hounds. Other versions of his offence were that he was *Zeus' rival with *Semele (our oldest authorities:

Stesichorus fr. 236 Davies, *PMGF*; Acusilaus fr. 33 Jacoby), or that he boasted that he was a better huntsman than Artemis (Eur. *Bacch.* 339–40), or that he wished to marry Artemis (Diod. Sic. 4. 81. 4). After his death his hounds hunted for him in vain, howling in grief, until the *Centaur Chiron made a lifelike image of him to soothe them (Apollod. 3. 4. 4).

Actaeon torn by hounds is found in many works of art from the 6th cent. In earlier pictures he sometimes wears a deerskin (as apparently in Stesichorus), but the first vases on which he sprouts antlers are after the middle of the 5th cent. Artemis surprised bathing appears first in Pompeian paintings. See L. Guimond, *LIMC* 1/1. 454–69.   H. J. R.; J. R. M.

Acte See CLAUDIA ACTE.

Actium (Ἄκτιον), a flat sandy promontory at the entrance to the Ambracian Gulf, forming part of the territory of Anactorium, as well as the NW extremity of *Acarnania. A cult of Apollo was located here as early as the 6th cent. BC to judge from the torsos of two archaic *kouroi* found on the cape in 1867. At this time, or soon thereafter, a temple stood on a low hill near the tip of the promontory where games were celebrated in honour of the god as late as the end of the 3rd cent. BC. In 31 BC the cape was the site of M. *Antonius (2)'s camp, and gave its name to the naval battle, fought just outside the gulf, in which he was defeated by *Octavian (2 September). A few years later, when Octavian founded *Nicopolis (3) on the opposite (northern) side of the strait, he took care to enlarge Apollo's sanctuary at Actium by rebuilding the old temple and adding a monumental naval trophy. In ship-sheds constructed in the sacred grove at the base of the hill, he dedicated a set of ten captured warships, one from each of the ten classes that had fought in the battle (Strabo 7. 7. 6). He also revitalized the old Actian Games by transferring them to a new venue outside Nicopolis. The quinquennial games, called Actia, were modelled on the Olympian festival, and were later imitated by several other Greek cities (see AGŌNES). An Actian 'era' was established, whose initial date is variously placed between 30 and 28 BC.

> P–K, *GL* 2. 380–1; *PECS* 28; W. M. Murray, *Octavian's Campsite Memorial* (1989) 125–55.   W. M. M.

actors See COMEDY (GREEK); COMEDY, LATIN; DIONYSUS, ARTISTS OF; THEATRE STAGING, GREEK; TRAGEDY, GREEK and LATIN.

Acts of the Apostles The second of two volumes which continues the story of the rise and spread of *Christianity begun in the gospel of Luke. Its textual history poses peculiar interpretative problems as it is extant in two versions, the longer in Codex Bezae. Its narrative starts with Jesus' ascension in Jerusalem and ends with *Paul preaching in Rome, where he had been taken after his appeal to Caesar (i.e. the emperor). The focus of the material on the earliest Jerusalem church around Peter and, later in the book, on the Christian career of Paul shows the concern of the author to relate the Jewish and Gentile missions and to demonstrate their basic unity. Only occasional glimpses are offered of the conflict in early Christianity which is evident in the Pauline corpus (e.g. Acts 6: 1 and 15). Acts has for a long time been a cause of great controversy between those who maintain the substantial authenticity of its historical account (while allowing for its apologetic interests) and those who see the document as a work of skilful narrative propaganda whose historical value is negligible. Knowledge of contemporary Graeco-Roman institutions should not mask the difficulties in accepting the historicity of Acts, a particular problem being the reconciliation of the accounts of Paul's career in Acts, Gal. 1–2, and the Corinthian correspondence. The references to Paul's theology indicate a markedly different set of ideas from what we find in the letters to the Romans and Galatians. For this and other reasons Acts has proved to be disappointing to the historian of Christian origins as a source for early Christian history. The history of the Jerusalem church after the start of the Pauline mission is only touched on in so far as it helps the author explain Paul's career as apostle to the Gentiles. Whereas Luke's gospel portrays Jesus as a Palestinian prophet with a controversial, indeed subversive, message for Jewish society, there is little in Acts (apart from the idealized accounts of the common life of the Jerusalem church) of that radicalism. The antagonism to *Jews and the sympathetic account of Roman officials evident in the gospel of Luke is continued in Acts, and a conciliatory attitude towards Rome has been suggested. Jews in Acts are regarded as responsible for the harassment of nascent Christianity, though there are occasional glimpses of more openness to Judaism elsewhere in the book than the concluding verses would indicate.

Various suggestions have been made with regard to its (and the related gospel of Luke's) purpose. These have included an apologia for Christianity to the Roman state, an explanation for the delay of the Parousia (Second Coming) by stressing the role of the church in the divine purpose, an essay in anti-Jewish polemic, and a defence of Paul when his case was heard in Rome. Like his contemporary *Josephus the author of Acts seeks to demonstrate that divine providence is at work, though for the latter there is nothing in the emergence of a strange Jewish messianic movement to contradict the Jewish tradition, since it is rather the inevitable continuation of it.

H. Conzelmann, *Acts of the Apostles* (1987); P. Esler, *Community and Gospel in Luke-Acts* (1987); W. Gasque, *A History of the Criticism of the Acts of the Apostles* (1975); E. Haenchen, *The Acts of the Apostles* (1971); M. Hengel, *Acts and the History of Earliest Christianity* (1979); F. J. Foakes Jackson and K. Lake, *The Beginnings of Christianity* (on the text of Acts) (1926); G. Ludemann, *Early Christianity according to the Traditions in Acts* (1989).   C. C. R.

Acts of the Pagan (or **Heathen**) **Martyrs** is the name given by modern scholars to about a dozen fragments of Alexandrian nationalist literature, preserved on papyri mostly written in the 2nd or early 3rd cent. AD. The majority of the fragments give, in dramatic form, reports of the hearing of Alexandrian embassies and of the trials of Alexandrian nationalist leaders before various Roman emperors. The episodes related, of which the dramatic dates range from the time of *Augustus to that of *Commodus, are probably basically historical and the accounts appear to be derived to some extent from official records. But they have been coloured up, more in some cases than in others, for propaganda purposes, to caricature the emperors, to stress the fearless outspokenness of the Alexandrians, who are sometimes surprisingly rude to the emperors, and to represent their punishment, usually execution, as martyrdom in the nationalist cause. This literature is in general bitterly hostile to Rome, reflecting the tensions between *Alexandria (1) and her overlord during the first two centuries of Roman rule. These included antagonism between the Greeks and Rome's protégés, the *Jews, and three episodes concern their quarrels. But despite the violent hatred expressed

by the Greeks for the Jews, anti-Semitism is only a subsidiary feature in these primarily anti-Roman compositions.

H. Musurillo, *The Acts of the Pagan Martyrs, Acta Alexandrinorum* (1954), with comm.; also Teubner text (1961).   E. M. S.; M. T. G.

Acusilaus, of Argos, lived 'before the *Persian Wars' (Joseph. *Ap.* 1–13) and compiled *genealogies, translating and correcting *Hesiod, with ingenious conjectures but no literary merit.

FGrH 2.

Ada, *satrap (see MAUSOLUS) of the Persian province of *Caria, youngest child of *Hecatomnus, sister of *Mausolus and of *Idrieus, to whom she was incestuously married and with whom she was co-ruler of Caria until his death in 344 BC. (See L. Robert, *Hellenica* 7 (1947), 63 ff., an interesting inscription from *Sinuri, which also shows that the Ptolemaic tax called the *apomoira* was of *Achaemenid Persian origin.) She then ruled alone (344–341) until displaced by her brother *Pixodarus. But *Alexander (3) the Great reinstated her in 334, and she adopted him as her son: Arr. *Anab.* 1. 23.

Strab. 14. 2. 17; Tod 161; L. Robert, *Le Sanctuaire de Sinuri*, 1 (1945), 94 ff.; A. B. Bosworth, *Historical Commentary on Arrian's History of Alexander* i *Commentary on Books i–iii* (1980), 152 ff.; S. Hornblower, *Mausolus* (1982), inscriptions at 364 ff.; S. Ruzicka, *Politics of a Persian Dynasty: The Hecatomnids in the Fourth Century BC* (1992).   S. H.

adaeratio, the procedure whereby dues to the Roman state in kind were commuted to cash payments. The related word *adaerare* first appears in AD 383 (*Cod. Theod.* 7. 18. 8) and the practice is characteristic of the later Roman empire. But it is attested for certain dues supplementary to the standard form of *taxation in Cicero's *Verrines* and Tacitus' *Agricola*, along with its attendant abuses. In the later Roman empire the procedure was also applied to distributions by the Roman state in kind. The transaction was sometimes official, sometimes unofficial, and might be made on the initiative of the government, the tax-collector (see PUBLICANI), or the taxpayer in the case of levies, or of either party in the case of distributions. The rate might be settled by bargaining, or fixed by the government at the market price or at some arbitrary sum. The range of commodities involved was large. Just as dues and distributions in kind had assumed greater importance because of the collapse of the coinage system in the 3rd cent. AD, so a consciousness of the existence of a stable gold coinage after Constantine led to a slow move back to transactions in money, normally gold, over the late 4th and 5th cents.

Jones, *Later Rom. Emp.* see index.   A. H. M. J.; M. H. C.

Adamklissi, the site of three Roman monuments in the Dobrudja plain (South Romania): (1) an altar (16.2 m. (53 ft.) square and *c.*6 m. (20 ft.) high) recording legionary and auxiliary casualties, probably from *Trajan's first Dacian campaign (AD 101/2) rather than that of *Domitian; (2) a circular mausoleum or *tropaeum* (*c.*40 m. (131 ft.) diam.) standing on the crest of the hill, built of the same local stone as the altar, and perhaps also linked with Trajan's first Dacian war (AD 101/2); (3) a circular *tropaeum* (*c.*30 m. (100 ft.) diam.) in the better-quality Deleni stone dedicated in AD 108/9 (*CIL* 3. 12467; cf. E. Doruțiu-Boilă, *Dacia* (1961), 345 ff.) surmounted by a hexagonal column and victory *tropaeum*, dominating the hill and visible from the Danube more than 40 km. (25 mi.) away. See TROPHIES. The surviving metopes portray scenes of conflict with Dacians and others but in a different style from the continuous relief of *Trajan's Column in Rome. A small city named after the monument (*Municipium Tropaeum Traiani*) grew up in the valley below. (See DACIA.)

F. Bobu Florescu, *Monumentul de la Adamklissi*, 2nd edn. (1961), Ger. edn., *Das Siegesdenkmal von Adamklissi* (1965); I. A. Richmond, *PBSR* 1967, 29 ff.; A. Poulter, *Studien zu den Militärgrenzen Roms* 3 (1986), 523–6.   J. J. W.

adeia, 'immunity', sometimes in Greece offered to men accused of involvement in a crime who were willing to inform on others (e.g. *Andocides in Athens' religious scandals of 415 BC). In Athens the term is used also of a special vote by the assembly permitting itself to discuss a subject which otherwise it would be forbidden to discuss (e.g. to levy the tax called *eisphora* or more generally to override an 'entrenchment clause' in an earlier decree forbidding discussion of a matter without a vote of immunity. Such clauses were intended to prevent over-hasty decisions by requiring two votes at separate meetings of the assembly before action could be taken on an entrenched matter.

D. M. Lewis, φόρος ... *B. D. Meritt* (1974), 81–9.   A. W. G.; P. J. R.

Adiabene (mod. Halab), district of the two Zab rivers in north *Mesopotamia. Possibly a Seleucid hyparchy, it became a vassal kingdom, later a satrapy, of *Parthia, and was constantly involved in her internal disputes and her wars with Rome. One of the dynasties of Adiabene embraced Judaism (Joseph. *AJ* 20. 17–37). *Trajan's army overran Adiabene in AD 116 and *Caracalla's in 216, but neither campaign had more than a momentary effect on the status or allegiance of the country. It was absorbed into the Sasanid empire at the time of the final collapse of Parthia.

M. S. D.; E. W. G.; S. S.-W.

adlection A man acquired the right of speaking in the Roman senate (*ius sententiae dicendae*; see SENATE) by holding a magistracy, the quaestorship; he became a full member when his name was placed on the senatorial roll (*album*) ('a censoribus ... allectum', Val. Max. 2. 2. 1). *Caesar, *dictator or *praefectus morum* (overseer of public morals), and the *triumvirs adlected men directly into the senate, presumably as *quaestorii*. (Adlection into the patriciate began with Caesar (Suet. *Iul.* 41. 2).) This unpopular proceeding was avoided by emperors until *Claudius, *censor in AD 47–8, admitted men *inter quaestorios* and *tribunicios* (*ILS* 968); *Vespasian anticipated his censorship (Tac. *Hist.* 2. 82), but in 73–4 did the same (*ILS* 1024 = MW 321, *inter praetorios*). After *Domitian (life censor) men were routinely adlected. Adlection *inter consulares* first appears in AD 182, was practised by *Macrinus, and disliked (Cass. Dio 79. 13. 1); with *Diocletian it became common.   J. P. B.; B. M. L.

Admetus See ALCESTIS.

Adonis (Ἄδωνις). Name given by the Greeks to a divine personage whom they thought to be eastern in origin (Semitic *Adon* = 'Lord'), but whose eastern prototypes (Dumuzi, Tammuz, Baal, Ešmun) are very different from the picture which became established in Greece. In mythology, Adonis is born from the incest of an easterner, whose name is variously given as Agenor, Cinyras, Phoenix, and Theias, and of *Myrrha or Smyrna. He aroused the love of *Aphrodite, who hid him in a chest and entrusted him to *Persephone, but she, captivated in her turn, refused to give him back. Then *Zeus decreed that the young man should spend four months of the year in the Underworld (see HADES) and four months with Aphrodite—whom Adonis chose also for the final four months, left to his own decision. He was born from a myrrh tree, and dying young in a hunting accident, was changed into an anemone, a flower without scent ([Apollod.] 3. 14. 3–4; Ov. *Met.* 10. 300–559, 708–39). A festival for the young god, known

as Adonia, is attested only at Athens, Alexandria (1), and Byblos. In 5th cent. BC Athens, women sowed seed at midsummer in broken pots and placed these on the roof-tops, so that germination was rapidly followed by withering (Ar. *Lys.* 708–39 with scholia). In this lively, noisy celebration, which has been brought into opposition with the *Thesmophoria, mourning is secondary; at Byblos, the ritual involves the whole population, expressing at two different times mourning and laments, and resurrection and joy, but there is no trace of the 'gardens of Adonis' (Lucian, *Syr. D.* 7). The festival at Alexandria (Theoc. 15), like that of Athens, presents a picture of a women's ritual including mourning, but above all rejoicing centred on the couple, Aphrodite and Adonis.

Starting from a vast comparative study, Sir James Frazer saw in Adonis an image of the succession of the seasons and of agricultural tasks, a sort of 'vegetation spirit'. Marcel Detienne, on the other hand, uses a structural analysis to demonstrate that the Greek picture of Adonis, far from being a divinization of agriculture, suggests rather the impermanent, the fragile, and the barren. Aphrodite's young lover has thus inspired a lively debate, and is still the focus of methodological problems, notably those centred on the Greek interpretation of eastern data, an issue studied in particular by S. Ribichini.

J. G. Frazer, *Adonis, Attis, Osiris* (1907); W. Atallah, *Adonis dans la littérature et l'art grec* (1966); B. Soyez, *Byblos et la fête des Adonies* (1977); M. Detienne, *The Gardens of Adonis* (1977, 2nd edn. 1994, with endnote; Fr. orig. 1972, 2nd edn. 1989); S. Ribichini, *Adonis: Aspetti 'orientali' di un mito greco* (1981); S. Ribichini (ed.), *Adonis: Relazioni del colloquio in Roma* (1984); B. Servais-Soyez, *LIMC* 1 / 1 (1981) 222 ff.

V. P.-D., A. Mot.

adoption

Greek Greeks counted on their heirs for support in old *age, and for continuation of their *oikoi* (families) and tendance of their tombs after death. But high mortality ensured that many had no surviving children. Adoption was a common recourse, probably encouraged by the great variation in fertility characteristic of populations with unreliable means of *contraception. The fullest accounts can be provided for *Gortyn and *Athens in the Classical period.

The law code of Gortyn apparently modifies prior practice. It permits an adult male to adopt anyone he chooses, including someone without full membership in the community, even if he already has legitimate children; however, the inheritance of those adopted in such circumstances is less than it would be if they were natural children. Adoptive fathers are to announce the adoption to a citizen assembly and make a stipulated payment to their *hetaireia* (in this context, a kind of kinship group analogous to the *phratry); they may also publicly disavow the adoption, and compensate those adopted with a set sum. Neither women nor minors may adopt.

At Athens, we hear of three forms of adoption, differing chiefly in the manner in which those adopted entered into their inheritance. These involved living parties (*inter vivos*), a will (testamentary adoption, said to have been introduced by *Solon), or the provision of an heir for a man already deceased. (Such posthumous adoptions did not require the prior agreement of the adoptive father.) As at Gortyn, only adult male citizens could adopt. However, Athenians' freedom of action was more limited: they could adopt only in the absence of legitimate sons, and then no one other than (male) citizens. Magistrates could not adopt or be adopted until their accounts had been rendered; those who were *atimoi* (subject to civic disability) could not be adopted. In addition, adopted sons could not themselves adopt in some or all cases. But fathers with daughters only could adopt; they might also marry their daughters to their adopted sons. In practice, adopters tended to choose adults, as these were more likely to survive and (according to the orators) had already given good evidence of their character, and sons were preferred to daughters. Those adopted would often have inherited anyway by the laws governing intestacy; adoptions of others were likely to be challenged by closer kin. Their claims might be furthered by the belief, apparent in other contexts as well, that adoption did not generally forge links of loyalty and intimacy equal to those of blood (e.g. Pl. *Leg.* 9. 878 a; Dem. *Epitaphius* 4). Adoptions by will could also be attacked on the legal grounds that the adopter had acted when mad or senile, under the influence of drugs, illness, or a woman, or under coercion. Adopted children severed their connections with their natural fathers, though not their mothers. They could return to their *oikos* of birth if they left a natural son as heir to their adoptive *oikos*.

Adoption at Athens has often been viewed in the context of the community's concern for the survival of individual *oikoi*, a concern thought to be reflected in the responsibilities of the eponymous archon (see ARCHONTES). Other Greek *poleis* (see POLIS) provide parallels: the role of the kings in adoptions at *Sparta (Hdt. 6. 57), the tradition that Philolaus, the lawgiver of *Thebes (1), used adoption to maintain the number of *klēroi* (Arist. *Pol.* 2. 1274ᵇ5). However, recent scholarship tends toward contrary conclusions: the *polis* was not concerned to maintain separate *oikoi* through adoption, though individuals certainly were; adoption was essentially a private matter, regulated by the phratries and *demes into which adopted children were introduced, in which the archon took no initiative; heirs had no legal obligation to continue an *oikos* through posthumous adoption. Furthermore, arguments (based on the disappearance of testamentary adoption) that continuation of the *oikos* ceased to be a goal of adoption after the 4th cent. probably read too much into the silence of our literary sources.

Almost all our evidence from adoption in the Hellenistic and Roman periods comes from numerous inscriptions from throughout the Greek world, especially Rhodes. These reveal a bewildering inconsistency in terminology, even within the same community, perhaps attesting to differences in formal procedures and consequences now unclear. They also indicate that Greeks might change their names on adoption.

L. Gernet, *Droit et société dans la Grèce ancienne* (1955), 121–49; A. R. W. Harrison, *The Law of Athens* 1 (1968); L. Rubinstein, *Adoption in IV. Century Athens* (1993); L. Rubinstein and others, *C&M* 1991, 139–51; M. S. Smith, *CQ* 1967, 302–10. M. G.

Roman Adoptio is a legal act by which a Roman citizen enters another family and comes under the *patria potestas* of its chief. Since only a *paterfamilias* (see PATRIA POTESTAS) could adopt, women could not (except in later law by imperial grant). When the adopted person, male or female, was previously in the paternal power of another, the act was *adoptio*; when a male who was not in paternal power but himself the head of a family, it was *adrogatio*. Women could not be adrogated. Both acts involved a *deminutio capitis minima*, a reduction of legal status.

Adrogatio fused two families, for with the adoptee (*adrogatus*) all under his power (*potestas, manus*) and his property pass into the family of the adopter (*adrogator*). In early times *adrogatio* was publicly validated by a vote of the curiate assembly, preceded (since it extinguished a family and its cult) by an investigation by the pontiffs; by the time of Cicero, 30 lictors represented the *curiae* (see CURIA (1)). Since the assembly met only in Rome, *adrogatio* could take place only there, until (by Diocletian's time at latest) imperial rescript replaced the vote.

Adoptio of a person in power (of any age) was a more private act performed before a praetor or governor. Its form was the same as that of *emancipation (*emancipatio*, the release of a child from power), except that after the third sale the buyer did not free the child but collusively claimed that he/she was in his power. Under Justinian, these formalities were replaced by a declaration before a magistrate.

The effect of both *adoptio* and *adrogatio* was to place the adopted person for all legal purposes in the same position as if he/she had been a natural child in the power of the adopter. The adoptee took the adopter's name and rank and acquired rights of succession in his new family, losing those held in the old family. 'Adoption imitates nature' (*Inst. Iust.* 1. 11. 4), so an adoptive relationship barred marriage and the adopter had to be older than the adoptee (a rule allegedly flouted by the adoption of P. *Clodius Pulcher). Bachelors and men physically incapable of reproduction (except if they had been castrated) could adopt. Adoption could be reversed by emancipation.

Adoption (of both kinds), since it created paternal power and continued the agnatic family, was originally the prerogative of men only. Adoption by women, 'to console them for the loss of children', was allowed by later emperors, as was adrogation of women: this shows a new conception. Safeguards grew up, especially for young children and their property.

Since adoption destroyed the adoptee's succession rights in the old family and a subsequent emancipation would destroy rights in the new family, Justinian drastically changed *adoptio* to allow the adoptee to retain rights in the old family, except where the adopter was a close relative, e.g. maternal grandfather.

The testamentary adoptions recorded in non-legal sources in the late republic and Principate apparently created only an obligation (from which the praetor could give dispensation) to take the testator's name. So T. *Pomponius Atticus inherited from his mother's brother Caecilius and became formally Q. Caecilius Q. f. Pomponianus Atticus (Cic. *Att.* 3. 20); the future emperor Ser. Sulpicius *Galba for some time bore a name taken from the family of his stepmother, Livia Ocellina: L. Livius Ocella (Suet. *Galb.* 3–4). Caesar's adoption of his great-nephew C. Octavius (see AUGUSTUS) was ratified by a posthumous *adrogatio*.

Adoption of adult men was a convenient recourse for childless aristocrats and for emperors in need of successors.

Gell. *NA* 5. 19; Gai. *Inst.* 1. 97–107; *Inst. Iust.* 1. 11; *Dig.* 1. 7.
A. B.; B. N.; S. M. T.

Adrastus (1), described in the *Iliad* as former king of *Sicyon (2. 572), was worshipped there at least until the 6th cent. (Hdt. 5. 67). Best known as the leader of the first Argive expedition against *Thebes (1) (and possibly the second as well), he was the only one to survive, escaping on the semi-divine horse *Arion (1) (*Il.* 23. 346–7; *Thebaid* fr. 6 Davies). He had undertaken the expedition to restore one son-in-law, Polynices, to the throne, and was to have done the same for the other, *Tydeus of Calydon (Hutchinson, on Aesch. *Sept.* 575).

The tradition which made Adrastus king at *Argos (2) may owe something to the interpolation of a patrilineal descendant into a matrilineal regal line (Finkelberg). His connections with cult sites other than Sicyon (Colonos Hippios, *Eleusis, *Megara) derive from the influence of the epic.

Adrastus

Some have sought a Mycenaean origin for the Theban wars (e.g. Brillante, see bibliog. below). The motif of 'seven' aggressors is found in near eastern sources (Burkert). There is no canonical list of champions (Homer names only Adrastus, *Amphiaraus, *Capaneus, Tydeus, possibly Mecisteus): perhaps the tradition of '*Seven against Thebes' was concocted to match the seven gates of Boeotian Thebes (*Il.* 4. 406, *Od.* 11. 263, as opposed to Egyptian, 100-gated, *Thebes (2): *Il.* 9. 381–3). The story was certainly well known to Homer's audience, and *Tyrtaeus alludes to Adrastus' eloquence as a byword (fr. 12 West, cf. Pl. *Phdr.* 269 a). The predominant role of Argos, the absence of a Corinthian champion, and the refusal of the Mycenaeans to participate (*Il.* 4. 376–81) suggest that the tradition developed after the Mycenaean period and before the rise of Corinth, but after that of Argos.

C. Brillante, *Studi micenei ed egeo-anatolici* 1980, 309–40; W. Burkert, *The Orientalizing Revolution* (1992; Ger. orig. 1984), 106; M. Finkelberg, *CQ* 1991, 308–12; G. O. Hutchinson (ed.), Aeschylus, *Septem contra Thebas* (1985), 134; I. Krauskopf, *LIMC* 1 (1981), 231–40.   A. Sch.

Adrastus (2), (*RE* 7) of Aphrodisias, *Peripatetic philosopher (2nd cent. AD). His influential writings included commentaries on the order of *Aristotle's works (mainly philological); on *Nicomachean Ethics* and *Theophrastus' *Characters* (historical and literary); on *Categories* and on *Physics*; and on *Plato (1)'s *Timaeus* (mathematical and scientific, relating Pythagorean and Aristoxenian harmonics and contemporary astronomy to Platonic cosmology (see ARISTOXENUS; PYTHAGORAS (1)).

P. Moraux, *Der Aristotelismus bei den Griechen* 2 (1984); A. Barker, *Greek Musical Writings* 2 (1989); H. P. F. Mercken, in R. Sorabji (ed.), *Aristotle Transformed* (1990).   A. D. B.

Adria See ATRIA.

Adrianus (Hadrianus), of Tyre (*c.* AD 113–93), sophist, pupil of *Herodes Atticus; held the chairs of rhetoric at Athens and Rome. One short *declamation attributed to him survives. See SECOND SOPHISTIC.

Philostr. *VS* 2. 10 (589–90); comm. S. Rothe (1989), 92. *Polemonis declamationes*, ed. Hinck (1873), 44.   M. B. T.

Adriatic Sea (Gk. ὁ Ἀδρίας; Lat. *Mare adriaticum* or *superum*), used as an alternative to '*Ionian sea' for the waters between the Balkan peninsula and Italy, and like 'Ionian', sometimes extended to include the sea east of Sicily. In neolithic times seafarers from the south settled around the gulf of Valona at the entrance to the Adriatic (*c.*80 km. (50 mi.) north of Corcyra). In the bronze age there is evidence for trade in Baltic *amber and perhaps in Bohemian *tin while weapons apparently came by sea from the north to Italy and to Greece, with ports of call in between. Seafarers from the Adriatic occupied the Nidhri plain in *Leucas, where they built tumulus burials like those known from Albania in the Middle Helladic period. In historical times, Greek exploration of the Adriatic was said to be the work of the Phocaeans (see PHOCAEA), who penetrated to its upper end by 600 BC (Hdt. 1. 163).

Greek *colonization was directed from *Corinth and *Corcyra in the late 7th and the 6th cent., their major foundations being *Apollonia and *Epidamnus. Further north, off the Dalmatian coast, emigrants from *Cnidus occupied Corcyra Nigra (mod. Curzola), and the *Syracusans (probably refugees from Dionysius I) took possession of Issa (modern Lissa). In Italy, *Rhodes and *Cos founded Elpiae among the Apulian *Daunians (Strab.

14.2.10) and, in central Italy, refugees from *Dionysius I settled *Ancona. At ports like *Adria and Spina at the Po estuary (see PADUS), Greeks and *Etruscans exchanged goods from the late 6th cent. onwards. Coin finds from the Po valley indicate Tarentine trade up the Adriatic during the 4th cent. (See TARENTUM.)

Although Adriatic commerce and colonization were harassed by Illyrian pirates who inhabited the South Dalmatian coast, a growing number of shipwrecks (over 150) reveals a continuing trade (see ARCHAEOLOGY, UNDERWATER), even during periods of piracy. *Piracy was nevertheless a serious nuisance that the Romans repeatedly tried to suppress, finally succeeding when Pompey tackled the problem in 67 BC. From the time of Augustus, the Adriatic was patrolled by a regular police flotilla. (See NAVIES.) To judge from *shipwrecks, the Adriatic experienced an increase of trade during these peaceful years.

R. L. Beaumont, *JHS* 1936, 159 ff.; Hammond, *Epirus* 326–31; H. Dell, *Hist.* 1967, 344–58.   M. C.; W. M. M.

Adulis or **Adule,** on the west coast of the Red Sea (at Zulla in Annesley Bay near Massawa), was used by Ptolemy II and III for elephant-hunts (see ELEPHANTS), and became an important export-mart for African and re-exported Indian wares, a caravan-route leading thence inland. Greeks and Indians frequented it. When the Aksumite kingdom rose (1st cent. AD, see AXUMIS) Adulis became its main port and base (for voyages to East Africa and *India), surpassing all others in the 3rd cent. AD. Two famous inscriptions (combined in *OGI* 54) are among its monuments.

Periplus Maris Erythraei, ed. L. Casson (1989), 4; Plin. *HN* 6. 172; Ptol. *Geog.* 4. 7. 8, 8. 16. 11; Cosmas, ed. E. O. Winstedt (1909), 101b ff.   R. G. M.

adultery

Greek At Athens, a law (attributed to *Draco or *Solon) allowed a man who killed another he found in the sexual act with his wife, mother, sister, daughter, or concubine held for the purpose of bearing free children, to plead justifiable homicide; such adulterers might also be held for ransom. It is probable that there was also a *graphē* against adulterers, possible that those caught in the act were delivered to the *Eleven for summary execution or trial. Adulterous wives had to be divorced, and were excluded from public sacrifices. As for unmarried women, Solon supposedly permitted a κύριος ('controller', male representative at law) to sell a daughter or sister into slavery if he discovered she was not a virgin. No instances are known, however, and indeed some husbands too probably preferred to respond (or not) to adultery without recourse to the law, so avoiding public dishonour. Many states are said to have allowed adulterers to be killed with impunity (Xen. *Hiero* 3. 3). But the law code of *Gortyn envisages adulterers paying ransoms, varying with the status of the parties and the setting of the acts, and pecuniary penalties are stipulated in some marriage contracts from Hellenistic Egypt. Punishments in other (mostly later) communities stress public humiliation. Laws at both Athens and Gortyn provided protection against entrapment and false accusations. There was allegedly no Lycurgan (see LYCURGUS (2)) law against adultery at Sparta, a tradition informed by the custom by which Spartans could share their wives with fellow citizens for procreative purposes. (See MARRIAGE LAW (Greek)).

S. G. Cole, *CPhil.* 1984, 97–113; G. Hoffman, *Le Châtiment des amants dans la Grèce classique* (1990); D. Cohen, *Law, Sexuality and Society* (1991).   M. G.

Roman Roman tradition ascribed to fathers and husbands great severity in punishing illicit sexual behaviour by daughters or wives. Such misconduct was *stuprum* in married or unmarried women, an offence against chastity (*pudicitia*); *adulterium* described sexual intercourse between a married woman and a man other than her husband. Until the legislation of Augustus, regulation was chiefly in the hands of the family: adultery probably always justified divorce; a family council might advise the *paterfamilias* (husband or father in whose power the woman was (see PATRIA POTESTAS)) on this and other sanctions, possibly including execution. The immediate killing of adulterers/adulteresses taken in the act was defensible (morally and in court) but probably not legally prescribed. Other physical violence against the adulterer is a literary commonplace. Adultery in the late republic, like the seduction or rape of an unmarried woman, entitled the father or husband to sue the man for damages (for *iniuria*, insult) and not only to divorce the wife but to retain part of her dowry. Magistrates occasionally proceeded against adulterers/adulteresses.

*Augustus, in the Julian law on repression of adulteries (*lex Iulia de adulteriis coercendis vel sim.*, *Dig.* 48. 5), passed apparently shortly after the marriage law of 18 BC, made illicit sexual intercourse (extramarital intercourse by and with a respectable free woman) a crime, to be tried by a special court under a praetor (in practice, often the senate). The law detailed restricted circumstances in which homicide by father or husband was justifiable. The normal judicial penalty for adulterers was *relegatio* (banishment) to different islands, and partial confiscation of property and dowry (one half). The husband with clear evidence had to divorce or be liable to a charge of procuring (*lenocinium*; penalties similar). On divorce, husband or father might bring an accusation within 60 days, or anyone within the next four months. A woman might not be accused while married.

Penalties were increased by Christian emperors. Constantine I introduced the death penalty (which Justinian confirmed), but allowed only the husband or the wife's relatives to prosecute.

Adultery by the husband was not *adulterium* (unless his partner was a married woman), but his intercourse with a respectable unmarried woman (or male) constituted *stuprum* and in the 5th cent. AD (*Cod. Iust.* 5. 17. 8) his adultery in the matrimonial home or with a married woman entitled his wife to divorce him without incurring the penalties then imposed for unjustified divorce. (See MARRIAGE LAW (Roman).)   A. B.; B. N.; S. M. T.

advocacy This article considers advocacy as a profession. For advocacy in its wider sense and in particular for its techniques, see RHETORIC.

A party to a Roman trial might entrust the presentation of his case to an advocate (*advocatus*, *patronus*, *causidicus*). These men, who appear as a class in the late republic under the influence of Greek rhetoric, and of whom *Cicero and the younger *Pliny (2) are prominent representatives, were orators rather than *lawyers. They would necessarily have, or acquire, some knowledge of law (Cicero evidently knew a lot), but their reputations were founded on their skill in forensic rhetoric. They and the jurists regarded each other as distinct classes, with different (and in the eyes of the other class inferior) functions, though occasionally an advocate might become a jurist. Advocates were forbidden to accept any reward for their services, but this rule was evidently often ignored and by the end of the 2nd cent. AD imperial recognition was given (*Dig.* 50. 13. 1. 9 ff.) to claims for an *honorarium* (or *palmarium*, if payment was conditional on the case being won). In the later empire, the advocates, at least in the east, are

no longer merely orators, but are qualified lawyers, who have studied at a law school and form a privileged corporation. Their number is limited, their fees are regulated, and they are attached to a particular court. The majority of the compilers of the *Digest* (see JUSTINIAN'S CODIFICATION) were advocates.

Advocates must be distinguished from legal representatives. In the earliest procedure, *per legis actiones*, the parties had in general to be present in person; under the formulary procedure they might appoint representatives (*cognitores*, *procuratores*). But in either case they might also employ the services of an advocate.

F. Schulz, *Roman Legal Science* (1946), 43 ff., 108 ff., 268 ff.; J. A. Crook, *Legal Advocacy in the Roman World* (1995).   B. N.

Aeacus (*Aἰακός*), ancestral hero of *Aegina, whose eponymous nymph bore him to *Zeus; to give him company, Zeus turned the island's ant population into humans, transforming *murmēkes* into 'Myrmidons' (Hes. fr. 205 M–W; cf. Ov. *Met.* 7. 517–660). As a primeval figure, he was naturally close to the gods, and unlike e.g. *Tantalus or *Ixion he retained their favour; according to Pindar (a sedulous propagator of Aeginetan legends) he helped *Apollo and *Poseidon build the walls of *Laomedon's Troy (*Ol.* 8) and even settled disputes between the gods themselves (Isoc. 8. 24). Famous for his justice and piety in life, he became a judge in the Underworld (Pl. *Ap.* 41 a, *Grg.* 524a; Isoc. 9. 14 f.; cf. Ar. *Ran.* 464 ff.). He was the founder of the warrior clan of the Aeacidae: his sons *Peleus and *Telamon (1), exiled for the murder of their brother *Phocus, fathered *Achilles and Ajax (see AIAS (1)) respectively.

M. L. West, *The Hesiodic Catalogue of Women* 162 ff.; J. Boardman, *LIMC* 1 (1981), 311–12.   A. H. G.

Aecae, *Daunian city 25 km. (15½ mi.) south-west of Foggia. A Roman ally, it defected to Hannibal in 216 BC but was recaptured. Colonies were founded under Augustus and Septimius Severus, and it became a stage on the *via Traiana. Aerial photography shows a large area of *centuriation nearby.

E. Greco, *Magna Graecia* (1981).   K. L.

Aedepsus (mod. Loutra Aidepsou), Euboean coastal town dependent on *Histiaea, famous in antiquity for its hot springs, known to Aristotle (*Mete.* 2. 366ᵃ) and still in use. It prospered in imperial times as a playground for the wealthy, equipped with luxurious swimming-pools and dining-rooms (Plut. *Mor.* 487 f, 667c). By AD 340 Aedepsus had attained city status (*IG* 12. 9. 1234b), replacing Histiaea as the chief city of northern Euboea. There are extensive Roman remains.

T. E. Gregory, *GRBS* 1979, 255–77.   A. J. S. S.

Aedesius (RE 4) (d. *c.* AD 355) of *Cappadocia, *Neoplatonist, pupil of *Iamblichus (2) and teacher of *Maximus (3) Chrysanthius, Priscus, and Eusebius Myndius. He set up a school of philosophy in Pergamum. No writings survive.

Eunap. *VS* 6. 461 (Loeb trans. by W. C. Wright).   A. D. S.

aediles, Roman magistrates. The aediles originated as two subordinates of the tribunes of the *plebs* whose sacrosanctity they shared. Their central function was to supervise the common temple (*aedes*) and cults of the *plebs*, those of *Ceres and *Diana on the *Aventine, but they also acted as the executives of the tribunes. With the addition in 367 BC of two *aediles curules*, elected from the patricians, the aedileship became a magistracy of the whole people, but the subsequent functions of both sets of aediles can be chiefly explained as patronage of the urban *plebs*. After the admission of plebeians the curule magistracy was held alternately by either order, but in the empire was omitted by patricians. Aediles were elected annually, the *plebeii* in the *concilium plebis*, the *curules* in the *comitia tributa*. *Curules* ranked below praetors, *plebeii* at first below tribunes but eventually with the *curules*. The office was not essential in the *cursus honorum*, but it was the first office to confer full senatorial dignity and the *ius imaginum* (see IMAGINES). The main duties of all aediles were the *cura urbis*, *cura annonae*, and *cura ludorum sollemnium*. *Cura urbis* meant care for the fabric of the city and what went on in it, including the streets of Rome, public order in cult practices, the water supply, and the market. In addition they acted as protectors of the common people against the usurpation of public land, extortionate money-lending, rape, and insults to the *plebs*, prosecuting offenders for a financial penalty before the assembly. Furthermore, Cicero claimed (*Verr.* 2. 1. 14) that, when aedile, he could prosecute C. *Verres for violation of the *provocatio laws, while P. *Clodius Pulcher used his position as aedile to accuse T. *Annius Milo of violence. Fines exacted went to separate chests for *plebeii* and *curules*. Out of the *cura urbis* developed the *cura annonae*, the maintenance and distribution of the corn supply. (See FOOD SUPPLY, ROMAN.) *Caesar created special *aediles Ceriales* for this duty, which passed under Augustus to the *praefectus annonae* and other officials. An important aspect of the urban administration was the public games (*ludi*). Here the growth of wealth and political rivalry in the later republic encouraged the aediles to spend an increasing amount of their own money to gain electoral advantage. The *ludi Romani* and the *Megalensia* fell to the *curules*, the *ludi Ceriales* and *Plebeii* to the plebeians. Augustus, however, transferred the games to the praetors. Under Caesar's dictatorship and the Principate the aediles lost most of their quasi-police functions, but retained their concern for the market and related issues, such as the operation of sumptuary laws. The curule aediles acquired formal jurisdiction over cases relating to sales. Aediles are also found as officials in all Roman municipalities (see MUNICIPIUM), and in corporate bodies such as *vici* or *collegia*.

Mommsen, *Röm. Staatsr.* 2³. 470 f.; Lintott, *Violence*; D. Sabbatucci, *L'edilità romana* (1954); L. Garofalo, *Il processo edilizio* (1989).
A. N. S.-W.; A. W. L.

aedituus (older form, **aeditumnus**), the keeper or sacristan of a consecrated building in Rome (*aedes sacra*). The word was applied to a wide range of officials, including both men of high rank charged with control of the building and those who carried out the lowly tasks of cleaning etc.

Wissowa, *RK* 476–7.
H. J. R.; J. A. N.

Aëdon (Ἀηδών), in mythology, daughter of *Pandareos, the son of Hermes and Merope. She married Zethus and had two children, Itylus and Neïs. Envying *Niobe, Amphion's wife, for her many children, she planned to kill them, or one of them, at night; but Itylus was sleeping in the same room as they and she mistook the bed and so killed him. In her grief she prayed to be changed from human form, and became a nightingale (ἀηδών).

Schol. *Od.* 19. 518. Rose, *Handb. Gk. Myth.* 282 and 340; H. Touloupa, *LIMC* 7 (1994) 527 ff.
H. J. R.

Aedui, a highly developed *Celtic people who occupied most of modern Burgundy. They appealed to Rome against the *Arverni and *Allobroges (121 BC) and received the title of *fratres consanguineique*. During the Gallic War they gave valuable though not whole-hearted support to Caesar, and when they finally joined *Vercingetorix in 52 BC their support was lukewarm. Under the

empire, though involved in the revolts of *Iulius Sacrovir (AD 21) and *Vindex (68), their aristocracy became highly Romanized. The hill-fort *Bibracte was abandoned for *Augustodunum; *duoviri* replaced the *vergobretus* as magistrates; and, under Claudius, the Aedui were the first northern Gallic nation to furnish Roman senators.

E. Thevenot, *Les Eduens n'ont pas trahi* (1960); B. Buckley, in A. King and M. Henig (eds.), *The Roman West* (1981). See also AUGUSTODUNUM.
J. F. Dr.

Aegae (Vergina) in northern Pieria, overlooking the coastal plain of Macedonia. Founded by the first of the Temenid kings and thereafter the site of their tombs, it has been made famous by Manolis Andronikos, who excavated a pre-Temenid cemetery of tumuli and then, in 1977, three royal tombs of the 4th cent. BC. Two were intact. The frescos, the offerings in gold, silver, ivory, and bronze, and the weapons were of the highest artistic quality. Tomb II was almost certainly that of *Philip (1) II (for an alternative view, that *Philip (2) Arrhidaeus was buried here, see E. Borza, *In the Shadow of Olympus* (1990), 256 ff.). Earlier and later burials have also been found. Theatre, palace, and acropolis stand above the cemetery area. Excavations continue.

M. Andronikos, *Vergina: The Cemetery of Tumuli* (1969; in Greek); *Vergina: The Royal Tombs and the Ancient City* (1984); *BSA* 1987; *Vergina II: The Tomb of Persephone* (1994); Hammond, *BSA* 1991.
N. G. L. H.

Aegean Sea, between Greece and Asia Minor. To it the modern name Archipelago was originally applied, but the ancient Greeks derived the name Aegean variously from *Theseus' father *Aegeus, who drowned himself in it; from Aegea, Amazonian queen (see AMAZONS), who was drowned in it; from *Aegae city. They subdivided it into *Thracian*, along Thrace and Macedonia to the north coast of *Euboea; *Myrtoan*, south of Euboea, Attica, Argolis, west of the *Cyclades; *Icarian*, along (Asiatic) coasts of *Caria and Ionia; *Cretic*, north of *Crete. Some, like *Strabo, treated the last three as separate, ending the Aegean at *Sunium in Attica. The whole Aegean contains many islands in three groups: along the Asiatic coast, including *Lesbos, *Chios, *Samos, *Rhodes; a small group off *Thessaly; Euboea and the Cyclades, a continuation or reappearance of the mountains of the Greek mainland.

Cary, *Geographic Background*, chs. 1. and 2.
E. H. W.

Aegeus, Athenian hero, father of *Theseus. As son of *Pandion and brother of *Pallas (2), *Nisus (1), and *Lycus (1), he received at the division of *Attica the area around Athens, although in Beazley, *ARV*² 259. 1 his place is taken by Orneus, indicating that he may be a latecomer in this group. When king of Athens, he consulted the *Delphic oracle about his childlessness, but failing to understand the reply (a figurative injunction to abstain from sex until his return home) fathered Theseus on *Aethra, daughter of Pittheus, king of Troezen. Later he married *Medea, who attempted to poison Theseus on his arrival in Athens, and was therefore driven out by him. When Theseus returned from Crete, he or his steersman forgot to raise the agreed sign on the ship, and Aegeus, thinking his son was dead, threw himself off the acropolis or into the sea (in this version called 'Aegean', Αἰγαῖον πέλαγος, after him).

Aegeus had a sanctuary in Athens, and was connected with the cults of both Apollo Delphinius and Aphrodite Urania; he was also one of the tribal *eponymoi (see PHYLAI). But his popularity in the 5th cent. was largely due to his position as father of Theseus. He was the subject of tragedies by *Sophocles (1) (*TrGF* 19–25) and *Euripides (frs. 1–13 Nauck²), as well as appearing in the latter's *Medea*, and of a comedy by *Philyllius (*PCG* 1–2). For Aegeus in vase-painting, see Kron below.

Kron, *Phylenheroen* 120–40, 264–9, and *LIMC* 1. 1359–67.　　　E. Ke.

Aegimius, a legendary king, son (or father, schol. Pind. *Pyth*. 1. 121) of Dorus, eponym of the *Dorians. Being attacked by the *Centaurs, he asked *Heracles to help him, and in gratitude for his aid adopted *Hyllus and made him joint heir with his own sons.

Aegina, island in Saronic Gulf, inhabited from late neolithic times and in contact with Minoan Crete and Mycenae. Early in the first millennium BC it was resettled by Greeks from Epidaurus (Hdt. 8. 46, 5. 43); protogeometric pottery indicates links with Attica and the Argolid. Aegina belonged to the Calaurian *amphictiony (Strabo 8. 6. 14; see CALAURIA). It was not a great colonizing power, though Aeginetans participated at *Naucratis (Hdt. 2. 178), settled on Crete (Hdt. 3. 58 f.), and are said to have colonized Italian Umbria (Strabo 8. 6. 16; see ATRIA; SPINA). Certainly Aeginetan connections with central Italy are attested *c.*500 BC by a dedication at Gravisca (Etruria) by the wealthy Sostratus of Aegina (Jeffery, *LSAG*² p. 439 + Hdt. 4. 152). The scale of Aegina's trade is indicated by its population of *c.*40,000 on territory which could support only 4,000 from its own agricultural resources. Like other prosperous places (Thuc. 1. 13) Aegina had a tyrant, *Pheidon. It struck coins early.

In the 6th cent. BC Aegina and Athens came to blows, a naval war which simmered on during the Persian War period (when however Aegina fought well on the Greek side), and ended only with Aegina's forcible incorporation (paying a steep 30 talents annual tribute) into the *Athenian empire in 458/7. This was a watershed in 5th-cent. Greek history given that Aegina was Dorian, as *Pindar often stresses. His *Eighth Pythian* of 446 may be a reproach to Athens for its recent treatment of Aegina and a warning not to go too far. But Athens went further, evicting the Aeginetans from Aegina in 431 BC (Thuc. 2. 27) alleging that they were 'chiefly responsible for the war', a reference to Aeginetan complaints at Sparta that their *autonomy under 'the treaty'— the *Thirty Years Peace of 446 rather than the terms of the 458 incorporation—had been infringed (Thuc. 1. 67). Athenian cleruchs (see CLERUCHY) were installed. This is the effective end of independent Aeginetan history, though *Lysander restored the island to the Aeginetans in 405 (Xen. *Hell*. 2. 2. 9). Aegina was used as a pirate base (see PIRACY) in the 4th cent. by Athens' enemies (Xen. *Hell*. 5. 1. 1 ff., 6. 2. 1). Macedonian in the Hellenistic period, it was conquered by the Romans in 211 and given by them to the Aetolians who sold it to *Attalus II of Pergamum (Polyb. 22. 8. 10, and see *OGI* 329 for Cleon, Attalid governor of Aegina). It passed to Rome again under *Attalus III's will in 133 BC, suffered from pirates again in the early 1st cent. (*IG* 4. 2), and was one of the Greek places said by Ser. *Sulpicius Rufus in 45 BC to be desolate (Cic. *Fam*. 4. 5; overdone). M. *Antonius (2) (Mark Antony) gave it to Athens but Augustus later reversed this (App. *BCiv* 5. 30; Cass. Dio 54. 7. 2). It seems to have been 'free' thereafter.

Aegina is of artistic interest chiefly for the relevant odes of *Pindar and the temple of *Aphaea. The building of the latter has traditionally been put *c.*510 BC but a date after the Persian Wars now seems possible.

T. Figueira, *Aegina, Society and Politics* (1981), and *Athens and Aegina* (1991); Jeffery, *CAH* 4² (1988), 364–7; J. Barron, *JHS* 1983, 1 ff.; P.

Graindor, *Athènes sous Auguste* (1927), 6 f. Temple of Aphaea: D. Ohly, *Ägina, Tempel und Heiligtum der Aphaia* (1978); U. Sinn, *AM* 1987, 131–67; D. Gill, *BSA* 1988, 169 ff.; 1993, 173 ff.; H. Bankel, *Der spätarchaische Tempel der Aphaia auf Aegina* (1993).　　　S. H.

aegis, divine attribute, represented as a large all-round bib with scales, fringed with snakes' heads and normally decorated with the *gorgoneion* (see GORGO). In Homer *Zeus' epithet *aigiochos*, and the story (*Il*. 15. 308–10) that the aegis was given to him by *Hephaestus suggest a primary association with Zeus, who lends it to *Apollo (*Il*. 15. 229–30). It is unclear whether Athena's aegis is also borrowed (cf. *Il*. 5. 736–8; cf. schol. *Il*. 15. 229). In post-Homeric times the aegis is most closely associated with *Athena, who is commonly shown wearing it over her dress; Zeus is very rarely shown with the aegis. At *Il*. 2. 446–9 the aegis is ageless and immortal, with a hundred tassels; its tasselled nature is reflected in its epithet *thysanoessa*. At *Il*. 5. 738–42 it is decorated with the Gorgon's head and the allegorical figures Phobos (Fear), Eris (Strife), Alke (Strength), and Ioke (Pursuit). Its shaking by Zeus (*Il*. 17. 593–6) or Apollo (*Il*. 15. 229–30, 304–22) brings victory to the side the god supports and fear to its enemies. It protects from attack; not even Zeus' thunderbolt can overpower it (*Il*. 21. 400–1). In later versions Aegis was a monster killed by Athena who then wore its skin (cf. Diod. Sic. 3. 70. 3–5), or the aegis was the skin of *Amalthea, the goat that had suckled Zeus, which Zeus used in the Titanomachy (see TITAN) (cf. e.g. Eratosth. [*Cat*.] 13. 102; *POxy*. 3003 col. 2. 15). Herodotus (4. 189) argued that Athena's dress and aegis imitated the goatskin garments of Libyan women. Starting with *Alexander (3) the Great, the aegis became an element in the iconography of Hellenistic rulers and then of Roman emperors. In Athens there was probably a sacred aegis, a cult object carried by the priestess of Athena on certain ritual occasions (*Suda*, entry under 'aigis'; *Paroemiographi*, ed. E. L. Leutsch and F. G. Schneidewin (1839), 1. 339).

Stengel, *RE* 1. 970–1; G. A. Mansuelli, *EAA* 3. 237–8; E. Saglio, in Dar.–Sag. 1. 101–4; G. S. Kirk, *The Iliad: A Commentary*, 1 (1985), 161–2; R. Janko, *The Iliad: A Commentary*, 4 (1992), 260–1.　　　C. S.-I.

Aegisthus, in mythology the son of Thyestes who survives to avenge the deaths of his brothers at the hands of *Atreus. In Aeschylus he is only a baby when Atreus kills the other boys, and perhaps for this reason survives (*Ag*. 1583–1606). A version apparently Sophoclean (see Dio Chrys. 66. 6; cf. Apollod. *Epit*. 2. 14; Hyg. *Fab*. 87 and 88. 3–4) makes him the incestuous offspring of Thyestes and his daughter Pelopia after the murder of the elder sons; an oracle had advised that a son thus born would avenge their deaths. In connection with this story, it was said that the baby Aegisthus (his name suggesting the word αἴξ, goat) was exposed and fed by a she-goat (Hyg. ibid. and 252). When he grew up he learnt the truth, and avenged the murder of his brothers by killing Atreus and later, with *Clytemnestra, *Agamemnon. All this is post-Homeric: in the *Iliad* there is harmony between the brothers Atreus and Thyestes (2. 100–8), and in the *Odyssey* Aegisthus is a baron with an estate near the domains of Agamemnon, and no reason is given for Agamemnon's murder except Aegisthus' relationship with Clytemnestra, whom he had seduced despite a warning from the gods (see 1. 29–43, 3. 249–75, 4. 524–37). In all versions Aegisthus rules the kingdom securely for some years after Agamemnon's death, until he in his turn is killed in revenge by Agamemnon's son, *Orestes. By Clytemnestra, Aegisthus had a daughter, *Erigone (Apollod. *Epit*. 6. 25; cf. Soph. *El*. 589).

Aegium

The death of Aegisthus is a favourite subject in Archaic and Classical art: see R. M. Gais, *LIMC* 1/1. 371–9; A. J. N. W. Prag, *The Oresteia: Iconographic and Narrative Tradition* (1985).

H. J. R.; J. R. M.

Aegium, Achaean port 40 km. (25 mi.) east of *Patrae, beneath the modern town of Aigion. It was settled from neolithic times, with particularly extensive activity during the late Helladic and Classical periods (when the city was walled). Classical sources refer to a shrine of Eileithyia, a *temenos* of Asclepius, and temples of *Athena and *Hera. The roadside shrine of *Artemis or Hera at Ano Mazaraki may have been controlled by Aegium.

Aegium gained political importance after the destruction in 373 BC of Helice (whose citizens, along with those of Rhypes, it absorbed). The city expanded from the 4th cent., with a large agora and shrine complex. The nearby sanctuary of Zeus Homarius was the cult centre of the *Achaean Confederacy after 276. By the late 3rd cent., Aegium held the league archive and received ambassadors. The biennial league assembly of all Achaean citizens met here until 189 BC. Under Roman control the city thrived, with many major building projects.

A. Papadopoulos, *Excavations at Aigion 1970* (1976); L. Papakosta, in A. Rizakis (ed.), *Achaia und Elis in der Antike* (1991), 235–40. C. A. M.

Aegosthena, fortified place in the territory of *Megara, at the easternmost point of the Corinthian Gulf. The remnants of the Spartan army which was defeated at *Leuctra joined a relieving force at Aegosthena on their way back to Sparta (Xen. *Hell.* 6. 4. 26). The fortifications are (despite earthquake damage in the early 1980s) among the best preserved in Greece, but the history of the site is ill known, and their date is uncertain: they are probably Hellenistic, and were perhaps constructed by *Demetrius (4) Poliorcetes. Aegosthena went into the *Achaean Confederacy when Megara joined in 243/2 BC, and over to *Boeotia in 224; it remained Boeotian when Megara returned to Achaea. Under Rome it was an autonomous *polis. See FORTIFICATIONS. (Greek).

RE 1 (1893) and Suppl. 12 (1970), 'Aigosthena'; *PECS* 21; A. Lawrence, *Greek Aims in Fortification* (1979), see index. J. B. S.

Aegritudo Perdicae, an anonymous Latin *epyllion narrating the calamitous love of Perdicas for his mother, Castalia. Its ascription to *Dracontius is unwarrantable, though it almost certainly belongs to his period (i.e. 5th cent. AD), and probably to Africa, although Spain is suggested too.

Ed. L. Zuhrli (Teubner, 1987). A. H.-W.; A. J. S. S.

Aelian (Claudius Aelianus) (AD 165/70–230/5), according to the *Suda* a freedman born in Praeneste (Palestrina), learned his Greek from the sophist Pausanias of Caesarea and was an admirer of *Herodes Atticus. After a brief career as a sophistic declaimer he turned to writing. His *Indictment of the Effeminate* (a posthumous attack on *Elagabalus), *On Providence* and *On Divine Manifestations* are now lost; fragments of the last show them to have been collections of stories designed to reveal the operations of divine forethought and justice. *On the Nature of Animals* (extant, 17 books) similarly claims to be illustrating the reality of divine providence in the animal kingdom, though its examples of paradoxical and extraordinary characteristics go far beyond his self-imposed programme. Extraordinary facts about animals also occur in the *Miscellany* (*Varia Historia*, 14 books), though there the emphasis falls rather on (generally 'improving') anecdotes from human life and history. The *Rustic Letters* is a co-ordinated set of 20 vignettes of life in the Attic countryside of 5th- and 4th-cent. BC literature (in the manner of *Alciphron). Aelian writes throughout with an extreme, mannered simplicity (ἀφέλεια), and was much admired in later antiquity for the purity of his Attic diction. He was widely read and drawn on by Christian writers.

Philostr. *VS* 2. 31 (624–5). *NA*: R. Hercher (1864), A. Scholfield (Loeb, 1958–9); *VH, Ep., Frs.*: R. Hercher (1866); *VH*: M. Dilts (1974); N. G. Wilson (Loeb, forthcoming); *Ep.*: A. Benner and F. Forbes (Loeb (*Alciphron*), 1949). W. Schmid, *Atticismus*, 3 (1893). M. B. T.

Aelianus (1st–2nd cent. AD), author of a Greek *Tactica*, on the tactics of the Hellenistic *hoplite phalanx, heavily indebted to earlier military writers.

TEXT H. Köchly and M. Rustow, *Griechische Kriegschriftsteller* (1855). M. B. T.

Aelius (*RE* 144), **Lucius** (also called 'Stilo' and 'Praeconinus': Suet. *Gram.* 3; Pliny, *HN* 33. 39, 37. 9), the first important Roman scholar, born at Lanuvium about 150 BC, of equestrian rank and a professed Stoic. His studies, which embraced Latin literature, antiquities, semasiology, and etymology, profoundly influenced contemporary and later scholars, including *Varro, *Cicero (cf. *Brut.* 205–7), and *Verrius Flaccus. His known endeavours include: an interpretation of the *Carmen Saliare; comments on sacral language and the usage of the *Twelve Tables; employment of critical signs (*notae*) in the study of literary texts; a tract on propositions (*proloquia* = ἀξιώματα: Gell. *NA* 16. 8. 2 f.), a topic of Stoic dialectic related to syntactic analysis; and a list (*index*) of the 25 genuine plays of *Plautus (Gell. *NA* 3. 3. 1, 12). Another noted Plautine scholar, Ser. Clodius, was his son-in-law. He also composed speeches for various Roman notables, though he was not an orator himself. All his works are lost.

Funaioli, *Gramm. Rom. Frag.* 51–76; Herzog–Schmidt, § 192. R. A. K.

Aelius Antipater, sophist, of Phrygian Hierapolis, *ab epistulis Graecis* ('secretary for Greek correspondence') of *Severus, teacher of the emperor's sons, was made a senator with consular rank and governed Bithynia. He wrote a history of Severus. Took his own life after the murder of *Geta.

Philostr. *VS* 2. 24–5; *PIR*² A 137. A. R. Bi.

Aelius Aristides See ARISTIDES, PUBLIUS AELIUS.

Aelius Caesar, Lucius, *Hadrian's first choice as successor, formerly L. Ceionius (*RE* 7) Commodus, son and grandson of the homonymous consuls of AD 78 and 106, was himself consul in 136, probably aged 32; in the same year he was adopted by Hadrian, given the *tribunicia potestas*, and sent to govern the two Pannonias with proconsular *imperium*, becoming consul for the second time in 137. After his sudden death on 1 January 138, his son (later called L. *Verus) and prospective son-in-law (the future Marcus *Aurelius) were adopted by Hadrian's second choice as heir, *Antoninus Pius.

SHA *Hadr., Ael., Ver.*; Cass. Dio 69. *PIR*² C 605; *BM Coins, Rom. Emp.* 3; R. Syme, *Athenaeum*, 1957, 306 ff. (= *RP* 1 (1979), 325 ff.); A. R. Birley, *Marcus Aurelius* (1987), 41 ff. A. R. Bi.

Aelius (*RE* 59) **Gallus,** prefect of Egypt after C. *Cornelius Gallus and before C. Petronius (see EGYPT (Roman)). Influenced by prevalent and exaggerated reports of the wealth of Arabia Felix, *Augustus instructed him to invade it. The expedition, which lasted two years (26–25 or 25–24 BC), failed; blame was conveniently laid upon the treachery of the Nabataean Syllaeus. Aelius Gallus wrote on medical topics and was a friend of *Strabo the geographer. He very probably adopted the son of the distinguished Roman knight L. Seius Strabo (see AELIUS SEIANUS, L.).

S. Jameson, *JRS* 1968, 71 ff.; G. Bowersock, *Roman Arabia* (1983); R. Syme, *The Augustan Aristocracy* (1986), see indexes.   R. S.; B. M. L.

Aelius (*RE* 88) **Marcianus,** a lawyer of the early 3rd cent. AD, probably from the eastern provinces. Mainly a teacher, he does not seem to have given *responsa* (consultative opinions). His extensive knowledge of the rescripts (replies to petitions) of Severus and Caracalla might be explained by a connection with *Ulpianus, whose style is similar, and of whom he may have been a pupil. He is not known to have held public office. Author of several monographs and commentaries published after Caracalla's death in 217, he is best known for his large-scale teaching manual, sixteen books (*libri*) of *Institutiones*. Though other lawyers do not seem to have cited him, Justinian's compilers admired his clarity and measured judgement and selected over 280 passages from his work for the *Digesta* (see JUSTINIAN'S CODIFICATION).

Lenel, *Pal.* 1. 639–90; *PIR*² A 215; *HLL* 4, § 428. 1; Kunkel 1967, 258–9; W. W. Buckland, *Studi Riccobono* 1 (1936), 273–83; Honoré 1981, 67–70.   T. Hon.

Aelius (*RE* 93, Suppl. 4) **Melissus,** grammarian contemporary with A. *Gellius (*NA* 18. 6. 1–3), who derides his work on semantics (*De loquendi proprietate*).

*PIR*² A 222.   R. A. K.

Aelius (*RE* 105) **Paetus, Sextus,** a Roman lawyer nicknamed 'Catus' (clever) for his shrewd pragmatism, was consul in 198 BC. He was the author of *Tripertita*, so called because it contained three elements: the law of the Twelve Tables, an account of their interpretation, and the formulas for use in litigation and possibly private transactions (*legis actiones*, 'actions in law'). He has some claim to have been the first professional legal author (see LEGAL LITERATURE) and his work, praised by Sextus *Pomponius as a cradle of the law (*cunabula iuris*), was used in the later republic, for example for the text of the *Twelve Tables.

Wieacker 1988, 536–8; Watson 1974, 135–6.   T. Hon.

Aelius (*RE* 117) **Promotus,** physician from Alexandria (1), probably belonging to the period between Hadrian and Pertinax (AD 138–93). He wrote a book on curative methods called *Potency* (Δυναμερόν), sections of which remain, largely unedited.

Aelius (*RE* 133) **Seianus, Lucius (Sejanus),** d. AD 31, of *Volsinii (mod. Bolsena). Sejanus' father was an *eques*, L. Seius Strabo, his mother the sister of Q. *Iunius Blaesus, suffect consul AD 10, and connected with Aelii Tuberones and Cassii Longini. Sejanus, who had attended Augustus' grandson C. *Iulius Caesar (2) in the east, was made Strabo's colleague as prefect of the guard by *Tiberius in AD 14, and soon, on his father's appointment as prefect of Egypt, became sole commander; by 23 he had concentrated the guard in barracks near the porta Viminalis. After the death of Tiberius' son Drusus *Iulius Caesar (1) in 23 (murder was later imputed) his influence was paramount; a succession of prosecutions eliminated opponents (chiefly adherents of the elder *Agrippina). Tiberius allegedly refused to allow a marriage with Drusus' widow *Livia Iulia (25), but retired from Rome in 26, further increasing Sejanus' influence (he allegedly encouraged the move); honours and oaths were offered to him as to Tiberius. In 29 Agrippina and her eldest son Nero *Iulius Caesar were deported; her second, Drusus *Iulius Caesar (2),

was imprisoned in 30. That year Sejanus was elected consul for 31 with Tiberius amid engineered demonstrations; proconsular *imperium* followed, and he hoped for tribunician power. In October, however, Tiberius, allegedly warned by his sister-in-law *Antonia (3), sent a letter to the senate which ended by denouncing him (certainly for plotting against *Germanicus' youngest son, *Gaius (1) 'Caligula' (the future emperor)). Sejanus was arrested, the guard having been transferred to *Macro, 'tried' in the senate, and executed; the punishment of Livia Iulia and of adherents, real or alleged, followed; even his youngest children were killed. Tiberius acted quickly and in fear of the outcome. Sejanus has been suspected of planning a coup against him; more probably he intended a gradual accession to partnership, involving Livia Iulia's son Ti. *Iulius Caesar Nero 'Gemellus'.

Syme, *Tacitus* 401 ff.; A. Boddington, *AJPhil.* 1963, 1 ff.; D. Hennig, *L. Aelius Seianus*, Vestigia 21 (1975) (review, R. Seager, *JRS* 1977, 185); B. Levick, *Tiberius the Politician* (1976), 148 ff.; R. Syme, *The Augustan Aristocracy* (1986), 300 ff. (stemma, table 23).   J. P. B.; B. M. L.

Aelius (*RE* 150) **Tubero, Lucius,** boyhood friend and relative by marriage of Cicero and legate of Q. *Tullius Cicero (1) 61–58 BC. At some point (perhaps before this) he was praetor. Assigned Africa by the senate in 49, he was not admitted by Q. *Ligarius and P. *Attius Varus and, with his son (see next article) joined *Pompey. Both were pardoned by *Caesar. He was interested in Academic philosophy and wrote *annales* (see ANNALS, ANNALISTS), but we have no secure reference to them.   E. B.

Aelius (*RE* 156) **Tubero, Quintus,** son of Lucius (above), accompanied his father 49–48 BC and fought at *Pharsalus, but was pardoned by *Caesar. In 46 he prosecuted Q. *Ligarius (whom Cicero successfully defended) for alleged co-operation with *Juba (1) I in 49. His failure in this is said to have turned him away from a public career. He wrote *annales* (see ANNALS, ANNALISTS) and books on law and is later cited in both fields. The *annales* may have imitated *Thucydides (2)'s style (he was the dedicatee of *Dionysius (7)'s *On Thucydides*). His history, written in the 30s, covered Roman history from its origins to his own day in at least fourteen books, probably many more. Like *Licinius Macer, he consulted the 'linen books' (Livy 4. 23. 1–3, cf. 10. 9. 10). His role as a historical source of *Livy and Dionysius is disputed. As a jurist, he was unusual in combining expertise in public and private law, writing for example monographs on the senate and the duties of a judge. According to Sex. *Pomponius, his archaic language (*antiquus sermo*) was held against him. (Pompon. *Dig.* 1. 2. 2. 46, cf. Gell. *NA* 14. 7–8). He married a daughter of Ser. *Sulpicius Rufus and their sons were consuls 11 BC and AD 4.

Peter, *HRRel.* 1² ccclxvi and 308; Cichorius, *Röm. Stud.* 226 ff.; Ogilvie, *Comm. Livy 1–5* 16 ff.; T. P. Wiseman, *Clio's Cosmetics* (1979), 135–9.   E. B.; T. Hon.; C. B. R. P.

Aemilianus See AEMILIUS AEMILIANUS, M.

Aemilius (*RE* 24) **Aemilianus, Marcus,** emperor AD 253. Against imperial policy, while governor of Moesia he dealt harshly with the *Goths, and was proclaimed emperor by his army. He marched on Italy, overthrew *Trebonianus Gallus, but was soon killed by his own troops, panicked by the approach of *Valerian. The civil strife of 253 exposed Greece to Gothic invasion.

B. Gerov, *Beiträge zur Geschichte der römischen Provinzen* (1980).
     J. F. Dr.

Aemilius Asper

Aemilius (*RE* 29) **Asper** (2nd cent. AD) wrote (lost) commentaries on *Terence, *Sallust, and *Virgil, perhaps with a separate discussion of Virgilian grammar. The fragments (ed. Wessner, 1905) suggest a learned and sensible critic; Aelius *Donatus (1) borrowed freely from him. *Priscian cited him as an authority *de verbo*, but the extant *artes* (see ARS) attributed to an 'Asper' (Keil, *Gramm. Lat.* 5. 547–54; H. Hagen (ed.) *Anecdota Helvetica, quae ad grammaticam Latinam spectant* (1870), 39–61) cannot be his.

A. Tomsin, *Étude sur le commentaire virgilien d'Aemilius Asper* (1952); Herzog–Schmidt, § 443. R. A. K.

Aemilius Laetus, Quintus, praetorian prefect AD 190–3, from Thaenae in Africa. Appointed after the downfall of M. *Aurelius Cleander, Laetus was responsible for L. *Septimius Severus becoming governor of Upper Pannonia in 191. Obliged to attend *Commodus' gladiatorial performances, which aroused increasing alarm, Laetus organized, with Commodus' concubine *Marcia and chamberlain Eclectus, Commodus' murder and replacement by *Pertinax (31 December 192). Although retained in office by Pertinax, Laetus did not resist the mutiny which led to Pertinax' death. He was dismissed by *Didius Severus Iulianus and murdered on his orders.

*PIR*² A 358; *AE* 1949, 38 (origin); A. R. Birley, *The African Emperor Septimius Severus* (1988). A. R. Bi.

Aemilius (*RE* 63) **Lepidus, Manius,** probably a grandson of M. *Aemilius Lepidus (3), the triumvir, and of Faustus *Cornelius Sulla and Pompeia, daughter of *Pompey, was consul AD 11, defended his sister Lepida in 20 and was appointed proconsul of Asia (21–2) despite objections on the score of his poverty and inactive disposition. His daughter Lepida married *Galba, the future emperor.

R. Syme, as cited under AEMILIUS LEPIDUS (5), M. T. J. C.; R. J. S.

Aemilius (*RE* 68) **Lepidus** (1), **Marcus,** was a member of the embassy sent to the east in 201–200 BC, during the course of which he delivered the Roman ultimatum to *Philip (3) V at Abydos; the story (Val. Max. 6. 6. 1; Just. 30. 3. 4) that he was sent to Egypt as *tutor* (guardian) to the young Ptolemy (1) V should be rejected, though it is true that Lepidus later developed close ties with Egypt. He was curule aedile in 193, praetor in Sicily in 191, and reached the consulship in 187, having been defeated in the two previous years, due, he believed, to the influence of his bitter opponent M. *Fulvius Nobilior. As consul he attacked Fulvius' conduct at Ambracia and attempted to block his triumph. He fought successfully in Liguria, and built the *via Aemilia from *Placentia (Piacenza) to *Ariminum (Rimini)— the modern region of Emilia Romagna through which it runs preserves his name. He returned to the area in 183 as a commissioner to found the colonies of *Mutina (Modena) and *Parma. A pontifex since 199, he was elected pontifex maximus (chief *pontifex) in 180 and in the following year became censor with M. Fulvius Nobilior; the two men were publicly reconciled. He held a second consulship in 175, again campaigning in Liguria, and in 173 was one of ten commissioners who made individual allotments of land in Liguria and Gaul. He was *princeps senatus from his censorship until his death in 152.

Scullard, *Rom. Pol.* 180–1; Briscoe, *Comm. 31–33, 56–7.* J. Br.

Aemilius (*RE* 72) **Lepidus** (2), **Marcus,** descendant of M. *Aemilius Lepidus (1), whose Gallic connections he inherited. After serving under Cn. *Pompeius Strabo, he was probably aedile in *Sulla's absence, joined Sulla (divorcing a wife related

to L. *Appuleius Saturninus) and enriched himself in the *proscriptions. Elected consul 78 BC, with *Pompey's support and against Sulla's wishes, with Q. *Lutatius Catulus (2) as colleague, he agitated against Sulla's settlement and after Sulla's death prepared to attack it. As proconsul he held Cisalpina through M. *Iunius Brutus (1), collected forces in Transalpina and made contact with *Sertorius in Spain. Marching on Rome, he was defeated by Catulus and fled to Sardinia, where he was defeated by the legate Triarius and died. His followers, under M. Veiento *Perperna, ultimately joined Sertorius.

The first to realize the strategic importance of a unified province of Gaul, he lacked the military ability to profit by his insight. *Caesar, though sympathetic, refused to join him, but remembered his example.

N. Criniti, *M. Aimilius Q. f. M. n. Lepidus* (1969; in Italian); L. Hayne, *Hist.* 1972, 661 ff. E. B.

Aemilius (*RE* 73) **Lepidus** (3), **Marcus** (the triumvir), younger son of M. *Aemilius Lepidus (2). As praetor 49 BC, he supported *Caesar, then governed Hither Spain (48–7), intervening in the dissensions in Further Spain (see CASSIUS LONGINUS, Q.) and returning to triumph. He was consul (46) and Caesar's *magister equitum (46–44). On Caesar's death he gave armed support to M. *Antonius (2) (Mark Antony), who in return contrived his appointment as *pontifex maximus in Caesar's place. He then left to govern the provinces assigned him by Caesar, Gallia Narbonensis and Hither Spain. When, after the war of *Mutina, Antony retreated into Gaul, Lepidus assured Cicero of his loyalty to the republic but on 29 May 43 joined forces with Antony and was declared a public enemy by the senate. At *Bononia (1) in October he planned the Triumvirate with Antony and *Octavian, accepting Further Spain with his existing provinces as his share of the empire; and demanding (or conceding) the proscription of his brother L. *Aemilius Paullus (3). After triumphing again *ex Hispania* ('from Spain') he held a second consulship (42) and took charge of Rome and Italy during the campaign of *Philippi. After their victory his colleagues deprived him of his provinces, on the rumour of a collusion between him and Sextus *Pompeius, but nothing serious was proved; and after helping Octavian ineffectively in the war against L. *Antonius (Pietas), he was allowed by Octavian to govern Africa, where he had sixteen legions and won an imperatorial salutation. Kept out of the discussions at Tarentum over the renewal of the Triumvirate (37) and ignored in the arrangements, he asserted himself when summoned by Octavian to aid in the war against Sextus Pompeius. He tried to take over Sicily, but Octavian won over his army, ousted him from the Triumvirate and banished him to *Circeii, though he later contemptuously allowed him to enter Rome. He kept his title of pontifex maximus until his death in 13 or 12, when Augustus took it over. Superior to his two partners in social rank and inherited connections, he lacked their ability to organize support and their total dedication to the pursuit of power.

Syme, *RR* and *AA*, see indexes; R. D. Weigel, *Lepidus, the Tarnished Triumvir* (1992); E. Badian, *Arctos* 1991, 5 ff. For the coins see *RRC* 494, 495; Weigel 76 f. G. W. R.; T. J. C.; E. B.

Aemilius (*RE* 74) **Lepidus** (4), **Marcus,** son of M. *Aemilius Lepidus (3) the triumvir, plotted in 30 BC to assassinate *Octavian on his return to Rome, but was detected by *Maecenas (Vell. Pat. 2. 88 and App. *BCiv.* 4. 50 216 ff.). His wife Servilia, perhaps the Servilia once betrothed to Octavian, committed suicide. Either he or another son of Lepidus the triumvir had earlier been promised to *Antonia (1).

Syme, *RR*, see index, and *AA* 35; R. D. Weigel, *Lepidus, the Tarnished Triumvir* (1992), 96 f.   T. J. C.; E. B.

Aemilius (*RE* 75) **Lepidus** (5), **Marcus,** probably elder son of Paullus *Aemilius Lepidus and Cornelia, daughter of *Scribonia and a Scipio. He was consul AD 6, then served under *Tiberius in the Pannonian rebellion (receiving *ornamenta triumphalia* in 9), and probably Dalmatia afterwards for a number of years. In 14 he was governor of *Tarraconensis (we do not know for how long) and in 21 he prudently declined the proconsulship and army of Africa, which went to Q. *Iunius Blaesus. He later accepted the proconsulship of Asia, which had no army (probably 26–8). In 22 he resumed the family's restoration of the Basilica Aemilia. He died in 33. *Augustus, on his death-bed, is said to have judged him 'capable (of becoming emperor), but disdaining it' (Tac. *Ann.* 1. 13. 2). Tacitus stresses his prudence and moderation. His children included Aemilia Lepida, wife of Drusus *Iulius Caesar (2)—who in 30 helped to bring about Drusus' fall and committed suicide when accused of adultery with a slave in 36 (Tac. *Ann.* 6. 40. 3; cf. *ILS* 1848)—and M. *Aemilius Lepidus (6).

R. Syme, *Ten Studies in Tacitus* (1970), 30–49 (rescuing his name from confusion in the manuscripts of Tacitus), 141 f., and *AA* 128–40, cf. *RP* 6. 252.   T. J. C.; E. B.

Aemilius (*RE* 76) **Lepidus** (6), **Marcus,** son of M. *Aemilius Lepidus (5), last of the family, married *Iulia Drusilla, was promised the succession by *Gaius (1) ('Caligula') and was executed when charged with participation in the conspiracy of Cn. *Cornelius Lentulus Gaetulicus.   T. J. C.; E. B.

Aemilius (*RE* 82) **Lepidus, Paullus,** son of L. *Aemilius Paullus (3), was proscribed in 43 BC (see PROSCRIPTION) and may be the 'Lepidus' who won Crete for *Brutus in 42. He later joined *Octavian whom he accompanied in the war against Sextus *Pompeius in 38. He was made suffect consul in 34, then governed either Syria or Macedonia as proconsul, and was made censor 22 with L. *Munatius Plancus, with whom he quarrelled until both resigned. He completed the restoration of the Basilica Aemilia begun by his father. His first wife was Cornelia, daughter of *Scribonia and a Scipio; her premature death is the subject of a consolatory elegy by Propertius (4. 11), which also mentions their two sons, L. *Aemilius Paullus (4) and M. *Aemilius Lepidus (5). He later married the younger Marcella, daughter of C. *Claudius Marcellus (1). He was an augur and perhaps a *frater arvalis* (SEE AUGURES; FRATRES ARVALES).

Syme, *RR* and *AA*, see indexes; *RP* 6. 247–68.   T. J. C.; E. B.

Aemilius Macer, a poet from Verona who died in 16 BC. Some fragments remain of his *Ornithogonia* and *Theriaca*; these drew on (but did not translate) works by *Bolus and *Nicander (whose *Alexipharmaca* is also imitated in some fragments quoted without title). Ovid in his youth heard him reciting at an advanced age (*Tr.* 4. 4. 43–4).

*PIR*² A 378; H. Dahlmann *AAWM* 1981, 6; J.-P. Néraudau *ANRW* 2. 38. 3. 1708; Courtney, *FLP* 292.   E. C.

Aemilius (RE 105) **Papinianus,** a leading lawyer of the Severan age and a close associate of the emperor *Septimius Severus, probably came, like him, from Africa and had some exposure to Hellenistic culture. He was assessor to a praetorian prefect, then from AD 194 to 202, to judge from their style, composed rescripts (replies to petitions), often of a highly technical character, for Septimius, latterly at least as a *libellis* (secretary for petitions). On the fall of C. *Fulvius Plautianus in AD 205 he became praetorian

prefect along with Q. *Aemilius Laetus, but on the death of Septimius in February 211 was dismissed by Caracalla (see M. AURELIUS ANTONINUS (1)). After the murder of Caracalla's brother and joint emperor P. *Septimius Geta (2) in 212 he was prosecuted by the praetorians and, without protest from Caracalla, put to death, an event which entered into legend as the martyrdom of a just man.

Leaving aside some perhaps early writings on Greek road officials (*astynomikoi*) and adultery, Papinianus is best known for 37 books of *Quaestiones* ('Problems'), which belong to the 190s and, between 206 and 212, nineteen books of *Digesta responsa* ('Ordered Opinions'), not confined to his own practice but drawing on a wide range of sources. His efforts to explore the ethical basis of legal rules goes along with a more crabbed style than is usual with Roman lawyers, but when properly understood his reasoning is as impressive as his technical mastery. Papinianus was long regarded as the greatest Roman lawyer, and Constantine I declared invalid the (at times critical) notes of *Paulus and *Ulpianus on his work. The Law of Citations of 426 gives him the leading position among the five writers of authority and a casting vote in case they are equally divided. Third-year law students, who had to study his work, were called Papinianists, but Justinian, while preserving this custom, rehabilitated Paulus' and Ulpianus' notes on Papinianus and esteemed *Iulianus more highly.

Lenel, *Pal.* 1. 803–946; *PIR*² A 388; *HLL* 4, § 416; Kunkel 1967, 224–9; Honoré 1981, 56–9; Syme, *RP* 2. 790–804, 3. 1393–414; V. Giuffrè, *ANRW* 2. 15 (1976), 632–66.   T. Hon.

Aemilius (*RE* 118) **Paullus** (1), **Lucius,** was consul in 219 BC with M. *Livius Salinator, when they defeated *Demetrius (7) of Pharos in the Second Illyrian War; both triumphed, but when Livius was convicted of *peculatus* (embezzlement) Paullus came close to sharing his fate. Consul again in 216, he was killed in the disaster at *Cannae. The decision to engage *Hannibal in another pitched battle was taken by the senate and fully supported by Paullus. If there was disagreement between Paullus and his colleague C. *Terentius Varro, it was purely tactical; but Polybius was probably misled by the Scipionic family (Paullus' daughter married *Scipio Africanus) into believing that the decision to engage was taken by Varro against the advice of Paullus.

Walbank, *Polybius*, 1. 24–5, 330–1, 435–49; *CAH*, 8² (1989), 51–2, 69 (J. Briscoe), 91–4 (R. M. Errington).   J. Br.

Aemilius (*RE* 114 (?)) **Paullus** (2), **Lucius,** became an augur in 192 BC and governed Further Spain as praetor in 191, with command prorogued for 190 and 189. A defeat in 190 was retrieved by a victory in the following year. Later in 189 he went to Asia as one of the ten commissioners who administered the settlement after the defeat of *Antiochus (3) III. On his return in 187, with a majority of the commission, unsuccessfully opposed the granting of a triumph to Cn. *Manlius Vulso. Despite several attempts he did not reach the consulship until 182, when he operated in *Liguria; his command was prorogued for 181 when, despite having been besieged in his camp, he eventually forced the Ligurian Ingauni to surrender. In 171 he was one of the patrons chosen by the peoples of Spain to represent their complaints against Roman governors. He was elected to a second consulship for 168, and ended the Third Macedonian War by his victory at *Pydna. His triumph was marred by the death of his two young sons; his two elder sons, by his first wife Papiria, had been adopted and became Q. *Fabius Maximus Aemilianus and P. *Cornelius Scipio Aemilianus. He was elected censor in 164 and died in 160, by no means a rich man; of the booty from the war against *Perseus (2) he had kept for himself nothing but Perseus' library. Paullus had a great interest in Greek culture, giving his sons a Greek as well as a traditional Roman education, and undertaking an archaeological tour of Greece after the war with Perseus (see EDUCATION, GREEK and ROMAN; TOURISM). That did not prevent him from willingly carrying out the senate's order to sack *Epirus, and from sanctioning other acts of brutality by Roman troops. See also PORCIUS CATO (1) M.

P. Meloni, *Perseo* (1953), 319–437; J.-L. Ferrary, *Philhellénisme et impérialisme* (1988), 531–65.   J. Br.

Aemilius (*RE* 81) **Paullus** (3), **Lucius,** elder son of M. *Aemilius Lepidus (2) and brother of M. *Aemilius Lepidus (3), the triumvir, accused *Catiline *de vi* (of violence) in 63 BC. While quaestor in Macedonia in 59 he was absurdly accused by the informer L. *Vettius of conspiring to murder *Pompey. In 56, as curule aedile, he began to rebuild the Basilica Aemilia. He was praetor 53 and consul 50. Previously a consistent *optimate, he was now bought by *Caesar for 1,500 talents which he needed for the basilica, gave him at least passive support in 50, and remained neutral during the ensuing Civil War. During the war of *Mutina he negotiated for the senate with Sextus *Pompeius and later joined in declaring his brother a public enemy; he was named first in the *proscriptions, but allowed to escape. He went to *Brutus in Asia, and continued to live at *Miletus, though pardoned at *Philippi.

Syme, *RR*, see index.   A. M.; T. J. C.; E. B.

Aemilius (*RE* 115) **Paullus** (4), **Lucius,** younger son of Paullus *Aemilius Lepidus and Cornelia, daughter of *Scribonia and a Scipio, and husband of *Iulia (4), was consul in AD 1. Towards AD 8 he conspired against *Augustus and was executed; the engagement between his daughter Lepida and the youthful *Claudius (the future emperor) was broken off in consequence of this and of Iulia's disgrace (later she married a M. Silanus, probably M. *Iunius Silanus (3), the consul of AD 19: for two of their children, 'abnepotes Augusti' ('great-grandchildren of Augustus'), see Tac. *Ann.* 13. 1).

E. Hohl, *Klio*, 1937, 339 ff.; Syme, *RR*, see index, and *AA* 123 ff.
                                                                                         T. J. C.; R. J. S.; E. B.

Aemilius (*RE* 127) **Regillus, Lucius,** praetor in 190 BC, defeated *Antiochus (3) III's fleet at Myonnesus; he celebrated a naval triumph in 189. During the battle he vowed a temple to the *Lares permarini*, which M. *Aemilius Lepidus (1) dedicated in 179; the text of the dedicatory tablet, badly corrupted, is preserved by Livy (40. 52).

Briscoe, *Comm. 34–37*, 313–37, and Teubner edn. of Livy 31–40, 773.
                                                                                                                  J. Br.

Aemilius (*RE* 139) **Scaurus, Mamercus,** the last male member of the distinguished family of Aemilii Scauri, was a man of unsavoury character, but a distinguished orator and advocate (Sen. *Controv.* 10 pref. 2–3; Tac. *Ann.* 6. 29). Though disliked by *Tiberius, he was a suffect consul in AD 21, but did not govern a province. Twice prosecuted for *maiestas, in 32 and 34, on the second occasion he committed suicide.

Syme, *AA*, see index.   J. P. B.; R. J. S

Aemilius (*RE* 140) **Scaurus** (1), **Marcus,** of patrician, but recently impoverished and undistinguished family, according to Cicero had to work his way up like a *novus homo*. He amassed wealth (not always reputably), gained the support of the Caecilii

Metelli, and became consul (with a Metellus) 115 BC, defeating P. *Rutilius Rufus. As consul he humiliated the praetor P. *Decius Subulo, triumphed over Ligurian tribesmen and was made *princeps senatus* by the censors (one a Metellus) although probably not the senior patrician alive. He also began building a road (*via Aemilia Scauri) linking the *via Aurelia and the *via Postumia. Increasingly powerful in the senate, he married *Caecilia Metella (1) and became the leader of the Metellan family group, then at the height of its glory. Though himself suspect because of his negotiations with *Jugurtha, he became chairman of one of the tribunals set up by C. *Mamilius Limetanus. Censor 109, he refused, until forced, to resign on the death of his colleague M. *Livius Drusus (1). About 105, he received a *cura annonae*, superseding the quaestor L. *Appuleius Saturninus. In 100 he moved the *senatus consultum ultimum* against Saturninus and his supporters. In the 90s he went on an embassy to Asia and on his return may have brought about the mission of Q. *Mucius Scaevola (2). After Rutilius' conviction (92) he avoided prosecution by Q. *Servilius Caepio (2) and became one of the chief advisers of M. *Livius Drusus (2). Attacked by Q. *Varius, he crushed him with a haughty reply. He was dead by late 89, when Metella married *Sulla. Throughout his life he was involved in numerous trials, not always successful in prosecution, but never convicted. He was the last great *princeps senatus*: 'his nod almost ruled the world' (Cic. *Font.* 24).

He wrote an autobiography, perhaps the first, but it was soon forgotten. (See BIOGRAPHY, ROMAN.) Cicero's admiration for him has coloured much of our tradition, but a very different view is found in (e.g.) Sallust, *Iug.*

See Asc. pp. 21 ff. C, with Marshall, *Asconius Comm.* Gruen, *Trials*, see index. Recent critical biography by R. L. Bates, *Proc. of the Amer. Philos. Soc.* 1986, 251 ff.   E. B.

Aemilius (*RE* 141) **Scaurus** (2), **Marcus,** son of M. *Aemilius Scaurus (1) and *Caecilia Metella (1), hence stepson of L. *Cornelius Sulla. Quaestor under *Pompey *c.*65 BC, he intervened in Judaea and Nabataea, chiefly for his personal profit. As aedile 58 he issued coins (*RRC* 422), together with his colleague P. *Plautius Hypsaeus, commemorating his inglorious campaign against the king of the Nabataeans as a victory. He also gave extravagant games, spending his enormous wealth. As praetor 56 he presided over the trial of P. *Sestius, then governed Sardinia (55), where he tried to recoup his fortunes. Prosecuted *repetundarum* (see REPETUNDAE) in 54 (before *Cato (Uticensis)), he was defended by *Cicero and other eminent men and was acquitted. Standing for the consulship of 53, he was accused (like the other candidates) of *ambitus*, defended by Cicero, but convicted through the hostility of Pompey, whose divorced wife *Mucia he had married. He went into exile.

Asc. pp. 18 ff. C, with Marshall, *Asconius Comm.*   E. B.

Aeneas, character in literature and mythology, son of *Anchises and the goddess Aphrodite. In the *Iliad* he is a prominent Trojan leader, belonging to the younger branch of the royal house, (13. 460–1, 20. 179–83, 230–41), and has important duels with *Diomedes (2) (5. 239 ff) and *Achilles (20. 153 ff.), from both of which he is rescued by divine intervention. His piety towards the gods is stressed (20. 298–9, 347–8), and *Poseidon prophesies that he and his children will rule over the Trojans (20. 307–8).

This future beyond the *Iliad* is reflected in the version in the lost cyclic *Iliu Persis* (see EPIC CYCLE) that Aeneas and his family left Troy before its fall to retreat to Mt. Ida, which led later to accusations of his treachery (e.g. *Origo gentis Romanae* 9. 2–3). The departure of Aeneas from Troy is widely recorded, and the image of Aeneas' pious carrying of his father *Anchises on his shoulders in the retreat is common in Greek vases of the 6th cent. BC found in Etruria, and occurs in 5th- and 4th-cent. Attic literature (Soph. fr. 373 Radt, Xen. *Cyn.* 1. 15). The further story of Aeneas' voyage to Italy may have existed as early as the 6th or 5th cent. BC (Stesichorus fr. 205 Davies; Hellanicus, *FGrH* 4 F 84), but seems well established by the 3rd cent. (Timaeus, *FGrH* 566 F 59). Following recent excavations at *Lavinium, claims have been made for *hero-cult of Aeneas there as early as the 4th cent. BC, but these must remain unproven; it is not easy to link this with other attestations of cult for Aeneas as Jupiter Indiges (e.g. Dion. Hal. *Ant. Rom.* 1. 64. 5; Livy 1. 2. 6).

The list of Aeneas' westward wanderings towards Italy is already long and contradictory by the 1st cent. BC (cf. Dion. Hal. 1. 44–64), including cities and cults supposedly named after him in Thrace, Chalcidice, Epirus, and Sicily, and visits to Delos and Crete. A visit to Carthage, possibly involving a meeting with *Dido, is certainly part of the itinerary by the time of *Naevius' *Bellum Punicum* (3rd cent. BC), where it is seen as an ancestral cause of the enmity between Rome and *Carthage. As Rome confronted a Greek-speaking Mediterranean world in the 3rd cent. BC, it found it politically and culturally useful to claim as its founder Aeneas, famous through his appearance in Homer but also an enemy of the Greeks; a particular stimulus was the invasion of Italy by *Pyrrhus of Epirus (280 BC), who claimed descent from Achilles and saw Rome as a second Troy (Paus. 1. 12. 2). In consequence, Roman poets (e.g. Ennius), historians (e.g. Cato (Censorius)), and antiquarians (e.g. Varro) stressed the Trojan origins of Rome; considerations of chronology eventually led to the view that Aeneas founded not Rome but a preceding city, Lavinium, and that Rome's eponymous founder *Romulus was his distant descendant.

*Virgil's version of the Aeneas-legend in the *Aeneid* aims at literary coherence rather than antiquarian accuracy. Aeneas' wanderings, apart from the stay at Carthage, are compressed into a single book (*Aeneid* 3); his war in Latium is the subject of the second half of the poem, and he appears there and at other times to have some typological link with *Augustus (cf. *Aen.* 8. 680 and 10. 261), who claimed him as ancestor (1. 286–8). The Virgilian Aeneas' central traits of *pietas and martial courage continue his Homeric character, but he is also a projection of the ideal patriotic Roman, subordinating personal goals to national interest. And yet he never renounces his human vulnerability; he is in despair in his first appearance in the poem (1. 92 ff), he is deeply affected by love for Dido (4. 395, 6. 455), and the poem ends not with his triumphant apotheosis, anticipated earlier (1. 259–60, 12. 794–5), but with his emotional killing of Turnus in a moment of passion.

The success of the *Aeneid* meant that few innovations were made in the Aeneas-legend by later writers; subsequent Aeneas-narratives are clearly crafted from existing materials, principally Virgil (e.g. Ov. *Met.* 13. 623 – 14. 608, *Origo gentis Romanae* 9. 2 – 15. 4).

J. Perret, *Les Origines de la légende troyenne de Rome* (1942); G. K. Galinsky, *Aeneas, Sicily and Rome* (1969); N. M. Horsfall, in J. N. Bremmer and N. M. Horsfall, *Roman Myth and Mythography* (1987); F. Canciani, *LIMC* 1, 'Aineias'; E. Gruen, *Culture and National Identity in Republican Rome* (1992).   S. J. Ha.

Aeneas (Aineias) Tacticus, probably the Stymphalian general of the Arcadian *koinon* (see ARCADIAN LEAGUE) in 367 BC (Xen.

Hell. 7. 3. 1); anyway the earliest(-surviving) and most historically interesting of the ancient military writers (*tactici*). Of several treatises only his 'Siegecraft (*Poliorcetica*) is extant, internally datable to the mid-4th cent. via the clustering of contemporary illustrations of its precepts (and linguistically important for its embryo form of the *koinē*). Concerned more with defence against than prosecution of siege-warfare, it offers unique insights into the stresses of life in small communities with warfare and revolution constantly threatening. See SIEGECRAFT, GREEK.

The best critical text is the Budé by A. Dain (1967) which, together with renewed study of content since the 1960s, is reflected in the full commentaries-cum-translation by D. Whitehead (1990; no text) and M. Bettalli (1990); but still valuable are the Loeb (1923) and Hunter–Handford (1927) edns. Language: B. A. van Groningen, *Mnemos.* 1938, 329 ff. (with earlier bibliog.). Lexicon: D. Barends (1955).   D. W.

Aenesidemus of Cnossus, sceptical philosopher, revived Pyrrhonism (see PYRRHON) in the 1st cent. BC, probably as a reaction to the decline of scepticism in the Academy under *Philon (3) of Larissa. He taught at some point in Alexandria (1). His works are lost, but versions of his 'Modes of Inducing Suspension of Judgement' (Τρόποι τῆς ἐποχῆς) are preserved by Philon (4) Judaeus, Diogenes Laertius, and Sextus Empiricus. Photius (*Bibl.* cod. 212) has a summary of his Πυρρώνειοι λόγοι ('Pyrrhonian Arguments') in eight books, dedicated to L. *Aelius Tubero, an Academic and friend of Cicero. Sextus also ascribes to Aenesidemus a set of modes of argument against causal explanation.

F. Decleva Caizzi, *CQ* 1992; J. Annas and J. Barnes, *The Modes of Scepticism* (1985). See also bibliog. under SCEPTICS.   G. S.

Aenianes, a people situated east of *Dodona in the Homeric Catalogue (*Il.* 2. 749) who moved later into the upper Spercheios valley. There they developed into a tribal state and belonged to the Pylaic and then the Delphic *amphictiony. Dependent on the *Aetolians from 272–167 BC, they continued as an independent *koinon* into Roman times.

IG 9. 2. 3 ff.; R. Flacelière, *Les Aitoliens à Delphes* (1937); Y. Béquignon, *La vallée du Spercheios* (1944): P-K, *GL* 1. 243 ff. and elsewhere; Hammond, *Epirus*, 375 f. and elsewhere; L. Moretti, *Iscrizioni Storiche Ellenistiche* 2 (1975), no. 92; B. Helly, *Rev. Ét. Grec.* 1993, 507 (*BÉ* 291).   P. S. D.

Aenus, a flourishing Greek city, originally an Aeolic foundation (Hdt. 7. 58. 3), just east of the river Hebrus (Alc. fr. 29 Lobel) on the coast of *Thrace. The modern Enez is on the site of the ancient city. Like Abdera, Aenus owed its wealth to its geographical situation. Not only did it command the trade that descended the Hebrus valley, but also it provided a route alternative to the Bosporus (1) and the Dardanelles for trade that wished to reach the Aegean from the Black Sea; merchandise could be disembarked at Odessus, sent overland to the Hebrus valley and then down to Aenus. Thus Aenus lay at the entrance to the natural route to the rich cornlands, ranches, forests, and fruit-producing regions of eastern and central Thrace. It also derived considerable revenue from its fisheries. As a tributary state, it paid a large sum, twelve talents, to the *Delian League, in 454 BC. The subsequent lowering of the tribute was due partly to the rise of Odrysian power (see THRACE), and partly the Athenian development of the sea-route from the Black Sea, which diverted commerce from the land-route by the Hebrus valley. Possibly, after the rise of the Odrysian power, Aenus passed out of Athenian control, but this was later re-established; thus Aenus supplied *peltasts at Pylos in 425 BC, and was an ally of Athens in Sicily in 415 BC. (Thuc. 4. 28. 4; 7. 57. 5). Between 341 and 185 BC Aenus passed through the hands of the Macedonian, Egyptian, and Pergamene kings, until

Aeoliae insulae

in 185 BC it was declared a '*free city' by the Romans (Plin. *HN* 4. 43). The coin types of Aenus reached perfection in the third quarter of the 5th cent. BC.

S. Casson, *Macedonia, Thrace and Illyria* (1926); J. M. F. May, *Aenus, its History and Coinage, 474–431 BC* (1950).   J. M. R. C.; N. G. L. H.

Aeoliae insulae, the volcanic Aeolian islands, 40 km. (25 mi.) north-east of Sicily, had a flourishing neolithic culture based on the obsidian industry and well represented in the Diana plain and Castello (Lipari), a natural fortress with a succession of neolithic, bronze age, Greek, and Roman settlements. The islands took full commercial advantage of their position between east and west in the early bronze age, when the local Capo Graziano culture is equated by Bernabò Brea with the Aeolians of Greek legend and imported Mycenaean pottery provides the first absolute dates in the prehistory of western Europe. Aegean contact continued in the middle bronze age (Milazzese culture): contact with the peninsular *Apennine culture recalls the Liparus legend (Diod. Sic. 5. 7) and gave rise to the late bronze age–early iron age *Ausonian culture, with its parallels at Milazzo for the proto-*Villanovan urnfields of the mainland. The Cnidian–Rhodian colony of Lipara was founded in 580–576 BC, and conquered in 252 by Rome; under the empire it had the status of a small provincial town with Roman citizenship. The islands produced obsidian, sulphur, alum, pumice, and coral.

BTCGI 3–9 (1984–91), 'Alicudi (Ericusa)', 'Basiluzzo (Basilidin)', 'Filicudi (Phoenicusa)', 'Lipari (Meligunis)', and other islands forthcoming; L. Vagnetti (ed.), *Magna Grecia e mondo miceneo*, exhib. cat. (Taranto, 1982); L. Bernabò Brea, *Gli Eoli e l'inizio dell'età del bronzo nelle isole Eolie e nell'Italia meridionale* (1985); L. Bernabò Brea and M. Cavalier, *Meligunis-Lipára*, 1–4 (1960–91).   D. W. R. R.

Aeolis, the territory of the northernmost group of Greek immigrants to the western coast of Asia Minor, covering the coastal strip from the entrance of the Hellespont to the mouth of the Hermus—a linguistic and ethnological, not a geographical unit. Near the end of the second millennium BC the Aeolians, deriving from *Boeotia and *Thessaly, planted their first settlements in *Lesbos, and thence expanded northwards to Tenedos, and along the mainland coast to the east and the south. There must have been considerable racial fusion with the local *barbarian inhabitants, but the Aeolians brought with them their own dialect (see DIALECTS, GREEK) and created a distinctive style of architectural decoration. Most of the Aeolian cities derived their livelihood from agriculture, commerce being of minor importance in Lesbos. The settlements in the south may have formed a league, whose religious centre was the temple of *Apollo at Gryneum. The chief city was *Cyme; other members probably included Aegae, Cilla, Larissa (where the Archaic settlement has been excavated), Pitane, *Smyrna (later resettled by *Ionians) and Temnus. The northern Aeolian settlements occupied the coastal part of *Troas.

J. M. Cook, *The Greeks in Ionia and the East* (1962); E. Kirsten, *Kl. Pauly* 1. 180–3; P. P. Betancourt, *The Aeolic Style of Architecture* (1977).
D. E. W. W.; S. M.

Aeolus, (1) the Homeric ruler of the winds (*Od.* 10. 1–79). Unlike Virgil (*Aen.* 1), Homer makes him a human by suppressing the idea that winds are minor deities. (See WIND-GODS) He lives in Aeolia, a floating island, in the furthest west. His six sons and six daughters have married one another. Already the 5th cent. found this incest intolerable: *Euripides (*Aeolus*) made Aeolus force his daughter *Canace to commit suicide because of her love for her brother *Macareus; Ovid (*Her.* 11) paints the drama in shrill colours. In Hellenistic times he was worshipped by the Liparaeans (Diod. Sic. 20. 101. 2).

(2) The son of *Hellen and eponym of the Aeolians occurs first in Hesiod (frs. 9, 10 M–W) but is clearly presupposed by Homer (*Il.* 6. 154; *Od.* 11. 236 f.). His original home is the north of Greece, where many of his descendants are located. (3) Son of *Poseidon and Melanippe, who is exposed together with his brother Boeotus. Their fate is the subject of Euripides' *Melanippe Desmotis* and *Melanippe Sophe*. Confusion between the various Aeoli arose early and they were accommodated into one genealogical scheme by Diod. Sic. 4. 67.

K. Tümpel, *RE* 1, 'Aiolos'; F. Giudice, *LIMC* 1, 'Aiolos'; G. Huxley, *Riv. Fil.* 1992, 385–7 (Italian connection).   J. N. B.

Aepytus, name of three Arcadian heroes. (1) Aepytus son of Hippothoüs entered the *abaton* of *Poseidon at *Mantinea, and was blinded and killed by the god. (2) Youngest grandson of (1), Aepytus son of Cresphontes, king of *Messenia, was exiled when his father and brothers were murdered, but returned to avenge them and take power. (3) Aepytus son of Elatus reigned over Arcadia and was buried at the foot of Mt. Cyllene.   M. J.

Aequi, simple Italic tribe inhabiting the valleys of the Himella, Tolenus, and upper *Anio); their dialect probably resembled Oscan (see OSCAN AND UMBRIAN). Expanding from the highlands towards Latium, by 500 BC they held the mountains behind *Tibur and *Praeneste, and for 70 years, despite their small numbers (Livy 6. 12), they proved even tougher enemies to the *Hernici, Latins (see LATINI), and Romans than their Volscian allies. They established themselves on the Alban hills and were not expelled until 431 (see ALGIDUS). Thereafter, however, Aequi are only casually mentioned until 304, when they apparently occupied their original central Italian area. Rome now almost exterminated them; she established Latin colonies at *Carsioli and *Alba Fucens, gave the surviving Aequi *civitas sine suffragio* and rapidly romanized them (Livy 9. 45, 10. 1. 9). The Aequian nation thus disappeared, although a *municipium Aequiculorum sive Aequiculanorum* is still recorded after 90 BC (Plin. *HN* 3. 106); its name survives in the district Cicolano north of the Fucine lake.

G. Devoto, *Gli antichi Italici* (1951), 127 ff.; *CAH* 7²/2 (1989), see index.
E. T. S.

aerarii, payers, were a class of Roman citizens who had incurred the *censors' condemnation for some moral or other misbehaviour. They were required to pay the poll-tax (*tributum*) at a higher rate than other citizens. The origin of the class is obscure. Mommsen argued that a payer was originally one who had no landed property and was therefore disqualified from certain public rights such as voting and military service but had to pay the poll-tax in proportion to his means.

Mommsen, *Röm. Staatsr.* 2³. 392 ff.; P. Fraccaro, *Athenaeum* 1933 (= *Opuscula* 2. 149 ff.).   A. D. E. L.

aerarium, derived from *aes*, denotes 'treasury'. The main *aerarium* of Rome was the *aerarium Saturni*, so called from the temple below the Capitol, in which it was placed. Here were kept state documents, both financial and non-financial (including *leges* (see LEX (1))) and *senatus consulta which were not valid until lodged there), and the state treasure, originally mainly of bronze (*aes*) but including also ingots of gold and silver and other valuables. The *Tabularium (1) was built near it in 78 BC.

The *aerarium* was controlled by the quaestors under the supervision of the senate, with a subordinate staff of *scribae*, *viatores*, etc. The *tribuni aerarii*, men of a property-class a little below the knights, were probably concerned with making payments from the tribes into the treasury. The *aerarium sanctius* was a special reserve, fed by the 5 per cent tax on emancipations. Treasure was withdrawn from it in 209 BC and on other occasions. Caesar in 49 BC seized the reserve for his own uses.

Caesar placed two aediles in charge of the *aerarium*, Augustus two *praefecti* (28 BC) and then two praetors (23). Claudius (AD 44) placed it again under the quaestors, Nero, finally, in AD 56 under two *praefecti*. These officials are last attested in the mid-4th cent. In the earlier empire at least the *aerarium* remained the official repository for state documents and cash; payments from it could be ordered by the senate and, in practice, by the emperor. *Bona caduca* (property without an heir), *bona damnatorum* (property of the condemned), and other public revenues were increasingly diverted to the *fiscus. The details of this process remain obscure.

The *aerarium militare*, also situated on the Capitol, was founded by Augustus in AD 6 to provide for the pensioning of discharged soldiers. Augustus provided for it a capital sum of 170,000,000 sesterces from his own funds and an income from the *centesima rerum venalium* (1% tax on sales by auction) and the *vicesima hereditatum* (5% tax on inheritances). It was administered by three ex-praetors (*praefecti aerarii militaris*), at first chosen by lot, later by the emperor.

O. Hirschfeld, *Die kaiserlichen Verwaltungsbeamten* (1905), 13 f.; A. H. M. Jones, *Studies in Roman Government and Law* (1960), ch. 6; F. Millar, *JRS* 1964, 33 ff.; M. Corbier, *L'aerarium Saturni et l'aerarium militare* (1974).
G. P. B.

Aerope, daughter of *Catreus, king of Crete, and given by her father to *Nauplius (2) to be sold overseas. She married *Atreus (or, in some versions, Pleisthenes) and gave birth to *Agamemnon and *Menelaus (1). While married to Atreus, she committed adultery with his brother Thyestes, to whom she secretly gave the golden lamb which allowed him to claim the throne. But *Zeus expressed disapproval by reversing the course of the sun (Eur. *El.* 699–746; Apollod. *Epit.* 2. 10–12). J. R. M.

aes, bronze, also more loosely copper or brass, hence (a) money, coinage, pay, period for which pay is due, campaign; (b) document on bronze. The earliest Roman monetary system involved the weighing out of bronze by the pound or its fractions (see WEIGHTS); transactions *per aes et libram*, by bronze and balance, became fossilized in Roman private law as a formal means of transferring ownership. Sums recorded in the sources as 'so many *aeris* (*gravis*, heavy, or *rudis*, raw)' are to be taken as intended to mean so many pounds of bronze and then so many coins weighing (more or less) a pound and called asses. In the late 140s BC, the Roman state changed from reckoning in asses to reckoning in sestertii = ¼ denarius = 4 asses each; at this point certain valuations were probably transferred from *asses* to the same number of sestertii, although the real value was different.

Aes alienum = debt; *aes equestre* = money assigned to an *eques* for the purchase of a horse; *aes hordiarium* = annual sum assigned to an *eques* for the maintenance of his horse. (*Aes signatum* in antiquity meant ordinary struck coinage, not, as some Italians suppose, the early Roman (and Italian) currency bars which have been misleadingly called *aes signatum* by numismatists from the 19th cent. onwards.)

M. H. Crawford, *RRC*, chs. 2, 6, and *Coinage and Money under the Roman Republic* (1985), chs. 2–3, 10. M. H. C.

Aeschines (1) (*c.*397–*c.*322 BC), Athenian orator whose exchanges with *Demosthenes (2) in the courts in 343 and 330 provide a large part of the evidence for the relations of Athens and Macedon in the 340s and the 330s. His origins were sufficiently obscure to allow Demosthenes' invention full play. He probably did not receive the usual formal training in rhetoric, but after hoplite service of some distinction in the 360s and early 350s, and a period as an actor, he embarked on a public career as a supporter first briefly of *Aristophon and then of *Eubulus (1), during whose supervision of the city's finances Aeschines' brother, Aphobetus, was a theoric commissioner (see THEŌRIKA). In 347/6 both Aeschines and Demosthenes were members of the *boulē and their disagreements led to sixteen years of enmity. Early in 346 (though many have dated the affair to 348/7) when alarming news reached Athens of the extension of Macedonian influence to *Arcadia, Eubulus supported by Aeschines took the lead in urging Athens to protest to Arcadia and to seek to organize a Common Peace, which would provide for common action against aggressors and so make it unnecessary for any state to seek Macedonian help. Aeschines was sent on an embassy to *Megalopolis where he sought to dissuade the assembly of the Arcadians from dealings with *Philip (1) II. Whether through the indifference of the Greek states or through the new threat to Greece caused by the refusal of the Phocian tyrant, *Phalaecus, to permit access to *Thermopylae, the key-point for the defence of Greece, the initiative of Eubulus and Aeschines proved abortive. An embassy of ten, including Aeschines and Demosthenes, was hastily sent to negotiate peace terms with Philip. Their return to the city was closely followed by a Macedonian embassy, and on the 18th and 19th Elaphebolion, when the peace was debated and voted, Aeschines played a notable if ineffectual part. Demosthenes, realizing that peace was essential and that the only form of peace which Philip would accept was a plain alliance with Athens and her allies of the *Second Athenian Confederacy, made himself responsible for getting the decree of *Philocrates passed: Aeschines strove without success for a *Common Peace open to all the Greeks. The ten ambassadors then set off again to secure Philip's oath to the treaty which he did not render until his forces were in position to attack Phocis. When the ambassadors returned with this alarming news, it was decided in the *boulē* to recommend an expedition to save Phocis, but by 16th Skirophorion, when the people met, it was known that Philip had occupied Thermopylae; Demosthenes' proposal was not even read out and he was himself shouted down. Aeschines then made a speech, which Demosthenes chose to regard as proof that Aeschines had been won over by Macedonian bribery. The truth was probably far different; since Phocis could not be saved, Aeschines sought to reconcile the Athenians to the fact by reporting vague suggestions of Macedonian proposals for central Greece which were very much what Athens was seeking.

From that day Demosthenes was implacably opposed to Aeschines as well as determined to destroy the Peace, while Aeschines was gradually won over to support it and seek its extension into a Common Peace. In 346/5 Demosthenes with the support of Timarchus began a prosecution of Aeschines for his part in the peace negotiations; Aeschines replied by charging Timarchus with breach of the law forbidding those whose misconduct was notorious from addressing the assembly; the *Against Timarchus* was successful and Demosthenes was forced to recognize that the time was not ripe to attack Aeschines. By mid 343 the mood of Athens had clearly begun to change; early in the year Philocrates had been successfully prosecuted by *Hyperides and

Aeschines Socraticus

in the *De falsa legatione* Demosthenes attacked Aeschines, the advocate of merely amending a discredited peace, as if he had been the orator really responsible in 346 for Athens' accepting the Peace. Aeschines replied in a speech of the same title and, supported by Eubulus and *Phocion, was narrowly acquitted. Aeschines continued to have some influence in the assembly, and in 340/39 was sent as one of Athens' representatives to the Amphictionic Council (see AMPHICTIONY), on which occasion he appears to have displayed a serious lack of judgement in relation to the affairs of central Greece: at a time when the war against Philip had recommenced and there was a clear need to avoid exacerbating the divisions of Greece, Aeschines replied to Locrian charges against Athens with such a vigorous attack on the conduct of the Amphissans that hostilities began and Philip was the more easily able to intervene.

Aeschines was a member of the embassy sent to negotiate with Philip after the battle of *Chaeronea, but from then on he withdrew from politics only to re-emerge on two occasions when circumstances seemed favourable for an attack on Demosthenes. The first was in early 336 when Ctesiphon proposed that Demosthenes should be crowned in the theatre at the *Dionysia for the excellence of his services to the city: earlier Demosthenes had been similarly honoured without protest but, at a time when Demosthenes' gloomy predictions after Chaeronea seemed mocked by the opening of the Macedonian invasion of Persia, Aeschines indicted the decree under the *graphē paranomōn*. However, the murder of Philip made the future too uncertain for Aeschines to be confident of success, and he decided not to proceed with the indictment for the moment. In 330 after the defeat of Persia at *Gaugamela and the failure of *Agis III's revolt, which Demosthenes had chosen not to support, Athens was in almost complete isolation with no prospect of liberation from Macedon, and Aeschines thought the moment suitable for him to proceed with his prosecution of Ctesiphon. In the *Against Ctesiphon*, after adducing minor, if perhaps valid, legalistic considerations concerning the details of the original decree, he reviewed the career of Demosthenes, somewhat selectively, and sought to show that Demosthenes was unworthy of the crown. In the *De corona* Demosthenes replied with all the devastating effect that his great rhetorical gifts could command, and Aeschines failed to secure the necessary fifth of the jury's votes to save him from a fine and the limitation of the right to prosecute. He chose to retire from Athens to Rhodes, where he taught rhetoric.

The supremacy of Demosthenes as an orator has to a large extent beguiled posterity into the opinion that he alone fully appreciated the menace of Macedon and correctly diagnosed the causes of Philip's success, and Aeschines has been represented as an opportunist with little judgement and less principle. In fact, there was no obvious way of saving Athens and Greece, and it is probable that Aeschines no less than Demosthenes sought to maintain his city's power and independence.

Speeches The only genuine speeches of Aeschines known to the critics of the Roman period were the three that we have: a fourth, concerning Delos, was rejected by *Caecilius (1). Aeschines was a man of dignified presence and fine voice, who deprecated the use of extravagant gestures by an orator, preferring a statuesque pose. Proud of his education, he displays it by frequent quotation of poetry. In the use of historical argument he cannot compare with Demosthenes, but in a battle of wits he more than holds his own. His vocabulary is simple but effective, though occasional obscurities may be found in his sentences. Ancient critics ranked

him lower than he deserves; the fact is that he was not aiming at literary perfection; his object was to produce a powerful effect on his audiences, and he was justified by the result.

TEXTS Blass (Teubner, corr. Schindel, 1978); with Eng trans., Adams (Loeb); with Fr. trans., Martin and Budé (Budé).

INDEX Preuss (1896).

G. Ramming, *Die politischen Ziele und Wege des Aischines* (1965); *HM* 2, see index under 'Aeschines'; R. Lane Fox, in R. Osborne and S. Hornblower (eds.), *Ritual Finance Politics* (1994), ch. 8; E. M. Harris, *Aeschines and Athenian Politics* (1995). For general bibliography, see ATTIC ORATORS; DEMOSTHENES (2).   G. L. C.

Aeschines (2) **Socraticus** (4th cent. BC), of the *deme of Sphettus in Attica, a devoted follower of *Socrates, was present at his trial and death. He wrote speeches for the lawcourts and taught oratory, but fell into poverty and took refuge at the court in *Syracuse, returning to Athens after the expulsion of *Dionysius (2) II in 356. Best known as the author of Socratic dialogues which resemble *Xenophon (1)'s more than *Plato (1)'s, Aeschines was apparently not an original thinker, and his Socrates expounds common ethical views. Although only fragments survive today, seven dialogues were considered genuine in antiquity: *Alcibiades, Axiochus, Aspasia, Callias, Miltiades, Rhinon, Telauges*. The first of these was partly intended to defend Socrates against charges of corrupting the young *Alcibiades. The dialogues of Aeschines were highly esteemed for their style and their faithfulness to Socrates' character and conversational manner.

G. C. Field, *Plato and his Contemporaries* (1930). Fragments: H. Dittmar, *Aischines von Sphettos* (1912); G. Giannantoni, *Socratis et Socraticorum Reliquiae* 2. 593–629.   M. Ga.

Aeschylus (*RE* 13), Athenian tragic dramatist

Life (?525/4–456/5 BC) Aeschylus was probably born at *Eleusis in 525/4 BC (*Marm. Par.*). He fought at the battle of *Marathon (*Marm. Par.*; *Vita* 4, 11) and probably at *Salamis (*Ion (2) of Chios, *FGrH* 392 F 7). His first tragic production was in 499 (*Suda* αι 357 with π 2230), his first victory in 484 (*Marm. Par.*); thereafter he may have been almost invariably victorious, especially after the death of *Phrynichus (1) *c.*473 (he gained thirteen victories altogether, *Vita* 13). Of his surviving plays, *Persians* was produced in 472 (his *chorēgos* being the young *Pericles (1)) and *Seven against Thebes* in 467. *Suppliants*, part of a production which won first prize over *Sophocles (1) (*POxy.* 2256. 3), must be later than *Seven* (despite the predominant role of the chorus and other features once thought to prove it very early); its exact date is uncertain. The *Oresteia* (comprising *Agamemnon*, *Choephori* ('Women Bearing Drink-offerings') and *Eumenides*, with the lost satyr-play *Proteus*) was Aeschylus' last production in Athens, in 458. He had already visited Sicily once, possibly twice, at the invitation of *Hieron (1) of Syracuse, composing *Women of Aetna* in honour of Hieron's newly founded city of Aetna (*Vita* 9) and producing *Persians* at Syracuse (ibid. 18; Eratosth. in schol. Ar. *Frogs* 1028); after the production of the *Oresteia* he went there again, dying at *Gela in 456/5. *Prometheus Bound*, if by Aeschylus (see below), may have been composed in Sicily and produced posthumously. His epitaph (*Vita* 11) makes no reference to his art, only to his prowess displayed at Marathon; this estimate of what was most important in Aeschylus' life—to have been a loyal and courageous citizen of a free Athens—can hardly be that of the Geloans and will reflect his own death-bed wishes (cf. Paus. 1. 14. 5) or those of his family.

Two sons of Aeschylus themselves became dramatists, *Euphorion (1) (who also restaged many of his father's plays) and Euaeon. A nephew, *Philocles, was the founder of a dynasty of tragedians that lasted over a century.

Works (° denotes a known satyr-play). Aeschylus' total output is variously stated at between 70 and 90 plays. Seven plays have survived via medieval manuscripts, of which *Prometheus Bound* is of disputed authenticity (it was possibly composed by Euphorion and produced by him as Aeschylus' work). In addition there survive substantial papyrus fragments of °*Netfishers (Diktyoulkoi)* and °*Spectators at the Isthmian Games (Theōroi* or *Isthmiastai)*.

Many of Aeschylus' productions were connected 'tetralogies', comprising three tragedies presenting successive episodes of a single story (a 'trilogy') followed by a satyr-play based on part of the same or a related myth. This seems to have been common practice in his day, though the production of 472 (*Phineus, Persians, Glaucus of Potniae* and °*Prometheus the Fire-kindler*) is an exception. Four tetralogies are securely attested: (1) the *Oresteia* (see above); (2) *Laius, Oedipus, Seven against Thebes*, °*Sphinx*; (3) *Suppliants, Egyptians, Danaids*, °*Amymone*; (4) a *Lycurgeia* comprising *Edonians, Bassarids, Young Men (Neaniskoi)* and °*Lycurgus*. At least seven other tetralogies can be reconstructed with a fair degree of probability: (5) *Myrmidons, Nereids, Phrygians* (satyr-play unknown), based on *Iliad* 16–24; (6) *Ghost-Raisers (Psychagōgoi), Penelope, Bone-Gatherers (Ostologoi)*, °*Circe*, based on the *Odyssey* but apparently with an innovative ending; (7) *Memnon, The Weighing of Souls (Psychostasia), Phrygian Women* (satyr-play unknown), based on the cyclic *Aethiopis*, ending with the funeral of Achilles; (8) *The Award of the Arms (Hoplon Krisis), Thracian Women, Women of Salamis* (satyr-play unknown), centring on the death of Ajax; (9) *Semele, Wool-Carders (Xantriai), Pentheus*, and perhaps °*The Nurses of Dionysus*, on the birth of Dionysus and his conflict with Pentheus (cf. Euripides' *Bacchae*); (10) *Eleusinians, Women (?) of Argos, Epigoni*, and perhaps °*Nemea*, on the recovery of the bodies of the *Seven against Thebes and their sons' war of revenge; (11) *Lemnian Women, Argo, Hypsipyle*, °*Cabiri*, on the story of *Hypsipyle and *Jason (1). In some cases two tragedies seem to be connected but no third related one can be identified: (12) *Prometheus Bound* and *Prometheus Unbound* (if, as is likely, the title *Prometheus the Fire-bearer (Pyrphoros)* is no more than a variant form of °*Prometheus the Fire-kindler (Pyrkaeus)*); (13) *Phorcides* and *Polydectes* (with °*Netfishers*), with *Perseus (1) as hero; (14) *Mysians* and *Telephus*.

Aeschylean plays not mentioned above include *Archer-Nymphs (Toxotides)*, on the death of Actaeon; *Athamas; Atalanta; Callisto; Carians* or *Europa*; °*Cercyon; Chamber-makers (Thalamopoioi); Children of Heracles; Cretan Women* (on the story of Polyidus); *Daughters of the Sun (Heliades); The Escort (Propompoi); Glaucus the Sea-god; °Heralds (Kerykes); Iphigenia; Ixion; °The Lion; Niobe; °Oreithyia; Palamedes; Perrhaebian Women* (whose central character was Ixion); *Philoctetes* (see Dio Chrys. *Or.* 52); *Priestesses (Hiereiai);* °*Sisyphus the Runaway* and *Sisyphus the Stone-roller* (if these two are different plays).

Technique Aeschylus was the most innovative and imaginative of Greek dramatists. His extant plays, though covering a period of only fifteen years, show a great and evolving variety in structure and presentation.

The three earlier plays (*Persians, Seven*, and *Suppliants*) are designed for a theatre without a *skēnē* but containing a mound or elevation (tomb of Darius, Theban acropolis, Argive sanctuary, the two latter with cult-images on them). There are two actors only; the main interactions are less between character and character than between character and chorus (often expressed in

'epirrhematic' form, i.e. dialogue between singing chorus and speaking actor), and in two cases the chorus open the play in marching anapaests. There is a wide variety of structural patterns, some of them (like *Sept.* 375–676, with its seven pairs of speeches punctuated by short choral stanzas) probably unique experiments, but all built round the basic framework of a series of episodes framed by entries and exits and separated by choral songs. The pace of the action is usually rather slow.

By 458 the dramatist had available to him a *skēnē* and probably an *ekkyklēma* and *mēchanē* also, as well as a third actor. Aeschylus makes imaginative, and once again very varied, use of the new opportunities. After composing the first half of *Agamemnon* entirely in his old style (with no actor–actor dialogue whatever), he centres the play on a verbal trial of strength between *Agamemnon and *Clytemnestra, meanwhile keeping *Cassandra long silent and then making her narrate Agamemnon's death prophetically before it happens. The house and its entrance are firmly controlled throughout by the 'watchdog' Clytemnestra. In the second half of *Choephori* the action increasingly accelerates as the climax approaches, and then abruptly slows as Clytemnestra for a time staves off her doom with brilliant verbal fencing. In *Eumenides* a series of short scenes, full of surprises and changes of location, and including a trial-scene with some virtuoso four-sided dialogue, leads to a conclusion mainly in the old epirrhematic mode for one actor and chorus (with a second chorus at the very end).

Aeschylus' plots tend to be characterized, not by abrupt changes of direction (*peripeteiai*), but by a build-up of tension and expectation towards a climax anticipated by the audience if not by the dramatis personae. He was quite capable of contriving *peripeteiai* when he wished, as witness *Seven against Thebes* where the whole action pivots on Eteocles' discovery that he has unwittingly brought about a combat between himself and his brother and thus fulfilled his father's curse; the trilogy form, however, encourages sharp changes of direction and mood between plays rather than within them.

In general the central interest in Aeschylean drama is in situation and event rather than in character. Even quite major figures in a play (like *Pelasgus or *Orestes) can be almost without distinctive character traits: if their situation gives them effectively no choice how to act, their personal qualities are irrelevant and are ignored. On the other hand, characters who make (or have previously made) decisions vitally affecting the action, when alternative choices were possible, are portrayed as far as is necessary for illuminating these decisions: Eteocles is usually calm and rational but can be carried away by strong emotions, Agamemnon is one who values prestige above all other considerations. The character most fully drawn is Clytemnestra, because the plot requires her to be a unique individual, 'a woman with a man's mind'. In the *Oresteia* several minor characters are drawn with marked vividness, less perhaps for their own sake than to focus special attention on what they have to say.

For similar reasons, Aeschylean choruses nearly always have a strong and distinctive personality. Their words are often of the utmost importance in drawing attention to the deeper principles underlying events (even when they do not themselves fully understand these principles or their implications) and, together with their music and dance, in establishing the mood and theme of a whole play. The women of *Seven*, dominated almost throughout by fear, contrast sharply with the Danaids, utterly determined in their rejection of marriage and coercing Pelasgus by a cool threat of suicide; the Argive elders of *Agamemnon*, enunciators of profound moral principles yet unable to understand how these principles doom Agamemnon to death, share a trilogy with the Erinyes, hellish bloodsuckers yet also divine embodiments of these same principles. Aeschylus' choruses often have a substantial influence on the action; the Danaids and the Erinyes are virtually the protagonists of their plays, the women's panic in *Seven* causes Eteocles' promise to fight in person, while in *Choephori* it is the chorus who ensure that Aegisthus is delivered unguarded into Orestes' hands. Sometimes a chorus will surprise the audience near the end of a play (as when the Argive elders defy Aegisthus); it is a distinctly Aeschylean touch in *Prometheus Bound* when the hitherto submissive Oceanids resolve to stay with Prometheus despite Hermes' warning of apocalyptic destruction impending.

Aeschylus' lyric style is smooth and flexible, and generally easier of immediate comprehension than that of *Pindar or Sophocles, provided the listener was attuned to a vocabulary that tended towards the archaic and the Homeric. In iambic dialogue, where he had fewer models to follow, he sometimes seems stiff compared with Sophocles or Euripides, though he can also create an impression of everyday speech through informal grammar and phraseology. He excels at devising patterns of language and imagery, elaborating them down to minute detail, and sustaining them all through a play or a trilogy.

Patterns of metre (and presumably of music) are likewise designed on a trilogic scale; in the *Oresteia* ode after ode ponders the workings of justice in syncopated iambics and lecythia, with variations and deviations to suit particular contexts (epic-like dactyls for the departure of the expedition to Troy, ionics for Helen's voyage and her welcome by the Trojans). Aeschylus' lyrics are mostly simple and perspicuous in structure, here too resembling *Alcman or *Stesichorus more than Pindar or Sophocles. He makes extensive use of marching anapaests as preludes to (and occasionally substitutes for) choral odes, and also in quasi-epirrhematic alternation with lyrics. The regular speech-verse is the iambic trimeter, but the trochaic tetrameter (characteristic of early tragedy according to Arist. *Poet.* 1449ᵃ22) appears in *Persians* and *Agamemnon*.

Aeschylus is consistently bold and imaginative in exploiting the visual aspects of drama. The contrast between the sumptuous dress of Atossa at her first, carriage-borne entry and the return of Xerxes alone and in rags; the chaotic entry of the chorus in *Seven*; the African-looking, exotically dressed Danaids and their confrontation with brutal Egyptian soldiers; the purple cloth over which Agamemnon walks to his death, and the display of his corpse in the bath-tub with Cassandra beside him and Clytemnestra 'standing where I struck' (a scene virtually repeated in *Choephori* with a different killer and different victims); the *Erinyes presented anthropomorphically on stage (probably for the first time), yet tracking Orestes like hounds by the scent of blood; the procession that ends the *Oresteia*, modelled on that at the Great *Panathenaea—these are far from exhausting the memorable visual images in only six or seven plays, quite apart from numerous careful touches of detail (e.g. at the end of *Agamemnon* where Aegisthus, that 'woman' of a man, alone of those on stage has neither weapon nor staff in his right hand).

Thought Aeschylus, like all truly tragic writers, is well aware of, and vividly presents, the terrible suffering, often hard to justify in human terms, of which life is full; nevertheless he also believes strongly in the ultimate justice of the gods. In his surviving work (leaving aside *Prometheus*), all human suffering is clearly traceable,

directly or indirectly, to an origin in some evil or foolish action— Xerxes' ill-advised decision to attempt the conquest of Greece; Laius' defiance of an oracular warning to remain childless; the attempt by the sons of Aegyptus to force the Danaids to be their wives; the adultery of Thyestes with Atreus' wife; the abduction of Helen by Paris. The consequences of these actions, however, while always bringing disaster to the actors, never end with them, but spread to involve their descendants and ultimately a whole community; some of these indirect victims have incurred more or less guilt on their own account, but many are completely innocent. In some of Aeschylus' dramas, like *Persians* or the Theban trilogy, the action descends steadily towards a nadir of misery at the end. In the *Oresteia*, however, presumably also in the Odyssean trilogy, and not improbably in the Danaid trilogy, it proves to be possible to draw a line under the record of suffering and reach a settlement that promises a better future; each time a key element in the final stages is the substitution of persuasion for violence, as when in the *Oresteia* a chain of retaliatory murders is ended by the judicial trial of Orestes, and the spirits of violent revenge, the Erinyes, are persuaded to accept an honoured dwelling in Athens.

In dramas of the darker type described above, the gods are stern and implacable, and mortals often find themselves helpless prisoners of their own or others' past decisions; though they may still have considerable freedom to choose how to face their fate (compare the clear-sighted courage of Pelasgus or Cassandra with Xerxes or Agamemnon). Elsewhere, especially perhaps in Aeschylus' latest work, a different concept of divinity may appear. In the *Oresteia* ethical advance on earth, as the virtuous Electra and an Orestes with no base motive succeed the myopic Agamemnon and the monstrous Clytemnestra, is presently answered by ethical advance on Olympus as the amoral gods of *Agamemnon* and *Choephori* turn in *Eumenides* into responsible and even loving (*Eum.* 911, 999) protectors of deserving mortals. Something similar may well have happened in the Prometheus plays.

Aeschylus is intensely interested in the community life of the *polis*, and all his surviving genuine works have strong political aspects. He seems to be a strong supporter of democracy (a word whose elements first appear together in the phrase δήμου κρατοῦσα χείρ 'the sovereign hand of the people', *Supp.* 604) and of Athens' wars of the early 450s, while recognizing the overriding importance of avoiding civil conflict by conciliating rival interests (*Eum.* 858–66, 976–87). To later generations, who from time to time continued to see his plays (cf. Ar. *Ach.* 10), Aeschylus, who may have come of age in the year of *Cleisthenes (2)'s reforms and whose death coincided with the peak of Athenian power, was (as in Aristophanes' *Frogs*) the poet of Athens' greatness, of the generation of Marathon where he had lived what to him was the supreme day of his life. See also TRAGEDY, GREEK.

LIFE AND WORKS R. P. Winnington-Ingram, *Studies in Aeschylus* (1983); A. J. Podlecki, *The Political Background of Aeschylean Tragedy* (1967); H. Hommel (ed.), *Aischylos, Wege der Forschung* (1974); E. Petrounias, *Funktion und Thematik der Bilder bei Aischylos* (1976); M. Gagarin, *Aeschylean Drama* (1976); O. P. Taplin, *The Stagecraft of Aeschylus* (1977); T. G. Rosenmeyer, *The Art of Aeschylus* (1982); W. C. Scott, *Musical Design in Aeschylean Theater* (1984); S. Ireland, *Aeschylus* (1986); A. Lebeck, *The Oresteia: A Study in Language and Structure* (1971); S. D. Goldhill, *Aeschylus: The Oresteia* (1992); M. Griffith, *The Authenticity of Prometheus Bound* (1977); A. Wartelle, *Bibliographie historique et critique d'Éschyle 1518–1974* (1978). On the textual tradition, R. D. Dawe, *The Collation and Investigation of Manuscripts of Aeschylus* (1964), and *Reper-*

tory of Conjectures on Aeschylus (1965); M. L. West, Studies in Aeschylus (1990).

TEXT H. Weir Smyth (Loeb, 1926): vol. 2 repr. 1957, with appendix of major new fragments by H. Lloyd-Jones; D. L. Page (OCT, 1972); M. L. West (Teubner, 1990); fragments in S. L. Radt, TrGF 3 (1985); scholia in O. L. Smith, Scholia in Aeschylum (Teubner, 1976–). Also G. Italie, Index Aeschyleus, 2nd edn. (1964), with addenda by S. L. Radt.

COMMENTARIES Persians, H. D. Broadhead (1960); Seven, L. Lupaş and Z. Petre (1981), G. O. Hutchinson (1985); Suppliants, H. Friis Johansen and E. W. Whittle (1980); Oresteia, G. Thomson (1966); Agamemnon, E. Fraenkel (1950), J. D. Denniston and D. L. Page (1957); Choephori, A. F. Garvie (1986); Eumenides, A. H. Sommerstein (1989), A. J. Podlecki (1989); Prometheus, M. Griffith (1982).

TRANSLATIONS R. Lattimore and others in The Complete Greek Tragedies (1954–6; comm. by J. C. Hogan, 1984); P. H. Vellacott (1956–61); Oresteia: R. Fagles (1977); H. Lloyd-Jones, 2nd edn. (1979).

A. H. S.

Aesculapius The miraculous transferral of the god of healing *Asclepius from *Epidaurus to Rome and the origin of the important healing-cult of the Tiber island there in 292 BC constituted significant moments in Roman narratives of the history of their religion (Val. Max. 1. 8. 2: Ovid made it his final Metamorphosis, Met. 15; 622–745); the summoning of a prestigious god from Greece, in accordance with the Sibylline Books (see SIBYL) and perhaps after a consultation of the *Delphic oracle, to remedy a Roman crisis (pestilence), represented a stage in the domestication of external religion and acted as a prototype for the closely related tale of the summoning of the Magna Mater in 204 BC. (See CYBELE.) In fact the cult was becoming widely diffused at that time everywhere (even our Rome-centred stories preserve some consciousness of the contemporary importance of the cult at nearby *Antium). The therapeutic tradition on the island is well attested (e.g. Suet. Aug. 59; Claud. 25), and survived to the point where it could be transferred to the tutelage of St Bartholomew, whose hospital there still functions. By the imperial period, in Italy and the provinces, a Roman cult is hard to disentangle from the very popular and varied combinations of healing deities blending local cults with a broadly Asclepian tradition.

H. Scullard, Festivals and Ceremonies of the Roman Republic (1981), 54–6.
N. P.

Aesepus, god of the Mysian river of that name, Hesiod, Theog. 342.

Aesernia (mod. Isernia), a strong site near the upper Volturnus river, controlling NW *Samnium. Originally a Samnite town, a Latin colony (see IUS LATII) established here after the Samnite Wars (263 BC) was staunchly pro-Roman until *Social War (3) insurgents captured it (90 BC) and made it their capital. It became a flourishing *municipium (80 BC) of c. twelve ha. (30 acres).

A. Viti, Res publica Aeserninorum (1982); F. Valente, Isernia (1982).
T. W. P.

Aesop, as legendary a figure as Homer. What we now call *fables (Gk. αἶνοι, μῦθοι, λόγοι), i.e. stories clearly fictitious (often about speaking animals), which illustrate a point or support an argument, are first alluded to by Hes. Op. 202–12 and Archil. fr. 174 West, but by the 5th and 4th cents. such fables in prose are regularly attributed to Aesop (Ar. Vesp. 566, Av. 471; Arist. fr. 573 Rose; a black-figured portrait of Aesop with talking fox, Beazley, ARV² p. 916 no. 183, K. Schefold, Die Bildnisse der antiken Dichter, Redner und Denker (1943) 57.4). Hdt. 2. 134–5 places him in the 6th cent. BC as the slave of Iadmon, a Samian later murdered by Delphians (cf. Ar. Vesp. 1446–8); Plato Com. fr. 70 KA has his soul

returning from the grave (cf. Plut. Sol. 6); the legend suggests a ritual scapegoat (φαρμακός).

A biography, serving as a context for the fables he told, may have existed already in the 5th century, but the extant biography, written no earlier than the Roman empire, is a romance on these themes. Beginning with a miracle (Isis grants him speech, the Muses give him inspiration in storytelling) and concluding with a martyr's death (Delphic priests kill him because he denounces their greed), it is largely a repository of slave-savant anecdotes about Aesop and his hapless Samian master, the 'philosopher' Xanthus, followed by Aesop's career as adviser to *Croesus and the king of Babylon (cf. the Assyrian Ahiqar).

The first known collection of Aesopic fables was made by *Demetrius (3) of Phaleron (Diog. Laert. 5. 5. 80). The medieval tradition (which includes moral epilogues) is in three parts, of which the oldest (Collectio Augustana) dates to the 3rd cent. AD, or even earlier. For the writings themselves see FABLES.

Editions (on different principles): E. Chambry, Aesopi fabulae, 2 vols. (1925–6); A. Hausrath and H. Hunger, Corpus fabularum Aesopicarum, 1/1, 2nd edn. (1970), 2 (1959; all published).

For testimonia, Life, and comparative material, B. E. Perry, Aesopica: Studies in Text History of Life and Fables of Aesop, 1 (1952; all published). Translation: L. R. Daly, Aesop Without Morals (1961; contains the Life). On the early biography: M. L. West, in F. R. Adrados (ed.), La fable, Entretiens Hardt (1983); A. Wiechers, Aesop in Delphi (1961). J. S. R.

Aesopus (1st cent. BC), tragic actor, 'dignified' (Hor. Epist. 2. 1. 82), contemporary of Q. *Roscius (Quint. Inst. 11. 3. 111 'Roscius is livelier, Aesopus more dignified'). He gave *Cicero lessons in elocution (Auct. ad Her. (3. 21. 34) suggests that he was greatly his senior) and supported Cicero's recall from exile (Sest. 120–3); he returned to the stage for *Pompey's *ludi, 55 BC, without much success (Fam. 7. 1. 2). See Div. 1. 80; Tusc. 4. 55; QFr. 1. 2. 14. His son, M. Clodius Aesopus, was rich enough to be a wastrel (Hor. Sat. 2. 3. 239; Plin. HN 9. 122). G. C. R.; M. T. G.

aesthetics Since its coinage in the mid-18th cent., 'aesthetics' has come gradually to embrace philosophies of both art and beauty (whether natural or created). Antiquity lacked any explicit tradition of thought which directly matched such categories. But it would be tendentious, for at least two reasons, to conclude that there was no ancient aesthetics. First, aesthetics has scarcely established a theoretical self-sufficiency for itself; its issues cut across the domains of psychology, ethics, and politics, and can be elucidated by thinkers who do not overtly acknowledge a sui generis aesthetic realm. Secondly, the modern development of aesthetics has repeatedly addressed texts and ideas deriving from Greek and Roman culture. An illuminating history of aesthetics would have much to say about ancient roots and influences.

Materials for aesthetics can be traced in at least four kinds of writing: philosophy, literary criticism, art criticism (on painting, sculpture, architecture), and rhetoric. While the separate ramifications of these traditions are complex, they combine to demarcate a particular group of activities (poetry, music, dance, the visual arts) as sharing a mimetic/representational status, and to explore questions—often posed by inter-artistic comparisons—concerning the creation, content, form, style, and effects of the products of these arts. Though this demarcation is not identical to the modern category of '(fine) art', the disparity should not be exaggerated; modern conceptions have grown from 18th-cent. theories, especially Batteux's, which attempted to remodel classical principles of mimesis. Nor have subsequent challenges to these principles, or shifts towards expressionism in definitions of art, broken the threads linking modern aesthetics to antiquity. Whether understood as a process engaged in by artists, or as a facet of what is communicated by their works, expression is certainly perceived by ancient thinkers: it is evinced, for example, by applications of mimeticist language to music, to the 'speaking' qualities of visual artefacts, and to the translation of mental/imaginative ideas into artistic form (e.g. Cic. *Orat.* 8–10; Plotinus, *Enn.* 5. 8. 1).

As this suggests, mimesis provides a supple concept of representation. It has scope to cover a large range of modes of depiction and symbolism, to cater for variations running from imitative realism to imaginative idealism (the latter being a recurrent strain in ancient mimeticism), and to encompass different accounts—circling around polarities of nature and craft, inspiration and technique—of artists' relationships to their works. Ancient attitudes to mimetic art correspondingly contain many distinctive configurations of emphasis: the psychologically and politically grounded moralism of *Plato (1), which denies aesthetic autonomy yet recognizes the potently heightened experiences made possible by artistic resources; the carefully poised arguments of *Aristotle's *Poetics*, with their attention to genre and structure, but also their guiding concern for mimetic significance and its emotional implications; the richly metaphorical stylistic terms of a long tradition of art criticism, now chiefly to be glimpsed in the summaries of *Pliny (1) *HN* bks. 34–6, as well as in the rhetorical descriptions of works of art in the *Philostrati and *Callistratus (5); the earnest reflections of *'Longinus', *On the Sublime*, where categories of rhetorical analysis are simultaneously employed and yet transcended by an emphasis on the capacity of language to transmit the emotional, intellectual, and imaginative insight of creative minds; and the metaphysical theses of *Plotinus, who adjusts Platonic categories so as to grant to (some) artistic images the power to convey intimations of transcendent truth, and who constructs a unitary, spiritual concept of 'beauty' which discards conventional notions of order/symmetry, and traces manifestations of the beautiful back to the ultimate source of being and goodness.

This compressed selection of references spans matters stretching from the sensory features to the social and religious significance of works of art. Yet the list merely hints at some of the points at which aesthetics, *qua* general views of the nature of the arts and of beauty, emerges from the currents of ancient thought. The fertility, and capacity for further development, of these views is attested by historical influence: Pliny's critical vocabulary provided a paradigm for 15th-cent. Italian art criticism; Aristotle's *Poetics* became canonical for literary theory from the 16th to the 18th century, and continued thereafter to provide a contested model for philosophizing about art; ps.-Longinus stimulated the 18th cent.'s meditations on sublimity, which were in turn a precursor of Romanticism; Plato and Plotinus, separately and in synthesis, informed versions of aesthetic idealism in the Renaissance, among the Romantics, and for 19th-cent. philosophers such as Schopenhauer and Hegel.

It would be wrong to pretend that ancient thinkers had discovered all the concerns of modern aestheticians; but equally mistaken to suppose that there is a chasm between the two. Proponents of aesthetic autonomy are sometimes dismissive of the strong ancient tendency to connect both art and beauty to more general accounts of human needs and values. But it is part of the importance of this tendency that, notwithstanding its many internal modulations, it marks out a vital alternative to doctrines of aesthetic self-sufficiency: an alternative which rests on the conviction that a historically sensitive aesthetics should engage with the intricate network of factors—psychological, ethical, religious, political—underlying the practices and categories of human culture.

M. C. Beardsley, *Aesthetics from Classical Greece to the Present* (1966); D. Cooper (ed.), *A Companion to Aesthetics* (1992). F. S. H.

Aeternitas The notion of *aeternitas*, designating perpetuity or eternity, first appears at Rome in *Cicero's day, under the influence of philosophic speculation (notably that of *Stoicism) on αἰών (eternity). From the beginning of the 1st cent. AD, *aeternitas* became an imperial virtue, advertising both the perpetual glory of the ruler and his power, parallel to the *aeternitas populi Romani*, and a promise of immortality. Assuming the iconography of the *Aion of Alexandria, 'Aeternitas Augusta' or 'Augusti' appears on coins and, in 66, Aeternitas even received a sacrifice after the discovery of a plot against Nero. Aeternitas is usually depicted as a veiled woman holding sceptre, globe, and phoenix, or the sun and moon (referring to eternity). But Aeternitas can also be associated with male figures.

M. Charlesworth, *Harv. Theol. Rev.* 1936; M. Quet, *La Mosaïque cosmologique de Merida* (1981); J. Martin, *Providentia Deorum* (1982), 278 ff. J. Sch.

Aethra, in mythology daughter of *Pittheus, king of Troezen, and mother of *Theseus by *Aegeus. Since Theseus was often said to be son of *Poseidon, various explanations were given: Aethra was sent by *Athena (hence called Apaturia, 'the Deceitful') to the island of Hiera or Sphaeria, where Poseidon came to her (Paus. 2. 33. 1); Poseidon visited her the same night as Aegeus (Apollod. 3. 15. 7, Hyg. *Fab.* 37. 1); it was a tale invented by Pittheus to save her reputation (Plut. *Thes.* 6). In the *Iliad* (3. 144) she is mentioned as waiting-maid to *Helen; a story as old as the *Epic Cycle (*Iliu Persis* fr. 4 Davies) and illustrated on the chest of *Cypselus (Paus. 5. 19. 3) says that she was carried off by the *Dioscuri when they came to rescue Helen from her abduction by Theseus (Apollod. 3. 10. 7, *Epit.* 1. 23). Her grandsons, *Demophon (1) and *Acamas, took her home when Troy fell (*Iliu Persis* fr. 4 Davies; Apollod. *Epit.* 5. 22; cf. Paus. 10. 25. 7–8).

Aethra is depicted in various scenes in art from the 6th cent. BC on: she is pursued by Poseidon, rescued from Troy by her grandsons, and, in a scene unknown to surviving literature, threatened by Theseus with a sword: see U. Kron, *LIMC* 1/1. 420–31. H. J. R.; J. R. M.

Aëtius (1), probably late 1st cent. AD, author of a comprehensive survey of the contrasting views of Greek philosophers on questions in natural philosophy. Hermann Diels convincingly argued that this lost work (the *Placita*) was reproduced in the ps.-Plutarchean *Epitome* and in *Stobaeus' *Eclogae*; and that it in turn derived indirectly, augmented e.g. with Stoic and Epicurean material, from *Theophrastus' *Physical Tenets*: hence its value as a source especially for Presocratic philosophy. Recent scholarship offers improved understanding of the purposes and development of the compilations which underlie Aëtius.

Diels, *Dox. Graec.* (includes reconstructed text); D. Runia, *Phronesis* 1989, 245 ff.; J. Mansfeld, *ANRW* 2. 36. 4 (1990). M. Sch.

Aëtius (2), of Amida, physician, fl. *c.* AD 530–60 in *Alexandria (1) and Constantinople. He wrote an extant medical encyclopaedia, called the *Tetrabiblon* from its division into four sections. Beginning with a summary of drug theory (see PHARMACOLOGY), which simplifies many obscurities in *Galen and *Oribasius, the

Tetrabiblon compacts pharmacy, *dietetics, general therapeutics, hygiene, bloodletting, cathartics, prognostics, *pathology, fevers, urines, cranial ailments, eye problems (see OPHTHALMOLOGY), *cosmetics, and *dentistry (bks. 1–8). Unavailable are well edited editions of bks. 9–16, containing important accounts of toxicology (bk. 13), and *gynaecology and obstetrics (bk. 16; see CHILDBIRTH).

TEXTS A. Olivieri, *Libri medicinales*, 2 vols. (1935, 1950); J. V. Ricci, *Aetios of Amida: The Gynaecology and Obstetrics of the VIth Century* AD (Eng. trans. 1950).

GENERAL LITERATURE J. Scarborough, *DOP* 1984, 224–6, M. J. Harstad, *Pharmacy in History* 1986, 175–80. J. Sca.

Aetius, Flavius (d. AD 454), a Roman patrician and distinguished general, was born at Durostorum (near Silistra in Bulgaria), the son of Gaudentius, a high-ranking military officer. He won profound influence with *Valentinian III and became the effective ruler of the western empire, being consul three times (432, 437, 446), an unprecedented distinction for one who was not a member of the imperial house. Appointed *patricius* in 435 he fought successfully thereafter against barbarians and rebels in Gaul, his main achievement being the destruction of the kingdom of the *Burgundians centred on the city of Worms. In 446 the Britons appealed to him in vain for help against the barbarian invaders of their island. In 451 he joined forces with the Visigoths (see GOTHS) and defeated *Attila and the Huns in the battle of the Catalaunian Plains, but could do little to oppose Attila when the Huns invaded Italy in 452. He was assassinated at the instigation of Petronius Maximus, the later emperor.

PLRE 2. 21–9; *The Oxford Dictionary of Byzantium*, ed. P. Kazhdan and others, 1 (1991), 31. E. A. T.; A. J. S. S.

Aetna, Latin *didactic poem of unknown authorship. It attempts to explain the volcanic activity of Mt. Etna (see AETNA (1)).

The poem is ascribed to Virgil in our earliest MSS and included amongst his juvenilia by the *Vita Donati*, where, however, doubt is expressed about its authenticity. Few, if any, would now maintain this ascription, or any of the other attributions that have been suggested. The poem predates the eruption of *Vesuvius in AD 79, for it describes the volcanic activity of the Naples region as extinct. It is generally agreed to postdate Lucretius, and allusion to Virgil and M. *Manilius is likely. Because of resemblances to Seneca's *Natural Questions*, and because Seneca shows no knowledge of the poem, a late-Neronian or Vespasianic date is perhaps probable, but an earlier date cannot be ruled out.

Rejecting mythological explanations, the author argues that the controlling force behind eruptions is wind operating at high pressure in narrow subterranean channels, and that the volcanic fire, produced by friction, gets a nutritive material especially in the lava-stone (*lapis molaris*). The poem's immediate scientific sources cannot be established, but direct or indirect influence of *Theophrastus and, more especially, of *Posidonius (2) is probable.

The devotion of an entire work to Aetna seems to have been original. A programmatic introduction and a conclusion frame a tightly structured scientific argument, which is enlivened by frequent personification and vivid imagery—particularly drawn from warfare, law, and handicrafts. A gigantomachy (41–73; see GIANTS), praise of physical science (222–81), and the concluding story of two brothers who rescued their parents during an eruption (603–45), contrast with the scientific material. Yet *Aetna* makes hard reading, because the text is extremely corrupt, the subject-matter is unfamiliar, and the author sometimes strains

after brevity and allusiveness. But he writes with vigour, confidence, and enthusiasm, and deserves to be read.

TEXTS *PLM* 1, Vollmer/Morel (Teubner, 1930); F. R. D. Goodyear (in OCT *Appendix Vergiliana* 1966); with comm. and index verborum: F. R. D. Goodyear (1966).

GENERAL F. R. D. Goodyear, *ANRW* 2. 32. 1. 344–63. H. M. H.

Aetna (1), Europe's highest active volcano (3,326 m. (10,912 ft.) in 1966), lying between *Tauromenium and *Catana in eastern Sicily. The lower slopes are remarkably fertile, principally today in vines, olives, lemons, and oranges, and are thickly populated; woods and scrub cover the middle slopes; the upper are desolate. Eruptions were attributed to a giant (*Typhon or Enceladus) beneath the mountain. The Sicans traditionally transferred westwards because of them. Few ancient eruptions are recorded, those of 475, 396, and 122 BC. being the most notable; Etna has apparently been more active in modern times. The mountain is the subject of an anonymous poem, *Aetna*, probably late Augustan. Ancient tourists known to have climbed the mountain include the emperors *Gaius (1) and *Hadrian. Etna basalt was widely used, in Sicily and further afield, for corn *mills (Strabo 6. 2. 3; cf. *Aetna*, 400–1).

Sources: E. Manni, *Geografia fisica e politica della Sicilia antica* (1981) 79–82; D. K. Chester, A. M. Duncan, J. E. Guest, and C. R. J. Kilburn, *Mount Etna, the Anatomy of a Volcano* (1985). A. G. W.; R. J. A. W.

Aetna (2), the name given to *Catana when *Hieron (1) I settled a colony there. In 461 BC these colonists were expelled, and transferred themselves to Sicel Inessa. *Ducetius captured Inessa-Aetna in 451, but it subsequently became a Syracusan stronghold. *Dionysius (1) I garrisoned it with Campanians whom *Timoleon had difficulty in dislodging. It suffered at *Verres' hands, but continued to be a place of some importance in the early empire, when, as a town on the Catana–Centuripae road (*It. Ant.* 93. 6), it served as the starting-point for excursions to the summit of Mt. Etna (Strab. 6. 2. 3; see AETNA (1)). Its location has never been satisfactorily identified on the ground. Sites proposed include Poira, Città (both near Paternò), Paternò itself, and S. Maria di Licodia.

BTCGI 8 (1990), 286–303; Dunbabin, *Western Greeks*, 131–2; G. Rizza, *PP* 1959, 465–74; D. Adamesteanu, *Kokalos* 1962, 169–74; K. Miller, *Itineraria Romana* (1916), 404; R. J. A. Wilson, *Sicily under the Roman Empire* (1990), 410 n. 79. A. G. W.; R. J. A. W.

Aetolia, a region in west-central Greece roughly shaped like a triangle with its base on the Corinthian Gulf, its apex at Mt. Tymphrestus, and its sides along the lower and middle *Acheloüs river-valley on the west, and a series of mountains from Mt. Oxya to Mt. Gkiona on the east. The topography of the region is rugged, a factor that played a significant role in Aetolia's history, serving as a natural deterrent to invading armies, and contributing to the widespread practice of *brigandage. Along the region's southern coast there are few harbours, although the area was settled from early times. Towns like *Pleuron, Olenus, Pylene, Calydon, and Chalcis are all known to Homer (*Il.* 2. 638–44).

Politically and economically Aetolia remained backward into the 5th cent. BC. *Thucydides (2) mentions settlements at Potidania, Crocylium, Tichium, Aegitium, and Proschium, but he describes them as small unfortified villages. During this period, Aetolia was organized as an *ethnos* (see ETHNICITY), consisting of at least three major territorial groups: the Ophioneis, the Apodoti, and the Eurytanes. These were further divided into smaller tribal units, some of which are known: the Callieis, Bomieis, and Thestiae. The religious centre of the *ethnos* was located at *Thermum, where, from the Archaic period (and perhaps earlier), a cult of Apollo flourished until the site's sack by *Philip (3) V in 218 BC. Territorially, Aetolia fell into two divisions: 'old' and 'acquired' (Strab. 10. 2. 3), distinctions which must have had something to do with the extension of Aetolian power.

The earliest record of a united *ethnos* dates to 426 BC, when the Aetolians temporarily joined together to repel the Athenian invasion of *Demosthenes (1) (Thuc. 3. 94–8). After 370, the formation of the *Aetolian Confederacy unified the region, and its territory was soon augmented in 338 by a gift from *Philip (1) II, the excellent harbour of *Naupactus, long coveted by the Aetolians. The primary period of Aetolian expansion occurred in the 3rd cent. with the annexation of Delphi and western Phocis. The league appropriated the territories of its neighbours (Amphilochia, southern Acarnania, and Malis) and extended its influence into Thessaly and the western Peloponnese. The Hellenistic period also witnessed the building of fortified cities in Aetolia, including those at Calydon, Pleuron, Lysimacheia, and Arsinoeia. After its defeat by Rome in 189 BC, Aetolia was reduced to its original dimensions and experienced a slow loss of population over the following 150 years. Finally, after 31 BC, a significant portion of the remaining population was sent to *Nicopolis (3) and *Patrae while others preferred to migrate to *Amphissa.

W. J. Woodhouse, *Aetolia* (1897); P-K *GL* 2. 299–367; S. Bommelje and P. Doorn, *Aetolia and the Aetolians* (1987); C. Antonetti, *Les Étoliens: Image et religion* (1990). W. M. M.

Aetolian Confederacy The looser tribal organization of the Aetolians of NW Greece gave way during the 4th cent. BC to a *federal state, or league, which soon acquired considerable power. This increased dramatically in the first part of the 3rd cent. BC, owing to the Aetolians' role in the victory over the invading Gauls (280/79) and their control of the Delphic *amphictiony which soon followed (from 277). Normally hostile to Macedon, they became allies of Rome against *Philip (3) V of Macedon in 212 or 211 BC, Rome's first allies in mainland Greece. After a period of estrangement they allied themselves with Rome against Philip once again (199 BC), but such was their feeling of ill-treatment at the hands of the Romans in the aftermath of Philip's defeat at *Cynoscephalae (197 BC) that they went on to make common cause with the Seleucid king *Antiochus (3) III. This proved their downfall, and in 189 the Aetolians were compelled to accept a treaty as subject allies of Rome. The confederacy was not dissolved, but external influence was gone and problems of debt and civil conflict soon ensued.

At the head of the confederacy was a general elected annually. The primary assembly had two regular meetings a year and could be summoned for special sessions. In this body votes seem to have been counted by heads and not, as in some federal states, by cities. The council (*boulē* or *synhedrion*), in which the cities were represented in proportion to population, contained some thousand members. Hence, particularly in time of war, much of the leadership fell to the *apoklētoi* (of whom there were more than 30), probably a committee of the council. The cities contributed to the federal treasury in proportion to their number of representatives in the council. At no time did the leadership of the confederacy pass out of the hands of the Aetolians proper. This was in no small part because more distant cities were not made regular members, but were instead bound to the confederacy by *isopoliteia*, which involved civic rights, protection, and potential citizenship but no active participation in federal affairs.

Grants of *asylia* (freedom from plundering) by the Aetolians were not infrequent and were highly prized on account of their practice of right of reprisal and *piracy.

G. Klaffenbach, introd. to *IG* 9². 1, with references to the widely-scattered sources; R. Flacelière, *Les Aitoliens à Delphes* (1937); J. A. O. Larsen, *Greek Federal States* (1968), 78 ff.; G. Nachtergael, *Les Galates en Grèce et les Sôtéria de Delphes* (1977); J. Scholten, *The Politics of Plunder* (2000). P. S. D.

Aetolian cults and myths Relatively isolated, after the Archaic period Aetolia had the reputation of a rough and violent region. In cult the massive conflagration of live birds and wild animals for Artemis Laphria at *Patrae (originally at Calydon, Paus. 7. 18. 8–13) has seemed to characterize Aetolian barbarism. But archaeological evidence permits a more temperate assessment. Aetolian religion had, none the less, some distinctive, conservative features. *Artemis is a great goddess, with exceptionally comprehensive concerns, including human and natural fertility, while her male partner, usually *Apollo, is a lesser figure. This has been taken to be a continuation of a bronze age pattern. There are important early temples in pairs, a larger one usually for the goddess and a smaller one for her companion, at Calydon, Taxiarchis (the modern site name), *Callipolis, and *Thermum, where alone Apollo is more prominent. At Calydon *Dionysus is associated with this pair, and he is important in local myth. *Zeus is relatively insignificant, *Poseidon unknown. Other figures are mostly female and can be seen as forms of the region's great goddess.

In myth, *Aetolus, the eponymous ancestor of the people, and the family of *Oeneus, Althaea, *Meleager (1) (who killed the Calydonian boar), and *Deianira, are prominent. Stories of *Heracles have him taming savage nature.

C. Antonetti, *Les Étoliens: Image et religion* (1990). M. H. J.

Aetolus, eponym of the Aetolians. *Endymion, king of *Elis, had three sons: Paeon, Epeius, and Aetolus. He set them to race at Olympia, promising the kingship to the winner. Epeius won, hence the ancient name Epeii for the people of the district. Paeon left the country and gave his name to the district of Paeonia. When Aetolus was forced to leave Elis because of a blood-feud, he went to the country of the *Curetes and gained control of the region which thereafter took his name (Paus. 5. 1. 3–8). W. M. M.

Aezani (mod. Çavdarhisar) was the most important city of northern *Phrygia in Roman times. The well-preserved ruins of the site are dominated by the peripteral (colonnaded) Ionic temple of *Zeus, built in the second quarter of the 2nd cent. AD. According to local legend Zeus was born in the Steunos cave which overlooked the river Pencalas near the city (the site has been identified and excavated). There were extensive sacred lands around the city, which were used to settle military colonists from the Attalid and Bithynian kingdoms. A long dispute over the revenues from this land was settled by Roman proconsul of Asia in the 120s, and this appears to have unleashed a period of great prosperity in the 2nd cent. AD. During this time Aezani was transformed from a modest agricultural town (there are traces of late Hellenistic buildings and it may have been the minting centre for the people of Phrygia Epictetus) into an imperial architectural show-piece, with a theatre, a stadium, a large bath-house, several bridges across the river Pencalas which flowed through the city, and cemeteries full of elaborately decorated tombs. Aezani was an enthusiastic member of the *Panhellenion at

Athens, where its best-known citizen and civic benefactor, M. Ulpius Appuleius Eurycles, served as Panhellene (AD 153–7). During this time it was also made one of the assize centres of the Asian province. The monuments and inscriptions suggest that its importance was much reduced in the late empire.

MAMA 9, introd.; F. Naumann, MDAI(I) 1985, 217–26; R. Naumann, Der Zeustempel zu Aizanoi (1979); Arch. Rep. 1984–5, 97–8; 1989/90, 127; M. Wörrle, Chiron 1992, 336 ff.   S. M.

Afghanistan See AI KHANOUM; ALEXANDRIA (3); BACTRIA.

Afranius (1) (RE 5), **Lucius,** author of fabulae togatae in the second half of the 2nd cent. BC, the most famous and best represented author of this genre, with over 40 titles and 400 lines surviving; perhaps also an orator, but the implications of Cicero, Brut. 167 are disputed. He praised *Terence and admitted borrowing material from *Menander (1) (but also from other authors, both Greek and Latin), and his plays included pederastic themes; see TOGATA.

CHCL 2. 820 f.; and see TOGATA.   P. G. M. B.

Afranius (2) (RE 6), **Lucius,** a *novus homo born in *Picenum (ILS 878), served under *Pompey against *Sertorius. He was praetor (probably 72 or 71 BC) and proconsul in either Cisalpine or Transalpine Gaul, winning a triumph (Cic. Pis. 58), and again served as a legate of Pompey against *Mithradates VI (66–61). As consul 60 he was overshadowed by his colleague Q. *Caecilius Metellus Celer, and was therefore ineffective on Pompey's behalf. His consular province was one of the Gauls, probably Cisalpina (see CISALPINE GAUL), but there is no evidence that he ever proceeded to it. From c.53 he governed Hither *Spain as Pompey's legate with three legions, and in 49 commanded at *Ilerda. Pardoned by *Caesar, he returned to Pompey, though charged with treachery by other Pompeians. He escaped from *Pharsalus, but was captured and executed after Thapsus.   G. E. F. C.; E. B.

Afranius (RE 8) **Burrus, Sextus** equestrian *procurator of *Livia Drusilla, *Tiberius, and *Claudius, came from Gallia Narbonensis (ILS 1321, showing him patron of Vaison). As favourite of *Iulia Agrippina, he was appointed sole prefect of the praetorian guard (see PRAEFECTUS PRAETORIO) by Claudius in AD 51 and retained his post under *Nero. He was Nero's adviser for many years, and, with the younger *Seneca, was responsible for the first period of Nero's government. In 55 he survived an unfounded charge of conspiracy; in 59 he managed Nero's relations with the public after the murder of his mother. He opposed Nero's divorce from *Octavia (3), which only took place after his death in 62. That he was poisoned is asserted by Suetonius and Cassius Dio, but regarded by Tacitus (Ann. 14. 51) as unproven.
                                                           A. M.; M. T. G.

Africa (*Libya), exploration Africa was distinguished from Asia as the third continent by c.500 BC, with the Nile, later usually the Red Sea, as divider; but its interior and, even at the most extended period of knowledge, its coasts south of Cape Delgado on the east and Cape Yubi on the west, remained substantially unknown, locations of marvels and geographical features uncertainly identifiable (Ptol. Geog. 4). Some believed it circumnavigable (Hdt. 4. 42) and triangular in shape (Strabo 17. 3. 1), but no circumnavigation is satisfactorily attested (see HANNO (1); EUDOXUS (3)), and there are modern scholars who think it impracticable for ancient ships; pure theorizing could account for the traditions. An inconsistent belief in a land bridge from Africa to Asia in fact prevailed (Ptol. 7. 3. 6).

In Egypt, and to some extent in Cyrenaica, Greeks could supplement autopsy with local information, cf. Herodotus on the Nile valley (2. 29–31), the inland route therefrom, via oases, possibly to the Atlas (4. 181–3), and a Libyan foray perhaps reaching the Niger, more probably Chad (not the Nile as he supposed; 2. 32–3). Extended knowledge of the *Red Sea and NE coasts came from *Alexander (3) the Great's Indian expedition, more under Ptolemaic rule in Egypt and still more in Roman times as a result of increasing trade with India (see especially, Peripl. M. Rubr.; Ptol. Geog. 4). Penetration up the Nile valley was furthered under Augustus by the campaign of C. Petronius against the Ethiopians (Strabo 17. 1. 54) and an investigative mission which probably reached southern *Nubia in Nero's reign (Sen. QNat. 5. 8. 3–5); but it was checked by swamps; *Ptolemy (4), however, recorded lakes sighted by a sailor driven off course near Zanzibar, which he took to be the source of the Nile (Geog. 1. 9; presumably Victoria and Albert Nyanza) and had also heard of the Mountain of the Moon whose snows fed them (Geog. 4. 8. 2; perhaps Mt. Kilimanjaro).

In the north-west, local knowledge, both of the coastal hinterland and of the west coast, may have been less readily available before the fall of Carthage. What became known then (see HANNO (1)) was soon supplemented by Roman exploration, often undertaken for military purposes. Already in 146 BC Scipio Aemilianus had despatched *Polybius (1) with a fleet down the west coast (Plin. HN 5. 9, 10). Later landmarks were the Jugurthine War (but Sallust's account is disappointing); campaigns by L. *Cornelius Balbus (2) under Augustus and Valerius Festus under Vespasian against the Garamantes in the Fezzan (Pliny, HN 5. 36–8), and by Suetonius Paulinus under Claudius in the Atlas mountains (ibid. 5. 14–5); investigative missions, probably under Domitian, attributed to Iulius Maternus and Septimius Flaccus (perhaps identical events), from Tripolitania via the Garamantes, possibly to Chad (Ptol. Geog. 1. 8. 4).

Archaeological evidence, constantly accruing, is not always easy to interpret since artefacts might penetrate further than travellers in the packs of native traders and raiders; but a scatter of recently reported inscriptions may suggest Mediterranean contacts further south than expected, e.g. in the Fezzan, the Hoggar mountains of Algeria, the Canaries while the announcement of Roman pottery found on Zanzibar accords with the literary record. See GEOGRAPHY; MAPS.

STUDIES AND TEXTS E. H. Bunbury, A History of Ancient Geography (1883; repr. 1959); Cary–Warmington, Explorers; R. K. Sherk, ANRW 2. 1 (1974), 537–43; P. Pédech, La Géographie des Grecs (1976); J. Desanges, L'Activité des Méditerranéens aux confins de l'Afrique (1978), and in H. Durchardt, J. A. Schlumberger, and P. Segl (eds.), Afrika, Entdeckung und Erforschung eines Kontinents (1989); L. Casson, The Periplus Maris Erythraei: Text with Introduction, Translation and Commentary (1989); S. M. Burstein, Agatharchides of Cnidos: On the Erythraean Sea (1989).
ARCHAEOLOGY General: R. E. M. Wheeler, Rome Beyond the Imperial Frontiers (1954). East Coast: M. C. Smith, H. T. Wright Azania 1988, 115–41; J. Desanges, E. M. Stern, P. Ballet, Sur les routes antiques de l'Azanie et de l'Inde, Mémoires des inscriptions et belles-lettres (1993); M. Reddé, JRA 1994, 454–6. West Coast: R. Rebuffat Antiquités Africaines 1974, 25–49; J. Onrubia Pintado, Encyclopédie Berbère 11 (1992), 1731–55 'Canaries (Îles)'. Interior: M. Reddé and J.-C. Golvin, Karthago (1986–7), 59–63; W. Y. Adams, Journal of the American Research Centre in Egypt 1983, 93–104 (for biennial reports on discoveries at Primis (Qasr Ibrim) see Reports to the Members of the Egypt Exploration Society, most recently 1991–2, 12–13); C. M. Daniels Libyan Studies 1989, 45–61; R. Rebuffat, CRAcad. Inscr. 1982, 188–99; notes on a Latin inscription in Sahara (Milan) 1990, 112, 1991, 154 with plate before p. 33, and V. Beltrami, Africa Romana 1994.   J. M. R.

Africa, Roman

Africa, Roman The *Punic Wars made Rome heir to the Carthaginian empire. In 146 BC she left most territory in the hands of *Masinissa's descendants, but formed a new province (Africa) in the most fertile part. This covered about 13,000 sq. km. (5,000 sq. mi.) of north and central Tunisia, north-east of a boundary line (the *fossa regia*, 'the royal ditch') from Thabraca to *Hadrumetum; it was governed by a praetor from Utica. Except for *Utica and six other towns of Phoenician origin which had supported Rome rather than Carthage in the Punic Wars, most of the land became *ager publicus*. Although the attempt by Gaius C. *Sempronius Gracchus to found a *colonia* at Carthage failed, Roman and Italian traders and farmers settled in the province in large numbers, and many of C. *Marius (1)'s veterans settled west of the *fossa regia*. After the battle of Thapsus in 46 BC *Caesar added to the existing province (thenceforth called Africa Vetus, 'Old Africa') the Numidian territory of Juba I (Africa Nova, 'New Africa'). Caesar's colonial foundations in Africa included Clupea, Curubis, and Neapolis, and his intention to colonize Carthage afresh was carried out by Octavian. A substantial territory in Numidia based on *Cirta was given to Caesar's supporter P. *Sittius.

Under Augustus, after various boundary changes, the united province, now called Africa Proconsularis, extended from Arae Philaenorum, on the western edge of Cyrenaica, to the river Ampsagas (Rhummel) in eastern Algeria. At least eleven colonies were founded in Proconsularis, in addition to the thirteen colonies settled on the coast of Mauretania (the rest of which was ruled by the client king *Juba (2) II). Africa Proconsularis was governed from Carthage by a proconsul, who (unusually for the governor of a province not controlled by the emperor) also commanded the Legio III Augusta, then stationed at *Ammaedara. Under Gaius (1) command of the legion was handed over to an imperial *legatus* who became responsible for the government of Numidia and the frontier districts. The provincialization of North Africa was completed by Claudius with the creation of two provinces in *Mauretania. Resistance to Roman rule on the fringes of the Sahara and in the mountainous regions such as the Kabylie and Aurès was no more than sporadic, and for over three centuries the whole area from Cyrenaica to the Atlantic was protected by only a single legion and auxiliaries. The southern frontier ran approximately from Arae Philaenorum through Cydamus (Gadhamès), Nefta, Vescera (Biskra) and Auzia (Aumale) to the Atlantic south of Volubilis.

Urban life in North Africa was of pre-Roman origin, both Punic and (under Punic influence) Numidian. In spite of the destruction of Carthage, a number of towns of Phoenician or Carthaginian origin survived on the coast, such as *Hadrumetum and *Lepcis Magna; further west, Icosium (Algiers), Iol (*Caesarea (3)), *Tingis, and Lixus appear to have been pre-Roman settlements of some size. In a few places Carthaginian language and institutions survived into the 2nd cent. AD, as inscriptions demonstrate; spoken Punic lasted much longer and was still being used, at least in rural areas, in *Augustine's day (*Ep.* 66. 108. 14, 209. 3). Over large areas of the interior the influence of Carthaginian civilization on the indigenous tribes was profound, especially in central Tunisia and in the region of Cirta where Numidian kings had encouraged it. Under Roman control, however, urbanization occurred on a vastly increased scale, and refounded Carthage became the largest city in the western empire after Rome (see URBANISM (Roman)). Over 600 communities ranked as separate *civitates*, of which a large number in due course obtained the rank of *municipium* or *colonia*.

The area of densest urbanization was around Carthage and the Bagradas valley, where some of the towns were only a dozen miles apart. Some, like Ammaedara and Theveste, were established on the sites of early legionary fortresses; *Lambaesis grew out of the settlement outside the final fortress chosen for Legio III Augusta; others, like Timgad and Diana Veteranorum, were settled as colonies for retired legionaries. Roman *equites* of African origin are known from the mid-1st cent. AD, soon followed by senators. During the 2nd cent. African senators (the best known being the orator *Cornelius Fronto) formed the largest western provincial group. The influence of Africans reached its height under *Septimius Severus, who was born at Lepcis Magna.

The wealth of Africa was proverbial throughout the Roman period, and consisted largely of agricultural products. Of these corn was certainly the most important and with Egypt Africa replaced Sicily as Italy's major supplier during the empire (see FOOD SUPPLY (Roman)). The Bagradas valley and the region around Cirta and Sitifis were productive corn-growing districts, but polyculture throughout North Africa was common. Especially from the 2nd cent. *olive-growing and the production of oil for export became an increasingly important part of the African economy, especially in the drier regions of Proconsularis, around Cillium and Sufetula in central Tunisia, and near *Thysdrus and Sullecthum in eastern Tunisia, as well as further west in Numidia and Mauretania. *Wine was also exported from Tripolitania, Proconsularis, and Mauretania, although on a much smaller scale (see AMPHORAE, ROMAN). The maintenance of irrigation systems, some clearly of pre-Roman origin, and the efficient collection and conservation of what little rain-water there was, were essential to successful cultivation. Africa was famed as a place where large estates in the hands of a few men were commonplace, the largest landowner being the emperor, but there were plenty of medium-sized estates as well, the majority of them owned not by Italians but by prosperous members of the Romano-African urban élite, whose wealth was so conspicuously displayed in the showy public monuments they paid for in their home towns. Our knowledge of the administration of imperial estates, and the relationship between tenants (*coloni*) and lessees (*conductores*), is best known from a series of 2nd and early 3rd century inscriptions from the Bagradas valley. Other exports from Africa included fish-pickle (*garum*), especially from Proconsularis (see FISHING); *marble, especially the prized yellow *marmor Numidicum* from Simitthus; wood, especially the citrus-wood for furniture making from Mauretania (see TIMBER); dyes, for which the island of Mogador off western Morocco was famous (see DYEING); an orange-red pottery ('African red slip-ware'), which despite its simplicity gained a Mediterranean-wide export market at the zenith of its production in the 4th and 5th cents. (see POTTERY, ROMAN); and wild animals destined for *amphitheatres in Italy and elsewhere, including lions, leopards, and *elephants, the capture of which is featured on a number of African mosaics (e. g. from Hippo Regius and Carthage). The arts flourished, with several vigorous local schools of sculptors working in both limestone and marble, while *mosaic *officinae*, in response to the demand for elaborate polychrome figured mosaics in both private houses and public buildings such as baths, adopted from the second quarter of the 2nd cent. onwards an original and creative approach to mosaic design which by the 4th cent. had left its influence on mosaic floors in Italy and several other provinces as well.

During the 3rd century the African provinces continued to prosper, and suffered less from imperial usurpations than most provinces of the Roman west; the failure of *Gordian I had, however, serious repercussions. Christianity established itself more firmly than in any other western province, first in the cities, but making rapid strides in Numidia after c.200. The works of *Tertullian and *Cyprian were of considerable importance in the development of Latin Christianity.

In *Diocletian's administrative changes, the provinces of Tripolitania, Byzacena, Numidia, Mauretania Sitifensis, and Mauretania Caesariensis formed the diocese of Africa, Africa Proconsularis being strictly outside the diocesan system, and Mauretania Tingitana forming part of the diocese of Spain. The military forces of the area were put under a comes Africae, and the frontier was divided into districts each under a praepositus limitis, a system unique in the empire (see LIMES).

Throughout the 4th and early 5th cent., North Africa was affected by serious divisions among Christians; the *Donatists, condemned as schismatics by imperial legislation from Constantine onwards, were particularly strong in rural areas of Numidia and Mauretania, where social discontent was growing and where central government's authority was increasingly in decline. Nevertheless the area remained prosperous in comparison with the devastated provinces of northern Europe, and the collapse of Africa to the *Vandals (Carthage was captured in 439) was a grievous blow, not least for the corn supply. The invaders found Africa easy prey, since the defensive system was designed for policing work and the suppression of sporadic tribal revolts rather than full-scale invasion.

ATLASES Atlas archéologique de la Tunisie, 1st ser., E. Babelon and others (1892–1913), 2nd ser., R. Cagnat and A. Merlin (1914–32); A. Piganiol, Atlas des centuriations romaines de Tunisie, 3rd edn. (1959); S. Gsell, Atlas archéologique de l'Algérie (1911).

INSCRIPTIONS CIL 8 and Suppls.; R. Cagnat, A. Merlin, and L. Chatelain, Inscriptions latines de l'Afrique (1923); A. Merlin, Inscriptions latines de la Tunisie (1944); S. Gsell, Inscriptions latines de l'Algérie 1 (1923); H. G. Pflaum, Inscriptions latines de l'Algérie 2 pts. 1 and 2 (1957–76); M. Euzennat, J. Marion, and J. Gascou, Inscriptions antiques du Maroc 2: Inscriptions latines (1982); Z. B. ben Abdallah, Catalogue des inscriptions païennes du Musée du Bardo (1986); Z. B. ben Abdallah and L. Ladjimi Sebai, Index onomastique des inscriptions latines de la Tunisie (1983).

PRINCIPAL STUDIES S. Gsell, Histoire ancienne de l'Afrique du Nord, 8 vols. (1914–29); T. R. S. Broughton, The Romanisation of Africa Proconsularis (1929); R. M. Haywood, in Frank, Econ. Survey 4 (1938), 1–119; B. H. Warmington, The North African Provinces from Diocletian to the Vandal Conquest (1954); C. Courtois, Les Vandales et l'Afrique (1955); P. Romanelli, Storia delle province romane dell'Africa (1959); B. E. Thomasson, Die Statthalter der römischen Provinzen Nordafrikas, 2 vols. (1960); L. Teutsch, Das römische Städtwesen in Nordafrika (1962); L. Thompson and J. Ferguson (eds.), Africa in Classical Antiquity (1969); I. M. Barton, Africa in the Roman Empire (1972); M. Benabou, La résistance africaine à la Romanisation (1976); J. M. Lassère, Ubique Populus (1977); D. Fushöller, Tunesien und Ostalgerien in der Römerzeit (1979); C. Lepelley, Les Cités de l'Afrique romaine au Bas-Empire (1979); P. MacKendrick, The North African Stones Speak (1980); W. H. C. Frend, The Donatist Church, 3rd edn. (1986); D. P. Kehoe, The Economics of Agriculture on Roman Imperial Estates in North Africa (1988); P. A. Février, Approches du Maghreb romain, 2 vols. (1989–90); G. C. Picard, La Civilisation de l'Afrique romaine, 2nd edn. (1990); J. Kolendo, Le Colonat en Afrique sous le Haut-Empire, 2nd edn. (1991); S. Raven, Rome in Africa, 3rd edn. (1993).

BIBLIOGRAPHIES Bibliographie analytique de l'Afrique antique (Paris), an annual review of published work. D. J. Mattingly and R. B. Hitchner, JRS 1995, 165 ff.

CONFERENCE PROCEEDINGS Africa Romana 1– (Sassari, 1984–) (annually); Histoire et archéologie de l'Afrique du Nord (biennially, at different locations in France since 1981; first published in Bulletin archéologique du Comité des Traveaux, but since the Third

Congress (1985) as separate volumes); C. M. Wells (ed.), L'Afrique romaine: Les Conférences Vanier 1980 (1982); L'Afrique dans l'occident romain 1er siècle av. J.-C.–IVe siècle ap. J.-C. (1990).

EXHIBITION CATALOGUES De Carthage à Kairouan (1982); A. ben Abed ben Khader and D. Soren (eds.), Carthage: A mosaic of ancient Tunisia (1987); M. Seefried Brouillet (ed.), From Hannibal to Saint Augustine: Ancient Art of North Africa from the Musée du Louvre (1994); Carthage: l'histoire, sa trace et son écho (1995).

CULTS G. C. Picard, Les Religions de l'Afrique antique (1954); M. LeGlay, Saturne africain, 2 vols. (1966); M. Bassignano, Il flaminato nelle province romane dell'Africa (1974); V. Brouquier-Reddé, Temples et cultes de Tripolitaine (1992).

ART AND ARCHITECTURE S. Gsell, Les Monuments antiques de l'Algérie (1901); M. Wheeler and R. Wood, Roman Africa in Colour (1966); A. Lézine, Architecture romaine d'Afrique (1981); P. Février, L'Art de l'Algérie antique (1971); K. M. D. Dunbabin, Mosaics of Roman North Africa (1978); K. Schmelzeisen, Römische Mosaiken der Africa Proconsularis (1992). Pottery: J. W. Hayes, Late Roman Pottery (1972), and Supplement to Late Roman Pottery (1980); A. Carandini, in P. Garnsey and others (eds.), Trade in the Ancient Economy (1983), 145–62.

THE ARMY IN AFRICA R. Cagnat, L'Armée romaine d'Afrique, 2nd edn. (1912); J. Baradez, Fossatum Africae (1949); N. Benseddik, Les Troupes auxiliaires de l'armée romaine en Maurétanie Césarienne sous le Haut Empire (1982); Y. Le Bohec, Les Unites auxiliaires de l'armée romaine en Afrique proconsulaire et Numidie sous le Haut Empire (1989), and La Troisième Légion Auguste (1989). W. N. W.; B. H. W.; R. J. A. W.

Africanus See CAECILIUS AFRICANUS, SEX. (jurist); CORNELIUS SCIPIO AFRICANUS, P.; IULIUS AFRICANUS; IULIUS AFRICANUS, SEX.

after-life See ART (FUNERARY); DEATH, ATTITUDES TO; ELYSIUM; HADES; ISLANDS OF THE BLEST; ORPHISM; TARTARUS; TRANSMIGRATION.

Agamemnon, in mythology son of *Atreus (or, occasionally, of Atreus' son Pleisthenes), brother of *Menelaus (1), and husband of *Clytemnestra; king of *Mycenae, or *Argos (2), and, in Homer, commander-in-chief of the Greek expedition against Troy, taking with him 100 ships, the largest single contingent (Il. 2. 569–80). He had a son, *Orestes, and three daughters, Chrysothemis, Laodice, Iphianassa (Il. 9.145); *Iphigenia, whom Homer does not mention, seems to be a later substitution for Iphianassa, as does *Electra (3) for Laodice (Xanthus, fr. 700 PMG).

Homer depicts Agamemnon as a man of personal valour, but lacking resolution and easily discouraged. His quarrel with *Achilles, who withdrew in anger and hurt pride from battle when Agamemnon took away his concubine *Briseis, supplies the mainspring of the Iliad's action, with Achilles' refusal to fight leading to tragedy. The Odyssey (1. 35 ff., 4. 512 ff., 11. 405 ff., 24. 96 f.) tells how, on Agamemnon's return home, *Aegisthus, Clytemnestra's lover, treacherously set on him and his men at a banquet and killed them all, Clytemnestra also killing his Trojan captive *Cassandra, daughter of *Priam. Eight years later Orestes came from Athens and avenged his father's murder (1. 304 ff.). This whole story became a favourite one among later authors, who retold it with various elaborations and changes. Aeschylus, for instance, makes Clytemnestra a powerful and awe-inspiring female who, quite alone, kills Agamemnon after she has pinioned him in a robe while he is unarmed in his bath (Ag. 1379–98).

The Cypria (see EPIC CYCLE) is the earliest evidence of the sacrifice of Agamemnon's daughter Iphigenia. Agamemnon caught a stag, then boasted that he was a better huntsman than *Artemis, whereupon the offended goddess held the Greek fleet wind-bound at Aulis. *Calchas told them to appease her by sacrificing Iphigenia, whom they sent for on the pretext of marriage to Achilles. Here the guilt for the killing seems to be laid on the

Aganippe

Greeks in general; moreover Iphigenia was snatched away and made immortal by Artemis, who left a deer on the altar in her place (as in Euripides' *Iphigenia in Tauris*). But again matters are very different in Aeschylus, where Iphigenia is simply a child, dead, and Agamemnon himself her killer, for which Clytemnestra never forgave him.

In historic times Agamemnon had a cult at *Laconia, *Tarentum, *Clazomenae, and *Chaeronea: see Farnell, *Hero-Cults* 321 and n. 55; also Mycenae. Agamemnon appears occasionally in art from the 7th cent. BC in a variety of scenes, mostly relating to the war at Troy: see O. Touchefeu and I. Krauskopf, *LIMC* 1 / 1. 256–77; also A. J. N. W. Prag, *The Oresteia: Iconographic and Narrative Tradition* (1985). Agamemnon in Homer: O. Taplin in C. Pelling (ed.), *Characterization and Individuality in Greek Literature* (1990). H. J. R.; J. R. M.

Aganippe, in mythology, daughter of the river-god Permessus (Paus. 9. 29. 5: spelling 'Ter-'), nymph of the spring of that name on *Helicon (Callim. fr. 696 Pf.), sacred to the *Muses.

Agapenor (Ἀγαπήνωρ), in mythology, leader of the Arcadian contingent against Troy (*Il.* 2. 609); son of *Ancaeus. On the way back from Troy he arrived at Cyprus (Lycoph. 479 ff.), where he founded *Paphos and a temple of *Aphrodite and settled (Paus. 8. 5. 2).

Agasias (1), Ephesian sculptor, son of Dositheus, active *c*.100 BC. He signed the Borghese Warrior from Anzio, now in the Louvre, a nude figure striding forward to parry an attack from above. Its 'flayed' anatomy and attenuated proportions look back to the school of *Lysippus (2).

> J. Marcadé, *Recueil de Signatures* (1957), 2. 2 f.; A. F. Stewart, *Greek Sculpture* (1990), 224 f., figs. 710 f. T. B. L. W.; A. F. S.

Agasias (2), Ephesian sculptor, son of Menophilus, active on *Delos *c*.100 BC. A fallen Celt is often associated with one signed base, dedicated by C. Marius; attributions include the bronze 'Worried Man.'

> J. Marcadé, *Recueil de Signatures* (1957), 2. 4 ff.; A. F. Stewart, *Greek Sculpture* (1990), 227 f., figs. 838, 842. A. F. S.

Agatharchides, of Cnidus (*c*.215 to after 145 BC). Greek historian, geographer, and *Peripatetic who lived most of his adult life in *Alexandria (1), eventually leaving, perhaps in flight to Athens after 145. He was not, as previously believed, regent to *Ptolemy (1) IX but was in the service of *Heraclides (3) Lembus. His major works, for which there are fragmentary remains, include: *Asian Affairs* (Τὰ κατὰ τὴν Ἀσίαν), probably a universal history that extended to the *Diadochi; *European Affairs* (Τὰ κατὰ τὴν Εὐρώπην), perhaps to his own time; and *On the Red Sea* (Περὶ τῆς Ἐρυθρᾶς θαλάσσης) in five books (some preserved by Diodorus, bk. 3, and Photius). These large-scale histories, interlaced with *anthropology and *geography, provided a model for *Posidonius (2). He attacked the Asianic prose style, and *Photius calls him a worthy disciple of *Thucydides (2) in expression. He may have voiced hostility toward the Ptolemies, from whom he may have fled.

> *FGrH* 86; *GGM* 1. liv–lxxiii, 111–95; P. M. Fraser *Ptol. Alex.* 1. 515 f., 539–50; S. M. Burstein, *Agatharchides of Cnidus: On the Erythraean Sea*, trans. and comm. (1989). K. S. S.

Agatharchus, painter, of Samos. He was the first to make a *skēnē*, for Aeschylus (probably for a revival at the time of the *Peloponnesian War), and wrote a book on '*skēnē*-painting', which inspired *Anaxagoras and *Democritus to write on per-spective (Vitr. *De arch.* 7 pref. 11). He was the first painter to use perspective on a large scale (isolated instances occur on vases from the mid 6th cent. BC), probably in architectural backgrounds for plays. His quick work is contrasted with *Zeuxis (1)'s slowness (Plut. *Per.* 13. 3). Plutarch (*Alc.* 16. 4), Demosthenes (21. 147), and Andocides (4. 17) say he was compelled by *Alcibiades (*c*.430 BC?) to paint his house (with perspective scenes?). The story is of interest not least for suggesting that private houses were usually not painted. See PAINTING, GREEK. K. W. A.

Agathias, also referred to as **Agathias Scholasticus** ('lawyer'), historian and poet in *Constantinople, *c*.AD 532–*c*.580. A native of Myrina in Aeolis, where his father was a rhetor, he was educated at *Alexandria (1) and Constantinople, where he later practised law, a profession about whose conditions he complains in his *Histories*. His poetic activity began early, with a lost *Daphniaca*, amatory hexameters, and he is the author of numerous *epigrams in classical style on personal and traditional subjects, including love poems; *Nonnus was a major influence in style, vocabulary, and versification. Many of these, as well as poems by his contemporaries, including Paul the Silentiary (see PAULUS) and other officials, were included by him in a collection known as the *Cycle*, compiled, or at any rate completed, in the early years of Justin II (AD 565–78), and modelled on the earlier *Garland* of *Meleager (2) (see ANTHOLOGY). The epigrams of the *Cycle* reflect the technical literary accomplishments of members of the office-holding élite in Constantinople in the latter part of the reign of Justinian (AD 527–65), as well as their classicizing tastes. Agathias' *Histories*, a continuation in five books of *Procopius' *History of the Wars*, covers only the years AD 553–9, and is likewise highly literary and rhetorical, an aim which Agathias defends himself (*Hist.* 3. 1), including also digressions and speculative passages about the meaning of the events narrated. The work is important also for its long excursuses on the *Franks and the *Sasanids, each of which draws on good information, however much imbalance they introduce to the work as a whole. Though apparently a Christian and a moralist, Agathias' work is literary and secular. Unlike Procopius, he was not a participant in the events he describes, nor did he have military experience. Nevertheless, his work made sufficient impact for it to be continued by Menander Protector, and to take its place in the line of early Byzantine secular historians.

> TEXT *Histories*, ed. R. Keydell (1967); Eng. trans. J. D. Frendo (1975).
> LITERATURE A. Cameron, *Agathias* (1970); M. Whitby, in A. Cameron and L. I. Conrad (eds), *The Byzantine and Early Islamic Near East* 1: *Problems in the Literary Source Material* (1992), 25–80; A. and A. Cameron, *JHS* 1966, 6–25; A. Mattsson, *Untersuchungen zur Epigrammsammlung des Agathias* (1942); A. Cameron, *The Greek Anthology from Meleager to Planudes* (1993), esp. 69–75. A. M. C.

Agathinus (*RE* 8; Suppls. 1, 3) **(Claudius Agathinus),** a Spartan doctor of the 1st cent. AD, associated with the medical sect of the *Pneumatists. He was a pupil of *Athenaeus (3) of Attaleia, and was linked with the Stoic philosopher L. *Annaeus Cornutus. He may have taught the physicians *Archigenes and *Herodotus (2). Fragments of his doctrines are reported by *Galen and *Oribasius, amongst others. He wrote influential works on pulsation (grudgingly praised by Galen, 8. 748 Kühn), on semi-tertian fevers, and on the use of hellebore; little is now known of their contents.

> TEXT There is no collection of the ancient testimonia, but there is an incomplete list in Susemihl, *Gesch. gr. Lit. Alex.*
> LITERATURE M. Wellmann, *Phil. Unters.* 1895; F. Kudlien, *RE* Suppl. 2. 1097–9. J. T. V.

Agathocles (1), tyrant, later king of *Syracuse, born 361/0 BC in Thermae, Sicily. His father Carcinus, an exile from *Rhegium, received Syracusan citizenship under *Timoleon 343/2 and owned a large pottery manufactory. The young Agathocles took part in various military enterprises and early on nurtured political ambitions. The oligarchy of six hundred that ruled Syracuse after Timoleon's death distrusted the active young man with popular tendencies and he was banished c.330. During his exile he attempted to obtain a power base in southern Italy, operating as a *condottiere* in *Croton or *Tarentum. He successfully relieved Rhegium when it was besieged by the six hundred, thereby toppling the oligarchy. Recalled by the people in Syracuse he was exiled again after the oligarchs had been reinstated. Subsequently he threatened the oligarchs and their Carthaginian allies (see CARTHAGE) with a private army of mercenaries from the Sicilian inland. Hamilcar changed sides and through his mediation Agathocles was able to return to Syracuse and in 319/8 was made '*stratēgos* with absolute power in the cities of Sicily' (*FGrH* 239 B 12). A military coup in 316 (cf. Diod. Sic. 19. 5. 4–9, from *Timaeus (2)) resulted in the murder and banishment of the six hundred and to Agathocles was entrusted 'the generalship with absolute power and the care of the city' (Diod. Sic. 19. 9. 4). The new rule, chiefly reliant on mercenaries, was a *tyranny in all but in name.

During the following years Agathocles concentrated on the cities that had given refuge to the banished oligarchs, especially *Acragas, *Gela, and *Messana. Messana appealed to Carthage for help and in 314 concluded a peace treaty with Agathocles; Hamilcar again acted as mediator. Carthage retained the 'epicraty' (area of control) west of the Halycus (mod. Platani), Syracuse the hegemony over the otherwise autonomous Greek cities (Schmitt, *SdA* 3, no. 424). When Agathocles in contravention of the treaty invaded Carthaginian territory he suffered a crushing defeat at the southern Himera in the summer of 311. While the Carthaginians were advancing against Syracuse Agathocles entrusted the city's defence to his brother Antander and made his way through the enemy blockade to Africa (14 August 310). His objective was to defeat the Carthaginians in their own country and to make them withdraw troops from Sicily (Diod. Sic. 20. 3–5). He burned his ships, defeated the enemy in the field, and advanced against Carthage. In Sicily Antander was holding out against the Carthaginians, but Acragas had organized an alliance of Greek cities promising them their liberty. Agathocles in Africa had been in contact with *Ophellas, the governor of *Cyrene, since 309. Ophellas was planning a great North African empire (Diod. Sic. 20. 40). On his assassination his army enlisted with Agathocles, who in 308/7 returned to Sicily where matters had been deteriorating. Soon afterwards the army in Africa was almost completely wiped out. Agathocles returned to Africa for a short time only to abandon the rest of his soldiers and to flee back to Sicily. The peace of 306 again named the Halycus as the border between the Carthaginian epicraty and Greek Sicily (Schmitt, *SdA* 3, no. 437). Agathocles later defeated the exiles' army and ruled Greek Sicily—with the exception of Acragas. In 305 he assumed the title of king (Diod. Sic. 20. 54, 1) and not long afterwards married Theoxene, one of *Ptolemy (1) I's stepdaughters.

From c.300 he concentrated his efforts on southern Italy (Diod. Sic. 21. 4 ff.). In two campaigns he briefly brought Bruttium under his control and supported Tarentum in 298/7 against the native Lucanians and the Messapians (See LUCANIA; MESSAPII). He conquered Croton 295 and concluded alliances with other cities

in southern Italy; he even captured *Corcyra (Diod. Sic. 21. 2) and held it for a short time. Agathocles' aim seems to have been the union of Sicilian and south Italian Greeks under his rule. His preparations for another campaign against Carthage were cut short when he was assassinated in 289/8. His attempt to establish a dynasty failed owing to family rivalries, he therefore 'restored to the people their self-government' (Diod. Sic. 21. 16. 5). Agathocles was on no account the popular tyrant often depicted by historians (Mossé; see bibliog. below), but rather a cruel careerist and an unscrupulous adventurer. Modern historians have frequently overestimated his historical importance: he achieved nothing of lasting impact—on the contrary, immediately after his death anarchy erupted both in Syracuse, where a *damnatio memoriae* was decreed (Diod. Sic. 21. 16. 6), and other places (Diod. Sic. 21. 18).

> Chief source: Diod. Sic. 19. 5–31. 17 (mainly based on Timaeus, who had been banished by Agathocles and hence wrote with a strong negative bias—cf. esp. Diod. Sic. 21. 17. 1–3 = Timaeus, *FGrH* 566 F 124d). H. Berve, *Die Herrschaft des Agathokles* 1953), and *Die Tyrannis bei den Griechen*, 2 vols. (1967); C. Mossé, *La Tyrannie dans la Grèce antique* (1969); S. Consolo Langher, in R. Romeo (ed.), *Storia della Sicilia* 2 (1979); K. Meister, *CAH* 7^2/1 (1984), ch. 10.   K. M.

Agathocles (2), of Cyzicus, grammarian, c.275/65–200/190 BC, quite possibly to be identified with the local historian (*FGrH* 472). He was a pupil of *Zenodotus. A small number of fragments attest an interest in myth and cosmology in *Homer.

> Ed. F. Montanari (1988).   N. G. W.

Agathon, son of Tisamenus of Athens, was the most celebrated tragic poet after the three great masters. (See TRAGEDY, GREEK.) He won his first victory at the *Lenaea in 416 BC, and the occasion of *Plato (1)'s *Symposium* is a party at his house in celebration of that victory. Plato emphasizes his youth in the *Symposium* and portrays him as a boy in the *Protagoras* (315d), of which the dramatic date is about 430, so he must have been born after 450. In the *Protagoras* he is seen in the company of the *sophist *Prodicus, and he appears to have been influenced in style by *Gorgias (1). In 411 he heard and approved *Antiphon (1)'s speech in his defence (Arist. *Eth. Eud.* 3. 5)—this suggests antidemocratic sentiments—and in the same year he was caricatured in *Aristophanes (1)'s *Thesmophoriazusae*. The play ridicules him for effeminacy and passive homosexual tastes (see HOMOSEXUALITY), and Plato, portraying him as the long-term boyfriend of one Pausanias, partly confirms the charge. Before 405 he left Athens (like *Euripides) for the court of *Archelaus (2) of Macedon (Ar. *Ran.* 83–5 and other sources), and he died there, probably before 399.

The parody of his lyrics at Ar. *Thesm.* 101–29 is elaborately decorative, and his speech at Pl. *Symp.* 194e–197e is a florid rhetorical exercise in the manner of Gorgias. His fragments (less than 50 lines) are in a pointed, epigrammatic style, probably due to sophistic influence. *Aristotle says that he wrote a tragedy (probably *Antheus* rather than *Anthos*) in which all the characters were invented, not taken from legend (*Poet.* 9); that he wrote a tragedy which failed because he tried to include too much material, as if writing an epic (*Poet.* 18); and that he was the first to write choral odes that were mere interludes, unconnected with the plot (*Poet.* 18). All these developments can be seen as exaggerations of tendencies found in the later work of *Euripides; and one of Agathon's fragments (fr. 4, where an illiterate character describes the letters $ΘΗΣΕΥΣ$) is an attempt to cap a virtuoso Euripidean passage (fr. 382 Nauck). He is also said to have introduced the chromatic scale into the music of tragedy (Plut. *Quaest. conv.* 3. 1. 1).

TrGF 1². 155–68; *Musa Tragica*, 96–109, 282–3; B. Snell, *Szenen aus griechischen Dramen* (1971) 154–8.　　　　　　　　　　A. L. B.

Agathos Daimon (Ἀγαθὸς δαίμων), 'good god/destiny/ fortune'. He is particularly closely associated with the proper use of *wine (cf. modern toasts such as 'cheers', 'good luck'): he received small libations of unmixed wine after meals, and in *Boeotia sacrifice was made to him before the new vintage was broached. But the idea expressed in his name could also be understood more broadly, as is clear from the later-attested practice of dedicating houses and small temples to him, often in association with Agathe Tyche (Good Luck); like other protective figures he was sometimes represented as a *snake. His role as a protector of houses became particularly prominent in Greek Egypt.

F. Dunand, *LIMC* 'Agathodaimon'　　　　　　　　　　R. C. T. P.

Agave See PENTHEUS.

Agdistis, a form of the Phrygian mother-goddess; at *Pessinus *Cybele was called Agdistis (Strabo 469, 567). According to the myth (see ATTIS), she was originally androgynous. Her cult spread to various parts of Anatolia, to Egypt (by 250 BC), to Attica (with that of Attis in Piraeus 4th–3rd, cents., *IG* 2². 4671; at *Rhamnus, 83/2 BC), *Lesbos, and *Panticapeum. At Lydian *Philadelphia (2) her private shrine (1st cent. BC) enforced a strict moral code (*Syll.*³ 985; O. Weinreich, *Sitz. Heidelberg* 1919). There and elsewhere Agdistis appears with *theoi sōtēres*. See ANATOLIAN DEITIES.

H. Hepding, *Attis* (1903); Hiller von Gaertringen, *ARW* 1926. Rhamnus inscription: K. A. Rhomaios, Ἑλληνικά 1928; P. Roussel, *Rev. Et. Anc.* 1930; M. Meslin, in *Hommages M. J. Vermaseren, EPRO* 68/2 (1978), 765 ff.; D. Cosi, *Casta Mater Idaea: Giuliano Apostata e l'etica della sessualità* (1986); R. Turcan, *Les Cultes orientaux dans l'empire romain* (1989), 38 ff.　　　　　　　　　　F. R. W.; J. Sch.

age The division of life into age-groups was prominently adhered to in antiquity, though there was considerable disagreement as to their precise identification. The Pythagorean philosophers (see PYTHAGORAS) identified four (Diod. Sic. 10. 9. 5), whereas Hippocratic writers (see HIPPOCRATES (2)) acknowledged seven ages of man, each seven years in length (Poll. 2. 4). Since adult society was primarily organized on a two-generational principle, a threefold division probably served most practical purposes, viz. παῖς, νέος, and γέρων in Greek, *puer*, *iuvenis*, and *senex* in Latin. Mental ability was judged to be strictly a function of ageing, as indicated by the fact that there were minimum age qualifications for administrative and executive posts. So an Athenian councillor had to be 30 years old, as, probably, did a Spartan *ephor (see also AGE CLASSES). Similarly the Roman *cursus honorum* or ladder of office prescribed minimum ages for all magistracies. Belief in the magical power inherent in certain *numbers, notably seven and three, meant that certain ages were believed fraught with danger. *Augustus is said to have expressed considerable relief 'at having survived my climacteric, the sixty-third year' (Gell. *NA* 15. 7. 3). *Censorinus' *De die natali* (*On Birthdays*) provides an invaluable compilation of information about age terminology, etc.

There is little evidence with which to estimate the age struc-

ture of the population of ancient Rome, and even less that of ancient Greece because Greek funerary monuments, unlike Roman ones, rarely record age at death except in the case of extreme youth and extreme longevity. What follows must therefore be treated with extreme caution, as must any such model. It is estimated that in Rome 'more than a quarter of all live-born Roman babies died within their first year of life' (Hopkins). About one-third of the children who survived infancy were dead by the age of 10. Upper-class females in their early teens tended to marry males who were at least ten years older. In Rome, however, the legal age for marriage was 12 and 14 for females and males respectively (see MARRIAGE LAW). Sepulchral inscriptions, no doubt biased in favour of the upper classes, suggest that in the Roman world the median age of death was 34 years for wives and 46.5 for husbands. The study of skeletal remains from Classical Athens has produced comparable results, viz. 35 for women and 44 for men. Life expectancy was appreciably lower for *women at all social levels, largely because of the debilitating and often lethal effects of *childbirth. Probably less than one per cent of the population attained the age of 80 and anyone who did so was judged remarkable, as [Lucian's] catalogue of octogenarians in *Macrobii* suggests. Notwithstanding the brevity of human life, threescore years and ten still constituted the proper quota of years (cf. Solon 27. 17 f. West, *IE*²). Maximum life-span, viz. about 100 years, appears to have been the same in antiquity as it is today. Old age is commonly described as hateful and detestable in classical literature and many lives would have been characterized by increasing incapacitation and loss of mobility from the beginning of the third decade onwards. (The study of skeletal remains at the Romano-British cemetery at Cirencester indicates that 80 per cent of the population suffered from osteoarthrosis). Particularly disadvantaged and scorned were spinsters and *widows. Certain races had a reputation for extreme longevity, notably the long-lived Ethiopians, whose life-span was put at 120 years. Many Greeks and Romans would only have had an approximate notion of their exact age in years, as the expression *P(lus) M(inus)* 'more or less', which is frequently found on Roman tombstones, indicates. See MENOPAUSE; POPULATION.

R. S. J. Garland, *The Greek Way of Life* (1990); K. Hopkins, *Population Studies* 1966, 246–64; T. Parkin, *Demography and Roman Society* (1992). 　　　　　　　　　　R. S. J. G.

age classes A method of social and political organization in *Sparta and Crete in the Classical period. Traces of analogous institutions in other Greek states permit the hypothesis that age-class systems played an important role in the development of the *polis throughout the Greek world in earlier periods. In the Spartan *agōgē (educational system) boys were removed from their parents at the age of 7 and allocated in annual age classes (*bouai*, 'herds') to tutors who were responsible for their upbringing. At 12 the boys entered pederastic relationships with young adults (e.g. *Agesilaus and *Lysander). The *krypteia, a head-hunting ritual with a police function, occurred at initiation into adulthood, after which all members of each age class married simultaneously. Age-class control of marriage, along with segregation of the sexes until the age of 30, probably had important demographic consequences linked to Sparta's manpower problems. Completion of the various stages of the system, which also provided the basis for military organization, conferred political rights and duties. In old age some individuals obtained considerable political power through membership of the *gerousia (council of elders).

J. R. Sallares, *The Ecology of the Ancient Greek World* (1991); A. Brelich, *Paides e parthenoi* (1969); N. M. Kennell, *The Gymnasium of Virtue* (1995).
J. R. S.

Agennius Urbicus (perhaps 5th cent. AD), writer on surveying (see GROMATICI) produced commentary on *Frontinus' treatise *On Land Disputes*.
J. B. C.

Agenor, Phoenician king. When his daughter, *Europa, disappeared, he sent his sons—*Phoenix (1), Cilix, and *Cadmus—to find her. They failed (*Zeus having abducted her to Crete), but founded respectively the Phoenician and Cilician peoples and Boeotian *Thebes (1) (Apollod. 3. 1. 1, with Frazer's notes).

Apollod. *The Library,* trans. J. G. Frazer (Loeb, 1921). A. Sch.

agentes in rebus The detested *frumentarii* (see POSTAL SERVICE) were abolished by *Diocletian, but were soon replaced by 'agents' perhaps purposely ill-defined, who likewise served as couriers between the court (*comitatus*) and the provinces. They were civilians, but they enrolled as troopers and rose by seniority through the same grades as non-commissioned soldiers. As they became more senior, they served as *curiosi* supervising the public post, and finally as chiefs of staff (*principes*) to the praetorian prefects, urban perfects (see PRAEFECTUS PRAETORIO; PRAEFECTUS URBI), proconsuls, *vicarii*, and eastern *duces* (see DUX). Their duties included making reports on the provinces, and they gained a reputation as secret police (Aur. Vict. *Caes.* 39. 44) and for extorting illicit tips (Lib., *Or.* 14. 14), but their real role was to be the trusted emissaries of the central government. Pontianus, a pious Christian instrumental in the conversion of St *Augustine, was an *agens in rebus*; Augustine's friend and fellow-townsman Evodius was another. By the mid-4th cent. AD they formed a college (*schola*) under the *magister officiorum, hence their name (in Greek) as 'the master's men'. They were practically abolished by *Julian, but under his successors they reached an establishment of more than a thousand. There were many applicants for the career, and they were carefully selected. By the time of the *Theodosian Code (and probably earlier), freedmen, Jews, and heretics were excluded; relatives of *agentes* had preference for entry, and various dignitaries had limited rights of nomination.

Jones, *Later Rom. Emp.* 578–82. A. H. M. J.; R. S. O. T.

ager publicus, public land, comprised lands acquired by Rome by conquest from her enemies or confiscation from rebellious allies. By tradition there was, as early as the 5th cent. BC, dispute between patricians and plebeians as to whether such lands should be retained in public ownership but open to exploitation on lease by wealthy *possessores* (possessors; see POSSESSION, LEGAL) or distributed in private ownership amongst the poorer classes. In practice much of this land seems to have been assigned to the use of Roman and, after 338, Latin colonies (see IUS LATII). The Licinio-Sextian laws of 367 BC (see LICINIUS STOLO, C.) purported to limit the amount of public land possessed by any one citizen to 500 *iugera* or 140 ha. (350 acres).

Public land continued to be acquired during subsequent centuries; the conquest of *Cisalpine Gaul added large areas of land which were either distributed amongst colonies or offered to citizens as smallholdings on permanent lease. Elsewhere, particularly in the south of Italy, large tracts remained in the hands of the state and were regularly leased out by the *censors to wealthier citizens in return for large rents. There is evidence that in these distributions the legal limits were ignored and the collection of dues was lax.

The agrarian reforms associated with the *Gracchi aimed at redistributing much of these large properties as smallholdings. In 133 BC (see SEMPRONIUS GRACCHUS (3), TI.) a commission was established to identify those lands possessed in excess of the legal limits. Much land was resumed by the state as a result and redistributed. A similar scheme was revived by C. *Sempronius Gracchus in 123 but the new distribution eventually ceased, following his violent death in 122; the whole exercise threatened the economic position of the wealthier landowners. The Gracchan reforms had also envisaged the establishment of further colonies on public land, one of which at least was successfully planted.

In 111 BC an agrarian law was passed which in effect privatized all the Gracchan smallholdings, abolishing the rent which had been previously imposed and turning the lessees into owners. There remained some public lands in Italy which continued to be leased by the censors but subsequently acquired lands, for example those seized by L. *Cornelius Sulla from the cities which opposed him, were usually distributed to veterans immediately. *Caesar in 59 gave much of the surviving censorial lands to *Pompey's soldiers. Thereafter the only significant public land in Italy, other than inalienable property such as parks in Rome and roads, comprised the property of individual municipalities and common pasture.

The gradual disappearance of public lands in Italy was in contrast to the position in the provinces. All provincial land was, in legal theory, owned either by the people of Rome or the emperor. In practice nearly all was effectively in the hands of permanent possessors and the theory affected only the remedies by which they might seek to protect their property. Truly publicly owned property was limited to lands seized from conquered communities and the like but there was a tendency to redistribute these, for example to colonies, rather than retain them in public keeping, so that, as in Italy, such land as remained public was in the hands of *municipia* (see MUNICIPIUM).

M. Weber *Römische Agrargeschichte* (1891); G. Tibiletti, *Athenaeum* 1948, 1949, and 1950; M. H. Crawford, *Athenaeum* 1989. See AGRARIAN LAWS AND POLICY.

A. D. E. L.

Agesilaus II (*c*.445–359 BC), Spartan king of the junior, *Eurypontid line. Son of *Archidamus II by his second wife, he was not expected to succeed his older half-brother *Agis II and so went through the prescribed educational curriculum (*agōgē*) like any other Spartan boy. In 400 he unexpectedly secured the succession, with the aid of his former lover *Lysander, ahead of Agis' son Leotychidas, whose parentage was suspect (rumour had it that his true father was the exiled *Alcibiades).

The first king to be sent on campaign in Asia, where his proclaimed aim was to liberate the Greeks from Persian suzerainty, Agesilaus achieved some success against the Persian viceroys *Pharnabazus and *Tissaphernes in 396–5 before his enforced recall to face a coalition of Sparta's Greek enemies in central and southern Greece. The battle of *Coronea (394) was a Pyrrhic victory, and, despite some minor successes of his around *Corinth and in *Acarnania (391–388), the coalition was defeated not on land by Agesilaus but at sea by the Spartan nauarch *Antalcidas with a Persian-financed fleet. Agesilaus, however, threw himself wholeheartedly behind the Peace of Antalcidas, or *King's Peace (386), which he interpreted to suit what he took to be Sparta's best interests. Pro-Spartan oligarchs were brought to power in *Mantinea, Phlius, and *Olynthus, but the most flagrant violation of the autonomy clause of the peace was the occupation of *Thebes (1) (382). By condoning that breach and securing the

Agiads

acquittal of Sphodrias (father of his son's beloved), who was on trial for an illegal attempt to seize the *Piraeus (378), Agesilaus provoked a further anti-Spartan coalition supported by Persia. Despite some success of Agesilaus in Boeotia in 378 and 377, the Thebans and their Boeotian federation (see BOEOTIAN CONFEDERACY) eventually proved too strong for an enfeebled Spartan alliance at *Leuctra in 371. The Theban ascendancy of 371 to 362, presided over by *Epaminondas and *Pelopidas, and the consequent liberation of *Messenia from Sparta, are directly attributable to Agesilaus' unremitting hostility to Thebes. Agesilaus nevertheless did not lose face or influence at home, and continued to direct Spartan counsels in the years of his city's humiliation. He organized the defence of the city against Epaminondas' coalition in 370 and 362, and sought to augment the state's revenues by foreign service as a mercenary (in Asia Minor with the Persian satrap Ariobarzanes in 364, and in Egypt with King Nectanebis II in 361–59). He died in Cyrenaica on the return journey from Egypt, aged about 84.

Though born lame in one leg, and displaying a streak of romanticism, Agesilaus was typically Spartan in his qualities and limitations. He was an efficient soldier, but a better tactician than strategist, who failed to understand the importance of siegecraft and sea power. At home, no Spartan king ever exploited better than he the resources of charisma and patronage available to a blue-blooded Heraclid king (see HERACLIDAE). But the narrowness of his personal loyalties and political sympathies dissipated those moral assets by which alone Sparta might have maintained her Greek hegemony, in the face of a sharply dwindling citizen population and the constant hostility of the *helots at home and Sparta's Greek and non-Greek enemies beyond her borders.

PB no. 9; P. Cartledge, *Agesilaos and the Crisis of Sparta* (1987); C. D. Hamilton, *Agesilaus and the Failure of Spartan Hegemony* (1991).

P. A. C.

Agiads The Agiads were the senior royal house at Sparta, descended mythically from the elder of Heraclid twins (Hdt. 6. 52; see HERACLES); the junior was known as the *Eurypontids. The origins of the Spartan dual kingship are unknown, but the office was entrenched in the 'Great Rhetra' ascribed to the lawgiver *Lycurgus (2) (Plut. *Lyc.* 6) and persisted until the end of the 3rd cent. BC. Distinguished Agiads included *Cleomenes (1) I, his half-brother *Leonidas (1), and *Cleomenes (2) III. The latter effectively terminated the traditional dyarchy in c.227 by installing his brother on the formerly Eurypontid throne.

P. A. Cartledge, *Sparta and Lakonia* (1979); P. Carlier, *La Royauté en Grèce avant Alexandre* (1984); C. Calame, in J. Bremmer (ed.), *Interpretations of Greek Mythology* (1987), ch. 8.

P. A. C.

Agis II, Spartan king of the *Eurypontid house (the first to be given a name belonging naturally to the *Agiads) from c.427 to 400 BC; he was son of *Archidamus II by his first wife. He achieved widespread prominence in 418, as nominal victor of the battle of *Mantinea, a success that both stilled powerful domestic criticism of his leadership and restored Sparta's authority in the Peloponnese and outside. In 413, perhaps glad to escape scandal on his own doorstep, he was appointed general commanding the Peloponnesian forces in central Greece, and permanently occupied a fortified base actually within Athens' borders at *Decelea. The centre of the *Peloponnesian War, however, shifted to Asia, and Agis' role in the eventual reduction of Athens by siege in 404 was subsidiary to that of *Lysander. In the aftermath of victory Agis voted for the condemnation of his Agiad fellow king *Pausanias (2) on a charge of high treason. Pausanias was acquitted,

but Agis was entrusted with the task of punishing Sparta's notoriously disloyal ally, *Elis, and did not scruple either to enlist Zeus of Olympia on his side or to exploit his personal connections in Elis (402–400). His death due to illness occasioned the succession dispute that brought *Agesilaus to the throne.

PB no. 26.

P. A. C.

Agis III, king of Sparta (338–?330 BC), *Eurypontid. Ascending the throne at a time of humiliation, when Sparta had lost her borderlands to *Philip (1) II of Macedon, he devoted himself to reviving his city's fortunes. Inconclusive intrigues with the Persian commanders in the Aegean (333) led to intervention in *Crete, where he attracted 8,000 Greek mercenaries, refugees from *Issus. With their support he declared open war in the Peloponnese during (it seems) summer 331. *Elis, *Tegea, and the *Achaean Confederacy joined his cause, but the Athenians fatally stood aloof. *Antipater (1) was able to raise a coalition army 40,000 strong, profiting from the common detestation of Spartan expansionism, and relieved the siege of *Megalopolis. Agis suffered a crushing defeat. He died heroically, but left Sparta enfeebled beyond redemption.

Berve, *Alexanderreich* 2, no. 15; E. Badian, *Hermes*, 1967, 170 ff., and in I. Worthington (ed.), *Ventures into Greek History* (1994), 258 ff.; A. B. Bosworth, *Conquest and Empire* 198 ff.

A. B. B.

Agis IV (c.262–241 BC), son of Eudamidas, ascended the *Eurypontid throne in c.244, at a time of domestic crisis. Concentration of estates in a few hands, heavy indebtedness of the majority, depletion of citizen numbers, and desuetude of the ancient civic regimen were ills he proposed to remedy by an alleged return to the aboriginal 'Lycurgan' order (see LYCURGUS (2)). But the cure proved as dangerous as the diseases. Opposition was overcome by impeaching and forcing into exile his fellow king Leonidas, driving an uncle into exile, and unprecedentedly deposing a board of *ephors. The reforms were apparently passed but could not be implemented before Leonidas staged a counter-coup while Agis was abroad assisting his allies of the *Achaean Confederacy against Aetolia (see AETOLIAN CONFEDERACY) and had him executed by the ephors on his return. High-minded but impractical, he fell before more astute political operators. His death became the legend around which a new generation rallied (see CLEOMENES (2) III). His life was written up by *Phylarchus in the romantic style of the day, a source upon which *Plutarch drew heavily for his extant biography.

Plut. *Agis* (comm. G. Marasco (1981)). E. Gabba, *Athenaeum* 1957, 3–55, 193–239; P. Cartledge and A. J. S. Spawforth, *Hellenistic and Roman Sparta* (1989).

P. A. C.

Aglaurus Daughter of the Athenian king *Cecrops, Aglaurus makes her best-known appearance in myth and art alongside *Pandrosus and Herse; disobeying *Athena's instructions, the sisters opened the chest where the child *Erichthonius was kept, and what they saw caused them to hurl themselves off the Acropolis to their deaths. But there are clear signs that Aglaurus' origins are separate from her sisters. She had an independent sanctuary at the east end of the Acropolis, and unlike Pandrosus she was linked more closely with adolescents and young fighters (the *ephēboi) than with babies. Her divine connections cover both *Ares, by whom she had a daughter Alcippe (see HALIRRHOTHIUS), and Athena, being associated especially with the goddess's festival, the *Plynteria.

U. Kron, *LIMC* 1/1. 283–98; R. Merkelbach, *ZPE* 9 (1972) 277–83;

G. Dontas, *Hesp.* 1983, 48–63; E. Kearns, *Heroes of Attica* 23–7, 57–63, 139–40; P. Brulé, *La Fille d'Athènes* (1987), 28–34. E. Ke.

Agnodice appears in *Hyginus (3) (*Fab.* 274) in a list of discoverers and inventors. She is described as an Athenian girl who lived at a time when there were no *midwives, because women and slaves were forbidden to learn medicine; this scenario matches no known historical period. Disguising herself as a man, Agnodice studied medicine under 'a certain Herophilus', and then practised medicine at Athens successfully, challenging the professional monopoly on the part of male doctors. Accused by her jealous rivals of seducing her patients, Agnodice demonstrated her innocence by performing the gesture of *anasyrmos*, lifting her tunic to expose her lower body. This revelation led to a charge of practising medicine unlawfully, but she was saved when the wives of the leading men lobbied the *Areopagus in her defence. Hyginus claims that Athenian law was then changed so that freeborn women could study medicine.

This story, variously argued to be an historical account, a novella, or a myth, had enormous influence in the history of medicine from the Renaissance onwards, being used as a precedent both for a female monopoly on midwifery and for women doctors.

C. Bonner, *AJPhil.* 1920, 253–64; H. King, *PCPS* 1986, 53–77; D. Nickel, *Int. Congress Hist. Med.* 1981, 2. 170–3; RE 1 / 1. 831. H. K.

agōgē, the Spartan public upbringing. The Classical *agōgē*, supervised by the *paidonomos* ('boy-herdsman'), embraced males aged 7–29. Only the immediate heirs to the kingships (see AGIADS; EURYPONTIDS) were exempt. There were three general stages, the *paides*, *paidiskoi*, and *hēbōntes*, probably representing ages 7–17, 18–19, and 20–29; several individual year-classes were separately named. The *paides* were trained in austerity, obedience, and mock battles by older youths within companies (*ilai*), subdivided into herds (*agelai*) of age-mates with their own internal leadership. At age 12 they entered an institutionalized pederastic relationship with a young adult (see HOMOSEXUALITY). The *paidiskoi* were army reservists and (probably a select group) participants in the *krypteia*. The *hēbōntes* joined the *syssitia and army, could marry, but remained in barrack life, competing for places among the 300 *hippeis*, the kings' bodyguard (see HIPPEIS § 3). Separating boys from their families, the *agōgē* inculcated conformity and the priority of collective interests, but also promoted the emergence of future élites. A diluted version of physical training existed for females.

The post-Classical *agōgē* underwent several changes: initial decay; reconstruction in the 220s BC under *Cleomenes (2) III; abolition by *Philopoemen in 188; finally, a 'revival' after 146 BC, with further augmentation in the later 1st cent. AD. The Roman *agōgē* was essentially an ephebic (see EPHĒBOI) training for males aged 14–19, supervised by the *bideioi* ('overseers') and *patronomos* ('guardian of law'), and based on the citizen-tribes (*phylai*). In a team structure added under the Flavians a *boagos* ('herd-leader') commanded his fellow ephebes. The status of *kasen* enabled poorer youths to be sponsored through the training, which included song, dance, athletic and military exercises, and probably intellectual instruction. A traditional veneer was provided through archaizing terminology and inscriptional language, training for females, and supposedly ancestral events such as the endurance contest at the sanctuary of Artemis Orthia (see SPARTAN CULTS).

S. Hodkinson, *Chiron* 1983, 245–51; P. Cartledge, *Agesilaos and the Crisis of Sparta* (1987), ch. 3; P. Cartledge and A. Spawforth, *Hellenistic and Roman Sparta* (1989), esp. 167–8, 201–7; N. M. Kennell, *The Gymnasium of Virtue* (1995). S. J. Ho.

agōnes 1. The term *agōn* (ἀγών) and its derivatives can denote the informal and extempore competitive struggles and rivalries that permeated Greek life in the general fight for success and survival (cf. Hes. *Op.* 11–26), especially philosophical, legal, and public debates; action between opposing sides in war; medical disputes. Competitive behaviour in this last area is illustrated by the Hippocratic work (see HIPPOCRATES (2)) *On Joints*, which at one point (*Art.* 70) envisages a medical assistant, in his struggle to realign a dislocated thigh, enjoying an *agōn* or contest with the patient (cf. also *Art.* 58: medical rivalry in producing prognoses). A corollary of the agonistic drive was the prominence as a motive for action of *philotimia (love of honour), which could turn into over-ambition and jealous rivalry, and, in its worst form, lead to *stasis (strife) and political upheaval (cf. Pind. fr. 210 Snell–Maehler; Thuc. 3. 82. 8).

2. Gatherings of people, usually for formal contests in honour of a god or local hero.

Before 300 Prior to the 8th cent. BC they seem to have been small-scale events, centring round a shrine or sanctuary. But the *agōn* at *Olympia came to acquire a special status: traditionally founded in 776 BC, by the end of the 8th cent. it was, because of the wide range of *athletics contests it offered and its lack of political ties, attracting increasing numbers of foreigners (especially from among the athletic Spartans) and was organized as a Panhellenic *agōn* (see OLYMPIAN GAMES; PANHELLENISM). With interstate relationships assuming increased importance during the 7th cent., local *agōnes* were reorganized at other places too. The *Pythian Games became Panhellenic in 582 BC; its range of athletics events followed the Olympian model, but it preserved its identity and associations with *Apollo through its emphasis on musical competitions. With the reorganization of the *Isthmian (c.581) and *Nemean Games (c.573), a group of four Panhellenic *agōnes* came to form an athletics circuit (*periodos*), as the Olympics, World Championships, European, and Commonwealth Games do for some athletes nowadays. At Athens the Great *Panathenaea (founded 566) was also Panhellenic, but for athletes never achieved the status of the other four. Despite this development, local *agōnes* with athletics contests continued to flourish: *Pindar's victory-odes mention more than 20 local games (cf. *Ol.* 13. 107–13; also Simon. *Epig.* 43 Page), and a 5th-cent. Laconian inscription records 72 victories won by Damonon and his son Enymacratidas at eight *agōnes* in the Peloponnese (*IG* 5. 1. 213, trans. Sweet 145–6: see bibliog. below).

Contests were often in athletics, but music, poetry, and equestrian events were also popular. *Hesiod won a poetry-singing competition in Chalcis (*Op.* 657); the Pythian Games included three types of musical contest (singing to the accompaniment of cithara or aulos, and solo aulos) and a painting competition (Pliny *HN* 35. 58). In Athens tragedies, comedies, and dithyrambs (choral songs) were performed in competitions at the City *Dionysia, and at the Panathenaea *rhapsodes competed in Homer-reciting contests. *Horse- and chariot-races were mainly entered by wealthy individuals who paid charioteers or jockeys to ride on their behalf, and hoped for political prestige from good performances (cf. Alcibiades' boast, Thuc. 6. 16. 2). The chariot-race was often long (about 14 km. (nearly 9 mi.) at the Olympian Games) and dangerous (Pind. *Pyth.* 5. 49–51: the victor was the only one of 40 starters to finish with chariot intact). Beauty

Agonium

contests, drinking contests, and even a wool-carding contest are also recorded.

At the four major Panhellenic *agōnes*, victors were honoured with a wreath: olive at Olympia, laurel at the Pythian Games, varieties of *selinon* (parsley or celery) at the Isthmus and Nemea (but cf. hyp. c *Nem.*, hyp. b *Isthm.*; Paus. 8. 48. 2). At other venues wreaths were made of date-palms (Paus. 8. 48. 2) or myrtle (Pind. *Isthm.* 4. 88). The victor might also be showered with leaves (*phyllobolia*). On returning home he could receive more substantial rewards: free meals (*sitēsis*), the privilege of a front seat (*prohedria*) when spectating at *agōnes*, and gifts. Athens was especially generous to victors: *Solon passed legislation to award Athenian victors at Olympia 500 drachmae (Plut. *Sol.* 23; monetary prizes are however anachronistic at this early date—see COINAGE, GREEK), and at the Great Panathenaea in the 4th cent. BC money, gold crowns, bulls, and large numbers of amphorae containing olive oil were awarded as prizes (IG 2² 2311, trans. Miller 80–3 (see bibliog. below); 100 amphorae, *c*.4,000 l. (880 gal.), for a victor in the men's *stadion* race, a very valuable prize). Local *agōnes* also awarded prizes: silver cups at *Sicyon (Pind. *Nem.* 10. 43), a bronze shield at *Argos (2), and a thick cloak at Pellene (Pind. *Ol.* 7. 83, 9. 97–8).

To lose in a contest was shameful, and the incidence of failure-induced depression and mental illness is likely to have been high (cf. Pind. *Ol.* 8. 68–9, *Pyth.* 8. 81–7; Paus. 6. 9. 6).

After 300   The spread of 'periodic' contests in the Greek style is a defining feature of post-Classical *Hellenism. In the 3rd and 2nd cents. BC they were sponsored by kings (the Alexandrian Ptolemaea and Pergamene Nicephoria) and leagues (the Soteria of *Delphi, by the *Aetolian Confederacy) as well as cities great and small (e.g. the plethora of Boeotian *agōnes* by *c*.50 BC: A. Gossage, *BSA* 1975, 115 ff.). Under the Roman Principate this expansion continued; provincial cities founded new games as late as AD 275–6; by the 3rd cent. they were celebrated from *Carthage to *Zeugma. At Rome they were first introduced under *Nero, followed by *Domitian (the Capitolia of 86), *Gordian III (the *agōn* for Athena Promachos of 242) and *Aurelian, whose *agōn* of *Sol (274) was still celebrated under *Julian. Frowned on by Christianity, Greek games (shorn of pagan ritual) none the less survived until at least 521, when *Justinian banned the Olympia of *Antioch (1).

The distinctiveness of 'sacred' games, celebrating a deity (often poliad or, under Rome, the *ruler-cult) and (at first) offering only a symbolic prize (typically a crown, *stephanos*), is fundamental. In the Hellenistic age the recognition of new 'sacred' games required cumbersome interstate diplomacy by the promoter (best attested with the Leucophryena of *Magnesia (1) ad Maeandrum (*I. Magn.* 16–87)). From 30 BC Roman emperors decided 'the gift of a sacred contest', weighing up cost, a city's record of loyalty and, in 3rd-cent. *Cilicia, its support for imperial troop-movements. An élite group of 'iselastic' games emerged, often named after one of the famous games of the 'ancient circuit' (*archaia periodos*), and distinctive for the privileges which victors could demand of their home cities, notably a triumphal entry, pension (*opsonion*), and tax-immunity (*ateleia*). Otherwise there were prize-games (*thematitai*, *themides*), also subject to Roman control.

'Sacred' contests comprised a sacrifice, to which other Greek cities sent representatives (*theōroi* or more often, under Rome, *synthutai*), and a profane festival (*panēgyris*), often incorporating *markets and fairs, as well as the contests proper, supervised by an *agōnothetēs*. Funding of new contests relied heavily on civic *euergetism; infrequently emperors—notably *Hadrian (C. P. Jones, *JRA* 1990, 487)—stepped in. From the 2nd cent. AD the *pantomime, and from the 3rd the *mime, joined the more traditional events.

Whatever the qualitative view taken of post-Classical agonistic culture (for contests in ruler-encomium see A. Hardie, *Statius and the Silvae* (1983)), its power in the shaping of later Hellenism is undeniable, and the limits of its diffusion suggest the limits of Hellenism. See ATHLETICS; COMEDY (GREEK); MUSIC; THEOROI; TRAGEDY, GREEK.

SOURCES L. Moretti, *Iscrizioni agonistiche greche* (1953); W. Sweet, *Sport and Recreation in Ancient Greece: A Sourcebook with Translations* (1987); M. Wörrle, *Stadt und Fest in kaiserzeitlichen Kleinasien* (1989): major Hadrianic inscription from Oenoanda, Eng. trans. S. Mitchell, *JRS* 1990, 183 ff.; S. Miller (ed.), *Arete: Greek Sports from Ancient Sources*, 2nd edn. (1991); C. Roueché, *Performers and Partisans at Aphrodisias* (1993): inscriptions, translations, discussion.

MODERN LITERATURE B. Biliński, *Agoni ginnici: Componenti artistiche ed intelletuali nell'antica agonistica greca* (1979); L. Robert, *Actes du VIIIe Congrès International d'Épigraphie Grecque et Latine à Athènes* (1984), 35 ff.; D. Young, *The Olympic Myth of Greek Amateur Athletics* (1984); W. Burkert, *Greek Religion* (Eng. trans. 1985); C. Morgan, *Athletes and Oracles* (1990).   S. J. I., A. J. S. S.

Agonium, name for 9 January, 17 March, 21 May, and 11 December in the Roman calendar; also Agonalia (Ov. *Fast.* 1. 324; possibly Agnalia at 1. 325), Agonia (Varro, *Ling.* 6. 14), and Dies agonales (Varro, *Ling.* 6. 12), when the *rex sacrorum sacrificed in the *Regia (Festus 9 Lindsay and Ov. *Fast.* 1. 317–38 with F. Bömer's notes). It had no associated god and the January celebration has no character letter in extant calendars; Macrobius (*Sat.* 1. 16. 6–8) makes it a fixed public festival (*feriae publicae stativae*).

Inscr. Ital. 13. 2. 393–4; *Kl. Pauly,* 1. 140; Latte, *RR* 135; R. Palmer, *Roman Religion and Roman Empire* (1974), 144–5.   C. R. P.

agora, Greek term for an area where people gather together, most particularly for the political functions of the *polis, normally sited centrally in cities (as at *Priene), or at least central to the street lines where the actual centre may be occupied by other features (such as the Acropolis at Athens); the area was sacred, and could be treated like a *temenos. In unplanned cities its shape depends on the nature of the available site, irregular at Athens, on low-lying ground bordered by rising land to west (the Kolonos Agoraios) and south (the slopes of the Acropolis). In planned cities the required number of blocks in the regular grid plan are allocated, giving a strictly rectangular shape. (See LAND DIVISION (GREEK); URBANISM (GREEK AND HELLENISTIC).)

Architecturally, the agora need be no more than the space defined by marker stones rather than buildings, as, originally, at Athens. When spectacular buildings develop for the various functions of the agora, they are placed along the boundary, which they help to define, rather than in the agora space. These include lawcourts, offices, and meeting-places for officials (and the formal feasting which was part of their office). These may be integrated with extended porticoes—*stoas—and it is these that come to dominate the architecture of the agora, often with long lines of rooms behind them, though not infrequently as colonnades pure and simple. Such colonnades, extended along the boundaries, define the agora more obviously than marker stones and are normal in the developed (and particularly the planned) agoras of the 4th cent. BC and the Hellenistic period (see STOA).

In unplanned agoras, streets normally run through the open area; thus the 'Panathenaic Way' enters the Athenian agora at its north-west corner, and leaves at the south-east. As the buildings on the borders develop, the agora tends more and more to be closed off, streets being diverted to pass outside the surrounding stoas, with perhaps one main street being allowed through (though by Roman times this may have to pass through formal, and closable, gateways).

The central area of the agora was the locality for special monuments and dedications, statue groups such as the Tyrannicides (see ARISTOGITON) at Athens, the line of exedrae at Priene. So long as the space was needed for crowds (all those voting in an *ostracism at Athens, as an extreme example) it had to remain open; it was only in the restricted political life of Greek cities in the Roman period that it might include large buildings such as the *odeum of Agrippa at Athens. See ATHENS, TOPOGRAPHY.

R. Martin, *Recherches sur l'agora grecque* (1951). On the sanctity of the agora: G. de Ste. Croix, *Origins of the Peloponnesian War* (1972), 282 ff. (on Pl. *Laws* 871a), 397 ff.; R. Parker, *Miasma* (1983), 19, 25.   R. A. T.

Agoracritus, Parian sculptor, active *c*.440–400 BC. A pupil of *Phidias, he made a bronze Athena Itonia and Zeus/Hades for *Coronea in Boeotia, a marble Mother of the Gods for the Metroon in the Athenian agora (see ATHENS, TOPOGRAPHY), and a colossal marble *Nemesis for *Rhamnus. Pausanias (1. 33. 3), who erroneously attributes the Nemesis to Phidias, describes it in detail, and fragments in Rhamnus, Athens, and London have led both to the recognition of copies and to the partial reconstruction at Rhamnus (along with its base) of the original. Nemesis was standing, holding an apple-branch in one hand and a phiale in the other, and wearing a crown embellished with *nikai* and deer. The base showed *Leda presenting the goddess's daughter, *Helen, to her in the presence of *Tyndareos and his children. Forecasting Helen's abduction and the Trojans' eventual punishment, this scene may also have hinted at Sparta's responsibility for both the Trojan and the *Peloponnesian War.

A. F. Stewart, *Greek Sculpture* (1990), 165, 269 ff., figs. 403 ff.; K. Shapiro Lapatin, *Hesp.* 1992, 107 ff.   A. F. S.

agoranomoi, overseers of the *market, an office known in many Greek states. In Athens there were ten, five for the city and five for the *Piraeus. They kept order in the market, saw to the quality of goods, and collected market dues (*Ath. pol.* 51. 1); but at Athens there were separate measures magistrates (*metronomoi*) responsible for weights and measures, and magistrates responsible for the corn trade. They could inflict penalties for minor offences; for more serious offences they initiated prosecutions before a jury-court and presided at the trial. In the post-Classical age they played an important part in ensuring the civic *food-supply, and might subsidize its cost themselves (see EUERGETISM; LITURGY).   A. W. G.; P. J. R.

agrarian laws and policy Allocation of land by the community is attested in the Greek world at the times of new city foundations (colonies; see COLONIZATION, GREEK), and when land was annexed (*cleruchies). There is also some evidence for legislation restricting the disposal of allotments by sale or inheritance, in order to maintain the original land-units which sustained the households. On the other hand, there developed strong resistance to the notion of redividing the city's territory so as to change the proportions of private landholdings: a promise not to propose anything of the kind was included in the oath of the Athenian jurymen. See also SPARTA.

At Rome agrarian legislation played a large part in the history of the republic and the struggles between the aristocracy and the *plebs. It is hard to know how far we should trust the evidence about the early republic, since often the details of the narratives in *Livy and *Dionysius (7) seem to have been elaborated in the light of late-republican experience. However, we can be confident that there were laws about land and it is highly probable that they were connected, as Roman tradition maintained, with plebeian discontent. Legislation arose originally from annexation of land after Roman military expansion. It thus concerned land which was the public territory of the Roman people (see AGER PUBLICUS), not land belonging to private individuals (private land remained free from interference by the community except where it could be shown that a public right existed over it, such as access to a water supply). One type of law established new cities (colonies) with their associated land, a second assigned new allotments in a wide tract of territory, such as those in the Sabina and the *ager Gallicus* in *Picenum, a third (*de modo agrorum*) did not positively assign land to anyone but restricted the exploitation at will of unassigned public land by reference to area occupied or number of beasts grazed. The first known law of the last type, the *lex Licinia* of 367 BC, was probably a response to the opportunities created by the acquisition of all the land of *Veii. During the middle republic, when Italy and *Cisalpine Gaul were gradually subjected to Roman power, land demands were satisfied by new allocations. However, in the late 2nd cent. BC, with a rising number of landless and a shortage of new land available for distribution in the peninsula, the Gracchi passed laws which sought to recover what was still technically public land from wealthy men who were exploiting it illegally to excess, and to redistribute it to the poor. This was regarded by wealthy landholders as a radical and subversive move. Nevertheless the Gracchan programme (see SEMPRONIUS GRACCHUS (3), TI. and SEMPRONIUS GRACCHUS, C.) was largely completed and such redistribution seems to have remained part of agrarian policy until the death of M. *Livius Drusus (2) (tribune of the Plebs 91 BC), though settlements were also made in territory acquired by conquest abroad (we know of land-assignment in Africa, the Balearics, Corsica, Greece, and Gaul, both Cisalpine and Transalpine). The Social and Civil Wars followed by *Sulla's proscriptions led *de facto* to great changes in landholding in Italy, which favoured the greater landholders against the peasants. (See SOCIAL WAR (3).) Some attempt was made to return to Gracchan policies in the late republic (P. *Servilius Rullus' bill, *Caesar's legislation of 59 BC), but the chief means of public acquisition of land in Italy now had to be purchase from private individuals. The proscriptions by the triumvirs (see TRIUMVIRI) after Caesar's murder made land available for distribution to their soldiers, but *Augustus returned to purchase in order to secure land for his *veterans after Actium.

A. J. Toynbee, *Hannibal's Legacy: The Hannibalic War's Effects on Roman Life* (1965); P. A. Brunt, *Italian Manpower 225 BC–AD 14* (1971); A. W. Lintott, *Judicial Reform and Land Reform in the Roman Republic* (1992).   A. W. L.

Agri Decumates, a territory comprising the Black Forest, the basin of the Neckar, and the Swabian Alp, annexed by the Flavian emperors to shorten communications between the Rhine and the Danube, and attached to Upper Germany. It may earlier have been settled by the landless poor of Gaul. Though the imperial authorities' prime concern was the *limes, they took pains to establish several artificial civilian communities on the Gallic

model, e.g. the *civitas Ulpia Sueborum*, administered from Laden-
burg. The meaning of 'Agri Decumates' has been much disputed;
today it is generally translated as 'Ten Cantons'. The area was
lost *c.* AD 260 and in the 4th cent. was occupied by the *Alamanni.

Tac. *Germ.* 29. D. Baatz, *Der römische Limes* (1975); L. D. Baatz and
F. R. Herrman, *Die Römer in Hessen* (1982); J. G. F. Hind, *Britannia*,
1984, 187 ff.   J. F. Dr.

Agricola See CALPURNIUS AGRICOLA, SEX.; IULIUS AGRICOLA, CN.

agricultural implements

Greek The *technology of Greek *agriculture was simple, and
apparently underwent little development. Breaking up the
ground, which was fundamental to sowing, weed-control, and
preservation of moisture, was achieved by simple symmetrical
ploughs, which did not turn the soil, or by mattock and hoe.
Ploughs and mattocks occasionally appear on vases and the (all
wood) plough is described at length in Hesiod (*Op.* 427 ff.).
Cereals were reaped with a curved sickle, and vines and olives
pruned with an implement which is scarcely distinguishable.

The processing of crops required more sophisticated equipment. Threshing cereals required a stone floor on which the
grain was threshed by animal hoofs or perhaps animal-drawn
sledges, the runners of which may have been toughened by the
addition of obsidian flakes; winnowing was by basket and shovel.
Pressing grapes could be done by human feet in a basket, vat, or
stone press-bed, but olives had to be crushed (see OLIVE). The
earliest (archaeological) evidence for an olive *mill is late 5th-
cent. BC; it is not clear how olives were crushed before that time.
An Archaic Attic vase shows an olive press which exploits leverage
and counterweights, and vessels specially constructed to facilitate
the separation of oil and water survive from the late bronze age.
Screw presses seem to be a Hellenistic innovation.

S. Isager and J. E. Skydsgaard, *Ancient Greek Agriculture* (1992), 44–66.
                                                                 R. G. O.

Roman Roman agricultural implements comprised slaves (see
SLAVERY), animals, and tools (Varro, *Rust.* 1. 17. 1). Only the third
category is reviewed here. The essential similarity between the
inventories in M. *Porcius Cato (1) (*Agr.* 10, 11) and *Palladius
(1. 42) some 600 years later indicates technological stability or
stagnation, depending on one's point of view. (This very stability
has enabled researchers working in Mediterranean areas little
affected by mechanized agriculture to interpret with some security the growing archaeological evidence, the ancient representations in art, and the Roman agricultural writers.) Yet while
innovations such as the Gallic reaping machine (Pliny, *HN* 18.
296; Palladius, 7. 2. 2–4) were rare, improvements in design were
common. Examples include: in arable cultivation, the plough
(e.g. Pliny, *HN* 18. 171–2) and threshing sledge (Varro, *Rust.* 1. 52.
2); and, in arboriculture, the vine-dresser's knife, trench-measur-
ing devices (Columella, *Rust.* 4. 2. 5, 3. 13. 11), and wine- and oil-
presses (Pliny, *HN* 18. 317). Different varieties of basic tools
existed (e.g. twelve types of *falx*) due to regional custom (cf.
Varro, *Rust.* 1. 50. 1–3), agricultural conservatism despite the
introduction of new designs, and the needs of diverse soils and
crops. While a *villa estate might keep different varieties of each
basic implement for specialized uses (e.g. Varro, *Rust.* 1. 22. 5),
the subsistence cultivator would fully exploit one multi-purpose
implement. Such was the *rastrum*, thought to characterize
peasant agriculture (Verg. *Aen.* 9. 607–8), which was used for
clearing rough land, for turnip cultivation, and for breaking up
clods of earth left after ploughing (Columella, *Rust.* 3. 11. 3, 2.

10. 23; Pliny, *HN* 18. 180). While some improved designs resulted
from the desire for elevated production, implements like the
reaping machine, the long-handled scythe, and, perhaps, the
harrow, developed as a result of labour shortage (Pliny *HN* 18.
296, 261, 180). Wooden equipment might be home-made, but
metal and stone implements were purchased, thus stimulating
the local economy (Cato, *Agr.* 22. 3–4, 135; Varro, *Rust.* 1. 22).
See AGRICULTURE, ROMAN; MILLS; PLOUGHING; TECHNOLOGY.

K. D. White, *Agricultural Implements of the Roman World* (1967), and
Farm Equipment of the Roman World (1975); S. Rees, *Agricultural Implements in Prehistoric and Roman Britain* (1979); J. Kolendo, *L'agricoltura
nell'Italia romana* (1980), and *Opus* 1985, 111–24; R. Pohanka, *Die
eisernen Agrargeräte der römischen Kaiserzeit in Österreich* (1986); M. S.
Spurr, *Arable Cultivation in Roman Italy c. 200 BC–c. AD 100* (1986).
                                                                 M. S. Sp.

agricultural leases See LEASES, AGRICULTURAL.

agricultural writers Agricultural manuals, written by practising landowners, flourished at Rome from M. *Porcius Cato (1)
(*c.*160 BC) to *Palladius (*c.*mid 5th cent. AD), enjoying higher
status than other technical literature. Greece had produced
notable works (*Varro knew more than 50, *Rust.* 1. 1. 8–11), but
written mostly from a philosophical or scientific viewpoint; and
an influential (non-extant) Punic work by Mago had been translated into both Greek and Latin (Varro ibid.; Columella *Rust.* 1.
1. 13). Agriculture, as gradually defined and systematized (earlier
Greek, Punic, and Roman writers had wandered off the topic:
Varro *Rust.* 1. 2. 13), embraced, in Varro's work (*c.*37 BC), arable
cultivation, livestock, arboriculture, market gardens, luxury
foods, slave management, and villa construction. A century later,
*Columella doubted whether one man could know it all (*Rust.* 1.
praef. 21; 5. 1. 1), and, from the early empire onwards, specialized
works appeared, such as *Iulius Atticus' monograph on vines
(Columella *Rust.* 1. 1. 15). While Varro criticized the Greek writer
*Theophrastus for excessive theory (*Rust.* 1. 5. 2), modern
scholars in their turn have doubted the practicality of the Roman
writers. Recent rural archaeology has given grounds for greater
confidence. The excavated *villa at *Settefinestre in Etruria has
substantiated in remarkable detail the recommendations of Varro
and Columella, as has the discovery of a large vineyard at
*Pompeii. But the agricultural writers describe not just one ideal
type of estate. Crop by crop they discuss a variety of methods of
cultivation, according to species, soil, topography, and custom—
a regional diversity confirmed by archaeological survey. See also
AGRICULTURE, ROMAN; GARGILIUS MARTIALIS, Q.; IULIUS ATTICUS.

H. Gummerus, *Der römische Gutsbetrieb, Klio Beiheft 5* (1906; repr.
1979); M. Fuhrmann, *Das systematische Lehrbuch* (1960); R. Martin,
Recherches sur les agronomes latins (1971); K. D. White, *ANRW* 1. 4 (1973),
440–97; E. Rawson, *PBSR* 1978, 12–34; A. Carandini and A. Ricci (eds.),
Settefinestre: Una villa schiavistica nell'Etruria romana (1985);
W. F. Jashemski, *The Gardens of Pompeii* (1979); D. Flach, *Römische
Agrargeschichte* (1990); S. Isager and J. E. Skydsgaard, *Ancient Greek
Agriculture* (1992); S. B. Pomeroy, *Xenophon: Oeconomicus* (1993).
                                                                 M. S. Sp.

agriculture, Greek The agriculture of Greece in the historical
period shared the basic cultigens and techniques of most of the
other contemporary civilizations of the Mediterranean. Life was
sustained by barley and wheat, sown mostly in the autumn as
field crops dependent on rainfall between autumn and spring.
Hulled barley (two- and six-row) and hulled wheat (emmer and
einkorn), introduced to the Aegean from the near east in the
neolithic period, remained important crops. Naked wheats,

especially tetraploid, durum wheat, evolved in the first millennium BC, but hexaploid bread wheat, better in colder climates, was imported from the north shores of the Black Sea. Cultivation with a simple wooden plough (ard), sometimes tipped with iron, to break up the surface of the soil for receiving seeds in autumn, is treated as normal by ancient sources but recently doubts have arisen as to whether smallholders could produce enough to feed a pair of plough-oxen in addition to their own households. For them hand cultivation by spade and hoe must have been common (see AGRICULTURAL IMPLEMENTS).

The practice of leaving half the land in uncultivated fallow is also regarded as normal by our sources while repeated ploughing of the fallow was desirable. But again, smallholders may have been forced to risk long-term depletion of the soil by resting much less than half their land each year. Some leguminous field crops (broad beans and various lentils (pulses)) were known in Mycenaean times and in *Homer. By the 4th cent. BC they were recommended as partial alternatives to fallow (either as crops in their own right or as green manure to be ploughed under); it is not clear how early or how widely they were employed in rotation with wheat and barley. The moisture and soil requirements of wheat made it an often unreliable crop in the Greek *climate. Barley, somewhat less nutritious and much less esteemed, was probably grown more widely. (See CEREALS.) Frequent local crop failures required supplementation through trade with less affected neighbours or over longer distances. While it is unlikely that overseas settlements of the 8th and 7th cents. BC had as a prime goal assistance to the grain supply of the mother cities, once established in *Magna Graecia and *Sicily or, later, on the northern Black Sea coast and its approaches (see EUXINE), the existence of surpluses in the new settlements at times of shortage in the old lessened the chances of famine and set in motion rhythms of trade with far-reaching consequences. How early the larger Greek towns came to depend on imported grain is disputed. Some have seen Athenian colonies on the *Hellespont in the later 6th cent. as established on the route of the city's grain supply but for Athens explicit evidence comes only in the late 5th cent. Meanwhile by c.470 BC the Ionian city of *Teos included interference with the city's grain supply among the targets of public curses (ML 30; Fornara, no. 63).

Other crops, chiefly olives, grapes, and the vegetables and fruits grown in irrigated gardens (kēpoi), supplemented the largely cereal diet. *Olive oil and *wine also permitted *trade, not least for the acquisition of grain in times of shortage. Greek settlement was rarely at elevations or latitudes too cold for the olive. Since the trees matured slowly (in ten to fifteen years), they were planted for long-term benefits and not in large numbers everywhere. Olive cultivation was not demanding once young trees had been established and no longer needed *irrigation, but harvesting and, with only primitive *technology (though improved in the 4th cent. BC and again in Roman times), oil production required much labour. By contrast, vines grew fast and demanded much hard work from the start.

For the Greeks improvement of agricultural property meant, after the creation of suitable plots of land, investment in trees and vines (see ARBORICULTURE) together with the necessary equipment, including store-rooms and containers for storing and shipping oil and wine. However, interplanting of cereals, pulses, vines, and trees in a single plot, or polyculture using separate plots, were probably always more common than specialization in a single crop.

Animal husbandry on a small scale (plough-oxen and mules,

donkeys as pack animals, some sheep, goats, and pigs) probably had a place on all but the smallest properties. Larger herds were moved to mountain pastures in the summer (see PASTORALISM; TRANSHUMANCE). The value of manuring was appreciated and organic wastes were collected conscientiously from settlements and applied especially to trees and vines. But the amount available in the absence of lush pastures and large numbers of cattle close to the farms limited its effect.

Nowhere in old Greece did the geography and the nature of the agriculture favour large, unitary estates farmed by a large labour-force, though properties increased in size in Hellenistic and especially Roman times. The wealthy usually owned several parcels of land whose environmental diversity may have been advantageous. Poorer farmers were more limited. The particular agricultural regimes in use varied with local social and economic conditions as well as with geography. *Thessaly's extensive good grain land was long controlled by a small upper class and farmed by a large population of serfs, as were *Laconia and *Messenia, less suited to grains but probably slow to develop crops for trading. The islands of *Chios and Corcyra had rich estates concentrating on vines and olives and cultivated by unusually large numbers of slaves (see SLAVERY).

*Attica up to the *Peloponnesian War was also known for its fine country houses, a measure of rural prosperity (Thuc. 2. 65. 2). Its relatively large landless (or inadequately landed) population were not primarily farm labourers, and significant use of slave labour by the top three property classes is indicated. But for all except the rich, hired or slave labour only supplemented that of the landowner and his family.

The range of possibilities open to the Greek farmer for increasing production were restricted and most required additional labour. Intensity and efficiency of agricultural production were neither uniform nor static, nor independent of social and economic factors, even if the ideal of self-sufficiency (autarkeia) was prevalent and other relevant concepts were largely unexamined. The agricultural information in *Xenophon (1)'s Oeconomicus, informative for us, was no doubt banal. But beginning in the 4th cent. BC an extensive technical literature developed (cf. references in *Theophrastus' botanical writings) which was used by Roman writers (see AGRICULTURAL WRITERS) but is almost entirely lost to us.

M.-C. Amouretti, Le Pain et l'huile dans la Grèce antique (1986); A. Burford, Land and Labor in the Greek World (1993); T. Gallant, Risk and Survival in Ancient Greece (1991); P. Garnsey, Famine and Food Supply in the Graeco-Roman World (1988); S. Hodkinson, in C. R. Whittaker (ed.), Pastoral Economies in Classical Antiquity (1988); S. Isager and J. E. Skydsgaard, Ancient Greek Agriculture (1992); R. Osborne, Classical Landscape with Figures (1987); W. Richter, Die Landwirtschaft im homerische Zeitalter, Archaeologia Homerica 2:H (1968); R. Sallares, The Ecology of the Ancient Greek World (1991); B. Wells (ed.), Agriculture in Ancient Greece (1992). M. H. J.

agriculture, Roman By modern standards Roman agriculture was technically simple, average yields were low, transport was difficult and costly, and storage was inefficient. This limited urbanization (and hence 'industrialization') and obliged the bulk of the population to live and work on the land. Nevertheless, in the late republic and earlier Principate agriculture and urbanization (see URBANISM (Roman)) developed together to levels probably not again matched until the late 18th cent. Roman agriculture broadly fits the ahistoric pattern which is commonly seen as characteristic of the Mediterranean region: based on the triad of *cereals, vines (see WINE) and *olives, at the mercy of a semi-arid *climate with low and unreliable rainfall, and dominated by small farms practising a polyculture aimed principally at self-sufficiency and safety. But two factors—the geophysical diversity of Italy (let alone of Rome's provinces), and the effects of political and social developments—led to historically important variations between areas and across time in the organization and practice of agriculture. The last 40 years have seen an enormous growth in archaeological research—surface survey of rural areas, excavations of farmsteads, study of the ancient environment (through pollen, seeds, bones)—which is taking our knowledge and understanding of Roman agriculture far beyond what could be discovered from the evidence of the literary sources.

In archaic Rome the land seems to have been controlled by the élite, and the majority of Romans were dependant labourers (*nexi*). The concept of private ownership of land (*ager privatus*) had probably developed by the late 6th cent. BC, and by the later 4th cent. Rome had become a state of citizen-smallholders. The political aim behind this development was the creation of a large conscript army of smallholders who could afford to arm themselves (the *assidui*); as this army defeated Rome's Italian neighbours the Roman state annexed tracts of their territories which were often distributed in small plots to create more *assidui*, although some was left as nominally 'public' land (*ager publicus*) and appears to have been dominated by the élite who now used enslaved enemies as their main agricultural workforce. This cycle of conquest, annexation, and settlement continued, almost without interruption, into the early second century BC, and settlement schemes, albeit thereafter using confiscated land, continued into the early Principate. The face of Italy was changed: forests were cleared and drainage schemes undertaken, as in south Etruria and in the Po valley; the territories of the ubiquitous Roman colonies were divided into small farms of similar size by rectangular grids of ditches, banks, and roads (*centuriation) which are often still traceable today; these examples and the obligation on most of Rome's Italian allies to supply infantry on the Roman model encouraged the wider diffusion of this pattern of peasant smallholding.

Rome's massive overseas expansion in the 2nd and 1st cent. BC boosted agricultural developments which had already begun in the 3rd cent. The large and long-serving armies of conquest required huge supplies of grain, wine, wool, and leather, the Celtic aristocracy under and beyond Roman rule enthusiastically adopted wine-drinking as a mark of status, and the city of Rome swelled as the capital of an empire and the centre for conspicuous consumption and display by its increasingly wealthy leaders. The boom in demand for agricultural produce, and the continuous supply of cheap slave labour, encouraged the élite to expand their landholdings and to invest in market-oriented production. A significant differentiation between larger and smaller farms emerges in the archaeological record, and also regional patterns of types of agriculture. While in southern Italy relatively extensive forms of agriculture, that is cereal cultivation using chaingangs of slaves and large-scale stockbreeding with seasonal movement between upland summer pastures and winter stations in the coastal plains (*transhumance), were probably predominant, central western Italy (the semicircle around Rome and her main ports) was dominated by the so-called '*villa system', that is intensive production on medium-sized estates (around 25 to 75 ha.; 60 to 180 acres) of wine, olive oil, and other cash crops, including wheat (see CEREALS), vegetables, fruit (see FOOD AND DRINK), and also small game and poultry, with a permanent nucleus of skilled slave labour topped up at seasonal peaks with casual labour hired from the free rural poor. These forms of agriculture flourished into the 2nd cent. AD with some reorientation: consumption by the frontier-based armies of the Principate and the Celtic aristocracy was increasingly met by the development of local Roman-influenced agricultural production, but the growth of Rome and general urbanization of Italy in the Augustan period greatly increased domestic demand in Italy. Roman estate owners showed considerable interest in technical and technological improvements, such as experimentation with and selection of particular plant varieties and breeds of animal, the development of more efficient presses and of viticultural techniques in general, concern with the productive deployment and control of labour, and, arguably, a generally 'economically rational' attitude to exploitation of their landholdings (see TECHNOLOGY). A technical literature of estate management emerged, drawing on Carthaginian and Hellenistic predecessors, which is represented to us principally by the manuals of *Cato (Censorius), *Varro, and *Columella (see AGRICULTURAL WRITERS).

The development of this estate agriculture put pressure on the peasant smallholders, although military needs led to some dramatic and bitterly opposed attempts to revive an independent peasantry in central Italy, notably the Gracchan programme (see SEMPRONIUS GRACCHUS (3), TI. and SEMPRONIUS GRACCHUS, C.) of the later 2nd cent. and the settlement schemes for veterans in the 1st cent. BC. The decline of the peasantry should not be exaggerated: excavated small farms show that some peasants too produced for and profited from the same markets as the large estates, and in hillier areas and the Po (Padus) valley the peasantry remained strong. But as the Roman army became mercenary and then, under Augustus, professional and more cosmopolitan, the political will to maintain an independent peasantry in Italy gradually evaporated, and it seems that peasants increasingly became tenants rather than owners of small farms. The problems of the 3rd cent. AD reduced the inflow of imperial revenues to Rome and Italy, and as the level of urbanization and demand for agricultural produce declined, so did intensive farming. Large estates were becoming more concentrated in the hands of a fewer noble families (and the Church), and the legal standing of the poor declined further. The result was a tendency, not general but widespread, to move to more extensive agriculture based on the labour of tied tenants (see COLONI), although paradoxically this was the period in which Roman-influenced estate agriculture flourished most in some of the less troubled provinces, notably Britain and Egypt. See AGRICULTURAL IMPLEMENTS; FARM-BUILDINGS; LATIFUNDIA; PASTORALISM; PEASANTS; PLOUGHING.

GENERAL K. D. White, *A Bibliography of Roman Agriculture* (1970); K. D. White, *Roman Farming* (1970); W. E. Heitland, *Agricola: A Study of Agriculture and Rustic Life in the Graeco-Roman World from the Point of View of Labour* (1921); A. J. Toynbee, *Hannibal's Legacy: The Hannibalic War's Effects on Roman Life* (1965); P. A. Brunt, *Italian Manpower 225 BC–AD 14* (1971); A. Sirago, *L'Italia agraria sotto Traiano* (1958); L. Cracco Ruggini, *Economia e società nell'Italia annonaria: Rapporti fra agricoltura e commercio dal IV al VI secolo d.C.* (1961).

ARCHAEOLOGY T. W. Potter, *The Changing Landscape of South Etruria* (1979); K. Greene, *The Archaeology of the Roman Economy* (1986); G. Barker and J. Lloyd (eds.), *Roman Landscapes: Archaeological Survey in the Mediterranean Region* (1991); J. Percival, *The Roman Villa* (1976); A. Carandini (ed.), *Settefinestre: Una villa schiavistica nell'Etruria romana* (1985); R. Hingley, *Rural Settlement in Roman Britain* (1989); M. K. Jones and G. Dimbleby (eds.), *The Environment of Man: The Iron Age to the Anglo-Saxon Period* (1981).

SPECIFIC TOPICS K. D. White, *Agricultural Implements of the Roman*

World (1967); K. D. White, *Farm Equipment of the Roman World* (1975); J. Kolendo, *L'agricoltura nell'Italia romana* (1980); A. Tchernia, *Le Vin de l'Italie romaine* (1986); M. S. Spurr, *Arable Cultivation in Roman Italy* (1986); E. Gabba and M. Pasquinucci, *Strutture agrarie e allevamento transumante nell'Italia romana (III–I sec. a.C.)* (1979); J. M. Frayn, *Sheep-Rearing and the Wool Trade in Italy during the Roman Period* (1984); P. W. de Neeve, *Colonus: Private Farm-Tenancy in Roman Italy during the Republic and Early Principate* (1984); J. M. Frayn, *Subsistence Farming in Roman Italy* (1979); D. W. Rathbone, *Economic Rationalism and Rural Society in Third-Century AD Egypt* (1991).   D. W. R.

Agrippa, Pyrrhonist *sceptic; dates unknown, but later than *Aenesidemus. Diogenes Laertius (9. 88) ascribes to him a set of five modes (τρόποι) of argument introduced to supplement or replace the older Modes of Aenesidemus, and frequently used by *Sextus Empiricus.

J. Barnes, *The Toils of Scepticism* (1990).   G. S.

Agrippa See VIPSANIUS AGRIPPA, M.

Agrippa I–II, Herodian kings. See IULIUS AGRIPPA (1–2), M.

Agrippa Postumus See IULIUS CAESAR, AGRIPPA.

Agrippina See IULIA AGRIPPINA ('the younger Agrippina'); VIPSANIA AGRIPPINA (1); VIPSANIA AGRIPPINA (2) ('the elder Agrippina').

Agroecius, bishop of Sens (*c*. AD 470) and associate of *Sidonius Apollinaris, wrote a treatise on spelling, *De orthographia* (ed. Keil, *Gramm. Lat.* 7. 113–25), dedicated to Eucherius of Lyons, as a supplement to *Flavius Caper.

PLRE 2, 'Agroecius' 2 and 3; Schanz–Hosius 4/2. 206–7.   J. D. H.

Agyrrhius (fl. *c*.405–373 BC). Athenian politician, introduced payment of one obol for attending the assembly (see EKKLESIA), and later increased it from two obols to three; sometimes, but probably wrongly, thought to have introduced the *theōrika. He spent some years in prison as a debtor to the state, but must have resumed political activity afterwards, since a corn law proposed by him in 374/3 has recently been discovered. *Callistratus (2) was his nephew.

PA 179; *APF* 277–80.   P. J. R.

Ahhiyawa Country attested in the *Hattuša archives (alternative and older spelling, *Ahhiya*), as a foreign land, often associated with Arzawa, i.e. western Anatolia. References mention kings, persons, ships, and deities of Ahhiyawa, and in so far as they are datable, span the period *c*.1400–1220 BC. At least one king of Ahhiyawa was ranked as a 'Great King', thus the equal of the Hittite and Egyptian kings. Location and identification remain controversial: the identification as 'Achaean' (Mycenaean) Greece by Forrer in 1920 has been much disputed. Arguments against emphasize the difficulty both of seeing an early form of *Achaea* in *Ahhiyawa*, and of identifying archaeologically a political entity in Greece or the Aegean islands which could correspond to the character of Ahhiyawa. Some also seek to locate Ahhiyawa on the Anatolian mainland. Arguments in favour, which have been regaining ground since *c*.1980 with the increasing evidence for a Mycenaean presence in western Anatolia, emphasize principally the improbability that the *Hittites, with their interest in western Anatolia, should never have mentioned the Mycenaeans. The location of Ahhiyawa across the sea from Anatolia, following the natural interpretation of the references, is also adduced. See MYCENAEAN CIVILIZATION.

T. R. Bryce, *OJA* 1989, 297–310.   J. D. Ha.

Ahuramazda, ('Ωρομάσδης, 'Ωρομάζης), 'the Wise Lord' or 'Lord Wisdom', Iranian supreme deity in the Avesta and in OP inscriptions. He is the wise, benevolent god, invoked as the creator and the upholder of *aša* ('rightness, truth') by Zarathuštra (*Yasna* 31. 8) and as the creator of heaven and earth by the Persian kings. In almost all inscriptions he is the only god and the special protector of kingship. Greeks equated him with *Zeus (Hdt. 1. 189). Greek. 'Ωρομάζης is first attested in the 4th cent. BC (Pl. *Alc.* 1. 122a). See RELIGION, PERSIAN.

M. Boyce, *Enc. Ir.* 1. 684–7, 'Ahura Mazda'; F. B. J. Kuiper, *JIJ* 1976, 25–42. See RELIGION, PERSIAN.   H. S.-W.

Ai Khanoum, Greek Hellenistic city excavated (1965–78) by the French archaeological delegation in Afghanistan, is situated in the eastern part of *Bactria, at the junction of the river *Oxus (mod. Amu Darya) and a tributary of the left bank, the Kokcha river, at the frontier between Afghanistan and the former Soviet Union. The Greek name of the city is uncertain. It seems to have been built as a fortified frontier town, to guard against the nomadic tribes to the north and the mountain peoples to the east (the Badakhshan range). It was founded, commanding a fertile plain, by the end of the 4th cent. or in the early 3rd cent. BC, in an area where there had been earlier settlement, as indicated by an irrigation system and an Achaemenid fortress. Ai Khanoum passed from Seleucid control to that of the so-called Indo-Bactrian kings, certainly by the reign of *Eucratides (*c*.172–155 BC) of Bactria. In *c*. the mid-2nd cent. BC it was destroyed by invasions from the Saca tribes. The buildings discovered include administrative quarters, a *temenos, a *gymnasium, a theatre, several rich private dwellings, a citadel where a garrison was installed, a palace built on the Persian style, and two temples built to Mesopotamian plan and decorated in Mesopotamian style. The site was surrounded by vast, impressive fortifications.

P. Bernard, *CRAcad. Inscr.* 1976, 287 f.; 1978, 421 f. and *Fouilles d'Ai Khanoum* (1973–); P. Bernard and others, *BÉFEO* 1980, 1–87; C. Rapin, *Rev. Arch.* 1987, 41 f. (bibliog.); S. Sherwin-White and A. Kuhrt, *From Samarkhand to Sardis* (1993).   S. S.-W.

Aias (Αἴας, Lat. Aiax). (1) Son of *Telamon (1), king of *Salamis (1), hence Aias Telamonius. He brought twelve ships from Salamis to Troy (*Il*. 2. 557). In the *Iliad* he is of enormous (πελώριος) size, head and shoulders above the rest (3. 226–9), and the greatest of the Greek warriors after *Achilles (2. 768–9). His stock epithet is 'bulwark (ἕρκος) of the Achaeans', and his characteristic weapon a huge shield of seven-fold ox-hide. He clearly has the better of *Hector in a duel (7. 181–305) after which the heroes exchange gifts, Aias giving Hector a sword-belt in return for a sword; and he is at his memorable best when with unshakeable courage he defends the Greek wall and then the ships (see esp. 15. 676–88, 727–46, 16. 101–11). He is also a member of the Embassy to Achilles, when he gives a brief but effective appeal to Achilles on friendship's grounds (9. 624–42). At *Patroclus' funeral games he draws a wrestling match with *Odysseus, strength against cunning (23. 708–39).

The *Aethiopis* told how after Achilles' death Aias carried his body off the field of battle while Odysseus kept back the Trojans (cf. *Od*. 5. 309f.). The *Little Iliad* (Proclus) told how the arms of Achilles were then adjudged to Odysseus instead of Aias, who went mad with anger, killed the herds of the Greeks, believing them to be the Greek leaders, and then committed suicide. See EPIC CYCLE. *Sophocles (1) dramatizes these later events in his *Ajax*, but at the end of the play Aias is taken to an honourable burial, in marked contrast to his treatment in the *Little Iliad* (fr. 3

Davies) where he is denied the customary burial honours (see J. R. March, *BICS* 1991–2, 1–36). In the *Odyssey*, when Odysseus is in Hades, he meets the shade of Aias who, in anger at his loss of Achilles' arms, refuses to speak and stalks away in magnificent *silence (11. 543–64).

In the Hesiodic *Great Ehoiai* (fr. 250 M–W) and thence in Pindar (*Isthm.* 6. 35 ff.) *Heracles visits Telamon and, standing on the lion-skin, prays that his new-born son may be as stout (ἄρρηκτος) as the skin; *Zeus, in answer, sends an eagle, αἰετος, and hence the baby is named Aias. From this develops the story (Lycoph. 455 ff.; cf. Aesch. *Thracian Women*, fr. 83 Radt) that Aias was invulnerable save at one point, where the skin had not touched him when (in this version) he was wrapped in it. It was later said that when he killed himself his blood flowed on the ground and there sprang up the iris (ὑάκινθος) which also commemorates the death of *Hyacinthus; hence the markings on its petals recall the hero's name (Αἴας—αἰαι; see Ov. *Met.* 13. 394 ff.). Aias had a cult in Salamis, Attica, Megara (?), the Troad, and Byzantium: see L. R. Farnell, *Greek Hero Cults* (1921), 305 ff. and n. 58.

Scenes from Aias' life popular in art, some from the 7th cent. BC, are combats with Hector and others, dicing with Achilles, lifting Achilles' body, the argument and voting about Achilles' arms, and (an especial favourite) his suicide: see O. Touchefeu, *LIMC* 1/1. 312–36.

(2) Son of Oïleus or Ileus, the Locrian chieftain. In Homer Aias leads the Locrian contingent to Troy with 40 ships (*Il.* 2. 527 ff.). He is 'much lesser' than Telamonian Aias (hence often called the Lesser Aias), quick-footed, and often paired with his great namesake as a brave fighter. He can, however, be an unpleasant character, on occasion grossly rude (23. 473 ff.), hated by *Athena (*Od.* 4. 502), and finally drowned by *Poseidon for blasphemy against the gods while scrambling ashore after shipwreck (*Od.* 4. 499–511).

In the *Iliu Persis* (Proclus) he dragged *Cassandra away from the statue of Athena to rape her, and in so doing loosened the statue from its plinth. This is a favourite scene in Archaic and Classical art: see O. Touchefeu, *LIMC* 1/1. 339–49. In historic times the Locrians sent two virgins annually to serve in the temple of Athena at *Ilium in expiation of this crime, the Locrians maintaining that this penalty was imposed for 1,000 years.

H. J. R.; J. R. M.

Aidōs See NEMESIS; SHAME.

Aion (Αἰών) was for late antiquity the personification and god of indefinitely extending time. In early Greek αἰών means 'life' (often in the sense of 'vital force'), 'whole lifetime', 'generation'. It was perhaps through application to the *kosmos*, the lifetime of which is never-ending, that the word acquired the sense of eternity (cf. Pl. *Ti.* 37d; Arist. *Cael.* 279ᵃ23–8). There is no good evidence for cult of Aion in the Classical or Hellenistic periods. The transition from philosophy to religious practice is first suggested by a statue of Aion dedicated at *Eleusis (at some time in the 1st cent. BC or AD) by three brothers 'for the power of Rome and continuation of the mysteries' (*Syll.*³ 1125): Aion is celebrated as 'ever remaining by divine nature the same' and closely linked with the single unchanging *kosmos*. Numerous developments occurred in the imperial period: Aion was identified with the power ruling the *kosmos* (so regularly in the *Corpus Hermeticum*, and sometimes in magical papyri, see MAGIC), with the sun (magical papyri), perhaps with the eternity of Rome and the

emperors (see AETERNITAS), and much else besides; in a festival at *Alexandria (1), probably of late foundation, an image was brought out of the inner sanctuary of the Koreion, with the announcement that 'the Maiden has brought forth Aion' (Epiph. *Adv. haeres.* 51. 22–3). But, though 'the word was widespread and clearly exercised a certain fascination', it 'did not carry with it any very definite connotation' (Nock). The identification of the lion-headed god of Mithraism (see MITHRAS) as a type of Aion remains controversial; so too does any possible influence exercised by the Iranian concept of Zurvān or primordial Time.

A. D. Nock, *Harv. Theol. Rev.* 1934, 78–99 (= *Essays on Religion and the Ancient World* (1972), 1. 377–96); D. Levi, *Hesp.* 1944, 269–314; A. J. Festugière, *La révélation d'Hermès Trismégiste* 4 (1954), 152–99; R. Beck, *ANRW* 2. 17. 4 (1984), 2086–9 (Mithraism); M. le Glay, *LIMC* 1. 399–411; G. Zuntz, *Aion: Gott des Römerreichs*, Abh. Heidelberg 1989/2 (cf. *CR* 1992, 212–13); R. R. R. Smith, *The Monument of C. Julius Zoilos* (1993), 45–8.
R. C. T. P.

aisymnētēs, according to *Aristotle (*Pol.* 1285ᵃ), a supreme ruler appointed by some early city-states in times of internal crisis, for life, for a prescribed period, or till the completion of the task, e.g. *Pittacus. Aristotle defines the office as an elective *tyranny; *Dionysius (7) of Halicarnassus (5. 73) compares the Roman *dictator. If Aristotle's account is accurate (and his definition has been questioned), these *aisymnētai* have affinities with the early lawgivers (*Solon, *Zaleucus, *Demonax, etc.), the difference presumably being one of local nomenclature. Inscriptions (*Syll.*³ 38, 57, 272, 642, 955) show regular magistrates so called in Teos, Miletus, Naxos, Megara, Selinus, and Chalcedon. The word first occurs in *Od.* 8. 258, meaning a referee (see Hainsworth's note; cf. also *Il.* 24. 347 with Richardson's note for the related word αἰσυμνητήρ).

F. Romer, *AJPhil.* 1982, 25 ff.; M. Gagarin, *Early Greek Law* (1986) 59 f.
P. N. U.; S. H.

Aither (Αἰθήρ), personification of the purer upper stratum of air (approximately the stratosphere), next to or identical with the sky; son of Erebus and Night (see NYX) (Hesiod, *Theog.* 124–5); of *Chaos and Darkness (Hyg. *Fab. pref.* I); husband of Day and of Earth (ibid. 2–3). See also TARTARUS.
H. J. R.

aius locutius (or **loquens**), the divine voice, 'sayer and speaker', that shortly before the battle of the *Allia warned of the Gauls. The warning was not heeded. As expiation a precinct (*templum*) and *altar (*ara*) were established near Vesta's shrine, on the via Nova, where the voice was heard.

Cic. *Div.* 1. 101, 2. 69 (with Pease's comm.); Livy 5. 32. 6, 50.5; Platner–Ashby, 3 f.
H. J. R.; J. L.

Ajax See AIAS.

Akkadian (1) Term used until 1869 for the language now known as *Sumerian. (2) Term used since 1869 for the East Semitic language that is also known by its northern and southern dialects as Assyrian and Babylonian. The language is first attested from personal names of the mid-3rd millennium when it began to supersede Sumerian. It was written on clay, stone, and waxed writing boards in *cuneiform script. A few late records preserve transcriptions into Greek. The latest datable records come from the early 1st cent. AD. As a spoken language it was gradually replaced by *Aramaic from *c.*800 BC onwards.

E. Reiner, *A Linguistic Analysis of Akkadian* (1966); T. B. Jones (ed.), *The Sumerian Problem* (1969).
S. M. D.

Alabanda, a city in northern *Caria, on the Marsyas, a tributary of the *Maeander, at the point where the road from *Tralles branches westward to *Halicarnassus and south to the coast opposite *Rhodes. Its site (now Arabhisar) between two hills is likened by Strabo to a pack-saddle. In the province of Asia it was a *civitas libera* (*free city). It was proverbial for its opulence and comfort, although claiming a Spartan ancestry. (See SPARTA.)

G. E. Bean, *Turkey beyond the Maeander* (1971), 180 f.
W. M. C.; S. S.-W.

alae In the republic *alae sociorum* were two bodies of Roman allies, including cavalry and infantry, each equivalent in size to a *legion, which fought on the wings (*alae*) of the battle-line. After the *Social War (3) (91–87 BC) the Romans increasingly recruited cavalry from native peoples, and *Caesar used Gallic and German cavalry units to great effect, usually placing them under their own commanders (*praefecti equitum*). During the Civil Wars some native contingents were used by the military dynasts under the command of Roman officers or veteran soldiers. In *Augustus' reorganization of the army, many non-Roman infantry and cavalry units were incorporated into the formal structure of the army as *auxilia. *Alae* (now used exclusively for cavalry) normally consisted of about 480–500 men divided into sixteen troops; probably from Flavian times, milliary *alae* with about 800–1,000 men divided into 24 troops were introduced. *Alae* were commanded by equestrian prefects, who in the three posts often held by equestrian officers (*tres militiae*) ranked above the prefects of auxiliary cohorts and military tribunes. Cavalrymen of the *alae* probably received 1,050 sesterces a year under Augustus, equivalent to the pay of a legionary cavalryman and more than that of a legionary infantryman (see STIPENDIUM). *Alae* were originally enlisted from ethnic groups and although this racial character was subsequently diluted by wider recruiting including the admission of some citizens, they often retained their regional titles (e.g. 'first *ala* of Spanish'); a few bore personal names indicating the officer who had first raised or commanded them (e.g. '*ala Agrippiana*'); many were named after an emperor as a mark of honour or because he had recruited them; and some titles indicated methods of fighting. A combination of these can produce very long designations (e.g. 'third Augustan *ala* of Thracian archers, Roman citizens').

Alae survived into the later empire as cavalry units among the frontier troops, ranking below cavalry *vexillationes*.

See bibliography under AUXILIA.
J. B. C.

Alamanni (Alemanni), 'All Men', a Germanic people, forming a loose confederation of tribes in western Germany in the 3rd and later cents. AD. The Iuthungi are often mentioned as participating in their activities. Their raids on the Roman provinces became serious from the 250s. In the 4th cent. they exploited Roman abandonment of the *Agri Decumates to settle south of the river Main. They frequently harassed Gaul, but their chief danger to the empire lay in their ability to invade Italy from over the Alps; it was against this threat that Aurelian walled Rome (*wall of Aurelian). The diffusion of political power (among many kings and princes) ensured that, though often defeated in battle, the Alamanni could never be broken by Rome. They remained troublesome throughout the 4th cent. In the 5th cent., though they moved into Alsace and northern Switzerland, they were eclipsed by other Germanic invaders: *Visigoths, *Burgundians, and, most notably, *Franks.

R. Roeren, *JRGZM* 1960, 214 ff.
J. F. Dr.

Alans, *nomadic pastoralists who lived in the northern *Pontus in the early cents. AD, operating politically in a number of separate subgroups. They often tried to cross the Caucasus—*Arrian, when governor of *Cappadocia, beat off one such attack—but Roman emperors from *Nero onwards fortified the region's western exits against them. In the late 4th cent., the *Huns overran their territory, conquering some groups, and driving others westwards. These crossed the Rhine on 31 December 406, some subsequently being absorbed into the Hasding *Vandal monarchy in Spain, others reaching accommodations with the Roman state in Gaul.
P. J. H.

Alaric, Gothic leader *c.* AD 395–410 who created the *Visigoths. By 408 he had united the Tervingi and Greuthungi who had crossed the Danube in 376 with survivors of Radagaisus' force which had invaded Italy in 406. He approached the Roman state with a mixture of force and diplomacy to extract an advantageous, but above all permanent, settlement. In search of this, he switched the focus of his operations from the Balkans and the eastern half of the empire, to Italy and the west (first in 402, then permanently after 408). He sacked Rome on 24 August 410 when the emperor *Honorius refused to negotiate; he died a few months later, after briefly threatening to transfer his Goths to Africa.

H. Wolfram, *History of the Goths* (1988), pt. 2; W. Liebeschuetz, *Barbarians and Bishops* (1990), ch. 3; P. J. Heather, *Goths and Romans 332–489* (1991), chs. 5–6.
P. J. H.

Alastor, avenging deity or *daimōn. Personification of the *curse which falls on a family through guilt. The *alastōr* exacts punishment for murder by causing new bloodshed and ensuring continuity of guilt as in the successive generations of *Atreus' family. After killing her husband *Agamemnon, *Clytemnestra identifies with 'the ancient bitter avenger (*alastōr*)' of *Atreus (Aesch. *Ag.* 1501), that is the 'spirit (*daimōn*) thrice glutted' on the blood of Thyestes, Atreus, and Agamemnon (*Ag.* 1476–7). She dies in turn at the hands of her son, who as *alastōr* becomes both curse and victim (Aesch. *Eum.* 236). *Oedipus describes his own *alastōr* as the curse that lies on his land (Soph. *OC* 788). *Alastōr* therefore is a suitable epithet for the *Erinyes. But the divine spirit of retribution can also work outside the family and lead *Xerxes to destruction at Salamis (Aesch. *Pers.* 354). By the 4th cent. BC *alastōr* had sunk to a common term of abuse meaning 'scoundrel' or 'wretch' (Dem. 18. 296, 19. 305).

In Homer's *Iliad* three minor characters are called Alastor. One is a follower of *Nestor (*Il.* 4. 295), and the other two on the Trojan side. The first is a Lycian killed by *Odysseus (*Od.* 5. 677), and the other father of Tros who is killed by *Achilles (*Od.* 20. 463).
H. J. R.; B. C. D.

Alba Fucens, a Latin colony of 6,000 (see IUS LATII) founded by Rome in 303 BC, on a hill above the *Fucine lake in central Italy. It was connected to Rome by the *via Valeria, a route of great antiquity. Alba usually supported the Roman government, e.g. against *Hannibal, the *socii* (90 BC; see SOCIAL WAR (3)), *Caesar, and M. *Antonius (2) (Mark Antony). In the 2nd cent. BC, dethroned kings such as *Syphax were confined here. The walls, which extend for nearly 3 km. (1¾ mi.), originated in the 3rd cent. BC, and the town saw substantial replanning in the 1st cent. BC. Extensive excavations have revealed the forum, basilica, shops, temples, theatres, amphitheatre, etc. Decline began in the 3rd cent. AD, and the place is not mentioned after 537 when Justinian's troops were stationed here.

Alba Longa

J. Mertens, *Alba Fucens* 1–2 (1969); F. de Ruyt, *Alba Fucens*, 3 (1982).
T. W. P.

Alba Longa, on the *Albanus mons, near modern Castel Gandolfo, traditionally founded *c.*1152 BC by *Ascanius (*Aen.* 3. 390 f.), and supposed founder of other Latin cities. There are rich cemeteries of the Latian culture, extending back to the 10th cent. BC. Apparently it once headed a league (of Prisci Latini? see Festus 253 Lindsay), the nature and members of which cannot be exactly determined: lists in Diodorus Siculus (7. 5), Dionysius (*Ant. Rom.* 4. *Rom.* 92, 5. 61), and Pliny (*HN* 3. 69), like surviving lists of Alban kings, are untrustworthy. Alba lost its primacy in Latium perhaps in the 7th cent. BC, allegedly through its destruction by Rome: some families are said to have migrated to Rome (Iulii, Tullii, etc.: Livy 1. 29 f.; Tac. *Ann.* 11. 24), while others joined neighbouring *Bovillae and preserved Alban cults and memorials until late times (*Albani Longani Bovillenses: ILS* 6188 f.). Alba was never rebuilt, but modern Albano preserves its name (from *Albanum* = Domitian's Alban *villa, which became a legionary camp under *Septimius Severus and subsequently the nucleus of today's town). Alban *wine and building stone (*peperino*) were famous.

F. Dionisi, *La scoperta topografica di Alba Longa* (1961); P. G. Gierow, *The Iron Age Cultures of Latium*, 1 (1966), 2/1 (1964); G. Lugli, *La villa di Domiziano* (1918), and *Ausonia* 10 (1921), 211 ff.; E. Tortorici, *Castra Albana* (1975); A. P. Anzidei and others, *Roma e il Lazio* (1985), 150 f.
E. T. S.; T. W. P.

Albania (Transcaucasian), the land between *Iberia and the *Caspian, to the north of *Media Atropatene: it now lies largely within northern Azerbaijan and Daghestan. Albania comprises an extensive and quite dry plain, with the eastern spur of the main Caucasus to the north: pastoralism was widespread, though archaeology indicates agriculture and significant settlements (so too notably *Ptolemy (4)). Through Albania, past Derbend, lay the easiest and most-frequented route south across the Caucasus. In extant manuscripts of classical texts the Albani are often confused inextricably with the *Alans across the mountains to the north. The Albani are first mentioned in the context of Alexander III's campaigns. Pompey brought them within the Roman sphere in 65 BC: a mythical link with *Alba Longa was claimed.

K. V. Trever, *Ocherki po istorii kul' tury Kavkazskoy Albanii* (1959); K. Aliev, *Kavkazskaya Albania (Iv. do n.e.–Iv.n.e.)* (1974); G. A. Koshelenko (ed.), *Drevneishiye gosudarstva Kavkaza i Srednei Azii* (1985) 93–105; A. A. Akopian, *Albania-Aluank v greko-latinskikh i drevnearmyanskikh istochnikakh* (1987).
D. C. B.

Albanus lacus (mod. Lago Albano), 'Alban Lake', a crater lake in the *Albanus mons near Rome. Its wooded banks in imperial times were studded with *villas, e.g. *Domitian's. Lacking natural outlets, its waters reach the Rivus Albanus, and thence the Tiber, via a tunnel, 1,800 m. (1,968 yds.) in length, through the crater rim built *c.*397 BC. The Romans reputedly excavated this *emissarium* to ensure the fall of *Veii which, an oracle prophesied, awaited the overflowing of the lake (Livy 5. 15–19). Actually their motive was to carry off the waters rapidly for *irrigation purposes (Cic. *Div.* 2. 69); otherwise seepage through the porous subsoil would have waterlogged the districts below.

Ogilivie, *Comm. Livy 1–5*, 658 ff.; G. Lugli, *La villa di Domiziano* (1918).
E. T. S.; T. W. P.

Albanus mons, the Alban hills and more specifically their dominating peak (Monte Cavo, 950m. (3, 115 ft)), 21km. (13 mi.) south-east of Rome. Until *c.*1150 BC the Albanus mons was an active volcano, discouraging dense population in *Latium; the volcano, however, has been inactive in historical times. On the summit stood the Latin federal sanctuary of Jupiter Latiaris where Roman consuls celebrated the *feriae Latinae* (Dion. Hal. 4. 49; the antiquity of the festival probably is underestimated). Remains exist, not indeed of the temple, but of the via Triumphalis leading to it; here at least five Roman generals celebrated *ovations after being refused regular *triumphs in Rome (e.g. M. *Claudius Marcellus (1) in 211 BC: Livy 26. 21).

On the iron age in the Alban hills generally, see P. G. Gierow, *The Iron Age Culture of Latium* 2/1 (1964); A. M. Bietti Sestieri, *The Iron Age Community of Osteria dell'Osa* (1992), 221 ff. E. T. S.; D. W. R. R.

Albinovanus, Celsus, secretary of *Tiberius, whom he accompanied to Armenia in 21–20 BC, and friend of *Horace (*Epist.* 1. 3. 15–20, 8. 1), who gently rebukes him for writing excessively imitative poetry.

*PIR*² A 478.
E. C.

Albinovanus Pedo, a well-known wit and raconteur (Sen. *Ep.* 122. 15; Quint. *Inst.* 9. 3. 61) who exercised his wit in writing epigrams; *Martial often mentions him as one of his models. He also wrote epic, a *Theseid* (Ov. *Pont.* 4. 10. 71) and a poem from which the elder Seneca (*Suas.* 1. 15, to illustrate the theme 'Alexander debates whether to sail the Ocean') quotes 23 lines about *Germanicus' North Sea expedition in AD 16. Pedo himself probably served as *praefectus* under *Germanicus (Tac. *Ann.* 1. 60. 2); the piece is loaded with melodramatic rhetoric and topics applied by declaimers (see DECLAMATION) to *Alexander (3) the Great. Pedo was a friend of Ovid and known personally to the younger Seneca (*Ep.* 122. 15; Sen. *Controv.* 2. 2. 12).

*PIR*² A 479; Courtney, *FLP* 315.
E. C.

Albinus (emperor) see CLODIUS SEPTIMIUS ALBINUS, DECIMUS.

Albinus (1), Platonist philosopher, pupil of *Gaius (2). Taught at Smyrna, where Galen heard him lecture in AD 151–2. The only extant writing which is certainly his is a brief preface to Plato's dialogues (*Prologos* or *Eisagōgē*), concerned with their classification and the order in which they should be studied. He also published a collection of the lectures of his master Gaius, which has been lost. The attribution to him by J. Freudenthal in 1879 of the *Didaskalikos*, or 'Handbook of Platonism' of Alcinous has recently been convincingly impugned. See ALCINOUS (2).

Text in C. F. Hermann's Teubner edn. of Plato (1853), 6. 147 ff.
J. M. D.

Albinus (2), writer on music, geometry, and dialectic, probably identical with Ceionius Rufius Albinus (*PLRE* 1 'Albinus' 14), the consul of AD 335, and perhaps with the poet of works entitled *De metris* and *Res romanae*; one fragment of each survives.

PLRE 1. 33 f.; Teuffel–Kroll, § 407. 5; Herzog–Schmidt, § 492; Courtney, *FLP* 425; Kaster, *Guardians*, 382 f. E. C.; R. A. K.

Albion, ancient (Celtic or pre-Celtic) name for the largest of the British Isles, first recorded in the 1st cent. AD, by when it had been superseded (among Romans) by 'Britannia': ps.-Arist. *Mund.* 393ᵇ12 (50 BC–AD 100?); Pliny, *HN* 4. 102. A reference to Albiones, an island-people two days' coasting from the tin-isles of the Oestrymnides in the *Sea Coast* of *Avianus (4th cent. AD), taken over from the earlier Greek *periploi*, was once thought to reflect Archaic Greek knowledge of Britain. In fact it perpetuates an earlier error of Greek geography (by *Ephorus?) which transferred to a British context a description of the tin-bearing region around Portugal's Cape Finisterra (see TIN).

C. Hawkes, *Pytheas: Europe and the Greek Explorers*, 8th Myres Memorial Lecture (1977).   E. H. W.; A. J. S. S.

Albucius (*RE* 2), **Titus**, senator and orator, who in youth had studied in Athens. *Lucilius (1) satirized the absurdities of his Graecomania (88–93 Marx), and *Cicero called him 'learned in Greek letters, or rather virtually a Greek' (*Brut.* 131). Despite being an Epicurean (see EPICURUS), he held magistracies and became governor of *Sardinia *c.*106 or 104 BC. Condemned for extortion there, he spent his *exile in philosophical study at Athens (Cic. *Scaur.* 40; *Tusc.* 5. 108).

Broughton, *MRR* 1. 556, 560, 3. 14.   C. J. F.; M. T. G.

Albucius Silus, Gaius, Augustan orator and teacher of rhetoric, from Novaria (Novara) in *Cisalpine Gaul. His life is summarized by Suetonius (*Gram. et Rhet.* 30 Brugnoli). The elder Seneca, who regarded him as one of the four outstanding declaimers of his day (see DECLAMATION), gives a vivid picture of a vulnerable personality (*Controv.* 7 pref.).

PIR² A 489; Schanz–Hosius, § 336. 4; W.-D. Lebek, *Hermes* 1966, 360–72.   M. W.

album An *album* was a whitened board or tablet on which information could be published in writing. Such tablets were widely used in Roman public life, for example to publicize the *praetors' edicts. *Album* was also the standard term for a published list or register. The *album senatorium* was the official list of members of the *senate which was publicly posted outside the senate-house from the time of *Augustus. See also ANNALES MAXIMI.   T. J. Co.

Albunea, sulphurous spring and stream near *Tibur with a famous waterfall, and its homonymous nymph (cf. Hor. *Carm.* 1. 7. 12), classed as a *Sibyl by *Varro (Lactant. *Div. Inst.* 1. 6. 12) and fancifully identified by etymology with the sea-goddess *Ino-Leucothea (Servius on Verg. *Aen.* 7. 83). The spring is the Latin equivalent of Greek poetic springs like Castalia (see DELPHI) and Hippocrene (see HELICON); it is usually identified with the modern Acque Albule. In Virgil's *Aeneid* Albunea is the site of the incubation-oracle of *Faunus (7. 81–102), but this is otherwise unattested. The name derives from the white (*albus*) appearance of the spring's sulphurous water. (See SPRINGS, SACRED.)

F. Castagnoli, *Enc. Virg.* 'Albunea'.   S. J. Ha.

Alcaeus (1), lyric poet, of *Mytilene on Lesbos. Probably born *c.*625–620 BC, since he was old enough to participate in the struggle against Athens for *Sigeum in the Troad in the last decade of the century in which *Pittacus distinguished himself (fr. 428; Hdt. 5. 95; Diog. Laert. 1. 74; Strabo 13. 1. 38). Lesbian politics at this period were violent and confused. The ruling dynasty, the Penthilidae, who traced their descent from *Orestes, were weakened and finally overthrown by two successive coups (Arist. *Pol.* 1311ᵇ26, 29). Power passed to a tyrant named Melanchrus, who was overthrown by a faction headed by Pittacus and Alcaeus' brothers *c.*612–609 (*Suda*, entry under Πιττακός; Diog. Laert. 1. 74); Alcaeus (perhaps too young—fr. 75) was not involved (Diog. Laert. 1. 74). A new tyrant, Myrsilus, emerged, who was opposed unsuccessfully by a faction of exiles including Pittacus and Alcaeus (frs. 129, 114); Pittacus subsequently allied himself with Myrsilus, while his former comrades continued the struggle in exile (frs. 129, 70). After Myrsilus' death the people elected Pittacus *aisymnētēs (dictator) to ward off Alcaeus' faction (frs.

70, 348; Arist. *Pol.* 1285ᵃ35 ff.). Internal divisions within the faction contributed to its failure to oust Pittacus (fr. 70). Pittacus' marriage alliance with the Penthilidae probably belongs to this period (fr. 70), as may Alcaeus' journey to Egypt and his brother Antimenidas' service abroad (frs. 432, 350). An ancient critic (*POxy.* 2506. 98) indicates at least three periods of exile. Alcaeus' poetry is full of attacks on and abuse of Pittacus, for perjury and faithlessness, low birth (probably false), drunkenness, unbridled ambition, and physical defects (frs. 72, 129, 348; Diog. Laert. 1. 81). Popular opinion was with Pittacus, as in general is that of posterity. The tradition that Pittacus subsequently pardoned Alcaeus (Diog. Laert. 1. 76) is suspect.

Alcaeus' poetry was divided by the Alexandrians into at least ten books. It was monodic, and was composed in a variety of lyric metres in two- or four-line stanzas, including the alcaic stanza, named after him. The dialect is predominantly Lesbian vernacular, but epicisms are admitted. His range is rivalled only by *Archilochus in the Archaic period. He dealt with politics, war, wine, love, hymns to the gods, moralizing, and myth (though possibly both moralizing and myth were always subordinated to specific contexts). There is considerable variety in the treatment of each theme. Politics may be dealt with through personal abuse or the grandeur of myth and ritual or both (frs. 72, 129, 298; Diog. Laert. 1. 81); the invitation to drink may be supported by myth (fr. 38A) or the imperatives of the weather (frs. 338, 347). He is open to a range of influences. In his use of lyric for abuse he blurs the difference between lyric and iambus. His hymns are influenced by the rhapsodic tradition (see RHAPSODES). Fr. 347 recasts a passage of *Hesiod in lyric form. He has a vivid descriptive power and an impressive vigour, particularly in his arresting openings; his control of form and mood (the developed contrasts of frs. 42 and 338, the changes of mood and register in fr. 129, the extended metaphor of storm for civil strife in fr. 326, the accelerating tempo of the list in fr. 140) is often underrated. He was popular at Attic *symposia and a favourite with *Horace (*Carm.* 1. 32. 5 ff., 2. 13. 26 ff.).

TEXTS E. Lobel and D. L. Page, *Poetarum Lesbiorum Fragmenta* (1955); E. M. Voigt, *Sappho et Alcaeus* (1971); D. A. Campbell, *Greek Lyric* 1 (1983), 206–437.
TRANSLATION D. A. Campbell, *Greek Lyric* 1 (1983), 206–437.
CRITICISM D. L. Page, *Sappho and Alcaeus* (1955), 149 ff.; A. P. Burnett, *Three Archaic Poets* (1983), 107 ff.; *RE* Suppl. 11. 8 ff.   C. C.

Alcaeus (2) is called by the *Suda* a comedian of the Old Comedy (see COMEDY (GREEK), OLD) (κωμικὸς τῆς ἀρχαίας κωμῳδίας) and author of ten plays. His *Pasiphae* took the fifth (last) prize in 388 BC (hyp. 4 Ar. *Plut.*). Fragments of seven other plays survive; the titles suggest that he specialized in mythological burlesques.

PCG 2. 3 ff. (*CAF* 1. 756 ff.).   K. J. D.

Alcaeus (3), of Messene (fl. 200 BC), author of 22 epigrams from the *Garland* of *Meleager (2) on various themes, notably political attacks on *Philip (3) V of Macedon (who replied to one of them; Plut. *Flam.* 9). Also wrote abusive iambics (now lost).

F. W. Walbank, *CQ* 1942, 134–45; 1943, 1–13; A. Momigliano, *JRS* 1942, 53–8; C. Edson, *CPhil.* 1948, 116–21; T. B. L. Webster, *Hellenistic Poetry and Art* (1964), 233; Gow–Page, *HE*.   A. D. E. C.

Alcamenes, Athenian (or Lemnian) sculptor, active *c.*440–400 BC. *Phidias' favourite pupil, he made numerous statues of divinities in Athens and Boeotia, in gold and ivory, bronze, and marble. The sole survivor, from the Acropolis, is a group of Procne preparing to kill Itys, which Pausanias (1. 24. 3) says he dedicated.

Alcathous

Copies exist of his Hermes Propylaeus and Hecate Epipyrgidia, also for the Acropolis, establishing him as a pioneer of the archaizing style (see RETROSPECTIVE STYLES). Pausanias (5. 10. 8) also gives him the west pediment of the temple of Zeus at Olympia, carved in the 460s, but this is presumably a mistake: for a solution to the problem, see PAEONIUS. Val. Max. 8. 11, ext. 3 describes his bronze Hephaestus in the Hephaesteion at Athens, but attempts to identify it and its accompanying Athena in copy remain controversial.

A. F. Stewart, *Greek Sculpture* (1990), 164 f., 267 f., figs. 399 f.　A. F. S.

Alcathous, son of *Pelops and *Hippodamia, was exiled from his homeland for fratricide; finding that the kingship of *Megara was on offer to whoever could kill the ferocious lion of Cithaeron, he claimed the prize (keeping the beast's tongue as proof, like *Peleus). He subsequently built the city's walls with help from *Apollo and was honoured with memorial games as a founding hero (Pind. *Isthm.* 8. 74). See Paus. 1. 41 f. and the account of the local historian *Dieuchidas (*FGrH* 485 F 10, from schol. Ap. Rhod. 1. 516–18).　A. H. G.

Alcestis, in mythology, daughter of *Pelias, wife of Admetus king of *Pherae (Thessaly), who is prepared to die in his place.

Pelias promised Alcestis to whoever could yoke a lion and boar to a chariot (Apollod. 1. 9. 15). Admetus was assisted in this feat by his lover (Soph. fr. 851 Radt) Apollo (cf. *Poseidon, *Pelops, and *Hippodamia), who had been punished by serfdom to Admetus for killing the *Cyclopes (Hes. *Catalogus mulierum* frs. 51–7 M–W) or the Pythian snake. But at his marriage Admetus forgets to sacrifice to *Artemis and finds the bridal chamber full of snakes. On *Apollo's advice he appeases Artemis and even obtains from the Fates the concession that someone may die in his place. In the event, only Alcestis will, but Kore (*Persephone) sends her back from death or (in tragedy) *Heracles rescues her by wrestling with Death (*Thanatos).

Though neither Admetus nor Alcestis receives cult directly, they are intertwined with Apollo and Artemis in cult and myth. The local Artemis, Brimo or Pheraea ('of Pherae'), was a *chthonian goddess, and hints of an earlier story lie in Alcestis' marriage to 'Insuperable' (Admetus) and her Persephone-like descent and return. Admetus founded Apollo's temple at Euboean *Eretria (there was a Thessalian Eretria too) and his name is frequent amongst the Aegeidae clan who administered the cult of Apollo Carneus on *Thera (see Pfister, below). Alcestis (Eur. *Alc.* 449) will be sung at Apollo's Carnea festival in *Sparta—as also at Athens (*Alc.* 452, but see Jacoby on *FGrH* 325 F 26).

Alcestis' self-sacrifice, with its hints of suttee, belongs with a sequence of folk-tale functions (see Megas, below): (*a*) a young man faces early death; (*b*) he can only be saved if another will die for him; (*c*) only his wife will; (*d*) the lord of life and death grants life to this wife. Admetus' task is even more loosely connected with other motifs (Stith Thompson H 335, H 1149).

Alcestis is mentioned for her beauty and offspring at *Iliad* 2. 714 and *Hesiod *Cat.* fr. 37. 20, but then the tradition is silent till *Phrynichus (1)'s play *Alcestis*. The myth is best known from Euripides' *Alcestis* (438 BC). Very few depictions of Alcestis in art antedate this play. The Roman age was fond of Heracles leading Alcestis back from death, with its soteriological overtones.

G. Megas, *ARW* 1933, 1–33; F. Pfister, *Reliquienkult* (1909), 90–1; C. Robert, *Die griechische Heldensage* (1920 (4th imp.)), 29–34; M. Schmidt, *LIMC* 1 (1981), 533–44; B. Sergent, *Homosexuality in Greek Myth* (1986).　K. D.

alchemy

Sources Of ancient texts on Greek alchemy there survive two papyri, three vast corpora of differing date and content, and a few isolated treatises. (*a*) Papyrus X from Leiden and the Stockholm papyrus can be dated by handwriting to the early 4th cent. AD. They are two parts of the same collection of recipes for gold, silver, precious stones, and purple, compiled from older works and, in particular, citing *Democritus. (*b*) Corpus M, the MS Marcianus graecus 299, now in Venice, was copied in the 11th cent., probably in Constantinople. Damaged, although a full table of contents survives, it is a compilation of texts probably formed at the court of the emperor Heraclius (7th cent.) on the initiative of one Theodorus, a court dignitary and associate of Stephen of Alexandria. (*c*) Corpus B, the MS Parisinus graecus 2325, now in the Bibliothèque Nationale in Paris, from the 13th cent., of unknown provenance: a collection of texts perhaps formed in the time of *Psellus (11th cent.). These texts mostly recur in M; at least a part of B was copied from M after mutilation of M. The collection relates chiefly to operational techniques; its purpose was evidently practical. (*d*) Corpus AL, the MS Parisinus graecus 2327 of the Bibliothèque Nationale, was copied in Heraklion (Crete) in 1478 by Theodore Pelecanus. In two parts, the first corresponds faithfully to (*c*) above; the second is a collection of texts, some certainly ancient, albeit of unknown origin. Ordered differently, the same content recurs—and must either be a copy or a twin—in the Florentine MS Laurentianus graecus pluteus 86, 16 (= L), copied in 1492 by Antony Dranganas in an unknown location. (*e*) The isolated treatises are mainly late collections of recipes inspired by Latin works on alchemy. The best known is the Anonymous of Zuretti (MS Vaticanus graecus 1134), copied in 1376 at Oppido Mamertina (in Calabria), which makes use of the classics of Latin alchemy.

Numerous Greek MSS on alchemy preserved in European and American libraries derive from the three corpora M, B, and AL. Of no interest editorially, they reveal the infatuation with Greek texts on alchemy in the hermetist circles of the 16th and 17th cents. The Greek alchemists were also translated very early on into Syriac and Arabic. Although numerous, MSS of these translations are not yet explored. They will certainly enable gaps in the Greek tradition to be filled.

Authors and works In the three corpora, texts of very diverse date follow each other seamlessly. But by internal and external criteria a relative chronology can none the less be established.

(*a*) The ancient authors. The alchemists were unanimous in recognizing as the oldest text *Physika kai mystika* or 'Natural and Initiatory Matters', ascribed to Democritus. Now fragmentary, the treatise must once have comprised four books on gold, silver, precious stones, and purple. The date is difficult to establish. L. *Annaeus Seneca (2) and *Pliny (1) knew of the alchemical recipes of Democritus, perhaps indicating a date in the early 1st cent. AD. The link with the pseudo-Democritean forgeries produced by *Bolus (*c.*150–100 BC?) is uncertain. A fifth book, dedicated to *Leucippus (3), is a separate, but perhaps contemporary, work.

Several 'ancient authors', allegedly contemporary with Democritus, have left fragments or brief treatises: the Persian magus Ostanes, teacher of Democritus; Pammenes; Pibechius (the name is Egyptian); Mary the Jewess, author of an important work on apparatus; Comarius (from the Syriac *komar*, 'high priest'); and others who are pseudonyms, like the queen Cleopatra, the divinities *Agathos Daimon or *Hermes Trismegistus, or even

Isis, whose *Letter to Horus* was inspired by the *Physika*. The *Chemistry of Moses*, of the same period, is a recipe-collection related to the *Physika*.

(*b*) Zosimus of Panopolis (mod. Ahmim), in Upper Egypt, fl. *c*. AD 300, the author of a large work entitled *Imouth* (Imhotep) in 28 books, each designated by a letter of the alphabet. In the corpora there survive some fairly lengthy sections (the so-called 'authentic memoirs') and some short chapters (*kephalaia*) reorganized on a didactic principle by a Byzantine compiler (some dedicated to Theodore, others to Eusebius). The titles of some sections are known: 'On Excellence' (preferable to 'On Virtue'); 'According to Energy'; 'On the Letter Omega'; 'On Apparatus and Furnaces'; 'On Divine Water'; the 'Book to Sophe' (i.e. the pharoah Cheops); and 'Final Account'. The place of these sections in the original work is problematic. Zosimus achieved the synthesis of all his predecessors with Greek philosophy, religious hermetics, and above all *Gnosticism; there are very many parallels with the Gnostic texts from Nag Hammadi.

(*c*) The commentators. From the 4th to the 7th cents., the writers after Zosimus were above all exegetical. Synesius (perhaps the later bishop of Cyrene; at any rate fl. 4th cent.), wrote a commentary for Dioscorus, priest of the temple of *Sarapis in Alexandria (1), on the beginning of the book of Democritus; Olympiodorus, perhaps the 6th-cent. Neoplatonist, commented on the 'Book of Energy' of Zosimus, which he juxtaposes with a doxographical account of the Presocratics. The Christian Philosopher and the Anonymous Philosopher belong to the 6th or 7th cent.; subject by subject they address the views of their predecessors and so are valuable above all as a source of earlier fragments. At the court of Heraclius, the nine *Lectures* (set speeches) of Stephen of Alexandria are essentially rhetorical commentaries on Zosimus, as are the four poems ascribed to Heliodorus, Theophrastus, Hierotheus, and Archelaus.

Doctrines and practices The origin and evolution of Greek alchemy were determined by the interaction between theory and practice.

(*a*) Origins. There are five main strands of Greek alchemy: (1) the technical achievements of artisans in Hellenistic and Roman Egypt in producing convincing imitations of gold, silver, precious stones, and purple; (2) the doctrine of *mimēsis*, according to which the point of *technē* (craftsmanship) was to reproduce nature, with the ultimate aim of matching, if not excelling, it; (3) the decline of Greek rationalism and the complementary rise in the power of revelation: renouncing hope of learning the truth by reason alone, men turn to revelation; (4) the theory of 'universal sympathy' renewed by *Stoicism: everything in the cosmos is linked by occult ties of 'sympathy' and 'antipathy'—a world-view integrating astrology and magic; (5) the intuition of the unity of matter.

(*b*) The Democritean tradition. The *Physika kai mystika* combine these elements. In a temple in Memphis, Democritus and his friends put the recipes to work without achieving transmutation. They summon from the shadows the ghost of their teacher Ostanes who reveals that the books are in the temple. There a column opens up, revealing the formula of 'universal sympathy': nature plays with nature (sympathy), nature vanquishes nature (antipathy), and nature dominates nature (neutralization).

The procedures are in fact a variation of artisanal recipes according to the sympathies revealed by connections of colour. Their aim is to realize a *baphē* (tincture), that is, a change in physical properties, which should be complete (*katabaphē*) and resistant to the test of fire (*apheukton*): gilding and silver-plating of base metals, low-grade alloys superficially enriched, coloured alloys, veneering, vegetal tincture, steeping, impregnation with a mordant, etc.

(*c*) The tradition of Mary. In parallel, the tradition attributes to Mary the first step in the study of sublimation and distillation, and of the fixed and the volatile: certain bodies (those based on mercury, sulphur, and arsenic) are transformed into vapours (*aithalai*) which can congeal (sublimation), condense (distillation), or fix themselves to metals and tint them. These new processes correspond to new apparatus. For distillation, the classic alembic with its cucurbit (*lōpas*), head (*bikos*), and discharge-pipe (*sōlen*). For sublimation, the aludel (*phanos*), a pot topped with a conical lid. For colouration, the *kērotakis*, derived from the headed palette of encaustic painters (see PAINTING (TECHNIQUES)): a closed vase where metal sheets are exposed to the tinting action of circulating vapours. The chief ingredient is 'Divine Water' or sulphur-water (*theion hudōr*), which can be either a sulphurous solution, mercury, or a theoretical entity.

(*d*) Zosimus. His originality is hard to grasp in view of the fragmentary character of the older texts, above all Mary, and the lack of evidence for the contemporaries with whom he disputed. According to Zosimus, alchemy—an art both sacred and divine—was revealed to woman by rebellious angels.

Matter is one in its cycle of transformations (one is all, from one all is derived, and towards one all advances). 'Divine Water' (perhaps mercury) is the basis of this unity, the constituent of beings (the all in everything). Therefore according to Zosimus the process of transformation consists in a return to the undifferentiated state, eager for transmutation, and in the reincorporation of a transmuting principle. This agent is the *pneuma, an ambiguous notion since it means both the spirit and the volatile part of the substances given off in sublimation and distillation. It has to be freed from the body (*sōma*) of the metals, or these bodies have to be transformed into spirits, and then these spirits have to be embodied or incorporated (bodily matter has to be spiritualized and spiritual matter embodied). The *pneuma* in this way is assimilated to the tincture (*baphē*). These operations, which take place in the *kērotakis*, are described in the form of 'visions', where the metals are tortured, killed, and revived. It seems that Zosimus was the first to establish a homology between the transformation of metals and that of the human operator. Carnal man, prey to the daimons of destiny, works the timely tinctures, linked to astrological conditions (*kairoi*). By his infallible method, calqued on the progress of nature, man of the spirit liberates himself from material determinism and can be reunited with the divine. Olympiodorus (above) amplified the philosophical aspects of Zosimus and stressed the agreement between 'Divine Water' and the 'one beginning' (*archē mia*) of the Presocratics.

MANUSCRIPTS *Catalogue des manuscrits alchimiques grecs*, under the direction of J. Bidez, F. Cumont, J. L. Heiberg, and O. Lagercrantz, 8 vol. (1924–32).

EDITIONS M. Berthelot and C. E. Ruelle, *Collection des anciens alchimistes grecs*, 3 vols. (1888; repr. 1967); R. Halleux, *Alchimistes grecs* 1: *Papyrus de Leyde, Papyrus de Stockholm, Recettes* (1981); M. Mertens, *Zosime de Panopolis, mémoires authentiques* (Diss. Liège, 1992); A. Colinet, *L'Anonyme de Zuretti* (Diss. Louvain, 1992).

STUDIES A. J. Festugière, *La Révélation d'Hermès Trismégiste* 1: *L'Astrologie et les sciences occultes*, 2nd edn. (1950); J. Lindsay, *The Origins of Alchemy in Greco-Roman Egypt* (1970); G. Fowden, *The Egyptian Hermes: A Historical Approach to the Late Pagan Mind* (1986). R. Ha.

Alcibiades

Alcibiades (451/0–404/3 BC), son of Cleinias, Athenian general and politician. Brought up in the household of his guardian *Pericles (1), he became the pupil and intimate friend of *Socrates. A flamboyant aristocrat, he competed in politics with the new-style *demagogues, and his ambitious imperialism drew Athens into a coalition with *Argos (2) and other enemies of *Sparta. This policy, half-heartedly supported by the Athenians, was largely discredited by the Spartan victory at *Mantinea (418). Though Alcibiades temporarily allied with *Nicias (1) to avoid *ostracism, the two were normally adversaries and rivals, and when Alcibiades sponsored the plan for a major Sicilian expedition, Nicias unsuccessfully opposed it. Both were appointed, together with *Lamachus, to command this expedition (415). After the mutilation of the *herms, Alcibiades had been accused of involvement in other religious scandals, and soon after the fleet reached Sicily he was recalled for trial. He escaped, however, to Sparta, where he encouraged the Spartans to send a general to Syracuse, and to establish a permanent Spartan post at *Decelea in Attica (which was eventually done in 413).

In 412 he was involved in Sparta's decision to concentrate on the Aegean rather than the Hellespont, but he soon lost the confidence of the Spartans and fled to the Persian satrap *Tissaphernes. He tried to secure his return to Athens by obtaining the support of Persia and bringing about an oligarchic revolution, but the negotiations with Persia were unsuccessful. The Athenian fleet at *Samos appointed him general, and for several years he skilfully directed operations in the Hellespont, winning a brilliant victory at *Cyzicus in 410. On returning to Athens in 407 he was cleared of the religious charges hanging over him and was appointed to an extraordinary command; but when a subordinate was defeated by *Lysander at Notium (406) he withdrew to Thrace, and his approach to the Athenians before Aegospotami was rebuffed (405). After he had taken refuge with the Persian *Pharnabazus, he was murdered in *Phrygia through the influence of the *Thirty Tyrants and Lysander.

Alcibiades was a competent military leader and a master of intrigue, but his personal ambition and the excesses of his private life aroused the distrust of the Athenians, and he was not given the chance to show whether his ambitious policies, carried out under his leadership, could bring about success.

PA 600; APF 9–22. Thuc. bks. 5–8; Xen. Hell. bk. 1; Pl. Alc. 1 and Symp.; Plut. Alc. J. Hatzfeld, Alcibiade, 2nd edn. (1951); W. M. Ellis, Alcibiades (1989). H. D. W.; P. J. R.

Alcidamas (4th cent. BC), rhetorician and sophist, was born in Elaea in Aeolis, studied with *Gorgias (1) and taught in Athens. His professional rivalry with *Isocrates and his school emerges in On the Writers of Written Speeches, in which he argues for the primacy of the skills of the practising, extemporizing orator. The Museum, a rhetorical textbook, survives only in fragments, but seems to have contained the germ of the later Contest of Homer and Hesiod. More philosophical interests are perhaps indicated by the condemnation of *slavery reportedly delivered in the Messenian Oration.

TEXTS G. Avezzù (1982); L. Radermacher, Artium Scriptores (1951), 132.
Cf. M. Narcy, in Dictionnaire des philosophes antiques, 1 (1989) 101; N. O'Sullivan, Alcidamas, Aristophanes and the Beginnings of Greek Stylistic Theory (1992). M. B. T.

Alcidas, Spartan commander in the early part of the *Peloponnesian War, failed to help *Mytilene in its revolt from Athens 428–7 and treated prisoners brutally (Thuc. 3. 17, 29–33) so creating doubts about Sparta's role as 'liberator' (the role: Thuc. 2. 8). He reappears as commander at *Corcyra, though with *Brasidas as 'adviser' (3. 69–80); and finally as a *founder of *Heraclea (4) in Trachis, perhaps chosen because of his religiously appropriate name (Alcides = *Heracles), though *Thucydides (2) characteristically does not say so. But the colony failed, not least because of Spartan harshness—another hit at Alcidas (Thuc. 3. 92–3, echoing 3. 32. 2, cf. 5. 52; Thucydides' repeated language makes the point that behaviour like Alcidas' damaged Sparta's image).

J. Roisman, Hist. 1987, 385 ff.; E. Badian, From Plataea to Potidaea (1993), 35 (both favourable); S. Hornblower, HSCP 1992, 189. S. H.

Alcinous (1) (Ἀλκίνοος), in mythology, son of Nausithous (Od. 7. 63), husband of Arete, his niece (7. 66), king of the Phaeacians in Scheria (6. 12, etc.), father of *Nausicaa. He received *Odysseus hospitably and sent him to Ithaca on one of the magic ships of his people (13. 70 ff.), though he had had warning of the danger of such services to all and sundry (13. 172 ff.). In the Argonautic legend (see especially Ap. Rhod. 4. 993 ff.) the *Argonauts visit Scheria (here called Drepane) on their return from Colchis; the Colchians pursue them there and demand *Medea. Alcinous decides that if she is virgin she must return, but if not, her husband *Jason (1) shall keep her. Warned by Arete, she and Jason consummate their marriage. For a *temenos of Alcinous on *Corcyra see Thuc. 3. 70. 4 with Hornblower, Comm. on Thuc.

H. J. R.

Alcinous (2), accredited in the MSS as author of the Didaskalikos, or 'Handbook of Platonism', a summary of *Plato (1)'s doctrines designed as a handbook for the general public. He was long identified with the 2nd-cent. AD Platonist *Albinus (1); but this identification has recently been impugned on palaeographical grounds, and it seems better to preserve the original name, admitting ignorance of the author's identity or dating (though a 2nd-cent. date still seems reasonable). Long since rejected as an accurate account of Plato's own views, by reason of its incorporation of many Aristotelian and even Stoic doctrines and terminology (see ARISTOTLE; STOICISM), the work has now come to be valued for what it is, a summary of the doctrine of at least one school of the Platonism of the period. Alcinous attributes Aristotle's categories and syllogistic to Plato; he equates Plato's Demiurge with Aristotle's Unmoved Mover; he interprets Plato's transcendent Forms as thoughts of God. However, despite an interesting distinction between a primal god and a world-mind, Alcinous has no doctrine of a supra-intellectual One, such as is characteristic of *Neoplatonism.

TEXT J. Whittaker (Budé, 1990), with Fr. trans.; C. F. Hermann's Teubner edn. of Plato (1853), 6. 147 ff.
COMMENTARY J. Dillon (1993), with Eng. trans. J. M. D.

Alciphron (2nd or 3rd cent. AD), sophist (see SECOND SOPHISTIC), whose Letters, supposedly written by Athenians of the 4th cent. BC (fishermen, farmers, '*parasites', courtesans (*hetairai)) attest his wide reading in classical literature and preserve many reminiscences of New Comedy, especially of *Menander (1). See also LETTERS, GREEK.

Loeb text and trans.: A. Benner and F. Fobes (1949; with letters of Aelian and Philostratus). Rohde, Griech. Roman (1876), 343 ff.

M. B. T.

Alcmaeon (1), the son of *Amphiaraus and Eriphyle, who killed his mother in revenge for his father's death. Bribed by Polynices with the necklace of Harmonia, Eriphyle gave a judgement in favour of *Adrastus against her husband when adjudicating between them as to whether Amphiaraus should join the expedition of the *Seven against Thebes despite his prophetic knowledge that all the participants except Adrastus would die. Amphiaraus ordered Alcmaeon to avenge him with death; alternatively, the *Delphic oracle advised him to kill his mother. In some variants Eriphyle endangered also Alcmaeon's life, by persuading him to participate in the expedition of the *Epigoni, having been bribed by Polynices' son with Harmonia's peplos. After murdering his mother Alcmaeon became mad and wandered about pursued by the *Erinyes. In one version the oracle advised him to settle in a land that had not existed when he had killed his mother; he settled in a place silted up by *Acheloüs, and the land was named *Acarnania after Alcmaeon's son *Acarnan. In a more elaborate version he was purified by *Phegeus king of Psophis whose daughter *Alphesiboea or Arsinoë he married. But the earth became barren and the oracle advised Alcmaeon to go to Acheloüs, who purified him and gave him in marriage his daughter Callirrhoë; she demanded the necklace and peplos of Harmonia which Alcmaeon had given to Alphesiboea. He returned to Psophis to retrieve them, claiming that he would be cured once he had dedicated them at the Delphic sanctuary. But Phegeus and his sons found out the truth and the latter killed him. A miracle turned Alcmaeon's sons from Callirrhoë into fully grown men and they avenged their father by killing Phegeus and his sons—and then dedicated the necklace and peplos to Delphi and settled Acarnania. (Cf. esp. Thuc. 2. 102–5; Asclepiades, FGrH 12 F 29; Soph., TGF 4. 149–50; Ephorus, FGrH 70 F 96; Apollod. 3. 6. 2, 7. 5–7; Paus. 8. 24. 7–10.)

I. Krauskopf, LIMC 1. (1981), 546–52, 'Alkmaion'; M. Delcourt, Oreste et Alcméon (1959); C. Sourvinou-Inwood, Theseus as Son and Stepson (1979), 8–11, 62 nn. 24–6; R. Parker, Miasma (1983), 377.　C. S.-I.

Alcmaeon (2) of Croton (5th cent. BC) wrote a philosophical book dedicated to a group of Pythagoreans (see PYTHAGORAS (1)), and known to *Aristotle and *Theophrastus. It mostly concerned the nature of man. Alcmaeon explained the human condition by the interplay of opposites, e.g. health as 'equal rights' of hot and cold, wet and dry, etc., disease as 'monarchy' of one of them. He held that 'passages' linked the sense-organs to the brain, which, followed by *Plato (1), he took to be the seat of understanding (but Calcidius' statement that Alcmaeon discovered this by dissection merits scepticism). And he compared the immortality of the soul to the endless circling of the heavenly bodies.

TEXT DK no. 24.
DISCUSSION/TRANSLATION Guthrie, Hist. Gk. Phil. 1; G. E. R. Lloyd, Methods and Problems in Greek Science (1991), ch. 8.
G. E. L. O.; M. Sch.

Alcmaeonidae, a noble Athenian family prominent in politics. Its first eminent member was Megacles, who as archon (see ARCHONTES), perhaps in 632/1 BC, involved it in a hereditary *curse (see CYLON). This led to an immediate, first expulsion of both the family and its ancestral bones (Thuc. 1. 126). The family fortunes were haunted by this curse, so later traditions are tendentious, but its importance should not be underplayed. Lacking a family cult (Davies), they were particularly vulnerable and apparently counteracted the damage ingeniously by other means, including later claims to be 'tyrant-haters'. They are already back with Alcmaeon, Megacles' son and their eponymous ancestor, who commanded the Athenian contingent in the First *Sacred War. Herodotus relates (perhaps with mischievous irony: Strasburger) how Alcmaeon was rewarded handsomely by *Croesus for assisting him at *Delphi (6. 125) and was thus

able to win a chariot victory at *Olympia (592?); *Megacles, his son, further enhanced family renown by marrying the daughter of *Cleisthenes (1), tyrant of Sicyon, but his attempt to marry his own daughter to *Pisistratus backfired, partly because of the curse (Hdt. 1. 61). Any family exile on Pisistratus' third return (c.546) was at an end by 525/4, the archonship of Megacles' son *Cleisthenes (2). They were, however, in exile in the last years of *Hippias (1)'s rule (after 514), and tried and failed to fortify Leipsydrion. Accounts of the expulsion of the tyrants are much affected by later claims. According to our best source, Herodotus (5. 55 ff.), the family gained the contract for rebuilding Apollo's temple at Delphi and bribed the oracle to tell Sparta to free Athens (see DELPHIC ORACLE). Cleisthenes returned to Athens and initiated reforms (508/7) but the family was expelled again as accursed by *Cleomenes (1) I. Later traditions present a more improving and patriotic tale.

In 490 (see PERSIAN WARS) they were suspected of collusion with the Persian invaders (Hdt. 6. 121), and this, along with their pro-Persian politics after 507 (Hdt. 5. 73) may explain the almost total eclipse in our evidence of the male line after 480. The early victims of *ostracism included another Megacles, nephew of Cleisthenes (2) (486), and *Xanthippus (1), husband of Megacles' sister Agariste (484). A few individuals flourish in the 5th cent., but any collective family role was diminished by the democracy. *Pericles (1), son of Xanthippus and Agariste, could ignore the Spartan invocation of the curse in 432/1, and *Alcibiades, despite his Alcmaeonid mother, escaped it altogether.

Hdt. 5. 55–72, 6. 125–31. APF 9688, 11811; R. Thomas, Oral Tradition and Written Record in Classical Athens (1989), ch. 5; H. Strasburger, Hist. 1955, 1 ff. (repr. in W. Marg (ed.), Herodot, WdF (1965)); W. G. Forrest, CQ 1960, 232 ff.　R. T.

Alcman, lyric poet, active in the mid- to late 7th cent. BC in *Sparta. His birthplace was disputed. Some believed him a *Laconian, while a number of ancient authors made him a *Lydian (Anth. Pal. 7. 18, 19, 709; Ael. VH 12. 50; Suda, entry under Ἀλκμάν, POxy. 2389, 2506, 3542; Vell. Pat. 1. 18. 2); the latter version (derived from fr. 16) was further embroidered to make him a freed slave (Heraclid Pont. Excerp. Polit. 9). The Suda credits him with six books of lyric songs (μέλη, melē); a group called 'Diving women'/'Swimming women' (κολυμβῶσαι, kolymbōsai), of which no certain trace survives, may have made up one of these or a seventh book. The lyric songs, mostly choral, included maiden-songs (παρθένεια, partheneia), which were probably arranged into two books by Alexandrian scholars (Steph. Byz. entry under Ἐρυσίχη). We also hear of hymns and wedding-songs (ὑμέναιοι, hymenaioi). The Suda credits him with love-poetry, and fragments with erotic content survive (58, 59a).

The most important surviving works are fragments of two maiden-songs found on papyri. The first (fr. 1) shows many features of the developed choral lyric: a myth (1–35), gnomic moralizing (36 ff.), and (probable but not certain, since the opening is lost) framing reference to the present occasion. An account of the death of the sons of *Hippocoon is followed by a gnomic transition (36 ff.) on divine punishment and mortal limitation. The rest of the fragment is devoted to praise of two females who play a major role in the ritual (Hagesichora and Agido) and description (with humorous self-deprecation) of the chorus. The song was performed at dawn (41 f., 60 ff.). The identity of the goddess honoured (87, Aotis, lit. 'the goddess at the dawn') is unclear (conjectures include *Helen, *Artemis Orthia, Phoebe daughter of Leucippus (see DIOSCURI)), likewise the nature of the festival, though many scholars detect a reference to a rival choir (60 ff.); there is uncertainty about the details of the myth and its relevance to the occasion. The second (fr. 3), more fragmentary, poem also concentrates on the actions of the leading figure (Astymeloisa). Both poems share a richness of sensuous imagery and a pronounced homoerotic tenor. There is an evident taste for puns, and a proliferation of proper names, many of significance only to the original audience. Alongside this parochiality we find a taste for the distant and exotic (1. 59, 100; cf. frs. 90, 148 ff.). Together the two songs show a gaiety and humour not usually associated with Sparta. Some other fragments come from maiden-songs (16, 26, 29, 38, 59b, 60), but many defy classification. Alcman's descriptive power is shown in an account of the sleep of nature (fr. 89, context unknown). Mythic narrative is attested by a number of fragments (e.g. fr. 69 *Niobe; fr. 77 addressed to *Paris; fr. 69 the stone of *Tantalus; fr. 80 *Odysseus and *Circe). The songs are composed in the Laconian vernacular, with intermittent epic and aeolic forms. The poetry had achieved classic status by the late 5th cent. (Ar. *Lys.* 1247 ff.).

TEXTS Page, *PMG*; C. Calame, *Alcman* (1983); Davies, *PMGF.*

COMMENT AND CRITICISM D. L. Page, *Alcman, the Partheneion* (1951); D. A. Campbell, *Greek Lyric Poetry* (1967); D. E. Gerber, *Euterpe* (1970); C. Calame, *Les Chœurs de jeunes filles en Grèce archaïque* 2 (1977); *RE* Suppl. 11. 19 ff.

TRANSLATIONS D. A. Campbell, *Greek Lyric* 2 (1988), M. L. West, *Greek Lyric Poetry* (1993). C. C.

Alcmene, mother of *Heracles. Her father was Electryon, who was accidentally killed by her husband *Amphitryon; she followed Amphitryon into exile in *Thebes (1), but refused to sleep with him until he had avenged the death of her brothers on the Taphians and Teleboans. *Zeus came to her in Amphitryon's shape a little before the latter's return, and she gave birth to twins—Heracles by Zeus, *Iphicles by Amphitryon. *Hera in jealousy obstructed the birth, thus ensuring that *Eurystheus was born before Heracles and so became king of *Argos (2). After the death of Heracles, Alcmene with the rest of his family was persecuted by Eurystheus, and in *Euripides' *Heraclidae* took refuge with them in Athens, insisting on Eurystheus' death after his defeat in battle. At her own death she was taken to the *Islands of the Blest to marry *Rhadamanthys, and a stone substituted in her coffin. The stone was revered in her heroon at Thebes (Pherecydes, *FGrH* 3 F 84). Alternative traditions gave her tombs at *Megara (Paus. 1. 41. 1) and at *Haliartus (Plut. *Mor.* 577e, apparently a bronze age burial). She also received widespread cult in Attica, though always in connection with others in the circle of Heracles.

A. D. Trendall, *LIMC* 1 1. 552–6; J. Schwartz, *Rev. Arch.* 1958, 1. 76–83. E. Ke.

alcoholism

Greece The ancient Greeks were unfamiliar with modern concepts of alcoholism, but they were well aware of self-destructive drinking and the effects of habitual drunkenness. In the *Odyssey*, *Homer makes a speaker note that wine is a bane to those who drink it excessively, and identify overindulgence as the cause of the *Centaur Eurytion's vile behaviour (21. 293–8). In *Hades, Homer's Elpenor admits that heavy drinking was a key factor in his fatal plunge from *Circe's roof (*Od.* 11. 61). *Pythagoras (1) is credited with the dictum that drinking to achieve drunkenness is a training-ground for madness, and he advises drunkards to take an unflinching look at their inebriate behaviour if they wish

to alter it (Stob. *Flor.* 3. 18. 23, 33). In the *Republic*, *Plato (1) writes about men who welcome any excuse to drink whatever wine is available (475a). *Aristotle's treatise *On Drunkenness* has been lost, but his extant works confirm an abiding interest in wine's pernicious effects. *Plutarch's *Moralia* deplores the vicious cycle exhibited by habitual drunkards who seek wine in the morning to remedy their hangovers, noting that wine not only reveals the character but can alter it as well (127f, 799b–c). The value of abstention was recognized by the ancient Greeks, and *Athenaeus (1) devotes considerable attention to water drinkers in *The Deipnosophists* (2. 44b–f); abstainers, however, were rare in Greek antiquity. Athenaeus and *Aelian discuss those groups— the Macedonians, for example—who drank with heroic intensity. *Cleomenes (1) I, *Alcibiades, *Philip (1) II of Macedon, *Alexander (3) the Great, *Dionysius (2) II, and *Demetrius (4) Poliorcetes can be counted among the most renowned topers of the ancient Greek world. In classical antiquity, however, allegations of intemperance often serve as vehicles for character assassination; thus, each case must be considered on its own merits.

Rome The ancient Romans were as interested in the harmful effects of excessive drinking and chronic intoxication as their Greek counterparts. In *On the Nature of Things*, *Lucretius writes that wine's fury disturbs the soul, debilitates the body, and provokes quarrels (3. 476–83). The younger *Seneca warns that habitual drunkenness so weakens the mind that its consequences are felt long after the drinking has stopped (*Ep.* 83. 26). He notes that some men become so tolerant of wine that even though they are inebriated they appear to be sober (*Ep.* 83. 11). Seneca also suggests that drunkenness tends to disclose and magnify character defects (*Ep.* 83. 19–20). In his *Natural History*, *Pliny (1) the Elder finds irony in the fact that men spend hard-earned money on something that can damage the mind and cause madness (14. 137). Like the Greeks, Pliny comments on truth in wine ('*in vino veritas*'), but emphasizes that the truths therein revealed are often better left unspoken (*HN* 14. 141). Seneca's and Pliny's descriptions of the psychological and physical effects of chronic intoxication presage modern observations: memory loss, identity confusion, narcissistic self-indulgence, antisocial behaviour, impaired speech and vision, distended stomach, halitosis, quivering, vertigo, insomnia, and early death (Sen. *Ep.* 83. 21, 95. 16; Plin. *HN* 14. 142). *Sulla, *Cato (Uticensis), M. *Tullius Cicero (2) (son of the orator), Mark Antony (M. *Antonius (2)), *Iulia (3) (daughter of Augustus), and the emperors *Tiberius, *Claudius, *Vitellius, and *Commodus are among the prominent Romans accused of notorious tippling.

The alcoholic beverage of choice for both the ancient Greeks and Romans was *wine, customarily diluted with water, except perhaps in the case of the Macedonians who were reputed to drink their wine *akratos*, or unmixed. Distilled spirits, such as brandy and whisky, had not yet been invented, and beer was looked upon as a swinish potation better left to barbarians.

G. A. Austin, *Alcohol in Western Society from Antiquity to 1800* (1985); V. D. Hanson, *The Western Way of War* (1989), 126–31; O. Murray (ed.), *Sympotica* (1990); J. M. O'Brien, *Alexander the Great: The Invisible Enemy* (1992); J. H. D'Arms, 'Heavy Drinking and Drunkenness in the Roman World: Four Problems for Historians', in O. Murray (ed.), *In Vino Veritas* (1995). J. M. O'B., B. L. R.

Alesia, a hill-fort of the Mandubii, modern Alise-Ste Reine, where, in 52 BC, Caesar besieged and captured *Vercingetorix. The site was not abandoned, but developed as a thriving township, which survived until the later 4th cent. Archaeologically it is of great importance. Its Gallic walls and Roman siege-works were uncovered in the 19th cent. Modern research has concentrated on the public and private buildings of the Gallo-Roman period, and has exposed impressive remains. Literary evidence for the production of high-quality metalwork here has been confirmed by archaeological finds.

> J. Le Gall, *Alésia* (1980); M. Mangin, *Alésia: Un quartier de commerçants* (1981). J. F. Dr.

Aletes (1) Son of *Aegisthus, killed by *Orestes in Mycenae (Hyg., *Fab.* 122, perhaps from the Attic tragedy *Aletes, TrGF* 3. 2. fr. 1b). His name ('Wanderer') may suggest an aetiological connection with the *aletis* rite at the Attic festival *Anthesteria, linked in mythology with his sister *Erigone. (2) Son of Hippotas, who in accordance with an oracle became king of *Corinth after having been given a clod of earth when he asked for bread on a festival day (schol. Pind. *Nem.* 7. 155). E. Ke.

Aletrium (mod. Alatri), town of the *Hernici 70 km. (43 mi.) south-east of Rome. Always loyal to Rome after 358 BC, Aletrium became a prosperous *municipium* (Cic. *Clu.* 46) and remained such (reject *Lib. colon.* 23). Its massive polygonal walls have survived almost intact, those surrounding the citadel being particularly remarkable. There is also an early *aqueduct of *c.*100 BC, built by L. Betilienus Varus.

> L. Gasperini, *Aletrium 1: I documenti epigrafici* (1965); G. Lugli, *La tecnica edilizia romana* (1957), 131 ff. E. T. S.; T. W. P.

Aleuadae, princely family of *Larissa in *Thessaly. The military and political organization of the federal Thessalian state goes back to Aleuas the Red (second half of the 6th cent. BC). The Aleuad Thorax and his brothers instigated Thessalian *Medism, but paid the price in lost influence after the *Persian Wars. In the 4th cent. the family opposed the tyrants of *Pherae and invited the Macedonian kings (fellow-Heraclids) to intervene in Thessaly. An Aleuad rebelled against *Philip (1) II of Macedon; thereafter the family disappears from Thessalian history. See also SIMONIDES.

> H. D. Westlake, *Thessaly in the Fourth Century* BC (1935); M. Sordi, *La lega tessala fino ad Alessandro Magno* (1958); B. Helly, *L'état Thessalien: Aleuas le Roux, les tétrades et les tagoi* (1995). B. H.

Alexander (1) I, 'the Philhellene', king of Macedon *c.*498–454 BC. Subject to Persia from 492 and related by marriage to the Persian noble Bubares, he used his influence to extend his territory eastwards to the mines of Mt. Dysoron (Krousia), which provided the silver for his impressive coinage; and in 480/79 he was active in the campaigns of *Xerxes and *Mardonius. The tradition in Herodotus that he was responsible for the murder of Persian envoys (*c.*512) and maintained secret relations with the Hellenic leaders in 480 is certainly propaganda to preserve his position and to broadcast his overtly philhellene policies. Acknowledged even before 480 as *proxenos* and benefactor of the Athenians, he was allegedly recognized (in 476?) at Olympia as Hellenic ruler of a barbarian people; and he fostered the myth that his ancestors were Temenids (see TEMENUS) from *Argos (2) (and gave sanctuary to refugees from *Mycenae, *c.*464). The propaganda no doubt helped him preserve his independence against Athenian expansion in the wake of Xerxes' invasion.

> N. G. L. Hammond and G. T. Griffith, *A History of Macedonia* 2 (1979); E. N. Borza, *In the Shadow of Olympus* (1990); E. Badian, in S. Hornblower (ed.), *Greek Historiography* (1994), ch. 4. A. B. B.

Alexander (2) II, eldest son of *Amyntas (1) III and Eurydice,

and king of Macedon 370–368 BC. His short and turbulent reign was bedevilled by rivalry and open war with his brother-in-law, Ptolemy of Alorus. An intervention in Thessaly in support of the *Aleuadae of Larissa (369) ended ingloriously when his garrisons were ejected by *Pelopidas and he himself was forced into alliance with *Thebes (1). Shortly afterwards he was murdered at Ptolemy's instigation. A. B. B.

Alexander (3) **III** ('the Great') of Macedon, 356–323 BC, son of *Philip (1) II and *Olympias. As crown prince he was taught by *Aristotle (from 342); he was his father's deputy in Macedon (340) and fought with distinction at the battle of *Chaeronea (338). Philip's last marriage created a serious rift, but a formal reconciliation had been effected by the time of his death (autumn 336), and Alexander was proclaimed king against a background of dynastic intrigue, in which his rivals (notably Amyntas, son of Perdiccas, and the faction of Attalus) were eliminated. A show of force in southern Greece saw him acknowledged Philip's successor as *hēgemōn* of the League of *Corinth; and in 335, when the Thebans took advantage of his absence campaigning on the Danube and rebelled, he destroyed the city and enslaved the survivors. The exemplary punishment enabled him to leave the Greek world under the supervision of *Antipater (1) with little fear of revolt, while he turned to the war of revenge against Persia.

2. In early 334 Alexander led his grand army across the Hellespont. In all some 43,000 foot and 5,500 horse (including the expeditionary force under *Parmenion), it was the most formidable array ever to leave Greek soil. The Macedonians were its indispensable nucleus. The infantry phalanx, *c.*15,000 strong and armed with the fearsome six-metre (19½-foot) pike (*sarisa*), comprised a guard corps (hypaspists) and six regionally levied battalions (*taxeis*); and the cavalry, originally 1,800 strong, was also divided into regional squadrons (*ilai*). In pitched battle the *phalanx, in massed formation, was practically unbreakable on level ground, and Alexander was able to generate a cavalry charge from the flank which had decisive momentum. The men of the hypaspists, usually supplemented by Agrianian javelin-men and the corps of archers, were deployed in rapid-moving columns along with the cavalry, and were an irresistible combination in mountain warfare. These units were far superior to any they encountered (except arguably the armoured cavalry of *Bactria), and, supplemented by a large reserve of secondary troops (Thracians, Illyrians, and the hoplites of the Corinthian League), they gave Alexander an overwhelming military advantage.

3. Alexander's superiority was immediately asserted at the *Granicus (334), where a composite satrapal army was outmanoeuvred and its large mercenary phalanx exterminated. That allowed him to march directly to occupy *Sardis, *Ephesus, and *Miletus. The most serious threat came from a superior Persian fleet, which sustained the stubborn defence of *Halicarnassus, and Alexander took the gamble of demobilizing his own fleet and abandoning the coast. He moved east via *Lycia, *Pamphylia, and *Phrygia (where he 'cut' the Gordian knot, fulfilling a presage of empire), and largely ignored a major Persian counter-offensive in the Aegean, which—fortunately for him—the Great King (*Darius III) crippled by withdrawing a large segment of the fleet to swell his royal army (summer 333). Alexander made Cilicia his base for the critical campaign and lured the vast Persian army into the narrow coastal plain south of *Issus, where its numbers were ineffective. He disrupted the front line with his standard cavalry charge from the right and gradually forced the

entire Persian army into panic retreat. This overwhelming victory (c. November 333) gave him control of the near east as far as the Euphrates. There was some resistance, notably at *Tyre and *Gaza, which he crushed in exemplary fashion, preferring protracted and costly sieges (seven months at Tyre) to diplomacy and negotiation. All challenges were met directly, whatever the human cost.

4. After a winter (332/1) in Egypt, which was surrendered peacefully, he invaded Mesopotamia and won his crowning victory at *Gaugamela (1 October 331). Darius' forces were outmanœuvred again, on chosen ground and unrestricted plain; Alexander sacrificed his left wing, leaving it to be enveloped while he extended the enemy line to the right, created a gap and drove inwards at the head of his cavalry. Again a general rout ensued, and Mesopotamia in turn lay open to him. *Babylon and *Susa fell without resistance, and he forced the Persian Gates against determined opposition to occupy the heartland of Persis (winter 331/0). At *Persepolis he acquired the accumulated financial reserves of the Persian empire and incinerated its great palace during (it would seem) an orgiastic *symposium, subsequently representing it as the final act of the war of revenge. That in effect came during the summer of 330 when Darius fled from his last refuge at *Ecbatana, to be murdered by his closest entourage (led by Bessus, *satrap of Bactria). Alexander honoured his rival's body and closed the war by discharging his Hellenic troops en masse.

5. A new challenge arose when Bessus, who had withdrawn to his satrapy, proclaimed himself King of Kings under the regnal name *Artaxerxes (5) v. He appointed counter-satraps in central Asia and fomented revolt. Alexander left his satraps to cope with the insurgency, while he moved in a great swathe through Areia, Drangiana, and Arachosia (east Iran and west Afghanistan) and crossed the Hindu Kush to invade Bactria (spring 329). Bessus was soon gone, arrested in his turn by his nobles and surrendered to Alexander for exemplary punishment. Shortly afterwards, when Alexander reached the north-eastern limit of the empire (the Syr-Darya), a new uprising began in Sogdiana (Uzbekistan), rapidly spreading south to Bactria. One of Alexander's (non-Macedonian) columns was ambushed by the insurgents' nomad auxiliaries west of *Marakanda (Samarkand), a military and moral reverse which impressed the need for slow, systematic pacification. The conquest of the area fortress by fortress witnessed deliberate massacre, enslavement, and transplantation of recalcitrant populations, and, when the revolt ended (spring 327), the north-eastern satrapies were left exhausted under a large garrison of mercenaries and a network of new city foundations, in which a Hellenic military élite was supported by a native agrarian work-force—the invariable model for the dozens of Alexandrias he founded in the eastern empire.

6. From Bactria Alexander moved into *India at the invitation of the local dynasts of the Kabul valley and Punjab. He was nothing loath to reaffirm the traditional Achaemenid claims to the Indus lands. Resistance was treated as rebellion, and his progress through Bajaur and Swat was marked by massacre and destruction, as in Sogdiana. Even the remote rock-fortress of Aornus (Pir-sar) was reduced by siege at the cost of prodigious hardship, to demonstrate that there was no escape from his dominion. The spring of 326 saw him at Taxila, east of the Indus, poised for a campaign against *Porus, who held the Jhelum (*Hydaspes) against him. After a series of diversionary manœuvres he crossed the river under cover of a spring thunderstorm and defeated Porus, whose war *elephants could not com-

pensate for his cavalry inferiority. The victory was commemorated in two city foundations (Bucephala and Nicaea), and a remarkable issue of silver decadrachms depicts Alexander (crowned by victory) in combat with Porus and his elephant. Alexander continued eastwards, crossing the rivers of the Punjab in the face of an increasing *monsoonal deluge, until his troops' patience was exhausted. They refused to cross the Hyphasis (Beas) and invade the Ganges river system, and Alexander reluctantly acceded. A river fleet (commissioned in the summer) was ready at the Hydaspes by November 325, and the army proceeded by land and water to the southern Ocean. The journey was marked by a singularly vicious campaign against the Malli, unprovoked except for their failure to offer submission, and Alexander's impetuousness cost him a debilitating chest wound. Further south the kingdoms of Sambus and Musicanus were visited with fire and slaughter when their allegiance wavered, and, as he approached his base in the Indus delta (Patalene), the natives fled in terror (July 325).

7. Alexander now returned to the west, deputing *Nearchus to take his fleet across the southern coastline while he led the main army through the Gedrosian desert (Makran), in emulation—so Nearchus claimed—of *Cyrus (1) and *Semiramis. The horrors of heat and famine which ensued were considerable, but perhaps exaggerated in the sources, which attest no great loss of life among the Macedonian army. Reunited with the fleet in Carmania (c. December 325), he returned to Persepolis and Susa (March 324), where some 80 of his staff joined him in taking wives from the Persian nobility. For the next year there was a lull in campaigning (except for a punitive expedition against the Cossaeans of the Zagros), but there were grandiose preparations in the Levant, where he commissioned a war fleet allegedly 1,000 strong, some of which was conveyed to Babylon in summer of 323. The first stage of conquest was certainly the *Persian Gulf and Arabian littoral, which Alexander intended to conquer and colonize, but the sources, in particular the memoranda (hypomnēmata) reported by *Diodorus (3) Siculus, refer to projects of conquest in the western Mediterranean aimed at Carthage and southern Italy—and plans are even alleged of a circumnavigation of Africa. The reality is perhaps beyond verification, but it is likely enough that Alexander conceived no practical limit to his empire.

8. Alexander's monarchy was absolute. From the outset he regarded Asia Minor as liberated territory only in so far as he displaced the Persians, and he announced the fact of possession by imposing his own satraps upon the erstwhile Persian provinces. By 332 he regarded himself as the proper ruler of the Persian empire, and after Gaugamela he was acclaimed king of Asia. From 330 his status was displayed in his court dress, which combined the traditional Macedonian hat (kausia) and cloak with the Persian *diadem, tunic, and girdle. He used Persian court ceremonial and promoted Persian nobles, but there is no evidence of a formal 'policy of fusion' with Persians and Macedonians assimilated into a single ruling class. Except for a brief moment at Opis the Macedonians were entrenched in a position of superiority. The Susa marriages would indeed give rise to a mixed offspring (as would the liaisons of his soldiers with native women), but in both cases the ultimate aim was probably to counter the regional and family loyalties which had been the curse of both Persian and Macedonian monarchs. At another level he had cut across the traditional regional basis of his army and introduced Iranians even to the élite *Companion cavalry. There was to be a single loyalty—to the crown.

9. Alexander naturally experienced opposition in various forms. His Macedonian troops proved increasingly reluctant to be enticed into further conquest. He gave way once, at the Hyphasis, but at Opis (324) he confronted their contumacious demands for repatriation with summary executions and a devastating threat to man his army exclusively from Persians. He had deliberately made his Macedonians dispensable and demonstrated the fact. The same ruthlessness marked his reaction to opposition at court. He isolated and struck down Parmenion because of his resistance to imperial expansion, and the adolescent pages, who seriously threatened his life for reasons which are obscure (but probably based on antipathy to the new absolutism), were tortured and stoned to death. Insubordination was as intolerable as conspiracy. Alexander's return to the west in 325/4 witnessed a spate of executions of satraps who had exceeded their authority or arrogated power (e.g. Astaspes in Carmania, Orxines in Persis). Misgovernment as such was a secondary consideration, as is shown by his remarkable offer of pardon to *Cleomenes (3). Relations with the Greek world became increasingly strained. At first the machinery of the Corinthian League was effective; and the challenge by *Agis III had limited support and was quickly crushed (? spring 330). But Alexander undermined the provisions of the league by his Exiles' Decree (324), which threatened Athens' possession of *Samos and gave almost every city the problem of repatriating long-term exiles. The last year of his reign was punctuated by tense and heated diplomacy, and his death was the catalyst for general war in southern Greece.

10. Given Alexander's uncompromising claims to sovereignty it can be readily understood how he came to conceive himself divine. A Heraclid by lineage, he believed himself the descendant of *Heracles, *Perseus (1), and (ultimately) *Zeus, and by 331 he had begun to represent himself as the direct son of Zeus, with dual paternity comparable to that of Heracles. He was reinforced in his belief by his pilgrimage (in 331) to the oracle of *Ammon (recognized as a manifestation of Zeus at *Siwa), and thereafter styled himself son of Zeus Ammon. But divine sonship was not divinity, and by 327, after conquest had followed conquest, Alexander was encouraged (particularly in the liberated atmosphere of the symposium) to believe that his achievements deserved apotheosis at least as much as Heracles'. *Proskynēsis*, the hierarchical prostration of inferior to superior, was *de rigueur* at the Persian court, but Alexander attempted to extend it to Macedonians and Greeks, for whom the gesture was an act of worship. The experiment failed, thanks to the resistance of *Callisthenes, but the concept remained, and there is an anecdotal (but probable) tradition that he wrote to the cities of Greece in 324, suggesting that it would be appropriate for divine honours to be voted him along with a *hero-cult for his deceased favourite, *Hephaestion (1). Cults were certainly established, predominantly in Asia Minor, and persisted long after his death, eclipsing the largely ephemeral worship of his successors.

11. Portraits of Alexander tend to follow the model created by his favourite sculptor, *Lysippus (2), who perpetuated the leftward inclination of his neck and the famous *anastolē* (hair thrown back from a central parting). His profile, first illustrated on the 'Alexander sarcophagus' (311), appears repeatedly on coins, most strikingly on the commemorative tetradrachms of *Lysimachus. His personality is far more elusive, thanks to the tendency in antiquity to adduce him as a moral example of good or evil and the propensity of moderns to endue him with the qualities they would admire in themselves. His reputation for invincibility, which he studiously fostered, has been a source of fascination (notably for *Pompey, *Trajan, and Napoleon), mostly for ill. The process began when he died (10 June 323) after a ten-day illness (which contemporaries ascribed to poison), and the marshals who sought to emulate him rapidly dismembered his empire.

The few inscriptions from Alexander's reign are edited by A. J. Heisserer, *Alexander the Great and the Greeks* (1980); see also P. Harding, *From the End of the Peloponnesian War to the Battle of Ipsus* (1985), nos. 101 ff.; C. T. Schwenk, *Athens in the Age of Lycurgus* (1985). The coinage by contrast is voluminous, but its richness is an embarrassment and there remain intractable problems of dating and mint attribution: see the copious study by M. J. Price, *The Coinage in the Name of Alexander the Great and Philip Arrhidaeus* (1991). The extant portraits are described and analysed by B. G. Ridgway, *Hellenistic Sculpture* 1 (1990) 108 ff. and A. F. Stewart, *Faces of Power: Alexander's Image and Hellenistic Politics* (1993); and there is a useful introduction to the archaeological discoveries in the east in Sir Mortimer Wheeler's *Flames over Persepolis* (1965).

Much of the history of Alexander depends upon source analysis. The rich crop of first-generation historians, including *Callisthenes, *Nearchus, *Ptolemy (1) I, *Aristobulus (1), and *Cleitarchus, is known only from secondary citations (collected in *FGrH* 117–53; for general discussion see L. Pearson, The *Lost Histories of Alexander the Great* (1960)), and our knowledge is based upon the derivative later tradition. *Arrian who based his account upon the works of Ptolemy and Aristobulus, is supplemented by *Strabo (who uses similar material, principally Aristobulus and Nearchus), but tends to conflict with the 'vulgate tradition', the common source of large passages of Q. *Curtius Rufus, Diodorus Siculus bk. 17, Justin bks. 11–12, and the late *Metz Epitome*, which is usually and credibly identified as Cleitarchus. For recent and very different approaches to the problem see N. G. L. Hammond, *Three Historians of Alexander the Great* (1988); A. B. Bosworth, *From Arrian to Alexander* (1988).

Modern literature revolves about certain classic studies of Alexander, beginning with the definitive panegyrical account by J. G. Droysen, *Geschichte des Hellenismus* 1 (1877). Other biographies of considerable influence include U. Wilcken, *Alexander the Great* (ed. Borza, 1967; Ger. orig. 1931); G. Radet, *Alexandre le Grand* (1931); W. W. Tarn, *Alexander the Great* (1948); F. Schachermeyr, *Alexander der Grosse* (1973). Detailed and itemized bibliography is provided by J. Seibert, *Alexander der Grosse* (1972), and *Das Zeitalter der Diadochen* (1983). Additional items may be found in recent general histories. See particularly A. B. Bosworth, *Conquest and Empire* (1988) and *CAH* 6² (1994), chs. 16 and 17; and for the north-east F. L. Holt, *Alexander in Bactria* (1988). A. B. B.

Alexander (4) **IV** (323–?310 BC), posthumous son of *Alexander (3) the Great and *Roxane. Already designated to the kingship at Babylon, he was elevated by *Perdiccas (3) (322) to join *Philip (2) Arrhidaeus as joint ruler of Alexander's empire. He was insignificant until 317, when his grandmother, *Olympias, used him in the power struggle for Macedon, and with Olympias he fell into *Cassander's hands in spring 316. Interned at Amphipolis, he was murdered after the pact of 311 and secretly buried (yet the spectacular Tomb III in the Great Tumulus at Vergina has been confidently claimed for him; see AEGAE). In Babylon and Egypt it was a convenient fiction to continue his regnal years to 306/5. A. B. B.

Alexander (5) **of Pherae,** 'tyrant' 369–358 BC. He achieved power by the murder of his uncle, Polyphron, and throughout his reign he attempted to restore the dominant position in *Thessaly which *Jason (2) had won for *Pherae, struggling against the Thessalian League created to counter his ambitions. Theban intervention under *Pelopidas forced him into alliance with Athens (368); but the combination against him was too strong, and in 364 after two significant defeats he became a subject ally of Thebes (1). By 362 he reasserted himself, raiding the Cyclades and subsequently worsting an Athenian fleet at *Peparethos. Athens and the Thessalian League united against him (361/0), but he contrived to remain in power until 358, when he was eliminated by a court conspiracy.

The ancient tradition (owing much to *Callisthenes' *Hellenica*) represents him as a monster of immoderation and cruelty, no doubt in part to create a foil for Pelopidas; but the picture recurs in the anti-Theban *Xenophon (1) and will have a nucleus of truth.

M. Sordi, *La lega tessala* (1958), ch. 8; J. Buckler, *The Theban Hegemony* (1980), ch. 5. A. B. B.

Alexander (6) **I,** king of Molossia in *Epirus (342–330/29 BC). Brother of *Olympias, he grew up at the court of *Philip (1) II and was placed on the Molossian throne by force in 342. Ties with Macedon were strengthened when he married Cleopatra, Philip's daughter (336). Late in 334 he answered an appeal from *Tarentum and intervened with a small expeditionary force in the war against the Lucanians (see LUCANIA). After initial successes in south Italy (and an alleged treaty with Rome) he came to grief at *Pandosia (late 331). His death made Epirus a protectorate of Macedon.

Berve, *Alexanderreich* 2. no. 38; Hammond, *Epirus* 534 ff.; R. Werner, in W. Will (ed.), *Alexander der Grosse* (1987), 335 ff. A. B. B.

Alexander (7) **II,** son of *Pyrrhus and king of Molossia 272–c.240 BC. During the Chremonidean War (see CHREMONIDES) he invaded Macedonia (c.262/1) but was routed and deposed by *Antigonus (2) Gonatas. Restored (c.260) with Aetolian help, he later (?243) divided *Acarnania with the Aetolians.

Hammond, *Epirus* 588 ff.; P. Cabanes, *L'Épire de la mort de Pyrrhos à la conquête romaine* (1976), 77 ff. A. B. B.

Alexander (8) (*RE* 84), **of** *Pleuron, 'the Aetolian' (he is the only known Aetolian poet), *grammaticus and poet, born c.315 BC, contemporary with *Callimachus (3) and *Theocritus. Around 285–283, he undertook for *Ptolemy (1) II Philadelphus the *diorthosis* (correction of the copies) of the tragedies and satyr plays collected for the Library at *Alexandria (1) (*Lycophron (2) handled the comedies). Later (c.227) he was, with *Aratus (1) and *Antagoras, called to the court of *Antigonus (2) Gonatas.

Fragments, mostly slight, survive of his epyllia (e.g. a *Halieus* or 'Fisherman', cf. Theoc. *Id.* 21), elegy, epigrams, ribald Ionic poems (learnedly imitating *Sotades (2)). He also wrote a *Phaenomena* (on constellations, like Aratus and many others), but was best known for his tragedies and was counted one of the '*Pleiad', the seven star Alexandrian tragedians. Little is known of the tragedies except that *Astragalistai* ('Knucklebone-Players') dealt with the young *Patroclus' manslaughter of an opponent (*Il.* 23. 85–8). His elegy *Apollo* assembled fashionably unhappy love-stories in the form of a series of prophecies uttered by *Apollo himself: 34 lines survive from the story of Antheus and Cleoboea, written in a learned, distanced style (fr. 3 Powell, *Parth. Amat. Narr.* 14). Another elegy, *Muses*, contained literary history, as also seen in striking, if contorted, tetrameters contrasting *Euripides' miserable personality with his irresistible poetry (fr. 7, Gell. *NA* 15. 20).

Powell, *Coll. Alex.* 121–30; Diehl, *Anth. Lyr. Graec.* 2. 227–32; Snell, *TrGF* 1. 278–9. Christ–Schmid–Stählin 2/1. 173–4 (§ 435). K. D.

Alexander (9) (c.290–c.245 BC), son of *Craterus (2) and his successor as viceroy of *Corinth and *Euboea, declared himself independent in 249 (rather than 252) and allied himself with the *Achaean Confederacy. A short war with *Argos (2) and Macedonian forces from Athens ended with *Antigonus (2) Gonatas' recognition of his usurpation. He died (by poison, it was rumoured) around 245, and his widow accepted Gonatas' son, Demetrius, in marriage.

R. Urban, *Wachstum and Krise des achäischen Bundes* (1979); Walbank, in *HM* 3. 300 ff. A. B. B.

Alexander (10) **Balas** (d. 145 BC), pretended (or bastard) son of *Antiochus (4) IV, usurped the Seleucid throne after the defeat and death of *Demetrius (4) I. He was a pawn of Pergamum and Egypt and had support from the Roman senate, which feared a revival of Seleucid power; as a king he was ineffective. His reign (153/2–145 BC) was ended by his expulsion and death; it is important mainly as initiating dynastic instability, which in conjunction with Parthian expansionism hastened the disintegration of the *Seleucid empire.

H. Volkmann, *Klio* 1925, 373 ff; E. Will, *Histoire politique du monde hellénistique* 2, 2nd. edn. (1982), 373 f. G. T. G.; S. S.-W.

Alexander (11) (*RE* 88) **'Polyhistor',** Greek polymath and ethnographer. Born c.105 BC at *Miletus, he was captured in the Mithradatic Wars (see MITHRADATES VI) and came to Rome as a slave of an unidentifiable Cornelius Lentulus; he was freed and given Roman citizenship by *Sulla (c.80 BC). He later taught C. Iulius Hyginus (see HYGINUS (1)). His vast literary output (*FGrH* 273) included compilations of geographical material and wonder-stories of various lands and peoples, including five books on Rome and works on Delphi, Egypt, the Chaldaeans, and the Jews. He also wrote works on the history of philosophy, and commentaries on the place-names in *Alcman and possibly on *Corinna. His encyclopaedic industry is evident; nothing suggests any concern for originality.

E. Rawson, *Intellectual Life in the Late Roman Republic* (1985), see index; L. Troiani, *Due Studi di storiografia e religione antiche* (1988). C. B. R. P.

Alexander (12) (2nd cent. AD), son of *Numenius, wrote a *Rhetoric* (Τέχνη) and an influential treatise *On Figures* (Περὶ σχημάτων), which discussed the distinction between 'natural' and 'figured' thought.

Spengel–Hammer 1. 352; Spengel, *Rhet.* 3. 1 and 9. T. Schwab, *Alexandros Numeniu* (1916); D. Russell, *Criticism in Antiquity* (1981), 176.

M. B. T.

Alexander (13) **of Abonuteichos** in *Paphlagonia. He was a contemporary of *Lucian whose bitterly hostile account, *Alexander or the False Prophet*, remains the most important source of information, although it must now be read against the evidence of inscriptions, coins, and works of art.

Alexander claimed to have a new manifestation of *Asclepius in the form of a snake called Glycon. A number of statues and statuettes have been discovered showing Glycon as a serpent with human hair—applied by Alexander, according to Lucian. Coins reveal that the birth of Glycon, described in detail by Lucian, took place in the reign of Antoninus Pius (Robert, 397–9: see bibliog. below) and that his cult gained very rapid acceptance. According to Lucian, this was the result of the oracles that Glycon provided in a variety of forms. After the cult was established, Alexander, who served as Glycon's prophet, or interpreter, created mysteries from which unbelievers, especially Christians and Epicureans, were excluded. Marcus *Aurelius recognized the cult by conferring status on Abonuteichos (thereafter known as Ionopolis) and Lucian mentions several consultants from the ranks of the imperial aristocracy, including Servianus, governor of Cappadocia in AD 161, and Rutilianus, governor of Moesia around 150 and Asia between 161 and 163. Alexander also sent Marcus Aurelius an oracle of Glycon at the beginning of the German Wars (probably in 168). The cult seems to have been particularly important around the Black Sea and in the Balkans. Alexander himself married the daughter of Rutilianus, and seems to have fathered at least one child by a woman of Caesarea Trochetta. He died probably in the 170s. Lucian's attack on him dates to the reign of *Commodus, while inscriptions and excavation show that Glycon continued to be honoured well into the 3rd, and, possibly the 4th, cent. AD.

C. P. Jones, *Culture and Society in Lucian* (1986); R. J. Lane Fox, *Pagans and Christians* (1986); L. Robert, *A travers de l'Asie Mineure* (1980), and *CRAcad. Inscr.* 1981, 512–37. D. S. P.

Alexander (14) (*RE* 94) **of Aphrodisias,** commentator on *Aristotle. Appointed public teacher of Aristotelian philosophy, probably though not certainly in Athens, at some time between 198 and 209 AD (his treatise *On Fate* being dedicated then to *Septimius Severus and *Caracalla); referred to by later writers as '*the commentator*' on Aristotle. Commentaries on *Metaphysics A–Δ*, *Prior Analytics* 1, *Topics*, *Meteorologica*, and *De sensu* survive; others are extensively quoted by later writers. The commentaries on *Metaph. E–N* and on *Sophistical Refutations* are, in their present form, spurious. In a number of short treatises (*On the Soul, On Fate, On Mixture* surviving in Greek; *On Providence* in Arabic translation) Alexander presents as Aristotelian his own developments of Aristotelian material. There are also numerous short discussions, some preserved in Greek (*Quaestiones, Ethical Problems*) and others only in Arabic, which seem linked with his teaching activity but whose authenticity is debatable. The *Medical Puzzles and Physical Problems* (ed. J. L. Ideler, *Physici et Medici Graeci Minores* (1841)), *(Unpublished) Problems* (ed. U. C. Bussemaker, *Aristotelis Opera* (1857) 4. 291; H. Usener (1859)), and *On Fevers* (ed. Ideler, as above) are certainly spurious.

Alexander explained Aristotle in Aristotelian terms; he is better at producing ingenious explanations of particular points than at seeing the broader implications. He has been accused—perhaps unjustly—of a tendency to materialistic and mechanistic explanations, and to nominalism; but he recognizes the specific forms of things that possess matter as real, though separable from the matter only in thought. He denied individual immortality, and identified the Aristotelian Active Intellect with God, an interpretation adopted by Averroes but rejected by Aquinas. The (differing) explanations of how God can be the source of our understanding in his *On the Soul* and in the short piece *On the Intellect*, immensely influential in the Middle Ages but doubtfully authentic, are suggestive rather than convincing. Providence he interprets as the influence of the heavens on the sublunary world, ensuring the continuity of physical change and the survival of species, while denying any divine concern for individuals as such. In emphasizing the dependence of time on thought he was closer to Aristotle than were *Straton (1) or *Boethus (4) of Sidon, who made time exist in its own right.

Texts in *Commentaria in Aristotelem Graeca* 1–3 (1883–1901) and *Supplementum Aristotelicum* 2 pts. 1–2 (1887–1892). Translations (most with commentary): *On the Soul*, A. P. Fotinis (1979); *On Fate*, R. W. Sharples (1983), P. Thillet (Budé, 1984); *On Mixture*, in R. B. Todd, *Alexander on Stoic Physics* (1976); other works (including sections of the commentaries) in the series *Ancient Commentators on Aristotle*, ed. R. Sorabji (in progress). For texts and translations of the works preserved in Arabic see the bibliographies in Sharples (1987) (below) and in R.

Goulet (ed.), *Dictionnaire des philosophes antiques* 1 (1989) (with M. Aouad). Latin translations from the Arabic: G. Théry, *Bibliothèque Thomiste* 7 (1926). Other literature (a selection): K. Flannery, *Ways into the Logic of Alexander of Aphrodisias* (1995); P. Moraux, *Alexandre d'Aphrodise* (1942), and (ed. posth. J. Wiesner), *Der Aristotelismus*, (forthcoming); P. Merlan, *Monopsychism* (1963); R. W. Sharples, *ANRW* 2. 36. 2 (1987) (full bibliography and summary of current scholarship), and in R. Sorabji (ed.), *Aristotle Transformed* (1990). R. W. S.

Alexander (15) **Philalethes** ('Truth-lover'), a physician (fl. later 1st cent. BC?), succeeded *Zeuxis (3) as leader of the Asian branch of *Herophilus' 'school'. Alexander's views on digestion, on various diseases, and on invisible ducts (πόροι) dispersed throughout the body have much in common with those of *Asclepiades (3) of Bithynia, as the Anonymus Londinensis and the Methodists recognized. However, only one problematic later Latin source explicitly identifies Alexander as a 'pupil' (*discipulus*) of Asclepiades. In his *Gynaecia* Alexander asserted that there are no diseases peculiar to women, thus siding with both Herophilus and Asclepiades on this controversial issue (see APOLLONIUS (10) MYS; DEMETRIUS (21) OF APAMEA; ERASISTRATUS). He agreed with Herophilus and Aristotle that male 'seed' (σπέρμα) has its origin in the blood. In his doxographic work Τὰ ἀρέσκοντα ('Opinions'), he made an influential distinction between an 'objective' and a 'subjective' definition of the pulse. He argued for a modified 'objective' version of the pulse definitions advocated by the Herophileans *Bacchius, *Zeno (7), and *Chrysermus.

Ed., trans., and comm.: H. von Staden, *From Andreas to Demosthenes Philalethes* (1995), ch. 12. Cf. H. von Staden, *Herophilus* (1989) 532–9. H. v. S.

Alexander (16), of *Tralles, physician, AD 525–605, died in Rome. The author of an extant encyclopaedia of practical medicine, Alexander shows his continual adaptation of Graeco-Roman texts in light of his actual practice. He wrote the justly famous *Letter on Intestinal Worms*, a fundamental work in the history of early parasitology; excellent are his accounts of *ophthalmology, angina, pulmonary diseases, urology, gout, and *pharmacology, the last scattered throughout his writings.

TEXTS T. Puschmann, *Alexander von Tralles*, 2 vols. (1878–9; repr. 1963). Fr. trans. F. Brunet, *Œuvres médicales d'Alexandre de Tralles*, 4 vols. (1933–7).
LITERATURE J. Duffy and J. Scarborough, *DOP* 1984, 25–7, 226–8. J. Sca.

'Alexander Severus' See AURELIUS SEVERUS ALEXANDER, M.

'Alexander Romance' See PSEUDO-CALLISTHENES.

Alexandra See CASSANDRA; LYCOPHRON (2(*b*)).

Alexandria (1) was founded by *Alexander (3) the Great in 331 BC when he took *Egypt from the Persians. It was developed principally by the first two Ptolemies, who made it the capital of their kingdom and the main Mediterranean port of Egypt (see PTOLEMY (1)). It was founded as a theoretically autonomous city (*polis*) of the traditional Greek type, modelled in several respects on Athens: it had an exclusive hereditary citizenship organized by *demes, probably with an assembly (*ekklēsia*), council (*boulē*), and annually elected magistrates, it had its own territory, restricted to citizen-owners and exempt from direct royal taxation, its own coinage, and its own laws. Its founding citizens were recruited from all over the Greek world; there were also numerous non-citizen residents of Egyptian and other ethnic origin, including a large Jewish community which acquired special privileges though not full citizenship. Alexandria soon became one of the largest and grandest cities of the Mediterranean world, famed for the monumental magnificence of its two main intersecting streets, its palace-quarter with the tomb of Alexander and the *Museum and *Library, its Serapeum (see SARAPIS), *gymnasium, and Pharus, the *lighthouse at the entrance to its two capacious artificial harbours. As a royal capital Alexandria could not be a normal *polis*: its coinage and, probably, its laws were used throughout Egypt; in the course of the dynastic struggles of the later Ptolemies, in which its citizens naturally took a prominent part, Alexandria was, it seems, punished with the loss of its *ekklēsia* and *boulē*, and its magistrates became more like royal officials. These struggles also ignited the notorious antagonism between the 'Greek' citizen-body and the Jewish community, which continued to flare up in the Roman period (see JEWS).

When Egypt came under Roman rule the citizens of Alexandria retained most of their surviving privileges; they were also used extensively in the new administration of the province, and only they, in Egypt, could acquire Roman *citizenship. Despite several appeals to the Julio-Claudian emperors, Alexandria only regained a *boulē* in AD 200/1 when Septimius Severus granted councils to all the cities of Egypt; this development, and the universal grant of Roman citizenship in AD 212, undermined Alexandria's political primacy in Egypt, but not her Mediterranean-wide economic and cultural importance. With over 500,000 inhabitants, Alexandria was the second city of the Roman empire; it was also the main port of the eastern Mediterranean for state and private shipping, straddling the luxury trade between India and Rome. Fine public and private buildings continued to be erected, and the arts and crafts and intellectual pursuits flourished: notable were glassware manufacture (see GLASS) and *medicine. In the 3rd cent. AD the reputed see of St Mark the evangelist became one of the main centres of the Christian church, revitalizing Alexandria's claims to intellectual, artistic, political, and economic prominence within and beyond Egypt.

GENERAL Fraser, *Ptol. Alex.*; A. Jähne, *Klio* 1981, 63–101; D. Delia, *Alexandrian Citizenship during the Principate* (1991)

REMAINS E. Breccia, *Alexandrea ad Aegyptum*, 2nd edn. (1922); A. Adriani, *Repertorio d'arte dell'Egitto greco-romano* (1961–6); M. Rodziewicz, *Alexandrie 3: Les Habitations romaines tardives d'Alexandrie* (1984).   D. W. R.

Alexandria (2) **'near Issus',** close to Iskenderun (Alexandretta) on the gulf of Issus, a city founded by *Alexander (3) the Great or *Seleucus (1) I near the site of the battle (of *Issus where Alexander defeated *Darius III in 333 BC. Despite its strategic position below the approaches to the *Amanus mountains it was eclipsed by its north Syrian neighbours *Antioch (1) and *Seleuceia (2) in Pieria.   S. M.

Alexandria (3) **'of the Arachosians',** founded by *Alexander (3) the Great in 329 BC on the strategic site of the *Achaemenid capital of Arachosia (Old Kandahar). Besides a Graeco-Aramaic edict of *Ashoka (*SEG* 20. 326), a statue-base with a Hellenistic inscription has been found there (*SEG* 30. 1664).

P. Bernard, *StIr* 1974, 171–85; P. M. Fraser, *Afghan Studies*, 1 (1979) 9–21 and *Cities of Alexander the Great* (1996) 101, 132–40.   P. B.

Alexandria (4) **'of the Arians',** founded by *Alexander (3) the Great near Herat, on a different site from Artakoana. Important staging-point on route leading to Kandahar and India.

Bosworth, *HCA* 1 (1980), 356–7.   P. B.

Alexandria (5) **Eschate** ('the farthest'), founded close to Cyreschata (mod. Leninabad/Khodjend) on the Syr-Darya (*Jaxartes), the largest of seven *'Achaemenid' fortresses seized by *Alexander (3) the Great in this region. Renamed Antioch by *Antiochus (1) I.

F. L. Holt, *Alexander the Great and Bactria* (1988), 54–9.   P. B.

Alexandria (6) 'among the Paropamisadae', founded on the strategic site of Begram, about 80 km. (50 mi.) north of modern Kabul. (Also known as Alexandria in Caucaso, see Arrian *Anab.* 3. 28. 14 and 4. 22. 4, with Bosworth, *HCA*.)

P. Bernard, *Journ. Sav.* 1982, 217–42; P. Goukowsky, *Mélanges P. Lévêque* 2 (1989), 235–66.   P. B.

Alexandria (7) **Troas** was originally founded in 310 BC as Antigoneia by *Antigonus (1) but renamed soon after by *Lysimachus. The site lies on the coast of *Troas opposite Tenedos, and through the *synoecism of several surrounding communities it became the most important city of the region. It was refounded as a Roman colony under Augustus and flourished under the empire. Ti. *Claudius Atticus Herodes (1), *procurator of Asia under *Hadrian, supervised the construction of an *aqueduct there: the costs rose so high that he was obliged to underwrite them in person rather than draw on imperial revenues. A large bathhouse on the site dates to this period and can be associated with the project. See QUINCTILIUS VALERIUS MAXIMUS, SEX.

A. G. C. Smith, *Anat. St.* 1979, 23–51.   S. M.

Alexandrian Term used for the culture (esp. literary) of *Alexandria (1).

Alexandrianism, Latin See HELLENISTIC POETRY AT ROME.

Alexis, *c.*375–*c.*275 BC, poet of Middle and New Comedy (see COMEDY (GREEK), MIDDLE and NEW), born at *Thurii (*Suda* α 1138), but apparently living most of his long life in *Athens. He wrote 245 plays (*Suda*); the first of his two, three, or four *Lenaean victories came probably in the 350s (six after *Eubulus (2), four after *Antiphanes in the victors' list, *IG* 2². 2325. 150 = 5 C 1 col. 3. 11 Mette), and he won a victory in 347 at the *Dionysia (*IG* 2². 2318. 278 = 1. 14. 64 and 3 B 1 col. 2. 119 Mette). The good anonymous tractate on comedy (2. 17 p. 9 Kaibel, 3. p. 10 Koster) makes *Menander (1) a pupil of Alexis—a relationship more plausible than that of blood alleged in the *Suda*. About 140 titles and 340 fragments survive, but it is difficult to assess from them the part played by Alexis in the transition from Middle to New Comedy. However, four interesting points emerge: some signs of influence on Menander (e.g. the comparison of life to a carnival, Alexis fr. 222 KA = 219 K, Menander fr. 416 Körte–Thierfelder) are suspected but not proved; Alexis used both the older form of chorus which could be addressed by an actor (fr. 239 KA = 237 K) and the later form familiar from Menander (fr. 112 KA = 107 K); the παράσιτος (*parasite) almost certainly received this name from Alexis (fr. 183 KA = 178 K); and Alexis' *Agonis*, dating probably to the 330s, was an early example of the type of plot especially associated with New Comedy, involving a love affair with a courtesan, and probably a confidence trick and recognition. The fragments sometimes show a lively imagination and beauty of language: e.g. 70 KA and K, carnal passion a crime against real Love; 222 KA = 219 K; 230 KA = 228 K, old age as life's evening. Pleasant wit is revealed in frs. 107 KA = 102 K and 168 KA = 163 K (cf. W. G. Arnott, *Hermes* 1965, 298 ff.). Of interest also are frs. 46 KA = 45 K, a verbally clever comparison of man and wine; 103 KA = 98 K, a long description of aids to female beautification; 113 KA = 108 K, part of a postponed prologue of New-Comedy type; 129 KA = 124 K, a cook's cure (in pseudomedical language) for burnt pork; 140 KA = 135 K (from the *Linus*, one of about a dozen mythological burlesques in Alexis), Heracles' teacher with a library of classical Greek authors; 247 KA = 245 K, a man philosophizing about the nature of Eros.

Alexis' fame continued down to Roman times. A. *Gellius (*NA* 2. 23. 1) notes that his plays were adapted by Roman comedians; *Turpilius used Alexis' *Demetrius* as a model, and *Plautus' *Poenulus* may derive at least in part from his *Carchedonius*.

> FRAGMENTS The authoritative text is now Kassel–Austin, *PCG* 2. 21–195, although earlier scholars use the numbering in Kock, *CAF* 2. 297–408, 3. 744. Commentary by W. G. Arnott (1996).
>
> INTERPRETATION Meineke, *FCG* 1. 374 ff.; G. Kaibel, *RE* 1/2. (1894), 1468 ff. 'Alexis' 9; A. Olivieri, *Dioniso* 1939, 279 ff.; L. Gil, *Estudios Clásicos* 1970, 311 ff. (speculative); H.-G. Nesselrath, *Die attische Mittlere Komödie* (1990), *passim*; W. G. Arnott, *PCPS* 1970, 1 ff.; *La critica testuale greco-latina, oggi* (1981), 355 ff.; *Studi di filologia classica in onore di Giusto Monaco* 1 (1991), 327 ff.   W. G. A.

Alfenus Senecio, Lucius, from *Cuicul in Numidia, either the son of a procurator of the same names who became governor of Mauretania Caesariensis (see CAESAREA (3)), or perhaps identical with him—in which case he was promoted to the senate. Senecio was legate of Syria Coele (see SYRIA) in AD 200 and of *Britain between 205 and 208. Nine inscriptions from forts in the northern Pennines, Hadrian's Wall, and the outpost of Risingham, record rebuilding under his governorship. A dedication to Victory at Benwell suggests that he may have conducted a campaign shortly before Severus came to Britain.

> *PIR*[2] A 520–1; A. R. Birley, *The Fasti of Roman Britain* (1981) 157 ff.
>   A. R. Bi.

Alfenus (*RE* 8) **Varus, Publius,** suffect consul 39 BC. Born at *Cremona, he was the first Cisalpine to gain a consulship, and the only one under Augustus. (His son, consul AD 2, was presumably born in Rome, and of consular descent.) *Porphyrio, on Hor. *Sat.* 1. 3. 130, identifies *Alfenus vafer*, a cobbler who has given up his trade, with Alfenus Varus from Cremona. The identification is doubtful, but the scholiast (see SCHOLIA) knew Varus' origin. In 41 Varus, with two other men, was concerned with confiscating land in northern Italy, or extorting money in lieu of land, for distribution to *veterans. His title is variously given by different scholiasts, and there is no other information. He was harsh in treating Virgil's *Mantua (see the anxious flattery of *Ecl.* 9. 26 ff.), but may have aided Virgil in regaining his land or getting compensation. *Ecl.* 6. 6 f. shows that Varus (it must be Alfenus) had been an officer in a war, which was to be expected, in view of his extraordinary promotion. (The scholiast's 'explanation' is useless.) He studied law under Ser. *Sulpicius Rufus and became an eminent jurist: he composed 40 books of *Digesta* ('Ordered Abstracts'), a title he was the first to employ. Of this work 70 excerpts survive in Justinian's compilation of the same name (see JUSTINIAN'S CODIFICATION), the earliest coherent passages of legal writing to be preserved (see LEGAL LITERATURE). Citing consultative opinions (*responsa*) of his teacher Servius along with his own, Alfenus lacks logical rigour but is prepared to see legal remedies extended to new situations. He analyses the facts of the cases in which he is consulted in greater detail than do later lawyers.

> The obvious identification is frequently accepted, but was rejected by E. Fraenkel, *Horace* (1958) 89 f. and doubted by Syme (*AA* 386 n. 17). For the officers concerned in the confiscations see Broughton, *MRR* 2. 377 f. (full evidence and discussion).
>
> Alfenus as jurist: Lenel, *Pal.* 1. 38–54; Bremer 1. 280–330; Wieacker 1988, 607–9; Kunkel 1967, 29; Watson 1974, 162–7.   E. B.; T. Hon.

Alfius (Alphius) Avitus wrote *Libri rerum excellentium*, a gallery of famous deeds in Roman history, in iambic dimeters. He seems to have lived in the first half of the 3rd cent. AD.

> *PIR*[2] A 530; A. D. E. Cameron, *Harv. Stud.* 1988, 144; S. Mattiacci, *I frammenti dei 'Poetae Novelli'* (1982), 207; Courtney, *FLP* 403.   E. C.

Algidus, the easternmost section of the outer edge of the *Albanus mons, famous for its temples of Diana and Fortune and its fashionable villas (Hor. *Carm. saec.* 69; Livy 21. 62; Sil. 12. 536). The rim of the Albanus mons is here pierced by a narrow pass which the *Aequi seized in the 5th cent. BC. (Diod. Sic. 11. 40 implies the date 484). This pass, which the *via Latina later used, dominated the route to the *Hernici; consequently *Cincinnatus and other Roman generals strenuously tried to dislodge the Aequi, *Postumius Tubertus finally succeeding in 431.

> E. T. S.; T. W. P.

alimenta The purpose of the alimentary foundations in the Roman empire was to give an allowance for feeding children, and this was achieved by the investment of capital in mortgage on land, the mortage-interest being paid to, and administered by, cities or state-officials. The system originated in civic *euergetism, the earliest known benefactor being the senator T. Helvius Basila at *Atina in the late Julio-Claudian period (*ILS* 997). A later benefactor, the younger Pliny, who gave a similar endowment to *Comum, has recorded his reasons for doing so (*Ep.* 7. 18). Inscriptions record similar private benefactions both in Italy and in the provinces, the east included. Gifts from the imperial *fiscus to Italian towns for this purpose were first made by *Nerva and *Trajan. The evidence for the imperial scheme in Italy (continuing at least until the early 3rd cent. AD) comes mainly from honorific inscriptions set up by the beneficiaries and two alimentary tables from Veleia and Ligures Baebiani (*ILS* 6675; 6509). These show that local landowners pledged property to the value of roughly 12 and a half times a lump-sum loan from the emperor, on which they had to pay annual interest of five per cent into an alimentary fund. The total received annually in interest at Veleia was 55,800 sesterces, which was distributed among 263 boys, 35 girls, and two illegitimate children. The boys received 16 sesterces a month, the girls 12, and the illegitimate children 12 and 10 respectively. The imperial largess was widely advertised by Trajan, on the arch at *Beneventum (K. Fittschen, *Arch. Anz.* 87, 742 ff.) and on coins with the legend *Alim(enta) Ital(iae)* (Mattingly–Sydenham, *RIC* 2. 240). Pliny (*Pan.* 26) linked the system to Rome's manpower needs. One late-antique author ([Aur. Vict.] *Epit.* 12. 4) explicitly states its purpose as poor-relief, although it is not clear how needy the recipients in fact were, and food-distribution generally had a long-standing place in the symbolics of private and imperial *patronage. There is no reason to think that the landowners needed or even welcomed the loans (which placed a perpetual charge on their property). Hadrian extended the scheme to at least one provincial city (*Antinoöpolis).

> J. Patterson, *PBSR* 1987, 124 ff.; C. P. Jones, *JHS* 1989, 189 ff.; G. Woolf, *PBSR* 1990, 196 ff.   J. P. B.; A. J. S. S.

Alinda (mod. Karpuzlu), town in *Caria (SW Asia Minor), possibly of great antiquity (the name may occur in Hittite documents). It paid tribute to the 5th-cent. Athenian empire (see DELIAN LEAGUE) and was in *Mausolus' sphere of influence, though there is no direct evidence for Hecatomnid control before Mausolus' sister *Ada who occupied Alinda after being expelled from *Halicarnassus by her brother *Pixodarus (Arr. *Anab.* 1. 23.

8, calling it a strong Carian fortress). *Alexander (3) the Great may have re-founded it as Alexandria ad Latmum. The theatre and remarkable market-building are Hellenistic.

ATL 1. 468; G. E. Bean, *Turkey Beyond the Maeander*, 2nd edn. (1980), ch. 16; S. Hornblower, *Mausolus* (1982), 314.   S. H.

Aliso, a fort on or near the Lippe established during the wars of *Drusus, possibly the one mentioned by Cassius Dio (54. 33. 4) as set up in 11 BC 'at the point where the Lupia and the Elison unite'. The garrison resisted the advancing Germans after the defeat of P. *Quinctilius Varus in AD 9 and regained the Rhine (Vell. Pat. 2. 120). *Germanicus, in 15, refortified all the posts between Aliso and the Rhine and restored the road (Tac. *Ann.* 2. 7). The important fort-complex excavated at Haltern may be its remains.

C. M. Wells, *The German Policy of Augustus* (1972).   J. F. Dr.

Allectus, probably finance minister (*rationalis summae rei*) of the usurper *Carausius, whom he succeeded by assassination in AD 293. His coinage and the archaeological evidence of ambitious building-work in *Londinium contrast with the negative picture given by a panegyric of *Constantius I, who finally organized a successful invasion of Britain in 296, in which the praetorian prefect Asclepiodotus defeated and killed Allectus.

P. J. Casey, *Britannia* 1977, 283–301; N. Shiel, *The Episode of Carausius and Allectus* (1977); A. Burnett, *British Numismatic Journal* 1984, 21–40; T. Williams, in V. A. Maxfield and M. J. Dobson (eds.), *Roman Frontier Studies* (1989), 132–41.   R. S. O. T.

allegory, Greek

Allegorical expression Elements of allegory are present in Greek literature from the earliest stage: in *Homer, in Phoenix' Prayers (Λιταί, *Il.* 9. 502–12), and *Achilles' image of *Zeus' jars (*Il.* 24. 527–33); in *Hesiod, the fable of the hawk and the nightingale (*Op.* 204–12) and the personifications of Aidos, *Nemesis, and *Dike (1) (*Op.* 197–201, 256–62). If an ancient interpretation is accepted, *Alcaeus (1) frs. 6 and 326 LP presented political exhortation through nautical imagery. Larger-scale allegorical tableaux and narratives begin to be composed in the late 5th and early 4th cents.: *Prodicus' Choice of *Heracles (Xen. *Mem.* 2. 1. 21), and *Plato (1)'s myths (esp. *Phd.* 108e ff.; *Resp.* 524a ff., 614b ff.; *Phdr.* 246a ff.). Thereafter, literary allegory remains largely the territory of philosophers and moralists (e.g. *Cleanthes in Cic. *Fin.* 2. 69; Dio Chrys. *Or.* 1. 58 ff. and 5; *Plutarch *De gen.* 590a ff.).

In the visual arts, though images of deified abstractions (*Eros, *Fates, Graces (see CHARITES)) are found early and are well established e.g. in Hesiod on the literary side, the possibilities of allegorical representation do not apparently begin to be exploited systematically until the Hellenistic era, with such works of sculpture as *Lysippus (2)'s Opportunity and the Archelaus relief in honour of Homer, and of painting as *Apelles' Calumny and Aetion's Alexander and Roxane (Lucian, *Cal.* 5; *Herodotus* 4–6). Visual and literary traditions converge in readings of (real or fictitious) works of art such as *Lucian's, or the moral allegory of the *Tabula Cebetis* (see CEBES).

Allegorical interpretation (allegorēsis) Allegorical reading of works of literature—above all the mythological poems of Homer and Hesiod, decoded as accounts of the physical world or the truths of morality—seems to begin as early as the 6th cent. BC and to be an established (if controversial) practice by the end of the 5th. *Theagenes (2) of Rhegium, *Anaxagoras, and his pupil *Metrodorus (2) of Lampsacus are all named as pioneers (Schol.

Il. 20. 67; Diog. Laert. 2. 3. 11), and there is evidence for allegorical exegesis among the sophists (Richardson, *PCPS* 1975). Plato, though ready to construct allegories in his myths, treated allegorical interpretation as either trivial (*Phdr.* 229e) or pernicious (*Resp.* 378d). Throughout this early period it is hard to be sure what the balance was between 'defensive' allegoresis (rescuing the poets and their myths from charges of intellectual naïvety and impiety) and 'positive' allegoresis (claiming the poets' authority for the interpreter's own doctrines). In either case, the underlying motive force was (and would continue to be) the cultural need to maintain the authority of the revered classics in the face of new (philosophical) traditions of thought.

In the Hellenistic and Roman periods, 'defensive' allegoresis became chiefly the territory of grammarians, in a vein now best represented by the relatively late works of Heraclitus (*Homeric Questions*) and ps.-Plutarch (*Life and Poetry of Homer*). *Crates (3) of Mallus, working in Pergamum, within a Stoic frame of reference, seems to have been a particularly influential figure in this tradition. Not all grammarians allegorized, however: Crates' Homeric interpretations were stoutly contested by his *Alexandrian contemporary *Aristarchus (2).

In the sphere of 'positive' allegoresis, special importance is normally attached to the work of the Stoics (now best represented by the treatise of *Cornutus, 1st cent. AD): see e.g. Philodemus, *De piet.* 15–16. *Zeno (2), *Chrysippus, and others (see STOICISM) undeniably provided a rich set of readings and techniques for later allegorists to work with. They may, however, have thought of themselves as recovering the beliefs of early man about the world, as transmitted (and distorted) by the poets, rather than as interpreting the minds and the words of the poets themselves. It would then be only with the *Neopythagoreans and *Neoplatonists, in the 2nd cent. AD and subsequently, that the philosophical tradition produced strongly 'positive' allegorical readings, presenting the poets themselves (Homer above all) as the first and greatest philosophers (Numenius, frs. 30–2 Des Places; Porphyry, *Cave of the Nymphs*; Proclus *Comm. on Plato Resp.* 2, 3, and 10). Homer was by this stage being built up, as a figure of authority to resist the rival claims of Moses and Christ, on behalf of pagan Greek culture.

Terminology Earlier allegorists tend to speak of an author's ὑπόνοια ('covert meaning'). The term ἀλληγορία (ἀλληγορέω) seems only to have emerged in the Hellenistic era; when it is formally defined as a rhetorical trope (e.g. Tryphon, 3. 193 Spengel), its scope is broad, including metaphor, gnomic utterance, and riddle as well as 'allegory' in the modern sense. αἰνίττομαι and αἴνιγμα ('hint', 'riddle', etc.) are also used to signal allegorical procedures.

TEXTS Heraclitus, F. Buffière (1962); Ps.-Plutarch, J. Kindstrand (1990); Cornutus, C. Lang (1881).
STUDIES J. Joosen and J. Waszink, *RAC* 1 (1950) 'Allegorese'; J. Tate, *CR* 1927, 214; *CQ* 1929, 41, 142; 1930, 1; 1934, 105; F. Buffière, *Les Mythes d'Homère* (1956); J. Pépin, *Mythe et allégorie*, 2nd edn. (1976); N. Richardson, *PCPS* 1975, 65; J. Onians, *Art and Thought* (1979), ch. 3; H. A. Shapiro, *Boreas* 1986, 4; D. Russell, *Criticism in Antiquity* (1991), 95; R. Lamberton, *Homer the Theologian* (1986); G. Most, *ANRW* 2. 36. 3 (1989), 2014; R. Lamberton and J. Keaney, *Homer's Ancient Readers* (1992), chs. 2–3; D. Dawson, *Allegorical Readers* (1992).   M. B. T.

allegory, Latin An awareness of the Greek traditions of allegory (see ALLEGORY, GREEK) entered Rome with the Hellenization of Roman culture; *Ennius and *Varro adopted Greek methods with the Roman gods, and the Stoic in *Cicero's *De natura deorum*

(2. 62–9) supplies examples of 'etymological' allegorism on these lines, deriving e.g. *Neptunus* from *nare*. *Lucretius engages extensively with physical and moral allegories of the gods and of the Underworld; *Virgil's imitation of Homer seems to reveal an awareness of the allegorical interpretations typical of the Pergamene school (for example of the Shield of Achilles). *Horace defends the claims of poetry with allegorizing interpretations of the *Odyssey* (*Epist.* 1. 2) and of the tales of *Orpheus and *Amphion (*Ars. P.* 391 ff.). *Apuleius works a Platonizing psychological allegory into his fable of Cupid and Psyche (*Met.* 4. 28 ff.). The word ἀλληγορία first appears in a Roman author (Cicero), although it has a restricted use, as a term of rhetoric. The author of one of the surviving Greek handbooks of allegory, *Cornutus, was an associate of *Lucan, *Persius, and L. *Annaeus Seneca (2), although the last is dismissive of allegory.

Personification allegory, which goes back to *Homer and *Hesiod, is developed, as in Virgil's figure of *Fama* (*Aen.* 4. 173 ff.), and in *Propertius' explanation of the attributes of *Amor* (2. 12); it was much extended by *Ovid in his picturesque Palace of the Sun, House of Sleep, etc. (*Met.* 2. 1 ff.; 11. 592 ff.), establishing a tradition that goes through *Statius to *Prudentius' *Psychomachia* and the fully-developed medieval use of continuous personification allegory.

Some allegories come directly from the Greek: *Horace reworks *Alcaeus' Ship of State (*Odes* 1. 14); *Silius adapts the Choice of *Heracles in the Dream of Scipio (*Pun.* 15. 18 ff.). Allegories from the Greek historiographical tradition are reworked in Tarquin's message to his son (see TARQUINIUS SUPERBUS) and *Menenius Agrippa's fable on the belly and other limbs (Livy 1. 54; 2. 32). The most novel tendency was the allegorical representation of contemporary persons and events: the shepherds of Virgil (and of his imitators) correspond, intermittently and in complex ways, with real persons, thus paving the way for the thorough allegory of later *pastoral. The legendary characters in the *Aeneid* are vehicles for some characteristics and actions of historical personages. Virgil's suggestive allusiveness is transformed into a rigidly schematic allegorization of persons and concepts by the line of Virgilian commentators passing through *Donatus (1) and *Fulgentius.

J. Whitman, *Allegory: The Dynamics of an Ancient and Medieval Technique* (1987); C. S. Lewis, *The Allegory of Love* (1936); D. C. Feeney, *The Gods in Epic* (1991), see index under 'allegory', 'personifications'; D. L. Drew, *The Allegory of the Aeneid* (1927); G. W. Most, *ANRW* 2. 36. 3 (1989), 2014–65; D. Comparetti, *Vergil in the Middle Ages* (trans. of 1st edn. of 1895).

J. T.; P. R. H.

Allia, a stream flowing into the *Tiber on the east bank, 18 km. (11 mi.) north of Rome (probably modern Fosso della Bettina), where the Romans, unable to defend the lightly fortified city, confronted, and were overwhelmed by, a Gallic war-band (18 July 390 BC). The related but differing accounts of the battle in our sources are probably later reconstructions.

CAH 7²/2 (1989), 302 ff. A. D.

alliance (Greek) Fundamentally, an agreement between states to fight together (*symmachein*) against a common enemy, so that the standard term is *symmachia*. Such alliances might be made either for a limited period or for all time. *Thucydides (2), 1. 44. 1, 5. 48. 2, distinguishes between a *symmachia*, as a full offensive and defensive alliance, and an *epimachia*, as a purely defensive alliance; but that use of the two terms is not widespread, and, for instance, the prospectus of the *Second Athenian Confederacy,

which was a defensive alliance, consistently uses *symmachein* and cognate words (*IG* 2². 43 = Tod 123). In a full offensive and defensive alliance it was commonly stated that the participating states were to 'have the same friends and enemies': that formulation might be used when the alliance was on an equal basis, but it could be adapted to circumstances in which one participant was inferior to the other, as in 404 BC when *Athens undertook both to have the same friends and enemies as *Sparta and to follow Sparta's lead.

The *Peloponnesian League, built up by Sparta in the second half of the 6th cent. BC, was the first instance of a league of allies united for purposes of foreign policy. Such leagues tended to be formed with a dominant state as leader (*hēgemōn*), influential through possession of executive power even if not formally privileged in decision-making, and with a council which played a part in decision-making and enabled representatives of the member states to express opinions and vote. Other examples were the *Delian League, the Second Athenian Confederacy, the league centred on *Thebes (1) in the 360s and after, and the League of Corinth (see CORINTH, LEAGUE OF) organized by *Philip (1) II of Macedon. In the Delian League Athens came to interfere in various ways with the *autonomy of the members; and to win support for her Second Confederacy she gave undertakings that such interference would not be repeated. In the Hellenistic period *federal states which expanded beyond their core membership, such as the *Achaean Confederacy and the *Aetolian Confederacy, took the place of leagues centred on a *hēgemōn*.

SOURCES For 770–338 BC, *Die Staatsverträge des Altertums* 2², ed. H. Bengtson; for 338–200 BC, *Die Staatsverträge des Altertums* 3, ed. H. H. Schmitt (1969).

MODERN LITERATURE W. S. Ferguson, *Greek imperialism* (1913), chs. 1–3, 7; G. Busolt, *Griechische Staatskunde* 3rd edn., 2 (1926), pt. 3; V. Martin, *La Vie internationale dans la Grèce des cités* (1940), pt. 2 ch. 1; I. Calabi, *Ricerche sui rapporti tra le poleis* (1953), chs. 2, 3, 5; V. Ehrenberg, *The Greek state*, 2nd edn. (1969), pt. 1 ch. 3; K. Tausend, *Amphiktyonie und Symmachie*, Hist. Einzelschr. 73 (1992). P. J. R.

alliance (Roman) See AMICITIA; FOEDUS; SOCII.

Allifae, mountain town overlooking the *Volturnus the gateway between *Samnium and *Campania: modern Castello d'Alife (with interesting museum in nearby Piedimonte d' Alife). Strategic Allifae changed hands repeatedly in the Samnite Wars. Under Rome it descended to lower ground and became a flourishing town (mod. Alife, with well-preserved Roman walls, etc.).

BTCGI 3 (1984) 'Alife'. E. T. S.; D. W. R. R.

Allobroges, a developing iron age people of central Gaul. They were annexed to Rome in 121 BC by Cn. *Domitius Ahenobarbus (2) and Q. *Fabius Maximus (Allobrogicus). An attempted revolt was crushed by C. Pomptinus (61). On the other hand, they rejected *Catiline (63) and *Vercingetorix (52). Under the empire they were attached to Narbonensis, and became highly Romanized, producing the province's first consul, D. *Valerius Asiaticus. In the later empire their territory was divided, and administered from *Vienna (the original capital, now an important episcopal centre), Geneva, and Grenoble.

A. L. F. Rivet, *Gallia Narbonensis* (1988). J. F. Dr.

Al Mina, a port at the mouth of the river *Orontes in Turkey, excavated by Sir Leonard Woolley in 1936–7. It was established as a trading-post (*emporion*) by 800 BC and visited by Cypriots and Greeks (mainly Euboeans and islanders). The Greek interest became dominant, with east Greeks and carriers of Corinthian pottery replacing the islanders in the 7th cent. After an interval under Babylonian domination the port revived under the Persians, now with a strong Phoenician element (coinage); it flourished until eclipsed by the foundation of *Seleuceia (2) in 301 BC. The old identification with the Greek foundation at Posideum now seems unlikely, since the latter was almost certainly at mod. Ras el-Basit, 40 km. (25 mi.) further south.

DCPP, entry under 'Al Mina'; L. Woolley, JHS 1938; S. Smith, Arch. Journ. 1942; J. Boardman, The Greeks Overseas, 3rd edn. (1980), 61 ff.; J. Elayi, StPhoen 1987.

J.-F. S.

Aloadae, in mythology, Otus and *Ep(h)ialtes (2), sons of Iphimedia and not in fact Aloeus but *Poseidon (Od. 11. 305; Hes. Catalogus mulierum. fr. 19 M–W). After nine years they were 9 cubits broad and 9 fathoms tall (Od. 11. 310–11). They imprisoned *Ares in a bronze vessel for thirteen months, but *Hermes got him out (Il. 5. 385–91). To reach heaven, they piled *Ossa on *Olympus (1) and *Pelion on Ossa, filling the sea with mountains and making land into sea (Apollod. 1. 7. 4, and perhaps Hes. Catalogus mulierum fr. 21 M–W). They also had designs on *Artemis and *Hera; but Artemis changed into a deer in their midst and they shot each other—an event somehow orchestrated by *Apollo on *Naxos (1) (Apollod 1. 7. 4; Od. 11. 305, 310–11; Pind. Pyth. 4. 88 and schol., fr. 163 Snell–Maehler; Hyg. Fab. 28). Matching this story, their graves were found in their precinct on Naxos (IG 12. 5. 56; Diod. Sic. 5. 5. 1). They might account too for the discovery of oversize bones, whether in *Crete or *Thessaly (Philostr. Her. 289 K).

F. Pfister, Der Reliquienkult in Altertum (1909), 425–6.   H. J. R.; K. D.

Alphabet, Greek In early Greece various forms of alphabet were current but all derived from a *Phoenician (Semitic) source, which must have reached the Aegean in the earlier 8th cent. (before our earliest Greek examples of c.740). Recent arguments dating the transfer much earlier are not supported by any material evidence. The alphabet was taken in the order of the Semitic model: $ABΓΔEFΙHΘIKΛMNΞOΠMϘPΣT$; not all states used all letters, but all probably retained them in the mechanically repeated order. Certain states found no use for F ('vau', u̯), others for $Ξ$ (properly, perhaps, a more complicated sibilant than is implied by our x), or $Ϙ$ ('qoppa', the k before o and u); and for s some used $Σ$, but others preferred M ('san', perhaps corresponding to the English pronunciation of z). The most striking feature in the Greek adaptation of the Phoenician model is that by altering (consciously or unconsciously) the original significance of $AEIO$ and adding Y Greek, unlike Phoenician, achieved an independent representation of vowel-sounds. $YΦXΨΩ$ are all Greek additions. Y, from its sound and shape, appears to be a variant of F, a vowel u derived from the semivowel u̯; evidently it belongs to the very early stage of adaptation, for no local alphabet lacks it. $Ω$, an Ionic invention, is also a doublet, formed by breaking the O. Received Semitic shapes were generally 'tidied up' in Greece—with verticals and horizontals conditioning the appearance of individual letters; hence a number of 'indeterminate' Semitic shapes yielded different Greek versions, e.g. $Γ$ and $Λ$ from gimel and $Λ$ or V from lamed. The exact origin of the three double-consonant letters $ΦXΨ$ is disputed, but they all appear early. Another non-Phoenician letter T ('sampi') was used in eastern Ionian areas for the sibilant rendered elsewhere as $ΣΣ$ or TT. Other Greek states also produced occasionally their own symbol for some sound not covered by the common alphabet, e.g. ↗ for psi in parts of central Greece and the Achaean colonies, but they too have a restricted use.

An early form of the Greek alphabet is preserved in the Archaic inscriptions of the Dorian islands, Thera, Melos, and in particular Crete. We find F, $Ϙ$ and M, as in many other 'epichoric' or local scripts, but Cretan lacks the aspirate and H stands for eta (as in Ionia) and the non-Phoenician additions $Φ$, X, and $Ψ$ are lacking, with $Π$ (or $ΠH$), K (or KH) and $ΠM$ used instead. Omega is $⊙$ or $⊚$. Other states adopt various forms of xi, chi, and psi. 'Blue' alphabets (after Kirchhoff's coloured map) use X for kh and $Ψ$ for ps (if they used a letter for ps at all; otherwise $ΦΣ$); also $Ξ$ (if not $XΣ$) for x. 'Red' alphabets used $Ψ$ for kh and X (occasionally $XΣ$) for x. A rough division is 'blue' = eastern, 'red' = western, though 'blue' Corinth and 'red' Rhodes are among the exceptions. Most colonies used the script of their metropolis (e.g. the colonies of Euboea and Achaea); but some may not have, e.g. Megara's western colonies and Syracuse; lack of early material from Megara itself and from Syracuse raises uncertainties.

One variety of the eastern alphabets, namely the East Ionic, eventually became predominant. In the Ionic dialect (as in many others) short e possibly had a close quantity [e] (see PRONUNCIATION, GREEK), but there were two forms of long e, one open and the other close: [e:] and [ɛ:]. Through the absence of the h-sound in Ionic pronunciation, the aspirate-letter H in this script stood not for an emphatic h with its (apparent) following vowel-sound e, but only for a lengthened vowel-sound [ɛ:]; again, it is uncertain whether this was originally a conscious or unconscious alteration. The East Ionic alphabet appears also to have originated the new symbol $Ω$ (see above) to represent [ɔ:]. [e:] and [o:] continued for a time to be denoted by E and O like the short vowels, but before 400 BC the development of the original diphthongs ei and ou into simple long vowels of close quality made it possible to use EI and OY not only for the original diphthongs but also for the [e:] and [o:] that had never been diphthongal (e.g. εἰμὶ κοῦρος, older EMI $KOPOΣ$).

The East Ionic alphabet was officially adopted by Athens in the archonship of Euclides (403–402 BC), but had infiltrated fully into private script by then. Its acceptance by the whole Greek world was complete by about 370. A few non-Ionic elements like F lingered locally for some time. When the Ionic H was used for eta a modification was introduced in some areas to express the rough breathing, ⊢; it gave rise to the later sign '.

Many changes in letter shape were also introduced, largely in the late 4th and 3rd cents., from writing in ink, so-called 'cursives'; they present rounded, simplified forms, C from $Σ$, $ϵ$ from E, $ω$ from $Ω$ and the like.

A Kirchhoff, Studien zur Geschichte des griech. Alphabets (1887); C. D. Buck, Comparative Grammar of Greek and Latin (1932), 68 ff., and The Greek Dialects (1955), 17 ff.; G. Klaffenbach, Griechische Epigraphik (1957); A. G. Woodhead, The Study of Greek Inscriptions (1959); M. Guarducci, Epigrafia greca 1 (1967); A. Heubeck, Schrift (1979); M. Guarducci, L'Epigrafia Greca dalle Origini al Tardo Impero (1987); Jeffery, LSAG; C. Baurain, C. Bonnet, and V. Krings (eds.) Phoinikeia Grammata (1992).

J. W. P.; L. H. J.; A. W. J.

alphabet, Latin See ALPHABETS OF ITALY.

alphabets of Italy There is no evidence for any form of writing in Italy before the arrival of Greek colonists in the 8th cent. BC. The Euboean alphabet brought by settlers at *Pithecusae (mod. Ischia) and *Cumae was borrowed by the *Etruscans, who acted as intermediaries for the spread of writing throughout much of the peninsula. Only in southern regions adjacent to other Greek settlements was the Greek alphabet again borrowed directly, as in *Lucania (for writing *Oscan) and the Sallentine peninsula (with some modifications, for writing *Messapian).

An alphabet learnt as such (the theoretical alphabet) may contain more letters than are in practice used. So a number of 7th-cent. Etruscan abecedaria (written-out alphabets) adhere to the Greek model and include letters such as *b*, *d*, or *o* that are not found in texts: *abcdevzhθiklmnšopśqrstuśφχ*. (Here *c* is the Greek gamma but with the value /k/; *v* is the sign *F*, the Greek digamma, with the value /w/.) Later abecedaria show a reduced inventory corresponding to the letters actually in use (*acevzhθiklmnpśqrstuφχf*), but when the Etruscan alphabet was adapted for writing other languages, there would often still have been the fuller resources of the original theoretical alphabet to draw on. New alphabets were created by selection from the available letters, sometimes with revised values, and by invention of further letters (normally added at the end).

There are several versions of the Etruscan alphabet. Many differences concern the shapes of letters, but more important are the variations in the system. The notation of /f/ changes with time: in the absence of an appropriate sign in the Greek alphabet, at first a digraph *vh* was used but from the mid-6th cent. this was displaced by a single letter 8 = *f*, of disputed origin, added at the end of the alphabet, as abecedaria show. There is also regional variation, especially between northern and southern alphabets. In the south /k/ was represented by different letters distributed according to the quality of the following vowel, so *ce*, *ci* but *ka* and *qu*, with later generalization of *c*; in the north, *k* was used to the exclusion of *c* and *q*. Etruscan distinguished two sibilants which were written with the letters *s* and *ś*, but the values of these are reversed between north and south. Exclusively southern is the syllabic punctuation in use from the late 7th cent. through to the mid-5th.

The Latin alphabet shared several developments with the Faliscan (see FALISCANS) alphabet. It was based on a southern Etruscan type, as is shown by the use of *c* for /k/ (and in early inscriptions the alternation *c* ~ *k* ~ *q* before different vowels, reflected in the letter names *cē*, *kā*, *qū*). This use of *c* meant that while *b* and *d* (as well as *o*) could be recovered from the theoretical alphabet with their Greek values, there was no sign for /g/: in the third century the letter G, a modification of C, was invented for the Latin alphabet and, unusually, was not added at the end but took the place of otiose *z*, attested in a 4th-cent. abecedarium. (The addition of *y* and *z* in final position took place only in the 1st cent. BC as an aid to the proper rendering of Greek words.) The letter X, the rarely used *ś* of the Etruscan alphabet, regained its Euboean value /ks/. A very early Latin innovation was the use of F alone, by simplification of the original digraph *vh*, to write /f/ (in the Faliscan alphabet a sign ↑ is found); this was accompanied by the use of *u* for /w/ as well as /u/. The Latin alphabet was thus: *abcdefghiklmnopqrstux* (*yz*). Several peoples of Italy in due course adopted the Latin alphabet for writing their own language, which could involve alterations: for instance, the Umbrians used a diacritic to distinguish between S and Ṡ, the latter representing a sound resulting from the palatalization of /k/; in Paelignian inscriptions there is a letter Ð, differentiated from D but of uncertain value.

The Oscan alphabet was created in Campania, probably in the late 5th cent. BC; a few mainly fragmentary abecedaria give the order: *abgdevzhiklmnprstufiú*. The letter forms show that its basis was the local version of the Etruscan alphabet, but the presence of *b*, *g*, *d* in their original position indicates knowledge of the theoretical alphabet; there is, however, no *o*, and *u* does

duty for both /u/ and /o/. The alphabet once ended with *f*, and the earliest inscriptions are written with this set of letters, but in the 4th cent. two new signs were added at the end: Ⱶ = *í*, to write a front vowel distinct from those written with *e* and *i*, and V̇ = *ú* with the value /o/.

The Umbrian (see OSCAN AND UMBRIAN) alphabet (as attested at *Iguvium, see TABULAE IGUVINAE) is derived from a northern Etruscan alphabet and consists of: *abřevzhiklmnprstufç* (there are no abecedaria to confirm the number of letters or their order). As with the early Oscan alphabet, *u* stands for both /u/ and /o/. Original *d* is still used for /d/ in an inscription of *c*.400 BC (from Todi), but acquired a new value after a change affecting intervocalic /d/ gave a sound represented by *rs* in the Latin alphabet, whence the conventional transcription of the Umbrian letter as *ř*; henceforth /d/ was written with *t*, which also stood for /t/. Perhaps by analogy with this, *p* could be used in place of *b* for /b/; there is no trace of a separate letter for /g/. A new letter *ç* was created to indicate the sound represented in the Latin alphabet by *Ṡ* (see above).

There is evidence from the 6th cent. for the *Venetic alphabet, which derives in the first instance from a northern Etruscan source, early enough for /f/ to be still written with the digraph *vh* rather than 8. Southern Etruscan influence, however, is to be seen in the subsequent introduction of syllabic punctuation. From the outset *o* is present, presumably taken from the theoretical model; its surprising position at the end of the alphabet, according to later abecedaria, would then be the result of secondary reordering. Unusually, *φ* and *χ* are used for /b/ and /g/; in the earliest texts *θ* stands for /t/ and *t* for /d/, but there are later local variations in the notation of dentals, e.g. at Este *z* is used for /d/. Dedications in the form of writing tables give abecedaria, as well as lists of letter groups, etc. that reveal methods of scribal training.

Amongst other alphabets of Etruscan derivation in northern Italy, the Lepontic alphabet, devised for writing a Celtic language and attested from the 6th cent. on, resembles the Venetic alphabet in having *o* and in using *θ* ~ *t* to mark the opposition /t/ ~ /d/ in early inscriptions. For /g/, *χ* is found, but not consistently; there is no early evidence for /b/. In later inscriptions, *p* stands for /p/ and /b/, and *t* is used for both /t/ and /d/, yielding a remarkably reduced alphabet (the order of letters is not known): *aeiklmnpśrstuχo*.

M. Lejeune, *Rev. Ét. Lat.* 1957, 88 ff.; H. Rix, in M. Cristofani (ed.), *Gli Etruschi: Una nuova immagine* (1984), 210 ff.; R. Wachter, *Altlateinische Inschriften* (1987); G. Fogolari and A. L. Prosdocimi, *I Veneti antichi* (1988); M. Pandolfini and A. L. Prosdocimi, *Alfabetari e insegnamento della scrittura in Etruria e nell'Italia antica* (1990).   J. H. W. P.

Alphesiboea, in mythology, daughter of *Phegeus of Psophis and wife of *Alcmaeon (1). According to Propertius 1. 15. 15, she and not Callirhoë's children avenged him; perhaps a mere blunder, perhaps an unknown variant.   H. J. R.

Alpheus (Ἀλφειός), the largest river of the *Peloponnese, rises in south *Arcadia near Asea and flows past *Olympia to the Ionian Sea. Its main tributaries are the Arcadian Ladon and Erymanthus; the Cladeus joins it at one corner of the ancient sanctuary at Olympia. As early as Homer (*Il.* 11. 727) Alpheus was also a river-god, son of *Oceanus (Hes. *Theog.* 338); in later sources he drowns himself in the river named after him either from unrequited love for Arethusa or remorse over his fratricide. Late cult for him is attested at Olympia and Sparta (Paus. 5. 14. 6, 3. 12. 9).

R. Baladié, *Le Péloponnese de Strabon* (1980), see index. In art: *LIMC* 1, 'Alpheios'.   T. J. D.; R. J. H.; A. J. S. S.

Alps Although the passes of the Alps had been used for trans-European commerce since prehistoric times, the early Greeks had no knowledge of these mountains, though a vague notion of them may lurk in their speculations about the *Hercynian Forest and the *Rhipaei montes; in Herodotus (4. 49) 'Alpis' is a tributary of the Danube. By the 4th cent. Greek travellers in north Italy and Provence brought information about a 'pillar' or 'buttress' of the north (Ephorus, in Scymn. 188); but *Apollonius (1) Rhodius (4. 627 f.) could still believe that the Rhône (Rhodanus) and Po (*Padus) were interconnected. The Roman conquest of *Cisalpine Gaul and Hannibal's invasion of Italy (Polyb. 3. 50–6; Livy 21. 32–7; the pass remains unidentified) brought more detailed knowledge, and *Polybius (1) gave a good description of the western Alps, though he thought that they extended uniformly in a west–east direction. The campaigns of *Caesar in Gaul, and of *Tiberius in Switzerland and Austria, opened up the Alps thoroughly, and in the first two centuries AD at least five paved roads (Little and Great St Bernard, Splügen, Maloja, and Brenner passes) were built across them. Strabo defined the curve of the Alps with substantial correctness, and graphically described their vegetation and the predatory habits of the valley populations.

The Romans distinguished the following chains: Alpes Maritimae, Cottiae (from Monte Viso), Graiae (the St Bernard section), Poeninae (Mont Blanc–Monte Rosa), Raeticae (Grisons), Noricae (Tyrol), Carnicae, and Venetae. They also gave the name of 'Alps' to the Austrian and Dalmatian mountains.

Roman Provinces Augustus reduced the area north of Nice (*Nicea (2)) on both sides of the Var and constituted it as the province of Alpes Maritimae in 14 BC: it was governed by a *praefectus, later by a *procurator, and the conquest was commemorated by the construction of the Tropaeum Alpium at La Turbie (see TROPHIES), above Monaco, in 7 or 6 BC. The district further north, after pacification, was left under the rule of M. *Iulius Cottius; later it was annexed by *Nero and known as Alpes Cottiae. These two little provinces formed buffers between Italy and Gaul. After *Diocletian Alpes Cottiae was restricted to an area east of the Alps, extended eastwards, and included in the diocese (*dioecesis) of Italy under a praeses. Alpes Maritimae was limited to west of the Alps and extended; it was united to the Gallic diocese. In the second century a third Alpine province had been created, Alpes Atrectianae et Poeninae, comprising part of *Raetia; it included the vallis Poenina (upper Rhône valley, today Valais) with its centre at Octodurum (Martigny) and was under a procurator. Diocletian renamed it Alpes Graiae et Poeninae.

L. Pauli, *The Alps: Archaeology and Early History* (1984); N. Lamboglia, *La Trophée d'Auguste à la Turbie* (1964); N. Christie, *JRA* 1991, 410 f.
H. H. S.; T. W. P.

altars Indispensable adjunct of *sacrifice in ancient religion.

Greek The chief type was the raised *bōmos* ($\beta\omega\mu\acute{o}\varsigma$) on which a wood fire was lit for the cremation of the victim's thigh-bones and spit-roasting of the entrails; *hero-cults by contrast commonly employed the *eschara* ($\grave{\epsilon}\sigma\chi\acute{\alpha}\rho\alpha$), a low altar onto which the victim's blood was made to flow; the domestic altar was for bloodless offerings (natural produce, *cakes, etc.). In Greek *sanctuaries monumental open-air *bōmoi*, usually of dressed stone (the ash altar of Zeus at *Olympia seems to have been unusual), are well attested archaeologically from the 6th cent. BC onwards; they were typically rectangular and sometimes approached by a flight of steps. Independent altars on a spectacular scale are a feature of the Hellenistic age—e.g. the so-called Great Altar of *Pergamum (early 2nd cent. BC), incorporating a sculptured frieze *c.*120 m. (130 yds.) long; the tradition was continued in the Roman east with the so-called Great Antonine Altar of *Ephesus (begun *c.* AD 166). In Greek myth and real life altars were traditionally places of refuge, the suppliants protected by the deity to whom the altar belonged (see also ASYLIA).

Roman The Latin terms *altaria* (plur.) and *ara* (variously explained by Roman antiquarians) derive from the roots denoting 'burning' (of sacrificial offerings). Normally of stone, of varying size, from small *cippi* (stone-markers) to large structures (as the *Ara Pacis), most often quadrangular (occasionally round), and decorated with reliefs, they were dedicated to a particular deity, and stood either separately or in front of temples (inside only for incense and bloodless offerings). A separate category consists of funerary altars (also cinerary urns often had the shape of altars).

GREEK C. G. Yavis, *Greek Altars* (1949); R. Tomlinson, *Greek Sanctuaries* (1976) 37 ff.; R. Étienne and M.-T. Le Dinahet (eds.), *L'Espace sacrificiel* (1991); H. van der Meijden, *Terrakotta-Arulae aus Sizilien und Unteritalien* (1993).
ROMAN W. Altmann, *Die römischen Grabaltäre der Kaiserzeit* (1905); H. C. Bowerman, *Roman Sacrificial Altars* (1913); W. Herrman, *Römische Götteraltäre* (1961); B. Candida, *Altari e cippi nel Museo Nazionale Romano* (1979); M. Hano, *ANRW* 2. 16. 3 (1986), 2333 ff. (altars of Lares); D. Boschung, *Antike Grabaltäre aus den Nekropolen Roms* (1987); D. Kleiner, *Roman Imperial Funerary Altars with Portraits* (1987); G. Gamer, *Formen römischer Altäre auf der hispanischen Halbinsel* (1989).
F. N. P.; J. B.; A. J. S. S., J. L.

Althaemenes, in mythology, son of *Catreus, king of Crete. Warned by an oracle that he would kill his father, he left Crete for Rhodes. Long after, his father came to seek him; Althaemenes took him for a pirate and killed him (Diod. Sic. 5. 59; Apollod. 3. 12–16).   H. J. R.

Altinum (mod. Altino, near Venice), from the 5th cent. BC a centre of the *Veneti (2), and later a Roman *municipium. It prospered as a highway junction, where the *via Postumia, *via Popillia, *via Annia (1), and transalpine via Claudia Augusta met, and was a fashionable resort with rich *villas (Mart. 4. 25. 1). It declined from the 3rd cent. AD, was sacked by *Attila in 452 and, although still occupied in the 7th cent., was succeeded by Torcello and Venice. Excavations have been extensive, especially in the cemeteries.

B. M. Scarfi and M. Tombolani, *Altino, preromana e romana* (1987).
E. T. S.; T. W. P.

Alyattes, fourth *Lydian king (*c.*610–560 BC), of the house of *Gyges and father of *Croesus, finally drove back the *Cimmerians, extended Lydian control to the *Halys, and made war on Cyaxares the Mede (585), during which occurred a solar eclipse (supposedly foretold by *Thales). Peace was concluded with the marriage of Alyattes' daughter to Astyages. He continued Lydian campaigns against *Ionia, captured *Smyrna, but failed against *Clazomenae and *Miletus. Lydia prospered, electrum coinage was used for the first time (see COINAGE, GREEK), and there was increasing interaction with the Greeks. Alyattes built two temples to Athena near *Miletus and sent offerings to *Delphi; he has been seen as the founder of the Lydian empire. His vast burial mound, the largest at Bin Tepe, was praised by Herodotus (1. 93) and Strabo (13. 627), and is now excavated.

Hdt. 1. 16–26, 73–4, 3. 48. J. Boardman, *The Greeks Overseas*, 2nd. edn. (1980); M. Mellink, *CAH* 3²/2 (1991), 647 ff. See GYGES.   R. T.

Alypius (3rd or 4th cent. AD), the author of an extant Εἰσαγωγὴ μουσική (Musical Introduction), the fullest source of our knowledge of Greek musical scales. See MUSIC §9.

Ed. C. Jan, *Musici Scriptores Graeci* (1895), 357–406.

Amadocus, name of two Thracian kings (see THRACE). (1), Odrysian Thracian king who offered Athens military support against Sparta (405 BC)—fruitlessly since Athenian generals refused cooperation with his intermediary, *Alcibiades. Associated with him was Seuthes, a protégé who, still loyal in 400 (when he employed *Xenophon (1)), became over-ambitious, but was reconciled when *Thrasybulus made both him and Amadocus Athenian allies (390/89).

Amadocus (2) fought with *Cersobleptes and Berisades for control of the Odrysian kingdom after Cotys' death, apparently established himself immediately east of the Nestos, and was finally eliminated by *Philip (1) II after 354 BC.

RE 1, 'Amadokos' 2, 3; on Amadocus (2) see *CAH* 6² (1994), ch. 9e (Z. Archibald) and ch. 14 (J. Ellis).   C. J. T.

Amafinius, Gaius, older contemporary of Cicero, popularized the philosophy of *Epicurus in Latin. Cicero refers to him disparagingly (*Fam.* 15. 19. 2; *Acad. Post.* 1. 5. Cf. *Tusc.* 1. 6, 2. 7, 6, 7).

Schanz-Hosius, § 157 b.

Amalthea, the goat that suckled *Zeus after his birth, when he was hidden in a cave to prevent his father *Cronus from devouring him (Callim. *Hymn* 1); later, rationalizing versions made the goat into a nymph. The myth was connected by Ovid (*Fast.* 5. 111–28) with another, perhaps originally independent, tradition about a '(bull's) horn of plenty' of the nymph Amalthea (Pherec. *FGrH* 3 F 42). According to Zenobius, in his collection of proverbs (2. 48, cf. 1. 26), Zeus turned the goat into a *constellation.

H. Stoll, Roscher, *Lex.* 'Amaltheia'; M. Henig, *LIMC* 1 'Amaltheia'.   J. N. B.

Amanus, the name applied to the mountain horseshoe of Elma Dağ above Alexandretta (see ALEXANDRIA (2)), together with Giaour Dağ which trends north-eastwards. It is separated from *Taurus by the deep gorge of the Jihun. It is crossed by great passes, the Amanid Gates (Baghche Pass from the Cilician plain to *Zeugma), and the Syrian Gates (Beilan Pass) carrying a Roman road from *Tarsus into Syria. The part of Mt. Amanus which *Cicero reduced to order (*Att.* 5. 20. 3) must be the heights that end in Ras-el-Khanzir.   E. H. W.

Amarantus, of Alexandria (1) (1st–2nd cent. AD), an older contemporary of *Galen (Gal. 14. 208; Ath. 8. 343 f.), was the author of a commentary on *Theocritus (*Etym. Magn.* 156. 30, 273. 41), perhaps based on the notes of *Theon (1), and of a work Περὶ σκηνῆς ('On the Stage'), which probably gave historical and biographical accounts of stage performances and performers (Ath. 8. 343 f. and 10. 414e).   J. F. L.

Amaseia (mod. Amasya), capital of the kings of *Pontus until soon after 183 BC, birthplace of *Mithradates VI Eupator, and home of the geographer *Strabo, who provides a detailed description of the site (12. 3. 39, 561 C); it lay in a defile of the river Iris between massive heights, with a magnificent fortress commanding the river valley and the chief Pontic roads. It was one of the cities of Pontus founded by *Pompey in 63 BC and the centre of a large territory including the so-called 'Chiliocomon', plain of a thousand villages. In 3/2 BC it was attached to the province of *Galatia as the centre of the district called Pontus Galaticus. *Trajan assigned it to *Cappadocia around AD 112. In the 2nd cent. it received the titles *mētropolis, *neōkoros, and first city (of Pontus). It had a strategic position in the road system leading to the NE frontier, became a garrison town, and was an important source of recruits to the legions. The site is still dominated by Hellenistic and Byzantine fortifications, and by the grave monuments of the Pontic kings.

F. Cumont, *Studia Pontica* 2 (1906), 146–71; 3 (1910), 109–48; Magie, *Rom. Rule Asia Min.*, see index.   S. M.

Amasis became pharaoh (see EGYPT, PRE-PTOLEMAIC; SAITES) in 570 BC as champion of the native Egyptians against *Apries. Though initially restricting Greek activities (e.g. channelling all trade through *Naucratis), he rapidly came to a *rapprochement* with the Greek world, allying himself with *Lydia, *Samos, *Cyrene, and perhaps *Sparta, and making gifts to major Greek shrines. This stance was dictated by the rise of *Persia, which overthrew Egypt in 525, shortly after Amasis' death. His long reign was recalled as a time of peace and prosperity attested by numerous great buildings (now largely lost), and Amasis himself was remembered as a great but unconventional and sometimes undignified figure.

Hdt. 1–3. G. Maspero, *Popular Stories of Egypt* (1915), 218 ff.; F. K. Kienitz, *Die politische Geschichte Ägyptens vom 7. bis zum 4. Jahrhundert vor der Zeitwende* (1953), 30 ff.; A. B. Lloyd, in B. Trigger and others, *Ancient Egypt: A Social History* (1992), see index, and *Herodotus Book II* 3 (1988), 174 ff.; T. G. H. James, *CAH* 3², see index; de Meulenaere, *Lexikon der Ägyptologie* 1. 181 f.   A. B. L.

Amathus, a major coastal city of *Cyprus, on a hill near mod. Ayios Tychonas, 10 km. (6 mi.) east of Limassol, surrounded by extensive and much excavated cemeteries, and immediately adjacent to its built harbour. Its foundation on a virgin site in the 11th cent. BC without nearby bronze age predecessors accords oddly with its alleged autochthonous identity. As late as the 4th cent. BC it used the Cypro-Minoan syllabary to write an unknown language (Eteo-Cyprian: see PRE-ALPHABETIC SCRIPTS (GREECE)). But it stood apart from the other cities in 498, refusing to join the *Ionian Revolt; Onesilus of *Salamis (2) therefore besieged it. A series of coins has been attributed to its 5th- and 4th-cent. kings, the last of whom, Androcles, fought with his ships for *Alexander (3) the Great at *Tyre. Recent excavation has located its famous *Aphrodite sanctuary.

P. Aupert and others, *Amathonte* 1: *Testimonia* 1 (1984); A. Hermary, *Kinyras: L'Archéologie française à Chypre* (1993), 167 ff; O. Masson, *Les Inscriptions chypriotes syllabiques*, rev. edn. (1983), 201 ff.   H. W. C.

Amazons, mythical race of female warriors. The name was popularly understood as 'breastless' (*maza*, 'breast') and the story told that they 'pinched out' or 'cauterized' the right breast so as not to impede their javelin-throwing (Apollod. 2. 5. 8, Strabo 11. 5. 1). No real etymology is known.

Epic Amazons exist in order to be fought, and ultimately defeated, by men in an Amazonomachy ('Amazon-battle'). Already in the *Iliad* we hear of *Bellerophon killing them in *Lycia (6. 186), their defeat at the river Sangarios (near *Pessinus, 3. 189), and a tomb of Myrrhine outside Troy (2. 814, cf. Strab. 12. 8. 6). In *Arctinus' *Aethiopis* their Thracian queen, *Penthesilea 'daughter of Ares', arrives to help the Trojans, but *Achilles kills her (and *Thersites for alleging Achilles loved her). *Heracles' ninth labour was to fetch the girdle of the Amazon queen, Hippolyte, resulting in another Amazonomachy (Apollod. 4. 16). *Theseus joined Heracles and as a result had to defeat an Amazon invasion of *Attica, a story told in a late 6th-cent. BC *Theseid* (story in Plut. *Thes.* 26).

Cult/commemoration Amazon tombs are frequent in central Greece, presumably because of local Amazonomachy myths. They are found at *Megara (Paus. 1. 41. 7), *Athens (Paus. 1. 2. 1), *Chaeronea and *Chalcis—as well as in *Thessaly at Scotussa and *Cynoscephalae (Plut. *Thes.* 27). There was an Amazoneum (shrine of Amazons, implying tombs and cult) at *Chalcis and Athens. At Athens there were annual sacrifices to the Amazons on the day before the Thesea. Many Asia Minor settlements were founded by Amazons: Amastris, *Sinope, *Cyme, Pitana, *Priene, *Mytilene (Lesbos), *Ephesus, *Smyrna, *Myrina (Diod. Sic. 3. 55. 6, Strab. 11. 5. 4). At Ephesus Hippolyte and her Amazons set up a *bretas* (old wooden statue) of Artemis and established an annual circular dance with weapons and shields (Callim. *Hymn* 3. 110; Pind. fr. 174 Snell–Maehler), as performed in historical times by maidens.

Ethnography Amazons, appropriately for a group inverting normal Greek rules, live at the edge of the world. Their usual homeland is next to a river Thermodon in the city of Themiscyra in remote Pontic Asia Minor (Aesch. *PV* 723–5, Pherec. *FGrH* 3 F 15), see PONTUS. Real Amazons would need men for procreation. *Diodorus (3) Siculus' Amazons at the Thermodon cripple their male children (2. 45), but his second sec. in Libya (3. 53–4), have house-husbands to whom they return (like Greek males) after their period of military service. In *Pseudo-Callisthenes, *Alexander Romance* (2. 25), they keep men across a river. It is part of the mythologizing of *Alexander (3) the Great that stories were quick to surface that he had met Amazons and threatened (Arr. *Anab.* 7. 13; Plut. *Alex.* 46) or pleasured (Diod. Sic. 17. 77) their queen.

Matriarchy and Message Especially since J. J. Bachofen's *Mutterrecht* (1859), Amazons have been used as evidence for an actual *matriarchy in prehistoric times. This has seemed an attractive counter to modern male prejudices, but mistakes the nature of myth. Women warriors and hunters are quite frequent in myth and folk-tale (Stith Thompson F 565) and inversely reflect the actual distribution of roles between the sexes. It may be that such inversion in Greece goes back to rituals of the initiation of maidens (cf. Ephesus) and youths (cf. the Thesea), where the definition of gender roles is at issue.

Art Amazonomachies and genre studies of Amazons are represented copiously in art from the late 7th cent. on, propelled by their special importance at Athens. *LIMC* catalogues 819 items.

P. Devambez, *LIMC* 1 (1981), 586–653; W. B. Tyrrell, *Amazons: A Study in Athenian Mythmaking* (1984); J. Blok, *The Early Amazons* (1995); K. Dowden, *Rh. Mus.* 1997. K. D.

Ambarvalia, Roman private and public field *lustration in May. The name appears only in Festus 16 Lindsay, *SHA Aurel.* 20. 3; Strab. 5. 3. 2. Private rite: Cato, *Agr.* 141; Verg. *Ecl.* 5. 75, *G.* 1. 338 ff. with Serv. on 1. 341; Tib. 2. 1; P. Pöstgens, *Tibulls Ambarvalgedicht* (1940). The rustic calendars (*menologia rustica*) for May note: *segetes lustrantur* ('crops are purified').

The public rites symbolically lustrated all fields and are sometimes connected with the pontifices (Strabo), sometimes with the arval brethren's May 29 worship of *Dea Dia (Festus):

Wissowa, *RK* 562 and E. Norden, *Aus altrömischen Priesterbüchern* (1939), 161 ff.; *contra*: Latte, *RR* 65. Other Italic communities had similar rites: J. Poultney, *The Bronze Tablets of Iguvium* (1954), 1 b 20–3.

A. Momigliano, *JRS* 1963, 100 ff.; U. Scholz, *Studien zum altitalischen und altrömischen Marskult und Marsmythos* (1970), 64 ff. C. R. P.

amber, a fossil resin, has a wide natural distribution in northern Europe and is also found in Sicily: so far as is known, the amber from the classical Mediterranean was Baltic. It has been found at Ras Shamra (*Ugarit) and Atchana, and also appears in the *terremare* (see TERRAMARA) in northern Italy. The earliest amber from the classical world comes from the Shaft-Graves at *Mycenae; amber is rare in Minoan Crete. J. M. de Navarro first deduced that during the early and middle bronze age amber travelled from west Jutland across Germany along the rivers to the Po (Padus) and the head of the Adriatic. The trade was probably conducted by central European middlemen who could exchange metal for amber for onward transmission both to the east Mediterranean and westwards to Britain. Amber beads were common throughout bronze age Europe, and reached Brittany, central France, and the Iberian peninsula; a gold-bound amber disc from Isopata (LM III A) and a crescentic necklace from Kakovatos in *Elis (LH II A) have striking British affinities. In the iron age a route starting from the east Baltic conveyed amber to Italy, particularly to the east coast, where *Picenum reached its peak as a centre of an indigenous amber industry in the 6th cent. BC. Amber was common in Archaic Greece, but not after *c.*550 BC, and it is seldom mentioned by Greek authors; *Thales was the first to note its power of attraction. The main centre of amber carving under the Roman empire was *Aquileia: amber was by then a fashionable luxury and played an important part in imperial trade with the free Germans: see Pliny, *HN* 37. 30–51 and Tac. *Germ.* 45, quoted by Cassiodorus in the 6th cent. AD in a letter of thanks for a large gift of Baltic amber sent to Theoderic (1).

J. M. de Navarro, *GJ* 1925, 481 ff.; A. Spekke, *The Ancient Amber Routes* (1957); D. E. Strong, *Catalogue of the Carved Amber in the British Museum* (1966); *Studi e ricerche sulla problematica dell'ambra* (1975); J. M. Coles and A. F. Harding, *The Bronze Age in Europe* (1979). D. W. R. R.

Ambiorix, chief of the Eburones, a Gallic tribe between the Meuse and the Rhine who were freed by *Caesar from dependence on the Atuatuci. However, in 54 BC Ambiorix revolted against Caesar: through treachery he destroyed the camp and forces of Titurius Sabinus at Atuatuca. He then induced the *Nervii to besiege the winter camp in their territory which Q. *Tullius Cicero (1) commanded. It was relieved only by Caesar's arrival. Ambiorix continued to resist (53–51) and though the land of the Eburones was devastated he evaded capture.

H. H. S.; J. F. Dr.

ambitus, a 'going round', is related to *ambitio*, the pursuit of public office, but always, unlike *ambitio*, denotes reprehensible activity which has been declared illegal.

Specifically it refers to obtaining electoral support (see ELECTIONS AND VOTING (Roman)) through gifts, favours, or the promise of these. According to *Polybius (1), the Romans had made the manifest use of money to buy votes a capital offence, but we have no other evidence for this in the last two centuries of the republic (the early books of Livy refer to laws in 432, 358, and 314 BC, the last two of which at least may have some historical substance). In 181 BC a *lex Cornelia Baebia* instituted a system of non-capital trials, which was developed in the late republic by further laws about *ambitus* and related matters—the use of bribery agents, associations, and expenditure on public dinners. These laws seem to have been a response to greater competition for office. However, Roman tradition did not discourage the cultivation of voters through material benefits (see especially the *Commentariolum Petitionis* and Cicero, *Pro Murena* (see LICINIUS MURENA)). What established politicians disliked was the stealing of votes by new men (see NOVUS HOMO) who outbid former patrons and the damage this caused to traditional claims of *patronage. In the late republic the distortion of politics by massive expenditure became scandalous in spite of the new legislation. Under the Principate, in so far as genuine competition for office persisted, *ambitus* remained an issue both in Rome and, perhaps more importantly, in the municipalities (see MUNICIPIUM) throughout the empire. The fact that penalties do not seem to have been very severe (Suet. *Aug.* 40. 1) suggests toleration of traditional behaviour. See also CORRUPTION.

Mommsen, *Röm. Strafr.* 865 ff.; L. Fascione, *Ambitus* (1984); A. W. Lintott, *JRS* 1990.   A. W. L.

Ambivius (*RE* 4) **Turpio, Lucius,** actor and theatre-director; produced plays by *Caecilius Statius and (the *didascaliae* record) all of *Terence's.

Ter. *Hecyra*, prologue 2; C. Garton, *Personal Aspects of the Roman Theatre* (1972).   P. G. M. B.

Ambracia (mod. Arta), situated on the river Arachthus, 18 km. (11 mi.) from its harbour Ambracus on the north shore of the gulf of Arta. Founded as a Corinthian colony (see CORINTH) *c.*625 BC, it owned fertile land, fisheries, and ship-timber, and it exported the produce of *Epirus. When it tried to expand its control southwards, it suffered a crippling defeat at the hands of Athens, *Amphilochia, and *Acarnania in 426 BC. It resisted the advance of *Philip (1) II with help from Corinth and Athens, but was compelled to accept a Macedonian garrison. It was ceded in 294 BC by *Cassander's son to *Pyrrhus, who made it his capital and spent lavishly on its adornment. With the fall of the Molossian monarchy it became a centre of conflict between Macedonia and Aetolia, and in 189 BC it surrendered after a long siege to Rome, which later declared it a '*free city'.

Hammond, *Epirus*; P. Cabanes, *L'Épire de la mort de Pyrrhos à la conquête romaine* (1976).   N. G. L. H.

Ambrose (Ambrosius) Born *c.* AD 340, son of a praetorian prefect of Gaul, Ambrose was well educated and achieved official success under the patronage of the great prefects Sex. Claudius *Petronius Probus and Q. Aurelius *Symmachus (2). Until his early death, his brother Uranius Satyrus showed equal promise. His sister Marcellina became well known for her practice of consecrated virginity, dating from the time of Liberius, bishop of Rome (AD 352–66). Ambrose was appointed governor of Aemilia and Liguria in 374. Already experienced, therefore, in the affairs of Milan (Mediolanum), he was chosen to be the city's bishop in the same year, while intervening in what had become a disputed election. He died in 397 (see Paulinus of Milan, *Life of St Ambrose* 3–5 for his early career and, more generally, *PLRE* 1. 52 'Ambrosius' 3).

Ambrose is famous for his confrontations with the emperor *Theodosius (2) I. Imperial orders to rebuild in 388 a synagogue at Callinicum destroyed by a Christian mob were rescinded after his intervention (*Epp.* 40, 41); and in 390 he excommunicated the emperor, following the calculated massacre of thousands in the circus at *Thessalonica (*Ep.* 51 provides more reliable information

than Paulinus). But those triumphs reflected force of personality without precedent or institutional significance. Nor is it easy to judge what direct contribution Ambrose made to Theodosius' laws against *paganism. His earlier relationships with Gratian and Valentinian II, close and affectionate, did more to form and reflect his attitudes to civil authority, as also did his embassies to Trier during the usurpation of Maximus, 383–4 and 386 (*Ep.* 24). His abiding preoccupations in the public sphere were the defeat of *Arianism (which brought him into famous conflict with the empress Justina in 386: see *Ep.* 20) and the inhibition of pagan cult (symbolized by his successful encouragement of imperial resistance to Symmachus over the restoration of the altar of Victory in the senate-house in 384, recorded in *Epp.* 17 and 18).

Ambrose was a master of oral instruction. Deeply learned in Greek traditions—both those stemming from *Plotinus and those indebted to *Philon (4) and *Origen (1)—and familiar with his near-contemporary *Basil of Caesarea, he made his own contribution to theological development by binding both exegesis and philosophy more closely to sacramental cult. Not content with mere typology, his 'mystagogic' skills harnessed the erudition of the Church to its growth as a community through baptism and homily. *Augustine was the most famous example of his success. His preaching was reinforced by a keen appreciation of ceremonial, hymnody, and architecture, together with veneration for the martyrs. He also devoted enormous energy to the spiritual health and ecclesial discipline of other churches in north Italy, not least through his correspondence and his attendance at synods. His sympathetic morality is revealed in his writings on virginity (closely associated with his sister) and in his *De officiis*.

WORKS Variously available in *PL* (14–17), *CSEL*, and *CCSL*. Beware more than one system of numbering for his *Letters*.
    LIFE Paulinus, *Vita di Cipriano, Vita di Ambrogio, Vita di Agostino*, ed. A. A. R. Bastiaensen (1975); Eng. trans. in F. R. Hoare, *The Western Fathers* (1954).
    STUDY N. McLynn, *Ambrose of Milan* (1994).   P. R.

ambrosia (lit. 'immortality', *a-mr̥t-ia*) and **nectar** are the food and drink of eternal life—usually in that order, though nectar is for eating in Alcman (fr. 42 Page, *PMG*) and Sappho thinks of ambrosia as a drink (fr. 141 LP). They are thus properly reserved for the gods, as traditional stories emphasize: see *Od.* 5. 196–9 on *Odysseus' meals with *Calypso. *Heracles was formally served with a draught of immortal spirit by Athena on his assumption into Olympus, but the dying *Tydeus was refused the same favour at the last moment when the goddess found him devouring his enemy's brains (Pherec. *FGrH* 3 F 97). One version of *Tantalus' crime claims that, having tasted divine food himself, he tried to smuggle some away for others who were not so privileged (Pind., *Ol.* 1. 60 ff.). Those who ingest such rarefied substances naturally have not blood but a special fluid called *ichor* coursing through their veins (*Il.* 5. 340, 416). As the ultimate preservative, ambrosia may also be administered by goddesses to their favourites by external application: it is used by *Thetis to keep *Patroclus' corpse fresh (*Il.* 19. 38f.; cf. 23. 186) and to sustain the fasting *Achilles (19. 347 ff.), and by Athena as a face cream to beautify *Penelope (*Od.* 18. 192f.). Its natural fragrance is employed by Eidothea to insulate *Menelaus (1)'s men from the stench of her father's seals (*Od.* 4. 445 f., see PROTEUS). At *Od.* 12. 63 doves are said to ferry it (from where?) to *Zeus.

A. H. G.

Ambrosiaster

Ambrosiaster (i.e. pseudo-Ambrose), the author of the *Commentary on Thirteen Pauline Letters* (except Hebrews) which has been handed down under the name of *Ambrose. Attempts at identifying the author have not yet yielded conclusive results. The commentary was written under Pope *Damasus (AD 366–84) in Rome and is regarded as an important witness to the Latin text of St *Paul prior to the *Vulgate and as an instructive example for the pre-Augustinian interpretation of Paul. The pseudo-Augustinian *Quaestiones Veteris et Novi Testamenti* probably also stem from his pen. In addition, some minor texts have been attributed to this author.

EDITIONS *Commentary* in *CSEL* 81 / 1–3 (H. J. Vogels); *Quaestiones* in *CSEL* 50 (A. Souter).

A. Pollastri, *EEC* 1 (1992), 30; A. Stuiber, *Theologische Realenzyklopädie* 2 (1978), 356 ff. W. K.

Amburbium, *lustration for Rome, seldom so named (Serv. on Verg. *Ecl.* 3. 77; SHA *Aurel.* 20. 3), usually linked with the *Ambarvalia's lustration of the fields (Festus 16. 9 Lindsay; Servius; SHA). Since it appears in no *calendar it may have been a movable festival (L. Delatte, *Ant. Class.* 1937, 114–17) or, based on the infrequent references, all late, it may have been a rarely performed lustration (cf. Ogilvie on Livy 1. 44. 2, and *JRS* 1961, 39) which anachronistically received its name by analogy with Ambarvalia. H. Usener placed it (*Weihnachtsfest*, 2nd edn. (1911), 1. 314–28) on 2 February as ultimately Christianized into Candlemas, unpersuasively despite Wissowa, *RK* 142 n. 12. Lucan (1. 592–638) describes an *amburbium*—but clearly an extraordinary ceremony.

RE 1 / 2 (1894), 1816–17; U. Scholz, *Studien zum altitalischen und altrömischen Marskult und Marsmythos* (1970), 59–63; J. Scheid, *Romulus et ses frères* (1990), 26 ff. C. R. P.

Ameipsias, Athenian comic poet, contemporary with *Aristophanes (1). His *Connus* (see PHRYNICHUS (2)) was placed second to *Cratinus' *Pytine* and above *Aristophanes (1)'s *Clouds* in 423 BC (hyp. 5 Ar. *Nub.*). Connus was *Socrates' music-master, and the play may have had a similar character to *Clouds*. Socrates himself was a character (fr. 9 quoted by Diog. Laert. 2. 28, without naming the play) and the chorus consisted of *phrontistae*, i.e. *sophists (cf. the *phrontistērion* in *Clouds*). *Comastae* ('Revellers'; see PHRYNICHUS (2)) won the first prize, defeating Aristophanes' *Birds*, at the City *Dionysia in 414 (hyp. 1 Ar. *Av.*). We have seven titles.

Kassel–Austin, *PCG* 2. 197 ff. (*CAF* 1. 670 ff.). K. J. D.

Amelesagoras, pseudonymous author of an *Atthis (*c.*300 BC), who seems to have presented himself as an Eleusinian prophet (see ELEUSIS), the name may be connected with Ameles, an Underworld river (Plato, *Resp.* 10. 621a). *Callimachus (3) seems to have used this book in his *Hecale* for the story of *Athena and the crow (cf. A. S. Hollis, *Callimachus: Hecale* (1990), 226–32).

FRAGMENTS *FGrH* 330 (with comm., *FGrH* 3b, Suppl. 598–607). R. L. Hu.

Amelius (or Amerius) Gentilianus (3rd cent. AD), from Etruria, was *Plotinus' pupil 246–69. He wrote extensively, mainly presenting and defending Plotinus' philosophy, which he did not always understand and with which he sometimes differed.

L. Brisson, *ANRW* 2. 36. 2 (1987), 793 ff. D. O'M.

Ameria (mod. Amelia), hill-town of southern *Umbria. Although very ancient (Plin. *HN* 3. 114), it is first mentioned by Cicero (*Rosc. Amer.* 15, 19, 20, 25), in whose day it was a prosper-

ous *municipium. It remained such in imperial times. Its massive polygonal walls are still well preserved. E. T. S.; T. W. P.

amicitia, friendship in Roman political terminology. The relationship might be between Rome and either another state or an individual (see CLIENT KINGS), or between individuals. *Amici populi Romani* were recorded on a *tabula amicorum*. Although *amicitia* involved no treaty or formal legal obligations, the term was often associated with alliance (*societas*) and might describe strong ties and indeed dependency. In Roman political and social life the *amici* of an eminent man acted as his advisers in public and personal matters and might form a group of devoted political adherents (though the word suggests equality of status such men might well be subordinates). Ideally *amicitia* involved genuine trust and affection (Cic. *Amic.*), in practice it might only be an alliance to pursue common interests. Such friendships frequently conflicted. Nevertheless, their making and breaking were formal. Under the Principate the friends of the emperor formed, with his kinsmen and freedmen, his court (see AMICUS AUGUSTI). Loss of this friendship was close to condemnation as a criminal. See also CLIENS.

E. Badian, *Foreign Clientelae* (1958); P. A. Brunt, *The Fall of the Roman Republic* (1988), esp. ch. 7. H. S.; A. W. L.

amicus Augusti Drawing on the institutionalized *philoi* (friends) of Hellenistic rulers, political leaders of the 1st cent. BC made friendship a technical term of Roman political life (*popularis politicians were held to have introduced it to grade their *clientelae*, Sen. *Ben.* 6. 34; see AMICITIA; CLIENS). The emperors adopted the term *amicus* to identify, essentially as courtiers under the nascent monarchic system, favoured members of the equestrian and senatorial *ordines*, and as an increasingly formal label for the inner circle who made up their advisory *consilium*. See COMITES for a similar semantic development.

J. Crook, *Consilium Principis* (1955); F. G. B. Millar, *The Emperor in the Roman World* (1977), 110–22. N. P.

Amisus (mod. Samsun), a 6th-cent. colony of *Miletus or *Phocaea, was built on a peninsula site on the Black Sea coast, the best harbour between *Sinope and *Trapezus, at the head of a commercial route into *Pontus and *Cappadocia. Athenians from the Piraeus joined the settlement in the mid-5th cent. Freed from the Persian empire by *Alexander (3) the Great, it was part of the kingdom of Pontus from around 250 BC, and became a royal residence of *Mithradates VI. L. *Licinius Lucullus (2) captured and restored the city in 71 BC, giving it freedom and additional territory, and it was one of the cities of *Pompey's Pontic province. Antony (M. *Antonius (2)) gave it to a tyrant but Augustus confirmed its status as a free and allied city within the province of Pontus and *Bithynia. The territory included the fertile coastal plain of Themiscyra and stretched west of the mouth of the *Halys. *Olives were an important crop and oil was widely exported. Its abundant coinage and the wide dispersal of its citizens attest a commercial importance which remains today.

Strabo 12. 3. 14, 547 C; F. Cumont, *Studia Pontica* 2 (1906), 111 ff.; 3 (1910), 1 ff.; Jones, *Cities E. Rom. Prov.*, see index; D. R. Wilson, *PECS* 49. S. M.

Ammaedara (mod. Haidra), a Roman city in western Tunisia on the Carthage–Theveste trunk road, 36 km. (22 mi.) north-east of the latter. The first fortress of the Legio III Augusta was established here in Augustan times on a virgin site close to the oued Haidra. The exact position of the fortress is unknown, but it is assumed to lie under the Byzantine fortress at the heart of the site; legionary tombstones from a necropolis to the east demonstrate the presence of the legion. When the fortress was moved to *Theveste *c.* AD 75, a town was founded as *colonia Flavia Augusta Aemerita Ammaedara* (*CIL* 8. 308). Imposing ruins, including those of a capitolium (see CAPITOL), a theatre, baths, an arch of Septimius Severus (195), and several mausolea, are spread out over an area of some 1,400 × 600 m. (1,500 × 650 yds.), but little excavation has been conducted. Ammaedara was a notable Christian centre, with bishops at least from 256; five churches of the 4th–6th cents. have been identified. A large Byzantine fortress (200 × 110 m.: 220 × 120 yds) dominates the centre of the site.

PECS 50; F. Baratte and N. Duval, *Les Ruines d'Ammaedara-Haidra* (1974); F. Baratte, *Recherches archéologiques à Haidra: Miscellanea* 1 (1974); N. Duval, *Recherches archéologiques à Haidra* 1: *Les Inscriptions chrétiennes* (1975); 2: *La Basilique dite de Melléus ou de Saint-Cyprien* (1981); and *ANRW* 2. 10. 2 (1982), 633–71.   R. J. A. W.

Ammianus Marcellinus (*c.* AD 330–95), the last great Latin historian of the Roman empire, was born at Syrian *Antioch (1). His early entry, *c.*350, into the élite corps of *protectores domestici* may indicate family connections with the imperial service at Antioch, in which case an early acquaintance with the Latin language could be inferred, as well as the Greek which formed the base of his literary education. Assigned by *Constantius II to the personal staff of the general Ursicinus, Ammianus saw service in north Italy, Gaul, and Germany (the early campaigns of *Julian), Illyricum and Mesopotamia. It was here, in the siege and capture by the Persians of Amida (mod. Diarbekir) in 359, that the first phase of Ammianus' military career came to an end. He escaped from the city, but Ursicinus was dismissed from office in the aftermath of its fall. Ammianus seems to have returned to Antioch, but subsequently participated in the disastrous Persian campaign of Julian (363). In later years he travelled—to the Black Sea and Egypt, southern Greece, possibly to a Thracian battlefield from the Gothic invasions of 376–8—before he came to Rome in the mid-380s. It was here that he completed his history. The work is composed in 31 books, of which the first thirteen, covering the period from Nerva to 353, seem from the nature of a reference to them by the grammarian Priscian already to have been lost by the early 6th cent. The earlier of the lost books were apparently not very full or original, but the scale of the narrative enlarged as Ammianus approached his own day. The surviving books describe in great detail the events and personalities of Ammianus' active lifetime through a period of just 25 years, covering the reigns of Constantius II and Julian (353–63), the brief tenure of Jovian (363–4), the joint reigns of Valentinian I (364–75) and Valens (364–78), and the usurpation of Procopius (366). The culmination of the work is the Gothic invasions of 376–8 (see GOTHS) and the battle of Adrianople (9 August 378) at which Valens was killed. The period from 378 to the time of publication is alluded to only in passing references which are, however, of value in judging the date of composition of the work; the latest datable events referred to are of 390 and 391, and the history was probably completed very soon after this.

In the earlier books, narrating his service under Ursicinus, Ammianus' own experiences form a major element, and events are largely seen through the often biased eyes of his patron; with their vivid narrative of sometimes very detailed events and the subjectivity of their judgements, these books have seemed to readers to resemble personal memoir rather than formal history. Despite his own participation—which was at a less privileged level than his experiences with Ursicinus—his narrative of the

Persian campaign of Julian is less personally involved, relying sometimes on written sources, and the books on Valentinian and Valens are less detailed, and despite moments of intense involvement, not focused on the author's own experiences. The centre-piece of the history was the government, first in Gaul as Caesar and then in the east as sole Augustus, of Julian the Apostate. Ammianus deeply admired Julian, particularly for his military and administrative abilities. He was openly critical of other aspects of Julian's regime, not least his religious policies.

Himself a *pagan of a more traditional cast, Ammianus disliked Julian's intolerance, and was hostile to the emperor's devotion to excessive sacrifice, and of his submission to the influence of philosophers who, in the end with disastrous results, indulged Julian's interest in Neoplatonic techniques of *divination. The extent to which Ammianus was himself a polemical writer is debated. He did not adopt the openly ideological stance against *Christianity taken by his younger contemporary *Eunapius (whose work he seems to have used from time to time). He is however scathing, in satirical fashion, about the ostentation of the bishops of Rome, criticizes those of *Alexandria (1) for their ambition, and ironically refers to the failure of Christianity to live up to its 'pure and simple' professions.

Ammianus' elaborate, individual, and often very intense style is notable for its strong pictorial sense and for its ability to portray character, in which it displays the influence of physiognomical writing (see PHYSIOGNOMY) and exploits often very vivid comparisons of human character with that of wild beasts. It contains many passages, especially of military narrative, in which individuals are shown at close quarters and in situations of personal stress and great danger. It is influenced too by the language of *satire, as when Ammianus denounces the behaviour of the nobility and common people of Rome, or the behaviour of lawyers. The subject-matter is wide, and the history contains many geographical and ethnographical digressions (describing the non-Roman as well as the Roman worlds), as well as scientific and antiquarian excursuses, in which the author's Greek culture is acknowledged, sometimes with quotations of Greek words in which Ammianus refers to Greek as his 'own' first language. The sources for the lost books are not known, except that Ammianus' back-references do not indicate the large-scale use of Greek sources that would have been possible for him, and there are occasional traces of the lost Latin history known as 'Enmann's Kaisergeschichte' which can be seen in other Latin writers of the period such as *Aurelius Victor and *Eutropius (1). For the contemporary period, Ammianus' narrative was based on personal knowledge and the accounts of eyewitnesses—those 'versati in medio' referred to in the preface of book 15; some of these, such as the eunuch Eutherius and the senator *Praetextatus can be convincingly identified. Ammianus does not mention the orator Symmachus (2), and was certainly not the anonymous historian addressed by Symmachus in *Epistolae* 9. 110. In general, his affinities with Roman 'senatorial' circles have been much exaggerated by historians.

Ammianus' work, justly admired by Gibbon, is a classic of Latin historiography, though whether the influence of *Tacitus is more than formal (it would explain the starting-point at the reign of Nerva) is debated. The influence of *Sallust is indicated from time to time, but the most persuasive literary influence is clearly that of *Cicero, whose writings are constantly referred to and alluded to. Greek authors, like *Herodotus, *Thucydides (2), and *Polybius (1), are acknowledged at suitable moments but do not seem otherwise to have exercised any real influence upon

Ammon

Ammianus' manner. *Homer and *Virgil are effectively used to give epic scale and colour to the narrative. Affinities with contemporary Latin prose writers are not obvious or extensive; the most obvious, both as to style and content, is perhaps the imperial legislation collected in the *Theodosian Code—a comparison by which Ammianus, a lover of settled government and respect for institutions, might not have been offended. See HISTORIOGRAPHY, ROMAN.

EDITIONS W. Seyfarth, 4 vols. (1970–1) and 2 vols. (1978); J. C. Rolfe, 3 vols. (Loeb, 1935–40; repr. 1956–8); J. Fontaine and others (Budé, 1968–84; proceeding).
COMMENTARY P. de Jonge, J. den Boeft, D. den Hengst, and H. C. Teitler (1935–91; proceeding).
TRANSLATION W. Hamilton, with introd. and notes by A. Wallace-Hadrill (1986).
SELECTED STUDIES E. A. Thompson, *The Historical Work of Ammianus Marcellinus* (1947); A. Cameron, *JRS* 1964, 15 ff.; H. T. Rowell, *Ammianus Marcellinus: Soldier-Historian of the Late Roman Empire* (Semple Lectures 1, 1967); R. Syme, *Ammianus and the Historia Augusta* (1968); R. C. Blockley, *Ammianus Marcellinus: A Study of his Historiography and Political Thought* (1975); G. Sabbah, *La Méthode d'Ammien Marcellin: Recherches sur la construction historique dans les Res Gestae* (1975); R. Seager, *Ammianus Marcellinus: Seven Studies in his Language and Thought* (1986); J. F. Matthews, *The Roman Empire of Ammianus* (1989) (with full bibliographies). J. F. Ma.

Ammon (Ἄμμων), *Hellenized name of Amun, the great god of Egyptian *Thebes (2) and chief divinity of the developed Egyptian pantheon; thus naturally identified with *Zeus (so first in Pindar, who composed a hymn to the god and is supposed to have commissioned an image for his temple in (Greek) Thebes (1) from the sculptor *Calamis; Paus. 9. 16. 1). Greek interest, probably mediated through the city of *Cyrene (on whose coins his head is shown from the early 5th cent. with the typical ram's horns) centred on the oracular cult at the oasis of *Siwa, in the Libyan desert; Herodotus assumes its fame, and Plutarch claims consultations by several prominent 5th-cent. Greeks including *Cimon, *Lysander, *Alcibiades, and *Nicias (1). In the 4th cent., in line with the growth of foreign cults, his worship is attested at Athens (where one of the two sacred triremes was renamed 'Ammonias' in his honour) and elsewhere in the Greek homeland; but it was above all *Alexander (3) the Great's visit in 331, after his victory at the *Issus, which caught the ancient imagination—even if the story of Zeus Ammon's acknowledgment of his own paternity of the young king, and so of Alexander's divinity, is a later elaboration.

H. W. Parke, *The Oracles of Zeus* (1967), ch. 9; J. Boardman, *The Greeks Overseas*, 3rd edn. (1980), 137; A. B. Lloyd, *Herodotus Book II*, 2. 195 ff. A. H. G.

Ammonius (1) (2nd cent. BC), pupil and successor of *Aristarchus (2) (schol. *Il.* 10. 397; *Suda*, entry under the name), wrote besides a commentary on Homer (*POxy.* 2. 121), other works on the Homeric poems, e.g. a treatise on *Plato (1)'s borrowings from Homer ([Longinus], *Subl.* 13. 3), and essays in defence of Aristarchus' recension of the Homeric text (schol. *Il.* 10. 397); these formed a valuable source for *Didymus (1). For his commentary on Pindar (schol. *Ol.* 1. 122 c) he used Aristarchus' work, but made independent additions (schol. *Nem.* 3. 16 b). The work on Aristophanes (schol. *Vesp.* 947), sometimes entitled Κωμῳδούμενοι (schol. *Vesp.* 1239), probably discussed the individuals attacked in Old Attic Comedy. He is not the author of the extant *De adfinium vocabulorum differentia* (ed. K. Nickan, 1966).

H. Erbse, *Beitr. zur Überlieferung der Iliasscholien* (1960), 295 ff.; R. Pfeiffer, *History of Classical Scholarship: From the Beginnings to the End of the Hellenistic Age* (1968), 216–17. J. F. L.; N. G. W.

Ammonius (2) **Saccas,** of *Alexandria (1), Platonist philosopher, active in first half of 3rd cent. AD, famous as the teacher of *Plotinus, who studied under him 232–42, as well as of *Origen (1) the Christian, *Origen (2) the pagan, *'Longinus', and others. According to Porphyry (in Eus. *Hist. Eccl.* 6. 19) he was brought up as a Christian but reverted to paganism as soon as he began to think for himself. The epithet θεοδίδακτος ('taught of God') and the nickname Saccas (sack-carrier? wearer of sackcloth?) would seem to imply a humble origin, though other interpretations have been proposed. He wrote nothing, and no distinctive features of his teaching can be inferred with any certainty from the few references to it in Nemesius, *Nat. hom.* 2 and 3, and Hierocles in Photius, cod. 251. Even the story of the vow of secrecy which his pupils, like those of Pythagoras, took and subsequently broke (Porph. *Vit. Plot.* 3. 24) is not entirely free from doubt. Nevertheless the teacher who evoked from Plotinus the cry τοῦτον ἐζήτουν ('this is the man I was looking for') and retained him as a disciple for eleven years has some claim to be considered the Socrates of *Neoplatonism.

Zeller, *Phil. d. Gr.* 3. 2⁵. 500 ff.; H. Dörrie, *Hermes* 1955, 439 ff.; E. R. Dodds and others, *Les Sources de Plotin*, Entretiens Hardt 5 (1960), 24 ff.; M. Baltes, *RAC* Suppl. 3 (1985), 323–32 'Ammonios Saccas'. E. R. D.; J. M. D.

amnesty To propose or demand the recall of *exiles was common throughout the Greek world, and attempts by such exiles to recover confiscated property frequently provoked further strife (e.g. Xen. *Hell.* 5. 3. 10–17). Far less common was an amnesty in the formal sense of an act of state, though cf. *Ptolemy (1) VIII's indulgences in 118 BC (*PTeb.* 5. 1–9) and perhaps also the so-called amnesty law of *Solon (Plut. *Sol.* 19). The most famous ancient 'amnesty' was not a legislative act (despite *Plutarch's use of the word *amnēstia* to suggest a Roman parallel, *Cic.* 42) but part of an agreement at Athens in 403 BC between opponents and former supporters of the *Thirty Tyrants; the (incomplete) text at *Ath. Pol.* 39 prohibits *mnēsikakein* ('remembering wrongs', sc. in a lawcourt) against all except specified oligarchic officials. Narrative sources present this agreement as the successful achievement of democratic magnanimity, though it was evidently imposed by the Spartan king *Pausanias (2). Several forensic speeches suggest that fear of Spartan retaliation may have persuaded prosecutors to dress up attacks on the amnesty as calls for it to be reinterpreted against their opponents.

T. C. Loening, *The Reconciliation Agreement of 403/402 BC in Athens*, Hermes Einzelschr. 53 (1987). S. C. T.

amoebean verse, a stylistic form found mainly in bucolic poetry (adapted in Catull. 62, Hor. *Carm.* 3. 9), consists of matching groups of verse assigned alternately to two characters usually in singing contests, which probably have roots in folk-poetry. Each theme introduced by one character has to be closely 'capped' by the other; sometimes an umpire decides the result.

A. S. F. Gow, *Theocritus* (1952), 2. 92; R. Merkelbach, *Rh. Mus.* 1956, 98; W. Froleyks, *Der Agon Logon* (1973), 87. E. C.

Amorgos, a narrow mountainous island (124 sq. km.: 48 sq. mi) in the SE *Cyclades. Its location makes it an attractive staging-point for shipping. Having flourished in the early bronze age, its later prehistory is obscure. During the Ionian migration three cities were founded c.900 BC, Arcesine in the west, Minoa in the centre, and Aegiale in the east. Naxians (see NAXOS (1)) were the original colonists, with Samians led by the poet *Semonides arriving in the later 7th cent. Dialect, script, and art indicate a Naxian presence at Arcesine and a Samian one at Minoa. Amorgos may have remained a Samian possession until 439 BC, appearing in the Athenian *tribute lists from 433 BC paying one talent. Under the *Second Athenian Confederacy Arcesine received a garrison. There were further Hellenistic settlements of Samians at Minoa, Milesians at Aegiale and, perhaps, Naxians at Arcesine (first attested in the imperial period). Though a place of *exile under the Julio-Claudians, its cities survived until late antiquity. The association between Amorgos and the fine cloth called *amorginon* is disputed.

RE 1/2 (1894), 'Amorgos'; PECS 50–1; IG 12. 7; AJArch. 1929, 27 ff; Les Cyclades (1983), 113–34; ΠΑΕ 1981– ; BSA 1989, 177 ff.   R. W. V. C.

Ampelius, Lucius (3rd–4th cent. AD), dedicated his 50-chapter *Liber memorialis* to a Macrinus still sometimes identified with the emperor M. *Opellius Macrinus, but language and intellectual level are those of late-antique compendia: moreover, there are far more errors and absurdities than can be blamed on later copyists. Subjects covered are cosmography, geography, marvels (some not found elsewhere), religion (from a Euhemeristic standpoint; see EUHEMERUS), and history; the Roman items are almost exclusively republican. Some items derive, even if indirectly, from *Nigidius Figulus, *Nepos, and the Roman historians, but several sources, at least one Greek, remain unknown.

TEXTS E. Assmann (Teubner, 1935); M.-P. Arnaud-Lindet (Budé, 1993).
TRANSLATION A. M. Lashbrook (1960).
BIBLIOGRAPHY HLLA 5. 177–9.
STUDIES E. Assmann, Philol. 1941, 197–221, 303–29; PIR² A 566.
L. A. H.-S.

Amphiaraus, seer descended from *Melampus (1), resident at *Argos (2), whence he participated in the expedition of the *Seven against Thebes. In one tradition, he died with all the other champions save *Adrastus (1) (Od. 15. 243–55). Since he knew that the expedition was doomed, Amphiaraus was unwilling to go, but—as pre-arranged with Adrastus—he was obliged to obey the judgement of his wife Eriphyle (sister of Adrastus), who had been bribed by Polynices with the necklace of Harmonia.

There is another version, perhaps originating with the epic *Thebaid* (fr. 9 Davies), that Amphiaraus was not killed at Thebes, but, while fleeing from the city, was swallowed up live, chariot and all, in a cleft made by *Zeus' thunderbolt.

It can be assumed that at some time between the development of the story of the Seven, and the first reference to his survival, Amphiaraus was associated with an underground oracular deity. A similar motif—pursuit, swallowing up live by the earth, and subsequent operation as an underground oracle—figures in the *aition* of *Trophonius at Lebadea, with whom Amphiaraus shared another characteristic, direct consultation (see ORACLES).

Amphiaraus' major sanctuary was near *Oropus, in disputed territory between Attica and Boeotia. Whether or not there was—as Strabo 9. 2. 10 states—another sanctuary of Amphiaraus nearer Thebes, later abandoned in favour of Oropus, is open to question (Hubbard, a partisan of the latter position, gives a good account of the arguments on both sides: 103–7, see bibliog.)

The oracle was one of those consulted by *Croesus and Mys (for *Mardonius) according to Herodotus (1. 46. 2, 1. 52, 8. 134). Amphiaraus gave Croesus the right answer.

The sanctuary at Oropus became popular during the *Pelo-

ponnesian War, when the Athenians invested Amphiaraus with healing powers on the model of *Asclepius. Consultation was by incubation: the consultants/patients bedded down on a ram-skin on the ground, and were visited by Amphiaraus as they slept.

The sanctuary, which has been excavated and is a charming place, was popular in the 4th cent. under the Athenians, under the Hellenistic Boeotian Confederacy (when that body used it as a show-case for the display of *proxeny decrees), and under the Romans, thanks to the impetus given by *Sulla, who granted it tax-free status (the inscription IG 7. 413 is worth reading in this regard; for translation see Sherk, Augustus no. 70).

C. W. J. Eliot, PECS 656, 'Oropos'; T. K. Hubbard, Harv. stud. 1992, 101–7; I. Krauskopf, LIMC 1 (1981), 690–713; A. Schachter, Cults of Boiotia 1 (1981), 19–26.   A. Sch.

amphictiony (from *amphiktiones*, 'dwellers around') is the name given to Greek leagues connected with *sanctuaries and the maintenance of their cults. Most were concentrated in the locality of the sanctuary, but the most important, such as the amphictiony of Anthela and *Delphi, came to include representatives from much of Greece. They could punish those who offended against the sanctuary, and the Delphic amphictiony could even declare a *Sacred War against an offending state. See CALAURIA.

G. Busolt, Griechische Staatskunde, 3rd edn., 2 (1926), 1280–1310; V. Ehrenberg, The Greek State, 2nd edn. (1969), 108–11; K. Tausend, Amphiktyonie und Symmachie (1992).   J. A. O. L.; P. J. R.

Amphidromia See NAMES, PERSONAL, GREEK.

Amphilochi, a tribe of NW Greece, occupying the wooded hill-country east of the gulf of Ambracia and controlling the narrow passage above the coast from *Acarnania and *Aetolia to *Ambracia. The only town, Amphilochian *Argos (3), claimed as its founders *Amphilochus, *Alcmaeon (1), or *Diomedes (1). Amphilochia was the scene of many campaigns.

Hammond, Epirus, 246 ff.   N. G. L. H.

Amphilochus, in mythology, brother of *Alcmaeon (1), and, in some accounts (as Apollod. 3. 82 and 86), his comrade in the expedition of the *Epigoni and helper in slaying Eriphyle. After Homer he takes part in the Trojan War (e.g. Quint. Smyrn. 14. 366), and is celebrated as a diviner. He and *Calchas left Troy together by land and came to *Claros (Strabo 14. 1. 27). A number of local tales (or constructions of Greek historians) connect Amphilochus with the origins of places and peoples in Asia Minor, as Poseideion on the borders of Syria and Cilicia (Hdt. 3. 91. 1), the Pamphylian nation (Hdt. 7. 91. 3), but above all the famous mantic shrine in Mallus (Strabo 14. 5. 16). Apollo killed him in Soli (Hes. fr. 279 M–W).

I. Krauskopf, LIMC 1/1 (1981), 713 ff.   H. J. R.

Amphion and **Zethus,** sons of *Zeus and *Antiope: they founded and walled seven-gated *Thebes (1) (Od. 11. 260–5).

The story is fleshed out by Sophocles (Niobe) and Euripides (Antiope). The brothers were born in a cave on Cithaeron and were said to have ruled Eutresis before coming to Thebes. Their mother, having been maltreated by *Dirce, was avenged by her sons. Amphion married *Niobe, with unfortunate issue; Zethus, an altogether more shadowy figure (Amphion's name can at least be connected with his walking around the site of Thebes playing his lyre and charming the stones into a wall), married the equally vague Thebe, or possibly *Aëdon (Heinzel 20, see bibliog. below). A prehistoric burial-mound immediately north of the

Amphipolis

Cadmea is probably the site variously identified as the tomb of one or the other or both.

Apollod. *The Library*, trans. J. G. Frazer (Loeb, 1921) 3. 5. 5–6; J. S. Barrett, in R. Carden (ed.), *The Papyrus Fragments of Sophocles* (1974), 171–235; E. Heinzel, *JÖAI Beiblatt* (1989); J. Kambitsis (ed.), *L'Antiope d'Euripide* (1972); A. Schachter, *Cults of Boiotia* 1 (1981), 28–9; F. Heger, *LIMC* 1/1 (1981) 718 ff.   A. Sch.

Amphipolis, on the east bank of the Strymon, which surrounds the city on three sides (hence its name), 5 km. (3 mi.) from its seaport Eïon; it was originally the site of a Thracian town, Ennea Hodoi ('nine ways', Hdt. 7. 114; see THRACE). After two unsuccessful attempts in 497 and 465 BC, it was colonized by the Athenians, with other Greeks, under Hagnon, son of Nicias, in 437–436 BC. It owed its importance partly to its strategic position on the coastal route between northern Greece and the Hellespont, and partly to its commercial wealth as the terminal of trade down the Strymon valley, a depot for the minerals of *Pangaeus and a centre for ship-timber (Thuc. 4. 108). In 424 BC Amphipolis surrendered to the Spartan *Brasidas. It remained independent until 357 BC, when it was captured by *Philip (1) II who gave it a favoured status in the Macedonian kingdom. *Alexander (3) the Great made it the chief mint in his domains. Under the Romans as an important station on the *via Egnatia it was declared a '*free city'. Excavation has revealed the wooden piles of the bridge, the remarkably strong fortification-walls, and the fine public buildings, of which the Hellenistic '*gymnasium' is of special importance. See also RHESUS.

S. Casson, *Macedonia, Thrace and Illyria* (1926); J. Papastavrou, *Amphipolis: Geschichte und Prosopographie*, Klio Beiheft 37 (1936); W. K. Pritchett, *Studies in Ancient Greek Topography* (1965), 30; D. K. Samsares, *Historical Geography of East Macedonia in Antiquity* (1976; in Greek); SNG 5, pt. 3 (1976); *AEMΘ* 1987 and 1989; D. Lazaridis, *Amphipolis* (1994).

    J. M. R. C.; N. G. L. H.

Amphis, Middle *Comedy poet. His 28 titles come chiefly from mythology or daily life, but *Gynaecocratia* ('Government by Women') sounds like an Aristophanic theme, and *Dithyrambus* ('*Dithyramb') may have dealt with musical innovations (cf. fr. 14); fr. 6 refers to 'the Good in Plato' (see PLATO (1)).

FRAGMENTS Kassel–Austin, *PCG* 2. 213–35, although earlier scholars use the numbering in Kock, *CAF* 2. 236–50.
    INTERPRETATION Meineke, *FCG* 1. 403 ff.; G. Kaibel, *RE* 1/2 (1894), 1953 f. 'Amphis' 2.   W. G. A.

Amphissa, 'the largest and most famous city of the [western, Ozolian] Locrians' (Paus. 10. 38. 2; see LOCRIS). Its traditional policy being enmity with *Phocis and alliance with *Thebes (1), Amphissa played a leading part in the Third *Sacred War, and was reduced to dependence by *Onomarchus in 353 BC. After the collapse of Phocis, it initiated moves that resulted in the Fourth *Sacred War in which *Philip (1) II of Macedon captured the city and destroyed its walls (338). Amphissa joined in the defence of *Delphi against the Gauls in 279 and thereafter became Aetolian until freed by the Romans in 167. After *Actium (31 BC), the city was inhabited by Aetolian refugees and claimed henceforth to be Aetolian and not Locrian. The ancient city is securely identified with remains at modern Salona.

L. Lerat, *Les Locriens de l'ouest* (1952), 1. 15–18, 174–80; *Lexikon der historischen Stätten* 110–11.   W. M. M.

amphitheatres The earliest surviving permanent amphitheatres are found in *Campania, the well-preserved example at

*Pompeii, called *spectacula* by its builders (*CIL* 10. 852), being the only closely datable example (*c*.80 BC). At Rome, although gladiatorial games were held in the *forum Romanum from an early date with spectators accommodated in temporary wooden stands, the first permanent building was erected by T. *Statilius Taurus in the *Campus Martius only in 29 BC. Nero built a much larger wooden structure there, destroyed by the fire of AD 64. Rome finally gained a permanent, monumental amphitheatre with the *Colosseum. Amphitheatres are common in the western provinces from the late republic but are rarer in the east, where from the 2nd cent. AD onwards many *theatres were instead adapted for this purpose. The use of gladiatorial techniques for training the Roman army led to small amphitheatres also becoming a normal adjunct of military *camps, the earliest surviving examples being Augustan. These and many of the minor amphitheatres in the provinces were cut into the natural rock or formed from simple earth mounds; wooden structures also continued to be built (Tac. *Ann.* 4. 62). The earliest masonry arenas such as Pompeii and Mérida (8 BC; see EMERITA AUGUSTA) had retaining walls to support earth mounds; self-contained monumental masonry structures (e.g. Arles (*Arelate), El Djem), combining radial and annular vaulted passages to solve problems of access and circulation for large numbers of spectators, mainly appear under the inspiration of the Colosseum. The amphitheatre should be distinguished from the *ludus* (see LUDI) or gladiators' training-school, generally having much less seating and a proportionately larger arena. See GLADIATORS; VENATIONES.

J.-C. Golvin, *L'Amphithéâtre romain* (1988).   I. A. R.; J. D.

Amphitryon, son of Alcaeus king of Tiryns. He and his fiancée *Alcmene (daughter of Electryon king of *Mycenae) were forced to flee to *Thebes (1) after he had accidentally killed Electryon. After helping the Thebans to rid themselves of the Teumessian fox, he set out to fight the Teleboans (who had killed eight of Alcmene's nine brothers), and defeated them. In his absence, *Zeus lay with Alcmene, who bore him *Heracles (*Il.* 14. 323–4); in the same accouchement she bore *Iphicles to Amphitryon.

Amphitryon led the Thebans successfully in war against the Euboeans (Paus. 9. 17. 3, 8. 15. 6; Plut., *Amatoriae narrationes* 3 (774c)), but was less fortunate against the *Minyans, fighting whom he died (Heracles subsequently freed the Thebans from their oppression). Amphitryon was buried at Thebes, jointly with *Iolaus (Schachter 1. 30–1; 2. 18, 64–5, see bibliog. below). He seems to have been a local Theban warrior hero (the tomb is attested from the 5th cent.), whose role was partially usurped by Heracles.

A. Schachter, *Cults of Boiotia* 1–2 (1981–6); A. D. Trendall, *LIMC* 1 (1981), 735–6.   A. Sch.

amphorae and amphora stamps, Greek The amphora is one of the most versatile and long-lived pot shapes. A two-handled jar (*amphi-phoreus*, 'carried on both sides'), it can vary enormously in size, detail of shape, and manner of decoration. Broadmouthed jars, plain or decorated, were generally known as *kadoi* or *stamnoi* in antiquity. Plain or part-decorated jars, more often termed *amphoreus*, were used widely for storage and transport; we see them often in vase scenes, and literary and epigraphic texts fill out the picture. The average capacity of Classical and Hellenistic jars is 20–25 lt. (4½–5½ gal.); earlier types are regularly larger (up to 95 lt. (21 gal.)), betraying their derivation from the static storage pithos. Early transport amphorae (late 8th cent., esp. Attic and Corinthian) probably contained oil; later, wine becomes the major commodity; jars supplement, then supplant skins. Other commodities which we know to have been transported in amphorae include pitch and dried fish. Stoppers were of various material, though few survive; clay is best attested, both as basic material and sealer, though resin was also used for the latter purpose.

From the Archaic period we have significant series, often with clear distinguishing characteristics of shape or decoration, from *Corinth (two types), *Chios, *Samos, *Lesbos, *Miletus, *Cyprus. The Attic oil jar disappears from the export market *c*.575 BC, but many of these centres continue production into the Classical and Hellenistic periods (esp. Chios and Samos). By then we find new exporters, *Thasos, *Mende, *Cnidus, *Rhodes, and several Black Sea colonies, and their amphorae predominate from the 4th to the 1st cent. Distinct varieties are also found in south Italy. It should be stressed that there are many other less frequent types, whether localized by modern scholarship or not, some clearly imitations of major series, giving an intricate pattern of distribution. Shapes tend to the slim and elongated, more easy to store on ship, while the original foot turns into a stem to facilitate handling; however, the trend is neither rapid nor uniform.

A. W. J.

Stamps Stamps were impressed on plain pottery amphorae, usually on their handles, before firing in the kiln, though not all amphorae were stamped. The stamps were evidently control stamps, which seem to have endorsed the jars as of standard capacity, each according to its geographical class and particular size. Amphorae produced by different local centres are distinguishable by special features of shape, and the stamped ones most specifically by their stamps.

Typical Greek amphora stamps contain a name in the genitive, most usually that of the endorsing potter or pottery manufacturer; plus a name, sometimes with a title, introduced by the preposition *epi*, presumably a dating authority (in the most numerous class of stamps, the name of the month made the date more precise); plus sometimes an ethnic adjective ('Thasian', 'Cnidian', etc.); and/or an identifying device, which may be the arms of the issuing state, as the 'rose' characteristic of the coins of Rhodes is common also in stamps on Rhodian amphorae. Some amphorae were stamped with a single name or device only; a few on the other hand named in their stamps other magistrates in addition to the presumed dating authority.

Stamped containers were issued by a limited number of Greek states, which were important as producers of *wine (a few, e.g. Samos, of *olive oil), or as large-scale commercial handlers. For instance, the elaborately stamped early Thasian amphorae were made at a time of close state-control of the production and sale of the famous wine of *Thasos, both wine and control being well attested in ancient literature and in epigraphical texts of the late 5th and early 4th cents. BC. In contrast, Rhodian wine is very little mentioned by the ancients; and yet Rhodian amphora stamps are by far the most numerous class known to modern study. Presumably the standard Rhodian container facilitated the collection of port taxes which were the main source of revenue of the state of *Rhodes. The wine contained was of ordinary grade consumed in bulk, for instance by the troops of Hellenistic times. Perhaps not much of it was made in Rhodes.

Although the original purpose of dating amphorae was no doubt to fix more closely the responsibility for their being standard containers, one effect must have been to date the contents, identifying the age or special vintage of the finer kinds of wine,

and the freshness of the cheaper which was not worth drinking after a year. An incidental benefit is that to modern archaeological studies: as the chronology of these objects becomes better established, their very commonly found fragments quite often provide the best evidence available for dating an excavated deposit of the 4th to the 1st cent. BC.

Since 1970, much progress has been made towards a precise and reliable chronology of amphora stamps, especially those of the 3rd cent. BC: here the stamps have helped to adjust by about 35 years an earlier tentative dating of Hellenistic pottery, for certain discoveries in Koroni in Attica provide an historical fixed point—the Chremonidean War, *c*.265–260 BC, see CHREMON-IDES—thus enabling us to fix the Rhodian and Thasian amphora series that had previously been wrongly or very vaguely dated.

Also since 1970, newly found amphorae and their stamps have been reported in great numbers from the whole of the Mediterranean and Black Sea areas, including many pottery sites where amphorae were made.

AMPHORAE *Lexicon Vasorum Antiquorum*, 1 (1992), entry under 'amphorae'.

STAMPS Introductory: *Excavations of the Athenian Agora, Picture Book No. 6: Amphoras and the Ancient Wine Trade*, rev. edn. (1979). New chronology: V. R. Grace, *MDAI(A)* 1974, 193–200, and *Hesp.* 1985, 1–54 (also contains updates on various amphora studies).

FACTORY SITES See notably Y. Garlan, *BCH.* Suppl. 5 (1979), 213–68: thorough investigation and prompt publication of a large ancient factory of amphorae in Thasos, with a surprising and convincing interpretation of the finds.

New publications in this field are now being noticed at five-year intervals by J.-Y. Empereur and Y. Garlan in a very useful bulletin: see now *Rev. Ét. Grec.* 1987, 58–109 (covering 1980–6), and 1992, 176–220 (covering 1987–91). These contain not only bibliography, but also summaries and comment, in French—particularly valuable to those who do not know Russian. We owe the French versions of Russian articles to Jacqueline Garlan.

V. R. G.

amphorae and amphora stamps, Roman Amphorae, ceramic coarseware jars used for transporting a range of goods, provide the most abundant and meaningful archaeological data on the nature, range, and scale of Roman inter-regional trade in commodities such as *olive oil, *wine, marine products and fish sauces (see FISHING), preserved fruits, etc. Amphorae were most heavily used in long-distance transport, especially maritime and riverine, and are thus an effective guide to regional economic activity. The contents were clearly intended to be recognizable from the distinctive outward appearance of the most common amphora types, though painted inscriptions were sometimes added to the jar. The epigraphic evidence associated with amphorae (stamps on the vessel and on the stoppers (see below), painted inscriptions) adds further to their value in studies of the economy. Most amphorae share a number of common features: a narrow mouth, two opposed handles, thickish walls for strength, a tapering base (often a spike, though some amphorae had flat bottoms) to facilitate pouring and stacking in ships. Size and weight were important; amphorae were designed to be portable by one or at most two individuals. The classification of amphorae is an important area of Roman *pottery research and the diagnostic characteristics, fabrics, provenance, date-range, contents, and outline distribution patterns are now reasonably well established for numerous examples. Classificatory names for amphorae are derived variously from pioneers in amphora studies (Dressel 1; Lamboglia 2), important sites (Ostia LXVI; Benghazi ER 1) or region of origin (Africana I, Tripolitanian II). Underwater finds from *shipwrecks, frequently intact and representative of cargo consignments, are of particular significance.

Current research on amphorae stresses the need for quantitative studies of pottery assemblages, fabric analysis to differentiate between amphorae of the same form but produced in different areas (the most successful forms were imitated), and the need for further investigation at kiln sites as well as at the centres of consumption (*Rome, *Ostia, etc.).

Stamps Stamps, variously applied to handle, rim, neck, or spike of the vessel, provide important evidence for the Roman economy. They can help establish elements of distribution pattern and provenance, as in the case of the Italian wine amphorae stamped 'SES', exported in the late republic from *Cosa to northern Spain and central/southern Gaul. Most stamps contain personal names, often abbreviated to the initials of the *tria nomina* (see NAMES, PERSONAL, ROMAN), primarily commemorating people involved in the production of the amphorae. Some give the names of those who owned potteries (*figlinae*), others the names of the workshop managers (*officinatores*). There was no empire-wide consistency in the use of stamps; the majority of olive oil amphorae from *Baetica were stamped, compared to a minute proportion of African ones. Indeed, the purpose of stamps is uncertain (and may have varied), whether intended as self-advertisement, as a potter's guarantee of quality, as a fiscal measure for assessing customs dues, as a commercial device to discourage fraud, or simply as an internal control system on production in the largest potteries.

AMPHORAE D. P. S. Peacock and D. F. Williams, *Amphorae and the Roman Economy* (1986); *Recherches sur les amphores romaines* (1972); *Méthodes classiques et méthodes formelles dans l'étude des amphores romaines* (1977); *Amphores romaines et histoire économique* (1989); A. Giardina, *Società romana e impero tardo-antico 3: Le merci, gli insediamenti* (1986); F. Laubenheimer, *Le Temps des amphores en Gaule* (1990); A. Parker, *Ancient Shipwrecks of the Mediterranean and Roman Provinces* (1992); J. Paterson, *JRS* 1982; *Producción y commercio del aceite en la Antigüedad 1–2* (1980–3); A. Tchernia, *Le Vin de l'Italie romaine* (1986).
STAMPS W. V. Harris, *The Inscribed Economy* (1993); D. Manacorda, *JRS* 1978; D. P. S. Peacock and D. F. Williams, *Amphorae and the Roman Economy* (1986).　　　　D. J. Ma.

Ampius Balbus, Titus, called by his enemies 'the trumpet of Civil War' (Cic. *Fam.* 6. 12. 3), was tribune (63 BC), pro-Pompeian, and proconsul in *Asia in 58 and possibly of *Cilicia after (Broughton, *MRR* 3. 15; cistophori in his name were minted at Ephesus etc.). After raising troops at *Capua (49) he served as *legatus pro praetore* in Asia. Exiled by *Caesar, he was recalled (47/6) through *Cicero's influence. He wrote biographies or memoirs (Suet. *Iul.* 77).　　　　H. H. S.; E. B.

ampliatio means 'a further hearing' and is known to us as a feature of procedure in some *quaestiones* and trials before *recuperatores* under the republic. When a certain proportion of the jury regarded the evidence of guilt of the accused as insufficient for condemnation or acquittal, they declared or voted 'non liquet' ('it is not clear') and the president, by pronouncing 'amplius', decreed a further hearing. Although normally one *ampliatio* might be expected to have been sufficient, the system lent itself to abuse by an unscrupulous jury: thus in 138 BC, when L. Aurelius Cotta (Consul 144) was prosecuted by *Scipio Aemilianus *de repetundis*, proceedings are said to have been repeated seven times. The *lex repetundarum* (see REPETUNDAE) of C. *Sempronius Gracchus imposed penalties on jurors who declared 'non liquet' more than twice and more than one third

had to do so for a new hearing to take place. C. *Servilius Glaucia later eliminated *ampliatio* from the *quaestio de repetundis*, substituting *comperendinatio*, the compulsory division of a trial into two parts. There is no evidence that the latter was used in other *quaestiones*. The length of legal proceedings seems to have been cut down drastically under the Principate and it may well be that our lack of evidence for *ampliatio* is the result of its formal abolition.

J. P. Balsdon, *PBSR* 1938; A. W. Lintott, *Judicial Reform and Land Reform in the Roman Republic* (1992).　　　　A. B.; B. N.; A. W. L.

amulets (*amuletum, -a*) were magically potent objects worn (hence the Greek names: περίαμμα, περίαπτον) for protection against witchcraft, illness, the evil eye, accidents, robbery, etc. (hence the Greek name: φυλακτήριον); also to enhance love, wealth, power, or victory. Houses, walls, and towns could be protected in the same way. Any kind of material might be employed: stones and metals as well as (parts of) animals and plants, since to every sort of material could be attributed an inherent 'magical' virtue (see MAGIC); also parts of human bodies (especially of people who had suffered a violent death: *gladiators, executed criminals, victims of *shipwreck etc.) were used as amulets. Their efficacy might be enhanced by engraved figures, e.g. deities or symbols, especially on stones and gems in rings. Powerful names taken from exotic (especially Egyptian and Hebrew) myth and cult were popular: Abraxas, Solomon (e.g. in the formula: 'sickness be off, Solomon persecutes you'), magical words (e.g. *abracadabra*) and formulae (e.g. the *Ephesia Grammata*), the 'great name' (e.g. Sebaoth), or lists of vowels understood as names of archangels (see ANGELS). Just as amulets could be applied without inscription, magical inscriptions could be effective in themselves. Signs with the inscription, 'sickness be off, Heracles lives here', could be seen on house doors. Apotropaic charms of this type have also been found in papyri.

Forms of amulets varied greatly: modern collections show hundreds of different types. Notable are *rings (with *gems), nails, knots, Egyptian scarabs, a hand showing an obscene *gesture, *phallus, vulva, eye, etc. Instructions for obtaining and preparing materia medica include attention to the correct time (midnight, early morning), circumstance (stellar *constellations), and place (crossways, burial places). Both materials and formulae are marked by a wide range of variation, arbitrariness, and free association. Plin. *HN* 28 ff. gives an extensive survey, which can be supplemented by charms from later antiquity as collected by Heim (see bibliog. below).

Belief in amulets remained active in Greece and Italy in all classes of the population throughout antiquity and into modern times.

R. Heim, *Jahrb. f. cl. Phil.* Suppl. 19 (1892), 463–576; C. Bonner, *Studies in Magical Amulets Chiefly Graeco-Egyptian* (1950); F. Eckstein and J. H. Waszink, *RAC* 1 (1950), 397–411; R. Kotansky, in C. A. Faraone and D. Obbink (eds.), *Magika Hiera: Ancient Greek Magic and Religion* (1991) 107–37; C. A. Faraone, *Talismans and Trojan Horses* (1992).　H. S. V.

Amyclae, an 'Achaean' centre on the right bank of the Eurotas river *c.*5 km. (3 mi.) south of Sparta, mentioned in the Homeric *Catalogue* as in the domain of *Menelaus (1). Accounts vary of its resistance to the *Dorians but not later than *c.*750 BC it, and consequently the rest of southern *Laconia, fell. It was incorporated in Spartan territory as an *oba* (see SPARTA); in the 1st cent. BC it had its own village-administration (*IG* 5. 1. 26). Remains of the famous sanctuary (from the 8th cent. BC) and throne of *Apollo Amyclaeus (see HYACINTHUS) have been excavated on the hill of H. Kyriaki; a deposit of over 10,000 archaic votives shows that Alexandra-*Cassandra was worshipped near by.

Paus. 3. 18. 7–19. 6; P. Calligas, in J. Sanders (ed.), *Philolakon* (1992), 31 ff.   A. M. W.; W. G. F.; A. J. S. S.

Amycus, in mythology, king of the Bebryces, a savage people of *Bithynia. He was of gigantic strength and compelled all comers to the land to box with him, the loser to be at the absolute disposal of the winner. When the *Argonauts arrived in his country, Polydeuces accepted his challenge, and being a skilled boxer overcame Amycus' brute force. In the fight Amycus was killed (*Apollonius (1)), or knocked out (*Theocritus), and made to swear to wrong no more strangers, or, having lost the fight, was bound by Polydeuces (Epicharmus and *Pisander (1) in schol. Ap. Rhod. 2. 98).

Ap. Rhod. 2. 1 ff.; Theoc. *Id.* 22. 27 ff. G. Beckel, *LIMC* 1/1 (1981), 738 ff.   H. J. R.

Amymone (Ἀμυμώνη), in mythology, daughter of *Danaus. While at *Argos (2) she went for water, was rescued from a satyr, and seduced by *Poseidon, who created the spring Amymone in commemoration (Apollod. 2. 14; Hyg. *Fab.* 169, 169a).

E. Simon, *LIMC* 1/1 (1981) 742 ff.   H. J. R.

Amynander, king of the *Athamanes, perhaps already from 220 BC (if he is the Amynas of Polyb. 4. 16. 9), and for many years junior partner in the kingship with Theodorus. An able diplomat, his policy was aimed at maintaining unity within his kingdom and independence from Macedon. In 209 he negotiated on behalf of the Aetolians with *Philip (3) V and in 205 was instrumental in arranging the Peace of Phoenice between Rome and Philip. In 200/199 he joined the Romans against Philip, helped to bring the *Aetolian Confederacy back into alliance with Rome, joined in T. *Quinctius Flamininus' diplomacy after the conference at Nicaea (1) (198/7), and fought at *Cynoscephalae (197). Feeling threatened, like many, by Rome's subsequent *rapprochement* with Philip, Amynander joined *Antiochus (3) III and the Aetolians against Rome (192/1). Driven from his kingdom by Philip (191), he fled to *Ambracia, persuaded the Ambraciotes to surrender to Rome, and regained his kingdom and peace with Rome (189). He disappears from the record shortly thereafter, whether because of death or irrelevance is unclear.

RE 1, 'Amynandros' 2; C. B. Welles, *Royal Correspondence in the Hellenistic Period* (1934), no. 35; D. C. Braund, *CQ* 1982, 350 ff.; M.-F. Baslez, in P. Cabanes (ed.), *L'Illyrie méridionale et l'Épire dans l'Antiquité* (1987), 167 ff. (with bibliog.).   P. S. D.

Amyntas (1), dynastic name in the royal house of the Macedonians. The most famous bearer of the name, Amyntas III, king of Macedon *c.*393–370 BC, increased the power of his kingdom by withstanding the pressure of the Illyrians and the Dardanian king, *Bardylis I, and by astute diplomacy. He managed to ally himself with whatever Greek state became his most powerful neighbour: the Chalcidic Confederacy (Tod no. 111; see CHALCIDICE), the Spartans who destroyed the Chalcidic Confederacy, the Athenians when they replaced Sparta (Tod no. 129) and then *Jason (2) of Pherae. His consolidation of Macedonia and his example in diplomacy were important factors in the success of his son *Philip (1) II. See MACEDONIA.

HM 2. (1979), see index.   N. G. L. H.

Amyntas (2), a dependent king (see CLIENT KINGS) of the Romans in Asia Minor. Secretary of *Deiotarus, he commanded the Galatian auxiliaries of the Liberators in 42 BC, but deserted after the first battle of *Philippi. After Deiotarus' death (39 BC) Mark Antony (M. *Antonius (2)) gave him a kingdom in northern *Pisidia and neighbouring *Phrygia to which in 36 he added *Galatia and parts of *Lycaonia and *Pamphylia. In 35 Amyntas received the surrender of Sextus *Pompeius. He accompanied Antony to *Actium, but deserted before the battle. Octavian enlarged his kingdom further by adding *Isauria and *Cilicia Tracheia. He successfully attacked Cremna and the dynast Antipater of Derbe but in 25 was killed campaigning against the Homonadeis on Lake Trogitis. Though he left sons, most of his kingdom was annexed and made into the province of Galatia.

B. Levick, *Roman Colonies in Southern Asia Minor* (1967); A. Hall, *Anat. Stud.* 1971, 125–66; D. Braund, *Rome and the Friendly King* (1984); R. Sullivan, *Near Eastern Royalty and Rome, 100–30* BC (1990); S. Mitchell, *Anatolia* (1993), see indexes.   M. C.; T. J. C.; B. M. L.

Amyzon, remote but important *sanctuary in *Caria, north of *Mylasa. Greek inscriptions have been found there dating from the time of the 4th-cent. BC Hecatomnid *satrap *Idrieus, also of *Philip (2) Arrhidaeus (in which Iranians are honoured, showing their social survival after the end of the *Achaemenid empire), and of the Ptolemaic and Seleucid periods of control in the 3rd century, esp. documents of *Antiochus (3) III and *Zeuxis (4) at the end of the century.

J. and L. Robert, *Fouilles d'Amyzon en Carie* (1983).   S. H.

anabolē, musical term (see MUSIC), used of the striking-up of a musical instrument (esp. of the lyre, *Od.* 1. 155, 8. 266: ἀνεβάλλετο), a prelude serving as a signal to dancers and singers (Pind. *Pyth.* 1. 4). In the *dithyramb of the 5th cent. BC it denotes the elaborate instrumental intermezzi introduced by *Melanippides (2), *Cinesias, and *Timotheus (1), or the dithyramb as a whole (Arist. *Rh.* 3. 9. 1; Ar. *Av.* 1385)

M. West, *Ancient Greek Music* (1992); G. Comotti, *Quaderni urbinati di cultura classica* 1989, 107–17.   C. M. B.; E. Kr.

Anacharsis, a largely legendary *Scythian prince who came to exemplify the wise barbarian. Sometimes presented as an admirer of Greek ways (esp. those of *Sparta), he later typifies *barbarian criticism of Greek customs. (For Sparta see *Lucian's *Anach.*) He is said to have travelled extensively in Greece and elsewhere in the 6th cent. BC and gained a high reputation for wisdom. On his return to Scythia he was put to death for attempting to introduce the cult of Magna Mater (see CYBELE) to the Scythians. So much we are told by our earliest source, *Herodotus (1) (4. 76 f.), but even at this early date it is impossible to distinguish what, if anything, is historical in this legendary material. Later he was given a Greek mother and made a friend of *Solon (Diog. Laert. 1. 101–5), and was sometimes included among the *Seven Sages. Ten letters from the Hellenistic period and some 50 sayings, a few perhaps from the Archaic period, are attributed to him. The letters especially extol the ideal simple life of the Scythians. They were much relished: *Cicero translated one of them (*Tusc.* 5. 90) and the figure of Anacharsis as the 'noble savage' was popularized by Abbé Barthélemy's *Voyage du jeune Anacharsis en Grèce* (1788).

TEXTS Sayings: J. F. Kindstrand, *Anacharsis* (1981), with comm. Letters: F. H. Reuters, *De A. epistulis* (Diss. Bonn, 1957), with comm.; trans. A. J. Malherbe, *The Cynic Epistles* (1977).   M. Ga.

Anacreon, lyric poet, native of *Teos. Little is known of his life. Born perhaps *c.*575–570 (Eusebius gives his *floruit* as 536/5), he probably joined in the foundation of *Abdera in Thrace by the Teans fleeing before the threat of the Persian general Harpagus

Anacreontea

in 545 (Strabo 14. 1. 30; Aristox. fr. 12 Wehrli, Hdt. 1. 168). He joined the court of *Polycrates (1), tyrant of Samos (Hdt. 3. 121), the most illustrious Greek of the day; *Strabo claims that his 'whole poetry is full of mention of Polycrates' (14. 1. 16), though there is no reference in surviving fragments. Tradition made Anacreon and Polycrates rivals for the love of a Thracian boy, Smerdies, whose hair Polycrates cut off in a fit of jealousy (Stob. 4. 21. 24; Ath. 12. 540e; Ael. VH 9. 4); this may be false inference from Anacreon's poetry. After the murder of Polycrates by the Persian satrap Oroetes he joined the Pisistratid court at Athens (see PISISTRATUS); allegedly *Hipparchus (1) sent a warship to fetch him ([Pl.] Hipparch. 228c). According to Plato (Chrm. 157e) he praised the family of Critias (grandfather of the oligarch *Critias), whose lover he was (schol. Aesch. PV 128). After Hipparchus' murder he may have gone to Thessaly (Anth. Pal. 6. 136, 142, if correctly attributed). The fragments suggest that he lived to old age, though the figure of 85 years ([Lucian] Macr. 26) cannot be verified. The tradition that he died by choking on a grape (Val. Max. 9. 12) displays the mythopoeia typical of ancient *biography.

He composed in elegiac distichs, iambic and trochaic rhythms, lyric stanzas consisting of glyconics with pherecratean clausula, and ionics (including a form with anaclasis named Anacreontic after him) (see METRE, GREEK). The dialect is Ionic vernacular with some epicisms. The range of what survives is narrow. Wine and love (both homosexual and heterosexual) figure prominently. His control of form produces an appearance of effortlessness. Many poems have an epigrammatic quality. Words are positioned with great effect, as in the fr. 357, a prayer to *Dionysus, with the play on the beloved's name and closing revelation that this is a love poem; 358 with the contrast between the fluent first and staccato second half reflecting the move from enchantment to rejection; 395 with its closing wordplay; and 360 with the closing image of the beloved boy as charioteer of the poet's soul. Striking images for love abound (396, 398, 413). Delicacy, wit, paradox, irony, and self-mockery are prominent, as in 417, addressed to a coy girl, represented as a reluctant filly, 347 which laments the loss of a boy's hair in mock-epic terms, the bathos of 359, the idea of riotous decorum in 356a. He also produced biting abuse in the iambic tradition (346, 372, 388) (see IAMBIC POETRY, GREEK). Later sources ascribe maiden songs to him (Ath. 13. 600d); a possible fragment survives (501). His work was edited by the Alexandrians into at least six books. His wit inspired a corpus of frivolous imitations in and after the Hellenistic period, the *Anacreontea, which until the 19th cent. were believed to be his work.

> TEXTS Page, PMG; B. Gentili, Anacreon (1958); D. A. Campbell, Greek Lyric 2 (Loeb, 1988), 22–161; West, IE², and Carmina Anacreontea (Teubner, 1984).
> TRANSLATION D. A. Campbell, Greek Lyric 2 (Loeb, 1988).
> CRITICISM B. Gentili, Anacreon (1958); G. M. Kirkwood, Early Greek Monody (1974), 150 ff.; RE Suppl. 11. 30 ff.   C. C.

Anacreontea, a collection of some 62 Greek poems preserved in the MS of the Palatine Anthology under the heading 'Anacreon of Teos' Sympotic Hemiambics'. Some of them refer to *Anacreon or actually adopt his persona; they are all in metres derived from him, and their main subjects are wine and love. There is no depth in them, but they are often delightful. Some of them were already current under Anacreon's name in the time of Aulus *Gellius (NA 19. 9. 4–6). Following their first publication by Stephanus in 1554 they were widely acclaimed as Anacreon's work and frequently edited and translated as 'the Odes of Anacreon'; they exercised extensive influence on European lyric

poetry. By the early 19th cent. it was clear to scholars that the poems all dated from long after Anacreon's time. They show very various levels of technical competence, and must have been composed at different dates between about the 1st cent. BC or AD and the 5th or 6th AD.

> TEXT M. L. West (Teubner, 1984); D. A. Campbell, Greek Lyric 2 (Loeb, 1988), with trans.
> CRITICISM M. L. West, in O. Murray (ed.), Sympotica (1990); P. A. Rosenmeyer, The Poetics of Imitation (1992).   M. L. W.

Anactorium, a joint colony of Corinthians and Acarnanians (see CORINTH; ACARNANIA) was founded c.620 BC on the south coast of the gulf of *Ambracia. It sent troops to fight in the battle of *Plataea against the Persians. In 425 Anactorium was absorbed into *Acarnania.

> Hammond, Epirus, 62 and 425 f.   N. G. L. H.

Anagnia (mod. Anagni), chief town of the *Hernici (Aen. 7. 684), in the fertile Sacco valley, with well-preserved walls. In 306 BC Anagnia became a civitas sine suffragio (see MUNICIPIUM) which *Pyrrhus and *Hannibal later ravaged (Livy 9. 42 f., 26. 9; App. Sam. 10). In the 2nd cent. it acquired full citizenship (Festus 155 Lindsay) and remained a municipium under the empire (reject Lib. Colon. p. 230). Vitellius' general *Fabius Valens and Commodus' concubine *Marcia were born here (Tac. Hist. 3. 62; ILS 406). The numerous temples near Anagnia were still celebrated in Marcus *Aurelius' time (Fronto, Ep. 4. 4); some have been identified, including one that dates back at least to the 6th cent. BC.

> M. Mazzolani, Anagni (1969); S. Gatti, Stud. Etr. 1986, 345 ff; Arch. Laz. 1988, 218 ff.   E. T. S.; T. W. P.

anagnōstēs, a reader, often an educated slave, whose duty in Roman houses was to entertain his master and guests at table by a recitation in Greek and Latin. *Cicero (Att. 1. 12. 4) mentions his distress at the death of his young reader Sosthenes. *Atticus kept very good readers whom he thought indispensable at dinner parties (Nep. Att. 13. 3 and 14. 1). Aulus *Gellius (3. 19) records similar entertainment at dinner with the philosopher *Favorinus. The anagnōstēs was also a civic functionary in the Greek east, as with the 'reader of the people' (ἀναγνώστης τοῦ δήμου) at Hellenistic Smyrna (JÖAI 28, Beiblatt, 121 ff.).

> J. W. D.; A. J. S. S.

Anahita (Anaitis, Ἀναῖτις), Persian goddess of the fertilizing waters (Avesta Yašt 5). *Artaxerxes (2) II (404–358 BC) introduced the use of cult-images into the major cities of his empire (Berossus in Clem. Al. Protr. 5. 65. 3) and invoked her with *Ahuramazda and *Mithras in royal inscriptions (A²Sa, A²Sd, A²Ha). Anahita is not mentioned in the *Persepolis administrative texts. No images of Anahita from Iran are known until Sasanid times. The cult spread to *Armenia, *Cappadocia, *Pontus, and *Lydia. In Armenia sacred *prostitution was practised (Strabo 11. 14. 16). In *Lydia she was assimilated to *Cybele and *Artemis, called Artemis Anaitis and Anaitis Meter in numerous monuments and inscriptions, and worshipped in temples at *Sardis, Hierocaesarea, Hypaepa, and elsewhere. The name Anahita means 'undefiled, immaculate'; in Greek Anahita is sometimes equated with Aphrodite or Athena (Plut. Artaxerxes 3). See RELIGION, PERSIAN; SYNCRETISM.

> M. Boyce, Enc. Ir. 1. 1003–11 'Anāhīd'; I. M. Diakonoff, Babesch 1979, 139–88.   H. S.-W.

Anakes (Ἄνακες), old by-form of ἄνακτες, 'lords', 'kings' (the latter being the meaning of *anax* in Linear B). This is the surprising title under which the *Dioscuri were invariably worshipped in Attica (as sometimes in *Argos (2)), often in the dual form Ἄνακε; an inscription has recently confirmed that these Anake / Dioscuri could be associated in cult with *Helen (*SEG* 33. 147. 37–8.). Some infer from the deep embeddedness of the title in Attica that the Anakes were originally independent deities, perhaps three in number. Actual traces, however, of Anakes who are not identified with Dioscuri are faint and uncertain (Paus. 10. 38. 7; Cic. *Nat. D.* 3. 53).

B. Hemberg, *ΑΝΑΞ, ΑΝΑΣΣΑ und ΑΝΑΚΕΣ* (1955).   R. C. T. P.

analogia, De, *Caesar's lost treatise inspired by the teaching of *Antonius Gnipho, written on a journey across the Alps (55 or 54 BC) and dedicated to *Cicero. It defended the principle of *analogy and a reformed *elegantia* founded on everyday speech. Aulus *Gellius (1. 10. 4) quotes from its first book the famous advice 'avoid, as you would a rock, the rare and obsolete word' (see H. Dahlmann, *Rh. Mus.* 1935, 258 ff.; E. Rawson, *Intellectual Life in the Late Roman Republic* (1985), 122 f.).   J. W. D.

analogy and anomaly were the titles of two themes in the investigation of the Greek and Latin languages in the classical era. They turned on the question, to what extent can regularity (*analogia*, analogy) be recognized in rules and classes (e.g. *scribo:scribens* (I write, writing); *lego:legens* (I read, reading); *equus* (one horse), *equi* (more than one)) and how far must exceptions (*anomalia*, anomaly) be accepted (e.g. *bonus, melior, optimus* (good, better, best); *Zeús, Zēnós* (Zeus, of Zeus); *Athēnai*, formally plural, the city of Athens). In part this related to the contemporaneous discussion on the natural or the conventional origin of language.

The topic arose in the Greek world in Hellenistic times, and was part of the context in which grammatical science itself developed. The Stoics (see STOICISM), especially *Chrysippus and *Crates (3), favoured anomaly, and the Alexandrian scholars argued for analogy in the establishing of correct texts in the Homeric poems and in the teaching of Greek. Only on the evidence of analogies could the apparent disorderliness of language be brought into order. In an early statement on the objectives of grammar (*c.*100 BC) the 'working out of analogies' was given an explicit place.

In the Roman world *Caesar wrote a (lost) treatise on analogy (*De *analogia*), but our most extensive and detailed treatment of the subject comes from books 8, 9, and 10 of *Varro's *De lingua Latina* (*On the Latin Language*; 1st cent. BC). In it both approaches to language are set out in separate sections as a formal debate. Traditionally (e.g. by Steinthal, see bibliog. below) this was seen as a formal struggle (*Kampf*), but recent reconsiderations have led scholars to think that Varro overformalized the actual course of the argument. He certainly made use of analogy in ordering the paradigmatic inflections of Latin nouns and verbs, and his series of corresponding case forms led later Latin grammarians to establish the five declensions by the end of antiquity.

Varro, *Ling.* bks. 8–10 (Loeb, 1938). H. Steinthal, *Geschichte der Sprachwissenschaft* (1891; repr. 1961), 71–161; F. H. Colson, *CQ* 1919, 24–36; J. Collart, in *Varron*, Entretiens Hardt 9 (1962), 117–40; D. Fehling, *Glotta* 1956, 214–70; 1958, 48–100.   R. H. R.

Anatolia See ASIA MINOR (Classical).

Anatolian deities Deities of prehistoric Anatolia may be inferred from such monuments as the painted shrines of neolithic Çatal Hüyük, or the figurines and 'standards' of early bronze age Alaca Hüyük, but only with the advent of writing, *c.*2000 BC, is a more complete picture available. In the Old Assyrian colony period (*c.*2000–1800 BC), deities appear as figurines or on seals, sometimes as family groups, sometimes as recognizable figures—the weather-god, the hunting-god, the nude goddess, etc., with their familiar animals, bull, stag, birds, etc. The Hittite kingdom (*c.*1650–1200 BC) (see HITTITES) provides the fullest evidence, where the iconography of seals, reliefs, figurines, etc., is amplified by the extensive texts of the *Hattuša archives relating to mythology and cult. At Hattuša, overlapping pantheons are attested: the autochthonous Hattian, with that of the Hittites evolved locally, and later the imported Hurro-Mesopotamian, which gradually gained ground over the other two. The proliferation of deities reflects the need to create a national pantheon from a multitude of local cults. Weather-gods and sun-gods head the pantheons, followed by such figures as the grain-god, the stag- (hunting-) god, etc., ending with natural phenomena such as mountains and rivers, etc. Male deities are provided with female consorts, listed separately and not strongly characterized except for an Ištar figure, who may also appear in the male list.

The end of the Hittite kingdom removes this documentation which is only partially replaced by the inscriptions of the Neo-Hittite states of SE Anatolia and north Syria (*c.*1100–700 BC). Details of cult are lacking. The Hurro-Hittite weather-god and his consort continue to be worshipped, and the stag-god becomes more prominent, as do Kubaba from Carchemish and the moon-god from Harran. At this period, limited evidence may be drawn from the *Phrygian monuments and inscriptions, principally relating to 'mother Kubile' (Kubaba), represented on stone monuments as a figure in a *polos* ('cylindrical head-dress') and long robe, standing in a small shrine or *naiskos* (see CYBELE).

O. R. Gurney, *Some Aspects of Hittite Religion*, Schweich Lectures, 1976 (1977); M. N. van Loon, *Anatolia in the Second Millennium BC; Anatolia in the Earlier First Millennium BC* Iconography of Religions 15, pts. 12 and 13 (1985–90).   J. D. Ha.

Anatolian languages In the course of this century new evidence has emerged for a family of closely related languages attested in Anatolia (Turkey) from the 16th cent. BC and indirectly known two or three centuries earlier; the evidence for the group spans two millennia and ends with the Roman empire. The best attested language is Hittite, which was spoken by a dynasty which moved from Neša (= Kaneš = mod. Kültepe in central Anatolia, north-east of Kayseri) to *Hattuša, modern Boğazköy or Boğazkale (east of Ankara), the future capital of the Hittite empire, which eventually dominated most of Anatolia and part of Syria (see HITTITES). The word *nešili*, literally 'in the language of Neša', means 'in Hittite', while Hittite (our term is based on a biblical form) was originally derived from the name of the previous non-Indo-European inhabitants of the area, the Hatti. The Boğazköy archives yielded a very large number of *cuneiform tablets with texts (historical, religious, etc.) which we can now classify as Old Hittite (*c.*1570–1450) or Middle Hittite (*c.*1450–1380) or Neo-Hittite (*c.*1380–1220); after B. Hrozný in 1915 argued that Hittite was *Indo-European, the grammar and lexicon have become quite well known and we now understand most texts. The same archives also provided cuneiform evidence for two other related languages, introduced in the Hittite texts by the words *palaumnili* 'in Palaic' and *luwili* 'in Luwian'. Palaic is the language of the Pāla territory, located in north-western Anatolia. Probably it died before the Neo-Hittite period; there are only a few imperfectly understood texts, but the affiliation of the language is not in doubt. Cuneiform Luwian, also attested on clay tablets mostly of religious nature, is slightly better known and was probably the language of the southern and western part of Anatolia. It survived longer than Palaic and had strong influence on Hittite, especially in the later period, as shown by the numerous lexical borrowings. In the first millennium the family is best represented by Hieroglyphic Luwian (also called Hieroglyphic Hittite), a Luwian dialect, written in a special syllabic script, rich in logograms, which was developed in the second millennium, possibly for monumental purposes. Most of the inscriptions were set up by the kings of the small states of south Anatolia and Syria which in the first millennium BC survived the collapse of the Hittite empire, until at the end of the 8th cent. they were defeated by the Assyrians. The youngest known members of the Anatolian family are *Lycian and *Lydian, two languages written in an alphabet derived from Greek, mostly in the 5th and 4th cent. BC. In addition three very poorly attested languages, all written alphabetically, may belong to the family: Carian (see CARIA), has a slightly higher number of texts dating from the 7th to the 4th cent. BC, but the decipherment of the script is not yet complete; Sidetic (named from *Side) is documented by a very few inscriptions from *Pamphylia (3rd cent. BC), and Pisidian has some inscriptions (mostly names) from the 3rd cent. AD. (See PISIDIA.)

The languages listed above, all of which must derive from a non-attested Proto-Anatolian, show regular correspondences with the ancient Indo-European languages. Part of the lexicon can be easily etymologized: cf. *watar* 'water' (Gr. ὕδωρ), *genu* 'knee' (Lat. *genu*), *newa-* 'new' (Gr. νέϝος), *wett-* 'year' (Gr. ϝέτος), *ed-* 'eat' (Lat. *edō*), and see also paradigms like *ešmi* 'I am' *ešši* 'you are (sing.)', *ešzi* 'he/she/it is' vs. Greek εἰμί (< †*esmi*), ἐσσί, ἐστί or Skt. *ásmi*, *ási*, *ásti*, etc. Hittite, Palaic, and Cuneiform Luwian have *a* where reconstructed Indo-European has *o* and use -*h*- or -*hh*- in correspondence with the Indo-European 'laryngeals', which were later lost in all Indo-European languages. It is now clear that the original Anatolian language had an accent distribution similar to that of Indo-European. Morphologically the most striking features are the conservativism of the case system (seven or perhaps eight cases in Old Hittite), but also the absence of a contrast between masculine and feminine (there is a neuter and a common gender) and the organization of the verbal system based on two conjugations with contrasts of past and present marked by different sets of endings. There are only two tenses (no imperfect and future, no aspectual distinction of aorist and perfect) and two moods (indicative and imperative, but no subjunctive and optative). The syntax is characterized by long chains of enclitic particles which follow the first word of the sentence and by the final position of the verb. The problem arises whether Proto-Anatolian is simply a branch, however early, of the Indo-European family which has lost some of the original categories, or is a sister rather than a daughter of Indo-European. This last view was supported by the American scholar Edgar Sturtevant, who spoke of an Indo-Hittite protolanguage; his demonstration is no longer accepted, but recent contributions are moving in the same direction though more on the basis of morphology and syntax than on that of phonology.

O. R. Gurney, *The Hittites*, 2nd edn. (1990); A. Kammenhuber, *Hethitisch, Paläisch, Luwisch und Hieroglyphenluwisch*, in B. Spüler (ed.), *Handbuch der Orientalistik* 1/2. 1–2. 2: *Altkleinasiatische Sprachen* (1969), 119–357; J. Friedrich, *Hethitisches Elementarbuch* 1 (1960); J. Puhvel, *Hittite Etymological Dictionary* (1984–); H. C. Melchert, *Anatolian Phonology* (1995).　　　　　　　　　　　　　　　　　　A. M. Da.

anatomy and physiology

I The examination of the parts of the body, their forms, location, nature, function, and interrelations (to adapt the list provided by A. *Cornelius Celsus in the proem to book 1 of the *De medicina*)—whether through dissection (ἀνατομία, the title of several ancient medical works, and of a lost work by *Aristotle) or as part of more abstract speculation about natural causes (φυσιολογία)—was a concern not only for doctors. Physiology did not have the restricted range it has today; in antiquity it covered all kinds of speculative investigation into nature—in areas ranging from the search for the *soul and its physical location in the body to the explanation of organic processes in animals and plants. This means that ancient medical writers often paid close attention to the work of those whom we might regard today as having quite different concerns. Much early Greek cosmology, for example, was concerned (directly or indirectly) with problems surrounding the nature and origins of life, and the relations between the macroscopic structures of the universe and the microscopic structures of the body. Several Presocratic philosophers of nature advanced speculative models to explain physiological and pathological processes in terms of the transformation and balanced arrangement of one or more types of principal matter which they believed to constitute the universe as a whole. (Ideas of balance and imbalance, democracy and tyranny, symmetry and asymmetry can be seen shaping many different areas of Greek thought, cosmological, political, and physiological.) The influence, both positive and negative, of early cosmological models on Hippocratic physiological theories (see HIPPOCRATES (2)) was often profound—so much so that the author of the Hippocratic treatise *On Ancient Medicine* directed a strong attack on those doctors who borrowed unverifiable hypotheses from the philosophers (see ELEMENTS; HYPOTHESIS, SCIENTIFIC).

Modern critics of Greek medicine—particularly those with scientific or medical backgrounds themselves—are often struck by the lack of agreement (even amongst ancient specialists) over the description of the human body's internal structures. And it is true that even in the Hippocratic corpus there is no single, dominant anatomical or physiological treatise. In fact there is little unambiguous, early evidence for dissection as an investigative tool either in the study of anatomy or in the development of physiological theories. It does seem surprising to find Aristotle noting towards the end of the 4th cent. (after the bulk of the Hippocratic treatises were written) that 'the internal parts of the body, especially those of man, are unknown. We must as a result refer to the parts of other creatures with a nature similar to that of humans' (*HA* 494ᵇ). Even *Galen several hundred years later was still relying on dissections of the Barbary ape for his knowledge of some aspects of human anatomy—yet Galen himself was struck by the lack of interest in anatomy amongst the earliest Greek doctors.

The reasons for this state of affairs (which seemed as surprising to many later Greek medical authorities as it does to some of us today) are extremely complex and this article aims merely at summary and general description. (There now exist several detailed guides to the anatomical and physiological theories of individual ancient doctors, and a selection is listed at the end of this article.) Galen's explanation was simple: The earliest doctors treated medicine as a craft, and medical knowledge was handed down from father to son. There seemed little point in writing down information which could more readily be obtained by direct inquiry. In contrast, conventional modern explanations of the situation have tended to focus on the widespread ancient taboos against dissection—especially human dissection—which persisted throughout antiquity. Such taboos there certainly were, however surprising this may seem in societies which otherwise tolerated the murder of men and women in the name of public entertainment. In spite of evidence that the dissection of animals played an increasingly important role in the study of human medicine after Aristotle, it is not at all easy to assess the status of the early, pre-Aristotelian evidence.

While it is widely believed that early in the 5th cent. BC *Alcmaeon (2) of Croton pursued anatomical studies of animals, there is little agreement (modern or ancient) as to just how far he went. Later ancient witnesses attribute to him pioneering work on the anatomy of the eye and its communication with the brain, the ear, the nasal passages, and the embryo, and more controversially the blood-vascular system (DK 24 A 5–18). As none of his own work survives intact, we are hardly in a position to judge just how far his research was based on autopsy, let alone its general motivations. The judgement of the early evidence is further complicated by the problem of the lack of technical anatomical vocabulary. Much apparently technical information may have been more or less common knowledge. At Aristophanes' *Frogs* 134 for instance, the comic Dionysus fears that by jumping off a tall building he will 'destroy two rissole wrappers of his brain'; should this metaphor have occurred in a medical treatise, we might immediately assume that it displayed more or less specialized autoptic experience of the brain. In fact it is not until Hellenistic times that a detailed anatomical vocabulary develops in earnest, and even then it grows by naming parts of the body through analogy with familar external objects. This is the procedure which had already been advocated by the author of the Hippocratic treatise *On Ancient Medicine* (22) to aid the comprehension of the functions of internal parts, of which he had only the vaguest idea: 'It is necessary to learn about [internal structures] from external ones which are evident to us,' he notes. The problem of anatomical nomenclature, its poverty and the lack of standardization was still so serious in the 2nd cent. AD that *Rufus of Ephesus and Galen himself devoted several treatises specifically to this subject.

Acute observations of physiological processes such as respiration, sensation, digestion, and excretion, were often incorporated into highly speculative theories without these observations themselves being the subject of practical verification. It seems that traditional anatomical models could also take on authoritative status in some quarters. Scenes of wounding in the Homeric epics point to the existence of traditional models to describe the internal structure of the body which became part of the furniture for some medical writers. For instance, *Il.* 13. 545–9: 'Antilochus watched Thoon as he turned around, and then rushed at him, thrusting. He severed the whole vein (*phleps*) which runs right up the back to the neck—he severed the whole of it. Thoon fell back and lay in the dust, stretching out both his hands to his friends.' In some cases it was a long time before this kind of literary tradition was displaced by the results of autopsy. A much later ancient commentator on this Homeric passage noted that 'here the poet is an anatomist. He refers to the so-called "hollow vein" [*koilē phleps*, the Greek term for the *vena cava*] which runs from the right of the spine, from the liver, passes over the diaphragm to the heart and from there to the neck.' Homer is a special case, of course, and the non-medical writers often preserve important observations which were never taken up at all. The phenomenon of contagion, for example, described by *Thucydides (2) in his account of the great *plague at Athens in 430 BC (2. 47), and hinted at in the first choral ode of Sophocles' *Oedipus*, was not examined in detail by the very doctors who Thucydides tells us were the first to suffer.

II Much early work on the structure of the body focused on the skeleton and the vascular system. One of the earliest surviving accounts of the way in which parts communicate with each other is preserved by Aristotle; it is striking for the few signs it shows of close acquaintance with the physical appearance of the structures it describes. Aristotle reports (*HA* 512ᵃ4 ff.) that *Diogenes (1) of Apollonia in the 5th cent. had posited a blood-vascular system of ducts (*phlebes*) distributed throughout the body, divided into two independent networks each serving one side of the body. The network on the right originated in the liver, and was probably called *hēpatitis*, while that on the left, *splēnitis*, came from the spleen. It is likely that surface anatomy (especially in connection with parts like the neck where internal structures stand out) played a part in the establishment of models such as this one; perhaps experience derived from the practice of therapeutic measures such as venesection was also relevant. Most significant, perhaps, is the underlying assumption here that the bilateral symmetry exhibited by the body externally should in some way be reflected internally.

Vessels, pores, and ducts, visible and theoretical, figure prominently in many ancient physiological theories. It is not clear from Aristotle's account of Diogenes exactly what the vessels carried, nor what function his model played in his physiological theory. One late doxographical source (*Aëtius (1), DK 64 A 29) reports that they carried air. (Air was known to be necessary to life and vital for the functioning of the senses; it was not known until much later, of course, exactly what happened to inspired air. A large group of ancient theorists, many of them still active in Galen's day, believed that inspired air passes from the lungs via the heart into the arteries (see PNEUMA)). Diogenes' 'ducts' probably carried a variety of fluids around the body, including air. Diogenes may or may not have been a doctor himself; certainly he was a cosmologist, and it seems likely that his physiological and anatomical work was related to his cosmology, and in particular to his idea that air has some kind of elemental status, and is to be associated with the cognitive faculties in animals.

Aristotle mentions two other similar early models of internal anatomical structures; one he attributes to the otherwise unknown Syennesis of Cyprus, and the other to *Polybus (3), supposed by many to have been the son-in-law of Hippocrates. An account similar to that of Polybus appears in the Hippocratic treatise *On the Nature of Man* (ch. 11); it might be noted that the surviving Hippocratic accounts of vascular anatomy are not as a rule as detailed as these three cited by Aristotle. (Although as exceptions, one should note the little-known Hippocratic treatises *On the Nature of Bones*, *On Anatomy*, *On Fleshes*, and the later (4th-cent.) work *On the Heart*.)

Along with early work on the anatomy of the vascular system comes speculation about the seat of cognition, and the ways in which the senses communicate with each other and the so-called 'command centre' of the body. Some early authorities, including in all probability Alcmaeon of Croton, Diogenes of Apollonia, and by implication the author of the Hippocratic *Sacred Disease*, argued for the brain's primary role here, but *Plato (1) moved the command centre to the heart (*Ti.* 70a ff.), followed by Aristotle and *Diocles (3) of Carystus. The debate continued until Galen reasserted the very early primacy of the liver in the 2nd cent. AD.

anatomy and physiology

In the Hippocratic writings, then, pathological commentary and physiological theory tend to be more detailed than empirical knowledge of internal anatomy. The author of *Sacred Disease*, famous for the argument that epilepsy has a natural cause, offers a convenient example of the priority of theory, even in cases where autopsy is brought to the fore. He insists that epilepsy has its origin in the brain; assuming that the human brain is fundamentally the same as the brain in all other animals, he describes the examination of the brain of a similarly afflicted goat. 'On opening the head', he claims, 'the brain will be found to be wet, full of fluid and foul-smelling—persuasive proof that the disease and not a deity is causing the harm.' Adherents of humoral theories similarly tended to locate the source of the humours in specific organs which seemed a priori to be appropriate. Typically for many Hippocratic authors, bile comes from the liver and phlegm from the head (see HUMOURS). External examination of the state of the most prominent vessels which allowed the communication of these fluids through the body could be an important part of a general assessment of the state of the body.

III With *Aristotle, there is much stronger evidence that physiological theory can be related to empirical investigation. (Some modern scholars hold that Aristotle may even have dissected a human embryo, but the evidence (*HA* 583^{b}14) is inconclusive. It seems unlikely, on balance, that Aristotle dissected human subjects.) In the first book of the treatise *On the Parts of Animals*, Aristotle stresses the importance of autopsy as a preliminary to theory, however disagreeable this may be. In the *History of Animals*, he went on to provide detailed, observationally based accounts of the vascular system and the internal geography of the body, and a whole range of physiological theories explaining digestion, respiration, etc. in the treatises which make up the so-called *Parva naturalia*. See ANIMALS, KNOWLEDGE ABOUT § II.

IV After Aristotle, it seems that more and more doctors began to employ animal dissection—including *vivisection—but human dissection probably remained the exception and not the rule. Diocles of Carystus (credited by Galen with having composed the first anatomical handbook (fr. 23 Wellmann)) made important observations about the anatomy of the womb (fr. 27 Wellmann). *Praxagoras of Cos is traditionally credited with drawing the distinction between veins and arteries, and doing important work on neural anatomy. As the teacher of *Herophilus of Chalcedon, Praxagoras stands at the beginning of one of the most fruitful periods of anatomical investigation in the history of medicine. Herophilus' and *Erasistratus' work in dissection—notably human dissection–led to a dramatic development of anatomical knowledge. Celsus reports that they were given condemned criminals and performed vivisections on them; although the evidence for this has been questioned in some quarters, most modern scholars seem to accept its plausibility, and, at the very least, it seems likely that Herophilus was one of the first physicians to make systematic use of human dissection. He made important discoveries about the anatomy of the eye, the male and female reproductive systems, and the blood-vascular system. Most famous perhaps, was his work on the nerves; it seems likely that he was the first to discern them, and perhaps the first to make the distinction between motor and sensory nerves.

In Hellenistic physiological theory we find the marriage of physics and anatomy developing in many ways. Erasistratus, credited by Galen with new anatomical work on the structure of the heart and the blood-vascular system, developed a theory which explained the origins of the body in terms of agglomerations of an elemental complex of vein, artery, and nerve. *Asclepiades (3) of Bithynia seems to have taken this type of idea further, reducing the body's component parts to elementary corpuscles and pores whose constant motion accounted for the change and unpredictability of physiological and pathological phenomena. The Asclepiadean theory, with its insistence that health and disease—indeed all physiological processes—can be understood in terms of the proper movement of these corpuscles in the pores, had the effect of dampening commitment to anatomical investigation amongst his many intellectual progeny. But not all; although the Methodists argued that the study of anatomy was rather beside the point, given their insistence that all the doctor needed to know about disease could be learned from the phenomenal presentation of two or three morbid states in the body, *Soranus of Ephesus made a considerable contribution to female anatomy in his *Gynaecology*. At the beginning of this work, Soranus notes that 'since we are now about to pass to the section on gynaecological hygiene, it will first be necessary to explain the nature of the female parts. Some of this can be learned directly, some from dissection. And since dissection, although useless, is nevertheless studied for the sake of profound learning, we shall also teach what has been discovered by it' (1. 2. 5, trans. O. Temkin). There follows a remarkably detailed account of the anatomy of the female reproductive system. (See GYNAECOLOGY).

Not all doctors placed anatomy at the service of physiology. Another group, active from the 2nd cent. BC onwards, associated themselves more or less directly with a current in Pyrrhonian scepticism (see PYRRHON), and marshalled powerful arguments against the value of physiological speculation in the practice of medicine. Pointing to the kinds of disagreements amongst dogmatic exponents of medical theories which had so frustrated even the Hippocratic author of *On Ancient Medicine* (see HYPOTHESIS, SCIENTIFIC), it was argued that experience was the only true teacher in medicine. Medical empiricism placed restrictions on the amount of research it was sensible for a doctor to pursue given the futility of theory-building, although anatomical investigation of accident victims remained—as it always had been—a valid way of gathering knowledge.

V *Galen's very importance as anatomist and physiologist makes any detailed treatment here quite impossible, and any summary treatment would be misleading. Best simply to quote Galen's own advice to the intending student of his anatomical and physiological theories, adapted from his work *On the Order of his Own Books*. '. . . *On Bones, for Beginners*. This is the first part of the course of anatomy; . . . then . . . approach the *Anatomical Administrations*. This work teaches the parts revealed in anatomy, their size, position shaping, interrelations, appearance, and similarities with each other. The man who is experienced in the observation of these things through anatomy will then go on to learn about their activities—their natural activities, written about in three books of comment entitled *On the Natural Faculties*. The faculties of the soul, as they are called, are dealt with in several other works, of which *On the Anatomy of the Dead* [lost] comes first, and then two books *On the Anatomy of the Living* [lost], and besides these, two more *On Anatomical Disagreements* [lost]. Next after these come three books *On the Motion of the Abdomen and the Lungs* [lost], two *On the Causes of Respiration*, and four books *On the Voice*. In the same category comes the work *On the Movement of the Muscles*. I have set out my investigations into the "ruling part", and all the other inquiries into physical and psychical activities in a number of books which I wrote *On the Doctrines of Hippocrates and Plato*. Next comes the specialized work *On the Seed*, and then *On the Anatomy of Hippocrates*. The treatise *On the Usefulness of the Parts* follows on all these.

'The material origins of the generation of all things in existence lie in the four elements, which are naturally mixed completely with one another, and which act on one another. This is proved in the first book of *On [Medical] Names*, and in *On the Elements according to Hippocrates*. I do not cover everything relating to the proof of the elements in this little book, but only those features of it which were used by Hippocrates. For the most complete account of the science of the elements of the body the reader is referred to what I said in book 13 of *On Demonstration* [lost], and in books 5 and 6 of *On the Doctrines of Asclepiades* [lost]. . . . Three books of comments *On Mixtures* follow the work *On the Elements according to Hippocrates*, and after these the treatise *On the Faculties of Simple Drugs*, followed by the treatise *On Compound Drugs*. In the first books the mixtures present in animals are discussed along with the special features of each, and in the third book the discussion is about the mixture of drugs. If you like, whether after two or after three books, you may read about the *Best Constitution of the Body* [lost], *On the Good State of Being*, and *On Anomalous Bad Temperament*, in that order . . .'

Galen's own work, and his summary of his predecessors' work, played the dominant role in preserving ancient anatomical and physiological knowledge for the Middle Ages and Renaissance. See MEDICINE.

For detailed accounts of the anatomical work of the individual medical writers mentioned above, see the individual entries.

TEXTS (selection only): Hippocratic works: *On Anatomy*, ed. É. Littré, *Œuvres complètes d'Hippocrate* (1839–63; repr. 1961–2), 8. 538–40; *On Fleshes*, ed. K. Deichgräber, *Hippokrates über Entstehung und Aufbau des menschlichen Körpers* (1935); *On the Nature of Bones*, ed. Littré, 9. 168–96; *On Ancient Medicine, On the Sacred Disease, On the Nature of the Child* are translated in the Pelican volume, *Hippocratic Writings*, ed. G. E. R. Lloyd (1978). There are several modern editions of Aristotle's anatomical works; their translation is most conveniently collected in *The Complete Works of Aristotle*, ed. J. Barnes, 2 vols. (1984). For Hellenistic anatomy, the best guide is H. von Staden, *Herophilus: The Art of Medicine in Early Alexandria* (1989), with full references to the work of Herophilus' immediate predecessors and successors. Galen's anatomy and physiology is best approached through W. L. H. Duckworth, *Galen on Anatomical Procedures, the Later Books* (1962) and *On the Usefulness of the Parts of the Body*, trans. with a useful introductory essay by M. T. May, 2 vols. (1968). See also the works on respiration and the blood-vascular system ed. and trans. in D. J. Furley and J. S. Wilkie, *Galen on Respiration and the Arteries* (1984). Several modern guides to texts and translations of Galen's works are available; the most recent is by J. A. López Ferez in *Galeno: Obra, Pensamiento e Influencia* (1991), 309–29. Rufus of Ephesus' anatomical work is edited, with Fr. trans. by C. Daremberg and C. É. Ruelle, *Œuvres de Rufus d'Éphèse* (1879).

LITERATURE C. Daremberg, *La Médecine dans Homère* (1865); L. Edelstein, 'The History of Anatomy in Antiquity', repr. in O. Temkin (ed.), *Ancient Medicine*, 2nd edn. (1987), 247–301; C. R. S. Harris, *The Heart and the Vascular System in Ancient Greek Medicine* (1973); M.-P. Duminil, *Le Sang, les vaisseaux, le coeur, dans la collection Hippocratique* (1983); G. E. R. Lloyd, *Science, Folklore and Ideology* (1983), with full references to earlier work, and 'Alcmaeon and the Early History of Dissection', repr. in *Methods and Problems in Greek Science* (1991); F. Kudlien, *RE* Suppl. 2. 38–48, 'Anatomie'. J. T. V.

Anaxagoras (probably 500–428 BC), son of Hegesibulus, and a native of *Clazomenae; the first philosopher known to have settled in Athens. The evidence for his biography, although relatively plentiful, is confused and confusing. The best critical study

(by Mansfeld) has him arrive in Athens in 456/5 in the archonship of Callias and philosophize there for 20 years or so, until his prosecution and trial on a charge of impiety (dated by Mansfeld to 437/6). He resettled in *Lampsacus, probably with the aid of his patron *Pericles (1). There he died and was buried with high honours. His name was associated with the fall of a large meteorite at Aegospotami in *Thrace (c.467); his explanations of other physical phenomena are already reflected in Aeschylus' *Supplices* (c.463) and *Eumenides* (458).

*Simplicius preserves extensive fragments of Anaxagoras' one book, which famously began with the words: 'All things were together' (fr. 1 DK). The longest and most eloquent surviving passage explains how our differentiated *kosmos* was created from the original *mélange* by the action of mind, an entirely discrete principle, unmixed with any other substances but capable of ordering and controlling them (fr. 12). Anaxagoras' most striking and paradoxical claim is the thesis that, despite the consequent separation of dense from rare, hot from cold, etc., 'as things were in the beginning, so now they are all together' (fr. 6): 'in everything—except mind—a portion of everything' (fr. 11). Ancient commentators (e.g. Arist. *Ph.* 187^{a}36–^{b}7) supplied examples: what we call black contains a predominance of portions of black (cf. fr. 12 end.), but portions of white also, for how else could water turn into snow? Similarly sperm contains flesh, hair, and indeed everything else, for hair cannot come from not-hair, flesh from not-flesh (fr. 10), etc.

If analysis or division were thoroughgoing, would it not be possible to reach particles of pure flesh or pure black? This idea is explicitly rejected by Anaxagoras: 'the small is unlimited' (there are no theoretical minima), and as complex as the large (frs. 3 and 6). The ultimate constituents of the world never exist as discrete physical entities, only as stuffs or powers of which—hence the designation 'portions'—such entities consist. When Anaxagoras talks of an infinity of 'seeds' both in the beginning and now in our world (fr. 4), we should probably think not of particles but of the potentiality of latent portions to become manifest.

To Anaxagoras is attributed the maxim: 'The appearances are a sight of what is not apparent' (fr. 21a). Infinite variety in phenomena reflects infinite variety in seeds; things as we perceive them are very like things as they really are. This position is far removed from Parmenidean metaphysics and epistemology. (See PARMENIDES.) Yet engagement with *Eleatic ideas is evidently responsible for some key features of Anaxagoras' thought, e.g. the doctrine of the fundamental homogeneity of reality, his 'all together' echoing Parmenides' own words (fr. 8. 5), and the explicit rejection of the concepts of birth and death in favour of mixture and dissolution (fr. 17) (see ELEATIC SCHOOL; PARMENIDES). Modern scholars have been fascinated by the subtlety with which these ontological principles are applied in Anaxagoras' system. By contrast his cosmology is perceived as a mere reworking of *Anaximenes (1)'s, even if the claim that the sun is a huge incandescent stone shocked contemporary opinion (Diog. Laert. 2. 12). More original is Anaxagoras' theory of mind, as both Plato (*Phd.* 97b ff.) and Aristotle (*Metaph.* 984^{b}15 ff., 985^{a}18 ff.) recognize, while lamenting its failure to offer teleological explanations of natural processes.

TEXTS DK no. 59; D. Lanza, *Anassagora* (1966).
DISCUSSION/TRANSLATION Guthrie, *Hist. Gk. Phil.* 2. Also: R. E. Allen and D. J. Furley (eds.), *Studies in Presocratic Philosophy* 2 (1975); J. Mansfeld, *Mnemos.* 1979, 39 ff.; 1980, 17 ff.; M. Schofield, *An Essay on Anaxagoras* (1980). M. Sch.

Anaxandrides (4th cent. BC), Middle Comedy poet (see COMEDY (GREEK), MIDDLE), possibly of Rhodian birth (Ath. 374b; see RHODES), won the first prize ten times (*Suda*, entry under the name), three times at the *Lenaea (IG 2². 2325. 142). His first victory was in 376 (*Marm. Par.* 70), and he was active at least as late as 349 (*IG* 14. 1098. 8). Forty-one titles have survived, and over 80 citations; some of the titles look back to Old Comedy (e.g. *Cities*, *Huntsmen*; see COMEDY (GREEK), OLD), some forward to New Comedy (e.g. *Madman*, *Samia*; see COMEDY (GREEK), NEW), and many are mythological (e.g. *Anchises*, *Protesilaus*). The longer citations reveal a moralizing strain which earned him a place in anthologies.

Kassel–Austin, *PCG* 2. 236 ff. (*CAF* 2. 135 ff.). K. J. D.

Anaxarchus (mid- to late 4th cent. BC), of *Abdera, a Democritean philosopher (see DEMOCRITUS) and teacher of *Pyrrhon (the putative founder of Scepticism). He accompanied *Alexander (3) the Great on his Asian campaigns—a relationship which generated numerous anecdotes. He wrote a treatise on *kingship—an early representative of what became a major Hellenistic genre. His familiar title, 'Anaxarchus of the happiness school (ὁ εὐδαιμονικός)' probably encapsulated an ethical stance. His sceptical leanings were advertised by his famous comparison of reality to a stage-painting.

Testimonia in DK 2. 235 ff. D. N. S.

Anaxilas (1) (*RE* 1), tyrant of *Rhegium (mod. Reggio), 494–476 BC. Of Messenian descent (see MESSENIA); seized and recolonized Zancle on the death of *Hippocrates (1), renaming it *Messana (Messina). Leagued with Terillus of Himera and (*c.*483) Carthage against the growing power of *Gelon and *Theron, he was reconciled with Gelon after the defeat of *Hamilcar (1), his daughter marrying *Hieron (1). He was restrained from attacking *Locri Epizephyrii (477) by Hieron. A just and moderate ruler.

D. Asheri, *CAH* 4² (1988), ch. 16; H. Berve, *Die Tyrannis bei den Griechen*, 1 (1967), 155–7. B. M. C.

Anaxilas (2) (4th cent. BC), Middle Comedy poet (see COMEDY (GREEK), MIDDLE), can be dated to the middle of the 4th cent. BC by the fact that in three of his plays (Diog. Laert. 3. 28) he ridiculed *Plato (1). We have nineteen titles and some 40 citations, the longest of which (fr. 22 KA, from *Neottis*) characterizes well-known *hetairai.

Kassel–Austin, *PCG* 2. 279 ff. (*CAF* 2. 264 ff.). K. J. D.

Anaximander, of *Miletus (died soon after 547 BC), said to be an associate or disciple of *Thales, was the first Greek to write a prose treatise 'On the Nature of Things' (*Peri physeōs*). He thus initiated the tradition of Greek natural philosophy by elaborating a system of the heavens, including an account of the origins of human life, and by leaving his speculation behind in written form. He was the first to make a *map of the inhabited world; some sources also credit him with a *sphairos* or plan of the heavens.

Anaximander's view of the cosmos is remarkable for its speculative imagination and for its systematic appeal to rational principles and natural processes as a basis for explanation. The origin of things is the *apeiron*, the limitless or infinite, which apparently surrounds the generated world and 'steers' or governs the world process. Symmetry probably dictates that the world-order will perish into the source from which it has arisen, as symmetry is explicitly said to explain why the earth is stable in the centre of things, equally balanced in every direction. The world process

begins when the opposites are 'separated out' to generate the hot and the cold, the dry and the wet. By a process that is both biological and mechanical, earth, sea, and sky take shape and huge wheels of enclosed fire are formed to produce the phenomena of sun, moon, and stars. The size of the wheels was specified, corresponding perhaps to the arithmetical series 9, 18, 27. The earth is a flat disc, three times as broad as it is deep. Mechanical explanations in terms of the opposites are offered for meteorological phenomena (wind, rain, lightning, and thunder) and for the origin of animal life. The first human beings were generated from a sort of embryo floating in the sea.

The *apeiron* is ageless, deathless, and eternal; unlike the anthropomorphic gods, it is also ungenerated. The cosmos, on the other hand, is a world-order of coming-to-be and perishing according to a fixed law of nature, described in the one quotation from Anaximander's book (perhaps the earliest preserved sentence of European prose): out of those things from which beings are generated, into these again does their perishing take place 'according to what is needful and right; for they pay the penalty and make atonement to one another for their wrongdoing (*adikia*), according to the ordinance of time'.

DK 2. 81 ff.; Guthrie, *Hist. Gk. Phil.* 1. 72 ff.; Kirk–Raven–Schofield, *Presocratic Philosophers*, 100 ff.; C. H. Kahn, *Anaximander and the Origins of Greek Cosmology* (1960; repr. 1985); J. Barnes, *The Presocratic Philosophers*, 1 (1979), 19 ff.; J. Engmann, *Phronesis* 1991, 1 ff. C. H. K.

Anaximenes (1), of *Miletus (traditional *floruit* 546–525 BC) followed in the footsteps of *Anaximander in composing a treatise in Ionian prose in which he developed a world system on the basis of an infinite or unlimited principle, which he identified as *aēr*. His system differed from that of his predecessor in several respects. Instead of suspending the earth in the centre of the universe by cosmic symmetry, he supported it from below by cosmic air. And instead of leaving the infinite starting-point for world formation indeterminate in nature, he specified it as elemental air, which he probably conceived as a kind of vital world-breath that dominates the world order as our own breath-soul rules over us. Anaximenes also offered a mechanistic explanation for world formation and change in terms of the condensation and rarefaction of the air. Air becomes fire by rarefaction; by motion it becomes wind; by condensation it becomes water and, by more condensation, earth and stones.

It was the Milesian cosmology as reformulated by Anaximenes that became standard for Ionian natural philosophy in the 5th cent. *Heraclitus reacts against this system by replacing air with fire. *Anaxagoras and *Democritus follow Anaximenes in regarding the earth as a flat disc supported by air. *Diogenes (1) of Apollonia, the most conservative 5th-cent. physicist, retains the cosmic air as divine principle of life and intelligence, controlling the world-order.

DK 1. 90 ff.; Burnet, *EGP* 72 ff.; Kirk–Raven–Schofield, *Presocratic Philosophers*, 143 ff.; Guthrie, *Hist. Gk. Phil.*. 1. 115 ff.; J. Barnes, *The Presocratic Philosophers*, 1 (1979), 43 ff. C. H. K.

Anaximenes (2), of Lampsacus (*c.*380–320 BC), historian and rhetorician, a pupil of *Zoïlus. His historical work (*FGrH* 72) comprised *Hellenica*, *Philippica*, and a work on *Alexander (3) the Great. An 'answer to a letter of Philip' ([Dem.] 11) was believed in antiquity to be his; so perhaps is the 'letter' itself ([Dem.] 12). He also wrote on Homer. The *Rhetorica ad Alexandrum*, first attributed to him by *Victorius Marcellus, on the ground of Quintilian, *Inst.* 3. 4. 9, is the sole surviving pre-Aristotelian manual of *rhetoric.

TEXTS Rhetorical fragments in L. Radermacher, *Artium Scriptores* (1951), 200 ff. *Rhetorica ad Alexandrum*: M. Fuhrmann (1966); trans.: E. S. Forster (rev. in J. Barnes (ed.), *The Complete Works of Aristotle* (1984)).

V. Buchheit, *Das Genos Epideiktikon* (1960), 189–231 (against Anaximenes' authorship of the *Rhetorica*). D. A. R.

Anaxippus, New Comedy poet (see COMEDY (GREEK), NEW), 'in the time of Antigonus and Demetrius Poliorcetes' (*Suda*). Four comedies are plainly attributed to Anaxippus; and one fragment (49 lines) of another is assigned to '(X)anthippus'—possibly a mistake for Anaxippus—the verbose but humorous speech of a cook who elevates the gastronomic art (see H. Dohm, *Mageiros* (1964), 156 ff.).

Kassel–Austin, *PCG* 2. 299 ff. W. G. W.

Ancaeus, in mythology, (1) son of Lycurgus from *Tegea in Arcadia. *Pausanias (3) identifies him with the father of *Agapenor who led the Arcadians at Troy (8. 4. 10). He joined the *Argonautic expedition, and was the strongest after *Heracles. His traditional weapon was the axe (πέλεκυς). He was killed during the Calydonian boar-hunt (Bacchyl. 5. 117; Pherec. *FGrH* 3 F 36, etc.; see MELEAGER (1)), and his death was depicted on a famous pediment by *Scopas on the temple of Athena at Tegea (Paus. 8. 45. 5–7). (2) Another Argonaut, son of *Poseidon and Astypalaea, who took over the job of steersman after the death of Tiphys (Ap. Rhod. 2. 894). The two namesakes are often confused, and the same story explaining the proverb 'many a slip between cup and lip' is told of both (Arist. fr. 571 Rose; Lycoph. *Alex.* 486–90).

Toepffer, *RE* 1. 2218–19; F. Bömer on Ov. *Met.* 8. 315. R. L. Hu.

'ancestral constitution' See PATRIOS POLITEIA.

Anchises, character in literature and mythology, son of Capys, father of *Aeneas, and member of the Trojan royal house. He does not appear in person in *Homer's *Iliad*, but the *Homeric *Hymn to Aphrodite* recounts his union with that goddess on the slopes of Mt.Ida. He was warned by *Aphrodite not to reveal her identity as the mother of the resulting child, Aeneas (*Hymn. Hom.* 5.286 ff), but disobeyed; as punishment, he was lamed by a thunderbolt (Verg. *Aen.* 2. 648–9) or blinded (Servius on *Aen.* 2. 35). Most versions of the Aeneas-legend tell how Anchises was carried on his son's back from Troy (e.g. Soph. fr. 373 Radt, Xen. *Cyn.* 1. 15); some state that he went with Aeneas to Carthage and Italy (Servius on *Aen.* 4. 427), but in the *Aeneid* he dies in Sicily before reaching either place (3. 707–15). Anchises' character in *Aeneid* bks. 2–3 is that of a frail and wise counsellor and priest-like religious authority; mutual affection between him and Aeneas is evident, especially when Aeneas descends to the Underworld to see his dead father (6. 106–9, 684–702), who offers both a philosophical revelation and a pageant of the future of Rome.

E. Flores, *Enc. Virg.* 'Anchise'. S. J. Ha.

Ancona, an important Picene town (see PICENUM), occupied from at least as early as the 9th cent. BC, and with the only good harbour on the central east coast of Italy. The colony was founded in 387 BC by Greek refugees from *Dionysius (1) I of Syracuse. It prospered under the republic, and became the main port of embarkation for Dalmatia. *Trajan rebuilt the harbour and erected a commemorative arch about it (AD 115), which still stands. The town was destroyed in the 6th cent. AD.

R. Pavia and E. Sori, *Ancona* (1990). M. C.; T. W. P.

Ancus Marcius See MARCIUS.

Ancyra (mod. Ankara), a settlement in the part of central Asia Minor occupied by the Galatian Tectosagan tribe, which became the most important city of the province of *Galatia after 25 BC. The Roman city was built on the west side of a strong acropolis, still dominated by fine Byzantine fortifications. Its buildings include the temple of Rome and Augustus, which carries a virtually complete text of the *Res gestae* of Augustus (the Monumentum Ancyranum), a theatre, and a large gymnasium of the early 3rd cent. It was an important military centre and became particularly important in late antiquity.

E. Bosch, *Quellen zur Geschichte der Stadt Ankyra im Altertum* (1967); C. Foss, *DOP* 1977; D. Krencker and M. Schede, *Der Tempel in Ankara* (1936); S. Mitchell, *Anatolia* (1993), see indexes. S. M.

Andocides (*c.*440–*c.*390 BC), a member of a distinguished aristocratic family, whose grandfather had been one of the ten Athenian envoys who negotiated the *Thirty Years Peace of 446. In 415, shortly before the great expedition to Sicily was due to depart, the Athenians were greatly dismayed one morning to discover that in the night the statues of *Hermes around the city (see HERMS) had been mutilated: Hermes being the god of travellers, this act was presumably intended to affect the progress of the expedition, but it was also taken, curiously, as a sign that the democracy itself was in danger. In the subsequent accusations the young Andocides and his associates in a club, which probably suspected of oligarchic tendencies (see HETAIREIAI), were named as having shared both in the mutilations and in the profanation of the Eleusinian mysteries (see DEMETER; ELEUSIS), and were arrested. Andocides, to secure immunity and, as he claimed, to save his father, confessed to a share in the mutilations and gave an account of the whole affair which, though it may have been far from the truth, was readily accepted by the Athenians. This secured his release, but shortly afterwards, when the decree of Isotimides, aimed at him especially, forbade those who had confessed to an act of impiety to enter temples or the *Agora, Andocides preferred to leave the city and began to trade as a merchant, in which role he developed connections all over the Aegean and in Sicily and Italy. In 411, seeking to restore himself to favour at Athens, he provided oars at cost price to the fleet in Samos, and shortly afterwards returned to Athens to plead for the removal of the limitation on his rights. Unfortunately for him, the revolution of the *Four Hundred had just installed in power the very class of citizens whom his confession had affected, and he was put into prison and maltreated. Released, perhaps at the fall of the Four Hundred, he returned to his trading, in the course of which he was for a while imprisoned by *Evagoras, the king of Cyprus. At some time after the re-establishment of the democracy in 410, he returned to the city to renew his plea (the speech *De reditu* belongs to this occasion) but he was again unsuccessful. Returning finally under the *amnesty of 403, he resumed full participation in public life, and in 400 (or 399) successfully defended himself in the *De mysteriis* against an attempt to have him treated as still subject to the decree of Isotimides: the sixth speech of the Lysian corpus (see LYSIAS), *Against Andocides*, was delivered by one of his accusers. In 392/391 he was one of the Athenian envoys sent to Sparta to discuss the making of peace, and on his return in the debate in the assembly he delivered the *De pace* urging acceptance of the proffered terms, which were in fact very similar to those of the *King's Peace of 387/386. The Athenians, however, rejected the peace, and Andocides and the other envoys were prosecuted by the young *Callistratus (2). Andocides anticipated condemnation by retiring into exile, and we hear no more of him.

Andreas

Speeches In addition to the three speeches mentioned above, there is a fourth speech, *Against Alcibiades*, preserved under his name, which purports to be concerned with an *ostracism in 415; most scholars regard this as a forgery. Fragments of four other speeches are preserved.

Greek and Roman critics discovered in Andocides faults which, according to their canons, were serious; and admittedly the faults are there. He sometimes carries the use of parenthesis to absurd extremes; he cannot keep to one point at a time; his style is so loose that the argument is hard to follow. On the other hand, this inconsequential method of expression is at times effective, giving the impression of an eagerness which outruns premeditated art. He possessed a natural gift of expression, a fine flow of words, and a good narrative style. He was not a professional rhetorician, and if he neglected scholastic rules, it can at least be claimed for him that he was successful on his own unconventional lines.

For general bibliography see ATTIC ORATORS.

TEXT Blass–Fuhr (Teubner, 1913).

TEXT AND TRANSLATION Dalmeyda (Budé, 1930), Maidment, *Minor Attic Orators*, 2nd edn., 1 (Loeb, 1953).

COMMENTARIES *De mysteriis* and *De reditu*, E. C. Marchant (1889); *De mysteriis*, D. Macdowell (1962); *De reditu*, U. Albini (1961); *De pace*, U. Albini (1964).

INDEX (to Andocides, Lycurgus, and Dinarchus). L. L. Forman (1897).

SPECIAL STUDY A. Missiou, *The Subversive Oratory of Andocides* (1992).

On the *Against Alcibiades* see P. J. Rhodes in R. Osborne and S. Hornblower (eds.), *Ritual Finance Politics* (1994), ch. 5.   G. L. C.

Andreas (d. 217 BC), physician and court doctor of *Ptolemy (1) IV (Philopator), follower of *Herophilus. Works: Νάρθηξ (a pharmacopoeia, with descriptions of plants and roots); Περὶ δακέτων (on snake-bites); Περὶ τῶν ψευδῶς πεπιστευμένων (against superstitious beliefs); Περὶ στεφάνων (on wreaths: all lost except for fragments). *Eratosthenes berated him as a 'literary *Aegisthus' (*Etym. Magn.* , entry under βιβλιαίγισθος)

Fraser, *Ptol. Alex.* 370 f.   A. J. S. S.

Andriscus, of Adramyttion (d. *c*.148 BC), pretender to the Macedonian throne, claimed to be Philip, son of *Perseus (2), hence called 'Pseudophilip'. *Demetrius (10) I of Syria, whom he asked for assistance, sent him to Rome, but he escaped to Asia Minor and received some encouragement from the Macedonian wife of the Pergamene prince Athenaeus. In Thrace he raised some troops from the chieftains Teres and Barsabas, with which he invaded Macedonia and quickly took control (149). Rejecting negotiations with P. *Cornelius Scipio Nasica Corculum, he defeated the praetor P. Iuventius Thalna but was crushed in 148 by Q. *Caecilius Metellus Macedonicus.

Polyb. 36. 10; Diod. Sic. 31. 40a, 32. 15; Zonar. 9. 28; Livy, *Per.* 48–50.   R. M. E.

Androgeos (Ἀνδρόγεως), son of *Minos, who died an untimely death in Attica, either treacherously killed by his defeated rivals in the Panathenaic Games (see PANATHENAEA), or sent by *Aegeus against the Marathonian bull and killed by it. To avenge him Minos besieged Athens, and was only appeased by an annual tribute of seven youths and seven maidens to be thrown to the Minotaur (see THESEUS). He was variously identified with the hero Eurygyes at the *Ceramicus or with the 'hero at the stern' in *Phaleron.

C. Calame, *Thésée et l'imaginaire athénien* (1990), 79–81; Kearns, *Heroes of Attica* 40.   E. Ke.

Andromache, daughter of *Eëtion king of Thebe in the Troad (see TROAS), and wife of *Hector (*Il.* 6. 395 ff.). Her father and seven brothers were killed by *Achilles, and her mother ransomed for a large sum (6. 414 ff.). After the fall of Troy her son *Astyanax was killed by the Greeks and she herself became *Neoptolemus (1)'s slave and concubine (*Little Iliad*, fr. 20 Davies; *Iliu Persis*). She bore him three sons, Pergamus, Pielus, and Molossus, eponym of the Molossi (Paus. 1. 11. 1 f.). According to Euripides' *Andromache*, she was threatened with death by Neoptolemus' wife *Hermione during the visit to Delphi in which he was killed, but was protected by *Peleus, Neoptolemus' aged grandfather. After Neoptolemus' death (Eur.) or on his marriage (Verg. *Aen.* 3. 327–9) she was handed over to Hector's brother *Helenus, lived with him in Epirus, and bore him a son, Cestrinus. After Helenus' death, Andromache went to Mysia with Pergamus, where she conquered Teuthrania and founded *Pergamum (Paus. 1. 11. 1 f.).

Andromache in scenes at Troy is sometimes found in art: see O. Touchefeu-Meynier, *LIMC* 1 / 1. 767–74.   J. R. M.

Andromeda, in mythology, the daughter of *Cepheus, king of the Ethiopians, and his wife Cassiepeia or Cassiope. The following, founded on Apollod. 2. 4. 3–5, is the usual legend. Cassiepeia boasted that she was more beautiful than the Nereids (see NEREUS); they complained to *Poseidon, who flooded the land and sent a sea-monster to ravage it. On consulting *Ammon, Cepheus learned that the only cure was to offer up Andromeda to the monster, and she was accordingly fastened to a rock on the sea-shore. At this point *Perseus (1) came by on his way from taking the head of *Medusa. He fell in love with Andromeda, and got her and her father's consent to marry her if he could kill the sea-beast. This he did; but Cepheus' brother Phineus, who had been betrothed to Andromeda, plotted against him (or attacked him by open force, Ov. *Met.* 5.1 ff.). Perseus showed him and his followers the head of Medusa, turning them all to stone. He and Andromeda stayed for a time with Cepheus, and left their eldest son, Perses, with him; from Perses the Persian kings were descended. They then went on to Seriphus, then to *Argos (2) and *Tiryns. Their other children were Alcaeus, Sthenelus, Heleius, Mestor, Electryon, and a daughter Gorgophone.

Andromeda, Perseus, Cepheus, Cassiepeia, and the monster were all turned into *constellations bearing their names (the monster is Cetus). This may have been foretold in Euripides' lost tragedy *Andromeda* (see [Eratosth.], Cat. 15–17, and T. B. L. Webster, *The Tragedies of Euripides* (1967), 192–9). If so, it is one of the very few Greek star-myths which can be traced back to an earlier date than the Alexandrian period.

Andromeda being rescued by Perseus is a popular scene in art from the late 6th cent.: see K. Schauenburg, *LIMC* 1 / 1. 774–90.

H. J. R.; J. R. M.

Andron (b. *c*.440 BC), son of Androtion, was a wealthy member of the Athenian intelligentsia; father of the atthidographer *Androtion (see ATTHIS). He is usually identified with Andron, one of the *Four Hundred, who initiated the prosecution of *Antiphon (1) and others in 410 (Plut. *Mor.* 833 d–f). Perhaps he was later imprisoned as a state-debtor (Dem. 22. 33–4).

P. E. Harding, *Androtion and the Atthis* (1994).   P. E. H.

Andronicus, (*RE* 25) of Rhodes, Peripatetic philosopher, who recalled the attention of the school to the works of *Aristotle and *Theophrastus (see PERIPATETIC SCHOOL). With the assistance of the grammarian *Tyrannio (1) he arranged the works of both in an order whose influence can still be seen in modern editions. He wrote a treatise in at least five books on the order of Aristotle's works with discussion of their contents and authenticity, an account of his life, and a transcript of his will. The exact date of Andronicus' editorial work (between 70 and 20 BC) is debated, as is whether he became formal head of a Peripatetic school at Athens. He defined the soul as a power resulting from the mixture of the bodily elements, and located emotion in an irrational part of the soul. The work *On the Emotions* (ed. A. Glibert-Thirry (Gk. and Lat.), *Corpus Latinum Commentariorum in Aristotelem Graecorum* 7 vols. (1957–1981) Suppl. 2 (1977)) is however spurious.

M. Plezia, *De Andronici Rhodii studiis Aristotelicis* (1946); I. Düring, *Aristotle in the Ancient Biographical Tradition* (1957), 244, 413 ff.; P. Moraux, *Der Aristotelismus* 1 (1973), 1–141; F. Wehrli in Ueberweg–Flashar, 593, 598–9. H. Gottschalk, *ANRW* 2. 36. 2 (1987), at 1083–1115 and 1130–1. R. W. S.

Andros, the most northerly and (after *Naxos (1)) second largest (380 sq. km; 147 sq. mi.) of the *Cyclades, its windswept, mountainous landscape mitigated by sheltered, fertile valleys. Gaureion in the north-west is the only safe harbour. Its prehistory is obscure. Settled by Ionians c.900 BC, it had connections with the Thessalo-Euboean region in the geometric period. The fortified town of Zagora, occupying a bleak headland on the SW coast, first occupied c.900 BC, was largely deserted c.700 BC; a small temple still survived c.400 BC. The close-packed buildings may have housed a population as large as 2,500. Besides the evidence for 8th-cent. domestic architecture, much may be learnt about Zagora's economy and contemporary society. The Classical city of Andros on the south coast (mod. Palaiopolis) occupied the steep slopes of a mountainside, served by an inadequate harbour. Although the earliest remains are late Archaic, it was probably first settled early in the 7th cent., perhaps by the inhabitants of deserted geometric towns such as Zagora. Late in the century Andros founded colonies at *Acanthus, *Stagira, and Sane in *Chalcidice and at Argilus in east Macedonia. After the battle of *Salamis the city was besieged unsuccessfully by the Greek allies for contributing ships to the Persian fleet. Under the *Athenian empire the imposition of a *cleruchy in 450 BC caused its tribute to be reduced from twelve to six talents. The presence of a Macedonian garrison from the mid-3rd cent. did not prevent Andros submitting to *Attalus I in 200 BC. An almost intact Hellenistic round tower survives at Agios Petros.

RE 1/2 (1894), 'Andros'; *PECS* 57; *IG* 12. 5; T. Sauciuc, *Andros* (1914); A. Cambitoglou and others, *Zagora* 1–2 (1971–88); A. Cambitoglou, *Archaeological Museum of Andros* (1981). R. W. V. C.

Androsthenes, of Thasos, companion of *Nearchus, subsequently (324 BC) explored Bahrain and the Arabian coast. His *Circumnavigation of India* (*FGrH* 711) was exploited by *Eratosthenes, and *Theophrastus drew on its vivid description of the flora of Bahrain. A. B. B.

Androtion (c.410–340 BC), son of *Andron, was a wealthy Athenian politician and atthidographer (see ATTHIS). Before his entry into politics (c.385) he studied under *Isocrates. His long political career involved service to Athens in many capacities: as *bouleutēs* (twice; see BOULĒ); as tax-commissioner; as governor of Arcesine on *Amorgos (358–356) during the *Social War (1); and as ambassador to *Mausolus of Caria (355/4). He proposed a motion regarding sacred vessels (*IG* 2². 216/7) and another honouring the sons of the *Spartocid ruler Leucon of *Panticipaeum (*IG* 2².

212); see also BOSPORUS (2). He was prosecuted for an unconstitutional proposal in 354/3 by personal enemies. *Demosthenes (2) wrote one of the speeches (Dem. 22). Despite efforts to define his career no consistent ideology can be shown. For some reason he ended his life in exile (after 344/3) in *Megara, where he wrote his *Atthis*. This eight-book work was more concerned with contemporary events than earlier *Atthides*; the last five books covered the period 404–c.340. We have 68 fragments. These show the usual chauvinism of a local historian, moderated by a scholarly concern for accuracy of detail. His work was a main source for *Philochorus' *Atthis* and was one of the sources for the Aristotelian *Athenian Constitution* (see ATHĒNAIŌN POLITEIA).

FGrH 324; P. E. Harding, *Androtion and the Atthis* (1994). P. E. H.

angels (ἄγγελοι), 'messengers'. *Hermes was considered the messenger of Zeus, and named Angelos (once Euangelos). *Iris was ascribed the same function; for *Plato (1) (*Cra.* 407e, 408b) the two are the divine *angeloi*. *Hecate was an 'angel' because she had contact with the lower world and the dead (Sophron in schol. Theoc. 2. 12); in the early empire Hermes is once named the 'messenger of *Persephone (*Epigr. Gr.* 575. 1, 1st–2nd cent. AD). By the 3rd cent. AD, with angels playing a large part in contemporary Judaism and *Christianity, they became important too for paganism as intermediaries (along with lesser gods and demons) of the true God, not just in *Gnosticism and *Neoplatonism but also in 'mainstream' belief: thus an oracle from *Claros inscribed at *Oenoanda (c. AD 200?) represents even Apollo as an angelic 'small part' of God. In the 2nd–3rd cents. AD abstract divinities called angels were worshipped in Egypt and Asia Minor (Lydia, Caria, and Phrygia) under such cult-titles as the Angelic Divine (Θεῖον Ἀγγελικόν) and Good Angel (Ἀγαθὸς Ἄγγελος).

T. Hopfner, *Griechisch-ägyptischer Offenbarungszauber* (vols. 21–2 of Wesseley's *Studien zur Paläographie und Papyruskunde* (1922–4)), 1, paras. 135 ff.; H. Leclercq in Cabrol–Leclercq, *Dict. d'arch. chrétienne* 1/2. 208 ff. 'Anges'; F. Sokolowski, *Harv. Theol. Rev.* 1960, 225 ff.; L. Robert, *CRAcad. Inscr.* 1971, 597 ff. (oracle); A. Sheppard, *Talanta* 1980–1, 77 ff. S. E.; A. J. S. S.

Angerona, Roman goddess, worshipped on 21 December (*Divalia or Angeronalia) in the Curia Acculeia (Varro, *Ling.* 6. 23), or the Sacellum Volupiae, where there stood on the altar a statue of Angerona with her mouth bound and sealed (Macrob. *Sat.* 1. 10. 8 ff., *fasti Praenestini*). The ancients connected her name with *angina* (Festus 16 Lindsay) or *angor* (Masurius in Macrob. 1. 10. 8 ff.); Mommsen with *angerere*, 'to raise up', sc. the sun after the solstice, with reference to a fragmentary section of the *fasti Praenestini* (*CIL* 1/2. 337–8).

Inscr. Ital. 13. 2. 541 ff.; Latte, *RR* 134; Roscher, *Lex.* 1. 348 ff.; Wissowa, *RK* 241. C. R. P.

Angitia, or the **Angitiae,** *Marsian goddess (es) principally worshipped on the *Fucinus lacus at Lucus Angitiae (cf. Verg. *Aen.* 7. 759 with Serv. on 750) at *Sulmo (*CIL* 9. 3074), where the plural of the name appears. Her native name was Anagtia; inscriptional evidence makes her a popular goddess of healing; she was subject to Hellenistic mythologizing (Cn. Gellius 9 Peter).

Conway, *Ital. Dial.* 182, 289 ff.; Roscher, *Lex.* 1. 351; Wissowa, *RK* 49. C. R. P.

Anicetus (*RE* 'Aniketos' 5), freedman and tutor of *Nero, who used him when prefect of the fleet at *Misenum to murder *Iulia Agrippina. Subsequently induced to confess himself the

Anicia Iuliana

paramour of *Claudia Octavia, he was exiled to Sardinia in AD 62, where he lived in comfort and died.　　　　A. M.; M. T. G.

Anicia Iuliana (*c*. AD 461–527/8), a Constantinopolitan aristocrat (see CONSTANTINOPLE) of western senatorial family (the Anicii) and imperial descent (*Valentinian III, grandfather; Olybrius, father); she was a staunch Chalcedonian Christian. In 512 rioters attempted to proclaim her husband Areobindus emperor instead of the Monophysite Anastasius. A generous ecclesiastical patron, she lavishly reconstructed the church of St Polyeuctus.

PLRE 2. 635–6; M. Harrison, *A Temple for Byzantium* (1989).　L. M. W.

Anicius Faustus, Quintus, from Uzappa near Mactar in Africa, as legate of Legio III Augusta from 197–201 was responsible for extending the network of forts in southern Numidia and Tripolitania, from Castellum Dimmidi to Gholaia (Bu-Ngem). Consul in 199, he later governed Upper Moesia, and was proconsul of Asia under *Macrinus. He founded a family which, after intermarriage with the *Acilii Glabriones, was regarded as the noblest in the senate; descendants include *Boethius and the consul of AD 541, Flavius Anicius Faustus Albinus Basilius. See also ANICIA IULIANA.

PIR[2] A 595; *PLRE* 1–2 (stemmata); *AE* 1969–70, 647 (origin).　A. R. Bi.

animals, attitudes to This was the subject of a huge debate among the philosophers. Already in the 6th and 5th cents. BC *Pythagoras (1) and *Empedocles had attacked the killing or maltreatment of animals, partly on the grounds that *transmigration made us literally akin to them. But vegetarianism was made difficult by the mutual interconnections between religious sacrifice and meat-eating. Justice was treated as a gift of God to benefit humans, not animals, both by *Hesiod and in the myth ascribed to *Protagoras in *Plato (1)'s *Protagoras*. Little was conceded by *Democritus' extending considerations of criminal justice to dangerous animals.

The decisive step, however, was taken not by the Presocratics, but by *Aristotle, who denied reason and belief to animals. Compensatingly, he allowed them a rich perceptual life, which he carefully disentangled from reliance on reason or belief. In ethics, he surprisingly combined the view that animals can be praised and blamed for their voluntary acts with the view that we owe them no justice, because we have nothing in common, and can conduct a just war against them. Aristotle's successor *Theophrastus, disagreed. We are, in an extended sense, akin (*oikeioi*) even in reasonings, and killing non-dangerous animals is unjust.

The Epicureans and Stoics (see EPICURUS; STOICISM) sided with Aristotle in denying reason to animals, and hence justice. Only *Plutarch was to ask 'why not kindness, if not justice?' The Epicurean rationale, clearest in *Hermarchus, is that justice is owed only where there is a contract, hence only among rational agents, *pace* Democritus. The Stoics denied that animals, as non-rational, could be treated as belonging (*oikeiōsis*: lit. a welcoming into the household)—and that despite the prevalence of animal pets. Hence justice could not be extended to them. Unlike Aristotle, they denied animals memory, emotion, foresight, intention, and voluntary acts.

From then on, the philosophical debate turned on animal rationality. Animal pain and terror were seldom cited before *Porphyry. Pythagoras and *Apuleius exploited them only in the case of humans transformed into animals. Outside philosophy, attitudes were sometimes broader. The Athenians punished a man for flaying a ram alive. When *Pompey staged a slaughter of *elephants, the public was more concerned for the terrified

elephants, the Stoic L. *Annaeus Seneca (2) for the loss of human life. The philosophers' praise of animals is sometimes only to downgrade humans (the *Cynics) or glorify the Creator (*Augustine), while vegetarianism was often based merely on ascetic or medical grounds.

The chief defenders of animals, in response to the Stoics, were the Neopythagoreans and certain Platonists. Defences are recorded in *Philon (4) *De animalibus* and *Origen (1) *Against Celsus*. Plutarch's *Moralia* contains three treatises in defence. But by far the most important work is Porphyry's *On Abstinence from Animal Food*. Of its four books, the first records the case against animals, but forbids meat on ascetic grounds; the second rejects animal sacrifice; the third claims rationality and justice for animals; the fourth is an anthropology of vegetarian nations. But Porphyry's probable pupil *Iamblichus (2) felt it necessary to reinstate sacrifice. To defend this, he reinterpreted Pythagoras' and Plato's belief in transmigration of human souls into animals, the first as excluding sacrificial animals, the second as metaphorical. He denied a rational soul to animals, and his pupil Theodore insisted that human souls could act on animals only by remote control, not by genuine transmigration.

The western Christian tradition was fatefully influenced by Augustine who ignored the pro-animal side of this debate and backed the Stoic ground for killing animals, thus departing from such predecessors as *Arnobius and *Lactantius, who had allowed animals rationality.

Given the extensive use of animals in antiquity, it would have been as hard to give up killing them as to give up slaves, and one of the justifications offered was that civilization would break down.

See also ANIMALS, KNOWLEDGE ABOUT; ANIMALS IN CULT; CRATES (1); HUNTING; PETS; PRISCILLIANISTS; SACRIFICE, GREEK and ROMAN; SEMONIDES; and particular animals (CAMELS; DOGS; ELEPHANTS; HORSES).

Porphyry, *On Abstinence from Animal Food*, ed. and trans. Bouffartigue and Segonds (Budé, 1977–　). R. Sorabji, *Animal Minds and Human Morals* (1993).　　R. R. K. S.

animals, knowledge about

1 Animals are the mirror of nature, claimed *Epicurus (quoted in Cic. *Fin.* 2. 32), echoing a view widely held in different ways throughout antiquity. But others added that animals mirror culture as well; Greek and Roman writing and thinking about animals was as often ethical as what we might call scientific in character. Hardly surprisingly, the archaeological record provides ample evidence that animals were closely observed by artists, and further evidence for the ancient study of animals comes from early medical observations about the role of animals and animal products in human regimen. Yet the term ζῳολογία seems not to occur in any surviving classical work, and the earliest English uses of 'zoology' refer more often than not to the study of the medicinal uses of animal products.

In the Homeric epics, animals exemplify many types of human qualities. Lions are brave, deer are prone to flight, bees swarm like crowds of people, dogs tread the treacherous path between loyalty and servility. (The story of Odysseus' dog, who died of joy on recognizing the scent of his long-lost master, was regarded by the later medical Empiricists as a miracle of diagnosis.) A great many similar examples can be found in the early Greek lyric poets. In the late 7th cent. BC, *Semonides of Amorgos wrote a poem comparing animals with different types of women; the only good woman is like a bee, the best of a terrible collection.

Specific qualities retain their associations with specific animals. *Herodotus' story of *Arion (2)'s rescue from pirates by a dolphin stands at the head of a long line of similar tales about these intelligent and compassionate creatures. Much later, *Plutarch marvelled at the society of ants in their anthills, and in a series of treatises (including the *De sollertia animalium*, *De esu carnium*, and *Bruta animalia ratione uti*) considered the problems of whether animals have souls and the capacity for reason, and feeling. (The debate about the minds of animals, the morality of killing them for sport and food, or even using them as beasts of burden, was a lively one.) If Plutarch allowed animals some degree of intellect, the opposing view that animals possessed vitality (*anima*) without rationality (*animus*) was perhaps dominant; thus man and animals were kept apart. The ethical, metaphorical, use of animals to explain the organization of human society reaches its fullest expression in the anecdotal zoology of *Aelian, which was composed in the time of Hadrian, in the Aesopic collection of *Fables, and ultimately in the medieval bestiaries.

Animals were also organized physically. The Romans in particular collected animals from all over the world in zoos and menageries, often preserving monstrous creatures from unnatural births as aids to *divination.

Early philosophers of nature were not innocent of these ethical concerns. There was a considerable amount of cross-fertilization between what we might call ethical (or psychological) and 'scientific' zoology; *Aristotle for instance makes frequent observations about the social behaviour of animals in the *Historia animalium*, and throughout the zoological works he cites poets, dramatists, and historians as well as less 'high' literary sources. Yet the question of the physiological origins of animal life was, of course, a central concern for many Presocratic cosmologists, and fragments survive of a number of biological theories. Amongst the earliest surviving accounts is that of *Anaximander, who is reported to have claimed that living creatures were generated in moisture, perhaps slime, protected by thorny bark, and that they grew drier and more self-supporting with age. Animals are soon able to sustain themselves, he claimed, but man alone, born initially inside some kind of fish, lacks self-sufficiency and needs prolonged nursing. Anaximander's account is notable for the importance it accords the animal's environment in its development. In *Empedocles' theory on the other hand, blood, bones, and flesh arose out of combinations of the elements. They then formed solitary limbs which wandered the earth in search of other parts with which to combine. The evidence for Empedocles refers to monstrous creatures, men with the faces of oxen, and oxen with the faces of men, which lived during the early stages of the development of man. (see ANATOMY AND PHYSIOLOGY; ANTHROPOLOGY; EMBRYOLOGY).

Early evidence for the systematic study of animal physiology is sparse, and signs of attempts at zoological taxonomy still more so. In one well-known early case, the author of the Hippocratic treatise (see HIPPOCRATES (2)) *On Regimen* 2 organizes the (mainly edible) animals which concern him into land, sea, and air creatures (2. 46–8), with further subdivisions on the basis of whether they are wild or domestic. Medical writers continued to preserve and amplify observations about the dietary and pharmaceutical properties of animals and animal products including hair, urine, and excrement.

Non-medical authors had their own interests. *Plato (1) is particularly associated with the use of a method (variously applied) which involved the progressive division of objects into typical pairs. Setting up patterns based on pairs of opposed *differentiae*, he might divide animals into 'walking' or 'aquatic', and aquatic in turn into 'winged' and 'water dwelling', and so on. It is not at all clear how far Plato developed this way of thinking in the direction of animal taxonomy, and the main Platonic texts (*Soph.* 220a–b, *Plt.* 264d, *Leg.* 823b) offer far from consistent examples of the uses to which division might be put. On the other hand, Aristotle seems to have Plato's method of division in mind at several points where he is himself apparently dealing with the problems of animal classification (e.g. in *Top.* 6). Plato's successor as head of the Academy, *Speusippus, is credited in a few fragments with having written a work *On Similarities*, in which animals with similar appearances may have been grouped together (see Ath. 105b). Speusippus is also credited with some new coinages in which some scholars see signs of taxonomical concerns—the word *malakostraka*, for instance, to describe soft-shelled creatures is particularly associated with him. On balance, however, very little is known about Speusippus, and the motivations behind Plato's method of division are certainly not linked primarily to zoological taxonomy.

II The earliest surviving systematic studies of the physical nature of animals are those of Aristotle—many would insist that no one in antiquity after Aristotle rivalled the breadth and depth of his interests. The biological treatises account for well over 20 per cent of the surviving Aristotelian corpus, and lists of Aristotle's works preserved by *Diogenes (6) Laertius and *Hesychius suggest that there is much more that has not survived. In spite of the amount of material, there is little agreement today even about the aims of Aristotle's zoological investigations. It is probably fair to say—though some are reluctant to go even this far—that he was the first to devise a detailed zoological taxonomy and that this formed an important part of his general study of the *physics of the sublunary sphere. (His pupil *Theophrastus carried this work further, applying Aristotelian methods to botany.)

In his famous exhortation to the study of animals, (*De partibus animalium* 1. 5), Aristotle speaks of the low status enjoyed by the enterprise—some philosophers, he says, considered the subject matter trivial or even disagreeable—but he maintains that the study of even the meanest of creatures is worth while if only because the means to discover their beauty, form, and purpose are close at hand. Modern disagreement about the nature of Aristotle's zoological enterprise is due in part to the difficulty of arranging the relevant treatises in a clear chronological sequence. (In particular, it is very difficult to decide exactly when most of Aristotle's empirical research was done. Some scholars feel that much must have been done during his stay on the island of Lesbos, in his middle years; others argue that the practical investigation was done late in life, after he had laid the theoretical foundations of his philosophy.) Aristotle himself would have us approach his work on animals as an example of his scientific method in action and in this briefest of summaries it is convenient to follow, albeit cautiously, Aristotle's own plan.

In the treatises which make up the so-called *Organon* (in particular, the *Posterior Analytics*), Aristotle set out the goals of scientific inquiry. He stressed the importance of firm, logically tested scientific knowledge, and elaborated the deductive apparatus for its achievement. In practice, Aristotle's method meant that he could begin an investigation into animals, for example, by collecting the relevant material—observations, information from others, along with the results of a preliminary assessment of these data, all of which go to make up what he calls the 'phenomena', together with the opinions of earlier authorities. Not all the phenomena are the result of autopsy—Aristotle himself acknowledges debts to all kinds of people, and the elder *Pliny (1) noted that with the help of *Alexander (3) the Great, Aristotle was able to order thousands of fowlers, fishermen, beekeepers, hunters, and herdsmen to inform him about every creature they encountered (*HN* 8. 44). None the less, Aristotle's commitment to personal, autoptic research, often through dissection, must not be forgotten.

The results of the first step in Aristotle's zoological investigation are set out in the *Historia animalium* ('Researches into Animals'). The range covered is extraordinary—the lives, breeding habits, and structure of some 540 different genera. Modern students of the Life Sciences tend to highlight certain areas of practical research in which Aristotle was ultimately deemed by modern standards to have been particularly successful. The following (traditional) list is far from complete. (*a*) Investigations of the developing chick, the classical embryological subject ever since. (*b*) Detailed descriptions of the habits and development of octopuses and squids. (*c*) Anatomical accounts of the four-chambered stomach of ruminants, of the complex relations of the ducts, vessels, and organs in the mammalian generative system, and of the mammalian character of porpoises, dolphins, and whales, all unsurpassed until the 17th cent. (*d*) Accounts of exceptional modes of development of fish, among them a dog-fish (*Mustelus laevis*), the young of which is linked to the womb by a navel cord and placenta much as in a mammal. The accuracy of Aristotle's observations was only confirmed a century ago.

Such a huge amount of raw material needed to be organized in some provisional way; listing the 'differences' between animals, Aristotle arranged his evidence in the *Historia animalium* under preliminary headings. He drew a broad distinction, for example, between bloodless and blooded creatures. Bloodless animals (of which he enumerates around 120 altogether) are of four main types, usually rendered in the following way: cephalopods (*malakia*), crustacea (*malakostraka*), testacea (*ostrakoderma*) and insects (*entoma*). Blooded animals include man, viviparous quadrupeds and cetacea, oviparous quadrupeds and animals without feet, birds, and fish. This is seen in itself as an exercise in taxonomy by many modern scholars, but while taxonomy is certainly implicit throughout the work, Aristotle himself seems quite clear about his own goals. At *Hist. An.* 1. 1–6, he offers a list of very broad genera into which animals can be placed, but does not explain the list, remarking at 1. 6 that his talk of animal genera at this stage in the inquiry is a 'kind of sample of the range of subjects and attributes which we will need to think about. We will go into these problems in detail later on.'

In the *De partibus animalium* ('On the Parts of Animals') problems of division are addressed in detail, as are other theoretical questions about the relative importance of the various causal factors which all need to be understood if an animal's existence is to be properly explained. In general, Aristotle advocates investigating the attributes common to a group of animals, then explaining their existence ultimately in terms of their purpose (the Final Cause). He also includes accounts of the matter from which they come (the Material Cause), the process which led to their generation (the Efficient Cause), and their shape (the Formal Cause). The parts of animals are divided into those whose division yields a part which can be called by the same name as the whole—flesh, hair, bone, blood, marrow, milk, cartilage, etc.— sometimes called *homoiomeria* or 'uniform' parts (dealt with especially at *Hist. an.* 3. 2–17, and *Part. an.* 2. 1–9), and those whose

division yields something with a different name—hands for instance, whose parts cannot be called 'hands', faces, skeletal structures, the internal organs, and so on. These are the *anhomoiomeria* or 'non-uniform' parts, and they are chiefly described and their functions discussed at *Hist. an.* 1. 7–14, 2. 8–12, 3. 1–11, and *Part. an.* 2–4. Concentrating attention exclusively on these characteristics as a prelude to explanation is not enough, and Aristotle criticizes certain of his predecessors for privileging the matter of an animal, and the material aspects of its generation, over its *raison d'être*. Empedocles, for example, is criticized for explaining the articulation of the spine in man by arguing that the foetus is twisted in the womb. Aristotle on the other hand argued that the vertebrae exist because they existed in the father, because they allow movement, and because without them the offspring could not become a man. Aristotelian explanation in zoology is dominated by questions of purpose and function.

Aristotle's licence to study the biological world was bought partially by insisting that the kind of reality which Plato would only allow his perfect Forms exists in the forms of things around us. While the Creator of Plato's physical world strives to copy the Forms with varying degrees of success, Aristotle argued that the good of a particular animal, or part of an animal, is explicable in terms of that animal's contribution to its own survival, or the survival of its species. This does not lead to inflexibility; some things may be necessarily so without any obvious purpose—the colour of one's eyes, the existence of breasts in men, and so on— but Aristotelian teleological explanation can deal even with them as instances of natural necessity. (The discussion of so-called 'inessential characteristics' occupies much of *De generatione animalium* 5).

At the beginning of book two of the *Parts of Animals*, then, Aristotle is able to say, 'I have set forth the parts out of which each of the animals is composed, and their number, in the *Researches into Animals*. Now I must examine the causes by which each animal has the nature it does, leaving aside what was said in the *Researches*.' In the following three books, Aristotle proceeds to develop his classification, and in particular his ideas about how different groups and subgroups can be practically distinguished. The language Aristotle uses to describe these different groups and types varies somewhat. Terms like γένος ('kind') and εἶδος (often translated 'species') are to some extent context-relative, even if the Aristotelian species are themselves fixed and unchanging.

Problems related to the origins and means of animal locomotion are investigated in the *De motu animalium* ('On the Movement of Animals') and the *De incessu animalium* ('On the Progression of Animals'). But how does the soul move the body? What is the ultimate source of movement? Aristotle elaborates his ideas about the 'unmoved mover' in many different contexts, but the specific problems raised here lead into the detailed investigation presented in the *De anima* ('On the Soul'). Physiological and psychological problems—the nature of respiration, life and death, dreams, perception, etc.—are investigated in the nine short treatises which make up the *Parva naturalia*.

The temptation to portray Aristotle as a proto-Linnaeus, held back only by his speculative understanding of physiological processes, has proved a very strong one. Others are so keen to resist this temptation that they seek quite different motivations behind the zoology. They argue that Aristotle's central concern in gathering all the biological data is to test practically the theoretical and logical devices he developed in the *Organon*. It seems more reasonable to tread a middle path, which allows a proper appreciation of the striking amount of highly detailed, empirical research of great quality which is preserved in the Aristotelian zoological treatises, whilst also keeping in mind the role of Aristotle's conception of science and scientific method in guiding his eyes.

III Zoological research of the type pursued by Aristotle seems subsequently to have been pursued with little commitment, although there is evidence to suggest that *Diocles (3) of Carystus performed animal dissections. Where botanical research (see BOTANY) often yielded important benefits in areas such as pharmacy (see PHARMACOLOGY), the pure study of animals attracted remarkably few students, and later, non-ethical, work on animals tends either to be practical—for example, in the form of anatomical studies for doctors who were fundamentally concerned with humans but unable to dissect them freely—or related to sport. There survive a number of prose and verse works on *hunting, shooting, and *fishing in the style of *Xenophon (1)'s Cynegetica, or the hexameter poetry of *Oppian. There also survives a considerable corpus of veterinary writings in both Greek and Latin.

Pliny's Natural History contains the most extensive collection of zoological and botanical material after Aristotle and *Theophrastus. In fact, much of it comes ultimately from Aristotle and Theophrastus, although the material is not organized according to the same kinds of principles. Pliny begins his (often anecdotal) account of animals with those that live on land (book 8). First comes the elephant, a creature which possesses a variety of human characteristics, or qualities that closely resemble them, including language, memory, sense of honour, and piety. Pliny evinces a romantic sympathy for many creatures; he relates the story of a literate elephant who was able to trace in Greek on the sand 'I, the elephant, wrote this' (8. 6). Creatures in the sea form the subject of book 9; birds and insects are dealt with in book 11, which ends with an enumeration of creatures notable for their small size. Animals, for Pliny, have their own worlds, their own societies, their own discoveries, which they make by accident, lacking the ratio—power of reasoning—necessary to solve their problems by deliberation. It might reasonably be said that this was the animal world which antiquity handed on to the Middle Ages. See also SOSTRATUS.

TEXTS See bibliogs. under entries for individual authors. For the ancient veterinary writings, see VETERINARY MEDICINE.
GENERAL O. Keller, Die antike Thierwelt, 2 vols. (1909–13); G. Loisel, Histoire des ménageries, 3 vols. (1912); D'Arcy W. Thompson, A Glossary of Greek Birds, 2nd edn. (1936), and A Glossary of Greek Fishes (1947); G. E. R. Lloyd, Science, Folklore and Ideology (1983).
On Presocratic zoogonies, see Kirk–Raven–Schofield, Presocratic Philosophers. The literature on Aristotle's zoology is copious, tendentious, and complex: the work of G. E. R. Lloyd provides a balanced, accessible, modern introduction, with full references to earlier work; see especially 'The Development of Aristotle's Theory of the Classification of Animals', Phronesis, 1961, 59–81, repr. with new introduction in Methods and Problems in Greek Science, (1991); and (in the same work) 'Aristotle's Zoology and his Metaphysics: The status quaestionis', with references to the work of influential modern scholars like Furth, Gotthelf, Lennox, and Pellegrin. The work of D. M. Balme is of central importance: amongst his most important contributions are "Γένος and εἶδος in Aristotle's Biology", CQ 1962, 81–98; 'Aristotle and the Beginnings of Zoology', Journal of the Society for the Bibliography of Natural History, 1970, 272–85; 'Aristotle's Use of Teleological Explanation in Nature', inaugural lecture, Queen Mary Coll. London, 1965. T. E. Lones, Aristotle's Researches in Natural Science (1912) remains important; M. Beagon, Roman Nature (1992) provides a useful introduction to Pliny.　　　　J. T. V.

animals in cult Numerous features of Greek religion attest links between animals and gods, usually between one animal or group of animals and one divinity. Thus *Athena is associated with various birds (in Athens especially the owl); *Dionysus is called 'bull' in an Elean hymn (Plut. Mor. 299b; see ELIS) and seen as a bull by *Pentheus (Eur. Bacch. 920–2). There are traces, too, of a closer identification, in which gods (and / or their worshippers) appear in animal or part-animal form. *Arcadia was in historical times the special home of theriomorphic deities (see ARCADIAN CULTS AND MYTHS); here we find a myth of *Poseidon's rape of *Demeter in equine form along with Pausanias' reference (8. 42. 4) to a horse-headed statue of Demeter, and the animal-headed figures decorating the robes of the cult-statues of Lycosura seem also to be related. But rituals involving the imitation of animals are found in other parts of the Greek world, the best-known example being probably the arkteia of *Brauron, where little girls played the part of bears in a ceremony for *Artemis.

By far the most important religious role of real animals in both Greece and Rome was that of sacrificial victim (see SACRIFICE). Animals for sacrifice were normally domesticated; pigs, sheep, goats, and cattle were the commonest species used, and it is likely that throughout antiquity most of the meat consumed from these animals would have been sacrificial meat. Deviant sacrifices, as of horses, fish, and also of wild animals more normally killed in hunting, are recorded in special contexts, but they are rare. Other sacred animals (which might also be sacrificed if appropriate) were those living in sacred enclosures and considered as consecrate to the deity: cattle, sheep, but also *snakes (like that on the Athenian acropolis, Hdt. 8. 41), dogs (in the cult of *Asclepius), or geese (*Juno Moneta on the Capitoline). Some of these creatures had a more general religious significance: snakes were widely perceived as sacred, while dogs were normally considered impure in a religious context. The actions of some animals (especially *birds) were frequently seen as supplying omens, and prophecy from the entrails of sacrificial victims was also practised, in Greece, but more especially by the Etruscans and thence the Romans (see DIVINATION). See also ANIMALS, ATTITUDES TO.

J. Prieur, Les Animaux sacrés dans l'antiquité (1988); L. Bodson, Ἱερὰ ζῷα (1975).　　　　E. Ke.

Anio (mod. Aniene), a river of Italy rising in the Sabine country (see SABINI) and separating it from *Latium (Plin. HN 3. 54). After flowing 120 km. (75 mi.) west-south-west it joins the *Tiber at the site of Antemnae just north of Rome. Landslides in AD 105 and later have changed but not destroyed its spectacular cascades at *Tibur (Hor. Carm. 1. 7. 13; Plin. Ep. 8. 17). It supplied two *aqueducts, Anio Vetus (272 BC) and Anio Novus (AD 52), and below Tibur was navigable (Strabo 5. 238). It was an important route for *transhumance from prehistoric times.

G. Colasanti, L'Aniene (1906); T. Ashby, Aqueducts of Ancient Rome (1935), 54, 252; G. Barker, Proc. Prehist. Soc. 1972, 199 f.
　　　　E. T. S.; T. W. P.

Anius, son of Apollo and king of *Delos. He prophesied that the Trojan War would last ten years. His mother Rhoeo (Pomegranate) was descended from *Dionysus through her father Staphylus ('Grape'). Anius married Dorippa and had three daughters, the Oenotrophoi ('Rearers of Wine'): Oeno ('Wine'), Spermo ('Seed'), and Elaïs ('Olive-tree') who supplied Agamemnon's army before Troy. According to the myth (first in Cyclic Epic), he received *Aeneas (Aen. 3. 80; Ov. Met. 13. 633; Lycoph. 170 and schol.). A votive marble relief (2nd / 1st cent. BC) with a dedication to Anius and with a typical funerary banqueting-scene was found near the hero's sanctuary on Delos (Delos Mus. 3201).

P. Bruneau, *LIMC* 1 / 1 (1981), 794 'Anios'. H. J. R.; B. C. D.

ankhisteia (ἀγχιστεία), a kinship group, extending to second cousins, or perhaps only to first cousins once removed. In Athenian law the nearest relatives within this group had the right to inherit property (see INHERITANCE, GREEK); if a person was killed, it was their duty to prosecute the killer. Relatives on the father's side took precedence over those on the mother's.

A. R. W. Harrison, *The Law of Athens* 1 (1968), 143–9; D. M. MacDowell, *CQ* 1989, 10–21. D. M. M.

Anna Perenna, Roman goddess with a merry festival on 15 March (Ov. *Fast.* 3. 523–696 with Bömer's notes). This date on the Ides and the first full moon of the year by archaic reckoning (1 March being New Year's Day) imply a year-goddess; hence her name from the prayer *ut annare perennareque commode liceat* ('for leave to live in and through the year to our liking': Macrob. *Sat.* 1. 12. 6), but cf. the evidence from satire and mime (below) with F. Altheim, *Terra Mater* (1931), 91–108, and H. J. Rose, *JRS* 1931, 138–9. Ovid tells three stories, one identifying her with Anna, sister of *Dido (*Fast.* 3. 545–656), the second with an old woman of *Bovillae named Anna, who fed the plebeians during the secession to the *mons Sacer (663–74); the third, after her apotheosis (675–96), provides an aetiology for ribald verses via an encounter with *Mars Gradivus (cf. Ribbeck, *CRF* 2. 279; Latte, *RR* 138; Varro, *Sat. Men.* 506 Buechler).

Kl. Pauly 1. 357–8; W. Otto, *Wien. Stud.* 1912, 322–31; Wissowa, *Ges. Abh.* 167–71; *LIMC* 1 (1981), 794–5. C. R. P.

Annaeus Cornutus, Lucius (1st cent. AD), Stoic philosopher, grammarian, and rhetorician whose pupils included *Lucan and *Persius (who honoured him in *Sat.* 5, and whose *Satires* he reportedly revised after the poet's death); exiled by Nero. His Life, now lost, was the last in Diog. Laert. 7; the description Λεπτίτης (*Suda*), denoting a citizen (not merely native) of *Lepcis Magna, refutes the common supposition that he was the younger Seneca's freedman, though patronage remains plausible. His one extant work (conjectural title Ἐπιδρομὴ τῶν κατὰ τὴν Ἑλληνικὴν θεολογίαν παραδεδομένων, 'Summary of the Traditions concerning Greek Mythology'), addressed to a young child, uses *etymology and also *allegory to derive philosophical insights from divine names and myths. Lost writings included a critique of Aristotle's *Categories*, reviewing a previous Stoic treatment of the subject; a treatise on spelling, favouring contemporary usage over ancient and balancing the claims of etymology and pronunciation; and commentaries on Virgil (one addressed to *Silius Italicus). He combines sensible comments (e.g. that at *Aen.* 9. 672 *commissa* = 'closed', not 'entrusted') with propensities to criticize passages as improper (his comment on *Aen.* 8. 406 disgusted Gell. *NA* 9. 10) and judge Augustan diction by Neronian usage (at *Ecl.* 6. 76 *vexasse*, which had subsided from 'ravage' to 'disturb', seemed too weak); he took the death-rite at *Aen.* 4. 696–705, already found in Euripides, for a Virgilian invention 'like the Golden Bough'.

TEXTS Ἐπιδρομή C. Lang (Teubner, 1881); minor works: R. Reppe, *De L. Annaeo Cornuto* (1906); A. Mazzarino, *Gramm. Rom. Frag.* 1. 167–71 (testimonia), 171 ff. (fragments).
TRANSLATION R. S. Hays (Ph.D. Diss. Univ. of Texas at Austin, 1983).
STUDIES A. D. Nock, *RE* Suppl. 5. 995–1005; G. W. Most, *ANRW* 2. 36. 3 (1989), 2014–65; *PIR*[2] A 609. L. A. H.-S.

Annaeus Lucanus, Marcus, the poet **Lucan** (AD 39–65), was born at Corduba (mod. Córdoba), 3 November AD 39. His father, M. *Annaeus Mela, was a Roman knight and brother of L. *Annaeus Seneca (2). Mela came to Rome when his son was about eight months old. There Lucan received the typical élite education, ending with the school of rhetoric, where he was a great success (see EDUCATION, ROMAN); he probably also studied Stoic philosophy under L. *Annaeus Cornutus, a connection of Seneca. He continued his studies at Athens, but was recalled by *Nero, who admitted him to his inner circle and honoured him with the offices of quaestor and augur. In AD 60, at the first celebration of the games called Neronia, he won a prize for a poem in praise of Nero. In AD 62 or 63 he published three books of his epic on the Civil War. Growing hostility between him and Nero, for which various reasons are given, finally led the emperor to ban him from public recitation of his poetry and from speaking in the lawcourts. Early in AD 65 Lucan joined the conspiracy of C. *Calpurnius Piso (2), and on its discovery was forced to open his veins in April 65; as he died he recited some of his own lines on the similar death of a soldier.

Works Lucan was a prolific writer. Of the many titles fragments exist of the *Catacthonia* ('Journey to the Underworld'), *Iliaca*, *Orpheus*, and epigrams. The surviving epic *De bello civili* (the alternative title *Pharsalia* is probably based on a misunderstanding of 9. 985) contains ten books covering events in the years 49–48 BC beginning with *Caesar's crossing of the Rubicon; the poem breaks off, almost certainly unfinished, with Caesar in *Alexandria (1). The historical sources include *Livy's (lost) books on the period and Caesar's own *On the Civil War*, but Lucan freely manipulates historical truth where it suits his purpose, e.g. in introducing Cicero in *Pompey's camp on the eve of the battle of Pharsalus in book 7. The epic has no single hero; the three main characters are Caesar, an amoral embodiment of Achillean (see ACHILLES) and elemental energy; Pompey, figure of the moribund republic and shadow of his own former greatness; and *Cato (Uticensis), an impossibly virtuous specimen of the Stoic saint (see STOICISM).

The Civil War is narrated as a tale of unspeakable horror and criminality leading to the destruction of the Roman republic and the loss of liberty; this message sits uneasily with the fulsome panegyric of Nero in the proem, unless that is to be read satirically or as the product of an early stage of composition before Lucan fell out with the emperor. From the moment when Caesar is confronted at the Rubicon by a vision of the distraught goddess Roma, in a scene that reworks Aeneas' vision of the ghost of Hector on the night of the sack of Troy, Lucan engages in continuous and detailed allusion to *Virgil's *Aeneid*, the epic of the birth and growth of Rome, in order to construct the *De bello civili* as an 'anti-*Aeneid*', a lament for the death of the Roman body politic as Roman military might is turned in against itself. Lucan's rhetorical virtuosity is exploited to the full to involve the audience (defined in the proem as Roman citizens, i.e. those most nearly concerned by the subject of civil war) in his grim tale. In an extension of tendencies present already in Virgil, an extreme of pathos is achieved through the use of lengthy speeches, apostrophe of characters in the narrative, and indignant epigrammatic utterances (*sententiae); in contravention of the objectivity associated with Homeric *epic, Lucan as narrator repeatedly intrudes his own reactions, as in the shocked meditation on the death of Pompey in book 8. Related to the goal of *pathos* are the features of hyperbole and paradox. Hyperbole is expressive both of the vast forces involved in the conflict, presented as a 'world war', and of the greatness of the crimes perpetrated. Lucan's use of paradox is rooted in the conceptual and thematic anti-structures of civil war, in which legality is conferred on crime, and the greatest exemplars of Roman military virtue, such as the centurion Scaeva in book 6, are at the same time the greatest criminals; but in this topsy-turvy world paradox also extends to the physical, as in the sea-battle at the end of book 3 which turns into a 'land-battle' because the ships are so tightly packed. Realism is not a goal; Lucan's notorious abolition of the traditional epic divine machinery is not determined by the desire for a historiographical plausibility; rather, Lucan replaces the intelligibility of the anthropomorphic gods of Homer and Virgil with a darker sense of the supernatural, in a world governed by a negative version of Stoic Providence or Fate. *Dreams, *portents, and *prophecies abound, as in the list of omens at Rome at the end of book 1, or in Appius *Claudius Pulcher (3)'s consultation of the long-silent Delphic oracle in book 5; the Gothick atmosphere reaches a climax with the consultation in book 6 by Sextus *Pompeius of the witch Erictho and her necro-mantic resurrection of a corpse. Death fascinates Lucan, in both its destructive and its heroic aspects; a recurrent image is *suicide, viewed both as the symbol of Rome's self-destruction and as the Stoic's praiseworthy exit from an intolerable life (the paradoxes are explored in the Vulteius episode in book 4). The Roman spectacle of ritualized killing in the amphitheatre is reflected in the frequent gladiatorial imagery (see GLADIATORS) of the epic. In all of these features Lucan shows a close affinity with the writings, above all the tragedies, of his uncle the younger Seneca.

Lucan displays his learning in mythological episodes, such as the story of *Hercules and *Antaeus in book 4, in the geography and ethnography of the catalogues of books 1 and 3 and the description of Thessaly in book 6, and in the 'scientific' passages on the snakes of Libya in book 9 and on the sources of the Nile in book 10; but these 'digressions' usually have a further thematic and symbolic purpose. It is true that Lucan's style lacks the richness and colour of Virgil's, but his limited and repetitive range of vocabulary, often prosaic in tone, is deliberately geared to the bleak, remorseless, and unromantic nature of the subject-matter; a similar response may be made to the criticism of the monotony of Lucan's metre. Stylistic and metrical narrowness as a purpose-ful inversion of Virgilian norms finds an analogy in the device of 'negative enumeration', the listing of things that do not happen, but which might in normal circumstances be expected to happen, as in the description of the funereal remarriage of Cato and Marcia in book 2.

Lucan's epic was avidly read and imitated for centuries after his death; his admirers include *Statius (whose mythological epic on civil war, the Thebaid, is permeated with echoes of Lucan), Dante, Goethe, and Shelley. After a period of critical condemna-tion and neglect, the sombre baroque brilliance of the work is once more coming to be appreciated.

CRITICAL TEXTS A. E. Housman, 2nd edn. (1927); D. R. Shackle-ton Bailey (1988).

TRANSLATIONS J. D. Duff (Loeb, 1928); S. E. Braund (1992).

COMMENTARIES C. E. Haskins (1887), with introd. by W. E. Heitland; R. J. Getty, Book 1, 2nd edn. (1955); E. Fantham, Book 2 (1992); V. Hunink, Book 3 (1992); P. Barratt, Book 5 (1979); R. Mayer, Book 8 (1981)

LITERARY HISTORY AND CRITICISM R. Pichon, Les Sources de Lucain (1912); M. P. O. Morford, The Poet Lucan (1967); F. M. Ahl, Lucan: An Introduction (1976); W. D. Lebek, Lucans Pharsalia: Dichtungsstruktur und Zeitbezug (1976); J. M. Masters, Poetry and Civil War in Lucan's Bellum Civile (1992).

PIR² A 611.   W. B. A.; P. R. H.

Annaeus (RE 11) **Mela, Lucius** (or **Marcus**), youngest son of the elder Seneca (L. *Annaeus Seneca (1)) and father of Lucan M. *Annaeus Lucanus, was an imperial procurator of equestrian status. Claiming Lucan's property after his death in the Pisonian conspiracy of AD 65 (see CALPURNIUS PISO (2), C.), he was himself implicated and committed suicide (Tac. Ann. 16. 17).

E. P. B.; M. T. G.

Annaeus (RE 12) **Novatus** (later **L. Iunius Gallio Annaeanus**), brother of the philosopher L. *Annaeus Seneca (2), was adopted (between 41 and 52) by the orator and senator L. Junius Gallio, by which name he was then known. As procon-sul of Achaia c. AD 52 (Syll.³ 2. 801) he refused to consider the case put by the Jews against St *Paul (Acts 18: 12). He was suffect consul in 55 or 56. Seneca dedicated some works to him. After his brother's ruin he was compelled to commit suicide.

F. Jackson and K. Lake, Beginnings of Christianity 5 (1933), 462; E. Groag, Röm. Reichsbeamten von Achaia (1939), cols. 32 ff.; Syme, Tacitus, 589 ff.; M. Griffin, Seneca: A Philosopher in Politics (1976).   A. M.; M. T. G.

Annaeus (RE 16) **Seneca** (1), **Lucius**, writer on *declamation, was born of equestrian family at *Corduba (mod. Córdoba) in Spain about 50 BC. Of his life we know little; he was certainly in Rome both as a young man and after his marriage, and his knowledge of the contemporary schools of rhetoric implies that he spent much time in the capital. His family wealth was increased by his marriage to Helvia, a fellow countrywoman, by whom he had three sons, L. *Annaeus Novatus (Gallio), L. *Annaeus Seneca (2), the philosopher, and M. *Annaeus Mela, the father of the poet *Lucan. He died around AD 40, after the death of Tiberius and before the exile of his second son.

His history of Rome 'from the start of the civil wars almost up to the day of his death', is lost. The partly preserved Oratorum et rhetorum sententiae divisiones colores, written for his sons in his old age, originally comprised ten books devoted to controversiae, each with a preface, and at least two devoted to suasoriae. Only five books (1, 2, 7, 9, and 10) of the Controversiae (together with seven of the prefaces) and one of the Suasoriae have survived more or less in full: an abridgement made later for school use (perhaps 4th cent.) gives us some knowledge of the missing books of controversiae. As the cumbersome title suggests, the material is grouped under three rubrics. For each theme, striking and epigrammatic extracts from various speakers are followed by the author's analysis of the heads of their arguments and by remarks on their colours or lines of approach to the case (see COLOR). Extracts from Greek declaimers are often placed at the end, and the whole is spiced with comments and anecdotes of Seneca's own.

Seneca's sons were primarily interested in *epigram, and his book is biased towards smart sayings. Only in Controv. 2. 7 does he seem to have set himself to reproduce a complete speech, and that is cut short by our manuscripts. The accumulated *sententiae, vividly illustrative of an important aspect of Silver Latin, tend to cloy. Relief is provided by the excellent prefaces, which sketch with graphic detail the characters of the major declaimers on whom Seneca, relying (it seems) only on a phenomenal memory, primarily drew. Elsewhere Seneca's own stories and digressions give priceless information on declamatory practice and on the literary scene of the early empire. His literary criticism is conservative and somewhat mechanical, and he is out of sympathy with a good deal of what he preserves for us (see LITERARY CRITICISM IN ANTIQUITY para. 8). High points include the assessment of the orator *Cassius Severus and his comparative failure as a declaimer (*Controv.* 3 pref.); the sections on *Ovid in the school of *Arellius Fuscus (ibid. 2. 2. 8–12); and a series of accounts of the death of Cicero, including a fine extract from the poet *Cornelius Severus (*Suas.* 6. 16–26).

See RHETORIC, LATIN.

> EDITIONS H. J. Müller (1887; repr. 1963); L. Håkanson (1989).
> TRANSLATIONS (with text): H. Bornecque, rev. edn. (1932); M. Winterbottom (Loeb, 1974).
> COMMENTARY *Suas.* W. A. Edward (1928).
> GENERAL S. F. Bonner, *Roman Declamation* (1949), indispensable; L. A. Sussman, *The Elder Seneca* (1978); J. A. Fairweather, *The Elder Seneca* (1981). On his life, M. T. Griffin, *JRS* 1972, 1–19.
> PIR² A 616.   C. J. F.; M. W.

Annaeus Seneca (2), **Lucius,** was born at *Corduba (mod. Córdoba) in southern Spain between 4 BC and AD 1. He was born into a wealthy equestrian family of Italian stock, being the second son of the elder Seneca (no. 1 above) and Helvia; his brothers were L. *Annaeus Novatus, later known as Iunius Gallio after his adoption by the orator of that name, and L. *Annaeus Mela, the father of the poet Lucan (see ANNAEUS LUCANUS, M). He was happily married to a woman younger than himself, Pompeia Paulina; the evidence for an earlier marriage is tenuous. He had one son, who died in 41.

He was brought to Rome by his mother's stepsister, the wife of C. Galerius, prefect of Egypt from 16 to 31. Little is known about his life before AD 41. In Rome by AD 5, he studied grammar and rhetoric and was attracted at an early age to philosophy. His philosophical training was varied. He attended lectures by Attalus the Stoic and by Sotion and Papirius Fabianus, both followers of *Sextius who had founded the only native Roman sect a generation before: Seneca was to describe it as a type of Stoicism. It is not known when he met *Demetrius (19) the Cynic, whom he was to write about in his Neronian works. At some time he joined his aunt in Egypt, who nursed him through a period of ill health. About 31 he returned with her, survivors of a shipwreck in which his uncle died. Some time later, through her influence, he was elected quaestor, considerably after the minimum age of 25. By the reign of *Gaius (1), he had achieved a considerable reputation as an orator, perhaps also as a writer (if some of the lost works can be dated so early), and in 39, according to a story in *Cassius Dio, his brilliance so offended the emperor's megalomania that it nearly cost him his life (political motives have been conjectured). In 41 under *Claudius he was banished to Corsica for alleged adultery with *Iulia (5) Livilla, a sister of Gaius, and remained in exile until 49, when he was recalled through the influence of the younger *Agrippina and made praetor. He was appointed tutor to her son *Nero, then 12 years old and ready to embark on the study of rhetoric. In 51 *Burrus, who was to become Seneca's congenial ally and colleague during his years of political influence, was made prefect of the praetorian guard (see PRAEFECTUS PRAETORIO); and with Nero's accession in 54, Seneca exchanged the role of tutor for that of political adviser and minister.

During the next eight years, Seneca and Burrus managed to guide and cajole Nero sufficiently to ensure a period of good government, in which the influence of his mother was reduced and the worst abuses of the Claudian regime, the irregularities in jurisdiction and the excessive influence and venality of the court, were corrected. Though he ensured that Nero treated the senate with deference, and was himself a senior senator, having held office as suffect consul for the unusual term of six months in 55 or 56, he did not regularly attend senatorial meetings. Nor is Dio's conception of his role as initiating legislation and reform plausible. Rather, as *amicus principis,* writing the emperor's speeches, exercising patronage, and managing intrigue, Seneca's power was ill-defined but real. His relatives received important posts, as did the *equites* to whom he addressed most of his works. *De clementia* probably gives some idea of the way in which Nero was encouraged to behave himself, but Seneca's reputation was tarnished by Nero's suspected murder of *Britannicus in 55 and certain murder of his mother in 59. As Nero fell under the influence of people more willing to flatter him and to encourage his inclination to seek popularity through exhibitionism and security through crime, Seneca's authority declined and his position became intolerable. In 62 the death of Burrus snapped his power, and Seneca asked to retire and offered to relinquish his vast wealth to Nero. The retirement was formally refused and the wealth not accepted until later; in practice he withdrew from public life and spent much time away from Rome. In 64, after Nero's sacrilegious thefts following the Great Fire in July, Seneca virtually retired to his chamber and handed over a great part of his wealth. He devoted these years to philosophy, writing, and the company of a circle of congenial friends. In 65 he was forced to commit suicide for alleged participation in the unsuccessful Pisonian conspiracy (see CALPURNIUS PISO (2), C.); his death, explicitly modelled on that of *Socrates, is vividly described by Tacitus (*Ann.* 15. 62–4) who, though sympathetic, clearly found it rather histrionic and preferred the ironic behaviour of *Petronius (2) a year later.

Seneca's extant works comprise, first, the ten ethical treatises which are found in the Ambrosian MS (C. 90 inf.) under the name *dialogi.* They are, with the exception of the *De ira* ('on anger'), comparatively short, and their general content is readily inferred from their traditional titles; the dating is in many cases controversial. They comprise (in the manuscript order): *De providentia* ('on providence'), undatable and dedicated to C. *Lucilius (2) (Iunior), maintaining that no evil can befall the good man; *De constantia sapientis* ('on the constancy of the wise man'), addressed to Annaeus Serenus, written sometime after 47 and probably before 62; *De ira* in three books, dedicated to Seneca's brother Novatus, probably in the early years of Claudius's reign (before 52); *Ad Marciam de consolatione* ('to Marcia, on consolation'), a belated and politically inspired attempt to console the daughter of A. *Cremutius Cordus for the death of her son, probably his earliest extant work written in 39 or 40; *De vita beata,* incomplete, addressed to Novatus (now called Gallio) and probably in part an apologia, dating to after the attack on Seneca by P. *Suillius Rufus in 58 (Tac. *Ann.* 13. 42); *De otio,* of which only eight chapters survive, dating before 62, if addressed to Serenus (whose name has been erased in the MS), like *De tranquillitate animi* ('on tranquillity of mind'), which begins with Serenus describing his moral conflicts; *De brevitate vitae* ('on the brevity of life'), addressed to Paulinus, *praefectus annonae* under Claudius and Nero and (now or later) Seneca's father-in-law, dated by some to 49, more plausibly to 55; *Ad Polybium de consolatione,* written about 43 to Claudius' freedman (see POLYBIUS (2)), in hopes of flattering him into supporting Seneca's recall from exile; *Ad Helviam de consolatione,* addressed to his mother who is consoled on his exile.

Beside the Ambrosian *dialogi,* we have four other prose works.

De clementia recommends the practice of the virtue to Nero in December 55/56 (after many suspected he had murdered Britannicus): of the original three books, only the first (which has affinities with Hellenistic essays *On *kingship*) and the beginning of the second (a technical philosophical analysis of the virtue) survive. The codex Nazarianus (Vat. Pal. 1547), the fundamental source for the text of this treatise, also contains the *De beneficiis*, an elaborate work in seven books, often dry but informative about the Roman social code. It is addressed to Aebutius Liberalis and was written sometime after the death of Claudius, with 56 as a *terminus post quem* for book 2, and before *Ep.* 81. 3 (summer of 64). The *Natural questions*, dedicated to Lucilius and written during the period of Seneca's retirement, deals mainly with natural phenomena, though ethics often impinge on physics, and is of great scientific and some literary interest. The text is corrupt and broken, and the original books, apparently eight in number, have a disturbed sequence. To the same period belongs the longest of the prose works, the *Epistulae morales*, consisting of 124 letters divided into 20 books; more were extant in antiquity. Their advertised recipient is again Lucilius, but the fiction of a genuine correspondence is only sporadically maintained. Though the form was inspired by *Cicero's letters to *Atticus (cited by Seneca), their antecedents are to be found rather in the philosophical letters of *Epicurus and *Horace and in the tradition of popular philosophical discourse (sometimes misleadingly called *'diatribe'). Despite the artificiality of the letter-form, the variety and informality of these essays have made them the most popular of Seneca's prose works at all times.

In a category of its own is the obscurely entitled *Apocolocyntosis*, a *Menippean satire written in a medley of prose and verse. It is an original and amusing skit on the deification of Claudius, containing serious political criticism and clever literary parody (even of Seneca himself).

Other prose works have been lost, for the titles or fragments of over a dozen survive. These included letters and speeches, a *Vita patris*, some ethical works, geographical treatises on India and Egypt, and books on physics and natural history.

The bulk of Seneca's prose work is philosophical in content and an important source for the history of *Stoicism. He put his literary skills, human experience, and common sense at the service of his protreptic and paedagogic purpose: though orthodox in doctrine and sometimes learned and technical, his works aim primarily at moral exhortation. The moralizing is given all the force which an accomplished rhetorician can provide and is enlivened by anecdote, hyperbole, and vigorous denunciation. The style is brilliant, exploiting to the full the literary fashions of the day while remaining essentially individual, and has an important place in the history of European prose. Non-periodic and highly rhythmical, antithetical, and abrupt, it relies for its effect on rhetorical device, vivid metaphor, striking vocabulary, paradox and point; the point, a product of the philosophical as much as the rhetorical tradition, is at times refined to excess by the unflagging ingenuity of the writer. Aimed at immediate impact, the structure is often deliberately loose and need not imply an inability to develop a sustained theme. Seneca's contribution to forging a philosophical vocabulary in Latin (see LUCRETIUS) was considerable. The ultimate beneficiaries were the Latin Church Fathers.

His most important poetical works are his tragedies: the corpus contains *Hercules [furens]*, based generally on the *Hercules furens* of *Euripides; *Troades*, combining the sacrificial plot-elements from Euripides' *Troades* and *Hecuba*; *Phoenissae*, an unfinished text without choral odes whose two long acts recall both *Sophocles' *OC* and Euripides' *Phoenissae*; *Medea*, close in action and characterization to Euripides' *Medea*; *Phaedra*, the Euripidean myth, but with a Phaedra both more shameless and more repentant than in the *Hippolytus Stephanephorus*; *Oedipus*, close in action to Sophocles' play; *Agamemnon*, unlike *Aeschylus' play in the role played by Aegisthus, the scenes between Cassandra and the Trojan chorus, and the final act; *Thyestes*, with no known model; and *Hercules Oetaeus*, a pagan passion-play whose derivative language and overextended action suggest rather an imitator than Seneca himself. A tenth drama (the only surviving *praetexta), *Octavia*, based on the events of AD 62, can hardly be by Seneca, who is a character of the drama. Absent from the oldest MS (Etruscus), it implies knowledge of events that occurred after Seneca's death, and lacks Seneca's richness of verbal invention and dramatic development.

Recent scholarship has argued against judging the tragedies in relation to their famous Greek predecessors, realizing that Seneca did not adapt individual Greek tragedies, but drew inspiration from the whole tragic corpus, especially from *Euripides. More significant is his debt to Roman poetry: he did not admire and probably did not use the now lost republican tragedians; it is more likely that he learned from the metrical and dramatic techniques of *Varius Rufus' *Thyestes* or *Ovid's *Medea*. There is unmistakable influence from Ovid's *Heroides* (*Medea*, *Phaedra*) and from episodes of violence and passion in the *Aeneid* and *Metamorphoses*: thus *Troades* makes full use of *Aeneid* 2, and *Thyestes*, while it may reflect Ennius' or Varius' lost versions of the myth, undoubtedly adapts the language and psychology of Ovid's *Tereus* in *Met.* 6.

The tragedies cannot be dated absolutely, though the parody of the lament from *Hercules furens* in *Apocolocyntosis* implies dating of that early play before 54: Fitch's relative dating based on metrical practice (*AJPhil.* 1981, 289–307) suggests that at least *Thyestes* and *Phoenissae* may be Neronian.

Seneca largely observes a post-classical pattern of five acts, opening with an expository monologue or prologue scene. Acts are divided by choral odes in anapaests, sapphics, or asclepiads: lyric is also used for special scenes, such as the glyconics of the wedding procession and Medea's own polymetric incantations in *Medea*, and the anapaestic monodies of Hippolytus' hymn to Artemis and Andromache's supplication. While the plays show many features of post-classical stagecraft (cf. Tarrant, *Harv. Stud.* 1978, 213–63), and could be staged, discontinuity of action, with unanswered speeches and unexplained exits, suggests rather that they were primarily intended to be recited (wholly or in excerpts) or read. This is also consistent with Seneca's variable practice in indicating when the chorus is a witness to or absent from dialogue scenes and specifying its group identity: *Agamemnon* and *Hercules Oetaeus* have two different choruses.

The plays have been called 'rhetorical': certainly their most conspicuous feature is the passionate rhetoric of the leading characters, displayed both in terse stichomythia and extended harangues. They have been claimed as Stoic, since the dominant theme is the triumph of evil released by uncontrolled passion and the spread of destruction from man to the world of nature around him. Certainly Seneca both praises the beneficial persuasive effect of poetry (*Ep.* 108. 9, citing *Cleanthes on the power of verse to concentrate the impact and brilliance of a thought) and exonerates drama from the charge of fostering harmful emotions (*De ira* 2. 2. 5, distinguishing the audience's emotional response as preliminary or conditional). However, although the plays reflect

Stoic psychology, ethics, and physical theories, their predominantly negative tone and representation of life makes it unlikely that they were composed as Stoic lessons (*contra* Marti *TAPA* 1945, 216–45.)

The tragedies exercised a powerful influence over the Renaissance theatres of Italy, France, and Elizabethan England, where the 'Tenne Tragedies' adapted from Seneca by various translators coloured the diction and psychology of Marlowe, Shakespeare, and Ben Jonson. Compared with both life and entertainment in the late 20th cent. the violence and extravagance of Senecan as of Elizabethan tragedy no longer seem as shocking, grotesque, or incredible as they did to readers in earlier generations.

Besides the tragedies we have 77 epigrams, a few handed down under Seneca's name, and others attributed to him. Apart from the three epigrams specified as Seneca's in the Codex Salmasianus, their authenticity is highly dubious.

Seneca was a talented orator, statesman, diplomat, financier, and viticulturist, a prolific and versatile writer, a learned yet eloquent philosopher. Yet his style can weary us, as it did the generation of *Quintilian and *Tacitus (1), and as a man, he has continued to be criticized as a hypocrite as he was in antiquity: he preached the unimportance of wealth but did not surrender his until the end; he compromised the principles he preached by flattering those in power and by condoning many of Nero's crimes. Yet, as he says himself, effective exhortation can include preaching higher standards than can be realistically expected, and most moral teachers have urged attention to their words rather than to their example. Moreover, his teaching is more subtle and complex than is sometimes appreciated: he does not require the sacrifice of wealth, only the achievement of spiritual detachment from worldly goods; he advocates giving honest advice to rulers, while avoiding offence and provocation. Moreover, he confesses to having abandoned his youthful *asceticism, to giving in on occasion to grief and anger, to being only on the first rung of moral progress. Above all, he conveys, as few moralists have, a sympathy with human weakness and an awareness of how hard it is to be good. For his disciples, then and later, Seneca's power as a healer of souls has more than made up for his shortcomings as a model of virtue.

TEXTS AND EDITIONS *Dialogues*, M. C. Gertz (1886), E. Hermes (Teubner, 1905), A. Bourgery and R. Waltz, 4 vols. (Budé, 1922–42), L. Castiglioni and I. Viansino, 3 vols. (Paravia, 1946–63, *Dial.* 3–6, 9–12 only). *De clementia* and *De beneficiis*, M. C. Gertz (1876), C. Hosius, 2nd edn. (Teubner, 1914), F. Préchac (Budé, 1921, 1927). *Natural Questions*, A. Gercke (Teubner, 1907), P. Oltramare (Budé, 1929). *Epistulae*, O. Hense, 2nd edn. (Teubner, 1914), A. Beltrami, 2nd edn. (1931), F. Préchac, 5 vols. (Budé, 1945–64), L. D. Reynolds (OCT 1965). *Apocolocyntosis*, F. Bücheler–G. Heraeus, 6th edn. (1922), R. Waltz, 2nd edn. (Budé, 1961), C. F. Russo, 5th edn. (1965). Various commentaries, including those of J. D. Duff (*Dial.* 10–12, 1915), C. Favez (*Dial.* 6 (1929) and 12 (1918)), H. Dahlmann (*Dial.* 10, 1949), P. Grimal (*Dial.* 2 (1953) and 10 (1959)), P. Faider, C. Favez, P. van de Woestijne (*Clem.* 1, 1928, 2, 1950), W. C. Summers (*Select Letters*, 1910), O. Weinreich (*Apocol.*, 1923), P. T. Eden (*Apocol.*, 1984).

GENERAL STUDIES *PIR*[2] 617; R. Waltz, *Vie de Sénèque* (1909); M. Griffin, *Seneca: A Philosopher in Politics* (1976; repr. with postscript, 1991); P. Grimal, *Sénèque ou la conscience de l'Empire* (1978); survey chapters on various aspects in *ANRW* 2. 32. 2 (1985); 2. 36. 3 (1989); P. Faider, *Études sur Sénèque* (1921); F. Giancotti, *Cronologia dei 'Dialoghi' di Seneca* (1957); A. Bourgery, *Sénèque prosateur* (1922); E. Albertini, *La Composition dans les ouvrages philosophiques de Sénèque* (1923); B. Axelson, *Senecastudien* (1933), and *Neue Senecastudien* (1939); C. Martha, *Les Moralistes sous l'Empire romain* (1865). There is a critical bibliography of the *Apocolocyntosis* for the years 1922–58 by M. Coffey

in *Lustrum* 1961, 239 ff., and a survey of recent scholarship on the prose works, 1940–57, by A. L. Motto, *CW* 1960, 13 ff., 37 ff., 70 ff., 111 f., and on the prose works 1968–78 in *CW* 1982, 69–123; F. R. Chaumartin gives a bibliog. of the philosophical works for 1945–85 in *ANRW* 2. 36. 3. 1545 ff.

TRAGEDIES
Text: F. Leo, 2 vols. (1878–9; repr. 1963); G. C. Giardina, 2 vols. (1966); O. Zwierlein (1987). Cf. O. Zwierlein, *Prolegomena* (1983), and *Kritischer Kommentar* (1986).
Commentaries: *Hercules furens*, Fitch (1987); *Troades*, Fantham (1982), Boyle (1994); *Medea*, Costa (1973); *Phaedra*, Coffey–Mayer (1990); *Agamemnon*, Tarrant (1976); *Thyestes*, Tarrant (1985).
Studies: E. Lefèvre (ed.) *Senecas Tragödien* (1972), and *Der Einfluss Senecas auf das europaische Drama* (1978); A. J. Boyle, (ed.), *Seneca Tragicus* (1983); N. T. Pratt, *Seneca's Drama* (1983); D. and E. Henry, *The Mask of Power* (1985); D. F. Sutton, *Seneca on the Stage* (1986); C. Segal, *Language and Desire in Seneca's Phaedra* (1986); A. L. Motto and J. R. Clark, *Senecan Tragedy* (1988); T. G. Rosenmeyer, *Senecan Drama and Stoic Cosmology* (1989); P. J. Davis, *Shifting Song: The Chorus in Seneca's Tragedies* (1993).
EPIGRAMS *Anth. Lat.* 1. H. Bardon, *Rev. Ét. Lat.* 1939, 63 ff.

L. D. R.; M. T. G., E. F.

annales maximi, a chronicle kept by the *pontifex maximus. Under the Roman republic the pontifex maximus used to keep an annual record, and to publish a version of it outside the *Regia on a whitened board which was probably repainted every year. The chronicle contained the names of magistrates, and apparently registered all kinds of public events (*Schol. Dan. Aen.* 1. 373). Although *Cato (Censorius) (*Orig.* 4. 1 Chassignet) was irritated by its frequent references to food shortages and eclipses, it was an important source for the earliest Roman historians, who also adopted its plain style and perhaps also its chronicle form (Cic. *De or.* 2. 52). The *annales maximi*, as the annual records were called, continued to be compiled until the time of P. *Mucius Scaevola, who was pontifex maximus in the time of the *Gracchi. By then the chronicle had no doubt become an anachronism; but enough material had already been amassed to fill 80 books (*Schol. Dan. Aen.* 1. 373). The early books apparently dealt with legendary events (*Origo gentis Romanae* 17. 1–3, 1–6; 18. 2–3: the kings of *Alba Longa!), and were evidently the product of secondary elaboration; but genuine records went back to at least 400 BC (Cic. *Rep.* 1. 25), and perhaps to the beginning of the republic.

J. E. A. Crake, *CPhil.* 1940, 375–86; E. Rawson, *CQ* 1971, 158–69 (= *Roman Culture and Society* (1991), 1–15); B. W. Frier, *Libri annales pontificum maximorum* (1979); R. Drews, *CPhil.* 1988, 189–99.　　T. J. Co.

annals, annalists The Latin word *annales* ('yearbooks', 'annals') became the standard term for historical records in a general sense, and was frequently used by historians as a title for their works, probably in imitation of the *annales maximi*. The first Latin writer to call his work 'Annals' was *Ennius, which proves that already in his time the term could be applied to any kind of historical work, even if, like Ennius' poem, it was not in the form of a year-by-year chronicle. Whether the earliest Roman historians, who wrote in Greek, adopted a year-by-year arrangement is disputed; the fact that later writers refer to (e.g.) Q. *Fabius Pictor's history as 'Greek annals' (*Graeci annales*: Cic. *Div.* 1. 43) is hardly decisive. Pliny (*HN* 8. 11) even calls the work of *Cato (Censorius) *annales*, even though Cato did not use the chronicle form, ridiculed the *annales maximi* (4. 1 Chassignet), and gave his work the distinctive title *Origines*.

Later Roman historians, including L. *Calpurnius Piso Frugi, Cn. *Gellius, *Valerius Antias, C. *Licinius Macer, Q. *Claudius

Quadrigarius, and Q. *Aelius Tubero, all seem to have followed a year-by-year 'annalistic' arrangement, and their works are frequently referred to as *annales*. It is these historians that modern scholars call 'annalists'. The situation is confused, however, because extant historians such as *Livy and *Tacitus (1) also arranged their material annalistically, but neither called his work *annales* (the title 'Annals' for Tacitus' well-known work has no ancient authority), and they are never called annalists by scholars.

The confusion arises partly from a distinction made by the ancients themselves between annals (*annales*) and histories (*historiae*). This distinction was first made in the period of the *Gracchi, when some Roman historians rejected the traditional practice of recounting the history of Rome from its origins and turned instead to contemporary political history in the manner of *Thucydides (2) and *Polybius (1), giving their works the Greek title *historiae*. The earliest exponents were *Sempronius Asellio and perhaps C. *Fannius, who were followed by L. *Cornelius Sisenna *Sallust, and *Asinius Pollio. This caused Roman critics, such as *Verrius Flaccus, to go beyond the conventional view that 'annals' meant simply histories in chronicle form, and to suggest that the term 'histories' should properly be applied only to accounts of contemporary events (Gell. *NA* 5. 18). But some historians went further, and made a qualitative distinction; thus Sempronius Asellio (doubtless influenced by his contemporary Polybius) argued that whereas annals merely chronicled events, histories offered serious critical analysis (Gell. *NA* 5. 18).

Modern scholars have given their own twist to this debate, and use the term 'annalists' for historians such as Valerius Antias and Claudius Quadrigarius, whom they consider to have been simple-minded, uncritical, and mendacious. Since their works do not survive, the quality of these historians is difficult to judge. In any event, the modern habit of disparaging particular historians by the use of the term 'annalists' has no basis in the ancient evidence, and should be avoided as unhelpful and misleading.

M. Gelzer, *Hermes* 1934, 46–55 (= *Kl. Schr.* 3 (1964), 93–103); A. Klotz, *Livius und seine Vorgänger* (1940); M. L. W. Laistner, *The Greater Roman Historians* (1947); E. Badian, in T. A. Dorey (ed.), *Latin Historians* (1966), 1–38; J. Briscoe, *Comm. on Livy 31–33* (1973), 2–12; T. P. Wiseman, *Clio's Cosmetics* (1979); T. J. Cornell, in I. S. Moxon and others (eds.), *Past Perspectives* (1986), 67–86; and see HISTORIOGRAPHY, ROMAN.   T. J. Co.

Annia (*RE* 'Annius' 123) **Aurelia Galeria Lucilla,** daughter of M. *Aurelius and *Annia Galeria Faustina (2), was born on 7 March AD 150 and betrothed in 161 to L. *Verus, whom she married at Ephesus in 164, becoming Augusta. Widowed early in 169, she was obliged by her father to marry Ti. *Claudius Pompeianus. There were children from both marriages. Unhappy at her reduced prominence under *Commodus she was involved in a plot against him in 182, exiled, and then executed.

A. R. Birley, *Marcus Aurelius*, 2nd edn. (1987); M. T. Raepsaet-Charlier, *Prosopographie des femmes de l'ordre sénatorial* (1987), no. 54.   A. R. Bi.

Annia Galeria Faustina (1) (*RE* 'Annius' 120), daughter of M. *Annius Verus (3rd consulship AD 126) and Rupilia Faustina, aunt of Marcus *Aurelius, was married to the future Emperor *Antoninus Pius and bore him two sons and two daughters, one of whom, the younger Faustina (see next entry), became wife of Marcus. Faustina became Augusta after Antoninus' accession in 138 and was deified on her death in 140.

PIR[2] A 715; A. R. Birley, *Marcus Aurelius*, 2nd edn. (1987).   A. R. Bi.

Annia Galeria Faustina (2) (*RE* 'Annius' 121), younger daughter of *Antoninus Pius and the elder Faustina (see previous entry),

was betrothed at *Hadrian's wish to the future L. *Verus in AD 138; this was set aside by Antoninus after Hadrian's death in favour of his wife's nephew M. *Aurelius. The marriage took place in 145, probably the earliest possible date, when Faustina was aged about 15. Her first child, Domitia Faustina, was born on 30 November 147 (*Fasti Ostienses*) and she at once became Augusta. She bore Marcus at least a dozen children, six of whom survived her, five daughters (the eldest being *Annia Aurelia Galeria Lucilla) and a son, *Commodus. The latter was alleged to be illegitimate; Faustina's loyalty as well as her marital fidelity were subject to question, not least in reports that she encouraged the rebellion of C. *Avidius Cassius. But Marcus, who gave her the title 'mother of the camp' (*mater castrorum*) in 174, ignored these rumours and had her deified on her death late in 175 at Halala in *Cappadocia (renamed Faustinopolis).

PIR[2] A 716; *BM Coins, Rom. Emp.* 4; K. Fittschen, *Die Bildnistypen der Faustina minor und die Fecunditas Augustae* (1982); A. R. Birley, *Marcus Aurelius*, 2nd edn. (1987).   A. R. Bi.

Annianus, a poet of Hadrian's time and friend of Aulus *Gellius, owned a Faliscan farm (Gell. *NA* 20. 8) and composed verse on country themes, probably entitled *(carmina) Falisca*, and *Fescennini, perhaps part of the same work; his nine surviving lines employ paroemiacs and miuric dactylic tetrameters.

PIR[2] A 623; S. Mattiacci, *I Frammenti dei 'Poetae Novelli'* (1982), 81; Courtney, *FLP* 387.   E. C.

Anniceris, 4th cent. BC philosopher of the *Cyrenaic school. He, *Hegesias (1), and Theodorus 'the godless' became leaders of three divergent branches of the school, his own originality consisting, so far as we know, in stressing the importance of the pleasures of friendship (see LOVE AND FRIENDSHIP). He is said to have ransomed *Plato (1) when the latter was sold into slavery on the occasion of one of his visits to *Syracuse, but the authenticity of the event is doubtful.

A. Laks, in J. Brunschwig and M. C. Nussbaum (eds.), *Passions and Perceptions* (*Proc. of the 5th Symposium Hellenisticum*) (1993).   C. C. W. T.

Annius (*RE* 49) **Gallus, Appius,** *suffect consul between AD 62 and 69; sent by *Otho against the Vitellians in NE Italy; in 70 he was legate of Upper Germany, against C. *Iulius Civilis.   J. B. C.

Annius (*RE* 67) **Milo, Titus,** of a prominent family of *Lanuvium, as tribune 57 BC worked for *Cicero's recall from exile and, with P. *Sestius, organized armed gangs to oppose those led by P. *Clodius Pulcher which had long prevented it. Fighting between Clodius and Milo in the city continued for several years, since— short of the *senatus consultum ultimum*, impossible to pass—there was no legitimate way of using public force to suppress it. Both Milo and Clodius ascended through the official career (see CURSUS HONORUM), at times unsuccessfully prosecuting each other for *vis*, until Milo's men met and defeated Clodius' near *Bovillae in January 52. Clodius, wounded in the fighting, was killed on Milo's orders, chiefly to clear the way for Milo's candidacy for the consulship of 52, elections for which had been prevented by Clodius with *Pompey's support. After continued rioting Pompey was made sole consul and passed legislation including a strict law on *vis*, under which Milo was prosecuted. Cicero, intimidated by Pompey's soldiers guarding the court, broke down and was unable to deliver an effective speech for the defence. (The speech we have was written later.) Milo was convicted and went into *exile at *Massalia, where he ironically professed to enjoy the mullets. *Caesar, in part out of loyalty to Clodius' memory, refused to recall him along with other political exiles, and in 48, while Caesar was away in the east, Milo joined M. *Caelius Rufus in an attempt to raise rebellion among the poor in Italy and was killed.

Cic. *Mil.*, with Asconius' comm. on the speech and Marshall, *Asconius Comm.*; Gruen, *LGRR*, see index. E. B.

Annius Verus, Marcus, grandfather of Marcus *Aurelius, from Ucubi (mod. Espejo) in *Baetica, became a patrician under *Vespasian, and was *suffect consul in AD 97. He was influential under *Hadrian, to whom he was probably related, being city prefect (*praefectus urbi*), and holding a second ('ordinary') consulship (see CONSUL) in 121, and a third in 126. Verus' attractive personality was combined with an astute matrimonial policy: his wife Rupilia Faustina belonged to the republican nobility; one daughter-in-law was the heiress Domitia Lucilla the younger, M. Aurelius' mother; a son-in-law was the future *Antoninus Pius. Still alive when Antoninus was adopted by Hadrian, Verus was remembered with affection by M. Aurelius, who had grown up in his house.

M. Aur. *Med.*; Cass. Dio 69; SHA., *M. Ant.*; *PIR*² A 695; A. R. Birley, *Marcus Aurelius*, 2nd edn. (1987), 243 f. A. R. Bi.

Annius (*RE* 98) **Vinicianus,** son of L. Vinicianus who conspired in AD 42, and son-in-law of Cn. *Domitius Corbulo, was legate (see LEGATUS) of Legio V Macedonica under him in 63 when he was not yet quaestor. In 65 he escorted *Tiridates (4) to Rome. He gave his name to a plot against *Nero at *Beneventum (summer 66).

M. Griffin, *Nero: The End of a Dynasty* (1984), 177 ff. A. M.; B. M. L.

annona See FOOD SUPPLY (Roman).

Anonymus Antatticista (Ἀνταττικιστής), a contemporary opponent of *Phrynichus (3) the Atticist, who cites from good, but not always Attic, writers many words which Phrynichus condemns.

Anecd. Bekk. 1. 77. M. B. T.

Anonymus Seguerianus (3rd cent. AD) wrote a treatise on the formal style (πολιτικὸς λόγος), which contains frequent references to the work of *Alexander (12) son of Numenius.

Spengel–Hammer 1. 352; G. Kennedy, *Art of Rhetoric* (1972), 616. M. B. T.

Anser (1st cent. BC), a salacious erotic poet (Ov. *Tr.* 2. 435); nothing remains of his works. He probably profiteered from *Antony's exactions (Cic. *Phil.* 13. 11), and there seems to be a punning uncomplimentary reference to him at Verg. *Ecl.* 9. 36.

Teuffel–Kroll, § 233. 3; Schanz–Hosius, § 246. E. C.

Antaeus (Ἀνταῖος), in mythology, a giant, son of *Poseidon and Earth (*Gaia), living in Libya; he compelled all comers to wrestle with him and killed them when overcome (Pind. *Isthm.* 4. 56 ff. and schol. Plato, *Tht.* 169b). He was defeated and killed by *Heracles. That he was made stronger when thrown, by contact with his mother the Earth (Apollod. 2. 115), seems a later addition to the story.

Antaeus in art: *LIMC* 1 / 1 (1981) 800–11. H. J. R.

Antagoras of Rhodes (first half of 3rd cent. BC) wrote an epic *Thebais*, epigrams, and other poems (fr. 1 Powell, verses in hymnal style on Eros, seems to be echoed by *Callimachus (3),

Hymn 1. 5). Like *Aratus (1), Antagoras visited the court of *Antigonus (2) Gonatas, and the fragments also reveal familiarity with the Athenian *Academy.

Powell, *Coll. Alex.* 120–1; Gow–Page, *HE* 2. 29–31; P. von der Mühll, *MH* 1962, 28–32. R. L. Hu.

Antalcidas (occasional deviant version, **Antialcidas),** Spartan statesman. He came from a prominent family and was probably related by marriage to King *Agesilaus II. He first appears as Sparta's representative at the Graeco-Persian conference at *Sardis in 392 BC. He negotiated a Sparto-Persian alliance with *Artaxerxes (2) II in 388 and, as admiral (*nauarchos*), blockaded the Hellespont with Persian naval assistance, forcing the Athenians and their allies to agree to the *King's Peace (or Peace of Antalcidas) in 387/6. Its terms abandoned the Greek cities of Asia to Persia and established peace (probably the first officially named '*Common Peace') in mainland Greece and the Aegean based upon the principle of autonomy, although the practical effect was the establishment of Spartan hegemony. Although the tradition of his long-standing enmity with Agesilaus is doubtful, he reproved the king for his unrelenting hostility towards Thebes (1) in the 370s. He successfully negotiated Persian support in 372/1 and was elected *ephor for 370/69. He undertook a further diplomatic mission to Persia sometime in the 360s, the failure of which led to his suicide.

RE 1. 2344–6; PB no. 97; D. Whitehead, *LCM* 1979, 191–3; P. Cartledge, *Agesilaos and the Crisis of Sparta* (1987), see index. S. J. Ho.

Antenor (1), in mythology, an elderly and upright counsellor in Troy during the siege, who advised the return of *Helen to the Greeks, and in return for this (or, according to much later accounts, for betraying the city) was spared by the victors. Pindar says his descendants held *Cyrene; but in the story current in Roman times he took with him the Eneti from Paphlagonia (who had lost their king at Troy) and, settling in Venetia at the head of the Adriatic, founded *Patavium. (See VENETI (2).).

For his image in art see *LIMC* 1 / 1 (1981) 811–15. R. A. B. M.

Antenor (2), Athenian sculptor, active c.530–500 BC. According to Pausanias (1. 8. 5), he made the first bronze group of the tyrannicides Harmodius and *Aristogiton for the Athenian agora; Pliny (*HN* 34. 70) dates it to 510. *Xerxes I took it to Persia in 480, but the Athenians soon asked *Critius to replace it. *Alexander (3) the Great, *Seleucus (1) I, or *Antiochus (1) I returned it, and thereafter it stood beside Critius' group. Antenor's only extant work is the monumental *korē* (Acropolis Museum 681) dedicated by the potter Nearchus; the *korai* of the east pediment of the temple of Apollo at *Delphi are stylistically similar, and perhaps attributable to his workshop.

A. F. Stewart, *Greek Sculpture* (1990), 60, 86 ff., 124, 249 ff., figs. 154, 199 ff. A. F. S.

Anthedon, harbour town on the NE coast of *Boeotia, known for the legend of *Glaucus (4) the fisherman. The remains of circuit-walls and harbour installations can still be seen. Generally a part of Theban territory, it probably served as one of the bases of *Epaminondas' ephemeral fleet during the Theban Hegemony. Heraclides Criticus (1. 23–4; trans. Austin, 83) gives a brief description of the city, which *Sulla destroyed in 86 BC. Quickly rebuilt, the harbour was still in use in the 6th cent. AD. See HARBOURS.

Paus. 9. 22. 5. H. Schläger, D. J. Blackman, and J. Schäfer, *Arch. Anz.* 1968, 21 ff.; 1969, 299 ff. J. Bu.

Anthemius, western Roman emperor (AD 467–72), son-in-law of Marcian, eastern emperor, was imposed on *Ricimer by the eastern court. Though praised by *Sidonius Apollinaris in a panegyric, he lacked support in the west and the defeat of the imperial fleet by the *Vandals in 468 undermined his position. In 472, he was besieged by Ricimer in Rome, defeated and beheaded.

PLRE 2. 96–8 'Anthemius' 3.   J. D. H.

Anthesteria, a festival of *Dionysus which despite its name (suggesting *anthos*, flower) was associated particularly with the new wine. It was celebrated in most Ionian communities, but details are known almost exclusively from Athens, where it was of an importance comparable perhaps to modern Christmas. It was celebrated in the correspondingly named month Anthesterion, roughly late February. On the evening of the first day, 'Jar-opening' (*Pithoigia*), *pithoi* of the previous autumn's vintage were taken to the sanctuary of Dionysus in the Marshes, opened, offered to the god, and sampled. On the following day, drinking-parties of an abnormal type were held: participants sat at separate tables and competed, in silence, at draining a *chous* or five-litre (nine-pint) measure (whence the day's name *Choes*); slaves too had a share. Miniature *choes* were also given as toys to children, and 'first Choes' was a landmark. The third day was called *Chytroi*, 'Pots', from pots of seed and vegetable bran (*panspermia*) that were offered, it seems, to the dead. On the basis of a proverb 'Away with you, Keres, it is no longer Anthesteria', it is often supposed that souls of the dead were conceived as wandering at the festival; but this is problematic, since *Kēres* are normally spirits of evil, not souls, and the proverb is also transmitted in the form 'Away with you, Carians (*Kares*)'. It was almost certainly during the Anthesteria that the wife of the *basileus* was somehow 'given as a bride' to Dionysus (who may have been escorted to her in image on a 'ship-chariot', a rite known from vases). A series of vases which show a mask of Dionysus on a pillar, in front of which women draw wine from mixing-bowls while others dance, may evoke a part of the same ceremony.

The main problem posed by the festival is to see how its different elements relate to one another. Recent critics have stressed the idea of 'reversal' as a unifying factor: it is clear at all events that the Anthesteria is not just an amalgam of a well-lubricated wine festival and a glum commemoration of the dead, as the Choes rite itself is marked by traits of abnormality and reversal.

A. W. Pickard-Cambridge, *The Dramatic Festivals of Athens*, 2nd edn. rev. by J. Gould and D. M. Lewis (corr. edn. 1988) 1–25; W. Burkert, *Homo Necans* (1983; Ger. orig. 1972), 213–43; J. Bremmer, *The Early Greek Concept of the Soul* (1983), 108–22; F. Frontisi-Ducroux, *Le Dieu-masque* (1991); R. Hamilton, *Choes and Anthesteria* (1992).   R. C. T. P.

Anthimus was a Greek doctor attached to the court of the emperor Zeno (AD 474–91) who was involved in treasonable relations with the Ostrogothic king *Theoderic (2) Strabo in 481. He fled Roman territory and took refuge in Italy at the court of *Theoderic (1) the Great, who later sent him on a diplomatic mission to the Franks. He wrote some time after 511 a short Latin handbook of *dietetics—*De observatione ciborum ad Theodoricum regem Francorum epistula*. The interest of this curious text, half medical textbook, half cookery book, is twofold: first, it provides a detailed and vivid picture of the eating and drinking habits of a Germanic people of the Völkerwanderung: beer and mead are drunk for pleasure, wine as a medicine; second, since Anthimus learnt his Latin from the lips of the common people and had no contact with the literary and grammatical tradition, the *De*

observatione ciborum is a specimen of the popular Latin of late antiquity, deviating from classical norms in vocabulary, morphology, and syntax, and of great value to the Romance philologist.

Ed. E. Liechtenhan, *CML* 8/1, 2nd edn., with Ger. trans. (1963); N. Groen, *Lexicon Anthimeum* (1926).   R. B.

Anthologia Latina, a modern invention gradually created in print and not intrinsically distinct from *Poetae Latini minores* or the *Appendix Vergiliana*, gathers poems mostly short that have no better home. Riese's arrangement by date of attestation has fewest drawbacks.

The largest block, found in the corrupt and mutilated Codex Salmasianus (8th–9th cent.), was compiled in Vandal Africa, on which it sheds interesting light. In numbered sections of unequal length it embraces a *liber epigrammatōn* in various metres by *Luxorius (Riese 287–375), which yields a date after AD 533; another collection probably by one African poet (R. 90–197); Virgilian *centos; couplets that end as they begin, or are repeated in reverse; epigrams attributed to the younger *Seneca; snippets of *Propertius, *Ovid, *Martial; *Symphosius' 100 *riddles; and longer pieces such as the *Pervigilium Veneris*. A Claudian and Neronian block in the Codex Vossianus (*c*.850) ends with epigrams attributable to *Petronius (3) (R. 464–79). From late sources Riese forgivably took poems since proved humanistic.

Though Riese segregated *Carmina epigraphica* (ed. Buecheler, 1895–7), some literary poems in the *Anthologia Latina* originated as inscriptions, e.g. on bath-houses or mosaics, and others had an epigraphical history still unclarified (e.g. R. 392–3).

See D. Schaller and E. Könsgen, *Initia carminum latinorum saeculo undecimo antiquorum* (1977) for bibliog. on single poems; V. Tandoi, *Enc. Virg.* 1, 'Antologia latina'; on the Salmasianus, M. Spallone, *IMU* 1982, 1–71; *Texts and Transmission*, 9–13. D. R. Shackleton Bailey (vol. 1, 1982) is emending Riese's 2nd edn. (1894–1906).   M. D. R.

anthology (ἀνθολόγιον), not used in the modern sense before *Diogenianus (2). Many Hellenistic poets published books of epigrams: *PMil. Vogl.* inv. 1295 and *PKöln* 104 are from collections by *Posidippus (2) and *Mnasalces, and a number of papyri of the 3rd–2nd cent BC contain epigrams (*P. Firmin Didot*, *SH* 961, 974, 985, 986, 981, *PColon*. 128). Florilegia of all sorts were common from an early period (H. Chadwick, *RAC* 'Florilegium'; J. Barns, *CQ* 1950–1), but the first artistically arranged anthology of epigrams still seems to be the *Garland* (Στέφανος) of *Meleager (2), *c*.100 BC. We now have at least three papyri of the *Garland* (*POxy*. 662 and 3324, *BKT* 5. 1. 75–6), all apparently abridged redactions or extracts. But our fullest source of information for both contents and arrangement remains the so-called *Palatine Anthology* (Pal. gr. 23 + Par. suppl. gr. 384 = *Anth. Pal.*), which preserves (*a*) Meleager's own preface (*Anth. Pal.* 4), listing every poet included; and (*b*) in *Anth. Pal.* 5–7, 9, and 12 a series of more or less unbroken blocks of epigrams by poets named in the preface. Parallels of arrangement between the sequence of erotica in *POxy*. 3324 and *BKT* 5. 1. 75–6, and *Anth. Pal.* 5 and 12 give some idea of Meleager's erotic book.

*Philippus (2) of Thessalonica compiled under *Nero another *Garland*, arranged (as the blocks in *Anth. Pal.* reveal) by alphabetical order of the first word of each poem and thematic arrangement inside the letter groups. The literary quality of the second *Garland* is generally lower, less love and more rhetoric. So far we have no papyri, but *POxy*. 3724 contains an *incipit* list of (mainly) epigrams by *Philodemus. Under (probably) Hadrian *Straton (3) produced his own collection of pederastic epigrams, and under Justin II (*c*.567/8) *Agathias a *Cycle* (Κυκλός) of epigrams by his contemporaries, arranged like Meleager's *Garland*.

Around AD 900 a Byzantine schoolteacher called Constantine *Cephalas put together a massive collection based on all these earlier collections, including those of Diogenianus, *Palladas, and much other material from a variety of sources, in particular a large number of inscriptional epigrams collected from various parts of Greece and Asia Minor by his contemporary Gregory of Campsa. Around 940 a scholar known as J (probably Constantine the Rhodian) produced in *Anth. Pal.* an amplified redaction of Cephalas (some 3,700 epigrams in all), adding much Christian and ecphrastic poetry. To this MS and its scholia we owe almost our entire knowledge of Greek epigram from Meleager to Agathias.

The epigrammatic contents of *Anth. Pal.* are conventionally identified as follows. 1, Christian epigrams; 2, an *ekphrasis of statues in a bath in Constantinople by *Christodorus; 3, epigrams from a Cyzicene temple; 4, prefaces of Meleager, Philippus, and Agathias; 5, erotica; 6, anathematica; 7, epitaphs; 8, epitaphs by *Gregory of Nazianzus; 9, epideictica; 10, protreptica; 11, convivial and satirical epigrams; 12, pederastica; 13, poems in various metres; 14, oracles, *riddles, and problems; 15, a miscellaneous appendix, including figure poems (*technopaignia) in the shape of an egg, axe, and wings. Blocks from Meleager, Philippus, and Agathias alternate with sections compiled and arranged by Cephalas himself.

Finally in 1301 Maximus Planudes produced in Marc. gr. 481 (his signed and dated autograph) a much reduced anthology based on an abridged Cephalas (not *Anth. Pal.* as sometimes held), but systematically rearranged in seven books with elaborate subdivisions. Book 6 is followed by extensive addenda taken from another source (also an abridged Cephalas, as the numerous duplications prove). Fortunately these two sources preserve 380 ecphrastic epigrams apparently omitted from the source of *Anth. Pal.* (misleadingly printed in modern editions as *Anth. Pal.* 16). Planudes deliberately omitted what he considered improper, and bowdlerized many erotica he included, using a knowledge of classical metre not possessed by Cephalas and J. But it is too simple to assume that all divergences between *Anth. Pal.* and Planudes are Planudean emendations. In particular, alternative author ascriptions have to be decided on an individual basis.

Many manuscript copies were made of Planudes' *Anthology* before it was finally printed by Janus Lascaris in 1494 (A. Turyn, Ἐπετηρὶς Ἑταιρείας Βυζαντινῶν Σπουδῶν 1972/3, 403–50; E. Mioni, *Scritti . . . C. Diano* (1975), 263–307). The sequence of epigrams in these MSS varies according to how Planudes' addenda were incorporated into his seven original books (Cameron, *Greek Anthology*, 345–62). *Anth. Pal.* was unknown during most of the Renaissance (lurking in London and Louvain), not brought to the attention of scholars till 1606 and not finally published till the 19th cent. Till then *Anth. Plan.* was *the* Greek Anthology, and exercised enormous influence throughout the Renaissance (J. Hutton, *The Greek Anthology in Italy* (1935) and *The Greek Anthology in France and . . . the Netherlands* (1946)).

The Greek Anthology is one of the great books of European literature, a garden containing the flowers and weeds of fifteen hundred years of Greek poetry, from the most humdrum doggerel to the purest poetry.

TEXTS H. Stadtmueller, *Anth. Pal.* 1–9. 563, 3 vols. (1894–1906); W. R. Paton, 5 vols. (Loeb, 1916–18); P. Waltz and others, 11 vols. with two still to appear (Budé, 1926–80); H. Beckby, 4 vols. with Ger. trans.,

notes, and excellent indexes, 2nd edn. (1967–8; the only complete edition based on *Anth. Pal.* and *Anth. Plan.*).

STUDIES C. Preisendanz, *Anth. Pal. phototyp. ed.* (1911); A. Wifstrand, *Studien z. gr. Anthologie* (1926); A. S. F. Gow, *The Greek Anthology: Sources and Ascriptions* (1958); A. S. F. Gow and D. L. Page, *Hellenistic Epigrams*, 2 vols. (1965), and *Garland of Philip*, 2 vols. (1968); D. L. Page, *The Epigrams of Rufinus* (1978); A. Cameron, *The Greek Anthology* (1993). See also EPIGRAM, GREEK.   A. D. E. C.

anthropology It is probably misleading, though not entirely inappropriate, to use this word to describe the ancient study of man and society. Misleading, because anthropology did not really exist as the kind of discrete discipline it is today (see ANTHROPOLOGY AND THE CLASSICS). What follows here is a very brief summary of some central anthropological themes from antiquity, gathered from a variety of sources and contexts, ethical, scientific, and literary.

The Greeks and Romans developed a range of ideas about their own identity and the identity of others; about the nature of human societies, their history, and organization. It is well known that many Greeks designated non-Greek speakers '*barbarian',—after the Greek verb for 'babble'—and language of course remained an important index of racial and cultural difference. (*Herodotus (1)'s *History* introduced many Greeks to foreigners and their customs for the first time: Hdt. 4. 183 notes that the Egyptian *Trogodytae 'squeak like bats'; elsewhere, e.g. Aesch. *Ag.* 1050, Hdt. 2. 57, Theoc. *Id.* 15. 87 ff., etc., strange tongues are likened to the language of birds.) Language served equally to differentiate Greek-speaking groups—the various Greek dialects had their own distinctive written as well as spoken forms. But thought was also given by poets, philosophers, doctors, and others to defining what it is to be human (an ἄνθρωπος), what separates mankind from animals and gods, men from women, men and women from children, and so on. Amongst many possible examples, one might mention the use of animal similes and metaphors in the Homeric epics (see HOMER) as aids to understanding human behaviour, *Semonides' misogynistic poem attributing various animal characteristics to different kinds of women (see ANIMALS, KNOWLEDGE ABOUT), the Hesiodic *Works and Days* (see HESIOD) where man is distinguished from brute beasts through his possession of justice, and medical works concerned with issues such as the physiological difference between male and female, and the validity of using the study of animal physiology and anatomy to illuminate the human body (see ANATOMY AND PHYSIOLOGY; EMBRYOLOGY; MEDICINE). To develop only the last point, many medical theories were formulated against a background of the assumed inferiority of the female sex. The natural world of *Aristotle—to take just one example—has man as opposed both to woman and mankind firmly placed in the centre; several hundred years later, the Methodist physician *Soranus in his *Gynaecology* was still investigating the implications for the study of pathology of his belief that there are diseases specific to *women (see GYNAECOLOGY).

Moreover, there was widespread and sustained interest throughout Graeco-Roman antiquity in explaining the progress and evolution of human—not just Greek—civilization, language, culture, and behaviour. Modern scholars have tended to condense the variety of ancient models of human history into two broad lines of argument. One line is represented most clearly by the Homeric and Hesiodic poems, and argues nostalgically that human society declined from an ancient 'golden age' through other ages of increasing metallic baseness to the present. The *'golden age' type of model is especially common in poetry (both

Latin and Greek) from *Pindar to *Juvenal and beyond. The other type of argument has it that civilization gradually progressed through the discovery of technological, political, and linguistic benefits. A fragment of the Presocratic philosopher *Xenophanes offers a convenient illustration of this type of position: 'The Gods did not show everything to mortals from the beginning, but through investigation mortals have discovered over time what is better' (DK 21 B 18). On this view, man has some control over his progress.

Two distinct threads have in turn been discerned in this developmental model of human society. One, which has something in common with an influential strain of ancient empiricism, is represented ultimately by *Lucretius (especially book 5 of *On the Nature of the Universe*), *Diodorus (3) Siculus, *Vitruvius, and parts of *Pliny (1), *Natural History* 7, and its origins are thought by many to lie with *Democritus of Abdera. This group tends to the view that accidental discoveries like that of *fire, the use of metals (see METALLURGY), links between diet and health, and so on provided the impetus for most major changes in society. On the second thread, the teleological view is taken that mankind's weakness in the face of a hostile world led to the development of essential means of protection. This 'challenge and response' model is associated with *Protagoras (in Plato's dialogue of that name), with *Plato (1) himself (who mapped out the ideal way forward in the *Republic*), *Aristotle, and to some extent the Stoic *Posidonius (2) of Apamea.

Behind this apparently straightforward dichotomous summary there lies much that is not at all straightforward. For a start, there was no single, orthodox 'Myth of the Golden Age' in which life for mankind becomes progressively worse with time. (Note, for example, the highly elaborate myth of ages set before the young Socrates at Pl. *Plt.* 269c–d.) Baser metallic ages, even in Hesiod, still have their good points, and Hesiod's golden age is apparently devoid of normal humans altogether—only godlike creatures remote and free from toil and grief (*Op.* 110–20). And the Roman encyclopaedist A. *Cornelius Celsus held (*On Medicine* 1, proem 1) that in the distant past medicine was only necessary for the treatment of wounds and other injuries because men lived virtuous and moderate lives. Yet the development of medicine, he suggests, has gone a long way towards counteracting the effects of the decline in moral standards.

Generalization, then, is difficult. Certain philosophical models which allow that human society is capable of improvement often insist that this improvement is dependent on men embracing the appropriate philosophical way of life. (This is as true of *Epicureans like Lucretius as it is of Plato.) Moreover, it should be added that even those who saw social institutions and the arts constantly progressing had no place for progress on the part of nature herself—say, by suggesting that animal species too might be in a state of constant development. On the contrary, philosophers and natural scientists from *Anaximander to Aristotle and beyond seem to have held that the successful adaptation of animals to their environment was simply the result of one-off changes in their form. See RACE.

The literature is copious. The most important ancient texts are discussed in T. Cole, *Democritus and the Sources of Greek Anthropology*, 2nd edn. (1990). See also L. Edelstein, *The Idea of Progress in Classical Antiquity*, (1967); G. E. R. Lloyd, *Science, Folklore and Ideology* (1983), and *The Revolutions of Wisdom* (1987), both with full bibliog.; J. P. Vernant, *Mythe et pensée chez les grecs* (1965; trans. *Myth and Thought Among the Greeks* (1983)).

J. T. V.

anthropology and the classics currently enjoy a fairly good relationship, but one which has never been stable. In the 19th cent. the interest of evolutionary anthropology in a 'savage' period through which all societies must pass meant that studies of contemporary simple societies could be used to illuminate the classical past. After the First World War, classicists reacted against what were perceived as the excesses of the work of Jane Harrison and the Cambridge school, in which it was claimed that knowledge of 'things primitive' gave a better understanding of the Greeks. Meanwhile, in social anthropology, the rise of the static structural-functional paradigm and an insistence on an identity as 'the science of fieldwork' combined to cause a rejection of history. In the last 50 years, the divorce between the subjects has been eroded from both sides, with comparative studies increasingly valued as enabling us to escape from our intellectual heritage and the specific—though, to us, self-evident—ways it has formulated questions and sought answers.

Anthropology is a comparative science, and in this sense the classical scholar may draw on specific comparisons between societies in order to show the range of possible responses to an issue, especially one which to us seems particularly in need of explanation, such as the Athenian epiclerate (see INHERITANCE, GREEK) or the Spartan system of *age classes. By examining other societies with a similar feature, it is possible to discover how it functions. It may be possible to extrapolate from this, filling in—if only hypothetically—some of the gaps in the ancient record.

It is, however, no longer the case that classicists only turn to anthropology in desperation, when faced with a strange custom which fails to make any sense. Current work which makes use of anthropology tends to be theoretically sophisticated, and has the advantage of making theory explicit, rather than working from assumptions which, because they are left unstated, the reader cannot criticize or modify. Such work may treat the surviving sources like the anthropologist's fieldwork informants, whose words cannot be taken at face value; the fieldworker may observe one thing but be told the opposite. A fuller integration of the classics and anthropology promises a more sophisticated approach to evidence as well as a challenge to the traditional boundaries between disciplines within classics.

There remain dangers for classicists; for example, adopting concepts from anthropology after they have ceased to be used there, or failure to appreciate the disciplinary context within which a particular anthropologist's work falls. This warning also applies to the tendency in recent work to concentrate on comparisons with present-day Mediterranean societies, perceived as appropriate because of similar patterns of public/private, male/female, honour/shame; in fact, the concept of a 'Mediterranean' society has itself been questioned in anthropology, as too homogenized, taking little account of variation. To date, more use has been made of anthropology in Greek studies, but the most recent work includes some on kinship patterns and family relationships in Roman society.

M. Bettini, *Anthropology and Roman Culture* (1991; It. orig. 1988); D. Cohen, *Law, Sexuality and Society* (1991); B. S. Cohn, *Comparative Studies in Society and History*, 1980, 198–221, and *Journal of Interdisciplinary History*, 1981, 227–52; E. R. Dodds, *The Greeks and the Irrational* (1951); M. I. Finley, *Use and Abuse of History* (1975), and *The World of Odysseus*, 2nd edn. (1962); J. E. Harrison, *Themis* (1912); S. C. Humphreys, *Anthropology and the Greeks* (1978); R. Redfield, *Arion* 1991, 5–23; J. Winkler, *The Constraints of Desire* (1990).

H. K.

Anticato or (probably less correctly) **Anticatones**, *Caesar's two-book contribution to the propaganda exchanges following the death of M. *Porcius Cato (2) in 46 BC. Laudations came first from *Cicero, then from *Brutus and *Fabius Gallus. *Hirtius replied to Cicero; Caesar's work followed, probably in speech form. He wrote it in Spain in early 45. A few fragments survive.

H. J. Tschiedel, *Caesars 'Anticato'* (1981).　　　　C. B. R. P.

Anticlea, daughter of *Autolycus (1), wife of Laertes, and mother of *Odysseus and Ctimene. Her ghost tells Odysseus how she died of longing for him (*Od.* 11. 84–5, 152–224; cf. 15. 353–65). She appeared in *Polygnotus' picture of the Underworld at Delphi (Paus. 10. 29. 8). *Sisyphus is often said to have been Odysseus' father by her (Aesch. fr. 175 Radt; Soph. *Aj.* 189, *Phil.* 417, etc.).

J. Escher, *RE* 1. 2424, 'Antikleia' 1; *LIMC* 1/1. 828–30.　　N. J. R.

Anticleides, of Athens (fl. early 3rd cent. BC), wrote a history of *Alexander (3) the Great (containing a long digression on Egyptian antiquities), a substantial mythological work reaching into historical times, perhaps as far as *Pisistratus, and an account of Delian antiquities (see DELOS). He favoured unusual versions and rationalizations of legends (like the atthidographers (see ATTHIS) and *Palaephatus) and invented romantic details of the Trojan War; some fragments show *Peripatetic influence.

FGrH 140; Pearson, *Lost Histories of Alexander* 251 ff.　F. W. W.; K. S. S.

Anticyra, an excellent Phocian port in the gulf east of *Cirrha, known for the hellebore (a medicinal plant) that grew nearby. Identified by Pausanias (10. 36. 5–10) with Homeric Cyparissus, it shared the history of *Phocis, being destroyed in 346 BC by *Philip (1) II, then rebuilt, and finally captured by T. *Quinctius Flamininus in 198 BC. Inscriptions and temple remains confirm its modern location at Palatia near Aspra Spitia.

PECS 60; *Lexikon der historischen Stätten* 119–20.　　W. M. M.

Antidorus (c.300 BC), of Cyme, may have been the first to abandon the name κριτικός and to call himself γραμματικός (Clem. Al. *Strom.* 1. 16. 79). He wrote a work on Homer and Hesiod, of which the form and content are unknown, and a treatise on λέξις, which was either a lexical study, perhaps of Homeric expressions, or a work on style (schol. Dion. Thrax, 3, 7, 448 Hilgard; schol. *Il.* 23. 638–9).

R. Pfeiffer, *History of Classical Scholarship: From the Beginnings to the End of the Hellenistic Age* (1968), 157–8.　　J. F. L.; N. G. W.

antidosis (ἀντίδοσις, 'exchange') in Athens was a legal procedure concerned with *liturgies. Liturgies were supposed to be performed by the richest men. If a man appointed to perform one claimed that another man, who had not been appointed and was not exempt, was richer than himself, he could challenge him either, if he admitted being richer, to perform the liturgy or, if he claimed to be poorer, to exchange the whole of his property for that of the challenger, who would then perform it. If the challenged man failed to fulfil either alternative, the case went to trial (*diadikasia*) by a jury, who decided which man should perform the liturgy; this was probably the most usual upshot, though actual exchanges of property sometimes did take place.

V. Gabrielsen, *C&M* 1987, 7–38; M. R. Christ, *TAPA* 1990, 147–69.　　D. M. M.

Antigenes (5th cent. BC), Attic *dithyrambic poet, who wrote a dedicatory poem for tripods won at the Dionysian competition (see DIONYSIA) by the Acamantis tribe (see PHYLAI). The poem, preserved at *Anth. Pal.* 13. 28, is written in Dionysiac language and composed in couplets (Archilochean, i.e. dactylic tetrameter

and ithyphallic; and cretic, surrounded by ancipitia, and Alcaic decasyllable).

TEXT D. F. Sutton, *Dithyrambographi Graeci* (1989), 19 f.
LITERATURE K. von Jan, *RE* 1/2. 2399; D. L. Page, *Further Greek Epigrams* (1981), 11–15; B. Zimmermann, *Dithyrambos* (1992), 40.

B. Z.

Antigone (1), daughter of *Oedipus and Iocasta, sister of *Eteocles, Polynices and Ismene.

*Sophocles (1)'s *Antigone* deals with events after the Theban War, in which Eteocles and Polynices killed one another (see SEVEN AGAINST THEBES). Antigone's uncle *Creon (1), the new king of Thebes, has issued an edict forbidding anyone to bury the body of the traitor Polynices. Antigone, despite efforts at dissuasion by Ismene, insists on defying the edict. She is arrested and brought before Creon, and proudly defends her action. He decrees that she should be imprisoned in a tomb and left to die, although she is engaged to his son *Haemon (3). Creon is left unmoved by Haemon's arguments against such punishment, but is finally made to change his mind by the prophet *Tiresias, who reveals that the gods are angry at the exposure of Polynices and the burial of Antigone. He buries Polynices but arrives at Antigone's tomb too late: she has hanged herself, and Haemon, who has broken into the tomb, kills himself in front of his father. Creon's wife Eurydice also commits suicide, leaving Creon a broken man.

Antigone's role in the play has been the subject of endless dispute, with some critics claiming that she is wholly in the right, others that she and Creon are equally right and equally wrong. Most would now agree that she is no saint (she is harsh and unfair to Ismene, and her defiance of male authority would have shocked an Athenian audience), but still find her somehow admirable. The dispute, and the fascination, will continue.

While her story is unlikely to be pure invention by Sophocles, there is no definite evidence as to her earlier history. Facts that may be relevant are:

1. We are told that in the epic *Oidipodeia* (fr. 2 Davies) Oedipus had children, not by his mother Iocasta, but by a woman called Euryganeia. The epic may have named the children of this union as Antigone, Ismene, Eteocles, and Polynices; certainly *Pherecydes (2) of Athens later did so (*FGrH* 3 F 95).

2. *Mimnermus (fr. 21 West) told a story about Ismene which is also mentioned in the Pherecydes fragment and illustrated on vases, but which is incompatible with her role in Sophocles (she was killed by *Tydeus, one of the attackers of Thebes). He may or may not have mentioned Antigone.

3. The *Seven against Thebes* of *Aeschylus, as we have it, ends with Antigone and Ismene mourning their brothers and Antigone defying a herald's edict against burying Polynices. But the role of the sisters in this play is thought to be a spurious addition influenced by Sophocles and by *Euripides' *Phoenissae.*

4. According to a dithyramb by *Ion (2) of Chios (fr. 1 Page), Antigone and Ismene were burnt to death in the temple of Hera by Eteocles' son Laodamas. It is uncertain whether this is earlier than Sophocles' play.

5. *Pausanias (3) (9. 25. 2) was shown a place at Thebes where Antigone was supposed to have dragged the body of Polynices, and this has been seen as reflecting a tradition older than Sophocles' play (in which the body is not moved); but such reasoning is unreliable.

Euripides too wrote an *Antigone*, according to which Antigone had a son, Maion, by Haemon. This must have some connection with a story in *Hyginus (3) (Fab. 72). Here Antigone, with the help of Polynices' widow Argeia, drags his body to the pyre of Eteocles. Antigone is arrested and Creon entrusts Haemon with the task of executing her, but instead Haemon lodges her with shepherds and pretends that she is dead. She bears him a son. Years later the son comes with her to Thebes to compete in some games, and Creon recognizes him as one of the Spartoi (descendants of the first Thebans) by a birthmark. In the end Haemon (evidently condemned by Creon) kills Antigone and himself. Probably Euripides' play dealt with the earlier part of this story (including Haemon's rescue of Antigone), while the later part (with Maion as a grown youth) comes from some later play, perhaps the *Antigone* of the younger *Astydamas. We also have fragments of an *Antigona* by *Accius.

Sophocles portrayed Antigone again in *Oedipus at Colonus*, where she accompanies her blind father in his exile. She is also a character in Euripides' *Phoenissae*, *Seneca's *Phoenissae*, and *Statius' *Thebais*.

LIMC 1, 'Antigone'; R. P. Winnington-Ingram, *Sophocles: An Interpretation* (1980); G. Steiner, *Antigones* (1984). A. L. B.

Antigone (2), daughter of Eurytion son of Actor, king of Phthia (see PHTHIOTIS). *Peleus was purified by her father after the murder of *Phocus and married her, with a third of the country for her dowry. Later she hanged herself out of jealousy (ps.-Apollod. 3. 13). A. L. B.

Antigone (3), daughter of *Laomedon, king of Troy. Because she vied in beauty with *Hera, the latter turned her hair into snakes. Afterwards Hera, or the other gods, turned her into a stork, which preys on snakes (Ov. *Met.* 6. 93–5 and late mythographers). A. L. B.

Antigonus (1) **I** (*c*.382–301 BC), 'the One-eyed' (Monophthalmos), Macedonian noble, was prominent under *Philip (1) II and governed Greater *Phrygia for *Alexander (3) the Great (334–323). Victorious in three battles over Persian refugees from *Issus (332), he remained unchallenged in his satrapy until he fell foul of the regent *Perdiccas (3) whom he denounced to *Antipater (1) in Macedon (322), unleashing the First Coalition War. For his services he was given command of the campaign against *Eumenes (3) and the remnants of the Perdiccan factions. In 319 he defeated both groups spectacularly, and Antipater's death, on the heels of his victories, encouraged him in his supremacist ambitions. He supported *Cassander against the regent *Polyperchon, and took the war against Eumenes (Polyperchon's appointee as royal general) into central Asia. The victory at Gabiene (316) gave him control of territory from the Hindu Kush to the Aegean, but his success brought immediate war with his erstwhile allies: Cassander, *Lysimachus and *Ptolemy (1) (315). The 'Peace of the Dynasts' (summer 311) briefly ratified the status quo, but it was a dead letter from the first. *Seleucus (1) I invaded Babylon in 311 with Ptolemy's support, provoking full-scale war, and Ptolemy resumed hostilities in 310. Antigonus directed his attention to the Greek world, broadcasting his predilection for freedom and autonomy, and ultimately reactivated the Corinthian League (see CORINTH, LEAGUE OF) of Philip II as a weapon against Cassander (303/2). Athens welcomed him and his son, *Demetrius (4) with open arms and exaggerated honours (307), and in the following year the two had themselves proclaimed kings (*basileis*; see BASILEUS). But the achievements belied the propaganda. The invasion of Egypt (306) was abortive, as was Demetrius' year-long siege of *Rhodes (305/4). Finally the

coalition of 315 was reforged. At *Ipsus (in Phrygia) the combined Antigonid forces were defeated decisively and Antigonus died in battle. His ambitions had been too patent, his resources inadequate to contain the reaction they provoked.

R. A. Billows, *Antigonus the One-Eyed* (1990); P. Briant, *Antigone le Borgne* (1973); Heckel, *Marshals*, 50 ff. A. B. B.

Antigonus (2) (*c*.320–239 BC), king of Macedonia (*c*.277/6–239 BC), son of *Demetrius (4) I and Phila, nicknamed 'Gonatas' (meaning unknown). He served under his father in Greece in 292, commanded his possessions there from 287, and took the royal title on Demetrius' death in 282, though he failed to gain Macedonia until 277/6. Before then his military ability won widespread recognition, not only in Macedonia, through a major victory near Lysimacheia in 277 over *Celts who had overrun Macedonia and Thrace. Cassandreia still resisted him for ten months but his dynastic alliance with *Antiochus (1) I, whose sister Phila he married, ended Seleucid competition. *Pyrrhus occupied western Macedonia and Thessaly in 274 but his death in 272 removed this threat. In Greece Demetrius' old naval bases—*Piraeus, *Chalcis, *Corinth, and *Demetrias—guaranteed Antigonus' influence, and although an alliance led by Athens and Sparta and supported by *Ptolemy (1) II Philadelphus tried to eject the Macedonians (in the '*Chremonidean War' of *c*.267–261), Athens finally had to capitulate. Subsequently Antigonus, in alliance with *Antiochus (2) II, took the offensive in Ptolemy's preserve, the SE Aegean—a naval victory near *Cos (perhaps 254) caused a modest spread of Macedonian influence which was reinforced by Antigonus' son *Demetrius (6)'s marrying Antiochus II's sister Stratonice. In Greece Antigonus became notorious for controlling cities by supporting tyrants, a practice which saved garrison troops but provoked serious local opposition, especially in the Peloponnese, where the *Achaean Confederacy exploited dissatisfaction to extend its influence, even taking Corinth in 243. Nevertheless Demetrias, Chalcis, and the Piraeus remained Macedonian. In Macedonia Antigonus seems to have aimed at restoring the court tradition of *Philip (1) II. In particular his own intellectual interests, fostered in his youth in southern Greece, led to frequent visits to Pella by historians, poets, and philosophers. The larger cities of the kingdom—at least *Amphipolis, *Pella, Cassandreia and *Thessalonica—encouraged by the stable conditions, acquired some limited rights of self-government, which were widely recognized before Antigonus' death. Antigonus also helped establish his dynasty by regulating the succession. His son Demetrius (6) played a major part, from the 260s onwards, both in military and civil capacities; some historians even think he used the royal title in Antigonus' last years. Antigonus' long period of rule—37 years—and cautious policies provided a desperately needed consolidation for Macedonia. Characteristic for his later reputation is his reported comment, even if not authentic, that kingship is honourable servitude.

W. W. Tarn, *Antigonos Gonatas* (1913); *HM* 3; R. M. Errington, *A History of Macedonia* (1990; Ger. orig. 1986); C. Habicht, *SCI* 1996, 131–4. R. M. E.

Antigonus (3) (*c*.263–221 BC), nicknamed 'Doson', 'the man who will give', regent and king of Macedonia 229–221. Son of *Demetrius (5) 'the Fair', who was half-brother of *Antigonus (2) Gonatas, Antigonus ruled at first as regent for *Demetrius (6) II's young son Philip (later *Philip (3) V), but after some initial military successes against invading Dardanians and Aetolians and rebellious Thessalians he was granted the royal title. He had already married Philip's mother Chryseis and adopted the boy, so dispelling suspicions that he might wish to usurp Philip's ultimate claim to succeed. Doson's reign is characterized by careful restorative diplomacy, in *Thessaly, where he allowed the Thessalian League to be reconstituted, but especially in the Peloponnese, leading to the restoration of Macedonian influence, which had largely vanished during Demetrius II's reign. He also visited *Caria around 227 and constructed a position of influence in the area around *Mylasa—his reasons are obscure—which Philip V could inherit. In the Peloponnese the *Achaean Confederacy was so oppressed by the Spartan king *Cleomenes (2) III that *Aratus (2) felt forced to approach Antigonus in 226. It was a fine opportunity for Antigonus to regain the Acrocorinth, which Aratus duly promised. In 224 Antigonus marched south, organized his allies into a Hellenic League under Macedonian presidency, restored Achaean influence in Arcadia and in 222 invaded Laconia. At Sellasia he crushed Cleomenes' army, occupied Sparta and supervised the reorganization of the revolutionary city. His sudden death, after bursting a blood vessel in battle with Dardanians in 221, left Macedonia to the 17-year-old Philip V; but before his death Antigonus arranged for experienced advisers to occupy the most important functions of state, thus confirming his reputation as a careful administrator who put public interests first.

N. G. L. Hammond and F. W. Walbank, *A History of Macedonia 3* (1988); R. M. Errington, *A History of Macedonia* (1990; Ger. orig. 1986); S. le Bohec, *Antigone Doson* (1993). R. M. E.

Antigonus (4), of Carystus (fl. *c*.240 BC), writer and bronzeworker, lived at Athens and (apparently) at *Pergamum.

Works An inferior anecdotal collection survives: (*a*) Ἱστοριῶν παραδόξων συναγωγή, collection of paradoxical stories (see PARADOXOGRAPHY) (*Rer. nat. scr. Graec. min.* 1. 8 f.); *Diogenes (6) Laertius and Athenaeus (1) use (*b*) *Lives of Philosophers*; (*c*) treatises on sculpture and painting (Plin. *HN* 1. 33, 34; 34. 84; etc.); (*d*) Περὶ λέξεως, on diction (Ath. 3. 88a; 7. 297a: probably this Antigonus).

A reliable biographer (see BIOGRAPHY, GREEK) with a flowing, periodic style, Antigonus achieved considerable popularity. His art-historical writing analysed style and authorship (e.g. Plin. *HN* 35. 67; [Zen.] 5. 82), and he was among the sculptors the Attalids (see ATTALUS 1–111) selected to celebrate their Celtic victories.

U. von Wilamowitz-Moellendorff, *Antigonos von Karystos* (1881); A. F. Stewart, *Greek Sculpture* (1990), 21, 269 f., 301 f. F. W. W.; A. F. S.

Antilochus, in mythology, son of *Nestor, mentioned several times in the *Iliad* as a brave warrior and a fine runner (e.g. 15. 569–70). He brings *Achilles the news of *Patroclus' death (18. 2 ff.), drives cleverly in the chariot-race (23. 402 ff.), and courteously cedes the second prize to *Menelaus (1) (596). His death is mentioned (*Od.* 3. 111); it took place (*Aethiopis*, whence *Pindar, *Pyth.* 6. 28 ff.) while he was defending his father against *Memnon (1), when *Paris had killed one of Nestor's horses and he called Antilochus to his help.

In art: *LIMC* 1 / 1 (1981), 830–8. H. J. R.

Antimachus, of Colophon, Greek poet and scholar (fl. 400 BC). He may have been taught by *Stesimbrotus of Thasos; Plutarch, *Lys.* 18. 8 says he competed at the Lysandreia festival in Samos in *Lysander's presence (therefore before 395 BC); his younger friend and admirer *Plato (1) sent *Heraclides (1) Ponticus (fr. 6 Wehrli) to Colophon to collect his poems.

Works Small fragments survive: the *Thebais* was an epic, prob-

ably in 24 books, narrating the first expedition against Thebes, and exhibiting a wide knowledge of earlier poetry. *Lyde* was a narrative elegy in at least two books, allegedly composed after the death of his wife or mistress Lyde. It included very diverse mythological episodes, e.g. the Argonautica, *Demeter's wanderings, *Oedipus, and *Bellerophon; unhappy love may have been one of its connecting themes. Other poems, *Deltoi, Artemis*, and *Iachine* (the title is probably corrupt), are mere names to us. Antimachus also produced an edition of *Homer and wrote on his life, claiming him as a fellow Colophonian; Homeric glosses, along with scholarly neologisms and obscure periphrases, are prominent in his poetry. In his combination of the roles of scholar and poet Antimachus is the precursor of the great Hellenistic poets of the next century, who however took very varied views of his work. *Callimachus (3) criticized the *Lyde* as 'fat and inelegant' (fr. 398 Pf.), but the form of his own *Aetia* may be in part modelled on it; *Posidippus (2) and *Asclepiades (2) (both of whom were allegedly among the '*Telchines' whom Callimachus attacked) praised it. *Apollonius (1) Rhodius alluded to his poems in the *Argonautica*, and explained one of his rare words in a scholarly work. But it appears that Callimachus' condemnation prevailed, and Antimachus' works were apparently not frequently read in antiquity: though *Quintilian 10. 1. 53 commends him, with reservations, as a writer of epic, the admiration felt for the *Thebais* by the emperor *Hadrian (Cass. Dio 69. 4. 6 = test. 31 Wyss) was clearly eccentric. (The tendency to use Antimachus' name as the antithesis to another poet, usually Homer, admired by the author does not necessarily imply familiarity with Antimachus' works.)

TEXT B. Wyss, *Antimachi Colophonii Reliquiae* (1936); *Lyde* frs.: West, *IE*² 2. 37–43; new frs. in *Suppl. Hell.* 52–79. Cf. R. Pfeiffer, *History of Classical Scholarship* 1 (1968), 93–5. F. W.

Antinoöpolis (mod. Sheik Abāda), a nome capital (see NOMOS (1)) of Middle Egypt east of the Nile, founded in AD 130 by Hadrian in memory of *Antinous (2) on a necropolis containing a temple of Rameses II. The via Hadriana linked it to the Red Sea. Its Greek constitution, modelled on that of *Naucratis, gave exemption from *liturgies elsewhere. Veterans and Hellenes from *Ptolemais (2) were enrolled. *Diocletian made it capital of the Thebaid. Considerable remains of public buildings survived in 1800. See ALIMENTA.

E. Jomard, *Description d'Égypte* 2 (1818), ch. 15, 1–44; A. Gayet, *Ann. Mus. Guimet*, 1897, 1902, 1903; J. Johnson, *JEg. Arch.* 1914; *ASAE* 1940–1; *Antinoe (1965–1968)—Missione Archeologica in Egitto dell'Univ. di Roma* (1974); *Antinoopolis Papyri* 1–3 (1950–67); A. Bernand, *Les Portes du désert* (1984), review in *Chron. d'É.* 1984, 359–70; E. Kuhn, *Antinoopolis* (1913); M. Zahrnt, *ANRW* 2. 10. 1 (1988), 669–706. W. E. H. C.

Antinous (1), son of Eupeithes (*Od.* 1. 383), ringleader of *Penelope's suitors, and first to be killed by *Odysseus, whose kingship he is said to have wished to usurp (*Od.* 22. 8–53).

K. Wernicke, *RE* 1. 2438–9 'Antinous' 1; O. Touchefeu-Meynier, *LIMC* 6/1. 631–4, 'Mnesteres' 2. N. J. R.

Antinous (2) (*RE* 5), from Claudiopolis (Bithynium) in Bithynia, born perhaps *c*. AD 110, was *Hadrian's companion on his longest provincial tour and generally regarded as the emperor's 'beloved': his death by drowning in the Nile in October 130, claimed by some to have been suicide or a ritual sacrifice, was mourned extravagantly by Hadrian. Antinous was deified, the city of *Antinoöpolis was founded near the place of death, and statues, cults, and festivals proliferated. See HOMOSEXUALITY.

R. Lambert, *Beloved and God* (1984); H. Meyer, *Antinoos* (1991); M. Zahrnt, *ANRW* 2. 10. 1 (1988), 669 ff.   A. R. Bi.

Antioch (1), in *Syria, one of the Seleucid royal capitals, on the left bank of the *Orontes, some 24 km. (15 mi.) from the sea, was founded in 300 BC by *Seleucus (1) I, in a favourable position between his Anatolian and eastern possessions, on the edge of a large and fertile plain. *Seleuceia (2), at the mouth of the Orontes, became its harbour. The king transferred thither the 5,300 Athenian and Macedonian settlers whom *Antigonus (1) I had planted at Antigoneia nearby in 307, and his successors enlarged the city and adorned it with splendid buildings. Little of Seleucid Antioch has survived, but it is known to have been laid out on a grid plan (see URBANISM). It contained a large Aramaic-speaking and also a Jewish community, whose privileges were said to go back to Seleucus I. The Antiochenes played a large part in the dynastic struggles of the later Seleucid era. After an interlude of Armenian rule (83–66 BC) it was annexed by *Pompey (64 BC) and became the capital of the province of Syria; it was made an autonomous city by Caesar (47 BC). Having sided with *Pescennius Niger it was in AD 194 degraded by *Septimius Severus, but in 201 restored to its former rank, to which *Caracalla added the title of colony. Antioch administered an extensive territory. With a population of around 250,000, it was the third city of the east, after *Alexandria (1) and *Seleuceia (1) on the Tigris, and later *Constantinople. Its wealth was derived above all from its being a centre of civil, military, and later ecclesiastical administration of much of the near east, but also from its position on the commercial road from Asia to the Mediterranean, and the production of wine and olive oil. Rivalry of the patriarchates of Antioch and of Alexandria and the conflicting theologies of the two sees contributed to the Christological controversies, which after the council of Ephesus (431) and Chalcedon (451) resulted in the establishment of separate Nestorian and Monophysite churches, and greatly reduced the influence of the patriarchs of Antioch. In the 6th cent. Antioch was weakened by earthquakes and plague. It was sacked by the Persians (540), and occupied by them 611–28. Deprived of its administrative role after being captured by the Arabs (641), Antioch survived, a smaller but still major city. For Antioch's personification in art see *LIMC* 1 / 1 (1981), 840–51.

K. O. Müller, *Antiquitates Antiochenae* (1839); G. W. Elderkin and R. Stillwell (eds.), *Antioch on the Orontes* 1–5 (1934–72); G. W. Downey, *History of Antioch* (1961); A. J. Festugière, *Antioche païenne et chrétienne* (1959); W. Liebeschuetz, *Antioch* (1972); *PECS* 61 ff. (archaeology); D. S. Wallace Hadrill, *Christian Antioch* (1985); J. D. Grainger, *The Cities of Seleucid Syria* (1990); H. Kennedy, in J. Rich (ed.), *The City in Late Antiquity* (1992), 181–98.   A. H. M. J.; H. S.; W. L.; S. S.-W.

Antioch (2) (Pisidian, or more correctly 'near Pisidia'), a city in Phrygia Paroreius north of *Pisidia, to be distinguished from the other Phrygian Antioch on the Maeander. It was a Seleucid foundation, peopled by colonists from *Magnesia (1) on the Maeander, occupying a strong site in the foothills of Sultan Dağ close to modern Yalvaç. Its fertile territory extended east to Lake Eğridir. The principal Hellenistic remains are at the nearby hilltop sanctuary of *Mēn Askaēnos, where there is an Ionic peripteral temple of the 2nd cent. BC. The temple estates were used to provide land for Roman *veterans of Legions V and VII when the city was refounded as Colonia Caesareia after the creation of the province of *Galatia in 25 BC. It was linked with the other Augustan colonies of the region and with the south coast by a military road, the *via Sebaste.

Antioch was the most important Roman colony in Asia Minor and the home of several senators and equestrians in the 1st cent.

AD, including L. Sergius Paullus, the proconsul of *Cyprus, whose advice may have caused St *Paul to pick Antioch as the main target of his first missionary journey in Asia Minor (Acts 13: 13–52). By the time of Paul's visit (*c.* AD 47) the city centre was dominated by an enormous imperial sanctuary, comprising a temple, porticoes, and a triumphal arch which celebrated Augustus' victories over the Pisidians and displayed a copy of the *Res Gestae*. Surviving structures of the imperial period include an aqueduct which fed a *nymphaeum and a large bath-house, a theatre, a decorated city gate, and the main street system (see URBANISM). From the time of Diocletian Antioch was the metropolis of the new province of Pisidia. Two large churches of the 4th cent. are still to be seen.

B. Levick, *Roman Colonies in Southern Asia Minor* (1967), and *RE* Suppl. 11. 49 ff.; S. Mitchell, *Anchor Bible Dictionary* 1 (1992), 264–5 and *Anatolia*, 2 vols. (1993), see indexes.   S. M.

Antioch (3) **Margiana** (southern Turkmenistan, 30 km. (18 mi.) east of modern Merv), situated in the narrow, fertile valley of the Murghab river, separated by the Kopet Dağ mountains on the west from *Parthia and bounded in the north by the Karakum mountains. Routes to it led from Aria (Herat) and from *Bactria, and thence to central Asia. *Antiochus (1) I (Strab. 11. 10. 2) reconstructed a foundation of *Alexander (3) the Great in the settlement area of the Achaemenid period. Soviet excavations revealed something of the layout of the site (Gyaur-Kale), which had been refounded in a large quadrangular pattern, crossed by two principal streets, intersecting at right angles; the Achaemenid citadel was taken within the fortification and seems to have served as the citadel of the new foundation. The excavations also discovered large sections of the surrounding walls, described by Strabo, though the date, Seleucid or Parthian, is at present uncertain. See URBANISM.

S. Sherwin-White and A. Kuhrt, *From Samarkhand to Sardis* (1993), 82 f. (with bibliog.).   E. H. W.; S. S.-W.

Antioch (4) **-Persis,** probably mod. Bushir, on the Persian Gulf, or perhaps Achaemenid Taoke (mod. Borazjan, 32 km. (20 mi.) from Bushir, on the main route inland to Shiraz and *Persepolis). Probably founded by *Seleucus I, it was recolonized by *Magnesia (1) ad Maeandrum for *Antiochus (1) I (OGI 233). It was a *polis, with characteristic Greek administrative and political institutions. It retained cult links with its mother city, Magnesia (OGI 233).

J.-F. Salles, *Proc. Sem. Arab. Studies*, 1981, 69–70; D. T. Potts, *The Arabian Gulf in Antiquity*, 2 (1991), see index; S. M. Sherwin-White and A. Kuhrt, *From Samarkhand to Sardis* (1992), see index.   W. W. T.; S. S.-W.

Antiochus (1) **I** (Soter) (*c.*324–261 BC), eldest son of *Seleucus (1) I and the Bactrian *Apame, crown prince (*mār šarri*) in Babylonia before he became co-regent with Seleucus I (292–281/0); then held responsibility for the 'Upper Satrapies', when he married Seleucus' second wife, *Stratonice, daughter of *Demetrius (4) Poliorcetes, for political as well as romantic reasons, since Demetrius still posed a threat. This apparent division of royal power (coins from the eastern satrapies, e.g. *Bactria, were still minted under the names of both Seleucus and Antiochus, and in inscriptions Seleucus' name took precedence) perhaps indicates both Seleucus' perception of the importance of the eastern part of the empire and of the need for royal authority there, and also of Antiochus' potential acceptability there as a half-Iranian king.

Antiochus was, with Seleucus I and *Antiochus (3) III, one of the most dynamic and successful of the Seleucid kings and played a crucial part in consolidating the empire, both territorially and institutionally. His huge colonizing and consolidating activity through the Seleucid empire, apart from many city foundations in Anatolia, include in the east, the oasis city of *Antioch (3) (Strabo 11. 10. 2), Soteira in Aria (region of Herat), and continued input for foundations such as *Ai Khanoum and *Antioch (4) - *Persis (see COLONIZATION, HELLENISTIC).

Antiochus' continuation of Seleucus I's work in Babylonia, using the Babylonian kingship as a political and religious focus for support is mirrored in the famous building inscription from the temple of Esida in *Borsippa, near Babylon (268), which also refers to the rebuilding of the temple of Esagila at *Babylon, in the rituals of which Antiochus also took part. The note of concord with Babylonian traditions and with Babylonian gods can be understood as intentional Seleucid policy of using Babylonian kingship as a vehicle for rule in *Babylonia, the core of the empire.

At his accession (281), Antiochus had to restore control of his father's empire, by military force, in many regions, e.g. revolts in Syria and in Anatolia, where dynasts in Bithynia and Pontus became independent, and reinforce Seleucid claims to *Thrace, which the kingdom continued to reiterate until the reign of Antiochus III. In this period *Sardis in Lydia became one of the Seleucid royal capitals (besides *Antioch (1) in Syria, *Seleuceia (1) on Tigris in Babylonia), as a base for political and military operations in the western parts of the empire. Antiochus was the first of the Hellenistic kings to organize an army to deal with the incursions into Anatolia of the Celts (Galatians) and their disruption of life in country and city. He is famous for his decisive victory over the Celts at the battle of Elephants, penning them back to a small area in the Halys region (see GALATIA). Antiochus was also in conflict with *Ptolemy (1) II over Coele-Syria and Phoenicia, but by the end of the 270s, peace had been restored with Coele-Syria and Phoenicia remaining under Ptolemy's rule and the Seleucid eastern empire apparently under control.

A. Kuhrt and S. Sherwin-White, *JHS* 1991, 71–86; S. Sherwin-White and A. Kuhrt, *From Samarkhand to Sardis* (1993). G. T. G.; S. S.-W.

Antiochus (2) **II** (*c*.287–246 BC), second son of *Antiochus (1) I and *Stratonice. His reign (commencing 261) is obscure because the sources are so limited. Involved in the 'Second Syrian War' (260–252), he tried to gain southern Syria, Palestine, and Phoenicia from *Ptolemy (1) II unsuccessfully, but maintained Antiochus I's possessions in Asia Minor (e.g. Lydia, Phrygia, Cilicia), while facing the independent development of the kingdom of Pergamum and the expanding empire of Ptolemy II. His marriage to *Berenice (2), daughter of Ptolemy II (252) and repudiation of *Laodice (2) with her children led, after his death, to war with Ptolemy (1) III and a dynastic struggle over the succession.

E. Will, *Histoire politique du monde hellénistique* 1 (1978), see index. G. T. G.; S. S.-W.

Antiochus (3) **III** ('the Great') (*c*.242–187 BC), second son of *Seleucus (2) II, succeeded to the *Seleucid throne as a young man, after the assassination of his elder brother, *Seleucus (3) III. He faced many problems within the empire: in the east, a rebellion in *Media led by the satrap Molon (222), with the support of the satrap of Persis, Alexander (brother of Molon); Molon invaded Babylonia, seized the royal capital, *Seleuceia (1) on Tigris, and took the title 'king'. In the west, *Achaeus (3), viceroy of Seleucid Asia Minor, was in revolt and in control of the royal capital of *Sardis. The Ptolemies still retained control of *Seleuceia (2) -Pieria in north Syria.

Within the next 25 years, Antiochus, 'restitutor orbis', overcame the revolt of Molon (Polyb. 5. 51–4), regained Seleuceia-Pieria (219), re-established control over Sardis (213), and in 212 began his *anabasis* to the 'Upper Satrapies', bringing *Commagene and *Armenia under direct Seleucid rule; he restored Seleucid suzerainty over *Parthia and *Bactria (210–206), renewed links with the *India of the *Mauryas (Polyb. 11. 39. 11–12) and, on his return, mounted a naval expedition to the *Persian Gulf, where the Seleucids controlled the island of *Icaros (2), and waged a campaign against *Gerrha, but in the end agreed a treaty that allowed the former status of the Gerrhaeans as independent to continue (Polyb. 13. 9. 4–5). It was as a result of these campaigns that Antiochus was given the epithet *megas* (Great), the *terminus ante quem* of which is 202 BC. In campaigns (202–198) Antiochus finally established lasting Seleucid control over southern Syria, Phoenicia, and Judaea after initial invasions (221, 219, 217, when he was defeated by *Ptolemy (1) IV at the battle of *Raphia). Then (198) Antiochus launched an onslaught against Ptolemaic possessions in *Lycia and *Caria, which he took over (new inscriptions attest to the disruption and turmoil that this caused to the local populations). He moved thence to *Thrace (197/6), where he refounded Lysimachea (Livy, 33. 38; App. *Syr.* 1). The campaign into Thrace, always (since Seleucus I) claimed as Seleucid, brought Antiochus up against the imperialistic Roman republic. In the protracted diplomatic exchange of 196–193, he and the senate were at cross purposes, and finally he invaded Greece. He was defeated by the Romans in two land battles, at Thermopylae in Greece and at Magnesia (see MAGNESIA, BATTLE OF) in Asia Minor (190). He also lost a naval campaign to them.

By the peace of Apamea (188), Antiochus ceded Seleucid satrapies in Anatolia, north of the *Taurus (e.g. *Lydia, *Phrygia, Mysia, Caria), retaining in southern Anatolia *Pamphylia and Rough and Smooth *Cilicia. He still ruled a huge realm, from southern Turkey, through Syria and Palestine to Babylonia, Iran, and central Asia. After his defeat by Rome, Antiochus was again on campaign to the 'Upper Satrapies,' where, disastrously, he pillaged the temple of Bel/Zeus in *Elymais, and died from his injuries.

Antiochus stands out as one of the most dynamic and successful of the Seleucid kings. The centrality of *Babylon (and so of Babylonia) and of his eastern empire is mirrored in a newly published Babylonian astronomical diary (188/7), which shows Antiochus participating in rituals in the temple of Esagila (Babylon), before he embarked on his ill-fated, second *anabasis*.

Antiochus was married (221) to *Laodice (3), daughter of Mithradates of Pontus, who gave Antiochus four sons, of whom *Seleucus (4) IV and *Antiochus (4) IV ruled as kings.

His reign was marked by continuous military campaigns to reconsolidate the Seleucid empire. He was also the first Seleucid to have organized, on a satrapal basis, a state *ruler-cult for the king, the *progonoi* (his ancestors) and, by 193, his queen, Laodice.

H. H. Schmitt, *Untersuchungen zur Geschichte Antiochos' des Grossen und seiner Zeit* (1964); E. Will, *Histoire politique du monde hellénistique* 2, 2nd edn. (1982); S. Sherwin-White and A. Kuhrt, *From Samarkhand to Sardis* (1993). See also ZEUXIS (4). G. T. G.; S. S.-W.

Antiochus (4) **IV** (Epiphanes) (*c*.215–164 BC), third son of *Antiochus (3) III, became king in 175. He sought actively to reconsolidate the remaining huge *Seleucid empire, from Cilicia and Syria eastwards, after the Peace of Apamea (188) had precluded the Seleucids from their possessions north of the *Taurus. His attempt to incorporate Ptolemaic Egypt and Cyprus (170–169/8) failed because Rome's victory over Perseus (2) of Macedon enabled Rome to order Antiochus from Egypt. His intervention in *Jerusalem, overturning Antiochus III's 'charter for Jerusalem' (following Antiochus III's capture of it from the Ptolemies), guaranteeing the worship of Yahweh and the extensive privileges of all those involved in the cult, in co-operation with an 'hellenizing party,' has, from the viewpoint of Seleucid historiography, resulted in a distorted and hostile picture of the king, presented in Maccabees 1–3 (see MACCABEES), whereas in reality Judaea was strategically and economically of minor importance. Antiochus was active as a benefactor of cities of Aegean Greece and of indigenous cities within the Seleucid empire. The great resources of military manpower remaining are reflected in accounts of the famous procession mounted by him at *Daphne (166/5), prior to his *anabasis* to the 'Upper Satrapies', a major military campaign, in which he met his death.

C. Habicht, *CAH* 8² (1989), 187 f.; O. Mørkholm, *Antiochus IV of Syria* (1966); S. M. Sherwin-White and A. Kuhrt, *From Samarkhand to Sardis* (1993), 218 f.   G. T. G.; S. S.-W.

Antiochus (5) V (Eupator) (*c.*164–162 BC), infant, son of *Antiochus (4) IV, reigned less than two years through the regent Lysias, and was put to death in *Antioch (1) when *Demetrius (10) I seized the throne. Importantly, he re-established Antiochus III's 'charter for Jerusalem'.   G. T. G.; S. S.-W.

Antiochus (6) VI (Epiphanes) (*c.*148–138 BC), infant, son of *Alexander (10) Balas and Cleopatra Thea (daughter of Ptolemy (1) VI). In the revolt at Antioch (1) against *Demetrius (11) II he was put forward by the general Diodotus (later called Tryphon) as heir to the throne formerly usurped by his father. Tryphon soon deposed (142) and killed him (138).

E. Will, *Histoire politique du monde hellénistique* 2 (1982), 404 f.
                    G. T. G.; S. S.-W.

Antiochus (7) VII (Sidetes) (*c.*159–129 BC) second son of *Demetrius (10) I, succeeded his brother *Demetrius (11) II, who had become a prisoner in Parthia (130). Able and dynamic, he quickly defeated and killed the pretender Tryphon in *Antioch (1) (138), reconquered Palestine (135–134) and recovered Babylonia from Parthia (130). But Mithradates I of Parthia's final defeat of him in battle and his death enabled Mithradates to annex the Seleucid empire east of the Euphrates.

C. Habicht, *CAH* 8² (1989), 162 f.; E. Will. *Histoire politique du monde hellénistique*, 2 (1982), 410 f.   G. T. G.; S. S.-W.

Antiochus (8) Hierax (*c.*263–226 BC), second son of *Antiochus (2) II and *Laodice (2), co-regent with *Seleucus (2) II, became independent ruler of Seleucid Anatolia when his brother fought the 'Third Syrian War' (246–242). He defeated Seleucus' attempt to recover Anatolia ('War of the Brothers,' *c.*239–236), allying himself with traditional enemies of the Seleucid dynasty, Pontus, Bithynia, and Galatians, and marrying a Bithynian princess, daughter of Ziaelas and sister of *Prusias (1) I. The Galatian alliance, however, embroiled him with the rising power of *Attalus I of Pergamum, who drove him from Asia Minor (230–228). After an unsuccessful attempt to raise Syria and the east against Seleucus, he became an exile (227) and died by violence in Thrace.

H. Heinen, *CAH* 7²/1 (1984), 418 f.; E. Will, *Histoire politique du monde hellénistique* 1 (1982), 294f.   G. T. G.; S. S.-W.

Antiochus (9), the name of some kings of *Commagene:

Antiochus I (full title, *Theos Dikaios Epiphanēs Philorhōmaios kai Philhellēn*), son of Mithradates Callinicus and Laodice (daughter of the Seleucid king Antiochus VIII Grypus), reigned in Commagene from *c.*69 to *c.*36 BC. After the Roman victory over *Tigranes (1) of Armenia, *Pompey recognized Antiochus' kingdom (64) and added strategic holdings across the Euphrates (e.g. Seleuceia-on-the Eulaeus). As a cautious statesman Antiochus tried to find his own way in the Roman civil war and in the Romano-Parthian Wars: He announced the Parthian invasion of 51 to *Cicero in Cilicia, only nominally supported Pompey at Pharsalus (48), but later went over to the Parthian side (his daughter Laodice was the wife of the Arsacid king *Orodes II). After the defeat of the Parthian prince Pacorus (38), Antiochus was besieged in Samosata by P. *Ventidius and Antony (M. *Antonius (2)); he defended his capital successfully and got a favourable agreement. To his son and successor Mithradates II he left a strong and well-prepared kingdom. Antiochus created a *ruler-cult and a Graeco-Persian religious *syncretism which granted a place in the pantheon to him and secured his deification. Inscriptions and especially the archaeological remains of the sepulchral places of worship in *Arsameia-on-the-Nymphaeus (for Mithradates I Callinicus), at the Karakuş (for the royal women), and on top of the *Nemrut Dağ (for himself) prove the king's cultic reforms, the religious and artistic syncretism, and his appeal to his Persian and Macedonian royal ancestors.

R. D. Sullivan, *ANRW* 2. 8 (1977), 732 ff., and *Near Eastern Royalty and Rome* (1990), 193 ff.; J. Wagner, *MDAI (I)* 1983, 177 ff.; S. Şahin and B. Jacobs, *EA* 1991, 99 ff.   J. Wi.

Antiochus (II ?), son of I (above), was summoned to Rome in 29 BC by Octavian and executed for having murdered an envoy of his brother Mithradates II to Rome.

R. D. Sullivan, *ANRW* 2. 8 (1977), 775 ff.   J. Wi.

Antiochus IV enjoyed the friendship of the emperor *Gaius (1) in Rome, was installed by him in Commagene in AD 38, but was deposed soon afterwards. *Claudius restored his kingdom in 41 and he reigned until 72. His son Epiphanes was betrothed to Drusilla, the daughter of King *Agrippa I. Antiochus proved himself to be a loyal *client king to the Romans: He protected Cilicia against the Cietae (52), supported Cn. *Domitius Corbulo against the Parthians (54, 58) and in return received part of Armenia (60). Despite his help in 69–70, especially in the Jewish Revolt, he was deposed by *Vespasian in 72 at L. *Caesennius Paetus' initiative for having intrigued with Parthia. Antiochus ended up honourably detained and subsidized in Rome, where his sons joined him. See IULIUS ANTIOCHUS EPIPHANES PHILOPAPPUS, C.

R. D. Sullivan, *ANRW* 2. 8 (1977), 785 ff.   J. Wi.

Antiochus (10), of *Syracuse, probably the oldest of the western Greek historians (see HISTORIOGRAPHY, GREEK), active in the 5th cent. BC, after *Herodotus (1) but before *Thucydides (2). He wrote: 1. *Sicelica*, in nine books from King Cocalus to the congress at *Gela (*FGrH* 555 T 3). Thucydides' archaeology of Sicily (6. 2–5) including the dates for the foundation of the Greek colonies is probably based on Antiochus (this suggestion goes back to A. Woelfflin, *Coelius Antipater und Antiochus von Syrakus* (1874)). 2. *On Italy*, one book (*FGrH* 555 F 2–13); accounts of the foundations of several Greek cities in southern Italy, namely *Elea, *Rhegium, *Croton, *Heraclea (1), *Metapontum, *Tarentum (F 8–13), preserved in *Strabo. His historical method was the collection or rather selection of oral traditions recording the most credible versions (F 2).

Antiochus

FGrH 555. K. J. Dover, in H. Herter (ed.), *Thukydides* (1968), 344 ff.; F. W. Walbank, *Kokalos* 1968/9, 476 ff. L. Pearson, *The Greek Historians of the West: Timaeus and his Predecessors* (1987); K. Meister, *Die griechische Geschichtsschreibung* (1990); O. Lendle, *Einführung in die griechische Geschichtsschreibung* (1992). K. M.

Antiochus (11), of Ascalon (b. *c*.130 BC), Academic philosopher (see ACADEMY) who studied under *Philon (3) of Larissa, but later founded his own school. He joined L. *Licinius Lucullus (2) on a mission to *Alexandria (1) and the eastern provinces in 87/6. Cicero heard Antiochus' lectures at Athens in 79 and held him in high esteem throughout his life. Antiochus died in 69/8 BC, shortly after the battle of Tigranocerta, which he witnessed, again in the company of Lucullus.

According to Cicero, Antiochus left Philon's Academy because of its scepticism (see SCEPTICS), and embraced a version of dogmatism hardly distinguishable from Stoic doctrine (see STOICISM). Antiochus himself maintained that the Stoics, together with the *Peripatetics, were the legitimate heirs of *Plato (1)'s philosophy, while the scepticism of the Academics from *Arcesilaus (1) on had been an aberration. He therefore called his school the Old *Academy.

Antiochus is known to have written a work on epistemology in two volumes (Κανονικά); the *Sosus*, probably a dialogue, in which he argued against the thesis of his teacher Philon that the tradition of the Academy had been uninterrupted throughout its sceptical period; and a book about the gods. Cicero tells us that he also wrote on other subjects, notably ethics. While Antiochus' epistemology was undoubtedly Stoic (see Cicero's *Lucullus*), he adopted some Peripatetic views in his ethics (Cicero, *Fin.* 5), claiming that the difference between Stoic and Peripatetic ethics was merely terminological.

His school does not seem to have continued beyond the time of his brother and successor Aristus. It is not clear whether Antiochus had any influence on the newly developing Platonism of his time.

SOURCES see H. J. Mette, *Lustrum* 1986/7.
DISCUSSION J. Glucker, *Antiochus and the Late Academy* Hypomnemata 56 (1978); J. Barnes, in M. Griffin and J. Barnes, *Philosophia Togata* (1989). G. S.

Antiochus (12), of Athens (not later than AD 300), author of a popular compilation of astrological lore. See ASTROLOGY.

Ed. A. Olivieri, *Catalogus Codicum Astrologorum Graecorum* 12 vols. (1898–1953) 1. 108, and F. Boll, ibid. 7. 128. *RE* 1. 2494 and Suppl. 4. 32.

Antiochus (13) **Chuzon,** chief architect of the *Theodosian Code of AD 438, was a lawyer from Antioch (1). He was quaestor to *Theodosius (3) II from March 427 to April 430, praetorian prefect in 430–1, and consul in 431. A member of the commission set up to prepare the Code in 429, he presided over its second phase from 435 to 438 and was praised when it was promulgated as 'distinguished in all things' (*cuncta sublimis: Nov. Theod.* 1. 39). As praetorian prefect he reformed the tax system and he or his grandson of the same name rebuilt the city walls of Antioch. He died between 438 and 444.

PLRE 2, 'Antiochus (Chuzon 1)' 7; T. Honoré, *Zeitschrift der Savigny-Stiftung für Rechtsgeschichte* 1990, 183–9; J. Harries (ed.), *Essays on the Theodosian Code* (forthcoming). T. Hon.

Antiope, mother of *Amphion and Zethus, whom she bore to *Zeus and/or *Epopeus of *Sicyon. In *Odyssey* 11. 260–2 she is daughter of Asopus. This would locate her firmly in southern *Boeotia, and fits the traditions which give her native town as Hyria (Hes. fr. 181 M–W), the place where she gave birth at Eleutherae (Apollod. 3. 5. 5), and the place where her sons lived before *Thebes (1) as Eutresis (Strabo 9. 2. 28 (411 C)). A second version—related with variations by *Euripides, in *Antiope*, and *Apollodorus 3. 5. 5—makes her daughter of Nycteus, brother of Lycus (see LYCUS (1), end). The two brothers, descended from Chthonius, one of the *Spartoi, returned from exile in Hyria when Lycus became regent for Laius. Antiope was impregnated by *Zeus, her father took umbrage, and she fled to Sicyon where she married Epopeus. Nycteus died, Lycus attacked and slew Epopeus, and led Antiope back to Thebes. *En route*, at Eleutherae, she bore her sons, who were reared by a cattleman. Antiope was imprisoned by Lycus and his wife *Dirke, but years later escaped and was reunited with her sons, who then punished Dirke and Lycus.

Subsequently Antiope was married to *Phocus and was buried at Tithorea (Paus. 9. 17. 3: scene of a regular agricultural ritual): it is thought that this pairing is depicted on an Attic red-figure vase of the late 5th cent. (*LIMC* 1. 856), which suggests a possible Euripidean origin for this (perhaps even the *Antiope*: Hermes is *deus ex machina* and also on the vase). It is to be noted that the name Phocus reappears at Glisas, east of Thebes, but in an apparently entirely different context (Plut. *Am. narr.* 4 (774e)).

The connection with Epopeus is one of several legendary threads binding Thebes to Sicyon, home of *Adrastus (1). There was also a river Asopus in the territory of Sicyon (Paus. 2. 5. 2–3), which may have helped.

Apollod. *The Library*, trans. J. G. Frazer (Loeb, 1921); J. Kambitsis (ed.), *L'Antiope d'Euripide* (1972); E. Simon, *LIMC* 1 (1981), 854–7. A. Sch.

Antipater (1) (?397–319 BC), Macedonian statesman. Trusted lieutenant of *Philip (1) II, he represented the king at Athens in 346 and 338, and governed Macedon during the Danubian campaign of *Alexander (3) the Great (335). From 334 he acted as viceroy in Europe and in 331/0 dealt competently with a revolt in *Thrace and the subsequent war in the Peloponnese which *Agis III of Sparta instigated. Later his relations with Alexander were soured, and in 324 *Craterus (1) was sent to replace him in Macedon. Alexander's death (323) resolved the tension but unleashed the *Lamian War in which a formidable Hellenic coalition, headed by the Athenians and Aetolians, came close to victory. The advent of Craterus and his veterans redressed the balance, and the critical victory at *Crannon (August 322) allowed Antipater to impose the settlement which brought oligarchy and a Macedonian garrison to Athens. At the news of *Perdiccas (3)'s dynastic intrigues he declared war and invaded Asia Minor with Craterus (321). After Perdiccas' death he presided over the conference at Triparadeisus where—in turbulent circumstances—he assumed the regency and returned to Europe early in 319 with the kings in his custody. His death shortly afterwards left a legacy of civil war, thanks to his preference of *Polyperchon over his own son, *Cassander.

Berve, *Alexanderreich* 2 no. 94; R. A. Billows, *Antigonus the One-Eyed* (1990); Heckel, *Marshals*, 38 ff. A. B. B.

Antipater (2), of Tarsus (2nd cent. BC), Stoic, succeeded *Diogenes (3) of Babylon as head of the Stoa at Athens, and taught *Panaetius. His basic positions differed little from those of *Chrysippus, apart from his definition of the final good (Arius Didymus quoted in Stob. *Ecl.* 2. 76. 13–15) in terms of choosing rather than attaining natural advantages; it does not seem to have been influential (see Plut. *De communibus notitiis adversus stoicos* 1071a–1072f for criticisms). He wrote on subjects such as marriage, and argued against *Carneades' criticisms.

Testimonia in von Arnim, *SVF* 3. 244 ff.   J. A.

Antipater (3), of Sidon, author of about 75 mainly funerary or ecphrastic epigrams in the Greek Anthology (see ANTHOLOGY). *Anth. Pal.* 9. 151 commemorates the sack of *Corinth (146 BC). An inscriptional epigram on *Delos may be as late as 105 (G. Mancinetti Santamaria, *Delo e l'Italia* (1982), 79–89). He spent his last years in Rome, where Q. *Lutatius Catulus (1) knew him as a fluent improviser (Cic. *De or.* 3. 194).

Gow–Page, *HE*; T. B. L. Webster, *Hellenistic Poetry and Art* (1964), 204–8.   A. D. E. C.

Antipater (4), of Tyre (1st cent. BC), who introduced *Cato (Uticensis) to Stoic philosophy, died shortly before 44 BC. He wrote on physical, metaphysical, and ethical issues.   J. A.

Antipater (5), of Thessalonica, wrote (at Rome) 80-odd graceful epigrams included in the *Garland* of *Philippus (2), ecphrastic, dedicatory, and funerary. A client of L. *Calpurnius Piso (2), consul 15 BC; datable poems range between *c.*11 BC and AD 12.

Gow–Page, *GP*; Cichorius, *Röm. Stud.* 325 f.; G. Williams, *Change and Decline* (1978), ch. 3.   A. D. E. C.

Antipater (6), father of *Herod (1) the Great, dominated the politics of Palestine for a generation and paved the way for Herod. A wealthy Idumaean, he had close contacts with the monarchy of the *Nabataeans. From 67 BC, he promoted Hyrcanus, the heir to the kingdom of the *Hasmoneans, who had abandoned his claim in favour of his brother Aristobulus, but who, after civil war, was in 63 installed as high priest by Pompey. Services to Roman generals culminated in 48 in Antipater's provision, to Caesar at *Alexandria (1), of Jewish, Arab, and Syrian troops, as well as personal military assistance. Antipater's reward was to be *procurator in *Judaea and a Roman citizen. His sons, Phasael and Herod, governed *Jerusalem and *Galilee. In 43, he helped C. *Cassius Longinus (1) to raise money in Judaea, but was poisoned at the instigation of the Arab Malichus.   T. R.

Antiphanes, poet of Middle Comedy (see COMEDY (GREEK), MIDDLE), exhibited his first play about 385 BC (Anon. *De com.* 45 p. 10) and won thirteen victories (*Suda*, entry under the name), eight of them at the *Lenaea (IG 2². 2325. 146). The number of plays attributed to him in antiquity ranged between 260 and 365; we have 134 titles and over 330 citations, many of them extensive. Several titles suggest mythological burlesque (including Ἀνθρωπογονία); others are evidently drawn from the plot of the play (e.g. Ἀκοντιζομένη, Ἁλιευομένη); others, again, refer to types or professions (e.g. Ἄγροικος ('Rustic'), Ἀκέστρια ('Sempstress'), Φιλοθήβαιος ('Thebes-lover')—this last may have been political in character, but not necessarily to be dated to the time at which *Demosthenes (2) was arguing for an alliance with *Thebes (1)). Like all poets of Middle Comedy, Antiphanes is often cited by *Athenaeus (1) for his references to food and drink, but he is also the source of many gnomic passages in *Stobaeus' anthology (e.g. frs. 54, 86, 121 KA). Among other citations of exceptional interest are frs. 120 (on metaphysics), 189 (on the difference between the tragedian's art and the comic poet's), and 207 (on music).

Kassel–Austin, *PCG* 2. 312 ff. (*CAF* 2. 12 ff.).   K. J. D.

Antiphilus, of Byzantium, author of 50 epigrams in the Greek Anthology (see ANTHOLOGY), from the *Garland* of *Philippus (2). Some are ingenious paradoxes or descriptions of freak accidents, many are devoted to the sea, especially around his native city. *Anth. Pal.* 9. 178 thanks Nero for restoring the liberty of *Rhodes in 53 AD.

K. Müller, *Die Epig. des A. von Byzanz* (1935); Gow–Page, *GP.*   A. D. E. C.

Antiphon (1) (*RE* 14), of the *deme of *Rhamnus (*c.*480–411 BC), the first Attic orator whose works were preserved. From a prominent family, he participated in the intellectual movement inspired by the *sophists, taking a particular interest in law and rhetoric; he reportedly taught *Thucydides (2), among others. Many (though not all) scholars are now inclined to identify him with *Antiphon (2) 'the Sophist' (Xen. *Mem.* 1. 6), fragments of whose work *Truth* are concerned with the nature of justice and the relationship between *nomos* ('law, convention') and *phusis* ('nature').

Thucydides (8. 68) praises Antiphon highly for ability (*aretē*), intelligence, and power of expression, adding that he stayed in the background himself but made his reputation giving advice to others. He credits Antiphon with planning the oligarchic coup that overturned the democratic constitution of Athens for a few months in 411 BC (see FOUR HUNDRED). When democracy was restored, most leaders of the coup fled, but Antiphon and Archeptolemus remained to stand trial for treason; both were convicted and executed. Antiphon's speech in his own defence, a small papyrus fragment of which survives, was the finest speech Thucydides knew. When congratulated by *Agathon on its brilliance, Antiphon replied that he would rather have satisfied one man of good taste than any number of common people (Arist. *Eth. Eud.* 1232^b 7).

Antiphon was apparently the first to compose speeches for other litigants and thus the first to write them down. His clients included well-known political figures and foreign allies of Athens. We have six complete works: three courtroom speeches and three *Tetralogies*. All concern homicide cases, though the fragmentary speeches treat many other issues. The courtroom speeches and the datable fragments come from the last two decades of Antiphon's life (430–411). In *Against the Stepmother* (1) a young man accuses his stepmother of having employed a servant-woman to poison his father. He may have brought the case from a sense of duty, for he offers little evidence. In *The Murder of Herodes* (5) a Mytilenean is accused of murdering Herodes during a sea voyage: Herodes went ashore one stormy night and never returned. He defends his innocence by appeal both to facts and to probabilities (εἰκότα), and accuses his opponent of trumping up the charge for political reasons and personal gain. In *On the Chorus Boy* (6) a *chorēgos* (see CHORĒGIA) is accused of the accidental death of a boy who was given a drug to improve his voice. The *chorēgos* argues that he was not even present at the time and that the prosecution is politically motivated.

The *Tetralogies* are Antiphon's earliest works. Their authenticity is disputed, but their arguments concerning probability, causation, and similar issues fit the period and Antiphon's interests. Using the sophistic method of contrasting arguments (cf. *Protagoras' Antilogiae*) and displaying a self-conscious virtuosity, the *Tetralogies* illustrate methods of argument that could be applied to a wide variety of cases. Each consists of four speeches for hypothetical cases, two on each side. In the *First Tetralogy* (2) a man is murdered and circumstantial evidence points to the accused, who argues that others are more likely (εἰκός) to be the

Antiphon

killers. In the *Second Tetralogy* (3) a boy is accidentally killed by a javelin; the defence argues that the boy himself, not the thrower, is guilty of unintentional homicide because he was the cause of his own death. In the *Third Tetralogy* (4) a man dies after a fight and the accused argues that the victim is to blame because he started it.

Antiphon stands at the beginning of the tradition of literary Attic prose. He is an innovator and experimenter; he is fond of antithesis (in both word and thought), poetic vocabulary, the use of participles, and occasionally extreme asyndeton. In comparison to successors like *Lysias, Antiphon lacks grace of expression, clarity of organization, and the vivid presentation of character, but the force and variety of his arguments may account for his success.

> For general bibliography see ATTIC ORATORS.
> TEXTS Blass–Thalheim (Teubner, 1914); Decleva Caizzi, *Tetralogiae* (1969); Gernet (Budé, 1923), with Fr. trans.; Maidment, *Minor Attic Orators* 1 (Loeb, 1941), with Eng. trans.
> TRANSLATION Morrison, in R. K. Sprague (ed.), *The Older Sophists* (1972): includes testimonia, speeches, and fragments of both orator and sophist.
> INDEX F. L. van Cleef (1895).
> See also K. J. Dover, *CQ* 1950; E. Heitsch, *Antiphon aus Rhamnus* (1984). M. Ga.

Antiphon (2), of Athens (5th. cent. BC), *sophist. Scholars are divided on whether he was identical with the orator (see ANTIPHON (1)). Works attributed to him include *Concord* and *Truth*; of the latter some papyrus fragments survive (DK B 44), critical of conventional morality from a standpoint of self-interest.

> Testimonia and fragments in DK 2. 334–70; Eng. trans. in R. K. Sprague (ed.), *The Older Sophists* (1972) (add P. Oxy 3647); Guthrie, Hist. *Gk. Phil.* 3; T. J. Saunders, *Proc. of the Aristotelian Soc.* 1977–8; D. J. Furley, in G. B. Kerferd (ed.), *The Sophists and their Legacy*, Hermes Einzelschr. 44 (1981); J. Barnes, *The Presocratic Philosophers* (1982), ch. 23 (a); F. Decleva Caizzi, in F. Adorno and others (eds.), *Corpus dei papiri filosofici greci e latini* (1989), 176 ff.; M. Ostwald, in M. Griffith and D. J. Mastronarde (eds.), *Cabinet of the Muses: Essays . . . T. Rosenmeyer* (1990), 293 ff. C. C. W. T.

Antiphon (3), tragic poet put to death by *Dionysius (1) I of Syracuse (Arist. *Rh*. 2. 6). Anecdotes belonging to him are attached to *Antiphon (1) in the biographical tradition (Philostr. *VS* 1. 15. 3, etc.).

> *TrGF* 1². 193–6; *Musa Tragica* 128–33, 286–7. A. L. B.

anti-Semitism See SEMITISM, ANTI-.

Antissa, small coastal *polis in NW *Lesbos; birthplace of the poet *Terpander. A bronze age site has been explored; the Classical town originated in the early geometric period. Three apsidal buildings (possibly temples), stretches of a probable city wall, and remains of a harbour mole have been identified. The Mytileneans strengthened the defences during their revolt of 428 BC (see MYTILENE). *Thrasybulus captured the town *c*.389; later it joined the *Second Athenian Confederacy. The Romans destroyed it in 166 BC because of its links with *Antiochus (4) IV, and its territory was given to *Methymna. In medieval times it moved inland.

> W. Lamb, *BSA* 1930–2; N. Spencer, *BSA* 1995; *IG* 12, Suppl. p. 32; *RE* 1/2 (1894), 2535–6. D. G. J. S.

Antisthenes (1) (mid-5th–mid-4th cent. BC), associate of *Socrates, one of those named by *Plato (1) as having been present at his final conversation. A professional teacher, he continued the sophistic tradition by writing voluminously on many subjects,

including ethics, politics, natural philosophy, epistemology, language, literature, and rhetoric, and in a variety of genres, including Socratic dialogues, declamations, and *diatribes against various people, including Plato.

He followed Socrates in holding that virtue can be taught and that it is sufficient for happiness, 'requiring nothing more than Socratic strength' (Diog. Laert. 6. 11). Consequently he stressed the austerity of the Socratic lifestyle, and was vehemently hostile to pleasures except those of a hard and simple life. This emphasis on the self-sufficiency and detachment of the virtuous agent was taken up by the Stoics (see STOICISM) and (with special emphasis on physical austerity) the Cynics; later writers treat Antisthenes as the founder of the Cynic tradition. See CYNICS; STOICISM.

He shared with *Cratylus, *Prodicus, and others an interest in the nature of language and its relation to reality (see ETYMOLOGY). He is among those (including *Protagoras and Prodicus) reported as having denied the possibility of contradiction. *Aristotle represents him (*Metaph*. 1024^b 32–4) as having derived this thesis from the view that anything can be referred to only by a unique formula specifying its nature. Aristotle also ascribes to 'followers of Antisthenes' (*Metaph*. 1043^b 23–32) the theory that only complex things can be defined, whereas simple entities are indefinable (a theory criticized in Plato's *Theaetetus*).

Following *Xenophanes and others, he was critical of conventional religion, maintaining that while in common belief (*kata nomon*) there are many gods, in reality (*kata phusin*) there is only one.

> F. Decleva Caizzi, *Antisthenis Fragmenta* (1966); G. Giannantoni, *Socraticorum Reliquiae* (1983); Guthrie, *Hist. Gk. Phil.* 3; H. D. Rankin, *Sophists, Socratics and Cynics* (1983); N. Denyer, *Language, Thought and Falsehood in Ancient Greek Philosophy* (1991), ch. 3. C. C. W. T.

Antisthenes (2), of *Rhodes (fl. early 2nd cent. BC), wrote a history, perhaps of Rhodes, down to his own time (used by *Polybius (1) via *Zeno (4)). He is probably the Peripatetic philosopher who wrote a history of the philosophical schools (Διαδοχαὶ φιλοσόφων). An important oracle, predicting the fall of Rome and preserved by *Phlegon, is attributed to him.

> *FGrH* 508; J. D. Gauger, *Chiron* 1980, 223–61. K. S. S.

Antistius Adventus Postumius Aquilinus, Quintus, senator from Thibilis in *Numidia, held important posts under M. *Aurelius. Decorated for service as a legionary legate in the Parthian War (AD 162–6), he became governor of Arabia and consul. Probably in AD 168, at the outset of the Marcomannic War, he held a special command over 'the defence zone (*praetentura*) of Italy and the Alps'. He later governed Lower Germany and Britain, being attested in the latter province only by an altar at Lanchester (*RIB* 1083). His son or nephew, Burrus, married M. Aurelius' youngest daughter.

> *PIR*² A 754, 757; A. R. Birley, *The Fasti of Roman Britain* (1981), 129 ff. A. R. Bi.

Antistius (*RE* 2) **Labeo, Marcus,** whose family came from *Samnium, was a leading Roman lawyer of the age of *Augustus and died between AD 10 and 22. His father Pacuvius, also a lawyer, was killed fighting for the republican cause. As a member of a commission to reconstitute the senate in 18 BC he showed his independent spirit. Out of sympathy with the new order, his political career stopped at the praetorship: the consulship belatedly offered him by Augustus he refused. Sextus *Pomponius (*Dig*. 1. 2. 2. 47) and Tacitus (*Ann*. 3. 75) contrast his attachment to republican principle with the obsequiousness of his contemporary C. *Ateius Capito (2). Taught by his father, C. *Trebatius Testa and others, he acquired expertise not only in law but in dialectics, language, literature, and grammar, which he brought to bear on legal problems. Author of many innovations, he divided his time equally between teaching in Rome and writing in the country, and composed in all some 400 books. He drew a line, as it were, under republican jurisprudence, which was henceforth cited largely through him. He was also, after C. *Aquillius Gallus, the first important figure to devote himself to legal science to the exclusion of political concerns. Sextus Pomponius speaks of him as the founder of the Proculian school, presumably because of his intellectual breadth and attachment to principle. In time his works were superseded, so that, though much cited by *Ulpianus, Justinian's compilers (see JUSTINIAN'S CODIFICATION) had available for excerpting only his *Pithana* ('Persuasive Views') and *Posteriora* (posthumous works) selected and edited by *Iavolenus Priscus.

Lenel, *Pal.* 1. 501–58; Bremer 2. 9–261; *PIR*² A 760; A. Pernice, *Marcus Antistius Labeo: Römisches Privatrecht im ersten Jahrhunderte der Kaiserzeit* (1873–1900); Kunkel (1967), 32–4; E. Seidl, *Studi Volterra* 1 (1971), 63–81; M. Bretone, *Tecniche e ideologie dei giuristi romani* 2 (1982).   T. Hon.

Antistius (*RE* 47) **Vetus, Gaius,** under whose father *Caesar had served in Further Spain as quaestor (69 BC), was Caesar's quaestor *pro praetore* in Syria (45–4). He opposed Q. *Caecilius Bassus (see CORNIFICIUS, Q.), but in 44 joined the Liberators (legate of *Brutus in 43: high praise in Cic. *Ad Brut.* 1. 11). He next appears as legate of *Octavian, tackling the *Salassi (35–34?), duly became consul (suffect 30), and, as consular legate, fought the *Cantabri (26–24). He was made *patrician, probably in 29 (*ILS* 948). His son was consul in 6 BC and his grandsons Gaius and Lucius in AD 23 and a few years later; L. *Antistius Vetus was his great-grandson.

Syme, *Rom. Rev.* and *AA*, see indexes.   T. J. C.; B. M. L.

Antistius (*RE* 53) **Vetus, Lucius,** of a patrician family from Gabii, consul with *Nero in AD 55, was legate of Upper Germany (55–6), but was recalled when planning a waterway to connect the Rhine (Rhenus) with the Rhône (Rhodanus). In 62 he vainly urged his son-in-law *Rubellius Plautus to take up arms against Nero. Proconsul of Asia (63/4), he anticipated condemnation by suicide (65). He was perhaps a source for *Pliny (1), *HN* 3–6.

W. Eck, *Die Statthalter der Germanischen Provinzen von 1.–3. Jahrhundert* (1985), n. 9 (pp. 23–4); Schanz–Hosius, 2. 653.   A. M.; M. T. G.

Antium (mod. Anzio), in *Latium. It was occupied from at least the 8th cent. BC by people with a material culture resembling that of Rome itself. It was certainly Latin in the 6th cent. BC (Dion. Hal. *Ant. Rom.* 1. 72; Polyb. 3. 22), but shortly thereafter *Volsci captured it, and for 200 years Antium was apparently the principal Volscian city. In the 4th cent. BC it was the centre of Volscian resistance to Rome, that ended only when C. *Maenius captured the Antiate fleet and made possible the establishment of a citizen colony (see COLONIZATION, ROMAN), 338 BC (Livy, bks. 2–8; Dion. Hal. *Ant. Rom.* bks. 4–10). Antiate pirates, however, continued active even after 338 (Strab. 5. 232). After being sacked by C. *Marius (1), Antium became a fashionable resort (Augustus had a villa here), with celebrated temples (App. *BCiv.* 1. 69, 5. 26; Hor. *Carm.* 1. 35) and an important *harbour. This was rebuilt by *Nero (who, like *Caligula, was born here); Nero also created a new colony, and there was an imperial villa. It was finally abandoned in the early medieval period.

M. Guaitoli, in *Quad. Ist. Top. Roma* 1981, 83 ff.; L. J. F. Keppie, *PBSR* 1984, 86 ff.   E. T. S.; T. W. P.

Antonia (1) (*RE* 'Antonius' 112), daughter of M. *Antonius (2) and Antonia, daughter of C. *Antonius 'Hybrida', in 44 BC was engaged to M. *Aemilius Lepidus (4), but the engagement was broken after the disgrace of Lepidus' father M. *Aemilius Lepidus (3), and her father gave her to Pythodorus, a wealthy notable of *Tralles. We hear no more about her, but their daughter married *Polemon (1) I of Pontus and, after his death, *Archelaus (5) of Cappadocia.   A. M.; T. J. C.; E. B.

Antonia (2) (*RE* 'Antonius' 113), elder daughter ('maior', Suet. *Ner.* 5. 1; wrongly 'minor', Tac. *Ann.* 4. 44, 12. 64) of M. *Antonius (2) (Mark Antony) and *Octavia (2), born in 39 BC, was the wife of L. *Domitius Ahenobarbus (2). Their children were Gnaeus, consul AD 32 (the father of *Nero), Domitia (wife of C. Passienus Crispus) and Domitia Lepida (mother of *Valeria Messallina).   T. J. C.; R. J. S.

Antonia (3) (*RE* 'Antonius' 114), younger daughter ('minor', Suet. *Calig* 1. 1; *Claud.* 1. 6) of M. *Antonius (2) (Mark Antony) and *Octavia (2), born 31 January 36 BC, married Nero *Claudius Drusus; their children were *Germanicus, Livilla (*Livia Iulia), and *Claudius (cf. *IG Rom.* 4. 206). After Drusus' death in 9 BC she refused to marry again, and after *Livia Drusilla's death brought up her grandchildren *Gaius (1) (the future emperor Caligula) and *Iulia Drusilla. Gaius, on his accession, conferred numerous honours upon her, including the name Augusta (see AUGUSTUS, AUGUSTA, AS TITLES), but soon found her criticisms irksome and, it was said, drove her to suicide (1 May 37). Claudius rehabilitated her memory.   T. J. C.; E. B.

Antonia (4) (*RE* 'Antonius' 115), daughter of *Claudius and Aelia Paetina, married in AD 41 Cn. Pompeius Magnus and afterwards Faustus Cornelius Sulla. Her first husband was put to death by Claudius, the second by *Nero. A story retailed by the elder *Pliny (1) that she was to accompany the conspirator C. *Calpurnius Piso (2) when he entered the praetorian camp after Nero's murder was rejected by *Tacitus (1) (*Ann.* 15. 53), probably rightly as she was not punished with the other conspirators. But later Nero had her killed as a revolutionary, though *Suetonius (*Ner.* 35) gives as the real reason her refusal to marry Nero after *Poppaea Sabina's death in 65. These stories reflect the threat posed by any husband of hers to Nero, especially as he had no heir.   A. M.; M. T. G.

Antonine emperors and period See ANTONINUS PIUS; AURELIUS, M.; COMMODUS; ROME, HISTORY 2.2.

Antoninus Liberalis, *mythographer, probably of Antonine times, published a Μεταμορφώσεων συναγωγή ('Collection of Metamorphoses') based on Hellenistic sources, e.g. *Nicander.

TEXT E. Martini, *Mythographi graeci* 2. 1, 61: E. Oder, *De Antonino Liberali* (1886); M. Papathomopoulos (ed. and trans.), *Antoninus Liberalis: Les métamorphoses* (1968).

Antoninus Pius, Roman emperor AD 138–61, born at Lanuvium in Latium in 86, was the son of T. Aurelius Fulvus (consul 89) and grandson of another Aurelius Fulvus (consul 70 and 85), from Nîmes (Nemausus). His mother Arria Fadilla was daughter of *Arrius Antoninus (consul 69 and 97), whose names he bore as well as Boionius from his maternal grandmother: T. Aurelius Fulvus Boionius Arrius Antoninus. He married *Annia Galeria Faustina (1), and became consul in 120. Apart from the traditional magistracies, his only posts were those of imperial legate in Italy (an innovation of *Hadrian), in his case in Etruria and Umbria, where he owned land, and proconsul of Asia (135–6).

His links with the Annii Veri, combined with his wealth, popularity, and character, led *Hadrian to choose him as adoptive son and successor on the death of L. *Aelius Caesar. Given *imperium and the *tribunicia potestas* (see TRIBUNI PLEBIS) on 25 February 138, he became Imperator T. Aelius Aurelius Antoninus Caesar and at Hadrian's wish adopted both the young son of L. Aelius (the future L. *Verus) and his nephew by marriage M. Annius Verus (Marcus *Aurelius). His accession at Hadrian's death, 10 July 138, was warmly welcomed by the senate, which overcame its reluctance to deify Hadrian at Antoninus' insistence and named him Pius in acknowledgment of his loyalty. His wife Faustina was named Augusta (see AUGUSTUS, AUGUSTA, AS TITLES) and his only surviving child, also *Annia Galeria Faustina (2), was betrothed to M. Aurelius Caesar, his nephew and elder adoptive son. Pius became consul for a second term and *Pater Patriae in 139, consul for a third term in 140 with M. Aurelius as colleague, and held one further consulship, in 145, again with M. Aurelius, whose marriage to the younger Faustina took place the same year. On the birth of a child to this couple in late 147, M. Aurelius received *tribunicia potestas* and Faustina (whose mother had died in 140) became Augusta. The dynastic succession thus clearly established—but, despite Hadrian's intention, the younger adoptive son received neither any powers nor the name Caesar—Antoninus' longevity and steady hand made 'Antonine' a byword for peace and prosperity. This impression is largely influenced by P. Aelius *Aristides' *To Rome*, delivered in 143 or 144, by the portrayal of the tranquil life of the imperial family, entirely confined to Italy, in *Fronto's *Letters*, by the impressive tribute to Antoninus in M. Aurelius' *Meditations*, and by the uniformly favourable attitude of the scanty historical sources.

Hadrian's policies were rapidly changed in some areas: the consular legates for Italy, unpopular with the senate, were abolished, and southern Scotland reconquered by the governor Q. *Lollius Urbicus, Hadrian's Wall being replaced by the '*wall of Antoninus' between Forth and Clyde. This campaign, for which Antoninus took the acclamation 'Imperator' for the second time in late 142, was the only major war, but Moorish incursions in North Africa were dealt with by sending reinforcements to Mauretania in the 140s, minor campaigns kept the peace in Dacia, a show of force at the beginning of the reign deterred a Parthian invasion, and in the late 150s a minor extension of territory in Upper Germany was marked by the construction of a new 'outer' *limes. Direction of military policy (and much else) was doubtless left to the guard prefect M. *Gavius Maximus, who held office for almost the entire reign. The statement in the SHA (*Ant.* 5. 3) that he kept 'good governors in office for seven or even nine years' seems to be mistaken; the senatorial *cursus honorum*—and other parts of the imperial system—settled down in a stable pattern, contributing to the emperor's popularity with the upper order. Two conspiracies against him are mentioned in the SHA (*Ant.* 7. 3–4), the second, that of Cornelius Priscianus, 'who disturbed the peace of the province of Spain' being thus referred to in the *fasti Ostienses* for 145, but no further details are known. A highlight of the reign was the celebration of Rome's 900th anniversary in 148, when Antoninus' otherwise thrifty financial policy was relaxed (by a temporary debasement of the silver coinage). He cut down on excess expenditure, although relieving cities affected by natural disasters, and left a surplus of 675 million denarii at his death. In spite of his conservatism and sceptical

attitude towards Greek culture, Greeks advanced to the highest positions in his reign (Ti. *Claudius Atticus Herodes (2), consul 143, being the best-known case); other provincials also rose, not least from Africa, helped by the prominence of Fronto, a native of Cirta. The long, peaceful reign allowed the empire a breathing-space after Trajan's wars and Hadrian's restless travels. Antoninus' last watchword for the guard, 'equanimity', sums up his policy well; but he was angry with 'foreign kings' in his last hours and clouds were looming. He died at Lorium near Rome on 7 March 161 and was deified 'by universal consent'.

SOURCES Literary: the short Life in the SHA is largely trustworthy; Cassius Dio's bk. 70, which covered his reign, was already lost in Byzantine times; the 4th-cent. epitomators add little, except the *Epit. de Caes.*, probably based, as the SHA, on Marius Maximus' *Vitae Caesarum*. Aelius Aristides' *To Rome*, ed. and trans. J. H. Oliver (1953), 871 ff., is important; further, Fronto's *Letters* and M. Aur. *Med.*; Philostratus, *VS* Inscriptions: the valuable collection by W. Hüttl, *Antoninus Pius 2* (1933), remains useful. Coins: *BM Coins, Rom. Emp.* 3 (1936); 4 (1940); Strack, *Reichsprägung 3*.
LITERATURE W. Hüttl, *Antoninus Pius 1* (1936); M. Hammond, *The Antonine Monarchy* (1959); E. Champlin, *Fronto and Antonine Rome* (1980); A. R. Birley, *Marcus Aurelius*, 2nd edn. (1987); Syme, *RP* 4. 325 ff.; 5. 668 ff.
A. R. Bi.

Antonius (*RE* 20), **Gaius,** second son of M. *Antonius (Creticus). *Caesar's legate in 49 BC, he was blockaded by a Pompeian fleet (see POMPEIUS MAGNUS (1), CN.), on Curicta in the Adriatic and forced to surrender. After his praetorship in 44 he went to Macedonia; the senate rescinded the appointment late in that year. He was besieged and captured in Apollonia by *Brutus (March 43); *Cicero urged Brutus to execute him. He tried to incite Brutus' troops to mutiny and was put under guard; when Brutus heard of the *proscriptions, he was executed (early 42).
G. W. R.; B. M. L.

Antonius (*RE* 22), **Iullus,** second son of the Triumvir Mark Antony (M. *Antonius (2)) and *Fulvia, born 43 BC, was brought up in Rome by *Octavia (2) and married in 21 to her elder daughter by C. *Claudius Marcellus (1) (consul 50 BC). Praetor (13), consul (10), and proconsul of Asia (7/6?), he was condemned (2 BC) for adultery with *Iulia (3), entailing designs on the Principate, and committed suicide. His son Lucius, last of the male line, died in AD 25. Iullus wrote verse, including an epic *Diomedeia* in 12 books; Horace addressed *Carm.* 4. 2 to him.

Syme, *AA*, see index; K. M. T. Atkinson, *Hist.* 1958, 327; Schanz–Hosius 2. 273.
T. J. C.; B. M. L.

Antonius (1) (*RE* 28), **Marcus,** praetor *pro consule* 102 BC, then proconsul, fought against the Cilician pirates (see CILICIA; PIRACY), triumphed late in 100, after participating in the action against L. *Appuleius Saturninus, and became consul 99. A friend of C. *Marius (1), with Arpinate connections, he delayed Q. *Caecilius Metellus Numidicus' return. As censors 97–96, he and L. *Valerius Flaccus (2) admitted Italians as citizens, thus prompting the *lex (2) Licinia Mucia (95). He defended M'. *Aquillius (2) and C. *Norbanus, was prosecuted under the law of Q. *Varius but acquitted, and served as a legate in the *Social War (3). Having turned against Marius, he was killed after Marius' return (87). He and L. *Licinius Crassus were the leading orators of their age, heard by *Cicero, who later drew idealized portraits of them, particularly in *Brutus* and *De oratore*. He professed disdain for Greek studies, and his oratory was simple, effective mainly through *actio* (delivery). His rhetorical treatise (the first in Latin after that of M. *Porcius Cato (1)) was left incomplete, and he did not publish his speeches.

ORF⁴ 221 ff.; E. Badian, *Chiron* 1984, 122 ff. (with references); U. W. Scholz, *Der Redner M. Antonius* (1963). For his epigram at *Corinth see S. Dow, *Harv. Stud.* 1951, 83 ff.   E. B.

Antonius (2) (*RE* 30), **Marcus**, 'Mark Antony', Roman statesman and general. The truth of his career and personality has been heavily overlaid by legend, as first hostile propaganda presented him as a villain, then romantic biography turned him into a figure of tragic self-destruction.

2. Eldest son of M. *Antonius (Creticus), he was born in 83 (or, less likely, 86) BC. His youth was allegedly dissipated. He distinguished himself as cavalry commander under A. *Gabinius (2) in Palestine and Egypt (57–4), then joined *Caesar in Gaul, where, apart from an interval in Rome (53–2), he remained till the end of 50; in 51 he was *quaestor. As tribune (see TRIBUNI PLEBIS) in 49 he defended Caesar's interests in the senate, fled to his camp when the 'last decree' was passed (see SENATUS CONSULTUM ULTIMUM), took part in the fighting in Italy, and was left in charge of Italy during Caesar's Spanish campaign. In 48 he served in Greece and commanded Caesar's left wing at *Pharsalus. Caesar then sent him to impose order on Italy as his *magister equitum (till late in 47), but he was only partly successful, and he held no further post till 44 when he was Caesar's consular colleague. On 15 February 44 he played a prominent role in the incident of the *Lupercalia, offering a *diadem which Caesar refused.

3. After the Ides of March he at first played a delicate game, combining conciliation of the Liberators with intermittent displays of his popular and military support. He acquired and exercised a strong personal dominance, but this was soon threatened by the emergence of *Octavian, and the two locked in competition for the Caesarian leadership. Octavian deftly acquired support and allies, and by early 43 Antony faced an armed coalition consisting of D. *Iunius Brutus Albinus, whom he was blockading in *Mutina, the consuls A. *Hirtius and C. *Vibius Pansa Caetronianus, both moderate Caesarians, and Octavian, backed by the senate's authority and Cicero's eloquence. In April he was compelled by reverses at Forum Gallorum and Mutina to retreat into Gallia Narbonensis. He was however joined there by the governors of the western provinces, M. *Aemilius Lepidus (3), C. *Asinius Pollio, and L. *Munatius Plancus, and subsequently reconciled with Octavian.

4. By the *lex Titia* (November 43) Antony, Lepidus, and Octavian were appointed 'triumvirs for the restoration of the state' for five years. (See TRIUMVIRI.) The *proscription of their enemies (especially the wealthy) was followed in 42 by the defeat of *Cassius and *Brutus at Philippi, which firmly established Antony's reputation as a general. By agreement with Octavian he now undertook the reorganization of the eastern half of the empire; he also received Gaul, strategically vital if there were to be any renewal of fighting in the west. In 41 he met *Cleopatra VII at Tarsus and spent the following winter with her in Egypt. Their twins Alexander Helios and Cleopatra Selene were born in 40. The defeat of his brother L. *Antonius (Pietas) in the Perusine War (see PERUSIA) compelled him to return to Italy early in 40, despite the Parthian invasion of Syria (see LABIENUS, Q.); but a new agreement was reached at Brundisium whereby Antony surrendered Gaul, which Octavian had already occupied, and married Octavian's sister *Octavia (2). The division of the empire

into east and west was becoming more clear-cut. At Misenum in 39 the triumvirs extended their agreement to Sextus *Pompeius, after which Antony returned with Octavia to the east. By 38 his lieutenant P. *Ventidius had expelled the Parthians from Syria. In 37, new differences between Antony and Octavian were settled at Tarentum, and the Triumvirate was renewed for another five years; but this time he left Octavia behind when he left for the east, and renewed his association with Cleopatra on a firmer basis. Their third child Ptolemy Philadelphus was born in 36.

5. This liaison had political attractions. Egypt was one of several important kingdoms which Antony strengthened and expanded; nor did he grant all that Cleopatra wished, for he refused to take territory from *Herod (1) of Judaea, another able and valued supporter. The allegiance of the east was courted by religious propaganda. By 39 he had already presented himself as *Dionysus in Athens, and he and Cleopatra could now be presented as *Osiris and *Isis (or *Aphrodite), linked in a sacred marriage for the prosperity of Asia (cf. Plut. *Ant.* 26). But in 36 Antony's Parthian expedition ended in a disastrous reverse, while the defeat of Sextus Pompeius and the elimination of Lepidus correspondingly strengthened Octavian. It still seems to have been some time before Antony accepted that a decisive clash with Octavian was inevitable. At first he continued to concentrate on the east, planning a further invasion of Parthia and annexing Armenia in 34: this was marked in *Alexandria (1) by a ceremony (hostile sources regarded it as a sacrilegious version of a Roman *triumph) after which Cleopatra and her children—including *Caesarion, whom Antony provocatively declared to be Caesar's acknowledged son—were paraded in national and regal costumes of various countries, just as if they might inherit them dynastically. The *propaganda exchanges with Octavian intensified in 33, then early in 32 Octavian intimidated many of Antony's supporters, including the consuls Cn. *Domitius Ahenobarbus (4) and C. *Sosius, into leaving Rome. Antony divorced Octavia; then Octavian outrageously seized and published Antony's will, in which he allegedly left bequests to his children by Cleopatra and requested burial in Alexandria. Octavian proceeded to extract the annulment of Antony's remaining powers and a declaration of war against Cleopatra: Antony would now seem a traitor if he sided with the national enemy.

6. The spring and summer of 31 saw protracted military engagements in western Greece. Antony's initial numerical superiority was whittled away by *Agrippa's skilful naval attacks, then during the summer Antony was deserted by most of his most influential Roman supporters, including Plancus, M. *Titius, and Domitius Ahenobarbus: they had allegedly been alienated by Cleopatra's presence. In September 31 Cleopatra and Antony managed to break the blockade at *Actium and escape southwards, but the campaign was decisively lost, and their supporters defected to Octavian in the following months. Antony committed suicide as Octavian entered Alexandria (August 30).

7. For all its romanticism, much of Plutarch's portrayal of Antony carries some conviction—the great general, with unusual powers of leadership and personal charm, destroyed by his own weaknesses. But it is easy to underestimate his political judgement. True, Octavian won the war of propaganda in Italy, but till a late stage Antony continued to have strong support from the east and from influential Romans (many old republicans preferred him to Octavian). He looked the likely winner until the Actium campaign itself, and it is arguable that military rather than political considerations sealed his downfall. His administra-

tive arrangements in the east were clear-sighted, and most were continued by Augustus.

8. His only literary publication was a pamphlet of c.33, 'On his own Drunkenness', evidently a reply to Octavian's aspersions rather than a tippler's memoir. Specimens of his epistolary style can be seen in *Cicero's correspondence, the thirteenth *Philippic*, and *Suetonius' *Augustus*.

9. Antony was married ?(1) to Fadia, though this is more likely to have been a careless affair; (2) to his cousin Antonia, daughter of C. *Antonius 'Hybrida', whom he divorced in 47; (3) in 47 or 46, to *Fulvia; (4) in 40, to Octavia. By Antonia he had a daughter *Antonia (1); by Fulvia two sons, M. *Antonius Antyllus and Iullus *Antonius; by Octavia two daughters, *Antonia (2) *maior* and *Antonia (3) *minor*, through whom he was the ancestor of the emperors *Gaius (1), *Claudius, and *Nero. His 'marriage' to Cleopatra would not have been seen as such by an Italian audience.

> Most of the source-material comes from Plutarch, *Antony* (see comm. of C. B. R. Pelling (1988)); Appian, *BCiv.* bks. 2–5 (see comms. of D. Magnino (1984) on bk. 3, and E. Gabba (1970) on bk. 5); and Cassius Dio bks. 41–51 (see comm. of M. Reinhold (1988) on bks. 49–52; other volumes are expected in the same series). The studies of J. Kromayer in *Hermes* 1894, 1896, and 1899 are still very valuable, esp. on military matters. On diplomacy and administration, see esp. H. Buchheim, *Die Orientpolitik des Triumvirn M. Antonius* (1960); on the politics of 44–30 R. Syme, *The Roman Revolution* (1939), is still unequalled. Modern biographies: R. F. Rossi, *Marco Antonio* (1959); H. Bengtson, *Marcus Antonius, Triumvir und Herrscher des Orients* (1977); E. G. Huzar, *Marcus Antonius: A Biography* (1978); F. Chamoux, *Marc Antoine* (1987).
>
> C. B. R. P.

Antonius (*RE* 32) **Antyllus, Marcus,** whose *cognomen* recalls Hercules' son Anto, the family's Tiburtine ancestor, was elder son of the triumvir Mark Antony (M. *Antonius (2)) and *Fulvia. In 37 BC at *Tarentum he was betrothed to *Iulia (3). He assumed the toga of manhood after *Actium and was executed by *Octavian after the capture of *Alexandria (1) (30).   G. W. R.; B. M. L.

Antonius Castor, perhaps a freedman of M. *Antonius (2), was one of the elder *Pliny (1)'s sources for botany (*HN* 25. 9). Pliny mentions that he possessed his own botanical garden.

> Schanz–Hosius, § 495. 3.

Antonius (*RE* 29) **(Creticus), Marcus,** son of M. *Antonius (1) and father of Mark Antony (M. *Antonius (2)) and of L. *Antonius (Pietas), an easy-going man, dominated by his wife Iulia, *Caesar's sister. As praetor (74 BC) he received an *imperium* rhetorically described as *infinitum* against the pirates (see PIRACY). Unsuccessful in western campaigns and oppressive in requisitioning (Cic. 2 *Verr.* 3. 213), he was disastrously defeated by Cretans in a naval battle and made a treaty with them (Diod. Sic. 40. 1). He died soon after.

> J. Linderski, *ZPE* 80 (1990), 157 ff.   E. B.

Antonius Diogenes, Greek writer of 'The Incredible Things Beyond *Thule' (Τὰ ὑπὲρ Θούλην ἄπιστα), a novel (see NOVEL, GREEK) in 24 books known only from *Photius' confusing epitome (*Bibl. cod.* 166) and some fragments. Quotation by *Porphyry dates him before c.AD250, papyri require no earlier date, and if, like Morgan, we reject parody by *Lucian any early imperial date remains open. Among many novelistic conventions (e.g. false deaths) Antonius carries to extremes that of presenting narrative through characters' stories: seven levels of subordination can be traced, and the whole was allegedly written on tablets by the protagonist Deinias and found in his grave during *Alexander (3) the Great's siege of *Tyre. Sorcery, travel (even to or near the moon), and *Neopythagoreanism bulk larger than love in this encyclopaedic novel.

> STANDARD EDITIONS S. A. Stephens and J. J. Winkler, *Ancient Greek Novels: The Fragments* (1993); M. Fusillo (1990) (both with comm.).
> TRANSLATION G. N. Sandy, in B. P. Reardon (ed.), *Collected Ancient Greek Novels* (1989).
> CRITICISM Rohde, *Griech. Roman* 269 ff; W. Schmid, *RE* 1 (1894), 2615–16, 2/2. 'Antonius (49) Diogenes'; Christ–Schmid–Stählin 2/2⁶. 819 ff; A. Lesky, *A History of Greek Literature* (1966), 862; E. L. Bowie, *CHCL* 1. 686 (=paperback: 1/4 (1989), 126); K. Reyhl, *Antonios Diogenes: Untersuchungen . . . Lukian* (Diss. Tübingen, 1969); G. Anderson, *Studies in Lucian's Comic Fiction* (1976), 1–7; J. R. Morgan, *CQ* 1985; J. S. Romm, *The Edges of the Earth in Ancient Thought* (1992).   E. L. B.

Antonius (*RE* 59) **Gnipho, Marcus,** a teacher of grammar and rhetoric (Suet. *Gram.* 7). After tutoring the young *Caesar, he set up school in his own house, where *Cicero heard him lecture on rhetoric in 66 BC. Suetonius refers to 'numerous' writings, and a commentary on *Ennius' *Annals* is independently attested, though his pupil L. *Ateius Philologus claimed that only two books *On the Latin Language* were authentic.

> Herzog–Schmidt, § 279.   R. A. K.

Antonius (*RE* 19) **'Hybrida', Gaius,** son of M. *Antonius (1). An officer under *Sulla in Greece and rewarded in his *proscriptions, he was prosecuted and escaped conviction by appealing to the tribunes. The *lex* (2) *Antonia de Termessibus* was passed in his tribunate. Expelled from the senate by the censors (70), he became praetor (66) with *Cicero's help, but in 64 made an election compact with *Catiline and was assailed by Cicero. As consul 63, he was bribed by his colleague Cicero with the province of Macedonia, agreed to march against Catiline, but left the fighting to M. *Petreius. Oppressive and unsuccessful in Macedonia, he was prosecuted *repetundarum* (see REPETUNDAE), vigorously defended by Cicero, but convicted. Recalled from exile by *Caesar, he became censor 42 under the Triumvirate.

> Asconius 82 ff., with Marshall, *Asconius Comm.* Gruen, *LGRR*, see index.   E. B.

Antonius (*RE* 79) **Musa,** physician to *Augustus whom he cured of a grave illness (Suet. *Aug.* 59). *Pliny the Elder links him with *Themison and his hydropathic therapies may place him in the tradition of *Asclepiades (3) of Bithynia. He also wrote on *pharmacology; nothing survives, but he is cited by *Galen (e.g. 12. 737–8 Kühn) and *Aetius (2) of Amida. Two works which are preserved under his name—*De herba botanica* ('on botanical herbs') and *De tuenda valetudine ad Maecenatem* ('on preserving health'; dedicated to *Maecenas)—are almost certainly spurious.   J. T. V.

Antonius Pallas, Marcus, freedman of *Antonia (3) and financial secretary (*a rationibus*) of her son, the emperor Claudius; brother of (?Claudius) *Felix. His wealth, success, and arrogant temper made him deservedly unpopular. Devoted to *Iulia Agrippina and alleged to be her lover, he successfully promoted her candidature in the competition after the execution of Messalina; he also hastened Claudius' adoption of her son. The senate voted him *ornamenta praetoria* and a sum of money: he refused the money and received public commemoration for virtue and frugality (Tac. *Ann.* 12. 53; cf. Plin. *Ep.* 7. 29. 2; 8. 6. 1, who indignantly quotes the senatorial decree inscribed on the tomb of Pallas on the via Tiburtina). After the accession of Nero, Pallas, like Agrippina, was gradually and firmly thrust aside from power. Compelled to resign his office, he stipulated that no questions should be asked, that his accounts be regarded as balanced. Finally, he was put to death by Nero, because of his wealth, it is said (AD 62). A papyrus attests his Egyptian estates.

PIR² A 858; S. I. Oost, *AJPhil.* 1958, 113 ff.　　　　　R. S.

Antonius (*RE* 23) **(Pietas), Lucius,** third son of M. *Antonius (Creticus), was quaestor in Asia 50 BC and in charge of the province for part of 49. As tribune 44, he carried a law allowing Caesar to appoint half the magistrates except for consuls; after Caesar's death he allowed Octavian to address a *contio* and later was made chairman of a commission to distribute public land (see AGER PUBLICUS) to *veterans and the poor. For his work on this (later annulled by the senate) he was made patron of the 35 tribes (see TRIBUS) and of the ex-military tribunes; he also (we do not know why) became patron of the *equites* and of the bankers (see BANKS) and was honoured with statues in the Forum (Cic. *Phil.* 6. 12 ff.). He served as a legate under his brother M. *Antonius (2) ('Mark Antony') in the war of *Mutina and, as consul 41, in co-operation with *Fulvia and, at least initially, with Antony's support (as the coins show), worked in Antony's interest against Octavian, trying to impress Antony's partisans by assuming the *cognomen* 'Pietas'. ('Pius' had been pre-empted by Sextus *Pompeius.) When he championed Italian cities against Octavian's veterans, Octavian, after securing the neutrality of Antony's commanders, attacked him. He was besieged at *Perusia and forced to surrender (40). Octavian pardoned him and sent him to a command in Spain, where he died.

Cic. *Phil.*; Cass. Dio 48; App. *BCiv.* 5; *RRC* nos. 516 f. (the coins); *ILLRP* 1111–12 (Perusia sling bullets).　　　　　E. B.

Antonius (*RE* 89) **Primus, Marcus,** born *c.* AD 20 at *Tolosa (Toulouse) in Narbonese Gaul, was according to *Tacitus (1) 'energetic, eloquent, skilled in stirring up feeling against others, effective in time of civil war and discord, rapacious, generous, a baleful influence in peacetime, but a great asset in war' (*Hist.* 2. 86). In AD 61 he was convicted of participating in the forgery of a will, but regaining his senatorial rank as a partisan of Galba, was given command of Legio VII Gemina in Pannonia. In 69 he declared for Vespasian, won over the Danubian armies, and ignoring exponents of a cautious strategy, led the invasion of Italy with dashing bravery, capturing *Aquileia, winning the second battle of *Bedriacum, and capturing Rome on 20 December. He was briefly in complete control, but C. *Licinius Mucianus outmanœuvred him by promising a provincial governorship, and broke his influence. Primus retired quietly to Tolosa and was still alive in 95 (Mart. 9. 99, 10. 23).　　　　　J. B. C.

Antonius (*RE* 96; Supp. 1) **Saturninus, Lucius,** *suffect consul AD ?82, commander of the army of Upper Germany, revolted at *Mogontiacum (probably 1 January AD 89). Hearing the news *Domitian marched north from Rome. Meanwhile, however, the governor of Lower Germany, *Lappius Maximus, who remained loyal, defeated and killed Saturninus in battle by the Rhine (perhaps near Coblenz). The usurper's German allies were said to be unable to cross to his assistance because of a sudden thaw (Suet. *Dom.* 6 f.; Cass. Dio 67. 11; Mart. 4. 11, 9. 84; *CIL* 6. 2066 = MW 15 (Arval Acts)). Saturninus was a *novus homo* (new man), and the causes of his action are a mystery. It marks a turning-point in the reign of Domitian, preceding other executions.

R. Syme, *JRS* 1978, 12 ff. (= *RP* 3. 1070 ff.); B. Jones, *The Emperor Domitian* (1992), see index.　　　　　R. S.; B. M. L.

Antony See ANTONIUS (2), M.

Antyllus (*RE* 3), 2nd cent. AD, physician, one of the *Pneumatists. He lived after *Archigenes, probably after Galen, and wrote treatises on *surgery, *dietetics, and therapeutics, none of which survives. Some of his work is cited by *Paul of Aegina, *Oribasius, and *Aetius (2) of Amida.　　　　　J. T. V.

Anubis, one of several local divine guardians of the dead in Egypt, originally in the form of a jackal, later as a human figure with a dog's head. As lord of the necropolis, he supervised embalmment, and conducted the judgement of the dead. In Hellenistic times, identified with *Hermes, as Hermanubis (Plut. *De Is. et Os.* 61 (375e)). Linked to the ideal funeral of *Osiris, he entered the cult of *Isis; in the inscriptions of the Serapeum at *Delos (3rd–2nd cent. BC) he has no association with death. In the Principate, he stands for the absurdity or wickedness of Egyptian religion (Verg. *Aen.* 8. 696–700; Joseph. *AJ* 18. 3. 4), later for its pious strangeness (Apul. *Met.* 11. 11).

J. C. Grenier, *Anubis alexandrin et romain* (1977).　　　　　R. L. G.

Anxur See TARRACINA.

Anyte of *Tegea (fl. early 3rd cent. BC), an Arcadian poetess, much admired in her time and thereafter. About eighteen of her Doric epigrams, mostly funerary, are in the Greek Anthology, and one is cited by Pollux 5. 48. Her lyrics are lost, but she translated some of *Sappho's spirit into her sensitive elegiac quatrains. She wrote epitaphs for animals, and was one of the first to write pastoral descriptions of wild nature (e.g. *Anth. Pal.* 16. 228).

Gow–Page, *HE* 1. 35 ff. (texts), 2. 89 ff. (comm.); *Suppl. Hell.* 33.　　　　　G. H.; A. J. S. S.

Anytus, a wealthy Athenian and democratic leader, best known as a prosecutor of *Socrates (399 BC). General in 409, he failed to prevent the loss of *Pylos (*Ath. pol.* 27. 5); at his trial he reportedly bribed the entire jury. After 403 BC he was a respected, moderate leader of the restored democracy. *Plato (1) (*Meno* 91) introduces him as a passionate enemy of the *sophists. His prosecution of Socrates for impiety was probably motivated less by religious concerns than by anger at Socrates' disdain for democratic politicians. We hear nothing of Anytus after 395; but there is no good reason to believe later reports that the repentant Athenians banished him for the prosecution of Socrates.

APF 1324.　　　　　M. Ga.

Aornos, a mighty 'eagles' nest' in the land of the Assacenae, located by Sir Aurel Stein at Pir Sar, beside a bend of the upper Indus on the border of Swat. Two great ridges, Pir-Sar and Una-Sar, converge at right angles; the 'rock' is Bar-sar ib Pir-Sar, cut off from the Una ridge by the Burimar ravine. The inhabitants of the surrounding towns (Massaga, Bazira, Ora) took refuge here. *Alexander (3) the Great took it by assault in spring 326 BC, though according to tradition the local *Heracles had failed to do so (Arr. *Anab.* 4. 25–30).

P. H. L. Eggermont, *Journal of Central Asia* 1984, 73–123; Bosworth, *HCA* 2 (1995), 178 ff.　　　　　P. B.

apadana, 'the public part of a royal palace'. Only attested at Susa, the Old Persian word is usually applied to the large multi-columned halls in the palaces at *Susa and *Persepolis, perhaps linked to the earlier architectural style of the Zagros (e.g. Hasanlu).

Apame

E. Herzfeld, *Iran in the Ancient East* (1941), 352; E. Porada, *Cambridge History of Iran 2* (1985), 793–809.
M. V.

Apame, name of several Iranian noblewomen. The best known was the daughter of Spitamenes, a Bactrian-Sogdian noble and opponent of *Alexander (3) the Great. Apame was married to Alexander's Companion (see HETAIROI) *Seleucus (1) I at *Susa in 324 BC (Arr. *Anab.* 7. 4. 6.). She bore him two sons, *Antiochus (1) I and Achaeus. Despite Seleucus' marriage to *Stratonice, daughter of *Demetrius (4) Poliorcetes, *c*.300, she retained a prominent position, shown by a Milesian inscription of 299 (*IDidyma* 480). Several of Seleucus' city-foundations commemorate her, the best known being *Apamea on the Orontes. Recent evidence shows that the name continued to be used in the Seleucid family: Antiochus II named a son Apames (Bab. Apammu, cf. Sachs–Hunger 1989, no. 245).

L. Robert, *BCH* (1984), 467–72; A. Mehl, *Seleukos Nikator und sein Reich* (1986); *Enc. Ir.* 'Apame' 3; S. Sherwin-White and A. Kuhrt, *From Samarkhand to Sardis* (1993), 25–27.
A. T. L. K.

Apamea, a city on the *Orontes, *Syria, which replaced the Macedonian military colony of Pella. It was founded by Seleucus I (or perhaps Antiochus I). It was the military headquarters of Seleucid Syria, and the place where Seleucid breeding of *elephants (for war) is attested (Strabo. 16. 2. 10). During the Principate it ruled a large territory; its citizen population numbered 117,000 under Augustus. Excavation has revealed mainly buildings and finds of the imperial period. See APAME.

J. D. Grainger, *The Cities of Seleucid Syria* (1990), see index; J.-P. Rey-Coquais, *PECS*, 66–7.
A. H. M. J.; S. S.-W.

aparchē, 'first-fruits', a gift to the gods consisting in a part representing the whole, and hence named 'from the beginning' (Gk. *ap-archai*, Lat. *primitiae*, Hebr. *bikkurim*). The swineherd *Eumaeus, having killed a pig for *Odysseus, cuts 'beginnings from the limbs' and burns them (*Od.* 14. 414–53). 'First-fruits' are a step from nature to culture: one renounces 'firsts' for the sake of 'Those who are First'. *Aparchai* could be either burnt, deposited at sacred spots, or sunk in water. They could consist of seasonal agricultural gifts (*hōraia*), or those vowed ad hoc. Measures of wheat, barley, wine, and meat could be stipulated as gifts to temples (as the Panhellenic *aparchai* in *Eleusis, *LSCG* 5) and could serve, in turn, for public festivals. See also FIRST-FRUITS.

Stengel, *RE* 1. 2666–8; W. H. D. Rouse, *Greek Votive Offerings* (1902; repr. 1976), 39–94; Burkert, *GR* 66–8.
I. M.

Apaturia, an *Ionian festival. (*Apellai (2) was a partial Dorian/Boeotian equivalent.) According to Herodotus (1. 147), Ionians are all those who 'derive from Athens and celebrate the festival Apaturia. All Ionians celebrate it except Ephesians and Colophonians.' Details are known almost exclusively from Athens. It is unique among Greek festivals in its special association with a particular social grouping, the *phratry: the phratries celebrated it, in the autumn month Pyanopsion, at their separate centres throughout Attica, and its main function was to enrol new phratry members (who by this registration acquired a title to *citizenship). It lasted three days, called (schol. Ar. *Ach.* 146) (1) Δορπία, from the 'dinner' the phratores held together on assembling in the evening; (2) Ἀνάρρυσις, from the 'drawing back' of the necks of the victims sacrificed to *Zeus Phratrios and *Athena Phratria that day; (3) Κουρεῶτις, the day of admission-sacrifices brought by the relatives of prospective new members: if the phratores ate of the animal, the candidate was thereby acknowledged. Three types of admission sacrifice are known, the occasions of which appear to have been: μεῖον, 'lesser', a preliminary offering made during early childhood; κούρειον, 'hair-cutting', on entry to the ephebate (see EPHĒBOI); γαμηλία, 'marriage offering', brought by newly-married phratores on behalf of their wives. Whether women other than wives (mothers of future phratores) were acknowledged by phratries is uncertain.

D. Roussel, *Tribu et cité* (1976), 133–44, 153–4; H. W. Parke, *Festivals of the Athenians* (1977), 88–92; S. G. Cole, *ZPE* 55 (1984), 233–8.
R. C. T. P.

Apellai (1) was a festival of *Apollo at Sparta and elsewhere, the orthography deriving from the Doric form (*Apellōn*): see APELLAI (2). At Sparta, the festival was monthly, on the seventh, and it was on this day that the stated meetings of the Spartan assembly were held. From this coincidence has arisen the erroneous modern notion that the assembly was called the *apella*. Actually, its name was the *ekklēsia*, as is corroborated by the existence of a 'little *ekklesia*' (*mikra ekklēsia*: Xen. *Hell.* 3. 3. 8). The identity and competence of the latter can only be guessed. The main *ekklēsia* comprised all Spartiate male citizens in good standing. With the concurrence of the *gerousia, and under the presidency of an *ephor, it had the right to vote on laws, decide on peace or war and the conclusion of treaties, elect ephors and other officials and members of the *gerousia*, appoint military commanders and emancipate *helots—all normally by shouting, not the counting of individual votes (Thuc. 1. 87).

Arist. *Pol.* 1273ª; Thuc. 1. 79–87; Plut. *Lyc.* 6, 26; *Agis* 8–11; Diod. Sic. 11. 50. G. E. M. de Ste. Croix, *The Origins of the Peloponnesian War* (1972), 346–9.
P. A. C.

Apellai (2) The principal annual celebration of this *Dorian festival of Apollo corresponded to the Ionian *Apaturia, at which new members of the *phratry and tribe (see PHYLAI) were formally admitted. The religious *calendars of many Dorian states contained the month Apellaios, as did that of *Delphi (*Syll.*² 438, inscription of the Labyadai phratry).

Nilsson, *GGR* 1³. 556; A. E. Samuel, *Greek and Roman Chronology* (1972); E. J. Bickerman, *Chronology of the Ancient World* (1980); M. Pettersson, *Cults of Apollo at Sparta: The Hyakinthia, the Gymnopaidiai and the Karneia* (1992).
P. A. C.

Apelles, painter, of Colophon, later of Ephesus (sometimes called Coan because of the Coan 'Aphrodite'). He is mentioned more frequently, and generally considered better, than any other painter. *Pliny (1) the Elder dates him 332 BC (from the portrait of *Alexander (3) the Great). He was taught first by Ephorus of Ephesus, then by *Pamphilus (1) of Sicyon. When in the Sicyonian school, he helped *Melanthius (2) to paint the victorious chariot of the tyrant Aristratus. He painted portraits of *Philip (1) II, Alexander (who allowed no other artist to paint him), and their circle, and a self-portrait (probably the first). Anecdotes connect him with Alexander, *Ptolemy (1) I, and *Protogenes. He died in *Cos while copying his 'Aphrodite', probably early in the 3rd cent.

About 30 works are recorded. He showed Alexander mounted and with a thunderbolt; also with the Dioscuri and Victory; and in triumph with War personified as a bound captive. Thus he fully reflected the eastern aspects of Alexander's rule in a Greek medium. His 'Aphrodite Anadyomene' (rising from the sea wringing out her hair) was in Cos, later in Rome. 'Sacrifice', also in Cos, was described by Herodas (4. 59). He is probably the Apelles who painted the 'Calumny' described by Lucian. The tone of his pictures was due to a secret varnish. He wrote a book on painting: he claimed to know when to take his hand from a picture (unlike Protogenes, his friendly rival), and that his works had charm, *charis* (unlike Melanthius'). His 'Nude Hero' was said to challenge nature herself; horses neighed only at Apelles' horses. See PAINTING, GREEK.   K. W. A.

Apennine culture is the term used to describe the material aspects (mainly ceramic) of the mixed economy attested along the Apennine chain between the Bolognese and the south-east tip of peninsular Italy from the middle (16th cent. BC) to the recent bronze age (13th cent.: 'sub-Apennine'). Particularly significant concentrations have been recovered in south-east Emilia, the Marche, Etruria and *Latium Vetus, Campania, Apulia, and on Lipari (where the Apennine material finds its closest stylistic affinities with that from the northern rather than the southern sites of the mainland). The chronological range, established by associations with imported Mycenaean pottery, sees an early preference for semi-nomadic pastoralism succeeded by stock-raising and settled agriculture; this development is accompanied by the abandonment (particularly notable in Apulia and Etruria) of coastal areas in favour of the interior, by the disappearance of decoration on the pottery, and by the spread of the cremation rite, adopted with varying degrees of alacrity. In its closing stages, the story of the Apennine culture is closely linked with that of the *terremare* (see TERRAMARA).

D. H. Trump, *Proc. Prehist. Soc.* 1958, 165 ff., and *PBSR* 1963, 1 ff.; S. M. Puglisi, *La civiltà appenninica* (1959); M. A. Fugazzola Delpino, *Testimonianze di cultura appenninica nel Lazio* (1976); G. Barker, *Landscape and Society: Prehistoric Central Italy* (1981).   D. W. R. R.

Apennines, Italy's limestone mountain backbone, branch off from the Alps near Genoa (*Genua). At first they are of moderate height (900–1,200 m.; 3,000–4,000 ft.), and run eastwards forming the southern boundary of *Cisalpine Gaul (Northern Apennines); then, near *Ariminum, they turn south-east, follow the line of the Adriatic coast and attain great altitudes – 2,921 m. (9,583 ft.) at the Gran Sasso (Central Apennines); approaching *Lucania they become lower again, swing south and occupy virtually all SW Italy (Southern Apennines: the granite Sila mountains of the Bruttian peninsula (see BRUTTII), although geologically distinct, are generally reckoned a prolongation of the limestone Apennines). Italy's volcanic mountains, however— *Albanus, *Vesuvius, Vultur—are independent of the Apennine system). The 1,300-km. (800-mi.) Apennine chain is not continuous and unbroken, but consists of tangled mountain masses of varying width, interspersed with numerous upland passes and fertile valleys suitable for agriculture or summer pasturage. Offshoots are numerous, e.g. Apuan Alps (Liguria; see LIGURIANS), Volscian mountains (*Latium); some are completely separated from the main range, e.g. mons *Garganus (Apulia). The Apennines feed most Italian rivers except the Po (*Padus) and some of its tributaries, but, not being perennially snow-capped, supply inadequate amounts of water in summer, when consequently the rivers become mere rills or torrent-beds. The Apennines contain numerous mineral springs but little mineral wealth. In antiquity their cheeses, wolves, bears, goats, extensive forests, and brigands were famous.

Polyb. 2. 16, 3. 110 includes Maritime Alps in the Apennines; Strab. 2. 128; 5. 211; Luc. 2. 396–438; Varro, *Rust.* 2. 1. 5,16; Plin. *HN* 11. 240, 16. 197.; D. S. Walker, *A Geography of Italy* (1967); G. Barker, *Landscape and Society: Prehistoric Central Italy* (1981), 11 ff.   E. T. S.; T. W. P.

Aper (*RE* 1), **Marcus,** an advocate (see ADVOCACY) of Gallic origin who rose to the praetorship in the middle of the 1st cent. AD and visited Britain. He is known only from *Tacitus (1)'s *Dialogus*, where he is portrayed vigorously defending forensic oratory in the modern style against poetry and older fashions.

PIR[2] A 910; Schanz–Hosius, § 428 γ; Syme, *Tacitus*, app. 91.

G. C. W.; M. W.

apex, a special kind of cap worn by Roman *flamines, *Salii, and some other priests. The word is said originally to have meant not the whole cap, but the spike or twig at the top of it, tied on with wool. The lower part of the head-dress was called the *galerus* and that of the *flamen Dialis* was the *albogalerus*, the white *galerus*, made of the skins of white victims sacrificed to *Jupiter. The *galerus* was a tight-fitting conical cap, visible in representations of *flamines* on reliefs. The *apex* achieved notoriety because *flamines* were obliged to resign if it fell off during a *sacrifice; such occasions were recorded.

Latte, *RR* 404.   H. J. R.; J. A. N.

Aphaea (Ἀφαία), a goddess worshipped in *Aegina, where the ruins of her temple (famous for its pedimental sculptures, now in Munich) are extant. She was identified with *Britomartis (Paus. 2. 30. 3); i.e. she was of similar character to *Artemis. For bibliography on the temple on Aegina see AEGINA.

H. J. R.; S. H.

Aphrodisias (mod. Geyre), was a *Carian city, probably established in the 2nd cent. BC as the political centre of 'the Plarasans and Aphrodisians' (Plarasans dropped from the description under Augustus); site of vigorous prehistoric and Archaic communities honouring a mother-goddess, called Aphrodite perhaps from the 3rd cent. BC and later identified with Roman Venus. That identification encouraged a special relationship with Rome and with the family of *Caesar; so Aphrodisias resisted *Mithradates (6) VI in 88 BC and the Liberators after Caesar's death, earning privileges which Rome conferred in 39 BC and confirmed up to the late 3rd cent. AD. The wall-circuit, c.3.5 km. (2.2 mi.) long and containing many inscribed blocks reused, a stadium, and columns have always been visible; excavation has now uncovered civic buildings and much sculpture, which is sometimes distinguished and often technically interesting—see APHRODISIAS, SCHOOL OF. Intellectual pursuits were prized too—famous Aphrodisians included the novelist *Chariton, the philosophers *Adrastus (2) and *Alexander (14), and, in the late 5th cent. AD, Asclepiodotus. Numerous inscriptions, including an 'archive' of official communications from Rome inscribed on a wall in the theatre, throw important light on Roman history, late antiquity, ancient entertainments, and the Jewish Diaspora.

It was associated with the province of Asia to the mid-3rd cent. AD, then became part, perhaps capital, of Phrygia-Caria, and, under Diocletian, capital of Caria, from which it derived its modern name.

K. T. Erim, *Aphrodisias: City of Venus Aphrodite* (1986), with extensive earlier bibliography. Selected recent work: J. de la Genière and K. T. Erim (eds.), *Aphrodisias de Carie* (1987); C. Roueché and K. T. Erim (eds.) *Aphrodisias Papers* (1990); R. R. Smith and K. T. Erim (eds.), *Aphrodisias Papers 2* (1991); C. Roueché and R. R. Smith (eds.), *Aphrodisias Papers 3* (1994). Sculpture: R. R. Smith, *JRS* 1987, 88–138; 1988, 50–77; 1990, 127–55; *Aphrodisias 1: The Monument of C. Julius Zoilos* (1993). Inscriptions: J. Reynolds, *Aphrodisias and Rome* (1982); J. M. Reynolds and R. F. Tannenbaum, *Jews and Godfearers at Aphrodisias* (1987); C. M. Roueché, *Aphrodisias in Late Antiquity* (1989), and *Perform-*

Aphrodisias, school of

ers and Partisans at Aphrodisias (1993). Coins: D. J. Macdonald, *The Coinage of Aphrodisias* (1993).   J. M. R.

Aphrodisias, school of The existence of an Aphrodisian sculptural school was first proposed in 1943, on the basis of numerous statues in Roman and other museums signed by sculptors bearing the ethnic 'Aphrodisieus'; examples include two centaurs from Hadrian's villa at *Tibur by Aristeias and Papias, now in the Capitoline Museum at Rome, and an *Antinous relief by Antonianus. Excavations at *Aphrodisias, begun in 1961, have confirmed a rich sculptural tradition beginning in the 1st cent. BC and lasting into the 5th cent. AD. Production on a large scale was facilitated by the existence of quarries of fine white *marble two kilometres (just over a mile) away. Portraits, architectural marbles (both narrative and decorative), *sarcophagi, copies, and small-scale versions of classical originals constitute the school's main output. Eclectic in style and highly proficient technically, the sculpture makes much use of polish and drill, and also of coloured marble for pictorial effect. Not only were the finished products widely exported, but Aphrodisian sculptors were much in demand in the cities of the eastern Mediterranean.

M. Squarciapino, *La Scuola di Afrodisia* (1943); J. M. C. Toynbee, Coll. *Latomus* 6 (1951), 29 ff.; K. T. Erim, *Aphrodisias* (1986); D. E. E. Kleiner, *Roman Sculpture* (1992), 243 f., figs. 133 f., 209.; C. Roueché and K. Erim, *PBSR* 1982, 102 ff.   A. F. S.

Aphrodisius See SCRIBONIUS APHRODISIUS.

Aphrodite (Ἀφροδίτη). Born from the severed genitals of *Uranus according to *Hesiod (*Theog.* 188–206), or in the Homeric version (see HOMER) daughter of *Zeus and *Dione (*Il.* 5. 370–417), Aphrodite is the representative among the gods of an ambivalent female nature combining seductive charm, the need to procreate, and a capacity for deception, elements all found in the person of the first woman, *Pandora (Hes. *Op.* 60–8). There is no agreement on her historical origins; the Greeks themselves thought of her as coming from the east (Hdt. 1. 105, Paus. 1. 14. 7), and in literature she is frequently given the name Cypris, 'the Cyprian'. (See CYPRUS.) The double tradition of her birth shows how the Greeks felt Aphrodite to be at the same time Greek and foreign, but also, on the level of mythology, that they perceived her as a powerful goddess whom it would be prudent to place under the authority of Zeus.

Aphrodite's cults extend very widely over the Greek world, though her temples and festivals cannot compete with those of the other great figures of the pantheon. *Cyprus is the home of her most famous cults, for instance at *Paphos and *Amathus. There, probably in the Archaic period, the name Aphrodite became attached to an indigenous goddess who was also subject to numerous oriental influences. In Greece itself, one or more cults of Aphrodite are known in every region. She was worshipped above all as presiding over sexuality and reproduction—necessary for the continuity of the community. Thus in many cities girls about to be married sacrificed to Aphrodite so that their first sexual experience might be propitious (e.g. Paus. 2. 32. 7, 34. 12). This is the particular sphere of Aphrodite, compared with other goddesses involved in marriage like *Hera and *Demeter, a function especially emphasized in the Argolid (see ARGOS (2)) by the mythological connections between cults of Aphrodite and the story of the Danaids (see DANAUS). The close bond which the Greeks felt to exist between human fertility and the fruitfulness of the land lies behind Aphrodite's connections with vegetation and the earth in general: as Melainis at *Corinth

(Paus. 2. 2. 4) and *Mantinea (Paus. 8. 6. 5) the 'black' Aphrodite shows her power over the 'black earth' as well as her links with the powers of the night. In Athens, Aphrodite ἐν κήποις, 'in gardens', was worshipped together with Athena at the *Arrhephoria, a rite concerned with fertility and with the sexuality of the *arrhephoroi* as future wives of citizens (Paus. 1. 27. 3). This Aphrodite was also worshipped by prostitutes. Epithets such as Hetaira ('courtesan', see HETAIRAI) and Porne ('prostitute') show her as protectress of this profession, whose essential stock-in-trade was seduction. Corinth was particularly well known for the beauty and luxurious living of its prostitutes, who certainly revered the local Aphrodite. All the same, it is unlikely that her sanctuary on Acrocorinth was the location of an institutionalized form of what is usually called 'sacred prostitution'. The only source for such a remarkable practice in a Greek context, *Strabo (8. 6. 21 (378–9 C)), places it in a vague past time, and is surely influenced by the eastern practices with which he was familiar. Herodotus also mentions a similar practice in several parts of the Mediterranean area, and his silence in regard to Corinth should invite caution. See PROSTITUTION, SACRED and SECULAR.

If Aphrodite was worshipped primarily by women, men also took part in her cult, notably in connection with her role as patron of seafaring (Aphrodite Euploia, Pontia, Limenia: e.g. IG 2². 2872, Paus. 2. 34. 11). Aphrodite is also concerned with magistrates in their official capacity, being the deity of concord and civic harmony. The title Pandemos, which is hers conspicuously in Athens (IG 2². 659), indicates her protection of the whole citizen body, but she can also be linked with a particular civic office (e.g. as Stratagis in *Acarnania (IG 9². 1. 2. 256), and as Epistasie on *Thasos (J. Pouilloux, *Thasos* 1, no. 24)). In this context, she is frequently associated with *Hermes, *Peitho, and the *Charites. Thus *Plato (1)'s interpretation of the epithets Urania and Pandemos as indicating respectively exalted and common love (*Symp.* 180^d–181) is completely unfounded. The title Urania, 'heavenly', occurs frequently in cult and refers to the power of the goddess who presides over every type of union. It is with this epithet that the name Aphrodite is used as the Greek designation of foreign goddesses, a process found already in *Herodotus (1) and which accelerates with the *syncretisms of the Hellenistic period. The title also expresses one of Aphrodite's ambiguities, making her simultaneously 'daughter of Uranus' and 'the goddess who has come from elsewhere'. According to Pausanias, there were several statues showing an armed Aphrodite, particularly at Sparta (3. 15. 10; 3. 23. 1). Considering the special characteristics of the upbringing of Spartiate girls, it is not too surprising that the goddess of femaleness should be given male attire, but the actual examples of the type scarcely permit us to see in her a war-goddess, except in connection with a protecting role such as she has at Corinth. Her association with *Ares, prominent in the literary tradition, has more to do with a wish to bring opposites together than with any similarity of function.

From *Sappho to *Lucretius, literature celebrates the power of love and the dominion of Aphrodite. Ares, *Adonis, Hermes, and *Dionysus are all at various times given as her lovers, as is the mortal *Anchises, but apart from a few isolated examples these associations do not appear in cult.

Farnell, *Cults* 2. 618 ff. (for the sources); W. F. Otto, *The Homeric Gods* (1955; Ger. orig. 1929), 91–103; A. Delivorrias and others, *LIMC* 2. 2–151; Burkert, *GR* 152–6; V. Pirenne-Delforge, *Les Cultes d'Aphrodite en Grèce* (Diss. Liège, 1992), and *L'Aphrodite grecque*, Kernos Suppl. 4 (1994).   V. P.-D., A. Mot.

Ap(h)thonius (*RE* 2), **Aelius Festus,** name under which is transmitted a metrical treatise in four books: composed (probably) in the first half of the 4th cent. AD, the work was merged with the *Ars grammatica* of Marius Victorinus by the mid-5th cent. (Keil, *Gramm. Lat.* 31–173). The name 'Ap(h)thonius' may be a corruption of '*Asmonius'.

Cf. Herzog–Schmidt, § 525. 1. *PLRE* 1. 335.　　　　R. A. K.

Apicius, proverbial cognomen of several Roman connoisseurs of luxury, especially in food, in particular M. Gavius Apicius (*PIR*[2] G 91), notorious resident of the resort of *Minturnae in the Tiberian period, i.e. early 1st cent. AD (he wrote on sauces and claimed to have created a *scientia popinae* ('eating-house cuisine'): Sen. *Helv.* 8). The collection of recipes (*De re coquinaria*) known by his name, is however 4th cent. (see COOKERY).

EDITIONS J. André (Budé, 1974); M. E. Milham (Teubner, 1969); L. M. Tromaras (1988).

TRANSLATIONS and practical interpretations: B. Flower and E. Rosenbaum (1958; reissued); J. Edwards (1984; repr. 1988).　　N. P.

Apion (fl. 1st cent. AD), son of Posidonius, a Greek (or Graeco-Egyptian) born in El Kargeh oasis, where he studied under *Didymus (1) and succeeded *Theon (1) as head of the *Alexandrian school. He lectured in Rome and elsewhere. In AD 40 he was part of the delegation sent by the Greeks of *Alexandria (1) to *Gaius (1) (Caligula) after the anti-Jewish riots; Josephus attacked him at length in bk. 2 of *Contra Apionem*. He wrote on Egypt (see Gell. *NA* 5. 14 for the story of Androcles and the lion); he called up (so he said) *Homer's spirit to ascertain the poet's parentage and birthplace, but published no account of the proceedings (Plin. *HN* 30. 6. 18) and compiled, *inter alia*, an alphabetically arranged Homeric *glossary, based, as was usual, on *Aristarchus (2), and preserved only in fragments and in the derivative work of *Apollonius (11) Sophista.

EDITIONS *FGrH* 616; S. Neitzel (1977).　　P. R. B. F.; N. G. W.

Apis, the sacred bull at *Memphis in Egypt, oracular 'herald' of *Ptah (cf. Plin. *HN* 8. 185), with distinctive markings (Hdt. 3. 28; Ael. *NA* 11. 10). The cult probably goes back to the earliest Old Kingdom. When the bull died, the body was embalmed and borne in procession to the subterranean 'great chambers' at Saqqara. Thousands of invocations found there, requesting Apis to bless life and name, testify to the cult's appeal to Egyptians. The embalmed bull was termed Osiris-Apis (Diod. Sic. 1. 85. 4; cf. Plut. *De Is. et Os.* 43 (368c)), from which in the Ptolemaic period was developed the Alexandrian cult of *Sarapis.

D. J. Thompson, *Memphis under the Ptolemies* (1988), 190–207, 284–96; G. J. F. Kater-Sibbes and M. J. Vermaseren, *Apis*, 3 vols. (1975–7) (catalogue only).　　R. L. G.

apocalyptic literature The apocalyptic literature composed by Jews and Christians in antiquity purports to offer information of God's purposes by means of revelation. In the apocalypses, understanding of God and the world is rooted in the claim to a superior knowledge in which insight of the divine through vision or audition transcends the wisdom of human reason. While an apocalyptic dimension has always formed a part of Jewish religion (evident in the material in the biblical literature which speaks of the prophet's access to the heavenly council), the writing of the extant Jewish apocalypses, most of which were preserved by Christians rather than Jews (mostly in Greek or in translations from the Greek), took place in a period which roughly spanned the career of *Alexander (3) the Great to the end of the *Bar Kokhba Revolt and may best be seen as the form

the prophetic tradition took at the end of the Second Temple period. The apocalypses are linked to the prophetic writings of the Hebrew Bible (the book of Daniel is an example), though their emphasis on heavenly knowledge and the interpretation of dreams links them with the mantic wisdom of the seers of antiquity. All the apocalyptic texts are distinguished from the prophetic by the range of their imagery and the character of the literary genre. Most apocalypses are pseudonymous (Revelation in the New Testament seems to be exceptional in this respect) and contain heavenly revelations mediated in different ways (heavenly ascents as the prelude to the disclosure of divine mysteries, an angelic revealer descending to earth to communicate information to the apocalyptic seer). Because in most of the extant apocalypses there is a particular focus on the destiny of the world, it is often stated that they offer evidence of an imminent expectation of the end of the world accompanied by the irruption of a new order. This is said by some scholars to contrast with a more material eschatology found in the rabbinic literature in which the future order of things evolves within history. This distinction is to be rejected as all the extant Jewish apocalypses offer an account of a hope for the future of the world which differs little from other non-apocalyptic sources.

The earliest apocalyptic material is probably found in the Enoch tradition, particularly in the collection of material known as 1 Enoch, many fragments of which have been discovered at Qumran (see DEAD SEA SCROLLS) and which may date from at least the 3rd cent. BC. That apocalypse contains material from a variety of sources and periods and includes legends about antediluvian heroes, revelations about astronomical calculations, geographical information, and heavenly journeys, all of which was to become typical of much of the apocalyptic literature. There was a flowering of apocalyptic literature after the First Jewish Revolt (2 Esdras, the Syriac Apocalypse of Baruch, and the Apocalypse of Abraham being examples), when discussion of *theodicy is added to the other interests of the apocalyptists, reminiscent in many ways of the book of Job.

In the rabbinic tradition (see RABBIS) the perspective of apocalyptic was severely circumscribed by confining the study of certain biblical texts with cosmological and theosophic content to well-trained interpreters, though it appears to have been more widespread than our sources suggest. The contrast between the apocalyptic literature and rabbinic literature is not as great as may appear at first sight. Care needs to be taken before drawing conclusions from the content of different types of text about the existence of ideological conflicts between rabbis and apocalyptists, as the genre of the literature explains the absence of the minutiae of law from the latter. Because apocalyptic has been so consistently linked with eschatology its visionary and mystical elements have been ignored, but the mystical element of apocalyptic literature continued to be a central component of rabbinic religion. In Christianity apocalyptic was initially central to primitive Christianity, as the central role which visions and revelations played in the various accounts of the Christian Church's emergence in the New Testament make plain. It fell out of favour as a result of its importance in some Gnostic and Montanist circles (a fact which led to suspicion of the book of Revelation; see GNOSTICISM; MONTANISM), though the distinctive dualism of apocalyptic theology lies at the heart of *Augustine's *City of God*.

J. H. Charlesworth, *The Old Testament Pseudepigrapha*, 2 vols. (1983); E. R. Dodds, *Pagan and Christian in an Age of Anxiety* (1965); M. Hengel, *Judaism and Hellenism* (1974); C. Rowland, *The Open Heaven* (1982); M. Stone, *Jewish Literature of the Second Temple Period* (1984).　　C. C. R.

apodektai ('receivers'), at Athens, a board of officials who received the state's revenues and, in the 5th cent. BC, paid them into the central state treasury, in the 4th, apportioned them (*merizein*) as directed by law among separate spending authorities. They were appointed by lot, one from each of the ten tribes or *phylai* (*Ath. pol.* 47. 5–48. 2).   P. J. R.

apographē See LAW AND PROCEDURE; ATHENIAN.

apoikia, 'a settlement far from home, a colony' (LSJ), and hence a Greek community regarded as distinct from the kind of trading-post conventionally known as an *emporion*. In effect, an *apoikia* may be defined as a *polis* established abroad by a *polis* (or *metropolis*: 'mother city') at home: the official processes required the appointment of a leader/founder, and are well described (for Sicily) in the early chapters of Thuc. 6. The development of the *polis* at home in Greece coincided chronologically, and clearly interacted conceptually, with the colonizing movement that was in progress between *c.*734 and 580 BC. Given the continuing importance of trade to the main colonizing cities, it follows that the distinction between *apoikia* and *emporion*—the settlement type characteristic of the pre-colonial phase—is in some cases more apparent than real. Certain *apoikiai* could well have been considered in effect as *emporia* first and *poleis* second; and the sheer size and population-density of at least one early *emporion*, *Pithecusae, seemingly established on a typically pre-colonial ad hoc basis, soon brought about a degree of social organization that might reasonably be expected of a 'true' *apoikia*. See CITY-FOUNDERS; COLONIZATION, GREEK.

A. J. Graham, *Colony and Mother City in Ancient Greece*, 2nd edn. (1983).
D. W. W. R.

Apollinarius (*RE* 'Apollinaris' 12), astronomer (fl. ?1st cent. AD). From references in *Galen, *Vettius Valens, and others, he appears to have been one of the most important figures in Greek *astronomy between *Hipparchus (3) and *Ptolemy (4). He constructed lunar tables, based on the 248-day period used by the Babylonian astronomers, which became standard in Greek astronomy until superseded by Ptolemy's. A long quotation from a theoretical work is preserved in an astrological compilation, and treatises by him on solar *eclipses and *astrology are also cited.

A. Jones, *TAPhS* 1990, and *Archive for History of Exact Sciences* 1983, 1–36; G. J. Toomer, *Archive for History of Exact Sciences* 1985, 193–206.
G. J. T.

Apollo (Ἀπόλλων, Dor. also Ἀπέλλων), Greek god, son of *Zeus and *Leto, brother of *Artemis, for many 'the most Greek of Greek gods' (W. F. Otto). Among his numerous and diverse functions healing and *purification, prophecy, care for young citizens, for poetry, and music are prominent (see Pl. *Cra.* 404d–405e). In iconography, he is always young, beardless, and of harmonious beauty, the ideal ephebe (see EPHEBOI) and young athlete; his weapon is the bow, and his tree the laurel.

His name is absent from Linear B (while Paean, his later epiclesis and hymn, appears as *Paiawon* in the pantheon of Mycenaean Cnossus). In *Homer and *Hesiod, his myth and cult are fully developed, and his main centres, *Delos and *Delphi, are well-known (Delian altar of Apollo, *Od.* 6. 162; Delphic shrine, *Il.* 9. 405 and *Od.* 8. 80; stone of Cronus, *Theog.* 499) though none goes back to the bronze age: Apollo's cult must have been introduced and brought to Panhellenic importance during the Dark Age. Epic poetry, where Apollo is prominent, had its decisive share in this development. The key document is the

*Homeric *Hymn to Apollo*; it consists of two aetiological parts, a Delian part which tells the story of Apollo's birth and a perhaps earlier Delphic part about the foundation of the oracular shrine in Delphi; opinions about structure and date vary, though a date in the 7th cent. BC for the Delian, and one slightly later for the Delphic part are also possible.

The origins of Apollo are debated; after earlier theories explaining the god from the sun (following an identification as old as the 5th cent., and adding the linguistic argument that the epiclesis *Lykeios* would derive from the stem *luc-*, as in latin *lux*), partisans of an Anatolian, esp. Lycian, origin relied upon the same epiclesis and upon his mother's name being Lycian and connected with *lada*, 'earth' (see LYCIA); the French excavations in Lycian *Xanthus proved both assumptions wrong. More promising is the connection with Dor. ἀπέλλα 'assembly', i.e. annual reunion of the adult tribesmen which also introduces the young men into the community (W. Burkert, *Rh. Mus.* 1975, 1–21; see APELLAI). This explains his widespread role as the divinity responsible for the introduction of young initiated adults into society: he receives the first cut hair at the end of *initiation (Hes. *Theog.* 347, mentioning Apollo together with Κοῦραι, 'Girls', i.e. *nymphs, and rivers), and his cult has to do with military and athletic training (for Apollo Lycius at Athens, M. Jameson, *Archaiognosia* 1980, 213–35; the 'Wolf-Apollo' has to do with Archaic wolf-warriors) and with the citizen-right of the sons (for Apollo Delphinius, F. Graf, *MH* 1979, 2–22). His cult on the lonely island of Delos, where Leto gave birth after long search, became the religious focus of Archaic Ionia (*Hymn. Hom. Ap.* 147) at least from the late 8th cent. onwards; before this date, archaeology shows a more regional, Cycladic influence. While a Delian temple of Artemis was present already in the 8th cent. (bronze age origin and continuity are contested), a temple of Apollo was built only in the mid-6th cent.; his cult centred around the famous altar of horns (parallels from Archaic Drerus on Crete, from *Ephesus, and from Boeotian Hyampolis, are now archaeologically attested).

Apollo's interest in music and poetry could derive from the same source, music and poetry having an educational role in Greece (see EDUCATION, GREEK). Apollo's instrument is the lyre whose well-ordered music is opposed to the ecstatic rhythms of flute and drums which belong to *Dionysus and *Cybele; according to the *Homeric Hymn to Hermes*, he received it from Hermes, its inventor. He is, together with the *Muses, protector of epic singers and cithara-players (Hes. *Theog.* 94); later, he is Musagetes, 'Leader of the Muses', in Pindar (fr. 91c Snell-Maehler) and on Archaic images. When philosophy takes over a similar educational function, he is associated with philosophy, and an anecdote makes him the real father of *Plato (1).

His own song, the *paean (παιάν; see L. Käppel, *Paian*, 1993), is sung and danced by the young Achaeans after the sacrifice to Apollo when bringing back *Chryseis to her father (*Il.* 1. 473): even if not necessarily a healing-song in this passage, it was understood as such later and was accordingly transferred to Asclepius as well. In the *Iliad*, Paieon could still be understood as an independent healing god (5. 401); later, it is an epiclesis of Apollo the Healer. The Ionian Apollo Ἰατρός ('Healer') had cult in most Black Sea cities, and as *Medicus* Apollo was taken over by the Romans during a *plague in the 5th cent. (Livy 4. 25. 3, see below). Only the rise of *Asclepius in the 5th and 4th cents. eclipsed this function, though in *Epidaurus, where Apollo took over a bronze age hill-sanctuary of Maleatas, Apollo Maleatas preceded Asclepius in official nomenclature until the imperial period. In *Iliad* 1 he is responsible both for sending and for averting the plague. The image of a god sending plague by shooting arrows points to the ancient near east where Reshep 'of the arrow' is the plague-god in bronze age *Ugarit/Ras Shamra and on Cyprus; details of iconography point to a transfer from Cyprus to Spartan *Amyclae—and in the Archaic Dorian world of Crete and Sparta, the paean is first attested as an individual poetical genre (Plut. *De mus.* 9. (1134c)); both in *Il.* 1. 473 and in the cultic reality of the Spartan Apollo, paean and κοῦροι ('young men') are closely connected.

Disease is the consequence of impurity, healing is purification—in myth, this theme later crystallized around Orestes whom Delphic Apollo cleansed of the murder of his mother, and of the concomitant madness. Oracular Apollo (see ORACLES) is often connected with purification and plague; he decreed the Cyrenean purification laws (6th cent., R. Parker, *Miasma* (1983), 332–51) and the setting up of his statue to avert the Athenian plague of 430 BC (Paus. 1. 3. 4, 10. 11. 5). But this is only a small part of the much wider oracular function which Apollo had not only in his shrines at Delphi and the *Ptoion on the Greek mainland, and at Branchidae (see DIDYMA), *Claros, and Gryneum (see MYRINA) in Asia Minor, but also in his relationship with the *Sibyl(s) and other seers like *Bacis or *Cassandra; while the Sibyls are usually priestesses of Apollo (e.g. *Erythrae, *PL* 8. 450, or *Cumae, Verg. *Aen.* 6. 77), Cassandra refused Apollo as a lover. Apolline prophecy was usually ecstatic: the Delphic Python was possessed by the god (in NT Greek, πυθών is 'ventriloquist'), as were the Sibyls (see Verg. *Aen.* 6. 77–80), Cassandra, young Branchus (Callim. fr. 229 Pf.), and Bacis; and the priest of Claros attained ecstasy through drinking water (Tac. *Ann.* 2. 54). Apollo's supreme wisdom is beyond human rationality.

In Archaic and Classical Greece, Delphi was the central oracular shrine (see the quest of *Croesus, Hdt. 1. 46). Though his cult had grown out of purely local worship in the 8th cent., myth saw its foundation as a primordial event, expressing it in the theme of dragon-slaying (*Hymn. Hom. Ap.* 287–374; see J. Trumpf, *Hermes* 1958, 129–57, and J. Fontenrose, *Python* (1959)); alternative myths gave an even longer prehistory to Apollo's taking over and his temple building (C. Sourvinou-Inwood, *'Reading' Greek Culture* (1991), 192–216, 217–43). Like isolated Delos, marginal Delphi achieved international political importance in Archaic Greece simply for being marginal. But from his role as a political adviser, Apollo acquired no further political functions—and only a marginally moralistic character.

In Italy, Apollo's arrival in Rome during a plague in 433 BC was due to a recommendation of the Sibylline Books (Livy 4. 25. 3): to avert the plague, a temple of Apollo Medicus was vowed and built just outside the *pomerium, where there had already been an *Apollinar*, presumably an open cult-place of the god (Livy 3. 63. 7, for the year 449). In Etruria, no cult of Apollo is attested, though his name, in the form *Aplu*, is read in mythological representations (with a Greek iconography): the form shows that the name was taken over from Latin *Apollo*, not directly from the Greek (A. Pfiffig, *Religio Etrusca* (1975), 251). Until the time of Augustus, the temple of Apollo Medicus was the only Roman temple of the god, and healing his main function; the Vestals addressed him as 'Apollo Medice, Apollo Paean' (Macrob. *Sat.* 1. 17. 15). Mainly in response to Mark Antony's adoption of Dionysus (see ANTONIUS (2), M.), and perhaps already stimulated by the victory of Philippi which Caesar's heirs had won in the name of Apollo, *Augustus made Apollo his special god (P. Zanker, *The Power of Images in the Age of Augustus* (1988), 48–53).

In 31 BC, Augustus vowed a second temple to Apollo in Rome after the battle of Actium, where, from his nearby sanctuary, the god was said to have helped against Mark Antony and Cleopatra; the temple was built and dedicated in 28, close to the house of Augustus on the Palatine, with a magnificent adjoining library. See DIVINATION; ORACLES.

For Greek Apollo, see esp. Burkert, *GR* 143–9 (with bibliog.); L. Bruit Zaidman and P. Schmitt Pantel, *Religion in the Ancient Greek City* (1992; Fr. orig. 1989), 191–8; sanctuaries of Delphi and Delos: E. Østby, in N. Marinatos and R. Hägg (eds.), *Greek Sanctuaries: New Approaches* (1993), 203–6, 217–19; M. Petterson, *Cults of Apollo at Sparta* (1992); oracles: H. W. Parke, *The Oracles of Apollo in Asia Minor* (1985); Rome: J. Gagé *Apollon romain: Essai sur le culte d'Apollon et le développement du 'ritus Graecus' à Rome des origines à Auguste* (1955); iconography: W. Lambrinoudakis, *LIMC* 2. 183–237 'Apollon'; I. Krauskopf, ibid. 335–63 'Aplu'; E. Simon and G. Bauchhenss, ibid. 363–464 'Apollo'. F. G.

Apollodorus (1) (*RE* 'Apollodoros' 9) (*c*.394–after 343 BC), the elder son of the Athenian banker *Pasion, was a minor politician and assiduous litigant. He is the speaker of seven speeches, wrongly attributed to *Demosthenes (2), which provide much information about him and his family. He repeatedly quarrelled with his step-father *Phormion (2) over money, and in *c*.349 made an unsuccessful attempt to prosecute him for embezzlement (see Dem. 36, 45, and 46). His early political affiliations are unclear, but in 348, possibly at the instigation of Demosthenes, he made an unsuccessful attempt to divert the budgetary surplus from the theoric (see THEŌRIKA) to the military fund. In the late 340s he prosecuted Neaera, the wife of a political opponent, for illegal usurpation of Athenian *citizenship (see Dem. 59). She was a former courtesan, and the speech is a rich source of information about the Athenian *demi-monde* (see HETAIRAI). It is likely that Apollodorus was the author of all but one of the speeches he delivered (see also Dem. 49, 50, 52, 53): these are rich in narrative, but slackly argued and often anacoluthic in style. His colourful but ultimately unsuccessful public career well demonstrates the pitfalls facing an ambitious *nouveau riche* at Athens.

APF 11672; C. Carey (ed.), *Apollodoros Against Neaira [Demosthenes] 59* (1992); J. Trevett *Apollodoros the Son of Pasion* (1992), with earlier bibliog. J. C. T.

Apollodorus (2), of *Gela, New Comedy poet (see COMEDY (GREEK), NEW), contemporary of *Menander (1) (*Suda* α 3405). He has sometimes been identified with *Apollodorus (3) of Carystus, but quoters (Ath. 3. 125a, 11. 472c; Poll. 4. 19, 10. 93, 138) and inscriptional evidence (cf. E. Capps, *AJPhil.* 1900, 45 ff.) prove his separate existence.

FRAGMENTS Kassel–Austin, *PCG* 2. 502 ff.
INTERPRETATION Meineke, *FCG* 1. 459 ff.; E. F. Krause, *De Apollodoris comicis* (Diss. Berlin, 1903). W. G. A.

Apollodorus (3), of Carystus, New Comedy poet (see COMEDY (GREEK), NEW), more famous than *Apollodorus (2) of Gela, and sometimes referred to as 'the Athenian' (which may imply the grant of Athenian *citizenship). He wrote 47 plays and won five victories (*Suda* α 3404). A contemporary of *Posidippus (1), he produced his first play *c*.285 BC. His Ἑκύρα ('Mother-in-law') and Ἐπιδικαζόμενος ('Claimant') were respectively the models for *Terence's *Hecyra* and *Phormio*. These Latin adaptations seem to indicate that Apollodorus was greatly influenced by *Menander (1), and that one of his characteristics was a fussy attention to detail in the organization of his plots. Fr. 5: the folly of Greek fighting Greek.

Apollodorus

FRAGMENTS Kassel–Austin, *PCG* 2. 485 ff., although earlier scholars use the numbering in Kock, *CAF* 3. 280–8.

INTERPRETATION Meineke, *FCG* 1. 462 ff.; G. Kaibel, *RE* 1/2 (1894), 2852 f. 'Apollodoros' 57; E. Capps, *AJPhil.* 1900, 45 ff.; E. F. Krause, *De Apollodoris comicis* (Diss. Berlin, 1903); M. Schuster, *De Apollodoris poetis comicis* (1907); W. E. J. Kuiper, *Two Comedies by Apollodorus of Carystus: Terence's Hecyra and Phormio* (1938): too speculative; M. R. Posani, *Atene e Roma* 1940, 141 ff.; K. Mras, *Anz. Österreich. Akad.* 1948, 184 ff.; T. B. L. Webster, *Studies in Later Greek Comedy*, 2nd edn. (1970) 225 ff.; D. Sewart, *Hermes* 1974, 247 ff; A. Taliercio, *Orpheus* 1988, 38 ff. W. G. A.

Apollodorus (4) (*RE* 'Apollodoros' 69), of Alexandria (1), physician and zoologist of the beginning of the 3rd cent. BC. His major work, *On Poisonous Animals*, was a source for pharmacologists and toxicologists in later antiquity (e.g. *Numenius, *Heraclides (4) of Tarentum, *Nicander, *Sostratus, Sextius Niger, *Pliny (1), *Dioscorides (2), *Archigenes, *Aemilius Macer, and probably *Philumenus; see PHARMACOLOGY). The scholiasts on *Nicander quote from a second tract by Apollodorus, *On Poisonous Drugs*.

FRAGMENTS See O. Schneider, *Nicandrea* (1856), 181–201.

LITERATURE J. Scarborough, *Pharmacy in History* 1977, 3–23. J. Sca.

Apollodorus (5), of Pergamum, was the rhetor chosen by *Caesar to take charge of the education of C. Octavius, the future *Augustus, in 45 BC (Suet. *Aug.* 89). His 'Art of Rhetoric' ($\tau\acute{\epsilon}\chi\nu\eta$) was translated into Latin by C. *Valgius Rufus (Quint. *Inst.* 3. 1. 18). The emphasis of his teaching seems to have been on firm argument and rather restrictive rules of composition: he insisted that all forensic speeches must consist of proem, narrative, proofs, and epilogue, in that order (see RHETORIC). *Theodorus (3) of Gadara was his younger rival. Our knowledge of the doctrines of both of them is mainly derived from the *Anonymus Seguerianus (Spengel, *Rhet.* 1. 352–98).

G. A. Kennedy, *The Art of Rhetoric in the Roman World* (1972), 337–40; J. Graeven, *Cornuti Artis Rhetoricae Epitome* (= Anonymus Seguerianus) (1891). D. A. R.

Apollodorus (6), of Athens (c.180–after 120 BC), studied in Athens with the Stoic *Diogenes (3) of Babylon, collaborated with *Aristarchus (2) in Alexandria, perhaps fled (in 146 ?), probably to *Pergamum, and later lived in Athens. A scholar of great learning and varied interests, he was the last of a series of intellectual giants in *Alexandria (1).

Works 1. *Chronicle* ($X\rho o\nu\iota\kappa\acute{a}$) was based on the researches of *Eratosthenes, although it extended coverage beyond the death of *Alexander (3) the Great to Apollodorus' time. Written in comic trimeters which made it easy to memorize, it covered successive periods of history, philosophical schools, and the life and work of individuals from the fall of Troy (1184) to 146/5; later it was continued to 119 or 110/9 BC. Apollodorus frequently synchronized events and used archon lists for dating. *Diodorus (3) Siculus employed it, but *Castor's $X\rho o\nu\iota\kappa\acute{a}$ became more popular in the Roman period. 2. *On the Gods* ($\Pi\epsilon\rho\grave{\iota}\ \theta\epsilon\hat{\omega}\nu$), a rationalistic account of Greek religion, much used by later writers, including *Philodemus. 3. A twelve-book commentary on the Homeric *Catalogue of Ships* based on Eratosthenes and *Demetrius (12) of Scepsis which accounted for Homeric geography and subsequent changes. *Strabo used it extensively in books 8 to 10 in discussing contemporary sites. His several other possible works include commentaries and perhaps critical editions of the comic poets *Epicharmus and *Sophron and an *etymology, perhaps the first by an Alexandrian grammarian.

Although some of his works display a rationalizing tendency, it is doubtful whether he was a Stoic (see STOICISM).

Apollodorus' authority gave rise to forgeries: a geographical guidebook ($\Gamma\hat{\eta}\varsigma\ \pi\epsilon\rho\acute{\iota}o\delta o\varsigma$) in comic trimeters (1st cent. BC) and the extant *Bibliotheca*, a study of Greek heroic mythology which presents an uncritical summary of the traditional Greek mythology (1st or 2nd cent. AD). See TIME-RECKONING; MYTHOGRAPHERS.

FGrH 244; F. Jacoby, *Apollodors Chronik* (1902); R. Pfeiffer, *A History of Classical Scholarship* (1968), 253 ff. *Bibliotheca*, ed. and trans. J. G. Frazer (Loeb, 1921); M. van der Valk, *Rev. Ét. Grec.* 1958, 100 ff. K. S. S.

Apollodorus (7), of *Damascus, building-expert (*architektōn*) to whom are attributed the *forum Traiani and baths of *Trajan (Cass. Dio 69. 4: he may therefore be responsible for *Trajan's Column) and Trajan's bridge over the *Danuvius (Procop. *Aed.* 4. 6. 13). He is said to have disagreed with *Hadrian, having mocked his innovative architectural interest in 'pumpkins'—the complex vaulted structures that were to be so characteristic of the imperial villa at *Tibur—and to have been banished and later killed for criticizing the emperor's temple of Venus and Rome. His is one of the few names associated with imperial building-projects, but the scope of his expertise in design, engineering, management, and planning is not precisely recoverable, and like *Vitruvius he seems to have had a background in military machinery, on which he wrote a treatise.

TEXT *Poliorcetica*, ed. R. Schneider (1908); *PIR*² A 922. N. P.

Apollodorus (8), of Seleuceia (1) on Tigris, Stoic philosopher (see STOICISM), the author of an *Ethics* and a *Physics* cited by Diog. Laert. 7. 102, 129; 125, 135. He also wrote logical works. Testimonia in von Arnim, *SVF* 3. 259–61.

Apollonia, the name of several Greek cities. The chief of these was in Illyria, founded c.600 BC where the river Aous enters the coastal plain, with relatively easy communications across the Balkan range. It was founded as a Corinthian colony (see CORINTH; COLONIZATION, GREEK) by 200 settlers (Steph. Byz.) and grew rapidly in size and prosperity, until it was able to destroy one of its neighbours, Thronium, by the middle of the 5th cent. In the Hellenistic period its strategic position and its wealth attracted the Macedonian, Molossian, and Illyrian kings and also *Corcyra. It joined Rome in 229 BC, was treated as a *free city and prospered greatly as the main base of Roman armies in the wars against Macedon. After 146 it was one of the terminal points of the *Via Egnatia, and it was *Caesar's headquarters in the campaign of Dyrrhachium (48). In 45–44 Caesar gathered an army at Apollonia for his eastern campaigns, and at his death his grand-nephew Octavian was stationed there as a cadet.

Excavation reports in *Iliria*. M. C.; N. G. L. H.

Apollonius (1) **Rhodius,** a major literary figure of 3rd-cent. *Alexandria (1), and poet of the *Argonautica*, the only extant Greek hexameter *epic written between *Homer and the Roman imperial period.

Life Our main sources are: *POxy.* 1241, a 2nd-cent. AD list of the librarians of the Royal Library at Alexandria; two Lives transmitted with the manuscripts of *Argon.* which probably contain material deriving from the late 1st cent. BC; an entry in the *Suda.* (1) All four state that Apollonius was from Alexandria itself, though two 2nd-cent. AD notices point rather to *Naucratis. The most likely explanation for the title 'Rhodian' is thus that Apollonius spent a period of his life there, which would accord well with what we know of his works (cf. below), though it remains possible that he or his family came from *Rhodes. (2) Apollonius served as librarian and royal tutor before *Eratosthenes (*POxy.* 1241), and probably in succession to *Zenodotus, thus *c.*270–45. It is to this period that the *Argonautica* should be dated. (3) All four sources make him a pupil of *Callimachus (3), which probably reflects beliefs about the indebtedness of his poetry to Callimachus (cf. below). (4) The *Lives* give confused and contradictory accounts of withdrawal to Rhodes after a poor reception for his poetry in Alexandria. Nothing of value can be retrieved from these stories, which may well be fictions based on the existence of a text of at least *Argon.* 1 which differed significantly from the vulgate, the *proekdosis*, cited six times by the scholia to *Argon.* 1). (5) Very flimsy ancient evidence has been used by some scholars to construct a 'quarrel' between Apollonius and Callimachus concerning poetic questions, particularly the value and style of epic. The many striking parallels between the works of Callimachus and the *Argonautica*, however, argue against, rather than for, any serious dispute; moreover, Apollonius does not appear in the list (*PSI* 1219) which seeks to identify Callimachus' opponents, the *Telchines, and Roman poets clearly align Apollonius with, rather than against, Callimachus. Two episodes in the *Argonautica* handle the same material as two poems of *Theocritus (Hylas, cf. *Id.* 13; Amycus and Polydeuces, cf. *Id.* 22), and this offers no reason to doubt the dating derived from other sources.

Lost works (1) Poems (cf. Powell, *Coll. Alex.* 4–8). *Canobus*: choliambic poem on Egyptian legends. *Foundation Poems* in hexameters on *Caunus, Alexandria, *Naucratis, Rhodes, and *Cnidus; poems of this type reflect the deep Alexandrian interest in local history and cult. Many other lost poems may also be assumed, including probably epigrams (cf. Ant. Lib. *Met.* 23); an extant epigram attacking Callimachus (*Anth. Pal.* 11. 275) is very doubtfully ascribed to Apollonius. (2) Prose Works. Apollonius' scholarly interests were reflected in many works (cf. R. Pfeiffer, *History of Classical Scholarship* 1 (1968) 144–8), including a monograph on Homer (*Against Zenodotus*). *Archilochus and *Hesiod were also among the poets discussed by Apollonius; he defended the authenticity of the *Shield of Heracles* (hypothesis A to the poem (see HYPOTHESIS, LITERARY)) and probably rejected Hesiodic authorship of the *Ornithomanteia* which was transmitted after *Works and Days* (corrupt scholium to *Op.* 828).

Argonautica Hexameter epic on the Argonautic legend (see ARGONAUTS) in four long books totalling 5,835 preserved verses. Fifty-two manuscripts are known, and a large body of papyri attests to the popularity of the poem in later antiquity. It was very important at Rome, where it was translated by the neoteric P. *Terentius Varro Atacinus, is a major influence on *Catullus 64 and *Virgil's *Aeneid*, and, with the *Aeneid*, forms the basis of C. *Valerius Flaccus' *Argonautica*.

Books 1–2 deal with the outward voyage, to recover the golden fleece, from *Iolcus in Thessaly to the Colchian city of Aia at the extreme eastern edge of the Black Sea (in modern Georgia, see COLCHIS), which is ruled over by Aeëtes, the cruel son of *Helios. The major events of this voyage are a stay at *Lemnos where the local women, who have murdered the entire male population, seize the chance for procreation, and *Jason (1) sleeps with Queen *Hypsipyle (1. 609–910); the loss of *Heracles from the expedition (1. 1153–1357); a boxing-match between *Amycus, king of the Bebrycians, and Polydeuces (see DIOSCURI) (2. 1–163); meeting with the blind prophet *Phineus whom the Argonauts save from the depredations of the Harpies (see HARPYIAE) and who, in return, tells them of the voyage ahead (2. 168–530); passage through the Clashing Rocks (*Symplegades) which guard the entrance to the Black Sea (2. 531–647); meeting on the island of Ares with the sons of Phrixus, who fled Greece on the golden ram (2. 1030–1230). In Book 3 Jason asks Aeëtes to grant him the fleece; this the king agrees to do on the condition that Jason ploughs an enormous field with fire-breathing bulls, sows it with dragon's teeth, and slays the armed warriors who rise up from the ground. Jason succeeds in this, because, at the instigation of Jason's protector Hera, the king's daughter, *Medea, falls in love with the hero and supplies him with a magic salve to protect him and give him superhuman strength. In Book 4 Medea flees to join the Argonauts and secures the fleece for them from the grove where it is guarded by a sleepless dragon. The Argonauts flee via a great river (the *Danube) which is pictured as flowing from the Black Sea to the Adriatic; at the Adriatic mouth, Jason and Medea lure her brother, Apsyrtus, who commands the pursuing Colchians, to his death, a crime for which Zeus decides that they must be purified by Medea's aunt *Circe who lives on the west coast of Italy. They reach Circe via rivers (the Po (*Padus) and the Rhône) imagined to link NE Italy with the western Mediterranean. From there they sail to Drepane (Corfu), Homer's *Scheria, where Jason and Medea are married, and are then driven to the wastes of Libya where they are again saved by divine intervention. They finally return home by way of Crete, where Medea uses her magic powers to destroy the bronze giant *Talos (1) who guards the island.

The central poetic technique of Apollonius is the creative reworking of *Homer. While the Hellenistic poet takes pains to avoid the repetitiveness characteristic of Archaic epic, Homer is the main determinative influence on every aspect of the poem, from the details of language to large-scale *narrative patterns, material culture, and technology (e.g. sailing) which is broadly 'Homeric' (but note 'Hellenistic' architectural features at 3. 215 ff.). This is most obvious in set scenes such as the Catalogue of Argonauts (1. 23–233), corresponding to Homer's Catalogue of Ships, the description of the cloak Jason wears to meet Hypsipyle (1. 721–67), corresponding to the Shield of *Achilles, the meeting of *Hera, *Athena, and *Aphrodite on *Olympus at the start of book 3 which finds many forerunners in Homer, the scenes in the palace of Aeëtes, corresponding to the scenes of the *Odyssey on Scheria, and the voyage in the western Mediterranean, corresponding to *Odysseus' adventures on his way home. These scenes function by contrast: the Homeric 'model' is the base-text by which what is importantly different in the later poem is highlighted. Individual characters too owe much to Homeric predecessors, while also being markedly different from them: e.g. Jason/*Odysseus, Medea/*Nausicaa and Circe. After Homer, the two most important literary influences are Pindar's account of the Argonauts (*Pyth.* 4) and Euripides' *Medea*; the events of the tragedy are foreshadowed in a number of places in the epic—perhaps most strikingly in the murder of Apsyrtus who goes to his death 'like a tender child' (4. 460)—and in one sense the epic shows us that the events of the tragedy were 'inevitable', given the earlier history of Jason and Medea.

A fundamental principle of composition for Apollonius is discontinuity, a feature shared with the poetics of Callimachus. The *Argonautica* is constantly experimental. This shows itself, for example, in the organization of the narrative both within books (e.g. book 2 where scenes of action—Amycus, the Harpies—stand in sharp contrast to long passages of ethnography and geography, and book 4 where different Argonauts and Medea take turns to play leading roles) and between books (thus book 3 stands apart as a tightly-knit drama of its own). Apollonius' principles of characterization have also frequently been misunderstood; the two main sides of Medea's character—impressionable virgin and dangerous sorceress—are only confusing if viewed from the perspective of that 'consistency' which *Aristotle prescribed for dramatic character. Apollonius is rather interested in the similarities and differences between the power of love, the power of persuasion, and the power of drugs, and this interest is explored through the presentation of Medea, whose character is thus a function of the narrative. Jason's character, on the other hand, brings persuasion and stratagem to the fore (cf. esp. his testing (*peira*) of the crew after the passing of the Clashing Rocks (2. 607–49), and the praise of *muthos* and *mētis* at 3. 182–93). His story is of the familiar type of *rite of passage (cf. *Orestes, *Theseus, etc.) in which a young man must accomplish a dangerous set of tasks before assuming his rightful position (in this case a kingship which had been usurped by *Pelias); that Jason seems often overwhelmed (*amēchanos*) by the enormity of what he must do and only finally accomplishes it through Medea's help finds many parallels in related stories, but also marks the difference between his exotic story and that of the Homeric heroes. With the partial exception of some of Odysseus' adventures, magic and fantasy have little role in Homer, whereas they had always had a prominent position in the Argonautic myth and are very important in the *Argonautica*. Discontinuity is also seen in the divine element of the epic where different Olympian gods—Athena, *Apollo, and Jason's main protector, *Hera—and other minor divinities are all prominent at one time or another.

In common with other Alexandrian poetry, the aetiology of cult and ritual is very important in the *Argonautica*. Apollonius' scholarly learning, visible also in his detailed manipulation of earlier texts, here emphasizes how the Argonautic voyage is in part a voyage of acculturation establishing Greek tradition. The repeatedly positive evaluation of Greek culture (including cult and ritual) should be connected with the Ptolemaic context of the work; the Ptolemies (see PTOLEMY (1)) promoted themselves as the true heirs and champions of Classical Greek culture, and this strain should not be overlooked in the epic. It is even possible that the characters of King *Alcinous (1) and Queen Arete owe not a little to *Ptolemy (1) II Philadelphus and his sister/wife. Just as Ptolemaic ideas are thus inscribed into prehistory, Apollonius also mixes the temporal levels of his poem in other ways too. One is by emotional authorial 'intrusions' (e.g. 1. 616–19, 2. 542–5, 4. 445–9) which strongly differentiate the *Argonautica* from the 'impersonal' Homeric poems; these are one manifestation of the strong literary self-consciousness of an epic which is much concerned with displaying the problems of *how* one writes epic poetry. Another is by reflections of Hellenistic science within the mythical material of the poem; Aphrodite bribes her son with a ball which is also a cosmic globe of a kind familiar in Apollonius' time (3. 131–41), Medea's suffering reflects contemporary physiological theories (3. 762–3), and Mopsus' death from snakebite (4. 1502–36) is a very typical mixture of Alexandrian medicine and myth.

The language of Apollonius is based on that of Homer, constantly extended and varied by analogy and new formation, but Apollonius also draws upon the vocabulary of the whole high poetic tradition. Metrically, his hexameter shows similar developments to Callimachus' and Theocritus', and dactylic rhythm is more predominant than in Homer. Complex, enjambed sentences and syntactically sophisticated indirect speech reveal the possibilities open to the poet of written, rather than oral, epic.

The *Argonautica* is a brilliant and disturbing achievement, a poem shot through with intelligence and deep ironies. Its reception at Rome is in stark contrast to its reception by modern critics who have tended to see it as a failed attempt to write like Homer; more recently, however, it has become the subject of serious literary study, and is thus coming into its own.

TEXT H. Fränkel (OCT, 1961); F. Vian (Budé, 1974–81). Scholia in C. Wendel, *Scholia in Apollonium Rhodium Vetera* (1935); Index verborum: M. Campbell (1983).

COMMENTARIES Whole poem: G. W. Mooney (1912); F. Vian (Budé 1974–81); cf. also H. Fränkel, *Noten zu den Argonautika des Apollonios* (1968). Individual books: bk. 1, A. Ardizzoni (1967); bk. 3, M. M. Gillies (1928), F. Vian (1961), R. L. Hunter (1989), cf. also M. Campbell, *Studies in the Third Book of Apollonius Rhodius' Argonautica* (1983); bk. 4, E. Livrea (1973).

TRANSLATION R. L. Hunter (1993).

LITERATURE C. R. Beye, *Epic and Romance in the Argonautica of Apollonius* (1982); A. W. Bulloch, in *The Cambridge History of Classical Literature* 1 (1985), 586–98; M. Campbell, *Echoes and Imitations of Early Epic in Apollonius Rhodius* (1981); J. F. Carspecken, *YClS* 1952, 33–143; M. Fantuzzi, *Ricerche su Apollonio Rodio* (1988); D. C. Feeney, *The Gods in Epic* (1991); M. Fusillo, *Il tempo delle Argonautiche* (1985); S. Goldhill, *The Poet's Voice* (1991); P. Händel, *Beobachtungen zur epischen Technik des Apollonios* (1954); M. W. Haslam, *ICS* 1978, 47–73; H. Herter, in Bursian, *Jahresb.* 1955, 213–410, and *RE* Suppl. 13. 15–56, 'Apollonius, der Epiker'; M. Hügi, *Vergils Aeneis und die hellenistische Dichtung* (1952); R. L. Hunter, *The Argonautica of Apollonius: Literary Studies* (1993), and *Jason and the Golden Fleece (the Argonautica)* (1993); A. Hurst, *Apollonios de Rhodes, manière et cohérence* (1967); G. Hutchinson, *Hellenistic Poetry* (1988); G. Paduano, *Studi su Apollonio Rodio* (1972); A. Rengakos, *Wien. Stud.* 1992, 39 ff.; U. von Wilamowitz-Moellendorff, *Hellenistische Dichtung* (1924). R. L. Hu.

Apollonius (2) (*RE* 112), of *Perge, mathematician (fl. 200 BC). Born at Perge in Pamphylia, he composed the first version, in eight books, of his *Conics* in *Alexandria (1) 'somewhat too hurriedly' (*Conics* 1 pref.). He visited *Ephesus and *Pergamum, where he stayed with the Epicurean Eudemus, to whom he subsequently sent the first three books of the revised version of the *Conics*. After Eudemus' death the remaining books were sent to Attalus (perhaps Attalus of Rhodes).

Of the *Conics* (Κωνικά) the first four books survive in Greek and the next three in Arabic translation; the eighth is lost. Apollonius states (*Conics* 1 pref.) that the first four books form an elementary introduction, while the remainder are particular extensions (περιουσιαστικώτερα). He claims no originality for the content of *Conics* 1–4, but says that he expounds the fundamental properties 'more fully and generally' than his predecessors. This is fully justified: earlier writers on conics, including *Archimedes, had defined them as sections of a right circular cone by a plane at right angles to a generator, and hence the parabola, ellipse, and hyperbola were called 'section of a right-angled cone', 'of an acute-angled cone', and 'of an obtuse-angled cone' respectively. Apollonius generates all three sections from the most general type of circular cone, the double oblique, and defines the fundamental properties by the 'application of areas' familiar from *Euclid, using the terms παραβολή, ἔλλειψις, and ὑπερβολή, according to whether the applied figure exactly fits, falls short of, or exceeds that to which it is applied.

Apollonius did for conics what Euclid had done for elementary geometry: both his terminology and his methods became canonical and eliminated the work of his predecessors. Like Euclid, too, his exposition follows the logical rather than the original sequence of working. Investigation of the latter has revealed how 'algebraic' his methods are. His silence on some features of conics (e.g. the focus of the parabola) is not due to ignorance, but to the elementary nature of the treatise; the specialized investigations of books 5–7 cover only a selection of possible topics, but book 5 in particular reveals Apollonius as an original mathematical genius.

Commentaries to the *Conics* were written by *Serenus and *Hypatia. That by Eutocius on books 1–4 is extant but superficial. *Pappus provides lemmata, including some to the lost book 8.

Of other works by Apollonius there survives only the λόγου ἀποτομή ('Cutting-off of a Ratio'), in two books, in Arabic translation. Pappus (bk. 7) describes incompletely the contents of five other lost works: (1) χωρίου ἀποτομή ('Cutting-off of an Area'); (2) διωρισμένη τομή ('Determinate Section'); (3) ἐπαφαί ('Tangencies'); (4) νεύσεις ('Inclinations'); (5) τόποι ἐπίπεδοι ('Plane Loci'). Apollonius also wrote works on the *Cylindrical Helix* (*Proclus on Euc. 105), the *Comparison of the Dodecahedron and Eicosahedron* (*Hypsicles, *Euclid bk. 14*, 2), and on unordered irrationals (Pappus on *Euc. 10*, 218 Junge–Thomson). In his ὠκυτόκιον ('Quick Delivery') he calculated limits for π closer than those of Archimedes (Eutocius on Arch. 258). His καθόλου πραγματεία ('General Treatise') dealt with the foundations of geometry (Marinus on *Data Euc.* 234). Pappus (bk. 2) gives excerpts from a work in which Apollonius sets out a system for expressing large numbers by, in effect, using 10,000 instead of ten as a base (cf. Archimedes' *Sand-reckoner*). The ascription to Apollonius of a work *On the Burning-Mirror* is probably a mistaken attribution of the extant work of *Diocles (4).

Apollonius did important work in theoretical *astronomy. Ptolemy, *Almagest* 12. 1 gives a theorem of Apollonius for establishing the stationary points of planets from the epicyclic/eccentric hypothesis. He also worked on lunar theory, but references to his 'lunar tables' arise from scribal confusion with the later astronomer *Apollinarius.

DATE Evidence in G. J. Toomer, art. 'Apollonius of Perga', *Dict. Sci. Biog.* 1. 179–80.

EDITIONS AND TRANSLATIONS Critical text of *Conics* 1–4, with Lat. trans., Eutocius' comm., and Gk. frs. of lost works, by J. L. Heiberg (Teubner, 1891, 1893). Arabic text of bks. 5–7 with transl. by G. J. Toomer, 2 vols. (1990). The translation of the whole by T. L. Heath, *Apollonius of Perga* (1896; repr. 1961), is much adapted, but has a useful introduction. For bks. 1–4 the best translation is the French by P. Ver Eecke, *Les Coniques d'Apollonius de Perge* (1923; repr. 1963). Λόγου ἀποτομή: no edition of Arabic; Lat. trans. by E. Halley (1706); Eng. trans. by E. M. Macierowski, *Apollonius of Perge: On Cutting off a Ratio* (1987).

COMMENT H. G. Zeuthen, *Die Lehre von den Kegelschnitten im Altertum* (1886; repr. 1966). Heath, *Hist. of Greek Maths.* 2. 126 ff. (very full summary, includes references to attempts to restore the lost works). O. Neugebauer, *Quellen und Studien zur Geschichte der Mathematik* B2 (1933), 215–54. J. P. Hogendijk, *Archive for History of Exact Sciences* 1986, 187–253. On Apollonius' astronomical contributions see *HAMA* 267–70. G. J. T.

Apollonius (3) (3rd cent. BC) served *Ptolemy (1) II as chief minister (*dioikētēs*) in Egypt and is best known as holder of a 10,000-*aroura* (2,750-ha: 6,800-acre) crown-gift estate near Philadelphia (1) in the *Fayūm. This estate formed the centre of a series of agricultural experiments (in *arboriculture, viticulture, crops, and livestock) and was managed by Zenon, a Carian immigrant from *Caunus, who came to the Fayūm in 256 and stayed on in the area after leaving Apollonius' service in 248/7. The collection of Zenon's papyri is the largest from the period and is now scattered throughout European and North American collections. It illustrates these and Apollonius' other interests:

*textile-manufacturing at *Memphis, his contacts in *Alexandria (1), and commercial dealings, including slave-trading, in the Levant (see SLAVERY).

C. Préaux, *Les Grecs en Égypte* (1947); C. Orrieux, *Zénon de Caunos* (1985); P. W. Pestman, *A Guide to the Zenon Archive* (1981). D. J. T.

Apollonius (4) (2nd cent. BC), of *Alabanda, called ὁ μαλακός ('soft', 'cissy'), a pupil of Menecles, founded a school of rhetoric at Rhodes, visited by Q. *Mucius Scaevola (1) and M. *Antonius (1).

Cic. *De orat.* 1. 75, 126, 130. M. B. T.

Apollonius (5), ? 2nd cent. BC, author of *Historiai thaumasiai*, a *paradoxographical compilation from earlier writers, preserved in Palatinus Graecus 398.

TEXT *Rer. nat. scr. Graec. min.* 1. 43–56. R. L. Hu.

Apollonius (6) (1st cent. BC), son of Archias, Athenian sculptor. A copyist and a member of a sculptor-dynasty alternating the names Apollonius and Archias, he was author of a herm (see HERMS) of the Doryphorus of *Polyclitus (2) and perhaps of other bronzes from the Villa of the Papyri at *Herculaneum.

A. F. Stewart, *Greek Sculpture* (1990), 160, 230, 309, figs. 380 f. A. F. S.

Apollonius (7), sculptor, son of Nestor, of Athens, signed the Belvedere torso in the Vatican (Winter, *KB* 394. 2). The supposed signature on the bronze boxer in the Terme is apparently an illusion (M. Guarducci, *Ann. della Scuola archeol. di Atene* 1959–60, 361). Apollonius may also have made the cult statue of *Jupiter Capitolinus, dedicated 69 BC, which is reflected in small bronzes.

T. B. L. W.

Apollonius (8), of Citium (*c.*90–15 BC?), Alexandrian physician. Extant in an illustrated 10th-cent. manuscript, his commentary on the Hippocratic (see HIPPOCRATES (2)) treatise Περὶ ἀρθρῶν ('On Joints'), offers invaluable evidence of the early state of the Hippocratic text, of orthopaedic *surgery, and of Empiricist polemics. His works on Hippocratic lexicography and on therapeutics are lost.

Ed. and trans.: J. Kollesch, F. Kudlien, and D. Nickel (1965). H. v. S.

Apollonius (9) **Molon** (1st cent. BC), of *Alabanda, rhetor and grammarian, was a pupil of Menecles; he lectured at Rhodes and visited Rome (87 and 81 BC), teaching *Cicero and other Romans, and was also successful as an advocate (see ADVOCACY).

Cic. *Brut.* 307, etc.; Diog. Laert. 3. 34. G. Kennedy, *The Art of Persuasion in Greece* (1963), 326. M. B. T.

Apollonius (10) **Mys** (fl. later 1st cent. BC?), Alexandrian physician of the 'school' of *Herophilus. Numerous fragments of his influential Εὐπόριστα ('Common Remedies'), *Unguents*, and *The School of Herophilus* survive, some on papyrus.

Ed., trans., and comm.: H. von Staden, *From Andreas to Demosthenes Philalethes* (1995), ch. 13; cf. von Staden, *Herophilus* (1989), 540–54.

H. v. S.

Apollonius (11) **Sophista** (*c.* AD 100) compiled a *Lexicon Homericum* which is extant in an abridged form (ed. I. Bekker, 1833). A fragment of the unabridged work survives in a Bodleian papyrus. He used especially the commentaries of *Aristarchus (2), on whose critical method he throws valuable light, and the glossary of *Apion.

F. Martinazzoli, *Hapax legomenon* 1. 2 (1957); H. Erbse, *Beitr. zur Überlieferung d. Iliasscholien* (1960), 206 ff.; H. Schenk, *Die Quellen des Homer-Lex. des A. Soph.* (1961). J. F. L.; R. B.

Apollonius of Tyana

Apollonius (12), **of Tyana** (Ἀπολλώνιος ὁ Τυανεύς), a Neopythagorean holy man (see NEOPYTHAGOREANISM), whose true history and persona it is scarcely possible to grasp. According to the only full account, the highly untrustworthy 'biography' of Philostratus (see PHILOSTRATI), he was born at Tyana in *Cappadocia at the beginning of the 1st cent. AD and survived into the reign of *Nerva. He led the life of an ascetic wandering teacher (see ASCETICISM), visited distant lands (including India), advised cities (e.g. Sparta), had life-threatening encounters with Nero and Domitian, whose death he simultaneously prophesied (Philostr. 8. 25–6; cf. Cass. Dio 67. 18), and on his own death underwent heavenly assumption. He was the object of posthumous cult attracting the patronage of the Severan emperors; pagan apologists compared him favourably to Jesus. An epigram from Cilicia (SEG 28. 1251; 31. 1320, not before the 3rd cent. AD) describes him as 'extinguishing the faults of men' (ἀνθρώπων ἔσβεσεν ἀμπλακίας). Of his writings there survive some doubtfully authentic letters and a fragment of his treatise On Sacrifices.

E. Bowie, ANRW 2. 16. 2 (1978), 1652 ff.; G. Anderson, Sage, Saint and Sophist (1994), passim. H. J. R.; A. J. S. S.

Apollonius (13), son of Mnesitheus, nicknamed **Dyscolus**, of *Alexandria (1) (2nd c. AD). Of his life little is known; apart from a short visit to Rome, he did not leave Alexandria, and it is not certain that he taught in a school. His works are distinguished, even among grammarians, for obscurity of style and asperity of manner; but his method is genuinely critical, and his zeal for correcting errors extends to his own (cf. Syntax, p. 231. 15 Bekker). For the history of grammar from *Dionysius (15) Thrax, to his own day he is our chief source of information, especially for Stoic linguistic philosophy. See GRAMMAR, GRAMMARIANS, GREEK.

Of some 20 works, mostly on syntax, named in the Suda, four survive (thanks to a single MS, Paris. gr. 2548): on the Pronoun, Conjunction, Adverb, and Syntax. A conspectus of his doctrines is given in the Syntax, which deals mainly with article, pronoun, verb, preposition, and adverb, successively. He approaches syntax from the parts of speech, not the sentence, beginning with the establishment of the 'correct' order of these, assuming that there must be a proper order for them as there is, in his view, for the alphabet; and he has much argument disproving such current opinions as that the function of the article is to distinguish genders, and that ὦ is its vocative. As a result, although he correctly settles many details, acutely arguing from function, not form, he nevertheless achieves no comprehensive, organic, system of syntax. His work is marked by a constant quest for principle. 'We must investigate what produces solecisms, and not merely adduce examples.' 'Why do some verbs take the genitive, not the accusative?' In discussing forms and constructions he makes much use of alleged ἀναλογία (see CRATES (3) OF MALLUS; ANALOGY AND ANOMALY), e.g. insisting on ἷμι, not εἷμι, by 'analogy' from the plural and dual; also τεθείκωμαι (pf. pass. subj.). He also makes use of what he recognizes to be false analogy (συνεκδρομή), as when he explains that the usage γράφει τὰ παιδία (nominative) is permitted because it sounds the same as when παιδία is accusative, in which case the syntax is normal.

He himself writes Hellenistic κοινή (standard Greek; see LANGUAGE, GREEK), as befitted a technical writer; Atticism was confined to belles-lettres. So we find such typical turns of syntax as ἐὰν with indicative, εἰ with subjunctive, ἐπεὶ μή, etc. Apollonius takes no thought for style, and his work is marked by frequent pleonasm, anacoluthon, etc. He had a wide knowledge of literature and was familiar with Latin. Inevitably he falls short of the comparative and historical methods available today. But it is notable that he achieved an understanding of the difference between time and aspect in non-indicative moods of the verb. He had great influence on later Greek and Latin grammarians, notably *Priscian, who called him, 'maximus auctor artis grammaticae'.

Edition, by Uhlig and Schneider in Teubner's Grammatici Graeci; P. Mass, De pronomine, pars generalis (1911); E. Egger, Apollonius Dyscole: Essai sur l'hist. d. théories gramm. dans l'antiquité (1854); A. Thierfelder, Abh. d. sächs. Akad. d. Wiss. 43 / 2 (1935); H. Erbse, Beitr. zur Überlieferung der Iliasscholien (1960), 311 ff.; D. L. Blank, ANRW 2. 34. 1 (1993), 708–30 and Ancient Philosophy and Grammar (1982). Translation of the Syntax: F. W. Householder (1981). P. B. R. F.; R. B.; N. G. W.

Apollonius (14), of Tyre, hero of an anonymous *novel, extant as the Latin Historia Apollonii Regis Tyrii (5th or 6th cent. AD); modern editors agree that it is preserved in three main and slightly divergent recensions. Scholars differ on whether or not it is a direct translation of a Greek original and on whether or not it is an epitome, both possible inferences from its linguistic Graecisms and disjointed narrative. The work must ultimately derive from a Greek model; it relates closely to the literary tradition of the Greek novel, from which it draws much of its romantic plot of the colourful adventures of a couple and their daughter, and some of its casual details suggest an original historical context for the story in the Greek world of the 2nd or 3rd cent. AD. It was very influential in the Middle Ages and Renaissance, notably on Shakespeare's Pericles.

TEXT G. Kortekaas (1984); G. Schmeling (Teubner, 1988).
CRITICISM B. E. Perry, The Ancient Romances (1967); T. Hägg, The Novel in Antiquity (1983); E. Archibald, Apollonius of Tyre: Medieval and Renaissance Themes and Variations (1991). S. J. Ha.

Apollophanes, Athenian Old *Comedy poet with one victory at the *Lenaea (IG 2². 2325. 132 = 5 C 1 col. 2. 6 Mette). In his Κρῆτες (Cretans) one character spoke Doric (fr. 7 KA = 6 K) (see DIALECTS, GREEK).

FRAGMENTS Kassel–Austin, PCG 2. 518–23, although earlier scholars use the numbering in Kock, CAF 1. 797–9.
INTERPRETATION Meineke, FCG 1. 266 f.; G. Kaibel, RE 2/1 (1895), 165, 'Apollophanes' 11. W. G. A.

apologists, Christian The modern collective term appears to go back to F. Morel (Corpus Apologetarum, 1615) and P. Maran (1742; cf. PG 6). The idea as such, however, is much older, as can be seen from the codex Paris. gr. 451 (written in 914 by the scribe Baanes by order of Arethas, archbishop of *Caesarea (1) in Cappadocia) which contains a collection of apologetic writings. The term designates a number of Christian Greek and Latin authors of the 2nd and early 3rd cents. who defended the Christian faith against attacks from their pagan contemporaries. Apologists in this sense, whose writings are partly or fully preserved, are Quadratus, Aristides, *Justin Martyr, *Tatian, *Melito, *Athenagoras, and *Theophilus (2) of Antioch, who all wrote in Greek, and the Latin authors *Minucius Felix and *Tertullian. Nothing is left of the works of Miltiades and Apollinaris of Hierapolis. They all wrote at a time when the legal position of the new religious groups was unclear and the Christians were under continuous threat from their *pagan environment (see CHRISTIANITY). In a wider sense, however, later writers such as Hermias, the author of the *Epistle to Diognetus, *Clement of Alexandria, ps.-Justin, *Commodianus, *Arnobius, *Lactantius, and *Firmicus Maternus are also called apologists. Moreover, there are numerous writings by authors not labelled thus, which, nevertheless, serve apologetical purposes. In addition, the term is sometimes also understood to include authors writing against Gnostics and Jews. This is, however, misleading, because these anti-Gnostic and anti-Jewish works imply other historical settings and differ considerably in content and style from the writings against pagans. The apologists proper wrote in various styles and literary genres, among which mention must be made of the *Apology*, a fictional forensic defence which may have originated in petitions to the Roman emperor(s), and the *Oration to/against the Greeks/Pagans* the precise real-life context of which is unclear. Minucius Felix composed a dialogue (*Octavius*). Likewise, the individual rhetorical strategies of these authors vary considerably. Some of them harshly attack anything non-Christian, whereas others seek to accommodate pagan ideas and concepts. The apologists had to defend themselves against popular charges such as 'Thyestean banquets' (*cannibalism) and 'Oedipean intercourse' (*incest) and against philosophical criticisms (*atheism and novelty and, therefore, by implication, political subversion as well). They responded by setting out their doctrine of God and Christian ethics and emphasizing their antiquity and their loyalty towards the Roman authorities. At the same time, they returned the charges brought against them and accused the pagans of idolatry and immorality. In particular, they criticized Greek and Roman myths and pointed out the contradictions among philosophers. In practice, therefore, many of these tracts go beyond pure apologetics and also serve protreptic and missionary purposes. They attempt to 'translate' the Christian faith into Greek philosophical categories and thus to make it acceptable to the pagan élite. It is not known, however, whether this literature had an immediate impact. In any case, the apologists, for the first time, tackled a variety of theological issues (e.g. the oneness of God, but also the relation between God the Father and Son (Logos), demonology, eschatology, and the immortality of the souls) and are, therefore, important for the history of Christian dogma.

R. M. Grant, *Greek Apologists of the Second Century* (1988).   W. K.

apophrades were 'impure' days of the Athenian *calendar, days associated with inauspicious rites (as e.g. of the *Plynteria (Plut. *Alc.* 34; Poll. 8. 141)), homicide trials in the *Areopagus court, and, perhaps, more generally with the 'moonless' times at the end of the month. Because *pollution was thought to be abroad, temples were closed and major undertakings were avoided. The term was later used to translate Roman *dies nefasti* and *dies atri* which were, in fact, somewhat different from the Attic *apophrades*.

J. D. Mikalson, *AJPhil.* 1975, 19–27; R. Parker, *Miasma* (1983), 158–9.   J. D. M.

apparitores, salaried officials who attended Roman magistrates and priests, attested from the 4th cent. BC to the 3rd cent. AD. They constituted one of the few resources of executive agency and administrative expertise available to magistrates, and gained power which they not infrequently abused. Appointed by the patronage of the magistrates, they served for more than their patron's year of office (except in the case of the *accensi*, who were personal assistants of consuls in office). These officials held the highest public appointment open to non-senators under the republican system, and constituted a status-category (*ordo*), entry to which provided a reflection of social promotion for *freedmen and people from outside Rome; during the empire the social standing of the grander *apparitores* was little lower than the

equestrian order (see EQUITES). Their standing was reflected in a complex organization into corporations (called *decuriae*) according to function, which seems to have been reordered in the early empire, when new grades serving the emperor as magistrate were created. The *scribae* (broadly 'clerks', though serving also as accountants and cashiers) were the highest in prestige (Horace was at least briefly *scriba* to the quaestors who ran the treasury, see AERARIUM), followed by the *lictores who carried the insignia of *imperium*, the *fasces, and acted as a bodyguard, the *viatores or general errand-runners, and the *praecones* or announcers. *Lictores curiati* served the higher priests, like the other staff in charge of the performance of ritual (for instance *pullarii* and *tibicines*). The magistrates of cities outside Rome used similar staffs.

E. Badian, *Klio* 1982, 582–603; B. Cohen, in C. Nicolet (ed.), *Des Ordres à Rome* (1984), 24–60; N. Purcell, *PBSR*, 1983, 125–73.   N. P.

appeals See LAW AND PROCEDURE, ROMAN § 2. 14.

Appendix Vergiliana, a collection of Latin poems of varied provenance and genre traditionally ascribed to *Virgil. According to *Donatus (2) (whose source is *Suetonius) Virgil wrote in his youth *Catalepton*, *Priapea*, *Epigrammata*, *Dirae*, *Ciris, *Culex*, and *Aetna. Servius adds the *Copa*. The 9th-cent. library catalogue of Murbach mentions a Virgilian MS containing also the *Moretum* and the post-Virgilian *Elegiae in Maecenatem*. The *Epigrammata* are included in the *Catalepton*. Later MSS include in the *Appendix* three other short poems: *De institutione viri boni*, *De est et non*, *De rosis nascentibus*.

(1) The *Catalepton* (κατὰ λεπτόν, (?) 'Trifles') contains fifteen epigrams differing in metre and content. Few believe in Virgilian authorship for the whole collection. Four poems dedicated to Virgil's friends may be authentic: 1 (to *Plotius Tucca, later Virgil's editor), 7 (an erotic piece dedicated to *Varius Rufus, the second editor), and 4 and 11, both dedicated to Octavius Musa, a historian (cf. Hor. *Sat.* 1. 10. 82). Two autobiographical poems, 5 and 8, in which Virgil's teacher Siro appears, are well written but unlikely to be authentic, similarly 3, 9 (on *Valerius Messalla Corvinus' triumph over the Aquitani), and 13 (close to Horace's *Epodes* in style and metre); 14 and 15 are usually thought spurious.

(2) Three *Priapea, in various metres, possibly alluded to by the younger Pliny (*Ep.* 5. 3. 2), Augustan in date and bucolic in style, but probably not by Virgil.

(3) *Dirae* ('Maledictions'), called down by an unknown poet upon an estate from which he was expelled by a veteran, Lycurgus, when the arable land was distributed. Their model is Callimachean (ἀραί; see CALLIMACHUS (3), who wrote this sort of 'curse poetry', cf CURSES), but they obviously relate to *Eclogues* 1 and 9. Date and authorship are elusive.

(4) *Lydia*, a love-lament (the manuscripts unite with the preceding poem), in which the poet, not necessarily the same as the writer of the *Dirae*, mourns the absence of his beloved. Metrical features point to the Augustan age. Debts to *Cornelius Gallus have been suspected in the connection of amatory, bucolic, and mythological themes.

(5) *Ciris*, a hexameter epyllion, relating how Scylla, daughter of King *Nisus (1) of Megara, became the cause of her father's death, because she had fallen in love with Minos, her country's enemy. The gods changed her into a sea-bird called Ciris. The emphasis on the love-motive in this version (contrast Aesch. *Cho.* 615–22, with Garvie's comm.) is typically Hellenistic. See also separate entry.

(6) *Culex*. A shepherd kills a gnat that has stung him to warn

him against a snake. Later on, the insect's ghost blames him for his ingratitude and explains the torments and the blessing of the nether world in a detailed νέκυια ('ghost-questioning'). A tumulus is erected in memory of the gnat. Lucan, Statius, and Martial mention a Virgilian *Culex*. Donatus claims that Virgil wrote the *Culex* at the age of 16, but the epyllion's nature as a post-Virgilian parody is revealed by numerous echoes of the *Aeneid* and Ovid's *Metamorphoses*.

(7) *Copa* ('The Hostess'), a short poem with numerous appeals to the virtues of drinking as a remedy against thoughts of mortality, can be connected both with Virgil's second *Eclogue* and with *Theocritus' *Idylls* 7 and 11. Allusions to *Propertius 4 eliminate the possibility of Virgilian authorship, and unawareness of Ovidian metrical and stylistic predilections suggests a date close to Virgil's death.

(8) *Moretum* ('The Salad'), relates in 124 hexameters the way in which a farmer, Simulus, prepares his breakfast on a dark winter morning. Its overall tone is Alexandrian (cf. Callimachus' *Hecale*). Metre (especially the very low number of elisions) and vocabulary (non-Virgilian to a noticeable extent) exclude Virgilian authorship.

(9) *Aetna*: see separate entry.

(10) *Elegiae in Maecenatem*, two (?) elegies on *Maecenas' death, of interest for ancient constructions of his character. See HELLEN-ISTIC POETRY AT ROME.

TEXTS *PLM* 1, Vollmer/Morel (Teubner, 1930); Giomini, 2nd edn. (1962); Salvatore (1957–60); OCT (1966). On the text: Courtney, *BICS* 1968; Reeve, *Maia* 1975 and 1976 and *Text and Transmission* (1983).

SURVEYS K. Büchner, *RE* 8 A; J. A. Richmond, *ANRW* 2. 31. 2. *Dirae*: Fraenkel, *JRS* 1966; Goodyear, *PCPS* 1971. *Culex*: Ross, *Harv. Stud.* 1975. *Copa*: Westendorp Boerma, *Mnemos.* 1958; Tarrant, *Harv. Stud.* 1992.; *Ciris*: Munari, *Atti Acc. d'Italia* (1944); Lyne, *CQ* 1971 and comm. (1978). *Catalepton*: Birt, comm. (1910); Westendorp Boerma, comm. (1949–63). *Moretum*: Perutelli, comm. (1983); Kenney, comm. (1984). *Aetna*: Goodyear, comm. (1965).; *Elegiae in Maecenatem*: Schoonhoven, comm. (1980); Esteve-Forriol, *Die Trauer- und Trostged-ichte in der römischen Literatur* (1962); Kenney, *CR* 1965; Cairns, *Generic Composition in Greek and Roman Poetry* (1972), 90–1. There are articles on all the poems in *Enc. Virg.*

A. Schi.

Appian (Ἀππιανός) of Alexandria, Greek historian. Born in *Alexandria (1) at the end of the 1st cent. AD, he experienced the Jewish rising of AD 116/7, became a Roman citizen, moved to Rome as an advocate and eventually gained, through the influence of his friend M. *Cornelius Fronto, the *dignitas* of a *procurator under *Antoninus Pius, which enabled him to devote his time to writing a Roman History. After the preface and book 1 on early Rome in the period of the kings, this work is arranged ethnographically, dealing with the individual peoples as Rome conquered them: book 2, Italians; 3, Samnites; 4, Celts; 5, Sicilians; 6, Iberians; 7, *Hannibal; 8, Carthaginians (Libyans and Nomads); 9, Macedonians and Illyrians; 10, Greeks and Ionians; 11, Syrians (Seleucids) and Parthians; and 12, *Mithradates VI.; 13–17 treat the Civil Wars; 18–21, the wars in Egypt; 22, the century up to *Trajan; 23, Trajan's campaigns against Dacians, Jews, and Pontic peoples; and 24, Arabians. A survey of Rome's military and financial system was apparently not yet written when Appian died in the 160s. The preface, books 6–9, and 11–17 survive complete, apart from 8b on the Nomads and 9a on the Macedonians (of which only fragments exist) as well as 11b on the Parthians (11b was perhaps unfinished at Appian's death; the textual tradition preserves a Byzantine fake instead); 1–5 are fragmentary, 10 and 18–24 lost.

In order to accommodate a millennium of Roman history in a single work, Appian greatly, but not always successfully, reduced the material he chose from a variety of Greek and Latin authors, among them *Hieronymus (1) of Cardia, *Polybius (1), and Roman annalists like C. *Asinius Pollio, *Caesar, and *Augustus. Since some of his valuable sources, especially on the Civil Wars, are otherwise lost, his work gains historical importance for us, even though it does not simply reproduce these sources. Recent research has stressed Appian's own conscious contribution not only in choosing, reducing, and organizing the material, but also in the independent composition of speeches, in the introduction of episodes from the rhetorical repertoire, and in detailed interference with the sources in view of his avowed aims: a proud citizen of Alexandria, Appian makes events in Egypt the climax of his work; a convinced monarchist, he explains, not always correctly, Roman republican institutions to his Greek audience (papyri show that his work was read in Dura-*Europus); a stout conservative, he regards a lack of popular concord, as witnessed in the Civil Wars, as cataclysmic; unusually interested in administration and finance, he preserves more social and economic information than most historiographers; above all, an ardent admirer of Rome, Appian explains her success through reference to the Romans' good counsel, endurance, patience, moderation, and, especially, overall virtue.

TEXT Bks. 1–12 and frs.: P. Viereck and A. G. Roos (1939; rev. E. Gabba, 1962); bks. 13–17: L. Mendelssohn and P. Viereck (1905); a new OCT by K. Brodersen is in preparation.

TRANSLATION H. White (Loeb, 1912–13).

LITERATURE E. Gabba, *Appiano e la storia delle guerre civili* (1956); B. Goldmann, *Einheitlichkeit und Eigenständigkeit der Historia Romana des Appian* (1988); A. M. Gowing, *The Triumviral Narratives of Appian and Cassius Dio* (1992); K. Brodersen, *ANRW* 2. 34. 1 (1993), 339–63.

K. B.

Appuleius (*RE* 21) **Decianus, Gaius,** son of P. *Decius Subulo, apparently adopted by a relative of L. *Appuleius Saturninus, as tribune 99 BC prosecuted P. Furius (tribune 100), incidentally expressing regret at Saturninus' death. For this he was convicted and went into *exile in Asia, where his son became a *negotiator.

Cic. *Flac.*

E. B.

Appuleius (*RE* 'Apuleius' 29) **Saturninus, Lucius,** of praetorian family and a good popular orator, as quaestor at *Ostia (probably 105 BC) was superseded in his *cura annonae* by M. *Aemilius Scaurus (1) and turned against the ruling oligarchy. As tribune 103 he sought the favour of C. *Marius (1) by passing a law assigning land to his African veterans (see IULIUS CAESAR STRABO, C.). Probably in that year, but possibly in 100, he passed a grain law against violent opposition by *optimate tribunes and a law setting up a permanent *quaestio* on *maiestas, directed (if in 103) against unpopular *nobiles*. He and C. *Servilius Glaucia continued turbulent action in 102 and 101. Q. *Caecilius Metellus Numidicus tried, as censor, to expel them from the senate, but was prevented by his colleague. Tribune again in 100, he again co-operated with Marius by proposing to settle the veterans of his German war in Transalpine Gaul and to give Marius a limited (and probably traditional) right to enfranchise non-Roman colonists. An oath of obedience, to be taken by all magistrates and senators, was attached to the law. Marius found an evasive formula allowing senators to swear it without disgrace, but Metellus refused and went into exile. Marius and Saturninus were later suspected of conspiring to bring this about. With the help of Glaucia, now praetor and supported by the *equites because of his *lex (2) Servilia de repetundis, Saturninus also proposed colonies and land assignments for Roman and Italian veterans of other armies that had fought in Thrace and Sicily and of *proletarii. Re-elected tribune for 99, he hoped to have Glaucia as consul, but Marius, now suspicious of their ambitions, rejected Glaucia's candidacy as illegal. After having C. *Memmius (1), a hostile candidate, murdered in the electoral assembly, Saturninus, by massive use of force in the *concilium plebis, tried to pass a law allowing Glaucia's candidacy. In the resulting riot, the senate, on the motion of the *princeps senatus M. Scaurus, passed the *senatus consultum ultimum—its first use against a tribune in office—and Marius organized an attack on the agitators. On receiving an official promise (fides publica) of safety, they surrendered to him and were imprisoned in the senate-house, but were murdered by a mob without receiving any protection from Marius (probably autumn 100). This embittered their surviving adherents against Marius. Saturninus' colonies were not founded, but his land assignments seem to have been recognized.

In foreign policy he has been (implausibly) suspected of having tried to start a major war in the east in which Marius could command. More credibly, the law found at Cnidus and Delphi has been ascribed to his circle. (See LEX (2): lex de provinciis praetoribus.) He or a relative adopted a son of P. *Decius Subulo, and a relative of his married M. *Aemilius Lepidus (2).

Broughton, MRR 3. 20 ff.; T. J. Luce, Hist. 1970, 161 ff.; J.-L. Ferrary, MÉFRA 1977, 619 ff.; E. Badian, Chiron 1984, 101 ff.　　　E. B.

Apries (OT Hophra), a 26th Dynasty pharaoh (589–570 BC) (see SAITES), campaigned with some success against Phoenician cities and Cyprus with the assistance of Carian and Ionian mercenaries, but his attack on Cyrene was disastrous, leading to a nationalist rising which set *Amasis on the throne. He was killed in an attempt to re-establish himself with Chaldaean help in 567 but was nevertheless buried in the royal cemetery at Sais.

Hdt. 2. 161 f., 4. 159.; Diod. Sic. 1. 68. F. K. Kienitz, Die politische Geschichte Ägyptens vom 7. bis zum 4. Jahrhundert vor der Zeitwende (1953), 27 ff., 161 ff.; A. B. Lloyd, in B. Trigger and others, Ancient Egypt: A Social History (1983), see index; A. B. Lloyd, Herodotus Book II 3 (1992), 169–206; H. de Meulenaere, (W. Helck, E. Otto, and W. Westendorf (eds.)) Lexikon der Ägyptologie (1975–1986) 1. 358 ff.; T. G. H. James, CAH² 3.2 (1991), see index.　　　A. B. L.

Apronius, Lucius (suffect consul AD 8), served as legate on *Germanicus' German campaign (15), receiving triumphal ornaments; similarly honoured as proconsul of Africa (18–21) in the war against *Tacfarinas. While governing Lower Germany, he campaigned unsuccessfully against the *Frisii (28); his son-in-law, C. *Cornelius Lentulus Gaetulicus, simultaneously governed Upper Germany.　　　J. B. C.

Apsines, of Gadara (3rd cent. AD), Athenian rhetor and rival of a Fronto of Emesa; author of On Figures, Investigations, and Declamations. His Rhetoric (Τέχνη), now heavily interpolated, drew extensively on *Hermogenes (2); it is the latest such work to survive complete.

Spengel–Hammer 1. 217.　　　M. B. T.

Apuleius, writer and orator, born c. AD 125 of prosperous parents (Apol. 23) at *Madaurus in Africa Proconsularis, and educated in Carthage, Athens, and Rome (Flor. 18, 20, 16); at Athens he gained enough philosophy to be called philosophus Platonicus by himself and others. He claims to have travelled extensively as a young man (Apol. 23), and was on his way to *Alexandria (1) when he arrived at *Oea, probably in the winter

of AD 156. The story from that point is told by Apuleius himself in his Apologia, no doubt in the most favourable version possible; at Oea he met an ex-pupil from Athens, Pontianus, who persuaded him to stay there for a year and eventually to marry his mother Pudentilla in order to protect her fortune for the family. Subsequently, Apuleius was accused by various other relations of Pudentilla of having induced her to marry him through magic means; the case was heard at *Sabratha, near Oea, in late 158 or early 159. We can deduce from the publication of the Apologia (see below) that he was acquitted. The Florida (see below) make it clear that Apuleius was active as a public speaker and philosophical lecturer in Carthage in the 160s AD, and he seems to have been made priest of the imperial cult for his province (Flor. 16); nothing is known of him after 170, though the disputed De mundo and De Platone (see below) are both addressed to the (unnamed) writer's son Faustinus. Of Apuleius' undisputed writings, only the Apologia and the Florida can be dated with any accuracy; scholars disagree on whether the Metamorphoses is a late or early work, though more think it late than early.

Works (1) The Apologia, Apuleius' speech of defence against charges of *magic (see above), sometimes called De magia in older editions and later MSS, is an extraordinary rhetorical tour de force. In rebutting the charges Apuleius digresses hugely in order to show a vast range of literary and other learning, and presents himself as a committed intellectual and philosopher. The title recalls *Plato (1)'s Apology, the argumentation Cicero at his most colourful.

(2) The Metamorphoses, sometimes called the Golden Ass, is the only Latin *novel which survives whole. On an epic scale (eleven books) and full of narratological cleverness, erotic, humorous, and sensational by turns, it is a remarkable and fascinating work. The basic story is that of the young man Lucius, who through his curiosity to discover the secrets of witchcraft is metamorphosed into an ass and undergoes a variety of picaresque adventures before being retransformed through the agency of the goddess *Isis. This plot is punctuated by a number of inserted tales, which have in fact a close thematic relation to the main narrative; the most substantial and best-known of them is that of Cupid and Psyche ('Soul' in Greek, see PSYCHE), which parallels the main story of Lucius by presenting a character (Psyche) whose disastrous curiosity causes troublesome adventures before her rescue through divine agency. The last book provides a much-discussed and controversial double twist: after his rescue by Isis, Lucius' low-life adventures are interpreted in a new religious and providential light (11. 15. 1–5), and the identity of the narrator seems to switch from Lucius to Apuleius himself (11. 27. 9), a final metamorphosis. The novel's literary influences are various, including much Greek and Latin poetry; the main ass-tale is partly paralleled by the Onos dubiously ascribed to *Lucian (which has no Isiac conclusion or inserted tales but is evidently an epitome), and the two may well have a common source in the lost Greek Metamorphoses of 'Lucius of Patrae' (Phot. Bibl. cod. 129). Many of the stories may derive from the tradition of bawdy Milesian Tales (see ARISTIDES (2)), and that of Cupid and Psyche, with its element of Platonic allegory, may owe at least something to a Greek source (cf. Fulg. Myth. 3. 6).

(3) The Florida are a short collection, derived from a longer one, of choice excerpts from Apuleius' showy *declamations given at Carthage in the 160s, containing passages of narrative, description, and anecdote which show considerable rhetorical and stylistic talent.

(4) The *De deo Socratis* is a declamation on the *daimonion* of *Socrates, probably based on a Greek original (note Plutarch's similar *De genio Socratis*), showing Apuleius' Platonic interests as well as his oratorical skills. For the *daimonion* see SOCRATES.

(5) Lost works: collections of speeches from which the *Florida* are a selection, other speeches and poems, *Ludicra* (minor poems), *De proverbiis*, *Hermagoras* (another novel), *Phaedo* (version of Plato), *Epitome historiarum*, *De republica*, *De medicinalibus*, *De arboribus*, *Eroticus* (cf. ps.-Lucian *Amores*), *Quaestiones conviviales*, works on astronomy, zoology, agriculture, music, and arithmetic.

(6) Disputed works: controversy continues on the authenticity of two extant works ascribed to Apuleius. (*a*) *De dogmate Platonis* or *De Platone*, two books of mediocre exposition of the philosophy of Plato. The extant Περὶ ἑρμηνείας (On Interpretation), a treatise on formal logic, has been by some ascribed to Apuleius as the third book of this work, but many regard it as spurious. (*b*) *De mundo*, a translation of the pseudo-Aristotelian Περὶ κόσμου.

(7) Spurious works: *Asclepius*, *Herbarius*, *De remediis salutaribus*, *Physiognomonia*. Of these the *Asclepius* has some interest as a Latin version of a Hermetic treatise.

The style of Apuleius is admired by many; it owes little to his African origin (the idea of 'African Latin' is now largely discredited), but is the apex of '*Asianism' in Latin, full of poetic and archaic words and apparent coinages, rhythmical and rhyming cola, and coloured with colloquialism and Graecisms; it is best seen in the great set pieces of the *Metamorphoses* (e.g. 11. 1–6). His literary personality is strongly projected in all his works, and in the extraordinary range they cover: proud of his abilities as a speaker and writer, possessed of certitude and a vast if indiscriminate and vicarious learning, he is best seen as a Latin sophist, matching in the Roman west the extraordinarily extrovert and self-promoting characters who were his contemporaries in the Greek *Second Sophistic. Some of his subsequent fame is initially owed to St *Augustine, his fellow-African, who was aware of Apuleius' prestige in his home province and was careful to attack him, but the *Metamorphoses* have been deservedly popular from the early Renaissance on.

TEXTS AND TRANSLATIONS *Metamorphoses*: D. S. Robertson and P. Vallette, 3 vols. (Budé, 1940–5); R. Helm (Teubner, 1908); J. A. Hanson, 2 vols. (Loeb, 1989); P. G. Walsh (1994), trans. only. *Apologia* and *Florida*: P. Vallette (Budé, 1925); R. Helm (Teubner, 1910); Eng. trans., H. E. Butler (1909).; *De deo Socratis* and doubtful works: J. Beaujeu (Budé, 1973); C. Moreschini (Teubner, 1991); the last includes *Asclepius*, also ed. A. D. Nock in *Hermès Trismégiste* 2 (1945).

COMMENTARIES *Met.* bk. 1, A. Scobie (1975); bk. 2, B. J. de Jonge (1941); bk. 3, R. T. van der Paardt (1971); bk. 4. 1–27, B. J. Hijmans and others (1977); *Cupid and Psyche* [bk. 4. 28–6. 24] E. J. Kenney (1990); bk. 6. 25–7, B. J. Hijmans and others (1981); bk. 8, B. J. Hijmans and others (1985); bk. 11, J. Gwyn Griffiths (1975). *Apol.* A. S. Owen and H. E. Butler (1914). The Budé texts of *Flor.* and *Apol.* contain useful short notes.

STYLE M. Bernhard, *Der Stil des Apuleius von Madaura* (1927); L. Callebat, *Sermo Cotidianus dans les Métamorphoses d'Apulée* (1968). *Index Apuleianus*, ed. W. Oldfather and others (1934).

GENERAL CRITICISM *Met.*: P. G. Walsh, *The Roman Novel* (1970); J. Tatum, *Apuleius and the Golden Ass* (1979); J. J. Winkler, *Actor and Auctor: A Narratological Reading of Apuleius'* Golden Ass (1984); C. C. Schlam, *The Metamorphoses of Apuleius* (1992); as history: F. Millar, *JRS* 1981, 63–75.; *Flor.*: K. Mras, *Apuleius' Florida im Rahmen ähnlicher Literatur* (1949). Disputed works: J. Redfors, *Echtheitskritische Untersuchung der apuleischen Schriften* De Platone *und* De Mundo (1960); B. J. Hijmans, *ANRW* 2. 36. 1 (1987), 393–475. Influence: H. Hagendahl, *Augustine and the Latin Classics* (1967); E. Haight, *Apuleius and his Influence* (1927).

BIBLIOGRAPHIES C. C. Schlam, *CW* 1971, 285–309; S. J. Harrison, *JRS* 1993, 59 ff.

S. J. Ha.

Apulia (mod. Puglia), a region of SE Italy corresponding to Augustan *Regio II, bounded by the valleys of the Bradano and Tiferno. Regio II also included a part of *Samnium which was not Apulian in culture (Plin. *HN* 3. 99–104). It is geographically diverse, with lagoonal and marshy coastal regions and a high plateau, the Tavoliere, in the north. Ethnically, it included the *Daunians, Peucetians, and *Iapygians (Lat. Sallentini). These were Messapian in language and culture (see MESSAPIC; MESSAPII), and part of a cultural *koinē which included strong Greek and Illyrian influences. Many cities have Greek foundation legends, issued Greek-style coinage and adopted Greek styles and techniques in architecture and civic development. Some of the northerly Daunian cities also show Oscan influence. The Apuli, after whom the region is named, were a distinct group settled near mons *Garganus, who had cultural similarities with their Daunian neighbours but were Oscan-speakers (Strabo 6. 3. 11). Apulia was one of the most densely urbanized regions of Italy. Economically, southern Apulia was reliant on agriculture and trade with Greece and Illyria, while the Tavoliere was a *wool-producing area.

C. D. Smith, *Daunia Vetus* (1978). K. L.

Aquae Mattiacae (mod. Wiesbaden), developed in the 1st cent. AD as an auxiliary-fort (see AUXILIA), first as a Rhine-bridgehead and then as part of the *limes. From the early 2nd to the mid-3rd cent., following the removal of the garrison, the site continued to flourish as the *civitas*-capital of the local tribe, the Mattiaci, and, thanks to its thermal springs (cf. Plin. *HN* 31. 20), as a spa.

H.-G. Simon, *Germania* 1963, 328 ff. J. F. Dr.

Aquae Sextiae (mod. Aix-en-Provence), the first Roman foundation in Transalpine *Gaul, was established as a fort by C. *Sextius Calvinus in 123 BC after his defeat of the Salluvii and in 102 BC was the scene of C. *Marius (1)'s great victory over the *Teutones. Under Caesar it was refounded as a Latin colony (see IUS LATII); under Augustus it was made a full colony, *Colonia Iulia Augusta Aquis Sextiis*; and under Diocletian it became the capital of the province of Narbonensis Secunda. No major monuments survive, but the courses of four aqueducts are known and significant discoveries have been made under the cathedral.

H. Ambard, *Aix romaine* (1985). J. F. Dr.

Aquae Sulis (mod. Bath), attributed by *Ptolemy (4) to the *civitas Belgarum* (see BELGAE). The hot springs, perhaps used in the iron age, were developed from the Neronian period and attained great elaboration, rivalling the largest Gallic establishments. The hot spring was enclosed in a polygonal reservoir in the SE corner of a colonnaded precinct within which stood the prostyle temple with its altar axially in front. The temple carried the famous Gorgon pediment. South of the precinct the spring connected with the principal suite of baths. The defences (constructed in the late 2nd cent.) enclosed other less well-known structures within their 9.3 ha. (23 acres). Outside was an extensive extra-mural settlement. Many inscriptions record visitors from Britain and abroad (*RIB* 138–78), whilst excavation of the sacred spring has produced 130 curse-tablets (see CURSES), the most important such archive for Romano-Celtic religion yet published. The site was deserted in Saxon times, the ruins being described in an 8th-cent. poem.

B. W. Cunliffe, *Roman Bath* (1969); B. W. Cunliffe and P. Davenport, *The Temple of Sulis Minerva at Bath* 1, *The Site* (1985); 2 (ed. B. Cunliffe), *The Finds from the Sacred Spring* (1988).   M. J. M.

aqueducts In a Mediterranean climate, correcting the accidents of rainfall distribution through the management of water-sources transforms *agriculture by extending the growing-season through the dry summer by means of *irrigation, allows agglomerations of population beyond the resources of local springs or wells, eases waterlogging through drainage in the wetter zones, and protects against floods caused by violent winter rainfall. The societies of the semi-arid peripheries had long depended on water-strategies such as irrigation drawn from perennial rivers, or the qanat (a tunnel for tapping ground-water resources).

Hydraulic engineering was therefore both useful and prestigious. It was quickly adopted by the nascent cities of the Greek world and their leaders: ground-level aqueducts bringing water from extra-mural springs into Greek cities were at least as old as the 6th cent. BC: notable late-Archaic examples are at Athens, using clay piping (see ATHENS, TOPOGRAPHY), and on *Samos, where the water was channelled by rock-hewn tunnel through the acropolis—a remarkable engineering feat on which Herodotus (3. 60) comments. In the Classical period, an aqueduct system is attested for the refounded city of *Priene, presumably when it was moved to its new site in the 4th cent. BC. Water from springs at a distance of 2 km. (1¼ mi.), and above the level of the city, was fed through a terracotta pipe 25 cm. (10 in.) in diameter set in a trench covered with marble slabs and leading to a distribution tank within the city walls.

A more elaborate system was constructed in the 2nd cent. BC by *Eumenes (2) II at *Pergamum. A copious spring 25 km. (15½ mi.) (in a direct line) north of the city was brought through an extended pipeline, following the contours. This was constructed in various materials. It led to a basin from which it flowed under pressure through iron pipes (supported by stone blocks at intervals) to the top of the citadel. The basin is at a height of 386 m. (1,266 ft.) above sea-level: at its lowest point, the pipe crossed a valley at only 175 m. (574 ft.) before rising to the citadel at c.330 m. (1,083 ft.) (Vitruvius (8. 6. 5) says the Greeks call this system a *koilia*). This system may have helped inspire the first important aqueduct at Rome, the aqua Marcia of 144 BC.

The city was, however, already served by two water-leats, for the most part in underground tunnels, called aqua Appia (312 BC) and aqua Anio Vetus (272); both were prestige works like the first generation of public roads, with which they had associations, and in the case of the Anio Vetus drawing to Rome the water of the river *Anio from its upper course a considerable distance away. The ease of tunnelling in the volcanic tufa of Rome's neighbourhood had combined with the problems of water management on a relatively wet west-facing coast to create an indigenous tradition of hydraulic engineering in Etruria, where extensive networks of land drains (*cuniculi*) were developed.

A supply of copious clean water was needed for a steadily increasing population. Most aqueducts, moreover (more or less legally), provided some water for irrigation in the market-garden belts in and around city walls, while some were used to turn water-*mills (notably at Barbégal near Arles). But the growing popularity of water-intensive services such as *baths and fountains (see NYMPHAEUM) also promoted the development of the aqueduct system, while there was considerable kudos to be gained by such spectacular reworkings of the dispositions of nature. By the imperial period, aqueducts became a widespread status symbol, and the great bridges (like the Pont du Gard on

the Nîmes aqueduct (see NEMAUSUS) or that at Segovia) which are so famous today owe something to the need for visibility and show.

Imperial benefaction created the most ambitious projects. As a sign of Rome's status as world-capital and to supply their elaborate waterworks Agrippa and Augustus added three aqueducts to its supply (the first after the aqua Tepula of 125 BC), and established an administrative infrastructure for maintaining the system. Aquae Iuliae or Augustae became standard in the repertoire of what favoured cities in Italy might receive: the longest of all was that which conveyed the water of the Serino spring to the cities of Campania. The Claudian aqueducts at Rome, aqua Claudia and Anio Novus, were also on the most ambitious scale, with very long sections on arches to maintain the head of water necessary for access all across the city of Rome. Further additions to the network were made under Trajan and Caracalla (for his baths): we know less about the period after the work of Sex. *Iulius Frontinus, our outstandingly detailed description of Rome's aqueducts in about AD 100. Dues were payable for private use of water, but no attempt was made in any city to cover the cost of the system, which always remained a public benefaction. See WATER.

A. T. Hodge, *Roman Aqueducts and Water Supply* (1992); T. Ashby, *The Aqueducts of Ancient Rome* (1935); Steinby, *Lexicon* 60 ff.; J. Coulton in S. Macready and F. H. Thompson, *Roman Architecture in the Greek World* (1987), 72 ff.   R. A. T.; N. P.

Aquila (*RE* 10) **Romanus,** perhaps of 3rd cent. AD, whose treatise *On Figures of Thought and Speech* survives. Its main source is a Greek work by Alexander Numenius (preserved in epitome), but it contains illustrations from Cicero, often misquoted from memory.

Ed. Halm, *Rhet. Lat. Min.* 22–37; Schanz–Hosius, § 837. *PIR*² A 983.   J. F. M.; M. W.

Aquileia, a city a few kilometres from the head of the Adriatic. In 186 BC Transalpine Gauls occupied this fertile site, which controls roads across the Julian Alps. Rome ejected them and founded a Latin colony (181 BC; see IUS LATII) to forestall similar intrusions and to exploit neighbouring gold-mines (Livy 39. 22, 54; 40. 34). Aquileia became a great military, commercial, and industrial stronghold; its *amber trade was especially important (Strab. 4. 207 f.; 5. 214). In imperial times it was a *colonia*, sometimes dubbed *Roma secunda*, the capital of Venetia et Istria, and one of the world's largest cities, with a population that perhaps approached 100,000. It had major harbour facilities, and important early Christian basilicas. When the city was sacked by *Attila in 452, many fled to the neighbouring lagoons of Venice. It was however an important medieval patriarchate, especially from the 9th cent. Ancient remains are numerous.

A. Calderini, *Aquileia romana* (1930); S. Panciera, *La vita economica di Aquileia* (1957); M. Verzár-Bass, *Scavi di Aquileia* 1 (1988).   E. T. S.; T. W. P.

Aquilius (*RE* 34) **Regulus, Marcus,** of aristocratic background, recouped his family fortunes after his father's exile by securing under *Nero the conviction of three consulars on capital charges, receiving seven million sesterces and a priesthood. In AD 70 his conduct was unsuccessfully questioned in the senate. Under *Domitian he helped prosecute Q. *Iunius Arulenus Rusticus, whom he described as a 'Stoic ape', afterwards publishing his speech and incurring *Pliny (2)'s hostility. Although Pliny

Aquillius or Aquilius

recognized that Regulus valued oratory, he quotes with approval the comment that he was 'the most evil fellow on two legs'. *Herennius Senecio, described him as 'a bad man, unskilled in speaking', the reverse of M. *Porcius Cato's definition of an orator (Plin. *Ep.* 1. 5; 2. 20; 4. 2, 7; 6. 2). Regulus published a biography of his dead son and was a patron of *Martial, who speaks of him in complimentary terms.   J. B. C.

Aquillius or **Aquilius** (*RE* 3), supposed Latin author of *Boeotia*, a *fabula* *palliata* which Varro attributed to Plautus.

> J. Wright, *Dancing in Chains* (1974); A. S. Gratwick, *CQ* 1979, 308 ff.
>   P. G. M. B.

Aquillius (1) (*RE* 10), **Manius,** consul 129 BC, succeeded M. *Perperna (1) in Asia and completed the war against the allies of *Aristonicus (1). With the help of a senatorial commission he delimited and organized the province, built roads in it (*ILLRP* 456) and gave it its constitution (Strabo 14. 1. 38 (646 C)). He triumphed (126), was accused *repetundarum* (see REPETUNDAE) and, although guilty, acquitted (App. *BCiv.* 1. 22. 92).   E. B.

Aquillius (2) (*RE* 11), **Manius,** son of (1), chief legate of C. *Marius (1) against the *Cimbri, and his colleague as consul 101 BC. He crushed the slave revolt in Sicily, personally killing the rebel leader. He celebrated an *ovatio* (99?), was later (95?) prosecuted *repetundarum* (see REPETUNDAE) and, although guilty (Cic. *Flac.* 98), acquitted, through the efforts of Marius and M. *Antonius (1). As head of a mission to Asia (90), he restored *Ariobarzanes I to Cappadocia and *Nicomedes (4) IV to Bithynia, then forced Nicomedes to attack *Mithradates VI, thus starting the First Mithradatic War. Defeated by Mithradates, he was captured and killed amid public humiliation.   E. B.

Aquil(l)ius (*RE* 23) **Gallus, Gaius,** a lawyer of equestrian family and a leading pupil of Q. *Mucius Scaevola (2), was praetor in 66 BC but thereafter retired to Cercina and devoted himself to legal study. A man whose probity won him popular esteem, he is praised by *Cicero, his colleague as praetor (*Off.* 3. 14. 60; *Nat. d.* 3. 30. 74), for introducing the formulae on bad faith (*de dolo malo*). This refers in particular to the formula (*actio de dolo*) by which a person who had suffered loss through the bad faith of another could sue the latter. Aquillius held that bad faith existed when pretence was at variance with reality (*aliud simulatum, aliud actum*), a definition which later proved too wide. He also invented a form (*stipulatio Aquiliana*), useful in settling accounts, by which one person could give another a complete discharge of all debts due. No writings survive.

> Lenel, *Pal.* 1. 55–6; Bremer 1. 111–21; Wieacker *RRG* 1, 600–1; Kunkel 1967, 21–2; Watson 1974, 72–5.   T. Hon.

Aquincum, on the Danube at Budapest, was the centre of the Illyrian-Celtic Eravisci, whose settlement lay on the Gellért hill, later the provincial capital of Lower Pannonia. Throughout the Roman period it was a key military base against the *Quadi and the Sarmatian *Iazyges. From *Vespasian it was an auxiliary cavalry station (see AUXILIA) and under *Domitian (c. AD 89) an earth and timber fortress was constructed by Legio II Adiutrix. After serving in *Trajan's Dacian and Parthian wars (when it was replaced by X Gemina) the legion returned as a permanent garrison at Aquincum, except for two further periods of detachment, 161–7 and under *Septimius Severus, when its place was taken by IV Flavia Felix. Around the camp a *canabae* developed its own administration, while the city of Aquincum, a *municipium* (*Aelium*) under Hadrian and *colonia* (*Septimia*) under Severus

extending over 50 ha. (124 acres), developed quite separately on a site 3¼ km. (2 mi.) north of the legionary fortress. Aquincum was abandoned along with the rest of *Pannonia (c.400), its last mention being Sid. Apoll. 5. 107.

> Military base: Z. Visy, *Der pannonische Limes in Ungarn* (1985), 80 ff.; civil town: K. Póczy, in A. Lengyel and G. T. B. Radan (eds.), *The Archaeology of Roman Pannonia* (1980), 255 ff.   F. A. W. S.; J. J. W.

Aquitania, a name originally applied to the area bounded by the Garonne, the Pyrenees, and the bay of Biscay. The Aquitani are described as differing from the other Gauls in speech, customs, and physique, and archaeologically their culture is distinguished by several simple Hallstatt survivals. They were divided into many small tribes which were defeated in 56 BC by P. *Licinius Crassus (2) and finally subdued after campaigns in 38 and 27 BC. Augustus made Aquitania an imperial province (see PROVINCIA), but extended it to include the Celtic tribes to the Loire. It was eventually governed from *Burdigala (mod. Bordeaux). Under the later empire the Augustan province was divided into three: Aquitania Prima and Secunda (capitals at Bourges and Bordeaux respectively), and Novempopulana (the original Aquitania, with its capital at Eauze). Greater Aquitania soon became famous for its wealth, based on agriculture and trade. Through the works of *Ausonius and modern archaeological discoveries we are particularly well informed about the sophisticated upper-class lifestyle of the 4th cent. AD, when large landowners divided their time between the cities and their expensive villas. The settling of the Visigoths (see GOTHS) in Aquitania Secunda in 418 appears to have done little to disturb this Romano-Gallic culture.

See BURDIGALA.   J. F. Dr.

Arabia (see ARABS). Greeks of the Classical period were familiar with the coast of Arabia and with Arabia Petraea. They knew less about the other divisions into which by *Ptolemy (4)'s time they had divided the peninsula—Arabia Felix in the south and Arabia Deserta. The Romans of the empire took account, as the organization of the southern sector of the *limes* shows, of the historical role of the Arabs, their steady pressure on the settled lands of the north (see NOMADS), their infiltration into the Syrian end of the Arabian peninsula, their seasonal movements of *transhumance between the Desert and the Sown.

In the north confrontation with, and partial subjection to, the great powers of *Mesopotamia and *Babylonia are attested on the monuments of the Assyrian kings from Shalmaneser III (853 BC) to Tiglath Pileser III (745–727 BC), and Esarhaddon (680–669 BC) and Babylonian Nabonidus visited Taima in person. The Persian king *Darius I recorded the tributary status of Arabaya (cf. Hdt. 7. 69; 3. 97). An *Achaemenid presence is also attested in the Omani peninsula, home of the Makā people of OP texts, where archaeology has revealed a flourishing iron age culture from c.1300 to 300 BC.

For the Greeks knowledge really began with *Alexander (3) the Great, whose last plans included the conquest of the eastern Arabian coast (Arr. *Anab.* 7. 19. 5), in preparation for which he sent naval expeditions into both the *Persian Gulf and *Red Sea. Early Seleucid interest in the Indian and Arabian trade (see the gifts of imported incense by *Seleucus (1) I to *Didyma: *RC* no. 5) is reflected in the Hellenistic Greek presence at Bahrain (*Tylos) and above all Failaka (*Icaros (2): see *SEG* 35. 1476–8), where a Seleucid fortress has been excavated, and in *Antiochus (3) III's expedition to *Gerrha in the Saudi interior. Ariston explored down to Bab-el Mandeb for *Ptolemy (1) II, who, to punish the hostile Nabataeans of Petra, tapped the incense route south of them by a trade-arrangement with the Lihyanites of Dedan (Al-'Ula); *Miletus settled for him a colony, Ampelone, as a seaport for Dedan. The 4th–3rd-cent. kingdoms in the south were Minaea on the Red Sea, Katabania at the Straits, and Sabaea, the Hadramaut, and Mahra along the south coast; by the 2nd cent. BC Minaea had vanished, and a Sabaean-Homerite confederacy (Himyarites) dominated Yemen.

In the north much was achieved by the Nabataean Arabs; their territories as far as the Negev and Transjordan were developed with the aid of skilful water-conservation (see NABATAEANS). The interior was unknown at this stage. Arabia's importance for Greeks and Macedonians lay chiefly in its *incense (see COSTUS; MYRRH) and *spices, but also *gold and *gems, and in its role as middleman for the Indian trade. The principal routes were from Sabaea through Medina, Dedan, and *Petra to *Syria, and routes from Dhofar to Gerrha, from Gerrha across to Petra, and from Egypt to Babylonia via Jauf. These routes became less important with the discovery of the *monsoon, allowing direct voyages from Roman Egypt to southern Arabia and India.

Augustus sent a military expedition under *Aelius Gallus to Arabia Felix (Sabaea) which failed; but Roman naval predominance in the Red Sea was secured and the reduction of Aden (Arabia Eudaemon) in the early Principate eased the movement of Roman merchantmen between Egypt and India (*Peripl. M. Rubr.* ed. Casson 26). In the north the evolution of a military frontier-in-depth (see LIMES) from the Black to the Red Sea involved absorption of the client-Nabataeans into the Roman provincial system, achieved under *Trajan, who sent *Cornelius Palma to annex the Nabataean kingdom and turn it into a new province (Arabia); he also built a great road through it from Aela on the Red Sea to *Damascus (in provincial Syria). The provincial era started on 22 March AD 106; the surprisingly rapid *Romanization of local legal procedure is revealed by the *Babatha archive. Of the two chief cities, *Bostra and Petra, the former was garrisoned by Legio III Cyrenaica during the 2nd cent. Slightly enlarged to the north under Septimius Severus, the province under *Diocletian was divided into (1) the part around Bostra, retaining the name Arabia, and (2) the rest, later incorporated in Palaestina but (by c.358) appearing as Palaestina Salutaris. In response to the Saracen threat, the *limes* was strengthened in the 4th–5th cents., but had fallen into decay by the 6th., thus offering no obstacle to the Muslim Arab invasions of the early 7th. Greek material culture, its impact on Arabs beyond the *limes* revealed in excavations at the Saudi site of Faw (3rd cent. AD), left traces in Arabia as late as the Ummayyad and even Abbasid periods.

G. Bowersock, *Roman Arabia* (1983), and *Hellenism in Late Antiquity* (1990), ch. 6; F. Millar, *The Roman Near East 31 BC–AD 337* (1993), ch. 11; D. Potts, *The Arabian Gulf in Antiquity* (1990); M. Speidel, *ANRW* 2. 8 (1977), 687 ff. (Roman army); S. Thomas Parker, *Romans and Saracens* (1986) (*limes*); B. Thomasson, *Laterculi Praesidum* 1 (1984), 327 ff. (Roman governors); J.-F. Salles, in A. Kuhrt and S. Sherwin-White (eds.), *Hellenism in the Near East* (1987) 75 ff., and (ed.), *L'Arabie et ses mers bordières 1: Itinéraires et voisinages* (1988); M. Rice, *The Archaeology of the Arabian Gulf c.5000–323 BC* (1994).

W. W. T.; E. W. G.; A. J. S. S.

Arabs, ancient tribes and peoples who lived in, and around the modern Arabian peninsula. The earliest references from the Neo-Assyrian annals and the Bible date back to the 9th–7th cents. BC; there was no relation at that time between the Arabs (sometimes confused with the Aramaeans) and the country of *Arabia. The

texts refer to nomadic tribes in the Sinai, in Jordan and Syria, and even along the banks of the Euphrates. *Herodotus (1) was acquainted with the Arabs of southern Palestine and the Sinai, and mentions the Arabs of the frankincense region—but the term Arab does not appear before the 2nd cent. BC in the inscriptions of Yemen. More information comes from *Diodorus (3) Siculus (using *Agatharchides and reflecting the findings of *Alexander (3) the Great's expeditions in the *Red Sea) and *Strabo (using Hellenistic sources and *Aelius Gallus' campaign in Arabia under Augustus, who refers to Arabs in Mesopotamia (along the Euphrates), in Egypt (Sinai and Red Sea), southern Jordan (the *Nabataeans) and the Syrian steppe and even in eastern Arabia (the people of *Gerrha). For classical authors the defining features of the Arabs (in the Bible as well) are nomadism (see NOMADS), pastoralism, and the camel-based caravan trade. However, their military strength is already mentioned in early (Assyrian) sources, and becomes prominent in Roman times.

I. Eph'al, *The Ancient Arabs* (1982); P. Briant, 'Les Arabes et le Proche Orient', *États et pasteurs* (1982), 113–79; H. I. MacAdam, in T. Fahd (ed.), *L'Arabie préislamique* (1989), 289–320.

J.-F. S.

Arachne ('Spider'), daughter of a Lydian dyer who challenged *Athena to a weaving contest. No doubt her story was originally a cautionary tale like those of *Thamyris and *Marsyas (1), warning against the inevitable failure and dire consequences of such presumption; but in the only extant literary version (Ov. *Met.* 6. 5–145) the emphasis is all on the insolent brilliance of the tapestry she weaves. Her catalogue of the sexual outrages of the gods, clearly designed to provoke the virgin goddess, outclasses Athena's routine effort and drives her to destroy Arachne's work and attack her. Only after the girl has hanged herself in distress does Athena transform her into a spider, fated to re-enact her compulsive web-making for ever after. It is possible that a Corinthian aryballos of c.600 BC may already show the competition scene; otherwise no other ancient representations are known.

G. D. and S. S. Weinberg, in S. Weinberg (ed.), *The Aegean and the Near East: Studies . . . Hetty Goldman* (1956), 262–7; J. G. Szilágyi, *LIMC* 1.

A. H. G.

Arachosia see ALEXANDRIA (3).

Aradus the main city of north Phoenicia, on the island of Awad, whose kings in the 5th cent. BC, allied to the Persians, ruled a large area on the mainland from the plain of Antioch (1) to Simyra: a major sanctuary to Heracles-Melqart and Eshmun stood at Amrith (Marathus). Autonomous under the Seleucids after conquest by *Alexander (3) the Great, the city was organized as a federation, including Antaradus (Tartous), opposite the fortified island (the fortifications are of uncertain date), and its former dominions (Gabala, Carne, Marathus, Simyra). The federation gradually dissolved, but Aradus remained an important harbour for eastern trade. In the mountains are the ruins of the main Aradian high place, the temple of *Zeus Baetocaeces.

DCPP, entry under the name; H. Seyrig, *RN* 1964; J.-P. Rey-Coquais, *Arados et sa Pérée* (1974); M. Yon and A. Caubet, *Transeuphratène 6* (1993).

J.-F. S.

Arae Flaviae (mod. Rottweil), on the Neckar. In AD 74 the Roman Rhine–Danube frontier was shortened by carrying a road south-eastwards from Strasburg (*Argentorate) to the *Danube. A fort was built at the point where another road coming up from Vindonissa joined it. At the same time a civilian settlement, 'The Flavian Altars', was developed as a centre of the imperial cult devoted to the ruling dynasty (see RULER-CULT). It was, perhaps, very early given municipal status (see MUNICIPIUM). Though the garrison was withdrawn around AD 100, the town prospered until the mid-3rd cent.

W. Schleiermacher, in (*Gymnasium*) *Germania Romana* 1: *Römerstädte in Deutschland* (1960), 59 ff.; A. Rüsch, *ANRW* 2. 5. 1 (1976), 560 ff.

J. F. Dr.

Aramaic, a *Semitic language, was used in the ancient near east from early in the 1st millennium BC and through the Roman period. Originating in upper Mesopotamia, it is first known through royal inscriptions from Syria and was used widely by the Assyrian and Persian administrations. After the fall of the Persian empire Aramaic continued to be used in the Hellenizing cities (see HELLENISM) of *Palmyra, *Edessa, *Petra, etc., as well as in the *Parthian east. There are many Greek–Aramaic bilingual inscriptions, the best known being the long Palmyrene Tariff. The Edessan dialect of Aramaic, later called Syriac, became the main language of the Christian Church of the middle east. Another late dialect of Aramaic, Mandaic, was used for the sacred writings of the Gnostic pagan sect of the Mandaeans or Sabians in southern Iraq.

K. Beyer, *The Aramaic Language: Its Distribution and Subdivisions*, trans. J. F. Healey (1986; Ger. orig. 1984); J. A. Fitzmyer, *A Wandering Aramean: Collected Aramaic Essays* (1979).

J. F. H.

Ara Pacis, a monumental altar erected in the northern *Campus Martius near the via Lata (Corso), considered one of the major products of Augustan public art. It was voted in 13 BC by the senate, as *Augustus records in his Testament (see RES GESTAE), to commemorate his safe return from Gaul and Spain; and finished in 9 BC. The altar proper was surrounded by a walled precinct (11.6 × 10.6 m.; 38 × 34¾ ft.) with entrances to east and west, and decorated with sculptured reliefs on two tiers. Internally there were festoons slung from ox-heads above and fluting below; externally the lower frieze was filled with complex acanthus scrolls, above which on the east and west were mythological panels, on the north and south a religious procession showing the imperial family, lictors, priests, magistrates, and representations of the Roman people. Smaller reliefs on the inner altar showing Vestals (see VESTA), priests, sacrificial animals, etc., continue the procession on the outer walls. The event represented by this procession has been much disputed, a *supplicatio* (formal period of public rejoicing) of 13 BC being recently proposed rather than the consecration of the altar itself.

Several of the sculptured slabs were brought to light about 1568, others in 1859 and 1903. In 1937–8 the site was thoroughly explored and the monument reconstructed, with most of its surviving sculptures, between the Mausoleum of Augustus and the Tiber. See SCULPTURE, ROMAN.

G. Moretti, *L'Ara Pacis Augustae* (1938); G. Koeppel, *Bonner Jahrb.* 1987, 101 ff.; 1988, 97 ff.; R. Billows, *JRA* 1993, 80 ff.; D. Castriota, *The Ara Pacis Augustae* (1995).

J. D.

Araros (Ἀραρώς), son of *Aristophanes (1), produced (after 388 BC) two of his father's plays, *Kokalos* and *Aiolosikon* (hyp. 4 Ar. *Plut.*). The first play of his own was produced in 375; we have citations from five plays, and six titles.

Kassel–Austin, *PCG* 2. 524 ff. (*CAF* 2. 215 ff.).

K. J. D.

Aratea, Latin poems translated from *Aratus (1) (his work was sometimes divided into *Phaenomena* and *Diosemeiai*) by the following. (1) P. *Terentius Varro Atacinus. (2) M. *Tullius Cicero (1) (see section on his poems): 480 continuous lines and about 70 in quotations are extant from the *Phaenomena*, 27 are quoted as

from *Prognostica* = *Diosemeiai*. Cicero wrote this work as a young man; he commits factual errors, but his concern was less scientific accuracy than meeting the challenge of conveying Aratus in Latin (he avoids Greek nomenclature wherever he can). The style is stiff and the versification rigid. (3) *Iulius Caesar Germanicus: the complete *Phaenomena* in 725 lines. He made better use than Cicero of commentators on Aratus and corrected a number of errors. There are also over 200 lines not based on Aratus about sidereal influences on weather; Germanicus may have intended these as part of a separate work. (4) *Avienus: a version expanded by over 700 lines from the Greek through verbal padding; he is more influenced by Germanicus than by Cicero.

W. Leuthold, *Die Übersetzung der Phaenomena durch Cicero und Germanicus* (1942); H. E. Richter, *Übersetzen und Übersetzungen in der römischen Literatur* (1938), 16. (1) J. Soubiran, *Cicéron, Aratea* (1972); K. Büchner, *RE* 7 A, 1237; G. Townend in T. A. Dorey (ed.), *Cicero* (1965), 109. (2) D. B. Gain, *The Aratus Ascribed to Germanicus* (1976); A. Le Boeuffle, *Germanicus, les Phénomènes d'Aratos* (1975); G. Maurach, *Germanicus und sein Arat* (1978); A. Traglia in *ANRW* 2. 32. 1. 321. (3) J. Soubiran, *Aviénus, les Phénomènes d'Aratos* (1981); D. Weber, *Aviens Phaenomena* (1986).

E. C.

Aratus (1) (*RE* 6), *c.*315 to before 240 BC, poet. Born at Soloi in Cilicia, he was taught by the grammarian *Menecrates (2) of Ephesus, and studied at Athens, where he probably first became acquainted with *Callimachus (3) and the philosophers *Timon (2) of Phlius and *Menedemus (1). He there imbibed *Stoicism from *Zeno (2) and was introduced to *Antigonus (2) Gonatas of Macedonia, who invited him to the court at Pella. There he celebrated the king's marriage to Phila, half-sister of the Seleucid *Antiochus I, and composed a *Hymn to *Pan* glorifying Antigonus' victory over the Celts (277). Later he migrated to Antiochus' court in Syria, where he is said to have undertaken editions of *Homer's *Odyssey* and *Iliad*. Returning to Macedonia, he died there some time before the death of Antigonus (240/39).

Aratus' best-known work, and the only one extant, is a poem entitled *Phaenomena*, undertaken at the suggestion of Antigonus. The first and longest part of this is a versification of a prose treatise by *Eudoxus (1) of Cnidus which gave a detailed description of the make-up and relative positions of the *constellations. After a proem to *Zeus (1–18), Aratus describes the poles and the northern constellations (19–318), the southern constellations (322–453), refuses to describe the five planets, enumerates the principal circles of the celestial sphere (462–558), and lists the simultaneous risings and settings of many combinations of the constellations, supposedly for telling the time at night (559–732). The second part of the poem (733–1154) deals with weather signs. Although it has a separate title (Διοσημεῖαι), and is derived from a different source (perhaps a work of *Theophrastus), it is an integral part of the poem. After enumerating the days of the lunar month, and mentioning the seasons and *Meton's 19-year calendarical cycle, Aratus gives weather prognostications, not only from the celestial bodies, but also from terrestrial phenomena and animal behaviour. The poem is enlivened by frequent mythological allusions and picturesque digressions, the longest being the descriptions of the *golden age (98–136) and of storms at sea (408–35). The author's Stoicism is apparent especially in the proem, where 'Zeus' is the Stoic all-informing deity.

The *Phaenomena* achieved immediate fame (cf. *Anth. Pal.* 9. 25 (Leonidas of Tarentum); Callim. *Epigr.* 27), and lasting popularity beyond the circle of learned poets: it became the most widely read poem, after the *Iliad* and *Odyssey*, in the ancient world, and was one of the very few Greek poems translated into Arabic.

Latin translations were made by P. *Terentius Varro Atacinus, Cicero, Germanicus, and Avienus (see ARATEA). It was read more for its literary charm than its astronomical content, but some of the numerous commentaries on it criticized the many grave astronomical errors which it contains, especially the commentary of *Hipparchus (3) (which, alone of his works, has survived, because of its connection with this popular poem).

Aratus wrote many other poems, all lost except for two epigrams preserved in the Greek *Anthology (Gow–Page, *HE* 760–7); for new fragments see *Suppl. Hell.* 83–120. A collection entitled Τὰ κατὰ λεπτόν gave its name to the *Catalepton* attributed to Virgil (see APPENDIX VERGILIANA).

TEXTS AND TRANSLATIONS OF THE *PHAENOMENA*: E. Maass (1893); G. R. Mair (Loeb, 1921); J. Martin (1954), with Fr. trans.

GENERAL For the ancient Lives see *Suda*, ed. A. Adler, 1. 337–8, and the Lives in E. Maass, *Commentariorum in Aratum reliquiae* (1898; repr. 1958). On the lost works see Maass, *Aratea* (1892), 211–48. On iconography H. Ingholt, *Berytus* 1968, 143–78; J. Martin, *Histoire du texte des phénomènes d'Aratos* (1956); M. Erren, *Die Phainomena des Aratos von Soloi* (1967). G. J. T.

Aratus (2) (271–213 BC), *Sicyonian statesman. He fled to *Argos (2) after the murder of his father Cleinias in 264 and was educated there. In 251 he expelled the tyrant Nicocles from *Sicyon and joined the city to the *Achaean Confederacy. From 245 on he occupied a dominant position amongst the Achaeans, normally holding the generalship of the confederacy in alternate years. His policy was for long based upon opposition to Macedon, especially Macedonian influence in the *Peloponnese, and co-operation with Egypt, where he visited *Ptolemy (1) II Philadelphus and whence he obtained substantial subsidies. He seized the Acrocorinth from a Macedonian garrison in 243 and joined Corinth to the Achaean Confederacy. In 241 he defeated *Antigonus (2) Gonatas' Aetolian allies at Pellene and thereafter, in alliance with Aetolia against Macedon (239–229), frequently attacked Athens and Argos; in 229 Argos was brought into the Achaean Confederacy and Athens, with Aratus' help, was freed from Macedonian control. These years also saw the addition of *Megalopolis (235) and *Orchomenus (2) to the confederacy. The growth of Spartan power under *Cleomenes (2) III changed much, especially against the backdrop of Aratus' failure to organize a strong Achaean army. After defeats by Cleomenes in 227, Aratus opened negotiations with *Antigonus (3) Doson of Macedon. The arrival of Doson in the Peloponnese in 224 and victory over Cleomenes at Sellasia (222) preserved the Achaean Confederacy from disruption but at the price of a Macedonian garrison on the Acrocorinth and the re-establishment of Macedonian influence in the Peloponnese. On the accession of *Philip (3) V, Aratus called in Doson's Hellenic League against Aetolian aggression (220). In the ensuing *Social War (2) he exposed the treachery of the Macedonian court cabal under Apelles, and after the Peace of Naupactus (217) resisted Philip's anti-Roman policy and proposed seizure of Ithome in Messenia. His death (213), probably from consumption, was widely blamed upon Philip. His ability as a guerrilla leader early on and his success at diplomacy (both within and without the Peloponnese) establish his reputation as the real architect of the Achaean Confederacy. He wrote *Memoirs* ('Υπομνηματισμοί: Polyb. 2. 40), pro-Achaean and apologetic in tone, and less reliable than Polybius claims (cf. Plut., *Arat*. 3).

Polyb. 2. 37–71; bks. 4–5; Plut. *Agis, Cleomenes, Aratus; FGrH* 231. *RE* 2, 'Aratos'. 2. F. W. Walbank, *Aratos of Sicyon* (1933); W. H. Porter (ed.), *Plutarch's* Aratus (1937), introd.; R. Urban, *Wachstum und Krise des*

achäischen Bundes: Quellenstudien zur Geschichte des Bundes von 280 bis 222 v. Chr. (1979). P. S. D.

Arausio, a town in Gallia Narbonensis (mod. Orange). Near here the *Cimbri defeated Cn. Mallius and Q. *Servilius Caepio (1) with huge losses (105 BC). Under Octavian a colony for *veterans of Legio II Gallica (*Colonia Firma Iulia Arausio Secundanorum*) was established on land taken from the federation of the Cavares (which included the Tricastini) and neighbouring peoples. Fascinating details of the *centuriation are preserved on marble tablets, of which many fragments have been recovered. Several important monuments survive, including the magnificent theatre, with an enigmatic semicircular structure adjoining, two temples, and the triumphal arch (possibly associated with the suppression of the rebellion of Florus and *Iulius Sacrovir in AD 21, though this remains controversial) which stands outside the north gate.

Grenier, *Manuel* 3. 172 ff. (general), 398 ff. (temples), 754 ff. (theatre); A. Piganiol, *Les Documents cadastraux de la colonie romaine d'Orange* (1962; Suppl. to *Gallia*); J. C. Anderson, *BJ* 1987, 159 ff.; A. L. F. Rivet, *Gallia Narbonensis* (1988), 272 ff. A. L. F. R.; J. F. Dr.

Araxes, properly the Armenian river now called Aras, Ras, or Yerash, rising in Bin Geul Dağ, then flowing eastwards across Erzerum and the Mogan Steppe. Until AD 1897 it joined the Kur (ancient Cyrus), but now flows separately into the Caspian. Swift and turbulent now, in Graeco-Roman times it marked a trade-route from the Caspian and the Cyrus to *Artaxata and Asia Minor. *Herodotus (1) confuses the Aras with the *Jaxartes or the *Oxus. Xenophon (1) calls it Phasis, his Araxes being probably the Khabur. The 'Araxes in Persis' is probably the Bendamir or Kum Firuz. E. H. W.

arbitration

Greek The submission of disputes to a neutral person or body, whose verdict the disputants agreed in advance to accept, was recognized among Greeks from earliest times. Many states (e.g. Sparta, Gortyn, Ephesus, Lampsacus) had public arbitrators, but we know details only about Athens. There private διαιτηταί (arbitrators), not necessarily citizens, were often used to settle claims on an equitable rather than legal basis (Arist. *Rh.* 1. 13); public arbitrators, appointed from citizens in their sixtieth year, settled claims involving more than ten drachmas; *Ath. pol.* 53. Such cases were referred to arbitrators by the 'Forty' (four magistrates from each of the ten *phylai or tribes). Once accepted by both parties, the arbitration was binding, but appeal to the *dikastēria (lawcourts) was still possible, so to that extent the διαιτηταί were strictly mediators, not arbitrators.

Hellenistic states often invited friendly neighbour-states to send a 'foreign tribunal' or 'sent-for judges' (ξενικὸν δικαστήριον, δικασταὶ μετάπεμπτοι, usually numbering three or five), to judge civil and sometimes criminal cases affecting their citizens. The visiting judges first tried to settle disputes 'out of court', but pronounced judgement if conciliation (σύλλυσις) failed. Rhodian judges (see RHODES) were particularly sought after (cf. Polyb. 28. 7. 8–10 with M. Holleaux, *Études* 1. 441 ff.), but inscriptions show that the institution, hardly mentioned in literary sources, was enormously widespread. The great French epigraphist Louis Robert (1904–85) threw light on very many such texts. Foreign *judges became a regular, not just an emergency, procedure, and are not necessarily a sign that Greek society was in acute stress. It is noticeable that central and southern Greece, perhaps because of their traditions of independence, resorted to foreign judges later than e.g. Asia Minor and the islands.

arboriculture

Interstate arbitration was important and is found early. *Periander arbitrated between *Athens and *Mytilene over *Sigeum (Hdt. 5. 95). The Persian settlement of western Asia Minor after the *Ionian Revolt (494) included a provision for arbitration, Hdt. 6. 42, cf. Tod 113 of *c*.390 BC. In *c*.450 BC *Argos (2) tried to reconcile Cnossus and Tylissus (ML 42 = Fornara 89). *Thucydides (2) records treaties binding the parties to accept arbitration (4. 118; 5. 18. 4, 79. 4, and see THIRTY YEARS PEACE) but such clauses were neglected because it was hard to find suitable arbitrators. (*Delphi was sometimes specified, Thuc. 1. 28. 1; but not often; perhaps because of whimsical procedures like that at Diod. Sic. 15. 18. *Olympia might have been more suitable). Athens may have arbitrated between members of its empire (Plut. *Per.* 25), like some later leagues, though it is disputed whether the arbitration in e.g. Tod 179 (4th-cent. Argive arbitration between Melos and Cimolos, in accordance with a decision of the League of Corinth (see CORINTH, LEAGUE OF)) was optional or compulsory. Boundary-disputes were always a prime cause of attested disputes. Again, inscriptions are the chief source of knowledge for all aspects; see e.g. the attempts by *Lysimachus and later Rhodes to arbitrate between Samos and Priene (*OGI* 13, *Syll.*³ 599, 688); see also *Syll* 471, 546 b, 588, 674, 679, 683, 685; *IDélos* 1513; A. Wilhelm, *Griechische Inschriften Rechtlichen Inhalts* (1951), reprinted in Wilhelm's *Akademieschriften zur griechischen Inschriftenkunde 3* (1974), 391–506, (1951), 60–74; *SEG* 29. 1130 *bis*, 30. 1119, 35. 665; and the collection by L. Piccirilli, *Gli arbitrati interstatali greci 1* (1973).

On διαιτηταί (private): A. R. W. Harrison, *Law of Athens* (1971) 2. 64 ff.; (public): P. J. Rhodes, *CAAP* on ch. 53. Foreign judges & arbitration: M. N. Tod, *International Arbitration amongst the Greeks* (1913), and *Sidelights on Greek History* (1932), 37 ff.; L. Robert, *Epigraphik der klassischen Welt* (1970), 26 ff., & *Opera Minora Selecta 5* (1989), 137–54; A. J. Marshall, *ANRW* 2. 13 (1980), 626–61; J. K. Davies, *CAH* 7²/1 (1984), 313; S. Ager, Interstate Arbitrations in the Greek World (1996).   M. N. T.; S. H.

Roman The history of Roman arbitration begins with the intervention of Rome as a great power in the politics of the Hellenistic world. Rome took the place of the kings who had often acted as international arbitrators between the free cities and leagues of the Greeks. Such disputes were referred to the senate, which decided the general issue, but sometimes left particular points to a third party with local knowledge for settlement. Rome did not, in the earliest period, enforce the acceptance of her arbitral awards. While not abusing her influence, Rome tended to accept the state of affairs at the time when the appellants first came under her influence as the standard of reference. This practice tended, as her authority increased, to merge into the defence of the privileges of her allies. With the formation of provinces and the consolidation of the empire, arbitration lost its international character, since, except by special permission, which was sometimes allowed, notably in Sicily, the subject peoples could not turn elsewhere, even if they wished to, although Rome tolerated the Greek institution of 'foreign judges' until well into the 2nd cent. AD (see Greek section, above). Senatorial adjudication of disputes between provincial communities of all categories continued to be frequent till the 3rd cent. of the empire. Such arbitration tended to merge with the general provincial administration, and was gradually replaced by the activity of special commissioners such as the *curatores reipublicae* and *correctores civitatum*. Its existence illustrates the lively political self-consciousness of the cities of the Roman empire.

ANCIENT SOURCES Polybius, Livy bks. 30–45. Documents in

F. F. Abbott and A. C. Johnson, *Municipal Administration in the Roman Empire* (1927).

MODERN LITERATURE Abbott and Johnson, ch. 11; E. de Ruggiero, *L'arbitrato pubblico presso i Romani* (1893); E. Badian, *Foreign Clientelae* (1957), chs. 4, 7; A. J. Marshall, *ANRW* 2. 13 (1980) 641 ff.
A. N. S.-W.; A. J. S. S.

arboriculture, tree cultivation. In the first millennium BC there was a remarkable expansion of fruit-tree cultivation in the Mediterranean from east to west. The productivity of Mediterranean *agriculture was significantly increased because trees were often intercropped with cereals and legumes, increasing total yields per unit area. These developments laid the economic foundations for the prosperity of Greek and Roman civilization and made diets more diverse and more nutritious. The most important of the trees in question were the *olive, vine (see WINE), *fig, apple, pear, plum, pistachio, walnut, chestnut, carob, date-palm, peach, almond, pomegranate, sweet and sour cherry-trees. The cultivation of many of these species of trees depended on the spread of the technique of grafting. The date of the establishment of citrus trees in the Mediterranean is disputed. They were probably not important until after the end of the classical period. The Roman agronomists provide us with information about arboriculture. Trees were also very important in the ancient economy for *timber. It was required for shipbuilding, houses, firewood and many other purposes. *Theophrastus describes the uses of different types of timber in the *Inquiry into Plants* (Eng. trans., A. F. Hort (1916)). The demand for timber sometimes resulted in deforestation. Its scale is disputed. Sometimes natural regeneration of forests followed it. Aleppo pine (*Pinus halepensis*) was an important coloniser of disturbed terrain.

R. Meiggs, *Trees and Timber in the Ancient Mediterranean World* (1982); J. R. Sallares, *The Ecology of the Ancient Greek World* (1991); J. V. Thirgood, *Man and the Mediterranean Forest* (1981).   J. R. S.

Arcadia, the central region of the Peloponnese, reaching the sea only in the SW (territory of Phigalia). It is separated by mountains from its neighbours (less so in the west towards *Elis and in the south towards Sparta), and divided internally by mountains into upland valleys. The area is mainly drained by the river *Alpheus and its tributaries, but in the east and north-east closed basins with no overground drainage were until recently liable to flooding. The valleys offer limited fertile areas, and grazing for sheep and goats; Arcadia was the home of the goat-god *Pan. Limited economic resources left Arcadia as a relatively poor area of Greece, and emigrant Arcadian *mercenaries were well known in the 5th and 4th cents. BC. Known Mycenaean sites in Arcadia are few but interesting (notably the LH IIIB/C cemetery at Palaiokastro in west Arcadia). The Arcadian dialect, resembling Cypriot, differed markedly from other Peloponnesian dialects. Arcadians shared a common Arcadian identity, expressed in myth (e.g. their common ancestor *Arcas), but also in the 5th-cent. *Arkadikon*-coinage and in statues of Arcas and his relatives dedicated in the 4th-cent. at *Delphi (*FD* 3. 1. 3–11, cf. 3. 4. 142–4 of the 5th cent.); such sentiment led to Arcadian federation, notable especially in the 360s (see ARCADIAN LEAGUE). None the less Arcadian communities developed as independent states (notably *Tegea, *Mantinea, and *Orchomenus (2) in the east, Cleitor in the north, Heraea in the west, and—after *Leuctra—*Megalopolis in the south-west); the larger communities developed as *poleis*, but the state-forms of some smaller communities (e.g. the Maenalians and Parrhasians) may have been looser. In the Classical and Hellenistic periods the larger Arcadian communities tended to absorb the smaller. From the mid-6th cent. the Arcadian communities were dominated by Sparta and, despite occasional disaffection, members of the *Peloponnesian League; routes through Arcadia were of major importance for Sparta's access to the north Peloponnese and beyond. Freed from Spartan control after Leuctra, the Arcadians formed a federation, briefly powerful, but the particular ambitions of individual communities were generally more important after the 360s. External forces, notably Macedon from *Philip (1) II onwards and later the *Aetolian and *Achaean confederacies, also operated in Arcadia. In the second half of the 3rd cent. the Arcadian communities gradually joined the Achaean Confederacy, of which Megalopolis was a notable member. Later both *Strabo and *Pausanias report that the region was in serious decline; Pausanias' description of Arcadia (bk. 8) is none the less of prime importance for our knowledge of the area in his day and earlier.

RE 2. 1118–37, 'Arkadia' 1; F. Hiller von Gaertringen, *Inscriptiones Graecae* 5. 2 (1913): assembles literary references for Arcadian history; M. Jost, *Sanctuaires et cultes d'Arcadie* (1985): with valuable coverage of archaeological sites; C. Callmer, *Studien zur Geschichte Arkadiens* (1943); L. Dubois, *Recherches sur le dialecte arcadien* (1988); J. A. O. Larsen, *Greek Federal States* (1968).   J. R.

'Arcadia' See PASTORAL POETRY, GREEK and LATIN; VIRGIL (section on 'Eclogues').

Arcadian cults and myths Apart from *Hephaestus, all the gods common to the Greeks are found in Arcadia. But certain deities are peculiar to the region, such as Alea, who was for a long time an independent goddess, and who even when associated with and finally assimilated to *Athena always kept her importance. The same is true of *Despoina, 'the Mistress', worshipped at *Lycosura, and of Anytus, her foster-father, while the Great Goddesses have their origin around *Megalopolis. Some cult groupings have a distinctive composition (*Poseidon and *Demeter), while others are characteristically Arcadian in the relative importance of the individual deities (thus the daughter, *Despoina or Kore (see PERSEPHONE) is dominant over Demeter). Different deities are preponderant in different areas. In the region of *Megalopolis, *Zeus Lycaeus, who is worshipped on Mt. Lycaeon, becomes the god of the *Arcadian League, while a pair of goddesses (Despoina and Demeter, or the Great Goddesses) are the most important female element. In Azania, Demeter is predominant; in the Pheneus area, *Hermes, worshipped on Mt. Cyllene. In eastern Arcadia, *Artemis, as goddess of marshy areas, is at the forefront in Stymphalus, *Orchomenus (2), and Caphyae; Poseidon Hippius is lord of *Mantinea; and Athena Alea rules over *Tegea and its hinterland. *Pan is worshipped on every mountain.

The most striking cults and aetiological myths are the complex associated with Mt. Lycaeon, where human sacrifice is evoked, and those which suggest an ancient pattern of divinities in animal shape. On the peak of Lycaeon, there was an altar of Zeus Lycaeus consisting of a mound of earth and ashes, and a *temenos into which entry was forbidden (*abaton*); transgressors would lose their shadow and would die within the year or be stoned to death (Plut. *Quaest. Graec.* 39; Paus. 8. 38. 6). Human sacrifice, instituted by *Lycaon (3), was practised at the altar; this is attested by Plato (*Resp.* 8. 565d), in the pseudo-Platonic *Minos*, in *Theophrastus (quoted in Porph. *Abst.* 2. 27. 2), and in Pausanias (8. 38. 7). Anyone who ate human flesh at the sacrificial feast was changed into a wolf (see LYCANTHROPY). This seems to be a genuine vestige, unique in Greece, of a ritual *cannibalism whose exact meaning

escapes us. The second characteristically Arcadian feature is the appearance of theriomorphic gods; thus we find the half-animal form of *Pan, with his goat's head and feet, as well as metamorphosis into animal shape and rites using animal masks. The phenomenon is illustrated in cult by the statue of Demeter Melaina ('Black') near Phigalia, who was shown with a horse's head, her hair adorned by snakes and other wild animals, and again in the same area by that of Eurynome, whose lower half was that of a fish (Paus. 8. 42. 1–13; 8. 41. 4). Part of the sculptured veil of Despoina found in the temple at Lycosura shows figures with animal masks and animal paws, dancing in honour of a goddess who has strong links with the animal world. See ANIMALS IN CULT. In myth, there is the story of Demeter's attempts at Phigalia and at Thelpusa to escape Poseidon by turning herself into a mare; to thwart this ploy, Poseidon turned himself into a stallion, and from their union was born the horse *Arion (1) and a daughter, Despoina (Paus. 8. 25. 4–7; 8. 42. 1–13). At Mantinea, where there was an ancient and important sanctuary of Poseidon Hippius, the god's epithet gave rise to a myth in which at his birth his mother Rhea gave *Cronus a foal to swallow, instead of the rock she used later at the birth of Zeus (Paus. 8. 8. 2). A further type of myth particularly well developed in Arcadia was that of the divine birth (Zeus, Hermes, Pan, Athena). See also BASSAE.

M. Jost, *Sanctuaires et cultes d'Arcadie* (1985), and in S. Alcock and R. Osborne (eds.), *Placing the Gods* (1994), 217 ff.   M. J.

Arcadian League Common ethnic identity led to Arcadian federation (see FEDERAL STATES), particularly in the 4th cent. BC. The coin-legend *Arkadikon* suggests federal ambitions in the 5th cent. BC, and the Spartan king *Cleomenes (1) I tried to unite the Arcadians against Sparta, but there is no clear evidence of a functioning Arcadian League in the 5th cent.

After *Leuctra an anti-Spartan democratic movement in Arcadia, led initially by *Mantinea and *Tegea, produced a federal state; most, if not all, Arcadian states joined, willingly or not, by 369 BC. Despite poor information the constitution's main elements are known. There was a large primary assembly (the 'Ten Thousand') and a council. An inscription (IG 5. 2. 1) lists 50 *dāmiorgoi* (see DEMIOURGOI), apparently appointed in rough proportion to their home state's size (10 from *Megalopolis, 5 each from seven other states, 3 from Maenalia, and 2 from Lepreum); the date of the inscription (though 4th cent.) is not clear, nor is it easy to see why some Arcadian communities are omitted. The federal magistrates were headed by a *stratēgos*, presented as a powerful leader. The league initially maintained a standing army (*eparitoi* in *Xenophon (1), presumably the *epilektoi* of *Diodorus (3) Siculus), whose troops strongly supported federal democracy. The league's constitution differs significantly from the contemporary Boeotian constitution (e.g. the powerful sole *stratēgos*). In the 360s, as Sparta weakened and Boeotia failed to exercise continuing decisive influence, the league was influential in the Peloponnese, participating vigorously in warfare and diplomacy. Internal disagreement, however, particularly between Mantinea and Tegea, disbanded the original *eparitoi* and split the league by 362, when Arcadians fought on both sides at the battle of *Mantinea. The league then declined, and its later history is obscure. Incidental references show that it continued (or re-emerged) in some form, doubtless with fluctuating membership, into the 3rd cent. BC. If still surviving, it will have disappeared finally when Arcadian states joined the *Achaean Confederacy in the later 3rd cent.

J. A. O. Larsen, *Greek Federal States* (1968); R. T. Williams, *The Confeder-*

ate Coinage of the Arcadians in the 5th Century BC (1965); D. M. Lewis, *CAH* 5² (1992), ch. 5 (on the 5th cent. BC); S. Dusanic, *The Arcadian League of the 4th century BC* (1970; in Serbian with Eng. résumé; J. Roy, *CAH* 6² (1994), ch. 8.   J. R.

Arcadius (1), of Antiocheia, a grammarian, of the later empire, who wrote a (lost) Ὀνοματικόν (table of noun inflexions). To him is falsely ascribed an extant epitome from *Herodian (1), probably made by Theodosius (end of 4th cent. AD), to which a spurious conclusion was added in the 16th cent.

EDITIONS (Hdn. Epitome): M. Schmidt (1860); E. H. Barker, *Arcadius Grammaticus* (1970; repr. of 1820 edn.).   P. B. R. F.; R. B.

Arcadius (2), **Flavius,** eastern Roman emperor (AD 383–408), was the elder son of *Theodosius (2) I. Weak and irritable, he filled the essential role of emperor, while policy was made by a succession of strong ministers, *Rufinus (1), *Eutropius (2), and Anthemius. The independence of civilian government in the east was maintained in the face of pressure from the west under *Stilicho, and of Gothic federate bands led respectively by *Alaric and Gainas.

A. D. Cameron and J. Long, with L. Sherry, *Barbarians and Politics at the Court of Arcadius* (1993).   E. A. T.; W. L.

Arcadius Charisius, Aurelius, a Roman lawyer and *magister libellorum* (master of petitions) of the age of *Diocletian, was assigned by some earlier scholars to the time of *Constantine or later, partly because of his ornate rhetorical style; but closer study, confirming the views of other scholars, shows that the imperial rescripts (replies to petitions) of mid-290 to 291 AD closely resemble the texts from his monographs in style and outlook, so that he is likely to have been Diocletian's *magister libellorum* in those years. Apart from more than a hundred rescripts, his work has survived in the form of six passages taken by Justinian's compilers (see JUSTINIAN'S CODIFICATION) from his monographs, the last of this genre. Each of them breaks new ground: on witnesses (*De testibus*), public duties (*De muneribus civilibus*), and the office of praetorian prefect (*De officio praefecti praetorio*). As a lawyer Arcadius stands in the pragmatic tradition of *Ulpianus and *Modestinus.

Lenel, *Pal.* 1. 57–60; *HLL* 5, § 508. 1; Liebs 1987, 21–30, 131–3; A. Dell'Oro, *Studi Betti* 2 (1962), 331–46; Honoré 1981, 115–19; E. Pólay, *Scritti Guarino* (1984) 2395–408.   T. Hon.

Arcas, eponymous hero of *Arcadia, whose name suggests 'bear' (ἄρκτος). He was the son of *Callisto and *Zeus, and when his mother was transformed into a she-bear he was saved by Hermes, who entrusted him to *Maia (1). The episode is located around Mt. Cyllene, and is shown on the reverse of 4th-cent. silver tetradrachms of Pheneus. Other elements of the tradition relate to Mt. Lycaeon. Some texts make Arcas the child offered to Zeus by *Lycaon (3) in a cannibalistic feast intended to test the god's divinity. Restored to life, Arcas as an adult failed to recognize his mother in the bear Callisto and pursued her into the interior of the *abaton* (forbidden enclosure) of Mt. Lycaeon. Zeus changed him into the *constellation Boötes (Hes. fr. 163 M–W; Ov. *Met.* 2. 409 ff).

Arcas succeeded Nyctimus as king of the *Pelasgians. He introduced agriculture, which he learned from *Triptolemus, and taught the arts of making bread and clothes. He gave his name to the land, Arcadia. His wife was the nymph Erato, his sons Azan, Apheidas, and Elatos. After his death, the oracle at Delphi (see DELPHIC ORACLE) ordered that his bones be moved to Mantinea, where they were the focus of a *hero-cult (Paus. 8. 9. 3–4). A sculpture dedicated at Delphi by the *Arcadian League in 369

BC showed Arcas, his mother Callisto, and his sons (Paus. 10. 9. 5).

A. D. Trendall, *LIMC* 2. 609–10; P. Borgeaud, *The Cult of Pan in Ancient Greece* (1988); M. Jost, *Sanctuaires et cultes d'Arcadie* (1985), see index.   M. J.

Arcesilas I, II, III, IV, second, fourth, sixth, and eighth kings of the Battiads, who ruled *Cyrene from its foundation (c.630 BC) for some 200 years. Information on their reigns comes almost entirely from *Herodotus (1) and from *Pindar and his scholiasts (see SCHOLIA). In detail the chronology is uncertain. Arcesilas I (c.591?–c.575?) seems to have followed closely in the founder's footsteps. Arcesilas II, the Cruel (after 570), quarrelled with his brothers, who seceded and founded Barca. They stirred up the Libyans against him, and he was defeated by them, and then murdered by his brother Learchus. He is the Arcesilas depicted supervising the loading of merchandise on the famous cup in Paris (E. Simon and M. and A. Hirmer, *Die Griechischen Vasen* (1976), pl. 15). Arcesilas III (before 525–after 522) succeeded to a monarchy stripped of its powers by the reform of Demonax of Mantinea (Hdt. 4. 161 f.). He seems to have tried to establish a demagogic *tyranny, was forced into exile, collected mercenaries on Samos with the help of *Polycrates (1), and regained power in Cyrene, only to be murdered later at Barca. In the meantime he had submitted to *Cambyses when the latter conquered Egypt. Arcesilas IV (before 462–c.440?) employed Pindar to celebrate his victory in the chariot-race at Delphi (462), but a democratic revolution led to his fall and the end of the dynasty.

Hdt. 4. 159–67, 200–5; Pind. *Pyth.* 4, 5 and scholia. F. Chamoux, *Cyrène sous la monarchie des Battiades* (1953); L. H. Jeffery, *Hist.* 1961, 142 ff.; B. M. Mitchell, *JHS* 1966, 99 ff.; S. Applebaum, *Jews and Greeks in Ancient Cyrene* (1979); A. J. Graham, *CAH* 3²/3 (1982), 136 ff.   A. J. G.; S. H.

Arcesilaus (1) or **Arcesilas** (both forms given in the sources), of Pitane in *Aeolis, 316/5–242/1 BC, head of the *Academy from c.268. In his youth, Arcesilaus studied mathematics with *Autolycus (2) at Pitane. His older brother wanted him to study rhetoric, but Arcesilaus escaped to Athens to study philosophy. He first attended the lectures of *Theophrastus, but then formed a close friendship with *Crantor, whom he followed to the Academy. There he also met *Polemon (2) and Crates. On the death of Crates, Socratides, an older member of the school, resigned in favour of Arcesilaus, and he was elected scholarch. *Diogenes (6) Laertius' biography (4. 28–45) describes him as a kind and urbane man, respected and admired by his contemporaries.

From the 1st cent. BC on Arcesilaus was known as the founder of the Middle Academy (Diog. Laert. 1. 14; Sext. Emp. *PH* 1. 220)—the philosopher who introduced scepticism (see SCEPTICS) into Plato's school. We do not know whether he was influenced in this by his older contemporary *Pyrrhon of Elis, though the famous satirical line of the Stoic *Ariston (1), 'Plato in front, Pyrrhon behind, in the middle Diodorus' (Diog. Laert. 4. 33) shows that people recognized some similarities. Arcesilaus, who is said to have owned a private copy of *Plato (1)'s dialogues, seems to have appealed to the examples of *Socrates and Plato. Like Socrates, Arcesilaus would examine or argue against any given thesis and make no assertions of his own. His professed attitude of withholding assent (ἐποχή) was adopted to avoid error and rashness of judgement. Stories about his alleged esotericism, according to which he taught the positive doctrines of Plato to an inner circle of advanced students (Sext. Emp. *PH* 1. 234; August. *contra Academicos* 3. 20. 43), are certainly later inventions.

Arcesilaus published nothing, and what we learn about his arguments must have been handed down in the Academy or through the writings of his opponents.

Arcesilaus' most influential and famous argument was directed against the Stoic theory of knowledge (see STOICISM). He argued that given the definition of the Stoic criterion of truth, the so-called cognitive impression (καταληπτικὴ φαντασία), one could show that nothing could be grasped or apprehended, since it was impossible to find an impression of such a kind that it could not be false. For any true and clear impression one could describe a situation in which an otherwise indistinguishable impression would be false. Since the Stoics held that the wise man would never assent to a false impression, it followed that the Stoic sage must withhold judgement on all matters. To the Stoic objection that suspension of judgement would make action, and hence life, impossible, Arcesilaus replied that it was possible to act without assenting to anything, and that in the absence of certain knowledge a wise man could be guided by 'what is reasonable' (τὸ εὔλογον).

The thesis that 'nothing can be grasped' (ἀκαταληψία) has been described by ancient as well as modern authors as a doctrine of the sceptical Academy, but this is a mistake: Arcesilaus and his successors down to *Carneades insisted that they did not know or assert that nothing could be known, any more than they knew or asserted any other philosophical thesis (Cic. Acad. 1. 45; Acad. post. 28).

SOURCES See H. J. Mette, Lustrum 1984, 41–94.

MODERN DISCUSSIONS A. A. Long and D. N. Sedley, The Hellenistic Philosophers (1987), chs. 68–9; P. Couissin, Rev. Ét. Grec. 1929, 373 ff., Eng. trans. in M. Burnyeat (ed.), The Skeptical Tradition (1983); A. M. Ioppolo, Opinione e scienza (1986).   G. S.

Arcesilaus (2) (1st cent. BC), successful Greek sculptor working in Rome, friend of L. *Licinius Lucullus (2), highly regarded by *Varro. His major public commission was the statue of *Venus Genetrix for the temple dedicated by *Caesar in 46 BC. He also supplied private collections: *Centaurs carrying *Nymphs, for *Asinius Pollio; and a lioness with Cupids for Varro. His models, proplasmata, were sold at a high price. Probably a versatile adapter of existing genres.

Overbeck 2268–70; A. F. Stewart, Greek Sculpture 2 (1990), 307 f.
T. B. L. W.; A. J. S. S.

archaeology, classical, properly the study of the whole material culture of ancient Greece and Rome, is often understood in a somewhat narrower sense. *Epigraphy, the study of inscriptions on permanent materials, is today more widely seen as a branch of historical rather than of archaeological enquiry; while numismatics, the study of coins (see COINAGE), has become a largely independent discipline. The chronological limits are also open to debate. In the case of the Greek world, it has become common to distinguish 'ancient' from 'prehistoric', and to treat the archaeology of early Greece—at any rate down to the late bronze age—as lying outside the scope of classical archaeology. For Italy, the same is true down to a later date, after the beginning of the iron age. There is wider agreement in treating the collapse of pagan civilization as the terminus at the lower end.

No less important than these explicit divisions are the unwritten, yet widely accepted constraints on the range of material culture accepted as appropriate for study. These constraints, which have helped to maintain an intellectual distance between classical and other archaeologies, have privileged the study of works of representational art and monumental architecture as the core, sometimes almost the entirety, of the subject. A second prominent attitude, one which indeed inspired the study of the material remains of antiquity in the first place, has been attention to the surviving ancient texts, with the aim of matching them with material discoveries. These assumptions can be traced back to the earliest stages of the history of the discipline; topographical exploration, which also began very early, understandably shared the same deference to the texts. The collection of works of art, a prerogative of wealth rather than of learning, helped to confer on the subject in its early years a social prestige at least as prominent as its intellectual. From Renaissance times in Italy and France, from the early 17th cent. in England, and from somewhat later in other parts of northern Europe and North America, these forces propelled the subject forward. Such excavation as took place before the mid-19th cent. was usually explicitly directed towards the recovery of works of art, with the textual evidence serving as a guide or, where it was not directly applicable, as a kind of arbiter. Once the volume of available finds reached a certain critical mass, a further motive came into play: that of providing models for the better training of artists and architects.

Textual evidence, collectors' preference, and the frequency of recovery combined to make *sculpture pre-eminent among the visual arts. It has retained this place even when the reaction against classicism has deprived it of virtually any bearing on contemporary artistic practice. From 1500 on, the finds from Rome and other Italian sites furnished an increasingly rich body of material. To J. J. Winckelmann (1717–68) belongs the credit for first attempting a systematic organization of this evidence, the limitations of whose range were hardly yet suspected. Only in the opening years of the 19th cent., with the transport of the *Parthenon, *Bassae, and *Aegina (see also APHAEA) sculptures to London and to Munich, did even the learned world begin to glimpse the true range of classical sculpture. From then on, leadership in this field passed to Germany: art history played a prominent part in university education there, and a German Institute in Rome was established as early as 1829. Over the next hundred years, the rate of new discoveries was on its own enough to maintain the vitality of this branch of study, with Adolf Furtwängler (1853–1907) as its most distinguished exponent. A period of consolidation then kept it alive until a series of new finds, some of them from underwater exploration, brought about a further revival of interest in the late 20th cent. (See ARCHAEOLOGY, UNDERWATER).

With classical *painting, the natural starting-point was the rich series of murals excavated at *Herculaneum, *Pompeii, and other sites from the Vesuvian destruction of AD 79, in the years from 1739 on. Some reflection of lost Greek masterpieces was recognized in these, but in this case there was no salvation to come from the later recovery of the originals. Instead, attention was diverted to Greek painted vases which (though not yet recognized as Greek) had begun to appear in numbers in Italian graves in the 1720s (see POTTERY, GREEK). Then, later in the same century, the foundations were laid for a branch of classical archaeology which, for the first time, owed almost nothing to the surviving textual evidence. Interest was at first directed to the interpretation of the figured scenes on the vases. Late in the 19th cent., there was a shift to the increasingly detailed study of classification, chronology, and, above all, attribution of the works to individual artists. This phase, with which the name of Sir John Beazley (1885–1970) is inseparably associated, lasted for three generations and absorbed the energies of some of the most distinguished figures in the history of the discipline. With Beazley's death, the unique authority of his attributions was no longer available and there was a marked reversion to the study of the content of the scenes (see IMAGERY). Two other strong directions in recent ceramic studies have been laboratory work on the composition of the clay and the closer investigation of the contexts in which the vessels were made, used, and exchanged (see POTTERY, SCIENTIFIC ANALYSIS). Meanwhile Roman wall-painting and *mosaic came to be increasingly treated as manifestations of Roman culture in its own right, rather than as reflections of lost Greek work. The interaction of such art with its architectural setting has become a particular object of research. The study of classical *architecture itself, a central pillar of the discipline during its formative, 'instructional' period, has become a progressively more specialized field, with a largely separate group of practitioners.

The modern history of fieldwork in the Greek world—that is, its redirection towards the goal of recovery of the entire range of the preserved material culture—began with the adoption of a more systematic strategy in the excavation of Pompeii from 1860 on, and received its greatest single stimulus from the discoveries of Schliemann at *Troy, *Mycenae, and *Tiryns in the 1870s and 1880s. The revelation that the soil could still hold secrets on the scale of whole civilizations—those of the bronze age Aegean—whose existence had not previously been suspected, acted as a spur to many other large-scale projects. In Greece, these have primarily been directed at the great sanctuaries, with the German expedition to *Olympia (1875–) giving a notable lead, followed by the Greek excavations on the Athenian Acropolis (1882– ; see ATHENS, TOPOGRAPHY), the French missions to *Delphi (1892–) and *Delos (1904–), and a number of others. Large areas of major settlement-sites have also been excavated, notably by the Americans at *Corinth (1896–), *Olynthus (1928–38), and the *Agora of Athens (1931–). Many of these projects are still in progress, adding vastly to knowledge and providing a training-ground for future practitioners. In Italy, the work has had a broader focus throughout, inspired perhaps by the continuing success of work at the Vesuvian sites. The greatest single focus of interest has naturally been Rome itself, where the discoveries cover almost every aspect of ancient urban life and span a chronological range of many centuries. By far the most extensive field of activity, however, involving intensive work in at least thirty modern countries, has been the archaeology of the Roman empire. While continental Europeans integrated this work into the study of classical antiquity of the historical period, English-speaking archaeologists were quick to turn to the possibilities opened up in the field of Aegean prehistory, in the *Cyclades and, after Evans's sensational discoveries at *Cnossus, in Crete (see MINOAN CIVILIZATION). Thus, within the space of a couple of generations, classical archaeology came to adopt an entirely new role as an instrument of general historical enquiry.

The most prominent recent innovation in fieldwork has been the introduction of intensive surface survey, first in central and southern Italy, then in the Aegean area and certain provinces of the Roman empire. This technique involves the systematic searching of a tract of landscape, without discrimination in favour of 'likely' locations, to find traces of the pattern of past settlement and activity, sometimes of a specific period but more often of all periods. In contrast with excavation, it is directed at the acquisition of regional knowledge, especially for the rural sector. In all these activities, the use of scientific techniques—for determining the provenance of manufactured objects, for the fuller classification of organic matter, for detection of buried features, and especially for dating—has become increasingly common. In the last-

named field, the most striking progress has been made by dendro-chronology which, by building up a sequence from a series of trees extending backwards in time, makes it possible to offer absolute dates for tree-rings in structural timbers and other large wooden objects.

Classical archaeology is probably the fastest-changing branch of Classical Studies. One symptom of this is that it is no longer possible to secure universal assent to any definition of its role, either within the study of the Classics or within world archaeology. But pluralism, at least in this case, is a sign of vitality.

I. Morris (ed.), *Classical Greece: Ancient Histories and modern Archaeologies* (1994); P. MacKendrick, *The Mute Stones Speak*, 2nd edn. (1983).

A. M. S.

archaeology, underwater The potential richness of the sea for salvage or accidental finding of sunken valuables was recognized from earliest times, but the possibility of defining meaningful groups of wrecked material or of interpreting submerged sites scarcely predates the widespread adoption of underwater breathing-apparatus in the 20th cent. Standard apparatus, supplied with compressed air from the surface, as used by sponge divers, enabled the discovery and partial excavation of rich 1st-cent. BC cargoes at Antikythera (1900–1) and Mahdia (1908–13), but the unwieldy equipment, reliance on untrained working divers, and exclusion of archaeological direction from involvement under water remained serious limitations on progress. Self-contained breathing-apparatus (the aqualung) came into widespread use after 1945, and resulted in the growth of diving for sport and pleasure; many ancient wrecks were discovered, especially in southern France, and the importance of this resource was recognized by F. Benoit. However, he did not direct operations under water, and his main underwater project, the excavation at the islet of Le Grand Congloué (1952–7), has subsequently been shown to have confused two superimposed Roman wrecks. *In situ* recording and interpretation were developed especially by P. Tailliez at the Roman wreck of Le Titan, southern France (1957), but the combination of these techniques with archaeological project-design and report-preparation did not mature until the establishment of a French national underwater archaeological service in 1967, which, beginning with A. Tchernia (1967–70), has developed both field techniques and also regular publications. In Italy, N. Lamboglia recognized the value of wreck sites in the 1940s, and established an underwater archaeological institute which carried out important excavations, e.g. at Albenga, though until recent years there remained a gap between the archaeological director (who dived only in an observation bell) and the excavation team of technicians. Meanwhile, British and American field-archaeology traditions resulted in the impact of H. Frost and P. Throckmorton on underwater sites, especially in the emphasis on methodical observation and recording before any excavation; this found expression in the successful Cape Gelidonya project (*Lycia) led by G. F. Bass, which finally established underwater archaeology as a respectable, worthwhile branch of the discipline. Subsequently, work on shipwrecks has developed successfully not only under the aegis of foreign expeditions, notably those of the Institute of Nautical Archaeology, but also through the growth of national and university institutes in Israel, Greece, Italy, France, Spain, and Croatia. Important developments have included the integration of excavation, post-excavation, conservation and reconstruction of wrecks (notably at Kyrenia, Cyprus), and the development of remote sensing and of remotely operated or piloted submersibles for survey below the effective free-diving limit (50–70 m.; 160–230 ft.). Meanwhile, the study of sea-level change and submerged settlement sites, notably by N. C. Flemming, has emphasized the significant information which can be recovered from underwater sites (e.g. the plan of the bronze age settlement on the isle of Elaphonisos, off SE Peloponnese), and the importance of underwater investigation for understanding ancient *harbours, not least *Caesarea (2) (by A. Raban). See RIACE WARRIORS; SHIPWRECKS, ANCIENT.

J. du P. Taylor (ed.), *Marine Archaeology: Developments during Sixty Years in the Mediterranean* (1965); P. A. Gianfrotta and P. Pomey, *Archeologia Subacquea* (1981); K. Muckelroy (ed.), *Archaeology under Water: An Atlas of the World's Submerged Sites* (1980); P. Throckmorton (ed.), *History from the Sea: Shipwrecks and Archaeology* (1987); A. J. Parker, *Ancient Shipwrecks of the Mediterranean and the Roman Provinces* (1992); A. Raban, *The Harbours of Caesarea Maritima: Results of the Caesarea Ancient Harbour Project, 1980–1985* 1, *The Site and the Excavations* (1989).

Journals and serial publications: *International Journal of Nautical Archaeology and Underwater Exploration* (London); *Archaeonautica* (Paris); *Cahiers d'Archéologie Subaquatique* (Fréjus); *Archeologia Subacquea* (*Bollettino d'Arte*, Suppl.) (Rome); *Forma Maris Antiqui* (*Rivista di Studi Liguri*) (Bordighera).   A. J. P.

archaism in Latin Archaism is the employment of obsolete or obsolescent diction intended as such (not the conservative retention of the language with which one grew up, nor the colloquial preservation of expressions eliminated from literary use). Its normal tendency, reinforced by Roman respect for antiquity, was to impart solemnity, even when the usage had not been solemn while still current: characteristic of epic diction ever since *Livius Andronicus admitted to his *Odyssia* forms not found in his dramatic fragments (e.g. -*ās* gen., *topper*), it also expressed the mock-grandeur of the Plautine slave (see PLAUTUS), and became a feature of historical prose in *Coelius Antipater.

During the late republic, educated speech evolved so fast that the early writers' language seemed markedly old-fashioned. The purism of *Caesar and the mature *Cicero excludes obsolescent usages along with the poetic or informal. This did not exclude the judicious use of an occasional archaism to confer solemnity (Cic. *De or.* 3. 153), and poets were accorded greater licence; but whereas the didactic poet *Lucretius freely employs such Ennian uses (see ENNIUS) as first-declension genitives in -*āī* and passive infinitives in -*ier*, other poets, especially the 'Alexandrian' school, are more restrained.

Although the puristic prohibitions were subsequently relaxed, that on archaism generally retained its force, except in history: *Sallust developed a style based on pre-classical writers and in particular the elder *Cato (Censorius); even *Livy, especially in his early books, admits such archaic uses as the 3 pl. perfect in -*ēre* and the naïve pronominal parataxis *is . . . is . . . ab eo* (1. 3. 6– 7). *Virgil makes judicious use of Ennian language in the *Aeneid*; thereafter writers in search of choice or solemn diction turned to Virgil (historians also to Sallust) rather than to Early Latin literature, for which the great Silver authors had little respect; the younger Seneca even deplores its imitation by Cicero and Virgil. Nevertheless, we hear mostly scornful reports of persons who enjoyed the old tragic poets, or affected honesty by imitating the apparent artlessness of the early orators; and *Valerius Probus brought with him the old-fashioned tastes of colonial *Berytus.

In the early 2nd cent., a revolution in sentiment restored pre-Ciceronian literature to favour; the movement, already so strong that even Suetonius employs such expressions as *miscellus* and *nemo quisquam*, was encouraged by *Hadrian's liking for Early Latin writers; furthermore, a cult of antique virtue is evident in Aulus *Gellius, though not in M. *Cornelius Fronto or in *Apuleius. Early authors (and with them Sallust) were read both for their own sakes and as sources for words and constructions to revive: the parallel with Atticism is imperfect, for wholesale pastiche was not attempted (see ASIANISM AND ATTICISM).

Unlike earlier archaists, the 2nd-cent. mannerists did not necessarily intend to convey solemnity; often they meant to avoid the obvious (a principle explicitly stated by Fronto), to demonstrate their learning (both Fronto and Gellius warn against the obscurity that might result), or to restore correct Latin usage (i.e. republican, including Ciceronian) against the corruptions of the Silver Age and current speech (though vulgar usages were admissible if found in early authors). This motive is particularly strong with Gellius, far less so with *Apuleius, for whom archaism is no more than one means to make a show; another is the coining of new words, also indulged by Gellius but disapproved by Fronto, who though in later eyes the chief exponent of the archaizing style was neither its inventor nor its arbiter. Ornamental archaism remained available for later authors (above all the Lucretianizing *Arnobius); but when usages reminiscent of Early Latin appear in subliterary texts they are simply vulgarisms that refined language had proscribed. See CLASSICISM; RETROSPECTIVE STYLES.   L. A. H.-S.

Archedemus, of Tarsus, Stoic philosopher (see STOICISM), probably a pupil of *Diogenes (3) of Babylon.

Testimonia in von Arnim, *SVF* 3. 262–4.

Archedicus, New *Comedy poet, who slandered *Demochares, nephew of *Demosthenes (2) (fr. 4 and Polyb. 12. 13).

FRAGMENTS Kassel–Austin, *PCG* 2. 533–6.
INTERPRETATION Meineke, *FCG* 1. 458 f.; G. Kaibel, *RE* 2/1 (1895), 441, 'Archedikos' 2.   W. G. A.

archēgetēs Denoting genealogical origins, political beginnings, and leadership, *archēgetēs* was a cult-title of heroic progenitors of families or tribes (*Ath. pol.* 21. 6; see HERO-CULT), and of heroized city-*founders (Battos: *LSCG* 115, l. 22; Euphron: Xen. *Hell.* 7. 3. 12). Named or anonymous tutelary hero-*archēgetai* protected entire lands (Plut. *Aristides* 11. 3; Paus. 10. 4. 10). *Apollo, the political god sanctioning and sharing in city foundation, was universally worshipped as *archēgetēs*, e.g. in Sicily (Thuc. 6. 3. 1: at *Naxos (2), by both Dorians and Ionians). At Sparta (and Thera? *IG* 12. 3. 762) *archēgetai* probably signified 'kings' (Plut. *Lyc.* 6). Cf. CINEAS (1).

I. Malkin, *Religion and Colonization in Ancient Greece* (1987), 241–50.   I. M.

Archelaus (1), philosopher (fl. 5th cent. BC), probably of Athenian birth, was a pupil of *Anaxagoras and followed him in the main, but in some details adhered to the views of the Ionians and *Empedocles. The tradition is consequently confused: he is credited both with accepting Anaxagoras' original 'mixture' of elements, from which the hot and the cold are first separated out, and also (improbably) with generating everything, as *Anaximenes (2) had, by condensation and rarefaction from air. He is said to have taught *Socrates, but it is improbable that he anticipated Socrates by engaging in ethical speculation.

DK no. 60.   W. D. R.

Archelaus (2), Macedonian king (413–399 BC). A legitimized son of *Perdiccas (2) II, he gained the throne by murder and was eventually assassinated by two male lovers. His reign, for which see esp. Thuc. 2. 100. 2, is notable for co-operation with Athens

Archelaus

(supply of shipbuilding materials; capture of Pydna), increasing security (fortress- and road-building; improvement of infantry and cavalry; matrimonial alliances), increasing wealth (resumption of silver coinage), transfer of major residence to *Pella because of the primary importance of north-eastern frontiers, and a 'Hellenizing' policy (theatre festival at Dium; patronage of *Zeuxis (1), *Timotheus (1), *Choerilus (2), *Agathon, and *Euripides) whose pretensions perhaps promoted the Athenian hostility reflected e.g. in Plato's *Gorgias*.

RE 2, 'Archelaos' 7; HM 3, see index; E. N. Borza, *In the Shadow of Olympus* (1990).   C. J. T.

Archelaus (3) (fl. 1st cent. BC), distinguished Greek general of *Mithradates VI, perhaps from *Sinope or *Amisus. After overrunning Bithynia and most of central Greece ('First Mithradatic War', 88–85 BC), he was twice defeated by *Sulla, and commissioned by Mithradates to negotiate a peace. Falling under suspicion of treasonable dealings with Sulla, on the renewal of war (83) he deserted to Rome, and he assisted L. *Licinius Lucullus (2) early in the third war (74). *Archelaus (5) was his great-grandson.

App. *Mith.* 18 ff.; Plut. *Sull.* 11 ff. For army figures, see esp. Memnon (fr. 22, FGrH 3b, no. 434).   G. T. G.

Archelaus (4), following the will left by his father *Herod (1), was appointed by Augustus ethnarch of the southern part of Herod's kingdom—*Judaea, *Samaria, and *Idumaea. Archelaus married (scandalously) Glaphyra, daughter of *Archelaus (5) of Cappadocia, previously the wife of his own half-brother, as well as of King *Juba (2) of Mauretania. In response to delegations of both Jews and Samaritans, in AD 6, Augustus banished Archelaus to Vienna (mod. Vienne) and put his territory under direct Roman rule.   T. R.

Archelaus (5), great-grandson of *Archelaus (3), last king of *Cappadocia from 36 BC when M. *Antonius (2) (Mark Antony) installed him. Augustus not only continued him in his kingdom but apparently saved him from a pretender (Val. Max. 9. 15. ext. 2) and in c.25 added Rough Cilicia and in 20 Lesser Armenia. The young *Tiberius, perhaps honouring a family connection, defended Archelaus before *Augustus at a trial (Suet. *Tib.* 8), but Archelaus was later brusque and ungrateful when Tiberius was living in Rhodes. Tiberius lured him to Rome in AD 17 and had him tried before the senate. Archelaus died when in Rome and his kingdom was turned into a procuratorial province (Tac. *Ann.* 2. 42; Cass. Dio 57. 17). Archelaus is an interesting figure who, in a good royal Hellenistic tradition of authorship, wrote an account of the territories covered by *Alexander (3) the Great: FGrH 123. His second wife was the widow of *Polemon (1) I and daughter of *Antonia (1), and a daughter of his married a son of *Herod (1).

Jones, *Cities E. Rom. Prov.*, 2nd edn. ch. 7; G. W. Bowersock, *Augustus and the Greek World* (1965) app. 3; B. M. Levick, *CQ* 1971; R. D. Sullivan, *Near Eastern Royalty and Rome 100–30 BC* (1990), 182–5; S. Mitchell *Anatolia* 1 (1993), 97 f. Coins: B. Simonetta, *Coins of the Cappadocian Kings* (1977), 45 f.   S. H.

Archermus, 6th-cent. Chiot sculptor (see CHIOS). According to Pliny, HN 36. 11–14, son of Micciades, grandson of Melas, and father of Bupalus and Athenis (fl. 540–537 BC), all sculptors; worked on *Delos and *Lesbos. Melas was a mythical hero of Chios, but a base from Delos mentioning his, Micciades', and Archermus' names, and a winged marble woman found nearby,

may bear out a scholiast's note (schol. Ar. *Av.* 573) that Archermus invented the winged *Nike. Unfortunately, the inscription is battered and the adjoining part of the statue lost. Though Archermus also signed a base on the Acropolis c.530, the 'Chiot School' remains elusive.

K. Sheedy, *AJArch.* 1985, 619 ff.; A. F. Stewart, *Greek Sculpture* (1990), 116, 243 f., fig. 92.   A. F. S.

archers (Greek and Hellenistic) Archaeological evidence shows that both the 'self' (i.e. made of one piece) and the 'composite' bow were known to bronze age Greece, and the considerable quantities of arrow-heads—flint, obsidian, and bronze—suggest that it was used for more than hunting; a bronze tablet from Cnossus alone (see MINOAN CIVILIZATION) records 8,640. Fewer arrow-heads are known from the early iron age, but late geometric Attic vases show that the bow was important again by the 8th cent. BC.

In *Homer's *Iliad* it is only used by one or two heroes on either side, and there is some suggestion that archers were despised. *Pandarus' bow was clearly composite since horn was used in its construction (cf. 4. 105 ff.), and the epithet 'back-springing' ($\pi\alpha\lambda\acute{\iota}\nu\tau\sigma\nu\sigma\varsigma$) applied to this and other bows is also appropriate to this type. Horn was also used in the construction of *Odysseus' bow (*Od.* 21. 395), and it is possibly significant that he apparently strings it sitting down, for such a bow was easier to string if one end could be anchored under a leg.

In historical times, archery continued to flourish in *Crete, and Cretan archers frequently figure as *mercenaries down to Roman times. But bowmen rarely appear among the troops of other Greek states, though vase-paintings suggest that the tyrants of Athens had *Scythian bowmen in the 6th cent., and *Polycrates (1) of Samos had 1,000, probably Samians, *Gelon of Syracuse 2,000 (Hdt. 3. 45. 4, 7. 158. 4). Athens also had some presumably native archers at the battle of *Plataea (Hdt. 9. 22. 1, 60. 3), and by 432 both mounted and foot-archers (Thuc. 2. 13. 8); four regularly served on Athenian *triremes, but seem to have been of little importance in actual fighting at sea. Even Sparta raised a force of archers in 424 (Thuc. 4. 55. 2).

Despite the respect accorded to Persian archers, they evidently had little effect on *hoplites. At the battle of *Marathon the Greek charge at the double was probably intended to leave the Persian archers as little time to shoot as possible, but at Plataea, although the Spartans and their comrades allegedly endured their fire for some time, casualties were slight. This probably explains why Greek states did not bother to raise organized forces of archers to any significant extent.

The rise of *Macedonia ushered in an era when all arms were integrated into more complex forces, and archers played a somewhat more important role, *Alexander (3) the Great, for example, using both Cretan and Macedonian archers. But even in Hellenistic warfare, archers were never battle-winners, and in general it is surprising how unimportant they were throughout Graeco-Roman times. Only, perhaps, at *Carrhae in 53 BC, when *Crassus was overwhelmed by the *Parthians, was a large-scale battle won by archery fire, and this was in very exceptional circumstances.

The extreme range of the ancient bow has been estimated to be between 300 and 250 m. (328 and 273 yds.), but its effective range was probably only up to 150–200 m. (164–219 yds.). Thus, at the double, advancing infantry would only have been under fire for about two minutes, allowing archers perhaps between twenty and thirty volleys.

H. Hommel, *RE* 2/1, τοξόται; A. M. Snodgrass, *Arms and Armour of the Greeks* (1967); W. McLeod, *Phoenix* 1965, 26; 1972.   J. F. La.

arches In Greek architecture openings are normally covered by horizontal lintels or beams. The first description of arched construction using voussoirs locked into place by a keystone is attributed to *Democritus by the younger *Seneca, referring to *Posidonius (2). The earliest attested vaults in Greek architecture are those of the Macedonian tombs, from the mid-4th cent. BC onwards; earlier dating is improbable. Arched gateways occur (but infrequently) thereafter, particularly in the Hellenistic period.

Arches (and vaults) have been attributed to the *Etruscans in Italy, though again early dates are unprovable, and a borrowing from 4th-cent. and Hellenistic Greece seems more likely. Apart from the free-standing *triumphal arch (and the architecturally similar arched gateways in city walls) the most significant Roman use of the arch is in continuous arcading, combined with engaged half-columns supporting an overall entablature, first attested in the *Tabularium (1) at Rome, and later used as the normal system for external walls of *amphitheatres and theatre auditoria.

T. D. Boyd, *AJArch.* 1978, 83 ff.; M. Andronikos, *BSA* 1987, 1 ff.; R. A. Tomlinson, *BSA* 1987, 305 ff.; A. Wallace-Hadrill, *PCPS* 1990, 143 ff.
R. A. T.

Archestratus, of *Gela, mid-4th-cent. BC poet. Some 340 hexameters are preserved by *Athenaeus (1) from the *Hēdupatheia* (also cited as *Gastronomia Deipnologia*, and *Opsopoiia*), a culinary tour of the Mediterranean, which *Ennius was later to adapt. The poem imitates *Hesiod's *Works and Days* in the use of an addressee (Moschus) and a constant imperative tone, and occasionally borrows phraseology from Hesiod, but it is not specifically parodic (contrast *Matron).

FRAGMENTS *Suppl. Hell.* 132–92; J. Wilkins and S. Hill, *Archestratus: The Life of Luxury* (1994).   R. L. Hu.

Archias See LICINIUS ARCHIAS, A.

Archidamian War is the name given to the first decade (431–421 BC) of the main *Peloponnesian War. The name derives from King *Archidamus II of Sparta, who had, however, opposed the war. *Thucydides (2) called this war the 'ten-years' war' (5. 25. 1); the earliest attested use of the title 'Archidamian' is in *Lysias (*Harpocration, entry under *Archidameios polemos*), in a speech which does not survive. See PELOPONNESIAN WAR for the further subdivision 'Pachetian', part of the Peloponnesian War (used by Strabo of the first half of Thuc. 3).

Thuc. 1–5; Busolt, *Gr. Gesch.* 3². 854 n. 1.   S. H.

Archidamus, 'leader of the *damos*', was the name of several *Eurypontid kings of Sparta, of whom the most notable were:

Archidamus II,

who married an aunt and reigned for over 40 years (?469–427 BC), in succession to *Leotychidas II. He first distinguished himself by his resolute response to the great *earthquake of 464, which had prompted a massive revolt of the *helots aided by a couple of the communities of the *perioikoi in Messenia. But even his seniority was insufficient to dissuade the Spartan assembly from voting for war with Athens in 432, and he led the allied forces in invasions of Attica on three occasions (431, 430, 428); in 429 he inaugurated the siege of *Plataea. Twice married, he was allegedly fined on the first occasion for marrying a too short wife (the mother of *Agis II); his second marriage produced *Agesilaus II.

Thuc. 1–2; Diod. Sic. 11. 63–4. PB no. 157; P. Cartledge *Agesilaos and the Crisis of Sparta* (1987).

Archidamus III,

son of *Agesilaus II and lover of the son of Sphodrias, reigned from 360/59 to 338 BC. He was born about 400 but did not fight at *Leuctra (371), after which disastrous defeat he was charged with escorting back to Sparta the remnant of the Spartan army. He commanded troops successfully against the Arcadians (see ARCADIA; ARCADIAN LEAGUE) in 368 and 365, and distinguished himself in the defence of Sparta against *Epaminondas in 362. In the Third *Sacred War he took the Phocians' part against Thebes (1), but withdrew Spartan forces in disgust at the duplicity of their commander *Phalaecus (346). Now that Sparta had lost an empire and failed to find a role, he aped his father's later career as a mercenary, responding to an appeal from Sparta's Italian daughter-city *Tarentum against the non-Greek Lucanians (c.342; see LUCANIA). But in 338, when other Greek leaders were preoccupied with the threat of *Philip (1) II of Macedon, Archidamus died in battle at Manduria in southern Italy. If the *Archidamus* of *Isocrates (a speech placed in the mouth of the then crown prince at a dramatic date of 366) is to be credited, Archidamus like his father was an irredentist believer in Sparta's futile mission to regain *Messenia.

Xen. *Hell.* 5–7; Theopompus, *FGrH* 115 F 232; Diod. Sic. 15–16; Plut. *Ages.* 19, 33–4; Paus. 3. 10. 3–5; 6. 4. 9. PB no. 158.   P. A. C.

Archigenes, of Apamea in Syria, pupil of *Agathinus; well-known physician at Rome in the time of Trajan (AD 98–117). He was an eclectic, but was chiefly influenced by the doctrines of the Pneumatic school (see PNEUMATISTS). The leading principle of his therapeutics was to combat the eight δυσκρασίαι (bad temperaments). *Galen's theory of the pulse was borrowed from that of Archigenes, while at other points Galen reacts against his teaching. Works: Περὶ τῶν κατὰ γένος φαρμάκων; Περὶ τόπων πεπονθότων; Περὶ καστορίου χρήσεως (On drugs, arranged by kinds; on affected parts; on the use of castor); eleven bks. of letters of medical advice; and many others: all lost except for frs.

W. D. R.; V. N.

Archilochus, Greek iambic and elegiac poet, from *Paros. He mentioned *Gyges, who died c.652 BC (fr. 19), and a total solar eclipse which was almost certainly that of 6 April 648 (fr. 122); a memorial to his friend Glaucus, son of Leptines (fr. 131), in late 7th-cent. lettering, has been found on *Thasos, where Archilochus spent part of his life (*SEG* 14. 565). His poetry was concerned with his personal affairs and with contemporary public events—politics, shipwrecks, war, etc. Its tone varied widely, from grave to gay, from pleasantly bantering to bitter. Archilochus was famous throughout antiquity for the stinging wit with which he lashed his enemies and sometimes his friends, and for what appeared to be carefree admissions of outrageous conduct such as fleeing from battle and abandoning his shield (fr. 5), or compromising young ladies. He repeatedly attacked one Lycambes, who had (or so the ancients understood) betrothed his daughter Neobule to Archilochus but later revoked the agreement. The vengeful poet then produced a series of poems in which he recounted in the most explicit detail the sexual experiences that he and others had enjoyed with both Neobule and her sister. This (so the legend goes) induced Lycambes and his daughters to hang themselves for shame. We have several fragments from sexual narratives (e.g. frs. 30–48). However, in the 'Cologne Epode' discovered in 1974 (fr. 196a) Neobule is represented as available for Archilochus but he dismisses her as over-

Archimedes

blown and promiscuous, while gently seducing the younger sister. The whole business has to be considered against the background of the Ionian *iambos* (see IAMBIC POETRY, GREEK) and its conventions of bawdy narrative and abuse of individuals.

The ancients arranged Archilochus' work in four sections: Elegiacs, (iambic) Trimeters, (trochaic) Tetrameters, and Epodes, with a couple of inauthentic pieces (frs. 322–4) tagged on at the end. Most celebrated were the Epodes, songs in simple strophes usually made up of a hexameter or iambic trimeter plus one or two shorter cola. Most famous of all was the first Epode, in which Archilochus remonstrated with Lycambes using the fable of the fox and the eagle (frs. 172–81). He used an animal fable in at least one other Epode (frs. 185–7). The lubricious material is concentrated in the Trimeters, though they also contained some serious pieces. The Tetrameters and Elegiacs were also of mixed character, but Archilochus clearly favoured tetrameters for elevated subjects such as accounts of battles (e.g. frs. 94, 98) and warnings of political dangers (frs. 105–6). Several of the elegiac fragments (8–13) lament men drowned at sea.

TEXT West, IE^2.

TRANSLATION West, *GLP.*

GENERAL A. Hauvette, *Archiloque, sa vie et ses œuvres* (1905); *RE* Suppl. 9. 136 ff.; A. P. Burnett, *Three Archaic Poets* (1983); *CHCL* 1. 117 ff.
M. L. W.

Archimedes, mathematician and inventor (*c.*287 to 212 or 211 BC). Born at *Syracuse, son of an astronomer Phidias, and killed at the sack of the city by the Romans under M. *Claudius Marcellus (1), he was on intimate terms with its king *Hieron (2) II. He visited Egypt, but lived most of his life at Syracuse, corresponding with *Conon (2), *Eratosthenes, and others. Popular history (see Plut. *Marc.* 14–19) knew him as the inventor of marvellous machines used against the Romans at the siege of Syracuse, and of devices such as the screw for raising water ($\kappa o \chi \lambda \acute{\iota} a s$); for his boast 'give me a place to stand and I will move the earth' (Simpl. *In phys.* 1110. 5); for his determination of the proportions of gold and silver in a wreath made for Hieron ($\epsilon \H{\upsilon} \rho \eta \kappa a$, $\epsilon \H{\upsilon} \rho \eta \kappa a$, 'Eureka! I have discovered it!' Vitr. 9 pref. 9–12); for his construction of two 'sphaerae' (a planetarium and a star globe) which were taken to Rome (Cic. *Rep.* 1. 21–2); and for his tomb, which by his wish depicted a cylinder circumscribing a sphere, with the ratio 3:2 which he discovered between them (Cic. *Tusc.* 5. 64–6).

His extant works, with the principal features of each, are, in Greek: (1) *On the Sphere and Cylinder*, two books: formulae for the surface-area and volume of a sphere and any segment of it. (2) *Measurement of the Circle*: by inscribing and circumscribing regular polygons of 96 sides, upper and lower limits of $3\frac{1}{7}$ and $3\frac{10}{71}$ are found to the value of π; Archimedes incidentally gives a rational approximation to the square root of 3 and of several large numbers. (3) *On Conoids and Spheroids*: determination of the volumes of segments of solids formed by the revolution of a conic about its axis. (4) *On Spirals*: properties of tangents to the 'Archimedean' spiral and determination of its area. (5) *Equilibriums of Planes* or *Centres of Gravity of Planes*, two books: the theory of the lever is propounded and the centres of gravity of various rectilinear plane figures (bk. 1) and of segments of conics (bk. 2) are established. (6) *Quadrature of the Parabola*: the area of a parabola is determined first by 'mechanical' (see below) and then by geometrical means. (7) *The Sand-reckoner*: description of a system for expressing enormously large numbers in words (in effect a notation in which 100,000,000 is used as a base as we use 10). Archimedes employs it to express the number of grains of sand

which, on certain assumptions, the universe is calculated to contain. It is the only surviving work of Archimedes touching on astronomy, and is our best source for the heliocentric system of *Aristarchus (1). (8) *Method of Mechanical Theorems*: description of the method invented by Archimedes for finding by 'mechanical' means the areas and volumes of the parabola, sphere, etc. (9) *On Floating Bodies*: deals with the positions which segments of a solid of revolution can assume when floating in a fluid; for this Archimedes invented a science of *hydrostatics *ab ovo*. The Greek text of the latter two works was discovered only in 1906, although *On Floating Bodies* was already known in Latin translation.

Extant works in Arabic translation are: (1) *On the Heptagon in a Circle*: geometrical construction of the regular heptagon. (2) *Book of Lemmas* (available only in Latin translation). (3) *On Touching Circles*. (4) *Book of Assumptions*. All of these have undergone alteration in transmission, and the authenticity of the last three is doubtful.

The most notable characteristic of Archimedes' mathematical work is its freedom from the trammels of traditional Greek mathematics. It is true that in the *proofs* of those theorems for which the integral calculus is now used (e.g. those determining the surface-area and volume of a sphere or the area of a parabola) he uses the standard Greek method of bypassing infinitesimals (invented by *Eudoxus (1) and employed in Euclid bk. 10, misnamed 'method of exhaustion' in modern works). But the *Method* (no. 8 above) reveals that for the *discovery* of these theorems he used a technique which consists of dividing two figures into infinitely thin strips, weighing these strips against each other, and then summing them to get the ratio of the two whole figures. This is analogous to the practice of the developers of the integral calculus in the 17th cent., but unlike them Archimedes recognized its lack of rigour, and used it only as a heuristic procedure. The same freedom of thought appears in arithmetic in the *Sand-reckoner*, which shows an understanding of the nature of a numerical system immeasurably superior to anything else from antiquity. It is this breadth and freedom of vision, rather than the amazing ingenuity which Archimedes displays in the solution of particular problems, which justifies calling him the greatest mathematician of antiquity. His work in *hydrostatics (see (9) above) was epoch-making (although the effect in antiquity was negligible). The same is true of *statics, though here he probably had predecessors.

All of his work in *astronomy is lost except for an ingenious method of finding the sun's apparent diameter described in the *Sand-reckoner*, and a passage giving the distances of the heavenly bodies preserved in Hippolytus (*Haer.* 41. 18 ff. Wendland). This corrupt passage suggests that he had no mathematical theory of astronomy. However, his construction of a planetarium implies the reverse. On this he wrote a work ($K a \tau \grave{a}$ $\tau \grave{\eta} \nu$ $\sigma \phi a \iota \rho o \pi o \iota \acute{\iota} a \nu$, Pappus 8. 3), now lost. Other lost works include treatises on the semi-regular polyhedra (Pappus 5. 34), on elementary mechanics ($\Pi \epsilon \rho \grave{\iota}$ $\zeta \upsilon \gamma \hat{\omega} \nu$ or $\Pi \epsilon \rho \grave{\iota}$ $\acute{\iota} \sigma o \rho \rho o \pi \iota \hat{\omega} \nu$, Pappus 8. 24) and on reflection in mirrors ($K a \tau o \pi \tau \rho \iota \kappa \acute{a}$, *Theon (4), comm. on Ptolemy's *Almagest* 1. 347 f.). An epigram preserves a 'cattle-problem' attributed to Archimedes; this poses a problem in indeterminate analysis with eight unknowns. There is no evidence that Archimedes found the solution. Fragments of a work entitled $\Sigma \tau o \mu \acute{a} \chi \iota o \nu$, dealing with a square divided into fourteen pieces for a game, are preserved in Greek and Arabic.

Commentaries by Eutocius to *Sphere and Cylinder, Measurement of the Circle*, and *Equilibriums of Planes* survive.

EDITIONS Critical text of Greek works (with Lat. trans.), fragments, some Arabic works in Latin translation, and Eutocius' commentaries, J. L. Heiberg, 2nd edn., 3 vols. (Teubner, 1910–15; repr. 1972). For earlier editions see Heath's translation, pp. xxix ff. Arabic versions: for *On the Regular Heptagon* see J. P. Hogendijk, *Archive for History of Exact Sciences* 1984, 197–330; *On Touching Circles*: ed. Y. Dold-Samplonius and others, *Archimedis Opera Omnia* 4, (Teubner, 1975), Arabic text with Ger. trans.; *Book of Assumptions*: Y. Dold-Samplonius, *Book of Assumptions by Aqāṭun* (Diss. Amsterdam, 1977). For the texts of Archimedes available in the Islamic world and the Latin west, M. Clagett, *Archimedes in the Middle Ages*, 5 vols. (1964–84).

TRANSLATIONS T. L. Heath, *The Works of Archimedes* (1897) and *The Method of Archimedes* (1912), repr. in one vol. (1957); French: P. Ver Eecke, *Les Œuvres complètes d'Archimède*, 2nd edn. (1960), includes commentaries of Eutocius.

COMMENT Heath, *Hist. of Greek Maths.* 2. 16 ff.; E. J. Dijksterhuis, *Archimedes*, 2nd edn. (1987), best detailed account of the works. I. Schneider, *Archimedes* (1979), in German: good account of recent literature. On the semi-regular polyhedra: I. S. Papadatos, *ΑΡΧΙΜΗΔΗΣ, τὰ 13 ἡμικανονικὰ Πολύεδρα* (1978). On the catoptrics: A. Lejeune, *Acad. Royale de Belgique, Mémoires Lettres*, 1957. On the mechanical inventions: A. G. Drachmann, *The Mechanical Technology of Greek and Roman Antiquity* (1961). G. J. T.

Archippus, Athenian comic poet. We have six titles, and four other plays were variously attributed to Archippus or *Aristophanes (1). Archippus may have been the man of that name denounced in 415 BC for profanation of the *mysteries (see ANDOCIDES; ARISTOMENES). In *Fishes* (after 403, as the reference to the archon Euclides (2) in fr. 27 KA shows) he exploited an idea similar to that of Aristophanes' *Birds*; fr. 27 concerns a treaty between Athens and the fishes. *Rhinon* no doubt satirized the man of that name who came into prominence in 404/3 (*Ath. pol.* 38. 3 f.).

Kassel–Austin, *PCG* 2. 538 ff. (*CAF* 1. 679 ff.). K. J. D.

architects The names of architects are preserved in literary sources as well as inscriptions. Theodorus, architect of the temple of Asclepius at *Epidaurus, is paid at only double the level of the ordinary craftsmen, suggesting a similar status, but this may be misleading, representing expenses rather than a living wage. *Vitruvius records treatises written by architects, such as Chersiphon and Metagenes, who built the Archaic temple of Artemis at Ephesus, *Ictinus and Carpion on the Parthenon, and the man whose writings profoundly influenced him, *Hermogenes (1); this suggests comparability with other educated men (as indeed, the *De architectura* requires). Roman architects are mostly anonymous; an exception is *Apollodorus (7).

From the inscriptions, in particular, their role is extensive. In Classical Greece they have to prepare the design (probably not detailed, scale plans, but possibly including full-size *paradeigmata*, examples to be copied) and to draw up specifications to be submitted to the appropriate commissioning bodies (in Athens, ultimately, the assembly), as well as calculating the quantities of material to be ordered, including stone, and the exact dimensions of blocks to be delivered from the *quarries. Though details are lacking from the Roman period, it is clear that the more important of the architects would have to be masters of design, which included the complex calculations needed for planning the structure of major concrete buildings such as the *Pantheon.

During construction, they would have to supervise the laying out of buildings, calculating the exact positioning of different elements (such as the columns in temples) on the spot. Important Greek buildings sometimes reveal layout marks to facilitate this. They also supervised on a day-to-day basis; the architect named on inscriptions for the work of any year may not be the original

designer, especially if construction was protracted over many years. See ARCHITECTURE; ARTISANS AND CRAFTSMEN.

J. J. Coulton, *Greek Architects at Work* (1977); A. Burford, *Craftsmen in Greek and Roman Society* (1972); W. Muller, *Architekten in der Welt der Antike* (1989). R. A. T.

architecture

Greek The forms of Greek architecture evolved essentially in the 7th and 6th cent. BC. After the collapse of *Mycenaean civilization, construction methods relapsed into the simplest forms of mud-brick and timber, mostly in small hut structures, the main exception being the great 10th-cent. apsidal building at *Lefkandi, over 45 m. (150 ft.) in length and flanked by wooden posts, supporting a thatched roof, a form echoed also in early structures at *Thermum.

The development of the Archaic period centred on temples, which in terms of size and expense always constituted the most important building type in the Greek world. Some of the earliest examples such as the little temple of *c.*750 BC at *Perachora retained the apsidal form, while one at *Eretria (the early temple of *Apollo Daphnephoros) was curvilinear. This soon gives way to the rectangular cella, in major buildings entered by a porch at one end, balanced by a similar but false porch at the back (west Greek temples omit this in favour of an adytum, an internal room at the back of the cella) and surrounded by a colonnade. Such temples of the first part of the 7th cent. BC as that to Poseidon at *Isthmia, and to *Hera at the Argive and Samian *Heraia were, like Lefkandi, 'hundred-footers' (*hekatompeda*), with steps and wall-footings of cut stone (at Isthmia the walls imitated timber-reinforced mud-brick but were constructed entirely in limestone), but with wooden columns. It is assumed these were already anticipating the forms of the Classical *orders of architecture though there is no material proof of this.

Construction in stone, employing the Doric or Ionic orders, developed in the late 7th cent. BC, when the Greeks began to have direct experience of Egypt, learning the methods of quarrying and working stone. The architectural form of temples built early in the 6th cent. BC, the temples of *Artemis at *Corcyra (Doric), and the House of the Naxians on *Delos—probably a temple of Apollo—(Ionic), shows that the arrangements and details of the orders were established by then, and in the case of Doric, these clearly imitate forms evolved from the earlier wooden structures. Thereafter architecture as applied to temples is a matter of refinement and improvement, rather than radical development and change. Ionic architects (especially in the *Cyclades) were already using *marble in the early 6th cent. Limestone remained the normal material in the Peloponnese, even for major temples such as that of *Zeus at *Olympia (*c.*470 BC), and in the temples of Sicily and Italy, but the opening of the quarries of *Pentelicon in the late 6th cent. led to the splendid series of Athenian marble temples of the 5th century.

Refinement concentrated on detail: the balance of proportions in all parts of the structure, in the precise form of column, capital, entablature, and above all the decorative mouldings. Colour was also used, now generally lost from temples and other normal buildings but well preserved on the façades and interiors of the built Macedonian vaulted tombs of the 4th cent. and later (such as the royal tombs at Vergina; see AEGAE). Here the façades, which imitate temple and related architectural forms, have their painted decoration perfectly preserved because they were buried immediately after the decoration was added. In Doric, clearly, this also evolved with the wooden buildings, whose structural divisions it emphasizes. The colours are harsh, positive blues and reds, with some patterning in contrasting yellow and gold. Refinement of architectural form involves the use of subtle curves rather than straight lines for the profiles of the columns: these evolve from the cruder curvature of early Doric, perhaps itself derived from the naturalistic curvature of Egyptian plant-form columns, and curvature of the temple base or crepis carried up to the entablature may be intended to correct optical illusion, as also the slight inward inclination of columns. Ionic buildings always used slender columns; Doric, very massive at first, becomes more slender—though the continued refinement into the Hellenistic period suggests that the 5th-cent. marble forms of Periclean Athens were not recognized as ideal and *Ictinus' interest in the mathematical relationship of various parts, particularly the ratio $2^2:3^2$, demonstrated in the *Parthenon, is not generally imitated.

The procedures of design employed by *architects are uncertain. Scale plans are known in Egypt, but their use in Greece was probably restricted by lack of drawing material and the limitations of the Greek numerical system, particularly for fractions. Procedures were more likely based on experience and tradition, details of layout being worked out in situ. 'Examples' (paradeigmata), probably full-scale, of detailed elements would be supplied to the *quarries and craftsmen as necessary. Structural systems were simple, based on the principle of post and beam, and dimensions were restricted by the size of available timber beams, generally not more than 12 m. (39 ft.); more complex woodworking systems may have been used in Macedon, where the palace at Vergina has rooms with a free span of more than 16 m. (52½ ft.). Macedon also developed the vault in the 4th cent. BC but this was not utilized generally in Greek architecture except for the Macedonian tombs and, in Hellenistic times, for gateways in *fortifications. In temple architecture there is no complexity of plan, apart from the totally exceptional *Erechtheum at Athens.

Other building forms evolve more slowly, and are always influenced by concepts employed in temples. Usually they are less lavish, and economy in construction is an important factor. Colonnades, which had developed largely as a decorative or prestige factor, could be employed extensively in more utilitarian structures, either as free-standing buildings (stoas) or extended round courtyards, both providing scope for adding rooms behind the resulting portico, which could be put to a variety of purposes (see STOA). As a result, a new principle of architectural design emerges. Temples were essentially free-standing buildings, viewed from the surrounding space. Buildings based on the courtyard principle, which by the 6th cent. had been adapted as the normal arrangement for Greek *houses, were intended to be seen from within, from the space they surrounded. These developments are seen in more progressive places, such as Athens in the 5th cent. BC, particularly in the buildings surrounding the Agora. *Theatre structures were still relatively undeveloped, and the theatre at Athens did not attain architectural form until the construction of the stone-seated auditorium in the second half of the 4th cent. Buildings might now be more complex in plan, though simple rectangles, or rectangular courtyards, were still preferred, with single roof levels. Curvilinear forms are rare, restricted to a few circular buildings (such as the *tholos, and the curvilinear auditorium of theatres). Some complex plans exist, such as the *Propylaea to the Athenian acropolis (436–432 BC), or the near contemporary *Erechtheum, but even here it can be seen that the architect is constrained to think in terms of the juxtaposition of rectangular blocks, though using different roof levels, rather than a fully integrated overall design.

It is the Hellenistic age which sees the widest application of Greek architectural forms, with developed arrangements, based on courtyard principles, for exercise grounds and planned agoras. Much structure remained in mud-brick and timber, but there was now more application of stone construction, with columns, to buildings other than temples. Here the simpler Doric order was generally preferred to Ionic. There are some distinctive regional or local developments such as the tall tenement houses of *Alexandria (1), of which some footings, in regular ashlar blocks, have been discovered. In *Pergamum idiosyncratic architectural forms evolve, employing the local stone, trachyte, not generally used in Greek architecture; but more significant here are the variations in traditional styles, such as the introduction of a palm-leaf capital, and walls formed from inner and outer skins of squared stone with rubble packing, as well as variations in the details of the conventional orders. In the Hellenistic period generally there is some impact of non-Greek architectural form; and although in Ptolemaic Egypt there is a distinctive separation between the Greek form and the continuation of an Egyptian tradition, the development of the more ornate Corinthian order, in the Seleucid kingdom particularly, may well reflect the influence of a local taste derived from earlier architectural usage.

The establishment of Roman authority over the former Hellenistic kingdoms did not lead to any abrupt change in forms of architecture. The troubled years of the early 1st cent. BC must have imposed something of a moratorium on building; but with the establishment of the Augustan Principate conditions favourable to construction returned. (There was something of a false dawn under *Caesar.) Buildings in Athens are either developed from Hellenistic prototypes (the *Odeum of Agrippa) or conceived as Classical derivatives (the temple of Rome and Augustus on the Acropolis, based on the details of the Erechtheum). In Asia Minor the distinctive pulvinated masonry style of the 2nd cent. BC continues into the 1st cent. AD. Many of the public buildings of Ephesus were reconstructed in the 1st cent. AD in Hellenistic form. Temples in the Greek areas were normally built with a stepped crepis (though they may well employ the Corinthian order); only 'official' Roman buildings such as the temple of Trajan at Pergamum are based on podia with steps only at the front. In the 2nd cent. this gives way to a more universal Roman style, ornately decorated, habitually using column shafts of smooth, coloured marbles and other stones. Even so, the construction did not employ Roman concrete techniques, though mortared work, and brickwork, occur more regularly. See ATHENS, TOPOGRAPHY; BUILDING MATERIALS; NYMPHAEUM; URBANISM.

D. S. Robertson, Greek and Roman Architecture (1943); W. B. Dinsmoor, The Architecture of Ancient Greece 3 (1950); A. W. Lawrence, Greek Architecture⁴, ed. R. A. Tomlinson (1983); R. Martin, Manuel d'Architecture grecque (1965); J. J. Coulton, Greek Architects at Work (1977); H. Lauter, Die Architektur des Hellenismus (1986); F. Sear, Roman Architecture (1989); W. L. MacDonald, The Architecture of the Roman Empire 1, 2nd edn. (1982); 2 (1986); S. Macready and F. Thompson (eds.), Roman Architecture in the Greek World (1987); S. Walker and A. Cameron (eds.), The Greek Renaissance in the Roman Empire (1989); J. B. Ward-Perkins, Roman Imperial Architecture, 2nd edn. (1981). R. A. T.

Roman Roman architecture represents the fusion of traditional Greek elements, notably the trabeated orders, with an innovative approach to structural problems resulting in the extensive exploitation of the arch and vault, the evolution of a new building material, concrete, and, probably, the development of the roof truss. While the *orders remained synonymous with the Greek-inspired architecture of temples and porticoes, it was the structural experiments which facilitated the creation of new building types in response to the different political, social, and economic conditions of Rome's expanding empire.

The importance of the orders reflects the early pre-eminence of temple architecture in central Italy, where the Tuscan order evolved probably under the inspiration of Archaic Greek Doric. By the 2nd cent. BC distinctive Italian forms of Ionic and Corinthian were also in widespread use beside more purely Hellenistic Greek forms. The fully Roman form of Corinthian, distinguished by the scroll-shaped modillions of the cornice, probably of Alexandrian origin, emerged as a concomitant to the growing use of marble in public building during the Augustan age. Among the numerous variants on the Corinthian capital, the most successful was the Composite, combining the acanthus-clad bell of the Corinthian with the diagonal volutes of the Italic Ionic. A purely decorative use of the orders, incorporating many features later to be associated with the Italian 'baroque', was particularly common in the 2nd and 3rd cents. AD, gaining impetus from the increasing availability of various precious marbles. Monumental columnar façades, two to three storeys high, decorated theatre stages throughout the empire, and the device was also employed in the eastern empire and at Rome for public fountains (see NYMPHAEUM), *libraries, and large bath-buildings (see BATHS). Colonnaded streets also became popular.

New building types evolved in the 3rd and 2nd cents. BC, some, such as the *amphitheatre, purely Roman, while *baths and *theatres, for example, showed more influence from Hellenistic Sicily and Magna Graecia. Sophisticated timberwork allowed for the roofing of large spans in the *basilica, covered theatre (*odeum), and atrium house (see HOUSES, ITALIAN), while the adoption of barrel-vaulting for terracing structures such as villa platforms and monumental sanctuaries (e.g. sanctuary of Fortuna at *Praeneste) provided the basic structural system later used in utilitarian buildings such as the Porticus Aemilia and in free-standing theatres and amphitheatres. The high status of the orders in Roman architectural thought led to them being applied as decorous adjuncts to arcuated façades already by the late republic (e.g. the Forum façade of the *Tabularium (1)), a motif which found full expression in buildings such as the theatre of Marcellus and the *Colosseum and which was to have a strong influence on Renaissance and later architecture.

The decisive developments in Roman concrete architecture in the early imperial period also took place in the context of domestic or non-traditional building types, such as Nero's *Domus Aurea, *Domitian's palace on the Palatine, and Hadrian's villa at *Tibur as well as the great imperial baths, which in turn influenced the later Basilica of Maxentius; the *Pantheon, as a temple, is exceptional. The flexibility and structural properties of the new material were used to create an architecture in which the dominant factor was not the solid masonry but the space which it enclosed. Instead of the structural rationality and sculptural quality of Classical Greek architecture, this was an architecture of illusion and suggestion, inspired by the ephemeral pavilions of Hellenistic palaces, in which subtly curvilinear forms based on complex geometries in plan and elevation, splendidly lit and clothed in light-reflecting material such as marble veneer and coloured-glass mosaic, contrived to negate the solidity of the structures themselves. Here too the columnar orders often formed an integral part of the visual effect, e.g. in the *frigidaria* of the imperial bath-buildings, although their structural role was generally negligible. Treatment of exteriors remained simple and traditional, often decorated in either veneer or stucco imitation of ashlar, although in the later empire the curves of the vaults were often allowed free expression outside as well as inside (e.g. the Hunting Baths at *Lepcis Magna). It was this exploitation of interior space which found its logical conclusion in the architecture of Byzantium and remains the most important Roman contribution to all subsequent architectural thought. See ARCHES; BRICKSTAMPS; BRIDGES; BUILDING MATERIALS; MARBLE; TRIUMPHAL ARCH.

A. Boethius, *Etruscan and Early Roman Architecture* (1978); J. B. Ward-Perkins, *Roman Imperial Architecture* (1980); W. L. MacDonald, *The Architecture of the Roman Empire* 1, 2nd edn. (1982); 2 (1986); L. Crema, *L'architettura romana* (1959); M. Lyttelton, *Baroque Architecture in Classical Antiquity* (1974). J. D.

archives

Greek (τὰ δημόσια γράμματα and variations; ἀρχεῖον is mainly Hellenistic). In Archaic Greece, documentation was minimal, laws being the most important public documents; lists of officials and agonistic victors (see AGŌNES) were evidently recorded (and later published), but the public inscriptions themselves were probably the 'stone archives' (see RECORDS AND RECORD-KEEPING). Temples were safe deposits from early on (e.g. *Heraclitus deposited in a temple a copy of his own book), and might contain public inscriptions: hence they often came to house the archives of the city: e.g. the Athenian Metroon, also a shrine; archives of 2nd-cent BC *Paros. Documents were also kept separately by the officials concerned, or in their offices (on wooden tablets (*pinakes*), or whitened boards (*leukōmata*), or papyri, e.g. the Athenian cavalry archive (see HIPPEIS § 2), the records of the *pōlētai (*Ath. pol.* 47–8), and there was little centralization. Athens acquired a central archive, the Metroon, in the late 5th cent. BC; manned by slaves, this housed official documents of the *boulē and assembly (*ekklēsia), i.e. mainly decrees, some foreign letters, and treaties with other cities (previously kept in the *bouleutērion or on stone); the laws were probably not kept there until the late 4th cent., nor were private documents like *Epicurus' will. Even after the creation of the Metroon, public inscriptions are regarded as authoritative texts. There is a general increase in documentation and hence of archive use from the 4th cent., though the extent and sophistication of archives in Egypt must be exceptional (cf. the piecemeal organization in 2nd-cent. Paros, *Chiron* 1983, 283 ff.). Public archives are increasingly used, and sometimes compulsory (Arist. *Pol.* 1321b), for private documents (contracts etc.) in the Hellenistic period. The registration of property and documentation of other transactions is particularly elaborate in Ptolemaic and Roman *Egypt.

Roman (*tabularia*, from *tabulae* as 'records'). Rome's early records were rudimentary: lists of magistrates (*fasti), copies of treaties, and priestly records, which were not systematically organized till the late 4th cent. (see ANNALES MAXIMI; ANNALS, ANNALISTS). The main archive was the *aerarium, in the temple of Saturn, established in the early republic and supervised by urban *quaestors. It contained copies of laws (see LEX (1)) and *senatus consulta, which were not valid until properly deposited (Suet. *Aug.* 94; Plut. *Cat. Min.* 16–18); also *acta senatus (later), public contracts, records of official oaths, lists of public debtors, and Marcus *Aurelius' new register of Roman births. It is unclear how strictly the archives were separated from the *aerarium*'s financial functions; the closely associated monumental complex nearby on the slopes of the Capitol certainly contained a *tabularium (*CIL* 1². 737), though its conventional identification as a Public Record Office is incorrect (it may in fact be the Atrium Libertatis). Romans continue to speak of records going into the *aerarium* (e.g. Tac. *Ann.* 3. 51). Access was not always straightforward (SEE RECORDS AND RECORD-KEEPING). Another archive was used by the *plebs* in the temple of Ceres (holding *plebiscita* and *senatus consulta*); censors' records went into the temple of the Nymphs and Atrium Libertatis; and private archives, e.g. of ex-officials, were also commonly kept (cf. Cic. *Sull.* 42). Inscriptions, like the bronze tablets of laws visible on the Capitol, formed a public source of reference. Under the empire, the focus is increasingly on the emperor's archival records, often called the *tabularium principis*: the emperor's *commentarii* included imperial edicts and letters (cf. Plin. *Ep.* 10. 65, 66); *commentarii* recording grants of Roman *citizenship (recorded in the *tabula Banasitana*) were established by *Augustus (*JRS* 1973, 86 ff.).

A. L. Boegehold, *AJArch.* 1972, 23 ff. (Metroon); R. Thomas, *Oral Tradition and Written Record in Classical Athens* (1989), ch. 1; G. Klaffenbach, *Bemerkungen zum griechischen Urkundenwesen* (*Sitz. Akad. Berlin*, 1960); W. E. H. Cockle, *JEg. Arch.* 1984, 106 ff., and F. Burkhalter, *Chiron* 1990, 191 ff., for Egypt.
ROMAN E. Posner, *Archives in the Ancient World* (1972); Mommsen, *Röm. Staatsr.* 2³. 1. 545 ff.; M. Corbier, *L'Aerarium Saturni et l'Aerarium militare* (1974), 674 ff.; F. Millar, *JRS* 1964, 33 ff. (*aerarium*); R. Talbert, *Senate of Imperial Rome* (1984), ch. 9; F. Millar, *The Emperor in the Roman World*, 2nd. edn. (1991), 259 ff.; M. Corbier, in *L'Urbs: Espace urbain et histoire* (1987), 267 ff.; C. Williamson, *Cl. Ant.* 1987, 160 ff. (on laws); P. Culham, *CPhil.* 1989, 100 ff.; N. Purcell, *PBSR* 1993, 125 ff.   R. T.

archontes ('rulers'), the general Greek term for all holders of office in a state. But the word was frequently used as the title of a particular office, originally at least the highest office of the state. *Archontes* are found in most states of central Greece, including *Athens, and in states dependent on or influenced by Athens.

In Athens by the 6th cent. BC there were nine annually appointed archons. The powers of the original hereditary king (*basileus*) came to be shared among three officials: the *basileus*, who retained particularly the religious duties; the *archōn*, who became the civilian head of state; and the *polemarchos ('warruler'), who commanded the army. (The Athenians believed that there had been a gradual transition from kings through life archons and ten-year archons to annual archons; annual archons allegedly began c. 683/2 BC). Six *thesmothetai ('statute-setters'), judicial officials, were added to the original three; and in the 5th or 4th cent. the board was made up to ten with the addition of the secretary to the *thesmothetai*, so that one could be appointed from each of *Cleisthenes (2)'s ten tribes (*phylai*). Whether direct election was retained throughout the 6th cent. is disputed; from 487/6 the method used was *klērōsis ek prokritōn*, allotment from an elected short list; and at a later date allotment replaced election for the first stage. See SORTITION. By the early 5th cent. the two highest property classes (*pentakosiomedimnoi and *hippeis (4)) were eligible for appointment, and in 457/6 eligibility was extended to the third class, the *zeugitai. Almost certainly, a man could only be a member of the board of archons once in his life; after his year of office he became a member of the council of the *Areopagus for the remainder of his life.

In the 6th cent., and presumably before, the archons and in particular the one entitled *archōn* were the most important officials of the Athenian state. *Solon was *archōn* when he was commissioned to reform the state in 594/3, and it is a sign of continuing trouble afterwards that there were years when no *archōn* was appointed and that an *archōn* called Damasias refused

to retire at the end of his year. *Hippias (1) was *archōn* in the first available year (526/5) after the death of his father *Pisistratus. However, the creation by Cleisthenes of ten *stratēgoi ('generals'), appointed annually by election and eligible for re-election, began a process by which in the 5th cent. the generals became the most important Athenian officials while the archons became routine officials.

In the later 5th and 4th cent. the archons' duties were particularly religious and judicial: earlier they had given verdicts on their own account, but now they conducted the preliminary enquiry (*anakrisis*) and presided in the jury-court which decided the verdict. The *archōn* was responsible for a number of religious festivals, and for lawsuits concerning family matters. The *basileus* was responsible for the largest number of religious matters, and for homicide suits. The *polemarchos* was responsible for some festivals, including the games in honour of those who had died in war, and for lawsuits involving non-citizens. The *thesmothetai* were responsible for the system of jury-courts as a whole, and for most 'public' lawsuits (in which any citizen might prosecute). In the elaborate organization of the court system developed in the 4th cent. all ten members of the board were involved in the selection of the jurors who were to serve each day, each supervising the procedure in his own tribe.

By the end of the 5th cent. it had become standard practice to identify each year by its *archōn*, and so he is sometimes referred to as the eponymous *archōn*, but that expression is not found in Greek texts until the Roman period.

Ath. pol. 3; 8. 1–2; 22. 5; 26. 2; 55–9; 63–6. R. K. Sinclair, *Democracy and Participation in Athens* (1988); D. L. Stockton, *The Classical Athenian Democracy* (1990), 108–11; M. H. Hansen, *The Athenian Democracy in the Age of Demosthenes* (1991).   A. W. G.; P. J. R.

Archytas (fl. *c*.400–350 BC), Pythagorean philosopher and mathematician from *Tarentum. He was elected general seven times and sent a ship to rescue *Plato (1) from *Dionysius (2) II of Syracuse in 361. He figures prominently in several Platonic letters whose authenticity is controversial, but he is never directly mentioned in the dialogues. Fragments 1–3 are probably authentic, but other fragments preserved in his name are commonly regarded as spurious. There is little evidence of his general philosophical principles. He argued that study of μαθήματα ('sciences') such as astronomy, geometry, arithmetic, and music was crucial to the understanding of reality (fr. 1) and his reference to them as 'sisters' may have influenced Plato (*Resp.* 530d). *Aristotle (*Metaph.* 1043ᵃ21) reports that he accepted definitions that combined form and matter. In fragment 3 he praises 'correct calculation' (λογισμός) as the source of political harmony. He was most famous as the founder of *mechanics and for solutions to specific mathematical problems such as the doubling of the cube. His proof that numbers in a superparticular ratio $(n + 1/n)$ have no mean proportional has relevance for ancient music theory as does his work with the arithmetic, geometric, and harmonic means (fr. 2). He gave mathematical accounts of the diatonic, enharmonic, and chromatic scales and developed a theory of *acoustics. See MUSIC; PYTHAGORAS (1).

DK 6; trans. in K. Freeman, *Ancilla* (1971). Generally: N. Purcell, *CAH* 6² (1994), 389 f. On Plato and Archytas: G. E. R. Lloyd, *Phronesis*, 1990. On fr. 1: C. Huffman, *CQ* 1985. On music: A Barker, *Greek Musical Writings* 2 (1989). On spurious fragments: H. Thesleff, *Pythagorean Texts* (1965).   C. A. H.

Arcisius (Ἀρκείσιος), in mythology, father of Laertes and grandfather of *Odysseus; his own parentage is variously given. In one story, his mother was a she-bear (Ἀρκείσιος—ἄρκτος, 'bear'), Aristotle in *Etym. magn.* 144. 25.

Arctinus, of Miletus, shadowy poet to whom several poems of the *Epic Cycle were sometimes ascribed. Chronographers give the worthless datings 775 and 744/1 BC.   M. L. W.

Ardea, a city of the Rutuli, a Latin people. Although 4.5 km. (3 mi.) from the sea, it served as a port for *Latium. First settled in the bronze age, its elaborate defences and rich temples that long served as federal sanctuaries for the Latin League confirm the tradition that Ardea was once an important city, worthy of signing a separate treaty with Rome (444 BC). In 442 a Latin colony (see IUS LATII) strengthened Ardea against the *Volsci and in 390 M. *Furius Camillus, it was said, set out from here to repel the Gauls. Apparently, too, Ardea remained loyal in the Latin War (Livy 8. 12). A Samnite raid *c.*315 BC and subsequently malaria caused Ardea to decline. However, the erection of numerous villas and possibly the dispatch of a Hadrianic colony prevented the village from entirely disappearing. In republican times Ardea served as a state prison; later its fields supported the imperial *elephants.

A. Andrén, *Opuscula Romana* 1 (1954), 1 ff. (acropolis excavations); 3 (1961), 1 ff.; C. Morselli and E. Tortorici, *Ardea* (*Forma Italiae* 1/16) (1982); *Ardea: Immagine di una ricerca,* exhib. cat. (1983); F. Melis and S. Quilici Gigli, *Arch. Class.* 1982, 1 ff.   E. T. S.; T. W. P.

Areithous (Ἀρηΐθοος), a mythological character, surnamed Κορυνήτης, i.e. Club-man, because he fought with a club of iron; his armour had been given him by *Ares. Lycurgus the Arcadian caught him in a narrow road where he had no room to swing his club, ran him through with a spear, and took his armour (*Il.* 7. 138 ff.).   H. J. R

Arelate, a town in Gallia Narbonensis, modern Arles-sur-Rhône. Literary references to its Greek origins have been confirmed by archaeology. It became important with the construction of the 'Fossae Marianae' and was used as a naval base by Caesar against *Massilia (49 BC). A colony of veterans of the sixth legion (*Colonia Iulia Paterna Sextanorum Arelate*) was founded here in 46 BC on land taken mainly from Massilia. Arelate was much enlarged by Augustus, to whom the earliest surviving town-wall and probably the still visible east gate are due, and further significantly developed by the Flavians. Early buildings still visible are the forum, magnificent *amphitheatre (136 m. × 107 m. (446 × 351 ft.) externally), and theatre. An extensive suburb, linked by a bridge, developed at Trinquetaille. The original importance of Arelate was due to its position as a port of transhipment for seagoing vessels. In the Later empire it gained hugely in status as an occasional imperial residence: *Constantine I ordered the first Christian council here in 314. In the 4th cent. AD the city was given major new buildings, and accommodated a mint. Though the area within the walls was reduced, *Ausonius (*Ordo Nob. Urb.* 10) attests the city's continuing prosperity. In the 5th cent. it became the seat of the praetorian prefecture of the Gauls, displacing Trier (*Augusta Treverorum) as the capital of the west. In the 440s its bishop could claim supremacy in Gaul. After various vicissitudes it was annexed by the *Visigoths in 476.

Grenier, *Manuel* 1. 289 ff.; 2. 493 ff.; 3. 157 ff.; A. L. F. Rivet, *Gallia Narbonensis* (1988), 190 ff.   J. F. Dr.

Arellius (*RE* 3) **Fuscus,** Augustan teacher of rhetoric, perhaps

from Asia Minor. The elder *Seneca, who thought him one of the four best declaimers of his day (see DECLAMATION), was critical of his uneven style (*Controv.* 2 pref. 1). Among his pupils were Ovid and the philosopher *Papirius Fabianus.

*PIR*² A 1030; Schanz–Hosius, § 336. 6.   M. W.

Areopagus, the 'Hill of Ares' (Ἄρειος πάγος) at *Athens, northwest of the Acropolis, and the ancient council associated with it. There are no substantial remains on the hill; the council's meeting-place may have been on a terrace on the north-east side rather than on the summit. Probably the council was called simply *boulē* ('council') at first, and was named after the hill when a second council from which it had to be distinguished was created, probably by *Solon.

In early Athens the membership of the council will have been aristocratic. By the time of Solon, if not earlier, it came to comprise all ex-archons (see ARCHONTES), who entered it at the end of their year of office and remained members for the rest of their lives. The annual entry of nine new members in middle life maintained a strength of about 150. Changes in recruitment depended on changes in the recruitment of the archons: based on wealth rather than family from the time of *Solon; including the *zeugitai, the third property class, from 457/6 BC; and no longer attracting the men with the highest political ambitions from the first half of the 5th cent., when the archonships became routine offices.

It is likely that the council began as a body advising first the king and later the archons (though this view has been challenged); and it certainly had acquired some jurisdiction, in homicide cases *inter alia,* before the time of Solon. Descriptions of it as guardian of the state or of the laws gave expression to its powerful position in early Athens, and may have been exploited as a basis for exercising new powers not formally conferred on it. Solon gave it or confirmed for it the right to try *eisangeliai, charges of major offences against the state, but his creation of a new council to prepare business for the assembly began the decline in the powers of the Areopagus.

There may have been no further formal change in its powers until the reform of *Ephialtes (4) in 462/1. By this time the archons were appointed by lot from an elected short list, to an office which was overshadowed by the generalship (see STRATĒGOI), so a powerful Areopagus was coming to seem an anachronism; and practice in participating in *Cleisthenes (2)'s political machinery was giving the Athenian citizens the taste for controlling their own destiny. That Athens was dominated by the Areopagus after the *Persian Wars may be an invention of later writers to explain why reform of the Areopagus was necessary, but if the Areopagus had been exercising its judicial powers to the advantage of *Cimon that may have provoked Cimon's opponents to attack it.

Ephialtes is said to have taken away the judicial powers which gave the Areopagus its guardianship of the state: these probably included the trial of *eisangeliai (if they had not been taken away earlier), and procedures which enabled it to control the magistrates, such as *dokimasia, the vetting before they entered office, and *euthynai, the examination of their conduct when they left office. The Areopagus retained the right to try cases of homicide, wounding, and arson (and the *ephetai, 'referees', who tried some categories of homicide cases were probably members of the Areopagus), and also some religious cases. The reform was contentious—Cimon was ostracized (see OSTRACISM), Ephialtes was murdered, the Areopagus as a homicide court was featured in

*Aeschylus' *Eumenides* of 458—but it held, and for a time the council ceased to be a politically important body.

A proposal to make the council guardian of the revised code of laws in 403/2 seems to have been ineffective; but it enjoyed a resurgence in the middle of the 4th cent. *Isocrates in his *Areopagiticus* of *c*.355 focused on a powerful Areopagus as a feature of Athens' more glorious past; from the 340s in judicial and in other matters it was able to submit a report (*apophasis*) to the assembly on the assembly's initiative or its own, and this could lead to action by the assembly or a trial in a jury-court; after the battle of *Chaeronea it was enabled to act as a court to try men accused of deserting the Athenian cause. Many of its decisions were to the advantage of *Demosthenes (2), and probably Demosthenes' opponents were responsible for a law of 337/6 threatening the Areopagus with suspension if the democracy were overthrown (*SEG* 12. 87); but it retained its enhanced position, and reported against Demosthenes when it enquired into the affair of *Harpalus in 323.

Under *Demetrius (3) of Phalerum (317–307) the Areopagus may have been given new powers in the area of morals (Philochorus, *FGrH* 328 F 65). In 305/4 and perhaps again in 230/29 it was involved in raising money for resistance to Macedon (*IG* 2². 1492B, 7. 2405/6); in the late 2nd cent. its judicial powers included cases concerning weights and measures (*IG* 2². 1013). In the Hellenistic period it again became common for ambitious men to serve as archons, and afterwards to join the Areopagus, and the prestige of its members will have added to the prestige of the council. Possibly after *Sulla's capture of Athens the Areopagus seems to have been involved in a codification of the laws (*SEG* 26. 120). Under the Roman Principate it ranked with the *boulē* and the assembly (*ekklēsia*) as one of the major corporations of Athens, and its herald became one of the state's major officials: it probably still comprised all living former holders of any of the archonships. In the 2nd cent. AD it acquired a panhellenic stature with its honours for Greek men of culture (e.g. *IGRom*. 3. 733; J. Crampa, *Labraunda* 3. 2 (1972), no. 66). It still existed in the 4th cent. AD, when it seems to have been primarily a judicial body.

Ath. pol. 3. 6; 8. 4; 25; 27. 1; 35. 2; 57. D. M. MacDowell, *Athenian Homicide Law in the Age of the Orators* (1963); D. J. Geagan, *The Athenian Constitution after Sulla*, Hesp. Suppl. 12 (1967); R. W. Wallace, *The Areopagos Council, to 307 BC* (1989); M. H. Hansen, *The Athenian Democracy in the Age of Demosthenes* (1991), chs. 3, 12.   T. J. C.; P. J. R.

Ares (Ἄρης, Aeol. Ἄρευς), the Greek war-god as embodiment of the ambivalent (destructive but often useful) forces of war, in contrast to Athena who represents the intelligent and orderly use of war to defend the *polis*.

The name is perhaps attested on Linear B tablets from *Cnossus and, in a theophoric name, from *Thebes (1). In *Homer's *Iliad*, his image is mostly negative: he is brazen, ferocious, 'unsatiable with war', his cry sounds like that of 'nine or ten thousand men', Zeus hates him (*Il*. 5. 890 f.), he fights on the Trojan side, his attendants are Deimos 'Fear' and Phobos 'Panic', and he is often opposed to *Athena (see esp. *Il*. 15. 110–42). On the other hand, a brave warrior is 'a shoot from Ares', and the Danai are his followers. In epic formulae, his name is used as a noun ('the frenzy of fighting'); this must be metonymy, although the god's name could have originated as a personification of the warrior's ecstasy (Ger. *wuot*). As with the ecstatic *Dionysus, the myth of his Thracian origin (*Il*. 13. 301; see THRACE) illustrates this position outside the ordered, 'Greek' world of the *polis* and has no historical value.

Mythology makes Ares the son of *Zeus and *Hera (Hes. *Theog*. 922, together with their daughters *Hebe and *Eileithyia), thus inscribing him in Zeus' world-order, and the lover of *Aphrodite (*Od*. 8. 267–366) whose eroticism is at least as liable to subvert the *polis* order (as her birth-legend and some rites suggest). Offspring of Ares and Aphrodite are Deimos and Phobos (Hes. *Theog*. 934), *Eros (Simonides, 575 *PMG*; it underlines the subversive aspect of Eros), the artificial Anteros (Cic. *Nat. D*. 3. 60), and Theban Harmonia. Among other children of Ares, unruly and disruptive figures abound (*Diomedes (1) the Thracian, *Cycnus (1) the brigand, *Phlegyas the eponym of the ferocious Phlegyans). See also ASCALAPHUS.

Cults of Ares are rare, and details for ritual lacking; what we know confirms the god's functions, and his marginality. Temples are known chiefly from Crete (Cnossus, Lato, Biannos, perhaps Olus) and the Peloponnese (Argos, Troezen, Megalopolis, Therapne, Geronthrae, Tegea), but also from Athens and Erythrae. Cretan towns offer sacrifices to Ares and Aphrodite (*ML* 42), who appear in interstatal and ephebic oaths; their combination seems to be typical for Archaic bands of warriors (see Plut. *Pel*. 19 who associates them with the homosexual bond among young warriors). See EPHĒBOI; HOMOSEXUALITY. The Tegean women (see TEGEA) sacrifice to Ares γυναικοθοίνας, 'Who feasts the women' (Paus. 8. 48. 4), in a ritual of reversal which fits the nature of Ares. In Athens, he has a temple in *Acharnae and a priest together with Athena Areia, and the two figure in the ephebic oath as the warlike protectors of the city's young soldiers, together with the pair Enyo and Enyalius.

In Thebes (1), mythology makes him the ancestor of the town (Aesch. *Sept*. 105): *Cadmus slays the dragon whom some authors declare to be the offspring of Ares (schol. Soph. *Ant*. 126) and marries Harmonia, the daughter of Ares and Aphrodite. Actual Theban cult, however, is extremely reticent about Ares: again, he as well as Harmonia seem to belong to the Archaic heritage of warfare (see above); given his nature, it would be impossible to make him the central deity of a town.

In literature from Homer onwards, Ares is identified with Enyalius (e.g. *Il*. 13. 519 and 521, 17. 211, but see *Il*. 2. 651, etc.) whose name Homeric formulae also use as a noun and who is attested in Mycenaean Cnossus. In cult, the two are functionally similar but distinct war-gods, sometimes with cults in the same town; Enyalius is especially common in NE Peloponnese, but receives a marginal dog-sacrifice in Sparta (Paus. 3. 14. 9) where his cult statue was fettered (Paus. 3. 15. 7).

In Rome, Ares was identified with *Mars; the Augustan temple of Ares on the Athenian Agora (perhaps the transferred 4th-cent. temple of Acharnae) meant Mars as the ancestor of Rome; Greek Ares would have been unthinkable on an agora.

In early art, Ares appears exclusively in mythological scenes, together with the other gods (divine assemblies, as for the wedding of Peleus and Thetis or on the Parthenon frieze). First a bearded warrior, he is later shown naked and young (Parthenon frieze), as a warlike ephebe with whom not only the Athenians connected him. See MARS.

Farnell, *Cults* 5. 396–414; F. Schwenn, *ARW* 1923–4, 224–44; Burkert, *GR* 169–70; F. Graf, *Nordionische Kulte* (1985), 265–9; P. Bruneau, *LIMC* 2 (1984), 479–92 'Ares'.   F. G.

Aretaeus, of *Cappadocia, medical author, a contemporary of *Galen (*c*. AD 150–200), wrote in Ionic in imitation of Hippocrates (2). Works (extant but incomplete): *On the Causes and Symptoms of Acute and Chronic Diseases*; *On the Cure of Acute and Chronic*

Diseases; (lost) *On Fevers; On Female Disorders; On Preservatives; Operations*. His main merit is that he builds on the solid foundations of *Archigenes. See PNEUMATISTS.

Ed. K. Hude, *CMG* 2 (1923); F. Kudlien, *Unters. zu A. von. Kapp.* (1964).
W. D. R.

aretalogy See MIRACLES.

Aretas, the name of several kings of the *Nabataeans (Nabataean Aramaic form *ḥrtt*).

Aretas I reigned in the early 2nd cent. BC.

Aretas II (*c.*120–96 BC) in 96 tried to help *Gaza against the attack of Alexander Jannaeus (see HASMONEANS), who was defeated by his successor, Obodas I (*c.*96–87) probably *c.*93.

Aretas III 'Philhellen' (*c.*87–6 BC) defeated Jannaeus and briefly occupied Damascus. He supported Hyrcanus II (see HASMONEANS) and in 66 besieged Jerusalem, until he was compelled to leave by M. *Aemilius Scaurus (2), who in 62 advanced to Petra but in return for 300 talents recognized Aretas as king of the Nabataeans.

Aretas IV (9 BC–AD 39, perhaps interrupted 3–1 BC). On the death of Obodas III (30–9 BC) Aretas IV (originally called Aeneas according to Josephus) was recognized by Augustus after some delay caused by the self-promoting intrigues of Syllaeus, the vizier of Obodas III. Aretas, who took the Aramaic throne-name 'lover of his own people' (= Philodemus/Philopatris), presided over a period of great Nabataean prosperity: many buildings and inscriptions are ascribed to his reign. He sent help to P. *Quinctilius Varus against the Judaean rebels after Herod (1)'s death (4 BC). His daughter married *Herod (2) Antipas, ruler of Galilee and Peraea, who later, *c.* AD 27, divorced her. Aretas, without consulting Rome, invaded Peraea and defeated Antipas. Aretas was saved from punitive Roman attack because L. *Vitellius withdrew when he heard of the death of Tiberius. Aretas apparently had brief control of Damascus at the time of St *Paul's escape from the city (*c.* AD 40), since the city was under a Nabataean ethnarch appointed by the king (2 Cor. 11: 32).

Ancient sources: Joseph. *AJ*; Strabo, *Geography*.

G. W. Bowersock, *Roman Arabia* (1983); A. Negev, *ANRW* 2. 8 (1977), 520–686; R. Wenning, *Boreas*, forthcoming.
J. F. H.

Areus, self-styled 'king of the Spartans', was the first Spartan king to hold an elaborate court and to issue silver coins (using types of *Alexander (3) the Great of Macedon). He was the addressee of a begging letter purportedly written by the high priest of Jerusalem, who based his appeal in part on the alleged kinship of the Spartans and the Jews. His long reign (*c.*309–265 BC) witnessed some notable successes. In 280 he invaded *Aetolia, after organizing a Peloponnesian coalition against the Greeks' Macedonian suzerain. In 272 he was abroad assisting Gortyn in Crete when King *Pyrrhus of Epirus attacked Sparta, but returned in time to repulse Pyrrhus before assisting in his destruction at *Argos (2). But his reign also coincided with the incipient collapse of the famed Spartan domestic regimen (see AGŌGĒ), and he fell in battle outside Corinth in 265, having failed to force the Macedonians' Isthmus lines during the *Chremonidean War.

A. S. Bradford, *A Prosopography of Lacedaemonians from the Death of Alexander the Great, 323 BC, to the Sack of Sparta of Alaric, AD 396* (1977), 43–4; P. A. Cartledge and A. J. S. Spawforth, *Hellenistic and Roman Sparta* (1989).
P. A. C.

Argas (first half of the 4th cent. BC), citharode and poet. According to the Peripatetic *Phaenias (fr. 10 Wehrli) he could not achieve the quality of *Terpander or Phrynis (cf. Alexis fr. 19; Anaxandrides fr. 16. 4 and 42. 17 KA).

O. Crusius, *RE* 2/1. 687 f.; West, *Greek Music* (1992), 372.
B. Z.

Argei On 16 and 17 March in Rome a procession went to the shrine of the puppets (*itur ad Argeos*: Ov. *Fast.* 3. 791), i.e. to the 27 shrines (*sacraria*) of the Argei (Varro, *Ling.* 5. 45–54) situated at various points in the four Servian regions of Rome. On 14 May the celebrants hurled the puppets from the pons Sublicius into the Tiber (Ov. *Fast.* 5. 621 ff.; Varro, *Ling.* 7. 44). This much is clear, but uncertainty surrounds almost all else. The ancients debated the number of *sacraria* (27 or 30; cf. A. Momigliano, *JRS* 1963, 99 ff.), the god involved (if any), and commonly explained the rituals as a surrogate for human sacrifice. Wissowa agreed (*RE* 2. 689 ff.), seeing a symbolic burial of Rome's then (3rd-cent. BC) enemies, Greeks and Gauls (Livy 22. 57); he dubiously supported it by seeing Greek etymologies. Others suggested a vegetation rite, unlikely because of the number of figures: L. Deubner, *ARW* 1925, 299 ff. Frazer suggested (*Fasti of Ovid* (1929), 4. 91 ff.) that the puppets were offerings to pacify the river-god and induce him to spare those approaching the stream. L. Holland, *Janus and the Bridge* (1961), 313 ff., rationalized it as distorted traditions about the *Vestals while D. Harmon, *ANRW* 2. 16. 2 (1978), 1446 ff. saw a relation with the Vedic fire-god Agni. These accounts lack plausibility from their misuse of anthropological parallels and theorizing. Perhaps most plausible is Latte, *RR* 412 ff., who saw the March setting of the puppets as gathering the city's moral pollution, which is then symbolically discharged in May; his analysis of the festival's two stages and relation with the puppets of the Compitalia accounts for more than the others.
C. R. P.

Argentarius, witty Greek rhetor in Augustan Rome (Sen. *Controv.* 9. 3. 12–13), disciple of L. *Cestius Pius. Perhaps identical with the next.
A. D. E. C.

Argentarius, Marcus (?Augustan), author of 36 elegant, witty epigrams included in the *Garland* of *Philippus (2), influenced by the best Hellenistic epigrammatists (*Leonidas (2), *Callimachus (3), *Asclepiades (2), and especially *Meleager (2)), but no slavish imitator. The most versatile and graceful of Philippus' contributors.

R. del Re, *Maia* 1955, 184–215; S. G. P. Small, *YClS* 1951, 65 f.; Gow–Page, *GP*.
A. D. E. C.

Argentorate (mod. Strasburg). Perhaps first occupied as one of *Drusus' *castella*, it was garrisoned *c.* AD 12–43 by Legio II Augusta, then by legionary detachments including one of XXI Rapax, who constructed the first basalt wall. Legio VIII was transferred here *c.*80. Its 2nd-cent. fortress (606 × 300 m.; 663 × 328 yds.)) was defended by an earth bank with a 90-cm. (35-in.) thick revetment wall of small blocks and brick borders. From the 3rd cent. Argentorate was exposed to barbarian attack, and in the mid-4th cent. its original wall was fronted by another, 2.5 m. (8.2 ft.) thick, of reused masonry with bastions *c.*25 m. (82 ft.) apart. In this period the *canabae, previously important, were given up as the civil population crowded into the fortress.

C. M. Wells, *The German Policy of Augustus* (1972), 147 ff.; J. J. Hatt, in P.-M. Duval and E. Frézouls, *Thèmes de recherche sur les villes antiques* (1977), 217 ff.; S. Johnson, *Late Roman Fortifications* (1983), 142 f.
J. F. Dr.

Arginusae, small islands between Lesbos and the mainland (now Garipadasi and Kalemadasi), scene of a battle between the

Argolic Gulf, Argolid

Athenian and Spartan fleets in 406 BC. There is some doubt about dispositions, but Sparta's 120 triremes were probably in a single line abeam, Athens' 150 in a double line abeam, possibly on either side of the westernmost island. *Xenophon (1) says the Athenians, on this occasion having the inferior fleet, adopted this formation in order to prevent the enemy breaking through their line in the manœuvre known as the '*diekplous', and then swinging round to attack from the stern. The result was a victory for the Athenians, but this was marred by the failure to pick up survivors from their crippled ships, when a storm arose.

RE 2/1, Ἀργινοῦσαι; Xen., Hell. 1. 6. 24 ff.; Diod. Sic. 13. 97–100; A. Andrewes, Phoenix 1974; D. Kagan, Fall of the Athenian Empire (1987).
J. F. La.

Argolic Gulf, Argolid See ARGOS (2).

Argonauts, one of the earliest (cf. Hom. Od. 12. 69–72) and most important Greek sagas, set in the generation before the Trojan War and involving heroes particularly associated with *Thessaly, central Greece, and the *Peloponnese. The main Greek literary sources are *Pindar's Fourth Pythian, the Argonautica of *Apollonius (1), and *Apollodorus (6) 1. 9. 16–26 (largely based on *Pherecydes (2) and Apollonius); certain incidents were treated by *Callimachus (3) in the Aitia.

King *Pelias of Iolcus sought to rid himself of the threat to his kingship posed by the legitimate heir, *Jason (1), by sending the young man off to recover the fleece of a golden ram upon which Phrixus had fled to the fabulous kingdom of the sun, Aia, ruled over by King Aeëtes. At least as early as the *Epic Cycle Aia was identified with the kingdom of *Colchis at the eastern end of the Black Sea. With Athena's help Jason had a marvellous ship, the Argo, built; the tradition that the Argo was actually the first ship is first found in *Euripides (Andr. 865, cf. Herter, Rh. Mus. 1942, 244–9). The greatest heroes of the age gathered to join Jason on the voyage. Lists differ widely, but among the most prominent Argonauts in many versions were *Heracles, who in some versions did not complete the voyage, *Orpheus, the *Dioscuri, the steersman Tiphys, Lynceus who could see even beneath the earth, *Telamon (1), *Peleus (father of *Achilles), the sons of the north wind *Boreas, and *Theseus. The supernatural powers of many of the Argonauts differentiate the story markedly from the Homeric epics. The main protecting goddess for the voyage was *Hera who wished to punish Pelias for neglecting to honour her. The principal events of the outward voyage were: a stop on *Lemnos where the women lured the Argonauts to sleep with them in order to repopulate the island (Pindar places this on the return voyage); the mistaken killing (by Jason) of the prince of *Cyzicus in the *Propontis; the loss to the expedition of Heracles when his beloved squire, *Hylas, is snatched away by *nymphs and Heracles takes off to find him; a boxing-match between Polydeuces (see DIOSCURI) and King *Amycus of the Bebrycians; a meeting at Thracian Salmydessus with the blind prophet *Phineus who offers information about their voyage (cf. *Circe and *Tiresias in the Odyssey) in return for ridding him of the foul *Harpyiae (Harpies) who refuse to allow him to eat; the passage through the *Symplegades ('Clashing Rocks') at the mouth of the Black Sea, safely accomplished (on Phineus' advice) by sending a dove through first to test the way. As a result of the Argo's passage, the rocks were finally fixed fast and ceased to clash together. In Aia, Jason requests the fleece from Aeëtes, but the king sets him challenges to accomplish: he must plough with fire-breathing bulls, sow dragon's teeth, and kill the armed warriors which spring up from the ground (cf. *Cadmus). Jason succeeds with the help of Aeëtes' daughter *Medea who supplies him with protecting potions and helps him take the fleece from the grove where it is guarded by a dragon.

Accounts of the return voyage vary widely. In some the Argonauts return by the same route (e.g. Soph. fr. 547 Radt; Callim. fr. 9 Pf.); in some they pass from the Colchian river *Phasis into the streams of *Oceanus and around into the Mediterranean again. Apollonius combines various accounts into an extraordinary voyage across the Black Sea to a river system ('the Danube') which takes them to the Adriatic; from there they travel by a combination of 'the Po' (*Padus) and 'the Rhône' (*Rhodanus) to the western Mediterranean, then back down the west coast of Italy, across to Corfu, thence to North Africa, then Crete and finally back to Thessalian Iolcus. Important events of the return voyage include the killing of Medea's young brother Apsyrtus, adventures in Libya during which the Argonauts carry their ship through the desert—they were intimately connected with the foundation legends of *Cyrene—and the encounter with the bronze giant *Talos (1) who protected Crete.

The saga is of a common folkloric quest type, but also clearly expresses, and was used by Greek writers to reflect, the confrontation between what was Greek and what 'other' and hence the very qualities which represented 'Greekness'. Ancient scholars themselves saw the story as a reflection of the age of colonization and expansion or, more banally, the search for gold (Strabo 1. 2. 39, 11. 2. 19).

K. Meuli, Odyssee und Argonautika (1921); Jessen, RE 2. 743–87; F. Vian, Apollonios de Rhodes, Argonautiques (1974–81); B. K. Braswell, A Commentary on the Fourth Pythian Ode of Pindar (1988); R. L. Hunter, The Argonautica of Apollonius: Literary Studies (1993), and Jason and the Golden Fleece (the Argonautica) (1993); P. Dräger, Argo Pasimelousa (1993); D. Braund, Georgia in Antiquity (1994), esp. ch. 1.
R. L. Hu.

Argonauts in art Argonauts generally appear in individual episodes. Boreads pursue Harpies (see HARPYIAE) on an Attic bowl (c.620 BC), later Archaic vases and an ivory from Delphi, and a Lucanian vase. The Argo appears on the Sicyonian treasury, Delphi (c.560 BC), Classical vases, Etruscan gems, Roman reliefs and coins. The Classical Niobid crater may show *Hylas lost. *Amycus is most famously depicted on a Lucanian vase (c.420–400 BC), and the Etruscan Ficoroni cista (c.300 BC). Jason and the fleece appear on Classical vases, an early imperial glass vessel, and a late imperial relief. Duris' early Classical cup showing the dragon regurgitating Jason is an otherwise unattested variation. Lost representations include the Archaic chest of *Cypselus and throne at *Amyclae (Paus. 3. 18. 15; Boreads), and a painting in Athens (see MICON). Pliny (HN 35. 130) details paintings by Cydias, and (34. 79) a statue group by Lycius, both Classical.

LIMC 2/1. 591–9; M. Vojatzi, Frühe Argonautenbilder (1982). K. W. A.

Argos (1), in mythology: (a: RE 18) son of Zeus and the Argive Niobe (daughter of *Phoroneus), eponym of the city of *Argos (2) (Apollod. 2. 1. 1), part of archaic Argive mythological propaganda. His grave, not far from that of his 'brother' *Pelasgus (Paus. 2. 22, cf. Apollod. 2. 1. 1–2), was in a dense sacred grove (Hdt. 6. 78–80). (b: RE 19) Argos 'Panoptes' ('All-seeing'), monster born of no agreed parents—perhaps even earthborn (Aesch. PV 567), with multiple eyes: four (the Aegimius, Hes. fr. 294 M–W), an extra eye in the back of the head and unsleeping (Pherec. FGrH 3 F 67), or covered in eyes (Eur. Phoen. 1116, perhaps Aesch. PV 678). *Hera has him guard *Io, but he is tricked and killed by *Hermes, who thus acquires his epithet 'Argeiphontes' (supposedly 'Argos-slayer', already in Hes. Catalogus mulierum, fr.

126 M–W). In later tradition, at death he turns into a peacock (Moschus 2. 58) or his eyes are added to its plumage (Ov. *Met.* 1. 722). (*c: RE* 20) An *Argonaut, builder of the Argo (Ap. Rhod. 1. 19, 226; Diod. Sic. 4. 41. 3), a favourite of Roman artists, *LIMC* 2 / 1 (1984), 600–2. (*d: RE* 27) 'Swift', *Odysseus, dog (*Od.* 17. 291).

K. Dowden, *Death and the Maiden* (1989), ch. 6.   K. D.

Argos (2), a city in the southern part of the Argive plain 5 km. (3 mi.) from the sea, at the foot of the Larissa hill which was occupied from prehistoric, through Classical and Hellenistic, to Frankish and Turkish times. A low hill, the Aspis, which has remains of earlier bronze age occupation, formed part of the city. Middle bronze age remains have been found over a wide area (the Deiras ridge, and the South Quarter), and a Mycenaean cemetery with chamber-tombs on the Deiras. Mycenaean Argos appears to have been at its height in Mycenaean IIIA–B (roughly later 14th–13th cents.) at which time the Aspis was fortified; these fortifications were rebuilt in the Classical period. After the disintegration of *Mycenaean civilization, a community continued to live on the Aspis, burying its dead in the Deiras cemetery. By the end of the 10th cent. a new community had grown up on the flanks of the Larissa, and it seems sensible to associate this with the settlement at Argos of a population of *Dorians. This remained the chief area of the city, which developed on the lower slopes and flatter ground below the Larissa. On these slopes is a substantial theatre, with an adjacent small theatrical structure, and below this, on the flat ground, the remains of the agora, with an angled stoa dated to the mid-5th cent. BC. Between the agora and theatre are large public baths (Hadrianic).

In *Homer's *Iliad* Argos was the kingdom of *Diomedes (2), who acknowledged *Agamemnon's leadership; Argos was also, in a wider sense, Agamemnon's empire. In the Dorian invasion Argos fell to Temenus, the eldest of the *Heraclidae. Early in the 7th cent. perhaps, a strong king, *Pheidon, defeated the Spartans, presided in person over the Olympian Games, and made Argos the first power in Greece. Though *Herodotus (1) attributed to him the giving of weights and measures to the Peloponnese, he cannot have been responsible for the introduction of silver coinage, now generally agreed not to have happened until the 6th cent. BC (the reference may be a confusion with a younger Pheidon; see COINAGE). In the 6th cent., Argive power receded in the face of the growth of Sparta (see CYNURIA). Henceforth Argos maintained a suspicious neutrality, fighting once a generation with Sparta. Her heaviest defeat was *c.*494 BC, when *Cleomenes (1) was barely repelled from the walls by the women of Argos, rallied by the poetess *Telesilla. In 480–479 the Argives observed a benevolent neutrality towards Persia. Shortly afterwards they set up a form of democracy. They were repeatedly allied with Athens against Sparta (461, 420, 395), but remained an ineffective power, except at the beginning of the *Corinthian War, when an attempt at a political amalgamation with Corinth was briefly successful. Argos sided with *Philip (1) II of Macedon and was one of the last cities to join the *Achaean Confederacy, after a period of rule by tyrants. Included in the province of *Achaia and a fierce rival of colonial Corinth in the 1st cent. AD, Roman Argos received new amenities from *Hadrian (including an aqueduct and baths) and enjoyed a certain standing as host of the Heraean and *Nemean Games and mother-city to numerous self-styled colonies in the Roman east.

The territory of Argos in Classical times included *Mycenae, *Tiryns, Nauplia, *Asine, and other strongholds in the Argive plain, but not the cities of the Acte east of Argos, nor Phlius and Cleonae in the northern hills. The great Argive goddess was *Hera, worshipped at the *Heraion 10 km. (6 mi.) north of Argos. The minor arts were important in the earlier period, but from the 7th cent. BC they shared in the general decline. Argive sculptors of the early Classical period were pre-eminent; the greatest was *Polyclitus (2).

The graves of the new settlement (especially in the area to the south of the town) have produced considerable quantities of the distinctive Argive geometric pottery, dated to the 9th and 8th cents. BC, which however dies out, subsiding into a dull subgeometric style or a short-lived figure style in the course of the 7th. Also amongst these burials was the important 'panoply' grave of the late 8th cent., with bronze corselet and a helmet.

The extent to which Argos controlled a wider area at these early times is uncertain; Herodotus attributes to the loss of an early Peloponnesian empire the later growth of hostility between Argos and Sparta. This may be a projection back; hostility probably came about as both states expanded their influence until they met, in the 7th and 6th cents.

South of Argos lies the important early bronze age site of *Lerna.

R. A. Tomlinson, *Argos and the Argolid* (1972); T. Kelly, *A History of Argos to 500 BC* (1976); M. Wörrle, *Untersuchungen zur Verfassungsgeschichte von Argos* (1964).; Roman Argos: A. Spawforth and S. Walker, *JRS* 1986, 101 ff.; A. Spawforth, *Hesp.* 1994.   R. A. T.; A. J. S. S.

Argos, Cults The main cult of the *polis* of Argos (2) was that of *Hera (already 'Argive' in Homer, *Il.* 4. 8 = 5.908), based c. 10 km. (6 mi.) north-east of the city across the Argive plain, between *Mycenae and *Tiryns. Argive ownership of this *Heraion—emphasized by an annual festival which began with a procession from the city across the plain to the sanctuary—symbolized the state's control of the territory between the two points (de Polignac, see bibliog.).

At the NW corner of Argive territory was Nemea, sacred to *Zeus and the original site of the *Nemean Games. Control of this sanctuary, originally belonging to Cleonae, passed to Argos in the 5th cent. BC. In the border area with Arcadia were a number of limitary sanctuaries of *Artemis. In the Argive countryside were several sanctuaries of *Demeter, and the grove of the eponymous hero *Argos (1(*a*)).

Within the city itself, major sanctuaries were clustered around the two heights of the acropolis, around the agora, and by the gates. Thus on the Deiras were adjoining sanctuaries of *Apollo Pythaeus or Deiradiotes and *Athena Oxyderces, and on Larissa sanctuaries of Athena Polias and Zeus Larissaeus. Part way up Larissa was a sanctuary of Hera Acraea. A dedication to Enyalius (see ARES) (7th cent. BC) was found on this peak. Around the agora were sanctuaries of Apollo Lyceus (where public notices were posted), of *Aphrodite, Demeter, and others, including an enclosure sacred to the heroes who had died at Thebes (*c.*550 BC: *SEG* 37. 283; Pariente), see SEVEN AGAINST THEBES. The east gate of the city was named after the nearby sanctuary of *Eileithyia; not far away was a sanctuary of the *Dioscuri (addressed as *Anakes in inscriptions of the 6th and 5th cent. BC).

A. Foley, *The Argolid 800–600 BC* (1988), 135–8; T. Kelly, *A History of Argos to 500 BC* (1976), 51–72; A. Pariente, *BCH* Suppl. 22 (1992); F. de Polignac, *Cults, Territory and the Origins of the Greek City-state* (1995) 41 ff.   A. Sch.

Argos (3) **Amphilochicum,** traditionally founded by *Amphil-

ochus after the Trojan War, on the eastern shore of the Ambraciote Gulf. In its struggles against *Ambracia (Thuc. 2. 68) it was
helped by Athens and *Acarnania, and played its part in Athenian
operations in NW Greece in the early years of the *Peloponnesian
War. It maintained its independence, was the capital of the
Amphilochi, and issued coins of Pegasus type *c*.350–250 BC.

P–K, *GL* 2. 1. 194 ff.; Hammond, *Epirus*.   N. G. L. H.

argumentum (1) An account of the background to the plot of
a play, in *Plautus' plays (as in *Menander (1)'s) addressed direct
to the audience by the speaker of the prologue, and frequently
also indicating the outcome of the plot. Sometimes a brief statement, sometimes a fuller account, it is an element in all Plautus'
prologues except those to *Asinaria*, *Trinummus*, and (apparently)
Vidularia (and not all his plays have prologues). *Terence never
includes an *argumentum* in his prologues.

(2) A plot-summary prefixed in the manuscripts to the plays
of Plautus, like the hypotheses to Greek plays (see HYPOTHESIS,
LITERARY) and *Sulpicius Apollinaris' *periochae* of Terence's plays.
*Acrostic and non-acrostic *argumenta* are found, written in verse
(iambic senarii) in the imperial era.

(1) R. L. Hunter, *The New Comedy of Greece and Rome* (1985), 24–35.; (2)
G. E. Duckworth, comm. on Plaut. *Epidicus*, p. 93.   P. G. M. B.

Ariadne, daughter of *Minos and Pasiphaë. In Cnossus *Daedalus built her a dancing-floor (*Il*. 18. 592), perhaps the Daidaleion
on Linear B tablet KN Fpl. She fell in love with *Theseus and
gave him a thread of wool to escape from the *Labyrinth after
killing the Minotaur. Theseus fled with Ariadne but abandoned
her on *Naxos (1) either by choice or because the gods commanded him. *Dionysus found and married her there. In another
version, Ariadne was already married to Dionysus when she
followed Theseus and was killed by Artemis on Dia (Naxos) (*Od*.
11. 321–5; Hes. *Theog*. 947–9). Ariadne also had a tomb in the
temple of Cretan Dionysus in *Argos (2) (Paus. 2. 23. 7–8).
According to one tradition (Paeon of Amathus in Plutarch, *Thes*.
20) she came to Cyprus pregnant by Theseus who left her there.
She died in childbed and was buried in the grove of Ariadne
Aphrodite. At a curious annual rite in her honour at *Amathus,
a young man imitated a woman in labour. Originally Ariadne
was a Minoan goddess of nature whose invocatory name ('Very
Holy') suggests that she was expected to appear to her worshippers in *epiphany. Her myth centres on marriage and death,
combining the sorrowful and happy aspects of the annual decay
and renewal of vegetation. Each part is celebrated in her two
festivals on Naxos, and both elements are preserved in the Attic
*Anthesteria. On the second day of the spring festival (Choes)
the king (*archōn basileus*) like Theseus surrenders his wife
(*basilinna*) to Dionysus for the Sacred Marriage. But the third
(Chytroi) was a day of death with sacrifices to chthonian
*Hermes.

Ariadne's desertion by Theseus on Naxos/Dia, her rescue
by, and marriage to, Dionysus are popular themes in literature
(Catull. 64. 50 ff.; Ov. *Her*. 10), and particularly in vase-painting
from the early 5th cent. BC through all periods of Greek and
Roman art until the 3rd cent. AD. Other parts of the myth
occurred in the painter's repertoire as early as the 7th cent. BC.
She appears assisting Theseus against the Minotaur; and on the
François vase she is shown facing Theseus who leads the dance
of Athenian youths and maidens whom he has rescued from the
Minotaur. She can be seen with her children; or, in a Pompeian
mural, sitting beside *Daedalus (?). In *Polygnotus' famous

'Nekyia' in the Lesche (hall) of the Cnidians (see CNIDUS) at
*Delphi, Ariadne even appeared sitting on a rock in the Under-
world gazing at her sister Phaedra (Paus. 10. 29. 3).

Nilsson, *MMR*[2] 523–8; *GGR* 1[3]. 314 f; Burkert, *GR* 239 f.; E. Simon, *Die
Götter der Griechen*, 2nd edn. (1980); M. Robertson, *History of Greek Art*
(1975), 2, fig. 35b; cf. 1. 125, 441, 535, 579, 596 (deserted by Theseus),
421, 483, 572, 599 f. (with Dionysus); W. A. Daszewski and M. L.
Bernhard, *LIMC* 3 / 1 (1986), 1052–70.   H. J. R.; C. M. R.; B. C. D.

Arianism, the principal Christian heresy of the 4th cent. Strictly
it denotes the subordinationist teaching of *Arius concerning the
Son. The council of *Nicaea (1) (325) condemned this, affirming
that the Son was 'of the same substance' (*homoousios*) as the
Father. While generally acceptable in the west, this formula was
suspect to many easterners as suggesting that Father and Son
were not distinct hypostases but an indifferentiated unity. In the
prolonged debates which followed the term was applied not only
to Anomoeism (from *anomoios*, or 'unlike'), the extremist Arian
view that Father and Son were wholly unlike, and the watered-
down Homoean (from *homoios*, or 'like') compromise that they
were similar, but also to basically anti-Arian interpretations
aimed at meeting the difficulties of the Nicene *homoousion*. Chief
among these were (*a*) the teaching of the council of *Antioch (1)
(341), which repudiated Arius and emphasized Christ's divinity
in the framework of a three-hypostases theology, but ignored the
homoousion; (*b*) the (misleadingly labelled) Semi-Arian teaching
that Father and Son were 'alike in substance' (*homoiousioi*).

Apart from 350–61, when *Constantius II was sole emperor,
Arianism made little headway in the west. In the east he and
*Valens promoted the imprecise Homoean doctrine as likely to
be most widely acceptable. With the accession of *Theodosius
(2) I Arianism soon found itself proscribed everywhere. It
received fresh life, however, through the fact that *Ulfila, missionary to the *Goths, had brought Christianity to them in a radically
Arian form. From the Goths it spread to other Germanic peoples,
who took it with them (it had become a badge of their
nationalism) when they invaded and set up their kingdoms in
the west.

R. P. C. Hanson, *The Christian Doctrine of God: The Arian Controversy,
318–381* (1988).   J. N. D. K.

Ariaramnes (*c*.280–*c*.230 BC). An early member of the Cappadocian ruling house, eldest son of Ariarathes II. It is generally
believed that either he or his son *Ariarathes III, whom he
appointed joint ruler, was the first to declare *Cappadocia fully
independent.

For bibliography, see ARIARATHES.   B. C. McG.

Ariarathes Ancestral name of the Hellenistic kings of *Cappadocia in Asia Minor. They were an Iranian family claiming
descent from *Cyrus (1) the Great, or one of the seven Persians
who slew the Pseudo-Smerdis.

Ariarathes I–III We know little of the early members of the
family, Ariarathes I (d. *c*.322 BC) and Ariarathes II (d. *c*.280), but
they ruled under Persian and then Macedonian sway, and it was
only in the mid-3rd cent. that *Ariaramnes, or his son and co-
ruler Ariarathes III (*c*.255–*c*.220), was able to declare Cappadocia
independent. Ariarathes III married Stratonice, daughter of the
Seleucid king *Antiochus (2) II.

Ariarathes IV–VI The link with the Seleucids was strengthened
when Ariarathes IV Eusebes (*c*.220–*c*.163) married Antiochis,
daughter of *Antiochus (3) III, and fought for Antiochus against
Rome at the battle of *Magnesia in 190. With the help of his new

son-in-law, *Eumenes (2) II of Pergamum, he won a reduction in his war indemnity, and became a 'friend and ally' of Rome. In the war against *Pharnaces I of *Pontus (c.183–179), he sided with the anti-Pontic coalition, and further showed his loyalty to Rome by sending help against *Perseus (2) in the Third Macedonian War. He successfully resisted the troublesome Galatians.

His son Ariarathes V Eusebes Philopator (c.163–c.130) was the most Hellenized of his family (see HELLENISM), and gained a reputation for Cappadocia as a haven for men of culture. He may have been educated at Athens, and was certainly honoured there as a patron of the arts. In his loyalty to Rome he refused a marriage alliance with the sister of Demetrius I of Syria (see DEMETRIUS (10)), but received scant reward when the senate divided Cappadocia between him and his brother Orophernes, who was laying claim to the throne. He expelled Orophernes with the help of his ally *Attalus II of Pergamum, but remained loyal to Rome: he met his death fighting for the Roman cause against *Aristonicus (1), and was posthumously rewarded when the territory of *Lycaonia was granted to Cappadocia.

His formidable wife Nysa allegedly murdered five of her six sons, leaving only the youngest, Ariarathes VI Epiphanes Philopator (c.130–c.116) alive. The stronger Pontic kingdom now becomes dominant in the increasingly complicated affairs of Cappadocia (in which the royal coin issues play a highly controversial role). Taking advantage of the internal dissension, *Mithradates V Euergetes invaded, and married his daughter Laodice to Ariarathes VI. *Mithradates VI Eupator is said to have been behind the assassination of Ariarathes by a Cappadocian noble called Gordius, in about 116.

Ariarathes VII–X For a time Laodice controlled Cappadocia as regent for her young son Ariarathes VII Philometor (c.116–c.101), but when *Nicomedes (3) III of Bithynia invaded, she decided to marry him. Foiled in his wish to help his sister Laodice, Mithradates decided instead to help his nephew: he expelled Laodice and Nicomedes, and restored Ariarathes to the throne. The latter proved ungrateful and unreliable—he refused to receive back Gordius, and prepared for war against Pontus—but at a private meeting Mithradates murdered him treacherously, installing his own son as Ariarathes IX Eusebes Philopator (c.101–c.86), with Gordius as regent.

The rule of Ariarathes IX was not popular and the Cappadocians invited back a brother of Ariarathes VII. This man is counted as Ariarathes VIII, although he was immediately driven off by Mithradates and died soon after. When Nicomedes III and Laodice put up a false pretender to the Cappadocian throne in about 96, the senate rejected his claims, and those of Ariarathes IX, and declared Cappadocia free. The Cappadocians wanted a king, however, and were allowed to choose *Ariobarzanes I. From here events are difficult to follow and much disputed. *Tigranes (1) II of Armenia, Mithradates' newest ally, expelled Ariobarzanes, presumably to make way for Ariarathes IX, but in about 95 the senate ordered the propraetor *Sulla to lead an expedition to restore Ariobarzanes. When the *Social War (3) broke out in Italy, Mithradates again expelled Ariobarzanes from Cappadocia (and Nicomedes IV from Bithynia), and reinstalled Ariarathes IX, only to have the situation immediately reversed, at the end of 90 or beginning of 89, by a Roman delegation under the leadership of *Manius Aquillius (2). With the outbreak of the First Mithradatic War in 89, however, Cappadocia was overrun, and Ariarathes IX returned to the throne. He presumably maintained his position until the end of the war, although he is some-

times identified (probably incorrectly) with the Pontic general Arcathias, who died in Macedonia in 87.

Ariarathes X Eusebes Philadelphos (c.42–36) succeeded to the throne when his brother *Ariobarzanes III was murdered, but Mark Antony (M. *Antonius (2)) deposed and killed him, replacing him with Sisines, who took the name Archelaus. See ARCHELAUS (5).

Diod. Sic. 31. 19–22, 28, 32; Strab. 12 (533–40 C). T. Reinach, *Trois Royaumes de l'Asie Mineure* (1888); B. Niese, *RE* 2 (1896), 'Ariarathes'; Magie, *Rom. Rule Asia Min.*; B. Simonetta, *The Coins of the Cappadocian Kings* (1977); O. Mørkholm, *Num. Chron.* 1979; R. Sullivan, *ANRW* 2. 7. 2 (1980). B. C. McG.

Aricia (mod. Ariccia), at the foot of the Alban hills (see ALBANUS MONS), 25 km. (16 mi.) south-east of Rome, on the edge of a fertile volcanic depression (vallis Aricina); the impressive viaduct, of Augustan date, which carried the *via Appia across this (Juv. 4. 117) survives). There are traces of early iron age occupation and, c.500 BC, Aricia was temporarily the leading city of *Latium: under Turnus Herdonius it organized resistance to *Tarquinius Superbus, helped *Aristodemus (2) of Cumae to crush the Etruscans (c.505 BC), supplied the Latin League with a meeting-place, and had a prominent role in the Lake *Regillus battle and ensuing *foedus Cassianum* (499–493). In 446 Aricia quarrelled with *Ardea over boundaries. After participating in the Latin War it received Roman *citizenship (Festus 155 Lindsay represents this, probably inaccurately, as partial citizenship), and became a prosperous *municipium. Such it remained, despite its sack by C. *Marius (1) (Livy, *Epit.* 80; *Lib. colon.* 230). Aricia was the birthplace of Augustus' mother *Atia (1), and is celebrated for its wealthy temple of *Diana Nemorensis, whose ruins still exist nearby in the woods surrounding Lake Nemi; its presiding priest was a runaway slave who had murdered his predecessor (see REX NEMORENSIS).

Strabo 5. 239; Verg. *Aen.* 7. 761 f.; Livy 1. 50 f. A. E. Gordon, *Cults of Aricia* (1934); T. F. C. Blagg, *Mysteries of Diana: The Antiquities from Nemi* (1983); F. Coarelli, *I santuari del Lazio* (1987). E. T. S.; T. W. P.

Arimaspeans, a fabulous one-eyed tribe from the distant north whose name (Ἀριμασποί) *Herodotus (1) claims to be able to derive from Scythian *arima* 'one', *spou* 'eye' (4. 27; cf. 3. 116 and 4. 13). He and *Aeschylus (PV 803–6) know them as a people engaged in a perpetual attempt to steal a hoard of gold guarded by griffins—just as the Indians try to take that of the giant ants (Hdt. 3. 102). The story apparently goes back to the epic *Arimaspea* ascribed to *Aristeas. A. H. G.

Ariminum (mod. Rimini), on the Adriatic, was an *Umbrian and Gallic settlement, which became a Latin colony (see IUS LATII) in 268 BC (Vell. Pat. 1. 14). An important harbour and road-centre, Ariminum was the key to *Gaul (Cisalpine), controlling the bottle-neck between Apennines and Adriatic (Polyb. 3. 61, etc.; Livy 24. 44, etc.; Strab. 5. 217). It remained loyal to Rome against *Hannibal (Livy 27. 10) and obtained Roman *citizenship c.89 BC (Plin. HN 3. 115). Surviving sack by *Sulla, occupation by *Caesar, confiscation and colonization by the *triumvirs, attacks by Flavians (AD 69) and Goths (538), it became one of five towns composing the *pentapolis maritima* under the Ravenna exarchs (App. *BCiv.* 1. 67, 4. 3; Plut. *Caes.* 32; Tac. *Hist.* 3. 41; Procop. 2. 10). Surviving monuments include the arch of Augustus, marking the end of the *via Flaminia, and a Tiberian bridge. Excavations have revealed rich late-Roman houses.

Ariobarzanes

P. G. Pasini, *L'arco di Augusto* (1974); G. Susini and A. Tripponi, *Rimini analisi* (1980), 15–51.   E. T. S.; T. W. P.

Ariobarzanes, the name of some kings of *Cappadocia:

Ariobarzanes I Philoromaios (*c*.95–63/2), a Cappadocian noble whom the Cappadocians chose in preference to *Ariarathes IX when the previous dynasty came to an end. His career consists almost entirely of a series of expulsions and restorations. Installed by *Sulla (*c*.95), driven out by *Tigranes (1) II of Armenia, and restored by M'. *Aquillius (2) (90/89 BC), driven out again the following year, and restored by C. *Scribonius Curio (1) at Sulla's command in 85/4, he had to retire before Tigranes again in 78, suffered the ravages of the Third Mithradatic War, and the renewed attacks of Tigranes in 67. *Pompey increased his kingdom to include, in the east, Sophene and *Gordyene, and, in the west, Cybistra, restored his capital Mazaca, and gave him large loans. Yet in 63 or 62 (his coins have the numbers of at least 32 regnal years) he abdicated in Pompey's presence in favour of his son.

Ariobarzanes II Philopator (63/2–*c*.52), son of Ariobarzanes I and Athenais, and married to Athenais, a daughter of *Mithradates VI, had an uneasy reign, requiring the help of A. *Gabinius (2) in 57 to crush his enemies, and was assassinated shortly before Cicero became governor of Cilicia in 51, probably by members of a pro-Parthian faction. Years 7 and 8 are numbered on his coins.

Ariobarzanes III Eusebes Philoromaios (52–42 BC), son of Ariobarzanes II, recognized by the senate as king and commended to Cicero, who found him in 51 beset by enemies in his kingdom, including his mother, and by heavy debts to Pompey and other Roman nobles; he remained loyal to Rome and aided Pompey in the war with Caesar. Caesar, however, confirmed him and added Lesser *Armenia to his kingdom. C. *Cassius Longinus (1) had him killed in 42 for refusing aid. Years 9 and 11 are numbered on his coins.

R. Sullivan, *ANRW* 2. 7. 2 (1980), 1125 ff., and *Near Eastern Royalty and Rome 100–30 BC* (1990), 54 ff.   T. R. S. B.; A. J. S. S.

Arion (1) (Ἀρείων). In Homer (*Il*. 23. 346–7), Arion is the 'swift horse', 'divine in origin', of *Adrastus (1). His mythological origins lie in *Arcadia. According to Pausanias (8. 25. 5), he was born at Thelpusa from the union of *Demeter and *Poseidon: Demeter transformed herself into a filly to escape Poseidon, who then changed himself into a horse to unite with her. Arion belonged successively to Poseidon himself, to Copreus, *Heracles and *Adrastus (1) (schol. *Il*. 23. 346). He is shown on the reverse of some Thelpusan coins, as a horse prancing towards the right.

L. Lacroix, in *Études d'archéologie numismatique* (1974); I. Krauskopf, *LIMC* 2. 477–9.   M. J.

Arion (2), a citharode from *Methymna in Lesbos, spent most of his life at the court of the Corinthian tyrant *Periander, who ruled from about 625 to 585 BC. He was said to have been thrown overboard while returning from a profitable visit to Italy and Sicily, but to have returned to *Corinth after being taken by a dolphin to *Taenarum (1) (Hdt. 1. 23–4). He seems to have transformed the *dithyramb from an improvised processional song into a formal stationary one (*Suda*, entry under Ἀρίων; Hdt. 1. 23). This may have been regarded, perhaps rightly, as a step towards the creation of tragedy, which was itself attributed to Arion in the *Suda* and perhaps even by *Solon (fr. 30a West).

Nothing survives of his work, and a piece attributed to him by Aelian (*NA* 12. 45) is spurious.

Pickard-Cambridge–Webster, *Dithyramb*[2] 97–100; J. Schamp, *Ant. Class.* 1976, 95–120.   R. A. S. S.

Ariovistus, king of the *Suebi, invaded Gaul *c*.71 BC at the invitation of the Sequani, defeated the *Aedui, and withstood a combined Gallic attempt to eject him. The senate ratified his conquests by the title of 'friend'. In 58, however, Caesar, exploiting the hostility of Gallic chiefs (see GALLIC WARS), picked a quarrel with him, and finally routed him in the plain of Alsace. Ariovistus' exploits are of particular interest in the study of the evolution of the Germanic peoples (see GERMANS), and their relationship to *Celts and Romans.

Caes. *BGall*. 1. 31–53, 5. 29; Cic. *Att*. 1. 19. 2. C. E. Stevens, *Latomus* 1952, 166 ff.; G. Walser, *Caesar und die Germanen* (1956).
C. E. S.; J. F. Dr.

Arisbe, name of two Greek cities: (1) in *Troas, a colony of *Miletus, subordinate to neighbouring *Abydos by the 3rd cent. BC (Polyb. 5. 111), but apparently surviving as a community under Roman rule, since as 'Baris' it is listed as the seat of an early Byzantine bishopric; (2) in *Lesbos, from Arisbe, daughter of *Macar; it had been subjugated by neighbouring *Methymna by the time of Herodotus (1. 151); remains are extant.   A. J. S. S.

Aristaeus, Greek culture-hero or demigod, with a bewildering number of associations. His imminent birth to *Apollo and the nymph Cyrene is prophesied by Chiron (see CENTAURS) in *Pindar, *Pyth*. 9. 59 ff., celebrating him as 'a *Zeus, a pure Apollo; a delight to his friends, close escort of sheep, Hunter and Herdsman'. Scraps of evidence for his cult and myth link him to Phthia (see PHTHIOTIS), *Arcadia, and *Boeotia (where he was known as *Actaeon's father) and in particular to the Aegean island of *Ceos, where he was worshipped as the mediator to mankind of apiculture (see BEE-KEEPING) and *olive oil and invoked as bringer of the cooling Etesian winds in high summer (Ap. Rhod. 2. 500–27, repeating the Pindaric titles Ἀγρέα καὶ Νόμιον, with schol. on 498; Callim. fr. 75. 33–7 Pf.). Virgil ends the *Georgics* by telling at length the story of how once all Aristaeus' bees died; his mother referred him to *Proteus for an explanation, and he was told that this was punishment called down by *Orpheus for the death of *Eurydice (1), who had been bitten by a snake when trying to escape Aristaeus' attentions. He carries out a propitiatory sacrifice, and after nine days the carcasses of the bulls and heifers, left to fester, have spontaneously generated new swarms by the process of *bougonia.

B. F. Cook, *LIMC* 'Aristaios' 1; Burkert, *HN* 109–11; L. Burn, *AK* 1985, 93–105.   A. H. G.

Aristagoras (1), deputy tyrant of *Miletus *c*.505–496 BC in *Histiaeus' absence and influential rebel with too many causes. Trying to extend Miletus' Aegean power, he promoted a joint Ionian-Phoenician expedition of 100 ships against prosperous, independent *Naxos (1) in 500 (Hdt. 5. 30). Failing in the four-month siege, facing large military debts, and perhaps contemplating an independent east Aegean empire, he arrested and deposed fellow autocrats before demobilization (and thereby curried favour with ordinary Greeks along the coast), seized the Persians' Ionian fleet, abdicated Histiaeus' *de iure* tyrannical powers at Miletus, and promoted revolt against *Persia from the Black Sea (see EUXINE) to *Cyprus (Hdt. 5. 37–8). Control of land and sea was quickly achieved. Seeking allies and cash, Aristagoras sailed to Europe (499/8). Spartans declined, Athenians and Eretrians (see ERETRIA) briefly enlisted, but, faced with Phoenician sea-power and Persian access by land, the *Ionian Revolt faltered. Although Aristagoras superficially united Ionian communities during the six-year revolt, his authority over Miletus and allied forces remained anomalous. As financial support diminished and allies bickered, he secured refuge and resources in strategically important Myrcinus, Histiaeus' base of operations (Hdt. 5. 124; 497/6 BC). While expanding power and revenues there, he was ambushed and killed by *Thracians (5. 126).

Herodotus calls Aristagoras the originator of the Ionian Revolt. He scored impressive early successes, but he later proved an easy scapegoat for self-justifying survivors, victims of Persian retribution, and Athenian and Spartan self-glorification. Subsequent events confirmed his belief (5. 49) in the possibility of Anatolian Greek independence, but his revenues, diplomatic skills, and strategic planning proved inadequate. History vilifies losers and tyrants, especially when exemplified in one man.

Hdt. bk. 5. P. Manville, CQ 1977, 80.   D. G. L.

Aristagoras (2), comic writer of uncertain date. His Μαμμά-κυθος ('Simpleton') was possibly a revision of *Metagenes' Αὖραι ('Breezes').

FRAGMENTS Kassel–Austin, PCG 2. 558–9.
INTERPRETATION Meineke, FCG 1. 218 ff.; G. Kaibel, RE 2/1 (1895), 849, 'Aristagoras' 11.   W. G. A.

Aristarchus (1) (RE 25), of Samos, astronomer, is dated by his observation of the summer solstice in 280 BC. He was a pupil of the Peripatetic *Straton (1) of Lampsacus. He is famous as the author of the heliocentric (see GEOCENTRICITY) hypothesis, that 'the fixed stars and sun remain unmoved, and that the earth revolves about the sun on the circumference of a circle, the sun lying in the middle of the orbit' (Archimedes, Sand-reckoner 4–5); he also assumed that the earth rotates about its own axis (Plut. De fac. 6). His only extant treatise, On the Sizes and Distances of the Sun and Moon, is, however, on the geocentric basis. Starting with six 'hypotheses', the treatise has eighteen propositions displaying the author's facility in both geometry and arithmetic. The ratios of sizes and distances which have to be calculated are equivalent to trigonometric ratios, and Aristarchus finds upper and lower limits to their values starting from assumptions equivalent to well-known theorems in geometry. The results are grossly discrepant from reality: this is due not only to Aristarchus' method, which, though mathematically correct, is ill suited for its purpose (see HIPPARCHUS (3)), but also to errors in the hypotheses, notoriously a figure of $2°$ for the moon's apparent diameter. He probably wrote the treatise more as a mathematical exercise than as practical astronomy. He is said to have invented a type of sundial known as the σκάφη (Vitr. 9. 8), and to have estimated the year-length as $365\frac{1}{4} + \frac{1}{1623}$ days (a value which he must have derived from Babylonian astronomy). See CLOCKS; TIME-RECKONING.

Text, transl., and comm. in T. L. Heath, Aristarchus of Samos (1913; repr. 1959): Aristarchus' life and work are discussed at 299 ff. See also Pappus, Synagoge 6. 69–73.
HAMA 2. 603, 634–43; B. Noack, Aristarch von Samos (1992).
G. J. T.

Aristarchus (2), of *Samothrace (c.216–144 BC), belonged to the school of *Aristophanes (2) of Byzantium at *Alexandria (1) and was tutor of Ptolemy VII son of Ptolemy Philometor (see PTOLEMY (1)). He succeeded Apollonius ὁ εἰδογράφος ('classifier of literary genres') as head of the Alexandrian Library (see LIBRARIES) (c.153 BC). On the accession of Ptolemy VIII (145 BC)

he left Alexandria for *Cyprus, where he died. With him scientific scholarship really began, and his work covered the wide range of grammatical, etymological, orthographical, literary, and textual criticism. He was styled ὁ γραμματικώτατος, 'extremely scholarly', (Ath. 15. 671 f.), and for his gift of critical divination was nicknamed μάντις ('seer') by *Panaetius (Ath. 14. 634c). His name has often been used to typify the complete critic (e.g. Cic. Att. 1. 14. 3. Hor. Ars P. 450). In matters of language he was an Analogist and an opponent of *Crates (3) of Mallus. The school which he founded at Alexandria and which lasted into the Roman imperial period had many distinguished pupils, e.g. *Apollodorus (6) and *Dionysius (15) Thrax. He was the first scholar to write numerous commentaries, and the first to write about prose authors. His writings fall into three main groups:

1. Critical recensions (διορθώσεις) of the text of *Homer, *Hesiod, *Archilochus, *Alcaeus, *Anacreon, *Pindar. For his recension of the Iliad and Odyssey, and elsewhere, he used symbols to indicate his suspicions of the genuineness of verses, wrongful repetition, confused orders of verses, etc. (see SCHOLARSHIP, ANCIENT (Greek)). The disiecta membra of his commentaries surviving in medieval scholia often enable us to reconstruct his apparatus of critical signs. In his treatment of textual problems in Homer he was more cautious than his Alexandrian predecessors and sought to remove corruption, conjecture, and interpolation by scrupulous regard for the best manuscript tradition, by careful study of the Homeric language and metre, by his fine literary sense, by emphasis on the requirements of consistency and appropriateness of ethos, and by his practice of interpreting a poet by the poet's own usage (Ὅμηρον ἐξ Ὁμήρου σαφηνίζειν). He avoided allegorical interpretation, as practised by the Stoics. But his work seems to have had comparatively little influence on the traditional text of Homer.

2. Commentaries (ὑπομνήματα) on Homer, Hesiod, Archilochus, *Alcman, Pindar, *Aeschylus, *Sophocles, *Aristophanes (1), *Herodotus (1), and perhaps *Euripides and *Ion (2).

3. Critical treatises (συγγράμματα) on particular matters relating to the Iliad and Odyssey, e.g. the naval camp of the Greeks; and polemics against other writers and scholars, e.g. against *Philitas and the 'chorizontes' (who ascribed the two poems to separate authors), especially Xenon.

K. Lehrs, De Aristarchi studiis Homericis, 3rd edn. (1882); A. Ludwich, Aristarchs homerische Textkritik (1884–5); R. Pfeiffer, History of Classical Scholarship: From the Beginnings to the End of the Hellenistic Age (1968), 210–3.   J. F. L.; R. B.; N. G. W.

Aristarchus (3), of *Tegea, tragic poet, dated by *Eusebius to 454/3 BC (date of first victory?) and called a contemporary of *Euripides by the *Suda, which says that he wrote 70 plays and won two victories. His plays included Tantalus, Achilles (adapted by *Ennius), Asclepius (said by the Suda to have been a thank-offering for recovery from illness). No precise meaning can be attached to the Suda's statement that he 'was the first to establish the present length for plays'.

TrGF 1². 89–92; Musa Tragica 56–61, 273–4.   A. L. B.

Aristeas, of Proconnesus in the *Propontis. Like *Abaris and *Zalmoxis, a legendary wisdom-figure associated with the cult of *Apollo, reflecting early Greek contacts with *Scythian culture. Herodotus (4. 13 ff.) knew him as the author of a hexameter poem called Arimaspea which told of the tribes in the far north, including the eponymous *Arimaspeans; he goes on to report marvellous tales of his shamanistic feats, including the disappearance of his 'corpse' in his home town while he was seen alive elsewhere, his subsequent reappearance after seven years (cf. EPIMENIDES); and even a rematerialization 240 years later in southern Italy, during which he informed the inhabitants of *Metapontum that he had been accompanying his god in the form of a raven.

J. D. P. Bolton, *Aristeas of Proconnesus* (1962); J. N. Bremmer, *The Early Greek Concept of the Soul* (1983), 25 ff.   A. H. G.

Aristeas, Letter of, is the Alexandrian Jewish story of the making of the Greek translation of the Law (Torah) for the library of *Ptolemy (1) II Philadelphus, at the instigation of his librarian, *Demetrius (3) of Phaleron. Aristeas, a courtier, describes to his brother Philocrates his mission on this subject to Eleazar, the high priest at Jerusalem. Eleazar expounded the rationale of the Law, and then supplied 72 scholars, six from each tribe. At a seven-day banquet, they discussed kingship and impressed the king with their philosophical wisdom. In a residence on the island of Pharus (see ALEXANDRIA (1)), they completed their work in 72 days, harmonizing their independent versions; they then gave a recitation. The Letter has a historical kernel: the ascription of the commissioning of the *Septuagint to Ptolemy Philadelphus is generally accepted; and the description of *Jerusalem is perhaps not wholly schematic. But traditional motifs are evident, especially in the discussion on *kingship; and the persistent apologia for Judaism gives rise to some imaginative claims. A date in either the early or the late 2nd cent. BC is likely. Josephus paraphrases the Letter in *Antiquities* 12. See JEWISH-GREEK LITERATURE; SEPTUAGINT.

M. Hadas, *Aristeas to Philocrates* (1951); Schürer, *History* 3/1, 677–87.   T. R.

Aristias, tragic poet, son of *Pratinas of Phlius. In 467 BC he won second prize with plays of his father's when competing against *Aeschylus (hyp. Aesch. *Sept.*). He probably won his first victory *c.*460. Like his father he was a noted composer of satyr-plays (see SATYRIC DRAMA).

TrGF 1². 85–7; *Musa Tragica* 54–7, 73.   A. L. B.

Aristides (1) 5th-cent. BC Athenian politician, probably cousin of the rich and well-born *Callias (1) son of Hipponicus and friend of *Cleisthenes (2), and not as poor as generally alleged in antiquity. He was probably archon (see ARCHONTES) in 489/8, less probably general in 490 at the battle of *Marathon (*AO* 56 f.). Famously just, he is often represented as an upright and 'aristocratic' foil to duplicitous and 'democratic' *Themistocles; but the contrast is bad and another tradition (Callaeschrus, *Ep. Gr.* p. 743) called him 'more fox by nature than by *deme', μᾶλλον τῷ τρόπῳ Ἀλωπεκῆθεν ἢ τῷ δήμῳ. His *ostracism was in 483/2: *Ath. Pol.* 22. 7. Surviving ostraca accuse him of *Medism ('brother of *Datis') and spurning suppliants: ML 21 = Fornara 41 D. He returned from exile under an act of recall, and at the battle of *Salamis in 480 led a hoplite engagement on the island of Psyttaleia (Hdt. 8. 76, 95). He commanded at *Plataea and after the Persian Wars helped Themistocles fool the Spartans over the building of Athens' city walls. He assessed the initial tribute of *Delian League members (Plut. *Arist.* 24; Thuc. 5. 18) and is not reliably heard of after that, unless he opposed a plan by 'the Samians' (or '[hellēno-]*tamiai' if we emend Plut. *Arist.* 25) to move the tribute to Athens from *Delos. He died *c.*467.

Plut. *Aristides* ed. Sansone. *APF* 48 ff., 256 f.; Rhodes, *CAAP* 22. 7; Meiggs *AE* 42; C. Fornara, *JHS* 1966, 51 ff. (Psyttaleia); A. Raubitschek, *School of Hellas* (1991), ch. 18 (ostraca); G. Huxley, *Riv. Fil.* 1990, 319 ff. (move of tribute).   S. H.

Aristides (2) Greek writer (origin unknown) of *Milesian Tales*

(Μιλησιακά). A copy was allegedly found in a Roman officer's kit after the battle of *Carrhae (Plut. *Crass.* 32. 4–6). This story, and the translation of Aristides into Latin by *Sisenna (Ov. *Tr.* 2. 443–4, cf. 413–14: ten fragments in F. Buecheler, *Petronii Saturae*⁴ (1862), 239 f.), probably the historian, praetor in 78 BC, gives Aristides a conjectural date of *c.*100 BC. Only one fragment survives (Harpocration, p. 88 Dindorf) but Ovid and Plutarch (as cited above) and *Apuleius, *Met.* 1. 1 (cf. Arr. *Epict. Diss.* 4. 9. 6; ps.-Lucian, *Amores* 1; SHA *Clod.* 11. 8, 12. 12), show that *Milesiaca* were short and lewd erotic tales, probably so named after their conventional setting (*Miletus). They presumably influence inset tales in the Lucianic Ὄνος (*Ass*) and Apuleius' *Metamorphoses*; also *Petronius Arbiter's *Ephesian Widow* (*Satyrica* 111–12) and *Pergamene Boy* (ibid. 85–7), though here subversive satire may be Petronius' contribution. Apuleius' 'I shall weave together diverse tales in that Milesian discourse that you know' (*sermone isto Milesio*) hints that Aristides set his *Milesiaca* in a narrative frame, and if the MSS of ps.-Lucian, *Amores* 1 are right Aristides presented himself as the tales' hearer, one of few features shared with 'ideal' Greek *novels (cf. openings of *Iamblichus (1), *Longus, *Achilles Tatius (1)). Aristides was notorious enough to be basis of the bogus Aristides of Miletus' *Italica* etc., much 'cited' by the ps.-Plut. *Parallela minora* (*FGrH* 286).

CRITICISM W. Schmid, *RE* 2 (1896), 885 'Aristeides' 23; Christ–Schmid–Stählin 2/1⁶. 481 ff.; S. Trenkner, *The Greek Novella* (1958), 172 ff.; P. G. Walsh, *The Roman Novel* (1970), 10–18.   E. L. B.

Aristides, Publius Aelius (AD 117–after 181), sophist (see SECOND SOPHISTIC) and man of letters. Born at Hadrianotherae in Mysia, he was a pupil of Alexander of Cotiaeum and studied in Athens and *Pergamum. At the age of 26, he suffered the first of a long series of illnesses, which ended his hopes of a great public career and drove him to spend much of his time as a patient at the Asclepieum (see ASCLEPIUS) of Pergamum. The rest of his life was passed mainly in Asia Minor, where he made his home in *Smyrna and in the intervals of illness occupied himself in writing and lecturing.

His many-sided literary output (built on an intimate knowledge of the Classical literary heritage) made him a giant in his own day and, through its subsequent popularity, a 'pivotal figure in the transmission of Hellenism' (Bowersock). It includes addresses delivered on public and private occasions, declamations on historical themes, polemical essays, prose hymns to various gods, and six books of *Sacred Discourses* (Ἱεροὶ λόγοι). Two rhetorical treatises transmitted under his name (ed. Schmid, 1926) are wrongly attributed. Among the public addresses, *To Rome* (26 Keil) paints an impressive picture of the Roman achievement, as seen by an admiring provincial, while the *Panathenaic Oration* (1 K) provides a potted history of Classical Athens, much used as a Byzantine school text. The historical declamations (the *Sicilians*, 5–6 K, and the *Leuctrians*, 11–15 K) show an equal facility with Classical oratorical style and with the fine details of 5th and 4th cent. BC history. Of the polemical works, the most interesting are *On Rhetoric* (2 K) and *In Defence of the Four* (3 K), which answer *Plato (1)'s attack on rhetoric and orators (politicians) in the *Gorgias*. The prose hymns (37–46 K), though Aristides did not invent the genre, revealed new possibilities in both a Platonizing and an Isocratean vein (see ISOCRATES), and were an influential model for later writers. The *Sacred Discourses* (47–52 K), finally, are in a class apart. A record of revelations made to Aristides in *dreams by the healing god Asclepius, and of his obedience to the god's instructions, they are of major importance, both as evidence for the practices associated with temple medicine (see MEDICINE § 2), and as the fullest first-hand report of personal religious experiences that survives from any pagan writer.

TEXT W. Dindorf (1829; repr. 1964); B. Keil (1898), nos. 17–53; F. Lenz and C. Behr (1976–80), nos. 1–16. Eng. trans., C. Behr (1981–6).

COMMENTARY J. Oliver, *The Ruling Power* (1953), on 36, and *The Civilizing Power* (1968), on 1; *Hymns*: J. Amann (1931), Zeus; A. Höffler (1935), Sarapis; A. Uerschels (1962), Dionysus.

STUDIES W. Schmid, *Atticismus* 2 (1889); A. Boulanger, *Aelius Aristide* (1923); G. Bowersock, *Greek Sophists* (1969), ch. 3; C. Behr, *Aelius Aristides* (1968); L. Pernot, *Les Discours siciliens* (1981); D. Russell, *Antonine Literature* (1990), ch. 8.   E. R. D.; M. B. T.

Aristides (*RE* 25) **Quintilianus** (3rd cent. AD ?), author of a lost *Poetics* and an ambitious *De musica*. Musical issues are classified as theoretical ('technical' and 'physical') and practical. Book 1 (technical) expounds harmonics, rhythmics, and metrics, mainly from Aristoxenian sources (see ARISTOXENUS), incorporating valuable material otherwise unknown. Book 2 (practical) discusses music's educational and psychotherapeutic uses with verve and style, ingeniously integrating older ideas (some attributed to *Damon (2)) with engaging reflections of Aristides' own, notably on solmization and on the *soul. Book 3 (physical), exploiting Pythagorean harmonic analyses, links musical phenomena through numerology, mathematics, and natural science with the overall structure of reality. The work is impressively detailed, and unified, despite inconsistencies, by a near-Neoplatonist vision (see NEOPLATONISM) of cosmos, soul, and music as manifestations of a single divine order. See MUSIC §§ 5–6.

TEXT R. P. Winnington-Ingram (1963).

TRANSLATIONS WITH COMMENTARY T. J. Mathiesen, *Aristides Quintilianus: On Music* (1983); A. Barker, *Greek Musical Writings* 2 (1989).   A. D. B.

Aristion, Athenian citizen and partisan of *Mithradates VI, with the backing of *Archelaus (3) made himself tyrant of *Athens in 87 BC in succession to Athenion, a *Peripatetic philosopher elected hoplite-general in 88 BC on a pro-Mithradates, anti-Rome, platform (*Posidonius, *FGrH* 87 F 36—highly coloured), whereupon he disappears from the historical record. Besieged by *Sulla on the Acropolis, Aristion was executed on his surrender. Since the 18th cent. he and Athenion have sometimes been confused: for their separate identities see I. Kidd, *Posidonius: The Commentary* 2 (1988), 884 ff. and in M. Griffin and J. Barnes (eds.), *Philosophia Togata* (1989), 41 ff.; also C. Habicht, *Athen: die Geschichte der Stadt in hellenistischer Zeit* (1995), ch. 13 esp. 304 n. 20.

App. *Mith.* 28, 38 f.; Plut. *Sull.* 12–13, 23; Strab. 9. 1. 20.   A. J. S. S.

Aristippus (1), from *Cyrene, an associate of *Socrates. His writings are said to have included dialogues and historical works, and he is said to have been the first of Socrates' associates to charge a fee for teaching. Much of the ancient evidence concerns his worldly and luxurious mode of life, and *Xenophon (1) represents him as a champion of sybaritic hedonism, whom Socrates admonishes with *Prodicus' fable of the Choice of *Heracles. He is said to have been the founder of the Cyrenaic school (see CYRENAICS), but this may be through confusion with his grandson of the same name (see below). While it is impossible to determine which, if any, of the specific doctrines of the school were held by the elder Aristippus, it is plausible to see the school as developing a general position laid down by him.

(2), grandson of the above, son of his daughter Arete, herself a leading member of the school, whence his nickname Μητροδί-δακτος ('Mother-taught').

G. Giannantoni, *I Cirenaici* (1958), and *Socraticorum Reliquiae* (1983); E. Mannebach, *Aristippi et Cyrenaicorum Fragmenta* (1961); C. J. Classen, *Hermes* 1958; Guthrie, *Hist. G. Phil.* 3, ch. 14; J. C. B. Gosling and C. C. W. Taylor, *The Greeks on Pleasure* (1982); H. D. Rankin, *Sophists, Socratics and Cynics* (1983); K. Döring, *Der Sokratesschüler Aristipp und die Kyrenaiker* (1988).   C. C. W. T.

Aristius (*RE* 2) **Fuscus, Marcus,** friend of *Horace and addressee of *Ode* 1. 22 and *Epist.* 1. 10; also mentioned in *Sat.* 1. 9. 60 ff. and 1. 10. 83. Said by *Pomponius Porphyrio to have been an eminent *grammaticus and an author of comedies, he may have had Stoic leanings, see STOICISM (S. J. Harrison, *CQ* 1992, 543–7).

PIR[2] A 1048. M. Hubbard and R. G. M. Nisbet on Horace, *Odes 1* (1970), 261–2.   P. G. M. B.

Aristo See TITIUS ARISTO.

Aristobulus (1) of Cassandreia, historian of *Alexander (3) the Great, served with the king as a minor officer and in his old age, after *Ipsus (301 BC), wrote an influential history of the reign. Known only from fragments, it was a major source for *Strabo on India; and for *Arrian it is subsidiary only to *Ptolemy (1) I (and occasionally given preference). Aristobulus was indicted in antiquity as a flatterer and did apparently give a eulogistic portrait of Alexander, at times with a blatant *suggestio falsi* (he states that *Philotas and *Callisthenes actually conspired and repeatedly denies Alexander's predilection for strong drink). In some cases (e.g. the Gordian Knot and the murder of *Cleitus (1)) his version is contrasted with the rest of the tradition and is clearly eccentric. On the other hand he gives invaluable chronological data (particularly for the Indian campaign) and recorded a wealth of geographical and botanical detail.

FGrH 139; L. Pearson, *Lost Histories of Alexander* (1960); P. Pédech, *Historiens compagnons d'Alexandre* (1984).   A. B. B.

Aristobulus (2), an *Alexandrian Jew, probably of the second half of the 2nd cent. BC, author of a commentary on the Pentateuch which is known only through quotations by *Clement of Alexandria, Anatolius, and *Eusebius. This has been thought by some scholars to be a much later work (of the 3rd cent. AD) falsely ascribed to Aristobulus; but this conclusion is not necessary. If the earlier date be accepted, the book is the earliest evidence of contact between Alexandrian Jewry and Greek philosophy. Its object was twofold, to interpret the Pentateuch in an allegorical fashion and to show that *Homer and *Hesiod, the Orphic writings (see ORPHIC LITERATURE), *Pythagoras (1), *Plato (1), and *Aristotle had borrowed freely from a supposed early translation of the OT into Greek. Though Aristobulus toned down the anthropomorphism of the OT, his thought remained Jewish and theistic; it did not accept the pantheism of the Stoics nor anticipate the Logos-doctrine of *Philon (4). See JEWISH–GREEK LITERATURE.

Zeller, *Phil. d. Gr.* 3. 2[4]. 277 ff.; Schürer, *History* 3 / 1. 579 ff., with bibliog. on p. 587.   W. D. R.; S. H.

Aristocles of Messene (Sicily or Peloponnese?), Peripatetic philosopher conventionally dated to 2nd cent. AD and identified with the teacher of *Alexander (14) of Aphrodisias, but perhaps belonging to 1st cent. BC/AD. His *On Philosophy* seems to have been an attempt at a critical history. He also wrote rhetorical treatises, an *Ethics*, a work On *Sarapis, and a comparison of *Homer and *Plato (1).

FRAGMENTS H. Heiland (1925).
S. Follet in *Dict. des philos. ant.* 1 (1989), 382.   M. B. T.

aristocracy

aristocracy ('power in the hands of the best'). The term is applied by modern scholars to the regimes of early Greece in which states were ruled by the noble families which had emerged from the Dark Age with the most landed property and political power, but the word *aristokratia* is not found before the 5th cent. BC, perhaps coined in response to '*democracy'. Thereafter it was the preferred term of those wishing to give a favourable picture of oligarchy. In *Plato (1)'s *Republic* aristocracy is the name given to the ideal form of constitution when there are several rulers rather than one; in the threefold classification of monarchy (*kingship), *oligarchy, and democracy aristocracy is the good form of oligarchy.

W. G. Forrest, *The Emergence of Greek Democracy* (1966); M. T. W. Arnheim, *Aristocracy in Greek Society* (1977); C. G. Starr, *The Aristocratic Temper of Greek Civilization* (1992).   V. E.; P. J. R.

aristocracy, attitudes to Élites in Greek and Roman societies were identified in a number of ways, of which the most important and inclusive was the sharing in the appreciation, discussion, and propagation of the cultural values in ideas, literature, and the visual arts which have left us the material that we call 'Classical'. Occasions for the display of these shared but competitive values, such as the religious *festival, the family celebration, or the shared meal (see SYMPOSIUM; CONVIVIUM), became central to ancient society.

Against this background, more selective definitions of widely variable kinds identified the politically powerful from time to time; no aristocratic group survived for long without a connection with the practice of government. Power-élites of whatever kind usually however included the whole kin-group of the practitioners of public, political life, and were therefore prone to regard the qualities—especially *aretē, virtus*—which they saw in themselves as justifying their status and its rewards as moral and as hereditary: in this they resemble the blood-aristocracies of other cultures. But the difficulties of self-replacement in the demographic circumstances of antiquity entailed a high incidence of élite vacancy, and upward social mobility to fill the gaps, which further encouraged genealogical pride, real or fictitious, and familial inclusiveness, as well as fostering a culture of intense competitiveness among individual aristocrats along with a very strong sense of personal honour (*timē, *philotimia*). This in turn entailed that *wealth in theory did not usually provide a sufficient entrée to membership of the élite, and encouraged the fostering of the intellectual culture which justified the claims of the hereditary good, *chrēstoi, kalokagathoi, boni,* *optimates, to their elevated position.

That culture, for that reason, seriously played down the claims of wealth and its creation, to the great detriment of our understanding of the ancient world. But in practice wealth was often a sufficient means of acquiring a political following, and of achieving, through *patronage, some place in the world of high culture, so that replacement of the supposedly hereditary élite did in fact take place in many cases through its acquisition. Whether for this reason or for others, moreover, the qualitative gap between élite and outsiders was much harder to maintain than in some historical societies, and it was almost always a feature of ancient social life that non-élite groups, whether an effective *dēmos* or simply people of moderate standing or influence (and particularly experts in the intellectual pursuits which contributed to aristocratic identity), formed an important part of the system too, and so acted to modify the development of aristocracy as such (see also GENEALOGY; PATRONAGE; WEALTH, ATTITUDES TO).

M. T. W. Arnheim, *Aristocracy in Greek Society* (1977); O. Murray, *Early Greece* (1980), 38–56, 192–208; M. Gelzer, *The Roman Nobility*, trans. R. Seager (1969); R. Saller, *Personal Patronage under the Early Empire* (1982), 119–43; C. G. Starr, *The Aristocratic Temper of Greek Civilization* (1992).   N. P.

Aristodemus (1), the traditional hero of the First Messenian War (c.735–715 BC; see SPARTA). When the Messenians had withdrawn to their stronghold of *Ithome in the fifth year of the war, he offered his daughter for sacrifice to the gods below, in response to a *Delphic oracle. Eight years later he was elected king, and after carrying on guerrilla warfare for five years, signally defeated the Spartans. But in the following year he slew himself in despair on his daughter's grave.

Paus. 4. 9–13. For the value of his traditions, see ARISTOMENES (1); MESSENIA.   A. M. W.

Aristodemus (2) **Malacus** ('the Effeminate'), tyrant of *Cumae, 504–c.490 BC. An account of the career of this colourful tyrant in *Dionysius (7) of Halicarnassus (7. 3–11) derives, probably via *Timaeus (2) from local Cumaean sources, and is important because it refers to the defeat of the forces of Lars *Porsenna at *Aricia by the Latins and their Cumaean allies. It thus provides independent confirmation of a famous episode of the early Roman republic, and dates it to the first year of the 69th Olympiad (= 504 BC). Aristodemus was a popular general (he had defeated a barbarian attack on Cumae in 524 BC) who led the Cumaean forces at *Aricia and then used his popularity to make himself tyrant. Later he gave refuge to the exiled Roman king *Tarquinius Superbus.

A. Alföldi, *Early Rome and the Latins* (1965), 50 ff.; M. W. Frederiksen, *Campania* (1984), 95 ff.   T. J. Co.

Aristodemus (3), of unknown date (4th cent. AD ?), compiled a history of Greece which included at least the period 480–431 BC, perhaps as a handbook for students of rhetoric. Aristodemus drew on a pro-Athenian tradition and included *Ephorus among a variety of sources; but the work is inaccurate, lacking in chronology, and makes no significant addition to the historical evidence. The fragments suggest that its value was negligible.

FGrH 104.   G. L. B.; K. S. S.

Aristogiton (Ἀριστογείτων), Athenian tyrannicide. He and Harmodius, both of the family of Gephyraei, provoked, according to *Thucydides (2), by amorous rivalry, plotted along with others to kill the tyrant *Hippias (1) at the Panathenaic festival of 514 BC (see PANATHENAEA) and end the tyranny. The plot miscarried, only *Hipparchus (1) was killed, and the 'tyrannicides' were executed.

After the expulsion of Hippias in 510 by Sparta and the *Alcmaeonids, the 'tyrannicides' were elevated as heroes. Bronze statues of them by *Antenor (2) were erected, probably quite early (Pliny, *HN* 34. 16–17, gives 510/9); carried off by *Xerxes in 480, they were replaced in 477/6 by a second group by *Critius and Nesiotes; the epigram inscribed on the base was composed by *Simonides (fr. 76 Diehl; *SEG* 10. 320). Their tomb was placed in the *Ceramicus; the *polemarchos sacrificed annually to them, and their descendants received free meals in the *prytaneion. Certain *scolia were sung claiming that they brought Athens *isonomia (freedom or democracy) (Page, *PMG* nos. 893–6). It was thus a popular belief, famously rebutted by Thucydides (1. 20, 6. 53 ff.), that Hipparchus was the tyrant at the time. Other conflicting claims clustered round the role of the tyrannicides, but Jacoby's view that 5th-cent. popular tradition literally thought they, rather than Sparta and the Alcmaeonids (as in Hdt. 5. 55–65), ended the tyranny, is undermined by Thucydides (6. 53) and comedy. It is likely that all parties concerned concurred in honouring them from early on as a convenient, simple, and patriotic symbol for the defeat of tyranny. Later, they are seen as having ended the tyranny.

Thuc. 1. 20, 6. 53 ff.; Hdt. 5. 55–65. R. Thomas, *Oral Tradition and Written Record* (1989), ch. 5; M. W. Taylor, *The Tyrant Slayers*, 2nd. edn. (1991); C. Fornara, *Philol.* 1970, 155 ff.; G. Vlastos, *AJPhil.* 1953, 337 ff.; F. Jacoby, *Atthis* (1949), 158 ff.; V. Ehrenberg, *Wien. Stud.* 1956, 57 ff.; G. M. A. Richter, *Sculpture and Sculptors of the Greeks* (1950), 199 ff. and figs. 565 ff.   R. T.

Aristomenes (1), a traditional hero of *Messenian resistance to Sparta, usually assigned to the Second Messenian War of *c*.650 BC but sometimes associated with a possible Messenian revolt of *c*.490 ('the *Rhianus hypothesis'). He is supposed to have won a major victory at Stenyclarus, but was defeated in the battle of 'The Great Trench'. For eleven years he held out in the stronghold of Eira (or Hira), twice escaping after capture. His legend was a central ingredient of nostalgic Messenian patriotic myth, which was given literary expression—or invented—after the (re)foundation of *Messene in 369.

Paus. 4. 14–24 (after *Rhianos of Crete, 3rd-cent. BC poet). F. Kiechle, *Messenische Studien* (1959), 72 ff., 86 ff.; L. Pearson, *Hist.* 1962, 397–426; H. T. Wade-Gery, in E. Badian (ed.), *Ancient Society and Institutions: Studies presented to V. Ehrenberg* (1966), 289–302; P. Cartledge, *Sparta and Lakonia* (1979).   P. A. C.

Aristomenes (2), Athenian comic poet, competed *c*.440 BC (*IG* 2². 2325. 120), and probably the poet whose plays span the period 440–390 in *IG* 14. 1097. 10 ff. He may also be the man of that name denounced for profanation of the *mysteries in 415 (see ANDOCIDES; ARCHIPPUS). We have five titles in all, and sixteen citations.

Kassel–Austin *PCG* 2. 562 ff. (*CAF* 1. 690 ff.).   K. J. D.

Ariston (1), of Chios, Stoic, pupil of *Zeno (2), developed Zeno's ideas in a way later regarded as unorthodox after *Chrysippus' writings had established a Stoic orthodoxy. He enjoyed a wide but brief popularity. He uncompromisingly focused on ethics, rejecting physics and logic. Within ethics he was also uncompromising, stressing the unity of the virtues, and the virtuous person's non-rule-governed discernment of the right thing to do. He stressed the importance of the virtuous person's point of view, to the extent of denying the significance of general distinctions of value made independently of it. The virtuous person is like an actor playing Agamemnon or Thersites: his material does not matter, only what he does with it. See STOICISM.

Testimonia in von Arnim, *SVF* 1. 75–90.   J. A.

Ariston (2), (*RE* 52) of *Ceos, *Peripatetic, probably succeeded *Lyco as head of the Lyceum *c*.225 BC. *Diogenes (6) Laertius appears to have derived from him the wills of *Aristotle and his successors, and a bibliography of *Straton (1). Gercke and Moraux assign to him Diogenes' bibliography of Aristotle, traditionally attributed to *Hermippus (2). Some reports may relate to him or to his Stoic namesake *Ariston (1) of Chios; a distinction between rational and non-rational soul seems to be his.

Works Characters; Lives (mainly anecdotal) of philosophers; *On Making Light of Arrogance*; *Tithonus, or On Old Age*; *Lycon*; *Erotic Parallels*; a supplement to Theophrastus' *On Waters*.

TEXTS F. Wehrli, *Die Schule des Aristoteles* 6, 2nd edn. (1968), 27–67.

STUDIES F. Wehrli, *RE* Suppl. 11 (1968), 156–9, and in Ueberweg–Flashar 579–82; P. Moraux, *Listes anciennes des ouvrages d'Aristote* (1951), 237 ff.; G. Movia, *Anima e intelletto* (1968), 150–5; A. M. Ioppolo, *Aristone di Chio* (1980), 272–8.   R. W. S.

Ariston (3), of Alexandria (1), philosopher, pupil of Aristus the brother of *Antiochus (11) of Ascalon. He later became a *Peripatetic and may be identical with the Ariston mentioned by *Simplicius as a commentator on Aristotle's *Categories*.

SOURCES In I. Mariotti, *Aristone d'Alessandria* (1966).

DISCUSSION P. Moraux, *Der Aristotelismus bei den Griechen* 1 (1973), 181–93.   G. S.

Aristonicus (1) (d. 128 BC), perhaps illegitimate son of *Eumenes (2) II of Pergamum, led an insurrection in *Asia Minor (133–129) after *Attalus III's death. He issued Attalid coins, 'cistophori' ('basket-bearers'), which asserted his royal claim, motivated the Attalid fleet at Leucae near *Smyrna to support him, and gained successes at Colophon, *Samos, and Myndos before being defeated by the Ephesians. He then tried to mobilize lower classes, slaves and non-Greeks, whom he called 'Heliopolitae' ('Sun-citizens'), according to *Strabo who attaches no significance to the name (14. 38. 1). Moderns have liked to imagine social-revolutionary motives unknown to the sources, but the mainspring was probably desperation after failing to mobilize the major cities. With these troops he captured Stratonicea in Mysia, Apollonis, and Thyateira; *Phocaea and Leucae remained loyal. When Roman troops arrived (131) he achieved some successes, even killing the consul P. Licinius Crassus, but was defeated by M. *Perperna (1) (130) and put to death in Rome.

J. Hopp, *Untersuchungen zur Geschichte der letzten Attaliden* (1977); A. N. Sherwin-White, *Roman Foreign Policy in the East* (1984).   R. M. E.

Aristonicus (2), son of Ptolemaeus, an Alexandrian grammarian (see ALEXANDRIA (1)) of the Augustan age (Strabo 1. 2. 31). Much of his chief work—on the Aristarchan recensions of *Homer (see ARISTARCHUS (2))—is preserved in our scholia (cf. *Nicanor (2)). He also wrote *On Ungrammatical Words*, commentaries on *Hesiod and *Pindar, and *On the *Museum at Alexandria*.

FRAGMENTS L. Friedlander (1953); O. Carnuth (1869).

CRITICISM M. van der Valk, *Researches on the Text and Scholia of the Iliad* 1 (1963), 553 ff.   P. B. R. F.; R. B.

Aristonous (mid-4th cent. BC), Corinthian citharode. On a stele found at Delphi (*BCH* 1894, 563 ff.) the Delphians (see DELPHI) give to him and his descendants privileges because of his *hymns. Two hymns are preserved in inscriptions: a *paean to Apollo written in regular eight-lined stanzas of glyconics and pherecrateans and a hymn to Hestia written in dactylo-epitrites. The style and language of the hymns show characteristics of the new *dithyramb.

TEXT Powell, *Coll. Alex.* 162, 164; L. Käppel, *Paian* (1992), 384 ff.

LITERATURE O. Crusius, *RE* 2/1. 967, and *Die delphischen Hymnen* (1894); West, *GM* 139 ff.   B. Z.

Aristonymus, comic writer and contemporary of *Aristophanes (1), whom he ridicules (fr. 3 KA).

FRAGMENTS Kassel–Austin, *PCG* 2. 571–4, although earlier scholars use the numbering of Kock, *CAF* 1. 668 f.

INTERPRETATION Meineke, *FCG* 1. 196 ff.; G. Kaibel, *RE* 2/1 (1895), 968, 'Aristonymos' 8.   W. G. A.

Aristophanes (1), the greatest poet of the Old Attic Comedy (see COMEDY (GREEK), OLD), was the son of Philippus and the father of *Araros. It has been inferred (wrongly, perhaps) from *Ach.

Aristophanes

652 ff. that he lived, or owned property, on *Aegina. Since he considered himself too young in 427 BC (Ar. *Nub.* 530 f. with schol.) to produce a play himself, he is unlikely to have been born earlier than 460 and may have been born as late as 450. He died in or shortly before 386. Eleven of his plays survive; we have in addition 32 titles (some of them alternative titles, and some certainly attributed to other authors) and nearly a thousand fragments and citations. The surviving plays, and the datable lost plays (°) are:

427: °*Banqueters*, produced by *Callistratus (1). It contained (frs. 198 and 222 and *Nub.* 529 with schol.) an argument between a profligate son and his father and also between the profligate and a virtuous young man.

426 (City *Dionysia): °*Babylonians*, produced by Callistratus. Dionysus was a character in the play (fr. 70), and by its 'attacks on the magistrates' it provoked a prosecution—apparently unsuccessful—by *Cleon (schol. Ar. *Ach.* 378).

425 (*Lenaea, first prize): *Acharnians* ('*Ach.*'), produced by Callistratus; the 'hero' makes, and enjoys to the full, a private peace-treaty.

424 (Lenaea, first prize): *Knights* ('*Eq.*'), produced by Aristophanes himself; Cleon is savagely handled and worsted in the guise of a favourite slave of Demos, and a sausage-seller replaces him as favourite.

423 (City Dionysia, bottom prize): *Clouds* ('*Nub.*'), ridiculing *Socrates as a corrupt teacher of rhetoric. We have only the revised version of the play, dating from the period 418–416; the revision was not completed and was never performed (schol. *Nub.* 552).

422 (Lenaea, second prize): *Wasps* ('*Vesp.*'), produced by *Philonides (1), ridiculing the enthusiasm of old men for jury-service.

421 (City Dionysia, second prize): *Peace* ('*Pax*'), celebrating the conclusion of peace with Sparta.

414 (Lenaea): °*Amphiaraus*, produced by Philonides (hyp. 2 Ar. *Av.*).

414 (City Dionysia, second prize): *Birds* ('*Av.*'), produced by Callistratus, a fantasy in which an ingenious Athenian persuades the birds to build a city in the clouds and compels the gods to accept humiliating terms.

411: *Lysistrata* ('*Lys.*'), produced by Callistratus, in which the citizens' wives in all the Greek states compel their menfolk, by a 'sex strike', to make peace; and *Thesmophoriazusae* ('*Thesm.*')—datable in relation to *Euripides' *Helena* and *Andromeda*, and by political references—in which the women at the *Thesmophoria plan to obliterate Euripides, and an elderly kinsman of his takes part in their debate, disguised as a woman.

408: the first °*Plutus* (schol. Ar. *Plut.* 173).

405 (Lenaea, first prize): *Frogs* ('*Ran.*'), in which *Dionysus goes to *Hades to bring back Euripides, finds that he has to be the judge in a contest between *Aeschylus and Euripides, for the throne of poetry in Hades, and ends by bringing back Aeschylus.

392: *Ecclesiazusae* ('*Eccl.*'); the date depends on a partially corrupt scholium (on *Eccl.* 193, see SCHOLIA) and on historical references, and a case can be made for 391. In this play the women take over the running of the city and introduce community of property.

388: the second *Plutus* ('*Plut.*'), in which the god of wealth is cured of his blindness, and the remarkable social consequences of his new discrimination are exemplified.

After 388: °*Aiolosikon* and °*Cocalus*, both produced by Aristophanes' son Araros (hyp. 4 Ar. *Plut.*). *Cocalus* anticipated some

of the characteristics of *Menander (1), according to *Vit. Ar.* 1 pp. 1, 3.

In the first period, down to 421, Aristophanes followed a constant procedure in the structure of his plays, particularly in the relation of the parodos (entry of the chorus) and the parabasis (address by the chorus to the audience) to the rest of the play. From *Av.* onwards we see significant changes in this procedure, culminating, in *Eccl.* and *Plut.*, in the introduction of choral songs irrelevant to the action of the play (indicated in our texts by the word χοροῦ), and in *Plut.* the chorus seems, for the first time, something of an impediment to the unfolding of the plot (see COMEDY (GREEK), MIDDLE). At the same time *Eccl.* and *Plut.* show a great reduction (though not a disappearance) of strictly topical reference. The evidence suggests that Aristophanes was a leader, not a follower, in the changes undergone by comedy in the early 4th cent. BC. Aristophanes' language is colourful and imaginative, and he composes lyric poetry in every vein, humorous, solemn, or delicate. He has a keen eye and ear for the absurd and the pompous; his favoured weapons are parody, satire, and exaggeration to the point of fantasy, and his favourite targets are men prominent in politics, contemporary poets, musicians, scientists, and philosophers, and—as is virtually inevitable in a comedian writing for a wide public—manifestations of cultural change in general. His sympathetic characters commonly express the feelings of men who want to be left alone to enjoy traditional pleasures in traditional ways, but they are also ingenious, violent, and tenaciously self-seeking in getting what they want. Having been born into a radical democracy which had been created and strengthened by his father's and grandfather's generations, Aristophanes nowhere advocates oligarchic reaction, least of all in 411, when this reaction was an imminent reality. His venomous attack on Cleon in *Eq.* is adequately explained by Cleon's earlier attack on him (see above), and his treatment of other politicians does not differ significantly from the way in which 'we' satirize 'them' nowadays. No class, age-group, or profession is wholly exempt from Aristophanes' satire, nor is the citizen-body as a whole, and if we interpret his plays as moral or social lessons we never find the lesson free of qualifications and complications. In *Eq.* Cleon is worsted not by an upright and dignified man but by an illiterate and brazen cynic who beats him at his own game. In *Nub.* Socrates' 'victim' is foolish and dishonest, and in the contest between Right and Wrong, Right, who is characterized by bad temper, sexual obsession, and vacuous nostalgia, ends by 'deserting' to the side of Wrong. In *Thesm.* Euripides, sharply parodied in much of the play, triumphs in the end. In *Ran.* the end of the contest between Aeschylus and Euripides finds Dionysus in a state of complete irresolution. Modern sentiment admires the heroine of *Lys.*, but possibly Aristophanes and his audience found preposterous much in her which seems to us moving and sensible. Aristophanes' didactic influence (as distinct from his influence in raising the intellectual and artistic standards of comedy) does not seem to have been significant. Plato (*Ap.* 18bc, 19d) blames him for helping to create mistrust of Socrates. On the other hand, *Ach.* and *Lys.* do not seem to have disposed the Athenians to negotiate for peace (*Pax* did not mould public opinion, but fell into line with it), and Cleon was elected to a generalship shortly after the first prize had been awarded to *Eq.* The fact that Aristophanes survived not only Cleon's attacks but also (with other comic poets) two oligarchic revolutions (see FOUR HUNDRED; THIRTY TYRANTS) and two democratic restorations should not be forgotten.

Aristophanes was intensively studied throughout antiquity,

and the plays which are now lost, as well as those which have survived, were the subject of commentaries (cf. schol. Ar. *Plut.* 210).

See also COMEDY (GREEK), OLD and MIDDLE; LITERARY CRITICISM IN ANTIQUITY, paras. 2, 3.

TEXT Coulon (Budé), frs. Kassel-Austin, *PCG* 3 (2).

COMMENTARIES All plays: van Leeuwen (1892–), Rogers (1902–19), Sommerstein (1980–): most recent vol. is *Thesm.* (1994); *Ach.*: Starkie (1909); *Eq.*: Neil (1901); *Nub.*: Starkie (1911), Dover (1968); *Vesp.*: Starkie (1897), MacDowell (1971); *Pax*: Platnauer (1964); *Av.*: N. Dunbar (1994); *Lys.*: Wilamowitz (1927), Henderson (1987); *Ran.*: Radermacher, 2nd edn. (1954), Stanford, 2nd edn. (1963), Dover (1993); *Eccl.*: Ussher (1973); *Plut.*: Holzinger (1940). Scholia: Dübner (1842), Koster and others (1960–). Index: Todd (1932; repr. 1962). Concordance: H. Dunbar (1883; rev. Marzullo, 1970).

GENERAL K. J. Dover, *Aristophanic Comedy* (1972); V. Ehrenberg, *The People of Aristophanes*, 2nd edn. (1951); H.-J. Newiger, *Metapher und Allegorie* (1957), and (ed.), *Aristophanes und die alte Komödie* (1975); C. F. Russo, *Aristofane autore di teatro*, 2nd edn. (1984); J. Taillardat, *Les Images d' Aristophane* (1962); E. Handley, *CHCL* 1. 355–409; J. Henderson, in J. Winkler and F. Zeitlin (eds.), *Nothing to do with Dionysos* (1990), 271–313.   K. J. D.

Aristophanes (2) of Byzantium (probably *c*.257–180 BC) succeeded *Eratosthenes as head of the Alexandrian Library (*c*.194 BC). He was a scholar of wide learning, famous for his linguistic, literary, textual, and scientific researches, and he is credited with the innovation of writing Greek accents.

His edition of *Homer's *Iliad* and *Odyssey* made a distinct advance on the work of *Zenodotus and *Rhianus. Despite some capriciousness and boldness of treatment, due to a subjective method of criticism, his work showed much critical acumen; e.g. he was the first to put the end of the *Odyssey* at 23. 296. In his textual criticism he used symbols to show his doubts of the genuineness or satisfactoriness of verses (see SCHOLARSHIP, ANCIENT).

Besides editions of *Hesiod's *Theogony*, *Alcaeus, and *Alcman, he produced the first properly ordered edition of *Pindar, in seventeen books; in his texts of the lyric poets Aristophanes used signs to mark the ends of metrical *cola*; but *PLille* 76a and 73 of *Stesichorus prove that his predecessors had recognized the importance of *cola*. *Scholia and papyri (see PAPYROLOGY) attest his work on *Sophocles and *Euripides; he also compiled the first critical edition of the comedies of *Aristophanes (1); but to a later date belong the metrical ὑποθέσεις, traditionally ascribed to him, on seven of these comedies (see HYPOTHESIS, LITERARY). He may have proposed a somewhat unsatisfactory grouping of fifteen dialogues of *Plato (1) in trilogies.

His select lists of the best Classical poets seem, along with those of *Aristarchus (2), to have provided the basis for the classification of writers in the Alexandrian canon. He corrected and supplemented the biographical and literary information contained in the *Pinakes* of *Callimachus (3). Introductions (attributed to Aristophanes) to some plays of *Aeschylus, Sophocles, and Euripides, based on the *Didascaliae* of Aristotle (see DIDASKALIA) and on Peripatetic research, are extant in an abbreviated form (see HYPOTHESIS, LITERARY). In the Περὶ προσώπων he treated the character-types in Greek Comedy. His interest in *Menander (1) led him to compile the treatise Παράλληλοι Μεν ἄνδρου τε καὶ ἀφ' ὧν ἔκλεψεν ἐκλογαί ('Parallels between Menander and the people he stole from'), possibly the first treatise on *plagiarism.

Of his lexicographical works the most important was the Λέξεις (or Γλῶσσαι), which perhaps consisted of a series of

special studies classified according to dialect or to subject and dealt with prose as well as verse. He produced two books of proverbs in verse (schol. Soph. *Aj.* 746) and four in prose (schol. Ar. *Av.* 1292). See PAROEMIOGRAPHERS.

The work Περὶ ζῴων appears to have been based on the ('on animals') studies of Aristotle, Theophrastus, and the *Paradoxographers. Excerpts survive in Byzantine miscellanies. There is no good reason to attribute to him a grammatical treatise Περὶ ἀναλογίας ('on *analogy').

R. Pfeiffer, *History of Classical Scholarship: From the Beginnings to the End of the Hellenistic Age* (1968), 171–209; W. J. Slater, *Aristophanis Byzantii fragmenta* (1986); C. K. Callanan, *Die Sprachbeschreibung bei Aristophane von Byzanz* (1989).   J. F. L.; N. G. W.

Aristophon (*c*.435–*c*.335 BC), Athenian politician, whose activities, extending from 403/2 to the late 340s, brought him into opposition first to the party of *Callistratus (2) over relations with Thebes (1), and later to *Eubulus (1) over finance and, perhaps, foreign policy. He successfully prosecuted *Timotheus (2) for his part in the *Social War (1) (357–355). In 346 he opposed the abandonment of Athens' claim to *Amphipolis in the Peace of *Philocrates (*FGrH* 115 F 166). He was attacked 75 times (never successfully) under the *graphē paranomōn, and, although the evidence for his life mainly concerns the period 363–350, the chance references to him in the orators show that he was a figure of the first importance.   G. L. C.

Aristotle (384–322 BC) was born in *Stagira in *Chalcidice. His father Nicomachus, a member of the medical guild of the Asclepiadae (see ASCLEPIUS), was court physician to *Amyntas II of Macedonia, and Aristotle may have spent part of his childhood at the court in *Pella. Although his interest in biology may have developed early because of his father's career, there is no evidence that he began systematic study. Asclepiad doctors taught their sons dissection, but Aristotle probably did not receive this training, since both of his parents died when he was extremely young.

2. At the age of 17 he travelled to Athens and entered *Plato (1)'s *Academy, remaining until Plato's death in 348/7 BC. Plato's philosophical influence is evident in all of Aristotle's work. Even when he is critical (a great part of the time) he expresses deep respect for Plato's genius. Some scholars imagine that no dissent was tolerated in the Academy; they therefore conclude that all works in which Aristotle criticizes Plato must have been written after Plato's death. This is implausible. Plato's own work reveals a capacity for searching self-criticism. Frequently these criticisms resemble extant Aristotelian criticisms. An attractive possibility is that the arguments of his brilliant pupil were among the stimuli that led Plato to rethink his cherished positions.

3. At Plato's death Aristotle left Athens, probably because of political difficulties connected with his Macedonian ties. (He may also have disapproved of the choice of *Speusippus as Plato's successor.) Accepting an invitation from *Hermias (1), ruler of *Assos and Atarneus in the Troad and a former fellow student in the Academy, he went to Assos, where he stayed until Hermeias' fall and death in 345, marrying his adopted daughter Pythias. While at Assos, and afterwards at *Mytilene on Lesbos, he did the biological research on which his later scientific writings are based. (The treatises refer frequently to place-names and local species of that area.) His observations, especially in marine biology, were unprecedented in their detail and accuracy. (His work remained without peer until the time of Harvey (1578–1657), and was still much admired by Darwin.)

4. Invited by *Philip (1) II of Macedon to Pella in 342 BC, he became tutor to Philip's son *Alexander (3) the Great. His instruction focused on standard literary texts, but probably also included political theory and history. Aristotle's opinion of his pupil's philosophical ability is unknown, but in later years their relationship was distant. In the *Politics* Aristotle writes that rule by a single absolute monarch would be justified only if the person were as far superior to existing humans, in intellect and character, as humans are to beasts. He conspicuously fails to mention any case in which these conditions have been fulfilled.

5. In 335, after a brief stay in Stagira, Aristotle returned to Athens. As a resident alien (*metic) he could not own property, so he rented buildings outside the city, probably between Mt. Lycabettus and the Ilissus. Here, in what was called the Lyceum, he established his own school. (The school later took its name from its colonnade or *peripatos*.) He delivered some popular lectures, but most of his time was spent in writing or lecturing to a smaller group of serious students, including some, such as *Theophrastus and *Eudemus, who achieved distinction. He amassed a considerable library, and encouraged his students to undertake research projects, especially in natural science and political history (where he projected a collection of historical and comparative descriptions of 158 regimes).

6. Pythias died early in this period; they had one daughter. For the rest of his life Aristotle lived with a slave-woman named Herpyllis, by whom he had a son, *Nicomachus (1). Although in his will Aristotle praises Herpyllis' loyalty and kindness, he freed her from legal slavery only then. On the death of Alexander in 323 BC, an outbreak of anti-Macedonian feeling forced Aristotle to leave Athens once again. Alluding to the death of *Socrates, he said that he was leaving to prevent the Athenians from 'sin[ning] twice against philosophy'. He retired to *Chalcis, where he died in 322 of a digestive illness.

7. Aristotle left his papers to Theophrastus, his successor as head of the Lyceum. *Strabo reports that Theophrastus left them to Neleus of Scepsis (in Asia Minor), whose heirs hid them in a cellar, where they remained unused until a rich collector, Apellicon, purchased them and brought them to Athens early in the first century BC. This is seriously misleading. There is copious evidence that some of Aristotle's major works were used by his successors in the Lyceum, as well as by *Epicurus and numerous Alexandrian intellectuals (see ALEXANDRIA (1)). At this stage the works were not edited in anything like the form in which we know them. A list of Aristotle's works, probably dating from the 3rd cent. BC, appears to cover most of the major extant texts under some description, as well as a number of works now lost. Among the lost works are dialogues, some of which were still well known in *Cicero's Rome. Apparently their style was different from that of the extant works: Cicero describes it as 'a golden river'. We can reconstruct portions of several lost works through reports and citations.

8. When *Sulla captured Athens (86 BC), Apellicon's collection was brought to Rome, where it was edited around 30 BC, by *Andronicus of Rhodes, whose edition is the basis for all subsequent editions. Andronicus grouped books into works, arranged them in a logical sequence, and left copious notes about his views on authenticity. We possess most of the works he considered genuine and important, in manuscripts produced between the 9th and 16th cents. The transmission during the intervening period is represented by several papyrus fragments, plus the extensive papyri from which the (dubious) *Athenaion politeia* has been edited. Several of the Greek commentaries produced

between the 3rd and 6th cents. AD show evidence of access to now lost elements of the manuscript tradition, and can prove useful in establishing the text.

9. The extant works may be classified as follows:

(*a*) Logic and Metaphysics: *Categories, De interpretatione, Prior Analytics, Posterior Analytics, Topics, Sophistici elenchi* (= *Top.* 9), *Metaphysics.*

(*b*) Nature, Life, and Mind: *Physics, De caelo, De generatione et corruptione, Meteorologica* (bk. 4 of dubious authenticity), *Historia animalium, De partibus animalium, De motu animalium, De incessu animalium, De generatione animalium, De anima, Parva naturalia* (including *De sensu, De memoria, De somno, De somniis, De divinatione per somnum, De longitudine et brevitate vitae, De iuventute, De respiratione*).

(*c*) Ethics, Politics, Art: *Eudemian Ethics, Nicomachean Ethics, Politics; Magna moralia* (probably not written up by Aristotle, but closely based on Aristotelian lectures); *Athenaion politeia* (authorship disputed); *Rhetoric; Poetics.*

Of the works surviving only in fragments, the most important and substantial is *Peri ideōn* (*On the Forms*), a critical discussion of Plato's theories; also significant are the dialogues *On Philosophy* and *On the Good*, and the *Protrepticus.*

Clearly spurious works transmitted along with the corpus include *De mundo, De spiritu, De coloribus, De audibilibus, Physiognomonica, De plantis, De mirabilibus auscultationibus, Mechanica, Problemata* (a compilation of materials from the school), *De lineis insecabilibus, Ventorum situs, De Melisso, Xenophane, Gorgia, De virtutibus et vitiis, Oeconomica, Rhetorica ad Alexandrum.*

10. Many questions have been raised about the status of the 'Aristotelian corpus'. The most plausible view is that the extant treatises are written lectures. The exact wording of most of the material is Aristotle's. We cannot rely on the order of books within a treatise as Aristotelian, or even the grouping of distinct books into a single treatise. All titles and many introductory and concluding sentences are likely to be the work of later editors. Cross-references may be genuine if well integrated with their context. Throughout we are faced with textual problems, some of which require the transposition of substantial passages for their solution. Some sections, furthermore, may have been left poorly organized by Aristotle himself, and are best regarded as assorted notes that were never worked into a finished discussion (for example, *De anima* 3. 6–7). The most serious philosophical problems raised by the state of the corpus come from its duplications: (*a*) multiple discussions of a single problem, and (*b*) a single discussion repeated in more than one context. There are many cases of the first type; here we must ask whether differences amount to incompatibility or are best explained by a difference of perspective or starting point. Doublets of the second type may be very brief, or they may be several books long; sometimes repetition is verbatim, sometimes with changes. *Metaphysics* 1 and 13 have many chapters in common, with small but significant changes. *Metaphysics* 11 compiles material from other books of the *Metaphysics* and the *Physics*. Books 5–7 of the *Nicomachean Ethics* also appear as books 4–6 of the *Eudemian Ethics*. In each case, we must ask how likely it is that Aristotle himself would have put the repeated portion in both contexts himself. If such a hypothesis creates problems with the overall argument of the work, we should ask whether it is clear that Aristotle himself must have noticed those problems.

11. The medieval tradition led us to view Aristotle's work as a closed, consistent system without internal chronological development. This view of the corpus was overthrown early in the

20th cent. by Werner Jaeger's important work, which convincingly presented evidence of development and stressed the flexible undogmatic character of Aristotle's philosophizing (whether or not one agrees with Jaeger's particular chronological story). Thereafter, however, scholars sometimes went to an opposite extreme, hastily assuming incompatibility and making irresponsible use of developmental explanations. In general, it is crucial to recognize the extent to which Aristotle's problems and questions in a particular work dictate his approach to an issue.

12. Aristotle was the first Greek philosopher to attempt a general account of validity in inference. The *Prior Analytics* is thus a towering achievement; though displaced in the Hellenistic period by Stoic propositional logic, it became the dominant account of formal logic from the early Middle Ages until the early 20th cent. The *Topics* and the *Sophistici elenchi* show Aristotle's keen interest in methods of dialectical argumentation and in the analysis of common fallacies and paradoxes; they give us a vivid picture of the philosophical culture of Aristotle's time.

13. In the *Posterior Analytics* Aristotle sets out the conditions under which scientific demonstration will convey genuine understanding (*epistēmē*). Conclusions must be deducible, ultimately, from first principles that are true, basic, necessary, and explanatory of the other conclusions of the science. The scientist has understanding when he is able to show how the more basic principles of his science explain the less basic. (In this sense, understanding must always be of the universal, since particulars cannot become part of a deductive explanatory structure of this sort; this does not mean, however, that Aristotle thinks our grasp of particulars shaky or prone to sceptical doubt.) *Posterior Analytics* 2. 19 argues that understanding is based on the experience of many particulars, and requires the achievement of *nous* concerning the first principles. Although *nous* has often been taken to be a special faculty of mind that grasps first principles a priori, it is probably best understood to be mental insight into the explanatory role of principles that the thinker knows and uses already on the basis of experience. Thus Aristotelian science does not require an a priori foundation.

14. In *Metaphysics* 4, Aristotle undertakes the defence of two especially basic logical principles: the Principle of Non-Contradiction and the Principle of the Excluded Middle. Non-Contradiction, which is called 'the most basic starting point of all', is established not by a proof from other principles, but by an 'elenctic demonstration', i.e. one that establishes that the opponent who challenges this law actually must rely on it if he is to think and speak at all. For to say anything definite he must rule something out—at the least, the contradictory of what he sets forth.

15. Throughout his work Aristotle is intensely concerned with experience, including the record of experience contained in what people say. It is common for an inquiry, in science as well as in ethics, to begin by 'setting down the *phainomena*', the 'appearances', which usually include perceptual observation and the record of reputable belief, frequently as embodied in language. Aristotle clearly believes that scientific inquiry involves examining common conceptions as well as looking at the world; indeed the two frequently interpenetrate, as in the inquiries into time and place in the *Physics*. Aristotle is also very careful to survey the views of the reputable thinkers who have approached a problem. As he states at the start of his inquiry into number in *Metaphysics* 13, he can hope in this way to avoid making the same mistakes, and can perhaps hope to progress a little beyond what the tradition has already accomplished. Although we may find fault with his treatment of one or another previous thinker, he

was the first Greek thinker to make engagement with the books of others a central part of his method.

16. 'Metaphysics' is not an Aristotelian term (it refers to the placement of that work 'after the *Physics*' in ancient editions), but Aristotle's study of the most general characteristics of things gives subsequent metaphysics its agenda. Aristotle holds that the central question about that which is (*to on*), for both his predecessors and himself, has been a question about *ousia*, usually translated 'substance'. Since *ousia* is a verbal noun formed from the participle *on*, this is not a perspicuous statement. But from Aristotle's procedures we can get a better idea of his problem. Two questions appear to drive the search for substance: a question about *change*, and a question about *identity*. Since a central part of our experience of nature is that of change—the cycle of the seasons, changes in living bodies—an account of nature needs to find a coherent way to speak about process. Following Plato's *Theaetetus*, Aristotle holds that this, in turn, requires the ability to single out some entities as (relatively) stable 'subjects' or 'substrates' (*hupokeimena*) of change, things to which the change happens. At the same time, discourse about the world also requires asking and answering the question 'What is it?' about items in our experience. This means being able to say what it is about an individual that makes it the very thing it is, and to separate that aspect from more superficial attributes that might cease to be present while the individual remained the same. This question, Aristotle holds, leads us to search for (what we now call) the thing's 'essence' (here we borrow a Ciceronian rendering of Aristotle's odd yet homely term, *to ti ēn einai*, 'the what it is to be'). The two questions might seem to point in opposite directions: the first in the direction of matter as the basic substance, since that persists while animals and people are born and die; the second in the direction of the universal, since 'human being' or 'tree' seem promising accounts of the 'what is it' of particulars. But it is Aristotle's view that in reality the two must be held closely together and will ultimately converge on a single account of the basic substances. For any adequate theory of change must single out as its substrates items that are not only relatively enduring, but also definite and distinct; and any account of the essence of a particular should enable us to say what changes it can undergo while still remaining one and the same. Aristotle pursues the two prongs of his question through several treatises, with results that appear to undergo development and are always difficult to interpret.

17. In the early *Categories*, Aristotle argues that the 'primary substances' and substrates of change are physical individuals, such as 'this human being' and 'this horse' (as contrasted both with individual qualities, quantities, relations, etc., and also with universals of all types). On the other hand, we can only individuate and identify them via 'secondary substances', species universals such as 'human being' and 'horse'. Unlike Platonic forms, secondary substances have no existence apart from physical individuals, but they are fundamental to our grasp of them. In *Physics*, and *Gen. corr.*, Aristotle brings matter into the picture and asks about its relation to form or organization. Although he ultimately rejects the notion that a thing's matter is substance, and more basic than its organization, he is apparently driven to grant that some cases of change—the comings-to-be and passings-away of substances—have to be explained with reference to material substrates.

18. Aristotle's culminating inquiry into substance, in *Metaph.* 7–8, is the subject of endless interpretative controversy. On one plausible reading, Aristotle concludes that the most basic sub-

strates are also the essences of things, and that both of these are identical with the *form* (*eidos*) of a thing as a member of a certain species, for example, the humanness (characteristic human organization) of Socrates. This form is a particular in the sense that Socrates is a distinct human being from Coriscus; on the other hand, the account of Socrates' essence or form mentions only those features he shares with other species members. In other words, what Socrates really is, and what must remain the same about him while other attributes change, is his characteristic species organization.

19. Other major topics in Aristotle's metaphysical work include *potentiality* and *actuality* (concepts linked to substance and invoked in explaining the forms of living things); *number* (Aristotle attacks the Platonist separation of numbers from things); *unity* (organic living beings have more than artefacts); and the nature of the *study of being* itself (it may become a general study with substance as its focal point). In *Metaphysics* 12, Aristotle articulates his idea of god as an eternally active and unaffected substance, whose activity is thinking and who inspires movement in the heavenly spheres by becoming an object of their love.

20. The *Metaphysics* describes the development of philosophy as a search for explanations of natural events that inspire wonder. In the *Physics* Aristotle describes the types of explanation a natural philosopher should be prepared to give. He begins from the question 'Why?' (*dia ti*)—asked either about a thing or a complex state of affairs; he suggests that there are four basic ways in which we can answer such a 'why' question. First, we may cite the materials of which a thing is composed. This answer is inadequate on its own, since we need to be able to pick out the thing as a structure of a certain sort before we can enumerate its constituents. Second, we may mention a thing's form or characteristic organization. Third, we may mention some agent or event that made the event or thing come about—this sort of answer is called by Aristotle 'the origin of change', and by the tradition 'the efficient cause'. Finally, we may mention 'the end' or 'that for the sake of which' a thing is. Aristotle insists frequently that we should explain processes or subsystems of creatures by showing how they contribute to the overall functioning of the creature. The characteristic organization of a species is in that sense an 'end' towards which processes should be seen as contributing. Whether Aristotle invokes teleological explanations to relate one species to another species is highly uncertain, as is the question whether such explanations apply to the non-living. The *Physics* also contains valuable discussions of place, time, and the nature of change.

21. Aristotle's work on *psychē* (*De anima*) is a general study of life and the living. After criticizing materialist and Platonist accounts of *psychē*, he defends the view that *psychē* is the substance of a living thing; he argues that this substance will be not its material constituents but its species-form. His working definition is that *psychē* is the 'first entelechy of a natural organic body'. 'First entelechy' takes the place of 'form' in order to stress the fact that it is not actual functioning (e.g. seeing or thinking) that is the *psychē*, but the organization-to-function. 'Organic' seems to mean 'equipped with materials that are suitable for performing these functions'. Aristotle goes on to give more concrete accounts of self-nutrition, reproduction, perceiving, imagining, and thinking; these inquiries are further developed in the *Parva naturalia* and, in some cases, the biological writings.

22. Aristotle's ethical treatises search for an adequate account of *eudaimonia*, a term usually translated 'happiness', but which might more perspicuously be understood as 'human flourishing'. There is general agreement that *eudaimonia* is the 'target' of human choice, and that it involves being active. Reflection, Aristotle holds, will show common candidates such as pleasure and honour to be inadequate accounts of what *eudaimonia* is; it must be understood as 'activity of soul in accordance with complete excellence'. This complex end has many constituent elements; Aristotle investigates a long list of excellences of character (such as courage, moderation, generosity, justice), which are, in general, stable dispositions to choose activities and to have responses that are neither excessive nor deficient in each area of choice; this 'mean' standard is given by looking to the choices of the 'person of practical wisdom', i.e. to paradigms of human excellence. Excellence of character requires and is required by practical wisdom, an excellence of the intellect.

23. Aristotle stresses the fact that practical wisdom requires a grasp of many particulars, which must be derived through experience. Like medicine and navigation, good judgement (in law as well as in ethics) requires a grasp of rules laid down in advance, but also the ability to adjust one's thinking to the complex requirements of the current situation. His account of 'equity' (*epieikeia*) in public judgement is continuous with reflections on that theme in the Greek orators; it has had enormous influence in the history of western law. Closely connected with Aristotle's accounts of practical wisdom are his reflections on voluntary action and excusing factors, and on choice (*prohairesis*), which is involved, it seems, in the specification of *eudaimonia* into its constituent parts as well as in more concrete operations.

24. Friendship (*philia*), Aristotle holds, is one of the most important elements in a good human life. Even if one were free of need and doing well in all other respects, one would still view life as not worth living without friends. Aristotle seems to hold that any genuine friendship requires mutual awareness and mutual activity seeking to benefit the other for the other's own sake. Friendships, however, come in different types, according to the characteristics of the parties that are the ground or basis for the friendship. There are friendships of pleasure, of utility, and of character, the last being both the most stable and the richest.

25. In two separate discussions Aristotle argues that pleasure is not equivalent to the good. (His accounts of pleasure differ, and may not be compatible.) In the final book of the *Eth. Nic.* he then goes on to praise the life that is devoted to contemplating the eternal. He appears to praise this activity not just as one among the other constituents of *eudaimonia*, but as something of supreme value, to which maximal attention should be given where possible. Scholars have long disagreed about whether these chapters are consistent with the more inclusive picture of *eudaimonia* that appears to emerge from the rest of the work; incompatibilist interpretations have much force. But however we resolve these questions, the chapters give evidence of Aristotle's high evaluation of the contemplative life, and complicate the task of describing the relationship between Aristotle's ethical thought and Plato's.

26. The investigation of human flourishing is a part of the science of politics, since legislators need to know about human ends in order to design schemes that promote these ends. But *political theory requires, in addition, a critical and empirical study of different regimes, and an attempt, on that basis, to consider what the best form of government would be. In the process, Aristotle makes Greek philosophy's most distinguished contribution to *economic theory.

27. Aristotle's great rhetorical treatise argues, against Platonic strictures, that rhetoric can be a systematic science. Defining rhetoric as 'the capability of recognizing in each case the possible means of persuasion', he argues for its autonomy and offers a comprehensive discussion of persuasion through speech. The work includes many discussions of broader interest, including a survey of ordinary beliefs about many ethical topics, and an analysis of the major emotions (see RHETORIC, GREEK).

28. Aristotle's *Poetics* should be read in close connection with his ethical writings, which insist, against Plato, that good people can sometimes fall short of *eudaimonia* through disasters not of their own making. Tragic action, Aristotle holds, inspires two emotions in its audience: *pity* (a painful emotion felt at the undeserved and serious suffering of another person), and *fear* (a painful emotion felt at the thought of serious disasters impending). We pity the tragic hero as someone undeserving of his misfortune, and fear for him, seeing him as someone similar to ourselves. (Plato's *Republic* had argued that both of these emotions are pernicious: literature that inspires them should be removed.) In this way, poetry proves more philosophical than historical narration, since it presents universals, things 'such as might happen' in a human life. Like other forms of representation (*mimēsis*), it gives rise to the pleasure of learning and recognition. The tragic hero's reversal inspires pity if it is due not to wickedness of character but rather to some *hamartia*, by which Aristotle seems to mean some error in action, sometimes blameworthy and sometimes not. Scholars will never agree on the proper interpretation of the *katharsis* through pity and fear that is the result of watching tragic action. But it should be observed that 'purgation' is only one possibility, and a problematic one; another possibility, perhaps more in keeping with the rest of Aristotle's argument, is that the emotional experience, by removing obstacles to our recognition of the mutability of human life, 'cleans up' or 'clears up' our muddled view of human fortunes. The central concepts of this work remain disputed and in need of close scholarly argument.

29. Aristotle's achievements have been fundamental to a great deal of the subsequent history of western philosophy. His undisputed greatness has produced at times an attitude of deference that he probably would have deplored. On the other hand, few if any philosophers have so productively stimulated the inquiries of other distinguished philosophers; few philosophers of the remote past, if any, are so conspicuously alive in the range of questions they provoke and in the resourcefulness of the arguments they offer.

See ANATOMY AND PHYSIOLOGY; ANIMALS, KNOWLEDGE ABOUT; BOTANY; EXPERIMENT; HYPOTHESIS, SCIENTIFIC; LOGIC; LOVE AND FRIENDSHIP; METEOROLOGY; MUSIC; PERIPATETIC SCHOOL; PHYSICS.

TEXTS 1. Bekker, *Aristotelis Opera* (1831); Teubner edns. of most works, OCTs of many, and texts in Oxford commentaries by Ross; also: *Mete.*, ed. F. Fobes (1919); *Gen corr.*, ed. H. H. Joachim (1922); *Cael.*, ed. P. Moraux (Budé, 1965); *Topi.*, ed. J. Brunschwig (Budé, 1967); *Rh.*, ed. R. Kassel (1976); *De motu an.*, ed. M. Nussbaum (1978).

TRANSLATIONS *The Complete Works of Aristotle*, ed. J. Barnes (1984); many works in Clarendon Aristotle Series; Loeb versions of biological and scientific works useful. Also: *Metaphysics* 7–8, M. Furth (1985); *Nicomachean Ethics*, T. H. Irwin (1985).

COMMENTARIES *Commentaria in A. Graeca* (1822–1909, with *Supplementum Aristotelicum*, 1882–1903); Aquinas, on many works (1882–6); W. D. Ross, on *Prior* and *Posterior Analytics*, *Physics*, *Metaphysics*, *Parv. nat.*, *De an.*; many works in Clarendon Aristotle Series. Also: *On Ideas*, G. Fine (1993); *Topics*, J. Brunschwig (1967); *Cael.* P. Moraux, (1965); *De an.*, G. Rodier (1900), R. D. Hicks (1907); biological works, extensive notes in Loeb vols. by Peck and Balme; *Metaph.* 7, M. Frede and G. Patzig (1987); *Eth. Nic.*, R.-A. Gauthier and J.-Y. Jolif (1970), A. Grant (1870), J. Stewart (1892); H. H. Joachim (1955), F. Dirlmeier (1966); *Pol.*, W. Newman (1887–1902), F. Susemihl and R. D. Hicks (1894), Barker (1966); *Poet.*, G. Else (1957), D. W. Lucas (1968), S. Halliwell (1987); *Ath. pol.*, P. J. Rhodes (1981).

GENERAL W. Jaeger, *Aristotle* (trans. 1948); I. Düring, *Aristoteles* (1966); W. D. Ross, *Aristotle* (1923); G. E. R. Lloyd, *Aristotle* (1968); J. Barnes, *Aristotle* (1982); J. L. Ackrill, *Aristotle the Philosopher* (1981); collections of articles in J. Barnes and others (eds.), *Articles on Aristotle* (1979), with extensive bibl.; essays in G. E. L. Owen, *Logic, Science, and Dialectic*.

PARTICULAR TOPICS I. Düring, *Aristotle in the Ancient Biographical Tradition* (1957); H. Cherniss, *Aristotle's Criticism of Plato and the Academy* (1944); G. Patzig, *Aristotle's Theory of the Syllogism* (1969); J. Lear, *Aristotle and Modern Logic* (1980); M. Burnyeat, in E. Berti (ed.), *Aristotle on Science* (1981); T. H. Irwin, *Aristotle's First Principles* (1988); E. Hartman, *Substance, Body and Soul* (1977); J. Owens, *The Doctrine of Being in the Aristotelian Metaphysics* (1978); C. Witt, *Substance and Essence in Aristotle* (1989); F. Solmsen, *Aristotle's System of the Physical World* (1960); S. Waterlow (now Broadie), *Nature, Change, and Agency in Aristotle's Physics* (1982), *Passage and Possibility* (1982); M. Nussbaum and A. Rorty (eds.), *Essays on Aristotle's De Anima* (1993); R. Sorabji, *Necessity, Cause, and Blame* (1979); K. J. Hintikka, *Time and Necessity* (1973); D. Charles, *Aristotle's Philosophy of Action* (1984); J. L. Austin, in his *Philosophical Papers* (1961); J. Cooper, *Reason and Human Good in Aristotle* (1976); W. F. R. Hardie, *Aristotle's Ethical Theory*, 2nd edn. 1980); A. Rorty (ed.), *Essays on Aristotle's Ethics* (1980); R. Kraut, *Aristotle on the Human Good* (1989); S. Broadie, *Ethics with Aristotle* (1991); A. Kenny, *The Aristotelian Ethics* (1978), and *Aristotle's Theory of the Will* (1979); J. Gosling and C. C. W. Taylor, *The Greeks on Pleasure* (1982); D. Keyt and F. Miller (eds.), *A Companion to Aristotle's Politics* (1991); D. Furley and A. Nehamas (eds.), *Aristotle's Rhetoric* (1993); S. H. Halliwell, *Aristotle's Poetics* (1986); A. Rorty (ed.), *Essays on Aristotle's Poetics* (1992).

M. C. N.

Aristoxenus, of *Tarentum (b. *c.* 370 BC), best known for musical writings but also a philosopher, biographer, and historian. He was trained in *music, possibly to professional standards, by his father Spintharus and Lampon of Erythrae (perhaps while living in *Mantinea). Later, probably at Athens, he studied with the Pythagorean (see PYTHAGORAS) Xenophilus, pupil of *Philolaus, before joining *Aristotle's Lyceum. Here his success made him expect to inherit the headship; and when Aristotle bequeathed it to *Theophrastus instead, his remarks about Aristotle (according to the *Suda*, our main biographical source) were memorably rude. The waspishness of criticisms levelled at others in his writings makes this believable; but his intellectual orientation is unmistakably Aristotelian, and his one surviving reference to Aristotle (*Harm.* 31. 10–16) is also the one unqualified compliment paid to anyone in that work. Nothing is known of him after 322 BC. Perhaps he devoted himself to writing: much of his enormous output (453 books, on the *Suda*'s reckoning) may come from this period. We are equally in the dark about the date and place of his death.

Works Aristoxenus' known works can be divided into five groups.

(*a*) Writings on harmonics, of which three incomplete books survive under the title *Elementa harmonica*. Repetitions, along with shifts in style and conceptual apparatus, suggest that book 1 belonged to a different work from books 2–3 (for a contrary view see Bélis (1986), in bibliog. below): the hypothesis, based on references in *Porphyry, that the former was called *Principles* (Ἀρχαί), the latter *Elements* (Στοιχεῖα) is uncertain. Aristoxenus saw himself as pioneering a wholly new and scientific approach to harmonics. Pythagoreans had conceived pitches as quantities, and studied their mathematical relations. Earlier empiricists had sought merely to tabulate various forms of attunement and scale. Aristoxenus takes his subject, melody ($\mu\acute{\epsilon}\lambda o\varsigma$) or attunement ($\tau\grave{o}\ \dot{\eta}\rho\mu o\sigma\mu\acute{\epsilon}\nu o\nu$), to be a 'nature' existing solely in the audible domain; and he holds that the science must therefore represent it as it appears to the ear, not through a physicist's conception of sounds as movements of the air, since sounds are not heard in that guise, and specifically harmonic or musical properties attach only to what is heard. (This explains, among other things, his treatment of notes as points in a quasi-spatial continuum of pitch accessible to the ear, not, like the Pythagoreans, as magnitudes of some physical variable; for it is not as such magnitudes that notes become elements in melody.) The main task of harmonics is to identify the components of audible $\mu\acute{\epsilon}\lambda o\varsigma$, to abstract the principles governing their relations, and to demonstrate that aesthetic distinctions between melodic and unmelodic sequences and structures are determined by these principles. Harmonics is to be a science of the sort analysed in Aristotle's *Posterior Analytics*: Aristoxenus' conceptions of melodic movement, continuity, space, and much else have an equally Aristotelian pedigree. Books 1–2 discuss basic components and structures (intervals, notes, genera, etc.), and introduce the fundamental principles governing harmonic organization: both books, especially book 2, offer challenging reflections on method. Book 3 derives from the principles a set of theorems about melodic sequences. Gaps exist in all three books, and the third breaks off in mid-flow. Aristoxenus' works on harmonics were very influential: much that is missing from *Harm.* can be reconstructed from later sources, especially *Cleonides, *Baccheius Geron, and *Aristides Quintilianus.

(*b*) Writings on rhythmics. Part of book 2 of an *Elementa Rhythmica* survives. It argues that rhythm is a temporal structure imposed on, not inherent in, what is 'rhythmized' ($\tau\grave{o}\ \dot{\rho}\upsilon\theta\mu\iota\zeta\acute{o}\mu\epsilon\nu o\nu$); and it defines rhythmic forms, by reference to a 'primary duration' ($\pi\rho\hat{\omega}\tau o\varsigma\ \chi\rho\acute{o}\nu o\varsigma$), in terms of the ratio between arsis ($\check{\alpha}\nu\omega\ \chi\rho\acute{o}\nu o\varsigma$, up-beat) and thesis ($\kappa\acute{\alpha}\tau\omega\ \chi\rho\acute{o}\nu o\varsigma$, down-beat). Another fragment on rhythm is *POxy.* 2687: later authors including Baccheius, Aristides Quintilianus, and the 11th-cent. Byzantine Michael *Psellus preserve further Aristoxenian material. A work *On the Primary Duration* is quoted by Porphyry (*On Ptolemy's Harmonics* 78. 21–79. 28).

(*c*) Other works survive only in brief quotations. Musical treatises included *On Music*, *On Melodic Composition* (each in at least four books, Ath. 619d; Porph. *On Ptol. Harm.* 125. 24), *On Listening to Music*, *On Tonoi*, *On Auloi and Instruments*, *On the Boring of Auloi*, *On Auletes*, *On Tragic Poets*, *On Tragic Dancing*, and perhaps *Praxidamanteia*. Aristoxenian passages in the pseudo-Plutarchan *De musica* (see PLUTARCH) show that he worked extensively on musical history.

(*d*) Biographies, including Lives of at least four philosophers, Pythagoras, *Archytas, *Socrates, and *Plato (1). Fragments of the latter two (frs. 25–30, 33) are scurrilous and vituperative; but his work on Pythagoras probably underlies much of the later tradition, and substantial reports about Archytas drawn from *Didymus (3) by *Ptolemy (4) and Porphyry may originate with him.

(*e*) Other writings. Recorded titles demonstrate the variety of Aristoxenus' interests: *Educational Customs* (or 'laws', $\nu\acute{o}\mu o\iota$), *Political Nomoi* in at least eight books (Ath. 648d), *Pythagorean Maxims*, *Historical Notes*, *Brief Notes*, *Miscellaneous Notes* in at least

sixteen books (Phot. *Bibl.* 176), *Random Jottings* ($T\grave{\alpha}\ \sigma\pi o\rho\acute{\alpha}\delta\eta\nu$), *Miscellaneous Table Talk*.

Aristoxenus' assorted memoranda left only minor traces in later historical gossip. In musicology, especially harmonics, he remained authoritative throughout ancient times. Harmonic theory became polarized into two main camps, 'Aristoxenian' and 'Pythagorean', but even Pythagorean and Platonist writers drew freely on his analyses. His conservative attitude to musical history became canonical, and authors of the imperial period still echoed his nostalgia for the pure styles of the Greek 5th cent. long after their sounds had died. See MUSIC §§ 5, 6, 8.

TEXTS, TRANSLATIONS, AND COMMENT Harmonics: good critical text, It. trans., notes, and testimonia, R. da Rios, *Aristoxeni Elementa Harmonica* (1954); text, Ger. trans., and comm., R. Westphal, *Melik und Rhythmik* (1883–93); text, Eng. trans., and comm., H. Macran, *The Harmonics of Aristoxenus* (1902); Fr. trans., C. E. Ruelle, *Collection des auteurs grecs* 1 (1871); Eng. trans. and notes, A. Barker, *Greek Musical Writings* 2 (1989). Rhythmics: texts, Ger. trans., and comm., R. Westphal, *Melik und Rhythmik* (1893); more complete texts and It. trans., G. B. Pighi, *Aristoxeni Rhythmica* (1969); critical texts, with passages from Psellus and elsewhere, Eng. trans., and comm., L. Pearson, *Aristoxenus: Elementa Rhythmica* (1990); Eng. trans. of remnant of *El. Rhythm.* bk. 2, A. Barker, *Greek Musical Writings* 2 (1989). Fragments: F. Wehrli, *Die Schule des Aristoteles* 2 (1945).

FURTHER DISCUSSION L. Laloy, *Aristoxène de Tarente* and *Lexique d'Aristoxène* (1904); A. Barker, *Ancient Philosophy* 1984; A. Bélis, *Aristoxène de Tarente et Aristote* (1986); M. Litchfield, *Journal of Music Theory* 1988.
A. D. B.

Arius (*c*.AD 260–336) was the most important of early Christian heretics. Probably a Libyan by birth and a pupil of Lucian, presbyter of *Antioch (1), he became a leading presbyter at *Alexandria (1). In 318 or 320/1 he began propagating subordinationist views about Christ's person. Controversy flared up, and he was condemned at the council of *Nicaea (1) (325). Though rehabilitated *c*.335 through the influence of Eusebius of Nicomedia, he died shortly after. Three important letters and some fragments of his *Thalia* (verse and prose popularizations of his doctrines) survive. His characteristic teaching was that the Son or Word was a creature, created before time and superior to other creatures, but like them changeable and distinct in essence from the Father. See ARIANISM.

R. Williams, *Arius: Heresy and Tradition* (1987). J. N. D. K.

Arius Didymus (1st cent. BC), of Alexandria (1), philosopher and adviser to *Augustus; *procurator of Sicily. He wrote a now lost consolation for the death of Nero *Claudius Drusus, addressed to *Livia Drusilla. His doxographical work (see DOXOGRAPHERS) is represented by two long fragments on Stoic and Peripatetic ethics, preserved by *Stobaeus (*Ecl.* 7, vol. 2, pp. 37–152 Wachsmuth); fragments on physics were edited by H. Diels (*Dox. Graec.* 445–72).

D. Hahm, *ANRW* 2. 36. 4 (1990), 2935–3055. B. I.

Arkas See ARCAS.

Armenia (see URARTU), a mountainous region of eastern Anatolia, north of Syria and Mesopotamia, bounded on the east by *Media Atropatene (mod. Azerbaijan) and on the west by *Cappadocia and *Commagene. The region, known after *Pompey's settlement of Asia Minor as Greater Armenia, was situated east of the upper *Euphrates, and included in the north extensive areas round Lake Van, along the valley of the river *Araxes (which empties into the Caspian Sea), and north to Lake Sevan (south of the river Kur) and the southern borders of the small kingdom of *Iberia (2) in the lower Caucasus. The great altitude of Armenia insulated the country from its neighbours, especially from the Mesopotamian lowlands. The main point of entry from Mesopotamia was in the SW corner (Sophene: southern Armenia) and from the crossing of the Euphrates at Tomisa in SE Cappadocia. The chief importance of this area for the *Achaemenid kings (and earlier, e.g. Assyrian, rulers) had been levies of horses (and military forces, e.g. Arr. *Anab*. 3. 8. 5; Strabo 11. 14. 9) that the Armenians bred on their pastures. This asset was also exploited by the Seleucids, as attested in the reign of *Antiochus (3) III, whose expedition against Xerxes of southern Armenia (Sophene) (Polyb. 8. 23) both enforced the payment of arrears of tribute and secured the contribution of horses and pack-animals useful for his *anabasis* to the 'Upper Satrapies'. *Xenophon (1) saw and described Armenia after the return of the failed campaign of *Cyrus (2) the Younger to usurp the Achaemenid throne.

Strabo (11. 14. 1–16; 15. 1) indicates that *Alexander (3) the Great ruled it after the Achaemenids, though without military conquest; *Seleucus I claimed possession of 'Armenia' (App. *Syr.* 57). In the northern bloc, it looks as though the old Iranian dynasty of the Orontids may have survived the change from Achaemenid to Seleucid rule. There is little doubt from Antiochus' later handling of the Armenian region (Polyaenus, 4. *Strat.* 17; Polyb. 8. 23) that the kingship was in the Seleucids' gift. From 212 BC, Antiochus III brought north Armenia, after the death of one Orontes, the 'last to rule' (Strabo 11. 14. 11), under direct satrapal rule with the establishment of two satraps, Artaxias (Artaxerxes) and Zariadris. After Antiochus' defeat by Rome (190), they asserted their independence, assuming the royal title. Zariadris was given south Armenia (Sophene), following Xerxes' assassination at Antiochus' behest, for reasons that are unknown, at some point after his confirmation in power (212).

It is probably in the reign of Antiochus III that a group of seven Greek rock inscriptions are to be dated (*c.*200 BC). These are carved on the rock-face of the southern slope of a hill at Armavir (mod. Echmiadian), in the fertile plain of the river Araxes, and include, for example, a fragmentary text referring to *Hesiod, a compilation of extracts of Greek dramatic verses, the official Seleucid calendar, and a letter from a king of the Armadoeiroi (unknown) to 'Orontes, king'. Although the functions of these texts are uncertain, they appear to attest much earlier evidence of patronage of (and learning about) Greek culture in north Armenia than was previously indicated, i.e. the era of the famous Armenian king, *Tigranes (1) II the Great (*c.*95–*c.*56 BC) who was famed in literary sources for his politics of philhellenism (cf. *Tigranocerta).

The imperialistic ambitions of Tigranes and his alliance with *Mithradates VI, king of Pontus, brought him into conflict with Rome; after the campaigns of L. *Licinius Lucullus (2) and *Pompey Armenia became a Roman protectorate. *Augustus, and the emperors who succeeded him, were dedicated to maintaining the *status quo*. Armenia became the subject of a tug-of-war between Rome and *Parthia (and its successor, Sasanid Persia), each seeking to keep control. A dynasty of Arsacid princes founded by *Tiridates (3) generally managed to maintain a balance, remaining Parthian in sympathy while professing friendship to Rome. Trajan temporarily reversed Roman policy by annexing the region.

Meanwhile Lesser Armenia had suffered a bewildering succession of rulers between the time of Pompey and Nero: it was granted by Rome to various neighbouring kings. Under *Deio-

tarus of Galatia in Pompey's day, it was later seized by *Pharnaces II but after *Zela it was given by Caesar to *Ariobarzanes III of Cappadocia (47 BC). Antony (M. *Antonius (2)) gave it to *Polemon (1) I of Pontus (37?) but after Actium Octavian installed *Artavasdes (2), a former king of Media; later, in 20 BC, it went to *Archelaus (5) of Cappadocia. Perhaps annexed by *Tiberius, it was granted by *Gaius (AD 38) to Cotys (grandson of Polemon I of Pontus). On the latter's death it was held by a son of Herod of Chalcis (54–72) and then was incorporated by *Vespasian in the Roman province of Cappadocia.

Armenia was the first kingdom officially to adopt *Christianity, and the new religion and its persecution by the Sasanids fostered a nationalistic spirit. In AD 387 the country was divided between Persia and Byzantium. The Arabs conquered it *c.* AD 653.

Rulers of Armenia Tigranes I, son of Artaxias I; Artavasdes (I) (*c.*114 BC); *Tigranes (1) the Great (*c.*95–*c.*56 BC); *Artavasdes (1) II (*c.*53–34); Artaxes son of Artavasdes (1) (*c.*34–20); *Tigranes (2) III, also son of Artavasdes (1) (*c.*20–6); *Tigranes (3) IV and Erato (*c.*6–1 BC); Ariobarzanes (*c.* AD 2); Addon (*c.* AD 3); Artavasdes III (*c.* AD 4–before 12); Tigranes V (*c.*12–13); Vonones (*c.*14–15/16); Orodes (*c.*15/16–18); Zeno (called Artaxias by Armenians) (18–35); Arsaces, son of Parthian *Artabanus II (AD 33–51/2); *Tiridates (4) (51/2–60); *Tigranes (4) VI (60–3); Tiridates (4), restored (63–after 72); Tiridates (–110); Axidares (110–   ); Meherdates (112); Parthamasiris (113–14); Sanatruces? (113/16); Vologases (116–40); Aurelius Pacorus (–163); Sohaemus (163–5/75?); Tiridates (175?); Tiridates (*c.*215); Arsaces II (*c.*220); Tiridates 'III' (*c.*287–330).

A. Christensen, *L'Iran sous les Sassanides* (1936); C. Burney and D. M. Lang, *The Peoples of the Hills: Ancient Ararat and the Caucasus* (1971); M. Colledge, *Parthian Art* (1977); M. Chaumont, *ANRW* 2. 9. 1. (1978), 71 f.; A. N. Sherwin-White, *Roman Foreign Policy in the East* (1984); M. Schottky, *Media Atropatene und Gross-Armenien in hellenistischer Zeit* (1989); S. Sherwin-White and A. Kuhrt, *From Samarkhand to Sardis* (1993), 190 f.   M. S. D.; E. W. G.; S. S.-W.

armies, Greek and Hellenistic Apart from what little archaeology can tell us, our earliest evidence comes from *Homer, but it is uncertain how far the poems can be taken as depicting real warfare. To some extent, what happens on Homeric battlefields is dictated by the nature of the poetry. However, with the possible exception of those from *Locris (*Il.* 13. 714 ff.), all troops are implied to be of the same type, and there is no cavalry, even the chariots not being organized as a separate force and only rarely being used for a massed charge (e.g. 15. 352 ff.), despite *Nestor's advice (4. 303 ff.). Nestor also recommends subdivision into *phylai* ('tribes') and *phratries (2. 362 f.), and other passages suggest organization into lines and files (e.g. 3. 77, 4. 90), but the constant use of the throwing-spear implies a loose formation except in particular circumstances (e.g. 16. 211 ff.).

By *Tyrtaeus' time, the fundamental distinction between 'heavy' infantry fighting hand-to-hand and 'light', missile-armed infantry, has appeared, at any rate in *Sparta, but the chariot has disappeared, and there is still no cavalry. What organization there is, is based on the three *Dorian *phylai*. Archaeological evidence confirms that by the mid-7th cent. BC *hoplites had appeared, and thereafter, for some three centuries, they dominated the battlefield, though some states (e.g. *Macedonia and *Thessaly) relied more on cavalry and the *Boeotians also had fine cavalry (see HIPPEIS § 2) in addition to hoplites. Some of the less urbanized areas (e.g. *Aetolia) also still tended to make more use of light, missile-armed troops, and all states probably had them. Most armies seem to have been recruited on a local basis. For instance, after the reforms of *Cleisthenes (2), Athenian hoplites were divided into ten units (*taxeis*) based on the ten *phylai*, and the cavalry was similarly divided into two groups of five units.

Most Greek troops were essentially militia. Cavalry and hoplites were drawn from the more well-to-do since they mostly provided their own equipment. Possibly for this reason, there appears to have been little or no training at least until the 4th cent., and very little organization. The smallest unit in the Athenian army, for example, seems to have been a *lochos*, probably consisting of several hundred men, and the same may have been true of the Argive and Theban armies (see ARGOS (2); THEBES (1)).

The exception was Sparta. Not only were Spartan soldiers trained from boyhood (see AGŌGĒ) and liable for service from 20 to 60, but their army was highly organized, giving it an ability to manœuvre that other armies lacked, At the beginning of the 5th cent. it may have consisted of five *lochoi*, but these were possibly already subdivided into *enōmotiai* (cf. Hdt. 1. 65. 5), and by 418 BC at the latest, when there were at least six *lochoi*, possibly twelve, each was subdivided into four *pentēkostyes* and sixteen *enōmotiai*, with a proper chain of command (Thuc. 5. 66. 3, 68. 3).

By *Xenophon (1)'s time the largest unit was the *mora*, of which there were again six, but it is not certain how many subunits each contained. Xenophon (*Respublica Lacedaemoniorum* 11. 4) appears to imply 4 *lochoi*, 8 *pentēkostyes*, and 16 *enōmotiai*, but it is possible that there were really 2, 8, and 32. It is thus also not possible to determine the strength of a *mora*, for which the sources give totals varying from 500 to 1,000: if each contained sixteen *enōmotiai*, its total strength was 640, if thirty-two, 1,280. By Xenophon's time the cavalry was also organized into *morai*, of unknown size, with the rich providing the horses, but not as in other states actually serving.

The Spartan ideal was clearly an army of citizen-hoplites (*homoioi*, lit. 'equals', see SPARTA § 2), but by 425 it appears that they only made up *c*.40 per cent, and there were fewer still by the time of *Leuctra. It is usually assumed that the numbers were made up by *perioikoi, but it is possible that Spartans who had lost their full citizenship (*hypomeiones*) continued to serve in the army, and that the *perioikoi* were always separately brigaded.

The defeat of the Spartan army at Leuctra ushered in a short period of Theban dominance, and saw the beginnings of a new form of warfare, in which the traditional hoplite *phalanx was combined with cavalry and other arms. These changes culminated in the army of *Alexander (3) the Great, but it is possible that the chief innovator was his father, *Philip (1) II. Macedonia had long had good cavalry, known as '*hetairoi' (i.e. 'companions' of the king), but it was possibly Philip who first raised and organized the '*pezetairoi*' or 'foot companions', who, with the '*hypaspistai*' (lit. 'shield-bearers'), possibly derived from the old royal guard, constituted the heavy infantry. By Alexander's time the *pezetairoi* were divided into *taxeis* of 1,500 men, subdivided down to files of sixteen men, though still called 'decads'; the hypaspists into *chiliarchai* of 1,000 men, then possibly subdivided in a similar way to the *pezetairoi*.

But what marked Alexander's army out from its predecessors was the number of different types of unit all interacting with each other—*pezetairoi* and hypaspists, light infantry armed with missiles, heavy and light cavalry. Alexander's conquests owed as much to his soldiers' ability to cope with any situation, as to his own strategic and tactical skills.

Under his successors there was a tendency for the cavalry to decline, with a corresponding increase in the importance of the phalanx. The latter's unwieldiness was sometimes compensated for by interspersing more mobile infantry units among the heavy infantry, notably by *Pyrrhus in his Italian campaigns, and the vulnerability of the phalanx to flank attacks was also sometimes offset by drawing up a second line. But, in the end, the Macedonian-type army proved no match for the Roman *legions, and manpower problems, particularly in Macedonia itself, meant that its kings could not afford to lose even a single battle, whereas the Romans could survive even the most appalling defeats.

J. K. Anderson, *Military Theory and Practice in the Age of Xenophon* (1970); W. K. Pritchett, *Greek State at War*, 1–5 (1971–91); J. F. Lazenby, *The Spartan Army* (1985); A. B. Bosworth, *Conquest and Empire* (1988).

J. F. La.

armies, Roman

Monarchy–3rd cent. AD Traditionally, King Servius *Tullius (*c*.580–530 BC), made the first attempt to channel the resources of the Roman state into military organization by dividing the citizens into wealth groups, so that the weapons they could afford determined their military role, with the richest serving as cavalry. Below these groups were the *capite censi* ('assessed by a headcount'),—men with no property, who were excluded from the army. Military service, therefore, although integral to the duties of citizenship, was also a privilege. This organization of the citizens probably emerged gradually and not through the act of an individual, but there is little clear evidence for the early army until *Polybius (1) in the 2nd cent. BC. By *c*.400 BC a small allowance had been introduced for each soldier to help pay his expenses on active service. The body of infantry was called the *legio* ('levying', *legion) and by 311 had been divided into four legions; these were supported by contingents of Rome's Italian allies (*socii) and subjects, grouped in formations comparable in size to the legions and commanded by Roman officers. Archers and other specialist fighters were supplied by *mercenaries.

The *Punic Wars stretched Roman manpower resources to the limit. The system of recruitment had been designed for a small city-state fighting short annual campaigns in Italy. Rome now waged long wars, sometimes overseas, and after the defeat of *Carthage in 201 BC, began to acquire provinces that needed a permanent military presence. Consequently, there was a reduction in the property qualification for military service. The annual levy selected citizens of military age (17–46), who were expected to serve for up to six consecutive campaigns but be available for enlistment for up to sixteen years, or ten years in the case of a cavalryman. The army was commanded by the chief magistrates, the consuls.

Throughout the 2nd cent. there was increasing discontent with the levy as Rome faced a series of foreign wars, and the property qualification was further reduced. Then in 107 BC the consul C. *Marius (1) extended this practice by accepting volunteers from the propertyless and had them equipped at the state's expense for the war in Africa (see JUGURTHA). Undoubtedly conscription along the normal lines still continued, but many volunteers probably chose to serve for sixteen years, and this contributed to the development of a professional, long-term army. The consequences of the *Social War (3) (91–87 BC) were also far-reaching, since Rome's defeated Italian allies were absorbed into the citizen body, significantly increasing the reservoir of manpower. Non-Italians now provided auxiliary forces of cavalry (see AUXILIA). But the state had no policy of granting appropriate discharge payments to its troops. Generals, often holding long-term commands, used their reputation, and promises of generous benefits, to recruit men with whom they then built up a personal rapport. Increasingly soldiers owed their allegiance to their commander rather than to the Roman state, and became instruments of violent political change. The precedent set by *Sulla in 88 BC of seizing power by military might was not to be expunged, and the republic succumbed to the rival mercenary armies of military dynasts.

*Augustus united these fragmented legions in loyalty to his person and created a fully professional, standing army. This was not revolutionary in itself, but his detailed provision for the troops' service conditions and emoluments (see AERARIUM; STIPENDIUM; VETERANS), the incorporation of the non-citizen *auxilia* into the formal military structure, the establishment of a personal bodyguard (*praetorians), the permanent policing of Rome (see COHORTES URBANAE), and the apportionment of legions and *auxilia* as permanent garrisons of individual provinces, shaped Roman military thinking until the 3rd cent. AD and made military organization an integral part of imperial policy. The most striking development in the command of the Roman army was that from the end of the 1st cent. AD onwards, the emperor, who in his nomenclature and public portrayal bore the attributes of a Roman general, took personal charge of all major campaigns.

H. M. D. Parker, *The Roman Legions*, 2nd edn. (1958); R. E. Smith, *Service in the Post-Marian Roman Army* (1958); J. Harmand, *L'Armée et le soldat à Rome de 107 à 50 avant notre ère* (1967); G. R. Watson, *The Roman Soldier* (1969); P. Connolly, *The Roman Army* (1975); E. Luttwak, *The Grand Strategy of the Roman Empire* (1976); J. C. Mann, *JRS* 1979, 175; L. Keppie, *The Making of the Roman Army* (1984); G. Webster, *The Roman Imperial Army*, 3rd edn. (1985); Y. Le Bohec, *L'Armée romaine* (1989).

J. B. C.

Late empire The army of the late empire is brilliantly described by *Ammianus Marcellinus, and its order of battle (c.AD 395) survives in the *Notitia Dignitatum, but its evolution is obscure. As pressure upon the frontiers grew, *Septimius Severus increased the number of legions and, by recruiting the praetorian guard from them, protected himself from other usurpers and formed a strategic reserve. This was supplemented on campaign by the usual frontier detachments. Emperors assumed personal command and, if they proved incompetent like *Severus Alexander, the army replaced them. Promotion of professional soldiers culminated in *Gallienus' exclusion of senators from military service, and the premium on mobility in his creation of a separate cavalry force.

This 'élite', as *Aurelian's army is called, was used by *Diocletian to reinforce frontier armies now increasingly commanded by professional *duces* (see DUX). But despite his emphasis on fixed defences, Diocletian retained a small mobile army of new units like the *comites* cavalry and the *Ioviani* and *Herculiani* legions. Units though numerous were comparatively small, and were conscripted from German prisoners and volunteers, as well as from soldiers' sons and peasants. Soldiers still received a cash *stipendium*, but it was supplemented by free rations and regular donatives (see DONATIVUM) in gold and silver. *Constantine I, however, was the true innovator who greatly enlarged the mobile army with new units like the Germanic *auxilia and by reducing the frontier armies. He disbanded the praetorian guard, and replaced its prefects as his lieutenants-general with a master of infantry (*magister militum*) and a master of cavalry (*magister equitum*). He created the distinctive strategy of the 4th cent.— frontiers garrisoned by *limitanei*, *comitatenses held in reserve— which was crippled by the Goths' defeat of *Valens at Adrianople (378). So many *comitatenses* were lost here that the western empire was ultimately unable to preserve the logistic base its army required.

Jones, *Later Rom. Emp.* ch. 17; D. Hoffmann, *Das Spätrömische Bewegungsheer* (1969–70); E. N. Luttwak, *Grand Strategy of the Roman Empire* (1976); R. S. O. Tomlin, in J. Hackett (ed.), *Warfare in the Ancient World* (1989), and in *Guinness Encyclopaedia of Warfare* (1991), 46 ff.

R. S. O. T.

Armilustrium, Roman festival on 19 October to *Mars which purified (see LUSTRATION) the army (Varro, *Ling.* 5. 153, 6. 22); this took place at the *Aventine's Armilustrium (Livy 27. 37. 4, Plut. *Rom.* 23. 3), which contained an altar (Festus 17 Lindsay), and involved the *Salii. Perhaps connected with the *Quinquatrus (19 March), which opened the campaign season: Wissowa, *Ges. Abh.* 165 ff.

Latte, *RR* 120; *Inscr. Ital.* 13. 2. 523.

C. R. P.

Arminius (*RE* 1, with Suppl. 1, p. 139), born c.19 BC, war-chief of the *Cherusci, son of Sigimer. He had Roman citizenship, and served long in the auxiliary forces, attaining equestrian rank. In AD 9 he lured P. *Quinctilius Varus with three legions into difficult country near the saltus *Teutoburgiensis between Ems and Lippe (Tac. *Ann.* 1. 60. 3; Barenau-Wiehengebirge and the neighbourhood of Detmold have been canvassed) and destroyed them. In 15 he fought Segestes, leader of the pro-Roman faction, whose daughter Thusnelda he had married. Segestes was helped by *Germanicus and Thusnelda fell into Roman hands. In 16, though beaten by Germanicus and wounded, Arminius again thwarted Roman expansion. In 17, helped by the Semnones and Langobardi, he weakened the neutral king *Maroboduus but was deserted by his uncle Inguiomerus; when he aspired to kingship, he faced rebellion. *Tiberius rejected the offer of a Chattan (see CHATTI) chief to poison him in 19, but he was soon killed by his own kinsfolk. He was a prudent tactician and a master of surprise attack, whose greatness was recognized by *Tacitus (1): 'beyond doubt the liberator of Germany' (*Ann.* 2. 88). Much has been written, but little established, about his name, the period of his service in the Roman forces, and the exact site of the defeat of Varus: there are no solid grounds for the improbable suggestion that it gave rise to the legend of Siegfried.

Strabo 291 f.; Vell. Pat. 2. 118 f.; Tac. *Ann.* 1 f.; Cass. Dio 56. 19–22. L. Schmidt, *Gesch. d. deutschen Stämme* 1, 2nd edn. (1938), 100 ff.; K. Weerth, *Über neue Arminius- und Varusforschungen* (1951); H. Glaesener, *LEC* 1954, 31 ff.; O. Höffer, *Siegfried, Arminius und die Symbolik* (1961); E. Thompson, *The Early Germans* (1965), see index; von Petrikovits, *BJ* 1966, 175 ff.; D. Timpe, *Arminius-Studien* (1970).

A. M.; T. J. Ca.; B. M. L.

arms and armour

Greek Most Homeric references to arms and armour are best interpreted in connection with Minoan and Mycenaean armaments, known from such representations as those on the shaft-grave daggers (see MYCENAE). The characteristic armour here is a figure-of-eight-shaped shield made from a single ox-hide and swung from the neck by a strap. The only other protection was a helmet. The chief weapon was a long rapier-like sword. Towards the end of the bronze age this style was displaced by the use of a much smaller round shield carried on the arm; a change which involved the addition of a breastplate and greaves, while the sword became shorter and was used for cut as well as thrust. In the Homeric poems the champions begin by throwing spears at each other, and when these are gone they proceed to close combat with swords.

The standing type of the Archaic and Classical soldier was the *hoplite, ultimately derived from the soldier of the transition to the iron age. The trend now was towards heavier armour and fighting based on weight of manpower. Shields were made of bronze and leather, and spears and swords of iron. In addition hoplites wore breastplates, greaves, and helmets as defensive armour. The spear as used by hoplites and cavalry (see HIPPEIS § 2) had become a pike for thrusting, not throwing, and was usually some 2 m. (c. 7 ft.) in length. Only light-armed troops and some light cavalry used instead the throwing-spear (ἀκόντιον). Along with the use of the spear as a pike, the sword (at least of the Athenian hoplite) had developed a short, straight-edged blade; it could only be used for very close fighting.

The 4th cent. saw the evolution of a more flexible type of equipment than the hoplite's. Experiments were first made with the *peltast, but the final change was the establishment of the Macedonian type as employed in the *phalanx. The spear (σάρισα) was increased still more in length to a maximum of just over 5 m. (17 ft.), and the shield reduced to a small target carried on the arm. The different ranks of the phalanx used different lengths of spear. The equipment for light-armed infantry and light- and heavy-armed cavalry was also specialized at this period. At all periods, soldiers competed over the excellence of their armour (e.g. Thuc. 6. 31. 3), some of which might be highly decorated. See WAR, ART OF, GREEK.

A. M. Snodgrass, *Early Greek Armour and Weapons* (1964), *JHS* 1965, 110 ff. (hoplite), and *Arms and Armour of the Greeks* (1967).

H. W. P.; M. V.

Roman Artistic representations, military treatises, other literary and subliterary references, and archaeological artefacts are the main sources of information. Pre-imperial artefacts are sparse and come mainly from siege sites. Imperial finds are most plentiful, associated mainly with ordered dismantlement-deposits in frontier installations. Late Roman equipment is again sparse, final site-abandonments being less ordered. Roman military equipment represented a constantly evolving and adapting *mélange* of cultural traits.

In the regal and early republican periods the Roman infantry was equipped on the Greek *hoplite model. A long thrusting-spear (*hasta*) was the chief offensive weapon, and the defensive armour varied with individual wealth, the richest men having cuirasses (*loricae*), round shields, greaves, and helmets of Greek or Italic form.

By the mid-2nd cent. BC, however, the heavy javelin (*pilum*) replaced the *hasta* in the first two legionary lines (*hastati* and *principes*; see LEGION). A short sword was used for close fighting, a Spanish form of which became dominant. Men of all three lines carried a long, curving, oval shield of Italic origin with a Celtic boss and central spine. Helmets were of the Celtic 'Montefortino' type. A bronze plate (*pectorale*) was worn by the poorer soldiers, and a coat of mail (*lorica hamata*) by the richest. The legionary light infantry (*velites*) had a small round shield, light javelins, sword, and helmet. The legionary cavalry wore a helmet and cuirass, and carried a round shield and spear. The allies (*socii*) were probably armed in corresponding fashion. During the last century of the republic (if not before) the *pilum* became universal for legionary infantry, a change associated perhaps with cohort organization (see COHORS), relaxing property qualifications, and increased state equipment supply.

In the first two centuries AD new forms of helmets developed

from Celtic models. The legionary shield continued to be large and curving, but oval, sub-oval, and rectangular variants were in contemporary use. Scale, mail, and articulated-plate cuirasses were current. The latter (modern usage: 'lorica segmentata') consisted of steel plates articulated on leather strips, and developed from the first half of the 1st cent. AD into the 3rd. Additional arm- and leg-armour was also sometimes worn. Spears and light javelins were carried by some legionaries instead of *pila*, and all continued with the short sword. Auxiliary infantry and cavalry (see AUXILIA) were also armoured in mail or scale (not plate), but large flat shields of varying shapes were carried. Infantry used short swords, cavalry the long Celtic *spatha*. The majority carried spears and/or javelins, while specialist units carried composite bows or lances (cavalry). Horsemen used Celtic saddlery, wore special helmet types, and had sports armour for training and displays.

The 3rd cent. saw distinctions between legionary and auxiliary and infantry and cavalry equipment disappear—all now carried slightly dished, oval shields (not curved), and wore mail or scale (the 'lorica segmentata' eventually going out of use). Cavalry helmet forms were adopted by infantry. The legionary *pilum* was generally replaced by a variety of spears and light javelins. Short swords continued in use but *spathae* took over as the main bladed weapon.

Increased emphasis on cavalry involved the use of heavily armoured mounted troops (*catafractarii, clibanarii*) on the Parthian/Sasanid model. Into the late Roman period infantry continued to be armoured; some troops carried flat, round Germanic shields; but a major change came with the introduction of simple, mass-produced infantry and cavalry 'Ridge' helmets *c.* AD 300.

In all periods the *mercenaries, allies, native levies, etc, valued for their specialized fighting skills, used their own ethnic military equipment.

Military status, especially during the imperial period, was defined by the right to carry arms and especially by military waist-belts. Fittings on the latter constantly evolved but were usually decorative and noisy.

Equipment was manufactured in cities and was largely a matter of individual acquisition and ownership before the 1st cent. BC. Thereafter, the state organized production, manufacture, and supply (individual ownership continued in the Principate), based principally on legionary *fabricae* and craftsmen. Army expansion necessitated the establishment of additional, city-based, state arms factories from *c.* AD 300 onwards.

P. Connolly, *Greece and Rome at War* (1981); L. Keppie, *The Making of the Roman Army* (1984); M. C. Bishop and J. C. N. Coulston, *Roman Military Equipment from the Punic Wars to the Fall of Rome* (1993); *Journal of Roman Military Equipment Studies*. J. C. N. C.

Arnobius, a teacher of rhetoric at *Sicca Veneria in Proconsular Numidia, said by *Jerome to have taught *Lactantius and to have suddenly become a Christian (c.295); see CHRISTIANITY. A year or two later, at his bishop's instance, he wrote seven books, *Adversus nationes*, as a proof of full conversion. He attacked those who argued, like the later opponents of Augustine, that 'ever since the Christians have been on earth, the world has gone to ruin' (*Adv. nat.* 1. 1), and that Christ was a mortal magician, not superior to *Apollonius (12) of Tyana or *Zoroaster (1. 52–3). His answer, although conventional in tenor, is not so in content, since he amasses much valuable antiquarian learning, designed to prove that Roman institutions were subject to change, and that therefore Christianity was not bad because it was new. Incidentally he reveals something of pagan beliefs current in Africa. He does not look for prefiguration of the Gospel even in the Old Testament. His attack on the *viri novi* in book 2 shows him abreast of recent developments in Platonism (see NEOPLATONISM); but, while he cites several dialogues and applauds *Plato (1)'s notion of God, he (characteristically) rejects the hypothesis of innate ideas. His own teaching on the soul may be of Stoic origin (see STOICISM). He cites the New Testament little, and indeed, apart from hope of his soul's salvation through Christ and his hostility to pagansim, Arnobius shows little trace of Christian theology. Writing before the council of Nicaea, he speaks of Christ as a secondary deity. His easy and fluent Latin yields the first use of the word *deitas* and of *atheus* as applied to Christianity.

EDITIONS A. Reifferscheid, *CSEL* 4; C. Marchesi (1934); H. Le Bonniec (1982–).

LITERATURE P. Monceaux, *Histoire littéraire de l'Afrique chrétienne* 3 (1906), 241 ff.; F. Gabarrou, *Le Latin d'Arnobe* (1921); H. Hagendahl, *La Prose métrique d'Arnobe* (1937); A.-J. Festugière, in *Mém. Lagrange* (1949), and *Vig. Chr.* 1952; P. Courcelle, *Rev. Ét. Grec.* 1953, and in A. Momigliano (ed.), *The Conflict between Paganism and Christianity in the Fourth Century* (1963), ch. 7.   W. H. C. F.; M. J. E.

Arpi, in Italy, Argos Hippion or Argyrippa, the largest of the *Daunian cities, in the Tavoliere of Apulia. It was in existence from at least as early as the 6th cent. BC, and made a treaty with Rome in 326 BC (Livy 9. 13). Thenceforth it flourished. It surrendered to *Hannibal, who wintered there in 215 BC, and lost its port when the Romans built the colony of *Sipontum in 194 BC. It then went into decline, and was of little significance by imperial times. Excavations have revealed extensive buildings of the Hellenistic period, with 13 km. (8 mi.) of defences.

G. D. B. J.; T. W. P.

Arpinum, in Italy, a Volscian hill-town (see VOLSCI) in the *Liris valley, modern Arpino, with interesting polygonal walls. Rome captured Arpinum from its Samnite conquerors and gave it *civitas sine suffragio* (see CITIZENSHIP, ROMAN), 305–303 BC (Diod. Sic. 20. 90; Livy 9. 44, 10. 1). After 188 it enjoyed full citizenship, being administered as a *praefectura* and, after 90, as a *municipium* (Livy 38. 36; Festus 262 Lindsay; Cic. *Planc.* 20). Subsequently Arpinum is seldom mentioned. *C. Marius (1) and *Cicero were both born on its territory (Juv. 8. 237 f.); remains, possibly of Cicero's villa, still exist nearby.

L. Ippoliti, *Il luogo di nascita di Marco Tullio Cicerone* (1936), with bibliography; Castagnoli, *Stud. urb.* 21 ff.   E. T. S.; D. W. R. R.

Arrhephoria Athenian festival, at which a rite is performed by the *arrhēphoroi*, two or four girls between the ages of 7 and 11, chosen by the *basileus* (see ARCHONTES) to serve *Athena Polias (cf. e.g. schol. Ar. *Lys.* 642; Harp. entry under 'arrhēphorein'; *Suda*, 'arrhēphoria'; *Etym. Magn.* 149, 14–23). They lived on the *Acropolis, they played a ritual game of ball, and they participated in the weaving of the *peplos* offered to Athena at the *Panathenaea. They helped the priestess of Athena Polias. At the Chalkeia they and the priestess set up the loom for the *peplos*. They are probably represented with the priestess in the central scene on the *Parthenon frieze. At the rite marking the end of their service (Paus. 1. 27. 3), at night, they put on their heads covered baskets given them by the priestess who knew no more than the girls what they contained, and through an underground passage they descended to the precinct of *Aphrodite in the Gardens, where they left what they were carrying and took and brought to the Acropolis something else covered up. After this they were replaced by others. This rite is thought to have originated in an initiatory ritual; but it is also possible that it may always have been a cultic office limited to a selected few, though connected with a particular age band and the transition out of it.

Deubner, *Attische Feste* 9–15; A. Brelich, *Paides e parthenoi* (1969), 231–7, 268–70; E. Simon, *Festivals of Attica* (1983), 39–46; H. W. Parke, *Festivals of the Athenians* (1977), 141–3; Burkert, *HN* 150–4, and *Wilder Ursprung* (1990), 40–59; P. Brulé, *La fille d'Athènes* (1987), 83–99, 118–23.   C. S.-I.

Arretium (mod. Arezzo) north-easternmost of the cities of Etruria (see ETRUSCANS) and one of the latest founded. It is not certain when it passed under Roman rule, but in the 3rd cent. BC it was an important base for Roman operations in north Italy, and it acquired additional importance in the mid-2nd cent. from the construction of the *via Cassia, of which it was the first terminal. It became a *municipium in the 2nd cent. BC and a colony under Sulla, and again under Caesar. From it comes a fine series of archaic and later bronzes, notably the Chimaera (cf. also Livy 28. 45, where Arretium supplies large quantities of bronze weapons for *Scipio Africanus' African expedition); and for nearly a century after *c.*30 BC its red-gloss table wares, both plain and relief-moulded, dominated the markets of the Roman world (see POTTERY, ROMAN).

BTCGI 3 (1984), entry under 'Arezzo'   J. B. W.-P.; D. W. R. R.

Arria (1) (*RE* 39) the Elder, the wife of A. Caecina Paetus, celebrated for her courage and self-control. Thus when her husband was condemned by *Claudius for his part in the conspiracy of L. *Arruntius Camillus Scribonianus (AD 42), she stabbed herself and, handing him the dagger, said, 'It doesn't hurt, Paetus' (Plin. *Ep.* 3. 16; Mart. 1. 13).   A. M.; M. T. G.

Arria (2) (*RE* 40) the Younger, daughter of *Arria (1), was wife of P. *Clodius Thrasea Paetus, mother of Fannia (who became the wife of *Helvidius Priscus), and relative of *Persius. She wished to die beside her condemned husband in AD 66 but he dissuaded her. Banished by *Domitian, she returned to Rome under *Nerva, and died in the reign of *Trajan, mourned by her friend *Pliny (2) the Younger in *Ep.* 7. 19. 9–10.   A. M.; M. T. G.

Arrian (Lucius Flavius Arrianus), *c.* AD 86–160. Born in *Nicomedia in *Bithynia, he held local office and pursued studies with *Epictetus, whose lectures he later published (allegedly verbatim) as the *Discourses* and summarized in the *Encheiridion* ('Manual'). In Greece between 108 and 112 he attracted the friendship of *Hadrian, who later adlected him to senatorial rank (see ADLECTION) and after his consulate (?129) employed him for six years (131–7) as legate of *Cappadocia. Subsequently he retired to Athens, where he held the archonship (145/6), and perhaps survived into the reign of Marcus *Aurelius.

One of the most distinguished writers of his day, Arrian represented himself as a second *Xenophon (1) and adopted a style which fused elements of Xenophon into a composite, artificial (yet outstandingly lucid) diction based on the great masters, *Herodotus (1) and *Thucydides (2). The *Cynegeticus* is an explicit revision of Xenophon's monograph in the light of the revolution in *hunting brought by the Celtic greyhound; and Xenophon's influence is demonstrable in the short essays he wrote in Cappadocia: the *Periplus* (*c.*131), the *Essay on Tactics* (136/7), and, most remarkable, the *Order of Battle against the Alans*, which expounds his tactics to repel the incursion of the *Alans (135) in the style of Xenophon's *Cyropaedia*.

Arrius Antoninus

Celebrated as a philosopher in his lifetime, Arrian is today principally known as a historian. Works now lost include the eight-book *Bithyniaca*, the history of his native province from mythical times to its annexation by Rome, and the seventeen-book *Parthica* with its detailed narrative of *Trajan's campaigns (probably the source for *Cassius Dio). His most famous work deals with the age of *Alexander (3) the Great. The period after Alexander's death (323–319 BC) was covered expansively in the ten books of *Affairs after Alexander* (significant fragments of which survive on palimpsest and papyrus). The only extant history is the so-called *'Anabasis of Alexander'*, a history of Alexander the Great in seven books from his accession to his death. A short companion piece, the *Indike*, provides a digest of Indian memorabilia, based explicitly upon *Megasthenes, *Eratosthenes, and *Nearchus, and recounts Nearchus' voyage from south India to *Susa. Arrian's work is conceived as a literary tribute to Alexander's achievements, to do for him what *Homer had done for *Achilles, and the tone is eulogistic, mitigating standard criticisms and culminating in a panegyric of extraordinary intensity. The sources Arrian selected were *Ptolemy (1) I and *Aristobulus (1), contemporaries and actors in the events and appropriately favourable to Alexander; and the narrative is in the main worked up from material they provided, supplemented by *logoi* ('stories'), mostly from late rhetorical sources and chosen for their colour. Arrian's priority was excellence of style, not factual accuracy. Consequently his account is rich in detail and eminently readable, but is marred by demonstrable errors and misunderstandings.

TEXTS A. G. Roos, rev. G. Wirth (Teubner, 1967); P. A. Brunt (Loeb, 1976–83).

STUDIES P. A. Stadter, *Arrian of Nicomedia* (1980); A. B. Bosworth, *A Historical Commentary on Arrian's History of Alexander* (1980, 1995), and *From Arrian to Alexander* (1988); H. Tonnet, *Recherches sur Arrien* (1988).

A. B. B.

Arrius (*RE* 9) **Antoninus,** maternal grandfather of the emperor *Antoninus Pius, was suffect consul in AD 69, proconsul of Asia under *Vespasian, and consul again in 97 under his friend, the emperor *Nerva. He is addressed in three letters by the younger *Pliny, who says that his Greek verses recalled *Callimachus (3) and *Herodas. Probably, like his son-in-law Aurelius Fulvus, he came from *Nemausus: his wife Boionia Procilla, to judge from her *gentilicium*, was of Celtic origin.

PIR[2] A 1086; Syme, *Tacitus*, app. 32, 87. G. E. F. C.

Arrius (*RE* 36) **Varus,** a Roman knight, served with distinction as *praefectus cohortis* under *Corbulo, but later is said to have defamed his old commander to Nero. In AD 69, when a *primipilus* in one of the Danubian legions, he lent vigorous help to M. *Antonius Primus on the Flavian side in the invasion of Italy, being rewarded after the final victory with the office of *praefectus praetorio*. C. *Licinius Mucianus, however, soon arrived at Rome, put a check upon his ambitions (cf. the treatment of Antonius Primus), and reduced him to the post of *praefectus *annonae*. He is not heard of afterwards. R. S.

Ar(r)uns, the Latinized form of a common Etruscan *praenomen*, widely attested in Etruscan inscriptions in the form *arnθ*. A legendary Arruns appears in the *Aeneid* (11. 759 f.) among the Etruscan allies of *Aeneas, and several Etruscans of this name figure in historical accounts of early Rome (e.g. Livy 2. 14. 5, 5. 33. 3; see ETRUSCANS). T. J. Co.

Arruntius (1) (*RE* 7), **Lucius,** of non-senatorial family from

Atina, was proscribed in 43 BC (see PROSCRIPTION), but escaped to Sextus *Pompeius. He returned to Italy in 39 after the treaty of *Misenum and commanded a division of *Octavian's fleet at *Actium. An able orator, Arruntius also wrote a history of the (First?) *Punic War in Sallustian style (see SALLUST). He made a resplendent marriage, was consul in 22 BC, and as *quindecimvir sacris faciundis* took part in the *Ludi Saeculares* (see SECULAR GAMES) in 17. In spite of his wealth Arruntius was noted for his simple, severe life.

T. P. Wiseman, *New Men in the Roman Senate 139 BC–14 AD* (1971); Syme, *AA*, see indexes; Peter, *HRRel*. 2. 41 f.; Schanz–Hosius 2. 327 ff.

G. W. R.; B. M. L.

Arruntius (2) (*RE* 8), **Lucius,** consul AD 6 and son of *Arruntius (1), also an orator. Wealth, connections, energy, accomplishments, and integrity made him one of the most influential senators of his time, but the story that *Augustus, on his deathbed, said that he was both worthy of the supreme power and capable, if the chance came, of seizing it, is a later fiction. Arruntius aroused the enmity of *Tiberius' ministers, but enjoyed the trust of Tiberius himself. Appointed governor of Nearer Spain, he was allowed to remain in Rome and administer his province by legates (see LEGATI) for ten or more years (from 23?). In 31 a charge brought against him by creatures of *Sejanus, was quashed; in 37, accused of *maiestas and adultery through the contrivance of *Macro and without the knowledge of Tiberius, he committed suicide. L. *Arruntius Camillus Scribonianus was his son by adoption.

Syme, *Tacitus* 380 f., 442 f., and *AA*, see index. T. J. C.; B. M. L.

Arruntius (*RE* 14) **Camillus Scribonianus, Lucius,** consul AD 32. Adopted son of L. *Arruntius (2), and descended from *Sulla and *Pompey, he was legate of *Dalmatia under *Gaius (1) and *Claudius. In 42, instigated by *Annius Vinicianus and many senators and knights, he persuaded his legions, VII and XI, to revolt. After four days they abandoned him and his watchwords 'liberty and the republic'. He was murdered; accomplices were tried in the senate and executed; the legions received the titles 'Claudia Pia Fidelis'.

Syme, *AA*; B. Levick, *Claudius* (1990), see indexes. J. P. B.; B. M. L.

Arruntius (*RE* 16) **Celsus,** grammatical authority of uncertain date (before mid-3rd cent. AD) cited by *Iulius Romanus (in Charisius), *Diomedes (3), *Consentius, *Priscian, and (perhaps) the scholiasts (see SCHOLIA) to Virgil's *Georgics*.

PIR[2] A 1141; Kaster, *Guardians* 390; Herzog–Schmidt, § 392. R. A. K.

Arruntius (*RE* 21) **Scribonianus, Lucius (Furius),** son of L. *Arruntius Camillus Scribonianus but spared by *Claudius, claimed descent from Pompeius Magnus, i.e. *Pompey (*ILS* 976), and was banished in AD 52 for consulting astrologers on Claudius' fate. He died soon after.

B. Levick, *Claudius* (1990), see index. J. P. B.; B. M. L.

Arruntius (*RE* 26) **Stella, Lucius,** *suffect consul AD 101 or 102 (*CIL* 6. 1492; Mart. 12. 3. 10). Born in Padua (*Patavium), he became *quindecimvir sacris faciundis* and was in charge (as aedile?) of the celebrations for *Domitian's Dacian triumph in 89 (Stat. *Silv.* 1. 2. 177 ff.) and (as praetor?) of those for the return of Domitian from the Sarmatian campaign in 93 (Mart. 8. 78). Rich and cultured, he was the chief figure in non-imperial literary *patronage in the Flavian period. He was a friend and patron both of *Martial, who mentions him in nineteen epigrams (from AD 85–6 to 102) and of *Statius, who dedicates to him the first book of the *Silvae* and a long epithalamium for his marriage to the rich Neapolitan widow Violentilla (*Silv.* 1. 2). He wrote love elegies celebrating Violentilla under the name of Asteris, and poems in imitation of *Catullus (Stat. *Silv.* 1. 2, Mart. 1. 7, 5. 11, 7. 14. 5 f.)

PIR[2] A 1151; P. White, *Harv. Stud.* 1975.   M. Ci.

ars, Gk. *technē*, 'art', came to have the concrete sense 'treatise'. Handbooks whose titles incorporated this word were often concerned with grammar or rhetoric. *Ovid's *Ars amatoria* playfully extended the genre. *Horace's *Ars poetica* is first so named by *Quintilian (8. 3. 60).

M. Fuhrmann, *Das systematische Lehrbuch* (1960).   M. W.

Arsacids, the Iranian royal dynasty with its original centre in *Parthia, ruling *c*.250 BC–AD 224; named after the tribal chieftain Arsaces, who had invaded the former Seleucid satrapy of Parthia from the north and killed its independent ruler Andragoras. Arsaces' kingly successors later claimed descent from, and the political heritage of, the *Achaemenids. They successfully drove the *Seleucids from Iran and Mesopotamia and from 92 BC on were neighbours and rivals to Rome on the Euphrates–Armenian border. Despite temporary successes in their fights against Rome and the nomad invasions from the north-east and their—on the whole—prudent policy towards their ethnically, socially, and culturally diverse groups of subjects, their power was again and again threatened or weakened by dynastic conflicts and quarrels with the higher aristocracy, ambitious governors, and 'vassal' kings. Although able to secure a status quo in foreign affairs, Arsacid rule in Iran and Mesopotamia was brought to an end by the former petty kings of Persis of the dynasty of the *Sasanids who successfully rebelled against the last Parthian king Artabanus IV. Members of the Arsacid clan were—with occasional interruptions—kings of Armenia until AD 428.

List of Parthian kings Arsaces I, *c*.247–217 BC; Arsaces II, 217–191; Priapitius, 191–176; Phraates I, 176–171; Mithradates I, 171–139/8; Phraates II, 139/8–128; Artabanus I, 128–124/3; Mithradates II, 124/3–88/7; Gotarzes I, 91/0–81/0; Orodes I, 81/0–76/5; Sinatruces, 78/7 (?)–71/0; Phraates III, 71/0–58/7; Mithradates III, 58/7; *Orodes II, 58/7–38; *Phraates (1) IV, 38–3/2; *Phraates (2) V, 2 BC–AD 2; Orodes III, 4–6; Vonones I, 8/9; *Artabanus II, 10/1–38; Vardanes I, 38–45; Gotarzes II, 43/4–51; Vonones II, 51; *Vologeses I, 51–76/80; Pacorus II, 77/8–114/5; Vologeses II, 77/8; Artabanus III, 79–81; Osroes, 108/9–27/8; Vologeses III, 111/2–47/8; Vologeses IV, 147/8–91/2; Vologeses V, 191/2–207/8; Vologeses VI, 207/8–226; Artabanus IV, 213–24. Tiridates, brother and successor to Arsaces I (Arr. *Parthica* fr. 1), is legendary.

SOURCES Inscriptions—Ostraca from Nisa: I. M. Diakonov and V. A. Livsic, *Dokumenty iz Nisy* 1 (1960); I. M. Diakonoff and V. A. Livshits, *Parthian Economic Documents from Nisa* (1976–9). Papyri and Parchments from Dura: C. B. Welles (ed.) *Excavations at Dura-Europos: Final Reports* 5/1 (1959). Avroman Parchments: E. H. Minns, *JHS* 1915, 22 ff. Other inscriptions: cf. P. Gignoux, *Glossaire des Inscriptions Pehlevies et Parthes* (1972), 43 f.; Heracles with inscription from Seleucia: D. S. Potter, *ZPE* 88 (1991).
Coins: M. Alram, *Enc. Ir.* 3 (1989), 536 ff.; D. G. Sellwood, *An Introduction to the Coinage of Parthia* 2 (1980).
Archaeology: K. Schippmann, *Enc. Ir.* 2 (1987), 297 ff.; M. A. R. Colledge, *The Parthian Period* (1986); T. S. Kawami, *Monumental Art of the Parthian Period in Iran* (1987).
Classical texts: App. *BCiv.* 2. 83. 110, 4. 88. 133; *Mith.* 15, 87, 104, 106, 117; *Syr.* 51, 65, 67 f, 359; Arr. *Parthica* (fr.); Cass. Dio *passim*; Isid.

Charac. *Stat. Parthica.*; Joseph. *AJ passim*; *BJ passim*; Lucian, *Hist. conscr.* esp. 15, 18–21, 29, 31, 37 f, 40; Philostr. *VA* 1. 21, 28, 31; Plut. esp. *Ant.*, *Crass.*, *Pomp.*; Polyb. 10. 28–31; Strab. esp. bks. 6, 11, 14–16; Amm. Marc. 6. 23 f., 23. 6. 2–6, 24 5. 3; Hor. *Carm. passim*; Epist. *passim*; Just. *Epit.* esp. bks. 12, 32, 36, 38 f. 41 f.; Oros. bks. 5–7; Pliny, *HN* bks. 2, 6, 30; Tac. *Ann.* esp. bks. 2, 6, 11, 14; Vell. Pat. 2. 24, 78, 82, 91, 100 f.
Chinese texts: F. Hirth, *China and the Roman Orient* (1885); J. J. M. de Groot, *Chinesische Urkunden zur Geschichte Asiens* (1921–6).
Babylonian cuneiform texts: cf. J. Oelsner, *Materialien zur babylonischen Gesellschaft und Kultur in hellenistischer Zeit* (1986); K. Kessler, *MDAI (B)* 1984, 273 ff.
GENERAL HISTORIES N. C. Debevoise, *Political History of Parthia* (1938); K. Schippmann, *Grundzüge der parthischen Geschichte* (1980); M. Karras-Klapproth, *Prosopographische Studien zur Geschichte des Partherreiches* (1988).
Parthia and Rome: K. H. Ziegler, *Die Beziehungen zwischen Rom und dem Partherreich* (1964); E. Dabrowa, *La Politique de l'état parthe à l'égard de Rome* (1983).   J. Wi.

Arsameia Name of two cities in *Commagene: (1) Arsameia by the Euphrates (mod. Gerger); (2) Arsameia by the Nymphaeus (mod. Eski Kahta), identified by remarkable inscriptions (with a rock relief) recording the tomb and cult centre (*hierothesion*) set up for his father, Mithradates Callinicus, by Antiochus I of Commagene (see ANTIOCHUS (9); NEMRUT DAĞ).

F. K. Dörner and others, *Arsameia am Nymphaios* (1963); E. Akurgal, *Ancient Civilizations and Ruins of Turkey*, 3rd edn. (1973), 347 f.; W. Hoepfner, *Arsameia am Nymphaios* 2 (1983).   E. W. G.; S. S.-W.

Arsinoë (*RE* 25) **I** (b. *c*.300 BC), daughter of *Lysimachus and his first wife Nicaea, was married to *Ptolemy (1) II, perhaps in 285 BC when he became co-regent; they had three children: *Ptolemy (1) III, *Berenice (2) (who married the Seleucid king *Antiochus (2) II), and Lysimachus. Falling victim to dynastic struggles, she was succeeded by *Arsinoë II.   D. J. T.

Arsinoë (*RE* 26) **II Philadelphus** ('Brother-loving') (*c*.316–270 BC), daughter of *Ptolemy (1) I and his mistress *Berenice (1), was married first (300/299) to *Lysimachus whom she aided in his bid for the Macedonian throne. Following Lysimachus' death at Corupedium, she next married (281/280) her half-brother Ptolemy Ceraunus; he murdered her younger sons. Arsinoë fled to Samothrace and then to Egypt where (mid-270s) she finally married her full brother *Ptolemy (1) II. This royal couple set a precedent for later Ptolemaic brother–sister marriages (see INCEST); the dynastic cult they instituted strengthened the monarchy. In her lifetime Arsinoë was granted a priestess ('basket-bearer', *kanēphoros*) in the Alexandrian dynastic cult (see ALEXANDRIA (1)); the couple were later incorporated as *Theoi Adelphoi* ('Sibling Gods'). In 270 Arsinoë became the first Ptolemaic ruler to enter the Egyptian temples as 'temple-sharing goddess'. Whatever its nature, Arsinoë's influence on her brother was internationally recognized (*Syll.*[3] 434–5. 15). In her honour, the *Fayūm was renamed the Arsinoite nome (see NOMOS (1)) and *Philadelphia (1) so named. Her career was marked by ambition and political deftness, her death memorialized by *Callimachus (3) (fr. 228 Pf.) and the festival of the Arsinoeia. A recent attempt to redate her death to 268 (Grzybek, *Calendrier macédonien* (1990) 103–20) has not met universal acceptance.

J. Quaegebeur, in H. Maehler and V. M. Strocka, *Das ptolemäische Ägypten* (1978), 245–62; S. M. Burstein, in W. L. Adams and E. N. Borza, *Philip II* (1982), 197–212.   D. J. T.

Arsinoë (*RE* 27) **III** (b. *c*.235 BC), daughter of *Ptolemy (1) III and *Berenice (3) II, married her brother *Ptolemy (1) IV Philopator (see INCEST). Her murder, during the palace coup in

Arsinoë

205, strengthened the opposition to Sosibius and Agathocles.

D. J. T.

Arsinoë (1), the capital city of the Arsinoite nome (the *Fayūm), earlier named Crocodilopolis and Ptolemais Euergetis. Originally drained and developed in the Twelfth Dynasty, the Fayūm was again expanded and settled in the Ptolemaic and Roman periods. Arsinoë, on the main Fayūm canal, served as administrative and cultural centre. Strabo (17. 1. 38) describes its sacred lake where the cult crocodile Souchos formed a tourist attraction. The élite of Roman Arsinoë, numbering 6,475, enjoyed privileges with administrative responsibilities. The extensive ruins of Arsinoë lie beneath modern Medinet el-Fayūm.

D. J. T.

Arsinoë (2), also called Cleopatris, lay near modern Suez where the canal from the Pelusiac branch of the Nile entered the Red Sea. Despite shoals and south winds, with *Myos Hormos and *Berenice, Arsinoë became an important port for *Red Sea trade. *Trajan's garrison at Clysma stood nearby.

B. Bruyère, *Fouilles de Clysma* (1966); S. E. Sidebotham, *Roman Economic Policy in the Erythra Thalassa* (1986). D. J. T.

art, ancient attitudes to

Artists and their work The Greeks regularly equated art with craft, τέχνη, which *Aristotle defined as the 'trained ability (ἕξις) of making something under the guidance of rational thought' (*Eth. Nic.* 1140ᵃ9–10). Until the late Hellenistic period, there is no evidence that sculpture and painting were viewed as fundamentally different from shoemaking or any other profession which produced a product. Although a number of writers betray an instinctive recognition of a qualitative difference between the visual arts on the one hand and utilitarian crafts on the other, no formal distinction was ever made between the 'fine arts' and other arts in Greek thought.

From an aristocratic point of view artists were regarded as social inferiors because they were obliged to do physical work for others, and this type of life was held to have a degrading effect on their bodies and minds (Xen. *Oec.* 4. 2–3; Arist. *Pol.* 1281ᵇ 1–3; Lucian, *Somnium* 6–9). Although this aristocratic prejudice is documented throughout antiquity, there is also evidence that not everyone adhered to it. Artists like *Phidias, *Polyclitus (2), *Parrhasius, and *Zeuxis (1) were clearly respected in their own time, and the quality and value of their work was recognized (Xen. *Mem.* 1. 4. 3; Isoc. *Antidosis* 2). Respect for the art of painting in particular seems to have grown during the Classical period, and in the late 4th cent. BC, under the influence of the prestigious painter *Pamphilus (1), painting was added to the normal curriculum of Greek education (Plin. *HN* 35. 77).

The modest position of artists in most Greek social and philosophical thought did not prevent some of them from attaining considerable prestige and even wealth. Phidias was part of *Pericles (1)'s inner circle; the painter *Polygnotus, whom Plutarch describes as 'not just one of the common workmen' (*Cim.* 4. 6), served as Cimon's artistic impresario; the family of the sculptor *Praxiteles belonged to the upper level of Athenian society in the 4th cent., and one of Praxiteles' sons, the sculptor *Cephisodotus (2) the Younger, undertook costly *liturgies (*trierarchies) for the city; and in the Hellenistic period a number of sculptors are recorded to have held magistracies and been the recipients of honours in various Greek cities. The reputation and influence of artists was further enhanced by the *patronage of Hellenistic monarchs. *Alexander (3) the Great gave special status to *Lysippus (2) and *Apelles, for example; *Demetrius (4) Poliorcetes

treated the painter *Protogenes with special favour; and the early Ptolemies (see PTOLEMY (1)) invited prominent artists to their court.

In the late Hellenistic period a new theory of artistic creativity was developed in which certain artists, especially Phidias, were recognized as inspired visionaries whose insight (φαντασία) and creative ability surpassed that of ordinary people and made them sages of a sort. This '*phantasia* theory', which grew out of an amalgam of *Stoicism and Platonic idealism (see PLATO (1)), left its mark on a variety of Roman and late Greek writers (e.g. *Cicero, *Dio Cocceianus or Chrysostom, and *Plotinus) but was never part of the mainstream of Greek thought about art.

Evolving uses of art, Greek There was a significant distinction in the Greek world between public and private art. The major arts of sculpture and painting fall primarily, if not exclusively, into the category of public art, which had two subdivisions: works with a religious purpose, such as cult images, temple sculptures, and votive offerings; and works with a political or cultural commemorative function, such as portraits of civic leaders, personifications of political ideas, paintings of famous battles, and victory monuments connected with public competitions (see AGONES). Funerary sculpture, although usually privately commissioned, was essentially public in function and also belongs to the commemorative category. Although public monuments usually had a decorative aspect, there seems to have been hardly any public art that was designed to be purely decorative. Even stage paintings in the theatre were created for public religious festivals.

Small-scale works of art which had a primarily decorative purpose, such as paintings on *pottery, engravings on *gems, and jewellery, belong to the category of private art. Some *terracotta statuettes may fall into this class, although the majority of these were probably votive. In the 4th cent. BC figural *mosaic pavements became an increasingly common decorative element in private houses, and Plutarch's story of *Alcibiades' efforts to compel the painter *Agatharchus to decorate his house (*Alc.* 16) suggests that mural paintings could also be part of domestic decoration, at least in aristocratic circles.

Over time there were two major shifts of emphasis within these categories. First, beginning in the 5th cent. BC, the line between religious and commemorative-political art became blurred as traditional subjects were adapted to convey political meanings (e.g. the Amazonomachy, the *Gigantomachy; see AMAZONS; GIANTS). The sculptures of the *Parthenon and the great altar and other Attalid dedications at *Pergamum are notable examples of this trend. Second, as the idea of acquiring works of art for private delectation developed among Hellenistic monarchs, the major arts of sculpture and painting gradually also became part of the world of private art.

Evolving uses of art, Roman Art in Rome had the same functions that it had in Greece, but private patronage of artists played a much wider role in the Roman world, and the commemorative aspect of public art tended to have a different emphasis.

The formation of private art collections was a distinctive phenomenon of the later Roman republic and was apparently first stimulated by the vast quantities of Greek art taken as *booty by the Romans in the 3rd and 2nd cent. BC. Captured sculptures and paintings were first used to adorn triumphal processions and subsequently to decorate villas and houses of the triumphators. In time, possessing an art collection became a badge of cultural sophistication, and the drive to acquire collections spread beyond the world of victorious generals. When the supply of looted works of art dried up, the demand created by collectors was met by Greek artists who migrated to Rome, and some of them, like the sculptor *Arcesilaus (2), were able to command huge prices for their work (Plin. *HN* 35. 155–6). By the 1st cent. BC a lively 'art world' had taken shape, populated not only by artists and collectors but also by dealers (see COSSUTII) and even forgers. One significant outcome of this development was the creation of Europe's first public art galleries, in which extensive private collections could be exhibited.

Although historical subjects were occasionally depicted in Greek art, the Romans were much more consistently interested than the Greeks in using the arts to record the details of specific historical events. Public buildings, for example, frequently bore inscriptions celebrating the largess and achievements of the prominent citizens who had built them, and both paintings and relief sculptures documented military campaigns and important public ceremonies. See ADAMKLISSI; ARA PACIS; TRAJAN'S COLUMN.

A fusion of this deep-seated historical self-consciousness with the growing importance of private patronage in late republican Rome resulted in a significant expansion of the scope of ancient *portraiture. The Greeks had produced portraits only of prominent public figures (e.g. military men and civic leaders). By the early empire, however, Roman portraits came to be commissioned not only by rulers and aristocrats but also by citizens of relatively humble status, such as freedmen.

Art criticism Ancient criticism of the visual arts was of four kinds. (*a*) Professional criticism, that is, criticism current among artists themselves. This focused on various technical achievements and improvements and was often propagated through professional treatises, like the *Canon* of Polyclitus. A number of these were used and cited by *Pliny (1) and *Vitruvius. The idea for such treatises seems to have originated among architects in the 6th cent. BC and was adopted by sculptors and painters in the Classical period. In the 3rd cent. the principles of professional criticism were incorporated into the first histories of sculpture and painting, which described these arts as progressing through a series of technical improvements towards a state of formal perfection. (*b*) Moralistic aesthetics. In Classical Greek philosophy the visual arts were viewed as forms of imitation, *mimēsis*, and their value was assessed on the basis of the moral and intellectual value of what they imitated (e.g. Plato's criticism of painting for its failure to imitate reality, *Resp.* 10. 596e–597e, and Aristotle's praise of 'moral' painters like Polygnotus in *Poet.* 1450ª23 and 1448ª1). The *phantasia* theory of the late Hellenistic and Roman periods, the essence of which is best preserved in *Philostratus, *VA* 6. 19, perpetuated this moralistic tradition in criticism but shifted its emphasis from *mimēsis* to the artist's spiritual insight. (*c*) Popular appreciation of *mimēsis*. Throughout antiquity there was a tradition of informal criticism which praised works of art for imitating nature so closely that the viewer was deceived into thinking that the work of art was 'real'. In the Archaic period this may have involved attributing magical qualities to works of art (as in the folk-tales about the works of *Daedalus preserved in *Diodorus (3) Siculus, 4. 76. 1–6). Later, in the hands of writers like Pliny, the *Philostrati, and *Callistratus (5) the marvellous power of illusionism is the dominant theme. (*d*) Stylistic analogy with rhetoric and literature. Cicero, *Brut.* 70, Quintilian, *Inst.* 12. 10. 1–10, and *Dionysius (7) of Halicarnassus in his essays on orators used the developmental histories that grew out of professional criticism as analogies for the stylistic development of rhetoric, prose, and poetry. This type of criticism is of particular interest

in art history because it took note of the importance of personal styles in sculpture and painting and approached the idea of style with sympathy and understanding.

See ART, FUNERARY, GREEK and ROMAN; ARTISANS AND CRAFTSMEN; EKPHRASIS; IMAGERY; PAINTING, GREEK and ROMAN; RETROSPECTIVE STYLES; SCULPTURE, GREEK and ROMAN

B. Schweitzer, *Zur Kunst der Antike: Ausgewählte Schriften* (1963), 11–164; H. Philipp, *Tektonon Daidala: Der bildende Künstler und sein Werk in vorplatonischen Schrifttum* (1968); A. Burford, *Craftsmen in Greek and Roman Society* (1972); J. J. Pollitt, *The Ancient View of Greek Art* (1974); A. Stewart, *Greek Sculpture, an Exploration* (1990), 33–73; C. Janaway, *Images of Excellence* (1995).   J. J. Po.

art, funerary, Greek This article covers both architecture and art made specifically to mark and monumentalize the grave; for grave goods (which may be of any sort, and in Greece were rarely, it seems, custom-made for the tomb): see CEMETERIES; DEAD, DISPOSAL OF.

Bronze age (*c*.3000–*c*.1100 BC). The earliest monumental funerary architecture occurs in the Mesara plain of Crete, where hundreds of circular stone tholos-tombs were erected during the third millennium, each housing multiple burials. Late Minoan rulers were occasionally buried in sumptuous built tombs, like the Royal Tomb at Isopata and the Egyptian-style Temple Tomb at *Cnossus. On the mainland, the 16th-cent. shafts of Grave Circle A at *Mycenae were surmounted by limestone *steles showing battles and hunts from chariots, and from *c*.1400 the élite were buried in corbelled tholos-tombs, of which several hundred are known from all over Greece; the largest and most famous is the so-called Treasury of *Atreus at Mycenae.

Early iron age and geometric period (*c*.1100–*c*.700). Greek monumental tomb-architecture stopped with the destruction of the Mycenaean palaces *c*.1200. Until recently, the subject's history would have resumed in the 8th cent., when large vases became popular in Athens as tomb-markers. In 1981, however, two rich 10th-cent. burials were discovered at *Lefkandi in Euboea, surmounted by an apsidal building 10 m. wide and 50 m. long (11 × 55 yds.): the earliest Greek hero-shrine or heroon (see HEROCULT). Such heroa were eventually to become a common feature of the Greek landscape. They assumed a wide variety of forms, from the simple triangular enclosure above the graves of seven late 8th-cent. heroes of Eretria to the heroon that Cimon built at Athens shortly after 474 to receive *Theseus' bones, lavishly embellished with frescos by *Micon. See RELICS.

Earth mounds topped by undecorated stone slabs were popular as grave-markers in many geometric communities, but at Athens and *Argos (2) large vases performed this function after *c*.800. At Athens, massive craters stood on men's graves and amphorae on women's, decorated with multifigured battles and funerals. Despite attempts to identify these scenes as episodes from Homer, they are probably all taken from contemporary life. The Argive vases are no less monumental, though quite different iconographically: their repertoire of birds, horses, fish, water, and men apparently reflects the landscape and inhabitants of the Argive plain. In other communities, most notably on Crete, the bronze age practice of burial in tholoi persists or is intentionally revived.

Archaic period (*c*.700–*c*.480). The period's chief innovations were the funerary statue and carved gravestone. *Kouroi* (standing, usually nude, youths) marked graves on *Thera by *c*.630, and some argue that the type was introduced for this purpose. Funerary *korai* (standing, draped, young women) appear shortly after

600, as do painted and sculptured gravestones. At Athens, these steles soon became extremely lavish, until banned by sumptuary legislation (Cic. Leg. 2. 26. 64), apparently c.490. Athletes, warriors, hunters, and elders are common subjects; women and children far less so. The less wealthy or less pretentious continued to favour earth mounds, though built tombs of stone or brick appeared around 600. These were sometimes embellished with clay plaques painted with mourning scenes; sets survive signed by Sophilus, Lydus, Execias, and others.

In other areas, funerary art varied widely. *Kouroi* rarely stood over graves in central and southern Greece, but often did so in *Miletus and *Samos. These cities' rich traditions of funerary sculpture also included *korai*, seated figures, and lions. *Sarcophagi were popular in east Greece: Rhodians favoured plain stone ones, Clazomenians lavishly-painted clay ones. Aeolians and Macedonians liked large tumuli, Thessalians preferred tholos-tombs; and so on.

Classical period (c.480–c.330). At Athens, the legislation mentioned above decreed that no tomb could be made by more than ten men in three days. So whereas high-quality grave-steles with single figures in relief remain in vogue in the Cyclades and Thessaly, until c.430 Attic funerary art is restricted to white-ground lecythi: small, clay oil-flasks usually painted with domestic or mourning scenes in applied colour. Some show scenes at the tomb itself, complete with lecythi standing on the stepped bases of the simple stone slabs that now served as tomb-markers.

Around 430, for reasons perhaps relating either to the outbreak of the *Peloponnesian War (431) or the plague (430), grave-steles began to reappear in Athens. At first echoing Cycladic models, they soon developed a standard repertoire of subjects: athlete, warrior, mistress and maid, father and son, married couple, family group, funeral banquet, and so on. Though most are in the form of *naiskoi* in high relief, low-relief slab-steles furnished a cheap alternative; stone lecythi were also popular, and unmarried women received marble *loutrophoroi*. Dead and living are often linked by a handshake, and the mood is usually sombre. During the 4th cent., the steles became larger and more elaborate, until *Demetrius (3) of Phalerum banned them in 317; they were often imitated elsewhere in Greece.

In Asia Minor, Greek architects and sculptors built sumptuous tombs for local rulers. In *Lycia, the most elaborate is the 'Nereid Monument' from *Xanthus, now in the British Museum. Constructed c.380, it consisted of a square podium embellished with battle-reliefs and surmounted by a small Ionic temple; Nereids stood between the columns, and other friezes, a sculptured pediment, and acroteria decorated its entablature, cella, and roof. The Carian ruler *Mausolus used many elements of this design for his *Mausoleum at Halicarnassus. Begun around 365, this most grandiose of all sculptured tombs was widely imitated.

Hellenistic period (c.330–c.30). *Alexander (3) the Great's sumptuous hearse, described by *Diodorus (3) Siculus (18. 26 ff.) set a new standard in funerary magnificence. His own mausoleum at *Alexandria (1), the so-called Sema, has disappeared, but other royal tombs have survived. In Macedonia, kings and aristocrats were buried in vaulted chambers painted with a wide variety of subjects: hunts, Amazonomachies, Centauromachies (see CENTAURS), *Hades and *Persephone, chariot-races and so on. The most famous of these, tomb II at Vergina (see AEGAE), was probably constructed for King *Philip (2) Arrhidaeus and Eurydice (d. 317/6), not *Philip (1) II (d. 336), as proposed by its excavator. Sculptured monuments range from the 'Alexander

Sarcophagus' from *Sidon (probably made for Abdalonymus, Alexander's puppet king), through the mausoleum at Belevi near *Ephesus (perhaps constructed for *Lysimachus, d. 281), to *Antiochus (9) I of Commagene's hierothesion at *Nemrut Dağ in eastern Turkey (c.40).

The extinction of the Attic gravestone industry in 317 prompted an exodus of sculptors to Rhodes, Macedonia, and *Alexandria (1), where painted or carved imitations of Attic steles continued into the 3rd cent. Thereafter, Alexandrians interred their dead in underground *necropoleis*, decked out like houses with colonnaded or pilastered façades, and often painted inside. In *Cyrene, faceless female busts set over rock-cut tombs probably represent Persephone. A rich local stele tradition develops in the Asian cities around 200, featuring either funeral banquets or family groups where the dead are overtly heroized. Inscriptions also tell of built heroa with bronze funerary statues of the deceased, but few examples (and no statues) survive. In Tarentum, *naiskoi* embellished with reliefs of heroic fights, Achilles' last journey, and so on, are popular from c.330–250. See IMAGERY.

D. Kurtz and J. Boardman, *Greek Burial Customs* (1971); A. M. Snodgrass, *An Archaeology of Greece* (1987), 148 ff., 182 ff.; A. F. Stewart, *Greek Sculpture* (1990), 49 ff. and *passim*.   A. F. S.

art, funerary, Roman Early republican tombs at Rome have none of the decorative features of contemporary Etruscan funerary art (see ETRUSCANS), but by the mid to late republic some aristocratic tombs show a desire for elaboration (e.g. the sarcophagus of L. *Cornelius Scipio Barbatus and the façade of the tomb of the Scipio family, painted and decorated with statues in niches). From the last years of the republic onwards funerary art ceased to be the prerogative of the rich: even *freedmen and slaves decorated their tombs and bought funerary monuments. Several media were used to decorate the tomb outside and inside, and to provide memorials for the dead. The exterior might have decorations in relief (stone or terracotta) alluding to the deceased's offices or profession (e.g. fasces and curule chair for a magistrate, or a scene of everyday business such as the baking depicted on the tomb of the baker M. Vergilius Eurysaces). Portraits of the deceased, represented in the round or in relief, were also popular, especially with freedmen in the late republic and early empire. Inside the tomb there were sculptured free-standing monuments, including the containers for the remains of the deceased—ash-chests in the early empire and, increasingly from c. AD 100 onwards, *sarcophagi. There were also commemorative monuments such as grave *altars or *cippi*. The interior of the tomb itself might be decorated with stucco, *painting, and mosaic. Stucco provided architectural and figured decoration for niches in the walls (e.g. the first tomb of the Caetennii and the tomb of the Valerii in the *Vatican cemetery), and was also used on the ceilings, which could be subdivided into a complex pattern of smaller fields by stucco mouldings, each containing a painted or stuccoed motif (e.g. tombs 'of the Pancratii' and 'of the Valerii' on the via Latina, Rome). Painting provided colour, but also a variety of motifs placed inside niches, on ceilings and on walls. In the *catacombs painting was the dominant form of decoration, but here biblical stories and Christian symbols replaced the pagan ones in use elsewhere. *Mosaic was used primarily for the floors of tombs, but also appears on ceilings and walls (the most spectacular being the ceiling decoration of the small tomb of the Iulii—tomb M—in the Vatican cemetery, with Christ/Helios in his chariot amid a design of vines on a gold background).

Outside Rome, different areas of the empire developed their

own types and styles of funerary monument and art: tombs of many kinds were decorated with sculpture, both statues and reliefs (e.g. the tomb of the Secundinii at *Augusta Treverorum (Trier), with its scenes both of everyday life and of mythology). Tombstones or grave steles were also used in many areas to mark the grave and commemorate the deceased (e.g. the numerous tombstones of both soldiers and civilians from Roman Britain).

The iconographic repertoire of Roman funerary art is particularly rich. Motifs might refer directly to the deceased: *portraiture, whether full-length or in bust form, was popular throughout the imperial period, and portraits are found both on the façades of tombs and on a variety of monuments such as sarcophagi, where they can appear both in relief on the chest and as a reclining figure on the lid. The deceased might also be represented engaged in an everyday activity, on their death-bed, or in heroized and idealized form, with the attributes of a deity or hero, and women might be represented with the beauty and attributes of *Venus. Battle and hunt scenes, designed to show the deceased's manliness, were widely used on sarcophagi, as were other scenes designed to suggest his virtues. Mythological scenes were extremely popular, and a wide selection of episodes from Greek mythology was used in all contexts, but again especially on sarcophagi. Motifs from the natural world (plants, birds, and animals) abound, possibly reflecting the desire to have one's tomb surrounded by a luscious garden teeming with life. In addition there was a host of other motifs, such as cupids, seasons, sphinxes, and griffins, which could be combined in a number of different ways. Clearly some of these designs had a significance beyond their surface meaning, and alluded allegorically to beliefs in and hopes for an after-life existence: however, this is an area of much scholarly disagreement, some maintaining that virtually all motifs used in funerary contexts have an eschatological meaning, others remaining more sceptical (e.g. some think that scenes of *Tritons and Nereids (see NEREUS) swimming through the sea allude to the *soul on its journey to the *Islands of the Blest, while others deny the motif any such significance). As the imperial period progressed the mystery religions (see MYSTERIES), with their promise of salvation, gained in popularity, and Bacchic themes (see DIONYSUS) and *Hercules (paradigm of a mortal attaining immortality) appeared more frequently in funerary art.

Much of the private, non-state art of Rome was funerary, and the production of sarcophagi in particular became a major industry (see MARBLE; QUARRIES), with partially carved chests travelling considerable distances. Although some individual choice of design was possible, and some highly idiosyncratic pieces survive, for most purposes, standardized motifs taken from pattern books were used, personalization being achieved by the addition of an inscription or portrait. Nevertheless, commemoration of the dead, on as lavish a scale as could be afforded, was a major concern for most Romans of the imperial period. See CEMETERIES; DEAD, DISPOSAL OF; DEATH, ATTITUDES TO; IMAGERY; SCULPTURE, ROMAN.

J. M. C. Toynbee, *Death and Burial in the Roman World* (1971); J. M. C. Toynbee and J. Ward-Perkins, *The Shrine of St Peter and the Vatican Excavations* (1956); S. Walker, *Memorials to the Roman Dead* (1985); F. Sinn, *Stadtrömische Marmorurnen* (1987); F. Cumont, *Recherches sur le symbolisme funéraire des romains* (1942); R. Bianchi Bandinelli, *Rome: The Centre of Power* (1970), and *Rome: The Late Empire* (1971).   G. D.

Artabanus II, king of the Parthian dynasty AD 10/1–38, an *Arsacid on his mother's side, gained the throne in a struggle against Vonones who fled to Armenia. When *Iulius Caesar Germanicus installed Artaxias (Zeno) in *Armenia (18), Arta-

banus acquiesced and renewed friendship with Rome. After strengthening his rule and his kingdom (a letter of his to Susa survives: see *RC* 299 ff.) Artabanus challenged Rome by installing his son Arsaces on the Armenian throne (35) and by claiming to be heir to Achaemenian territories in the west (Tac. *Ann.* 6. 31). Urged by Artabanus' aristocratic opponents, Tiberius replied by encouraging rivals to the thrones of both Armenia and Iran. Artabanus also faced an Iberian invasion of Armenia which he failed to stem, and a revolt of a section of the Parthian nobility which forced him to retire to Hyrcania (36). Later he recovered his power and, in a meeting with L. *Vitellius on the bank of the Euphrates in the spring of 37, he promised non-interference in Armenia and was granted the *status quo ante*. New pressure from Parthian nobles forced him to flee again, but he was restored with the help of Izates, king of Adiabene. He died soon after.

E. Dabrowa, *La Politique de l'état parthe à l'égard de Rome* (1983); U. Kahrstedt, *Artabanos und seine Erben* (1950).   J. Wi.

Artabazus (*c*.387–*c*.325 BC), son of *Pharnabazus, *satrap of *Dascylium, and Apame, daughter of *Artaxerxes (2) II; *c*.361/0 he succeeded his half-brother, Ariobarzanes, who had been executed for rebellion (see SATRAPS' REVOLT). When he in turn revolted against Artaxerxes II, he fled to the Macedonian court (352), before returning in 343. Like his son, Pharnabazus, he remained loyal to *Darius III; he only joined *Alexander (3) the Great after the murder of the Persian king and was given the Bactrian satrapy (see BACTRIA), which he resigned soon after (327). He died a short time later.

Berve, *Alexanderreich*, no. 152; M. Weiskopf, *The So-called 'Great Satraps' Revolt'*, Hist. Einzelschr. 63 (1989).   P. B.

Artaphernes or **Artaphrenes**, but only the former is correct: cf. El. *Irdapirna* and OP †*Rta-farnah-*. (1) Full brother of *Darius I and satrap of Sardis, who put down the *Ionian Revolt. He figures in two Persepolis tablets (official journeys starting from *Sardis: PF 1404, 1455). (2) His son, who accompanied *Datis in 490 BC and was in *Xerxes I's army in 480.   P. B.

Artas See MESSAPII.

Artavasdes (1) **II** of *Armenia (55/4–34 BC) succeeded his father *Tigranes (1) II, and was Rome's ally when *Crassus invaded Mesopotamia; but *Orodes' simultaneous invasion of Armenia brought him over to Parthia's side, and he married his sister to Orodes' son Pacorus. When the news of the Roman defeat at *Carrhae together with Crassus' head reached Artaxata, the two kings were attending a performance of *Euripides' *Bacchae*. From then until 36 Artavasdes tried a policy of strict neutrality between Rome and Parthia before joining Mark Antony's expedition (see M. *Antonius (2)) against the Parthians and the king of *Media Atropatene. He deserted in the critical battle, and in 34 Antony, in revenge, entered Armenia with an army and captured the king and his family. Artavasdes was taken to Egypt and put to death by order of *Cleopatra (VII), on the eve of the Actium campaign.

P. Asdourian, *Die politischen Beziehungen zwischen Armenien und Rom* (1911), 52 f.; H. Bengtson, *Zum Partherfeldzug des Antonius* (1974).   J. Wi.

Artavasdes (2), king of *Media Atropatene, whose land and capital, Phraaspa, were attacked by M. *Antonius (2) in 36 BC. Enmity with the Armenian *Artavasdes (1) and a quarrel with the Parthian king, *Phraates (1) IV, soon swung him to Antony's side. In 33 Artavasdes and Antony met on the Araxes river, on which occasion Antony's son Alexander and the king's daughter

Iotape were betrothed to one another. At first victorious, Artavasdes was finally overcome by the Parthians about 31/0 and took refuge with Octavian (see AUGUSTUS), who received him amicably and granted him Lesser *Armenia. He died shortly before 20 BC (cf. his epitaph: *CIL* 4. 1. 1798). J. Wi.

Artaxata, a royal city in *Armenia, in the district of Ararat, *c*.32 km. (20 mi.) SW of Erivan. It was founded by Artaxias I, traditionally with the advice of *Hannibal (Strabo 11. 538; Plut. *Luc.* 31). The Romans captured it several times during invasions of Armenia; the Roman general, *Corbulo, burnt it in AD 58 (Tac. *Ann.* 13. 41); it was rebuilt by *Tiridates (3) and renamed Neronia (Cass. Dio 63. 7), but reverted to its old name. Statius Priscus (AD 163) seized it when he invaded Armenia. He did not destroy it, but founded a new city, Caenopolis (later, Valarshapat) not far away. Artaxata was still important in the 4th and 5th cent. AD.

C. Burner and D. M. Land, *The Peoples of the Hills* (1971).
M. S. D.; E. W. G.; S. S.-W.

Artaxerxes (1) **I** (465–424 BC) (OP *Rtaxšaçā*), one of *Xerxes' and Amestris' sons, who came to power in the obscure situation following his father's murder (August 465). The Egyptian Revolt, helped by Athens, ended with the reimposition of *Achaemenid control (454); fighting in Asia Minor seems to have finished with a serious Persian set-back—but the historicity of the Peace of Callias (449/8; see CALLIAS, PEACE OF) remains debated. According to one chronological reconstruction, it was in his reign that first Ezra (458), then Nehemiah (445), carried out their missions in Jerusalem. The latest El. tablets and other documents attest to work carried out at *Persepolis and *Susa.

Briant, *HEA* ch. 14. P. B.

Artaxerxes (2) **II** (405/4–359/8 BC), eldest son of *Darius II and Parysatis, Arsu/Arses succeeded his father smoothly in 405/4. His reign is usually seen as initiating a period of accelerated decline. This vision, based on an uncritical reading of the polemical, 4th-cent. Greek sources, is not confirmed by a more balanced assessment of the longest reign in *Achaemenid history. The extensive building-works and the development of cults of Mithra (see MITHRAS) and *Anahita show the continued vitality of politico-religious ideology, too often and wrongly perceived as unchanging.

Briant, *HEA* ch. 15. P. B.

Artaxerxes (3) **III** 359/8–338 BC), Ochos (*Umakuš* in Bab. texts), one of *Artaxerxes (2) II's sons, proclaimed king with the name Artaxerxes (359/8). Apart from the relatively unimportant *Satraps' Revolt in Asia Minor (see ARTABAZUS), the great achievement of Artaxerxes' reign was the reconquest of Egypt in 343, following the crushing of the revolt of the Phoenician cities (345).

Briant, *HEA* ch. 15. P. B.

Artaxerxes (4) **IV** (338–336 BC), throne-name of Arses, one of *Artaxerxes (3) III's sons. The *Aramaic version of the famous trilingual inscription from *Xanthus is dated to the first year of an Artaxerxes who can only be Arses.

E. Badian, *Festschrift F. Schachermeyr* (1977), 40–50; R. J. van der Spek, *BiOr* 1993, 96. P. B.

Artaxerxes (5) **V** Now that Arses is known to have taken the regnal name *Artaxerxes (4) IV (see E. Badian in *Festschrift F. Schachermeyr* (1977)) it follows that Bessus, satrap of *Bactria

and pretender to the Persian throne after *Darius III's murder, was (self-styled) Artaxerxes V. See ALEXANDER (3) III, THE GREAT.
S. H.

Artaxerxes (6) (*Ardashir*), the name of several *Sasanid kings, the greatest being Artaxerxes I (d. AD 241), son of Pabag, founder of the Sasanian empire. Taking advantage of the Parthian preoccupation with Roman attacks to assume the kingship of Istakhr, and then to conquer the neighbouring provinces one by one, he finally defeated the *Arsacid king Artabanus IV in battle (28 April 224). After further campaigns his empire included Iran, Babylonia, Mesopotamia, and parts of NE Arabia. Though major changes in political, social, and religious affairs in later Iranian tradition are attributed to him, Ardashir actually owed a great deal to the Parthian legacy. He tried to present himself as a devout Mazda-worshipper and a worthy scion of his 'forefathers' both in his inscriptions and his rock reliefs. He fought an indecisive campaign against *Severus Alexander (230–2), but in a second invasion of Roman Mesopotamia (237/8–40) captured Carrhae, Nisibis, and Hatra. Towards the end of his reign his son *Sapor is believed to have become co-regent.

J. Wiesehöfer, *Enc. Ir.* 2 (1987), 371 ff.; M. H. Dodgeon and S. N. C. Lieu (eds.), *The Roman Eastern Frontier and the Persian Wars AD 226–363*, (1991), 9 ff. J. Wi.

Artemidorus (1), of Tarsus (2nd and 1st cents. BC), grammarian. For his edition of the bucolic poets he wrote *Anth. Pal.* 9. 205. See also GLOSSA, GLOSSARY, GREEK.

Artemidorus (2) (fl. 104–101 BC), a Greek of *Ephesus, voyaged along Mediterranean shores, outer Spain (and Gaul?), and in *Alexandria (1) wrote eleven geographical books (Περίπλους, Τὰ γεωγραφούμενα, Γεωγραφίας βιβλία), often quoted. His records, especially of distances in western regions, including (misapplied) use of Roman measurements, were fair, with errors and confusions (K. Miller, *Mappaemundi* (1898), 6. 127 ff.). For eastern waters and Ethiopia Artemidorus relied on *Agatharchides, adding distances and details as far as Cape Guardafui; for India, on *Alexander (3) the Great's writers and *Megasthenes. He made two calculations of the inhabited world's length and two of its breadth, without determining positions by latitude and longitude. He was an important intermediary source between Agatharchides and *Strabo.

GGM 1. 74 ff. Berger, *Gesch. d. wiss. Erdkunde d. Gr.* 4. 38 ff. E. H. Bunbury, *Hist. of Anc. Geog.* 2 (1879), 61 ff; Fraser, *Ptol. Alex.* i 173, 549 f. E. H. W.; S. H.

Artemidorus (3) (mid/late 2nd cent. AD), of *Ephesus but called himself 'of Daldis' after his mother's native city in Lydia, whose chief deity *Apollo instigated his work on predictive *dreams. His *Onirocritica*, the product of travels to collect dreams and their outcomes and of study of the numerous earlier works on the subject, is the only extant ancient dream-book. It is of interest both for its categories of dream interpretation and for its religious and social assumptions. It was influential both in the Arab world, and in Europe from the Renaissance onwards. Artemidorus also wrote *Oeonoscopica* (but probably not the *Chiroscopica* ascribed to him).

TEXT R. A. Pack (1963); trans. R. J. White (1975).
LITERATURE C. Blum, *Studies in the Dream-Book of Artemidorus* (Diss. Uppsala, 1936); S. R. F. Price, *P&P* 1986, 3–37. S. R. F. P.

Artemis Daughter of *Zeus and *Leto, *Apollo's elder twin sister, a very important Olympian deity, a virgin and a huntress, who presided over crucial aspects of life. She presided over women's transitions (see RITES OF PASSAGE), most crucially their transformation from *parthenos* (virgin) to (fully acculturated and fully 'tamed') woman (*gynē*), and over *childbirth and *kourotrophein* (the rearing of children). She was also concerned with male activities, often (as at Sparta, see below) with their rites of transition to adulthood, also *hunting and certain aspects of war. Like all deities, she had different cults in the different parts of the Greek world, but the above-mentioned concerns are part of her panhellenic persona and recur commonly in local cults; the same is even more strongly the case with her firm association with the wild and her persona as protector of young animals as well as of *hunting. It is possible to perceive that the core of her personality is a concern with transitions and transitional marginal places, such as marshes, junctions of land and water and so on, and marginal situations. There is some merit in this, but since such classifications are inevitably culturally determined, we cannot be sure whether this was indeed a core aspect of Artemis or a culturally determined construct created by our own assumptions and preferred conceptual schemata at a time when transitions and things marginal are at the forefront of scholarly discourse—especially since deities were complex beings and did not begin with one function which was then expanded.

In the Classical period Artemis' iconography crystallized into a particular version of the iconographical schema 'young *parthenos*', a version that includes several variants; usually she has a bow and arrow, and she is often associated with a deer. One of Artemis' epithets, it should be noted, is Elaphēbolos (the 'Shooter of Deer'), after which was named the month Elaphebolion. Sometimes, especially in the Archaic period, she was represented through the schema of *Potnia Thērōn*, 'Mistress of the Animals', usually winged, flanked by animals. Very rarely she is shown with wings but not as a Potnia Thērōn, that is, not flanked by animals. Many, but not all, scholars believe that her name appears in the Linear B tablets of *Pylos (PY Es 650. 5; Un 219. 5). One of the religious nexuses that contributed to the making of the divine persona that crystallized in the figure of the historical Greek goddess Artemis is the 'Potnia Thērōn' facet of a Minoan goddess. It is for this reason, that Artemis sometimes became associated or identified with another 'later transformation' of that goddess, *Britomartis/Dictynna.

In *Homer, Artemis was, like Apollo, on the side of the Trojans. She was a death-bringing deity, for she sent sudden death to women (cf. e.g. *Od*. 11. 171–3), as Apollo did to men. Apollo and Artemis together killed the children of *Niobe, who had boasted about the large number of children she had in comparison to Leto's two. She or Apollo, or both, killed *Tityus who had tried to rape Leto (or, in Euphorion fr. 105 Powell, Artemis herself). Some of the more important myths assigning her the role of punishing deity are that of *Actaeon (whom she transformed into a stag and had torn apart by his own hounds), that of her companion *Callisto (for having lost her chastity to Zeus), and her demand that *Iphigenia be sacrificed. According to one version of his myth she killed the hunter *Orion for insulting her.

In Attica her most important cults are those of Artemis Brauronia, Munichia, Tauropolos, and Agrotera. As Brauronia and Munichia she was above all concerned with female transitions, especially that from *parthenos* to *gynē*. At her sanctuaries at *Brauron and *Munichia (1) little girls between the ages of 5 and 10 served Artemis as *arktoi* (bears), a pre-menarche ritual that turned girl-children into marriageable *parthenoi*. Artemis Brauronia was, in general, a women's goddess, and she included a strong kourotrophic function. Artemis Munichia was also a *kourotrophos*, and in addition she was also concerned with *ephēboi*; at her festival, the *Munichia (2), ephebes sailed from Zea to the harbour of Munichia in 'the sacred ships', and held races at sea. Then they processed for Artemis and sacrificed, celebrations said to be in commemoration and thanksgiving for the battle of *Salamis. The cult of Artemis Phosphoros was also associated with that of Munichia at Munichia, while the torch-bearing Artemis, the iconographical representation of Artemis as Phosphoros, is one of the most frequently encountered types among the votives, especially votive reliefs, found at Brauron (L. Kahil, *AK* 1977, 86–98, and in W. G. Moon (ed.), *Ancient Greek Art and Iconography* (1983), 231–44; L. Palaiokrassa, *To hiero tēs Artemidos Mounichias* (1991), and *MDAI (A)* 1989, 1–40; C. Sourvinou-Inwood, *Studies in Girls' Transitions* (1988); P. Brulé, *La Fille d'Athènes* (1987), 179 ff.). The cult of Artemis Tauropolos at Halai Araphenides (E. Attica) appears to have been associated with a boys' initiation ceremony, reflected in the rite described at Eur. *IT* 1439 ff. as having been ordained by Athena. She ordered *Orestes to take Artemis' Tauric statue to Athens, and set it up in a sanctuary that he was to found at Halai. There Artemis was to be worshipped as Tauropolos, and at her festival (as a compensation for the aborted sacrifice of Orestes) the sword was to be held to a man's throat and blood spilled. (F. Graf, *Antike Welt* 1979, 33–41; H. Lloyd-Jones, *JHS* 1983, 87–102.)

Artemis Agrotera had some involvement with war. The Spartans sacrificed a goat to her before battle, while the Athenians, we are told, before the battle of *Marathon vowed to sacrifice to Artemis Agrotera as many goats as enemies killed. In the event they could not find enough goats, so they vowed to sacrifice 500 a year, which they did, on her festival on 6 Boedromion, which thus involved a strong element of thanksgiving for Marathon. This festival included a procession to the temple in which the ephebes took part. The sanctuary of Artemis Agrotera was peri-urban, at Agrae. The overwhelming (though not universal) scholarly opinion is that the temple of Artemis Agrotera is to be identified with the so-called Ilissus temple, built by *Callicrates (1). (On Artemis and war cf. Burkert, *HN*, 65–7; J.-P. Vernant, *Mortals and Immortals* (collected essays ed. F. I. Zeitlin) (1991), 244–57, and *Figures, Idoles, Masques* (1990), 162–81; H. W. Parke, *Festivals of the Athenians* (1977); P. Ellinger, *Arch. Anz.* 1987, 88–99 and *Quaderni urbinati di cultura classica* 1978, 7–35.)

In some places, including Athens, Artemis' role as protector of women in childbirth is expressed through her epithet Loch[e]ia (cf. e.g. Eur. *IT* 1097, *Supp.* 958; *IG* 2². 4547; Sokolowski, *LSCG* 154 A 16–17 (*Cos)). Elsewhere it is expressed in her identification with *Eileithyia (cf. e.g. Artemis Eileithyia at *Thebes (1), *Orchomenus (1), *Thespiae, *Chaeronea, *Tanagra, *Thisbe, *Anthedon: A. Schachter, *Cults of Boeotia* 1 (1981), 94, 98, 101–6); cf. on both epithets Plut. *Mor.* 658f. It has been suggested that in *IG* 2². 4547 Eileithyia is not a separate deity but belongs with *Artemidi Lochiai* as a second epithet (M. Guarducci, in D. W. Bradeen and M. F. McGregor (eds.), *Phoros* (1974), 60)).

At Sparta Artemis had several cults, the most important of which was that of Artemis Orthia (see SPARTAN CULTS), a cult closely associated with the *agōgē*, the long process through which Spartan boys became élite warriors and citizens, though Artemis Orthia also had other functions, not least ones pertaining to female concerns, and there was clearly a close association between Artemis Orthia and Eileithyia since many dedications to Eileithyia were found in this sanctuary. (R. M. Dawkins (ed.),

Artemisia

The Sanctuary of Artemis Orthia (1929); C. Calame, Les Chœurs de jeunes filles en Grèce archaïque (1977), 276–97; J.-P. Vernant, Mortals and Immortals (1991), 225–43; R. Parker, in A. Powell (ed.), Classical Sparta (1989), 151–2.)

A ritual practice broadly comparable to the Attic arkteia (but in much closer proximity to marriage) has been convincingly reconstructed (P. Clement, Ant. Class. 1934, 393–409) as having been associated with the cult of Artemis Pagasitis at *Pagasae-Demetrias and the cult of Artemis Throsia at *Larissa, the nebreia, which consisted of the consecration of girls to Artemis for a certain period during which they were called nebroi (fawns). (Cf. also K. Dowden, Death and the Maiden (1989), 41–2; P. Brulé, La Fille d'Athènes (1987), 191.)

At *Patrae the festival Laphria in honour of Artemis Laphria included a procession in which the virgin priestess rode in a chariot drawn by deer and the holocaust sacrifice of many animals; these were thrown alive into the altar enclosure, and included wild animals such as deer and boar, which were not normally sacrificed in Greek religion (cf. Paus. 7. 18. 8–13; G. Piccaluga in Le Sacrifice dans l'antiquité, Entretiens Hardt 27 (1981), 243–77).

The cult of Artemis at Ephesus (on which cf. A. Bammer, Das Heiligtum der Artemis von Ephesos (1984)) includes Asiatic elements; but this does not make Artemis an eastern goddess.

Artemis was often identified with other goddesses whose name she sometimes bore as an epithet, for example, besides Artemis Eileithyia referred to above, Artemis *Hecate (cf. e.g. Aesch. Supp. 675–7).

Farnell, 2. 425–86, 520–48, 448–607; L. Kahil, LIMC 2 (1984), 618–753; Nilsson, GGR 1³. 481–500; 179 ff. Nilsson, Feste Burkert, GR 149–52; E. Simon, Die Götter der Griechen (1985), 147–78; P. Ellinger, 'Artemis', Dictionnaire des Mythologies (1981); J.-P. Vernant, Figures, Idoles, Masques (1990), 137–207; C. Calame, Les Chœurs de jeunes filles en Grèce archaïque (1977); A. Schachter, in Le Sanctuaire grec, Entretiens Hardt 37 (1992), 1–57.   C. S.-I.

Artemisia (1), early 5th-cent. BC ruler, under Persian suzerainty, over *Halicarnassus, *Cos, *Nisyrus, and *Calymnos: Hdt. 7. 99 (which implies 6. 43 is exaggerated: 'democracies' installed in Ionia (see IONIANS) after the *Ionian Revolt). In the *Persian Wars Artemisia accompanied Xerxes' expedition with five ships. According to the Halicarnassian *Herodotus she was a 'warner' figure, who unsuccessfully urged Xerxes not to fight at Salamis, but fought bravely and escaped by sinking a ship in her way. The ship was Calyndian (not Calymnian), from a place on the border between Caria and *Lycia. Xerxes remarked 'my men have become women and my women men' (Hdt. 8. 88). Afterwards she urged him to retreat and transported part of his family to *Ephesus. Her son or nephew or grandson Lygdamis was still in power at Halicarnassus c.465–450 (ML 32 = Fornara 70).

S. Hornblower, Mausolus (1982), 22–6.   P. T.; S. H.

Artemisia (2), daughter of *Hecatomnus, ruled *Caria with her full brother and incestuous husband *Mausolus (see INCEST) in the mid-4th cent. BC: I. Labraunda (1972), no. 40, joint decree in Greek ('it seemed good to Mausolus and Artemisia') conferring *proxeny on *Cnossus. He certainly used the Persian title *satrap and she probably did too. At his death in 353 (when she succeeded him, ruling until 351) she was grief-stricken, supposedly drank his ashes (Gell. NA 10. 18), and organized a rhetorical funeral competition at which *Theodectes, *Theopompus (3) (the winner), and others performed; but the participant 'Isocrates' may not be the famous man. She held down Rhodes, already

absorbed into the Hecatomnid sphere of influence by Mausolus, and was the target of *Demosthenes (2)'s speech 15 (351) 'On the Freedom of the Rhodians', urging an attack on Caria to free the Rhodian democrats. She should share with her satrapal brothers and sister (Mausolus, *Idrieus, *Pixodarus, *Ada) the responsibility for spreading *Hellenism in Caria, while retaining the native cultural element, in the generation before *Alexander (3) the Great.

S. Hornblower, Mausolus (1982): on the whole family; inscriptions at 364 ff.; S. Ruzicka, Politics of a Persian Dynasty: The Hecatomnids in the Fourth Century BC (1992).   S. H.

Artemisium, a promontory on the NE coast of *Euboea, so called from a temple of Artemis Proseoa on this site. The place is perhaps to be identified with the village of Potaki near the bay of Pevki. An ancient shipwreck yielding bronze statuary was found in the 1920s. For the naval battle of 480 BC see ARTEMISIUM, BATTLE OF.

J. Lazenby, The Defence of Greece (1993), ch. 6; A. Parker, Ancient Shipwrecks (1992), 57.   P. T.; A. J. S. S.

Artemisium, battle of (480 BC). Pevki bay near *Artemisium on *Euboea was probably the base of the Greek fleet during the three days of fighting which coincided with the battle of *Thermopylae. With fewer and slower ships, the Greeks nevertheless took the initiative for two days, though careful to fight towards evening so that they could break off if necessary. But on the third day, perhaps to coincide with the final assault on Thermopylae, the Persian fleet came out at midday, and although still technically the victors, the Greeks had so many ships damaged that they were already considering withdrawal when the news of what had happened at Thermopylae reached them. Though indecisive, Artemisium, as *Pindar said (Plut. Them. 8. 2), was where the Greeks 'laid the shining foundation of freedom'. See PERSIAN WARS.

RE 2/2, 'Artemision' 1; Hdt. 7. 175–95, 8. 1–18; C. Hignett, Xerxes' Invasion of Greece (1963); J. F. Lazenby, The Defence of Greece (1993).
                                                                                            J. F. La.

Artemon (1) (probably not later than 2nd cent. BC), sometimes identified with *Artemon (2) of Cassandreia or *Artemon (3) of Pergamum, edited the letters of Aristotle with notes on the art of letter-writing.

Demetr. Eloc. 223; David on Arist. Cat. 24ª28 (Comment. in Arist. Graeca 8. 2 (1904), ed. A. Busse).   M. B. T.

Artemon (2), of Cassandreia (perhaps 2nd or 1st cent. BC), wrote two bibliographical treatises (perhaps part of a single work): (1) On Collecting Books, (2) On Using Books, in the second book of which he discussed the three types of drinking-song (skolion; see SCOLIA); also a work On the Dionysiac Guild (see DIONYSUS, ARTISTS OF.)

FHG 4. 342.   M. B. T.

Artemon (3), of Pergamum, also styled 'the historian', perhaps identical with *Artemon (2) of Cassandreia, Cassandreia being his birthplace, Pergamum the scene of his literary activity. He is mentioned several times in the scholia to Pindar for explanations of historical, geographical, and mythological problems.

FGrH 569.   J. D. D.; K. J. D.; M. B. T.

Artemon (4), of Miletus, wrote, under Nero, a work in 22 books on *dreams and their consequences, with special reference to cures by *Sarapis. He is criticized by *Artemidorus (3), see 1. 2, 2. 44, etc.

FHG 4. 340; D. Del Corno, *Graecorum de re onirocritica scriptorum reliquiae* (1969).   M. B. T.; S. R. F. P.

Artemon (5), of Magnesia (date uncertain), author of a *Famous Exploits of Women*, from which *Sopater (2) made excerpts.

Phot. *Bibl.* 161, p. 103a37.   M. B. T.

artillery Evidence for Greek and Roman artillery comes from the surviving technical treatises, incidental historical and subliterary references, and, most importantly, finds of both machine-fittings and projectiles. The latter at present date from the 2nd cent. BC to the 4th cent. AD.

In 399 BC artificers of *Dionysius (1) I apparently invented the first artillery piece (Diod. Sic. 14. 42. 1). The *gastraphetēs* shot arrows only, and somewhat resembled an early medieval crossbow. Propulsion force was supplied by a composite bow, which, being too powerful for a man to draw by hand, was bent by means of a slide and stock. Later *gastraphetai*, some of which were stone-throwers, used a winch and had a stand.

Torsion catapults appeared around 340 BC, possibly invented by *Philip (1) II's engineers. Stock, winch, and base remained much the same, but two springs, bundles of rope made from animal sinew, horsehair, or human hair, and held at high tension in a metal-plated wooden frame, now provided propulsive power. Torsion machines improved continuously in efficiency through the Roman period. From c.270 BC a technical literature of calibrating formulae and standard dimensions developed (see CTESIBIUS; HERON; PHILON (2)). However, torsion catapults did not supersede the large non-torsion types before the later 3rd cent. and small composite machines continued into the late Roman period.

The torsion *katapeltēs oxybelēs* shot bolts only (main calibres: one to four bolt), the *lithobolos* hurled stone-shot (weights of ten *minae* to three talents). Both types had a maximum effective range well in excess of 300 m. (330 yds.). Schramm reached 387 m. (423 ft.) with a full-size reproduction of a two-cubit (approx. 100-cm./40-in.) machine employing horsehair springs. Modifications devised between 200 and 25 BC are reflected in machines described by *Vitruvius, and by fittings from *Ephyra, Mahdia, and Ampurias.

Each imperial Roman legion had integral artillery specialists and workshops to design, manufacture, repair, and deploy its c.70 *catapultae* and *ballistae* (Cf. 1st-cent. AD *Cremona finds; also *ILS* 2034). The small but powerful engines illustrated on *Trajan's Column and described by *Heron of Alexandria (*chiroballistra*), with all-metal frames, were probably developed in the 1st cent. AD. They continued in use into the late Roman period, as evidenced by finds from Lyons, Gornea, and Orsova, and the accounts of *Vegetius, *Procopius, and Mauricius. By the 4th cent. AD the one-armed, stone-throwing *onager* was also developed.

Artillery figured most prominently in sieges, especially those associated with Rome's eastern wars, and its use spread to the *Sasanids through Roman contacts. Whilst *Onomarchus and *Alexander (3) the Great used artillery in the field, lack of mobility restricted it before the Roman period. Long range made artillery a valuable naval weapon (e.g. *Demetrius (4) off *Salamis (2) and *Agrippa at Naulochus). See FORTIFICATIONS; SIEGECRAFT, GREEK and ROMAN; WAR, ART OF, GREEK and ROMAN.

E. W. Marsden, *Greek and Roman Artillery: Historical Development* (1969) and *Greek and Roman Artillery: Technical Treatises* (1971); D. Baatz, introd. to E. Schramm, *Die antiken Geschütze der Saalburg* (1980); P. Connolly, *Greece and Rome at War* (1981), 279–83, 302–3; M. C. Bishop

and J. C. N. Coulston, *Roman Military Equipment from the Punic Wars to the Fall of Rome* (1993).   J. C. N. C.

artisans and craftsmen (see ART, ANCIENT ATTITUDES TO; CLUBS, GREEK and ROMAN; INDUSTRY; MARKETS AND FAIRS). In Greece the prejudices of the (largely landowning) citizen-élites against the activities of 'mechanics' (*banausoi*), often slaves, *freedmen, or *metics, subjected artisans to formal handicaps in the oligarchic *polis, including limitation of political rights (Ptolemaic *Cyrene: *SEG* 9. 1, para. 8, unfortunately corrupt), restriction of their freedom of movement (Thessalian cities: Arist. *Pol.* 7. 12, 1331ª31–5), and exclusion from the *gymnasium (Beroea in the 2nd cent. BC: P. Gauthier and M. Hatzopoulos, *Meletemata* 1994, 21, line 29), although in the Athenian *democracy their social standing was higher, notwithstanding the condescension of Athenian 'intellectuals'. Craftsmen themselves could be proud of their products, if the 'signatures' on painted *pottery are really those of their makers, as too of their occupations, to judge from the Athenian artisans who stated them in their dedications, including a 'washerwoman' (πλύντρια) (A. Raubitschek, *Dedications from the Athenian Acropolis* (1949), 464–5), the last a reminder of the considerable involvement of women in the humbler crafts, especially *textile production (see *IG* 2². 1553–78 with M. Tod, *Epigraphica* 1950, 3 ff.). Although entrepreneurs could prosper through artisanal activity, craftsmen as a group were largely powerless, since the citizen-group, beyond taxing sales and charging rents for market- and workshop-space, had no interest in promoting industry as such.

The larger scale of the Roman economy gives greater visibility to the entrepreneurial artisan in Roman society, such as the contract-baker M. Vergilius Eurysaces, whose grandiose tomb at Rome still stands (Richardson, *Topog. Dict. Ancient Rome*, entry under Sep. Eurysacis), although there is little clear evidence for manufacturing enterprises of more than local significance (but see AMPHORAE (ROMAN) and LAMPS) and—apart from the exceptional case of brick production (see BRICKSTAMPS)—the Roman élite cannot easily be linked with manufacture. On the other hand, upper-class disdain for the crafts, as at Cic. *Off.* 1. 42, hardly encouraged the open admission of such links, which certainly accounted for some of the wealth of successful Roman *freedmen. Roman craftsmen are widely attested in rural villages as well as cities.

A. Burford, *Craftsmen in Greek and Roman Society* (1972); J. Morel, in A. Giardina (ed.), *L'Uomo romano* (1989), ch. 8 (Eng. trans., *The Romans* (1993)).   A. J. S. S.

artists of Dionysus See CLUBS, GREEK; DIONYSUS, ARTISTS OF.

Arusianus Messius (late 4th cent. AD), rhetorician, compiled an alphabetical list of nouns, adjectives, verbs, and prepositions that admit more than one construction (*Exempla elocutionum*: ed. Keil, *Gramm. Lat.* 7. 449–514, superseded by A. della Casa (1977)). Beyond two citations of the orator *Symmachus (2), the compilation is based exclusively on the four main school authors, *Virgil, *Terence, *Cicero, and *Sallust.

PLRE 1. 600; Herzog-Schmidt, § 615.   R. A. K.

arval brethren See FRATRES ARVALES.

Arverni, an advanced iron age people, occupying modern Auvergne, who contested the primacy of Gaul with the *Aedui (Caes. *BGall.* 1. 31. 3). In 207 BC they treated with *Hasdrubal (2) (Livy 27. 39. 6), and in the next century, under Luernius and his son Bituitus, they commanded an extensive empire (Strabo 4. 2.

3). Bituitus was, however, defeated by Cn. *Domitius Ahenobarbus (2) and Q. *Fabius Maximus (Allobrogicus) (121), and the Arvernian empire was reduced to suzerainty over some neighbouring tribes. In 52 *Vercingetorix, son of a former Arvernian king, led the Gallic revolt against *Caesar, and defeated an attempt upon the hill-fort capital, *Gergovia. After the fall of Vercingetorix, the Arverni lost their powers of suzerainty, but obtained the position of *civitas libera* (see FREE CITIES), and became prosperous and Romanized. Under Augustus their capital was moved to Augustonemetum (Clermont-Ferrand). Their territory accommodated a major centre of pottery production at Lezoux, and their principal temple, on the Puy-de-Dôme, was famous for a statue costing forty million sesterces (Plin. *HN* 34. 45). Following *Alamannic devastation of the region in the 3rd cent. AD Clermont was reduced in size but under the late empire remained an important centre. The Arverni were ceded to the Visigoths in 475, after a heroic struggle led by their bishop, *Sidonius Apollinaris.

> C. Jullian, *Hist. de la Gaule* 2. 546 ff., 3. 1 ff.; D. Nash, *Settlement and Change in Central Gaul c. 200–50 BC* (1978). J. F. Dr.

Aryan, the name by which the peoples of ancient *India and Iran designated themselves; it is also used for the branch of very closely related *Indo-European languages spoken by them (*i.a.* Avesta, Vedic, *Old Persian, Scythian). The linguistic concept 'Aryan' gradually acquired racist connotations, and 'Indo-Iranian' is now usually employed instead.

> R. Schmitt, *Enc. Ir.* 2 (1987), 684–7, 'Aryans'; J. Wiesehöfer, in *Achaemenid History 5: The Roots of the European Tradition* (1990), 149–165.
> H. S.-W.

Ascalabus, in mythology, son of Misme, an Attic woman. His mother gave *Demeter, who was looking for *Persephone, a vessel of water, meal, and pennyroyal; he laughed at her for drinking it greedily, and she threw what was left of it over him, whereat he became a spotted lizard.

> Ant. Lib. 24, citing Nicander; Ov. *Met.* 5. 446 ff. H. J. R.

Ascalaphus, in mythology, (1) son of *Ares; (2) son of Orphne (Ov. *Met.* 5. 539), or Gorgyra (Apollod. 1. 33), and Acheron. When *Persephone was in *Hades, *Zeus agreed that she could return if she had eaten nothing. Ascalaphus had seen her eat a few pomegranate-seeds and betrayed her; Persephone turned him into an owl (Ovid), or *Demeter did, when the stone which she had put over him was lifted by *Heracles (Apollod.). See ASCALABUS. K. C.

Ascanius, character in literature and mythology, son of *Aeneas. Not mentioned in Homer, he appears in the Aeneas-legend by the 5th cent. BC, at first as one of several sons of Aeneas (Hellanicus, *FGrH* 4 F 24, 31). His mother in the cyclic *Cypria* (see EPIC CYCLE § 4 (6)) was Eurydice (Paus. 10. 26. 1); in Virgil and Livy and thereafter she is *Creusa (2), daughter of Priam; Livy also mentions a further version, that he was the son of Lavinia (Livy 1. 3. 2–3). The *gens Iulia* claimed him as eponymous founder with an alternative name of 'Iulus', variously derived (cf. *Aen.* 1. 267–8 with Servius). In the *Aeneid* he is a projection of typical and sometimes ideal Roman youth, but still too young to play a major part; other versions tell of his subsequent career as king of *Lavinium and founder of *Alba Longa, the city from which Rome was founded (e.g. Livy 1. 3. 1–5; Dion. Hal. *Ant. Rom.* 1. 65–9). He is depicted in both Greek and Roman art: *LIMC* 2/1 (1984), 860–3.

> Ogilvie, *Comm. Livy 1–5*, 1. 3. 2; E. Flores, *Enc. Virg.* 'Ascanio'. S. J. Ha.

asceticism The Greek word *askēsis* is as old as Homer and implies disciplined and productive effort. (The Romans admired ascetic practice but chiefly by absorbing the values of Greek philosophy.) At first physical by allusion—to the skill of the craftsman and the vigour of the athlete—it quickly acquired a moral sense also, clear in *Xenophon (1) (e.g. *Mem.* 1. 2. 19). He contrasted the ascetic with the self-willed amateur (*Cyr.* 1. 5. 11), stressing submission to a tradition of instruction, and he made a connection with self-mastery (*Mem.* 2. 1. 1), overlaying with that positive moral note the more general notion of *labour. The ascetic improved upon nature, remaining in that sense a craftsman.

Asceticism was associated thereafter with philosophical rather than religious practice. Philosophers rejected ritual as a guarantee of liberation or virtue. Their moderation was distinct from the self-denial of priests, initiates, and devotees, even when that involved *fasting or sexual restraint.

Linked thus with philosophy, asceticism adopted forms dictated by different schools. With Platonism ascendant, its general aim veered naturally towards truth and knowledge understood in increasingly exalted and visionary senses. Followers of *Pythagoras (1), believing a divine element was imprisoned in the body, recommended release through *silence as an aid to contemplation, with fasting an added option (perhaps more symbolic than effective). Some Cynics may have furthered the ascetic cause, particularly when, like *Crates (2), they advocated simplicity and detachment. The *sophists developed at their best a complex system of personal formation, in which asceticism, together with education and natural talent, had its part. Balance was called for, linked with a formal theory of the virtues, particularly prudence. The Stoics (see STOICISM) armed themselves against what they called 'passion' and relinquished some goods to safeguard others: sound judgement, therefore, mattered more than will-power. No less, in their way, the disciples of *Epicurus chose some goods over others in pursuit of true happiness and should be allowed the title of 'ascetic' in a strict sense. Finally, *Neopythagoreanism from the 1st cent. BC on prompted more severe criticism of cult as a moral tool and emphasized the inner quality of true piety—an emphasis that would mirror if not reinforce the suspicion of some Christian ascetics about the usefulness of sacramental religion. By the time of admirers such as Philostratus (see PHILOSTRATI) and *Iamblichus (2), those different elements had begun to conflate—a process confirmed within *Neoplatonism.

Not surprisingly, therefore, asceticism made its appearance in a Christian context precisely when Christians opened themselves fully, during the 2nd cent., to the classical philosophical tradition. There was early promise, for example, in the *Second Epistle of Clement* (linking self-mastery with the Christian understanding of conversion); but the chief exemplars are *Clement and *Origen (1) of Alexandria. (The Greek term *askēsis* occurs in the NT once only, at Acts 24: 16. In the Septuagint related words occur only in *Maccabees and 'self-mastery' in an ascetic sense is rare, e.g. Ecclesiasticus 26: 15.) Clement inherited his understanding of both concepts (e.g. *Strom.* 1. 5. 31) from *Philon (4), who was influenced here by Neopythagorean and sophistic traditions (presenting Jacob as the typical ascetic, e.g. *Legum Allegoriae* 2. 89). Origen connected asceticism firmly with 'purity' and 'virginity' understood in a fully Christian sense (*c. Cels.* 7. 48) but only because such ideas appealed to him on other grounds.

The chief Christian theorists of asceticism sprang precisely from that Alexandrian school: Evagrius of Pontus in the late 4th cent. AD and John *Cassian in the early 5th. Their teaching, however, was modified or augmented by NT values, particularly that of renunciation. The classic and influential example occurs in the *Life of Antony* 2, a text owing much to Alexandrian tradition and marked by a surprising number of philosophical debts and allusions. There Antony, the archetype of the Christian ascetic, responds to the call of Matt. 19: 21 to sell all, give to the poor, and follow Jesus. It was during the later 4th cent. that reference to the word *ascesis* began to appear in Latin texts, instantly connected with 'monk' (*monachus*) and associated terms. *Itinerarium Egeriae* betrays a need to explain the correspondence, 3. 4, 10. 9, 20. 5). Thus the monk inherited the mantle of the philosopher and dictated thereafter the acceptable style of strenuous self-improvement.

Pagan attitude and practice is best traced within each philosophical school. For specifically Christian developments: H. von Campen-hausen, *Die Askese im Urchristentum* (1949); W. Völker, *Das Vollkom-menheitsideal des Origenes* (1931); A. Vööbus, *History of Asceticism in the Syrian Orient*, 2 vols (1958–60); D. J. Chitty, *The Desert a City* (1966). P. R.

Asclepiades (1) (*RE* 27), of Tragilus (4th cent. BC), wrote an account of Greek *mythology as told in *tragedy, the six books of *Tragodoumena* (*FGrH* 12), just as earlier *mythographers (e.g. *Acusilaus, *Pherecydes (2)) had based such accounts on epic and lyric. He was a source for *Apollodorus (6) but is mainly known to us from scholiasts, esp. on Homer. Like *Theopompus (3) and *Ephorus, he was a pupil of *Isocrates ([Plut.] *X orat.* 837c), from whom he derived a synoptic and traditional vision, together with a relatively elegant periodic style. K. D.

Asclepiades (2), of Samos, also called Sicelides (fl. 300–270 BC). Inventor of the Alexandrian erotic *epigram (see ALEXANDRIA (1); MUSEUM), distinguished by concise and witty treatment with the paraphernalia of fire and Erotes that were to be so characteristic of later erotic epigram. A strong influence on *Callimachus (3), *Posidippus (2), and *Hedylus. He praised the *Lyde* of *Anti-machus (*Anth. Pal.* 9. 63), which Callimachus had attacked (fr. 398 Pf.), and is listed among the latter's literary enemies (schol. Flor. p. 3 Pf.). Spoken of by *Theocritus as a master (7. 40). He may have published a collection of epigrams jointly with *Posidippus (2) and *Hedylus (A. D. E. Cameron, *Greek Anthology* (1993), 369–76).

Gow and Page, *HE*; A. Cameron, in H. P. Foley (ed.), *Reflections on Women in Antiquity* (1982), 275–302; S. L. Tarán, *The Art of Variation in Hellenistic Epigram* (1979); G. O. Hutchinson, *Hellenistic Poetry* (1988), 264–76. A. D. E. C.

Asclepiades (3) (*RE* 39), of Prusias ad Mare in Bithynia, physician. He spent at least some of his career in Rome, and died sometime in the 1st cent. BC. He is best known for his theory that the body is made out of fragile corpuscles (ἄναρμοι ὄγκοι). (Although these corpuscles were not what a modern biologist might mean by the term, the word ὄγκος ('lump') did have medical connotations in antiquity.) The corpuscles were envisaged as moving through ducts (πόροι) distributed throughout the body; when their movement is hindered or altered, morbid effects ensue. The origins of Asclepiades' theory have been traced variously to *Epicurus, the Platonist *Heraclides (1) Ponticus, the Peripatetic *Straton (1) of Lampsacus, or to a combination of them all. There are strong indications, however, that the theory arose out of a reaction to the physiological system of *Erasi-stratus. Asclepiades was attacked fiercely by *Galen for the conse-

quences of his theory, especially for denying the role of teleological activity in nature.

In his therapy Asclepiades is associated with the use of non-invasive treatments—wine, massage, bathing, etc.—and with the judicious rather than wholesale use of drugs. He seems to have achieved considerable fame in his own lifetime, but his ideas were assimilated into the medical Methodism of figures like *Themison and *Thessalus (2).

TEXT No works survive; some of the ancient testimony is collected in C. G. Gumpert, *Asclepiadis Bithyniae Fragmenta*, (1794). New edn. by J. T. Vallance in preparation.
LITERATURE A. Cocchi, *Discorso primo . . . sopra Asclepiade* (1762); E. Rawson, *CQ* 1982, 358–70; J. T. Vallance, *The Lost Theory of Asclepiades of Bithynia*, (1990), and *ANRW* 2. 37. 2 (1993). J. T. V.

Asclepiades (4), of Myrleia in *Bithynia (1st cent. BC), worked in Spain, and wrote on the history of Bithynia, and of scholarship; on Homer and Theocritus; and, as Atticist analogist, Περὶ ὀρθογραφίας, 'On Orthography'. It is either he or the homonymous doctor (no. 3 above) whom *Sextus Empiricus quotes in the *Adv. grammaticos* as stating that grammar was a *technē* or craft.

FGrH 697; W. Slater, *GRBS* 1972, 317–33; G. Rispoli *Lo spazio del verisim-ile: Il racconto, la storia e il mito* (1988), 170–204. P. B. R. F.; K. S. S.

Asclepiodotus (1st cent. BC), probably the pupil of *Posidonius (2), wrote an account of the Greek *phalanx and other branches of the army, which after *Aeneas Tacticus is the earliest extant example of a treatise on military practice. His account of the organization and disposition of an ideal phalanx of 16,384 men is theoretical and highly technical. He may be reproducing a lost work of Posidonius, with some material possibly derived from *Polybius (1), or earlier textbooks; items of historical interest are occasionally preserved, e.g. that the Thessalian cavalry fought in rhomboid formation (7. 2).

TEXT AND DISCUSSION *Aeneas Tacticus, Asclepiodotus, Onasander* (Loeb, 1923). J. B. C.

Asclepius (Ἀσκληπιός, Dor.-Aeol. Ἀσκλαπιός, Boeot. also Ἀσχλαπιός, Αἰσχλαβιός; Lat. *Aesculapius), hero and god of healing.

In *Homer's *Iliad*, he is a hero, the 'blameless physician' (formula in *Il.* 4. 194, 11. 518), taught by the *Centaur Chiron (*Il.* 4. 219); his two sons, the physicians *Machaon and Podalirius, lead a contingent from Tricca in *Thessaly (*Il.* 2. 729–33). Late Archaic authors fit him into two different genealogies: in a Thes-salian version alluded to in a Hesiodic poem (fr. 60 M–W; see HESIOD) and narrated more fully in *Pindar (*Pyth.* 3), he was the son of *Apollo and *Coronis, daughter of *Phlegyas. Coronis had become Apollo's beloved, but then married the mortal Ischys; when a raven denounced the girl to the god, he (or his sister *Artemis) killed her, but snatched the unborn baby from the pyre, and entrusted him to Chiron (see CENTAURS). When grown up, Asclepius became a great healer who even raised men from the dead, which provoked *Zeus into killing him with his thunderbolt. Angered, Apollo retaliated by killing the *Cyclopes who had made the thunderbolt; in order to punish him, Zeus sent him into servitude with Admetus, king of Pherae (see ALCESTIS). In the Hesiodic *Catalogues*, however, Asclepius is the son of Arsinoë, daughter of Messenian Leucippus (Hesiod fr. 50 M–W; see MESSENIA), although the story must have followed about the same course as in Pindar, with Asclepius' death by lightning and Apollo's anger and servitude (frs. 51, 52, 54b, c). Thus, already in the 6th cent. BC two local versions of the myth

are well attested and show a very early double location of Asclepius; in both, Apollo is already present. A later, Epidaurian
version retained 'the daughter of Phlegyas' (Coronis or Aigle) as
mother but made *Epidaurus his birthplace, where the baby was
exposed, nurtured by a goat, and protected by a dog (Paus. 2. 26.
3; hence the sacred dogs and the prohibition of goat sacrifice in
Epidaurus).

The two early local myths complicate the question of his local
origin. It seems prudent to assume two Archaic foci of a healer-
cult of Asclepius, in Tricca in Thessaly and in Messenia. Unlike
ordinary heroes, Asclepius must have been very early emancipated from the attachment to a local grave; this allowed him
to develop a god-like stature, though in most places he stayed
attached to his father Apollo. Tricca had 'the oldest and most
famous sanctuary' of Asclepius (Strabo 9. 5. 17, p. 437) which is
still archaeologically unknown, while the Asclepieum of
*Messene has revealed an important Hellenistic complex of
inner-city sanctuaries briefly described by Pausanias (4. 31. 10),
whose pre-Hellenistic roots are still unknown.

Expansion of Asclepius must have begun in late Archaic times;
both Cos and Epidaurus became famous during the 5th cent.
*Cos was the home of a school of physicians which was organized
in a pseudo-gentilicial way (i.e. as if it was a *genos): following
the lead of the Homeric Ἀσκληπιαδαί, they all called themselves
the descendants of Asclepius or Asclepiadae (Pl. Phdr. 270c). Local
tradition insisted on a Triccan origin (Herod. 2. 97). The site of
an early sanctuary is uncertain; when, in 366/5 BC, the city of
Cos was rebuilt, Asclepius received a sanctuary in a grove of
Apollo Cyparissius (LSAM 150 A, dated 325–300 BC); the famous
oath, sworn to Apollo, Asclepius, (his daughters) *Hygieia and
*Panacea, 'and all gods and goddesses', belongs to the same
period. At Epidaurus, Asclepius must have arrived in about 500
BC when his first sanctuary was built below the hill-sanctuary of
Apollo Maleatas where cult went back to the bronze age (first
ex-voto: Jeffery, LSAG 180). Epidaurus became the centre for later
expansion. Already in the 5th cent., Asclepius had come to
*Sicyon, brought on a mule cart and in the form of his snake
(Paus. 2. 10. 3). Similarly, the god sent his snake to Athens where
he arrived in 420/19, coming by sea to his sanctuary in the
*Piraeus (see the account in the Telemachus monument, recon-
structed by L. Beschi, ASAA 1967/8, 381–436 and AAA 1983, 31–
43); not long after, he was transferred by cart, together with
Hygieia, to his main city sanctuary on the west slope of the
Acropolis, well above the theatre of Dionysus. Perhaps already
in the 4th cent. BC, a certain Archias who had found healing in
Epidaurus, brought the cult to *Pergamum (Paus. 2. 26. 8 f.). To
cure a plague in 293 BC, the Sibylline books (see SIBYL) caused the
Romans to fetch the god's snake by ship from Epidaurus to
Rome, where the snake chose the Tiber island as its home (Livy
10. 47. 7), but a 5th-cent. dedication from Tuscany points to
much earlier acquaintance with the cult elsewhere in peninsular
Italy, and the architectural layout of the Hellenistic Asclepieum at
*Fregellae shows Coan influence (F. Coarelli, Fregellae 2 (1986)).
Epidaurian foundations might in their turn become foci for
further Asclepiea, like the one in Cyrenean Balagrae from which
derives the sanctuary on Crete at Lebena, or Pergamum mother
of the Smyrnaean sanctuary (Paus. 2. 26. 9). The origins of many
other Asclepiea are less well documented, but not necessarily
late—the Olympian dedication of Micythus of Rhegium who
lived in *Tegea after 467 BC dates Asclepius' Tegean cult not
much later than the Coan or Epidaurian one (Paus. 5. 26. 2); this
sanctuary, as many others in the Peloponnese, might derive from

Messenia, not from Epidaurus—though later combinations
obscure the picture, like the cult of Machaon in Messenian
Gerenia (Paus. 3. 26. 9).

The success of Asclepius was due to his appeal to individuals
in a world where their concerns became more and more removed
from polis religion and even from the healer Apollo, whose appeal
still was discernible in his expansion to Rome in 433 BC (see
AESCULAPIUS) and in his popularity in the Black Sea towns (see
EUXINE): with the one exception of Asclepius' transfer to Rome,
it was individuals who were responsible for the expansion. The
hero, 'best of the physicians', son of Apollo but still enough of a
human to try to cancel death, the fundamental borderline
between man and god in Greek thinking, was more easily accessible than Apollo who could proclaim lofty indifference towards
man and his destiny (Il. 21. 462–6); even as a god, Asclepius was
never so distant (see the very personal attachment of P. Aelius
*Aristides in the 2nd cent. AD to Pergamene Asclepius).

Most Asclepiea share common features. The children of
Asclepius, his sons Machaon and Podalirius and his daughter
Hygieia, have cult in most, as has Apollo whom official inscriptions from Epidaurus always name before Asclepius. Most sanctuaries contain a sacred snake, some—like Epidaurus—also
sacred dogs. A central feature of the cult is *incubation, the
receiving of dreams in which the god prescribes the healing; such
dreams are preserved in the long 'Sacred Discourses' ('Ιεροὶ
λόγοι) of Aelius *Aristides and in the accounts of more or less
miraculous healings inscribed in Epidaurus, Pergamum, Lebena,
and Rome (M. Guarducci, Epigrafia greca 4 (1978), 143–66; H.
Müller, Chiron 1987, 193–233). Often, actual medical therapy
followed the dream: Asclepiea developed into sacred hospitals
and nursing-homes, but, owing to their wide appeal, also constituted meeting-places for local intellectuals and places of philosophical instruction (as in Cilician Aegae, Philostr. VA 1. 7).
Besides the healing rites, other rituals are possible (initiatory
dedications of ephebic hair in *Paros (IG 12. 2. 173); burnt sacrifices in Titane (Paus. 2. 12. 7), with archaic cult images). Most
Asclepiea were situated outside the town, sometimes on the
seashore or in a lone valley, or at least in a marginal position in
town. They share such sites with oracular shrines; both constituted places where man could meet the divine directly (in his
sanctuary, Asclepius 'reveals himself in person to man', Philostr.
VA 1. 7).

In iconography, Asclepius generally appears as a mature,
bearded man, similar to Zeus, but with a milder expression; a
beardless Asclepius, as portrayed by *Calamis and *Scopas, is the
exception. His most constant attributes are the staff (see ritual
'putting up the staff' at Cos, [Hippoc.] Ep. 11. 778 Kühn) and the
snake, often coiled about the staff. Generally, the god is standing;
in the famous chryselephantine statue from Epidaurus (Paus. 2.
27. 2, see coins), the god is seated, the staff in his left hand, his
right extended above the head of a serpent, and beside the throne
lies a dog.

E. J. and L. Edelstein, Asclepius: A Collection and Interpretation of the
Testimonies (1945); R. Martin and H. Metzger, La Religion grecque (1976),
62–109; A. Semeria, Ann. S. N. Pisa 1986, 931–58; F. Graf, in O. Reverdin
and B. Grange (eds.), Le Sanctuaire grec (1992), 159–99. Iconography:
B. Holtzmann, LIMC 2 (1984), 863–97.   F. G.

Asconius Pedianus, Quintus (AD 3–88: probable meaning of
Jer. Chron. on 76, his death coming 12 years after the onset of
blindness; the earliest reference to his activities may be Servius'
remark (on Ecl. 4. 11) that C. *Asinius Gallus (d. AD 33) told
Asconius that *Virgil's fourth Eclogue was written in his honour);

from Padua (*Patavium) (*Livius noster* p. 77. 4 Clark; also Quint. 1. 7. 24). It is not known whether he had a public career, although he was certainly familiar with senatorial practice (e.g. 43. 27). His intimate knowledge of the city of Rome indicates that he spent many years there and possibly also composed his written work there. The only surviving work is part of a commentary (written AD 54–7) on *Cicero's speeches, preserved in the order *Pis., Scaur., Mil., Corn., Tog. Cand.*, and apparently much abbreviated. It is not known precisely how many speeches received such attention, but it was certainly a considerable number. This commentary was written for his two sons, in preparation for public life. The sources used include Cicero himself (some speeches now lost) and the invaluable *acta* for speeches after 59 BC. Although his reliability has occasionally been impugned (most notably by Marshall, 62–77), the consensus still regards him as a priceless resource, both for his chronological proximity to Cicero and for the variety of important sources accessible to him. Other works attributed to Asconius are: (1) *Vita Sallustii* (ps.-Acron on Hor. *Sat.* 1. 2. 41); (2) a work possibly entitled *De longaevorum laude* or *Symposium* (Pliny, *HN* 7. 159; *Suda*, entry under Ἀπίκιος); (3) *Contra Vergilii obtrectatores* (Donat. *Vit. Verg.* 191, ed. C. Hardie, OCT). The manuscripts of the commentary on Cicero also contain a mainly grammatical work on *Verr.*, but this has been shown by Madvig to be a 5th-cent. compilation.

LIFE AND WORKS *PIR*[2] A 1206; J. N. Madvig, *De Q. Asconii Pediani et Aliorum Interpretum in Ciceronis Orationes Commentariis* (1828); B. A. Marshall, *A Historical Commentary on Asconius* (1985); S. Squires, *Asconius: Commentaries on Five Speeches of Cicero*, with trans. (1990).

TEXTS Kiessling–Schöll (1875); A. C. Clark (OCT, 1907); T. Stangl, *Ciceronis Orationum Scholiastae* (1912); C. Giarratano (1920); see also M. D. Reeve, in L. D. Reynolds (ed.), *Texts and Transmission* (1983), 24–5.   P. K. M.

Ascra (local form: Askre), a Greek village in the territory of *Thespiae, founded by Diocles and the *Aloadae, best known as the home of *Hesiod, who defamed it forever by describing it as 'bad in winter, hard in summer, but never good' (*Op.* 640). Located in the Valley of the Muses on Mt. *Helicon, the site of the village is still marked by a stone tower. Although the Thespians destroyed it at some point, it survived until the Hellenistic period, only to decline afterwards. Archaeological survey shows that it revived markedly in the 4th–6th cents. AD.

J. Bintliff and A. Snodgrass, *Antiquity* 1988, 60 ff., and in H. Beister and J. Buckler (eds.), *BOIOTIKA* (1989), 285 ff.   J. Bu.

Asculum Picenum, the capital of *Picenum, strongly placed amid imposing mountains near the Adriatic on the river Truentus (Strab 5. 241); modern Ascoli Piceno, with numerous ancient remains. Rome captured Asculum in 268 BC and continued the *via Salaria to it (Florus 1. 14). The *Social War (3) broke out here, but the Romans recovered the town after a two-year siege and grimly punished it (App. *BCiv.* 1. 38, 47, 48). In imperial times it was a *colonia* (Plin. *HN* 3. 111). See also A(U)SCULUM SATRIANUM
E. T. S.

Asellio See SEMPRONIUS ASELLIO.

Ashoka, the major king of the Mauryan dynasty ruling *c.*268–232 BC over almost all the Indian subcontinent (see MAURYAS). His edicts were inscribed on pillars and rock surfaces and were largely composed in Prakrit and written in Brahmi although some in the north-west were in Greek and *Aramaic. Apart from being the earliest deciphered epigraphs in Indian history, they provide details of his reign and of his attempts, inspired by Buddhism, to persuade his subjects to conform to values of social well-being. He makes mention of five contemporary Hellenistic kings: *Antiochus (2) II, *Ptolemy (1) II Philadelphus, *Antigonus (2) Gonatas, Magas of Cyrene, and Alexander of either Epirus or Corinth.

R. Thapar, *Asoka and the Decline of the Mauryas*, 2nd edn. (1973).
R. Th.

Asia, Roman province *Attalus III of Pergamum bequeathed his kingdom to the Romans. After his death in 133 BC it was constituted as *provincia Asia* by M'. *Aquillius (1). Originally it consisted of Mysia, the Troad (*Troas), *Aeolis, *Lydia, Ionia (see IONIANS), the islands along the coast, much of *Caria, and at least a land corridor through *Pisidia to *Pamphylia. Part of *Phrygia was given to Mithradates V Euergetes and was not made part of the province until 116 BC. *Lycaonia was added before 100 and the area around Cibyra in 82 BC. After 80 BC, the SE portion was removed and joined to the new province of Cilicia, as were the Phrygian assize-districts of Laodicea, Apamea, and Synnada between 56 and 50 BC. Under the empire Asia included all the territory from Amorium and Philomelium in the east to the sea; it was bounded in the north by Bithynia, in the south by Lycia, and on the east by Galatia.

The province of Asia was rich in natural resources and in the products of agriculture and industry. Woollen fabrics were a speciality of the interior. Long-established trade routes ran from the interior along the valleys of the *Hermus and the *Maeander to the harbours of the Aegean. Roman republican governors and capitalists exploited the new province with predatory rapacity and aroused widespread hatred, which was exploited by *Mithradates VI when he stirred up much of Asia to revolt between 88 and 85 BC. Allegedly 80,000 Italians were murdered in a single day at his instigation. After defeating Mithradates *Sulla reorganized the province in 85/4 BC. and revised the administrative pattern into eleven assize-districts. This occasion marked the beginning of a new era for many cities, especially in the interior regions of Lydia and Phrygia. Methods of taxation were taken over from the Attalids, but Roman innovations included new customs arrangements introduced by a law of 75 BC, which, with several revisions, was still in force in AD 62 (see PORTORIA). Asia continued to suffer from heavy taxation and arbitrary exactions through the civil wars of the late republic. The province had the misfortune to pick the losing side in the wars between Mithradates and Rome, between *Pompey and *Caesar, between the tyrannicides and Antony (M. *Antonius (2)), and between Antony and *Octavian. Neither victors nor losers in these wars hesitated to milk its rich resources. The principate of Augustus brought relief and was welcomed with genuine hope and enthusiasm, which is reflected above all in the organization of *ruler-cult, both at provincial and civic level, throughout the province.

Asia was now governed by a proconsul (see PRO CONSULE), who normally served for one year, assisted by three legates (*legati*) and a quaestor. He traditionally landed at *Ephesus, the headquarters of the republican *publicani* and later of the imperial *procurators, but spent much of his time visiting the assize centres (*conventus) of the province according to a fixed rotation, where he heard cases and conducted other judicial business. The structure of the assize-districts is illustrated by an inscription of the Flavian period from Ephesus, which lists the assize centres and the smaller cities which were subordinate to them. Ephesus eclipsed the old Attalid capital of *Pergamum, although these cities and *Smyrna remained locked in rivalry for the rank of

leading provincial city. The other assize centres included Adra-
myttium, *Cyzicus, *Synnada, Apamea, *Miletus, *Halicarnassus (*JRS* 1975, 64–91).

Under the Principate new cities were created in the interior
regions of Mysia, Lydia, and Phrygia; the province thus comprised a conglomeration of self-governing cities on which the
Roman system of provincial government depended. The cities
were responsible for local administration, for their own finances
and building (sometimes under the supervision of an outside
curator (see CURATOR REI PUBLICAE)), for law and order on their
territories, and for tax collection. The province was represented
as a unity by the council (*koinon*) of Asia, a general assembly of
representatives from all the cities and other communities, which
met annually in one of the five provincial cities (Ephesus, Smyrna,
Pergamum, *Sardis, and Cyzicus) and organized the provincial
imperial cult (see CONCILIUM). The high priests (*archiereis*) of Asia
are probably to be distinguished from other provincial officials
called Asiarchs, but the relationship of the two posts remains
controversial. Progress towards provincial unity, however, was
always hampered by inter-city rivalry, particularly among the
communities of the west coast and the Maeander valley.

Asia was supposedly one of the ungarrisoned provinces of
the empire. No full legions were stationed there, but legionary
detachments were present at various periods at the Phrygian
cities of Apamea and Amorium, there was an auxiliary cohort
stationed at Phrygian Eumeneia, and smaller contingents of soldiers were regularly used to patrol routes through mountainous
areas. During the 3rd cent. AD soldiers were increasingly present
in hitherto peaceful rural areas, leading to conflict and bitter
complaints from the rural civilian population.

In the first two centuries AD the cities of Asia enjoyed great
prosperity, attested by splendid ruins and handsome monuments,
and reflected, for instance, in the panegyric speeches of P. Aelius
*Aristides. The wealth of inscriptions, locally minted coins, and
material remains makes Asia one of the best documented of all
Roman provinces. The cities had changed from autonomous
city-states into administrative centres, but countless inscriptions
attest the eagerness of members of the city aristocracies for public
service, their generosity in providing civic amenities (doubtless at
the expense of the rural populations which they exploited), and
the entry of many families into the senatorial and equestrian
orders. The glittering and extravagant society of the coastal cities,
with their wealthy rhetors and sophists, contrasts with the traditional, rural-based society of the Anatolian interior. Urbanization brought Graeco-Roman culture up-country, but the basic
Anatolian character of the population of regions such as Lydia
and Phrygia was of enduring importance and was particularly
conspicuous in their religious cults. The strict, self-disciplined
morality of Anatolian pagan belief in the hinterland of the province of Asia provided fertile ground where Jewish and early
Christian groups flourished. Much of the interior had apparently
converted to Christianity before the beginning of the 4th cent.

In the 3rd cent. AD the province suffered not only from the
indiscipline of the soldiery and a general decline in voluntary
civic generosity, but also from a collapse in security prompted by
*Gothic invasions of the 250s and 260s, which led many cities to
pull down their public buildings to provide material for hastily
improvised fortifications. As the political and strategic emphasis
shifted away from the Aegean to the Anatolian plateau and to
the overland routes between the Balkans and the eastern frontier,
Asia lost some of its former prominence and was divided into
seven smaller provinces by *Diocletian. In the political order of

the 4th cent. the leading cities which served as new provincial
capitals—such as Ephesus, Sardis, and *Aphrodisias—retained
much of their former glory, but most of the cities of the interior
declined until they were barely distinguishable from villages.

> T. R. S. Broughton, in Frank, *Econ. Survey* 4; Jones, *Cities E. Rom. Prov.*
> ch. 2; Magie, *Rom. Rule Asia Min.*; S. Mitchell, *Anatolia: Land, Men, and
> Gods in Asia Minor*, 2 vols. (1993); C. Habicht and G. P. Burton, *JRS*
> 1975, 64–91, 92–106 (the assize system); S. R. F. Price, *Rituals and Power:
> The Roman Imperial Cult in Asia Minor* (1984).
>
> W. M. C.; E. W. G.; S. M.

Asia, south-east known as *Chrysē*, 'the Golden Land' to Pomponius Mela (3. 70) and Pliny (*HN* 6. 54, 80). The *Peripl. M. Rubr.*
(63. 20) refers to it as a place for regular trade on the edge of the
inhabited world, but only a few coins, glass, seals, and bronzes
from the Roman world are known. To the finds from Oc-éo
in southern Vietnam, and the bronze lamp from Pong Tuk in
Thailand, can be added a coin of the usurper *Victorinus found
near U-Thong in western Thailand.

Direct contact between *India and south-east Asia is shown
by the appearance of iron in the mid-1st millennium BC as seen
at Ban Don Ta Phet in western Thailand and the Sa-Huynh
culture of Vietnam. Imports from India include glass, semi-
precious stone beads, carnelian lion pendants as found in early
Buddhist reliquaries, and 'etched' beads. Bronzes, with scenes of
people, houses, horses, cattle, and buffaloes, resemble those on
the Kulu vase from Gundla, India, and knob-base vessels are
paralleled by one in an early Buddhist reliquary at Taxila.

Indo-Roman rouletted ware in Java, Bali, and Vietnam is evidence for indirect trade between the Mediterranean and south-
east Asia via India, where it is found at Arikamedu, identified as
Podukeē of the *Periplus*, along with imported Roman Arretine
ware, seals, and amphorae from the Mediterranean.

> V. Begley and R. D. De Puma (eds.), *Rome and India—the Ancient Sea
> Trade* (1991); L. Casson, *The Periplus Maris Erythraei* (1989); I. C. Glover,
> *Early Trade between India and South-East Asia*, Occ. Paper 16, Hull:
> Centre for South-East Asian Studies (1990); L. Malleret, *L'Archéologie
> du Delta du Mekong* (1960–2).   I. C. G.

Asia Minor

Pre-Classical Palaeolithic and mesolithic occupation was in caves
and rock-shelters and has left simple paintings. The neolithic
(*c.*8000–6500 BC) brought settlement in plains and valleys, growth
of villages, and the domestication of plants and animals. Vigorous
wall-paintings at Çatal Hüyük and clay statuary at Hacılar
emphasize hunting, virility, fertility, and childbirth. Painted
pottery first appears in the chalcolithic (*c.*6500–3400 BC). An
economic upsurge in the early bronze age (*c.*3400–2000 BC) was
made possible by developments in metallurgy, attested in metalwork from Troy and from royal burials at Alaca Hüyük, and
was perhaps stimulated by Mesopotamian demand for native
Anatolian metals. Greater wealth led to universal fortification of
settlements and the rise of citadels (e.g. *Troy) and of palaces
(e.g. Norşun Tepe). By the middle bronze age (*c.*2000–1700 BC)
Assyrians had trading-stations in central Anatolia on which indigenous rulers at (e.g.) Kültepe, Alişar, and Acemhöyük imposed
levies. *Cuneiform writing was introduced. In the late bronze
age (*c.*1700–1200 BC) the *Hittites dominated central Anatolia
from *Hattuša (mod. Boğazköy). Extreme western and northern
regions remained largely independent, but a north Syrian province was administered from Carchemish. Famine and Sea-
Peoples are thought to have been responsible for extinguishing
the state *c.*1200 BC, but the royal line continued at Carchemish

and in other north Syrian kingdoms, where Hittite culture survived into the iron age (c.1200–700 BC). Central Anatolia was dominated by the Phrygians (capital at *Gordium) and eastern Anatolia by the kingdom of *Urartu.

*CAH*³ 1, chs. 7b, 18, 24; 2, chs. 6, 15, 21, 24, 30; 3, chs. 8, 9; J. Mellaart, *The Archaeology of Ancient Turkey* (1978).   D. F. E.

Classical The geographical term Asia Minor is used to denote the westernmost part of the Asian continent, equivalent to modern Turkey between the Aegean and the Euphrates. The western and southern coastal fringes were part of the Mediterranean world; the heartland of Asia Minor lay in the interior of Anatolia, comprising the hilly but fertile uplands of *Phrygia, the steppic central plateau, and the rugged and harsh country of *Cappadocia. These areas were framed by the Pontic ranges which rise steeply from the Black Sea in the north, and the long range of the *Taurus which snakes through southern Anatolia from Lycia to the Euphrates and separates Asia Minor from Syria. In the Graeco-Roman period the region's history is illuminated by an almost limitless flood of historical information, which makes it possible to identify the separate languages, cultures, and religious traditions of its various regions—*Bithynia, Mysia, *Lydia, *Caria, *Lycia, *Pisidia, *Cilicia, *Cappadocia, *Galatia, *Paphlagonia, and *Pontus—and also to document the influence of external powers and cultures, above all of Persia, Greece, and Rome. Asia Minor was one of the economic powerhouses of the Persian empire. Much of the population of eastern Anatolia had strong Iranian connections, and Persian settlements were also widespread in the west after the mid-6th cent. BC. Many endured until late antiquity. Greek influence—*Hellenism—was naturally strongest in the coastal areas, where Greeks had established settlements between c.1100 and 600 BC. The cultural process, however, was not one-way, and the Greeks of Caria and *Pamphylia were also much influenced by pre-existing Anatolian cultures. During the 4th cent. BC Hellenization spread to the indigenous inhabitants of Pisidia and Lycia in the south-west; most of the interior, however, was barely touched before the 1st cent. BC. Roman rule made the strongest impact. In the time of Hadrian Asia Minor was divided into six provinces: Asia, Pontus and Bithynia, Galatia, Lycia and Pamphylia, Cilicia, and Cappadocia, although provincial boundaries and administrative arrangements were more flexible in Anatolia than in almost any other part of the empire. The creation of an all-embracing road network, the universal *ruler-cult, the founding of cities to act as administrative centres, a permanent military presence, and the creation of far-reaching systems of *taxation forged a new society in Asia Minor, which was as much Roman as it was Anatolian.

The indigenous regional cultures of Asia Minor, however, survived until the end of antiquity, preserving their native languages and their religious practices (see ANATOLIAN DEITIES; ANATOLIAN LANGUAGES), above all in the rural parts of the interior and in the mountains. These were only finally erased by the spread of Christianity, which became strongly rooted as early as the 3rd cent. and extended, except for obstinate, usually urban, pockets of paganism, across the whole of the peninsula by the end of the 4th century. Neither Christianity nor the introduction of Islam by the Turks between the 11th and 14th centuries obliterated the basic patterns of Anatolian life, which were rooted in a traditional rural economy. There was a continuity of population and settlement pattern which can be observed even in contemporary Turkey, where the modern peasant is manifestly the descendant of his Hittite or, indeed, neolithic forebears.

Magie, *Rom. Rule Asia Min.*; L. Robert, *A travers l'Asie Mineure* (1980);

S. Mitchell, *Anatolia*, 2 vols. (1993); R. Syme (ed. A. Birley), *Anatolica* (1995).   S. M.

Asianism and Atticism The Greek orators of Asia Minor during the Hellenistic period developed a new style of oratory, marked by wordplay, emotional effect, bombast, and rhythm; some idea of it can be obtained from the scanty fragments of *Hegesias (2) and from some of the Greek declaimers excerpted by L. *Annaeus Seneca (1). There was an inevitable reaction, seen clearly in the work of the Augustan critics *Dionysius (7) of Halicarnassus and *Caecilius (1) of Caleacte, in favour of the stylistic and lexicographical norms of 5th-cent. Attic oratory (see ATTIC ORATORS). Later this reaction was to set an enduring mark on Greek prose right up to the Byzantine era. The confrontation of styles is best known from its Latin repercussions. *Cicero, with his Greek educational background and florid manner, was criticized as an 'Asian' by what he represents in the *Brutus* and the *Orator* as a minority of extremists who even thought the style of *Thucydides (2) appropriate in a Roman court. These polemics may cover a clash between Cicero and his rival, C. *Licinius Calvus, over the title of Roman Demosthenes (see DEMOSTHENES (2)). The controversy was in any case short-lived at Rome, and it was never particularly meaningful in Roman circumstances. The tendencies of Silver Latin might be thought to suggest an 'Asian' victory in the west; in the east, the admirers of Attic prose were able to suppress the productions of their rivals (see RHETORIC; SECOND SOPHISTIC).

U. von Wilamowitz-Moellendorff, *Hermes* 1900, 1–52 is the classic exposition; E. Norden's *Die Antike Kunstprosa* (1898; repr. with suppls., 1909) is a rich source of material, though he may be thought to overuse the concept of Asianism. For Atticism, W. Schmid, *Der Atticismus* (1887–96).   M. W.

Asine, a town in the Argolid, on the coast, south-east of Nauplion. Excavations by Swedish expeditions have revealed occupation extending from the early bronze age, succeeded by an important middle Helladic settlement.

Late bronze age remains centre on a promontory acropolis, whose *fortification, though much rebuilt in later times, was probably laid out in this period. Inhabited areas extend beyond this, particularly to the east, in the protogeometric and subsequent periods. There are substantial Hellenistic fortifications. Historically, Asine was subjugated by the Argives (see ARGOS (2)), probably in the 8th cent. BC when the inhabitants are said to have been given a refuge by the Spartans in *Messenia. Occupation of the site, however, continued unbroken into the Classical period.

O. Frodin and A. W. Persson (ed. A. Westholm), *Asine [1]: The results of the Swedish Excavations* (1938); I. and R. Hagg, *Excavations in the Barbouna Area at Asine* (Boreas 4 / 1–2, 1973–8); G. C. Nordquist, *A Middle Helladic Village: Asine in the Argolid* (Boreas 16, 1987); various authors, *Asine II* (1976–).   R. A. T.

Asinius (*RE* 15) **Gallus, Gaius,** son of C. *Asinius Pollio, born in 41 BC, was consul 8 BC and proconsul of Asia 6–5 BC. He had married *Vipsania Agrippina (1) when *Tiberius had to divorce her in 12 BC, and the marriage produced five sons. A friend of *Augustus, who (in a fictitious anecdote) judged him ambitious enough to aim at the Principate, though not equal to it (Tac. *Ann.* 1. 13), he angered Tiberius with proposals in the senate designed to enhance the emperor's power. He was arrested in AD 30 and died of starvation after three years in custody; Tiberius alleged a sexual intrigue with *Vipsania Agrippina (2), and his name was erased from public monuments. A fine orator, he also wrote epigrams, and *A Comparison of Cicero and my Father*, criticizing *Cicero's style.

Syme, *AA*; B. Levick, *Tiberius the Politician* (1976), see indexes; coin portrait: M. Grant, *From Imperium to Auctoritas* (1946), 387.

R. S.; B. M. L.

Asinius Pollio, Gaius (76 BC–AD 4), supported *Caesar, as praetor in 45, commanding in Spain in 44, and then joined Antony (M. *Antonius (2)); in Cisalpine Gaul in 41 he saved *Virgil's property from confiscation. Consul in 40, he celebrated a triumph over the Parthini of Illyria in 39; from the booty he built the first public *library in Rome. Then, with full honours, he retired from politics to devote himself to literature, organizing the first public recitations.

In youth an associate of *Catullus, he later enjoyed the friendship of Horace (*Carm.* 2. 1) and Virgil (*Ecl.* 4). His own work included poetry, tragedy, and oratory in Atticist style (see ASIANISM AND ATTICISM), but he was above all an historian. The *Historiae* treated the period from 60 BC to the battle of Philippi in 42; analytical, critical, and serious, they were used by Plutarch and Appian. A sharp critic, he corrected Cicero and Caesar, Sallust for *archaism, and Livy for provincialism (*Patavinitas*); and he maintained his republican independence even against Augustus.

*PIR*² A 1241; G. Zecchini, *ANRW* 2. 30. 2 (1982), 1265 ff. (with bibliography).

A. H. McD.; A. J. S. S.

Asinius Quadratus, Gaius, author of the *Thousand Years* (Χιλιετηρίς), a fifteen-book history of Rome from the beginnings to Severus Alexander with a Greek slant (it was written in Ionic Greek and equated Rome's foundation with the first Olympiad in 776 BC), and a Parthian history in at least nine books. Probably the same as C. Asinius Protimus Quadratus (*PIR*² A 1244; P. Herrmann, *Chiron* 1993, 233 ff.), Severan suffect consul; if so, of Asiatic Greek origin.

*PIR*² 1. 508; E. Bowie, in M. Finley (ed.), *Studies in Ancient Society* (1974), 176.

H. H. S.; A. J. S. S.

Asisium (mod. Assisi), birthplace (probably) of *Propertius, *municipium* of *Umbria on the western slopes of the Apennines. It played little part in history until captured by Totila *c.* AD 545 (Procop. 7. 12). Its early imperial temple of 'Minerva' serves today as a church.

L. Temperini, *Assisi romana e medievale* (1985). E. T. S.; T. W. P.

Asius, of Samos (?6th cent. BC), wrote genealogical hexameter poetry (see GENEALOGY) concerning the legendary history of *Samos and other parts of Greece; also some elegy.

Davies, *EGF* 88 ff.; Bernabé, *PEG* 1. 127 ff.; G. L. Huxley, *Greek Epic Poetry* (1969), 89–98.

M. L. W.

askoliasmos (ἀσκωλιασμός), a country sport in Attica. The players tried to keep their balance while jumping on an inflated and greasy wine-skin (ἀσκός). It was probably played at many festivals, and despite Verg. *G.* 2. 384 should not be particularly connected with the Rural *Dionysia in Attica. Its origin was discussed by *Eratosthenes.

*DFA*³ 45; Fraser, *Ptol. Alex.* 2. 904 note 202.

H. J. R.; S. H.

Asmonius (4th cent. AD), grammarian cited by *Priscian as the author of a (lost) *ars dedicated to the emperor *Constantius II and of a treatise on metre. The latter may survive under the name '*Ap(h)thonius'.

Cf. Herzog-Schmidt, § 525. 1.

R. A. K.

Aspasia, Milesian-born mistress of *Pericles (1) from *c.*445 BC

when he divorced his wife. She is said to have taught rhetoric (*Suda*), and to have had discussions with *Socrates (Plut. *Per.* 24). She was the target of attacks and jokes in comedy because of her supposed influence over Pericles: Ar. *Ach.* 515 ff. blames her for the main *Peloponnesian War. The story that *Hermippus (1) the comic poet prosecuted her for impiety (Plut. *Per.* 32) probably rests on a misunderstanding of some passage in one of his comedies: it is not saved even by other traditions 'circumstantially' reporting Pericles' pathetic behaviour at the trial. Her (subsequently legitimated) son by Pericles, also a Pericles, was one of the generals put to death after *Arginusae. After Pericles' death in 429 Aspasia allegedly took up with another *demagogue, Lysicles, until he died in 428. See also EPITAPHIOS.

G. Busolt, *Gr. Gesch.* (1893–1904), 3. 505 ff.; I. F. Stone, *The Trial of Socrates* (1988), 233 ff.; K. J. Dover, *The Greeks and their Legacy* 2 (1988), ch. 13; P. Stadter, *Plut. Per. Comm.* (1989); M. Henry, *Prisoner of History* (1994).

S. H.

Aspasius (*RE* 2) (*c.* AD 100–50), Peripatetic. His commentaries on *Aristotle's *Cat.*, *Int.*, *Metaph.*, *Ph.*, and *Cael.*, and his *Treatise on the Natural Emotions* are lost. His commentary on the *Nicomachean Ethics* survives in part (ed. G. Heylbut, *Comm. in Arist. Graec.* 19 / 1 (1889)). The treatment of the *Nicomachean Ethics* rather than the *Eudemian* as the authoritative Aristotelian ethical work begins with this commentary. Aspasius continued the process of removing Stoic formulations from the Peripatetic doctrine of emotion.

H. Gottschalk, *ANRW* 2. 36. 2 (1987), 1156–8; A. Kenny, *The Aristotelian Ethics* (1978), 29–36; P. Moraux, *Der Aristotelismus*, 2 (1984), 226–93; F. Becchi, *Prometheus* 1983, in *Studi Barigazzi* 1 (1984), and *ANRW* 2. 36. 7 (forthcoming).

R. W. S.

Aspendus, a city in *Pamphylia whose inhabitants claimed kinship with the Argives (see HELLENISM; ARGOS (2)). Linguistic evidence shows that most of the inhabitants were of Anatolian origin (see ANATOLIAN LANGUAGES). The city issued coins in the 5th cent. BC which preserve its Anatolian name Estvediys, to be identified with the Asitawandas named on inscriptions of the second millennium BC from Karatepe. Although assessed as a member of the *Delian League, it preferred Persian rule, even resisting *Alexander (3) the Great. It was alternately under Ptolemaic and Seleucid rule until 189 BC, and later came under Roman control. Situated 13 km. (8 mi.) from the present mouth of the *Eurymedon, which was navigable as far as the city, it had an important harbour from which grain was exported. The remains include *market buildings and a council-house of the Hellenistic period, as well as many important Roman public buildings, above all the magnificently preserved *theatre and long stretches of *aqueduct.

S. Jameson, *RE* Suppl. 12. 99–109; K. Lanckoroński, *Städte Pamphyliens* 1 (1890), 85 ff.

S. M.

Asper, Aemilius See AEMILIUS ASPER.

assembly See EKKLESIA.

assembly, Macedonian Mass assemblies are known from Macedonia under the monarchy only in times of crisis; since Macedonian crises were usually directly military or connected with a military operation, those assembling were soldiers or soldiers and camp-followers, who were asked to support a decision already taken by the king or (if the king was dead) by leading barons and officers. There is no ancient evidence for an assembly ever having met at regular intervals, either in peacetime or in war. Reported meetings are always ad hoc and reflect a temporary weakness of the leading persons (whether the king or other leaders) caused by extreme circumstances which momentarily created an unusual level of dependence on the army by the leader(s), and necessitated the acquisition of practical support for an unusual, difficult, or even dangerous decision by those immediately affected by it. Modern historians writing about Macedonia have often been dissatisfied with merely describing the subtle and unsystematic workings of this state dominated by its kings and barons, who, however, were in practice dependent on maintaining the support of the army for their extravagant military operations. Some have tried to explain what they found by extrapolating from the loosely structured play of political forces which the sources report a more developed, more civilized, and more systematic assembly system. Picking up tiny hints from writers of the Roman empire, who were either interpreting a particular political situation in Roman terms for their Roman readers (e.g. Q. *Curtius Rufus 6. 8. 25) or making a trivial rhetorical contrast in a constructed speech (Arr. *Anab.* 4. 11. 6), inspired moreover by the 20th-cent. *Zeitgeist* to seek legalism and modernistic 'constitutionality' (*Staatsrecht*) in ancient state structures, historians have constructed various models of a Macedonian assembly. The two main variants are those of F. Granier, who made an 'Army Assembly' (*Heeresversammlung*) responsible for recognizing a new king and for holding treason trials, and of P. Briant, who, acknowledging that there is no support in the sources for Granier's construction (even as later emended by A. Aymard, who tried to refute the devastating criticism of P. de Francisci), postulated instead a 'People's Assembly' with the same functions, but for which there is even less evidence. These modern constructs, unknown to all ancient writers, confuse ad hoc support-seeking within a delicate and continually changing balance of practical influence and power with a modernizing legalistic constitutionality. But they continue to attract some modern writers.

For: F. Granier, *Die makedonische Heeresversammlung* (1931); A. Aymard, *Études d'histoire ancienne* (1967); P. Briant, *Antigone le Borgne* (1973); N. G. L. Hammond, *The Macedonian State* (1989). Against: P. de Francisci, *Arcana Imperii* 2 (1948); R. M. Errington, *Chiron*, 1978, and *A History of Macedonia* (1990; Ger. orig. 1986); E. Borza, *In the Shadow of Olympus* (1990). R. M. E.

assizes See CONVENTUS (2).

associations See CLUBS.

assonance, Greek Assonance is a technical term of modern literary analysis, used of a perceptible repetition of a sound or sounds within a verbal sequence. We may distinguish: (1) consonantal repetition, generally called 'alliteration', especially if word-initial (βράγχος καὶ βῆχες καὶ βαρυφωνίη Hippoc. *Aer.* 8; κακῶν ... κῦμα Aesch. *Sept.* 758) or stem-initial (δυσκύμαντα ... κακά Aesch. *Ag.* 653); (2) vocalic repetition (ἄγριον ἄνδρα Il. 8. 96, λαμπρὸν φάος [α-ο/α-ο] Il. 1. 605); (3) syllabic repetition, or near-repetition, of stem syllables (πάθει μάθος Aesch. *Ag.* 177, σῶμα ... σῆμα Pl. *Grg.* 493a), and of (4) final syllables (i.e. rhyme or near-rhyme: γέροντας ὄντας Ar. *Ach.* 222, στρόφου καὶ ψόφου Hippoc. *VM* 10, γιγνόμενος ἀναίσθητος θάνατος Thuc. 2. 43. 6, κρείων Ἀγαμέμνων Il. 1. 130).

In ancient stylistics assonance is rarely discussed and inconsistently labelled. Types (3) and (4) are sometimes referred to as *paronomasia* (Cic. *De or.* 2. 256), *parhomoiōsis* (Arist. *Rh.* 3. 9. 9), *homoioteleuton* (Quint. *Inst.* 9. 3. 77), (1) and (2) as *homoioprophoron* (Martianus Capella 5. 13), *homoiokatarkton* (Phld. *Rh.* 1. 162), or

merely designated by sound ('the Euripides *sigma*': Plato Com. 29 *PCG*). In Greek literary practice, however, all four types are common, especially in verse, though none is as systematically exploited as (say) alliteration in early Latin, or rhyme in later European, verse. Type (4) is ubiquitous because of the inflectedness of the Greek language, but (except in sophistic-oratorical prose) is rare as a significant stylistic resource. Type (3) is less common, but usually significant. Types (2) and (1) are much commoner, especially in verse, but are often low in perceptibility because the collocation is conventional (as ἄγριον ἄνδρα: contrast κακῶν ... κῦμα).

The main uses of these patterns (not necessarily mutually exclusive) are as follows. (*a*) To link the constituent items: most of the above examples belong here. (*b*) As emotional intensification of the word-group that carries the assonance. Pure instances (usually involving multiple alliteration) are rare but striking: τυφλὸς τά τ' ὦτα τόν τε νοῦν τά τ' ὄμματ' εἶ (Soph. *OT* 371), ἀμφ' Ὀδυσῆι δαΐφρονι δαίεται ἦτορ | δυσμόρῳ, ὃς δὴ δηθὰ φίλων ἄπο πήματα πάσχει (*Od.* 1. 48–9: δδ ... ππ ...). (*c*) For mimetic (loosely, 'onomatopoeic') effect: ἐν ὀρφναῖσιν πέτρας | φοίνισσα κυλινδομένα φλὸξ ἐς βαθεῖαν φέρει πόντου πλάκα σὺν παταγῷ (Pind. *Pyth.* 1. 23–4: a noisy π/φ pattern for the eruption of *Aetna (1)). Instances of (*b*) tend to (*c*) when associated with violent action: ἔσσευε κούρα κάπρον ἀναιδομάχαν | ἐς καλλίχορον Καλυδῶν(α) (Bacchyl. 5. 104–7: κκ ... χχ ... καλ). (*d*) As an organizing principle in a great variety of contexts: to point parallel phrases, as often in 'Gorgianic' oratory (ταῖς ψυχαῖς διαφέρειν ἢ ταῖς ἰδέαις ἐλλείπειν Lys. 2. 4), but also often elsewhere (ὦ πῦρ σὺ καὶ πᾶν δεῖμα καὶ πανουργίας | δεινῆς τέχνημ' ἔχθιστον Soph. *Phil.* 927–8), or simple metrical units (e.g. the halves of an elegiac 'pentameter': ἴσχει γὰρ χαλεπῆς πείρατ' ἀμηχανίης Thgn. 140), or larger units (and larger thoughts: Aesch. *Cho.* 935 ff., strophe ἔμολε μὲν δίκα ... ἔμολε δ' ἐς δόμον ..., antistrophe ἔμολε δ' ᾇ μέλει ... ἔθιγε δ' ἐν μάχᾳ; for antiphonal lament (—δορὶ δ' ἔκανες—δορὶ δ' ἔθανες | —μελεοπόνος—μελεοπαθής Aesch. *Sept.* 962–3) or antiphonal insult (—τυφογέρων εἶ κἀνάρμοστος—καταπύγων εἶ κἀναίσχυντος Ar. *Nub.* 908–9). In (*d*) as in (*a*) there is often a sense of linking, especially where assonance enforces a simple parallel or opposition: ἅμ' ἔπος, ἅμ' ἔργον (prov. in [Zen.] 1. 77); οὔτε σώμασιν οὔτε χρήμασιν εὐδαιμονοῦσιν ἄνθρωποι, ἀλλ' ὀρθοσύνῃ καὶ πολυφροσύνῃ (Democr. 40); τῆς δόξης μᾶλλον ἢ τοῦ δέους ἀπηλλάγησαν (Thuc. 2. 42. 4); μήτε πολὺ μήτε παχύ (Hippoc. *Acut.* 19). (*e*) To mark off a whole passage as special (usually by multiple assonance). First in Hesiod (Μοῦσαι Πιερίηθεν ἀοιδῇσι κλείουσαι, | δεῦτε, Δί' ἐννέπετε, σφέτερον πατέρ' ὑμνείουσαι *Op.* 1–2); often in early aphoristic prose (πόλεμος πάντων μὲν πατήρ ἐστι Heraclit. 53; κατήγμασι δὲ σπληνῶν μήκεα, πλάτεα, πάχεα, πλήθεα Hippoc. *Off.* 12, πᾶσι πάντοθεν πολὺς πλάδος Hippoc. *Epid.* 1. 5, both complete sentences); flaunted, as a demonstration of the emotive power of words, in Gorgianic-sophistic prose (ἐπειράθην καταλῦσαι μῶμον ἀδικίαν καὶ δόξης ἀμαθίαν, ἐβουλήθην γράψαι ... Gorg. *Hel.* 21), and parodied as such by Plato in Agathon's sophistic praise of love, *Symp.* 197de, ἐν πόνῳ, ἐν φόβῳ, ἐν πόθῳ, ἐν λόγῳ, κυβερνήτης, ἐπιβάτης, παραστάτης. (*f*) For euphony: καὶ Χλῶριν εἶδον περικαλλέα *Od.* 11. 281, with predominant λ ν ρ (an example noted by Dion. Hal. *Comp.* 16). Such an instance is arguably a subtype of (*c*). Euphony, however, often involves no assonance: cf. e.g. the melodious five-vowel opening phrases of Pindar's *Ol.* 1 (ἄριστον μὲν ὕδωρ) and *Pyth.* 1 (χρυσέα φόρμιγξ).

In Greek literature, as in other literatures, (*a*) and (*d*) are the predominant functions, though (*a*) in particular is often ignored by ancient theorists and modern classical commentators.

Norden, *Ant. Kunstpr.* 810 ff.; J. D. Denniston, *Greek Prose Style* (1952), 124 ff.; W. B. Stanford, *The Sound of Greek* (1967); M. S. Silk, *Interaction in Poetic Imagery* (1974), 173 ff., 224 ff.   M. S. Si.

assonance, Latin Assonance, the recurrence of sounds in proximity, is a common feature of language, observable in all periods of Latin.

Alliteration The repetition of initial sounds appears in formulaic language of all levels in (*a*) idioms and proverbs: 'purus putus', 'fortes fortuna iuuat', 'domo doctus dico'; (*b*) prayers: 'quod felix faustum fortunatumque siet', 'utique tu fruges frumenta uineta uirgultaque grandire beneque euenire siris, pastores pecuaque salua seruassis' (Cato *Agr.* 141); (*c*) legal formulae: 'per lancem liciumque' (Gell. *NA* 11. 18. 9).

Alliteration is well attested in early Latin, perhaps aided by word stress on initial syllables. In the native *Saturnian verse, it can characterize one half-line (e.g. *Naevius' epitaph beginning 'inmortales mortales si foret fas fere', Gell. 1. 24. 2) or link two in the manner of Anglo-Saxon versification (e.g. 'prima incedit Cereris Proserpina puer', Naev. 29(31)). Sometimes a single alliteration extends over a line in comic accumulation 'Cerconicus, Crinnus, Cercobulus, Collabus' (Plaut. *Trinummus* 1020) or epic intensity 'machina multa minax minitatur maxima muris' (Enn. *Ann.* 620 S). *Lucretius continues this tradition (e.g. 1. 199–202), but alliterative groups of more than three words are rare among neoteric and Augustan authors. Found more often are sequences of alliterative pairs, often dividing or framing the line: 'motum ex Metello consule ciuicum' (Hor. *Carm.* 2. 1. 1) and 'fataque fortunasque uirum moresque manusque' (*Aen.* 6. 683). Cicero also uses this sequential pattern for humour ('lacerat lacertum Largi mordax Memmius', *De orat.* 2. 240).

Conspicuous alliteration often suggests archaic imitation: 'censuit, consensit, consciuit' (Livy 1. 32. 13); 'ita mihi saluam ac sospitem rem publicam sistere in sua sede liceat' (Suet. *Aug.* 28). *Sallust, *Tacitus, and *Apuleius especially favour alliterative pairs for their gnomic capacity or archaic tone: 'fluxa atque fragilis' (*Cat.* 1. 4); 'spes in uirtute, salus ex uictoria' (*Ann.* 2. 20. 7); 'pugnisque pulsatus et calcibus contusus' (*Met.* 7. 25) (see ARCHAISM IN LATIN).

Homoeoteleuton The repetition of final sounds is an almost inevitable consequence of Latin inflection, e.g. 'excitatus senatus, inflammatus populus Romanus' (Cic. *Phil.* 12. 15). Its effectiveness in fixing formulaic language is seen in idiomatic ('mel et fel', 'spes atque opes') and religious language ('macte isto ferto esto', Cato, *Agr.* 134). Because final syllables are generally unstressed, forceful homoeoteleuton usually involves long vowels or multiple syllables.

Homoeoteleuton reinforces rhetorical balance, as in 'atque superbiam atque ferociam augescere atque crescere' (Cato in Gell. *NA* 6. 3. 14) or 'non scripta, sed nata lex, quam non didicimus, accepimus, legimus, uerum ex natura ipsa arripuimus, hausimus, expressimus, ad quam non docti, sed facti, non instituti, sed imbuti sumus' (Cic. *Mil.* 4. 10). Extreme use was faulted by C. *Lucilius (1) (Gell. *NA* 18. 8) and *Cicero (*Orat.* 38), who regularly demonstrates variety in the use of repetitive case endings. Republican poets, high and low, enjoy this effect: 'sparsis hastis longis campus splendet et horret' (Enn. var. 14 Vahlen); 'macesco consenesco et tabesco' (Plaut. *Capt.* 134); 'naufragiis magnis multisque coortis' (Lucr. 2. 552); 'deliciae meae puellae' (Catull. 2. 1), and 'cum puero ut bello bella puella cubet' (Catull.

78. 4), where it is combined with alliteration. But examples involving adjacent words in *Horace and *Virgil are much less common (chiefly neuter plurals).

Rhyme Latin inflexion also facilitates occasional rhyme, which reinforces syntactic or metrical boundaries. In prose, it is especially noticeable in Apuleius ('spirant flamina, nutriunt nubila, geminant semina, crescunt germina', *Met.* 11. 25). Early drama exploits this, 'haec omnia uidi inflammari, | Priamo ui uitam euitari, | Iouis aram sanguine turpari' (Enn. *Trag.* 92–4 Jocelyn), as do Cicero's hexameters (*Div.* 1. 20). Although there are fewer cases of two-syllable rhyme in Virgil than Lucretius, rhymes of one syllable are fairly common in each. Conspicuous poetic rhymes include: 'ruebant | . . . tenebant' (Verg. *Aen.* 9. 182–3); 'uolentia rura | . . . ferrea iura' (*G.* 2. 500 f.); 'sunto | . . . agunto' (Hor. *Ars Am.* 99 f.). Longer chains can be found at Lucr. 3. 745–7, Verg. *Aen.* 1. 517–19 and 2. 443–64, but are parodied in the Cyclops' speech (Ov. *Met.* 13. 787–800).

Over one-fifth of elegiac pentameters display internal rhyme, between the two halves of a line, almost always involving an adjective and noun in agreement (with long series at Prop. 2. 34. 85–90 and Ov. *Fast.* 2. 533–9). Leonine rhyme, the internal rhyming of two syllables (e.g. 'quot caelum stellas, tot habet tua Roma puellas', Ov., *Ars Am.* 1. 59), occurs only occasionally in classical hexameters (e.g. Lucr. 1. 318; Verg. *Ecl.* 8. 80; Ov. *Met.* 6. 247), but becomes one of the regular medieval rhyming schemes.

Other effects These include syllable repetition (e.g. 'neglegens gens', Livy 5. 46. 3; 'morerere recuruo', Ov. *Her.* 10. 71); anagrams ('parua aut praua', Ter. *Eun.* 575); puns ('amens amansque', Plaut. *Merc.* 82); onomatopoeia ('at tuba terribili sonitu taratantara dixit', Enn. *Ann.* 451 S); etymological wordplay ('callida musa | Calliope', Lucr. 6. 93 f.); and sound symbolism.

Euphony The Roman rhetorical and grammatical writers followed Greek traditions in urging restraint or even abstinence in these major sound effects. Thus, *Ennius' alliterative line 'O Tite tute Tati tibi tanta tyranne tulisti' seemed excessive (*Rhet. Her.* 4. 12. 18); even slight homoioteleuton was labelled a vice (Serv. on *Aen.* 4. 504 'at regina pyra'); and the repetition of sounds at the end of one word and the beginning of another was criticized by *Quintilian (9. 4. 37 ff. on 'ars studiorum' and Cicero's 'O fortunatam natam'). In so far as some of these phenomena are plentiful in Latin literature, rules of euphony usually reflect the canons of the critical tradition rather than the practices of prose or poetry.

J. B. Hofmann and A. Szantyr, *Lateinische Syntax und Stilistik* (1965), 699–714 (with thorough bibliography); J. Cousin, *Bibliographie de la langue latine* (1951); E. Wölfflin, *Zur Alliteration* (1881), repr. in *Ausgewählte Schriften* (1933); K. Polheim, *Die lateinische Reimprosa* (1925); J. Marouzeau, *Traité de stylistique appliquée au latin* (1935); F. J. E. Raby, *Christian Latin Poetry*, 2nd edn. (1953), 20 ff. (on rhyme); L. P. Wilkinson, *Golden Latin Artistry* (1963).   R. G. A.; J. E. W.

Assos, an impregnable site in the southern Troad (*Troas), facing south towards *Lesbos (it was originally colonized from *Methymna) and controlling the coast road. The *harbour is artificial. The public buildings, including a council-house, market stoas, and temple grouped around the Hellenistic agora, rose in steep terraces up to the acropolis, where the remains of a peripteral Doric temple of the 6th cent. BC can be seen. The impressive fortifications date back to the 4th cent. BC, when the city housed an important philosophical school founded by the Platonist *Hermias (1). *Aristotle lived in Assos from 348 to 345 BC, when it was part of the Persian empire, and it was later the birthplace of the Stoic philosopher *Cleanthes.

Kl. Pauly 1. 1542–4; *PECS* 104–5; J. T. Clarke, F. R. Bacon, and R. Koldewey, *Investigations at Assos 1882–1883* (1921); Ü. Serdaroglu and others, *Ausgrabungen in Assos: Asia-Minor-Studien* 2 (1990).   S. M.

Assyria 1. Land of the patron god Aššur, the kingdom in the Upper Tigris region in modern Iraq, centre of an important state in the middle bronze age and then of two great empires in the late bronze, and early iron ages, ending 612 BC. Royal cities included Assur, *Nimrud, Khorsabad, and *Nineveh.

2. Region including *Babylonia with former Assyria from the *Achaemenid period; the province of Assyria formed by Trajan in 116 AD and abandoned by Hadrian (Eutr. 8. 2; Ruf. Fest. 14 and 20) corresponds to the later Sasanid 'Asorestan' with a new royal city at *Ctesiphon. The former heartland of Assyria was called (*Media) Adiabene in the Parthian period, when the city of Assur enjoyed a revival.

T. Nöldeke, *Hermes* 1871, 443–68; W. Andrae, *Das wiedererstandene Assur*, rev. B. Hrouda (1977).   S. M. D.

Asteria, sister of *Leto and mother, by Perses, of *Hecate (Hes. *Theog.* 409–12). The fact that she is Leto's sister must be connected with the fact that Asteria (meaning 'starry') is also given as an ancient name for *Delos (Pindar, fr. 52e. 42, etc. Snell–Maehler). According to *Callimachus (3), *Hymn* 4. 36–40, and others, she leapt into the sea to escape the amorous pursuit of *Zeus, and so gave her name to the island.

LIMC 'Asteria' 1; M. L. West on Hes. *Theog.* 409.   A. L. B.

astragali, knucklebones (ἀστράγαλοι), a popular pastime with Greeks and Romans of all ages. They also served as dice: the four long faces of the knucklebones were of different shapes, one flat, one irregular, one concave, and one convex, and in dicing these had the value respectively of 1, 6, 3, 4.

R. Hampe, *Die Stele aus Pharsalos im Louvre* (1951).   F. A. W.; M. V.

astrology, the art of converting astronomical data (i.e. the positions of the celestial bodies) into predictions of outcomes in human affairs. Astrology developed in the Hellenistic age, essentially as an import from Babylon, which equally furnished many of its astronomical parameters. *Alexandria (1) was its major centre. By the 1st cent. BC, it had emerged as a sophisticated technical art, commanding widespread credence and respect. So it remained until the late empire, when its incompatibility with *Christianity led to its formal suppression (though not extinction).

There are several branches of astrology, of which the most important is genethlialogy, the art of foretelling an individual's life from the positions of the stars (i.e. sun, moon, planets, and fixed stars) at birth or conception; see CONSTELLATIONS. The basic astronomical data for calculating a 'nativity' (i.e. a horoscope) are (*a*) the positions of the seven known planets (including sun and moon) relative to one another (their 'aspects') and to the twelve signs of the zodiac, and (*b*) the position of the circle of the zodiac (and thus of the planets moving round it) relative to a second circle of twelve 'places' (mod. 'houses') whose cardinal points ('centres') are the rising- and setting-points on the horizon and the zenith and nadir. The whole may be likened to a complex clock whose seven hands (the planets) turn counter-clockwise at various mean speeds (from the moon's month to Saturn's almost 30 years) against a dial whose twelve hours are the signs of the zodiac; simultaneously, the dial and its hands together rotate

clockwise (in a 24-hour period corresponding to the apparent daily revolution of the heavens) against a second, fixed dial which is the local frame of reference for the nativity, itself divided into twelve sectors (the 'places') with the rising and setting points at 9 and 3 o'clock and the zenith and nadir at about 12 and 6. The astrologer reads this clock at the time of birth and then assigns meanings, in terms of the 'native's' destiny, character, and occupation, to the various positions and relationships in the 'nativity'. In antiquity, as now, astronomical tables rather than direct observation were used.

Actual horoscopes survive from antiquity, both simple (as in papyrus fragments) and complex (as in professional treatises, e.g. the *Anthologies* of *Vettius Valens). Astrology was popular with all classes; similarly, astrologers spanned a wide social and intellectual range. At the pinnacle were men such as Ti. *Claudius Thrasyllus and his son Ti. *Claudius Balbillus who were theoreticians and practitioners of the art, confidants and functionaries of emperors from *Tiberius to *Vespasian, and connected by marriage both to powerful Romans (*Sejanus and *Macro) and to the Greek client kings of *Commagene. Because it was so widely believed, astrology was potentially subversive of public order. Accordingly, astrologers were periodically expelled from Rome, and Augustus forbade both consultations in private and those concerning deaths (AD 11).

From a modern perspective it is the postulated link, causal or semiotic, between celestial and terrestrial events that renders astrology suspect. Most ancients took that link for granted, under a belief in a 'universal sympathy' which connects all parts of the cosmos in a harmoniously functioning whole. *Stoicism legitimized divination of all sorts, and the worship of the stars, especially the sun (see HELIOS; SOL), added further authority to astrology, as did the common belief in the *soul's celestial origin and destiny. Many intellectuals accordingly accepted and justified the art, including such astronomers as *Ptolemy (4) who makes a well-reasoned case (*Tetrabiblos* 1. 1–3) that astrology is but the application of *astronomy, in a necessarily fallible way, to the sublunary environment. There were, however, sceptics and critics, among the most cogent being *Sextus Empiricus (*Math.* bk. 5) and *Favorinus of Arles (reproduced in summary by Gell. *NA* 14. 1); and low-grade practitioners preying on the superstitious attracted inevitable scorn.

The most important extant astrological writings are, in chronological order, Marcus *Manilius' *Astronomica, c.* AD 14 (ed. and trans. Goold (1977)); the poem of *Dorotheus of Sidon transmitted in Arabic, 1st cent. AD (ed. and trans. Pingree (1976)); Ptolemy's *Tetrabiblos*, mid-2nd cent. (ed. and trans. Robbins (1940)); the *Anthologies* of Vettius Valens, late 2nd cent. (ed. Kroll (1908); bk. 1 ed. and trans. Bara (1989)); the *Mathesis* of *Firmicus Maternus, mid-4th cent. (ed. Kroll–Skutsch–Ziegler (1913), trans. Forbes (1970), ed. and trans. Monat (1992); and the *Apotelesmatica* of Hephaestion of Thebes, *c.*415 (ed. Pingree (1973)). There is much otherwise unpublished material in *CCAG*. Extant horoscopes are collected in O. Neugebauer and H. van Hoesen, *Greek Horoscopes* (1959). The fundamental modern treatment remains A. Bouché-Leclercq, *L'Astrologie grecque* (1899). See also F. Boll, C. Bezold, and W. Gundel, *Sternglaube und Sterndeutung*, 6th edn. (1974); F. H. Cramer, *Astrology in Roman Law and Politics* (1954); F. Cumont, *Astrology and Religion among the Greeks and Romans* (1912); W. and H. G. Gundel, *Astrologumena* (1966); S. J. Tester, *A History of Western Astrology* (1987); T. S. Barton, *Ancient Astrology* (1994).   R. L. B.

astronomical instruments Although the introduction of an astronomical instrument (the gnomon, an upright stick for measuring shadow-lengths) is credited to *Anaximander in the 6th cent. BC, reliable information on the form of such instruments comes only from the later Hellenistic era, with extant examples (mostly sundials; see CLOCKS) and detailed descriptions in the works of *Vitruvius, *Heron, *Ptolemy (4) and his commentators. As early as 432 BC *Meton observed the solstice at Athens with a *heliotropion*, but this may have been no more than an upright pillar fixed on a level platform to mark the shortest shadow. We know nothing about the instruments used by successors of Meton, such as *Callippus in the 4th cent., to determine the times of solstice and equinox, nor of those used by *Timocharis and other early Hellenistic astronomers to measure stellar declinations. Perhaps the earliest instrument, apart from sundials, of which we have a detailed description is the device constructed by *Archimedes (*Sand-reckoner* 11–15) for measuring the sun's apparent diameter; this was a rod along which different coloured pegs could be moved. However the 'equatorial armillary' at *Alexandria (1) described by Ptolemy (*Almagest* 3. 1) may be even earlier: it certainly predates *Hipparchus (3). This was a bronze, ungraduated ring fixed permanently in the plane of the equator, which displayed the time of equinox by the crossing of the sun's shadow.

Hipparchus is the first Greek who certainly used instruments employing the Babylonian division of the circle into 360 degrees. He is also known to have employed the 'four-cubit dioptra' mentioned in *Almagest* 5. 14 and described by *Pappus and *Proclus. This was a device for measuring the apparent diameter of sun and moon. Hipparchus also had some instrument for determining the angular distance between heavenly bodies, but this need not have been as elaborate as the 'armillary astrolabe' constructed for that purpose by Ptolemy (*Almagest* 5. 1), which is a representation of the principal celestial great circles by connected, pivoting, graduated bronze rings. Some type of graduated sighting instrument akin to that described by Heron in *Dioptra* would have sufficed (although Heron's instrument was intended principally for terrestrial surveying). It is probable that Hipparchus devised the plane astrolabe, the purpose of which was to tell the time at night from the stars' positions: although the earliest surviving description of this is from the 6th cent. AD (*Philoponus), the underlying mathematical theory of stereographic projection is expounded in Ptolemy's *Planisphierium*.

Other instruments described in the *Almagest* are the meridian ring (a graduated circle) and the plinth (a graduated stone quadrant), for measuring the sun's declination (1. 12), and a 'parallactic instrument' (similar to the medieval 'triquetrum') for determining the moon's zenith distance (5. 12). While none of these was elaborate, great skill and precision in making and fitting the parts and graduating the arcs must have been demanded of the craftsman, in order to attain the accuracy which Ptolemy expected from observations (agreement to within 10 minutes of arc with calculated values). Extant artefacts from the Hellenistic period demonstrate that a high level of craftsmanship was attained, notably the 'Anticythera instrument' (which is a device for representing, rather than observing, the relative motions of sun and moon).

GENERAL: D. J. Price and A. G. Drachmann, in C. Singer and others (eds.), *A History of Technology*, 3 (1957), 582–619.

ARCHIMEDES' INSTRUMENT: A. Lejeune, *Annales de la Société Scientifique de Bruxelles*, 1947, 27–47.

ARMILLARY ASTROLABE: A. Rome, *Annales de la Société Scientifique de Bruxelles*, 1927, 77–102.

PLANE ASTROLABE: O. Neugebauer, *Isis*, 1949, 240–56.

ANTICYTHERA INSTRUMENT: D. Price, *TAPhS* 64/7 (1974).
G. J. T.

astronomy The use of the heliacal rising and setting of prominent stars or star-groups to mark points in the year is found in the earliest literature of the Greeks (*Homer and *Hesiod, e.g. *Op.* 619 ff.), and no doubt goes back to prehistoric times. This 'traditional' Greek astronomy continued (with some refinements borrowed from 'scientific' astronomy) to the end of antiquity. It was embodied in the 'astronomical calendars' (or παραπήγματα, so called from the practice of sticking a peg to mark the current day in holes along the sides) which began with *Meton and *Euctemon in the 5th cent. BC and of which several examples are preserved in manuscript and on stone. These mark important points of the year (including solstices and equinoxes), and use the risings and settings of stars as a basis for weather predictions (the latter already in Hesiod).

2. Scientific astronomy in Greece hardly predates the 5th cent. BC. The cosmological speculations of the earlier Presocratics are irrelevant, and the scientific feats attributed to some of them (e.g. *Thales' prediction of an eclipse) by later writers are unworthy of belief. However, some of the basic concepts necessary to later astronomy were enunciated in the course of the 5th cent. *Parmenides (A 44 DK) mentioned the sphericity of the earth and stated that the moon receives its light from the sun (B 15). *Empedocles went beyond this to infer the cause of solar eclipses (B 42), as did *Anaxagoras. Yet how unfamiliar this was even to an educated man of the late 5th cent. is shown by the remark of *Thucydides (2) (2. 28) that solar eclipses *seem* to occur only at new moon. There seems to have been general ignorance about the planets: *Democritus, according to Seneca (*QNat* 7. 3. 2) said that he *suspected* that there were several (*plures*) planets but gave neither number nor names. Significant for the future development of Greek astronomy is the transmission of elements from *Babylonia (which had a tradition of observational astronomy going back to the 8th cent. BC): the twelve signs of the zodiac appear in Greece perhaps as early as the late 6th cent. (if the lines quoted from Cleostratus of Tenedos (DK 6) are genuine); certainly the nineteen-year luni-solar cycle of Meton was derived from Babylon; but this, like Meton's solstice observations, is still directed towards the goals of 'traditional' astronomy.

3. The 4th cent. saw the introduction of the most characteristic Greek contribution to astronomical theory, the idea that the apparently irregular motions of the heavenly bodies should be explained by geometrical models based on uniform circular motion. Later sources attribute this to *Plato (1) (*Simplicius on Arist. *Cael.* 219ᵃ23), but although it is not inconsistent, in a general sense, with views expressed in his dialogues, the only certainty is that the first system embodying this idea was constructed by Plato's contemporary *Eudoxus (1). It is significant that Eudoxus was also the first to establish axiomatic rigour in geometry: we may conjecture that it was this success which led to the notion of extending the explanatory power of geometry to other fields, including the heavens. Eudoxus' system of 'homocentric spheres', centred on the fixed, spherical earth, and rotating with uniform motions about different poles, combined simplicity with mathematical ingenuity, and was able, in principle, to account for the retrogradations of the planets and the latitudinal deviations of all bodies, including the moon. The observational elements involved were few, namely crude synodic and sidereal periods for the planets and the moon. Yet even these represent a considerable advance over the ignorance prevalent 50 years earlier: Eudoxus is the first Greek who is *known* to have recognized all five planets (the passages in Plato *Resp.* 616d–617b and *Ti.* 38c ff, where the five planets are hinted at, may well have been written later than

Eudoxus' book). Here again we may suspect Babylonian influence in the observational data, particularly since there are Mesopotamian elements also in the description of the *constellations which Eudoxus published. For all its mathematical elegance, Eudoxus' system exhibited serious discrepancies from easily observable facts. In particular no homocentric system could account for the obvious variations in size and brightness of e.g. the moon and Venus. Nevertheless *Callippus modified Eudoxus' model to eliminate some of the grosser discrepancies, and this revised model has come down to us because *Aristotle accepted it (*Cael.*, *Metaph.* 1073^{a}14–1074^{b}14), transforming what had probably been for Eudoxus a purely geometrical scheme into a physical mechanism with contiguous solid spheres. Scientific astronomy in the 4th cent. remained at this purely theoretical level: practical astronomy was concerned with traditional topics, the calendar (Eudoxus' *Octaeteris* and Callippus' 76-year cycle), and the risings and settings of stars. The earliest extant astronomical works, those of *Autolycus (2) and *Euclid, are little more than a treatment of the latter in terms of elementary geometry.

4. At an unknown date, probably not long after Callippus, the epicyclic and eccentric hypotheses for planetary motion were proposed. These provided a remedy for the most glaring defect of the homocentric system, by producing variation in the distance of a heavenly body, while at the same time giving a simple representation of the 'anomalies' (variations in speed and direction) of the bodies; they became the standard models used in Greek theoretical astronomy. No doubt the complete geometric equivalence of epicyclic and eccentric forms (under suitable conditions), which was assumed in the planetary theory of *Apollonius (2) (*Ptolemy (4), *Almagest* 12. 1), was discovered soon after these models were proposed. One might conjecture that it was in examining the transformation of one to the other that *Aristarchus (1) of Samos (*c.*280 BC) came to the realization that one can transpose the geocentric universe to a heliocentric one, and so put forward his famous hypothesis (see GEOCENTRICITY). This, like the earlier suggestion of *Heraclides (1) Ponticus that the earth rotates on its axis, appears never to have been taken seriously by practising astronomers, although the grounds for rejecting it were 'physical' rather than astronomical. The 3rd cent. probably saw much astronomical activity, but our knowledge of it, derived mostly from incidental remarks in the *Almagest*, is slight. There was more observation, of solstices by Aristarchus and *Archimedes, of the declinations of fixed stars (presumably for delineating a star-globe) by Aristyllus and *Timocharis, and of the moon (including eclipses) by Timocharis. But theoretical astronomy remained at the stage of explaining the phenomena by means of geometrical models and deriving the mathematical consequences. This is evident in Apollonius' use of the epicyclic/eccentric hypothesis to determine stationary points on planets' orbits, and also in the single astronomical work surviving from this time, Aristarchus' treatise on the distances of the sun and moon: this is a mathematical exercise showing how the limits for those distances can be derived from certain numerical assumptions (about the inaccuracy of which the author appears unconcerned, although it must have been obvious). The topic of the distances of the heavenly bodies was much discussed, by Archimedes and Apollonius amongst others, but no-one before Hipparchus devised a reliable method of computing even the moon's distance.

5. Astronomy was transformed by *Hipparchus (3) between *c.*145 and 125 BC. His great innovation was the idea of using the geometrical models, which his predecessors had developed to *explain* the phenomena, in order to *predict* or calculate them for a given time. He did not himself fully succeed in this (we are specifically informed that he renounced any attempt at constructing a theory of the planets), but he contributed several essential elements, including the development of *trigonometry, ingenious methods for the application of observational data to geometrical models, and the compilation of observations, not only of his own and other Greeks, but especially from the massive Babylonian archives (to which he seems to have had privileged access). Although sporadic Mesopotamian influences appear in Greek astronomy from at least the time of Meton, it is apparently Hipparchus who was the main conduit to the Greek world of Babylonian astronomy, including not only observations, but also astronomical constants (e.g. very accurate lunar periods), the sexagesimal place-value notation for expressing fractions, and methods of calculation. The latter were sophisticated arithmetical procedures for predicting celestial phenomena, and now that the original *cuneiform documents have been analysed, it seems likely that it was the Babylonian success in applying mathematical methods to astronomical prediction which inspired Hipparchus to attempt the same within the Greek theoretical framework. He got as far as constructing a viable epicyclic model for the moon, and made many other individual advances, including the discovery of the precession of the equinoxes, to which he was perhaps led by noticing the discrepancy between the year-length which he had derived from observations of equinoxes (the tropical year) and that used by the Babylonians (which was in fact a sidereal year). He also recorded a large number of star positions to be marked on his star-globe.

6. The history of astronomy in the 300 years between Hipparchus and Ptolemy is very obscure, because the unchallenged position of the *Almagest* in later antiquity resulted in the loss of all earlier works on similar topics. However, the evidence from Indian astronomy (the *siddhāntas* based on lost Greek treatises from late Hellenistic times) and from Greek papyri shows that the process begun by Hipparchus was continued by his successors, who produced predictive mathematical models for all the heavenly bodies. This undoubtedly contributed to the enormous growth in genethlialogical *astrology (which requires calculating the celestial positions for a given time) in the period following Hipparchus. But theoretical astronomy was characterized by a bewildering profusion of Babylonian arithmetical methods (which Hipparchus himself had not hesitated to use, even in his lunar theory), combined with geometrical planetary models which, although producing numerical results, lacked logic and consistency. This situation satisfied the professional needs of astrologers such as Ptolemy's contemporary *Vettius Valens, but was repugnant to the scientific purism of *Ptolemy (4) himself. In his magisterial *Almagest* (*c.* AD 150) he ignores (apart from an occasional contemptuous aside) the work of his immediate predecessors, singling out Hipparchus as the sole peer worthy of his imitation and criticism. Starting from first principles, and rigidly excluding arithmetical methods, he constructed an edifice of models for sun, moon, planets, and fixed stars based on a combination of epicycles and eccentrics employing uniform circular motions, the numerical parameters of which he determined by rigorous geometrical methods from carefully selected observations. These were supplemented by tables allowing the computation of all celestial positions and phenomena pertinent to ancient astronomy, to a suitable accuracy (Ptolemy regarded agreement with observation within 10' of arc as acceptable). The

result is a work of remarkable power and consistency, which dominated astronomy for 1,300 years.

7. Ptolemy himself regarded his work as provisional, but it was treated as definitive by his ancient successors, who produced nothing of significance in astronomy, confining themselves to explicating the *Almagest* (and other treatises by him), despite the fact that there were serious defects in it even by ancient standards, notably in the solar theory, producing errors which increased with the lapse of time. That these were completely unnoticed in later antiquity is an indication both of the lack of independent observation and of the state of the science after Ptolemy. However, important corrections to the solar theory and other individual details of Ptolemaic astronomy were made after it experienced a revival through its transmission to the Islamic world (the *Almagest* was translated into Arabic *c.* AD 800), but even there the edifice as a whole remained undisturbed, and criticisms of Ptolemy were concerned mainly with his alleged violation of the principle of uniform circular motion in introducing the equant. Ancient astronomy did not begin to become obsolete until Copernicus, and the process was not completed until Kepler.

8. The astronomy of the Greeks covered only a part of what is now comprised in the term. It can be considered the most successful of the ancient applied sciences, if one accepts the ancient view that its task is confined to describing and predicting observed motions by means of a consistent mathematical model. Physical astronomy, however, remained at a very low level (like physics in general). But it is not entirely ignored even in the *Almagest*, and in his *Planetary Hypotheses* Ptolemy attempted to fit the kinematical models of the *Almagest* into a unified physical system. This was based on Aristotelian notions, including the crucial thesis that nature is not wasteful. In it Ptolemy describes a universe in which each planetary 'shell' is contiguous with that of the bodies immediately above and below it. This system enabled him to compute the absolute dimensions and distances of all parts of the universe out to the sphere of the fixed stars, which he found to be less than 20,000 earth-radii from the central earth (less than the distance from the earth to the sun by modern computation). This vision of a small and completely determined universe, although not universally accepted even in late antiquity, became the canonical view in the Middle Ages, in both east and west, and is enshrined in biblical exposition and learned poetry as well as in the works of professional astronomers. It was a strong argument against consideration of the heliocentric hypothesis, which entailed a vastly larger universe in which the fixed stars were at enormous distances.

For special studies see the articles on the ancient authors referred to. *HAMA*, which makes earlier general discussions obsolete, is essential for particular topics too. On Greek calendars see the series *Griechische Kalender*, ed. F. Boll and others, *Sitz. Heidelb. Akad. Phil.-hist. Kl.* 1910.16, 1911.1, 1913.3, 1914.3, 1920.15; also Rehm, *RE* 18. 1295 ff. 'Parapegma', and (for the fragments on stone) Diels and Rehm, *Sitz. Berlin Akad. Phil.-hist. Kl.*, 1904, 92 ff., 752 ff. For cosmological and astronomical views of the prescientific period see T. L. Heath, *Aristarchus of Samos* (1913; repr. 1959), introd. On Babylonian influences: A. Jones, *Isis* 1991, 441 ff. On Arabic translations of the *Almagest*: P. Kunitzsch, *Der Almagest* (1974). G. J. T.

Astures, a group of at least twelve peoples situated on the Cantabrian coastline and interior between the Callaeci and Cantabri. Before the Augustan conquest they shared the social and economic characteristics of the *Cantabri and lived in small hilltop enclosures. Pliny's census, *HN* 3. 28, estimated 240,000

free men divided between the Transmontani of the north and the Augustani of the south. Pacified by Roman legions (26–19 BC), the Astures furnished auxiliary troops and horses. *Gold was extracted on a huge scale (see MINES AND MINING) and transported by a comprehensive road system. They formed an imperial *conventus* with the capital at Asturica Augusta (mod. Astorga). Pliny's description of this as a 'splendid city' ('urbs magnifica') has been substantiated by excavation. The Legio VII Gemina was stationed at Legio (mod. León) from AD 74. Late Roman walls survive in both towns.

A. Schulten, *Los Cantabros y Astures* (1943); A. Tranoy, *La Galice romaine* (1981); N. Santos, *El ejército y la romanización de los Astures* (1981); R. Jones, *JRS* 1976, 45 ff. S. J. K.

Astyanax, or **Scamandrius** (*Il.* 6. 402), young son of *Hector and *Andromache. At the capture of Troy he was flung from the walls by *Neoptolemus (1) (*Little Iliad* fr. 20 Davies) or killed by Odysseus (*Iliu Persis*). His death is a major motif of Euripides' *Trojan Women*. In Archaic and Classical art his death is often shown together with that of *Priam at the sack of Troy: see O. Touchefeu, *LIMC* 1/1. 929–37. *Polygnotus in his painting of Troy at Delphi showed Priam dead but Astyanax still alive, a child at his mother's breast in the Greek camp (Paus. 10. 25. 9).

H. J. R.; J. R. M.

Astydamas, the name of two tragic poets of the 4th cent. BC, father and son. The father was the son of Morsimus, son of *Aeschylus' nephew Philocles. It appears that some of the information attached to the father in our sources properly belongs to the son. In that case all we know of the father is that he produced his first play in 398 and lived to be 60 (Diog. Laert. 4. 43. 5); and it was the son who was said to have been a pupil of *Isocrates before turning to tragedy, to have written 240 tragedies (but the number can hardly be right), and to have won fifteen victories.

The younger Astydamas was one of the most successful poets of his day. He won his first victory in 372, and others are recorded in inscriptions. After the success of his *Parthenopaeus* (340) the Athenians honoured him with a statue in the theatre (part of the base survives), but he was not allowed to inscribe on it the conceited epigram that made him a byword for vanity (D. L. Page, *Further Greek Epigrams* (1990), 33–4). *Aristotle (*Poet.* 14) tells us that his *Alcmaeon* made the hero kill his mother unwittingly (when the usual version makes him do so deliberately). An especially famous play was the *Hector*, based on parts of *Homer's *Iliad*: it is believed to be depicted on an Apulian vase and attested in three papyri, and *Plutarch speaks of it (*De glor. Ath.* 7) in the same breath as Aeschylus and *Sophocles (1).

TrGF 1². 198–207; *Musa Tragica* 134–45, 287–8; B. Snell, *Szenen aus griechischen Dramen* (1971), 138–53. A. L. B.

astynomoi ('city magistrates'), an office found mostly in the Ionian states (see IONIANS). In *Athens there were five for the city and five for the *Piraeus, appointed by lot for one year. Their principal duties were to keep the streets and sanctuaries clean and free from obstructions, and they enforced certain sumptuary laws (*Ath. pol.* 50. 2). In many states they also had harbour and market duties. An inscription of the 2nd cent. AD gives a law governing the duties of the *astynomoi* at *Pergamum, enacted in the 2nd cent. BC (*SEG* 13. 521). A. W. G.; P. J. R.

Astyoche, in mythology sister of *Priam and daughter of *Laomedon (Apollod. 3. 146). She married *Telephus (1)) (Quint. Smyrn. 6. 135) and bore Eurypylus who came to the Trojan War and was killed by *Neoptolemus (1) with many of his people, 'thanks to gifts made to a woman' (*Od.* 11. 521). This the commentators explained as the gift either of a wife (Hermione) by *Menelaus (1) to Neoptolemus, or by Priam to Astyoche of the golden vine which was given Tros by Zeus as compensation for the loss of *Ganymedes (*Little Iliad*, fr. 6 Allen), etc. See Eust. *Od.* 1697, 30 ff. In art she appears on Attic vases: *LIMC* 2/1 (1984), 938–9.   H. J. R.

Astyochus, Spartan admiral, 412/411 BC, whose inadequacies at a critical early stage of the Ionian War (see PELOPONNESIAN WAR) hindered Sparta's cause. Lacking adequate resources, he failed to sustain the revolt of *Lesbos. Following a quarrel he refused *Chios' requests for help; complaints from their *harmost Pedaritus prompted a commission to scrutinize him and share control of policy. His subsequent unwillingness to engage the Athenians without overwhelming superiority and inability to extract sufficient pay from *Tissaphernes caused serious grievance among his fleet and (probably unfounded) accusations of bribery.

RE 2. 1873, 'Astyochos' 3; PB no. 169; Thuc. 8. 20–85; H. D. Westlake, *Individuals in Thucydides* (1968), ch. 15.   S. J. Ho.

asylia was freedom from others' right of self-help by seizure of one's goods (συλᾶν); see SYLE. Such seizure could be exercised not only against the offender but against other citizens and *metics of the offender's state. When *asylia* was granted to individuals (e.g. *Syll.*[3] 644) it meant that whatever claims there were against the individual's state, the personal property of that individual was safe from seizure by citizens and residents of the *asylia*-granting state. *Asylia* could be given to entire states.

But *asylia* in this sense of freedom from legalized reprisals came to mean in effect general freedom from acts of *piracy and *brigandage; the 3rd-cent. BC *Aetolians granted such freedoms, perhaps only to get safe bases for further piracy. (But the Aetolians were not as uniquely bad as *Polybius (1) makes out.) A more specific, and perhaps original, meaning was inviolability of shrines: Hellenistic cities often asked for and usually got recognition of *asylia* for sanctuaries in their territory, cf. *SEG* 12. 373 (*Cos) or the long series from *Magnesia on Maeander (*IMagn.*). Such sanctuaries were used for refuge; hence the later meaning of 'asylum'.

E. Schlesinger, *Die griechische Asylie* (1933); P. Gauthier, *Symbola* (1972), ch. 5; F. W. Walbank and J. K. Davies, *CAH* 7[2]/1 (1984), 234 f., 288 ff.; U. Sinn, in Marinatos and Hägg (eds.), *Greek Sanctuaries* (1993), ch. 5; K. J. Rigsby, *Asylia* (1996).   J. A. O. L.; S. H.

Atalanta, a mythical heroine, daughter of Schoeneus, *Iasus, or Maenalus. According to *Apollodorus (6) (3. 9. 2) she was exposed at birth and nursed by a bear before being brought up by hunters. When she reached maturity she chose to remain a virgin and to spend her time hunting as a companion of *Artemis (cf. CALLISTO). She killed the centaurs Rhoecus and Hylaeus, who had tried to rape her, she took part in the hunt of the Calydonian boar, where *Meleager (1) fell in love with her, and at the games held in honour of *Pelias she defeated *Peleus in wrestling. Later, when her father wished to give her in marriage, she promised to marry the man who could defeat her in a foot-race. After several young men were defeated and put to death, Hippomenes (or Melanion, or Hippomedon) was victorious in the test, having dropped some golden apples on the track, which Atalanta stopped to pick up (cf. already Hes. frs. 72–6 M–W; Apollod. 3. 9. 2; Hyg. *Fab.* 185. 2). Near Methydrion in *Arcadia were shown

'racetracks of Atalanta' (Paus. 8. 35. 10). From the marriage was born *Parthenopaeus. During a hunt, the couple made love in a sanctuary of *Zeus (or *Cybele) and as punishment for their impiety they were changed into lions (Apollod. 3. 9. 2; Hyg. *Fab.* 6; Ov. *Met.* 10. 686).

In art Atalanta is shown sometimes as a huntress at Calydon (vases from 580 BC onwards, 4th-cent. pediment from Tegea), sometimes as an athlete at the games for Peleus. In the first type, she is usually shown wearing a short garment and sometimes an animal hide; in the second, she wears, in the 5th cent., a bodice. The episode of the foot-race is not found in art.

J. Boardman, *LIMC* 2. 940–50.   M. J.

Atargatis (Aramaic 'Atar-'Ata), the goddess of Hierapolis-Bambyce in Syria whose usual name among Greeks and Romans was the 'Syrian goddess' (Συρία θεά, *dea Syria*); a mother-goddess, giver of fertility. Her temple, rebuilt *c.*300 BC by *Stratonice, wife of *Seleucus I, was plundered by *Antiochus IV and by *Crassus, but was still in Lucian's day one of the greatest and holiest in Syria; its site has yet to be found. Her consort was Hadad; his throne was flanked by bulls, that of Atargatis by lions. At Ascalon, Atargatis was represented as half woman, half fish. Fish and doves were sacred to her; the myth records that, having fallen into a lake, Atargatis was saved by the fish ([Eratosth.] *Cat.* 38), or, in another version, that Atargatis was changed into a fish, and her daughter *Semiramis into a dove (Diod. Sic. 2. 4. 2–6; 2. 20. 1–2; Ov. *Met.* 4. 44–8). Late in the 3rd cent. BC her cult appears in Egypt, Macedon, and, with civic status, at Phistyon in *Aetolia and (early 2nd cent.) at Thuria in *Messenia. Citizens of Hierapolis founded a shrine on *Delos in 128–127, of which Athens soon took control. Atargatis was worshipped also in a number of other Greek cities and in Rome, where Nero favoured her for a while; Roman troops took her cult to the Danubian provinces and Britain. Astrologers identified her with the constellation Virgo, and a 3rd-cent. 'creed' found in England (*RIB* 1791) accepts the *dea Syria* as one of several names or manifestations of the universal goddess. At Thuria her cult included mysteries. Lucian, *De dea Syria*, describes the cult in Syria; Apuleius, *Met.* 8–9, the life of her wandering Galli. See EUNUCHS (religious); FISH, SACRED; METRAGYRTES.

M. Hörig, *ANRW* 2. 17. 3 (1983), 1581 ff.; *LIMC* 'Dea Syria' (with bibliog.).   F. R. W.; A. J. S. S.

Ate, mental aberration, infatuation causing irrational behaviour which leads to disaster. A hero's *atē* is brought about through psychic intervention by a divine agency, usually *Zeus, but can also be physically inflicted (*Il.* 16. 805). *Agamemnon blames Zeus, *Fate, and the *Erinyes for his delusion that made him take *Briseis and lead the Achaeans to the brink of defeat (*Il.* 19. 87 f., cf. 2. 111, 8. 237, 11. 340; *Od.* 12. 371 f., etc.). Ate is personified as the daughter of Zeus whom he expelled from Olympus to bring harm to men (*Il.* 19. 90–4, 126–31). A similarly pessimistic notion of divine punishment for guilt underlies *Homer's Parable of the Prayers. In this early allegory swift-footed Atē outruns the slow Prayers and forces men into error and punishment (*Il.* 9. 502–12). In another moralizing personification Ate becomes the daughter of *Eris (Strife) and sister of Dysnomia (Lawlessness) (*Theog.* 230; cf. Solon 3. 30–5); but *Hesiod also used *atē* impersonally in the sense of punishment for hubris (Hes. *Op.* 214 ff.; *Theog.* 205 f.). *Aeschylus draws a powerful picture of *atē* both as a daemonic force (see DAIMON) and instrument of ruin (*Ag.* 1124, 1433; *Cho.* 383, 956 ff.).

Ateius Capito, Gaius

E. R. Dodds, *The Greeks and the Irrational* (1951).   H. J. R.; B. C. D.

Ateius (*RE* 7) **Capito** (1), **Gaius,** of undistinguished family, was tribune 55 BC. He opposed the consuls *Pompey and *Crassus, and stigmatized the latter's proposed attack on Parthia as a war of unjust aggression. Unable to prevent Crassus' departure by announcing adverse prodigies (see PORTENTS), he solemnly cursed him as he left the city (November). In 50 he received a *nota* (mark of condemnation) from the censors on the ground that he had invented the prodigies: the punishment was, in Cicero's view, illogical (*Div.* 1. 29 f.). He is probably the Capito who was concerned in distributing land to veterans by Caesar's appointment in 44 (Cic. *Att.* 16. 16 c, f). He served in some capacity under L. Plotius Plancus, praetor 43.   T. J. C.; E. B.

Ateius (*RE* 8) **Capito** (2), **Gaius,** a lawyer of modest senatorial family, was a follower of Ofilius, became consul in AD 5 and was supervisor of the water supply (*curator aquarum,* see CURA(TIO)) from AD 14 to 22, when he died. A writer on public law, sacred and constitutional, he supported Augustus but from a conservative standpoint. Sex. *Pomponius and *Tacitus (*Ann.* 3. 75) attest his standing as a lawyer, but contrast him as a legal conservative with *Antistius Labeo, who was a republican politically but an innovator in legal matters. Pomponius regards Capito as the originator of the Cassian or Sabinian school (*secta*) of lawyers (see C. *CASSIUS LONGINUS (2); MASURIUS SABINUS). His work has not survived and he is only once cited by another lawyer, perhaps because he took the Augustan 'restoration' too seriously.

Lenel, *Pal.* 1. 106; Bremer 2. 261–87; *PIR*^{2} A 1279; Kunkel 1967, 114–15; Wieacker, *RRG* 1.   T. H.

Ateius (*RE* 11) **Philologus, Lucius,** a noted scholar of the Ciceronian age and a teacher of both *grammar and *rhetoric (Suet. *Gram.* 10). Born at Athens, he was enslaved (probably in 86 BC) and later manumitted. He took the name Philologus as a mark of his varied learning and claimed to have written 800 books on all kinds of subjects. None survives, but sources refer to an epitome of Roman history composed for *Sallust, stylistic precepts composed for *Asinius Pollio, a work on rare or obsolete words (*Liber glossematorum*), a literary catalogue (*Pinakes*), and a treatise on the question 'Did Aeneas love Dido?'

Funaioli, *Gramm. Rom. Frag.* 136–41; Herzog–Schmidt, § 279.   R. A. K.

Atella, *Campanian city, in the Clanis valley. The site was inhabited from the 7th cent. BC and urbanized in the 4th. Atella was a Roman ally (see SOCII) by 338 but defected in 211. It was flourishing in the empire, but abandoned in the 11th cent. There are remains of walls, street plan, republican and imperial baths and houses, and a Hellenistic / Roman cemetery.   K. L.

Atellana (sc. *fabula*), in origin a native Italian farce, named after *Atella in Campania but doubtless common in Oscan towns, and probably early known in Rome, where it was normally performed in Latin. (Livy 7. 2 and Val. Max. 2. 4. 4 provide evidence for the amateur status of actors in *Atellana*; the implications are disputed.) It was a masked drama, largely improvised, with stock characters: Bucco ('the fool'), *Dossennus ('the glutton'), Maccus ('the clown', the most frequently occurring name in titles of *Atellanae*), Manducus ('the chewer', an ogre or bogeyman, thought by many to be an alternative name for Dossennus), Pappus ('the old gaffer'). It became a literary form for a short time in the period of *Sulla, its principal exponents being L. *Pomponius and *Novius. Other named authors are Aprissius

(one line survives) and perhaps Sulla himself (if this is what his 'satyric comedies' were); and a Mummius is said by Macrobius to have revived the genre later (three short fragments survive). *Atellanae* continued to be performed at least until the time of *Juvenal. They seem to have been primarily low-life comedies, often in coarse language, set in a small Italian town and giving a humorous portrait of rustic and provincial life; the familiar characters were shown in a variety of situations (titles include *Maccus the Soldier, Maccus the Innkeeper, Maccus the Girl, Pappus the Farmer*). The literary fragments are in verse, using the same iambic and trochaic metres as *palliata and *togata, and occasionally also the same titles and dramatic motifs; disguise and masquerade were elements of many plots. Some titles suggest parodies of tragedies (e.g. Pomponius, *The Fake Agamemnon, The Dispute over the Armour*; Novius, *Andromache*). *Atellanae* were short, and sometimes used as *exodia* ('after-pieces') to tragedies, like *satyric drama at Athens, and these parodies may have been inspired by such occasions (if they were not actually satyr-plays); but the influence of *phlyakes* may also have been a factor. Novius' title *Debate between Death and Life* is intriguingly different from the rest. See COMEDY, LATIN.

Fragments: Ribbeck, *CRF*; P. Frassinetti, 2nd edn. (1967); F. Leo, *Hermes* 1914, 169 ff. = *Ausgewählte kleine Schriften* (1960), 1. 257 ff; Schanz–Hosius, 1. 245 ff, 2. 824; W. Beare, *The Roman Stage*, 3rd edn. (1964), 137 ff; P. Frassinetti, *Fabula Atellana* (1953).   P. G. M. B.

Ateste (mod. Este) has given its name to one of the principal iron age cultures of northern Italy, lasting from the 9th cent. BC until its peaceful annexation by Rome in 184 BC. Until AD 589 it stood on the Adige, now some miles south, and throughout its history thus combined natural advantages for sea-trade, presumably coming through *Atria, with easy access to the land routes round the gulf. Already by the late 7th–early 6th cents. its products were not only reaching *Felsina and the head of the Adriatic, but were also crossing the Alps to Carniola and the Tyrol. Noted for its production of sheet-bronze, particularly of situlae, Ateste was for 800 years the most important commercial and artistic centre of Venetia (see VENETI (2)): its commercial position led to the incorporation of foreign (e.g. oriental) elements, via Greek and Etruscan intermediaries, into a distinctive indigenous art-style.

BTCGI 7 (1989), 'Este'; F. R. Ridgway, *IBR* 419 ff.; *Atti XI Convegno Studi Etruschi, Este-Padova 1976* (1980); A. M. Chieco Bianchi and L. Calzavara Capuis, *Este* 1 (*Mon. Ant.* 1985). Situla art: L. Bonfante, *Out of Etruria* (1981), 14 ff.   D. W. R. R.

Ath. pol. See ATHĒNAIŌN POLITEIA.

Athalaric, (Ostro-)*Gothic king of Italy AD 526–34, grandson of *Theoderic (1) son of Amalasuentha and Eutharic (consul 519). After Eutharic's death, Athalaric was Theoderic's heir though still a minor. His succession was difficult, and subsequent Gothic political disputes centred on controlling him, one particular issue being his education. Said by *Procopius to have turned early to dissolution, he died while still a youth.   P. J. H.

Athamanes, a tribal group inhabiting the area between the Arachthus and the western slopes of Pindus, notionally descended from *Athamas. After the end of the Epirote kingdom in the 230s BC, it seems, they developed an influential monarchy under Theodorus and *Amynander and continued as an independent *koinon* into the early 1st cent. BC.

P–K, *GL* 2. 1. 216 ff.; Walbank, *Polybius* 1, on 4. 16. 9; Hammond,

Epirus, 682 f. and elsewhere; L. Moretti, *Iscrizioni Storiche Ellenistiche* 2 (1975), no. 91; and see the bibliog. to AMYNANDER. P. S. D.

Athamas, a figure of Boeotian and Thessalian myth. In the best-known story, he was king of Boeotian *Orchomenus (1), husband of Ino (see INO-LEUCOTHEA) and father of Phrixus, *Helle, *Melicertes and Learchus. The first two were the children of Nephele ('Cloud'), Athamas' first wife; their stepmother Ino concocted a bogus oracle demanding their deaths in sacrifice in order to restore the fertility of the land, but they were borne away on a golden ram (see HELLE). Later, Ino and Athamas brought up the child *Dionysus, in revenge for which *Hera drove them mad. Athamas killed their son Learchus, and Ino ran from him carrying Melicertes and jumped into the sea, where mother and son were transformed into deities, Leucothea and Palaemon. In one version, Athamas was then exiled and settled in Thessaly, where he married Themisto. But another tradition places Athamas originally in Thessalian (H)alos, where he himself proposes to sacrifice Phrixus to Zeus Laphystius. The motif of human sacrifice is altogether clearer here, since in Herodotus' rather confusing account (7. 197) Athamas himself is later nearly sacrificed. Both stories probably have to do with the cult of Zeus Laphystius; the Thessalian one explained why a descendant of Athamas must be sacrificed if he set foot in the *prytaneion.

Apollod. 1. 9. 1–2; 3. 4. 3. C. Schwanzar, *LIMC* 2. 950–3. E. Ke.

Athanaric, Gothic leader, made a treaty with *Valens in AD 369 but c.376 failed to hold off a Hunnic attack on his territories and withdrew to a refuge in the Carpathian mountains, yielding Gothic leadership to *Fritigern. He later visited Constantinople and died there on 25 January 381. His father had also been a Gothic leader, to whom Constantine is said to have raised a statue at Constantinople. See GOTHS; HUNS.

P. J. Heather, *Goths and Romans, 332–489* (1991). J. F. Ma.

Athanasius (c.AD 295–373) was an outstanding theologian and Church leader, and as a deacon played an influential part at the council of *Nicaea (1) (325). Appointed bishop of *Alexandria (1) in 328, he vigorously championed the Nicene doctrine of the consubstantiality (ὁμοούσιον) of Father and Son against *Arianism, being five times deposed and exiled. Two of his exiles he spent in the west, to which he introduced monasticism. In the last decades of his life he developed the doctrine of the divinity and personality of the Holy Spirit, and did much to promote understanding between the different anti-Arian groups in the Church. His surviving writings include apologetic, dogmatic, and ascetic treatises, historical essays, and letters.

Migne, *PG* 25–8. Crit. edn. (incomplete), H. G. Opitz (1934–41). J. N. D. K.

atheism The Greek for atheism is 'not to recognize (νομίζειν) the gods' or 'deny that the gods exist' or, later, 'to remove (ἀναιρεῖν) the gods'. (The old doctrine that θεοὺς νομίζειν never means to 'believe in' but always to 'pay cult to' the gods is wrong; but it is true that borderline cases exist.) The Greek word ἄθεος can be applied to atheism (Pl. *Ap.* 26c), but in the earliest instances it means 'impious, vicious' or 'hated, abandoned by the gods', and these senses persist along with the other; so too with ἀθεότης. Thus Christians and pagans were to swap charges of ἀθεότης, by which they meant 'impious views about the divine' (A. von Harnack, Texte und Untersuchungen 28. 4 (1905), 3–16; A. D. Nock, *Sallustius* (1926), p. lxxxviii).

The gods of popular polytheism were rejected or drastically reinterpreted by all philosophers from the 6th cent. BC onwards, but most preserved a divine principle of some kind (as in different ways *Plato (1), *Aristotle, and *Stoicism were to do). Radical atheism is hard to detect, and was never an influential intellectual position in the ancient world. *Anaxagoras and *Thucydides (2) have been suspected of it, because of their silences; a character in *Critias' satyr-play *Sisyphus* famously argues that gods are an invention of a 'wise lawgiver' to deter secret crime (*TrGF* 43 F 19); on the other hand *Democritus, whose overall system is compatible with atheism, appears to speak of gods in some fragments, and *Prodicus did not necessarily reject the divine in every form merely because he offered a rationalizing account of the origin of human belief in the gods of myth (DK 84 B 5). Much the most important testimony to the reality of atheism is Plato's in *Laws* 10, where he speaks of contemporary thinkers who hold that the world is governed by nature or chance, not god, that morality is man-made and the best life is that according to nature (889ᵃ–890ᵃ). Who Plato had in mind is disputed (W. de Mahieu, *RBPh* 1963, 5–24; 1964, 16–47); he goes on to say that such radical atheism was already on the wane (967a–b).

Much less helpful are the claims often made in later antiquity that this or that earlier thinker (often linked together in an 'atheist list') had 'removed the gods'. Some typical atheists of these catalogues (cf. M. Winiarczyk, *Philol.* 1984, 157–83) are *Protagoras, Prodicus, *Diagoras of Melos, *Theodorus (2) of Cyrene (who probably acquired the sobriquet ἄθεος in his lifetime), *Euhemerus, and *Epicurus. Too much oversimplification and polemical distortion lies beyond the lists for them to have authority: Protagoras, for instance, was a declared agnostic (DK 80 B 4), a position incompatible with atheism.

A second view combated by Plato in *Laws* 10 is that the gods exist, but are indifferent to the doings of mankind (885b, 899d ff.). Such 'practical atheism' had doubtless always existed, and became the declared position of Epicurus (who however urged that the gods should still be honoured); philosophical opponents asserted that only fear of public opinion had restrained Epicurus from 'abolishing the gods' altogether (Cic. *Nat. D.* 1. 85, 121, 123).

A. B. Drachmann, *Atheism in Pagan Antiquity* (1922); W. Fahr, ΘΕΟΥΣ ΝΟΜΙΖΕΙΝ (1969); M. Winiarczyk, *Rh. Mus.* 1990, 1–15; on *Sisyphus*, M. Davies, *BICS* 1989, 16–32; and see the bibliog. to PRODICUS. R. C. T. P.

Athena In *Iliad* 5. 733–7, *Homer describes how Athena took off the finely-wrought robe 'which she herself had made and worked at with her own hands' and 'armed herself for grievous war'. This incident encapsulates the paradoxical nature of a goddess who is as skilled in the preparation of clothes as she is fearless in battle; who thus unites in her person the characteristic excellences of both sexes. At the greater *Panathenaea in Athens, she was presented with a robe, the work of maidens' hands (see ARRĒPHORIA), which traditionally portrayed that battle of the gods and giants in which she was the outstanding warrior on the side of the gods.

Her patronage of crafts is expressed in cults such as that of Athena Erganē, Athena the Craftswoman or Maker; it extends beyond the 'works' of women to carpentry, metalworking, and technology of every kind, so that at Athens she shared a temple and a festival with *Hephaestus and can, for instance, be seen on vases seated (in full armour!) in a pottery. Her love of battle is seen, as we saw, in myth, and also in such cults as that of Athena Victory (*Nike); she is regularly portrayed fully armed, one leg purposefully advanced, wearing her terror-inducing *aegis.

She is also closely associated with the masculine world in her mythological role as a helper of male heroes, most memorably seen in her presence beside Heracles on several of the metopes of the temple of *Zeus at *Olympia. Indeed her intervention in battle often takes the form of 'standing beside' a favourite (e.g. *Il*. 10. 278–94). (She has accordingly been seen as every man's ideal elder sister, in contrast to the tomboy Artemis and sexy Aphrodite (P. Friedrich, *The Meaning of Aphrodite* (1978)); but these modern western categories scarcely fit the Greek family.) Her virginity is a bridge between the two sides of her nature. Weaving is a characteristic activity of ordinary young girls, but a perpetual virgin, who is not subject to the distinctively feminine experience of *childbirth, is a masculine woman, a potential warrior.

The warlike Athena is scarcely separable from Athena Polias, the goddess of the Acropolis (see ATHENS, TOPOGRAPHY) and protectress of cities. 'City-protecting' was most commonly performed by goddesses rather than gods; and the other great protectress was the other great warrior-goddess of the *Iliad*, Athena's close associate *Hera. Athena exercised this function in many cities besides Athens, including Sparta and (in the *Iliad*) Troy. Athens was unique only in the degree of prominence that it assigned her in this role.

A few cult titles and festivals of Athena seem to indicate interests other than those discussed so far; and it has often been suggested that her familiar classical functions have been pared down from a much broader original competence. But this is too much to deduce from stray allusions to cults the details of which are usually very little known. The 'Athena Mother' of *Elis (Paus. 5. 3. 2) is a puzzle; and Athena's limited intrusions upon the preserves of other gods at Athens—the cult of Athena of Health (*Hygieia) for instance—may simply reflect a tendency of city-protecting gods to have a finger in every pie.

Athena is unique among Greek gods in bearing a connection with a city imprinted in her very name. The precise linguistic relation between place and goddess is teasingly difficult to define: the form of her name in early Attic inscriptions is the adjectival *Ἀθηναία*, which suggests that she may in origin be 'the Athenian' something, the Athenian Pallas for instance (*Παλλὰς Ἀθηναίη* being a regular Homeric formula). But this account still leaves the shorter name-form Athena unexplained. Athenians themselves, of course, stressed the goddess's association with their city enthusiastically. She was foster-mother of the early king *Erechtheus/*Erichthonius, and had competed, successfully, with Poseidon for possession of Attica. In Panhellenic mythology, however, she shows no special interest in Athens or in Athenian heroes. The association with Athens does not appear to affect her fundamental character.

Her most important myth is that of her birth from the head of Zeus. It stresses her unique closeness to Zeus, a vital quality in a city-protecting goddess, and at the same time the gap that divides her, a child without a mother, from the maternal side of femininity. In the oldest version (Hes. *Theog.* 886–90) Zeus became pregnant with Athena after swallowing *Metis; she was thus also a kind of reincarnation of *mētis* (*μῆτις*), 'cunning intelligence'.

It has in fact been suggested that Athena's characteristic mode of action, a mode that unifies her apparently diverse functions while differentiating them from those of other gods with which they might appear to overlap, is the application of *mētis*. Her *mētis* appears obviously in her association with crafts and in her

love (Hom. *Od.* passim) for wily *Odysseus; more obliquely, it is argued, it is for instance to be seen in her title Hippia, 'of horses', which she acquires via a product of *mētis*, the bridle, whereas *Poseidon Hippius embodies the animal's brute strength. In warfare she would express rational force, *vis temperata*, in contrast to the mindless violence of Ares. One may doubt, however, how fundamental the opposition to Ares and the role of *mētis* in fact are in defining her military function.

Precursors of Athena have been identified in Mycenaean military or palace-protecting goddesses; the only solid evidence is a tantalizing reference in a Linear B tablet from Cnossus to A-ta-na po-ti-ni-ja.

Burkert, *GR* 139–43; M. Detienne and J.-P. Vernant, *Cunning Intelligence in Greek Culture and Society* (1978; Fr. orig. 1974); P. Demargne and H. Cassimatis, *LIMC* 'Athena'. R. C. T. P.

Athenaeum, *Hadrian's famous institution for the study of Greek *rhetoric and letters in the centre of Rome. In the 4th cent. AD it was the setting for public *declamation in Latin as well. Its location is uncertain.

E. Harleman, *Eranos* 1981, 57 ff.; M. Boatwright, *Hadrian and the City of Rome* (1987). A. J. S. S.

Athenaeus (1) (fl. *c.*AD 200), of *Naucratis in Egypt. His only extant work, *Δειπνοσοφισταί* ('The Learned Banquet'), was probably completed in the years immediately following the death of *Commodus in AD 192; other chronological inferences are uncertain. It belongs to the polyhistoric variety of the symposium form (see SYMPOSIUM LITERATURE), practised earlier by *Aristoxenus and *Didymus (1). It is now in fifteen books (originally perhaps 30); there is also an Epitome, which covers existing gaps. At the 'banquet', which extends over several days, philosophy, literature, law, medicine, and other interests are represented by a large number of guests, who in some cases bear historical names (most notably *Galen); a Cynic philosopher is introduced as a foil. The Roman host, Larensis, probably the author's patron, is attested epigraphically (*CIL* 6. 212). The sympotic framework, if not devoid of occasional humour, is subordinate in interest to the collections of excerpts which are introduced into it. These relate to all the materials and accompaniments of convivial occasions; they are drawn from a vast number of authors, especially of the Middle and New *Comedy, whose works are now lost; they are valuable both as literature and as illustrating earlier Greek manners. The order of these extracts sometimes suggests the use of lexica (Didymus (1), *Pamphilus (2)) or of *διδασκαλίαι* (see DIDASKALIA), as well as of lists of *κωμῳδούμενοι* (people made fun of in comedy); but Athenaeus has collected much independently from the great writers; he cites some 1,250 authors, gives the titles of more than 1,000 plays, and quotes more than 10,000 lines of verse.

TEXT G. Kaibel (Teubner, 1887–99); Epitome: S. P. Peppink (1937–9).
TEXT AND TRANSLATION C. B. Gulick (Loeb, 1927–413), 7 vols.
COMMENTARY J. Schweighäuser (1801–7).
CRITICISM R. Hirzel, *Dialog* (1895) 2. 352. F. Rudolph, *Philol.* Suppl. 6 (1891) (sources); K. Mengis, *Stud. Gesch. Kult. Alt.* 1920 (composition); C. A. Bapp, *Leipz. Stud.* 1885 (music and lyric); K. Zepernick, *Philol.* 1921 (trustworthiness); G. Zecchini, *La cultura storica di Ateneo* (1939); D. Braund and J. Wilkins (eds.), *Athenaeus and his World* (2000).
W. M. E.; R. B.; N. G. W.

Athenaeus (2) **Mechanicus,** author of an extant work on siege-engines (Περὶ μηχανημάτων; see ARTILLERY; SIEGECRAFT), may probably be dated in the 1st cent. BC.

Ed. R. Schneider, *Abh. d. Gesellsch. d. Wissensch. zu Göttingen* (Phil.-hist. Kl.) NF 12 (1912). E. W. M.

Athenaeus (3) of Attaleia in Pamphylia was the founder of a school of physicians, the *Pneumatists. Imbued with Stoic ideas but well trained in philosophy in general, Athenaeus assumed as basic elements the four qualities, together with the *pneuma as the fifth. Health and disease he explained through their *eukrasia* (good temperament) and *dyskrasia* (bad temperament). His physiology (see ANATOMY AND PHYSIOLOGY) was dependent on Aristotle. Details of his *pathology are unknown. His system was important in its speculative formulation rather than in its practical consequences, although his followers produced important studies of pulsation and heart disease. Athenaeus, who considered medicine as part of general education, devised most elaborate *dietetic rules, in which he included pedagogical as well as medical precepts, differentiated according to the different stages of life. The ideas of Athenaeus were highly esteemed by *Galen.

His dates are controversial. Galen in *De causis contentivis* makes him a pupil of the Stoic *Posidonius (2), from which Kudlien, *Hermes*, 1962, 419 ff., concluded that he lived in the middle years of the 1st cent. BC. But if the reputation of Athenaeus and his pupils was as great as Galen suggests, the silence of *Celsus and *Pliny (1) the Elder, writing a century later, is somewhat strange. It may thus be preferable to revert to the older dating, which placed his activity around AD 50, and to treat Galen's reference to a link with Posidonius as reflecting intellectual rather than personal dependence.

TEXT Fragments from Oribasius in *Veterum et Clarorum Medicorum Graecorum Opuscula*, C. F. Matthaei (1808), incomplete.
LITERATURE M. Wellmann, *Phil. Unters.* 1895, and *RE* 2. 2034; F. Kudlien, *Hermes*, 1962, 419 ff.; cf. also T. C. Allbutt, *Greek Medicine in Rome* (1921); for the history of Pneumatism, see F. Kudlien, *RE* Suppl. 11 (1968), 1098 ff. L. E.; V. N.

Athenagoras, Christian *apologist from Athens and author of two extant works, *The Resurrection of the Dead*, and the *Legatio*. The latter is a defence of Christianity composed in the form of a letter to the emperors Marcus *Aurelius and *Commodus. This work is an extremely important, early assertion of Christian propriety against commonplace charges that Christians were atheists and cannibals (see ATHEISM; CANNIBALISM). One of its most interesting features is the extensive use of classical literature to justify or explain Christian practice.

Ed. W. R. Schoedel, *Athenagoras* (1972). D. S. P.

Athēnaiōn politeia ('Athenian constitution', Aristotelian). *Aristotle is credited with works on the constitutions of 158 states: a papyrus containing all but the opening few pages of the *Athenian constitution* was acquired by the British Museum, and was published in 1891. About the first two thirds (chs. 1–41) give a history of the constitution to the restoration of the democracy after the regime of the Thirty (see THIRTY TYRANTS). This part derives from a mixture of sources, and is of uneven merit, but at its best it contains valuable information which does not survive in any other text. The remaining third (42–69) gives an extremely useful account of the working of the constitution in the author's time, and appears to be based on the laws of Athens and the author's own observation.

There has been much argument as to the authorship of the work: it was regularly attributed in antiquity to Aristotle, and was written (in the 330s BC, with some revision in the 320s) when he was in Athens; there are some striking agreements between the *Athēnaiōn politeia* and Aristotle's *Politics* (e.g. that *Solon should not be blamed for the extreme *democracy which was built on his foundations), but also some striking disagreements (e.g. on Solon's provisions for the appointment of the *archontes); except in a few passages the style is different from that of the Aristotelian corpus, but this is a different kind of work from those in the main corpus. Some scholars believe that Aristotle himself wrote the *Athēnaiōn politeia*; but Aristotle can hardly himself have written all the works attributed to him, and he was neither an Athenian nor an admirer of the Athenian democracy, so the work is more probably to be attributed to a pupil. Its value to historians is considerable, whether Aristotle was the author or not.

TEXTS *Editio princeps*: F. G. Kenyon (1891); M. H. Chambers (Teubner, 1986).
COMMENTARIES P. J. Rhodes (1981); M. H. Chambers (1991; Ger.).
TRANSLATION P. J. Rhodes (1984).
LITERARY STUDY J. J. Keaney, *The Composition of Aristotle's Athenaion Politeia* (1992). P. J. R.

Athenian Constitution, Aristotelian See ATHĒNAIŌN POLITEIA.

Athenian empire See DELIAN LEAGUE.

Athenodorus, of Tarsus, son of Sandon, Stoic, a friend of *Cicero and *Strabo, and, like *Arius Didymus, a court philosopher to Augustus; he addressed a work to *Octavia (2). (He is to be distinguished from Athenodorus Cordylion.) He probably came to Rome with the then Octavian in 44 BC; in old age he was sent by Augustus to expel Boethus, Antony's ruler in Tarsus, where he then became the chief citizen. He was probably a pupil of *Posidonius (2), and sent a summary of some of the latter's views to Cicero, who wanted them for his *De officiis*. He wrote a work against Aristotle's *Categories*, an account of *Tarsus, and, like Posidonius, *On the Ocean*. The younger *Seneca used his ethical writings.

FGrH 746; Philippson, *RE* Suppl. 5. 47 ff. J. A.

Athens (Ἀθῆναι)

Prehistory The more substantial remains of later periods have largely effaced prehistoric settlement evidence, apart from subterranean features like tombs and wells, whose distribution suggests that the characteristic settlement pattern from early times was a nucleus around the Acropolis and a wider spread of hamlets and farms. The settlement's earlier history is obscure, but it clearly became one of the more significant Mycenaean centres (see MYCENAEAN CIVILIZATION), as indicated by wealthy 14th-cent. BC tombs and the later 13th cent. BC fortification and water-supply system on the Acropolis. Twelfth-cent. remains are scanty, but cemetery evidence indicates a wide spread of communities, mostly small, by the Submycenaean phase; overall, the evidence offers no support for the theory that Athens attracted large 'refugee' groups.

History Tradition held that *Theseus was responsible for the *synoecism, in the political rather than physical sense, of the Athenian (Attic) state. More prosaically put, this would imply a unified kingdom, centred on Athens, in the late bronze age. But if there was any such kingdom it did not survive the collapse of Mycenaean civilization and the synoecism is now generally put *c*.900 BC after a tumultuous period in which refugees from Attica

Athens

settled in Ionia (see IONIANS) from c.1050 BC onwards. Athenian imperial *propaganda later exaggerated the organized character of this process, turning it into a movement of *colonization which would justify the *metropolis making hegemonical demands of the 'daughter-cities'. Another later propaganda item was the myth of 'autochthony' (Attica had 'always had the same inhabitants'). This was false, but useful for scoring off the *Dorian 'newcomers'. See AUTOCHTHONS.

The Attic countryside was settled from the centre in the 8th cent. by 'internal colonization': Athens was not among the first genuinely colonizing states. The early Attic state was aristocratic and politically hardly distinctive. There was nothing even embryonically democratic about the annual *archontes who began in 684/3 BC and were the chief officers of state: Thuc. 1. 126, correcting Hdt. 5. 72 which says an obscure group ran Athens, the '*prytaneis of the naukraries', a title which implies ships (ναυ-); see NAUKRARIAI. But early Athenian naval activity is plausible, because Attica's long coastline is one of the features which did make it exceptional. Others were an imposing city acropolis, with its own water-supply; a mountain-system which formed a first line of defence for Athens itself; and valuable resources in the silver-bearing *Laurium region of east Attica.

In 632 'the Athenians', a collective noun now first used as a political agent, resisted *Cylon's attempt at a *tyranny; there is no reason to link this rejection of constitutional upheaval with *Draco's law-code in the 620s. Athens' first overseas settlement at *Sigeum in c.610 may be an indicator of economic restlessness of the kind which produced *Solon. His economic and political reforms in the 590s created an Attica of smallholders; enhanced Athenians' sense that they were a political élite; and widened eligibility for political office. But proper democracy was still in the future and Solon could not save Athens from the tyranny, later in the 6th cent., of *Pisistratus and sons. The tyranny was not oppressive until shortly before the end (510), and did more for Athens' later military and naval prominence than 5th-cent. historians allowed.

It was *Cleisthenes (2) in 508 who, after a short phase of aristocratic struggle, established the democracy which provoked Persia by helping the *Ionian Revolt, and then defeated Persia at *Marathon and ten years later at *Salamis. The Cleisthenic state was however aristocratic in many ways and full democracy did not arrive until the 460s and the reforms associated with *Ephialtes (4) and *Pericles (1). But meanwhile Athens had in 478/7 become an imperial city: see DELIAN LEAGUE. Against a background of increasing tension with Sparta, the displaced leader of Greece, the Athenians now capitalized on their Persian War achievement. Military successes against Persia culminated in the battle of the *Eurymedon in the early 460s, and more subject-allies were brought under Athenian control (see DELIAN LEAGUE); art and architecture, poetry and rhetoric continued to insist on the Persian Wars theme in a way hardly guessable from the history of *Thucydides (2). The Athenian empire survived the First *Peloponnesian War of c.461–46, though the *Thirty Years Peace of 446 ended Athens' ten-year control of *Boeotia. But increasing Athenian expansionism in the early 430s alarmed Sparta and the outbreak in 431 of the 27-year *Peloponnesian War ended the *Pentekontaetia* or 50-year period from the Persian Wars; this was the period of maximum Athenian cultural achievement.

In the *Archidamian War, the Spartans failed in their programme of 'liberating' Greece from the tyrant city, Athens. Nor did Athens' catastrophic Sicilian Expedition of 415–413 or the

oligarchic regime of the *Four Hundred (411), or even the definite commitment of wealthy Persia to the Spartan side (407) end the war, which included Athenian successes like Cynossema (411), Cyzicus (410), and *Arginusae (406) before the final defeat at Aegospotami in 405. Athens became a subject-ally of Sparta and a second, Spartan-sponsored oligarchy took power in 404, the *Thirty Tyrants.

But by a recovery even more remarkable than that of 413, Athens climbed back to independent and even semi-imperial status in the early 4th cent. Fifth-century Athens had been an imperial, Hellenistic Athens was a university, city; 4th-cent. Athens was something in between. Democracy was restored in 403 and the constitution was mildly reformed, though not in a way which can be associated with any named reformer. From now on the democracy was more efficient but noticeably less radical (see DEMOCRACY, ATHENIAN). In foreign affairs, Athens soon dared to confront the Spartans as one of the coalition which fought the *Corinthian War of 395–386 and, remarkably, included Sparta's recent backer Persia. The battle of Cnidus of 394 was a naval victory over Sparta, won by a Persian-sponsored fleet but with an Athenian commander, Conon. The *King's Peace of 386 (see GREECE, HISTORY) ended this first phase of Athenian recovery. But Spartan aggressions and unpopularity enabled Athens to launch a *Second Athenian Confederacy in 378.

Initially the confederacy was successful and welcome: its members included Thebes, now a rising power. Athens defeated Sparta at Naxos and Alyzia in the mid-370s. But Thebes' defeat of Sparta at *Leuctra in 371 led to a *rapprochement* between Athens and Sparta in the 360s. Meanwhile Athenian attempts to turn their empire into something more like its 5th-cent. predecessor, especially attempts to recover *Amphipolis and the *cleruchy put in on *Samos in 366, were unpopular. Major island allies rebelled in the *Social War (1) of 357–355. Because of distractions like this and the Third *Sacred War, not to mention sheer short-sightedness, it was not until 351 that Athens and *Demosthenes (2) realized the threat posed by *Philip (1) II of Macedon. A brief war (early 340s) ended with the Peace of *Philocrates (346); Athens now acknowledged the loss of Amphipolis. The end, militarily, to Athenian great-power status came in 338 at *Chaeronea, though modern historians rightly insist that this did not signal either the death of the *polis* generally or of Athens in particular.

The Athens of *Eubulus (1) and *Lycurgus (3) pursued, in the 330s and 320s, ostensibly backward-looking policies of retrenchment which actually anticipate Athens' Hellenistic role as cultural centre. Athens did not openly resist *Alexander (3) the Great, but when at the end of his life he restored Samos to the Samians, Athens embarked on and was defeated in the Lamian War of 323–322 (naval battles of Abydos and Amorgos, land battle of Crannon), after which democracy was suppressed. There were however later democratic restorations and reactions, the first as early as 318 (democracy installed by *Polyperchon).

Under *Cassander, Athens was ruled tyrannically by *Demetrius (3) of Phalerum (318–307), a period of peace but imposed cultural austerity. He was expelled by the rapturously welcomed Antigonid Macedonian *Demetrius (4) Poliorcetes. Another Cassander-supported tyrant *Lachares seized power in 300; the hoplite general Charias resisted him unsuccessfully in 296 in the name of democracy. (See also OLYMPIODORUS (1).) Lachares fell in 294 and Athens submitted to the Antigonids for much of the century until the 220s; the exceptions were a precarious period of freedom in the 280s/early 270s (a period associated with the name of the patriot commander Olympiodorus) and the *Chremonidean War of the 260s, which ended with Athens' surrender in 262. In the 220s, under the regime of Euryclides and Miccion, Athens managed to stay on good terms with the Ptolemies as well as with Macedon, as Rome's shadow lengthened over Greece.

Roman (see ACHAIA; GREECE, ROMAN). Friendly with Rome from 229 BC (Polyb. 2. 12. 8), Athens was rewarded for her support against *Perseus (2) with the gift of *Delos (166 BC), its possession fuelling an economic boom, peaking by 100 BC (S. Tracy, *Harv. Stud.* 1979, 213 ff.) and linked with (if not prompting) a copious ('New Style') silver coinage. In 88 BC, under the tyrant *Aristion, Athens enthusiastically supported *Mithradates VI; the city was sacked as a result by *Sulla (86 BC), and a timocratic constitution imposed (see AREOPAGUS), but it retained 'free' status (Strab. 9. 1. 20). From the 50s BC on *philhellenism prompted Roman nobles, then emperors, to become benefactors of the city. *Hadrian transformed it with a lavish building programme and made it the seat of the *Panhellenion. Thereafter it flourished culturally as a centre of Greek rhetoric (see SECOND SOPHISTIC), and it remained a bastion of philosophy, above all (from c. AD 400) *Neoplatonism, until c.530. Damaged by the *Heruli (267) (see P. *HERENNIUS DEXIPPUS) and besieged by *Alaric (396), the city acquired major new buildings in the 5th cent., notably the vast 'Palace of the Giants'. *Christianity was slow to make inroads; the *Parthenon may not have become a church before the 6th cent.

PREHISTORY *GAC* F 1; *LH Citadels*, 73 ff.; J. Whitley, *Style and Society in Dark Age Greece* (1991), 61, 87 ff. (on Submycenaean).
O. T. P. K. D.
HISTORY See relevant chs. of *CAH*² vols. 3/3 (1982); 4 (1988); 5 (1992); 6 (1994); 7/1 (1984). The most important work to have appeared since the conclusion in 1994 of the Greek volumes of *CAH* is C. Habicht, *Athens from Alexander to Antony* (1997, Germ. orig. 1995).
S. H.
ROMAN D. J. Geagan, *ANRW* 2. 7. 1 (1979), 371–437 (with older bibliog.); J. H. Oliver, *The Civic Tradition and Roman Athens* (1983); P. Castrén (ed.), *Post-Herulian Athens* (1994); M. Hoff and S. Rotroff (eds.), *The Romanization of Athens* (1997).
A. J. S. S.

Athens, topography

Acropolis, the central fortress and principal sanctuary of *Athena, patron goddess of the city. In the later 13th cent. BC the steep hill was enclosed by a massive wall. Within, there are Mycenaean terraces, perhaps once supporting traces of 'the strong house of *Erechtheus' (Hom. *Od* 7. 81). The first monumental temples and sculptural dedications date to the 6th cent. BC. Two large Doric temples of limestone with marble trim were built, along with a half-dozen small temples or treasuries. Later quarrying has obliterated the foundations of all but one of the peripteral temples (c.510 BC) which stood on the north side of the hill, just south of the later Erechtheum. A marble temple, the Older Parthenon, was under construction on the south half of the hill in 480 BC when the Persians took and sacked the city. The debris from this devastation was buried on the Acropolis and no major construction took place for about a generation. In the 450s a monumental bronze statue of Athena Promachus was set up to celebrate victory over the Persians and in the second half of the 5th cent. four major buildings were constructed at the instigation of *Pericles (1), with *Phidias as general overseer. First came the *Parthenon (447–432); the *Propylaea (437–432), gateway to the Acropolis, occupied the western approaches to the citadel. Soon after, an old shrine of Athena Nike (Victory) was refurbished and a small temple of the Ionic order, tetrastyle amphiprostyle in

plan, was built just outside the Propylaea. Finally, the *Erechtheum was constructed during the last quarter of the 5th cent. Only a few buildings were added to the Acropolis in later times: a sanctuary of Brauronian *Artemis (see BRAURON) and the Chalkotheke, where bronzes were stored. A tall pier built just outside the Propylaea in the 2nd cent. BC first carried statues of *Eumenes (2) II and *Attalus II, kings of Pergamum and benefactors of Athens, later replaced by one of Agrippa. The Roman presence in Greece is reflected on the Acropolis by the construction after 27 BC of a small round temple dedicated to Roma and Augustus and built in an Ionic order closely copying the Erechtheum.

Environs of the Acropolis Numerous sanctuaries clustered around the base of the Acropolis rock. The sanctuaries of 'the nymph' (7th cent. BC), *Asclepius (420 BC), and *Dionysus (c.500 BC) were on the south slope. The theatre of Dionysus was built of limestone and marble in the 330s BC and renovated several times in the Roman period. To the west was a stoa built by King Eumenes II of Pergamum (197–159 BC) and beyond that the local millionaire Ti. *Claudius Atticus Herodes (2) built a huge *odeum in memory of his wife Regilla (c. AD 160). The ground east of the theatre was taken up by the odeum of Pericles (c.443 BC), a replica of the tent of Xerxes, captured by the Greeks at the battle of *Plataea (479 BC). A broad street lined with tripods set up by victorious *chorēgoi* (producers) in the choral lyric contests led from the theatre around the east end and north side of the Acropolis. The small Corinthian Lysicrates monument (335 BC) is the best-preserved surviving tripod base. In this eastern area were to be found several other cults (*Aglaurus, *Dioscuri, *Theseus), as well as the *Prytaneion*, hearth of the city (all unexcavated). The north side of the Acropolis sheltered cults of *Aphrodite and *Eros, *Pan, *Apollo, and *Demeter and *Persephone (Eleusinium). The *Areopagus, a low hill north-west of the Acropolis, was the seat in early times of a council and lawcourt as well as a shrine of the Eumenides (Furies; see ERINYES). St *Paul addressed the court of the Areopagus, though by the 1st cent. AD the council almost certainly met in the lower city and not on the hill.

Agora, the civic centre of Athens, was located north-west of the Acropolis on ground sloping down to the Eridanus river. Traversed by the Panathenaic Way, the Agora was a large open square reserved for a wide variety of public functions, lined on all four sides by the principal administrative buildings of the city. First laid out in the 6th cent. BC, it remained a focal point for Athenian commerce, politics, and culture for centuries, surviving the Persian sack of 480 BC and the Sullan siege of 86 BC (see CORNELIUS SULLA FELIX, L.). Here in the Classical period were to be found the *bouleutērion* (council-house), the Tholos (dining-hall for the *prytaneis), the Metroon (archives), mint, lawcourts, and magistrates' offices (Royal Stoa, and South Stoa I), along with sanctuaries (Hephaisteion, Altar of the Twelve Gods, Stoa of Zeus Eleutherius, Apollo Patrous), fountain-houses, and stoas (*Stoa Poecile, Stoa of the Herms). More large stoas (Attalus II, Middle Stoa, South Stoa II) were added in the 2nd cent. BC. To the 2nd cent. perhaps should be dated (controversial) the elaborate octagonal marble water-clock known today as the Tower of the Winds, built some 200 m. (220 yds.) east of the Agora. This eastern area was later occupied by the market of Caesar and Augustus, which supplanted many of the commercial functions of the old Agora. In the 2nd cent. AD a huge peristyle court with library was built by Hadrian just to the north of the Roman market. Roman additions to the Agora also reflect Athenian prominence in cultural and educational affairs: an odeum given by *Agrippa (c.15 BC) and a library dedicated by Pantaenus (c. AD 100). Badly damaged and partially abandoned as the result of the sack by the *Heruli in AD 267, the Agora was finally destroyed by *Alaric and the Visigoths in AD 395.

Pnyx, the meeting-place of the Athenian assembly (*ekklēsia), was built on a low ridge west of the Acropolis. Originally laid out in either c.500 or 462/1 BC, and remodelled in 403 under the *Thirty Tyrants (Plut. *Them.* 19), the final phase was built in c.340 BC. This third phase consists of a rock-cut speaker's platform (bēma) and a massive curved retaining wall for the auditorium. Stoas were laid out on the ridge above but never finished. By the Hellenistic period most meetings took place in the theatre of Dionysus, and a small open-air sanctuary of Zeus *Hypsistos was established just south-east of the bēma in the Roman period. North of the Pnyx the ridge was given over to the worship of the Nymphs, while the south end of the ridge (the Museum) was the site first of a Macedonian garrison fort in Hellenistic times and then the marble tomb of C. *Iulius Antiochus Epiphanes Philopappus (d. AD 114/16).

South-east Athens In this quarter of town were to be found the oldest cults of the city: Dionysus in 'the Marshes', Olympian Zeus, Gē (Earth), and Pythian Apollo (Thuc. 2. 15). Best preserved is the colossal *Olympieum. The centre of *Hadrian's worship in the Greek world, it was approached through an arch bearing inscriptions delimiting the old town of Theseus from the new Athens built by *Hadrian (IG 2². 5185). Nearby, to the north, a gymnasium with a sanctuary of Apollo Lyceus gave its name to *Aristotle's school, the Lyceum. Other shrines and the old Enneakrounos fountain-house lay further out, along the banks of the Ilissus river. Across the river lay the Panathenaic stadium, built by *Lycurgus (3) (338–326 BC), rebuilt in marble by Ti. Claudius Atticus Herodes (2) (AD 139–44), and restored in 1896.

Fortifications An Archaic city wall was replaced in 479 BC, immediately after the Persian sack, by a new expanded circuit, hastily constructed at the behest of Themistocles (Thuc. 1. 90). Its length of 6½ km. (4 mi.) was pierced by at least fifteen gates, the principal one being the *Dipylon, to the north-west. Moats and outer walls were added in the 4th cent. in response to threats from Macedonia, and a large extension was added to the east in Roman times. Destroyed in AD 267, the walls were replaced in part by a new, much more constricted, circuit, though the outer wall was eventually refurbished as well. Communication between Athens and the harbours of *Piraeus was assured by means of three *Long Walls.

Cemeteries Burials were made outside the city walls, all around the circuit. The principal cemetery, known as the *Ceramicus, lay along the two major roads leading north-west from the city. It was used as a burial ground from c.1100 BC until the 6th cent. AD, and excavations have recovered hundreds of graves, along with sculptured and inscribed grave-markers. In this same vicinity lay the dēmosion sēma, the state burial ground for the war-dead as well as other notables. Further on lay the *Academy.

GENERAL Pausanias, bk. 1 with Frazer's comm., W. Judeich, *Topographie von Athen*, 2nd edn. (1931); W. B. Dinsmoor, *The Architecture of Ancient Greece*, 3rd edn. (1950); R. E. Wycherley, *The Stones of Athens* (1978); J. Travlos, *Pictorial Dictionary of Athens* (1971), *The Development of the City Plan of Athens*, 2nd edn. (1993; in Greek), and *Bildlexikon zur Topographie des antiken Attika* (1988), 23–33; J. Binder, *The Topography of Athens: A Sourcebook* (forthcoming).

ACROPOLIS AND ENVIRONS Plutarch, *Pericles*. O. Jahn and A. Michaelis, *Arx Athenarum a Pausania descripta*, 3rd edn. (1901); W. B. Dinsmoor Jr., *The Propylaia* 1 (1980); M. Brouskari, *The Acropolis Museum* (1974); J. A. Bundgaard, *The Parthenon and the Mycenaean City on the Heights* (1976); E. Berger (ed.), *Parthenon-Kongress Basel*, 2 vols (1984); A. W. Pickard-Cambridge, *The Theatre of Dionysus in Athens* (1946); S. Aleshire, *The Athenian Asklepieion* (1989).

AGORA R. E. Wycherley, *The Athenian Agora 3: Literary and Epigraphical Testimonia* (1957); J. Camp, *The Athenian Agora* (1986); J. Camp (ed.), *The Athenian Agora Guide*, 4th edn. (1990); J. von Freeden, *Oikia Kyrrestou: Studien zum sogenannten Turm der Winde in Athen* (1983).

PNYX H. H. A. Thompson, *Hesp.* Suppl. 19 (1982), 133–47.

SOUTH-EAST ATHENS J. Travlos, *Pictorial Dictionary of Athens* (1971), *passim*; J. P. Lynch, *Aristotle's School* (1972); D. Willers, *Hadrians Panhellenisches Programm* (1990).

FORTIFICATIONS J. Travlos, *Pictorial Dictionary*, 158–79; D. Conwell, *The Athenian Long Walls* (Diss. Univ. Penn., 1992).

CERAMICUS U. Knigge, *The Athenian Kerameikos* (1991).

J. McK. C.

athletics

Greek At the core of Greek athletics was an individual's hard physical struggle in order to gain victory over an opponent; hence, it included not only (as 'athletics' implies nowadays) track and field events but also *boxing, *wrestling, and equestrian events (see HORSE- AND CHARIOT-RACES), and excluded team competitions, fun-running, and performances aimed at setting records (cf. the derivation of 'athletics' from the root ἀθλ- denoting struggle, competition for a prize, and misery). Athletics was a popular activity; valuable contemporary evidence for it is provided by vase-paintings and the victory odes of *Pindar and *Bacchylides.

The first substantial description of Greek practice comes from *Homer's account of the funeral games for *Patroclus (Il. 23. 262–897; cf. Od. 8. 120–30). Eight events are mentioned there (chariot-racing, boxing, wrestling, running, *javelin, an event similar to fencing, throwing the weight, and archery); the five in italics regularly formed the central part of all later games.

From the middle of the 5th cent. the four major venues for athletics competitions were the *Olympian, *Pythian, *Nemean, and *Isthmian Games. The running-races were the *stadion* (a length of the stadium, 192 m. (210 yds.) at Olympia), *diaulos* (there and back), and *dolichos* (twelve laps at Olympia). There was no marathon or event of similar length, although according to Herodotus (6. 105) *Phidippides, who ran from Athens to Sparta, trained as an ultra-distance runner for the purpose of delivering messages. A race in armour, derived from military training, was introduced into athletics programmes at the end of the 6th cent., and there was a *pentathlon consisting of long-jump, *stadion*, *discus, javelin, and wrestling. At the Olympic and Pythian Games there were separate events for men and boys, while at the Nemean and Isthmian Games there was also an intermediate category for youths (ἀγένειοι, lit. 'beardless').

Training took place in the *gymnasium, or *xystos* (covered colonnade); for the running events, especially the *dolichos*, long training-runs must have been done outside the confines of these buildings. The need for athletes to have a suitable diet was widely recognized (Hippoc. VM 4; Arist. Eth Nic. 2. 6. 7; Pl. Resp. 410b; Paus. 6. 7. 10). Sometimes an athlete's father would act as his coach (Pind. Isthm. 6. 72–3); often, past victors became coaches (Melesias of Athens, Pind. Ol. 8. 54–64; see THUCYDIDES (1); Iccus of Tarentum, Paus. 6. 10. 5). Before the Olympia, the wise precaution was taken of making competitors swear by Zeus that for the previous ten months they had trained properly (Paus. 5. 24. 9). When training or competing, athletes covered their bodies with olive oil to keep off the dust and were generally naked, though there is some disputed evidence pointing to the use of loincloths (e.g. Thuc. 1. 6. 5 and the Perizoma group of vases, Beazley, *ABV* 343–6; see M. McDonnell, *JHS* 1991, 182–93). Male sexual interest in young athletes, admired for their physique, was commonplace (e.g. Xen. *Symp.* 1. 2–10; Aeschin. *In Tim.* 156–7; see HOMOSEXUALITY).

Women competed at Olympia in separate games, the Heraea in honour of *Hera; there was just one event, a shortened *stadion*-race (Paus. 5. 16. 2–3). During the men's athletics, married women were forbidden to watch, but virgin girls were permitted (Paus. 6. 20. 9), a custom perhaps derived from a conception of the games as an occasion for girls to meet future husbands.

It is hard to evaluate athletics performances, because running-races were not timed, and distances in field events not measured (but see PHAYLLUS (1)); one indication that standards may have been low is the fact that Pausanias records many examples of men who had been able to win in several different types of event (cf. Paus. 6. 3. 7, 6. 13. 3, 6. 15. 8–9).

Roman At Rome colourful *circus spectacles (especially chariot-racing) and *ball games were the most popular sporting activities. But Augustus promoted traditional athletics, staging athletics competitions in the Campus Martius and exhibition-running in the Circus (Suet. *Aug.* 43. 1–2); he himself was keen on watching boxing (45. 2). Ultra-distance running was also practised: 'Some men can do 160 [Roman] miles in the Circus' (Plin. *HN.* 7. 84). Interest in athletics was maintained by the establishing of Greek-style games at Rome and elsewhere. In (?)4 BC *Tiberius won the chariot-race at the Olympian Games; from then on, Romans (mostly either eastern provincials with Roman citizenship, or those with sufficient authority to bend the rules, as Nero did in AD 67) won at Olympia with increasing regularity. See AGONES.

> ANCIENT SOURCES Epinician odes of Pindar and Bacchylides; Pausanias bks. 5 and 6; Philostratus *Peri gymnastikes.* W. E. Sweet, *Sport and Recreation in Ancient Greece: A Sourcebook with Translations* (1987); S. G. Miller (ed.), *Arete: Greek Sports from Ancient Sources*, 2nd edn. (1991).
>
> MODERN LITERATURE E. N. Gardiner, *Greek Athletic Sports and Festivals* (1910); M. I. Finley and H. W. Pleket, *The Olympic Games* (1976); T. F. Scanlon, *Greek and Roman Athletics: A Bibliography* (1984); *Nikephoros: Zeitschrift für Sport und Kultur im Altertum* (1988–); O. Tzachou-Alexandri (ed.), *Mind and Body: Athletic Contests in Ancient Greece* (1989); J. P. V. D. Balsdon, *Life and Leisure in Ancient Rome* (1969), 159–68, 314–26; Museo della Civiltà Romana, *Lo sport nel mondo antico* (1987). S. J. I.

Athos, a headland on the easternmost of the Chalcidian promontories (see CHALCIDICE), with a conspicuous pyramid-shaped peak rising sheer from the sea to 1,935 m. (6,350 feet). In 492 BC a Persian fleet was destroyed near it by a storm. To avoid the passage round Mt. Athos, *Xerxes dug a *canal through the neck of the promontory (483–481). This had a length of 2.4 km. (1½ mi.), a breadth of 20–30 m. (65–100 ft.), and a depth of 2–3 m. (6–10 ft.) (Hdt. 7. 22–24; Strabo 7. 331). Despite the doubts expressed by ancient and modern writers, the canal was completed; the cutting is visible in places. The mountain was sacred to Zeus (Aesch. *Ag.* 289) and cast its shadow on *Lemnos at sunset (Soph. fr. 709 Radt).

> S. Isserlin, *BSA* 1991, 83 ff. and 1994, 277 ff. (canal). M. C.; N. G. L. H.

Atia (1) (*RE* Attii 34), daughter of M. *Atius Balbus and of Iulia, *Caesar's sister, was the wife of C. *Octavius and the mother of C. Octavius (the future *Augustus) and of *Octavia (2). After her husband's death she married L. *Marcius Philippus (2) in 58 BC.

She died in 43 in her son's consulship and received a public funeral. The legend that she had given birth to Augustus by *Apollo had some circulation. A. M.; T. J. Ca.

Atia (2) (*RE* Attii 35), sister (presumably younger) of Atia (1). She married her sister's stepson, L. *Marcius Philippus (3), and had a daughter Marcia. T. J. C.

Atilius (*RE* 2–3), author of *fabulae palliatae*, perhaps earlier than *Caecilius Statius (one title and nineteen words survive); noted for his harsh style, but praised by *Varro for stirring the emotions. Probably identical with the Atilius who translated *Sophocles' *Electra* (badly, according to Cicero *Fin.* 1. 5; an extract was chanted at Caesar's funeral), perhaps not with L. Atilius of Praeneste, named in the Terentian *didascaliae* as a director of (probably revivals of) Terence's plays. See PALLIATA.

> Ribbeck, *CRF*; Schanz-Hosius, 1. 161–2; J. Wright, *Dancing in Chains* (1974). P. G. M. B.

Atilius (*RE* 36) **Caiatinus (or Calatinus), Aulus,** grandson of Q. *Fabius Maximus Rullianus, consul 258 and 254 BC, censor 247. He enjoyed mixed fortunes in Sicily in 258 but celebrated a triumph in 257, probably as praetor (Broughton, *MRR* s.a.). *Polybius (1) (1. 38. 6 ff.) credits the capture of Panormus in 254 to both consuls but only Cn. Cornelius Scipio Asina was awarded a triumph. Atilius was the first dictator to take an army outside Italy—to Sicily in 249. He dedicated temples to *Spes in the forum Holitorium and *Fides on the Capitol. Cicero (*Sen.* 61, etc.) preserves part of his epitaph.

> Walbank, *HCP* 1. 81 f., 98 f. A. D.

Atilius (*RE* 39) **Fortunatianus** (date uncertain, before 4th cent. AD?), grammarian and author of a metrical handbook (*ars) dedicated to a former pupil of senatorial family. The first part of the *ars* deals with general principles (Keil, *Gramm. Lat.* 6. 279–94), the second with Horatian metres (ibid. 294–304). The work depends largely on earlier authorities, especially *Caesius Bassius.

> Herzog–Schmidt, § 525. 2. R. A. K.

Atilius (*RE* 51) **Regulus, Marcus,** consul in 267 and 256 BC (suffect). In 267 both consuls triumphed for successes against the Sallentini and the capture of *Brundisium. In 256 he and L. *Manlius Vulso Longus defeated the Carthaginians in the naval battle of Ecnomus and took the war into Africa, seizing Aspis / Clupea. After Vulso's return to Rome Regulus defeated the Carthaginians at Adys and captured *Tunis, but offered unacceptable peace terms. In spring 255 he was defeated on ground chosen by *Xanthippus (2) and was captured. He died in captivity, probably of natural causes. The later legend (unknown to *Polybius (1) but already found in C. *Sempronius Tuditanus fr. 5 Peter, cf. Hor. *Carm.* 3. 5) of his return to Rome to negotiate an exchange of prisoners (or peace terms), his successful opposition to any concession, and consequent brutal death at Carthage may have been invented to palliate his widow's torturing of two Punic prisoners in revenge for his death (cf. Diod. Sic. 24. 12). See PUNIC WARS.

> Walbank, *HCP* 1. 82 ff.; M. Fantar, in H. Devijver and E. Lipiński (eds.), *Punic Wars* (1988), 75 ff.; F. Vallançon, *Archives de philosophie du droit* 1989, 305 ff. A. D.

Atilius (*RE* 60) **Serranus, Aulus,** curule aedile 194 BC, praetor 192 and 173, consul 170. Atilius and his colleague, L. Scribonius Libo, were said to be the first *aediles to hold scenic games (see LUDI) at the Megalesia. In 192–191 Atilius commanded the fleet against *Nabis and *Antiochus (3) III; his dedication of a gold crown to Delian Apollo during this time was one of the earliest made by a Roman. In 172 he was a member of Q. *Marcius Philippus' notorious embassy to Greece, and in 171 served there under the consul C. Licinius Crassus. His consular command was in Liguria.

Broughton, *MRR* (with Suppl. p. 27); T. Homolle, *BCH* 1884, 75 ff.
P. S. D.

atimia, in a Greek state, the loss of some or all rights. It originally amounted to outlawry, total loss of rights *vis-à-vis* the individual or community the man made *atimos* had wronged; later it came usually if not always to denote loss of civic rights (including the right to go to law to protect one's personal rights). In Athens *atimia* could be temporary (men in debt to the state lost their rights until the debt was discharged), and it could be limited to specific disabilities (soldiers who stayed in Athens under the *Four Hundred lost the rights to serve in the council and to speak in the assembly, see EKKLĒSIA).

A. R. W. Harrison, *The Law of Athens* 2 (1971), 169–76.
A. W. G.; P. J. R.

Atina (mod. Atene Lucana), in Italy, *Lucanian city in the Valle di Diano. *Oscan and Greek inscriptions indicate a Hellenized (see HELLENISM) Oscan settlement from the 5th cent. BC, but it was not prominent before the Roman period. It may have had either praefectural or municipal status (see MUNICIPIUM; PRAEFECTURA). Inscriptions indicate a flourishing settlement and strong connections with nearby *Grumentum and *Volcei. K. L.

Atius (*RE* 11) **Balbus, Marcus,** of a good senatorial family of *Aricia and related to *Pompey, was the husband of *Caesar's sister Iulia and the father of *Atia (1), *Augustus' mother. Praetor before 59 BC, he was a commissioner under the *lex (2) Iulia agraria*. E. B.

Atlantis, i.e. '(the island of) *Atlas', 'the island lying in the Atlantic'; the oldest surviving wonderland in Greek philosophy. *Plato (1) is the earliest and chief source for the story, said to have been told to *Solon by Egyptian priests, of a huge and wealthy island of this name outside the Pillars of Heracles which once ruled 'Libya . . . as far as Egypt' and 'Europe as far as Tyrrhenia [= Etruria]' until, in an expedition to conquer the rest, its rulers were defeated by the Athenians, the island shortly after sinking overnight beneath the Atlantic after 'violent earthquakes and floods' (*Ti.* 24e ff.); the unfinished *Critias* describes the island's constitution (similar to the ideal *polis of Plato's *Republic*) and layout of its chief city (a series of concentric circles of alternating land and water). *Crantor is said to have accepted the truth of the tale, an indicator of ancient controversy about Atlantis as early as *c.*300 BC (Procl. *In Ti.* 76; cf. Strabo 2. 3. 6). Modern speculation continues that the massive eruption of the volcano on Santorini (see THERA) in the late bronze age, resulting in the loss of most of the island's land mass, provided the basis for the legend. Major discrepancies in the Platonic tale (size, date, and position) offer serious obstacles to this view, however.

J. Luce, *The End of Atlantis* (1969); E. Ramage (ed.), *Atlantis: Fact or fiction?* (1978); P. Forsyth, *Atlantis* (1980); P. Vidal-Naquet, *The Black Hunter* (1986), ch. 13. H. J. R.; A. J. S. S.

Atlas (Ἄτλας), probably 'very enduring' (τλᾶν), the *Titan son of *Iapetus and brother of *Prometheus. In the *Odyssey* he is the 'deadly minded' father of *Calypso, 'who knows the depths of the whole sea, and holds the tall pillars which hold earth and

heaven apart' (1. 52–4, cf. S. West's comm.; Aesch. *PV* 348–50). In *Hesiod he lives at the edge of the world beside the *Hesperides and holds up the heaven (*Theog.* 517–20). The 'rationalizing' identification of the Titan with the *Atlas mountains is first found in *Herodotus (4. 184. 3; cf. Verg. *Aen.* 4. 246–51 who strikingly combines the mythical and rationalizing versions); a story in which he was a shepherd turned to rock by *Perseus (1) with the Gorgon's head (Ov. *Met.* 4. 627–62) may go back to the 5th cent. BC (cf. *PMG* 837). Atlas was the father of various *constellations, notably the Pleiades, and is sometimes conceived as a wise man who founded the science of *astronomy; *Plato (1) makes him the eponymous first king of *Atlantis (*Criti.* 114a–d). From an early date Atlas was associated with Heraclean legends. Sent to fetch the golden apples of the Hesperides, *Heracles—on the advice of Prometheus—asked Atlas to get them while he held up the sky; Atlas refused to take back the sky but Heracles tricked him into doing so (Pherec. *FGrH* 3 F 17, where the story is apparently set in the north). Nevertheless, Atlas is often omitted from accounts of Heracles and the Hesperides, and *Euripides (*HF* 403–7) seems to make the Hesperides and Atlas two separate Heraclean 'labours'.

Lesky, *Gesammelte Schriften* (1966), 363–8; Wernicke, *RE* 2. 2118–33; Bond on Eur. *HF* 394–9. R. L. Hu.

Atlas in art Atlas is depicted in art from the mid-6th cent. BC, usually with Heracles in the Garden of the Hesperides, notably on the early Classical metope from *Olympia. In Hellenistic and Roman art he supports the globe with great effort. Pausanias notes him on the chest of *Cypselus (5. 18. 4), and the throne of *Amyclae (3. 18. 10); Philostratus (*Imag.* 2. 20) describes a painting of him. From the 5th-cent. temple of *Zeus at *Acragas begins the use of 'atlantes' as architectural supports, continuing into Roman times (Vitr. 6. 7. 6).

LIMC 3/1. 2–16. K. W. A.

Atlas mountains, the great range which formed the backbone of Roman Africa. Its highest peaks are in the Great Atlas to the west, in present-day Morocco (the loftiest is Djebel Toubkal, 4,167 m. (13,671 ft.) above sea level), and Greek legend converted them into the bowed shoulders of the god who held up the heavens (see ATLAS). The chain slopes eastwards through the Middle Atlas (maximum altitude 3,290 m. (10,794 ft.)) and the Little Atlas (up to 2,531 m. (8,304 ft.)) to the Aurès. Strabo (17. 3. 2) makes it clear that the term Atlas referred to the whole chain of mountains and hills down to the Lesser *Syrtis. On the north the Atlas buttresses the Tell or fertile coastal plain. Southwards the mountains slope down to the Saharan desert. Between Tell and Sahara are the High Plateaux with much good grazing land; in the centre and the east lie the shottes or salt lakes. The Atlas range was an important source of timber ('the blessed woods, the gift of Atlas': Mart. 14. 89); especially prized was the *citrus*-wood used for making *furniture (*Ptolemy (2) of Mauretania had a table four and a half feet wide (1.37 m.): Plin. *HN* 13. 94). *Suetonius Paulinus was the first Roman general to cross the summit of the Atlas range, in AD 42 (Plin. *HN* 5. 14–15; Cass. Dio 60. 4).

A. N. Sherwin White, *JRS* 1944, 1–10. Timber: R. Meiggs, *Trees and Timber in the Ancient Mediterranean World* (1982), 286–91.
W. N. W.; R. J. A. W.

atomism Ancient philosophers developed a rich variety of atomistic theories. The best way to approach this tradition is by recognizing that ἄτομον means 'indivisible', and then considering what 'indivisibility' might mean and why some thinker might advocate it.

Thus, *Leucippus (3) and *Democritus were particularly concerned to counter Eleatic arguments denying the possibility of plurality and change (Arist. *Gen. corr.* A 8). *Zeno (1) had argued that since what is, is all alike (a thesis the atomists accept), it contains no differentiations permitting a merely finite division. But the alternative, divisibility anywhere, was supposedly equivalent to divisibility everywhere, and this was taken to yield the absurdity that being divides into nothing. Thus what is, is indivisible. The atomists responded by insisting, paradoxically, that what is not, is: divisibility everywhere is still absurd, but what is, is divided up to a point, with portions of nothing or void differentiating the structure of reality and separating off individual atoms which are internally indivisible because solid or homogeneous. 'What is not is' sounds like a blatant contradiction; how might the atomists have defended it? Perhaps void was not empty space itself, but rather 'the empty', a negative occupant of space. Qua nothing, void is not; but qua occupier of a place—wherever there are no atoms—it is. The existence of not-being also accounts for change, albeit in a limited sense. The Eleatic (see ELEATIC SCHOOL) *Melissus had identified not-being with void and contended that it is a necessary but unfulfillable condition for the occurrence of change: the atomists' place-occupying nothing fulfils it.

A third Eleatic argument, again from Melissus, may well have radically constrained the atomists' conceptions of these elements and their possible relations. Elaborating his denial that change occurs, Melissus argued that 'the arrangement which was earlier does not perish, nor does an arrangement which is not come into being' (DK 30 fr. 7). As a result, no group subject to rearrangement of its constituent members can exist, because such rearrangement would involve impossible change. Thus, the familiar objects of the apparent macroscopic world cannot truly exist, since such objects suffer rearrangement. Contrary to traditional interpretations, however, it is arguable that the atomists could not have identified macroscopic objects with microscopic collections of atoms and void. Such groupings would be equally vulnerable to Melissus' attack, for *ex hypothesi* arrangements of atoms and void can alter no more than collections of anything else. The microscopic world comprises individual atoms, not groups of them; change permitted by the introduction of void is only relative change in position, not in any intrinsic feature of the atoms. Numerous reports in fact have Leucippus and Democritus asserting that atoms and the void alone are real, and that no authentic unity can emerge from plurality. The striking pessimism about what can be known which marks the first phase of Greek atomism, usually described as a sceptical evaluation of the reliability of the senses, is the proper reaction to a stark world where every appearance of real change or aggregation is a delusion.

Democritus may have had a mathematical argument for atomism too (Plut. *Mor.* 1079e). When a cone is cut parallel to the base, if the surfaces produced are equal, the 'cone' will be a cylinder; if unequal, a ziggurat. Possibly Democritus, choosing the second horn of the dilemma, maintained that these mathematical steps would be atomic magnitudes. Less conjectural evidence of finitist mathematics is to be found in the Platonic tradition. The report that *Plato (1) identified indivisible lines as the source of the line (Arist. *Metaph.* 992ᵃ 19–22) does not determine whether they are physical or ideal. But later Platonists, perhaps *Xenocrates (1), deployed arguments whose ontological

commitments are precise, e.g. that the Forms of Line, Surface, and Body are indivisible, as otherwise their parts would be prior to them ([Arist.] *Lin. ins.* 968ᵃ9–13).

The brilliant dialectician *Diodorus (2) Cronus transformed philosophical conceptions of indivisibility and profoundly influenced the future course of atomic theory. Perhaps under the influence of Aristotle (*Ph.* 6. 1–4, 10), Diodorus argued that although it is never true that anything is moving, things have moved (Sext. Emp. *Math.* 10. 119–20). If something moves, it is moving now, at the present instant, and thus in the present time. Since any division in the present would divide it without remainder into past and future, it must be partless and so atomic. Movement must thus take a certain whole number of time-atoms. Now a thing can occupy only a single place in a partless time; so, a finite number of places equinumerous with the time-atoms will have been traversed, provided no intervals between the starting- and stopping-points were skipped. Hence, movement in partless time entails traversal of partless places. Finally, these spatial atoms require atoms of matter: were some matter smaller than its atomic space, that space would be part empty, and so not partless. A material atom gets into different places when it occupies successive spatial atoms for the duration of successive temporal atoms. Partless matter fills partless space throughout partless segments of time; accordingly, it never moves, but nevertheless has moved. Significantly, Diodorus insisted on 'very small and partless body' rather than 'atom' as the technical designation for bits of matter (frs. 116–17 Giannantoni), and his material 'atoms' are a consequence of very different arguments from those which provoked Leucippus and Democritus. True, his partless bodies are indivisible, because division would be into the parts they lack; but partlessness rather than indivisibility is their defining characteristic.

It was on grounds of explanatory economy that *Epicurus contended that the totality of things is body and void; everything else which might seem to be in its own right, such as qualities, events, and time, cannot exist apart from body, but is one or another attribute of it (Lucr. 1. 449–82). Void, again the precondition for motion, is the exception, being identified as place, which when empty exists independently of body. Thus if it is correct to attribute the conception of void as a place-occupying nothing to the earlier atomists, Epicurus may rank as the first Greek thinker explicitly to articulate the idea of space as extension pure and simple.

Only at this juncture does Epicurus introduce atomism. The ultimate constituents of compound bodies must be atomic and unalterable, since otherwise everything would be pulverized into nothing (*Ep. Hdt.* 40–1). The indivisible atoms themselves consist of minimal parts reminiscent of and perhaps prompted by Diodorus' 'small and partless bodies' (*Ep. Hdt.* 57). Two major considerations lead to the postulation of minimal parts. First, in a Zenonian spirit, an infinite division of a finite body would yield an infinity of particles each possessing magnitude and together constituting a body of infinite size—thus contradicting the premise that it is finite. The limit of division is parts themselves indivisible, because partless. Second, a conceptual argument: were the mind to scan an infinite collection of parts, it would reach infinity, which is impossible. In obedience to the linkage between varieties of atomism pioneered by Aristotle and Diodorus, Epicurus also advocated temporal atoms (Sext. Emp. *Math.* 10. 142–54).

As *Lucretius amply demonstrates, atomic features and events are intended to explain causally a great many macroscopic phenomena. Much modern scholarship thus supposes that Epicureanism was a reductive theory which identifies without remainder familiar objects and occurrences with what happens on the atomic level. Yet Epicureans believe that free volition, an attribute of the macroscopic mind, directly influences atomic matter (Lucr. 2. 251–83). Although Epicurus is a thoroughgoing materialist—there is nothing but body and void—he does not believe there is nothing but atoms and void, and we have strong evidence that the bodies which are our minds exert a causal influence downwards which is not subject to the laws of atomistic motion, but rather interrupts them.

Even this partial and skeletal survey suffices to prove that the rubric 'Greek atomism' covers a bewilderingly rich range of alternative theories; ironically, the only stimulus not to be found is the first to occur to a modern reader, the evidence of empirical experiment. Leucippus and Democritus inaugurated atomism in reaction to Eleatic arguments against plurality and change; 'atomicity', that is, 'indivisibility', is truly the focal point of their system. In sharp contrast, Diodorus argued for temporal, spatial, and material partlessness; his scheme does indeed yield indivisibility, but only as a by-product of his argument against ongoing movement. Again, Epicurus' case for both atomicity and partlessness is sensitive to yet other considerations, and his philosophy as a whole is better regarded as 'materialistic' rather than 'atomistic', to avoid the danger of mistaking his theory for a reductive one. The debate over finitist mathematics is sensitive to a further, distinct set of arguments.

This diversity has been often obscured by a tendency to assimilate all these thinkers to a standard list of atomistic commitments, which usually includes a desire to provide comprehensive reductive explanations, especially in psychology. If Leucippus and Democritus denied reality to all arrangements, they were not in the position to explain them, reductively or not. Diodorus did not engage in any project of scientific explanation taking him beyond his argument for partlessness. Epicurus did entertain explanatory ambitions, but they were antireductionist. Many of the most celebrated doctrines associated with these philosophers are not atomistic *per se*. Democritus argued against the reliability of the senses by adducing their conflict, rejecting relativism, and thus denying that we have perceptual access to truth; while this epistemology neatly complements his atomism by leaving rational rather than empirical investigation of microscopic reality unassailed, there is no logical connection within his metaphysics. Likewise, no convincing case has been made for any link between Epicurus' atomism and his theological and ethical views. What is crucial for his brief against immortality and divine intervention in human affairs is that the soul is a temporary physical compound and that there is a naturalistic mechanism to account for 'supernatural' visions. That the soul is made of atoms and that *dreams are explained in atomistic terms are both incidental to his fundamental materialism. Since divisibility arguments and the possibility that materialism carries reductive implications continue to provoke deep philosophical disputes, the legacy of ancient atomism retains perennial interest.

S. Makin, *Archiv für Geschichte der Philosophie*, 1989; D. Sedley, *Phronesis*, 1982; R. Wardy, *Archiv für Geschichte der Philosophie*, 1988; R. Sorabji, *Time, Creation and the Continuum* (1983); N. Denyer, *Prudentia*, 1981; D. Sedley in J. Barnes and M. Mignucci (eds.), *Matter and Metaphysics* (1988).   R. B. B. W.

Atrebates (1), a people of Gallia Belgica (see BELGAE), conquered by *Caesar in 57 BC. However, in 53 they contributed 4,000 men to the Gallic forces at *Alesia, under *Commius, and revolted

again in 51. Under the empire their centre was transferred from the hill-fort at Etrun to Nemetacum (Arras), on an important road junction. Though they will have been disturbed by the Germanic invasions of the late 3rd cent. (Arras was reduced in size), their high-quality woollens still figured in *Diocletian's Price Edict of 301.

E. M. Wightman, *Gallia Belgica* (1985).   J. F. Dr.

Atrebates (2), an offshoot of a Gaulish tribe which had probably entered Britain before 54 BC and occupied a region between the Thames, the Test, and West Sussex. Successive rulers recorded by coins were *Commius, *Tincommius, Eppillus, and Verica; the last three appear to have had treaties with Rome. After AD 43 part at least of the area was ruled by Ti. *Claudius Cogidubnus, but eventually three *civitates were created: (a) of the Atrebates with its capital at *Calleva Atrebatum (Silchester), (b) of the *Belgae with its capital at Venta (Winchester), (c) of the *Reg(i)ni with its capital at Noviomagus (Chichester). An imperial tileworks of the reign of Nero existed at Pamber. Silchester was the site of a pre-Roman *oppidum* founded in the Augustan period and Chichester also lay within iron age earthworks. Evidence for immediately pre-Roman occupation at Winchester is less certain.

S. S. Frere, *Britannia*, 3rd edn. (1987).   S. S. F.; M. J. M.

Atreus, in mythology, son of *Pelops and *Hippodamia and brother of Thyestes. In *Homer there is harmony between the brothers (*Il.* 2. 100–8), but from late epic on (*Alcmaeonis* in schol. Eur. *Or.* 995) they had shared an implacable feud. Atreus married *Aerope, but she committed adultery with Thyestes and secretly gave him the golden lamb which carried with it claim to the kingship. *Zeus, however, expressed disapproval by reversing the course of the sun (Eur. *El.* 699–746; Apollod. *Epit.* 2. 10–12). Atreus banished Thyestes; but later, when he learnt of Aerope's adultery, he pretended a reconciliation with his brother and at a feast served up to him the flesh of the latter's own sons. At the end of the meal Atreus showed his brother the heads and hands of his sons, then once more banished him (Aesch. *Ag.* 1590 ff.; Apollod. *Epit.* 2. 10–12; Seneca, *Thyestes*, passim). By Aerope Atreus was father of *Agamemnon and *Menelaus (1); or, by another genealogy, their grandfather, who brought them up when his son and their father, Pleisthenes, died young. Atreus was finally killed by *Aegisthus, Thyestes' only surviving son.

J. R. M.

Atria (mod. Adria), a coastal city in the north of the Po delta (see PADUS), now nearly 20 km. (12½ mi.) from the sea. From the late 6th cent. BC onwards it was an important entrepôt for Greek and *Etruscan trade with the Po valley and Europe. Epigraphy suggests that the city was an originally Aeginetan foundation that came under Etruscan control in the 5th cent. (cf. Livy 5. 33. 8). Varro (*Ling.* 5. 161) derives *atrium* from Atria.

BTCGI 3 (1984), entry under 'Adria'; G. Colonna, *Rivista storica dell'antichità* 1974, 1 ff.   D. W. R. R.

Atrium Vestae, the whole ancient precinct next to the *Regia, east of the *forum Romanum, including the temple and sacred grove of *Vesta and the house of the Vestal virgins, although the term is now commonly used for the latter alone. Remains of its republican predecessor underlie the existing structure, built on a different orientation during *Nero's reorganization of the *via Sacra. Trajan added the eastern suite and probably a second storey, installing hypocausts in some rooms. There were further modifications under *Hadrian, while the enlargement of the central peristyle court is Severan. Later additions were minor.

Steinby, *Lexicon* 138 ff.; Nash, *Pict. Dict. Rome* 1. 154 ff.   J. D.

Attaleia (mod. Antalya), a city of *Pamphylia founded by *Attalus II and perhaps intended as a focus of Attalid political influence in southern Asia Minor. Its coins show that it claimed kinship with Athens. In 79 BC it was mulcted of territory by *Servilius Vatia Isauricus for its complicity with the pirate leader Zenicetes (see PIRACY). These lands were probably used by Augustus for settling *veterans of Italian origin, who dominated local politics in the early empire. The ruins include an impressive tomb of Italian style built above the harbour for a man of consular status in the early empire, and a triple-arched gate built through the still-surviving city walls to honour *Hadrian's visit in AD 129. Attaleia became a colony in the 3rd cent.

K. Lanckoroński, *Städte Pamphyliens* 1 (1890), 7 ff.; S. Jameson, *RE* Suppl. 12. 109–29; R. Stupperich, *MDAI (I)* 1991 (tomb).   S. M.

Attalus I (269–197 BC), ruler of *Pergamum (241–197), the first Pergamene to use the royal title. Cousin and adopted son of *Eumenes (1) I, Attalus expanded and consolidated his kingdom through active self-defence policies, successfully fighting against some of the *Galatians before c.230 (to whom he had first refused customary payments) and against *Antiochus (8) Hierax before 227, a success which temporarily brought all Seleucid Asia Minor north of the Taurus into his sphere of influence. Most of this he lost again to *Seleucus (3) III and *Achaeus (3) from 223–212, though an agreement with *Antiochus (3) III against Achaeus (216) seems to have recognized Attalus' rights to Mysia and Aeolis, where Pergamene rule was re-established or consolidated. Friendly contacts with cities in Ionia and Hellespontine Phrygia were established, though hostility to the Bithynian kingdom was permanent. In Pergamum itself victories were celebrated by Attalus' taking the title '*Soter' ('Saviour') and with monuments of spectacular expense and artistic quality (e.g. the 'Dying Gaul'); demonstrative investment at *Delphi (a prominent stoa might be connected with these victories) brought friendship with *Aetolia, where he financed at least one fort before 219. At Athens he dedicated on the Acropolis a series of statues setting his Galatian victory into the Greek context of victory against Giants, Amazons, and Persians (though this dedication might be later). These Greek connections involved him with Aetolia and Rome in the First Macedonian War. He provided ships, gained *Aegina (209), became honorary *stratēgos* (chief magistrate) of the Aetolian Confederacy and was included among Roman friends in the Peace of Phoenice (205). He instrumentalized his Roman connection when *Philip (3) V developed his Aegean policy after 204, largely at the expense of Pergamum and Rhodes. Attalus' appeal (with Rhodes) helped bring Rome back to Greece for the Second Macedonian War (200–197), in which Attalus personally and his fleet actively participated. His diplomacy brought Athens (where a tribe was named Attalis after him), the Achaeans, and Sparta into alliance with Rome. He died suddenly at *Thebes (1) while courting *Boeotia (spring 197). He left four sons, *Eumenes (2) II, *Attalus II, *Philetaerus (2), and Athenaeus.

E. Hansen, *The Attalids of Pergamon*, 2nd edn. (1971); R. E. Allen, *The Attalid Kingdom* (1983).   R. M. E.

Attalus II (220–138 BC), king of *Pergamum (158–138), second son of *Attalus I, called 'Philadelphus' ('Brother-loving'). Attalus served under his brother *Eumenes (2) II as loyal general against *Antiochus (3) III, the *Galatians, *Prusias (1) I, and Pharnaces

I, and as diplomat, especially in Rome, where after 167 some senators favoured him against Eumenes. As king—he bore the title already in Eumenes' lifetime—he married Eumenes' widow Stratonice and adopted her son Attalus. He recognized Roman paramountcy and acted accordingly: he restored *Ariarathes V to Cappadocia, supported *Alexander (10) Balas against *Demetrius (10) I in Syria (153–150), *Nicomedes II of Bithynia against *Prusias (2) II (149), whom with Roman help he had recently defeated, and sent troops against *Andriscus (148) and to *Corinth (146). He founded *Philadelphia (2) in Lydia and *Attaleia (Antalya) in Pamphylia, continued Eumenes' building programme at Pergamum and the tradition of magnificent gifts to Greek cities and shrines (e.g. the 'Stoa of Attalus' at Athens).

E. Hansen, *The Attalids of Pergamon*, 2nd edn. (1971); J. Hopp, *Untersuchungen zur Geschichte der letzten Attaliden* (1977).   R. M. E.

Attalus III (c.170–133 BC), son of *Eumenes (2) II, last king of Pergamum (138–133), who bequeathed his kingdom to Rome. Called 'Philometor' ('Mother-lover') because of his close relationship to Stratonice, he was allegedly unpopular and had a reputation for being brutal and uninterested in public affairs, though given early experience by *Attalus II, devoting himself rather to scientific study, especially botany and pharmacology. His will, modelled on that of *Ptolemy (1) VIII, may have been a dramatic attempt by the childless king to curb opposition, which however broke out with violence under *Aristonicus (1) after Attalus' premature natural death in 133.

J. Hopp, *Untersuchungen zur Geschichte der letzten Attaliden* (1977).   R. M. E.

Atthis was the title given in post-*Alexandrian scholarship to the genre of Greek *historiography that narrated the local history of *Attica. The title, derived from the name of the daughter of the mythical king Cranaus (Strab. 9. 1. 8), was probably invented by *Callimachus (3) for cataloguing purposes. The authors themselves used a variety of titles (*Protogonia, Attika, Attikē Syngraphē*) or none. The genre was probably created by *Hellanicus (1) in the late 5th cent., though *Pausanias (3) (10. 15. 5) credits *Cleidemus. It was most popular in the 4th cent. when *Atthides* were written by Cleidemus, *Androtion, *Phanodemus, and perhaps *Melanthius (3). *Demon and *Philochorus, the last and most respected atthidographer, wrote in the 3rd. Later *Ister compiled an epitome of these *Atthides*.

In structure the *Atthis* was a chronicle, based upon a hypothetical list of kings (for the mythical period) and, after 683/2 BC, on the eponymous archons. In the case of the latter the entries began with the archon's name, followed by his patronymic or demotic, and then the formula, 'in the time of this man such and such happened'. Within an entry, material was also organized chronologically, but the structure was not conducive to showing relationship between events or cause and effect. The subject-matter of an *Atthis* was typical of a local history, covering such diverse material as the origins of religious *festivals and cults, etymology of place-names, geography, ethnography, and the creation of financial and political institutions. In short, the *Atthis* was a blend of mythical fantasy and accurate historical detail, the latter especially as the account came closer to the historian's own day. The style was 'monotonous and hard for the reader to stomach' (Dion. Hal. *Ant. Rom.* 1. 8. 3). The tone was patriotic, though more chauvinistic in some than others.

Serious study of the *Atthis* was begun by Wilamowitz in his investigation of the sources of the *Athenian Constitution* attributed to Aristotle (*Aristoteles und Athen* (1893)). Felix Jacoby elevated the *Atthis* into an independent genre of historiography. Even so, his theory that the individual atthidographers wrote to vindicate their own political ideology was an effort to explain the biases in the *Athenian Constitution*. Recently emphasis has been on the scholarly nature of atthidography.

> Jacoby collected the fragments in *FGrH* 3b, with comm. in 3b Suppl. 1 and 2; see also his *Atthis* (1949) and P. E. Harding, *Androtion and the Atthis* (1994). P. E. H.

Attic From or relating to *Attica or *Athens; see also ASIANISM AND ATTICISM.

Attic cults and myths Most Greek states honoured most Greek gods; the differences between them are of emphasis and degree. As characteristic Athenian emphases one might mention: the extraordinary prominence of *Athena, unusual even for a city-protecting goddess; the international standing of the Mysteries of *Demeter and Kore (*Persephone) at *Eleusis; the rich development of *deme religion, and the related abundance of *hero-cults; the honours acquired in the second half of the 5th cent. by *Hephaestus, usually a minor figure; the comparatively modest role of *Hera.

According to one 5th-cent. observer (*Republica Atheniensium* 3. 2, see OLD OLIGARCH), Athens had more *festivals than any other Greek state; only a selection can be mentioned here. The great show-pieces, which attracted foreign visitors, were the *Panathenaea, the City *Dionysia (when tragedies and comedies were performed), and the Eleusinian *mysteries. Further major landmarks of the domestic year, each lasting several days, were the *Thesmophoria (Demeter and Kore), the most important women's festival; *Anthesteria, the new-wine festival; *Apaturia, the phratry festival. The other 'literary festivals' (*Lenaea, Rural Dionysia, Dionysia in Piraeus, *Thargelia) were also very popular. Other traditional festivals that were widely or universally celebrated (sometimes impinging on domestic life, through the custom of preparing special food) or that affected many families from time to time were the *Diasia (Zeus *Meilichios), Cronia (when slaves dined with masters), *Pyanopsia (Apollo), Scira (see SCIROPHORIA) (Demeter: another women's festival), *Hieros Gamos* (*Zeus and Hera) and several initiatory festivals of Artemis, chief among them the Brauronia (see BRAURON). 'Spectator festivals'—a newer type, on the whole—marked by competitions or an abundance of free meat, included Olympieia, Dipolieia, and Diisoteria (all for Zeus, the third in *Piraeus), Epitaphia (games for the war-dead, see EPITAPHIOS), Thesea, Asclepieia, Hephaestea, Bendidea; we should note here too an important procession in honour of the Semnai Theai (see ERINYES). Of several festivals of Demeter closely related to the agricultural year, the most widely diffused was Proerosia, 'pre-ploughing'. A number of other well-known festivals—the *Haloa (Demeter and others), *Arrephoria and *Plynteria (Athena), *Oschophoria (Dionysus and Athena), had restricted numbers of actual participants, symbolically important though they might be for the entire state.

The most important Attic myths concerned: the conflict of Athena and *Poseidon for possession of Attica; the birth from earth of the two first kings *Cecrops and *Erechtheus/*Erichthonius, which founded symbolically the Athenians' claim to be 'autochthonous'; the adventures of the daughters of these two kings, which acquired important aetiological associations; the arrival in Attica of *Dionysus and, especially, Demeter (the latter event being the origin of the Eleusinian mysteries); the mission of *Triptolemus, who distributed wheat worldwide; the self-sacrifice of *Codrus; and above all the varied career of *Theseus. A distinctive canon of four Athenian achievements was shaped in the special context of the Funeral Speech (see EPITAPHIOS) for the war-dead: the war of Erechtheus against *Eumolpus of Eleusis and his Thracian allies; the war of Theseus against the invading *Amazons; succour in the cause of right given by the Athenians to the *Heraclidae and to the mothers of the *Seven against Thebes. In contrast to these public and patriotic myths is the rich cycle attaching to the misfortunes of *Cephalus and *Procris.

> Deubner, *Attische Feste*, from which H. W. Parke, *Festivals of the Athenians* (1977) and E. Simon, *Festivals of Attica* (1983) derive; Burkert, *HN*; P. Brulé, *La Fille d'Athènes* (1987): women's festivals; R. Parker, in J. Bremmer (ed.), *Interpretations of Greek Mythology* (1987); Kearns, *Heroes of Attica* (1989). R. C. T. P.

Attic Orators By the time of *Hermogenes (2) (*On Ideas* 2. 11) writing in the 2nd cent. AD there was a list of ten Athenian orators (*Lysias, *Isaeus (1), *Hyperides, *Isocrates, *Dinarchus, *Aeschines (1), *Antiphon (1), *Lycurgus (3), *Andocides, *Demosthenes (2)) whose classic status was recognized; the same selection figures in the *Lives of the Ten Orators* falsely ascribed to *Plutarch. This follows a tendency typical of the Hellenistic period, to produce select lists for different genres (see CANON). The number ten apparently goes back at least to *Caecilius (1) of Caleacte (Augustan period), who (*Suda*, entry under Κεκίλιος) wrote a treatise *On the Style of the Ten Orators*. However, even if Caecilius' ten were the same as Hermogenes', the selection was slow to acquire canonical status. There is evidence for alternative lists. His contemporary *Dionysius (7) (*On Imitation* 5) lists six orators worthy of imitation (Lysias, Isocrates, Lycurgus, Demosthenes, Aeschines, Hyperides), while at *On the Ancient Orators* 4, Isaeus replaces Lycurgus. Quintilian (*Inst.* 10. 1. 76–80) lists Demosthenes, Aeschines, Hyperides, Lysias, and Isocrates, and elsewhere (*Inst.* 12. 10. 20 ff.) refers to ten orators (Lysias, Andocides, Coccus, Isocrates, Hyperides, Lycurgus, Isaeus, Antiphon, Aeschines, Demosthenes), though it is unclear whether he thinks of this list as exclusive. Dio Chrysostom 18. 11 lists Demosthenes, Lysias, Hyperides, Aeschines, Lycurgus.

> Blass, *Att. Ber.*; R. C. Jebb, *The Attic Orators from Antiphon to Isaeus*, 2nd edn. (1893); G. Kennedy, *The Art of Persuasion in Greece* (1963). C. C.

Attica, the territory of *Athens, consisting in a triangular promontory some 2,400 sq. km. (930 sq. mi.) in area divided from the rest of the Greek mainland by the mountain range of *Parnes. Attic topography is extremely varied, with fertile upland valleys, waterlogged lowland valley-bottoms, more or less barren mountain slopes and productive coastal and inland plains. Practically the whole peninsula falls below the 400 mm. (16 in.) isohyet, making agriculture a particularly precarious occupation. The rugged hills of southern Attica were a source of silver and lead, exploited from the bronze age (*Laurium), and the mountain ranges of *Hymettus and *Pentelicon were a source of fine quality *marble used from the 6th cent.

The earliest human settlement belongs to the neolithic, when a considerable number of mainly coastal sites were occupied, and occupation seems to have extended to the whole area in the early bronze age. Attica has large numbers of toponyms of 'pre-Greek' form. It is not clear, even in the late bronze age, how Attica was organized politically and there has been much modern discussion about what period, if any, is reflected in the myths according to which *Theseus 'synoecized' Attica (see SYNOECISM). In terms of material culture Attica seems marked by uniformity throughout.

Athens is the only place in Dark Age Attica where continuity of occupation can be clearly demonstrated, and some archaeologists see the Archaic and Classical settlement pattern in Attica as resulting from 'internal colonization' from Athens. By the end of the 8th cent. there are archaeological traces of human occupation at many sites which were later to be Classical demes.

Archaic Attica is remarkable for outstanding dedications and burials, marking an élite well rooted in the countryside; this is consistent with the traditions about the Solonian crisis (see SOLON) and about the locally based factional struggles which led to the tyranny of *Pisistratus. Local factions are notably absent from the Classical historical record, presumably as a result of *Cleisthenes (2)'s reforms, which institutionalized a voice for some 139 or 140 local communities (*demes) on his new council of five hundred (see BOULĒ). The continued vigorous life of these demes is testimony to the extent to which Athenians' lives continued to be rooted in the countryside.

Continued investment in the countryside is marked by 5th-cent. building at all the major rural *sanctuaries (*Eleusis, *Sunium, *Rhamnus, *Brauron, Cape Zoster). Extension of *agriculture into marginal areas, along with the apparent agricultural base of most élite wealth, suggests that even when Athens had the financial ability to become reliant on imported foodstuffs this did not lead to any exodus from the land. In the Hellenistic period evidence for rural occupation declines; by Roman times much of Attica is in the hands of relatively few landowners.

Some forts constructed along Attica's northern border in the 5th cent., and forts on the coast were added during the latter stages of the *Peloponnesian War, but only in the 4th cent. was a system of forts constructed, and garrison duty became part of military training. Fighting in and over Attica in the 3rd cent. is marked by a series of rubble fortifications associated with the Chremonidean War (see CHREMONIDES).

MAPS E. Curtius and J. A. Kaupert (eds.) *Karten von Attika* (1881–1903)

GEOGRAPHY P–K, *GL* 1.

ARCHAEOLOGICAL DESCRIPTION A. Milchhoeffer, *Karten von Attika: Erläuternder Text* (1883–1900); J. Travlos, *Bildlexikon zur Topographie des antiken Attika* (1988)

SETTLEMENT R. G. Osborne, *Demos* (1985); G. Fowden *JHS* 1988, 48–59

BUILDING HISTORY J. Boersma, *Athenian Building Policy* (1970)

DEFENCE J. Ober, *Fortress Attica* (1985).   R. G. O.

Atticus See POMPONIUS ATTICUS, T.

Atticus (*c.* AD 150–200), Platonist (see PLATO (1)), opposed the infiltration of *Peripatetic elements into Platonism, but himself introduced into it certain doctrines proper to *Stoicism. Like *Plutarch, he insisted on a literal interpretation of Plato's *Timaeus*, as regards the temporal beginning of the cosmos.

TEXT E. des Places (Budé, 1977), with trans. and notes.

PHILOSOPHY J. M. Dillon, *The Middle Platonists* (1977), ch. 5; P. Moraux, *Aristotelismus*, 2. 564–82.   J. M. D.

Attila, king of the *Huns (AD 435/440–53), at first ruled jointly with his brother Bleda whom he murdered in 445. Member of a dynasty which had united previously separate Hunnic groups around itself, together with many subject peoples (the majority Germanic) to create a substantial empire in central Europe. His major military campaigns were those of 442–3 and 447 against

the Balkan provinces of the eastern empire; that of 451, when he invaded Gaul but was defeated at the Catalaunian plains by Roman and allied (especially Visigothic) forces under Flavius *Aetius; and that of 452, when he invaded Italy and sacked several important cities. He intended to invade the east again in 453, but died during the night after his marriage to a girl called Ildico. His campaigns were pursued in support of a diplomatic policy whose main aim seems to have been the extraction of money.

E. A. Thompson, *A History of Attila and the Huns* (1948); O. J. Maenchen-Helfen, *The World of the Huns* (1973).   P. J. H.

Attis, in mythology, the youthful consort of *Cybele and prototype of her eunuch devotees. The myth exists in two main forms, with many variants. According to the Phrygian tale (Paus. 7. 17. 10–12; cf. Arn. *Adv. nat.* 5. 5–7), the gods castrated the androgynous *Agdistis; from the severed male parts an almond tree sprang and by its fruit Nana conceived Attis. Later Agdistis fell in love with him, and to prevent his marriage to another caused him to castrate himself. Agdistis is clearly a doublet of Cybele, though Arnobius brings them both into his account. Ovid (*Fast.* 4. 221–44) and others change many details, but keep the essential aetiological feature, the self-castration. In a probably Lydian version Attis, like *Adonis, is killed by a boar. The story of Atys, son of *Croesus, who was killed by the Phrygian Adrastus in a boar-hunt (Hdt. 1. 34–35) is an adaptation of this, and attests its antiquity, though the Phrygian is probably the older version.

In Asia Minor Attis bears his native name only in the Neo-Phrygian inscriptions, though the high priest and, under the empire, all members of the priestly college at *Pessinus had the title Attis. Attis is sometimes called Papas or Zeus Papas.

Whatever his original character, vegetation-god or mortal lover of Cybele, in the early cult he remains a subsidiary figure, whose death is mourned but who is not, apparently, worshipped. Attis rarely appears in Greece, but was present at Rome from the time of Cybele's introduction, even if the evidence for him only becomes plentiful from *c.* AD 150.

Under the later empire he was invested with celestial attributes, and became a solar deity, supreme, all-powerful, and sometimes it seems a surety of immortality to his initiates. In art he is generally represented as an effeminate youth, with the distinctive Phrygian cap and trousers. See ANATOLIAN DEITIES; EUNUCHS (RELIGIOUS).

H. Hepding, *Attis* (1903); Nilsson, *GGR* 2. 640 ff.; H. Graillot, *Le Culte de Cybèle* (1912); M. J. Vermaseren, *Cybele and Attis* (1977); G. Sfameni Gasparro, *Soteriology and Mystic Aspects in the Cult of Cybele and Attis* (1985); F. Coarelli, in U. Bianchi (ed.), *Soteriologia dei culti orientali* (1982), 40 ff.; P. Borgeaud, in C. Calame (ed.), *Métamorphoses du mythe* (1988), 87 ff.; *LIMC* 3/1 (1986), 'Attis'.   F. R. W.; J. Sch.

Attius Labeo, a translator of both *Iliad* and *Odyssey* (see HOMER) into Latin, attacked for his lack of learning by his contemporary *Persius Flaccus (*Sat.* 1. 4, 49 with *scholia).   S. J. Ha.

Attius (*RE* 32) **Varus, Publius,** of undistinguished family, praetor and then governor of Africa before 51 BC, took the side of *Pompey in the Civil War. In 49, after failing to hold *Caesar in *Picenum, he established himself in his old province of Africa (see LIGARIUS). Assaulted by C. *Scribonius Curio (2) at Utica he was relieved by *Juba (1). After *Pharsalus he had to yield the supreme command to Q. *Caecilius Metellus Pius Scipio, and served under him in the Thapsus campaign, from which he escaped to Spain. He fell at Munda.   T. J. C.; E. B.

Audax (*RE* 2), compiler of a derivative school-grammar in question-and-answer format (*De Scauri et Palladii libris excerpta*: Keil, *Gramm. Lat.* 7. 320–62). He perhaps was a correspondent of Augustine (*Ep.* 260. 61).

Herzog–Schmidt, § 522. 2. R. A. K.

Aufidius (*RE* 6), **Gnaeus,** praetor in 107 BC, wrote a 'Graeca historia' (i.e. history in Greek), probably of Rome (Cic. *Tusc.* 5. 112).

FGrH 814; E. Rawson, *Intellectual Life in the Late Roman Republic* (1985), 92, 222 n. 39. S. H.

Aufidius (*RE* 15) **Bassus,** 1st-cent. AD Roman historian, admired for his eloquence (Tac. *Dial.* 23; Quint. *Inst.* 10. 1. 103). His health was uncertain, which perhaps prevented a public career; his death was approaching *c.* AD 60 (Seneca, *Ep.* 30, praising his Epicurean fortitude). He wrote (1) a 'German War', (*Bellum Germanicum*), probably treating the campaigns of AD 10–16 as a unity; and (2) a general History, which began early enough to treat *Cicero's death (Sen. *Suas.* 6. 18, 23). It was continued by the elder *Pliny (1) under the title 'From the Conclusion of Aufidius Bassus' (*A fine Aufidii Bassi*), which seems to indicate an inconspicuous closing date; this was not earlier, and perhaps not much later, than AD 31. *Tacitus may well have used him.

Fragments in Peter, *HR Rel.* 2. cxxv–vii, 96–8. Syme, *Tacitus* 274–5, 288, 697–700; D. Timpe, *Der Triumph des Germanicus* (1968), 8–23; E. Noè, *Storiografia Imperiale Pretacitiana* (1984), see index. C. B. R. P.

Aufidius (*RE* 30) **Modestus** (late 1st cent. AD), an authority on Virgil and Horace (if the Horatian scholar is not *Iulius Modestus).

PIR² A 1390; Herzog–Schmidt, § 392. R. A. K.

Aufidius Victorinus, Gaius, a senator from Umbria, son-in-law of the orator *Fronto and close friend of M. *Aurelius, is often mentioned in the former's *Letters*, and by Cassius Dio and the *Historia Augusta*. *Suffect consul in AD 155, he had a long career in imperial service, being sent to Upper Germany in 162 to deal with a threat from the Chatti and to Spain in 170 following a Moorish invasion. Prefect of the city in the first years of Commodus' reign and consul for the second time (as *ordinarius*; see CONSUL) in 183, he died in the following year. His sons were both consul under Severus.

PIR² A 1393; G. Alföldy, *Fasti Hispanienses* (1969), 38 ff.; E. Champlin, *Fronto and Antonine Rome* (1980). A. R. Bi.

Aufidus (mod. Ofanto), the most important river of southern Italy. A powerful stream in winter and sluggish creek in summer, it rises near the Tyrrhenian Sea but flows into the Adriatic, through the territories of Hirpini (see SAMNIUM) and Apuli (see APULIA), past *Canusium and *Cannae. *Horace, a native of nearby Venusia, often mentions it. E. T. S.; D. W. R. R.

Auge See TELEPHUS (1).

augures, official Roman diviners. They formed one of the four great colleges of priests (see COLLEGIUM), instituted (so the tradition) in the regal period; originally made up of three (patrician) members, the complement was increased to nine in 300 BC when the plebeians were admitted (five plebeians, four patricians), to fifteen by *Sulla, and sixteen by *Caesar. New members were admitted (for life) through co-optation; from 103 BC through popular election by the assembly of seventeen tribes (see TRIBUS) from the candidates nominated by two college members. Etymology disputed: traditionally derived from 'directing the birds' (*avi* + *ger* (*o*)), but probably connected with the root *aug* (*eo*), denoting increase and prosperity (cf. *augustus*).

We have to distinguish between the functions of the individual augurs and those of the college. As a college they were a body of experts whose duty was to uphold the augural doctrine (variously described as *disciplina*, *ars*, *scientia*, or law: *ius augurium* or *augurale*) which governed the observation and application of the auspices (see AUSPICIUM) in Roman public life (Cic. *Nat. D.* 1. 122; *Leg.* 2. 20–1). They passed decrees (*decreta*) either on their own initiative (mostly concerning theoretical aspects of the doctrine) or more frequently responding to questions posed by the senate or the magistrates (*responsa*). These 'replies' often dealt with cases of ritual fault (*vitium*) which would nullify the auspices or with the removal of *religio*, a ritual obstacle to an action. The senate was free either to accept or to reject the advice. Individual augurs were both experts (*periti*) and priests (*sacerdotes*). They could give *responsa* (to be distinguished from those of the college); in their capacity as priests they celebrated various rites known as *auguria*, and also (when asked) performed inaugurations of priests and temples (*templa*). They could assist the magistrates in taking the auspices (although this happened much less frequently than is generally assumed) and, in particular, an augur had the right of making a binding announcement (*nuntiatio*) of adverse unsolicited (oblative) omens, especially at the popular assemblies (Cic. *Leg.* 2. 31; *Phil.* 2. 79–84).

J. Linderski, *ANRW* 2. 16. 3 (1986), 2146 ff. J. L.

Augurinus, Sentius See SENTIUS AUGURINUS.

augurium canarium, a ceremony so called by Pliny (*HN* 18. 14, quoting the *commentarii pontificum* (pontifical records), see LIBRI PONTIFICALES), and *canarium sacrificium* by *Ateius Capito (2), who says that reddish (*rutilae*) bitches were sacrificed for crops (*pro frugibus*) to 'deprecate' the fierceness of the dog-star (Festus, *Gloss. Lat.* 386). This dog sacrifice (*sacrum canarium*, formed from *canis*, 'dog') was performed by public priests (*publici sacerdotes*, *Schol. Dan. G.* 4. 424); it took place near the porta Catularia, apparently late in the summer, when the crops were yellowing (*flavescentes*, Festus (Paulus 147)). On the other hand the day or days (*dies*) for the sacrifice were to be fixed (Pliny) 'priusquam frumenta vaginis exeant' ('before the corn comes out of the sheath'), hence in the spring. As it was both augury and sacrifice, the *augures probably fixed the day for the ceremony (or in their parlance, inaugurated it), and the pontiffs performed the sacrifice itself. The ceremony appears to have belonged to the category of apotropaic rites to prevent calamities (*uti avertantur mala*, Serv. *Dan. Aen.* 3. 265).

L. Delatte, *Ant. Class.* 1937, 93 ff; P. Catalano, *Contributi allo studio del diritto augurale* (1960); J. Linderski, *ANRW* 2. 16. 3 (1986), 2222. J. L.

augurium salutis, an augural inquiry as to whether it was permissible (for the magistrates) to pray for the safety of the people. This (annual) prayer could be said only on a day free of all wars. It was attempted in 63 BC, and revived by Augustus (Cass. Dio 37. 24–5, 51. 20. 5; Cic. *Div.* 1. 105; *ILS* 9337).

J. Linderski, *ANRW* 2. 16. 3 (1986), 2254 ff. J. L.

Augusta Praetoria (mod. Aosta) a colony founded with 3,000 *praetorians in Cisalpine Gaul (see GAUL (CISALPINE)) by Augustus (24 BC); it was here that A. *Terentius Varro Murena had encamped the previous year when subjugating the *Salassi (Strabo 4. 206; Cass. Dio 53. 25). Standing at the Italian end of the Great and Little St Bernard passes (see ALPS), Augusta became and still is the capital of this whole region. Notable remains include the Augustan walls of a rectangular *castrum*, and Augustus' arch.

V. Viale and M. Viale Ferrero, *Aosta romana e medievale* (1967); I. A. Richmond, *Roman Archaeology and Art* (1969), 240 f.   E. T. S.; T. W. P.

Augusta Raurica (mod. Augst, near Basle), a colony founded by L. *Munatius Plancus in 44 BC in the territory of the Raurici. Strengthened by Augustus, with *Augusta Praetoria and *Augusta Vindelicorum it helped protect the upper Rhine and Danube valleys, and the Alpine route from Italy. It flourished in the 2nd and 3rd cents. as is demonstrated by the impressive remains: forum, temples, theatre, amphitheatre, basilica, baths, *curia*, dwellings. In the 3rd cent. it proved vulnerable to *Alamannic attack. The city wall, begun then, remained uncompleted, and in the 4th cent. the settlement was moved a little north, to the fortified site of Castrum Rauracense (Kaiseraugst).

F. Stähelin, *Die Schweiz in römischer Zeit*, 3rd edn. (1948), 95 ff., 597 ff.; R. Laur-Belart, *Führer durch Augusta Raurica*, 4th edn. (1978); M. Martin, *Römermuseum und Römerhaus Augst* (1981).   J. F. Dr.

Augusta Taurinorum (mod. Torino, Turin), an important Augustan colony (*c.*25 BC) in Cisalpine Gaul (see GAUL, (CISALPINE)), at the confluence of the Dora and Po (*Padus) rivers (which here became navigable: Pliny, *HN* 3. 123). Originally the capital of the Taurini, who were probably Celticized *Ligurians, it is apparently identical with the Taurasia captured by Hannibal, 218 BC (App. *Hann.* 5). Tacitus (*Hist.* 2. 66) records its burning in AD 69, but it is otherwise seldom mentioned. The modern city preserves the ancient street plan (in the form of a rectangular *castrum*); one gate, the porta Palatina (? of Augustan date) is notably well preserved.   E. T. S.; T. W. P.

Augusta Traiana or **Beroe** (mod. Stara Zagora, Bulgaria) was a Roman city of *Thrace founded by Trajan to replace the Thracian-Hellenistic Beroe in the north of the Thracian plain, controlling a huge territory extending from the Haemus range (Stara planina) in the north to the Rhodope mountains in the south. The 2nd-cent. walls enclose an area of 48.5 ha. (120 acres), within which several streets and public buildings have been excavated. In the late empire the city was again known as Beroe and is described by Ammianus (27. 4. 12) as one of the 'spacious cities' (*amplae civitates*) of Thrace. After being sacked by the *Huns, by the 6th cent. (according to Procop. *Aed.* 4. 11. 19) it was in need of repair and was fortified with a massive new double wall. It was again sacked, by the *Slavs or Avars, around 600.

R. F. Hoddinott, *Bulgaria in Antiquity* (1975), 199 f., 312 f.   J. J. W.

Augusta Treverorum (mod. Trier), *civitas*-capital of the *Treveri, developed from a settlement around a fort established under Augustus to guard a crossing of the Moselle. In the early empire Trier became the seat of the imperial procurator of Belgica and the Germanies (see BELGAE; GERMANIA), and eventually also that of the governor of Belgica. It soon (probably under Claudius) gained colonial status. Later, the advantages of its position brought it even more success. *Postumus chose it as his capital; the *tetrarchs based the Gallic prefecture there; and throughout the 4th cent. AD it accommodated various emperors and usurpers. Its bishop enjoyed great influence with the resident rulers. From 395, however, emperors ceased to visit the German frontier and the Gallic prefect was transferred to Arles (*Arelate). Early in the 5th cent. Trier was frequently sacked by the *Franks, and went into decline.

Roman Trier covered well over 280 ha. (690 acres). Impressive ruins from all periods have survived—e.g. a bridge, an amphitheatre, bath-buildings, the 'porta Nigra' gateway, the cathedral, and an imperial audience hall ('basilica'). Its environs are also unusually rich in remains—e.g. a temple quarter, pagan and Christian burials and monuments, villas, late-imperial palaces, and a hunting-park. The city's wealth came not only from public spending: private trade—especially in pottery, cloth, and wine—made a significant contribution too.

E. M. Wightman, *Roman Trier and the Treveri* (1970); H. Heinen, *Trier und das Trevererland in römischer Zeit* (1985).   J. F. Dr.

Augusta Vindelic(or)um (mod. Augsburg), probably originated in a civil settlement around an Augustan military base protecting an important crossroads-site, and was designated capital of *Raetia by *Tiberius. Its early prosperity was noted by Tacitus (*Germ.* 41). *Hadrian raised it to municipal status (see MUNICIPIUM), and after reorganization under *Diocletian it remained the civil capital of Raetia Secunda. It became the seat of a bishop. Nothing of Roman Augsburg remains above ground, but numerous sculptures and smaller objects have been found.

C. Wells, *The German Policy of Augustus* (1972), 87 ff.; G. Gottlieb, *Das römische Augsburg*, 2nd edn. (1984).   J. F. Dr.

Augustales, members of a religious and social institution common in the cities of the western Roman empire. There are numerous variations on the title, which taken together appear in some 2,500 inscriptions. The two most common are *Augustalis* and *sevir Augustalis*. These represent two separate organizations, rarely found in the same town but characterized by the same general features; the simple title of *sevir*, on the other hand, usually represents a very different institution. The vast majority of *Augustales* were *freedmen (85–95% of those attested in inscriptions), as well as Trimalchio and his friends, the only *Augustales* depicted in literature (Petron. *Sat.* 30, etc.). They often acted as benefactors (see EUERGETISM), funding public entertainments and building-projects as well as paying entry fees. In return, they enjoyed the prestige of their office, which functioned almost as a magistracy. *Augustales* were entitled to honorific insignia and were often selected by the town councillors. As their title indicates, their formal responsibilities may have centred on the imperial cult (see RULER-CULT), in the context of which they probably organized sacrifices and games. They generally performed these duties for a year, after which they retained membership in an order (*ordo*), sometimes organized like a *collegium, whose members held a rank just below that of the local council. The institution thus provided wealthy freedmen, who were legally barred from holding civic magistracies, with opportunities for public display and prestige.

R. Duthoy, *Epigraphische Studien* 11, 143–214, and *ANRW* 2. 16. 2 (1978), 254–309; S. E. Ostrow, *Hist.* 1985, 64–101; A. Abramenko, *Die Munizipale Mittelschicht in kaiserzeitlichen Italien* (1993).   J. B. R.

Augustine, St (Aurelius Augustinus) (AD 354–430), was born at Thagaste (mod. Souk Ahras, Algeria), son of Patricius, a modest town councillor of pagan beliefs, and a dominant Catholic mother, Monica. Educated at Thagaste, *Madauros, and Carthage, he taught rhetoric at Thagaste, Carthage, and Rome and (384–6) as public orator at Milan, then the capital of the emperor Valentinian II. Patronized at Rome by *Symmachus (2), the pagan orator, he hoped, by an advantageous marriage (to which he sacrificed his concubine, the mother of a son, Adeodatus—d. *c.*390) to join the 'aristocracy of letters' typical of his age (see AUSONIUS). At 19, however, he had read the *Hortensius* of *Cicero. This early 'conversion to philosophy' was the prototype of successive conversions: to *Manichaeism, a Gnostic sect promising Wisdom, and, in 386, to a Christianized *Neoplatonism patronized by *Ambrose, bishop of Milan. Catholicism, for Augustine, was the 'Divine Philosophy', a Wisdom guaranteed by authority but explored by reason: 'Seek and ye shall find', the only scriptural citation in his first work, characterizes his life as a thinker.

Though the only Latin philosopher to fail to master Greek, Augustine transformed Latin *Christianity by his Neoplatonism: his last recorded words echo *Plotinus. Stimulated by abrupt changes—he was forcibly ordained priest of Hippo (Bone, Algeria) in 391, becoming bishop in 395—and by frequent controversies (see DONATISTS; PELAGIUS), Augustine developed his ideas with an independence that disquieted even his admirers. He has left his distinctive mark on most aspects of western Christianity.

Augustine's major works are landmarks in the abandonment of Classical ideals. His early optimism was soon overshadowed by a radical doctrine of grace. This change was canonized in an autobiographical masterpiece, the *Confessions* (c.397–400), a vivid if highly selective source for his life to 388 and, equally, a mirror of his changed outlook. *De doctrina Christiana* (begun 396/7) sketched a literary culture subordinated to the Bible. *De Trinitate* (399–419) provided a more radically philosophical statement of the doctrine of the Trinity than any Greek Father. *De civitate Dei* (413 to 426) presented a definitive juxtaposition of Christianity with literary paganism and Neoplatonism, notably with *Porphyry. After 412, he combated in Pelagianism views which, 'like the philosophers of the pagans', had promised men fulfilment by their unaided efforts. In his *Retractationes* (427) Augustine criticized his superabundant output of 93 works in the light of a Catholic orthodoxy to which he believed he had progressively conformed—less consistently, perhaps, than he realized.

Letters and verbatim sermons richly document Augustine's complex life as a bishop; the centre of a group of sophisticated ascetics (notably *Paulinus of Nola), the 'slave' of a simple congregation, he was, above all, a man dedicated to the authority of the Catholic Church. This authority had enabled his restless intellect to work creatively: he would uphold it, in Africa, by every means, from writing a popular song to elaborating the only explicit justification in the early Church of a policy of religious persecution (see DONATISTS).

WORKS Migne, *PL* 32–47 and in many separate editions; C. Andresen, *Bibliographica Augustiniana*, 2nd edn. (1973). See esp. the translation of the *Confessions* by H. Chadwick (1991) and the commentary by J. J. O'Donnell, 3 vols. (1992); also G. Clark, *Augustine: The Confessions* (1993).

Consult also J. Burnaby, *Amor Dei* (1938); H.-I. Marrou, *St Augustin et la fin de la culture antique*, 4th edn. (1958); P. Courcelle, *Recherches sur les Confessions de St Augustin* (1950), and *Les Confessions de St Augustin dans la tradition littéraire* (1963); R. Holte, *Béatitude et Sagesse* (1962); F. van der Meer, *Augustine the Bishop*, Eng. trans. (1961); G. Bonner, *St Augustine of Hippo: Life and Controversies* (1963); P. Brown, *Augustine of Hippo* (1967); H. Chadwick, *Augustine* (1986); C. Kirwan, *Augustine* (1989). J. F. Ma.

Augustodunum ('Augustusville': mod. Autun), *civitas*-capital of the *Aedui, was founded *c.*12 BC in the plain of the Arroux to replace the hill-town of *Bibracte and demonstrate Roman cultural superiority. Its massive walls enclosed an unusually large (*c.*200-ha. (500-acre)) area. Though never completely built-up, the city was among the most populous in Gaul. It became a centre of higher education and, in the 4th cent. emerged as the seat of an important bishopric. Though it suffered for its

resistance to the Gallic emperor *Victorinus (1), it was restored under Constantine I. Important buildings (including two town gates, a large theatre, and a Celtic temple) survive.

Grenier, *Manuel* 3. 234 ff.; P.-A. Février and others, *Histoire de la France urbaine* 1 (1980); Musée Rolin, *Autun, Augustodunum* (1987). J. F. Dr.

Augustus (63 BC–AD 14), the first emperor at Rome, who presided over the inception of much of the institutional and ideological framework of the imperial system of the first three centuries AD. The long survival of his system, and its association with a literary milieu that came to be regarded as the *golden age of Latin literature, make him a uniquely important figure in Roman history, but no narrative history of his lifetime survives except for the account of *Cassius Dio (incomplete 6 BC–AD 14), and the rest of the evidence is very deeply imbued with partisan spirit of various kinds. An estimation of his personal contribution is hard to achieve.

Son of a *novus homo* (C. *Octavius, praetor 61, d. 59) from *Velitrae in the Alban Hills, C. Octavius was typical enough of the milieu of junior senators in the third quarter of the 1st cent., perceiving that the way to success lay through the support of the great dynasts for their agents and followers. In this he had a head start: his mother *Atia (1) (of a family from *Aricia, next door to Velitrae) was the daughter of *Caesar's sister, which made C. Octavius one of the closest young male relatives of the dictator, a connection emphasized when in 51 BC he gave the funeral oration for his maternal grandmother. In 47 he was made *pontifex; with Caesar in Spain in 45, he was enrolled as a patrician, and when the dictator drew up his will (13 September 45) he adopted the 17-year-old Octavius and made him his heir. The young man spent the winter in study at *Apollonia in Illyricum, but reacted with decision and alacrity when Caesar was murdered and the will read. Over the next months he consolidated his position as the leader of the friends of Caesar, commemorating his adoptive father, and wooing his veterans; a course of action which brought him into conflict with Antony, (M. *Antonius (2)), and support of the cause against him which was victorious at *Mutina (April 43), after which he seized the consulship by force. At Bononia the differences between him, Antony, and M. *Aemilius Lepidus (3) were resolved and the *Triumvirate established. The next years were marked by the crushing of L. *Antonius (Pietas) and *Fulvia at *Perusia, with singular violence, the settling of *veterans, on confiscated land, and the *proscriptions, in which he was as ruthless as the others. He married *Scribonia as a gesture to Sex. *Pompeius, and she bore his only child *Iulia (3) (in 39 he divorced her to marry *Livia Drusilla); to seal the political dispositions made at Brundisium in October 40 Antony married his sister *Octavia (2). All the politicians of the time made use of *imperium, one of the only surviving constitutional principles of any potency, and Caesar's heir now took the first name Imperator.

Over the 30s, events combined with astute responses enabled Imp. Caesar to represent himself as defender of an Italian order. His principal local rival for this position, Sex. Pompeius (finally defeated at Naulochus in 36), he represented as a pirate-leader. He took advantage of his control of the ancient centre of *imperium and (especially through the singular post-consular aedilate of *Agrippa in 33) maintained the favour of the disaffected and volatile *populus* who still in theory granted it. After a half-hearted attempt to attain some military reputation against a foreign enemy (the Illyrians) he turned to representing Antony in *Alexandria (1) as alien, immoral, and treacherous. In 32 a formal oath expressed the mass loyalty of Italy to his cause. The advantages of this policy were not wholly symbolic. Italy offered material resources, manpower, and the land with which to reward its loyalty. Imp. Caesar and his close supporters of these years and afterwards (especially M. *Vipsanius Agrippa, T. *Statilius Taurus, and C. *Maecenas) were victorious against Antony, whose pro-Egyptian policy and failure in *Armenia had lost him much of his eastern support. The battle of *Actium (31 BC) was the turning-point; the capture of Alexandria in the next year ended the war and led to the incorporation of Egypt in the *imperium*. Victory in the east, the vindication of his political promises in Italy, and the booty of the Ptolemies gave him an unassailable position, soon expressed in terms of divinity.

From his consulship of 31 (he held it every year down to 23) there began a down-playing of the irregularity of the triumviral system, which culminated in a formal *restitutio* of the *res publica*, a restoration in the sense of repair or revival rather than a return to a different constitution. He returned to Rome in mid-29, triumphed, beautified the city by the dedication of important temples, and signalled an end to war by the closing of the temple of *Janus. Agrippa was his colleague in the consulship for 28 and 27: at the beginning of 27 he made the formal gesture of reinstating the magistrates, senate (reduced in numbers through a purge of undesirable elements), and people in their old constitutional role. In return he received a major grant of proconsular *imperium*, and many honours, including the name Augustus (see AUGUSTUS, AUGUSTA, AS TITLES), and departed to carry out the military duties of his new command.

Before 7 BC Augustus spent a great deal of time in the provinces (only in 23, 18, 17, and 12 did he spend the whole year in Rome, and he was absent for the whole of 26/5, 21/0, and 15/4). The Civil Wars had shown that power at Rome was to be won in the provinces, and with ever greater numbers of Roman citizens outside Italy, Augustus had to form an empire-wide system. The creation of a huge proconsular *provincia* on the model of the commands of Pompey and the triumvirs, which gave Augustus *imperium* over most of the *milites* of the *res publica*, was the core of this, and the most important part of the 'settlement' of 27. Delegation was essential in so unwieldy an entity, and, like his predecessors, Augustus appointed senatorial legates and equestrian prefects to serve his *imperium*. If these men ran units which were analogous to the *provinciae* of the proconsuls who continued to be sent to the parts of the Roman dominion that lay outside Augustus' command, that is not to say that the settlement envisaged two types of province. Such an innovation would have been far less subtle than the skill with which the legal flexibility of the assignment of proconsular commands and the convenient precedents of the previous generation were adapted to Augustus' purpose.

There were difficulties, since holders of *imperium* had been accustomed to a greater independence than Augustus could afford to allow them. Already in 30 the claim of M. *Licinius Crassus (2) to the *spolia opima* had tested the limits of self-determination; this bid for an antique honour was, characteristically, thwarted by a display of greater erudition from Augustus. Egypt's temptations proved too much for even the equestrian prefect C. *Cornelius Gallus (26). M. Primus came to grief because his informal instructions were inconsistent (c.24). In 23, again following the precedent of *Pompey, the proconsular *imperium* was clearly labelled *maius* (superior), which also clarified the position of the other holders under Augustus of wide-ranging commands, such as Agrippa and C. *Iulius Caesar (2).

The maintenance of the loyalty of the soldiers finally depended on Augustus' capacity to pay them. That in turn depended on the organization of revenues so that they would regularly accrue to him directly. A simple fiscal logic thus operated which transformed the empire: previously, the maintaining of cash flows to the centre, where they might be squandered by one's enemies, was of little interest to provincial governors. Now, the efficiency of the exaction system was the only guarantee of the survival of the new order. The whole world was enrolled, and noticed it (Luke 2: 1, even if the process was not so sudden as the experience of *Judaea implied). Taxation was reformed and new provinces made so that their tribute might swell Augustus' takings. The enthusiastic imposition of such burdens caused rebellion and disaster, especially in Germany. A military treasury on the Capitol announced the theoretical centrality of the fiscal arrangements to the whole *imperium* from AD 6 (see AERARIUM).

The incorporations of this period doubled the size of the provincial empire: NW Spain and the provinces of the Alps and the Alpine foreland, *Raetia, *Noricum, and *Pannonia, with *Germania and *Moesia beyond them, saw most of the military aggression, the provincialization of *Galatia and *Judaea being relatively peaceful. A reasonably high level of military activity was a sensible ingredient in Augustan political strategy, and provided the *gloria* which fuelled the *auctoritas* of the ruling cadre. Some of this took the form of expeditions which bore no fruit in terms of the all-important taxation, either directly (or in some cases ever): like Augustus' own trip to the Danube (35–33 BC), *Aelius Gallus' Arabian campaign (25–24), and the wars in southern Egypt of C. Cornelius Gallus (29) and C. Petronius (25). The main point of such trips was the glamour of the geography and ethnography, celebrated in poetry and on Agrippa's *map, which propagated the belief that Augustus' Rome ruled the whole inhabited world. This impression was reinforced by Augustus' generally successful use (continued in the east from Antony's careful practice) of the traditional diplomatic relations with local magnates, kings, or communities, in places outside the direct *imperium* of a Roman governor. Ritual courtesies on both sides could suggest that the empire included *India or *Britain, and had a practical role in settling outstanding issues with *Parthia in 20 in a negotiation which Augustus made a great deal of. When a serious military threat appeared, in the shape of the Pannonian Revolt, 'the worst war since those against Carthage', or the German war that followed the massacre of *Quinctilius Varus and his three legions, the system all but collapsed.

For all his absences, Rome itself was at the heart of Augustus' vision. City-foundations in the provinces, and benefactions to existing *coloniae* and *municipia, encouraged the imitation of the metropolis and the recognition of that constituency of Italians spread across the Mediterranean world that had played such a vital part in the Civil Wars. He could not avoid a real concern for the urban populace of Rome itself, who caused major disturbances of the traditional kind at intervals throughout his ascendancy. In 23, the choice of *tribunicia potestas* (see TRIBUNI PLEBIS) as the 'indication of the highest station', and the way in which Augustus counted the years of his 'reign' thereafter, signalled also his descent from the *populares* (see OPTIMATES) of the late republic, many of whose policies he continued (albeit sometimes with a show of reluctance): he made provision against famine, fire, and flood, and reorganized the districts of the city (spreading his own cult in the process). The popular assembly duly ratified his legislation, and was represented *en masse* in displays of loyalty at important moments.

Augustus, Augusta, as titles

*Varro had taught the Romans to be at home in their own city, and Augustus was an eager interpreter of the process. The ancient messages of cult and civic ritual offered many opportunities, which he was making use of already in the 30s. After Actium the serious development of the cult of Palatine Apollo as a parallel for Capitoline Jupiter, and the restoration of dozens of Rome's ancient sanctuaries; after 12 (when he finally became *Pontifex Maximus on the death of Lepidus) the formation of the House of the *Pater Patriae, in 2 BC the inauguration of a replacement forum (see FORUM AUGUSTUM), to which many state ceremonies were removed; throughout the creation of a 'suburb more beautiful than the city' on the *Campus Martius, for the amenity of the populace: the reduplication of Rome's glories cleverly allowed him to be a new founder without damaging the old system, and to surpass all past builders and benefactors without the solecism of departing from or belittling their precedent. He thus underlined his relationship with the previous centuries of Roman history in a Roman Whig history that culminated in his ascendancy.

His management of *lex* was equally historic: giving his name to far more *leges* than any legislator before him (see LEX (2) for *leges Iuliae*), and announcing his control of the legislative assembly in the process, he became the city-founding lawgiver of the new Rome. The control of religion, that mirror of the *res publica*, was the interpretative vehicle of much of this, and learning, interpretation, and doctrine, of law or ritual precedent, history or geography, were the indispensable servants of all these projects. Hence the cultural and literary acme that later generations of Romans perceived at this epoch. These processes came together in the pivotal years 19–17 BC, when he had made the last modifications to his position in the *res publica*, settled the eastern and western provinces, and acquired his first grandson (C. *Iulius Caesar (2), the child of *Iulia (3) and Agrippa). Now came the ethical and social laws, and in 17 the great celebration of the divine diuturnity that the Fates had given to Rome by making her populace virtuous and therefore fecund, in the *ludi saeculares*, see SECULAR GAMES.

His concern for the institutions of state allowed him to insert himself into the annals of Roman history as a continuator or reformer rather than as an intruder or revolutionary, while the inherent flexibility of the institutions gave him a wonderful repertoire of gambits both for shaping opportunities for political success for his supporters and for social promotion, of which the most important form of all was the identification of a successor to his office. The very happy accident of his long life allowed readjustment of many of his innovations in a process of trial and error, a refining process which explains the success and long survival of many of them: the city prefect (see PRAEFECTUS URBI), the public *postal service, the *vigiles, and so on.

The arrangement of a successor proved the most difficult task of all. The calculation of *auctoritas* in which he excelled, and which his very name evoked, entailed that no merely dynastic principle could be guaranteed; it would belittle his own carefully constructed practical reputation for real ability to have a successor who owed everything, as he had done, to a name. At the same time he had been unable (and had perhaps not wanted) to avoid accumulating honours for his family, and using for that very consolidation of *auctoritas* the image of a Father and the model of the state as a super-household, one conducted like his own and under his benign but omnicompetent tutelage. There was in the end a dissonance between the role of those who had to be permitted to acquire the necessary *auctoritas* to maintain

the image of effective governance, especially through largely factitious military escapades, and the need to rely on his own blood-line to keep alive the charisma of his own divine associations. Agrippa was a compliant assistant in the public sphere, and Livia happy and expert at propagating the necessary pictures in the private; but *Tiberius and *Drusus, Livia's children by her first marriage, were not good at being second fiddle, and Iulia, his daughter and only child, on whom the whole dynastic construction relied, nearly wrecked the whole thing by probably calculated sexual misbehaviour. This called into question the credentials of the model family, the legitimacy of her offspring, and the feasibility of using ethics as a constitutional strategy, while potentially irradiating her partners (who included Antony's son Iullus *Antonius) with her share of the ancestral charisma.

The dynastic policy was not overtly monarchic either, however, and what saved Augustus was the fact that he had (since he did not have the option of destroying them wholesale) re-created the Roman aristocracy and given them a new role in his social system. As an antidote to the Civil War social mobility was to be curbed; freedmen were discouraged from promotion, the *plebs* was indulged but controlled; the two upper classes were encouraged to procreate, and each had its precise place in the religious system, at the theatre, and in government. As an ornament to the whole thing, and to camouflage the prerogatives that he ascribed to his own family, survivors of the great lines of the historic Roman past were encouraged to live up to their ancestors' images, and given an honorific but circumscribed part to play in a system whose regulation, through his censorial function, it was Augustus' job to manage. Hence—and the power derived also from his fatherly pretensions—the ethical content of much of his legislation, which did the nobility the credit of thinking them worthy of the past while giving their arbiter a useful way of coercing them if they failed to live up to it. The seeds of the disastrous use of the laws on *adultery and *maiestas* over the next generations were therefore sowed by Augustus, who was not himself faced by any very coherent opposition.

Later authors dated the establishment of the imperial monarchy to 31 or 27 BC. In many ways, as Augustus probably saw, and Tacitus appreciated, the new arrangements, many times modified, and threatened by diverse instability, could not be regarded as established until someone had succeeded to them, and then shown himself willing to continue their essentials. Although the *optimus status* was in most respects in place by the climax of the legislative phase and the announcement of the *saeculum* in 17, and the pinnacle of *auctoritas* was commemorated in 2 BC, the Augustan empire could have been dissolved in AD 14. The achievement of Augustus lay in the flexibility with which he and his advisers responded to a period of striking social change in the Mediterranean world, the legacy of the Roman/Italian diaspora of the previous century. But in controlling a dynamic process there is more continuity and less revolution than is usual in the foundation of a monarchy, and that may well help to account for the stability of the system that Augustus' successors developed out of his innovations. See also ROME, HISTORY, § 2.1; APOLLODORUS (5).

Syme, *Rom. Rev.* and *AA*; F. Millar and E. Segal, *Caesar Augustus, Seven Aspects* (1984); K. A. Raaflaub and M. Toher, *Between Republic and Empire: Interpretations of Augustus and his Principate* (1990); P. Zanker, *The power of images in the age of Augustus* (1988); C. Nicolet, *L'Inventaire du monde* (1988).   N. P.

Augustus, Augusta (Gk. Σεβαστός, Σεβαστή), **as titles** Republican usage was religious (first in Enn. *Ann.* 502: 'augusto augurio'). On 16 January 27 BC *Octavian received the title from the senate, and he intended *Tiberius also to take it. Tiberius did not formally accept, but it was used in official documents and taken by all later emperors (*Vitellius delayed). Denied to other male members of the dynasty, it became the imperial title *par excellence*, and so was transmitted to military units and cities (some, e.g. Augst, Sivas, still bear it). The title 'Augusta' was conferred on the emperor's wife (*Livia Drusilla, in Augustus' will, the first), exceptionally on other relatives (*Antonia (3)).

J. P. B.; B. M. L.

Aulis, small Greek city near *Tanagra, on a rocky peninsula between two bays. Its most famous monument is the temple of Artemis and its neighbouring buildings. The best harbour in northern *Boeotia, Aulis is most famous as the point of assembly for the Achaean expedition against Troy. Here *Iphigenia was sent to be sacrificed for a safe voyage of the fleet, a theme developed by *Euripides. *Hesiod (*Op.* 651 ff.) sailed thence to *Euboea. Strabo (9. 2. 3) states that an Aeolian fleet sailed from it to Asia. *Agesilaus attempted to sacrifice there in 396 BC, before his expedition to Asia (Xen. *Hell.* 3. 4. 4), but the Boeotians interrupted the ceremony. It was the principal base for *Epaminondas' unsuccessful naval ambitions in 364 BC. In 312 BC *Antigonus (1)'s admiral Ptolemaeus docked 150 ships there in the conflict with *Cassander (Diod. Sic. 19. 77. 4). L. *Aemilius Paullus (2) visited Aulis in 167 BC to view the anchorage of the Achaean fleet.

J. Buckler, in US Naval Academy (ed.), *New Aspects of Naval History* (1985). J. Bu.

Aurelia (*RE* 'Aurelius' 248), of the family of the Cottae, was the mother of C. *Iulius Caesar (1). She watched over the conduct of his wife *Pompeia and detected P. *Clodius Pulcher at the Bona Dea ceremony. She died in 54 BC. E. B.

Aurelian (Lucius Domitius (*RE* 36) **Aurelianus)** (*c.* AD 215–75), a man of humble origin from the Danubian region, achieved high military rank under *Gallienus, but helped organize the plot that destroyed him. Appointed by *Claudius II to the chief command of the cavalry, he served with distinction against the *Goths. Though Aurelian was the obvious successor to Claudius, he did not immediately declare himself on the latter's death, allowing the throne to pass to Quintillus. However, it was not long before he was hailed as emperor by his troops and disposed of his rival (*c.* September 270).

Barbarian invasions first claimed his attention. He defeated the *Vandals in Pannonia and then repulsed a dangerous incursion into Italy by the *Alamanni and Iuthungi, pursuing the latter over the Danube. On his return to Rome, he surrounded the city with walls to protect it against further barbarian attacks (*wall of Aurelian). With characteristic ruthlessness, he also disposed of early political opponents to his rule.

He next dealt with Palmyra. *Zenobia, ruling for her young son, *Septimius Vaballathus, had recently exploited Roman civil war to occupy Egypt and Asia Minor up to Bithynia (autumn 270). Coins and papyri show that she was now calling Vaballathus Imperator, but not Augustus, and was projecting him as the—albeit junior—colleague of Aurelian. Aurelian tolerated the compromise for only as long as he had to; early in 272 he marched east. Following defeat at *Antioch (1) on the Orontes, Zenobia withdrew south, and proclaimed Vaballathus Augustus (spring 272). Aurelian pursued the rebels to Emesa, broke their main strength, and forced them to take refuge in Palmyra, which he

then besieged. In summer 272, Zenobia was captured on her way to seek aid from Persia, and Palmyra surrendered.

Marching back westward, Aurelian defeated the Carpi on the Danube, but was recalled by a further revolt in *Palmyra (spring 273). He quickly crushed the uprising, and then proceeded to Egypt to suppress violent disturbances possibly associated with the rebellion in Palmyra.

Aurelian now turned west and ended the Gallic empire at Châlons, defeating *Tetricus (early 274). Tetricus and Zenobia headed the captives from all Aurelian's victories in a magnificent triumph.

Early in 275 Aurelian set out against Persia, but was murdered at Caenophrurium, near *Byzantium, in a household plot. Some time passed before *Tacitus (2) was appointed to succeed him—the army offering the choice to the senate, the senate shirking the dangerous responsibility.

Aurelian's energy and military talents restored the unity of the empire after a decade of division; and he was more than just a successful general. Towards the end of his reign (274) he had the courage to abandon the old province of *Dacia—by now reduced to the Transylvanian highlands—and relocate its garrison, civilian administrators, and those of the rest of the population able and willing to join the evacuation, south of the Danube. He sought to reform the silver coinage, much damaged by 40 years of continual debasement. And, with the help of the booty won from Palmyra, he attempted to establish the worship of Sol Invictus—with himself as this deity's chosen vicegerent—at the centre of Roman state religion (see ELAGABALUS, DEUS SOL INVICTUS). Thus in many ways he pioneered the work of Diocletian and Constantine I; yet he lacked the originality to bring the period of 'crisis' to its conclusion. His murder was followed by a further ten years of uncertainty.

PLRE 1. 129 f.; L. Homo, *Essai sur le règne de l'empereur Aurélien* (1904); R. Syme, *Emperors and Biography* (1971); A. Bodor and others, *Dacoromania. Jahrbuch für östliche Latinität* 1973; G. Sotgiu, ANRW 2. 2 (1975), 1039 ff.; G. H. Halsberghe, ANRW 2. 17. 4 (1984), 2181 ff.; E. Kettenhofen, *Tyche* (1986), 138 ff.; M. Peachin, *Roman Imperial Titulature* (1990). J. F. Dr.

Aurelius, Marcus, emperor AD 161–80, was born in 121 and named M. Annius (*RE* 94) Verus. His homonymous grandfather, M. *Annius Verus, from Ucubi (Espejo) in Baetica, consul for the third time (as *ordinarius*) in 126 and city prefect, a relative of *Hadrian and an influential figure, brought him up after his father's early death. His mother Domitia Lucilla inherited the fortune created by Cn. *Domitius Afer. From early childhood Marcus was a favourite of Hadrian, who nicknamed him *Verissimus*. At the age of 15 he was betrothed at Hadrian's wish to Ceionia Fabia, daughter of the man Hadrian adopted as L. *Aelius Caesar. In 138 Hadrian ordered his second heir *Antoninus Pius, whose wife was Marcus' aunt Annia Galeria Faustina (1), to adopt Marcus along with Aelius' son Lucius: he now became M. (Aelius) Aurelius Verus Caesar. When Hadrian died, Marcus was betrothed to Antoninus' daughter, his own cousin *Annia Galeria Faustina (2), instead of Ceionia. Quaestor in 139, first elected consul in 140 and again in 145, he married in the latter year; his first child was born on 30 November 147; the next day he received *tribunicia potestas* (see TRIBUNI PLEBIS) and *imperium* and Faustina became Augusta (*fasti Ostienses*). Marcus was educated by a host of famous teachers, one being the orator *Fronto; many of their letters survive. His leaning to philosophy, already manifest when he was 12, became the central feature of his life. He was much influenced by Q. *Iunius Rusticus (elected to a second consulship

219

in 162), son or grandson of the Stoic 'martyr' (see STOICISM) of AD 93, and by the teaching of *Epictetus. Although Marcus is called a Stoic, his *Meditations* (see below) are eclectic, with elements of Platonism and Epicureanism as well. Further, he was much indebted to Antoninus, who receives a lengthier tribute than anyone else in the *Meditations* (1. 16; another version, 6. 30). His tranquil family life is vividly portrayed in his correspondence and recalled with affection in the *Meditations*. Faustina bore him further children; several died in infancy, but the couple had four daughters when Marcus succeeded Antoninus on 7 March 161; and Faustina was again pregnant.

Marcus at once requested the senate to confer the rank of co-emperor on his adoptive brother Lucius, as Hadrian had intended. Lucius took Marcus' name *Verus, while Marcus assumed that of Antoninus. There were thus two Augusti for the first time, equal rulers, except that only Marcus was Pontifex Maximus and he had greater *auctoritas*. The coinage proclaimed the *concordia Augustorum*, L. Verus was betrothed to Marcus' eldest daughter *Annia Aurelia Galeria Lucilla, and the *felicitas temporum* was further enhanced when Faustina gave birth to twin sons on 31 August, their names honouring Antoninus (T. Aurelius Fulvus Antoninus) and Lucius (L. Aurelius Commodus). But Antoninus' death had unleashed trouble on the frontiers: in Britain, dealt with by Sex. *Calpurnius Agricola; Upper Germany, to which Marcus' close friend *Aufidius Victorinus, Fronto's son-in-law, was sent; along the Danube; and, most seriously, in the east. The Parthians seized Armenia and defeated the governor of Cappadocia, who took his own life, and invaded Syria. It was decided that an expeditionary force was needed, to be led by L. Verus, with an experienced staff. Verus left Italy in 162 and was based at Antioch (1) until 166 (with a visit to Ephesus in 164 to marry Lucilla), but was merely a figurehead. After the expulsion of the Parthians from Armenia by Statius Priscus (163), he took the title Armeniacus (accepted by Marcus in 164), crowning a new king, Sohaemus. Other generals, notably *Avidius Cassius, defeated the Parthians in Mesopotamia: Ctesiphon was captured and Seleuceia (1) on the Tigris sacked at the end of 165. Verus became Parthicus Maximus, Marcus following suit after a short delay. In 166 further success led to the title Medicus. But plague had broken out in the eastern army; the threat in the north was becoming acute—the despatch of three legions to the east had weakened the Rhine–Danube *limes. Verus was obliged to make peace, celebrating a joint triumph with Marcus (12 October 166). Each became *Pater Patriae and Marcus' surviving sons, *Commodus (whose twin had died) and Annius Verus (b. 162), became Caesar.

Marcus planned a new campaign to relieve the Danube frontier. New legions, II and III Italicae, were raised in 165; V Macedonica, formerly in Lower Moesia, was moved to Dacia on its return from the east. But the *plague, reaching Rome in 166, delayed the expedition until spring 168; meanwhile Pannonia and Dacia were both invaded. The emperors went to the Danube in 168 and reinforced the frontier, stationing the new legions in western Pannonia under Q. *Antistius Adventus (*ILS* 8977). They wintered at Aquileia, where the plague broke out; the praetorian prefect *Furius Victorinus was a victim and *Galen, the imperial physician, refused to stay. At Verus' insistence, he and Marcus also left in January 169, but Verus had a stroke on the journey and died a few days later. Marcus deified him and obliged the widowed Lucilla to marry the Syrian *novus homo* Ti. *Claudius Pompeianus, who had distinguished himself in Pannonia. In spite of further bereavement—his younger son Verus died—he pressed

on with preparations, auctioning imperial treasures to raise funds, and returned north, to Sirmium, in autumn 169.

Apparently planning to annex territory beyond the Danube, he launched an offensive in spring 170, but incurred a severe defeat. The *Marcomanni and *Quadi of Bohemia and Slovakia invaded, outflanked Marcus and swept over the Julian Alps, sacking Opitergium (Oderzo) and besieging Aquileia. It was the worst such crisis since the German invasions at the end of the 2nd cent. BC. Desperate measures, led by Pompeianus and P. *Helvius Pertinax, cleared Italy, Noricum, and Pannonia. The Marcomanni were defeated as they tried to recross the Danube with their booty. But the Balkans and Greece were invaded by the Costoboci, requiring further emergency measures, and Spain was ravaged by the Moors, dealt with by Marcus' friend Victorinus. Marcus, based at Carnuntum, first used diplomacy to detach some tribes from the 'barbarian conspiracy'; some peoples were settled within the empire. The offensive, resumed in 172, is depicted at the start of the Aurelian column in Rome. In spite of the death of the praetorian prefect Vindex, the Marcomanni were defeated: victory was claimed, with the title Germanicus. In a battle against the Quadi Roman troops were saved by a 'rain miracle', shown on the column, later claimed to have been achieved by the prayers of Christian legionaries; Marcus gave the credit to the Egyptian Hermes 'Aerius'. In 173 he pacified the Quadi, moving to Sirmium in 174 to take on the Sarmatian *Iazyges of the Hungarian plain. After some successes, he was obliged to make an armistice when Avidius Cassius, who had had special powers in the east, was proclaimed emperor. The revolt collapsed after three months, but Marcus, now Sarmaticus, toured the east, taking Faustina, who died in late 175 and was deified, and Commodus. He went through Asia and Syria to Egypt, returning via Athens to Rome. Here he held a triumph (23 December 176) and raised Commodus to Augustus. In summer 178, renewed warfare in the north took him northwards again. He remained, evidently planning to annex Marcomannia and Sarmatia, until his death (17 March 180).

Marcus has been universally admired, as a philosopher-ruler, to the present day, criticized only for leaving his unworthy son as successor. This no doubt seemed the best way to ensure stability, and he left Commodus experienced advisers, including his numerous sons-in-law. Despite Marcus' lack of military experience he took personal command against the first wave of the great *Volkerwanderung* that ultimately destroyed the empire, setting an example that inspired his contemporaries in the view of *Ammianus (31. 5. 14).   A. R. Bi.

Meditations Marcus is most famous for a work his subjects never saw, the intimate notebook in which he recorded (in Greek) his own reflections on human life and the ways of the gods, perhaps before retiring at night. The title *Meditations* is purely modern: τὰ εἰς ἑαυτόν ('to himself'), found in our MSS, may not go back to the author, but is surely accurate. Internal evidence suggests that he was past his prime when he wrote (2. 2, and other references to his age or imminent death), and that at least parts were composed during his lengthy campaigns against the German tribes. It seems to have survived almost by accident; it was unknown to the writers of his time and for long afterwards, but seems to have surfaced in the 4th cent. (Them. *Or.* 6. 81c, not a certain allusion). In general the closest analogies for the thought are with *Epictetus, but Marcus is interested less in sustained exposition. The style, often eloquent and poetic, can also be compressed, obscure, and grammatically awkward. All of this is understandable if he was writing memoranda for his eyes alone.

Although divided by moderns into twelve 'books', the work seems not to have a clear structure. Brief epigrams are juxtaposed with quotations (usually of moral tags, occasionally of longer passages: esp. 7. 38–42, 11. 30–9) and with more developed arguments on divine providence, the brevity of human life, the necessity for moral effort, and tolerance of his fellow human beings. Frustratingly, these *pensées* are almost invariably generalized: we do not learn Marcus' secret thoughts about his family, members of the court, or military policy. We do, however, get some idea of his personality and preoccupations.

The first book of the *Meditations* is a different matter, being more coherent than the others; it may have been composed independently. Here Marcus goes through a list of his closer relatives and several teachers, recording what he owes to each—in some cases a specific lesson, but more often a general moral example. This list culminates in two long passages on what he owes to his predecessor *Antoninus Pius, and to the gods (1. 16 and 17). Though often allusive and obscure, these give us unique access to the mind of an ancient ruler, and the whole book is a precious personal document.

In the rest of the work, though technical discussion of Stoic doctrine is avoided, certain recurrent themes stand out: the need to avoid distractions and concentrate on making the correct moral choice; the obligation of individuals to work for the common good (e.g. 6. 54: 'What does not benefit the hive does not benefit the bee'); the unity of mankind in a world-city (4. 4; cf. G. R. Stanton, *Phronesis* 1968, 183 ff.); insistence on the providence of the gods, often combined with rejection of the Epicurean alternative that all is random movement of atoms (e.g. 6. 17, 8. 39). Duty and social responsibility are strongly emphasized; Marcus was keenly aware of the temptations of power (e.g. 5. 16, 6. 30 'do not be Caesarified'). Thoughts of providence lead him to contemplate the vastness of time and space, and the guiding pattern that according to the Stoics gives order to the universe (e.g. 10. 5). There is also a more melancholy note, of resignation and pessimism. Though determined to persevere in his moral efforts, the author is often resigned to their futility (8. 4; 9. 29 'who will change men's convictions?'). Hymns to the grandeur and order of the universe (4. 23, 5. 4) can give way to revulsion and disgust (8. 24). Above all, Marcus is fascinated by life's transience and the way in which all great men, even philosophers and emperors, pass on and are forgotten (4. 32, 33, 48, 50, etc.). His most lasting achievement is a work which has inspired readers as different as Sir Thomas Browne, Matthew Arnold, and Cecil Rhodes.

WRITINGS Correspondence in *Fronto: Letters*, ed. M. P. J. van den Hout (1988); Eng. trans. by C. R. Haines, 1919–20; see also bibliog. to CORNELIUS FRONTO, M.

Meditations, ed. J. Dalfen (Teubner, 1979, 1987²); commentaries: A. S. L. Farquharson, with trans. (1944), rev. trans. published separately; W. Theiler (1951). Studies: P. A. Brunt, *JRS* 1974, 1–20; E. Champlin, *Fronto and Antonine Rome* (1980); R. B. Rutherford, *The Meditations of M. Aurelius: A Study* (1989), with Brunt, *JRS* 1990, 218–19; E. Asmis, *ANRW* 2. 32. 3 (1989), 2228–52. On Marcus and Christianity see Brunt, in C. Deroux (ed.), *Studies in Latin Literature and Roman History* 1 (1979), 483–520.

ANCIENT SOURCES Literary: Cass. Dio 71–3; SHA *Hadr.*, *Ant. Pius*, *M. Ant.*, *Verus*, *Comm.*; Philostr. *VS*; *Corpus Iuris*, cf. W. Williams, *JRS* 1976. Coins: *BM Coins, Rom. Emp.* 4. Column: W. Zwikker, *Studien zur Markussäule* 1 (1941); C. Caprino, *La colonna di M. Aurelio* (1955).

MODERN LITERATURE G. Alföldy, *Konsulat und Senatorenstand unter den Antoninen* (1977); A. R. Birley, *Marcus Aurelius*, 2nd. edn.

(1987); J. H. Oliver, *Marcus Aurelius: Aspects of Civic and Cultural Policy* (1970); E. Champlin, see above.   R. B. R.

Aurelius Achilleus, according to the literary sources usurper in Egypt, AD 296–7, although papyri style him as *corrector* under another usurper, L. Domitius Domitianus, conquered by *Diocletian in person early in 297. He may have assumed leadership of the revolt after the (hypothetical) death of Domitianus.

PLRE 1, 'Achilleus' 1. T. Barnes, *The New Empire of Diocletian and Constantine* (1982), 12.   H. M.; A. J. S. S.

Aurelius (*RE* 46) **Antoninus** (1), **Marcus** (AD 188–217), nicknamed **Caracalla,** emperor AD 198–217. Elder son of L. *Septimius Severus, originally called Septimius Bassianus; renamed after M. Aurelius and made Caesar in 195. Augustus in 198, he was consul for the first time with his father in 202 and for the second time with his brother P. *Septimius Geta (2) in 205, when he had his hated father-in-law C. *Fulvius Plautianus killed. Consul for the third time in 208, again with Geta, whom he also hated, he accompanied his father to *Britain, sharing command against the Caledonians. When Severus died, he and Geta abandoned Scotland, making the *wall of Hadrian the frontier again, and returned to Rome. After having Geta killed (26 December 211), a drastic purge followed. To conciliate the soldiers, he raised their pay, creating financial problems. One solution was the 'Antonine *constitution'; he simultaneously doubled the inheritance tax paid only by citizens, which funded the *aerarium militare. In 215 a new coin was struck, the so-called *antoninianus*, evidently tariffed at two denarii, but weighing only 1.5: this was to lead to inflation.

In 213 he fought the *Alamanni (the first time they are mentioned), evidently gave the Raetian *limes a stone wall, and became Germanicus Maximus. In 214 he attacked the Danubian Carpi and reorganized Pannonia, each province now having two legions (Britain was split into two provinces at this time; Hither Spain was also subdivided). Obsessed by *Alexander (3) the Great, he raised a Macedonian phalanx and went east in his footsteps, through Asia and Syria to *Alexandria (1), where large numbers who had mocked him were killed. When his offer to marry a Parthian princess was rejected, he attacked Media. While preparing a further campaign he was murdered near Carrhae (8 April 217). *Macrinus deified him as Divus Antoninus Magnus.

Cass. Dio 77–8; Hdn. 4; SHA *M. Ant.*; *RIC* 4. 1; A. N. Sherwin-White, *The Roman Citizenship* 2nd. edn. (1973); A. Mastino, *Le titolature di Caracalla e Geta* (1981).   A. R. Bi.

Aurelius Antoninus (2), **Marcus,** the emperor (AD 218–22) **Elagabalus** (*RE* 'Varius (10) Avitus'), was the son of Sex. *Varius Marcellus and *Iulia Soaemias Bassiana, niece of *Iulia Domna. Born probably in 203, as Varius Avitus Bassianus, he was holding the priesthood, hereditary in his mother's family, of the presiding deity of *Emesa in Syria, in 218, when his mother and grandmother *Iulia Maesa used him as figurehead of a rebellion against *Macrinus. He was proclaimed to be son of his mother's cousin M. *Aurelius Antoninus (1) (Caracalla) and renamed after him. After the victory, he took the cult of the god by whose name he is known to Rome, which he reached in July 219. In late 220 his intention to make *Elagabalus ('deus Sol invictus') supreme god of the empire aroused open hostility at Rome when he divorced his first wife Julia Paula and married the Vestal virgin Aquilia Severa, a 'sacred marriage' to match the union of the god with Juno *Caelestis. He was forced to adopt his cousin Alexianus, renamed Alexander (26 June 221), and to divorce Aquilia in favour of a descendant of M. Aurelius, Annia Faustina; but by the end of 221 took Aquilia back and tried to get rid of Alexander. This provoked renewed outrage, which came to a head with his murder on 11 March 222 and replacement by Alexander. His flouting of conventions in the choice of officials, combined with disgust at the orgiastic ceremonial of the Syrian cult had proved too much for senate, praetorians, and *plebs* alike. See AURELIUS SEVERUS ALEXANDER, M.; VALERIUS COMAZON, P.

Cass. Dio 78–9; Hdn. 5; SHA *Heliogab.* (largely fiction from 18. 3 onwards). *BM Coins, Rom. Emp.* 5. E. Kettenhofen, *Die syrischen Augustae* (1979); M. Frey, *Untersuchungen zur Religion und zur Religionspolitik des Kaisers Elagabal* (1989). A. R. Bi.

Aurelius Cleander, Marcus, a freedman of Phrygian origin, chamberlain (*a cubiculo*) of *Commodus in succession to Saoterus, exercised effective power over the emperor from AD 185, when the praetorian prefect Perennis was overthrown. Cleander even became prefect himself, with two colleagues and the additional title 'bearer of the dagger' (*a pugione*), but was sacrificed to the angry *plebs* during a food shortage in AD 190.

PIR[2] A 1481; H.-G. Pflaum, *Les Carrières procuratoriennes équestres* (1960–1), no. 180 *bis*, cf. 178 *bis*. A. R. Bi.

Aurelius (*RE* 96) **Cotta, Gaius,** brother of the two following and nephew of P. *Rutilius Rufus, was a distinguished orator and, with M. *Livius Drusus (2) and P. *Sulpicius Rufus, one of the circle of ambitious young nobles around L. *Licinius Crassus. Exiled by Q. *Varius' commission, he returned with *Sulla. Consul 75 BC and described by Sallust as 'from the centre of the noble clique' (see G. Perl, *Philol.* 1965, 77 f.), he yet repealed Sulla's law disqualifying tribunes from higher offices when faced with starvation and discontent. (Another legal reform was abandoned.) He governed Cisalpine Gaul, but died before he could triumph. In *Cicero's *De natura deorum* he champions the Academic philosophy. (See ACADEMY.)

Malcovati, *ORF*[4] 286. E. B.

Aurelius (*RE* 102) **Cotta, Lucius,** brother of Gaius (above) and Marcus (below), as praetor 70 BC participated in the partial reversal of *Sulla's settlement by a law dividing criminal juries equally among senators, *equites*, and *tribuni aerarii*. In 66 he successfully prosecuted the consuls designate, P. *Autronius Paetus and P. *Cornelius Sulla, for *ambitus* and himself became consul 65, then censor 64. He supported Cicero against *Catiline and later in his exile, but remained neutral in the Civil War, though a relative of *Caesar. Just before Caesar's death he was expected to propose, as a *quindecimvir*, that Caesar should be called king outside Italy, in accordance with a reported command by the sacred books. After Caesar's death he withdrew from politics. E. B.

Aurelius (*RE* 107) **Cotta, Marcus,** brother of the two preceding, as consul 74 BC was sent to defend newly annexed *Bithynia against *Mithradates VI. Defeated by land and sea near *Chalcedon, he was rescued by L. *Licinius Lucullus (2). He remained in Bithynia and after a long siege sacked *Heraclea (3). At first enthusiastically welcomed in Rome and called 'Ponticus', he was later prosecuted, convicted, and disgraced.

Memnon, *FGrH* 434, chs. 27–39. J. Linderski, *AJAH* 1987 [1995] 148 ff. E. B.

Aurelius (*RE* 176) **Opillus** (late 2nd–early 1st cent. BC), a freedman who taught philosophy, rhetoric, and grammar, and accompanied P. *Rutilius Rufus into exile at Smyrna (Suet. *Gram.* 6).

He was cited by *Varro and *Verrius Flaccus as an authority, especially on Plautine diction; his (lost) works included a nine-book miscellany (*The Muses*) and a catalogue (*Pinax*) of the plays doubtfully attributed to *Plautus. See GRAMMAR, GRAMMARIANS, LATIN.

Funaioli, *Gramm. Rom. Frag.* 86–95 (cf. Mazzarino, *Gramm. Rom. Frag.* 385 f.). Herzog–Schmidt, § 193. R. A. K.

Aurelius (*RE* 221) **Severus Alexander, Marcus,** Roman emperor AD 222–35. Son of *Iulia Avita Mamaea by her second husband, the procurator Gessius Marcianus of Arca Caesarea in Syria, b. *c*. AD 209, his names were Gessius Alexianus Bassianus until his adoption in 221 by his cousin M. *Aurelius Antoninus (2) (Elagabalus), when he became M. Aurelius Alexander Caesar. Made emperor on Elagabalus' murder in March 222, he took the further name Severus and was called 'son of the deified Antoninus' (Caracalla). His mother, under whose influence he remained throughout his reign, set out to recreate a 'senatorial regime', with a council of sixteen. Elderly senators such as *Marius Maximus and *Cassius Dio were prominent. The jurist *Ulpianus became praetorian prefect but, at latest in early 224, was killed by the guard; Dio was obliged to hold his second consulship (229) outside Rome to avoid the same fate and expressed concern at growing military indiscipline at the end of his *History* (bk. 80). Alexander was married in late 225 to Cn. Seia Herennia Sallustia Orba Barbia Orbiana Augusta, whose father may even have been made Caesar; but she was banished two years later when her father attempted a coup. A major new threat resulted from the collapse of Parthia and the revival of Persia under the *Sasanids, *c*.224–5. In 231 Alexander launched a Persian expedition. The war, in which he took only a nominal part, ended in 233; although not a great success, it maintained Roman control over the province of Mesopotamia. Meanwhile the *Alamanni were threatening Upper Germany and Raetia. A further expedition was necessary. Alexander wintered in Germany in 234–5, but before the campaign could begin was murdered outside Mainz, with his mother, in an uprising led by the equestrian commander C. *Iulius Verus Maximinus (February or March 235). His memory was condemned (see DAMNATIO MEMORIAE), but he was deified in 238 after Maximinus' death.

Cass. Dio 79–80; Hdn. 5–6; SHA *Heliogab.* 13–17, *Sev. Alex.* (largely fiction); *RIC* 4. 2. R. Syme, *Emperors and Biography* (1971); E. Kettenhofen, *Die syrischen Augustae* (1979); D. Kienast, *Römische Kaisertabelle* (1990). A. R. Bi.

Aurelius Victor, Sextus, an African, governor of Pannonia Secunda, AD 361, and *praefectus urbi*, 389, published *De Caesaribus* ('On the Caesars'), probably after 360, from Augustus to Constantius II (360). Based on *Suetonius, this imperial history treated biographical material after a moralizing fashion, in the tradition of *Sallust and *Tacitus (1); the writer is pagan, interested in prodigies. The *Origo gentis Romanae* ('Origin of the Roman Race') and *De viris illustribus* ('On Distinguished Men', republican biography) associated with the *Caesars* in a three-part history are not by his hand.

TEXTS F. Pichlmayr (1911); P. Dufraigne (Budé, 1975); trans. and comm., H. Bird (1994). *Origo Gentis Romanae*: G. Puccioni, (1958); J.-C. Richard (Budé, 1983).
PLRE 1, 'Victor' 13. H. Bird, *Sextus Aurelius Victor: A Historiographical Study* (1984). A. H. McD.; A. J. S. S.

Aureolus benefited from *Gallienus' patronage of talented soldiers, becoming commander of the cavalry corps in Milan

(Mediolanum). He helped Gallienus overcome various rebels, though failed against *Postumus (AD 265). The first of Gallienus' generals to show dissatisfaction with his regime, he mutinied while the emperor was fighting the *Goths (268). He was besieged in Milan by Gallienus and, when the latter was assassinated, at first declared himself Augustus and then surrendered to *Claudius II. He was killed by the troops.

PLRE 1. 138. H. G. Simon, *Kölner historischer Abhandlungen* 1980, 435 ff.
J. F. Dr.

aurum coronarium Gold *crowns were offered to rulers and conquerors in the ancient near east and in the Hellenistic world. Similar offerings were made from the early 2nd cent. BC to Roman generals (e.g. Plut. *Aem.* 34. 5) and rapidly came to be exacted by them. A law of *Caesar (59 BC) enacted that it should not be demanded until a *triumph had been formally decreed. Under the empire, *aurum coronarium* went to the emperor alone and was exacted with increasing frequency, not only for triumphs (see *Res gestae* 21; Plin. *HN* 33. 54) but on imperial accessions, anniversaries, adoptions, and so forth, and then became an irregular form of taxation on communities.

Millar, *ERW* 140 ff.
F. G. B. M.

Aurunci, neighbours of the *Sidicini in the Latium–Campania border region. Servius (on *Aen.* 7. 727) identifies them with the Ausones (= *Oscans), who may once have occupied a large part of southern Italy (called Ausonia). About 313 BC Rome conquered the Aurunci, who lived mainly in dispersed farmsteads and hamlets.

P. Arthur, *Romans in Northern Campania* (1991), 24 f.
T. W. P.

A(u)sculum Satrianum, *Daunian city, 28 km. (17 mi.) SW of Foggia. It was an important city in the 4th–3rd cent. BC, but suffered after its revolt and consequent sack in 89 BC. Its territory was confiscated and allocated to Caesarian veterans. Traces of Gracchan and Caesarian *centuriation remain, and coinage and inscriptions attest Greek and *Oscan influence.
K. L.

Ausonian culture, the name introduced in 1956 by Bernabò Brea for the culture of the late bronze age in the *Aeoliae insulae, is closely related to the later *Apennine culture of the peninsula, with which the islands had previously traded. The archaeological evidence coincides with the legend (Diod. Sic. 5. 7) that Liparus, son of the king of the Ausonians (see AURUNCI) in central Italy, founded a city on the island named after him. 'Ausonian I' is virtually confined to the Lipari acropolis. 'Ausonian II' is represented by villages and cremation cemeteries at Lipari and Milazzo (Mylae in NE Sicily); the cemetery at Milazzo has much in common with Protovillanovan cemeteries on the mainland (see VILLANOVAN CULTURE).

L. Bernabò Brea, *Sicily before the Greeks*, 2nd edn. (1966); E. Gabba and G. Vallet (eds.), *La Sicilia antica* 1/1 (1980); R. Leighton, *Morgantina Studies* 4 (1993), 134 ff.
D. W. R. R.

Ausonius, Decimus Magnus, of Bordeaux (*Burdigala), statesman, teacher, and writer, enjoyed one of the more meteoric careers of the 4th cent. AD. The son of a humble doctor, he taught grammar and rhetoric for 30 years before being appointed tutor of the emperor's son and heir and summoned to Trier (Augusta Treverorum) in the mid-360s. When in 375 Valentinian I died and *Gratian duly succeeded, Ausonius enjoyed a remarkable political ascendancy, placing family and friends in positions of influence and gaining for himself a praetorian prefecture and the consulship of 379. Most of his retirement he spent cultivating

literary friendships in Aquitaine and writing poems which shed interesting light on his outlook and environment.

His rather obscure politics have always attracted less attention than his writings, which apart from a panegyric of Gratian and a few of his letters and dedications, are all in verse. His longest and most famous poem is the *Moselle*, a lively and colourful description relatively untouched by contemporary tendencies to flatter or plagiarize. Experiences in Trier supposedly also inspired *Cupido cruciatus* ('Cupid in Torment') based on a wall-painting, and the *Bissula*, both (for him) mildly erotic. The later *Ordo urbium nobilium* ('Catalogue of Famous Cities') shows in an extreme form his tendency to enumerate, as do his *Caesares* and *Fasti* (on the Roman consuls). Works such as the *Technopaegnion*, the *Ludus Septem Sapientum* ('Play of the *Seven Sages'), *Griphus ternarii numeri* ('Riddle of the Number Three'), and the so-called *Eclogues*, may derive from classroom practice. He compiled an ingenious and provocative Virgilian 'nuptial *cento', and his epigrams include translations from the Greek and a few Greek compositions of his own. More solemn are various poems about his close family, a commemoration of deceased relatives in the *Parentalia*, and the obituaries of local teachers in the *Professores*. The *Ephemeris* ('Daily Round') is a kind of self-portrait, but one more notable for its literary colour and metrical variety than any intimate personal detail; consul or not, Ausonius likes to put on the traditional guise of the easily contented man. The long and powerful Christian prayer embedded in this work is by no means the only evidence of a Christian allegiance, evidently combined with a lively interest in the traditional Graeco-Roman deities.

Ausonius often asks to be read in a jovial spirit and small doses. Together with great wit and originality, he shows a strong local patriotism and an appreciation of his classical heritage unsurpassed in late antiquity.

Ed. and comm., R. P. H. Green, *The Works of Ausonius* (1991); Eng. trans., H. G. Evelyn White (Loeb, 1919–21).

PLRE 1. 140 f. H. Sivan, *Ausonius of Bordeaux* (1993); M. K. Hopkins, *CQ* 1961, 239–49; R. P. H. Green, *CQ* 1985, 491–506.
R. P. H. G.

auspicium, literally 'watching the birds' (*avis*, *specio*), but the term was applied to various types of *divination. Festus (Paulus, *Gloss. Lat.* 367) records five types of auspical signs: from the sky (*ex caelo*, mostly thunder and lightning), from birds (*ex avibus*; observed were the number, position, flight, cries, and feeding of birds), from sacred chickens, the *pulli* (*ex tripudiis*; they were kept hungry in a cage; if food dropped from their beaks when they were eating, this was an excellent sign, *auspicium sollistimum*), from quadrupeds (*ex quadrupedibus*, e.g. a wolf eating grass), and from unusual, threatening occurrences (*ex diris*). They were either casually met with (*oblativa*) or specially watched for (*impetrativa*). The first two categories could be both oblative and impetrative, the third only impetrative, the fourth and fifth only oblative. Through the auspices the gods did not foretell the future but only expressed their approval or disapproval of an action either contemplated or in progress (the latter only through the *oblativa*). They were valid for one day only, and thus pertained solely to the time of an action, not to its substance. If denied, the approval for the same undertaking could be sought again on the next day. Here resides the technical difference (often disregarded in colloquial speech) between auspices and auguries: the latter were the auspices that pertained not only to timing but also to substance. At inaugurations of priests and temples the deity gave approval not only for the day of the ceremony but also for the person or the place (*locus*) to be inaugurated. The *auguria* had no time limit, and to remove their effects a special ceremony of *exauguratio* was necessary. The auguries could be conducted only by the augurs (see AUGURES); any person could use the auspices, hence the division into private and public auspices. The former largely fell into desuetude, though remaining in use for weddings (Cic. *Div.* 1. 28); the *auspicia publica* were administered by the magistrates. All public acts were conducted *auspicato*, after a consultation of impetrative auspices, e.g. elections, census, military operations (cf. the phrase *ductu auspicio imperio*). The auspices of the magistrates were divided into *minora*, 'lesser' (of the lesser magistrates) and *maiora*, 'greater' (of consuls, praetors, and censors, Gell. *NA* 13. 15. 4).

P. Catalano, *Contributi allo studio del diritto augurale* (1960); J. Linderski, *ANRW* 2. 16. 3 (1986), 2146 ff.　　　　　　　　　　　　　J. L.

autobiography See BIOGRAPHY, GREEK and BIOGRAPHY, ROMAN.

autochthons (αὐτόχθονες), in myth, are figures born literally from the earth, with no human parents. While the idea of 'mother' Earth is influential here, autochthony is not normally presented as the origin of humanity in general (the story of *Deucalion and Pyrrha comes closest to this) but rather serves to make a statement about a particular group of people. True autochthons (as opposed to the merely earthborn, γηγενεῖς) remain in the land where they were born. Thus the autochthonous ancestor, like the founder-figure, expresses and forms the group's sense of its identity, making an implicit claim to superiority over non-autochthonous groups. The *Spartoi, the autochthonous 'sown men' of *Thebes (1), may at one time have represented a special class in the city, while the autochthon *Erichthonius expressed the claim of all Athenians to be the true original inhabitants of *Attica. There were probably very many local claims to autochthonous ancestors across the Greek world (Paus. 2. 12. 4 is a typical example). See also PROPAGANDA.

A. Brelich, *Gli eroi greci* (1958), 138; N. Loraux, *The Children of Athena* (1993; Fr. orig. 1981), 37–71; J. Peradotto, *Arethusa* 1977, 92–101; V. Rosivach, *CQ* 1987, 294 ff.; F. Vian, *Les Origines de Thèbes* (1963), 158–76, 216–25, 234–6.　　　　　　　　　　　　　E. Ke.

Autocrates, Athenian comic poet, ἀρχαῖος ('Old'; see COMEDY (GREEK), OLD), according to the *Suda*, which adds 'he wrote also many tragedies'. Τυμπανισταί (or Τυμπανίστριαι, Hsch.) is the only title we have.

Kassel–Austin, *PCG* 4. 18 f. (*CAF* 1. 806).　　　　　　　K. J. D.

Autolycus (1), in mythology, maternal grandfather of *Odysseus. He 'surpassed all men in thievery and (ambiguous) swearing', by favour of *Hermes (whose son he is in later accounts), *Od.* 19. 394 ff.; one of his thefts, *Il.* 10. 267; later stories in von Sybel in Roscher's *Lexikon*, entry under the name.

LIMC 3/1 (1986), 55–6.　　　　　　　　　　　　　H. J. R.

Autolycus (2) (*RE* 9), of Pitane, astronomer (fl. late 4th cent. BC), author of two works on elementary spherical astronomy, among the earliest Greek mathematical treatises that have come down to us entire: (1) *On the Moving Sphere* (Περὶ κινουμένης σφαίρας) treats of the poles and principal circles of the sphere. Many of its propositions are also used in the *Phaenomena* of *Euclid, but the priority cannot be determined. (2) *On Risings and Settings* (Περὶ ἀνατολῶν καὶ δύσεων), dealing with risings, settings, and visibility periods of stars, is in two books, which are in fact different versions of the same work. In a lost work (Simpl. in *Cael.* 504 f.) Autolycus criticized the system of concentric spheres of *Eudoxus (1) on the ground that it did not account

for the differences in the apparent sizes of some heavenly bodies at different times, and attempted to remedy this.

EDITION critical text by J. Mogenet (1950). See 22 ff. of this for history of the text and editions, and 5 ff. for Autolycus' life and works. See also Pappus 6. 33 ff.

TRANSLATIONS English (poor) by F. Bruin and A. Vondjidis (1971); German by A. Czwalina, Ostwalds Klassiker no. 232 (1931).

COMMENT *HAMA* 2. 748–67.　　　　　　　　　　　G. J. T.

Automedon, in mythology, *Achilles' charioteer, son of Diores (*Il.* 17. 429 and often); hence by metonymy, any charioteer, as Juvenal 1. 61.

autonomy (Gk. αὐτονομία). In internal affairs it means the state of affairs where a community is responsible for its own laws; in this sense it is opposed to *tyranny (Hdt. 1. 96. 1) and means self-determination, whereas *freedom (*eleutheria*) means absence of external constraint. But *autonomia* is also regularly used in the context of interstate relations, where it indicates a limited independence permitted by a stronger power to a weaker; that is, external constraints are relevant to *autonomia* too. The term first occurs (in the adjectival form 'autonomous', αὐτόνομος, and in a personal and metaphorical sense) at Soph. *Ant.* 821, a play usually but not certainly dated 443 BC.; and it is a plausible hypothesis that 'autonomy' was first used in interstate contexts in the *Delian League. It may have been generally guaranteed in the *Thirty Years Peace of 446. Certainly *Aegina's complaint about infringed autonomy was an issue at the beginning of the *Peloponnesian War. In the 4th cent. autonomy formed part of Sparta's *propaganda in Asia Minor (390s) and it was (together with freedom) promised to all Greek states by the *King's Peace and the *Second Athenian Confederacy. In the Hellenistic period 'freedom and autonomy' continue to be coupled (e.g. Tod 185; Welles, *RC* 1 = letter of *Antigonus (1) the One-eyed to Scepsis; Polyb. 21. 19. 9) and the autonomy of the Greek cities was frequently underwritten by the kings. In this period and the Roman, the word certainly did not mean complete independence or 'autonomy' in our sense, but nor had it done under 5th-cent. Athens. See FREE CITIES.

E. J. Bickerman, *RIDA* 1958, 13 f.; M. Ostwald, *Autonomia: Its Genesis and Early History* (1982), with H. D. Westlake, *CR* 1984, 85 f.; E. Levy, *Revue philosophique de la France et de l'étranger*, 1983, 249–70; K. Raaflaub, *Die Entdeckung der Freiheit* (1985), 193–207; A. B. Bosworth, *Stud. Ital.* 1992, 122–52; E. Badian, *From Plataea to Potidaea* (1993), ch. 4; D. Whitehead, in R. Rosen and J. Farrell (eds.), *Nomodeiktes* (1994), 321 ff.; M. Hansen, in Hansen and K. Raaflaub (eds.) *Studies in the Ancient Greek Polis* (1995), 21 ff.　　　　　　　　　　　S. H.

Autronius (*RE* 7) **Paetus, Publius,** quaestor (with *Cicero) 75 BC, legate in Greece 73, was elected consul with P. *Cornelius Sulla for 65, but both were convicted of *ambitus and lost the consulship to their competitors. Involved in the 'First Catilinarian Conspiracy' and in that of 63 (see SERGIUS CATILINA, L.), he is said to have plotted *Cicero's death, was convicted of *vis in 62 and went into exile in Epirus.　　　　　　　　　　　　E. B.

auxilia In the 1st cent. BC Rome often employed men recruited outside Italy as cavalry and light infantry, or in specialist roles, and during the Civil Wars Gallic and German cavalry and the forces of local kings, especially in Asia Minor and Syria, were important. Some of these were temporary formations serving under their own leaders near their homeland in accordance with their treaty obligations to Rome, and this practice continued, e.g. the Batavians (see BATAVI) serving under C. *Iulius Civilis.

But *Augustus formally incorporated many ethnic auxiliary units into the army; they comprised non-citizens from the less developed provinces, and often took their title from a district or tribe (*Britannorum*, 'of British'), or a city (*Antiochensium*, 'of the people of Antioch'), or from their armament (*Sagittariorum*, 'of archers'), sometimes with the addition of an imperial name (e.g. *Flavia*). Subsequently men were recruited to supplement existing units, firstly from areas with plentiful manpower, especially Belgica (see GAUL (TRANSALPINE)), *Pannonia, and *Thrace, and then locally from areas close to the camps of the *auxilia* units, or from adjacent provinces. Consequently, the ethnic character of the *auxilia* was gradually diluted, except in the case of a few units with specialist functions, like Syrian archers. There was a small number of citizen auxiliary regiments, whose origin is obscure. In the 1st cent. AD, although many *auxilia* were volunteers, most were probably conscripted.

Despite the extensive evidence of *diplomata* (see DIPLOMA), it is difficult to calculate the total number of *auxilia*; when fresh units were raised from a particular district they were numbered anew, not consecutively after their predecessors. By the Flavian period they probably numbered about 180,000, rising to over 220,000 in the mid-2nd cent. The *auxilia* consisted of infantry cohorts and cavalry wings (*alae*) of about 480–500 men, and part-mounted cohorts (*cohortes equitatae*) containing 120 cavalry and 480 infantry (see ALAE; COHORS). Probably in the Flavian era larger regiments (milliary) were created containing between 800 and 1,000 men. Regular auxiliary regiments were commanded by Roman officers of equestrian rank, either tribunes or prefects, and the most senior was the prefect of an *ala*; subordinate officers were centurions and decurions, commanding centuries and troops (*turmae*) respectively.

Auxiliary infantrymen were probably paid at five-sixths the rate of a legionary, receiving 750 sesterces a year under Augustus, with proportionally higher rates for cavalrymen (see STIPENDIUM). Service-time was eventually established at 25 years, and by the early 2nd cent. all *auxilia* were receiving citizenship on discharge for themselves and their children. It is not clear if the *praemia* (cash or land allocations) enjoyed by legionary *veterans were eventually extended to the *auxilia*.

Gradually more citizens began to enlist in auxiliary units and the distinction between auxiliaries and legionaries became blurred as the former took an increasingly important part in fighting and in maintaining provincial garrisons. By the time of *Constantine I new infantry formations in the field army were designated as *auxilia*, and also some units in the frontier districts, while in certain areas *alae* and cohorts served as part of the frontier troops.

G. L. Cheesman, *The Auxilia of the Roman Imperial Army* (1914); K. Kraft, *Alen und Kohorten an Rhein und Donau* (1951); E. B. Birley, *Corolla Memoriae Erich Swoboda Dedicata* (1966), 54; D. B. Saddington, *ANRW* 2. 3 (1975), 176; *The Development of the Roman Auxiliary Forces from Caesar to Vespasian* (1982); P. A. Holder, *Studies in the Auxilia of the Roman Army from Augustus to Trajan* (1980); Y. Le Bohec, *Les Unités auxiliaires de l'armée romaine en Afrique Proconsulaire et Numidie* (1989); K. Dixon and P. Southern, *The Roman Cavalry* (1992); M. A. Speidel, *JRS* 1992, 87. J. B. C.

Auximum (mod. Osimo) with well-preserved ancient walls, hill-town of *Picenum, 17 km. (10½ mi.) from the Adriatic. Becoming a Roman colony (128 BC?), it developed into a flourishing place, which supported *Caesar against *Pompey. Much later it and four other cities constituted the Pentapolis under the *Ravenna Exarchate.

E. T. Salmon, *Roman Colonisation under the Republic* (1970), 122 ff.
E. T. S.; T. W. P.

Avaro-Slav invasions Slavs and Avars were the Roman empire's main enemies on the Danube frontier in the late 6th and early 7th cents. AD. The Slavs arrived first, agriculturalists with rudimentary social organization who gradually filtered south from Poland in family or village groups. They reached the Danube *c*.500 and, often in conjunction with Bulgar groups, began to ravage the empire. Their pressure was particularly difficult to handle, because they lacked recognized leaders whom Roman diplomacy could target, adapted to the forests or swamps on the margins of civilized life, and quickly acquired military skills from their neighbours.

The Avars, nomadic warriors whose hegemony in central Asia was overturned by the Turks, first contacted Justinian in 558. They rapidly dominated the area north of the Black Sea and Danube and by 570 controlled *Pannonia; under their leader the Chagan, a ruthless fighter and unscrupulous diplomat, they established a powerful federation whose military technology and organization were imitated by their Roman opponents. During Maurice's reign (582–602) Avars and Slavs jointly and independently ravaged much of the Balkans, capturing or isolating most inland cities, reaching the Peloponnese, and even subjecting *Constantinople to a fierce siege in 626.

M. Whitby, *The Emperor Maurice* (1988). L. M. W.

Aventicum, *civitas*-capital of the *Helvetii, modern Avenches, destroyed by the *Alamanni in the 3rd cent. AD. Vespasian established a colony of *veterans here (*Colonia Pia Flavia Constans Emerita Helvetiorum Foederata*); the relationship of *coloni* and *incolae* is disputed. Much survives, including defences (of the Flavian colony), east gate, theatre, forum, amphitheatre, baths, and private houses.

F. Stähelin, *Die Schweiz in römischer Zeit*, 3rd edn. (1948); D. van Berchem, *Les Routes et l'histoire* (1982); H. Bögli, *Aventicum* (1984).
J. F. Dr.

Aventine, the southernmost hill of Rome, overlooking the Tiber and separated from the other hills by the Murcia valley, had legendary associations with *Remus. Temples here included those dedicated to *Diana, patroness of a Latin League, and to Juno Regina following her *evocatio* from *Veii (392 BC). Until AD 49 the hill was outside the *pomerium, which may explain why 'foreign' deities were established here. The temple of *Ceres, Liber (see LIBER PATER), and Libera (493 BC) was headquarters of the plebeian aediles; the hill itself was *ager publicus* given to the *plebs* for settlement in 456 BC, and it remained a cosmopolitan centre of popular politics under the late republic. C. *Sempronius Gracchus was besieged here in 121 BC. Under the empire, however, it became principally a centre of élite housing. To the south-west lay the Emporion and *Monte Testaccio, a hill 36 m. (120 ft.) high composed of discarded fragments of oil-amphorae.

Coarelli, *Roma* 338–52; Richardson, *Topog. Dict. Ancient Rome* 47; M. Andreussi, in Steinby, *Lexicon* 147–50. I. A. R.; J. R. P.

Avernus, a deep volcanic crater, now a lake, near *Puteoli. Its appearance inspired the belief that it led to the Underworld (Strabo 5. 244, etc.). *Hannibal made a sacrifice there, and M. *Vipsanius Agrippa built a *canal linking it with a new port, which soon silted up. Associated monuments include the so-called Sibylline cave and 'temple of *Apollo' (a bath-building).

M. Pagano and others, *MÉFRA* 1982, 271 ff; P. Amalfitano (ed.), *I Campi Flegrei* (1990), 170 ff. T. W. P.

Avianus or Avienus

Avianus or **Avienus** (the MSS give both forms), Roman fabulist (fl. *c*. AD 400). He dedicated his 42 fables in elegiacs to one Theodosius, who is generally agreed to be *Macrobius (Macrobius Ambrosius Theodosius); it is possible (though not more) that he is the Avienus who appears in the latter's *Saturnalia* (who is certainly not the geographical writer *Avienus). His chief source is the Greek fabulist *Babrius, though whether he used Babrius direct or via the Latin prose paraphrase of the 3rd-cent. rhetorician *Iulius Titianus or some other intermediary is debated. He made little use of *Phaedrus (4). As a poet Avianus leaves much to be desired. He is imprecise in expression, and lacks the dramatic instinct of the good story-teller. His language and syntax display features characteristic of late antique Latin, which sit uncomfortably with the many echoes of Virgil, themselves often inappropriately deployed. The metre is broadly Ovidian (see OVID), though there are examples of non-classical prosody. Paraphrases, scholia, and quotations show that Avianus was popular in medieval schools, and at least some of the *promythia* and *epimythia* which introduce or follow particular fables in order to point a moral may have originated in the medieval period. See FABLE.

TEXTS A. Guaglianone (1958); F. Gaide (1980); with comm., R. Ellis (1887); with trans., Duff, *Minor Lat. Poets*.
STUDIES A. Cameron, *CQ* 1967, 385–99; J. Küppers, *Die Fabeln Avians* (1977); S. Döpp, *Hermes* 1979, 619–32 (against Cameron).
J. H. D. S.

Avidius Cassius, Gaius, son of C. Avidius Heliodorus, *ab epistulis* of *Hadrian, of Cyrrhus in Syria, was born in Egypt presumably AD 130 while his father was there with Hadrian; like many sons of successful equestrians he entered the senate and as legionary legate contributed greatly to Roman victories in L. *Verus' Parthian War (162–6), capturing Ctesiphon and sacking Seleuceia on Tigris. His prowess was praised by *Fronto (*Ad amicos* 1. 6), whom he provided with memoranda on the war (*Ad Verum* 2. 3) for a projected History. He became consul at the end of the war (166) and at once governor of Syria, with enhanced responsibility for the entire east at latest in 172, when he crushed the revolt of the Bucoli in Egypt. In spring 175, on a false report of M. *Aurelius' death on the Danube, he was proclaimed emperor and controlled much of the east, including Egypt, for some three months. But his colleague P. *Martius Verus in Cappadocia remained loyal to Marcus and Cassius was murdered by a centurion. His family and supporters were pardoned, although some were later killed by Commodus.

SHA *M. Ant.*; *Avidius Cassius* (largely fiction); Cass. Dio 71; *SB* 10295, identified as a letter of his by A. K. Bowman, *JRS* 1970; M. L. Astarita, *Avidio Cassio* (1983); A. R. Birley, *Marcus Aurelius*, 2nd edn. (1987), 184 ff.; Syme, *RP* 5. 689 ff.
A. R. Bi.

Avidius Nigrinus, Gaius, nephew of *Avidius Quietus, was suffect consul AD 110 and shortly afterwards imperial legate of *Achaia, replacing the normal proconsul, going on to be legate of the recently conquered Dacia. Perhaps still there at *Trajan's death in 117, he was replaced and in 118 put to death at Faventia, his home, for alleged conspiracy against *Hadrian, who had supposedly intended him as his successor (SHA *Hadr.* 7. 1). His stepson and son-in-law L. Ceionius Commodus was adopted as heir by Hadrian in 136 (as L. *Aelius Caesar), perhaps the result of remorse.

*PIR*² A 1408; Syme, *RP* 1. 325 ff.
A. R. Bi.

Avidius Quietus, Titus, from Faventia, legate of Legio VIII Augusta, proconsul of *Achaia, and suffect consul AD 93, a Stoic and disciple of P. *Clodius Thrasea Paetus; he supported *Pliny (2) in the senate in 97 and shortly afterwards became governor of Britain (*CIL* 16. 43); he and his brother *Avidius Nigrinus were friends of *Plutarch.
A. R. Bi.

Avienus or **Avienius** (the latter form is found in an inscription, but there are good arguments against accepting it as correct), **Postumius Rufius Festus,** Latin poet (fl. mid-4th *c*. AD). A member of a senatorial family from Volsinii in Etruria, and himself proconsul of Africa and Achaia, Avienus wrote three *didactic poems which survive in whole or part: (1) *Descriptio orbis terrae*, an adaptation in hexameters of the Greek geographical poem of *Dionysius (9) 'Periegetes', with omissions, additions, and amplifications, and describing noteworthy things in physical and political geography while reproducing much ancient ignorance which learned contemporaries could have corrected; (2) *Ora maritima*, a description in iambics of the Atlantic, Mediterranean, and Black Sea coasts, written after the *Descriptio*, to which it refers. The surviving part deals mainly with the coast between Marseilles (Massilia) and Cadiz (Gades); though poorly organized, this preserves important early material for our knowledge of ancient geography and seafaring, perhaps collected in a Greek text which was Avienus' immediate source; (3) *Aratea phaenomena*, sometimes divided into *Phaenomena* and *Prognostica*, an astronomical poem in hexameters based on the Greek original of Aratus (1), on which Avienus expands. Also extant is a short occasional poem addressed to one Flavianus Myrmeicus; a lost iambic version of *Vergilii fabulas* ('Tales from Virgil') is recorded by Servius (on *Aen.* 10. 272). Avienus' interest in antiquities is typical of his class and time. He writes in a classical manner, but his verse is short on inspiration.

TEXTS A. Holder (1887); *Descriptio orbis terrae*: P. van de Woestijne (1961); *Ora maritima*: A. Berthelot (1934), A. Schulten, 2nd edn. (1955), D. Stichtenoth (1968; Ger. trans.), all with notes or comm. *Aratea Phaenomena*: J. Soubiran (1981), with Fr. trans. and substantial notes.
STUDIES A. Cameron, *CQ* 1967, 385–99; J. Matthews, *Hist.* 1967, 484–509; J. Küppers, *Die Fabeln Avians* (1977), 20–5. *PLRE* 1. 336 f.
J. H. D. S.

Avillius Flaccus, Aulus, schoolfellow of C. *Iulius Caesar (2) and L. *Iulius Caesar (4) and a friend of Tiberius and *Macro. In AD 29 he prosecuted *Vipsania Agrippina (2). As prefect of Egypt (32–8) he was friendly to the Greek elements there, and so anti-Jewish. *Philon (4) attacked him in his *Against Flaccus*. In 38 he was unexpectedly arrested, condemned at Rome, perhaps on a charge of plotting with Ti. *Iulius Caesar Nero Gemellus and Macro, banished to *Andros, and later put to death on *Gaius (1)'s instructions.

*PIR*² A 1414. Philon, *In Flaccum*, ed. H. Box (1939); Schürer, *History* 1. 389 ff.; 3. 859 ff.
A. M.; T. J. C.

Avitus, Eparchius, Roman emperor (AD 455–6). He enlisted Visigothic support against *Attila (451) then, following the Vandal sack of Rome (455), was proclaimed emperor in Gaul by the *Visigoths and the Gallic aristocracy, Arrived in Italy, he was not recognized by the east, fell foul of *Ricimer and, lacking Visigothic military support, was murdered.

His career reflects the willingness of Gallic nobles to participate in imperial careers and politics at a time when their country was becoming increasingly marginalized, and the emergence of the Visigoths as a great power in the region.

PLRE 2. 5. C. E. Stevens, *Sidonius Apollinaris* (1933).   J. F. Dr.

Axionicus, Middle Comedy poet (see COMEDY (GREEK), MIDDLE), perhaps late in the period (fr. 2 mentions Gryllis, a *parasite of one of *Alexander (3) the Great's generals). Fr. 4 parodies a Euripidean lyric (cf. U. v. Wilamowitz–Moellendorff, *Griechische Verskunst* (1921) 410 n. 1).

FRAGMENTS Kassel–Austin, *PCG* 4. 20–7.
INTERPRETATION Meineke, *FCG* 1. 417 f.; G. Kaibel, *RE* 2/2 (1896), 2628.   W. G. A.

axones ('axles'). At Athens the laws of *Draco and of *Solon were inscribed on numbered *axones*; the term *kyrbeis* (of unknown origin), used of Solon's laws, is thought by some to refer to a different set of objects, but is more probably an alternative name for the same objects. They were probably three- or four-sided wooden pillars, mounted on a vertical axis so that readers could turn them. Probably they could still be read and studied in the 4th cent.; in the time of *Plutarch small fragments survived.

Ath. pol. 7. 1; Plut. *Sol.* 25. E. Ruschenbusch, Σόλωνος νόμοι, *Hist. Einzelschr.* 9 (1966); R. S. Stroud, *The Axones and Kyrbeis of Drakon and Solon*, U. Calif. Pub. Cl. Stud. 19 (1979).   V. E.; P. J. R.

Axumis (mod. Aksum), from the 1st to the 7th cent. AD the eponymous capital of a kingdom of northern *Ethiopia which covered the modern provinces of Tigre and Eritrea. Through their port *Adulis, the Aksumites traded busily with Arabians, Greeks, Romans, and Indians. Aksum was the earliest tropical African state to adopt coinage. By the 2nd cent. their power extended to Somalia and parts of southern *Arabia, and they controlled much of the traffic to *India from that time until far in the Byzantine era. Aksumite military activities in the west probably contributed to the collapse of *Meroe. Fragments of their history are known from inscriptions and classical references. The summit of Aksumite influence was in the 4th and 5th cents. Converted to Christianity in the 4th cent., the city of Aksum remains one of the most important centres for the Ethiopian Church.

Y. M. Kobishanov, *Axum* (1979).   R. G. M.

Babatha, the owner of an archive of personal documents found in the Judaean desert. Babatha was a Jewish woman who lived in the province of *Arabia in the first half of the 2nd cent. AD. Her documents, composed in Nabataean, *Aramaic, Hebrew, and Greek, were discovered hidden in a leather pouch in a cave near the Dead Sea. The date of the documents ranges from AD 96 to 134. It is probable that Babatha died in the cave after taking refuge there during the *Bar Kokhba Revolt (132–5). The documents include marriage contracts, property transfers, and papers concerning a protracted lawsuit over the custody of Babatha's son by her first marriage. They are a precious source of evidence for the history of the region in the last years of the *Nabataean kingdom and the early years of the *provincia* Arabia, and for the cultural and legal history of *Jews in this period.

Y. Yadin, *IEJ* 1962, 231–6, and in N. Lewis (ed.), *Documents from the Bar Kokhba Period in the Cave of Letters: Greek Papyri* (1989); F. Millar, *The Roman Near East* (1993), see index.   M. D. G.

Babrius, Valerius (?), probably from Syria or Asia Minor, composed not later than the 2nd cent. AD (*POxy.* 1249) Μυθίαμβοι Αἰσώπειοι, 'Fables of *Aesop in Iambics', being versions in choliambic metre of existing *fables, together perhaps with some additions or adaptations of his own. The work is more likely to have been originally in two books (*Avianus, proem) than in ten (*Suda*); 144 fables survive. The choliamb seems by this period to have lost its satirical overtones and to have been associated with chatty entertainment. Babrius' language is basically *koinē Greek, but has an admixture of high poeticisms. The literary and artistic claims made in his two extant proems are such as to suggest that, despite the apparent artlessness of his style, he wrote for the delectation of an educated public rather than for the schoolroom. His collection enjoyed great popularity, and was paraphrased in prose and verse in the Middle Ages.

TEXTS O. Crusius (Teubner, 1897); M. J. Luzzatto and A. La Penna (Teubner, 1986); B. E. Perry (Loeb, 1965); W. G. Rutherford, comm. (1883).

CRITICISM O. Crusius, *Leipz. Stud.* 1879; B. E. Perry, *TAPA* 1962, 287–346 (sources); M. J. Luzzatto, *ASNP* 1985, 17–97 (vocab.).   N. H.

Babylon The ruins of the city extend over several mounds in the vicinity of modern Hillah (*c*.80 km. (50 mi.) south of Baghdad); the most important are Babil, Kasr, Merkes, Homera. Babylon is attested as a settlement from the third millennium BC to the early Islamic period. It became politically important under Hammurabi (1792–1750 BC); but its time of greatest splendour was as capital of the Neo-Babylonian empire (605–539 BC). Most of its famous buildings date from this period. Babylon was an important centre for the *Achaemenid and *Seleucid rulers, who supported its cults (in which they sometimes participated

personally) and continued to use and maintain its palace. Contrary to later classical writers (e.g. App. *Syr.* 58; Plin. *HN* 6. 122), Babylon did not decline following the foundation of *Seleuceia (1) on Tigris.

R. Koldewey excavated the site 1899 to 1917; an Iraqi team explored further in the 1970s and 1980s. The city area inside the double fortifications (described by Hdt. 1. 178 ff.) was *c*.400 ha. (990 acres). Eight gates pierced the walls; the summer palace (Babil) and New Year Festival temple lay outside them to the north. The ancient course of the *Euphrates, crossed by a stone-built bridge, divided the city in half; the citadel with palace (Kasr) lay on the east bank on the northern edge of the city. Next to the palace lay the Ishtar gate, decorated with brilliantly coloured glazed-brick reliefs; from here southwards ran the similarly decorated processional way to the ziggurat (the temple-tower of Etemenanki) and central sanctuary of Bel-Marduk (Esagila). East of Etemenanki, lay the dwelling quarters, Merkes and Homera; a Greek theatre in Homera, built *c*.300 BC, may have been the focus of the small Greek community, probably installed in the early 3rd cent. In the Parthian period, Babylon still had a city-governor and a *gymnasium. Most of the thousands of *cuneiform texts from Babylon have come from illicit excavations.

EXCAVATION R. Koldewey, *Das wiedererstehende Babylon* (1912; 5th edn. by B. Hrouda, 1990); *Iraq* 1983, 207.

ANCIENT DESCRIPTIONS E. Unger, *Babylon, die heilige Stadt* (1931; 2nd edn. by R. Borger, 1970); A. George, *Babylonian Topographical Texts* (1992); and *Antiquity* 1993, 734–46; R. Rollinger, *Herodots Babylonischer Logos* (1993).

ACHAEMENID PERIOD E. Haerinck, *IrAnt* 1973), 108–32; A. Kuhrt and S. Sherwin-White, in H. Sancisi-Weerdenburg and A. Kuhrt (eds.), *Achaemenid History* 2 (1987), 69–78

HELLENISTIC PERIOD E. Schmidt, *AA* 1941, 786–844; F. Wetzel and others, *Das Babylon der Spätzeit* (1957); G. J. P. McEwan, *Priest and Temple in Hellenistic Babylonia* (1981); S. Sherwin-White *ZPE* 47 (1982), 51–70; J. Oelsner, *Materialien zur babylonischen Gesellschaft und Kultur in hellenistischer Zeit* (1986), 112–26; A. Kuhrt and S. Sherwin-White, *JHS* 1991, 71–86, and *From Samarkhand to Sardis* (1993); A. Kuhrt and S. Sherwin-White (eds.), *Hellenism in the East* (1987), chs. 1–3.   A. T. L. K.

Babylonia, country in south Iraq, stretching from modern Baghdad to the Arab-Persian Gulf, drained by the *Euphrates and *Tigris rivers. Settlement (dependent on irrigation) is first attested in the sixth millennium BC. The population was mixed; non-Semitic *Sumerian dominates the literary record in the third millennium, gradually replaced by Semitic *Akkadian in the second millennium, which in turn was displaced by *Aramaic in the later first millennium.

Babylonia's political pattern until the 15th cent. BC was one of contending city-states, some of which succeeded in imposing control on their rivals (e.g. Agade: 2340–2200; Third Dynasty of Ur: 2100–2000; Babylon: 1760–1595). From then on, Babylonia formed a territorial state with *Babylon as its capital. Babylonia was subject to *Assyria from the late 8th cent. until the Babylonian general, Nabopolassar, fought back the Assyrians and, with Median help, destroyed Assyria's empire (626–609). Nabopolassar founded the Neo-Babylonian empire, stretching from Palestine to the Iranian frontier, ruled from Babylon. The most famous Neo-Babylonian king was his son, Nebuchadnezzar II (604–562), who rebuilt Babylonia's cities extensively and sacked Jerusalem (587). The last Neo-Babylonian ruler, Nabonidus (555–539), was defeated in battle at Opis by *Cyrus (1) the Great of Persia (559–530), who turned Babylonia's imperial territory into a single satrapy of the Achaemenid empire (see PERSIA). It was divided early in *Xerxes I's reign (486–465) into two provinces: the satrapy of Babylonia stretched from the Persian Gulf to Assyria and north-west to the east bank of the Euphrates. *Alexander (3) the Great conquered Babylonia in 331, detaching its northern region (*Mesopotamia); he planned to turn Babylonia into one of his chief bases. *Seleucus (1) I and *Antigonus (1) I disputed, and fought for, control of Babylonia (316–309) and it became a core-region of the Seleucid empire. After lengthy struggles (141–127), Babylonia came under Parthian control in 126, and henceforward formed part of the empires of the *Arsacids, then the *Sasanids. Babylonia's strategic location on north–south and east–west routes and its legendary fertility (Hdt. 1. 193; Strabo 16. 1. 14) meant that it continued to play an important role in the Persian, Seleucid, Parthian, and Sasanian periods. Important royal centres were founded by Seleucus I at *Seleuceia (1) on Tigris and by the Parthians at *Ctesiphon.

Babylonian learning, writing, cultic, and literary traditions proved tenacious, and survived alongside the increased use of new languages (such as Aramaic, Persian, and Greek). The latest *cuneiform text dates to AD 78. Classical writers frequently confused Babylonia with Assyria, to which *Berosus objected with little effect. Babylonia was perceived by Greeks and Romans as the source of astronomical and astrological lore. They associated this activity with 'Chaldaeans'—the name of a number of tribal groups in Babylonia. There is no evidence that Babylonians ever linked any particular learning with these tribes. *Astronomy and *mathematics were an important and highly developed part of Babylonian scholarship; most of the latest preserved cuneiform texts are of this scientific nature. To what degree Babylonian astronomy and mathematics influenced Greek science is debated. See ASTROLOGY; ASTRONOMY §5; MATHEMATICS.

SOURCES A. K. Grayson, *Assyrian and Babylonian Chronicles* (1975); Sachs–Hunger, 1–2 (1988–9).

HISTORY General: J. Oates, *Babylon* (1978; 2nd edn. 1986). Archaeology: R. McC. Adams, *Heartland of Cities* (1981). Assyrian, Neo-Babylonian, Achaemenid: *CAH*² 3, chs. 7, 21, 25, 27, 28a; 4 (1988), ch. 3a; 6, ch. 11; H. Sancisi-Weerdenburg (ed.), *Achaemenid History* 1 (1987), 139–81; H. Sancisi-Weerdenburg and A. Kuhrt (eds.), *Achaemenid History* 4 (1990), 177–205. Hellenistic: J. Oelsner, *Materialien zur babylonischen Gesellschaft und Kultur in hellenistischer Zeit* (1986); A. Kuhrt and S. Sherwin-White (eds.), *Hellenism in the East* (1987), chs. 1–4; and *From Samarkhand to Sardis* (1993). In Classical writers: A. Kuhrt, in H. Nissen and J. Renger (eds.), *Mesopotamien und seine Nachbarn* (1982), 539–53.

BABYLONIAN LITERATURE AND LEARNING O. Neugebauer, *The Exact Sciences in Antiquity* (1952; 2nd edn. 1957); *CAH*² 3, chs. 28b, 28c; *Reallexikon der Assyriologie* (1928–   ), 7. 531–85, 'Mathematik'; H. Galter, (ed.), *Die Rolle der Astronomie in den Kulturen Mesopotamiens* (1993).
A. T. L. K.

Bacaudae (or **Bagaudae), a name of Celtic origin, possibly

meaning 'the warriors', first applied to the followers of Aelius and Amandus, suppressed in Gaul by *Maximianus in AD 285, and later given to those involved in more varied extra-legal activities (from banditry to regional rejection of imperial authority) in northern Gaul and NE Spain in the first half of the 5th cent. AD. The sources are very fragmentary and difficult; the most detailed, on the later period, is *Salvianus' *On the Government of God* (5. 21–7), but even this has to be treated with great care. There is little doubt that the Bacaudae appeared at times of severe military, political and social disruption, but the wide differences in modern interpretations of the phenomenon (e.g. class-warfare between peasants and landlords, efforts at self-help by local aristocrats, hostile reaction to the imposition of state authority) suggest that it has no single explanation. See BRIGANDAGE.

E. A. Thompson, *P&P* 1952; B. Czúth, *Die Quellen der Geschichte der Bagauden* (1965); R. MacMullen, *Enemies of the Roman Order* (1966); J. F. Drinkwater, *Classical Views* (1984); R. van Dam, *Leadership and Community in Late Antique Gaul* (1985); J. F. Drinkwater and H. Elton (eds.), *Fifth-Century Gaul* (1992).
J. F. Dr.

Bacchanalia can be used to mean either 'Bacchic festival' or 'Bacchic places of worship', but usually translates the Greek *mysteries (*orgia*), with special reference to the worship suppressed by the Roman authorities in 186 BC. We have an account of the suppression in Livy (39. 8–18) and an inscribed version of the senatorial decree (*ILLRP* 511) against the cult, in the form in which it was circulated to the allied states of Italy. These sources can be supplemented by references in *Plautus' plays and now by archaeological evidence to show that the Bacchic cult, perhaps of south-Italian Greek origin, was widespread in Italy, central and south, decades before the senate chose to act against it. The form of the Italian cult seems to differ from other Hellenistic examples in admitting men as well as women to the mysteries and in increasing the frequency of meetings. It is a matter of debate how far the cult's followers were forming a movement of protest against the Roman authorities.

The surviving decree concentrates on the structure of Bacchic cells—their oaths of loyalty, their organization and funding, their membership, their property. This suggests that it was the power of cell-leaders over worshippers, cutting across traditional patterns of family and authority, that disturbed the senate, rather than alleged criminal actions or orgiastic rites; but any allegation would have helped in the discrediting of a powerful and well-embedded cult; Livy's vivid account has valuable elements, and in substance shows knowledge of the decree itself; but its highly literary elaboration shows the influence of the senate's propaganda against the cult.

The senate's persecution succeeded at least in removing the cult from prominence, though artistic evidence shows its long-sustained influence. Later Italian evidence, especially the great Bacchic inscription of Agripinilla, shows a domesticated, family version of the cult, well subordinated to élite authority.

See DIONYSUS.

L. Gallini, *Protesta e integrazione nella Roma antica* (1970); J. A. North, *PCPS* 1979, 85–103; J.-M. Pailler, *Bacchanalia. La Répression de 186 av. J.-C. à Rome et en Italie: Vestiges, images, tradition* (1988) (very full bibliography and sometimes speculative discussion); on the Agripinilla inscription: J. Scheid, in *L'Association dionysiaque dans les sociétés anciennes* (1986), 275–90.
J. A. N.

Baccheius Geron (3rd–4th cent. AD) wrote an informative *Introduction to the Art of Music* in question-and-answer form, giving pithy harmonic and rhythmic analyses, mainly Aristoxenian (see

ARISTOXENUS) but with later additions and modernized perspectives.

Ed. C. von Jan, *Musici Scriptores Graeci* (1895), repr. with It. trans. in L. Zanoncelli, *La Manualistic musicale greca* (1990); Eng. trans. by O. Steinmayer, *Journal of Music Theory* 1985.   A. D. B.

Bacchiadae, aristocrats of *Corinth, claimed Heraclid (see HERACLIDAE) descent from King Bacchis. After suppressing the kingship *c.*750 BC they ruled, 200 in number, until *Cypselus overthrew them *c.*657. Corinth's western interests were established under them; they founded *Syracuse and *Corcyra, and were allies of *Chalcis in the Lelantine War (see GREECE, Archaic period). They married only among themselves (see ENDOGAMY), and were more exclusive than most Greek *aristocracies; that was the main reason for their fall. Their flight to Corcyra probably began the long enmity between Corinth and her colony. Bacchiadae in exile are said to have founded royal families in Lyncestis (Upper *Macedonia)—and in Rome (see CITIZENSHIP, ROMAN; DEMARATUS (1); TARQUINIUS PRISCUS).

J. B. Salmon, *Wealthy Corinth* (1984).   J. B. S.

Bacchius, of Tanagra (275–200 BC?), physician, member of the *Alexandrian 'school' of *Herophilus. Bacchius' influential Hippocratic lexicon (*Lexeis* 1–3; see HIPPOCRATES (2)), of which Epicles of Crete produced an abridged version and against which the Empiricists *Philinus (1) and *Heraclides (4) wrote polemical treatises, was one of the earlier author-specific Alexandrian lexica. His glosses on about 60 words from at least eighteen treatises in the Hippocratic corpus (see HIPPOCRATES (2)) survive, preserved mainly by *Erotian. They offer valuable evidence concerning Alexandrian philology and concerning the availability of Hippocratic texts in early *Alexandria (1). To explain individual words, Bacchius drew extensively on Hippocratic treatises and on *Aristophanes (2) of Byzantium's *Lexeis*. His other works on Hippocratic texts included commentaries (on *Epidemics* 6, *Aphorisms*, and *In the Surgery*) and an 'edition' of *Epidemics* 3. He also made significant contributions to sphygmology, *pathology, *pharmacology, and doxography (*Memoirs on Herophilus and the Members of his House*).

Ed., trans., and comm.: H. von Staden, *From Andreas to Demosthenes Philaletus* (1995), ch. 4. Cf. H. von Staden, *Herophilus* (1989), 484–500, and in *Tratades Hipocráticas* (1992), 549–69.   H. v. S.

Bacchus See DIONYSUS.

Bacchylides (*c.*520–450 BC), lyric poet, of Iulis in *Ceos, son of Midon (or Midylus, *Etym. Magn.* 582, 20), nephew of *Simonides (Strabo 486, *Suda*, entry under Βακχυλίδης). His floruit was given as 480 by *Chron. Pasch.* 162b (304. 6), as 467 and 451 by *Eusebius–Jerome (the entry in Eusebius, *Chron.* Ol. 87.2 = 431 BC), refers to a flute-player Bacchylides mentioned by the comic poet *Plato (2) in his *Sophistai*, fr. 149 KA, *PCG* 7. 494, see G. Fatouros, *Philol.* 1961, 147). The assumption that he was younger than *Pindar (Eust. *Prooem. ad Pind.* 25 = schol. Pind. 3, p. 297. 13 Dr.) is unfounded and unlikely in view of the early date of his poem in praise of the young prince *Alexander (1), son of Amyntas (fr. 20b Snell–Maehler), who succeeded his father as king of Macedon in *c.*494. Although Bacchylides was one of the canonical nine lyric poets (*Anth. Pal.* 9. 184 and 571; schol. Pind. 1, p. 11. 20 Dr.), and although he was well known in Hellenistic and Roman times (imitated by Horace *Carm.* 1. 15, quoted by *Strabo, *Plutarch, [*'Longinus'], *Subl.* and by the emperor *Julian who 'enjoyed reading him', as Amm. Marc. 25. 4. 3 says), only a handful of lines had survived in quotations when a papyrus

containing his book of victory odes almost complete and the first half of his book of *dithyrambs was found at Meīr, near Al-Kussīah, south of *Hermopolis Magna, in 1896 and published by F. G. Kenyon in 1897. Since then, remains of fifteen more papyri have been attributed to him, and two papyri contain scholia on his epinician odes and dithyrambs. The known dates of his epinician odes are: 476 (5, for *Hieron (1)'s horse-race victory at Olympia, also celebrated by Pindar, *Ol.* 1), 470 (4, for Hieron's chariot victory at Delphi, for which Pindar sent *Pyth.* 1), 468 (3, for Hieron's chariot victory at Olympia), and 452 (6, for Lachon's sprint victory as a boy at Olympia); likely dates are: *c.*485 (13) and 454 or 452 (1 and 2); the Third Dithyramb (17, 'The Youths' or 'Theseus') seems to date from the early 490s; it is really a paean sung by a Cean choir at *Delos. Bacchylides spent some time in exile in the Peloponnese (Plut. *De exil.* 14). Like Simonides and Pindar, he may have stayed at *Syracuse as Hieron's guest (Ael. *VH* 4. 15), but the alleged rivalry between him and Pindar seems to be a figment of some ancient biographers.

His patrons, apart from Hieron of Syracuse, included athletes from Ceos, *Aegina, *Phlius, *Metapontum, and *Thessaly; a poem in honour of a magistrate of Larissa seems to have been added at the end of the book (14b, cf. Pindar's *Nem.* 11). Several of his dithyrambs were composed for competitions at Athens (15?, 18, 19, 23?), one for Sparta (20). The Alexandrian editors gave them titles and arranged them in alphabetical order. Stylistically, his dithyrambs are like ballads, using lively narrative, often allusive and selective, as well as direct speech. They exploit the pathetic potential of the myths, as do those epinician odes which contain a mythical narrative as their centre-piece. *Dith.* 2 (16, 'Heracles' or 'Deianira' ?) appears to assume familiarity with *Sophocles (1)'s *Trachiniai*; *Dith.* 4 (18, 'Theseus') is unique in being a dialogue between the chorus as people of Athens and the chorus leader, their king, *Aegeus; this may have been influenced by Attic drama (plays like Aesch. *Supp.* or *Pers.*), rather than being an archaic form of dithyramb. Bacchylides also wrote hymns (frs. 1–3), paeans, of which fr. 4 + 22 contains a fine eulogy of peace, processional songs (frs. 11–13), maiden-songs (Plut. *De mus.* 17), dancing-songs (hyporchemata, frs. 14–16), songs about love (erotica, frs. 17–19), and songs of praise (encomia?, frs. 20–20f). *Didymus (1) wrote a commentary on the epinician odes and probably also on other books. The textual transmission must have broken off sometime in the Roman period; later authors like *Athenaeus (1) and *Clement of Alexandria seem to quote from anthologies.

TEXT B. Snell and H. Maehler (Teubner 1970; repr. 1992).
COMMENTARIES, WITH TEXT AND TRANS. R. C. Jebb (1905); H. Maehler, *Die Lieder des Bakchylides 1: Die Siegeslieder* (1982); 2: *Die Dithyramben und Fragmente* (1997).
LITERATURE A. Koerte, *Hermes* 1918, 113–47, and *RE* Suppl. 4. 58–67; E. D. Townsend, *Bacchylides and Lyric Style* (1956); B. Gentili, *Bacchilide* (1958); A. P. Burnett, *The Art of Bacchylides* (1985); W. M. Calder and J. Stern (eds.), *Pindaros und Bakchylides* (1970); H. Maehler, *MH* 1991, 114–26 (on 17); W. S. Barrett, *Hermes* 1954, 421 ff. (on fr. 4 + 22); B. Snell, *Hermes* 1952, 157–63 (= *Ges. Schr.* 105–11) (on fr. 20a).   H. Ma.

Bacis, a Boeotian chresmologue (oracle-collector) 'maddened by the *Nymphs' (Paus. 4. 27. 4) whose *oracles were known from the 5th cent. BC onwards (e.g. Hdt. 8. 20. 77 and 9. 43, referring to the invasion of *Xerxes, and Paus. 4. 27. 4 to the rebuilding of *Messene); collections are still known in the 2nd cent. AD (Lucian. *De mort. Peregr.* 30). To cope with the mass of oracles from manifestly different dates, later authors assumed several Bacides (ps.-Arist. *Pr.* 954[a]36; Plut. *De Pyth. or.* 10. 399a). Bacis shares both *possession (religious) by the *Nymphs and wavering between singular and plural with the *Sibyl, with whom he is sometimes combined; both belong to the world of rather shadowy, non-official ecstatic prophecy known since the late Archaic age. See PROPHECIES.

A. Bouché-Leclerq, *Histoire de la divination dans l'antiquité* 4 vols. (1879–1882), 2, 105–10; Rohde, *Psyche*, 292.   F. G.

Bactria, Enormous region lying (roughly) between the *Oxus (Amu-Darya) to the north and the Hindu Kush to the south; the term occasionally also includes Sogdiana to the north (Tadjikistan / Uzbekistan). The Achaemenid satrapy (Bāxtriš) is cited several times in the *Persepolis tablets. Because of the silence of the classical sources, Bactrian history only becomes more fully recoverable with *Alexander (3) the Great, who had to fight tough battles here. Recent excavations have profoundly enhanced our knowledge, especially excavation of the site of *Ai Khanoum, a Hellenistic city, (possibly) founded by Alexander himself, on the upper Oxus (Alexandria Oxiana?). Surveys in eastern Bactria, on both banks of the Oxus, have revealed that the agricultural prosperity, for which the country was famed, goes back to the bronze age. From this time on, networks of irrigation canals were constructed, which were maintained and extended throughout the *Achaemenid and Hellenistic periods. Under the early *Seleucids, Bactria was extensively colonized, and Bactra (mod. Balkh) served as a temporary residence for Antiochus (the future *Antiochus (1) I), son of *Seleucus (1) I. Inscriptions found on several Bactrian sites have provided new insights into Iranian and Greek settlement and into the process of acculturation. A Graeco-Bactrian kingdom was created by Seleucid breakaway satraps. This secession is generally thought to have been achieved by *Diodotus (1) *c.*230 BC, linked to the invasion by the Parni (see PARTHIA) of the Iranian plateau, but this chronology is debated. In 206, following a campaign by *Antiochus (3) III, the Graeco-Bactrian king *Euthydemus (2) I accepted Seleucid supremacy. In the reign of *Eucratides I, people from beyond the Oxus invaded Bactria and destroyed the city of Ai Khanoum *c.*145 BC. At the end of Heliocles' reign (*c.*130 BC), another invasion virtually obliterated the Greek presence in Bactria.

P. Briant, *L'Asie Centrale et les royaumes proche-orientaux* (1984); P. Bernard, *Fouilles d'Aï-Khanum* 4 (1985); S. Sherwin-White and A. Kuhrt, *From Samarkhand to Sardis* (1993); cf. *Topoi: Orient-Occident* 1994; J. Rea and others, *ZPE* 104 (1994), 261 ff.   P. B.

Baebius (*RE* 41) **Tamphilus, Gnaeus,** was praetor in 199 BC, when he suffered a defeat in northern Italy, and was sent back to Rome in disgrace by the consul L. *Cornelius Lentulus. He eventually reached the consulship in 182, when he fought successfully in Liguria, and returned to Rome to hold the elections at which his brother Marcus (below) was chosen as consul.
                                                                          J. Br.

Baebius (*RE* 1, 16, 44) **Tamphilus, Marcus,** was praetor 192 BC, when he took an advance force to Greece shortly before the invasion by *Antiochus (3) III. In 191 he conducted operations in Thessaly, in co-operation with *Philip (3) V, until the arrival of the consul M'. *Acilio Glabrio (1). Consul in 181, he and his colleague P. Cornelius Cethegus carried the first law on *ambitus: Livy 40. 19. 11. This may also be the *lex Baebia* providing that only four praetors be elected in alternate years: Livy 40. 44. 2. (The provision was repealed by 175.) Both consuls commanded in Liguria and in 180 transferred the Apuani to Samnium (*ILS*

6509). Despite having engaged in little fighting, they were awarded *triumphs.

On the *lex Baebia Cornelia* see Scullard, *Rom. Pol.* 172–3; on the political position of the Baebii, Briscoe, *Comm.* 31–33, 70–1.   J. Br.

Baetica, the heart of the province originally (197 BC) called Further Spain, comprising a range of sophisticated and urbanized peoples formerly controlled by *Carthage. As Roman territory increased, an administrative division between Hither and Further Spain was formed: this began at the Mediterranean south of *Carthago Nova (mod. Cartagena) and ran west-north-west to the Guadiana and thence northwards to the Tajo. In 27 BC the old settled province east and south of the Anas was assigned to the senate as Hispania Baetica. It was divided for judicial purposes into four *conventus centred at Gades (Cadíz), Corduba (Córdoba, the capital), Astigi, and Hispalis (Seville: Plin. *HN* 3. 7). Moreover, Caesar and Augustus created many colonies in this heavily urbanized province, while their grants of municipal status (see MUNICIPIUM) to native communities were greatly extended by Vespasian. Baetica was one of the richest provinces in the Roman west, exporting metals (see GOLD), *olive oil, and fish sauce (see FISHING; FOOD AND DRINK) to Rome and the northern frontiers. Baetica was lost to the *Vandals in AD 411 and, after a period of control by the *Suebi, eventually passed into *Visigothic hands in the mid-5th cent. AD. Its southern sector became a Byzantine province between 552 and the early 7th cent.

R. Thouvenot, *Essai sur la province romaine de la Bétique* (1940). S. J. K.

Baiae, dependency of *Cumae, said to have been named after Baios, a companion of *Odysseus. It never became a *municipium*, but flourished as a fashionable spa and resort, thanks to volcanic hot springs. By the mid-1st cent. BC, many of the Roman élite owned houses there. Several imperial palaces were built and it remained fashionable until the 3rd cent. AD, when *earthquakes and malaria (see DISEASE) sent it into a decline. Medieval interest in the medical properties of the springs and the historical associations caused a resurgence of popularity. Extensive remains of *bath complexes and parts of the imperial palaces have been excavated.

S. De Caro and A. Greco, *Campania* (1981).   K. L.

Balbinus See CAELIUS CALVINUS BALBINUS, DECIUS.

Balbus wrote a surveying treatise on measurements and geometrical shapes. He undertook military surveying during the Dacian campaigns of an emperor, either *Domitian or *Trajan. See GROMATICI.   J. B. C.

Balbus, Cornelius See CORNELIUS BALBUS (1) and (2), L.

Baleares et Pithyusae insulae The name Gymnesiae (Γυμνησίαι), used by early Greek voyagers, was replaced by Baliares or Baliarides. The spelling was changed to Baleares under Augustus. Roman names of each island were Maiorca (formerly Columba), Minorca (formerly Nura), Capraria, Menaria, Tiquadra, and Cunicularia (formerly Hannibalis). On Maiorca towns included native Tucis, Bocchoris, and Guium, with Latin colonies at Palma and Pollentia. Minorca had native Sanisera as well as Punic(?) Mago and Iamo. The Greek name of Pithyusae became Roman Ebusus (Ibiza) and Colubraria (Formentera), and there was a Punic colony at Ebusus. Although the islands were officially Roman by 202 BC, they were not pacified until 121 by Q. *Caecilius Metellus Baliaricus. The islands formed part of the *conventus Carthaginiensis* (Hispania *Tarraconensis). Iamo, Mago, and Ebusus (part of *Baetica) were granted municipal rights under

ball games

Vespasian and the latter issued coins under Tiberius and Gaius. In the countryside native megaliths (talayots) continued well into the imperial era. In AD 395 the islands constituted an independent province and also hosted dye-works (bafii, see DYEING) for the state. They were seized by the *Vandals in AD 455 and by the Byzantines in 534 (?). Throughout this time the rural population was strongly Christianized and the islands maintained important trading links with North Africa.

A. Arribas, *La romanitzacio de les Illes Balears* (1983); J. Ramon, *El baix imperi i l'epoca bizantina a les Illes Pitiuses* (1986); A. Tovar, *Iberische Landeskunde 3: Tarraconensis* (1989), 269 ff.   S. J. K.

ball games Playing with a ball (σφαῖρα) was at least as old as *Homer (*Od.* 6. 100, 8. 370). It is shown in Athenian art, notably two late Archaic reliefs, one (Athens 3476) apparently showing a throw-in from the touch-line in a team game, the other (Athens 3477) what looks like a hockey match; a black-figure vase (London B182a) depicts ball-play by piggyback. Sparta was credited with the invention of ball-play (Ath. 1. 14); a Spartan wrote a lost work on the subject (Ath. 1. 15c), and the ephebes of imperial times fielded 14-strong teams of ball-players (sphaireis) in an annual tournament perhaps akin to American football (P. Cartledge and A. Spawforth, *Hellenistic and Roman Sparta* (1989), 205 ff.). In other Greek cities ball-play was not an important part of athletic training; the sphairistērion of the Hellenistic *gymnasium was probably a boxing-ring, not a ball-ground (so H. Delorme, *Gymnasion* (1960), 281 ff.; Harris *contra*). Various Roman balls and ball games are alluded to by *Martial. *Galen recommended ball-play as a cheap and safe way of keeping fit in his extant work *On Exercise with the Small Ball* (*Scripta minora* 1. 93). Late authors describe a team-game called episkyros (ἐπίσκυρος) with a superficial resemblance to Rugby except (significantly) that no kicking, only throwing, is mentioned (Poll. 9. 104; Eust. *Od.* 1601, 30).

H. Harris, *Sport in Greece and Rome* (1972), ch. 3.   F. A. W.; A. J. S. S.

Ballista (or **Callistus),** praetorian prefect of Macrianus junior and Quietus, the boy emperors established in the east by their father, *Macrianus, following the capture of *Valerian (AD 260). Ballista consolidated the regime by halting the main Persian advance into Asia Minor, but, with Quietus, was killed in Emesa by *Septimius Odaenathus after the defeat of the Macriani on the Danube (261).

E. Kettenhofen, *Die römisch-persischen Kriege* (1982), 107 ff.   J. F. Dr.

banks in antiquity supplied a selection of the services familiar from their modern counterparts. None the less, the essential banking function, receipt of deposits which might then be lent at interest to a different set of customers, appears only fleetingly in ancient texts (Dem. 36. 11). Many temples, both Greek and Roman (e.g. *Apollo on *Delos, *Castor and Pollux at Rome) took deposits and even lent money; but deposits remained untouched and cash was lent from the temple's own funds. Similarly, moneylenders who lent from their own resources, even on a regular basis, were not bankers; nor were usurers, specializing in short-term, high-interest loans of small sums—the common Greek term is obolostatēs ('a lender of obols'). Banking in the Greek world appears to have evolved out of professional money-changing: a response to the multiplicity of state coinages (trapezitēs or 'banker' refers to the trapeza or changer's table). Changers, and presumably bankers, existed all over the Classical and Hellenistic Greek worlds, but our knowledge is concentrated in Athens, where, from the 4th cent. BC, the names are known

of some twenty bankers. Money-changing remained important; otherwise, the emphasis and impact of the services provided by Athenian bankers is disputed. Modernizing approaches treat banks as central not only to fringe economic activity, but to the whole *polis: primarily through the linked taking of deposits and extension of credit. Alternative readings, stressing differences between ancient and modern economies, see bankers (often themselves non-Athenians) as more marginal to the citizen-structure of the polis, providing a peripheral range of *credit and other services (including acting as witnesses and guarantors). The majority of their clients would then be persons themselves not fully integrated into the koinōnia (community) of the polis: traders, other visitors to Athens, and a minority of citizens who urgently needed money or the support of specialist banking skills. Not disputed is the wealth of the most successful Athenian bankers. *Pasion, beginning as a bankers' slave, gained his freedom, took over control of his former masters' bank, and eventually became a citizen. Remarkably, his own banking slave, *Phormion (2), followed an almost identical path from rags to riches (Isoc. 17; Dem. 36, 45, [46], [49], [52]). Bankers from the Greek world seem to have operated in isolation; there is no clear evidence for any integrated banking system. A letter of credit is introduced to an Athenian jury as something needing explanation (Isoc. 17. 35 ff.). This is in contrast to Ptolemaic Egypt, where surviving papyri reveal a complex system of giro payments and bills of exchange. There was a range of banking institutions, changing through time: a network of royal or state banks (based on *Alexandria (1) with branches in local capitals, banks operated on license, private banks, and logeutēria (royal treasuries). By the 2nd cent. BC, and into the Roman period, the scene was dominated by state and private banks.

For the Roman west, literary evidence for banking operations is unsystematic. The basic problem is distinguishing between wealthy men of affairs who might offer financial services, including credit (e.g. T. *Pomponius Atticus) and professional dealers in money. Whereas the former might be wealthy through ownership of land, the latter were generally of lower status, made most of their living through financial transactions, and might be organized into collegia (see CLUBS, ROMAN). Three identifiable groups had banking interests: argentarii, coactores argentarii, and *nummularii. The earliest testimony from Rome and Italy (down to c.100 BC) mentions only argentarii, who resembled Greek trapezitai in offering a range of functions: changing, deposit, and credit. Specialization is evident from the 1st cent. BC, with argentarii continuing to take deposits and lend, but money-changing becoming the province of the nummularii. There also emerge from c.50 BC the coactores argentarii, who offered credit facilities to those purchasing goods at auction. This marks a possible partial break with the tendency for credit in antiquity to be economically non-productive. Against this (as for the Greek world), there is no hard evidence for Roman bankers lending in *maritime loans. Though possibly prosperous, none of these financiers came from the upper end of society: Antony (M. *Antonius (2)) could insult *Octavian by claiming his grandfather was an argentarius (Suet. *Aug.* 2. 6; cf. 4. 2 for nummularius). Nor did they number among their clients the Roman élite, who generally had their own safe deposits and sources of credit. As in Athens, Italian bankers regularly crop up in connection with the affairs of merchants (as indicated by the affairs of *Caecilius Iucundus, Pompeian auctioneer). This tripartite system of finance was restricted to the western empire, and possibly only to Italy. Even there, from AD 200, distinctions begin to disappear, with a return to the idea of the all-embracing *argentarius*. A final (if problematic) perspective on Roman banking from the 6th cent. AD is provided by the *Digest*. See NEGOTIATORES.

N. Platon, *Revue historique de droit français et étranger*, 1909, 7 ff., 1911, 158 ff.; R. Bogaert, *Les Origines antiques de la banque de dépôt* (1966), *Banques et banquiers dans les cités grecques* (1968), *Grundzüge des Bankwesens im alten Griechenland* (1986), *Hist.* 1984, 181 ff., *MH* 1986, 19 ff., *ZPE* 68 (1987), 35–75; 69 (1987), 107–41; P. Millett, *Lending and Borrowing in Ancient Athens* (1991); E. Cohen, *Athenian Economy and Society* (1992); J. Trevett, *Apollodorus, the Son of Pasion* (1992); C. Préaux, *L'Économie royale des Lagides* (1939); F. Preisigke, *Girowesen im griechischen Ägypten* (1910; repr. 1971); J. Andreau, *Les Affaires de Monsieur Jucundus* (1974), *La Vie financière dans le monde romain* (1987), and in E. Frézouls (ed.), *Le Dernier Siècle de la république romaine et l'époque augustéenne* (1978), 47 ff.; C. T. Barlow, *Bankers, Moneylenders and Interest Rates in the Roman Republic* (1978).   P. C. M.

Bantia, *Lucanian city on the border with Apulia (25 km. (15½ mi.) south of Venosa). It flourished in the 4th-3rd cents. BC, and became a *municipium* in 89 BC. The material culture shows strong Greek and *Daunian influence. The *tabula Bantina* was found there, as was an augural temple.   K. L.

barbarian Social groups frequently assert their cohesiveness by emphasizing the differences between themselves and 'outsiders'. Individuals belong to a range of groups, and which they choose to emphasize will depend on particular historical situations. While we associate Classical culture primarily with emphasis on *citizenship (membership of a *polis*), Classical Greek literature also assigns considerable importance to defining a common Greek identity and creating the figure of the 'barbarian' in contrast.

That contrast was not important in Archaic literature. The factors that brought it to the fore were (*a*) the imposition of Persian control over western Asia Minor from the mid-6th cent. BC and the successful armed resistance to Persia by many Greek states in 480/79 BC (see PERSIAN WARS); (*b*) justification of Athenian hegemony over the *Delian League on the grounds that Greeks should unite to continue resistance against Persia; and (*c*) the appearance of considerable numbers of non-Greek slaves at Athens (where the economic exploitation of the indigenous poor had been curtailed by *Solon's *seisachtheia* (alleviation of *debt)).

With *Aeschylus' *Persians* (performed 472 BC), a consistent image of the barbarian appears in Athenian literature and art. Apart from a lack of competence in Greek (e.g. Ar. *Thesm.*), the barbarian's defining feature is an absence of the moral responsibility required to exercise political freedom: the two are connected, since both imply a lack of *logos*, the ability to reason and speak (sc. Greek) characteristic of the adult male citizen. Barbarians are marked by a lack of control regarding sex, food, and cruelty. In *Homer, the breaking of such taboos had been associated with super-human heroes; in Classical thought, they were 'barbarous' (the myth of Tereus, thought originally to have been a Megarian hero (see MEGARA), includes rape, tearing out a tongue, a mother's murder of her own child, and *cannibalism: consequently Tereus had to be reclassified as a Thracian king; see THRACE). Absence of political freedom entails rule by tyrants, and frequently women, and the use of underhand weaponry like bows and poison; the absence of moral self-control entails the wearing of wasteful and 'effeminate' clothing, drinking wine neat, and enjoying emotional ('Lydian' or 'Ionian') music. Somatic differences might be used by writers (or vase-painters) to reinforce the image of the barbarian, but it did not matter whether the typology was black African or Thracian.

The Greek/barbarian polarity continued to be a major element in Greek literature throughout antiquity; it compensated for the military and political powerlessness of Greek cities in the Hellenistic and Roman periods. Along with other elements of Greek culture, it became part of the ideological baggage of Latin literature. Its importance in practical terms is less clear: 'barbarians' were excluded from the *Olympic Games and other religious ceremonies, e.g. at *Eleusis, and a 4th-cent. BC lawcourt speech could make capital out of an opponent's alleged 'barbarian' descent (Dem. *Meid.* 149 f.). Roman rhetoric, too, could represent opponents, both non-Roman and Roman, as either 'barbarians' or 'barbarous' (Cic. *Font.*, etc.; representations of *Cleopatra (VII) or *Boudicca), though such language masked much more real distinctions (principally that between the Roman citizen and the non-citizen), and Roman moral discourse symbolized disapproval in different terms (e.g. Etruscan luxury). While some Greek intellectuals stretched the polarity to its limits (Isoc. *Paneg.* and *Philippus*; Arist. *Pol.* 1. 2–7 and 3. 14 on barbarians being slaves 'by nature'), others questioned the usefulness of the concept (Pl. *Resp.* 262de). The polarity might be associated with a more universal distinction between 'us' at the centre of the world and 'them' at the periphery: the barbarians who inhabited the 'edge' of the world might be savages without laws, settled homes, or agriculture (see NOMADS), but alternatively they might have created an earthly paradise (the *Hyperboreans, the 'Kingdom of the Sun' in the Indian Ocean). Like kings, women, children, old people, or slaves, some barbarians might be closer to the divine world than the adult male citizen (Celtic Druids, Persian magi, Indian gymnosophists; cf. the Christian *Salvianus' positive judgement of 5th-cent. AD Germanic invaders).

In the Hellenistic period, the distinction between Greek and barbarian came to be seen as insignificant even by some of those imbued by the literary culture (*Stoicism); its irrelevance was explicitly expressed by Christians (Colossians 3: 11; 1 Corinthians 7: 21; cf. Acts 8: 27). Nevertheless the prejudice against 'barbarians' remained latent in the literary tradition, to be exploited by late antique Christians like *Prudentius (*c. Symm.* 2. 807–19) as well as non-Christians such as Ammianus when they wished to parade their scholarship. With the rediscovery of *Aristotle in the 12th cent., it became one of the roots of western self-definition first against Muslims and the 'orient', and later against subject populations around the globe. See ORIENTALISM; RACE.

P. Cartledge, *The Greeks* (1993); Y. Dauge, *Le Barbare: Recherches sur la conception romaine de la barbarie et de la civilisation* (1981); E. Hall, *Inventing the Barbarian* (1989); F. Hartog, *The Mirror of Herodotus: The Representation of the Other in the Writing of History*, Eng. trans. (1988); A. N. Sherwin-White, *Racial Prejudice in Imperial Rome* (1967); F. M. Snowden, *Before Color Prejudice* (1983).   T. E. J. W.

Barcino (mod. Barcelona), *Colonia Iulia Augusta Paterna Faventia*, founded by Augustus on a coastal branch of the via Augusta, possibly around 15 BC. There was no earlier native occupation and excavations have revealed traces of its early walls, street-grid (see URBANISM), the *mosaic floors of houses, an early imperial cemetery, and part of an *aqueduct. Inscriptions reveal names of wealthy citizens (viz. Pedanii, Herennii). The city walls were rebuilt in the 4th or 5th cent. AD and an early Christian basilica has been discovered. Literary and archaeological sources point to the growing importance of the city from the 5th cent.

A. Balil, *Las murallas romanas de Barcino* (1961), and *Colonia Iulia . . . Faventia Barcino* (1964); J. Oriol Granados, in *Los foros romanos de las provincias occidentales* (1987).   S. J. K.

Bardylis I

Bardylis I founded a powerful kingdom early in the 4th cent. BC which threatened to destroy the Molossian and Macedonian kingdoms. The former was saved by Sparta and the latter by *Philip (1) II of Macedon. The centre of Bardylis' kingdom lay north of Lake Lychnitis, and his immediate subjects were probably Dardanians; but he controlled many Illyrian tribes and disposed of large and warlike forces (see DARDANI; ILLYRII).

F. Papazoglu, *Hist.* 1965, 143 ff.; N. G. L. Hammond, *BSA* 1966, 243 f.; Hammond and Griffith, *HM* 2 (1979), see index; N. G. L. Hammond, *CAH* 6² (1994), 428 f.   N. G. L. H.

Barea Soranus See MARCIUS BAREA SORANUS, Q.

Barium (mod. Bari), a Peucetian city and port. Despite a strategic position it was of only minor importance in antiquity, and was economically dependent on *fishing. There are traces of Greek influence, and it had municipal status (see MUNICIPIUM) after 89 BC. It became a diocesan capital (see DIOECESIS) in AD 374.
K. L.

Bar Kokhba, 'son of a star', is the name commonly used to denote the leader of the second Jewish revolt in Palestine (AD 132–5), to whom was applied, allegedly by Rabbi Akiba, the Messianic prophecy in Num. 24: 17. The precise form of his real name, Shim'on (Simon) ben or (in Aramaic) bar Cosiba, which often appears in distorted form in rabbinic literature, has been given by the discovery of his letters and other documents from his camp, which designate him 'Nasi (prince) of Israel' and are dated by the era of his 'liberation of Israel'. This era, apparently dated from 1 Tishri (October) 131, is used also on the coins struck by the rebels. Little is known of the course of the revolt, but there is epigraphic evidence that a large legionary force was needed to suppress it. The rebels relied mainly on guerrilla tactics, with their focus in *Judaea. While the letters show that En Gedi was an important base, and archaeology suggests that the caves of the region were put to military use, whether the rebels ever held Jerusalem is unclear. The last stand was made at Bethar, in the sack of which Bar Kokhba was killed.

Cass. Dio 69. 12–14; Euseb. *Hist. Eccl.* 4. 6. L. Mildenberg, *The Coinage of the Bar Kokhba War* (1984); B. Isaac and A. Oppenheimer, *Journal of Jewish Studies* 1985, 44–9; Y. Yadin, *Bar Kokhba* (1981); P. Schäfer, *Der Bar Kokhba-Aufstand: Studien zum zweiten jüdischen Krieg gegen Rom* (1981); S. Applebaum, *Prolegomena to the Study of the Second Jewish Revolt* (AD 132–5) (1976); Schürer, *History* 1. 534–57.   E. M. S.; T. R.

Barygaza (*Bhrigukaccha/Bharukaccha* in Indian sources, now Broach) near the mouth of the Narmada on the gulf of Cambay. The navigational use of the *monsoon winds, erroneously associated with *Hippalus, led to ships financed by traders from the eastern Mediterranean and Egypt sailing to Barygaza direct from the *Red Sea and Aden; conducted by pilots, they were towed from the coast to the port. They brought merchandise, presents, and Roman coins. To Barygaza were brought Indian and Chinese products (see SERES) from the north through Modura (Mathura) and Ozene (Ujjain), and merchandise from central India and the Deccan through Tagara (Ter) and Paethana (Paithana). Indian ships sailed from Barygaza to the Gulf, the southern Arabian coast, and the Horn of Africa. It was also important to the Persian trade.

Ptol. *Geog.* 7. 1. ff.   E. H. W.; R. Th.

Basil of Caesarea (*Cappadocia), c. AD 330–79 (the dates are debated but not disproved). He is honoured as the chief architect of monastic life in the Greek Church. His early education was completed at Athens, where he came under the influence of *Himerius and *Prohaeresius. He was also instructed briefly by *Libanius. Those experiences marked him out for a teaching career, upon which he may have embarked. However, the influence of Eustathius of Sebaste and of travel in the eastern provinces inclined him to the practice of asceticism, which he undertook in the company of his friend *Gregory (2) of Nazianzus. His education bore fruit, nevertheless, in his *Address to Young Men*, which discussed the adaptation of the classical curriculum to Christian use and enjoyed lasting influence. His ascetic experience was distilled chiefly in his *Long Rules* and *Short Rules*.

A growing interest in Church affairs drew him into the moderate party of Basil of Ancyra and encouraged him in lifelong loyalty to Meletius of Antioch. Within the general context of the Arian controversy, those associations made him less acceptable to both *Alexandria (1) and Rome. Nevertheless, he was remembered for his courageous resistance to the Arian emperor *Valens and he did much to damage the reputation of the Arian theologian Eunomius. See ARIANISM.

He spent the whole of his priestly and episcopal career in *Caesarea (1). In spite of his orthodoxy, he attracted the favour of Valens, who supported financially his extensive works of charity and sent him on an important mission to Armenia in 373. As a churchman, he strongly advocated and worked for unity but in conservative terms that were less convincing to ambitious peers.

His numerous letters are an important source for eastern provincial life at the time and reveal a man of delicacy, insight, and power. His homilies are much neglected and show a skilful combination of learning, style, and clarity. His crowning achievement was his *Hexaemeron*, which *Ambrose paraphrased.

WORKS Migne, *PG* 29–32. Other modern editions: *Basilio di Cesarea, Discorso ai Giovani (Oratio ad adolescentes)*, ed. M. Naldini (1984); Eng. trans. in *Saint Basil, The Letters*, 4. 379–435 (see below). Rufinus' Latin translation of *Rules: Basili regula a Rufino latine versa*, ed. K. Zelzer (*CSEL* 86, 1986); Eng. trans. of all *Rules*: *The Ascetic Works of Saint Basil*, trans. W. K. Lowther Clarke (1925); *Basil of Caesarea, Ascetical Works*, trans. M. M. Wagner (1950); *Basile de Césarée, Contre Eunome, suivi de Eunome, Apologie*, trans. Bernard Sesboüé and others, 2 vols. (SC 299, 305, 1982–3). *Basile de Césarée, Sur le baptême*, ed. U. Neri and trans. J. Ducatillon (SC 357, 1989). *Basile de Césarée, Sur le Saint-Esprit*, ed. and trans. B. Pruche, 2nd edn. (SC 17 bis, 1968); *St Basil the Great on the Holy Spirit*, trans. B. Jackson, rev. D. Anderson (1980). Letters: *Saint Basile, Lettres*, ed. and trans. Y. Courtonne, 3 vols. (1957–66); *Saint Basil, The Letters*, trans. R. J. Deferrari, 4 vols (Loeb, 1950–53). Homilies: *Basile de Césarée, Homélies sur l'Hexaéméron*, ed. and trans. S. Giet, 2nd edn. (SC 26 bis, 1968); *Saint Basil, Exegetic Homilies*, trans. A. C. Way (1963); *Basile de Césarée, Sur l'origine de l'homme (Homélies X et XI de l'Hexaéméron)*, ed. and trans. A. Smets and M. van Esbroeck (SC 160, 1970).

STUDIES P. J. Fedwick (ed.), *Basil of Caesarea: Christian, Humanist, Ascetic*, 2 vols. (1981). S. Giet, *Saint Basile: Évangile et église*, 2 vols. (1984); P. Rousseau, *Basil of Caesarea* (1994).

DATING P. Maraval, *Rev. Ét. Augustiniennes* 1988, 25–38.   P. R.

Basile, a cult figure worshipped in Athens and elsewhere in Attica. Her city shrine was held in common with *Neleus and (probably later) *Codrus, and as her name suggests one of her 'meanings' may have been that of sovereignty, especially perhaps in connection with the claim of Athens to Ionian primacy. Nothing is known of her mythology.

H. A. Shapiro, *ZPE* 63 (1986), 134–6.   E. Ke.

basileus, basileia See KINGSHIP; for the basileus (an official) at Athens see ARCHONTES; LAW AND PROCEDURE, ATHENIAN.

basilica, the name applied to a wide range of Roman building forms, most commonly and characteristically to the large, multi-purpose public halls which regularly accompanied the *forum in the western half of the Roman world, and corresponded roughly in function to the Greek and Hellenistic *stoa. The earliest known was built in Rome by M. *Porcius Cato (1) in 184 BC. The name came, by extension, to be used for any large covered hall in domestic (Vitr. *De arch.* 5, 5, 2; Sid. Apoll. *Epist.* 2, 2, 8), commercial (*basilica vestiaria, basilica argentaria*), military (Vegetius, *De re militari* 2. 23), or religious (Basilica Hilariana, *CIL* 6. 30973) use.

The origin is uncertain. The name suggests the Greek area, and the first basilicas may have been the administrative halls of the Hellenistic kings. There is an enclosed hall, the roof supported by an internal row of columns, called the Basilike Stoa on *Thera, put up in the period of Ptolemaic control. A structure similar to the Roman basilica, with a clerestory-lantern, the roof supported by a rectangle of columns, open to the front, is the Stoa of Poseidon (wrongly nicknamed in modern times the 'Hypostyle hall') on *Delos. The earliest surviving Italian basilica is probably that at *Pompeii.

A typical basilica is a rectangular building, open either along one side or at one end, with the roof in two sections, the central part being raised over a clerestory supported on an internal colonnade. A platform, often in an apsidal niche at one end, or, less frequently, the middle of one side, contained the tribunal for magistrates. This plan can be elaborated by doubling the internal colonnade, adding a gallery (Basilica Ulpia in the *forum Traiani which also has a projecting apse at both ends). Basilicas can be free-standing buildings (early examples in the Roman colony at *Corinth), or placed along one side of the enclosed fora. The roofs of basilicas are supported by timber beam construction. This, and the large number of columns required to support them, are a required feature of basilical architecture. The great basilica added to the forum Romanum by *Maxentius (and completed by *Constantine I) of brick-faced concrete, with concrete-vaulted roofs is exceptional, and derives its form from the great central hall of the Roman imperial thermae. See BATHS.

Basilicas of traditional type continued to be built in the 3rd cent. AD (the Severan basilica at *Lepcis Magna). Since they were designed to hold large numbers of people they responded to the needs of Christian worship following the official recognition of *Christianity, and the early *churches at Rome and elsewhere are essentially basilicas with the apisidal tribunal, using the prestigious columns and timber form of construction.

J. B. Ward-Perkins, *Roman Imperial Architecture*, 2nd edn. (1981).
R. A. T.

Bassae, in SW Arcadia, near Phigaleia, the site of one of the best-preserved Greek temples. This was dedicated to *Apollo the Helper (*Epikourios*). *Pausanias (3) says it was the work of *Ictinus, but this attribution is now doubted. It dates to the latter part of the 5th cent. BC with an interruption due to Spartan occupation of the area during the *Peloponnesian War. The greater part of the temple is in the local limestone, with carved decoration applied in marble. The *orientation, followed also by its predecessor, was towards the north instead of the east, and the early sunlight, instead of entering through the main doorway, was admitted to the adytum through an opening in the eastern side-wall. Ten engaged Ionic columns decorated the side walls of the cella internally, with a single central Corinthian column—one of the earliest of its kind, and one of the most beautiful (see ORDERS)—between the cella and the adytum. The sculptured frieze is now in the British Museum. The arrangement and order of its slabs are uncertain.

Apollo with the epithet *Epikourios* may be regarded as the protector of Arcadians serving as *mercenaries. The alternative explanation, that he was a helper against disease, and specifically the Athenian *plague at the beginning of the Peloponnesian War, is unlikely (the plague would not have affected Bassae), though this idea has led to an excessively early date for the temple.

C. R. Cockerell, *The Temples . . . at Aegina and . . . Bassae* (1860); F. E. Cooper, *The Temple of Apollo at Bassai* (1978); C. Hofkes-Brukker and A. Mallwitz, *Der Bassai Fries* (1975). R. A. T.

Bassaeus Rufus, Marcus, praetorian prefect under M. *Aurelius, an Italian of humble origin, rose from the centurionate and primipilate (see CENTURIO; PRIMIPILUS) to hold four procurator-ships, and the prefecture of the *vigiles and of Egypt, before commanding the *praetorian guard from AD 168 until his death some ten years later. He was honoured for his service in the Marcomannic War (*ILS* 1326) and is mentioned by Cassius Dio and Philostratus.

PIR[2] B 69; H.-G. Pflaum, *Les Carrières procuratoriennes équestres* (1960–1), no. 162 + *add.*; B. Dobson, *Die Primipilares* (1978), no. 134.
A. R. Bi.

Bastarnae, a roving tribe which first appeared on the lower Danube *c.*200 BC. They were enlisted by *Philip (3) V and *Perseus (2) of Macedon against their enemies in the northern Balkans, and by Mithradates VI against the Romans. They defeated C. *Antonius 'Hybrida' (*c.*62 BC), but were subdued by M. Licinius Crassus (2) (29–28 BC; cf. Cass. Dio 51. 23. 2–27. 3), and henceforth they generally appear as subject allies of Rome, on one occasion under *Nero having hostages recovered and returned to them by the Roman governor of *Moesia (*CIL* 14. 3608). One hundred thousand were transferred across the Danube into *Thrace (SHA *Probus* 18. 1), and *Diocletian settled others in Pannonia. Their German *ethnicity may be deduced from Strabo (7. 3. 17), Pliny (*HN* 4. 100), and Tacitus (*Germ.* 46. 1). They appear to have been the first of the race to travel the migration route from the Baltic to the Black Sea, and their movement is recalled on the *Peutinger Table, where the Carpathians are called 'Alpes Bastarnicae'.
M. C.; J. J. W.

Batavi, a Germanic people, living on the lower Rhine. Though an offshoot of the *Chatti, they helped *Drusus against the Germans in 12 BC, and frequently thereafter provided military support for Rome. Remaining incorporated in the empire after the withdrawal to the Rhine in AD 9, they paid no taxes, and helped *Germanicus attack their fellow Germans in 16. Their warriors formed auxiliary regiments (see AUXILIA), by the mid-1st cent. serving under their own chiefs; and until 68 they are also found in the personal bodyguard of the emperors. It was they, under the leadership of C. *Iulius Civilis, who headed the great revolt of 69–70. Thereafter they were not prominent in Roman history; and their relationship to the *Franks, who later occupied their territory, is obscure.

C. Rüger, *Germania Inferior* (1968); R. Brandt and J. Slofstra (eds.), *Roman and Native in the Low Countries* (1983); R. Urban, *Der 'Bataveraufstand'* (1985). J. F. Dr.

Bath See AQUAE SULIS.

baths, one of the most characteristic and widely distributed types of Roman buildings, had their origins in the Greek world where public baths were common from at least the 4th cent. BC.

Bato

Surviving 3rd-cent. Greek baths centre on a series of hip-baths arranged around the walls of one or more rooms, often circular (*tholoi*), with niches above the tubs, and were furnished with hot water which was poured over the seated bather. Baths of this type are found in southern Italy (e.g. Stabian baths, *Pompeii, first phase) and Sicily, where, together with local traditions of therapeutic baths at volcanic springs and fumaroles, they were instrumental in the development of the purely Roman type. These replaced the individual tubs with communal pools, and often incorporated the dry sweating-rooms (*laconica*) and exercise grounds (*palaestrae*) of the Greek *gymnasium in the same establishment (Stabian baths, later phases; Republican baths at Regio VIII, 5, Pompeii). The basic features of these early Roman baths were a changing-room (*apodyterium*), an unheated *frigidarium* with a cold-water basin, an indirectly heated warm room (*tepidarium*) sometimes containing a tepid pool, and a strongly heated room (*caldarium*) containing a hot plunge pool and a separate water-basin on a stand (*labrum*). The evolution of the *hypocaust and wall-heating systems after *c*.100 BC, replacing the less efficient braziers, and the introduction of window-glass in the 1st cent. AD permitted the development of an elaborately graded system (Sen. *Ep.* 90. 25; Celsus, *Med.* 1. 4, 2. 17) often with the incorporation of several wet and dry sweating-rooms (*sudatoria*). With increasingly assured water supply to towns (see AQUEDUCTS), large cold and even heated swimming-pools (*piscina, natatio*) also became common adjuncts.

Public baths, often located near the *forum, were a normal part of Roman towns in Italy by the 1st cent. BC, and seem to have existed at Rome even earlier. The baths in the Campus Martius donated to the Roman people by *Agrippa *c*.20 BC set new standards of luxury and architectural elaboration, and heralded a new civic role for the baths in the towns of the empire. At Rome they were followed by the baths of *Nero, *Titus, and *Trajan, the latter being the first of the truly monumental complexes set in a vast enclosure containing gardens, lecture-halls, libraries, and other cultural facilities, reflecting the influence of the Hellenistic gymnasium. The symmetrical plan of the bathing-block, perhaps originating with the baths of Nero, centred on a triple cross-vaulted *frigidarium*, and incorporating a large *natatio* and twin colonnaded *palaestrae*, sometimes interpreted as basilical halls, was highly influential both at Rome (baths of *Caracalla and *Diocletian) and in the provinces with such buildings as the Antonine baths at *Carthage, the Barbara baths at *Augusta Treverorum (Trier), and the Hadrianic baths at *Lepcis Magna. Even when the architectural form was not imitated so closely, the influence of the 'imperial' type can be seen in the increased size and elaboration of many baths in the provinces from the late 1st cent. onwards, along with an increase in the amount of space devoted to non-bathing functions. Regional variations developed, central Italy and North Africa producing many buildings of highly complex curvilinear plan (e.g. at Hadrian's villa near *Tibur and Thenae in Tunisia). Roman-style baths were widely adopted in the eastern provinces, forming a distinctive type in Asia Minor (e.g. at *Ephesus and *Miletus) where they were assimilated to the Hellenistic gymnasium.

Bathing occupied a central position in the social life of the day; by the 2nd cent., any community of any substance, civil and military, had at least one set of public baths, while private baths are common in country *villas and in wealthier town houses. Larger towns often had one or more substantial buildings (*thermae*) which were show-pieces for the community as well as

a number of smaller, privately owned *balnea* to serve everyday needs. See HOUSES, ITALIAN; WATER.

I. Nielsen, *Thermae et Balnea* (1990); F. K. Yegül, *Baths and Bathing in Classical Antiquity* (1992); R. Rebuffat, in *Les Thermes romains. Actes de la table ronde . . . Rome, 11–12 Nov. 1988* (1991), 1 ff.; J. DeLaine, in H.-J. Schalles and others (eds.), *Die römische Stadt im 2. Jahrhundert n. Chr.* (1992), 257 ff.   J. D.

Bato (1), chief of the Daesitiates, raised rebellion in *Illyricum in AD 6, raided the Dalmatian coast, and fought against the Romans in the Sava valley, and, after the capitulation of his Pannonian allies in AD 8, retreated southwards. After vainly defending several forts against the Romans, he surrendered and was interned at Ravenna (AD 9).

PIR^2 B 94. E. Koestermann, *Hermes* 1957, 345 ff.   R. S.

Bato (2), the Pannonian, like his Dalmatian namesake (above), revolted, tried to capture *Sirmium (AD 6), and shared in the subsequent fighting, but surrendered in AD 8 at the river Bathinus. Soon after, however, his namesake captured and killed him.

PIR^2 B 93.   R. S.

Baton, New Comedy poet (see COMEDY (GREEK), NEW), mid-3rd cent. BC; an anecdote links him (if his name is rightly conjectured at Plut. *Mor.* 55c; cf. J. Traversa, *Index Stoicorum Herculensis* (1952) col. 22 = *SVF* 1, fr. 471 von Arnim) with *Cleanthes (d. *c*.231) and *Arcesilaus (1) (d. 241). Frs. 3 and 5 travesty *Epicurus' teaching about 'the good' and pleasure.

FRAGMENTS Kassel–Austin, *PCG* 4. 28–35.

INTERPRETATION Meineke, *FCG* 1 480 f.; G. Kaibel, *RE* 3/1 (1897), 143, 'Baton' 6; I. Gallo, *Teatro ellenistico minore* (1981), 15 ff. (a later version of *Vichiana* 1976, 206 ff.).   W. G. A.

battle, battles See under names of individual battles; also ARMIES (both entries); HOPLITES; PHALANX; WAR, ART OF (both entries).

Baubo belongs to the main Orphic version of the Rape of *Persephone (Asclepiades of Tragilus, *FGrH* 12. 4; Orph. frs. 49–52 Kern; see ORPHISM). She resembles *Iambe in the *Homeric Hymn to Demeter*. She and her husband Dysaules receive *Demeter at Eleusis during her search for Persephone, and their children *Eubouleus and *Triptolemus give her information about the rape. Like Iambe Baubo gives Demeter a refreshing drink (the *kykeōn*), and when she refuses it Baubo by an indecent exposure makes her laugh and accept it. (Her name can be used of the female sexual organs.) The story may be an *aition* for a ritual at the *Thesmophoria. Her cult is found on *Naxos in the 4th cent. BC (*SEG* 16. 478) and *Paros in the 1st cent. BC (*IG* 12. 5. 227).

O. Kern, *RE* 3. 150–1; Karagiorgha–Stathacopoulou, *LIMC* 3/1. 87–90; F. Graf, *Eleusis und die orphische Dichtung Athens in vorhellenistischer Zeit* (1974), 165–71; N. J. Richardson, *The Homeric Hymn to Demeter* (1974), 79–82, 215–16, 322; M. Olender, *Rev. Hist. Rel.* 1985, 3–55.   N. J. R.

Baucis (Βαῦκις) and her husband Philemon were a pair of elderly peasants who entertained *Zeus and *Hermes with the resources of their meagre larder when the gods paid an incognito visit to *Phrygia (compare the story of *Orion's birth); for their piety they were spared, like Lot and his wife in Genesis ch. 19, from the flood which drowned their less hospitable neighbours. They lived out the rest of their lives as priests of the temple into which their humble shack was transformed, and were themselves finally transfigured into an oak and a linden-tree springing from the same trunk. The tale, which has genuine roots in ancient Anatolian tree-cult (see TREES, SACRED), has its first and canonical telling in Ovid, *Met.* 8. 618–724, though a Hellenistic Greek treatment along the lines of *Theseus' stay in the hut of *Hecale or the entertainment of *Heracles by Molorcus (both recounted by *Callimachus (3)) probably lies behind it.

A. S. Hollis, *Ovid: Metamorphoses Book VIII* (1970), p. 106 ff.

A. H. G.

beards See COSMETICS; PORTRAITURE, ROMAN.

Bedriacum (or Betriacum), near modern Calvatone midway between *Verona and *Cremona in Cisalpine Gaul, gave its name to two decisive battles in AD 69. *Vitellius' troops defeated *Otho's in the first, but were themselves defeated by *Vespasian's in the second some months later. Both battles were apparently fought nearer Cremona than Bedriacum.

E. T. S.; T. W. P.

bee-keeping had the same importance for antiquity that sugar production has now. Honey-gathering preceded the culture of bees which began perhaps in the mesolithic period. The evidence for bee-keeping in classical antiquity is mainly literary, ranging in time from Hesiod onwards and in content from incidental allusions to codifications of the practical experience of Greek, Roman, and Carthaginian bee-masters (Arist. *Hist. An.* 5. 21–2, 9. 40; *Gen. an.* 3. 10; Varro, *Rust.* 3. 16; Verg. *G.* 4; Columella, *Rust.* 9. 2–16; Plin. *HN* 11. 4–23); Hellenistic monographs (e.g. Aristomachus of Soli, Philiscus of Thasos) are lost. *Solon introduced regulations for bee-keepers (Plut. *Sol.* 23. 8). Greek cities (*Teos, Theangela in *Caria) and Ptolemaic Egypt had taxes on bee-keeping and stimulated honey-production. Varieties of breeds and methods were developed, especially in Hellenistic times. Attica (Hymettus), Theangela, *Cos, *Calymnos, *Rhodes, *Lycia, Coracesium, *Thasos, *Cyprus, *Syria, *Sicily (*Megara Hyblaea), *Liguria, *Noricum, and southern *Spain produced and exported the best honey. A hive could produce 1–3 *choes* (3–9 l.: 5–16 pt.) at one harvesting. Archaeological evidence from Egypt (tomb paintings) and Greece (terracotta hives) now supplements literature. Hives were of various materials, perishable (cork, bark, wood, reeds, basketwork) and permanent (terracotta), and set generally horizontally (the existence then of upright bar-hives is debatable). Pottery hives have been widely found in Greece (Athens, Attica, Corinthia, Crete), many grooved or combed internally, and often associated with combed extension rings or cylinders, detachable for easy harvesting of 'unsmoked' honey (Strabo 9. 1. 23). See also HONEY.

H. M. Fraser, *Beekeeping in Antiquity* (1931; 2nd edn. 1951); Forbes, *Stud. Anc. Technol.* 5², 80–111; J. E. Jones and others, *BSA* 1973; J. E. Jones, *Archaeology* 1976; E. Crane, *The Archaeology of Beekeeping* (1983); *Bee World* 1975; Crane and Graham, ibid. 1985; H. Mussche and others, *Thorikos* 1990, 63–71.

J. E. J.

Behistun See BISITUN.

Belgae According to *Caesar, a population-group of this name occupied lands to the north of the Seine and Marne. They were the fiercest inhabitants of Gaul and boasted of their German blood (cf. Strabo 4. 196). Certain tribes, he says, had settled in *Britain, and Belgae are located there by Ptolemy (4). The Gallic Belgae were subdued by Caesar in 57 BC, but continued to give trouble for 30 years more. The archaeology of the province of Gallia Belgica shows little uniformity, with the area towards the Rhine mouth less developed than areas further south and west.

Despite Caesar's statement that groups of Belgae settled in Britain before his time, there is no agreement about their identification through archaeology. SE England shares a number of cultural features with northern Gaul, and coins of Gallo-Belgic type are found from *c.*120 BC. Other features, like cremation burial and wheel-made pottery, are introduced from Gaul throughout the 1st cent. BC; so Caesar's reference is best seen as an indicator of close contacts rather than any major migration of people. There is evidence for a number of individual tribal leaders moving between Gaul and Britain up to AD 43.

The *civitas* of the Belgae, with its capital at Venta (Winchester), is assumed to have been a Roman creation carved out of the kingdom of Ti. *Claudius Cogidubnus. Winchester has an iron age antecedent, and was possibly the site of an invasion-period auxiliary fort. The town was enclosed within a late 2nd-cent. defence of 55 ha. (136 acres), but its archaeology is comparatively little known. An important late Roman cemetery has been excavated at Lankhills.

N. Roymans, *Tribal Societies in Northern Gaul* (1990); B. W. Cunliffe, *Iron Age Communities in Britain*, 3rd edn. (1991); M. Biddle, in *Proc. Brit. Acad.* 1983.

M. J. M.

Belisarius (*c.* AD 500–65), *Justinian's famous general, is known primarily through the writings of his assessor *Procopius. Native of Germania in Thrace, he served in Justinian's bodyguard during Justin's reign. His career as commander began against the Persians, with mixed success: defeat near Callinicum (531) outweighed victory outside Dara (530), prompting demotion and recall, but at *Constantinople in January 532 his bodyguard helped suppress the Nika Riot. Back in *Justinian's favour Belisarius was appointed to command the expedition to reconquer Africa; the Vandals were soon defeated and their king, *Gelimer, captured (533–4). Belisarius was awarded the exceptional honour of a triumph, held the ordinary consulship of 535 in magnificent style, and then returned west to recapture Ostrogothic Italy. Rapid occupation of Naples and Rome preceded much hard fighting, but the surrender of King Vitigis and the Gothic capital *Ravenna marked the apex of Belisarius' military career (540). Subsequent campaigns against Persians and Goths were disappointing, relations with Justinian became tense, partly through the machinations of Theodora and Belisarius' wife Antonina, but in 562 he defended Constantinople against Zabergan's Cutrigurs.

PLRE 3. 181–224.

L. M. W.

Bellerophon (Βελλεροφῶν, Βελλεροφόντης). In *Homer's account (*Il.* 6. 152–202) he is son of *Glaucus (2) (or, according to *Hesiod, *Poseidon: fr. 43. 81 f. M–W) and grandson of *Sisyphus, and a native of Ephyre (generally identified with *Corinth). *Proetus, king of Tiryns, had a wife Anteia (Stheneboea in later versions) who fell in love with Bellerophon and tried to seduce him. When he rejected her advances she falsely accused him of trying to rape her. So Proetus sent him to Iobates, king of Lycia and Anteia's father, with a sealed letter containing instructions to kill the bearer. Iobates set Bellerophon tasks likely to bring about his death, sending him to kill the *Chimaera, and to fight the Solymi and the *Amazons. When Bellerophon returned triumphant from all these tasks, and survived an ambush laid for him by Iobates, the king married him to his daughter and gave him half his kingdom. In versions after Homer, Bellerophon accomplished his tasks with the help of the winged horse *Pegasus, which *Athena helped him to catch (Pind. *Ol.* 13. 63 ff.). According to *Euripides, he also used Pegasus to take vengeance on Stheneboea (Eur. *Stheneboea*), and offended the gods by trying to fly on him to Olympus (Eur. *Bellerophon*). In Homer, although there is no direct mention of

Bellona

Pegasus, Bellerophon became 'hated by all the gods' (*Il.* 6. 200), which presumably was caused by the attempt to reach Olympus.

Bellerophon on Pegasus attacking the Chimaera is found in art from before the mid-7th cent. BC, where it appears first in Corinthian vase-painting: see Brommer, *Vasenlisten*³, 292–8, and *LIMC* 7, 'Pegasus'.　　　　　　　　　　　　　　　J. R. M.

Bellona (older form Duellona), Roman goddess of war. She had no *flamen* (see FLAMINES) and no festival in the calendar, unlike the major ancient deities; she acquired her temple as late as the 290s BC (Livy 10. 19. 17); but the presence of her name in the ancient formula of *devotio* (Livy 8. 9. 6) suggests that she was nevertheless an archaic Roman goddess, whether or not belonging to the circle of Mars. Her temple was built in the Campus Martius, outside the *pomerium*, and was a frequent meeting-place of the senate when dealing with generals returning from war. In front of it was the area used by the *fetiales* in declarations of war. Bellona was successively identified with Nerio, the cult-partner of *Mars; with Enyo, the Greek war-goddess; and with Mā, the Mother Goddess of *Cappadocia.

> Wissowa, *RK* 151–2; her temple: L. Chiotti in Steinby, *Lexicon* 190–3.
> 　　　　　　　　　　　　　　　　　　　　　　H. J. R.; J. A. N.

Bellum Africum, a record of *Caesar's war in Africa (winter 47–46 BC). Its 98 chapters have some literary pretensions and merit, though the military narrative is too slow and painstaking for modern tastes. Its authorship was uncertain even in antiquity (Suet. *Iul.* 56. 1). The style has some colloquialism and little variety, but suggests some education; the content points to a trained soldier who took part in the campaign, though not a man in Caesar's confidence. The attribution to A. *Hirtius (see BELLUM ALEXANDRINUM) is impossible.

> TEXTS R. du Pontet (OCT, 1901); A. Klotz, 3rd edn (Teubner, 1982).
> COMMENTARY R. Schneider (1905).
> TRANSLATIONS A. G. Way (Loeb, 1955); A. Bouvet (Budé, 1949); J. F. Mitchell (1967).　　　　　　　　　　　　　　　　C. B. R. P.

Bellum Alexandrinum ('Alexandrian War'), a work continuing *Caesar's commentary on the Civil War. Only the first 33 chapters deal with the war at *Alexandria (1); then follow the campaign of Cn. *Domitius Calvinus against *Pharnaces II (chs. 34–41), the war in Illyricum (42–7), the disturbances during Q. *Cassius Longinus' tenure in Spain (48–64), and finally Caesar's campaign against Pharnaces (65–78) ending in the victory at Zela (2 August 47). One view in antiquity (Suet. *Iul.* 56. 1) made *Hirtius the author of this work and also of the *Bellum Africum and the *Bellum Hispaniense*; Hirtius himself writes, perhaps in anticipation, of completing a continuation down to Caesar's death (preface to *Bellum Gallicum* 8). For this work, though not for the other two, stylistic comparison with *BGall.* 8 makes his authorship quite possible.

> TEXTS R. du Pontet (OCT, 1901); A. Klotz, 3rd edn (Teubner, 1982).
> COMMENTARIES R. Giomini (1956); G. B. Townend, chs. 1–33 only (1986).
> TRANSLATIONS A. G. Way (Loeb, 1955); J. Andrieu (Budé, 1954); J. F. Mitchell (1967).
> STUDY K. Barwick, *Caesar und das corpus Caesarianum*, *Philol.* Suppl. 31 (1938).　　　　　　　　　　　　　　　　　　　C. B. R. P.

Bellum Civile ('Civil War'), title of three works. (1) *Caesar's commentaries on the war begun in 49 BC: Caesar is unlikely to have used the title himself. (2) Lucan's epic (see ANNAEUS

LUCANUS): this, or *De Bello Civili*, is the best-attested ancient title, though the popular alternative *Pharsalia* (cf. 9. 980–6) is regaining some scholarly fashion. (3) The poem of 295 hexameters introduced into *Petronius Arbiter's *Satyricon* (119–24). Some criticism of Lucan is clearly suggested, especially his suppression of divine machinery; but interpretation is not straightforward, given the satirical characterization of the speaker Encolpius.
　　　　　　　　　　　　　　　　　　　　　　　　　C. B. R. P.

Bellum Gallicum See IULIUS CAESAR (1), C.

Bellum Hispaniense ('Spanish War'), an account of the campaign which ended at Munda (45 BC). Its author was an eyewitness, certainly not A. *Hirtius (see BELLUM ALEXANDRINUM), but clearly from *Caesar's army. His level of education was not high, and his Latin is an intriguing blend of colloquialism and literary pretension, even including quotations from *Ennius. The text is lamentable, but many obscurities may spring from the author's incapacity to express complexity. His closeness to the events produces a clear impression of the atrocities of war.

> TEXTS R. du Pontet (OCT, 1901); A. Klotz, 3rd edn. (Teubner, 1982).
> COMMENTARIES A. Klotz (1927); G. Pascucci (1965), cf. *ANRW* 1. 3 (1973), 596–630.
> TRANSLATIONS A. G. Way (Loeb, 1955); J. F. Mitchell (1967).
> 　　　　　　　　　　　　　　　　　　　　　　C. B. R. P.

Belus (*Βῆλος*), Hellenized form of the Levantine god Ba'al and Babylonian Bel (both meaning 'lord'). Ba'al is attested from the third millennium BC on at *Ebla and *Ugarit. In *Babylonia, Bel describes Marduk (earlier Enlil), god of *Babylon and head of the pantheon certainly by the 12th cent. BC (cf. Hdt. 1. 181. 2). Bol of *Palmyra also came to be called Bel. For classical writers, Belus is often a way of describing an eastern supreme deity or legendary figure, sometimes seen as the founder of dynasties (e.g. Hdt. 1. 7. 2; Ov. *Met.* 4. 213).

> *Reallexikon der Assyriologie* 7. 360–74, 'Marduk'; *DCPP*, 55, 'Baal'; J. Teixidor, *The Pagan God* (1977).　　　　　　　　　　A. T. L. K.

bematists, the surveyors of *Alexander (3) the Great. Of known bematists Philonides of Crete was a celebrated distance runner, and others (notably Baeton and Diognetus) had literary aspirations. Their measurements of key distances in the empire comprised an archive, later controlled by *Seleucus (1) I. Individual bematists published their observations in monographs termed *Stathmoi* ('Stages'), which combined precise calculations of distance with more exotic reports of the flora, fauna, and customs of the empire. The latter tended to the outrageous, but the measurements were of lasting value and provided *Eratosthenes with the framework for his geography of Asia.

> *FGrH* 119–22; Berve, *Alexanderreich* 2, nos. 198, 800.　　A. B. B.

Bendis, a Thracian goddess. Little is known of the character of her cult; Strabo says—but does he know?—that it was orgiastic (10. 3. 16). Greek artists represented her as a booted huntress, rather like Artemis; she is sometimes described as *δίλογχος*, twin-speared. Her cult was introduced to Athens in two stages: by 430/29 BC she shared with the Phrygian Adrasteia a small treasury under the control of the Treasurers of the Other Gods; and a decree of (probably) 413/2 (*IG* 1³. 136) assigned her a priestess and founded the great festival in the *Piraeus known from the opening of *Plato (1)'s *Republic*, at which twin processions, of native Thracians and of Athenians, were followed by a torch-race on horseback and an 'all-night celebration' (*παννυχίς*). The role played by Thracians in the Athenian public cult is confirmed by decrees issued by a body of Thracian '*orgeōnes of Bendis' in the 3rd cent. BC; in one, the origin of this unique honour is traced back to an oracle of *Dodona (IG 2². 1283). The immediate motivation for the introduction of the goddess's cult is unknown; at bottom, the Athenians' interest in Bendis must be a product of their preoccupation with Thrace, which goes back to the 6th cent. See RELIGION, THRACIAN; THRACE.

Z. Gočeva and D. Popov, LIMC 'Bendis' and 'Deloptes'; R. Garland, Introducing New Gods (1992). R. C. T. P.

beneficiarii were junior officers in the Roman army below the rank of centurion (see CENTURIO). They were appointed through the favour (beneficium) of their commander (Vegetius, 2. 7), and the title existed at least from the time of *Caesar. In the imperial period a beneficiarius ranked among the principales, who received pay at one-and-a-half times or twice normal legionary rates (see STIPENDIUM), and performed administrative duties. Normally a man was promoted beneficiarius after serving as an immunis (a soldier on basic pay who performed a specialist function for which he received exemption from routine duties), and then holding one or more posts in the century—officer in charge of the watch (tesserarius), standard-bearer (signifer), or orderly (optio). More senior grades of beneficiarii were eventually established (commentarienses and corniculariii). The rank of each beneficiarius depended on the status of the official to whose office he was attached (these included senior military officers, procurators, provincial governors, the prefect of the city, the praetorian prefects), and he could often expect promotion to the centurionate.

R. MacMullen, Soldier and Civilian in the Later Roman Empire (1963); D. J. Breeze, JRS 1971, 130; BJ 1974, 245. J. B. C.

Beneventum (mod. Benevento in southern Italy) was originally a stronghold of the Hirpini Samnites (see SAMNIUM) named Malventum. It fell sometime after 300 BC to the Romans, who made it a Latin colony (see IUS LATII), changing its ill-sounding name to Beneventum, 268 BC (Vell. Pat. 1. 14; Festus 25 Lindsay). Thereafter Beneventum flourished. Under the republic it was a military base, later an opulent *municipium; under the empire a colonia and road-centre (*via Appia, *via Traiana). In AD 571, it became an important *Lombard duchy. *Trajan's arch (AD 114) is particularly notable, and there is evidence of a cult of *Isis, including an Egyptian obelisk (erected AD 88).

I. A. Richmond, Roman Archaeology and Art (1969), 229 ff.; H.-W. Müller, Il culto di Iside nell'antica Benevento (1971); M. Rotili, L'arco di Traiano a Benevento (1972), and in I Longobardi (1990), 131 ff. E. T. S.; T. W. P.

Berenice, the name of several Ptolemaic dynastic foundations. Among the best known are: (a) Berenice (mod. Benghazi), the westernmost Cyrenaican city, founded in the mid-3rd cent. BC (exact date and circumstances disputed) after the abandonment of Euhesperides (whose harbour had silted up) and named for *Berenice (3) II who gave a city-wall. It was the starting-point of M. *Porcius Cato (2)'s march across the Syrtica to Thapsa and birthplace of Andronicus, opponent of *Synesius. Inscriptions highlight pirate raids in the 1st cent. BC and its self-governing Jewish community; excavations reveal the development of a suburb in considerable detail. See PENTAPOLIS.

RE 3 (1899), 282, no. 8; J. A. Lloyd (ed.), Excavations at Sidi Khrebish, Benghazi 1 (1977), 2 (1979), 3 (1985); A. Laronde, Cyrène et la Libye hellénistique (1987), 382 f., 463 f., in part contested by T. V. Buttrey, Libyan Studies 1994. J. M. R.

(b) Berenice of the *Trogodytae (mod. Medinet al-Harrās), on the western shore of Foul Bay (Ras Banās peninsula) and the starting-point of a caravan route (with cisterns and stations) through the eastern desert to *Coptus. This formed the most important port for eastern trade.

(c) Berenice Panchrysos, on the African coast of the *Red Sea near the gold mines of Jebel Allaki.

(d) Berenice Epideiris on the same coast at the Straits of Bab el-Mandeb, a cargo-point perhaps for *elephants.

D. J. T.

Berenice (1) **I,** first mistress and then wife of *Ptolemy (1) I Soter, came to Egypt with her aunt Eurydice whom she supplanted as queen. By her first marriage (to Philippus, a Macedonian), she was mother to Magas, king of Cyrene and Antigone, wife of *Pyrrhus of Epirus. Her later children were *Arsinoë II, *Ptolemy (1) II, and Philotera. Her influence at the Ptolemaic court was notable (Plut. Pyrrh. 4. 4). *Theocritus (Id. 15) records the *Adonis-festival in her honour; with Soter she was celebrated in the Ptolemaieia.

RE 'Berenike' 9. D. J. T.

Berenice (2) 'the Syrian', daughter of *Ptolemy (1) II and *Arsinoë I (b. c.280 BC), was Ptolemy III's sister. *Antiochus (2) II married her after the 'Second Syrian War' (252). At Antiochus' death (246), *Laodice (2), his divorced first wife, murdered Berenice and her son by Antiochus before Ptolemy III could intervene.

F. M. H.; S. S.-W.

Berenice (3) **II,** daughter of Magas of Cyrene and Apama II, was born c.273 BC. Following the murder that she initiated of her mother's candidate Demetrius, her marriage in 246 to *Ptolemy (1) III Euergetes returned *Cyrene to Ptolemaic control. She survived into the reign of her son *Ptolemy (1) IV, falling a victim to palace intrigues in 221. In the dynastic cult she and Euergetes were the Benefactor Gods; the Egyptian-style deification of their daughter Berenice is recorded in the Canopus decree of 238 BC. She is perhaps best known for 'The Lock of Berenice' commemorated by *Callimachus (3) (fr. 110 Pf.) and *Catullus (66). Coloured faience 'queen-vases' bearing her depiction were probably used in cult.

RE 'Berenike' 11. D. J. T.

Berenice (4) (b. AD 28), daughter of M. *Iulius Agrippa I, was married to Marcus, brother of Ti. *Iulius Alexander in 41, and then in 46 to her uncle Herod, king of Chalcis. From his death (48) she lived with her brother, M. *Iulius Agrippa II. To quieten rumours of incest, she persuaded Polemon, priest-king of Olba in Cilicia, to marry her (53/54), but the marriage did not last long. She played some part in public affairs: in 66 she tried, at first single-handed and then with Agrippa, to prevent the Jewish Revolt, and in 69, in Agrippa's absence, she supported the Flavian cause. *Titus fell in love with her while he was in Judaea (67–70), and when she visited Rome with Agrippa (75) he openly lived with her, perhaps for some years. He deferred, however, to public opinion and did not marry her, and on his accession (79) he dismissed her with regret on both sides (Suet. Tit. 7) and ignored her when she visited Rome again.

J. A. Crook, AJPhil. 1951, 162 ff.; D. Braund, Hist. 1984, 20 ff. E. M. S.; M. T. G.

Beros(s)us (Βηρωσός; Babylonian dialect of Akkadian, Bel-re'ušu; fl. 290 BC); Babylonian scholar and author of Babylonian history (Βαβυλωνιακά) in three books, presented to *Antiochus

(1) I, now only preserved in fragments. Using Babylonian sources, book 1 described the country and creation; book 2 covered history before and after the flood down to Nabonassar (747–734); book 3 contained a detailed political history to *Alexander (3) the Great. Berosus stressed the distinction between *Babylonia and *Assyria, confused by many Greek writers on the east.

> *FGrH* 680; S. M. Burstein, *The Babyloniaca of Berossus* (1978); A. Kuhrt, in A. Kuhrt and S. Sherwin-White (eds.), *Hellenism in the East* (1987), 32–56.   A. T. L. K.

Berytus (mod. Beirut), a *Phoenician city mentioned in the letters of el-Amarna (14th cent. BC) and also attested in the Persian period. From *Antiochus (4) IV on it issued a coinage as Laodicea in Phoenice, but with the old name of Canaan inscribed in Phoenician. The reverse shows *Poseidon, the tutelary god of the city, also known from the wealthy colony of the Poseidoniasts of Berytus in Hellenistic *Delos. In *c.*16 BC, it became a Roman colony with the *ius Italicum*, *veterans of two legions being settled there by Agrippa. A great trading-town, it was also famed for its wine and linen, and, from the end of the 3rd cent AD, for its school of Roman law.

> *DCPP*, entry under the name; R. Mouterde and J. Lauffray, *Beyrouth, ville romaine* (1952).   A. H. M. J.; H. S.; J.-F. S.

betrothal,

Greek ἐγγύη, was a contract between two men, the groom and the bride's father (or other κύριος, 'controller', male representative at law) which established that a union was a fully valid marriage. In Classical Athens, this contract was oral, more or less formulaic (judging from examples in *Menander (1)), aimed at assuring the legitimacy of children, and accompanied by an agreement concerning dowry; the bride herself need not be present, or even of an age to understand the proceedings, and the celebration of the marriage and cohabitation might be long delayed or in the end not take place (*Demosthenes (2)'s sister was betrothed at 5 to a man she never married). Marriages at Sparta too might involve betrothal; sources speak as well of another custom, abduction marriage (conceivably with the complicity of the bride and her family). Scattered references to betrothal in Hellenistic documents from a number of cities go some way towards confirming the suggestion that most Greeks practised ἐγγύη (Diod. Sic. 9. 10).

> C. Vatin, *Recherches sur le mariage et la condition de la femme mariée à l'époque hellénistique* (1970); C. B. Patterson, in S. B. Pomeroy (ed.), *Women's History and Ancient History* (1991), 48–72; D. M. MacDowell, *Spartan Law* (1986).   G. W. W.; M. G.

Roman Sponsalia in the republic consisted of reciprocal *sponsiones*, and breach-of-promise actions (in the form of actions for damages) existed. The movement of classical Roman law was in the direction of removing constraint, and the term *sponsalia* came near to an informal agreement to marry, voidable at will (except that the intending husband was required to return such dowry as had been given to him and the intending bride was expected to return the much more usual gift from her intending husband, the *donatio ante nuptias*, for gifts after marriage were excluded). The betrothal was solemnized with a kiss and the intending husband put an iron *ring (*anulus pronubus*) on the third finger of his partner's left hand; it was the occasion for a party (also called *sponsalia*).

See also MARRIAGE LAW, Greek and Roman.

> S. Treggiari, *Roman Marriage* (1991), esp. 138 ff.; J. Gardner, *Women in Roman Law and Society* (1986), 45 ff.   G. W. W.; A. J. S. S.

biblical epic See EPIC, BIBLICAL.

Bibracte (mod. Mont-Beuvray), a hill-fort, the original capital of the *Aedui, where in 52 BC supreme command was conferred upon *Vercingetorix. Though its inhabitants were later transferred to *Augustodunum, the site retained a religious significance. Bibracte is much cited in modern research as the best example of indigenous Celtic urbanization in central Gaul during the late iron age (see CELTS). Excavations have revealed buildings and artefacts which suggest various distinct zones of settlement (religious, artisanal, aristocratic) and increasing economic, social, and political sophistication; but the picture is obscured by the continued occupation of Bibracte into the Roman period.

> P.-A. Février and others, *Histoire de la France urbaine* 1 (1980), 203 ff., 226 ff.   J. F. Dr.

bidental When lightning struck, the Etruscan and Roman ritual prescribed that the bolt be buried (often inscribed *fulgur conditum*), and the place enclosed (Luc. 1. 606–8; 8. 864). The ancients derived the name from the sacrificial victim (*bidens*, 'having two teeth'), but it may be a rendering of the Etruscan word for the bolt.

> C. O. Thulin, *Die etruskische Disciplin* (1905); P. Mingazzini, in *Gli Archeologi Italiani in onore di A. Maiuri* (1965) 317 ff.   J. L.

bilingualism Widespread bilingualism at some level was characteristic of the ancient world, whether we look for (*a*) bilingual *communities*, in which two languages are in use (e.g. official and popular languages, written and non-written, formal and informal), or (*b*) bilingual individuals who know two languages at some level. Perfect capacity in two languages, a modern ideal, was probably both rare and unnecessary, and, despite Hdt. 8. 144 on Greek (see GREEK LANGUAGE), the close modern identity of language and nation seems to have been relatively unimportant. But bilingualism implies language choice: according to context, the associations of each language, or social ambition. Latin and especially Greek, were the languages of culture and education (in the Roman empire, Latin was the language of law and army), as well as power, so that while many other languages coexisted alongside Latin and Greek, neither Greeks nor Romans ever had to impose their language on others. Greek and Roman writers tended to be uninterested in other languages, or they were never written down, so our evidence (written) is slight and misleading (e.g. we learn about Getic in *Tomis from *Ovid's complaints (e.g. *Pont.* 4. 13, 17 ff.), not from inscriptions.

Greek unwillingness to learn other languages, linked to their assurance of cultural superiority, is well known (Momigliano). *Herodotus learned no other languages (and suffered at interpreters' hands: e.g. 2. 125), Greek thinkers say little about foreign languages or revealingly categorize languages simply as Greek or *barbarian (e.g. *Plato (1), *Cratylus*). Yet this monolingualism may be more characteristic of the literary élite and of high culture. Other Greeks must have acquired other languages: e.g. the Ionian and Carian *mercenaries in Egypt in the Archaic period, the Greeks in Persian service, e.g. *Democedes (see D. M. Lewis, *Sparta and Persia* (1977), 12–15), traders and colonizers—*Massalia was still trilingual in the 1st cent. BC—and often married non-Greek women (cf. for the reverse, the unfortunate Scylas, Hdt. 4. 78 ff., with Scythian father and Greek mother). The *orientalizing period of Greek culture is hard to envisage with merely monolingual Greeks. Late 5th-cent. Athens has a mixture of customs and languages 'from all the Greeks and barbarians' (*Old Oligarch 2. 8). However, by the Classical period, the bilinguals in a Greek city would be mainly foreigners, traders, and slaves, i.e.

outsiders (e.g. Scythian archers, Ar. *Eccl.* 1001–225).

The picture becomes more complex with *Alexander (3) the Great's conquests of large non-Greek speaking areas. The idea that Greek was always imposed as the language of administration in the Hellenistic kingdoms is increasingly doubtful. In the Seleucid empire, there is a mixture of Greek and *Aramaic in the administration and, at least east of Asia Minor, evidence for bilingual Greeks. In Ptolemaic Egypt, Greek did become the language of administration; the extent to which Egyptians learnt Greek and became bilingual, however, or Greeks integrated at all into Egyptian society, is extremely difficult to gauge, and some recent work stresses bilingualism and at least limited interaction. There is evidence for individuals with double names, one Egyptian, one Greek, and for scribes fluent in both demotic and Greek. So the weight of administrative documents in Greek may hide greater Egyptian participation. Individual bilingualism, especially among prominent and ambitious Egyptian officials, must have been widespread.

The Roman empire was bilingual at the official, and multilingual at the individual and non-official, level. With the increasing Hellenization of Rome itself (see HELLENISM), educated Romans were expected to be bilingual in Latin and Greek, especially from the 1st cent. BC, at least for cultural purposes (there were tensions: *Juvenal complains about women who irritate their husbands by speaking Greek, *Sat.* 6. 184 ff.). *Quintilian advised that children start learning Greek before Latin (*Inst. Or.* 1. 1. 12–14). Greek was widely used in diplomatic activity from the republic: P. Licinius Crassus, proconsul of Asia in 131 BC who spoke five Greek dialects (Val. Max. 8. 7. 6) was exceptional, but by Cicero's time, interpreters were not always needed for Greek in the senate (Cic. *Fin.* 5. 89, with *Div.* 2. 131). *Tiberius tried, too late, to discourage Greek in the senate, a rare case of Latin chauvinism (Suet. *Tib.* 71: this failed). Most Roman emperors were fluent in Greek: Marcus *Aurelius, despairing of Latin, wrote his private *Meditations* in Greek; while *Septimius Severus may have been trilingual (Lat., Gk., Punic), *Severus Alexander perhaps better at Greek than Latin (SHA *Alex. Sev.* 3. 4).

The Romans made remarkably little attempt to impose Latin on the empire. The language of administration in the west was certainly Latin, and ambitious provincials simply had to acquire it themselves (Brunt). In the Greek-speaking east, administration was mostly conducted in Greek, mainly from pragmatism, and edicts, imperial constitutions, and letters sent by Rome to Greek cities were usually translated into Greek first (and inscribed in Greek). Greek speakers were markedly unenthusiastic about learning Latin, and Roman colonies in the east were linguistically quickly absorbed. However the extent of bilingual inscriptions implies there was no strict single language policy (see Kaimio). Decisions of the Roman courts were probably always given in Latin, and Latin was necessary in law for certain documents for Roman citizens. With the widening of Roman *citizenship (AD 212), *Severus Alexander (222–35) allowed Greek in the wills of Roman citizens. From the 4th cent., Latin was increasingly used in government and court when the government transferred to the east; this was deplored by educated Greeks. Greek became less widely known even in educated circles in the west from the 4th cent. (cf. Symmachus, *Epistolae* 4. 20).

The many other languages in the Roman empire tend to be submerged in our evidence because they were unwritten, or non-literary, and many gain prominence with Christian preoccupations, but must always have been there: e.g. Gallic, Getic, neo-*Phrygian, *Aramaic, Coptic, and Syriac which develop as literary languages after AD 200, Iberian, Thracian, Punic (noted by St Augustine), not to mention Hebrew. Romanized provincials presumably knew the 'vernacular' as well as Latin, and the languages each had their own milieu. The Roman army in particular brought together a multilingual force where the lingua franca was Latin (cf. Tac. *Hist.* 2. 37, 3. 33, for problems of polyglot armies). This substratum is indicated by the later adaptation of Roman law to the extension of Roman citizenship: Ulpian allowed 'even Punic, Gallic, Syriac, and other languages' for certain transactions (trusts) under Roman law (*Dig.* 32. 11 pref.). See also TRANSLATION.

A. Momigliano, *Alien Wisdom: The Limits of Hellenization* (1975); J. Kaimio, *The Romans and the Greek Language* (1979); C. W. Müller and others, *Zum Umgang mit fremden Sprachen in der griechisch-römischen Antike* (1992). For other languages in the Roman empire: R. Mac-Mullen, *AJPhil* 1966, 1 ff.; F. Millar, *JRS* 1968, 126 ff. and *The Roman Near East 31 BC–AD 337* (1993); W. Harris, *Ancient Literacy* (1989), 175 ff.; P. Brunt, *Imperial Themes* (1990), 267 ff. (full bibliography); Jones, *Later Rom. Emp.*, ch. 24; A. Kuhrt and S. Sherwin-White, *From Samarkhand to Sardis* (1993). For Egypt: W. Clarysse, *Aegyptus* 1985, 57 ff.; W. Peremans, *Anc. Soc.* 1973, 59 ff. R. T.

biography, Greek 1. Biography in antiquity was not a rigidly defined genre. *Bios*, 'life', or *bioi*, 'lives', could span a range of types of writing, from *Plutarch's cradle-to-grave accounts of statesmen to *Chamaeleon's extravagant stories about literary figures, and even to *Dicaearchus' ambitious *Life of Greece*. Consequently the boundaries with neighbouring genres—the encomium, the biographical novel on the model of *Xenophon (1)'s *Cyropaedia*, the historical monograph on the deeds of a great man like *Alexander (3) the Great—are blurred and sometimes artificial. One should not think of a single 'biographical genre' with acknowledged conventions, but rather of a complicated picture of overlapping traditions, embracing works of varying form, style, length, and truthfulness.

2. The impulse to celebrate the individual finds early expression in the *dirge and the funeral oration (see EPITAPHIOS); organization of a literary work around an individual's experiences is as old as the *Odyssey* (see HOMER), and various *Heracleids* and *Theseids* seem to have treated their subjects' deeds more comprehensively. In the 5th cent. biographical interest was pursued in various ways. *Ion (2) of Chios gossiped about contemporary figures in his 'Visits' (*Epidemiai*), while *Stesimbrotus wrote colourfully on *Themistocles, *Thucydides (1) son of Melesias, and *Pericles (1). The historian *Thucydides (2) included selective sketches of several figures, notably *Pausanias (1) and Themistocles. In the 4th cent. appeared two influential encomia, *Isocrates' *Evagoras* (see EVAGORAS), enumerating its subject's qualities in a loosely chronological framework, and Xenophon's *Agesilaus* (see AGESILAUS), giving first a focused narrative of achievements, then a catalogue of virtues. Xenophon's *Cyropaedia* also set the model for the idealizing and largely fictional biographical novel, while his 'Socratic Memoirs' (*Memorabilia*), along with the Platonic corpus, developed the personality of Socrates in different literary forms.

3. *Aristotle gave biography a new impetus. Under his influence interest in ethical and cultural history encouraged the writing of more generalized *bioi*. Dicaearchus and *Clearchus (3) treated different lifestyles; *Theophrastus' *Characters* are clearly related; while Dicaearchus' three-volume *Life of Greece* traced the origins of contemporary Greek culture. *Aristoxenus wrote Lives of philosophers, in which an interest in lifestyle combined with malicious stories about *Socrates' irascibility and *Plato (1)'s

plagiarism. This anecdotal style heralds a distinctive style of biography of cultural figures. Chamaeleon's Lives of various poets were notable for their wild inferences of biographical data from an author's work, and his model was followed by *Hermippus (2) of Smyrna, *Satyrus (1) (who adopted dialogue form), and *Sotion (1), who presented in thirteen books a διαδοχή, 'succession', of great philosophers. This tendency to collect Lives in series became a standard mode of presenting intellectual history, and the 'succession' of teachers and pupils was a helpful idiom for explaining influences. Little can be said of the literary form of these works, except that it varied.

4. Biography of political figures is more problematic. Dicaearchus presented philosophers as men of action as well as intellectuals, and the active life was prominent in discussion of lifestyles; several monographs also approximated to biographies or to series of biographical sketches, such as *Theopompus (3)'s *Philippica*, *Phaenias' *On the Sicilian Tyrants*, and *Idomeneus (2) *On the (Athenian) Demagogues*. Both Phaenias and Idomeneus also wrote on the Socratics, and other works similarly spanned politicians and intellectuals: Hermippus of Smyrna included (often mythical) lawgivers in his series, and Satyrus treated *Philip (1) II. But political history had an adequate alternative mode of presentation in the various forms of *historiography, which themselves increasingly stressed human personality.

5. Rather than clear-cut political *bioi*, we thus have works with biographical affinities. The impact of *Alexander (3) the Great was here important. Such early monographs as those of *Cleitarchus, *Ptolemy (1) I and *Aristobulus (1) centred on the king's person; the fragmentation of the Hellenistic world into dynasties encouraged monographs on other kings, such as *Duris' four-volume *History of Agathocles* (see AGATHOCLES), and perhaps the works on Agathocles and *Pyrrhus which formed a four-volume supplement to *Timaeus (2)'s *History*. The biographical novel on the model of *Cyropaedia* also revived, with its typical emphasis on a king's upbringing. *Onesicritus' *How Alexander Was Brought Up* belongs here, and so later does *Nicolaus of Damascus' *On Augustus' Life and Education*. This genre overlapped with encomium, which also flourished: *Polybius (1) 10. 21 mentions his earlier three-volume work on *Philopoemen, and distinguished the 'inflation' appropriate to that work from the truthfulness required of continuous history. The monographs may not have been full on childhood, and ranged beyond their subject's personal achievements; the novels (see NOVEL, GREEK) were largely idealized and partly fictional. But the biographical interest of these works is still strong, and the dividing line from biography is not clear.

6. About 240 BC *Antigonus (4) of Carystus displayed a new accuracy in describing contemporary philosophers; and in the scholarly atmosphere of *Alexandria (1) there developed a different style of biography, revaluing the findings of the *Peripatetics and re-establishing their chronological data. Commentaries and epitomes called for biographical introductions, which generally avoided chronological narrative: between the particulars of birth and death short notes elucidated the mode of life, friends, students, works, etc. Typical of this school is *Posidonius (2)'s pupil Jason of Nysa; later *Didymus (1)'s *On Demosthenes* collects many learned items in conjunction with a commentary on the *Philippics* of *Demosthenes (2). The artistic pretensions of this tradition are not great.

7. A type of autobiography goes back to early lyric poetry, to Xenophon's *Anabasis*, and to such self-defences as Isocrates' *Antidosis*, Demosthenes' *On the Crown*, and Plato's *Seventh Letter*.

By the 3rd cent. men of action were elaborating the memoir: *Aratus (2) was here most influential. With Nicolaus of Damascus' *Autobiography* the technique extends to an intellectual figure; he finds a follower in *Josephus.

8. The Christian Gospels have points of contact with the Greek tradition, with their charismatic hero and their anecdotal narrative texture. A different moral earnestness is found in Plutarch's *Parallel Lives*, which mark a considerable new achievement. Their scale, ambition, and historical sobriety are hard to parallel in the antecedent traditions; so is the depth of characterization. Important here is the technique of comparison of a Greek and Roman hero, drawing attention to nuances of personality. The moralizing is sometimes subtle; the psychological interest is uneven, but can be penetrating.

9. *Philostratus' *Life of Apollonius* (see APOLLONIUS (12)) veers towards hagiography: readers would probably not have taken it as literal truth. *Eunapius broke up the Alexandrian form. More learned were the Neoplatonist biographies of *Porphyry and *Marinus. The first book of Marcus *Aurelius provides a more exploratory form of intellectual autobiography. *Galen is similar but less perceptive, while *Lucian's *Dream* is more playful; *Libanius goes back to the model of Isocrates' *Antidosis*. *Diogenes (6) Laertius exemplifies the abridging and synthesizing of the materials of literary biography.

Much of Greek biography is lost; the range and richness of its remains are still striking. See also CHARACTER.

F. Leo, *Die griech.-röm. Biographie nach ihrer litt. Form* (1901); G. Misch, *A History of Autobiography in Antiquity* (1950); A. Dihle, *Studien zur griechischen Biographie*, 2nd edn. (1970); A. Momigliano, *The Development of Greek Biography*, 2nd edn. (1993); I. Gallo, *Frammenti biografici da papiri 1–2* (1975–80; vol. 3 forthcoming); M. R. Lefkowitz, *The Lives of the Greek Poets* (1981); J. Geiger, *Cornelius Nepos and Ancient Political Biography*, (1985), with J. L. Moles, *CR* 1989, 229–33; B. Gentili and G. Cerri, *History and Biography in Ancient Thought* (1988); R. A. Burridge, *What are the Gospels?* (1992).   C. B. R. P.

biography, Roman Roman biography did not wholly derive from its Greek equivalent: their own political and family customs led Romans to value the recording of the deeds of their great men. We hear of songs at banquets praising the famous, of dirges (*nenia) at funerals, and of a native tradition of funeral laudations (*laudatio funebris). Such laudations were preserved and kept among the family records, together with the likenesses (*imagines) of distinguished ancestors: Cicero (*Brut.* 62) complains about the inaccuracies of these laudations. Sepulchral inscriptions were important too, and became very elaborate, often giving details of private as well as public matters (cf. the 'laudations' of Murdia and Turia, *CIL* 6. 2. 10230 and 1527, 31670, see 'LAUDATIO TURIAE'). The flavour of such formal memorials is as recurrent in Roman biography as that of encomium in the Greek counterpart; it is, for instance, one of the elements detectable in *Tacitus (1)'s *Agricola*.

2. The competitive quest for glory also stimulated writers to self-justification and self-defence. The award of a triumph might depend on the bulletins sent home by generals; such writing naturally goes back to an early period. More elaborate apologetic or propagandist autobiography found a natural home in Rome: examples were the three books of M. *Aemilius Scaurus (1), the five or more of P. *Rutilius Rufus, and Q. *Lutatius Catulus (1)'s single book *On his Consulship and his Achievements*. The twenty-two books of *Sulla's memoirs owed something to the Greek precedent of *Aratus (2). *Caesar's *Commentaries* presented a particularly nuanced form of self-projection; *Cicero too wrote

about his own career and achievement both in Latin and in Greek. Under the Principate, it was especially members of the imperial family who wrote political memoirs: *Augustus, *Tiberius, *Iulia Agrippina, *Hadrian, *Septimius Severus.

3. Justification was not limited to autobiography. C. *Sempronius Gracchus' two books To Pomponius presented a picture of his brother Ti. *Sempronius Gracchus (3) which similarly contributed to contemporary debate. Equal generosity, even when the political point was less immediate, was surely to be found in the memoirs written by clients or freedmen of the great, M. *Tullius Tiro on Cicero and Plotus (= L. *Voltacilius (?) Pilutus or Pitholaus) on the Pompeii (Suet. Rhet. 6, cf. Peter, HRRel. 1. cclxxxiii–cclxxxiv). Such works can be hard to distinguish from the historical monograph: in his letter to L. *Lucceius (Fam. 5. 12) Cicero seems to assume that such a monograph will naturally centre on a single person and his achievements, and playfully pleads for a liberal attitude to the truth. *Sallust's extant monographs notably avoid such a sharp focus on *Jugurtha or *Catiline, but C. *Oppius (2)'s work on Caesar may belong here.

4. The political heat of the late republic produced further writings designed to praise and defend, or sometimes attack, not only political actions but private character or philosophy. The influence of forensic rhetoric, so often describing the life of client or opponent, is here strong. The death of M. *Porcius Cato (2) inspired works by Cicero and *Brutus, which were answered first by A. *Hirtius, then by Caesar's own counterblast the *Anticato; this in its turn was countered by Munatius Rufus. L. Calpurnius Bibulus wrote on the other philosopher-statesman, Brutus. These works represent the beginnings of a considerable literature, a blend of martyrology and ideological propaganda, which came to cluster around the Stoic opponents of the 1st-cent. Principate (see STOICISM). Deaths of Famous Men, such as C. Fannius' three books on *Nero's victims, dwelt especially on the theatrical martyrdoms: Q. *Iunius Arulenus Rusticus' Life of *Thrasea Paetus and *Herennius Senecio's of *Helvidius Priscus are mentioned by Tacitus in the preface to his Agricola, and this must have been a further influence on that work. Agricola too explores political life under a tyrant, though it praises restrained collaboration rather than ostentatious martyrdom; its use of an individual's life to sketch a political ambience is most deft.

5. Jerome named *Varro, *Cornelius Nepos, *Hyginus (1), *Santra, and *Suetonius in a canon of biographers (De vir. ill. 2. 821 Vull.). The contributions of Hyginus and Santra are obscure, but the list still brings out the range of literary form which the genre could accommodate. Varro may be named for his On Poets or for his Imagines ('Likenesses', a work which added some sort of brief description to a series of 700 portraits), or even for his Life (Vita) of the Roman People, a Roman imitation of *Dicaearchus. Besides longer works on M. *Porcius Cato (1) and on Cicero, Nepos wrote sixteen or eighteen books containing some 400 short Lives: the series On Foreign Generals survives, together with Cato (an abbreviation of the longer version) and the more elaborate and eulogistic Atticus, both it seems from the series On Roman Historians. His enterprise owed something to Greek writing 'On Famous Men', and Nepos was perhaps trying to make the great men of history accessible to a wider Roman audience. Suetonius' Caesars pointedly reduce the element of historical narrative, instead providing a learned survey of an emperor's character and behaviour under a series of headings. There is some generic similarity with his lives of grammarians and rhetors, but the scale and ambition is much greater. The style of the Caesars proved congenial as spectators increasingly saw Roman history in terms

of the ruling personality, and biography supplanted historiography as the dominant mode of record: *Marius Maximus and then the *Historia Augusta continued Suetonius and followed his model.

6. There is little intimacy in Roman biography. Much Latin poetry is self-revealing and self-analytical, but the most ambitious formal autobiography and biography centred on public figures, and exploration of spiritual life is felt as inappropriate. Cicero (Brut. 313 ff.) does tell us something of his education and development, analysing his debt to various teachers; but there are no Latin pieces of self-exploration comparable with Marcus *Aurelius' Εἰς Ἑαυτόν ('To himself') until we reach St *Augustine.

F. Leo, Die griech.-röm. Biographie nach ihrer litt. Form (1901); G. Misch, A History of Autobiography in Antiquity (1950); W. Steidle, Sueton und die antike Biographie, 2nd edn. (1963); W. Kierdorf, Laudatio funebris (1980); E. Rawson, Intellectual Life in the Late Roman Republic (1985); J. Geiger, Cornelius Nepos and Ancient Political Biography (1985), with J. L. Moles, CR 1989, 229–33; A. Dihle, Sitz. Heidelberg 1986.3; R. G. Lewis, ANRW 2. 33. 5. 3623–74.   C. B. R. P.

biology See ANATOMY AND PHYSIOLOGY; ANIMALS, KNOWLEDGE ABOUT; BOTANY; EMBRYOLOGY; GYNAECOLOGY; PHARMACOLOGY.

Bion (1), of Borysthenes (Olbia) (c.335–c.245 BC), popular philosopher. His own account of his early life (Diog. Laert. 4. 46–7) is problematic. His disreputable parents (an ex-prostitute and a freedman who sold salt fish) strain credulity; his father's financial disgrace and his own enslavement suspiciously recall alleged events in the biography of *Diogenes (2) the Cynic. Bion reached Athens c.315 and, while classed as Academic by *Diogenes (6) Laertius 4. 46–58, probably associated variously with *Xenocrates (1) the Academic, *Crates (2) the Cynic, Theodorus the Cyrenaic, and *Theophrastus the Peripatetic. He subsequently wandered throughout the Greek world giving public lectures and teaching for money. When old, he became a court philosopher of *Antigonus (2) Gonatas. Cynic in his theatrical deportment, caustic wit, rhetoric, literary style, dismissal of traditional education, rejection of all philosophy except ethics, and in much of his ethics, Bion nevertheless followed the *Cyrenaics in accepting the legitimacy of different social and political roles, including that of kings, and in interpreting the tag 'use the things that are present' to include riches as well as poverty. His serio-comic writings, of which *Teles and *Diogenes (6) Laertius preserve some substantial fragments, greatly influenced the 'diatribe' tradition and *Horace's Satires. See also CRATES (2); CYNICS; DIATRIBE.

R. Heinze, De Horatio Bionis imitatore (1889); O. Hense, Teletis Reliquiae, 2nd edn. (1909); J. F. Kindstrand, Bion of Borysthenes (1976).   J. L. Mo.

Bion (2), of Smyrna, listed in the Suda as the third bucolic poet in succession to *Theocritus and *Moschus; probably late 2nd cent. BC. A lament for him composed by a disciple from Italy, the Epitaphios Bionos—traditionally if wrongly edited as 'Moschus III'—claims, perhaps only rhetorically, that his death was brought about by poison (109 ff.). The reference in the same piece to *Aphrodite's last kiss for her lover *Adonis (68 f.) makes it likely that the 'Lament for Adonis' transmitted in the bucolic MSS was a composition by Bion himself; this 98-line hexameter poem ('Bion I') describes in extravagantly emotional fashion the distress of the goddess, and of the whole natural world, as news of the gory death of the Assyrian hunter is spread abroad. The debt to Theocritus' account of the death of Daphnis (Theoc. 1. 66 ff.; cf. 15. 100 ff.), including the elaborately varied refrains, is clear; but there is a new sentimentality and what Webster (*Hellenistic Poetry and Art* (1964), 203) called a 'luxury of lamentation'.

Seventeen other pieces, amounting to a little over 100 hexameter lines, are preserved, all but one in Stobaeus; most are mildly erotic or pastoral in tone, some are complete poems. There is no particular reason to accept Orsini's ascription of the *Epithalamium for Achilles and Deidameia* (conventionally 'Bion II') to the poet, though it fits his smooth but unadventurous Theocritean style well enough.

TEXT A. S. F. Gow, *Bucolici Graeci* (1952).

TRANSLATION A. S. F. Gow, *The Greek Bucolic Poets* (1953).

COMMENTARY On the *Lament for Adonis*: M. Fantuzzi, *Bionis Smyrnaei Adonidos Epitaphium* (1985); N. Hopkinson (ed.), *A Hellenistic Anthology* (1988). A. H. G.

Biottus, Greek comic poet of the 2nd cent. BC, mentioned only in didascalic lists (see DIDASKALIA). His Ποιητής ('Poet') was produced in 167, his Ἀγνοῶν ('Man in Ignorance') in 154 (*IG* 2². 2323. 212, 238 = 3 B 3 col. 4a 23, 5a 24). No fragments survive.

Kassel–Austin, *PCG* 4. 36. W. G. A.

birds, sacred Though the Greeks and Romans did not consider any bird actually divine, many birds, like other animals, were closely associated with the gods, and all birds could bring messages from the gods by omens (see PORTENTS). *Divination from the activities of birds (often eagles or other birds of prey) is well attested in *Homer (e.g. *Il.* 12. 200 ff.) and in tragedy (especially interesting is Aesch. *PV* 488–92, which indicates a well-developed science). In Rome, observation of birds was one of the chief forms of divination (see AUGURES). Not only was the behaviour of wild birds watched for signs, but on military expeditions chickens were kept for the purpose.

Numerous special divine associations developed in Greece. The eagle as the bird of *Zeus was almost universal. *Athena takes the form of several different birds in Homer and local myth; her connection with owls seems to be post-Homeric and is particularly linked with Athens. *Apollo was associated with the falcon and the swan, *Hera with the peacock; this last pairing must be of relatively recent date, since the peacock was still a novelty to Greeks in the 5th cent. BC. None of these birds was considered inviolate by virtue of association with a god. In fact, the association was occasionally sacrificial: doves, which along with sparrows were *Aphrodite's sacred bird, were frequently sacrificed to her (*Hesp.* 1984, 76–7, cf. 37–40). Most of these traditions were taken over when the Roman gods were identified with Greek counterparts; there were also some native Italian associations of birds with gods, such as that of the woodpecker with *Mars (see PICUS).

J. E. Pollard, *Birds in Greek Life and Myth* (1977). For individual species, D'A. W. Thompson, *Glossary of Greek Birds* 2nd edn. (1936). E. Ke.

birthday (γενέθλιος ἡμέρα; *natalis dies*). Among the Greeks the birthdays of several major Olympian deities (e.g. of *Artemis on the sixth, *Apollo on the seventh, and *Poseidon on the eighth) were in early times assigned to days of the month (e.g. *Hesiod, *Op.* 771) and were treated as sacred. Throughout Greek history these 'monthly' birthdays continued to be recognized and were often the focal points of the deities' annual festivals. For humans the day of birth itself was marked by congratulatory visits and presents from relatives and friends, but in the Archaic and Classical periods there seems to have been no recurring monthly or annual celebrations of the day. Birthdays of humans first attained significance for the Greeks when they began to assimilate rulers and outstanding individuals to gods (see RULER-CULT). *Plato (1), for example, shared Apollo's birthday (7 Thargelion: Diog. Laert. 3. 2), and after his death his followers gave him special veneration each year, probably on his birthday. In his will *Epicurus endowed an annual banquet for his followers on his birthday (10 Gamelion: Diog. Laert. 10. 18). So too after his death the birthday of the Hellenistic statesman *Aratus (2) of Sicyon (Plut. *Arat.* 53) was celebrated annually. Under the influence of Egyptian and Asian customs (Pl. *Alc.* 121), the birthdays and accession days of the Ptolemies (see PTOLEMY (1)), *Seleucids, and Attalids were publicly fêted during their lifetimes throughout their kingdoms, both monthly and annually, often with offerings and games (e.g. that of Ptolemy V by the Egyptians: *OGI* 90. 47).

The Romans, unlike the Greeks, marked only anniversaries and from earliest times annually celebrated their own birthdays and those of family members, friends, and patrons with gifts, offerings, prayers, vows, and banquets. Roman poets developed a specific type of poem (*genethliacon*) for the occasion (e.g. Hor. *Carm.* 4. 11 and Mart. 9. 52) and may have inspired a similar type of Greek poetry in the Roman period (e.g. *Anth. Pal.* 6. 227 and 261). The rituals of the Roman birthday formed part of the cult of the *genius* of a man or the *iuno* of a woman (e.g. Tib. 2. 2. 5–6; see GENIUS). Under the empire the people celebrated annually, as an important part of imperial cult, the birthdays of past and present emperors and members of the imperial family. The Romans also marked with rituals and festivals the annual *natales dies*, or foundation days, of cults, temples, and cities.

W. Schmidt, *Geburtstag im Altertum* (1908); K. Argetsinger, *Cl. Ant.* 1992, 175–93. J. D. M.

Bisitun (mod. Behistun; Βαγίστανον ὄρος (Ctesias in Diod. Sic. 2. 13. 1)), a cliff 30 km. (18½ mi.) east of Kermanshah, with a relief and a long trilingual inscription (*Elamite, Babylonian, *Old Persian) by *Darius I. The three versions differ in minor (though significant) details. Cols. 1–4 report on his victories over the usurper Gaumata and other rebel kings in his first regnal year. The inscription was carved in stages; the OP version was added last. Copies were sent out (DB 4. 88 ff.) and parts have been found at Elephantine (*Aramaic) and *Babylon. Bisutun is the only narrative OP text. Cols. 1–4 follow models from *Mesopotamia and *Urartu. Col. 5, on Darius' second and third years, (OP only) is similar to the ahistoric style of the later OP inscriptions.

H. Weissbach, *Die Keilinschriften der Achämeniden* (1911), with El., Bab., and OP text; R. G. Kent, *Old Persian*, (1953); E. N. von Voigtlander, *The Bisitun Inscription of Darius the Great: Babylonian Version* (1978); J. C. Greenfield and B. Porten, *The Bisitun Inscription of Darius the Great: Aramaic Version*, (1982); R. Schmitt, *SÖAW* 561 (1990); H. Luschey and R. Schmitt, *Enc. Ir.* 4. 289–305, 'Bīsotūn'. H. S.-W.

Bithynia, a territory in NW Asia Minor, originally confined to the peninsula of Chalcedon, but gradually extending eastward to *Heraclea (3) and *Paphlagonia, and southward across the Propontis to Mysian Olympus. Although much of the land is mountainous and covered with forest, the *Sangarius river with its tributaries and the valleys that run back from the Propontis form fertile plains and provide relatively easy communications. It was economically one of the richest regions of *Asia Minor, producing good timber, excellent pasturage, and all manner of fruits and grains, possessing fine marble quarries and good harbours, and crossed by the main roads to the Anatolian plateau and to Pontus.

The Bithynians were of Thracian origin (see THRACE) and long retained their ethnic identity. They were often at war with the Greek colonies of the coast, preserved a measure of autonomy under their own rulers during the Persian regime, and in 298/7 BC founded a dynasty beginning with King Zipoetes. By a combination of aggressive policies and judicious alliances (especially with the *Galatians, whom they invited into Asia in 278/7) the Bithynian kings protected themselves against the Seleucids and their rival Heraclea and extended their power to inner Paphlagonia, to the fertile basins round *Nicaea (1) and Prusa, and eventually over the cities of the coast. Their kings, especially Nicomedes I and II and Prusias I, were active founders of cities and promoted Greek culture. Despite some loss of territory to Pergamum in the 2nd cent. BC, there were few changes until 75/4 BC when Nicomedes IV bequeathed his kingdom to Rome (see NICOMEDES I–IV; PRUSIAS (1) I and (2) II).

In organizing the province of *Pontus and Bithynia in 63 BC *Pompey divided the land between eleven cities for convenience in maintaining order and collecting taxes. Much of the land, especially in the large territory of Nicaea (1), was split up into large estates. Despite heavy exploitation by the *publicani in the 1st cent. BC, which led much land to be transferred to Italian owners, the region was to become very prosperous under the Roman empire. Pontus and Bithynia was at first governed by proconsuls, but the importance of the highways to the eastern frontiers and to Syria and of the maritime connections in the Black Sea led imperial procurators to assume greater responsibilities than usual under the Julio-Claudian emperors; and special imperial legates replaced proconsuls under *Trajan and *Hadrian (*Pliny (2), C. *Iulius Cornutus Tertullus, C. Iulius Severus), a practice which became permanent from the time of Marcus *Aurelius. The conditions of city life in Bithynia in the early 2nd cent. AD are unusually well documented, with the correspondence of Pliny (2) the Younger and *Trajan c. AD 110 and the speeches of *Dio Cocceianus revealing peculation by magistrates, unwise and extravagant building, bitter rivalries between the cities, and social discontent. They appear to be symptoms of booming but uncontrolled civic prosperity.

M. I. Rostovtzeff, BSA 1918, 1 ff.; Jones, Cities E. Rom. Prov. 148 ff.; G. Vitucci, Il Regno di Bitinia (1953); S. Mitchell, Acts of the 8th Int. Congress of Greek and Latin Epigraphy (1984), 120–33; B. Levick, G&R 1979, 119–31.　　　　T. R. S. B.; S. M.

Biton (Βίτων) (3rd or 2nd cent. BC), the author of a small extant work on siege-engines, Κατασκευαὶ πολεμικῶν ὀργάνων καὶ καταπαλτικῶν ('The Construction of War-machines and Catapults'; see ARTILLERY; SIEGECRAFT), and of a lost work on *optics.

Ed. E. W. Marsden, Greek and Roman Artillery 2 (1971), 61 ff. (with trans.).　　　　S. H.

Black Sea See EUXINE.

Blaesus, of Capreae (? 2nd or 1st cent. BC), author of σπουδογέλοια (whether comic or satiric is uncertain).

M. Gigante, Rintone e il teatro in Magna Grecia (1971), 82–3.　　　　J. S. R.

Blossius (RE 1), **Gaius**, of Cumae, descendant of a prominent anti-Roman family of Hannibalic *Capua and a student of Stoic philosophy (see STOICISM), was a friend of Ti. *Sempronius Gracchus (3), after whose death he joined *Aristonicus (1). After Aristonicus' defeat he killed himself. His philosophical influence on both these men is difficult to gauge.

D. R. Dudley, JRS 1941, 94 ff.　　　　E. B.

Bocchus I (RE 1), king of *Mauretania and father-in-law or son-in-law of *Jugurtha. His offer of alliance, early in the Jugurthine War, was rejected by Rome. He later joined Jugurtha, receiving western *Numidia as his price. With Jugurtha, he twice nearly defeated C. *Marius (1), but was finally induced by *Sulla to surrender Jugurtha. He became a 'friend of the Roman People' and retained part of Numidia. The surrender of Jugurtha to Sulla, with whom Bocchus maintained a close connection, was depicted on Sulla's signet ring, to Marius' irritation, and in a controversial group of statues dedicated by Bocchus on the Capitol in 91 BC (Plut. Mar. 32. 4). It is shown on a coin of Faustus *Cornelius Sulla, Sulla's son. (See RRC 426/1.)

Sallust, Iug., is the main source. For the coins see Mazard.　　　　E. B.

Bocchus II (RE 2), king of *Mauretania jointly with *Bogud (his brother), ruling the later Caesariensis. In the Civil War he joined P. *Sittius and supported *Caesar against *Juba I. He was rewarded with part of *Numidia, but lost it after Caesar's death. He supported Octavian's commanders against *Antony's and Bogud, whom he expelled, and he received the undivided kingdom from Octavian. He died in 33 BC. Augustus later gave the kingdom to *Juba II.

Cass. Dio, bks. 48–50, is the main source. For the coins see Mazard.　　　　E. B.

body The history of the body is a discipline which emerged in the 1980s; it questions the extent to which the body is 'natural', and asks whether all societies have experienced the body in the same way. The combined classical and Christian heritage of western civilization has assigned the body a subordinate place in its value systems, but dichotomies such as mind/body and soul/body are by no means universal. The subject is associated in particular with the work of Foucault, although his studies of the classical world have been criticized for relying unduly on élite philosophical texts, neglecting Rome, and ignoring female sexuality.

It is in medical texts that the differences between ancient and modern experiences of the body are perhaps most obvious. For many centuries, Graeco-Roman *medicine included the belief that the womb could move around the body, and debate existed on such issues as the seat of consciousness (the liver, the heart, and the brain were suggested) and the origin of male seed (from the brain, the blood, or the whole body). The female body was seen as unstable; strong affinities existed between the top and bottom, so that defloration deepened the voice, while menstrual blood could come out of the nose (see EMBRYOLOGY; GYNAECOLOGY).

Another clear distinction between our own society and the ancient world concerns nakedness. Clothing was one of the features believed to set humanity apart from the animals. In Homer, nakedness is associated with vulnerability and shame; Odysseus covers himself before Nausicaa (Od. 6. 126–9). For the Greeks of the Classical period, however, nudity becomes the costume of the citizen; because male nudity is seen as normal, only *barbarians are represented as feeling shame when a man is seen naked (Hdt. 1. 10. 3 on the Lydians). Female nudity, meanwhile, continues to be associated with vulnerability and shame; the girls of *Miletus are persuaded to end a mass suicide epidemic by the threat of exposure after death (Plut. Mor. 249bd). Nudity is also associated with *initiation (e.g. *Brauron) and fertility. In Athenian vase-paintings, men are represented naked in outdoor scenes, never in private domestic space. Women are generally shown naked only in private scenes when nudity is to be expected—for example, when washing—or when they are about to be killed or raped. In Etruscan art, in contrast, men wear shorts or loincloths in situations when Greek men would be shown naked—for instance when exercising. In Roman art, nudity continues to be the costume of the male hero.

From childhood, the body needed to be controlled. Roman child-nurses were advised on how to mould the shape of the body, by swaddling and massage (Sor. *Gynaeceia* 2. 15, 32). For men, correct control of the body was a further part of the costume of a good citizen. The orator, in particular, was advised on every aspect of presentation of self (e.g. Cic. *Off.*; Quint. *Inst.* 11. 3) (see RHETORIC, LATIN; GESTURES). The state too had a role in controlling the body, by instilling obedience through *education and, above all, through military training (see EPHĒBOI). *Physiognomy used the body to reveal character, but recognized that individuals could learn to conceal their faults by changing their outward appearance. From *Pandora's adornment by the gods onwards, women were represented as deceptive and frivolous, their elaborate clothing, wigs, and make-up concealing the vices underneath. Both Greek and Roman sources praise the unadorned woman (e.g. Xen. *Oec.* 10. 2–13; Seneca, *De consolatione* 16), while Roman sumptuary legislation tried to set limits on the expense of women's clothing (see COSMETICS; DRESS).

*Augustine (e.g. *De civ. D.* 19. 13) draws a parallel between the ordered arrangement of the parts of the body and the ordered arrangement of the appetites of the soul. Peace and health consist of both. Within the order of nature, the soul must control the body and reason the appetites, just as master controls slave and man controls woman. Some Christians positively valued neglect of the body—seen in abstinence from food and sex (see CHASTITY), or lack of interest in one's appearance—as evidence of a proper rejection of this world, whereas Graeco-Roman philosophy urged the care of the body as evidence of the virtue of *enkrateia* or self-control.

The body is also a central metaphor for political and social order. In Livy, *Menenius Agrippa uses the body as an analogy for the body politic; the rest of the body revolts against the stomach (i.e. senate), perceived as idle, but soon weakens and has to recognize its dependence (2. 32). Disease in the body politic was a way of expressing social disorder.

General bibliography: B. Duden, *Body History* (1990). General survey: R. Porter, in P. Burke (ed.), *New Perspectives on Historical Writing* (1991), 206–32. M. Arthur-Katz, *Metis* 1989, 155–79; L. Bonfante, *AJArch* 1989, 534–70; P. Brown, *The Body and Society* (1988); M. Feher and others (eds.), *Fragments for a History of the Human Body*, pts. 1–3 (1989); M. Foucault, *The History of Sexuality* (1978–86; Fr. orig. 1976–84); D. Halperin and others, *Before Sexuality* (1990); E. Keuls, *The Reign of the Phallus* (1985); D. Konstan and M. Nussbaum (eds.), *Differences* 2/1 (1990); T. Laqueur, *Making Sex* (1990); *Source: Notes in the History of Art* 12/2 (1993); R. Padel, *In and Out of the Mind* (1992); A. Richlin, *Helios* 1991, 160–80; M. Wyke, in L. J. Archer and others (eds.), *Women in Ancient Societies* (1994), 134–51. H. K.

Boedromia, literally 'festival of running to help in response to a cry for aid' (or of the god associated therewith), a minor Attic festival of *Apollo. Both the associated month-name Boedromion and Apollo's title Boedromios are widely attested, the festival only at Athens, and only faintly even there: in the only allusion to it in a surviving Classical text, *Demosthenes (2) seems to imply (3. 31) that in the 4th cent. BC it was an optional element in the festival programme. It was probably military in flavour, being linked aetiologically with aid brought in battle. The only

rites mentioned are *sacrifice and a *procession (Dem. 3. 31; Plut. *Thes.* 27).

F. Jacoby, note on Philochorus, *FGrH* 328 F 13. R. C. T. P.

Boeotia and Boeotian Confederacy Boeotia was a region in central Greece, bounded in the north by *Phocis and Opuntian *Locris. The east faces the Euboean Gulf, and Mts. Parnes and Cithaeron form the southern boundary with Attica. On the west Mt. *Helicon and some lower heights separate a narrow coastline from the interior. Lake *Copais divided the region into a smaller northern part, the major city of which was *Orchomenus (1), and a larger southern part dominated by *Thebes (1). Geography and the fertility of the soil encouraged the growth of many prosperous and populous cities and villages. Although now there is indication of palaeolithic and mesolithic habitation, numerous findings prove a dense neolithic population. Thucydides (1. 12) states that the region was originally named Cadmeis, but that the *Boiotoi* gave it its present name 60 years after the Trojan War. Yet the Catalogue of Ships (*Homer, *Iliad* 2) knows of Boeotians already living in Boeotia before the war. Archaeology also proves both continuity of culture before the putative Trojan War and the decline of population during LH III, probably owing to mass migrations to the east. This late Helladic period was none the less prosperous enough to sustain Mycenaean palaces at Thebes, Orchomenus, and *Gla.

Boeotia enters history only with *Hesiod of *Ascra, whose *Works and Days* indicates an agricultural society of smallholdings. In his time several *basileis* in *Thespiae possessed the judicial power to settle inheritances. Evidence also indicates that other large cities exercised power over their smaller neighbours, *Plataea, *Tanagra, and Thebes among them. The result was the development of well-defined political units that formed the basis of an early federal government. The union of these cities in a broader political system was aided by their common culture, ethnicity, language, and religion. By the last quarter of the 6th cent. BC some of these cities formed the Boeotian Confederacy, doubtless under the hegemony of Thebes (see FEDERAL STATES). The Boeotians, as a people, not as a confederacy, were early members of the Delphic *Amphictiony.

From the outset of the *Persian Wars until the *Pax Romana*, Boeotia was the 'dancing-floor of war' in Greece. Boeotian reaction to the Persian invasion was mixed. Plataea, Thespiae, and some elements in Thebes originally favoured the Greeks, but after the battle of *Thermopylae only Plataea remained loyal to the Greek cause. The Persian defeat entailed the devastation of Boeotia. A truncated confederacy may have survived, but the region was politically unimportant. In 457 BC Boeotia allied itself with Sparta, which resulted in the battles of Tanagra and Oenophyta, the latter a major Boeotian defeat. Afterwards, Athens held control of Boeotia until the battle of *Coronea in 447 BC. Thereafter, Boeotia rebuilt its confederacy, and remodelled its federal government along the lines described by the *Hellenica Oxyrhynchia* (see OXYRHYNCHUS, THE HISTORIAN FROM).

Boeotia supported Sparta in the *Peloponnesian War, with Thebes helping to inflame it by its siege of Plataea. Boeotia defeated Athens at the battle of *Delion in 424 BC, and contributed substantially to its eventual defeat. After the peace treaty of 404 BC relations between Boeotia and Sparta cooled to the point where they broke in 395 BC, when Boeotia joined Athens, *Corinth, and *Argos (2) to oppose Sparta in the *Corinthian War. Sparta's victory and the *King's Peace resulted in the political fragmentation of the region. A Spartan attack on Thebes in

382 BC further weakened Boeotia, until 378 BC, when Thebes revolted and re-established the Boeotian Confederacy, which ultimately led to confrontation at the battle of *Leuctra. There the Boeotian army under *Epaminondas defeated Sparta and created a period of Theban ascendancy that lasted until the Third *Sacred War. Weakened by the devastation of that war, Boeotia allied itself with *Philip (1) II. The alliance, always uneasy, ended with its decision to join Athens to oppose him at *Chaeronea in 338 BC. During the Hellenistic period the region was often the battleground of monarchs and leagues alike. Only with *Sulla's victory at *Chaeronea in 86 BC did Boeotia enjoy peace under Rome. Forming part of *Achaia from 27 BC, Roman Boeotia is evoked, with much convincing detail (F. Millar, JRS 1981, 63 ff.), in *Apuleius' Golden Ass (mid-2nd cent. AD). It was not entirely a backwater: Lebadea (see TROPHONIUS) and Thespiae hosted Panhellenic cults and festivals; and the family and circle of *Plutarch reveal men of culture among Boeotia's landowners. Archaeological survey shows a strong recovery from earlier depopulation in the 4th-6th cents. AD, when Thebes re-emerged as Boeotia's natural centre.

R. Buck, *History of Boeotia* (1979), and *Boiotia and the Boiotian League 423–371 BC* (1994); P. Roesch, *Thespies et la confédération béotienne* (1965), and *Études béotiennes* (1982); O. Rackham, *BSA* 1983, 291 ff. (historical ecology), and *La Béotie antique* (1985); J. Fossey, *Topography and Population of Ancient Boeotia* (1988); H. Beister and J. Buckler (eds.), *Boiotika* (1989); J. Bintliff, in G. Barker and J. Lloyd (eds.), *Roman Landscapes* (1991). J. Bu.; A. J. S. S.

Boeotia, cults of The Linear B archive at *Thebes (1) (Spyropoulos and Chadwick, Piteros and others, see bibliog. below) refers to a number of deities, four of whom were worshipped in the Hellenic period: Potnia (later Demeter of Potniae, southern suburb of Thebes, of which *Demeter Thesmophoros was *poliouchos*), *Hera, *Hermes (the chief deities of the Hellenic *poleis* of Plataea and Tanagra respectively), and the goddess of a place near Thebes called Hapha/e (therefore [H]aphaea, possible precursor of Leucothea; see INO). *Homer knows of *Poseidon at Onchestus, Athena of Alalcomenae, the Thebans *Dionysus, *Heracles, and *Ino-Leucothea (all, save the last, in the *Iliad*). It is possible that the Poseidon Heliconius of the *Ionians was derived from the god who controlled the pass at Onchestus, at the NE foot of the *Helicon massif: his cult in Boeotia may therefore go back to the bronze age. Like the god at *Calauria (where Minyan Orchomenus (1) was a member of the *amphictiony) Poseidon at Onchestus was served by a priestess.

*Athena Alalcomeneïs gave her name to the limitary sanctuary at the eastern end of the territory of Coronea; at her sanctuary just outside the town of Coronea she bore the epithet Itonia, revealing the Thessalian origins of her worshippers (see THESSALY). From the middle of the 6th cent. BC, Itonia shared her sanctuary with a male god, first depicted later as *Zeus Caraeus/Ceraeus/Acraeus ('of the mountain-tops'), Laphystius ('devourer', describing his character), and Basileus ('king', referring to the range of his powers). He was the ethnic god of the *Minyans of Orchomenus and eastern Thessaly (Acraeus and Laphystius east and west of Iolcus respectively). The date at which worshippers of this Zeus and Athena moved into Boeotia is uncertain (there is reason to prefer a bronze age over a 'dark age' date: for example, the place-name Thebes, found in both Boeotia and Achaea-Phthiotis (see THESSALY), occurs in Linear B at Thebes). However, the two may have been combined—possibly for political reasons—in the middle of the 6th cent. Later, particularly under the Hellenistic Boeotian Confederacy, Athena Itonia and Zeus

Caraeus were the official gods of the confederacy: the Boeotian year began and ended (at the winter solstice) with months sacred to Zeus (Boukatios) and Athena (Alalkomenios).

Cults of *Apollo can also be traced back to the early Archaic period. He took over, directly or indirectly, a set of oracles of the same type around the Copais (*Ptoion, *Tegyra, Thurium, Tilphossa, Lebadea; see TROPHONIUS). One of these, the oracle of Trophonius at Lebadea, like that of *Amphiaraus near *Oropus, belonged to an underground oracular god who was approached directly by the consultant.

Another pan-Boeotian deity whose worship covered all of Boeotia and extended across the strait to Euboea was the bi-form *Demeter, of whom traces are found as Achaea, (Demeter and Kore) Thesmophoros, Eleusinia, Megalartos/Megalomazos. She too must have belonged to a very early stratum, as did several groups of cults, known under different names in different places: female trinities, female and male pairs, warrior groups, boys who drowned (Schachter 1972).

The worship of *Artemis must also be extended back to a very early period (*Aulis): her function in time of war is reflected in the epithet Euclea, which apparently she bore in every Boeotian agora.

Several Boeotian sanctuaries were regularly frequented by non-Boeotians: Amphiaraus at Oropus, *Trophonius and Zeus at Lebadea, Apollo at the Ptoion, the *Muses at the foot of Helicon. Others—*Hera called Cithaeronia (worshipped as such on Mt. Helicon as well), Demeter Achaea, Athena Itonia, Zeus Caraeus—were more important within Boeotia itself, while here and there were cults on whom the local population lavished worship and expense, but whose popularity was strictly local: *Eros at Thespiae, the hero Ptoios at *Acraephnium, the *Cabiri west of Thebes (the last no doubt brought to Boeotia from Asia Minor, possibly in the 8th cent.).

C. Piteros and others, *BCH* 1990, 103–86; A. Schachter, *Teiresias*, Suppl. 1 (1972), 17–30; A. Schachter, *Cults of Boiotia*, 5 vols. (1981–); T. G. Spyropoulos and J. Chadwick, *Minos*, Suppl. 4 (1975). A. Sch.

Boeotian Confederacy See BOEOTIA; FEDERAL STATES.

Boeotius, treaty of, modern name for an important moment in Spartan–Persian diplomacy in the late 5th cent. BC (Xen. *Hell.* 1. 4), by which Sparta in 408 BC may have secured the *autonomy of the Asia Minor Greeks provided they paid tribute to Persia. The treaty is only a hypothesis but would explain why the definite revival of the autonomy issue caused so little surprise in the 390s. (Xen. *Hell.* 3).

D. M. Lewis, *Sparta and Persia* (1977), 122–5, and *CAH* 6² (1994), 24 n. 2; C. Tuplin, *Achaemenid History* 2 (1987), 133 ff. S. H.

Boethius, Anicius Manlius Severinus (c. AD 480–c.524). The Ostrogothic king *Theoderic (1) appointed this leading nobleman consul (510), and *magister officiorum* (?522). He resisted official oppression, was implicated in a senatorial conspiracy, imprisoned, and executed. His *De consolatione philosophiae* is a prison dialogue with Philosophy, a *Menippean mixture of prose and verse, owing much to *Martianus Capella and *Augustine. It justifies providence on a Stoic and Neoplatonic basis (see STOICISM; NEOPLATONISM), without overt *Christianity; its reconciliation of free will and divine prescience is philosophically notable; it shows high literary genius, and an astounding memory for classical texts under trying conditions. Boethius' Greek scholarship was rare in Italy; he planned introductions and translations for the mathematical and logical disciplines, and complete translations of *Plato (1) and *Aristotle. The project was never completed, and much is lost or fragmentary. Survivors: *De arithmetica* and *Institutio musica* (on which see below); a commentary on *Cicero's *Topics*, translations and commentaries for *Porphyry's *Isagoge*, and Aristotle's *Prior Analytics*, *Categories*, and *Perihermeneias*; translations of Aristotle's *Topics* and *Sophistici elenchi*. Five treatises give Boethius' own introduction to Peripatetic logic. Literal translation and repetitive explanation made the philosophic corpus inelegant but serviceable; excepting *De syllogismis hypotheticis*, it is generally unoriginal. Boethius owed much to *Alexandrian and Athenian Neoplatonists (especially *Ammonius (2)), but personal contact is unprovable. Involved in Christological controversies which had divided Rome and Constantinople, he wrote five theological *Tractates*; the fifth, the most original, favours the Theopaschite formula, aimed at reconciling Monophysites. Undervalued in his own day, Boethius wielded vast influence from Carolingian times onward, especially on Abelard; *De consolatione* was translated by King Alfred, Chaucer, and Elizabeth I.

TEXTS, COMMENTARIES, TRANSLATIONS Migne, *PL* 63–4 (including *spuria*); *De consolatione*, ed. L. Bieler, *CCSL* 94 (1957), comm., J. Gruber (1978); *Tractates*, ed. R. Peiper (1871); *De cons.* and *Tractates*, ed. with Eng. trans., E. K. Rand, H. F. Stewart, and S. J. Tester (1973); *De arithmetica* and *De musica*, ed. G. Friedlein (1867); Eng. trans. of *De arith.*, M. Masi (1983), Eng. trans. of *De mus.*, C. M. Bower (1989); *De syllogismis Hypotheticis*, ed. L. Obertello (1969); *Geometriae* (supposed), ed. M. Folkerts (1970); Aristotelian translations: trans. of Porphyry's *Isagoge*, and comm. on *Prior Analytics* in *Aristoteles Latinus*, ed. L. Minio-Paluello and B. Dod (1961–75); comm. on *Isagoge*, ed. S. Brandt, *CSEL* 48 (1906), on *Peri hermeneias*, ed. C. Meiser (1877–80), on Cicero's *Topics* in *Ciceronis Opera* 5. 1, ed. J. C. Orelli and J. G. Baiter (1834); *De Topicis Differentiis*, Eng. trans. with comm., E. Stump (1978).

LITERATURE P. Courcelle, *Late Latin Writers and their Greek Sources* (1969; Fr. orig. 1948); M. T. Gibson (ed.), *Boethius* (1981); H. Chadwick, *Boethius* (1981). S. J. B. B.

Musical writings Boethius' *Institutio musica*, mainly paraphrased from Greek sources, deploys Pythagorean harmonics (see PYTHAGORAS), within the quadrivium, to promote understanding of music's extraordinary powers. Books 1–3 (introduction and mathematical demonstrations) and possibly book 4 (divisions of the monochord, modes) derive from a lost work by *Nicomachus (3). Book 5 (incomplete) renders *Ptolemy (4) *Harm.* 1, very selectively: perhaps *Harm.* 2–3 were intended to follow. Boethius' eloquent but difficult text became the foundation of medieval music theory.

Ed. G. Friedlein (1867); Eng. trans. with notes, C. M. Bower, *Fundamentals of Music* (1989). A. D. B.

Boethus (1) and (2) (2nd cent. BC), metalworkers, of *Chalcedon. Members of a family of artisans alternating the names Boethus and Athenaeon. Made portraits at *Lindus and *Delos between 184 and 126, a bronze *herm found in a ship wrecked off Mahdia in Tunisia (c.100), and a child strangling a goose (Plin. *HN* 34. 84), perhaps preserved in copy; also expensive couches and silver tableware. A bronze statue of Agon (Eros Enagonios) found in the Mahdia wreck may go with the herm. Not to be confused with either the sculptor (?) of the Elgin throne (Malibu, Getty Mus.) or Boethus son of Apollodorus of Carthage, known from a single signature from *Ephesus.

J. Marcadé, *Receuil de signatures* (1957), 2. 28 ff; A. F. Stewart, *Greek Sculpture* (1990), 229 f., 305 f., figs. 847, 850. A. F. S.

Boethus (3), of Sidon (2nd cent. BC), Stoic, pupil of *Diogenes (3) of Babylon. He held unorthodox positions in some areas of Stoic physics: he rejected the *ekpurōsis* and derived *soul from air

and fire. He devoted much attention to details of Stoic cosmology, writing a commentary on *Aratus (1)'s *Phaenomena* and works *On Nature* and *On Fate*. At Diog. Laert. 7. 54 he is said to have admitted several *kritēria*: intelligence, perception, desire, and knowledge. Despite far-reaching theories of basic unorthodoxy based on this passage, its significance is unclear, since the candidates are probably not offered as *kritēria* in the same sense, or for the same thing. See STOICISM

Testimonia in von Arnim, *SVF* 3. 265–7. J. A.

Boethus (4), of Sidon, Aristotelian philosopher of the time of Augustus, *Andronicus of Rhodes' pupil and successor, it seems, as head of the *Peripatetic school at Athens. He pursued Andronicus' work of explaining *Aristotle: his commentaries, now lost, were used by later Greek commentators. His learned and subtle interpretation and defence of Aristotle's *Categories* is best documented.

P. Moraux, *Der Aristotelismus bei den Griechen* 1 (1973), 143 ff.; H. Gottschalk, *ANRW* 2. 36. 2 (1987), 1079 ff. D. O'M.

Bogazkoy See HATTUSA.

Bogud (*RE* 1–2), king of Mauretania jointly with *Bocchus II, ruling the later Tingitana. (Both were sons of *Bocchus I.) He fought for *Caesar in Spain and Africa and played a major part at Munda. After Caesar's death he fought for M. *Antonius (2) against Octavian's commanders in Spain, but his subjects rebelled and Bocchus, who had supported Octavian, seized his kingdom. He joined Antonius in the *Actium campaign and was killed defending Methone against *Agrippa.

Cass. Dio 48–50, is the main source. For the coins see Mazard. E. B.

Boii, Gauls who are traditionally thought to have entered Italy c.400 BC (reputedly via the Great St Bernard) and established themselves between the Po (*Padus) and the Apennines, ousting *Etruscans and *Umbrians. However, it is now clear that the existing population was already predominantly Celtic (see CELTS). The Etruscan town of *Felsina (later *Bononia (1), mod. Bologna) was one of a number of centres, with richly furnished graves. Defeated by Rome c.282 BC, they signed a 45-year truce. They were conquered again at *Telamon (2) (225) and submitted until *Hannibal's arrival encouraged them anew; with Ligurian and other allies they continued fighting Rome until they were subjugated, massacred, and mulcted of half their territory in 191. Military roads and colonies (Bononia, *Parma, *Mutina) consolidated the Roman victory and the Boii disappeared from Italy through either expulsion or assimilation (Livy 5. 35, 21–35; Polyb. 2. 17 f., 3). Boii are also recorded in Gaul, where they supported the Helvetii, were defeated at *Bibracte (58 BC), and settled on Aeduan territory (Caes. *BGall.* 1. 5. 28, 7. 9). Bohemia, which preserves their name, likewise contained Boii from early times until their extermination by *Burebistas the Dacian c.50 BC.

The relationship of these various Boii is commonly but somewhat unconvincingly explained as follows (Strabo 5. 213): large numbers left the parent Gallic stock, entered Italy, were expelled thence after 191 BC and settled in Bohemia.

For bibliography see CISALPINE GAUL, and *The Celts*, exhib. cat. (1991), 220 f. E. T. S.; T. W. P.

Boio, short form of a woman's name (based on 'Boiotian' ?). (1) Legendary Delphian (see DELPHI) author of a *hymn mentioning *Hyperboreans and the prophet *Olen (Paus. 10. 5. 7–8). (2) Either Boio (fem.) or Boios (masc.), author of the Hellenistic

Ornithogonia ('Origins of Birds', cf. 'Theogony') used by *Ovid in his *Metamorphoses*. The two are generally conflated.

Powell, *Coll. Alex.* 23–5. *RE* 3 (1899), 633–4; F. Jacoby, *FGrH* 3b (Suppl.) on Philochorus, 328 F 214. K. D.

Bola (or Bolae), town in Latium, which often changed hands between Romans and *Aequi in the 5th cent. BC. It disappears from history after 389 BC (Livy 6. 2. 14; Diod. Sic. 14. 117. 4). Its site was somewhere near *Algidus. E. T. S.; T. W. P.

Bolus (*RE* 3, Suppl. 1), from Mendes in Egypt, contemporary of *Callimachus (3) (3rd cent. BC), a writer on *magic and *pharmacology. A work of his entitled *On Sympathies and Antipathies* was somehow attributed to *Democritus of Abdera, and as a consequence Bolus is sometimes referred to as pseudo-Democritus. Only fragments of his works survive; one apparently contained a materia medica in which drugs were divided into artificial and natural substances (Χειρόκμητα and Φυσικὰ δυναμερά). He also wrote a work *On Marvels* (Θαυμάσια) and was the first in a considerable tradition of *paradoxographers. The *Suda* reports the existence of two men called Bolus, one a philosopher and follower of Democritus, and the other a Pythagorean from Mendes, but they are now thought to be identical.

FRAGMENTS DK 68 B 300 and *FGrH* 263.
LITERATURE K. Ziegler, *RE*, 'Paradoxographoi'. J. P. Hershbell, *Ambix* 1987, 5–20, contains full references to earlier critical work on Bolus and a controversial assessment of his identity. D. J. F.; J. T. V.

Bona Dea (the Good Goddess—this is her title, not name, which is uncertain), an Italian goddess, worshipped especially in Rome and Latium. In Rome, she had an annual nocturnal ceremony held at the house of a chief magistrate, from which men were rigorously excluded (See CLODIUS PULCHER, PUBLIUS); it was led by the women of the magistrate's family with the help of the *Vestal virgins (Cic. *Har. resp.* 37; Plut. *Caes.* 9). It was a state ritual, performed in secret, for the welfare of the Roman people (*pro salute populi Romani*). Some detail is recorded: the room was decorated with vine-branches and other plants; wine was brought in contained in a covered jar, but it was called milk and the jar a honey-pot. The epigraphic record presents a picture quite distinct from this secret aristocratic rite: there is no sign of secrecy; the worshippers are often slaves or freed persons; men are not infrequent dedicants. The inscriptions are quite widespread within Italy, but rare outside. The Romans evidently had their own version of the cult; it is not clear whether theirs was the original one.

H. H. J. Brouwer, *Bona Dea: The Sources and a Description of the Cult* (1989). J. A. N.

Bonifacius (or Bonifatius), Roman general (d. AD 432), after long service in North Africa (as *tribunus* in 417 and *comes Africae* in 423–5) was appointed *comes domesticorum* in 425 (see COMITES), but remained in Africa to wage war against the indigenous barbarian tribes. He was widely believed in 428/9 to have invited the *Vandals to cross from Spain to assist him against the government at Ravenna, from which, despite his longstanding support for Galla *Placidia, he had become estranged through rivalry with Flavius *Aetius. Unable to rid the country of its new allies, he was reconciled to the government but died in Italy of a wound received when trying to overcome Aetius. His office as *magister utriusque militiae* (see MAGISTER MILITUM) was inherited (the legalities are obscure) by his son-in-law Sebastianus. He is repeatedly praised by the historian *Olympiodorus (3).

PLRE 2. 237–40, 'Bonifatius' 3. J. F. Ma.

Bonna (mod. Bonn). Auxiliary troops (see AUXILIA) were first stationed at Bonna *c*.20/10 BC and remained in garrison there into the 3rd cent. The legionary fortress dates from the reign of Claudius and was rebuilt several times. It was in use in the 4th cent., very probably still by a military garrison. As well as the *canabae there was also a separate civil settlement.

H. Schönberger, *JRS* 1969, 144 ff. P. S.; J. F. Dr.

Bononia (1) (mod. Bologna) in Cisalpine Gaul (see GAUL, CISALPINE) has always been a place of consequence. First settled *c*.1000 BC, about 500 BC the Etruscans founded *Felsina there. Felsina became the chief Etruscan city north of the Apennines (Plin. *HN* 3. 115), but fell first to the *Boii, then to Rome (196 BC), and acquired the name Bononia (Livy 33. 37). Subsequently as Latin colony (see IUS LATII), *municipium, or imperial *colonia*, Bononia maintained its importance (Livy 37. 57; Festus 155 Lindsay; Tac. *Ann.* 12. 58; Procop. *Goth.* 3. 11). As a centre of the north-Italian road-system (Strabo 5. 216 f.), Bononia flourished and was able to survive a conflagration in AD 53 and *Alaric's attack in 410 (Tac. *Ann.* 12. 58; Zos. 6. 10). It later became part of the Byzantine exarchy, and was taken by the *Lombards in 727.

(2) See GESORIACUM.

F. Bergonzoni and G. Bonora, *Bologna romana* (1976). E. T. S.; T. W. P.

Bonus Eventus, personified god of the good outcome of agricultural labour (Varro *Rust.* 1. 1. 6), and, by extension, other human activity. A *porticus* near the baths of *Agrippa at Rome dedicated to him was probably associated with a temple (Amm. Marc. 29. 6. 19): inscriptions suggest that the cult was popular.

Steinby, *Lexicon*, entry under the name. N. P.

books, Greek and Roman Books existed in *Egypt long before they came into use in Greece. Systems of writing had been invented and developed for administrative purposes in both Egypt and *Mesopotamia by *c*.3000 BC. While the Sumerians (see SUMERIAN) and Babylonians used clay tablets for their *cuneiform scripts, the Egyptians used *papyrus. A blank sheet of papyrus was found in the tomb of the vizier Hemaka in Saqqara of *c*.3000 BC. The oldest surviving inscribed papyrus texts are the temple accounts of Abusir of *c*.2450 BC. A number of fine statues of seated scribes of the same period suggests that this profession was already well established and that writing had been practised for centuries, long enough for the 'hieratic' script to develop through the adaptation of hieroglyphs to the use of reed-brush and papyrus. The hieroglyph for 'book-roll' is first attested in the first dynasty (*c*.3000–2800 BC), and Egyptian literature was supposed to have begun with the writings of Imhotep, the architect of the first pyramid under King Djoser in the third dynasty (*c*.2600 BC). Religious books were kept in temples; although temple 'libraries', i.e. chambers designated for the storage of books, have survived only in Ptolemaic temples (Edfu, Philae, ed-Tod), literary references to books and libraries suggest their existence in the Middle Kingdom (thirteenth dynasty, *c*.1700 BC), and *Diodorus (3) (1. 47, using the account of *Hecataeus (2)) describes the library in the Ramesseum at *Thebes (2).

The papyrus plant (*Cyperus papyrus*) grew mainly in the swamplands of lower Egypt and especially the Nile delta. It was used for many purposes: to make ropes, sandals, baskets, boats, and—most importantly—writing material. The Greeks called it βύβλος or βίβλος (see below), later πάπυρος (first attested in Theophr. *Hist. pl.* 4. 8. 2), believed to be derived from Egyptian

books, Greek and Roman

pȝ-n-pr-ʿ, 'that of Pharaoh', which suggests that its manufacture and marketing were a royal monopoly. The *locus classicus* describing its manufacture is Plin. *NH* 13. 74–82 (translation and discussion in Lewis, 34–69, see bibliog. below). The triangular-sectioned stem is cut into segments *c*.30–40 cm. (12–16 in.) long, from which the outer hull is then removed; the white pith is sliced lengthwise into thin strips, which are placed vertically parallel to each other on a plane surface; over these, a second layer of strips is placed horizontally, and the ends squared off. They are then pressed in presses (*prelis*); the plant's natural juice glues the layers firmly together. After drying, the sheet is smoothed with a stone or a sea-shell. According to *Pliny (1) the Elder, twenty sheets (κολλήματα, *plagulae*) were then glued together to form a roll (χάρτης, *charta*), on average 6–8 m. (20–26 ft.) long (in Pharaonic times, too, papyrus rolls of twenty sheets had been standard). If a longer roll was required, it had to be manufactured specially. The narrow edge (κόλλησις, 'gluing') of a sheet which, in Greek books, overlaps that of the sheet to its right is usually 20–25 mm. (¾–1 in.) wide. In rolls of Egyptian texts, however, the right-hand sheet overlaps the one to its left, so that the scribe, writing from right to left, had his reed brush travelling 'downhill' over the joins. If this was the way in which rolls were originally manufactured, Greek scribes turned them upside down, so that they, too, could write 'downhill' over the joins. The sheets on the inside of the roll show horizontal fibres; in this way the joins are better protected from being pulled apart. Only the first sheet of the roll has its vertical fibres on the inside, at right angles to those of the following sheets; this is the 'protocol' (πρωτόκολλον) which protected the outside of the book when it was rolled up; it was sometimes a parchment sheet (cf. [Tib.] 3. 1. 9), or reinforced with parchment. Whether the ends of rolls were similarly reinforced is not clear; the surviving ends of book-rolls show no sign of an *eschatocollion* (Mart. 2. 6. 3). Rollers (*umbilici*, Hor. *Epist.* 14. 8; Mart. 4. 89) with decorative knobs (*cornua*, Mart. 11. 107) attached to the last sheet survive in some rolls from *Herculaneum but none have been found in Egypt.

As the pen runs more smoothly along the fibres than across, the scribes normally used the inside of the roll first where the glued join (κόλλησις) runs at right angles to the fibres; this is conventionally called 'recto', its back 'verso', but these terms should only be used with regard to codices ('recto' = right-hand page), whereas for rolls the terms 'front'/'back', or 'inside'/'outside' are preferable. In some rolls, however, the writing runs across the fibres on the inside, parallel to the joins, in long lines from edge to edge. Such rolls (*rotuli*) were employed only for Greek and Latin documents, never for literary texts which were designed for continuous reading. Documents, on the other hand, were often glued together to form rolls, the blank backs of which could then be used for literary texts (for private use, not for sale). As the inside of the roll was nearly always used first, a dated document may provide a *terminus post quem* for the literary text; the reverse case (document on the back of a book roll, cf. Mart. 8. 62) is relatively rare. Papyrus rolls were dressed with cedar-oil (κεδρία, *cedrium*) to protect them against worms (Vitr. *De arch.* 2. 9. 13).

A papyrus roll would take a book of *Thucydides (2), or a play of *c*.1500 lines, or two to three books of *Homer. The length of the books of *Apollonius (1)'s *Argonautica*, or the books of *Polybius (1), *Strabo, or *Diodorus (3), may have been determined by this standard format. The text is arranged in columns (σελίδες, *paginae*); the number of lines per column, usually between 25 and 45, varies with the height of the column and the size of the writing. The length of the lines also varied; in hexameter and trimeter poetry it was determined by the verse, but lyric poetry and prose were (at any rate, from the 2nd cent. BC onwards) written in shorter lines of between 5 and 10 cm. (2–4 in.), with an average of between 18 and 25 letters per line. Some book rolls have wide upper and lower margins as well as generous spaces between columns. Sometimes a line accidentally omitted from the text is added in the upper or lower margin, usually with a reference mark.

Apart from papyrus, leather was also used in Egypt to produce rolls for literary texts. The *Annals* of Thutmosis III were written on leather rolls and deposited in the temple of Amūn at Karnak. The inscription in the library of the Edfu temple also lists leather rolls. In the ancient near east, leather was widely used as a writing material. *Ctesias (in Diod. Sic. 2. 32. 4) describes the 'royal hides' (βασιλικαὶ διφθέραι) which the Persians used for their chronicles; from Persia, leather rolls may have come into use in Ionia and then in other parts of Greece. In Italy, too, animal hides were used at an early stage (Dion. Hal. 4. 58). While leather had to be tanned, vellum or parchment was manufactured by placing the hide in slaked lime for some days; then flesh and hairs were scraped off and the hide was rubbed with calcium oxide, stretched in a frame, and finally smoothed with pumice. The name 'parchment' (περγαμηνή, *pergamena*) is derived from *Pergamum, which became a centre of production and export in the 2nd cent. BC when papyrus from Egypt was in short supply. The earliest extant Greek documents on vellum (parchment), however, prove that the manufacturing process had been known earlier.

In the production of books parchment played only a minor role compared with papyrus, which remained the dominant writing material throughout Greek and Roman antiquity. In *Crete, papyrus may have been used as early as the second millennium BC, as strands of papyrus have been found baked into Minoan clay sealings. Egyptian papyrus was also exported to Phoenicia (see PHOENICIANS) and beyond; the story of Wen-Amūn (11th cent. BC) mentions 500 rolls of finished papyrus sent to Byblos in return for timber. The fact that in Greek (Aesch. *Supp.* 947, Hdt. 2. 100, etc.) byblos means 'papyrus roll' suggests that originally it may have been imported from *Byblos, Phoenician Gubla. So it is at least possible that papyrus as a writing material was known in the Greek world in Mycenaean times, but there is as yet no firm evidence for its use as a vehicle for Greek literature before *c*.500 BC when book-rolls of papyrus first appear on Attic vases. Herodotus' remark (5. 58) that the Ionians had used leather rolls at a time when papyrus was scarce, and hence kept the word διφθέρα ('hide') for 'book' (βύβλος), does not rule out early acquaintance with papyrus. In the 8th cent. BC, papyrus is mentioned in cuneiform texts in Assyrian accounts as 'reeds from Egypt', and an 8th-cent. palimpsest papyrus written in Hebrew has come to light near Murabba'at on the Dead Sea (*PMur.* 17 = *Discoveries in the Judaean Desert* (1960) 2 pp. 93–100).

Although writing may have been employed early on in the composition of Greek poetry (and the complex structure of both *Iliad* and *Odyssey* is hardly conceivable without it), the performance of poetry continued to be oral throughout the Archaic and Classical periods. When *Archilochus describes himself as a 'woeful messenger-stick' (ἀχνυμένη σκυτάλη, fr. 185 W) he does not necessarily imply that his epode was transmitted on a piece of papyrus or leather, wrapped round a stick (see SKYTALE). On the other hand, much of early epic poetry is reflected in both lyric poetry and black-figure vase-painting, Corinthian and Attic, and it seems doubtful whether this can be accounted for by oral transmission (by itinerant *rhapsodes and choirs) alone. It is therefore reasonable to assume that book-rolls played a part in the transmission of Greek poetry in the 7th and 6th cent., if only as *aides-mémoire* to the performers. In the 6th cent., the tyrants *Polycrates (1) of Samos and *Pisistratus of Athens are said to have been admired for their collections of books (Athen. 1. 3a). Pisistratus is credited with a revision of the texts of Homer which until then had been 'confused' (Cic. *De or.* 3. 137); he is also said to have inserted lines about *Salamis (1) and *Theseus into the texts (*Il.* 2. 558, *Od.* 11. 631). On the other hand, [Pl.] *Hipparch.* 228b says that Pisistratus' son *Hipparchus (1) brought the poems of Homer to Attica and forced the singers at the *Panathenaea to perform them—in preference, perhaps, to other parts of the *Epic Cycle. In any case, there clearly was, in the later 6th cent., an authoritative text of Homer which served as a basis for rhapsodic recitals at the Panathenaea.

From *c*.500 onwards, book-rolls (evidently of papyrus) appear on Attic vases; as far as the writing can be identified, they all contain poetry. The Duris cup in Berlin of *c*.485 BC (Beazley, *ARV²* 431. 48) illustrates the use of book-rolls in schools, and Ar. *Nub.* 961–72 describes the 'ancient education' (ἀρχαία παιδεία), i.e. in the schools of *c*.500 BC, where the children were made to memorize epic poetry and to sing it in the traditional mode. Reading books for pleasure is mentioned in Eur. *Erechtheus* (fr. 369 N, of 422 BC?), and in Ar. *Ran.* 52 f. (405 BC) *Dionysus says he read *Euripides' *Andromeda* on board ship. The earliest references to booksellers are in *Eupolis (fr. 327 KA, *PCG* 5. 485) and in *Plato (1) (*Ap.* 26d), where *Socrates says that a copy of *Anaxagoras could be bought 'from the orchestra' (in the Agora of Athens?) for one drachma 'at most'. The term 'bookseller' (βιβλιοπώλης) is first attested in *Theopompus (2) the comic poet (fr. 77 Kock). *Xenophon (1) (*An.* 7. 5. 12–14) refers to 'many written books' being exported on ships from Athens to the Black Sea (see EUXINE), and in *Mem.* 4. 2. 10 *Socrates asks Euthydemus whether he wants to become a rhapsode, having bought the complete works of Homer.

The intellectual revolution of the *sophists and the interest in dithyrambs and tragedy boosted demand for books in Athens, where book production and the book trade flourished in the 4th cent. BC. It made the vast collecting activities of *Aristotle and his pupils possible and led to the formation of *libraries, notably that of Aristotle himself (Strabo 13. 608).

The oldest surviving specimens of literary papyrus rolls date from the second half of the 4th cent. The *Timotheus (1) papyrus (*PBerol.* 9875, *Persians*), found at Abusir north of *Memphis, written in long lines in large, clumsy letters, may antedate *Alexander (3) the Great's conquest of Egypt. The carbonized papyrus roll found at Derveni, near *Thessalonica, a commentary on an Orphic cosmogony, is written in small letters (*c*.2 mm. (¹⁄₁₀ in.) high) in a careful, skilled hand which makes the columns look almost like *stoichedon* inscriptions (i.e. exactly aligned vertically). Given the regularity and elegance of Attic writing on vases and also of private letters on lead tablets, such as the letter of Mnesiergus in Berlin (*Syll.*³ 1259), the Derveni papyrus has a far stronger claim to being a typical representative of a 4th-cent. book. From the beginning of the Ptolemaic period through to the 8th cent. AD, an uninterrupted series of book-rolls and, later, codices chiefly from Egypt illustrates the development of Greek (and, to a lesser extent, Latin) books and their scripts.

The *Museum and the *Library at *Alexandria (1), founded by *Ptolemy (1) I Soter, became the most important centre of

scholarship, and literary criticism in particular, for centuries to come. The work of the Alexandrian scholars led to a standardization in the formats of Greek books and in the layout of the texts. While in early 3rd-cent. BC texts of poetry, verse (other than hexameters and trimeters) is not written metrically, books from the 2nd cent. BC onwards show lyric passages arranged in short metrical units or *kōla*; their colometry is preserved in the medieval manuscripts of *Pindar's *epinikia* and the choruses of Attic drama (see TRAGEDY; COMEDY). Prose texts are usually set out in fairly narrow columns in lines of equal length. Aids to the reader, such as spaces between sentences, punctuation, or horizontal dashes (*paragraphoi*) in the left-hand margin or between line-beginnings, very rare at first, become more frequent in the 2nd and 1st cent. BC and increasingly common during the Roman period, as do accents and breathings. *Aristarchus (2) devised a system of critical reference signs to alert the reader to textual problems and their discussions in commentaries; most of these appear in book-rolls, though not always with the functions assigned them by Aristarchus. Commentaries (ὑπομνήματα) were written in rolls separate from the texts on which they comment, but the rolls carrying texts often have notes or excerpts from commentaries in the margins, although they are rarely as copious as in the Louvre papyrus of *Alcman's *Partheneion*.

Greek book-rolls continued the Egyptian tradition of book illumination; the surviving illustrated papyri are mostly scientific or mathematical books, or magical papyri; fragments of illustrated papyrus rolls of Homer or drama are very rare. Book illumination becomes more common only in the later Roman period, with the victory of the codex (see below). Titles, too, were added, either in the left-hand margin against the opening line, or at the end of a book under its last line. Title-tags (*sillyboi*) were sometimes appended to book-rolls. Book titles first came into use with Attic drama, because the titles of plays had to be entered for the competition. While the older lyric poems are usually referred to by their opening lines, *Aristophanes (1) (*Nub.* 553 f.) quotes *Eupolis' *Marikas* by title and then his own play, the *Knights* (τοὺς ἡμετέρους Ἱππέας). *Dithyrambs, too, may have been entered for competitions by their titles, perhaps as early as the 6th cent., if Herodotus' statement that *Arion (2) 'gave his dithyrambs names' (ὀνομάσαντα, 1. 23) is to be trusted. Prose works in the 5th and 4th cents. BC generally do not seem to have had titles, even though Plato (*Politicus* 284b) refers to his dialogue *Sophist* by this title (ἐν τῷ Σοφιστῇ). Normally, prose works, too, are referred to by quoting their opening words, a practice which may have been promoted by *Callimachus (3)'s catalogue of the Alexandrian library, the *Pinakes* ('Panels'). The division of longer works into books must be attributed to the Alexandrian scholars who edited them.

Rolls were kept on shelves, or in boxes or buckets (τεῦχος, *capsa*, *scrinium*). Sometimes rolls were kept in a vellum cover (διφθέρα, *paenula*) with a coloured label. The vellum label with Πίνδαρος ὅλος ('The Complete Pindar', *PAntinoop.* 1. 21) may have been attached to a box or bookcase containing the seventeen books of the Alexandrian edition. While private libraries had boxes or movable cases, as did the library of *Eumenes (2) II of Pergamum, the great public libraries of early imperial Rome had bookcases inserted in niches (θυρίς, *fenestra*) in the walls. This is a feature of both Egyptian temples (Edfu, Philae, ed-Tod: see above) and Coptic monasteries; it seems probable that *Caesar saw them in Alexandria (in the Serapeum library?) and hence planned to introduce them in Rome's first public library, a plan which *Asinius Pollio carried out after Caesar's death in the

Atrium Libertatis, thus creating the model for Augustus' library on the Palatine.

The most important innovation in the shape of the book was Roman in origin. The codex was created when the wooden panels of writing-tablets fastened together with thongs were replaced by parchment (*membrana*). At first used as notebooks (Hor. *Sat.* 2. 3. 2; Quint. *Inst.* 10. 3. 31), parchment codices had come into use for classical literature by the 1st cent. AD (Mart. 14. 184–92 advertises them as cheap pocket editions), while the normal form of the book was, in the Latin west as in the Greek east, the papyrus roll. What eventually established the codex was its adoption by the Christians; the vast majority of biblical and NT texts from the early 2nd cent. onwards are in codex form. Pagan classical authors appear in parchment and papyrus codices from the 2nd cent. AD and more frequently in the 3rd; by the 4th cent., three out of four literary texts were in codex form.

Codices were assembled from quires consisting of wide sheets folded vertically in the middle and then stitched together along the fold. Quires of four or five sheets (*quaterniones, quiniones* = 8 or 10 leaves) are common, thinner or thicker quires are exceptional and may be early experiments. Sheets of papyrus were often placed so that on facing pages the direction of the fibres was the same (recto pages with horizontal and vertical fibres alternating), but the alternative arrangement (i.e. vertical facing horizontal fibres, and vice versa) is not uncommon. Vellum sheets were usually arranged with hair sides facing and flesh sides facing. While papyrus sheets in Greek book-rolls, and in codices of the 2nd and 3rd cents., rarely exceed 35 cm. (13½ in.) in height and 23 cm. (9 in.) in width, wider sheets (30–35 cm.: 12–13½ in.) were often used in Greek and Coptic codices of the 4th, 5th, and 6th cents., when large parchment codices were also common. Small formats (even miniature codices like the Cologne parchment codex of the life of Mani with pages of 38×45 mm. ($1\frac{1}{2} \times 1\frac{3}{4}$ in.)) are also found in this period.

The text was written before the sheets were stitched together, usually in one column per page, prose texts sometimes in two narrow columns like those in rolls (more frequently in parchment than in papyrus codices). Pagination is frequent; sometimes quires are also numbered on their first pages. Codices were bound between wooden panels covered in leather. Papyrus codices remained common in Egypt until the late 6th cent.; elsewhere, parchment codices begin to prevail from the later 3rd cent. onwards. For codices, the advantages of parchment over papyrus are obvious: less fragile folds, greater durability, greater capacity, and they are easier to use. Constantine ordered 50 parchment copies of the Scriptures for the churches in Constantinople, and Jerome records that the papyrus manuscripts in the library of *Caesarea (2), having become worn by use, were replaced by parchment codices.

Little is known about the book trade in the Greek world, probably because the private copy always remained the commonest form of book production. In the 4th cent. there seem to have been itinerant booksellers who 'carried around' bundles of *Isocrates' speeches (Dion. Hal. *Isoc.* 18). More information is available on the book trade in Rome from the 1st cent. BC onwards, and some publishers like *Cicero's friend *Atticus, or the Sosii, Horace's publishers, or *Martial's and *Quintilian's publisher, Tryphon, are well attested; the younger *Pliny (2) (*Ep.* 11. 11. 2) was surprised to learn that booksellers in Lyons (*Lugdunum (1)) were selling his books. The evidence for book prices is scanty and contradictory; on the whole, it seems that in Rome books were not expensive: Martial quotes 5 denarii as the price of a luxury edition of his poems (1. 117), while a cheap one would cost 6 to 10 sesterces (1. 66). Palimpsests, i.e. texts written on reused papyrus or parchment after the original writing had been rubbed or washed off, were cheaper still (Catull. 22).

N. Lewis, *Papyrus in Classical Antiquity* (1974); J. Černy, *Paper and Books in Ancient Egypt* (1947); W. Schubart, *Das Buch bei den Griechen und Römern*, 2nd edn. (1921); G. Cavallo, *Libri, editori e pubblico nel mondo antico* (1975); E. G. Turner, *The Typology of the Early Codex* (1977); C. H. Roberts and T. C. Skeat, *The Birth of the Codex* (1983); E. G. Turner, *Greek Manuscripts of the Ancient World*, 2nd edn., rev. P. J. Parsons (1987), with excellent bibliography; H. Blanck, *Das Buch in der Antike* (1992). H. Ma.

books, poetic The accelerated rise of the book-roll in the 4th and 3rd cents. BC has artistic consequences which are first strongly felt in the Alexandrian Library. The scholar-poets who classify and collect into books the literature of the past apply the same principles of editorial organization in the publication of new poetry. Anthologies of epigrams, whether by one hand or by several, proliferate. *Callimachus (3), who has an early involvement in the classification of *Pindar's epinicians (fr. 450), gathers his own *Iambi* into a poetry book, and perhaps also his six *Hymns*; analyses of the fragmentary *Aetia* indicate considerable sophistication in its book-construction. *Antimachus' *Lyde* and *Philitas' *Paegnia* may have exploited the book as an artistic unit before Callimachus; not so the archaic elegies of Theognis' *Gnomology to Cyrnus* (19–254), whose arrangement (at least as we know it) seems to be Hellenistic (M. L. West, *Studies in Greek Elegy and Iambus* (1974), 40 ff.). Early glimpses of the gathering of poems into books at Rome are to be sought in the fragments of *Lucilius (1) and *Laevius.

As well as collecting short poems, books subdivide long ones. In this latter field at least, prose writers may have been ahead of poets: the first known writer to divide his own text into books (30 of them, each with a preface) is the 4th-cent. BC historian *Ephorus (Diod. Sic. 5. 1. 4, 16. 76. 5). The editorial division of the Homeric epics into 24 books may or may not be pre-Alexandrian; the authorial use of the book as a unit of epic composition is first visible to us in *Apollonius (1)'s four-book *Argonautica*. Subdivision encourages patterning. *Virgil's *Aeneid* falls easily into two six-book halves (the *Odyssean* and *Iliadic* portions), or three four-book thirds (Carthage, arrival in Italy, fighting in Italy), with the individual book strongly marked as an artistic unit (so esp. *Aen.* 4, with its structuring repetitions of *at regina*, 'but the queen . . .', at 1, 296, 504). Such effects can be intertextual. The invocation of Erato which inaugurates the second half of the *Aeneid* picks up the invocation of Erato which inaugurates the second half of the *Argonautica*. Here, however, the norm of careful arrangement allows for planned inconcinnity: the second half of the *Aeneid* starts 36 lines 'late', with the displacement of the invocation throwing strong emphasis on to the book-bridging demise of Aeneas' nurse Caieta.

The book of collected poems puts on display both the unity and the variety of a body of work which shares a genre, a theme or an author (or more than one of these). To all intents and purposes, the poet who gathers his own poems into a book obeys the same set of artistic imperatives which govern the editor who collects the poems of others. In the polymetrics of *Catullus (1), the poet's own arrangement seems to be overlaid by the arrangement of a later editor; it is in principle impossible to use aesthetic criteria to disentangle the two events. Nowhere can the art of book-arrangement be more closely studied than among the Augustans; and no collection has been so analysed in recent years for its symmetries and contrasts of structure and theme as *Virgil's book of *Eclogues*. At times a sequence of poems within a book asks to be read almost as a single unfolding poem (note that the opening poem's *incipit*, or initial word(s), can function as a title for a whole book): never more so than in *Propertius, in whom, as is reflected in continuing editorial controversy about poem-division, the breaks in argument between adjacent poems are sometimes no more (or less) abrupt than the breaks between parts of a single poem. It is in Propertius and his Augustan elegiac colleagues, with their sustained focus on erotic autobiography, that the invitation to read a book of poems as a kind of narrative, albeit an artfully disordered narrative, is most marked.

The arrangement of the book itself becomes a subject for poetry, as the author (or anthologist: see *Anth. Pal.* 4) builds in editorial prefaces and epilogues: we see him rounding off his book (Ov. *Tr.* 1. 11), deciding on a dedicatee (Catull. 1), rearranging his poems for a second edition (Ov. *Am. epigr.*). From the ostentatious care of editorial arrangement characteristic of Augustan poetry derive the (disingenuous) denials of such care by the exiled Ovid (*Pont.* 3. 9. 51–4) and by *Statius (*Silv.* 1 pref.). *Martial uses an editorial book-preface to discuss the decorum of the editorial book-preface (2 pref.). The book turns up as a character—personified, sent to seek its fortune (Hor. *Epist.* 1. 20; Ov. *Tr.* 1. 1), even given a voice to tell the tale of its own reception (*Tr.* 3. 1).

The collected poem is doubly framed, finding one set of contexts as a single bounded poem which may encode a time, a place, an addressee, and another set of contexts as its boundary dissolves into the larger unit of the book, calling the primacy of those points of reference into question and acknowledging larger worlds of reception which may always have been implied within the poem's occasionality. In another sense, the book is itself a kind of surrogate for the immediacy of that unattainable primary performance, offering as it does a new 'performance' in which a group of poems cumulatively reveals a set of attitudes, a voice, a life—an author, in short, constructed (or deconstructed) by the unfolding text.

Future discussions will take their bearings from N. Krevans, *The Poet as Editor: The Poetic Collection from Callimachus to Ovid* (1996). See also J. van Sickle (ed.), *Augustan Poetry Books, Arethusa* 13 / 1 (1980); W. Kroll, *Studien zum Verständnis der römischen Literatur* (1924), 225 ff.; and cf. D. P. Fowler, *MD* 1989, 75 ff.   S. E. H.

booty 'It is a law established for all time among all men that when a city is taken in war, the persons and the property of its inhabitants belong to the captors' (Xen. *Cyr.* 7. 5. 73). This universal ancient conception is reflected in the wide range of meanings of the ancient terminology for 'booty' (notably λεία, λάφυρα, and ὠφέλεια in Greek, *praeda* and *spolia* in Latin). It referred not just to movable and inanimate objects (e.g. precious metals), but could also include animals and livestock, human beings, and even whole cities and territory. War, for instance, was one of the major suppliers of the slave trade (see SLAVERY). It was rare after *Homer for wars to be fought solely and openly for acquisitive purposes. But it was always assumed that success in war would lead to appropriation by the victor of the property and persons of the vanquished, and sometimes of territory as well. Hence the largest sudden transfers of wealth in the ancient world were the result of successful warfare: for example *Sparta's conquest of *Messenia and the Messenians in the late 8th cent. BC, the *Persian Wars and their sequels, *Alexander (3) the Great's conquest of the Persian empire and the wars of the Successors, who all

regarded their conquests as 'spear-won territory', and the numerous wars of the expanding Roman republic. On a smaller scale raiding between neighbouring states was endemic, as were *piracy at sea and *brigandage on land, except when a stronger power was able to impose peace in its sphere of influence (Athens in the 5th cent., Rhodes in the Hellenistic period, Rome under the empire). Throughout antiquity, it was also assumed that armies would sustain themselves from the territory in which they operated.

W. K. Pritchett, *The Greek State at War* 1 (1971), chs. 3–5, and 5 (1991), ch. 2 (very full collection of material); E. Bickerman, *RIDA* 1950, 99–127; Y. Garlan, *Guerre et économie en Grèce ancienne* (1989); W. V. Harris, *War and Imperialism in Republican Rome 327–70 BC* (1979); M. M. Austin, *CQ* 1986, 450 ff.   M. M. A.

Boreas, the North Wind, which brings to the Greeks an icy blast from Thrace (see the fine description at Hesiod, *Op.* 506 ff.); 'King of the Winds' for Pindar (*Pyth.* 4. 181), and the most strongly personified of the *wind-gods. This vivid characterization is owed to the story of his forcible seizing of the Athenian princess Oreithyia, daughter of *Erechtheus, from the banks of the Ilissus (Pl., *Phdr.* 229cd); from the marriage he fathered the flying heroes *Calais and Zetes. The legend dates—if we may assume that Pausanias (5. 19. 1) was mistaken in identifying the subject on the chest of *Cypselus—from the early 5th cent. BC, when a crop of vase-paintings showing the god as a rough and hirsute winged figure (sometimes with spiky, Jack Frost hair) attest the sudden popularity of the kidnap story. Herodotus (7. 189) provides a possible explanation: the northerly gale which wrecked the Persian fleet before Artemisium is supposed to have been summoned up by Athenians praying to 'their son-in-law' for aid, and they are said to have founded a cult by the Ilissus in gratitude. One might also link the tale to the marriage of the Athenian magnate *Miltiades to Hegesipyle, daughter of the Thracian king Olorus (Hdt. 6. 39), as a kind of justificatory reverse *aition*. Athenian influence has sometimes been detected in the description of Boreas' coupling with the mares of the Trojan king 'Erichthonius' at *Il.* 20. 219 ff.

S. Kaempf-Dimitriadou, *LIMC* 'Boreas'.   A. H. G.

Borsippa (mod. Birs Nimrud), *c.*20 km. (12½ mi.) SW of *Babylon, cult-centre of Nabu, god of wisdom. The 47-m.- (154-ft.-) high ruins of its temple-tower (ziggurat) have attracted archaeologists: the main temple complex (Ezida) was explored by H. Rassam and R. Koldewey (1879–80; 1902), the ziggurat by Austrians in the 1980s. Borsippa flourished from *c.*2000 BC to the early Islamic period; *Antiochus (1) I rebuilt Ezida; Strabo (16. 1. 7) described it as a centre of *linen manufacture.

GENERAL E. Unger, *Reallexikon der Assyriologie* (1928–), 1. 402–29, 'Barsippa'.

EXCAVATION H. Rassam, *Asshur and the Land of Nimrod* (1897); R. Koldewey, *Die Tempel von Babylon und Borsippa* (1911), 57; *Iraq* 1980, 105–16; 1985, 219; 1987, 236–7.

HELLENISTIC PERIOD J. Delsner, *Materialien zur babylonischen Gesellschaft und Kultur in hellenistische Zeit* (1986), 110–11. Antiochus I and Borsippa: A. Kuhrt and S. Sherwin-White, *JHS* 1991, 71–86.
A. T. L. K.

Borysthenes, a river of *Scythia (the modern Dnieper). According to Herodotus (4. 53) it was the largest river after the Nile and the Ister (Danube) and was navigable for 40 days from the Black Sea (Euxine). Herodotus seems to have been unacquainted with its upper course, but his praise of its fisheries and meadows is well founded. The Borysthenes was a principal route into the hinterland of Scythia and beyond. However, archaeology indicates that little of the goods that passed up the Borysthenes proceeded beyond Kiev.   M. C.; D. C. B.

Boscoreale, former hunting-reserve of the Angevin kings of Naples (*Neapolis) and part of the Naples conurbation, 2 km. (1¼ mi.) from Pompeii, is famous for the excavation of several *villae rusticae*, buried in the eruption of *Vesuvius in AD 79. They combine efficient equipment for investment-agriculture (especially oil and wine), and clear evidence of slave-labour, with comfortable appointments: from one ('Pisanella') came the 94 pieces of silver plate known as the Boscoreale treasure (in the Louvre); from another, perhaps once an estate of *Agrippa Postumus, came the fine paintings in the Metropolitan Museum in New York. The recently excavated Villa Regina preserves the fittings and surroundings of a more modest farm in eloquent detail. See VILLA.

> R. Etienne, in K. Schefold (ed.), *La regione sotterrata dal Vesuvio: Studi e prospettive* (1982); V. Kockel, *Arch. Anz.* (1985), 495–571; P. H. Blanckenhagen and M. Alexander, *The Paintings from Boscotrecase* (1962); R. R. R. Smith, *JRA* 1994.   N. P.

Bosporus (1), **the Thracian,** a narrow strait 27 km. (17-mi.) long connecting the Black Sea (see EUXINE) with the sea of Marmara (see PROPONTIS). Together with the Hellespont the Bosporus separated Asia from Europe and provided a marine passage between the Black Sea and the eastern Mediterranean. Despite a strong current that runs from the Black Sea towards the *Aegean, the Bosporus was navigable in antiquity, and was not a barrier to the armies that occasionally crossed it from one continent to the other. The Scythian rivers that flowed into the Black Sea provided food for the spawning mackerel and tuna that migrated through the Bosporus into the sea of Marmara. Phoenicians and Greeks exploited these rich fishing areas (see FISHING), and the Greeks developed extensive trade between native towns and their own coastal colonies along the Black Sea (see PONTUS). The Bosporus thus added the Black Sea to the history of the eastern Mediterranean world.

> E. C. Semple, *The Geography of the Mediterranean Region* (1932).
>   E. N. B.

Bosporus (2), **the Cimmerian,** the straits of Kerch', connecting the Black Sea (*Euxine) and the sea of Azov (Maeotis). The straits were the centre of a major kingdom, which was known, accordingly, as the Bosporan kingdom or simply the Bosporus. Its main cities were *Panticapaeum on the western shore (the Crimea) and Phanagoreia on the eastern (the Taman' peninsula). Other cities of the kingdom include, in the west, Theodosia, Nymphaeum, Myrmecium, Tiritace, Porthmium, Iluratum, Cimmericum, Cytae; in the east, Hermonassa, Gorgippia, Cepi, Patraeus, Tyrambe, Toricus.

The Bosporus was ruled by the *Spartocids from 438 BC, who extended their authority to east and west. At first archons, they soon claimed the right to royalty. The Spartocid dynasty flourished until c.250, when relations with the peoples of the hinterland, always uncertain, became still less manageable. Ultimately, *Mithradates VI's general, Diophantus, was needed to protect the cities of the Bosporus and when the last Spartocid died c.110 BC, the region was brought within Mithradates' developing Pontic empire.

Upon the death of Mithradates VI, *Pompey had his treacherous son, *Pharnaces II, recognized as king of the Bosporus. When Pharnaces was defeated by *Caesar in 47 BC at the battle of

Zela, the Bosporus was granted to Mithradates of Pergamum. However, Mithradates was left to establish his own authority in the region, while Rome was engrossed with more pressing problems of its own. In consequence, Mithradates failed, defeated and killed by Asander, who won recognition from Antony and then Augustus. Asander ruled the Bosporus until his death in 17 BC, and was succeeded by his widow Dynamis, daughter of Pharnaces II, who was married to *Polemon (1) I of Pontus with imperial approval. However, Polemon's position in the Bosporus was only secured with the support of a Roman expedition led by Agrippa in 14 BC. Polemon had a particular reason to rename Phanagoreia as Agrippeia.

But Polemon and Dynamis soon quarrelled. While Polemon married Pythodoris, Dynamis sought the help of Aspurgus, whom she married. Aspurgus, from a power-base in the hinterland, defeated Polemon. Augustus accepted the situation and recognized Dynamis as queen until her death in AD 8. Aspurgus assumed control upon her death and received recognition and Roman citizenship from the emperor *Tiberius in AD 14. Aspurgus ruled until his death in AD 37/8, leaving two sons, Mithradates and Cotys. Despite *Gaius (1)'s apparent award of the Bosporus to Polemon II, grandson of Polemon I, it was held by Aspurgus' second wife, Gepaepyris, and Mithradates (VIII).

Mithradates VIII won the recognition of *Claudius in 41, but was soon denounced to the emperor by his brother Cotys as disloyal. After fighting and negotiation, Cotys received the throne, while Mithradates was brought to Rome and displayed as a captive. However, he seems to have been left to enjoy a form of retirement at Rome. He brought with him information about the still obscure regions to the north of the Black Sea and is cited as an authoritative source by the elder *Pliny (1).

*Nero took an active interest in the Black Sea region: in AD 63/4 Polemon II's kingdom on the SE shore was annexed and Nero set in train a campaign to the Caspian Gates, only forestalled by civil war. In this context it has often been claimed that Nero annexed the Bosporan kingdom too, c. AD 62, largely on the basis of dubious inferences from coinage. It is quite possible that Cotys remained king. At any rate, Cotys' son Rhescuporis held the kingdom from AD 68/9 until c. AD 90. The dynasty persisted, bolstered by Roman subsidies. But in the 3rd cent. AD, the Bosporans could not withstand pressures from the hinterland: the Roman frontier was no longer secure in this region.

The kings of the Bosporus were unusual among Rome's *client kings in the explicit fervour with which they proclaimed their Roman citizenship through their nomenclature and in their overt enthusiasm for the imperial cult. While the kings were not unconscious of their Hellenic roots, they were also much influenced by the cultures of *Scythia and evidently they were more accepting than other eastern dynasties of their new-found Roman identities.

> N. A. Frolova, *The Coinage of the Kingdom of Bosporus, AD 69–238* (1979); V. F. Gajdukevich, *Das Bosporanische Reich* (rev. trans. 1971); V. V. Struve (ed.), *Corpus inscriptionum regni Bosporani* (1965).   D. C. B.

Bostra (Semitic *Buṣrā*) was a commercial and administrative city of the *Nabataean kingdom at the northern end of the *Wādī al-Sirḥān* trade route. It was refounded by *Trajan as the capital of the province of Arabia and became the camp of the Legio III Cyrenaica. It was made a colony by *Severus Alexander and was sacked by *Zenobia. Its well-preserved remains include a fine theatre and an archway which has been identified on stylistic grounds as Nabataean. See ARABS.

R. E. Brünnow and A. von Domaszewski, *Die Provincia Arabia* 3 (1909); M. Sartre, *Bostra: Des origines à l'Islam* (1985); G. W. Bowersock, *Roman Arabia* (1983).
J. F. H.

botany From earliest times, Greeks and Romans had expert familiarity with plants and their growth cycles; agriculture dominates, alongside acute command of medicinal herbs, including production of oils and perfumes. Exact nomenclatures were quite irrelevant; everyone 'knew' plants and flowers carpeting fields and mountain valleys in season; flower metaphors became common in *Homer and the lyric poets. There is nothing esoteric about early botanical lore; locals understood their plants—from various wheats and vegetables to the widespread poisons (hemlocks, mandrake, the opium poppy, etc.)—and they spoke of parts (roots, seeds, flowers, stems, leaves) *as* plants providing particulars: food, medicines, poisons, oils, beverages (wine, beer).

Botany figures in Mycenaean Greek texts, suggesting a sophisticated perfume and perfumed oil industry at *Pylos, Cnossus, and elsewhere (see MINOAN CIVILIZATION). Few species are imported exotics, and Homer's flowers are likewise local, e.g. the saffron crocus (*Il.* 14. 348: *Crocus sativus* L.), galingale (*Il.* 21. 351; *Od.* 4. 603: *Cyperus longus* L.), lotus (*Il.* 14. 348: *Lotus corniculatus* L.), the bluebell (*Il.* 14. 348: *Cyclamen graecus* Link), the asphodel (*Od.* 11. 359, 24. 13: *Asphodelus ramosus* L.), the laurel or bay (*Od.* 9. 183: *Laurus nobilis* L.), and others. Homer mentions the opium poppy and its sleep-inducing latex (*Il.* 8. 306–7; *Od.* 4. 220–30: *Papaver somniferum* L.), but the poet credits it to Egypt, an anomaly since *P. somniferum* is native to Asia Minor. Influence also came from herbalists of Assyrian origin; *Aristotle's *dēmiourgos* (*Pol.* 1282ᵃ3) mirrors a hoary tradition of skilled rootcutters (the *rhizotomoi*) who gained their craft and plied their trade in the countryside. Interwoven with medical botany is religion and myth, and typical is Homer's 'gift' of the unknown *moly* to Odysseus (*Od.* 10. 305) to ward off *Circe's evil drug (*Od.* 10. 394), a gift from *Hermes, long celebrated as the deity who gave herbs to man: 'O Hermes, benefactor, discoverer of drugs' (*PGM* 8. 27 f.). Moderns need not untangle this medley of beliefs about botany: the ancient mind did not wall *magic away from pure philosophy, any more than there were strict divisions between botany and herbal lore. Deep traditions speak through the poetry of *Sappho and *Theognis, using flowers and herbs in metaphor with telling effect; Sappho speaks of cassia (*Supp.* 20c2: *Cinnamomum cassia* Blume), roses blooming, the tender chervil, and flowery melilot (all no. 96. 11. 13–14 (Loeb 1, p. 120)), along with edible chickpeas (no. 143 (Loeb, 1, p. 156)). Locals knew what plants were like nettles, and Theognis (537) knows the nasty effects of squill (*Urginea maritima* (L.) Baker), long storied in tales of what a community *pharmakos* endured. Not coincidental is *pharmakos* = 'scapegoat' and the neuter *pharmakon* usually = 'drug' or 'magical spell'.

Debate began early about the nature of plants in relationship to other forms of life. Aristotle, *De an.* 410ᵇ22, in noting faulty Orphic notions on how plants breathe, indicates how old was this discussion; speculation on *Medea's *pharmakon* (lulling to sleep the golden fleece's guardian reptile) also was quite early: *Musaeus (1), semi-legendary and pre-Homeric, stated that Medea used a drug with *arkeuthos*, the prickly juniper, *Juniperus oxycedrus* L. (schol. on Ap. Rhod. 4. 156), faithfully reproduced by *Apollonius (1) in his *Argonautica* many centuries later. Musaeus wrote poems on healing plants: Theophrastus (*Hist. pl.* 9. 19. 2) cites Musaeus and *Hesiod on the properties of *tripolion*, the sea starwort (*Aster tripolium* L.), encapsulating folk tradition with accuracy in citation and current use: 'It is useful for every good

treatment, and they dig it up at night, pitching a tent there.' *Pindar (*Pyth.* 3. 51–3) says that traditional medical treatments of *Asclepius were incantations, surgery, soothing potions, and amuletic drugs, reflecting *medicine's dual therapies, herbal drugs and surgery. Athenian playwrights record well-known herbs and plants with some frequency; e.g. *Sophocles' lost *Rhizotomoi* ('Rootcutters' = Macrob. *Sat.* 5. 19. 9–10) noted the professional status of rootcutters and herbal experts, even as Medea uses *thapsia*, the deadly carrot (*Thapsia garganica* L.), to induce frenzy; *Aristophanes (1)'s *Peace* (712) and *Lysistrata* (89) show the commonplace use of pennyroyal (*Mentha pulegium* L.) as a female contraceptive; these examples could be severally multiplied.

Striking is the *mélange* of herbal lore and specific plants indicated for women's ailments (see GYNAECOLOGY) in the Hippocratic *Diseases of Women* and similar tracts (see HIPPOCRATES (2)); there are over 300 identifiable species, collected expertise of *midwives (also recorded by the gifted *Soranus of Ephesus in his *Gynaecology* (c. AD 117)). Analogy was crucial: the Hippocratic *Nature of the Child* and the shorter *Seed* liberally employ agricultural terms (see HIPPOCRATES (2)); the author (probably mid or late 4th cent. BC) is well acquainted with growth patterns in plants, from seed through germination into seedling, a 'youth', followed by maturity and senescence. Aristotle incorporated plants into his scheme of living things, endowing them with three faculties of the *soul: nutrition, growth, reproduction, but not motion or perception. Pseudo-Aristotle, *Plants*, summarizes ideas on botany at the Lyceum, but it is *Theophrastus (c.370–288/5 BC) who provides the best Greek account of botany in *Inquiry into Plants* (*Hist. pl.*) and *Causes of Plants* (*Caus. pl.*); as Aristotle's foremost student, Theophrastus certainly echoed his mentor's paradigms of nature.

An acute observer of plants, Theophrastus distinguished long before modern botany between dicotyledons and monocotyledons, based on precise morphology; he is not ignorant of plant sexes (viz. *Hist. pl.* 2. 8. 1 on fertilization in figs; 2. 8. 4 on fertilization in date palms; cf. Hdt. 1. 193 on similar understanding about Assyrian figs and palm-trees), but chooses to tabulate by forms, flower to fruit, defining flowers as epigynous, perigynous, and hypogynous, showing that he understood the essential relation of flowering to fruiting; anticipating Dioscorides, Theophrastus notes geography to account for differences in shapes and properties of plants when used as medicines—and very good are his descriptions of plants and their parts (root, stem, leaves, flowers, seeds or fruits, and so on), their cultivation as crops or as pot-herbs—and he often quotes from the ubiquitous *rhizotomoi*, the special uses of plants, from medicines to quasi-magical potions and aphrodisiacs; Book 9 of *Hist. pl.* is a priceless document in its own right, the first herbal manual in Greek to survive.

Hellenistic botany extended its scope, resulting in part from the far-flung expeditions of *Alexander (3) the Great into India; many *spices trickled into Greek cooking and pharmacy owing to voyages to India, fairly common by 200 BC. Much Hellenistic botany and *pharmacology is lost excepting citations, especially by *Dioscorides (2) of Anazarbus (*fl. c.* AD 65), *Pliny (1) the Elder's marvellous pot-pourri, the *Natural History* of AD 77, *Galen of Pergamum (AD 129–after 210), and a few others. The *Preface* of Dioscorides' *Materia Medica* demonstrates use of earlier Greek texts, and through Dioscorides, Pliny, Galen, etc. we know of Iollas of Bithynia (? 250–200 BC), *Heraclides (4) of Tarentum (*fl. c.*100 BC), *Crateuas (*fl. c.*100 BC), *Asclepiades (3) of Bithynia (d. 92 BC.), *Andreas (d. 217 BC), as well as Dioscorides' near-contemporaries Sextius Niger, Julius Bassus, Niceratus, Petronius, Diodotus, and several more. Pliny's botany is good when he remains in Italy, but his polymathic curiosity led him to copy all non-Italian sources as being of equal merit; Pliny's plants compared with corollary passages in Dioscorides (both independently used Sextius Niger's lost works) display reasonable accuracy, and species and genera are often keyed with some assurance. Crateuas produced an illustrated herbal, but it is not ancestral to most later illuminated herbals (e.g. the Vienna Dioscorides of AD 512). Together, Pliny and Dioscorides provide details of about 600 species; Pliny gives much on various wheats and vines, vegetables, apples, olives (following in the steps of *Cato (Censorius), and *Varro), and several cultivars, while Dioscorides provides precise accounts—though not much morphology—of medically useful plants, arranged according to a drug affinity system (what the drug did when given to a patient for a particular ailment). Botanical drugs likewise figure heavily in the works of Galen of Pergamum, who quotes voluminously from earlier authorities, attempting (unsuccessfully) to organize his materials.

Among writers in Latin, *Cornelius Celsus' De medicina (c. AD 37) has a good account of medical plants, derived partially from Hellenistic sources, and *Scribonius Largus' Compositiones (AD 43 or later) details 242 botanicals (from abrotanum (Artemisia abrontanum L., a wormwood) to zea (Triticum spelta L., spelt)), 36 minerals, 27 animal products (beeswax, honey, eggs, beaver testicle, etc.); Scribonius carefully considers certain poisonous drugs (e.g. aconite, hyoscyamus, hemlock (Conium maculatum L.), various mushrooms, the opium poppy), crucial at the Roman imperial court (Scribonius was physician to *Claudius, who succumbed to mushroom poisoning in AD 54). Compositiones in turn became a source for several later Latin texts in medical botany, including the De medicamentis by Marcellus Empiricus (c. AD 400), a trove of Gallicisms creeping into Latin.

Characteristic of botanical and pharmacological texts is continuous adaptation of written documents to local conditions; numerous 'substitution lists' in Greek and Latin were circulating by AD 200, clearly seen in the Galenic tract by that title. By AD 400, the major lines of Graeco-Roman medical botany—as well as pure botany, best discerned in the works of Theophrastus—are well defined; certain flowering-plant families are well represented in folklore, agriculture, and botany: prominent among the dicotyledons are Labiatae, Umbelliferae, Boraginaceae, Ranunculaceae, Convolvulaceae, Compositae, Salicineae, Rosaceae, Cruciferae, Leguminosae, Solanaceae, and Coniferae; and frequently included among the monocotyledons are Liliaceae, Gramineae, and Orchideae; there is detailed expertise on trees and woods, as well as fungi, lichens, and algae. See AGRICULTURAL WRITERS; ARBORICULTURE; CONTRACEPTION; FIG; OLIVE; PHARMACOLOGY; TIMBER; WINE.

TEXTS See under individual authors. In addition: J. Chadwick and M. Ventris, Documents in Mycenaean Greek, 2nd edn. (1973), nos. 92–3, 98–107. K. Preisendanz and others (eds.), Papyri Graecae Magicae, 2nd edn., 2 vols. (1973–4); H. D. Betz, (ed.), The Greek Magical Papyri in Translation (1986) (botany, medicine, zoology, trans. J. Scarborough). V. Rose, Theodori Prisciani Euporiston (1894); T. Meyer, Theodorus Priscianus und die römische Medizin (1909; repr. 1967) (Ger. trans. and comm.). M. Niedermann and E. Liechtenhan, Marcellus über Heilmittel, 2 vols. (1968) (Ger. trans. by J. Kollesch and D. Nickel).

GENERAL LITERATURE E. H. F. Meyer, Geschichte der Botanik, 4 vols. (1854–7; repr. 1965), esp. vols. 1–2; B. Langkavel, Botanik der spaeteren Griechen (1866; repr. 1964); H. Stadler, 'Theophrast und Dioscorides', in Abh. aus dem Gebiet der klassischen Altertums-Wissenschaft: Wilhelm von Christ zum sechzigsten Geburtstag dargebracht von seinen Schülern (1891), 176–87; M. Wellmann, 'Die Pflanzennamen des Dioskur-

ides', Hermes 1898, 360–422; J. Sargeaunt, The Trees, Shrubs, and Plants of Virgil (1920; repr. 1969); T. A. Sprague, 'Botanical Terms in Pliny's Natural History', Kew Bulletin 1933, 30–40; O. Regenbogen, 'Theophrastos von Eresos', RE Suppl. 7 (1940), 1354–1562; R. Strömberg, Griechische Pflanzennamen (1940); N. Jasny, The Wheats of Classical Antiquity (1944); J. André, Notes de lexicographie botanique grecque (1958); J. Stannard, 'The Plant Called Moly', Osiris 1962, 254–307; E. Abbe, The Plants of Virgil's Georgics (1965); J. Stannard, 'Pliny and Roman Botany', Isis 1965, 420–5; K. Lembach, Die Pflanzen bei Theokrit (1970); C. Fabricius, Galens Exzerpte aus älteren Pharmakologen (1972); J. Stannard, 'Marcellus of Bordeaux and the Beginnings of Medieval Materia Medica', Pharmacy in History (USA) 1973, 47–53; F. Skoda, 'Associations d'idées et métaphores dans quelques dénominations de plantes en grec ancien', Annales de la Faculté des Lettres et Sciences humaines de Nice 1974, 131–9; J. Stannard, 'Squill in Ancient and Medieval Materia Medica', Bulletin of the New York Academy of Medicine 1974, 684–713; G. Maggiulli, Nomenclatura micologica latina (1977); J. Scarborough, 'Theophrastus on Herbals and Herbal Remedies', Journal of the History of Biology 1978, 353–85; S. Sconocchia, Per una nuova edizione di Scribonio Largo (1981); J. André, L'Alimentation et la cuisine à Rome (1981); A. G. Morton, History of Botanical Science (1981), esp. chs. 2–3; J. Scarborough, 'Beans, Pythagoras, Taboos, and Ancient Dietetics', Classical World 1982, 355–8; R. Meiggs, Trees and Timber in the Ancient Mediterranean World (1982); J. Stannard, 'Medicinal Plants and Folk Remedies in Pliny, Historia naturalis', History and Philosophy of the Life Sciences 1982, 3–23; J. Scarborough, 'Roman Pharmacy and the Eastern Drug Trade', Pharmacy in History (USA) 1982, 135–43; G. E. R. Lloyd, Science, Folklore and Ideology (1983), 119–49: 'Theophrastus, the Hippocratics and the Root-Cutters' and 'Pliny, Learning and Research'. E. L. Greene, Landmarks of Botanical History, ed. F. N. Egerton, 2 vols. (1983), esp. vol. 1, chs. 1–3; J. M. Riddle, Dioscorides on Pharmacy and Medicine (1985); G. Wöhrle, Theophrasts Methode in seinen botanischen Schriften (1985); J. André, Les Noms de plantes dans la Rome antique (1985); A. Tchernia, Le Vin de l'Italie romaine (1986); J. Scarborough, 'Pharmacy in Pliny's Natural History: Some Observations on Substances and Sources', in R. French and F. Greenaway (eds.), Science in the Early Roman Empire: Pliny the Elder, his Sources and Influence (1986), 59–85; J. D. Hughes, 'Theophrastus as Ecologist', A. Preus, 'Drugs and Psychic States in Theophrastus' Historia plantarum 9. 8–20', and A. Gotthelf, 'Historiae I: plantarum et animalium', all three in W. W. Fortenbaugh and R. W. Sharples (eds.), Theophrastean Studies: On Natural Science, Physics and Metaphysics, Ethics, Religion and Rhetoric (1988), 67–135; D. Brent Sandy, The Production and Use of Vegetable Oils in Ptolemaic Egypt (1989); J. Scarborough, 'Contraception in Antiquity: The Case of Pennyroyal', Wisconsin Academy Review, 35/2 (1989), 19–25; J. Raven, 'Plants and Plant Lore in Ancient Greece', Annales Musei Goulandris 1990, 129–80; M. Moisan, Lexique du vocabulaire botanique d'Hippocrate (1990); J. Scarborough, 'The Pharmacology of Sacred Plants, Herbs, and Roots', in C. A. Faraone and D. Obbink (eds.), Magika Hiera: Ancient Greek Magic and Religion (1991), 138–74.
J. Sca.

bottomry See MARITIME LOANS.

Boudicca (name uncertain, but 'Boadicea' has neither authority nor meaning), wife of *Prasutagus, who was established as client king of the *Iceni (East Anglia) by the Romans. On his death (AD 60/1) he had left the emperor co-heir with his daughters, but imperial agents maltreated his family. Under Boudicca the Iceni, assisted by the *Trinovantes, rose in rebellion while the governor, *Suetonius Paulinus, was occupied in the west. *Camulodunum (Colchester), *Londinium, and *Verulamium were successively sacked. Venturing a battle, however, with Paulinus' main force, Boudicca's troops were easily routed, and she herself took poison.

Tac. Ann. 14. 31–7; Agr. 16. 1–2; Cass. Dio 62. 1–12.; S. S. Frere, Britannia, 3rd edn. (1987).
C. E. S.; M. J. M.

boulē, in Greek states, a council; frequently the council which had day-to-day responsibility for the state's affairs. Its membership and powers could vary with the complexion of the regime: in the Homeric world it was a meeting of nobles called to advise the king; in an oligarchic state eligibility might be restricted, membership might be for a long term, and the council might be relatively powerful and the citizens' assembly relatively weak (cf. the *gerousia, council of elders, in *Sparta); in a democratic state eligibility would be broader, a limited term of office would ensure that more of the citizens served at some time, and the council would be the servant rather than the master of the assembly. The council would be involved in decision-making, administration and jurisdiction. Most states, except some of the very smallest, had a council of this kind. In the cities of *Boeotia in the Classical period one quarter at a time of the citizens with full rights served as the council. *Federal states and leagues of allies (see ALLIANCE (GREEK)) commonly had a council, known sometimes as *boulē*, sometimes by another word such as *synedrion* ('meeting').

In Athens the original council, the body which advised first the kings and subsequently the archons, and came to be composed of ex-*archontes, was the council of the *Areopagus. *Solon in 594/3 BC has been credited with the creation of a second council to perform the function of *probouleusis*, prior consideration of the assembly's business: a council of 400, one hundred from each of the four tribes (*Ath. pol.* 8. 4; Plut. *Sol.* 19. 1–2). Some have doubted its existence, but the evidence is as good as we could expect for a 6th-cent. institution, and there is a parallel in 6th-cent. *Chios, a council referred to emphatically as the people's (*dēmosiē*), with the implication that it has been created beside or in place of a more aristocratic council (ML 8).

In 508/7 BC *Cleisthenes (2) replaced this with a council of 500, fifty from each of the ten new tribes (*phylai*), and within each tribe appointed from the *demes in proportion to their size. Membership was open to all but the lowest of the four property classes (i.e. to *pentakosiomedimnoi, *hippeis, *zeugitai, but not *thētes); by the second half of the 5th cent., if not earlier, appointment was by lot for a year; and by the 4th cent. service was limited to two years in a man's life. The council met every day except holidays and days of ill omen; by the late 5th cent. members were paid, but service made heavy demands on a conscientious member's time, and the richer citizens seem to have served in more than due proportion. In the Hellenistic period, as extra tribes were created and abolished, there continued to be 50 members from each tribe; but when the creation of Hadrianis in AD 127 brought the number of tribes to thirteen again membership was reduced nominally to 500 and in fact to about 520. We are poorly informed on changes under the later Roman empire.

By the 450s BC if not from the time of Cleisthenes the 50 members from one tribe served as the *prytaneis ('presidents') for one tenth of the year (a smaller fraction when there were more than ten tribes), in an order determined by lot. They acted as a standing committee of the whole council; one of their number served as *epistatēs* ('chairman') for a single day, and he and the *prytaneis* from one *trittys remained on duty for the whole twenty-four hours. They also convened the council and assembly: at first the archons may have presided in both; at any rate from the 450s to the early 4th cent. the *prytaneis* presided; from the early 4th cent. this duty was transferred to a new board of *proedroi*, appointed for a day at a time and consisting of one councillor from each tribe except the prytany, one of the nine acting as *epistatēs*.

The function of Solon's council, inherited by Cleisthenes', was prior consideration of the assembly's business. In Athens the principle was interpreted so as to minimize the restriction imposed on the assembly: the assembly could not reach a decision on any subject until it had been considered by the council and placed on the assembly's agenda; but, although the council's *probouleuma* ('prior resolution') could incorporate a specific proposal, it did not have to do so, and in the assembly any citizen could propose a motion or an amendment; if a new topic emerged during the assembly's debate, the assembly could commission the council to produce a *probouleuma* for a later meeting. Only a member of the council could propose a *probouleuma*: a non-member who wanted to raise an item of business would commonly make a formal approach to the council through the *prytaneis*, or else arrange informally for a member to raise his business in the council.

This council probably began to acquire administrative and judicial powers with the reform of the Areopagus by *Ephialtes (4) in 462/1 BC. It became the general overseer of Athens' administrative machinery, supervising the work of the many boards appointed for specific duties and itself providing the members for several of them. Its responsibilities included the state's finances and the sacred treasuries, warships (*triremes) and naval equipment in general, the cavalry and their horses (see HIPPEIS § 2), prizes for the *Panathenaea, public buildings, and the invalids who were given a maintenance grant by the state.

In Greek states the administration was weak, and it was believed not that the lawcourts should be independent of the administration but that the administration should be subject to them but that administrative bodies needed to be strengthened with judicial powers. In Athens many of the council's judicial powers were concerned with officials and with the official duties of private citizens: it was involved in the *dokimasia (vetting before entry into office) of the *archontes* and the following year's councillors; it provided the interim *logistai ('accountants') who checked officials' financial accounts each prytany, and it could try charges against officials; and it provided the *euthynoi* ('straighteners', see EUTHYNA) who received accusations of non-financial offences against officials when they left office (but the annual *logistai* who checked officials' final accounts were not members of the council). It was also involved in the procedure of *eisangelia ('impeachment') for the trials of major offences against the state.

The council was the keystone of the democratic constitution, preparing business for the assembly and providing a focus between the assembly's meetings, and holding together the fragmented administration of the state. It was prevented from dominating by the fact that its members were appointed for a limited term and not from a limited class: the council could not easily acquire an interest different from that of the state as a whole.

In the revolutions of 411 BC the democratic council was replaced first by the *Four Hundred which had a monopoly of power, and then, under the intermediate regime, by a council of five hundred which was elected but was less powerful than the Four Hundred. In 404/3 the *Thirty Tyrants had a council of five hundred. See EKKLESIA.

GENERAL G. Busolt, *Griechische Staatskunde*, 3rd edn. (1920–6); V. Ehrenberg, *The Greek State*, 2nd edn. (1969); J. A. O. Larsen, *Representative Government in Greek and Roman History* (1955), and *Greek Federal States* (1968).

ATHENS *Ath. pol.* 43–9; P. J. Rhodes, *The Athenian Boule* (1972); R. K. Sinclair, *Democracy and Participation in Athens* (1988), chs. 3–5;

M. H. Hansen, *The Athenian Democracy in the Age of Demosthenes* (1991), ch. 10.   A. W. G.; T. J. Ca.; P. J. R.

Bouphonia The annual 'ox-slaying' at the Athenian festival of the Dipolieia. During this rite an ox was killed, the sacrificer fled, and the sacrificial knife was cast into the sea after being tried for murder. The slain ox was stuffed and yoked to a plough.

Burkert, *HN* 136–43; E. Simon, *Festivals of Attica* (1983), 8–12; J.-L. Durand, *Sacrifice et labour en Grèce ancienne* (1986); A. Henrichs, in F. Graf (ed.), *Symposium Karl Meuli* (1992), 152–60.   A. H.

Boutes, name of several mythological figures, the principal being (1) the family hero of the Attic *genos* Eteoboutadai and first priest of Poseidon Erechtheus; he was worshipped alongside Poseidon in the *Erechtheum. According to Apollodorus (3. 14. 8) he and his brother *Erechtheus divided their father *Pandion's power so that Boutes became priest and Erechtheus king. (2) Son of Teleon, an *Argonaut, who, charmed by the *Sirens' song, plunged into the sea, but was rescued and taken to *Lilybaeum by Aphrodite, by whom he became the father of Eryx.

LIMC 3/1 (1986), 152–3.   E. Ke.

Bouzyges, or 'Ox-yoker', in Athenian myth was the first to use oxen for ploughing, and his name was connected with one of the sacred ploughings performed in Attica. The name was also the title of the priest of Zeus Teleios, who ceremonially pronounced (proverbial) curses against the perpetrators of certain acts. It is likely that the mythical figure was the prototype of the priest.

C. Bérard, *LIMC* 3. 153–5; W. Burkert, *Zeitschrift für Religions- und Geistesgeschichte* 1970, 356–68.   E. Ke.

Bovianum Undecumanorum (mod. Boiano) capital of the Pentri Samnites and settled from at least the 7th cent. BC. It was prominent against Rome in the Samnite Wars (see SAMNIUM) but, in the *Social War (3), after being a temporary capital for the Italians, was sacked by Sulla. It was colonized under the triumvirs and under *Vespasian (by veterans from Legio XI Claudia), and remained important in late antiquity.

G. de Benedittis, *Bovianum ed il suo territorio* (1977), and in *Samnium* (1991), 233 ff.   E. T. S.; T. W. P.

Bovianum Vetus, a *colonia* in *Samnium (Plin. *HN* 3. 107), not now located. It has been erroneously associated with the sanctuary at *Pietrabbondante.

E. T. Salmon, *Samnium and the Samnites* (1967), 13; A. La Regina, *Rh. Mus.* 1966, 260 ff.   E. T. S.; T. W. P.

Bovillae, ancient town on the *via Appia, 17 km. (10½ mi.) from Rome. Here survivors from destroyed *Alba Longa allegedly found refuge: they included the *gens* Iulia which thereafter always maintained close associations with Bovillae. Here T. *Annius Milo killed Clodius, 52 BC. By then Bovillae had greatly dwindled, but it remained a *municipium*, whose inhabitants in imperial times were styled Albani Longani Bovillenses.

G. M. de Rossi, *Bovillae* (1979).   E. T. S.; T. W. P.

boxing In Greek and Roman boxing there was no classification of competitors by weight and so the advantage was generally with the heavier man.

The Greeks bound leather thongs (ἱμάντες) round their wrists and knuckles, to protect them rather than to increase the severity of the blow. Sometimes the fingers, or some of them, were left free, though this may have been the practice in the *pankration rather than specifically boxing. For training they used softer

padded gloves (σφαῖραι). Body-blows were not generally used and the face was always the principal target.

The Romans used the *caestus*, a glove weighted with pieces of iron and having metal spikes placed round the knuckles, and boxing was often more of a gladiatorial show than an athletic sport. See AGŌNES; ATHLETICS; GLADIATORS.

ANCIENT SOURCES Hom. *Il.* 23. 653–99; Theoc. *Id.* 22. 80–134; Verg. *Aen.* 5. 363–484.
MODERN LITERATURE M. Poliakoff, *Combat Sports in the Ancient World* (1987), 66–88.   R. L. H; S. J. I.

Brasidas (d. 422 BC), Spartan commander. He gained prominence through defending *Methone (2) from the Athenians in 431, held the ephorate (see EPHORS) in 431/0 and naval advisory positions in 429 and 427. Following distinguished action as a trierarch at *Pylos in 425, he was sent to northern Greece in 424 with a small force of helots and mercenaries. After saving *Megara *en route*, he rapidly gained several important cities, including *Amphipolis and *Torone, ignoring the armistice of 423 by supporting the revolts of *Scione and *Mende. Although unable to protect all his successes adequately, he permanently injured Athens' interests in the region. In 422 he defeated an Athenian army under *Cleon at Amphipolis, but was himself mortally wounded. Brasidas served as a prototype for Sparta's subsequent conduct of foreign campaigns through semi-independent Spartiate *harmosts commanding non-Spartiate troops, and his success encouraged her future use of *neodamōdeis*, *helots freed for military service.

RE 3. 815–18, 'Brasidas' 1; *RE* Suppl. 1. 258 no. 1a; PB no. 177; H. D. Westlake, *Individuals in Thucydides* (1968), ch. 10; Hornblower, *Comm. on Thuc.* 2 (1996).   S. J. Ho.

Brauron, site of a sanctuary of *Artemis on the east coast of *Attica at the mouth of the river Erasinos. It is included in *Philochorus' list of twelve townships united by *Theseus (*FGrH* 328 F 94). Archaeological evidence indicates human presence in the area of the sanctuary and the acropolis above it from neolithic times onwards, and there is an important late Helladic cemetery nearby. In the sanctuary itself there is a continuous tradition from protogeometric on, with a temple built in the 6th cent. (Phot. *Lexicon*, entry under Βραυρώνια) and an architecturally innovative *pi*-shaped *stoa with dining-rooms built in the later part of the 5th cent. Flooding in the early 3rd cent. BC led to the abandonment of the site. Some traditions associate the Pisistratids (see PISISTRATUS; HIPPIAS (1); HIPPARCHUS (1)) with Brauron (Photius, as above), or with the local residential centre called Philaidai which lay a short distance inland from the sanctuary (Pl. *Hipparch.* 228b).

Cult activity at Brauron was particularly associated with the *arkteia*, a ritual, known also at the sanctuary of Artemis *Munichia (1) in the Piraeus, in which young girls between the ages of 5 and 10 'became' bears. The aetiological myth for the *arkteia* related that this service was required of all Athenian girls before marriage because of an incident in which a bear belonging to the sanctuary had been killed after becoming savage with a young girl (schol. Ar. *Lys.* 645). Modern scholars suggest that the ritual was a *rite of passage which marked the physical maturation of pubescent girls and prepared them for taming by marriage by stressing their wildness. Some pottery vessels of a shape particularly used for dedications to Artemis (*krateriskoi*) excavated at Brauron show naked girls running and part of a bear, and scholars have suggested that these illustrate the ritual. The sanctuary included a cave sacred to *Iphigenia, and dedications were also made in celebration of successful *childbirth. The Brauronia was a quadrennial festival organized by *hieropoioi* appointed by the city by lot, and involved a procession from Athens out to Brauron. We also hear of a sacred hunt.

J. Travlos, *Bildlexicon zur Topographie des antiken Attika* (1988); R. Osborne, *Demos* (1985), 154–72; C. Sourvinou-Inwood, *Studies in Girls' Transitions* (1988); A. Antoniou, *Brauron* (1990; in Greek). R. G. O.

breast-feeding was a proof of maternal devotion and, according to some philosophers, a good woman's duty (there is a detailed discussion in Gell. *NA* 12. 1). It was acknowledged to be tiring, but it increased the mother's affection for the child, and the baby was thought to be morally, as well as physically, influenced by the milk it drank and the milk's provider: breast-milk was explained as a further transformation of the blood which had gone to form the embryo (see EMBRYOLOGY). Mothers who were unwilling to breast-feed might be blamed for laziness, indifference, or vanity about their breasts. But wet-nursing was a standard practice. The Greek and Latin words for 'nurse' (*titthē, trophos; nutrix*) have the primary meaning of someone who feeds the child; the bond between nurse and nursling was acknowledged to be strong and is often commemorated in inscriptions. There has been extensive recent discussion on the psychological effects of shared child-rearing.

*Soranus (*Gynaecology* 2. 11. 18) prefers that the mother should breast-feed, but advises the use of a wet-nurse if the mother is ill or may become exhausted. He recommends giving boiled *honey (the equivalent of glucose) with or without goat's *milk (which is closest in composition to human milk) for the first two days of a newborn's life, then, if possible, using a wet-nurse until the mother's body has stabilized after *childbirth and her milk is less heavy. (The manuscripts have the figure twenty for the number of days this takes; some editors correct to three.) Soranus notes that some doctors think breast-feeding should start at once. He devotes several chapters (2. 12. 19–15. 29) to the choice of a wet-nurse, explaining how to test her milk and to ensure that she leads a healthy life: in particular, she should not drink *wine, which affects the milk as well as making her incapable. He envisages a wet-nurse who lives in the household, and recommends employing several so that the child is not dependent on one. At 2. 17. 36–40 Soranus gives detailed instructions on how and when to feed the child: he does not approve of feeding on demand, but does not specify the number of feeds per day; 2. 21. 46–8, on weaning, suggests that the child will not be ready for solid food before the sixth month, or for complete weaning until the third or fourth half-year when the teeth can deal with food; the majority of wet-nursing contracts from Egypt (see below) also envisage breast-feeding for two years. In the section on childbirth, 2. 5. 7–8 offers treatments for engorged breasts and for suppressing lactation in women who do not intend to breast-feed. Plutarch (*Mor.* 609e) praises his wife for undergoing surgery to her nipple so that she could continue nursing. Some folk remedies for breast problems are included in Pliny's *Natural History* (28. 77. 250; 30. 45. 131).

Because breast-milk was explained as a transformation of surplus blood, which would otherwise be shed in *menstruation or used in the growth of an embryo, nursing women were advised (Soranus 2. 12. 19) to abstain from sexual activity: even if they did not become pregnant, intercourse might stimulate menstruation, and would in any case cause disturbance to the milk and the nursling. The contraceptive effect of lactation was thus reinforced. One motive for not breast-feeding may have been the mother's wish for more children.

Contracts with wet-nurses, which survive from Egypt, set out the rules of life which the wet-nurse must follow to safeguard her milk supply. Wages were low in comparison with those of a trained weaver, but the total cost of hiring a wet-nurse, for instance to rear a foundling child, was a large investment. Contracts include provision for the return of wages, and further penalty clauses, if the child dies or the nurse becomes unable to feed. The wet-nurse in these contracts may be free-born and living outside the household (if so, she must make regular vists for the child to be inspected), or may be a slave hired from another owner. Within households, slave mothers may have been obliged to hand over children to a wet-nurse so that they could return to work.

Several Greek deities have a title *Kourotrophos, meaning 'concerned with child-rearing', but no Greek or Roman goddess is specifically concerned with lactation and there are few examples in art of the 'nursing goddess'. See MOTHERHOOD.

Soranus, *Gynaecology*, trans. O. Temkin (1956; repr. 1991); K. R. Bradley, *Klio* 1980, 321–5, and in B. Rawson (ed.), *The Family in Ancient Rome* (1986); S. Dixon, *The Roman Mother* (1988); T. H. Price, *Kourotrophos: Cults and Representations of the Greek Nursing Deities* (1978). E. G. C.

Brennus (I), the Gallic chieftain who traditionally captured and destroyed Rome (in 390 BC or, according to *Polybius (1)'s more probable chronology, 387), and made the famous utterance: 'Woe to the vanquished', 'Vae victis.' The absence of any archaeological evidence for a destruction-level of this date suggests that his sack of Rome was superficial only.

T. Cornell, *CAH* 7²/2 (1989), 302 ff. P. T.

Brennus (2), leader of the *Galatian invasion in 279 BC. Following on the heels of another body of Gauls under Bolgius, Brennus overran Macedonia and invaded Greece in autumn. Checked by a Greek coalition at *Thermopylae, he sent a detachment to *Aetolia whereupon the Aetolian force withdrew from Thermopylae; he then turned the Greek position at Thermopylae, as the Persians had done in 480 BC (see PERSIAN WARS); and when the Greek forces scattered, he attacked *Delphi. The detachment in Aetolia and the main column under Acichorius were harassed by guerrilla tactics, while Brennus was wounded at Delphi. During the general retreat northwards the Gauls were attacked by the Thessalians; Brennus committed suicide, and few escaped.

G. Nachtergael, *Les Galates en Grèce et les Sôtéria de Delphes* (1977). N. G. L. H.

brevis brevians, 'abbreviation (of a long syllable) through the agency of a (nearby) short (syllable)'; the Latin term used by Louis Havet (1880) to denote a phenomenon in some forms of early Latin dramatic verse first clearly isolated by C. F. W. Mueller (1869) and dubbed by him *Iambenkürzung*, 'shortening of an iambic sequence'. The modalities of the phenomenon and its relationship to the prosodical features of the spoken language of the 3rd and 2nd cent. BC continue to be disputed. The cretic and bacchiac verses of drama, the *Saturnian verse and the dactylic hexameter of narrative poetry seem to have rarely, if ever, accepted the proffered licence. See METRE, LATIN.

O. Skutsch, *Prosodische und metrische Gesetze der Iambenkürzung* (1934); essays by S. Boldrini and M. Bettini in *Metrica classica e linguistica* (1990). H. D. J.

bribery, Greek Much of the Greek vocabulary for bribery is noticeably neutral ('persuade by gifts / money', 'receiving gifts'), although pejorative terms like 'gift-swallowing' are found as early as Hesiod (*Op.* 37 ff.). In Attic tragedy, we hear of accusations of bribery against e.g. seers like Tiresias (Soph. *OT* 380 ff.); Thucydides' *Pericles (1) (2. 60. 5, cf. 65. 8) finds it necessary to say that he has *not* taken bribes; clearly the normal expectation was that politicians did. Accusations of bribery are frequent in the 4th-cent. orators, partly because it was necessary to prove bribery in order to make a treason accusation (*eisangelia) stick: Hyp. 4. 29 f. Hyp. 5. 24 f. implies an Athenian distinction between bribes taken for and against the interests of the state; the latter type have been called 'catapolitical' (Harvey). See also CORRUPTION.

D. Harvey, in P. Cartledge and D. Harvey (eds.), *CRUX* (1985), 76 ff.
S. H.

bribery, Roman See AMBITUS, and cf. CORRUPTION.

brickstamps Roman Brickstamps bearing the names of kings occur already in ancient *Egypt. Stamped bricks began to be used in Rome during the 1st cent. BC. Except for the brickstamps of military units throughout the Roman empire, these inscriptions became historically and archaeologically important documents only after the fire of Rome in AD 64, when there was an unprecedented demand for fired bricks as a great rebuilding programme was instituted. For more than a century the building activity in the city made large-scale production of bricks profitable. The raw materials were available close at hand, especially in the lower Tiber valley on estates largely owned by members of distinguished Roman families, often of senatorial rank. From the mid-1st cent. AD the content of the stamps becomes more exact and more complex, indicating the *praedia* or *figlinae* where the bricks were produced, and eventually including the names of the *dominus* or owner, the foreman, and the workers employed there. In AD 110 the names of the consuls appear in a brickstamp for the first time (*CIL* 15. 18), on a brick produced at the *figlinae Brutianae* owned by M. Rutilius Lupus (*praefectus Aegypti* 113–17). This practice occurs periodically until 164, except in 123 when every brickstamp had to bear a date, presumably at the behest of the government. The stamps provided a system of accounting accreditation. Stamps make it possible to trace the ownership of brick-yards for generations; e.g. those of Cn. *Domitius Afer (consul AD 39) passed through inheritance and marriage to his descendant by law, the emperor Marcus *Aurelius. By the early 3rd cent. brick-production in Rome had become virtually an imperial monopoly. During the chaotic decades between *Caracalla and *Diocletian, brickstamps almost disappear, to be once more resurrected in Diocletian's reorganization of the brick industry, now part of the imperial bureaucracy (*c*.300). Two centuries later, *Theoderic (1)'s brickstamps, a fitting expression of the cultural aspirations of Ostrogoth rule, bring to a close the history of the ancient brick industry.

EDITIONS H. Bloch, *Supplement to CIL XV. I Including Complete Indices to the Roman Brick-Stamps* (1948); M. Steinby, *Indici Complementari ai Bolli Doliari Urbani* (1987).

STUDIES H. Bloch, *AJArch.* 1959, 225 ff; T. Helen, *Organization of Roman Brick Production* (1975); M. Steinby, *RE* Suppl. 15 (1978), 1489–1531, 'Ziegelstempel von Rom und Umgebung'. H. B.; H. D.

bridges Remains of causeway bridges are associated with bronze age road systems in the Argolid (see ARGOS (2)). Some of the bridges had water-passages with 'arches' composed of horizontal overlapping stones, and the type survived into the Classical period. Timber bridges must have been built from an early period, and stone bridges constructed on the pillar-and-lintel principle are known from the 5th cent. BC. The bridge over the sacred stream at *Brauron has five parallel rows of orthostats spanned by lintels

(*BCH* 1962, 681). A bridge on the military road to *Marathon, probably of the 4th cent. BC, is 5. 2 m. (17 ft.) wide and 14 m. (46 ft.) long, but the opening for the stream a mere 0.4 m. (1¼ ft.) wide by 1.4 m. (4½ ft.) high. It is built of well-fitted rubble. In the Hellenistic period bridges up to 300 m. (980 ft.) long were built, for instance, in northern Greece and in Asia Minor. There is a splendid example near *Cnidus. Piers of masonry, carefully built on the rocky bed, were so shaped as to create an efficient slipstream, and they carried a removable roadway of planking. It is uncertain whether any surviving example of a stone bridge with true arches dates from before the Roman period. The Etruscan 'bridges', as at *Veii and *Vulci, are tunnelled spurs of natural rock, the built structures in stone being in fact Roman. For, while the wooden bridge is associated with the very existence of Rome, the stone bridge is a relatively late development, the earliest dated example being the pons Aemilius (Livy 40. 51. 4) of 179 BC, given an arched superstructure in 142 BC, and followed by *pons Mulvius in 109 BC, and pons Fabricius in 62 BC. Typical of the state of affairs outside Rome is Strabo's description (4. 1. 12) of the Narbonese *via Domitia or the statement of Augustus (*RG* 20. 5): 'I repaired the *via Flaminia and all the bridges on it except the Mulvian and Minucian'. Nearly all monumental bridges thus belong to the imperial age. In Italy the most complete are those of Augustus at *Ariminum and of Hadrian at Rome, the most imposing those of Augustus at *Narnia and at *Asculum Picenum, the most curious the bold foot-bridge of Val de Cogne (*JRS* 1939, 149). But they are far outclassed in length by the Augustan bridge at *Emerita and in height by the famous bridge which several Spanish communities combined to erect over the Tagus gorge at Alcantara (AD 106). The tradition of wooden bridge-building, however, continued in the hands of military engineers (*PBSR* 1935, 34). *Caesar's description of his temporary wooden bridge on the Rhine (*BGall.* 4. 17) is famous (cf. *CR* 1908, 144). *Vegetius (1. 10) describes pontoon bridges of boats, anticipated, of course, by the bridge of boats *Xerxes had thrown across the *Hellespont, while many bridges of timber more durably constructed than these must have carried even the most important trunk roads. Bridges spanning powerful rivers, however, were usually built with stone piers and wooden superstructure, as the Flavian Rhine bridge at *Mogontiacum or *Trajan's Danube bridge, the latter some 1,120 m. (3,675 ft.) long, with stone piers and segmental arches of timber (see DANUVIUS). British examples are the Thames bridge at London, (*Londinium) the Tyne bridges at Corbridge (see CORIOSOPITUM) and Newcastle upon Tyne (Pons Aelius), where stone piers of the same kind are known to have been used. At *Arelate (Arles) there was a famous permanent bridge of boats (Auson. *Ordo nob. urb.* 77, p. 171 Green), figured in a mosaic at *Ostia (G. Becatti, *Scavi di Ostia* 4 (1961), pl. 184). Several Roman bridges constructed in stone, with stone arches, survive intact, because of the general strength and quality of their construction, and continued usefulness. Good examples are at Vaison and the beautiful Pont Flavien at St Chamas in Provence with its formal arches (a regular feature of such bridges) intact at both ends. See also AMPHIPOLIS.

P. Gazzola, *Ponti romani*, 2 vols. (1963); for bridges at Rome, Richardson, *Topog. Dict. Ancient Rome* 296 ff.; J. Ober, *Hesp.* 1982, 453; G. E. Bean and J. M. Cook, *BSA* 1952, 180. R. A. T.

brigandage (Gk. *lesteia*, Lat. *latrocinium*), the unlawful use of personal violence to maraud by land, was not condemned wholesale by the Classical Greeks. A carry-over from pre-state times, it remained a respectable occupation among some communities

(Thuc. 1. 5). In the 3rd cent. BC central Greece was dominated by the *Aetolians, whose confederacy protected, indeed quasi-institutionalized, their traditional way of life as bandits and pirates. As with Aetolia, brigandage was particularly prevalent in geographically more marginal zones, especially uplands, over which even the ancient empires exercised only nominal control (in the heart of the Persian empire note the Uxii, Arr. *Anab.* 3. 17. 1; *Isauria is the classic Roman case), and where pastoral mobility (see NOMADS; TRANSHUMANCE) facilitated illegal behaviour. With the Roman state's claim to the monopoly of force, *latrocinium* acquired a wider semantic range than modern 'brigandage' (it included e.g. 'feuding' and 'raiding'). The urban populations saw brigandage as such as an all-pervasive threat beyond the city gates (this was true even in Italy at the height of empire). In its attempts to control bandits (never permanently successful, not least because they often had the support of élite landowners), the Roman state relied on the army, including the occasional all-out campaign (as by Augustus in the Alps: Strabo 4. 6. 6), more usually on the uncoordinated efforts of local police and vigilantes (western cities had their *viatores*, 'road patrols', eastern ones their *diogmitai* commanded by irenarchs, lit. 'peace-keepers'), backed up by the most brutal forms of exemplary punishment of culprits. Whether antiquity knew the phenomenon of the 'social bandit' (Hobsbawm, below) is debated, although the admiring tales attached to a few 'super-brigands' (Iulius Maternus; Bulla Felix) suggest the ideological appeal of such a type. See BACAUDAE; PIRACY.

E. Hobsbawm, *Bandits*, 2nd edn. (1985); B. Shaw, *P&P* 1984, 3–52, and in A. Giardina (ed.), *The Romans* (1989; Eng. trans. 1993), ch. 11.

A. J. S. S.

Brigantes, the most populous tribe in Britain (Tac. *Agr.* 17) who held territory in northern England and had their capital at Isurium (Aldborough, North Yorks.). The tribal name is derived from the term 'high ones' or 'hill people'. Their lands included the legionary fortress of *Eburacum (York), forts at Olicana (Elslack?), Cataractonium (Catterick), Vinovium (Binchester), Camulodunum (Slack?) and Rigodunum (Castleshaw?). The major Iron Age *oppidum* at Stanwick (North Yorks.) was one of their centres and excavation has produced luxury Roman imports. Under Queen *Cartimandua early relations with Rome were friendly; later strife in the royal household compelled annexation by Q. *Petillius Cerialis and *Agricola in AD 71–9 (Tac. *Agr.* 17, 20). The Pennines and forests of Lancashire and Durham were intersected by garrisoned roads (Tac. *Agr.* 20) and lead-mining began by AD 81 (*RIB* 2404. 61). In the Ouse basin civil life gave rise to a town at Isurium and widespread villas, as at Well, Castledykes, Gargrave, or Dalton Parlours. The literary and archaeological evidence suggest a confederation of local groups rather than a centralized tribal organization. The eponymous goddess Brigantia won local fame (*RIB* 627, 628, 1131, 2066, 2091, cf. 623).

B. R. Hartley and L. Fitts, *The Brigantes* (1988). I. A. R.; M. J. M.

Brigantium, also called Brigantia, town in N.W. Spain (mod. La Coruña). Ptolemy (4)'s name, Brigantium Flavium, suggests it was a recipient of Vespasian's grant of the Latin right (see IUS LATII). There is no evidence, however, for municipal institutions even though tombstones are known and it appears as a *statio* on two *itineraries (*Ravenna Cosmography*). The *cohors Celtibera* was stationed there prior to the early 5th cent. A *lighthouse still stands 2 km. (1¼ mi.) to the north (*CIL* 2. 2559).

A. Tranoy, *La Galice romaine* (1981). S. J. K.

Brigetio, *O-Szőny* on the Danube, was first an auxiliary station, then a legionary fortress and city, in *Pannonia, in the territory of the Azali. Built by a *vexillatio* ('detachment') from three legions in the early 2nd cent. AD, it was occupied evidently in turn by Legio XI Claudia and XXX Ulpia Victrix until the end of *Trajan's reign, when I Adiutrix became its permanent garrison. The legionary *canabae developed its own quasi-municipal organization, but the separate civil town (*municipium*), created probably under Severus, is first recorded in 217 (*RIU* 377), and was subsequently promoted to a *colonia* (*RIU* 604).

Z. Visy, *Der Pannonische Limes in Ungarn* (1985), 53 ff. (plans and aerial photo); L. Barkóczi and A. Mocsy (eds.) *Die römischen Inschriften Ungarns*, 2 vols. (1972 and 1976) 2. 89 ff. J. J. W.

Brimo, name or title of a goddess, often identified with *Persephone (as *Etym. Magn.* 213, 49), *Hecate (as ibid.; Ap. Rhod. 3. 861), or *Demeter (as Clem. Al. *Protr.* p. 13, 4 Stählin). In the Eleusinian *mysteries (see ELEUSIS) the *hierophantēs proclaimed that she (viz. Demeter) had borne 'a holy child Brimos' (Hippol. *Haer.* 5. 8. 40 Marcovich), evidently *Plutus, but this does not imply a birth in the rite.

Clinton, *Iconography*; Graf, *Eleusis*, 130–1. K. C.

Briseis, in mythology, daughter of Briseus of Lyrnessus and widow of Mynes; *Achilles' slave-concubine, taken from him by *Agamemnon and afterwards restored (*Il.* 1. 392; 19. 60, 296, and contexts).

LIMC 3 / 1 (1986), 157–67. H. J. R.

Britain, Roman, the province of Britannia. The oldest name of the island known to us is *Albion; the earliest form of the present name, Πρεττανία, was used by the Greeks. The Latin *Britannia* was in use by the 1st cent. BC. It has no direct Celtic origin and is probably a Latin abstraction from an earlier form.

The iron age communities of Britain showed a variety of social organization, although all were agrarian peoples organized into tribal territories dominated by a range of enclosed settlement sites. Many were agriculturally sophisticated and had developed an impressive Celtic art style (see CELTS). The peoples of the south-east had a long history of shared culture with northern Gaul. The islands were known to the Mediterranean world from at least the 3rd cent. BC. After 120 BC, as trading contacts between Transalpine Gaul and areas to the north intensified, Britain began to receive goods such as wine *amphorae, and Gallo-Belgic coinage was introduced. Close political contacts with northern Gaul provided the pretext for *Caesar's expeditions in 55 and 54 BC and the context for the migration of the *Belgae to Britain which he mentions (*BGall.* 5. 12). His campaigns did not result in conquest although he imposed tribute on *Cassivellaunus before withdrawing. Contacts with the continent intensified with the *Romanization of Gaul from *Augustus onwards, and Rome maintained an interest in British affairs. Several burials of this period include luxury Roman goods probably sent as diplomatic gifts. Enhanced external contact stimulated internal political change culminating in the expansion of the *Catuvellauni who, under *Cunobelinus, obtained territorial dominance in the south-east.

Annexation had apparently been contemplated by Augustus and *Gaius (1) but was only achieved by *Claudius in AD 43. The army of four legions, with *auxilia*, quickly overran the territory of the Catuvellauni, with a set-piece battle at *Camulodunum

Britain, Roman

(Colchester). The army then moved west and north so that by the time of the *Boudiccan revolt (AD 60/1) the lowlands south of the Trent and much of Wales were held. Romanization was under way and towns were well established at *Londinium (London), *Verulamium (St Albans), and Colchester. The revolt was crushed but territorial expansion slowed for perhaps a decade. A succession of able Flavian governors enlarged the province by completing the conquest of Wales and pushing into Scotland (see CALEDONIA). The last of these, Cn. *Iulius Agricola (c. AD 77/8–83/4), advanced far into Scotland and defeated the Caledonians in a great battle at mons Graupius. Its location is unknown but camps associated with his campaigns have been identified as far north as the Moray Firth. After his withdrawal the rest of Scotland remained unconquered and there began a gradual retreat, eventually to the Tyne–Solway line (by the period of Trajan). The Stanegate road which marked this line became a *de facto* frontier until the construction of the *wall of Hadrian from c. AD 122. Although Scotland was again occupied first in the period c.139–64, when the *wall of Antoninus was the frontier, and then during *Septimius Severus' campaigns of 208–11, it was never successfully incorporated, and Hadrian's Wall remained the effective permanent frontier of the province.

Britain was an imperial province which contained a very substantial military garrison throughout the Principate. In the 2nd cent. the army comprised three legions – II Augusta at *Isca (2) (Caerleon), XX Valeria Victrix at *Deva (Chester), and VI Victrix at *Eburacum (York)—and perhaps 75 auxiliary units. These were predominantly based in the north and Wales and brought considerable wealth to these regions, which nevertheless remained less Romanized than areas to the south and east.

Local government was based on the Gallic cantonal system, with the following sixteen *civitates* known: the *Brigantes (capital at Aldborough), *Parisi (Brough-on-Humber), *Silures (Caerwent), *Iceni (Caistor-by-Norwich), *Cantiaci (Canterbury), Carvetii (Carlisle ?), Demetae (Carmarthen), *Reg(i)ni (Chichester), *Dobunni (Cirencester), *Durotriges (Dorchester, Dorset, and also later Ilchester), *Dumnonii (Exeter), *Corieltauvi (Leicester), Catuvellauni (Verulamium/St Albans), *Atrebates (2) (Silchester), Belgae (Winchester), and *Cornovii (Wroxeter). In addition there were four *coloniae* at Colchester (founded AD 49), *Lindum (Lincoln, 90–6), *Glevum (Gloucester, 96–8), and York (early 3rd cent.), together with Londinium which, although the provincial capital, is of uncertain status. The *civitates* were large and as many as seventy lesser urban centres served the countryside away from the principal towns. Although relatively large, none of the towns was well provided with public buildings. Most of those known are of later 1st- and 2nd-cent. date. During the 2nd and 3rd cents. most towns (including the lesser centres) were provided with defences, although there is debate over why these were built. In the 4th cent. the principal towns continued to be occupied but they became characteristically residential rather than productive centres. Although important as defended locations, none of them survived with urban characteristics for long into the 5th cent.

The single province of the Principate, governed from London, was divided in the early third century into Upper (with its capital at London) and Lower (capital York). A further subdivision into four provinces (Maxima Caesariensis, capital London; Flavia Caesariensis, capital Lincoln; Britannia Prima, capital Cirencester; and Secunda, capital York) took place under Diocletian. Valentia, known in northern Britain in the 4th cent., was probably the result of a further division of Secunda, although its location remains obscure.

The countryside was already extensively farmed before the conquest and agriculture remained the mainstay of the province with perhaps 90 per cent of the late Roman population of about 3.6 million living rurally. Most of these people continued to inhabit traditional farmsteads with only about one in a hundred sites becoming a *villa. Villa-building began soon after the conquest and continued steadily through the 2nd and 3rd cents. with a peak in both numbers and opulence during the 4th cent. The villas were generally modest by Mediterranean standards and most developed piecemeal through the aggrandizement of existing houses. *Mosaics were common by the 4th cent. and there is abundant evidence for the existence of a wealthy, rurally based aristocracy in southern Britain.

Other economic activities known from archaeology show growth to a peak of prosperity during the 4th cent. Metal extraction (for *gold, *silver, and *lead) began very soon after the conquest but did not become dominant. Local craft-based production was widespread, its success attested by the very abundant collections of objects found on most settlements. In the early empire there was great dependence on other provinces for the supply of consumer goods, imported initially through the military supply networks. Later local production grew to sustain the bulk of the province's needs and very substantial manufactures for items like pottery developed, especially in rural locations in the south and east (see POTTERY, ROMAN). None of these, however, became major exporters to other provinces.

Art and culture in Britain developed as a hybrid of Celtic and classical features. The religions of the Mediterranean spread to Britain with the army and administrators, but the Celtic gods were worshipped across most of the province (see RELIGION, CELTIC). However, they took on new forms, with the increased use of Romano-Celtic styles of temple architecture (first found at the end of the iron age) and the adoption of Latin epigraphy on altars and dedications. Particular gods are associated with certain regions and *civitates*. Many soldiers also adopted Celtic gods whom they identified with gods of the Roman pantheon (see SYNCRETISM). Christianity is found throughout the province in the 4th cent., although the extent of its acceptance is disputed. In art new materials (especially stone sculpture and mosaic) supplanted the metalwork used in the iron age La Tène styles. Not all the results are aesthetically pleasing today but some mosaics show an innovatory blend of ideas. Latin was widely adopted, although a study of the graffiti illustrates that writing was most used on military and urban sites (see VINDOLANDA TABLETS).

During the later empire Britain enjoyed relative peace compared with other provinces. A series of usurpers emerged from the province, D. *Clodius Septimius Albinus (193–6), *Carausius (286–93), *Allectus (293–7), *Magnus Maximus (383–8), and *Constantine III (407). Problems with raiders from across the North Sea may have led to the piecemeal construction of the *Saxon Shore forts from the middle of the 3rd cent. onwards. These and other coastal installations in the north and in Wales hint at increasing military threats, although the continued use of the traditional style of garrisons on Hadrian's Wall, combined with the general absence of the late Roman field army, implies that there were few serious military problems. In 367 there were concerted barbarian attacks from the north, which necessitated a military campaign, although the account by *Ammianus Marcellinus probably exaggerated these events. There is little else to suggest any serious military threats until early in the 5th cent. By then the depleted British garrison could not cope and the more pressing threats to Rome herself prevented aid from being sent. Britain, left to defend herself, gradually fell to the *Saxons.

S. S. Frere, *Britannia*, 3rd edn. (1987); A. R. Birley, *The Fasti of Roman Britain* (1981); *RIB* vol. 1 (1965), vol. 2 (1990–); M. J. Millett, *The Romanization of Britain* (1990); B. Jones and D. J. Mattingly, *An Atlas of Roman Britain* (1990); M. Henig, *Religion in Roman Britain* (1984); A. L. F. Rivet and C. Smith, *The Place-names of Roman Britain* (1979).

M. J. M.

Britannicus See CLAUDIUS CAESAR BRITANNICUS, TI.

Britomartis, Cretan goddess (see CRETE) of nature whose name means 'Sweet Virgin' (Hesychius; Solin. 11. 8). She had cults mainly in NE Crete, a festival at Olous, and cult image by *Daedalus (Paus. 9. 40. 3). In myth she was pursued by *Minos and jumped into the sea to escape him, was rescued by fishermen in their nets and afterwards called Diktynna (from *diktyon* 'net', Callim. *Hymn* 3. 189). The *aition* confused Britomartis with another goddess called Diktynna who received worship on the Rodhopou peninsula. Both Britomartis and Diktynna were related figures and, like *Aphaea ('Unseen') on Aegina, disappeared in the cult of *Artemis as minor satellites or epithets. See CRETAN CULTS AND MYTHS.

Nilsson, *MMR* 510–13, and *GGR* 1³ (1967), 311 f.; *LIMC* 3/1 (1984), 169–70.

H. J. R.; B. C. D.

Brizo, a goddess worshipped by women at *Delos, especially as protectress of sailing (*Semos of Delos in Ath. 8. 335a–b = *FGrH* 396 F 4). Her name is derived from βρίζειν, 'to sleep', and she was credited with sending prophetic *dreams. Bowls of all sorts of food, except fish, were offered to her in sacrifice.

J. D. M.

bronze The ancients used the words χαλκός, *aes*, indiscriminately for copper and for the harder and more fusible bronze, an alloy of copper and tin. Implements of bronze are found in Egypt and *Mesopotamia before 3000 BC. During the third millennium (the early Minoan period of Crete) the general use of bronze and the normal composition of the alloy (one part of tin to nine of copper) were established (see METALLURGY). Until the introduction of *iron, bronze was the sole metal for utilitarian purposes, and afterwards it continued in general use to the end of antiquity for sculpture, many domestic objects, and, after the 5th cent. BC, for small-denomination coins. Brass (ὀρείχαλκος, *orichalcum*, a mixture of copper and zinc) is not found before Roman imperial times, when *lead was also added to bronze in increasing quantities.

Copper is widely found in classical lands, where the principal sources of supply were, for Greece, *Chalcis in Euboea and *Cyprus, and for Italy, Bruttium, Etruria (see ETRUSCANS), and Elba, while under Roman rule *Spain produced largely. Tin may at first have come from Iran or beyond, and later Herodotus speaks of the metal as coming from the extremities of Europe (3. 115): Spain, Brittany, and Cornwall seem to have been the main sources. In comparison with the noble metals, bronze was inexpensive.

Several varieties of bronze were distinguished in antiquity—Corinthian, Delian, Aeginetan, Syracusan, Campanian—but these cannot be identified with any certainty. The technical processes employed were: hammering into plates which were riveted together (σφυρήλατον), used in the making of utensils, and, during the Archaic period, of statues; and casting with wax, either

solid (usually in the case of small statuettes or the handles, rims, and feet of vessels) or hollow over a core of clay or plaster (πρόπλασμα, *argilla*) to produce large-scale sculpture. Relief decoration was done in repoussé work (ἐμπαιστική); incised ornament is also common, especially on mirrors. Tin and copper solders were used in addition to riveting for joins. The dull patina of bronzes in museums is the result of time; ancient bronzes were kept bright to resemble gold, and the surface was often gilded, or variegated with damascening, inlay, or enamelling.

Pliny, *HN* 34. H. Blümner, *Technologie und Terminologie der Gewerbe und Künste bei Greichen und Römern* (1874–87), vol. 4; W. Lamb, *Greek and Roman Bronzes* (1929); C. Rolley, *Les Bronzes grecs* (1983); P. Bol, *Antike Bronzetechnik: Kunst und Technik antiker Erzbilder* (1985); D. E. L. Haynes, *The Technique of Greek Bronze Statuary* (1992); L. Pirzio Biroli Stefanelli and others, *Il bronzo dei Romani: Arredo e suppellettile* (1990).

F. N. P.; M. V.

Bructeri, a Germanic people, living north of the Lippe in the neighbourhood of modern Münster. A powerful people, they were allies of the *Cherusci, whom they assisted in resisting the invasions of Germany by *Germanicus. They also played a prominent part in the *Batavian revolt of AD 69–70, in which their priestess Veleda had much influence. Though heavily defeated (*c.*98) by the Chamavi and Angrivarii (Tac. *Germ.* 33) they survived, moved south of the Lippe, and retained their identity for a further two centuries before being absorbed by the *Franks.

E. A. Thompson, *The Early Germans* (1965). E. A. T.; J. F. Dr.

Brundisium (mod. Brindisi), a *Messapian city on the Adriatic coast, and an important harbour. Source-traditions of foundation by *Diomedes (2) or Phalanthus, or of Cretan colonists, probably do not indicate Greek colonization, but Greek influence is indicated by finds from a cemetery at Tor Pisani. Brundisium entered into alliance with *Thurii *c.*440 BC (*SEG* 16. 582), and produced coinage closely modelled on that of *Tarentum, but little is known about the Messapian city. In 244, a Latin colony (see IUS LATII) was founded there, and the *via Appia was extended from Tarentum to Brundisium. Thereafter, it was the principal route from Italy to Greece and the east. It was strategically vital during the Punic Wars and the conquest of the east, and was exempted from the *portoria by *Sulla. It was captured by *Caesar (49 BC), to cut off *Pompey's retreat, and besieged by Antony (M. *Antonius (2)) in 40. It was also the location for the Treaty of Brundisium, by which the *triumvirs came to an agreement (see M. ANTONIUS (2), para. 4). Despite its importance, archaeological evidence is limited.

K. L.

Bruttedius (Bruttidius) (*RE* 2) **Niger,** aedile AD 22; a gifted orator, pupil of *Apollodorus (5) of Pergamum (Sen. *Controv.* 2. 1. 35–6), and historian (Sen. *Suas.* 6. 20 f. reproduces his account of *Cicero's death), he prosecuted C. *Iunius Silanus (2) for extortion aggravated by *maiestas (Tac. *Ann.* 3. 66). Ambition tempted him to advance himself by delation, and he is probably the Bruttidius of Juv. 10. 83 who is involved in the downfall of *Sejanus.

Peter, *HRRel.* 2. 90–1. J. W. D.; B. M. L.

Bruttii, the inhabitants of the *Calabrian peninsula of Italy from the 4th cent. BC onwards. Earlier inhabitants are named as Oenotrians and Chones (Strabo 6. 1. 4–6), but there is no secure identification with the archaeological cultures of the region. The Lucanians began to make inroads on the region *c.*390, and it became politically and culturally Oscanized (see LUCANIA; OSCANS). In *c.*356, the inhabitants of the area revolted and established themselves as a politically independent group; their name derived from the Lucanian word for a runaway (Diod. Sic. 16. 15; Strabo 6. 1. 4; Just. *Epit.* 23. 1). They had few cities, their chief ones being *Petelia and *Consentia, and they seem to have been organized into a league, like many Oscan peoples. For most of the 4th and 3rd cents. they pursued an aggressive policy at the expense of the Greek cities along the coast, capturing a number of them. During the Pyrrhic war, they opposed Rome and became Roman allies after *Pyrrhus' defeat in 270. Half of the *Sila Forest, which occupied a large part of their territory, was confiscated and exploited by Rome for its timber. During the Hannibalic war, they revolted, seeking to wage war on both Rome and their long-standing enemies, the Greeks (see PUNIC WARS). During the 2nd cent., a number of colonies were founded along the Bruttian coast, but the mountainous and inaccessible nature of the hinterland attracted *brigandage and unrest, of which the most notable example was *Spartacus' revolt.

A. De Franciscis and O. Parlangeli, *Gli Italici del Bruzio* (1960); various authors in 'Studi sulla Calabria Antica' (*PP* 1974); C. Turano, *La Calabria Antica* (1977).　　　　K. L.

Bruttius Praesens, Gaius, a senator from *Lucania, was a friend of *Pliny (2). His career began under *Domitian but languished under Trajan until a successful legionary command in the Parthian War (AD 115–16, see TRAJAN) brought him to prominence. Governor of Cilicia when Trajan died there in 117, Praesens was favoured by *Hadrian, under whom he was legate of Cappadocia and Lower Moesia, proconsul of Africa, and legate of Syria. He held a second consulship in 139 as colleague of the new emperor *Antoninus Pius, and may have been city prefect. His granddaughter Crispina married *Commodus.

Pliny, *Epp. AE* 1950, 66; Syme, *RP* 5. 563 ff.　　　　A. R. Bi.

Brutus See IUNIUS BRUTUS (2), M.

Bryson (early 4th cent. BC), of Heraclea (3) Pontica, a sophist associated with the following of *Euclides (1) of Megara, he is criticized by Aristotle for an allegedly fallacious quadrature of the circle (*An. post.* 75^{b}4; *Soph. el.* 171^{b}16, 172^{a}3). The argument, whatever its original intent, employs a form of two-sided convergence of polygonal sequences to the circle, a procedure later exploited by *Archimedes in his measurement of the sphere.

Frs. and comm. in K. Döring, *Die Megariker* (1972), 62–7, 157–66; I. Mueller, in N. Kretzmann (ed.), *Infinity and Continuity in Ancient and Medieval Thought* (1982), 146–64; W. R. Knorr, *Ancient Tradition of Geometric Problems* (1986), 76–80.　　　　W. R. K.

Bubastis, the local cat-goddess of Bubastis (mod. Tell Basta), also worshipped elsewhere in Egypt (see Hdt. 2. 60, 66–7). Analysis of Ptolemaic cat-mummies has shown that cats bred for dedication were slaughtered at regular intervals. Egyptian animal-worship was puzzling to outsiders; *Diodorus (3) Siculus (1. 83. 8) recounts firsthand the near-disastrous fate of a visiting Roman who unwittingly killed a cat in Alexandria (1). See EGYPTIAN DEITIES.　　　　D. J. T.

Bucephalas, *Alexander (3) the Great's favourite Thessalian horse, bought for thirteen talents and broken in by Alexander himself; named after his ox-head brandmark. Alexander gave the name Bucephala to a city founded on the *Hydaspes (Jhelum) where Bucephalas died (326 BC). See HORSES.　　　　R. M. E.

bucolic See PASTORAL POETRY, GREEK; PASTORAL POETRY, LATIN.

building materials

Greek In its developed stages Greek *architecture was based on the use of finely dressed stone masonry, predominantly limestone. Where available either locally or transported, white *marble was used for the finest structures. The coloured marbles favoured in the late bronze age were not used. Transport costs were a major factor in the availability of stone: local stone would often be used as an economy and this occasionally tends to the use of abnormal materials such as trachite at *Pergamum. In major buildings the dressed blocks were regularly fastened with clamps and dowels of wood or metal, but without mortar; and although exceptionally almost entire buildings might be of marble, including ceilings of quite large span (e.g. the *Propylaea at Athens), considerations of cost frequently meant that the less conspicuous parts were built in local limestone. See QUARRIES. Inferior materials were regularly surfaced with fine marble stucco to resemble masonry, but the use of fine marble veneer was a Hellenistic innovation, as was the reintroduction of coloured and patterned marbles (other than grey). In some Hellenistic buildings such decorative stone facings were imitated in painted plaster and all but the best materials were plastered on the interior often to receive painted decoration (see PAINTING (TECHNIQUES); PAINTING, GREEK). In simpler buildings, walls were still built of mud-brick. Tiles were generally terracotta, occasionally marble. Similarly other roof elements such as antefixes and decorative revetments, especially on western Greek buildings, were normally terracotta. See TERRACOTTAS. *Bronze was used for many decorative purposes and facings (e.g. the temple of Athena Chalkioikos at Sparta). Waterproof cement was regularly used for hydraulic works and for floors which required frequent washing.

R. A. T.

Roman Roman building practice was everywhere based on locally available materials. The only building materials widely transported in the Roman empire were *marble and *timber for roofing. In Rome itself the plentiful local supplies of soft, easily dressed, volcanic tufa were used from the 6th cent. BC onwards and remained in use at all periods as a general-purpose building material (see QUARRIES). From the 2nd cent. BC travertine was quarried near *Tibur. This was a fine building stone, used particularly in the later republic until the large-scale use of marble was developed under Augustus. For much domestic architecture the use of timber-framed unfired brick (see BRICKSTAMPS) was widespread in Rome before the fire of AD 64. The major Roman contribution to architectural development was the exploitation and perfection of *opus caementicium*, Roman concrete. This comprised a hydraulic mortar laid in alternate courses with aggregate. It derived its unique strength from the use of the local volcanic deposits (*pozzolana,* Lat. *pulvis puteolanus,* from its first exploitation at *Puteoli in Campania). In Rome from the 2nd cent. BC onwards it was increasingly employed in monumental building, at first faced with small irregularly shaped stones (*opus incertum*) and later with small squared stones set diagonally (*opus reticulatum*). Building in concrete was flexible and cheap and allowed the construction of vaulted chambers on a large scale. The aggregate was often skilfully graded by weight, the supreme example here being the dome of the *Pantheon; from the time of Hadrian the vaulting-load might be further lightened by the incorporation of large jars. In Rome and central Italy concrete from the 1st cent. AD was faced with fired brick. Outside Italy local resources did not allow the use of concrete and other materials were developed; a tough mortared rubble, often strengthened with courses of brick, was used in Gaul, the Balkans, and Asia Minor, and in the eastern provinces vaulting was carried out in brick, anticipating Byzantine practice, as well as in cut stone. From the 1st cent. BC Roman *architecture made extensive use of white and coloured marble for columns, veneer, and paving (see CARRARA). Roof tiles were made of baked clay or stone, though gilt *bronze was used occasionally. Waterproof mortars and *lead and terracotta piping were regularly employed for hydraulic installations (see BATHS).   J. B. W.-P.; H. D.

Late Roman The bulk of materials used in buildings of the 4th to 6th cents. AD continued to be those most readily and cheaply available. The monuments of the two principal capitals, *Ravenna and *Constantinople, were mainly in brick; but other areas, such as much of Asia Minor and Syria, had a flourishing tradition of fine, cut stonework. Humbler buildings were often of more perishable materials, timber and wattle in the north, mud-brick in the south.

In the east, vaults and domes came to be built in brick; whereas in the west more traditional concrete was still used, sometimes lightened with interlocking hollow tubes of terracotta. In many parts of the empire *mosaics were common, both in rich private houses and in the new churches. For floors, mosaicists generally used stone cubes for their durability, while on walls they attained a richer sparkling effect through the use of gilt and coloured glass cubes.

As in earlier centuries, marble was the one building material regularly shipped over long distances. By far the most important marble in this period was the white stone of the island of Proconnesos in the sea of Marmara, which was extensively used in nearby Constantinople, and also shipped widely overseas, often already carved as standard fittings such as chancel screens. However, particularly in the west, including Rome itself, the period is also characterized by the extensive use of *spolia*, marble fittings (such as capitals) taken from older classical buildings and built into new buildings without reworking them.   B. R. W.-P.

GREEK I. R. Martin, *Manuel d'architecture grecque* 1 (1965).

ROMAN A. Boethius, *Etruscan and Early Roman Architecture*, rev. edn. (1978); J. B. Ward-Perkins, *Roman Imperial Architecture* (1980); J. P. Adam, *La Construction romaine* (1984).

LATE ROMAN J. Ward-Perkins, in D. Talbot Rice (ed.), *The Great Palace of the Byzantine Emperors: Second Report* (1959), 52–104; J.-P. Sodini, in *Hommes et richesses dans l'Empire byzantin* 1: *IVe–VIIe siècle* (1989), 163–86; F. W. Deichmann, *Die Spolien in der spätantiken Architektur* (1975).

Bulla Regia, a town in the Bagradas valley in North Africa. A large building of c.100/80 BC, a defensive circuit, and burials bear witness to the Numidian period (see NUMIDIA), when it was a royal capital (hence *Regia*); the earliest material goes back to c.300 BC. Later it came within Africa Proconsularis; a *free city under Augustus (Plin. *HN* 5.22), it received the *ius Latii* under Vespasian and became a colony under *Hadrian. Extensive Roman ruins survive, including the forum, temples of *Apollo and *Isis, the theatre, and substantial baths; particularly notable are its many mosaic-paved houses of late-Roman date, some with a complete underground storey to provide a pleasantly cool retreat from the summer heat.

PECS 171–2; A. Beschaouch, R. Hanoune, and Y. Thébert, *Les Ruines de Bulla Regia* (1977); *Recherches archéologiques franco-tunisiennes à Bulla Regia* 1/1: *Miscellanea* (1983), 2/1: *Les thermes memmiens* (1993), 4/1: *Les Mosaiques* (1980); pre-Roman background: M. Khanoussi, *Reppal 2* (1968), 325–35.   R. J. A. W.

Burdigala (mod. Bordeaux), capital of the Bituriges Vivisci and, eventually, of *Aquitania, was a busy international trading-port (with strong British links). Important remains include an amphitheatre (the 'Palais-Gallien'), a temple of Tutela, and instructive inscriptions and reliefs. In the late empire a reduced enceinte, c.700 × 450 m. (765 × 492 yds.), rectangular with bastions, was built, principally to protect the port. It was the birthplace (c. AD 310) of *Ausonius, who celebrated its university. Though it fell under Visigothic (see GOTHS) rule from c.418, it continued to prosper.

Grenier, *Manuel* 1. 410; R. Étienne, *Bordeaux antique* (1962); H. Sivan, in J. F. Drinkwater and H. Elton (eds.), *Fifth-Century Gaul* (1992).   C. E. S.; J. F. Dr.

bureaucracy (Greek) Because the Greek world remained a world of separate, small states, and because those states entrusted their administration as far as possible to individual citizens or boards of citizens, often appointed for a single year, rather than to professional administrators, bureaucracy in the Greek world is not a large subject. However, administrative machinery had to be kept in motion, documents had to be drafted, and records had to be kept and retrieved; and, even in the amateur culture of the Greek city-states, there were some opportunities for specialization in this kind of work.

Athens, as usual, is the state about which we are best informed. Inventories were compiled, and often inscribed, of the contents of temple treasuries and of dockyards; there were contracts for tax-collection, mine leases, and the like; there were records of decrees and of lawcourt verdicts. Some public slaves (*dēmosioi*) were used not for manual labour but for keeping records and producing them when required, and for assisting in the elaborate procedures of the jury-courts (*Ath. pol.* 47. 5–48. 1; 63–5; 69. 1); one inscription orders a named slave to record what is stored in the arsenal and the public secretaries to verify the record (*IG* 2². 120. 11–19). At a higher level Athens had a number of citizen secretaries and under-secretaries, and with the passage of time there was a tendency for secretarial posts to become less like magistracies, in which any public-spirited citizen might take his turn, and more like specialist posts which would be held by men with appropriate interests and skills. They were subject to the general rule that a man could hold a particular post only for one year, but several posts of this kind existed and it was possible for a man to hold several of them over a period.

See also ARCHIVES; RECORDS AND RECORD-KEEPING.   P. J. R.

Burebistas (*RE* 3. 2903–5, 4. 1958–60; Suppl. 1. 261–4), king of the Dacians (see DACIA), built up an extensive but impermanent empire in the Danubian lands (c.60–44 BC). With a priest called Cecaenos he carried out religious and moral reform in Dacia, pulling up all the vines (Strabo 303 f. C). In *Pannonia he took over the *Scordisci (56–50 BC), who became his mercenaries, and defeated the *Boii and Taurisci (c.45), taking control of the Hungarian plain. He harried the Pontic Greek cities and spread his power into *Thrace. *Pompey negotiated with him for assistance in 48 BC (cf. *Syll*³. 762: decree in honour of the ambassador Acornion of Dionysopolis). *Caesar was intending to march against him in 44. Burebistas himself was assassinated about this time and his empire broke up into four or five kingdoms, but the 'Dacian problem' was still alive under *Augustus.

A. Mócsy, *Pannonia and Upper Moesia* (1974), see index; M. Szabo, *Les Celtes de l'Est* (1992), 64 ff.   R. S.; B. M. L.

Burgundians (Burgundiones), a Germanic people who first appear on the Main soon after AD 250. They had little contact with the Romans until *c*.406, when they crossed the Rhine and established a kingdom in the province of Germania Prima (see GERMANIA) with their capital at Worms. In 436, following an unsuccessful attempt to occupy Belgica Prima, they were subjected to an appalling defeat by Flavius *Aetius and an army of Huns (an event commemorated in the *Nibelungenlied*). Aetius moved the survivors to Maxima Sequanorum, where the Burgundian kingdom recovered and played a significant role in sub-Roman Gaul, until it was overrun by the *Franks in 534.

H. Wolfram, *Das Reich und die Germanen* (1990), 351 ff.   J. F. Dr.

Burrus See AFRANIUS BURRUS, SEX.

Busiris, a legendary Egyptian king, the eponym of Busiris in the Delta, who, according to Ionian tradition, habitually slaughtered foreigners entering Egypt at the altar of *Zeus. He was finally slaughtered by *Heracles (Hdt. 2. 45, with A. B. Lloyd's, comm. (1976)). The tale was popular among classical artists and authors.

A.-F. Laurens, *LIMC* 3 / 1 (1986), 147–52, 'Bousiris'.   D. J. T.

Buthrotum (now Butrinto, uninhabited), founded traditionally by the Trojan *Helenus on a low hill at the seaward end of a narrow channel leading from a lake, possessed fine harbours and fisheries and was a port of call on the coasting route along *Epirus. It has prehistoric remains, a fine theatre, and strong Hellenistic fortifications. The centre of a tribal union, it later became a Roman colony. Recent excavation reveals cultural influence from Archaic *Corinth.

L. M. Ugolini, *Albania antica* 3 (1942); Hammond, *Epirus*, see index; *Studime Historike* 2 (Tiranë 1966), 143 ff.; excavation reports in *Iliria*; K. Arafat and C. Morgan, *Dialogos* 2 (1995), 25 ff.   N. G. L. H.

Buxentum (mod. Policastro), a Roman colony, founded in 194 BC on the Greek city of Pyxus, itself a colony of *Rhegium. Livy (34. 5. 1, 39. 23. 3) says that it was unsuccessful, despite a second deduction in 186, but archaeological surveys contradict this, showing an intensification of settlement in the region.

F. de Polignac and M. Gualtieri, in G. Barker and J. Lloyd (eds.), *Roman Landscapes* (1991).   K. L.

Byblos (mod. Jubayl, Lebanon), a major port of Phoenicia, deriving much of its prosperity from the export of timber (see the Egyptian story of Wen-Amon, 11th cent. BC). Allegedly the oldest city in the world (so *Philon (5) of Byblos), it was occupied from the fifth millennium. Egypt took an interest in Byblos from an early date and there is evidence for relations with bronze age *Crete, Greece, and *Mesopotamia. Excavations have yielded little of the Phoenician period, except for one early example of alphabetic writing, the sarcophagus of King Ahiram (10th cent. BC). Byblos was an independent kingdom with its own coinage under the Persians, when a massive fortress was erected. It developed as a centre for the cult of *Adonis and prospered in Roman times. The Greeks took from its name their word for papyrus (see BOOKS, GREEK AND ROMAN).

DCPP, entry under the name; M. Dunand, *Fouilles de Byblos* (1939, 1951, 1973).   J. B.; J.-F. S.

byssus (βύσσος, prob. = Akkad. *būṣu*, Hebr. *būṣ*), a conspicuously fine fibre, normally of plant origin. Aeschylus (*Sept.* 1039; *Pers.* 125) mentions fine tunics of βύσσος, probably *linen (flax) in this context; the Egyptian mummy bandages described by Herodotus (2. 86) as βύσσος were also linen. But later the term was extended to *cotton (explicitly in Poll. 7. 75–6) and even floss

*silk (Strabo 15. 1. 20). Pausanias' much-quoted references to *byssus*-growing in Elis (5. 5. 2, 6. 26. 6) are ambiguous. That *byssus* also covered the silky anchor-filaments of the giant mussel *Pinna nobilis* used by the Romans for special fabrics is unproven.

RE 3. 1108.   J. P. W.

Byzacium The name, of uncertain Libyan origin, applied in Roman times (Livy 33. 48. 1; Plin. *HN* 5. 24) to part of the province of Africa (see AFRICA, ROMAN), from the gulf of Hammamet to the gulf of Gabes, with the hinterland; it was probably the Βυσσᾶτις χώρα of Polybius (3. 23. 2). The chief town was *Hadrumetum. The area was extremely fertile in parts, renowned for both its cereals (Plin. *HN* 5. 24, 17. 41, 18. 94) and its olives; olive oil was exported from Sullecthum, Lepti Minus, and elsewhere. A procuratorial region was based on Hadrumetum. Under Diocletian it became a separate province with the name Valeria Byzacena.

J. Ferron, *Cahiers de Tunisie* 1963, 31–46 (pre-Roman); J. Desanges, ibid. 7–22 (Roman).   B. H. W.; R. J. A. W.

Byzantium, a famous city on the European side of the south end of the *Bosporus (1), between the Golden Horn and the *Propontis. The Greek city occupied only the eastern tip of the promontory, in the area now covered by the Byzantine and Ottoman palaces of Constantinople / Istanbul. The evidence of cults and institutions confirms the claim of the Megarians (see MEGARA) to be the main founders, but groups from the Peloponnese and central Greece probably also participated in the original colony, which is to be dated 668 (Hdt. 4. 144) or 659 BC (Euseb. *Chron.*). Little material earlier than the late 7th cent. has yet emerged from excavations. Except during the *Ionian Revolt the city was under Persian control from *Darius I's Scythian expedition until 478. In the Athenian empire (see DELIAN LEAGUE) it paid fifteen talents' tribute or more, deriving its wealth from tuna fishing and from tolls levied on passing ships. The city also had an extensive territory not only in European *Thrace but also in *Bithynia and Mysia in Asia. It revolted from Athens in 440–39 and 411–408. Although under Spartan control after the battle of Aegospotami (405) alliance coins show that it joined the anti-Spartan sea league formed after the battle of *Cnidus in 394. It became a formal ally of Athens from *c*.378 to 357 and also when resisting *Philip (1) II of Macedon in the siege of 340–39. *Hecate is supposed to have helped the besieged on this occasion and her symbols, the crescent and star (later adopted as the emblem of the Turkish state), appear on the city coinage. It suffered from the attacks and exactions of the *Galatians in the 270s but picked the winning side in Rome's Macedonian wars in the 2nd cent. BC. Byzantium's strategic position enabled it to enjoy privileged status under the Roman empire, which did not, however, protect the city from the depredations of passing armies and rapacious officials. All privileges were lost when it supported *Pescennius Niger against *Septimius Severus, and fell after a two-year siege (AD 193–5; *Cassius Dio, 75. 12. 1, gives a brilliant although exaggerated account). Severus reduced Byzantium to village-status and caused much destruction, but rebuilding soon followed and traces of the subsequent Severan restoration have been archaeologically identified. Constantine I refounded Byzantium as New Rome, *Constantinople, on 11 May 330, extending its bounds to new city walls and adorning it with magnificent new buildings.

W. L. Macdonald, *PECS* 177–9; J. Boardman, *The Greeks Overseas*, 3rd edn. (1980).   A. J. G.; S. M.

Cabiri, divinities at certain mystery sanctuaries, notably Boeotian *Thebes (1), *Lemnos, perhaps *Samothrace. The name is of Semitic origin from *kabir*, 'lord' (Schachter 96 n. 4 for refs., see bibliog. below). At the sanctuaries where there is adequate evidence, namely Thebes and Samothrace, it is clear that the role they play is subsidiary to that of the central deities. The latter were either a goddess and her consort, or a triad of goddess, consort, and child.

Cabiri are found throughout the northern Aegean, and on adjacent Asiatic and Thracian mainlands, and in two places in mainland Greece, both in *Boeotia (Thebes and *Anthedon). Their number and precise function varied with local customs and preoccupations. Thus, while numbers range from two to seven, at Thebes there were two, father and son (Cabirus and *pais* in inscriptions, *Prometheus and Aetnaeus in Pausanias, *Hermes and *Pan in art), a reflection of a common Boeotian dioscoric type (see DIOSCURI). Similarly, while at Lemnos they were smiths, at Thebes they promoted cattle-raising and viticulture as the agricultural economy developed.

Although much of the evidence for Cabiri in the Aegean and the Asian mainland is relatively late (Hemberg collects all that was available at the time), the cults at Lemnos and Samothrace were known to *Aeschylus and *Herodotus (1), respectively, and the Theban Cabiri are attested by name from the end of the 7th, and were probably established there by the 8th cent. BC.

GENERAL B. Hemberg, *Die Kabiren* (1950) (but for the Theban cult, nothing written before the renewed excavations of the 1950s and 1960s is reliable).

SPECIFIC SITES Lemnos: J. Boardman, *PECS* 496–7. Samothrace: G. Roux, *Bull. Assoc. G. Budé* 1981, 2–23. Thebes: A. Schachter, *Cults of Boiotia* 2 (1986), 66–110.   A. Sch.

Cacus For the Augustans (Verg. *Aen.* 8. 190–279; Livy 1. 7. 3–15, with Ogilvie's notes; Prop. 4. 9; Ov. *Fast.* 1. 543–86, with Bömer's notes, 5. 643–52) a savage fire-breathing monster inhabiting the *Palatine (*Aventine according to Virgil, but the Scalae Caci on the Palatine imply otherwise: Platner–Ashby, 465; Nash, *Pict. Dict. Rome* 2. 299) whose thieving terrified the locals; he stole some of Geryon's cattle from *Heracles, who killed him. This Hellenized version relied on Heracles traditions (cf. Hdt. 4. 8) and a false etymology from the Greek *kakos* (evil: Serv. on *Aen.* 8. 190), and provided an aetiology for the cult of Heracles at the Ara Maxima (Ogilvie on Livy 5. 13. 6). Originally a sister Caca (Lactant. *Div. inst.* 1. 20. 36, Serv.) makes him a bisexual deity, possibly *chthonian, connected with fire (Serv.). Dubious connection with Caeculus, founder of *Praeneste, of whom a miracle involving fire is related (Servius on *Aen.* 7. 678). Cn. *Gellius (fr. 7 Peter) knows him as an Etruscan killed by Heracles; cf. A. Alföldi, *Early Rome and the Latins* (1965), 228–30.

J. Fontenrose, *Python* (1959), 339–42; Latte, *RR* 60; F. Münzer, *Cacus der Rinderdieb* (1911); J. P. Small, *Cacus and Marsyas in Etrusco-Roman Legend* (1982); *LIMC* 3 / 1. 177–8.   C. R. P.

Cadmus, legendary Phoenician founder of Boeotian *Thebes (1), whose origins are still disputed: Phoenicia, Egypt. Mycenaean Greece, Archaic Greece, have all been proposed (see bibliog. below).

In *Homer, he appears indirectly, as father of *Ino-Leucothea (*Od.* 5. 333), and through the names Cadmeii, Cadmeiones given to the inhabitants of Thebes attacked by the Seven (see SEVEN AGAINST THEBES) and the *Epigoni (Cadmeii: *Il.* 4. 388, 391, 5. 807, 10. 288, *Od.* 11. 276; Cadmeiones: *Il.* 4. 385, 5. 804, 23. 680).

The generally accepted story (see Frazer) is that Cadmus was sent by his father *Agenor to find his sister *Europa, who had been abducted (by *Zeus, as it turned out). He failed in his search (Europa ended up in Crete, while Cadmus went to the Greek mainland), but was ordered by Delphi (see DELPHIC ORACLE) to be guided by a cow and establish a city where the animal lay down. Thus he founded Thebes, having killed a dragon, and peopled the place with men sprung from the dragon's teeth (*Spartoi). His dynasty ended with *Thersander, son of Polynices.

Apollod. *The Library* , trans. J. G. Frazer (Loeb, 1921), 3. 1. 1, 3. 4. 1–2, 3. 5. 4; M. Astour, *Hellenosemitica* (1967), 147–59; M. Bernal, *Black Athena* 2 (1991), esp. 497–504; R. B. Edwards, *Kadmos the Phoenician* (1979), *passim*; A. Schachter, in *La Béotie antique* (1985), 143–52; F. Vian, *Les Origines de Thèbes* (1963), chs. 2, 3, 11; *LIMC* 5 / 1 (1990), 863–82 (in art).   A. Sch.

Caecilia (*RE* 'Pomponius' 78) **Attica,** daughter of T. *Pomponius Atticus, mother of *Vipsania Agrippina (1). Born 51 BC, she is frequently mentioned as a child in *Cicero's letters to Atticus. In *c.*37, M. *Antonius (2) arranged her marriage to *Agrippa. Her education continued under *Caecilius Epirota, until he was dismissed on suspicion of improper relations with her. She is not heard of again, and Agrippa remarried in 28.

T. J. C.; E. B.

Caecilia (*RE* 'Caecilius' 134) **Metella** (1), daughter of L. *Caecilius Metellus Delmaticus, married M. *Aemilius Scaurus (1) and bore him two children. After his death she married *Sulla, marked out for a consulship (88 BC), to whom she bore twins, Faustus *Cornelius Sulla and Fausta, later wife of T. *Annius Milo. In 86 they all joined him in Greece. In his dictatorship (81), when she was dying of a disease probably caught from him, he divorced her and had her carried out of the house, to avoid ritual contamination.   E. B.

Caecilia (*RE* 'Caecilius' 136) **Metella** (2), daughter of Q. *Caecilius Metellus (Creticus) and wife of a Crassus, probably the elder (?) son of M. *Licinius Crassus (1) (*ILS* 881; cf. 9924, 9933). E. B.

Caecilius (1) (*RE* 2), of Caleacte in Sicily, rhetor and historian (1st cent. BC); said by some to have been a freedman of Jewish faith (see *Suda*). His range of interests and his literary outlook resemble those of *Dionysius (7) of Halicarnassus, who mentions him as a friend (*Pomp.* 3. 20). No fragments remain of his history of the slave wars (attested by Ath. 6. 272 f.), but there is a good deal of evidence for his rhetorical works. His book 'On the Sublime' ($\Pi\epsilon\rho\grave{\iota}$ $\mathring{\upsilon}\psi o\upsilon s$) was the target *'Longinus' attacked, and from which he no doubt drew many of his examples; his comparison of *Demosthenes (2) and *Cicero also attracted criticism (Plut. *Dem.* 3). A treatise on figures is often quoted by later writers, and the reported titles 'What is the Difference between the Attic and the Asianic Taste ($\zeta\mathring{\eta}\lambda os$)?' and 'Against the Phrygians' make his Atticist position clear (see ASIANISM AND ATTICISM). According to the *Suda he also wrote 'On the Style ($\chi\alpha\rho\alpha\kappa\tau\mathring{\eta}\rho$) of the Ten Orators', and many judgements on style and authenticity are cited by later writers; whether this book amounted to a systematic account of the 'canon' of the ten orators (see ATTIC ORATORS) is uncertain. Caecilius was an erudite rhetor; there is no reason to think he was a particularly intelligent critic.

Fragments (very uncritically collected): E. Ofenloch (1907). See, in general, commentaries on 'Longinus'; also A. E. Douglas, *Mnemos.* 1956, 30–40. D. A. R.

Caecilius (2) of Novum Comum, one of *Catullus' friends, composed a poem on Cybele (Catull. 35).

Caecilius (*RE* 29) **Africanus, Sextus,** a Roman lawyer of the mid-2nd cent. AD and pupil of *Iulianus probably came from Thuburbo Minus (mod. Tebourba) in Tunisia. He was dead when Gellius (*NA* 20. 1. 1–55) around 180 AD depicted a debate between him and the philosopher *Favorinus on the *Twelve Tables, in which Caecilius defended the ancient laws against the imputation of cruelty. He wrote nine books (*libri*) of *Quaestiones* ('Problems'), which deal with difficult cases, report Iulianus' views on them, and in rather clumsy language add comments of his own. Though hardly cited by later lawyers, Justinian's compilers (see JUSTINIAN'S CODIFICATION) excerpted 121 passages from his work.

Lenel, *Pal.* 1. 1–36, 2. 782; *PIR*² C 18; *HLL* 4, § 415. 2; Kunkel 1967, 172–4; A. Wacke, *ANRW* 2. 15 (1976), 455–496; F. Casavola, *Giuristi Adrianei* (1980), 75–105; D. Liebs, *ZRG* 1990, 371 f.; Honoré, 1962, 134–6. T. H.

Caecilius (*RE* 36) **Bassus, Quintus,** equestrian officer under *Pompey in the Civil War. After *Pharsalus he fled to Syria, took over two legions that had mutinied against their commander, and seized *Apamea, which he defended against Caesarian commanders while negotiating with *Deiotarus and the Parthians. After *Caesar's death both his troops and his besiegers soon joined C. *Cassius Longinus (1), who dismissed him unharmed. E. B.

Caecilius (*RE* 53) **Epirota, Quintus,** a freedman of T. *Pomponius Atticus and friend of *Cornelius Gallus, taught grammar under *Augustus. After Gallus' death (27 BC) he opened a select school for older pupils and was the first to lecture on *Virgil and other contemporary poets (Suet. *Gram.* 16).

Herzog–Schmidt, § 320; *PIR*² C 42. R. A. K.

Caecilius Iucundus, financial agent (*coactor argentarius*, see BANKS) at *Pompeii in the mid-1st cent. AD: an archive of 153 wax tablets reveals his lively involvement with auction sales.

*Freedmen were prominent in his milieu, and he also contracted with the Pompeii town council for the administration of some of its concerns. The evidence is valuable precisely because, though he was active and prosperous, Iucundus' wealth and rank were not outstanding.

J. Andreau, *Les Affaires de Monsieur Jucundus* (1974). N. P.

Caecilius (*RE* 72) **Metellus, Lucius,** consul 251 BC, served in Sicily where, in June 250, he won a great victory over the Carthaginians at *Panormus, capturing many *elephants (the coins of the Caecilii Metelli frequently portray an elephant). He was again in Sicily in 249 as *magister equitum* to the dictator A. *Atilius Caiatinus, and in 247 as consul for the second time. He was dictator to hold the elections in 224 and pontifex maximus from 243 until his death in 221. The story that he was blinded saving the *Palladium from the burning temple of *Vesta in 241 may be apocryphal.

Walbank, *HCP* 1. 100–3. J. Br.

Caecilius (*RE* 81) **Metellus, Quintus,** son of Lucius (above) and a pontifex from 216 BC, was one of the envoys who brought news of the *Metaurus in 207. He was elected consul for 206 under the presidency of one of the victors at the Metaurus, M. *Livius Salinator, who was then dictator with Metellus himself as *magister equitum*. Metellus and his colleague faced *Hannibal in southern Italy, regaining *Lucania. In 205 he held the elections as dictator. After this he consistently supported *Scipio Africanus against the latter's political opponents. He was one of the commissioners to assign land to Scipio's veterans in 201–200, and an ambassador to Greece in 185 and 183. In 179 he reconciled the censors M. *Aemilius Lepidus (1) and M. *Fulvius Nobilior. He was noted for his oratory and had a celebrated quarrel with the poet *Naevius (H. D. Jocelyn, *Antichthon* 1969, 32–47).

J. Briscoe, *CAH* 8² (1989), 73, and *ANRW* 2. 30. 1094. J. Br.

Caecilius (*RE* 82) **Metellus Baliaricus, Quintus,** son of Macedonicus (below), as consul 123 BC and proconsul conquered the *Baleares islands and settled 3,000 Italians from Spain at Palma and Pollentia. He triumphed 121 and was censor, with L. *Calpurnius Piso Frugi, 120. He is probably the *aedile who went to Thessaly at a time of acute scarcity of wheat and secured the Thessalian crop for Rome (around 130).

On the aedile in the Thessalian document see P. Garnsey and others, *JRS* 1984, 30 ff., with mistaken identification; corrected P. Garnsey and D. Rathbone, *JRS* 1985, 25. The error was first reproduced, then corrected, Broughton, *MRR* 3. 39. A date during the Sicilian slave war (135–131: perhaps 133) seems more suitable than 129, suggested in *JRS* 1985. E. B.

Caecilius (*RE* 83) **Metellus Calvus, Lucius,** brother of Macedonicus (below), followed his brother in the consulship (142 BC) and served on P. *Cornelius Scipio Aemilianus' embassy to the east. He was the father of Delmaticus and Numidicus (below), each of whom became consul and censor, and so, with Macedonicus, founded the greatness of the family. E. B.

Caecilius (*RE* 86) **Metellus Celer, Quintus,** grandson (by birth) of Q. *Caecilius Metellus Baliaricus and by adoption brother of Nepos (below), was perhaps tribune 72 or 68 BC and aedile 67 (Val. Max. 6. 1. 8—but this may be his adoptive father), then legate under *Pompey. As urban praetor 63 and augur, he ended the farce of the trial of C. *Rabirius (1). At Cicero's request, he received command against the Catilinarians (see SERGIUS CATILINA, L.), and the province of Cisalpine Gaul; yet he supported

Nepos against Cicero, whom he treated insultingly (see Cic. *Fam.* 5. 1–2). Consul 60, he turned against Pompey, who had divorced his sister *Mucia Tertia for flagrant scandals, and in 59 opposed *Caesar's programme. He died before going to his province (Transalpina). He was the husband of *Clodia.   E. B.

Caecilius (*RE* 87) **Metellus (Creticus), Quintus,** grandson of Macedonicus (below), became *pontifex as a young man, urban *praetor probably 73 BC (*MRR* 3. 38), and supported *Verres at his trial (70). Consul 69, with Q. *Hortensius Hortalus, who ceded his province of *Crete to him, he fought there successfully as proconsul, defeating the pirates and capturing several cities. When *Pompey received *imperium* equal to the proconsuls' (see GABINIUS, A. (2)), he sent a legate to supersede Metellus and accepted the surrender of some cities expecting favourable terms. Metellus humiliated the legate and Pompey prepared to confront him personally, but had to leave for Asia under the law of C. *Manilius. Metellus completed the conquest of Crete and organized a province (66–65?). After lengthy obstruction by Pompey's friends he triumphed 62 and assumed a victor's *cognomen*. After Pompey's return he was prominent among Pompey's opponents. He died in the late 50s.

Gruen, *LGRR*, see index.   E. B.

Caecilius (*RE* 91) **Metellus Delmaticus, Lucius,** son of Calvus (above) and brother of Numidicus (below), was attacked by C. *Marius (1) when, as consul 119 BC, he opposed his law on election procedure. As consul and proconsul he defeated the Delmatae (see DALMATIA), triumphing 117, and rebuilt two temples from the spoils. As pontifex maximus he tried three Vestals (see VESTA) accused of unchastity (114), acquitting two. (See CASSIUS LONGINUS RAVILLA, L.) He was probably censor 115 (see *Chiron* 1990, 403 n. 14). *Caecilia Metella (1) was his daughter.   E. B.

Caecilius (*RE* 94) **Metellus Macedonicus, Quintus,** son of Q. *Caecilius Metellus, fought under L. *Aemilius Paullus (2) and was on an embassy sent to announce the victory of Pydna to the senate. He was probably tribune in the late 150s BC, setting up a special court (Val. Max. 6. 9. 10). As *praetor 148, he was sent to Macedonia, probably with proconsular status, and remained until 146, defeating *Andriscus and perhaps another pretender (Zonar. 9. 28. 8) and at least beginning the provincial organization of Macedonia. Called away to deal with the rebellion by the *Achaean Confederacy, he won some successes, but had to hand over to L. *Mummius and returned to Rome. Although he triumphed and was awarded the victor's *agnomen* (unprecedented for a praetorian), he became consul only in 143, after two unsuccessful attempts. Sent to Hither Spain, he defeated a Celtiberian rebellion, but was said to have handed his army over in bad shape to his successor and enemy Q. *Pompeius. In 133 both of them were forced by the consul L. *Furius Philus to go to Hither Spain as his *legati*. In 133 he helped to suppress a slave rising and, although an enemy of P. *Cornelius Scipio Aemilianus, fiercely opposed Ti. *Sempronius Gracchus (3). In 131 he and Pompeius were the first plebeian pair of censors. In that office (probably) he built a *portico enclosing temples of Jupiter Stator and Juno Regina, the first temples in Rome faced with marble. A speech urging citizens to marry and raise children, assigned to Numidicus (below) by Gellius, is thought (probably correctly) to be one of his censorial speeches on account of a statement in a Livian *Periocha* (see *ORF* ⁴ p. 107). He was *augur for at least 25 years and died in 115, leaving four sons, all of whom became consuls

and two (Baliaricus (above) and Caprarius) *censors, as well as three daughters, all of whom married leading aristocrats. He thus, with Calvus (above), founded a dynasty that dominated Roman politics for over a generation.

M. G. Morgan, *Hist.* 1969, 422–46, and *Hermes,* 1971, 480–505.   E. B.

Caecilius (*RE* 96) **Metellus Nepos, Quintus,** brother of Celer (above), legate under *Pompey 67–?63 BC, as tribune 62 harassed *Cicero and, with *Caesar's support, tried to secure a special command against the Catilinarians for Pompey. (See SERGIUS CATILINA, L.) Suspended from office, he fled to Pompey, who (however) took no action. Praetor 60 and proconsul (province unknown), he was consul 57, agreed not to oppose Cicero's return while protecting P. *Clodius Pulcher, and proposed Pompey's *cura annonae*. As proconsul he called in on the three dynasts at *Luca on his way to Hither Spain. He died soon after his return.

On both Celer and Nepos, see Gruen, *LGRR*, index.   E. B.

Caecilius (*RE* 97) **Metellus Numidicus, Quintus,** son of Calvus (above) and brother of Delmaticus (above). Elected consul 109 BC to finish the war against *Jugurtha, he won two battles and stormed several towns, with the help of his legates C. *Marius (1) and P. *Rutilius Rufus, but made little progress in guerrilla war. He insulted Marius, who asked for leave to stand for a consulship, and Marius now intrigued against him in Numidia and in Rome until he was elected consul 107 and, by a special law, appointed to supersede Metellus, who left before Marius' arrival. In Rome he was prosecuted, but acquitted, and allowed to triumph in 106 and take a triumphal *cognomen*. As censor 102, he tried to expel L. *Appuleius Saturninus and C. *Servilius Glaucia from the senate, but was prevented by his colleague (and cousin) Q. Metellus Caprarius. In 100 he stubbornly refused to swear an oath to observe one of Saturninus' laws when the rest of the senate did and chose to go into exile. After Saturninus' death his return was long prevented by Marius and his friends, despite the pleas of his son (see Pius (below)) and other nobles. It was finally voted late in 99. He returned in glory, but henceforth kept out of politics.

See Sallust, *Iug.,* with Paul's comm., for his Jugurthine command. On his exile and return see E. Badian, *Chiron* 1984, 130 ff. His prosecution is best put in 107, on his return from Africa, not either in 106 or after his praetorship (thus Broughton, *MRR* 3. 40).   E. B.

Caecilius (*RE* 98) **Metellus Pius, Quintus,** son of Numidicus (above), acquired his last name for his efforts to secure his father's recall from exile. As praetor (89 or 88 BC) he enrolled enfranchised Italians, including his friend *Archias. In the *Social War (3) he defeated *Poppaedius. Unable to defend Rome against L. *Cornelius Cinna (1), he went into exile in Africa (87), retaining his *imperium*. After Cinna's death he collected a private army, was defeated by the governor, then joined *Sulla, thus bringing him the formal approval of the *optimates*, and conquered most of northern Italy for him. Made pontifex maximus and Sulla's colleague as consul 80, he was next sent to fight against *Sertorius in Further Spain, where his movements can be traced in places named after him: Metellinum (Medellin), Castra Caecilia (Cáceres), Vicus Caecilius (north of the Tajo). Unsuccessful until joined (probably against his will) by *Pompey in Hither Spain, he loyally co-operated with Pompey and won some victories in 76–75. He acquired many clients, some of whom he enfranchised, but became known for excessive luxury. Returning in 71, he

Caecilius Metellus Pius Scipio, Quintus

(unlike Pompey) dismissed his army, triumphed, and lived in retirement until *c*.63.

For his Spanish campaigns the main source is Plut., *Sert.*; see C. F. Konrad, *Plutarch's Sertorius: A Historical Commentary* (1993).   E. B.

Caecilius (*RE* 99) **Metellus Pius Scipio, Quintus,** consul 52 BC, was son of P. Cornelius Scipio Nasica (praetor 93; for the family see Cic. *Brut.* 211–12). He was adopted by Q. *Caecilius Metellus Pius, possibly by will. Probably *praetor 55, he was (although now a plebeian) *interrex in 53, and then became candidate for the consulship of 52. The elections were abortive, and *Pompey became sole consul. About the same time Pompey married Scipio's daughter (widow of P. *Licinius Crassus (2)). When Scipio was prosecuted for *ambitus, Pompey's personal intervention secured his acquittal, and in July Pompey made him his colleague. Thenceforward Scipio led the attack on *Caesar and proposed the decisive motion in January 49. The senate granted him Syria, whence in 48 he brought two legions to Thessaly; he commanded the centre at *Pharsalus. He escaped to Africa and became supreme commander in the African War. Caesar tried to bribe Scipio before Pharsalus, but detested him, and wrote a bitter passage about his activities in Syria (*BC* 4. 3. 31–3). Cicero extravagantly praised his great qualities inherited from distinguished ancestors (*Brut.* 212 f.) but despised his ignorance of his family tradition (*Att.* 6. 1. 17). His dying words in reply to the Caesarian soldiers who sought him out after Thapsus, 'Imperator se bene habet', 'the commander is well', passed into 'republican' legend (cf. Livy, *Per.* 114).   G. E. F. C.; E. B.

Caecilius (*RE* 25) **Statius,** author of *fabulae palliatae* (fl. 179 BC, d. 168, according to Jerome, who says he was an Insubrian Gaul, perhaps from Milan. He was taken to Rome as a slave and subsequently freed. *Terence, *Hecyra* 9–27, tells how his plays were produced by *Ambivius Turpio, who encouraged him after initial setbacks and helped him to succeed. He was highly regarded in antiquity: among others, *Volcacius Sedigitus ranked him first of the authors of *palliatae*, and *Varro praised his plot-construction and ability to stir the emotions. Cicero criticized his Latinity but assumed general familiarity with his works. Some 42 titles and about 280 lines survive, showing a style akin to that of *Plautus. Most important are three passages of *Plocium* ('The Necklace'), quoted by Gell. *NA* 2. 23 together with *Menander (1)'s original Greek, which show Caecilius to have adapted as freely as Plautus; until 1968 these were the only extended passages of Roman comedy that could be compared with their Greek original. In other ways he has been seen as a forerunner of Terence, above all in retaining a high proportion of Greek titles and in adapting perhaps sixteen plays by Menander; but *Plocium* shows these to be poor clues to his interests. See COMEDY, LATIN; PALLIATA.

FRAGMENTS E. H. Warmington, *Remains of Old Latin* 1 (Loeb, 1935); Ribbeck, *CRF*; T. Guardi (1974).
LITERATURE F. Leo, *Geschichte der römischen Literatur* (1913), 217 ff; J. Wright, *Dancing in Chains* (1974); *CHCL* 2. 115 f., 813 f.   P. G. M. B.

Caecina (*RE* 7), **Aulus,** a friend of Cicero (*Fam.* 6. 5–9) and a member of an old Etruscan family of *Volaterrae (mod. Cecina). Cicero had defended his father in an inheritance case in 69 BC (cf. Cic. *Caecin.*). Caecina supported *Pompey in 49 and wrote a pamphlet against *Caesar; consequently he was exiled after *Pharsalus (48); Cicero commended him to the governors of Sicily and Asia (*Fam.* 6. 9; 13. 66). He surrendered to Caesar in 46. Trained by his father, he was an expert in the *Etrusca disciplina*

(see HARUSPICES), on which he wrote; his work was used by *Pliny (1) the Elder (*HN* 2) and by *Seneca (*Quaest. Nat.* 2. 3. 9). He had some repute as an orator.

E. Rawson, *JRS* 1978 (= *Roman Culture and Society* (1991), 289 ff).   H. H. S.; M. T. G.

Caecina (*RE* 10) **Alienus, Aulus** (suffect consul AD 69) as quaestor of Baetica in 68 supported *Galba, being rewarded with a legionary command in Upper Germany. According to Tacitus, he was 'handsome, youthful, tall, vigorous, and eloquent' (*Hist.* 1. 53); however, threatened with prosecution for peculation, Caecina helped to instigate *Vitellius' bid for power, leading part of his army in the invasion of Italy. Honoured and enriched by *Vitellius, he was sent to block the Flavian advance, but was arrested by his army on suspicion of treachery. After the Flavian victory he won the friendship of *Vespasian, but was executed in 79 on Titus' orders, allegedly for conspiring with *Eprius Marcellus.   J. B. C.

Caecina (*RE* 24) **Severus, Aulus** (suffect consul 1 BC), from Volaterrae, had by AD 15 forty years' service as an officer or commander. As governor of Moesia in AD 6 he marched to defend Sirmium against the Pannonian rebels, before returning to protect his province against the Dacians and Sarmatians. Next year, sharing command of five legions with M. *Plautius Silvanus (2), he won a victory north-west of Sirmium and joined Tiberius at *Siscia. By 14 Caecina was governor of Lower Germany where he faced a serious mutiny. While campaigning with *Germanicus, by resolute leadership he extracted his troops from a dangerous situation on the return to the Rhine, winning *ornamenta triumphalia. In 21 he argued unsuccessfully in the senate that wives should not be permitted to accompany their husbands on provincial governorships (Tac. *Ann.* 3. 33).   J. B. C.

Caelestis, 'heavenly', the epithet of *Juno at Carthage, successor to, and inheritor of many aspects of, the Carthaginian Tinnit (Tanit). The cult, with an oracle, was important in Roman *Carthage, where it became an emblem of the province of Africa, and is found later at Rome and in other centres. Caelestis was closely linked with Baal, interpreted in Latin as *Saturnus, and had points of contact with many other cults including the Magna Mater. The patronage of *Septimius Severus was particularly important for the success of the cult, and *Iulia Domna was sometimes identified with her.

G. H. Halsberghe, *ANRW* 2. 17. 4 (1984), 2203–23.   N. P.

Caelius Calvinus Balbinus, Decius, and **Clodius Pupienus Maximus, Marcus,** members of a board of twenty *consulares* appointed by the senate for the defence of Italy against the emperor *Maximinus, were after the deaths of Gordian I and II in Africa chosen joint emperors by the senate (AD 238). Both had had long senatorial careers. Constitutionally, on the model of the consulate, they had equal powers, each being pontifex maximus; but Balbinus was entrusted with the civil administration and Pupienus with the command of the army. To placate the people, the boy *Gordian III was given the status of Caesar.

At the news of Maximinus' murder Pupienus proceeded to Aquileia and sent back the former's legions to their provinces, and with his German bodyguard returned to Rome to share a triumph with Balbinus and Gordian. For a few days the joint government worked smoothly, but the praetorians, who resented the senate's action, mutinied. The two emperors were dragged from their palace and murdered after ruling for three months.

*PIR*² C 126 and 1179; K. Dietz, *Senatus contra principem* (1980), nos. 16, 26.   H. M. D. P.

Caelius mons, the most south-easterly of the *seven hills of Rome, lay south of the *Esquiline. Originally named Querquetulanus, its name Caelius was derived by antiquarians from Caelius *Vibenna. Crossed by the *wall of Servius, it was densely populated in the republic; after a devastating fire in AD 27 (Tac. *Ann.* 4. 65) it was largely occupied by the houses and gardens of the wealthy. The chief buildings on the hill included the temple of Divus *Claudius, begun by his widow *Iulia Agrippina, which was largely destroyed by *Nero to build a monumental *nymphaeum as part of his *Domus Aurea, but restored by Vespasian; Nero's Macellum Magnum (AD 59), a new food-market; and barracks for several of the military units stationed in Rome, including *peregrini and *frumentarii*, *vigiles*, and the *equites singulares*, the mounted bodyguard of the emperor.

A. M. Colini, *Storia e topografia del Celio* (Mem. Pont. Acc. 1944); Coarelli, *Roma* 150–3, 164–76; Richardson, *Topog. Dict. Ancient Rome* 61–3; G. Giannelli, in Steinby, *Lexicon* 208–11.   H. H. S.; J. R. P.

Caelius (*RE* 35) **Rufus, Marcus,** born (probably) 88 or 87 BC at Interamnia (mod. Teramo), son of an *eques* (see EQUITES), did his *tirocinium fori* (see EDUCATION, ROMAN) under *Cicero and M. *Licinius Crassus (1). As one of a band of upper-class youths he was attracted to *Catiline, but did not join in his conspiracy. In 59 he successfully prosecuted C. *Antonius Hybrida for *repetundae*. Known for a dissolute and extravagant lifestyle, he was also active in politics and in 57/6 was somehow involved in the murder of an Alexandrian embassy opposing *Ptolemy (1) XII's restoration. For this he was prosecuted in 56 for *vis* by the son of L. *Calpurnius Bestia, whom he had unsuccessfully prosecuted; a P. Clodius, perhaps P. *Clodius Pulcher, joined as *subscriptor* (see QUAESTIONES). A vigorous orator, he defended himself and was defended by Crassus and (in a surviving speech) by Cicero, who depicted the prosecution as a plot hatched by *Clodia, with whom Caelius had had an affair. Caelius was acquitted and, in revenge, supported T. *Annius Milo as tribune 52, and after Milo's conviction joined Cicero in securing the acquittal of Clodius' actual murderer. During Cicero's proconsulate Caelius was aedile (50) and vainly hoped for Cilician panthers or money from Cicero, whom he informed, in a series of letters written in a delightful, informal style, of gossip and political events in Rome (Cic. *Fam.* 8). Joining *Caesar as the probable victor in civil war (see 8. 14. 3) and from contempt for *Pompey, he served in Spain (49) and became *praetor peregrinus* (see PRAETOR) 48. Against the opposition of the consul P. *Servilius Isauricus and the urban praetor C. *Trebonius, he proposed a radical programme of debt relief, was suspended from office, and, joined by Milo, raised an insurrection in which he was killed.

Cic. *Pro Caelio*, R. G. Austin, 3rd edn. (1960); Asc. pp. 33–7, 55 C, with Marshall, *Asconius Comm.* For his age and career see Sumner, *Orators* 146 f.; M. H. Dettenhofer, *Perdita Iuventus* (1992), 80 ff., 140 ff., 156 ff. He has often been identified with the Caelius and sometimes with the Rufus mentioned in various poems by Catullus.   E. B.

Caeneus (Καινεύς), a Lapith (see CENTAURS), of whom three principal stories are told. (1) He was invulnerable, and therefore the Centaurs disposed of him by hammering him into the ground (Pind. fr. 150 Bowra, cf. Hyg. *Fab.* 14. 4 with Rose). (2) He set up his spear to be worshipped (schol. on Ap. Rhod. 1. 57, on *Il.* 1.

264). (3) He was originally a girl, Caenis, loved by *Poseidon, who gave her (invulnerability and) a change of sex (*Aen.* 6. 448 and Servius there, and scholiasts as above). He was son of Elatus of Gyrtone (*Il.* 2. 746 and schol. 1. 264, Ap. Rhod. 1. 57). His final battle was often shown in ancient art: *LIMC* 5/1 (1990), 884–91.
                                                                                     H. J. R.

Caere (Gk. Agylla; Etr. χai[s]re; mod. Cerveteri), 48km. (30 mi.) north of Rome near the Tyrrhenian coast, was one of the oldest (Verg. *Aen.* 8.479 f.) and wealthiest of the twelve cities of Etruria (see ETRUSCANS), and the only one with its own 'treasury' at *Delphi (Strabo 5. 2. 3). Caere's cemeteries provide an unbroken sequence from the iron age to the early empire, and bear witness to the commercially successful local production in the 7th cent. BC of both painted Hellenizing wares and *bucchero* pottery. Continuing east Mediterranean contacts are attested by the 'Caeretan hydriae', presumably made by émigré east Greek craftsmen from *c.*530 BC, and by extensive Greek imports—among them Attic Nicosthenic *amphorae, aimed specifically at the promising Etruscan market after Caere and *Carthage had achieved the departure of the Phocaeans from Alalia in 540 (Hdt. 1. 167). From the 7th cent. onwards, tombs take the form of elaborate chambers under tumuli laid out in streets; the most important is still the Tomba Regolini-Galassi, which in 1836 revealed the splendours of Etruscan *orientalizing. See also PYRGI.

BTCGI 5 (1987), 'Cerveteri'; L. Pareti, *La Tomba Regolini-Galassi* (1947); R. Vighi and others, *Mon. Ant.* 1955; M. A. del Chiaro, *Etruscan Red-figured Vase-painting at Caere* (1974); T. Rasmussen, *Bucchero Pottery from Southern Etruria* (1979); *Gli Etruschi e Cerveteri*, exhib. cat. (Milan, 1980); J. P. Hemelrijk, *Caeretan Hydriae* (1984); M. Gras, *Trafics tyrrhéniens archaïques* (1985); H. Blanck and G. Proietti, *La Tomba dei Rilievi di Cerveteri* (1986); *Gli Etruschi di Cerveteri*, exhib. cat. (Milan, 1986); S. S. Leach, *Subgeometric Pottery from Southern Etruria* (1987).   D. W. R. R.

Caerites (Caeretans) were the inhabitants of the Etruscan city of *Caere. But the name was also applied to a category of Roman citizens, and occurs in the phrase *tabulae Caeritum* ('tables of the Caeretans'). These were official documents which listed the names of citizens whom the censors had deprived of their voting rights (see CENSOR; CENSUS). The fact that the lists were called *tabulae Caeritum* can be explained if there was a time when the only names they contained were those of actual Caeretans (i.e. inhabitants of Caere). This inference prompted the conclusion (Gell. *NA* 16. 13. 7) that Caere was the first community to be incorporated with the form of Roman *citizenship known as *civitas sine suffragio* ('citizenship without suffrage'). One suggestion (Strabo 5. 2. 3) is that Caere was given Roman citizenship (without suffrage) as a reward for helping Rome against the Gauls in 390 BC, but this is not in *Livy, who rather implies (7. 20) that the Caeretans were not yet Roman citizens in 353. It is more likely that they were incorporated after a revolt in 273 (Cass. Dio fr. 33). In that case the best explanation of the phrase *tabulae Caeritum* would be that of Brunt, namely that Caere was the last community of citizens without suffrage to obtain full citizen status.

A. N. Sherwin-White, *The Roman Citizenship*, 2nd edn. (1973), 51 ff.; A. J. Toynbee, *Hannibal's Legacy* (1966), 1. 410 ff.; P. A. Brunt, *Italian Manpower* (1971), 515 ff.; M. Humbert, *Municipium et civitas sine suffragio* (1978), 410 ff.; T. J. Cornell, *CAH* 7²/2 (1989), 313 f.   T. J. Co.

Caesar See IULIUS CAESAR (1), C.

Caesaraugusta (mod. Zaragoza), in NE central Spain. An Augustan *colonia* and early mint with rectangular layout

(895m. × 513m.: 979 × 561 yds.) and settled by *veterans of the Cantabrian Wars (IV, VI, and X Legiones; see CANTABRI). Excavations have uncovered the forum, the theatre, baths, mosaics, and the late Roman walls. Caesaraugusta retained importance in the Visigothic period (see GOTHS).

J. Arce, *Caesaraugusta, ciudad romana* (1979).   S. J. K.

Caesarea (1) **of Cappadocia** (formerly Mazaca, mod. Kayseri) was created by *Cappadocian kings to be their capital. The *philhellene *Ariarathes V gave it a Greek constitution (the laws of *Charondas) and the name Eusebeia by Mount Argaeus, which was changed to Caesarea by *Archelaus (5) in 12–9 BC. From AD 17 it became the chief city of the province of Cappadocia and housed an imperial mint. There are few remains of the ancient city, but wealthy tombs of the Roman period have been excavated nearby.

L. Robert, *Noms indigènes dans l'Asie Mineure gréco-romaine* (1963), 457–523; P. Weiss, *Jahrbuch für Numismatik und Geldgeschichte* 1985, 21–48.
A. H. M. J.; G. E. B.; S. M.

Caesarea (2) **in Palestine,** under its original name of Strato's Tower (after a king of *Sidon), was captured by the *Hasmonean king Alexander Jannaeus in 103 BC, attached to the province of Syria by Pompey in 63, and given to *Herod (1) by Octavian in 30. Between *c*.22 and 10 BC, Herod rebuilt the city on a lavish scale, renaming it after the emperor, and constructing a huge artificial *harbour. Tensions over the control of the constitution between the large Jewish minority and the Graeco-Syrian majority led to riots, and delegations were sent to Nero. His decision against the Jews was followed by attacks on the synagogue, and then the elimination of the Jewish population of 20,000, allegedly in a single day, sparked off the first Jewish revolt against Rome in AD 66. The city was the administrative capital of *Judaea under the procurators and again after 70. *Vespasian made it a Roman colony, and *Severus Alexander a *mētropolis. In the 3rd and 4th cents., it was a cosmopolitan cultural centre, home to well-known rabbis, to the great Christian library of *Origen (1), and, after him, to *Eusebius.

L. Levine, *Caesarea under Roman Rule* (1975); J. Ringel, *Césarée de Palestine* (1975); K. G. Holum and others, *King Herod's Dream: Caesarea on the Sea* (1988); Schürer, *History* 2. 115–18.   E. M. S; T. R.

Caesarea (3), mod. Cherchel, on the coast of Algeria. Probably founded as a Punic trading-station, known as Iol, the oldest finds date to *c*.500 BC. Defences were constructed towards the end of the 3rd cent. BC. Annexed by Rome in 33 BC, it was placed in the hands of the Berber prince *Juba (2) II, who called it Caesarea, and made it into a Graeco-Roman city as possible (theatre, amphitheatre, street-grid, etc. and a magnificent art collection). See URBANISM. In AD 40, it became the capital of the province of *Mauretania Caesariensis, and the residence of the *procurator; *Claudius made it a *colonia* (see COLONIZATION, ROMAN). It became a prosperous port town of *c*.20,000, with a belt of villas around it; its agricultural *mosaics are celebrated. Embellished in Severan times (see ROME, HISTORY), it had magnificent 4th-cent. houses, and the civic centre was refurbished around the time of the Vandal conquest (429), being abandoned for poor houses only in the period of the Byzantine reconquest (533).

P. Leveau, *Caesarea de Maurétanie* (1984); N. Benseddik and T. W. Potter, *Fouilles du forum de Cherchel* (1992).   T. W. P.

Caesarion See PTOLEMY (1) XV.

Caesellius (*RE* 2) **Vindex, Lucius** (early 2nd cent. AD), gram-

marian whose miscellany was criticized by contemporaries (e.g. Gell. *NA* 6. 2, 11. 15) and excerpted by later writers (extracts on orthography: Keil, *Gramm. Lat.* 7. 202–7).

*PIR*² C 167; Herzog–Schmidt, § 434.   R. A. K.

Caesennius (*RE* 9) **Paetus, Lucius (Iunius Publius),** consul AD 61, was ordered by *Nero in 62 as legate of Cappadocia to advance to Armenia. His mission failed and he capitulated to the Parthians on disgraceful terms in his camp at Rhandeia. Dismissed, but unpunished, in 70 he was appointed governor of Syria by *Vespasian (whose relative he probably was by virtue of his marriage to (Vespasian's niece?) Flavia Sabina (*ILS* 995)) and in 72/3 annexed the kingdom of *Commagene.

R. Syme, *JRS* 1977, 38 ff. = *RP* 3 1043 ff.   A. M.; M. T. G.

Caesius (*RE* 16–17) **Bassus** (1st cent. AD), a friend of *Persius Flaccus, who dedicated his sixth satire to him and whose poems he allegedly 'edited'. *Quintilian (10. 1. 96) thought Bassus' own lyric poems the only Roman examples of the genre worth reading besides Horace's odes. Later metricians (e.g. *Terentianus Maurus) relied upon his theoretical writings; these may be partly represented by an acephalous treatise falsely attributed to *Atilius Fortunatianus (Keil, *Gramm. Lat.* 255–72). The excerpts on metre printed at *Gramm. Lat.* 6. 305–12 are not his work.

*PIR*² C 192; Herzog–Schmidt, § 350 (cf. 525. 3); Morel–Büchner, *FPL* 158.   R. A. K.

cakes (flour-based sweetmeats or fancy breads) were given many names in Greek and Latin, of which the most general were πέμματα, πόπανα, *liba* (sacrificial cakes), and *placentae* (from πλακοῦντες). The Greeks especially had a vast number of different kinds, and several monographs were written on the subject (on these see Ath. 3. 109b–116a, 14. 643e–648c; Poll. 6. 72 ff.). Most were regarded as a luxurious delicacy, to be eaten with fruit after the main course at a special meal. Cakes were also very commonly used in *sacrifice, either as a peripheral accompaniment to the animal victim or as a bloodless sacrifice. Sacrificial cakes very often had a special form characteristic of the relevant divinity or rite; among the more spectacular examples are the Attic ἀμφιφῶν, stuck with lights and offered to *Artemis on the full-moon day, or the Sicilian μύλλος, shaped like female genitals and offered to the Two Goddesses, *Demeter and *Persephone.

Orth, *RE* 11. 2088–99; Lobeck, *Aglaoph.* 1060–85; E. Kearns, in R. Hägg (ed.), *Ancient Greek Cult Practice from the Epigraphical Evidence* (1994), 64–70.   E. Ke.

Calabria in antiquity referred to the Sallentine peninsula of SE Italy. It did not acquire its modern meaning of SW Italy (ancient Bruttium), until after the *Lombard invasion of AD 700. Ancient Calabria is a flat and arid region, noted mainly for cultivation of olives and vines. It was the territory of the *Messapii (Lat. Sallentini, Gk. Iapyges), whose culture was part of an Adriatic *koinē, showing signs of extensive contacts with Greece, Epirus, and Illyria. Mycenaean finds indicate the early development of contacts with the Aegean, and many of the coastal cities, such as Callipolis and *Hydruntum, maintained a flourishing trade with western Greece. The region became urbanized in the 5th and 4th cents. BC and contains a large number of cities. The region entered into Roman control in 270, after supporting *Pyrrhus in the Pyrrhic war, and most cities became allies (*socii) until 89 BC. Although many cities were very small, most were recognized as independent *municipia by Rome and continued to exist until late antiquity and beyond.

G. Susini, *Fonti per la Storia Greca e Romana del Salento* (1962); O. Parlangeli, *Studi Messapici* (1960); E. Greco, *Magna Grecia* (1981); F. d'Andria, *Archeologia dei Messapici* (1990); S. Settis (ed.), *Storia della Calabria antica* (1994). K. L.

Calais and Zetes, sons of *Boreas the god of the north wind and his Athenian wife Oreithyia, hence jointly the 'Boreadae'; winged like their father, they were able, as members of the Argonautic expeditionary force (see ARGONAUTS), to chase the Harpies (*Harpyiae) away from their persecution of the blind king *Phineus (Ap. Rhod. 1. 211 ff., 2. 240 ff.). After Heracles was left behind at Cios while searching for *Hylas, it was the Boreads who persuaded the heroes not to turn back for him; he revenged himself later by killing them both in *Tenos. One of their grave steles swayed in the breeze when the north wind blew (1. 1298 ff.). The scene of the Harpy pursuit is popular in 6th cent. art.

K. Schefold, *LIMC* 'Boreadai', and *Gods and Heroes in Late Archaic Greek Art* (1992; Eng. trans.) 192 f. A. H. G.

Calamis, Greek sculptor, active during the second quarter of the 5th cent. BC, to be distinguished from a second Calamis, sculptor and silversmith, working after *c*.400 BC. He worked in marble, bronze, and gold and ivory. His style was distinguished for its grace and refinement, and he was famous for his statues of horses. Pausanias (9. 16. 1) states that he made a statue of *Zeus *Ammon for *Pindar, and a *Hermes Criophorus for *Tanagra (9. 22. 1); the latter is reproduced on Roman coins of that city. His most ambitious work was a colossal bronze statue of Apollo, 30 cubits (15 m.: 50 ft.) high, which he made for Apollonia Pontica (Plin. *HN* 34. 39; Strabo 7. 319). It is perhaps reproduced on silver coins of that city. His Sosandra was praised by *Lucian (*Eikones* 6) for the simple and orderly arrangement of its drapery. His Apollo Alexikakos stood in the *Ceramicus of Athens (Paus. 1. 3. 4). An important figure for the art criticism of antiquity, he has not been securely identified as the originator of any surviving work.

Overbeck 508–32, 857; J. Pollitt, *Art of Ancient Greece* (1965), 46 ff. G. M. A. R.; A. J. S. S.

Calauria (now Póros), a Saronic island (23 sq. km.: 9 sq. mi.) adjacent to the Argolid, and its *polis*. The town lay near the island's summit (283 m.: 928 ft.); its remains, chiefly Hellenistic, include a probable heroon (see HERO-CULT) of *Demosthenes (2), who killed himself here.

The sanctuary of *Poseidon has Mycenaean tombs, 8th-cent. and later dedications, and cult buildings of *c*.520–320 BC. It was the focus of the Calaurian *amphictiony, whose members included Hermione, *Epidaurus, *Aegina, *Athens, and Boeotian *Orchomenus (1). The inclusion of Nauplia and Cynurian Prasiae, neither of them autonomous after *c*.650, implies an early foundation date. Rather than a military, political, or economic union, the amphictiony was probably a cultic association of mainly local, non-Dorian towns: the sanctuary's material apogee is not matched by any known political activity. By *Strabo's time the sanctuary had been sacked by Cilician pirates (see PIRACY) and the amphictiony no longer existed. See AMPHICTIONY; TROEZEN.

G. Welter, *Troizen und Kalaureia* (1941); K. Tausend, *Amphiktyonie und Symmachie* (1992); T. Kelly, *AJArch.* 1966; N. Pharaklas, Τροιζηνία, Καλαύρεια, Μέθανα (1972); *RE* 10/2 (1919), 1550–1, 2535–41. D. G. J. S.

Calchas, in mythology son of Thestor; a seer who accompanied the Greek army to Troy (*Il.* 1. 69 ff.). He reveals the reason for the plague on the camp (ibid.) and foretells the length of the war

(2. 300 ff.). After *Homer he is introduced into several episodes, such as the sacrifice of *Iphigenia (Aesch. *Ag.* 201 ff.), the building of the Wooden Horse (Verg. *Aen.* 2. 185, cf. Quint. Smyrn. 12. 3 ff.), and generally the actions by which it was fated that Troy should be captured. An oracle had foretold that Calchas would die when he met a diviner better than himself, and this occurred when he met a seer usually identified as *Mopsus, grandson of *Tiresias. An oracle in *Apulia was identified with his name (Paus. 6. 3. 9).

For Calchas in art, see V. Saladino, *LIMC* 5/1. 931–5. H. J. R.; J. R. M.

Calcidius See CHALCIDIUS.

Caledonia, the name used by *Tacitus and *Cassius Dio for the Scottish Highlands, beyond the river Forth. Others use the adjective, sometimes of inland Britain, mostly of north Britain, referring to its seas, its north cape and monument with Greek letters, its frosts, fauna, pearls, and people. Its wooded hills (*saltus*) were early famous but vaguely located until Ptolemy (*Geog.* 2. 3. 8) placed them south-west of Beauly Firth. The name survives (Watson, *Celtic Place-names of Scotland* (1926), 21) in Dunkeld, Rohallion, and Schiehallion. It occurs as a personal (*Eph. Epigr.* 6. 1077) and tribal (*ILS* 4576) name.

Cn. *Iulius Agricola defeated the Caledonii without conquering them. Forts associated with his campaigns are found as far north as the Moray Firth. A withdrawal took place in the 80s. In AD 197 the Caledonii broke a treaty with Rome, were reduced by *Septimius Severus in 209, but broke faith again in 210–11. Forts of the Severan campaigns are found in the same areas as those of Agricola and are similarly located to oversee the mouths of the highland glens. Cassius Dio (76. 12) divides non-Roman Britain between Caledonii and Maeatae.

A. L. F. Rivet and C. Smith *The Place-names of Roman Britain* (1979); W. Hanson and G. Maxwell, *Rome's North-West Frontier* (1983); D. J. Breeze, *The Northern Frontiers of Roman Britain* (1982). I. A. R.; M. J. M.

calendar, Greek There was no single Greek calendar. Almost every Greek community had a calendar of its own, differing from others in the names of the months and the date of the New Year. All were, at least originally, lunar. The months were named after festivals held or deities specially honoured in them. Dios and Artemisios, Macedonian months, were, for example, named after *Zeus and *Artemis; Anthesterion at Athens from the festival *Anthesteria. Such month names are found in Linear B and in literature as early as Hesiod (*Op.* 504). In much later times some states used ordinal numbers for their month names.

The Athenian calendar is best known. The year began, in theory, with the appearance of the first new moon after the summer solstice, and the months were Hekatombaion, Metageitnion, Boedromion, Pyanopsion, Maimakterion, Posideon, Gamelion, Anthesterion, Elaphebolion, Mounichion, Thargelion, and Skirophorion. All were named after festivals held in the month, some very obscure to us and probably to 5th- and 4th-cent. Athenians. Each month was in length 29 or 30 days; an ordinary year was 354 ± 1, a leap year 384 ± 1 days. A leap year was created by inserting a 'second' (δεύτερος) or 'later' (ὕστερος) month, usually a second Posideon. Despite some scholarly claims to the contrary, the Athenians appear not to have followed any regular scheme, such as the 'Metonic Cycle' (see METON) used by the Seleucids, in determining leap years.

The first day of the Athenian month was the 'new moon' (νουμηνία), determined in theory if not always in practice by the observation or expectation of the first visibility of the new moon.

The next nine days were of the 'waxing' month, and were numbered forward as with us: Βοηδρομιῶνος πέμπτη ἱσταμένου being Boedromion 5. The 11th and 12th were simply ἐνδεκάτη and δωδεκάτη. The 13th to the 19th were numbered forward in the style Βοηδρομιῶνος τρίτη καὶ δεκάτη, Boedromion 13. The 20th was called δεκάτη προτέρα and the 21st δεκάτη ὑστέρα. The next eight days, of the 'waning' month, were numbered backwards from the end of the month, in the style Βοηδρομιῶνος ἐνάτη φθίνοντος or later Βοηδρομιῶνος ἐνάτη μετ' εἰκάδας, Boedromion 22. In Athens the last day of the month was named ἔνη καὶ νέα, the 'old and new' day, but elsewhere in the Greek world was τριακάς (30th). In a 'hollow' month, having only 29 days, the omitted day was, most likely, δευτέρα φθίνοντος, the 29th.

In the 2nd cent. BC the Athenians occasionally distinguished between their purely lunar calendar (κατὰ θεόν) and their festival calendar (κατ' ἄρχοντα) which had been affected by the intercalation of individual days. Such a distinction may have been thought necessary because days were often intercalated for non-calendric purposes, as for example in 271/0 BC when four days were added between Elaphebolion 9 and 10, probably to allow additional time for preparations for the City Dionysia (SEG 14. 65). Dates given without the qualification κατὰ θεόν are those of the festival calendar.

In Athens a third calendar, the 'prytany' calendar, was used, either separately or in conjunction with the two other calendars, to date government documents. Since in the Classical period each prytany (see PRYTANEIS) served for one-tenth of the year, and since, at least in *Aristotle's time, the ten prytanies served terms of regular length (the first four 36 days each, the last six 35; Ath. pol. 43. 2), a day could be accurately dated by the name of the prytany and the number of the day within its term. Hence the formula for the 'civic' calendar was, for example, ἐπὶ τῆς Ἐρεχθηίδος ἐνάτης πρυτανείας, τρίτη καὶ εἰκοστῇ τῆς πρυτανείας, i.e. 'on the twenty-third day of the ninth prytany, that of the tribe Erechtheis'. That would be day 307 of the year. Inscriptions often give the date by both the 'prytany' and 'festival' calendar, and in IG 7. 4253 of 332/1 BC we find this day was also Thargelion 11 by the festival calendar. From the 4th cent. on, the festival and prytany years began on the same day, and calendar equations such as the above allow the determination of whether the year was a leap year or whether days had been intercalated.

Such calendars were used in Athens and elsewhere to date actions of legislative or other governmental bodies and, occasionally, events of historic importance. But the month names indicate the calendars were first invented to assure the timely performance of religious rituals and *festivals, and numerous sacred calendars, listing day, deity, sacrificial victim (see SACRIFICE, GREEK), and often costs, officials involved, and perquisites, survive from throughout the Greek world. Such calendars, from families, *demes, and states, were not records of past activities but were prescriptions for the future administration and performance of cultic activities.

A. E. Samuel, Greek and Roman Chronology (1972); M. P. Nilsson, Die Entstehung und religiöse Bedeutung des griechischen Kalendars (1962); S. Dow, BCH 1968, 170–86; W. Burkert, Greek Religion (1985), 225–7.
J. D. M.

calendar, Roman The original Roman calendar consisted of ten months only, the later March–December, and must therefore have had an uncounted gap in the winter, between years (cf. Ov. Fast. 1. 27–44, with J. G. Frazer's note). The republican calendar, represented for us by the fragmentary fasti Antiates (Inscr. Ital. 13. 2. 1–28) and literary descriptions (notably Censorinus, DN 20–2; Macrob. Sat. 1. 12–16, drawing ultimately on *Varro and *Verrius Flaccus), was believed by some to have been introduced from Etruria (see ETRUSCANS) by *Tarquinius Priscus (Iunius Gracchanus quoted in Censorinus 20. 4); indeed the month-name Iunius, pure Latin Iunonius, is connected with the Etruscan form of Juno's name, Uni. The introduction of this calendar, however, predates the Capitoline temple (traditionally dated after the expulsion of the kings, see CAPITOL), for of the feast-days which it marks with large letters none is connected with that cult. January, as containing the festival †Januar (presumably the *Agonium of later calendars, 9 January) of the god of gates who was on his way to be a god of all beginnings, must have been intended to be the first month, but the revolution which expelled the kings put a stop to this and March remained the first month of the year until 153 BC. From then the official year of the consuls and most other Roman magistrates began on 1 January; that of the *tribuni plebis began on 10 December. March, May, Quintilis (July), and October had 31 days each (Nones on 7th, Ides on 15th), February 28, and the rest 29 (Ides on 13th): total 355.

To intercalate, February was shortened to 23 or 24 days and followed by an intercalary month of 27 days. This intercalating was so clumsily done that by the time of *Caesar the civic year was about three months ahead of the solar. In his capacity as *pontifex maximus, he intercalated sufficent days to bring the year 46 BC to a total of 445 days, which was thus 'the last year of the muddled reckoning' (Macrob. Sat. 1. 14. 3). From the next year onwards the Egyptian solar calendar (see TIME-RECKONING) was adapted to Roman use, by inserting enough days in the shorter months to bring the total up to 365 and arranging for the insertion of a day, not a month, between 23 and 24 February, in leap year (thus 23 February occurred twice; the non-existent date '29 February' is a modern absurdity). No substantial change was made thereafter until the reforms of Pope Gregory XIII, promulgated in 1582 and gradually adopted as our normal 'Gregorian' calendar (in Britain only in 1752); today the Greek and Russian Orthodox churches continue to use the Julian calendar.

E. J. Bickerman Chronology of the Ancient World (revised edn. 1980); A. K. Michels, The Calendar of the Roman Republic (1967); P. Brind'Amour, Le Calendrier romain (1983); M. York, The Roman Festival Calendar of Numa Pompilius (1986); G. Radke, Fasti Romani (1990); M. Salzman, On Roman Time (1990); M. Maas, John Lydus and the Roman Past (1992), ch. 4; A. Grafton, Joseph Scaliger (1983–93); see also FASTI.
H. J. R.; S. R. F. P.

Cales (mod. Calvi), an *Auruncan city, c.47 km. (29 mi.) north of Naples. It was a strategic point, controlling communications between *Latium and *Samnium, and was occupied from the 7th cent. BC. In the aftermath of the Latin War (see LATIN I), it became a Latin colony (334 BC), counterbalancing Samnite-controlled *Teanum Apulum. It remained an important Roman base throughout the Samnite and *Punic Wars, but was one of the colonies which refused troops to Rome in 209 and was subsequently punished (Livy 27. 9). There was a second colonization in 184 BC, and it remained an important city. The territory was fertile and it was noted for its pottery. The *via Latina ran through the city. There are remains of the walls, theatre, baths, a temple, Roman and pre-Roman street patterns, and numerous burials and inscriptions.

W. Johannowsky, Boll. d'Arte (1963); S. de Caro and A. Greco, Campania (1981).
K. L.

Calidius (*RE* 5), **Marcus**, as praetor 57 BC helped to effect Cicero's return from exile and the recovery of his house; in 52 he supported T. *Annius Milo (Asc. p. 34 C). He stood unsuccessfully for the consulship of 50 and then unsuccessfully prosecuted C. *Claudius Marcellus (1), one of the successful candidates. He again unsuccessfully stood for the consulship of 49. He was sent by *Caesar to Cisalpine Gaul (see GAUL (CISALPINE)), probably as a legate for 48–7, and died there. He had a feud with the Gallii, played out in unsuccessful mutual prosecutions. He was a pupil of *Apollodorus (5) in oratory (Jer. *Chron.* for 64 BC). Cicero disliked him, but in *Brut.* 274 ff. praised him as an outstanding orator, though unemotional.

Malcovati, *ORF* [4] no. 140; Douglas, *CQ* 1955; Gruen, *LGRR*, see index; Shackleton-Bailey, *CLA* 3 (1968), 314 f.   S. H.

Caligula, Roman emperor. See GAIUS (1).

Calleva Atrebatum, mod. Silchester, on the Hampshire–Berkshire border. The Roman town was *civitas*-capital of the *Atrebates (2) and succeeded an enclosed iron age *oppidum*. This was founded in the Augustan period and shows a planned layout. The place-name 'CALLEV' is given on coins of Eppilus dated to *c.* AD 10. The land within the late 2nd-cent. earthen defences (rebuilt in stone *c.* AD 260–80) was excavated on a large scale in 1890–1909. Shops, a *dyeing industry, and some 60 houses were exposed, and of public buildings a forum with basilica, baths, a presumed *mansio*, five small temples, and a small Christian church. Recent excavations have exposed extensive iron age deposits beneath the basilica and discovered earlier phases of a timber forum, whilst also exploring the amphitheatre and defences. The population was perhaps *c.*6,000. The town was eventually deserted in circumstances still obscure.

G. C. Boon, *Silchester: The Roman Town of Calleva* (1974); M. G. Fulford, *Proc. Prehist. Soc.* 1987, and *Antiq. Journ.* 1985.   C. E. S.; M. J. M.

Callias (1), son of Hipponicus, of one of the richest families in 5th-cent. Athens; the family was also religiously important as one of the *genos* Kerykes, which supplied some of the priests for the mysteries at *Eleusis, including and above all the *dadouchos* ('torchbearer'); Callias himself was *dadouchos* (Plut. *Arist.* 5) and his family probably held the office on a hereditary basis (cf. Xen. *Hell.* 6. 3. 3 for *Callias (4)). Callias was cousin of *Aristides (1) and married Elpinice, sister of *Cimon. He distinguished himself at the battle of *Marathon; he is also said to have won the chariot-race at *Olympia three times, but this is suspect. His colossal wealth is however certain, and may derive from early exploitation of the *Laurium silver-mines. He supposedly negotiated the *Callias Peace of *c.*450 BC with Persia and was one of the negotiators of the *Thirty Years Peace with Sparta in 446 (but probably not the author of the alliances with Rhegium and Leontini, ML 63–4; see CALLIAS (3) son of Calliades). He was father of Hipponicus, a general in the *Archidamian War (Thuc. 3. 91) who allegedly died at *Delion in 424 (unless this is a confusion with Hippocrates), and grandfather of Callias (4). He was probably *proxenos of Sparta because Xenophon makes his grandson *Callias (4) say he inherited the role.

APF 254 ff., where he is Kallias II; R. Garland, *BSA* 1984, 97 ff. ('torchbearers').   T. J. C.; S. H.

Callias (2), Athenian comic poet, won first prize at the City *Dionysia in 446 BC (*IG* 2². 2318, col. 3), and was active at least until 430 (*IG* 14. 1097. 5 f.). We have eight titles (including Ἀταλάνται), and 40 citations; fr. 15 mentions *Socrates. 'Callias

the Athenian, a little earlier than *Strattis' (Ath. 453c) who composed a γραμματικὴ τραγῳδία, 'alphabet-revue' (cf. 448b, 276a), might be the same person.

Kassel-Austin *PCG* 4. 38 ff. (*CAF* 1. 693 ff.).   K. J. D.

Callias (3) son of Calliades, 5th-cent. BC Athenian politician, probably proposer of the 'Callias Decrees' which put Athenian finances on a war footing (ML 58 of probably 434/3, though later dates have been argued for), also of alliances with *Rhegium and *Leontini, 433/2 (ML 63, 64). He was killed 432 at the siege of *Potidaea (Thuc. 1. 61. 1 and 63. 3).

D. M. Lewis, *CAH* 5² (1992), 373; L. Kallet-Marx *CQ* 1989, 94 ff.   S. H.

Callias (4) (*c.*450–370 BC), Athenian nobleman, grandson of Callias (1), notorious for his wealth and extravagance. He was *dadouchos of the Eleusinian mysteries (see CALLIAS (1)). He was ridiculed by comic poets, and attacked by *Andocides, whom he accused of sacrilege. More sympathetic pictures of his house and life are given by *Xenophon (*Symp.*) and *Plato (1) (*Prt.*). He was general 391/0 in the *Corinthian War, and took part in a famous victory of *Iphicrates over Spartan *hoplites (Xen. *Hell.* 4. 5. 13). As an old man, he was a member of a three-man embassy sent to Sparta, whose *proxenos Xenophon says he was, in 371/0 (Xen. *Hell.* 6. 3. 3 ff.); the embassy successfully negotiated peace.

D. MacDowell, *Andokides on the Mysteries* (1963), 10 f.; *APF* 261 ff., where he is Kallias III; R. Seager, *CAH* 6² (1994), 180 f.; A. B. Bosworth, in I. Worthington (ed.), *Ventures into Greek History* (1994), 17 ff.
                                                           V. E.; S. H.

Callias (5), of *Syracuse, lived at the court of *Agathocles (1), tyrant of Syracuse (316–289 BC), and wrote a history of his reign in 22 books. It so favoured Agathocles that Callias was suspected of accepting bribes; so Diod. Sic. (21. 17. 4), who however probably knew Callias only through the medium of Agathocles' enemy *Timaeus (2). Callias' history had little influence on the tradition (which remained unfavourable to Agathocles), although, apart from the account written by Agathocles' brother Antandrus, it was the first important work on this subject. The fragments do not provide sufficient material to determine the contents of the work in detail.

FGrH 564; L. Pearson, *The Greek Historians of the West* (1987), 228 f.; K. Meister, *CAH* 7²/1 (1984), 384, 409, and *Die griechische Geschichtschreibung* (1990), 136 f.   G. L. B.; S. H.

Callias (6), of Sphettus (an Athenian *deme), Athenian in Ptolemaic service (see PTOLEMY (1)) but active in helping his home city. Callias was unknown, except as the name of the brother of *Phaedrus (2), until the publication in 1978 of an important long Athenian decree of 270/69 BC honouring him. It emerges that in 287/6, when Athens revolted from *Demetrius (4) Poliorcetes of Macedonia, Callias helped the Athenians on Ptolemy I's instructions by deploying on their behalf a Ptolemaic mercenary force on *Andros, and that he and his brother Phaedrus enabled them get in the harvest. (Cf. *IG* 2² 682, Athenian honours to Phaedrus). He continued to be diplomatically active on Athens' behalf in subsequent negotiations with Demetrius, and later still he mediated for the Athenians with *Ptolemy (1) II Philadelphus and procured grain for them. He also led the Athenian delegation to Philadelphus' new festival, the Ptolemaieia (see PTOLEMY (1) II PHILADELPHUS), and was Ptolemaic governor of *Halicarnassus. His politics were evidently somewhat different from those of his brother, who is now, however, regarded as much more moderate and less pro-Macedonian than used to be thought.

Callias, Peace of

T. L. Shear, *Kallias of Sphettos and the Revolt of Athens in 286 BC* (1978); M. Osborne, *ZPE* 35 (1979), 181 ff.; C. Habicht, *Untersuchungen zur politischen Geschichte Athens im 3 Jh. v. Chr.* (1979); P. M. Fraser, *CR* 1981, 240 f.　　　　　　　　　　　　　　　　　　　　　　　　S. H.

Callias, Peace of, a mid 5th-cent. treaty between Athens and Persia (Diod. Sic. 12. 4, from Ephorus). Its historicity is disputed, chiefly because *Thucydides (2) does not mention it explicitly, though some passages in his *History* are probably indirect evidence. The date of the Peace is disputed; some evidence points to 449 but other items suggest the 460s, and this may mean that the 449 agreement was a renewal. Certainly direct Athenian–Persian hostilities ceased in mid-century.

D. M. Lewis, *CAH* 5² (1992), 121–7; E. Badian, *From Plataea to Potidaea* (1993), ch. 1. Both give the extensive earlier literature.　　S. H.

Callicles, a character in *Plato (1)'s *Gorgias*, whose historicity is disputed. He attacks conventional morality as an inversion of true or natural morality, since the restrictions of conventional justice (*to nomōi dikaion*) violate the natural right (*to phusēi dikaion*) of the strong to exploit the weak.

E. R. Dodds, *Plato: Gorgias* (1959).　　　　　　　　　C. C. W. T.

Callicrates (1) Athenian *architect of the 5th cent. BC, responsible for work at the Nike sanctuary and the central long wall to the *Piraeus (see ATHENS, TOPOGRAPHY). He was associated with *Ictinus (see PARTHENON).

RE 10 'Kallikrates' 11; R. Carpenter, *The Architects of the Parthenon* (1970).　　　　　　　　　　　　　　　　　　　　　　　R. A. T.

Callicrates (2), son of Theoxenos of Leontion, (died 149/8 BC), Achaean politician, opponent of *Lycortas and *Polybius (1). As envoy to Rome in 180/79 he urged the senate to support its friends in the Greek states who put Roman interests first, by expressing its wishes unambiguously. The senate's praise boosted Callicrates' position at home, so that as *stratēgos* (chief magistrate) for 179/8 he restored the exiles to *Sparta and *Messene—the major issue on which Achaean politicians and Rome disagreed. Polybius (24. 10. 8–10) views Callicrates' speech as a turning-point for the worse in Roman relations with Achaea, though his own opposition and later experience coloured his view. Callicrates remained influential: in 168 he prevented Achaea from sending troops to Egypt, and after *Pydna he provided the Romans with a list of 1,000 Achaeans to be interned (including Polybius), which made him widely unpopular, not just with Polybius. He died during a diplomatic mission to Rome.

RE Suppl. 4, 'Kallikrates' 7g; E. S. Gruen, *The Hellenistic World and the Coming of Rome* (1984); P. S. Derow, *CAH* 8² (1989), 300 f.　R. M. E.

Callicratidas, Spartan admiral, who succeeded and quarrelled with *Lysander in 406 BC. After cowing *Lysander's partisans and refusing to wait for Persian money, he assembled a large fleet (140–70 ships) from Greek resources, defeating and blockading a squadron under *Conon (1) at Mytilene. He drowned in his subsequent defeat by the Athenian relief fleet off the *Arginusae islands. Later sources applaud his forthright manner and '*Panhellenism', contrasting him favourably with Lysander; *Xenophon (1) depicts him as blustering and militarily impetuous, underrating his contribution in stretching Athens' resources to the limit.

RE 10. 1641–2, 'Kallikratidas'; PB no. 408; V. Gray, *The Character of Xenophon's Hellenica* (1989), 22–4, 81–3; J. L. Moles, *JHS* 1994.
　　　　　　　　　　　　　　　　　　　　　　　　　S. J. Ho.

Callimachus (1), Athenian *polemarchos and (though this is

controversial) commander-in-chief in the campaign of *Marathon, 490. Herodotus (6. 109) says he was polemarch 'by lot' but the lot was not introduced for that or other archonships (see ARCHONTES) until 487; it has therefore been ingeniously suggested that for the twenty years after *Cleisthenes (2), archonships were elective but the particular posts were distributed by lot, Roman fashion. (See SORTITION.) But perhaps Herodotus was just wrong. In any case, Callimachus accepted *Miltiades' plan to meet the Persians in the field. His part in the actual battle, in the last stage of which he was killed, has been obliterated by the personality and achievements of Miltiades, but his share in the victory was fully recognized in the wall-paintings on the *Stoa Poecile (Painted Stoa), where he was portrayed among the Athenian gods and heroes (Paus. 1. 15). The inscription(s) ML 18 seems to be a memorial to or dedication by him but interpretation is hard, and it has even been doubted whether it refers to him at all (see refs. at ML addenda (1988), 309).

H. Berve, *Miltiades* (1937), 78 ff.; E. Badian, *Antichthon* 1971, 21 ff.; N. G. L. Hammond, *Studies* (1973), ch. 7, and *CAH* 4² (1988), ch. 9; E. D. Francis and M. Vickers, *BSA* 1985, 111; J. F. Lazenby, *The Defence of Greece* (1993), 57 f.　　　　　　　　　　　　　P. T.; S. H.

Callimachus (2), Greek sculptor, active *c*.430–400 BC. He made a golden lamp for the *Erechtheum, a set of bronze Laconian dancers, and a *Hera for *Plataea, and allegedly invented the Corinthian capital (Vitr. 4. 1. 9–10). He may also have invented the running drill (cf. Paus. 1. 26. 6–7), but over-elaboration spoiled his work (Plin. *HN* 34. 92). Some neo-Attic reliefs (see RETROSPECTIVE STYLES) apparently reproduce the dancers.

A. F. Stewart, *Greek Sculpture* (1990), 166, 168, 271f.　　A. F. S.

Callimachus (3) (*RE* 6), of *Cyrene, Greek poet and scholar, 'Battiades' (*Epigr.* 35), i.e. son (or descendant?) of Battus; his grandfather was a general (*Epigr.* 21). He flourished under *Ptolemy (1) II (285–246 BC) and continued into the reign of *Ptolemy (1) III (*Suda*); he mentions the Celtic invasion of 279 (*Hymn* 4. 171 ff.; fr. 379); the marriage (*c*.275) and apotheosis (270? 268?) of *Arsinoë II Philadelphus (frs. 392, 228); and the Laodicean War of 246/5 (fr. 110). Other work for *Berenice (3) II (*Epigr.* 51?, frs. 387–8, *Suppl. Hell.* 254 ff.), and perhaps the *Victory of Sosibius* (fr. 384), belong to the same late period. Callimachus stood close to the *Alexandrian court; it may be accident that we have no works datable between Arsinoë's death and the accession of Berenice (herself a princess of Cyrene).

Callimachus was credited with more than 800 books (*Suda*). Michael Choniates, *c*. AD 1200, may still have possessed copies of *Aetia* and *Hecale*. But, apart from the six hymns and some sixty epigrams, and a selection from the prose *Paradoxa* (fr. 407), only fragments now survive. The Milan *Diegeseis*, a papyrus of *c*. AD 100, contains summaries of the poems, in the order *Aetia*, *Iambi*, *Lyrica*, *Hecale*, *Hymns*.

Works 1. *Aetia*, in four books (some 4,000 lines in all?): a miscellany of elegiac pieces, from extended epigrams (fr. 64, on the tomb of *Simonides; fr. 114, on the Delian statue of *Apollo) to narratives of 100–200 lines (frs. 67–75, Acontius and Cydippe; *Suppl. Hell.* 254–69, *Victory of Berenice*). The common subject is 'origins': the origins in myth or history of Greek cults, festivals, cities, and the like. Episodes are chosen and rehearsed with antiquarian relish. In the 'prologue' (fr. 1) the poet answers the critics who complain that he does not compose a 'continuous poem' on the deeds of kings or heroes: poetry should be judged by art, not quantity; Apollo recommended the slender Muse, the untrodden paths; better be the cicada than the braying mule. Like *Hesiod, he had met the *Muses, in a dream, and they related the *Aetia* to him (fr. 2). Books 1 and 2 were structured, at least in part, by a dialogue between the poet-researcher and the Muses; books 3 and 4 are framed by the substantial court-poems *Victory of Berenice* and *Lock of Berenice*. Within books, poems may be grouped thematically. The 'epilogue' (fr. 112) recalls Hesiod's meeting with the Muses; and leads over to the 'pedestrian field of the Muses', i.e. (probably) to the *Iambi*. It is generally (but controversially) argued that the *Aetia* went through two editions: the poet in old age added 'prologue' and 'epilogue', and perhaps books 3–4 entire.

2. *Iambi*: thirteen poems, written in scazons or other iambic metres (see METRE, GREEK, § 4(a)). In the first, *Hipponax speaks, returned from the dead; in the last, the poet names Hipponax as the exemplar of the genre. Personal *invective (1–5), and the *fable (2, 4), play their part, as in the traditional *iambus* (see IAMBIC POETRY, GREEK). But these poems range much wider: 6 (the statue of *Zeus at *Olympia) reads as an epodic epigram, 8 as an iambic epinician; 7–11 record various *aitia*; 12 celebrates a birth. The framing poems continue literary polemic: in 1 against quarrelling scholars, in 13 against those who think that an author should confine himself to a single genre.

3. Miscellaneous poems include the lyric *Apotheosis of Arsinoë* (fr. 228), and the elegiac epinician for Sosibius (fr. 384).

4. *Hecale*, a hexameter narrative of something over 1,000 lines. *Theseus leaves Athens secretly to face the bull of *Marathon; a storm breaks; he takes shelter in the cottage of the aged *Hecale; he leaves at dawn and subdues the bull; he returns to Hecale, finds her dead, and founds the *deme Hecale and the sanctuary of Zeus Hekaleios in her memory. This heroic (but not Homeric) material was deviously elaborated, with Hecale rather than Theseus at the centre. The scene of rustic hospitality became famous; talking birds diversify the narrative; the action ends in another *aition*, perhaps drawn from the *Atthis.

5. The *Hymns* reanimate the traditional (Homeric) form (see HYMNS), but with no view to performance. The hymns to Zeus, *Artemis, and *Delos (nos. 1, 3, 4) elaborate the god's birth and virtues with quizzical learning and virtuoso invention. Those to Apollo (no. 2), *Athena (no. 5), and *Demeter (no. 6) are framed as dramas, in which the narrator-celebrant draws the hearer into an imagined ritual; 6 (Doric hexameters) and still more 5 (Doric elegiacs) deliberately cross generic boundaries (see GENRE).

6. The *Epigrams* (a selection preserved in *Meleager (2)'s anthology) cover the full range of literary, erotic, dedicatory, and sepulchral themes; scattered fragments (frs. 393–402) hint at more.

7. Callimachus wrote prose works on *nymphs; on athletic contests (see AGONES); on the foundation of *islands and cities; on winds, on rivers, on 'marvels', and on birds; on 'barbarian customs' and on local names of fish and of months. He was among the founders of lexicography and paradoxography (see ETYMOLOGICA; PARADOXOGRAPHERS). The *Pinakes* ('Tables of Those who have Distinguished themselves in Every Form of Culture and of What they Wrote') presented, in 120 books, a bibliography of Greek literature and a catalogue of the Alexandrian *Library, organized by subject ('rhetoric', 'laws', 'miscellaneous prose'); they included some biographical notes, and cited the first line of each work, and the number of lines. Callimachus also 'arranged' the poems of *Pindar and *Bacchylides (fr. 450, *Suppl. Hell.* 293).

Callimachus often states his preferences in poetry and among poets. He defends shorter (and discontinuous) poems (fr. 1), the

small drop from the pure spring (*Hymn* 2. 107 ff.), diversity of genre (πολυειδία) (fr. 203); 'a big book equals a big evil' (fr. 465), 'slim' poetry (fr. 1. 24) is better than 'thick' (fr. 398). This 'new' aesthetic (which might seem less novel if we had the poetry of the 4th cent.) quotes the example of past poets. Callimachus invokes Hesiod (frs. 2, 112; *Epigr.* 27), and condemns the *Epic Cycle (*Epigr.* 28); Homer is all-present, but formal emulation and verbal pastiche are rigorously avoided. From Pindar he borrows the critical images of the 'fine flower' (*Hymn* 2. 112, *Isthm.* 7. 18) and the 'carriage road' (fr. 1. 25–8, *Pae.* 7b. 11). *Mimnermus and *Philitas exemplify the short poem, *Ion (2) of Chios πολυειδία. *Antimachus, *Plato (1), and *Praxiphanes are variously dispraised (frs. 398, 589, 460). Of contemporaries, Callimachus commends *Aratus (1) (*Epigr.* 27, fr. 460); the story of his quarrel with *Apollonius (1) Rhodius (and of the *Ibis*, frs. 381–2) is now generally discounted.

Callimachus says little about Egypt (though some have tried to find Pharaonic ideology in *Hymn* 4). From *Alexandria (1) he looks to Greece, and the Greek past; he has a scholar's systematic knowledge of the Greek literary inheritance, an exile's feeling for the old country and its links (through *aitia*) with the contemporary world. His work often reaches out to the archaic world, crossing the centuries of drama and prose—to Hesiod, Hipponax, Pindar. But this past is transmuted. Verbal borrowing is rare; genres are shifted or mixed, myth transformed by mannerism, words and motifs juxtaposed in post-modern incongruities. *Victoria Berenices* may serve as an example. This epinician is also an *aition* (the foundation of the *Nemean Games). It borrows words from Pindar, and story from Bacchylides, in the wrong dialect (Ionic) and the wrong metre (elegiac). The narrative dwells not on *Heracles but on the rustic hospitality of the peasant Molorcus; Molorcus' war with the mice parallels Heracles' fight with the lion. Callimachus' poems are (by epic standards) short; various in style, metre, and genre; experimental in form, recondite in diction, polished in versification, devious, elaborate, allusive, and sometimes obscure (the earliest surviving papyrus, within a generation of Callimachus' death, includes an explanatory paraphrase). To Roman poets he became the exemplar of sophistication, *princeps elegiae* ('master of elegy': Quint. *Inst.* 10. 1. 58): *Catullus translated him (66), *Propertius invokes him (3. 1. 1). The *Aetia* in particular stands behind *Ovid's *Fasti* and Propertius 4; *Georgic* 3 begins with an allusion to it. But classicizing snobbery took him to represent technique without genius (Ov. *Am.* 1. 15. 14).

Callimachus commands an extraordinary variety of tone: tongue-in-cheek epic (*Hecale* fr. 74 Hollis), versified statistics (*Iambus* 6), classic pathos (*Epigr.* 19), Catullan elegance (fr. 401). The scholarship is integral to the poetry, which even quotes its own sources (frs. 75. 54, 92. 3, *Schol. Flor. Callim.* 35?). But irony and invention dominate.

TEXTS R. Pfeiffer, *Callimachus* 1–2 (1949–53); additional fragments, *Suppl. Hell.*; *Hecale*, A. S. Hollis (1990). Commentary on the *Epigrams*, Gow–Page, *HE*. Commentaries on the *Hymns*: 1, G. R. McLennan (1977); 2, F. J. Williams (1978); 3, F. Bornmann (1968); 4, W. H. Mineur (1984); 5, A. W. Bulloch (1985); 6, N. Hopkinson (1984).

GENERAL *RE* Suppl. 5. 386–452, 13. 184–266; P. M. Fraser, *Ptolemaic Alexandria* (1972); G. O. Hutchinson, *Hellenistic Poetry* (1988); Alan Cameron, *Callimachus and his Critics* (1995); L. Lehnus, *Bibliografia Callimachea* (1989); W. Wimmel, *Kallimachos in Rom* (1960).   P. J. P.

Callimachus (4) of Bithynia (?), Alexandrian physician (later 3rd cent. BC?), member of the 'school' of *Herophilus. He ascribed great value to semiotics, i.e. to the careful study of symptomatic

Callinus

signs (τὰ σημεῖα τὰ συμπίπτοντα) that 'signify' (σημαίνει) each affection (πάθος) and its cause (αἰτία), as a basis both for prognosis and for treatment. By contrast, he devalued attempts to question patients in order to ascertain antecedent causes (ἡγούμεναι προφάσεις) represented by the patient's regimen, lifestyle, or general physical condition. Famous for his treatise on the toxic effects of certain fragrant wreaths, he also wrote on various botanical drug ingredients, at times using idiosyncratic nomenclature. See BOTANY. Like many Herophileans, he contributed to the interpretation of Hippocratic works (including *Epid.* 6 and perhaps *Prognostic*), not hesitating to ridicule exegetical precursors, including the founding father of his own school, Herophilus. Such criticisms illustrate the dynamic, pluralistic, agonal relations that prevailed in Hellenistic medicine, even among adherents of the same medical 'school'.

Ed., trans., and comm.: H. von Staden, *From Andreas to Demosthenes Philalethes* (1995), ch. 3. Cf. von Staden, *Herophilus* (1989), 480–3.

H. v. S.

Callinus, Greek elegiac poet of the mid-7th cent. BC, from *Ephesus. The only extended fragment is a call to arms in defence of the city; it may have been delivered at a *symposium. Other fragments refer to Ephesus' war with *Magnesia (1) ad Maeandrum and to the hostile approach of the *Cimmerians and Treres (c.652 BC). Callinus apparently mentioned *Homer's name in connection with the legendary Theban War.

TEXT B. Gentili and C. Prato, *Poetae Elegiaci* 1 (Teubner, 1979); West, *IE²*.

TRANSLATION West, *GLP*.

COMMENT C. M. Bowra, *Early Greek Elegists* (1938); D. A. Campbell, *Greek Lyric Poetry* (1967).

M. L. W.

Calliphon, philosopher of uncertain date (probably not before *Ariston (1) of Chios and *Hieronymus (2) of Rhodes, who flourished c.250 BC). Cicero says he held that the supreme good consists in the union of pleasure and virtue.

Callipolis (also **Callion**), main city of the Aetolian tribe Callieis (a branch of the Ophiones), located in eastern *Aetolia on the upper Mournos river. Mentioned by *Thucydides (2) (3. 96. 3) in the 5th cent., the Callieis in the 4th cent. fortified their city, which prospered until it was attacked and destroyed by the Gauls (see GALATIA) in 279 BC (Paus. 10. 22. 2–4). Excavations at modern Palaiokastro, near Velouchovo, have revealed clear evidence for the city's wealth and for its destruction. An interesting cache of clay seals from the destroyed archives attests to the diplomatic and business connections of Callipolis before its destruction.

Lexikon der historischen Stätten, 294–5, 'Kallion'; P. Themelis, *AAA* 1979, 245–79.

W. M. M.

Callippus (*RE* 22), astronomer (fl. 330 BC), went with Polemarchus (pupil of *Eudoxus (1)) from *Cyzicus to Athens, where he associated with Aristotle. He corrected Eudoxus' theory of concentric spheres (Simpl. *in Cael.* 493, 5–8), by adding two more spheres in each case for the sun and moon, and one more for each of the planets (see Arist. *Metaph.* 1073^b 32–8; Simpl. *in Cael.* 497, 17–24). He proposed a year-length of 365¼ days, on which he based the 76-year cycle named after him, containing 27,759 days and 940 months (of which 28 were intercalary), as an improvement on *Meton's 19-year cycle (Geminus 8. 57–60); the first 'Callippic Cycle' began in 330–329 BC. Callippus also composed the first *parapēgma* (astronomical calendar) to demonstrate clearly the inequality of the seasons.

HAMA 2. 683 ff.; on the 'Callippic Cycle': F. K. Ginzel, *Handbuch der Chronologie* 2 (1911–14), 409 ff.; on the *parapēgma*: A. Rehm, *Parapegmastudien* (1941), esp. 42.

G. J. T.

Callirhoë, the name ('beautifully flowing') given to (1) a daughter of the river Acheloüs (for her story see ACARNAN, ALCMAEON (1)); (2) a virgin of Calydon vainly loved by Coresus, a priest of *Dionysus (Paus. 7. 21. 1–5); (3) a daughter of Oceanus, mother of Geryoneus (Hes. *Theog.* 287–8); (4) an Athenian spring, later called Enneakrounos ('Nine Spouts'), whose *water was favoured for ritual uses (Thuc. 2. 15. 5). Both the fountain-house and the personification of the spring appear in Attic art: *LIMC* 5/1 (1990), 937–9.

J. D. M.

Callisthenes, of *Olynthus, historian (d. 327 BC). Nephew of *Aristotle, he collaborated with the philosopher in compiling the official list of Pythian victors (see PYTHIAN GAMES), and by 336 he had produced a monograph on the Third *Sacred War and a ten-book *Hellenica*, which covered the period 386–356. His *Deeds of Alexander*, written in the entourage of *Alexander (3) the Great, covered events at least to 330 and had a strong eulogistic trait, glorifying the military achievements and propagating the king's claim to divine paternity. In early 327 he alienated Alexander by his opposition to *proskynesis* (see ALEXANDER (3) the Great § 10), was falsely implicated in the Pages' Conspiracy, and summarily executed. *Theophrastus lamented his death, but there is no evidence that it created a *Peripatetic tradition of hostility to Alexander. See PSEUDO-CALLISTHENES for the Alexander-Romance.

FGrH 124; Pearson, *Lost Histories of Alexander*; L. Prandi, *Callistene* (1985).

A. B. B.

Callisto, 'very beautiful', a mythical Arcadian princess or *nymph. (See ARCADIA.) She was daughter of *Lycaon, and a companion of *Artemis in the chase. Loved by *Zeus, she gave birth to *Arcas and was changed by Zeus (or Artemis or *Hera) into a bear. In some versions she was shot with an arrow and killed by Artemis, while in others she was changed into a *constellation (the Great Bear) by Zeus. Despite her links with Artemis Calliste, Callisto is not a divine hypostasis. She makes several appearances in the visual arts.

[Apollod.] 3. 100–1; ps.-Eratosth. 1, 8; Ov. *Met.* 2. 405 ff.; M. Jost, *Sanctuaires et cultes d'Arcadie* (1985), see index; I. McPhee, *LIMC* 5. 940–4.

M. J.

Callistratus (1), thought by some to have been a comic poet, but best known as the man under whose name *Aristophanes (1) produced his three earliest plays.

A. Körte, *RE* 10/2 (1919), 1737 'Kallistratos' 37; D. M. MacDowell, *CQ* 1982, 21 ff.; Kassel–Austin, *PCG* 4. 56; E. M. Carawan, *CQ* 1990, 138 n. 3.

W. G. A.

Callistratus (2), of the *deme of Aphidna, Athenian politician. A nephew of *Agyrrhius, he prosecuted ambassadors who favoured peace with *Sparta in 392/1 BC, but his ascendancy began with the *Second Athenian Confederacy, for which he devised a tribute system (*syntaxis*). In 372/1 he engineered a peace aligning Athens with Sparta and isolating *Thebes (1). The policy survived *Leuctra (371) and the need to save Sparta from destruction (370/69), though Callistratus had to deflect allied distaste. Loss of *Oropus in 366 activated similar pent-up feelings in Athens; he escaped exile only after a brilliant *apologia*, much admired by *Demosthenes (2). His view of Sparta and Thebes recovered ground, but after *Mantinea (362) and amidst other Athenian misfortunes he was impeached and retreated into exile.

He perhaps visited *Byzantium; he certainly helped Perdiccas III (ruled *Macedonia 365–359) to double Macedon's harbour-tax income ([Arist.] *Oec.* 1350ᵃ 16), plotted with an Athenian general in the north Aegean, and 'founded' Crenides (later *Philippi). A Delphic response (see DELPHIC ORACLE) promising 'just treatment' tempted him home to seek sanctuary at the Altar of the Twelve Gods, but he was executed—not least for involvement with the Macedonian enemy. Despite generalships in 378/7 and (after joining *Iphicrates in prosecuting *Timotheus (2)) 373/2–372/1, he was, unlike Iphicrates or Timotheus, essentially an orator and politician, noted for diplomatic offensives in the Peloponnese—and exposed to the obscenities of contemporary comedy.

RE 10, 'Kallistratos' 1; R. Sealey, *Essays in Greek History and Politics* (1965), 133 ff., *AO*, and *CAH* 6² (1994), see indexes.   C. J. T.

Callistratus (3), pupil of *Aristophanes (2) of Byzantium, commented on Homer and other authors, and wrote Σύμμικτα, quoted by *Athenaeus (1). He attacked his fellow-pupil *Aristarchus (2) for departing from his master's doctrines.

R. Pfeiffer, *History of Classical Scholarship: from the Beginnings to the End of the Hellenistic Age* (1968), 190; H.-L. Barth, *Die Fragmente aus den Schriften der Grammatikers Kallistratos zu Homers Ilias und Odyssee* (1984).   N. G. W.

Callistratus (4) (*RE* Suppl. 3 225–9), a provincial Roman lawyer of the reign of *Septimius Severus (AD 193–211) whose name points to a Greek background. Besides dealing with the provincial governor's edict (*Edictum monitorium*), he innovated by writing on tax law (*De iure fisci et populi*) and magisterial jurisdiction (*De cognitionibus*). His perspective is provincial, the sources cited being predominantly laws of the emperor and senate, seldom the opinions of lawyers, and the subject-matter criminal law and procedure, exemption from public duties, and related matters with a public aspect. Other legal writers do not cite him, but Justinian's compilers (see JUSTINIAN'S CODIFICATION) took 100 rather cumbrous passages from his works.

Lenel, *Pal.* 1. 81–106; *PIR²* C 231; *HLL* 4, § 430. 1; D. Liebs, *ANRW* 2. 15 (1976), 310–41; R. Bonini, *I 'libri de cognitionibus' di Callistrato* (1964).   T. Hon.

Callistratus (5) (3rd or 4th cent. AD), a sophist (see SECOND SOPHISTIC) who wrote *Descriptions* of fourteen statues (including Lysippus' Opportunity), in imitation of the *Images* of *Philostratus of Lemnos.

TEXT C. Schenkl and E. Reisch (Teubner, 1902).
TRANSLATION A. Fairbanks (Loeb, with Philostratus, 1931).
     M. B. T.

Callistus See IULIUS CALLISTUS, C.

Callixeinus (Καλλίξεινος), of Rhodes, probably 2nd cent. BC, wrote *On Alexandria* (see ALEXANDRIA (1)) in at least four books. Two extensive verbal quotations are preserved in *Athenaeus (1): F 2 = 5. 196a–203b on a grand *procession (πομπή) of *Ptolemy (1) II Philadelphus, presumably held to celebrate the victory in the First Syrian War 271/0(?); F 1 = 5. 203e–206c on the magnificent ships built by *Ptolemy (1) IV Philopator *c.*221–204 (including details of measurements, equipment, and technology). Neither local history nor a guidebook to Alexandria, it was rather a compilation of reports concerning extraordinary incidents; it was based on written sources and arranged thematically.

FGrH. 627. F. Jacoby, *RE* 10 (1919), 1751 ff.; H. Volkmann, *RE* 23 (1959), 1578 ff.; E. E. Rice, *The Grand Procession of Ptolemy Philadelphus* (1983); O. Lendle, *Einführung in die griechische Geschichtsschreibung* (1992) 270.   K. M.

Calpurnia (1) (*RE* 'Calpurnius' 126), daughter of L. *Calpurnius Piso Caesoninus, married *Caesar in 59 BC, cementing an alliance between her husband and father. Though Caesar was prepared to divorce her to marry *Pompey's daughter in 53, her affection for him was great, and she attempted to keep him from the senate on the Ides of March (Plut. *Caes.* 63). After the murder she handed his papers and 4,000 talents to M. *Antonius (2) (Mark Antony).   G. E. F. C.; R. J. S.

Calpurnia (2) (*RE* 'Calpurnius' 130), third wife of *Pliny (2) the Younger, whom she accompanied to *Bithynia (*Ep.* 10. 120–1). She was grand-daughter of L. Calpurnius Fabatus, a Roman knight of Comum (*ILS* 2721), to whom Pliny excused her miscarriage on grounds of her youth and inexperience (*Ep.* 8. 10–11). His affectionate letters to her (6. 4. 7; 7. 5) established the theme of conjugal love in Latin literature.

A. N. Sherwin-White, *The Letters of Pliny: A Historical and Social Commentary* (1966).   G. E. F. C.; M. T. G.

Calpurnius Agricola, Sextus, legate of Upper Germany in 158 and 'sent against the Britons' by M. *Aurelius in 162; inscriptions attest his activity at Ribchester, Hardknott, Carvoran, Vindolanda, and Corbridge. He later commanded an army, probably of Dacia, in the Marcomannic War.

W. Eck, *Die Statthalter der germanischen Provinzen* (1985), 65 ff.   A. R. Bi.

Calpurnius (*RE* 23) **Bestia, Lucius,** as a *Gracchan land commissioner distributed land in Africa (*ILLRP* 475). As tribune (120 BC ?) he secured the recall of P. *Popillius Laenas from exile. As consul 111, he was sent to *Numidia, with M. *Aemilius Scaurus (1) as one of his legates, to fight *Jugurtha. He concluded a peace, which was disavowed in Rome, was later condemned by the commission set up by C. *Mamilius Limetanus, and went into exile. He must have returned, but went into exile again to escape prosecution under the law of Q. *Varius.   E. B.

Calpurnius (*RE* 27) **Bibulus, Lucius,** son of the following by his first wife, studied in Athens, joined his stepfather M. *Iunius Brutus (2) in the Civil War and was proscribed. But he surrendered to M. *Antonius (2) (Mark Antony) after Philippi and was rehabilitated. Henceforth he served Antony as a mediator between him and Octavian and as a naval commander and was sent to aid Octavian against Sextus *Pompeius. He was praetor 35 and governed Syria for Antony 34–32, when he died there.

R. Syme (see following article).   E. B.

Calpurnius (*RE* 28) **Bibulus, Marcus,** *Caesar's colleague in the curule *aedileship and the *praetorship and finally, after a bribery fund had been set up for him by the *nobiles,* in the consulship of 59 BC, for which he defeated L. *Lucceius. After being forcibly prevented from vetoing Caesar's agrarian law, he attempted to invalidate all legislation of that year by remaining at his house and announcing that he was 'watching the heavens' for unfavourable omens—a device of doubtful legality. In the 50s he consistently supported the *optimates and was chosen to propose Pompey's sole consulate in 52. In 51–49 he governed Syria, where one of his officers won a minor success, for which he was awarded a triumph, largely through the efforts of his father-in-law M. *Porcius Cato (2). Assigned a naval command

Calpurnius Crassus Frugi Licinianus, Gaius

with a large fleet in 49, he was unable to prevent Caesar's crossing to Epirus and died in 48. He had three sons by a first wife (name unknown), two of whom were killed in *Alexandria (1) in 50 and one (L. *Calpurnius Bibulus), survived. He later married *Porcia, daughter of Cato, and had one son by her, who wrote a brief biography of M. *Iunius Brutus (2), Porcia's second husband (Plut. *Brut.* 13, 23). He was probably related to the Calpurnii Pisones.

Syme, RP 6. 193 ff.   E. B.

Calpurnius (*RE* 32) **Crassus Frugi Licinianus, Gaius,** of a family descended from *Pompey and *Crassus, was probably nephew of the L. *Calpurnius Piso Frugi Licinianus adopted by Galba, and should be identified with C. Calpurnius Piso Licinianus, suffect consul AD 87 (W. Henzen, *Acta Fr. Arv.* 118, line 64). Exiled to *Tarentum for conspiracy against *Nerva, he was removed to an island for allegedly plotting against *Trajan. Perhaps a victim of his illustrious lineage, he became suspect at the start of the reign of Hadrian, who was warned about him by P. *Acilius Attianus, and was killed by a procurator while trying to escape.

J. B. C.

Calpurnius (*RE* 40) **Flaccus,** of unknown date, author of *declamations from fifty-three which extracts survive.

Ed. L. Håkanson (1978); Schanz–Hosius, § 592.   M. W.

Calpurnius Piso, a contemporary of the younger *Pliny (2) (*Ep.* 5. 17), wrote an elegiac poem, 'Constellations', with a Greek title (Οἱ Καταστερισμοί). Probably identical with the consul of AD 111 C. Calpurnius Piso (*PIR*² C 285) or his brother. See CONSTELLATIONS.

PIR² C 281.   A. J. S. S.

Calpurnius (*RE* 63) **Piso** (1), **Gaius,** was *praetor urbanus* 72 or 71 BC after acquittal on *ambitus charges. As consul 67 he opposed *Pompey's friends, the tribunes C. *Cornelius and A. *Gabinius (2), and disqualified M. *Lollius Palicanus from a consular candidature. Pre-empting Cornelius with the senate's support, he passed an *ambitus* law. Assigned both Gauls, he remained as proconsul until 65 (or later in Cisalpine Gaul) and, exercising his legal rights, impeded Pompey's recruitment. He defeated the *Allobroges and repressed trouble in *Transpadana. (For this he was unsuccessfully prosecuted by *Caesar, who had an interest in the area.) He supported Cicero against the Catilinarians (see SERGIUS CATILINA, L.) and in 61 was called on to speak first in the senate by his kinsman M. *Pupius Piso, much to Cicero's chagrin. He is not heard of after 59.

Gruen, LGRR 213 ff. (and see index).   E. B.

Calpurnius (*RE* 65) **Piso** (2), **Gaius,** the figurehead of the great conspiracy against *Nero in AD 65, had been exiled by *Gaius (1), who compelled his wife Livia Orestilla to leave her husband in favour of himself and then accused the pair of adultery (probably AD 40). Under *Claudius, Piso became suffect consul, but he showed no real ambition. He lived in magnificent style and was one of the most popular figures in Rome, with his charming manners and oratorical gifts, which he put at the service of rich and poor alike. Already in 62 he was suspect to Nero's advisers (Tac. *Ann.* 14. 65), but in the actual conspiracy he proved a futile leader and after its betrayal had no thought for any action other than suicide.

His precise relationship to other members of his family is unknown, but his son Calpurnius Galerianus, who was executed

in 70, is described as cousin as well as son-in-law of L. *Calpurnius Piso (3) (Tac. *Hist.* 4. 49). It is probably his birth and talents which are celebrated in the *Laus Pisonis*.

R. L. J.; G. E. F. C.; M. T. G.

Calpurnius (*RE* 69) **Piso** (1), **Gnaeus,** suspected of complicity in *Catiline's 'first conspiracy', was sent to Spain as *quaestor pro praetore*, perhaps during a shortage of commanders, on the motion of *Crassus. Crassus no doubt hoped he would counter the entrenched influence of *Pompey there, but he was killed by adherents of Pompey (64 BC). He was the father of (2).

E. B.

Calpurnius (*RE* 95) **Piso** (2), **Gnaeus,** son of (1) and father of (3), coined *pro quaestore* for Pompey in 49 BC (*RRC* 446), joined the republicans in Africa, but survived. In 44 he joined the tyrannicides, but was pardoned. He refused to engage in public life until asked by Augustus to be his colleague in 23, when Augustus presumably intended to give up the consulship. When Augustus fell seriously ill before doing so, he handed his register of Roman finances and armies to Piso (Cass. Dio 53. 30. 2). He held no further public position, but his and L. *Sestius Quirinalis' acceptance of the consulship marks the acceptance of Augustus' new order by the old republicans.

Syme, Rom. Rev. 334 f.   E. B.

Calpurnius (*RE* 70) **Piso** (3), **Gnaeus** (consul 7 BC), who inherited from his father Cn. *Calpurnius Piso (2) a republican independence of temper, was appointed governor of Syria in AD 17, for the avowed purpose of lending counsel and assistance to *Germanicus when he journeyed to the east. His previous experience had lain in other lands: proconsul of Africa and legate of Hispania *Tarraconensis. After reciprocal bickering and open quarrel, Germanicus broke off his 'amicitia' (friendship) with Piso. Germanicus' death (19) was attributed by his friends to magical devices or poisoning by Piso and his wife *Munatia Plancina. Returning to Rome, Piso was prosecuted in the senate (20), but took his own life before the trial was terminated, protesting his innocence and his loyalty to Tiberius. The text of an important *senatus consultum* about Piso's trial and disgrace, including an account of his activities in Syria, was found in Spain in the 1980s.

Tac. Ann. 2–3; Syme, AA, see index. For the senatus consultum: W. Eck,
Cahiers du Centre Glotz 4 (1993), 189 ff.   R. S.; R. J. S.

Calpurnius (*RE* 74) **Piso** (1), **Lucius,** younger brother of Cn. *Calpurnius Piso (3), and known as 'augur' to distinguish him from L. *Calpurnius Piso (2), was consul 1 BC and proconsul of Asia. Like his father and brother a strong-minded man (Tac. *Ann.* 4. 21), in AD 16 he spoke out openly in the senate against the corruption of public life, and brought a suit against *Urgulania, a favourite of Livia's; in 20 he defended his brother. He was accused of *maiestas in 24, but died before trial.

R. Syme, JRS 1956, 17 ff. (= Ten Studies in Tacitus (1970), ch. 5), and
AA, see index.   R. J. S.

Calpurnius (*RE* 99) **Piso** (2), **Lucius** (consul 15 BC) was called 'the pontifex' to distinguish him from 'the augur', L. *Calpurnius Piso (1). Born in 48, son of L. *Calpurnius Piso Caesoninus, Piso inherited a prudent nature and philhellenic tastes: he was the patron of the poet *Antipater (5) of Thessalonica. According to *Porphyrio on Horace, *Ars P.* 1, that poem was dedicated to the sons of Piso. The cognomen 'Frugi' often attached to this Piso derived from two errors in the ancient evidence; and, as concerns the *Ars Poetica*, it is not possible to verify two sons (cf. R. Syme in *JRS* 1960, 20). Attested in Pamphylia in 13 BC (Cass. Dio 54. 34.

6), presumably as consular legate of the province of Galatia, he was summoned to *Thrace to put down a serious insurrection, a task which took three years and earned him the *ornamenta triumphalia* (Cass. Dio 54. 34. 6 ff.; Vell. Pat. 2. 98). Soon after this he may have been appointed proconsul of Asia (cf. *Anth. Pal.* 10. 25. 3 f.). Piso died in AD 32, after having been *praefectus urbi* for twenty years (Tac. *Ann.* 6. 11, if correct). He had enjoyed the unbroken confidence of *Tiberius; and his notoriously convivial habits impaired neither his efficiency nor his reliability (Sen. *Ep.* 83. 14).

Syme, *Rom. Rev.*, see index, and *RP* 2. 496 ff.　　　R. S.; R. J. S.

Calpurnius (*RE* 79) **Piso** (3), **Lucius**, grandson of Cn. Calpurnius Piso (3) and son of L. Calpurnius Piso, consul AD 27 (Plin. *Ep.* 3. 7. 12), was consul in AD 57 with *Nero. In 62 he was made member of an important financial commission; in 69 he was proconsul of Africa. Suspected in 70 of aspiring to the throne, he was murdered by C. Calpetanus Rantius Quirinalis *Valerius Festus, who was in touch with C. *Licinius Mucianus in Rome.

G. E. F. C.; M. T. G.

Calpurnius Piso (*RE* 90) **Caesoninus, Lucius,** in his youth probably served in Greece and rapidly rose to the consulate, which he held in 58 BC (with A. *Gabinius (2)) after marrying his daughter to *Caesar (consul 59). He refused to support *Cicero against P. *Clodius Pulcher, and as a reward was given the province of Macedonia by a law of Clodius. His administration there (57–55) was attacked by Cicero in two speeches (*Prov. cons.* and, after his return, *In Pisonem*). He was censor (50) and remained neutral in the Civil War, which he did his best to prevent. After Caesar's death he again tried to prevent civil war (against M. *Antonius (2)), but died soon after.

An Epicurean and friend of *Philodemus, he was open to conventional attack as a voluptuary; but he was (at least) no worse than many of his contemporaries, and his political influence was on the side of peace. He is generally regarded as the owner of a villa in *Herculaneum, where Epicurean papyri, including work by Philodemus, were discovered. He was the father of L. *Calpurnius Piso (2) the pontifex.

Asc. *Pis.* 1 ff. C, with Marshall, *Asconius Comm.*; Cic. *Pis.*, ed. R. G. M. Nisbet (1961); Syme, *Rom. Rev.*, see index.　　　E. B.

Calpurnius (*RE* 96) **Piso Frugi, Lucius,** earned his *agnomen* (which became hereditary) by his probity. As tribune 149 BC, he set up the first of the *quaestiones*: a standing committee of senators to hear *repetundae* cases. As praetor he may have fought in Sicily (unless Flor. 2. 7. 7 refers to his later service). As consul 133 he fought there with some success, taking *Morgantina and beginning the attack on the slaves' stronghold Henna. He became censor 120. He wrote *Annales* (seven books, going down to his own time), used by later historians. Cicero thought his style jejune, but Aulus *Gellius, who admired the archaic, commended it and quotes our only major fragment (on Cn. *Flavius). He pinpointed the beginning of Rome's moral decline in 154, as marked by an omen (Plin. *HN* 17. 244).

Peter, *HR Rel.* 1².　　　E. B.

Calpurnius (*RE* 100) **Piso Frugi Licinianus, Lucius,** was adopted by the emperor *Galba on 10 January 69 and killed with him in the Forum five days later. Born in AD 38, he was son to M. Crassus Frugi (consul AD 27), and to Scribonia, daughter of L. Scribonius Libo (consul AD 16) and great-granddaughter of Sextus Pompeius: his sister married L. *Calpurnius Piso (3), the son of

her father's consular colleague. This illustrious family had already met disasters under the later Julio-Claudians. Piso's eldest brother, Pompeius Magnus, was married to *Claudius' daughter *Antonia (4), but was executed along with both his parents in AD 46; a second brother, M. Crassus (consul 64), was forced to suicide during *Nero's last years; and Piso himself had been in exile for some time when Galba recalled him in 68. He was perhaps connected with a doctrinaire group in the senate, and as such was backed for the adoption by Laco the praetorian prefect (Tac. *Hist.* 1. 14; Suetonius (*Galb.* 17) says that Galba had long intended to leave him his property and his name. His critics found his personality forbidding, and he was totally unacceptable to the soldiers in the guard. His wife, daughter of Q. Veranius (consul 49), survived him for many years (Plin. *Ep.* 2. 20).

Tac. *Hist.* 1, esp. 14 and 48. The stemma in *PIR*² is in part corrected by R. Syme, *JRS* 1960, 12 ff. = *RP* 2. 496 ff.　　　G. E. F. C.; M. T. G.

Calpurnius Siculus The author of seven pastorals, Calpurnius may be dated with reasonable security to the Neronian age. The crucial pieces of evidence are *Eclogue* 1. 75 ff., which seemingly allude to the comet that foretold *Claudius' death and *Nero's accession in AD 54, and *Eclogue* 7, which celebrates the construction of a wooden amphitheatre in the *Campus Martius, and, almost certainly, the *Munus Neronis* (Neronian Games) which inaugurated it in 57. Nevertheless, attempts continue to ascribe Calpurnius to a later period, on internal, stylistic, metrical, and lexical grounds. Of the author's life virtually nothing is known: his cognomen *Siculus* may not refer to his homeland, but symbolize his debt to *Theocritus. He is sometimes credited with the *Laus Pisonis* ('Panegyric on Piso').

Of the *Eclogues*, 1, 4, and 7 are court-poems, dealing in ascending chronological order with the early years of *Nero's reign. All three contain extensive monologues. By contrast, 2, 3, 5, and 6 are in dialogue form, and are concerned with rustic matters of a more traditional kind. In 1, two shepherds, Ornytus and Corydon—who is generally identified with Calpurnius—discover verses inscribed by Faunus on the bark of a tree, prophesying a new golden age. In contrast to Calpurnius' model, Virgil *Eclogue* 4, the prophecy incorporates detailed references to contemporary politics. In 2, a shepherd and a gardener (an innovation in pastoral) sing without rancour of the love which they share for Crocale. *Eclogue* 3, which is structured around a parallel between a wayward woman and a wayward heifer, presents a contrasting view of love. In it Lycidas, an unpleasant personage as are several of Calpurnius' characters, attempts to recover the affections of Phyllis, whom he has beaten in a jealous rage. His pleas for forgiveness combine the roles of elegiac lover and shepherd-poet; he also exhibits resemblances to the elegist's *bête-noire*, the *dives amator* or rich rival. *Eclogue* 4, the longest and most fulsome of the poems, celebrates the pacifying and fructifying effect which the divine Nero has had on rural life. Corydon's opening statement that the times are now more propitious for literary endeavour is balanced by a concluding plea for imperial patronage. *Eclogue* 5 reports old Micon's advice on how to keep sheep and goats. Both the subject-matter and the insistence on hard work are georgic rather than pastoral. In *Eclogue* 6 a singing-contest is, unusually, aborted by the extreme quarrelsomeness of the competitors, Lycidas and Astylus, who stake prizes of a most unpastoral kind. *Eclogue* 7 describes Corydon's bedazzlement at the *Munus Neronis*, and his resultant alienation from his rural existence.

TEXTS C. H. Keene, *The Eclogues of Calpurnius and Nemesianus*

(1887), with comm.; C. Giarratano, *Calpurnii et Nemesiani Bucolica* (1924); D. Korzeniewski (ed.), *Hirtengedichte aus neronischer Zeit* (1971); *Bucoliques, Éloges de Pison*, ed. and trans. J. Amat (Budé, 1991).

TRANSLATION A. M. Duff, *Minor Latin Poets* 1 (1982)

STUDIES E. Champlin, *JRS* 1978, G. Townend, *JRS* 1980, T. P. Wiseman, *JRS* 1982, E. Champlin and D. Armstrong, *Philol.* 1986, E. Courtney *Rev. Ét. Lat.* 1987 (all on C.'s date); E. Cesareo, *La Poesia di Calpurnio Siculo* (1931); R. Verdière, *Eos* 1966, and *ANRW* 2. 32. 3 (1985); E. Leach, *Ramus* 1973 and 1975; R. Garson, *Latomus* 1974; P. Davis, *Ramus* 1987.

L. C. W.

Calvisius (*RE* 13) **Sabinus, Gaius,** of obscure and probably non-Latin family, served under *Caesar in Greece in 48 BC and became governor of Africa in 45. Praetor in 44, he tried to protect Caesar on the Ides of March. M. *Antonius (2) (Mark Antony) reappointed him to Africa (November 44), but this came to nothing (see CORNIFICIUS, Q.). He was consul 39. He commanded a fleet for *Octavian against Sextus *Pompeius (38) and was responsible for restoring order in Italy (36). Later he was governor in Spain and triumphed in May of 28. He was a *septemvir epulo* (see SEPTEMVIRI EPULONES) and served as *curio maximus* (see CURIA (1)). His son was consul 4 BC and his grandson consul AD 26.

Syme, *Rom. Rev.*, see index. T. J. C.; E. B.

Calvus See LICINIUS CALVUS, C.

Calymnos A Dodecanese island lying between *Cos and Leros to the west of the *Halicarnassus peninsula. Calymnos together with nearby islands whose identity is disputed are probably the 'Kalydnai isles' mentioned in Homer (*Il.* 2. 677). Caves and tombs reveal neolithic and Mycenaean occupation. The main Mycenaean citadel was probably at Perakastro near the modern capital Pothia. Herodotus (7. 99) states that Calymnos was later colonized by Dorians from Epidaurus. In historical times, Calymnian ships fought with the Carians during the Persian War (see ARTEMISIA (1)), and the island appears in the Athenian *tribute lists. At the end of the 3rd cent. BC it was absorbed by Cos and the population became *demes of the Coan state.

A sanctuary of *Apollo and theatre were found at the site of Christ of Jerusalem near Damos in the southern half of the island. Finds show that the cult existed there from archaic times onwards, and nearby cemeteries and walls attest ancient occupation in this area. The other main centre of occupation was around Vathy in the east, as an impressive fortification circuit wall at Embolas shows. There are Roman and Byzantine remains throughout the island as well as on the islet of Telendos to the west.

INSCRIPTIONS M. Segre, *ASAA* 1944–5.
LITERATURE G. E. Bean and J. M. Cook, *BSA* 1957, 127 ff.; R. Hope Simpson and J. F. Lazenby, *BSA* 1962, 172 ff. E. E. R.

Calypso ('Concealer'?), a nymph, daughter of *Atlas (*Od.* 1. 14, 52), possibly invented by *Homer. She lived on the island of Ogygie, 'where is the sea's navel' (*Od.* 1. 50), rescued *Odysseus when shipwrecked, and kept him for seven years, vainly promising immortality. Commanded by *Zeus and *Hermes to release him, she helped him to make a boat and let him go (*Od.* 5. 1–268, 7. 244–66). In *Hesiod, *Theog.* 1017–18, she has two sons by Odysseus, Nausithous and Nausinous, and in Hes. fr. 150. 31 M–W is perhaps mother of the Cephallenians by Hermes. Later she is mother by Odysseus or Atlas of Auson, eponym of Ausonia (southern Italy) (Scymn. 229 f., schol. Ap. Rhod. 4. 553, etc.). In Lucian (*Ver. Hist.* 2. 35) Odysseus writes to her after his death from the *Island of the Blest, regretting having left her and

promising to return, and in Hyginus (*Fab.* 243) she commits suicide for love of him. She is also an Oceanid (Hes. *Theog.* 359, *Hymn. Hom. Cer.* 422), Nereid (Apollod. 1. 2. 7), or Hesperid (vase by Asteas, *LIMC* 5/1. 399–400, no. 36), see HESPERIDES.

Lamer, *RE* 10. 1772–99; Rafa, *LIMC* 5/1. 945–8. N. J. R.

Camarina, a Syracusan (see SYRACUSE) colony founded *c*.599 BC at the mouth of the river Hipparis in southern Sicily, near modern Scoglitti. Its mid-6th cent. fortifications enclose a vast area of 145 ha. (358 acres), far larger than other Syracusan colonies. In constant dispute with the Syracusans, it was destroyed by them in 533 and again *c*.484 after refoundation by *Hippocrates (1) of Gela. Established once more in 461 by the Geloans, it supported the anti-Syracusan coalition in 427–4, but decided for Syracuse after 415 (cf. Thuc. 6. 75–88). Abandoned by *Dionysius (1) I in 405, but reoccupied from 396, it revived in the period of *Timoleon; several houses of this period have been uncovered. Extensive excavations since 1971 have transformed our knowledge of the topography of the city and its cemeteries. Estimates from the latter suggest that the 6th-cent. population was about 16,000. The agora with two stoas lay at the west end of the city overlooking the sea, and a 5th cent. temple of Athena is known at the summit of the hill near the centre of the city. A cache of over 140 inscribed lead sheets found in this temple in 1987 indicates that after the 461 refoundation the population was divided into three tribes, subdivided into at least fourteen *phratries. A 4th-cent. lead sale-document shows that the term *laura* (λαύρα) was used to denote different districts of the city. The supposition that Camarina was finally destroyed and abandoned in 258 BC (Diod. Sic. 23. 9. 4–5) is invalidated by the discovery of houses of Roman republican date, but this reoccupation was limited to the west quarter. Strabo (6. 2. 5) records the city as deserted.

PECS 434–5; *BTCGI* 4 (1985), 286–324; Gabba–Vallet, *Sicilia antica* 1. 509–27; F. Cordano, *Le tessere pubbliche dal tempio di Atena a Camarina* (1992). Sale contract: *SEG* 34. 940. Coinage: U. Westermark and K. Jenkins, *The Coinage of Kamarina* (1980). A. G. W.; R. J. A. W.

Cambyses (OP Kābujiya), eldest son of *Cyrus (1); acceded on the death of his father (530 BC). He completed his father's grand plan by conquering Egypt, where he was successful in promoting a policy of collaboration with the local élites. The Egyptian documents (Udjahorresnet inscription; Apis sarcophagi) contradict the information collected later by Herodotus on this point. *Babylonia is a good example in showing how Cambyses placed the great sanctuaries under tight control. The news of the revolt of his brother, Smerdis, forced Cambyses to leave Egypt in haste in 522; he died in Syria, possibly at Damascus.

Briant, *HEA* chs. 1–2. P. B.

camels, long domesticated in Arabia and neighbouring lands, were unfamiliar in Anatolia in 546 BC when *Cyrus (1)'s baggage-camels terrified the Lydian horses (Hdt. 1. 80). These may have been two-humped central Asiatic camels like those depicted at Persepolis; the one-humped Arabian camel was more generally known. *Herodotus (3. 103) thought a full description unnecessary; but the camels captured by *Agesilaus II in 395 BC were curiosities when brought to Europe (Xen. *Hell.* 3. 4. 24). In the Hellenistic and Roman periods camels were widely used in Asia and North Africa. *Antiochus (3) III's army at the battle of *Magnesia included Arab swordsmen mounted on fast camels (Livy 37. 40. 12), and the Romans employed *dromedarii*, but the chief military and civilian use of the camel was for transport.

J. K. A.

Camenae, goddesses of a spring (from which the *Vestals drew their daily water), meadow, and grove below the *Caelian hill just outside the porta Capena at Rome. They included *Egeria, and were linked traditionally with the inspiration of King *Numa and in turn were identified with the *Muses (at least from the time of Livius Andronicus (Liv. Andron. *Od.* fr. 1). There was a shrine and a festival (13 August); the place was embellished but lost its rural atmosphere as the city spread around it (Juvenal 3. 10).

Steinby, *Lexicon*, entry under the name.   N. P.

cameos Hardstones such as agate or sardonyx, shell, and glass were carved three-dimensionally into vessels, plaques, ring-stones, or pendants so as to take advantage of the contrasting colours of different layers of the material. The technique was first employed in the Hellenistic period, and reached its apogee under the Roman empire. The most elaborate surviving cameos are the Tazza Farnese (in Naples), the Gemma Augustea (in Vienna), and the Cameo of *Tiberius (in Paris); they carry complex figured scenes of a mythological and political nature. The cameo was a much favoured vehicle for portraiture; notable examples are the idealized superimposed heads of *Alexander (3) the Great and *Olympias (or of Ptolemies, see PTOLEMY (1)) on cameos in Vienna and St Petersburg. Large-scale cameos played a part in the circulation of imperial ideology; smaller ones reveal private devotion to a range of deities, carry scenes of everyday life, or bear inscriptions relating to love or health. Hardstone cameos were intrinsically valuable; less expensive items might be made in layered glass. The Portland vase is the most outstanding extant object in this category. See PORTRAITURE.

P. Zazoff, *Die antiken Gemmen* (1983); M. Henig and M. Vickers (eds.), *Cameos in Context* (1993).   M. V.

Camerinum (mod. Camerino), town of the *Umbrians midway between *Perusia and the Adriatic. Its inhabitants, known as Camertes, were sometimes mistaken for burghers of Etruscan *Clusium, whose earlier name was Camars. Camerinum signed a 'most equal' treaty with Rome before 300 BC and was favoured by her thereafter, even as late as imperial times.   E. T. S.

Camilla, a legendary Volscian maiden, whose father Metabus, in flight fastened her to a javelin, dedicated her to *Diana, and threw her across the Amisenus river. After life as a huntress she joined the forces of *Turnus (1), engaged in battle, and was killed by the Etruscan *Arruns. Virgil alone (*Aen.* 7. 803, 11. 539–828) relates her story.   A. S. P.

camillus, fem. **camilla,** the ancient name for acolytes in Roman cult; the normal term was *pueri et puellae ingenui patrimi matrimique.* They might be the children of the officiant, but must, as the phrase states, be below the age of puberty, be free-born, and have both parents alive.

Wissowa, *RK* 496; Latte, *RR* 407–8.   H. J. R.; S. R. F. P.

Camirus was one of the three independent Dorian cities on *Rhodes until the *synoecism with *Lindus and *Ialysus created the federal Rhodian state in 408/7. Camiran territory occupied the NW part of Rhodes, and the city lay near the coast 34 km. (21 mi.) from modern Rhodes town. Camirus lacked city walls and a fortified acropolis, but excavations have revealed excellently preserved remains of public and private areas from Archaic to Hellenistic date, including a *temenos* and temple, extensive remains of houses, and an agora with stoa, cistern, and temple of Athena. The nearby necropolis of Fikellura produced the distinctive Archaic pottery which bears its name.

Camirus was a member of the Dorian hexapolis (with Lindus, Ialysus, *Cos, *Cnidus, and *Halicarnassus), and appears in the Athenian *tribute-lists. It declined in political importance after the foundation of federal Rhodes, but continued to be inhabited and maintained its own civic and religious organization.

INSCRIPTIONS *IG* 12. 1; M. Segre and G. Pugliese Carratelli, *ASAA* 1949–51, 141 ff.; G. Pugliese Carratelli, *ASAA* 1952–4, 211 ff.

LITERATURE *Clara Rhodos* 1931; 1932–3; G. Konstantinopoulos, *Arhaia Rodos* (1986) (in Greek).   E. E. R.

Campania, region of west central Italy bounded by the river *Liris, the Apennines and the Sorrentine peninsula, in prosperity, political importance, and social organization closely tied to the region of Rome in the late republic and early empire (Augustus' First Region included both, and the name came to refer to the neighbourhood of Rome, the *Campagna*). The well-watered and mineral-rich plains and foothills (e.g. the *agri Campanus* and *Falernus,* the *Phlegraei campi*) and the numerous harbours and beach-heads combined to give it a wider Italian and Mediterranean significance.

Seaborne contacts of the bronze age and geometric periods were followed by the establishment of a sequence of *apoikiai, *Pithecusae on the island of Ischia, and its successor *Cumae on the mainland opposite, with its daughter-settlements Dicaearchia (later *Puteoli) and *Neapolis (Naples). Etruscan cultural influence shaped the principal cities of the interior, *Nola and *Capua, and the important centre of *Pontecagnano on the gulf of Salerno to the south. Political takeover by the peoples of the mountains in the later 5th cent., direct at Capua and Cumae, more subtle at Naples, led to the development of the area as a centre of the Italic/Hellenistic culture associated with the *Oscan language. Rome's conquest of the area, and the cultural developments that resulted, from the late 4th cent. played a vital role in the formation of the peninsula-wide Roman state and its institutions. Agricultural prosperity and the wealth of the ruling élites gave it a reputation for luxury which the Romans used to stigmatize their city's potential rival and occasional enemy (notably in the Hannibalic War), Capua. The wealth of Campania also made it a hotly contested location for the settlement of *veterans in the late republic. Cash-crop agriculture and the villa-resorts of the coast and the hot springs flourished throughout the Roman period, when the cities, especially Puteoli, Naples, and Capua, were among the most important in Italy. The richness of the archaeological record (even outside the special circumstances of the cities destroyed by *Vesuvius in AD 79) is outstanding.

K. J. Beloch, *Campanien,* 2nd edn. (1890); J. Heurgon, *Capoue préromaine* (1942); J. H. D'Arms, *Romans on the Bay of Naples* (1970); M. W. Frederiksen, *Campania* (1984).   N. P.

camps When *Polybius (1) (6. 27–32) described the construction of a military camp (*castra*) c.143 BC, he was referring to a well-established practice. *Livy, writing of 294 BC, assumes the existence of a fixed layout, without explaining it (10. 32. 9). The invention of castrametation by the Romans was probably connected with *orientation, town planning, and land division, which themselves were associated with augural practices. Land division, with its careful delineation of areas and use of boundary lines intersecting at right angles, was well suited to military planning. Roman camp-building techniques emphasize the professionalism of their military establishment.

Archaeological and aerial surveys have revealed about 400 marching-camps in *Britain, generally square or oblong in shape, protected by a ditch and rampart of turves surmounted by a palisade, and with at least four gates, often guarded by a ditch or curving extension of the rampart (*clavicula*). Some were construction, or practice camps (to teach soldiers building techniques); others were large enough to accommodate an army (e.g. a group in SE Scotland of 67 ha. (165 acres), perhaps associated with the campaigns of *Septimius Severus in AD 208). At *Masada in Judaea several siege camps with their internal stone walls have survived.

However, archaeological evidence rarely illuminates the internal layout of temporary camps. According to Polybius, when a consular army of two legions and an equal number of allies encamped, the general's tent (*praetorium*) was located in a central position, with an open space (*forum*) on one side, and the quaestor's tent (*quaestorium*) on the other. In front of these were the tribunes' tents. The main street (*via principalis*—about 30 m. (33 yds.) wide), ran parallel to the *praetorium*, being intersected at right angles by other streets along which were encamped the legions and allies. The most important of these streets was the *via praetoria* (about 15 m. (16½ yds.) wide), which formed a T-junction opposite the *praetorium*. The legionary cavalry was positioned in troops on either side of the *via praetoria*; then the legionary infantry (grouped respectively as *triarii*, *principes*, and *hastati*) in maniples, with the *triarii* back to back to the cavalry. In front of the *triarii* ran other roads parallel to the *via praetoria*, beyond which were positioned the *principes* back to back to the *hastati*. Beyond the *hastati* the allied cavalry and infantry were similarly encamped. The *via quintana*, running parallel to the *via principalis*, divided the first to fifth maniples from the sixth to tenth. Behind the *praetorium* were the élite allied infantry and cavalry, and local auxiliary troops. The camp was square, surrounded by a ditch, rampart, and palisade, with a space (*intervallum*) of about 60 m. (66 yds.) from the tents. Each of the two main roads of the camp led to fortified gates. Polybius perhaps refers to half of a four-legion camp, when both consular armies were camping together. In the complete layout they would be positioned back to back, in a camp of oblong shape, with the legions and allies at either end. However, when a two-legion army encamped alone, the layout was perhaps changed to accommodate the *praetorium* between the two legions, as apparently confirmed by a camp excavated in Spain, associated with Roman attempts to capture *Numantia in the 150s BC.

The *De munitionibus castrorum* ('On Camp Fortifications'), an anonymous treatise (probably 2nd cent. AD), is a theoretical work, presumably for the guidance of military surveyors, and differs significantly from Polybius' version. The tripartite rectangular layout contained a combined *praetorium* and *principia* (headquarters), in front of which ran the *via principalis*, intersected at right angles by the *via praetoria*; here in the *praetentura* (one-third of the layout), auxiliaries were encamped in centuries, and also behind the *praetorium* along the *via quintana* in the *retentura* (the remaining two-thirds, where the *quaestorium* was now situated; praetorians were encamped next to the *praetorium*, and legionaries next to the *intervallum* along the *via sagularis*, encircling the entire camp.

G. Webster, *The Roman Imperial Army*, 3rd edn. (1985), 167; Numantia: A. Schulten, *Numantia* 1–4 (1914–31); Britain: S. Frere and J. K. St Joseph, *Roman Britain from the Air* (1983); J. K. St Joseph, *JRS* 1969, 104; 1973, 214; 1977, 125; G. S. Maxwell and D. R. Wilson, *Britannia* 1987, 1; *De munitionibus castrorum*: see HYGINUS (4). J. B. C.

Campus Martius comprised most of the Tiber flood-plain bounded by the Pincian, Quirinal, and Capitoline hills. Taking its name from an altar to Mars, it was originally pasture outside the *pomerium, and therefore used for army musters and exercises and for the *comitia centuriata*; here too armies gathered before processing in *triumph through the city. As a result, the Campus and the Circus Flaminius (221 BC), a monumentalized open space just to the south through which the procession passed, were during the republic increasingly filled with temples, porticoes, and other monuments set up to commemorate (and thank the gods for) military victories, at the same time impressing the assembled electorate: for example the temples of the Lares Permarini (179 BC) and Fortuna Huiusce Diei (101 BC), in the Porticus Minucia Vetus (107 BC), modern Largo Argentina. The theatre of *Pompey (52 BC) with huge portico, foreshadows the immense buildings of the Augustan *viri triumphales* in both Campus and *Circus, including T. *Statilius Taurus' amphitheatre (29 BC), *Caesar's *Saepta Iulia, completed by *Agrippa (26 BC), who also built the Porticus Argonautarum (25 BC), *Pantheon, and *thermae* with water-gardens; and the theatres of M. *Claudius Marcellus (5) and L. *Cornelius Balbus (2) (the latter with *crypta*) of 13 BC. Dominating the north of the Campus were Augustus' mausoleum (28 BC), the *Solarium (10 BC), and the *Ara Pacis (9 BC) (Strabo 5. 3. 8). Imperial buildings gradually filled the remaining space in the Campus, which changed from being political and military in character to an area primarily concerned with imperial commemoration and entertainment. *Gaius (1) projected an amphitheatre; *Nero built *thermae* (AD 62–4) and *Domitian the Divorum (dedicated to *Vespasian and *Titus), a stadium (now Piazza Navona), and *odeum*. *Antoninus Pius honoured *Hadrian with a temple (AD 145), and is himself commemorated by the Column of Antoninus, with famous panels on its base; the Column of Marcus Aurelius is decorated with spiral reliefs of the Marcomannic wars. Eventually, the whole area was included within the *wall of Aurelian.

Coarelli, *Roma* 266–309; Richardson, *Topog. Dict. Ancient Rome* 65–7; T. P. Wiseman in Steinby, *Lexicon* 220–4. I. A. R.; J. N.; J. R. P.

Camulodunum (mod. Colchester, Essex). A large area, including the site of the later town, comprised an iron age *oppidum* from the Augustan period. It was surrounded by substantial earthworks and was the capital and mint of *Cunobel(l)inus. Captured in *Claudius' campaign of AD 43, a fortress of Legio XX Valeria was constructed beside it, and in 49 a colony (*colonia Victricensis*) was founded on the site of the fortress. This became the first provincial capital, with the temple of Divus Claudius and a theatre with an adjacent forum. This unwalled town was sacked by *Boudicca in AD 60/1 and was subsequently rebuilt to cover an area of c.43 ha. (106 acres). Its defences were a clay bank to which, it appears, a stone wall was added in the early 2nd cent. Outside the walls was an important Romano-Celtic sanctuary at Gosbecks and Samian pottery was made in an industrial suburb in the 2nd/3rd cent.

P. Grummy, in G. Webster (ed.), *Fortress into City* (1988); M. J. Millett *The Romanization of Britain* (1990). C. E. S.; M. J. M.

canabae, civil settlements which developed close to legionary bases, e.g. *Mogontiacum (Mainz), *Deva (Chester), sometimes subdivided into *vici*. They attracted *veterans, traders, and local women, with whom soldiers frequently formed liaisons; their children, if they enlisted, gave their origin as *castris* ('in the camp'). *Canabae* were administered by a legionary legate, although Roman citizens in them could act as *de facto* magistrates. Expansion sometimes led to the development of an adjacent related settlement, and during the 2nd–3rd cent. AD some acquired municipal or even colonial status (see COLONIZATION, ROMAN; MUNICIPIUM).

R. MacMullen, *Soldier and Civilian in the Later Roman Empire* (1963), 119; K.-V. Decker and W. Seltzer *ANRW* 2. 5. 1 (1976), 457; D. J. P. Mason, *Britannia* 1987, 143. J. B. C.

Canace (Κανάκη), tragic victim of the story presented in *Euripides' Aeolus. A daughter of the island-king *Aeolus (1), she was impregnated by her brother Macareus. When she gave birth and the affair came to light, her father sent her a sword with which she committed suicide; the guilty brother followed suit.

G. Berger-Doer, *LIMC*; T. B. L. Webster, *The Tragedies of Euripides* (1967), 157–60. A. H. G.

canals (*fossae*, διώρυγες). Drainage and *irrigation canals were widely used in antiquity. The oldest, in Iraq, date to the sixth millennium BC, while in *Egypt they were in use from the fourth millennium. Thenceforth, in both *Mesopotamia and *Egypt, irrigation canals came increasingly to be employed, although long-distance straight-line waterways are mainly a developement of the first millennium BC; Sennacherib's celebrated Jerwan aqueduct (691 BC), ran for over 80 km. (50 mi.) from the uplands to *Nineveh (1). But in Mesopotamia full state-controlled irrigation systems appeared only on Sasanian times (AD 226–640). In Greece, Lake *Copais was first reclaimed by the Mycenaeans (Strabo 9. 2. 40); Hellenistic works (by Crates of Chalcis: Strabo 9. 2. 18) and Hadrianic dykes are also attested; *Xerxes' canal through Mt. *Athos was for military ends. Projects (never realized) to pierce the Isthmus of *Corinth are intermittently attested from *Periander's time (see DIOLKOS). In Sicily, *Empedocles of Acragas drained low-lying terrain around *Selinus in 444 BC (Diog. Laer. 8. 59–60), and the port-city of *Spina, founded *c.*540 BC in NE Italy, had a 'grand canal', and a grid of other canals to create rectangular blocks, in which were buildings on wooden piles. The canals may have been constructed by the *Etruscans, whose skills in this area of engineering were noted (e.g. *Pliny (1), *HN* 3. 20); there are still conspicuous traces in southern Etruria (and also *Latium) of underground *cuniculi*—tunnels, for land reclamation. The level of the *Albanus lacus was also lowered by means of a *cuniculus*, 1,800 m. (1,968 yds.) in length, and a 24-km.-(15-mi.-)long canal, built in the 4th cent. BC (Livy 5. 15. 12).

The Romans used canals extensively, learning much from the Etruscans who, in the 6th cent. BC, did much to alleviate flooding problems in Rome itself (Livy 1. 38. 2). A canal was cut by M. Cethegus (consul 160 BC) through the *Pomptine Marshes which, although not particularly successful as a drainage measure, nevertheless proved successful as an alternative mode of travel to the via Appia (Hor. *Sat.* 5. 5.). In the Po valley (see PADUS), where land reclamation was, according to tradition, begun by the Etruscans (Plin. *HN* 3. 115), M. *Aemilius Scaurus (1) built the first Roman canals in 109 BC (Strabo 5. 1. 11); they were intended to be both navigable and for drainage, and led to a highly successful development of the region. Under Augustus, a canal was dug between *Ravenna and the Po estuary, creating an important harbour (Plin. *HN* 3. 119) and there were significant attempts to canalize the mouth of the *Tiber. *Claudius used 30,000 men for eleven years in an attempt to drain the *Fucinus lacus (Suet. *Claud.* 20. 1–2; 21. 6).

There were significant works of canalization in many provinces (e.g. by C. *Marius (1) at the mouth of the Rhône; by Drusus, and later Cn. *Domitius Corbulo, at the mouth of the Rhine; and the Car Dyke of the western Fens of Britain, probably

a Hadrianic catch-water system). But Egypt remained the principal country of canals. *Alexandria (1) was connected with the Nile by the 'Canopus Canal'; and though earlier Egyptian schemes for digging through the isthmus of Suez apparently failed, *Ptolemy (1) II, using some of their workings, built a canal from the Nile (near Heliopolis) to the Bitter Lakes, which he connected with *Arsinoë (2). Improved under *Trajan and *Hadrian, it enabled Alexandria to become the principal centre for seaborne trade between the east and the Mediterranean.

R. J. Forbes, *Irrigation and Drainage* (1955); R. M. Adams, *Land behind Baghdad* (1965); T. W. Downing and M. Gibson (eds.), *Irrigation's Impact upon Society* (1974); T. W. Potter in T. Rowley (ed.), *The Evolution of Marshland landscapes* (1981), 1 ff.; B. Isserlin and others, *BSA* 1994, 277–84 (Athos canal). E. B.; T. W. P.

candidatus, a candidate for a Roman magistracy. Officially named *petitor* (his rivals were therefore styled *competitores*), he was called *candidatus* because he wore a whitened toga when greeting electors in the forum. A slave (*nomenclator*) reminded him of the names of the electors, and he had a crowd of partisans (*sectatores*) from the *plebs* including his own freedmen and other clients, whose numbers were taken as an index of his likely success (these numbers were limited by a *lex Fabia* of 64 BC). In the late republic these activities frequently began a full year before the election, but the traditional period of canvass was over the last three market-days (*nundinae*); this brought the candidate's name to the notice of the presiding magistrate. Originally candidacies, even of those absent, might be accepted on election day, but such concessions were limited by laws of the late republic. Under the Principate names might be given to the presiding consul or to the emperor who would pass the names on, if he had no objection (*nominatio*). By the end of *Augustus' reign, however, some senior magistrates were *candidati Caesaris*, who were elected without the need to canvass or the risk of rejection. See ELECTIONS AND VOTING.

E. S. Staveley, *Greek and Roman Voting* 1972; B. M. Levick, *Athenaeum* 1981. P. T.; E. S. S.; A. W. L.

Canidius (*RE* 2) **Crassus, Publius,** of obscure family, served under M. *Aemilius Lepidus (3) in Transalpine Gaul and helped in the negotiations that led to Lepidus' joining M. *Antonius (2) (Mark Antony) in May 43 BC. He is probably the Crassus who led an army for Antony during the Perusine War (see PERUSIA). At the end of 40, after the Peace of Brundisium, he held a suffect consulship, and subsequently served Antony in the east. Early in 36 he subdued the Iberians (2) and Albanians in the region of the Caucasus, and then joined Antony's Parthian expedition. Probably left in command in Armenia, he brought his army to join Antony in 32, and took charge of all the land forces in the Actium campaign. After the battle he joined Antony in Egypt, was captured by Octavian and was either executed or committed suicide.

Syme, *Rom. Rev.*, see index. T. J. C.; E. B.

Caninius (*RE* 9) **Rebilus, Gaius,** of praetorian family, served as *Caesar's *legatus* in 52 BC against *Vercingetorix. In 49 he was sent by Caesar to *Pompey to arrange a compromise, and then fought under C. *Scribonius Curio (2) in Africa. In 46 he was in Africa again with the status of proconsul, taking part in the campaign of Thapsus; in 45 he served as a *legatus* in the campaign of Munda. On the last day of 45, on the sudden death of Q. Fabius Maximus, Caesar appointed him consul for the few remaining hours of the year (Cic. *Fam.* 7. 30). What happened to him after that is uncertain.

Syme, *Rom. Rev.*, see index; Broughton, *MRR* 3. 49.   T. J. C.; R. J. S.

Caninius (*RE* 13) **Rufus,** a wealthy landowner and benefactor of *Comum, and friend of *Pliny (2) the Younger, who wrote to him mainly about their shared literary interests (*Ep.* 1. 3; 2. 8; 3. 7; 6. 21; 7. 18; 8. 4; 9. 33). Rufus intended to write an epic poem in Greek celebrating *Trajan's conquest of *Dacia.   J. B. C.

Canius Rufus, from Gades, a poet and friend of *Martial, who alludes to his versatility and merriment in epigram 3. 20 (cf. 1. 61. 9; 1. 69).

P. Howell, *Commentary on Bk. 1 of the Epigrams of Martial* (1980), 252 f.

Cannae (mod. Canne), Apulian town on the right bank of the river *Aufidus (Ofanto), where *Hannibal defeated the Romans in 216 BC. The battle was probably fought downstream from the town and on the same side of the river, with the Carthaginian left and Roman right resting on its bank. The Romans probably outnumbered Hannibal in infantry (80,000 : 40,000?), though 15,000 may have been left to guard their camps, but had fewer cavalry (6,000 : 10,000). Hannibal threw his centre infantry forward, keeping back his Africans on both wings, and when the Roman infantry drove in his centre, they were outflanked by the Africans. Meanwhile, Hannibal's left-wing cavalry, having driven off the Roman cavalry, rode round to help his right-wing cavalry defeat the Roman allied cavalry, and then repeatedly charged the Roman rear. Virtually surrounded, the Roman army perhaps suffered higher casualties in a single day's fighting than any other western army before or since.

RE 3/2.; Polyb. 3. 107 ff.. Livy 22. 36 ff.. J. F. Lazenby, *Hannibal's War* (1978); J. Seibert, *Hannibal* (1993).   J. F. La.

cannibalism has been called 'for Greeks, one of those extreme pollutions, often imagined, though never experienced' (Parker). Such hard evidence as there is, e.g. Thuc. 2. 70. 1, Potidaea, tends to relate to sieges and is usually something the enemy does, not your own side. From Aegean prehistory, *Minoan civilization provides an isolated find of human bones from *Cnossus (*c.*1500 BC) said to bear butchery-marks.

R. Parker, *Miasma* (1983), 305; P. Garnsey, *Famine and Food Supply in the Graeco-Roman World* (1988), 28 f.; S. Wall and others, *BSA* 1986, 334–88.   S. H., A. J. S. S.

canon In Classical Greek the word *kanōn* (lit. 'rod') was used to mean 'rule' or 'standard'; hence its use as the title of a manual on proportions by the sculptor *Polyclitus (2) and as the name of a statue illustrating his principles. The word was later applied by Christian writers to what became the approved selection of books of the Bible, but it was not used in pagan antiquity in the sense of a list of chosen 'best authors'. (*Photius in the 9th cent. AD uses it of any individual author who represents the 'standard' of the genre or the model for another writer: e.g. *Thucydides (2) is the *kanōn* for *Cassius Dio, *Bibl.* 35b33.) The idea of compiling lists of the best writers in a particular genre, such as the Nine Lyric Poets, was attributed by Roman writers to Alexandrian scholars, particularly *Aristarchus (2) and *Aristophanes (2) of Byzantium (Quint. *Inst.* 10. 1. 54). This makes sense in so far as much of the scholarship of the time was devoted to the rescue, classification, and exegesis of earlier literature, and the Alexandrians could use the books in their Library, with *Callimachus (3)'s *Pinakes* as the major work of reference, to tell them which authors had stood the test of time (*qui vetustatem pertulerunt,*

Quint. *Inst.* 10. 1. 40). But they must also have been familiar with the much earlier lists of the type 'the Nine *Muses' or 'the *Seven Sages', and it is possible that (e.g.) the Nine Lyric Poets already formed a recognizable group.

The Alexandrians themselves seem to have used the term 'those included' (οἱ ἐγκριθέντες) for the select authors; in Latin the favoured term was *classici,* and *Quintilian used *ordo* and *numerus* to designate a selective list. The 'included' authors had a much better chance of survival than those not listed, partly because their works (or some of them) attracted scholarly commentary and were thus more easily studied, and more likely to be available for recopying, by successive generations. Papyrus discoveries have tended to confirm the influence of the Alexandrian lists: *Menander (1), *Bacchylides, and *Hyperides, all notable rediscoveries, are known to have been among the 'included' authors.

The choice of certain numbers, especially three and multiples of three, was no doubt useful as a mnemonic device, but it gives a misleading sense of authority and fixity to lists which were in fact subject to variation. Even the famous three great tragedians, familiar without further identification as early as the 4th cent. BC (Diog. Laert. 5. 88), could appear in a list with *Ion (2) of Chios and *Achaeus (2) as well as on their own (*TGF* 1² CAT A 3), and the ten *Attic orators are not always the same ten (or ten at all). Even the biblical canon, with its strong theological implications, has not always been defined in exactly the same terms, despite belief in its divine authority and unalterability. The pagan lists (of authors, not books) were certainly less authoritative, and the term 'canon' itself is probably best avoided, as Pfeiffer warned. It was first used in the modern sense by David Ruhnken in 1768, in an essay tracing the history of the ancient lists which displays a sharp awareness of their limitations. The most that can be said is that the ancients had a pragmatic sense of which were the 'best', or most useful or most famous, authors in the different genres, and that it was works by these authors that by and large formed the basis of the educational system in late antiquity. The very strong emphasis placed by ancient educators on speaking and writing skills, with rhetorical composition as the summit of achievement, gave pride of place to the imitation of admired models (see EDUCATION, ROMAN).

Out of the ancient works that were known or rediscovered during the Renaissance, markedly different 'canonical' selections have been made in different periods, and the changing process of reception continues, with new theoretical and political implications as western culture itself is held up to scrutiny.

D. Ruhnken, *Historia critica oratorum graecorum,* also contains text of Rutilius Lupus, *De figuris* (1768); R. Pfeiffer, *A History of Classical Scholarship* 1 (1968), with earlier bibliography; P. Ackroyd and C. Evans, *Cambridge History of the Bible* 1 (1970); *Critical Inquiry* (1983): *Canons;* A. and J. Assmann (eds.), *Kanon und Zensur* 1987; *Annals of Scholarship* 10/1 (1993): *Reinterpreting the Classics.* For Polyclitus: J. J. Pollitt, *The Art of Ancient Greece,* 2nd edn. (1990).   P. E. E.

Cantabri, a coastal and mountain people of NW Spain situated east of the *Astures. They lived in many dispersed fortified settlements of varying sizes and their society was organized in terms of *gentes* and family groups (*gentilitates*). They were finally reduced by the Romans in campaigns from 26 to 19 BC, led by *Augustus (26–25) and M. *Vipsanius Agrippa (19). Those who survived this Cantabrian War were either deported or remained under the supervision of Roman troops. Juliobriga (mod. Reinosa) was the major town before *Vespasian's colony of

Flaviobriga. The prime natural resource was *iron, although *lead and salt were also important.

J. González Echegarray, *Los Cantabros* (1986); Syme, *RP* 2, 825–54.
S. J. K.

Cantharus, Athenian comic poet, victorious at the *Dionysia in 422 BC (*IG* 2². 2318. 115 = 1 col. 8. 17 Mette).

FRAGMENTS Kassel–Austin, *PCG* 4. 57–62, but earlier scholars use the numbering of Kock, *CAF* 1. 764 ff.
INTERPRETATION Meineke, *FCG* 1. 251; A. Körte, *RE* 10/2 (1919), 1884 f., 'Kantharos' 3.
W. G. A.

Cantiaci, inhabitants of Kent who formed a *civitas* of Roman *Britain, the only one to adopt not a tribal but a geographical title (Cantion, cf. Caes. *BGall.* 5. 14) which perhaps goes back to *Pytheas. Kent received numerous immigrations in the later pre-Roman period, and *Caesar himself records four kings there (*BGall.* 5. 22). The Cantiaci, therefore, were probably an artificial grouping of these elements created by Rome for local government purposes. The *civitas*-capital was Durovernum (Canterbury), but Durobrivae (Rochester) was a secondary centre round which were many villas. Richborough (Rutupiae), Dover (Portus Dubris), and Lympne (Portus Lemanis) were important ports and bases of the fleet, the Classis Britannica, and later became forts of the *Saxon Shore, as did Reculver (Regulbium). Excavations have demonstrated that Canterbury was preceded by an iron age *oppidum* and developed into a major Roman town. The theatre, a temple, and public baths have been examined. A substantial pottery industry existed along the Thames estuary in the Upchurch Marshes and iron was worked in the Weald.

A. Deticas, *The Cantiaci* (1983).
S. S. F.; M. J. M.

cantica, the parts of a Latin drama with musical accompaniment, as contrasted with *deverbia* or *diverbia* (unaccompanied passages, in iambic senarii). Two types may be distinguished: (1) continuous sequences of long lines (septenarii or octonarii) in iambics, trochaics, or anapaests, generally known nowadays as 'recitative' lines; (2) passages in a variety of metres, known in antiquity as *mutatis modis cantica* ('cantica with changes of metre'), in Plautus generally including lyric metres, whereas Terence normally uses combinations of 'recitative' metres. Modern discussions tend to restrict the term to the second type, which is a particular feature of the comedies of Plautus. See METRE, LATIN.
P. G. M. B.

Canuleius (*RE* 2), **Gaius** According to *Cicero (*Rep.* 2. 63) and *Livy (4. 1 ff.), as tribune of the plebs in 445 BC he passed the plebiscite (*plebiscitum*) revoking the ban on legitimate *marriages between patricians and plebeians contained in the Twelve Tables (see MARRIAGE LAW). *Dionysius (7) of Halicarnassus (*Ant. Rom.* 11. 53 ff.) says nothing of this but he and Livy ascribe to Canuleius a leading role in agitation for plebeian access to the consulship that resulted in the creation of the consular tribunate (see CONSUL). This narrative is fiction, based on the false assumption that the consular tribunate was introduced as a political compromise. Canuleius' speech in Livy (4. 3–5) was used as a model by *Claudius (*ILS* 212).

Ogilvie, *Comm. Livy 1–5*, 527 ff.; J. Linderski, in K. Raaflaub (ed.), *Social Struggles in Archaic Rome* (1986), 244 ff.
A. D.

Canusium, (mod. Canosa) chief city of *Daunia (Plin. *HN* 3. 104, Procop. *Goth.* 3. 18). It was not a Greek foundation (Strabo 6. 3. 7), but there was extensive Hellenization (see HELLENISM)

from the 4th cent. BC onwards, in pottery styles, coinage, and language (Hor. *Sat.* 1. 10. 30). It became a Roman ally in 318 BC, but revolted during the *Social War (3). After 89 BC, it became a *municipium*, and was granted colonial status by Marcus *Aurelius. It was a station on the *via Traiana, and was noted for its wool production. Its prosperity is reflected in the rich grave-goods, monumental buildings, and large order of *decuriones (*CIL* 9. 338).

E. Greco, *Magna Grecia* (1981); M. Marin, *Topografia storica del Daunia antica* (1970).
K. L.

Capaneus (Καπανεύς), in mythology, son of Hipponous and father of Sthenelus (*Il.* 4. 367; Hyg. *Fab.* 70. 1); one of the *Seven against Thebes, see also ADRASTUS (1). As he climbed on the walls, boasting that not even *Zeus should stop him, he was destroyed by a thunderbolt: Aesch. *Sept.* 427; Eur. *Phoen.* 1172 ff. (from the cyclic *Thebais*? See EPIC CYCLE). In art he appears especially in Italy, above all Etruria: *LIMC* 5/1 (1992), 952–3.
H. J. R.

Capena, the centre of a small independent territory on the west bank of the Tiber. The original settlers were closely related to the *Faliscans and spoke a similar, near-Latin Indo-European dialect. Politically the city was closely associated with Etruscan *Veii and was annexed to Rome after the destruction of Veii in 396 BC, but culturally the remains of its cemeteries reveal strong affinities also with the Faliscan cemeteries of Falerii and *Narce, as well as with the Sabine territories. Though a *municipium*, the city was of small importance in Roman times and was eventually abandoned. It occupied the hill of Civitucola, 4 km. (2½ mi.) north of the modern Capena, and is known chiefly from the contents of its cemeteries. Near the SE border of its territory, at Scorano, lay the important early river-crossing, market-town, and sanctuary of *Lucus Feroniae.

Not. Scav. 1906, 1922, and 1953; G. D. B. Jones, *PBSR* 1962, 116 ff.; 1963, 100 ff.; T. W. Potter, *The Changing Landscape of South Etruria* (1979), *passim*.
J. B. W.-P.; T. W. P.

capitalism is a term freighted with heavy ideological baggage. For economists and historians working within a Marxist tradition (see MARXISM AND CLASSICAL ANTIQUITY) it has a specific reference to an advanced socio-economic formation in which value, profit, and rationality are determined according to the productive modalities and mentalities of large-scale competitive businesses and price-fixing markets. On this view, the economies of Greece and Rome would be classed as pre- or non-capitalist. For non-Marxists of various stripes, capitalism in the sense of the productive deployment, especially investment, of fixed or variable capital assets may occur within a wider range of political, social, and economic contexts, including the societies of Greece and Rome.

The disagreement is not only ideological. To define Greece and Rome as pre-capitalist may imply also, for instance, the view that 'the economy' as a separately instituted sphere did not exist in classical antiquity and that the ancients therefore did not, because they could not, practise economic analysis properly so called (see ECONOMY, GREEK); or that ancient economic institutions with apparent modern equivalents in fact functioned quite differently from their modern counterparts or namesakes—ancient *banks, for example, being seen as merely glorified money-changers and usurers rather than lenders of risk or venture capital for productive economic investment. Those who, in contrast, regard the economy of the ancient world or local sectors thereof as in some useful sense capitalist detect differ-

Capitol, Capitolium

ences of scale and sophistication rather than of fundamental nature.

Such ideological and pragmatic disagreements have a century-long pedigree within Ancient History, going back to the creative controversy between Karl Bücher and Eduard Meyer over the proper periodization of world history in economic perspective. They received a further injection of fuel in the second quarter of the 20th cent. from the anthropologically influenced theorist Karl Polanyi, whose outlook owed more to Max Weber than to Karl Marx. But his 'substantivist' views engendered an equal and opposite reaction from those who, without necessarily accepting the pejorative labels of 'formalists' or 'modernizers' that Polanyi and his followers had foisted upon them, nevertheless argued that the ancients were motivated by a recognizably capitalist rationality and to that end instituted processes of wealth-creation susceptible of analysis in the formal terms of neoclassical micro-economic theory, including such mathematical tools as Leontief-style input-output tables.

The dispute shows no sign of proximate resolution, and indeed cannot formally be resolved in the absence of the requisite quantities of the right types of evidence, above all data amenable to statistical or quasi-statistical analysis. But whereas for exponents of the 'capitalist' hypothesis that absence is merely an accident of non-survival, for the Marxist or Weberian 'primitivists' it is itself further evidence in support of their classificatory hypothesis.

K. Marx, *Precapitalist Economic Formations* (1964; Ger. orig. 1857–8); M. I. Finley (ed.), *The Bücher–Meyer Controversy* (1979); K. Polanyi, *Primitive, Archaic and Modern Economies* (1968); M. I. Finley, *The Ancient Economy* (1973; 2nd edn. 1985); S. T. Lowry, *The Archaeology of Economic Ideas: The Classical Greek Tradition* (1988); J. R. Love, *Antiquity and Capitalism: Max Weber and the Sociological Foundations of Roman Civilization* (1991); E. E. Cohen, *Athenian Economy and Society: A Banking Perspective* (1992).   P. A. C.

Capitol, Capitolium, or mons Capitolinus,

the smallest of the hills of Rome: an isolated mass with two peaks, conventionally known as Capitolium proper and Arx. Legend associated the hill with Saturn, and recent archaeological work has revealed traces of bronze age settlement. It is best known as the site of the great temple begun by the Tarquins (see TARQUINIUS PRISCUS and SUPERBUS) and dedicated, in the first year of the republic according to tradition, to Jupiter Optimus Maximus, Juno, and Minerva. At all periods, the hill was less an inhabited part of the city than a citadel and religious centre. It was successfully defended against the Gauls in 390 BC. Here the consuls sacrificed at the beginning of the year and provincial governors took vows before going to their provinces; a sacrifice here was the culmination of the triumphal procession (see TRIUMPH). The original platform of the temple (62 m. × 53.5 m. (68 × 58½ yds.) in area) still exists; but the original temple, often embellished, was burnt in 83 BC. The new temple of Q. *Lutatius Catulus (2) (69 BC), was renovated and repaired by Augustus; it was burnt down during the course of fighting on the hill in AD 69, while *Vespasian's temple perished in the fire of AD 80. The last rebuilding was undertaken by *Domitian. On the north summit of the hill, the *arx*, lay the temple of Juno Moneta (344 BC), the *auguraculum* (an augur's observation post with primitive hut) and the *Tarpeian Rock, which overlooked the *forum Romanum. On the col between the hills, known as *inter duos lucos*, lay the temple of Veiovis (192 BC) and the *asylum* associated with Romulus. The east face of the hill was occupied by a massive building usually identified as the *Tabularium (1) and the approach-road from the Forum (*clivus Capitolinus*), paved in 174 BC.

Both hill and the temple of Jupiter were reproduced in many cities of Italy and (especially the western) provinces, and either hill or temple or both in *Constantinople; *Jerusalem, as refounded by *Hadrian, was styled *Aelia Capitolina*. The right to erect such *capitolia* was at first probably reserved for Roman *coloniae*. See FORUM.

Coarelli, *Roma* 26–37; M. Cristofani (ed.), *La grande Roma dei Tarquini* (1990), 68–76; Richardson, *Topog. Dict. Ancient Rome* 68–70; G. Tagliamonte and C. Reusser, in Steinby, *Lexicon* 226–34.
A. W. V. B.; I. A. R.; J. N.; J. R. P.

Cappadocia at one time designated the whole region between Lake Tatta and the *Euphrates, and from the *Euxine Sea to *Cilicia; but the northern part became 'Cappadocian Pontus' or simply '*Pontus', and the central and southern part Greater Cappadocia. This last consists of a rolling plateau, almost treeless in its western portion, some broken volcanic areas in the centre and the west (the cone of Mt. Argaeus reaches 3,660 m.: 12,000 ft.), and the ranges, for the most part well watered and well timbered, of the *Taurus and Antitaurus. A rigorous winter climate limits production to hardy cereals and fruits. Grazing was always important; the *Achaemenid kings levied a tribute of 1,500 horses, 50,000 sheep, and 2,000 mules, and Roman emperors kept studs of race-horses there. *Mines are mentioned of quartz, salt, Sinopic earth (cinnabar), and silver. Since the passes were frequently closed in winter the country was isolated.

In the second millennium BC this region of small principalities and temple-states was penetrated by the Assyrians, and became subject to the Hittite rulers of Boğazköy (see ASIA MINOR, PRECLASSICAL). After their fall (c.1000 BC) it lay open to invasion and devastation by Phrygians and later *Cimmerians. The Achaemenid conquest (585 BC) and subsequent land-grants to Persians prompted some Persian cultural influence (see *CAH*[2] plates to vol. 4, no. 43 for a late 5th-cent. fire-altar from Bünyän). There also existed large territories owned by temples and ruled by priests, such as those of Ma at Comana and Zeus at Venasa (see ANATOLIAN DEITIES).

The *satrap *Ariarathes I refused to submit to *Alexander (3) the Great and was killed by *Perdiccas (3). His descendants, restored after 301, added Cataonia to their possessions and were recognized as kings from c.255 BC, although *Seleucus (1) I claimed to have conquered part of ('Seleucid') Cappadocia (App. *Syr.* 55); Seleucid possessions here were conquered by *Ariarathes II (Diod. Sic. 31. 19. 5), perhaps c.260 BC. *Ariarathes IV supported *Antiochus (3) III against Rome at Magnesia (190 BC), but he and his successors thereafter were pro-Roman. Even though Graeco-Macedonian settlers are hardly attested, a gradual Hellenization (see HELLENISM) took place under these philhellene rulers, reflected in the adoption of Greek personal names, cultural institutions (e.g. a *gymnasium at Tyana: *SEG* 1. 466), and civic organization (e.g. the 2nd-cent. BC decree from Hanisa published by Robert). Devastated by *Tigranes (1) of *Armenia in the Mithradatic Wars, Cappadocia was restored by Pompey. Antony replaced the royal line, which had proved disloyal in the Parthian invasion, with the energetic *Archelaus (5), who renamed Mazaca *Caesarea (1) and founded Archelais. Annexed in AD 17, Cappadocia was a procuratorial province until *Vespasian, when (72) it was joined with *Galatia under a consular legate until *Trajan, who, between 107 and 113, formed a new province of Cappadocia with Pontus which remained united to the time of

Diocletian. With Rome's *de facto* acceptance of the Euphrates as its eastern frontier, Cappadocia from Vespasian on was integrated into Rome's eastern *limes by the construction of roads and forts and the establishment of legionary garrisons at Satala and *Melitene; the system survived until beyond the reign of *Justinian, who repaired it. Roman Cappadocia remained chiefly a region of large estates (now including imperial properties), cities on the Greek model (in spite of Rome's interest in promoting *urbanism) hardly occupying a third of the territory. Political Romanization was slow too: before 200 only one senatorial family (from Tyana) is attested (H. Halfmann, *Die Senatoren aus dem östlichen Teil des Imperium Romanum* (1979) no. 130). See ARIARAMNES; ARIARATHES; ARIOBAZARNES.

> L. Robert, *Noms indigènes dans l'Asie Mineure gréco-romaine* 1 (1963), 457 ff.; B. Simonetta, *The Coinage of the Cappadocian Kings* (1977); C. P. Jones, *Chiron* 1982, 143 f.; *CAH* 7²/1 (1984), 426; R. Teja, *ANRW* 2. 7. 2 (1980), 1083 ff.; T. Mitford, ibid. 1169 ff. (*limes*); S. Mitchell, *Anatolia* 1 (1993). T. R. S. B.; A. J. S. S.

Capreae (now Capri), a precipitous small island off the Sirens' shrine on the Promontorium Minervae of the Bay of *Naples, and part of Naples' territory until Augustus appropriated it for a luxury estate: wild, secure, remote, and picturesque (the Roman coastal *villas' architecture made full use of the sheer cliffs, sea-caves such as the Blue Grotto, and views to the mainland). *Tiberius, whose lifestyle during his withdrawal here for most of AD 26–37 was the object of much speculation and anecdote at Rome, developed the estate, building twelve villas named after the gods (Tac. *Ann.* 4. 67), of which there are important remains at Marina di Capri, Damecuta, and (probably the principal residence, 'Villa Iovis') on the easternmost crag. The estate remained imperial, being used for political *exile under Commodus (Cass. Dio 72. 4).

> A. Maiuri, *Capri: Storia e monumenti* (1956). N. P.

Caprotina, title of *Juno, from Nonae Caprotinae ('Nones of the Wild *Fig') on 7 July, to whom freedwomen and female slaves sacrificed, then fighting a mock battle with fig-tree sticks (Varro, *Ling.* 6. 18; Macrob. *Sat.* 1. 11. 36 ff.). These activities do not appear in extant calendars. The connection of fig and Juno implies an original fertility ritual (cf. Plut. *Rom.* 29; Latte, *RR* 106 ff.).

> *Kl. Pauly* 1. 1046 ff.; *RE* 17. 849 ff.; J. Bremmer, *Roman Myth and Mythography* (1987), 76 ff.; R. E. A. Palmer, *Roman Religion and Roman Empire* (1974), 7 ff. C. R. P.

Capsa (mod. Gafsa), an oasis in southern Tunisia. Originally a considerable Libyan settlement (*Jugurtha used it as a treasury: Strab. 17. 3. 12), it was destroyed by C. *Marius (1) in 106 BC (Sall. *Iug.* 89 ff.). It later revived, becoming a *municipium under *Trajan and subsequently a *colonia*. Under the Byzantines, it was a centre of defence against the desert nomads, with a fort built by Justinian's general Solomon. The only visible monuments are two pools, dedicated to Neptune and the nymphs. The local museum contains a unique 4th-cent. AD mosaic, an unusually detailed depiction of athletic contests, from a settlement 60 km. (37 mi.) east of Capsa.

> *PECS* 195; C. Saumagne, *Cahiers de Tunisie* 1962, 519–31. Mosaic: M. Khanoussi, *MDAI(R)* 1991, 315–22. B. H. W.; R. J. A. W.

captatio benevolentiae This phrase—'fishing for good will'— has no ancient authority as a technical term, but well describes what the ancient rhetoricians advise for the exordium of a speech (see RHETORIC, ROMAN). The hearer is to be rendered 'attentive, teachable, and well disposed': and the prescription for this last requirement involves a display of modesty and good manners on the part of the speaker.

> See *Rhetorica ad Alexandrum* 29; Cic. *Inv. rhet.* 1. 16. 21, *De or* 1. 119; Quint. *Inst.* 4. 1. E. Curtius, *European Literature and the Latin Middle Ages* (1953; Eng. trans.), 409. D. A. R.

Capua (mod. S. Maria di Capua Vetere), settled in the 9th cent. BC. The early finds show a close resemblance to Villanovan artefacts from Etruria (see VILLANOVAN CULTURE). By *c*.600, Capua was an *Etruscan city, whose material culture supports *Velleius' foundation-date (Vell. Pat. 1. 7. 2), and one of the principal cities of *Campania. It was the head of a league of twelve cities, including *Atella, *Cales, *Casilinum, Calatia, *Suessula, and Acerrae. The entire surrounding area was known as the *ager Campanus*. After 474 BC, when the Etruscans were defeated by a combined force of Syracusans and Cumaeans (see SYRACUSE; CUMAE), Etruscan power in Campania began to wane. *Oscan expansion, which had hitherto taken the form of gradual peaceful settlement, became more rapid and aggressive, and in *c*.425 Capua was conquered, along with *Cumae (421), *Paestum (410), and most of inland Campania (Diod. Sic. 12. 31). Under Oscan rule, Capua became one of the most powerful cities in Italy. It became Oscanized, as shown by the material culture and inscriptions, and was proverbial in later authors for wealth and arrogance (Ath. 12. 36). Initial contacts with Rome developed *c*.343, Capua possibly seeking assistance against a fresh wave of Oscan invaders from *Samnium; Capua is central to the problem of the First Samnite War. In 338, the settlement after the Latin War (see LATINI) included citizenship for the *equites Campani* and *civitas sine suffragio* for the rest of the Campanians (Livy 7. 29–8. 14, see CITIZENSHIP, ROMAN). There was surprisingly little Capuan involvement in the Second and Third Samnite wars. It remained loyal to Rome, although there were pro-Roman and anti-Roman factions in most Campanian cities (Diod. Sic. 19. 76; Livy 9. 25). The construction of the *via Appia between Rome and Capua in 312 emphasized the growing links between Rome and Campania. In 216, however, the anti-Roman faction at Capua gained power and the city defected to Carthage, remaining an important ally of *Hannibal until its recapture in 211. The leaders of the revolt were executed and Capua deprived of both its territory and its political rights; it was now directly governed by a Roman praetor. A colony was founded there in 83, and it regained its civic rights in 58 BC. Part of the fertile *ager Campanus* was used for colonies, but most of it was rented out by the censors at considerable profit. Exempt from the Gracchan land reforms, (see SEMPRONIUS GRACCHUS (3) TI.) it was distributed to 20,000 colonists by Caesar (Cic. *Leg. agr.* 1. 7; Vell. Pat. 2. 44). Imperial Capua was a prosperous city, as reflected in many public buildings and inscriptions. It was still a leading city in the 4th cent. AD (Auson. *Ordo nob. urb.* 46 ff. = pp. 170–1 Green) but was sacked by *Vandals in 456 and finally destroyed by Saracens in 840. There is extensive and well-preserved evidence of Oscan and Roman tombs, houses, and public buildings; inscriptions set up by the *magistri Campani* give a valuable insight into the political and social structure. See CNOSSUS.

> J. Heurgon, *Capoue préromaine* (1942); E. T. Salmon, *Samnium and the Samnites* (1965); M. W. Frederiksen, *PBSR* 1959; *Campania* (1984); S. de Caro and A. Greco, *Campania* (1981). K. L.

Capys, (1) father of *Anchises (*Il.* 20. 239); (2) companion of Aeneas and founder of *Capua (*Aen.* 10. 145); (3) king of *Alba Longa (Livy 1. 3. 8).

> J. Heurgon and G. d'Anna, *Enc. Virg.* 'Capi'. S. J. Ha.

Caracalla

Caracalla See AURELIUS ANTONINUS (1), M.

Caratacus (the form Caractacus is found only in an inferior manuscript), son of *Cunobel(l)inus. He took part in the resistance in *Britain to the Roman invasion of AD 43 perhaps at Bagendon, near Cirencester, among his subjects the *Dobunni (so emend Cass. Dio's Βοδούννων) rather than in Kent and Essex, as Dio states. He was easily able to escape over the Severn to the *Silures of Monmouthshire, where he renewed hostilities against the governor *Ostorius Scapula, by whom, however, he was defeated somewhere in the hills of the Welsh border. He fled to *Cartimandua, who surrendered him to the Romans (51). Tacitus puts into his mouth a rhetorical speech delivered at Rome to *Claudius, who spared his life.

> Cass. Dio 60. 20. 1–2; Tac. *Ann.* 12. 33–7. S. S. Frere, *Britannia*, 3rd edition (1987). C. E. S.; M. J. M.

Carausius, Marcus Aurelius Maus(aeus?), a Menapian of humble origin, who had served as a helmsman, was given a command in AD 285 or 286 to suppress barbarian (Saxon) raiders in the English Channel. After allegedly being accused of retaining recaptured booty, he moved to Britain and proclaimed himself emperor, maintaining himself against attempts to dislodge him, striking coinage, from c.290 even claiming recognition from his 'brothers' *Diocletian and *Maximian, and gaining control of Gaul as far as Rouen. He is said to have used barbarian (Frankish) troops and may have constructed some of the *Saxon Shore forts. He was ejected from Boulogne by *Constantius I Caesar in 293, following which he was assassinated and replaced by *Allectus, his *rationalis* (finance minister).

> *Pan. Lat. Vet.* 10 (2); 8 (5); Aur. Vict. *Caes.* 39; Eutr. 9. 13 f.; *RIC* 5 2; *RIB* 2291. N. Shiel, *The Episode of Carausius and Allectus* (1977); A. R. Birley, *The Fasti of Roman Britain* (1981), 309 ff.; P. J. Casey, *Carausius and Allectus* (1995). A. R. Bi.

Carbo See PAPIRIUS.

Carcinus (1), son of Xenotimus of the Attic *deme of *Thoricus, a tragic poet who won a victory at the *Dionysia of 446 BC. He made a dedication as a *trierarch c.450, and served as a general on a naval expedition in 431 (Thuc. 2. 23. 2). He and his sons, who were dancers, are mocked by *Aristophanes (1) at *Clouds* 1260 f., *Wasps* 1497–1534, *Peace* 781–95, 864.

> *TrGF* 1² 128–31; A. H. Sommerstein on Ar. *Wasps* 1501; *APF* 283–5. A. L. B.

Carcinus (2), son of *Xenocles and grandson of *Carcinus (1), a tragic poet who is said to have written 160 plays (*Suda*). He competed at the *Lenaea c.376 BC, and won the first of his eleven victories at the *Dionysia shortly before 372. He paid several visits to the court of *Dionysius (2) II of Syracuse (Diod. Sic. 5. 1. 1). He was cited by *Lysias and *Menander (1), and *Plutarch (*De glor. Ath.* 7) speaks very highly of his *Aerope*. *Aristotle often refers to him: *Poet.* 16 (recognition scene in *Thyestes*), 17 (a fatal error of stagecraft in *Amphiaraus*), *Eth. Nic.* 7, 8 (the endurance of Cercyon in *Alope*), *Rh.* 2. 23 (an argument in *Medea*, apparently a version in which Medea did not kill her children), 3. 16 (arguments of Jocasta in *Oedipus*). Titles also included *Aias*, *Orestes*, *Semele*, and perhaps *Tyro*.

> *TrGF* 1². 210–15; *Musa Tragica* 146–55, 288–9; G. Xanthakis-Karamanos, *Studies in Fourth-Century Tragedy* (1980), 33–8, 87–9. A. L. B.

Carcinus (3), of Naupactus (?6th or 5th cent. BC), named by *Charon (2) of Lampsacus as author of the *Naupactia*, a genealo-gical epic (see GENEALOGY) elsewhere cited anonymously. It included the *Argonaut story.

> Davies, *EGF* 145–9; Bernabé, *PEG* 1. 123–6; G. L. Huxley, *Greek Epic Poetry* (1969), 68–73. M. L. W.

Cardia, a Greek city on the western shore of the Thracian *Chersonesus (1) near the head of the gulf of Melas. The exact location is unknown owing to the absence of excavation in the area, but it is probably located on Cape Bakla, where early 20th-cent. maps indicate ruins. Founded by *Miletus and *Clazo-menae in the late 7th cent. BC, Cardia received an influx of Athenian colonists led by the elder Miltiades (see MILTIADES), as the Athenians manifested a growing interest in the region. Recognizing Cardia's strategic position at the narrowest part of the peninsula, Miltiades strengthened its fortifications and built a wall across the neck of the isthmus. Miltiades' successors abandoned the city to the Persians in 493, but by the mid-5th cent. it was restored to Athenian influence. An object of continuing struggle between Athens and the Thracians and later between Athens and Macedon, Cardia became allied with *Philip (1) II in 352/1 and was ruled by the tyrant Hecataeus during *Alexander (3) the Great's reign. One of Alexander's successors, *Lysi-machus, destroyed the city and removed some of its inhabitants to the new foundation of Lysimacheia near by. Although Lysi-macheia remained important, Cardia's fortunes were restored, and by Strabo's time it was the largest city in the Chersonesus. The city produced two famous sons: *Eumenes (3) was secretary to Philip (1) and Alexander (3) of Macedon, and was a major figure in the wars of the Successors. *Hieronymus (1) was an eyewitness to the establishment of the early Hellenistic king-doms, and his account is our primary source for those events.

> B. Isaac, *The Greek Settlements in Thrace Until the Macedonian Conquest* (1986). E. N. B.

careers

Greek In virtually all the Greek-speaking areas, pressures to evolve clear career structures in public life were countered by social or political considerations, thereby preventing the emergence of recognizable *cursus honorum* on the Roman republican model. Though, for example, *Thucydides (2) (5. 66. 3–4) credited the Spartan army with a clear hierarchical command structure, promotions and careers within it were by appointment and co-optation rather than by election. Hence they were as much a matter of belonging to a notable lineage, or of influence with kings or ephors, as of merit. At Athens a simple hierarchy of military command in both infantry and cavalry is attested, while re-election to the generalship (see STRATĒGOI) was common and helped to provide a clear career path for professional soldiers, often interspersed with spells of mercenary command abroad. In contrast, careers in civilian office-holding in Classical Athens were effectively precluded by the short-term tenure and non-repeatability of office, by collegiality, and above all by selection by lot (see SORTITION). A young politician had to use the assembly (*ekklēsia*) rather than office-holding, and tended to begin by lawcourt advocacy or by serving a senior politician as his 'friend' or 'flatterer' (e.g. [Dem.] 59. 43) before establishing his own position and his own clique of followers. Public career structures in other Greek states are barely traceable for lack of detailed evidence.

The Hellenistic courts developed more of a career structure, alike for their ministers, envoys, and army commanders, ostensibly formalized by the growth of graded titles such as 'friend', 'first friend', 'companion', and 'relative' (of the king). (See FRIEND-SHIP, RITUALIZED.) However, here too patronage could easily override merit, status was precarious, and recruitment as much a matter of family succession as of individual promise.

Outside public life, some professions such as doctors or performing artists (see DIONYSUS, ARTISTS OF) formed guilds with their own procedures and officers, but little in the way of formalized career structures is perceptible.

E. Bikerman, *Institutions des Séleucides* (1938), 40–50; *DFA*[3], 279–321; J. K. Davies, *Wealth and the Power of Wealth in Classical Athens* (1981), 122–4; S. Hodkinson, *Chiron* 1983, 254–65; R. E. Allen, *The Attalid Kingdom* (1983), 129–35; J. F. Lazenby, *The Spartan Army* (1985), ch. 1.   J. K. D.

Roman Ancient society was not so organized as to provide a course of professional employment which affords opportunity for advancement. The Latin phrase normally translated as 'career' is the Ciceronian **cursus honorum*, which refers to the series of elective magistracies open to senators: those of *quaestor, held at 30 from *Sulla's legislation onwards, but five years younger under the Principate; of *aedile; of *praetor, held at 39 under the late Republic, but by some at 30 under the Principate; and of *consul, held at 42 after Sulla (cf. the career of *Cicero), by patricians at 33 under the Principate, and by new men (see NOVUS HOMO) at 38 or later (cf. the career of Cn. *Iulius Agricola). Successful election to these posts depended on birth and achievement (cf. Tac. *Ann.* 4. 4: high birth, military distinction, and outstanding gifts in civil life, i.e. forensic or political oratory, knowledge of the law: note the order). Success might be achieved not only in the magistracy that preceded but in preliminary offices civil and military (as one of the **vigintisexviri* or **tribuni militum*), and in positions held at Rome, in Italy, or the provinces, under the republic often involving command of troops, that normally followed the praetorship and consulship (propraetorships, -consulships, allocated by seniority and the lot, see PRO CONSULE, PRO PRAETORE); or that were devised under the Principate to get previously neglected work done (e.g. curatorships of roads in Italy; see CURA(TIO)). After AD 14 elections were effectively conducted in the senate and a man's success depended on the verdict of his peers or on his ability to strike bargains with his rivals' supporters; but *Augustus' *lex Iulia de maritandis ordinibus* (see MARRIAGE LAW, ROMAN) provided speedier advancement for men married with children, while the opinion of the emperor, known or surmised, was of great and increasing weight (cf. *ILS* 244. 4; Pliny, *Pan.* 66), hence too the favour of his advisers. Some posts, notably legionary commands and governorships of regions that were part of his 'province' (e.g. *Syria, *Gaul (Transalpine) outside Narbonensis), were in his direct gift, though the senate ratified such appointments (both types of officer were 'legates (**legati*) of Augustus'). The influence exercised by the emperor has given rise to the view that there was a special type of career 'in the Emperor's service' regularly involving particularly speedy advancement (especially between praetorship and consulship) enjoyed by 'military men' (*viri militares*). A more cautious hypothesis is that men advanced themselves using what gifts they had; those who took to army life necessarily were the appointees of the emperor. Each appointment was ad hoc and might depend on a number of factors, e.g. current needs, a man's availability, experience, record, current effectiveness of his supporters, but precedent was also relevant.

The word 'career' is often applied to the posts offered by the emperor to men of equestrian and lower status, whether in official positions (e.g. **praefectus praetorio* = prefect of the prae-torian guard, or *procuratores Augusti* in his provinces, supervising tax collecting) or as his private agents (also *procuratores*) managing his private estates (see PROCURATOR). But although such posts mostly had their distinctive standing, and were normally preceded by up to three military posts, and although (because of this) recognizable patterns of advancement developed (cf. the two Trajanic 'careers' *ILS* 1350 and 1352), appointments were again ad hoc, *ad hominem* (cf. *AE* 1962, 183), intermittent, and accepted on a basis of mutual goodwill, with character rather than professionalism the overt criterion. Imperial freedmen and even slaves who held subordinate positions in the organizations enjoyed lower standing, but their continuous service over long periods of time justifies the application of the term 'career' to their activities (see FREEDMEN; SLAVERY).

In the army below the rank of tribune it is legitimate to speak of a career, since the minimum period of service outside the praetorian guard was 20 years. Men frequently record their advance through minor posts of privilege (e.g. *tesserarius*, OC watchword) to (e.g.) one of the 60 centurionates of a legion, or upwards through legionary centurionates (e.g. *ILS* 2653) (see CENTURIO).

Elsewhere the word is inappropriate; outside the limited state apparatus the ancient world lacked the great organizations that now provide methodical advancement in business and industry.

Senators: A. Astin, *Latomus* 1958, 49 ff. (pre-Sullan rules); J. Morris, *Listy Filologické* 1964, 316 ff. (Principate); E. Birley, *Proc. Brit. Acad.* 1953, 197 ff. ('Emperor's service'); cf. B. Campbell, *JRS* 1975, 11 ff. *Equites*: H.-G. Pflaum, *Carrières procuratoriennes* (1960–1). Soldiers: G. R. Watson, *The Roman Soldier* (1969), 75 ff. Slaves: P. R. C. Weaver, *Familia Caesaris* (1972).   B. M. L.

Caria, mountainous region inhabited by Carians in SW Asia Minor south of the *Maeander, with Greek cities (*Cnidus and *Halicarnassus) occupying the salient peninsulas and mixed communities on the shores of the gulfs. Until the 4th cent. BC the pastoral Carians lived mainly in hilltop villages grouped under native dynasties (some of which paid tribute to the Athenian empire in the 5th cent.) and organized round sanctuaries, the principal seat being *Mylasa. The Carians claimed to be indigenous; but in Greek tradition they came from the islands, and the interior of Caria is in fact lacking in prehistoric sites. They preserved their language until Hellenistic times. We have some inscriptions (mostly from *Egypt) written in an alphabet, partly of Greek origin, which is now approaching a decipherment; it seems possible (though it is not yet fully demonstrated) that the language may be *Indo-European and belong to the Anatolian group. (See ANATOLIAN LANGUAGES.)

Carians were early associated with *Ionians in mercenary service (especially under the Pharaohs; Carians continued to live in Egypt even after the Persian take-over in 525 BC: Hdt. 2. 61 and archaeological evidence). Subjected by *Croesus and then by Persia, they joined in the *Ionian Revolt and ambushed a Persian army. The coastal communities joined the *Delian League at the time of the Eurymedon campaign. Under the rule of the Hecatomnids (*c.*395–after 334), and especially of *Mausolus, Carian Hellenism was intensively furthered and modern cities were planned to promote the Greek way of life (this Hecatomnid 'plan' for Caria is controversial); but the Hecatomnids also promoted the local element so that one can speak of an active and simultaneous policy of 'Carianization'. Thus the Hecatomnids put up *Greek* dedications at *Labraunda, *Amyzon, and *Sinuri, but made no big splash at the more famous panhellenic sanctuaries, preferring (it seems on present evidence) to patronize these Carian places. See also APHRODISIAS.

Strabo 14. 651 ff.; L. and J. (J. and L.) Robert, *La Carie* 2 (1954), and *Fouilles d'Amyzon* (1983); G. Bean, *Turkey Beyond the Maeander*, 2nd edn. (1980); S. Hornblower, *Mausolus* (1982), and *CAH* 6² (1994), ch. 8a; T. Linders and P. Hellström (eds.), *Architecture and Society in Hecatomnid Caria* (1989); N. Demand, *Urban Relocation in Archaic and Classical Greece* (1990), chs. 10–11; M. Mellink, *CAH* 3²/2 (1991), 662 ff.; S. Ruzicka, *Politics of a Persian Dynasty: The Hecatomnids in the Fourth Century BC* (1992). On Carian language: I.-J. Adiego, *Studia carica* (1993).

J. M. C.; A. M. Da., S. H.

Carinus, Marcus Aurelius, elder son of M. Aurelius *Carus, left by him as Caesar in the west, when he marched against Persia (AD 282). Made Augustus before his father's death, Carinus succeeded him as colleague of his brother *Numerianus and crushed the rebel '*corrector Venetiae', Iulianus, in battle near *Verona. Early in 285 Diocletian, appointed emperor to succeed Numerianus, ended a difficult campaign at the battle of the Margus in Moesia.

*PIR*² A 1473; M. Peachin, *Roman Imperial Titulature and Chronology, AD 235–284* (1990), 98 ff.

H. M.

Caristia (*cara cognatio*), Roman family festival on 22 February. Ovid (*Fast.* 2. 617–38) makes it a reunion of surviving family members after the *Parentalia's rites to the departed (February 13–21), and the presence of the ancestral spirits (*Lares: *Fast.* 2. 631–4) supports that. Valerius Maximus (2. 1. 8) adds that no outsiders were admitted and family quarrels were settled. It appears under the date in the calendars of *Filocalus and Polemius Silvius, under February in the *Menologia rustica*.

Inscr. Ital 13. 2. 414; Latte, *RR* 274 n. 3, 339 n. 2; F. Schneider, *ARW* 1920/1, 385–9.

C. R. P.

carmen, from *cano* (?), 'something chanted', a formulaic or structured utterance, not necessarily in verse. In early Latin the word was used especially for religious utterances such as spells and charms: the laws of the *Twelve Tables contained provisions against anyone who chanted a *malum carmen*, 'evil spell' (Plin. *HN* 28. 2. 18). *Carmen* became the standard Latin term for song, and hence poem (sometimes especially lyric and related genres: cf. C. O. Brink on Hor. *Epist.* 2. 2. 25, 59–60, 91), but the possibilities of danger and enchantment inherent in the broader sense continued to be relevant, and there is often play on the different senses (see e.g. Ov. *Met.* 7. 167).

O. Hey, *TLL* 'carmen'; J. Quasten, *RAC* 'carmen'; B. Neumeyr, in O. Hiltbrunner (ed.), *Bibliographie zur lateinischen Wortforschung* 3 (1988), 261–71; C. Thulin, *Italische sakrale Poesie und Prosa* (1906); E. Norden, *Ant. Kunstpr.* (1909), 160–1, and *Aus altrömischen Priesterbüchern* (1939).

P. G. F., D. P. F.

Carmen arvale, hymn sung during the sacrifice to *Dea Dia by the *fratres arvales* (arval brethren). Even if known only from an inscriptional copy of AD 218 (A. Gordon, *Album of Dated Latin Inscriptions* (1958), 44 no. 276), marred by errors of transcription, this hymn is of great interest, because at the least it is older than the 4th cent. BC (*Lases* for *Lares*). Norden believed that it revealed the influence of Greek poetry. In spite of the problems that it poses, the hymn is understandable. It is addressed to the *Lares, Semones (see SEMO SANCUS DIUS FIDIUS) and *Mars. The first two groups of deities are invoked three times one after the other, Mars three times thrice. The *carmen* culminates in a quintuple cry of triumph (*triumpe*). In the context of the sacrifice to Dea Dia, these divinities are requested to guarantee the integrity of the land and the harvest, so that Dea Dia can exercise her office there.

E. Norden, *Aus altrömischen Priesterbüchern* (1939); J. Scheid, *Romulus et ses frères: Le collège des frères arvales, modèle du culte publique dans la Rome des empereurs* (1990), 616 ff.

J. Sch.

Carmen de bello Aegyptiaco (or **Actiaco**) is the title given to a poem of which 52 more or less complete hexameters in eight columns and a number of fragments survive on PHerc. 817, published in 1809 by Ciampitti and attributed by him and many since for weak reasons to C. *Rabirius (2); it might be part of the *Res Romanae* of *Cornelius Severus. It deals with Octavian's Egyptian campaign after Actium and *Cleopatra VII's preparations for suicide.

EDITIONS G. Ferrara (1908), G. Garuti (1958).

On the papyrus see R. Seider, *Paläographie der Lat. Papyri* 2. 1 (1978), 4; E. O. Wingo, *Latin Punctuation* (1972), 54. See Courtney, *FLP* 334.

E. C.

Carmen de figuris, anonymous Latin poem (*c.* AD 400), dedicated to *Arusianus Messius, and describing figures of speech in 186 hexameters. Three lines are devoted to each figure, defining it and giving one or two examples. The material is taken from *Rutilius Lupus and *Alexander (12). The prosody is late, but aphaeresis of final *s* and ancient forms (e.g. *indupetravi*) imitate preclassical poetry.

PLM 3 272–85; for sources see Halm, *Rhet. Lat. Min.*, 63–70; Schanz–Hosius, § 1020.

O. S.; M. W.

Carmen de ponderibus et mensuris (perhaps *c.* AD 400), a Latin didactic poem in 208 hexameter verses, once ascribed to *Priscian, but now attributed to one Rem(m)ius Favinus (or Flav[in]us), sets out the several systems of *weights and *measures adopted in ancient Greece and Rome. It includes two interesting technical accounts: (1) a hydrometer for measuring the specific gravity of liquids (ll. 103–21), similar to the instruments attributed elsewhere to the Alexandrians *Menelaus (3), *Pappus, and *Hypatia; and (2) a method used by *Archimedes for solving the problem of the crown (to distinguish an alloy from pure gold or silver) by means of a hydrostatic balance (ll. 125–62), much like the instrument attributed to Archimedes by Menelaus.

F. Hultsch, *Metrologicorum scriptorum reliquiae* 2 (1866), 24–31, 88–98; M. Clagett, *Science of Mechanics in the Middle Ages* (1964), 85–93; W. R. Knorr, *Ancient Sources of the Medieval Tradition of Mechanics* (1982), 123–5; D. K. Raïos, *Archimède, Ménélaos d'Alexandrie et le 'Carmen de Ponderibus et Mensuris'* (1989).

W. R. K.

Carmen Nelei See NELEI CARMEN.

Carmen Priami ('The Song of Priam'), a poem in *Saturnian verse, of which *Varro, *Ling.* 7. 28 quotes one line; an archaizing composition, apparently written after and in reaction to *Ennius' *Annals*.

Courtney, *FLP* 44.

P. G. M. B.

Carmen Saliare or **Carmina Saliaria,** the ancient hymn(s) of the *Salii in *Saturnian verse, unintelligible (Hor. *Epist.* 2. 1. 85–6; Quint. *Inst.* 1. 6. 40) despite commentaries by L. *Aelius and others; the few fragments, already corrupt in antiquity, mostly illustrate obsolete diction (e.g. intervocalic *s* [z] = classical *r*). As transmitted, they include (fr. 1) the syncopated imperative *cante* 'sing' (= *canite*) and the title *diuom deo* 'god of gods' for Janus, (fr. 2) the unchanged Indo-European form *tremonti* '(they) tremble' (= *tremunt*, cf. Doric Greek -οντι) and the name *Leucesios* (or *Lucetios*: Macrob. *Sat.* 1. 15. 14) '(god) of light' for Jupiter; but text and interpretation remain speculative and controversial (one theory derives them from a misunderstood commentary).

TEXT Morel–Büchner, *FPL* 1–5.

DISCUSSION AND BIBLIOGRAPHY G. Radke, *Archaisches Latein* (1981), 115–23.   L. A. H.-S.

Carmentis or **Carmenta** (the latter Greek and seldom Latin, as Hyg. *Fab.* 277. 2), meaning 'full of *carmen* (divine incantation)'; see A. Ernout and A. Meillet, *Dictionnaire étymologique de la langue latine*² (1959), s.v. 'carmen'; A. Walde and J. B. Hoffmann, *Lateinisches etymologisches Wörterbuch* (1938–54), s.v. 'carmen'; Ogilvie, *Comm. Livy 1–5* 1. 7. 8, and, for other etymologies, Ov. *Fast.* 1. 619–20, Plut. *Quaest. Rom.* 56. Connected with *childbirth (cf. the two Carmentes, Prorsa and Postverta, in reference to the child's position in the womb: Varro, *ARD* frs. 103–4 Cardauns), prophecy (Serv. on *Aen.* 8. 51), or both (*fasti Praenestini*, 11 January), although the prohibition on leather (Ov. *Fast.* 1. 629; cf. Varro, *Ling.* 7. 84) implies childbirth. Mythologically a prophetess, mother of *Evander paralleling *Themis of the Greek tradition (Serv. on *Aen.* 8. 336), she (Hyg. *Fab.* 277. 2; Isid. *Etym.* 1. 4. 1, 5. 39. 11) or Evander (Tac. *Ann.* 11. 14) taught the aborigines writing. As a nymph (Serv. on *Aen.* 8. 51), she was perhaps a water-goddess; connection with divine incantation (*carmen*) and identification with the *Camenae associated her with poetry; thus Livius Andronicus began his translation of the *Odyssey* by implicitly equating 'Camena' with 'Muse', which later literary conceits of the spring of Hippocrene on Mt. *Helicon furthered; cf. Bömer on Ov. *Fasti* 1. 462. She had a *flamen* (Cic. *Brut.* 56, *CIL* 6. 31032; see FLAMINES), which implies the cult's antiquity (Latte, *RR* 36–7), a two-day festival (11 and 15 January), and a shrine at the foot of the Capitoline hill, near the Porta Carmentalis (Livy 2. 49. 8 with Ogilvie's notes; Platner–Ashby, 101, 405).

Wissowa, *RK* 219–21; *Inscr. Ital.* 13. 2. 394–6, 398; Cardauns on Varro, *ARD* 103–4.   C. R. P.

carmina triumphalia, songs sung, in accordance with ancient custom, by soldiers at a *triumph, either in praise of their victorious general or in a satiric ribaldry supposed to avert the evil eye from him.

Schanz–Hosius 1⁴. 21–2; Baehr. *FPR* 330–1, 383.   J. W. D.; S. R. F. P.

Carmo (mod. Carmona), some 40 km. (25 mi.) east of Hispalis (Seville) in Further Spain, had been an important centre of the *Tartessus cultural grouping. It was later walled by the Carthaginians and became the stronghold of the Iberian chief Luxinius. It was prominent in the Second *Punic War and in Ser. *Sulpicius Galba (1)'s operations of 151 BC; in 49 BC it declared for Caesar. Municipal status (see MUNICIPIUM) may not have been achieved before Gaius (1). Strength and prosperity, sustained into the Muslim period, are illustrated by standing Roman walls, an amphitheatre, and an extensive cemetery.

G. Bonsor, *Rev. Arch.* 1899, 1 ff.; A. Jiménez, *La puerta de Sevilla en Carmona* (1989); M. Bendala, *La necrópolis romana de Carmona* (1976).   S. J. K.

Carnea, the main Dorian festival, honouring *Apollo Carneius. We know little about its content except at *Sparta, where it took place in late summer and lasted nine days; and even here the evidence is fragmentary. The Spartan Carnea was above all a choral and musical festival of *Panhellenic importance. The most picturesque rite was that of the σταφυλοδρόμοι, 'grape runners', one of whom, draped in woollen fillets, was chased by the others: it counted as 'a good omen for the city' if he was caught. Carnea runners are also attested on *Thera and at *Cnidus. We also hear

that the Carnea was 'an imitation of the military way of life', at which men selected by *phratries camped out and dined together in huts (*Demetrius (12) of Scepsis in Ath. 141e). See SPARTAN CULTS.

Burkert, *GR* 234–6; W. F. Otto, *Das Wort der Antike* (1962), 76–84. See also bibliog. to HYACINTHUS (Petterson item).   R. C. T. P.

Carneades from Cyrene (214/3–129/8 BC), the most important representative of the sceptical *Academy, often called the founder of the New Academy as distinct from the Middle Academy of *Arcesilaus (1). He studied philosophy in the Academy under Hegesinus, but also took lessons in Stoic dialectic from *Diogenes (3) of Babylon. Carneades became scholarch some time before 155, when he was sent by Athens on an embassy to Rome together with the Stoic Diogenes and the Peripatetic *Critolaus. He resigned as head of the Academy in 137/6 and was succeeded by a younger namesake. Carneades was famous for his dialectical and rhetorical skills. He attracted many students, and his lectures drew large audiences, even from the schools of the orators. He left no writings, but his arguments were recorded in many volumes by his pupil *Clitomachus.

Carneades used the method of arguing for and against any given view to criticize all dogmatic philosophies, covering not only epistemology, but also physics, theology, and ethics. He also continued the debate between the Academy and the Stoa, whose doctrines had been defended against earlier sceptical objections by *Chrysippus. In the dispute about the criterion of truth, he expanded the argument about the impossibility of distinguishing between cognitive and non-cognitive impressions. Most influential became his reply to the standard objection that sceptical withholding of assent (ἐποχή) makes life impossible. He confronted the Stoics with a dilemma: if there is no cognitive impression, then either the wise man will hold opinions—an alternative abhorred by the Stoics—or else he will suspend judgement on everything. In the latter case, he will still be able to act, since it is possible to follow impressions without full assent, and the wise man may make reasonable decisions if he is guided by impressions that are plausible or convincing (πιθανόν, Lat. *probabile*) and checked for consistency with other relevant impressions. Carneades' account of the πιθανόν was introduced to refute the Stoic claim that life is impossible without cognitive impressions. But it also presented an attractive alternative to Stoic epistemology and was adopted by some of Carneades' successors as the basis of a new theory of fallibilism, which made it possible for the Academics to abandon strict suspension of judgement and develop their own doctrines. (see SCEPTICS; STOICISM.)

Carneades' criticisms of the belief in gods (see ATHEISM) and *divination were extensively used by Cicero (*Nat. D.*; *Div.*) and *Sextus Empiricus (*Math.* 9). In ethics, he is credited with a classification of all possible views about the highest good (*Carneadea divisio*), invented no doubt in order to argue that none of these options can be conclusively defended. Again his main target was *Stoicism, and echoes of the debate can be found e.g. in *Cicero and *Plutarch. On the occasion of the famous embassy to Rome, he gave speeches for and against justice on two consecutive days. Carneades' performance was so impressive that *Cato (Censorius) demanded a speedy departure of the Athenian delegation in order to protect Roman youths from the subversive influence of the philosophers.

SOURCES H. J. Mette, *Lustrum* 1985.

MODERN DISCUSSION A. A. Long and D. N. Sedley, *The Hellenistic*

Carneiscus

Philosophers (1987), chs. 68–70; see also bibliography under ARCESILAUS; SCEPTICS.   G. S.

Carneiscus, Epicurean of the 3rd or 2nd cent. BC, author of *Philistas*, a discussion of friendship in which *Praxiphanes was criticized.

Ed. W. Crönert, *Kolotes und Menedemos* (1906) 69; H. von Arnim, *RE* 10 (1917), col. 1993.

Carnuntum, on the Danube (*Danuvius) between Petronell and Deutsch-Altenburg, was an important Roman military base and the seat of government of *Pannonia (Upper). At first part of *Noricum, Carnuntum was probably added to *Pannonia *c.* AD 14 when Legio XV Apollinaris was transferred there from *Emona, but the legionary fortress was not constructed until Claudius. Some stone structures probably date from this time (*CIL* 3. 4591), and some rebuilding appears to have taken place in AD 73–6 (*CIL* 3. 11194–6). An auxiliary cavalry base was also established in the 60s a short distance to the west. The legion remained at Carnuntum, except for the years 62–71, until *c.*114, when it was replaced by XIV Gemina Martia Victrix, around whose fortress an extensive *canabae* developed. The civil settlement, which lay 5 km. (3 mi.) to the west, became a *municipium* (*Aelium*) under *Hadrian and a *colonia* (*Septimia*) under *Septimius Severus. It was visited by several emperors: thus M. *Aurelius wrote there the second book of his *Meditations*; *Diocletian, *Galerius, and *Maximian met there in 308; *Valentinian I stayed at Carnuntum in 375, and ordered the camp to be reconstructed. Carnuntum was flourishing in the 2nd cent. before its destruction in the *Marcomannic Wars, after which it was soon rebuilt. Under Septimius Severus the civilian town also flourished, but later diminished. Extensive remains of structures in both civilian and military areas have been revealed by excavation during the last century and, more recently, by aerial photography. Around the middle of the 4th cent. both fortress and city were severely damaged, apparently by earthquake.

M. Kandler and H. Vetters, *Der Römische Limes in Österreich* (1986), 202 ff.   F. A. W. S.; J. J. W.

Carpathos, known in medieval times as Scarpanto, is a Dodecanese island lying between *Rhodes and *Crete, bisected along its 48-km. (30-mi.) length by precipitous mountains. It preserves traces of Minoan and Mycenaean settlement. In historical times its cities were Carpathos (whose port was probably Potidaion at modern Pigadi), Arkaseia, and Brykous. The identity of inhabitants called the Eteocarpathioi in inscriptions is still disputed. The cities appear in the Athenian *tribute-lists, and at an uncertain date were absorbed by Rhodes and became *demes of the Rhodian city *Lindus. There was an important sanctuary of *Poseidon Porthmios in Tristomo Bay. The islet Saria to the north of Carpathos has extensive Byzantine ruins.

Inscriptions in *IG* 12. 1 (see also 1³ 1454); M. Segre, *Historia* (Milan) 1933, 577 ff.; M. Jameson, *Hesp.* 1958, 122 ff. P. M. Fraser and G. E. Bean, *The Rhodian Peraea and Islands* (1954); G. Susini, *ASAA* 1963–4, 203 ff.; R. Hope Simpson and J. F. Lazenby, *BSA* 1962, 159 ff.; 1970, 68 ff.   E. E. R.

Carrara, white *marble *quarries in NW Italy. Perhaps first exploited on a small scale by the *Etruscans, they were further developed after the foundation of the colony of *Luna in 177 BC, which acted as a port. Large-scale quarrying began in the 1st cent. BC. *Mamurra, *Caesar's *praefectus fabrum* (see FABRI), was the first to veneer the walls of his house with Carrara (Plin. *HN*

36. 7. 48), and may have opened up the quarries for Caesar's building programme, replacing the use of Attic white marbles (see PENTELICON). The reconstruction of the *Regia (37 BC) is often regarded as the earliest example of large-scale use of Carrara, and the industry (for buildings, sculpture, and *sarcophagi) reached its peak under Trajan, before giving way to the employment of marbles from the east Mediterranean. It was however partly revived in the 4th cent. AD.

E. Dolci, *Carrara: Cave antiche* (1980); J. B. Ward-Perkins, *Marble in Antiquity* (1992), with bibliography.   T. W. P.

Carrhae (mod. Harran), a city of north *Mesopotamia about 40 km. (25 mi.) south-west of *Edessa, at the junction of important trade routes. This site is the Haran of the OT and the Mari letters in which the temple of the moon-god is first mentioned in a tablet from *Mari of about 2000 BC. It was an important provincial capital, trading-city, and fortress in the Assyrian empire (the site yielded valuable inscriptions of Nabonidus in 1956). A Macedonian military colony under *Seleucid rule, it preserved its name in the Hellenized form 'Carrhae'. The Roman general M. *Licinius Crassus (1) was defeated near Carrhae in 53 BC. Carrhae was included in the territory annexed as a result of the eastern wars of M. *Aurelius and issued coins as a Roman city from his reign until that of *Gordian III. Severus gave it colonial status and additional titles attest further honours from *Caracalla, who was visiting the temple of Sin in 217 when he was assassinated. It was a fortress city, changing hands more than once during the centuries of frontier warfare between Rome and Byzantium and Sasanid Persia. At the time of its final capture by the Arabs in 639 the city was inhabited jointly by Christians and pagan Sabians.

The town walls survive, with principal gateways; but most visible remains, except a Christian *basilica, including the Great Mosque and the castle, are Islamic.

Jones, *Cities E. Rom. Prov.*² 217 f., cf. ch. 9; C. J. Gadd, *Anat. St.* 1958, 35 f.; J. B. Segal, in E. Bacon, *Vanished Civilisations* (1963), 20 ff.
                                                                  E. W. J.; S. S.-W.

carriages See TRANSPORT, WHEELED.

Carrinas (*RE* 1), **Gaius,** perhaps praetor 83 BC, commanded government levies against *Sulla and was repeatedly defeated in central and northern Italy. When Cn. *Papirius Carbo fled, Carrinas tried to relieve *Praeneste, but failed, and, with L. *Iunius Brutus Damasippus, turned towards Rome to join *Pontius Telesinus and his Samnites. They were defeated at the Colline gate and Carrinas was captured and executed.   E. B.

Carseoli (mod. Carsóli), 68 km. (42 mi.) east of Rome. A town of the *Aequi on the *via Valeria, it became a Latin colony in *c.*298 BC (see IUS LATII), and later a *municipium. It was abandoned in the 13th cent., but has been little studied.

A. Cederna, *Not. Scav.* 1951, 169 ff., and *Arch. Class.* 1953, 187 ff.
                                                                      E. T. S.; T. W. P.

Carsulae, on the *via Flaminia in Umbria, near *Narnia. It was rarely mentioned, but Vespasian's army stopped there in AD 69 (Tac. *Hist.* 3. 60). Extensive excavations have revealed the forum, basilica, temples, arches, and a theatre and amphitheatre.

G. Becatti, *Tuder-Carsulae* (1938); U. Ciotti, *San Gemini e Carsulae* (1976).
                                                                      E. T. S.; T. W. P.

Carteia, a town near San Roque on the coast of southern Spain in *Baetica. It was a naval base in the Second *Punic War and, in 171 BC it was made a *colonia Latina* (see IUS LATII), the first such foundation outside Italy in a permanent *provincia*. This comprised over 4,000 sons of Roman soldiers and Spanish women, their *liberti* (freedmen), and the Carteians themselves. The city issued bronze coinage from some time prior to 90 BC, while excavations have revealed the remains of the possible 1st-cent. BC *capitolium*. See CAPITOL.

F. Presedo and others, *Excavaciones arqueológicas en España* 120 (1982); R. Knapp, *Aspects of the Roman Experience in Iberia* (1977), 116 ff.

S. J. K.

Carthage (*Qrtḥdšt* (= 'New Town'); *Καρχήδων*; *Carthago*), a *Phoenician colony and later a major Roman city on the coast of NE Tunisia.

History According to tradition (Timaeus, *FGrH* 566 fr. 60) Carthage was founded from *Tyre in 814/3 BC, but no archaeological evidence has yet been found earlier than the second half of the 8th cent. BC. The site provided anchorage and supplies for ships trading in the western Mediterranean for *gold, *silver, and *tin, and soon outstripped other Phoenician colonies because of its position, its fertile hinterland, and its better harbour.

Trade was more important to Carthage throughout its history than perhaps to any other ancient state. Initially most of it was conducted by barter with tribes in Africa and Spain, where metals were obtained in return for wine, cloth, and pottery; but early contact with the Greek world is shown by the presence of Attic *amphorae in the earliest levels at Carthage. Voyages of exploration were undertaken along the Atlantic coast of North Africa and Spain. Carthage controlled much of the trade in the western Mediterranean, settling its own trading-posts in addition to those founded by the Phoenicians, so that Carthaginian influence extended from Tripolitania to Morocco, as well as to western Sicily, Sardinia, and southern Spain. From the 4th cent. Carthage also exported agricultural produce and was integrated into the wider Hellenistic economy of the Mediterranean world. Pottery from levels of the last Punic phase (first half of the 2nd cent. BC) shows significant quantities of imports from Greece, Italy, and the Iberian peninsula.

Carthage was ruled at first by a governor (*skn*), responsible to the king of Tyre; whether by the 7th cent. she had her own kings (*mlk*) is far from clear. At any rate by the 6th cent. the constitution had become oligarchic, headed by at first one, later two 'judges' (*špṭm*), called *suffetes* in Latin; they were elected annually on a basis of birth and wealth. Military commands were held by separately elected generals. There was a powerful 'senate' of several hundred life-members. The powers of the citizens were limited. A body of 104 judges scrutinized the actions of generals and other officials. Largely through this body the ruling class was successful in preventing the rise of *tyranny either through generals manipulating the mercenary armies or officials encouraging popular discontent. Military service was not obligatory on Carthaginians, whose population was too small to control a large citizen army; instead mercenaries were hired from various western Mediterranean peoples.

In the 5th cent., owing to setbacks in Sicily, Carthage occupied much of the hinterland of north and central Tunisia, and settled agriculture flourished. The native Numidian population in the areas to the west of Carthage adopted settled urbanism and other elements of Punic culture and religion from the late 3rd cent. onwards, and especially under enlightened rulers such as *Masinissa, so that considerable parts of North Africa outside formal Carthaginian control were already to a greater or lesser extent Punicized before the arrival of Rome.

The chief external policy of Carthage was control of the sea routes to the west. From *c*.600 BC it was clear that rival claims must lead to war between *Etruscans, Carthaginians, and Greeks. The westward thrust of *Phocaea and *Massilia was crushed off Alaia in Corsica by the Etruscan and Carthaginian fleets (*c*.535). This led to the consolidation of Carthaginian control of southern and western Sardinia and parts of southern Spain. Earlier *Malchus (1) had won successes in *Sicily, where the western end of the island remained in Carthaginian hands down to the 3rd cent. BC. For three centuries Carthaginians and Greeks fought intermittently for Sicilian territory and the allegiance of Sicans, Sicels, and Elymians. In 480 BC a great Carthaginian army under *Hamilcar (1) was defeated at Himera by the tyrants Gelon and Theron. His grandson Hannibal avenged the defeat by destroying Himera (409) and a succession of Greek cities on the south coast; but the ensuing wars with *Dionysius (1) of Syracuse ended with Carthaginian power confined to the far west of the island, and with the destruction of one of their three cities, *Motya (to be replaced by the new Carthaginian stronghold of *Lilybaeum). *Agathocles (1) later carried the war into Africa, but was defeated near *Tunis (307).

With Rome Carthage concluded treaties in 508 and 348, in which she jealously guarded her monopoly of maritime trade while refraining from interference in Italy. When *Pyrrhus attacked (280), her fleet helped Rome to victory. But sixteen years later Sicilian politics brought the two states into open conflict. Carthaginian intervention on the side of the Mamertines at Messina in 264 precipitated the first of the *Punic Wars, which ended in the destruction of Carthage (146 BC). Rome decreed that neither house nor crop should rise again. But Carthaginian blood survived, and the awesome pantheon still persisted: worship of Baal-Hammon, Tanit, Eshmoun, and Melqart was too deep-rooted in many parts of North Africa to die with the destruction of Carthage, and it was to continue, under a thinly Romanizing veneer, until the rise of *Christianity.

Carthage never developed a distinctive art of her own, but was content to copy and adapt styles imported from Egypt and Greece. She manufactured and exported carpets, rugs, *purple dyes, jewellery, pottery, lamps, tapestry, timber, and hides. Her agricultural skill, which made excellent use of the fertile Tunisian plains, profited her Roman conquerors: Mago's 32 books on scientific farming were translated into Latin; see AGRICULTURAL WRITERS.

The site of Carthage was too attractive to remain unoccupied for long. The attempt of C. *Sempronius Gracchus to establish the colony of Junonia on suburban land failed, but the city was colonized by Augustus in fulfilment of Caesar's intentions, and became the capital of Africa Proconsularis (see AFRICA, ROMAN). By the 2nd cent. AD Carthage had become the second city only to Rome in the western Mediterranean. A few urban troops and a cohort of the Third Augustan legion sufficed to keep order. But through his control of the vital African corn-trade, the proconsul was a potential danger to the emperor, as shown by the rebellions of *Clodius Macer and the Gordians (see GORDIAN I).

Carthage became an outstanding educational centre, especially famous for orators and lawyers. In the 3rd cent. the genius of *Tertullian and the devotion of *Cyprian made her a focus of Latin Christianity. Her bishop held himself the equal of the bishop of Rome, and Carthage played a great part in establishing western Christianity on lines very different from the speculation of the Greek churches. As a great Catholic stronghold she fought against the *Donatist heresy. When the Vandals overran Africa, she became the capital of *Gaiseric and his successors, who embraced the Arian version (see ARIANISM) of Christianity. After *Belisarius' victory Catholicism was restored on stricter lines. Carthage remained loyal to the eastern Roman empire and beat off the earlier Muslim invasions, until captured in 697.

Topography Carthage was founded on part of a large peninsula which stretched eastwards from lagoons into the gulf of Tunis; the isthmus linking it to the mainland further west is c.5 km. (3 mi.) wide at its narrowest point. Scanty remains of houses of the last quarter of the 8th cent. BC have been found, at one point up to 350 m. (380 yds.) from the shore, suggesting that the settlement then was already of considerable size; but the original nucleus, if there really was a colony here a century earlier to correspond with the traditional foundation date, has yet to be found. Little is known of the archaic urban layout, but surface evidence and cemeteries to the north and west suggest that it covered at least 55 ha. (136 acres). Pottery kilns and metal-working quarters have been identified on its fringes, and the *tophet*, where child sacrifice to Baal and Tanit took place, has been located on the south; this was in continuous use from the later 8th cent. down to 146 BC. Substitution of animal for child was practised from the start: one in three archaic sacrifices in the sector excavated in the 1970s were of animals, declining to one in ten in the 5th/3rd cent. BC.

In the late 5th cent. massive fortifications, 5.20 m. (17 ft.) wide, were erected with projecting towers and gates; Livy (*Epit.* 51) says they were 32 km. (20 mi.) long. Substantial houses, some with peristyles and simple *terrazzo* or tessellated floors, are known from the Hellenistic period, when the city reached its greatest extent: a new area of housing was laid out on the slopes of the Byrsa hill soon after 200 BC, covering an archaic necropolis. Also to the last Punic phase belong the two artificial harbours to the south near the *tophet*, one rectangular (later adapted into an elongated hexagon), the other circular around a central island. The first was the commercial harbour, and the latter housed the warships of the Carthaginian navy: *Appian reports a ship-shed capacity of 220 vessels here. Little is known of the disposition of the harbour(s) at an earlier date.

Roman Carthage has suffered greatly from stone-robbing, but the regular Augustan street grid centred on the Byrsa hill is known in detail, as well as the position of the principal public buildings, including the amphitheatre on the western outskirts, the circus on the south-west, the theatre, and the odeum. The 2nd cent. AD saw the apogee of the city's prosperity: a massive forum and basilica, the biggest known outside Rome, was erected on the Byrsa in Antonine times, and also Antonine is the huge and lavish bath-house down by the sea, designed on a symmetrical layout like the great imperial baths of Rome. It was probably to supply it that Carthage's 132-km. (82-mi.) aqueduct was constructed, the longest anywhere in the Roman world. The forum on the Byrsa is unlikely to have been the only one: recent work (since 1990) near the coast midway between the Antonine baths and the harbours, alongside the *cardo maximus*, has revealed part of what is probably the forum of the Augustan city; a Punic temple, perhaps that of *Apollo mentioned by Appian as bordering the Punic agora, has been located below. The 4th cent. and later saw a rash of extramural church-building, and c.425 a massive new defensive circuit was erected on the landward side against the *Vandal threat; despite it the city fell easily to the Vandals in 439. Several houses of the 5th and 6th cents. are known, when Carthage continued to prosper: survey work in the Carthaginian hinterland shows rural settlement at its densest

in the 5th and 6th cents., matching and even outstripping that of the 2nd and 3rd cents.

INSCRIPTIONS *CISem.* 1; M. G. Guzzo Amadasi, *Le iscrizioni fenicie e puniche delle colonie in Occidente* (1967); L. Ennabli, *Les Inscriptions funéraires chrétiennes de Carthage*, 3 vols. (1975–91).
COINAGE G. K. Jenkins and R. B. Lewis, *Carthaginian Gold and Electrum coins* (1963); G. K. Jenkins, *Sylloge Nummorum Graecorum* 42: *North Africa* (1969); E. Acquaro, *La monetazione punica* (1979).
POTTERY P. Cintas, *Céramique punique* (1950); A. M. Bisi, *La ceramica punica: Aspetti e problemi* (1970).
HISTORY S. Gsell, *Histoire ancienne de l'Afrique du Nord* (1914–28); O. Meltzer, *Geschichte der Karthager* 1–2 (1879–96); 3 (1913, by U. Kahrstedt); G. Picard, *Carthage* (1964; Fr. orig. 1956); G. and C. Picard, *La Vie quotidienne à Carthage*, 2nd edn. (1982; Eng. trans. of 1st edn. 1961); B. H. Warmington, *Carthage* (1960); W. Huss, *Geschichte der Karthager* (1985), and *Die Karthager* (1990); M. H. Fantar, *Carthage: Approche d'une civilisation*, 2 vols. (1993). Gracchan and Augustan colonization: L. Teutsch, *Das römische Städtewesen in Nordafrika* (1962), 2–4, 101–6; S. Lancel, *Carthage: A History* (1995); J. Rives, *Religion and Authority in Roman Carthage* (1995).
TOPOGRAPHY A. Audollent, *Carthage romaine, 146 avant J.-C.–698 après J.-C.* (1901); A. Lézine, *Carthage-Utique: Études d'architecture et d'urbanisme* (1968); P. Bertolini, *Le stele arcaiche del tophet di Cartagine* (1976); H. Benichou-Safar, *Les Tombes puniques de Carthage* (1982); E. Lipinski (ed.), *Studia Phoenica 6: Carthago* (1988); S. T. Stevens, *Bir el Knissia at Carthage: A Rediscovered Cemetery Church. Report no. 1* (1993); S. Lancel, *Carthage* (1994; Fr. orig. 1992). Results of the UNESCO-sponsored excavations since 1973: J. G. Pedley (ed.), *New Light on Ancient Carthage* (1980); J. H. Humphrey (ed.), *Excavations at Carthage 1975–1978*, 7 vols. (1976–82), and (ed.), *The Circus and a Byzantine Cemetery at Carthage* (1988); *Cahiers des études anciennes* 6–19 (1976–86); S. Lancel (ed.), *Byrsa* 1–2 (1979–82); P. Gros (ed.), *Byrsa* 3 (1985); H. R. Hurst and S. P. Roskams (eds.), *Excavations at Carthage: The British Mission* 1, in two parts (1984); F. Rakob (ed.), *Karthago: Die deutschen Ausgrabungen in Karthago* 1 (1991), and *MDAI(R)* 1991, 33–80; A. Ennabli (ed.), *Pour sauver Carthage* (1992). Hinterland: J. A. Greene, *Ager and 'Arōsōt: Rural Settlement and Agrarian History in the Carthaginian Countryside* (1990). W. N. W.; B. H. W.; R. J. A. W.

Carthago Nova, a town in Hither Spain, today Cartagena. It lay on a peninsula within one of the best harbours of the Mediterranean. Originally named Mastia, it was refounded as New Carthage by *Hasdrubal (1) in 228 BC as a base for the Carthaginian conquest of Spain. It was captured by *Scipio Africanus in 209, visited by *Polybius (1) in 133 (described in 10. 10), was made a colony (*colonia Urbs Iulia Nova Carthago*), probably by 42 BC, and was a mint from the mid-1st cent. BC until the reign of *Gaius (1). During the empire it was overshadowed by *Tarraco, although it became capital of Hispania Carthagininsis in the Diocletianic provincial reforms. Excavations have revealed the amphitheatre, theatre, streets, private houses, and the late Roman walls. It was famous for its *silver-mines (which brought the Roman treasury a daily revenue of 2,500 drachmae in the mid-2nd cent. BC), fish-pickle (see FISHING), and esparto grass. Sacked by the *Vandals, it became capital of the Byzantine province of Spania.

S. Ramallo Asensio, *La ciudad romana de Carthago Nova: La documentación arqueológica* (1989); M. J. Peña, *Estudios de la antigüedad* 1984, 74 ff. S. J. K.

Cartimandua, queen of the *Brigantes, whose treaty-relationship with *Claudius protected the early northern borders of Roman *Britain. In AD 51, true to her obligation, she handed over the fugitive *Caratacus, but was weakened by the resulting breach with her husband, the patriot Venutius, and twice required the help of Roman troops in the period 52–7. Later, planning to deprive him of support, she divorced Venutius and married his squire Vellocatus; but with the Roman world otherwise engaged in 68–9, Venutius seized his chance and drove her out. The result was the conquest of Brigantia under *Vespasian and its incorporation into the province.

S. S. Frere, *Britannia*, 3rd edition (1987). S. S. F.; M. J. M.

Carus, Marcus Aurelius (*RE* 77), praetorian prefect from Narbo, overthrew *Probus after rebelling in Raetia in AD 282. Leaving his elder son, *Carinus, as Caesar in the west, Carus marched against Persia with *Numerianus. He captured Ctesiphon, but, advancing further, was killed, perhaps by treachery (summer 283). He was the first emperor not to seek the senate's approval of his accession.

PLRE 1. 183; P. Meloni, *Il regno di Caro* (1948); K. Pink, *NZ* 1963, 5 ff.; R. Syme, *Emperors and Biography* (1971); H. W. Bird, *Latomus* 1976, 123 ff.; F. Kolb, *Diocletian* (1987). J. F. D.

Carvilius, freedman of Spurius Carvilius Maximus (consul 235 BC). 'The Romans were late in beginning to teach for payment, and the first of them to open an elementary school was Spurius Carvilius' (Plut. *Quaest. Rom.* 59). It is unlikely that Carvilius' school was the first to be opened at Rome, where literacy is attested *c*.450 BC (Livy 3. 44). *Cicero's statement, that boys in the early republic were required to learn the *Twelve Tables by heart, points to the probability that schools existed before 250. Carvilius probably was the first to open a school for pay, earlier teachers having depended on voluntary gifts from pupils.

According to *Plutarch, Carvilius was the first to differentiate between the letters C and G (*Quaest. Rom.* 54). Some scholars have attributed the distinction to Appius *Claudius Caecus. See also EDUCATION, ROMAN.

S. Bonner, *Education in Ancient Rome* (1977), 34 f. T. J. H.

Carvilius (*RE* 9) **Maximus, Spurius,** of non-senatorial origins, was consul twice (293; 272 BC) with L. *Papirius Cursor (2). Both secured triumphs for decisive victories in northern central *Samnium (293) and for ending the resistance of *Tarentum and her southern Italian allies (272). To commemorate his achievements in 293 Carvilius built a temple to Fors *Fortuna and erected statues of *Jupiter and himself together on the *Capitol. He was censor, probably in 289.

E. T. Salmon, *Samnium and the Samnites* (1967); *CAH* 7²/₂ (1989), 380; K.-J. Hölkeskamp, *Die Entstehung der Nobilität* (1987). A. D.

caryatides, a Greek term for column-shafts carved in the form of draped women; male equivalents were called Atlantides (see ATLAS). Apparently named after Caryae in *Laconia, where virgins danced to *Artemis Caryatis (Pratin. *Lyr.* 4; Paus. 3. 10. 7). Of near-eastern derivation (e.g. Tell Halaf), they appear in Greece around 550 BC, and are popular on late Archaic treasuries at *Delphi; the most famous are those of the Athenian *Erechtheum. The Erechtheum accounts, however, simply call them *korai*; in this case, perhaps, they were civic versions of the private *korē* dedications of the past. Copies of the Erechtheum caryatids embellished the *forum Augustum, the *Pantheon, and Hadrian's villa at *Tibur. Vitruvius (1. 1. 5) calls them 'images of eternal servitude', and connects them with Caryae's punishment for *Medism in the *Persian Wars, but since the type is unquestionably earlier and Caryae was destroyed much later (370; 222 BC), this must be an *aition* (explanation) invented after the fact.

A. F. Stewart, *Greek Sculpture* (1990), figs. 124, 188 f., 431 f.; D. E. E. Kleiner, *Roman Sculpture* (1992) figs. 83, 214 f. A. F. S.

Carystus See EUBOEA.

Casilinum, town in *Campania, where the *via Appia and *via Latina met and crossed the Volturnus: modern Capua (a name it acquired in AD 856 when the inhabitants of nearby ancient *Capua, fleeing the Saracens, settled here). Casilinum resolutely resisted, but finally fell to *Hannibal. It has always been a strategic keypoint. E. T. S.

Casinum (mod. Cassino), on the *via Latina. An *Oscan, *Volscian, Samnite (see SAMNIUM), and, from the late 4th cent. BC, Roman city (sacked by Hannibal in 208 BC), it became a flourishing *municipium*. The Ummidii were a prominent local family. It was destroyed by the *Lombards in the 6th cent. The forum, temples, theatre, and amphitheatre are known.

G. Carettoni, *Casinum* (1940). E. T. S.; T. W. P.

Caspian Sea (Κασπία θάλασσα, also called 'Hyrcanian' from Hyrcania, mod. Gurgan, the area at its SE corner). This large and brackish inland water was correctly described by Herodotus (1. 202) as a lake. In spite of partial exploration by Greeks, all subsequent writers thought that the *Oxus and *Jaxartes flowed into it; many believed that it was joined to the Black Sea (by the river Phasis), or to the sea of Azov; and the prevalent view was that a channel linked it with a not far distant northern Ocean. The first of these opinions may have had apparent support from the remains of a prehistoric channel between the Caspian and the Aral Sea, and the last may have been prompted by a vague knowledge of the Volga. About 285 BC *Patrocles sailed up both sides on behalf of the *Seleucids, but, failing to reach the north end, gave currency to the belief that one could sail from the Caspian to India by the northern Ocean. Renewed exploration after the reign of Tiberius led to the rediscovery of the Volga ('Rha' in Ptolemy), and *Ptolemy (4) restated the truth that the Caspian is a lake, though he got its shape wrong.

Cary–Warmington, *Explorers* (1929), 136 ff., (1963, Pelican) 166, 177, 185, 198; Thomson, *Hist. Anc. Geog.*, see index; Cary, *Geographic Background*, 177 f., 184, 189 ff., 198 f., 312. A. Herrmann, *RE* 10/2 (1919), 2275–90, 'Kaspisches Meer'. E. H. W.

Cassander (d. 297 BC), son of *Antipater (1), represented his father at Babylon (323), where *Alexander (3) the Great treated him with naked hostility. In the struggles of the Successors he first impinges at Triparadeisus (late 321), where he was appointed chiliarch (cavalry commander and grand vizier). Chiliarch he remained at Antipater's death (autumn 319), subordinate to the regent *Polyperchon; but he defected to *Antigonus (1) and with Antigonus' support established bases in *Piraeus and the *Peloponnese (318/7). An inconclusive invasion of Macedon (?early 317) was followed by a wholly successful one which overthrew the tyrannical dowager, *Olympias. From 316 he was master of Macedon and promoted the memory of *Philip (1) II (whose daughter, Thessalonice, he married) over that of Alexander. He ceremonially refounded *Thebes (1) (316), and had the young *Alexander (4) IV secretly killed at *Amphipolis (*c*.310). A leading figure in the coalition war against Antigonus (315–311), he secured recognition of his position as general in Europe in the 'peace of the dynasts' (311) and later (*c*.305) had himself proclaimed 'King of the Macedonians', subsequently his official title. When war resumed, he lost ground in southern Greece as the oligarchies he had supported (most notably at Athens) were undermined by Antigonus' propaganda of autonomy, and only the outbreak of war in Asia saved him from a devastating invasion at the hands of *Demetrius (4) (302). His death (?May 297) left Macedon temporarily stable, to be soon convulsed by the quarrels of his heirs.

HM 3.   A. B. B.

Cassandra or **Alexandra**, in mythology daughter of *Priam and *Hecuba. In *Homer she is mentioned as being the most beautiful of Priam's daughters (*Il.* 13. 365), and she is the first to see her father bringing home the body of *Hector (24. 699 ff.). The *Iliu Persis* (Proclus) adds that during the sack of Troy she took refuge at the statue of Athena, but *Aias (2) the Locrian dragged her away to rape her, and in so doing loosened the statue from its plinth. Perhaps Homer knew of this episode, for at *Od.* 4. 502 he says that Aias was 'hated by Athena'; but he makes no direct mention of it. Nor does he mention Cassandra's prophetic powers for which in later tradition she was famous. The *Cypria* (Proclus; see EPIC CYCLE) first mentions her prophecies. Aeschylus' *Agamemnon* (1203 ff.) tells how Apollo gave her the power of prophecy in order to win her sexual favours, which she promised to him. But she broke her word, so he turned the blessing into a curse by causing her always to be disbelieved. Later authors follow this form of the story; but there is another (schol. *Il.* 7. 44 and Eust. *Il.* 663, 40) which says that she and her brother *Helenus, when children, had their ears licked by Apollo's sacred serpents while asleep and so were given their prophetic gifts. Cassandra commonly appears, in tragedy and elsewhere, as forewarning of terrible events, like the evil fate which *Paris would bring on Troy or the disasters which the Wooden Horse would cause (as Verg. *Aen.* 2. 246), but having her warnings unheeded. On the basis of this, *Lycophron (2) (*Alexandra*) puts into her mouth a forecast of mythological and historical adventures of both Trojans and Greeks from the war to his own day. After the sack of Troy, Cassandra was given to *Agamemnon as his concubine, and on his return home *Clytemnestra killed them both. There is a memorable scene in Aesch. *Ag.* (1072 ff.) where Cassandra sings of the horrors which have already polluted the house of *Atreus and foretells her own death and that of Agamemnon.

A favourite scene in Archaic and Classical art is that of Cassandra clutching the image of Athena while Aias seizes her: see O. Touchefeu, *LIMC* 1 / 1. 339–49.   H. J. R.; J. R. M.

Cassian Born in what is now Romania in *c.* AD 360, Cassian had the advantage of a Latin upbringing in the Greek world. Like his master Evagrius of Pontus, he travelled through Syria, Palestine, and Egypt, making extensive contact with the masters of eastern *asceticism and gaining a thorough grounding in the theory of the ascetic life.

With the Egyptian condemnation of *Origen (1) in 399, he enjoyed the protection of John *Chrysostom in Constantinople, together with many other exiled admirers of the *Alexandrian master. After an obscure interval, he settled in southern Gaul in *c.*415 under the patronage, in particular, of Proculus of Arles. He served and moulded the ascetic enthusiasms of several bishops and founded two monasteries of his own near Marseilles.

For the resulting communities he wrote his *Institutes* and *Conferences*, which gained widespread and permanent influence in the west. The *Institutes* were more practical, important for liturgical detail and for their systematic treatment of the vices, reflecting eastern practice and the theology of Evagrius. The *Conferences* reported conversations with ascetics of northern Egypt and gave new Christian vigour to the dialogue form. Their setting appeared solitary but Cassian's intentions were coenobitic: he encouraged virtues and practices proper to community life. While respecting Egyptian tradition, he adapted it to the new monasteries of Gaul.

Cassian's writings were charged with an Alexandrian optimism. The ascetic was made in the image of God and perfection was in some sense a natural expectation based on the development of inherent qualities. Virtues formed a unity, so that any step forward would find its reward in an integrated drama of self-possession. The result was a genuine freedom—not only from inadequacy but from fear of submission to others. In making such emphases, Cassian had a role to play on a broader stage. He wrote a treatise on the Incarnation against Nestorius; and his views on freedom had a lasting influence in Gaul among those who sympathized more with *Pelagius than with *Augustine. His ascetic teaching was highly valued by Benedict and was mentioned explicitly in the latter's *Rule*. He died *c.*435.

WORKS Ed. M. Petschenig, *CSEL* 13 and 17; see also *Jean Cassien, Conférences*, ed. and trans. E. Pichery, 3 vols. (SC 42, 54, 64, 1955, 1958, 1959); *Jean Cassien, Institutions Cénobitiques*, ed. and trans. J.-C. Guy (SC 109, 1965).

STUDIES O. Chadwick, *John Cassian* (1950, 1968), the two editions differ instructively; P. Rousseau, *Ascetics, Authority, and the Church* (1978).   P. R.

Cassiodorus (Magnus Aurelius Cassiodorus Senator), politician, writer, and monk (*c.* AD 490–*c.*585). His Bruttian family had a tradition of provincial leadership and official service. He assisted his father, praetorian prefect of Italy, 503–7, under the Ostrogothic king *Theoderic (1). Writing Theoderic's diplomatic letters in 506, he was *quaestor sacri palatii* (rhetorical draftsman and legal adviser), 507–12. Consul in 514, in 523 he replaced his disgraced kinsman *Boethius as *magister officiorum* (but also with draftsman's duties); he served into 527, aiding the new reign of *Athalaric and Amalasuintha. Prefect of Italy from 533, he was again both administrator and royal draftsman. With Pope Agapitus (535–6), he planned an abortive school of Christian higher education at Rome. Remaining prefect under kings Theodahad and Witigis, and made patrician, he retired in 537/8 during the Gothic wars. Moving to Constantinople, he assisted Pope Vigilius in the Three Chapters controversy (550). Soon after, he withdrew permanently to his monastery of Vivarium on his ancestral estate at Scylacium. There he organized translations and manuscript copying, partly to support the Three Chapters against official condemnation, partly to promote Christian education. Vivarian texts soon circulated widely, but the monastery quickly shared in the decay of Italian civilization.

Among his works: (1) a short chronicle of the world and Rome, ordered by Theoderic's son-in-law Eutharic, when consul in 519. (2) A lost, tendentious Gothic history, extensively used in *Jordanes' *Getica* (*c.*551). Notable for its untrustworthy pedigree of Theoderic's Amal family and use of Gothic legend, it is the first known ethnic history from the barbarian kingdoms, integrating *Goths into the classical past. (3) Panegyrics (fragmentary) on Gothic royalties, last of the Latin prose genre. (4) *Variae*: twelve books of state papers, edited *c.*537, an invaluable source for Ostrogothic Italy, and the structures, culture, and ideology of late-Roman government. The collection was both an apology for the Ostrogoths and their Roman collaborators, and a moral, rhetorical, and practical guide for future rulers and ministers; Cassiodorus' blending of *ekphrasis* and learned digression into official discourse is remarkable. (5) The appended *De anima* grounded the *Variae* in religious reflections on human nature and society. (6) *Expositio Psalmorum*: this exegetical and literary commentary developed the Psalms as a Christian rhetorical handbook and encyclopaedia of liberal arts, superseding pagan classics. (7) *Institutiones*: an intellectual Rule for Vivarium (but also meant for a wider public), this short encyclopaedia and bibliography of Christian and secular studies renewed the project of Christian higher education, and depicted reading (including the liberal arts) and copying as central to monastic life. (8) *De orthographia*: a guide for Vivarian copyists. Among influential Vivarian translations were Josephus' *Antiquitates*, and the ecclesiastical *Historia tripartita*, combining *Socrates (2) Scholasticus, *Sozomen, and *Theodoret. Cassiodorus did not save classical culture, as is sometimes claimed; but, especially from Carolingian times, *Variae*, *Expositio*, and *Institutiones* were widely read, and helped to maintain and integrate the Christian and Roman inheritances in western Europe.

Ed. Migne, *PL* 59–70. *Variae, Chron.*, and Jordanes' *Getica*, ed. T. Mommsen, *MGH*, with panegyrics, ed. L. Traube; *Variae* also ed. Å. Fridh, *CCSL* 96 (1973), with *De Anima*, ed. J. Halporn; Eng. trans. of selected *Variae*, T. Hodgkin (1886), S. J. B. Barnish (1992). *Expositio Psalmorum*, ed. M. Adriaen, *CCSL* 97–8 (1958); Eng. trans., P. G. Walsh (1990). *Institutiones*, ed. R. A. B. Mynors (1937); Eng. trans., L. W. Jones (1946). *De orthographia* ed. H. Keil, *Grammatici Latini* 7 (1880). J. J. O'Donnell, *Cassiodorus* (1979); Barnish and Walsh, introductions; Barnish, *Latomus* 1989. S. J. B. B.

Cassiterides ('Tin Islands'), a name applied generically to all the north Atlantic tin lands, and often associated with Cornwall and the Scillies. They were said to have been known first by the *Phoenicians or Carthaginians (see CARTHAGE) from Gades. A Greek named Midacritus (c.600 BC ?) is recorded to have imported tin from Cassiteris island (Plin. *HN* 7. 197). The Carthaginians kept their tin-routes secret; hence Herodotus (3. 115) doubted the existence of the Cassiterides. *Pytheas visited the miners of Belerium (Land's End) and their tin depot at Ictis; but it was left to a Roman, probably P. *Licinius Crassus (1), governor in Spain c.95 BC, to make the tin-routes generally known. *Strabo, who enumerates ten Cassiterides, describes the tin- and lead-mines and the black cloaks and long tunics of the natives.

The unambiguous evidence about the location of the Cassiterides in the classical sources suggests that it was a partly mythologized generic name for the sources of *tin beyond the Mediterranean world and not a single place. The absence of archaeological evidence for any pre-Roman iron age trade with the tin-producing areas of SW England supports this.

M. Todd, *The South-West to AD 1000* (1987); A. L. F. Rivet and C. Smith, *The Place-names of Roman Britain* (1979); F. Haverfield, *RE* 10/2 (1919), 2328–32, 'Kassiterides'. E. H. W.; M. J. M.

Cassius (tyrannicide). See CASSIUS LONGINUS (1), C.

Cassius (1) (*RE* 3), a Roman physician of the time of Augustus and Tiberius (31 BC–AD 37). His specific for the relief of colic was famous in antiquity.

Cassius (2) (*RE* 8), doctor-sophist, the author of Ἰατρικαὶ ἀπο ρίαι καὶ προβλήματα φυσικά ('medical puzzles and problems of physics'), not earlier than the 3rd cent. AD.

Ed. J. L. Ideler, *Physici et Medici Graeci Minores* (1841) 1. 144. W. D. R.; V. N.

Cassius (*RE* 37) **Chaerea**, a centurion in Lower Germany in AD 14. In 41, as a tribune in the praetorian guard, he was mocked by *Gaius (1) (Caligula) for his supposed effeminacy. He played a leading part in the latter's murder (41). On *Claudius' accession he was executed. J. P. B.; R. J. S.

Cassius (*RE* 40) **Dio** (*c.* AD 164–after 229), Greek senator and author of an 80-book history of Rome from the foundation of the city to AD 229. His full name was perhaps L. Cassius Dio, as on M. M. Roxan, *Roman Military Diplomas* 2 (1985), no. 133 ('Cl.' on *AE* 1971, 430, could attest the further name 'Claudius', but is probably a stone-cutter's error; 'Cocceianus' may have been added in Byzantine times through confusion with Dio of Prusa). Dio came from a prominent family of *Nicaea (1) in Bithynia (modern Iznik). His father, Cassius (*RE* 27) Apronianus, entered the senate, attaining a consulship and several governorships. Dio's senatorial career was even more distinguished. He was praetor in 194 and suffect consul probably c.204. From 218 to 228 he was successively *curator* of *Pergamum and *Smyrna, proconsul of *Africa, and legate first of *Dalmatia and then of Upper *Pannonia. In 229 he held the ordinary consulship with *Severus Alexander as colleague and then retired to *Bithynia. Dio lived through turbulent times: he and his fellow senators quailed before tyrannical emperors and lamented the rise of men they regarded as upstarts, and in Pannonia he grappled with the problem of military indiscipline. These experiences are vividly evoked in his account of his own epoch and helped to shape his view of earlier periods.

Dio tells us (72. 23) that, after a short work on the dreams and portents presaging the accession of *Septimius Severus, he went on to write first a history of the wars following the death of *Commodus and then the *Roman History*, and that for this work he spent ten years collecting material for events up to the death of Severus (211) and a further twelve years writing them up. Nothing survives of the early works or of other historical writings attributed to Dio by the *Suda. The dates of composition of the *Roman History* are disputed, but the most natural interpretation of Dio's words is that he began work c.202. His plan was to continue recording events after Severus' death as long as possible, but absence from Italy prevented him giving more than a cursory account of the reign of Severus Alexander and he ended the history with his own retirement (80. 1–5).

The *Roman History* is only partially extant. The portion dealing with the period 69 BC to AD 46 (36. 1. 1–60. 28. 3) survives in various MSS, with substantial lacunae after 6 BC. For the rest we depend on excerpts and the epitomes of *Zonaras (down to 146 and 44 BC to AD 96) and Xiphilinus (from 69 BC to the end).

Like its author, the work is an amalgam of Greek and Roman elements. It is written in Attic Greek, with much studiedly antithetical rhetoric and frequent verbal borrowings from the classical authors, above all *Thucydides (2). The debt to Thucydides is more than merely stylistic: like him, Dio is constantly alert to discrepancies between appearances and reality. In its structure, however, the history revives the Roman tradition of an annalistic record of civil and military affairs arranged by the consular year (see ANNALS, ANNALISTS). Dio shows flexibility in his handling of the annalistic framework: there are many digressions, usually brief; external events of several years are sometimes combined in a single narrative cluster; introductory and concluding sections frame the annalistic narratives of emperors' reigns.

For his own times Dio could draw on his own experience or oral evidence, but for earlier periods he was almost entirely dependent on literary sources, chiefly earlier histories. Attempts to identify individual sources are usually futile. Dio must have read widely in the first ten years, and in the ensuing twelve years

Cassius Dionysius

of writing up he probably worked mainly from his notes without going back to the originals. Such a method of composition may account for some of the history's distinctive character. It is often thin and slapdash; errors and distortions are quite common, and there are some surprising omissions (notably the conference of *Luca). However, Dio does show considerable independence, both in shaping his material and in interpretation: he freely makes causal links between events and attributes motivations to his characters, and many of these explanations must be his own contribution rather than drawn from a source.

One notable feature of the work is the prominence of the supernatural: Dio believed that divine direction played an important part in his own and others' lives and he devoted much space to *portents. Another is the speeches, which are free inventions and sometimes on a very ample scale. Many of them are commonly dismissed as mere rhetorical set-pieces, but they generally have a dramatic function, often heavily ironic. In *Maecenas' speech of advice to *Augustus (52. 14–40) Dio combines an analysis of the problems facing Augustus and of the imperial system as it evolved under the emperors with a sketch of how he himself would have liked to see the empire governed.

The *Roman History* is dominated by the change from the republic to the monarchy of the emperors, repeatedly endorsed by Dio on the grounds that only monarchy could provide Rome with stable government. The late republic and the triumviral years (see TRIUMVIRI) are accorded much more space than other periods. Dio anachronistically treats the conflicts of the late republic as struggles between rival contenders for supreme power. His account of the settlement of 27 BC perceptively explores the ways in which it shaped the imperial system under which he still lived (53. 2. 6–21. 7). Dio's treatment of individual emperors' reigns reflects the values and interests of the senator: his overriding concern is with the respects in which emperors measured up to or fell short of senators' expectations.

TEXTS U. P. Boissevain (1895–1931), concordance in vol. 5; Budé edn., with Fr. trans. (in progress), bks. 50–1 so far published (1991); E. Cary, with Eng. trans. (Loeb, 1914–27); J. W. Rich, bks. 53–55. 9, with Eng. trans. and comm. (1990).

TRANSLATION Bks. 51–6, I. Scott-Kilvert (1987).

COMMENTARIES Bks. 49–52, M. Reinhold (1988); bks. 58–63 (selections, with trans.), J. Edmondson (LACTOR 15, 1992).

STUDIES F. Millar, *A Study of Cassius Dio* (1964); B. Manuwald, *Cassius Dio und Augustus* (1979); D. Fechner, *Untersuchungen zu Cassius Dios Sicht der römischen Republik* (1986); A. M. Gowing, *The Triumviral Narratives of Appian and Cassius Dio* (1992). J. W. R.

Cassius (RE 42) Dionysius of *Utica, wrote (1) (88 BC) a Greek translation (with additions) of the work of the Carthaginian Mago on agriculture, which became the standard work on the subject, used by all its successors in antiquity (see AGRICULTURAL WRITERS); (2) 'Ριζοτομικά, 'On Root-cutting', a compilation much used by *Pliny (1) the Elder.

E. Rawson, *Intellectual Life in the Late Roman Republic* (1985), 135. W. D. R.

Cassius (RE 47) Hemina, Lucius, Roman historian and antiquarian, one of the earliest to write in Latin. He treated Roman history from its Trojan and Italian origins (book 1) and the foundation (book 2) to the Second *Punic War (book 4, apparently written before 149 BC) and then beyond: fr. 39, presumably from a later book, treats 146 BC. The fragments show etymological and aetiological ingenuity, euhemeristic rationalism (see EUHEMERUS), and an interest in things Greek. The emphasis on Italian origins

suggests an affinity with M. *Porcius Cato (1)'s *Origines*.

Fragments in Peter, *HRRel.* 1². clxv–xxiii and 98–111. E. Rawson, *Roman Culture and Society* (1991), 245–57 (= *Latomus* 1976, 689–702); U. W. Scholz, *Hermes* 1989, 167–81. C. B. R. P.

Cassius Longinus, (c. AD 213–73), rhetorician and philosopher, who taught at Athens (see J. Bidez, *Vie de Porphyre* (1913), ch. 4) and, in the last few years of his life, became the principal adviser of the rulers of Palmyra, *Septimius Odaenathus and *Zenobia; he was executed when the city fell to *Aurelian (Gibbon, *Decline and Fall*, ch. 11, gives the classic English account). *Plotinus (*Vita* 14) spoke of Longinus as 'a lover of learning, but in no wise a philosopher'; though he wrote on philosophical subjects (Περὶ ἀρχῶν, commentary on *Plato (1)'s *Timaeus*), he was much more celebrated for his critical and rhetorical work; *Eunapius (*Vitae Sophistarum* 4) calls him 'a living library and walking museum'. For the attribution to him of Περὶ ὕψους, see 'LONGINUS'.

Fragments in J. Toup's edn. of Περὶ ὕψους (1778); rhetorical fragments in A. O. Prickard's (OCT, 1906). PLRE 1, 'Longinus' 2; L. Brisson and M. Patillon, *ANRW* 2. 36. 7 (1994), 5214 ff. D. A. R.

Cassius (RE 59) Longinus (1), Gaius, the tyrannicide (killer of *Caesar), was quaestor 54 BC and proquaestor under *Crassus in 53. He escaped from *Carrhae, collected the remnants of the army, and organized the defence of Syria, staying on as proquaestor till 51: in 52 he crushed an insurrection in Judaea and in 51 repelled a Parthian invasion. As tribune 49 he supported *Pompey and was appointed by him to a naval command; in 48 he operated in Sicilian waters but on the news of *Pharsalus abandoned the war and (perhaps at Tarsus, spring 47) obtained Caesar's pardon and the post of *legatus*. Praetor peregrinus 44, he played a leading part in the conspiracy against *Caesar. Soon after the deed he was forced by popular hostility to leave Rome, and was assigned by the senate in June the task of importing corn from Sicily, and later the unimportant province of *Cyrene. After quarrelling with M. *Antonius (2) (Mark Antony) he sailed instead for Asia (September or October) and from there to Syria, where, early in 43, the governors of Bithynia and Syria, Q. Marcius Crispus and L. *Staius Murcus, put their armies at his disposal. Q. *Caecilius Bassus, whom they had been besieging, followed suit; a force under A. Allienus on its way from Egypt to P. *Cornelius Dolabella (1) was intercepted and made to join him; and after the capture of (Syrian) Laodicea he took over Dolabella's army too. After *Mutina the senate had given him, with *Brutus, command over all the eastern provinces and probably also *imperium maius*; but in the autumn they were outlawed for the murder of Caesar under the law of Q. *Pedius. After raising more troops and money and subduing the Rhodians, who had refused their support, Cassius crossed with Brutus to Thrace in summer 42 and encountered Antony and *Octavian at *Philippi. In the first battle his camp was captured and, probably under the impression that the day was altogether lost, he killed himself.

More keen-sighted and practical than Brutus, Cassius seems nevertheless to have been less respected and less influential. He was a man of violent temper and sarcastic tongue, a strict disciplinarian, and ruthless in his exactions. The charge of covetousness may have been well founded; but there is no convincing evidence that he was influenced by petty motives in the conspiracy against Caesar. He married Brutus' half-sister Iunia Tertia (Tertulla), who survived till AD 22 (Tac. *Ann.* 3. 76).

R. Y. Tyrrell and L. C. Purser (eds.), *The Correspondence of M. Tullius Cicero* 6² (1933), 102 ff.; Syme, *Rom. Rev.*, see index; *RRC* 498 ff.

(revealing that he held a priesthood); E. Rawson, in I. Moxon and others (eds.), *Past Perspectives* (1986). T. J. C.; R. J. S.

Cassius (*RE* 60) **Longinus** (2), **Gaius,** a great-grandson (or nephew) of the tyrannicide *Cassius of the same name, and descended on his mother's side from Servius *Sulpicius Rufus, was a senator of rigorously conservative views (Tac. *Ann.* 14. 42 f.) and the leading Roman lawyer under Claudius and *Nero. After a career as praetor, suffect consul, and governor of Asia (Minor) and Syria he was, despite blindness, exiled to Sardinia after the discovery of C. *Calpurnius Piso (2)'s conspiracy in 65, but *Vespasian recalled him. A pupil of *Masurius Sabinus, his senior in age and superior in intellect but inferior in social status, he founded the Cassian school (*schola Cassiana,* a century later called the Sabinians), a group of lawyers who insisted on a traditional and pragmatic view of the law. His views are cited by other lawyers but none of his writing survives.

Lenel, *Pal.* 1. 110–26; Bremer 3. 9–79; *PIR*² C 501; *HLL* 3, § 326. 2; Kunkel 1967, 130–1; F. D'Ippolito, *Ideologia e diritto in Gaio Cassio Longino* (1969); D. Nörr, *Scritti Guarino* (1984), 2957–78; J. W. Tellegen, *ZRG* 1988, 263–311. T. Hon.

Cassius (*RE* 65) **Longinus, Lucius,** brother of *Cassius the tyrannicide, took *Caesar's side in the Civil War and in 48 BC held a proconsular command in Greece. Tribune 44, he took no part in the conspiracy against Caesar; he may have passed the *lex Cassia* enabling Caesar to create *patricians. He supported *Octavian against *Antony, and after their reconciliation in 43 fled to Asia, where Antony pardoned him in 41. C. *Cassius Longinus (2) was probably his great-grandson. T. J. Ca.; R. J. S.

Cassius (*RE* 70) **Longinus, Quintus,** probably cousin of the tyrannicide *Cassius, was *Pompey's rapacious quaestor in Further *Spain *c.*52 BC. In 49, as one of the two tribunes who supported *Caesar, he fled to his camp and in April summoned the senate on his behalf. Caesar made him governor of Further Spain, where he surpassed his conduct as quaestor. While preparing an expedition against *Juba (1) in 48 he was surprised by a rebellion of provincials and soldiers; peace was restored after the arrival of *Bogud and M. *Aemilius Lepidus (3), to whom he had sent for help. When his successor C. *Trebonius also arrived (early 47), he left with his treasures, but his ship was wrecked.

T. J. C.; R. J. S.

Cassius (*RE* 72) **Longinus Ravilla, Lucius,** as tribune in 137 BC passed a *lex tabellaria* extending voting by ballot to trials before the assembly, except for treason. (Cf. A. *Gabinius (1).) He was consul 127 and censor 125, when he and his colleague Cn. Servilius Caepio brought the Aqua Tepula (an inferior *aqueduct) to Rome. Renowned for severity as a *iudex* (called 'scopulus reorum', the rock on which the guilty foundered), he gained fame by formulating the question '*Cui bono?*' ('Who profited?') as a principle of criminal investigation. In 113, when three Vestals (see VESTA) had been accused of unchastity and two acquitted by the pontifex maximus L. *Caecilius Metellus Delmaticus, he was appointed a special investigator and condemned them and some men involved. E. B.

Cassius (*RE* 80) **Parmensis** (i.e. of Parma), **Gaius,** was, like *Cassius Longinus (1), among Caesar's murderers. *Horace (*Epist.* 1. 4. 3) thinks of Albius (*Tibullus) as writing poetry to surpass that of this Cassius (confused by the scholiasts with an inferior poet Cassius Etruscus, Hor. *Sat.* 1. 10. 61).

J. W. D.; R. J. S.

Cassius (*RE* 89) **Severus,** outspoken Augustan orator and wit. Some thought he marked a turning-point in Roman oratory (Tac. *Dial.* 19). A vivid picture is painted by the elder Seneca (*Controv.* 3 pref.). He was exiled on a charge of *maiestas under Augustus and his books were burned (Tac. *Ann.* 1. 72, 4. 21). He eventually died in Seriphos, apparently around AD 35.

*PIR*² C 522; Schanz–Hosius, § 336. 2; K. Heldmann, *Antike Theorien über Entwicklung und Verfall der Redekunst* (1982), 163–98. M. W.

Cassius (*RE* 91) **Vecellinus, Spurius,** is recorded in the *fasti as consul in 502, 493, and 486 BC, although the name Cassius is plebeian. According to tradition he negotiated the treaty (*foedus) between Rome and the Latins in 493, which established peace and a military alliance between the two parties. A copy of the treaty survived to the time of *Cicero (*Balb.* 53) and its terms are outlined by *Dionysius (7) of Halicarnassus (6. 95). In 486 Cassius is said to have proposed an agrarian law for the benefit of the *plebs,* but was accused of aiming at kingship and condemned to death. The surviving accounts make him a forerunner of the *Gracchi and contain many anachronisms, but it does not follow that the whole episode is invented.

E. Gabba, *Athenaeum* 1964, 29–41; Ogilvie, *Comm. Livy 1–5,* 337 ff.; A. N. Sherwin-White, *The Roman Citizenship,* 2nd edn. (1973), 20 ff.; A. Drummond, *CAH* 7²/2 (1989), 183 f.; T. J. Cornell, ibid. 274 ff.

T. J. Co.

Cassivellaunus, king presumably of the *Catuvellauni (Herts.), appointed supreme commander of the south-eastern Britons on the occasion of *Caesar's second invasion (54 BC). After an initial defeat in Kent, he endeavoured to avoid battle and hamper his enemies' foraging strategy with guerrilla tactics which much embarrassed Caesar, who was able, however, to capture his capital (perhaps Wheathampstead, Herts.). A peace was arranged through Caesar's agent *Commius, by which Cassivellaunus agreed to pay a tribute and allow the independence of the *Trinovantes (Essex). Following his submission, Caesar withdrew to Gaul. Subsequently the Catuvellauni expanded to become the dominant tribe in SE *Britain. No coinage can be certainly attributed to him.

Caes. *BGall.* 5. 2. S. S. Frere, *Britannia,* 3rd edn. (1987). S. S. F.; M. J. M.

Cassope, main city of the Cassopaeans, a Thesprotian people (see THESPROTI) who broke away around 400 BC to become an independent tribal state. An Epidaurian inscription (see EPIDAURUS) attests to the city's existence by the mid-4th cent., although it was probably not fortified this early. A member of the Epirote Alliance (343/2–232) and the League of *Epirus (232–168), Cassope supported *Perseus (2) against the Romans and suffered reprisals when the Romans punished Epirus following his defeat (168). Never totally abandoned, the city continued in existence until 31 BC when its inhabitants participated in the synoecism of *Nicopolis (3). Well-preserved remains of the city can be found above modern Kamarina and include a 3-km. (1¼-mi.) circuit wall, an agora, two theatres, a *katagōgion,* or 'guest house', and numerous Hellenistic houses.

PECS 440; *Lexikon der historischen Stätten* 307–8; Hammond, *Epirus* 553, 656. W. M. M.

Castor and Pollux, the temple of the *Dioscuri (*aedes Castorum* or even *Castoris*) at Rome, in the Forum, beside the Fountain of Juturna, was attributed (see especially Dion. Hal. *Ant. Rom.* 6. 13. 1–2) to the deities' miraculous intervention in 484 BC in the battle of Lake *Regillus in response to the vow of the dictator A.

Postumius (they brought the news of the victory to Rome in person). Recent excavation has shown that the first temple is indeed of about this date, and that it was little smaller than the rebuildings of L. *Caecilius Metellus Delmaticus (117) and Tiberius (dedicated AD 6), lavish though the last was. This was accordingly one of the first monumental structures in the vicinity of the Forum, and long the most imposing—testimony to the importance of the cavalry in the early Roman state: the function of the Dioscuri in other Latin towns, as attested by inscriptions (e.g. *ILLRP* 1271), and the link with the equestrian order (see EQUITES) and its annual parade, the *transvectio* of 15 July, which survived into the imperial period, leave little doubt that that was the principal association of the original cult. The temple on its high podium was a vantage-point in the Forum, and played an important part in the turbulent popular politics of the end of the republic. In the Augustan age, the brotherhood of the Dioscuri was an excuse for a display of *pietas* by Tiberius towards his dead brother Drusus. Some important remains of the architecture of this phase survive.

H. Scullard, *Festivals and Ceremonies of the Roman Republic* (1981), 65–8; Steinby, *Lexicon*, 'Castorum, aedes'. N. P.

Castor of Rhodes (1st cent. BC), rhetorician, author of a six-book *Chronological Tables* covering oriental, Greek, and Roman history from *Belus and Ninus to *Pompey (61/0 BC), subsequently used by *Varro, *Plutarch, Sex. *Iulius Africanus, and *Eusebius. Other historical and rhetorical works are also attested.

FGrH 250; Dahlmann, *RE* Suppl. 6 (1935), 1240. M. B. T.

Castra Regina (mod. Regensburg; or, from its Celtic name of Rataspona, Ratisbon), a Flavian military station in *Raetia, facing the confluences of the Regen and the Naab with the Danube (*Danuvius). Its auxiliary garrison was, under Marcus Aurelius, replaced by Legio III Italica, but Augsburg (Augusta Vindelicorum) remained the provincial capital.

H. Schönberger, *JRS* 1969, 144 ff. J. F. Dr.

Castulo, a major city and mint of the Oretani situated on the upper Guadalquivir (Baetis). It was a key centre during the Hannibalic War on account of its geographical situation and *silver-mines. It lay within Further Spain (in the Saltus Castulonensis), and exploitation of its mines by Rome probably began in the later 2nd cent. BC. It was probably made a *municipium under Caesar, and was absorbed by *Tarraconensis under Augustus.

J. M. Blázquez, *Excavaciones arqueológicas en España* 105 (1979). S. J. K.

catacombs, a term derived from κατὰ κύμβας, a locality close to the church of St Sebastian on the *via Appia, 3 miles south of Rome. The name may refer to the natural hollows across which the road passes or to an inn-sign, but was in use in the 4th and 5th cents. AD for the Christian cemetery associated with St Sebastian's in the form *ad catacumbas* or *catacumbae*. This famous cemetery was a series of narrow underground galleries and tomb-chambers cut in the rock. Their walls are lined with tiers (up to seven are known) of coffin-like recesses (*loculi*) for inhumation, holding one to four bodies apiece and sealed with a stone slab or tiles. The affinity to the *columbarium is evident, but the type itself seems to have been immediately derived from Jewish catacombs, where Jews, like Christians, remained a household of the faithful, united in death as in life. Catacombs were not confined to Rome: examples are known at Albano, *Alexandria (1), *Hadrumetum, Kertch', *Neapolis, Malta, and *Syracuse. All are associated with soft rocks, where tunnelling was easy.

The catacombs at Rome, however, are much the most extensive, stretching for at least 550 km. (340 mi.). Their distribution (some 50 are attested), along the main roads outside the city, is explained by their later growth out of, and side by side with, pagan cemeteries lying beyond the city boundaries in conformity with the law (see DEAD, DISPOSAL OF). That of St Priscilla, on the *via Salaria, was below a burial-ground of the Acilii Glabriones, although the old view that allegedly Christian members of this consular family were buried there is now doubted (M. Dondin-Payre, *Exercice du pouvoir et continuité gentilice*, etc. (1993), 203 ff.). The Domitilla catacomb, on the via Ardeatina, developed from the hypogeum of the Flavii. The official organization by the Church of public catacombs, mainly for the poor of Rome's Christian community, began *c.*200, when the then pope, St Zephyrinus, directed St Callixtus to provide τὸ κοιμητήριον or cemetery (see the 3rd-cent. Greek text known as the *Philosophumena*), which is represented by the oldest part of the catacomb beside the via Appia that bears St Callixtus' name today. Another important catacomb near the same road is that of Praetextatus.

In the tomb-chambers (*cubicula*) of the catacombs are altar-tombs and arched recesses (*arcosolia*) for the bodies of popes and martyrs. Walls and ceilings received paintings (see PAINTING, ROMAN) which represent the first development of Christian art and are executed in the same technique and style as contemporary pagan work. Their subjects are biblical (scenes from the OT far outnumbering those from the NT) or symbolic (the Good Shepherd, Christ-*Orpheus, Christ as lawgiver, eucharistic and celestial banquets, figures of *orantes*, etc.). A few motifs are drawn from daily life and some are frankly pagan. A remarkable and probably private catacomb, dating from the 4th cent. and discovered on the via Latina in 1955, has paintings which include a medical class and six episodes from the *Hercules-cycle (see HERACLES), as well as biblical scenes more elaborate and showing a much wider range of content than those in the official public catacombs. Furniture in the catacombs included carved *sarcophagi, lamps, pottery, and painted-glass medallions.

The presence of these large cemeteries is explained partly by the size of the Christian community in Rome and partly by the long periods of toleration. About a century after the official recognition of the Church, the catacombs fell into disuse and became centres of *pilgrimage.

O. Marucchi, *Le catacombe romane* (1933); L. Hertling and E. Kirschbaum, *Le catacombe romane e i loro martiri* (1949; Eng. trans. 1960); J. Stevenson, *The Catacombs* (1978); G. Bertonière, *The Cult-centre of the Martyr Hippolytus on the Via Tiburtina* (1985); A. Ferrua, *The Unknown Catacomb* (1991), on the via Latina complex. On the Jewish catacombs of Rome: G. Frey, *Rend. Pont.* 1937; E. Goodenough, *Jewish Symbols in the Graeco-Roman Period* 2 (1953), 3 ff.; 3 (1957), figs. 707–838; M. Williams, *ZPE* 101 (1994) 165 ff.

I. A. R.; J. M. C. T.; A. J. S. S.

Catana (Κατάνη, Lat. Catina, mod. Catania), founded from *Naxos (2) in 729 BC, lies on the sea at the SE side of Mt. Aetna; to the south and west stretches the fertile Catania plain, coveted by the Syracusans, whose superior power dominated Catana for much of its history. Its lawgiver *Charondas was its most famous citizen in its early period. *Hieron (1) I removed the Catanaeans to Leontini and renamed the city Aetna, repeopling it with Doric mercenaries. In 461 these were expelled and the old name restored. The Athenians used Catana as a base in 415–413. Captured by *Dionysius (1) I in 403, it from then on formed part of the Syracusan empire, with brief intervals of independence or subjection to *Carthage. After 263, when the Romans captured it, it became a *civitas decumana*, and it flourished under the Roman republic (Cic. 2 *Verr.* 3. 103), although it suffered damage in the First Slave War. A *colonia* under Augustus, it was extensively rebuilt under the empire: the theatre, odeum, amphitheatre, and three public bath-buildings are known, as well as the site of the forum and a possible circus. Part of the ancient city, however, disappeared beneath the lava flow from the eruption of 1669, which profoundly altered the ancient topography and obliterated the natural harbour. See AETNA (2).

PECS 442–3; BTCGI 5 (1987), 153–77; A. Holm, *Catania antica* (1925); G. Libertini, *Scritti su Catania antica* (1981); R. J. A. Wilson, *ANRW* 2. 11. 1 (1988), 123–36, and *Sicily under the Roman Empire* (1990), *passim*.
A. G. W.; R. J. A. W.

catapults See ARTILLERY; SIEGECRAFT, GREEK.

Catiline See SERGIUS CATILINA, L.

Catius (*RE* 1), **Titus**, an Insubrian from Cisalpine Gaul (see GAUL (CISALPINE)), is mentioned by Cicero (*Fam.* 15. 16) as a recently deceased writer on Epicureanism (see EPICURUS). He is also mentioned by *Quintilian (*Inst.* 10. 1. 24) and probably by *Pliny (2) the Younger (*Ep.* 4. 28), who supplies the praenomen.
Schanz–Hosius, § 157b.
M. T. G.

Cato (Censorius) See PORCIUS CATO (1), M.

Cato (Uticensis) See PORCIUS CATO (2), M.

catoptrics, a special field of *optics, is properly the geometric theory of the visual appearances of objects seen under reflection (*anaklasis*), but among the ancients also includes studies of refraction (*diaklasis*) and of burning mirrors (*pyria*). The basic principle that rays are reflected at equal angles is already understood in the 4th cent. BC (cf. Pl. *Ti.* 46ac; Arist. [*Pr.*] 16. 13). The earliest extant compilation of catoptrical theorems is *Euclid's *Catoptrica* (early 3rd cent. BC), a text whose authenticity is sometimes doubted. Euclid proves theorems on the location, size, and orientation of images in plane, convex, and concave mirrors, and proposes a false theorem on the convergence of rays in concave spherical mirrors. A version of some of the Euclidean results, with additional descriptions of deployments of trick mirrors, is in the catoptrics by *Heron of Alexandria (mid-1st cent. AD), extant only in a medieval Latin version, *De speculis*, misattributed to Ptolemy (4). Another treatment of catoptrics, extant in the *Optica* attributed to Ptolemy (mid-2nd cent. AD), surveys much the same material as Euclid and Heron, with a few additions, e.g. experimental verification and quantification of the principles of reflection and refraction. More sophisticated geometrically is the tract *On Burning-mirrors* by *Diocles (4) (late 3rd cent. BC), extant in its Arabic translation. Diocles proves how to reflect the parallel rays from the sun to a given point by means of a parabolic mirror and shows that spherical mirrors lack a coherent focal point (the phenomenon later called 'spherical aberration'). The principle of refraction, e.g. that rays are bent towards the normal when passing from air into water, is stated in Euclid's *Catoptrica* (post. 6), but not applied in the extant version of that tract. Extensions of this sort are reported by Apuleius as being in a catoptrical work he assigns to *Archimedes. This and two other ancient references to an Archimedean catoptrics, however, appear to be misattributions. Similarly, the legends of Archimedes' use of great burning mirrors to defend Syracuse against the Roman siege are the product of Byzantine imaginations.

J. L. Heiberg (ed.), *Euclidis Opera* 5 (1895); A. Lejeune (ed.), *Optique de Claude Ptolémée*, 2nd edn. (1989); G. J. Toomer (ed.), *Diocles: On Burning Mirrors* (1976); W. R. Knorr, *Isis* 1983, 53–73, and *Archives internationales d'histoire des sciences* 1985, 28–105; A. Jones, *Centaurus* 1987, 1–17.
W. R. K.

Catreus, in mythology, son of *Minos and Pasiphae, and father of *Althaemenes, Apemosyne, *Aerope, and *Clymene. Because of a prophecy that one of his children would kill him, Althaemenes and Apemosyne emigrated to *Rhodes, and Catreus gave Aerope and Clymene to *Nauplius (2) the navigator and slave-trader to sell overseas. Aerope married Pleisthenes, who in this version replaces *Atreus as father of *Agamemnon; and Clymene married Nauplius himself and bore *Palamedes and Oeax. Althaemenes killed Apemosyne because he did not believe her when she told him that she had been raped by *Hermes; and also killed Catreus when he visited Rhodes, believing him to be a pirate (Apollod. 3. 2).
H. J. R.; J. R. M.

Cattigara, port of the Sinae (see SERES) near the mouth of the river Cottaris. Marinus of Tyre mentions a sailor Alexander who, in the 1st cent. AD, sailed to Cattigara on a gulf inhabited by fish-eaters (Ptol. *Geog* 1. 14. 1). No archaeological site can be reliably identified, although Oc-éo near the Mekong Delta in southern Vietnam is a candidate.

L. Malleret, *L'Archéologie du Delta du Mekong* 3 (1963), 421–54; M. Raschke, *ANRW* 2. 9. 2 (1978), n. 1694.
I. C. G.

Catullus (1), **Gaius Valerius,** Roman poet, came from a distinguished propertied family of *Verona but spent most of his life in Rome. The dates of his life are incorrectly transmitted in the *Chronicle* of Jerome but can be approximately reconstructed. He was probably born in 84 BC or a little earlier, and probably died in 54 BC: at any rate, there is no trace in his work of events subsequent to 55 BC. Since he was sent to Rome as a young man, his family were probably thinking of a political career, but he seems to have had no great ambitions in this area. His only public activity, so far as we know, was service on the staff of the propraetor C. *Memmius (2), who was governor of Bithynia in 57–6 BC. In general, the political events of the turbulent decade he passed in Rome are little mentioned in his work. On one occasion his politically active friend C. *Licinius Calvus involved him in a literary campaign against the triumvirs, especially *Caesar (with his minion, *Mamurra), but this outburst of ill-humour did not last and when Caesar magnanimously offered him his hand in reconciliation, he did not refuse it (Suet. *Iul.* 73).

If Catullus was only marginally involved in politics, he was at the centre of the radical social change that marked the end of the republic. He lived in the circles of the *jeunesse dorée* (the *delicata iuventus* as Cicero called them) who had turned away from the ideals of early Rome and embraced Hellenistic Greek culture. This environment affected not only Catullus' outlook and views but also his language, which acquired a facility previously unknown in Roman literature. In a literary sense also Catullus was surrounded by like-minded individuals. A whole group of young poets, the so-called 'neoterics', shared the same rejection of traditional norms and the same search for new forms and content, and, as in their lifestyle, Hellenistic culture provided the most important model (see HELLENISTIC POETRY AT ROME). In these same aristocratic circles Catullus met the married woman whom he called 'Lesbia'. He depicts her as self-assured, beautiful, and cultured, and regards her becoming his lover as the peak of felicity. But when he realizes that she has been false to him with

Catullus

a succession of partners, his happiness turns to despair. The ups and downs of this affair provide Catullus with the central theme of his poetry. His love poetry is completely different from the light-hearted frivolity of Hellenistic literature, as presented in the epigrams of the *Greek Anthology*; he sought in love not sexual transport but a deep human union which would last a whole lifetime. Apuleius (*Apol.* 10) tells us that behind the name Lesbia was a Clodia, and this seems to offer a secure historical context, since we know of a Clodia with similar characteristics living in Rome at this time, the sister of P. *Clodius Pulcher and wife to the consul of 60 BC, Q. *Caecilius Metellus Celer. Cicero gives a picture of her in his *Pro Caelio* which for all its bias must have had some basis in life. The identity of Lesbia and Clodia was for a long time thought secure, but has often been questioned in the 20th cent. Nevertheless, even if the identification cannot be proved, Cicero's picture of the historical *Clodia is instructive for the social background to Catullus' poetry.

Catullus died young, and left behind only a slim corpus of work amounting to 114 poems of extremely varied length and form. The book is primarily ordered on metrical grounds. Sixty short poems in lyric or iambic metres are followed by poems 61–8, which are long poems in a variety of metres: the remainder of the book consists of *epigrams. Another structural principle groups the elegies and epigrams together—that is, all the poems in elegiacs (65–116). Within these major sections, the ordering is again not random. In the short poems, as far as possible, a succession of poems in the same metre is avoided: the only exceptions are the many poems in phalaecean hendecasyllables, which often of necessity must be placed together, and the two short closural poems, 59 and 60. In the long poems, the first and last are metrically related to the neighbouring shorter poems: poem 61 is in lyric metre, 65–8 in elegiacs. A series of cycles may also be noticed in the content; the most important of these is the Lesbia cycle at the beginning of the book (2, 3, 5, 7, 8, 11), telling the story of Catullus' love affair from their first courtship through the height of passion to estrangement and the final break up of the affair. It is then up to the reader to place the rest of the Lesbia poems, which are not ordered chronologically, within this framework. There is another Lesbia cycle in the epigrams (70–87), though it is more loosely constructed and not completely chronological. Further cycles of related poems include those dealing with the dubious pair of friends Furius and Aurelius (15–26) and with Gellius (74–91, and then 116). Other motifs, such as the trip to Bithynia, the Iuventius poems, and the invectives against Caesar, are distributed throughout the book. This apparently careless arrangement has led some to believe that Catullus did not order the book himself, but that it is the result of posthumous publication. The principles of ordering mentioned above, however, seem more likely to go back to the poet himself, and a similar variety may be discerned in various reconstructions of Hellenistic books, such as the *Garland* of *Meleager (2) (see BOOKS, POETIC).

The three major groupings of poems within the corpus differ considerably in their approach. The short poems (1–60) contain much that one might term 'social poetry' from a thematic point of view, though they also include expressions of stronger emotions. These poems are certainly not, as has sometimes been thought, artless productions of a moment's reflection: Catullus models himself in them on the elegance and facility of the shorter Hellenistic forms. The group of longer poems in more elevated style begins with two wedding poems (61–2): poem 63 describes the fate of a young man who has become a devotee of *Cybele,

the '*epyllion' 64 contrasts happy and unhappy love in the stories of *Peleus and *Ariadne, and 65–8 are a series of elegiac poems on various themes. Poem 66 (with the introductory poem 65) contains a translation of the *Lock of Berenice* which concludes *Callimachus (3)'s *Aetia*: 68 (possibly two connected poems), is often seen as a precursor of the love elegies of *Propertius and *Tibullus. The epigrams (69–116) differ radically from the other poems. Even when they deal with the painful circumstances of the poet's own life, they are never simply representations of a momentary emotion, but rather reflective analyses of a situation or the poet's own experience.

BIBLIOGRAPHY K. Quinn, *ANRW* 1. 3 (1973), 369–89; H. Harrauer, *A Bibliography to Catullus* (1979); J. P. Holoka, *Gaius Valerius Catullus: A Systematic Bibliography* (1985).
TEXTS R. A. B. Mynors (1958); H. Bardon, 2nd edn. (1973); G. P. Goold, with Eng. trans. (1983); G. Lee, with Eng. trans. (1991).
COMMENTARIES E. Baehrens (1885); R. Ellis, 2nd edn. (1889); W. Kroll, 5th edn. (1968); C. J. Fordyce (1961); H.-P. Syndikus, 3 vols (1984–90; German).
STUDIES E. A. Havelock, *The Lyric Genius of Catullus* (1967); K. Quinn, *Catullus: An Interpretation* (1972); R. O. A. M. Lyne, *The Latin Love Poets* (1980), 19–64; T. P. Wiseman, *Catullus and his World* (1985); J. K. Newman, *Roman Catullus and the Modification of the Alexandrian Sensibility* (1991). H. P. S.

Catullus (2) (*RE* 2), writer of *mime in or before the mid-1st cent. AD (Juv. 8. 185 ff., 13. 111; Mart. 5. 30. 3) whose lost works include *Phasma* ('The Ghost'), called *clamosum* ('noisy') by Juvenal, and *Laureolus*, the tale of a notorious bandit, whose crucifixion was staged live (Mart. *Spect.* 7. 4; Suet. *Calig.* 57, Joseph. *AJ* 19. 94). Despite *Cicero's reference to a mimographer Valerius in *Fam.* 7. 11. 3, Wiseman's arguments that the mime-writer Catullus was the poet Valerius *Catullus (1) cannot be proved.

T. P. Wiseman, *Catullus and his World* (1985), 192–8, 258; K. M. Coleman, *JRS* 1990, 44–73. E. F.

Catuvellauni, the most powerful southern British tribe, occupying parts of Herts., Beds., Cambs., Bucks., and Northants. *Cassivellaunus probably ruled this tribe; later kings were *Tasciovanus and his son *Cunobel(l)inus, who became the leading ruler in pre-Roman *Britain. After AD 43 a *civitas was created with its capital at *Verulamium, though this town itself may have possessed municipal status (see MUNICIPIUM). Building done by a corvée of this *civitas* is attested on Hadrian's Wall (*RIB* 1962). The region was mainly agricultural with an important cluster of villas around Verulamium. Large pottery industries were founded near Radlett (Herts.), in the Nene valley, and in Oxfordshire.

K. Branigan, *The Catuvellauni* (1985). S. S. F.; M. J. M.

Caucasus, a mountain range from the Black (*Euxine) Sea to the *Caspian. The Main Caucasus lies to the north, the Lesser Caucasus to the south: they are joined by the Likhi mountains which separate *Colchis and Transcaucasian *Iberia (2). Classical writers are regularly confused about the location of the Caucasus range, which is variously amalgamated with the Urals or the Hindu Kush. However, the significance of its passes was recognized as early as Herodotus, but their locations and names remained controversial even after *Pompey's Transcaucasian adventure in 65 BC and recurrent Roman military and diplomatic activity in the region thereafter (e.g. Plin. *HN* 6. 30–40; but cf. *IG Rom.* 1. 192). In the Graeco-Roman world, the Caucasus was best known as the site of *Prometheus' sufferings, which made it something of a tourist attraction.

D. C. Braund, *Georgia in Antiquity* (1994); *LIMC* 'Kaukasos'.   D. C. B.

Caudine Forks, the narrow defile where a Roman army was trapped by, and surrendered to, Gavius *Pontius 321 BC (Livy 9. 2–6). It lay in the territory of the Caudini Samnites, somewhere between *Capua and *Beneventum, but cannot be certainly identified. The Arienzo–Arpaia valley, the traditional site, contains the significantly named hamlet Forchia, but seems too small; an objection that applies also to the valley between S. Agata de' Goti and Moiano. The plain between Arpaia and Montesarchio, although large enough, does not fit Livy's description.

RE 3/2, 'Caudinae furculae'; P. Sommella, *Antichi campi di battaglia in Italia* (1967), 49 ff.   E. T. S.; T. W. P.

Caulonia, 7th-cent. BC *Achaean, possibly Crotoniate (see CROTON), colony. It flourished in the 6th cent. but was sacked by *Dionysius (1) I in 387 and became a Locrian dependency (see LOCRI EPIZEPHYRII). Independence was restored by *Dionysius (2) II but it suffered *Oscan and Hannibalic raids (see HANNIBAL), and was deserted by the 1st cent. BC.

H. Tréziny, *Kaulonia* 1 (1989).   K. L.

Caunus (mod. Dalyan), city in south-eastern *Caria, close to *Lycia. It was generally reckoned to be Carian, though *Herodotus (1) (1. 176. 3) says the Caunians imitated the Lycians in most respects, and the local script of Caunus is not quite like Carian (L. Robert, *Hellenica* 8 (1950), 20–1; cf. Hdt. 1. 172). It was captured by Harpagus for Persia in the 6th cent. BC (Hdt. 1. 176. 3), tributary to Athens in the 5th (see DELIAN LEAGUE), and within the sphere of influence of *Hecatomnus and his son *Mausolus (*SEG* 12. 470–1) in the 4th. Thereafter it can be considered a Greek city. It was controlled by various of the Hellenistic kings until Rhodes bought it for 200 talents from Ptolemaic Egypt in *c*.191 (Polyb. 30. 31. 6 with Walbank, *HCP*) so that it became 'the main city of the Rhodian Peraea' (Walbank on Polyb. 30. 5. 11; for the Peraea see RHODES). The Romans freed it in 167, but returned it, perhaps only temporarily, to Rhodes as a punishment for supporting *Mithradates VI in 88. Despite a history of malaria (see DISEASE), Caunus was prosperous (see the 1st-cent. AD customs inscription, *JHS* 1954, 97–105), not just from its maritime trade but from its fertile territory (it was famous for its figs and had good timber resources). Caunus had impressive public buildings and fortifications. The rock-cut tombs are notable.

Strabo 14. 651–2. G. E. Bean, *JHS* 1953, 10–35 and 1954, 85–110, and *Turkey Beyond the Maiander*, 2nd edn. (1980), ch. 14, also in *PECS* 443–4; P. Roos, *The Rock-tombs of Caunus* 1–2 (1972–4), and in T. Linders and P. Hellström (eds.), *Architecture and Society in Hecatomnid Caria* (1989), 63–8; S. Hornblower, *Mausolus* (1982), see index; *Arch. Rep.* 1970–1, 54; 1978–9, 83; 1984–5, 89; 1989–90, 109; L. Robert, *Documents d'Asie Mineure* (1987), 487–520 (the outstanding treatment).   S. H.

cavalry See AUXILIA; EQUITES; HIPPEIS § 2.

caves, sacred The Greeks associated caves with the primitive (see TROGODYTAE), the uncanny, and hence the sacred. In myth they witness divine births (Zeus on Mt. Dicte), are home to monsters (the *Cyclopes), and conceal illicit sex (see SELENE). Remote and wild, real caves attracted the cult of *Pan and the *Nymphs, for whom several dozen cave-sanctuaries are known (e.g. those of Attica; the Corycian Cave at *Delphi) or, as openings to the Underworld, oracles of the dead: note the 'cave-like shrine' at *Taenarum (1) (Paus. 3. 25. 4) and the vaulted crypt excavated

at *Ephyra. In Italy the most celebrated holy cave was the Lupercal on the Palatine (see LUPERCALIA). Of imported cults, the most associated with caves was Mithraism (see MITHRAS), whose rites were celebrated in real or make-belief caves because the cave was considered an 'image of the universe'. That thesis is also central to Porphyry's *On the Cave of the Nymphs* (best in Lamberton's translation, 1983), an allegorical interpretation of Homer's description in *Od*. 13 of the cave near which the sleeping Odysseus is set on his return to Ithaca. Because Homer's cave has two doors, one for men and the other for immortals, Porphyry's explication is much concerned with doctrines of the entry and exit of souls into and out of the world. The cave's moistness and its dedication to water-nymphs (naiads) are related to genesis into mortal existence.

R. Buxton, *Imaginary Greece* (1994), 104 ff.; J. Travlos, *Bildlexikon zur Topographie des antiken Attika* (1988), see index under 'Nymphen', 'Pan'; *L'Antre Corycien* 1–2, *BCH* Suppls. 7, 9 (1981–4).   R. L. B., A. J. S. S.

Cebes, of Thebes (1), like his compatriot *Simmias (1), is a main character in *Plato (1)'s *Phaedo*; he probably also shared with him long-standing membership of the Socratic circle (see *Cri.* 45b; Xen. *Mem.* 1. 2. 49, 3. 11. 17; see SOCRATES). Their having 'been together with' *Philolaus while he was in *Thebes (1) (*Phd.* 61d–e) is poor evidence of Pythagorean affiliations. *Diogenes (6) Laertius reports of him solely that he had three dialogues attributed to him, *Pinax*, *Hebdome*, and *Phrynichus*. An extant dialogue with the title Κέβητος Θηβαίου πίναξ (ed. K. Praechter, 1893) has Cynic/Stoic connections, and probably belongs to the 1st cent. AD. References to Cebes in [Plato] *Letter* 13 (363a) and Plutarch, *De genio Socratis* (?575e, 580e, 590a) reflect his literary role in the *Phaedo*.   C. J. R.

Cecrops, a mythical king of Athens. In most accounts (*Marm. Par.* A1 is an exception) he was not the first king, being son-in-law and successor to Actaeus, but Athenians clearly regarded him as their archetypal ancestral figure. No parents are recorded for him, and probably he was thought of as autochthonous (see AUTOCHTHONS). He was described as διφυής, 'double-natured', with reference to his form as half-man, half-snake—the normal style of his depiction on red-figure vases, where he is a popular figure in many Athenian scenes. Cecrops was the father of *Aglaurus, *Pandrosus, and Herse, and of one son Erysichthon, who died young. His deeds mark him out as a civilizing figure, the one who established monogamous marriage, writing, funeral rites (schol. Aristoph. *Plut.* 773, Tac. *Ann.* 11. 14. 2; Cic. *Leg.* 2. 63), and other customs which though diverse were perceived as important to contemporary, 'normal', society. The foundation of many religious cults was also ascribed to him. The historical tradition recognized a second King Cecrops, son of *Erechtheus; probably it was this Cecrops who was worshipped at *Haliartus in Boeotia, and he may also have come to be identified as the tribal eponym (see EPONYMOI).

B. Knittlmayer, I. Kasper-Butz, and I. Krauskopf, *LIMC* 6. 1084–91; Kron, *Phylenheroen* 84–103, 259–62; Kearns, *Heroes of Attica* 110–12, 175–6.   E. Ke.

Celeus, as ruler of *Eleusis in the *Homeric Hymn to Demeter* (96 ff.), accepts the disguised Demeter as nurse of his son *Demophon (2).

Kern, *RE* 11. 138–42; N. J. Richardson (ed.), *The Homeric Hymn to Demeter* (1974, 1979), pp. 176 ff.; R. Proskynitopoulou, *LIMC* 5. 981–3.   N. J. R.

Celsus

Celsus, jurist, see IUVENTIUS CELSUS; medical author, see CORNELIUS CELSUS, A. 'Library of Celsus' (Ephesus), see LIBRARIES.

Celsus, author of a comprehensive philosophical polemic against *Christianity, The True Doctrine, written probably between 175 and 181 (Origen, c. Cels. 8. 69, 71). The work is primarily known through *Origen (1)'s Contra Celsum, which preserves most of it through direct quotation. Celsus wrote from the perspective of a Middle Platonic philosopher, though in one section of his work he also appears to have adopted the criticism levelled against Christianity by a Jew (Origen, c. Cels. 1. 28). *The True Doctrine* is important evidence for knowledge of Christian doctrine among Gentiles, as well as for the difficulty outsiders had in determining the difference between 'orthodox' Christians and *Gnostic fringe groups (Origen, c. Cels. 5. 61 ff.). The importance of Celsus' book is suggested by the fact that Origen's massive refutation was written in the 240s.

Efforts to identify this Celsus with the Celsus who is the addressee of Lucian's *Alexander* are not convincing: the author of *The True Doctrine* was a Platonist, while the recipient of the *Alexander* was evidently an Epicurean.

R. Bader, Ἀληθὴς λόγος (1940); H. Chadwick, *Origen: Contra Celsum* (1965); R. J. Hoffman, *Celsus: On the True Doctrine* (1987).

W. D. R.; D. S. P.

Celtiberians, a name used by Graeco-Roman writers to describe several peoples (Arevaci, Lusones, etc.) living around the middle Ebro valley and in the eastern Meseta of Spain. The Celtic flavour of their script, religion, and elements of their material culture distinguishes them from their neighbours to the west and east (see CELTS). However their characteristic ceramics and richly decorated weapons were widely adopted by indigenous peoples in central and northern Iberia. Most of the population lived in *castros* (hill-forts). Towns were rare and appear after the 5th–4th cents. BC. After a first encounter with Cato (Censorius) (195 BC), wars against Rome occurred between 181 and 179 (peace of Ti. *Sempronius Gracchus (2)), 153 and 151, and finally 143 and 133 (the war of *Numantia). Pompey sacked the towns of Celtiberians who had supported *Sertorius (72 BC). The *tabula Contrebiensis* and settlements like Azaila suggest that *Romanization had begun in the early 1st cent. BC. The region was incorporated in the *conventus of Clunia.

I Symposium sobre los Celtiberos (1987); M. Salinas, *Conquista y romanización de Celtiberia* (1986).

S. J. K.

Celtic languages The Celtic branch of Indo-European is traditionally divided into Insular Celtic and Continental Celtic. The records of the Continental Celtic languages consist of names, occurring in profusion in Greek and Roman sources, and epigraphic remains from the Classical period; none of these languages can be shown to have survived beyond imperial times. The best known is Gaulish: in the Greek alphabet (borrowed from *Massalia) there are funerary and votive inscriptions on stone, mainly from Gallia Narbonensis (c.200–50 BC; see GAUL (TRANSALPINE)) but also from central Gaul (c.100 BC–AD 50), as well as graffiti on pottery. In the Latin alphabet, from the mid-1st cent. BC onwards, from most parts of Gaul, there are inscriptions on stone and a range of other texts, including substantial fragments of a late 2nd-cent. bronze calendar from Coligny, a sizeable corpus of graffiti in cursive script on pottery from La Graufesenque (c. AD 40–120), and cursive inscriptions on lead tablets, such as those from Chamalières and Larzac, that are not fully understood. There are also a few Gaulish inscriptions from

Italy, probably of the last two cents. BC, written in the Lugano alphabet (see ALPHABETS OF ITALY). Other short inscriptions in this alphabet, from c.550 to the 1st cent. BC, found in the region of the Italian lakes, are in a form of Celtic known as Lepontic: the differences between this and Gaulish seem slight. From Spain there are *Celtiberian inscriptions (see SPAIN, PRE-ROMAN SCRIPTS AND LANGUAGES). The Celts who, in the 3rd cent. BC, settled in central Anatolia and gave their name to *Galatia have left no remains of their language beyond names and glosses.

Within Insular Celtic, two language groups are recognized: Goidelic (Irish and its offshoots—Scots Gaelic and Manx) and British or Brittonic (Welsh, Cornish, and Breton). Their classification as Insular Celtic may be understood not simply as a geographical designation but also as implying a shared development from proto-Celtic: this has been challenged by those scholars who prefer to stress links between British and Gaulish.

The earliest evidence for Irish comes from short inscriptions in the Ogam alphabet, found in Ireland but also in South Wales and elsewhere in western Britain, and assigned mainly to the 5th and 6th cents. AD. Manuscript remains (in the Latin alphabet) first appear in the 7th cent, but it is the fuller evidence from the 8th and 9th cents. (principally glosses in Latin manuscripts) that represents classical Old Irish. Later manuscripts have also preserved early material, notably legal texts and sagas, but allowance has always to be made for scribal modernization of the language. There are extensive remains of Middle Irish (c.950–1200) and an unbroken attestation of Modern Irish from c.1200 down to the present day. Manx (now extinct) and Scots Gaelic apparently separated from Irish only in medieval times.

British was the language of almost the whole of Britain in the Roman period. Names found in Greek and Roman sources, more rarely in Latin inscriptions, are the earliest attestations (the only direct evidence may be provided by one or two unintelligible fragmentary texts on lead tablets). Following the Saxon incursions of the 5th cent. AD and the eventual confinement of the language to western regions, linguistic divisions resulted in separate languages: Cornish, extinct since the 18th cent.; Welsh, still spoken in many parts of Wales; Cumbrian, which apparently did not survive beyond medieval times. The form of the language taken across to Brittany by British settlers from the mid-5th cent. onwards developed into Breton (claims of Gaulish influence are doubtful). The first meagre manuscript remains of Old Welsh date from the 8th cent., those of Old Cornish and Old Breton from the 9th; more abundant testimony is available for subsequent stages.

Recueil des inscriptions gauloises (1985–); R. Marichal, *Les Graffites de La Graufesenque* (1988); M. Lejeune, *Lepontica* (1971); L. Weisgerber, in *Natalicium Johannes Geffcken* (1931), 151 ff.; D. MacManus, *A Guide to Ogam* (1991); R. Thurneysen, *A Grammar of Old Irish* (1948); K. Jackson, *Language and History in Early Britain* (1953); H. Lewis and H. Pedersen, *A Concise Comparative Celtic Grammar*, rev. edn. (1961). J. H. W. P.

Celts, a name applied by ancient writers to a population group occupying lands mainly north of the Mediterranean region from Galicia in the west to Galatia in the east. (Its application to the Welsh, the Scots, and the Irish is modern.) Their unity is recognizable by common speech and common artistic traditions. (1) Dialects of Celtic are still spoken (Ireland, Scotland, Wales, Brittany), or are attested by inscriptions, quotations, and place-names in this area. See CELTIC LANGUAGES. (2) The artistic unity is most apparent in the La Tène style (called from the Swiss type-site) which appears c.500 BC. It is a very idiosyncratic art of swinging, swelling lines, at its best alive and yet reposeful.

It is generally accepted that the primary elements of Celtic culture originated with the bronze age 'Urn-field people' of the upper Danube (13th cent. BC), who probably spoke a proto-Celtic language. From the 8th cent. bronze-working was gradually overtaken by iron-working, and as a result the 'Urn-field culture' was transformed into the 'Hallstatt culture' (from the Austrian type-site). It may have been the availability of iron weapons that allowed and encouraged cultures which we may term Celtic to appear in Spain and Great Britain as early as the 8th and 7th cents. Hallstatt society reached its highest point in the 6th cent., but fell victim to economic and political dislocation early in the 5th. However, Celtic development continued unabated with the emergence of La Tène culture, which was so strong that it gave Celtic warriors the power to break through the defences of the Classical world and reach the Mediterranean. In 390 they sacked Rome; and while in 279 one band raided *Delphi, in 278 another crossed the Hellespont and eventually settled the territory called *Galatia, where Celtic was still spoken in the 5th cent. AD. It was a developed Celtic La Tène society that *Caesar confronted and described in Gaul in the mid-1st cent. BC, and indeed the migration of the *Helvetii may be interpreted as the last great ancient Celtic population-movement. But by then the tide was running against the Celts. The ancients knew them as fierce fighters and superb horsemen, and noticed the savagery of their religious rites conducted by the priesthood, the Druids, who derived their doctrine from Britain. See RELIGION, CELTIC. Yet the Celts' political sense was weak, and they were crushed between the migratory Germans and the power of Rome, to be ejected (e.g. from Bohemia and southern Germany) by the former, and conquered outright by the latter. However, there was a notable revival of the Celtic warrior-spirit in the late Roman period, when western nobles either fought against the final wave of invaders or served their kings as counsellors and generals.

T. G. E. Powell, *The Celts* (1958); A. Ross, *Pagan Celtic Britain* (1967); S. Piggott, *The Druids* (1968); A. Momigliano, *Alien Wisdom* (1975), ch. 3; J. Untermann, *Kl. Pauly* 5 (1979), 1612 ff.; J. Collis, *The European Iron Age* (1984); H. D. Rankin, *Celts and the Classical World* (1987).   J. F. Dr.

cemeteries The organization of a formal cemetery, as a space reserved exclusively for the *disposal of the *dead, was an important dimension of the social definition of the ancient city. Burial within the settlement had been common in many parts of the Mediterranean world in the early iron age, but after the 8th cent. BC it was rare. Cemeteries normally lined the roads leading away from cities. They usually consisted of numerous small grave-plots, which were rarely used for more than two or three generations, although some cemeteries, such as the *Ceramicus at Athens, remained in use for over a millennium. Burial in a recognized cemetery was a primary symbol of *citizenship in Athens.

The spatial distinction between city and cemetery held fast throughout pagan antiquity, only changing as part of the broader transformation associated with the Christian take-over of the western Roman empire. There were two parallel developments. Starting in the 3rd cent., Christians began building *basilicas over the shrines of saints, which were normally in extramural cemeteries. By the 6th cent. some of these basilicas were forming the centres for new towns: 'the city has changed address', as Jerome (*Ep.* 107. 1) put it. Meanwhile, by the 4th cent. the population of many western cities was shrinking, leaving open areas within the walls. From Britain to Africa, city-dwellers started burying in these spaces in the 5th cent. At Rome, the last-dated known burial outside the city and the first epitaph from within

it both date to 567. By the 7th cent. the two processes were combining, as the first large churchyard cemeteries within settlements appeared, and by the 11th cent. this had been established as the medieval pattern.   I. Mo.

Cenchreae (mod. Kechries), eastern port of *Corinth on the Saronic Gulf. Natural protection was increased by moles of uncertain date. Little Classical or earlier has been recovered, but the place was fortified perhaps as early as 480 BC. Excavations show that major development (quays, warehouses) occurred in the 1st cent. AD following Corinth's refoundation as a *colonia*. *Apuleius has Lucius return from ass to human form during the festival of *Isis at Cenchreae. Structures can still be seen in the water, since the sea-level has changed. The most important finds, in the Isthmia museum, are the late-Roman glass panels (found in crates for shipment) depicting landscapes and figures such as *Homer and *Plato (1).

R. Scranton, *PECS* 446; excavations: *Kenchreai* 1– (1978–).
J. B. S.

Cenomani, Gauls, reputed to be Aulerci, who established themselves in *Gaul (Cisalpine) *c.*400 BC (Polyb. 2. 17; Strabo 5. 216). Their territory lay around Lake Garda. Chief towns: Brixia and probably *Verona and Bergomum (Livy 5. 35). The Cenomani usually supported Rome, e.g. in 225 BC against *Boii and *Insubres and in 218 against *Hannibal (Polyb. 2. 23, 24, 32; Livy 21. 55). In 200, however, they joined the Carthaginian general Hamilcar, but were quickly subjugated and Romanized, disappearing from history (Livy 31. 10; 32. 30). In 49 BC Gallia *Transpadana, including the Cenomani district, obtained Roman citizenship.

S. Sabatino and others (eds.), *The Celts* (1991), 244 ff.   E. T. S.; T. W. P.

censor, the title of one of a pair of senior Roman magistrates, elected by the centuriate assembly (see CENTURIA) to hold office for eighteen months. Although they lacked *imperium* and the right to an escort of lictors (*lictores*), the censors possessed considerable authority and influence owing to the range of their responsibilities. The censorship was established in 443 BC as a civil magistracy with the primary function of making up and maintaining the official list of Roman citizens (*census*), previously the task of the consuls (see CENSUS). The censors were initially exclusively patrician. One of the *leges Publiliae* of 339 required that at least one of the censors be a plebeian (see PUBLILIUS PHILO, Q.), but not until 131 BC were both censors plebeian. The office came to be regarded as the highest position in the *cursus honorum* and to be held as a rule only by ex-consuls. Censors were normally elected every four (later five) years, but practice varied greatly. After *Sulla, by whom the powers of the censors were for a time greatly reduced, election was very irregular, and no censors were elected after 22 BC. Thereafter the emperors themselves assumed responsibility for censorial functions or delegated them to lesser officials.

The powers of the censors extended well beyond the conduct of the census itself. At the most general level they exercised a supervision of the morals of the community (*regimen morum*). When the lists of citizens were drawn up the censors, if they agreed and stated the reason, might place a mark of censure (*nota*) against the name of a man whose conduct, public or private, they found reprehensible. The effect of this was to remove the man in question from his tribe (*tribus*), usually from all the tribes, in which case he became an *aerarius*, obliged to pay tax but not entitled to vote. The censors also revised the membership of the senate. Here the censorial *nota* meant exclusion from the senate. Initial admission to the senate was dependent upon the censors down to the time of Sulla, by whose legislation election to the quaestorship automatically brought membership of the senate. Of the *equites equo publico (the members of the equestrian centuries, who held the public horse) the censors conducted a review in the Forum. If the censors found an individual in any way unsuitable for service in the cavalry (or for the distinction it implied), they could deprive him of his horse and status.

The censors were the officials responsible for the leasing of revenue-producing public property (land, forests, mines, etc.), and it was they who made the contracts with the *publicani for the collection of the revenue arising (*vectigal), as for the collection of the harbour-taxes (*portoria) within Roman territory. The contract for the collection of the taxes of an entire province could also be sold to *publicani* by the censors at Rome, as was most notably the case with the province of Asia (from 123 or 122 BC). In addition, the censors were usually responsible for the letting of contracts for public works (roads, buildings, etc.); the amount available for these was determined by the senate. As Rome's dominion grew, so did the financial operations of the censors, giving rise both to potentially great fortunes for the *publicani* and to tension between the censors and senate on one side and the *publicani* and equestrian order on the other.

> Mommsen, *Röm. Staatsr.* 2³. 1. 331 ff.; F. Cancelli, *Studi sui censores* (1957); J. Suolahti, *The Roman Censors* (1963); H. F. Jolowicz and B. Nicholas, *Historical Introduction to the Study of Roman Law*, 3rd edn. (1972), 38 f., 51 ff.; A. Drummond, *CAH* 7²/2 (1989), 186 f. (with bibliog.). For the censorial *fasti*, see also Broughton, *MRR*. P. S. D.

Censorinus (3rd cent. AD), a Roman grammarian (Prisc. 1. 4. 17), wrote *On Accents* (*De accentibus*, lost), and 'a fine volume, on Birthdays' (*De die natali* volumen illustre) (Sid. Apoll. *Carm.* 14 pref. 3), dedicated to Q. Caerellius on his *birthday in AD 238, which is preserved. The first part deals with human life, particularly its origins, the second with time and its divisions. The work is derived from different sources, above all Varro, and also Suetonius ('On the Roman year'/*De anno Romanorum*), and is valuable for its mainly competent transmission of these. It is accompanied in the MSS by an anonymous and noteworthy collection of articles on various topics, e.g. the universe, geometry, metre (our earliest source for Roman metre, see METRE, LATIN), and *music, known (since L. Carrio's edition, Paris, 1583) as *fragmentum Censorini*. See also SCHOLARSHIP, ANCIENT, ROMAN.

> TEXTS O. Jahn (1845; repr. 1964); F. Hultsch (1867); N. Sallmann (1983). Schanz–Hosius 3. 219 ff. A. H.-W.; V. N.

censorship See INTOLERANCE, INTELLECTUAL AND RELIGIOUS.

census, a national register prepared at Rome, on the basis of which were determined voting rights and liability for military service and taxation. The census was held first by the king, then by the *consuls, and from 443 BC by the *censors. One was normally held every four (later five) years. Individuals were required to state their full name, age, name of their father or *patronus*, domicile, occupation, and the amount of their property (Livy 40. 51. 9; *tabula Heracleensis* 145). The names of women and children were not included in the census, but parents gave details about families (Dion. Hal. *Ant. Rom.* 4. 15). On the basis of the information received the censors registered citizens in tribes, *tribus (by domicile, except in the case of *freedmen who were, for most of the republic, registered in one or more of the four urban tribes), and centuries (see CENTURIA) (by property and age,

as most of the centuries were divided amongst five classes, each with a property qualification and each containing centuries of *iuniores* and *seniores*). The centuries of cavalry (see EQUITES) were registered separately, and those whose property did not qualify them for enrolment in one of the five classes were registered in a single century of *capite censi* ('counted by head'; see PROLETARII). The taking of a census was concluded with a religious ceremony of purification, the *lustrum* (*lustration). In the *tabula Heracleensis* the chief magistrates of towns in Italy are ordered to take a census simultaneously with the holding of one in Rome; how long (if at all) before Caesar registration could be done locally, and not at Rome, is not known. At the end of the republic the census was taken very irregularly, at least in so far as it was taken by the censors: the *tabula Heracleensis* envisages the possibility of it being taken by other magistrates. It was held three times by *Augustus. The last known census was held in Italy by *Vespasian and *Titus: taxation, conscription, and voting had ceased to be Italian concerns. In *Sicily locally elected censors are attested under the republic; their responsibility was the valuation of property on the basis of which taxes were paid (Cic. 2 *Verr.* 2. 131). This may have been the case elsewhere, too, but it is not until the reign of Augustus that provincial censuses were organized by the central government. In the less urbanized provinces this involved the creation of new machinery which sometimes provoked popular resistance (as in Gaul, where there were censuses in 27 and 12 BC and AD 14 and 61, and Judaea in AD 6). Responsibility for the census lay normally with the governor, but many other men of senatorial, and later equestrian, rank were involved (*ILS* 3, index, p. 351). Evidence is primarily epigraphical and comes mostly from the 'imperial' provinces. The census-return (*forma censualis*) included full details of the character and extent of cultivated land and number of slaves owned (*Dig.* 51. 15. 4), and of other forms of property, information necessary to those responsible for levying the *tributum soli* and *tributum capitis* (see TRIBUTUM). There appears to have been no generally prescribed census-period, and it is presumed that governors were charged with keeping the register up to date. Roman Egypt was unique in having a regular census-period (fourteen years), and numerous census returns are preserved on papyri, addressed to a range of different officials and giving full details of the property and occupants of individual households.

> A. H. J. Greenidge, *Roman Public Life* (1901), 221 ff., 429 ff.; S. L. Wallace, *Taxation in Egypt from Augustus to Diocletian* (1938), 96 ff.; G. Tibiletti, *Stud. Doc. Hist. Iur.* 1959, 93 ff.; G. Pieri, *L'Histoire du cens jusqu'à la fin de la république romaine* (1968); P. A. Brunt, *Italian Manpower* (1971, 1987), chs 1–5, 7–9; D. Rathbone, in H. Sancisi-Weerdenburg and others (eds.), *De Agricultura* (1993), 121 ff. P. S. D.

Centaurs (Κένταυροι; for the etymology, and their ancestry, see IXION), a tribe of 'beasts' (φῆρες, Aeol. for θῆρες, *Il.* 1. 268, 2. 743), human above and horse below; the wild and dangerous counterpart of the more skittish *satyrs, who are constructed of the same components but conceived of as amusing rather than threatening creatures. In both cases it is the very closeness of the horse to humanity that points up the need to remember that a firm line between nature and culture must be drawn. *Pirithous the king of the Lapiths, a *Thessalian clan, paid for his failure to absorb this lesson when he invited the Centaurs to his wedding-feast; the party broke up in violence once the guests had tasted *wine, that quintessential product of human culture (Pindar fr. 166 Snell–Maehler), and made a drunken assault on the bride (see the west pediment of the temple of Zeus at *Olympia). 'Ever since then', says Antinous in the *Odyssey* (21. 303), 'there has been conflict between centaurs and men.' Their uncontrolled lust, violence, and greed for alcohol (see ALCOHOLISM) challenge the hard-won and ever fragile rules of civilization, which are symbolically reasserted by the victories of *Heracles (whose wife *Deianira the Centaur Nessus tried to rape) and *Theseus (who sometimes fights alongside his friend Pirithous in the wedding-fight) over the savage horde. Centaurs belong to the forested mountains of *Arcadia and northern Greece, the fringes of human society, so it is natural that in the 'Centauromachies' so popular in Archaic art (e.g. the François vase) they fight with uprooted trees and boulders against armed and disciplined Greek heroes; it is with fir-trunks that they pound the invulnerable Lapith *Caeneus into the ground.

Their double-natured ambivalence is further emphasized in traditions which single out two of their number, Chiron and Pholus, as wise and civilized exceptions to the general rule. Pholus, it is true, eats his steak raw like an animal when entertaining Heracles in his Arcadian cave (Apollod. 2. 5. 4), but his self-control is shown by the fact that he is capable of holding his liquor—a specially aged vintage donated by Dionysus—until the other members of his tribe scent the bouquet of the wine, go berserk, and have to be shot down by Heracles. Chiron is a more complex character, blurring the human–animal boundary still further: vase-painters often make the point by giving him human rather than equine front legs and draping him in decorous robes. His bestial side is demonstrated by the way he feeds the baby *Achilles, deserted by his mother *Thetis, on the still-warm blood of the hares which in art he habitually carries over his shoulder as a portable game-larder (hence, in turn, the savagery of the hero); but he is also a source of wisdom on natural medicine (Il. 4. 219, 11. 831), and is recorded as an educator of *Jason (1) and *Asclepius as well as Achilles.

By the 5th cent. BC, Centaurs (like *Amazons) come to symbolize all those forces which opposed Greek male cultural and political dominance; on the *Parthenon metopes, with their heroically nude boxers and wrestlers, the triumph over Persia is a clear subtext. (See PERSIAN-WARS TRADITION.) Of later literary treatments, *Ovid's magnificently gory, over-the-top account of the Lapith wedding (Met. 12. 210 ff.) is not to be missed.

M. Gisler-Huwiler, LIMC 'Cheiron'; R. Osborne, in S. Goldhill and R. Osborne (eds.), Art and Text in Ancient Greek Culture (1994), 52–84.

A. H. G.

cento

Greek A cento is a poem or poetic sequence made up of recognizable shorter sequences from one or more existing poems, in Byzantine Greek called κέντρων (as Eust. Il. 1099. 51; schol. on Ar. Nub. 450 β Holwerda) from the later Latin use of 'cento' ('patchwork'). Examples of this whimsical genre are few before the imperial age; early anticipations include the mock-oracle at Ar. Pax 1090–3, which is based on (without strictly following) Homeric phrases. With some exceptions (e.g. the Byzantine *Christus Patiens, based on tragedy, and cf. Lucian, Symp. 17), later examples tend likewise to use Homer, as with the epigram at Anth. Pal. 9. 381, the anonymous 'parody' at Dio Chrys. Or. 32 (many parodies, so-called, are virtually centos), and the Ὁμηροκέντρωνες of the Byzantine empress Eudocia.

E. Stemplinger, Das Plagiat in der griech. Lit. (1912), 193 ff.; A. Tuilier, 'Le Χριστὸς πάσχων et l'art du centon', in Actes VI, Cong. Ét. Byz. (1950), 1. 403 ff.

M. S. Si.

Latin The Latin tradition of cento post-dated and largely used the poems of *Virgil, familiar to all educated Romans. Parodies

of Virgil are known early on (Donat. Vit. Verg. 43), and a brief cento is found at Petronius Sat. 132. 11. The earliest extant cento proper is the 461-line tragedy Medea usually ascribed to *Hosidius Geta (2nd cent. AD—cf. Tert. De praescr. haeret. 39), in which all the characters speak in Virgilian hexameters, and the choric lyrics consist entirely of final half-hexameters. There are eleven other pagan Virgilian centos from late antiquity, none longer than 200 lines; many are short epic narratives on mythological subjects (e.g. Mavortius' Iudicium Paridis), but some are amusing parodies on trivial topics (e.g. De alea and De panificio). The best known are the two epithalamian examples, the wittily obscene Cento nuptialis of *Ausonius, written c.374, and the slightly less risqué Epithalamium Fridi of *Luxorius (early 6th cent.); Ausonius describes his technique in an important prefatory letter, classifying his cento as 'frivolum et nullius pretii opusculum', 'a slight work, frivolous and worthless'.

Christian cento-writers had a more serious evangelistic purpose in blending pagan learning with Christian doctrine. The poetess *Proba used 694 Virgilian verses to paraphrase parts of the Old and New Testament about 360 AD (cf. Isid. Orig. 1. 38. 25, De vir. ill. 22), and three other shorter Christian centos are extant, mostly owing something to Proba and to be dated between the 4th and 6th cents.—De verbi incarnatione, De ecclesia, where the poet is hailed at the end as 'Maro Iunior' ('Younger Virgil'), and the Versus ad gratiam Domini of Pomponius, a Virgilian 'Eclogue' in which 'Meliboeus' is instructed in Christian doctrine. Pope Gelasius is said to have declared a centimetrum de Christo an apocryphal text in 494 (Migne, PL 59. 162); *Isidorus (2) claims this was Proba's cento (De vir. ill. 22), but both this and the authenticity of Gelasius' decree are disputed. Later Latin poetical texts up to the Renaissance include passages of cento from Horace, Ovid, and Christian poets as well as Virgil, but the literary form of full cento ceases in late antiquity.

TEXTS Complete: Baehrens, PLM 4. 191 ff. (pagan); Schenkl, in CSEL 16/1. 511 (Christian). Individual centos: Hosidius Geta, Medea, ed. G. Salanitro (1981), R. Lammacchia (Teubner, 1981); Ausonius, Cento Nuptialis, in R. P. H. Green's edn. of Ausonius (1991); Luxorius, Epithalamium Fridi, in edns. of Luxorius by M. Rosenblum (1961) and H. Happ (1988); Cento Probae, ed. and trans. E. A. Clark and D. F. Hatch (1981).

CRITICISM F. Ermini, Il centone di Proba e la poesia centonaria latina (1909); R. Lamacchia, Enc. Virg. 'Centoni'; M. Manitius, Geschichte der lateinischen Literatur des Mittelalters 1 (1911), see index under 'Zentonenpoesie'.

S. J. Ha.

centumviri (lit. 100 men), a special civil court at Rome, or, strictly, the panel from which a court (consilium) was chosen. The panel numbered in fact in the later republic 105 men (three taken from each *tribus) and in the empire 180. The number forming a consilium is not known, but in the empire there were usually four consilia, though the full court of 180 might sit for a particular case (Pliny, Ep. 4. 24, 6. 33). From the time of Augustus the presidents of the consilia were drawn from the *decemviri stlitibus iudicandis, and before then from among the ex-quaestors. The centumviri took only the second stage of the proceedings, in place of the more usual single *iudex. The first stage, before the praetor urbanus or peregrinus (Gai. Inst. 4. 31; see PRAETOR) was by legis actio sacramento (see SACRAMENTUM), even after legis actiones had otherwise been abolished. The extent of the court's jurisdiction is obscure. It plainly covered claims concerning inheritances; and the querela inofficiosi testamenti was probably developed by the court, but beyond this the evidence is unclear. Nor can we be sure whether the jurisdiction of the court, in the areas which it covered, was exclusive or concurrent, in the sense that the same case could be brought either in the centumviral court or before a single *iudex*. It is certain that inheritance cases could, in the classical law, be brought before a single *iudex*, but it has been conjectured by some that the explanation for this apparent concurrence is that cases before the centumviral court had to be of a certain minimum value. Certainly it was a court where *causes célèbres* were heard and the greatest orators might appear (Cic. *De or.* 1. 242, *Brut.* 144; Tac. *Dial.* 38; Plin. *Ep.* 4. 24, 6. 33). The first recorded case before the court was *c*.145 BC (Cic. *De or.* 1. 181, 238) and since the number of *tribus* was increased to 35 in 241 BC, the court cannot, in the form in which we know it, have existed before then, but its name suggests that there must have been an earlier time when the court actually had 100 members.

J. M. Kelly, *Studies in the Civil Judicature of the Roman Republic* (1976).
B. N.

centuria, literally a group of 100, was the smallest unit of the Roman legion; 60 centuries made up a legion. It was also the name given to the constituent units of the centuriate assembly (*comitia centuriata*). According to tradition, this assembly of the *populus Romanus* was founded by Servius *Tullius, fifth king of Rome, although many scholars have preferred to date its foundation to the middle or end of the 5th cent. BC. The bulk of the assembly was made up of eighteen centuries of horsemen (*equites*), of which six were known as the *sex suffragia*, and 170 of foot-soldiers (*pedites*). The *pedites* were divided into five *classes* according to their *census. The first class fell into 40 centuries of *iuniores* (from 17 to 45 years of age) and 40 of *seniores* (from 46 to 60; the upper limit for military service was not, however, maintained in the political assembly); the second, third, and fourth into 10 centuries of *seniores* and 10 of *iuniores* apiece; the fifth into 15 of each. There were in addition five centuries of non-combatants, of which four (of carpenters and musicians) were attached to one or other of the *classes*, and one (the *capite censi* or *proletarii*), made up of those whose property fell below the minimum required for the fifth *classis*, were ranked separately below all the rest. The voting order of the assembly was fixed: first the equestrian centuries, then the *classes*, then the *capite censi*.

At some point between 241 (when the number of tribes, *tribus*, was increased to 35) and 215 BC (when tribal centuries in the first *classis* are first attested) the distribution of the centuries underwent a reform. *Livy (1. 43. 12) and *Cicero (*Rep.* 2. 39–40) leave some room for doubt about the details of the change but show that the object was to correlate the centuries and the territorial tribes. It is certain that the first *classis* was now made up of 70 tribal centuries (35 each of *iuniores* and *seniores*). Some maintain that only the first *classis* was so affected, others that the second *classis* was similarly arranged, others still that each of the five *classes* now comprised 70 centuries. It seems certain, at all events, that the total number of voting units remained fixed at 193 and that the voting units were called centuries. Either *classes* two to five were rearranged to contain 100 centuries, each a voting unit, or the more numerous centuries of these *classes* were combined by some mechanism to produce a total of 100 voting units, also known as centuries. Adherents of the latter view appeal to the *tabula Hebana, which shows that *Augustus created a system of voting for the *destinatio of consuls and praetors in which senators and *equites* from 33 tribes voted in ten special centuries. There is, however, no evidence for any such practice under the republic and no evidence for centuries that are not

voting units or for voting units that are not individual centuries. The centuries of *equites* and non-combatants were apparently not affected by the reform. The voting order was, however, altered (either at the same time or later within the same period), and the privilege of casting the first vote was thereafter allotted to one of the centuries of the first *classis*.

The name *centuria* was also used for the block of 100 *heredia* (primary allotments, theoretically each of two *iugera*), which was the unit for the delimitation of the *ager publicus*.

G. W. Botsford, *The Roman Assemblies* (1909); L. R. Taylor, *Roman Voting Assemblies* (1966); E. S. Staveley, *Greek and Roman Voting and Elections* (1972); L. J. Grieve, *Hist.* 1985, 278 ff. (all with extensive bibliog.).
P. S. D.

centuriation, a system of marking out the land in squares or rectangles, by means of *limites*, boundaries, normally prior to distribution in a colonial foundation. (The units above and below the *centuria* are explained by Varro, *Rust.* 1. 10.) The practice appears with the second phase of Latin colonization beginning after 338 BC, perhaps at much the same time as apparently similar approaches in such cities of Magna Graecia as *Heraclea (1) and *Metapontum. (There is no good evidence that in the Roman world the earliest stage involved marking out only in strips, rather than in squares or rectangles.) Centuriation was widespread in Italy between the 4th cent. BC and the early empire, spreading to the provinces with the projected colony of *Carthage-Junonia in 122 BC. In so far as a single plot of land in a single location was distributed, the practice was not rational in the normal conditions of Mediterranean agriculture: peasant strategies probably depended then as now on farming scattered plots with different soils, altitudes, and aspects, and therefore minimizing the risk of total crop failure; and marriage and inheritance probably rapidly fragmented originally unitary holdings. Those centuriation systems which remain visible today are on the whole those in relatively homogeneous terrain, especially where the *limites* between lots were also ditches which served for drainage, as in the Po (*Padus) valley. *Limites* might otherwise be anything from a drystone wall to a row of markers. The *limites* which run east–west are usually known as *decumani*, those which run north–south as *cardines* or *kardines*. There is an abundant, if often desperately obscure, literature on centuriation and similar matters in the writings of the *gromatici* or *agrimensores*, land surveyors, dating from the 2nd cent. AD to the late empire and beyond. The identification, never mind dating, of centuriation systems known only from aerial photographs is often uncertain in the extreme.

J. S. P. Bradford, *Ancient Landscapes* (1957); O. A. W. Dilke, *The Roman Land Surveyors* (1971); *Misurare la terra*, exhib. cat. (Modena, 1983); O. A. W. Dilke, *Greek and Roman Maps* (1985); B. Campbell, *The Writings of the Roman Land Surveyors* (forthcoming).
M. H. C.

centurio The centurions were the principal professional officers in the Roman army. In the post-Marian army each of the ten cohorts (see COHORS; MARIUS (1), C.) had six centurions, whose titles, except in the case of the first cohort, were: (*secundus, tertius,* etc.) *pilus prior, pilus posterior, princeps prior, princeps posterior, hastatus prior,* and *hastatus posterior.* Between these centurions of the lower-ranking cohorts there was little difference in status apart from seniority. The first cohort had, probably from early in the empire, only five centuries and was double the size of the others. Its centurions were *primus pilus, princeps, hastatus, princeps posterior,* and *hastatus posterior.* This group constituted the *primi ordines*, and within it a strict seniority was observed, with the post of *primus pilus* as the final honour.

During the republic centuries were selected from the ranks; under the Principate, the majority of the centuries continued to be promoted legionaries, but some were *ex equite Romano*, i.e. men who had transferred from an equestrian career, or ex-praetorians (*evocati*). They were attracted by high pay (five times that of the praetorian soldier for the centurion, ten times for a member of the *primi ordines*), and good prospects on retirement. (See also PRIMIPILUS.)

Centurions are found also in the *auxilia and the *praetorians, but without the distinguishing titles of their legionary counterparts.

A. von Domaszewski, *Die Rangordnung des römischen Heeres* (1908; rev. 1967); B. Dobson, *ANRW* 2. 1 (1974), 392 ff.   H. M. D. P.; G. R. W.

Ceos, an island (131 sq. km.: 50 sq. mi.) in the NW *Cyclades. A final neolithic settlement existed at Kephala. Agia Irini, a fortified town in the north-west, was occupied throughout the bronze age. From *c*.2000–1500 BC Minoan influences increased, reflecting interest in the silver and copper at *Laurium in Attica. To this period belongs a series of large terracotta female figures from a temple which survived the town's decline after *c*.1500 BC and was still visited in the Hellenistic period. The four Classical cities (Iulis, Coressia, Carthaea, Poeessa) were *Ionian foundations of *c*.900 BC. Though independent city-states, they frequently acted in common and at times had a federal organization (see FEDERAL STATES). Ceos prospered in the late 6th and early 5th cents.; temples at Carthaea and Coressia and a *hestiatorion* (dining-room) on *Delos were built, Cean athletes competed at Panhellenic festivals, and *Simonides and *Bacchylides flourished. It contributed four ships to the Greek fleet in 480 BC. Under the Athenian empire its tribute was four talents (see TRIBUTE LISTS). A revolt from the *Second Athenian Confederacy *c*.363 BC was suppressed. Athens sought to control the export of Cean ruddle in the 4th cent. Coressia, renamed Arsinoë, was a Ptolemaic naval base during the *Chremonidean War. Coressia's incorporation by Iulis (like Poeessa's by Carthaea) betrays its later Hellenistic decline. Of its many towers one at Agia Marina survives almost intact.

L. Bürchner, *RE* 11/1 (1921), 182–90, 'Keos'; *PECS* 446–7; *IG* 12. 5; D. M. Lewis, *BSA* 1962, 1 ff.; *Hesp*. 1971, 359 ff.; *Keos* 1– (1977–); *Op. Ath*. 1980, 189 ff.; *JDAI* 1985, 361 ff.; J. F. Cherry and others, *Landscape Archaeology as Long-term History* (1991).   R. W. V. C.

Cephalas ('Big-head'), **Constantinus,** held an official post in the palace at Constantinople in AD 917. Some time before this he compiled an anthology of Greek epigrams, on which the Greek *Anthology was later based. Apparently he died or abandoned the task before completing it, since his collection is imperfectly edited and appears not to have been published in the normal way; but the material is invaluable.

A. Cameron, *The Greek Anthology from Meleager to Planudes* (1993), esp. 254–6.   G. H.

Cephallenia, the largest of the western Greek islands, located between *Leucas and *Zacynthus, due west of the entrance to the Corinthian Gulf. Inhabited as early as the neolithic period, Cephallenia preserves many Mycenaean tombs, and may have avoided the destructions at the end of the bronze age if one may trust an unbroken ceramic tradition. Many identify the island with Same or Dulichium of *Homer's poetry, although the recent discovery of a large *tholos near *Poros may hint that this formed the most important part of Odysseus' realm. In historical times, the island was a tetrapolis, containing the four states of Same,

Pale, Crane, and Proni (near mod. Sami, Lixouri, Argostoli, and Poros). Men from the island fought in the *Persian and *Peloponnesian Wars, joined the *Second Athenian Confederacy, and endured the attacks of *Philip (3) V and the Romans. After *Actium (31 BC), the island's citizenry were 'free', although *Hadrian later gave the island to the Athenians as a gift (Cass. Dio 69. 16. 2).

Kl. Pauly 3 (1969), 187–8; *Lexikon der historischen Stätten* 319–21.   W. M. M.

Cephalus, a famous mythical hunter known to the *Epic Cycle (*Epigoni* F 4, incert. loc. 1 Davies); a hero having mythological connections with *Attica, *Phocis and *Cephallenia. His cult is known only in Attica, where he seems to have originated from the *Thoricus area. Whether he was the son of Deion(eus) of Phocis, or of Hermes and an Athenian princess, he married *Procris daughter of *Erechtheus, but was abducted by *Eos, by whom he had a son usually named Phaethon. On returning to his wife, he disguised himself in order to test her fidelity, but found it wanting. Procris fled in shame, but on her return tried the same trick, with the same result. Cephalus accidentally killed Procris when she was spying on him as he went hunting, and was brought to trial at the *Areopagus by her father Erechtheus. Exiled from Attica, he took part with his invincible hound in the hunt of the Teumessian fox, and finally went to Cephallenia where he became the father of the eponyms of the four *poleis*.

Hes. *Theog*. 985–7; Pherec. *FGrH* 3 F 34; Hellanicus, *FGrH* 323a F 22; Apollod. 2. 4. 7, 3. 14. 3, 15. 1; Ant. Lib. 41; J. Fontenrose, *Orion* (1981), 86–111; Kearns, *Heroes of Attica* 177.   E. Ke.

Cepheus (Κηφεύς), name of four or five mythological persons, the best known being the father of *Andromeda. Though generally called an Ethiopian from *Euripides on, he and consequently the whole legend are very variously located; for particulars see Tümpel in Roscher's *Lexikon* 2. 1109–13.

LIMC 6/1 (1992), 6–10 (in art).   H. J. R.; A. J. S. S.

Cephisia, Attic *deme north-east of Athens at modern Kephisia. It was included in *Philochorus' list of twelve townships united by *Theseus (Philochorus, *FGrH* 328 F 94). Archaeological finds include late geometric pottery, a Classical deme decree honouring a man responsible for improving the *palaestra in association with which it was found, and many Roman remains. Cool and shady Cephisia became a fashionable resort in the Roman imperial period, and *Herodes Atticus had a villa here, celebrated in literature (Gell. *NA* 1. 2. 1–2, 18. 10. 1; Philostr. *VS* 2. 1. 30) and partially excavated.

ΑΔ 17B (1961–2), 29–30; 24A (1969), 6–7; 37B1 (1982), 63–6.   C. W. J. E.; R. G. O.

Cephisodorus (1), Old *Comedy poet active *c*.400 BC (*IG* 2². 2325. 69 = 5 B 1 col. 3. 3 Mette; Lys. 21. 4).

FRAGMENTS Kassel–Austin, *PCG* 4. 63–8.
INTERPRETATION Meineke, *FCG* 1. 267 ff.; A. Körte, *RE* 11/1 (1921), 227, 'Kephisodoros' 5.   W. G. A.

Cephisodorus (2) of Athens or Thebes (1), wrote a history of the Third *Sacred War.

FGrH 112.

Cephisodotus (1), Athenian sculptor, probably father of *Praxiteles and a brother-in-law of *Phocion. *Pliny (2)'s floruit of 372–369 BC (*HN* 34. 50) may relate to his most famous work, the bronze *Eirene and *Plutus (Peace and Wealth) in the Athenian

*Agora, perhaps commissioned to celebrate the *Common Peace of 371.

A. F. Stewart, *Greek Sculpture* (1990), 173 f., 275 f., figs. 485 ff.   A. F. S.

Cephisodotus (2), Athenian sculptor, son of *Praxiteles. Active between 344 and 293 BC. With his younger brother Timarchus, Cephisodotus inherited his father's workshop, his clientele, and his wealth. The two specialized in marble statues of divinities and in portraits, chiefly in bronze, of which the most famous was the *Menander (1) (d. 293/2) in the theatre of Dionysus at Athens (see PORTRAITURE, GREEK). Many copies of it survive, plus some statuettes in Praxitelean style from *Cos that may be part of their sculpture for the altar of *Asclepius. Attributions include a fine female head from Chios in Boston. His son Praxiteles (II) continued Cephisodotus' work; the *Hermes and *Dionysus group from *Olympia, which is now generally accepted as post-Praxitelean, is sometimes ascribed to him.

A. F. Stewart, *Greek Sculpture* (1990), 66 f., 198 f., 295 ff., figs. 604 ff., 610, 613.

A. F. S.

Cephissus (Κηφισός), the name of several rivers, the best known being the *Attic and the *Boeotian Cephissus. The Attic Cephissus was the main river of the plain of Athens, gathering all sources and streams of the mountains around, and emptying itself into the bay of Phaleron; its water, divided into many streams, irrigated the plain west of Athens (cf. Soph. *OC* 685); its clay-bed provided the material for Athenian *pottery (Greek). The Boeotian Cephissus springs from the northern Parnassus, near Lilaea, and waters the plains of *Phocis and northern *Boeotia, debouching into the lake *Copais. Both were worshipped as gods and furnished with genealogies; the former's cult-statue showed him as a man with bull's horns (Ael. *VH* 2. 33).

J. Knauss, *Kopais 2: Wasserbau und Siedlungsbedingungen im Altertum* (1987); in art: *LIMC* 'Kephisos'.   V. E.; J. Bu., A. J. S. S.

Ceramicus, *Kerameikos*, large and (in ancient authors) loosely defined district of NW Athens based on the potters' (*kerameis*) quarter. Within the Themistoclean wall it embraced the area from the *Dipylon gate up to and including the Agora, for which it could be a virtual synonym (Paus. 1. 2. 4 ff.), although Classical authors (esp. Thuc. 2. 34. 5; Xen. *Hell.* 2. 4. 33) used it above all of the famous extramural cemetery (including the *Dēmosion Sēma* or public burial-ground: see EPITAPHIOS) lining the routes which fanned out from the Sacred and Dipylon gates. Excavations since 1863 (the Germans from 1913) provide detailed information about Athenian mortuary practices over 1,500 years, from the earliest Submycenaean burials (*c.* 1100 BC) to late antiquity. Many fine funerary monuments, both ceramic and sculptured, are now displayed in the Athens archaeological museum (see ART, FUNERARY, GREEK). The Cleisthenic *deme *Kerameis* lay somewhere in this vicinity. See ATHENS, TOPOGRAPHY; CEMETERIES.

Paus. 1. 29. 2 ff.; *Kerameikos* 1– (1939–) (excavations); R. Wycherley, *Athenian Agora* 3 (1957), 221 ff. (testimonia), and *Stones of Athens* (1978), ch. 11; J. Travlos, *Pictorial Dictionary of Ancient Athens* (1971), 299 ff.; U. Knigge, *Der Kerameikos von Athen* (1988).   A. J. S. S.

Cerberus (Κέρβερος), monstrous hound who guards the entrance to the Underworld, often called simply 'the dog of Hades', 'the dog'. Hesiod makes him a child of *Echidna and *Typhon, 'brass-voiced and fifty-headed' (*Theog.* 311 f.); three heads are more normal in literary descriptions and in art, while Attic vase-painters usually make do with two. A shaggy mane runs down his back, and he may sprout writhing snakes. Despite his impressive appearance, however, he failed to keep out *Orpheus, who lulled him to sleep with music; while *Heracles (with Athena's help) even managed to chain him up and drag him away to the upper world, where in a rerun of the conclusion to the labour of the Erymanthian boar he terrified *Eurystheus with the captive beast. The scene was already depicted in Archaic art on the so-called 'Throne of *Amyclae' (Paus. 3. 18. 13); a Caeretan hydria in the Louvre handles the theme with magnificent exuberance.

S. Woodford and J. Spier, *LIMC* 'Kerberos'; K. Schefold, *Gods and Heroes in Late Archaic Greek Art* (1992) 129–32.   A. H. G.

Cercidas of *Megalopolis (fl. 225 BC), statesman, lawgiver, and poet. He negotiated *c.*226 with *Aratus (2) of Sicyon and *Antigonus (3) Doson to secure Macedonian support for the *Achaean Confederacy against *Cleomenes (2) of Sparta; he commanded 1,000 Megalopolitan infantrymen at the battle of Sellasia, 222; after the defeat of Sparta he framed a new constitution for his city. Anecdotes testify to his devotion to *Homer.

Works There are few book-fragments: from the *Iambi* only one choliambic line (fr. 14 Powell) survives from a poem apparently condemning loose living; other frs. are all from the *Meliambi* (poems lyrical in form but with satirical elements), of which substantial remains are also preserved in *POxy.* 1082. These poems are ethical in content, expressing concern for the poor, questioning conventional attitudes, and displaying impatience with speculative thought, features consistent with the label 'Cynic' applied to Cercidas in the papyrus; but in view of his involvement in public life, the extent and nature of his *Cynicism is problematic. (Fr. 1 Pow. expresses admiration for *Diogenes (2), but in semi-ironical terms.) The poems are innovative, written in literary Doric with bold neologisms, striking expressions, and forceful metre; they contain citations of Homer and *Euripides, and allude to a wide range of authors, a reminder that Alexandria (1) had no monopoly of learning. The suggestion of A. D. Knox that Cercidas was also the compiler of an anthology of moralizing verses is now generally rejected.

TEXTS Powell, *Coll. Alex.* 201–13; Diehl, *Anth. Lyr. Graec.* 3. 141–52; (with trans.) A. D. Knox, *Cercidas and the Choliambic Poets* (bound with Theophrastus, *Characters*) (Loeb, 1929; repr. 1993), 403–55; E. Livrea, *Studi cercidei* (1986); L. Lomiento (1993); ed. and comm. by E. Livrea and F. Williams (in preparation).

GENERAL D. R. Dudley, *A History of Cynicism* (1937), 74–84; J. L. López Cruces, *Les Méliambes de Cercidas* (1995).   F. W.

Cercops of Miletus (? 6th cent. BC), epic poet, to whom (or to Hesiod) is ascribed the *Aegimius* (on the Dorian hero *Aegimius who fought against the *Centaurs).

R. Merkelbach and M. L. West (eds.), *Fragmenta Hesiodea* (1967), 151 ff.   S. H.

cereals, the most important component of the diet (see FOOD AND DRINK). The Greeks and Romans cultivated wheat, barley, oats, rye, and millets, using dry-farming methods. Greek and Roman farmers did not understand wet-rice cultivation, which was practised in the near east in antiquity. Maize only reached Europe from America after Columbus. The botanical works of *Theophrastus, the Roman agronomists (see AGRICULTURAL WRITERS), and medical writers provide a lot of information on cereals. These sources may be supplemented with the evidence of palaeobotanical remains of cereals found on archaeological sites.

By the end of antiquity wheat was the most important cereal. Innovations such as the spread of the rotary grain-mill (see MILLS), from the 4th cent. BC onwards, and the use of finer sieves to separate grain from chaff, made it possible to produce purer flour, although it was still coarse by modern standards. Wheat came to be preferred to the other cereals because it contains a higher proportion of gluten (which raises loaves during baking) than other cereals. This development led to the gradual displacement of the original Greek and Latin words for wheat (πυρός and triticum) by the words for 'grain' in general (σῖτος and frumentum).

Several species of wheat were cultivated. These are classified into three main groups: diploids (14 chromosomes)—einkorn (Triticum monococcum); tetraploids (28 chromosomes)—emmer (T. dicoccum), durum (T. durum); hexaploids (42 chromosomes)—bread (T. aestivum), spelt (T. spelta). Among the tetraploids and hexaploids there is a major distinction between free-threshing wheats (durum and bread wheats), in which the grain is easily separated by threshing and winnowing from the glumes that enclose it, and husked wheats (emmer and spelt), in which the glumes cannot be detached from the grains by threshing. The husked wheats required a laborious process of parching and pounding to extract the grain. In spite of the difficulty of this process, the husked wheats predominated over the free-threshing wheats in many regions in antiquity because of their high productivity. Emmer was the commonest type of wheat in Mycenaean Greece in the second millennium BC, and in *Pompeii as late as the 1st cent. AD. It was the most important cereal crop in *Latium, around Rome, in the first half of the first millennium BC, while spelt, adapted to a colder climate, was the major crop of iron age Britain. In Hellenistic Egypt the Greek colonists introduced durum wheat to displace the emmer cultivated by the natives. The most important feature of the history of cereals in antiquity was the replacement of husked wheats by free-threshing wheats, principally durum in the Mediterranean and bread wheat further north. This process has been explained in terms of genetic changes which increased the apparent productivity of free-threshing wheats and made them easier to harvest.

Barley (Hordeum vulgare; Greek κριθή) was also very important. It was often made into μᾶζα, a kind of *cake. Barley needs less water than wheat and is better adapted to semi-arid environments. Its significance declined because it produces inferior bread. Barley was eaten by slaves and poor people in general. In Attica it was probably more important than wheat as late as the 4th cent. BC. The *helots paid a rent in barley to the Spartans. There were two main varieties of barley, two-rowed and six-rowed.

Oats, Avena sativa and A. byzantina (e.g. in Anatolia), and rye, Secale cereale (e.g. in *Macedonia) only started to become significant crops during the Classical period. The millets (Panicum miliaceum and Setaria italica) were cultivated on a small scale in areas where *irrigation was possible in summer. See also FOOD SUPPLY.

J. R. Sallares, Ecology of the Ancient Greek World (1991); M. S. Spurr, Arable cultivation in Roman Italy (1986).   J. R. S.

Ceres, an ancient Italo-Roman goddess of growth (her name derives from † ker- 'growth'), commonly identified in antiquity with *Demeter. Her name (*Oscan Kerri-, see the 'Curse of Vibia', Conway, Ital. Dial. 130, 1) suggests that of Cerus ('in carmine Saliari Cerus manus intellegitur creator bonus', Festus 109, 7 Lindsay), but in cult she is found associated not with him but with *Tellus. This is shown by the juxtaposition of their festivals (*Fordicidia, to Tellus, 15 April; Cerialia, 19 April) and the fact

that the feriae sementiuae ('sowing festivals') are celebrated in January in honour of both (Ov. Fast. 1. 657 ff., on which see Bayet, Croyances et rites (1971), 177 ff.). The occurrence of the Cerialia on the calendars and the existence of a flamen Cerialis testify to the antiquity of Ceres' cult at Rome, but her whole early history is extremely obscure, particularly her relations, if any, with non-Italian (Greek) deities; see, for some ingenious conjectures, F. Altheim, Terra Mater (1931), 108 ff. One of the many difficulties is to determine whether the rite of swinging attested by 'Probus' on Verg. G. 1. 385–9 as used at the feriae sementiuae is really, as he says, borrowed from the Attic αἰώρα (see ERIGONE) or an independent development. Another is the question whether the long list of minor deities invoked by the officiant on the same occasion (Servius on G. 1. 21) arises out of genuinely early ideas or is a relatively late priestly elaboration (see Wissowa, Ges. Abh. 304 ff.; H. J. Rose, JRS 1913, 233 ff.). There is, however, no doubt that Ceres' most famous cult, that on the *Aventine (introduced 493 BC), is largely under Greek influence, but it is difficult to reconstruct precisely the manner of this Hellenization (see HELLENISM). She is there worshipped with *Liber Pater and Libera, the triad apparently representing the Eleusinian group of *Demeter, Kore (see PERSEPHONE), and *Iacchus (but see Altheim, Terra Mater 15 ff.). The temple became a centre of plebeian activities (see PLEBS), was supervised by the plebeian aediles Cereris, and was connected with the ludi Ceriales which became a prominent feature of the Cerialia. To this Greek cult belongs also, no doubt, the annual festival conducted by the women in August, called Greek and an initiation by *Cicero (Leg. 2. 21); also probably Ceres' occasional association with the Underworld (as in the 'Curse of Vibia', above), the purely Roman goddess in this connection being Tellus (as Livy 8. 6. 10). See also MUNDUS.

Wissowa, RK 191 ff., 297 ff.; Altheim, Hist. Rom. Rel., passim; Latte, RR 71, 101, 161; H. Le Bonniec, Le Culte de Cérès à Rome (1958); Bayet, Croyances et rites (1971), 89 ff.; Ceres' temple in Rome: Nash, Pict. Dict. Rome 1. 227 ff.; B. S. Spaeth, The Roman Goddess Ceres (1996).

H. J. R.; J. Sch.

Cersobleptes (or **Cersebleptes,** IG 2. 65 b), the Odrysian king (see THRACE), son of Cotys I. Cersobleptes found himself, when he came to the throne in 360 BC, engaged in a war, which he had inherited from his father, with Athens, and with two pretenders to the throne, Berisades and *Amadocus (2). *Charidemus, the Athenian general, married Cersobleptes' sister, and continued to advise him, as he had done his father. In 359 BC the Athenian commander, Cephisodotus, was forced to make a treaty with Cersobleptes, which the Athenians repudiated. In the following year, Berisades and Amadocus joined forces, and, with Athenian help, forced Cersobleptes to sign a treaty dividing the kingdom of Cotys between the three princes, *Chersonesus (1) being ceded to Athens; Cersobleptes' share seems to have been the eastern part, Cypsela, *Cardia, and the *Propontis. Charidemus, however, persuaded Cersobleptes to renounce the treaty, and it was not till 357 that he was forced by the Athenian commander, *Chares (1), to surrender the Chersonese, and agree to the partition of Thrace. In the following years *Philip (1) II of Macedon proposed an alliance with Cersobleptes for the expulsion of the Athenians from the Chersonese, but nothing came of it. Meanwhile, through the agency of Charidemus, Athens secured Cersobleptes' goodwill, while his rival Amadocus (Berisades was now dead) turned to Philip. Philip invaded Thrace, and it was only his severe illness that prevented its subjection. In the peace of 346 BC between Athens and Philip, Cersobleptes was not included. The last war between Philip and Cersobleptes took place in 342 BC, and in that year or the next the Odrysian kingdom passed into the control of Macedonia. His name is inscribed on a silver vessel from *Rogozen (Bulgaria).

> Demosthenes, 23; Tod 151; Head, *Hist. Num.*[2] 257, 284; A. Hoeck, *Hermes* 1891, 76 ff.; Hammond and Griffith, *HM* 2, see index; Z. Archibald, *CAH* 6[2] (1994), ch. 9e, discussing the silver Rogozen treasure and its implications; see also J. Ellis, ibid. chs. 14 and 15.   J. M. R. C.; S. H.

Certamen Homeri et Hesiodi, Ἀγὼν Ὁμήρου καὶ Ἡσιόδου, abbreviation of Περὶ Ὁμήρου καὶ Ἡσιόδου καὶ τοῦ γένους καὶ ἀγῶνος αὐτῶν ('On Homer and Hesiod, their Ancestry and Their contest'), title of an anonymous treatise preserved in a Florence MS. It is a joint life of *Homer and *Hesiod, written round an account of a contest between them supposed to have taken place at *Chalcis (the circumstances inspired by Hes. *Op.* 650–60). Hesiod is adjudged victor, despite the crowd's acclamation of Homer, after each has recited 'the best' part of his poetry: the passages are chosen to show Homer as the poet of war, Hesiod as the poet of peace (cf. Ar. *Ran.* 1033–6). The story is familiar to Varro and later writers, ignored in the Lives of Homer. The treatise as we have it dates from the Antonine period, but much of it was taken bodily from an earlier source (it agrees closely with a papyrus fragment of the 3rd cent. BC, *Catalogue of the Literary Papyri in the British Museum*, ed. H. Milne (1927, 191), often thought to be the *Mouseion* of *Alcidamas, to which Stobaeus 4. 52. 22 ascribes two verses found in the *Certamen* (78–9), and which contained accounts of the deaths of Hesiod (cited in *Cert.* 240) and Homer (*PMich.* 2754, agreeing closely with the end of *Cert.*, but followed by what appears to be a transition to a new section). Some of the verses were current before this (78–9 = Thgn. 425, 427; 107–8 = Ar. *Pax* 1282–3), and the contest of verses and *riddles represents an early form (Rohde, *Kl. Schr.* (1901), 1. 103 f.); but it is not known whether Homer and Hesiod were matched before Alcidamas.

A fragment ascribed to Hesiod (357 M–W) referring to an earlier contest with Homer in *Delos is of uncertain origin and date.

> TEXT OCT, *Homeri opera* (1911–20), 5. 218 ff. (T. W. Allen); U. von Wilamowitz-Moellendorff, *Vitae Homeri et Hesiodi* (1916), 34 ff.
>
> CRITICISM K. Hess, *Der Agon zwischen Homer und Hesiod* (1960); M. L. West, *CQ* 1967, 433 ff.; R. Renehan and G. L. Koniaris, *Harv. Stud.* 1971, 85 ff.; N. J. Richardson, *CQ* 1981, 1 ff.; K. Heldmann, *Die Niederlage Homers im Dichterwettstreit mit Hesiod* (1982).   M. L. W.

Cervidius (*RE* 1) **Scaevola, Quintus,** a leading Roman lawyer of the later 2nd cent. AD, probably came from *Carthage and, through his wife, had a close connection with Nemausus (Nîmes). Perhaps a pupil of Sextus *Pomponius, he rose to be *praefectus vigilum* (chief of police) in Rome in 175–7. He was the chief legal adviser of Marcus *Aurelius, had a large consultative practice, with many clients from the eastern empire, and taught some eminent pupils, including *Paulus and Tryphoninus. He annotated the *Digesta* of *Marcellus and *Iulianus, published 20 books (*libri*) of *Variae quaestiones* ('Varied Problems'), and, most notably, is credited with 6 books of *Responsa* ('Opinions') and 40 of *Digesta* ('Ordered Abstracts'). These both purport to record Scaevola's views in reply to consultants but in the *Responsa* the opinions, stringently edited, are much shorter. The overlap between these collections has led to some sceptical views of their genuineness, but the likelihood is that the *Responsa* were published by Scaevola himself and later annotated by Paulus and

Tryphoninus, whereas the *Digesta* were published (perhaps by Tryphoninus, who annotated them) after the author's death. The cases Scaevola records are of great interest, but his opinions are at times disappointingly curt, and take forms such as 'there is no reason why not' (*nihil proponi cur non*). To *Modestinus he was one of the greatest lawyers; later his prestige slumped, but Justinian's compilers (see JUSTINIAN'S CODIFICATION) took more than 300 passages from his works.

> Lenel, *Pal.* 2. 215–322; *PIR*[2] C 681; *HLL* 4, § 415. 6; Kunkel 1967, 217–19; F. Schulz, *Symbolae Lenel* (1933), 143–236; R. Taubenschlag, *Opera minora* 1 (1959), 505–18.   T. Hon.

Cestius Epulo, Gaius, a senator, significant only as the builder of the conspicuous pyramid tomb beside the via Ostiensis at Rome (later built into the Porta S. Paolo). The tomb, with its grandiose Egyptian aspirations, and an inscription recording the execution of Cestius' will (*Agrippa was an heir), shows the pride and wealth of a *novus homo* in the Augustan system.

> *ILS* 917; *PIR*[2] C 686.   N. P.

Cestius (*RE* 9) **Gallus, Gaius,** son of a consul and himself suffect consul AD 42, was legate of Syria from 63 (or 65) to 67. In 66 he marched into Palestine to restore calm, but failed to occupy Jerusalem and on his withdrawal was defeated at Beth-horon. He died in 67.

> *PIR*[2] C 691; M. Griffin, *Nero* (1984), 117.   A. M.

Cestius (*RE* 13) **Pius, Lucius,** Augustan rhetor, from *Smyrna. He is frequently cited by the elder *Seneca, who comments on his outspoken wit. He was once flogged by Cicero's son (M. *Tullius Cicero (2)) for slandering the orator, to some of whose speeches he wrote replies.

> *PIR*[2] C 694; Schanz–Hosius, § 336. 8.   M. W.

Cetius Faventinus, Marcus, (3rd–4th cent. AD), made a revised abridgement of *Vitruvius for builders of private houses; his work was used by *Palladius (1) and *Isidorus (2).

> TEXTS AND COMMENT H. Plommer, with Engl. trans. (1973); A. Hevia Ballina (1979).   L. A. H.-S.

Ceyx (Κήυξ), son of the Morning Star, king of Trachis, friend of *Heracles, and father-in-law of *Cycnus (Hes. *Shield* 354); but most famous as husband of Alcyone. Their marriage was celebrated in the Hesiodic *Wedding of Ceyx* (frs. 263–9 M–W; see HESIOD), but nuptial bliss was short-lived: whether as punishment for the couple's temerity in calling each other '*Zeus' and '*Hera' (Apollod. 1. 7. 4), or because Ceyx drowned at sea and his wife's grief was inconsolable (an extended, bravura account by *Ovid, *Met.* 11. 410 ff.), the gods turned them into sea-birds. The semi-mythical 'halcyon' (traditionally identified with the kingfisher) is already associated with a plaintive, mourning cry at *Il.* 9. 563 (cf. Eur. *IT* 1089 ff.); the *kēx* (*Od.* 15. 478) for whom she calls may be intended as the male of the species, or as some other diving gull.

> D'A. W. Thompson, *A Glossary of Greek Birds* (1936), entries under κανάξ, ἀλκυών; R. Merkelbach and M. L. West, *Rh. Mus.* 1965, 300–17.   A. H. G.

Chabrias (*c*.420–357/6 BC), of Athens, a professional soldier who for over 30 years was frequently engaged in warfare for Athens (being a general at least thirteen times) and for the kings of *Cyprus and *Egypt in revolt from *Persia. His greatest achievements were the defence of *Boeotia in 378, during which he invented a useful method of defence against *hoplites, the decisive naval victory over Sparta near *Naxos in 376, and the extension of the *Second Athenian Confederacy. After 370 he fought in the Peloponnese, and his fortunes seem to be linked to those of *Callistratus (2), with whom he was prosecuted by Leodamas, the Boeotian sympathizer, in 366; like Callistratus he was restored to power shortly before the battle of *Mantinea, and, when soon afterwards Callistratus was in exile, Chabrias was with *Agesilaus in Egypt supporting King Tachos. After further campaigning as general for Athens in the Hellespont, he died, out of office, fighting gallantly for Athens at the battle of Chios in 357/6.

Nepos, *Chabrias*: Xen. *Hell.* 5. 1 ff.; Diod. Sic. 15. 29 ff.; Dem. 20. 75 ff.
W. K. Pritchett, *The Greek State at War*, pt. 2 (1974), 72–7. G. L. C.

Chaeremon (1), a tragic poet active about the middle of the 4th cent. BC. *Aristotle, *Rh.* 3. 12 = 1413ᵇ13 ff., says that his work was suitable for reading (rather than performance) and that he was 'precise like a speech-writer' (see LOGOGRAPHERS). Indeed one fragment of his work (fr. 14b) contains an *acrostic giving his name. Elsewhere (*Poet.* 1) Aristotle refers to his *Centaur* as 'a rhapsody combining all the metres', but *Athenaeus (1) calls this work a 'polymetric drama' (13. 608e), and in fact it was probably a satyr play (see SATYRIC DRAMA). Athenaeus also cites several fragments to show that Chaeremon was fond of flowers (13. 608d–f). The longest fragment (fr. 14), from the *Oeneus*, is a description of sleeping girls (probably *maenads), notable for vivid detail and erotic kitsch. Other fragments, however, are conventionally sententious.

TrGF 1². 215–27; *Musa Tragica* 154–7, 289–90; C. J. Collard, *JHS* 1970, 22–34; B. Snell, *Szenen aus griechischen Dramen* (1971), 158–69; G. Xanthakis-Karamanos, *Studies in Fourth-Century Drama* (1980), 71–84.
A. L. B.

Chaeremon (2) (*RE* 7), of *Alexandria (1), where he held a priesthood: Greek writer on Egypt. He taught the young *Nero. His writings treated Egyptian history, religion, customs, astrology, and hieroglyphic writings. A Stoic viewpoint is visible.

FGrH 618; A. Barzanò, *ANRW* 2. 32. 3, 1981–2001; M. Frede, *ANRW* 36. 3, 2067–103. Fragments edited by P. W. van der Horst (1984).
C. B. R. P.

Chaerephon (5th cent. BC), Athenian, of the *deme of Sphettus, a friend and enthusiastic admirer of *Socrates. With other democrats he was banished by the *Thirty Tyrants and returned with *Thrasybulus in 403, but died before Socrates' trial in 399. He is best known for reporting the *Delphic oracle's opinion that no-one was wiser than Socrates (Pl. *Ap.* 21a). The story is probably true, being related by both *Plato (1) and *Xenophon (1), but Chaerephon's motivation and the statement's meaning remain uncertain. The *Suda* refers to works of Chaerephon, but if there were any, they disappeared early.

TESTIMONIA G. Giannantoni, *Socratis et Socraticorum Rell.* 2. 632–3.
M. Ga.

Chaeris, a pupil of *Aristarchus (2), whose text of *Homer he defended, wrote also a commentary on *Pindar and *Aristophanes (1), and perhaps a Τέχνη γραμματική ('art of grammar'), all lost.

R. Berndt, *De Charete Chaeride Alexione grammaticis* (1902), 31–50.
N. G. W.

Chaeronea, city in NW *Boeotia commanding the small *Cephissus plain bordering *Phocis. Remains include a small theatre cut into the slopes of Petrachos and the restored Lion Monument above the *polyandreion* of the Theban dead who fell

at the battle there (see following entry) in 338 BC. A member of the Boeotian Confederacy, Chaeronea is most notable as the birthplace of *Plutarch and the scene of two major battles. The more famous is *Philip (1) II's victory over the Greeks in 338 BC. In 86 BC *Sulla defeated *Mithradates VI's general *Archelaus (3) there; one of his victory trophies has been found.

J. Camp and others, *AJArch.* 1992, 443 ff.; J. Fossey, *Topography and Population of Ancient Boeotia* (1988), 375 ff. J. Bu.

Chaeronea, battles of The town of *Chaeronea commands the route south down the *Cephissus valley. In 338 BC *Philip (1) II of Macedonia won a crushing victory over an alliance of southern Greek states, led by Athens and *Thebes (1), effectively putting an end, at one level, to the era of the independent *polis. It is not certain how the victory was won, but Philip possibly feinted withdrawal of his *phalanx on the right, encouraging the Athenians to pursue, and thus causing a gap in the allied line; the decisive charge into the gap was then perhaps delivered by Philip's son, the future *Alexander (3) the Great, at the head of the Macedonian cavalry on the left. The stone lion east of the modern village clearly commemorates the battle, but its precise significance is unknown: it possibly marks the resting place of the Theban élite '*Sacred Band'—254 skeletons were found in its vicinity. In 86 BC *Sulla also won a victory here over the army of *Mithradates VI of Pontus.

RE 3/2 'Chaironeia'; Diod. Sic. 16. 85–6; Polyaenus, *Strat.* 4. 2. 2; N. G. L. Hammond, *Studies in Greek History* (1973); G. L. Cawkwell, *Philip of Macedon* (1978). J. F. La.

Chalcedon, Megarian colony founded in 685 BC (so Euseb. *Chron.*) on the Asiatic side of the *Bosporus (1) opposite Byzantium (mod. Kadıköy). It was called the city of the blind (Hdt. 4. 144) because its founders missed the uncolonized site of *Byzantium, with which it was subsequently closely linked. Apart from stray tombs few ancient remains have survived.

G. E. Bean, *PECS* 216; R. Merkelbach, *Die Inschriften von Chalkedon* (1980). A. J. G.; S. M.

Chalcidice, the triple peninsula projecting from Macedonia, was inhabited originally by the Sithonians (Strabo 7, fr. 10), a branch of Edonian Thracians. Their name survived in 'Sithonia', the central promontory between the western 'Pallene' and the eastern 'Acte'. By the early 7th cent. BC the Bottiaei, displaced by the Argead Macedonians from the plain west of the Thermaic Gulf, 'Bottiaea' or 'Emathia', occupied the NW portion of the peninsula, thereafter known as Bottice. The first Greek colonists from *Chalcis in the 8th cent. dispossessed the Sithonians and founded around 30 settlements, perhaps giving the name 'Chalcidice' to the entire peninsula. Eretria founded colonies, e.g. at Dicaea and Neapolis; *Andros at Sane, *Acanthus, and *Stagira; and *Corinth at *Potidaea on the narrow isthmus of Pallene around 600 BC. The Pallene promontory also contained *Mende and *Scione.

Followers perforce of *Xerxes, the cities joined the *Delian League and became subjects of imperial Athens. Revolting in 432/1 they established a common capital at the former Bottic town *Olynthus, thus inaugurating οἱ Χαλκιδεῖς or the 'Chalcidic Confederacy', which became a most interesting specimen of ancient federalism. (See FEDERAL STATES.) The member cities shared a common citizenship and common laws (Xen. *Hell.* 5. 2. 12); the confederacy struck a magnificent silver coinage, circulating especially in the Balkans and copied there by non-Greek mints. In the 380s it extended its control to the north-west,

Chalcidius

depriving Macedonia of Anthemus and its capital *Pella. But at the request of Acanthus and other states Sparta intervened in 382 and forced the confederacy to capitulate in 379 and become subordinate allies (Xen. *Hell.* 5. 3. 26). The Chalcidians soon joined the *Second Athenian Confederacy (Tod, no. 123), but the creation of an Athenian *cleruchy at Potidaea (*c.*362) and other signs of Athenian ambition led to an unwise alliance in 356 with the Macedonian king *Philip (1) II (Tod, no. 158), who cynically ceded to the Chalcidians Anthemus and Potidaea. The sequel was war in early 349. Aid from Athens was ineffective, and the capital Olynthus, taken by means of treachery, was destroyed in 348. Thus ended a remarkable experiment in federal government.

Ancient authors (e.g. Dem. 9. 26) seem definitely to exaggerate the number of Chalcidic cities destroyed by Philip. Mecyberna, for instance, survived the destruction of Olynthus and continued to exist as an important port throughout the Hellenistic period, as did Acanthus, *Torone, Aphytis, and others. Land grants in Bottice were given by the kings to Macedonian nobles (Ditt. *Syll.*³ 332), and new cities were founded by them, notably Cassandrea, created by *Cassander in 316 on the site of the former Potidaea, which seems to have been the most important single city of Macedonia down to the Roman conquest. *Antigonus (2) II Gonatas founded Antigonea 'the Sandy' on the Bottic coast of the Thermaic Gulf and in all likelihood Stratonicea, probably the successor to Uranopolis, the curious creation of Cassander's eccentric brother Alexarchus. In 348–168 Chalcidice seems to have held a special place within the Macedonian realm, for the inscriptions reveal no instance of a citizen of any city in the peninsula being designated as a Macedonian.

Around 43 BC Q. Hortensius Hortalus, the proconsul of Macedonia, founded a colony of Roman citizens at Cassandrea, which did not, however, displace the older Greek city. By the reign of Augustus a *conventus of Roman citizens existed at Acanthus. In AD 268 Cassandrea successfully withstood a Gothic assault.

D. M. Robinson and P. A. Clement, *The Chalcidic Mint* (1938); A. B. West, *The History of the Chalcidic League* (1919); M. Zahrnt, *Olynth und die Chalkidier* (1971); M. B. Hatzopoulos, *Un donation du roi Lysimaque*, Meletemata 5 (1988); M. Hatzopoulos and L. Loukopoulou, *Recherches sur les marches orientales du royaume macédonien*, Meletemata 11 (1992).
C. F. E.; N. G. L. H.

Chalcidius (Calcidius is more correct), 4th-cent. AD Christian translator and commentator on *Plato (1)'s *Timaeus* (to 53c only), using earlier Platonic and Peripatetic exegetes, especially *Adrastus (2), Gaius, *Numenius and *Porphyry. He dedicated his work to Hosius, according to MS tradition Constantine's bishop of Corduba (d. 358), though a high Milanese official of *c.*395 has also been suggested. The silence of *Macrobius and *Isidorus (2) of Seville about Chalcidius proves little, as Augustine, who is certainly later, uses *Cicero's *Timaeus*. It was Calcidius' crabbed version, however, that was read in the west throughout the Middle Ages.

Ed. J. H. Waszink (1962). Waszink, *Studien zum Timaioskommentar des Calcidius* (1964). Epitaph of second Hosius: E. Diehl, *Inscriptiones Latinae Christianae Veteres* (1925–31), 83.
H. C.; M. J. E.

Chalcis, the chief city of *Euboea throughout antiquity, controlling the narrowest part of the Euripus channel and (after 411 BC) a bridge to the mainland. In the 8th cent. BC Chalcis, with its neighbour *Eretria, planted colonies in *Italy and *Sicily; its precise role in the Syrian *emporium* of *Al Mina is debated. In the later 8th cent. BC it disputed with Eretria possession of the Lelantine plain, which lay between them (see GREECE (HISTORY);

LEFKANDI). In the 7th cent. colonies were sent to the north Aegean. A centre of trade and manufacture, Chalcis was famous for its metalwork. In 506 it was compelled to cede part of its plain to Athenian cleruchs (see CLERUCHY). The city made common cause, however, with Athens during the invasion of *Xerxes. It led a revolt of Euboea against Athens (446) but was defeated (cf. ML 52) and became a tributary ally until 411. A member of the *Second Athenian Confederacy, from 350 it was a focus of Macedonian intrigues until 338, when, by imposing a Macedonian garrison, *Philip (1) II created here one of the three 'fetters' or 'keys' of Greece. The Hellenistic city was involved in the Macedonian and Syrian wars against Rome. For its participation in the *Achaean Confederacy's struggle against Rome, Chalcis was partly destroyed (146); 60 years later it served as a base for the Pontic general *Archelaus (3). On a continuously occupied site, the ancient city has left few remains. Instead we have a description (3rd cent. BC), stressing its many public buildings, the commerce of its agora, and intensive olive-cultivation in the hinterland (Heraclides Creticus 1. 27–30 = Austin 83).

Strabo 10. 445–8; *IG* 12 (9) 106 ff. J. Boardman, *CAH* 3²/1 (1982), ch. 18b; W. G. Forrest, *CAH* 3²/3 (1982), ch. 39d; J. Balcer, *The Athenian Regulations for Chalcis* (1978); G. L. Cawkwell, *Phoenix* 1978, 47 (the bridge); O. Picard, *Chalcis et la confédération eubéenne: Étude numismatique et d'histoire* (1979); S. Bakhuizen, *Studies in the Topography of Chalcis on Euboea* (1985).
W. A. L.; J. B.; S. H., A. J. S. S.

Chaldaean Oracles, these are conventionally attributed either to a certain Julian the Chaldaean, who is alleged to have flourished in the reign of *Trajan, or to his son, Julian the Theurgist, who lived in the reign of Marcus *Aurelius and, according to the *Suda*, was responsible for the rain miracle in Marcus' German wars. The traditional date in the 2nd cent. AD can be defended only on the dubious assumption that there are two allusions to the oracles in the work of *Numenius, who wrote no later than the second half of the 2nd cent. Otherwise there is no reference to these texts until the late 3rd cent., when *Iamblichus (2) quoted from them in his *On the Mysteries of the Egyptians*.

There is considerable evidence in the corpus, and from the way in which the oracles are cited by later Neoplatonists, that the text consisted of a series of oracles spoken by a variety of gods, of whom the most important was evidently *Hecate. However, at the beginning there also seems to have been a conversation between the elder 'Julian' and the soul of Plato (1) mediated by 'Julian' II. It also seems that the books provided some sort of explanation of the doctrines in the oracles. The doctrines appear to be based upon Platonic and Pythagorean speculation, cult, and *magic. (See PLATO (1); PYTHAGORAS.)

The oracles and commentary contained in the Chaldaean book not only offered a guide to the nature of the universe, they also appear to have acted as a guide to *theurgy.

FRAGMENTS E. des Places, *Oracles Chaldaïques* (1971); R. Majercik, *The Chaldaean Oracles: Text, Translation and Commentary* (1989).

DISCUSSION H. Lewy, *The Chaldaean Oracles and Theurgy*, 2nd edn. (1978); H. D. Saffrey, *Recherches sur le néoplatonisme après Plotin* (1990).
D. S. P.

Chalybes, a people of the SE coast of the Black (*Euxine) Sea, renowned in legend as the first workers of *iron and as the inventors of steel or carburized iron. Archaeology east of *Trapezus offers some confirmation of iron-working in this part of the Black Sea region early in the second millennium BC. *Xenophon (1) and *Strabo appear to place the Chalybes among the mountains south of Trapezus, but both seem also to mention iron-working Chalybes near Cerasus. The availability of iron and other ores on this coast, and early iron-working there, has been taken to account for Greek settlement at Trapezus.

D. C. Braund, *Georgia in Antiquity* (1994); R. Drews, *JHS* 1976, 18–32.
T. R. S. B.; D. C. B.

Chamaeleon (*RE* 1), of *Heraclea (3) Pontica (*c.*350–after 281 BC), Greek *Peripatetic writer; almost no biographical details exist. He wrote works on *satyric drama and comedy, and studies of a number of early poets, including *Homer, *Pindar, and *Aeschylus. These works, which were anecdotal and uncritical, are often cited by *Athenaeus (1): their hallmark was the deduction of biographical data from references in comedy and from the writers' own works, a technique already visible in the Aristotelian 'Constitution of Athens' (5–12): see ATHĒNAIŌN POLITEIA. Chamaeleon's philosophical writings, 'On Drunkenness', 'On Pleasure' (alternatively attributed to *Theophrastus), 'On the Gods', and his 'Speech of Encouragement' (Προτρεπτικός), also seem to have stood firmly in the Aristotelian tradition.

Fragments ed. with comm. by F. Wehrli, *Phainias von Eresos, Chamaileon, Praxiphanes* (1957), and by D. Giordano, 2nd edn. (1990; in Italian). G. Arrighetti, *Poeti, eruditi e biografi* (1987); *RE* Suppl. 11. 368–72.
C. B. R. P.

Chaones, name of a tribal state (ἁ πόλις ἁ τῶν Χαόνων) in north *Epirus which extended from the Dexari, probably near Berat (*FGrH* 1 F 103), to the river Kalamas (ancient Thyamis) in the 6th cent. BC but was eaten into later by the *Illyrii and the *Thesproti. The royal house claimed descent from Helenus of Troy, and in 429 BC its representatives commanded the army under an annual *prostateia*; the capital was probably at Phoenice. As a part of the Epirote Alliance and then of the Epirote Confederacy the Chaonian state shared the history of Epirus until 170 BC, when the Chaones and the Thesproti joined Rome and survived under the Roman settlement.

Hammond, *Epirus*; P. Cabanes, *L'Épire de la mort de Pyrrhos à la conquête romaine* (1976). N. G. L. H.

Chaos 'The very first of all Chaos came into being', says *Hesiod (*Theog.* 116); it is noteworthy that he implies by the verb (γένετο, not ἦν) that it did not exist from everlasting. What it was like he does not say; the name clearly means 'gaping void'. Later, presumably influenced by the ὁμοῦ πάντα ('all is together') of *Anaxagoras, it is described (Ov. *Met.* 1. 5 ff.) as a mixture of the 'seeds' (*semina*) or potentialities of all kinds of matter.
H. J. R.

character, in English, is a broad, non-technical term, which suggests an interest in recognizing patterns in human behaviour, and in analysing the psychological structures underlying these patterns. It is easy to point to ancient theories and practices which exhibit this interest; it is more difficult to define the salient differences between ancient and modern thinking on this topic.

Most of the relevant strands of ancient thought can be found in works ascribed to *Aristotle: *Rhetoric* 2. 12–17 contains evaluative sketches of the characteristic emotional responses of different social groups (young, old, etc.), a genre developed in *Theophrastus' collection of 'style-markers' (*Characters*) of defective ethical types; [*Physiognomics*] presents a typology of human characters based on popular thinking about the significance of facial and bodily shapes (see PHYSIOGNOMY); [*Problem.*] 30. 1 (on melancholy), provides evidence of the medical thinking that, by late antiquity, evolves into the theory of the four humoral temperaments (see HUMOURS).

The dominant interest in Aristotle (and in much ancient thought and literature) is in analysing ethically good and bad character, i.e. virtue and vice. The typical approach, found in Pl. *Resp.* 4, 8–9, Arist. *Eth. Eud.* 2–3, *Eth. Nic.* 2–4, Cic. *Off.* 1, consists of the tabulation of virtues and vices, conceived both as modes of human behaviour and as psychological structures. In the Aristotelian model, human beings are taken to be adapted by nature (*phusis*), to develop relatively stable patterns of emotion and desire ('dispositions', *hexeis*) which, in conjunction with value-laden beliefs and reasoning, form the basis for the choice-based actions and speeches in which people display their *ēthos* ('character', understood as 'ethical quality'). The social contexts of family, friendship-bond, city-state (and, for some, philosophical school) provide the informing framework for the development, as well as the definition, of these qualities. Other ancient philosophers emphasize an idea found also in Aristotle (*Eth. Nic.* 9. 4) that only the virtuous have real stability and cohesion of character and that the non-virtuous are dominated by 'unreasonable' and fluctuating desires or 'passions'. The ethical approach to character, more or less influenced by philosophical ideas, is evident in, e.g. *Horace's *Satires* and *Epistles, *Virgil's *Aeneid, *Plutarch's biographies, and Tacitus' histories.

Strikingly absent from the ancient thought-world is the interest in unique individuality and the subjective viewpoint which figures in modern western thinking about character. What is prominent, however, in ancient literature from Homer's *Iliad* onwards is the sympathetic presentation of abnormal and problematic psychological states and ethical stances. However, this is better understood as part of the communal exploration of the nature and limits of norms of good and bad character than as anticipating the modern preoccupation with individual subjectivity. See also BIOGRAPHY.

R. Klibansky and others, *Saturn and Melancholy* (1964); E. C. Evans, *TAPhS* 1969; C. Gill *CQ*, 1983–4, and *The Self in Dialogue* (1994); N. Sherman, *The Fabric of Character* (1989); C. B. R. Pelling (ed.), *Characterization and Individuality in Greek Literature* (1990). C. G.

Chares (1) (*c.*400–*c.*325 BC), famous Athenian soldier, probably more often general than any other Athenian of the 4th cent. except *Phocion, notorious for his treatment of the allies of the *Second Athenian Confederacy: *Isocrates' speech *De pace* was directed at him especially (Ar. *Rh.* 1418ᵃ32). He operated largely in the northern Aegean partly against *Cersobleptes and *Chersonesus (1), in 352 winning back *Sestus, and partly against *Philip (1) II, notably at *Olynthus and *Byzantium. His troops were generally *mercenaries, for whose payment he was largely left to provide himself. During the *Social War (1) (357–355) he was obliged to hire out the services of his mercenaries to the rebellious satrap *Artabazus and won a great victory, 'sister to *Marathon' as he claimed (schol. to Dem. 4. 19), but this precipitated the Persian ultimatum which abruptly ended the Social War. Chares fought in the campaign of *Chaeronea, and was one of those whose surrender was at first demanded by *Alexander (3) the Great in 335. Shortly after, he retired to *Sigeum and held command in *Mytilene during the Persian offensive in the Aegean in 333 and 332. He was with the mercenaries at *Taenarum (1) in the mid-320s, but died before 324/3.

W. K. Pritchett, *The Greek State at War* 2 (1974), 77–85. G. L. C.

Chares (2), of Mytilene, chamberlain (*eisangeleus*) of *Alexander (3) the Great. His voluminous *Histories of Alexander* contained rich and romantic detail, notably the experiment with *proskynēsis* (see ALEXANDER (3) the Great, § 10) and the mass marriage at *Susa. He was used by *Plutarch and colourful extracts are provided by *Athenaeus (1); but too little is known of his work for its influence to be defined.

FGrH 125; Pearson, *Lost Histories of Alexander* 50 ff.　　　A. B. B.

Chares (3), a writer of *Gnomai* (see GNŌMĒ), from which over 50 lines are preserved, in a mutilated state, in a papyrus of the early 3rd cent. BC.

S. Jaekel, *Menandri sententiae* (1964), 26–30.　　　J. S. R.

Chares (4), of *Lindus, Greek sculptor, active c.300 BC. A follower of *Lysippus (2), Chares was renowned for his bronze statue of *Helios for *Rhodes, the famous Colossus. Some 32 m. (105 ft.) high, it was financed by the sale of the equipment left behind by *Demetrius (4) Poliorcetes when he abandoned the siege of Rhodes in 305. It stood on a hill overlooking the city (not astride the harbour); it fell in an earthquake in 228 or 226 BC. See also SEVEN WONDERS.

A. F. Stewart, *Greek Sculpture* (1990), 298 f.　　　A. F. S.

Charidemus, mercenary general. Born (illegitimately) in Oreus (*Histiaea), his early career involved (sometimes rapid) switches between mutually hostile employers—*Athens (368–365, 365–362), *Olynthus (365), *Artabazus (361–360), Cotys of Thrace (365, 360), and *Cersobleptes (359–353)—and the attempted foundation of a personal principality in the Troad (*Troas) (c.360). Given Athenian citizenship (357) in a deal about *Chersonesus (1) between Athens and Cersobleptes (his brother-in-law), he was *stratēgos* in 351–348 (*Hellespont; Olynthus) and 338/7 (Attica, post-*Chaeronea). Strongly anti-Macedonian (perhaps because of Cersobleptes' fate at *Philip (1) II's hands), his surrender was demanded by *Alexander (3) the Great (335); he fled to *Darius III who executed him in over-hasty reaction to his calling the King's Friends cowards during an argument about strategy (330). A man of high personal courage, he was also accused of sexual and alcoholic excesses.

RE 3, 'Charidemos' 5; Berve *Alexanderreich*, no. 823; W. K. Pritchett, *The Greek State at War* 2 (1974).　　　C. J. T.

chariots See HORSE- AND CHARIOT-RACES; TRANSPORT, WHEELED.

Charisius (*RE* 8), **Flavius Sosipater** (late 4th cent. AD), compiled an *Ars grammatica* in five books (ed. K. Barwick, 1925), juxtaposing passages of basic school grammar with excerpts from more learned sources (e.g. *Remmius Palaemon, *Iulius Romanus): these borrowings both provide copious evidence for the earlier grammatical tradition and contain numerous fragments of early Latin authors. Bk. 1 (defective at the beginning) and bk. 2 survey the constituent elements of grammar (*de voce, de litteris,* etc.) and the parts of speech; bk. 3 deals with conjugation, bk. 4 (lacunose) with style and metre. Bk. 5, which dealt with the differences between Latin and Greek forms and constructions, is largely lost. See GRAMMAR, GRAMMARIANS, LATIN.

PLRE 1. 201; Herzog–Schmidt, § 523. 2.　　　R. A. K.

Charites, 'Graces', goddesses personifying charm, grace, and beauty. Like the *Nymphs and the *Horae, they vary in number, but are usually three from Hesiod (*Theog.* 907–9), who names them Aglaea (Radiance), Euphrosyne (Joy), and Thalia (Flowering) (cf. *Pindar, *Ol.* 14. 3–17; *Homer neither names nor numbers them, *Il.* 14. 267–8, 275). *Hesiod calls them daughters of *Zeus and Eurynome, and is followed by most writers, although the mothers vary. They are closely associated with

*Aphrodite in Homer (e.g. *Od.* 8. 364–6, 18. 193–4), and later. In Hesiod (*Theog.* 53–64; *Op.* 73–5), they and the Horae deck *Pandora. They enjoy poetry, singing, and dance (*Theog.* 64; Thgn. 15) and perform at the wedding of *Peleus and *Thetis. They make roses grow (Anac. 44. 1), have myrtles and roses as attributes, and the flowers of spring belong to them (*Cypria* fr. 4 Allen). They bestow beauty and charm, physical (*Anth. Pal.* 7. 600), intellectual, artistic, and moral (Pind. *Ol.* 14. 6). The Hellenistic poet *Hermesianax makes *Peitho (Persuasion) one (Paus. 9. 35. 5).

The Charites have no independent mythology, associating with gods of fertility, especially Aphrodite, whose birth they attend. Often they are shown standing, processing, or dancing, the latter sometimes in connection with *Hecate in the Hellenistic and Roman period. *Pausanias (3) details cults and depictions of the Charites, particularly at *Orchomenus (1) (9. 35. 1–7); they also occur throughout southern Greece and in Asia Minor. Athens had a Hellenistic cult of *Demos and the Charites. Pausanias notes regional variations in their number and names, and many depictions, from aniconic images at Orchomenus (9. 38. 1), to their use as decorations on the 'Amyclaean throne' (3. 18. 9–10) and on the Zeus at Olympia (5. 11. 8). They occur on a metope from *Thermum, vases, Athenian New Style coins, and neo-Attic reliefs. The Charites were originally draped (e.g. a painting by *Apelles at *Smyrna, Paus. 9. 35. 6), later naked. The familiar group of three naked women is Hellenistic in origin, and became standard in many Roman copies in several media.

RE 3 / 2, 'Charites, Charis'; LIMC 3 / 1. 191–203; B. MacLachlan, *The Age of Grace: Charis in Early Greek Poetry* (1993).　　　K. W. A.

charities See ALIMENTA; EUERGETISM; FOOD SUPPLY.

Chariton, Greek novelist, author of the eight-book *Chaereas and Callirhoë* (Τὰ περὶ Χαιρέαν καὶ Καλλιρόην). He opens by naming himself and his city, *Aphrodisias, claiming to be secretary to an orator Athenagoras. All three names have been suspected as appropriate fictions, but both personal names appear on inscriptions of Aphrodisias, Athenagoras recurring in two prominent families. Papyri date Chariton not later than the mid-2nd cent. AD, but although scholars agree in making his, or *Xenophon (2)'s, the earliest of the novels surviving complete, dates are canvassed between the 1st cent. BC and *Hadrian's reign. His use of a historical character (Callirhoë's father is *Hermocrates, victor over the Athenians in 413 BC) suggests an early stage in the genre's development. The historical *mise-en-scène*, much quotation of *Homer, and allusion to many other classical authors (notably *Thucydides (2) and *Xenophon (1)) show some literary ambition, confirmed by careful avoidance of hiatus; yet Chariton's diction does not Atticize (see ASIANISM AND ATTICISM); hence Papanikolaou (see bibliog. below) dated him in the 1st cent. BC.

Chariton begins at *Syracuse: Chaereas and Callirhoë, both outstandingly beautiful, fall in love and marry. Soon after marriage Chaereas, driven to jealousy by disappointed rivals, kicks his pregnant wife. Taken for dead she is buried, but tomb-robbers find her alive, and in *Miletus sell her to the rich and educated Dionysius. Chaereas learns of Callirhoë's abduction and, searching for her, is himself enslaved. Callirhoë marries Dionysius to protect the child she expects by Chaereas, but her beauty overwhelms the *satrap Mithradates, then Artaxerxes, the Persian king, at whose court Mithradates and Dionysius dispute their claims to her, and she and Chaereas again meet. Eventually the couple, reunited, return to Syracuse, to live happily ever after.

Chariton deploys traditional elements of the genre (travel,

false deaths, pirates, enslavements, shipwrecks, happy ending) in a clear, linear narrative whose components are adroitly joined; key twists he ascribes to Fortune ($T\acute{v}\chi\eta$), occasionally directing readers' responses by authorial comment (e.g. 8. 1. 4). See NOVEL, GREEK.

EDITIO PRINCEPS Villoison (Amsterdam, 1750).

STANDARD EDITIONS W. E. Blake (1938); G. Molinié (Budé, 1979; rev. A. Billault, 1990).

COMMENTARIES D'Orville (Amsterdam, 1750; 2nd edn. Leipzig 1783, with notes by Reiske and others). Good notes in German translations of K. Plepelits (1976) and C. Lucke and K.-H. Schäfer (1985).

ENGLISH TRANSLATIONS B. P. Reardon, in B. P. Reardon (ed.), Collected Ancient Greek Novels (1989); W. E. Blake (1939).

CRITICISM G. L. Schmeling, Chariton (1974); Rohde, Griech. Roman, 517 ff.; W. Schmid, RE 5 (1897), 2168–71, 'Chariton' 3; Christ–Schmid–Stählin 2/2⁶, 808 ff.; A. Lesky, A History of Greek Literature (1966), 862–3; E. L. Bowie, CHCL 1 (1985), 688–90 (= paperback 1/4 (1989), 128–30); S. Heibges, De clausulis Charitoneis (1911); B. E. Perry, AJPhil. 1930, and The Ancient Romances (1967), 96–148; W. Bartsch, Der Charitonroman und die Historiographie (1934); R. Petri, Über den Roman des Chariton (1963); T. Hägg, Narrative Technique in Ancient Greek Romances (1971), and The Novel in Antiquity (1983), 5–18; A. D. Papanikolaou, Chariton-Studien (1973); B. P. Reardon, YClS 1982; G. Anderson, Eros Sophistes (1982), 13–21, and Ancient Fiction (1984). E. L. B.

Charmadas (168/7–some time after 107 BC), member of the *Academy, pupil of *Carneades. Mentioned by *Sextus Empiricus (Pyr. 1. 220) as founder of the 'Fourth Academy' together with *Philon (3) of Larissa. He taught in the Athenian Ptolemaeum for a while, but later returned to the Academy. Charmadas was famous for his elegant style and is said to have had many students.

J. Glucker, Antiochus and the Late Academy (1979), 109–11. G. S.

Charmides (d. 403 BC), an Athenian of noble family, nephew and ward of *Critias, uncle of *Plato (1), and member of the Socratic circle. He is mentioned in Pl. Symp. 222b, Prt. 315a, Xen. Mem. 3. 6. 1, 7. 1–9, and plays a large part in the Platonic dialogue that bears his name. According to Xen. (Mem. 3. 7) he was encouraged by *Socrates to take up political life. He assisted Critias in the oligarchic revolution of 404 and fell with him in battle in 403, when the democrats returned under *Thrasybulus. W. D. R.

Charon (1), mythological ferryman, who ferries the shades across a river (usually *Acheron) or a lake (Acherusia) into *Hades proper. First attested in the epic Minyas (M. Davies, EGF fr. 1), his first known visual representations occur c.500 BC on two black-figure vases (LIMC nos. 1, 1a); a few decades later he became popular on Attic white-ground lecythi. *Polygnotus painted him in the Nekyia in the Lesche (hall) of the Cnidians at *Delphi (Paus. 10. 28. 1–2). In a katabasis (descent) ascribed to *Orpheus (cf. Serv. on Verg. Aen. 6. 392) Charon, out of fear, ferried Heracles, who had gone to fetch *Cerberus, into Hades, and was punished for this dereliction with a year in fetters.

C. Sourvinou-Inwood, LIMC 3 (1986), 'Charon' 210–25, and 'Reading' Greek Death (1995), ch. 5; O. Waser, Charon, Charun, Charos (1898); H. Hoffman, Visible Religion 4–5 (1986), 173–204; R. H. Terpening, Charon and the Crossing: Ancient, Medieval and Renaissance Transformations of a Myth (1985) (cf. the review by H. King, CR 1986, 355–6). On Charon's fee: S. T. Stevens, Phoenix 1991, 215–29. C. S.-I.

Charon (2), of Lampsacus, historian. Tradition (Dion. Hal. Thuc. 5, Pomp. 3. 7; Plut. Mor. 859b; Tert. De anim. 46 = T 4a–d) made him an older contemporary and source of *Herodotus. The Suda (entry under the name = T 1) confirms this dating (despite contradictory statements within the work) and lists the following works: Aethiopica, Persica in 2 bks., Hellenica in 4 bks., On

Lampsacus in 4 bks., Libyca, Chronicles (Oroi) of the Lampsacenes in 4 bks., Prytaneis of the Lacedaemonians, Kτίσεις πόλεων in 2 bks., Cretica in 3 bks., Periplus of the Area outside the Pillars of Heracles.

Historians operating with the traditional dating accepted only Yearbooks of Samos and the Persica as genuine, since neither the scale nor the subject-matter of the other works is compatible with an early date. Jacoby, however, dates Charon later and makes him a younger contemporary of *Hellanicus (1), mainly because of the similar subject-matter (so recently Lendle). Von Fritz does not commit himself on the issue of the dating: 'as far as the fragments are concerned Charon may just as well have been an older contemporary of Herodotus as a younger contemporary of Hellanicus.' Charon was no doubt older than Herodotus, but even so, it is impossible to prove that Herodotus used his account (cf. Moggi) or silently corrected it in his own work (thus Piccirilli). The Persica fragments suggest a less detailed treatment of events than Herodotus, but a similar interest in anecdote, legends, and local traditions. Style and presentation are archaic.

FGrH 262, 687b (Persica); F. Jacoby, Abhandlungen zur griechischen Geschichtsschreibung (1956), 178 ff.; A. Hepperle, in Festschrift O. Regenbogen (1956); K. von Fritz, Die griechische Geschichtsschreibung, 2 vols. (1967); R. Drews, The Greek Accounts of Eastern History (1973), 24 ff.; L. Piccirilli, ASNP 1975, 1239 ff.; M. Moggi, ASNP 1977, 1 ff.; O. Lendle, Einführung in die griechische Geschichtsschreibung (1992) 71 ff. K. M.

Charondas, the lawgiver of his native town *Catana and other Chalcidic colonies, especially *Rhegium. He is often associated with *Zaleucus, but he lived later, probably towards the end of the 6th cent. BC. Much of our information about him is legendary. More reliable are reports that he set very precise penalties for different offences and that he prohibited the extension of credit in commercial transactions.

Arist. Pol. esp. 1274ᵃ⁻ᵇ. A. Szegedy-Maszak, GRBS 1978; M. Gagarin, Early Greek Law (1986). M. Ga.

Charops, a pro-Roman leader in *Epirus, was educated at Rome; his grandfather, also Charops, had helped T. *Quinctius Flamininus against *Philip (3) V in 198 BC. During Rome's war against *Perseus (2) he undermined Rome's trust in his political rivals. *Polybius (1) (30. 12) denounced his character in such terms as to suggest that he might have encouraged Rome's devastation of Epirus: thereafter until his death c.159 BC he acted tyrannically in Epirus, but he was not overthrown although he had lost the favour of leading Romans.

H. H. Scullard, JRS 1945, 55 ff.; S. I. Oost, Roman Policy in Epirus (1954), 72 ff.; Hammond, Epirus, 626 ff.; Walbank, HCP 3. 314 on 27. 15. 3. H. H. S.

Charybdis, a sort of whirlpool or maelstrom in a narrow channel of the sea (later identified with the Straits of Messina, cf. JHS 1965, 172), opposite *Scylla (1) (Od. 12. 101 ff.); it sucks in and casts out the water three times a day and no ship can possibly live in it. Odysseus, carried towards it by a current when shipwrecked, escapes by clinging to a tree which grows above it and dropping into the water when the wreckage is cast out (432 ff.). Hence proverbially, a serious danger, as Horace, Carm. 1. 27. 19.

A. Heubeck, in A. Heubeck and A. Hoekstra, Comm. on Odyssey 2 (1989), 124; S. Hornblower, in Comm. on Thuc. (n. on 4. 24. 5). H. J. R.; S. H.

chastity

Before Christianity Chastity was not recommended in classical Greek *medicine before *Soranus. In pagan religion, certain goddesses chose to remain virgins (e.g. *Hestia/*Vesta,

*Artemis/*Diana) and some priestesses—not necessarily those serving virgin goddesses—remained life virgins (e.g. Artemis Hymnia in Arcadia, Paus. 8. 13. 1) while others could only hold the position until the age of marriage (e.g. *Poseidon at *Calauria, Paus. 2. 33. 3). They did not support their other human followers who emulated this behaviour (e.g. *Euripides' *Hippolytus (1)).

In contrast to the Hippocratics (see HIPPOCRATES (2)) who believed a girl must be 'opened up' for the sake of her health, Soranus recommended perpetual virginity as positively healthful for both men and women (*Gynaeceia* 1. 30–2). These chapters were omitted in the Latin versions of his work compiled in late antiquity. He argued that desire harms the body, while pregnancy and *childbirth exhaust the body. However, Soranus ends the section by conceding that intercourse is necessary for the continuance of the human race.

In contrast to Christian writers of the early Roman empire (see below), Soranus recommends virginity neither for spiritual health nor as part of rejecting the world, but to make the present life easier.

J. Rubin Pinault, *Helios* 1992, 123–39; A. Rousselle, *Porneia* (1988; Fr. orig. 1983); P. Brown, in D. Halperin and others (eds.), *Before Sexuality* (1990), 479–93.   H. K.

Christian Celibacy and *asceticism are endemic to *Christianity and are typical of the distinctive outlook on life which runs throughout much of early Christian literature. The lifestyle of John the Baptist and the canonical gospels' portrayal of the celibacy of Jesus and his eschatological message set the pattern for subsequent Christian practice. While the influence of Graeco-Hellenistic ideas cannot be ruled out, particularly Platonism (see PLATO (1)), the background to this form of religious observance is to be found in the ascetical practices of certain forms of sectarian Judaism. The level of purity demanded by the Qumran sect (see DEAD SEA SCROLLS) reflects the regulations with regard to sexual activity in Leviticus and the requirements laid upon men involved in a holy war in Deuteronomy (probably explaining the reference to virginity in Rev. 14: 4). Elsewhere there is evidence that asceticism was a central part of the mystical and apocalyptic tradition of *Judaism (e.g. Dan. 10). The centrality of eschatological beliefs for Christianity meant that from the earliest period there was a marked component of Christian practice which demanded a significant distance from the values and culture of the present age. The hope for the coming of a new age of perfection in which members of the Church could already participate placed rigorous demands on those who would join. Some evidence suggests that baptized men and women thought that they had to live like angels (cf. Luke 20: 35), putting aside all those constraints of present bodily existence which were incompatible with their eschatological state. *Paul's approach in 1 Cor. 7 in dealing with the rigorist lifestyle of the Corinthian ascetics is typical of the compromise that evolved, in which there is a grudging acceptance of marriage and an exaltation of celibacy. The emerging monastic movement, therefore, drew on a long history of ascetical practice which was taken to extremes in some Encratite circles.

P. Brown, *The Body and Society* (1988); H. Chadwick, *RAC* 5 (1962), 343–65; R. Lane Fox, *Pagans and Christians* (1986).   C. R.

Chatti, a Germanic people, who lived in the neighbourhood of the upper Weser and the Diemel. Although not mentioned by *Caesar, they were the most powerful enemies of Rome in western Germany throughout the 1st cent. AD. Overrun by

*Drusus in 12 BC, they took part in the revolt of AD 9 and were later attacked by *Germanicus, who in 15 burned their town of Mattium (exact site unknown), and by the generals of *Claudius. They fought a war in 58 against the Hermunduri for the possession of some salt-beds, and took part in the revolt of C. *Iulius Civilis in 69–70. They broke the neighbouring *Cherusci, but had to yield the Wetterau to Domitian. Their social and military organization was more highly developed than that of the other Germans. Their nobles took even less part in productive life than those of other Germanic peoples. They are occasionally mentioned as attacking the Roman empire in the later part of the 2nd cent., but from the early 3rd cent. we hear nothing more of them. Their name appears to have survived in that of Hessen.

E. A. Thompson, *The Early Germans* (1965).   E. A. T.; J. F. Dr.

Chauci, a Germanic people, living on the North Sea coast between the mouths of the Ems and the Elbe. Overrun in the Augustan conquest of western Germany, they apparently took no part in the revolt of *Arminius; but they more than once raided the Gallic coast from the sea during the 1st cent. AD. Little is known of their history; but Tacitus (*Germ.* 35) comments on their great numbers, and *Pliny (1) the Elder vividly describes the poverty-stricken lives of the coast-dwellers (*HN* 16. 2–4). Their relationship with the *Saxons, who lived on that same coast at a later date, is unclear.

E. A. T.; J. F. Dr.

chemistry See ALCHEMY; PHYSICS.

Chersonesus (1), Thracian, a long, narrow peninsula forming the European side of the *Hellespont (Dardanelles). Running generally in an east–west direction, it connects the sea of Marmara with the Aegean. It was noted in antiquity for its fertility and for its strategic location as a crossing between Europe and Asia. Several Greek cities lay along the protected southern (Hellespontine) shore, leaving no doubt about their ability to control sea traffic through the straits. It was settled by Aeolian and Ionian Greeks in the 8th and 7th cents. BC. Private Athenian interest commenced in the late 7th cent., with settlers involved in both local agriculture and trade and in the growing Greek commerce with the Black (*Euxine) Sea. By the 5th cent. the Athenian state took an official interest in protecting the grain trade, and a number of Chersonese cities became tributary states in the Athenian empire (see DELIAN LEAGUE). In the 4th cent. a wall 8 km. (5 mi.) long was built across the narrow neck of the peninsula as a defence against Thracian incursions. *Philip (1) II of Macedon ruled the area, and, after passing through the hands of *Alexander (3) the Great's successors, the Chersonesus became a part of *Pergamum's domain (189). Thence it passed into Roman hands (133) as *ager publicus, and was converted into an imperial estate under *Augustus. Because of its strategic importance in modern times, travel has been limited and excavation virtually non-existent, thereby forcing us to depend mainly upon ancient written sources for the history of the rich cities of the Chersonesus. See CARDIA; MILTIADES.

U. Kahrstedt, *Beiträge zur Geschichte der thrakischen Chersones* (1954); B. Isaac, *The Greek Settlements in Thrace until the Macedonian Conquest* (1986).   E. N. B.

Chersonesus (2), the Crimea, or Tauric Chersonese, named after the local Tauri of its mountainous south-west. Through the Archaic period, Greeks established settlements around its coast, notably at *Chersonesus (3) and *Panticapaeum. The Crimea offered the relative security of a peninsular region, rich fisheries, fertile land, abundant salt, and every opportunity for trade by sea or with the hinterland. The eastern portion of the Crimea constituted half of the Bosporan kingdom (see BOSPORUS (2)). The Crimea was renowned in antiquity as a source of grain, especially in the 4th cent. BC. See FOOD SUPPLY, GREEK.

G. A. Koshelenko, I. T. Kruglikova, and V. S. Dolgorukov (eds.), *Antichnye gosudarstva Severnovo Prichernomor' ya* (1984). D. C. B.

Chersonesus (3), city situated in the SW Crimea, near modern Sevastopol'. Literary evidence (*Strabo, *Pliny (1), etc.) suggests that it was founded from *Heraclea (3) Pontica, south across the Black (*Euxine) Sea. Until recently it was agreed that Heracleot settlement began *c*.420 BC, on the site of an earlier, small Ionian (Milesian?) site. But recent archaeology has been taken to show that the Heracleot settlement dates from no later than *c*.525 BC. It also attests a vigorous trade with the south coast of the Black Sea, which continued into the Byzantine period, when Pope Martin (7th cent. AD), exiled to the city, mentioned ships bringing grain there in search of salt. Under the Principate it received a Roman garrison, which seems to have developed the defended harbour at nearby Charax (Ai-Todor), manned by Roman forces from the 1st cent. AD to the middle of the 3rd cent.

V. I. Kadeyev, *Khersones v pervykh vekakh nashey ery* (1981); G. A. Koshelenko, I. T. Kruglikova, V. S. Dolgorukov (eds.), *Antichnye gosudarstva Severnovo Prichernomor'ya* (1984), 45–57; D. Kacharava and G. Kvirkvelia (eds.), *Goroda i poseleniya Prichernomor' ya antichnoy epokhi* (1991), 304–26. D. C. B.

Cherusci, a Germanic people, living around the middle Weser. They are the best known of the Germanic opponents of the Romans in the 1st cent. AD. Overrun in the Augustan conquest of western Germany, it was their chieftain *Arminius who led the revolt of AD 9, which resulted in the defeat of P. *Quinctilius Varus and his army. They successfully defended themselves against *Germanicus' punitive expeditions in 15–16, inflicting heavy losses on the Romans. They expelled king *Maroboduus from among the *Marcomanni (AD 17), and defeated the attempt of Arminius himself to set up a tyranny over them. Thereafter they weakened themselves by their internal struggles which, together with the hostility of the *Chatti, reduced them to comparative impotence by the time of *Tacitus (1). In later times they are rarely heard of.

E. A. Thompson, *The Early Germans* (1965). E. A. T.; J. F. Dr.

childbirth was generally the concern of women, either family and neighbours or experienced *midwives who were sometimes ranked as doctors, but male doctors expected to be called in for difficult cases. Several treatises in the Hippocratic corpus (see HIPPOCRATES (2)) include some discussion of childbirth. *On the Nature of the Child* ascribes the onset of labour to the movement of the foetus, which breaks the membranes. *Diseases of Women* says that prolonged and unsuccessful labour usually means a difficult presentation, stillbirth, or multiple birth. Suggestions include vigorous shaking to stimulate delivery, and drugs to speed labour (*ōkytokia*); if all else fails, the doctor may resort to embryotomy, the extraction by instruments of a foetus which is stillborn or impossible to deliver alive. The uterus is envisaged as a container rather than as a powerful muscle, and labour is described as pains not contractions. *Aristotle (*HA* 586^b) notes that pains can occur in the thighs and the lower back as well as the lower abdomen, and that women can help delivery by effort and correct breathing. Dissection by *Herophilus, in the 3rd cent. BC, revealed that the uterus is muscular, and Galen (*Nat. Fac.* 3.

3) argues that it has the power to retain or expel the foetus.

The most detailed account of labour and delivery is in the 1st-cent. AD handbook written by *Soranus for midwives, the *Gynaecology*. Soranus envisages delivery on a birthing-chair, or on a hard bed if the mother is weak. He does not discuss contractions or distinguish stages of labour, but does describe dilation of the cervix and the breathing-technique to be used in delivery. Pain relief is provided by warm cloths on the abdomen and sharp-scented things to smell, and Soranus emphasizes that the midwife and helpers must reassure the mother and be careful not to embarrass her. At the birth, the midwife signals whether the baby is male or female, then lays the baby on the ground and assesses whether it is 'worth rearing'. She judges when to cut and tie the umbilical cord, cleans and swaddles the baby, and puts it to bed.

Soranus invokes psychological and physical factors in the mother, as well as big babies, multiple births, and abnormal presentations, to explain difficult labour. He offers techniques for relieving a narrow or obstructed cervix (these do not include episiotomy) and for turning a foetus, but makes no mention of obstetric forceps or of Caesarean section as an alternative to embryotomy: a mother could not have survived the trauma of a Caesarean. He has no confidence in drugs, induced sneezing, and shaking to stimulate delivery of the baby or the placenta, and disapproves of cold baths, tight swaddling, and hard beds for newborns. He notes the belief that delivery is impeded if the woman's hair or belt is tied, and the reluctance of some midwives to cut the cord with iron.

Maternal mortality, like neonatal and infant mortality, is often assumed to have been high, but estimates of the maternal death rate range from 5 in 20,000 to 25 in 1,000. Women may have died from exhaustion and haemorrhage in a difficult delivery (especially if they had poor health or were very young) or from eclampsia, a kind of epilepsy which can now be detected early; puerperal fever occurred, but infection is relatively unlikely in home delivery.

In Greek tradition, childbirth ritually polluted those present because blood was shed, and delivery on sacred ground was therefore forbidden (see POLLUTION). Olympian goddesses are not represented as giving birth. The deities most often invoked in labour were *Artemis *Eileithyia (sometimes regarded as separate deities) or *Hera in Greece, *Juno Lucina in Rome. Roman childbirth rituals are briefly described by *Augustine (*De civ. D.* 6. 9), but his source is the antiquarian *Varro rather than common practice. There are also allusions to rituals in which the father lifts the child from the earth (*tollere liberum*) or carries the child round the hearth (*amphidromia*), but these would not always be practicable—for instance, in a house with no central hearth or when the baby was born on the upper floor of a tenement—and it was the name-day celebration, approximately ten days after the birth, which publicly acknowledged the child as a family member. See EMBRYOLOGY; MOTHERHOOD; POLLUTION.

Soranus, *Gynaecology*, trans. O. Temkin (1956; repr. 1991); V. French, in M. B. Skinner (ed.), *Rescuing Creusa* (1987); A. Hanson in S. B. Pomeroy (ed.), *Women's History and Ancient History* (1991); R. Jackson, *Doctors and Diseases in the Roman Empire* (1988). E. G. C.

children In Greece the decision whether to raise a child normally rested with the father except in *Sparta where 'elders of the tribes' were required to pronounce upon its fitness to live (Plut. *Lyc.* 16. 1). In Rome a law attributed to Romulus allegedly required all parents to 'bring up all their male offspring and the first-born of the girls' (Dion. Hal. *Ant. Rom.* 2. 15. 1). The exposure of infants is frequently commented upon in both Greek and Latin authors but this does not help us to determine how frequent it was in practice. Categories at high risk, however, include girls, those with a *deformity, illegitimate offspring, and slave offspring. Being less 'popular' than boys (e.g. *POxy.* 4. 744), many girls may have been undernourished (cf. Xen. *Respublica Lacedaemoniorum* 1. 3). Whether this led to a marked imbalance among the sexes, as has sometimes been alleged, is unknown. From the time of *Trajan onwards some families in Roman cities were given financial aid called *alimenta* to help defray the cost of raising their children.

A boy, like a slave, was a marginal figure, but unlike a slave his marginality was only temporary. Girls, however, even upon attaining adulthood, always remained under the supervision of a male. In Athens a ceremony called the *amphidromia*, held probably on the fifth day after birth, signalled a child's entry into the family. Soon afterwards boys were registered in hereditary associations known as *phratries. Boys and girls until aged about 6 spent most of their time in the women's quarters or γυναικεῖον. In *Sparta at this age boys left home and entered the public educational system called the *agōgē*, which was designed to produce a well-disciplined army (Plut. *Lyc.* 16). A variety of *rites of passage for males signalled the end of childhood in the Greek world. The Roman equivalent to the *amphidromia* was the *lustratio*, 'purification', which took place on the eighth or ninth day. There was no subsequent ceremony of incorporation for Roman children. Childhood ended for boys around 16 with the putting on of the plain white adult toga in place of the *toga praetexta* with purple border. There is no secure evidence of any puberty ceremonies for girls in either the Greek or Roman world, although it has been claimed that the *arkteia* functioned as such in Athens (see BRAURON).

In light of the probably high level of infant mortality there has been much speculation about the intensity of parental affect in antiquity. The keen desire for children that we observe both in literature and in the popularity of *adoption admittedly reflects in part the pragmatic acknowledgement that many parents in their old age were dependent upon offspring for support. A child's duty to its parents extended in the case of the Greeks to the legal requirement to maintain its parents in old age. No such ruling existed in the Roman world before the 2nd cent. AD.

Corporal punishment was frequently administered to children. The Roman *paterfamilias* or household head even had the right of life and death over his offspring (see PATRIA POTESTAS), though it was little exercised in the late republic and empire apart from cases of abandonment at birth and *adultery. The nurse and *paedagogus* (or child-minder), both slaves, were important figures in a child's upbringing. Since the age gap between fathers and children was about 30 years, many children would have come under the supervision of a guardian. The Greeks and Romans believed that intelligence was a function of age and hence tended to regard the child as intellectually inferior. Largely because of their ritual purity children played a significant role in religion, singing in choirs and even serving as priests (e.g. Paus. 7. 19. 1, 7. 24. 4). Especially important was the *pais amphithalēs* or *puer patrimus et matrimus*, a child whose parents were both still alive and so had not been polluted by contact with the dead.

Our perception of childhood in antiquity is based almost wholly on what unrepresentative adults such as *Plato (1) (possibly childless) and *Aristotle have chosen to record. The concept of play, for instance, receives prominent attention in the

Laws of Plato, who sees it as fulfilling a major role in the moulding of personality. It follows that *toys, commonly found in graves or depicted in vase-paintings, provide the most evocative picture of the world of the child. Evidence about games derives largely from late lexicographical sources. Representations of children in Greek art begin in the late-5th cent. BC and in Roman art at the beginning of the imperial era, possibly inspired by Augustus' programme for promoting the rearing of children. Roman children are frequently mentioned in funerary inscriptions and lawcodes. See AGE; AGE CLASSES; CHILDBIRTH; EDUCATION; MOTHERHOOD.

J. K. Evans, *War, Women and Children in Ancient Rome* (1991); R. S. J. Garland, *The Greek Way of Life* (1990); M. Golden, *Children and Childhood in Classical Athens* (1990); B. Rawson (ed.), *Marriage, Divorce, and Children in Ancient Rome* (1991); T. Wiedemann, *Adults and Children in the Roman Empire* (1989). R. S. J. G.

children's songs (Greek) Pollux (9. 94–129) lists eighteen παιδιαί, children's songs often accompanied with some sort of action, and adds details about χαλκῆ μυῖα, a kind of Blind Man's Buff, χελιχελώνη, a kind of Prisoner's Base, and (9. 113) χυτρίνδα, a kind of Catch. Another such game was ἄνθεμα (Ath. 629c).

TEXT Page, *PMG* 875–80; J. M. Edmonds, *Lyra Graeca* (1952) 3. 536–43. C. M. B.; E. Kr.

Chilon, Spartan *ephor (*c.*556 BC), whose wit and wisdom gained him an assured place among the '*Seven Sages' of Greece (Pl. *Prt.* 343a). Related by marriage to kings of both houses (see AGIADS; EURYPONTIDS), he was said to have been the first to 'yoke the ephors alongside the kings' (Diog. Laert. 1. 68), a possible reference to the monthly renewed compact between Spartan kings and *ephors. As ephor he may have helped to overthrow the tyranny at *Sicyon (*PRyl.* 18 = *FGrH* 105 no. 1), which in turn may have been part of a momentous change in Sparta's foreign policy leading to the establishment of the *Peloponnesian League. He was worshipped at Sparta after his death as a hero (Paus. 3. 16. 4, corroborated by an extant inscribed hero-relief; see HERO-CULT).

V. Ehrenberg, *Neugründer des Staates* (1925), 7–54; A. R. Burn, *The Lyric Age of Greece* (1960), 207–9; G. L. Huxley, *Early Sparta* (1962), 69 ff. and n. 486; P. Cartledge, *Sparta and Lakonia* (1979). P. A. C.

Chimaera (Χίμαιρα, 'she-goat'), bizarre monster slain by *Bellerophon, composed of 'lion in front, snake behind, and she-goat in the middle' (*Il.* 6. 179–82); in art the eponymous central head (sometimes a protome with forefeet) which protrudes uneasily from the lion's back may be made less risible by allowing it to perform the fire-breathing which Homer and Hesiod describe. The latter (*Theog.* 319 ff.) assigns it to the monstrous family of *Typhon and *Echidna, while Homer claims it was specially reared by 'Amisodarus' (*Il.* 16. 328).

A. Jacquemin in *LIMC*; M. L. Schmitt, *AJArch.* 1966, 341–7. A. H. G.

China, Chinese See SERES.

Chionides is treated by *Aristotle (*Poet.* 1448ᵃ33) as one of the two earliest Attic comic poets, and it is probable that he was the first recorded comic victor at the City *Dionysia, in 486 (*Suda*, entry under the name). Two plays ascribed to him, *Heroes* and *Beggars*, existed in Hellenistic times (Ath. [137e and 638d] doubts the authenticity of *Beggars*) and the *Suda* mentions also the title '*Persians or Assyrians*'. See COMEDY (GREEK), OLD, § 1.

Kassel–Austin, *PCG* 4. 42 ff. (*CAF* 1. 4 ff.). K. J. D.

Chios, an important *Ionian *polis on the large Aegean island of the same name (842 sq. km.: 325 sq. mi.), some 7 km. (4½ mi.) from Asia Minor. *Thucydides (2) calls it the greatest *polis* of Ionia and its citizens among the wealthiest Greeks (8. 24. 4, 40.1). The north and north-west comprise pine-clad limestone mountains (up to 1,297 m.: 4,255 ft.) and infertile schists; on the softer rocks of the SE lowlands mastic trees were (and are) grown for their valuable gum; but the plain beside the large eastern bay has supported the main settlement in all periods. Chios controlled the neighbouring islets of Oinoussai and modern Psara (an important bronze age site). Ionic Greek is spoken, though there were Aeolian cultural influences. Literary figures included *Homer (supposedly), *Ion (2), and *Theopompus (3); there was a distinctive artistic tradition.

Reputedly colonized from *Euboea in the 9th cent. BC (also the date of the earliest Greek burials), in Archaic times Chios was often at loggerheads with *Erythrae on the Asiatic mainland (where Chians had land) and with *Samos. The inscribed 'constitution' of *c.575–550 BC (if it is not, in fact, Erythraean) refers to a 'council of the people' and to the duties of officials, perhaps reflecting an oligarchic system. Transport *amphorae were exported as far afield as southern Russia, and archaeology suggests that early trade concentrated on the Black Sea, Egypt, and the west. The only major colony was at *Maroneia (Thrace), though Chians helped found the Hellenion at *Naucratis, where their pottery has been identified. They built an ostentatious altar at Delphi (late Archaic).

The Chians established a *modus vivendi* with *Croesus and *Cyrus (1), but later came under a Persian-backed tyrant. They played a leading part in the *Ionian Revolt, manning 100 ships at Lade. On the basis of that figure the free population is speculatively put at between 60,000 and 120,000, though slaves were numerous from an early date. Settlement was relatively dispersed: there are many Classical to Roman farmsteads and some important rural sanctuaries, notably Emborio (major bronze age site with Archaic–Roman temple and settlement) and Phaná (Archaic temple of Apollo).

The Chians encouraged Athens to set up the *Delian League, in which they were leading ship-contributors. Loyal to Athens during the Samian Revolt and Sicilian expedition, they revolted in 412, precipitating Athens' defeat by Sparta. Lysander installed a *harmost; after the Spartan withdrawal Chios was soon freed, and later became the first member of the *Second Athenian Confederacy. It revolted in the *Social War (1) and came under Hecatomnid domination (see MAUSOLUS). After *Alexander (3) the Great it was mostly independent, resisting *Philip (3) V and siding with Rome against *Antiochus III. Brought into *Mithradates VI's camp in 86, Chios was captured by *Sulla but became a *free city (*civitas libera*). *Tiberius visited it twice. By *Vespasian's day its privileges had been ended; but the town prospered in Roman and late Roman times, as numerous inscriptions and public buildings show.

J. Boardman and C. E. Vaphopoulou-Richardson (eds.), *Chios: A Conference at the Homereion* (1986); J. Boardman, *Excavations in Chios, 1952–55: Greek Emporio* (1967); P. Argenti, *Bibliography of Chios* (1940), updated by A. Tsaravopoulos, *Horos* 1986; [British Admiralty] Naval Intelligence Division, *Greece* 3 (1945), 514–32; *RE* 3/2 (1899), 2286–98.　D. G. J. S.

Chiron See CENTAURS.

Chloë, i.e. 'green', title of *Demeter as goddess of the young green crops. She had a shrine near the Acropolis at Athens (Paus. 1. 22. 3) and a festival, the Chloia, perhaps on Thargelion 6 (Deubner, *Attische Feste* 67).

Choerilus (1), an Athenian tragic poet, one of the earliest known. The *Suda* says that he competed first in 523–520 BC, wrote 160 plays (a most unlikely figure), won thirteen victories, and, 'according to some', made innovations in *masks and costumes. He is also said to have competed against *Aeschylus and *Pratinas soon after 500 BC and (doubtfully) to have lived to compete against *Sophocles (1). From his work we have only two bold metaphors and one play title (*Alope*). He is probably not the Choerilus described in an anonymous line as 'King among the Satyrs'.

TrGF 1². 66–8; *Musa Tragica* 37–9, 270; Pickard-Cambridge–Webster, *Dithyramb*² 68–9.　A. L. B.

Choerilus (2) of Samos, epic poet of the late 5th cent. BC, famed for his *Persica*. It was in more than one book, and contained a catalogue of the tribes that crossed the Hellespont with the Persians; it was still read in the 3rd cent. AD (*POxy*. 1399). Fragments show skill and originality. Choerilus may have also written *Samiaca*. *Lysander, when in Samos (*c.*404), cultivated him in the hope of epic immortality, and *Archelaus (2) paid him to move to Macedon, where he died.

P. Radici Colace, *Choerili Samii Reliquiae* (1979); Bernabé, *PEG* 1. 187 ff.; G. L. Huxley, *GRBS* 1969, 12 ff.　M. L. W.

Choerilus (3), of *Iasus, epic poet; travelled with *Alexander (3) the Great; was paid to celebrate him; a bad poet (Hor. *Epist.* 2. 1. 232–4, *Ars P.* 357–8; Porphyrion ad loc.).

Suppl. Hell. 154 ff.　S. H.

chorēgia At Athens the *chorēgia* was a *leitourgia* (*liturgy), or public service performed by a wealthy citizen for the *polis*. A *chorēgos* (literally 'leader of a chorus') was responsible for the recruitment, training, maintenance, and costuming of *choreutai* (members of a chorus) for competitive performance at a festival. The same system of individual contribution was used to provide the Athenian navy with its ships (*trierarchia*: see TRIERARCHY).

The *chorēgia* was central to the organization and funding of the dramatic *festivals in Athens and its demes. The actors were appointed and remunerated separately by the *polis*, but the chorus involved the main part of the expense in these productions. In the Great *Dionysia, the main dramatic festival held annually, choruses were required for each of the various genres of performance: five for comedy (with 24 *choreutai* in each), three for tragedy and satyr-play (see SATYRIC DRAMA) (12 or 15 *choreutai*) and ten each for the two categories of *dithyramb, men's and boys' (50 *choreutai*). The competition at these festivals was as much between rival *chorēgoi* and their choruses as between poets (Dem. *Meid.* 66; [Andoc.] 4. 21), and the efforts of a *chorēgos* could be a crucial factor for the success of a dramatic entry.

The date of the introduction of the *chorēgia* is uncertain, but its history roughly corresponds with the period of Athenian *democracy. For tragedy at the Great Dionysia it probably began about 501 BC, and about 486 for comedy, which may have been produced by volunteers before then (Arist. *Poet.* 1449ᵇ1). *Chorēgoi* for dithyramb at the Great Dionysia were chosen by the ten *phylai ('tribes') and the *chorēgos* represented his *phylē* in the competition. *Chorēgoi* for tragedy and, until the mid-4th cent., for comedy at the Great Dionysia were appointed by the *archōn eponymos*, for the *Lenaea by the *archōn basileus*, from the richest Athenians liable for the duty. After that time comic *chorēgoi* were chosen by the *phylai* ([Arist.] *Ath. Pol.* 56. 3). *Chorēgoi* were chosen several months in advance of the next festival (hyp. 2 Dem. *Meid.*; cf. Dem. 4. 36); this allowed for a long period of training and perhaps also for the possibility that a *chorēgos* might claim exemption or undertake an **antidosis*, a legal action instituted when a person nominated thought that another citizen should perform the duty. No one could be required to perform a major *leitourgia* such as a *chorēgia* in two consecutive years (Dem. *Lept.* 8), though wealthy men eager to secure the goodwill of their fellow citizens might volunteer to serve beyond what was officially required. In his speech *Against Meidias* *Demosthenes (2) presents himself as having saved the honour of his *phylē* by volunteering as its dithyrambic *chorēgos* after it had failed to appoint one for two years running. *Chorēgoi* belonged to the very highest socio-economic tier, roughly one per cent of the citizen population. The sums spent on *chorēgiai* show that the duty could elicit vast expenditure. One extremely enthusiastic *chorēgos* catalogues a list which represents the huge outlay of nearly two and a half talents (Lys. 21. 1–5). This includes a dithyrambic *chorēgia* at the Little *Panathenaea for 300 drachmae, and a tragic *chorēgia* for 3,000 dr. The latter figure is somewhere in the region of ten times what a skilled worker might have earned annually. This was probably for the Great Dionysia, whose prestige encouraged lavish outlay (cf. schol. Dem. *Lept.* 28), and where the tragic *chorēgia* covered the costs for a group of three tragedies and a satyr-play. In the same passage a comic *chorēgia* is said to have had 1,600 dr. spent on it, 'including the dedication of the equipment'; while a *chorēgia* for dithyramb at the Great Dionysia, with its 50 *choreutai*, was likely to be a costly undertaking (Dem. *Meid.* 156). The system was also widely adopted for festivals in the Attic *demes (especially the Rural Dionysia), though on a much smaller scale of expenditure.

Once chosen, the first duty of the *chorēgos* was to recruit the members of his chorus. Participation in choruses was confined to citizens, although it seems that *metoikoi* (*metics), resident aliens, were allowed to participate as *choreutai* and *chorēgoi* at the smaller and less prestigious Lenaea (schol. Ar. *Plut.* 953; cf. Lys. 12. 20; Dem. *Lept.* 18). For dithyramb, *choreutai* were drawn from the *chorēgos'* own *phylē*; for tragedy and comedy they were probably selected from the citizen-body as a whole, although personal connections formed at local levels may have influenced the choice; *choreutai* known for their skill must have been especially sought after. A *chorēgos* had some legal powers to facilitate recruitment, at least in the case of a boys' chorus, where parents may have been reluctant to hand over their son to the charge of the *chorēgos* (Antiphon 6. 11). The *chorēgos* for such a chorus was required to be over 40 years of age. (Aeschin. *In Tim.* 11–12). The *chorēgos* provided a place for the training of the chorus, and sometimes an expert trainer, who might be the poet himself. The *chorēgos* was also responsible for the general maintenance of his *choreutai* and for the provision of the masks and costumes of the chorus. It may have been possible to hire second-hand costumes (Poll. 7. 78), and in comedy *chorēgoi* are sometimes reviled for their meanness (Eup. fr. 329 KA; Ar. *Ach.* 1150 ff.) However, costumes afforded an opportunity for ostentatious display by the *chorēgos*: Demosthenes provided his 50 *choreutai* with gold crowns and robes (Dem. *Meid.* 22). Dramatic *chorēgoi* may also have been called on to furnish 'extras' and a secondary chorus when required (cf. Plut. *Phoc.* 19). Such arrangements were doubtless made in close consultation with the poets to whom the *chorēgoi* chosen for a festival were assigned by lot. (This was the case for dithyramb at the Thargelia: Antiphon 6. 11.) In dithyramb, where the musical accompaniment was especially important, the *chorēgoi* may have drawn lots for the choice of *aulētēs* (pipe-player).

A victorious *chorēgos* in dithyramb received a bronze tripod

from the *polis* which he frequently erected, often as part of a more elaborate monument, in a public place such as the street called 'Tripods' (Paus. 1. 20. 1) or in the general vicinity of the theatre. It is not clear whether victorious *chorēgoi* in drama received any prize beyond an ivy crown, but the spirit of competition and the desire for prestige were so strong among *chorēgoi* (cf. the term ἀντιχορηγός, 'rival *chorēgos*' e.g. Dem. *Meid.* 59) that the glory of a victory was its own reward (cf. Xen. *de Equitum magistro* 1. 26). Winners in drama often erected a commemorative inscription and may have commissioned to mark the occasion vases of the kind that survive with images related to theatrical productions. These could also serve as commemorations of the *epinikia* or victory-celebration which a victorious *chorēgos* was expected to give his 'team'. The *chorēgia* was at once a legal obligation on the rich and an opportunity for its practitioners to acquire a high public profile. Rich men would cite their glorious *chorēgiai* and other *leitourgiai* in public speeches with the explicit expectation of being shown political or forensic favour (χάρις) in return. On the other hand, some among the rich saw the system as a means of popular extortion (e.g. Theophr. *Char.* 26. 6). The '*Old Oligarch' complains (1. 13) that the *dēmos* (people) has spoilt musical activities and demands to be paid for its performances, an indication that *chorēgoi* may have been expected to remunerate their *choreutai* with direct cash payment and not simply maintenance. Yet service as *chorēgos* could also be a way of garnering glory at the expense of one's fellows in a fiercely competitive arena before a large civic audience. The stories of the *chorēgiai* of *Alcibiades indicate a desire for self-display and recognition that shows itself in behaviour of an aristocratic style and anti-democratic nature—such as the wearing of ostentatious purple robes (Ath. 12. 534c) and the physical assault of a fellow competitor ([Andoc.] 4. 20–1). See PHILOTIMIA.

Throughout the 4th cent., social and economic strains put pressure on the system. Doubts were raised about the value of the enormous expenditure on *chorēgiai* in view of the competing needs of military funding and in the absence of imperial wealth (Lycurg. *Leoc.* 139; Dem. *Lept.* 26; Isoc. 7. 54). In 405 at least, *chorēgiai* at the Great Dionysia were shared between two men (called *synchorēgoi*: schol. Ar. *Ran.* 404), but it was only in *c.*310 that *Demetrius (3) of Phalerum abolished the system of competitive *chorēgiai* as such. He instituted a single *agōnothetēs* in charge of the festivals who was evidently chosen for his great wealth and supplemented the funds allocated by the *polis*. In inscriptions of this period the *dēmos* is officially recorded as *chorēgos*.

Chorēgiai are well attested outside Athens, in many islands and cities of the mainland and Asia Minor. In some cases they may be modelled on the Athenian system.

A. Pickard-Cambridge, *The Dramatic Festivals of Athens*, 2nd edn. with addenda, rev. J. Gould and D. M. Lewis, (1988); H. J. Mette, *Urkunden dramatischer Aufführungen in Griechenland* (1977); H.-D. Blume, *Einführung in das antike Theaterwesen* (1978); J. K. Davies, *Wealth and the Power of Wealth in Classical Athens* (1981); P. J. Wilson, *The Athenian Institution of the Khoregia* (2000).   P. J. W.

chreia, a collection of witty or clever sayings, so called because designed for utility (χρησίμου τινὸς ἕνεκα, Hermog. *Prog.* c. 3); one of the varieties of *progymnasmata. Such collections were already being made in the 4th cent. BC, e.g. by Theocritus of Chios and *Demetrius (3) of Phalerum, and some biographies of philosophers, e.g. that of *Diogenes (2) by *Diogenes (6) Laertius, consist largely of *chreiai*; the ancestry of the genre may be seen in some parts of *Xenophon (1)'s *Memorabilia*. The greatest extant collection is the *Gnomologium Vaticanum*, published in

Wien. Stud. 1887–9. The moral tone of the *chreiai* is far from austere.

A. S. F. Gow, *Machon* (1965), 12 ff.   J. D. D.; K. J. D.

Chremonidean War See CHREMONIDES.

Chremonides, son of Eteocles, Athenian from the *deme of Aithaladai. An early associate of *Zeno (2), founder of *Stoicism, Chremonides was a leading democratic politician at Athens and negotiated the anti-Macedonian alliance with *Areus of Sparta and his allies, which he confirmed in a decree of 268/7 BC (IG 2². 686, 687). The ensuing long war (until 262/1), which despite help from *Ptolemy (1) II Philadelphus the alliance lost, was called the 'Chremonidean War'. Thereafter Chremonides and his younger brother Glaucon escaped to Egypt and entered Ptolemaic service, Chremonides commanding a fleet which was defeated by *Rhodes *c*.258.

J. Pouilloux, ed. J. Bingen and others, *Hommages C. Préaux* pp. 376–82 (1975); H. Heinen, *Untersuchungen zur hellenistischen Geschichte des 3. Jh. v. Chr.* (1972).   R. M. E.

Christianity Classicists have traditionally found interesting both the Christian cult itself and Christian attitudes to Greek and Roman culture and the imperial state. Recent research encourages equal attention to the *Jews. Christianity began as a Jewish sect and changed its relationship with the Jewish community at a time when both groups were affected by later Hellenism. Christians laid claim to an antiquity rooted in the history of ancient Israel, while at the same time they sought the tolerance, interest, and loyalty of the pagans around them.

The first followers of Jesus inhabited a political system, the Roman empire, that regarded Jews as singular. Strategic prudence had recognized in *Herod (1) the Great (confirmed as king of *Judaea in 40 BC) a useful ally against opponents of Roman expansion and against rivals for power in Rome itself. The Jews, monotheists who identified closely their religion and their ethnicity, survived thus in the Roman context only because exceptions were made: suspending in this instance a characteristic readiness to absorb the religion of an alien people, Rome allowed them a controlled political independence in several territories (although Judaea itself, after Herod's death, passed under direct administration).

Many Jews lived willingly with resulting contradictions. Yet such compromise had long caused division among them. Following the conquests of *Alexander (3) the Great, intercourse with Hellenistic culture (see HELLENISM) had seemed advantageous to some; but the resolution of the 'devout' and the revolt of the *Maccabees had shown that traditional values were far from dead. Now the encroachment of Rome gave new edge to revulsion from the Gentile world, and the frequent brutality of the conquerors strengthened the hand of those more dubious about the benefits of alliance.

Jesus lived, therefore, in a divided Palestine. The rule of Rome and the fortunes of her Jewish allies seemed secure; but the cruelty of Herod had kept alive strong forces of resistance and revolt. One cannot avoid asking where Jesus stood on issues of religious and political loyalty, although his native Galilee was subject to a tetrarch (see TETRARCHY) rather than a Roman governor during his lifetime.

It is likely that Jesus reflected several tendencies in the Judaism of his day. Followers saw him variously as a forerunner of the *rabbis, holy man, wonder-worker, rebel, and prophet. Attempts to decide how he saw himself have proved difficult. When we set side by side the NT (New Testament) reports and our knowledge of Galilee at the time, the wonder-working holy man appears his most likely guise. He emphasized the imminent ending of the visible world and the judgement of God upon it. He promoted also a sense of liberty, to be enjoyed by those willing to repudiate family, career, and a sense of 'sin'. That, and the number of his followers in the volatile atmosphere of *Jerusalem at pilgrimage time, was enough to set him at odds with the Jewish high-priestly establishment, wedded to the social order required by Rome.

Those who had not known Jesus well, if at all, were less simple and less dramatic in their interpretations. The NT reveals how they broadened the religious context within which he was seen as significant, in pagan as well as Jewish terms. They also postponed the consummation he had seemed to herald. Partly as a consequence, they felt it proper to debate the value and authority of the Roman dispensation and the contrasting force of Jewish tradition. They also passed judgement on Temple and synagogue. Those characteristic centres of Jewish cult did not differ entirely from other religious traditions. In spite of strident voices defending the unique and separate quality of their life, some elements of the religious practice of the Jews invited comparison with *paganism. Blood *sacrifice, priesthood, ritual purity, dietary law, the preservation and study of sacred texts, speculation about the nature and purposes of God and about human virtue—all took a Jewish form but also identified Judaism as a religion among others: for those categories of thought and practice were familiar to many in the ancient world. Thus Christian criticism, operating within the Jewish tradition, highlighted a potential for realignment, inviting the attachment of additional or alternative meanings to the religious practice of the Jews themselves.

At a time, therefore, when Jews were divided over the nature of their privilege and separation, one group among them began actively to seek recruits among the Gentiles. Distance from other Jews was not achieved simply. The destruction of the Temple in AD 70, occurring in the midst of the earliest Christian readjustment, was built into the Church's founding documents. The Jewish revolts of 115–17 and 132–5, however, attracted little Christian comment. The Church's distinctiveness, by then, was more obvious. Christian texts with a strong Jewish flavour, like *1 Clement* (*c*.96) and Hermas' *Shepherd* (early to mid-2nd cent.), gave way to more deliberate competition for both respectability and a claim on the past. The 'apologist' *Justin Martyr (d. *c*.165), while defending his new religion against the Roman élite, asserted also against Jews, in his *Dialogue with Trypho*, Gentile claims to the heritage of Israel and a natural alliance between the OT (Old Testament) and classical cosmology.

*Origen (1) of Alexandria (*c*.185–254) established in the next generation (especially after his move to *Caesarea (2) in 230) a new style of dialogue with Jews, all in pursuit of his own biblical research. The Jews in Palestine had by that time acquired new confidence, after the disasters of 66–73 and 132–5. Their rabbinic leaders had completed the publication of the *Mishnah; and, under the leadership of a Patriarch, a disciplined community had been set in place, contrasting markedly with enduring elements of Hellenistic Jewry elsewhere. Origen became the architect of a mature Christian biblical exegesis. His purpose was to demonstrate in Christianity the fulfilment of OT prophecy. He focused, as had Justin, more on the significance of Jesus than on the inadequacy of the Law. A 'spiritual' understanding was required to detect fulfilment, assisted to a limited extent by the allegory beloved of *Philon (4). Yet Origen remained dependent on the Jewish exegesis he hoped to undermine. His most notable attack

Christianity

on paganism, the *Against Celsus*, required extensive defence of Jewish thought. His more homiletic works addressed an enduring ambiguity in Christian life, affected by converts from Judaism only slightly less exaggerated or precise in their mixed loyalty than the Ebionites and Nazarenes of the age.

Origen's African contemporary, *Tertullian (*c.*160–225), is noted chiefly for rigorist theology (reflecting in part an admiration for the martyrs) and for attacks on *Gnosticism. Tertullian probably had little to do with real Jews. His work *Against the Jews* was chiefly directed against pagans. It was, rather, the gnosticizing Marcion (d. *c.*160) who led Tertullian to develop his views on the justice and providence of the OT God and the status of Jesus as Messiah. (Marcion, for his part, had appeared to reject the OT dispensation completely.) Displaying in the process some debt to *Melito of Sardis (d. *c.* AD 190) and *Irenaeus (d. *c.* AD 200), as well as to Justin, Tertullian thus transmitted a specifically western approach to OT exegesis that influenced his fellow Africans *Cyprian (d. 258) and *Augustine (354–430) and all Latin theology.

The real sense, however, of a seamless inclusion of the OT within the Christian tradition came with *Eusebius of Caesarea (*c.*260–*c.*340). He had been reared in the tradition of Origen. Famous for his *History of the Church*, which contributed much to a sense of continuity between the orthodox Christians of Constantine's reign and the faith and practice of the Apostolic age, his *Preparation of the Gospel* and *Demonstration of the Gospel* are no less significant for their Christian appropriation of the Hebrew past.

The toleration of Christianity by the Roman state made it less necessary to compete with Judaism for the favour of the state and heralded a sharp decline in Jewish–Christian relations. Yet the arrogant vitriol of John *Chrysostom (*c.*347–407) shows that a challenge from Jewish ideas was still perceived by Christians, at least at *Antioch (1), centuries after the death of Jesus. Unflagging antagonism remained a major engine of the Church's development, compelling it to adopt yet more distinguishing forms and attitudes of its own. The differences between Christianity and Judaism apparent or desirable in 4th-cent. eyes were, naturally, not those that had struck Hermas or Justin. Even *Jerome (d. 420), Scripture scholar though he was, found himself in circumstances very different from those of Origen. Yet the shifting quality of the debate implied a lasting insecurity of definition. Faced from within by new divisions and critics of its administration and discipline, the 4th-cent. Church was still not ready to label itself finally. Moreover, the confidence of the *Theodosian Code (that heresy was a thing of the past) proved laughable in the light of Monophysite secession and the persistent *Arianism of barbarians in the west.

In that long process of Christian self-definition in relation to Judaism, crucial in determining the character of Christianity itself, three sensitivities stand out, concerning sacrifice, text, and morality.

The interpretation of sacrifice separated Christians at an early stage. Jews retained an attachment to priest and victim, but in the context of the desert Tabernacle rather than the Temple (almost certainly by that time destroyed). From then on, Christians saw themselves as competing for the heritage of priesthood as well as of the synagogue tradition. The Church continued to emphasize the symbolic priesthood of the heavenly Jesus and developed its own priestly caste, which presided over a eucharistic cult with strong sacrificial elements. The word 'bishop' quickly acquired an official meaning (1 Tim. 3: 1); but clear priestly association with the Eucharist (absent in the *Didache*, where the bishop is seen as teacher and prophet, 15. 1, and vague in *1 Clement*, in spite of an asserted need for succession, 44) does not occur until Ignatius of Antioch (d. *c.*107), *Letter to the Philadelphians* 4 (which links 'bishop' with 'Eucharist' and 'altar'). Subsequent development was inexorable; but not every Christian assembly demanded the presence and action of a bishop or priest until the 3rd cent.

Priesthood and sacrifice implied atonement: for sacrifice had to have a purpose. *Paul had presented the execution of Jesus as an expiation for sin (Col. 1: 20, Rom. 3: 25)—the sin of Adam and the sin of individual men and women. Christianity thus adopted on its own terms the historical perspective of restoration to God's favour enshrined in the Jewish Scriptures, paying less attention to political or tribal triumph in a Messianic age and more to cosmic and psychological divisions between creatures and creator, the defeat of sin and the heavenly destiny of redeemed humanity.

Christians argued against the Jewish interpretation of the texts that they shared. Christian appropriation demanded a new sense of what drove the ancient writers. God's words and actions and the inspired utterances of prophets were now focused on Jesus. The evident meaning of older texts had often to be wrenched so far in a new direction that 'exegesis', methodical interpretation, took centuries to achieve a Christian maturity and depended in part on the literary skills of the pagan élite. Once again, Origen illustrates the process. The allegorical tradition, filtered to some extent through Philon, allowed him access to the 'spiritual' meaning of the Bible; but other traditional skills of criticism and analysis were required, which the rabbis were equally aware of, and which Origen just as keenly applied. Moreover, since Jesus was an historical figure, the prophecies typical of Scripture were, after the time of Jesus himself, robbed of further purpose. 'Prophecy' suddenly attracted suspicion in place of reverence. The most famous victims of that prejudice were the Montanists of the late 2nd and early 3rd cents. (see MONTANISM). Their combination of ecstatic prophecy, apocalyptic expectation, and ascetic rigour (which successfully attracted Tertullian) can be found thereafter in varying proportions among many movements both critical and schismatic. Opponents favoured a closed 'canon' of Scripture (finally achieved only in the 4th cent.): no documents later than a certain date were regarded as 'inspired'. Interpretation was no longer expected to yield surprise but simply reinforced a significance already totally achieved.

The attitudes that established a textual canon were also influential in defining authority: for one had to know who was entitled to expound the significance of Scripture. Agreement on that issue kept pace with the developing style of Christian priesthood: in the end, the bishop and his assistants claimed exclusive rights to exegesis, just as they claimed the right to preside over the sacrificial cult of the church.

Finally, Christians developed a new moral theory not based on the OT; and that, too, served to separate them from Jewish contemporaries. Their emphasis was on love, as opposed to law—such were the terms in which they explained themselves, though with little justice to the Jews. They tapped other ethical traditions also: later *Stoicism especially. Increasing sophistication can be traced through the *Shepherd*, the 2nd-cent. *Sentences of Sextus*, and the *Pedagogue* of *Clement of Alexandria (*c.*150–*c.*215). The Greek ascetic tradition made its appeal to the more committed. Surprise at a failure in love would be naïve: more significant was the enduring Christian attachment to law (which made anti-Jewish polemic a tortured enterprise). With the tolerance of Constantine, the church was ready to take advantage of the law of the state. For some time, however, it had been developing its own legal system, represented by the decrees of Church councils, of which the archetype is described in Acts 15. Other early councils, of the 2nd cent., were mustered against perceived errors such as those of Montanism (Euseb. *Hist. Eccl.* 5. 16) or in relation to the date of Easter—a sensitive issue *vis-à-vis* the Jews (Euseb. *Hist. Eccl.* 5. 24). Evidence of gathering momentum is provided by African practice in the 3rd cent. (beginning with allusions in Cyprian, *Ep.* 71. 4, 73. 3). Council decisions continued to focus mainly on ecclesiastical order; but moral prescriptions were frequently implied or stated and spilled inevitably into the lives of ordinary men and women.

The Christian cult acquired, under the same influence, an increasingly formal character. The development of a calendar (exemplified by the Chronographer of AD 354), particularly relating to the ceremonies of initiation during Lent and Easter, augmented by the celebration of Epiphany and, later, Christmas and by commemorations of the martyrs, enfolded Christians in a detailed regime. A series of strictures and public ceremonies impinged upon the wayward, involving a modicum of public shame and defining the steps whereby they might be reconciled to both God and their fellows. (An early model is presented in *1 Clement* 57. 1. Vague evidence accumulates in Clem. Al. *Strom.* 2. 13. Details emerge only with Tert. *De paenitentia* 8. 9. 4 and Cyprian *De lapsis* 29; *Ep.* 55. 29.) All Christians, to a greater or lesser degree, were exhorted to undertake a life of self-discipline, marked by traditionally habitual patterns of prayer, fasting, and generosity.

While thus strengthening its self-definition against Judaism, Christianity faced the task of relating to other cults. It presented itself from an early stage as a universal religion. It did not merely invite adherence but demanded it: all men and women were thought able to achieve their destiny only within its embrace. One possible response to so aggressive an invitation was resentment; and here we touch upon the so-called 'persecution' of Christianity by the Roman state. Legal proceedings against the Church were intermittent and often moderate; violent demonstrations outside the law were unusual. The heroism revered in the *Acts of the Martyrs* seems to have been invited as often as it was imposed. Nevertheless, we find occasional confrontation. The famous attack by *Nero on Christians in Rome in 64 had no lasting impact or significance. The traditionally accepted oppression by *Domitian in the 90s has gained its notoriety mostly from the misleading obscurity of Melito (Euseb. *Hist. Eccl.* 4. 26. 9 f.). More generally significant in political terms may have been the situation described in *Pliny (2)'s *Ep.* 10. 96 f. of 112; but *Trajan's insistence on the observance of legal procedure and the avoidance of harassment says as much as his governor's distaste. Christians in that period may have attracted suspicion partly through a presumed association with rebellious Jews. As the political hopes of the Jews began to fade and the self-effacing preoccupations of rabbinic society gathered strength, Christians were exposed as possible enemies of the state in their own right. It was then that famous martyrs made their names—*Polycarp of Smyrna and Justin Martyr in 165 and those condemned at *Lugdunum (1) in 177. Yet the pleas of Melito and *Athenagoras cannot disguise the local quality of such reversals. Outbursts under *Septimius Severus and Maximinus Thrax (see IULIUS VERUS MAXIMINUS, C.) were similarly limited. It was not until the middle of the 3rd cent. that forceful opposition was sanctioned

by central authority. Severe threats to the stability of the state had by that time fostered new anxieties about loyalty; but the growing strength of the Church made it less susceptible to intolerance. The short-lived brutality of *Decius (249–51) and the dissipated attacks of *Valerian (253–60) were foiled by that resilience—proven as much by the Church's readmission of the weak as by its admiration for the strong. The new confidence was even more evident under the Diocletianic persecution from 303 until *Galerius' deathbed surrender in 311.

Throughout the prior period, several paradoxes had been laid bare, connected with the universal vision of the Church, the analogous breadth of Rome's claims to government, and its desire to tolerate nevertheless a variety of religious beliefs and practices. State and Church faced similar problems: how should one balance universalist demands and individual variety? The state's solution was to demand, in the interest of unity, a minimum but inescapable conformity in religious practice and to display, when it came to controlling belief, a prudent reticence. The devotee of an alien cult should not oppose, at least, the gods of Rome. The difference between loyalty to the empire and enthusiasm for local deities was more easily made clear with the growth of the imperial (*ruler-) cult (which called for the simplest obeisance) and the extension of citizenship by the Antonine *Constitution of 212. Christians resolutely branded that policy a subterfuge, demanding particular rights for what they thought of in their case as absolute values, undermining at once the freedom of the individual and the authority of the state.

They pursued the same embarrassing tactics in their broader dialogue with the classical world. As they acquired the vocabulary and adopted the habits of Greek philosophy, so they began to make their own points on the issues that philosophy had traditionally addressed: the nature of the divine and the visible world, the significance of texts, the canons of moral education and behaviour, the uses of ritual, the shape of history, and the character of its major figures. Such usurpation made them eventually impossible to ignore. The stages of encroachment are represented by the very writers who composed polemic against the Jews—*1 Clement*, the *apologists, the *Alexandrians, and the Africans—and culminate in the added reflection that came with more assured success in the 4th cent. Cappadocians and the writings of *Ambrose and Augustine. Method counted for as much as ideas: for with genre—letter, dialogue, homily, or life—Christians absorbed models as well as techniques, which affected their notions of community and conviction as much as of virtue or divinity. Thus they invaded the classrooms, libraries, temples, and debating-chambers of their adversaries long before they gained positions of public authority and power. Infuriatingly, they began to impose peculiar meanings on what the majority of their fellows had long been accustomed to say: so, while they could appear reassuringly familiar and traditional as a Mediterranean cult among others, they were constantly found to be undermining that to which they appeared to subscribe.

Christian engagement with Jewish tradition and classical culture made a distinctive contribution to the religious life of the Mediterranean world. The Christian view of God was subtle. It combined attachment to transcendence and monotheism with a sense of personal dynamism in the godhead—potent, purposeful, and affectionate. Correspondingly, the relation of the individual to that divinity engaged every level of human experience, bodily and spiritual, from hunger, fear, and desire to insight and self-sacrifice. Such beliefs were made formal in the doctrines of the Trinity and the Incarnation, both in their way indebted to pagan and Jewish antecedents. There was also in Christianity a clear system of authority and leadership: the bishop was its own brilliant, proper, and lasting creation. Heir to Jewish priesthood and biblical learning, he provided both the focus and the generative impulse, through baptism and mission, for a stable community. The sacramental liturgy, reinforced by singing, processions, and the veneration of dead heroes and exemplars, enabled the Church to act out its beliefs through symbol and recollection. The past was especially valuable to the Christian, once correctly understood. The canon of sacred texts, the succession of priests, the interpretations of scripture, and the customs of discipline and worship all conspired to produce a vision of where time was leading the Church and rescued it from the disoriented ambiguities of Gnosticism. Finally, Christians developed their own morality, founded on the conviction that each person was created by God and destined for his lasting company; a morality that valued, therefore, the whole human being, refined by continence, expanded by selfless generosity, and rewarded by bodily resurrection.

Such, at least, was the 'orthodox' view; but it was never taken for granted. 'Orthodoxy' was established only slowly and was constantly challenged by men and women who claimed the title 'Christian'. The nature of their dissent or variety sprang in part from the fact that they had found other ways of relating to Jewish and pagan tradition. A more anthropomorphic view of God, indifference to sacramental worship, suspicion of the clergy and preference for charismatic leadership and personal inspiration, a love of myths and symbols in the place of literal history, mistrust of the *body and a corresponding desire for 'spiritual' experience and fulfilment—all such emphases diffracted the pattern of Christian development, yet seemed no less Christian for that. It is neither possible nor just to isolate groups that represented those tendencies precisely: that was the ploy of their enemies. What seemed clear choices in the cause of self-definition, especially when they attempted to exclude either pagans or Jews, were normally made in circumstances of confusion, which they by no means brought to an end. The tidy writings of Irenaeus and *Epiphanius of Salamis (d. 403) teem with supposedly undesirable eccentrics; but those 'heretics' may have seemed to others at the time no more than ordinary Christians. The image of the Gnostic or the Montanist, of the Encratite or rigorist ascetic, often the product of prejudice and horror, can disguise a more complicated variety that represented nevertheless the Christian norm.

We cannot content ourselves, therefore, with a straightforward account of Christian triumph over pagan and Jew. It was simply that certain answers to fundamental questions began to seem more acceptable to some Mediterranean people—answers in a debate pursued by some in all parties about the nature of creation, the destiny of the cosmos and the individual, the status of sacred texts, the substantiality of the visible world, the use of ritual and law, and the proper styles of religious authority. The new answers were thought to deserve the label 'Christian'; but what had happened was that the controlling element in a whole society had changed its mind about the meaning of history and experience.

Can we be sure about the scale of that development? It is impossible to judge the size of the Christian population at any one time. Surviving reports are marred by hyperbole, ignorance, and convention. Archaeology and inscriptions are statistically haphazard and impervious to individual sentiment. Suffice it to say that within certain urban communities, particularly in the

east, Christians formed a sizeable minority and occasionally even a majority in the late 3rd cent.. The difficult question is why. Breeding and friendship must have played a large part in the expansion of Christianity—perhaps always larger than that of convincing oratory. What remains textually of Christian address was not necessarily disseminated broadly. We know little more about the *reception of the Christian message than we do about that of any ancient document. With the advent of toleration, it is likely that expediency, laziness, and fear played as much a part then as they do now. Talk of 'superstition' is misleading. Features of religious life supposedly attractive to a superstitious mind had always been available in traditional cult. The change of allegiance demands more subtle explanations. See PAUL, ST; RELIGION, JEWISH.

W. H. C. Frend, *The Rise of Christianity* (1984); E. Sanders, *Jesus and Judaism*, 2nd edn. (1985); A. Segal, *Rebecca's Children* (1986); B. Metzger, *The Early Versions of the New Testament* (1977); J. Gager, *Kingdom and Community: The Social World of Early Christianity* (1975); W. Meeks, *The First Urban Christians: The Social World of the Apostle Paul* (1983); H. Shanks (ed.), *Christianity and Rabbinic Judaism* (1993); H. Jonas, *The Gnostic Religion*, 2nd edn. rev. (1992); W. Bauer, *Orthodoxy and Heresy in Earliest Christianity*, Eng. trans. ed. R. A. Kraft and G. Krodel (1972); W. Jaeger, *Early Christianity and Greek Paideia* (1962); H. Chadwick, *Early Christian Thought and the Classical Tradition* (1966); R. M. Grant, *Gods and the One God* (1986); R. Markus, *Christianity in the Roman World* (1974); R. Lane Fox, *Pagans and Christians* (1986). P. R.

Christodorus (5th–6th cents. AD), poet from *Coptus in Egypt. All that survives complete is an **ekphrasis* on the statues decorating the baths of Zeuxippus in *Constantinople, which in diction and metrical practice shows clear traces of the influence of *Nonnus, and two epigrams. He was, however, a prolific author; lost works include an epic on Anastasius I's Isaurian victory in 497, versified histories (*patria*) of *Thessalonica, Nacle, *Miletus, *Tralles, *Aphrodisias, and *Constantinople (*Suda*, entry under the name), and a poem on the pupils of *Proclus (Lydus, *Mag.* 3. 26). He may have written the fragmentary poems in *P. Vienna* 29788 A–C.

TEXTS *Anth. Pal.* bks. 2, and 7. 697–8; with trans., W. R. Paton, *Greek Anthology* (Loeb, 1916–18).
STUDIES F. Baumgarten, *De Christodoro poeta Thebano* (1881); R. C. McCail, *JHS* 1978, 38–40; R. Stupperich, *MDAI(I)* 1982, 210–35.
PLRE 2. 293. J. H. D. S.

Christus Patiens, a play in 2,610 verses describing the Passion of Jesus Christ, bearing the name of Gregory of Nazianzus (see ZONARAS), but now usually thought to have been written by a Byzantine of the 11th or 12th cent. (important evidence pointing to an earlier date has recently been assembled by A. Garzya in *Sileno* 1984, 237–40). It contains a very great number of lines from *Euripides, and some from *Aeschylus and *Lycophron (2). It is of doubtful use for the textual criticism of Euripides, but portions of the lost end of the *Bacchae* have been recovered from it (see E. R. Dodds's edition of *Bacch.* (1960), 243 ff.).

TEXT J. G. Brambs (Teubner, 1885); A. Tuilier (1969).
J. D. D.; K. J. D.; N. G. W.

Chronicon Paschale ('Easter Chronicle'), a universal history from Creation to *c.* AD 630. A particular concern is the establishment of chronological connections between Church feasts and the Creation and Incarnation; there are several computations and each year is dated by different methods. The anonymous narrative amalgamates Old and New Testament, Jewish, Christian, and secular material. *Malalas was an important source for mythological events and, increasingly, from *c.*400 to 532; between *c.*330 and 469 it uses the Constantinopolitan city chronicle also preserved in *fasti Hydatiani* and Marcellinus Comes, supplemented by Arian information paralleled in *Philostorgius. The fifth ecumenical council (553) dominates the sparse account of 532–602, but the 7th-cent. narrative constitutes an important witness to secular and ecclesiastical affairs until it breaks off in 628 in a letter from the emperor Heraclius describing Chosroes II's overthrow.

Ed. L. Dindorf (1831); Eng. trans. of AD 284–628: M. and M. Whitby (1989). L. M. W.

chronography, chronology See CALENDARS; CLOCKS; ECLIPSES; TIME-RECKONING.

Chryseis (Χρυσηΐς), in *Homer's *Iliad* the daughter of Chryses, priest of *Apollo at Chryse in the Troad (see TROAS), who has been captured and awarded to *Agamemnon. On Agamemnon's refusal to let Chryses ransom her, Apollo sends a plague on the Greek camp. *Calchas explains the situation and Chryseis is returned, but Agamemnon takes Achilles' concubine *Briseis for himself, thus causing *Achilles' anger (*Il.* 1. 11 ff.).

LIMC 3/1 (1986), 281–2. J. R. M.

Chrysermus (fl. mid-1st cent. BC?), Alexandrian physician of the 'school' of *Herophilus. The extant evidence, transmitted principally by *Galen and *Pliny (1) the Elder, concerns his pulse theory and his drug prescriptions. Like most Herophileans, he displayed independence from Herophilus, defining the pulse as a distention (διάστασις) and contraction (συστολή) of the arteries, when the arterial coat, through the agency of a vital and psychic faculty (ὑπὸ ψυχικῆς καὶ ζωτικῆς δυνάμεως), rises on all sides and then shrinks together again (Gal. 8, p. 741 Kühn). Unlike Herophilus, Chrysermus in his pulse definition omits mention of the heart. His addition of the distinction between 'psychic' and 'vital' probably was indirectly influenced by *Erasistratus and the Stoics (who, however, gave the distinction quite different applications). His elaboration and modification of Herophilus' model of the pulse became very controversial: accepted by Chrysermus' pupil Heraclides of *Erythrae, it was rejected by other Herophileans (e.g. by *Aristoxenus) and by *Galen.

Ed., trans., and comm.: H. von Staden, *From Andreas to Demosthenes Philalethes* (1995), ch. 10. Cf. von Staden, *Herophilus* (1989), 523–8. H. v. S.

Chrysippus, of Soli (*c.*280–207 BC), succeeded *Cleanthes as head of the Stoa in 232 (see STOICISM). He came to Athens about 260 and studied in the sceptical *Academy, learning the importance of argument for and against given positions. He studied under Cleanthes and adopted the Stoic position, defending it voluminously. He is said to have told Cleanthes that he needed only to know the positions, and would provide the proofs himself. Another saying has it that 'if there had been no Chrysippus there would have been no Stoa'; his extensive writings (we have a partial list in Diogenes Laertius) argued for all aspects of Stoicism so competently that his position became Stoic orthodoxy, eclipsing earlier Stoics other than *Zeno (2), whose views Chrysippus took pains to preserve and explain. Through him Stoicism became a well-argued position, with extensive resources for debate on many fronts. He developed Stoic logic in particular. Modern scholars have focused on areas of alleged disagreement between him and Zeno, but our evidence is scanty, and often indicates no more than a difference of emphasis.

TESTIMONIA von Arnim, *SVF* 2, 3. 3–205; Diog. Laert. 7. 179–202. J. A.

Chrysogonus See CORNELIUS CHRYSOGONUS, L.

Chrysostom, Dio See DIO COCCEIANUS.

Chrysostom, John (*c.* AD 354–407), bishop of Constantinople. Though educated at Antioch (1) by *Libanius, John turned to *asceticism at home and later became a hermit. Ordained deacon at Antioch in 381 and priest (386), and pre-eminently a preacher, he reluctantly became bishop of *Constantinople (398). Trouble with the empress Eudoxia, *Theophilus (2) of Alexandria, and Asiatic bishops resenting his extension of Constantinople's quasi-patriarchal authority, caused his deposition by the Synod of the Oak (403). He was banished, recalled, banished again to Armenia (404), and died in exile (407).

Most eloquent of preachers (hence his name Chrysostom, 'the golden-mouthed') but not an outstanding theologian, he expounded Scripture in the Antiochene tradition according to its historical sense, practically and devotionally. He has left commentaries on Genesis, the Gospels of Matthew and John, the *Acts of the Apostles and all the Epistles of *Paul. Denunciation of luxury, care for the poor, and interest in education are characteristic. The homilies *De statuis* throw light on an urban riot in 387. *De sacerdotio* gives his conception of clerical duties. The *Liturgy of Chrysostom* is not his work.

EDITIONS H. Savile (1612); B. de Montfaucon (Paris, 1718–38); Migne, *PG* 47–64.

Life by C. Baur, 2 vols. (1929–39; Eng. trans. 1959). See also J. A. de Aldama, *Repertorium Pseudochrysostomicum* (1965); J. H. W. G. Liebeschuetz, *Barbarians and Bishops* (1990); F. van de Paverd, *St. John Chrysostom, the Homilies on the Statues* (1991). S. L. G.; W. L.

chthonian gods, literally gods of the earth, χθών, a subdivision of the Greek pantheon. In this usage, *chthonios* gets its meaning from a contrast, implicit or explicit, with 'Olympian' or 'heavenly' gods. Gods can be chthonian in two ways.

1. *Chthonios* was applied as a cult-title to individual gods, notably *Hermes, *Demeter, *Hecate, *Zeus, and (once) Ge (*Gaia), Earth, herself. This usage goes back, in the case of Zeus, to *Homer and *Hesiod. The epithet was normally given to a god who was connected with both the upper and the lower worlds, and served to show that in a particular ritual context it was the chthonian aspect that was being appealed to. The case of Zeus Chthonios is more complicated, since in some contexts he seems to be less 'Zeus when active in the Underworld' than a distinct figure, 'the Underworld equivalent to Zeus', i.e. Hades (Hes. *Op.* 465, with M. L. West's note).

2. A general division between Olympian and chthonian gods is sometimes made (first in Aeschylus, *Supp.* 24–5, *Ag.* 89). In such references the *chthonioi* are not listed; if pressed to do so, unnaturally, a Greek would doubtless have named *Hades/Pluton, *Persephone, the Eumenides (see ERINYES), and similar figures, and probably the heroes too. Scholars often, more questionably, extend the list to include powers such as Zeus *Meilichios who are not explicitly associated with the earth but share characteristics with those which are.

In modern accounts, the Olympian/chthonian distinction is often elevated into a fundamental principle structuring the whole of Greek mythology and ritual. But the Olympio-chthonian gods of type (1) straddle the great divide; and the modern distinction between Olympian and chthonian forms of sacrificial ritual distorts a different distinction that the ancients drew, between 'divine' and 'heroic' forms of sacrifice. (Divergences from the standard type of sacrifice did indeed occur in the cult of the chthonians, but not always, and not there alone.) The point is not simply that the question 'Olympian or chthonian?' is sometimes unanswerable, but that in many contexts the Greeks might simply not have felt the need to ask it.

M. H. Jameson, *BCH* 1965, 159–65; Burkert, *GR* 199–203.   R. C. T. P.

churches (early Christian) The first Christians met in the private houses of the faithful. Gradually, as local Christian communities became more established both in numbers and in wealth, they might acquire their own church-houses, using them specifically as places of worship and for other religious activities, such as the granting of charity and the instruction of converts. Externally these buildings looked just like other private houses, though internally they might be adapted for their new function, for instance by combining rooms to create a large enough space for worship. The best example of an early church-house is that excavated at Dura-*Europus on the Euphrates: an ordinary town house, built around AD 200, adapted for Christian use before 231, and destroyed when the city walls were reinforced in 257. Before the conversion of Constantine I, and his conquest of the empire between 312 and 324, some Christian communities may already have commissioned halls specifically for worship, and certainly small shrines, such as the 2nd-cent. *aedicula* over the supposed tomb of St Peter in Rome (see VATICAN), were already being built over the bodies of the martyrs.

However, the accession of an emperor with Christian sympathies and the granting of security, wealth, and privileged status to the Church transformed church building. Large buildings were constructed inside towns, to serve as halls of worship for the rapidly expanding Christian community, and outside, to glorify the shrines of the martyrs and to serve as the focus for Christian burial-grounds. The pace of building differed according to circumstance. For instance, in Rome itself massive investment by Constantine rapidly gave the city one huge intramural church (St John Lateran) and a string of martyr-churches outside the walls (St Peter's, S. Agnese, S. Lorenzo, SS. Marcellino e Pietro, and the first church of St Paul). However, in many provincial towns the earliest substantial church buildings may often have been of the late 4th, or even of the 5th cent.

The Christians wished their buildings to look different from pagan shrines, and their principal need was for large halls that could contain many people worshipping together, unlike pagan temples which were mainly conceived of as homes for the gods and their statues, and internally as the focus of rituals involving few people at a time. The principal influence on early Christian architecture was, therefore, not the pagan *temple, but the great secular meeting-hall of antiquity, the *basilica. Christian basilicas varied greatly in detail (i.e. with or without aisles, galleries, apses, transepts, etc), but all shared in common the aim of containing many people at one time, with an architectural, decorative, and liturgical focus on one end of the building, where the clergy officiated at the altar (which in many cases was sited over the body of a saint). Alongside the prevalent rectangular basilicas, other types of church existed, such as centrally planned and domed churches, of which the most famous examples are the 4th-cent. S. Lorenzo in Milan (*Mediolanum), and the 6th-cent. S. Vitale in *Ravenna and S. Sophia in *Constantinople.

Probably because more happened inside churches than inside temples (which were often the backdrop to ceremonies performed outside), the main focus of decoration tended to be internal. Many late antique churches, like S. Vitale at Ravenna, are plain structural shells on the outside, but inside are lavishly decorated with marble fittings, veneer, and floor- and wall-mosaics; and would once also have been filled with gold and silver plate and fittings, and with drapes of precious fabrics.

R. Krautheimer, *Early Christian and Byzantine Architecture* (1965).
B. R. W.-P.

Chythri (mod. *Kythrea*), a small inland city of *Cyprus in a long-populated region, possibly the 'Kitrusi' of the Esarhaddon prism of 673/2 BC (an Assyrian text). 11th-cent. BC tombs give some credence to the supposed foundation by Chytrus, grandson of *Acamas. The largely unexcavated site (Ayios Dimitrianos) lies 14 km. (8½ mi.) NE of Nicosia, below Mt. Pentadaktylos on the northern fringe of the Mesaoria; it is close to the island's most abundant spring, Kephalovryso, whose waters were channelled to *Salamis (2)-Constantia, perhaps in Roman, certainly in Byzantine times. Syllabic texts come from a shrine of Aphrodite Paphia; an extramural sanctuary of Apollo Alygates is nearby at Voni. Inscriptions refer to a gymnasium; an over-life-size bronze statue of Septimius Severus is now in Nicosia.

J. C. Peristianis, *Γενική ἱστορία τῆς νήσου Κύπρου* (1910); K. Nikolaou, *RDAC* 1965, 30 ff.; O. Masson, *Les Inscriptions chypriotes syllabiques*, rev. edn. (1983), 258 ff.   H. W. C.

Cicero See TULLIUS CICERO (1), M.

Cilicia, a district of southern *Asia Minor. The name was applied to various regions at different periods but came ultimately to designate the eastern half of the south coast. The western portion (Cilicia Tracheia, Rugged Cilicia) is wild and mountainous, the eastern (Cilicia Pedias, Plain Cilicia) is rich plainland. Greek settlers brought with them the name of the Cilices, who were located by Homer in the northern Troad (*Il.* 6. 397), see *Troas. Their leader was *Mopsus the seer, whose name survived in the place-names Mopsuhestia and Mopsucrene and occurs as a personal name in later inscriptions. Identified partly or wholly with the Hilakku of Assyrian records and with the Egyptian Kelekesh, the Cilicians were subjects of the Assyrians in the 8th cent. BC. They were then ruled by a line of kings, at first independent then subject to the Persians, called Syennesis, whose palace was probably at *Tarsus. In the Hellenistic period the country was disputed between the *Seleucids and the Ptolemies (see PTOLEMY (1)); Olba in the eastern part of Tracheia, whose priest-rulers claimed descent from *Teucer (2) and *Aias (1), maintained itself as an independent dynasty for several centuries. The mountain region resisted outside control during most of its history and in the 2nd cent. pirates were well established on the coast of Tracheia (see PIRACY). Partly to secure the insecure mountain region the Romans around 80 BC created a second province in Asia Minor called Cilicia, which extended across southern Anatolia between Asia in the west and Syria in the east, and was to be governed by Cicero in 51/0 BC. The pirates had meanwhile been suppressed by Pompey's campaign of 67 BC and Cilicia Pedias was added to the province *c*.63 BC. The northern mountain fringes of Pedias around Hierapolis-Castabala, however, were assigned to the dynasty of Tarcondimotus, which survived until the time of Augustus. By then the Cilician province had been dismembered, divided between the new province of *Galatia, *Syria, and a series of client rulers in Tracheia. After further rearrangements by Vespasian, Cilicia became one of the parts of the Triple Province (with *Lycaonia and *Isauria) created under Antoninus Pius. Cilicia Pedias was strategically important during the 3rd cent. AD when its cities, particularly Tarsus, Anazarbus, and the naval port of Aegae, acted as staging-posts, supply bases, and winter quarters for armies engaged on the eastern front. Cilicia Pedias, traversed by two important rivers, the Pyramus and the Cydnus, was one of the most fertile parts of Asia Minor, producing flax, vines, olives, and corn. Tracheia offered woven products, ship timber (especially valuable to the Ptolemies and later to the pirates) and military recruits.

Jones, *Cities E. Rom. Prov.* ch. 8; R. Syme, *Anatolian Studies Presented to W. H. Buckler* (1939), 299 ff. = RP 1, 120 ff.; Magie, *Rom. Rule Asia Min.* chs. 11, 12, 17; B. D. Shaw, *Journal of the Social and Economic History of the Orient* 1989; R. Ziegler, *Städtisches Prestige und kaiserliche Politik* (1985).   G. E. B.; S. M.

Cilician Gates, the pass through the *Taurus mountains which connected the central Anatolian plateau with the Cilician plain and with *Syria. In Roman times this was one of the key routes of the eastern part of the empire, carrying almost all the overland traffic heading for *Antioch (1) and the Syrian regions. By the time of Caracalla the road, which had been traversed by Cicero as proconsul of Cilicia, was known as the via Tauri, and, apart from the *via Sebaste, was the only route between the highlands and the south coast of Asia Minor that was suitable for wheeled traffic.

R. P. Harper, *Anat. St.* 1970, 149–53.   S. M.

Cimbri, a German tribe from north Jutland. Towards the end of the 2nd cent. BC overpopulation and encroachments by the sea drove them to migrate in company with the *Teutones and Ambrones. From the Elbe they arrived, by a roundabout route, in Noricum, where they defeated a Roman consular army (113 BC). They then turned west and entered the Helvetian territory between the Main and Switzerland, where a few of them settled. (Vestiges of a Cimbric element in the population are perhaps implied by inscriptions to Mercurius Cimbrianus at Miltenberg and Heidelberg: *ILS* 4595, 4596, cf. 9377.) About 110 they entered the Rhône valley. In 109 they defeated M. Iunius Silanus, and then turned into the centre of Gaul. In 105 they were again in the south, where they won the great victory of Arausio (mod. Orange), and then entered Spain, whence they were expelled by the Celtiberians. They now moved towards Italy. C. *Marius (1) defeated the Teutones and the Ambrones, who took the western route, at Aquae Sextiae (Aix-en-Provence) in 102, and in 101 destroyed the Cimbri, who had travelled round the Alps and entered Italy by the north-east, near *Vercellae, in the Po (*Padus) valley. A few of the Germans had remained in northern Gaul; the later Aduatuci claimed to be their descendants. A remnant of the Cimbri was found in Jutland by the naval expedition sent by Tiberius in AD 5 (*RG* 26).

CAH 9¹ (1932), 139 ff. and 9² (1994), see index; E. Demougeot, *Latomus* 1978, 910 ff.   O. B.; J. F. Dr.

Ciminius mons, range of volcanic mountains rising to just over 900 m. (*c.*3,000 ft.), which separate southern from central Etruria. A crater lake (lacus Ciminius: Lago di Vico) nestles amongst them. Q. *Fabius Maximus Rullianus won fame by penetrating their awe-inspiring, thickly wooded slopes in 310 BC (Livy 9. 36–9). *Sutrium and *Nepete are keys to the region.

E. T. S.; D. W. R. R.

Cimmerians (Κιμμέριοι, Assyrian Gimirri, the 'Gomer' of Ezek. 38: 6; Gen. 10: 2), a people driven from south Russia by the nomad Scyths (Hdt. 1. 16 f.). They overthrew Phrygia under the last King *Midas (2) (*c.*676?), killed *Gyges, took the lower town of Sardis (*c.*644), and terrorized Ionia (Strabo 647, citing Callinus and Archilochus), but were gradually destroyed by epidemics and in wars with *Lydia and Assyria. Their name survived in the Cimmerian *Bosporus (2) (straits of Kerch') and some place-names thereabouts (though 'Crimea' itself is from Turkish *kirim*, a ditch, i.e. that across the isthmus of Perekop). In our *Odyssey* (11. 14 ff.) Cimmerians appear as a people on whom the sun never shines, near the land of the dead.

A. Heubeck, in A. Heubeck and A. Hoekstra, *Comm. on Odyssey* 2 (1989), 77 ff.; *CAH* 3²/2 (1991), 555–60 and see index.   A. R. B.; S. H.

Cimon, wealthy and noble 5th-cent. BC Athenian, son of *Miltiades and Hegesipyle, daughter of the Thracian king Olorus; Cimon and the historian *Thucydides (2), son of an Olorus, were thus related (*APF* 234 f.). His sister Elpinice married *Callias (1); an unpublished ostracon (among other evidence) alleges *incest between them ('let Cimon take his sister Elpinice and get out'). He married the *Alcmaeonid Isodice, and perhaps also an *Arcadian woman. His sons by one of these were: Lacedaemonius, Eleos / Oulios, Thettalus, programmatic names (he was *proxenos for Sparta and Thessaly, and the *Ionian name Oulios, see *SEG* 38. 1996 *bis*, recalls one justification of the *Delian League by stressing Ionianism); three other sons by Isodice are historically dubious. On Miltiades' death in 489 he paid his 50-talent fine. He joined an embassy to Sparta in 479 and thereafter was often *stratēgos (see *AO*). In 478 he helped *Aristides (1) bring the maritime Greeks into the Delian League and commanded most of its operations 476–463. He drove *Pausanias (1) out of *Byzantium; captured Eion-on-the-Strymon from the Persian Boges (?476/5); and conquered *Scyros, expelling the Dolopians (pirates), installing a *cleruchy, and bringing back the 'bones of *Theseus' to Athens. Cimon's greatest achievement was the *Eurymedon victory over Persia, *c.*466; this brought places as far east as *Phaselis into the league. It is possible that he negotiated peace with Persia about now, that his peace was rejected by his domestic enemies at the end of the decade, and that the 450 Peace of Cimon's brother-in-law Callias (see CALLIAS, PEACE OF) was a renewal of Cimon's peace. Next he subdued Thracian *Chersonesus (1) and reduced revolted *Thasos in 465–463 (hence the hostility of Thasian *Stesimbrotus, a source of *Plutarch), but was prosecuted on his *euthyna by *Pericles (1) for allegedly accepting bribes from *Alexander (1) I of Macedon; he was acquitted. He next persuaded Athens to send him (462) with a large hoplite force to help Sparta against the *helots, now in revolt. But the Athenians were sent humiliatingly home on suspicion of 'revolutionary tendencies', and Cimon's *ostracism followed (461). The exact connection between this and *Ephialtes (4)'s reforms is obscure, but Cimon was no hoplite conservative. True, he spent lavishly on entertainments and public works, as part of rivalry with radical leaders like *Themistocles, Ephialtes, and *Pericles (1). Again, some of Cimon's policies were reversed after his ostracism: his pro-Spartan policy and his peace with Persia (if he made it) were abandoned. But despite personal ties and sympathies with Sparta he was no enemy of the democracy or the empire: Eurymedon was as much the achievement of the naval *thētes as of hoplites; hoplites and *thētes admittedly competed for military glory in the post-Persian War period (ML 26, cf. *JHS* 1968, 51 ff.) but both were excluded from top office until 458 so that opposition is unreal; Sparta at least saw Cimon and his hoplites as revolutionaries, i.e. compromised by the reforms hatching back home; and Cimon approved the Ionian propaganda of the empire (cf. above on Oulios), expanded it as much as Pericles, and like him forcibly opposed secession from it.

In 458 Cimon tried to help fight for Athens against Sparta at *Tanagra but was rebuffed and not yet recalled from ostracism (though one tradition asserts this). When he did return at the end of the 450s he arranged a five-year truce with Sparta and fought Persia on Cyprus where he died.

> Thuc. 1. 98, 100, 102, 112, with Gomme, *HCT* and Hornblower, *Comm. on Thuc.*; Plut. *Cimon*, ed. Blamire (1989). W. R. Connor, *Theopompus and Fifth-Century Athens* (1968); *APF* 302–7; E. Badian, *From Plataea to Potidaea* (1993), chs. 1–2.   A. W. G.; T. J. C.; S. H.

cinaedic poetry, verses on sexual and scatological subjects, usually in ionic verse, and in post-Classical times recited or sung with appropriate gestures (cf. Strabo 14. 1. 41, Aristid. Quint. 1. 13, Ath. 14. 620e–f) by performers called *kinaedologoi*, often as entertainment at *symposia etc. These verses were given literary form in the first half of the 3rd cent. BC by *Sotades (2), *Timon (2) of Phlius and *Alexander (8) 'the Aetolian', but retained their probably original connection with the 'effeminate' east (cf. *POxy.* 3010), and the morals of the performers were assumed to match those of their verses (cf. Petron. *Sat.* 23. 3).

> W. Kroll, *RE* 'Kinaidos'.   R. L. Hu.

Cinaethon of Lacedaemon (?6th cent. BC), *epic-*genealogical poet, sporadically credited with the *Little Iliad*, *Oedipodia*, *Telegony* (see EPIC CYCLE), and a *Heraclea*.

> Bernabé, *PEG* 1. 115–17; G. L. Huxley, *Greek Epic Poetry* (1969), 86–9.   M. L. W.

Cincinnatus See QUINCTIUS CINCINNATUS, L.

Cincius (*RE* 5) **Alimentus, Lucius,** Roman senator and historian, was praetor in Sicily in 210/9 BC, and was captured by Hannibal (Livy 21. 38. 3). His history of Rome, written in Greek, set the foundation of the city in 729–728 BC and reached his own times. With the work of Q. *Fabius Pictor, it formed the basis of the senatorial historical tradition, especially of the Second Punic War. The constitutional antiquarian of the same name wrote towards Augustan times.

> Peter, *HR Rel.* 1², ci, 40; *FGrH* 810; Walbank, *HCP* 1, 29. E. Badian, in T. Dorey (ed.), *Latin Historians* (1966).   A. H. McD.; A. J. S. S.

Cineas (1), (?) Thessalian *founder of *Ai Khanoum (in modern Afghanistan) to whom, as *archēgetēs, *hero-cult was paid, on the evidence of an interesting verse inscription put up at the instance of *Clearchus (3) of Soli.

> L. Robert *CRAcad. Inscr.* 1968, 42 (= *OMS* 5 (1989), 510 ff.); cf. Austin 192 for translation of the text. F. W. Walbank, *The Hellenistic World*, 2nd edn. (1992), 60 f.   S. H.

Cineas (2) the Thessalian was an uncommonly able orator (he was a pupil of *Demosthenes (2)) and diplomat in the service of King *Pyrrhus of Epirus. Best known for his dealings with Rome during Pyrrhus' Italian venture (not least because he was adopted by the Roman tradition as an early Hellenic admirer of Rome), he also wrote an epitome of the tactical treatise of *Aeneas Tacticus of Stymphalus and a historical work, possibly focused upon Pyrrhus and *Epirus but dealing also with *Thessaly.

> *RE* 11, 'Kineas' 3; *FGrH* 603 (with comm.); P. Lévêque, *Pyrrhos* (1957), 346 ff.   P. S. D.

Cinesias (*c.*450–390 BC), of Athens, *dithyrambic poet. A victory is recorded at the Athenian *Dionysia (*IG* 2/3². 3028) for the early 4th cent. He was twice engaged in legal proceedings with *Lysias (Or. 21. 20; fr. 73). No fragments of interest survive. *Aristophanes (1) refers to him at *Av.* 1372 ff. as a typical representative of the New *Dithyramb (cf. also *Lys.* 860; *Ran.* 153, 1437; *Eccl.* 330; fr. 156. 10 K–A). *Pherecrates (fr. 155. 8 ff. K–A) regarded him as a corrupter of traditional dithyrambic composition. *Strattis (frs. 14–22 K–A) wrote a whole comedy against him.

> Maas, *RE* 11/1. 479 ff.; M. L. West, *Greek Music* (1992), 359; B. Zimmermann, *Dithyrambos* (1992), 118 ff.   B. Z.

Cinna See CORNELIUS CINNA (1), L.; HELVIUS CINNA.

Cinyras, legendary king of *Cyprus; in *Homer's *Iliad*, he is the donor of *Agamemnon's magnificent inlaid corslet (11. 20 ff.), and thereafter becomes a byword for wealth (Tyrtaeus, fr. 12. 6; Pind. *Nem.* 8. 18). Some authors (Strabo 16. 755; Apollod. 3. 14. 3) make him an immigrant from *Syria, and he is strongly associated with the cult of *Aphrodite at *Paphos, whose priests traced their descent back to him (Tac. *Hist.* 2. 3). His devotion to the goddess did not however save him from being tricked into bed by his daughter *Myrrha; though *Apollodorus (6) makes the child of that incestuous union, *Adonis, a legitimate son by his wife Metharme.   A. H. G.

Circe, powerful sorceress of mythology, daughter of *Helios and the Oceanid Perse (Hom. *Od.* 10. 135–9). *Homer places her island of Aeaea at the extreme east of the world (*Od.* 12. 3–4), but as early as *Hesiod, *Theog.* 1011–16 she is associated also with the west and frequently placed at Monte Circeo (see CIRCEII) on the coast of *Latium (so *Apollonius (1) of Rhodes and *Virgil; cf. Hunter on Ap. Rhod. *Arg.* 3. 311–13). In the *Odyssey*, Circe transforms a group of *Odysseus' men into pigs (though they retain human intelligence); Odysseus rescues them by resisting the goddess' magic, thanks to the power of the plant 'moly' which *Hermes gives him. Odysseus and his men stay with her for a year, after which she dispatches them to the Underworld to consult *Tiresias. On their return she gives them more detailed instructions as to how to confront the perils of the homeward journey. In the cyclic *Telegonia* (see EPIC CYCLE), her son by Odysseus, Telegonus, accidentally killed his father when raiding Ithaca, and she herself married *Telemachus (cf. M. Davies, *EGF* pp. 71–3). As Aeëtes' sister, she has a prominent role in Apollonius' *Argonautica* in which she cleanses *Jason (1) and *Medea after their treacherous killing of Medea's brother Apsyrtus (*Arg.* 4. 557–752); it is probable that Apollonius was not the first poet to associate her with the Argonautic voyage (see ARGONAUTS). Moralists frequently interpreted Circe as a symbol of luxury and wantonness, the pursuit of which turns men into beasts (cf. Hor. *Epist.* 1. 2. 23–6; Kaiser, *MH* 1964, 200–13).

> A. Lesky, *Gesammelte Schriften* (1966), 26–62; F. Canciani, *LIMC* 6.   R. L. Hu.

Circeii (mod. Circeo), a prominent mountain on the Tyrrhenian coast, south of Rome. A Latin colony (see IUS LATII) was established here in 393 BC, against the *Volsci, and polygonal walls survive. Later a *municipium, there are remains of the so-called sanctuary of Circe, another temple, and villas.

> G. M. de Rossi, *Il Circeo* (1973); *Enea nel Lazio* (1981), 70 ff.   E. T. S.; T. W. P.

circus, the Roman arena for chariot-racing. The most important at Rome was the Circus Maximus (*c.*650 × 125 m.: *c.*711 × 137 yds.), in the Murcia valley between the Palatine and Aventine, traditionally founded in the regal period and progressively adorned during the republic. The distinctive form with parallel sides and one semi-circular end fitted with tiered seating, and with twelve starting gates (*carceres*) at the open end, was created under *Caesar and preserved in the monumental rebuilding by *Trajan. The area was divided into two tracks by a long central barrier (*euripus* or *spina*), marked at the ends with conical turning-posts (*metae*) and decorated with Augustus' obelisk and other monuments, including the movable eggs and dolphins which marked the ends of the seven laps in each race. Four, six, eight or twelve teams of horses competed under different colours, red and white at first (Tert. *De spect.* 5, 9), then also green (Suet. *Calig.* 55) and blue (Suet. *Vit.* 7), *Domitian's purple and gold (Suet. *Dom.* 7) being temporary. Other circuses at Rome included the Circus Flaminius in the *Campus Martius, formalized *c.*220 BC but without permanent seating, and the Vatican Circus of *Gaius (1) and *Nero (Plin. *HN* 36. 74; 16. 201), the site of Christian martyrdoms, close to the later St Peter's basilica. Best preserved is the Circus of Maxentius outside the city on the via Appia, dedicated in AD 309 (*ILS* 673).

Circuses are found elsewhere in Italy and in many parts of the empire. In the east those of *Antioch (1) and *Alexandria (1) were famous, while Spain provides notable examples such as Merida (*Emerita Augusta) and *Urso, the latter famous for its racing-stables (Plin. *HN* 8. 166). In the late empire circuses became increasingly associated with the emperor and were built in connection with imperial residences as at *Constantinople and Milan (*Mediolanum). See HORSE- AND CHARIOT-RACES.

J. Humphrey, *Roman Circuses* (1986). J. D.

Ciris A poem from the *Appendix Vergiliana*. It is generally thought to be un-Virgilian; it contains many echoes of *Virgil. Its story is that of *Scylla (2), daughter of *Nisus (1), king of *Megara, who was metamorphosed into the *ciris* bird; the identity of this bird is not explained, but the name alludes (see l. 488) to Scylla's severing of Nisus' magic lock (Greek *keirein*), an action which betrayed Megara to the attacking *Minos with whom Scylla had fallen in love. In style and narrative technique the poem is heavily neoteric, and besides many visible imitations of *Catullus 64, it probably extensively imitates C. *Helvius Cinna's *Smyrna* and other neoteric poems.

EDITION AND COMMENTARY R. O. A. M. Lyne, *Ciris: A Poem Attributed to Vergil* (1978).
TRANSLATION H. R. Fairclough, *Virgil 2: Aeneid 7–12 and Minor Poems* (Loeb, 1934).
STUDIES R. F. Thomas *CQ* 1981, 371–80; C. Connor *CQ* 1991, 556–9. R. O. A. M. L.

Cirrha, a port to the east of Itea on the north coast of the gulf of *Corinth, owned tin-mines which were worked in prehistoric times. The site was occupied in the early Helladic period and in the transitional period between the middle Helladic and the late Helladic periods. It flourished in the latter part of the late Helladic period as the port of Mycenaean *Crisa and it was especially prosperous in the 7th cent. It was involved in the fate of Crisa, but it revived later as a port.

P-K, *GL* 1. 2. 686 ff. N. G. L. H.

Cirta (mod. Constantine in Algeria), a hill-top fortress perched on a dramatic site commanding the gorges of the Ampsaga (Rhummel), was the capital of *Syphax and then of *Masinissa, who encouraged the settlement of Italian merchants, and linked Cirta to the ports of Rusicade (Skikda) and Chullu (Collo). A sanctuary of Baal-Hammon with over 850 votive stelae and neo-Punic inscriptions is the principal witness of this *Numidian phase; the Numidian mausoleum at El-Khroub, 14 km. (8½ mi.) SE of Cirta, possibly that of Masinissa's son, Micipsa, shows by its silverware and Rhodian wine amphorae Numidian commercial contacts with the Greek Hellenistic world. *Jugurtha captured Cirta from Adherbal (112 BC) and massacred the Italian inhabitants. For help in overthrowing *Juba (1), P. *Sittius and his followers were granted Cirta and the surrounding country by Caesar (46 BC). Under the empire, the full name of Cirta was *Colonia Iulia Iuvenalis Honoris et Virtutis Cirta* and it was the centre of a unique confederation which included three other colonies, Rusicade, Chullu, and Milev; magistrates and the municipal assembly were those of the confederation, not of the individual cities. In Cirta's territory were a number of urban settlements dependent on it, including Castellum Tidditanorum (Tiddis), home of the Lollii Urbici whose circular family mausoleum erected by Q. *Lollius Urbicus still stands 4 km. (2½ mi.) east of their home town. Cirta's best known citizen was M. *Cornelius Fronto. Cirta lay within Africa Proconsularis until *Hadrian transferred the part of this province which included Cirta to Numidia, but the city did not become a provincial capital until *Diocletian made it head of his newly constituted province of Numidia Cirtensis. Damaged in the civil wars of the early 4th cent., it was restored by Constantine who renamed it Constantina, and it then became the capital of all Numidia. Remains of a bridge over the Rhummel and of an aqueduct south of the town are the only extant monuments.

PECS 224–5; S. Gsell, *Inscriptions latines de l'Algérie* 2 / 1 (1957), nos. 468–1941; L. Teutsch, *Das Städtwesen in Nordafrika* (1962), 65 ff., 176 ff. Sanctuary: A. Berthier and R. Charlier, *Le Sanctuaire punique d'El Hofra à Constantine*, 2 vols. (1955); F. Bertrandy and M. Sznycer, *Les Stèles puniques de Constantine* (1987). Mausoleum: H. G. Horn and C. B. Rüger (eds.), *Die Numider* (1979), 158–71, 287–382.
W. N. W.; B. H. W.; R. J. A. W.

Cisalpine Gaul See GAUL (CISALPINE).

cities See POLIS; URBANISM.

citizenship, Greek Greek citizenship stemmed from the fusion of two distinct but related elements, (*a*) the notion of the individual state as a 'thing' with boundaries, an ongoing existence, and a power of decision, and (*b*) the notion of its inhabitants participating in its life as joint proprietors. The first element was a product of the various processes of state formation which eroded personal chieftainship by centralizing power and exercising it through a growing number of offices or magistracies with limited length of tenure: at first denoted by an extended use of the word *polis (cf. ML 2), it later engendered the more abstract term *politeia*, 'polity', 'constitution', or 'commonwealth'. The second element developed from the informal but ineradicable roles which *epic already portrays as being played in communal life by the *dēmos* (the territory or settlement and its inhabitants) and the *laos* (the people in terms of roles—especially military—and relationships): reflected in various ways in early texts such as ML 2 (Dreros on *Crete), ML 8 (*Chios), or the Great Rhetra of *Sparta (Plut. *Lyc.* 6), it was formalized in the word *politēs* (citizen) and in the assembly (*ekklēsia, *apellai (1), etc.) as an institution. The fusion of the two elements was expressed in the fundamental phrase 'to have a share in the polity' (*metechein tēs politeias*), which is widespread in Greek texts. It implied that all citizens shared in public responsibilities (deciding, fighting, judging, administering, etc.) and in public privileges (access to land, distributions, or power) as if they were shareholders in a company.

Political pressures and political theory (cf. especially Arist. *Pol.* 3) crystallized round the questions 'Should shares be equal?' and 'Who should be a citizen?'. Aspirations towards equality, opposed by oligarchs, were expressed by terms such as *homoioi* ('peers', full Spartiates), *isēgoria* ('freedom to speak in assembly'), and *isonomia* ('equity of power between rulers and ruled'), by the diffusion of power among the citizenry, and by the notion of 'ruling and being ruled by turns' which shaped *Aristotle's functional definition of citizenship (*Pol.* 1277ᵃ27). In consequence, the boundary between citizen and non-citizen needed explicit definition. Some formulations admitted all free residents, as *Cleisthenes (2)'s reform in Athens probably did. Others required descent from a real or imagined founder or group, and therefore emphasized legitimacy of birth. Others envisaged 'those best able to help (the city) with their property and persons' (Thuc. 8. 65. 3), or (as in Sparta) disfranchised those unable to contribute fully to the common table. Such formulations tended to equate citizenship with the four abilities—to fight, to vote, to hold office, to own land—and thereby to make citizen bodies into closed, privileged, all-male corporations, outside which lay various inferior or adjunct statuses such as *perioikoi ('dwellers-round'), *metoikoi (*metics) or *paroikoi ('resident free aliens'), and *apeleutheroi ('freedmen'). However, need and advantage forced states to make individual exceptional enfranchisements, e.g. for men with particular resources or talents (cf. the seer Teisamenos, Hdt. 9. 33). Collective grants (e.g. ML 94) or amalgamations of citizenship also remained rare except as a product of *synoecisms such as *Rhodes or *Megalopolis.

Such exclusivity gradually broke down in the Hellenistic period, as citizenship became more an honour and a status than a function. The purchase of citizenship became a common practice, as did plural citizenship or the mutual permeability of citizenship represented by treaties of *isopoliteia. By the Roman period active citizenship in the Greek states required previous service in the upper-class *ephēbeia* (see EPHEBOI).

W. Gawantka, *Isopolitie* (1975); R. G. Mulgan, *Aristotle's Political Theory* (1977); J. K. Davies, *CJ* 1977–8, 105–21; R. Descat, *Rev. Ét. Anc.* 1979, 229–40; C. Mossé, *Rev. Ét. Anc.* 1979, 241–9; M. J. Osborne, *Naturalization in Athens* 1–4 (1981–3); W. G. Runciman, *Comparative Studies in Society and History* 1982, 351–77; P. B. Manville, *The Origins of Citizenship in Ancient Athens* (1990); S. D. Lambert, *The Phratries of Attica* (1993), ch. 1. J. K. D.

citizenship, Roman In both the Greek and the Roman world in the Archaic period, it seems that communities were open to the arrival of people from elsewhere, at all social levels, whether one thinks of Hesiod's father, *Demaratus (1) of Corinth in Tarquinii, the Tarquins (see TARQUINIUS PRISCUS; TARQUINIUS SUPERBUS), or Attus Clusus and his followers in Rome. Detailed rules for citizenship were of course developed in both civilizations, as the city evolved, in the 7th to 5th or 6th to 5th cents. BC. In the case of Rome, though the details are obscure, Roman citizenship clearly developed in dialogue with the citizenships of other Latin communities. It involved the observance of the Roman civil law; and the struggles of the plebeians gradually brought protection for citizens from magisterial *imperium.

At all events, Roman citizenship came to possess two features which distinguished it from *polis* citizenship and which later

surprised Greek observers: the automatic incorporation of freed slaves of Romans into the Roman citizen body; and the ease with which whole communities of outsiders could be admitted as citizens. By the time Rome faced the invasion of *Hannibal in 218 BC, she had a long history of giving citizenship to Italian communities, either with the vote (*optimo iure*) or without the vote (*sine suffragio*). (The latter communities, as with *Arpinum, the place of origin of C. *Marius (1) and *Cicero, were usually later granted the vote.) Apart from Roman communities of these two types and allies, *socii, Italy also contained numerous Latin communities, whose members shared a number of rights with Romans and whose citizenships were interchangeable with that of Rome, and vice versa, if the person concerned changed domicile. One of the rights shared with Romans was *conubium*. A child born to two Romans was a Roman; but so was a child born to a Roman father and a mother from a people possessing *conubium*. (See IUS LATII, LATINI, MUNICIPIUM.)

All citizens, after the abolition of the ban on *conubium* between patricians and plebeians, had *conubium*; they were also liable to *tributum and military service. If they had the vote, they were also eligible to stand for magistracies. (Individuals were occasionally deprived of the vote as a punishment, becoming *aerarii.) It is not certain whether communities without the vote were bound by the Roman civil law or not.

In the course of the 2nd cent. BC, grants of citizenship dried up, except for a few communities *sine suffragio* granted the vote; and Rome sought also to restrict the access of Latins to Roman citizenship. Attempts were made to respond to the desire of Latins and Italians alike for citizenship, by M. *Fulvius Flaccus in 125 BC, by C. *Sempronius Gracchus in 122 BC, and by M. *Livius Drusus (2) in 91 BC. The failure of Flaccus provoked the revolt of *Fregellae; and when the last attempt failed, most of the allies went to war with Rome to achieve their end, the so-called *Social War (3); and in order to ensure the loyalty of the rest, as also of the Latins, who had for the most part remained loyal, Rome granted them citizenship by the *lex Iulia* of 90 BC. Although the details of the process are obscure, citizenship was in fact also extended to former rebels. By the time of *Sulla, Italy south of the Po (*Padus) and former Latin colonies north of the Po were Roman, with the possible exception of the Ligurians; actual registration in the Roman *census, however, remained very incomplete.

The last generation of the Roman republic and the civil wars which followed witnessed demands for citizenship in those areas of Italy which still did not have it—demands which were satisfied by *Caesar—and the increasing spread of citizenship overseas as a reward for service of one kind or another, in the Greek world as well as in the west. In the established imperial system, Roman citizens enjoyed in theory and often in practice protection against the *imperium* of a provincial governor, and a relatively favourable tax status.

Roman citizenship continued to spread, for three principal reasons. (1) Communities were granted Latin status and their magistrates automatically acquired Roman citizenship, a right which was probably created after the Social War for new Latin communities north of the Po and perhaps in Liguria. (2) Citizenship was granted to auxiliaries and their families on discharge. (3) Legionaries were supposed to be recruited among citizens only, but were clearly also recruited among provincials and deemed to be citizens. Their families on their discharge—between *Augustus and *Septimius Severus serving soldiers could not marry—if their wives were of citizen status, helped to spread Roman citizenship. (4) In the East, from *Pompey on, citizenship was conferred on individuals, typically members of the provincial city-élites.

Citizenship was finally granted to virtually all the free population of the empire by *Caracalla, in the so-called Antonine *constitution. But by this time, the right to vote had long disappeared; provincial Romans had lost their exemption from taxation; and many of the most important personal privileges of citizenship had been restricted to the élite, the *honestiores, as opposed to the humiliores. And thereafter the essential distinction was between slave and free—which also in due course became less important with the depression of the status of the free tenant (see COLONUS)—and, within those who were still free men, between honestiores and humiliores.

A. N. Sherwin White, *Roman Citizenship*, 2nd edn. (1973); P. D. A. Garnsey, *Social Status and Legal Privilege in the Roman Empire* (1970); M. Humbert, *Municipium et civitas sine suffragio* (1978).   M. H. C.

city-founders See FOUNDERS, CITY.

Civil Wars, Roman See ROME, HISTORY.

civitas, 'citizenship, citizen community' (for the first, see CITIZENSHIP, ROMAN), term of Roman administrative law referring, like Greek *polis, to any free-standing community, and specifically, in the imperial period, to the lowest grade of autonomous member-community of the cellular provincial empire. In areas of the empire newly under Roman rule (as frequently in Gaul, Britain, Spain, and Africa in the early empire) such a *civitas* formed from a local ethnic or social unit, had a citizenry, council and magistrates, and a set of procedural rules adaptable to local custom. In many cases there was also encouragement to form a city to provide a physical setting for the new institutions. The next step might be the grant of full municipal status (see MUNICIPIUM). Meanwhile, the *civitas* could be relied on to carry out the *census and collect taxes, and its officials became the connection with representatives of the Roman *res publica* such as governors or procurators.   N. P.

Claros, *oracle and grove of *Apollo belonging to the city of Colophon. The oracle appears to have been founded by the 8th cent. BC, as stories about its foundation appear in the *Epigoni* (attributing the foundation to Manto), *Hesiod mentions the site in connection with a contest between the seers *Calchas and *Mopsus, and it is mentioned as a residence of Apollo in the Homeric *Hymn to Apollo*. The sanctuary was discovered 1907, and an excavation, begun under the direction of Louis Robert in the 1950s, turned up the oracular chamber under the temple and numerous inscriptions relating to its operation. On the basis of these inscriptions and literary texts, we know that there were 'sacred nights' upon which the consultations would take place, when there would be a procession of consultants to the temple of Apollo with sacrifices and singing of hymns. Consultants would then hand over questions to the priests who would descend into the adytum (innermost sanctuary), through the blue marble-faced corridors underneath the temple, to a place outside the room in which the divine spring flowed. Within this room the thespiōdos, a man, would drink from the spring and utter his responses to the questions of each consultant. These would then be written down in verse by the prophētēs and delivered to the consultants. An inscription of Hellenistic date confirms *Tacitus (1)'s statement that the Colophonians imported people of *Ionian descent to act as prophets (thespiōdoi),

though he confuses the issue by mentioning only one official instead of two.

Inscriptions are now revealing the nature of Claros' clientele among the cities of Asia Minor and further afield in greater detail. These inscriptions, along with various discussions in the literature of the empire, reveal that Claros was one of the most important oracular sites in Asia Minor from roughly the 3rd cent. BC to the mid-3rd cent. AD. A number of responses are preserved on inscriptions and in the *Tübingen Theosophy*.

Iambl. *Myst.* 3. 11; Tac. *Ann.* 2. 54. 2–3; Aelius Aristides, *Sacred Tales* 3. 10–11; H. Erbse, *Fragmente griechischer Theosophien* (1941); H. Parke, *The Oracles of Apollo in Asia Minor* (1985); J. and L. Robert, *Claros* 1 (1989), and *BCH* 1992.   D. S. P.

class struggle, as a concept and phrase, is indelibly associated with the Marxist tradition of socio-historical analysis and practical political endeavour. 'The history of all hitherto existing society is the history of class struggles', is the opening sentence of the first main section of *The Communist Manifesto* (1848). Karl Marx, moreover, did not only apply the phrase to the societies of Greece and Rome (among others) but also acknowledged his debt to the 'giant thinker' Aristotle for demonstrating, as he saw it, the general utility of the concept for historical analysis and explanation. See MARXISM AND CLASSICAL ANTIQUITY. Marx, however, nowhere in his voluminous writings gave an extended and coherent definition of 'class', which remains one of the most essentially contested terms of art in all socio-historical theory. His omission has been variously repaired by historians sympathetic to Marxist theory. Conversely, the very applicability and utility of any definition of class for the understanding of Greece and Rome have been equally passionately denied.

Economic class is an objective actuality, a relationship subsisting among persons similarly placed in an economic system. But when used as a dynamic term of historical analysis, or a fortiori as a political slogan, it may comport also a psychological ingredient of self-consciousness, so that membership of a certain economic class may crucially determine the members' conscious behaviour towards each other and towards members of another class or classes. Economic classes, moreover, in order properly to constitute classes, are usually thought of as being in some relation of hierarchy and antagonism towards each other. Definition of class-membership is difficult enough for any society, but it is often held that the societies of Greece and Rome raise peculiarly recalcitrant obstacles.

Suppose that people are classed according to their relationship to the means and labour of economic production: between those who do and do not own such means, between those who do or do not have to work for a living and/or for others. Are the richest Roman senator and the non-working owner of a relatively modest pottery manufactory therefore to be placed in the same class? Or consider ownership of land, always the most basic and coveted means of production. In most Greek cities at most periods non-citizens were normally debarred from legal ownership of land, even if they happened to possess the economic means to work it. That legal obstacle could be circumvented by leasing land from others, but would that place the lessee in the same class as the citizen lessor?

If class definition is problematic for the ancient world, so too is the identification of class struggle. In so far as chattel slaves were legally rightless and limitlessly exploitable productive labourers, they stood in a relationship of class to their masters and mistresses, but in what sense could they be said to have conducted a 'class struggle' against them? Outright slave revolts (see SLAVERY) were rare, and there is little or no sense of a shared consciousness of identity and purpose among them. On the other hand, the masters and mistresses may justly be held to have waged a constant class struggle against their slaves, with the aid of those free, non-slaveowners who identified their interests with the maintenance of the institution of slavery (as practically all ancient free people almost always did).

By contrast, in political struggles within the citizen estates of the Greek world (*stasis), as in the city of Rome under the late republic, there is no doubting the high degree of self-conscious solidarity between the two great antagonistic groups of the 'rich' and the 'poor' (otherwise known as 'the few' and 'the many', and a host of other binary terms). Since the root of their antagonism lay in differential ownership of the means of production, and the aim of their struggle was often the control of the organs of government, this looks very much like class struggle—except that the classes are defined not purely by economic but by a mixture of economic and legal criteria, and the solidarity of 'the poor' was less organic and more soluble than that of 'the rich'.

Arist. *Pol.* 5; J.-P. Vernant, *Myth and Society in Ancient Greece* (1980), 1–18; P. Vidal-Naquet, *The Black Hunter: Forms of Thought and Forms of Society in the Greek World* (1986), 159–67; M. I. Finley, *The Ancient Economy* (1973; 2nd edn. 1985); G. E. M. de Ste. Croix, *The Class Struggle in the Ancient Greek World: From the Archaic Age to the Arab conquests* (1981); A. Fuks, *Social Conflicts in Ancient Greece* (1984); H.-J. Gehrke, *Stasis* (1985); K. R. Bradley, *Slavery and Rebellion in the Roman World 140 BC–70 BC.* (1989). P. A. C.

classicism The modern use of 'classicism' to refer either to the art and literature of a period held to represent a peak of quality or perfection, or to the conscious imitation of works of such a period, derives from M. *Cornelius Fronto's use of *classicus* (lit. 'belonging to the highest class of citizens') to denote those ancient writers whose linguistic practice is authoritative for imitators (quoted in Gell. *NA* 19. 8. 5). The possibility of designating a period as 'classical', and of the consequent appearance of 'classicizing' movements, arises with the Hellenistic consciousness of the present as set off from, but heir to, a great past tradition, and with the self-conscious development of a theory of imitation (see IMITATIO). A full-blown classicizing movement emerges in 1st-cent. BC Rome, fostered by Greek writers like *Dionysius (7) of Halicarnassus who champion *Thucydides (2) as a model for historians and argue for the superiority of 'Attic' over 'Asianic' rhetorical models (see ASIANISM AND ATTICISM); in the visual arts there is a parallel movement to imitate Greek models of the 5th and 4th cents. BC (see RETROSPECTIVE STYLES). In modern scholarship on the ancient world 'Classical' has been used as a period term (often with evaluative overtones), opposed to 'Archaic', 'Hellenistic', 'baroque', etc., to refer in particular to the art and literature of 5th- and 4th-century BC Athens and of late republican and Augustan Rome. 'Classicism', referring both to the imitation of antique models and to more general stylistic choices, has been a key term in the cultural history of the 18th and 19th cents.

T. Gelzer, in *Le Classicisme à Rome*, Entretiens Hardt 35 (1979), 3–7; J. Stroux, in W. Jaeger (ed.), *Das Problem des Klassischen und die Antike* (1931), 1–14; G. M. A. Richter, *JRS* 1958, 10–15. P. R. H.

classis A *classis* ('class') was a group of Roman citizens who could meet a certain minimum wealth qualification. Servius *Tullius is supposed to have divided property owners into five *classes* for military purposes. The first three classes were equipped

as heavy infantry, the last two as light-armed skirmishers (Livy 1. 43; Dion. Hal. *Ant. Rom.* 4. 16; Cic. *Rep.* 2. 22). This system, together with the monetary values given in our sources to the levels of wealth required for membership of the various classes, belongs to the middle republic, and cannot be earlier than *c.*400 BC. But certain texts (Festus, entry under 'infra classem'; Gell. *NA* 6. 13) mention a simpler division between a single *classis* and the rest, who were defined as *infra classem* ('beneath the class'). It has been suggested that the institution of a *classis* of heavy infantry could go back to the 6th cent., when according to archaeological evidence *'hoplite' tactics and equipment were in use in central Italy, and that the tradition concerning Servius Tullius is to this extent based on fact.

In early times, then, the term *classis* signified Rome's armed forces; a vestige of this survived in the later use of *classis (navalis)* to mean 'navy'. It is also worth noting that the cognate term *classicus* ('belonging to the first rank') gives us the modern word 'classical', whence the title of this dictionary (see CLASSICISM).

The later republican division into five classes was instituted for fiscal purposes, as a means of taxing citizens on a sliding scale according to their wealth (see TRIBUTUM), and as the basis for distributing citizens into voting units in the *comitia centuriata*. By that time the army was recruited indiscriminately *ex classibus*, that is, from all those who could meet the minimum property qualification for membership of the fifth class, a qualification that seems to have been reduced at various stages during the 2nd cent. BC until the time of C. *Marius (1).

Momigliano, *Terzo contributo*, 593 ff., and *Quarto contributo*, 430 ff., 443 ff.; E. Gabba, *Republican Rome: The Army and the Allies* (1976), 1–19; R. Thomsen, *King Servius Tullius* (1980), esp. 176 ff. T. J. Co.

Clastidium (mod. Casteggio), town near *Placentia in Cisalpine Gaul. Here in 222 BC the Roman consul M. *Claudius Marcellus (1) engaged in person and slew the Celtic enemy chieftain Viridomarus—the one certainly historical instance of *spolia opima. E. T. S.

Claudia Acte (*RE* 399), freedwoman (see FREEDMEN, FREEDWOMEN) of *Nero (possibly already manumitted by Claudius), came from Asia Minor: hence her alleged descent from the Attalid kings of *Pergamum. In AD 55, encouraged by the younger *Seneca despite the opposition of *Iulia Agrippina, Nero made her his mistress, but from 58 onwards she was gradually supplanted by *Poppaea Sabina. Her wealth is attested by records of her household and estates in Italy and Sardinia. She deposited Nero's remains in the tomb of the Domitii.

Tac. *Ann.* 13. 12; Suet. *Ner.* 28, 50; Cass. Dio 61. 7. G. E. F. C.; M. T. G.

Claudia Octavia, daughter of *Claudius and Messallina, was born AD 40. She was betrothed in infancy to L. *Iunius Silanus, and in 49, after Silanus' repudiation and death, to Agrippina's son L. Domitius Ahenobarbus (*Nero), whom she married in 53. Nero, who disliked and neglected her, divorced her in 62 for sterility (a charge of adultery having failed) in order to marry *Poppaea Sabina, and sent her to live in Campania under military surveillance. When a rumour that she had been reinstated provoked demonstrations of popular approval, he contrived fresh charges of adultery and treason, banished her to Pandateria, and soon had her put to death (9 June). For the *praetexta* on her fate, see OCTAVIA.

PIR[2] C 1110; V. Rudich, *Political Dissidence under Nero* (1993), esp. 70–4.

Portraiture: V. Poulsen, *Opuscula Romana* 4 (1962), 107 ff.

G. W. R.; T. J. C.; A. J. S. S.

Claudian (Claudius Claudianus, b. *c.* AD 370), poet. A native of *Alexandria (1), he came to Italy *c.*394 and, turning from Greek to Latin, scored an instant success by eulogizing his young patrons, the consuls Probinus and Olybrius (January 395). Thereafter he became court poet under the emperor *Honorius and his minister *Stilicho, for whom he produced a series of panegyrics and other propagandist poems. His efforts won him the title *vir clarissimus*, a bronze statue in the forum Traiani (*CIL* 6. 1710), and a rich bride selected by Stilicho's wife, Serena. His death (*c.*404) may be inferred from his silence in the face of Stilicho's subsequent achievements.

Three of Claudian's *panegyrics were written on consulships held by Honorius in 396, 398, and 404; the consulships of *Mallius Theodorus in 399 and Stilicho in 400 were similarly recognized. The marriage of Honorius to Stilicho's daughter Maria in 398 was celebrated with four *Fescennini and an *epithalamium, doing propagandist work as well as fulfilling their traditional functions. *Invectives against *Rufinus (1) and *Eutropius (2), Stilicho's rivals at the eastern court of Arcadius, appeared in 396–7 and 399 respectively. The other main genre in which Claudian worked, the epic, is represented by *De bello Gildonico* (398), *De bello Getico* (402), and the unfinished mythological poems of uncertain date, *De raptu Proserpinae* and *Gigantomachia*.

Claudian's poetry belongs firmly to the classical tradition, though it does not necessarily follow that *Augustine and *Orosius (followed by many modern scholars) were right in supposing him a pagan. He is indebted particularly to the Greek rhetoricians of the later empire and to the Latin poets of the Silver Age; in diction and technique he is the equal of *Lucan and *Statius, in hyperbole he perhaps outdoes them. Set speeches and descriptions are the hallmark of his work. Though slanted in the propagandist manner, his writings are a valuable historical source for his period.

TEXTS J. B. Hall (1985); with trans., M. Platnauer (Loeb, 1922).

COMMENTARIES *IV Cons. Hon.*, J. Lehner (1984); *VI Cons. Hon.*, K. A. Müller (1938); *Cons. Stil.*, U. Keudel (1970); *De bello Gildonico*, E. M. Olechowska (1978); *De raptu Proserpinae*, J. B. Hall (1969), C. Gruzelier (1993); *In Eutropium*, P. Fargues (1933); *In Rufinum*, H. L. Levy (1971); *Panegyricus dictus Olybrio et Probino consulibus*, W. Taegert (1988).

STUDIES P. Fargues, *Claudien* (1933); D. Romano, *Claudiano* (1958); P. G. Christiansen, *The Use of Images by Claudius Claudianus* (1969); A. Cameron, *Claudian* (1970); S. Döpp, *Zeitgeschichte in Dichtungen Claudians* (1980); J. B. Hall, *Prolegomena to Claudian* (1986).

PLRE 2. 299 f..

J. H. D. S.

Claudius (Tiberius Claudius (*RE* 256) **Nero Germanicus,** 10 BC–AD 54), the emperor **Claudius I**, was born at *Lugdunum (1) (Lyon) (1 August), the youngest child of Nero *Claudius Drusus and of *Antonia (3). Hampered by a limp, trembling, and a speech defect all perhaps due to cerebral palsy, and by continual illnesses, he received no public distinction from Augustus beyond the augurate, and was twice refused a magistracy by Tiberius. Enactments of AD 20, the *tabula Siarensis (ZPE 55 (1984), 58 f., fr. 1, 11. 6 f.; 19–21.) and the *senatus consultum de Cn. Pisone patre* (ed. W. Eck and others, forthcoming) 1. 148, like Tac. *Ann* 3. 18. 4, illustrate his low position in the imperial family. Claudius retained the status of a knight until on 1 July 37 he became suffect consul with his young nephew, the emperor *Gaius (1); for the rest of the reign he received little but insults. What role, if any, he played in planning the assassination of Gaius in 41 is disputed. After the murder he was discovered in the palace by a soldier, taken to the

praetorian barracks, and saluted emperor while the senate was still discussing the possibility of restoring the republic. Senators did not easily forgive him for the way he came to power, but he had the support of the army: the revolt of L. *Arruntius Camillus Scribonianus in Dalmatia (42) was short-lived. Claudius stressed his bond with guard and legions and, making up for previous inexperience, briefly took a personal part in the invasion of *Britain (43). The capture of Camulodunum occasioned an impressive pageant, and Claudius made a leisurely progress back to Rome for his triumph (44). By the end of his principate he had received 27 salutations as *imperator*, more than any other emperor until *Constantine I. He was also consul four more times (42, 43, 47, and 51), and revived the office of censor, which he held with his favourite L. *Vitellius in 47–8.

Although he reverted from the pretentious absolutism of Gaius (whose acts, however, were not annulled wholesale), and stressed civility to the senate, the precariousness of his position made him liable to take sudden and violent action against threats real, imagined by himself, or thought up by advisers; offenders who were given a trial were often heard by few advisers in private. His early career and mistrust of the senate led him to rely on the advice of freedmen, especially *Narcissus (2) and M. *Antonius Pallas, whose influence and wealth were hated; but his dependence on his third and fourth wives *Valeria Messallina and *Iulia Agrippina was due as much to their political importance as to uxoriousness. Messallina was the mother of his only surviving son *Britannicus, born 41 (Claudius' earlier wives, Plautia Urgulanilla and Aelia Paetina, left him only with a daughter, *Antonia (4)). She was hard to dislodge for that reason, but fell in 48, in what looks like a struggle between freedmen on the one hand and senators and knights on the other. Agrippina, daughter of Claudius' popular brother *Germanicus, was a figure in her own right, and particularly desirable after the loss of face entailed by Messallina's fall. The son she brought with her was more than three years older than Britannicus, and in 50 he was adopted by Claudius as a partner for his own son to assure their joint accession to power; in 53 Nero married Claudius' daughter *Claudia Octavia. But while Nero's career was accelerated, with a grant of proconsular power outside Rome coming in 51, Britannicus was pushed aside. Claudius' death on 13 October 54 conveniently made it impossible for him to give his natural son the toga of manhood, but the story that he was poisoned by Agrippina has been questioned.

In youth Claudius wrote works on Etruscan and Carthaginian history (see ETRUSCANS; CARTHAGE). From *Livy he acquired a knowledge of Roman history, and he was steeped in religion and tradition, but his celebration of the *Secular Games (47), extension of the *pomerium, and taking of the *augurium salutis ('augury of security', 49) had the political purpose of reassuring the Roman people about the stability and success of his regime.

Claudius paid particular attention to the welfare of the populace. Building the harbour at *Ostia and draining the *Fucinus lacus were intended to secure or increase the grain supply, as was his offer of privileges to those who invested in the construction of grain ships.

Claudius' interest in government, from which he had been excluded, inclined him to intervene whenever he found anything amiss, and he berated senators who failed to take an active part in debate. He was particularly interested in jurisdiction, and was indefatigable, if emotional and inconsistent, in dispensing justice. Legislation had clear aims: to discourage sedition; to protect inheritance within the clan and the rights of individual property owners; more 'liberal' measures increased the rights of slaves, women, and minors. Arguments for his legislation invoked traditional *mores* and the upholding of status, but in his senatorial speech advocating the admission of Gauls to the senate, Claudius' preoccupation with the place of innovation in Roman life shows him coming to terms with changes in economy and society.

Claudius was noted for generosity with the citizenship, though his advisers also sold it without his knowledge. (See CITIZENSHIP, ROMAN.) A few widespread grants of Latin rights (see IUS LATII), along with his favourable response to the request of long-enfranchised Gallic chieftains for permission to stand for senatorial office (resented by existing senators), made him seem more generous than he was: proved merit was his own criterion for grants. Administrative changes have also been given undue weight, as also the influence of the *freedmen, who were emerging in previous reigns and have wrongly been claimed to have become the equivalent of modern 'ministers' as part of a policy of 'centralization'. Claudius' grant of additional jurisdiction to provincial *procurators, and the introduction of that title for equestrian governors of provinces, previously called 'prefects', simply relieved him of the job of hearing appeals and stressed the dependence of the governors upon their emperor.

Claudius added other provinces to the empire besides Britain, although that left few resources for an active policy against the Germans: the two *Mauretanias (whose last king, Ptolemy (2), had been executed by Gaius), *Lycia (43), and *Thrace (46); and he resumed overseas colonization. His dealings with *Judaea and the *Parthians, however, were inept. In Judaea the procurators who replaced the deceased King Agrippa I in 44 proved unsatisfactory, and by 54 Claudius' eastern governors had allowed the Parthians to gain control of Greater Armenia, a serious blow to Roman prestige.

Claudius was deified on death, enhancing his adoptive son's prestige, but in Nero's early years the failings of the regime (influence of women and freedmen, corruption, trials held in private, the bypassing of the senate, favour to provincials), were excoriated: the younger *Seneca's *Apocolocyntosis* reveals the tone. Under *Vespasian a more balanced view prevailed and Claudius' temple was completed, but *Tacitus (1), though he exploits Claudius' speeches, is merciless. Modern writers have overreacted, exaggerating his purposefulness in encouraging the development of the provinces; his accession and survival, preserving the imperial peace, and his recognition of social changes were his main domestic achievements.

ANCIENT SOURCES Tac. *Ann.* 11f.; Cass. Dio 59f.; Suet., *Divus Claudius*, ed. J. Mottershead (1986); Sen. *Apocolocyntosis*, ed. with trans. by P. Eden (1984); E. M. Smallwood, *Documents Illustrating the Principates of Gaius, Claudius and Nero* (1967), esp. 367–70 (trans. D. Braund, *Augustus to Nero: A Sourcebook of Roman History 31 BC–AD 68* (1985)).
MODERN LITERATURE V. M. Scramuzza, *The Emperor Claudius* (1940); A. Momigliano, *Claudius, the Emperor and his Achievement* (1934; repr. 1961) (bibliography); B. Levick, *Claudius* (1990) (bibliography).
J. P. B.; B. M. L.

Claudius II, 3rd-cent. AD emperor. See CLAUDIUS (II) GOTHICUS.

Claudius (*RE* 29), **Quintus,** was tribune of the *plebs* 218 BC, when he carried a law providing that no senator or son of a senator might own a ship capable of carrying more than 300 amphorae; C. *Flaminius (1) is said to have been the only senator to support Claudius. By Cicero's day (see *Verr.* 2. 5. 45) the law was disregarded.

Livy 21. 63. 3; J. Briscoe *CR* 1963, 323 (in review of Cassola).　J. Br.

Claudius (*RE* 31), **Tiberius** (or perhaps Tiberius Iulius), an important figure in the history of imperial administration in the 1st cent. AD. He was a freedman from Smyrna, was manumitted by *Tiberius, and served all the emperors from Tiberius to *Domitian. Under Claudius he became a procurator, and at some later date (possibly on *Vespasian's accession) was made *a rationibus* (in charge of financial accounts). Vespasian gave him equestrian rank. Banished by Domitian *c*.AD 82, he was recalled *c*.89 on the intercession of his son *Claudius Etruscus. He died in 92 aged nearly 90.

Stat. *Silv.* 3. 3, with the preface to the book; Mart. 7. 40. P. R. C. Weaver, *CQ* 1965, 145 ff. and *Familia Caesaris* (1972), see index under 'Claudius Etruscus, father of'.　G. E. F. C.; R. J. S.

Claudius Aristocles, Tiberius, of *Pergamum (2nd cent. AD), was a Peripatetic philosopher turned sophist who also held the consulship. As sophist he studied under *Herodes Atticus, taught in Pergamum and performed throughout Italy and Asia Minor. His works included two rhetorical textbooks, letters, and declamations.

Philostr. *VS* 2. 3 (567); *Suda* A 3918 Adler; Synesius, *Dio* 35c. M. B. T.

Claudius Atticus Herodes (1), **Tiberius** ('Atticus'), Athenian magnate, the first Roman consul of old Greek stock, father of Claudius Atticus Herodes (2). Son of the vastly rich Hipparchus disgraced by *Domitian, he recovered part of his inheritance under *Nerva. A military *diploma shows that he held a first (suffect) consulship around AD 130—a promotion he owed to the favour of *Hadrian, a great lover of Athens.

W. Ameling, *Herodes Atticus* 1 (1983), 21 ff.; A. R. Birley, *ZPE* 116 (1997), 209 ff. or M. M. Roxan, *Roman Military Diplomas 1985–1993* (1994) 159.
A. J. S. S.

Claudius Atticus Herodes (2), **Tiberius** (Lucius Vibullius Hipparchus Tiberius Claudius Atticus Herodes), 'Herodes Atticus' (*c.* AD 101–77), celebrated Athenian sophist and benefactor of Greek cities, ordinary consul AD 143; friend of M. *Aurelius, whom he taught (along with L. *Verus). A controversial public figure, he quarrelled with Fronto and the *Quintilii brothers, governors of Greece, and was accused of 'tyranny' by Athenian enemies (AD 174) before M. Aurelius, whose efforts to reconcile the two parties emerge from a long Athenian inscription published in 1970; his gifts of buildings, above all at Athens (see ATHENS, TOPOGRAPHY), were not always appreciated by fellow Greeks (see OLYMPIA). His declaiming style was straightforward, elegant, and restrained, recalling Critias and influencing a wide circle of pupils. His works included lectures and diaries; only a Latin translation of a *fabula* survives (Gell. *NA* 19. 12), apart from a symbouleutic speech whose attribution remains contested. Philostratus made him the centre-piece of his *Lives of the Sophists*. See CYNURIA; PHILOSTRATI; SECOND SOPHISTIC.

Philostr. *VS* 2. 1; ['Ηρώδου] περὶ πολιτείας, ed. Albini (1968); W. Ameling, *Herodes Atticus* 1 (1983).　E. L. B.; A. J. S. S.

Claudius (*RE* 82 and Suppl. 5) **Balbillus, Tiberius,** probably a son of Ti. *Claudius Thrasyllus and shared his astrological lore. (See ASTROLOGY.) He was ADC (*praefectus fabrum*, see FABRI) to *Claudius and tribune of Legio XX in the invasion of Britain in AD 43, winning decorations; he served as secretary dealing with Greek embassies and applications, and held posts in Egypt, including headship of the *Museum at *Alexandria (1). Favoured by *Iulia Agrippina, he was prefect of Egypt from 55 until her death in 59. He survived until the reign of *Vespasian, who allowed him honours from Ephesus; his daughter married Epiphanes of *Commagene and he was grandfather of *Iulius Antiochus Epiphanes Philopappus (suffect consul 109). Sen. *QNat.* 4. 2. 13 describes Balbillus as exceptionally gifted in every branch of literature; fragments of his *Astrologumena* are preserved (*CCAG* 8. 3. 103, 8. 4. 233). (The identity of astrologer and prefect was denied by A. Stein (*PIR*² C 813); whether the emissary sent to Claudius by Alexandria in 41 (*PLondon* 1912 = Smallwood, *Docs. . . . Gaius* 370, line 16) is connected with them is unclear.)

Magie, *Rom. Rule Asia Min.* 2. 1398 ff.; F. H. Cramer, *Astrology in Roman Law and Politics* (1954), 112 ff.; H.-G. Pflaum, *Les Carrières procuratoriennes* (1960), 34 ff.; Millar, *ERW* 86 f.   H. H. S.; B. M. L.

Claudius (*RE* 91) **Caecus, Appius,** censor 312 before holding other high office; consul 307 and 296, praetor 295: in the latter two years he fought in Etruria (see ETRUSCANS), *Campania, and *Samnium. In 280, now old and blind, he successfully opposed peace with *Pyrrhus after the Roman defeat at *Heraclea (1). It is not known whether the version of this speech known to Cicero was authentic. He is also credited with a work (probably in prose) containing a collection of moral essays.

Claudius has been rightly described as the first live personality in Roman history, and his censorship as sensational. As censor, he commissioned the building of the *via Appia from Rome to Capua and the first *aqueduct (aqua Appia). In drawing up the list of the senate he left out men regarded as superior to those included, even enrolling the sons of freedmen. He distributed the lower classes (*humiles*) through all the rural tribes, thus increasing their influence in the tribal assembly; the move was reversed by the censors of 304 (see CENSOR; CENSUS). He also transferred the cult of *Hercules from private to public superintendence. Claudius probably supported the action of the aedile Cn. *Flavius, also in 304, in publishing the details of legal procedure and a calendar of the days on which legal business could be conducted. He is said to have had a wide personal following (*clientela*; see CLIENS).

All this may look democratic, but in 300 he opposed the admission of plebeians to the two main priestly colleges (*pontifices and *augures) and on two occasions attempted to secure the election of an all-patrician college. These moves can be explained either as part of his political conflict with Q. *Fabius Maximus Rullianus or on the supposition that Claudius was trying to promote the interests of the people as a whole, not just those of the new plebeian nobility.

The above account largely follows T. J. Cornell, *CAH* 7²/2 (1989), 395–9; see also T. P. Wiseman, *Clio's Cosmetics* (1979), 85–9.   J. Br.

Claudius Caesar Britannicus, Tiberius son of *Claudius and *Valeria Messalina, born 12 February AD 41. His first surname was Germanicus; 'Britannicus' was added after Claudius' invasion of Britain. His stepmother *Iulia Agrippina induced Claudius in 50 to adopt her son L. Domitius (*Nero), who was three years older than Britannicus and so now took precedence over him; and she contrived to remove the tutors and officers of the guard who were loyal to Britannicus, thus ensuring Nero's accession on Claudius' death (54). Early in 55 Agrippina seems to have considered using Britannicus to prop up her failing influence, but he very soon died, almost certainly poisoned by Nero's order.

*PIR*² C 820; M. Griffin, *Nero* (1984); B. Levick, *Claudius* (1990), see index; V. Rudich, *Political Dissidence under Nero* (1993), esp. 8 f. Portraiture: V. Poulsen, *Acta archaeologica* 1951, 129 ff.

G. W. R.; T. J. C.; A. J. S. S.

Claudius (*RE* 102) **Caudex, Appius,** was consul 264 BC and the first Roman commander in the First *Punic War. According to *Polybius (1), following *Fabius Pictor, he defeated first *Hieron (2) and then *Hanno (2), and began the siege of Syracuse. *Philinus (2), however, said that he was defeated, and it has been suggested that the alleged victories of Caudex are in fact anticipations of those of his successor M'. *Valerius Maximus Messalla.

Polyb. 1. 11–12; Walbank, *HCP* 1, 66–7.   J. Br.

Claudius Charax, Aulus, of Pergamum, Greek historian and Roman senator. He held a legionary command in Britain, governed Cilicia, and was *suffect consul in AD 147 (*AE* 1961, 320). A well-known figure in the Greek cultural revival of his day (note *IG* 5. 1. 71, col. 3, lines 5, 8, 25: term as Spartan *patronomos*; see SECOND SOPHISTIC), he wrote a (lost) universal history (*Hellenica*) in 40 books. Full of *mythoi* or anecdotal digressions of a more or less fabulous nature, it was still read in the Byzantine Middle Ages.

FGrH 103. O. Andrei, *A. Claudius Charax di Pergamo* (1984).   A. J. S. S.

Claudius Cogidubnus, Tiberius (Cogidubnus), *client king of the British *Atrebates (2) *c.* AD 43–75. *Tacitus (*Agr.* 14) notes his loyalty, rewarded by rule over additional *civitates*. An inscription from Chichester dedicating a temple to *Neptune and *Minerva (*RIB* 91) records his title *Rex magnus Brit(anniae)*, 'Great King of Brit(ain)'. There are many signs of his successful philo-Roman policy. The Fishbourne villa may have been built for his old age. The *civitas Reg(i)norum* (see REG(I)NI) derives its name from his kingdom. See ROMANIZATION IN THE WEST.

J. E. Bogaers, *Britannia* 1979; S. S. Frere, *Britannia*, 3rd edn. (1987).   M. J. M.

Claudius (*RE* 123) **Crassus Inregillensis Sabinus, Appius,** was consul 471 BC. According to *Livy and *Dionysius (7) of Halicarnassus he was the leading member of the First *Decemvirate, which drew up the first ten of the *Twelve Tables. The story of the Second Decemvirate (450–449), when Claudius is said to have led a tyrannical regime, culminating in (1) his attempt to gain control of *Verginia; (2) the overthrow of the Decemvirate; and (3) the suicide of Claudius, should probably be rejected. The role ascribed to Claudius in Livy and Dionysius is part of the traditional picture of the innate violence and arrogance of the Claudii.

Cic. *Rep.* 2. 61–3; Livy 3. 33–58; Dion. Hal. *Ant. Rom.* 10. 54–11. 46. Ogilvie, *Comm. Livy 1–5*, 451–508, A. Drummond, *CAH* 7²/2 (1989), 227–30.   J. Br.

Claudius (*RE* 139; Suppl. 1) **Drusus, Nero,** second son of Ti. *Claudius Nero and *Livia Drusilla, younger brother of *Tiberius, later emperor, was born in 38 BC about the time of Livia's marriage to *Octavian (see *PIR*² D 857 for the circumstances); his *praenomen* was originally Decimus. After Ti. Nero's death in 33 he was brought up by Octavian. In 19 he was permitted to stand for magistracies five years before the legal ages, and in 18 was quaestor. In 15 BC with Tiberius he subdued the Raeti (see RAETIA) and *Vindelici, and established the later via Claudia Augusta over the Alps into Italy. In 13, left in charge of the Three Gauls, he organized a census and on 1 August 12 (or 10, Wells, p. 267) founded an altar to Rome and Augustus at *Lugdunum (1). Augustus entrusted the conquest of Germany to him, while Tiberius subdued the Balkans (12–9). His chief bases were on the

Claudius Etruscus

lower Rhine near Vechten, *Vetera, then *Mogontiacum. In 12, after routing the Usipetes and Sugambri, who had raided Gaul, he sailed along a canal dug for the purpose (Fossa Drusiana, probably the Vecht), through the lakes into the sea, won over the *Frisii, perhaps occupied Borkum at the mouth of the Ems, defeated the *Bructeri in a naval encounter upstream, and invaded the country of the *Chauci. His ships were stranded by the ebb tide but the Frisii helped him get away. He began the year 11 in Rome as urban praetor, then subdued the Usipetes, and after bridging the Lippe marched through the territory of the Sugambri and *Cherusci to the Weser; he left behind forts at *Aliso and among the *Chatti. After celebrating an *ovatio and receiving *ornamenta triumphalia he attacked the Chatti in 10 as proconsul, and returned to Rome with Augustus and Tiberius. In 9 as consul he fought the Chatti, *Suebic *Marcomanni, and Cherusci, and reached the Elbe; but died in camp after falling from his horse. Tiberius, hastening from *Ticinum, reached him before his death.

Drusus' conquests were extensive and well-garrisoned. (Florus' claim (2. 30. 26) of 50 forts on the Rhine alone has not been substantiated.) The senate bestowed on him and his descendants the surname of Germanicus; but the achievements in Germany were largely swept away with P. *Quinctilius Varus in AD 9. He was popular, and his views considered 'republican'; Tiberius disclosed to Augustus a letter expressing them. He was buried in Augustus' mausoleum; a cenotaph was built at Mogontiacum. An unknown poet wrote his mother the *Consolatio ad Liviam. His wife *Antonia (3) bore him *Germanicus—who, emulating his father, in AD 15–16 tried to recover Roman territory in Germany—*Livia Iulia, and *Claudius.

L. Schmitt, *Gesch. d. deutschen Stämme* 1, 2nd edn. (1938), 93 ff.; K. Christ, *Drusus und Germanicus* (1956); C. Wells, *The German Policy of Augustus* (1972), see index. Portraiture: L. Fabbrini, *BA* 1964, 304 ff.
A. M.; T. J. Ca.; B. M. L.

Claudius (*RE* 143) **Etruscus**, the wealthy son of Tiberius *Claudius and (Tettia?) Etrusca, possibly nephew of *Domitian's general L. Tettius Iulianus (consul 83), was probably made a knight by *Vespasian. He obtained from Domitian the recall of his exiled father. Martial 7. 40 and Statius' *Silvae* 3. 3 are addressed to him on the occasion of his father's death (he was patron of both; see PATRONAGE, LITERARY, LATIN).

S. Gsell, *Essai sur le règne de l'empereur Domitien* (1894), 219 ff.; P. Weaver, *CQ* 1965, 150 f.; B. W. Jones, *The Emperor Domitian* (1992), see index.
A. M.; B. M. L.

Claudius (*RE* 82) **(II) Gothicus, Marcus Aurelius,** emperor AD 268–70. An equestrian cavalry-general of modest Danubian stock, he owed his position to *Gallienus' encouragement of men of talent, but was probably involved in the plot that overthrew his patron, and made him emperor (late summer 268). He consolidated his rule by winning the support of both the ordinary troops and the senate—despite their quite different reactions to Gallienus' death and deification—by ridding himself of the usurper *Aureolus, and by routing Germanic raiders in northern Italy.

Indeed, Claudius' main concern was defence, and here he initially continued Gallienus' tactics, leaving the east to *Palmyra and the Rhine to the Gallic empire, while himself concentrating on expelling the *Goths from the Balkans. In this he was remarkably successful. His victory at *Naissus in 269 contributed significantly to removing the main Gothic threat for over a century: it is hardly surprising that *Constantine I later claimed him as an ancestor. On the other hand, his next move would surely have

been to reverse Gallienus' policy of *laissez-faire*, and attack either the Gallic empire (under *Victorinus, less predictable) or Palmyra (under *Zenobia, looking covetously at Egypt). However, before he could act he died of the plague in Sirmium (late summer 270).

PLRE 1. 209; P. Damerau, *Kaiser Claudius II Goticus* (1934); R. Syme, *Emperors and Biography* (1971), 209 ff.; H. Wolfram, *History of the Goths* (1988), 54 f.
J. F. D.

Claudius Mamertinus was the author of a speech delivered on 1 January AD 362 in *Constantinople, thanking the emperor *Julian for the gift of the consulship. Though highly eulogistic, his work is useful in reconstructing and assessing Julian's time as Caesar. He was disgraced in 368.

PLRE 1. 540 f.; E. Gallétier, *Panégyriques latins* 3 (1955).
J. F. Dr.

Claudius (*RE* 216) **Marcellus** (1), **Gaius,** first cousin of M. *Claudius Marcellus (4), was consul 50 BC. Frustrated in his efforts to procure *Caesar's recall, he called on *Pompey to take command of the two legions stationed at *Capua and to raise more troops (2 December). After the outbreak of war, however, he remained in Italy and obtained Caesar's pardon. He took no part in the dissensions of 44–42 and died in 40. By his wife *Octavia (2) he had three children, M. *Claudius Marcellus (5) and two daughters: the elder Marcella married, c.28 BC, M. *Vipsanius Agrippa and, after being divorced by him in 21, Iullus *Antonius; the younger Marcella, born in 40, was married to M. Valerius Messalla Appianus (consul 12 BC) and then to Paullus *Aemilius Lepidus.

Syme, *Rom. Rev.*, see index, and *AA* 147 ff.
G. W. R.; T. J. C.; R. J. S.

Claudius (*RE* 217) **Marcellus** (2), **Gaius,** brother of M. *Claudius Marcellus (4), was consul 49 BC. He supported *Pompey and crossed over to Greece with him; in 48 he was joint commander of the Rhodian section of his fleet. He probably died before the battle of *Pharsalus.
T. J. C.; R. J. S.

Claudius (*RE* 220) **Marcellus** (1), **Marcus,** one of Rome's most outstanding commanders, served in the First *Punic War, and at unknown dates thereafter became an augur, curule aedile, and praetor. As consul in 222 BC he campaigned successfully against the Insubrian Gauls, relieving Clastidium (mod. Casteggio) and winning the *spolia opima (spoils of honour) by killing the Gallic chief in single combat; with his colleague Cn. *Cornelius Scipio Calvus he captured *Mediolanum (Milan); he celebrated a triumph. Marcellus played an important part in the Hannibalic War; he supported the fundamental Fabian strategy (see FABIUS MAXIMUS VERRUCOSUS, Q.), but showed more initiative than Fabius in his willingness to engage *Hannibal when a favourable opportunity arose. He held a second praetorship in 216, successfully resisting Hannibal's attack on *Nola. He was elected suffect consul in 215, but abdicated when the augurs declared that his election had been faulty. Since he was replaced by Fabius and became consul the following year, it may be that he accepted his removal from office on the assurance of Fabius' support for 214. In both 215, when he received proconsular command, and in 214 he continued to resist Hannibal's attempts to take *Nola, and in the latter year he and Fabius captured *Casilinum. In the autumn of 214 he was appointed to command in Sicily, and in 213 began the siege of *Syracuse, which he captured in 212. Marcellus' treatment of the city was harsh, and he indulged his taste for Greek culture by carrying off to Rome large numbers of works of art (see BOOTY). After mopping-up operations against Carthaginian forces based at *Acragas (Agrigento) (211), he returned to Rome and celebrated an *ovatio* (minor triumph). As consul in 210 and proconsul in 209 he was eager to bring Hannibal to a fixed battle; when he succeeded, he was defeated. In 208, consul yet again, he and his colleague T. Quinctius Crispinus were aiming to recapture *Locri Epizephyrii, but were caught in an ambush near Venusia (Venosa); Marcellus was killed immediately and Crispinus fatally wounded.

J. Briscoe, *CAH* 8² (1989), 50, 53–5, 61–2, 70–1, 78.   J. Br.

Claudius (*RE* 222) **Marcellus** (2), **Marcus,** son of M. *Claudius Marcellus (1), tribune 204 BC (when he was sent with others to investigate the charges against *Scipio Africanus and Q. *Pleminius), curule aedile 200, and praetor in Sicily 198. Consul 196, he was defeated by the Boii, but defeated the Insubres near *Comum; the order of the two battles is uncertain. In 193 he served as legate in northern Italy under the consul L. Cornelius Merula; he sent letters to Rome criticizing Merula's conduct. In 189 he was *censor with *Flamininus; they restored citizen rights to the Campanians, perhaps giving them the right to vote. He was pontifex from 196 to his death in 177, when he was succeeded by his son.

Briscoe, *Comm.* 31–33, 318–19; M. Frederiksen, *Campania* (1984), 249–50.   J. Br.

Claudius (*RE* 225) **Marcellus** (3), **Marcus,** succeeded his father (M. *Claudius Marcellus (2)) as a *pontifex in 177 BC. As tribune of the *plebs in 171 he did not support veteran centurions who were appealing against being conscripted for the war with *Perseus (2), while as praetor in 169 he and a colleague took over the levy from the consuls; he governed both Hither and Further Spain, with command prorogued in 168. He was consul in 166 and 155, triumphing in both years for victories in northern Italy. In 152 he became the first man since the Hannibalic War (see PUNIC WARS) to hold a third consulship, doubtless because his military experience was needed for the war in Hither Spain. After military successes Marcellus recommended a negotiated peace on the terms established by Ti. *Sempronius Gracchus (2) in 179. The senate rejected this and voted for the war to continue. *Scipio Aemilianus supported the majority view, which accounts for the hostile attitude to Marcellus taken by *Polybius (1). Marcellus was drowned while on an embassy to *Masinissa.

Astin, *Scipio* 38–40; Walbank, *HCP* 3. 642–7.   J. Br.

Claudius (*RE* 229) **Marcellus** (4), **Marcus,** consul 51 BC, proposed a motion, declared illegal by the Caesarians, probably to recall *Caesar on 1 March 50. Pompey resisted this, but in October Marcellus carried various resolutions which, though some were vetoed, ensured that the question would be discussed on the ensuing 1 March. He also declared invalid the *lex Vatinia* authorizing Caesar to found a colony at Novum Comum, and had a citizen of *Comum flogged to prove that he did not consider him a Roman. Marcellus took no active part in the Civil War and after *Pharsalus retired to *Mytilene, but in September 46 Caesar allowed his return; *Cicero in gratitude delivered the *Pro Marcello.* But in May 45 Marcellus was murdered at *Piraeus near Athens, and Caesar, unjustly according to Cicero, was suspected of complicity (*Att.* 10. 1. 3).

E. G. Hardy, *Some Problems in Roman History* (1924) 126 ff.; Gruen, *LGRR* 460 ff. (and see index).   G. E. F. C.; R. J. S.

Claudius (*RE* 230) **Marcellus** (5), **Marcus,** son of C. *Claudius Marcellus (1) and of *Octavia (2), sister of *Augustus, was born in 42 BC. His betrothal in 39 to a daughter of Sextus *Pompeius

Magnus was brief. In 25 he and *Tiberius served in Spain under Augustus, whose preference for Marcellus was shown by Marcellus' marriage in the same year to *Iulia (3); and in 24 a more rapid anticipation of the normal *cursus honorum* was decreed for Marcellus than for Tiberius. In 23, as aedile, Marcellus gave exceptionally magnificent games. He began to be thought of as a rival to *Agrippa for the position of heir to the monarchy, and his ambition gave cause for concern (Plin. *HN* 7. 149), but he died late in 23. He was buried in Augustus' own mausoleum; Octavia named a library after him and Augustus a theatre. His death was lamented by Virgil (*Aen.* 6. 860–86) and Propertius (3. 18).

Syme, *Rom. Rev.,* see index. Library and theatre: Platner–Ashby 84 f., 513 ff.; Nash, *Pict. Dict. Rome* 2. 254 ff., 418 ff. Portraiture: V. H. Poulsen, *Acta archaeologica* 1946, 12, 22 ff.; L. Fabbrini, *Arch. Class.* 1961, 152 ff.   A. M.; T. J. Ca.; E. B.

Claudius Marcellus Aeserninus, Marcus, senator (praetor AD 19) and distinguished orator in the same class (so Tac. *Ann.* 11. 6) as his maternal grandfather, C. *Asinius Pollio, and M. *Valerius Messal(l)a Corvinus.

PIR² C 928.   A. J. S. S.

Claudius Maximus, Stoic senator and mentor of Marcus *Aurelius, was governor of Upper Pannonia from AD 150–4 and proconsul of Africa at the end of the 150s, in this capacity presiding over the trial at Oea (Tripoli) of *Apuleius, who addressed him as 'a man of austere principles and long military service'. M. Aurelius paid him a lengthy tribute in his *Meditations.*

PIR² C 933–4. Apul. *Apol.;* M. Aur. *Med.;* SHA, *M. Ant.*   A. R. Bi.

Claudius (*RE* 246) **Nero, Gaius,** served under M. *Claudius Marcellus (1) at Nola in 214 BC, and took part in the siege of Capua as praetor and propraetor (212/11). He was sent to Spain after the deaths of Cn. *Cornelius Scipio Calvus and P. *Cornelius Scipio (1), and succeeded in holding the situation until the arrival of *Scipio Africanus (211/0). He again served under Marcellus, at *Canusium in 209, and became consul 207 with M. *Livius Salinator, previously his enemy. He was appointed to face *Hannibal in the south, but when the messengers sent by *Hasdrubal (2) to Hannibal were intercepted, Nero took the bold decision to march rapidly north with part of his forces. The consuls defeated Hasdrubal at the *Metaurus, and Nero returned south immediately, announcing the victory by throwing Hasdrubal's head in front of Hannibal's outposts. In 204 Nero and Livius were censors, and their old enmity was renewed. In 201/0 he was one of the three ambassadors sent to the east before the Second Macedonian War.

Walbank, *HCP* 2. 267–74; J. Briscoe, *CAH* 8² (1989), 55, 59, 72.   J. Br.

Claudius (*RE* 254) **Nero, Tiberius,** *Cicero's choice for the hand of *Tullia (2) in 50 BC, was quaestor 48 and commanded *Caesar's fleet in the Alexandrian War (see BELLUM ALEXANDRINUM). In 46 he was entrusted with the settlement of veterans in Narbonese Gaul (see GAUL (TRANSALPINE)). In 44, however, he proposed that Caesar's murderers should be rewarded. Praetor 41, he supported L. *Antonius (Pietas) against *Octavian, and took part in the defence of *Perusia. Early in 40 he escaped, attempted in vain to procure a slave-rising in *Campania, and joined Sextus *Pompeius in Sicily with his wife *Livia Drusilla and infant son *Tiberius, the future emperor. Later, disagreeing with Sextus, he joined Antony in Greece, and returned to Rome after the Pact of Misenum (39). In January 38

Octavian persuaded him to divorce Livia so that he might marry her himself. His second son Nero *Claudius Drusus was born three months after the marriage. Nero died in 33.

Syme, *Rom. Rev.*, see index; W. Suerbaum, *Chiron* 1980, 337 ff.

T. J. C.; R. J. S.

Claudius (*RE* 282) **Pompeianus, Tiberius,** from *Antioch (1) in Syria, of equestrian origin, had a brilliant senatorial career; as governor of Lower *Pannonia (AD 167) he confronted the first barbarian invasions that developed into the Marcomannic War (see MARCOMA(N)NNI). Late in 169 he became M. *Aurelius' son-in-law, marrying *Annia Aurelia Galeria Lucilla, widow of L. *Verus. He played a major role throughout the Marcomannic War, clearing the invaders from Italy in 170 and serving on Marcus' staff; he was consul for the second time (as *ordinarius*) in 173, with another son-in-law of Marcus as colleague. Marcus had intended him to act as adviser to *Commodus but at latest in 182, after Lucilla's involvement in a conspiracy against Commodus, he retired from public life, pleading poor eyesight; but was in Rome when Commodus was murdered, rejecting appeals from both P. *Helvius Pertinax (his former protégé) and M. *Didius Severus Iulianus to accept or share the imperial position. His son by Lucilla, Aurelius Commodus Pompeianus, was ordinary consul 209, a presumed grandson ordinary consul 231.

PIR[2] C 973. Cass. Dio 71–2; Hdn. 1; SHA *M. Ant., Comm., Pertinax, Did. Iul.* A. R. Birley, *Marcus Aurelius*, 2nd edn. (1987).

A. R. Bi.

Claudius (*RE* 295) **Pulcher** (1), **Appius,** as consul 143 BC with difficulty defeated the *Salassi and, against the will of the senate, triumphed, protected against a *veto by his daughter who was a Vestal (see VESTA). Censor 136, he became *princeps senatus* and a leading statesman. An enemy of P. *Cornelius Scipio Aemilianus, he married a daughter to Ti. *Sempronius Gracchus (3), advised Tiberius during his tribunate and served on his agrarian commission until his own death (*c*.130). The suggestion that he was the subject of *ILS* 23 (see P. *Popillius Laenas) seems unlikely. (Accepted *CIL* 1[2]. 4 (1986), p. 923.)

Astin, *Scipio*, see index.

E. B.

Claudius (*RE* 296) **Pulcher** (2), **Appius,** son of (1), as praetor (89 or 88 BC) enrolled some foreigners enfranchised under the *lex Plautia Papiria* (see PLAUTIUS SILVANUS (1), M.). An enemy of L. *Cornelius Cinna (1), he left Rome in 87, was outlawed (see MARCIUS PHILIPPUS (1), L.) and struck off the senate list. He returned with *Sulla and, as consul 79, was assigned Macedonia. There, perhaps after being *interrex* (77), he won some victories despite illness, but died 76. He was the father of P. *Clodius Pulcher.

E. B.

Claudius (*RE* 297) **Pulcher** (3), **Appius,** eldest son of (2), served in the east under his brother-in-law L. *Licinius Lucullus (2) in 72–70 BC. As praetor 57 he supported his brother P. *Clodius Pulcher; from 56 to 55 he was governor of *Sardinia. Consul 54, he joined his colleague L. *Domitius Ahenobarbus (1) in a scandalous electoral compact with C. *Memmius (2) and Cn. *Domitius Calvinus, candidates for 53. After governing Cilicia (53–51) he was prosecuted by P. *Cornelius Dolabella (1) for *maiestas as a result of alleged misconduct in Cilicia, and for *ambitus in connection with his candidature for the censorship; but helped by *Pompey, *Brutus, and others he was acquitted on both counts and became censor (50) with L. *Calpurnius Piso (2), in which office he was severe (see CENSOR). In 49 he followed Pompey, and died in Greece early in 48. He wrote a work on

augural discipline dedicated to *Cicero, whose attitude towards this arrogant and unprincipled but influential aristocrat was understandably mixed (cf. e.g. *Fam.* 2. 13. 2). His wife was, it seems, a Servilia of the Caepio family and his daughters married Cn. *Pompeius Magnus (2) and Brutus.

Cic. *Fam.* 3. L. A. Constans, *Un correspondant de Cicéron, Ap. Claudius Pulcher* (1921); Syme, *Rom. Rev.*, see index.

T. J. C.; R. J. S.

Claudius (*RE* 300) **Pulcher, Gaius,** was an augur (see AUGURES) from 195 BC and praetor in 180, when he investigated an outbreak of poisoning. Consul in 177, he carried a law repatriating Latins (see LATINI) who, or whose parents, had come to Rome after 189. He was assigned the command in *Istria (2), but attempted to take over the army there without having performed the normal religious rites in Rome. His predecessors refused to recognize his authority, and he was forced to return to Rome to carry out the formalities. He then completed the war, crushed a Ligurian revolt, and returned to Rome to celebrate a triumph. He was, however, obliged to return to northern Italy in order to recapture *Mutina (mod. Modena), which had been occupied by the Ligurians. Censor in 169, he and his colleague Ti. *Sempronius Gracchus (2) assisted the levy for the war against *Perseus (2). The *censors reviewed the *equites and allotted contracts with such severity that Claudius was prosecuted for *perduellio (treason) and nearly convicted. In 168 he initially opposed, but eventually agreed to Gracchus' proposal to restrict freedmen to one urban tribe (*tribus). In 167 he was one of the commissioners who administered the settlement after the defeat of Perseus, and died soon afterwards.

J. Briscoe, *JRS* 1964, 76.

J. Br.

Claudius (*RE* 304) **Pulcher, Publius,** was consul 249 BC, when he attacked the Carthaginian fleet at Drepana and suffered a major defeat, losing 93 out of 123 ships. According to later writers (but not Polybius (1)) the defeat was the result of his contempt for the auspices (see AUSPICIUM): when told that the sacred chickens would not eat, he ordered them to be thrown into the sea 'so that they might drink'. On his return he was prosecuted, acquitted on a charge of *perduellio, but heavily fined.

Polyb. 1. 49–52. Walbank, *HCP* 1. 113–15.

J. Br.

Claudius (*RE* 308) **Quadrigarius, Quintus,** Roman annalist of the immediate post-Sullan period, wrote a history of Rome in at least 23 books, from the Gallic sack to his own times. The latest date preserved is 82 BC, the latest book 23. If he is the Claudius who translated C. *Acilius (Livy 25. 39. 12; 35. 14. 5), he presumably adapted the senatorial historian's material to his own annalistic form; the 'Examination of Chronology' by 'Clodius' (Plut. *Num.* 1) is scarcely his. He may have used rhetorical methods of narrative elaboration. This, however, was probably not exaggerated, as by *Valerius Antias. Claudius' style, as the fragments show, was simple, his vocabulary plain, with an archaic grace (Gellius 9. 13; 15. 1; 13. 29 (28)). He ranks with Valerius Antias as the leading annalist before *Livy, and Livy used him. See ANNALS, ANNALISTS.

Peter, *HRRel.* 1[2]. cclxxxv, 205; M. Gelzer, *Kl. Schr.* 3 (1964), 221 ff.; M. Zimmerer, *Der Annalist Q. Claudius Quadrigarius* (1937).

A. H. McD.; R. J. S.

Claudius Subatianus Aquila, Tiberius, from *Cuicul in *Numidia, was the first prefect of the new Severan province of *Mesopotamia, annexed in AD 197. He was prefect of *Egypt AD 206–11, and in this capacity persecuted Christians, according to *Eusebius (who, however, dates his governorship earlier).

Euseb. *Hist. Eccl.* 6. 3. 3; *AE* 1979, 625; *RE*, Suppl. 15 (1978), 569 f.

A. R. Bi.

Claudius Thrasyllus (*RE* 7), **Tiberius**, of *Alexandria (1), astrologer (d. AD 36), owed his great reputation to the emperor *Tiberius, who, meeting him in *Rhodes, brought him to Rome, trusted his predictions, and made him a Roman citizen. Thrasyllus produced a distinguished family, including his astrologer son Ti. *Claudius Balbillus. His interests were wide, including music (he wrote Περὶ τῶν ἑπτὰ τόνων, ('On the seven tones') and philosophy (the division of *Plato (1)'s dialogues into tetralogies is ascribed to him). He is frequently cited by *Vettius Valens and other astrologers. See ASTROLOGY.

For extracts from his epitomized work(s) on astrology see Συγκεφαλαίωσις τοῦ πρὸς Ἱεροκλέα Θρασύλλου πίνακος: CCAG 8. 3. 99 ff. Biography: F. Cramer, *Astrology in Roman Law and Politics* (1954), 92 ff.; W. and H. G. Gundel, *Astrologumena* (1966), 148 ff. (see 151 for his family stemma).

G. J. T.

clavus angustus, latus The *angustus clavus* was a narrow, the *latus clavus* a broad, purple upright stripe (possibly two stripes) stitched to or woven into the Roman *tunica*. The former indicated equestrian, the latter senatorial rank. Under the emperors the *latus clavus* was worn before admission to the senate, on the assumption of the *toga virilis*, by sons of senators as a right (see TOGA). The *latus clavus* could also be granted by emperors to men of non-senatorial origin; the award of the *latus clavus* gave such men the right to stand for senatorial office (so the future emperor Septimius Severus arrived at Rome at the age of 17 and successfully petitioned Marcus Aurelius for the *latus clavus*). Military tribunes (*tribuni militum*) in the legions were distinguished as *tribuni angusticlavii* or *tribuni laticlavii* according to whether they were pursuing an equestrian or senatorial career.

Millar, *ERW*, ch. 6.

G. P. B.

Clazomenae (mod. Klazumen), one of the twelve cities of the *Panionium, situated on the south shore of the gulf of Smyrna on a small island joined to the mainland by a causeway. The original settlement was on the mainland, where large numbers of the terracotta *sarcophagi peculiar to Clazomenae have been found. The move to the island came 'from fear of the Persians' (Paus. 7. 3. 9), apparently at the time of the *Ionian Revolt (500–494 BC). About 600 BC Clazomenae successfully repulsed an attack by the Lydians under *Alyattes, but later fell to *Croesus. In the *Delian League the city was at first assessed at one and a half talents, but during the *Peloponnesian War this was raised to six and even to fifteen talents; the reason for this is uncertain. By the *King's Peace (386 BC) Clazomenae came under Persian rule, which ended with *Alexander (3) the Great. Clazomenae continued to function as a *polis* through the Hellenistic and imperial periods. Distinguished Clazomenian philosophers were *Anaxagoras and *Scopelianus.

Little remains of the ancient monuments, apart from public and private inscriptions, except for part of the original wall of the island site and remains of the harbour.

G. E. Bean, *Aegean Turkey* (1980), 128 f.

G. E. B.; S. S.-W.

Cleanthes of Assos (331–232 BC), student of *Zeno (2) and his successor as head of the Stoa (see STOICISM). His religious spirit is distinctive; after the writings of *Chrysippus established a Stoic orthodoxy, this came to seem less central. We have a long fragment of his *Hymn to Zeus*, which allegorizes the active principle

of Stoic physics and displays a distinctive use of Heraclitean ideas (see HERACLITUS). He was interested in the detail of Stoic physics, and wrote on the nature of the cosmos, stressing the role of *fire. His version of ethics uncompromisingly stressed the distinctive value of virtue and downplayed the importance of factors like pleasure. He denied the usefulness of moral rules unless based on an understanding of basic principles, and even in consolatory writings urged the importance of understanding general principles, rather than their applications.

Testimonia in von Arnim, *SVF* 1. 103–39; Diog. Laert. 7. 168–76.

J. A.

Clearchus (1) (*c.*450–401 BC), Spartan officer. *Proxenos of *Byzantium, he held various commands, there and elsewhere, from 411 onwards. At Byzantium again in 403, he made himself tyrant, but was ejected by Spartan forces. He joined *Cyrus (2) the Younger, for whom he commanded the Greek *mercenaries in the attempt at the Persian throne. At the battle of *Cunaxa Clearchus' reluctance to expose his right flank permitted the decisive Persian cavalry charge. He subsequently held his troops together, but was arrested with his fellow officers at a conference with *Tissaphernes and executed by *Artaxerxes (2) II.

RE 11. 575–7, 'Klearchos' 3; *PB* no. 425.

S. J. Ho.

Clearchus (2), Middle *Comedy poet, won at least one victory at the *Lenaea *c.*335–330 BC (*IG* 2². 2325. 154). We have three titles and five citations.

Kassel–Austin, *PCG* 4. 79 ff. (*CAF* 2. 408 ff.).

K. J. D.

Clearchus (3) (*RE* 11) of Soli in *Cyprus, pupil of *Aristotle, Greek polymath. His writings included 'Lives' (not 'biographies', but 'ways of life' of various peoples), an encomium on *Plato (1) and a discussion of the mathematical passages in the *Republic*, zoological and mystical works, and collections of proverbs and *riddles. He travelled as far as *Bactria, where he erected a stele with his transcription of some 150 'Delphic maxims'. His works were full of learned curiosities, and showed a notable interest in eastern peoples; attacks on luxury fit the *Peripatetic background, but his enthusiasm for Plato was less typical. See also CINEAS (1).

L. Robert, *CRAcad. Inscr.* 1968, 416–57 (= *Opera Minora Selecta* 5 (1989), 510–51). Fragments in F. Wehrli, *Klearchos* (1948).

C. B. R. P.

Cledonius (5th cent. AD), grammarian of senatorial rank at Constantinople, where he wrote a treatise (Keil, *Gramm. Lat.* 5. 9–79) on the *Ars minor* and *Ars maior* of Aelius *Donatus (1). The work survives only in a lacunose and interpolated copy from the 6th or 7th cent. (E. A. Lowe (ed.) *Codices Latini Antiquiores* 11 vols. (1934–1971) 7. 864).

PLRE 2. 302; Herzog–Schmidt, § 702.

R. A. K.

Cleidemus, or **Cleitodemus** (fl. between 378 and 340 BC), expert in ceremonial ritual (*exēgētēs*), was considered in antiquity the first atthidographer (Paus. 10. 15. 5); see ATTHIS. His work was probably titled *Prōtogonia*. It comprised no more than four books. We have 25 fragments. Those from the first two books concern the mythical period to 683/2; the two from book three are on *Cleisthenes (2); the remainder continue the account to the *Peloponnesian War (fr. 10) and perhaps further. Like other atthidographers he wrote with a democratic and patriotic bias. His work was cited by *Plutarch (frs. 17, 18, 21, 22) and probably known to *Aristotle, but for the historical period was displaced by *Androtion's *Atthis*.

FGrH 323; J. McInerny, *Cl. Ant.* 1994, 17 ff.

P. E. H.

Cleisthenes

Cleisthenes (1), of *Sicyon, the greatest tyrant of the family of Orthagoras, which ruled for the record period of a century (probably *c.*665–565 BC). His reign (*c.*600–570) was allegedly marked by a movement against the Argive *Dorian ascendancy (see ARGOS (2)): the three traditional Dorian tribes (*phylai*) were given derogatory names while the non-Dorian was called *Archelaoi* ('ruling people'); Argive *rhapsodes were suppressed, an Argive hero was replaced by a Theban (see THEBES (1)), and a new festival of *Dionysus was established. His daughter Agariste (mother of the Athenian *Cleisthenes (2)) married the *Alcmaeonid *Megacles after a year-long house party for her suitors. In the First *Sacred War Cleisthenes was prominent on the winning side while neighbouring *Corinth was on the losing: he destroyed *Crisa, and won the chariot-race in the first *Pythian Games.

> Hdt. 6. 126–30; Arist. *Pol.* 1315ᵇ; Nicolaus of Damascus, *FGrH* 90 F 61; A. Andrewes, *The Greek Tyrants* (1956); H. Berve, *Die Tyrannis bei den Griechen* (1967); C. Mossé, *La Tyrannie dans la Grèce antique* (1969); A. Griffin, *Sikyon* (1982).   P. N. U.; P. J. R., R. T.

Cleisthenes (2), Athenian politician, of the *Alcmaeonid family, son of *Megacles and Agariste, daughter of *Cleisthenes (1) of *Sicyon. He was archon under the tyrant *Hippias (1) in 525/4 BC, but later in Hippias' reign the Alcmaeonids went into exile and put pressure on Sparta through the *Delphic oracle to intervene in Athens and overthrow the tyranny. In the power vacuum which followed, Cleisthenes and Isagoras were rivals for supremacy; Isagoras obtained the archonship (see ARCHONTES) for 508/7; but Cleisthenes appealed for popular support with a programme of reform. Isagoras appealed to King *Cleomenes (1) I of Sparta, who came to Athens with a small force, invoked the hereditary curse of the Alcmaeonids, and forced Cleisthenes and others to withdraw; but he met with strong popular resistance and was forced to withdraw in turn, taking Isagoras with him. Cleisthenes returned, and his reforms were enacted and put into effect.

Cleisthenes' main achievement was a new organization of the citizen body. The four *Ionian tribes (*phylai*) and other older units were left in existence but deprived of political significance. For the future each citizen was to be a member of one of 139 local units called *demes (*demoi*, see DEMOS), and the demes were grouped to form 30 new *trittyes ('thirds') and 10 new *phylai*; citizenship and the political and military organization of Attica were to be based on these units (e.g. *Solon's council, *boulē, of 400 became a council of 500, with 50 members from each tribe and individual demes acting as constituencies). The main purpose of the reform was probably to undermine the old channels of influence (and perhaps to give the Alcmaeonids an advantageous position in the new system); its main appeal to the ordinary citizens was perhaps the provision of political machinery at local level; and working this machinery educated the citizens towards democracy. (See DEMOCRACY, ATHENIAN.) The institution of *ostracism is almost certainly to be attributed to Cleisthenes.

In the 5th cent. Cleisthenes came to be regarded as the founder of the democracy, but in the political disputes at the end of the century the democrats looked further back, to Solon or even to *Theseus.

> PA 8526; APF 375–6. C. W. J. Eliot, *Coastal Demes of Attika* (1962); D. M. Lewis, *Hist.* 1963, 22–40; M. Ostwald, *Nomos and the Beginnings of the Athenian Democracy* (1969); J. S. Traill, *The Political Organization of Attica*, *Hesp.* Suppl. 14 (1975); P. Siewert, *Die Trittyen Attikas und die Heeresreform des Kleisthenes* (1982).   T. J. C.; P. J. R.

Cleitarchus, of (?) *Alexandria (1), son of the historian *Dinon and historian of *Alexander (3) the Great. His work, comprising at least twelve books, achieved great popularity and was apparently the model for the Roman historian, L. *Cornelius Sisenna. Its date is disputed (largely on the basis of a passing reference to a Roman embassy to Alexander); but it was most probably early (*c.*310 BC) and derived from firsthand information. Ancient critics denounced it as pretentious in style and unreliable in content, but little can be deduced from the few extant fragments. More important is the fact that Cleitarchus was the source of the so-called 'vulgate tradition' (the numerous passages of *Diodorus (3) Siculus, Q. *Curtius Rufus, *Justin, and the Metz Epitome which transmit the same information). This common tradition supplements and sometimes corrects the court-based account of *Arrian, notably in the vivid reports of the sieges of *Halicarnassus and *Tyre and the detailed narrative of operations in central Asia. There was a propensity for scenes of slaughter and suffering, perhaps exaggerated but revealing more sensitivity to the human cost of conquest than Arrian's somewhat sanitized account.

> *FGrH* 137; Pearson, *Lost Histories of Alexander*, ch. 8; J. R. Hamilton, in K. Kinzl (ed.), *Greece and the East Mediterranean* (1977), 126 ff.; N. G. L. Hammond, *Three Historians of Alexander the Great* (1983).   A. B. B.

Cleitus (1) 'the Black' (d. 328 BC), Macedonian noble and brother of the wet-nurse of *Alexander (3) the Great, commanded the royal Squadron of Companions (see HETAIROI) and saved Alexander's life at the *Granicus. In 330 he was raised to the command of the entire Macedonian cavalry alongside the royal favourite, *Hephaestion (1). Alienated by the absolutist trends at court, he lost control at a symposium (at *Marakanda (Samarkand) in summer 328), criticizing the king's divine aspirations and the fashionable denigration of *Philip (1) II, and was struck down by Alexander in a paroxysm of drunken fury. The murder became a standard example of royal immoderation in rhetoric and popular philosophy (see ALCOHOLISM).

> Berve, *Alexanderreich* 2, no. 427; Heckel, *Marshals* 34 ff.   A. B. B.

Cleitus (2) 'the White' (d. 318 BC), Macedonian officer, held senior infantry and cavalry commands under *Alexander (3) the Great (from 327) and returned to the west with *Craterus (1) and the veterans of Opis (324). As Craterus' admiral he won two (?) naval victories which sealed Athens' fate in the *Lamian War (322), and was rewarded for his continued loyalty in the war against *Perdiccas (3) (Justin falsely implies that he defected) with the satrapy of *Lydia (321). Expelled by *Antigonus (1) I (319/18), he assumed command of the fleet which *Polyperchon sent to check Antigonus' ambitions in the *Propontis. Initially successful, he was surprised and crushingly defeated by Antigonus. He died alone in *Thrace.

> Heckel, *Marshals* 185 ff.   A. B. B.

Clement of Alexandria (Titus Flavius Clemens) was born *c.* AD 150, probably at Athens and of pagan parents. He was converted to *Christianity and after extensive travels to seek instruction from Christian teachers received lessons from Pantaenus, whose catechetical school in *Alexandria (1) was then an unofficial institution giving tuition to converts. Clement affects a wide acquaintance with Greek literature, since his writings abound in quotations from *Homer, *Hesiod, the dramatists, and the Platonic and Stoic philosophers (see PLATO (1); STOICISM). However, comparison with ps.-Justin's *De monarchia* and *Cohortatio ad Graecos* shows that he made much use of florilegia.

His *Protrepticus* is a copious source of information about the Greek *mysteries, though his wish to represent them as a perversion of Scriptural teachings must have led to misrepresentation. After ordination he succeeded Pantaenus as head of the school some time before 200, and held the office till 202, when, on the eve of the persecution under *Septimius Severus, he left Alexandria and took refuge, perhaps with his former pupil Alexander, then bishop of *Cappadocia and later of Jerusalem. Clement died between 211 and 216.

Much of his writing is lost, but the following survive nearly complete: (1) The *Protrepticus* or 'Hortatory Address to the Greeks' (*c*.190), designed to prove the superiority of Christianity to pagan cults and way of life. (2) The *Paedagogus* or 'Tutor' (*c*.190–2), an exposition of the moral teaching of Christ, not only in general, but also with application to such details as eating, drinking, dress, and use of wealth. (3) The *Stromateis* or 'Miscellanies' (probably *c*.200–2) in eight books, the first seven attempting a construction of Christian philosophy with its centre in Christ the *logos* and the word of Scripture; book 5. 9, with its justification of allegory as a way of saying what cannot be spoken, points the way to negative theology; the eighth book is a fragment on logic. (4) The *Excerpta ex Theodoto*, which follow in one MS, is a collection of dicta by a Valentinian heretic, of whom Clement, who calls himself a Gnostic, seems not to disapprove (see GNOSTICISM). (5) *Eclogae propheticae* are also attached to this MS. (6) The *Quis dives salvetur?* is a homily urging detachment from (though not necessarily renunciation of) worldly goods. (7) The fragments of the *Hypotyposeis* ('Sketches') suggest an exegetical work consisting mainly of notes on passages from Scripture. Clement added little to dogma, but his philosophy points the way to *Origen (1), and, as in the case of the latter, prevented his being regarded as a saint.

TEXTS O. Staehlin, 4 vols (1905–36); *Exc. ex Theod.* R. P. Casey (1934), F. W. Sagnard (1947).

GENERAL LITERATURE C. Bigg, *The Christian Platonists of Alexandria* (1886; rev. 1913); H. Chadwick, *Early Christianity and the Classical Tradition* (1966); S. Lilla, *Clement of Alexandria* (1971); D. Dawson, *Allegorical Readers and Cultural Revision* (1991). M. J. E.

Clement of Rome, author of an epistle (*c*. AD 96) from the Roman Church, rebuking the Corinthian Church for arbitrarily deposing clergy. This letter is remarkable, in a largely pacifist Church, for its use of martial imagery. Clement has been identified improbably with *Flavius Clemens and more probably with Peter's successor as bishop of Rome. The *Clementina* say that he is of Caesar's household, but associate neither him nor Peter with Rome.

The chief of the numerous works attributed to him are (1) the *Second Epistle*, a mid-2nd-cent. sermon on virginity of uncertain origin; (2) *Apostolic Constitutions*, eight books of law and liturgy, *c*.375, of which the seventh contains Hellenistic–Jewish prayers; and (3) the *Clementine Romance*, which combines an apologetic dialogue featuring Clement as the adversary of *Apion with an account of Peter's legendary encounter with Simon Magus. The plot which brings the two together substitutes domestic separation and reunion for the erotic stereotypes of pagan novels. This romance survives in two 4th-cent. recensions of divergent character: the *Homilies* in Greek and the *Recognitions* in Syriac and Rufinus (2)'s Latin. Neither fully represents the original, which appeared between the 2nd and 4th cents.

Epistles, ed. and annotated by J. B. Lightfoot (1890). B. Altaner, *Patrology* (1960), 90 ff. *Clementina*, ed. B. Rehm (1965, 1975). H. C.; M. J. E.

Cleobis and **Biton,** the two Argive brothers (see ARGOS (2)) mentioned by *Solon to *Croesus, in *Herodotus' story (1. 31), as among the happiest of mortals. Their mother, presumably as *Cicero says (*Tusc.* 1. 47), a priestess of *Hera, found that her oxen were not brought in time for a festival, and they drew her cart the 45 stades (*c*.8 km.: 5 mi.) to the temple. She prayed to the goddess to grant them the greatest boon possible for mortals, and Hera caused them to die while they slept in the temple. The Argives honoured them with statues at *Delphi. A pair of *kouros*-statues from Delphi, long thought to be inscribed with their names, may, according to a controversial rereading, represent the *Dioscuri.

SIG 5 = Tod 3; SEG 3. 395, 35. 479. Cf. C. Picard, *Rev. Hist. Rel.* 1927, 365 ff.; *LSAG*[2] (1990), 154 ff., 168 no. 4; A. F. Stewart, *Greek Sculpture* (1990), 112, 342, figs. 56 f. W. K. C. G.; A. F. S.

Cleomedes (*RE* 3) wrote (perhaps *c*. AD 360) a treatise on astronomy, Κυκλικὴ θεωρία [μετεώρων] 'Elementary Theory [of the Heavens]'. Although disordered and often trivial, the work is valuable for what it preserves from earlier mathematical and philosophical writers, notably *Posidonius (2). It provides (1. 10) the most details for *Eratosthenes' 'measurement of the earth', although Cleomedes' account appears to be largely fictitious.

EDITION R. B. Todd (Teubner, 1990).
TRANSLATIONS Lat., H. Ziegler, with his 1891 Teubner edn.; Fr. (faulty), R. Goulart (1980).
COMMENT *HAMA* 2. 652–7, 959–65 (includes dating). G. J. T.

Cleomenes (1) I, *Agiad king of Sparta (reigned *c*.520–490 BC), son of Anaxandridas II by a second, bigamous union. His long, activist reign was one of the half-dozen most influential on record. He pursued an adventurous and at times unscrupulous foreign policy aimed at crushing *Argos (2) and extending Sparta's influence both inside and outside the Peloponnese. It was during his reign, but not entirely according to his design, that the *Peloponnesian League came formally into existence. He embroiled *Thebes (1) with Athens and frustrated Thebes' plans for a united *Boeotian federation by referring Plataea to Athens for alliance (probably in 519: Thuc. 3. 68). He intervened twice successfully in Athenian affairs, overthrowing the Peisistratid tyranny of *Hippias (1) in 510 and expelling *Cleisthenes (2) in favour of Isagoras in 508. But his attempt to restore Isagoras by a concerted expedition of Sparta's Peloponnesian and central Greek allies in *c*.506 was frustrated by the opposition of the Corinthians and of his Eurypontid fellow king *Demaratus (2). A further Spartan proposal to restore Hippias in *c*.504 is not specifically attributed to Cleomenes but was anyway blocked by majority vote of Sparta's allies in the first certain act of the Peloponnesian League proper. In 494 Cleomenes defeated Argos at Sepeia near Tiryns and unscrupulously capitalized on his victory by burning several thousand Argive survivors to death in a sacred grove, for which impiety he was tried at Sparta and acquitted.

But he disliked overseas commitments, refusing to interfere in the affairs of *Samos (*c*.515), or to support the *Ionian Revolt (499); and he showed no certain awareness of the Persian danger before 491 when his attempt to punish *Aegina for *Medism was thwarted by Demaratus. He thereupon bribed the *Delphic oracle to declare Demaratus illegitimate and had him deposed, but the intrigue came to light and he fled Sparta, possibly to stir up revolt among the *Arcadians. Recalled to Sparta, he met a violent end, perhaps at his own hands.

Hdt. 5. 39 ff. W. G. Forrest, *A History of Sparta 950–192 BC* (1968; repr.

1980), ch. 8; G. E. M. de Ste. Croix, *The Origins of the Peloponnesian War* (1972); P. Cartledge, *Sparta and Lakonia* (1979); G. L. Cawkwell, *Mnemos.* 1993, 506 ff.　　　　　　　　　　　　　　P. A. C.

Cleomenes (2) **III**, *Agiad king of Sparta (reigned *c.*235–222 BC). The son of Leonidas, he imbibed ideals of social revolution from his wife Agiatis, widow of his father's opponent *Agis IV. Before implementing those ideals at home (and they were not for export), he was active abroad. He first moved in 229, when he annexed *Tegea, *Mantinea, *Orchomenus (2), and Caphyae in Arcadia from the *Aetolian Confederacy. Then, having provoked the *Achaean Confederacy into war (228), he won victories at Mt. Lycaeum and Ladoceia (227). Now (winter 227/6) he seized quasi-despotic power at home and set up a 'Lycurgan' regime (see LYCURGUS (2)). Debts were cancelled, land was redivided, the citizen body was replenished from *perioikoi and foreigners. A refashioned educational cycle and mess-regimen were reinstated (see AGŌGĒ), the army re-equipped. The allegedly post-Lycurgan ephorate was abolished, the *gerousia* made subject to annual re-election, the dyarchy transformed into a *de facto* monarchy. Cleomenes' military successes against Achaea in Arcadia were followed by the capture of *Argos (2) (225) and siege of Corinth (224). These provoked *Aratus (2) into opening negotiations with the Greeks' notional suzerain, *Antigonus (3) Doson of Macedon, who reached the Isthmus, secured the revolt of Argos and placed Cleomenes on the defensive, though in winter 223 he took and destroyed Megalopolis. Despite a mass liberation of *helots, Cleomenes' new model army proved no match for Antigonus at Sellasia north of Sparta in July 222, and he fled to the court of his patron *Ptolemy (1) III Euergetes of Egypt. Imprisoned by Euergetes' successor, he broke out, tried in vain to stir up revolution in Alexandria (1), and committed suicide (winter 220/219).

Cleomenes' patriotism is not in doubt, and the ideals he proclaimed provoked eager support inside and outside Sparta, but it may be questioned how far he was a social and political reformer on principle.

Polyb. 2. 45–70; Plut. *Cleom.* (after Phylarchus; comm. G. Marasco, 1981), *Arat.* F. W. Walbank, *Aratus of Sicyon* (1933); T. W. Africa, *Phylarchus and the Spartan Revolution* (1961); P. Cartledge and A. J. S. Spawforth, *Hellenistic and Roman Sparta* (1989), ch. 4.　　　　P. A. C.

Cleomenes (3), of *Naucratis, financial administrator. In 332/1 BC *Alexander (3) the Great placed him in charge of the eastern sector of Egypt with responsibility for the fiscal system of the entire country. According to the Aristotelian *Oeconomica* he was adept at exploitation, and at a time of international famine he concentrated the entire grain surplus of Egypt in his hands, marketing it at an enormous profit. He accumulated a reserve of 8,000 talents and devoted considerable attention and expense to the public buildings of *Alexandria (1). That won him official recognition of his *de facto* position as *satrap and pardon for any excesses in his administration. The settlement of *Babylon (323) subordinated him to Ptolemy (1) I, who had him executed, suspecting him of sympathy for *Perdiccas (3).

Berve, *Alexanderreich* 2, no. 431; J. Seibert, *Untersuchungen zur Geschichte Ptolemaios' I* (1969), and *Chiron* 1972, 99 ff.　　　　　　　A. B. B.

Cleon, Athenian politician, the son of a rich tanner. He was perhaps involved in the attacks on *Pericles (1) through his intellectual friends in the 430s BC, and in the opposition to Pericles' strategy of refusing battle against the invaders in 431. In 427 he proposed the decree (overturned the next day) to execute all the

men of *Mytilene after the suppression of its revolt. In 426 he attacked the *Babylonians* of *Aristophanes (1) as a slander on the state. In 425, after the Athenians had got the better of the *Spartans at *Pylos, he frustrated the Spartan peace proposals, and later accused the generals in charge of the siege of Sphacteria of incompetence. *Nicias (1) offered to resign the command to him, and he was obliged to take it, and in co-operation with *Demosthenes (1), the general on the spot, he kept his promise and rapidly obtained the Spartans' surrender. In the same year he doubtless approved the measure greatly increasing the tribute paid by the allied states; and he was responsible for increasing the jurors' pay from two to three obols. In 423 he proposed the decree for the destruction of *Scione and the execution of all its citizens. In 422, as general, he led an expedition to the Thraceward area, and recovered *Torone and Galepsus, but he failed in an attack on *Stagira and was defeated by *Brasidas and killed in a battle outside *Amphipolis.

We have a vivid picture of Cleon in *Thucydides (2) and Aristophanes, both of whom had personal reasons for disliking him. He was an effective, if vulgar, speaker, and seems to have been given to extravagant promises and extravagant accusations against opponents. He was one of the first of a new kind of politician, who were not from the old aristocracy, and whose predominance depended on persuasive speeches in the assembly and lawcourts rather than on regular office-holding; when he did serve as general, the undisputed facts include both successes and failures. See also DEMAGOGUES, DEMAGOGY.

PA 8674; APF 318–20; W. R. Connor, *The New Politicians of Fifth-century Athens* (1971); B. Mitchell, *Hist.* 1991, 170–92.
　　　　　　　　　　　　　　A. W. G.; T. J. C.; P. J. R.

Cleonides (perhaps 2nd cent. AD). His *Introduction to Harmonics* is an unusually reliable compendium of *Aristoxenus' basic doctrines.

TEXT C. von Jan, *Musici Scriptores Graeci* (1895), repr. with It. trans. in L. Zanoncelli, *La Manualistica musicale greca* (1990); rev. text and Eng. trans., J. Solomon (1980).　　　　　　　　　A. D. B.

Cleonymus, Athenian politician of the 420s BC. He is mocked by *Aristophanes (1) as a glutton, a liar, and a coward, and he justified the last charge by running away after the battle of *Delion (424). He is attested epigraphically as the author of two decrees of 426/5, for Athens' ally Methone, and laying down more stringent rules for the collection of the *Delian League's tribute, and he was probably a member of the council (see BOULE) for that year. His political stance was probably similar to *Cleon's. See also DEMAGOGUES, DEMAGOGY.

PA 8680.　　　　　　　　　　　　　　　　P. J. R.

Cleopatra I (*c.*215–176 BC), daughter of *Antiochus (3) III and *Laodice (3) and wife (from 193) of *Ptolemy (1) V Epiphanes. On Epiphanes' death she acted as regent for her elder son *Ptolemy (1) VI, who on her death four years later took the title Philometor ('Mother-loving').

RE 'Kleopatra' 14.　　　　　　　　　　　　　D. J. T.

Cleopatra II (*c.*185–116 BC), daughter of *Cleopatra I and *Ptolemy (1) V and both sister and wife of first *Ptolemy (1) VI Philometor (from 175) and then (from 145) his successor (and brother) *Ptolemy (1) VIII Euergetes II. Her children (by Philometor) were Ptolemy Eupator, *Ptolemy (1) VII Neos Philopator, *Cleopatra III and Cleopatra Thea, and (by Euergetes) Ptolemy Memphites. Her long life was marked by dynastic strife in which she looked to the population of *Alexandria (1) for support. Supplanted in Euergetes' affection by her daughter, Cleopatra III, in 132–130 she engaged in a civil war against her bigamous husband-brother and his new wife. Euergetes fled to Cyprus with Cleopatra III and although he was back in control from 130 mother and daughter only reached an uneasy reconciliation in 124. The reconciliation of Euergetes and his two wives, Cleopatra mother and daughter, was marked by an amnesty decree in 118 (*PTeb.* 5). Cleopatra survived Euergetes' death in 116 to rule briefly with Cleopatra III and *Ptolemy (1) IX Soter II, but she died soon after. Her economic assets included a fleet of barges and land.

RE 'Kleopatra' 15.   D. J. T.

Cleopatra III, daughter of *Ptolemy (1) VI and *Cleopatra II, was seduced and married by *Ptolemy (1) VIII Euergetes II in 140/139 BC. She spent much of her life in conflict with her mother, whom she now joined as her uncle's wife. Following Euergetes' death (in 116) she ruled with first her elder (*Ptolemy (1) IX Soter II) and then (from 107) her younger son (*Ptolemy (1) X Alexander I). The drama of this final stage of her career, epitomized in 105/4 BC (*PColon.* 2. 81) when she served instead of the king as priest in the royal cult, is variously reported; all agree that different sons were favoured successively and that Cleopatra met a violent end (in 101 BC). New appointments in the dynastic cult (see RULER-CULT) reflect the troubled times; in 115 three new priestesses joined the cult of this powerful queen.

RE 'Kleopatra' 16.   D. J. T.

Cleopatra VII (69–30 BC), the final and best known of the Ptolemies, was daughter of *Ptolemy (1) XII (Auletes). On the latter's death in 51 she became queen, alone at first and subsequently with her younger brothers, first *Ptolemy (1) XIII (who opposed Caesar) and then (47–45) with *Ptolemy (1) XIV. A joint reign with *Ptolemy (1) XV Caesar (Caesarion, reputedly Caesar's son) is recorded from 45 BC. Her later children by Mark Antony were the twins Alexander and Cleopatra (born 40 BC after Antony's winter in *Alexandria (1)), and Ptolemy Philadelphus (born 36). In 37/6 she marked Antony's gift to her of Chalcis in Syria by instituting a double numeration of her regnal years (year 16 = 1). She died by her own hand (and the bite of a royal asp) soon after Octavian (see AUGUSTUS) took Alexandria on 3 August 30.

Best known for her successful relations first with Caesar (C. *Iulius Caesar (1)) who besieged and captured Alexandria in 48–47, and later with Antony (*M. Antonius (2)), following a colourful encounter at *Tarsus in 41, she managed to increase her kingdom territorially in return for financial support. Caesar restored *Cyprus to *Egypt and in 34, in a magnificent ceremony at Alexandria, Cleopatra appeared as *Isis to mark the division of the earlier kingdom of *Alexander (3) the Great between the royal couple and their children. Cleopatra ruled Egypt and Caesarion Cyprus as Queen of Kings and King of Kings; Antony's children Alexander Helios (the Sun) and Ptolemy Philadelphus were named kings east and west of the Euphrates respectively, with Cleopatra Selene (the Moon) queen of Cyrene. The symbolism of the ceremony was more important than any reality.

Internally Cleopatra was strong, using her position as pharaoh to gain backing from all the people. To her title of Philopator ('father-loving') was added Philopatris ('loving her country') (*BGU* 14. 2377. 1) and her support for the traditional Egyptian bull-cults is recorded at both Memphis and Armant. In the final struggle against Octavian however she confiscated temple lands. In Greek she was known also as Thea Neotera, 'the younger

goddess'. An expert linguist, she was reportedly the first Ptolemy to have known Egyptian, and *Plutarch reports it was her conversation rather than her looks which formed the secret of her success.

The legend of Cleopatra has proved even more powerful than her historical record. Thanks to her successful liaisons with men of power she was named as the author of treatises on hairdressing and cosmetics. Her exploitation of Egyptian royal symbolism with its eastern tradition of luxury was used against her by her antagonists; for Roman poets she was 'monster' and 'wicked woman'. Her visit to Rome in 46–44 achieved little but embarrassment for Caesar. Following his murder, her attempts to aid the Caesarians in 42 were thwarted by *Cassius, and by contrary winds. The summons to Tarsus by Antony followed. Her liaison with Antony formed the focus of Octavian's propaganda, based on fear of Egyptian wealth. Yet the skilful manipulation of power by this queen preserved Egypt from the direct rule of Rome longer than might otherwise have been the case. See ACTIUM; OCTAVIA (2).

RE 'Kleopatra' 20; H. Volkmann, *Cleopatra* (1953).   D. J. T.

Cleophon (1), Athenian politician. He was a son of Cleippides, general (see STRATĒGOI) in 429/8 BC; he is represented as a lyre-maker and his mother was alleged to be Thracian (see THRACE). He was already a public figure at the time of the ostracism of *Hyperbolus, and was the most prominent *demagogue, in the manner of *Cleon, after the democratic restoration in 410. He introduced the *diobelia*, a payment of two obols a day, possibly to citizens not otherwise receiving public funds. He attacked both *Critias and *Alcibiades, and was opposed to peace with *Sparta both after Athens' victory at *Cyzicus in 410 and after her defeat at *Aegospotami in 405 (see ATHENS (history)). His elimination on a charge of treason paved the way for the peace settlement negotiated by *Theramenes. See also DEMAGOGUES, DEMAGOGY.

PA 8638; E. Vanderpool, *Hesp.* 1952, 114–15; W. R. Connor, *The New Politicians of Fifth-century Athens* (1971), see index; A. Andrewes, *CAH* 5² (1992), ch. 11.   A. W. G.; T. J. C.; P. J. R.

Cleophon (2), an Athenian tragic poet according to the *Suda*, which lists ten play titles. However, as six of these are also attested for *Iophon, it is likely that Iophon is meant here. In that case the Cleophon mentioned by Aristotle at *Poet.* 2 (he portrays people as they are, not better or worse), 22, *Rh.* 3. 7, *Soph. el.* 15, may not have been a tragic poet at all.

TrGF 1². 246–7.   A. L. B.

cleruchy (κληρουχία), a special sort of Greek colony (see COLONIZATION, GREEK) in which the settlers kept their original citizenship and did not form a completely independent community. In Classical Greek history (see end of this article for the Hellenistic position) the term is confined to certain Athenian settlements founded on conquered territory (Greek and non-Greek) from the end of the 6th cent. BC, especially during the period of the *Delian League. It is often difficult to decide whether a settlement of the 5th cent. is a cleruchy, as ancient authors do not always distinguish cleruchies from other colonies (see APOIKIA), and because it seems that colonists did not forfeit their Athenian citizenship any more than did cleruchs. Perhaps in the 5th cent. 'cleruchy' was appropriate where (as at *Lesbos, Thuc. 3. 50) the original Greek inhabitants remained, 'colony' where they did not. (This does not work for 4th-cent. *Samos.) Another possibility is that cleruchic land was not heritable whereas land in a colony was.

cliens

The chief certain or probable cleruchies down to the end of the 5th cent. are: *Chalcis (506; it is now thought unlikely that Chalcis had one again c.446), *Naxos (1), *Andros, *Chersonesus (1), *Lemnos, and *Imbros (c.450), *Histiaea (c.446), *Aegina (431, status disputed by Figueira), Lesbos (427), *Melos (416). (For the late 6th- or early 5th-cent. installation of a cleruchy on *Salamis (1) see ML 14 = Fornara 44 B, though this cleruchy had some peculiar features. The status of *Scyros in the 5th cent. is uncertain.) These cleruchies did not survive Athens' defeat in 404. Later cleruchies are: Lemnos, Imbros, and Scyros (from the early 4th cent. until the Roman period, with intervals), Samos (c.365–322), *Potidaea (361–356), Chersonesus (1) (353/2–338).

The numbers in a cleruchy varied from 4,000 (Chalcis) to 250 (Andros). Settlers (κληροῦχοι) each received an allotment (κλῆρος) which maintained them as *zeugitai. The cleruchs probably resided in the cleruchies (rather than living in Athens as rentiers), and the cleruchies may sometimes have served the purpose of garrisons in addition to providing land for the poor. As Athenian citizens, cleruchs were liable for military service, paid war-tax (*eisphora), and took part in religious activity at Athens. But at Lemnos, remarkable epigraphic mentions of the '*dēmos of the initiated', a reference to the *mystery cult of the Great Gods (*Cabiri), show that here at least cleruchic religion was distinctive, and 'not quite like that of an ordinary Attic *deme' (Parker). Distance, moreover, forced cleruchs generally to create organs for local self-government on the Athenian model, *boulē, *ekklēsia, and magistrates (see MAGISTRACY, GREEK). In the 4th cent. at least cleruchies were supervised by officials sent out from Athens.

In the Hellenistic period, particularly in Ptolemaic *Egypt, we again find cleruchs, professional soldiers settled on holdings of land ('cleruchic' land). Some direct Athenian influence has been postulated: it has been ingeniously noted (Turner) that the Athenian cleruchs evicted from *Samos in 322 became available for *Ptolemy (1) I's recruiting agents at exactly the right time.

ATHENS A. J. Graham, *Colony and Mother City in Ancient Greece* (2nd edn., 1983), 166 ff.; P. Gauthier, *Rev. Ét. Grec.* 1966, 64 ff., and in M. I. Finley (ed.), *Problèmes de la terre* (1973), 163 ff.; W. Schmitz, *Wirtschaftliche Prosperität: Soziale Integration und die Seebundspolitik Athens* (1988), 298 ff.; T. J. Figueira, *Athens and Aigina in the Age of Imperial Colonization* (1991), with general discussion; P. A. Brunt, *Studies in Greek History and Thought* (1993), ch. 5; R. Parker, in R. Osborne and S. Hornblower (eds.), *Ritual, Finance, Politics* (1994), 339 ff. (religion, esp. Lemnos); J. R. Green and R. K. Sinclair, *Hist.* 1970, 515–27; J. Cargill, *Athenian Settlements of the Fourth Century BC* (1995).

HELLENISTIC PERIOD, esp. Egypt: C. Préaux, *L'Économie royale des Lagides* (1939), 477 ff.; M. Launey, *Recherches sur les armées hellénistiques* (1949–50), 45 ff.; E. G. Turner, *CAH* 7²/1 (1984), 124 f. and n. 13.

S. H.

cliens In Rome a client was a free man who entrusted himself to another and received protection in return. Clientship was a hereditary social status consecrated by usage and recognized, though not defined or enforced, by the law. The rules of the law were however far more binding in the special case of the freedman, who was *ipso facto* a client of his former owner (see FREEDMEN). Ordinary clients supported their patron (*patronus) in political and private life, and demonstrated their loyalty and respect by going to his house to greet him each morning (see SALUTATIO), and attending him when he went out. The size of a man's clientele, and the wealth and status of his individual clients, were a visible testimony to his prestige and social standing (and therefore to his political influence). In exchange clients received favours and benefits of various kinds, including daily subsistence in the form of food or money (such a payment was known as a *sportula*) and assistance in the courts.

This reciprocal exchange of goods and services between persons of unequal social standing is only one facet of a much wider phenomenon in Roman society, in which power and status at all levels depended on personal connections and the trading of benefits and favours. At the level of the élite, Roman grandees dispensed huge sums of money to favoured protégés (e.g. Plin. *Ep.* 1. 19; 6. 32), and obtained administrative and military appointments for them through personal contacts with high-ranking public officials, above all from the emperor himself. It has been suggested (R. Saller) that Roman nobles gained power and influence by acting as 'brokers' for imperial patronage. But it is a much debated question whether this general phenomenon should be described as clientage, and whether the recipients of such benefits are properly to be regarded as clients. Some have argued that clientage was a fundamentally important part of Roman political and social life (M. Gelzer, E. Badian, R. Saller), while others regard it as a marginal phenomenon of little importance (P. A. Brunt, F. Millar, N. Rouland). Two points can be briefly made. First, there is no doubt that in Rome political power and social prestige depended on the manipulation of personal connections and the exchange of favours and benefits between individuals of unequal standing. On the other hand, the language of clientage was restricted, and in literary sources the parties to exchanges of benefits tend to refer to each other as friends (*amici*; see AMICITIA), rather than as clients, which implied social inferiority. In authors such as Martial '*cliens*' is a pejorative term, effectively meaning parasite.

In the provinces (especially in Gaul) Roman clientship superimposed itself on pre-existing local forms of social ties. It is a controversial point whether the relations of certain foreign states with Rome are to be described as clientship. But there is no doubt that Roman individuals and families built up large *clientelae* among foreigners: whole communities could become clients, and obtained access to the centre of power through the mediation of individual patrons.

N. D. Fustel de Coulanges, *Histoire des institutions politiques de l'ancienne France* 5 (1890), 205 ff.; M. Gelzer, *The Roman Nobility* (1969; Ger. orig. 1912); L. Friedländer, *Darstellung aus der Sittengeschichte Roms*, 10th edn. (1922), 1. 223 ff., 2. 230 ff.; E. Badian, *Foreign Clientelae* (1958); N. Rouland, *Pouvoir politique et dépendance personnelle dans l'antiquité romaine* (1979); R. Saller, *Personal Patronage under the Early Empire* (1982); F. G. B. Millar, *JRS* 1984, 1–19, and 1986, 1–11; P. A. Brunt, *The Fall of the Roman Republic* (1988), 382 ff.; A. Wallace-Hadrill (ed.), *Patronage in Ancient Society* (1989). See also PATRONUS.

A. M.; T. J. Co.

client kings The term 'client kings' is conventionally used by scholars to denote a range of monarchs and quasi-monarchs of non-Roman peoples who enjoyed a relationship with Rome that was essentially harmonious but unequal. These were rulers under the patronage of the Roman state, but the less abrasive language of friendship was the norm. In fact, there is very little ancient authority for the term 'client king': the Roman state called such kings *rex sociusque et amicus*, 'king and ally and friend', in a formal recognition by the senate (*appellatio*). Grand ceremony seems often to have accompanied such recognitions, under republic and Principate alike. Although the practice of such relationships varied according to the relative power of the 'client king', Rome seems to have drawn few distinctions in theory.

From the 3rd cent. BC at the latest Rome developed such relationships with a view to the consolidation or expansion of her empire in Italy and beyond. *Hieron (2) II of Syracuse is often regarded as the first client king (c.263 BC), but he doubtless had predecessors, for example among the chieftains of northern Italy. And Rome continued to build and maintain relationships with client kings throughout her history, though it has often been claimed that Rome abandoned that mode of diplomacy around AD 200. Many kingdoms did indeed become provincial territory over the centuries, usually when Rome felt the need to step in to control local unrest: for example, where kings failed to manage their succession, where a dynasty ended, or where local conditions had changed. See PROVINCIA, PROVINCE.

Client kingdoms were usually located at the margins of Roman control, whether on the periphery of the empire or in an area which Rome would find difficult and expensive to administer directly (e.g. mountainous *Cilicia Tracheia). In consequence of their marginal position, client kings might be perceived as within the Roman empire or, occasionally, outside it. At the frontier, client kingdoms were important reservoirs of manpower, resources, and local knowledge. Rome expected client kings to meet her demands whenever she saw fit to make them, but client kings were not required to pay regular taxes. In return, client kings expected Rome to ensure their positions locally. The nearest Roman legions forestalled the movements of client kings' enemies, both internal and external, by their very presence. Where necessary, Roman forces came to the aid of client kings, who might ultimately take refuge on Roman territory. On occasion, Rome might prefer to come to an arrangement with the enemies of her client kings, but it was the unspoken promise of Roman support that kept client kings loyal to Rome (or loyal enough). One expression of that expectation was the occasional bequest by client kings of their kingdoms to Rome where no other acceptable successor was available to them (e.g. *Attalus III).

Client kings, like cities and others, exercised their relationship with Rome through more personal relations with leading individuals and families at Rome. Under the Principate such personal bonds continued to proliferate, but the emperor and his family now became the most attractive source of patronage for client kings, so that they became pre-eminent in royal relations as in all else. Augustus seems deliberately to have made kings more a part of the Roman empire, following a trend set by *Caesar and Antony (M. *Antonius (2)) in particular. Most client kings now held Roman citizenship: by AD 100 they had begun to enter the Roman senate (e.g. C. *Iulius Antiochus Epiphanes Philopappus). They regularly sent their sons to grow up at Rome, preferably with the imperial family (e.g. M. *Iulius Agrippa II). *Augustus is said to have encouraged marriages among client royalty (Suet. Aug. 48). In their kingdoms, client kings named their cities after the emperor or members of his family: they also celebrated the imperial (*ruler-)cult and a few kings (notably those of the Bosporan kingdom; see BOSPORUS (2)) were priests of that cult. The ruling emperor was depicted on royal coinage, though there is no indication that that was the result of Roman coercion. Coercion was not required: the relationship between client king and Rome, however unequal, was based upon mutual advantage.

D. C. Braund, *Rome and the Friendly King: The Character of Client Kingship* (1984); E. S. Gruen, *The Hellenistic World and the Coming of Rome* (1984); B. Isaac, *The Limits of Empire*, rev. edn. (1992); R. D. Sullivan, *Near Eastern Royalty and Rome, 100–30 BC*, Phoenix Suppl. 24 (1990).

D. C. B.

climate The ancient climate was very similar to the modern climate. The Mediterranean climate is characterized by cool, wet winters and hot, dry summers. There is a very high degree of interannual climatic variability, which makes farming (see AGRICULTURE) risky and sometimes causes *famines. The ordinary run of interannual climatic variability is taken for granted by literary sources. Only exceptional years stood a chance of being recorded. The rain, predominantly in winter, is usually adequate for dry-farming of cereals, and for evergreen trees resistant to the summer drought. However, it is not sufficient for dense coniferous or deciduous forests. Westerly winds bring most of the rain, so that areas in the rain shadow on the eastern side of Greece, e.g. *Attica, are much drier than regions in western Greece. Rainfall often takes the form of short, intense showers. It runs off the land and does not help plants. There are statistical correlations between cereal yields, total annual precipitation and the monthly distribution of rainfall during the year. The winters generally remain warm enough for plants like the olive-tree, with a low degree of frost tolerance, while the summers are hot enough to support subtropical vegetation. The Mediterranean climate and much of the flora associated with it is quite young in terms of geological time. For ancient views on the weather see *Aristotle's *Meteorologica*, and *Theophrastus, *On Weather Signs*.

Various methods are used to investigate the ancient climate. Palynology (pollen studies) enables us to make inferences about climate by examining the geographical distribution in antiquity of plants with known climatic requirements. Theophrastus' botanical works also indicate that the mean temperature c.300 BC was within a degree of modern values. In the future the most important source of information will probably be tree-ring studies. We can construct tree-ring chronologies (dendrochronology) reaching as far back as several thousand years ago, and then make inferences about climate in each year from the thickness of the ring. This technique has already been employed on subalpine conifers to show that the year 218 BC, when *Hannibal crossed the Alps, was a mild year, helping to explain the success of Hannibal's audacious enterprise. Information derived from tree-ring studies should eventually resolve a number of controversies among modern historians about the possibility that there were secular climatic variations in antiquity.

J. Neumann, *Climatic Change* 1992, 139–50; G. Panessa, *ASNP* 1981, 123–58; J. R. Sallares, *Ecology of the Ancient Greek World* (1991).

J. R. S.

Clitomachus (187/6–110/9 BC), Academic (see ACADEMY) sceptic. Clitomachus was a Carthaginian (see CARTHAGE), originally named Hasdrubal. He went to Athens at the age of 24 to study philosophy. *Diogenes (6) Laertius (4. 67) describes him as well versed in *Peripatetic and Stoic (see STOICISM) as well as Academic thought. At 28 he became the pupil of the sceptic *Carneades. From 140/39 he conducted his own school in the Palladium, but returned in 129/8 with many followers to the *Academy, of which he became head two years later.

Clitomachus was famous for his industry, allegedly writing over 400 books (rolls?), mainly recording the arguments of his teacher Carneades. Cicero, who used his Περὶ ἐποχῆς ('On withholding assent') in the *Lucullus*, tells us that Clitomachus insisted, against some other pupils of Carneades, that his teacher had never abandoned the attitude of strict suspension of judgement. Cicero also mentions two other books, dedicated to the Roman senator L. Censorinus and to the poet C. *Lucilius (1), apparently containing introductions to Academic scepticism. Clitomachus also wrote a work 'On Philosophical Sects' (Περὶ αἱρέσεων), and a 'Consolation', addressed to the Carthaginians on the destruction of their city, in which he used notes from a lecture by Carneades.

Sources in H. J. Mette, *Lustrum* 1985.　　　　　　G. S.

Clitumnus, a river near Trebiae in Umbria, famous for the white sacrificial cattle on its banks (Verg. *G*. 2. 146). It flowed into the Tinia, and subsequently into the *Tiber. Shrines of the personified Clitumnus and other deities adorned its source (called Sacraria in the *itineraries), attracting numerous tourists (Plin. *Ep.* 8. 8; Suet. *Calig.* 43).　　　　　　E. T. S.

Cloaca Maxima, originally a stream draining NE Rome from the Argiletum to the Tiber through the *forum Romanum and *Velabrum. According to tradition it was canalized by *Tarquinius Priscus or *Tarquinius Superbus, but, while traces of early construction remain, the main sewer is largely due to *Agrippa's overhaul in 33 BC with later repairs and extensions. See SANITATION.

Steinby, *Lexicon* 288 ff.　　　　　　J. D.

Cloatius (*RE* 2) **Verus,** Augustan lexicographer and antiquarian, wrote on the meanings of Greek words and on Latin words derived from Greek. He is probably the 'Cloatius' whom *Verrius Flaccus cites (with L. *Aelius) on Latin sacral terms.

*PIR*² C 1150; Herzog–Schmidt, § 283.　　　　　　R. A. K.

clocks The usual instrument for telling time in antiquity was the sundial. This employed the shadow of a pointer (γνώμων) cast on a plane, spherical, or conical surface marked with lines indicating the seasonal hours (one seasonal hour was $\frac{1}{12}$ of the length of daylight at a given place: hours of constant length were used only by astronomers). Although crude sundials may have been introduced into Greece in the 6th cent. BC (Hdt. 2. 109 says that the Greeks imported the γνώμων and twelve-part division of the day from the Babylonians), it was not commonly used until the 3rd cent., when the mathematical theory necessary for correctly drawing the hour-lines had been developed. None of the hundreds of preserved sundials predates the 3rd cent. Before then the popular way to tell time was a crude shadow-table, using the measured length of a man's own shadow.

At night the ancients used the water-clock (κλεψύδρα), which measured time by the flow of water from a vessel. A primitive form was in use in Athenian courts of the 5th cent. BC, but accuracy was not achieved until *Ctesibius (3rd cent.) invented a device to ensure a uniform flow. He also added many refinements, including a dial with a moving pointer, and 'side-effects' (moving figurines). This was the ancestor of the elaborate display clocks of Byzantine and Islamic times. A variation is the 'anaphoric clock' described by Vitruvius (9. 8), which indicated the varying seasonal hours by a rotating disc, driven by water-power, on which the constellations were engraved in stereographic projection; a fragment of such an instrument is preserved. See SOLARIUM AUGUSTI; TIME-RECKONING.

Sundials: S. Gibbs, *Greek and Roman Sundials* (1976) (includes lists of preserved sundials). Shadow tables: *HAMA* 2. 736 ff. Water-clocks: A. G. Drachmann, *Ktesibios, Philon and Heron* (1948), 16–41; P. Rhodes, *Commentary on the Aristotelian Athenaion Politeia* (1981), 719 ff.

　　　　　　G. J. T.

Clodia (*RE* 66), second of the three sisters of P. *Clodius Pulcher, born *c*.95 BC, had married her first cousin Q. *Caecilius Metellus Celer by 62 (Cic. *Fam.* 5. 2. 6). Her bitter enemy *Cicero (but gossip said she had once offered him marriage, Plut. *Cic.* 29)

paints a vivid picture of her in his *Letters* from 60 BC onwards, and above all in the *Pro Caelio* of April 56. Her affair with *Catullus—the identification with Lesbia is widely admitted—began before the death of Metellus in 59, which Clodia was said to have caused by poison: by the end of that year M. *Caelius Rufus was her lover. After the Caelius case her political importance ceases, but she may have been still alive in 45 BC (Cic. *Att.* 12. 38, etc.).

See CAELIUS RUFUS, M.　　　　　　G. E. F. C.; R. J. S.

Clodius (*RE* 38) **Macer, Lucius,** *legatus in Africa in AD 68, revolted from *Nero and cut off the corn-supply of Rome. Though inspired by messages from *Galba, he never recognized him; instead he called himself propraetor, minted coins, and raised a new legion I Macriana liberatrix. Galba had him executed in October.

P. Romanelli, *Storia delle province romane dell'Africa* (1959), 279 ff.

　　　　　　A. M.; G. E. F. C.; M. T. G.

Clodius (*RE* 48) **Pulcher, Publius,** youngest of six children of Ap. *Claudius Pulcher (2). He was born *c*.92 BC (since quaestor in 61). In 68 he incited the troops of his brother-in-law L. *Licinius Lucullus (2) to mutiny in Armenia. When prosecuting *Catiline in 65 he was, according to Cicero, in co-operation with the defence. On his return to Rome he had been apparently friendly with *Cicero (Plut. *Cic.* 29), but in May 61 Cicero gave damaging evidence against him when he was on trial for trespassing on the *Bona Dea festival disguised as a woman the previous December. However Clodius was narrowly acquitted by a jury said to have been heavily bribed. Next year, on returning from his quaestorian province of *Sicily, he sought transference into a plebeian *gens (see PLEBS): this was at first resisted, but in March 59 *Caesar as *pontifex maximus presided over the *comitia curiata* (see CURIA (1)) at which the adoption was ratified. There were suggestions of subsequent disagreements with Caesar and *Pompey and of his departure from Rome, but in the event he was elected tribune for 58. His measures included free corn for the *plebs,* restoration of *collegia* (see CLUBS, ROMAN), repeal or modification of the *Leges Aelia et Fufia,* grant of new provinces to the consuls A. *Gabinius (2) and L. *Calpurnius Piso Caesoninus, a bill exiling those who had condemned Roman citizens to death without popular sanction, a bill confirming the exile of Cicero (who departed in late March), the dispatch of *Cato (Uticensis) to *Cyprus, and grant of title of king and control of *Pessinus to Brogitarus ruler of the Galatian Trocmi. Clodius then turned against Pompey, allowing the escape of the Armenian prince Tigranes, threatening Pompey's life, and (Cic. *Dom.* 40; *Har. resp.* 48) suggesting that Caesar's acts of 59 were invalid because of M. *Calpurnius Bibulus' religious obstruction. These attacks on Pompey were continued in 57, especially over the question of Cicero's recall, and in the early part of Clodius' aedileship in 56; but after *Luca his attitude changed and by agitation and violence he helped to bring about the joint consulship of Pompey and *Crassus in 55. He still continued to control large sections of the urban *plebs* (*plebs urbana*). He stood for the praetorship of 52 but owing to rioting the elections had not been held when he was murdered by T. *Annius Milo on 18 January of that year. His clients among the *plebs* burned the senate-house as his pyre.

Clodius, who like two of his sisters used the 'popular' spelling of his name, probably saw the tribunate as a vital step in his political career: revenge on Cicero need not have been his main aim in seeking transfer to the *plebs,* nor (despite Cic. *Dom.* 41; *Sest.* 16) Caesar's aim in granting it. Moreover, the view that

Caesar was at any time his patron seems misconceived. In 58–56 he may have been allied with Crassus; but he was surely both opportunist and independent, for before as well as after Luca he was friendly with various *optimates* (Cic. *Fam.* 1. 9. 10, 19), and in 53 he was supporting the candidates of Pompey for the consulship (Asconius, 26, 42). The one consistent motif is his courting of the urban plebs and the promotion of its interests. The daughter of his marriage to *Fulvia was briefly married to Octavian (later *Augustus) in 42.

Lintott, *Violence* and *G&R* 1967; L. G. Pocock, *CQ* 1924; E. Badian, *JRS* 1965; E. S. Gruen, *Phoenix* 1966; E. Rawson, *Roman Culture and Society* (1991), 102 ff. (on Clodius' eastern *clientelae*; see CLIENS).

G. E. F. C.; A. W. L.

Clodius Pupienus Maximus, Marcus See CAELIUS CALVINUS BALBINUS, D.

Clodius (*RE* 52) **Quirinalis, Publius,** from Arelate (mod. Arles) in Gaul, said by *Jerome to have taught rhetoric at Rome *c.* AD 44.

PIR² C 1181; Schanz–Hosius, § 480. 3. M. W.

Clodius (*RE* 17) **Septimius Albinus, Decimus,** from *Hadrumetum (mod. Sousse) in Africa, won distinction as a legionary legate in Dacia in the 180s AD and was governor of Britain at the time of *Commodus' murder. He accepted the title of Caesar in return for supporting L. *Septimius Severus in spring 193, presumably assumed the name Septimius at this time and was regarded as junior colleague, while remaining in Britain. When Severus made his own son Caesar and renamed him M. *Aurelius Antoninus (1) in 195, after defeating C. *Pescennius Niger and the successful First Parthian War, Albinus' position became untenable. He crossed to Gaul and proclaimed himself Augustus, making *Lugdunum (1) his headquarters but failing to win over the Rhine legions. He was defeated and killed at the battle of Lugdunum on 19 February 197.

Cass. Dio 73–5; Hdn. 2–3; SHA *Pertinax, Did. Iul., Sev., Clod.* (the latter mainly fictional); *BM Coins, Rom. Emp.* 5; A. R. Birley, *The Fasti of Roman Britain* (1981), 146 ff., and *The African Emperor Septimius Severus*, 2nd edn. (1988). A. R. Bi.

Clodius (*RE* 58) **Thrasea Paetus, Publius** (suffect consul AD 56), Stoic (see STOICISM), renowned for his uprightness and belief in senatorial freedom. He composed a biography of *Cato (Uticensis), for which the biographer Munatius Rufus (1st cent. BC) was a source and which was used by *Plutarch for his *Cato Minor* (25, 37). He at first co-operated with *Nero but, after trying to stem senatorial servility, he showed opposition by abstention. Condemned under Nero in AD 66, he committed suicide in the presence of his son-in-law *Helvidius Priscus and the Cynic philosopher *Demetrius (19) but dissuaded his wife *Arria (2) from taking her life, as he had once tried to dissuade her mother.

Tac. *Ann.* 13. 49; 14. 12, 48–9; 15.20–1; 16.21–35; Plin. *Ep.* 3. 16. 10; 6.20; 8.22.; Syme, *Tacitus*, 556 ff.; M. T. Griffin, *Nero*; J. Geiger, *Athenaeum* 1979, 48 ff. G. C. W.; M. T. G.

Clodius (*RE* 59) **Turrinus,** a well-born Spanish declaimer, close friend of L. *Annaeus Seneca (1) (see esp. *Controv.* 10 pref. 14–16). His eloquence suffered from his cautious adherence to the doctrines of *Apollodorus (5). His son of the same name was treated by Seneca as one of his own children.

PIR² C 1188; Schanz–Hosius, § 337. J. W. D.; M. W.

Cloelia, a Roman girl given as hostage to *Porsenna. She escaped across the Tiber to Rome, by swimming or on horseback, but was handed back to Porsenna who, admiring her bravery,

freed her and other hostages. An equestrian statue on the via Sacra later celebrated her exploit. Critics who dismiss the story as legend believe that the statue was dedicated to a goddess (*Venus Equestris?) and that later Romans wrongly associated it with Cloelia.

Cf. Ogilvie, *Comm. Livy 1–5*, on Livy 2. 13. H. H. S.

closure, the sense of finality or conclusiveness at the end of a work or some part of it. In addition to the basic fulfilment of expectations raised by particular texts, some ancient genres show marked closural conventions; examples include the choral coda of Euripidean tragedy, the *plaudite* of Roman comedy (see COMEDY, LATIN), and the rhetorical peroration. We also find a variety of closural modes across genres: authorial self-reference, generalization, prophecy, prayer, motifs such as death, marriage, ritual, and departure. Our understanding of ancient closure is limited by what we have; some endings have been lost, some works were never finished, and some extant endings may be interpolations. Our uncertainties about ancient closural convention in turn lead us to disagree about whether in fact we do possess the actual endings of works such as *Herodotus' Histories*, *Euripides' Iphigenia at Aulis*, *Lucretius' De Rerum Natura*, and *Catullus 51. Even when we have the ending we may have difficulties in assessing closure. Closure may be unexpected or false, undercut or ironized; it is often hard to interpret the effect on closure of the audience's knowledge of later events in the continuing myths from which so many ancient narratives are taken. *Aristotle tells us in the *Poetics* that a plot must have an ending, which follows from something but from which nothing follows (ch. 7), and that different endings suit different genres (ch. 13); further discussion of closure may be found in the rhetorical tradition and in remarks on particular endings. But the most telling ancient comment on the interpretative significance of endings as the opportunity for what B. H. Smith calls 'retrospective patterning' is to be found in *Solon's advice at Herodotus 1. 32: that we call no one happy until death.

D. Fowler, *MD* 1989, 75–122; F. Dunn, D. P. Fowler, and D. H. Roberts (eds.), *Classical Closure* (1997); P. Hamon, *Poétique* 1975, 495–526; F. Kermode, *The Sense of an Ending* (1966); B. H. Smith, *Poetic Closure* (1968). D. H. R.

clubs, Greek The clubs here discussed may (but see Jones 1999, 27–33) be defined as voluntary associations of persons more or less permanently organized for the pursuit of a common end, and so distinguishable both from the state and its component elements on the one hand, and on the other from temporary unions for ephemeral purposes. Despite the large number and great popularity of clubs in the Greek world, both in the Hellenistic and in the Graeco-Roman period, literature makes surprisingly few references to them, and the available evidence consists almost entirely of inscriptions and, in the case of Egypt, papyri. These provide a picture which, if incomplete, is at least vivid and detailed.

Greek clubs, sacred and secular, are attested as early as the time of *Solon, one of whose laws, quoted by Gaius (*Dig.* 47. 22. 4), gave legal validity to their regulations, unless they were contrary to the laws of the state; and we hear of political clubs (*hetaireiai*) at Athens in the 5th cent. BC (Thuc. 3. 82; 8. 54; 65). In the Classical period the societies known to us are mostly religious, carrying on the cult of some hero or god not yet recognized by the state, such as the votaries (see ORGEONES) of Amynus, Asclepius, and Dexion, the heroized *Sophocles (1). In Hellenistic times, clubs become much more frequent and varied, and though many of them have religious names and exercise primarily religious functions, their social and economic aspects become increasingly prominent and some of them are purely secular. They are found throughout the Graeco-Roman world, but are specially common in the cosmopolitan trade-centres such as *Piraeus, *Delos, and *Rhodes, in *Egypt, and in the flourishing cities of *Asia Minor, and they appear to have played a valuable role in uniting in a common religious and social activity different elements of the population—men and women, slaves and free, citizens and aliens, Greeks and '*barbarians'. On the titles and aims of these guilds, their cults and festivals, their social and economic aspects, their membership and officials, their organization and finance, much light has been thrown by inscriptions, fully discussed by F. Poland (see below). See ERANOS; THIASOS.

From the multifarious societies so revealed, incapable of a wholly satisfactory classification, three groups may be singled out for mention.

(a) Among the religious guilds a leading place is taken by the Dionysiac artists (see DIONYSUS, ARTISTS OF).

(b) In various cities wholesale merchants (ἔμποροι) formed associations of their own (Poland, 107 ff.), and in Athens they combined, for some purposes at least, with the shippers (ναύκληροι). In the 2nd cent. BC two vigorous and wealthy societies, in which these two elements unite with the warehousemen (ἐγδοχεῖς), meet us on the island of Delos, the Heracleïstae of Tyre and the Poseidoniastae of Berytus (W. A. Laidlaw, History of Delos (1933), 212 ff. and L. Robert, in Études Déliennes (BCH Suppl. 1, 1973), 486 ff.); the large and well-appointed clubhouse of the latter, which apparently served religious, social, and commercial ends, has been completely excavated (C. Picard, Exploration archéologique de Délos, 6. 1921).

(c) Numerous guilds, some of which probably date from the Classical period, are composed of fellow workers in the same craft, industry, or trade. Their main function was religious and social rather than economic; and though we hear of troubles at *Ephesus in which the guilds play a leading part (Acts 19: 24 ff.; Anatolian Studies presented to W. M. Ramsay (1923), 27 ff.), their chief object was social, rather than to modify conditions of labour or to champion the interests of the workers against their employers. See ARTISTS AND CRAFTSMEN.

E. Ziebarth, Das griech. Vereinswesen (1896); J. Oehler, Zum griech. Vereinswesen (1905); F. Poland, Geschichte d. griech. Vereinswesens (1909); M. N. Tod, Sidelights on Greek History (1932), 69 ff; N. F. Jones, The Associations of Classical Athens (1999). For specific aspects or regions see M. San Nicolò, Aegyptisches Vereinswesen zur Zeit der Ptolemäer u. Römer (1913–15); P. Foucart, Des associations religieuses chez les Grecs (1873); F. Poland, RE 'Technitae'; M. Radin, Legislation of the Greeks and Romans on Corporations (1910). The decrees and laws of the Attic societies are collected in IG 2². 1249–1369; those of the Delian corporations in IDélos 1519–23; for a selection of inscriptions relating to clubs see Syll.³ 1095–1120, C. Michel, Recueil d'inscriptions grecques (1900–1927), 961–1018; for Egyptian religious associations A. D. Nock, etc., Harv. Theol. Rev. 1936, 39 ff. (partly repr. in Nock's Essays (1972), 414 ff.); J. K. Davies, CAH 7²/1 (1984), 283, 318 ff. (general); P. M. Fraser, Rhodian Funerary Monuments (1977), 58 ff.; DFA³ (1988), 279 ff., 365 (artists of Dionysus); W. Brasheer, Vereine im gr.-röm. Ägypten (1993).
M. N. T.; S. H.

clubs, Roman The Latin words corresponding most closely to the English 'club' are *collegium and sodalitas (see SODALES). The former was the official title of the four great priestly colleges, *pontifices, *septemviri epulones, *quindecimviri sacris faciundis, and *augures, and the word had religious associations even when the

object of the club was not primarily worship. Few, if any, collegia were completely secular. Some took their name from a deity or deities, e.g. *Diana et *Antinous (ILS 7212), *Aesculapius et Hygia (see HYGIEIA) (ibid. 7213), *Hercules (ibid. 7315, etc.), *Silvanus (ibid. 7317), and their members were styled cultores. Even when their name was not associated with a god, collegia often held their meetings in temples and their clubhouse (schola) might bear the name of a divinity (ILS 7218: Schola deae Minervae Aug.). The collegia illustrate the rule that all ancient societies from the family upwards had a religious basis. Collegia are associated with trades and professions (merchants, scribes, workers in wood and metal) and also with districts (vici) of the city of Rome. The annual festival of the districts was the Compitalia, held at the turn of the calendar year, which celebrated the *Lares of the Crossroads.

Plutarch (Num. 17) attributes to Numa *Pompilius the foundation of certain collegia but it is doubtful whether many existed before the Second Punic War. There were no legal restrictions on association down to the last century of the republic though the action taken by the senate against the Bacchanales (see BACCHANALIA) in 186 BC (Livy 39. 14 f.; ILS 18 or ILLRP 511) shows that the government might intervene against an objectionable association. Membership of many clubs came to be dominated by freedmen, and slaves were also admitted to plebeian clubs. In the Ciceronian age the collegia became involved in elections and other political action; many were suppressed in 64 BC and again by *Caesar, after a temporary revival by P. *Clodius Pulcher. Augustus created new associations in the city districts, associated with the cult of the emperor's *numen or *genius. On the other hand he also enacted by a Lex Iulia (probably AD 7, ILS 4966) that every club must be sanctioned by the senate or emperor. This permission is sometimes recorded on club inscriptions, and undoubtedly was freely given, though the policy of different emperors varied (*Trajan forbade the formation of clubs in Bithynia; Plin. Ep. 10. 34) and suspicion of clubs as a seed-bed of subversion remained. An extant *senatus consultum (ILS 7212) shows that general permission was given for burial clubs (collegia funeraticia), provided that the members met only once a month for the payment of contributions. In practice these clubs engaged in social activities and dined together on certain occasions, e.g. the birthdays of benefactors.

Although many collegia were composed of men practising the same craft or trade, there is no evidence that their object was to maintain or improve their economic conditions. In most cases they were probably in name burial clubs, while their real purpose was to foster friendliness and social life among their members. Many clubs of *iuvenes existed mainly for sport, and associations were formed among ex-service men (*veterani). Several lists of members survive (e.g. ILS 6174–6; 7225–7). These are headed by the names of the patroni (ILS 7216 f.), wealthy men, sometimes of senatorial rank, who often had made gifts to the clubs. The members bore titles recalling those borne by municipal officials. The presidents were magistri or curatores or quinquennales (who kept the roll of members). Below these came the decuriones, and then the ordinary members (plebs). The funds were sometimes managed by quaestores. In these clubs the humbler population (tenues) found some compensation for their exclusion from municipal honours. The fact that at the distributions of money or food a larger share was given to the officials or even to the patroni implies that the object of the clubs was not primarily philanthropic, though they no doubt fostered goodwill and generosity among their members.

J.-P. Waltzing, *Étude historique sur les corporations professionelles chez les Romains* vols. 1–2 (1895–6), 3–4 (1899–1900; repr. 1970); F. M. De Robertis, *Lavoro e lavoratori nel mondo Romano* (1963); Lintott, *Violence.*
G. H. S.; A. W. L.

Cluentius (*RE* 4) **Habitus, Aulus,** of a prominent family of *Larinum, in 76 BC charged his stepfather Oppianicus and others with attempting to poison him; they were convicted after notorious bribery on both sides. In 66 the case was reopened by Oppianicus' son, who charged Cluentius with the murder of the elder Oppianicus. Cicero conducted the defence and, by 'throwing dust in the eyes of the jury' (as he later boasted), won his case. The true facts cannot be disentangled.

Cic. *Clu.* G. S. Hoenigswald, *TAPA* 1962, 109 ff.   E. B.

Clunia, a town in the territory of the Celtiberian Arevaci and later in Roman *Tarraconensis, lay 40 km. (25 mi.) north-west of Uxama (mod. Osma). It was a *conventus* capital which had been granted municipal status (see MUNICIPIUM) under *Tiberius and was made a *colonia* (*Clunia Sulpicia*) by the future emperor *Galba. Excavations of the early imperial *forum, theatre (see THEATRES), and *baths suggest that the town may have entered a period of decline from the 3rd cent. onwards. It may have eventually ceded importance to Uxama.

P. de Palol and others, *Clunia* 1991.   S. J. K.

Clusium (Etr. *Clevsin-, Chamars*; mod. Chiusi), above the *via Cassia in the Val di Chiana, traditionally played an important role in early Roman history under *Porsenna; it did not pass into Roman hands until a comparatively late stage. Clusium was one of the twelve cities of Etruria (see ETRUSCANS), and one of the oldest in the north-east. The earliest finds are *Villanovan, the ossuaries developing in the orientalizing period into 'canopic urns' (i.e. images of the dead). One of the earliest of the numerous chamber tombs produced the François vase (see POTTERY, GREEK), and a number are painted. The city was an important centre of stone-carving and, from the 5th cent. BC, of decorative bronze-working. Its territory has produced an exceptionally large number of Etruscan inscriptions (*CIE* 475–3306). A man of Clusium, Arruns, invited the Gauls to cross the Alps into Italy (Livy 5. 33).

BTCGI 5 (1987), 'Chiusi'; R. D. Gempeler, *Die etruskischen Kanopen* (1974); M. Harari, *Il Gruppo Clusium nella ceramografia etrusca* (1980); J.-R. Jannot, *Les Reliefs archaïques de Chiusi* (1984); S. Steingräber, *Etruscan Painting* (1986), nos. 14–27.   D. W. R. R.

Cluvius (*RE* 12) **Rufus,** the imperial historian, consul probably before AD 41. *Nero's herald in the theatre, he became *Galba's governor of Hispania *Tarraconensis. He first supported *Otho, but later declared for *Vitellius, defending Spain. His *Historiae* may have begun with Gaius (1) and ended with Otho; but in any event the main part covered the reign of Nero. *Tacitus (1) (*Ann.* 13. 20, 14. 2) may have followed him in the *Annals.*

Peter, *HRRel.* 2. clxv and 114; P. Fabia, *Les Sources de Tacite* (1893), 171, 376; Syme, *Tacitus*, 178 ff., 293 ff., 675 ff.   A. H. McD.; M. T. G.

Clymene, name of a dozen different heroines (for one see CATREUS), the best known being the mother of *Phaethon, wife of Merops, king of Ethiopia. Meaning simply 'famous', it is a stopgap name, like Creusa, Leucippus, etc., used where there was no genealogical or other tradition.   H. J. R.

Clymenus (1) Euphemistic epithet ('Renowned') of *Hades/Pluton, esp. as the husband of Kore (see PERSEPHONE) (Philicus, *Hymn to Demeter, Suppl. Hell.* no. 676; Callim. fr. 285 Pf.; Damagetus, *Anth. Pal.* 7. 9. 7; Aristodicus, ibid. 7. 7. 189. 3; Ov.

Fast. 6. 757 f.). Pluton was worshipped by this title in his cult at Hermione in the Argolid (see ARGOS (2)); his temple stood opposite that of *Demeter Chthonia, whose foundation was ascribed to Clymenus, son of Phoroneus, and to his sister Chthonia (*IG* 4. 686–691. 715. 2; Lasus of Hermione, *Hymn to Demeter, PMG* fr. 702. 1 Page; Paus. 2. 35.4 f., 9 f.). The variant form Periclymenus appears to have been literary rather than cultic (Hes. fr. 136.11 M.–W., Hsch.). (2) Homonym shared by a dozen mythological figures. (*a*) The Argive (or Arcadian) Clymenus, son of Teleus (or Schoeneus), abducted and violated his daughter *Harpalyce just after her marriage to *Alastor. In revenge, she served the flesh of her younger brother, or that of the offspring from the incestuous union, to her father at a banquet. Harpalyce was transformed into a bird, the *chalkis*; Clymenus committed suicide (Euph., *Thrax* fr. 24a van Groningen = *Suppl. Hell.* no. 413 A 4–16 and the embellished prose version in Parth., *Amat. Narr.* 13; Nonnus, *Dion.* 12. 72 ff., cf. schol. T and Eust. *Il.* 14. 291). Hyginus has Harpalyce killed by Clymenus (*Fab.* 206, 238, cf. 242, 246). (*b*) *Boeotian, son of Presbon and king of the *Minyans at *Orchomenus (1). He was murdered by Theban brawlers at the festival of *Poseidon at Onchestus (Paus. 9.37.1–4; Apollod. *Bibl.* 2. 4. 11; for other versions of his death see *P Oxy.* 26. 2442 fr. 29. 4–8; cf. A. Schachter, *Cults of Boiotia* 2 (1986), 220). His son Erginus, an *Argonaut (Pind. *Ol.* 4. 19; R. Pfeiffer on Callim. fr. 668; M. W. Haslam on *P Oxy.* 53. 3702 fr. 2. 6 f.), attacked *Thebes (1) and was killed by *Heracles; his grandsons *Trophonius and Agamedes built the first stone temple for *Apollo at *Delphi (*Hymn. Hom. Ap.* 296 f.; Ian Rutherford on Pind. *Paeans* 8. 100–11; Paus. 10. 5. 13). (*c*) Son of Orchomenus (Hes. fr. 77 M–W), perhaps the same as the son of Presbon. (*d*) Father of Eurydice, *Nestor's wife (*Od.* 3. 452). Usually identified with the king of Orchomenus (cf. *b* and *c* above) in modern accounts. (*e*) Aetolian, son of Oeneus and Althaea (Hes. fr. 25. 16 M.–W.; Apollod. *Bibl.* 1. 8. 1; Ant. Lib. *Met.* 2). (*f*) Cretan, son of Cardys from Cydonia and founder of the Olympian Games (Paus. 5. 8. 1). (*g*) Other namesakes: see K. Latte and W. A. Oldfather, *RE* 11 (1921), 881.   A. H.

Clytemnestra (Clytaem(n)estra, Κλυταιμ(ν)ήστρα; the shorter form is better attested); daughter of *Tyndareos and *Leda; sister of *Helen and the *Dioscuri; wife of *Agamemnon; mother of a son, *Orestes, and of three daughters, named by *Homer Chrysothemis, Laodice, and Iphianassa (*Il.* 9. 145), although *Iphigenia, whom Homer does not mention, seems to be a later substitution for Iphianassa, as does *Electra (3) for Laodice (see Xanthus fr. 700 *PMG*). During Agamemnon's absence at Troy she took his cousin *Aegisthus as a lover, and on Agamemnon's return home after the ten-year war they murdered him, along with his Trojan captive, *Cassandra. Years later Orestes avenged his father's murder by killing both Clytemnestra and Aegisthus.

Her legend was a favourite one from Homer on, and given a variety of treatments. Homer makes her a good but weak woman led astray by an unscrupulous Aegisthus (*Od.* 3. 263 ff.), and 'hateful' (ibid. 310) or 'accursed' (11. 410) only in retrospect. Agamemnon is killed by Aegisthus, while Clytemnestra kills Cassandra (11. 422). Here there is no direct mention of her own murder by Orestes, although it is implied (3. 309 f.). *Stesichorus (fr. 223 Davies, *PMGF*) blames *Aphrodite, who made Tyndareos' daughters unfaithful because he had neglected her. But it is *Aeschylus' Clytemnestra, in his *Oresteia* of 458 BC, who dominates the extant literature which incorporates this legend. Prior to Aeschylus, Aegisthus and Clytemnestra were, as far as we can tell, joint partners-in-crime in Agamemnon's murder, with

Cnidus

Aegisthus taking the dominant role. In the *Agamemnon*, Clytemnestra has nursed grief and rage down the long years because of her husband's sacrifice of their daughter Iphigenia at Aulis (see esp. 1414–18, 1525–9, 1552–9), then on his return home kills him entirely on her own, and with a fierce joy, after netting him in a robe while he is unarmed in his bath (1379–98). Here she is an immensely powerful figure, a woman with the heart of a man (10 f.), while Aegisthus' role has dwindled into comparative insignificance, and he becomes a blustering weakling (cf. *Od.* 3. 310, ἀνάλκιδος Αἰγίσθοιο 'feeble Aegistheus') who appears on stage only at the end of the play (see in general J. R. March, *BICS* Suppl. 49 (1987), 81–98). *Sophocles (1) and *Euripides in their *Electras* still make her the more prominent figure, but tend to increase the relative importance of Aegisthus again; in Sophocles she is depicted as a truly evil woman, but Euripides treats her more sympathetically, making her (*El.* 1105–6) somewhat sorry for all that has happened. When the time comes for her death at Orestes' hands, in Aeschylus she tries to resist him (*Cho.* 889 ff.) and threatens him with the *Erinyes (924), whom her ghost afterwards stirs up against him (*Eum.* 94 ff.); in the two other tragedians she simply pleads for her life, although Euripides, unlike Sophocles, also introduces the Erinyes into the legend (*El.* 1252 ff.; *Or.* 34 ff.).

Her part in other legends is small: she brings Iphigenia to Aulis, supposedly to marry *Achilles (Eur. *IA* 607 ff.); and she gives advice to *Telephus (1) when he comes in search of Achilles to heal his wound, which enables him to get a hearing from the Greeks (Hyg. *Fab.* 101. 2; probably from Euripides).

Clytemnestra appears occasionally in art from the 7th cent. BC, though usually in scenes where she herself is not the main character, such as the murder of Aegisthus by Orestes; depictions of her own death are rare: see Y. Morizot, *LIMC* 6/1. 72–81; A. J. N. W. Prag, *The Oresteia: Iconographic and Narrative Tradition* (1985).   H. J. R.; J. R. M.

Cnidus, a *Dorian city, founded perhaps *c*.900 BC, and claiming descent from Sparta, was situated on a long peninsula (Reşadiye), in the gulf of *Cos (SW Asia Minor), and was a member of the Dorian Hexapolis. Originally set on the SE coast of the peninsula (modern Datça), the Cnidians moved probably (though this is controversial) in the 360s to a magnificent strategic and commercial site at the cape (Tekir). The fortifications and two protected harbours are still open to view. Failing in the attempt to convert their peninsula into an island, the Cnidians yielded to the Persians (after 546). After the Persian Wars they joined the *Delian League, but warmly espoused the Spartan cause after 413. Cnidus again came under Persian rule by the *King's Peace (386). Subjected to Ptolemaic control (see PTOLEMY (1)) in the 3rd cent. and perhaps Rhodian in the early 2nd, Cnidus was a *civitas libera* (*free city) under Roman rule from 129 BC. Notable citizens were *Ctesias, *Eudoxus (1) the astronomer, Sostratus (architect of the Pharus of *Alexandria (1)), and *Agatharchides. Cnidus was famous for its medical school, its wines, and the Aphrodite of *Praxiteles.

Archaeological remains excavated also include a Hellenistic house, a stoa, a round building, perhaps the famous temple of Aphrodite, a theatre, and a temple and stadium of the imperial period. See also OCNUS (for the Cnidian *lesche* or club-house at Delphi); POLYGNOTUS; TRIOPAS.

G. E. Bean, *Turkey Beyond the Maeander* (1980), 135 f.; I. Love, *PECS* 459; W. Blümel, *Die Inschriften von Knidos* 1 (1992).   J. M. C.; S. S.-W.

Cnossus (Greek and Roman), a town on Crete. It flourished

from the 9th to the 6th cent., to judge from the evidence of large numbers of tombs (protogeometric to orientalizing periods), but seems to have lost power in the 6th–5th cents. From the 4th cent. onwards it was again one of the principal cities of the island. Its main centre lay north-west of the *Minoan palace, but its buildings are poorly known; a shrine to *Demeter (protogeometric to 2nd cent. AD) lay just south of the palace. In the 4th–3rd cents. Cnossus frequently fought Lyttus, and then, after Lyttus' destruction, *Gortyn. Cnossus, which resisted the Roman invasion, lost out to Gortyn, and in 36 BC suffered the attribution to *Capua of valuable territory (Vell. Pat. 2. 81. 2; Cass. Dio 49. 14. 5); after 27 BC it was turned into a *colonia* (*Iulia Nobilis*), perhaps receiving settlers from Capua. From the Roman period a basilica is known, and houses, including the 'Villa Dionysus'. Despite a series of earthquakes, the city prospered until the 3rd cent. AD, extending by *c*.50–60 ha. (*c*.125–150 acres), but may have been largely abandoned after a major earthquake in mid-4th cent. Three basilica churches of the 5th–6th cent. were built outside the city. Perhaps from the 5th cent. the more easily defensible site of Heraklion became the dominant site of the region.

IC 1. 45–82, with testimonia; ML 42; Polyb. 4. 53–5; Strabo 10. 476–7; S. Hood and D. Smyth, *Archaeological Survey of the Knossos Area*, 2nd edn. (1981); I. F. Sanders, *Roman Crete* (1982); L. H. Sackett, *Knossos from Greek City to Roman Colony* (1992); D. Evely and others (eds.), *Knossos: A Labyrinth of History* (1994).   L. F. N., S. R. F. P.

Cocceius (*RE* 12) **Nerva, Lucius,** Roman politician. He was sent by *Octavian to Antony (M. *Antonius (2)), then in Syria, in 41 BC, returned with him to Italy in 40, and helped to negotiate the Pact of Brundisium (see ANTONIUS (2), M., para. 4). In 38 or 37 he accompanied C. *Maecenas to *Brundisium on another diplomatic mission, recounted by *Horace (*Sat.* 1. 5). He was brother of M. *Cocceius Nerva (1), and probably of C. Cocceius Balbus, suffect consul in 39. He himself is not known to have held any office.

Syme, *Rom. Rev.*, see index.   C. B. R. P.

Cocceius Nerva, Marcus, Roman emperor. See NERVA.

Cocceius (*RE* 13) **Nerva (1), Marcus,** Roman politician. He supported L. *Antonius (Pietas) in 41 BC. Pardoned by *Octavian, he held a command in the east, probably as governor of Asia (?38–7), and was consul in 36. He attended the *Secular Games in 17 BC as *quindecimvir sacris faciundis*.

Syme, *Rom. Rev.* and *AA*, see indexes.   C. B. R. P.

Cocceius (*RE* 14) **Nerva (2), Marcus,** probably grandson of M. Cocceius Nerva (1), was suffect consul and from AD 24 *curator aquarum* (official in charge of the water-supply; see AQUEDUCTS). A close friend of *Tiberius, he accompanied him into retirement in 26 but in 33, disgusted (it was said) by Tiberius' society and handling of the senators' financial problems of that year, he starved himself to death. A distinguished lawyer, he developed the school founded by M. *Antistius Labeo and later known as Proculian (see MASURIUS SABINUS); his son Marcus, father of the emperor *Nerva, also belonged to it.

Lenel, *Pal.* 1. 787 ff.; H. F. Jolowicz, *Historical Introduction to Roman Law*, 3rd edn. by B. Nicholas (1972), 378 ff.   T. J. C.; B. M. L.

codex, though it came to have a special meaning in legal contexts, denotes leaves of wood, papyrus, or (especially) parchment bound together in the form of a modern volume as opposed to a roll. (See BOOKS, GREEK AND ROMAN.) Christian Scriptures took this convenient form, which made it easier to find the passage one wanted. The earliest legal work to which the term was applied was the *Codex Gregorianus* of AD 291. This was a collection of imperial laws (constitutions) from the time of Hadrian onwards, divided into books (*libri*) and subject-headings (titles). The identity of the author Gregorius is uncertain; he may have been a western lawyer who served *Diocletian as master of petitions (*magister libellorum*). His *Codex* was composed largely of replies on behalf of emperors to petitions in writing on points of law (rescripts). Extracts from it have survived, mainly in Justinian's *Codex*. Then, about 295, *Hermogenianus, who served *Diocletian and *Maximian as *magister libellorum* from 293 to 295, published a second collection (*Codex Hermogenianus*). This work, divided into titles only, again consisted largely of rescripts to private individuals and apparently included all the eastern rescripts of the years 293 and 294 for which Hermogenianus had himself been responsible, with a few letters to officials and some western additions. It too survives only in extracts, mostly in Justinian's *Codex*. Both works were widely used, new editions quickly appeared, and the term 'codex' came in legal circles to mean a collection of imperial laws. The *Gregorianus* and *Hermogenianus* were not however exclusive collections; anyone was free to cite imperial laws which were not in them.

The next codex, that of Theodosius II (see THEODOSIAN CODE), was different. Theodosius himself directed it to be compiled. The collection was to be confined to general laws to the exclusion of rescripts. Moreover imperial laws of the period from Constantine (306 to 337) onwards were no longer to be cited if they were not in the collection. In 438 Theodosius officially promulgated the resulting *Codex Theodosianus* in sixteen books, which then became the exclusive source of imperial laws from Constantine to the end of 437. Ninety years later Justinian in his *Codex* of 529 (see JUSTINIAN'S CODIFICATION), of which there was a second edition in 534, continued the official collection of imperial laws from 438 to his own time. No longer limited to general laws, he embodied in it parts of the three previous collections; the parts not included were repealed. The earlier collections however remained in use in those areas of the west which the ambitious emperor failed to recapture. Though Justinian, unlike his predecessors, tried to harmonize the laws in his *Codex*, the result was not what would in modern terms count as a code. Containing some 5,000 laws, it is too bulky and, even so, has to be supplemented on any given topic by the private writings of authority contained in Justinian's *Digesta*.

P. Jörs in *RE* 4. 1 (1900) 'codex' cols. 161–7; P. Krüger, in *Collectio librorum iuris anteiustiniani* 3. 236–42); G. Rotondi, *Scritti Giuridici* 1 (1922), 110–265; A. Cenderelli, *Ricerche sul Codex Hermogenianus* (1965); Honoré 1981, 109–15, 119–32; Liebs 1987, 30–52, 134–44; *HLL* 5. § 504, 505. T. Hon.

Codrus, supposedly king of Athens in the 11th cent. BC. According to the story current in the 5th cent. (Pherec. *FGrH* 3 F 154; Hellanicus ibid. 4 F 125; cf. Lycurg. *Leoc*. 84–7) his father Melanthus, of the Neleid family, came to Attica when expelled from *Pylos by the *Dorians and, after killing the *Boeotian king Xanthus in single combat during a frontier war, was accepted as king of Athens in place of the reigning Theseid Thymoetes. During the reign of Codrus the Dorians invaded Attica, having heard from *Delphi that they would be victorious if Codrus' life was spared; a friendly Delphian informed the Athenians of this oracle. Codrus thereupon went out dressed as a woodcutter, invited death by starting a quarrel with Dorian warriors, and so saved his country. He was succeeded by his son Medon, and the kingship remained in the family until the 8th cent.; alternatively,

Codrus was the last king and his descendants were archons (*Ath. pol*. 3. 3). Other sons of Codrus, in particular Androclus (Pherec. F 155) and Neleus, led the colonization of Ionia from Athens. See IONIANS. This last detail makes Codrus a hinge-figure in the controversial tradition according to which the Pylians who colonized Ionia had gone there not direct but via Athens: the existence of this tradition, which is sometimes seen as essentially an Athenian imperial fiction of the 5th cent., in the century before is implied by *Herodotus' statement that the Pisistratids (see PISISTRATUS; HIPPIAS (1)) were, like Codrus and Melanthus, 'Pylians and Neleids' (5. 65). A sizeable shrine of Codrus, Neleus, and Basile in Athens is known from a decree of 418/7 BC (*IG* 1³. 84). A vase of *c*.450 (Beazley, *ARV*² 1268 no. 1: *LIMC* 'Ainetos' 1) shows the king, dressed as a hoplite, in conversation with Aenetus.

R. E. Wycherley, *BSA* 1960; B. Smarczyk, *Untersuchungen zur Religionspolitik und politischen Propaganda Athens im Delisch-Attischen Seebund* (1990), 328–59. R. C. T. P.

Coelius (*RE* 7) **Antipater, Lucius,** Roman historian. His seven books on the Second *Punic War marked an important artistic advance on his predecessors, as *Cicero recognized (*Leg*. 1. 6; *De or*. 2. 54); it also introduced to Rome, from Greek and Hellenistic models, the form of the historical monograph. The work, completed after 121 BC, was dedicated to the grammarian L. *Aelius Stilo Praeconinus. Coelius used not only Roman sources, including a funeral laudation (Livy 27. 27. 13), but also *Silenus of Caleacte's Carthaginian account (Cic. *Div*. 1. 49); it is possible, but unlikely, that he also used *Polybius (1). His style was elaborate, with extravagant hyperbata, rhythm, and recherché vocabulary; the narrative was sometimes sensational, he included speeches, and he had a taste for prophetic dreams (frs. 11, 49–50 P). He was used extensively by *Livy for his third decade. He was a legal expert and the teacher of L. *Licinius Crassus, but there is no evidence of a public career.

FRAGMENTS Peter, *HRRel*. 1². ccxi–ccxxxvii, 158–77; ed. with comm. by W. Herrmann (1979).
LITERATURE R. Jumeau, *Hommages à Jean Bayet* (1964), 324–33; E. Badian, in T. A. Dorey (ed.), *Latin Historians* (1966), 15–17; W. D. Lebek, *Verba Prisca* (1970), 217–23; H. Tränkle, *Livius und Polybios* (1977), 222–8. C. B. R. P.

Coelius (*RE* 12) **Caldus, Gaius,** as tribune (107 BC) extended vote by ballot to treason cases (cf. CASSIUS LONGINUS RAVILLA, L.). Praetor in Spain (see *RRC* 437/2a) and consul 94, though a *novus homo*, he probably governed the Gallic provinces till at least 87 (see Badian, *Stud. Gr. Rom. Hist*. 60 ff.). E. B.

coercitio, the right, held by every magistrate with *imperium, of compelling reluctant citizens to obey his orders and decrees, by inflicting punishment. Against this compulsion, which magistrates exercised not as judges but as holders of executive authority, *provocatio might be employed or an appeal to the tribunes. Moreover, the *provocatio* laws made it an offence to inflict capital punishment in face of appeal and banned the flogging of citizens, except in certain contexts, notably those of military service, the games, and the stage. Hence, where citizens were concerned, *coercitio* would usually take the form of imprisonment (see PRISON), fine, exaction of pledges, or *relegation from Rome.

Mommsen, *Röm. Staatsr*. 1³. 163 ff.; *Röm. Strafr*. 35 ff.; W. Kunkel, *Unters. z. Entwicklung d. röm. Kriminalverfahrens in vorsullanischer Zeit* (1962). P. T.; A. W. L.

Cogidubnus See CLAUDIUS COGIDUBNUS, TI.

cognomen See NAMES, PERSONAL, ROMAN.

cohors In the early Roman republic the infantry provided by the allies were organized in separate *cohortes* of varying strength, each under a Roman or native **praefectus*. In the legions the cohort was first used as a tactical unit by P. *Cornelius Scipio Africanus in Spain, but for over a century it was employed alongside the manipular organization (see MANIPULUS) before the latter was superseded in the field (perhaps in the Marian period). The cohort was made up of three maniples, or six centuries, the latter retaining manipular titulature into the Tetrarchic period. There were ten *cohortes* in a legion.

From the time of P. *Cornelius Scipio Aemilianus, the general's personal bodyguard was known as the *cohors praetoria*. By the middle of the 1st cent. BC, the term was used also to describe the group of personal friends and acquaintances which accompanied a provincial governor. Both these usages led to developments in the empire. This entourage was the origin of the emperor's *cohors amicorum* (see AMICUS AUGUSTI); the military *cohortes praetoriae* were formalized in the praetorian guard (see PRAETORIANS).

In the imperial *auxilia infantry were organized in *cohortes*, nominally 500 strong (*cohortes quingenariae*) under *praefecti*. Some had an additional cavalry component (*cohortes equitatae*). Larger units (nominally 1,000 men, *cohortes milliariae*) under **tribuni militum*, were used from the Neronian period onwards (see NERO). In Rome, the urban troops and the **vigiles* were also organized in *cohortes* under tribunes.

In the *Notitia Dignitatum certain units of the late frontier armies, commanded by *tribuni*, still retained the title of cohort.

L. Keppie, *The Making of the Roman Army* (1981).

H. M. D. P.; G. R. W.; J. C. N. C.

cohortes urbanae, the police force of Rome, established by *Augustus under the command of the **praefectus urbi* (prefect of the city). A permanent police force in Rome was an innovation and the first prefect M. *Valerius Messalla Corvinus resigned declaring that he did not understand how to exercise his powers. Originally there were three cohorts, each commanded by a tribune and six centurions, numbered X–XII in continuation of the praetorian sequence (see PRAETORIANS); under the Flavians there were four cohorts in Rome. Single 'urban' cohorts (so named because they were originally withdrawn from Rome) are found at *Puteoli, *Ostia, and *Carthage, presumably protecting the shipment of grain to Rome, and at *Lugdunum (Lyons), where there was an important mint. Each cohort contained 500 men, probably increased to 1,000 by *Vitellius, who added some legionaries. They were recruited from Italians, served for twenty years, were paid half the rate of praetorians, and had their base in the praetorian camp until the construction of a new camp for them in 270. Tribunes of the urban cohorts were often promoted to the praetorian guard (e.g. *ILS* 1379). Although in dynastic crises the prefect and his cohorts might take an independent line, as in 41 and 69, normally the soldiers of the *cohortes urbanae* would, like the praetorians, provide additional protection for the emperor. The force survived *Constantine's abolition of the praetorian guard in 312.

E. Echols, *CJ* 1961, 25; H. Freis, *RE* Suppl. 10 (1965), 1125, and *Die Cohortes Urbanae*, Epig. Stud. 2 (1967). J. B. C.

coinage, Greek

Definitions Coinage to the Greeks was one of the forms of *money available to measure value, store wealth, or facilitate exchange. Coins were made from precious metal such as *gold or *silver, or from a copper alloy; they were of regulated weight and had a design (type) stamped on one or both sides. Lumps of bullion too could be weighed to a standard and stamped with a design, but the stamp on a coin indicated that the issuing authority, normally a state or its representative(s), would accept it as the legal equivalent of some value previously expressed in terms of other objects, including metal by weight. Merchants and others therefore were expected to accept it in payment. A coin of precious metal might weigh the same as the equivalent value of bullion, but would normally weigh less, to cover minting costs and, in varying degrees, to make a profit for the mint: in other words, coins were overvalued relative to bullion (see WEIGHTS).

The scope of Greek coinage is wide, both geographically and chronologically. In the Archaic and Classical periods many of the Greek communities established around the Mediterranean and Black (*Euxine) Seas produced coins, and they often influenced their neighbours to do the same: Persians (see PERSIA) in western *Asia Minor, Carthaginians (see CARTHAGE) in North Africa and Sicily, *Etruscans in Italy, *Celts in western Europe. The coins of these peoples, although they usually bear images and inscriptions appropriate to their traditions, are in general inspired by Greek models, and they tend to be catalogued as part of Greek coinage. After 334 the conquest of the Persian empire by *Alexander (3) the Great inaugurated a massive extension of the area covered by coinage, in particular in the successor kingdoms, Syria, Egypt and so on. In effect the term Greek coinage includes most of the non-Roman coinage of the ancient world issued between the Straits of Gibraltar and NW India.

Beginnings Literary and archaeological evidence combine to show that coinage began in western Anatolia, at the point of contact between Greek cities on the Aegean coast and the Lydian kingdom in the interior. The first coins were of electrum, an alloy of gold and silver occurring naturally in the river Pactolus, which flowed into the Hermus to the west of *Sardis, the *Lydian capital. A date of *c.*600 BC or a little later for their introduction fits their appearance in a miscellaneous deposit of jewellery and figurines discovered in the foundations of the temple of Artemis at *Ephesus, and also the subsequent development of coinage in Asia Minor and the wider Aegean world. The first coins of electrum were followed in *Lydia by coins of pure gold and silver, with the type of confronting foreparts of a lion and of a bull. Such coins have traditionally been attributed to the Lydian king *Croesus (*c.*561–547), but hoard evidence suggests that most, if not all, are later than his reign and were part of the coinage issued in the area by the Persians.

Purpose In the modern world the role of coinage in everyday buying and selling is clear, but this does not mean that similar commercial reasons prompted its introduction. Coins were not necessarily advantageous in large transactions, and their usefulness in exchanges between cities was inhibited by various factors, including the diversity of weight-standards in the Greek world. For example, the weight of the drachma differed in cities as close together as *Aegina, *Corinth, and Athens. As for small transactions, few early coinages included the necessary range of small denominations. It is true that one of these was the electrum coinage produced in the 6th cent. in Ionia, but even the lowest known denomination ($\frac{1}{96}$) represented a large sum. Given the nature of the earliest coins—in particular their standardized weights and the lion's head that features on many of them—it is a plausible hypothesis that they were issued to make a large number of uniform and high-value payments in an easily portable and durable form, and that the authority or person making the payment, perhaps to *mercenaries, was the king of Lydia. For the original recipients coins were simply another form of movable wealth, but many pieces might thereafter be exchanged for goods or services and so pass into general circulation as money. But the progress towards a monetary economy was by no means straightforward or immediate. The fact that many of the early electrum coins are covered in small punch-marks suggests that it was some time before such coins were universally acceptable.

Minting Technique: Implications for Study The first task of the Greek moneyer was to create from metal of the required quality the blanks, or flans, of suitable shape and correct weight. Blanks were normally made by casting, that is, pouring the molten metal into moulds. (In the Greek world coins themselves were rarely made by casting.) To convert the blank into a coin it was struck with dies made from either toughened bronze or iron, and hand-engraved in negative (*intaglio*). One die, which was to produce the obverse, was set in an anvil. The blank was placed on top of it and the metal forced into the die beneath by a short stout bar (χαρακτήρ), its butt resting on the blank while its top was struck with a hammer. On the earliest coins the butt simply reproduced its own rough surface on the reverse; at a later stage, in many places by the end of the 6th cent., the practice arose of engraving the butt also with a device, thus creating a coin with types on both sides.

Minting was thus a relatively simple process, but at each stage there are implications for the modern study of its products. At the preparatory stage great care was generally taken to ensure both the purity of the metal and the accurate weight of the blanks: modern methods of non-destructive metal analysis can detect any significant differences in the composition of a metal alloy and thus help to classify the coins or to signal a change of monetary policy. Sometimes it was not—for whatever reason—convenient to prepare fresh blanks, and new types were overstruck on old coins. In cases where the undertypes were not totally obliterated by the restriking process, such 'overstrikes' can provide valuable evidence for relative dating and for the circulation of coins. When the blanks were being struck, the alignment of the two dies might be fixed or it might be variable: similarities or differences in the patterns of alignment may again help to classify or date some coins. Studies of the dies employed are of fundamental importance in modern numismatics. A single coin in isolation can provide a certain amount of information, but the significance of the information is immeasurably enhanced when two or more coins can be shown to have been struck from the same die(s). Coins sharing dies in this way must normally have been struck at the same place and at approximately the same time. Furthermore, since in practice the punch dies were more exposed to wear and/or damage than anvil dies and tended to be discarded more frequently, it is often possible to build up a sequence of issues sharing either an obverse or a reverse die. Finally, die-studies form the basis of attempts to estimate the size of a coinage. Using a variety of statistical methods, it may be possible to work out from a sample of dies the total number of dies used to produce a given coinage. To estimate the amount of bullion required, that total must be multiplied by the number of coins that were struck from each die. But in any individual case, that figure is elusive. There is no means of telling when a particular die was under-used, though conversely there is frequently evidence for the use of dies in an advanced stage of deterioration, and dies were sometimes recut, to repair them or to update

them. The size of an issue of coins depended on many factors, not least the availability of bullion.

Coin Types The type of a Greek coin is a mark of its origin, whether a community or an individual. The earliest coins, found in the temple of Artemis at Ephesus, had types only on the obverse and their variety makes it difficult to assign them to a specific minting authority. The commonest type, a lion's head, has been attributed to the kingdom of Lydia; others, such as a seal's head or a recumbent lion, may belong to Phocaea and Miletus respectively. The significance of the earliest types was not usually reinforced by any letter or inscription. On one coin from the Artemision with the type of two lions' heads the inscription WALWEL has been read. This cannot refer to king *Alyattes of Lydia (c.610–560) since another name, KALIL, has been identified on a similar issue. The identity of these persons remains unknown. Rather more revealing are the inscriptions on two early coins showing a stag. One has a simple name in the uncontracted genitive, Φανέος, 'of Phanes', the other reads Φανὸς ἔμι σῆμα 'I am the badge of Phanes'. The identity of the Phanes referred to is not known (a mercenary captain of that name from *Halicarnassus employed in Egypt in the 530s is too late for the coin), but with a different name and device the formula occurs on an archaic seal-stone probably from Aegina (J. Boardman, *Archaic Greek Gems* (1968), no. 176). The analogy makes clear the origin of a coin type in the personal seal or badge of the authority responsible for its issue. Apart from these examples coin legends are rare in the 6th cent. By its end the initial letter or letters of an ethnic might be introduced (as a *koppa* on coins of Corinth or *Athe* on those of Athens), and in course of time the tendency was to lengthen the inscription. When written out in full it was frequently in the genitive case, signifying [a coin] of whoever the issuing authority was.

After an initial period of variation the types of individual cities settled down and changed little: familiarity encouraged acceptability. Most coin types are connected with religion in the widest sense. Sometimes a divinity is represented directly, in other cases indirectly, through an animal or an attribute. Even some of the types illustrating a local product belong in this category: for example an ear of barley can symbolize Demeter, goddess of corn. Many types refer to local myths or religious traditions, for example those connected with the foundation of a city. Only rarely do types refer to historical events, at least in the Archaic and Classical periods. In this respect they share the preference of Greek art in general for the allusive and symbolic, rather than for direct and literal references to political matters.

The Spread of Coinage (*Archaic and Classical*) Electrum, with its variable content of gold and silver, did not last long as the primary metal for coining, and in the second half of the 6th cent., with a few exceptions such as *Cyzicus, *Phocaea, and *Mytilene, the coin-producing cities of Asia Minor turned exclusively to silver. Coinage in gold became a rarity both there and elsewhere, although from the early 5th cent. the Persians issued gold darics with the same type as their silver sigloi, a crowned figure representing the king of Persia. ('Darics' were so named by the Greeks after the Persian king *Darius I; 'siglos' is a Greek form of the Semitic 'shekel'.) These coins were issued for use in those parts of the Persian empire in closest contact with the Greeks, and the institution of coinage did not initially travel far to the east of its birthplace in western Asia Minor.

To the west and north the story was different. By *c*.550 coinage had crossed the Aegean to communities close to the isthmus of

Corinth—Aegina, Corinth and Athens—and not much later had taken root among the Greek cities and the tribes of the Thraco-Macedonian area (see THRACE; MACEDONIA). The rich metal resources of the latter gave rise to coinage in a remarkable range of denominations, including the heaviest of all Greek silver coins, the double octadrachm. Such coins travelled far, especially to the east, and may have been made for export. The first Athenian coins, the so-called *Wappenmünzen*, share some of the characteristics of the early coins of Asia Minor, notably their changing types, their lack of any indication of origin, and the use of electrum as well as silver for some issues. In the later part of the 6th cent., perhaps under the tyrant *Hippias (1), these issues were replaced by the famous 'owls', with obverse helmeted head of Athena, reverse owl, and the abbreviated name of the city. These coins too travelled a long way, another example of the export in the form of coin of silver mined in the territory of the issuing state.

From the Aegean area the medium of coinage spread rapidly to the western Greeks settled around the coasts of southern Italy and Sicily, France, and Spain. Early Corinthian coinage in particular influenced some of the first coinages in the west both in production technique and because imported Corinthian coins were often used as flans for overstriking. There was also a notable willingness to experiment: the first Italian coins were made using the sophisticated 'incuse' method, unique in the Greek world, in which the obverse type appears normally in relief, while on the reverse a closely similar version of the same type is struck in negative, the two types exactly aligned. To the western cities also belong the first bronze coins, at *Thurii from *c*.440, at *Acragas from *c*.430, and thus the development of the idea of fiduciary coinage in which the worth of a coin was not related to the intrinsic value of its metal content. The coins of the western Greeks attained the highest standards of artistic excellence and especially in the late 5th and early 4th cents. the careers of many of the artists can be traced from their signatures on dies.

Hellenistic

In the 4th cent. the Greek world of independent city-states began to give way in the eastern and western Mediterranean to the ambitions of individuals and the growing power of Rome. In the east the exploitation by *Philip (1) II of Macedon of the mines of *Pangaeus after 356 left a rich legacy of coinage in gold and silver which was adapted and expanded by his son *Alexander (3) the Great to cover the whole near east. He adopted the Attic weight-standard for both his gold and silver coinage, and struck coins with the same designs at more than one mint. After Alexander's death in 323, the currency system he had put in place remained remarkably stable. In the world of territorial states and kingdoms that emerged in the 3rd cent. only *Ptolemy (1) I in Egypt introduced major innovations in the types and weights of his coins, to produce an autonomous system of coinage. The change to larger political units, kingdoms, states, and leagues was reflected in the coinage. Many individual cities coined from time to time, but mostly in *bronze; only Athens and Rhodes coined continuously in silver down to the 1st cent. BC. Coins with Alexander's types played an important role as international currency, especially in Asia Minor, where 'posthumous Alexanders' were produced in quantity until 175 BC and even later.

The types of Hellenistic coins, like those of earlier periods, are for the most part religious in content; and although they display a strong historical consciousness in line with the culture of the time, they rarely refer directly to historical events. The major innovation was the introduction of the portrait of a ruler. Few

portraits of living persons have been recognized on Greek coins before Ptolemy I shortly after 305/4. A reverse of *Abdera in the last quarter of the 5th cent. realistically depicts a male head which might be the portrait of an individual (Pythagores) named on the coin. In the 4th cent. fine portraits occur on the coins of Persian satraps or Lycian dynasts in Asia Minor (e.g. *Pericles (2)). From the Hellenistic period we have a whole gallery of portraits of rulers in which idealized images of royal power are often combined with realism and insight into character. On the far eastern fringes of the Hellenistic world the kings of *Bactria are known to us largely through their brilliant coin-portraits. See PORTRAITURE.

In the last two centuries BC, as Roman power spread inexorably eastwards, Hellenistic coinage evolved new forms. League coinages had already played a leading role, for example those of the *Arcadian and *Achaean Confederacies in Greece. At Athens 'New Style' coinage began around 170, and *Pergamum at about the same time began to issue cistophoroi, so called from the adoption as their obverse type of a *cista mystica*, a basket used in the celebration of the rites of Dionysus. After the battle of Actium (31 BC) Rome's control over the eastern Mediterranean was complete and Greek coinage had virtually ceased. The subsequent plethora of city coinages with Greek legends and local types which were issued in the eastern provinces of the Roman empire (the so-called 'Greek imperials') until well into the later 3rd cent. AD are more Roman in appearance and conception; see COINAGE, ROMAN.

The standard handbook of Greek coinage is B. V. Head, *Historia Numorum*, 2nd. edn. (1911). I. Carradice and M. Price, *Coinage in the Greek World* (1988), provides an authoritative introduction to the field; for more detailed discussion see C. M. Kraay, *Archaic and Classical Greek Coins* (1976), and O. Mørkholm, *Early Hellenistic Coinage* (1991). Good surveys, with fine illustrations, in: M. Hirmer and C. M. Kraay, *Greek Coins* (1966); G. K. Jenkins, *Ancient Greek Coins*, 2nd. rev. edn. (1990). For Greek imperials see: A. Burnett, M. Amandry, and P. Ripollés, *Roman Provincial Coinage* (1992); C. Harl, *Civic Coins and Civic Politics in the Roman East* (1987); C. Howgego, *Greek Imperial Countermarks* (1985).
N. K. R.

coinage, Roman There are two related stories about Roman coinage, the one of its internal evolution, the other of its progressive domination of the Mediterranean world, its use throughout the Roman empire, and finally its fragmentation into the coinages of the successor kingdoms in the west and the Byzantine empire in the east.

Rome under the kings and in the early republic managed without a coinage, like the other communities of central Italy, with the episodic exception of some Etruscan cities; *bronze by weight, *aes rude* (see AES), with a pound of about 324 g. (11½ oz.) as the unit, served as a measure of value, no doubt primarily in the assessment of fines imposed by a community in the process of substituting public law for private retribution; this stage of Roman monetary history is reflected in the *Twelve Tables. The progressive extension of Roman hegemony over central Italy brought booty in the form of *gold, *silver, and bronze; the means to create a coinage on the Greek model were to hand. The stimulus was probably provided by Roman involvement with the Greek cities of *Campania, with the building of the *via Appia in the late 4th cent. BC; Rome had struck a diminutive coinage of bronze at Neapolis after 326 BC, with the legend *PΩMAIΩN*; she now struck a coinage of silver pieces worth two (probably) drachmas, with the legend ROMANO, otherwise indistinguishable from the Greek coinages of the south. But the continuing irrelevance of coinage to Rome emerges from the fact that there was nearly a generation before the next issue, probably contemporary with the Pyrrhic War. (See PYRRHUS.) From this point, there is a virtually unbroken sequence of Roman coinage to the end of the Roman Empire in the west.

To the basis of silver didrachms was added a token coinage in bronze; the curious decision was also taken to produce a cast bronze coinage, the unit (or *as*) of which weighed a pound; this coinage is now known as *aes graue*, though the Latin writers who spoke of the bronze coinage of early Rome as *aes graue* probably had little idea of what was involved. Bronze currency bars were also cast for a short time, in the period of the Pyrrhic and First *Punic Wars, now very misleadingly known as *aes signatum* (to a Roman, this phrase simply meant 'coined bronze'). It is striking that even now the coinage of Rome remained on a relatively small scale, compared with those of Carthage and the Greek cities of Italy.

The silver coinage with its token coinage in bronze (changing the ethnic in due course from ROMANO to ROMA) and the heavy cast bronze coinage went on side by side down to the outbreak of the Second *Punic War in 218 BC. It is probably in this period that Roman coinage penetrated the territories of the peoples of the central Apennines for the first time; and it is likely that, just as military needs may explain much of the production of Roman coinage in this period, so it was returning soldiers who carried it to Samnite and other communities.

The enormous strain of the war against *Hannibal led to a reduction in the metal content of the heavy cast bronze coinage, an emergency issue of gold and finally the debasement of the silver coinage. The first coinage system of Rome collapsed and in or about 211 BC a new system was introduced; it included a new silver coin, the denarius, which remained the main Roman silver coin until the 3rd cent. AD. The issue was financed initially by unprecedented state levies on private property, thereafter by booty as the war went better for Rome. The unit (or *as*) of the bronze coinage by this stage weighed only about two ounces (54 g.: 2 oz.), the denarius (or 'tenner') was worth ten of these; there were subsidiary denominations in both silver—including a piece known as the victoriatus, without a mark of value, weighing three-quarters of the denarius, but with a low and erratic silver content—and bronze and a short-lived issue of gold. The end of the war saw the virtual cessation of minting by other Italian communities; and coinage other than Roman on the whole disappeared rapidly from circulation in Italy. When the Italians produced a rebel coinage in 90–88 BC, it was modelled on the denarius, apart from a single issue of gold, in which they anticipated L. *Cornelius Sulla (see below).

Despite the creation of the denarius, bronze remained the most important element in the Roman monetary system for some years; a belief similar to those held by M. *Porcius Cato (1) even led to the virtual suppression for a decade of the silver coinage, a symbol of increasing wealth and of declining public morality. But the consequences of Rome's conquest of the world could not be suppressed for ever; the booty in silver *inter alia* which flowed into Rome from 194 BC onwards and the mines in *Macedonia which Rome controlled from 167 BC found expression in a vastly increased issue of silver coinage from 157 BC. It became normal for Rome to coin in a year as much as a Greek city might coin in a century; and it was only with Sulla that the mint abandoned the practice of producing a large part of what was needed each year as new coin; the mint then went over to what remained standard practice, to top up revenues already in the form of Roman coin with issues largely from newly mined

metal. In the years after 157 BC, the coinage came accurately to reflect the position of Rome as ruler of the world by omitting the ethnic: no identification was needed.

The relative unimportance of the bronze coinage after 157 BC led to the cessation of production of the as and to the production of its fractions on a very reduced weight standard; and in about 141 BC the bronze coinage was effectively devalued when the denarius was retariffed as the equivalent of 16, not 10, asses; its name, however, remained unchanged. By the end of the 2nd cent. BC, victoriati in circulation weighed only about half a denarius; and halves of the denarius, or quinarii, were henceforth intermittently struck, often for the Po valley (see PADUS) or Provence (see below).

The period after the Second Punic War saw the beginning of the process whereby Roman coinage came to be the coinage of the whole Mediterranean world. The denarius rapidly became the silver coin of Sicily, flanked both by Roman bronze and by bronze city issues. In Spain, the Romans permitted or encouraged the creation of silver and bronze coinages modelled on the denarius coinage, probably in the 150s BC. In the Po valley and in Provence, the Romans accepted for their own purposes the local monetary unit, equivalent to half-a-denarius, and indeed on a number of occasions struck such a unit for those areas. By way of contrast, the Greek east remained largely uninfluenced by Roman monetary structures until the 1st cent. BC. But as more and more of the Mediterranean world came under direct Roman rule and became involved in the civil wars that brought the republic to an end, so the use of Roman monetary units and Roman coins spread, to Africa, Greece and the east, and Gaul. Only Egypt, incorporated in 30 BC, remained monetarily isolated from the rest of the Roman world.

The military insurrection of Sulla in 84 BC had seen the production of a gold as well as a silver coinage, the availability of the metal combining with an urgent need for coinage to pay his soldiers; the precedent of Sulla was followed by *Caesar in this if in no other respect: the vast quantities of gold derived as booty from Gaul and Britain were converted in 46 BC by A. *Hirtius into the largest gold issue produced by Rome before the reign of *Nero; by 44 BC the distribution of gold coins, or aurei, to the troops was a normal occurrence. Caesar's rival *Pompey had become from the exploitation of the provinces of the east the wealthiest man of his time; in attempting successfully to outdo him in wealth as well as in prestige, Caesar in effect superseded the state as a minting authority.

The civil wars which followed the death of Caesar saw the production of coinage in a variety of metals—including bronze on more than one standard—by most of the rival contenders; unity of minting authority and uniformity of product returned when the last survivor of the civil wars finally suppressed the institutions of the free state and established an autocracy. The coinage of Caesar Octavianus (see AUGUSTUS) became the coinage of Rome.

Meanwhile, the types displayed by the Roman republican coinage had also come to mirror accurately the escalating internal conflict of the nobility. By 211 BC, the production of coinage was in the hands of men called moneyers, young men at the beginning of a political career. The possibilities offered by the coinage for self-advertisement gradually became apparent during the 2nd cent. BC and by the last third of the century the issue produced by a moneyer was as far as its types were concerned effectively a private concern; a moneyer might recall his town of origin, the deeds of his ancestors, eventually the contemporary achievements of a powerful patron; with Caesar, the coinage began to display his portrait, an overtly monarchical symbol; even *Brutus, the self-styled Liberator, portrayed on his last issue two of the daggers which had murdered Caesar on one side and his own portrait on the other side. In striking contrast to M. *Antonius (2) (Mark Antony), the future Augustus gradually suppressed on his coinage any reference to his lieutenants; and the coinage with which he paid the troops who defeated Antonius and *Cleopatra VII at the battle of Actium was already a coinage which displayed only the portrait and attributes of a single leader.

One important change in the structure of this coinage took place under Augustus: the silver fractions of the denarius, which had filled the gap between the denarius and the as, were largely replaced by *orichalcum* multiples of the as, the sestertii and dupondii which are among the most familiar components of the Roman imperial coinage. At the same time, the as and the smallest denomination now struck, the quadrans, or quarter, were produced in pure copper. The most probable view is that the letters SC on the new base metal coinage of Augustus reflect the fact that the new structure was endorsed by a decree of the senate (s(enatus) c(onsultum)); the reform perhaps involved the revaluation of surviving republican asses, heavier than Augustan asses, as dupondii.

The mainstream coinage of the Roman empire, then, consisted of aurei and denarii, at a ratio of 1 : 25, and base metal fractions. Although at all periods much, even most, was struck at Rome, this was not necessarily so: it is likely that between Augustus and the changes under *Nero most of the precious metal coinage was struck in Gaul. In addition, the empire continued in the east to produce coinages modelled on the earlier coinages of a number of areas, for instance cistophori in Asia till the 2nd cent. AD, tetradrachms in *Syria till the early 3rd cent. AD, tetradrachms in Egypt till *Diocletian. But the shift of minting from Gaul to Rome began a process of concentration of minting which lasted till the Severans (see ROME, HISTORY). Thereafter, the evolution of the empire saw an inexorable tendency for more and more of the mainstream coinage to be produced in the provinces, though there were ebbs and flows in the pattern. And the base metal coinage of the east consisted for a long time not of the familiar sestertii, dupondii, asses, and quadrantes of the mint of Rome, but of a range of provincial bronze coinages. The kaleidoscopic variety of the coinage of the empire was completed by hundreds of city coinages, in the west till *Claudius, in the east (the so-called 'Greek imperials') till the 3rd cent. AD. All these coinages, however, were probably based on, or compatible with, Roman monetary units. It is less clear how far the empire formed a single circulation area: the most probable view is that even mainstream coinage, once it had reached an area, tended to stay there, even in the 1st and 2nd cents. AD; but there is no doubt that the compartmentalization of circulation became even more marked with the shift from a monetary to a natural economy in the third century AD (see below).

The monetary system of the Roman Empire always operated on very narrow margins. It is possible to calculate that in normal times perhaps 80 per cent of the imperial budget was covered by tax revenues, the rest by the topping up of what came in with coins minted from newly mined metal. Prudent emperors managed; the less prudent did not.

In AD 64 Nero reduced the weight of the aureus and the weight and fineness of the denarius; and despite attempts under the Flavians (*Vespasian, *Titus, *Domitian) to reverse the trend, the next century and a half saw a slow decline in the silver content of the denarius, paralleled by a similar or worse decline in that of the provincial 'silver' coinages. *Commodus further reduced the weight of the denarius and *Septimius Severus drastically reduced its fineness; while *Caracalla chose to issue a coin, known to modern scholars as the antoninianus, with the weight of about one and a half denarii, but (probably) the face value of two. Since the imperial portrait bore a radiate crown, not the laurel wreath of the denarius, the coin may have been known as a 'radiate'. The tax-paying population of the Roman empire was not to be deceived and the state found its revenues increasingly arriving in the form of recent issues of poor quality, while older issues of better quality were hoarded or melted down. The combination of this process with the increasing demands on the empire as barbarian pressure increased led from AD 238 onwards to the complete collapse of the silver coinage: the denarius ceased to be produced and by AD 270 the antoninianus had ceased to contain more than a trifling percentage of silver. The weight even of the gold unit fluctuated, presumably as emperors divided what was in the kitty by the number of aurei it was necessary to pay out. In a sense, all that happened was that what had always been the underlying reality was revealed: an agricultural surplus supported an army and a bureaucracy. For on the whole taxes and payments were slow to catch up with the declining value of the coinage; and as the monetary circle—levies of taxes, payments to soldiers and others, payments to cultivators for grain for soldiers and others, providing the source for yet further levies of taxes—became increasingly meaningless, so it became ever more apparent that the 'real' wage of a soldier, for instance, was his ration of corn. And the institutional structures of the empire slowly changed to accommodate this fact.

At the same time, the sheer bulk of coinage produced and its appalling quality facilitated the production of imitations: the *nummularii*, whose profession it had been to test for forgeries, could not cope. A large part of the hoards of the late 3rd cent. AD, particularly in the west, is made up of coins known to modern scholars as 'barbarous radiates'.

By a series of reforms, the details of which remain obscure, Aurelian and the immediately subsequent emperors attempted to reform and stabilize the coinage. *Aurelian produced coins marked *XXI* or *KA* (in Greek), to indicate 5 per cent silver content; and there followed coins marked *XI* or *IA* (in Greek), to indicate 10 per cent silver content. The next major reform is that of Diocletian, who stabilized the gold coinage at 60 aurei to the Roman pound, restored a pure silver coinage at 96 units to the pound, and produced in addition a large bronze denomination with some silver content, known at the time as the nummus, and also small bronze pieces, doubles with a radiate head and no silver content, the ultimate descendants of Caracalla's double denarius, and singles with a laureate head. The gold unit was henceforth known as the solidus. Further adjustment was necessary in AD 301, the year of the Prices Edict, when Diocletian issued a revaluation edict, attested by the coins and by one of the two texts on a fragmentary inscription from *Aphrodisias. Diocletian also consolidated the distribution of production in twelve to fifteen mints distributed through most of the Roman empire; their products on the whole circulated in the areas where they were struck.

*Constantine (1) reduced the weight of the solidus to 72 to the Roman pound, but managed not to wreck the system completely; his gold coin remained standard for many centuries. A pure silver piece, however, never again played a major part in production or circulation, except to a certain extent between about AD 350 and 400. Nor did the Diocletianic nummus really survive, though some of the bronze issues of his successors approach it in diameter. Rather the coinage of the late Roman empire consists essentially of solidi and vast quantities of small bronze denominations of changing face value. There is a long series of reforms and revaluations, until some sort of stability is finally achieved in the 5th cent. AD, with the emergence of very small bronze nummi, followed by the substantial 'reforms' associated with the names of Anastasius and *Justinian. It is this pattern which is initially replicated by the coinages of the successor kingdoms of the west, before they develop the silver coinages characteristic of the Middle Ages. In the east, the coinages of the Arab successors to much of the territory of the Byzantine empire are likewise of silver. See FINANCE, ROMAN.

M. H. Crawford, *Roman Republican Coinage* (1974), *Coinage and Money under the Roman Republic* (1985), and *JRS* 1970, 40–8, 'Money and Exchange in the Roman World'; Mattingly–Sydenham, *RIC* (1923–67; 2nd edn. 1984–   ); H. Mattingly and others, *BM Coins, Rom. Emp.* (1923–   ); A. S. Robertson, *Roman Imperial Coins in the Hunter Coin Cabinet* 1–5 (1962–82) (much bibliography); D. R. Walker, *The Metrology of the Roman Silver Coinage* 1–3 (1976–8); A. Bay, *JRS* 1972, 111–22, 'The Letters SC on Augustan *aes* Coinage'; K. Hopkins, *JRS* 1980, 101–25, 'Taxes and Trade in the Roman Empire (200 BC–AD 400)'; R. Duncan-Jones, *Money and Government in the Roman Empire* (1994); M. Amandry, A. M. Burnett, and P. P. Ripollès, *Roman Provincial Coinage* (1992); C. J. Howgego, *Greek Imperial Countermarks* (1985); C. M. Kraay, in *Essays in Roman Coinage presented to Harold Mattingly* (1956), 113–36, 'The Behaviour of Early Imperial Countermarks'; A. Wallace-Hadrill, *JRS* 1986, 66–87, 'Image and Authority in the Coinage of Augustus'; M. H. Crawford, 'From Metal to Coinage in the Roman Empire', forthcoming, and *ANRW* 2. 2. 560–93, 'Finance, Coinage and Money from the Severans to Constantine'; M. H. Crawford and J. M. Reynolds (eds.), *The Revaluation Edicts from Aphrodisias* (forthcoming); J. P. C. Kent, in *Essays . . . Mattingly*, 190–204, 'Gold Coinage in the Late Roman Empire'; M. F. Hendy, *JRS* 1972, 75–82, 'Mint and Fiscal Administration under Diocletian, his Colleagues, and his Successors, AD 305–24', *Studies in the Byzantine Monetary Economy* (1985), and *Viator* 1988, 29–78, 'From Public to Private: The Western Barbarian Coinages as a Mirror of the Disintegration of Late Roman State Structures'.

Bibliographical surveys appear twice yearly in *Numismatic Literature*; quinquennial surveys in connection with the series of International Numismatic Congresses. M. H. C.

Colchis The triangular region on the east coast of the Black (*Euxine) Sea, fenced around by the mountains of the *Caucasus range. Colchis consisted of a coastal wetland, crossed by many rivers (see PHASIS), and a more elevated and fertile hinterland. Its extent was variously defined in antiquity, but the corners of its triangle were regularly located near Dioscurias (mod. Sukhumi) to the north-west, near Apsarus (mod. Gonio) or *Trapezus to the south-west and near Sarapanis (mod. Shorapani) inland to the east, towards *Iberia (2).

In myth, Colchis was the destination of Phrixus on the Golden Ram, of which the fleece was the object of the *Argonauts' quest. Colchis' king was Aeëtes, whose daughter *Medea fled with *Jason. Local kings traced their ancestry to Aeëtes, whose name remained current in the region throughout antiquity.

From the 6th cent. BC the coast of Colchis was settled by Greeks, sometimes described as Milesians (see MILETUS). The local population seems to have been fragmented: many peoples are known, though classical writers are usually satisfied with all-embracing terms, 'Colchi', 'Heniochi', and later 'Lazi'. The region paid regular tribute to the Persian empire (see ACHAEMENIDS; PERSIA), whose symbols proliferate there through the 5th

cent. BC, when Colchis enjoyed stability and prosperity. Hellenistic Colchis was less prosperous: at the periphery of the *Seleucid empire, Colchis lost much of its hinterland to Iberia.

*Nero annexed Colchis in AD 64, when Polemon II of *Pontus could no longer control endemic *piracy in the region. Colchis became part of Pontus Polemoniacus, itself part of the province of *Cappadocia, whose governor *Arrian toured its coast in AD 132 and composed a *periplus*. Rome established forts on the coast, possibly developing earlier royal positions: the first and most important seem to have been those at Dioscurias (renamed Sebastopolis) and Apsarus, followed by other forts at Phasis, Pityus, and elsewhere. Rome also nominated the kings of the several local peoples of the region.

By the Byzantine period Colchis was usually known as Lazica and its people as 'Lazi'. From the 2nd cent. AD onwards, Roman support seems to have elevated the Lazi from a local significance in SW Colchis to control of an empire in western Transcaucasia. During the 5th and 6th cents., the Lazi changed their allegiance from Byzantium to Persia and back again. Under Justinian there was large-scale warfare between the two empires in Lazica, not least for possession of the new fort at Petra (mod. Tsikhisdziri). *Procopius consistently misrepresents the history of Lazian foreign relations and the nature of the Lazian economy.

D. C. Braund, *Georgia in Antiquity* (1994). D. C. B.

Collatia, in *Latium about 16 km. (10 mi.) east of Rome (mod. Lunghezza?). Already under Roman control in regal times, it played a role in the Tarquin saga (see TARQUINIUS COLLATINUS, L.). Cicero (*Leg. agr.* 2. 96) records it as a village, Pliny (*HN* 3. 68) as non-existent. The via Collatina, however, long continued in use. E. T. S.

Collatio legum Romanarum et Mosaicarum was put together in Rome or Italy by a Jewish or Christian author with some knowledge, perhaps professional, of Roman law, in the 4th cent. AD. By juxtaposing biblical passages on the law of Moses with extracts from Roman imperial constitutions and juristic texts, the compiler aimed to demonstrate the compatibility of the older Mosaic law with its Roman counterpart. Although eccentric in its approach on occasion, the treatise is symptomatic of a general interest in assimilating Judaeo-Christian to Roman culture prevalent at the time, and contains legal material not found elsewhere.

Ed. with trans. and notes, M. Hyamson (1913). J. D. H.

collatio lustralis (χρυσάργυρον), a tax in gold and silver levied every five years (later four) on traders in the widest sense. It was instituted by *Constantine, and abolished in the east by Anastasius in AD 498; it continued to exist in the Ostrogothic and Visigothic kingdoms in the 6th cent. From the late 4th cent. it was levied in gold only. Not only were merchants liable, but moneylenders, craftsmen who sold their own products, and apparently anyone who received fees. Prostitutes paid, and the fact that the government thus profited from sin made the tax unpopular with Christians. Doctors and teachers were expressly exempted. Landowners and peasants selling their own products were also immune, and rural craftsmen were declared exempt in 374. Painters were also freed from the tax then, and clergy and veterans who practised crafts or trade were exempt if their assessment fell below a certain minimum. The tax was assessed on the capital assets of the taxpayer, including himself and his slaves and family. The rate of tax does not seem to have been heavy, but it caused grave hardship to poor craftsmen and shopkeepers. It was levied in each city by *mancipes* (i.e. contractors: see MANCEPS) chosen by the merchants on the tax-register (*matricula*). The revenue went into the *largitiones* (one of the financial departments), but the collection was organized by the praetorian prefecture.

Jones, *Later Rom. Emp.* 431 f.   A. H. M. J.; A. J. S. S.

collegium (1) Magisterial or priestly: a board of officials. (2) Private: any private association of fixed membership and constitution (see CLUBS, ROMAN).

The principle of collegiality was a standard feature of republican magistracies at Rome. Although in some cases the common status of colleagues did not exclude seniority (originally one *consul may have been superior to the other and the consuls as a whole were senior colleagues of the *praetors), the principle in general was to avoid arbitrary power by ensuring that every magistracy should be filled by at least two officials, and in any case by an even number. They were to possess equal and co-ordinate authority, but subject to mutual control. Thus a decision taken by one consul was legal only if it did not incur the veto (*intercessio*) of the other. This principle led to alternation in the exercise of power by the consuls each month. Under the Principate emperors might take as a colleague in their tribunician power (see TRIBUNI PLEBIS) their intended successors, who in many cases were co-emperors.

The name *collegium* was also applied to the two great priesthoods of the *pontifices and the *augures and to the *duoviri* (later *decemviri* and *quindecimviri*) *sacris faciundis*, who had charge of the Sibylline oracles (see SIBYL) and of what the Romans called the 'Greek ritual' (*ritus Graecus*) in general. The lesser priesthoods were known as *sodalitates* (see SODALES). Collegiality here had the added dimension of expertise in recondite lore and tradition.

Mommsen, *Röm. Staatsr.* 1³. 27 ff; E. S. Staveley, *Hist.* 1956; Wissowa, *RK.*   P. T., C. B.; A. W. L.

Colluthus (5th cent. AD), epic poet from Lycopolis in *Egypt. Author of several panegyrics, an account of the Persian war of Anastasius (506), and a *Calydoniaka* (*Suda*, entry under the name), now lost. His only surviving work is an *Abduction of Helen* (Ἁρπαγὴ Ἑλένης) in hexameters clearly influenced by *Nonnus, but not so strict in metrical practice.

TEXT A. W. Mair (Loeb, 1928) (together with Oppian and Triphiodorus); E. Livrea, with comm. (1968); P. Orsini (Budé, 1972).   A. D. E. C.

Colonia Agrippinensis (mod. Cologne), command-centre of the Rhine frontier (see RHENUS), and one of the most important cities of the western Roman empire.

In 38 BC *Agrippa transferred the *Ubii to the left bank of the Rhine. Around 9 BC their capital, *Oppidum Ubiorum*, was chosen to accommodate an altar for the imperial (*ruler-) cult, and was therefore renamed *Ara Ubiorum*. This probably signifies the Roman intention to make the city the capital of a new province of Germany. About the same time two legions were stationed close by. However, the defeat of P. *Quinctilius Varus returned the frontier to the Rhine, and the legions were subsequently transferred. The city was henceforth capital of Lower Germany. In 50 *Claudius founded a veteran colony (*Colonia Claudia Ara Agrippinensium*) in honour of *Iulia Agrippina his wife. A naval base, headquarters of the Rhine fleet, was established a little upstream. The colonists and the Ubii merged rapidly, and the latter adhered only unwillingly to C. *Iulius Civilis in 69–70.

Cologne enjoyed great prosperity. Various manufactures are attested, and its fine glassware was widely exported. A large mercantile port developed between the colony and the river. In the 3rd and 4th cents. the city's proximity to the frontier and the involvement of resident administrators and generals in imperial politics exposed it to barbarian attack and civil war, but it retained its importance. It fell to the *Franks *c.*456.

O. Doppelfeld, *ANRW* 2. 4 (1975), 783 ff.; P. La Baume and others, *Führer zu vor- u. frühgesch. Denkmälern* 37 / 1 (1980).   J. F. Dr.

colonization, Greek 'Colonization', in the language of a former imperial power, is a somewhat misleading definition of the process of major Greek expansion that took place between *c.*734 and 580 BC. In fact, the process itself was not so much 'Greek' as directed in different ways and for different reasons by a number of independent city-states (see POLIS). This at least emerges with relative clarity from both the historical and the archaeological evidence. For the rest, the mass of general and particular information that has accumulated under these two headings is only rarely susceptible to a single uncontroversial interpretation. Although the position has greatly improved since the 1930s, it is still only too true that archaeologists and ancient historians do not always appreciate each other's aims and methods—a problem that is exacerbated by the fact that on the subject of colonization ancient no less than modern authors are more than usually influenced by their own political agenda and accordingly more than usually liable to project the priorities, practices, and terminology of their own times onto the much earlier events they purport to describe.

The actual course of early Greek expansion is reasonably clear, in terms both of the areas colonized and of the identity of the chief colonizing cities: *Chalcis, *Eretria, *Corinth, *Megara, *Miletus, and *Phocaea. Of these, the *Euboean cities (Chalcis, Eretria) must rank as pioneers. Eretrian *Corcyra was the first Greek colony in the Adriatic, which suggests that it was intended mainly as a way-station on the route to the west; and the primarily Chalcidian foundation of *Cumae on the bay of Naples is the most northerly as well as the earliest (before 725) Greek colony on the mainland of southern Italy—known to later historians as *Magna Graecia. Cumae was a logical extension of the precolonial Euboean venture at the *emporion of *Pithecusae, itself a result of earlier commercial experience—not least in a Levant (*Al Mina) that had been aware of western resources (*Sardinia) since the bronze age. Chalcidians extended their reach to eastern Sicily with the foundation of *Naxos (2) in 734, soon followed by *Leontini and *Catana; on the straits of Messina (see MESSANA), they were joined by Cumaeans at Zancle, whence Mylae provided much-needed land, and control of the vital passage was completed at *Rhegium *c.*720. Nearer home, the *Chalcidice peninsula takes its name from the early and extensive Euboean presence on the northern shores of the Aegean, notably at *Torone (Chalcis; this is controversial) and at *Mende, founded by Eretria, as was *Methone (2) (for refugees from Corcyra) on the gulf of Salonica (*Thessalonica). The Euboean domination of this area, motivated by land hunger rather than commerce, was not broken until *c.*600, when Corinth established *Potidaea to trade with *Macedonia (and see SCIONE, founded by *Achaea). By then, Corinthians (and Corinthian pottery) had long enjoyed a substantial western presence, built on precolonial experience that had extended to expatriate ceramic production at Euboean Pithecusae. In 733, Corinth evicted the Eretrians from their port of call at Corcyra and founded *Syracuse, which had the best harbour in eastern Sicily and for long conditioned the history of nearby *Megara Hyblaea, founded by Corinth's near neighbour at home, *Megara—which elsewhere gained control by *c.*660 of the approaches to the Black (*Euxine) Sea with *Chalcedon and the superior site of *Byzantium.

Early Euboean and Corinthian achievements in the west concentrated the attention of others, both on the west itself and on other areas as yet unopened. Of the former, the Achaeans were responsible from *c.*720 for *Sybaris, *Croton, *Caulonia (founded from Croton), *Metapontum, and Poseidonia (i.e. *Paestum, probably founded from Sybaris)—the latter, on the Tyrrhenian coast, was situated at the end of an overland route from the south that provided a serious challenge to the well-established trade (ultimately with Etruria) through the straits. In the last decades of the 8th cent., *Sparta founded its only colony by taking possession of the finest port in south Italy, *Tarentum; Rhodians and Cretans (see RHODES; CRETE) combined to establish *Gela on the south coast of Sicily in 688; *Locri Epizephyrii is said to have been founded by settlers from *Locris in central Greece in 673, *Siris from Colophon in Ionia before 650. By now, daughter-foundations were a standard feature of the western scene: two of them, *Selinus and *Acragas, representing extensions into western Sicily by Megara Hyblaea and Gela respectively, boast temples that are no less magnificent than those of Greece itself.

At the other end of the Greek world, the literary evidence is less reliable than it is for the west, and excavation has been less extensive: but it is claimed that Miletus founded a great number of cities along the Turkish coast to *Trapezus (see COLCHIS), north from the *Bosporus (1) to the Danube, and in the Crimea. In a completely different direction, *Thera founded *Cyrene in North Africa *c.*630. And from *c.*600, Phocaeans safeguarded their far western trade by founding colonies on the Mediterranean coast on either side of the Rhône delta: *Massalia, *Nicaea (2), and Antipolis in what is now southern France, and the aptly named *Emporion in northern Spain. (See our other EMPORION entry.)

It is no exaggeration to say that by 580 all the most obvious areas in the then available world had been occupied to at least some extent by Greeks. The factors that influenced any given colonizing city, or indeed the foundation of any given colony, were inevitably many and various: it is not possible to compile a generally applicable assessment of the interlocking claims of overpopulation and land hunger at home, opportunities for commercial or social advancement abroad, 'internal' (Greek vs. Greek) rivalry and reaction to external pressure. No less various were the relations between colony and mother city, and the effects of Greek colonization on the indigenous inhabitants of the regions colonized. Many different natural resources were doubtless targeted for exploitation, and markets were accordingly made: but the cultural 'Hellenization of the *barbarians' (see HELLENISM) was at no time consciously planned, nor did all the 'barbarians' share the unswerving predilection for the Greek point of view displayed by all ancient and most modern commentators on colonial matters. It remains true that the history of the Greeks abroad is an indispensable element of the history of the Greeks at home.

See also APOIKIA; ARCHĒGETĒS; CLERUCHY; FOUNDERS, CITY; METROPOLIS.

T. J. Dunbabin, *The Western Greeks* (1948), and *The Greeks and their Eastern Neighbours* (1957); J. Bérard, *La Colonisation grecque de l'Italie méridionale et de la Sicile*, 2nd edn. (1957), and *L'Expansion et la colonisation grecques* (1960); A. J. Graham, *Colony and Mother City in Ancient Greece*, 2nd edn. (1983); J. Boardman, *The Greeks Overseas*, 3rd edn. (1980), and *CAH* 3² 3 (1982); I. Malkin, *Religion and Colonization in Ancient Greece* (1987); E. Hall, *Inventing the Barbarian* (1989); J.-P. Descœudres (ed.), *Greek Colonists and Native Populations* (1990); O. Murray, *Early Greece*, 2nd edn. (1993), ch. 7; G. Tsetskhladze and F. De Angelis (eds.), *The Archaeology of Greek Colonisation* (1994). New archaeological discoveries in Greek lands are regularly reported in *Arch. Rep.*   D. W. W. R.

colonization, Hellenistic *Plutarch, in the eulogy of his hero *Alexander (3) the Great (*De Alex. fort.*), made the foundation of cities the linchpin of the achievement of Alexander, who wished to spread Greek civilization throughout his realm. Although we must be mindful of the predictable ideology which has structured Plutarch's argument, as well as distrustful of the number of cities attributed to the conqueror (70!), it is nevertheless true that Alexander's conquest opened the countries of the middle east to Greek immigration. The Greeks, however, could only imagine life in cities with Greek-style houses, streets, public buildings, civic institutions, and a rural territory where the colonists could hold plots of land (*klēroi*; see CLERUCHY). Begun by Alexander, usually as military colonies rather than cities proper (*Alexandria (1) in Egypt is an exception), this policy was followed by his successors and developed further by the *Seleucids. Every region of their empire was included, but it is possible to distinguish four arenas in particular: *Babylonia (including Susiana and the *Persian Gulf), where *Seleuceia (1) on Tigris filled the role of royal residence (Akk. *āl šarrūti*), and the military colonists of the islet of *Icaros (2) (mod. Failaka) held land-grants; north *Syria, the 'new Macedon', sown with dynastic foundations (*Antioch (1), *Apamea, *Seleuceia (2) in Pieria, Laodicea-on-the-Sea); *Asia Minor, where new cities were planted on older sites (e.g. Celaenae/Apamea, *Laodicea-Lycus, etc.); and, last but not least, central Asia, where the best-documented example is *Ai Khanoum (perhaps originally an Alexandria). All the foundations received a Greek and/or Macedonian population, as the onomastic evidence shows; the Seleucids wanted, in effect, 'to create *Greek* colonies and to instal citizens of Greek cities in *Phrygia, in *Pisidia, and even in the Persian Gulf region' (L. Robert). When *Antiochus (1) I wanted to strengthen the city of *Antioch (4)-Persis, he asked *Magnesia (1) ad Maeandrum to send a contingent of new colonists. Even the most distant foundations remained in direct contact with their Aegean counterparts: we know, for example, that the philosopher *Clearchus (3) of Soli, a pupil of Aristotle, stayed at Ai Khanoum, leaving as evidence a copy of the Delphic maxims; the family of the Graeco-Bactrian king *Euthydemus (2) I (last quarter of the 3rd cent. BC) came from Magnesia ad Maeandrum, and influences from the Maeander valley are also detectable in a statuette found in the Bactrian sanctuary of Takht-i Sangin; the Greek inscriptions found in Arachosia use a language and syntax which imply regular links with the Aegean cities. However, the Graeco-Macedonian dominance in the new cities implies neither an enforced Hellenization of the local peoples nor their marginalization. (See HELLENISM.) In Babylonia, what is striking is the continuity and survival of traditional social, political, and religious institutions. Anu-uballit, governor of *Uruk in the reign of *Seleucus (2) II, is a specially interesting case: he had received permission from the Seleucid king to add to his Babylonian name the Greek 'Nikarchos'; at the same time he continued to watch over and care for the Babylonian sanctuaries of the city.

G. M. Cohen *The Seleucid Colonies* (1978); P. Briant *Rois, tributs et paysans* (1982), 227–90; A. Kuhrt and S. Sherwin-White (eds.), *Hellenism in the East* (1987); S. Sherwin-White and A. Kuhrt, *From Samarkhand to Sardis*

colonization, Roman

(1993); R. Billows, *Kings and Colonists: Aspects of Macedonian Imperialism* (1995).
P. B.

colonization, Roman The earliest colonies of Roman citizens were small groups of 300 families at *Ostia, *Antium (338 BC), and *Tarracina (329 BC). Others were added as the Roman territory expanded, through reluctance to maintain a permanent fleet. In 218 there were 12 such 'coloniae maritimae'. The older view that such small communities were to serve as garrisons guarding the coasts of Italy, and even their title, have been disputed and a more political 'Romanizing', or 'urbanizing' purpose envisaged. (See ROMANIZATION; URBANISM.) *Coloni* retained Roman citizenship because the early colonies were within Roman territory, and were too small to form an independent *res publica*; some colonies, such as those at Antium and *Minturnae (295 BC), seem to be part of a double community, rapidly assimilated, even if the relations between the two populations is obscure. Later 'double communities', though often doubted, are attested, as at *Interamnia Praetuttiorum (*ILLRP* 617 f.). Citizen colonies are distinct from Latin, which, though largely manned by Romans, were autonomous states established outside Roman territory and with acknowledged strategic aims, clear for the 6,000 sent to *Alba Fucens in 303 BC (see IUS LATII; LATINI); the two-*iugera* plots ascribed to Tarracina (however supplemented by access to undistributed land) were smaller than those allotted to Latin colonists (15 at Vibo Valentia (see HIPPONIUM) in 192 BC). 'Coloniae maritimae' seem to have been normally exempt from legionary service, though the exemption was revocable, and *coloni* were bound not to absent themselves by night from their colonies in time of war. (Arguments brought against this *vacatio militiae* are not wholly convincing.)

About 177 BC the system of citizen colonies was reorganized. They were assimilated to Latin colonies, and the use of the latter to all appearances abandoned. Henceforth citizen colonies were large—2,000–5,000 men—and were employed for the same purpose as Latin colonies formerly. It should not be assumed, however, that all the original Roman colonies remained small and static. *Puteoli (194 BC), though exceptional because of its position, was showing administrative complexity and magisterial jurisdiction in a public building contract of 105 BC (*ILLRP* 518). It is worth noting that the first deployment of large Roman colonies is in Cisalpina (2,000 at *Parma and *Mutina, 183 BC), where the strategic and cultural situation was different from that of 4th-cent. Latium. Generous allotments of land were given to the new colonies and their internal organization was changed also. They remained citizen colonies but received extensive powers of local government for their annual magistrates—*duoviri*, *praetores*, or *duoviri praetores*—and council (*consilium*). Not many of the new-style colonies were founded till the *Gracchan age, when a further change took place in their employment. Henceforth they were founded for social and political as much as for strategic reasons, either as emigration schemes for the landless or to provide for veteran soldiers. They could, as with the Sullan settlements in Etruria and *Pompeii (see CORNELIUS SULLA, L.), cause friction with the original inhabitants and give rise to unrest, notably the revolts of 78 and 63 BC.

The first foundation outside Italy was the Gracchan Junonia at *Carthage (122 BC). Its charter was revoked, but the *coloni* retained their allotments. In 118 BC *Narbo Martius in Provence was successful despite senatorial objections. In 103 and 100 BC, L. *Appuleius Saturninus and C. *Marius (1) proposed large-scale colonization in certain provinces, and effected a few settlements in Africa, Corsica, and Provence. But extensive colonization outside Italy became regular only under *Caesar and *Octavian, when, reflecting the change in the locus of political power, colonies began to adopt the names of their founders and benefactors as titles of honour (so *Colonia Claudia Ara Agrippinensium*, Cologne, AD 50; see COLONIA AGRIPPINENSIS). Some colonists were still being drawn from the civilian population, notably at the refounding of Carthage and *Corinth and at *Urso in Spain (all about 44 BC). Such exceptional colonies were known as *coloniae civicae*. Augustus, discharging his *veterans and avoiding Italy after 27 BC, established numerous colonies not only in Narbonensis (see GAUL (TRANSALPINE)), the Spanish provinces, *Africa, and *Mauretania, but also in the east. There had already been Caesarian foundations in Asia Minor (e.g. Apamea Myrlea). After *Philippi, Octavian gave veterans Italian land (Cass. Dio 49. 14 records the allocation to *Capua of Cretan territory in compensation; see CNOSSUS), but the Perusine war (see PERUSIA) showed that if not sent home (*RG* 16) they would have to be settled elsewhere, and the numbers of Antonian troops to be discharged indicated the east. (See M. *Antonius (2).) Augustan colonies were thickly scattered, mainly on the seaboard of Greece and NW Asia Minor. In *Pisidia (25 BC), surrounding the mountains that sheltered the rebellious Homanadenses, and at *Berytus (c.14 BC) they provided a military presence when legions could not be afforded. In the East an existing *polis* could survive colonization: at Iconium in *Phrygia and at Ninica in *Cilicia native communities continued; colonization may be seen as part of a movement in populations that included the individual settlement of Italian businessmen, soldiers, and others, as well as the creation of hybrids like *Nicopolis in *Epirus: colonization was sometimes unofficial in both east and west. In the later Republic, casual immigrants established the *pagus* and *conventus civium Romanorum* in native communities, thus forming the basis of future *municipia*. See also AGER PUBLICUS.

Eastern colonies used the standard constitution of *duoviri* and *ordo* (see below); where there was a genuine settlement the use of Latin for official purposes was persistent, and the eastern colonies were a fruitful source of senators and *equites*, for their size, but the overall picture, in language, constitution, religion, and architecture, is of a rich mix. To possess a Capitolium (see CAPITOL) was important, and some colonies, *Ariminum (268 BC and Augustan), *Puteoli, Pisidian *Antioch (2) (25 BC), were miniature Romes (Gell. *NA* 16. 13. 8 f.), even organized into seven districts (*vici*). If colonies sent to places where native communities already existed provided the latter with the model of how Romans and Italians lived, and brought some means of following it, that was incidental (see ROMANIZATION). None the less the original communities would often eventually receive citizenship and coalesce with the colony.

Eastern colonization continued under *Claudius and *Vespasian (*Ptolemais (1), AD 51; *Caesarea (2) Maritima, c. AD 70) but increasingly became a means of enhancing the status of existing cities (even though the concomitant privileges did not include exemption from tribute) rather than of finding homes for veterans or of constructing military outposts. *Colonia Aelia Capitolina* (*Jerusalem, AD 135) was a special punitive case. Claudius also began the regular colonization of the Balkan provinces and the northern frontier, which continued till *Hadrian. Thenceforth no new colonies were founded. Instead, the title colony with *ius coloniae* became a privilege increasingly sought out by *municipia* as the highest grade of civic dignity. The process began when Claudius conferred the title on the capital cities of certain Gallic

communities, but only became considerable in the 2nd cent. (see
IUS ITALICUM; MUNICIPIUM).

The arrangements for local government in Caesarian and
imperial colonies were a more complex development of the
earlier system. Colonial magistracies were always more standardized than municipal and eventually came to resemble a small-
scale replica of the Roman constitution; so the 300 families of
early Roman colonies echoed threefold divisions of the Romulan
state. (Hence the later popularity of the *ius coloniae*.) However,
the evolution of constitutions in Italy was very gradual. *Duoviri
iure dicundo* appear under the republic only at Pompeii and Ostia.
While there is evidence for standardization in Cic. *Leg. agr.* 2.
92 f., and Caesar was responsible for developments in connection
with his agrarian legislation, the *lex Mamilia Roscia Peducaea
Alliena Fabia* (FIRA 12, 138 no. 12), archaic elements persisted
('*manus iniectio*' occurs in the Caesarian law for Urso, 177 no. 21
(= Dessau, *ILS* 6087), 61). *Aediles and sometimes *quaestors
are also attested, the former before republic passed into empire:
at *Venusia the colony began electing quaestors in 34 BC (*fasti
Venusini*, CIL 9. 422). The census was taken by *duoviri quinquennales*, replaced in some Italian colonies by *censores*. Even under the
empire individuality was not wiped out: Abellinum had *censores*,
praetores duoviri, and *aediles duoviri*, the last apparently unique,
and some colonies in Narbonensis may have had *quattuorviri*
(A. Degrassi, *Scritti vari* 1 (1962), 127–143; aediles 179–83). Ex-
magistrates passed into the council of **decuriones*, sometimes
called *conscripti*. See CENTURIATION.

ANCIENT SOURCES References in Livy, Cicero (esp. *Leg. agr.* 2),
and Appian, *BCiv.* 1; inscriptions, esp. the *lex Ursonensis*; Strabo; Pliny
the Elder.

MODERN LITERATURE Beloch, *Röm. Gesch.*; E. Kornemann, *RE*
4 (1901), 511–88, 'Coloniae' (lists); A. N. Sherwin-White, *The Roman
Citizenship*, 2nd edn. (1973); physical aspects in O. Dilke, *The Roman
Land Surveyors* (1971). Italy: H. Rudolph, *Stadt und Staat im römischen
Italien* (1935); E. T. Salmon, *Roman Colonisation under the Republic* (1969)
(the long-lived foundation rituals 20–5, further refs., J. Rykwerts, *The
Idea of a Town* (1988) 117–24); P. A. Brunt, *Italian Manpower* (1971;
repr. 1987); H. Galsterer, *Herrschaft und Verwaltung im republikanischen
Italien: die Beziehung Roms zu den italischen Gemeinden vom Latinerfrieden
338 v. Chr. bis zum Bundesgenossenkrieg 91 v. Chr.* (1976), 41–64; L. Keppie,
Colonization and Veteran settlement in Italy 47–14 BC (1983); R. Meiggs,
Roman Ostia, 2nd edn. (1973); archaeological contributions also in A.
Frova, *Scavi di Luni* (1973, 1977); F. Coarelli, *Fregellae* (1981, 1986).
Provinces: F. Abbott and A. C. Johnson, *Municipal Administration in the
Roman Empire* (1926); E. Kornemann, *RE* 4 (1901), 1173–1200, 'Con-
ventus'; M. Grant, *From Imperium to Auctoritas* (1946); F. Vittinghoff,
Römische Kolonisation und Bürgerrechtspolitik (1952); T. R. S. Broughton,
The Romanization of Africa Proconsularis (1929); N. Mackie, *Hist.* 1983,
332–58 (Mauretania); A. H. M. Jones, *Cities E. Rom. Prov.*; B. Levick,
Roman Colonies in Southern Asia Minor (1967).

A. N. S.-W.; B. M. L., E. H. B.

Colonos, a small Attic *deme 2½ km. (1½ mi.) north of the
Acropolis, near Plato's *Academy. The deme seems to have been
particularly rich in sanctuaries of gods (*Poseidon Hippios,
*Athena Hippia, and probably *Demeter and the Eumenides,
see ERINYES) and of heroes (*Theseus, *Adrastus (1), *Pirithous,
*Oedipus), although we know of these only from literary sources
(Soph. *OC*, Paus. 1. 30. 4). The sanctuary of Poseidon may have
been a gathering place for members of the Athenian cavalry (cf.
Ar. *Eq.* 551 ff.), a group whose commitment to *democracy was
often felt to be suspect, and it was at Colonos in 411 BC that
the assembly was held which voted democracy out of existence
(Thuc. 8. 67); see FOUR HUNDRED. The natural beauty of the place,
now almost entirely lacking, was lovingly described by Colonos'

most famous demesman, *Sophocles (1) (*OC* 670 ff.).

E. Kirsten and W. Kraiker, *Griechenlandkunde*, 4th edn. (1962), 150 ff.

C. W. J. E.; R. G. O.

colonus (a) A member of a *colonia* (see COLONIZATION, ROMAN);
(b) a tenant farmer. *Ager publicus*, the municipal domains, were
normally let to *coloni*, as were the estates of private landlords
when slave gangs were abandoned in the 1st cent. BC (see
LATIFUNDIA), and also imperial estates. Private and imperial
estates were normally managed by bailiffs (*vilici*), often slaves
or freedmen of the owner, or farmers-general (see CONDUCTOR,
MANCEPS), who cultivated a home farm and let the other farms
to *coloni* and collected their rents. The rent was at first usually a
fixed sum of money, later generally a share of the crops; on
African estates the *coloni* also owed a few days' labour in the year
on the home farm. On some municipal estates the tenure was
perpetual, so long as a fixed rent charge (*vectigal*) was paid.
Nominally leases were for five years, but tenure tended to
become hereditary. Perpetual tenure by emphyteutic leases (see
EMPHYTEUSIS) was granted to *coloni* who reclaimed waste land. In
order to simplify the collection of taxes *Diocletian tied all the
rural population to the places where they were registered. Landlords, finding this rule convenient, persuaded the government to
enforce it against their tenants and to attempt to strengthen it,
although repeated imperial legislation on the subject suggests
that in practice *coloni* maintained more mobility than used to be
thought. The rule about *coloni* applied only to descendants of the
tenants first registered (*originales*, *adscripticii*), and other tenants
were free.

R. Clausing, *The Roman Colonate* (1925); Jones, *Later Rom. Emp.* 795 ff.;
W. Goffart, *Caput and Colonate* (1974); J. Kolendo, *Le Colonat en Afrique
sous le Haut-Empire* (1976); P. Veyne, *Rev. Hist.* 1980, 3 ff.; J. Carrié, *Opus*
1982, 351 ff., and 1983, 205 ff. (challenging the very existence of 'the
late-Roman colonate'); P. de Neeve, *Colonus* (1984); C. Whittaker,
Land, City and Trade in the Roman Empire (1993), esp. ch. 5; D. Rathbone,
Economic Rationalism and Rural Society in Third-century AD Egypt (1991),
404 ff.

A. H. M. J.; A. J. S. S.

color (Gk. *chrōma*), 'colour' was used generally of cast or complexion of style. But in *declamation it took on a specialized
sense of the 'gloss' put on a case argued in a *controversia*, usually
serving to palliate an offence. It is one of the main rubrics of L.
*Annaeus Seneca (1)'s collection, which gives many examples.
Colours could be far-fetched (*Controv.* 1. 6. 9) or plain silly (9. 4.
22). In the case of the virgin who survived being thrown for her
sins from the Tarpeian rock, *Iunius Otho suggested that 'she
prepared for her punishment and practised falling from the time
when she began her offence' (ibid. 1. 3. 11). The same Otho was
author of four books of colours, now lost. In Greek theory, *chrōma*
was equivalent to *metathesis aitias*, 'shift of cause'. See RHETORIC,
LATIN.

S. F. Bonner, *Roman Declamation* (1949), 55–6; D. A. Russell, *Greek
Declamation* (1983), 48–9. J. W. D.; M. W.

Colosseum, the medieval name of the Amphitheatrum
Flavium, near the colossus of Nero on the site of the lake of
Nero's *Domus Aurea. Begun by Vespasian, it was continued
by Titus, and dedicated in June AD 80. Domitian was probably
responsible only for the complex substructures of the arena. The
building measures 188 × 156 m. (205 × 170 yds.) along the axes,
and is 52 m. (170 ft.) high. The travertine façade has three storeys
of superimposed arcades framed by half columns of the Doric,
Ionic, and Corinthian orders, surmounted by a masonry attic
decorated with Corinthian pilasters on a low podium; there are

windows in the podium and in the spaces between the pilasters, alternating with bronze shields. There were also mast-corbels for the awning, worked by sailors. The seating, supported by concrete vaults, was in three tiers, with standing room above it. The arena was cut off by a fence and a high platform carrying marble chairs for guilds and officials, including boxes for the emperor and magistrates on the short axis. The arena was floored in timber, covering cages for beasts, mechanical elevators, and drains. Audiences, estimated at 50,000, were marshalled outside the building in an area bordered by bollards, and held tickets corresponding to the 76 numbered arcades, whence an elaborate system of staircases serviced all parts of the auditorium.

The amphitheatre was restored by Nerva and Trajan (*CIL* 6. 32254–5), Antoninus Pius (SHA *Ant. Pius* 8), after the fires of 217 (Cass. Dio 78. 25; SHA *Heliogab.* 17; *Alex. Sev.* 24; *Maximus et Balbinus* 1. 14) and of 250 (Jer. *Ab Abr.* 2268), after 442 (*CIL* 6. 32094), and in 523 (Cassiod. *Var.* 5. 42).

Steinby, *Lexicon* 30 ff.; *Anfiteatro Flavio: Immagini, testimonianze, spettacoli* (1988); G. Lugli, *Roma antica* (1946), 319 ff.; Nash, *Pict. Dict. Rome* i. 17 ff.
I. A. R.; D. E. S.; J. D.

Colotes (*RE* 1), of Lampsacus (*c*.310–260 BC), pupil and devoted follower of *Epicurus. He countered *Arcesilaus (1) (Plut. *Adversus Coloten* 1121e, 1124b; Diog. Laert. 9. 44) and the sceptical New Academy with Epicurean materialism and *atomism, and sought to discredit all thinkers who, as he or his opponents thought, had cast doubt on the plain evidence of the senses, among whom he included *Democritus, Cyrenaics, Arcesilaus and his followers, *Parmenides, *Empedocles (against whom the Epicurean *Hermarchus also wrote), *Socrates, *Melissus, *Plato (1), and *Stilpon. Several of his works are preserved among the fragments of the Epicurean library from *Herculaneum: *Against Plato's Lysis*; *Against the Euthydemus* (both ed. W. Crönert in *Kolotes und Menedemos*, 1906); *Against the Gorgias*; *Against the Republic*, from which Proclus (*in Platonis Rempublican commentarii* 2. 113. 12 f., 116. 19–21 Kroll) preserves Colotes' extensive attacks on Plato's use of myths: about Er in the *Republic*, Colotes wondered how a dead man can come back to life. *Macrobius (*Commentarius Ex Cicerone in Somnium Scipioni* 1. 9–2. 4) reports that *Cicero in consequence preferred to have his tale related by one roused from a dream. *Plutarch in *Adversus Coloten* gives a detailed if unfavourable report of Colotes' treatise with the ungainly long title Ὅτι κατὰ τὰ τῶν ἄλλων φιλοσόφων δόγματα οὐδὲ ζῆν ἔστιν, 'On the Point that it is not Possible Even to Live According to the Doctrines of Other Philosophers', in which he extended a refutation of the scepticism and suspension of belief in certain knowledge (ἐποχὴ περὶ πάντων) promulgated by the contemporary Arcesilaus in the New Academy, to a claim that no theory of knowledge other than the empiricism of *Epicurus affords a secure basis for practical life. Colotes uses an argument from ἀπραξία, 'inaction', a version of which Epicurus had already used against the ethical determinist in *On Nature* and which reappears in *Lucretius (4. 507–10, cf. *Adversus Coloten* 1122c), according to which to deny the truth of our impressions is to abolish knowledge, and without knowledge life itself becomes impossible. Thus he challenges the cognitive sceptic to show how suspension of belief is consistent with the requirements of life itself. See SCEPTICS.

R. Westman, *Plutarch gegen Kolotes* (1955); Eng. trans. with notes of Plut. *Adversus Coloten* by Einarson and De Lacy in the Loeb series, vol. 14; A. Concolino Mancini, *Cronache Ercolanesi* 1976, 61–7; G. Arrighetti, *Cronache Ercolanesi* 1979, 5–10; P. A. van der Waerdt, *GRBS* 1989, 225–67.
W. D. R.; D. O.

colours, sacred Three colours are especially important for sacral purposes in antiquity; they are white, black, and red, the last being understood in the widest possible sense, to include purple, crimson, even violet (cf. E. Wunderlich, 'Die Bedeutung der roten Farbe im Kultus der Griechen und Römer', 1925 (*RGVV* 20. 1), 1 ff.).

White is in general a festal colour, associated with things of good omen, such as sacrifices to the celestial gods (white victims are regular for this purpose in both Greece and Rome). See for instance *Il.* 3. 103, where a white lamb is brought for sacrifice to *Helios; the scholiast rightly says that as the Sun is bright and male, a white male lamb is brought for him, while Earth, being dark and female, gets a black ewe-lamb (cf. Verg. *G.* 2. 146 for the white bulls pastured along Clitumnus for sacrificial purposes). It is the colour of the clothing generally worn on happy occasions (e.g. Eur. *Alc.* 923, Martial 4. 2, on which see Friedländer); of horses used on great festivals such as (probably) that of Demeter and Persephone at Syracuse (Pind. *Ol.* 6. 95, cf. J. Rumpel, *Lex. Pindaricum*, 1883, entry under λεύκιππος, and cf. LEUCIPPUS). In Rome, white horses drew the chariot of a *triumphator* (J. Marquardt, *Röm. Staatsverw.* (1881–5), 2². 586).

Black on the contrary is associated with the *chthonian gods and mourning (Homer and Euripides, passages cited above, and see Xen. *Hell.* 1. 7. 3, the *Arginusae trial), and with the dead (hence the *Erinyes wear sombre clothing, φαιοχίτωνες, Aesch. *Cho.* 1049, as infernal powers). There are, however, exceptions. At Argos (2), white was the mourning-colour (Socrates of Argos in Plut. *Quaest. Rom.* 26); Plutarch's assertion that white was the colour of Roman mourning will hardly pass muster, see Rose, *Rom. Quest. of Plut.* (1924), 180. Hence to wear it at a festival was both ill-mannered and unlucky (Martial 4. 2, cf. Ov. *Ib.* 102 and the scholiast there). The above facts easily explain why 'white' and 'black' respectively mean 'lucky' and 'unlucky' when used of a day, etc. (See RACE.) The natural association of white with light and black with darkness is explanation enough, but it may be added that white garments are conspicuously clean (cf. *Od.* 4. 750 for clean clothes at prayer), black ones suggest the unwashed condition of a mourner; cf. DEAD, DISPOSAL OF. See further G. Radke, *Die Bedeutung der weissen und der schwarzen Farben* (Diss. Berlin, 1936), and Lintott, *Violence* 16 ff. (political use of 'squalor').

Red has more complicated associations, for which see Wunderlich, above. It would seem to suggest blood, and therefore death and the Underworld (hence, e.g., the use of red flags in cursing, Lysias 6. 51), but also blood as the source or container of life, wherefore a red bandage or wrapping of some kind is common in ancient, especially popular medicine, and also the ruddy colour of healthy flesh and various organs of the body, wherefore it is associated with rites of fertility on occasion (e.g. statues of Priapus, Hor. *Sat.* 1. 8. 5). Perhaps because red, or purple, is the colour of light, red is on occasion protective, e.g. the *praetexta* of Roman magistrates and children. But it is also associated with the burning heat of summer, cf. AUGURIUM CANARIUM. For red (and red hair) as a mark of shamelessness and evil see R. Parker, *Miasma* (1983), 335 (red he-goat specified in purificatory law from *Cyrene).

Other colours are of little or no sacral importance, but it may be noted that the veil (*flammeum*) of a Roman bride, often stated to be red, is distinctly called yellow (*luteum*) by Lucan (*Phars.* 2. 361) and Pliny (*HN* 21. 46).
H. J. R.; S. H.

columbarium (1), a Roman dovecot. These were sometimes small and fixed in gables (*columina*), sometimes very large tower-like structures (*turres*), fitted with nesting-niches in rows, perches, and running water.   J. D.

(2) Columbarium is also a type of tomb, popular in early imperial Rome, so called because of its similarity to a dovecot. Often totally or partially subterranean, such tombs had niches (*loculi*) arranged in rows in the walls with pots (*ollae*) sunk into them to contain the ashes of the dead. These provided comparatively cheap but decent burial for the poorer classes: the occupants of each niche could be identified by an inscription, and might be commemorated by more expensive memorials (such as a portrait bust or marble ash-chest). The largest columbaria could hold the remains of thousands and were built to accommodate the slaves and freedmen of the Julio-Claudian imperial households (e.g. the columbaria of the freedmen of Augustus and *Livia Drusilla on the *via Appia, now virtually destroyed, or the three well-preserved columbaria of the Vigna Codini). Smaller columbaria appear to have been built by speculators or burial clubs (see CLUBS, ROMAN), with the niches allocated to individuals not related to one another (as in the columbarium of Pomponius Hylas), though some, such as those in the Isola Sacra cemetery and at *Ostia, were family tombs. See ART, FUNERARY, ROMAN.

J. M. C. Toynbee, *Death and Burial in the Roman World* (1971), 113–18; Nash, *Pict. Dict. Rome* 2. 324–6, 333–9, 346–8.   G. D.

Columella, Lucius Iunius Moderatus (cf. *CIL* 9. 235) *fl.* AD 50, b. *Gades in Spain (*Rust.* 8. 16. 9; 10. 185) author of the most systematic extant Roman agricultural manual (written *c.* AD 60–5) in twelve books. Book 1: introduction, layout of villa, organization of slave workforce; 2: arable cultivation; 3–5: viticulture (mainly) and other arboriculture; 6, 7: animal husbandry; 8, 9: *pastio villatica* (e.g. specialized breeding of poultry, fish and game, and bees); 10: horticulture (in hexameter verse); 11: duties of *vilicus* (slave estate-manager), calendar of farm work and horticulture; 12: duties of *vilica* (female companion of *vilicus*), wine and oil processing and food conservation. Another surviving book (the so-called *Liber de arboribus*) probably belonged to a shorter first version of the subject, while his works criticizing astrologers (11. 1. 31) and on religion in agriculture (if ever written, 2. 21. 5) are not extant. Columella defends the intensive slave-staffed villa—characterized by capital investment (1. 1. 18), close supervision by the owner (1. 1. 18–20), and the integration of arable and animal husbandry (6 *praef.* 1–2)—against influential contrary views on agricultural management (1 *praef.* 1). His calculation of the profits of viticulture (3. 3. 8–15) has aroused lively modern debate. But that Columella treats vines at greater length than cereals reflects the complexity of viticulture not the supposed demise of Italian arable cultivation. He owned several estates near Rome (2. 3. 3; 3. 9. 2) but had firsthand knowledge of agriculture elsewhere in Italy (cf. 7. 2. 3) and in the provinces, especially southern Spain (cf. 2. 15. 4), Cilicia, and Syria (2. 10. 18). Continually aware of the effects of various climatic conditions, soils, and land formations (e.g. 2. 9. 2–7), he does not describe just one ideal estate. The serious nature of his work is further illustrated by the ample bibliography of Greek, Punic, and Roman authors (1. 1. 7–14), while his practical experience ensured a critical use of all sources. Columella's stylish prose, citations of Virgil, and book of verse were designed to give his work greater credibility among contemporary literary landowners, e.g. the younger Seneca and his brother Gallio (3. 3. 3; 9. 16. 2; see ANNAEUS SENECA (2), L., and ANNAEUS NOVATUS); they do not undermine its practical worth. See AGRICULTURAL WRITERS; AGRICULTURE, ROMAN; VILLA.

TEXTS W. Lundström and A. Josephson (1897–1968), with index by G. G. Betts and W. D. Ashworth (1971); H. B. Ash, E. S. Forster, and E. H. Heffner (Loeb, 1941–68); E. de Saint-Denis, Book 10 (Budé, 1969); R. Goujard, '*Les arbres*' (Budé, 1986); J. André, Book 12 (Budé, 1988); J. C. Dumont, Book 3 (Budé, 1993).
LITERATURE R. Martin, *ANRW* 2. 32. 3 (1985), 1959–79; A. Tchernia, *Le Vin de l'Italie romaine* (1986).   M. S. Sp.

Comanus, of Naucratis, grammarian. His work on *Homer provoked a response from *Aristarchus (2). He was also interested in *Hesiod and Demosthenes (2). A few fragments survive.

Ed. A. R. Dyck (1988).   N. G. W.

comedy, Greek, origins of In many preliterate cultures there are public occasions on which people pretend humorously to be somebody other than themselves, and it is a safe assumption that comedy, so defined, was of great antiquity among the Greeks (possibly of incomparably greater antiquity than tragedy). The word κωμῳδοί, 'κῶμος-singers', presupposes κῶμος, and a κῶμος (*kōmos*) is a company of men behaving and singing in a happy and festive manner. In the 4th cent. BC the City *Dionysia at Athens included 'procession, boys' (i.e. boys' chorus), 'κῶμος, comedy and tragedy' (Dem. 21. 10). The inscription which was erected in the 4th cent. to put on public view the records of victories at the City Dionysia from the beginning (*IG* 2². 2318) is headed ἀφ' οὗ (?) πρῶ]τον κῶμοι ἦσαν τῶ[ι Διονύσωι, and under each year the entries are in the order: boys' chorus, men's chorus, comedy, tragedy. It appears from these data that, so far as was known in the 4th cent., a humorous adult male chorus was an archaic feature of the City Dionysia, and it is probable that comedy was a specialized development from this. The question: 'when did the κῶμος first develop a *dramatic* character?' is not answerable. The practical question is: 'how far back, and to what parts of the Greek world, can each ingredient of Old Attic Comedy be traced?' (See ATTICA.) There are three categories of evidence which help to answer this question (A), and five more which are of doubtful value (B).

A. 1. An Attic black-figure amphora of the mid-6th cent. BC depicts men disguised as horses, with riders on their backs, accompanied by a flute-player. This shows that the animal-chorus so common in 5th-cent. comedy far antedates known comedies. Another Attic vase showing men dressed as birds is contemporary with the earliest known comedies.

2. During the 6th cent. BC vase-painters (especially on the Greek mainland, including Attica) commonly depict (*a*) dancers whose dress is exaggerated fore and aft for humorous effect—occasionally they wear a *phallus of exaggerated size—and (*b*) *satyrs of various types, sometimes hairy, phallic, and in general grotesque. The distinction between (*a*) and (*b*) is not absolute, for dancers may be found as participants in mythical scenes, and there is sometimes room for doubt whether the painter is depicting a satyr or a man dressed up. These facts suggest that in the Archaic period men dressed as satyrs in order to enact scenes and incidents from mythology (old or fresh) folklore. The most striking single item of evidence in this category is a Corinthian krater of the early 6th cent., in which we see both a dancer wearing a mask and some naked beings of abnormal proportions, indicated by names which suggest demons rather than mortals, engaged in activity with large jars. Unfortunately, the interpretation of this vase is controversial, but if it really depicts a humorous dramatic performance it antedates all comparable evidence from Attica.

3. *Archilochus in the 7th cent. and *Hipponax at the end

of the 6th composed many poems which contain unrestrained vilification and the grossest sexual humour. These elements in Attic Comedy thus have a distinguished literary ancestry, and it is not necessary to account for them by reference to Dionysiac ritual of any kind.

B. 1. The earliest and best-known theory about the origin of comedy is *Aristotle's (*Poet.* 1449ᵃ10): that it began ἀπὸ τῶν ἐξαρχόντων τὰ φαλλικά ('from the prelude to the phallic songs'). As it is hardly to be supposed that Aristotle had any information on the nature and content of phallic songs 200 years before his own day, it seems that having (reasonably) decided that the origins of both tragedy and comedy were to be sought in festivals of *Dionysus, and having derived tragedy from the ἐξαρχῶν–chorus relationship in the serious and heroic dithyramb, he looked for a similar relationship in something gay and ribald, and found it in the phallic songs of his own day (he says: 'the phallic songs which are still customary in many cities'). *Semos of Delos (quoted by Ath. 622c) speaks of 'phallus-bearers' or φαλλοφόροι (at *Sicyon?) who ridiculed members of their audience, and it is possible that the germ of the parabasis of Old Comedy lay in words or verses uttered in mockery of the public by men who accompanied the phallus in the procession in Dionysiac festivals at Athens. It must, however, be remembered that phallic songs as known to Aristotle and Semos may have been deeply influenced by literary comedy.

2. Equally, when *Sosibius (*FGrH* 595 F 7) speaks of 'an old type of comic sport' at Sparta, he is not necessarily speaking of anything as old as the 6th cent. BC. The clay models of grotesque masks found at the sanctuary of *Artemis Orthia are as old as that, but we do not know whether the masks were used for any dramatic purpose.

3. Although Aristotle (*Poet.* 1448ᵃ33) speaks of *Epicharmus as 'much earlier' than the earliest poets of Old Attic Comedy, *Chionides and *Magnes, an alternative tradition (*Marm. Par.* 71) made Epicharmus a contemporary of *Hieron (1), and references in frs. 98 and 214 support the latter tradition. Epicharmus may reasonably be ranked among the influences on Attic Comedy, but not among its ancestors.

4. The Megarians (see MEGARA) claimed to have originated comedy (Arist. *Poet.* 1448ᵃ31), and *Ecphantides fr. 3 KA, corrupt though it is, certainly says something derogatory about 'Megarian comedy'. This, however, only shows that some kind of comedy at Megara was contemporary with the earlier poets of Attic Comedy, and the Megarian claim recorded by Aristotle does not seem to rest on good grounds. The tradition that *Susarion was Megarian is later than the tradition which made him Attic.

5. Extrapolation from extant comedies—a line of inquiry on which much time and ingenuity has been spent—is perilous. Our earliest complete play, *Aristophanes (1)'s *Acharnians*, was produced in 425 BC. Very few of the citations from lost plays throw any light on the structure and composition of those plays, and, in any case, no citation can be dated with assurance earlier than 450 BC. Since the 5th cent. was a period of rapid change in the arts generally, it is irrational to suppose that the form of comedy remained essentially unchanged until the time of Aristophanes. The most we can glean from extant comedies is the fact that they contain two disparate elements which may have entirely separate ancestries: (*a*) a disguised chorus which addresses itself directly to its audience, and (*b*) dramatic scenes to which the chorus's disguise is irrelevant.

Pickard-Cambridge–Webster, *Dithyramb²*; L. Breitholtz, *Die dorische Farce im griechischen Mutterland* (1960). K. J. D.

comedy (Greek), Old For practical purposes, 'Old Comedy' is best defined as the comedies produced at Athens during the 5th cent. BC. An early form of comedy was composed in *Sicily (see EPICHARMUS), the connection of which with Attic comedy is hypothetical. At Athens itself no transition from Old to Middle Comedy occurred precisely in 400 BC, but the two extant plays of *Aristophanes (1) which belong to the 4th cent. differ in character from his earlier work, above all in the role of the chorus (see para. 2 below). The provision of comedies at the City *Dionysia each year was made the responsibility of the relevant magistrate in 488/7 or 487/6 BC ('eight years before the *Persian Wars', *Suda*, entry under Χιωνίδης; cf. *IG* 2². 2325); Aristotle's statement (*Poet.* 1449ᵇ2) that before then comic performances were given by 'volunteers' (ἐθελονταί) is probably a guess, but a good one (cf. COMEDY, GREEK, ORIGINS OF). Comedies were first included in the *Lenaea shortly before 440 BC. Before and after the *Peloponnesian War five comedies were performed at each festival; there is evidence that the number was reduced to three during the war, but this question is controversial. In the 4th cent. comedies were performed also at the Rural *Dionysia (cf. Aeschin. 1. 157), and it is likely, given the existence of early theatres in several Attic *demes, that such performances were widespread before the end of the 5th cent. No complete plays of any poet of the Old Comedy except *Aristophanes (1) survive, and he belongs to the last stage of the genre, but we have a great many citations from the work of his elders (notably *Cratinus) and contemporaries (notably *Eupolis). Some of these support generalizations about Old Comedy based on Aristophanes, but where support is absent or doubtful it is important to remember Aristophanes' date and not to assume that the structural features common to his earliest plays constitute, as a whole, a formula of great antiquity.

2. The chorus, which had 24 members (cf. Ar. *Av.* 297 ff., with scholia and on *Ach.* 211), was of primary importance in Old Comedy, and very many plays (e.g. *Babylonians, Banqueters, Acharnians*) take their names from their choruses. In Aristophanes (the practice may have been different in Cratinus) the chorus addresses the audience in the parabasis, which has a central position in the play, and again at a later stage. In parts of the parabasis the chorus maintains its dramatic role (as Acharnians, knights, clouds, jurymen, etc.), while in others it speaks directly for the poet; in the former case dramatic illusion is partly broken, in the latter case wholly. The entry of the chorus is sometimes a moment of violence and excitement; it may be (as in *Acharnians* and *Wasps*) hostile to the 'hero' of the play, and it has to be won over; thereafter it is on his side, applauding and reinforcing what he says and does. It is possible that the sequence hostility–contest–reconciliation between chorus and hero was a common formula.

3. The plots of Old Comedy are usually fantastic. In their indifference to the passage of time, the ease with which a change of scene may be assumed without any complete break in the action (places which in reality would be far apart can be treated as adjacent), and the frequency of their references to the audience, the theatre, and the occasion of performance, they resemble a complex of related charades or variety 'turns' rather than comedy as we generally understand the term. The context of the plot is the contemporary situation. In this situation, a character takes some action which may violate the laws of nature (e.g. in Aristophanes' *Peace* Trygaeus flies to the home of the gods on a giant beetle in order to release the goddess Peace from imprisonment and bring her back to earth) or may show a complete disregard for practical objections (e.g. in Aristophanes'

Acharnians Dikaiopolis makes a private peace treaty with his country's enemies and enjoys the benefits of peace). Events in Old Comedy are sometimes a translation of metaphorical or symbolic language into dramatic terms, sometimes the realization of common fantasies; they involve supernatural beings of all kinds and the talking animals familiar in folklore. The comic possibilities of the hero's realization of his fantasy are often exploited by showing, in a succession of short episodes, the consequences of this realization for various professions and types. The end of the play is festive in character (Aristophanes' *Clouds* is a striking exception), a kind of formal recognition of the hero's triumph, but the logical relation between the ending and the preceding events may be (as in Aristophanes' *Wasps*) very loose, as if to drown the question 'But what happened *then*?' in the noise of song and dance and to remind us that we are gathered together in the theatre to amuse ourselves and Dionysus by a cheerful show.

4. Men prominent in contemporary society are vilified, ridiculed, and parodied in Old Comedy. Sometimes they are major characters, either under their own names (e.g. '*Socrates' in *Clouds* and '*Euripides' in *Thesmophoriazusae*) or under a very thin disguise (e.g. the 'Paphlagonian slave' in *Knights*, who is *Cleon). Many plays, e.g. *Hyperbolus* and *Cleophon*, actually bore real men's names as their titles (see HYPERBOLUS; CLEOPHON (1)). The spirit in which this treatment was taken by its victims and by the audience raises (and is likely always to raise) the most difficult question in the study of Old Comedy. A man would hardly become a comic poet unless he had the sense of humour and the natural scepticism which combine to make a satirist, and prominent politicians are always fair game for satire. Equally, artistic or intellectual change is a more obvious and rewarding target for ridicule than traditional practices and beliefs. There is nothing in the comic poets' work to suggest that as a class they positively encouraged an oligarchic revolution, and their own art was characterized by elaborate and continuous innovation. There is some evidence (schol. Ar. *Ach.* 67, cf. schol. Ar. *Av.* 1297) for attempts to restrict the ridiculing of individuals by legislation; the evidence for their scope and effect is scanty.

5. Mythology and theology are treated with extreme irreverence in Old Comedy; some plays were burlesque versions of myths, and gods (especially Dionysus) were made to appear (e.g. in Aristophanes' *Frogs* and Cratinus' *Dionysalexandros*) foolish, cowardly, and dishonest. Yet the reality of the gods' power and the validity of the community's worship of them are consistently assumed and on occasion affirmed, while words and actions of ill-omen for the community are avoided. It is probable that comic irreverence is the elevation to a high artistic level (*Demodocus' tale of *Ares and *Aphrodite in *Od.* 8 may be compared) of a type of irreverence which permeates the folklore of polytheistic cultures. The essential spirit of Old Comedy is the ordinary man's protest—using his inalienable weapons, humour and fantasy—against all who are in some way stronger or better than he: gods, politicians, generals, artists, and intellectuals.

6. The actors wore grotesque masks, and their costume included artificial exaggeration (e.g. of belly and *phallus) for comic effect; the phallus may have been invariable for male roles until the 4th cent. No limit seems to have been set, in speech or action, to the humorous exploitation of sex (normal and unorthodox) and excretion, and the vocabulary used in these types of humour eschews the euphemism characteristic of prose literature.

7. Most of the extant comedies of Aristophanes require for their performance four actors and, on occasion, supernumeraries, whose responsibilities can be precisely defined. Performance by three actors plus supernumeraries is possible only if we give the latter a degree of responsibility which blurs the distinction between actor and supernumerary.

See also: ARISTOPHANES (1); CRATES (1); CRATINUS; EUPOLIS; MAGNES; TELECLIDES.

The fragments and citations are now available in Kassel–Austin, *PCG*, replacing *CAF*; the first collection, that of A. Meineke (*Fragmenta Comicorum Graecorum*, 1839–57, particularly vol. 1 (*Historia Critica Comicorum Graecorum*), was an outstanding work of scholarship; J. M. Edmonds, *The Fragments of Attic Comedy* (Old Comedy in vol. 1, 1957) is full of errors and absurdities.

P. Geissler, *Chronologie der altattischen Komödie*, 2nd edn. (1969); A. W. Pickard-Cambridge, *The Dramatic Festivals of Athens*, 2nd edn. (1988).

K. J. D.

comedy (Greek), Middle The term 'Middle Comedy' was coined by a Hellenistic scholar (? *Aristophanes (2) of Byzantium) as a convenient label for plays produced in the years between Old and New Comedy (*c*.404–*c*.321 BC). This was a time of experiment and transition; different types of comedy seem to have predominated at different periods; probably no single kind of play deserves to be styled 'Middle Comedy' to the exclusion of all others.

The defeat of Athens in 404 BC vitally affected the comic stage; the loss of imperial power and political energy was reflected in comedy by a choice of material less intrinsically Athenian and more cosmopolitan. In form at least the changes began early. *Aristophanes (1)'s *Ecclesiazusae* ('Assemblywomen': probably 393 BC) and *Plutus* ('Wealth': 388), now generally acknowledged to be early examples of Middle Comedy, reveal the atrophy of the comic chorus. The parabasis has disappeared; instead of lyrics specially composed for the chorus, interpolated pieces (ἐμβόλιμα) were used at points marked in the MSS by the word χοροῦ, '(song) of the chorus'. Already in the *Plutus* the lines expressly written for the chorus are virtually reduced to an entrance dialogue and duet. This decline of the chorus was probably gradual but not rectilinear. Throughout the period plays that took their titles from the chorus (e.g. *Eubulus's *Stephanopolides*, 'Garland-sellers', cf. Heniochus fr. 5) continued to be written, and examples can be found of choruses that still conversed with the actors (Aeschin. 1. 157, 345 BC; cf. Alexis fr. 239 KA = 237 K) or sang specially composed lyrics (Eubulus frs. 102, 103 KA = 104, 105 K). Yet the typical New-Comedy chorus, which took no part in the plot, must have become the norm by the end of the period, together with the five-act structure that its four unscripted interludes made possible.

The dangling phallus and grotesque padding of Old-Comedy costume were probably given up during the period, but it is uncertain whether this was the result of legislation (? *Lycurgus (3)'s theatrical reforms) or a change in popular taste.

Yet the specific flavour of Middle Comedy remains elusive. The pronouncements of ancient scholarship (e.g. Platonius 10–11 Kaibel = 50 ff. Perusino, emphasizing the lack of political criticism and the popularity of mythological burlesque; *Aristotle, *Eth. Nic.* 4. 6, 1128^{a}22 ff., claiming that contemporary comedy had replaced the foul language of Old Comedy with innuendo) seem reasonably accurate, provided they are not interpreted too rigidly. In the absence of any complete play (after the *Plutus*) judgements about Middle Comedy almost entirely depend on the interpretation of a large number of fragments, often quoted along with their play-titles, but it cannot be stressed too greatly that the bias of the main preserver of these fragments,

comedy (Greek), New

*Athenaeus (1), may give a distorted impression of the part that descriptions of food and drink played in Middle Comedy.

Even so titles and fragments, when carefully examined, can be very informative. The variety of subject, especially in contrast with New Comedy, is striking. Plays with political themes were still produced, mainly but not exclusively in the early part of the period (notable titles are Eubulus' *Dionysius*, *Mnesimachus' Philip*), and politicians such as *Demosthenes (2) and Callimedon were frequently ridiculed, if rarely criticized outright. As in Old Comedy, philosophers were pilloried and their views comically misrepresented; *Plato (1) and the Pythagorean sects (see PYTHAGORAS (1)) seem to have been the commonest victims. In the earlier part of the period mythological burlesque played a prominent role, doubtless continuing Old-Comedy traditions. There may have been two main types of such burlesque: straight travesty of a myth, with or without political innuendo, and parody of tragic (especially *Euripidean) versions. The aim was often to reinterpret a myth in contemporary terms; thus *Heracles is asked to select a book from *Linus' library of classical authors (*Alexis fr. 140 KA = 135 K), and *Pelops complains about the meagre meals of Greece by contrast with the Persian king's roast camel (Antiphanes fr. 172 KA = 170 K). Popular also were *riddles, long descriptions of food and feasting (often in extravagantly poetic language or anapaestic dimeters), and the comedy of mistaken identity (Middle-Comedy originals have been suggested for *Plautus' Menaechmi, 'The Brothers Menaechmus', and Amphitruo).

Numerous fragments and titles show that the presentation of contemporary types, manners, and pursuits (e.g. κιθαρῳδός/lyre-player and singer, μεμψίμοιρος/fault-finder, σκυτεύς/cobbler, φιλοθήβαιος/the 'I love Thebes' man) was a characteristic of Middle Comedy. This interest in the details of ordinary life may well have been associated with the development of one particular type of play, which dealt with a series of more or less plausible everyday experiences such as love affairs and confidence tricks, and featured a group of stock characters ultimately (though with the distortions of caricature) drawn from life. This was the type of play that later prevailed in New Comedy. Virtually all its stock figures (e.g. cooks, parasites, pimps, soldiers, courtesans, angry or avaricious old men, young men in love) can be identified in the fragments and titles of Middle Comedy. Although several of these characters can be traced back, at least embryonically, to Old Comedy (thus the braggart soldier has a prototype in the *Lamachus of Aristophanes' Acharnians; *Eupolis named one play Κόλακες, 'Flatterers', after its chorus; courtesans were title-figures in several of *Pherecrates' comedies), it is clear that the middle of the 4th cent. had the greatest influence on their typology. That was the time when, for instance, the cook began to receive his typical attributes of braggadocio and garrulousness, and the *parasite to be called regularly by this name (παράσιτος) in place of the older term κόλαξ.

Plots of the standard New-Comedy pattern can already be detected in the surviving fragments of Middle Comedy; Alexis' Agonis (datable to c.340–330 BC) featured a courtesan named Agonis, a young man in love, and probably too a confidence trick and recognition. Some of the typical plot elements (e.g. low trickery, the clever slave) go back to Old Comedy and probably beyond that to popular farce; others (e.g. recognition scenes) owe much to tragedy, especially Euripides. Although several of the sources are disputed, the part played by Middle Comedy in the complicated story of the development of the typical New-

Comedy plot must not be underestimated. Aristophanes is said to have introduced rape and recognition into comedy, but only in a mythological burlesque, the Cocalus, a late play written in the Middle-Comedy period. Rapes and recognitions are likely to have been themes of other Middle-Comedy burlesques such as Eubulus' Auge and Ion and *Anaxandrides' Helen, all perhaps incorporating parodies of Euripidean tragedies which were famous for their rapes and recognitions. Consequently, when the Suda (α 1982) claims that it was Anaxandrides who invented 'love affairs and the rapes of maidens', this probably means that this comic poet was the first to use them as incidents of contemporary life in a non-mythological framework.

To 57 poets Athenaeus attributes more than 800 plays. We know the names of about 50 poets, many of them non-Athenian but writing for the Attic stage. The most important are Alexis (who continued writing well into the New-Comedy period), Anaxandrides, *Antiphanes, Eubulus (2), and *Timocles.

The fragments of all the Middle-Comedy poets are superbly edited by Kassel and Austin, PCG 2, 3/2, 4, 5, 7; this supersedes the older editions by Meineke, Kock, and Edmonds, although Kock's numbering of the fragments was standard previous to Kassel and Austin, and Edmonds's edition (Middle Comedy in vol. 2, 1959) adds a lively but inaccurate English translation. Eubulus is edited also by R. L. Hunter (1983), Alexis by W. G. Arnott (1996).

E. Fraenkel, De media et nova comoedia quaestiones selectae (1912); A. Körte, RE 11/1 (1922), 1256 ff., 'Komödie (mittlere)'; F. Wehrli, Motivstudien zur griechischen Komödie (1936); K. J. Dover, chapter on 'Greek Comedy' in Platnauer (ed.), Fifty Years of Classical Scholarship (and Twelve) (1954; rev. edn. 1968), 125, 144 ff; H. Dohm, Mageiros (1964); T. B. L. Webster, Studies in Later Greek Comedy, 2nd edn. (1970); W. G. Arnott, G&R 1972, 65 ff.; F. H. Sandbach, The Comic Theatre of Greece and Rome (1977), 55 ff.; R. L. Hunter, ZPE 36 (1979), 23 ff.; E. W. Handley, CHCL 1. 398 ff.; H. G. Nesselrath, Die attische Mittlere Komödie (1990).
W. G. A.

comedy (Greek), New, comedy written from the last quarter of the 4th cent. BC onwards, but generally regarded as ending its creative heyday in the mid-3rd cent., composed mainly but not exclusively for first performance at Athens. At some stage the author of an anonymous treatise on comedy reckoned to know that there were 64 playwrights of New Comedy, of whom the most distinguished were *Philemon (2), *Menander (1), *Diphilus, *Philippides, *Posidippus (1) and *Apollodorus (3) (Prolegomena de comoedia, ed. W. J. W. Koster (1975), 10); the first three are commonly seen as the leading playwrights of the period, and above all Menander, who, though not the most successful in his own lifetime, was soon recognized as the outstanding practitioner of this type of drama. The volumes of Kassel and Austin, Poetae Comici Graeci include nearly 80 playwrights dated with some probability as active between 325 and 200, and over 50 later date; but many are simply names (or even fragments of names) found on inscriptions. A large number of fragmentary papyrus texts are believed to be from New Comedy (because of their similarity to identifiable texts), but they remain anonymous.

Texts of Menander (and perhaps others) circulated widely until the 7th cent. AD but were then completely lost; only with the discovery of papyri in the 20th cent. did it again become possible to form a picture of some plays at first hand (see PAPYROLOGY, GREEK). In the mean time, knowledge of the genre was based very largely on the Latin adaptations by *Plautus and *Terence, though there are also echoes in later Greek authors such as *Alciphron and *Lucian. Even now we have perhaps 8 per cent of Menander's total output and otherwise very little in Greek except scrappy fragments and short quotations. But there is

370

enough in common between the surviving Greek remains and the Latin adaptations for us to feel confident about picking out certain features as characteristic of the genre as a whole (see COMEDY (GREEK), MIDDLE).

Athens continued (at least at first) to be the magnet that attracted playwrights like Diphilus and Philemon from far away. But the plays themselves were quickly exported all over the Greek-speaking world, as is shown by the large number of terracotta *masks and other artistic representations that have been discovered and by the evidence for travelling companies of 'artists of Dionysus' (see DIONYSUS, ARTISTS OF). Although Athenian citizenship and marriage-laws are integral to many of the plays, the presentation of characters, situations, and relationships is true to such universal elements of human experience that the plays could be enjoyed then as now by audiences far removed from Athens. Political references are rare and subordinate to the portrayal of the private and family life of fictional individuals; there are social tensions (between rich and poor, town and country, citizens and non-citizens, free and slave, men and women, parents and children), but they are not specific to one time or place. Love or infatuation (always heterosexual) plays a part and is regularly shown triumphing over obstacles in a variety of contexts. But this is not the only ingredient; Menander excelled at the sympathetic portrayal of many kinds of personal relationship and of the problems that arise from ignorance, misunderstanding, and prejudice. These generate scenes that the audience can perceive as comic because of their own superior knowledge, enjoying the irony of the situation; but Menander often plays games with his audience's expectations as well. Menander may have been exceptional, both in the skill with which he handled all these elements and altogether in the elegance and economy of his plot-construction; but this is the type of play that is accepted as typical of New Comedy.

The playwrights' skill lay partly in their ability to give fresh treatment to familiar material. In some ways comedy had become simpler and tamer by the end of the 4th cent.: there was little metrical variety (and the chorus was reduced to performing interludes that marked the act-breaks in a standard five-act structure) and very little obscenity (the costume of male characters no longer included a phallus), and the exuberant fantasies of Old Comedy were not found. But there were boastful stock characters (such as cooks, *parasites, and soldiers), stock situations (such as the rediscovery of long-lost children), and familiar comic routines (such as the door-knocking scene which is central to the presentation of the main character in the third act of Menander's *Dyscolus* and can be traced back to Aristophanes' *Acharnians*). The terracottas show that there was also a standard repertoire of masks; some correspond closely with the descriptions in the list of 44 'masks of New Comedy' by Iulius *Pollux (*Onom.* 4. 143–54, 2nd cent. AD), but the status of that list is unclear since the repertoire must have evolved flexibly. It has been suggested that particular masks were attached to particular names and that in some sense the same character was seen to appear in play after play with the same name and mask; on the whole the evidence of the plays tells against this.

For bibliography see COMEDY (GREEK), MIDDLE; MENANDER (1); THEATRE STAGING, GREEK; and add L. B. Brea, *Menandro e il teatro greco nelle terracotte liparesi* (1981). Pending the appearance of vol. 8 of *PCG*, the anonymous papyrus texts are best consulted in C. Austin, *Comicorum Graecorum fragmenta in papyris reperta* (1973). P. G. M. B.

comedy, Latin This term has come to be synonymous with *fabula *palliata*, since the *palliatae* of *Plautus and *Terence are the only complete Latin comedies to have survived from antiquity. But there were other types of comedy in Latin (see ATELLANA; FABULA; MIME; TOGATA), and there was clearly some overlap of subject-matter, titles, and style between the various types. Varro praised *Titinius, Terence, and *Quinctius Atta for their character-drawing, combining authors of *palliata* and *togata* in the same list, and both types were influenced by *Menander (1). The creative heyday of the *palliata* is thought to have been from *Livius Andronicus to *Turpilius, that of the *togata* from Titinius to Atta; most productions cannot be dated, but the two types probably flourished side by side in the mid-2nd cent. BC. This may reflect a development within the *palliata*; at first happy to allow the inclusion of Roman elements in its Greek setting (as seen most clearly in the plays of Plautus), it came to favour greater consistency (see LUSCIUS LANUVINUS) and thereby perhaps encouraged the development of a separate type of comedy with an Italian setting.

Plautus and Terence continued to be performed, and new *palliatae* to be written, at least until the time of Horace, and *togatae* too were occasionally revived; but the comic stage came to be dominated by the coarser *Atellana* (still performed in Juvenal's day) and above all (for several centuries) the mime. The comedies of *Pomponius Bassulus and *Vergilius Romanus were doubtless written for recitation, like the *togatae* mentioned by Juvenal at about the same time.

Livy's account of the evolution of drama at Rome (7. 2; cf. Hor. *Epist.* 2. 1. 139 ff.) does not explicitly distinguish comedy from tragedy, and its value is questionable. But it does include an informal tradition of 'jests in improvised verse' (see FESCENNINI) as a relevant factor in the period before Livius Andronicus introduced plays with coherent plots. The Romans were doubtless also familiar with native Italian traditions such as the *Atellana* before they began to enjoy the *palliata*, and there are clear signs of the influence of the former on the latter, at least in our texts of Plautus; in turn, when the *Atellana* became scripted in the time of Sulla, it was influenced by the *palliata*. Furthermore, knowledge of Greek drama was widespread in southern Italy well before Livius Andronicus, and many Romans must have seen or heard of performances in Greek by travelling 'artists of Dionysus' (though perhaps not normally in Rome itself); such performances may themselves have influenced the native Italian traditions. See DIONYSUS, ARTISTS OF.

It is generally assumed that all actors were male, except in mimes. They certainly wore masks in *Atellana*, almost certainly in *palliata*, and perhaps also in *togata*, but not in mimes.

For an attempt to show that satyr-plays (see SATYRIC DRAMA) were written and performed at Rome, see T. P. Wiseman, *JRS* 1988 (and see POMPONIUS, L.).

See also AFRANIUS (1), L.; AMBIVIUS TURPIO, L.; ARISTIUS FUSCUS, M.; CANTICA; CONTAMINATIO; ENNIUS, Q.; FABULA; MAECENAS MELISSUS, C.; NAEVIUS, CN.; QUEROLUS; as well as the authors and genres mentioned above.

W. Beare, *The Roman Stage*, 3rd edn. (1964); S. M. Goldberg, *CW* 1981; E. Lefèvre (ed.), *Das römische Drama* (1978); E. Rawson, *PBSR* 1985.
P. G. M. B.

Cominianus (*RE* 2) (early 4th cent. AD), grammarian whose lost handbook (*ars*), compiled for school use, was excerpted by *Charisius and exploited (directly or indirectly) by other writers on grammar (e.g. *Dositheus (2)).

Herzog–Schmidt, § 523. 1. R. A. K.

comitatenses, collective term for units of the late Roman mobile army, so called because they were attached to the imperial court (*comitatus*), as distinct from units of the frontier armies (**limitanei*). This distinction existed earlier, but was completed by Constantine. *Comitatenses* were grouped into large armies commanded by the *magistri militum* (see MAGISTER MILITUM) and small armies commanded by **comites*.

Jones, *Later Rom. Emp.* 608 ff.; D. Hoffmann, *Das spätrömische Bewegungsheer* (1969–70). R. S. O. T.

comites, under the Principate, the 'companions' of the emperor on his journeys abroad. Constantine I gave the formal title *comes* ('count'), in three grades, to imperial emissaries and senior office-holders, since they were members of his court (*comitatus*). The title became attached to certain high offices, including later the command of small regional armies of mobile troops (**comitatenses*). The *comites* were also the senior cavalry unit of Diocletian's mobile army, an honorific incorporated in the titles of some 4th-cent. mobile cavalry units.

Jones, *Later Rom. Emp.* 52, 104–6. R. S. O. T.

comitia In Rome the **Comitium* was the place of assembly. *Comitia* is a plural word meaning an assembly of the Roman people summoned in groups by a magistrate possessing the formal right to convoke them (*ius agendi cum populo*). The convocation had to be on a proper 'comitial' day (*dies comitialis*), after the auspices had been taken, on an inaugurated site. When only a part of the people was summoned, the assembly was strictly a *concilium* (Gell. *NA* 15. 27). When the whole people was summoned, but not by groups, the assembly was a **contio*. In the *comitia* the majority in each group determined the vote of the group. The *comitia* voted only on proposals put to them by magistrates, and they could not amend them.

The three types of *comitia* were the *comitia curiata*, the *comitia centuriata*, and the *comitia tributa*, the constituent voting groups being, respectively, *curiae* (see CURIA (1), **centuriae*, and **tribus*. A special form of the *comitia curiata* and *centuriata* was the *comitia calata*, possibly summoned by the pontifices who played an important part in them. Resolutions of the *comitia* (and possibly of the *concilium plebis*) were subject to formal ratification by the patrician senators (see PATRUM AUCTORITAS) before they could become laws.

Comitia curiata. This was the earliest form of Roman assembly, and dated from the age of the kings. Its functions were progressively taken over by the *comitia centuriata*, although it continued throughout the republic to confirm the appointment of magistrates by a *lex curiata de imperio*, and witnessed the appointment of priests, adoptions, and wills, probably under the chairmanship of the **pontifex maximus*. The pontifices probably also announced each month to the *comitia curiata* the days on which the Nones were to fall. In **Cicero's time (*Leg. agr.* 2. 31) the 30 *curiae* were represented in the *comitia* only by 30 lictors.

Comitia centuriata. This was a timocratic (i.e. wealth-based) assembly, traditionally instituted by Servius **Tullius. The theory that it was not introduced until after 450 BC is no longer fashionable, but it is generally agreed that the complex system based on five graded property classes (as described by Livy 1. 43; Dion. Hal. *Ant. Rom.* 4. 16–18) cannot go back to the time of the kings. Its functions were to enact laws, to elect senior magistrates (consuls, praetors, censors), to declare war and peace, and to inflict the death penalty on Roman citizens who had exercised their right of appeal (see PROVOCATIO), or at least on those who were arraigned on political charges (the matter is much disputed). An interval (**trinundinum*—probably of 24 days) was observed after the notification of a meeting, during which preliminary discussions (*contiones*) of the proposals (*rogationes*) were held. In the judicial *comitia* a preliminary investigation before a *contio* had to be held, lasting for three days; after a *trinundinum* and perhaps a further *contio* the vote was taken. The *comitia centuriata* met outside the sacred boundary (**pomerium*) of the city, usually in the **Campus Martius*, and in military order. This reflects the military origins of the *comitia centuriata*, but in the later republic, probably from as early as *c*.400 BC, the voting centuries were no longer identical with tactical field units.

The voting centuries in the *comitia centuriata* numbered 193 in all, and were divided among the five property classes in such a way that the higher census classes, which were numerically the smallest, contained the largest number of centuries; at the bottom the proletarians (**proletarii*), who fell below the minimum property qualification for membership of the fifth class, were enrolled in a single century and were effectively disfranchised. Each class was also divided equally between centuries of seniors (men aged 46 and over) and juniors (men aged between 17 and 45), although the latter were far more numerous than the former. The result was that the rich could outvote the poor, and the old could outvote the young. A reform of the system in the 3rd cent. went only a little way towards redressing the balance, and the assembly retained an inbuilt conservative bias to the end of the republic.

Comitia plebis tributa. The assembly of the **plebs* was strictly a *concilium*, but after plebiscites acquired the force of law it too was generally called *comitia*. Thanks to a reform traditionally enacted by the tribune **Publilius Volero in 471 BC, the voting units in the plebeian assembly were the territorial tribes (Livy 2. 56. 2). The assembly elected plebeian tribunes and aediles, enacted plebiscites and held trials for non-capital offences; its procedures were quicker and less cumbersome than in the *comitia centuriata*.

The *comitia populi tributa* were founded in imitation of the plebeian assembly, at an uncertain date (probably before 447 BC). The procedure was the same, but the *comitia populi* were convoked by consuls or praetors, and patricians were admitted. The *comitia* elected quaestors, curule aediles, and military tribunes, enacted laws, and held minor trials.

From the 3rd cent. BC the pontifex maximus was elected by a special assembly of seventeen tribes chosen by lot. In 104 (by a *Lex Domitia*) this system was extended to the other pontiffs, the augurs and the *decemviri sacris faciundis* (it was temporarily abolished by **Sulla, but restored in 63 BC).

The Roman *comitia* were far from democratic. The centuriate assembly was blatantly weighted in favour of the propertied classes, while the tribal assembly, though ostensibly more democratic, in fact discriminated against both the urban *plebs*, who were confined to only four of the 35 tribes, and the rural population, who lived far from Rome to attend in person. The enfranchisement of Italy after the **Social War (3) only aggravated these problems. Attempts at reform were half-hearted and either abortive (Ps.-Sallust, *Epistulae and Caesarem senem* 8. 1) or too late (Suet. *Aug.* 46), and in the 1st cent. BC the assemblies ceased to be an effective means of expressing popular will. The election of magistrates was transferred to the senate by **Tiberius; only the declaration of the result (*renuntiatio*) was still performed before the people. The judicial and legislative functions of the *comitia* also lapsed in the early empire; the last known enactment is an agrarian law of AD 98. The *comitia* nevertheless continued a formal existence at least until the 3rd cent. AD.

Municipia and *coloniae* also had *comitia*, at which (in republican times and at least in the first century of the empire) magistrates were elected. In republican times they also passed legislation.

See also CENTURIA; CLASSIS; CURIA (1); DEMOCRACY (NON-ATHENIAN); LEX CURIATA; TRIBUS.

Mommsen, *Röm. Staatsr.* 3; A. H. J. Greenidge, *Roman Public Life* (1901); G. W. Botsford, *The Roman Assemblies* (1909); E. Meyer, *Röm. Staat u. Staatsgedanke*, 3rd edn. (1964); L. R. Taylor, *Roman Voting Assemblies* (1966); E. S. Staveley, *Greek and Roman Voting and Elections* (1972); F. de Martino, *Storia della costituzione romana*, 2nd edn., 1–5 (1972–5); C. Nicolet, *The World of the Citizen in Republican Rome* (1980; Fr. orig. 1976); *CAH* 7²/2 (1989), 436 ff. (E. S. Staveley), 8² (1989), 163 ff. (A. E. Astin), 9. 43 f. (A. W. Lintott).   A. M.; T. J. Co.

Comitium, the chief place of political assembly in republican Rome (Varro, *Ling.* 5. 155; Livy 5. 55) occupying an area north of the *forum Romanum at the foot of the Capitoline. It is associated with seven levels of paving from the late 7th to the mid-1st cent. BC, after which it ceased to exist as a recognizable monument owing to Caesar's reorganization of the area, although individual elements remained into the empire. Consecrated as a *templum*, it appears to have been originally rectangular in plan and orientated by the cardinal points, with the *Curia (2) to the north and the *Rostra and Graecostasis (place where foreign embassies awaited reception by the Senate) to the south. In the mid-3rd cent. this was replaced by a curved stepped structure, possibly circular in form and modelled on the Hellenistic *ekklēsiastērion*. The numerous monuments and statues which filled it have perished, except for the altar, truncated column, and archaic *cippus* (a stone marker), bearing a ritual inscription (*ILS* 4913), sealed below a black marble pavement (*lapis niger*) originally dating to the Caesarian alterations and subsequently incorporated into the Augustan paving.

F. Coarelli, *Foro romano* 1 (1983), 19 ff., 2 (1985), 11 ff.; P. Romanelli, *Monumenti antichi* 1984; E. Gjerstad, *Early Rome* 3 (1960), 217 ff.; Nash, *Pict. Dict. Rome* 1. 287 ff.   I. A. R.; D. E. S.; J. D.

Commagene, country on the west bank of the upper Euphrates, first known as the neo-Hittite kingdom of Kummuh with a capital of the same name at *Samosata. Its history can be partially reconstructed from Assyrian sources *c*.870–605 BC, and hieroglyphic Luwian inscriptions of its kings dating *c*.805–770 BC have been found. In 708 BC it was conquered and annexed to the Assyrian empire (see ASSYRIA), remaining a province until 607 BC.

It was incorporated into the *Seleucid empire by the reign of *Antiochus (3) III at the latest; it became an independent kingdom *c*.162 BC when its governor, Ptolemaeus, revolted against the Seleucids (Diod. Sic. 31. 19a). His son Samos was succeeded as king by Mithradates Callinicus (*c*.96–*c*.70). The latter's son, *Antiochus (9) I, submitted to *Pompey in 64 BC and was rewarded with a piece of Mesopotamia; he was deposed by Antony in 38 BC for abetting the Parthian invasion. On the death of Antiochus III, *Tiberius annexed the kingdom in AD 17, but it was restored by *Gaius (1) in AD 38 to King *Antiochus (9) IV, who, after being deposed by Gaius, was reinstated by *Claudius in 41 and reigned till 72, when *Vespasian, on account of his alleged Parthian sympathies, finally annexed the kingdom and incorporated it in Syria. The royal house claimed descent, through the satrapal dynasty of *Armenia, from *Darius (1) and, by a marriage alliance, from the Seleucids and *Alexander (3) the Great; its genealogy, its art and religion, these two likewise a mix of Iranian and Greek traditions, are illustrated by the grandiose funeral monument of Antiochus I at *Nemrut Dag and the cult

centre (*hierotheseion*) for his father at nearby *Arsameia. On annexation the country was divided into four city territories, Samosata (the royal capital, founded by King Samos *c*.150 BC), Caesarea Germanicia (founded by Antiochus IV in AD 38), Perrhe, and Doliche. Commagene remained a separate κοινόν (federation) within the province of Syria. For its kings see ANTIOCHUS (9).

E. Honigmann, *RE*, Suppl. 4. 978–90; J. D. Hawkins, *Reallexicon der Assyriologie* 6, 'Kummuh'; F. K. Dörner (ed.), *Kommagene: Geschichte und Kultur einer antiken Landschaft* (1975); R. Sullivan, *ANRW* 2. 8 (1977), 732 ff. (dynasty); F. Millar, *The Roman Near East 31 BC–AD 337* (1993), see index; papers by D. French and others in *Asia Minor Studien* 3 (1991).   A. H. M. J.; J. D. Ha.; A. J. S. S.

commendatio Under the Roman republic distinguished politicians influenced the elections of magistrates by open canvassing (*suffragatio*) on behalf of friends. This practice was continued by emperors (Suet. *Aug.* 56. 1), and, when done in absence, by letter or by posting a list of recommended candidates, was known as *commendatio* (cf. 'epistulae commendaticiae', Cic. *Fam.* 5. 5. 1). This method became normal when the emperor was infirm (Cass. Dio 55. 34. 20, AD 8), or absent (e.g. *Tiberius, AD 26 onwards). Such *candidati Caesaris* were normally sure of success; that made Tiberius careful to limit their numbers and delicate in his handling of the consulship (Tac. *Ann.* 1. 15. 1; 1. 81). However, *Vespasian, in order to give his candidates a better chance, had to have them voted on separately (*ILS* 244 = EJ 364). Any pretence that imperial influence was not decisive disappeared by the end of the 1st cent. (*Pliny (2), *Pan.* 77. 7).

B. Levick, *Hist.* 1967, 207 ff.   J. P. B.; B. M. L.

***commentarii*,** 'memoranda', were often private or businesslike, e.g. accounts, notebooks for speeches, legal notes, or teaching materials. Their public use (excluding the false '*commentarii* of the kings') developed in the priestly colleges (e.g. *pontifices, see LIBRI PONTIFICALES, and *augures), and with magistrates (*consuls, *censors, *aediles) and provincial governors. They apparently recorded decisions and other material relevant for future consultation: this could amount to a manual of protocol. Under the empire the 'imperial memoranda' (*commentarii principis*) provided an archive of official constitutions, rescripts (see MAGISTER LIBELLORUM), etc: entering a decision in the *commentarii* conferred its legal authority.

In the late republic a more literary usage developed, 'memoir' rather than 'memoranda'. Various records, handbooks, and other learned works were so described, but especially autobiographies, under the influence of such Greek works as *Aratus (2)'s 'memoirs' (ὑπομνήματα, the nearest Greek equivalent): thus perhaps the work of *Sulla, more certainly *Cicero's accounts of his consulship and above all *Caesar's *commentarii*. Such works favoured a plain style, ostensibly concentrating on content rather than the more obvious forms of rhetoric: they might purport to provide raw material for others to work up (Plut. *Luc.* 1. 4; Cic. *Att.* 2. 1. 2, *Brut.* 262; Hirtius *BGall.* 8 pr. 5), but that pretence was sometimes thin.

F. Bömer, *Hermes* 1953, 210–50; J. Rüpke, *Gymnasium* 1992, 201–26.   C. B. R. P.

Commentariolum petitionis An essay in epistolary form, *c*.5,000 words, on the technique of electioneering, purporting to be addressed by Q. *Tullius Cicero (1) to his brother Marcus *Tullius Cicero (1) on the occasion of the latter's consular candidature in 64 BC; the text is transmitted in the manuscripts of Cicero's letters

commerce

to Quintus, but is absent from the Mediceus (one of the best MSS). Its authenticity has been repeatedly impugned; the arguments against it are cumulatively rather than individually significant, but have not been generally accepted as conclusive. The level of contemporary reference implies, at all events, a considerable familiarity with the history of the period. The only plausible later context for the production of such a document would be that of a rhetorical exercise or *suasoria*. The content is divided into three sections: first, the means necessary to overcome the disadvantage of being a *novus homo*; second, methods of building up support, (*a*) through personal connections and (*b*) through canvassing the popular vote, the latter regarded as less important; third, a short section on how to prevent or counteract bribery. See ELECTIONS AND VOTING, ROMAN.

EDITIONS W. S. Watt (OCT 2nd edn., 1965); H. Kasten (1965); D. Nardo (1970); J. M. David and others, *ANRW* 1. 3. 239–77, surveying previous literature.   J. G. F. P.

commerce See TRADE.

commercium was the right of any *Latinus* (see LATINI) to own Roman land and to enter into contracts with a Roman that were according to the forms of Roman law and enforceable in Roman courts without recourse to the *ius gentium* (especially using conveyance by *mancipatio*).

This belonged to a *Latinus* by right (Romans possessed a reciprocal *commercium* in Latin communities) but might also be given as a privilege to foreigners. Without it a foreigner could only go to law through the actions granted by the peregrine praetor (see PRAETOR). Associated with *commercium* was *conubium*, the right to contract a legal marriage with a member of another state without either party forfeiting inheritance or paternity rights. Without *conubium* a Roman's children by a foreigner took the citizenship of the foreigner and could not be heirs to his property. These complementary rights formed an essential part of *ius Latii*. Their development, unparalleled in the ancient world until the later stages of some Greek cities, belongs to the period before the growth of large states in Latium, and was encouraged by the continental environment of the numerous small *populi* of the plain-dwelling Latini. In 338 BC Rome temporarily suspended these rights between certain Latin peoples, and again between certain *Hernici* in 308. This was only a temporary expedient in punishment for their revolts. The Latin colonies, including the so-called 'Last Twelve' founded between 268 and 181 BC, all shared these rights not only with Rome but with one another: being often contiguous and also adjacent to Roman colonies, they could not flourish without such connections. Under the empire *conubium* with Romans was sometimes withheld from *ius Latii*, but the spread of Roman *citizenship inside Latin communities rendered this rare. The grant of either to *peregrini*, however, remained exceptional. *Conubium cum peregrinis mulieribus* was thus given as a reward upon discharge to the *praetorian troops, when required, and also, along with the citizenship, to the auxiliary troops (see AUXILIA) drawn from the provinces.

These conceptions could also be applied to the relations between any communities of *peregrini*. Thus in 168 BC Macedonia was split up into four districts which were forbidden *commercium* or *conubium*, as an exceptional expedient to avoid the creation of a new province.

A. N. Sherwin-White, *The Roman Citizenship* (2nd edn., 1973); P. A. Brunt, *Italian Manpower* (1971, 1987).   A. N. S.-W.; A. W. L.

Commius, established in 57 BC as king of the Gallic *Atrebates (1) by *Caesar and employed in the invasion of *Britain in a diplomatic capacity. He also acted as a cavalry commander, but in 52 joined the Gallic rebellion, and, surviving attempts at assassination, eventually escaped to Britain, founding a dynasty among the British *Atrebates (2). Coins issued by Commius inscribed 'Commios', with a triple-tailed horse on the reverse, were probably the earliest inscribed British coins.   J. B. C.

Commodianus, Christian Latin poet, probably from 3rd-cent. Africa, but assigned by some to the 4th or 5th cent. and to other locations; perhaps of Syrian origin. In the *Instructiones*, 80 short poems mostly in *acrostic form, he attacks paganism and Judaism and admonishes Christians; the *Carmen apologeticum* or *De duobus populis* is an exposition of Christian doctrine with didactic intent. His language and versification have been much vilified; in particular, he shows scant regard for classical prosody. The character of his verse, however, is better attributed to a desire to innovate and write poetry with appeal for ordinary uneducated Christians than to incompetence.

TEXTS B. Dombart, *CSEL* 15 (1887); J. Martin, *CCSL* 128 (1960); A. Salvatore, with comm. and It. trans., *Instructiones* (1965–8), *Carmen apologeticum* (1977).
TRANSLATION (*Instructiones*). R. E. Wallis (1870) (Ante-Nicene Christian Library, vol. 18).   J. H. D. S.

Commodus, Lucius Aurelius (*RE* 89), sole emperor AD 180–92, one of twin sons born to M. *Aurelius and *Annia Galeria Faustina (2) in August 161, the first emperor 'born in the purple'. Given the title Caesar in 166, he was summoned to his father's side after the usurpation of *Avidius Cassius in 175, received *imperium* and *tribunicia potestas* at the end of 176, and was consul in 177, now Augustus and co-ruler. He was married in 178 to Bruttia Crispina (see BRUTTIUS PRAESENS, C.) and left Rome with Marcus for the second Marcomannic War. On his father's death on 17 March 180 he became sole emperor, taking the names M. Aurelius Commodus Antoninus, rapidly made peace, and abandoned the newly annexed territories, holding a triumph in October 180.

Major wars were avoided during the reign, the exception being in Britain, where, following a breach of the northern frontier, victories were won by Ulpius Marcellus, for which Commodus assumed the title Britannicus in AD 184. There were minor disturbances on the Danube frontier and in *Mauretania, and serious problems with banditry and deserters, as well as mutinies in the British army. Commodus at first retained his father's ministers, e.g. the guard prefect *Tarruttienus Paternus, but after an assassination attempt in 182, in which the emperor's sister *Annia Aurelia Galeria Lucilla was implicated, Paternus was dismissed and soon killed along with many others. The guard prefect *Tigidius Perennis effectively ran the government from 182 to 185, when he was lynched by mutinous troops. M. *Aurelius Cleander, the freedman chamberlain, was the next favourite to hold power, even becoming guard prefect. After his fall in 190, following riots at Rome, power was shared by the emperor's favourite concubine *Marcia, the chamberlain Eclectus, and (from 191) the guard prefect Q. *Aemilius Laetus. Commodus, by now obsessively devoted to performing as a *gladiator, appeared to be dangerously deranged. Proclaiming a new golden age, he shook off his allegiance to his father's memory, calling himself Lucius Aelius Aurelius Commodus, as well as eight other names, including Hercules Romanus: each month was given one of these names; Rome itself became the Colonia Commodiana.

Numerous senators had been executed; others feared the same fate, and Laetus, probably with the connivance of P. *Helvius Pertinax and others, had Commodus strangled in the night of 31 December 192. His memory was at once condemned (see DAMNATIO MEMORIAE), but was restored by L. *Septimius Severus in 195.

Cass. Dio 71–3; Hdn. 1–2; SHA M. Ant., Comm.; F. Grosso, La lotta politica al tempo di Commodo (1964); A. R. Birley, Marcus Aurelius, 2nd edn. (1987), and The African Emperor Septimius Severus, 2nd edn. (1988).
A. R. Bi.

Common Peace (κοινὴ εἰρήνη), the phrase used by *Diodorus (3) Siculus, following *Ephorus, and by some contemporaries (though not by *Demosthenes (2), *Isocrates, or *Xenophon (1)) to describe a series of peace-treaties in Greece in the 4th cent. BC, applicable to all cities on the basis of *autonomy. Such treaties were concluded in 387/6 (the *King's Peace), 375, 371 twice, 365 (possibly), 362/1, and 338/7 (see CORINTH, LEAGUE OF), and proposed on other occasions; their principles strongly influenced the foreign policies of leading cities between 387 and 338 and were used as the basis of their relations with Greece by *Philip (1) II, *Alexander (3) the Great, and *Antigonus (1) I the One-eyed.

T. T. B. Ryder, Koine Eirene (1965); M. Jehne, Koine Eirene (1994).
T. T. B. R.

communes loci (Gk. koinoi topoi), 'commonplaces'. Traced back as far as *Gorgias (1) and *Protagoras by *Cicero (Brut. 46–7), they were 'arguments that can be transferred to many cases' (Cic. Inv. rhet. 2. 48). They were practised at school among the *progymnasmata, and theorists laid down headings (e.g. Hermog. Prog. 6); declaimers made them part of their stock-in-trade. They were often directed against generalized targets, vices or the vicious, and they were a means of 'amplification' (Rhet. Her. 2. 47); but they could be less polemical, and might be legal (e.g. the credibility of witnesses), moral (e.g. the fickleness of fortune, with scope for historical examples), or philosophical (e.g. the gods). The types are well illustrated in the pages of L. *Annaeus Seneca (1), who often speaks simply of loci, thus approaching modern scholars' talk of topoi. The danger of commonplaces was that they might be dragged in regardless of strict relevance (see Quint. Inst. 2. 4. 27–32); and they made their mark on many genres of literature. The pejorative connotation of 'commonplace' is a 16th-cent. development. See TOPOS.

S. F. Bonner, Roman Declamation (1949), 60–2, and Education in Ancient Rome (1977), 263–4; M. Winterbottom (ed.), The Elder Seneca (1974), 635.
M. W.

communio See OWNERSHIP.

Companions See HETAIROI.

Comum (mod. Como), birthplace of the elder and the younger *Pliny, the latter of whom owned large properties there and was a notable benefactor. A flourishing centre of the south Alpine iron age Golaseccan culture, it came under Gallic rule in the 4th cent. BC and in 196 BC it passed within the Roman orbit. After 89 BC it received a first group of colonial settlers, and in 59 BC, at the hands of Caesar, a second group, under the name of Novum Comum. During the empire it became a *municipium, with territories bordering on those of *Mediolanum (Milan) and Bergomum. In late antiquity it was an important military base for the protection of north Italy. The chequer-board street plan of the Roman town, a rectangle 445 × 500 m. (486 × 546 yds.), is still reflected by the modern layout of roads (see URBANISM), and there

are traces of the baths and library erected by *Pliny (2) the Younger.

Como fra Etruschi e Celti (1986).
J. B. W. P.; T. W. P.

conciliabulum, term of Roman administrative law used to denote large villages in Italy in the republic. The rural population had been organized into tribus rusticae (see TRIBUS), which had become unwieldy when (in the 4th–3rd cents.) Roman territory greatly increased in size. The conciliabulum provided a focus for relations with the centre, but had few distinctive rights. The category became obsolete with the municipalization (see MUNICIPIUM) of Italy after the *Social War (3).
N. P.

concilium or commune, koinon in the east, the provincial council, an important element in the Roman system of provincial administration (see PROVINCIA). The councils held (? annual) meetings attended by representatives (local notables) from the constituent communities of part or all of a province or even several associated provinces (as with Gallia Comata; see GAUL (TRANSALPINE)). Their origins were chequered: some in the east had once been independent leagues (e.g. that of *Lycia or, in *Achaia, the koina of the *Achaeans, *Boeotians, *Euboeans, etc., see FEDERAL STATES); others were Roman initiatives (notably the concilium of the three Gallic provinces inaugurated in 12 BC by Drusus, Augustus' stepson); yet others emerge fully-fledged from hazy antecedents, as with the Sicilian commune known from *Cicero's Verrines or the most influential of all these bodies, the koinon of the Greeks of Asia, well established by the late republic. Their chief functions were (1) to represent their provinces to the centre (through their right to send embassies to the senate and emperor) not only diplomatically (e.g. to mark imperial accessions) but also on matters of substance, notably complaints against unsatisfactory governors (note Tac. Ann. 15. 20; CIL 13. 3162) but also routine requests for clarification of legal and administrative procedure (Dig. 5. 1. 37; 49. 1. 1. 1); and (2) to organize the provincial *ruler-cult, a function so central that the presiding official often doubled as imperial high priest (archiereus in the east, flamen or sacerdos in the west); the councils could orchestrate provincial oaths of loyalty, as with the Panachaean League in AD 37 (Oliver, no. 18, 5–6); they also brought to the emperor's attention (in the 2nd cent. AD through written testimonials, μαρτυρία) loyalist provincial magnates, as with *Opramoas (IGRom. 3. 735. 11). Useful tools of control, and as such encouraged by Rome, they acted to some extent as pressure groups for the provincial élites; in the east continuing polis-particularism could prompt fierce internal quarrels (as in the Achaean League: Spawforth, Hesp. 1994). Shorn of the imperial cult, the councils survived the reforms of *Diocletian and *Constantine into the 6th cent. AD, by when their membership included the provincial bishops.

J. Deininger, Die provinziallandtäge der römischen Kaiserzeit von Augustus bis zum Ende des dritten Jahrhunderts n. Chr. (1965); Jones, Later Rom. Emp. 2. 763 ff.; Millar, ERW 385 ff.
A. J. S. S.

concilium plebis See COMITIA.

Concordia The cult of personified harmonious agreement (Gk. *homonoia) within the body politic at Rome (a useful ideological slogan, as for instance concordia of the *senate and *equites in the politics of *Cicero) is an effective diagnostic of its absence. The first temple overlooking the *Forum from the lower slopes of the Capitoline was attributed to M. *Furius Camillus as peacemaker in the troubles associated with the Licinio-Sextian legislation of 367 BC (see LICINIUS STOLO, C.); a major rebuilding by L.

Condate

*Opimius in 121 commemorated the suppression of C. *Sempronius Gracchus and his followers, and the grandest rebuilding by *Tiberius (vowed 7 BC, dedicated as Concordia Augusta, AD 10, foreshadowing various usages under the empire, on coins (*concordia* of provinces, soldiers, or armies) and in municipal contexts (e.g. the monument of Eumachia at *Pompeii) to proclaim loyalty and political acquiescence in difficult times) was intended to celebrate a really elusive solidarity within *Augustus' household. Some remains of the lavish marble architecture of the last temple survive. There were other minor sanctuaries of this cult at Rome, also linked to republican political disturbances.

H. Scullard, *Festivals and Ceremonies of the Roman Republic* (1981), 167–8; B. M. Levick in *Essays H. Sutherland* (1978), 217–33; T. Hölscher, *LIMC* 5/1 (1990), 479–98.　　　　　　　　　　　　　　N. P.

Condate, a common place-name in the Celtic provinces of the Roman empire, meaning 'confluence', and perhaps reflecting the Celts' reverence for watercourses. See also LUGDUNUM (1).

A. Holder, *Alt-Celtischer Sprachschatz* (1897–1913): 30 examples cited.　　　　　　　　　　　　　　　　　A. L. F. R.; J. F. Dr.

conductor The Roman law of letting contracts (see LOCATIO CONDUCTIO) was central to the working of much public and private business. The *conductor* was the lessee, that is the person to whom the contract was let. The term is used of contractors for private building, and other private concerns (Vitr. 1. 1. 10; *Dig.* 19. 1. 52 pr., 40. 7. 40. 5), including agricultural *leases. More importantly, it covered the lessees of state building projects, and under the empire, those to whom the state farmed taxes, especially, at least in the 2nd cent., AD the *portoria, and the indirect taxes (*vectigal) due to local communities. It was also used of those who managed under lease imperial assets such as the Vipasca mines, storehouse complexes in Italy, and agricultural estates. In inscriptions from an estate of this kind in the late 2nd cent. AD, *conductores* are found acting as middlemen between the *procurator and the primary producers, and abusing their considerable powers. Both the system and the abuse continued in later antiquity.

J. Crook, *Law and Life of Rome* (1967); D. P. Kehoe, *The Economics of Agriculture on Roman Imperial Estates in North Africa* (1988), 117–53 with earlier bibliog.　　　　　　　　　　　　　　　　　N. P.

confarreatio See MANUS.

confederacies See FEDERAL STATES; and see under particular confederacies.

Confluentes (mod. Koblenz), lay where the Moselle joins the Rhine. A Julio-Claudian fort, probably securing a Moselle bridge, gave rise to a significant township. In the 4th cent. the site was again fortified and garrisoned; by the mid-5th cent. it was held by the *Franks. See CONDATE.

C. M. Wells, *The German Policy of Augustus* (1972), 137 f.; H. von Petrikovits, *JRS* 1971, 178 ff.　　　　　　　　　　　　　　J. F. Dr.

congiarium, from *congius* (a measure of capacity = 6 *sextarii* (see MEASURES)), a quantity of oil, wine, etc., distributed as a gift, later also the cash equivalent. From the time of Augustus onwards, *congiaria* were naturally an imperial monopoly, associated with accessions, birthdays, victories, etc. The recipients were identical with the *plebs frumentaria*, who received distributions of corn. See FOOD SUPPLY (ROMAN).

D. van Berchem, *Les Distributions de blé et d'argent à la plèbe romaine sous l'Empire* (1939), 119–76.　　　　　　　　　　　　M. H. C.

Conon (1), Athenian general. First attested at *Naupactus (414) (Thuc. 7. 31) and *Corcyra (411/0), he was re-elected *stratēgos*

on *Alcibiades' restoration (407/6) and after Notium reorganized the fleet. Blockaded in *Mytilene, he survived the witch-hunt after the resultant battle of *Arginusae (406). When *Lysander pounced at Aegospotami (405) he escaped, re-emerging from self-imposed exile with *Evagoras of Cyprus as a Persian fleet-commander (397). Despite financial problems (he protested personally to *Artaxerxes (2) II) operations flourished, culminating in Sparta's defeat at *Cnidus (394), and he returned home (393), bringing money for fortifications and mercenaries (cf. Tod 106, 107 = Harding 12 D, 17). Suspected of promoting Athenian imperial ambitions at Persia's expense, he was arrested by Tiribazus but escaped to Cyprus; see Tod 128, comm. He died shortly afterwards, leaving his son *Timotheus (2) a wealthy man.

RE 11, 'Konon' 3; *APF* no. 13700; D. Kagan, *The Fall of the Athenian Empire* (1987); B. Strauss, *Athens after the Peloponnesian War* (1986); *CAH* 5² (1992), ch. 11 (A. Andrewes), 6² (1994), ch. 4 (R. J. Seager); *AO*, see index.　　　　　　　　　　　　　　　　　C. J. T.

Conon (2) (*RE* 11), of *Samos (first half of 3rd cent. BC), mathematician and astronomer. After observing star-risings and weather phenomena in Italy and Sicily, he became famous by his identification (*c*.245 BC) of a group of stars near the *constellation Leo as the 'asterization' (Πλόκαμος, 'Coma Berenices'; see CONSTELLATIONS) of the lock of hair dedicated by Queen *Berenice (3) II to the victory of Ptolemy III (see PTOLEMY (1)). This flattery was celebrated by *Callimachus (3) (*Aetia* fr. 110) in a poem imitated by Catullus (Catull. 66). The story that Conon compiled observations of solar eclipses is dubious. In mathematics he wrote on intersecting conics (Apollonius, *Conics* 4 pref.) and was a correspondent of *Archimedes, who respected him and regrets his early death (e.g. *Quadratura parabolae, praefatio*).

HAMA 2. 572 n. 4.　　　　　　　　　　　　　　　　　G. J. T.

Conon (3), author of 50 mythical 'Narratives' (*Diegeseis*) dedicated to King *Archelaus (5) Philopator (or Philopatris) of Cappadocia (36 BC–AD 17). A summary is preserved by Phot. *Bibl.*, who calls him 'Attic in style, pleasant and charming in his constructions and phrases, often somewhat compressed and recondite'. Part of the original seems to be extant on a papyrus of the 2nd cent. AD. The stories are localized, and include foundation myths (*ktiseis*), love stories, and aetiologies of cults.

FGrH 26 F 1; Phot. *Bibl.* ed. Henry, vol. 3 pp 8–39; *POxy.* 52. 3648; A. Henrichs, in J. Bremmer (ed.), *Interpretations of Greek Mythology* (1987).　　　　　　　　　　　　　　　　　J. S. R.

conscripti The phrase *patres conscripti*, i.e. the *senate, is interpreted in ancient sources either as a single expression ('enrolled fathers') or as two distinct terms deriving from the addition to the pre-existing patrician senators (*patres*) of enrolled (*conscripti*) members (usually categorized as plebeian) in or immediately after the regal period. Both explanations are probably guesswork and modern attempts to link the second with alleged non-patrician *consuls in the early republican *fasti are precarious.

J.-C. Richard, *Les Origines de la plèbe romaine* (1978), 478 ff.; *CAH* 7²/2 (1989), 180 f.　　　　　　　　　　　　　　　　　A. D.

consecratio Roman law (civil and pontifical) distinguished between things belonging to gods and things belonging to humans (*res divini* and *humani iuris*); the former were subdivided into *res sacrae* and *res religiosae*. A third category was the *res sanctae* which were *quodammodo divini iuris*, only in a certain sense governed by divine law (Gai. *Inst.* 2. 2–10; Aelius Gallus in Festus, *Gloss. Lat.* 382–3; Trebatius in Macrob. *Sat.* 3. 3). 'Sacred (*sacrae*) things' belonged to a deity; they were transferred from the human into the divine sphere by the twofold act of *dedicatio and consecratio*, performed by a magistrate assisted by a pontiff. Things given to gods by private persons the pontifical law did not regard as (technically) sacred (*Dig.* 1. 8. 6. 3). Furthermore the *immobilia* (temples, altars) could be consecrated only on 'Italian soil' (*in agro Italico*); in the provinces (*in solo provinciali*) they were only *pro sacro* (Plin. *Tra.* 49–50). 'Religious (*religiosae*) things' were objects affected by *religio*, i.e. reverence or fear, in particular graves (Cic. *Leg.* 2. 58; *Dig.* 1. 8. 6. 4, 10. 3. 6. 6; Masurius Sabinus in Gell. *NA* 4. 8. 9). As examples of 'holy (*sanctae*) things' walls (*muri*) and gates (*portae*) are given, but (as shown by Valeton) all inaugurated places were *loca sancta*, i.e. all *templa* (see TEMPLUM), hence also city walls as they followed (at least originally) the line of *pomerium*, the inaugurated boundary. They were under divine protection, but they did not belong to a deity; in a broader sense all things protected by a sanction, divine or human, were described as *sancta* (*Dig.* 1. 8. 8–9). As most temples were consecrated and inaugurated, they were 'sacred', 'holy', and also 'religious'; the *Curia (2) and *Rostra (inaugurated but not consecrated) were 'holy' and 'religious'; graves were 'religious', and 'holy' only in so far as protected by a sanction. A thing (or person) was given to the deity as a permanent possession through *dedicatio* and *consecratio*, or could be forfeited to it for destruction through the ritual of *consecratio capitis* (without *dedicatio*), which proclaimed a person an accursed outlaw, *homo sacer*; also the goods of a (religious) offender could be consecrated by a tribune or magistrate (Cic. *Dom.* 123–4); he would pronounce the formula of *sacratio* with his head covered (*capite velato*), incense burning on a portable altar (*foculus*), and the flute-player drowning ill-omened sounds.

I. O. M. Valeton, *Mnemos.* 1892, 338 ff.; F. Fabbrini, *Novissimo Digesto Italiano* 1968, 510 ff.; A. Watson, *The Law of Property in the Later Roman Republic* (1968); G. Crifò, in *Du châtiment dans la cité* (Coll. de l'éc. fr. de Rome 79; a *table ronde*, 1984), 456 ff.; F. Salerno, *Dalla 'consecratio' alla 'publicatio bonorum'* (1990).   J. L.

Consentes Di Twelve deities (six male, six female), perhaps those worshipped at the *lectisternium* of 217 BC (Livy 22. 10. 9), whose gilded statues stood in the Forum in the late republic (Varro, *Rust.* 1. 1. 4), like the Twelve Gods whose altar stood in the Agora at Athens. The relationship of these to the modest monument on the slopes of the Capitoline hill, whose rebuilding in AD 367 is recorded in an inscription which calls it the 'Porticus Deorum Consentium', is not clear.   N. P.

Consentia (mod. Cosenza), the chief city of the *Bruttii, dominating land routes to inland *Calabria. It was founded before 400 BC, the date to which the first coins can be assigned, and was captured by the Bruttii *c*.350 BC. It entered the Roman alliance *c*.270 and changed sides several times in the Hannibalic War. Little is known of its later history, but there are Roman buildings in and around Consentia, and it may have been a Roman colony.

U. Kahrstedt, *Die wirtschaftliche Lage Grossgriechenlands unter der Kaiserzeit* (1960).   K. L.

Consentius (*RE* 3) (probably 5th cent. AD), grammatical authority of senatorial rank (perhaps from Gaul), whose extant treatises *De nomine et verbo* (*On noun and verb*) and *De barbarismis et metaplasmis* (*On barbarisms and 'metaplasmi'*; Keil, *Gramm. Lat.* 5. 338–85, 386–404) are excerpted from a larger work. His illustrations, drawn from the speech of his own times, make him valuable for the study of vulgar Latin. See GRAMMAR, GRAMMARIANS, LATIN.

PLRE 2. 310; Herzog–Schmidt, § 702.   R. A. K.

consilium principis A Roman magistrate was always at liberty to summon advisers in deliberation or on the bench. The fluctuating body of advisers summoned to the Roman emperors retained this semi-unofficial character, though the gathering of *amici* (see AMICUS AUGUSTI) was increasingly afforced by judicial and administrative personnel (the prefect of the praetorian guard was regularly a member) and its meetings must be distinguished from consultation of individuals. Rules of selection and procedure continued to be flexible, although under Marcus *Aurelius a grade of salaried legal experts, *consiliarii*, appears (Ulpian, *Dig.* 4. 4. 11. 2). Cassius Dio (52. 14. 3; cf. 15) makes *Maecenas advise *Augustus to put the management of affairs into the hands of himself and the best citizens, reflecting the interest of ruling circles in their role rather than the actual scope of the work done by the *consilium*. Hence the interest of other imperial writers in its composition: Suet. *Tib.* 55; SHA *Hadr.* 18. 1; SHA *Alex. Sev.* 16. 1 f. In fact the character of the *consilium* changed little in the 2nd and 3rd cents. Its functions remained largely judicial (Plin. *Ep.* 4. 22, 6. 22, 6. 31) or diplomatic; it met ad hoc (cf. Juv. *Sat.* 4), and most of its work was concerned with detail rather than the formulation of 'policy'. This *consilium* is to be distinguished from the *consilium* established by Augustus, and known as the *consilium semenstre*, consisting of the consuls, one of each of the other colleges, and fifteen senators chosen by lot, retaining membership for six months (Cass. Dio 53. 21. 4 ff.; Suet. *Aug.* 35. 3). This body prepared business for the senate in collaboration with the *princeps* (see the fifth Cyrene edict, *JRS* 1927, 36 = EJ 311; see CYRENE, EDICTS OF). Its composition was modified in AD 13 and any decision it made was given the force of a *senatus consultum*; but *Tiberius had no use for an institution that diminished the role of the senate (Suet. *Tib.* 55). See also CONSISTORIUM.

J. A. Crook, *Consilium Principis* (1955); A. N. Sherwin-White, *JRS* 1957, 252 ff., and *The Letters of Pliny* (1966); Millar, *ERW*, see indexes.
                J. P. B.; B. M. L.

consistorium, the name given to the imperial *consilium* from the time of *Diocletian, since the members no longer sat but stood in the emperor's presence. It functioned both as a general council of state and as a supreme court of law. Its membership depended on the emperor's choice but normally included the principal civil and military officers of the imperial court (*comitatus*), former holders of these offices, and appointed members known as *comites consistoriani* who held no office; these last included legal experts, mostly drawn from the Bar. Its minutes were kept by the imperial *notarii*, secretaries who might also serve as confidential emissaries and rise to high office, but in the 5th cent. their clerical duties passed to *agentes in rebus and subordinates of the *magister memoriae. Its sessions were called 'silences' (*silentia*), and its ushers *silentiarii*. The consistory was an active council of state during the 4th cent., but its time was increasingly filled by ceremonial business, and by the 5th cent. its proceedings appear to have become entirely formal.

Jones, *Later Rom. Emp.* 333 ff.   A. H. M. J.; R. S. O. T.

Consolatio ad Liviam, a poem of condolence in 474 elegiac lines, addressed to *Livia Drusilla, wife of Augustus, on the death of her son Nero *Claudius Drusus on campaign in Germany in 9 BC. It contains many of the commonplaces of ancient consolation. Date and authorship have been much discussed. The traditional ascription to *Ovid is clearly false, his imitator (as the poet is) not being equipped with his technical skills and imaginative power. Recent attempts at dating have set the piece variously in the principates of *Tiberius, *Claudius, and *Nero; some have seen it as a forgery, composed for propagandist purposes, but it may be simply a literary exercise, without hidden political intent. See CONSOLATION.

TEXTS F. W. Lenz, *P. Ovidii Nasonis Halieutica*, 2nd edn. (1956); with comm., A. Witlox (1934), H. Schoonhoven (1992) (useful bibliog.); with trans., J. A. Mozley, *Ovid: The Art of Love, and Other Poems*, 2nd edn. (Loeb, 1979).

J. H. D. S.

consolation The practice of offering words of comfort to those afflicted by grief is reflected in the earliest Greek poetry (e.g. Hom. *Il.* 24. 507–51). Later, under the twin influences of rhetoric and philosophy, a specialized consolatory literature began to develop, initiating a tradition which persisted throughout Graeco-Roman antiquity and into the Middle Ages. This literature took a number of forms. Philosophers wrote treatises on death and the alleviation of grief. Letters of consolation were written to comfort those who had suffered bereavement or some other loss-experience, such as exile or illness; these might be highly personal, or possess the more detached character of an essay. Funeral speeches (see LAUDATIO FUNEBRIS) frequently contained a substantial consolatory element. Poets sometimes wrote verse *consolationes*, which cannot always be clearly distinguished from *epicedia* (see EPICEDION). Greek cities voted prose-decrees of consolation for the kin of deceased worthies; inscribed examples survive (e.g. *IG* 4². 85–6).

Though writers varied their compositions with due regard to the individual addressed, the specific circumstances of the case, or their other purposes in the work, extant specimens of ancient consolatory writing tend to draw on a relatively narrow repertoire of arguments and approaches; the contributions of the different philosophical schools found their way into an eclectic melting-pot. Consolation proper is regularly associated with the expression of sympathy (in itself a form of consolation), and (importantly) with exhortation; eulogy of the deceased is also a frequent ingredient. Arguments typically employed include the following: all are born mortal; death brings release from the miseries of life; time heals all griefs; future ills should be prepared for; the deceased was only 'lent'—be grateful for having possessed him. Normally grief is regarded as natural and legitimate, though not to be indulged in.

The first figure of major importance in the tradition was the Academic (see ACADEMY) *Crantor, whose lost essay *On Grief* was deeply influential. Latin writers owed much to *Cicero's *Consolatio* (also lost), written to comfort himself on the death of his daughter *Tullia (2). The best examples of surviving pagan material are probably Ser. *Sulpicius Rufus' letter to Cicero on that occasion (Cic. *Fam.* 4. 5), Seneca's *Ad Marciam* (*Dial.* 6) and *Ep.* 63 and 99, and (though scoring low on literary merit) the *Consolatio ad Apollonium* of ps.-Plutarch. In *Boethius' *Consolation of Philosophy*, Philosophy herself consoles the author for his misfortunes. Continuity with the classical tradition can be seen in the work of Christian writers such as *Ambrose, *Jerome, and the Cappadocian Fathers, who make full use of pagan topoi (see TOPOS), but firm belief in a blissful afterlife and the wealth of relevant material available in Scripture ensured that consolation acquired a different character in Christian hands.

GENERAL K. Buresch, *Leipz. Stud.* 1886, 1–170; C. Favez, *La Consolation latine chrétienne* (1937); R. Kassel, *Untersuchungen zur griechischen und römischen Konsolationsliteratur* (1958); P. von Moos, *Consolatio* (1971–2) (on medieval *consolationes*).

SPECIFIC WORKS Cicero's *Consolatio*: K. Kumaniecki, *Annales de la Faculté de Lettres et Sciences humaines d'Aix*, *Sér. class.*, 1969, 369–402.

Seneca: comms. on *Ad Helviam* and *Ad Marciam* by C. Favez (1918, 1928); M. Coccia, *Rivista di cultura classica e medioevale*, 1959, 148–80. ps.-Plut. *Cons. ad Apoll.*: comm. by J. Hani (1972). Cappadocian Fathers: R. C. Gregg, *Consolation Philosophy* (1975). Ambrose: Y.-M. Duval, Entretiens Hardt 23 (1977), 235–91. Jerome: comm. on *Ep.* 60 by J. H. D. Scourfield (1993).

J. H. D. S.

Constans, Flavius Iulius Youngest son of *Constantine I, along with his two surviving brothers he became Augustus after his father's death in AD 337, assuming control of Italy, Africa, and Illyricum. In 340 he extended his rule over all the western provinces, having defeated and killed his brother *Constantine II near Aquileia when the latter invaded northern Italy. In 341–2 he successfully campaigned against the Franks, and the next year made a winter crossing of the Channel to visit Britain (the last legitimate Roman emperor to be seen there). His regime became unpopular with troops and civilians alike, and in January 350 he was overthrown and killed in a coup at Autun led by the general *Magnentius.

E. D. H.

Constantine I, 'the Great' (Flavius Valerius Constantinus (*RE* 2)) (c. AD 272/3–337), born at Naissus, was son of *Constantius I and Helena. When his father was appointed Caesar (293) Constantine remained as a tribune at the court of *Diocletian. He fought alongside *Galerius against Persia (298) and the Sarmatians (299), and was at Nicomedia in 303 and again in 305 when Diocletian abdicated. Constantius was now senior Augustus; his eastern partner Galerius reluctantly released Constantine for service with his father. Constantine, fearing interception by the western Caesar, Flavius Valerius *Severus, hastened to Britain to aid his father against the Picts.

When Constantius died at York (*Eburacum, 306), his troops proclaimed Constantine Augustus; Galerius gave this rank to Severus, but grudgingly conceded Constantine the title Caesar. Based mainly at Trier (*Augusta Treverorum), Constantine ruled his father's territories of Spain, Gaul, and Britain. At Rome *Maxentius usurped power; Severus and then Galerius failed to dislodge him. For Constantine an alliance with Maxentius was welcome. The usurper's father, the former emperor *Maximian, returned to power, visited Constantine in Gaul (307), and gave him the title Augustus and his daughter Fausta in marriage. Constantine sheltered Maximian when driven from Rome after failing to depose his son (308). At the conference of Carnuntum Galerius gave the title Augustus to *Licinius; like *Maximinus in the east, Constantine spurned the style *filius Augustorum* (son of the Augusti) and retained that of Augustus, which Galerius recognized (309/10). Meanwhile he defended the Rhine, warring against the Franks (306–7), raiding the territory of the Bructeri, and bridging the river at Cologne (Colonia Agrippinensis, 308). He was campaigning against the Franks (310) when Maximian tried to regain power. Constantine forced him to surrender and commit suicide. As the connection with the Herculian dynasty was now discredited, a hereditary claim to the throne was invented for Constantine: it was alleged that his father had been related to *Claudius II. On the death of Galerius (311), Maximinus and Licinius narrowly avoided war when partitioning his territories, and as Maximinus looked for support to Maxentius, Constantine looked to Licinius. In 312 Constantine invaded Italy. Victorious over Maxentius's northern forces near Turin and Verona, he marched on Rome. Maxentius gave battle at Saxa Rubra, was defeated, and was drowned near the *pons Mulvius. The senate welcomed Constantine as liberator and made him, not Maximinus, senior Augustus. He took over the rule of Italy and Africa, and disbanded the praetorian guard which had supported Maxentius.

Two years earlier it had been given out that Constantine had seen a vision of his tutelary deity the sun-god *Apollo accompanied by Victory (see NIKE; VICTORIA) and the figure XXX to symbolize the years of rule due to him. By the end of his life Constantine claimed to have seen a (single) cross above the sun, with words 'Be victorious in this'. At Saxa Rubra, Constantine as the result of a dream sent his soldiers into battle with crosses (and no doubt other symbols) on their shields; heavily outnumbered, he defeated Maxentius. No more, yet no less, superstitious than his contemporaries, he saw the hand of the Christian God in this, and the need to maintain such support for himself and the empire. (See CHRISTIANITY.) From that moment he not merely restored Christian property but gave privileges to the clergy, showered benefactions on the Church, and undertook a massive programme of church building. At Rome a basilica was provided for the Pope where the barracks of the mounted branch of the praetorians had stood, and other churches, most notably St Peter's, followed. His religious outlook may have undergone later transformations, and was affected by his encounters with problems in the Church. In Africa he confronted the Donatist schism: the *Donatists objected to the largest for their opponents and appealed to him. To the *vicarius of Africa, a 'fellow worshipper of the most high God', he wrote (314) of his fear that failure to achieve Christian unity would cause God to replace him with another emperor. Sincerity is not determinable by historical method; it is, in any case, not incompatible with a belief that consequential action may have political advantage. He had been present at Nicomedia when persecution began in 303; he knew that the problem with Christianity was that its exclusiveness stood in the way of imperial unity. If he threw in his lot with the Christians, there could be no advantage if they were themselves not united. Following a papal council in 313, his own council at Arles (Arelate) in 314, and his investigation into the dispute, he saw the refusal of the Donatists to conform as obtuse. From 317 he tried coercion; there were exiles and some executions. Totally failing to achieve his object, he left the Donatists to God's judgement (321). Weakness in the face of a movement widespread in Africa is seen when the Donatists seized the basilica Constantine built for the Catholics at Cirta; he left them in possession and built the Catholics another one.

At Milan (*Mediolanum, 313) he met Licinius, and gave him his half-sister Constantia in marriage. Back at Nicomedia, Licinius published regulations agreed with Constantine on religious freedom and the restoration of Christian property (the so-called Edict of Milan). Licinius struck down Maximinus, and the two emperors were left to rule in harmony. In 313 the Rhine frontier engaged Constantine's attention; in 314 after attending the council of Arles he campaigned against the Germans; in 315 he spent two months in Rome.

The concord with Licinius was unstable. A first war was decided in Constantine's favour by victories at Cibalae (316) and Campus Ardiensis. Licinius ceded all his European territories except for the diocese of Thrace. In 317 Crispus and *Constantine II, sons of Constantine, and Licinius II, son of Licinius, were made Caesars. Constantine spent 317–23 in the Balkans. Licinius became increasingly distrustful of him and suspicious of his own Christian subjects, whom he began to persecute. Constantine defeated a Gothic invasion (323) but was accused by Licinius of usurping his function; war followed. Constantine was victorious at Adrianople, in the Hellespont, and at Chrysopolis, and forced the abdication of Licinius at Nicomedia (324). Though his life was spared after his wife intervened with her brother, Licinius was later accused of plotting and executed, with his Caesar Martinianus (325); the Caesar Licinius II was executed in 326. Implication in the supposed plot may have been the excuse also for Constantine to remove one of the consuls of 325, Proculus. In a mysterious scandal, he even ordered the deaths of his son Crispus and his wife Fausta (326). Only one usurpation is recorded in the rest of his reign: Calocaerus in Cyprus (334), who was burnt alive by the emperor's half-brother Dalmatius.

On 8 November 324 Constantine made his third son *Constantius II Caesar and founded *Constantinople on the site of *Byzantium. The need for an imperial headquarters near the eastern and Danubian frontiers had been seen by Diocletian, who preferred Nicomedia; Constantine will have recognized the strategic importance of Byzantium in his war with Licinius. The city's dedication with both pagan rites and Christian ceremonies took place on 11 May 330. From the beginning it was 'New Rome', though lower in rank. Pagan temples and cults were absent, but other features of Rome were in time reproduced (Constantius II upgraded the city council to equality with the Roman senate). To speak of the foundation of a capital is misleading; yet a permanent imperial residence in the east did in the end emphasize division between the empire's Greek and Latin parts.

In a reunited empire Constantine was able to complete Diocletian's reforms and introduce innovations. The separation of civil and military commands was completed. A substantial field army was created under new commanders, *magister equitum and magister peditum, responsible directly to the emperor: its soldiers (*comitatenses) had higher pay and privileges than the frontier troops (*limitanei). The number of Germans seems to have increased, especially in the higher ranks. Praetorian prefects and vicarii (see PRAEFECTUS PRAETORIO; VICARIUS) now had purely civilian functions. In a reorganization of the government, the *magister officiorum controlled the imperial bureaux (scrinia), a new corps of guards (scholae) which replaced the praetorians, and a corps of couriers and agents (*agentes in rebus); the *quaestor sacri palatii was chief legal adviser; the comes sacrarum largitionum and the comes rei privatae handled those revenues and expenditures not controlled by the praetorian prefects. The Emperor's council (*consistorium) had the above as permanent members, as well as *comites. These at first were men who served at court or as special commissioners, but the title 'count' was soon given freely as an honour. He also resuscitated the title of patrician. He tried vainly to stop *corruption in the steadily growing bureaucracy. He gave senatorial rank freely, and reopened many civilian posts to senators who began to recover some of their lost political influence. From his reign survive the first laws to prevent tenant farmers and other productive workers, not to mention town councillors, from leaving their homes and work (see COLONUS). His open-handedness harmed the economy: taxation (mostly in kind) rose inexorably despite the confiscation of the vast temple treasures. He established a gold coinage of 72 solidi to the pound, but the other coinage continued to depreciate.

Resident now in the more Christianized east, his promotion of the new religion became more emphatic. He openly rejected *paganism, though without persecuting pagans, favoured Christians as officials, and welcomed bishops at court, but his actions in Church matters were his own. He now confronted another dispute which was rending Christianity, the theological questions about the nature of Christ raised by the Alexandrian priest *Arius. To secure unity Constantine summoned the council which met

Constantine II (Flavius Claudius Constantinus)

at *Nicaea (1) in 325 (later ranked as the First Ecumenical Council), and proposed the formula which all must accept. Dissidents were bludgeoned into agreement; but *Athanasius' view that his opponents had put an unorthodox interpretation on the formula was seen by Constantine as vexatious interference with attempts to secure unity. Even if his success in this aspect was superficial, he nevertheless brought *Christianity from a persecuted minority sect to near-supremacy in the religious life of the empire.

He spent the generally peaceful last dozen years of his reign in the east or on the Danube, though he visited Italy and Rome (326), and campaigned on the Rhine (328/9). Victory over the Goths (332) was followed (334) by a campaign against the Sarmatians, many thousands of whom were then admitted within the empire as potential recruits. In 336 he fought north of the Danube, even recovering part of the lost province of *Dacia. The empire's prestige seemed fully restored; a Persian war loomed but did not break out until after his death.

His youngest son *Constans gained (333) the title Caesar already held by Constantine II and Constantius II. A believer in hereditary succession, Constantine groomed these to succeed along with his nephews Dalmatius (Caesar 335) and Hannibalianus, hoping they would rule amicably after his death. Baptized when death approached (such postponement was common at the time), he died near *Nicomedia (22 May 337).

J. Burckhardt, *The Age of Constantine the Great* (1949; Ger. orig. 1898); A. H. M. Jones, *Constantine and the Conversion of Europe*, 2nd edn. (1962); T. D. Barnes, *Constantine and Eusebius* (1981), and *The New Empire of Diocletian and Constantine* (1982); R. Lane Fox, *Pagans and Christians* (1986); T. Grünewald, *Constantinus Maximus Augustus* (1990).

R. P. D.

Constantine II (Flavius Claudius Constantinus (*RE* 3)**),** second son of *Constantine I, was born at Arles (*Arelate) in AD 316 and proclaimed Caesar 1 March 317. After his father's death he became senior Augustus (9 September 337) and continued ruling Gaul, Britain, and Spain. He quarrelled with his youngest brother *Constans, invaded Italy and was killed at Aquileia in spring 340.

R. P. D.

Constantine III (*RE* 5), the last of three usurpers proclaimed in Britain (AD 406–7) by the army, with part of which he crossed to Gaul hoping to rescue it from barbarian invasions. He won over Spain, and was recognized as emperor (409) by *Honorius. He invaded Italy unsuccessfully, and fell out with his *magister militum*, the Briton Gerontius, who besieged him at Arles (Arelate) but fled when Honorius' generals approached; Constantine had himself ordained priest and surrendered to these, but was executed (411).

C. E. Stevens, *Athenaeum* 1957, 316–47.

R. P. D.

Constantinople Constantinople was founded by *Constantine I on the site of *Byzantium in AD 324, shortly after his victory over *Licinius near by. There are hardly any sources before the 6th cent., and these are already full of myths: e.g. that Constantine started to build at Troy and brought the *Palladium from Rome. When he claimed to 'bestow an eternal name' he probably meant his own! The city was styled 'New Rome' from the start, but it is not likely that Constantine had any thought of superseding Rome. He was simply building his own tetrarchic capital: the New Rome motif took on new significance after the sack of Rome (410) and the disappearance of the western empire.

Though not such an obvious site as has often been claimed

(being vulnerable from its hinterland and deficient in drinking-water), the new foundation grew rapidly in size and importance, though it did not become a regular imperial residence till the end of the century. By the reign of *Valens (373) an elaborate system of *aqueducts and conduits was installed to provide sufficient water for the growing population. The Constantinian walls were demolished in 413, and the present walls built about 1½ km. (1 mi.) further west. The area of the city was thus doubled, though many people lived in addition in the suburbs of Hebdomon and Sykae and the independent city of *Chalcedon. Like Rome, the city was divided into fourteen regions, though not till 413, with one of the regions across the Golden Horn and one outside the walls. As at Rome, there was also a free issue of corn, begun in 332 (probably necessary to support the expansion).

Though claimed by *Eusebius as a Christian foundation never stained by *pagan worship, several pagan temples were left untouched. But Constantine at once built a number of martyria and churches, notably the Holy Apostles, where he and many of his successors were buried. He also rebuilt the hippodrome and adorned the streets and squares with statues brought from all over the empire ('dedicatur Constantinopolis omnium urbium nuditate', *Jerome; 'Constantinople is dedicated by denuding every other city'). In 340 Constantius II created a senate, with quaestors, tribunes of the plebs, and praetors, but he did not manage to attract any of the old senatorial families from Rome. From 342 to 359 the city was administered by a proconsul, thereafter by a city prefect as at Rome.

The bishop of Constantinople soon acquired great prestige, and in 381 the council of Constantinople declared that 'he should have the primacy of honour after the bishop of Rome because it was the New Rome'. In 451 he acquired patriarchal jurisdiction over the dioceses of Thrace, Asiana, and Pontica. Already before the close of the 4th cent. we find the first stages in the growth of Byzantine monasticism.

In 425 a number of professorial chairs were established: five and three in Greek and Latin *rhetoric, ten in Greek and Latin *grammar, one in philosophy, and two in law. But it was a long time before Constantinople managed to attract scholars of the first rank. The prosperity of the city was largely due to the fact that it housed the imperial court, the senate, the palatine ministries, the praetorian prefecture of the east, and the two *magistri militum praesentales*. It was also the seat of the supreme courts of appeal with all their lawyers, and of the patriarchate with its numerous clergy, and thronged with petitioners and litigants, ecclesiastical, civil, and military.

The Notitia of the city, drawn up under *Theodosius (3) II, gives much valuable information: for example, that there were 20 public and 120 private bakeries; 9 public and 153 private baths; and 4,388 houses apart from blocks of flats. Of the buildings of the early period there survive the 'burnt column' of Constantine, the hippodrome with its two obelisks, the aqueduct of Valens, the Theodosian walls, the basilica of Studius, a mosaic floor from the Grand Palace, Justinian's churches of S. Sophia, S. Eirene, and SS. Sergius and Bacchus, the palace of *Justinian on the sea of Marmara, and several huge cisterns. See too ANICIA IULIANA.

R. Janin, *Constantinople byzantine*, 2nd edn. (1964); G. Dagron, *Naissance d'une capitale: Constantinople et ses institutions de 330 à 451* (1974), and *Constantinople imaginaire* (1984); C. Mango, *Le développement urbain de Constantinople (IVe–VIIe siècles)* (1985), and *Studies on Constantinople* (1993).

A. D. E. C.

Constantius I (*RE* 1), **Flavius Valerius** (perhaps Flavius Iulius before 293; nicknamed, not before the 6th cent., **Chlorus**), born no later than AD 250, of Illyrian stock; stories of his relationship with *Claudius II are fictions of *Constantine's propagandists. Constantius served as an army officer, as governor of Dalmatia, and possibly as praetorian prefect of Maximianus Augustus (*Maximian), whose daughter or stepdaughter Theodora he married, having put away Helena, the mother of Constantine I. On the establishment of the *tetrarchy *Diocletian appointed him Caesar, Maximian invested him at Milan (*Mediolanum, 1 March 293), and he took charge of Gaul, basing himself mainly at Trier (*Augusta Treverorum). His first task was to recover NE Gaul, held, with Britain, by the usurper *Carausius. In summer 293 he stormed Boulogne; but *Allectus, who murdered Carausius, retained Britain. Many of Carausius' defeated barbarian allies, Chamavi and Frisii, were settled within the empire. In 296, with Maximian guarding the Rhine, Constantius and his praetorian prefect, Asclepiodotus, took ship for *Britain. Asclepiodotus, landing near Clausentum (Bitterne), routed and killed Allectus; Constantius, separated from his prefect, came up the Thames to London in time to destroy the survivors of the beaten army. Constantius showed mercy to Britain and restored its defences. His other campaigns included a spectacular victory over the Alamanni at Langres (302). He failed fully to implement in his territories Diocletian's edicts against Christians (304), merely demolishing some churches. (See CHRISTIANITY.) On the abdication of Diocletian and Maximian (1 May 305) Constantius had Spain added to his territories but his rank as senior Augustus was curbed by the fact that both Caesars, Flavius Valerius *Severus and C. Galerius Valerius Maximinus, were creatures of *Galerius Augustus, who also held Constantine as a virtual hostage. Constantius crossed to Britain and asked that his son be released. Constantine was able to reach him fast enough to assist in his last victory, over the Picts, and to be proclaimed emperor by the army at York (*Eburacum) when Constantius died there (25 July 306). His premature death, and Constantine's proclamation, wrecked Diocletian's tetrarchic system. Constantinian propaganda bedevils assessment of Constantius, yet he appears to have been an able general and a generous ruler. By Theodora he had six children, half-siblings of Constantine; grandsons included *Gallus Caesar, *Julian, and the usurper (350) Nepotian.

R. P. D.

Constantius II, Flavius Iulius, (RE 4), third son of Constantine I, he became Augustus in the east after his father's death in AD 337; he spent much of his reign repelling Persian aggression in northern Mesopotamia. He marched westwards to defeat the usurper *Magnentius at the battle of Mursa in 351, having appointed his cousin *Gallus as Caesar in *Antioch (1). He subsequently (354) had Gallus deposed and executed on suspicion of treachery. Insecurity in the west led him to elevate Gallus' brother *Julian as Caesar in Gaul in 355. He was seen by contemporaries as a ruler dominated by his courtiers, and by a coterie of Arian (see ARIUS) bishops who influenced his sincere (but ultimately unsuccessful) attempts to achieve doctrinal unity in the Church. He died at Mobsucrenae in Cilicia on 3 November 361, while marching to confront the challenge of Julian, who had been declared Augustus in Gaul the previous year.

E. D. H.

Constantius III (RE 9). Successful against *Constantine III as *magister militum* of *Honorius, from then on (AD 411) he effectively ruled the west. Recovering Galla *Placidia from the Visigoths he married her (417); she bore him *Valentinian (3) III. He settled the Visigoths (see GOTHS) in Aquitania Secunda (418).

Made Augustus (February 421), he died seven months later.

R. P. D.

constellations and named stars From the earliest times the Greeks, like many other peoples, named certain prominent stars and groups of stars. Homer speaks of the Pleiades, the Hyades, Orion, Boötes, the Bear ('also called the Wain', *Od.* 5. 273), and the 'Dog of Orion' (i.e. Sirius, *Il.* 22. 29). Hesiod mentions all of these, and uses their heliacal risings and settings to mark the seasons and times for agricultural operations (e.g. the rising of the Pleiades for harvesting, and their setting for ploughing, *Op.* 383–4). This traditional 'agricultural calendar' was elaborated and codified in the later 'astronomical calendars' of *Meton, *Euctemon and their successors (see ASTRONOMY). The above are the only stars and star-groups known to have been named in archaic times, and although it is likely that some of the later constellations were identified before the 4th cent. BC (*Democritus, for instance, is said to have used Lyra, Aquila, and Delphinus for calendrical purposes), the division of the *whole* visible sky into constellations seems not to precede *Eudoxus (1). However, the twelve signs of the zodiac were introduced from *Mesopotamia long before then: the introduction is credited to Cleostratus of Tenedos (6th cent. BC), but it is disputed whether the verses attributed to him are genuine. However, the ultimate source is certain, since the iconography (see para. 4 below) and nomenclature of some of those constellations betray their Babylonian origin.

2. Eudoxus (c.360 BC) extended and codified the previously unorganized material into a description of the heavens, in which he divided the whole of that region of the sky visible from Greece into named constellations, which (with some minor changes and additions at later periods) became canonical. In doing so he subsumed some previously named star-groups (such as the Pleiades and Hyades) into larger constellations. Although the original has not survived, we have a good idea of the content of his work from its adaptation in the *Phaenomena* of *Aratus (1) and the commentary of *Hipparchus (3). From these it is clear that the constellations were conceived not merely as star-groups but as the outlines of actual figures in the heavens, on which the individual stars are located (e.g. 'the star on the right foot of the Great Bear (Ursa Major) is the same as the one on the tip of the left horn of the Bull (Taurus)'. Although the idea as such is found in much older Babylonian texts, the wording of Eudoxus surely implies the existence of a star-globe on which the figures representing the constellations were actually drawn and the most prominent stars too located. Representations of such globes survive from antiquity (e.g. the globe borne by the Farnese *Atlas), and *Ptolemy (4) (*Alm.* 8. 3) gives detailed instructions for constructing one. Later tradition ascribed the invention of this device to such heroic figures as *Atlas, *Thales, and *Anaximander, but it is very unlikely that it predates the 5th cent., and there is no certainty that it existed before Eudoxus himself. However, there undoubtedly were artistic representations of individual star-groups as mythological figures much earlier (cf. the stars on the shield of *Achilles, *Il.* 18. 486 ff.).

3. Like other peoples of antiquity, the Greeks identified some star-groups with mythological beings. Thus Hesiod calls the Pleiades 'daughters of Atlas'. This kind of identification was, at least in the system of Eudoxus, embedded in the very name of some constellations: for instance the whole *Perseus (1) myth is reflected in the names of the constellations Perseus, *Andromeda, Cetus, Cassiopeia, and *Cepheus. But it was only

in Hellenistic times that systematic attempts were made to connect all constellations with traditional mythology. Aratus already has numerous mythological excursuses and allusions, but the most influential work of this kind was the *Catasterisms* (Καταστερισμοί) of *Eratosthenes. A later epitome of this survives, which shows it to be the source of much in the similar work of *Hyginus (3), and of material both in the commentaries on Aratus by *Achilles Tatius (2) and others (see ARATEA) and in *Germanicus' Latin version of Aratus. Although we possess only a small part of the extensive ancient literature on astral mythology, even this is enough to show that there was no 'standard' version, but that different myths were often attached to the same constellation. For instance the sign Gemini, which gets its name from the Babylonian MAŠ-MAŠ ('twins'), was identified not only with the famous divine twins Castor and Pollux (see DIOSCURI), but also with the Theban heroic twins *Amphion and Zethus, and even with (the half-brothers) *Heracles and *Apollo, among others.

4. Connected with the mythology, but only partly determined by it, is the iconography of the constellations. This too was far from uniform, even among the professional astronomers (cf. Ptol. *Alm.* 7. 4, trans. Toomer 340). But there are certain traditional and unchanging characteristics, e.g. Taurus is always represented as only the forepart of a bull: it is probable that this is a relic of the Mesopotamian iconography of the constellation, as is certain for the representations of the zodiacal signs Capricorn (as a 'goat-fish') and Scorpius. The task of assembling and analysing all the scattered material on this subject, from the literary and astronomical descriptions, and from surviving ancient artefacts and medieval manuscripts (including not only the illustrations of Germanicus' *Aratea* but also, in the Arabic tradition, the drawings in aṣ-Ṣūfī's adaptation of Ptolemy's star catalogue), remains to be done.

5. The 48 canonical constellations, in the order in which they appear in Ptolemy's star-catalogue (essentially the same, but in slightly different order, already in Geminus 3. 8–13) are as follows.

(*a*) Northern constellations (i.e. north of the zodiacal belt):

(1) Ursa Minor (ἄρκτος μικρά, the Little Bear); also known as κυνόσουρα ('Dog's Tail').

(2) Ursa Major (ἄρκτος μεγάλη, the Great Bear); also known as the Wain (ἅμαξα). The old Roman name, independent of the Greek tradition, was 'Septemtrio' or 'Septemtriones', 'the Seven Threshing-oxen'.

(3) Draco (δράκων, the (great) Snake).

(4) Cepheus (Κηφεύς), the father of Andromeda, represented as an oriental monarch.

(5) Boötes (βοώτης, the Ox-herder); includes the bright star Arcturus (ἀρκτοῦρος, the Bear-ward).

(6) Corona Borealis (στέφανος βόρειος, the Northern Crown).

(7) *Hercules (ἐγγόνασιν, the figure 'On his Knees'). The identification with Hercules, which is the modern nomenclature, comes from later antiquity: in Aratus, Germanicus, and Ptolemy he is an anonymous kneeling man.

(8) Lyra (λύρα, the Lyre), usually depicted as a tortoiseshell, from the myth of Hermes' invention of the instrument. The bright star in Lyra has the same name as the constellation.

(9) Cygnus (ὄρνις, the Bird); the identification with a particular bird, the Swan, belongs to the later tradition, but agrees with most of the extant iconography.

(10) Cassiopeia (Κασσιεπεία, the mother of Andromeda), always represented as seated on a throne.

(11) Perseus (Περσεύς), represented with upraised scimitar in one hand and the Gorgon's head in the other.

(12) Auriga (ἡνίοχος, the Charioteer), includes the two stars named the Kids (ἔριφοι, Haedi) and the bright star Capella (αἴξ, the Goat).

(13, 14) Ophiuchus and Serpens (ὀφιοῦχος, the Snakeholder, represented as holding ὄφις, the Snake, known as ὄφις ὀφιούχου to distinguish it from Draco and Hydra).

(15) Sagitta (οἰστός, the Arrow).

(16) Aquila (ἀετός, the Eagle); the bright star in this constellation has the same name (Aquila).

(17) Delphinus (δελφίς, the Dolphin).

(18) Equuleus (ἵππου προτομή, the Bust of a Horse). This small constellation, for which no myths are known, seems to have been added by Hipparchus. The nomenclature 'Equuleus' is not ancient.

(19) *Pegasus (ἵππος, the Horse). Although called 'Horse' rather than 'Pegasus' in most ancient texts, the identification is supported by the iconography, which represents the front half of a winged horse.

(20) Andromeda (Ἀνδρομέδα), usually represented as chained (awaiting the sea-beast Cetus).

(21) Triangulum (τρίγωνον, the Triangle).

(*b*) Constellations of the zodiac:

(22) Aries (κριός, the Ram).

(23) Taurus (ταῦρος, the Bull). The name and iconography are of Mesopotamian origin. The constellation includes the old Greek star-groups of the Hyades (ὑάδες, Piglets) and Pleiades (meaning unknown, later assimilated to πελειάδες, Doves). The Romans identified and named the latter independently as 'Vergiliae'.

(24) Gemini (δίδυμοι, the Twins); the nomenclature is Mesopotamian, see para. 3 above.

(25) Cancer (καρκίνος, the Crab). This constellation, whose nomenclature is Babylonian, incorporated the old Greek star-groups of the two Asses (ὄνοι, Asini), and the Manger (φάτνη, Praesepe).

(26) Leo (λέων, the Lion). The name goes back to Mesopotamia. The bright star 'on the heart' had its own name βασιλίσκος (Regulus, 'Little King'). The star-group 'Coma Berenices' was given a separate name by *Conon (2).

(27) Virgo (παρθένος, the Maiden), represented with wings, having in her left hand the bright star Spica (στάχυς, the Ear of Corn), and on her right wing the star Vindemiatrix (προτρυγητήρ, the Harbinger of Vintage), both probably old Greek appellations.

(28, 29) Libra and Scorpius. In Mesopotamia these were represented together as a huge scorpion, of which the first sign was the claws and the second the body and tail. In Greek sources too the first sign is often called χηλαί, 'the Claws', and so represented. But the nomenclature ζυγός, 'the Scales' (of a balance) and the corresponding representation is also found. The second sign is accordingly either a whole or partial scorpion (σκορπίος or σκορπίων). The star Antares (so named because of its similarity to the planet Mars in redness) is in Scorpius.

(30) Sagittarius (τοξότης, the Archer), represented as a centaur with a bow, an iconography derived from Mesopotamia.

(31) Capricorn (αἰγόκερως, the Goathorn); the representation

as a mixture of goat and fish goes back to Mesopotamia.

(32) Aquarius (ὑδροχόος, the Water-carrier).

(33) Pisces (ἰχθύες, the Fishes). The constellation is called 'Fish' (singular) in Mesopotamia; the representation as two fishes joined by a line is probably a Greek innovation.

(c) Southern constellations (i.e. south of the zodiacal belt):

(34) Cetus (κῆτος, the Sea-monster), connected with the myth of Andromeda (see above).

(35) *Orion (Ὠρίων). The meaning of the name of this old Greek star-group is unknown; he was represented as a giant hunter.

(36) Eridanus (ποταμός, the River); the identification with a specific river Eridanus is at least as old as Aratus.

(37) Lepus (λαγωός, the Hare).

(38) Canis Major (κύων, the Dog), includes the brightest of all stars, Sirius (Σείριος, also called κύων).

(39) Canis Minor (πρόκυων, Harbinger of the Dog), named after the bright star Procyon which it includes.

(40) Argo (Ἀργώ, the ship of the *Argonauts). This huge constellation has in modern times been divided into three separate constellations, Puppis, Vela, and Carina; it includes the bright star Canopus (Κάνωβος, named after the Egyptian town).

(41) Hydra (ὕδρα or ὕδρος, the Water-snake).

(42, 43) Crater (κρατήρ, the Mixing-bowl) and Corvus (κόραξ, the Raven); both of these are represented as standing on Hydra.

(44) Centaurus (κένταυρος, the *Centaur), represented with a thyrsus in one hand and holding the Beast (see no. 45) dangling in the other.

(45) Lupus (θηρίον, the Beast); the identification with a wolf or another specific beast is found only in late sources.

(46) Ara (θυτήριον, the Altar, or θυμιατήριον, the Incense-burner).

(47) Corona Australis (στέφανος νότιος, the Southern Crown).

(48) Piscis Austrinus (ἰχθὺς νότιος, the Southern Fish).

The Milky Way (γαλαξίας, γαλακτίας κύκλος, or simply γάλα), which runs through many constellations, was named from its appearance at an early time. Among the many conjectures as to its nature, Democritus made the correct one.

6. Besides the above canonical constellations (known as the *Sphaera graecanica*) there existed from the late Hellenistic period a completely different *Sphaera barbarica*. These fanciful 'constellations' may reflect late Egyptian and Babylonian traditions, but our knowledge of them comes exclusively from the fragmentarily preserved Graeco-Latin astrological literature. The first evidence for the *Sphaera barbarica* is connected with *Nigidius Figulus (1st cent. BC), and it is found in the extant astrological works of M. *Manilius and *Firmicus Maternus. It had little influence on the astronomical tradition, but greatly affected Indian, Islamic, and medieval western astrology and its artistic representations.

Fundamental is F. Boll and W. Gundel, 'Sternbilder, Sternglaube und Sternsymbolik bei Griechen und Römern', in Roscher, *Lex.* 6. 867 ff., which includes some useful illustrations of the iconography. For the latter the best (though inadequate) collection remains G. Thiele, *Antike Himmelsbilder* (1898). On the Farnese Atlas star-globe see also V. Valerio in *Der Globusfreund* 35–7 (1987), 97 ff. On the history of the star-globe: A. Schlachter, *Der Globus* (1927). On the *Sphaera barbarica*: F. Boll, *Sphaera* (1903).   G. J. T.

constitution, Antonine (*constitutio Antoniniana*) is the name given to the edict of *Caracalla (Antoninus), probably of AD 212, which made all free men and women in the empire Roman

citizens (Ulpian, *Dig.* 1. 5. 17; Cass. Dio 78. 9), perhaps with minor exceptions. According to Dio, the emperor's motive was to increase the numbers liable to taxes imposed on citizens such as inheritance tax. A surviving papyrus (*PGiess.* 40) points to religious motives. In any event the concept of universal citizenship fitted the egalitarian outlook which the Severan dynasty (193–235), rooted in Africa and Syria, shared with such contemporaries as *Galen and *Ulpian. The effect of the enactment is disputed. The new citizens took Roman names and became subject to Roman law. But it has been argued that citizenship was at this period of minor importance in comparison with upper-class status (see HONESTIORES). In practice pre-existing law proved resistant to change, especially in Egypt, and Roman law was obliged to concede to local custom a greater force than it had previously possessed. In the long run the effect of the *constitutio Antoniniana* was profound, since it promoted in both east and west a uniform legal system and a consciousness of being Roman that lasted until the fall of the empire, and sometimes beyond it.

C. Sasse, *Die Constitutio Antoniniana* (1958); K. Bourazelis *Theia Dōrea: meletes panō stēn politikē tēs dynasteias tōn Severōn kai tēn constitutio Antoniniana* (1989).   T. Hon.

Constitution of the Athenians attributed to *Aristotle: see ATHENAION POLITEIA; attributed to *Xenophon (1): see OLD OLIGARCH.

constitutions (*constitutiones*), the generic name for legislative enactments by Roman emperors, took different forms. (a) Like all higher magistrates, emperors had the power to issue *edicts; imperial edicts were used for enactments of a general character (e.g. the *constitutio Antoniniana*, extending citizenship to the whole Roman world). (b) The emperor had great judicial powers. His decisions took the form of decrees (*decreta*). Although the Romans had no theory of binding precedent, such rulings, coming from the emperor, were regarded as authoritative for future cases and were freely quoted by the jurists. (c) The emperor received many petitions and requests for rulings from officials and from individuals. Rescripts (*rescripta*) were the written answers issued by the imperial chancery. They were of two main kinds. (1) *epistulae* (letters) were addressed to officials or public bodies, and were drafted by the department *ab epistulis*. (2) *Subscriptiones* (see SUBSCRIPTIONS), so called because the emperor validated them by writing at the end 'scripsi' or 'subscripsi' ('I have written underneath'), were drafted by the department *a libellis* in response to petitions (*libelli*) on a wide variety of subjects from private persons and (rarely) cities (see MAGISTER LIBELLORUM). A large number, dealing with points of law, are preserved in Justinian's *Codex* (see CODEX; JUSTINIAN'S CODIFICATION). (d) *Mandata* (instructions) were given by the emperor to officials, especially provincial governors. Since they were in form merely administrative, they were not strictly constitutions, but they created a number of important rules which could be relied on by private individuals.

H. F. Jolowicz and B. Nicholas, *Historical Introduction to Roman Law*, 3rd edn. (1972); T. Honoré, *Emperors and Lawyers* (1981; 2nd edn. 1994).   B. N.

consul, the title of the chief annual civil and military magistrates of Rome during the republic. Two consuls were elected annually for most, if not all, of the republic by the centuriate assembly (see CENTURIA) at a meeting called for the purpose, normally by a consul, exceptionally by a *dictator, *interrex, or military

Consus

tribune (see TRIBUNI MILITUM) with consular power. Before 153 BC their year of office began on 15 March (possibly earlier in the years before c.220), thereafter on 1 January.

According to tradition the dual annual magistracy succeeded immediately to the kingship. Most of the powers of the king (including military command and the right to summon the senate and the people, but excluding certain religious functions, reserved for the *pontifices and the *rex sacrorum) fell to a pair of annual magistrates, called originally praetors (Livy 3. 55. 12; Festus 249 Lindsay) and subsequently consuls, the powers now tempered by the principle of collegiality and limited tenure of office. Against this it has been held that the dual collegiate system must have been some time in developing, and scholars have pointed to the fact that for most of the years from 448 to 368 there were more than two chief magistrates (the military tribunes) and to Livy 7. 3. 5, where an 'ancient law' (lex vetusta) is referred to that mentions a praetor maximus, taken to refer to a sole (or pre-eminent) chief magistrate. The title *praetor (from prae-ire, to go before; the etymology of 'consul' is not clear) suggests military leadership, and many have seen in the praetor maximus the supreme magistrate of the early republic, with the fully collegiate magistracy appearing in its final dual form only much later, perhaps as late as 367. The traditional view that republic and dual magistracy were coeval is supported by the *fasti, which show a succession of two annual consuls in the years before 451, and was apparently in place by the time *Polybius (1) wrote (see 3. 22. 1–2). The testimony of the fasti has yet to be successfully impugned, and modern supporters of the traditional view have seen in Livy's praetor maximus a descriptive reference to the senior (but not more powerful) of the two collegial magistrates or an indication of the superiority of the their office. The Greek translations (στρατηγός for praetor and στρατηγὸς ὕπατος, or στρατηγός or ὕπατος alone, for consul) may be indicative, but they are not attested before the early 2nd cent. BC and seem more likely to reflect contemporary Greek perceptions than Roman antiquities.

As the highest office of state the consulship figured in the 'struggle of the orders' between patricians and plebeians. Analysis of the fasti, however, suggests that the tradition may have been wrong in regarding the consulship as an office from which plebeians were at one time excluded by law. Plebeian consuls were, nevertheless, few in the 5th cent., and it was not until 367 BC that a Licinian plebiscite (see LICINIUS STOLO, C.) required the election of at least one plebeian consul and not until 342 that this became regular in fact. The first entirely plebeian college held office in 172.

The consul's power, or *imperium, was effectively that of the king, limited by the period of office and the presence of a colleague with the same imperium. The importance of the principle of collegiality here is reflected in the fact that if a consul died or resigned, his colleague was bound to hold an election to fill his place for the remainder of the year (as *suffect consul). Over time, some functions were removed from the consuls. The conduct of the *census was taken over by the *censors from 443, and civil jurisdiction passed effectively to the praetor from 366. In the city consuls could exercise *coercitio, a general power of enforcing order and exacting obedience to their commands, but the extent of their power within the city (imperium domi) was subject from the earliest times to *provocatio. The power of the consul in the field (imperium militiae) was virtually unrestricted, as symbolized by the addition of the axe to the *fasces when the consul left the city on campaign. It was probably not until a law of *Cato

Censorius in the 190s that the citizen's right of provocatio was extended beyond the precincts of the city. The consuls could and usually did act together, for example in calling the senate or an assembly, and use of the veto (*intercessio) against one another was rare. When division of labour in the city was indicated, this might be arranged by agreement or by lot, or by use of the custom whereby each assumed duties (and the fasces) for a month at a time. When both consuls were on campaign together, the normal practice was for each to assume overall command for a day at a time.

Under the empire consuls continued, but in an appropriately attenuated way. With *Augustus consular imperium came to be part of the emperor's arsenal and to be held by the emperor independently of the office of consul itself. With the suppression of the centuriate assembly and popular election, the emperors either recommended the candidates (see COMMENDATIO) or held the office themselves. The position continued to confer honour, as is indicated by the increasing use of pairs of suffect consuls during the same year after the initial brief tenure of the consules ordinarii, who gave their name to the year as the republican consuls had done. The republican age limits (fixed initially by the lex Villia annalis of 180 BC (see VILLIUS, L.) and later by a law of *Sulla's dictatorship; in the late republic no one under 42 could be elected) were often disregarded as imperial relatives and protégés were signalled by the bestowal upon them of the consulship. In these circumstances children might become consuls, and *Honorius was made consul at his birth in AD 384. The consulship continued in the western empire for 150 years after that.

Mommsen, Röm. Staatsr. 2³. 74 ff.; M. Holleaux, Στρατηγὸς Ὕπατος (1918); A. E. Astin, The Lex Annalis before Sulla (1958); H. F. Jolowicz and B. Nicholas, Historical Introduction to the Study of Roman Law, 3rd edn. (1972) (with bibliography); A. Drummond, CAH 7²/2 (1989), 186 ff. (with bibliography); A. Lippold, Consules (1963) (on the consuls 264–201 BC); E. Badian, Chiron 1990, 371 ff. (on the consuls 179–49 BC). For the consular fasti: A. Degrassi, Insc. Ital. 13/1 (1947) (republican), and I Fasti consolari dell'impero romano (1952); also Broughton, MRR.

P. S. D.

Consus, a Roman god of the granary (from condere 'to store') whose festivals (Consualia) on 21 August and 15 December coincided, respectively, with the gathering of the harvest and the onset of winter. The ancients commonly supposed his name to have something to do with consilium (Varro ARD 140 Cardauns). Horses as funerary animals (Gell. NA 10. 15. 3, fasti Praenestini 15 December) were added under Etruscan influence (Dion. Hal. Ant. Rom. 2. 31) and led to a misidentification with Poseidon Hippios (Livy 1. 9. 6 with Ogilvie's notes; Latte, RR 72). He seems connected with two festivals of *Ops: Opiconsivia (25 August) and Opalia (19 December). Since corn was often stored underground, this may account for his subterranean altar in the Circus Maximus, uncovered only on his festival days (Varro, Ling. 6. 20; Dion. Hal. Ant. Rom. 2. 31); for its alleged inscription (Tert. De Spect. 5), A. Blumenthal, ARW 1936, 384 ff. and H. Rose, ARW 1937, 111 ff. He had a temple (Aedes Consi) on the Aventine, probably vowed or dedicated by L. *Papirius Cursor (2) about 272 BC (Platner–Ashby 141). His characteristic offering was first-fruits (Dion. Hal., ibid.). Horses and asses were garlanded and rested on his festival (Plut. Quaest. Rom. 48 with Rose's notes).

G. Dumézil, Idées romaines (1969), 289 ff.   C. R. P.

contaminatio, a word used by modern scholars to express the procedure of *Terence (and perhaps *Plautus) in incorporating material from another Greek play into the primary play which he was adapting. Terence tells us that he had done this in adapting *Menander (1)'s *Andria* (adding material from Menander's *Perinthia*), and that his critics had complained that he ought not to *contaminare* plays in this way (i.e. to 'spoil' them by adding alien material: *An.* prologue 9 ff.; at *Haut.* 17 he says he has been accused in a general way of 'contaminating' many Greek plays while writing few in Latin). Terence claims the precedent of *Naevius, Plautus, and *Ennius, we cannot tell how truthfully (though some have claimed to detect *contaminatio* in Plautus; the fragments of Naevius and Ennius are too meagre to judge). He followed the same procedure in *Eunuchus* and *Adelphoe* but was there accused of 'theft' (plagiarism from earlier Latin comedies), not *contaminatio*.

G. E. Duckworth, *The Nature of Roman Comedy* (1952), 202 ff.; G. Guastella, *La contaminazione e il parassita* (1988).   P. G. M. B.

contio (*conventio*, a coming together) was a public meeting at Rome from which no legal enactment actually emerged, even though it might form part of a longer formal procedure, such as a trial before the people. Hence it did not have to be held in a *templum*, an area hallowed by the taking of the auspices. It could be convened by a magistrate or a priest. Apart from trials, it was used among other things for preliminary discussion of legislation or simply as a means of providing a politician with a political platform to pronounce on matters of the moment. A magistrate could call away a meeting summoned by an inferior and a tribune could veto (see INTERCESSIO) the making of a speech at any meeting. The right of addressing the audience depended on the discretion of the convener. He addressed the gathering from a platform, to which he might summon speakers of sufficient importance, while others spoke from ground level. These meetings generally took place in the Forum or its neighbourhood, but could be held outside the *pomerium* so that a pro-magistrate might attend without losing his *imperium*. See COMITIA.

Mommsen, *Röm. Staatsr.* 1³. 191 ff.; G. W. Botsford, *The Roman Assemblies* (1909).   P. T.; A. W. L.

contraception played a minor role in Hippocratic medicine, where the emphasis was rather on helping women to conceive. (See HIPPOCRATES (2).) The exception is a substance called 'misy', possibly copper ore, recommended as having the power to prevent conception for a year (e.g. Hippoc. *Mul.* 1. 76 and *Nat. Mul.* 98). It was erroneously believed that the most fertile time of the month was just before or just after a menstrual period, when the womb was open to receive semen. Any attempt to use this information in reverse, in order to avoid conception, would thus in fact have led to intercourse at the most fertile days of the month.

However, it has been argued that many of the remedies given as general gynaecological cures (see GYNAECOLOGY) in the ancient medical tradition did in fact contain substances, mostly of plant origin, effective both as contraceptives and as early-stage abortifacients. Some substances were used as barriers; for example, sponges soaked in vinegar or oil, or cedar resin applied to the mouth of the womb. These could have acted as spermicides. Others could either be taken orally or used as pessaries, and included pomegranate skin, pennyroyal, willow, and the squirting cucumber, which forcefully ejects its seeds. The degree to which these would have been effective is, however, very difficult to assess. The widespread practice of polypharmacy, by which a combination of several different remedies were used at

once, together with the use of *amulets, other magical techniques, and non-fertile sexual positions would have made it difficult to judge which method was responsible in the event of a long period without pregnancy ensuing. There is considerable debate also over the use of coitus interruptus, which is not discussed in the sources (see however 'landing in the grassy meadows' in Archilochus, *PColon.* 7511 = SLG 478²) but which is nevertheless assumed by some modern commentators to have been widespread. *Soranus recommends a form of withdrawal by the female partner, in order to prevent the ejection of semen deep into the womb, as well as sneezing after intercourse, washing the vagina, and drinking cold water (*Gynaeceia* 1. 20).

An additional problem is that, although some distinction between *abortion and contraception was made in the ancient world—at least by Soranus (*Gynaeceia* 1. 20)—conception was often seen as a process, and any intervention in early pregnancy could thus be seen as 'contraceptive'. This confusion is heightened by the fact that the substances used as contraceptives or abortives would perhaps also work as emmenagogues. What was envisaged as action to bring on a delayed period could thus have been an early abortion—or, indeed, vice versa. See BOTANY; PHARMACOLOGY.

E. Eyben, *Anc. Soc.* 1980–1, 5–82; M.-T. Fontanelle, *Avortement et contraception dans la Médecine greco-romain* (1977); A. E. Hanson, in D. M. Halperin and others, *Before Sexuality* (1990), 309–38; K. M. Hopkins, *Comparative Studies in Society and History* 1966, 124–51; J. M. Riddle, *Contraception and Abortion from the Ancient World to the Renaissance* (1992).   H. K.

contract was one of the four branches of the law of obligations set out in Justinian *Inst.* 3. 13. However, it constituted a law of specific contracts rather than a law of contract based on a uniform set of principles. According to Gaius *Inst.* 3. 89 and Justinian *Inst.* 3. 13. 2 contracts fell into four classes. They could arise (*a*) *re*, by the handing over of a thing; (*b*) *verbis*, by formal words; (*c*) *litteris*, by written entries in the creditor's account book (*codex accepti et expensi*); (*d*) *consensu*, by mere informal agreement. The contract *litteris* became obsolete during the first centuries AD.

By far the most important of the verbal contracts was the stipulation (*stipulatio*); others were the promise of a dowry (*dotis dictio*) and a freed slave's promise of services (*promissio operarum*). Real contracts were of four kinds. (1) *Mutuum* was a loan for consumption, as a result of which the borrower was obliged to return an equal sum (in the case of money) or objects of the same kind, quantity, and quality (as far as things like wheat and oil were concerned). A claim for interest could not be enforced under the action arising from *mutuum* (i.e. the *condictio*); it required a separate contract, a stipulation, which also usually contained certain incidental provisions like time and place of repayment. From the end of the republic, interest was limited to 12 per cent a year (*centesimae usurae*). *Justinian reduced the ordinary maximum rate to 6 per cent. (2) *Commodatum* was a gratuitous loan of a thing for use. The borrower was required to return the very same thing borrowed. Since the contract was for his benefit, the borrower was subject to a strict type of liability (*custodia*) which went beyond fault (*culpa*) and excluded only acts of God. A counter action (*actio commodati contraria*) was available to the borrower to claim damages and expenses. (3) *Depositum*: here the object was handed over not to be used but to be kept in safe custody. Deposit, too, was gratuitous. Since it was the depositor who benefited, the depositee's liability was restricted to dishonesty (*dolus*) and gross fault (*culpa lata*), later, possibly, to showing less care than he did for his own property (*diligentia* *quam in suis*). As with *commodatum*, a counteraction was available to the depositee. (4) *Pignus* entailed the handing over of a thing in order to secure a debt. Apart from creating a contractual relationship between pledgor and pledgee, it also gave rise to a *ius in rem*, a (limited) real right of the pledgee over the property of the pledgor. *Pignus* was thus the paradigm of real *security.

Consensual contracts, too, were of four types. This limited class of contracts, concluded by mere consent (*nudo consensu*), comprised *sale (*emptio* or *venditio*), hire (**locatio* or *conductio*), *mandate (*mandatum*), and partnership (*societas*). The essence of partnership was the pooling of resources (capital, property, skill, or labour, or a combination of them) for a common purpose. The partners were free as to how they wished to allocate profits and losses between them. However, a partnership, in which one partner shared only in the loss and not at all in the profits (*societas leonina*) was inadmissible. The bringing of an *actio pro socio* (an action of one partner against another) terminated the partnership and entailed a general settlement of accounts.

Recognition of the consensual contracts was one of the most remarkable achievements of Roman jurisprudence. They were all based on the precepts of good faith (*bona fides*), and the jurists therefore had much leeway in determining the rights and duties of the respective parties in a flexible and equitable manner. Litigation concerning sale, in particular, provided the Roman lawyers with ample opportunity to develop a nucleus of general principles of contractual liability (as e.g. the effect of mistake, fraud, or coercion on a contract, principles of interpretation, invalidity due to immorality, illegality, impossibility). Contract in general was increasingly seen to be based on consent, and consent was taken to depend on a meeting of the minds. This had repercussions on the verbal and real contracts; they were gradually 'consensualized'.

Informal agreements that did not fit into the pigeon-holes of the Roman contractual scheme (*nuda pacta*) were unenforceable. Down to the time of Justinian, the general principle remained that a bare pact does not create an obligation (*nuda pactio obligationem non parit*). At the same time, however, a gradual erosion of this principle took place. Already in classical law, agreements attached to one of the recognized contracts (*pacta in continenti adiecta*) constituted an exception. Also, the praetor (hence: *pacta praetoria*) had recognized informal promises to pay an already existing debt (*constitutum*) and informal undertakings by arbitrators, bankers, carriers by sea, innkeepers, and stablekeepers (*receptum arbitri, argentarii* and *nautarum, cauponum, stabulariorum*). The emperors added to this list (*pacta legitima*, among them, particularly, gift (*donatio*) and reference to arbitration (*compromissum*)). Finally, where a party to an informal arrangement not enforceable as such had performed his side of the bargain, he came to be granted an *actio praescriptis verbis* (action with a preface explaining the facts) in order to enforce counter-performance. This remedy originated in classical law and led, by the time of Justinian, to the recognition of a new class of 'contracts' based on (agreement and) part-performance and referred to as innominate real contracts (even though some of them had acquired individual names, like exchange (*permutatio*), which did not fall under sale, and delivery on sale or return which was called *aestimatum*).

B. Nicholas, *Introd. to R. Law*, 1st edn. (1962), 159 ff.; S. E. Wunner, *Contractus* (1964); A. Watson, *The Law of Obligations in the Later Roman Republic* (1965); H.-P. Benöhr, *Synallagma* (1965); H. F. Jolowicz and B. Nicholas, *Historical Introduction to Roman Law,* 3rd edn. (1972), 279 ff.; C. A. Maschi, *Contratti reali* (1973); M. Kaser, *Römisches Privatrecht* 1, 2nd edn. (1971), 522 ff., vol. 2, 2nd edn. (1975), 360 ff.; G. Diósdi, *Contract* (1981); R. Zimmermann, *The Law of Obligations* (1990). R. Z.

contubernium meant a 'dwelling together', as of soldiers or animals, but referred especially to a quasi-marital union between slave and slave or slave and free. Since a slave lacked juristic personality, a *contubernium* was not a marriage but a factual situation, at the pleasure of the slave-owner, creating no legal consequences despite the use of such words as *uxor, maritus*, or *pater*, even in legal texts. Children were the property of the mother's owner; no slave-woman could be guilty of adultery; manumission of one or both parents need not extend to their issue. Sepulchral inscriptions indicate that *contubernia* were highly valued. But how widespread *de facto* slave 'families' were and which social contexts best favoured them cannot be accurately known. Slave-owners always retained the right to separate slave family members, and commonly did so to judge from records of slave sales and bequests.

For bibliography see MARRIAGE LAW; SLAVERY.   M. I. F.; K. R. B.

conventus, 'assembly', is technically used (1) for associations of Italians abroad; (2) for provincial assizes.

(1) By the early 2nd cent. BC Italians (especially in the east) united for religious and other purposes under elected *magistri*. In the late republic these associations (which came to be called *conventus civium Romanorum*) often gained a position of great political importance locally; the governor would rely on them for service on juries and on his council (*consilium*) and for advice on local conditions. In the Caesarian and Augustan period such associations often formed the nucleus for the foundation of new colonies and *municipia civium Romanorum*. Under the empire these associations sometimes passed decrees together with the Greek city authorities; in some areas they came to be organized under *curatores*. In the long term with the spread of *Romanization, especially in the west, these associations disappeared.

(2) In most provinces, by the late republic, assizes (where the provincial governor held court) were held in fixed centres. Under the Principate the status of assize centres became a much sought after privilege, comparable to that of being a centre for the imperial (*ruler-)cult, which was in the gift of the emperor. In the province of Asia for example, which had at least 300 urban communities, there were fourteen assize centres in the 2nd cent. AD. The annual assize-tour of the provincial governor constituted the practical framework within which he exercised all his routine administrative and jurisdictional duties.

E. Kornemann, *RE* 4. 1173 ff.; G. P. Burton, *JRS* 1975, 92 ff.   G. P. B.

conversion The term implies rejection of one way of life for another, generally better, after brief and intense insight into the shortcomings of self or the demands of circumstance. Ancient religious cult did not require such radical or sudden shifts. Devotees could embrace one allegiance without renouncing others. Observance was intensified by addition rather than by exchange, even in the case of initiation to a mystery. A. D. Nock made much of the account of Lucius in *Apuleius (*Conversion* 138–55—the allusions are to Isis). Lucius' *metamorphosis owed more to miracle, however, than to will-power, although the conversion of others may have been invited (Apul. *Met*. 11. 15).

It is common to suggest that only *Christianity, and to a lesser extent *Judaism, could muster a sharp sense of exclusive loyalty, so that adherence to either cult demanded rejection of some other practice. Two considerations undermine that view.

First, the characteristic word for conversion in the NT, *metanoia*, was used also by Classical philosophers. Its chief meaning was to come to one's senses in a new and different way. While Marcus Aurelius, for example (M. Aur. *Med.* 8. 10), and Plutarch (e.g. *Tim.* 6. 2; *Mar.* 10. 4) generally retained the narrow sense of inconstancy or regret, other texts are more dramatic—e.g. *Poimandres* 28 (*Corpus Hermeticum*, ed. Nock and Festugière 1. 16 f.) and the *Tabula* of Cebes, ed. K. Praechter 1893 (§§ 9–11). In the words used by *Hierocles, 'conversion is the beginning of philosophy' (*FPG* 1. 451 f.). Such writers could take their cue, in any case, from the classic insights of *Plato (1) (*Resp.* 7. 4).

Latin was strikingly weak in its corresponding word-power. *Conversio* remained resolutely wedded to its physical origins and even in a moral sense had more to do with association than with psychological attitude. Commonly quoted passages such as Cic. *Nat. D.* 1. 27 and Plin. *Ep.* 9. 13. 18 are ambiguous or narrow. There was among the Romans a contrasting admiration for *constantia*, in the sense of steadfastness, whereby those deserving moral approbation were as likely to maintain the gifts and inclinations of their breeding as to renounce their past in favour of novel commitments.

Second, the literature of Christian conversion frequently describes a change of heart based on existing association with the Church. The classic example of *Augustine (*Confessions* 8. 6–8, 12) echoes the experience of many men and women in the century before him (and L. *Annaeus Seneca (2)'s 'sudden change' is a striking anticipation, *Ep.* 6. 1 f.). Antony and *Basil were already sprung from pious Christian families. *Ambrose, by contrast, although similarly placed, was embarrassed to find himself on the verge of baptism and episcopacy with no respectable conversion to his name.

The perceived meanings of conversion, therefore, prompt us to attach equal importance to breeding or intimate friendship in the growth of the Christian community. Baptism, even when postponed because of its demands, was not identified with conversion. The term should be reserved for the experience of a narrower body of men and women, who felt a need to carry religious commitment to new heights not far removed from the ambitions of pagan philosophers. Mass attachment to the Church after Constantine, on the other hand, was more circumspect than passionate. The sermons addressed by bishops to their expanding flocks are telling in their exhortations. The level of intensity they recommended was clearly greater than their cautious hearers had achieved.

A. D. Nock, *Conversion* (1933), and *RAC* 2 (1954), 105–18.   P. R.

convivium The Roman *convivium* was modelled on the Etruscan version of the Greek *symposium. These Italian feasts differed from their Greek prototypes in four important respects: citizen women were present; equality was replaced by a hierarchy of honour; the emphasis was on eating and the *cena*, rather than on the *comissatio*, or later drinking session; the entertainment was often given by one man for his inferior *amici* and *clientes* (see CLIENS). The Roman *convivium* was therefore embedded in social and family structures, rather than largely independent of them; the difference is captured by the remark of *Cato (Censorius) in *Cicero, *Sen.* 13. 45, that the Romans were right to emphasize the aspect of 'living together' by calling a group of reclining friends a *convivium* rather than a *symposium*.

The differences between Greek and Roman customs produced some tensions. The presence of respectable women is archaeologically attested in Etruria (see ETRUSCANS) and early Rome, and

was already denounced by *Theopompus (3) (Athen. 12. 517–18); it led to a series of attempts by Roman antiquarians to explain that originally Roman women had been prohibited from drinking wine or reclining (Cato and *Varro in Gell. *NA* 10. 23; Plin. *HN* 14. 89–90; Isid. *Etym.* 20. 11. 9). Later moralists were obsessed with the consequent dangers of *adultery, which became a specifically Roman vice. Inequality and the tendency to excessive display of wealth gave rise to an emphasis on the need for moderate behaviour, and satires on vulgar ostentation (Hor. *Sat.* 2. 8; Juv. *Sat.* 5; Petronius). The activities of the *grassator* (*parasite) and pretensions towards Greek-style literary sophistication in private banquets were ridiculed, and contrasted with the public feasts given by politicians and emperors (Cato in Gell. *NA* 11. 2. 5; Cic. *Pis.* 65–7; Stat. *Silv.* 1. 6). The result was a complex convivial culture, whose literature was descriptive and moralizing, rather than designed for actual performance at the *convivium*, and was much concerned with differences between Greek and Roman customs (Plut. *Quaest. conv.*).

Roman religion involved special forms of the feast (*epulum*). In 399 BC the *lectisternium* was introduced, a ritual in which images of the gods were arranged as banqueters on couches, and for which the priestly college of the *epulones* seem to have had responsibility. Other *collegia* such as the *arval brethren dined together according to complex rituals. The Saturnalia (see SATURNUS) was a traditional carnivalesque feast of inversion.

The Roman *dining-room was based on the *triclinium* arrangement of couches, traditionally with three couches and nine participants (Vitr. *De arch.* 6. 5. 6). This produced a space for entertainment facing the diners, rather than enclosed by them, and encouraged displays that were more lavish than in Greece, but did not involve participation. In late antiquity the *triclinium* arrangement gradually gave way to the single semicircular *sigma*-couch or *stibadium*, often arranged in alcoves around a central space; this became the dominant form in the larger ceremonial dining-rooms of late antique palaces such as *Piazza Armerina.

S. de Marinis, *La tipologia del banchetto nell'arte etrusca arcaica* (1961); O. Murray, *Concilium Eirene* 1982, 47–52; *JRS* 1985, 39–50; J. H. D'Arms, *Échos du monde classique* 1984, 327–48; K. M. T. Dunbabin, in W. J. Slater (ed.), *Dining in a Classical Context* (1991); O. Murray (ed.), *Sympotica* (1990); *In Vino Veritas* (1994); E. Gowers, *The Loaded Table* (1993); Latte, *RR* 398 f.; J. Scheid, *Romulus et ses frères* (1990), 506–676.   O. Mu.

cookery The religious importance of *sacrifice gave cooking a powerfully expressive role in ancient society: the order of the exposing of meat to different sources of heat, especially boiling and roasting, mattered ritually. The public meat-cook (*mageiros*) was a man; other food preparation was among the private, household tasks of an adult woman (see HOUSEWORK). Food could be prepared at the hearth of the city and consumed as a public activity, like the meals of the Athenian *prytaneion*; it was more normally regarded as a household matter. But the staples of domestic diet (see MEALS), especially grains (of which there was a considerable variety, see CEREALS), could also be cooked in special forms as offerings (a wide range of sacred breads and *cakes is known).

Cereals could be boiled (like pulses, which were also important) or made into coarse or fine flours, which could also be boiled; the heat necessary for bread-making makes provision of communal ovens desirable outside very large households. The spread of bakeries is a part of a gradual, partial, controversial, and never very advanced displacement of cookery from the household, reaching its acme in the Roman tavern, with its cheap wine and cooked food a sign of the advantages available to urban populations (see INNS, RESTAURANTS). Even in urban settings much cooking was still done in the household on a brazier, using techniques like the sealed broiling of the *clibanus* or roasting-pot; samovar-like water-heaters, often highly ornamented, were also used. Casual finds and the kitchens of *Pompeii and *Herculaneum have provided copious information on practical technique, not for all that yet exhaustively studied.

The standard pattern of meals remained the combination of nutritious staples with tasty condiments (see SPICES). Quality in food reflected the excellence of these, and became—by 5th-cent. BC Athens if no earlier—an ingredient in social stratification. Raw materials were carefully calibrated: their places of origin acquired precise reputations. The preparation of speciality vegetables or meats through careful tending was part of the process. The combination of condiments, often exotic—for instance as sauces based on fish products (see FISHING), *wine and its derivatives, *olive oil, or the cooking juices of fish or meat—was also a matter for considerable ingenuity and skill, and this (rather than the precise execution of the cooking and serving of the food) was the base of the claim of the ancient connoisseur to knowledge of an *ars*.

Ancient *cuisine* did therefore become *haute*, and resembled the high style in the cooking of other élites in being to some extent regional (the specialities of the various homes of *truphē*, 'luxury', such as south Italy, are an example). There was therefore a considerable literature, much of it comic or semi-serious; but although *Athenaeus (1) provides a huge store of culinary anecdote and quotation from earlier sources, and the moral indignation of the Roman writers spices it with tales of culinary excess, reinforced by occasional description like Trimalchio's parody meal in *Petronius Arbiter's *Satyricon*, the reconstruction of *system* and *style*, as opposed to the understanding of individual recipes, in ancient cooking still rather eludes us, and the only surviving text on cookery [*Apicius] *De re coquinaria*, with its odd combination of the bizarre and the everyday, helps surprisingly little.

M. Detienne and J.-P. Vernant, *La Cuisine du sacrifice en pays grec* (1979); J. André, *L'Alimentation et la cuisine à Rome* (1971); E. Gowers, *The Loaded Table* (1993). N. P.

Copae, city situated on the northern shore of Lake *Copais in *Boeotia. The acropolis was seated on a small hill at the modern village of Topolia. Remains date it from the Mycenaean period to the Hellenistic. A contingent from Copae held the centre of the Boeotian line at the battle of *Delion in 424 BC. In 395 BC it formed one unit of the Boeotian Confederacy together with *Acraephnium and *Chaeronea, thus serving as a political buffer between *Orchomenus (1) and *Thebes (1). Mentioned in Homer's *Iliad*, *Pausanias (3) further notes that it possessed sanctuaries of *Demeter, *Dionysus, and *Sarapis.

S. Lauffer, *Kopais* 1 (1986); J. Fossey, ANRW 2. 1 (1979), 229 ff. J. Bu.

Copais, large lake in *Boeotia, now drained, that in antiquity divided the area into two regions, the eastern and larger dominated by *Thebes (1) and the western by *Orchomenus (1). Mentioned by both Homer and Hesiod, the lake was itself divided into two basins, the north-western perhaps named Cephisis and the other Copais proper. The lake, fed principally by the *Cephissus river and some streams from Mt. *Helicon, was a basin bounded by limestone mountains. Numerous *katavothra* (drains) in the stone allowed water from it to drain into the northern Euboean Gulf. The lake varied in depth during the year. A shallow marsh in summer, the western part was often dry enough to be cultivated. *Aristophanes (1) notes its fame for delicious eels, fish, and reeds used to make flutes. When flooded, it left only a narrow pass between the two basins and Mt. Helicon, which proved to be strategically important, as witnessed by the numerous battles fought there.

In the late Helladic period its most famous site was *Gla, which was then probably an island. Modern evidence proves that two attempts were made in antiquity to drain the lake. The first in the bronze age is the earliest drainage project in European history. Legend remembers that the *Minyans constructed a system of canals leading to a central canal that drew the water to sea. Strabo (9. 2. 18) states that Crates, an engineer working under the orders of *Alexander (3) the Great, cleared the obstructions to the existing system. Recent Bavarian research demonstrates that various cities and individuals along its rim consistently controlled the lake, most notably Epaminondas of *Acraephnium in the early empire and *Hadrian in AD 125, both of whom kept the dikes in repair.

S. Lauffer, *Kopais* 1 (1986); J. Knauss, *Kopais* 3: *Wasserbau und Geschichte Minysche Epoch–Bayerische Zeit* (1990). For the Coronea 'archive' of imperial letters detailing Hadrian's project see Oliver, nos. 118, 110 (with Engl. trans.). J. Bu.

Coptus (mod. Qift), a nome-capital of Upper *Egypt on the east bank of the Nile. The temple of Min, repaired by Ptolemy II (see PTOLEMY (1)), remained important until the Christian period. The focus of caravans to the *Red Sea, it conveyed Indian maritime trade to *Alexandria (1). In the first century AD Coptus exceeded *Thebes (2) in population, attracting *Palmyrene merchants. As the centre of *Aurelius Achilleus' revolt *Diocletian largely destroyed it c. AD 297. The tariff inscription of AD 90 is important.

W. M. F. Petrie, *Koptos* (1896); A. J. Reinach, *Bull. de la Soc. Fr. des fouilles archéologiques* 1910, 1–58; 1912, 47–82; A. Bernand, *Les Portes du désert* (1984) (review, *Chron. d'Ég.* 1984, 359–70); S. E. Sidebotham, *Roman Economic Policy in the Erythra Thalassa* (1986); *O. Leid.* 170–4; *PMich.* 3. 214–21; J. Bingen, *Chron. d'Ég.* 1984, 355–8; M. G. Raschke, ANRW 2. 9. 2. 1059–60; L. Casson, *ZPE* 84 (1990), 195–206. W. E. H. C.

Cora (mod. Cori), strongly placed at the NW angle of the Volscian mountains in *Latium. Latins and *Volsci disputed its possession before 340 BC. After 338 BC it was an ally of Rome and by 211 BC a *municipium* (Livy 26. 7). Fine remains exist of polygonal walls and two temples.

P. Vitucci, *Cori*; *Quad. Ist. Top. Roma* (1966), 13 ff. E. T. S.; T. W. P.

Corax, of *Syracuse (5th cent. BC) is said to have been the first teacher of *rhetoric, and to have given instruction on prooemia, argumentation, and epilogues, and discussed arguments from probability (εἰκός). *Aristotle (*Rh.* 2. 24. 1402ᵃ17) knew of an 'art' (τέχνη) of Corax, and later rhetors call him a 'technographer' (τεχνόγραφος); but it is far from certain that his teaching was systematic or expressed in a textbook. *Tisias was his pupil.

Evidence in L. Radermacher, *Artium Scriptores* (1951), A 5 and B 2; G. A. Kennedy, *The Art of Persuasion in Greece* (1963), 58 ff.; T. Cole, *The Origins of Rhetoric in Ancient Greece* (1991), 22 ff. (sceptical). D. A. R.

Corbilo, an important trading-port of the *Veneti (1) on the Loire, to which British *tin was shipped for conveyance across Gaul to the Mediterranean coast (the transit took 30 days). *Scipio Aemilianus (c.135 BC) met traders from Corbilo in southern Gaul, but failed to extract information about Britain from them. By the Roman period its role had passed to Portus Namnetum (Nantes).

Polyb. 34. 10. 6; Strabo 4. 2. 1; Diod. Sic. 5. 22. R. Dion, *Annuaire du Collège de France* 1968, 502 ff.   J. F. Dr.

Corbulo See DOMITIUS CORBULO, CN.

Corcyra (Κέρκυρα, Corfu), northernmost of the western Greek islands, located in the *Ionian Sea off the western coast of *Epirus. The island, measuring 62 km. (38½ mi.) from north to south, lies parallel to the coast with a strait of only 2 km. (1¼ mi.) separating its NE cape from the mainland. Verdant and remote, Corcyra was identified with *Homer's *Scheria (cf. Thuc. 1. 25. 4 and 3. 70. 4, see ALCINOUS (1)). Neolithic and early bronze age remains from the island's earliest inhabitants (at Aphiona and Cape Kavokephali in the island's north-west) reveal similarities with cultures in *Campania and *Apulia. In historical times, Corcyra served (as it does today) as an important port on the western sailing route between Greece and Italy. During the 8th cent. (traditionally in 734 BC), *Corinth established a colony on the island's east side under the *Bacchiad oecist or *founder Chersicrates (or perhaps Archias), and expelled a group of *Eretrians in the process (cf. Plut. *Mor.* 293a–b). Their city, named Corcyra (an Illyrian name, or perhaps a corruption of 'Gorgon', the demon routed by the Corinthian hero *Bellerophon), was built on the rocky Palaeopolis peninsula just south of the modern capital of the island. Commanding three *harbours (ps.-Skylax 29), the city prospered as a staging-point for voyages from Greece to the northern *Adriatic, Italy, and the western Mediterranean. Although Corcyra contributed to the general settlement of colonies in the region by Corinth (at *Epidamnus and *Apollonia, it was a co-founder), relations between colony and mother city were not always cordial. For example, Corcyra fought the Corinthians in a sea battle *c.*660 (Thuc. 1. 13) and may have contributed to the fall of the Bacchiad clan. (But on the date see Hornblower, *Comm. on Thuc.*) A generation later, the Cypselid tyrant *Periander temporarily reasserted Corinthian control over the colony, but after his death, Corcyra once again regained its independence. Thereafter, the colony offended Corinth in various ways—by not participating in the *Persian War (unlike *Leucas, *Anactorium, and *Ambracia), by opposing the spread of Corinthian influence in the Adriatic, and by staying aloof from Greek politics in general (Thuc. 1. 32, 37–8). Circumstances surrounding a civil war at Epidamnus eventually drew it into a war with Corinth and forced it to ally with Athens for protection. An Athenian fleet was sent to Corcyra in 433, and again in 427 and 425 when Corinthian fleets attempted to co-operate with disaffected elements on the island. These years saw Corcyra convulsed by a savage civil war or *stasis during which the democrats massacred hundreds of their oligarchic opponents (Thuc. 3. 69 ff.). In 410, Corcyra's democrats shook off their Athenian connection for a generation, but reallied with the city (perhaps separately from the *Second Athenian Confederacy) in 375 or soon thereafter when faced with the Spartan support of its oligarchic opponents. The island provided two ships for *Timoleon's expedition against *Dionysius (2) II of Syracuse in 344, and *c.*340 joined Athens in a vain attempt to prevent the intrusion of *Macedonia into Adriatic waters. After the death of *Alexander (3) the Great, the island became an object of dispute between various mainland dynasts: *Cassander, *Demetrius (4), and *Pyrrhus, and was occupied for a time by the Syracusan tyrant *Agathocles (1). In 229 Corcyra was captured by the Illyrians, but was speedily delivered by a Roman fleet and remained a Roman naval station until at least 189. At this period it was governed by a prefect (presumably nominated by the consuls),

but in 148 it was attached to the province of Macedonia. Corcyra backed *Pompey against *Caesar, and M. *Antonius (2) against *Octavian, although Octavian occupied the island during the spring of 31 and established a fleet station there. The island was later 'freed' by *Claudius.

Excavations, carried out on the Palaeopolis peninsula, have revealed something of the city's nature and extent, particularly of its sanctuaries. These include: a 7th-cent. Archaic temple (with a richly decorated terracotta roof) in the Mon Repos park; a late 6th-cent. temple (of Apollo?) near the Kardaki spring; a famous Archaic temple of Artemis (with its Gorgon pediment dated *c.*585) due west of Mon Repos near Agioi Theodoroi; a geometric to Classical period sanctuary (of Artemis?) at Kanoni on the southern tip of the peninsula; and a 6th-cent. temple (dedicated to Poseidon) at the Cloister of Panagia Kassiopitra. Remains from the ancient city have been found north-west of Mon Repos at the church of Agia Kerkyra, where Archaic to Roman levels have been excavated as well as traces of a Hellenistic *bouleutērion*, a bath dated *c.* AD 100, and a 5th-cent. AD basilica.

J. Partsch, *Die Insel Korfu* (1887); P–K, *GL* 2. 422–55; *Kl. Pauly* 3 (1969), 305–7; *Lexikon der historischen Stätten* 323–8; *PECS* 449–51.   W. M. M.

Corduba (mod. Córdoba), a native city on the middle Guadalquivir (Baetis), refounded by M. *Claudius Marcellus (3) in 169 or 152 BC. Excavations suggest it to have been a walled Roman and native *dipolis*. It became a *colonia* with the title *Patricia*, between 46 and 45 BC. It was sacked by *Caesar in 45 for its Pompeian allegiance, and settled with veterans by Augustus. It became capital of *Baetica and had a colonial and provincial forum and many temples. It was the chief centre of Roman intellectual life in Further and Hither Spain. Its republican poets were succeeded by the Senecas and Lucan. Important in the late Roman period, its bishop Hosius (Ossius) was the dominant figure of the western Church throughout the earlier 4th cent. Its wealth was sustained by olive oil and precious metals from near by.

R. Knapp, *Roman Córdoba* (1983); A. Stylow in *Stadtbild und Ideologie*, W. Trillmich and P. Zanker (eds.) (1990), 259 ff.   S. J. K.

Corfinium, town of the *Paeligni, on a strong site on the *via Valeria controlling a strategic bridgehead across the river Aternus near modern Corfinio: remains exist at the church of San Pelino (i.e. Paelignus). Corfinium is unrecorded until the *Social War (3) when the Italians made it their seat of government and renamed it Italia, intending it to become the permanent capital of Italy (90 BC). They were quickly obliged, however, to transfer their seat of government first to Bovianum and then to Aesernia. After the Social War Corfinium became a Roman *municipium*. In 49 BC garrisoned by L. *Domitius Ahenobarbus (1), it offered temporary resistance to *Caesar (Caes. *BCiv.* 1. 15 f.; App. *BCiv.* 2. 38; Suet. *Iul.* 33 f.; Luc. 2. 478 f.). Subsequently Corfinium received colonists on several occasions, but apparently was never styled *colonia* (*Lib. colon.* 228, 255). Inscriptions indicate that it remained a flourishing *municipium* in imperial times.

F. van Wonterghem, *Superaequum, Corfinium, Sulmo, Forma Italia* IV, 1 (1984).   E. T. S.; T. W. P.

Corieltauvi, a British tribe occupying part of the eastern Midlands (Leics., Notts., Lincs.), inaccurately known as the Coritani. The coins and other remains suggest a decentralized iron age society with several political centres. A *civitas Corieltauvorum* was created with its capital at *Ratae (Leicester); part of its land was reserved for the fortress of Legio IX (later II Adiutrix) at *Lindum

Corinna

(Lincoln) and subsequently used for a *colonia*. Industries included horse-breeding, and the production of *iron and building-stone. The countryside contained a large group of lesser urban sites or large villages in addition to numerous *villas.

> M. Todd, *The Coritani*, 2nd edition (1991); R. S. O. Tomlin, *Ant. Journ.* 1983.　　　　　　　　　　　　　　　　S. S. F.; M. J. M.

Corinna, lyric poet, native of *Tanagra in *Boeotia, less probably *Thebes (1) (Paus. 9. 22; *Suda*). Tradition made her a pupil of *Myrtis (*Suda*) and contemporary (perhaps older) and rival of *Pindar, whom she allegedly defeated (once, Paus. 9. 22; five times, Ael. *VH* 13. 25, *Suda*). *Aelian's statement that Pindar retorted by calling her a 'Boeotian sow' is a biographical fancy derived from Pindar (*Ol.* 6. 90), likewise *Plutarch's anecdote (*De glor. Ath.* 4. 347f–348a) presenting her as adviser to the young Pindar (cf. Pind. fr. 29). Her traditional date has been contested. No *Alexandrian scholar studied her work, and the earliest references to her belong to the 1st cent. BC (*Anth. Pal.* 9. 26; Prop. 2. 3. 21); the papyrus fragments consistently reflect the Boeotian orthography of the late 3rd cent. BC; her metre shows some affinities with *Attic drama and her simple style is unlike that of Archaic choral poetry; the papyrus presents sporadic *Atticisms. On present evidence the issue cannot be resolved. Her poetry was divided into five books. She was added by some as a tenth to the canon of nine lyric poets (e.g. *Anecd. Bekk.* 751; περὶ διαφορᾶς ποιητῶν 18 ff.). Though the *Suda* speaks of epigrams, surviving fragments consist of lyric narratives dealing (almost exclusively) with local legends; titles attested are *Boeotus, Seven against Thebes, Euonymia, Iolaus, The Return Voyage, Orestes*. The dialect is predominantly epic, with some Boeotisms. Fr. 655 suggests that the narratives were sung by choirs of local girls. The largest papyrus preserves two narratives: the first tells of a singing contest between Cithaeron and *Helicon, and the distress of the loser Helicon; the second contains a speech by the seer Acraephen to the river-god Asopus explaining the disappearance of the latter's nine daughters. The style is simple; fluent narrative, 'objective' in manner, with epithets sparse and unsurprising.

> TEXTS Page, *PMG* 326 ff.; (with trans.) D. A. Campbell, *Greek Lyric*, 4 (Loeb, 1992), 14 ff.
>
> COMMENTARIES AND CRITICISM D. A. Campbell, *Greek Lyric Poetry* (1967), 408 ff.; D. E. Gerber, *Euterpe* (1970), 394 ff.; J. M. Snyder, *The Woman and the Lyre* (1989), 41 ff.; *RE* 11. 1393 ff.　　　C. C.

Corinth

Greek and Hellenistic The city lies near the isthmus which joins central Greece to the *Peloponnese. Copious springs make the site extremely attractive, and it commands both the Isthmus and a proverbially rich coastal plain. Acrocorinth, the citadel, is too high to be a normal acropolis; the city was by the springs at its northern foot. Neolithic and early Helladic settlement was extensive; afterwards the site, although not deserted, was not heavily occupied until the iron age: development is continuous from the late 10th cent. BC. Corinthians exploited their unrivalled position for western voyages early. Pottery reached *Delphi in the early 8th cent. or before, and soon after *Ithaca and even inland *Epirus. Further west, it is found in the earliest levels at *Pithecusae; and when other colonies were established they became the core of a market for Corinthian painted pottery (see POTTERY, GREEK) which covered the whole Greek world until the mid-6th cent., when it gave way to Attic except at home. Corinthian agriculture always remained important, but the economy was remarkably diverse already in the 7th cent.: trade was extensive, and *Herodotus (1) observed (2. 167) that Corin-

thians despised craftsmen less than did other Greeks. Corinth played a large part in developing the Doric order (see ORDERS): it evolved in temples built at Corinth and Isthmia, and many in NW Greece on which Corinthians worked. Corinthian craftsmen were still employed in major projects in the 4th century at *Epidaurus and Delphi, and they built in exported Corinthian stone; this tradition was revived in the 2nd cent. AD (*FD* 111/4, no. 96).

A Corinthian king-list is preserved, but the early part is fictional; the aristocratic *Bacchiadae ruled until *Cypselus overthrew them *c.*657 BC; he passed the tyranny to his son *Periander, and the last tyrant fell *c.*585. An unusually narrow *oligarchy followed: the council of 80, with eight *probouloi*, was probably founded by the tyrants, but now became the main organ of government. Corinth became a *Spartan ally probably soon after 550, perhaps to secure protection against *Argos (2); they failed to overthrow *Polycrates (1) of Samos in a joint expedition *c.*525. During the reign of *Cleomenes (1), Corinth became alarmed at the growth of Spartan power and successfully led opposition among the allies to Spartan interventions in Athens. Corinth was inscribed with Athens and Sparta on the second coil of the serpent column at Delphi for its part in the defence of Greece against *Xerxes (see PERSIAN WARS). Corinthian aggression against *Megara led to the First *Peloponnesian War when the victim appealed to Athens for help; Corinth was extremely active and suffered heavily early in the war, but was satisfied with the balance established by the Thirty Years Peace, and took a leading role in preventing intervention against Athens when *Samos rebelled in 440. Since 480, the Corinthians had exploited fears of *Corcyra to win influence in north-western waters; when they thought their interests there were threatened by the Athenian alliance with Corcyra (433), they agitated energetically for war. Their success in procuring the *Peloponnesian War was matched by failure during it: their performance as Sparta's main naval ally was disastrous. The Corinthians voted against the Peace of *Nicias (1) because it required them to accept their war losses; their attempts to renew hostilities against Athens succeeded only in embarrassing Sparta. When Athens attacked *Syracuse, Corinth enjoyed unaccustomed success in defence of its colony, helped partly by technical improvements which reinforced the prows of its *triremes. In 404 Sparta's refusal to destroy Athens began a rapid deterioration in relations, and within a decade Corinth joined Argos, *Boeotia, and Athens to fight Sparta in the *Corinthian War, so called because much of the action was in Corinthian territory—which suffered extensively. Spartan sympathizers were killed during a religious festival, and their opponents, with popular support, devised novel constitutional arrangements which gave Argives rights at Corinth and vice versa (see ISOPOLITEIA). Sparta insisted on their dissolution under the *King's Peace; Corinthian loyalty was maintained until a withdrawal from hostilities was negotiated in 366. Corinth fought against *Philip (1) II at *Chaeronea. The Corinthian League (see CORINTH, LEAGUE OF) was established at a meeting held in the city, but its central location had another consequence: Acrocorinth became the seat of a Macedonian garrison. It was occupied by *Ptolemy I, and by *Demetrius (4) Poliorcetes and *Antigonus (2) Gonatas until it was famously captured in 243 by *Aratus (2), and Corinth joined the *Achaean Confederacy. Corinth went over to *Cleomenes (2) III of Sparta, but on Aratus' agreement with *Antigonus (3) Doson a Macedonian garrison returned. It gave place, after the Second Macedonian War, to a Roman successor which T. *Quinctius Flamininus ostentatiously withdrew to demonstrate the reality of Greek 'freedom'; L.

*Mummius destroyed Corinth in 146 to intimidate Greece into proper use of it.

See also CENCHREAE; ISTHMIA; LECHAEUM; PERACHORA.

RE Suppl. 4 (1924), 6 (1935), 12 (1970), 'Korinthos'; J. B. Salmon, *Wealthy Corinth* (1984); R. S. Stroud, *Chiron* 1994.

EXCAVATIONS H. S. Robinson, *PECS* 240 ff.; vols. of the *Corinth* series (1929–   ); annual reports and other studies in *Hesperia*.

TOPOGRAPHY J. Wiseman, *Land of the Ancient Corinthians* (1978).
J. B. S.

Roman Corinth was refounded (44 BC) as a Caesarian colony (see IULIUS CAESAR (1), C.), the agricultural aspect of which is stressed by new evidence for rural *centuriation. The original colonists were mainly Roman freedmen, swelled by an influx of Roman businessmen (see NEGOTIATORES). By the late 1st cent. AD the colony was a flourishing centre of commerce, administration (see ACHAIA), the imperial cult, and entertainment. At first a self-conscious enclave of *Romanitas*, it became progressively Hellenized (see HELLENISM); under *Hadrian it was admitted to the *Panhellenion and Greek replaced Latin as the language of official inscriptions. Lavishly equipped with public buildings, the city survived barbarian attacks by the *Heruli (267) and *Alaric (396) and severe earthquakes in 77 and 521. From the time of St *Paul it was the centre of early *Christianity in Greece.

J. Wiseman, *ANRW* 2. 7. 1 (1979), 428–540; M. Amandry, *Les duovirs corinthiens*, BCH Suppl. 14 (1988); T. Gregory (ed.), *The Corinthia in the Roman Period*, JRA Suppl. 8 (1993). A. J. S. S.

Corinth, League of, modern name for organization of Greek states created by *Philip (1) II of Macedon after the battle of *Chaeronea: the details were agreed at Corinth. Partly modelled on earlier *Common Peace agreements, it provided (despite various Macedonian garrisons) for the *autonomy of all signatories and required collective action against states which contravened its terms. New features reflected Philip's intention to use it as the basis for his relations with the Greek states. Signatories swore not to overthrow the kingdom of Philip and his descendants; there was a *synedrion* (meeting) to take decisions, and a *hēgemōn* (leader): Philip himself. The military obligations of members were determined by size; it is disputed whether their votes in the *synedrion* were too. Members swore to maintain existing constitutions at a time when pro-Macedonian parties were at an advantage; a specific clause against redistribution of land and cancellation of debts had an anti-democratic effect. Philip announced his planned invasion of Asia at the *synedrion*, and was elected commander for that war: it is unclear whether the members became his allies too. On Philip's assassination, *Alexander (3) the Great was elected in his place: he used the *synedrion* to decide the punishment of *Thebes (1) after its revolt. It has long been disputed whether the Greek cities of *Asia Minor joined; in any case the league had little significance by the end of Alexander's reign. A new but similar organization was established in 302 by *Demetrius (4) Poliorcetes, but *Ipsus rendered its purpose void.

G. T. Griffith in *HM* 2. J. B. S.

Corinthian cults and myths *Corinth, not having a *Mycenaean past, lacked a heroic tradition of its own, borrowing legendary figures from the Argolid (see ARGOS (2)) and the east (e.g. *Bellerophon(tes), *Medea: see Rose 269–71). None of the myths is intimately connected with the major gods of the *polis*, whose principal urban cults were those of *Aphrodite on Acrocorinth, *Apollo, and *Demeter Thesmophoros. The urban centre also possessed hero sanctuaries (their incumbents as yet unidentified, but probably connected with the founding families of the *polis*) and one or more sacred springs, of which Peirene is the best known (Steiner; Williams 1981).

The principal extra-urban cults were of *Hera Akraia at *Perachora (with an urban branch) and of *Poseidon at Penteskouphia (west of the city) and at Isthmia. The last became the site of one of the four panhellenic festivals of the so-called 'circuit' (*periodos*).

Strong eastern influence is to be seen both in the legends and especially in the nature of the urban cult of Aphrodite. Not only was she the *poliouchos* ('protecting the city'), but her cult at Corinth was notorious as a centre for sacred *prostitution (Williams (1986), 20). Also unusual was the relative prominence of *Helios in myth and cult.

Greek Corinth was destroyed in 146 BC, and no doubt much evidence for pre-Roman cult went with it. The Roman city continued to worship Aphrodite, Poseidon, and Demeter, to whom were added gods from Rome and Asia (Engels 93–107; Wiseman, 465–91 and 509–33, who gives good surveys of remains up 146 BC and after the refoundation).

See *Hesperia* for ongoing reports; C. K. Williams II in S. Macready and F. Thompson (eds.), *Roman Architecture in the Greek World* (1987), 26–37; H. J. Rose, *A Handbook of Greek Mythology* (1958); A. Steiner, *Hesp.* 1992, 385–408; C. K. Williams II, *Hesp.* 1981, 408–21, and in M. del Chiaro and W. Biers (eds.), *Corinthiaca* (1986), 12–24; J. Wiseman, *ANRW* 2. 7. 1 (1979); D. W. Engels, *Roman Corinth* (1990). A. Sch.

Corinthian War, 395 to 386 BC, fought against Sparta by a combination of Athens, *Thebes (1), *Corinth, Persia, and others. The surface cause was trouble between *Locris and *Phocis in which Thebes and Sparta intervened, the deeper cause was general fear of Spartan expansionism in Asia Minor, central and northern Greece (*Thessaly and perhaps *Macedonia), and even the west (cf. Isoc. 8. 99) where Spartan activity surely annoyed Corinth, *Syracuse's *metropolis. The war was fought at sea (where the battle of Cnidus, August 394, was a decisive blow to Sparta) and on land near Corinth, hence the name; but it is also relevant that the war was conducted by a 'council at Corinth', Diod. Sic. 14. 82. It was ended by the *King's Peace.

Xen. *Hell.* 4–5; *Hell. Oxy.*; Diod. Sic. 14; A. Andrewes, *Phoenix* 1971; R. Seager, *CAH* 6² (1994), chs. 3–4. S. H.

Coriolanus See MARCIUS CORIOLANUS, CN.

Coriosopitum (also known as **Corstopitum**), a Roman military post and town on the north bank of the Tyne near Corbridge, Northumberland. The name in its restored form suggests that it was a *pagus* centre of the *Brigantes. Here the road from York (Eburacum) to Scotland bridged the Tyne, branching to Carlisle and Tweedmouth. A supply base at nearby Redhouse constructed under Cn. *Iulius Agricola is the earliest military installation in the area. This was replaced at the Corbridge site with an auxiliary fort (rebuilt once) which was occupied *c*. AD 90–105. The unit in occupation may have been the *ala Petriana* (*RIB* 1172). A Trajanic fort, one of those on the Stanegate, replaced this *c*.105–20, being rebuilt *c*.120–30. A further reconstruction took place in the late 130s (*RIB* 1147–8), and again in the late 150s, with the fort sequence ending *c*.163. The site remained of considerable importance as a town serving the eastern part of the *wall of Hadrian. In addition to the civil functions, there were legionary work-compounds and temples. Late 4th-cent. silver plate, gold rings (*RIB* 2422. 1), and a gold coin-hoard attest prolonged use as an administrative centre.

M. C. Bishop and J. N. Dore, *Corbridge: Excavations of the Roman Fort and Town 1947–80* (1988).　　　　　　　　　　　　　M. J. M.

Coritani See CORIELTAUVI.

corn See CEREALS.

corn supply See FOOD SUPPLY.

Cornelia (1) (*RE* 'Cornelius' 407), second daughter of P. *Cornelius Scipio Africanus, married Ti. *Sempronius Gracchus (2). Of her twelve children only three reached adulthood: Sempronia, who married P. *Cornelius Scipio Aemilianus, and the two famous tribunes Ti. *Sempronius Gracchus (3) and C. *Sempronius Gracchus. After her husband's death she did not remarry (she is reported to have refused an offer by *Ptolemy (1) VIII Euergetes II), devoting herself chiefly to the education of her children. Traditions about her attitude to the tribunes' political activities vary, but she made Gaius abandon his attack on M. *Octavius (see Plut. *C. Gracch.* 4. 3). Some of her letters were admired by Cicero (*Brut.* 211), but Quintilian (1. 1. 6) no longer knew them. The authenticity of two fragments addressed to Gaius and preserved in *Nepos MSS must be regarded as uncertain. (See N. Horsfall, *Cornelius Nepos* (1989) 41 f.) After Tiberius' death she retired to a villa at *Misenum (where she heard of Gaius' death) and devoted herself to cultural pursuits and correspondence and conversation with distinguished men (Plut. *C. Gracch.* 19). She was dead by 100 BC. The base of a statue of her seen by Pliny (*HN* 34. 31) survives (see *ILLRP* 336) and has been much discussed. (See M. Kajava, *Arctos* 1989, 119 ff.)

B. Kreck, *Untersuchungen zur politischen und sozialen Rolle der Frau in der späten römischen Republik* (1975), 47 ff., collects all the evidence; Bauman, *WPAR* 42 ff.　　　　　　　　　　　A. E. A.; E. B.

Cornelia (2) (*RE* 'Cornelius' 417), the cultured daughter of Q. *Caecilius Metellus Pius Scipio, married P. *Licinius Crassus (2) in 55 BC and in 52 *Pompey. After Pharsalus she accompanied him to Egypt, where she saw him murdered. She returned to Italy.　　　　　　　　　　　　　　　　　G. W. R.; R. J. S.

Cornelius (*RE* 18), **Gaius,** quaestor under *Pompey and friend of A. *Gabinius (2), whose colleague and supporter he was as tribune in 67 BC. His attempts to introduce various reforms were resisted by the *optimates, but he succeeded in limiting the senate's power to grant dispensations from laws and in passing a law that for the first time required praetors (we do not know whether only in Rome or also provincial commanders) to administer justice in accordance with their edicts. He was tried for *maiestas in 65 and successfully defended by *Cicero, who wanted to please *Pompey.

Asconius, pp. 57 ff. C, with Marshall, *Asconius Comm.* 214–80; M. Griffin, *JRS* 1973, 196 ff.　　　　　　　　　　　　　　　E. B.

Cornelius Anullinus, Publius, from Iliberris (mod. Granada) in *Baetica, had a distinguished career under Marcus *Aurelius, being *consul *c.* AD 175 and governor of Upper Germany. Proconsul of Africa at the time of L. *Septimius Severus' capture of Rome in 193, he was summoned to take command of an army in the eastern wars, 193–5, and was then city prefect and consul for the second time in 199. He was a close friend of Severus, who enriched him.

Cass. Dio 74–5; Aurelius Victor, *Epit. de Caes.*; *PIR*² C 1322.　　A. R. Bi.

Cornelius (*RE* 69) **Balbus** (1), **Lucius,** was born in *Gades (Cadiz), a *civitas foederata* (i.e. it had a treaty with Rome), and distinguished as 'Balbus maior'. He acquired Roman citizenship

at *Pompey's instance in 72 BC. He moved to Rome, where his political sense and the wealth derived from his adoption (*c.*59) by *Theophanes of Mytilene gave him enormous influence. Part architect of the coalition of 60 BC, he gradually shifted his allegiance from Pompey to *Caesar, serving the latter as *praefectus fabrum* (officer of engineers; see FABRI) in 62 and 59, and later managing his interests in Rome. In 56 he was prosecuted for illegal usurpation of the citizenship, and was successfully defended by *Cicero in the extant speech *Pro Balbo*. In the Civil War he was outwardly neutral, and persistently tried to persuade Cicero and L. *Cornelius Lentulus Crus to join him. Actually he favoured Caesar, and after Pharsalus became, with C. *Oppius (2), Caesar's chief agent in public affairs. In 44 he supported *Octavian, though cautiously, and in 40 became Rome's first foreign-born consul. Author of a published diary (now lost), and recipient and editor of A. *Hirtius' commentaries, he had wide literary interests over which he constantly corresponded with Cicero. He bequeathed 25 denarii to every citizen of Rome.

Syme, *Rom. Rev.* and *RP* 1–3, see indexes; T. P. Wiseman, *New Men in the Roman Senate* (1971), no. 137 and see index. On the legal issue in the *Pro Balbo* see P. A. Brunt, *CQ* 1982, 136–47.　　　G. E. F. C.; R. J. S.

Cornelius (*RE* 70) **Balbus** (2), **Lucius,** nephew of L. *Cornelius Balbus (1) and distinguished as 'Balbus minor' in Cicero's letters, received the Roman *citizenship with his uncle. In 49 and 48 BC he undertook diplomatic missions for *Caesar; in 43 he was proquaestor in Further Spain under C. *Asinius Pollio, who complained of his tyrannical conduct at *Gades and of his absconding with the pay-chest. He was honoured by *Augustus with a pontificate and consular rank. Proconsul of Africa (21–20?), he defeated the Garamantes and other peoples and triumphed (27 March 19), a unique distinction for one not born a Roman. (See TRIUMPH.) He built a new town and docks at *Gades (Cadiz) and a theatre at Rome, which he dedicated in 13. He wrote a *fabula praetextata* (see FABULA) about his mission of 49, and lengthy Ἐξηγητικά (works of interpretation) of uncertain scope.

Syme, *Rom. Rev.*, *RP* 1–3, and *AA*, see indexes; P. Romanelli, *Storia delle province romane dell'Africa* (1959), 176 ff., 168 ff.; G. Funaioli, *Grammaticae Romanae Fragmenta* (1907), 540 f.; Schanz–Hosius 1, see index; F. della Corte and E. Paratore, *Riv. cult. class. e med.* 1960, 347 ff.; T. P. Wiseman, *New Men in the Roman Senate* (1971), no. 138.

T. J. C.; R. J. S.

Cornelius (*RE* 82) **Celsus, Aulus,** lived in the reign of *Tiberius (AD 14–37), and wrote an encyclopaedia on the *Artes*, including books on agriculture, military science, rhetoric (and perhaps on philosophy and jurisprudence). Of these only the books on medicine survive. The eight books of the *De medicina* include an historical introduction to Greek medicine and a discussion of origins of *dietetics and medical theory (bk. 1, with proem), *pathology and therapeutics (bk. 2), special treatments (bks. 3–4), drug-lore (bks. 5–6, see PHARMACOLOGY), *surgery (bk. 7), and skeletal *anatomy (bk. 8). Celsus has been linked with *Methodism and even Pyrrhonian scepticism (see PYRRHON), but attempts to connect him with a particular medical or philosophical sect have never been conclusive. Some have even doubted that he was a doctor himself, but his understanding of highly technical details of medical practice, especially in surgery, where he refers more than once to his own experience, militates against this. Surprisingly perhaps, his influence on medicine in later antiquity seems to have been negligible, and it was only when he was rediscovered in the Middle Ages that he came to be highly valued—as much for the quality of his Latin as for his medical knowledge. The proem to book 1 is one of the most important ancient sources for the history of Greek medicine, covering the period from the Homeric epics to Celsus' own day. See BOTANY; MEDICINE.

TEXT F. Marx, *CML* 1: *A. Cornelii Celsi quae supersunt* (1915); proem to bk. 1 (with comm. and modern bibliog.), P. Mudry, *La Préface du 'De medicina' de Celse* (1982). Eng. trans. by W. G. Spencer (Loeb, 1935).

J. T. V.

Cornelius (*RE* 97) **Cethegus, Publius,** of patrician (but not recently successful) family, fled with C. *Marius (1) in 88 BC, returned with him in 87 and stayed in Rome under the Marian government. He joined *Sulla in Italy and was active in the *bellum Sullanum* and the *proscriptions. In the 70s, though he held no high office, his knowledge of procedure and skill at intrigue gave him power equal to a consular's (Cic. *Brut.* 178). Men like M. *Antonius (Creticus) and L. *Licinius Lucullus (2) obtained their commands by courting him and his mistress.

A. Keaveney, *Lucullus* (1992), 67 ff.

E. B.

Cornelius (*RE* 101) **Chrysogonus, Lucius,** freedman of *Sulla, in collusion with two relatives of Sextus Roscius of Ameria (who had been murdered) placed the dead man's name on the proscription lists, to enable them jointly to buy his property at a nominal sum. He is the chief object of attack in Cicero's speech on behalf of Sextus *Roscius, whom Chrysogonus accused of his father's murder. When the case acquired political overtones, Sulla seems to have withdrawn his support.

Cicero, *pro Sexto Roscio Amerino.*

E. B.

Cornelius (*RE* 106) **Cinna** (1), **Lucius,** of patrician, but not recently distinguished, family, fought successfully in the *Social War (3) and, against the opposition of *Sulla, became consul 87 BC. Trying to rescind Sulla's legislation as passed by force, he was driven out of Rome by his colleague Cn. *Octavius (2) and illegally deposed; L. *Cornelius Merula was elected to replace him. Collecting Italians and legionaries, he was joined by Cn. *Papirius Carbo and Q. *Sertorius, and by C. *Marius (1) whom he summoned back to Italy. They marched on Rome and captured it late in 87 after the death of Cn. *Pompeius Strabo and Q. *Caecilius Metellus Pius' failure to relieve it. He punished those who had acted illegally, but tried (not very successfully) to stop indiscriminate violence on Marius' orders. Consul 86 with Marius and, after Marius' death, with L. *Valerius Flaccus (3), he sent Flaccus to fight against *Mithradates VI, while he restored ordered government in Italy. He gained the co-operation of the *equites* and the people by financial reforms (carried by Flaccus and M. *Marius Gratidianus), and that of eminent consulars by moderation and return to *mos maiorum* ('ancestral custom'), although he could not repair the economic disruption of Italy due to the Social and Civil Wars. Following Marius' precedent, he held the consulship again in 85 and 84 with Cn. *Papirius Carbo, owing to the emergency caused by the Mithradatic War and the threatening behaviour of Sulla, with whom he continued to negotiate. Embarking on a campaign in Liburnia early in 84, probably to train an army for a possible conflict with Sulla's veterans, he was killed in a mutiny. Sulla now rebelled and the government disintegrated. Our uniformly hostile accounts of him derive from *Sullani* or men who deserted him to join the victorious Sulla.

H. Bennett, *Cinna and his Times* (1923); Badian, *Stud. Gr. Rom. Hist.* 206 ff.; C. M. Bulst, *Hist.* 1964, 307 ff.

E. B.

Cornelius (*RE* 107) **Cinna** (2), **Lucius,** son of L. *Cornelius Cinna (1), took part in the revolt of M. *Aemilius Lepidus (2), joined Q. *Sertorius in Spain, and was allowed to return, along with other *Lepidani* (supporters of Lepidus), by a *Lex Plautia* passed (in 70 BC?) with the support of his brother-in-law *Caesar; but was still debarred by *Sulla's legislation from a public career, and reached the praetorship only in 44, after Caesar had reinstated the sons of the proscribed (49). As praetor he showed republican sympathies: he expressed approval of the murder of Caesar, and was attacked on his way to the senate (17 March) and rescued by M. *Aemilius Lepidus (3). He procured the restoration of the deposed tribunes L. Caesetius Flavus and C. Epidius Marullus, and on 28 November refused the province assigned to him by M. *Antonius (2) (Mark Antony). He married, perhaps at this time, *Pompey's daughter, widow since 46 of Faustus *Cornelius Sulla. He was probably proscribed in 43 (cf. Sen. *Clem.* 1. 9. 8). See PROSCRIPTION.

T. J. C.; R. J. S.

Cornelius (*RE* 108 and Supp. 1) **Cinna Magnus, Gnaeus,** son of L. *Cornelius Cinna (2), and grandson of *Pompey, consul in AD 5 (see TABULA HEBANA). He supported Sex. *Pompeius and M. *Antonius (2) (Mark Antony), and a rhetorical fable (Sen. *Clem.* 1. 9; Cass. Dio 55. 14–22) has him plotting against *Augustus during his absence in Gaul (possibly 16–13 BC), but pardoned at *Livia's behest. He left Augustus his sole heir.

R. Syme, *Rom. Rev.* and *AA*, see indexes; W. Speyer, *Rh. Mus.* 1956, 277 ff.

T. J. C.; B. M. L.

Cornelius (*RE* 112) **Cossus, Aulus,** a Roman commander who won the *spolia opima* by killing Lars Tolumnius, the king of *Veii, in a cavalry duel. The breastplate of Tolumnius, which Cossus dedicated to Jupiter Feretrius, bore an inscription which was taken by some, including the emperor *Augustus, to indicate that Cossus performed the feat as *consul (428 BC), although most of the literary tradition (Livy 4. 19–20; Dion. Hal. *Ant. Rom.* 12. 5) placed the event in 437, when Cossus was military tribune (see TRIBUNI MILITUM). A minority opinion dated it to 426, when Cossus was *tribunus militum consulari potestate* and *magister equitum* (Val. Max. 3. 2. 4; Frontin. *Str.* 2. 8. 9). The controversy about the date and Cossus' status (on which see Livy 4. 20) was important because of its relevance to the case of M. *Licinius Crassus (2).

Cf. Ogilvie, *Comm. Livy 1–5*, 563 f.

H. H. S.; T. J. Co.

Cornelius (*RE* 134) **Dolabella** (1), **Gnaeus,** after serving under *Sulla in the east, became consul 81 BC. He then governed Macedonia, triumphing in 78 (?). *Caesar, in a speech that became famous, unsuccessfully prosecuted him *repetundarum.*

E. S. Gruen, *AJPhil.* 1966, 385 ff.

E. B.

Cornelius (*RE* 135) **Dolabella** (2), **Gnaeus,** praetor 81 BC. As proconsul he plundered Cilicia with the help of his legate C. *Verres, who then helped M. *Aemilius Scaurus (2) convict him *repetundarum.* He lost his property and went into exile.

SEE CORNELIUS DOLABELLA (1), CN.

E. B.

Cornelius (*RE* 141) **Dolabella** (1), **Publius,** allegedly born 69 BC (App. *BCiv.* 2. 129. 539), but certainly earlier. After a dissolute youth (*Cicero twice defended him), he divorced his wife in 50 and, against Cicero's wishes, married *Tullia (2), embarrassing Cicero by (unsuccessfully) prosecuting Ap. *Claudius Pulcher (3). (Divorce followed in 46 and he never repaid the dowry.) After working for *Caesar before 49, he was defeated commanding a

393

fleet for him (49), then fought without distinction in Greece. Alleging illness, he returned, had himself adopted by a plebeian Lentulus (see D. R. Shackleton Bailey, *Two Studies in Roman Nomenclature* (1976) 29 ff.), and, as tribune 47, in Caesar's absence, provoked street fighting (which M. *Antonius (2) failed to suppress) by proposing cancellation of debts—largely to escape his own creditors. Forgiven by Caesar, he accompanied him to Africa (but is not mentioned at Thapsus), then fought for him in Spain, was wounded, and utterly charmed him. He was rewarded with confiscated estates and picked to become consul when Caesar left for the east; but Antonius blocked the election. On Caesar's death he seized the consulship and, securing recognition, courted the tyrannicides' supporters while negotiating with Antonius. He thus obtained Syria for five years (and Cicero considered accepting a position on his staff (*legatio*): *Att.* 15. 11. 4). Crossing to Asia, he brutally assassinated the proconsul C. *Trebonius and plundered the province. The senate now united to outlaw him (cf. Cic. *Phil.* 11). In May 43 he crossed into Syria, was soon besieged by C. *Cassius Longinus (1) in (Syrian) Laodicea, and when, despite support from *Cleopatra VII, he could not hold it, committed suicide. He was the grandfather of the following.

> Syme, *RP* 3. 1244 ff. (the suggestion that he was Caesar's illegitimate son is implausible); M. Dettenhofer, *Perdita Iuventus* (1992) 119 ff., 165 ff. For the stemma of the republican Dolabellae see E. Badian, *PBSR* 1965, 48 ff. E. B.

Cornelius (*RE* 143) **Dolabella** (2), **Publius,** probably grandson of (1), was consul in AD 10, and (14 to *c*.20) *legatus pro praetore* (see LEGATI) in Dalmatia, where he kept the legions quiet in 14 and built or rebuilt a number of military roads from *Salonae to the legionary camps and the mountainous country beyond. In 23/4, as proconsul of Africa, he ended the war against *Tacfarinas but was denied *ornamenta triumphalia* (see ORNAMENTA). He was known for excessive obsequiousness and tried to join Cn. *Domitius Afer in the prosecution of Dolabella's own relative P. *Quinctilius Varus (*Ann.* 4. 66. 2). His descendants held consulships in 86 and 113. T. J. C.; E. B.

Cornelius (*RE* 157) **Fronto, Marcus** (*c*. AD 95–*c*.166), orator, *suffect consul July–August 142; born at *Cirta (Constantine) in *Numidia; completed his education in Rome; a leading advocate under *Hadrian, he was appointed tutor by *Antoninus Pius to Marcus *Aurelius (Caesar) and his adoptive brother Lucius *Verus, remaining on intimate terms with them until his death, probably from the plague of 166/7.

Though famous for his oratory ('not the second but the other glory of Roman eloquence', *XII Panegyrici Latini* 8 (5). 14. 2, an allusion to *Cicero), Fronto is known today almost exclusively through his correspondence, chiefly with Marcus, but also with Pius, Lucius, and various friends. The letters expound and illustrate his stylistic theories: the orator must seek out the most expressive word in Early Latin texts, preferring the unusual to the commonplace provided it is not obscure or jarring (but new coinages are discountenanced); he must dispose his words in the best order and cultivate rhetorical figures, the *sententia*, and the image-like description (εἰκών). Among Fronto's favourite authors are *Cato (Censorius), *Plautus, *Ennius, and *Sallust; Cicero, though unsurpassed as a letter-writer, is criticized as an orator for taking insufficient pains to find 'unexpected and surprising words' (*insperata atque inopinata verba*, 57. 16–17). *Virgil is ignored, *Lucan and L. *Annaeus Seneca (2) the younger damned.

The letters also illustrate Fronto's distaste for *Stoicism, his distress at its hold on Marcus, his constant ill-health, his family joys and sorrows, and the difficulties of life at court. He complains (111. 17–20) that Romans have no capacity for affection (φιλοστοργία), nor even a name for it; Marcus, silent on Fronto's rhetorical tuition, acknowledges that he has learnt from him the hypocrisy of courts and the coldness of Roman patricians (M. Aur. *Med.* 1. 11). Their own correspondence is marked by extreme displays of affection.

A few declamations and fragments of speeches have also survived, as have a draft for a panegyrical history of the Parthian War. *Minucius Felix (*Oct.* 9. 6–7) quotes a speech alleging that *Christian ritual included incest and murder; despite the entire absence of political advice from Fronto's letters, some have seen in this *invective the origin of Marcus' persecution. At the opposite extreme, it has been dismissed as incidental forensic abuse; it might also have been a speech in loyal support of imperial policy.

Aulus *Gellius includes Fronto in five chapters of his *Attic Nights*; three are in book 19, perhaps making the connection seem closer than it was. His authority in questions of vocabulary is vividly conveyed, but the admiration expressed for Quadrigarius and Virgil is probably Gellius' own. Fronto reacts with dismay to a report that 'Gellius' (presumably Aulus) is trying to acquire and publish his works (182. 5–6).

Before his letters came to light in 1815, Fronto had been idealized as the wise counsellor of a philosophic emperor; afterwards an exaggerated reaction dismissed him as a futile twaddler. He was more remarkable for mastery of language and warmth of heart than for keenness of intellect or strength of purpose; but our few fragments of his speeches tend to justify his ancient fame.

> TEXT M. P. J. van den Hout, 2nd edn. (1988).
> TRANSLATION C. R. Haines (Loeb, 1919–20), based on an obsolete text.
> STUDIES *PIR*² C 1364; E. Champlin, *Fronto and Antonine Rome* (1980); R. Marache, *La Critique littéraire de langue latine et le développement du goût archaïsant au II* siècle de notre ère* (1952); P. V. Cova, *ANRW* 2. 34. 2. 873 ff.; P. Soverini, ibid. 919 ff. L. A. H.-S.

Cornelius (*RE* 158) **Fuscus,** surrendered his senatorial rank through distaste for the duties of office-holding. In AD 68 he brought his home town (perhaps in Narbonese Gaul) over to *Galba's side and was rewarded with the procuratorship of *Illyricum. A dashing and energetic man, he supported the Flavian commander M. *Antonius Primus in the invasion of Italy (Tac. *Hist.* 2. 86). Subsequently, as praetorian prefect, he was sent by *Domitian to conduct a campaign against the Dacians. Having invaded *Dacia he was defeated and killed in 86 or 87 (Cass. Dio 67. 6; Jord. *Get.* 13. 76). It is unlikely that the altar at *Adamklissi in Romania commemorating Roman casualties, should be associated with Fuscus.

> R. Syme, *AJPhil.* 1937, 7 (= *Danubian Papers* (1971), 73), and *Tacitus* (1958), 683. J. B. C.

Cornelius (*RE* 164) **Gallus, Gaius,** said (not altogether reliably; see below) to have been born 70/69 BC at *Forum Iulii, by which modern Fréjus is probably meant. In 43 he appears at Rome as a mutual acquaintance of *Asinius Pollio and Cicero (*Fam.* 10. 31. 6, 32. 5). In 41 he had some sort of supervision of the confiscations of land, which involved *Virgil's family farm, in Transpadane Gaul (Broughton, *MRR* 2. 377). In 30 as *praefectus fabrum* (see FABRI) he took an active military part in *Octavian's

Egyptian campaign after *Actium and laid out a Forum Iulium (this may have caused confusion about his birthplace) either in or near *Alexandria (1); this he recorded in an inscription (AE 1964, 255), erased after his downfall, on an obelisk that is now in front of St Peter's at Rome. Octavian made him the first *praefectus* of the new province of *Egypt. He suppressed a rebellion in the Thebaid, marched south beyond the first cataract, negotiated the reception of the king of *Ethiopia into Roman protection, and established a buffer-zone with a puppet king. He celebrated these achievements in a boastful trilingual inscription at Philae dated 15 April 29 (CIL 3. 14147 = ILS 8995) and in inscriptions on the Pyramids, and set up statues of himself all over Egypt. He was apparently recalled, and, because of the insolence to which his pride had encouraged him, was interdicted from the house and provinces of Augustus. He was then indicted (and condemned?) in the senate, and driven to commit suicide (27/6 BC).

He wrote four books of love-elegies, probably entitled *Amores*, addressed to Volumnia Cytheris, a freedwoman actress who had been the mistress of Antony (M. *Antonius (2)) 49–45 BC, under the pseudonym Lycoris. As well as one already-known pentameter, nine lines of these verses have been recovered from a papyrus, perhaps dating from the 20s BC, found in 1978 in a fortress in Egyptian *Nubia and perhaps containing an anthology of quatrains from Gallus. These verses confirm the position of Gallus as creator (Ov. *Tr.* 4. 10. 53) of the new genre of love-elegy and his influence, long suspected, on *Propertius; the appearance of the word *domina* also confirms the long-held view that it was Gallus who, developing *Catullus, created the basic situation for Augustan elegists of the inamorata's dominance over the enslaved and helpless lover. There also seems to be a reference to the intended Parthian expedition of C. *Iulius Caesar (1). Virgil in his tenth *Eclogue* (ll. 44 ff.—probably as far as 63), a consolation to Gallus on his desertion by Lycoris, according to *Servius adapts lines (employing topics which appear in later love-elegy) from Gallus' own elegiacs into hexameters; a misunderstanding of *Chalcidico versu* (l. 50), probably a reference to the alleged inventor of elegiac verse Theocles of Chalcis, as a reference to *Euphorion (2) is probably responsible for statements in ancient commentators that Gallus translated or imitated Euphorion, specifically a poem on the Grynean grove at Colophon (Serv. on *Ecl.* 6. 72). It is however likely that Gallus did occasionally imitate Euphorion and was introduced to him by his friend *Parthenius, who wrote his Ἐρωτικὰ παθήματα for the use of Gallus in epic (i.e. hexameter) and elegiac verse (in fact Gallus apparently wrote no hexameter verse, whereas Euphorion, with insignificant exceptions, wrote nothing else); this seems to indicate a Propertian-style interest in mythological *exempla*. The style of the papyrus fragment is very plain, with none of the recherché obscurity of Euphorion; Quintilian (*Inst.* 10. 1. 93) regards Gallus as 'durior' ('harder') than Propertius and Tibullus.

The statement by Servius (on *Ecl.* 10. 1; *G.* 4. 1) that the Georgics originally ended with *laudes Galli* is probably due to another misunderstanding. See ELEGIAC POETRY, LATIN.

PIR² C 1369. See in general J.-P. Boucher, *C. Cornelius Gallus* (1966); N. B. Crowther, *ANRW* 2. 30. 3 (1983), 1622; Courtney *FLP* 259, and *Quaderni urbinati di cultura classica* 1990, 103–10. On the papyrus Anderson–Parsons–Nisbet, *JRS* 1979, 125, L. Nicastri, *Cornelio Gallo e l'elegia ellenistico-romana* (1984); on the obelisk inscription F. Magi, *Studi Romani* 1963, 50, S. Mazzarino, *Quaderni catanesi di studi classici e medievali* 1980, 7; on the Philae inscription S. Mazzarino, *Rh. Mus.* 1982, 312; on his condemnation and suicide L. J. Daly and W. L. Reiter, in C. Deroux (ed.), *Studies in Latin Literature and Roman History* 1 (1979),

289, K. Raaflaub and L. J. Samons, in K. Raaflaub and M. Toher (eds.), *Between Republic and Empire* (1990), 423; on the *laudes Galli* W. B. Anderson, *CQ* 1933, 36, 73, E. Norden, *Kl. Schr.* (1966), 468.　　E. C.

Cornelius Labeo (? second half of 3rd cent. AD) wrote a (lost) history of Romano-Etruscan religion, the target of polemic from *Arnobius and St *Augustine.

PIR² C 1373.

Cornelius (*RE* 176) **Lentulus** (1), **Gnaeus**, was consul 201 BC, without having held the praetorship. His attempts to oppose peace with Carthage and to succeed *Scipio Africanus in Africa were rejected by the people. In 196 he was one of the ten commissioners for the settlement after the Second Macedonian War; he held a personal meeting with *Philip (3) V and urged him to seek an alliance with Rome. He died in 184, having been an augur (see AUGURES) since 217.

Scullard, *Rom. Pol.* 81, 279; J. Briscoe, *CAH* 8² (1989), 73–4.　　J. Br.

Cornelius (*RE* 181) **Lentulus** (2), **Gnaeus**, consul 14 BC, known as 'Augur' to distinguish him from Cn. Lentulus, consul 18 BC. Poor to begin with, he received a grant from *Augustus, and became extremely rich (Sen. *Ben.* 2. 27. 1 f.). He was proconsul of Asia (3–2 BC), was still alive in AD 22 (Tac. *Ann.* 3. 59), and died later in the reign of *Tiberius, whom he made his sole heir (Suet. *Tib.* 49. 1). He, and not his namesake, is very probably the Cn. Lentulus referred to by Tacitus (*Ann.* 1. 27, 2. 32, 3. 68, 4. 29, 44) as victor over the *Getae. He was governor of a Balkan province under Augustus and a close friend of *Tiberius. He accompanied *Drusus to Pannonia in AD 14, was ridiculously accused of *maiestas in 24 (cf. Cass. Dio 57. 24. 8), and died in 25, very rich after earlier poverty (see above).

PIR² C 1379; Syme, *Tacitus* 750, and *AA* 284–99 and see index.　　T. J. C.; E. B.

Cornelius (*RE* 188) **Lentulus, Lucius** He and L. Manlius Acidinus, though holding no office, were sent to Spain with consular *imperium* in 206 BC to succeed *Scipio Africanus and remained there until 201 and 200 respectively. In 205, when Livy (probably wrongly) says Lentulus held the curule aedileship in absence, they suppressed a revolt by Indibilis and Mandonius. On his return to Rome in 200 his claim to a triumph was rejected because he had not held an office before his proconsulship, but he was granted an *ovatio. Consul 199, he operated in northern Italy, and returned there for part of 198. In 196 he was sent as ambassador to mediate between *Antiochus (3) III and Egypt, and was one of the Roman representatives who met Antiochus at Lysimacheia.

Briscoe, *Comm.* 31–33, 108–9; Broughton, *MRR* 3. 66; Sumner, *Orators* 140 with stemma, 143, and *Arethusa* 1970, 89.　　J. Br.

Cornelius (*RE* 216) **Lentulus Clodianus, Gnaeus,** perhaps served under Cn. *Pompeius Strabo, left Rome during *Sulla's absence and returned with him (Cic. *Brut.* 311). He was an undistinguished orator (ibid. 234). As consuls 72 BC, he and L. *Gellius tried to prevent abuses by *Verres and passed a law enabling commanders to confer citizenship for valour, and one exacting payment from buyers of estates of the proscribed (see PROSCRIPTION). He was defeated by *Spartacus and recalled to Rome. As censors 70, he and Gellius severely purged the corrupt senate. He served as *Pompey's legate against the pirates, supported the law of C. *Manilius, and died soon after.　　E. B.

Cornelius (*RE* 218) **Lentulus Crus, Lucius,** praetor 58 BC, became consul in 49 as an enemy of *Caesar. Sent by the senate to govern Asia, he brought two legions from there to *Dyrrachium,

Cornelius Lentulus Gaetulicus, Gnaeus

where L. *Cornelius Balbus (1) vainly tried to bribe him to abandon Pompey. After *Pharsalus he fled to Egypt and there met his death a day after *Pompey. He is said by Caesar to have been made desperate by debt, and various sources (including at times *Cicero, whom he had supported in 58) describe him as lazy, luxurious, and pretentious. He was the brother of P. *Cornelius Lentulus Spinther.   E. B.

Cornelius (*RE* 220) **Lentulus Gaetulicus, Gnaeus,** was consul AD 26 and legate of Upper Germany, possibly in succession to his brother, in 30–9. As a lax disciplinarian he was popular with his own army and also with the Lower German legions, commanded by L. *Apronius, his father-in-law. An attempt to indict him in 34 as an associate of *Sejanus (his son had been engaged to Sejanus' daughter) failed. In 39 he was accused of leading a conspiracy by which the emperor *Gaius (1) was to be murdered at *Mogontiacum. Gaius claimed to have been forewarned of the plot, in which M. *Aemilius Lepidus (5) was said to be involved, and both were executed. He was an erotic poet, regarded by *Martial as one of his models. Nine epigrams in the Greek *Anthology may be by him.

Courtney, *FLP* 345 f. (the poetry); Syme, *AA*, see index and table 21.
J. P. B.; E. B.

Cornelius (*RE* 228) **Lentulus Marcellinus, Gnaeus,** descended from M. *Claudius Marcellus (1) and patron of Sicily, aided Cicero against *Verres. A legate under *Pompey (67 BC), he settled problems in Cyrenaica (see CYRENE and J. M. Reynolds, *JRS* 1962, 97 ff.). Praetor 60 and proconsul in Syria 59–58, he became consul 56 and vigorously opposed the three dynasts, especially their arrangements at *Luca, as well as the restoration of *Ptolemy (1) XII (Auletes), surpassing himself as an orator (Cic. *Brut.* 247). He probably died soon after.   E. B.

Cornelius (*RE* 238) **Lentulus Spinther, Publius,** elder brother of L. *Cornelius Lentulus Crus (see E. Badian, *Chiron* 1990, 407 n. 26), quaestor *c*.74 BC, aided *Cicero as aedile 63. Urban praetor 60, he became proconsul in Spain and (with *Caesar's support) a pontifex. Consul 57, he worked hard to restore Cicero from exile and helped him regain his property. As proconsul of *Cilicia from 56, he had been charged with restoring *Ptolemy (1) XII (Auletes), but this was prevented by religious chicanery. He triumphed 51. In the Civil War he was captured by Caesar at *Corfinium and dismissed, then after long hesitation rejoined *Pompey, fought at *Pharsalus and died shortly after, possibly executed by Caesar.   E. B.

Cornelius (*RE* 240) **Lentulus Sura, Publius,** an undistinguished orator (Cic. *Brut.* 235), returned to Rome with *Sulla (ibid. 311) and disgraced himself as quaestor 81 BC. *Praetor repetundarum* 74, he became consul 71, but was expelled from the senate by the censors in 70. Praetor for the second time in 63, he joined *Catiline and became head of the conspiracy in the city. Compromised by a letter to the Allobrogan envoys (see FABIUS SANGA, Q.), he was arrested and executed. He was buried by his stepson M. *Antonius (2).   E. B.

Cornelius (*RE* 272) **Merula, Lucius,** was made suffect consul by Cn. *Octavius (2) after his expulsion of L. *Cornelius Cinna (1), chiefly because as *flamen Dialis* (see FLAMINES) he could not be active in his consular duties. Prosecuted after Cinna's return, he committed suicide, first piously resigning his priesthood. He was briefly succeeded as *flamen Dialis* by *Caesar.   E. B.

Cornelius (*RE* 274) **Nepos,** the earliest extant biographer in Latin, lived *c*.110–24 BC. From Cisalpine Gaul, by 65 BC he was living in Rome and moving in literary circles: he corresponded with *Cicero and considered *Atticus a friend; Catullus dedicated verses to him. He kept out of politics.

Works (1) *De viris illustribus* ('On Famous Men'), at least sixteen books and with perhaps 400 lives, grouped according to categories (those of generals and historians are firmly attested), and including non-Romans. It was first published before the death of Atticus, probably in 34 BC; a second, expanded, edition appeared before 27 BC. Of this we have *De excellentibus ducibus exterarum gentium* ('On Eminent Foreign Leaders') and the lives of M. *Porcius Cato (1) and Atticus from his 'Roman Historians'. (2) Lost works: *Chronica*, a universal history in three books (Catull. 1); *Exempla*, anecdotes in at least five books (Gell. *NA* 6 (7). 18. 11); fuller lives of Cato (Nep. *Cato* 3. 5) and Cicero (Gell. 15. 28. 2); a work on geography, cited by *Pomponius Mela and *Pliny (1) the Elder. His light verse (Plin. *Ep.* 5. 3. 6) was probably never published.

'An intellectual pygmy' (Horsfall), Nepos probably took the idea of a parallel treatment of foreigners from *Varro's *Imagines*. His defects are hasty and careless composition (perhaps less marked in his first edition) and lack of control of his material. He is mainly eulogistic, with an ethical aim, but also gives information about his hero's environment. As historian his value is slight; he names many sources, but rarely used them at first hand. His style is plain. His intended Roman readership is hard to locate— but middlebrow, with, at best, only a slight knowledge of Greece. See BIOGRAPHY, ROMAN.

> LIFE AND WORKS N. Horsfall, *CHCL* 2.
> TEXTS E. Malcovati, 3rd edn. (1964); P. K. Marshall (Teubner, 1977).
> COMMENTARIES K. Nipperdey and K. Witte, 12th edn. (1962); M. Ruch, *Hannibal, Cato, Atticus* (1968); N. Horsfall, *Cato, Atticus* (1989).
> STUDIES E. Jenkinson, *ANRW* 1. 3 (1973), 703 ff. (with bibliog.); T. P. Wiseman, *Clio's Cosmetics* (1979), 154 ff.; J. Geiger, *Cornelius Nepos and Ancient Political Biography*, Hist. Einzelschr. 47 (1985); A. Dionisotti, *JRS* 1988, 35 ff.   J. C. R.; G. B. T.; A. J. S. S.

Cornelius (*RE* 279) **Palma Frontonianus, Aulus,** from *Volsinii, ordinary consul AD 99, was governor of Hispania *Tarraconensis *c*.100–3 when his administration was praised by *Martial (12. 9, written in 101). While governor of *Syria (104/5–8) he brought *Nabataea under Roman control in 106, creating a new province (coins celebrate 'the aquisition of Arabia'), and was honoured by Trajan with triumphal ornaments (*ornamenta*), a statue, and a second ordinary consulship in 109. Rich, powerful, and distinguished, at some point he apparently incurred the personal hostility of *Hadrian and was executed at the start of his reign along with three other consulars on the grounds that he was plotting against the emperor.

G. Alföldy, *Fasti Hispanienses* (1969), 24.   J. B. C.

Cornelius (*RE* 323) **Scipio** (1), **Lucius,** son of L. *Cornelius Scipio Barbatus, was curule *aedile, *consul (259 BC), and *censor (258). In 259 he attempted to use the new Roman fleet to deprive the *Carthaginians of a naval base against Italy: he captured Aleria and reduced *Corsica, but failed to storm Olbia in *Sardinia. Two inscriptions (*ILS* 2, 3; *ILLRP*, no. 310) record his career, but do not mention the triumph which the *fasti triumphales* assign to him. Near the porta Capena he dedicated a temple to the Tempestates which had spared his fleet; remains of his inscribed sarcophagus survive.   H. H. S.; A. J. S. S.

Cornelius (*RE* 325) **Scipio** (2), **Lucius,** younger son of P. *Cornelius Scipio Africanus, was captured during the war with *Antiochus (3) III (the sources vary as to when and where); he was well treated, and released by Antiochus shortly before the battle of *Magnesia. He was *praetor peregrinus* in 174 BC, but was expelled from the senate by the *censors elected in that year. The story in Valerius Maximus that a son of Scipio called Gnaeus was elected to the praetorship only because his father's secretary C. Cicereius (praetor 173) withdrew, and was prevented by his relations from fulfilling the duties of his office, may in fact refer to Lucius.

Broughton, *MRR* 1. 406 n. 2; Briscoe, *Commentary 34–37*, 339.   J. Br.

Cornelius (*RE* 330) **Scipio** (1), **Publius** (for family connections see CORNELIUS SCIPIO CALVUS, CN.) was consul in 218 BC. The senate initially despatched him to Spain, expecting to be able to fight *Hannibal there. Delayed by a Gallic uprising, he did not leave until July at the earliest and arrived by sea at the mouth of the Rhône in September; at the same time Hannibal crossed the river well inland. Returning to northern Italy with part of his forces, Publius had the worse of a cavalry skirmish at the Ticinus (mod. Ticino, near Pavia). He retreated eastwards to Placentia (Piacenza) where he was joined by his colleague Ti. Sempronius Longus. A little west of Placentia, at the river *Trebia, the Carthaginians won a major victory and over half the Roman army was destroyed. For Publius' part in subsequent events in Spain see CORNELIUS SCIPIO CALVUS, CN.

J. Briscoe, *CAH* 8² (1989), 46–9.   J. Br.

Cornelius (*RE* 331) **Scipio** (2), **Publius,** was the eldest son of P. *Cornelius Scipio Africanus and adoptive father of P. *Cornelius Scipio Aemilianus. (See next two entries.) He became an augur (see AUGURES) in 180 BC, but poor health prevented him from holding any other office. He wrote some short speeches which, according to *Cicero (*Brut.* 77) showed that if he had enjoyed good health, he would have been regarded as an outstanding orator, and also a historical work in Greek. The view that one of the inscriptions from the tomb of the Scipios (*ILLRP* 311) refers to him should be rejected.

Astin, *Scipio* 12–14, G. Bandelli, *Epigraphica* 1975, 84–99.   J. Br.

Cornelius (*RE* 335) **Scipio Aemilianus Africanus (Numantinus), Publius,** born 185/4 BC as second son of L. *Aemilius Paullus (2), adopted as a child by P. *Cornelius Scipio (2), son of P. *Cornelius Scipio Africanus, as his elder brother was by a Q. Fabius Maximus. In 168 he fought under Paullus at Pydna. Back in Rome, he met *Polybius (1), who became his friend and his mentor in preparing him for a public career. (See esp. Polyb. 31. 23 ff.) In 151, though asked by the Macedonians, as Paullus' son, to settle their problems that soon led to the war with *Andriscus, he instead volunteered for arduous service as a military tribune under L. *Licinius Lucullus (1) in Spain, thus persuading others to volunteer. In the fighting he won a major decoration, the *corona muralis* (see CROWNS AND WREATHS). When sent to request *elephants from *Masinissa, he renewed Africanus' patronal relations with him and vainly tried to mediate peace between him and *Carthage after a battle he had witnessed. In 149 and 148 he served as a military tribune under M'. *Manilius in Africa (see PUNIC WARS) and again distinguished himself both in the fighting, where he won a rare distinction, the *corona graminea* (Plin. *HN* 22. 6 ff., 13), and in diplomacy, persuading a Carthaginian commander to defect. After Masinissa's death he divided the kingdom among his three legitimate

sons according to the king's request. Coming to Rome to stand for an *aedileship for 147, he was elected *consul, contrary to the rules for the *cursus honorum*, by a well-organized popular demand that forced the senate to suspend the rules. He was assigned Africa by special legislation and, after restoring discipline and closing off the enemy's harbour, he overcame long and desperate resistance and early in 146 captured Carthage after days of street-fighting. After letting his soldiers collect the booty, he destroyed the city and sold the inhabitants into slavery. Anyone who should resettle the site was solemnly cursed. With the help of the usual senate commission he organized the province of Africa and after giving magnificent games returned to celebrate a splendid triumph, earning the name 'Africanus' to which his adoptive descent entitled him. He distributed some captured works of art among cities in Sicily and Italy (Cic. *Verr. passim*; *Syll.³* 677; *ILLRP* 326).

Probably in 144–3 he headed an embassy to the kings and cities of the east, perhaps even as far as the territory contested between Parthians and Seleucids (Lucil. 464 Marx), with *Panaetius as his personal companion. After his return he presumably guided senate policy in those areas, especially towards *Pergamum, the *Seleucids, and the *Jews. (We have no evidence on its formulation and little on its execution.) In 142 he was censor with L. *Mummius, who mitigated some of his severity. They restored the pons Aemilius (see BRIDGES) and adorned the *Capitol.

In 136 he secured the rejection of the peace in Spain negotiated for C. *Hostilius Mancinus by his cousin and brother-in-law Ti. *Sempronius Gracchus (3). This deeply offended Gracchus, even though Scipio saved him from personal disgrace. In 135, again by special dispensation and without campaigning for the office, he was elected consul 134 and sent to *Numantia, with an army consisting chiefly of his own clients (see CLIENS) because of the shortage of military manpower. He starved Numantia into surrender in just over a year, destroyed it, and sold the survivors into slavery, returning in 132 to celebrate a second triumph and acquire the (unofficial) name 'Numantinus'. By approving of Gracchus' murder he incurred great unpopularity. It was increased when, in 129, defending the interests of Italian clients holding public land, he was responsible for a senate decree that paralysed the agrarian commission by transferring its judiciary powers to the consuls, usually hostile or absent. When, soon after, he was found dead, various prominent persons, including his wife (Gracchus' sister) and *Cornelia (1) (Gracchus' mother), were suspected of responsibility, though the funeral laudation written by his friend C. *Laelius (2) specified natural death. (See E. Badian, *JRS* 1956, 220.)

His personal morality and civil and military courage made him an unlikely friend of M. *Porcius Cato (1). But he was a patron of poets and philosophers, with a genuine interest in literature (he was himself an able orator) and in Greek philosophy, as transmitted by Polybius, which he combined with a traditional aristocratic Roman outlook. He believed in the 'balanced constitution', with the people entitled to choose their leaders (Polyb. 6. 14. 4 and 8: hence his willingness to accept extraordinary appointments) and to take charge of criminal trials (Polyb. 6. 14. 5 ff.: hence his support for the ballot law of L. *Cassius Longinus Ravilla). But he could foresee the ultimate fall of Rome (Astin 251 f.; cf. Polyb. 6. 9. 12 ff.), which could be delayed by stopping signs of decay, especially the decline in aristocratic morality (see *ORF⁴* 21, esp. nos. 13, 17, 30, and cf. Polyb. 6. 8. 4 f.) and the danger of the democratic element, under the tribunes (cf. Polyb.

Cornelius Scipio Africanus, Publius

6. 16. 5 ff.), leading the state into anarchy and tyranny (cf. Polyb. 6. 9. 2 ff.—and an aristocratic Roman fear of a leader's excessive popularity producing *regnum*, 'monarchy'). Utterly ruthless towards Rome's enemies, he believed in loyal patronage (both for Rome and for himself) over client-friends, whether monarchs like *Attalus II and Masinissa or Italian allies. Cicero, in *De republica*, depicts him as the ideal Roman statesman (cf. also *De senectute* and *De amicitia*) and sets him in a group of aristocrats and their cultured clients (esp. *Amic.* 69) that modern scholars turned into the *Scipionic Circle.

> In addition to the sources cited in the text see esp. Polyb. 31–9, *passim*, and App. *Hisp.* 84, 363–98, 427; *Pun.* 71, 322–72, 330, and 98, 464–135, 642. Astin, *Scipio*; H. B. Mattingly, *CQ* 1986, 91 ff. (dating the embassy); H. Trofimoff, *RIDA* 1988, 263 ff. (some political ideas).   E. B.

Cornelius (*RE* 336) **Scipio Africanus** (the elder), **Publius,** son of P. *Cornelius Scipio (1) and nephew of Cn. *Cornelius Scipio Calvus, husband of the daughter of L. Aemilius Paullus (1), father of P. *Cornelius Scipio (2), L. *Cornelius Scipio (2), and of two daughters, married to P. *Cornelius Scipio Nasica Corculum and Ti. *Sempronius Gracchus (2), respectively. He was born in 236 BC and is said to have saved his father's life at the battle of the Ticinus in 218 and, as military tribune, to have rallied the survivors of the battle of *Cannae at Canusium. He was curule *aedile 213, and in 210 was appointed by the people to the command in Spain, the first person to have received consular *imperium* without having previously been *consul or *praetor. In Spain he resumed the aggressive policy of his father and uncle; in 209 he captured *Carthago Nova (mod. Cartagena), the main Carthaginian supply base in Spain, by sending a wading party across the lagoon, which, he had discovered, normally ebbed in the evening. In 208, employing tactics which marked a major break with traditional Roman practice, he defeated *Hasdrubal (2) Barca at Baecula (Bailen), north of the Baetis (Guadalquivir). When Hasdrubal escaped towards the Pyrenees and the route to Italy, he decided not to pursue him. In 206 he defeated *Mago (2) and *Hasdrubal (3) the son of Gisgo at Ilipa, just north of Seville. Thereafter only mopping-up operations remained in Spain; a mutiny in his army was quelled, and the ringleaders executed. Scipio crossed to Africa to solicit the support of *Syphax, and met *Masinissa in western Spain.

Elected *consul for 205, Scipio wanted to carry the war to Africa. Opposition in the senate was led by Q. *Fabius Maximus Verrucosus and Q. *Fulvius Flaccus (1), but he was assigned Sicily with permission to invade Africa if he saw fit. Denied the right to levy new troops, he crossed to Sicily accompanied only by volunteers, returning to southern Italy to recapture *Locri (Epizephyrii); the subsequent behaviour of *Pleminius briefly threatened Scipio's own position. In 204 he landed in Africa, began the siege of *Utica, and wintered on a nearby headland. Hasdrubal and Syphax encamped a few miles to the south; in the course of feigned peace negotiations Scipio discovered the details of their camps, which were made of wood or reeds, and in the spring of 203 a night attack led to their destruction by fire and the death of large numbers of Carthaginian troops. Later Scipio defeated Hasdrubal and Syphax at the battle of the Great Plains, *c*.120 km. (75 mi.) west of Carthage. He now occupied *Tunis, but was forced to use his transport ships to block a Carthaginian attack on his fleet at Utica, losing 60 transports. During an armistice, peace terms were agreed, and accepted at Rome, but in the spring of 202 an attack by Carthage on Roman ships, and subsequently on envoys sent by Scipio to protest, led to

the resumption of hostilities. Hannibal had now returned to Carthage, and after further abortive peace negotiations Scipio defeated him at the battle of *Zama; peace was concluded on Rome's terms. Scipio received the *cognomen* Africanus and returned to Rome to celebrate a triumph.

Scipio now had great prestige at Rome. The so-called 'Scipionic legend' (in its later form Scipio is the son of Jupiter) had already come into existence. The capture of Carthago Nova, when Scipio is said to have told his troops that *Neptune had appeared to him in a dream and promised him help, led to the belief that he was divinely inspired. The Iberians had saluted him as a king, but there is no evidence that he ever envisaged playing other than a traditional role in Roman politics. His success, however, meant that he had many enemies among the nobility, some alarmed by the stories circulating about him, others merely jealous of his success. He was elected *censor in 199 but his tenure of the office was unremarkable: he became *princeps senatus*, a position confirmed by the following two pairs of censors. Consul for the second time in 194, he wanted to succeed T. *Quinctius Flamininus in Greece, believing that a continued military presence was necessary as security against *Antiochus (3) III, but the senate voted that the army should be withdrawn. Scipio campaigned in northern Italy during his consulship, but achieved little. As an ambassador to Africa in 193 he failed, perhaps deliberately, to settle a dispute between Carthage and Masinissa; the story that he also went to Asia in that year and met Hannibal should be rejected. In 190 he volunteered to go to Asia as a legate under his brother L. *Cornelius Scipio Asiagenes. He rejected a bribe, which Antiochus offered him in order to secure a favourable peace; shortly before the battle of *Magnesia Antiochus returned his captive son L. *Cornelius Scipio (2). He took no part in the battle itself because of illness, but was chosen to present the Roman peace terms after Antiochus' defeat. At Rome there now began a series of conflicts between the Scipio brothers (and their allies) and their opponents, among whom M. *Porcius Cato (1) was prominent, culminating in the much debated 'trials of the Scipios'. The accusations involved the embezzlement of public funds and, perhaps, the taking of bribes from Antiochus. It is probable that Publius was attacked in the senate in 187, and Lucius put on trial (in what way and with what result is uncertain), and that Publius was accused in 184, but avoided trial by retiring into voluntary exile at *Liternum (in *Campania), where he died the following year.

> H. H. Scullard, *Scipio Africanus, Soldier and Politician* (1970); J. Briscoe, *CAH* 8² (1989) 59–65, 73–4; Walbank, *HCP* 1, 2, 3; Briscoe, *Comm. 31–33, 34–37*, see indexes under 'Scipio'; Scullard, *Rom. Pol.* 290–303 (trials); F. W. Walbank *PCPS* 1967, 54–69 = *Selected Papers* (1985), 120 ff. (legend).   J. Br.

Cornelius (*RE* 337) **Scipio Asiagenes** (see below), **Lucius,** brother of P. *Cornelius Scipio Africanus, under whom he served in Spain (207–206 BC), Sicily (205), and Africa (204–202). He was curule aedile (probably) 195, and praetor in Sicily 193. In 191 he served at Thermopylae under M'. *Acilius Glabrio (1), who, if Livy is right, sent him to Rome to report the victory. An unsuccessful candidate the previous year, he was elected consul for 190, receiving the command against *Antiochus (3) III; his brother Africanus served under him as legate. After making a truce with the Aetolians, he crossed to Asia and defeated Antiochus at the battle of *Magnesia in December 190. After concluding a provisional peace agreement he returned to Rome to triumph, and took the *cognomen* Asiagenes (or Asiagenus; Asiaticus does not occur before the Augustan period). For his part in the 'trials of the Scipios' see CORNELIUS SCIPIO AFRICANUS, P. The censors of 184, M. *Porcius Cato (1) and L. *Valerius Flaccus (1), deprived him of his public horse.

> J. P. V. Balsdon, *Hist.* 1972, 224–34; Briscoe, *Comm.* 34–37, see index; Sherk, *RDGE* nos. 35, 36 (letters of the Scipios to Greek communities in Asia).　　　　　　　　　　　　　　　　　　　　　　　J. Br.

Cornelius (*RE* 343) **Scipio Barbatus, Lucius,** consul 298 BC, censor ?280. His Hellenizing sarcophagus is the earliest from the tomb of the Scipios and its (later?) verse epitaph (*ILLRP* 309) claims that he captured Taurasia (and?) Cisauna in (eastern?) Samnium, subdued all 'Lucania' (which has been variously identified) and took hostages. This apparently refutes *Livy (10. 11 ff.), who records a Lucanian treaty and hostages but simply ascribes Barbatus successes in Etruria.

> E. T. Salmon, *Samnium and the Samnites* (1967), 260 f.; G. Radke, *Rh. Mus.* 1991, 69 ff.　　　　　　　　　　　　　　　　　　　　　　A. D.

Cornelius (*RE* 345) **Scipio Calvus, Gnaeus,** son of L. *Cornelius Scipio (1), brother of P. *Cornelius Scipio (1), and hence uncle of P. *Cornelius Scipio Africanus, father of P. *Cornelius Scipio Nasica. Consul in 222 BC, he and his colleague M. *Claudius Marcellus (1) defeated the Insubres and captured Mediolanum (Milan). In 218, after *Hannibal had crossed the Rhône, he was sent to Spain by his brother; the aim was to keep the Carthaginian forces there occupied and prevent reinforcements being sent to Hannibal. He brought the area north of the Ebro, both the coastal strip and the hinterland, under Roman control. In 217, now probably proconsul, he defeated the Punic fleet at the mouth of the Ebro, and followed this with lightning raids which took the Roman fleet south of *Carthago Nova (mod. Cartagena) and to Ebusus (Ibiza). He was now joined by his brother, and together they advanced to *Saguntum (Sagunto). In 216 they inflicted a serious defeat on *Hasdrubal (2) just south of the Ebro, which put an end to any prospect of his joining Hannibal in the near future. The events of the next four years are obscure, but in 212 Saguntum was recaptured. In 211, however, facing three separate Carthaginian armies, the brothers split their forces; Publius was caught by *Mago (2) and *Hasdrubal (3) the son of Gisgo, and killed in battle; Gnaeus attempted to retreat, but was pursued by all three armies and met his end near Ilourgeia, in the hinterland of Carthago Nova.

> J. Briscoe, *CAH*, 8² (1989), 56–9.　　　　　　　　　　　J. Br.

Cornelius (*RE* 30) **Scipio Nasica, Publius,** son of Cn. *Cornelius Scipio Calvus, was chosen to receive the sacred stone of the Magna Mater on its arrival in Italy from *Pessinus in 204 BC. (See CYBELE.) He was curule aedile 197 and as praetor 194 in Further Spain defeated a force of invading Lusitani near Ilipa, north of Seville. Defeated for 192, he was consul 191, when he completed the subjugation of the *Boii, and, after objections from a tribune, celebrated a *triumph. He stood unsuccessfully for the *censorship in both 189 and 184, was a commissioner for the settlement of *Aquileia (183–181), and in 171 one of the patrons chosen by the people to present their complaints against former Roman governors.

> J. Briscoe, *Comm.* 34–37, see index.　　　　　　　　　J. Br.

Cornelius (*RE* 353) **Scipio Nasica Corculum, Publius,** son of P. *Cornelius Scipio Nasica, son-in-law of P. *Cornelius Scipio Africanus, and father of P. *Cornelius Scipio Serapio, served with distinction under L. *Aemilius Paullus (2) in the *Pydna campaign in 168 BC, and wrote an account of the battle in a letter

to a king, glorifying his own role; the letter was used by *Plutarch (*Aem.* 15–22), perhaps not at first hand, as one of his sources for the battle. He was elected consul for 162, but after departing for their provinces the consuls were recalled and forced to abdicate because of a fault in their election (see SEMPRONIUS GRACCHUS (2), TI.). As *censor in 159 he and his colleague removed unauthorized statues from the Forum. Consul for the second time in 155, he completed the Dalmatian War and celebrated a triumph. He successfully opposed the plans of the censors of 154 to build a permanent theatre in Rome. In opposition to M. *Porcius Cato (1), he opposed the declaring of war on Carthage. As ambassador to Africa in 152 he persuaded *Masinissa to withdraw from disputed territory. In 150 he organized resistance to *Andriscus in Greece, and his report led to an army being sent in the following year. In 147 and 142 the censors appointed him *princeps senatus. He was a *pontifex for many years and became pontifex maximus 150. He was learned in the law and a renowned orator.

> Astin, *Scipio* 276–80.　　　　　　　　　　　　　　　J. Br.

Cornelius (*RE* 354) **Scipio Nasica Serapio, Publius,** son of Cornelius Scipio Nasica Corculum, may have been praetor 141 BC and, if so, the praetor defeated by the *Scordisci. As consul 138, with D. *Iunius Brutus Callaicus, he was involved in trouble about the army levy with some tribunes, who briefly held the consuls under arrest. In 133 he vigorously opposed his cousin Ti. *Sempronius Gracchus (3). When Tiberius mobilized a mob to seek re-election as tribune, he was accused of aiming at tyranny, but the consul P. *Mucius Scaevola saw no reason to take action. Scipio, calling on those who wanted to keep the republic safe to follow him, led a charge by senators and their clients (see CLIENS) against Tiberius in which the latter was killed. The deed was ever after applauded by *optimates and execrated by *populares (compare e.g. Cic. *Off.* 1. 76 and *Rhet. Her.* 4. 68). Sent to Asia as head of a mission in connection with the annexation of the province, but in part to remove him from popular fury, he died at *Pergamum. He was elected *pontifex maximus in his absence, perhaps as early as 141 (to succeed his father), but perhaps only in 132.

> M. G. Morgan, *Hist.* 1974, 183 ff. (the praetorship and the Scordisci).　　　　　　　　　　　　　　　　　　　　　　　　　E. B.

Cornelius (*RE* 369) **Severus,** Augustan epic poet. *Quintilian (*Inst.* 10. 1. 89) praises the quality of the first book of his poem on the Sicilian War of 38–36 BC. The poem about kings which his friend *Ovid (*Pont.* 4. 16. 9; cf. 4. 2. 1) ascribes to him may have been the first part of a long verse chronicle called *Res Romanae* (Probus, ed. Keil, *Gramm. Lat.* 4. 208, cites a half line under this title). The 25 lines on *Cicero's death quoted by the elder Seneca (L. *Annaeus Seneca (1)) (*Suas.* 6. 26) probably come from a later part of this work.

> *PIR*² C 1452; H. Dahlmann, *AAWM* 1975, 6; Courtney, *FLP* 320.　　E. C.

Cornelius (*RE* 374) **Sisenna, Lucius,** Roman historian. *Praetor in 78 BC, he defended C. *Verres (70) and was legate to *Pompey in 67, dying in Crete. His *Histories* ran at least to twelve books, perhaps to 23 (fr. 132). They touched on Roman origins but concentrated on a detailed account of the *Social War (3) and Sullan Civil War, certainly from 90 to 82, probably to *Sulla's death: they perhaps continued the work of *Sempronius Asellio, and were in turn probably continued by *Sallust's *Histories*. His model was *Cleitarchus, and the fragments suggest vividness and some flair, with speeches, digressions, omens, and dreams (though he was sceptical of their prophetic power). The style was mannered, the vocabulary recherché. Sallust admired him, but felt that he spoke of Sulla with 'insufficient freedom' (*Iug*. 95), a phrase suggesting prudent restraint rather than partisanship. In *Cicero's view his work easily outstripped any previous Roman history (*Brut*. 228, *Leg*. 1. 7), and *Varro used his name as title for a work on historiography (*Sisenna de historia*).

FRAGMENTS Peter, *HRRel* 1². cccxxxiv–xlix, 276–97; G. Barabino, *Studi Noniani* 1 (1967), with comm.

LITERATURE W. D. Lebek, *Verba Prisca* (1970), 267–86; E. Rawson, *Roman Culture & Society* (1991), 363 ff. (= *CQ* 1979, 327 ff.).   C. B. R. P.

Cornelius (*RE* 377) **Sulla, Faustus,** son of L. *Cornelius Sulla Felix and of *Caecilia Metella (1). His *praenomen* and that of his twin sister, Fausta, were given to symbolize their father's good fortune. As his father's heir he was repeatedly threatened with prosecution. Serving as military tribune under Pompey, he was the first to scale the walls of the Temple in Jerusalem. On his return, he gave magnificent games in his father's memory (60 BC), was made augur, and in 56 issued coins chiefly celebrating his father and Pompey (*RRC* 426). He was quaestor 54 and supported his half-brother M. *Aemilius Scaurus (2) and, in 52, his brother-in-law T. *Annius Milo in their trials. He was put in charge of the restoration of the senate-house destroyed after P. *Clodius Pulcher's death. In the Civil War he joined *Pompey, fled to Africa after *Pharsalus, and after Thapsus was captured and killed by P. *Sittius.

Gruen, *LGRR*, see index.   E. B.

Cornelius (*RE* 386) **Sulla, Publius,** relative of L. *Cornelius Sulla Felix, in whose *proscriptions he amassed wealth and on whose behalf he helped in founding a veteran colony at Pompeii. With P. *Autronius Paetus he was elected consul for 65 BC, but convicted of *ambitus* and expelled from the senate. He was said to have been involved in the 'First Catilinarian Conspiracy' (see SERGIUS CATILINA). Prosecuted as a Catilinarian in 62, he obtained massive aristocratic support, was defended by Q. *Hortensius Hortalus and *Cicero (whom he handsomely rewarded), and acquitted. In 54 he launched an *ambitus* prosecution against A. *Gabinius (2), apparently without success. In the Civil War he fought with some success for *Caesar, secured his rehabilitation, and enriched himself in the sales of Pompeian properties. He died *c*.45.

Cicero, *Pro Sulla* (ed. and comm. D. H. Berry, 1996) Gruen, *LGRR*, see index.   E. B.

Cornelius (*RE* 392) **Sulla Felix, Lucius,** born *c*.138 BC of an old, but not recently prominent, patrician family, after a dissolute youth inherited a fortune from his stepmother, which enabled him to enter the aristocratic career. Chosen by C. *Marius (1) as his *quaestor (107) he distinguished himself in the Numidian War, finally securing the surrender of *Jugurtha by *Bocchus I through diplomacy and thus ending the war. He again served under Marius against the Germans in 104 and 103, then joined the army of Q. *Lutatius Catulus (2), probably dispatched by Marius to advise Catulus, and enabled him to join in the final victory. Omitting the *aedileship, he failed to become *praetor for 98, but succeeded through lavish bribery in becoming *praetor urbanus* 97. He was assigned *Cilicia *pro consule*, then instructed to instal *Ariobarzanes (1) in *Cappadocia. He accomplished this largely with local levies and displayed Roman power to the eastern kingdoms, including (for the first time) *Parthia. A Chaldaean's prophecy that he would attain greatness and die at the height of good fortune influenced him for the rest of his life. He stayed in Cilicia for several years, perhaps until 92. On his

return he was prosecuted, but the prosecution was abandoned. In 91 the senate, promoting him against Marius, granted Bocchus permission to dedicate a group showing the surrender of Jugurtha on the Capitol. Marius' reaction almost led to fighting, but the *Social War (3) supervened (Plut. *Sull*. 6).

In the war Sulla distinguished himself on the southern front and in 89, promoted especially by the Metelli, gained the consulship of 88 with Q. *Pompeius Rufus, whose son married Sulla's daughter. Sulla himself married *Caecilia Metella (1), widow of M. *Aemilius Scaurus (1), and was now one of the leading men in the state.

Given the command against *Mithradates Eupator by the senate, he was deprived of it by the tribune P. *Sulpicius Rufus, who transferred it to Marius in order to gain Marius' aid for his political plans. Sulla pretended to acquiesce, but finding support among his troops, who hoped for rich booty in Asia, he marched on Rome and took the unprepared city by force. His officers, except for his quaestor (his relative L. *Licinius Lucullus (2)), deserted him, and his methods shocked even his supporters. He had Sulpicius killed in office and his allies hunted down (Marius escaped to Africa), then passed several laws by armed force. General opposition compelled him to send his army away and allow the election of his enemy L. *Cornelius Cinna (1) as consul 87, over his own candidate P. *Servilius Vatia; and he failed to gain control of the army of Cn. *Pompeius Strabo. Leaving Rome and ignoring a summons to stand trial, he embarked for Greece, where Q. Braetius Sura, a legate of the commander in Macedonia, had already driven the enemy back to the sea. Sulla's hope of safety lay in winning the eastern war: he ordered Sura to return to Macedonia and took charge of the fighting.

Outlawed, but not molested, under Cinna, he agreed (it seems) to refrain from attacking L. *Valerius Flaccus (3) on his march against Mithradates. He himself twice defeated *Archelaus (3) and sacked the Piraeus and (in part) *Athens. After Lucullus had saved Mithradates from C. *Flavius Fimbria, who had taken over Flaccus' army, he made peace with the king at Dardanus (85), granting him his territory, recognition as an ally, and impunity for his adherents in return for surrender of his conquests and support for Sulla with money and supplies. He then dealt with Fimbria, reconciled his own army (disgruntled at the peace with the enemy of Rome) by quartering it on the cities of Asia, which he bled of their wealth, and on hearing of Cinna's death abandoned negotiations with the government and openly rebelled (84). Invading Italy, he was soon joined by most aristocrats—especially Q. *Caecilius Metellus Pius, M. *Licinius Crassus (1), and *Pompey—and within a year defeated all the loyalist forces. Finding the Italians hostile, he swore not to diminish their rights of citizenship, but massacred those who continued resistance (especially the Samnites) and imposed severe penalties and confiscations on whole communities. After securing Rome through his victory at the Colline gate, he was appointed dictator under a law of the *interrex L. *Valerius Flaccus (2), whom he made his *magister equitum*, and was voted immunity for all his actions, past and future. He continued and legalized his massacres by publishing *proscription lists (sometimes fraudulently added to by subordinates: see CORNELIUS CHRYSOGONUS, L.).

During 81 he enacted a legislative programme designed to put power firmly in the hands of the senate, whose numbers (traditionally 300, but now much reduced) he raised to 600 by adlecting *equites* supporting him. In addition to minor reforms, he (1) curbed the tribunate by requiring the senate's approval for tribunician bills, limiting the veto (*intercessio) and debarring ex-tribunes from other magistracies, thus making the office unattractive to ambitious men; (2) restored the *quaestiones*, the number of which he raised to at least seven, to the enlarged senate; (3) increased the number of praetors to eight and that of quaestors to twenty, chiefly to ensure that tenure of provinces was not (in general) prolonged beyond one year; (4) laid down a stricter *cursus honorum*, making the quaestorship as well as the praetorship compulsory before the consulship could be reached at a minimum age of 42; (5) made quaestors automatically members of the senate, thus abolishing the censors' right of selection, and did away with the powerful post of *princeps senatus*; (6) subjected holders of *imperium* outside Italy to stricter control by the senate. His veterans were settled on confiscated land (especially in *Campania and Etruria, see ETRUSCANS) as guarantors of his order. Then, believing in the old prophecy that he now had not long to live, he gradually divested himself of power and restored constitutional government, becoming consul (with Metellus Pius) in 80 and returning to private status in 79. He retired to Campania, where he died of a long-standing disease in 78. His funeral was impressively staged to display the power of his veterans, especially in view of the agitation of the consul M. *Aemilius Lepidus (2). In fact, his constitutional settlement, weakened by concessions during the 70s, was overthrown in 70 by his old adherents *Pompey and *Crassus; but his administrative reforms survived to the end of the republic and beyond.

Despite his mystical belief in his luck (hence his *agnomen* and the *praenomina* of his twin children: see Faustus *Cornelius Sulla), despite his arrogance and ruthlessness, Sulla never aimed at permanent tyranny: he did not even put his portrait on his coins. He wished his settlement to succeed, and he thought it out carefully, no doubt with the help of his associates (some of the group that had supported M. *Livius Drusus (2)), to eliminate the 'two-headedness' (thus Varro) that C. *Sempronius Gracchus had introduced into the republic and to restore a strengthened senate to unchallenged power. His arrangements were consistent, practical, and neither visionary nor reactionary. Yet he had no appreciation of deep-seated problems: he made no attempt to remove the threat of client armies, such as had supported his own rebellion, by putting the senate in charge of providing for veterans, and he seems actually to have abolished the provision of corn to the poor at a controlled price. His own example not only set a precedent for the use of client armies against the republic, but helped to destroy the morale of those on whom resistance to an imitator would depend. After sparing the only powerful enemy of Rome for his personal advantage, he had prepared the ground for that enemy's resurgence by ruining the cities of Asia; he had weeded out those most loyal to the republic in Rome and Italy and rewarded and promoted those who, for whatever reason, had joined in his rebellion. A sense of duty and public service could not be expected of those now making up the senate who had welcomed the opportunities for power and enrichment provided by a rebel; and a generation later it became clear that Italy, having suffered for its loyalty to the republic, was unwilling to defend Sulla's beneficiaries and their corrupt successors against Caesar when he followed Sulla's example.

That example did instil a horror of civil war that lasted for a generation: his beneficiaries praised his rebellion that had brought them to power, but shuddered at his cruelty after victory. Yet that memory was bound to fade. His career and the effects of his victory ultimately made another civil war almost inevitable, and a politic *clementia* now made a successful rebel unobjectionable to the majority.

The main sources are *Plutarch's *Sulla* and *Appian (*Civil Wars* 1 and *Mithridatica*). Sulla's memoirs, edited by L. *Licinius Lucullus (2), pervade the tradition: both Plutarch and Appian's source read and to a considerable extent followed them. The tradition of those who joined Sulla on his return was conveyed in the widely-read history of L. *Cornelius Sisenna, traceable especially in Appian and historians based on Livy. For a sympathetic portrait of Sulla and recent bibliography, especially of the author's own numerous contributions, see A. Keaveney, *Sulla, the Last Republican* (1982). For the main problems of detail recently discussed, see Broughton, MRR 3. 73 ff. The date of his praetorship and proconsulate: T. C. Brennan, *Chiron* 1992, 103 ff. (with bibliography) supersedes earlier discussion. The date of his formal abdication of the dictatorship and assumption of the consulship still seems best put at the beginning of 80, rather than in the middle, especially since he is never given both titles. (For other recent views see Broughton, MRR 3. 73 ff. The older view that he remained dictator until 79 has been abandoned.) On his priesthoods see A. Keaveney, *AJAH* 1982, 150 ff. For the persistence of his reforms, U. Laffi, *Athenaeum* 1967, 177 ff., 255 ff.   E. B.

Cornificius (*RE* 5), **Lucius,** a friend of *Octavian, in 43 BC prosecuted the absent *Brutus for the murder of *Caesar. In 38 he was one of Octavian's naval commanders in the war against Sextus *Pompeius. In 36 he was cut off with three legions at Tauromenium, but extricated them and after a perilous march joined *Agrippa at Tyndaris. He was consul 35, and proconsul of Africa, triumphing on 3 December 32. He rebuilt the temple of *Diana on the *Aventine, and used to commemorate his march of 36 by riding to his dinner engagements on an elephant.

Syme, *Rom. Rev.*, see index; Platner–Ashby 149 f.   T. J. C.; R. J. S.

Cornificius (*RE* 8), **Quintus,** of recent senatorial family, was an orator and poet and a friend of *Catullus and *Cicero (cf. Catull. 38. 1, Cic. *Fam.* 12. 17–30). He wrote a lost *epyllion *Glaucus*. As *quaestor pro praetore* in 48 BC he recovered Illyricum for *Caesar and helped to defend it against the Pompeian fleet (see POMPEY). In 46 he was in charge of Cilicia, perhaps as *legatus pro praetore*; soon, however, Caesar assigned him to Syria and the war against Q. *Caecilius Bassus; what he did in this command is not known. He was praetor (probably) in 45, and in the summer of 44, probably in accordance with Caesar's appointment, he went as governor to Africa Vetus, and continued to hold it for the senate in disregard of the claims of C. *Calvisius Sabinus. In 43 the triumvirs (*Octavian, M. *Antonius (2) (Mark Antony), and M. *Lepidus (3)) proscribed him (see PROSCRIPTION) and assigned the province to T. *Sextius, governor of Africa Nova, who eventually defeated and killed him near Utica (42). He held an augurate. (See AUGURES.)

Syme, *Rom. Rev.*, see index; E. Rawson, *CQ* 1978, 188 ff. (= *Roman Culture and Society* (1991) 272 ff.); Courtney, *FLP* 225 ff. (the poetry). On the coins (*RRC* 509) see R. Fears, *Hist.* 1975, 592 ff.   T. J. C.; R. J. S.

Cornovii, a tribe of western Britain (Staffs., Cheshire, Shropshire), with its capital at *Viroconium (Wroxeter). Legionary fortresses existed in their territory at Viroconium and later at *Deva (Chester); auxiliary forts also were long maintained, whether because of tribal unrest or to control the Welsh metal mines. Few *villas occur, although there were a large number of less Romanized farmsteads in the Severn valley. Romanized settlement largely concentrated at Viroconium. Industries include salt (at Droitwich), copper, and lead workings. The Notitia records a Cohors I Cornoviorum at Newcastle-upon-Tyne.

G. Webster, *The Cornovii*, 2nd edn. (1991).   S. S. F.; M. J. M.

Cornutus

Cornutus, philosopher. See ANNAEUS CORNUTUS, L.

Coronea Town in west-central *Boeotia, scene of two battles. In the first (447 BC), a combined force of Boeotians, *Locrians, *Euboeans, and others, determined to rid central Greece of Athenian control, defeated an Athenian and allied army under Tolmides marching home after reducing *Chaeronea. As a result, the Athenians agreed to evacuate Boeotia. In the second (394 BC), *Agesilaus II of Sparta, returning from Asia Minor, encountered an army of Boeotians and others. *Xenophon (1), who was present, described this battle as 'like no other in my time', probably because after the Spartans had defeated the enemy left, they found the Thebans, who had similarly defeated their left, in their rear. Thereupon the Spartans countermarched their *phalanx and met the Thebans head on. After ferocious fighting, the Thebans managed to break through and rejoin their already defeated allies, but were unable to prevent Agesilaus from continuing his march.

RE 11/2; Xen. Hell. 4. 3. 15 ff.; J. F. Lazenby, The Spartan Army (1985).
J. F. La.

Coronis, daughter of *Phlegyas, and mother of *Asclepius according to the common tradition. She was loved by *Apollo; while pregnant with his child, she was (lawfully or not) united with Ischys, son of Elatus. A raven denounced them to Apollo in *Delphi and was turned from white to black (Pindar, however, says Apollo knew it by his omniscience); the god had Coronis and Ischys killed. But when she was on the funeral pyre, he took the unborn child from her and gave him to the *Centaur Chiron to bring up (Pind. Pyth. 3; Pherec. FGrH 3 F 3 + 35; Ov. Met. 2. 542–632; the famous Hesiodic 'Coronis Ehoie', reconstructed by Wilamowitz, has been deconstructed by M. L. West). The local *Epidaurian legend omits the union with Ischys and has 'the daughter of Phlegyas' expose her baby son in the woods of *Epidaurus where a dog finds and a goat nurtures him (Paus. 2. 26. 3; hence the sacred dogs and the prohibition on goat sacrifice in Epidaurus). See ASCLEPIUS.

M. L. West, The Hesiodic Catalogue of Women: Its Nature, Structure, and Origins (1985); E. Simon, LIMC 6 (1992), 104–6, 'Koronis'.
H. J. R.; F. G.

corrector In the eastern provinces correctores of the *free cities of a province, which were technically independent of the provincial governor, are first attested under *Trajan. He sent a praetorian senator to regulate the state of the *free cities of *Achaia. (*Pliny (2), Ep. 8. 24 gives him advice.) Fewer than twenty such senatorial officials (in Greek διορθωτής or ἐπανορθωτής) are known in the period up to *Diocletian; sometimes the regulatory and adjudicatory duties constitutive of this role were not restricted only to the free cities of a province. They possessed *imperium and their powers were more wide-ranging than those of curatores (see CURATOR REI PUBLICAE) appointed only to supervise the finances of individual cities.

In Italy various senatorial officials (such as *iuridici, imperial legates, and praepositi delegated to oversee specific regions) are attested in the 2nd and 3rd cents. AD. In the early 3rd cent. we find a consular corrector Italiae (ILS 1159), later several more, as well as correctores of Italian regions, where Diocletian established them as regular governors.

A. Premerstein, RE 4. 1646 ff.; B. Thomasson, Legatus (1991), 80 ff.
G. P. B.

corruption is a difficult term; its use largely a matter of perspective. Indeed, from a modern, western point of view, many prac-

tices widely accepted in antiquity seem both immoral and detrimental to good government. But beyond underlining the difference between classical societies and our own, the imposition of expectations or prescriptions derived from contemporary ideals does little to advance our understanding of the past.

Charges of corruption (fraud, *bribery, *ambitus, double-dealing, peculation, or the sale of offices) must always be viewed against the norms of the society in which the accusation is made. It should also be recognized that the majority of the surviving classical evidence comes from works whose primary purpose is denigration. Accusations of corruption—along with other vices and depravities—were part of a complex moralizing rhetoric of execration intended to damn an opponent in as many memorable ways as possible. These claims should be accorded the same degree of credibility as invective concerning dubious ancestry, sexual perversion, or physical *deformity.

It is within this framework that texts on corruption should be read. The insults traded between the 4th-cent. BC Athenian orators *Demosthenes (2) and *Aeschines (1) were an accepted part of their rivalry and their advocacy of competing political programmes (Dem. De cor. 126 ff.; Aeschin. In Ctes. 102 ff.). Such abuse was unexceptional. In his speech against C. *Verres (governor of Sicily, 73–71 BC) *Cicero included accusations of extortion, bribery, and taxation fraud (Cic. Verr. esp. 2. 3). These were aspects of a long, lurid, and highly rhetorical description of Verres' vices—indispensable elements in any properly constructed character assassination. More broadly, before accepting Cicero's version, it should be noted that provincial governorships were widely regarded as a legitimate source of income (Cicero himself did well while governor of Cilicia) and that very few cases of maladministration were ever successfully prosecuted in the Roman courts.

Of course, in the ancient world there were those who acted illegally or immorally. Sometimes they were caught and punished. In AD 38, the citizens of *Alexandria (1) secured the conviction of A. *Avillius Flaccus, a former prefect of Egypt, on charges of extortion (but see entry on him). He was exiled and later—in a display of imperial probity—executed on the orders of the emperor Caligula (see GAIUS (1); Philo, In Flacc. esp. 125 ff.). In the early 3rd cent. AD, the emperor *Severus Alexander discovered an official receiving money for his (apparently illusory) influence at court; a practice known colloquially as fumum vendere—selling smoke. In one of the blunter examples of imperial wit, Severus ordered a fire of wet logs to be made. The offender was suffocated to death (SHA Alex. Sev. 36). But, again, these incidents must be seen in context. On the whole, they represent isolated reactions. They are attempts to police particularly blatant or excessive abuses or to eliminate rivals, rather than evidence of any widespread condemnation of these practices themselves. No doubt the majority played safe, following the maxim of the emperors Septimius Severus and *Caracalla that governors should be careful to take 'neither everything, nor every time, nor from everyone' (Dig. 1. 16. 6. 3).

The continued acceptance of activities which we would regard as corrupt has been seen by some commentators as a sign of an unchecked moral and administrative malaise. These conclusions should be handled with care. It is not clear that officials who profited from their offices were any less reprehensible, or any less effective, than early modern tax farmers. For officials—otherwise unsalaried—the charging of fees for their services was a convenient way both of securing an income and of regulating the many demands on their time. Equally, in societies where access to power and position was dominated by networks of influential connections (see PATRONAGE (NON-LITERARY)), it may be that the payment of money offered an important, alternative channel of advancement. In turn, for *peasants, the payment of fees—albeit irksome—offered a simple and affordable means of mollifying a hostile and ever-threatening officialdom.

These are possibilities. But when dealing with highly emotive or unashamedly moralizing terms, they indicate the importance of viewing the classical world in its own context. Sweeping condemnations of the persistence or toleration of 'corruption' should be resisted. If we insist on judging the ancient world against contemporary standards, we will not achieve much—other than a misplaced smugness as to our own superiority.

W. Schuller (ed.), *Korruption im Altertum: Konstanzer Symposium Oktober 1979* (1982); R. MacMullen, *Corruption and the Decline of Rome* (1988); P. A. Brunt, *Hist.* 1961, 189 ff. (= *Roman Imperial Themes* (1990), 53 ff.); C. Collot, *Revue historique de droit français et étranger* 1965, 185 ff.; S. Perlman, *GRBS* 1976, 223 ff. C. M. K.

Corsica (Κύρνος), a rugged island in the Mediterranean off western Italy, consisting mostly of mountains that rise nearly 3,000 m. (9,000 ft.) and fall sheer into the sea on the west. The eastern coast, however, has good harbours. The tradition that Corsica's earliest inhabitants were Iberians mixed with Ligurians is credible but unprovable. About 535 BC *Etruscans, helped by Carthaginians (see CARTHAGE), expelled the colony which *Phocaeans had established at Alalia 30 years earlier. The island, which apparently fell under Etruscan control for some time, later came under Carthaginian influence. By sending expeditions in 259 and 231, Rome ousted the Carthaginians and organized Corsica with *Sardinia as one province (subsequently in imperial times, exactly when is unknown, Corsica became a separate province). Rome colonized Mariana and Aleria (which became the political and administrative capital) on the east coast, but exercised only nominal authority over the wild interior. Corsica produced shipbuilding *timber, bitter-tasting *honey, granite (see QUARRIES), cattle; the Romans did not work its mines. Vandals, Goths, Ravenna exarchs, and Saracens successively followed the Romans as masters of the island.

Strabo 5. 223 f.; Plin. *HN* 3. 80 (number of Corsican towns exaggerated); Hdt. 1. 165 f.; Diod. Sic. 5. 13 f.; Theophr. *Hist. pl.* 5. 8. 1; the younger Seneca's picture of Corsica as inhospitable and unhealthy (*Dial.* 12. 7 f.; *Epigr.* 1 f.) is untrustworthy: Corsica was his place of exile; see ANNAEUS SENECA (2), L. In general ancient authors seldom mention Corsica. F. von Duhn, *Italische Gräberkunde* (1924) 1. 112; E. Pais, *Storia della Sardegna e della Corsica* (1923); J. and J. Jehasse, *La Nécropole préromaine d'Aleria, Gallia* Suppl. 25 (1973). For *Theophrastus on Corsica see P. M. Fraser in S. Hornblower (ed.), *Greek Historiography* (1994) 185. E. T. S.; T. W. P.

Corstopitum See CORIOSOPITUM.

Cortona (Etr. *Curtun-*), 30 km. (18 mi.) south-east of *Arretium, was an important *Etruscan stronghold with a commanding view of the Val di Chiana. The archaeological evidence indicates that its '*Pelasgian' walls are no earlier than the 5th cent. BC; they are still largely extant, as are two earlier tumuli (*meloni*) and a Hellenistic mausoleum (the 'Tanella di Pitagora'). The most notable piece of local figured bronze-work in the Museo dell'Accademia Etrusca di Cortona (founded 1726) is a magnificent 5th-cent. lamp with sixteen lights, depicting a *gorgoneion*. After the defeat of the Etruscans in 311 BC by Q. *Fabius Maximus Rullianus, Cortona and the two other leading cities of the interior, *Pisa (2) and *Arretium, made treaties with Rome.

BTCGI 5 (1987), 'Cortona'; A. Neppi Modona, *Cortona etrusca e romana nella storia e nell'arte* (1977); D. Briquel, *Les Pélasges en Italie* (1984), 101 ff. D. W. R. R.

Coruncanius, Gaius and **Lucius,** were sent on an embassy to the Illyrian queen *Teuta in 230 BC, the senate's response to an appeal from the Greeks of Issa (Appian) or to Italian complaints about Illyrian *piracy (*Polybius (1)). The younger (Lucius?) was killed by Illyrian pirates, before they reached Teuta (*Appian, with the Issaean envoy Cleemporus as fellow victim) or on the queen's orders after a meeting during which he attacked Illyrian ways and exalted Roman ones (Polybius). The death of their envoy provided the Romans with an occasion for the First Illyrian War (both; see ILLYRICUM). Some combination of these accounts is possible; where it is not, Appian's is to be preferred.

App. *Ill.* 7; Polyb. 2. 8; *RE* 4, 'Coruncanius' 1 and 2; P. S. Derow, *Phoenix* 1973, 118 ff. (discussion of sources); R. M. Errington, *CAH* 8² (1989), 86 ff. (with bibliog.). P. S. D.

Coruncanius (*RE* 3), **Tiberius,** from *Tusculum, consul 280 BC, dictator (for elections) 246, died 243. As consul he celebrated a triumph over *Volsinii and *Vulci and was active with his colleague (P. Valerius Laevinus) against *Pyrrhus. Pontifex from an unknown date, he became (between 255 and 252) the first plebeian *pontifex maximus. As an early jurist, 'primus profiteri coepit' (Pompon. *Dig.* 1. 2. 2. 38), i.e. he was the first to admit members of the public to his consultations, thereby rendering *jurisprudence a profession instead of a mystery.

Broughton, *MRR*, vol. i, 190–91. P. S. D.

Corybantes, nature spirits, often confused with the *Curetes. Like them they danced about the new-born *Zeus, and they functioned together in *Despoina's cult at *Lycosura (Paus. 8. 37. 6). They guard the infant *Dionysus in Orphic myth (see ORPHISM), and dance to the sound of flutes in the orgiastic cults of *Dionysus (Strabo 10. 3. 11) and of *Cybele (Diod. Sic. 5. 49). B. C. D.

Corythus, the name of several obscure mythological persons, including (1) son of *Zeus and husband of *Electra (2) daughter of Atlas; his sons were Dardanus and Iasius (Iasion), see DARDANUS; Servius on *Aen.* 3. 167. (2) Son of *Paris and *Oenone. His story is variously told; the least unfamiliar account is in *Parthenius, *Er. Path.* 34, from *Hellanicus (1) and Cephalon of Gergis. He came to Troy as an ally; *Helen fell in love with him and Paris killed him. *Nicander, quoted by Parthenius, calls him son of Paris and *Helen. H. J. R.

Cos, a fertile island of the Sporades, situated in the SE Aegean, on the north–south trading route along the coast of Turkey and onwards to Cyprus, Syria, and Egypt. After Mycenaean occupation, the island was colonized, in the 'Dark Ages,' by *Dorians, perhaps from *Epidaurus, whose arrival may be identified with the establishment of the settlement attested by the cemeteries at the Seraglio (*c.*1050–*c.*750 BC). It was a member of the Dorian Hexapolis. The Doric dialect continued to be used into late antiquity (e.g. *POxy*. 2771: AD 323).

In the late Archaic period the island was subject initially to Persia and to the Lygdamid (see ARTEMISIA (1)) dynasty of *Halicarnassus, which faced Cos across the straits between the island and Turkey, and then to Athens. Cos is not attested as a member of the *Second Athenian Confederacy (founded 378 BC) and perhaps did not join. In 366 BC, an epochal date in Coan history, the Coans, previously organized in separate cities (e.g. Astypalaea, Halasarna, Cos Meropis) united to form one city-state (see SYNOECISM) after a revolution (Diod. Sic. 15. 76. 2), founding a new city on the NE coast (site of the modern town of Cos), which was fortified and where a good, artificial *harbour was built. The island fell under the control of *Mausolus and probably remained Hecatomnid until 'liberated' by *Alexander (3) the Great's admiral, Amphoterus, in 332 BC.

In the 3rd cent., apart from a period of subjection to *Antigonus (2) Gonatas, Cos was independent, an ally, not a subject, of the Ptolemies (see PTOLEMY (1)), enjoying, as inscriptions attest, a democratic constitution, and trading, political, and cultural links with *Alexandria (1); the poets *Philitas, *Theocritus, and *Herodas exemplify the literary ties. The rich corpus of Coan inscriptions also indicates the continuing vitality and importance of 'traditional' Greek cults through the Hellenistic period. The corpus attests too the continuing activity of Coan doctors, deriving from the local 'school of medicine' founded by *Hippocrates (2), in the 5th cent., whose services Greek states asked for, and gained, usually in times of famine, war or revolution.

With the establishment of Rome as arbiter of foreign policy in Greece and Asia Minor from c.200 BC on, Cos was loyal to the Romans and remained a *civitas libera* (*free city) until the end of the republic. In *Augustus' reign Cos was tributary and was incorporated in the province of Asia. In AD 53 the emperor *Claudius, influenced by his Coan physician, Gaius Stertinius Xenophon, granted the island *immunitas*. The status of Cos as a *civitas libera* ('free city'), attested in the reign of Caracalla, possibly dates back to AD 79. In the late Roman empire the island, incorporated in the *regio Cariae* and the *provincia insularum*, returned to tributary status.

There are rich archaeological remains on Cos, from e.g. the excavations of the famous Asclepium (see ASCLEPIUS), outside the city, to those of the agora, the port quarter, a gymnasium, the Hellenistic temple and altar of *Dionysus, and, in the Roman period, villas with fine mosaics, an odeum, and the so-called Western Excavations, including Roman houses with mosaics, baths, a gymnasium, and an early Christian basilica.

S. Sherwin-White, *Ancient Cos: An Historical Study from the Dorian Settlement to the Imperial Period*, Hypomnemata 51 (1978); K. Höghammar, *Sculpture and Society: A Study of the Connection between Free-standing Sculpture and Society on Kos in the Hellenistic and Augustan Periods*, Uppsala Studies in Ancient Mediterranean and Near Eastern Civilizations 23 (1993). W. A. L.; S. S.-W.

Cosa (mod. Ansedonia), situated on a commanding rocky promontory on the coast of Etruria, 6 km. (4 mi.) south-east of Orbetello. Excavation has revealed no trace of *Etruscan Cusi, which may have occupied the site of Orbetello itself. The surviving remains are those of the Latin colony founded in 273 BC (Vell. Pat. 1. 14. 7), to which belong the irregular circuit of walls, of fine polygonal masonry, and the neatly rectangular street-plan (see URBANISM). The majority of the individual buildings, including the arx and the forum, a basilica, and several temples, date from the town's period of maximum prosperity, in the 2nd cent. BC. Underwater *archaeology has yielded convincing evidence that the harbour of Cosa accommodated a large-scale fishery project (see FISHING).

Amer. Acad. Rome 1951 onwards (reports and pottery studies); E. T. Salmon, *Roman Colonization* (1969); F. E. Brown, *Cosa: The Making of a Roman Town* (1980); A. M. McCann, *The Roman Port and Fishery of Cosa* (1987). J. B. W.-P.; D. W. R. R.

Cosconius (*RE* 11), **Quintus** (early 1st cent. BC), wrote on law, language, and literary history. His works are lost.

Herzog–Schmidt, § 280. R. A. K.

Cosmas Indicopleustes, fl. AD 545, *Alexandrian merchant, Nestorian, and argumentative autodidact. His travels included *Ethiopia, but perhaps not the Indies. His self-illustrated *Christian Topography* (547–9) mixes astronomy, geography, and theology, with some personal observation and humour; it is informative on Ethiopia, India, and Ceylon. Scornfully rejecting classical cosmology and its Alexandrian Monophysite synthesis with *Christianity, Cosmas probably attacked John *Philoponus, who countered in *De opificio mundi* (557–60). Expounding a rectangular, vaulted universe, the model for the Tabernacle, he combines this oriental, Bible-based cosmology with Greek science. His literalistic exegesis follows the Nestorians of Nisibis and Theodore of Mopsuestia, who was controversially condemned in 544 and 553. Cosmas' attitude to classical science likewise belongs to contemporary disputes; he shares interests with John *Malalas (e.g. Christian historical teleology), and shows the cultural vitality of his world; his influence was prolonged and widespread.

Ed. W. Wolska-Conus (1968–73); Eng. trans. J. W. McCrindle (1897); W. Wolska, *La Topographie chrétienne de Cosmas Indicopleustés* (1962). S. J. B. B.

cosmetics Most of the aids to beauty known today were to be found in ancient times on a woman's dressing-table; and both in Greece and Rome men paid great attention to cleanliness, applying *olive oil after exercise and bathing (see BATHS), and scraping the limbs with strigils: dandies went further and would remove the hair from every part of their body with tweezers, pitch-plaster, and depilatories.

Many specimens have been found of ancient cosmetic implements, such as *mirrors, combs, strigils, razors, scissors, curling-tongs, hairpins, nail-files, and ear-picks. Mirrors were usually made of polished metal, rather than glass. Combs were of the tooth-comb pattern, with one coarse and one fine row of teeth. Razors, made of bronze, were of various shapes, the handle often beautifully engraved. Safety-pins (*fibulae*) and brooches had many forms elaborately inlaid with enamel and metal. Ear-picks (*auriscalpia*) were in general use at Rome.

Cosmetics and perfumes were freely used. Athenian women attached importance to white cheeks, as a marker of status; they applied white lead, and also used an orchid-based rouge. Roman women also had a great variety of salves, unguents, and hair-dyes kept in a toilet box with separate compartments for powders, paints, and toothpastes. Several recipes for these commodities are given by *Ovid in his mock-didactic poem *De medicamine faciei*, the strangest being one for a lotion, 'halcyon cream', made apparently from birds' nests and guaranteed to cure spots on the face.

Greek women usually wore their hair arranged simply in braids and drawn into a knot behind; and the same style was frequently adopted in Rome. But under the empire a fashion arose of raising a structure of hair on the top of the head, either in a wig or painfully arranged by a lady's maid. Blondes were fashionable in Rome, and brunettes could either dye their hair or use the false hair which was freely imported from Germany.

Men in early Greece and Rome wore beards and allowed the hair of the head to grow long. From the 5th cent. BC the Greeks cut the hair of their heads short, and from the time of *Alexander (3) the Great they shaved their chins. The Romans followed suit in the 3rd cent. BC, but from the time of Hadrian they again wore beards. See DRESS; PORTRAITURE, GREEK and ROMAN.

Ov. *Medic.*; B. Grillet, *Les Femmes et les fards dans l'antiquité grecque* (1975); M. Dayagi-Mendels, *Perfumes and Cosmetics in the Ancient World* (1989). F. A. W.; M. V.

Cossutii, a Roman family of architects, sculptors, and marble traders. The earliest known Cossutius was employed by *Antiochus IV of Syria (reigned, 175–164 BC) to build the *Olympieum at Athens (Vitr. 7 pref. 15 f.), and probably also on an aqueduct at *Antioch (1). Shortly thereafter, Cossutii appear at *Delos and other Aegean cities, apparently in connection with the *marble trade. Their freedmen were active sulptors: two neo-Classical statues of *Pan from *Lanuvium in the British Musuem are signed by 'Maarkos Kossoutios Kerdon freedman of Maarkos,' and a 'Maarkos Kossoutios Menelaos' signed a drapery fragment once in Rome: some identify him with the Menelaus pupil of Stephanus (pupil of *Pasiteles) who signed the group of *Orestes and *Electra now in the Museo Nazionale Romano (see also RETROSPECTIVE STYLES). Also in Italy, three Cossutii freedmen of the early imperial period were *marmorarii*, specializing in carving, restoration, and cutting inscriptions.

The family achieved equestrian rank during the late republic, but never sought political prominence, stopping at the office of moneyer (in 74 and 44 BC); *Caesar was briefly betrothed to a Cossutia in his adolescence, but repudiated her when he needed a patrician wife to become *flamen Dialis* (Suet. *Iul.* 1. 1).

E. Rawson, *PBSR* 1975, 36 ff. (= *Roman Culture and Society* (1991), 189 ff.); cf. G. M. A. Richter, *Three Critical Periods in Greek Sculpture* (1951), fig. 85 (Pan); A. F. Stewart, *Greek Sculpture* (1990), 221, 229 f., fig. 861 (Orestes and Electra). A. F. S.

costus, the root of *Saussurea lappa*, an Indian plant found mainly in Kashmir; from Skt. *kúṣṭhaḥ*, cf. Gk. κόστος (Theophr. *Hist. pl.* 19. 7. 3; *Peripl. M. Rubr.* 39, 49), Old South Arabian *qst*. Called simply *radix*, 'the root', by the Romans (Plin. *HN* 12. 25. 41), it was used as a spice, a perfume, and an ingredient in various ointments.

J. I. Miller, *The Spice Trade of the Roman Empire* (1969), 84–6; H. G. Rawlinson, *Intercourse between India and the Western World* (1926); F. Bron, *MH* 1986, 132. D. T. P.

Cotta See AURELIUS COTTA.

cotton is first attested from excavations in the Indus valley for the early second millennium BC; cotton plants were imported into *Assyria (1) by Sennacherib *c.*700 BC, who attempted to grow them at *Nineveh (1). Herodotus 3. 106 mentions cotton as an Indian crop. It spread during Hellenistic times into *Ethiopia, *Nubia and Upper *Egypt, and perhaps later into Indo-China. Early fibres seem to come from the tree *Gossipium arboreum* rather than the bush *Gossipium herbaceum*. The word cotton may perhaps be derived from West Semitic *ktn*, at first 'tunic' in general, later the linen tunic worn by priests. A connection with the early Akkadian textile or garment *kutinnu* is doubtful.

E. J. W. Barber, *Prehistoric Textiles* (1991). J. P. Brown, *Journal of Semitic Studies* 1980. S. M. D.

Cotys, Cotyto, a *Thracian goddess worshipped in her homeland and later in *Corinth and *Sicily with orgiastic, Dionysiac-type rites (see DIONYSUS) of music and dance (Aesch. fr. 57 Radt). In Athens *Eupolis made her Corinthian devotees and their notorious rites the subject of his comedy *Baptae* ('Baptists').

RE 11 (1922), 1549–51 'Kotys'. J. D. M.

council See BOULE.

craftsmen See ARTISANS AND CRAFTSMEN; INDUSTRY.

Cragus, a *Lycian god identified with *Zeus (Lycophron 542 and schol.), humanized into a son of Tremiles (eponym of the Tremileis or Lycians), after whom Mt. Cragus was named (Steph. Byz. entry under the name).

T. Bryce, *The Lycians* 1 (1986), 232.

Crannon, city occupying a depression in the middle of the hills between the east and west plains of *Thessaly. Occupied early on by the Thessalians, the city was governed by an aristocratic family, the Scopadae, rivals of the *Aleuadae. Around 515 BC the collapse of their palace, killing several family members, terminated their influence. The small extent of its territory and the proximity of *Larissa stunted the city's subsequent development. In the 4th cent. Dinias of Pherae became tyrant with the support of his home-city. In the *Lamian War *Antipater (1) defeated the allied Greeks near Crannon (322 BC). See also SIMONIDES. B. H.

Crantor of Soli in Cilicia (*c.*335–275 BC), philosopher of the early *Academy, and the first Platonic commentator. He studied under *Xenocrates (1), and cohabited with *Arcesilaus (1), whom he had won over to the Academy from the Peripatos. His influential commentary on Plato's *Timaeus* sided with those who denied a literal creation of the world. It included a detailed mathematical interpretation of the harmonic intervals constituting the world soul. His ethical writings were much admired. One famous passage depicted a contest between the various Goods, with Virtue the eventual winner. His *On grief* (Cicero's model for his own *Consolatio*) opposed the Cynic-inspired ideal of eradicating this emotion (see CONSOLATION). See also ATLANTIS.

H. J. Mette, *Lustrum* 1984, 7 ff. (testimonia and bibliography); H. Dörrie, *Der Platonismus in der Antike* 1 (1987). D. N. S.

Crassus See LICINIUS CRASSUS (1), M.

Craterus (1) (d. 321 BC), marshal of *Alexander (3) the Great. First attested in charge of a Macedonian infantry *taxis*, he commanded the left of the phalanx at *Issus and *Gaugamela. After the removal of *Philotas and *Parmenion, in which he played an unsavoury role, he assumed Parmenion's mantle and commanded numerous independent detachments during the campaigns in Sogdiana and India. At Opis (324) he was appointed viceroy in Europe in *Antipater (1)'s stead and commissioned to repatriate 10,000 Macedonian veterans. Alexander's death found him in Cilicia, and he could not participate in the Babylon settlement at which his role in Macedonia was (somewhat mysteriously) modified. In 322 he moved to Europe, where his forces were instrumental in winning the *Lamian War. The following year he co-operated with Antipater, now his father-in-law, in the invasion of Asia Minor, where he died heroically in battle against *Eumenes (3). A staunch defender of Macedonian tradition (and perhaps an uncomfortable figure at Alexander's court), he was intensely popular with the Macedonian rank and file, who cherished his memory.

Berve, *Alexanderreich* 2, no. 446; Heckel, *Marshals* 107 ff. A. B. B.

Craterus (2) (321–*c.*255 BC), son of *Craterus (1) and Phila, *Antipater (1)'s daughter, was appointed governor of Corinth and Peloponnese (*c.*280), and later viceroy of Attica and Euboea, by his half-brother, *Antigonus (2) Gonatas. In 271 he tried to assist Aristotimus, the Elean tyrant and in 266 checked *Areus of Sparta at the Isthmus.

Crates

It is open to question whether the same Craterus produced the Ψηφισμάτων συναγωγή, a collection of Athenian decrees in at least nine books, with extensive commentary (see EPIGRAPHY, GREEK). Arranged chronologically and concentrating on the 5th cent., the work came out of the same Peripatetic tradition that produced *Theophrastus' study of customs and the Aristotelian *Constitution of Athens*; see ATHENAION POLITEIA.

FGrH 342; CAH 7²/1 (1984).   F. W. W.; K. S. S.

Crates (1), Athenian comic poet, won three victories at the City *Dionysia, the first almost certainly in 450 BC (Jer. *Chron*. Ol. 82. 2, *IG* 2². 2325. 52); he was an actor before he was a poet (Anon. *De Com* 9. 8. 7). We have six titles. *Animals* depicted a situation in which animals refuse to be eaten by men. (See ANIMALS, ATTITUDES TO.) It seems to have contained a comic prophecy of an era in which all work will perform itself (see METAGENES and PHERECRATES). *Aristophanes (1) (*Eq*. 537 ff.) speaks of him affectionately, and *Aristotle (*Poet*. 1449ᵇ7) says that he was the first to discard ἰαμβικὴ ἰδέα and create plots which were 'general' (καθόλου), i.e. to advance beyond the ridiculing of real individuals.

Kassel–Austin, PCG 4. 83 ff. (CAF 1. 130 ff.).   K. J. D.

Crates (2), of *Thebes (1) (*c*.368/365–288/285 BC), *Cynic philosopher and poet. Having gone to Athens as a young man, he became a follower of *Diogenes (2) and gave his wealth to the poor. How far he maintained Diogenes' philosophy is disputed. He claimed to be 'a citizen of Diogenes', espousing a similar cosmopolitanism; notoriously enacted Diogenes' prescriptions regarding free and public sex in his relations with Hipparchia, with whom he shared a Cynic way of life; and often expressed ethical sentiments as extreme and intolerant as Diogenes'. But he did not insist on the complete renunciation of wealth or that everybody should become a Cynic, and he conceded a certain legitimacy to existing occupations; and the deployment of his considerable charm and kindliness in proclaiming his message, comforting the afflicted, and reconciling enemies, won him the titles of 'door-opener' and 'good spirit' and a reputation for humanity which endured throughout antiquity. Granted their obvious differences in personality and missionary approach, Crates seems himself to have followed Diogenes rigorously, while (sometimes) allowing greater latitude to others. This partial moral relativism makes him the link between 'hard' and 'soft' Cynicism; he is also, through *Zeno (2) (his most famous follower), the link between Cynicism and *Stoicism.

Of Crates' considerable poetic production the most important surviving fragments are witty and resourceful reworkings of passages from *Homer and *Solon, which the ancient tradition rightly interpreted as serio-comic Cynic statements rather than mere literary parodies.

For bibliography see CYNICS.   J. L. Mo.

Crates (3) of Mallus, son of Timocrates, was a contemporary of *Demetrius (12) of Scepsis (Strabo 14. 676) and *Aristarchus (2). He visited Rome as envoy of *Attalus II of *Pergamum, probably in 159 BC, when his lectures, during his recovery after breaking his leg in the *Cloaca Maxima, greatly stimulated Roman interest in scholarship (Suet. *Gram*. 2; see, however, Walbank, HCP 3. 415: the king may have been *Eumenes (2) II and the date 168). He may have helped king Eumenes II organize the library at Pergamum. He was mainly interested in *Homer, but we have no list of his writings. He also concerned himself with *Hesiod, *Euripides, *Aristophanes (1), and *Aratus (1), and laid claim to

the title of κριτικός ('critic'), which implied vastly wider interests than those of γραμματικός ('grammarian'). Strabo 2. 5. 10 reports that he constructed a sphere to represent the world, on which the map of the land mass could be shown.

The Pergamenes and the Alexandrians were divided on the rival principles of 'analogy' and 'anomaly' in language. (See ANALOGY AND ANOMALY.) *Aristophanes (2) and *Aristarchus (2), of *Alexandria (1), in editing Homer sought the correct form (or meaning) of a word by collecting and comparing its occurrences in the text, a procedure more novel in their age than in ours. Further, they tried to classify words by their types of form (cf. our declensions), in order by reference to the type to decide what was correct in any doubtful or disputed instance. Thus in Homer Aristarchus accented Κάρησος after Κάνωβος, πέφνων after τέμνων, οἰῶν after αἰγῶν; and similarly as to inflexions (see APOLLONIUS (13)). Crates, on the contrary, borrowed his linguistic principles from the Stoics (see STOICISM), and sought in literature a meaning which he already knew a priori. Not only words (see ETYMOLOGY) but literature likewise they thought a μίμησις θείων καὶ ἀνθρωπείων ('representation of things human and divine'; Diog. Laert. 7. 60), an accurate reflection of truth, and on this basis they carried to ludicrous extremes the allegorical method of interpretation, in order to secure the support of Homer for Stoic doctrines. In such features as inflexion they saw only confusion wrought upon nature's original products by man's irregular innovations and perversions. *Cleanthes had named this unruly principle of language ἀνωμαλία ('anomaly'), illustrating it without much difficulty from the Greek declensions. This term and doctrine, and the allegorical method, were adopted by Crates and his school, to whom, consequently, the Alexandrian classification of forms (Crates seems to have written chiefly on noun anomalies) seemed futile in practice and wrong in principle.

The controversy gained importance with the growth of purism (see GLOSSA), and its extension from Greek to Latin; it is reflected in *Varro's *De lingua Latina*. Compromises attempted by both Greek and Roman scholars left the problem unsettled. 'Quare mihi non invenuste dici videtur, aliud esse Latine, aliud grammatice loqui' ('Therefore, it seems to me that the remark, that it is one thing to speak Latin and another to speak grammar, was far from unhappy'.) Quint. *Inst*. 1. 6. 27.

H. Steinthal, *Geschichte d. Sprachwissenschaft bei den Griechen u. Römern*, 2nd edn. (1891), 121 ff.; H. J. Mette, *Parateresis: Untersuchungen zur Sprachtheorie des Krates von Pergamon* (1952); J. Collart, Entretiens Hardt, 9. 119 ff.; R. Pfeiffer, *History of Classical Scholarship: From the Beginnings to the End of the Hellenistic Age* (1968), 235, 238–46.

P. B. R. F.; R. B.; N. G. W.

Crateuas, medical botanist and personal physician of *Mithradates VI of Pontus (120–63 BC), after whom he named *mithridatia*, the mall, liliaceous *Erythronium dens-canis* L. (Plin. *HN* 25. 26. 62). Crateuas composed two or more tracts, known only by fragments: (1) a herbal, title not preserved, which featured coloured drawings of plants accompanied by botanical descriptions and specific instructions for medical employment (ibid. 25. 4. 8); (2) *Root Cutting and Gathering* (scholia on Nic. *Ther*. 681a (ed. A. Crugnola, 1971)), a book on the pharmacology of roots and medicinal plants, detailing preparation techniques. Crateuas' treatises were well known to *Dioscorides (2), whose *Materia medica* derived some details from *Root Cutting* and other works, indicated by occasional citations. Perhaps some of the botanical illuminations in the Anicia Juliana manuscript of AD 512 (cod. Vindobonensis med. gr. 1) are based on Crateuas' drawings, but recent opinion leans against direct borrowing (Riddle, *Dioscorides*

190–1). The Anicia Juliana codex also gives crabbed fragments from Crateuas' lost herbal. See also BOTANY; PHARMACOLOGY.

TEXT Frs. and testimonia, ed. M. Wellmann, *Pedanii Dioscuridis Anazarbei De materia medica* (1906–14), 3. 139–46.

GENERAL LITERATURE M. Wellmann, *Krateuas*, Abh. d. könig. Gesellschaft d. Wissenschaften zu Göttingen (Phil.-hist. Kl.) NF 2/1 (1897); F. E. Kind, *RE* 11/2, 1644–6, 'Krateuas' 2; G. Watson, *Theriac and Mithridatium* (1966), 33–7; J. Riddle, *Dioscorides on Pharmacy and Medicine* (1985), 181–91.

J. Sca.

Cratinus was regarded, with *Aristophanes (1) and *Eupolis, as one of the greatest poets of Old Attic Comedy (see COMEDY (GREEK), OLD). He won the first prize six times at the City *Dionysia and three times at the *Lenaea (*IG* 2². 2325. 50, 121). We have 27 titles and over 500 citations. The precisely datable plays are: *Cheimazomenae* at the Lenaea in 426 BC (hyp. 1 Ar. *Ach.*), *Satyrs* at the Lenaea in 424 (hyp. 1 Ar. *Eq.*), and *Pytine* at the City Dionysia in 423 (hyp. 6 Ar. *Nub.*). Three more are approximately datable: *Archilochi* treats (fr. 1) the death of *Cimon as recent, and therefore comes not long after 450; *Dionysalexandros* (see below) attacked *Pericles (1) for 'bringing the war upon Athens', and must belong to 430 or 429; and fr. 73 *Thraltae* suggests that Pericles has just escaped the danger of *ostracism (444/3). We do not know when Cratinus died; Ar. *Pax* 700 ff. speaks of him (in 421) as dead, but the context is humorous and its interpretation controversial. One category of titles is especially characteristic of Cratinus: *Archilochi, Dionysi, Cleobulinae, Odysses, Pluti,* and *Chirones* (see also TELECLIDES). In Ὀδυσσῆς it appears from fr. 151 that the chorus represented *Odysseus' crew; it is possible that the 'new toy' of fr. 152 was a model of his ship brought into the orchestra. The play is mentioned by Platonius (*Diff. com.* 7 and 12) as an example of 'Middle Comedy' ahead of its time, i.e. as containing no ridicule of contemporaries. There are papyrus fragments of *Pluti*, one of which indicates that the chorus explained its identity and role to the audience in the parodos. The hypothesis of *Dionysalexandros* is also largely preserved in a papyrus; in this play *Dionysus—as the title suggests—was represented as carrying *Helen off to Troy; there was a chorus of *satyrs. In *Pytine* Cratinus made good comic use of his own notorious drunkenness (cf. Ath. 39c), represented himself as married to Comedy, and adapted in self-praise the compliment paid to his torrential fluency and vigour by Ar. *Eq.* 526 ff.

Cratinus' language and style were inventive, concentrated, and allusive, and Aristophanes was obviously much influenced by him, but Platonius (*Diff. com.* 14) describes his work as comparatively graceless and inconsequential. It is clear from Ath. 495a, Hdn. 2. 945, and Galen, *Libr. Propr.* 17 that Cratinus was the subject of commentaries in Hellenistic times.

Kassel–Austin, *PCG* 4. 112 ff. (*CAF* 1. 11 ff.). K. J. D.

Cratippus of Athens, historian. A continuator and critic of *Thucydides (2), he has been identified with the historian from Oxyrhynchus (see OXYRHYNCHUS, THE HISTORIAN FROM), though there are difficulties.

FGrH 64; H. Bloch, *Harv. Stud.* Suppl. 1 (1940), 313; A. W. Gomme, *More Essays* (1962), 126 ff.; W. K. Pritchett, *Dionysius of Halicarnassus: On Thucydides* (1975), 67 f.; G. S. Shrimpton, *Theopompus the Historian* (1991), 183–95. S. H.

Cratylus, a younger contemporary of *Socrates. He pressed the doctrine of *Heraclitus to an extreme point, denying to things even the slightest fixity of nature. According to *Aristotle he was *Plato (1)'s first master in philosophy, and Plato drew the conclusion that since fixity does not exist in the sensible world

there must be a non-sensible world to account for the possibility of knowledge. Plato in his *Cratylus* makes Cratylus maintain that falsehood is impossible and that all words in all languages are naturally appropriate to the meanings with which they are used, and exhibits him as uncritically accepting Socrates' glib etymologies.

Testimonia in DK 65; D. J. Allan, *AJPhil.* 1952. W. D. R.

credit, the temporary transfer of property rights over money or goods, was central to the functioning of ancient society. The great majority of credit operations would have been informal transactions between relations, neighbours, and friends, marked by the absence of interest, security, or written agreement. Although under-represented in our sources, these day-to-day transactions, with their basis in reciprocity, created and strengthened bonds between individuals. Hence the hostility felt by *Plato (1) (*Leg.* 742c) towards formal credit agreements, implying as they did a lack of trust. In Athens (where a detailed construction is possible), the range of possible sources of credit extended beyond family and friends to include professional moneylenders, bankers, and usurers. In these latter cases, relationships between the parties would be more impersonal, justifying interest and formal precautions. From the Roman world, detailed testimony from the republic focuses on credit transactions between members of the élite, juggling their resources with an eye towards political advantage. *Cicero writes of the obligation to take over the debts of an *amicus* (*Off.* 2. 56; see AMICITIA). Those thrown back on formal sources of credit could turn to a range of specialist lenders: *argentarii, coactores argentarii,* and *nummularii.* See BANKS.

J. Korver, *De terminologie van het crediet-wezen en het Grieksch* (1934, repr. 1979); P. C. Millett, *Lending and Borrowing in Ancient Athens* (1991); E. Cohen, *Athenian Economy and Society* (1992); C. T. Barlow, *Bankers, Moneylenders and Interest Rates in the Roman Republic* (1978); M. W. Frederiksen, *JRS* 1966, 80 ff.; J. Andreau, in E. Frézouls (ed.), *Le Dernier Siècle de la république romaine et l'époque augustéenne* (1978), 47 ff.; J. Andreau, *La Vie financière dans le monde romain* (1987); D. Rathbone, *Economic Rationalism and Rural Society in Third-century AD Egypt* (1991). P. C. M.

Cremera (mod. Fossa di Formello, variously called Valca or Valchetta), stream flowing past *Veii to join the Tiber at *Fidenae. Three hundred members of the Fabian clan perished on its banks (477 BC), after establishing a blockhouse from which to raid Veientine territory. See GENS; VEII. E. T. S.

Cremona, a Latin colony (see IUS LATII), founded in 218 BC on the north bank of the Po in north Italy (Polyb. 3. 40; Tac. *Hist.* 3. 34). Cremona staunchly supported Rome against *Hannibal, although thereby it suffered so severely that it required additional colonists (Livy 21. 56; 27. 10; 37. 46). Its territory was confiscated for a colony of *veterans in 41 BC (Verg. *Ecl.* 9. 28). There was extensive *centuriation of its territory and it continued prosperous, although sacked (and then restored) by Vespasian in AD 69. It was an important military base, with a permanent parade ground, and the centre for a bishopric from the 5th cent., if not before.

G. Pontiroli (ed.), *Cremona romana* (1985); P. Tozzi, *Storia padana antica* (1972). E. T. S.; T. W. P.

Cremutius (*RE* 2) **Cordus, Aulus,** the historian, writing under *Augustus (Suet. *Tib.* 61. 3) and *Tiberius, treated the period from the Civil Wars to at least 18 BC (Suet. *Aug.* 35. 2). Refusing to glorify Augustus, he celebrated *Cicero, *Brutus, and *Cassius, 'the last Roman'. Prosecuted at the instigation of *Sejanus (Tac. *Ann.* 4. 34 f.), he committed suicide (AD 25). His work was burnt, but copies, preserved by his daughter, were published in abridged form under *Gaius (1) (Cass. Dio 57. 24. 4). *Pliny (1) the Elder and Seneca the Younger (L. *Annaeus Seneca (2)) used his work.

Peter, *HRRel.* 2. cxiii and 87; Syme, *Tacitus* 337 f.; R. Bauman, *Impietas in Principem* (1974), 99 ff.
               A. H. McD.; B. M. L.

Creon (1), of *Thebes (1), son of *Menoeceus (1), brother of Iocasta. (See OEDIPUS.) He offered her and the kingdom to anyone who would rid Thebes of the *Sphinx. After Oedipus' fall and again after the death of *Eteocles, he became king or regent of Thebes. During the attack by the *Seven against Thebes, he lost his son *Menoeceus (2). Another son, *Haemon (3), was either killed by the Sphinx or took his own life after the suicide of *Antigone (1), his espoused, or on a later occasion. Creon was almost as unfortunate in his daughters, whom he gave in marriage to *Heracles and *Iphicles. The former, Megara, was killed by Heracles in a fit of madness (the details in Apollod.: see Frazer's index under 'Creon'). Creon was killed by *Theseus in a battle over the burial of the Seven (Stat. *Theb.* 12. 773 ff.).

Creon (2), a king of *Corinth whom *Medea killed by magic and fled, leaving her children behind to be killed by the Corinthians. *Euripides has her kill Creon's daughter (*Jason's betrothed) with a poisoned costume (*Med.* 1136 ff.) and murder her own children (1273 ff.).

Although the name 'Creon' means simply the 'lord' or 'ruler', and is used to fill in gaps in genealogies, it is a measure of the skill and artistry of *Sophocles and *Euripides that they make these two figures into credible, if not lovable, human beings.

Apollod. *The Library*, trans. J. G. Frazer (Loeb, 1921). In art: *LIMC* 6/1 (1992), 112–17 (Creon (1)).
               A. Sch.

Cresilas, Greek sculptor from Cydonia in Crete, active c.440–410 BC. His statues of *Pericles (1) and Dieitrephes shot through with arrows (Plin. *HN* 34. 74; Paus. 1. 23. 3, 25. 1) stood on the Acropolis; their signed bases survive, plus a dedication to Athena and two more at Hermione (Argolid, see ARGOS (2)) and *Delphi; one of his works was later displayed at *Pergamum. According to Plin. *HN* 34. 53, his *Amazon for *Ephesus was placed third after those of *Polyclitus (2) and *Phidias. Copies of Pericles' head survive, and the Sciarra/Lansdowne-type Amazon is often ascribed to him.

J. Marcadé, *Recueil de signatures* (1953), 1. 62 ff.; A. F. Stewart, *Greek Sculpture* (1990), 78, 162 ff., 262, figs. 390, 397 f.
               A. F. S.

Cretan cults and myths Most reflect the island's important bronze age past. *Diodorus (3) records the tradition that the Greek gods had their origin in Crete and thence visited the world to confer their benefactions on mankind (Diod. Sic. 5. 46. 3; 64. 2; 77. 4; see EUHEMERUS). *Zeus Cretagenes was worshipped in the central Cretan cities of *Gortyn (IC 4. 183. 19), Lato, and Lyttus, and in the west. Legend placed his birth in a Cretan cave on Mt. Ida or Dicte (Psychro). He also died in Crete, and from Hellenistic times his tomb was shown on the island (Diod. Sic. 3. 61. 2), prompting *Callimachus (3)s' outburst that all Cretans are liars (Hymn 1. 8). The cult was old, since Zeus Dictaeus already appears on a Linear B tablet from Cnossus (Fp 1). Zeus Welkhanos represents the fusion with a native youthful male *paredros* of the Minoan goddess of nature. Coins from Phaestus (5th/4th cent. BC) show the young god sitting in a tree and holding a bird in his lap (B. Head, *Hist. Num.*[2] (1911), 473). The Theodaesia were celebrated in central and eastern Crete in honour of Zeus' periodic *epiphany. It was an occasion of renewal and of initiation of the youth to full citizenship. It recalls the renewal of *Minos' kingship by Zeus in a cave every nine years (Strabo 10. 4. 8; cf. Pl. *Minos* 319c; *Leg.* 624d; Hom. *Od.* 19. 179).

*Apollo Delphinius had cults in *Cnossus (Dor. Delphidios, *SIG* 712. 13), Hyrtacina, and Dreros. The connection with dolphins (Hymn Hom. Ap. 495) probably arose from the local adaptation of a pre-Greek name. The substance of the cult also concerned initiation of the young (F. Graf, *MH* 1979, 2–22). The Archaic Delphinium at Dreros combined the Minoan form of the bench-shrine with the interior sacrificial hearth of the Mycenaean megaron. The temple contained bronze figures of the trinity of *Leto, Apollo, and *Artemis. Leto's (Dor. *Lato*) cults at Gortyn and Phaestus (as Phytia) celebrated the withdrawal of young men from the *agela* on reaching manhood and marriageable age. At the Ecdysia festival they stripped off the girlish clothes of their childhood. The implications of sex change are reflected in myth (Ov. *Met.* 9. 666–797; Ant. Lib. *Met.* 17), while the attendant institutionalized *homosexuality gave much offence to other Greeks.

Three Minoan goddesses who were absorbed by Artemis but retained important cults in historic times are *Eileithyia in her cave at Amnisus, *Britomartis ('Sweet Maid') near Lyttus and at Olous, with a wooden image said to be by *Daedalus in her temple, and Dictynna at Lisus and Cydonia. Myths were told around Dictynna's graecised name: she either invented hunting nets (*diktya*) or fled into fishermen's nets to escape Minos' unwelcome attentions (Diod. Sic. 5. 76. 3). Athena's cult as Tritogeneia in Cnossus, and as Wadia ('Sweet Athena') in Castri, also had a Minoan background, as did that of Aphrodite and *Hermes at Kato Symi. *Asclepius' cult was popular in Crete in Hellenistic times. His main sanctuary at Lebena attracted visitors throughout Crete and from across the Libyan sea (Philostr. *VA* 4. 34).

*Demeter's sacred marriage with *Iasion in a thrice-ploughed field which produced the divine child Plutus preserved a Minoan sacred ritual (Hom. *Od.* 5, 125–8; Hes. *Theog.* 969–70). Similar origins accounted for the story of Europa's abduction by Zeus in the shape of a bull, and the myth of *Ariadne who died in more ways than any other heroine. Crete's best known legends of *Minos, of the Athenian Daedalus who built the labyrinth of Cnossus, and the annual Athenian tribute of seven youths and maidens until *Theseus slew the Minotaur, mirror Cretan influence in the Aegean during the bronze age. Minos built the first fleet (Thuc. 1. 4. 1), and when his grandson *Idomeneus (1) joined the Achaean expedition against Troy, there were 90 or 100 cities on the island (Hom. *Il.* 2, 649; *Od.* 19. 174; Strabo 10. 4. 15; Diod. Sic. 5. 79. 3–4). See MINOAN CIVILIZATION.

Minoan Crete pioneered the working of metal in the western Aegean giving rise to the myths about the Dactyles, *Curetes, and the bronze robot *Talos (1) who burnt Crete's enemies in his fiery embrace.

Nilsson, *MMR*; *GGR* 1³. 312–15, 319–24, 347–50, 554 f.; R. W. Hutchinson, *Prehistoric Crete* (1962); R. F. Willetts, *Cretan Cults and Festivals* (1962); F. Schachermeyr, *Die minoische Kultur des alten Kreta* (1964).
               B. C. D.

Crete, Greek and Roman (for prehistoric Crete see MINOAN CIVILIZATION). Evidence for the history of the island comes both from literary sources, inscriptions, and coins and from excavation and (increasingly) field survey. The transition from bronze to iron age is still not fully understood, but some sites go back into the Dark Ages (Dictaean cave; the Idaean cave—finds start in the 8th cent.; refuge sites, e.g. Karphi and Vrokastro), but in historical times the island was predominantly *Dorian (Eteocretan, a non-

Greek language, was used in places in the Archaic period, and traces survived into the 2nd cent. BC). Cretans prided themselves that *Zeus was born on Crete (see preceding article), they developed a peculiar temple form, and also eschewed the *hero-cults found on the Greek mainland. Of Homer's 'Crete of the hundred cities' over 100 names survive, but there seem to have been in the Classical and Hellenistic periods only about 40 city-states: Archaic Dreros, Prinias, and Axos, and 5th–2nd-cent. Lato, are well known archaeologically; *Cnossus, *Gortyn, and Lyttus were initially the most important, along with Cydonia and Hiera-pytna. The island's position on the sea-routes to and from *Cyprus, the Levant, and *Egypt secured it an important place in the development of Archaic Greek art: important innovations were attributed to the mythical Cretan *Daedalus. It had a reputation as the home of mercenary slingers and archers, and of lawgivers (see GORTYN; LAW IN GREECE). Aristocratic society persisted in the island, and the constitutions (though without kings) resembled that of *Sparta, which was said to have been derived from Crete, and impressed *Plato (1) and *Aristotle. In the Classical period the island lay outside the mainstream of Greek history. From the mid-3rd cent. her foreign relations centred on the new and unstable Cretan League, the Attalid dynasty (see PERGAMUM), and the intrigues of Macedon. In 216 BC the cities accepted *Philip (3) V as protector, but strife soon returned, both against Rhodes and still more between the cities, especially Cnossus and Gortyn. By this time Crete was reputed as a home of pirates second only to *Cilicia (see PIRACY). Their activities were encouraged by Philip, who realized his hope of thereby injuring Rhodes. The pirates supported Mithradates VI of Pontus against Rome, and when M. *Antonius (Creticus) intervened to punish them, he was beaten off Cydonia (71), but Q. *Caecilius Metellus (Creticus) crushed the islanders (69–67). Crete became a Roman province, united with Cyrene, under a senator of praetorian rank, and the old league became the provincial council; from the 4th to 7th cent. AD Crete formed a province on its own in the diocese of Macedonia. *Jews are known on Crete from the 1st cent. BC to the 5th cent. AD, and Christians from the earliest times (St Paul's Epistle to Titus). The prosperity of the island under Roman rule was disrupted by major earthquakes in the 4th cent., though between c.450 and 550 numerous Christian basilicas were built. From the early 7th cent. Crete was increasingly vulnerable to raids by Slavs and then Arabs, to whom it fell in AD 827–8. See also LANDSCAPES (ANCIENT GREEK).

Inscriptiones Creticae, ed. M. Guarducci, 4 vols. (1935–50); Arist. *Pol.* 2. 10; Polyb. 6. 45–7; Strabo 10. 474–84; A. C. Bandy, *The Greek Christian Inscriptions of Crete* (1970).; Coins: G. Le Rider, *Monnaies crétoises du V*ᵉ *au I*ᵉʳ *siècle av. J.-C.* (1966); J. N. Svoronos, *Numismatique de la Crète ancienne*, 2 vols. (1890), with *AE* 1889, 193–212; *RPC* 1992. J. Boardman, *CAH* 3²/3 (1982); *Creta antica* (1984); H. van Effenterre, *La Crète et le monde grec de Platon à Polybe* (1948); D. Gondicas, *Recherches sur la Crète occidentale* (1988); E. Kirsten, *Das dorische Kreta* 1 (1942); S. Kreuter, *Aussenbeziehungen kretischer Gemeinden zu den hellenistischen Staaten im 3. und 2. Jh. v. Chr.* (1992); E. I. Mikroyiannakis, *I Kriti kata tous ellinistikous chronous* (1967); S. P. Morris, *Daidalos and the Origins of Greek Art* (1992); L. F. Nixon, *Pepragmena tou ST' Diethnous Kritologikou Sinedriou* 1/2 (1990); A. Petropoulou, *Beiträge zur Wirtschafts- und Gesellschaftsgeschichte Kretas in hellenistischer Zeit* (1985); I. F. Sanders, *Roman Crete* (1982); C. Tiré and H. van Effenterre, *Guide des fouilles françaises en Crète*, 2nd edn. (1978); D. Tsougarakis, in N. M. Panagiotakis (ed.), *Kriti: Istoria kai politismos* (1987), and *Byzantine Crete from the 5th Century to the Venetian Conquest* (1988); R. F. Willetts, *Cretan Cults and Festivals* (1955), and *Ancient Crete: A Social History* (1965); J. Wilson Myers and others, *The Aerial Atlas of Ancient Crete* (1992).
W. A. L.; L. F. N., S. R. F. P.

Creusa (Latin form of Greek 'Kreousa'), the feminine form of *Creon, 'ruler'. The name is borne by several mythical characters. (1) Daughter of *Erechtheus of Athens, wife of *Xuthus, and mother of *Achaeus (1), *Ion (1), and Diomede (Hes. fr. 10a. 20–4 M–W). *Sophocles' *Creusa* presumably concerned this Creusa, and may have been identical with his *Ion*. She is also an important character in *Euripides' *Ion* (in which *Apollo was father of Ion by Creusa). (2) Daughter of *Priam, wife of *Aeneas, and mother of *Ascanius. According to Virgil she was lost in the flight from Troy and her ghost then prophesied the future (*Aen.* 2. 730–95). In earlier authors the wife of Aeneas had been called Eurydice and had escaped with him. (3) Alternative name for Glauce, daughter of the Corinthian *Creon (2), in Latin authors like Prop. 2. 16. 30.

LIMC 'Kreousa' 1–3; on Creusa (1) see R. Parker, in J. Bremmer (ed.), *Interpretations of Greek Mythology* (1987), 206 f.; on (3), L. Preller, revised by C. Robert, *Die Griechische Heldensage* (1921), 871 n. 3.   A. L. B.

Crimea See CHERSONESUS (2); SPARTOCIDS.

Crimissa (mod. Cirò), Crotoniate colony (see CROTON), founded c.600 BC, 30 km. (18½ mi.) north of Croton, by *Philoctetes traditionally. Nothing is known about the city, which may have been abandoned by the 4th cent. BC, but the nearby sanctuary of Apollo Alaios was in use until the Hellenistic period. Excavation has uncovered houses, cult buildings, and votive deposits.

K. L.

Crinagoras, *epigrammatist from *Mytilene. Mytilenean inscriptions document three embassies in which Crinagoras participated, to Caesar in 48/7 and 45 and to Augustus in 26/5 BC. The dates of his epigrams range between 45 BC and AD 11 and perhaps 15. Evidently he lived to a considerable age. M. *Claudius Marcellus (5), *Antonia (3), Cleopatra Selene, *Tiberius, and perhaps the elder *Iulia (3) are among his subjects. *Parthenius wrote a book called *Crinagoras* (*Etym. magn.* entry under ἅρπυς), now lost. Many of his 51 epigrams in the Greek Anthology were included in the *Garland* of *Philippus (2).

Gow–Page, *GP* 2. 210–60; A. Cameron, *LCM* 1980, 129–30.

A. D. E. C.

Crisa, on a spur close to the modern Chryso, controls the roads from the coast of the Crisaean Gulf to *Amphissa and to Delphi. It was a Mycenaean site of some importance, but its greatest prosperity was attained in the 7th cent. BC when it had a share in the foundation of *Metapontum. In the First *Sacred War Crisa was destroyed and its fertile plain was dedicated to Pythian *Apollo. The name Crisa and the name *Cirrha were often interchangeable as our sources show.

P-K, *GL* 1. 2. 686 ff. and 715 n. 63.   N. G. L. H.

Critias (c.460–403 BC), one of the *Thirty Tyrants at Athens. Born of an old wealthy family to which *Plato (1) also belonged (*APF* 8792) he, like his close friend *Alcibiades, was a long-time associate of Socrates. He is often included with the *sophists, and surviving fragments of his tragedies and other works evince an interest in current intellectual issues. Later scholars were uncertain whether some plays ascribed to him may have been the work of *Euripides (*Vit. Eur.*); there is still disagreement about the authorship of *Sisyphus*, which included a speech giving a rationalistic account of the origin of human belief in the gods (*TGF* 1. 43 F 19).

Critias was implicated in the mutilation of the *herms (415) but was released on the evidence of *Andocides. He played little

Critius

or no part in the oligarchic coup in 411. In perhaps 408 he proposed the recall of Alcibiades. The latter's second exile in 406 was probably linked to Critias' own exile; he went to *Thessaly where he may have assisted in a revolt by democratic forces. He was an admirer of *Spartan ways, about which he wrote several works, and upon the Spartan defeat of Athens in 404 he returned from exile to become one of the Thirty Tyrants. In *Xenophon (1)'s narrative (*Hell.* 2. 3–4) he appears as the leader of the extremists, violent and unscrupulous, who proposes the execution of his colleague *Theramenes; but the account in *Ath. pol.* (34–40) does not mention him. He was killed fighting against Thrasybulus in spring 403. His reputation did not recover after his death; but Plato honoured his memory in several dialogues.

Fragments: DK 88. Guthrie, *Hist. Gk. Phil.* 3; M. Ostwald, *Popular Sovereignty* (1986), 462–5.   M. Ga.

Critius, Athenian (?) sculptor, active *c.*490–460 BC. Author, with Nesiotes, of six dedications on the Acropolis, all bronzes. The two were famed for their bronze Tyrannicides (Harmodius and *Aristogiton), commissioned in 477/76 to replace those by *Antenor (2), stolen by *Xerxes in 480. Copies of them survive; they are often considered to represent the 'official birthday' of the early Classical style in Greek sculpture. Attributions include the 'Critius Boy' from the Acropolis.

A. F. Stewart, *Greek Sculpture* (1990), 133, 135 f., 251 f., figs. 219 f., 227 ff.   A. F. S.

Crito, doctor. See STATILIUS CRITO, T.

Crito (1), a wealthy and devoted friend of *Socrates, who in *Plato (1)'s *Apology* offers to stand surety for him, and in the *Crito* plans for Socrates' escape from prison. Seventeen dialogues are ascribed to him (Diog. Laert. 2. 121).

APF 8823. Testimonia: G. Giannantoni, *Socratis et Socraticorum Reliquiae* (1990) 2. 635–6.   M. Ga.

Crito (2), one of the latest poets of New Comedy (see COMEDY (GREEK), NEW); he won second prizes at the *Dionysia in 183 and 167 BC (IG 2². 2321. 151, 210 = 3 B 3 coll. 3b. 5, 4a. 21 Mette). From his Φιλοπράγμων ('Busybody') an eight-line fragment (3) survives, in which the Delians (see DELOS) are called '*parasites of the god (i.e. *Apollo).'

FRAGMENTS Kassel–Austin, PCG 4. 346–8.
INTERPRETATION Meineke, FCG 1. 484; A. Körte, RE 11/2 (1922), 1932, 'Kriton' 2.   W. G. A.

Crito (3), of *Argos (2), a *Neopythagorean philosopher, of whose *On Wisdom* Stobaeus (2, 157–8) quotes fifteen lines of Doric prose, about the mind as created by God so as to enable man to contemplate God.

H. Thesleff, *The Pythagorean Writings of the Hellenistic Period*, Acta Academiae Aboensis, humaniora 30/1 (1965), 109.   D. J. F.

Critolaus (RE 3), of *Phaselis, head of the *Peripatetic school. His dates are unknown, but he was probably an old man when he took part, with *Carneades the Academic (see ACADEMY) and *Diogenes (3) the Stoic (see STOICISM), in the philosophers' delegation to Rome in 156/5 BC. His headship of the school marks a renewal of its scientific and philosophical activities. The fragments of his writings show some acquaintance with Aristotelian doctrines, though much of it may be second-hand. He defended the Aristotelian doctrine of the eternity of the world against the Stoic periodic conflagration, and taught that the soul was made of the fifth element, i.e. the heavenly aether. In ethics he held the

highest good to be a composite of the goods of the soul, those of the body, and external goods, while emphasizing the far greater importance of the first. His criticisms of the Stoic distinction between 'passions' (πάθη) and 'good feelings' (εὐπάθειαι) reflect a general opposition to the monistic Stoic psychology. He was a severe critic of *rhetoric and refused to recognize it as a proper art; but he recognized the superiority of *Demosthenes (2), and may have invented the story that the latter learned his rhetoric from the *Rhetoric* of *Aristotle.

TEXT F. Wehrli, *Die Schule des Aristoteles* 10 (1959), 49–74.
STUDIES F. Wehrli, in Überweg-Flashar, 588–91; A.-H. Chroust, *Acta Antiqua Academiae Scientiarum Hungaricae* 1965, 369 ff.   R. W. S.

Croesus, last king of *Lydia (*c.*560–546 BC), son of *Alyattes. He secured the throne after a struggle with a half-Greek half-brother, and completed the subjugation of the Greek cities on the Asia Minor coast. His subsequent relations with the Greeks were not unfriendly; he contributed to the rebuilding of the Artemisium at *Ephesus and made offerings to Greek shrines, especially *Delphi; anecdotes attest his friendliness to Greek visitors and his wealth. The rise of *Persia turned Croesus to seek support in Greece and Egypt, but *Cyrus (1) anticipated him: Sardis was captured and Croesus overthrown. His subsequent fate soon became the theme of legend: he is cast or casts himself on a pyre, but is miraculously saved by Apollo and translated to the land of the *Hyperboreans or becomes the friend and counsellor of Cyrus.

Hdt. bk. 1; FGrH 90 (Nic. Dam.) F 65, 68; Bacchyl. 3. *British Museum Cat. Sculpture* (1928) 1/1. 38; *Louvre, Vases antiques gr.* 197 (= CAH 4², plates vol. (1988), no. 230); G. Radet, *La Lydie* (1893), 206 ff.; J. M. Cook, CAH 3²/3 (1982), ch. 39 a; M. Mellink CAH 3²/2 (1991), 651 ff.   P. N. U.; S. H.

Cronus, the youngest of the *Titans, sons of *Uranus (Heaven) and *Gaia (Earth). His mythology is marked by paradoxes. According to one myth he castrated his father at the instigation of his mother. From his marriage with his sister Rhea the race of the (Olympian) gods was born: *Hestia, *Demeter, *Hera, *Hades, *Poseidon, and *Zeus. Fearing to be overcome by one of his children he swallowed them on birth, save only the last, Zeus, saved by Rhea, who wrapped a stone in swaddling-clothes which Cronus swallowed instead. The infant Zeus was hidden in Crete, where he was protected by the *Curetes. Later, by the contrivance of Gaia, Cronus vomited up all his children and was overcome by them after a desperate struggle. He was incarcerated in Tartarus (Hes. *Theog.* 137–8, 154 ff., 453 ff.). Later authors give roughly the same story, differing mainly on his place of exile, clearly under the influence of the second group of Cronus myths.

In these Cronus is pictured as king of the *golden age (Hes. *Op.* 111), a utopian wonderland. He maintains this role in the hereafter at the borders of the earth (ibid. 169), as the ruler of the *Islands of the Blest (Pind. *Ol.* 2. 70). Another variant posits him on a far away island, asleep and inactive (Plut. *De def. or.* 420a). Later he becomes the model for the Italic god *Saturnus, civilizer of Latium and Italy.

The stark contradiction between the extreme cruelty manifested in the first version and the utopian blessings in the second has fostered conjectures concerning different origins. While Cronus as king of the golden age was supposed to have been an authentic Greek (or at least Indo-European) contribution, the cruel tyrant was assumed to have been derived from another culture. Indeed, similar myths of swallowing fathers can be found all over the world, but none as close as the Hurrian–Hittite myth

410

of Kumarbi, first published in 1945. Scholars generally agree that Hesiod must have (indirectly) borrowed the theme from this near eastern myth. This, however, does not suffice to explain the blatant inconsistencies in the presentation of one divine person in a single work by Hesiod, the more so since the same inconsistency returns in ritual.

Since Cronus is predominantly a mythical god, rites, cults, and cult-places are scarce. *Olympia boasted an ancient cult. His festival, the Cronia, celebrated in Athens and a few other places after the harvest, is a carnevalesque feast of exultation and abundance: masters and slaves feast together (Plut. *Mor.* 1098b; Macrob. *Sat.* 1. 10. 22). One source even reports that masters served their servants during the festival (Accius, *FPL* p. 34). However, other (legendary) cult practices involve horrible human sacrifices, while foreign gods associated with human sacrifice, like Bel, are consistently identified with Cronus. Though pre-Greek and *Asia Minor influences cannot be discarded, the central contradiction in both myth and ritual seems to reveal the very essence of their message and function; both refer to exceptional periods in which stagnation and reversal of the normal codes find expression in both positive and negative imagery.

W. Burkert, *The Orientalizing Revolution* (1992; Ger. orig. 1984); H. S. Versnel, in H. S. Versnel (ed.) *Transition and Reversal in Myth and Ritual* (1993), 89–135. *LIMC* 6/1 (1992), 142–7 (in art). H. S. V.

Croton (mod. Crotone), *Achaean colony in the 'toe' of Italy, founded *c.*710 BC. It flourished in the 7th and 6th cents., reaching its apogee after its destruction of *Sybaris in 510 BC. It was the hegemon of the Italiote League, which met at the Crotoniate sanctuary of *Hera Lacinia, and controlled a large territory. Pythagorean factions (see PYTHAGORAS) dominated politics but were ejected in the late 6th cent. Despite defeat by *Locri and *Rhegium (Strabo 6. 1. 10), Croton remained powerful until 379 BC, when it was captured by *Dionysius (1) I, remaining under his control for twelve years. Leadership of the Italiote League was lost to *Tarentum, and Lucanian and Bruttian raids caused strain. In 270, Croton became a Roman ally (see SOCII), but revolted during the Hannibalic War (see PUNIC WARS), and was not recaptured until 205/4. A Roman colony was founded (194 BC) and inscriptions and excavation show that the sanctuary of Hera was in use until the 3rd cent. AD. Archaeological evidence for Croton is slight, but surveys of the territory show declining settlement-density in the 4th cent., with a resurgence in the Roman period.

E. Greco, *Magna Grecia* (1981); M. Giangiulio, *Ricerche su Crotone arcaica* (1989); various authors, *Crotone, Atti di Convegno di Studi di Magna Graecia* 23 (1984); *Crotone e la sua storia tra IV e III secolo a.c.* (1993). K. L.

crowns and wreaths

Greek (στέφανος, στεφάνη). These were worn by Greeks for a variety of ceremonial purposes: by priests when *sacrificing, by members of dramatic choruses, orators and symposiasts (see SYMPOSIUM). They served as prizes at games and as awards of merit. Originally made from the branches of trees and plants, each having a specific connotation (e.g. olive/*Olympian victory, funerals; vine and ivy/*Dionysus; rose/*Aphrodite, symposium), crowns began to be made in gold and occasionally silver. Less solid examples were made for funerary use, and some are preserved in the archaeological record. Gold crowns occur frequently in the epigraphic sources relating to Athens and *Delos, where, however, the figures given represent their cost in silver drachmae rather than their weight in gold. The crown-

making stage was often bypassed, and the recipient simply pocketed the money.

Roman Crowns and wreaths were awarded by the Romans as decorations for valour, and in the republic the nature of the achievement dictated the type of award, the most distinguished being the *corona obsidionalis* or *graminea*, a crown of grass granted to a man who raised a siege. Pliny (*HN* 22. 4) lists only eight recipients, ending with *Augustus. The *c. civica* made of oak leaves was granted to anyone who had saved a comrade's life in battle. The *c. navalis* (also *classica* or *rostrata*—decorated with a ship's prow) was reserved for distinguished conduct in naval battles. A *c. muralis* or *c. vallaris* was awarded to the first man to scale a town or camp wall under assault. A gold crown (*c. aurea*) rewarded general acts of gallantry, as did a miniature spear (*hasta pura*), standard (*vexillum*), necklaces (*torques*), bracelets (*armillae*), and metal discs (*phalerae*) which could be attached to body armour. Commanders celebrating a *triumph wore a crown of laurel, those with the lesser honour of an *ovatio, a crown of myrtle. In the late republic rank rather than merit became the overriding factor in the type of award. This was developed in the imperial period and although the *corona civica* was open to all soldiers, most military decorations were granted on a fixed scale according to rank. For example, by the 2nd cent. AD senators of consular rank alone received the *corona classica*, and were entitled to four crowns, spears, and standards; men of praetorian rank received three of each; equestrians received a combination of one or two crowns, spears, and standards. Centurions and *primipili*, along with ordinary soldiers, received necklaces, bracelets, and discs, but might also be honoured with a crown or spear, or both.

GREEK Ath. 15. 669f–686c. E. Egger and E. Fournier, Dar.–Sag. 'Corona'; Kranz, *RE* 11. 1588–607; M. Blech, *Studien zum Kranz bei den Griechen* (1982).
ROMAN V. A. Maxfield, *The Military Decorations of the Roman Army* (1981). J. B. C.

crucifixion seems to have been a form of punishment borrowed by the Romans from elsewhere, probably *Carthage. As a Roman penalty it is first certainly attested in the *Punic Wars. It was normally confined to slaves or non-citizens and later in the empire to humbler citizens; it was not applied to soldiers, except in the case of desertion. *Constantine I abolished the penalty (not before AD 314). Two inscriptions of the 1st cent. AD from *Cumae and *Puteoli have been found containing the contract of the undertaker both of funerals and of executions of this kind (see LEX (2), 'lex libitinaria'). The general practice was to begin with flagellation of the condemned, who was then compelled to carry a cross-beam (*patibulum*) to the place of execution, where a stake had been firmly fixed in the ground. He was stripped and fastened to the cross-beam with nails and cords, and the beam was drawn up by ropes until his feet were clear of the ground. Some support for the body was provided by a ledge (*sedile*) which projected from the upright, but a footrest (*suppedaneum*) is rarely attested, though the feet were sometimes tied or nailed. Death probably occurred through exhaustion: this could be hastened through breaking the legs. After removal of the body the cross was usually destroyed. See also PUNISHMENT.

M. Hengel, *Crucifixion in the Ancient World*, chs. 4–10; L. Bove, *Labeo. Rassegna di diritto romano* 1, 1955–1967. G. R. W.; A. W. L.

Ctesias (late 5th cent. BC) of *Cnidus, Greek doctor at the court of *Artaxerxes (2) II, who wrote a history of *Persia (Περσικά) in 23 books, consisting mostly of romantic stories, based on either narrative oral traditions or court gossip, and now preserved only in fragments. Ctesias' claim that he consulted the royal records (Diod. Sic. 2. 32. 4) is not corroborated by the information he gives. Both in antiquity and modern times his work has been found unreliable, albeit entertaining. He also wrote the first separate work on *India (᾿Ινδικά) and a geographical treatise (Περίοδος).

FGrH 3c, 688; Fr. trans., J. Auberger, *Ctésias: Histoires de l'Orient*, (1991); F. Jacoby, *RE* 11/2. 2032–73; J. M. Bigwood, *Phoenix* 1978, 19–41; R. Drews, *The Greek Accounts of Eastern History* (1973); H. Sancisi-Weerdenburg, *Achaemenid History I: Sources, Structures, Synthesis* (1987), 33–46; J. Hofstetter, *Die Griechen in Persien* (1978), 111–13.　　H. S.-W.

Ctesibius, inventor (fl. 270 BC), was the son of a barber in *Alexandria (1), and employed by *Ptolemy (1) II. He was the first to make devices employing '*pneumatics', i.e. the action of air under pressure. His work on the subject is lost, but descriptions of some of his inventions are preserved by *Philon (2), *Vitruvius, and *Heron. These include the pump with plunger and valve (Vitr. 10. 7; Heron, *Pneumatics* 1. 28), the water-organ (Vitr. 10. 8), the first accurate water-clock (Vitr. 9. 8. 4 ff.; see CLOCKS) and a war-catapult (Philon, *Belopoeica* 43). No great theoretician, Ctesibius was a mechanical genius, some of whose inventions were of permanent value. It is probable that many of the basic ideas in the works of Philon and Heron on mechanical devices derive from him.

A. G. Drachmann, *Ktesibios Philon and Heron* (1948); Fraser, *Ptol. Alex.* 1 427 f., 431 ff.　　G. J. T.

Ctesiphon, on the river Tigris, c.96 km. (60 mi.) above *Babylon, was a village garrisoned by *Parthia from c.140 BC as an Asiatic stronghold opposite Hellenistic *Seleuceia (1), becoming (from c.50 BC?) a city and *Arsacids' residence within roughly circular walls. After Roman invasions (AD 116, 166) had damaged Ctesiphon but especially Seleuceia, Ctesiphon became *Babylonia's chief city, taken by *Septimius Severus (197–8), on whose arch at Rome (203) it may appear, domed. Ardashir (*Artaxerxes (4)) made it the new *Sasanid-empire capital. Successors built palaces and added suburbs; ruins of fortifications and an impressive brick-vaulted palace, Taq-e-Kesra ('Arch of Chosroes'), survive. In 636 Arabs took it.

M. Streck, *Alte Orient* 16, 3/4 (1917); *RE* Suppl. 4. 1102 ff.; O. Reuther, *Antiquity* 1929, 434 ff.; J. H. Schmidt, *Syria* 1934, 1 ff.; M. A. R. Colledge *Parthian Art* (1977), see index. Severus' arch: D. Strong, *Roman Art*, 2nd edn., rev. R. Ling and M. A. R. Colledge (1988), 200, pl. 154.
　　M. A. R. C.

Cuicul (mod. Djemila), a mountain town lying between *Cirta and Sitifis on the main road linking *Numidia and *Mauretania. Originally a *castellum* ('fortress'), dependent on Cirta, it became a *veteran colony under *Nerva. Originally a walled town of c.7 ha. (17 acres), it soon spread southwards in the 2nd cent. AD, when it received further settlers from elsewhere in Africa, including the Cosinii from *Carthage: agricultural prosperity increased and many public buildings were erected. A citizen of Cuicul, Claudius Proculus, was governor of Numidia AD 208–10. The extensive ruins, excavated between 1909 and 1958, include two fora, an arch of *Caracalla, an imposing temple to the *gens Septimia*, baths, and two Christian basilicas and a baptistery. Cuicul's prosperity in late Roman times is further demonstrated by the numerous figured *mosaics from its spacious houses, but after the 5th cent. the city went into rapid decline, and there are no records of Cuicul after 553.

PECS 249–50; P. A. Février, *Djemila* (1968); M. Blanchard-Lemée, *Maisons à mosaïques du quartier central de Djemila (Cuicul)* (1975).
　　W. N. W.; R. J. A. W.

cults See RELIGION (various entries).

culture-bringers, mythical figures who are credited with the invention of important cultural achievements. Around the 6th cent. BC the Greeks started to ascribe a number of inventions to gods and heroes. So *Athena Polias planted the first *olive-tree, and as Ergane she invented weaving (see TEXTILE PRODUCTION); *Demeter taught sowing and grinding corn; *Dionysus was connected with viticulture (see WINE), and *Apollo thought up the *calendar. Of the heroes, Argive *Phoroneus invented fire, and the Rhodian *Telchines metal-working; pan-Hellenic *Heracles founded the *Olympian Games. In Athens, *Prometheus became highly important; to him it owed politics, logic, architecture, meteorology, astronomy, arithmetic, literature, etc.—in short all *technai* (Aesch. *PV* 506).

In the 4th cent., interest shifted towards inventors of political traditions and finding new names for all kinds of inventors. The first development reflects the growing importance of philosophy, the latter the growing consciousness of local traditions.

Especially the sophists developed a great interest in the origin of culture, witness *Protagoras' lost *On the Original State of Man*. *Prodicus went so far that he considered Demeter and Dionysus to have been deified because of their inventions. His views were an instant success and he was followed by *Euhemerus, whose Zeus takes a great interest in 'inventors who had discovered new things that promised to be useful for the lives of men' (*FGrH* 63 F 20). Euhemerus was translated into Latin by *Ennius, but the Romans on the whole showed little interest in culture-bringers.

K. Thraede, *RAC* 'Erfinder' 2; A. Henrichs, *Harv. Stud.* 1984, 139–58 (Prodicus and Euhemerus).　　J. N. B.

Cumae (Gk. Cyme; mod. Cuma), *Euboean colony, founded c.740 BC, 16 km. (10 mi) north-west of Naples (Neapolis). This was the earliest colony on the Italian mainland, and dominated coastal *Campania from 700 to 474 BC, in turn founding *Neapolis, Dicaearchia, Zancle, Abella, and possibly *Nola. Under the rule of *Aristodemus (2) it came into conflict with the *Etruscans, but defeated them at *Aricia in 505 BC and again in 474, in alliance with *Syracuse. In 421, it fell to the *Oscans during their conquest of Campania (Diod. Sic. 11. 51; 12. 76). Although substantially Oscanized, Greek culture was never completely eradicated (Strabo 5. 4. 4). During the Archaic period, it enjoyed cordial relations with Rome, but these soured after the Oscan conquest. It became a *civitas sine suffragio* (see CITIZENSHIP, ROMAN) in 338, and remained loyal to Rome in the *Punic Wars. In 180 it adopted Latin as its official language, and probably obtained full citizenship soon after. The developing port of *Puteoli eclipsed Cumae economically, but it remained important. Many of the Roman élite had villas there, and the harbour and acropolis were sumptuously rebuilt by Augustus, who also granted Cumae colonial status (*CIL* 10. 3703–4). The Cumaean *Sibyl and cult of *Apollo were important in Augustan ideology (Virg. *Aen.* 6), and Cumae was popular among Roman aristocrats because of its Greek culture. During the 3rd–4th cents. AD, it declined, but the acropolis remained strategically important until the 8th cent.

M. W. Frederiksen, *Campania* (1984); N. K. Rutter, *Campanian Coinage* (1979); R. F. Paget, *JRS* 1968; E. Gàbrici, *Mon. Ant.* 1913; A. Maiuri, *The Phlegraean Fields* (1957); S. De Caro & A. Greco, *Campania* (1981).
　　K. L.

Cunaxa, a small town on the *Euphrates near Baghdad, where

*Cyrus (2), younger son of *Darius II of Persia, was defeated and killed by his elder brother, *Artaxerxes (3) II, in 401 BC. The battle is chiefly interesting for the ease with which Cyrus' Greek *mercenaries, on his right, defeated Artaxerxes' left, with the loss of only one man. *Xenophon (1), who was serving among the Greeks, has left us a vivid description of their charge at the double, shouting their war-cry—'Eleleu'—and some clashing their spears on their shields to frighten the enemy horses (*An.* 1. 8. 17–20). Even after Cyrus himself had been killed and the rest of his army had fled, the Greeks still managed to rout the remainder of Artaxerxes' army, in a second attack. It was after this battle, and the subsequent treacherous capture of their commanders, that the Greeks began the long march home which is the main subject of Xenophon's *Anabasis.*

Xen. *An.* 1. 8; Plut. *Artaxerxes* 7. 3 ff. J. K. Anderson, *Xenophon* (1974); J. M. Bigwood, *AJPhil.* 1983; H. D. Westlake, *Studies* (1989), ch. 17.
J. F. La.

cuneiform is wedge-shaped writing developed from impressions of clay tokens and incised pictograms by impressing the triangular cross-section of a reed upon clay. First used for *Sumerian, it was adopted also for proto-Elamite, *Akkadian, Hurrian, Hittite, Urartian (see URARTU), *Elamite, Old *Persian, and alphabetic *Ugaritic languages between *c*.3000 BC and *c*. AD 50. The script uses more than 500 signs to write syllables, logograms, determinatives, etc., each sign having various values, and was written on clay, stone, and waxed writing-boards. It was gradually replaced by alphabetic scripts.

D. O. Edzard, *Reallexikon der Assyriologie* 5 (1976–80), 544–68, 'Keilschrift'.
S. M. D.

Cunobel(l)inus, son of *Tasciovanus, king of the *Catuvellauni. He moved against the *Trinovantes and later Kent. Suetonius called him 'rex Britanniarum' (*Calig.* 44. 2). Under him *Camulodunum (Colchester) became a major *oppidum* and centre for Roman imports. His coins bear Latin inscriptions and emblems of mythology. He died before AD 43. See BRITAIN.

S. S. Frere, *Britannia*, 3rd edn. (1987).
C. E. S.; M. J. M.

Cupido amans, a poem of unknown authorship, in sixteen hexameters, on Cupid in love; post-Augustan.

TEXTS *Anth. Lat.* 240 Riese, 233 Shackleton Bailey; with trans., Duff, *Minor Lat. Poets.*
J. H. D. S.

cura(tio), curator Among many more general meanings these words refer to a specific duty inhering in a regular office; thus *Cicero (*Leg.* 3. 7) defines the *aediles as *curatores* of the city (i.e. its buildings, *sanitation, *policing, etc.), the *annona, and the games (see LUDI). As Roman commitments expanded, some tasks came to surpass the powers of annual magistrates. In 145 BC the praetor Q. *Marcius Rex (1) was prorogued in order to complete an *aqueduct. This was later avoided by the conferment of special *curae*, in principle detached from office, for time-consuming tasks. In particular, the far-flung network of *roads in Italy, or its constituent parts, frequently received *curatores* after 100 BC; thus *Caesar gained popularity by lavish spending as *curator* of the *via Appia *c*.67. Other *curae* were conferred as required. In 78 the consul Q. *Lutatius Catulus (1) was made *curator* for restoring the Capitol (Gell. *NA* 2. 10. 2), a task that dragged on for years. About 105 the *princeps senatus M. *Aemilius Scaurus (1) superseded the quaestor at Ostia L. *Appuleius Saturninus in the latter's regular charge of imports of corn. In 57, *Pompey, in a major innovation, received a *cura annonae* with *imperium *pro

consule for five years. *Augustus assumed a *curatio annonae* (*RG* 5. 2) based on this precedent at a time of famine. (He already had the *imperium*.) But he refused a *cura morum* (*RG* 6. 1), no doubt as reminiscent of Caesar's *praefectura morum*. Occasional *curationes* continue under the empire when required, e.g. the consular *curatores* for the restoration of *Campania appointed by *Titus after the great eruption of *Vesuvius (Suet. *Tit.* 8. 4). However, under Augustus many routine functions of magistrates came to be entrusted to boards of experienced (consular or praetorian) *curatores*. In 22, he established praetorian *curatores* for distributing corn, in 20 for the roads, in 11 for the city's water supply. The senate decree creating that office (copied by Frontinus, *Aq.* 2. 100) shows the regulations establishing the powers and duties of such boards. *Curatores* for public buildings and for monitoring and regulating the *Tiber followed in Augustus' lifetime, and several more such boards later. The system was at once imitated in Roman colonies and municipalities and for a long time ensured the smooth functioning of urban life.

RE 'cura, curatores'.
E. B.

curator rei publicae (or *civitatis*, etc.), in Greek λογιστής, was an official of the central government; the first certain example occurs under *Domitian (*ILS* 1017). *Curatores* normally were appointed by the emperor, of elevated social rank (senatorial, equestrian, or provincial notable) and by geographic origin foreign to the city (or cities) where they held office. The known chronological and geographic distribution, during the 2nd and 3rd cent., AD of this official is uneven. They are, for example, well attested in Italy and Asia (though many cities never received a *curator*, while the first known example in North Africa occurs only under *Septimius Severus. Their prime function was to investigate and supervise, on a short-term basis, the finances of individual civic communities; in the provinces they thus supplemented the administrative powers of provincial governors.

By the early 4th cent., probably as a result of the administrative reforms of *Diocletian, *curatores* were elected by local councils (though the nomination may have had to be confirmed by the emperor) and they were normally local politicians who had completed all the other magistracies of their city. The original distinguishing features of social pre-eminence, foreign origin, and appointment from above had disappeared and the *curator* had evolved into a senior magistracy *within* the civic community.

W. Lieberman, *Philol.* 1897, 290 ff; G. P. Burton, *Chiron*, 1979, 465 ff.
G. P. B.

Curetes, young, divine male warriors of *Crete. They attend upon Zeus, the *megistos Kouros* of the Dictaean Hymn of Palaiokastro who leads them (*daimones*, 1. 52) up Mt. Dicte. As nature spirits and associated with the mountain goddess Rhea (Eur. fr. 472 N; cf. the *Idaean Dactyls), they protect the fruit of the fields (Diod. Sic. 5. 65; Paus. 4. 31. 9). Their name is in fact identical with *kouroi* (*Il.* 19. 248), and they are the male equivalent of the *Nymphs, themselves often called *Kourai*. Curetes and Nymphs were born together (Hes. fr. 198 M–W) and acted as joint witnesses to Cretan oaths (*GDI* 5041).

In their best-known myth the Curetes are connected with the birth of *Zeus *Kretagenes* and dance noisily about his cave on Dicte (Apollod. 1. 1. 7; Diod. Sic. 5. 70), or Ida, while clashing their shields either to drown the infant's cries (Callim. *Hymn* 1. 52–4) or to frighten off his father *Cronus (Strabo 10. 3. 11). In the same manner the Curetes protect *Leto's children from jealous Hera (Strabo 14. 1. 20). Their lively armed dance, like

curia

Zeus' leaps in the Dictaean Hymn (*BSA* 1908/9, 339–56; *Syll.*³ 685), promoted the growth of fields and flocks.

The find of bronze shields (8th–6th cent. BC) in the Idaean cave suggests that human *kouroi* annually performed war dances there in a kind of initiation ritual of young men (cf. the role of the *Anakes, and *Dioskouroi* ('sons of Zeus', see DIOSCURI) who were identified with the Curetes in Phocis, Paus. 10. 38. 7). The dancers re-enacted Zeus' birth and death (the Curetes buried the god in his cave, Ister *FGrH* 334 F 48). The confusion with other collective divine groups such as *Cabiri and *Corybantes (Paus. 8. 37. 6), and an association with Dionysiac cult (Strabo 10. 3. 11; see DIONYSUS), hint at orgiastic elements in the armed initiatory rites. The number and names of Curetes varied in tradition, like their complex genealogy (Schwenn *RE* 11 (1922), 2203–6).

Ancient tradition also knew of an *Acarnanian or *Aetolian tribe Curetes (*Il.* 9. 529 and schol.; Strabo 10. 3. 1). See also CRETAN CULTS AND MYTHS.

H. Jeanmaire, *Couroi et Courètes* (1939); B. Hemberg, *Die Kabiren* (1950), 277, 297; M. L. West, *JHS* 1965, 155 f.; Burkert, *GR* 261 f.

H. J. R.; B. C. D.

curia (1) was the most ancient division of the Roman people, already existing under the kings. The *curiae* were 30 in number (ten for each Romulean tribe, see TRIBUS). Some bore local names (*Foriensis, Veliensis*), others personal ones (*Titia*). Membership of the *curiae* was determined by birth, but as they also seem to have been local groupings (Dion. Hal. *Ant. Rom.* 2. 7. 4), each with its own meeting-place, it is probable that originally they comprised the families resident in particular localities. The use of the term *curia* for a division of the people and for a meeting-place supports the etymology from †*co-viria* = 'gathering of men' (Kretschmer, *Glotta* 1920, 145–57). Each *curia* was headed by an official called the *curio*, aged at least 50 and elected for life. One of these leaders was chosen as head of all the *curiae*, the *curio maximus*. The post was held by patricians until 209 BC, when a plebeian was elected for the first time. This fact tends to confirm the view of our sources (Dion. Hal. 4. 12. 20; Asconius, p. 76 C) that the *curiae* included both *patricians and plebeians (see PLEBS).

The *curiae* were probably the basis of the oldest military organization and certainly the constituent elements of the oldest Roman assembly (see COMITIA); they had a special devotion for Juno Quiritis, and celebrated the annual festivals of the *Fornacalia and *Fordicidia. A comparable subdivision of the tribe seems to have existed at *Iguvium (Umbria).

Curia was also the name given to the assembly-places of many other corporations, and especially to the senate-house (see CURIA (2)). As constituent voting units of citizen assemblies, *curiae* are attested in Latium (*Lanuvium) and in many Italian and provincial *municipia and *coloniae*, of both Latin and Roman status. They were especially common in Africa. During the empire *curia* was also the usual name for a municipal senate, to which elections of magistrates were transferred from the people. It comprised mostly ex-magistrates chosen for life (at least in the west), and in the late empire turned into a hereditary caste, called the *curiales*, whose lives and property were under the control of the state as security for the collection of taxes. See also DECURIONES.

G. Humbert, Dar.–Sag. 1/2. 1627; Mommsen, *Röm. Staatsr.* 3. 99; P. De Francisci, *Primordia Civitatis* (1959), 572 ff.; A. Momigliano, *JRS* 1963, 108 ff. (= *Terzo Contributo*, 571 ff.); R. E. A. Palmer, *The Archaic Community of the Romans* (1970); J.-C. Richard, *Les Origines de la plèbe romaine* (1978), 197 ff. For the *curiae* in *municipia*, Jones, *Later Rom. Emp.* 2. 724.

A. M.; T. J. Co.

Curia (2), the senate-house of Rome. The original building on the north side of the *Comitium in the forum Romanum, ascribed to Tullus *Hostilius, was orientated by cardinal points. It was restored by Sulla after 81 BC, damaged following the funeral of P. *Clodius Pulcher in 52 and rebuilt by Faustus *Cornelius Sulla. Caesar began a new building, on a slightly different site and orientation in 44 as part of his forum, which was inaugurated by *Augustus in 29. Restored by *Domitian in AD 94, it was rebuilt by *Diocletian after the fire of 283, following the Caesarian plan. The sumptuous oblong hall (25.6 × 17.8 m.: 84 × 58 ft.) of brick-faced concrete decorated externally with imitation stucco ashlar, has a central door facing a magistrates' dais and lateral marble benches.

A. Bartoli, *Curia Senatus* (1963); Steinby, *Lexicon* 331 ff.; Nash, *Pict. Dict. Rome* 1. 301 ff.

J. D.

curialis See DECURIONES.

Curiatius (*RE* 7) **Maternus,** Roman dramatist. The host and main speaker in *Tacitus' *Dialogus*, he champions poetry against oratory and explains the decay of eloquence by appeal to historical circumstances. His (lost) plays included *praetextae* (see FABULA) on *Cato Censorius and a Domitius. He may be the 'sophist' (see SECOND SOPHISTIC) killed by *Domitian (Cass. Dio 67. 12. 5).

*PIR*² C 1604; Schanz–Hosius § 402; Syme, *Tacitus*, esp. app. 90.

M. W.

Curium, a coastal city of *Cyprus, built on a bluff 15 km. (9½ mi.) west of Limassol, near Episkopi, perhaps mentioned on the Esarhaddon prism (673/2 BC)—'Damasu king of Kuri . . .'. That its cemeteries point to an 11th-cent. origin, after the desertion of a bronze age town at Bamboula, 2 km. (1¼ mi.) east-north-east, echoes its traditional Argive foundation (see ARGOS (2)). Once aligned with *Paphos (both used the Paphian syllabary), it won autonomy from the Persians after its king Stasanor betrayed his *philhellene allies in the land battle at *Salamis (2) in 498. The last king, Pasicrates, fought with his ships for *Alexander (3) the Great at Tyre in 332. Excavated public buildings are chiefly Roman or early Christian. The extramural sanctuary of Apollo Hylates, 3 km. (1¼ mi.) west, was active from the 7th cent. BC to the 4th AD.

T. B. Mitford, *Inscriptions of Kourion* (1971); H. W. Swiny (ed.), *Ancient Kourion Area* (1982); S. Sinos, *The Temple of Apollo Hylates* (1990).

H. W. C.

Curius (*RE* 9) **Dentatus, Manius,** Roman soldier and statesman, consul in 290, 284 (suffect), 275, 274 BC. After ending the Third Samnite War (290) (see ROME (HISTORY)), he conquered the *Sabini (290), the *Senones (283), *Pyrrhus (275), and the *Lucani (274). He triumphed twice in 290, according to *Livy (*Per.* 11), and in 275. As *censor in 272 he commissioned Rome's second *aqueduct, the Anio vetus, but died in 270 while supervising the work. Rhetorical accounts of his incorruptibility and frugality resemble the tales told of C. *Fabricius Luscinus, and derive largely from M. *Porcius Cato (1) who idealized him.

G. Forni, *Athenaeum* 1953, 170–240.

E. T. S.; T. J. Co.

curses A curse is a wish that evil may befall a person or persons. Within this broad definition several different types can be distinguished, according to setting, motive, and condition. The most direct curses are maledictions inspired by feelings of hatred and lacking any explicit religious, moral, or legal legitimation. This category is exemplarily represented by the so-called curse tablets (Gk. κατάδεσμος, Lat. *defixio*), thin lead sheets inscribed with maledictions intended to influence the actions or welfare of persons (or animals). If a motive is mentioned it is generally inspired by feelings of envy and competition, especially in the fields of sports and the (amphi)theatre, litigation, love, and commerce. Almost without exception these texts are anonymous and lack argumentation or references to deserved punishment of the cursed person(s). If gods are invoked they belong to the sphere of death, the Underworld, and witchcraft (*Demeter, *Persephone, *Gaia, *Hermes, *Erinyes, *Hecate). In later times the magical names of exotic demons and gods abound. Spirits of the dead are also invoked, since the tablets were often buried in graves of the untimely dead as well as in *chthonian sanctuaries and wells. The tablets might be rolled up and transfixed with a needle and sometimes 'voodoo dolls' were added. These tablets first appear in the 6th cent. BC with often simple formulas ('I bind the names of . . .') and develop into elaborate texts in the imperial age. More than 1,500 have been recovered.

Also included in the well-known collections of *defixiones*, yet a distinct genre, are prayers for justice or 'vindictive prayers'. Often inscribed on lead tablets, but also in other media, they differ from the binding curses in that the name of the author is often mentioned, the action is justified by a reference to some injustice wrought by the cursed person (theft, slander), the gods invoked belong to the great gods (including for instance *Helios), and they are supplicated in a submissive way to punish the culprit and rectify the injustice. This variant becomes popular only in the Hellenistic and Roman periods and is found all over the Roman empire, but especially in *Britain.

Both these types of curse are concerned with past and present occurrences. Another type refers to future events. Conditional curses (imprecations) damn the unknown persons who dare to trespass against certain stipulated sacred or secular laws, prescriptions, treaties (e.g. the famous curses from Teos, *Syll.*³ 37–8). They are prevalent in the public domain and are expressed by the community through its representatives (magistrates, priests). The characteristic combination of curse and prayer, a feature they share with judicial prayer, is already perceptible in the Homeric term ἀρά. The culprit thus found himself in the position of a man guilty of sacrilege and so the legal powers could enforce their rights even in cases where only the gods could help. A special subdivison in this category is the conditional self-curse as contained in oath formulae. Here, too, the person who offends against the oath invokes the curse he has expressed himself and the wrath of the gods. Similar imprecations, both public and private, are very common in funerary inscriptions against those who violate graves, especially in Asia Minor. All these curses may be accompanied with ritual actions, and most of them have left traces in literature, especially in 'curse poetry'.

A. Audollent, *Defixionum Tabellae* (1904); W. Speyer, *RAC* 7 (1969), 1160–1288, 'Fluch'; D. R. Jordan, *GRBS* 1985, 151–97; J. H. M. Strubbe, in C. A. Faraone and D. Obbink (eds.), *Magika Hiera: Ancient Greek Magic and Religion* (1991), 33–59; H. S. Versnel, ibid. 60–106; L. Watson, *Arae: The Curse Poetry of Antiquity* (1991); J. G. Gager, *Curse Tablets and Binding Spells from the Ancient World* (1992).   H. S. V.

cursus honorum Down to the 3rd cent. BC there were perhaps few rules concerning the *cursus honorum* (career path) other than a requisite period of military service before seeking the political offices open to one's order, and some restrictions on iteration (cf. Livy 27. 6. 7). The senatorial establishment in the early 2nd cent. continued to support a loosely regulated *cursus* (Livy 32. 7. 8–12; cf. Cic. *De or.* 2. 261), surely because it facilitated use of private influence in elections. However, in or soon after 197, when the number of *praetors was set at six, a new law stipulated

that all *consuls be ex-praetors. Henceforth, the basic progression was *quaestor–praetor–consul. If the tribunate of the *plebs* and the aedileship were held, the former usually and the latter always followed the quaestorship; the censorship traditionally went to ex-consuls (see AEDILES; CENSOR; TRIBUNI PLEBIS). The *cursus* acquired further rigidity from the *lex Villia annalis* of 180 (see VILLIUS (ANNALIS), L.), which set minimum ages for each of the curule magistracies. L. *Cornelius Sulla added an age requirement for the quaestorship, which he made compulsory. In the early Principate the pattern was extended. The vigintivirate (see VIGINTISEXVIRI) became a prerequisite for the quaestorship; between these two offices it was customary (though not mandatory) to serve as military tribune. All except patricians were obliged to hold either the tribunate of the *plebs* or the aedileship before reaching the praetorship. Career patterns beyond the praetorship were less structured, though promotions to provincial governorships and the new non-magisterial posts show certain regularities. Established patterns of advancement eventually developed for equestrian careers, especially for the senior prefectures, but with greater variations than the senatorial *cursus*. A *cursus* was observed also in municipal magistracies. See CAREERS, ROMAN.

A. Astin, *The Lex Annalis Before Sulla* (1958); A. R. Birley, *The Fasti of Roman Britain* (1981), 4–35.   T. C. B.

Curtius (*RE* 7, 9), the hero of an aetiological myth invented to explain the name of lacus Curtius, a pit or pond in the Roman *Forum, which by the time of *Augustus had already dried up. Three Curtii are mentioned in this connection: (1) a *Sabine Mettius Curtius who fell from his horse into a marsh while fighting against *Romulus; (2) C. Curtius, consul of 445 BC who consecrated a site struck by lightning; (3) and most important, the brave young knight M. Curtius who, in obedience to an oracle, to save his country, leaped armed and on horseback into the chasm which suddenly opened in the Forum.

Ogilvie, *Comm. Livy 1–5*, 75 ff. For the lacus Curtius see Richardson, *Topog. Dict. Ancient Rome* 'Curtius'.   P. T.

Curtius (*RE* 21) **Montanus** was prosecuted under *Nero for his satiric poems, at the same time as *Thrasea Paetus and *Helvidius Priscus were condemned for treason. He was excluded from holding any public office and entrusted to the care of his father (Tac. *Ann.* 16. 28, 29, 33). The latter is probably the Curtius Montanus who in AD 70 attacked M. *Aquilius Regulus in a fierce speech in the senate (Tac. *Hist.* 4. 42). A connection with the younger *Pliny (2)'s addressee Montanus (*Ep.* 7. 29, 8. 6) has been suggested. Identification with *Juvenal's Montanus (4. 107) is less likely.

R. Martin, *JRS* 1967, 109 ff.; R. Syme, *RP* 5. 465.   M. T. G.

Curtius (*RE* 30) **Rufus**, suffect consul AD 43, of obscure origin and alleged by some to be the son of a gladiator, entered the senate and won the praetorship, with the support of *Tiberius, who considered that he was 'his own parent' (Tac. *Ann.* 11. 21). Legate (see LEGATI) of the Upper Rhine army in 47, he employed his troops with digging for silver in the territory of the Mattiaci and was rewarded with the *ornamenta triumphalia*. Later, as an old man, he was proconsul of Africa, fulfilling a prediction made to him in his humble beginnings (Tac. *Ann.* 11. 21; Plin. *Ep.* 7. 27. 2), and died in office. In *Tacitus (1)'s obituary he is an unamiable *novus homo*; the view that he was identical with Q. *Curtius Rufus, the historian of *Alexander (3) the Great, now holds the field. (See next entry.)

Curtius Rufus, Quintus

Syme, *RP*, see indexes; identity with the historian: J. Atkinson, *A Commentary on Q. Curtius Rufus, Books 3 and 4* (1980), 19 ff.; cf. U. Vogel-Weidemann, *Acta Classica* 1974, 141 f.   R. S.; B. M. L.

Curtius (*RE* 31) **Rufus, Quintus,** rhetorician and historian, wrote during the 1st or early 2nd cent. AD (under *Claudius remains the preferred choice). His ten-book history of *Alexander (3) the Great goes as far as the satrapy distributions at *Babylon. The first two books (down to 333 BC) are lost (and there are substantial lacunae elsewhere), and in what remains there are no statements of biography and few on method. His work is extremely rhetorical, close in tone to the *Suasoriae* of the elder Seneca (L. *Annaeus Seneca (1)); it contains many speeches of varied length and quality, and the narrative is suffused with moralizing comments and arbitrary attributions of motive. There is little consistency (after strong criticism in the body of the work the final appreciation of Alexander is pure encomium), and the exigencies of rhetoric determine the selection of source material. Consequently he switches arbitrarily from source to source and sometimes blends them into a senseless farrago. He has often been accused of deliberate fiction, but even in the speeches he used data from his regular sources and added an embroidery of rhetorical comment. He did not manufacture fact. He is by far the fullest derivative of *Cleitarchus and preserves much that is of unique value (particularly on *Macedonian custom; see ASSEMBLY, MACEDONIAN); and he also records material common to *Arrian and probably made direct use of *Ptolemy (1) I. But he very rarely names authorities and their identification in detail is hazardous. See also CURTIUS RUFUS.

Ed. E. Hedicke (Teubner, 1908); H. Bardon (Budé, 1961–5). J. Yardley and W. Heckel (eds.), *Quintus Curtius Rufus: The History of Alexander* (1984): trans. and notes; J. E. Atkinson, *A Commentary on Q. Curtius Rufus, Books 3 and 4* (1980).   A. B. B.

Cybele (*Κυβέλη*; Lydian form *Κυβήβη*, Hdt. 5. 102), the great mother-goddess of Anatolia, associated in myth, and later at least in cult, with her youthful lover *Attis. *Pessinus in Phrygia was her chief sanctuary, and the cult appears at an early date in *Lydia. The queen or mistress of her people, Cybele was responsible for their well-being in all respects; primarily she is a goddess of fertility, but also cures (and sends) disease, gives oracles, and, as her mural crown indicates, protects her people in war. The goddess of mountains (so *Μήτηρ ὀρεία*; Meter Dindymene), she is also mistress of wild nature, symbolized by her attendant lions. Ecstatic states inducing prophetic rapture and insensibility to pain were characteristic of her worship (cf. especially Catull. 63).

By the 5th century BC Cybele was known in Greece, was early associated with *Demeter (H. Thompson, *Hesp.* 1937, 206) and perhaps with a native 'Mother of the Gods', but except possibly for such places as *Dyme, *Patrae (Paus. 7. 17. 9; 20. 3), and private cult associations at *Piraeus, where Attis also was honoured, it is likely that the cult was thoroughly Hellenized. (See HELLENISM.) Cybele was officially brought to Rome from Asia Minor in 205–204 (for the conflicting legends see Graillot, below, ch. 1), but under the republic, save for the public games, the Megalesia, which were celebrated by the aediles and the old patrician families, and processions of the priests of Cybele with the participation of the *quindecimviri sacris faciundis (Lucr. 2. 624 f.; Luc. 1. 599 f.), she was limited to her Palatine temple and served only by oriental priests (Dion. Hal. *Ant. Rom.* 2. 19. 3 ff.). The consultation of the Sibylline books (see SIBYL) and the cult of Cybele were under the control of the *quindecimviri sacris faciundis. The cycle of the spring festival, mentioned in public documents from *Claudius' reign, while not fully attested till AD 354, began to take form then. The rites began on 15 March with a procession of the Reed-bearers (*cannophori*), and a sacrifice for the crops. After a week of *fastings and *purifications, the festival proper opened on the 22nd with the bringing of the pine-tree, symbol of Attis, to the temple. The 24th was the Day of Blood, commemorating the castration and probably the death of Attis. The 25th was a day of joy and banqueting, the *Hilaria, and after a day's rest the festival closed with the ritual bath (*Lavatio*) of Cybele's image in the Almo. The rubric for the 28th (*Initium Caiani*) is apparently unrelated. The relation of this spring festival to the Hellenistic mysteries of Cybele is uncertain. Of the later mysteries, in which Attis figured prominently, we again know little. The formulae preserved (Firm. Mat. *Err. prof. rel.* 18; Clem. Al. *Protr.* 2. 15) mention a ritual meal; the carrying of the *κέρνος*, a vessel used in the *taurobolium* ('bull-sacrifice') to receive the genitals of the bull; and a descent into the *παστός*, probably an underground chamber where certain rites were enacted; but one can also think in terms of a metaphor for *initiation.

The ritual of the *taurobolium* originated in Asia Minor, and first appears in the west in the cult of Venus Caelesta (i.e. -is) at Puteoli in AD 134 (*ILS* 4271, but cf. 4099 of AD 108). From the Antonine period, numerous dedications to Cybele and Attis record its performance in this cult 'ex vaticinatione archigalli' (i.e. with official sanction), on behalf of the emperor and the empire. From Rome the rite spread throughout the west, notably in *Gaul (Transalpine). It was performed also on behalf of individuals, and was especially popular during the pagan revival, AD 370–90. In the rite, the recipient descended into a ditch and was bathed in the blood of a bull, or ram (*criobolium*), which was slain above him (Prudent. *Perist.* 10. 1011–50). It was sometimes repeated after twenty years; one late text (*ILS* 4152) has 'taurobolio criobolioq. in aeternum renatus', 'reborn into eternity through the *taurobolium*, and *criobolium*' (a concept possibly borrowed from Christianity), but in general the act was considered rather a 'thing done' for its own value than as a source of individual benefits. There has been much speculation, ancient (e.g. Julian, *Or.* 5. 9. 168d f.) and modern, about Cybele and her cult, but these theories are either late allegorizations or in the latter case, inspired by the modern 'myth' of the Great Mother.

A belief in immortality was perhaps part of the cult from early times, and the after-life may at first have been thought of as a reunion with Mother Earth. Later, Attis became a solar god, and he and Cybele were regarded as astral and cosmic powers; there is some evidence that the soul was then thought to return after death to its celestial source.

Thanks to its official status and early naturalization at Rome and in *Ostia, the cult spread rapidly through the provinces, especially in Gaul and Africa, and was readily accepted as a municipal cult. Its agrarian character made it more popular with the fixed populations than with the soldiery, and it was especially favoured by women.

Cybele is generally represented enthroned in a *naiskos* ('shrine'), wearing either the mural crown or the *calathos* ('basket'), carrying a libation-bowl and drum, and either flanked by lions or bearing one in her lap.

See also AGDISTIS; ANAHITA; ANATOLIAN DEITIES; ATTIS; EUNUCHS; METRAGYRTES.

H. Hepding, *Attis* (1903); Cumont, *Rel. or.*; H. Graillot, *Le Culte de Cybèle* (1912); R. Duthoy, *The Taurobolium* (1969); M. Vermaseren, *Cybele and Attis* (1977); G. Sfameni Gasparro, *Soteriology and Mystic Aspects in the Cult of Cybele and Attis* (1985); R. Turcan, *Les Cultes ori-*

entaux dans l'Empire romain (1989), 35 ff.; E. Gruen, Studies in Greek Culture and Roman Policy (1990), 5 ff.; M. Beard, in N. Thomas and C. Humphrey (eds.), Shamanism, History and the State (1993), 164 ff.

F. R. W.; J. Sch.

Cyclades, an archipelago in the southern Aegean, comprising some thirty habitable islands, ranging in size from a few square kilometres to over 400 sq. km. (155 sq. mi.), and numerous small islands deserted through most of history. They offer a favourable route across the Aegean where land is always in sight and refuge close at hand.

The Cyclades are part of a sunken land mass extending southeast from Attica and Euboea, composed of metamorphic rocks (predominantly marble and schist) with igneous intrusions of granite and gneiss. *Thera, *Melos, and Cimolos are volcanic islands lying along the south Aegean arc. All are mountainous (1,000 m. (3,280 ft.) on *Naxos (1)) and lack extensive arable land, but are rich in minerals; iron ores are widespread, precious copper, lead / silver ores, and gold localized to Cythnos, Seriphos, *Siphnos, and Syros. Their *marble, particularly Parian (see PAROS) and Naxian, is among the finest. An extreme Mediterranean climate with low annual rainfall and strong winds prevails, increasingly arid towards the south-east. Climate and geology suggest that they were as barren in antiquity as now. Schistic soils are preferred to the derivitives from marble and igneous rocks for cultivation. Barley and vines fare best. Animal husbandry is restricted by scarce water resources.

Widespread permanent occupation began in the early bronze age, preceded by sporadic settlement from middle neolithic times. A distinctive Cycladic civilization emerged in the third millennium, influential in Attica and *Euboea. Important centres were Chalandriani (Syros) and Ceros. Towards its end populations clustered at fortified towns and some islands were deserted. Cities developed in the middle and earlier late bronze age (c.2000–1500 BC), perhaps in response to contact with Crete (see MINOAN CIVILIZATION). With the rise of the Mycenaean kingdoms many islands suffered decline and depopulation. Unsettled conditions elsewhere c.1200 BC occasioned a temporary revival. Fortified acropolis sites appeared only to be abandoned or destroyed in the 11th cent. Except Naxos, all were apparently deserted from c.1050–950 BC.

Ancient geographers defined the Cyclades, somewhat inconsistently, as the islands encircling *Delos (*Ceos, Cythnos, Seriphos, Siphnos, Paros, Naxos, Ios, Myconos, Syros, *Tenos, *Andros). From c.1000 BC these were settled by *Ionians with Delos as their cult centre. The southern Cyclades (*Melos, Cimolos, Pholegandros, Sicinos, *Thera, Anaphe), counted among the Sporades, were colonized from c.900 BC by *Dorians from the Peloponnese. In the geometric period the northern Cyclades were oriented towards the Thessalo-Euboean region, the remainder towards Attica, except Thera. From the 8th until the 5th cent. they flourished as independent states governed by wealthy aristocracies. Regional styles in sculpture, architecture, pottery, and other minor arts developed on the larger islands. From c.550 BC external interference increased, from mainland Greece and Asia Minor. During the *Persian Wars many submitted and contributed ships to the Persian fleet, the western string remaining loyal to the Greek allies. Afterwards the Ionian Cyclades joined the *Delian League; the Dorian islands remained independent until the Peloponnesian War. Many again joined the *Second Athenian Confederacy after 377 BC. *Antigonus (1) Monophthalmos founded the League of Islanders c.314 BC, again based on Delos. Subsequently the Cyclades, in the struggles between the Hellenistic kingdoms for control of the Aegean, frequently changed hands between Macedonians, Ptolemies (see PTOLEMY (1)), Attalids of *Pergamum, *Rhodes, and finally the Romans, who after 133 BC administered them as part of the province of Asia. *Piracy was a constant threat in the Hellenistic period. Many became bywords for small-state insignificance and poverty, later being used by the Julio-Claudians as places of *exile. Having suffered in the wars of the late republic, settled conditions under the empire allowed some prosperity to return to the larger islands where occupation continued at the ancient centres until late antiquity. See under individual islands.

L. Bürchner, RE 11.2 (1922), cols. 2308–20 ('Kykladen'); IG 12 (5), 7 ff.; A. Philippson, Die griechischen Landschaften 4 (1959), 61 ff.; C. Renfrew, The Emergence of Civilization (1972); GAC 304 ff.; W. Ekschmitt, Kunst und Kultur der Kykladen 1–2 (1986); R. Barber, The Cyclades in the Bronze Age (1987); R. Étienne, Ténos 2 (1990); N. H. Gale (ed.), Bronze Age Trade in the Mediterranean (1991), 249 ff.; AJArch. 1992, 699 ff.

R. W. V. C.

Cyclopes (Κύκλωπες) are one-eyed giants. In *Homer they are savage and pastoral, and live in a distant country without government or laws. Here *Odysseus visits them in his wanderings and enters the cave of one of them, Polyphemus, who imprisons him and his men and eats two of them raw, morning and evening, until they escape by blinding him while in a drunken sleep, and getting out among the sheep and goats when he opens the cave in the morning (Od. 9). Polyphemus is the son of *Poseidon, and the god, in answer to his prayer for vengeance, opposes the homecoming of Odysseus in every possible way, bringing to pass the curse that he may return alone and find trouble when he arrives (ibid. 532–5). The blinding is a popular theme of early vase-painting. Elsewhere (notably Theoc. 11) we find an amorous Polyphemus, who lives in *Sicily and somewhat ludicrously woos the nymph *Galatea, without success.

But in *Hesiod (Theog. 139–46, 501–6) the Cyclopes are three, Brontes, Steropes, and Arges (Thunderer, Lightener, Bright). They are divine craftsmen who make *Zeus his thunderbolt in gratitude for their release from imprisonment by their father *Uranus (Heaven; their mother is Earth). They often appear (as Callim. Hymn 3. 46–79) as *Hephaestus' workmen, and often again are credited with making ancient fortifications, as those of *Tiryns, and other cities of the Argolid (schol. Eur. Or. 965; see ARGOS (2)). Their only known cult is on the Isthmus of *Corinth, where they received sacrifices at their altar (Paus. 2. 2. 1). The story of the blinding of the one-eyed 'Polyfoumismenos dragon' in his cave is still told in Greece.

R. Mondi, TAPA 1983, 17–38; LIMC 6/1. 154–9 'Kyklops, Kyklopes'

R. A. S. S.

Cycnus, the Greek for 'swan' and the name of more than ten mythical figures. (1) A son of *Ares who robbed travellers bringing offerings to *Delphi. The pseudo-Hesiodic (see HESIOD) Shield of Heracles (57–121, 320–480) tells how *Heracles and *Iolaus encountered Cycnus and Ares in the sanctuary of *Apollo at *Pagasae, and, when Cycnus would not let them pass, did battle and killed him, with the encouragement of Athena. *Stesichorus's Cycnus added other details: the brigand had planned to build a temple (to Apollo, apparently, but this has been questioned) with the skulls of his victims, and Heracles fled before him as long as he was aided by Ares. The battle was a very popular subject in 6th-cent. art. (2) A son of *Poseidon killed by *Achilles at the start of the Trojan War. The episode was treated in the Cypria (see EPIC CYCLE, para. 4 (6)) and apparently in

*Sophocles' *Poimenes* ('Herdsmen'). *Ovid *Met.* 12. 71–145 provides details: Cycnus was invulnerable, so *Achilles strangled him, and he was transformed into a swan. (3) A king of the *Ligurians and relative or lover of *Phaethon. He lamented beside the Po (see PADUS) for Phaethon's death and was transformed into a swan (Phanocles fr. 6; Verg. *Aen.* 10. 189–93; Ov. *Met.* 2. 367–80). (4) Ovid has yet another Cycnus transformed into a swan at *Met.* 7. 371–9 (cf. Ant. Lib. 12).

LIMC 'Kyknos'.   A. L. B.

Cylon, an Athenian nobleman; winner at *Olympia, perhaps in 640 BC. He married the daughter of *Theagenes (I), tyrant of *Megara, and with his help and a few friends seized the Acropolis at Athens, with a view to a tyranny, in an Olympic year (632?, see OLYMPIAN GAMES). The masses, however, did not follow him, and he was besieged. He himself escaped; his friends surrendered and, though suppliants at an altar, were killed. Hence arose the ἄγος, or *curse, which attached to those said to be responsible, especially to Megacles the archon and his family, the *Alcmaeonidae.

Hdt. 5. 71, corrected by Thuc. 1. 126. P. J. Rhodes, *CAAP* 81; A. Andrewes, *CAH* 3²/3 (1982), 368 ff.; Hornblower, *Comm. on Thuc.* 1. 202 ff.; R. G. Osborne, *BSA* 1989, 313.   A. W. G.; S. H.

Cyme, the most important and powerful of the Aeolian cities (see AEOLIS) on the seaboard of *Asia Minor, occupying a naturally strong harbour site midway between the mouths of the Caicus and the *Hermus, and facing north-west towards *Lesbos. It was dominated successively by the Persians, the Athenians (to whose empire it belonged; see DELIAN LEAGUE), the *Seleucids, the Attalids of *Pergamum, and the Romans. A severe *earthquake devastated the city in AD 17 and it was rebuilt with help from the emperor *Tiberius. *Hesiod's father came from Cyme to *Boeotia and its most distinguished citizen was the historian *Ephorus. The inhabitants were noted for their easygoing temperament.

H. Engelmann, *Die Inschriften von Kyme* (1976) (with testimonia); *Arslantepe, Hierapolis* etc. (1993).   D. E. W. W.; S. M.

Cynaethus, of Chios, according to schol. Pind. *Nem.* 2. 1, was prominent among the later *Homeridae, composed the Homeric *Hymn to Apollo* (the Delian part? cf. l. 172), and initiated Homeric recitation at *Syracuse (504/1 BC). Partially true?

M. L. West, *CQ* 1975, 161–70; W. Burkert, in *Arktouros: Hellenic Studies presented to B. M. W. Knox* (1979), 53–62.   M. L. W.

Cynegirus, brother of *Aeschylus, fell at the battle of *Marathon (490 BC) while attempting to seize a Persian ship by the stern (Hdt. 6. 114). This exploit was immortalized in the *Stoa Poecile (c.460; cf. Ael. *NA* 7. 38), and was variously elaborated by historians (cf. Just. *Epit.* 2. 9. 16 ff.) and rhetoricians (e.g. *Polemon (4)).   A. H. S.

Cynics ('the dog-like'), term used of *Diogenes (2) 'the dog' (so called for his shamelessness) and his followers. The genesis, status, significance, and influence of Cynicism were anciently controversial and remain so. Interpretative problems arise from Cynic behaviour and sayings, from the loss of nearly all Cynic writings (though this matters less in the case of Cynicism than of other philosophies), and from diverse distortions in the ancient traditions (invention of sayings and anecdotes; artificial integration of Cynicism into a formal philosophical succession from Socrates to the Stoics; bowdlerization; polemical misrepresentation).

Cynicism was never a formal philosophical school but rather a way of life grounded in an extreme primitivist interpretation of the principle 'live according to nature'. Diogenes having discovered the true way of life, there was relatively little diversity or development within Cynicism, though 'hard' Cynics (rigorous exponents of the original prescription, found at all periods) can be distinguished from 'soft' Cynics (who compromised varyingly with existing social and political institutions), practical Cynicism from literary Cynicism (Cynicism as written or written about), and Cynics (in some sense) from those influenced by Cynicism.

'Hard' Cynicism was best expounded by Diogenes and (to some extent) *Crates (2). From 320–220 BC 'soft' Cynicism was diversely represented by *Onesicritus, whose *History* portrayed *Alexander (3) the Great as a Cynic philosopher-king; the eclectics *Bion (1) of Borysthenes, court philosopher of *Antigonus (2) Gonatas, and *Teles, schoolteacher; and *Cercidas, politician, lawgiver, and social reformer. Practical Cynicism declined in the 2nd and 1st cents. BC but revived in the early empire. Greek cities swarmed with Cynics. Cynicism produced remarkable individuals (*Demetrius (19), friend of the younger Seneca (L. *Annaeus Seneca (2)); Dio Chrysostom (*Dio Coccelianus); in the 2nd cent. AD *Demonax, Peregrinus, and Oenomaus). The Roman authorities inevitably clashed with 'hard' Cynics (qua anarchists). Later, Cynic and Christian ascetics were sometimes confused, sometimes distinguished. (Some scholars even claim Jesus as a Cynic.) Cynics are mentioned until the 6th cent. Continental European philosophy has shown some interest in Cynicism.

Cynicism greatly influenced Greek and Roman philosophy, rulership ideology, literature, and (later) religion. Crates' follower *Zeno (2) founded *Stoicism, a development of Cynicism with a proper theoretical grounding: Stoic ethics are essentially Cynic ethics, Stoic cosmopolitanism a development of Cynic; Diogenes' *Republic* influenced Zeno's and *Chrysippus'. The legitimacy of Cynicism was debated within Stoicism, reactions ranging from nearly total acceptance (*Ariston (1)) to partial acceptance (Zeno, Chrysippus), to rejection (*Panaetius), to bowdlerizing and idealizing redefinition (*Epictetus). More broadly, the very extremeness of Cynic positions on material possessions, individual ethics, and politics catalysed the definition of other philosophies' positions: apart from the Stoics, the Epicureans (see EPICURUS), though greatly influenced by Cynic ethics, polemicized against Cynicism. Diogenes and Crates are generally celebrated in popular philosophy. While the Cynic king is a moral concept wholly antithetical to the wordly king, Onesicritus (following *Antisthenes (1) and *Xenophon (1)) facilitated appropriation and redefinition of that concept by rulership ideology (as later in Dio Chrysostom's Kingship Orations); see KINGSHIP. Cynic ethics influenced Christian *asceticism.

To maximize their audience the Cynics (despite avowed rejection of literature) wrote more voluminously and variously than any ancient philosophical school: relatively formal philosophical treatises, dialogues, tragedies, historiography, letters, diatribes, various kinds of poetry and of literary parody, prose-poetry hybrids (*Menippus (1)). The Cynic *diatribe, anecdotal tradition, satiric spirit, and serio-comic discourse had enormous and varied philosophical and literary influence (e.g. on the diatribes of the younger Seneca and Plutarch; philosophical biography and the gospels; Roman satire; the epistles of Horace, St Paul, and Seneca; Lucian). See BION (1); CRATES (2); DIATRIBE; DIOGENES (2); OENOMAUS.

A. O. Lovejoy and G. Boas, *Primitivism and Related Ideas in Antiquity* (1935); D. R. Dudley, *A History of Cynicism* (1938; repr. 1967); R. Höistad,

Cynic Hero and Cynic King (1948); M. Billerbeck (ed.), Epiktet: Vom Kynismus (1978); M.-O. Goulet-Cazé, L'Ascèse cynique (1986); H. Niehues-Pröbsting, Der Kynismus des Diogenes und der Begriff des Zynismus, 2nd edn. (1988); L. Paquet, Les Cyniques grecs: Fragments et témoignages, 2nd edn. (1988); G. Giannantoni, Socrates et Socraticorum Reliquiae 2. 5 B–N; 4. 413–583 (1990); M. Billerbeck (ed.), Die Kyniker in der modernen Forschung (1991); F. G. Downing, Cynics and Christian Origins (1992); M.-O. Goulet-Cazé and R. Goulet (eds.), Le Cynisme ancien et ses prolongements (1993); J. L. Moles, in A. Laks and M. Schofield, Justice and Generosity (1994), ch. 5.   J. L. Mo.

Cynoscephalae (mod. Chalkodónion), hills north-east of Skotoussa in *Thessaly, scene of two battles. The first, in 364 BC, between *Alexander (5) of Pherae (Velestino) and a combined army of Thebans (see THEBES (1)) and *Thessalians commanded by *Pelopidas, ended in the former's defeat but the latter's death. The second, in 197 BC, between *Philip (3) V of Macedonia and the Romans under T. *Quinctius Flamininus, ended the Second Macedonian War. The two armies were marching west from Pherae, concealed by the hills, and clashed in wet and misty conditions. Encouraged by the early skirmishing, Philip decided to deploy on a ridge above the Romans, but although his right had some success, his left was caught deploying and routed, whereupon part of the Roman right managed to attack the Macedonian right in flank and rear and annihilate it. The battle illustrates the vulnerability of the *phalanx when faced by the more flexible legion.

RE 12/1 Κυνὸς κεφαλαί; Polyb. 18. 20 ff.; Livy 33. 7–10; Hammond in HM 3. 432 ff.   J. F. La.

Cynuria (Κυνουρία), land of the autochthonous Cynurii (Hdt. 8. 73), the coastal sub-region of the east Parnon foreland centred on the plain of modern Astros overlooking the Argolic Gulf; also known as the Thyreatis (Θυρεᾶτις) after Thyrea (site disputed), with Anthene its chief settlements. The area was border country contested between Argives (see ARGOS (2)) and Spartans, who took control after victory in the 'battle of the champions' (Paus. 2. 38. 5) c.545 BC, although Argos maintained its claim (see Thuc. 5. 41), with ultimate success, the region being Argive once more under Rome. In the 2nd cent. AD the 'Thyreatic land' was managed by a bailiff (SEG 13. 261) on behalf of the family or heirs of Ti. *Claudius Atticus Herodes (2), whose opulent villa 5 km. (3 mi.) west of Astros has been excavated.

P. Pharaklas, Ἀρχαῖα Κυνουρία (1985); W. Pritchett, Studies in Ancient Greek Topography, 3 (1980), ch. 4, and 4 (1982), chs. 3–4; S. Alcock, Graecia capta (1993) (villa).   A. J. S. S.

Cyparissus (Κυπάρισσος), i.e. Cypress, in mythology son of *Telephus (1), a Cean (Ov. Met. 10. 106 ff.), who grieved so much at accidentally killing a pet stag that the gods turned him into the mournful tree; or a Cretan, who was so metamorphosed while fleeing from the attentions of *Apollo, or *Zephyrus (Serv. on Aen. 3. 680).

LIMC 6/1 (1992), 165–6.   H. J. R.; A. J. S. S.

Cyprian (Thascius Caecilius Cyprianus), c. AD 200–58. Son of rich parents probably from the upper ranks of curial society (see DECURIONES) rather than of Roman senatorial rank, he became bishop of *Carthage (248) soon after baptism and was quickly beset by *Decius' persecution (248), for which his writings are a major source. His letters and tracts, from which much of the old Latin Bible can be reconstructed, deal mainly with difficulties within the Christian community resulting from the persecution, especially the terms and proper authority for restor-

ation of apostates and the avoidance of a split between the rival advocates of laxity and rigour. In 256–7 his theology led to a split with Rome, whose bishop Stephen recognized the baptism of *Novatianus' community (since 251 separated on rigorist grounds). In *Valerian's persecution (257) he was exiled to Curubis, but returned to Carthage and on 14 September 258 was executed there, the authorities treating him with the respect due to his class. More an administrator than a thinker, he writes with the effortless superiority of a high Roman official, liking correct procedure and expecting his clergy and plebs (and in practice his episcopal colleagues) to accept his authority. He speaks of bishops as magistrates, judges on behalf of Christ, and his language finds many analogies in Roman law. His application of juridical categories to the conception of the Church permanently influenced western Catholicism. His Life by his deacon Pontius, the earliest Christian biography, aims to show him as the equal of the glorious martyr Perpetua, pride of African Christianity.

EDITIONS W. von Hartel, CSEL 3; Letters: L. Bayard (1945); with introductions and trans., G. W. Clarke, 4 vols. (1984–9); Passio: R. Reitzenstein (1913); De unitate: M. Bévenot, The Tradition of MSS (1961).

STUDIES E. W. Benson, Cyprian (1897); H. Koch, Cyprianische Untersuchungen (1926); A. Beck, Römisches Recht bei Tertullian und Cyprian (1930); G. W. Clarke, Letters (1984–9).   J. F. Ma.

Cypriot syllabary See PRE-ALPHABETIC SCRIPTS, GREECE.

Cyprus, third largest Mediterranean island (9,282 sq. km.: 3,584 sq. mi.) was of strategic and economic importance to the Mediterranean and near eastern powers, and significant both to their relations with western Asia and with one another. It is vulnerable to the power politics of its neighbours, by one or other of whom it has often been occupied or governed, and whose mutual conflicts have sometimes been fought out on its soil or its seas. Though mountainous (the highest points on its Troödos and Kyrenia ranges are 1,951 and 1,023 m. (6,403 and 3,357 ft.) respectively), its central plain (Mesaoria) is fertile, while its extensive piedmont and river-valley systems are suited to crop and animal husbandry. The island suffers intermittently from serious seismic disturbance. Rainfall is uncertain, drought endemic, and fertility dramatically responsive to irrigation capacity. Copper ore, chiefly located in the Troödos foothills at the junction of igneous and sedimentary deposits, has been exploited since prehistory. Timber resources played a major role in the region's naval history.

The character of the first human traces, found with extinct pleistocene animal species at the Akrotiri, Aetokremnos rock-shelter, with a carbon-14 date of c.8000 BC, is uncertain, as is their relationship with the c.6000 BC pre-ceramic neolithic phase, best seen at the type-site, Khirokitia, but distributed at numerous other locations, coastal and inland. Successive phases of neolithic and chalcolithic settlement embrace a 3,500-year period; excavation has established the general character of several sites spanning this period, yet origins and interrelationships between its successive episodes are alike uncertain. The gradual introduction of metal technology during the third millennium greatly accelerated social and material development; the main stimulus may have been the disruption and dispersal of more advanced societies in adjacent Anatolia. The 1,500 years of the Cypriot bronze age (early, middle, and late) were marked by a progression from isolated rural communities linked by shared traits in material civilization (typifying the late third millennium) to what by the 13th cent. had become an urbanized hierarchical society, enriched by the international exchange systems in which raw copper played a major role (symbolized by the cargoes of the wrecked Ulu Burun and Cape Gelidonya ships off SW Turkey). This change saw a shift from the north and south piedmont of the Kyrenia mountains to the south and east coasts, to new towns founded at the end of middle Cypriot (17th cent.) at river mouths (Enkomi, Maroni, Palaepaphos) or on natural harbours (Citium, Hala Sultan Tekke). While Egypt and the cities of the Levant (notably *Ugarit) enjoyed regular exchanges with Cyprus, Minoan Crete played a part and, from c.1400 Mycenaean Greece was prominent, even dominant. The island was literate during late Cypriot, using the Cypro-Minoan script (see PRE-GREEK LANGUAGES). Objective proof of the identification of Cyprus with the 'Alasya' of Hittite, Egyptian, Ugaritic, and other documents remains elusive, for all its appeal. The final bronze age years (1200–1050) knew turbulence, violence—and remarkable prosperity, in which there was a fruitful coalescence of the native Cypriot with migrant Aegean and Levantine elements that produced a distinguished but short-lived material civilization whose ceramic design, metalwork, ivory carving, and glyptic were pre-eminent; perhaps iron technology was disseminated westward at this time. By 1050 virtually all the old settlements had been abandoned, in some cases to be replaced nearby by communities under the strongest Greek influence yet seen, including Mycenaean types of tomb and, very probably, the Arcadian dialect. This process may dimly be reflected in the legends, where figures from the *Nostoi* (see EPIC CYCLE, para. 4 (11)) are credited with the foundation of the later cities—*Teucer (2) at *Salamis (2), *Agapenor at Paphos, etc. Classical Cypriot script, adapted from Cypro-Minoan, lasted for some purposes almost to 200 BC (and was the vehicle too for the undeciphered Eteo-Cyprian of *Amathus).

The Iron Age settlement-pattern was based on a nexus of city-kingdoms (sometimes seen as a Mycenaean legacy)—Salamis, Citium, *Amathus, *Paphos, *Curium, Soli, Marion, Tamassus, *Idalium, *Chytri—which largely lasted throughout antiquity. Citium was for long a *Phoenician city (Phoenician influence was very strong elsewhere in the island), Amathus was 'Eteocypriot'. The kings ruled as autocrats; only at *Idalium may power have been shared with a '*dēmos'. The 8th- and 7th-cent. 'royal' tombs at Salamis suggest both the wealth and foreign connections of these rulers. From the late 8th cent., if no earlier, Cyprus was sucked into east Mediterranean politics; its kings acknowledged at least the nominal suzerainty of a succession of great powers. The Sargon II stela said to have been found at Citium (Larnaka) reports the submission of the kings to *Assyria in 709; the information is repeated on other Assyrian documents. While the 7th cent. seems to have been largely a period of independence, the island was dominated by *Egypt in the earlier 6th cent. In 545 came voluntary submission to Persia; there was Cypriot help for the Persians in the Carian War, the conquest of *Babylon and, in 525, their attack on Egypt. Sufficient independence remained for the kings to issue their own coinage, starting c.538 with Euelthon of Salamis (the same Euelthon to whom Pheretime of *Cyrene vainly appealed for help against her son *Arcesilas III— further symptom of independence). When *Darius I reorganized the empire, Cyprus found itself in the fifth satrapy with *Phoenicia and *Syria-Palestine; tribute was imposed, but the amount is unknown. The cities (except Amathus) joined the *Ionian Revolt, egged on, it seems, by dissidents who gained control in Salamis, where crucial land and sea battles were fought. Though the Ionian fleet was victorious, ashore the Cypriots were defeated, and their leader, Onesilus, killed. The cities were reduced by the Persians, Soli holding out the longest. The Cyp-

riots had an uncomfortable time in the subsequent long struggle between Greece and Persia; their ships fought poorly on the Persian side in 480–79. The island was constantly campaigned over during Athenian efforts under *Cimon to deny it to the Persians, but Cimon's death during the 449/8 campaign raised the siege and, temporarily, pro-Persian rulers became everywhere dominant; but the Teucrid king of Salamis, *Evagoras I (c.411–374) was conspicuously pro-Greek, in fact as well as theory. Later, the kings intervened decisively on behalf of *Alexander (3) the Great at the siege of *Tyre in 331, where their ships were badly mauled. The *Diadochi, usually violently, abolished the city-kings, and with them any pretence of an independent Cyprus. The island became part of the Ptolemaic share of Alexander's legacy (see PTOLEMY (1)) and thereby lost most of what remained of its idiosyncratic material civilization. In the 1st cent. BC the island passed to and fro between Roman and Ptolemaic rule until its final annexation after *Actium by *Octavian; in 22 BC it was ceded as a minor public province. Its Roman history was (apart from serious earthquakes and the Jewish revolt of 115/6) relatively tranquil and—to judge from surviving monuments at Salamis, *Curium, and Nea Paphos—prosperous.

G. Hill, *A History of Cyprus* (1940); K. Spyridakis, *Evagoras I von Salamis* (1935); J. R. Stewart, in *Handbook to the Nicholson Museum*, 2nd edn. (1948); E. Gjerstad, *SCE* 4/2: *The Geometric, Archaic and Classical Periods* (1948); O. Vessberg and A. Westholm, *SCE* 4/3: *The Hellenistic and Roman Periods* (1956); P. Dikaios and J. R. Stewart, *SCE* 4/1a: *The Stone Age and the Early Bronze Age* (1962); H. W. Catling, *Cypriot Bronzework in the Mycenaean World* (1964); H.-G. Buchholz and V. Karageorghis, *Altägäis und Altkypros* (1971); P. Åström, *SCE* 4/1b: *The Middle Cypriote Bronze Age* (1972), *SCE* 4/1c: *The Late Cypriote Bronze Age: Architecture and Pottery* (1972), and, with L. Åström, *SCE* 4/1d: *The Late Cypriote Bronze Age: Other Arts and Crafts. Relative and Absolute Chronology, etc* (1972); V. Karageorghis, *Kition* (1976); L. Hellbing, *Alasia Problem* (1979); N. P. Stanley-Price, *Early Prehistoric Settlement in Cyprus* (1980); V. Karageorghis, *From the Stone Age to the Romans* (1982), and *CAH* 3²/1 (1982), 511–33; 3²/3 (1982), 37–82 (1982); O. Masson, *Les Inscriptions chypriotes syllabiques*, 2nd edn. (1983); F. G. Maier, *Cypern: Insel am Kreuzweg der Geschichte*, 2nd edn. (1982) and *CAH* 6² (1994), ch. 8d; V. Karageorghis and J. D. Muhly (eds.), *Cyprus at the Close of the Late Bronze Age* (1984); C. Baurain, *Chypre et la Méditerranée orientale au Bronze Récent* (1984); O. Negbi in *RDAC* (1986), 97–121; A. Reyes, *Archaic Cyprus* (1994).
H. W. C.

Cypselus, tyrant of *Corinth, traditionally (and probably in fact) c.657–627 BC. He overthrew the *aristocracy of the *Bacchiadae, and established the earliest tyrant dynasty (see TYRANNY), and one of the longest lasting. *Herodotus' account, though its context is hostile, bears unmistakable signs of a favourable tradition in the folk-tale (which has eastern parallels) that his mother Labda, herself of Bacchiad descent, rescued him as an infant by hiding him in a *kypselē* (beehive) when the Bacchiadae tried to kill him. The story that he spent his youth in exile is probably invented: the Bacchiadae treated him as one of them, though his father Aetion was not; that enabled him to exploit discontent with their exclusive control. He drew active support only from wealthy Corinthians, but his popularity is reflected in Aristotle's view that he became tyrant 'through demagoguery' (see DEMAGOGUES): he had no bodyguard i.e. (perhaps) did not *need* one. His most important achievement was to remove the Bacchiadae: we hear little of his actions in power. He built a treasury at *Delphi: Herodotus preserves an early favourable *Delphic oracle. He founded colonies in north-west Greece with his bastard sons as founders and tyrants, and established a long-lasting Corinthian interest there: the most important was *Ambracia; *Anactorium and *Leucas, where he had a *canal dug through the spit which joins the mainland, were smaller foundations. He probably also devised the Corinthian tribal system (see PHYLAI), an early example of one based on domicile and not descent, upon which later institutions were based.

Hdt. 5. 92; *RE* 12, 'Kypselos' 2; O. Murray, *Early Greece* (1980); J. B. Salmon, *Wealthy Corinth* (1984).   J. B. S.

Cypselus, chest of, a chest of cedar-wood decorated with figures in ivory, gold, and wood, exhibited at *Olympia in the temple of Hera. It is said to have been the one in which the infant *Cypselus was hidden, and afterwards to have been dedicated by either Cypselus or his son *Periander. Nothing of this famous chest survives, but Pausanias' long description of the decorations (5. 17. 5) suggests that they were in the style of contemporary painted pottery, i.e. that of the 7th to 6th cent. BC. The shape of the chest was doubtless that of the *kibōtoi* that appear on Greek pottery vases from the 6th cent. down. A contemporary dedication by Cypselids is an inscribed gold bowl (Boston Museum).

M. Robertson, *History of Greek Art* (1975), see index.
S. C.; G. M. A. R.; M. V.

Cyranides, a Greek tract in five books, listing the magical and curative powers of stones, plants, and animals. Authorship, date, and title are uncertain, although the Cyranides bears affinity to works 'by' *Hermes Trismegistus, suggesting Egyptian—perhaps Coptic—origins in the 1st or 2nd cent. AD. The treatise says it is partly by Cyranus, king of Persia, and partly by Harpocration (the medical and astrological writer). Book 5 contains a number of parallel passages to *Dioscorides (2), indicating that both the *Cyranides* and Dioscorides drew from common and rather ancient traditions.

TEXT D. Kaimakis (ed.), *Die Kyraniden* (1976).
GENERAL LITERATURE R. Ganszyniec, *RE* 12/1. 127–34, 'Kyraniden'; F. Pfister, *RE* 19/2. 1446–56, 'Pflanzenaberglaube'; J. Pollard, *Birds in Greek Life and Myth* (1977), esp. ch. 14; J. Scarborough, in I. Merkel and A. G. Debus (eds.), *Hermeticism and the Renaissance* (1988), 19–44.   J. Sca.

Cyrenaica See PENTAPOLIS.

Cyrenaics, a school of philosophers reputedly founded by *Aristippus, influential in the later 4th and early 3rd cent. BC. Its best-known members were Theodorus, *Hegesias (1), and *Anniceris. Its main tenets were that sense-impressions are the only things which are knowable, and that the sensory pleasure of the present moment is the supreme good. The claim of pleasure to be the supreme good was supported by the argument that all living things pursue pleasure and shun pain, and bodily pleasure was characterized as a smooth motion of the flesh. The predominance of the pleasure of the moment was supported by the sceptical epistemology implied by the claim that only sense-impressions are knowable; since both past and future lie beyond the scope of present impressions, the wise agent will live only in and for the present. These doctrines may have had some influence on Epicureanism, partly by way of reaction.

G. Giannantoni, *I Cirenaici* (1958), and *Socraticorum Reliquiae* 1 (1983); E. Mannebach, *Aristippi et Cyrenaicorum Fragmenta* (1961); H. D. Rankin, *Sophists, Socratics and Cynics* (1983); K. Döring, *Der Sokratesschüler Aristipp und die Kyrenaiker* (1988).   C. C. W. T.

Cyrene (mod. Shahat), the major Greek colony in Africa (see COLONIZATION, GREEK), was founded from *Thera *c.*630 BC, and reinforced by later groups of colonists, who were, before the Hellenistic period, predominantly *Dorian. It gave its name to the surrounding territory (mod. Cyrenaica), apparently claiming authority (sometimes resisted) as *mētropolis of all Greek settlements there; it is not always clear whether ancient references to Cyrene are to the city or to this territory. Information about it has been significantly increased by 20th-cent. excavation; there is now material evidence from at least the 7th cent. BC to at least the 7th cent. AD, but its interpretation is often debatable.

For the foundation, the account in Herodotus (4. 150–8) is supplemented by an inscription purporting to give the substance of the Theraean decree which organized the colonial expedition (*SEG* 9. 3, 20. 714); after two initial failures, a site was found, with Libyan help, on the northern edge of the Gebel Akhdar, 621 m. (2,037 ft.) above and *c.*12 km. (7½ mi.) from the sea, in a fertile area with a freshwater spring and normally good rainfall, but shading into pre-desert southwards; other Greek settlements followed swiftly, for example a dependent port near by, the city of Taucheira further off. Communications with these and exploitation of the country required Libyan co-operation, which was withdrawn on arrival of a new wave of colonists in the 6th cent. Libyan/Egyptian opposition was defeated *c.*570 and Greek expansion continued, with more dependent settlements and the cities of Barca and Euhesperides. Evidence for the Libyan relationship is unsatisfactory. Within city territories they presumably provided dependent labour; outside them they were free, although in the adjacent pre-desert perhaps tributary, and, apparently, peaceable; Herodotus notes their Hellenization (see HELLENISM), as well as their cultural influence on Greeks (4. 170–1, 186, 189), there was intermarriage and, by the Hellenistic period, marked racial mixture. Hostile raiding, sometimes serious, may have been initiated by more distant tribes (Diod. Sic. 3. 49). Cyrene's own territory became unusually large for a *polis*, with organized villages reminiscent of Attic *demes; its cereals, vines, olives, and grazing were notable, and the grazing extended into the pre-desert, which was also the source of silphium, Cyrene's characteristic export and emblem (see PHARMACOLOGY); like silphium-collection, animal husbandry must often have been in the hands of Libyans. The horses were particularly famous, horse-drawn chariots became a feature of Cyrene's armies, and chariot-racing, with teams victorious in Greek games (Pind. *Pyth.* 4, 5), a predilection of the rich (see HORSE- AND CHARIOT-RACES). The resultant wealth financed buildings, sculptures, painting, and a tradition of learning and literature; if the great names (e.g. *Aristippus (1), *Carneades, *Callimachus (3), *Eratosthenes) cluster in the Classical and Hellenistic periods, Roman Cyrene made some contribution to Hadrian's *Panhellenion and in late antiquity produced *Synesius.

The *founder (Aristoteles Battus) and his heirs ruled as kings. The dynasty survived civic unrest and revolution as well as family infighting, submitted to *Persia in 525, but recovered independence in the 5th cent.; it was finally overthrown *c.*440. The subsequent republican régime is obscure; 4th-century monuments suggest a prosperous élite and further expansion, perhaps including an extension of influence, to Great Catabathmus (Sollum) in Marmarica, and Arae Philaenorum (Ras el Aali) in Syrtica; this, it has been suggested, would open access to trans-Saharan trade-goods. All Cyrenaica offered allegiance to *Alexander (3) the Great. After his death, and an attempted coup by the adventurer Thibron, it became a dependency of the Ptolemaic kingdom of Egypt (see PTOLEMY (1)). Ptolemy I gave Cyrene a moderately oligarchic constitution under which his own authority was ensured by his permanent office as *stratēgos* (*SEG* 9. 1). A date in 322–1 is now generally accepted for this, but almost all dates and many details after that are disputed. He and his successors aroused some local opposition, and their representatives tended to assert independence (*Ophellas, Magas); briefly, in the middle of the 3rd cent., there was, apparently, a free interlude when *Demophanes and Ecdelus established a federation of the cities; but it ended when Magas' daughter *Berenice (3) married Ptolemy III. Cyrene seems to have been the royal capital but must have lost prestige through Ptolemaic patronage of the other cities (*Berenice/Euhesperides, Arsinoë/Taucheira, Ptolemais/Barca), especially if it was a Ptolemy who raised her port to city-status as Apollonia (but the earliest evidence for this is of 67 BC); all cities presumably lost cohesion by the introduction of new colonists beholden to the Ptolemies (certainly Jews and probably ex-soldiers of the Ptolemaic army); while in the 2nd cent. Ptolemy Physcon (later Ptolemy VIII of Egypt) enlisted diplomatic support from Rome and reinforced it by bequeathing Cyrenaica to Rome should he leave no heir (*SEG* 9. 7). At his death in 116 there were in fact heirs, two of whom, as is now known, succeeded him in turn, Ptolemy IX of Egypt and Ptolemy Apion; but when Apion died in 96 the kingdom did pass to Rome, who accepted the royal property but gave the cities freedom.

Internal factions and external pressures (piratical assaults, perhaps coinciding with Libyan raiding) caused a breakdown of order; the senate authorized annexation in 75/4, but the organization of the new province is uncertain. *Pompey's defeat of the pirates (see PIRACY) in 67 relieved one pressure but the Roman Civil Wars brought others, especially severe when Antony (M. *Antonius (2)) garrisoned Cyrene and restored Cyrenaica to the Egyptian crown. After *Actium, Cyrenaica was combined with *Crete in a public province governed by an annual praetorian proconsul, whose main seat in Cyrenaica was at Cyrene, where the provincial council also met. (For the Augustan decrees found there see CYRENE, EDICTS OF.) The imperial-period monuments suggest modest prosperity, evoking standard signs of élite loyalty to Rome; but it was sharply interrupted c.2 BC–AD 2 by a Marmaric War, after which a small Roman garrison was introduced to guard the Syrtican approaches to Cyrenaica, again in 115–17 by a Jewish Revolt, after which legionary veteran colonists were sent to compensate for the casualties, and under *Claudius II Gothicus when there was another Marmaric War (*SEG* 9. 9), from whose effects Cyrene may have been slower to recover; that perhaps explains why Diocletian preferred Ptolemais as metropolis of his new province of Upper Libya. This was a loss of status to Cyrene which altered her civic character, but the life and works of Synesius seem to show that intellectual pursuits continued there; and, despite severe earthquake damage in the late 4th cent. and further Libyan raiding in the 5th, her Christian monuments are not negligible. Some life survived on the site after the Arab invasions in the 7th century. See MARMARICA; PENTAPOLIS; PTOLEMY (1).

HISTORY Jones, *Cities E. Rom. Prov.*[2] ch. 12; F. Chamoux, *Cyrène sous la monarchie des Battiades* (1953); A. J. Graham, *Colony and Mother-city in Ancient Greece*, 2nd edn. (1983) ch. 4 and app. 2; R. S. Bagnall, *The Administration of Ptolemaic Possessions Outside Egypt* (1976), ch. 3; A. Laronde, *Cyrène et la Libye hellénistique* (1987), and *ANRW* 2. 10. 1 (1988), 1006–2064; P. Romanelli, *La Cirenaica romana* (1943); S. Applebaum, *Jews and Greeks in Ancient Cyrene* (1979); G. Lüderitz, *Die Juden der Cyrenaika* (1993); J. M. Reynolds, *CAH* 10[2] (1996) ch. 13j and 11[2], forthcoming.

SITE R. G. Goodchild, *Cyrene and Apollonia: An Historical Guide* (1963), and *Kyrene und Apollonia* (1971).

ARCHAEOLOGY Surveys: S. Stucchi and others, *Da Batto Aristotele a Ibn el- 'As* (1987); A. Laronde and others, *Les Dossiers d'Archéologie* 167 (1992); D. White and others, *Expedition* 34/1. 2 (1992). Reports: S. Stucchi and others, *L'Agorà di Cirene* 1 (1965), 2/1 (1981), 2/4 (1983), 3/1 (1981); D. White, *The Extramural Sanctuary of Demeter and Persephone at Cyrene … Final Reports* 1 (1984), 2 (1985), 3 (1987), 4 (1990), current work appears mainly in the journals, *Libya Antiqua* (Tripoli), *Libyan Studies* (London), *QAL* (Rome).

INSCRIPTIONS (large groups only) *Corpus Inscriptionum Graecarum* (1825–1877) 3; *SEG* 9; G. Oliverio, *QAL* 1961, 3–54; G. Pugliese-Carratelli and D. Morelli, *ASAA* 1961–2, 217–375.

COINS E. S. G. Robinson, *Catalogue of the Greek Coins of Cyrenaica in the British Museum* (1927); L. Naville, *Les Monnaies d'or de Cyrenaïque* (1951); T. V. Buttrey, in C. N. L. Brooke and others (eds.), *Studies in Numismatic Method Presented to Philip Grierson* (1983), 23–46, in A. M. Burnett and, M. H. Crawford (eds.), *The Coinage of the Roman World in the Late Republic* (1987), 165–74, and *Libyan Studies* 1994. J. M. R.

Cyrene, edicts of, five edicts of *Augustus preserved in a Greek inscription from *Cyrene, published in 1927. The first four belong to 7–6 BC and apply to the public province of *Crete and Cyrene alone; the fifth, which introduces a *senatus consultum*, dates from 4 BC and applies to the whole empire. The documents definitively prove that Augustus received an *imperium maius* (see IMPERIUM) over the public provinces and demonstrate his ably balanced treatment of provincials.

In the first edict Augustus establishes the procedure that criminal cases involving a capital charge against a 'Greek' (i.e. a *Hellenized provincial, here and throughout the inscription) should be tried by mixed juries of Greeks and Roman citizens of a certain census, unless the accused preferred to have an entirely Roman jury. The system is modelled on the *quaestiones perpetuae* (see QUAESTIONES) of Rome. Roman citizens, except Greeks who had received Roman *citizenship, are not allowed to be accusers in cases involving murders of Greeks. The second edict approves the conduct of the governor towards certain Roman citizens. The third addresses the issue of double citizenship, establishing that the provincials who have obtained Roman citizenship should continue to undertake liturgies in their home-cities (see LITURGY; K. Atkinson, *Ehrenberg Studies* (1966), 21 ff. for a different view of 'liturgy' here), unless they had special privileges. Under the fourth, all legal actions between Greeks, other than capital ones, were to have Greek judges, unless the defendant preferred Roman judges. The fifth edict, in which Augustus acts jointly with the senate (see SENATUS), communicates a *senatus consultum* establishing that charges of extortion can be examined by five senatorial judges, after a preliminary examination by the whole senate (see REPETUNDAE; for the problem of this new procedure's relationship to the old, *RDGE* 31). This marks the beginning of the judicial function of the senate.

TEXT *SEG* 9. 8 = Riccobono no. 68 = Sherk, *Augustus* 102 (Eng. trans.); *RDGE* no. 31 (5th edict and *SC* and comm.); Oliver, nos. 8–12 (with Eng. trans. and comm).

F. de Visscher, *Les Édits d'Auguste découverts à Cyrène* (1940); J. Bleicken, *Senatsgericht und Kaisergericht* (1962); A. N. Sherwin-White, *Roman Citizenship*, 2nd edn. (1973), 334 ff.; A. Marshall, *ANRW* 2. 13 (1980), 658 ff.; A. Lintott, *Imperium Romanum* (1993), 64 f.

A. M.; A. J. S. S.

Cyril of Alexandria (d. AD 444), bishop from 412 after his uncle Theophilus. He continued Theophilus' suppression in Egypt of all error (*paganism, *Judaism, heresy), though his monks probably had not his approval for their murder of *Hypatia in 415. Polemic in his Old Testament commentaries presupposes the continuing vitality of pagan cult in Egypt. He replaced the Isis-cult at Menuthis by translating thither relics of SS. Cyrus and John. About 435–40 he wrote twenty books (only 1–10 extant in full) refuting *Julian point by point, so that his refutation is the principal source for reconstructing Julian's work, besides containing many quotations from *Porphyry, *Hermes Trismegistus, and other pagan sources. In 430–1 his zeal for orthodoxy and the honour of *Alexandria (1) led him to attack Nestorius of Constantinople, who was deposed at the council of Ephesus (431). But the resulting schism between *Antioch (1) and Alexandria could be healed (433) only by cautious concessions on Cyril's part, and in the controversy between the 'monophysites' and the defenders of the 'two-nature' Christology of the council of Chalcedon (451) both sides were able to appeal to his statements, the interpretation of which became an issue in theological debate under Justinian.

Ed. Migne, *PG* 68–77; J. Quasten, *Patrology* 3 (1960), 116 ff.; *Select Letters,* ed. and tr. L. R. Wickham (1983).   H. C.; J. F. Ma.

Cyril of Jerusalem, bishop from *c.* AD 350 to his death in 387 (although banished three times from his see). His 24 *Catechetical Lectures* are an important source for liturgical history and for the topography of 4th-cent. *Jerusalem. Cyril promoted the theological significance of holy places, and was instrumental in the development of a 'stational' liturgy; he was also a keen defender of the ecclesiastical status of Jerusalem as the prime see of Christianity, provoking opposition from the provincial metropolitan bishop of (Syrian) Caesarea.

Ed. W. K. Reischl and J. Rupp (1848–60); Eng. trans. L. P. McCauley and A. A. Stephenson (1969–70); P. W. L. Walker, *Holy City, Holy Places?* (1990).   E. D. H.

Cyrus (1) the Great (OP *Kuruš*), son of *Cambyses I, who became *c.*557 BC king of the small kingdom of Anshan in *Persia, at that time subject to the Median king. Beginning in 550 he fought extensive campaigns in which he conquered, respectively, *Media (550/49), *Sardis and *Lydia (546), *Babylonia, and the neo-Babylonian empire (539). At some point (before or after 539?) he conquered central Asia. He was thus the first Persian king to bring together territories into an imperial framework, to whose organization he contributed substantially. In general, the Greek (especially the *Cyropaedia* of *Xenophon (1)), Babylonian ('Cyrus cylinder'), and Judaean sources (Ezra) present him as a conqueror welcomed by the local inhabitants. This apologetic tendency reflects both the expectations nourished by certain groups (e.g. the Jews, who received permission to return to Jerusalem) and a policy continued by his successors: i.e. forging collaborative links with the local élites. This willingness to accommodate local conditions went hand-in-hand with tight control, as shown by the fact that land was confiscated to benefit the crown and Persian nobility. The royal administration also maintained a close watch over the fiscal obligations of the Babylonian sanctuaries. His achievement as founder of the empire was symbolized by the building of a royal residence in Persia, *Pasargadae, where his tomb was also constructed. He was buried here by his son, *Cambyses II, after his death in 530 following a campaign in central Asia.

Briant, *HEA* chs. 1–2.   P. B.

Cyrus (2) the Younger, second son of *Darius II and Parysatis. In 408 BC he was given an overarching command in Asia Minor to enable him to mount an effective fight against Athenian positions. When his ally *Lysander defeated Athens (405/4), he was actually at the Persian court for the coronation of his elder brother

Arsikes/Arses, who took the throne-name *Artaxerxes (2) II. Supported by his mother, he returned to Sardis where he put in train preparations for a *coup d'état.* He mounted his attack with an army of regular contingents from Asia Minor, reinforced by Greek mercenaries, in the spring of 401, thus taking full advantage of the problems faced by the Persians in Egypt, which was slipping from their control at this time. He led his army to Babylonia; a battle was fought at *Cunaxa in which Cyrus lost his life. The reasons for his defeat were primarily political. Contrary to assertions in apologetic literature (esp. Xen. *An.*), he failed to gain the adherence of the Persian nobility and the empire's élites, who remained by and large loyal to Artaxerxes II.

Briant, *HEA,* ch. 15.   P. B.

Cythera, an island off Cape *Malea (Peloponnese) with rich *murex* deposits (see PURPLE), which attracted an early Minoan settlement (MM II–LM I). Perhaps *c.*550 BC Sparta seized it from *Argos (2), installing a garrison and governor (Κυθηροδίκης); its inhabitants became *perioikoi. An obvious strategic threat to Sparta, 'better sunk beneath the sea' said *Chilon, it was captured by *Nicias (1) and held for Athens from 424 to 421 and again from 393 to 386. Lost to Sparta in 195 (see LACONIA) it was given by Augustus in 21 BC to C. *Iulius Eurycles; Hadrian returned the island to Sparta. In myth it was the birthplace of Aphrodite (Hes. *Theog.* 192), who had a sanctuary there (Hdt. 1. 105. 3).

G. L. Huxley and J. N. Coldstream, *Kythera* (1972); P. Cartledge and A. Spawforth, *Hellenistic and Roman Sparta* (1989).   W. G. F.; A. J. S. S.

Cythnos See CYCLADES.

Cytinium, city in *Doris constituting one part of the Tripolis, later the Tetrapolis. Located at the base of Mt. *Parnassus above the *Cephissus valley, it straddled the strategic pass between the Corinthian Gulf and the valley. The *Phocians attacked it in 457 BC, leading to its defence by Sparta and the subsequent confrontation between Sparta and Athens at *Tanagra. *Philip (1) II seized it before the battle of Chaeronea. It was a member of the Delphic *Amphictiony in the 4th cent. and a member of the *Aetolian Confederacy in the 3rd. A 108-line inscription from *Xanthus (*SEG* 38. 1476) details a (failed) Cytinian request for financial help (205 BC) to help rebuild city walls slighted by *Antigonus (3) Doson in (?)228 BC.   J. Bu.

Cyzicus, a colony possibly founded by *Corinthians in 756 BC and again by Milesians (see MILETUS) in 675 (a date partly confirmed by finds of early pottery) on the peninsula of Arctonnesus in the southern *Propontis, among a Myso-Phrygian population. The site rivalled *Byzantium in commercial importance and had the advantage of not being vulnerable to Thracian attacks. The city had an east and west harbour, probably linked through the neck of the peninsula by a navigable channel, and attracted almost all Propontic shipping which avoided the inhospitable northern shore. The city was the largest Propontic contributor, with a tribute of 9 talents, to the Athenian empire (see DELIAN LEAGUE). *Alcibiades won a naval victory over the Spartans here in 411. Its coinage of electrum staters, called Cyzicenes, became famous everywhere.

The commercial importance of the city continued in the 4th cent. and the Hellenistic period, and it acquired an enormous territory in Mysia, adjoining the kingdom of *Pergamum on the south. Relations with the Attalid kings were always good. It received further territory from Rome as a reward for courageous resistance to *Mithradates VI in 74 BC. Privileges were, however,

Cyzicus

lost in 20 BC and in AD 25, when Roman citizens were killed in disturbances and Cyzicus acquired a reputation for disloyalty. Amends were soon made. It became an assize-centre (see CONVENTUS) in the administrative structure of Roman Asia and an important centre of the provincial imperial (*ruler-)cult. *Hadrian provided funds for a huge temple; his bust dominated the pediment and the Cyzicenes regarded him as the thirteenth Olympian god. The foundations and some of the frieze blocks, commemorating Trajan's victories, have survived. As Cyzicus declined, marble was removed and used for buildings in *Constantinople.

Strabo 12. 575–6. F. W. Hasluck, *Cyzicus* (1910); *Arch. Rep.* 1959/60, 4; E. Akurgal, *PECS* 473–4; A. Schulz and E. Winter, *Asia-Minor-Studien* 1 (1990), 33–81 (temple of Hadrian).   T. R. S. B.; S. M.

Dacia was situated in the loop of the lower Danube (see DANUVIUS), consisting mainly of the plateau of Transylvania, but extending in a wider sense eastwards to the Sereth and north to the Vistula. The Dacians were an agricultural people, but under the influence of Celtic invaders (see CELTS) in the 4th cent. BC they absorbed Celtic culture and developed the gold, silver, and iron mines of the Carpathians. From c.300 BC they traded with the Greeks, who frequently confused them with the *Getae, by way of the Danube; from the 2nd cent. they also had relations with the Greek cities of Illyria (see ILLYRII) and *Epirus via Roman traders, seeking slaves. Their chief import was wine.

The separate Dacian tribes were united by *Burebistas c.60 BC and under him they conquered Celtic and Illyrian peoples to the south and west, threatening Roman Macedonia. After his death the power of Dacia declined because of internal struggles. For a time the Dacians were regarded as a serious threat. *Caesar was planning a campaign against them before his death (Suet. *Iul.* 44. 3). Some years later *Octavian (App. *Ill.* 23), also fearing a possible alliance between Antony (M. *Antonius (2)) and the Dacians, sought a marriage alliance with Cotiso, one of the rival Dacian kings (Suet. *Aug.* 63). Under Augustus the Dacians caused few problems, but their military power revived under *Decebalus with victories over Oppius Sabinus (AD 85) and *Cornelius Fuscus (86). After a Roman victory at Tapae (SW Transylvania) *Domitian made peace, recognizing Decebalus as a client ruler (see CLIENT KINGS). Conquest of Dacia was effected by *Trajan in the First and Second Dacian Wars (101–2, 105–6, cf. Cass. Dio 58. 6–14). Decebalus' stronghold Sarmizegethusa (mod. Gradiştea Muncel south of Oraştie, one of several Dacian citadels which have been explored) was taken and destroyed. These campaigns are depicted on the spiral frieze of *Trajan's Column.

Under *Hadrian (117–18) Dacia lost one of its legions while Roman auxiliary garrisons were withdrawn from the plains of the Banat to the west and Wallachia to the east. The remaining territory was divided into three provinces, *Upper Dacia* comprising the heartlands of Transylvania under a praetorian legate and two lesser commands under procurators, *Lower Dacia* in the south-east, and Porolissensis in the north-west. Later in the century (c.168) the provinces were joined again as Tres Daciae under a consular legate.

There was a great influx of people from other provinces into Dacia, especially from Illyricum. Some came as skilled miners, e.g. Dalmatians in the gold mines at Alburnus Maior (Roşia Montana). More than a dozen cities were established; the most important were the *coloniae* at Ulpia Traiana (Sarmizegethusa) and Apulum. As a result of the *Gothic invasions (mid-3rd cent.) Dacia was evacuated under *Aurelian (270), and the name transferred to a new province along the south bank of the Danube.

On Sarmizegethusa: C. and H. Daicoviciu, *Sarmizegethusa (Les Citadelles et les agglomerations daciques des Monts d'Oraştie)* (1963). Roman Wars and military organization: F. Lepper and S. Frere, *Trajan's Column* (1988). Civil settlements: P. Mackendrick, *The Dacian Stones Speak* (1975). Inscriptions: D. M. Pippidi and I. I. Russu, *Inscriptiones Daciae Romanae* 1– (1975–). I. Piso, *Fasti Provinciae Daciae* 1 (1993).

M. M.; J. J. W.

dadouchos, the torchbearer, the second most important priest of the *Mysteries (after the *hierophantēs*) at *Eleusis, was chosen for life from the hieratic clan of the Kerykes. He was distinguished by a headband with a myrtle wreath, a robe (probably) of purple, and his torches: his main task had to do with providing light, a central feature of the cult. The *dadouchoi* were frequently drawn from distinguished families; the appointment was considered a very great honour; and at times there was considerable competition for it. See ELEUSIS.

Clinton, *Sacred Officials.* K. C.

Daedalus, a legendary artist, craftsman, and inventor. *Homer calls artful works δαίδαλα and associates them with *Hephaestus (*Il.* 18. 372 ff., 479, 482, etc.). The Canaanite–*Ugaritic artisan-god Kothar (*ktr*) probably stands behind both. Homer locates Daedalus himself in *Crete (a precociously *orientalizing culture), ascribing to him the χόρος ('dancing-ground') of *Ariadne at *Cnossus (*Il.* 18. 590 ff.); the Cnossian Linear B *da-da-re-jo* ('Daedalus' place') may corroborate the association. Later sources add the Minotaur's *labyrinth, a statue of *Aphrodite, Ariadne's thread, and the bull that captivated Pasiphae—enraging her husband, *Minos, who imprisoned Daedalus.

His escape with his son Icarus on waxen wings may appear in Greece c.560 BC, on a vase from Athens, and in the west c.470, on an inscribed Etruscan gold *bulla* (a type of amulet). Icarus flew too close to the sun and his wings melted, but Daedalus crossed safely to *Sicily, where he was protected by King Cocalus, whose daughters boiled the pursuing Minos alive in a steam bath (Hdt. 7. 170; Diod. Sic. 4. 77–9). There Daedalus was credited with numerous marvels, including a fortress near *Acragas, the platform for Aphrodite's temple on Mt. *Eryx (where he also made a golden ram or honeycomb for the goddess), and his own steam bath at *Selinus. Greek encounters with *Phoenicians already in Sicily perhaps inspired these tales.

Attic 5th-cent. dramatists wrote satyr-plays (*Sophocles (1)) and comedies (*Aristophanes (1), *Plato (2), *Eubulus (2)) about his adventures, and *Aeschylus' *Theoroi* or *Isthmiastae* turned him into a maker of 'living' statues (fr. 78a Radt). Next he was credited with the invention of the walking pose for *kouroi*, whose Egyptian connections were soon noticed (cf.

425

Diod. Sic. 1. 97). Connoisseurs constructed a family tree of Greek and Sicilian pupils (Plin. *HN* 36. 9; Paus. 5. 17; etc.), and local pride labelled many primitive statues with his name (e.g. Paus. 9. 40. 3). His association with the 'Daedalic' style of sculpture is, however, purely modern (see SCULPTURE, GREEK).

By *c*.500, the Athenians had begun to claim him for themselves. *Cleisthenes (2) named a *deme of the tribe Cecropis after him, and *Cleidemus (in Plut. *Thes.* 19) had him escape to Athens, not Crete, and be protected by *Theseus. He was soon incorporated into Attic genealogy via *Erechtheus' son Metion; in Pl. *Euthphr.* 11c, *Socrates even calls him an ancestor. New legends appeared: jealous of his nephew *Talos (2) for inventing the saw, potter's wheel, and compass, he killed him, was tried by the *Areopagus, but escaped to Crete, whereupon his adventures with Minos began (Diod. 4. 76; Apollod. 3. 15, 65)!

A chameleon-like figure mutating with changing political and cultural circumstance, he gained a new lease of life in Rome, where his Sicilian flight caught *Ovid's imagination (*Met.* 8. 183 ff.; *Tr.* 2. 105 f.; etc.), and was popular in Roman painting. A source of inspiration into the 20th cent. (James Joyce and Michael Ayrton), this episode even prompted a self-proclaimed 'New Daedalus' to make the first human-powered flight from Crete to Thera in 1988.

LIMC 3.1 (1986), 313–21; A. F. Stewart, *Greek Sculpture* (1990), 240 ff.; S. P. Morris, *Daidalos and the Origins of Greek Art* (1992). A. F. S.

Daeira, an obscure Attic goddess associated with fertility and identified, in confusing testimonia, with *Persephone, other Underworld figures, or even *Demeter. She received cult in some Attic *demes, apparently had a shrine at *Eleusis, but was not worshipped in the *Mysteries.

P. Moraux, *Une imprécation funéraire à Néocésarée* (1959), 30–8; Clinton, *Sacred Officials*, 98. K. C.

Daimachus, of Plataea. There are two. The elder (before *c*.350 BC), is one of the first of many Boeotian historians, although Jacoby's identification of him as the author of the *Hellenica Oxyrhynchia* is unlikely. The younger was Antiochus I's ambassador to the court of Bindusāra and wrote a history of India. He, rather than the elder Daimachus, may also be the author of works on siege warfare and on piety. See PALIBOTHRA.

FGrH 65 and 716; F. F. Schwarz, in *Beitr. zur alten Geschichte: Festschrift für Franz Altheim* (1969), 1. 293–304. S. Hornblower, in *Proceedings of the Second International Congress of Boiotian Studies* (forthcoming) (defending Jacoby). K. S. S.

daimōn (δαίμων). Etymologically the term *daimōn* means 'divider' or 'allotter'; from *Homer onwards it is used mainly in the sense of operator of more or less unexpected, and intrusive, events in human life. In Homer and other early authors, gods, even Olympians, could be referred to as *daimones*. Rather than referring to personal anthropomorphic aspects, however, *daimōn* appears to correspond to supernatural power in its unpredictable, anonymous, and often frightful manifestations. Accordingly, the adjective δαιμόνιος means 'strange', 'incomprehensible', 'uncanny'. Hence *daimōn* soon acquired connotations of Fate. Hes. *Op.* 122 f., 126, introduced a new meaning: the deceased of the *golden age were to him 'wealth-giving *daimones*' functioning as guardians or protectors (φύλακες). This resulted in the meaning 'personal protecting spirits', who accompany each human's life and bring either luck or harm. A lucky, fortunate person was εὐδαίμων ('with a good *daimōn*': already in Hesiod),

an unlucky one was κακοδαίμων ('with a bad *daimōn*': from the 5th cent. BC).

*Plato (1) used all the earlier meanings of the term and introduced a new one. In *Phd.* 107 d–e, *Resp.* 617 d–e, *620* d–e, he describes guardian-*daimones* who accompany man during his life and after his death function as prosecutor or advocate. In a related sense the *daimōn* becomes a transcendental stake in man, his divine 'Ego', also identified with his *Nous* ('Mind'), which man receives from god, an idea already developed by *Empedocles. Completely new is Plato's concept (e.g. *Symp.* 202d–203a) of *daimones* as beings intermediate between god and men. This notion was adopted by all subsequent demonologies. A pupil of Plato, *Xenocrates (1) (frs. 23–5 Heinze), argued for the existence of good and evil *daimones*. This is essentially the picture accepted by the Stoa (see STOICISM) and in Middle and New Platonism (esp. *Plutarch, *Porphyry, and *Iamblichus (2)). In later antiquity the existence of semi-divine beings helped to solve problems connected with the emergence of monotheistic ideas and the inherent problems of *theodicy. It also offered a solution to the question of the true nature of the old polytheistic gods. They now acquired the status of (good) *daimones* (see ANGELS).

All three solutions were gratefully adopted by Christian theologians: the angels from their own biblical heritage took over the positive functions of good and beneficent intermediaries; all *daimones*, now revealing the true nature of the pagan gods, were interpreted as both the embodiment and the cause of evil and sin against the will of God.

C. Colpe and others, *RAC* 9 (1976), 546–797; J. Z. Smith, *ANRW* 2. 16. 1 (1978), 425–39; F. E. Brenk, *ANRW* 2. 16. 3 (1986), 2068–145. H. S. V.

Dalmatia, a Roman province on the east coast of the Adriatic north of Epirus, took its name from the Delmatae, a warlike Illyrian tribe, partly Celticized (see CELTS), who inhabited the region behind *Salonae. At one time they were subject to the Illyrian kingdom (see ILLYRICUM) but revolted from Gentius and maintained their independence after his defeat by the Romans (168 BC). Because of their attacks on Roman allies they were invaded by the Romans in 156/5 BC and their capital Delminium (mod. Županac near Duvno) was destroyed. More campaigns are recorded against them in 118/7 and 78/7; in 51 they defeated troops sent against them by *Caesar and during the Civil War they sided with the Pompeians and defeated Caesar's legates Q. *Cornificius and A. *Gabinius (2) (48/7 BC). After further fighting under P. *Vatinius (45/4), *Octavian occupied most of their territory (3/3). After more disturbances (16 BC), they were attacked by *Tiberius (11–9 BC), and finally beaten in the last campaign (*bellum Delmaticum*, *ILS* 3320; cf. Vell. Pat. 2. 115. 1) of the great rebellion of AD 6–9, begun by the Daesitiates of Bosnia (see BATO (1–2)). Illyricum was subsequently divided into two imperial provinces, known by the Flavian period as Dalmatia and *Pannonia. The former included all Illyricum south of the river Save and extended eastward almost to the Danube. It was governed by imperial legates of consular rank who resided at Salonae, of whom one, L. *Arruntius Camillus Scribonianus, revolted unsuccessfully in AD 42. In the mid-3rd cent. the senatorial legates were replaced by equestrian *praesides*. Under Diocletian Dalmatia was divided into Dalmatia, its capital at Salonae, and Praevalitana or Praevalis, its capital Scodra; the former was in the *dioecesis Pannoniarum*, the latter in *dioecesis Moesiarum*.

G. Alföldy, *Bevölkerung und Gesellschaft der Römischen Provinz Dalmatien*

(1965); J. J. Wilkes, *Dalmatia* (1969); M. Zaninović, *ANRW* 2. 6 (1977), 767–809.   F. A. W. S.; J. J. W.

Damascus, ancient oasis-city, almost certainly the centre of the Achaemenid province 'Beyond-the-River' (note its role in 333 BC: Q. *Curtius Rufus 3. 8. 12, 13. 1), and a capital of the later *Seleucids, under whom it issued coins (some in the name of Demetrias, assumed for Demetrius III). Annexed by *Pompey in 64 BC, it was granted by M. *Antonius (2) to *Cleopatra VII, reannexed by *Octavian, granted by Gaius (1) to the king of the *Nabataeans (see ARETAS), and finally annexed *c.* AD 62. In the 3rd cent. it was made a *colonia*. It derived its wealth from the products of its territory (notably figs: ps.-Julian, *Ep.* 80 Loeb), from its wool production and from the caravan trade. *Theodosius (3) II and *Arcadius (2) built a church in honour of St John the Baptist. It was taken for good in 635–6 by the Islamic Arabs. The chief extant remains belong to the sanctuary of *Zeus Damascenus, built during the 1st cent. AD.

C. Watzinger and K. Wulzinger, *Damascus* (1922); J.-P. Rey-Coquais, *PECS* 256 f.; F. Millar, *The Roman Near East* (1993), esp. 310 ff.
                                        A. H. M. J.; A. T. L. K., A. J. S. S.

Damastes, of *Sigeum, Greek geographer and historian in the 5th cent. BC, younger contemporary of *Herodotus (1) (*FGrH* 5 T 1) and pupil of *Hellanicus (1) (T 2). His works comprise *Events in Greece*; an ethnographical-geographical work based on *Hecataeus (1) (T 4), exact title unknown (*On Peoples* or *Catalogue of Peoples and Cities* or *Periplus*); *On Poets and Sophists* (*Peri poiētōn kai sophistōn*): lost, probably the first attempt to write a history of Greek literature; *Ancestors of Those who Fought at Troy* (T 1): in antiquity frequently ascribed to *Polus of Acragas, the pupil of *Gorgias (1) (*FGrH* 7), cf. T 3.

FGrH 5; K. von Fritz, *Die griechische Geschichtsschreibung*, 2 vols. (1967); A. Lesky, *History of Greek Literature* (1966).   K. M.

Damasus I, Pope AD 366–84. Damasus organized bloody riots to defeat his rival Ursinus. Elegant and vigorous, cultivated and unscrupulous, this 'matrons' earpick' increased the wealth and status of his church, but generally avoided confrontation with pagan senators. He requested his adviser *Jerome to begin the *Vulgate, and restored martyrs' tombs on which the calligrapher *Filocalus, his 'follower and admirer', engraved his epigrams. He advanced Rome's disciplinary and credal authority, basing it, against Constantinople's, on apostolic succession; his buildings and martyr-cults gave Rome new glory as the Christian capital.

Migne, *PL* 13. 347–418; *Epigrammata Damasiana*, ed. A. Ferrua (1942); *Collectio Avellana*, ed. O. Günther (1895–98) docs. 1, 5–13. E. Caspar, *Geschichte des Papsttums* 1 (1930); C. Pietri, *Roma Christiana* (1976).
                                                              S. J. B. B.

Damia and **Auxesia,** goddesses of fertility (cf. DEMETER and PERSEPHONE / KORE), worshipped at *Epidaurus, *Aegina, and *Troezen (Hdt. 5. 82–8; Paus. 2. 32. 2). Herodotus says that the cult at Epidaurus was instituted on the advice of Delphi (see DELPHIC ORACLE) after a crop-failure, and the cult statues were later stolen by the Aeginetans. The Aeginetan cult involved sacrifices and female choruses who sang ritual abuse against local women. The Epidaurian rites were similar. The Aeginetan statues were kneeling, probably as birth-goddesses. The *aition* for this was that they fell on their knees when the Athenians tried to carry them away unsuccessfully. Women dedicated their brooches to them. At Troezen Damia and Auxesia were Cretan

girls, stoned to death in a revolt, and honoured in the Lithobolia (stone-throwing festival). This and the ritual abuse resemble what occurred in other fertility cults (cf. N. J. Richardson, *The Homeric Hymn to Demeter* (1974), 216, 246). Damia was identified with the Italian *Bona Dea.

RE 2. 2616–18 (Dümmler) and 4/2. 2054 (Kern); *LIMC* 3/1. 323–4.
                                                              N. J. R.

damnatio memoriae After the deaths of persons deemed by the senate enemies of the state, measures to erase their memory might follow. Originally there was no set package, as the phrase implies (cf. Ulp. *Dig.* 24. 1. 32. 7) but a repertoire (Tac. *Ann.* 3. 17. 8–18. 1): images might be destroyed (*Sejanus; *Valeria Messal(l)ina), and their display penalized (L. *Appuleius Saturninus, 98 BC), the name erased from inscriptions, and a man's *praenomen* banned in his family (Livy 6. 20. 14; 384 BC!). With emperors their acts were abolished. *Claudius prevented the senate from condemning *Gaius (1) (Cass. Dio. 60. 4. 5); but decrees were passed against *Domitian (Suet. *Dom.* 23), *Commodus (*SHA Comm.* 20), and *Elagabalus (SHA *Heliogab.* 17).

P. Vittinghoff, *Der Staatsfeind in der röm. Kaiserzeit* (1936); R. Bauman, *Impietas in Principem* (1974), see index.   J. P. B.; B. M. L.

damnum iniuria datum was one of the four sources of delictual obligations mentioned in Gaius, *Inst.* 3. 182. It was based on the most important statutory enactment on Roman private law subsequent to the *Twelve Tables, the *lex Aquilia* of (probably) 286 BC. Its first chapter provided that if anyone wrongfully (*iniuria*) killed another's slave or livestock-quadruped he had to pay the owner the highest value which the thing had had in that year. Ch. 3 dealt with damage not covered by ch. 1 and done to another by unlawfully burning, breaking, or ruining (*urere, frangere, rumpere*) his property; liability was for 'as much as this affair will be in the next 30 days'. (Ch. 2 dealt with different matters and had become obsolete in classical law.) Some details of the actual text of the *lex* are uncertain and much speculation surrounds, in particular, the rather peculiar assessment clauses. The title 9. 2 of the *Digest* contains a wealth of cases concerning damage to property which show the Roman jurists ingeniously interpreting the provisions of the *lex Aquilia*, extending its scope of protection by granting, wherever appropriate, actions on the case (*actiones in factum*) or based on the policy of the statute (*actiones utiles*), and working their way towards more generalized requirements of delictual liability: self-defence, necessity, public authority, and consent as situations where the defendant's act could not be labelled unlawful (*non iure factum*); fault (which the Roman lawyers regarded as implicit in the term *iniuria*) as the basis of Aquilian liability; the effect of contributory negligence; compensation of the plaintiff for damage suffered. Protection was granted in cases of indirect causation (i.e. where the defendant's act could not, strictly speaking, be described as killing (*occidere*) or burning, breaking or ruining; where a non-owner had suffered damages; or where a son in power or a supposed slave who was really free had been injured (extension of Aquilian protection to damage to freemen in general appears to be due to Justinian's compilers)). According to prevailing opinion, the *actio legis Aquiliae* was 'mixed' in classical as well as Justinianic law: it was partly aimed at compensating the injured party for his loss; yet, at the same time it also had a penal character.

A. Pernice, *Zur Lehre von den Sachbeschädigungen* (1867); S. Schipani, *Responsabilità 'ex lege Aquilia'* (1969); U. von Lübtow, *Untersuchungen zur lex Aquilia* (1971); R. Wittmann, *Die Körperverletzung an Freien* (1972); G. MacCormack, *SDHI* 1975, 1 ff.; Lawson and Markesinis, *Tortious*

Damocles

Liability for Unintentional Harm 1 (1982); D. Nörr, Causa mortis (1986); H. Hausmaninger, Schadensersatzrecht der lex Aquilia, 4th edn. (1990); R. Zimmermann, The Law of Obligations (1990), 953 ff.　　R. Z.

Damocles (RE 6), courtier ('friend') and diplomatist of *Dionysius (2) II. The familiar (but ben trovato) story, of the sword suspended over his head as he banqueted, is wrongly attributed by *Cicero (Tusc. 5. 61) to the court of *Dionysius (1) I.　　B. M. C.

Damon (1) (RE 18), *Pythagorean, of *Syracuse. Went bail for Phintias (not Pythias), condemned by a *Dionysius ((1) or (2)); saved by Phintias' last-minute return. One of a series of 'friendship under *tyranny' stories: cf. Harmodius and *Aristogiton, Chariton and Melanippus.　　B. M. C.

Damon (2), pioneering Athenian musicologist, pupil of *Prodicus and teacher of *Pericles (1), admired by *Socrates and *Plato (1). He is said to have invented the 'relaxed Lydian' attunement. His views on *music's political significance, and on ethical effects of various rhythms (probably also of harmoniai, 'attunements') are reflected in Plato, Resp. 3: central doctrines in *Aristides Quintilianus, De mus. 2, may derive from him. If technical analyses underlay his work, their form is unknown but was probably non-quantitative.

Testimonia and fragments in DK no. 37. See also F. Lasserre, Plutarque: de la Musique (1954); A. Barker, Greek Musical Writings 1 (1984); R. Wallace, in R. Wallace and B. Maclachlan (eds.), Harmonia Mundi (1991), 30–53.　　A. D. B.

Damophon, Messenian sculptor, active early 2nd cent. BC. Repaired *Phidias' *Zeus at *Olympia and made marble cult statues for cities of the *Achaean Confederacy: Messene, Aegium, *Megalopolis, and *Lycosura in Arcadia. Substantial fragments of the last have survived, comprising *Demeter and Despoina enthroned, with *Artemis and the *Titan Anytus. They show that Damophon was an eclectic neoclassicist who attempted to update the style of Phidias while paying close attention to the needs of the cult's devotees. Pausanias thought his work important enough to describe at length (8. 37. 1–6, etc.); other connoisseurs ignored it.

A. F. Stewart, Greek Sculpture (1990), 94 ff., 221, 303 f., figs. 788 ff.; SEG 41 (1991), 332 (new 99-line inscription about the Damophon family).　　A. F. S.

Damoxenus, New Comedy poet (see COMEDY (GREEK) NEW), whose name implies non-Athenian birth, although the Suda (δ 50) calls him Athenian. Fr. 1 mentions Adaeus of Macedon, who perished at Cypsela in 353 BC; fr. 2 (68 lines long) a cook's claim to be a pupil of *Epicurus; and fr. 3 a youth playing ball.

FRAGMENTS Kassel–Austin, PCG 5. 1–7.

INTERPRETATION Meineke, FCG 1. 484 f.; G. Kaibel, RE 4/2 (1901), 2082, 'Damoxenos' 3; A. Giannini, Acme 1960, 167 f.; H. Dohm, Mageiros (1964), 161 ff.; I. Gallo, Teatro ellenistico minore (1981), 69 ff.　　W. G. A.

Danaë, in mythology daughter of *Acrisius, king of *Argos (2), and Eurydice. Acrisius imprisoned her, but *Zeus visited her in the form of a shower of gold, and Danaë gave birth to *Perseus (1). Acrisius cast mother and baby adrift in a chest, but they landed safely on the island of Seriphos (Apollod. 2. 4). In later years Perseus rescued Danaë from persecution by Polydectes, king of Seriphos, by turning him to stone with Medusa's head. Scenes of Danaë with the shower of gold, or with the chest, are found not infrequently in art: see J.-J. Maffre, LIMC 3/1. 325–37.　　J. R. M.

Danaus and **the Danaids** The family relationships of Danaus are given by *Pherecydes (2) of Athens (FGrH 3 F 21) and others. They make him the son of *Belus, the brother of Aegyptus, eponym of the Egyptians, and the brother-in-law of *Phoenix (1), eponym of the Phoenicians. He himself is the eponym of the Danaans (Δαναοί), a word of unknown origin used commonly by Homer and other poets to mean the Greeks.

He was the father of 50 daughters, the Danaids. They were the subject of a long epic poem, the Danais, of which we know little except that it described them preparing for a battle in Egypt (fr. 1). From other sources we learn that they were betrothed to their cousins, the 50 sons of Aegyptus, and that, to escape this marriage, they fled with their father to *Argos (2) (whence their ancestor *Io had fled to Egypt) and were received as suppliants by its king, *Pelasgus.

Their reception and their pursuit by the sons of Aegyptus are the subject of the Suppliants of *Aeschylus (see also PV 853–69). This is generally thought to have been the first play of a connected tetralogy of which the other plays were Egyptians, Danaids, and the satyric Amymone. It is uncertain how the story was treated in the rest of the tetralogy, since other sources contradict each other on many details. It is agreed, however, that Pelasgus failed to protect the Danaids from the Egyptians (probably they defeated and killed him in a battle), and that Danaus ordered his daughters to kill their new husbands on their wedding night. All obeyed except one, Hypermestra, who spared her husband Lynceus (probably out of love), and became the ancestor of subsequent kings of Argos. Surviving accounts of this story include Horace, Odes 3. 11 (a famous evocation of Hypermestra's heroism) and Ovid, Heroides 14 (a letter from Hypermestra to Lynceus), as well as treatments by scholiasts (see SCHOLIA) and *mythographers; and lost accounts include plays by *Phrynichus (1) (Egyptians, Danaids) and *Aristophanes (1) (frs. 256–76).

We do not know how Aeschylus resolved the issues, except that *Aphrodite had a role in Danaids and made a speech in favour of love (fr. 44). *Euripides (Or. 871–3) mentions a prosecution of Danaus by Aegyptus, and *Pindar (Pyth. 9. 112–16) says that Danaus found new husbands for his daughters by offering them as prizes in a foot-race. A frequent motif in Latin literature is that of the Danaids' punishment in the Underworld, where they continually pour water into a leaking vessel. But this is not demonstrably earlier than the Roman period ([Plat.] Ax. 371e need not be pre-Roman, and the water-carriers seen in earlier vase-paintings of *Hades need not be Danaids).

The myth of *Amymone and *Poseidon is a separate story, linked by their water-carrying to that of the other Danaids.

LIMC 3. 1 (1986), 341–3, E. Keuls, 'Danaides' and 'Danaos'; A. F. Garvie, Aeschylus' Supplices: Play and Trilogy (1969); E. Keuls, The Water Carriers in Hades (1974).　　A. L. B.

dancing From earliest times, the dance played an important role in the lives of the Greeks, and was sometimes regarded by them as the invention of the gods. It was generally associated with music and song or poetry in the art called μουσική, and frequently made use of a body of conventionalized *gestures, χειρονομία. The dance had a place in religious festivals, in the secret rites of *mysteries, in artistic competitions, in the education of the young, and even in military training, especially in Sparta. People danced at weddings, at funerals, at the 'naming-days' of infants, at harvests, at victory celebrations, in after-dinner merrymaking, in joyous dance processions (κῶμος) through the streets, in animal mummery, and even in incantations. Performances by professional dancers were enjoyed, especially at the *symposium; such dancers were almost all slaves and *hetairai.

Among particularly famous dances of the Greeks were the *geranos* (a nocturnal serpentine dance the name of which is probably derived from the root †ger-, 'to wind', and not from the word for 'crane'); the pyrrhic and related dances by men and boys in armour; the *partheneion*, a song-dance performance by maidens; the *hyporchēma*, a lively combination of instrumental music, song, dance, and pantomime; the skilful 'ball-playing' dance; and the uproarious *askōliasmos*, performed on greased wine-skins. In the worship of *Dionysus the wild *oreibasia*, or 'mountain-dancing' of frenzied women, by classical times was toned down into a prepared performance by a *thiasos, or group of trained devotees.

In the Athenian theatre, the *tyrbasia* of the cyclic choruses, the lewd *kordax* of comedy, the stately *emmelleia* of tragedy, and the rollicking *sikinnis* of the satyr-play were distinctive. The actors in the *phlyakes-plays of *Magna Graecia apparently at times burlesqued the dignified dances of the religious festivals.

The Romans were much more restrained than the Greeks in their use of the dance. Some of them, including *Cicero (*Mur.* 6. 13), openly expressed contempt for dancers. There are records of a few ancient dances used in religious ceremonies—e.g. the leaping and 'three-foot' dances (*tripudia*) of the armed *Salii and the *fratres arvales*, and the 'rope dance' of maidens in honour of *Juno (Livy 27. 37. 12–15). *Etruscan and Greek dancers, from the 4th cent. BC on, exerted some influence, and the introduction of various *oriental cults brought noisy and ecstatic dances to Rome. Dancing by professionals, usually slaves, often furnished entertainment at dinner-parties (see CONVIVIUM). With the coming of the *pantomime, popular interest in the dance became great. See MASKS; MIME; MUSIC.

Ath. 1. 25–7, 37–40; 14. 25–30; Lucian, Περὶ ὀρχήσεως (*On the dance*); Plato, *Leg.* 7. 814e–817e. L. B. Lawler, *The Dance in Ancient Greece* (1964), and *The Dance of the Ancient Greek Theatre* (1964); S. Lonsdale, *Dance and Ritual Play in Greek Religion* (1993).   L. B. L.; A. J. S. S.

Danuvius, ancient name of Celtic or Thracian origin for the Danube, originally denoted only the upper course down to the whirlpools and cataracts (Strabo 7. 3. 13) of the Iron Gates below Belgrade. This stretch remained unknown to the Greeks, long acquainted with the lower course down to the Black Sea as the *Ister, the sources of which long remained a matter of speculation (Hdt. 2. 33). By the 1st cent. BC, when a Roman army first reached the river probably under C. *Scribonius Curio (1) in 72/3 BC (Sall. *Hist.* 3. 79, cf. 49 and 50 Maurenbrecher), the identity of the two had been realized, though many Roman poets preferred the Greek name. Under Augustus the province of *Illyricum was extended to the Danube *c.*12 BC (*RG* 30) which, except for advances into Germany and Dacia (2nd–3rd cents. AD), remained the northern limit of the empire for four centuries. Revered locally as a deity (*CIL* 3. 3416, 11894), the river was held in awe by the Romans (Pliny, *Pan.* 16. 2: *Magnum est, imperator Auguste, magnum est stare in Danubii ripa*, 'A magnificent thing it is, august emperor, to stand on the Danube's bank'). It was bridged in AD 105 by *Trajan, a construction of the architect *Apollodorus (7) of Damascus depicted on Trajan's Column. This followed repair of the tow-path through the gorges (*CIL* 3. 1699 = 8267) in AD 100 and, in the following year, the excavation of a *canal to bypass the barrier of the Iron Gates and permit navigation between the upper and lower courses (J. Šašel, *JRS* 1973, 80: *ob periculum cataractarum derivato flumine tutam Danuvi navigationem fecit,*

'(Trajan) in view of the dangerous waterfalls made the Danube safe to navigate by diverting the river'). From the 1st cent. AD the river was controlled by two Roman fleets, the Pannonian based on the upper course at Taurunum above Belgrade and the Moesian on the lower at Noviodunum near the delta.

J. J. W.

Daphne ('Laurel'), daughter of a river-god (usually the Ladon, in *Arcadia; West on Hes. *Theog.* 344), a wild virgin huntress who caught *Apollo's eye. Failing to outrun the god in her attempt to avoid ravishment, at the point of capture she prayed for help from *Zeus (or her father) and was metamorphosed into a bay-tree; Apollo, clasping the trunk in frustrated passion, had to content himself with adopting her foliage as his cultic plant. *Ovid, *Met.* 1. 452 ff. is the classic treatment; see also *Parthenius, *Love Stories* 15, and Paus. 8. 20, who summarize a Hellenistic Greek version.   A. H. G.

Daphne, a park 9 km. (5½ mi.) south of *Antioch (1), at natural springs supplying the city's water. Its inviolate *temenos, with a temple of *Apollo and *Artemis, was dedicated by *Seleucus (1) I and served by priests appointed by the kings (see *RC* 44 = Austin, no. 175); it saw the celebrated festival and procession staged by *Antiochus (4) IV in 166 BC (*CAH* 8² (1989), 345). *Pompey enlarged its area, and under the Principate it seems to have been imperial property and, in the 4th cent. AD, the site of a palace. Famed for its natural beauties (the emperors protected its famous cypresses), it was a favourite and somewhat disreputable resort of the Antiochenes; in the 4th cent. a controversial festival (the Maiumas?) celebrated there was considered immoral by *Libanius (*Or.* 41. 16–17) and on one occasion banned. A theatre, several villas, and *mosaics have been excavated.

R. Stillwell (ed.), *Antioch on the Orontes* (1938); *PECS* 63.
A. H. M. J.; A. J. S. S.

Daphnis, a Sicilian herdsman, named from the laurel-tree (*daphnē), he was the son, or favourite, of *Hermes and loved by the nymph Echenais who demanded his fidelity. When he was made drunk by a princess and lay with her, the nymph blinded him. This version was attributed, probably wrongly, to Stesichorus (Ael. *VH* 10. 18, Davies, *PMGF* 280; cf. Timaeus, *FGrH* 566 F 83, Diod. Sic. 4. 84). Daphnis consoled himself by inventing pastoral music or perhaps was the first subject of the genre when other herdsmen sang of his misfortunes. In another version, he dies when *Aphrodite, angry because he will love no one, instils in him a powerful passion to which he refuses to yield (Theoc. 1. 64–142).

G. Berger-Doer, *LIMC* 3 (1986), 'Daphnis'   M. H. J.

Daphnis and Chloe See LONGUS.

Dardani, an Illyrian people (their name may derive from the same root as *dardhë*, the Albanian for 'pear') but also linked with Thracians and with Asia Minor, inhabited the upper Vardar valley and the Kosovo region in the southern Balkans. They were neighbours of Macedon on the north-west, with whose kings they fought several major wars between the 4th and 2nd cent. BC and subsequently with Roman proconsuls, until they were finally defeated perhaps by M. *Antonius (2) in 39 BC or M. *Licinius Crassus (2) in 29/8 BC. 'They are so utterly wild that they dig caves beneath their dunghills and live there; but still they have a taste for music and are always playing musical instruments, both flutes and strings' (Strabo 7. 5. 7); they are also known to have had some knowledge of medicinal plants, according to Pedanius

Dardanus

*Dioscorides (2). They were included in the Roman province *Moesia and, after the late 1st cent. AD, in Upper Moesia. Under the Flavians a *colonia* was settled in their territory at Scupi (mod. Skopje). They were still notorious as bandits in the following century (SHA *Marc.* 21. 7). In the late empire it was the homeland of several emperors, notably *Constantine I and *Justinian, the latter marking his birthplace with the new city Justiniana Prima (now located at Caričin Grad in southern Serbia).

> J. Wilkes, *The Illyrians* (1992), 144 ff.   J. J. W.

Dardanus, ancestor of the Trojan kings. In *Iliad* 20. 215 ff. we have the genealogy *Zeus–Dardanus–Erichthonius–Tros, and thereafter

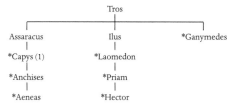

According to *Homer, Dardanus was Zeus' favourite of all his sons by mortal women (*Il.* 20. 304–5). Later authors give two accounts of him. (*a*) He was from *Samothrace, the son of Zeus and *Electra (2), daughter of *Atlas, and brother of *Iasion. Either because he was driven out by *Deucalion's flood (Lycoph. 72–3 and schol.) or because Iasion was killed by a thunderbolt for assaulting *Demeter (Apollod. 3. 12. 1; cf. *Od.* 5. 125 ff.) Dardanus left Samothrace and came to the mainland. Here King *Teucer (1) welcomed him and gave him part of his kingdom and the hand of his daughter Batia in marriage. After Teucer's death Dardanus called the country Dardania (Apollod. 3. 12. 1). (*b*) He lived in Italy, and was son of Electra (2) and *Corythus (1) and brother of Iasius (Iasion). Either the brothers separated, Iasius going to Samothrace and Dardanus to the Troad (*Troas), or Dardanus killed Iasius. Servius on Verg. *Aen.* 3. 167 mentions three other accounts, that he was an Arcadian, a Cretan, and a native of the Troad. The constants are that he was Electra (2)'s son and founded Dardania.

> *LIMC* 3 / 1 (1986), 352–3 (in art).   H. J. R.; J. R. M.

Dares of Phrygia, Trojan priest of *Hephaestus in the *Iliad* (5. 9) and supposed author of a pre-Homeric account of the Trojan War (Ael. *VH* 11. 2). The extant *Daretis Phrygii de excidio Troiae historia* (5th or 6th cent. AD) is represented in a fictional prefatory epistle from *Sallust to *Cornelius Nepos as a translation of this work by the former. It is undistinguished and derivative, but was much read in the Middle Ages.

> Ed. F. Meister (Teubner, 1873). A. Beschorner, *Untersuchungen zu Dares Phrygius* (1992).   S. J. Ha.

Darius I (OP *Dārāyavauš*); son of Hystaspes, a Persian of noble lineage already known in the reigns of *Cyrus (1) and *Cambyses. He seized power after a bloody struggle against an individual said by him to have been the magus Gaumata. It is quite possible that the person he in fact assassinated was Bardiya (Gk. Smerdis), the brother of Cambyses (522 BC). He then had to quell numerous revolts by subject peoples and deal with the insubordinate Oroites, satrap of Sardis. His achievements were commemorated for posterity, in text and picture, on the rock of *Bisitun in Media. To mark what he presented as a refoundation of the empire, he created two new royal residences: *Susa in *Elam and *Persepolis

in *Persia. He also extended the empire in the east (Indus valley) and west (*Thrace). Soon after his brutal crushing of the *Ionian Revolt (*c*.500–493), he put *Datis in command of an army which conquered the Aegean islands, before meeting a setback at the battle of *Marathon (490). Until his death in 486, Darius worked to perfect the administration and tributary structure of the empire, as shown by a famous passage in *Herodotus (1) (3. 89–97). It is illustrated even better by the thousands of Elamite tablets found in the treasury and fortifications of Persepolis. See ACHAEMENIDS; PERSIAN WARS.

> H. Koch, *Es kündet Dareios der König* (1992); P. Briant, *HEA* chs. 2–12, and *Darius, les Perses et l'Empire* (1992).   P. B.

Darius II (Ochus), who ruled *Persia from 424 to 404 BC, was one of *Artaxerxes (1) I's bastard sons; he acceded to the throne after a struggle with his brother, who was killed. Dissension between *Pharnabazus and *Tissaphernes in western Asia Minor meant that the Persians had not regained their former position in the region; this was why Darius sent his younger son, *Cyrus (2), there with exceptional powers. The documents from the centre of the empire are not very informative for Darius' reign, but Egypt and Babylonia are better known due to the *Aramaic documents and the Murashû archives respectively; for the latter see M. Stolper, *Entrepreneurs and Empire* (1985) and *CAH* 6² (1994), ch. 8 b.

> Briant, *HEA* ch. 14.   P. B.

Darius III A descendant of a collateral branch of the royal family, Artashata (not Codomanus) acceded to the throne after the assassination of *Artaxerxes (4) IV and took the name Darius (336 BC). Since antiquity Darius has been judged very negatively—a serious distortion of what was in fact a complex reality. His dynastic legitimacy is well established; he prepared himself well for the confrontation with *Alexander (3) the Great; to the last he adhered to a coherent strategy—unfortunately unsuccessful—in coping with an exceptional opponent. He died in 330 as a result of a plot, when his struggle against Alexander had definitively failed.

> Briant, *HEA* chs. 17–18.   P. B.

Dascylium was the seat of the Persian *satrap of Hellespontine *Phrygia on the shore of Lake Dascylitis (mod. Manyas Göl) and famous for its hunting-park (Xen. *Hell.* 4. 1. 15; *Hell. Oxy.* 17. 3; Strabo 12. 8. 10, 575C). The 1950s excavations of the site at Hisartepe near Ergili have recently (1989) been continued. Several Graeco-Persian relief sculptures have been found in the region and the dig has produced Greek pottery from the early 7th cent. BC, an Old Phrygian and *Aramaic inscriptions, Achaemenid clay seals of Xerxes' reign, and a Babylonian cylinder seal of the second millennium BC. There was another settlement called Dascylium on the sea of Marmara east of the mouth of the Rhyndacus, which appears in the Athenian *tribute lists and was a custom-station of Roman *Asia.

> J. A. R. Munro, *JHS* 1912, 57 ff.; K. Bittel, *Arch. Anz.* 1953, 1 ff.; E. Akurgal, *PECS* 259; S. Mitchell, *Arch. Rep.* 1989/90, 89; M. Nollé, *Studien zur graeco-persischen Kunst: Denkmäler vom Satrapensitz Daskyleion* (1991); T. Corsten, *EA* 1988, 53–76, and 15 (1990), 19–46 (the coastal Dascylium).   D. J. B.; S. M.

Datames, born *c*.405 BC, son of Camisares, allied to the main family of *Paphlagonia. His career is known mainly from the Life by *Cornelius Nepos and his coins. He was satrap of *Cappadocia and rebelled against *Artaxerxes (2) II in the 360s; he died in the ensuing turmoil.

> N. Sekunda, *Iran* 1988; Briant, *HEA* ch. 15.   P. B.

Datis, a Mede (see MEDIA), Persian commander of the 490 BC *Marathon campaign; *en route* he made dedications at *Delos (Hdt. 6. 97) and Rhodian *Lindus: *FGrH* 532 D 1 and perhaps also F 1 32 (+ D 1 for his ?earlier divinely foiled attack). A *Persepolis tablet attests him already in 494, ? in the *Ionian Revolt. He featured derisively in Athenian popular mythology ('song of Datis': Ar. *Peace* 289 ff.), perhaps because of his arrogant letter at Diod. Sic. 10. 27. See also ARISTIDES (1).

D. M. Lewis, *JHS* 1980, 194 f.; A. Raubitschek, *School of Hellas* (1991), ch. 18.   S. H.

Daunians are identified by Greek authors and archaeological evidence as the inhabitants of northern *Apulia; like the Peucetians and *Messapians to the south, they emerge after *c.*700 BC as a distinct tribe of the *Iapygians. The alleged Illyrian origins (see ILLYRII) of the latter receive archaeological support from the iron age graves at Monte Saraceno (Mattinata); there too, certain stone *sēmata* clearly stand in a genetic relationship to the characteristic Daunian steles of the 7th and 6th cents., notable for the intricacies of their incised geometric patterns and erotic and other figured scenes. Relations with the other side of the Adriatic are again apparent in the distribution of Daunian pottery in the 6th and 5th cents. (when Daunian territory also extended to the Melfese, in modern Basilicata). Close contacts with Greek *Tarentum were notable from the late 5th century, while its fall in 272 BC brought prosperity to the Daunian 'princes' allied to Rome, reflected in the rich painted tombs and in the houses with pebble mosaics at Canosa, *Arpi, and other centres.

E. M. De Juliis, *La ceramica geometrica della Daunia* (1977), and *Gli Iapigi* (1988); M. L. Nava, *Stele daunie 1* (1980); R. Cassano (ed.), *Principi imperatori vescovi: Duemila anni di storia a Canosa* (1992).   D. W. W. R.

De rebus bellicis, an anonymous treatise preserved with the *Notitia Dignitatum, recommending to the emperors (probably *Valentinian I and *Valens, AD 364–75) plans for reforming the imperial financial policy, the currency, provincial administration, the army, and the law. The author also describes proposed military machines and equipment, of which coloured illustrations survive in the MSS.

E. A. Thompson, *A Roman Reformer and Inventor* (1952); M. W. C. Hassall and R. I. Ireland (eds.), *De rebus bellicis* (1979).

E. A. T.; R. S. O. T.

Dea Dia, a goddess worshipped by the *fratres arvales, who celebrated her main festival in May. Her function and character are, in many respects, obscure. The etymology of 'Dia' suggests an original connection with the brightness of the sun; but she was also connected with agricultural prosperity.

R. Schilling, *Rites, cultes et dieux de Rome* (1979), 366–70; J. Scheid, *Romulus et ses frères* (1990), 664–9.   M. B.

dead, disposal of Correct disposal of the dead was always a crucial element in easing the *soul of the deceased into the next world. However, the forms of burial varied enormously. Great significance was attached to the choice of inhumation, cremation, or some other rite (e.g. Hdt. 3. 38; Lucr. 3. 888–93), but there is rarely any reason to see a direct correlation between specific methods and specific racial, class, or religious groups.

Greece In prehistory there was enormous variation. An inhumation burial is known from mesolithic times in the Franchthi cave (Argolid), while in Thessaly cremation cemeteries go back to early neolithic. In the early bronze age rich grave goods were sometimes used, particularly in the multiple inhumation tombs of the *Cyclades and *Crete. In the late bronze age, there was for the first time considerable uniformity on the mainland, with multiple inhumations in rock-cut chamber-tombs being the norm. In early *Mycenaean times a few people were buried in spectacular tholos-(beehive) tombs. Very large cemeteries of chamber-tombs have been found at *Mycenae and other sites. This pattern extended as far north as *Thessaly, but in *Macedonia and *Epirus individual inhumation in stone-lined cist-graves, grouped together under mounds of earth, was normal. After the destruction of the Mycenaean world *c.*1200 BC, regional variations returned in the 'Dark Age'. Inhumations in cists with the body contracted were normal at Argos (2); cremation on a pyre with just a handful of the ashes scattered in the grave at *Lefkandi; on Crete, chamber-tombs with multiple inhumations until about 1000, and then multiple cremations with the ashes placed in urns. At Athens, adult rites changed frequently—inhumations in cists in the 11th cent.; cremations with the ashes in urns, *c.*1000–750; inhumations in earth-cut pit-graves, *c.*750–700; cremations in the grave itself, *c.*700–550; and then inhumations in pit-graves, tile-covered graves, or *sarcophagi from about 550 onwards. Early archaeologists associated both cist burial and cremation with the Dorian invasion at various times, but these correlations are not convincing.

There were, however, a few generally observed rules. Cremation with the ashes placed in a metal urn (usually bronze), in the Homeric style, tended to be associated with warrior burials throughout antiquity. Children were rarely cremated, and in most places infants were buried inside amphoras or storage pots. Starting in the 6th cent. there was a general trend towards simpler burials, which may have been accompanied by sumptuary laws. Inhumation in pit-graves or tile graves was adopted for adults in most parts of Greece by the 6th or 5th cent. The main exception was western Greece, where adults were inhumed in giant storage pots from the Dark Age to Hellenistic times.

Rich grave goods and elaborate tomb markers went out of style everywhere for most of the 5th cent., but returned around 425. There was a great flowering of funerary sculpture at Athens in the 4th cent. Funerary spending escalated still further after 300, and in the 3rd–1st cents. BC the massive 'Macedonian'-style vaulted tombs, often with painted interiors, are found all over Greece. The most spectacular of these are the late 4th-cent. royal tombs, possibly of *Philip (1) II and his court, at Vergina in Macedonia (see AEGAE). Athens was an exception to this general pattern. Cicero (*Leg.* 2. 66) says that *Demetrius (3) of Phalerum banned lavish tombs, probably in 317, and indeed no monumental burials are known from Attica between then and the 1st cent. BC. Lucian (*On Mourning* 21) called cremation a 'Greek custom', but he was probably thinking in purely literary terms, drawing on classical passages such as Hdt. 3. 38. In Roman times inhumation was the strict rule throughout the whole Greek east, although the precise forms varied—from tile graves at Athens to chamber-tombs at *Cnossus, built tombs at Dura *Europus, and spectacular rock-cut tombs at *Petra. Greek settlers in the near east, from Egypt to Bactria, generally adopted rites very similar to the local population's practices.

Rome Burial customs in prehistoric Italy were as varied as those in Greece. The earliest graves found at Rome date to the 10th cent. BC, and include both urn cremations and inhumations. There is, however, no reason to see these as belonging to different racial groups. Roman burials were until about 100 BC generally rather simple, in marked contrast to their neighbours the *Etruscans, who built complex chamber-tombs which often housed cremations in unusual urns, accompanied by rich grave goods. From the 8th cent. on the customs of southern Italy were heavily influenced by Greek settlers, and inhumation generally replaced cremation. Impressive local traditions of tomb-painting developed, particularly in *Campania.

At Rome itself, few burials are known from republican times, suggesting that rites were so simple as to leave few archaeological traces. Across most of Europe in the 5th–3rd cents. the bulk of the population was disposed of relatively informally, often by exposing the body on platforms. In Italy there is some evidence for mass burial of the poor in huge open pits. The use of these *puticuli* at Rome in the late republic is mentioned by *Varro (*Ling.* 5. 25; cf. Hor. *Sat.* 1. 8; Festus, entry under 'puticuli'), and a few were excavated in the 1880s. By the 3rd cent. BC some of the rich were being cremated with their ashes placed in urns and buried in communal tombs. By the 1st cent., cremation was the norm, and according to *Cicero (*Leg.* 2. 57) and *Pliny (1) the Elder (*HN* 7. 187) even the ultra-conservative Cornelii gave up inhumation in 78 BC. At about the same time, Roman nobles began building very elaborate tombs modelled on those of the Greek east, with monumental sculptures and elaborate stone architecture.

The spiralling cost of élite tombs ended abruptly under Augustus, who built himself a vast mausoleum. Other nobles were careful to avoid being seen as trying to rival the splendour of the imperial household (but see CESTIUS EPULO, C.). Simpler tombs, organized around modest *altars, came into fashion for the very rich, while the not-quite-so-rich and the growing number of funerary clubs (see CLUBS, ROMAN) (*collegia*) adopted the *columbarium* (2) (a word meaning 'dovecot', coined by modern scholars). The earliest example dates to *c.*50 BC, but they became common after *c.* AD 40. They were barrel-vaulted brick and masonry tombs with niches for urns, usually holding 50–100, although one example found at Rome in 1726 held 3,000 urns.

Urn cremation was adopted all over the western empire in the 1st and 2nd cent. AD, although there were always significant local variations. By about AD 150, the empire can be divided into a cremating, Latin-using west and an inhuming, Greek-using east. But during the 2nd cent. members of the Roman élite adopted inhumation, probably as a conscious emulation of Hellenistic practices, and in the 3rd cent. this rite gradually swept across the whole west. The change has no obvious links to *Christianity or any other religious movement. However, it was certainly convenient for the spread of Christianity, which generally opposed cremation, which destroyed the body and posed difficulties for some visions of the day of resurrection. By the late 4th cent., certain practices found widely in western cemeteries—an east–west orientation, the use of lime on the walls of the grave, and the decline of grave goods—might indicate the presence of Christians. At Rome itself, there was a general shift around 300 away from traditional cemeteries in favour of *catacombs and burial within *basilicas.

See further ART, FUNERARY, GREEK and ROMAN; CEMETERIES; DEATH, ATTITUDES TO.

D. Kurtz and J. Boardman, *Greek Burial Customs* (1971); J. Fedak, *Monumental Tombs of the Hellenistic Age* (1990); I. Morris, *Death-Ritual and Social Structure in Classical Antiquity* (1992); J. Toynbee, *Death and Burial in the Roman World* (1971); R. Reece (ed.), *Burial in the Roman World* (1977); H. von Hesberg and P. Zanker (eds.), *Römische Gräberstrasse* (1987). I. Mo.

Dead Sea Scrolls, documents made of leather and papyrus, and, in one case, of copper, found between 1947 and 1956 in caves near Qumran by the Dead Sea. The scrolls, written by Jews, are mostly in Hebrew and *Aramaic, but a small number are in Greek. Many are fragments of biblical texts from the Old Testament and from Jewish religious compositions otherwise only preserved through Christian manuscript traditions. The scrolls were written in the last centuries BC and 1st cent. AD.

Of particular significance in the study of *Judaism in this period are the texts composed by sectarians, who are probably to be identified with Jews who used the nearby site at Qumran as a religious centre. These texts include community rules, hymns, liturgical texts, calendars, and works of bible interpretation. Among this last group is found the *pesher* type of interpretation, characteristic of this sect and rarely found elsewhere in Jewish literature, in which the real meaning of scriptural passages is alleged to lie in hidden allusions to more recent events.

The Community Rule (1QS, also called the Manual of Discipline), a composite work found in various manuscripts in different caves, laid down the rules for initiation into the community and for living within it. The Rule of the Congregation or Messianic Rule (1QSa) gives regulations for the eschatological integration of the 'congregation of Israel' into the sectarian community. The Damascus Rule (CD) is also attested in a medieval manuscript (the Zadokite Fragments) discovered in Cairo in 1896. The War Rule (1QM) is a rather different text which regulates the behaviour of the 'sons of light' in the eschatological war against the 'sons of darkness'. The Temple Scroll (11QT) contains a systematic statement of the regulations pertaining to the Temple cult, derived from the Pentateuch but with frequent non-biblical additions which are presented as the direct words of God. Numerous fragments of the scrolls are still unedited and it is certain that more sectarian material will be recognized in the remaining material.

How many of those documents were originally composed by adherents of one particular sect is debated. If the scrolls were deposited in the caves for safe keeping, they may have been placed there by more than one group, perhaps after the destruction of the Jerusalem Temple in AD 70. The contents of the Copper Scroll (3Q15), a prosaic list of the hiding-places of an immensely valuable treasure, might support this hypothesis, but finds of multiple copies of some sectarian texts in different caves may suggest that only one sect was responsible for placing them there. In that case doctrinal differences between texts must be accounted for by supposing either variant branches of the sect or a gradual development of the sect's ideas over time.

Many attempts have been made to connect the scrolls to the Jewish groups of this period known from other sources. Most such attempts assume that the scrolls were deposited by the inhabitants of the site at Qumran, where excavation revealed a small community, isolated in the desert, with a deep concern for ritual purity. The most plausible of such identifications is with the *Essenes, who are known primarily from descriptions by *Philon (4), *Josephus, and *Pliny (1) the Elder. However, the classical evidence is equivocal and contradictory, and some aspects of the Essene society depicted there do not fit the evidence from the scrolls, so that those who hold this hypothesis have to consider the scrolls community as Essenes of a peculiar type. It may be better to take the sectarian material in the scrolls as evidence of a type of Judaism otherwise unknown. See RELIGION, JEWISH.

Editions in series *Discoveries in the Judaean Desert* (1955–) (for other editions, see bibliographies); facsimile edition (1992). Translation: G. Vermes, *The Dead Sea Scrolls in English*, 4th edn. (1994). General introduction in G. Vermes, *The Dead Sea Scrolls: Qumran in Perspective* (1977). Bibliography in J. A. Fitzmyer, *The Dead Sea Scrolls: Major Publications and Tools for Study*, 2nd edn. (1977); Schürer, *History* 3 / 1. 380–469. On the site at Qumran, see R. de Vaux, *Archaeology and the Dead Sea Scrolls* (1973). Numerous studies and reviews can be found in *Revue de Qumran*, *Journal of Jewish Studies*, and in *Dead Sea Scrolls Discoveries*.

M. D. G.

deae matres, 'mother goddesses', whose cult is widely attested in monuments and inscriptions of the Celtic and Germanic regions of the Roman empire, from northern Italy to Britain. Their role as fertility goddesses is suggested not only by their titles but also by their most common attribute, baskets of fruits and other provisions. There was, however, considerable local variation both in epithets and in iconography, indicating that their general character took many particular forms. The most distinctive representation is of a triad, typical of Celtic thought, although individual goddesses, pairs, and groups of four or more are also common. In some cases they are associated with springs, while in others they are depicted nursing infants. The title *matronae* ('matrons') was preferred in northern Italy and on the lower Rhine, while their epithets, found in many parts of the empire, often incorporate tribal or local names. See RELIGION, CELTIC.

G. Bauchheiss and G. Neumann, *Matronen und verwandte Gottheiten* (1987).

J. B. R.

death, attitudes to

Greek The Greek attitude towards *Hades is best summed up by *Achilles, 'I'd rather be a day-labourer on earth working for a man of little property than lord of all the hosts of the dead' (*Od.* 11. 489–91). The Homeric dead are pathetic in their helplessness, inhabiting draughty, echoing halls, deprived of their wits (*phrenes*), and flitting purposelessly about uttering batlike noises (*Od.* 24. 5 ff.). Athenian lawcourt speeches urge the jury to render assistance to the dead as if they were unable to look after their own interests (e.g. Lys. 12. 99). The precise relationship between the living body and the *psychē* (spirit of the dead) is unclear, since the latter is only referred to in connection with the dead. The necessity of conducting burial rites (e.g. *Il.* 23. 71) and the insult to human dignity if they are omitted (cf. Soph. *Ant. passim*) are frequently mentioned in literature. Except in philosophy and *Orphism (cf. Pind. *Ol.* 63–88; Pl. *Resp* 2. 363c–e, *Phd.* 113d–114c), belief in a dualistic after-life is largely absent from Greek eschatology. In Homer the Underworld judge *Minos merely settles lawsuits between the litigious dead (*Od.* 11. 568–70). Only gross sinners (e.g. *Tantalus, *Tityus, and *Sisyphus) receive retributive punishment (see TARTARUS), while the favoured few end up in the Elysian Fields (4. 561 ff.; see ELYSIUM). Fear of the after-life was therefore largely absent (but cf. Pl. *Resp.* 1. 330d). Though powerless in themselves the dead had access to the infernal powers, notably Pluto (Aedoneus) and Persephone, for which reason folded lead plaques (*katadesmoi*) inscribed with *curses bearing the name of the person to be 'bound down' were occasionally placed in graves.

The deceased's journey to the next world was effected by elaborate ritual conducted by the relatives of the deceased, primarily women. The funeral, from which priests were debarred for fear of incurring *pollution, was a three-act drama which comprised laying out the body (*prothesis*), the funeral cortège (*ekphora*), and the interment. We only rarely hear of undertakers (*nekrothoptoi, nekrophoroi*) and other 'professionals'. We know of

no burial 'service' as such. Cremation and inhumation were often practised concurrently in the same community, with no apparent distinction in belief. From *c.*500 BC intramural burial was forbidden in Athens (cf. Plut. *Lyc.* 27 for Sparta). No tomb-cult was practised in early times, but in Classical Athens women paid regular visits to the grave. Offerings included cakes and *choai*, i.e. libations mainly of pure water. The attention that the dead received from the living in this period was judged to be so important that it constituted a reason for adopting an heir (Isae. 2. 36, 7. 30). In the Archaic period a funeral provided a perfect showcase for the conspicuous display of aristocratic wealth, power, and prestige, and many communities passed legislation designed to limit its scope and magnificence (e.g. [Dem.] 43. 62 and Plut. *Sol.* for *Solonian legislation; *Syll.*³ 1220 for *Delphi).

Funerary ritual was substantially modified for those who died in their prime, the unburied dead, victims of murder, suicides, heroes, etc. Special sympathy was felt towards women who died at a marriageable age but unmarried. To underline their pathos, a stone marker in the form of a *loutrophoros* (i.e. vase used in the nuptial bath) was placed over the grave. Victims of murder were vengeful and malignant, as indicated by the grisly practice of cutting off their extremities (see MASCHALISMOS). Most powerful were the heroic dead, who even in *Plutarch's day still received blood sacrifice (Plut. *Aristides* 21).

Geometric vases depict only the *prothesis* and *ekphora*, whereas Athenian white-ground *lēkythoi* (oil flasks) frequently depict tomb-cult. *Hades is rarely represented in Greek art (but cf. Paus. 10. 28–31 for *Polygnotus' lost painting, the *Nekyia*) or in literature (*Od.* 11 and Ar. *Frogs* are notable exceptions; cf. too '*Orphic gold leaves). Though the belief in Hades as the home of the undifferentiated dead predominated and never lost its hold over the popular imagination (cf. its persistence as a theme in epitaphs), other concepts include the transformation of the dead into stars (e.g. Castor and Pollux), their absorption into the upper atmosphere or aether (e.g. *IG* 1³. 1179), the Pythagorean (e.g. DK 14, 8a) and Platonic (e.g. *Phd.* 107d) belief in *transmigration, and the indistinct 'blessedness' promised to initiates in the mysteries of *Eleusis. See AITHER; PLATO (1); PYTHAGORAS.

Roman In the Roman tradition death is conceived of essentially as a blemish striking the family of the deceased, with the risk of affecting all with whom it had contact: neighbours, magistrates, priests, and sacred places. For this reason ritual established a strict separation between the space of the deceased and that of the living. Cypress branches announced the blemished house, and on days of sacrifices for the dead sanctuaries were closed.

The time of death spanned above all the period when the deceased's corpse was exposed in his or her home, its transport to the cemetery, and its burial. These operations were usually completed after eight days. The transformation of the corpse was achieved in the course of 40 days. The deceased did not, in the course of the funerary ritual, arrive at life eternal, but joined, as it were, a new category: those members of the community, the di *manes, who lived outside towns on land set aside for this purpose and managed by the pontifices. The legal status of these tombs was that of the *religiosum* (see RELIGION, ROMAN, TERMS RELATING TO). The *di manes* were thought of as an undifferentiated mass or (rather) a collective divinity (Romans spoke of the *di manes* of such-and-such a person), and received regular cult during the *Parentalia of 13–21 February and at other times. The immortality which they enjoyed was conditional on the existence of descendants, or at least of a human presence (a proprietor of the land on which the tomb was located, or a funerary *collegium*: see CLUBS, ROMAN), since it was the celebration of funerary cult, in the form of sacrifices, which ensured the deceased's survival.

The unburied dead were called *lemures* and thought of as haunting inhabited areas and disturbing the living. Usually anonymous (being no longer integrated into any social context) they none the less received cult at the *Lemuria in May, supposedly to appease them.

Along with these forms of survival, conceived generally as menacing and undesirable, there existed a third belief about life after death—deification. Combining Roman tradition with Hellenistic practices and ideas deriving from Hellenistic philosophy, the deification of exceptional individuals was instituted at Rome after *Caesar's assassination. Thereafter elevation to the status of a god (*divus*) by a *senatus consultum* became the rule for emperors and some members of their families (SEE RULER-CULT).

To these traditions was added, from the last centuries of the republic on, a series of Hellenistic concepts, ranging from speculation about the immortality of the soul to images of hell. Verse epitaphs prove that these ideas were rarely exclusive and coherent. We are dealing with speculations rather than beliefs capable of shaping a person's whole existence.

See CEMETERIES; CONSOLATION; DEAD, DISPOSAL OF; EPIGRAM.

GREEK M. Alexiou, *The Ritual Lament in Greek Tradition* (1974); C. M. Antonaccio, *An Archaeology of Ancestors* (1995); J. Bremmer, *The Early Greek Concept of the Soul* (1983); D. C. Kurtz and J. Boardman, *Greek Burial Customs* (1971); R. S. J. Garland, *The Greek Way of Death* (1985); S. C. Humphreys and H. King, *The Anthropology and Archaeology of Death: Transience and Permanence* (1982); I. Morris, *Death-Ritual and Social Structure in Classical Antiquity* (1992); E. Rohde, *Psyche* (Eng. trans. 1925); C. Sourvinou-Inwood, *'Reading' Greek Death* (1995); E. Vermeule, *Aspects of Death in Early Greek Art and Poetry* (1979).

ROMAN A. Brelich, *Aspetti della morte nelle iscrizioni sepolcrali dell'impero romano*, Diss. Pannonicae 1/7 (1937); G. Sanders, *Lapides memores. Païens et chrétiens faces à la mort: le témoignage de l'épigraphie funéraire latine* (1991); F. Cumont, *After-Life in Roman Paganism* (1922), and *Recherches sur le symbolisme funéraire des Romains* (1942); J. Toynbee, *Death and Burial in the Roman World* (1971); A. Fraschetti (ed.), *Annali dell'Istituto universitario orientale di Napoli, Sezione di archeologia e storia antica* (1984); J. Scheid, *Klio* 1993; A. D. Nock, *Harv. Theol. Rev.* 1932; P. Boyancé (ed.), in *Études sur la religion romaine* (1972); I. Morris, *Death-Ritual and Social Structure in Classical Antiquity* (1992).

R. S. J. G., J. Sch.

debt, the creation of obligations in cash or kind, existed at all levels of society throughout the ancient world: from loans of seed and implements between peasants (Hes. *Op.* 396 ff., 453 ff.) to lending of small sums and household objects between city-dwellers (Theophr. *Char. passim*), from borrowing to cope with unforeseen crises (Dem. 53. 4 ff.) to substantial cash loans between the wealthy to support an élite lifestyle (Ar. *Nub.*; Plut. *Mor* 827 ff.). More generally, the partly random testimony of papyri from Ptolemaic and Roman Egypt hints at the likely frequency of loan transactions in other times and places, largely concealed by the perspective of surviving sources. The part played by debt in funding trade and commerce (see MARITIME LOANS) is disputed; but always to the fore were the socio-political implications of widespread indebtedness, plausibly linked with the so-called 'Solonic Crisis' (see SOLON) in Archaic Athens and the 'Struggle of the Orders' in early *Rome. In time of siege or revolution, the indebted could be a force to be reckoned with (Aen. Tact. 5. 2, 14. 1; Thuc. 3. 81.). Athens after Solon was exceptional in its successful prohibition of loans secured on the person (*Ath. pol.* 6. 1); debt-bondage and other forms of debt-dependence were common throughout the remainder of the Greek and Roman worlds. Frequent laws intended to regulate debt were rarely enforceable and generally had only limited or temporary effect. Forms of debt-bondage continued in Rome long after the *lex Poetelia de nexis* (326 BC, see POETELIUS LIBO VISOLUS, C.), which reputedly prohibited imprisonment for debt. Wider implications of indebtedness were also apparent at the upper end of society. Wealthy Athenians risked their status by raising loans on the security of property to fulfil *eisphora (tax) and prestigious *liturgy obligations. In the late Roman republic, indebtedness was intertwined with élite politics: the massive debts incurred by politicians in the pursuit of power could result in credit crises (49 BC, on the eve of the Civil War) and, in extreme cases, point the way to revolution (the conspiracy of *Catiline). A possible alternative was exploitation of the provincials: *Cicero, while governor in Cilicia, records with more dismay than surprise loans at usurious rates of interest by *Brutus to the nearby city of *Salamis (2) on *Cyprus, and by *Pompey to *Ariobarzanes III, king of neighbouring *Cappadocia (*Att* 5. 21; 6. 1).

M. I. Finley, *The Ancient Economy* (1973; 2nd edn. 1985), *Land and Credit in Ancient Athens 500–200 BC* (1951; repr. 1985), and *Economy and Society in Ancient Greece* (1981), 150 ff.; J. A. Crook, *Law and Life of Rome* (1967); G. E. M. de Ste Croix, *Class Struggle* (1981); P. C. Millett, *Lending and Borrowing in Ancient Athens* (1991); D. Asheri, *Studi classici e orientali* 1969, 5 ff.; H. A. Rupprecht, *Untersuchungen zum Darlehen im Recht der graeco-aegyptischen Papyri der Ptolemäerzeit* (1967); M. Frederiksen, *JRS* 1966, 128 ff.; D. Braund, in A. Wallace-Hadrill, (ed.), *Patronage in Ancient Society* (1989), 137 ff.; J. Andreau, *La Vie financière dans le monde romain* (1987); J. P. Royer, *Revue historique de droit français et étranger* 1967, 191 ff., 407 ff.; S. Mrozek, *Hist.* 1985, 310 ff.   P. C. M.

decaproti (δεκάπρωτοι) first appear in AD 66 and become common throughout the eastern provinces of the Roman empire in the 2nd and early 3rd cents.; the office was abolished in Egypt and probably elsewhere in AD 307–8. *Decaproti* were probably in origin a finance committee of the city council, concerned with civic revenues and endowments. By the 2nd cent. they were collecting imperial taxes and levies, and in the 3rd this was their chief function; in Egypt they were responsible for the imperial land revenue. They were liable to make good deficits from their own property. Normally ten in number, the board had a varying membership, sometimes increasing to twenty. They were elected, and probably held office for five years. See FINANCE, ROMAN.

T. Schwertfeger, *Olympia Bericht* 1981, 251 ff. (with bibliog.).   A. H. M. J.; A. J. S. S.

decarchies were juntas, literally 'ten-man rules', established under the aegis of *Lysander in parts of the former Athenian empire (see DELIAN LEAGUE) following Sparta's victory in the *Peloponnesian War. They were non-responsible, absolute dictatorships (*dunasteiai* in Greek parlance), sometimes supported by a garrison under a Spartan commander known as a *harmost. They collected their city's share of the war-tax levied by Sparta (*Ath. pol.* 39. 2) and in other ways functioned as instruments of Sparta's nasty, brutish, and short-lived Aegean empire. Best-attested, and most notorious, were the *Thirty Tyrants at Athens, who ruled with the aid of the Piraeus Ten. But their overthrow in 403 BC was soon followed by the abolition of many other decarchies, especially in the Asiatic cities, in 403–2; the rest fell either after Sparta's defeat at sea off *Cnidus (394) or at the conclusion of the *King's Peace (386).

A. Andrewes, *Phoenix* 1971, 206–26; P. Rahe, (Diss. Yale, 1977); J.-F.

Bommelaer, *Lysandre de Sparte: Histoire et traditions* (1981); P. Cartledge, *Agesilaos and the Crisis of Sparta* (1987), 90–1.   P. A. C.

Decebalus, king of *Dacia, a shrewd and resourceful military leader, led several campaigns against Rome (AD 85–9) in which a governor of Moesia, Oppius Sabinus, and later Domitian's praetorian prefect, *Cornelius Fuscus, were killed. Although the Dacians were defeated at Tapae in 88, *Domitian, faced with military rebellion in Germany and offensive moves by the *Marcomanni and *Quadi on the Danube, concluded a generous peace by which Decebalus was established as a king friendly to Rome (see CLIENT KINGS), was granted the assistance of Roman engineers, and received an annual subsidy. *Trajan, suspicious of Decabalus' power and eager for military glory, invaded Dacia (101–2) and after a tough campaign imposed a peace settlement which left Roman garrisons there. In 105 Trajan went to war again, apparently in response to Decebalus' infractions of the treaty. Sarmizegethusa, the capital, was captured, Decebalus, ruthlessly pursued, committed suicide, and the province of Dacia was created (106).

M. Speidel, *JRS* 1970, 142 ff. (inscription, about Decebalus' captor).   J. B. C.

Decelea, a small Attic *deme with its centre at Tatoi in the foothills of Mt. *Parnes and extensive views over the Attic plain. It is included in *Philochorus' list of twelve townships united by *Theseus (Philochorus, *FGrH* 328 F 94). Archaeological remains here date from the late bronze age onwards, including a 4th-cent. BC Athenian fort and some remains which may be associated with the Spartan garrison stationed there between 413 and 404 BC (Thuc. 7. 19, 27–8). The most famous and important Attic *phratry inscription, the Demotionid decree (*IG* 2². 1237), was found at Tatoi.

Th. A. Arbanitopoulou, Δεκέλεια (1958); J. Ober, *Fortress Attica* (1985), 141–4.   C. W. J. E.; R. G. O.

Decelean War See PELOPONNESIAN WAR.

decemprimi, the ten senior members of the local council of a Latin or Roman municipality (**municipium*), formed with the yearly magistrates a group which in times of crisis represented the community in dealings with the central government. They are mentioned in the republican period only, but in the fully developed empire a similar group of **decaproti* emerges as specially liable to Rome for the collection of the imperial taxes. The connection between the two groups is obscure. See DECURIONES.   A. N. S.-W.

Decemvirates, First and Second According to the developed Roman tradition, after prolonged plebeian agitation for the compilation of a law code, all regular magistracies (including the plebeian tribunate) were suspended for 451 BC and replaced by a board of ten with consular powers (and not subject to appeal (**provocatio*)). Consisting largely of ex-consuls, this board drew up ten tables of laws but was replaced for 450 by a second, similar decemvirate. This second board drew up two further tables (including a ban on legitimate marriages between patricians and plebeians) but, led by Ap. *Claudius Crassus Inregillensis Sabinus, became increasingly tyrannical and refused to relinquish office (in the Varronian chronology it holds office only for one year, but other chronologies usually assign it two). The fall of the Second Decemvirate, reversal to the consulship and legislation of L. *Valerius Poplicola Potitus and M. Horatius Barbatus was precipitated by Claudius' attempted seizure of Verginia and the

resultant Second Secession. The members of the Second Decemvirate committed suicide or went into exile; the tables of laws were set up publicly as the *Twelve Tables.

Much of this narrative is implausible and incoherent, particularly that of the Second Decemvirate, whose history borrows central motifs from the overthrow of *Tarquinius Superbus and the First *Secession and hence is used by *Cicero (*Rep.* 2. 61 ff.) as exemplifying the decline of aristocratic rule into oligarchic oppression. The explanation offered for its appointment (rather than the continuation of the first board in office) is inadequate and its apparent inclusion of five patricians and five plebeians is at odds with the entirely patrician composition of the first board and its own supposed reinforcement of patrician exclusivity. The First Decemvirate is more credible (if the Twelve Tables are genuinely mid-5th cent.) but the varying annalistic accounts of its prehistory, purpose, and operation have no secure basis and are in part contradicted by the tables themselves. If historical, the Decemvirate will represent a special magisterial commission in the Greek style, charged with the compilation and publication of key provisions, particularly of civil law. However, the (rival) stories of an embassy to Athens and other Greek cities to collect laws in 454 or of assistance by Hermodorus of Ephesus in compiling the Twelve Tables will be fictions, probably designed in part to explain supposed Greek borrowings in the Tables.

CAH 7²/2 (1989), 114 f., 227 ff., 718 ff. (bibliog.).   A. D.

decemviri sacris faciundis See QUINDECEMVIRI SACRIS FACIUNDIS.

decemviri stlitibus iudicandis ('Board of ten for judging lawsuits'). Sex. Pomponius (*Dig.* 1. 2. 2. 29) implies that this minor magistracy (belonging to the **vigintisexviri*) was established between 242 and 227 BC but some scholars interpret a supposed *lex Valeria Horatia* of 449 (Livy 3. 55. 7 (see VALERIUS POPLICOLA POTITUS, L.)) as referring to a plebeian forerunner. In the late republic the *decemviri* certainly judged suits to decide whether a man was free or slave but *Augustus probably transferred this function to **recuperatores* and made the *decemviri* presidents of the *centumviri. They are last attested in the mid-3rd cent. AD.

J. M. Kelly, *Studies in the Civil Judicature of the Roman Republic* (1976), 66 ff.; J.-C. Richard, *Les Origines de la plèbe romaine* (1978), 564.   A. D.

Decidius (*RE* 4) **Saxa, Lucius,** constantly attacked in *Cicero's *Philippics* and described as a foreigner 'from the furthest reaches of Celtiberia' (11. 12), but in fact of Italian (probably Samnite) descent. After serving as an officer under *Caesar in the Civil War he was made tribune by Caesar (perhaps 44 BC). After Caesar's death he joined M. *Antonius (2) and served under him in Italy and at Philippi, then governed Syria for him and was killed in the Parthian invasion (40). His army joined Q. *Labienus.

Syme, *RP* 1. 31–41.   R. S.; E. B.

decision-making (Greek) A Greek state was the community of its citizens, and at any rate the most important decisions were made by an assembly of the citizens. *Democracies and *oligarchies differed not over that principle but over its application: how many of the free adult males were full citizens, entitled to participate in the assembly; which decisions were reserved for the assembly and which could be made by 'the authorities' (the magistrates and/or a council). The widespread principle of *probouleusis,* 'prior consideration' by a council of business for the assembly, provided further scope for variation. In democratic

Athens the council (see BOULE) had to approve items for the assembly's agenda, and could, but did not have to, propose a motion; but in the assembly any citizen could speak, and could propose a motion or an amendment to a motion already proposed. In more oligarchic states proposals might be allowed only from the magistrates and / or the council, and the right to address the assembly might be limited to magistrates and members of the council.

Larger organizations often entrusted decisions to a representative council. The Delphic *Amphictiony was a body of Greek peoples and had a council in which the peoples were represented: that was the main decision-making body, though there were sometimes meetings of an assembly. Federal Boeotia (see BOEOTIAN CONFEDERACY) in the late 5th and early 4th cents. BC. had a council of 660 (sixty from each of eleven electoral units), within which one quarter played a probouleutic role; the revived federation of the 370s had an assembly. In leagues of allies the leading state might be a voting member of the council (as probably in the *Delian League), or be outside the council, interacting with it (as in the *Peloponnesian League and the *Second Athenian Confederacy). The *Aetolian and the *Achaean Confederacy of the Hellenistic period had both councils and assemblies.

A. Andrewes, *Probouleusis* (1954); J. A. O. Larsen, *Representative Government in Greek and Roman History* (1955); P. J. Rhodes, *The Athenian Boule* (1972), ch. 2. P. J. R.

Decius (emperor). See MESSIUS QUINTUS DECIUS, C.

Decius (*RE* 15) **Mus** (1), **Publius,** is first mentioned as a military tribune (see TRIBUNI MILITUM) in the First Samnite War (343 BC; Livy 7. 34 f.; see SAMNIUM). As consul in 340 he fought against the Latins at Veseris in *Campania (probably near Monte Roccamonfina: M. W. Frederiksen, *Campania* (1984), 185), and lost his life by 'devoting' himself and the enemy forces to the gods of the Underworld; riding headlong into the opposing ranks he brought about their destruction along with his own. The fact that a similar act of *devotio* was later performed by his son (see (2) below) does not necessarily mean that the story is unhistorical. For the possibility that his family originated in Campania, see J. Heurgon, *Capoue préromaine* (1942), 260 ff.; F. Càssola, *Gruppi politici* (1962), 152 ff. T. J. Co.

Decius (*RE* 16) **Mus** (2), **Publius,** son of (1) above, *consul in 312, 308, 297, 295 BC; *censor in 304, was one of the leading political figures of his generation and a close ally of Q. *Fabius Maximus Rullianus, his colleague as censor and in his last three consulships. At *Sentinum in 295 he commanded the Roman forces together with Rullianus, and his act of self-sacrifice (*devotio*: see DECIUS MUS (1), P.) turned the battle in the Romans' favour.

K.-J. Hölkeskamp, *Entstehung der Nobilität* (1987), 131 ff.; T. J. Cornell, *CAH* 7²/2 (1989), 377 ff. T. J. Co.

Decius (*RE* 17) **Mus** (3), **Publius,** son of (2) above. As consul in 279 BC he led an army against *Pyrrhus but was defeated and killed at *A(u)sculum Satrianum. The suggestion that he, like his father and grandfather, 'devoted' himself (see DEVOTIO) in the battle is unknown to the sources; there are no good grounds for supposing that such a story appeared in *Ennius.

O. Skutsch, *Annals of Ennius* (1985), 353–5, and *CQ* 1987, 512–14; T. J. Cornell, *JRS* 1986, 248–9, and *CQ* 1987, 514–16. E. T. S.; T. J. Co.

Decius (*RE* 9 + Suppl. 3. 327) **Subulo, Publius,** a dissolute man but a good orator, moved in Gracchan circles and as tribune

120 BC unsuccessfully prosecuted L. *Opimius. Accused *repetundarum*, he was acquitted, no doubt because of his popularity. *Praetor in 115, he was humiliated by the consul M. *Aemilius Scaurus (1). He probably died soon after. His son was C. *Appuleius Decianus.

E. Badian, *JRS* 1956, 91 ff. E. B.

declamation (Lat. *declamatio*, Gk. *meletē*) was over a very long period the main means employed by teachers of rhetoric to train their pupils for public speaking. It was invented by the Greeks, who brought it to Rome and the Roman world generally. Its developed forms were known in Latin as the *controversia*, a speech in character on one side of a fictional law case, and the *suasoria*, a deliberative speech advising a course of action in a historical, pseudo-historical, or mythological situation; the first trained for the courts, the second for the political assembly or committee room.

The *sophists of the 5th cent. BC regarded it as their principal task to teach rhetoric. Surviving display speeches from this period, apparently intended as models for students, are clear forerunners of the *controversia*. *Antiphon (1)'s *Tetralogies*, arranged in speeches for and against, exemplify techniques of argument. In particular, *Gorgias (1)'s *Palamedes* displays a clear articulation that marks off parts of the speech and stages in the argument, and is clearly intended to train the student in systematic exposition. For *Philostratus (*VS* 481), sketching the so-called *Second Sophistic, it was the orator *Aeschines who, after his exile to Rhodes, introduced the use of stock characters, poor man and rich man, hero and tyrant. We are poorly informed about the Hellenistic period, but it must have been then that the characteristic form of the *controversia* evolved. The master would lay down a law, or laws, often imaginary, to govern the case, together with a *theme* detailing the supposed facts and stating the point at issue (cf. e.g. Sen. *Controv.* 1. 5: 'A girl who has been raped may choose either marriage to her ravisher without a dowry or his death. On a single night a man raped two girls. One demands his death, the other marriage'). The case would be fictional, and names would be given only if it concerned historical circumstances. The speaker, whether pupil or rhetor, would take one side or the other, sometimes playing the part of an advocate, usually that of a character in the case. Thus training was given in all branches of rhetoric. Attention was paid to the articulation of the speech and to the forging of a persuasive argument; style would be inculcated by precept and example; memory was trained too, for speeches were not read out, and delivery (experience of an audience was given by the occasional introduction of parents and friends). Particularly important was the 'invention' (finding) of arguments. The *stasis* system, which owed much to *Hermagoras of Temnos (*c.*150 BC), enabled a speaker to establish the type of the case (e.g. 'conjecture', did X do Y?) and draw on a check-list of topics appropriate to that type (e.g. in the case of conjecture, motive and opportunity) with their associated arguments. The rhetor would teach the rhetorical system in abstract and exemplify it in his own model speeches, as we see in the Latin *Minor Declamations*, attributed to *Quintilian (see DECLAMATIONES PSEUDO-QUINTILIANEAE), and in the Greek collection of *Sopater (2).

These practices are presupposed by the earliest Latin rhetorical handbooks, *Cicero's *De inventione* and the anonymous *Rhetorica ad Herennium*, both based on Greek teaching. For some time we are largely dependent on Latin sources. The Elder Seneca (L. *Annaeus Seneca (1)) is the most familiar, but he probably gives a distorted picture: he is most interested in epigram and the clever slanting of a case, not at all in the technicalities of the *stasis* system or the elaboration of a complex argument. Quintilian, though critical (*Inst.* 2. 10) of the unreality of contemporary practice (as were *Petronius Arbiter (*Sat.* 1–4) and *Tacitus (*Dial.* 35)), never questions the basis of declamation, and his book is a handbook for the declaimer as well as for the orator. The *Minor Declamations* seem to reflect his procedures. Later, the *Major Declamations* look more like display pieces for the special occasion. Later still, *Ennodius testifies to the popularity of declamation as late as the 6th cent. AD.

Meanwhile the Greek evidence becomes important. The Greek declaimers excerpted in the elder Seneca seem often to employ the so-called Asianic rhetoric, overfond of emotional effect, wordplay, bombast, and rhythm. But a rather more austere impression is given by the preserved declamations of *Polemon (4), *Lucian, P. Aelius *Aristides, *Libanius, and the 6th-cent. Choricius; they are '*Attic' not only in the classicism of their language but also in the comparative moderation of their style, though declaimers eventually succumbed to the accentual rhythms that succeeded to the metrical clausulae of earlier declaimers. All of these spoke for display. But we are taken into the workshop of declamation by the important book of Sopater (late 4th cent. AD?), the *Diairesis zētēmatōn* or 'Division of Problems'. The author gives advice on the treatment of no less than 82 fictional cases, ordered according to their *stasis*, on a system related to that evolved by *Hermogenes (2) of Tarsus; there are model excerpts in direct speech.

Sopater does not deal with the *suasoria*, though he is interested in historical themes: indeed, Greek theory seems to have subsumed deliberative oratory under the *controversia*. See ASIANISM AND ATTICISM; DIVISIO; RHETORIC, GREEK and LATIN.

Fundamental: S. E. Bonner, *Roman Declamation* (1949); D. A. Russell, *Greek Declamation* (1983). See also the bibliography for ANNAEUS SENECA (1), L. For Quintilian, M. Winterbottom, *Hommages à Jean Cousin* (1983), 225–35; for Sopatrus, D. C. Innes and M. Winterbottom, *Sopatros the Rhetor* (1988), with an introduction covering declamation more generally.   M. W.

Declamationes pseudo-Quintilianeae, two sets of rhetorical pieces ascribed to *Quintilian. (1) The *Declamationes minores* ('Minor Declamations') are the last 145 of a collection originally numbering 388. Each has a theme and a treatment (the length varies greatly). Their derivation from some rhetorical school is ensured by the frequent presence of *sermones* ('chats'), giving a master's hints on the treatment of the *controversia*. That the master was Quintilian himself is quite possible but hardly provable. (2) The *Declamationes maiores* ('Major Declamations') were already by the late 4th cent. AD circulating under the name of Quintilian, as quotations in Servius and Jerome prove; and there is evidence that they were 'edited' by scholars of that period. These highly coloured pieces can hardly come from the hand of Quintilian (for whose views on unreal declamation see *Inst.* 2. 10), but date and author(s) remain quite uncertain. See DECLAMATION.

Schanz–Hosius § 485. *Minores*: Ed. M. Winterbottom (1984), with comm.; D. R. Shackleton Bailey (1989). See generally J. Dingel, *Scholastica Materia* (1988), showing how the declamations were used to teach the *stasis* system. *Maiores*: Ed. L. Håkanson (1982). Trans. B. A. Sussman (1987), with some notes. C. Ritter, *Die Quintilianischen Declamationen* (1881; repr. 1967) is dated but remains valuable. M. W.

decuma In Italy, by the 2nd cent. BC, one-tenth of the grain harvest (and one-fifth of the fruit harvest) on *ager publicus* was paid to the state; it was collected by *publicani*. In the provinces the Romans on the whole took over any form of taxation they found. In Sicily, probably Carthage and certainly King *Hiero (2) II had collected a tithe on the harvest. This was appropriated by Rome. Under the reorganization of P. *Rupilius, the whole of Sicily was put under Hiero's system. All land not *ager publicus* or belonging to free cities (see SOCII; PROVINCIA) was *decumanus*. The tax was sold to contractors at Syracuse and they made contracts (*pactiones*) with individual tax-farmers under the supervision of the governor. The cities themselves sometimes bought the contracts. In 75 BC the sale of the tithe on fruit was transferred to Rome. Sardinia, taken over from Carthage, may have paid a tithe, we do not know how collected. A further tithe of grain could be requisitioned by the governor against assessed payment, when needed by Rome. This seems to have happened quite frequently and provided opportunities for chicanery and exploitation. By the late republic, most of the *free cities were liable to this tax. In Asia, the tithe inherited from *Attalus III was sold in Rome under five-year contracts by the censors, under a law of C. *Sempronius Gracchus. (See PUBLICANI.) Collection was by *pactiones* with the cities. In Bithynia and Pontus, as well as Syria, the kings had probably employed a system similar to that of the Attalids and Hiero. When *Pompey organized those provinces, he seems to have extended the Asian system of collection to them. Caesar converted the Asian tax, at a reduced level, to a fixed *stipendium* collected by the quaestor. In Sicily a fixed tax paid in money had taken the place of the *decuma* by the time of Augustus, and in other provinces under the tithe system the development was similar.

Cicero's *Verrines* give full details for Sicily. See *RE* 'decuma'; J. Carcopino, *La Loi d'Hiéron et les Romains* (1914). On provincial taxes in general, see L. Neesen, *Untersuchungen zu den direkten Staatsabgaben der römischen Kaiserzeit (27 v. Chr.–284 n. Chr.)*, esp. 25 ff., 104 ff., 150 f. for the *decuma* and the terms for fixed taxes.   E. B.

decuriones were the councillors who ran Roman local government in both colonies and municipalities (see MUNICIPIUM), Latin and Roman. They did so as members of the local council (*senatus*, in the later empire *curia (1)); hence *decuriones* were then also called *curiales*. They were recruited mainly from ex-magistrates and held office for life. The list of councillors was revised every five years. The qualifications included criteria of wealth, age, free birth, and reputation. The minimum age was 25, reduced by *Constantine I to 18. Members of influential families could however be made honorary members even if they lacked the standard qualifications. The number of councillors varied, but was often 100. They controlled the public life of the community, its administration, and finances, including the voting of honorary decrees and statues. They had charge of its external relations, including the sending of embassies and petitions to the emperor or provincial governor. The local popular assemblies did little apart from electing magistrates.

In the course of time the class of *decuriones* became hereditary, membership descending in the male line; and nomination to office replaced popular election. *Decuriones* were privileged. Their toga had a purple stripe (*clavus*) and, more important, they counted as *honestiores* and so were exempt from certain degrading punishments. Indeed their privileged position was essential to the running of the empire, since they were responsible for collecting imperial taxes in the local area and for performing a number of other public duties (*munera*; see MUNUS); and they were personally liable for default. From the 3rd cent. AD these duties became increasingly burdensome and many

dedicatio

councillors sought exemption from the status of *decurio*. Roman senators and equestrians were excused local office and so were farmers of state lands and taxes, shippers of corn, doctors, professors, and some others. From *Diocletian onwards the government made strenuous efforts to prevent *decuriones* evading their duties, for example by fleeing or joining the imperial service. These efforts were not however fully effective, and the class was gradually drained of its wealthier members.

Jones, *Later Rom. Emp.*; see also bibliog. for MUNICIPIUM.

A. N. S.-W.; A. H. M. J.; T. Hon.

dedicatio Transfer of a thing from the human into the divine sphere was accomplished through the act of *dedicatio* and *consecratio*, the former indicating surrender of an object into divine ownership, the latter its transformation into a *res sacra*. Dedications of temples, places, and altars (*aedes, terra, ara*) were legally binding only if performed by competent authorities: (*a*) the magistrates with *imperium*; (*b*) with respect to temples, the board of two men acting in their stead (*duumviri aedi dedicandae*) elected by the people (often appointed as duumvirs were the magistrates who had vowed the temple while in office, or their relatives); (*c*) the *aediles, but only from the fines imposed by them (*pecunia multaticia*); (*d*) any person specifically (*nominatim*) selected by the people or *plebs, as stipulated by a *lex Papiria*, perhaps of 304 BC (Cic. *Dom.* 127–8, 130–6; *Att.* 4. 2. 3; Livy 9. 46. 6–7). At dedications of temples, the dedicant held a doorpost (*postem tenere*) and pronounced (without interruption, hesitation, or stumbling) a formula dictated to him by a pontiff (*pontifice praeeunte*), with other pontiffs often present (Cic. *Dom.* 117–41; Varro, *Ling.* 6. 61; Plin. *HN* 11. 174; Servius on *G.* 3. 16). It contained a precise description of the object, the ground on which it stood, and the conditions of its use, with a written record as the title-deed (*lex dedicationis*; *ILS* 112, 4906–14; *Inscr. Ital.* 4. 1. 73).

R. G. Nisbet, comm. on Cicero, *De domo sua* (1939); R. E. A. Palmer, *Roman Religion and Roman Empire* (1974); A. Ziolkowski, *The Temples of Mid-Republican Rome* (1992).   J. L.

dedications

Greek A literary dedication is a symbolic presentation of a work or collection to a dedicatee as a mark of affection or respect. It is usually embodied in a formal opening (or near-opening) address. The first attested instance is *Dionysius (6) Chalcus' elegy to a friend (fr. 1 West): 'accept this poem as a toast (προπινομένην). I present it to you first (πέμπω σοι πρώτῳ) ... Take it as a gift (λαβὼν τόδε δῶρον) and toast me back in song (ἀοιδὰς ἀντιπρόπιθι)'. The phraseology is prefigured in Pindar, *Nem.* 3. 76–9, 'drink this song that I present to you' (τόδε τοι πέμπω ... πόμ' ἀοίδιμον); but in Pindar poetry is not the poet's gift but the 'gift of the Muses' (*Ol.* 7. 7), and an opening address is reserved for divinities like the Muse herself (*Nem.* 3. 1, etc.). Dedication implies secularization. In the 4th cent. BC dedication becomes more matter-of-fact (e.g. Isoc. 1. 2, 'I have sent you this discourse as a gift'); and in Hellenistic and imperial Greece it becomes commonplace—among poets (e.g. Meleager, *Anth. Pal.* 4. 1), *littérateurs* (e.g. Dion. Hal. *Comp.*), and especially writers of plain prose. Thus Archimedes' *Psammites* is dedicated to Gelon, son of *Hiero (2) II, his *Method* to *Eratosthenes. *Onasander's *Strategicus* (pref. 1) takes it as axiomatic that 'works on horsemanship, hunting, fishing, or farming' should be 'dedicated to the devotees of those activities'.   M. S. Si.

Latin Honorific reference to a particular person in a work of prose or poetry, or in one part of a work, is extremely common in Latin literature. This is clearly connected with the important role played by the relationships of patronage (see PATRONAGE, LITERARY, LATIN) and friendship in the production and circulation of Latin literary texts. Dedication, by once and for all connecting the literary text with a particular person, is in itself an act of great honour, and it is also usually accompanied by explicit expressions of praise. It is generally placed at the beginning of the work, or shortly after the beginning: in works in more than one book, a dedication to the same person is often repeated at the beginning of some (e.g. *Quintilian) or all (e.g. *Columella) of the books. Alternatively, the various books may be dedicated to different people: for example, each of the three books of *Varro's *De re rustica* is addressed to a different dedicatee, while in his *De lingua Latina* 2–4 are dedicated to Septimius, 5 onwards to *Cicero. Dedication is often presented as a gift-offering of the book (sometimes concretely as a physical copy of the work, *Catullus 1), within a framework of personal relations in which the author wishes to express his gratitude to a friend or patron for the help or encouragement that he has received. On occasions there is also the suggestion that the dedicatee will help the reception and dissemination of the work with the prestige of his name or with concrete acts of support. This element is absent—and the element of homage is also less relevant—when the work is dedicated to a close friend or relative, such as a wife (Varro *Rust.* 1) or son (Cato, *Ad fil.*; Cic. *Off.*; Sen. *Controv.*). There is a general presupposition that the dedicatee has a specific interest in the work dedicated to him, and it is very common, especially in rhetorical and technical works, to declare that the work has been written at the request of the dedicatee, a request that the author, despite the difficulties of the task, could not refuse because of the duty of friendship and courtesy he owes the dedicatee (e.g. *Rhet. Her.*; Cic. *De or., Orat., Top.*). This commonplace is found already in the dedications of Hellenistic works, and although it is mostly purely conventional, it gives to the work the appearance of being an exchange of courtesies between author and dedicatee, written entirely for the dedicatee to meet his or her needs. It also functions as justification for any deficiencies in the work, or as a subtle reminder of the difficulties the author has overcome.

Even when the dedication is limited to an initial address to the dedicatee, by placing the work within a framework of personal relationships between the author and an eminent friend it tends to confer on the literary discourse an atmosphere of intimacy and personal conversation. It may thus contrast more or less significantly with the general stylistic level of the text as a whole, and for this reason it is not found equally in all genres. It is commonest in those genres which have an element of address, as for instance the didactic, where the author directly addresses a disciple. In these cases the addressee may easily be identified with a particular dedicatee, chosen for reasons of personal homage, and named both at the beginning of the work and throughout: so C. *Memmius (2) in *Lucretius is both didactic addressee and dedicatee, and one can compare the dedicatees of various technical and philosophical works in prose, which often explicitly aim at the instruction of a particular individual, either the dedicatee or someone connected with him. Lyric and elegy, with their origins in Archaic Greece, are similarly 'allocutive' genres which in Latin are often addressed to friends whom the poet honours by dedicating a single poem or a collection to them. Satire often presents itself as a conversation (*sermo*) addressed to an interlocutor, and sometimes takes the form of a letter: the epistolary form naturally brings with it a specific addressee, and the genre may develop into an entire treatise in letter form addressed to specific individuals under instruction (cf. Hor. *Ars P.*; Cicero's *De officiis* is addressed to his absent son and concludes with an epistolary farewell). In contrast, narrative works (epic, historiography, and, naturally, drama) tend to lack dedications, though the situation begins to change in the imperial period, when dedications were extended to historiographical works (already A. *Hirtius, author of [= Caes.] *BGall.* 8; Vell. Pat.) and the opportunity or duty of rendering homage to the emperor led to the introduction of dedications to him of all sorts of literary work. Despite the obviously necessary deference, dedications to the emperor could take the usual form of a personal conversation with an interlocutor with whom the author was on personal terms (Hor. *Epist.* 2. 1 and *Vitruvius to *Augustus, and with a larger panegyrical element the younger Seneca (L. *Annaeus Seneca (2)), *Clem.* to *Nero, and *Pliny (1), *HN* to the future emperor *Titus). More commonly, however, dedications to the emperor resembled rather invocations of divinities, and might coexist with a personal dedication to a friend: in epic, they might substitute for or supplement the traditional invocation of an inspiring deity. The emperor takes on this role for the first time in *Virgil, *Georgics* 1, where the invocation of Augustus is accompanied by the personal dedication to *Maecenas (here distinct from the didactic addressee, in contrast to Memmius in Lucretius), and we then find it in *Ovid, *Fasti* 1. 3 ff., in the didactic poems of *Germanicus and M. *Manilius, in *Calpurnius Siculus (4. 86 ff.), in the epics of *Lucan (1. 63–6) and *Valerius Flaccus Setinus Balbus, and also in prose in *Quintilian (where the invocation of *Domitian in *Inst.* bk. 4 is inserted within a personal dedication to Quintilian's friend Victorius Marcellus) and *Valerius Maximus. A non-imperial figure who plays a similar role is M. *Valerius Messalla Corvinus in *Tibullus 2. 1. 35. Solemn invocations of the emperor are also found in the epics of Statius (*Thebaid* and *Achilleid*).

In the case of lyric, elegy, and satire there may be little or no connection between the dedicatee and the content of the work (e.g. P. *Alfenus Varus in Verg. *Ecl.* 6, which then turns to praise of *Cornelius Gallus, or the address to Tullus in Prop. 1. 1. 9), but it is much more common for the addressee to be in some way connected with the themes of the work. The convention was that a collected work was dedicated to the person to whom the first item was dedicated, but much more complicated and refined strategies can be seen in *Horace, and also in elegy, *Martial, *Statius (*Silv.*), and *Pliny (2) the Younger (*Ep.*): dedications to others, to the emperor, and at times to the general reader are brought into relief by their positioning. The privileged positions (especially in Horace) are, apart from the opening, the place after the opening, the end, the opening of the second half of the collection, and immediately before the final envoi. Often the initial element with the dedication develops programmatic or autobiographical motifs, with the whole activity of the author, his choices in life and art, related to those of the dedicatee (cf. e.g. Hor. *Odes* 1. 1, *Epist.* 1. 1, and Prop. 2. 1, all addressed to Maecenas). Another honorific act related to the dedication is to make a contemporary an actual protagonist in a work, as *Cicero makes Varro a character in the *Academica*, or to insert him in the content of a poem.

The personal character of the dedication expresses itself most clearly in the form of the dedicatory epistle. This is found already in Greek didactic works, and at Rome begins with Hirtius and L. *Annaeus Seneca (1)'s *Controversiae* and is then extended to all sorts of work. Prose letters are also prefaced to collections of poetry such as the epigrams of Martial and the *Silvae* of Statius. Even in works from the 1st cent. BC and later, where the main method of publication was through the impersonal medium of the book trade, the dedication preserved the formulae derived from its origins in private circulation; introductory epistles written as prefaces for the general public continue to present themselves as gift-offerings of private copies, complete with requests for corrections and advice, just like the letters of Cicero or Pliny the Younger accompanying provisional versions of their works or presentation copies (cf. Cic. *Fam.* 9. 8, a private letter accompanying a copy of the *Academica* sent to *Varro, not part of the published work). The dedication continued to suggest, with more or less conviction, an atmosphere of private intimacy between an élite of producers and receivers of literature, even when literary discourse was addressed primarily to the general public, and to a future audience still unknown to the author.

R. Graefenhain, *De more libros dedicandi apud scriptores Graecos et Romanos obvio* (1892); F. Stephan, *Quomodo poetae Graecorum Romanorumque carmina dedicaverint* (1910); J. Ruppert, *Quaestiones ad historiam dedicationis librorum pertinentes* (1911); T. Janson, *Latin Prose Prefaces* (1964); P. White, *JRS* 1974, 88–92; M. Citroni, *Maia* 1988.

M. Ci.

dediticii, originally, persons who have made a *deditio in fidem*, an unconditional surrender, to Rome; the normal consequence in the case of a whole community was that Rome regulated their status, usually by restoring them to their position before their surrender. The *lex Aelia Sentia* of AD 4 created a category of freed slaves, who had been guilty of certain offences, who were free 'with the same *condicio* as the *condicio* of foreigners who have made a *deditio*' (Gai. *Inst.* 1. 13–15). The precise nature of this *condicio* remains obscure, but presumably the essence was that the liberty was precarious and could be ended at will by a Roman magistrate. *Dediticii* were excluded from one of the provisions of the Antonine *constitution: it is disputed whether the provision in question is the grant of citizenship or a condition attaching to this grant.

A. N. Sherwin-White, *Roman Citizenship*, 2nd edn. (1973), 280–94.

M. H. C.

defamation See INIURIA.

defensor civitatis, 'defender of the municipality', an office revived by *Valentinian I and *Valens in *c.* AD 365 to protect *peasants against local landowners. The praetorian prefect was to appoint retired officials without local ties, their duty being to hear minor lawsuits quickly and cheaply. However, by the 390s the *defensor* was chosen by his town, and seems to have been absorbed into the local network of patronage.

Jones, *Later Rom. Emp.* 144–5.

R. S. O. T.

deformity Malnutrition, *disease, and certain social practices contributed to the prevalence of congenital deformity in antiquity, though palaeopathology can tell us nothing about the level of incidence of any specific deformity. Far fewer congenitally deformed persons would have survived infancy than is the case today, however, because the Greeks and Romans would have had little compunction about withholding the necessities of life from those they deemed incapable of leading an independent life. In *Sparta the abandonment of deformed infants was a legal requirement (Plut. *Lyc.* 16. 1–2). Likewise *Aristotle (*Pol.* 7. 1335^{b}19–21) recommended that there should be a law 'to prevent the rearing of deformed children'. A law attributed to Romulus permitted the exposure of a monstrous infant on condition that five witnesses approved the decision (Dion. Hal. *Ant. Rom.* 2. 15. 1–2). Table 4 of the *Twelve Tables instructed the *paterfamilias* to 'Quickly kill a dreadfully deformed child' (cf. Cic. *Leg.* 3. 19). L. *Annaeus Seneca (1) claims that the fathers of such infants 'chuck them out instead of exposing them' (*Controv.* 10. 4. 16). In *Justinian's *Digest* Iulius *Paulus (1. 5. 14) excludes from his definition of children 'those abnormally procreated in a shape different from human form', yet according to Ulpian (*Domitius Ulpianus) parents were entitled to claim *alimenta* privileges for childbearing even if the child was grossly deformed (50. 16. 135). *Soranus provides criteria for determining whether a child was fit to be raised (*Gynaeceia* 2. 6. 5). The incidence of individuals suffering from postnatally acquired disabilities and deformities must have been extremely high. Slaves in particular ran an extremely high risk of becoming crippled, bow-backed, or otherwise deformed as a result of hard labour (cf. Arist. *Pol.* 1. 1254^{b}27–31).

The belief that the birth of a congenitally deformed infant was an expression of divine ill will is already present in *Hesiod (*Op.* 235). Oath-breaking was supposedly punished by the birth of a deformity (e.g. Tod 2. 204. 39–45). However, there is no evidence to indicate that any Greek community took official notice of abnormal births, nor that such births constituted a distinctive category of *divination. By contrast the Romans regarded the birth of a deformed child or animal as portentous in the extreme, as is demonstrated by the fact that *monstrum* ('portent') is etymologically related to *monere* ('to warn'). Prodigies were recorded on a yearly basis in the pontifical records and have survived both in the writings of *Livy and in *Obsequens' *Prodigiorum liber*. According to Livy 'the most abhorred *portents of all' were the hermaphrodites (see HERMAPHRODITUS), for whom distinctive rites of expiation were introduced in 207 BC (27. 11. 4).

Few individuals of whom we have record are known to have been congenitally deformed. One is the Spartan king *Agesilaus II, both diminutive and congenitally lame (Plut. *Ages.* 2. 2). It is unclear whether the emperor *Claudius was actually deformed or merely disabled (Sen. *Apocol.* 5; Suet. *Claud.* 3. 2). Given the ideological emphasis upon physical wholeness, it would hardly be surprising if the deformed were stigmatized as second-class citizens, like the hunchbacked *Thersites (*Il.* 2. 217 f.). The absence of physical blemish was a requirement for holding both Greek and Roman priesthoods (cf. Pl. *Leg.* 6. 759c; Sen. *Con.* 4. 2; Dion. Hal. *Ant. Rom.* 2. 21. 3; Gell. *NA* 1. 12. 3) (see PRIESTS). *Plutarch states that the demand for freak slaves was so great in Rome that there even existed a 'monster market' (*Mor.* 520c), and there are abundant references in the late republican and early imperial period to their popularity as household *pets (e.g. Plin. *HN* 7. 75; Sen. *Ep.* 50. 2; Quint. *Inst.* 2. 5. 11; Mart. 8. 13). Hunchbacks, cripples, dwarfs and obese women were popular entertainers at drinking-parties, as numerous artistic representations indicate (cf. also Lucian, *Symp.* 18). The majority of the chronically deformed probably either begged or claimed the indulgence of a well-to-do relative. Seneca conjures up the nightmarish image of a vile racketeer who deliberately deformed children so that he could live off their earnings (*Controv.* 10. 4).

From earliest times reports of persons exhibiting gross deformities were widely circulated, as the name of the *Cyclops Polyphemus ('much talked about') suggests, though we should note that *Homer never specifically describes the giant's celebrated synophthalmia (see CYCLOPES). Book 8 of *Pliny (1)'s *Natural History* supplies a bizarre catalogue of human deformity, which has been fittingly compared to *The Guinness Book of Records*. Book 4 of Aristotle's *Generation of Animals* provides the most illuminat-

ing discussion of the classification and aetiology of congenital deformity to be undertaken in the west before the middle of the 17th cent. Topics covered include disproportionality, redundancy and deficiency of parts, doubling of organs, situs inversus (i.e. irregular positioning of organs), imperforate anus, hypospadias, and dwarfism. His most significant contribution to the subject was his insistence that deformities, though unusual and irregular, were an integral and necessary part of nature (767^{b}13–15). See CHILDBIRTH.

R. S. J. Garland, *The Eye of the Beholder: Deformity and Disability in the Graeco-Roman World* (1995); A. P. Kozloff and D. G. Mitten, *The Gods Delight: the Human Figure in Classical Bronze* (1988), nos. 19, 20, 25, 28, 56, and 57. R. S. J. G.

Deianira, in mythology daughter of *Oeneus and Althaea, and wife of *Heracles, won by him in combat from another suitor, the river *Acheloüs. Originally she may well have been a bold-hearted and aggressive character who deliberately murdered Heracles (see J. R. March, *The Creative Poet*, BICS Suppl. 49 (1987), 49–77); but *Sophocles, in his *Trachiniae*, portrays her as a gentle, timid and loving woman who unintentionally brings him to death. Once, years earlier, when the *Centaur Nessus assaulted her, Heracles shot him with an arrow poisoned with the Hydra's blood. Dying, Nessus told Deianira to gather some blood from around his wound, assuring her that it was a potent love-charm. She did so and kept it for years, during which she bore Heracles several children. Now, in the play, Heracles brings Iole home as his concubine, and Deianira, to regain his love, sends him a robe smeared with the 'love-charm'. He is carried home, dying from the poison, and she kills herself. Deianira with Nessus is a popular scene in art from the 7th cent. BC: see F. Díez de Velasco, *LIMC* 6/1. 838–47. H. J. R.; J. R. M.

Deiotarus (RE 2), Hellenized tetrarch of western *Galatia, was attacked by *Mithradates VI and became a loyal Roman ally. *Pompey greatly increased his territory and the senate, perhaps adding more to it outside Galatia, and gave him the royal title. He came into conflict with his son-in-law Brogitarus, in eastern Galatia, who was supported by P. *Clodius Pulcher. In 51 BC he put his forces at the disposal of *Cicero and M. *Calpurnius Bibulus. In the Civil War he followed Pompey, joined *Caesar after *Pharsalus, and assisted Cn. *Domitius Calvinus in his Pontic campaign, incidentally seizing all of Galatia. Caesar made him give up some territory, but confirmed him. On Caesar's final return to Rome (45), Deiotarus' enemies accused him before Caesar and Cicero defended him (*Pro rege Deiotaro*). On Caesar's death he reoccupied his lost territories, bought recognition from M. *Antonius (2), but then joined M. *Iunius Brutus (2). After the death of C. *Cassius Longinus at Philippi he deserted to the triumvirs and escaped punishment, dying peacefully in 40. He had organized two legions on the Roman model, one of which became XXII Deiotariana.

For geographical and social background see S. Mitchell, *Anat. St.* 1974, 61 ff., esp. 74 f. and *Anatolia* (1993), see index. E. B.

Deiphobus, in mythology, son of *Priam and *Hecuba, and one of the more powerful Trojan fighters (*Il.* 13. 156 ff., 402 ff.). *Athena impersonated him so as to deceive *Hector and bring about his death (22. 227 ff.). After *Paris was killed, Deiphobus married *Helen; he went with her to examine the Wooden Horse (*Od.* 4. 274 ff.); and after the capture of Troy, *Menelaus (1) and *Odysseus went first to his house, where the fighting was hardest (8. 517 ff.). He was killed and mutilated by Menelaus after being, according to *Virgil, betrayed by Helen (*Aen.* 6. 494 ff.). Deiphobus is sometimes found in art in scenes of the war at Troy: see L. Kahil, *LIMC* 3 / 1. 362–7.   J. R. M.

Deiphontes (Δηϊφόντης), in mythology, a descendant in the fifth generation of *Heracles. He married *Hyrnetho, daughter of *Temenus king of *Argos (2), and was favoured by him above his own sons, who therefore murdered their father and strove with Deiphontes, with results variously described by different authors (collected by Stoll in Roscher's *Lexikon*).   H. J. R.

deisidaimonia (δεισιδαιμονία). Although originally the term had a positive meaning ('scrupulousness in religious matters', *Xenophon (1) and *Aristotle), it is predominantly used in a derogatory way and denotes an excessive pietism and preoccupation with religion, first and most explicitly in *Theophrastus' sixteenth *Character*. He defines *deisidaimonia* as 'cowardice vis-à-vis the divine' and gives the following characteristics: an obsessive fear of the gods, a bigoted penchant for adoration and cultic performance, superstitious awe of *portents both in daily life and in *dreams, and the concomitant inclination to ward off or prevent possible negative effects by magical or ritual acts, especially through continuous *purifications. Later, *Plutarch (*De superst.*) gives largely the same picture, tracing its origin to erroneous or defective knowledge about the gods. This is also the opinion of Roman observers like *Lucretius, *Cicero, and the younger Seneca (L. *Annaeus Seneca (2)), who use the Latin word *superstitio*, which *Ennius and *Plautus had already associated with negative notions such as private *divination, *magic, and more generally *prava religio* ('bad religion').

The latter notion in particular forbids us from simply identifying *deisidaimonia* and *superstitio* under the collective label 'superstition'. To a far greater extent than its Greek pendant, Latin *superstitio* became a judgemental term used by the dominant 'orthodox' religion to classify 'other', especially foreign and exotic, religions of which it disapproved (e.g. Juv. 6. 314 ff., 511 f. on foreign, esp. Egyptian, rites, and 14. 96 on Jewish rites). It acquired the function of a social marker through pejorative reference to the other's 'bad religion'. This use was adopted (and reversed) by the Christians especially in their condemnation of the retention of *pagan beliefs and of the magical application of Christian myth and ritual. See ORIENTAL CULTS AND RELIGION.

P. J. Koets, *Deisidaimonia: A Contribution to the Knowledge of the Religious Terminology in Greek* (1929); H. Bolkestein, *Theophrastos' Charakter der Deisidaimonia* (1929); S. Calderone, *ANRW* 1. 2 (1972), 377–96; C. R. Phillips III, *ANRW* 2. 16. 3 (1986), 2677–773.   H. S. V.

Delian League, modern name for the alliance formed 478 / 7 BC against the Persians. ('Athenian empire' might be a better title for this article, but not all students of *imperialism admit that Athens had an empire in the full sense). In 478 the Greeks, led by the Spartan *Pausanias (1), campaigned in *Cyprus and secured *Byzantium; but Pausanias abused his power and was recalled to Sparta. At the request of the allies, who pleaded Pausanias' behaviour and '*Ionian kinship' (Thuc. 1. 95. 1), Athens accepted leadership. The Peloponnesians acquiesced (some evidence suggests reluctance), and a new alliance was formed with its headquarters on the sacred island of *Delos—a traditional Ionian festival centre but with an appeal to Dorian islanders also. Athens provided the commander of the allied forces and settled which cities were to provide ships and which money; the treasurers also, ten *hellēnotamiae, were Athenians, and the Athenian *Aristides (1) made the first assessment. But at the outset policy was determined at meetings on Delos at which every member, including Athens, had just one equal vote. The nucleus of the alliance was formed by the Ionian cities of the west coast of *Asia Minor, the *Hellespont, and the *Propontis, and most of the Aegean islands. *Chios, *Samos, *Lesbos, and some other states with a naval tradition provided ships; the remainder brought annual tribute to the treasury at Delos. Members took permanently binding oaths of loyalty.

At first the anti-Persian objectives were vigorously pursued. Persian garrisons were driven out of *Thrace (except at Doriscus on the Hebrus) and *Chersonesus (1); Greek control was extended along the west and south coast of Asia Minor; new members joined until there were nearly 200. The climax was *Cimon's victory at the *Eurymedon (466). Meanwhile Carystus in *Euboea was forced to join (c.472), *Naxos (1) tried to secede and was forced back in (c.467), and in 465 wealthy *Thasos revolted because of Athenian encroachment on Thasian mainland holdings. Thasos surrendered 462 and stiff terms were imposed, but nearby on the Strymon a large colony of Athenian allies was wiped out by the local inhabitants. If Cimon made a first peace of Callias (see CALLIAS, PEACE OF) after Eurymedon it ended with his *ostracism and fighting against Persia resumed in 460, when a strong Athenian force sailed to *Cyprus but was diverted to Egypt to support Inarus, a *Libyan prince in revolt from Persia. The Egyptian expedition ended in disaster for Athens in 454, and in that year the treasury was moved from Delos to Athens (?for security in this moment of peril; but the date of the move is not absolutely certain). See TRIBUTE LISTS, ATHENIAN. But Athenian power spread in Greece and the Aegean: Dorian *Aegina was coerced in 458, and the First *Peloponnesian War gave Athens control over *Boeotia 457–446: it now seems *Orchomenus (1) and *Acraephnium were actually tributary members of the league, which should therefore not be regarded as purely maritime. At sea Cimon, back from ostracism, led a force to Cyprus but this phase of resumed expansion ended with his death at the end of the 450s. Meanwhile Athens exploited the propaganda potential of *Apollo's sanctuaries at Delos and *Delphi; a struggle took place throughout the century between Athens and the Peloponnesians at this level as well as the military (see DELPHI).

The main Callias Peace of 450 (see CALLIAS, PEACE OF), if historical, restricted Persian movement west of *Phaselis and outside the Euxine, and Persia made other concessions. The removal of the original justification of the league led to restlessness among Athens' allies, but this was checked and tribute-levying (perhaps discontinued for a year) was resumed. *Cleruchies and other repressive institutions were now imposed, though the greater bulk of epigraphic evidence after mid-century creates a risk of confusing first occurrence with first attestation. The first known cleruchy was at Andros 450, also perhaps Naxos and Euboea (Carystus); Chersonesus (1) was settled by *Pericles (1) in 447. By now only Chios, Samos, and Lesbos contributed ships, the rest paid tribute and had no effective means of resisting. Epigraphic evidence suggests a shift to harsher terminology, 'the allies' being replaced by 'the cities which the Athenians rule'; and the greater proliferation of visually and symbolically formidable imperial inscriptions in allied states may itself have functioned increasingly as a repressive device in the years after 460. This sombre league-into-empire picture of gradually increasing oppression (*ATL*, Meiggs) has been challenged (Finley), less by the offering of a more cheerful one than by the insistence that Athenian behaviour had never been anything but harsh (see CIMON for the coercion of *Scyros etc. in the 470s). In favour of the 'gradual deterioration' view is Thuc. 1. 99, an important chapter. Equally serious is the questioning of traditional criteria for dating of Attic inscriptions; techniques of laser enhancement have been used to downdate ML 37 (Athenian alliance with Sicilian Segesta) from 458/7 to 418, see SEG 39. 1. If this dating wins general acceptance, not only does important evidence for early Athenian ambitions in the west disappear, not to mention possible damage done to the credit of *Thucydides (2), but some fundamental epigraphically-based assumptions about the development of Athenian imperial policy may have to go. But at time of writing the issue is open. The new technique needs to be more generally tested, not just applied to one fragmentary and desperately disputed text.

Boeotia revolted in 447 or 446, Athens was defeated at *Coronea, and the ensuing crisis—revolts by *Megara and Euboea, and a Spartan invasion—was settled by the *Thirty Years Peace. In 440 Samos defied Athens, was besieged and subdued and forced to pay a large indemnity. Whether or not a technical democracy was now installed or an *oligarchy tolerated is uncertain; it was perhaps more important to Athens, here and elsewhere, that the governing group should be pro-Athenian (see DEMOCRACY, NON-ATHENIAN). Back at Athens, the people's courts or *dikastēria* (see LAW AND PROCEDURE, ATHENIAN) played a major part in the control of empire.

When the *Peloponnesian War began, this Athenian control was firm; Spartan hopes for large-scale revolt from Athens were disappointed, nor did the Spartans make best use of their opportunities, e.g. on Lesbos, which Athens crushed. In 425 the Athenians increased the tribute assessment to nearly 1,500 talents (the original asessment is said to have been 460 talents). In 416 when *Melos refused to join the alliance, Athens reduced the island, executed the men, and enslaved the women and children, a small-scale atrocity but one long remembered against Athens. After the Sicilian disaster of 415–413 Chios, *Miletus, *Thasos, Euboea, and other key places revolted, but even this wave of revolt was contained, partly because of Persian behaviour and Spartan limpness, partly because Athens had learned to avoid counter-productive reprisals.

The Athenian empire brought benefits to the poorer cities: *piracy was suppressed to the great advantage of trade, and the Athenian navy offered well-paid service, particularly attractive to the population of the *islands. Pride in Athenian imperial success and cultural achievement may not have been confined to Athens' own citizens, though these are not aspects on which our main source Thucydides dwells. He does not even bring out the extent to which the upper classes at Athens benefited (as inscriptions like *Hesperia* 1953, 225 ff. attest) from overseas territorial possessions in the empire, acquired in defiance of local rules. But such possessions help to explain why there was so little principled objection to the empire, and the democracy which ran it, on the part of the Athenian social and intellectual élite. They also show that the literary picture of solidarity between the Athenian demos and the demos in the allied states is too simple. Thucydides or rather one of his speakers hints that the allies would prefer independence from either Athens or Sparta. Nevertheless, and in Athens' favour, the same chapter (8. 48) is surely right to acknowledge that at worst, arbitrary judicial process and violent killings could be expected from the oligarchies which Sparta had to offer instead.

The allies did not in fact make much contribution to the defeat of Athens, and when Sparta took Athens' place the cities soon had reason to regret the change. In less than 30 years they again

united under Athenian leadership (see SECOND ATHENIAN CONFEDERACY). But it is a significant indicator of the reasons for Athenian unpopularity in 431 (Thuc. 2. 8) that in 377 Athens repudiated cleruchies, garrisons, and overseas possessions.

Thuc. with Gomme, *HCT* and Hornblower, *Comm. on Thuc.*; LACTOR 1³, *The Athenian Empire* (1984; translated. sources); *ATL* 3; Meiggs, *AE*; M. Finley, *Economy and Society in Ancient Greece* (1981), ch. 3; D. Lewis, 'Democratic Institutions and their Diffusion', *Proc. 8th Epig. Congress* (1984), 55 ff.; *CAH* 5² (1992), chs. by P. J. Rhodes, D. Lewis, and A. Andrewes; P. J. Rhodes, *G&R* New Survey 17² (1993); R. Thomas, in A. K. Bowman and G. Woolf (eds.), *Literacy and Power in the Ancient World* (1994), 43 ff.   R. M.; S. H.

Delion, temple of *Apollo on the NE coast of *Boeotia (now Dhilesi), where the Boeotians defeated the Athenians in 424 BC. The Athenians, with 7,000 *hoplites and some cavalry, but no proper light troops, had fortified the temple and were caught returning to Attica by a Boeotian army also of 7,000 *hoplites, but with more than 10,000 light troops, 500 *peltasts, and some cavalry. The battle provides the first example of the Boeotian tactic of deploying hoplites in a deep *phalanx—here the Thebans (see THEBES (1)) on the right were 25 deep, whereas the Athenians were only eight deep. The Thebans defeated the Athenian left, and although the Athenian right was at first successful, it fled in panic at the sudden appearance of Boeotian cavalry, sent round behind a hill to support their left. Athenian losses, at over 14 per cent, were perhaps the worst ever suffered by a hoplite army.

Thuc. 4. 90 ff.. *RE* 4/2, 'Delion' 5; D. Kagan, *The Archidamian War* (1974).   J. F. La.

Delium See DELION.

Dellius (*RE* 1), **Quintus,** deserted P. *Cornelius Dolabella (1) for C. *Cassius Longinus (1), then Cassius for M. *Antonius (2), under whom he served in diplomatic missions and as an officer until, just before *Actium, he joined Octavian. M. *Valerius Messalla Corvinus, whose career was not dissimilar, called him *desultor* (a trick rider changing horses) of the Civil Wars. He was the addressee of a Horatian ode and wrote an account of Antonius' Parthian War that was probably used by Plutarch in his *Antony.*

R. G. M. Nisbet and M. Hubbard, *A Commentary on Horace: Odes Book II* (1978), 51 f.   E. B.

Delos, a small island (3 sq. km.: 1.2 sq. mi.) between Myconos and Rheneia, regarded in antiquity as the centre of the *Cyclades. Composed of gneiss and granite, it is barren and almost waterless and was incapable of supporting its inhabitants.

Delos, the only place to offer shelter to *Leto, was the birthplace of *Apollo and *Artemis, as recounted in the Archaic *Homeric Hymn to Apollo*. This was the basis of its historical importance. It was also the burial-place of the *Hyperboreans. *Anius was its heroic founder, son and priest of Apollo, later associated with the Trojan cycle.

Early bronze age occupation on Mt. Cynthus was succeeded by a Mycenaean settlement on the low ground later occupied by the sanctuary. Two Mycenaean graves were later identified as the tombs of the Hyperborean maidens (the Theke and the Sema). Continuity of cult into historic times is unlikely.

Delos was colonized by *Ionians *c.*950 BC but the sanctuary's prominence originates in the 8th cent. It became the principal cult centre of the Ionians of the Cyclades, Asia Minor, Attica, and Euboea, and was perhaps the centre of an Ionian *amphictiony. *Naxos (1) and *Paros were its most conspicuous patrons in the early Archaic period. In the later 6th cent. first *Pisistratus and then *Polycrates (1) of Samos asserted their authority. The Athenians purified the island by removing burials within view of the sanctuary and perhaps built a temple of Apollo (the *pōrinos naos*). Polycrates dedicated Rheneia to Apollo, providing the basis for the sanctuary's subsequent wealth. Delos emerged unscathed from the *Persian Wars and subsequently became the meeting-place and treasury of the *Delian League. After their removal to Athens in 454 BC the Athenians assumed administration of the sanctuary but did not impose tribute. In 426 BC Athens carried out a second purification, clearing all burials and depositing their contents in the Purification Trench on Rheneia. Henceforth women about to give birth and the dying had to be removed to Rheneia. They also reorganized their quadrennial festival (the Delia), celebrated with particular splendour by *Nicias (1) in 417 BC, perhaps to inaugurate the new temple of Apollo. In 422 BC the Delians were expelled by Athens on a charge of impurity but were soon recalled. Its independence following liberation in 405 BC was short-lived, administration of the sanctuary reverting to Athens from 394 BC.

Athenian domination lasted until *Antigonus (1)'s foundation of the League of Islanders in 314 BC, championed by the Ptolemies in the early 3rd cent. but redundant after the *Chremonidean War. For a century and a half Delos was independent and functioned as a normal city-state, with an archon as its chief magistrate and the sanctuary's administration entrusted to a board of *hieropoioi* (religious officials). This was a period of extensive new public building, some provided by foreign patrons (e.g. the stoas of *Antigonus (2) II Gonatas and *Philip (3) V). These and the festivals instituted by successive Hellenistic kings were more a display of religious patronage than an assertion of political domination. Although Delos' population remained relatively small (*c.*3,000–4,000) it began to develop as a commercial centre, attracting foreign bankers and traders, Italians prominent among them.

Independence ended in 166 BC when Rome handed control of Delos to Athens. Its inhabitants were expelled and replaced by Athenian *cleruchs. Delos was made a free port to the detriment of Rhodian commerce. In conjunction with its commercial growth in the later 2nd and early 1st cent. its population expanded enormously and it became increasingly cosmopolitan, merchants and bankers from Italy and the Hellenized East forming distinct communities (see NEGOTIATORES). Delos became the most important market for the slave trade (see SLAVERY). Although Athenians filled the civic posts (chief magistrate, the *epimelētēs*), guilds and associations of the foreign communities and trading groups administered their own affairs. Sacked in 88 BC by *Archelaus (3), *Mithradates VI's general, and again in 69 BC by pirates (see PIRACY), Delos never recovered its former greatness. By the end of the 1st cent. BC its importance as a sanctuary as well as a commercial centre were lost. Its decline, which became a *topos in Roman literature, owed as much to shifts in trading-patterns as the destructions. A small community survived into late antiquity.

The cults of Apollo, Artemis, and Leto were naturally the most prominent and among the most ancient, though none need be earlier than the 8th cent. Apollo was the focus of the annual Ionian festival (the *panēgyris*) celebrated with games, singing, and dancing. Individual cities sent delegations to the major festivals and some, such as *Andros, *Ceos, and Carystus, had their own *oikoi* (buildings) within the sanctuary. It was administered by boards of officials responsible for managing the property of Apollo and guarding the temple treasures, as well as maintaining the buildings of the officially recognized cults. However, as in any normal *polis, the gods charged with other communal concerns were given due attention, each having its own cult and annual festival. From the late 3rd cent. and especially after 166 BC foreign cults multiplied, reflecting the cosmopolitan character of the city. Most were of oriental origin, such as *Sarapis, *Isis, and the Syrian gods Hadad and *Atargatis, but Italian divinities, such as the *Lares compitales*, also occur and, from the early 1st cent. BC, a synagogue served the Jewish community. Many were the concern of private groups and not officially recognized.

Among the more curious cult rituals were the sacred offerings sent to Delos by the Hyperboreans, passed from city to city along a fixed route, apparently modified under Athenian influence to pass through Attica. The 'crane' dance (*geranos*; see DANCING; PYGMIES), initiated by *Theseus and the Athenian youths returning from *Crete, was performed at the Altar of Horns. *Callimachus (3) alludes to self-flagellation around the altar and gnawing the trunk of the sacred olive.

The archaeological exploration of Delos, conducted by the French school since 1873, has unearthed the sanctuary and large parts of the ancient city. Its public buildings, commercial installations, and residential quarters, combined with a mass of epigraphic documentation from the 4th cent. BC, give a detailed picture of its political, religious, social, and economic history. Nevertheless, the identification of many of the monuments is disputed.

Most of the ancient cults lay in the low ground on the sheltered west side of the island. Here were the temples of Apollo, the Artemision, and, to the north, the Letoon, as well as the Dodekatheon (sanctuary of the twelve gods) and others not securely identified. In the same area are the *oikoi* of various cities, *dining-rooms, and the altars; the site of the Altar of Horns (the *keratinos bōmos*), reputedly built by Apollo himself, is debated. The Heraion, one of the earliest temples, stood apart at the foot of Mt. Cynthus, whose peak was crowned by a sanctuary of Zeus and Athena. The cult of Anius was housed in the *archēgesion* in the north-east. Originally the sanctuary was approached from the north, passing the Lion Terrace, but subsequently it was entered from the south. The later cults, especially those of oriental origin, were for practical and religious reasons concentrated below Mt. Cynthus and around its peak. The synagogue, on the NE coast, was isolated from the other sacred areas. Many of the associations named after a particular divinity (e.g. the Poseidoniasts of *Berytus and the Hermaists) combined cult with commercial and social functions (see CLUBS, GREEK).

The sanctuary of Apollo was also the focus for the city's political institutions, housing the *prytaneion, the *bouleutērion*, and *ekklēsiastērion*. Associated with the social and religious life of the city were the hippodrome, stadium, and gymnasium on the low ridge north-east of the sanctuary. North of the Sacred Lake were two palaestras and on the lower slopes of Cynthus, in the old town, was the theatre. Around the sanctuary and encroaching on the sacred precincts were many of the commercial establishments, such as the markets of the Delians and the Italians. Warehouses fringed the shore south of the port. Residential areas surrounded the sanctuary on the north, east, and south. No trace of the early city remains. The old town of the 3rd cent., with its unsystematic plan of winding streets and irregular houses, lay to the south at the base of Mt. Cynthus. The expansion of habitation in the later 2nd and early 1st cent. matched the increase in population after 166 BC. Houses of this period are larger, more regular, and organized on a rectilinear street grid. Their affluence testifies to the wealth of the city. Many contain mosaics and traces of wall-paintings and the largest have colonnaded courts. Some 15,000 clay sealings found in one house are all that remains of a private archive. Delos remained unwalled until 69 BC when, following the pirate sack, Triarius constructed a wall encompassing the main sanctuary and the residential areas to its north and south. The city's vast necropolis covered the SE shore of Rheneia.

The Homeric Hymn to Apollo; Callim. Hymn to Delos, with comm. by W. H. Mineur (1984). L. Bürchner, V. von Schoeffer, RE 4. 2 (1901), cols. 2459–2502; PECS 261–4; IG 11 (2) and (4); IDélos (1926–72); F. Durrbach (ed.), Choix d'Inscriptions de Délos 1 (1921); Exploration archéologique de Délos 1– (1909–); many articles in BCH; P. Roussel, Les Cultes égyptiens à Délos (1915–16), and Délos: Colonie athénienne (1916); J. Hatzfeld, Les Trafiquants italiens dans l'Orient hellénique (1919; repr. 1975); W. A. Laidlaw, A History of Delos (1933); R. Vallois, L'Architecture hellénique et hellénistique à Délos 1–2 (1944, 1966), and Les Constructions antiques de Délos (1953); J. Kent, Hesp. 1948, 243 ff.; M. Gallet de Santerre, Délos primitive et archaïque (1958); P. Bruneau, BCH 1968, 633 ff.; J. Marcadé, Au musée de Délos (1969); P. Bruneau, Recherches sur les cultes de Délos à l'époque hellénistique et à l'époque impériale (1970); Études déliennes (BCH suppl. 1, 1973); M.-F. Baslez, Recherches sur les conditions de pénétration et diffusion des religions orientales à Délos (1977); P. Bruneau and J. Ducat, Guide de Délos, 3rd edn. (1983); M.-F. Boussac and others, Les Sceaux de Délos 1– (1992–); N. K. Rath, The Sacred Bonds of Commerce (1993); G. Reger, Regionalism and Change in the Economy of Independent Delos (1994). R. W. V. C.

Delphi (See also DELPHIC ORACLE; PYTHIAN GAMES). Delphi, one of the four great *panhellenic *sanctuaries (the others are *Isthmia, *Olympia, *Nemea), is on the lower southern slopes of *Parnassus, c.610 m. (2,000 ft.) above the gulf of *Corinth.

Before 300 BC There was an extensive Mycenaean village in the *Apollo sanctuary at the end of the bronze age; the area was resettled probably during the 10th cent., and the first dedications (tripods and figurines) appear c.800. The settlement was probably relocated after the first temple was built (late 7th cent.). The first archaeological links are with Corinth and Thessaly. The 6th-cent. Homeric *Hymn to Apollo says Apollo chose *Cretans for his Delphic priests, and early Cretan metal dedications have been found, but Cretan material could have come via Corinth, and Cretan priests may have been invented because Crete was distant i.e. this is a way of stressing the end of local domination. The first *Pythian Games were held in either 591/0 or 586/5.

The sanctuary, for which our main literary evidence is Pausanias 10, consisted of a *temenos enclosed by a wall. Inside it were the monuments dedicated by the states of Greece to commemorate victories and public events, together with about twenty 'treasuries' (the oldest are those of Cypselid Corinth (see CYPSELUS; PERIANDER); *Sicyon, c.560; *Cnidus, c.550; and *Siphnos, c.525), a small theatre, and the main temple of *Apollo to which the Sacred Way wound up from the road below. The *Persian Wars were architecturally celebrated with special panache, and heroes like *Miltiades were commemorated more assertively here (Paus. 10. 10) than was possible back at democratic Athens. The first temple was destroyed by fire in 548 BC; debris, including many votives (notably chryselephantine statuary), was buried under the Sacred Way. This destruction led to an architectural reorganization of the temenos. The great new temple was constructed in the late 6th cent. with help from the *Alcmaeonids, and was itself destroyed by earthquake in 373. A new temple was built by subscription. The physical organization of the *Delphic oracle is controversial.

Delphi was attacked by the Persians in 480 and by the Gauls in 279 BC, but suffered little damage. Excavations were begun by

French archaeologists in 1880, when the village of Kastri was moved from Delphi to its present site some way away. Apart from the revelation of the main buildings of the enclosure and the remains of numerous buildings (such as the base of the Serpent Column and *Lysander's victory-monument for Aegospotami), there have been notable finds of sculpture: the metopes of the Sicyonian building and the metopes of the Athenian treasury, the frieze of the Siphnian treasury, pedimental sculptures of the 'Alcmaeonid' temple, the bronze Charioteer, and the remnants of? *Lysippus (2)'s memorial for a Thessalian dynast (the 'Daochos monument'). Below the modern road and the Castalian Spring are public buildings (palaestra, etc.), the mid-7th-cent. temple of Athena Pronaia, the 4th-cent. *tholos, and the treasury of *Massalia (c.530), in the area called the Marmaria, where there are also boulders which have fallen from the rocks above (the Phaedriades).

The affairs of the sanctuary were administered by an ancient or ostensibly ancient international organization, the Delphic *Amphictiony. Influence at Delphi could be exercised in various ways and (mostly) via this amphictiony: by imposing fines for religious offences, by declaring and leading *sacred wars, and by participation in prestigious building projects. Thus from the age of Archaic *tyranny to the Roman period, Delphi (like other pan-Hellenic sanctuaries but more so, because of its centrality and fame) was a focus for interstate competition as well as for contests between individuals (see PYTHIAN GAMES). The four *sacred wars are therefore only the moments when such competition flared up into overt military clashes. But even 'conventional' wars like the *Peloponnesian Wars had a religious aspect: Sparta's foundation of *Heraclea (4) Trachinia during the *Archidamian War was arguably an attempt to increase Sparta's influence in the amphictiony. And at all times in Greek history, control of *Thessaly was desirable because Thessaly had a built-in preponderance of amphictionic votes. In the 3rd cent. BC the power of *Aetolia was linked to its possession of Delphi, and significantly Rome's first alliance with a Greek state (212 or 211) was with Aetolia.

Delphi was also a *polis*, which issued decrees that survive on stone. But one decree (CID 1, no. 9) suggests abnormality in that the *phratry of the Labyadae is found handling some of the business (e.g. rules about conduct of funerals) which would elsewhere have been the concern of the *polis* proper rather of a kinship group.

Finally, Delphi had military importance as a place of muster in central Greece (e.g. Thuc. 3. 101).

After 300 BC New Hellenistic powers used patronage of Delphi to gain legitimation; the *Aetolian Confederacy certainly, and perhaps *Attalus I of *Pergamum, made dedications promoting their victories against the Gauls as pan-Hellenic services (see SOTERIA). The appropriation (168 BC) by the victorious L. *Aemilius Paullus (2) of a monument destined for King *Perseus (2) announced de facto Roman domination of the sanctuary. Although *Augustus reformed the amphictiony (mainly to serve the interests of *Nicopolis (3)) and *Domitian repaired the temple (AD 84), the only emperor to take a real interest in Delphi was *Hadrian, who held the city's archonship twice, toyed with enlargement of the amphictiony (ending up instead founding the *Panhellenion), and sponsored building (Syll.³ 830); whether the orchestrator (καθηγεμών) of Roman Delphi's beautification in a debated passage of *Plutarch (De Pyth. or. 409c) is Hadrian or the author himself, a Trajanic priest of Apollo, is debated. A regional Greek interest in the cult endured into the 3rd cent. AD, but international attention was now confined largely to *tourism and the Pythian Games. Delphi was still a 'sacred city' (ἱερὰ πόλις) under *Constans (Syll.³ 903 D); the steps in the installation of *Christianity remain obscure.

Fouilles de Delphes 1902– (multi-vol. publication of French excavations); BCH Suppl. 4 (1977); G. Rougemont and others, Corpus des inscriptions delphiques (1977–) 1 (1977); G. Daux, Delphes aux IIᵉ et Iᵉ siècles (1936); R. Flacelière, Les Aitoliens à Delphes (1937); G. Roux, L'Amphictionie, Delphes et le temple d'Apollon au IVᵉ siècle (1979); H. J. Schalles, Untersuchungen zur Kulturpolitik der pergamenischen Herrscher (1985), 104 ff. (Attalids); J.-F. Bommelaer, Guide de Delphes: Le Site and Le Musée (1991); C. Morgan, Athletes and Oracles (1990), and in N. Marinatos and R. Hägg (eds.), Greek Sanctuaries: New Approaches (1993), 27–32; S. Swain, Hist. 1991, 318 ff. (Hadrian); S. Hornblower, HSCP 1992, 169–97; M. Maass, Das antike Delphi (1993); J. Davies, in S. Hornblower (ed.), Greek Historiography (1994), ch. 7. Further bibliog.: E. Østby in Greek Sanctuaries (above), 203 ff.

C. A. M., S. H., A. J. S. S.

Delphic oracle *Oracle of *Apollo. Its origins are dated to the very end of the 9th cent. BC and eventually it developed into the most important Greek oracle. It was consulted by poleis (see POLIS) as well as individuals, and played an important guiding role in the formation of the Greek poleis and in *colonization; it gave guidance on *pollution, 'release from evils', (rarely) laws, and, above all, cult. The story that Apollo was not the original owner of the oracle, but replaced an earlier deity (different versions naming different deities, but all including *Gaia or *Themis, or both) does not reflect cult history; it is a myth, expressing the perception that at Delphi the *chthonian, dangerous, and disorderly aspects of the cosmos have been defeated by, and subordinated to, the celestial guide and lawgiver. Apollo's oracle has tamed the darker side of the cosmos—both at the theological (Gaia's defeat) and at the human level: it therefore gives men divine guidance through which they can cope with this side of the cosmos.

The earliest temple for which there is evidence belongs to the second half of the 7th cent. The temple whose remains are visible was built in the 4th cent. Its predecessor was built in the last quarter of the 6th cent. after the earlier temple had been burnt down in 548/7. The oracular consultation took place in the adytum (innermost sanctuary), in which stood the *omphalos marking the centre of the world as determined by Zeus, who released two eagles, one from the east and one from the west, which met at Delphi (cf. Pind. fr. 54). Another story makes the omphalos *Python's or *Dionysus' tomb. Also in the adytum grew a laurel-tree, but the chasm with the vapours is a Hellenistic invention. The enquirer had to pay a consultation tax called pelanos (which had begun as a bloodless offering and kept the name when it became a monetary contribution). At the altar outside the temple was offered the preliminary sacrifice before the consultation, the prothysis, which on regular consultation days was offered by the Delphic polis on behalf of all enquirers. On other days it was offered by the enquirer—to be more precise, on behalf of the enquirer by the *proxenos of his city: non-Delphians were treated at the Delphic oracle as xenoi, foreigners, worshipping at the sanctuary of another polis. If the preliminary ritual was successful, i.e. if the animal had reacted as it should when sprinkled with water (cf. Plut. Mor. 437a, 438a–b), it was sacrificed, and the enquirer entered the temple, where he offered a second sacrifice, depositing either a whole victim or parts of one on a trapeza, offering-table, at the entrance of the adytum. He then probably went with the prophētai (interpreters) and other

cult personnel to a space from which he could not see the Pythia (see below) in the adytum. The Pythia, who had prepared herself by *purification at the Castalian Spring, burnt laurel leaves and barley meal on the altar called hestia inside the temple (which came to be seen as the common hearth of Greece); crowned with laurel, she sat on the tripod, became possessed by the god, and, shaking a laurel, prophesied under divine inspiration—a state which may correspond to what in non-religious explanatory models would be considered a self-induced trance. Her pronouncements were then somehow shaped by the prophētai. Exactly what form the Pythia's pronouncements took and what the prophētai did are matters of controversy. One possibility is that she felt that she received partial signs transmitting fragmentary visions—not gibberish—and that the prophētai interpreted these, shaping them into coherent, if ambiguous, responses; this was not an attempt to hedge their bets, but a result of the ambiguity inherent in the god's signs and the Greek perception that ambiguity is the idiom of prophecy, that there are limits to man's access to knowledge about the future: the god speaks ambiguously, and human fallibility intervenes and may misinterpret the messages.

The most important of the oracle's religious personnel (consisting of Delphians) were: the Pythia, an ordinary woman who served for life and remained chaste throughout her service; the prophētai; the hosioi, who participated in the ritual of the consultation and shared tasks with the prophētai, and the priests of Apollo. The Pythia is not mentioned in the oldest 'document' informing us about the Delphic cult and oracle, the Homeric *Hymn to Apollo, where the god gives oracular responses 'from the laurel-tree' (393–6), an expression that corresponds closely to that ('from the oak-tree') used in the Odyssey (14. 327–8; 19. 296–7) for the prophecies at *Dodona, where the oak-tree spoke the will of *Zeus, which was interpreted by priests. A similar practice involving the laurel may perhaps have been practised at Delphi at an early period. Whether *divination by lot was practised at Delphi as a separate rite is a matter of controversy. Control of the oracle was in the hands of the Delphic *Amphictiony, run by the amphictionic council, whose duties included the conduct of the pan-Hellenic *Pythian Games, the care of the finances of the sanctuary, and the upkeep of the temple. The amphictiony, we are told, fought a war against Crisa and defeated it; this is the First *Sacred War, the historicity of which has been doubted, but the traditional date for its end (c.590 BC) coincides with the beginning of a period of transformation, a serious upgrading of the sanctuary, not the least of its manifestations being the building of several treasuries. The first Pythian Games were held to celebrate the amphictiony's victory. Other Sacred Wars took place subsequently, of which the fourth ended in 338 with the victory of *Philip (1) II of Macedon at the battle of *Chaeronea. It is not true that the oracle's influence had diminished as a result of its suspect position in the *Persian Wars. Its influence continued, only its 'political' role inevitably diminished in the radically changed circumstances of the Hellenistic and Graeco-Roman world.

H. W. Parke and D. E. W. Wormell, The Delphic Oracle (1956); G. Roux, Delphes: Son oracle et ses dieux (1976); P. Amandry, La Mantique apollinienne à Delphes (1950); R. Parker, in P. Cartledge and F. D. Harvey (eds.), Crux (1985), 298–326; J. Fontenrose, The Delphic Oracle (1978); S. Price, in P. E. Easterling and J. V. Muir (eds.), Greek Religion and Society (1985), 128–54; C. Rolley, in R. Hägg (ed.), The Greek Renaissance of the Eighth Century BC (1983), 109–14; I. Malkin, Religion and Colonization in Ancient Greece (1987); C. Morgan, Athletes and Oracles (1990), and

Demades

in N. Marinatos and R. Hägg (eds.), *Greek Sanctuaries: New Approaches* (1993), 18–44; C. Sourvinou-Inwood, *'Reading' Greek Culture: Texts and Images, Rituals and Myths* (1991), 192–243.   C. S.-I.

Demades (c.380–319 BC) Athenian statesman, of major importance in the two decades following the Greek defeat at the battle of *Chaeronea (338 BC). Of his early career nothing sure can be said, but by 338 he must have made his mark; taken prisoner in the battle, he was chosen by *Philip (1) II of *Macedonia as an envoy and used by the Athenians to negotiate the so-called Peace of Demades. From then on he was regularly called on by the city to get it out of troubles caused by those who did not share his view that Macedon was too strong militarily for the Greeks to revolt with a real chance of success. Having counselled against supporting *Thebes (1)'s revolt of 335, he was able to dissuade *Alexander (3) the Great from persisting in his demand for the surrender of *Demosthenes (2), *Hyperides, and other advocates of war. He opposed involvement in the revolt of *Agis III (331), at which date he was treasurer of the military fund (ταμίας τῶν στρατιωτικῶν) (IG 2². 1493). He seems to have sought the suspension of the Exiles' Decree in 324 by proposing a flattering decree that Alexander be voted a god (which earned him a ten-talent fine), but his greatest service was successfully to negotiate with *Antipater (1) the end of the *Lamian War. In 319 he went on an embassy to Antipater to request the withdrawal of the garrison from Munichia, but *Cassander had him executed, a letter to *Perdiccas (3) having come to light in which Demades urged him to move from Asia against Antipater and save the Greeks.

His policies of appeasement leagued him frequently with the prudent *Phocion. Stories of his greed are dubitable, and the fact that, like Demosthenes, he was found guilty of appropriating some of the money deposited by *Harpalus by no means proves that he had actually done so. All in all, he served Athens well and deserved the statue that had been erected in the Agora (Din. 1. 101).

He began life as a rower and received no formal training in rhetoric. He developed his great natural talent by speaking in the assembly. *Theophrastus opined that as an orator Demosthenes was worthy of the city, Demades too good for it. He published no speeches (cf. Cic. *Brut.* 36 and Quint. *Inst.* 12. 17. 49)—the fragment of a speech *Concerning the Twelve Years* ('Υπὲρ τῆς δωδεκαετίας) is generally agreed not to be genuine—but many striking phrases were remembered.

P. Treves, *Athenaeum* 1933, 105 ff.; V. de Falco, *Demade Oratore, Testimonianze e frammenti*, 2nd edn. (1954); A. N. Oikonomides, *Platon* 1956, 105 ff.; P. Treves, *Rend. Ist. Lomb.* 1958, 327 ff.; J. O. Burtt, *Minor Attic Orators* 2 (1954) (for 'Υπὲρ τῆς δωδεκαετίας).   G. L. C.

demagogues, demagogy (δημαγωγοί, δημαγωγία) 'leader(ship) of the people', a phenomenon particularly associated with Classical Athens in the 5th cent. BC, though the 4th cent. had its (less extreme) demagogues too. Unlike their English counterparts, the Greek words were not initially or necessarily disparaging (K. Dover (ed.), Ar. *Frogs* (1993), 69 n. 1), i.e. the root meaning was 'leader' not 'misleader'; and they are fairly rare: *Thucydides (2) uses 'demagogue' and 'demagogy' once each (4. 21; 8. 65). That 'demagogue' came to be bad is however beyond doubt, see e.g. Xen. *Hell.* 5. 2. 7 for 'troublesome demagogues' at *Mantinea, or Arist. *Pol.* 1313ᵇ40: demagogues as flatterers of the people. The role of demagogues, a term which should be extended to include 'respectable' figures like *Pericles (1) and *Nicias (1) as well as more obvious ones like *Cleon and *Hyp-

erbolus, was important in Athenian *democracy. (Plato, *Gorgias*, makes Pericles flatter the people, contrast Thuc. 2. 65, etc.) On the most favourable view, demagogues were the 'indispensable experts', particularly on financial matters, whose grasp of detail kept an essentially amateur system going. Certainly inscriptions, our main source of financial information about Classical Athens, help correct the hostile picture in Thucydides and *Aristophanes (1). But it has been protested that demagogues worked by charisma not expertise.

In antiquity, *Theopompus (3), in his *Philippica* book 10, and *Idomeneus (2) wrote on the Athenian demagogues.

A. Andrewes, *Phoenix* 1962, 83; W. R. Connor, *New Politicians of Fifth-Century Athens* (1971); M. I. Finley, in M. I. Finley (ed.), *Studies in Ancient Society* (1974), 1 ff. and *Politics in the Ancient World* (1983), 76 ff.; W. Thompson, *Classical Contributions ... McGregor* (1981), 153 ff.; P. J. Rhodes, *JHS* 1986, 132 ff. See also HYPERBOLUS and other names mentioned above.   S. H.

Demaratus (1), of *Corinth was widely recognized in antiquity not only as the father of *Tarquinius Priscus, the first Tarquin king of Rome (Polyb. 6. 11a. 7, the oldest written source), but also as a *Bacchiad refugee who, having traded successfully with Etruria, took up residence at *Tarquinii after the events of 657 BC (Dion. Hal. *Ant. Rom.* 3. 46. 3–5; Livy 1. 34. 2). He was accompanied there by three Corinthian craftsmen (Eucheir, Diopus, and Eugrammus), who transmitted *plastikē* to Italy (Plin. *HN* 35. 43. 152). Demaratus is best seen as essentially a lay-figure, exemplifying Rome's traditional liberality in the matter of accepting foreigners (cf. *Syll.*³ 543) by his status as the effective patriarch of the Tarquin dynasty. The extent and early establishment (e.g. at *Pithecusae) of Corinthian trade with the west made it possible to evoke a rich Corinthian merchant of the mid-7th cent., and to credit him with a major role in the 'Hellenization of Etruria'—a term that in (archaeological) fact conceals a much more complex story of economic and social interaction between 7th-cent. Greeks and *Etruscans. See HELLENISM.   D. W. W. R.

Demaratus (2), *Eurypontid king of Sparta (reigned c.515–491 BC). He twice obstructed his Agiad co-king *Cleomenes (1) I, first on the invasion of Attica (c.506) and again when he prevented the arrest of the Medizing faction (see MEDISM) on *Aegina (491). Dethroned on a false charge of illegitimacy manipulated through Delphi by Cleomenes, he himself Medized by fleeing to *Darius I. He accompanied *Xerxes in 480, presumably in hopes of recovering his throne, but served in *Herodotus (1) as a tragic warner of his city's die-hard resistance. Herodotus had possibly talked with Demaratus' descendants in the Troad (*Troas), where Demaratus had been rewarded for his services to Persia with four cities.

Hdt. 5. 75 ff.. P. Cartledge, *Sparta and Lakonia* (1979).   P. A. C.

demes, dēmoi (δῆμοι), local territorial districts—villages, in effect—in Greece and, by extension, the inhabitants or members thereof. The first of these twin meanings has been detected in the Linear B tablets, and both of them occur in *Homer (Whitehead (below), app. 1, with D. M. Lewis in O. Murray and S. Price (eds.) (1990), *The Greek City* 260 ff.); the first remains common thereafter, but of greater significance is the second, which at local level—*dēmos as the word for an entire citizen-body being a related but separate story—expresses the fact that a Classical or Hellenistic state's dēmoi sometimes served as its official, constitutional subdivisions, besides sustaining internally organized communal functions of their own. Jones (below) assembles evidence, mainly epigraphic, concerning one or the other or both of these roles in 24 places altogether. Some of them manifest deme systems apparently *sui generis* (e.g. *Calymnos, *Chalcis, *Cos, *Elis, *Eretria, *Histiaea, *Rhodes, *Stratonicea) but more than half betray the impact, direct (*cleruchies) or indirect (e.g. *Miletus: M. Piérart, *MH* 1983, 1 ff, and 1985, 276 ff), of the most richly documented deme system of all, that of post-Cleisthenic Athens (see CLEISTHENES (2)). There 139 *dēmoi*, encompassing the city itself and the Attic countryside, became the building-blocks of Cleisthenes' three-tier civic structure. As natural units of nucleated settlement they varied enormously in size, from tiny hamlets to substantial towns like *Acharnae or *Eleusis, but equalizing mechanisms operated at the levels of *trittyes* and *phylai*, including proportional representation on the *boulē* of 500. Deme membership (proclaimed by a *dēmotikon* or deme name, usually adjectival) was hereditary in the male line, irrespective of any changes of residence, and served as guarantee of membership of the *polis* itself. Registration of 18-year-olds, occasionally others, as demesmen was thus the most far-reaching of the many functions supervised by the *dēmarchos*, the one official to be found in any and every deme. (Other such functions are attested in fiscal, military, and religious areas.) Besides the demarch, though, a deme assembly could devise and appoint whatever officials it liked, as one instance of the high degree of self-determination it enjoyed generally. To its own (resident) members their deme felt like a *polis* in miniature (cf. Thuc. 2. 16. 2), and where possible it behaved as such, levying and spending income, organizing local cults and *festivals, and commemorating its decision-making on the inscriptions from which much of our evidence derives. Ambitious Athenians might occasionally see their deme as a stepping-stone to higher things, but prosopographical evidence more strongly indicates the microcosm(s) and macrocosm as separate spheres, with life in the small pool remaining rewarding enough for many a big fish.

GENERAL V. von Schoeffer, RE 5/1 (1903), 1–131; N. F. Jones, *Public Organization in Ancient Greece* (1987), *passim*.

ATHENS B. Haussoullier, *La Vie municipale en Attique* (1884), still valuable; J. S. Traill, *The Political Organization of Attica* (1975), partially modified by *Demos and Trittys* (1986); R. Osborne, *Demos* (1985); D. Whitehead, *The Demes of Attica* (1986). D. W.

Demeter, the Greek goddess of corn, identified in Italy with *Ceres. The second part of her name means 'mother', and δη (or δα) was thought to mean 'earth' in antiquity, but the Greeks had a separate goddess of the Earth, and Demeter came later in the pantheon, as granddaughter of Ge (*Gaia) and sister of *Zeus. An alternative modern theory connects δη with δηαί, the Cretan word for 'barley' (cf. ζειά, 'spelt'), but this is linguistically doubtful. She is, however, certainly the goddess who controls all crops and vegetation, and so the sustainer of life for men and animals. In early epic corn is called 'Demeter's grain' (Δημήτερος ἀκτή), and in a Homeric simile 'blonde Demeter' herself winnows grain from chaff (*Il.* 5. 500 f.). Her daughter by Zeus, *Persephone (Attic Pherrephatta), was called simply Κόρη, 'the Girl', and the two were so closely linked that they were known as 'the Two Goddesses' (τὼ Θεώ) or even sometimes as 'the Demeters' (Δημήτερες). Because the life of plants between autumn and spring is one of hidden growth underground, Persephone was said to have been carried off by her uncle *Hades, lord of the Underworld, and compelled to spend the winter months with him as his wife, returning to the upper world with the flowers of spring. Thus as Kore she was a deity of youth and joy, the leader of the *Nymphs, with whom she looked after the growth of

the young, but as Hades' wife she was also queen of the dead, governing the fate of souls, and thus an awesome and dread goddess.

As deities of *agriculture and growth, associated with a settled rhythm of life, Demeter and Kore were regarded as important influences in the development of civilization. Their title Thesmophoros was traditionally interpreted as due to their role as givers of law and morality. The Greek religious calendar was closely linked to the farmer's year, and many of their festivals coincided with the seasonal activities of ploughing, sowing, reaping, threshing, and storing the harvest. One of the most important and widespread, the *Thesmophoria, normally took place in autumn (11–13 Pyanopsion in Athens), near to sowing-time, and included ceremonies intended to promote fertility. Like many festivals of Demeter, it was secret and restricted to women. Their secrecy seems to have been due primarily to the sense of awe and fear generated by contemplation of the powers of the earth and Underworld.

The most important festivals of Demeter and Kore were the ceremonies of initiation known as '*mysteries', the most famous of which were those of *Eleusis. By guaranteeing to initiates the favour of the goddesses, they offered above all the promise of a better fate after death, but they also promised him prosperity in life, personified by *Plutus (Wealth), who was the child of Demeter, born from her union with the Cretan hero *Iasion 'in a thrice-ploughed field' (Hom. *Od.* 5. 125–8; cf. Hes. *Theog.* 969–74, *Hymn. Hom. Cer.* 486–9).

Many legends told how, when Demeter was searching for her daughter after Hades had carried her off, she received information or hospitality from the local inhabitants of different places in Greece, and in gratitude taught them how to practise agriculture and to celebrate her rituals. The chief claimants for this honour were Eleusis and *Sicily, her most important cult centres. The oldest and best-known version of the myth is the *Homeric Hymn to Demeter* (see HYMNS), an epic poem probably of the Archaic period. This tells how, after Kore was carried off, Demeter wandered the earth in search of her, disguised as an old woman, until she came to Eleusis where she was welcomed by the family of King *Celeus. She became the nurse of his baby son *Demophon (2), and tried to immortalize him by anointing him with *ambrosia and holding him in the fire at night to burn away his mortality. She was interrupted by *Metanira, Celeus' wife, and so prevented from making him immortal. Instead, she revealed her true identity, promised Demophon heroic honours after death, and ordered the Eleusinians to build her a temple and altar. She then withdrew to her new temple and caused a universal famine, until Zeus was forced to order Hades to release her daughter. Hades, however, gave Persephone a pomegranate seed to eat, and because she had tasted food in the Underworld she was compelled to spend a third part of every year there, returning to earth in spring. Demeter then restored the fertility of the fields and taught the princes of Eleusis how to perform her mysteries, whose absolute secrecy is stressed. The poem closes with the promise of divine favour to the initiates both in life and after death.

The Great Mysteries at Eleusis were celebrated in early autumn (Boedromion), and were preceded by the Lesser Mysteries at Agrae, just outside Athens, in spring (Anthesterion). Some modern scholars have rejected the predominant ancient view which connected Persephone's absence with winter, arguing that her descent should coincide with the storing of seed-corn in underground granaries after harvest, during the period of summer dryness, to be taken out in autumn for sowing. This fits some near eastern myths of a similar type about a disappearing deity, but the story was never understood in this way by the Greeks, and the traditional explanation agrees much better with the agricultural condition of Greece itself.

The famine, in the *Homeric Hymn*, reflects another form of the belief that the death of vegetation has a divine cause. Persephone's absence and Demeter's anger and grief both combine to create sterility. The hymn assumes the existence of agriculture already before the Rape, but the Athenians in the Classical period claimed that Demeter had given to *Triptolemus, one of the princes of Eleusis, the gifts of corn and the arts of agriculture, and that he then travelled over the world teaching these to other nations (see CULTURE-BRINGERS).

Sicily was always regarded as especially consecrated to the Two Goddesses, and in the Hellenistic and Roman periods versions of the myth of Kore which placed her Rape and Return here became popular. She was said to have been carried off from a meadow near Enna in the centre of the island, and to have disappeared underground at the site of the spring Cyane (*Κυάνη*) near *Syracuse, where an annual festival was held. Other major festivals took place at the times of harvest and sowing.

In Arcadia Demeter was worshipped with *Poseidon. The Black Demeter of Phigaleia and Demeter Erinys of Thelpusa were both said to have taken the form of a mare and to have been mated with by Poseidon in horse-shape, and at Phigaleia she was shown as horse-headed. Their offspring were *Despoina ('the Mistress') and (at Thelpusa) the horse *Arion (1). At Phigaleia she was also said to have caused a universal famine because of her anger both with Poseidon and over the loss of her daughter (Paus. 8. 25 and 42).

These motifs of Demeter's anger and a consequent famine recur in the story of *Erysichthon, who incurred her wrath by trying to cut down a grove sacred to her, although warned by the goddess in disguise not to do so. She punished him with an insatiable hunger which ruined all his household (Callim. *Hymn* 6).

A unique genealogy of Demeter makes her the mother of *Artemis (Aesch. fr. 333 Radt): Herodotus says that this was due to *syncretism with Egyptian mythology (2. 156. 5–6).

In art Demeter is shown both on her own and with Persephone, with related figures of cult such as Hades and *Triptolemus, and in groups with the other Olympian deities. Particularly popular scenes are those of the Rape and Return of Persephone, and the Mission of Triptolemus. She carries a sceptre, ears of corn and a poppy, or torches, and she and her daughter are often portrayed as closely linked and similar in iconography.

Kern, *RE* 4. 2713–64; Farnell, *Cults* 3. 29–279; Nilsson, *GGR* 1³. 456–81; Deubner, *Attische Feste* 40–92; Burkert, *GR* 159–61; G. Zuntz, *Persephone* (1971), N. J. Richardson, *The Homeric Hymn to Demeter* (1974, 1979). G. Sfameni Gasparro, *Misteri e culti mistici de Demetra* (1986); A. C. Brumfield, *The Attic Festivals of Demeter* (1981); K. Clinton, *Iconography*.; S. E. Cole, in S. Alcock and R. Osborne (eds.), *Placing the Gods* (1994), 199 ff.; In art: *LIMC* 4/1. 844–908.　　　　　N. J. R.

Demetrias, Magnesian city in the gulf of Volos, sited on a promontory (Pefkakia) occupied from the neolithic to the late bronze age (see IOLCUS). Traces of Classical settlement found near the Hellenistic theatre are sometimes identifed as *Pagasae. In 293 *Demetrius (4) Poliorcetes founded Demetrias by *synoecism, turning the site into a fortified stronghold; in the 3rd cent. BC it was one of the 'fetters of Greece', i.e. it enabled Macedon to control Greece; and a great commercial centre, with a fortified

palace dominating an orthogonal residential area and public buildings.

Rome, victorious over *Philip (3) V, 'liberated' Demetrias; after 191 it reverted to Macedon until the defeat of *Perseus (2) in 168. In decline from the 1st cent. BC, it emerged as an important early-Christian centre, with two ports and two basilicas.

F. Stählin and others, *Pagasai und Demetrias* (1934); papers on the antiquities by B. Helly and P. Marzolff in *Actes du colloque international sur la Thessalie antique en mémoire de D. Théocharis* (1992), 337 ff.
　　　　　B. H.

Demetrius (1), Old *Comedy poet (Diog. Laert. 5. 85). Fr. 2 refers to the destruction of the Athenian walls in 404 BC (see LONG WALLS).

FRAGMENTS Kassel–Austin, *PCG* 5. 8–10.
INTERPRETATION Meineke, *FCG* 1. 264 ff.; G. Kaibel, *RE* 4/2 (1901), 2805 f. 'Demetrios' 74.　　　　　W. G. A.

Demetrius (2), of Alopece, Athenian sculptor, active *c*.400–370 BC. Maker of portrait-bronzes renowned for their realism (Quint. *Inst.* 12. 10. 9, etc.). His subjects included the aged priestess Lysimache and the horse-breeder Simon; Lucian's account of his Pellichus (*Philops.* 18), a Corinthian general, is probably a comic invention. See PORTRAITURE, GREEK.

A. F. Stewart, *Greek Sculpture* (1990), 173, 274 f.　　　　　A. F. S.

Demetrius (3), of *Phaleron (b. *c*.350 BC), son of Phanostratus, Athenian *Peripatetic philosopher (pupil of *Theophrastus) and statesman, began his political life in 325/4 and was probably elected *stratēgos for many of the next few years. He escaped death as a pro-Macedonian in 318, and *Cassander made him absolute governor at Athens, where he held power for ten years. As *nomothetēs he passed comprehensive legislation (317/6–316/5); military and other service was limited, various forms of extravagance were curbed, measures were taken to regularize contracts and titles to property and *nomophylakes were set up. When *Demetrius (4) Poliorcetes took Athens (307), Demetrius fled to *Boeotia, and was later librarian at *Alexandria (1) (297). He died in disgrace under *Ptolemy (1) II Philadelphus.

Works Moral treatises, popular tales, declamations, histories, literary criticism, rhetoric, and collections of letters, fables, and proverbs. Though an outstanding orator, Demetrius produced mainly a superficial amalgam of philosophy and rhetoric. He assisted his fellow Peripatetics, and under him Athens enjoyed relative peace.

Collections of fragments: *FGrH* 228; F. Wehrli, *Demetrios von Phaleron* (1947). See also W. S. Ferguson, *Hellenistic Athens* (1911); S. Dow and A. H. Travis, *Hesp.* 1943, 144 ff.; H.-J. Gehrke, *Chiron* 1978, 149 ff.
　　　　　A. B. B.

Demetrius (4) **I** of Macedonia, 'Poliorcetes', 'Besieger of Cities' (336–283 BC), son of *Antigonus (1) I, was reared at his father's court in Phrygia and fled with him to Europe (322). He was married (321/0) to Phila, daughter of *Antipater (1), widow of *Craterus (1) and a potent political asset, and rapidly acquired military distinction, commanding Antigonus' cavalry at Paraetacene and Gabiene (317/6). His independent commands began inauspiciously at Gaza (312), where he lost an army to *Ptolemy (1) I, and subsequently (311) failed to displace *Seleucus (1) I from Babylonia. However, in 307 he led the Antigonid offensive in Greece, liberating Athens from the regime of *Demetrius (3) of Phaleron, and in 306 his victory over a Ptolemaic fleet off *Cyprus inspired his father to claim kingship for them both. These laurels were tarnished by setbacks in Egypt and, above all, Rhodes, where an epic year-long siege (305–4), which won Demetrius his reputation as 'the Besieger', was ended by negotiation. He was more effective as Antigonus' lieutenant in Greece (304–2), extending the alliance to Boeotia and Aetolia and reconstituting the League of Corinth (302) (see CORINTH, LEAGUE OF). Consequently he retained a base in the Isthmus when Antigonus' empire crumbled away after the defeat at *Ipsus (301).

From this nadir his position strengthened when Seleucus married his daughter, *Stratonice, and ceded *Cilicia (299/8). Demetrius then reappeared in Greece (?295) to 'liberate' Athens from the tyranny of *Lachares and defeated the Spartans. At this juncture he was invited to intervene in the dynastic turmoil in Macedon, where (thanks to Phila) he had himself proclaimed king after murdering the young Alexander V. He now held the throne for seven years (294–287) and devoted much of his energy to extending his control in central Greece (*Thebes (1) was twice besieged) and the west. But his primary ambition was the reconquest of Antigonus' empire, and by 288 a massive fleet of 500 ships was in preparation. At the news Seleucus, *Lysimachus and Ptolemy I allied against him, and his army refused to fight as Macedonia was invaded from east and west. Expelled from Macedon, he could not contain southern Greece, where the Athenians expelled his garrison from the city (but not Piraeus). Ptolemy arbitrated over a peace (287) and encouraged Demetrius to contest Asia Minor yet again. Plague and famine decimated his army, and he surrendered himself to Seleucus. The last two years of his life he spent in captivity, where drink and despondency accelerated his death. In his youth he was affable, accessible, the embodiment of Antigonus' propaganda of liberation. Later he fostered an aura of regal majesty (without his father's vindictive savagery), and his absolutist pretensions encouraged some of the most extreme manifestations of the *ruler-cult. His chequered fortunes are a mirror of his age, when kingship meant conquest.

C. Wehrli, *Antigone et Démétrios* (1968); *HM* 3; R. A. Billows, *Antigonos the One-Eyed* (1990). A. B. B.

Demetrius (5) (*RE* 35) 'the Fair', son of *Demetrius (4) Poliorcetes and half-brother of *Antigonus (2) Gonatas. On the death of Magas of *Cyrene (c.250 BC) was invited by Magas' widow Apama, doubtless in agreement with Gonatas, to take over Cyrene and marry her daughter *Berenice (3), engaged to the future *Ptolemy (1) III. Demetrius, however, transferred his affections from Berenice to Apama, and was murdered at Berenice's instance.

Just. *Epit.* 26. 3; E. Will, *Histoire politique du monde hellénistique*, 2nd edn. (1979) 1. 243–6. J. Br.

Demetrius (6) (*RE* 34) **II** of Macedon, son of *Antigonus (2) Gonatas and Phila, born c.276 BC. On succeeding Gonatas in 239 he divorced Stratonice, daughter of *Antiochus I, and married Phthia, daughter of Olympias of Epirus, when Olympias appealed to him for help against the *Aetolian Confederacy, then seeking to annex the Epirote part of *Acarnania. The Aetolians immediately allied themselves with the *Achaean Confederacy against Macedon. The events that followed are obscure. Demetrius probably saved Acarnania, assisted *Argos (2) against Achaea, and detached *Boeotia (perhaps together with the Megarid, part of *Phocis, and Opuntian *Locris) from Aetolia. His general Bithys defeated *Aratus (2). About 233, however, the Epirote monarchy was overthrown and the new republic joined the two confederacies. Demetrius made an alliance with Agron

king of the *Illyrii to protect Acarnania, now independent, but was defeated resisting Dardanian invasion and died in 229, leaving one son by Phthia, later *Philip (3) V. Demetrius' cousin *Antigonus (3) Doson became king as Philip's guardian.

E. Will, *Histoire politique du monde hellénistique*, 2nd edn. (1979), 348–54. J. Br.

Demetrius (7) (*RE* 44a (Suppl. 1)), of Pharos surrendered *Corcyra to Rome in 229 BC, during Rome's First Illyrian War. He was rewarded by being made dynast of part of Illyria, but his influence increased considerably when he became guardian of Pinnes, successor of *Teuta. He fought with *Antigonus (3) Doson against *Cleomenes (2) III of Sparta at Sellasia (222). In 220 he sailed south of Lissus (Lesh), attacking *Pylos and some of the *Cyclades; but *Polybius (1) is probably wrong to regard these actions as proof that he, rather than Rome, was the aggressor in the ensuing Second Illyrian War. He sold his services to Macedon against the Aetolians, and on his return began ravaging some of the Illyrian cities under Roman protection. The Romans sent the consuls of 219 against him, but Demetrius escaped and fled to *Philip (3) V of Macedon. In 217 he urged Philip to make peace with Aetolia and cross to Italy. In 215 he unsuccessfully urged Philip to seize *Ithome, and in 214 died in an attack on *Messene. Polybius describes him as foolhardy and totally lacking judgement.

Polyb. 2. 10–11, 3. 16–19, 5. 101–8, 7. 12, with Walbank, *HCP*; Badian, *Stud. Gr. Rom. Hist.* 1–33. J. Br.

Demetrius (8) **I,** Graeco-*Bactrian king c.186–170 BC. He helped to negotiate a treaty ending the war between his father, *Euthydemus (2) I, and *Antiochus (3) III; to reward his services, Antiochus betrothed a daughter to him (c.206 BC). Later in his father's reign, he apparently led an invasion across the Hindu Kush mountains into Arachosia, Drangiana, and NW India. His conquests were marked by the founding of a city, Demetrias, in Arachosia, and coins showing him wearing the scalp of an Indian elephant. Just. *Epit.* refers to him as 'rex Indorum', a title later echoed by Chaucer in 'The Knight's Tale'. He succeeded his father as king of this enlarged empire in c.186, but his reign was probably cut short by the rise of the usurper *Eucratides I. He is distinguished from his probable son, *Demetrius (9) II, by coin-type.

F. L. H.

Demetrius (9) **II,** Graeco-Bactrian king c.145–140 BC. Probably a son of *Demetrius (8) I, his coins replace the Heracles types of *Euthydemus (2) I, *Euthydemus (3) II, and Demetrius I with Athena holding shield and spear. He briefly ruled part of the *Oxus valley after the death of *Eucratides I, as hoard evidence shows. Some scholars consider him the 'rex Indorum' who was defeated by Eucratides I. F. L. H.

Demetrius (10) **I** of Syria (187–150 BC), second son of *Seleucus (4) IV. Roman hostage for sixteen years until 162, when he escaped, helped by friends, among them *Polybius (1). He established himself, despite Roman support for his opponents within and without the kingdom, by executing his young cousin *Antiochus (5) V and defeating the powerful satrap of Media Timarchus (161 or 160)—whereupon Demetrius took the title 'Soter' ('Saviour')—and the rebellious Jews in Palestine. Despite these successes, tolerated but never formally recognized by Rome and opposed by Rome's friends, he fell in battle against *Alexander (10) Balas, who had Pergamene, Ptolemaic, and Roman support (150).

CAH 8² (1989). R. M. E.

Demetrius II

Demetrius (11) **II** of Syria (c.161–125 BC), eldest son of *Demetrius (10) I. He successfully opposed *Alexander (10) Balas with mercenary and Ptolemaic support (145), asserted Seleucid rule in Palestine and against Diodotus Tryphon (142), but was captured by the Parthian Mithradates I (139). When *Antiochus (7) VII Sidetes attacked Parthia, Demetrius was freed (129) and ruled again until he was killed near Tyre in a war he had himself provoked by attacking Egypt, against Alexander Zabinas, whom *Ptolemy (1) VIII had set up (125).

C. Habicht, *CAH* 8² (1989), 362 ff.   R. M. E.

Demetrius (12), of *Scepsis in the Troad (b. c.214 BC), was a student of local topography and wrote a work in 30 books on the 62 lines in *Iliad* 2 which catalogue the Trojan forces.

R. Pfeiffer, *History of Classical Scholarship: From the Beginnings to the End of the Hellenistic Age* (1968), 249–51.   N. G. W.

Demetrius (13) **Ixion** (2nd cent. BC), a grammarian, contemporary with *Aristarchus (2), who seceded from *Alexandria (1) to *Pergamum and disputed Aristarchan textual principles. He also compiled an *Atticist Lexicon.

Demetrius (14) (*RE* 115), of Laconia (c.100 BC), Epicurean pupil of Protarchus of Bargylia and younger contemporary of *Philodemus' teacher *Zeno (5) of Sidon. He refuted *Carneades' attack on the possibility of proof, and expounded *Epicurus' epiphenomenal doctrine of time as an 'accident of accidents'. *Aëtius (1) (1. 18. 3 p. 316, 4 Diels) includes him, along with *Leucippus (3), *Democritus, and *Metrodorus (1), in a list of those who think that atoms (see ATOMISM) are infinite in number and that void is infinite in extent. Philodemus in *On Signs* records that he lectured on inference from similarities. Several of his works are preserved in the Epicurean library from *Herculaneum, together with those of Philodemus, from whom he differs markedly in style (being more taut and concise), including treatises in multiple books on poetics, on gods, and on the philology and textual criticism of Epicurean texts. He was willing to argue that the school's philosophical shortcomings were sometimes due to faulty textual transmission.

TESTIMONIA Collected by M. Gigante, in E. Puglia, *Demetrio Lacone: Aporie testuali ed esegetiche in Epicuro* (*PHerc. 1012*), La scuola di Epicuro 8 (1988), §§ ii–xii; discussion by P. and E. A. De Lacy, *Philodemus, On Methods of Inference*, 2nd edn., La scuola di Epicuro 1 (1978); D. Sedley, in M. Griffin and J. Barnes (eds.), *Philosophia Togata* (1989), 97–119.

WORKS Ed. W. Crönert, in *Kolotes und Menedemos* (1906), 100; V. de Falco (1923). On poetry: C. Romeo, *Demetrio Lacone, La Poesia* (*PHerc. 188 e 1014*), La scuola di Epicuro 9 (1988). On gods: E. Renna, *Cronache Ercolanesi* 1982, 43–9; and *Cronache Ercolanesi* 13 (1982), 25–8. On Epicurean philology: E. Puglia (as cited above). On signs: De Lacy and De Lacy (as cited above).   W. D. R.; D. O.

Demetrius (15) (probably 2nd or 1st cent. BC), author of a short guide to letter-writing which enumerates 21 types of letter, with one or two models for each.

Ed. V. Weichert (1910).   M. B. T.

Demetrius (16), of Magnesia (fl. 50 BC), friend of T. *Pomponius Atticus, wrote in Greek on concord (Περὶ ὁμονοίας), and on homonymous towns and writers; much of his biographical detail was transmitted to *Diogenes (6) Laertius. See HOMONOIA.

FHG 4. 382.   J. S. R.

Demetrius (17). The treatise 'On Style' (Περὶ ἑρμηνείας) is traditionally ascribed to *Demetrius (3) of Phalerum. This is

most unlikely to be right. The author probably belongs to the late Hellenistic or early Roman period, though no indications are decisive. After an introductory section on sentence-structure and the period, the book proceeds to a discussion of four types (χαρακτῆρες) of style—grand, smooth, slight, and forceful (μεγαλοπρεπής, γλαφυρός, ἰσχνός, δεινός: see LITERARY CRITICISM IN ANTIQUITY, para. 5)—and the ways of achieving these and avoiding their 'corresponding faults'. Much of the material is *Peripatetic; the examples come from poets and historians as well as orators, and among the orators *Demosthenes (2) has not the dominant position which later rhetoric usually assigned to him; many minor 4th-cent. writers are also quoted. Particularly noteworthy parts of 'On Style' are the sections on letter-writing (§§ 223–35) and on humour and charm (χάρις, §§ 131–70, in the discussion of the 'smooth' style).

EDITIONS L. Radermacher (1901); W. Rhys Roberts (1902).
TRANSLATIONS W. Rhys Roberts (Loeb, 1927), revision by D. C. Innes forthcoming; G. M. A. Grube (1961), with extensive introduction and notes; T. A. Moxon (1934).
LITERATURE Besides discussions in surveys listed at *literary criticism in antiquity, see D. M. Schenkeveld, *Studies in Demetrius* (1964); F. Solmsen, *Hermes* 1931, 285–311 (repr. (with other relevant articles) in R. Stark, *Rhetorica* (1968)).   D. A. R.

Demetrius (18), of Tarsus (1st cent. AD), a grammarian, one of the characters in *Plutarch's *De def. or.*, where he is said (ch. 2) to be on his way home from *Britain to Tarsus. Perhaps identical with a Demetrius who dedicated two tablets with Greek inscriptions, now in the York museum (*IG* 14. 254 f.), and possibly also *Demetrius (17). See W. Rhys Roberts, in Loeb *Demetrius*, 272 ff.   J. S. R.

Demetrius (19) the *Cynic lived in Rome under *Gaius (1), *Nero, and *Vespasian and was friendly with the Stoic philosopher L. *Annaeus Seneca (2). He was probably exiled to Greece under Nero (AD 66) but returned in the time of Vespasian. He was criticized for defending the Stoic philosopher Egnatius Celer when he was accused by C. *Musonius Rufus of having given false testimony against his friend *Barea Soranus. Demetrius was subsequently deported by Vespasian to an island for criticizing the regime.

M. Billerbeck, *Der Kyniker Demetrius* (1979); J. F. Kindstrand, *Philol.* 1980, 83 ff.; J. L. Moles, *JHS* 1983, 103 ff.   M. T. G.

Demetrius (20), of Troezen (probably 1st cent. AD), wrote works on literary history. The only known title is that of his work on philosophers, *Against the Sophists*.

Ath. 1. 29a; Diog. Laert. 8. 74.   M. B. T.

Demetrius (21), of Apamea (2nd cent. BC?), physician of the 'school' of *Herophilus. No Herophilean was more famous for his contributions to *pathology. In *On Affections* 1–12 and in *Signs* (or *Semiotics*) he discussed the symptoms and causes of numerous mental and physical disorders, including priapism, satyriasis, mania, hydrophobia, lethargy, cardiac disorders, phrenitis, dropsy, pneumonia, and pleurisy. Like Herophilus, he also had a strong interest in *gynaecology: he discussed the causes of difficult *childbirth (δυστοκία), inflammation of the uterus, and seven kinds of vaginal discharge. Displaying the scientific independence characteristic of the Herophilean school, he directly contradicted Herophilus by asserting that there are diseases peculiar to women. Therapeutics represent a further attested interest of Demetrius. Although also known from an anonymous papyrus, Demetrius is the only Herophilean whose views are transmitted mainly by Methodist sources (*Soranus, Caelius Aurelianus); this perhaps is an indication of the esteem in which his 'practical' contributions were held, also by non-Herophileans.

Ed., trans., and comm.: H. von Staden, *From Andreas to Demosthenes Philalethes* (1995), ch. 6. Cf. *Herophilus* (1989), 506–11.   H. v. S.

dēmiourgoi, 'public workers', are in *Homer such independent craftsmen as metalworkers, potters, and masons, and also seers, doctors, bards, and heralds. *Plato (1) and *Xenophon (1) use the word thus. More generally in Classical Greece the word is used sometimes in that sense, sometimes as the title of major officials in a state; though perhaps of greatest antiquity in *Elis and *Achaea, they are most often found in Dorian states. In the *Achaean Confederacy they formed a council of ten, who assisted the *stratēgos; the *Arcadian League imitated this organization, based originally on local representation. Outside mainland Greece, *dēmiourgoi* are found in *Crete and several Aegean islands, and in the Roman period in *Asia Minor. In Athens there are references to a division of the citizen body into *eupatridai, farmers, and *dēmiourgoi*, and to the involvement of those classes in the appointment of the archons after 580 BC (*Ath. pol.* frs. 2–3; 13. 2), but the farmers and *demiourgoi* are probably the result of 4th-cent. speculation.

Mycenaean world: L. R. Palmer, *TAPA.* 1954, 18–53b; K. Murakawa, *Hist.* 1957, 385–415. Archaic Greece generally: L. H. Jeffery, *Arch. Class.* 1973–4, 319 ff. Crete: M. Guarducci, *Riv. Fil.* 1930, 54–70. Athens: Rhodes, *CAAP* 71–2, 182–4. The evidence for *dēmiourgoi* as officials in various states is mainly *epigraphical.   F. W. W.; P. J. R.

Democedes, of *Croton (6th cent. BC), one of the most famous doctors (see MEDICINE) of his time (Hdt. 3. 125), and origin of *Croton's medical reputation (Hdt. 3. 131), practised in *Aegina, *Athens, and then for *Polycrates (1) of Samos. After the murder of Polycrates in *c.*522, he won great repute at the Persian king *Darius I's court (Hdt. 3. 129–38), but the picturesque Herodotean story of his escape back to Croton, and marriage to the daughter of *Milon the wrestler, may be a romanticized later folk-tale.

Testimonia in DK no. 19; A. Griffiths, in H. Sancisi-Weerdenburg and A. Kuhrt (eds.), *Achaemenid History* 2 (1987), 37 ff.   R. T.

Demochares (*c.*360–275 BC), Athenian orator (the nephew of *Demosthenes (2)), historian, and statesman, rose to power after the expulsion of *Cassander's agents in 307. During the 'Four Years' War' against Cassander (307–304) he fortified Athens and made an alliance with *Boeotia. Exiled probably in 303, he returned in Diocles' archonship (288/287?), and recovered *Eleusis from Macedon. He secured financial aid from *Lysimachus, *Antipater (1), and *Ptolemy (1) I; and in 280–279 had a decree passed honouring Demosthenes. Sincere and patriotic, he consistently opposed Macedonian control of Athens and *Demetrius (3) of Phaleron. His written works consisted of speeches, a biography of *Agathocles (1), and a contemporary history, mainly of Athens, in over 21 books. It was highly rhetorical, and Demochares probably used it to attack opponents including the Macedonian *Demetrius (4); it may be an important source for *Plutarch's *Demetrius*.

FGrH 75; T. L. Shear, Jr., *Kallias of Sphettos and the Revolt of Athens in 286 BC* (1978); R. A. Billows, *Antigonos the One-Eyed and the Creation of the Hellenistic State* (1990), 337–9.   F. W. W.; K. S. S.

democracy, Athenian Athenian democracy from 508/7 to 322/1 BC is the best known example in history of a 'direct' democracy as opposed to a 'representative' or 'parliamentary' form of democracy.

1. Ideology Today democracy is invariably a positive concept, almost a buzz-word, whereas *dēmokratia* in ancient Greece was a hotly debated form of constitution, often criticized by oligarchs and philosophers alike. The Athenian democrats themselves, however, connected *dēmokratia* with the rule of law (Aeschin. 1. 4–5) and, like modern democrats, they believed that democracy was inseparably bound up with the ideals of liberty and equality (Thuc. 2. 37). Democracy was even deified, and in the 4th cent. BC offerings were made to the goddess Demokratia (IG 2². 1496. 131–41).

Dēmokratia was what the word means: the rule (*kratos*) of the people (**dēmos*), and decisions of the assembly were introduced with the formula *edoxe tō dēmō* (IG 2². 28). When an Athenian democrat said *dēmos* he meant the whole body of citizens, irrespective of the fact that only a minority turned up to meetings of the assembly (Aeschin. 3. 224; Thuc. 8. 72). Critics of democracy, on the other hand, especially the philosophers, tended to regard the *dēmos* as a class, i.e. the 'ordinary people' (Arist. *Pol.* 1291^{b}17–29; *Ath. pol.* 41. 2) or the 'city poor' who by their majority could outvote the minority of countrymen and major propertyowners (Pl. *Resp.* 565a).

The fundamental democratic ideal was liberty (*eleutheria*, see FREEDOM), which had two aspects: political liberty to participate in the democratic institutions, and private liberty to live as one pleased (*zēn hōs bouletai tis*) (Arist. *Pol.* 1317^{a}40–^{b}17; Thuc. 7. 69. 2). The most important aspect of liberty was freedom of speech (*parrhēsia*) which in the public sphere was every citizen's right to address his fellow citizens in the political assemblies, and in the private sphere was every person's right to speak his mind (Dem. 9. 3). The critics of democracy, especially the philosophers, took democratic *eleutheria* to be a mistaken ideal that led to a deplorable pluralism and prevented people from understanding the true purpose in life (Pl. *Resp.* 557b–558c).

The democrats' concept of equality was not based on the view that all are equal (although the philosophers wanted to impute this view to the democrats, Arist. *Pol.* 1301^{a}28–35). The equality advocated by the democrats was that all should have an equal opportunity to participate in politics (**isonomia*, Hdt. 3. 80. 6; Eur. *Supp.* 353, 408, 441), especially an equal opportunity to speak in the political assemblies (*isēgoria*, Hdt. 5. 78; Dem. 15. 18) and that all must be equal before the law (*kata tous nomous pasi to ison*, Thuc. 2. 37. 2). The concept of equality was purely political and did not spread to the social and economic sphere of society.

2. Institutions A description of the political system must focus on the 4th cent. BC, especially on the age of *Demosthenes (2) (355–322) where the sources are plentiful enough to allow a reconstruction of the democratic organs of government.

Political rights were restricted to adult male Athenians. Women, foreigners, and slaves were excluded (Dem. 9. 3). An Athenian came of age at 18 when he became a member of his father's *deme and was enrolled in the deme's roster (the *lēxiarchikon grammateion*, Aeschin. 1. 103); but, as *ephēboi, most young Athenians were liable for military service for two years (*Ath. pol.* 42) before, at the age of 20, they could be enrolled in the roster of citizens who had access to the assembly or *ekklēsia (the *pinax ekklēsiastikos*, Dem. 44. 35). And full political rights were only obtained at the age of 30 when a citizen was allowed to present himself as a candidate at the annual sortition of magistrates (Xen. *Mem.* 1. 2. 35) and jurors (*Ath. pol.* 63. 3) (who served as both legislators and judges).

The citizen population totalled some 30,000 adult males over

18, of whom some 20,000 were over 30 and thus in possession of full political rights. The population of Attica—citizens, foreigners, and slaves of both sexes and all ages—may have amounted to some 300,000 persons. (See POPULATION, GREEK.)

Any citizen over 20 had the right to speak and vote in the people's assembly (*ekklēsia*) (Xen. *Mem.* 3. 6. 1). The people met 40 times a year (*Ath. pol.* 43. 3), mostly on the *Pnyx (Aeschin. 3. 34); a meeting was normally attended by at least 6,000 citizens, the quorum required for (among other things) ratification of citizenship decrees (Dem. 59. 89), and a session lasted a couple of hours only (Aeschin. 1. 112). The assembly was summoned by the 50 *prytaneis and chaired by the nine *proedroi (*Ath. pol.* 44. 2–3). The debate consisted of a number of speeches made by the politically active citizens, and all votes were taken by a show of hands (*cheirotonia*), assessed by the *proedroi* without any exact count of the hands (ibid. 44. 3) (see ELECTIONS AND VOTING). The Athenians distinguished between laws (general and permanent rules, called *nomoi*) and decrees (temporary and/or individual rules, called *psēphismata*, Andoc. 1. 87); see LAW AND PROCEDURE, ATHENIAN. The assembly was not allowed to pass *nomoi* but did, by decree, make decisions on foreign policy and on major issues of domestic policy (*Ath. pol.* 43. 6). Furthermore, the people in assembly were empowered (*a*) to elect the military and financial magistrates (ibid. 43. 1, 44. 4); (*b*) to initiate legislation (*nomothesia*) by appointing a panel of legislators (*nomothetai*, Dem. 3. 10–3); and (*c*) to initiate a political trial (*eisangelia eis ton dēmon) by appointing a panel of judges (a *dikastērion*, *Ath. pol.* 43. 4).

Citizens over 30 were eligible to participate in the annual sortition of a panel of 6,000 jurors (*hoi omomōkotes*, Ar. *Vesp.* 662) who for one year served both as legislators (Dem. 24. 21) and as judges (ibid. 148–51). When a *nomos* was to be enacted, the assembly decreed the appointment, for one day only, of a board of e.g. 1,000 legislators (*nomothetai) selected by lot from the 6,000 jurors (Dem. 24. 20–38; Aeschin. 3. 38–40). Having listened to a debate the *nomothetai* decided by a show of hands all amendments to '*Solon's laws', i.e. the Solonian law code of 594/3 as revised and codified in 403/2 (Andoc. 1. 82–5). Boards of *nomothetai* were appointed only infrequently, and to legislate once in a month was considered excessive (Dem. 24. 142).

Jurisdiction was much more time-consuming. The popular courts (*dikastēria*) met on roughly 200 days in a year. On a court day members of the panel of 6,000 jurors showed up in the morning in the *Agora, and a number of courts were appointed by *sortition from among those who presented themselves. These courts consisted of 201 or 401 judges each in private actions and 501 or more in public actions. Each court was presided over by a magistrate and in a session of some eight hours the judges had to hear and decide either one public action or a number of private actions (*Ath. pol.* 63–9). The two most important types of political trial were (i) the public action against unconstitutional proposals (*graphē paranomōn), brought against proposers of decrees (Aeschin. 3. 3–8), and (ii) denunciation to the people in assembly (*eisangelia eis ton dēmon*, Hyp. 3. 7–8), used most frequently against generals charged with treason and *corruption (Dem. 13. 5).

In addition to the decision-making organs of government (*ekklēsia, nomothetai, dikastēria*) Athens had about 1,200 magistrates (*archai*), elected from among citizens over 30 who presented themselves as candidates (Lys. 6. 4). About 100 were elected by the *ekklēsia* (Aeschin. 3. 14) whereas the other 1,100

were chosen by lot (Dem. 39. 10), viz. 500 councillors and *c*.600 other magistrates, often organized in boards of ten with one representative from each tribe (*IG* 2². 1388. 1–12). The period of office was restricted to one year and a magistrate selected by lot could only hold the same office once whereas elected magistrates could be re-elected (*Ath. pol.* 62. 3). Before entering office magistrates had to undergo an examination (*dokimasia) before a *dikastērion* (ibid. 55. 2–5) and, on the expiration of their term of office, to render accounts (*euthynai) before another *dikastērion* (ibid. 54. 2; 48. 4–5).

The magistrates' principal tasks were to summon and preside over the decision-making bodies, and to see to the execution of the decisions made (Arist. *Pol.* 1322ᵇ12–17). Apart from routine matters, the magistrates could not decide anything but only prepare the decisions (ibid. 1298ᵃ28–32). The council of five hundred prepared business for the *ekklēsia* (*Ath. pol.* 45. 4) and the *nomothetai* (Dem. 24. 48), the other magistrates for the *dikastēria* (Aeschin. 3. 29).

By far the most important board of magistrates was the council of five hundred (*hē* *boulē hoi pentakosioi). It was composed of 50 persons from each of the ten tribes who for a tenth of the year (a prytany of 36 or 35 days) served as *prytaneis*, i.e. as executive committee of the council, which again served as executive committee of the assembly. The council met every day except holidays in the *bouleutērion* on the Agora to run the financial administration of Athens and to consider in advance every matter to be put before the people (*Ath. pol.* 43. 2–49. 5).

Of the other boards of magistrates the most important were the ten generals (*stratēgoi) who commanded the Athenian army and navy (ibid. 61. 1–2), the board for the Theoric Fund (*hoi epi to* *theōrikon) who in the 350s under *Eubulus (1) supervised the Athenian financial administration (Aeschin. 3. 24–5), and the nine archons (see ARCHONTES), who in most public and private actions had to summon and preside over the popular courts and supervised the major festivals, e.g. the *Panathenaea and the *Dionysia (*Ath. pol.* 55–9).

In all matters the initiative was left to the individual citizen, in this capacity called *tōn Athenaiōn ho boulomenos hois exestin* (*SEG* 26. 72. 34). At any time about 1,000 citizens must have been active as speakers and proposers of *nomoi* and *psēphismata* or as prosecutors and *synēgoroi* before the people's court. But it was always a small group of about twenty citizens who more or less professionally initiated Athenian policy. They were called *rhētores* (Hyp. 3. 4, 8) or *politeuomenoi* (Dem. 3. 29–31), whereas the ordinary politically active citizen is referred to as an *idiōtēs* (Dem. *prooem.* 13). There were no political parties and the people did not just vote according to the crack of their leaders' whip. But by persuasion and charisma major political leaders sometimes succeeded in dominating the political assemblies for a longer period, as did *Pericles (1) from 443 until his death in 429 (Thuc. 2. 65. 10), and *Demosthenes (2) in the period 341–338 (Dem. 18. 320).

The ordinary citizens were reimbursed for their political activity as *ekklēsiastai*, or *nomothetai* or *dikastai* or *bouleutai* (*Ath. pol.* 62. 2; Dem. 24. 21). Very few of the magistrates were paid on a regular basis, but many obtained perquisites instead (Isoc. 7. 24–7). Speakers and proposers in the political assemblies were unpaid, and those who attempted to make a profit out of politics were regarded as *sycophants and liable to punishment (Dem. 59. 43).

The council of the *Areopagus was a survival of the Archaic period and in the period 461–404 mainly a court for cases of homicide (Philochorus, *FGrH* 328 F 64). In the 4th cent., however, the activity of the Areopagus was again progressively enlarged in connection with the attempts to revive the 'ancestral' or 'Solonian' democracy (Din. 1. 62–3; Lycurg. 1. 52).

3. *History* In 510 BC the Pisistratid tyrants (see PISISTRATUS; HIPPIAS (1)) were expelled from Athens, but the revolution ended in a power struggle between the returning aristocrats led by *Cleisthenes (2) and those who had stayed behind led by Isagoras. With the help of the ordinary people (the *dēmos*) Cleisthenes successfully opposed Isagoras (Hdt. 5. 66–73) and, reforming the Solonian institutions of 594 BC, he introduced a new form of popular government which was in fact arising in several Greek city-states at the time. The term *dēmokratia* can be traced back to c.470 (*SEG* 34. 199; Aesch. *Supp.* 604) and may go back to Cleisthenes' reforms of 508/7 (Hdt. 6. 131. 1). Cleisthenes' major reforms were to divide Attica into 139 municipalities (*demes or *dēmoi*) which, in turn, were distributed among ten tribes (*phylai*). Citizen rights were linked to membership of a deme, and a council of 500 (*boulē*) was introduced, with 50 representatives from each of the ten tribes, and a fixed number of seats assigned to each of the demes (*Ath. pol.* 21. 2–6). Finally, to avoid a repeat of the power struggle of 510–507 Cleisthenes introduced *ostracism (ibid. 22. 1, 3–4).

During the next century the new democracy was buttressed by other reforms: in 501 command of the army and navy was transferred from the polemarch to a board of ten popularly elected generals (*stratēgoi*) (*Ath. pol.* 22. 2). In 487/6 the method of selection of the nine archons was changed from election to selection by lot from an elected short list (ibid. 22. 5). *Ephialtes (4)'s reforms of 462 deprived the council of the Areopagus of its political powers which were divided between the assembly, the council of five hundred, and the popular courts (ibid. 25. 2). Shortly afterwards, on the initiative of Pericles, political pay was introduced for the popular courts (Arist. *Pol.* 1274ᵃ8–9) and the council or *boulē* (*IG* 1³. 82. 20), so that even poor citizens could exercise their political rights. Athenian citizenship became a much-coveted privilege, and in 451 Pericles had a law passed confining *citizenship to the legitimate sons of an Athenian mother as well as father (*Ath. pol.* 26. 4).

The defeats in the *Peloponnesian War resulted in a growing opposition to democracy and twice the antidemocratic factions succeeded for some months in establishing an *oligarchy, in 411 a moderate oligarchy led by the council of *Four Hundred (Thuc. 8. 47–98, *Ath. pol.* 29–33) and in 404–3 a radical oligarchy under a junta which fully earned the name 'the *Thirty Tyrants' (Xen. *Hell.* 2. 2–4; *Ath. pol.* 35–8; Diod. Sic. 14. 3. 7). In 403/2 democracy was restored in a modified form. Legislation (in 403) and all jurisdiction in political trials (in c.355) were transferred from the people in assembly to the panel of 6,000 jurors acting both as legislators (*nomothetai*) and judges (*dikastai*). In the 330s a kind of minister of finance was introduced (*ho epi tē dioikēsei*) (*SEG* 19. 119). He was elected for a four-year period and could be re-elected, and for twelve consecutive years the administration of Athens was entrusted to *Lycurgus (3) (Hyp. fr. 139 Sauppe). These and other reforms were allegedly a return to the 'ancestral' or 'Solonian' democracy (Andoc. 1. 83; Aeschin. 3. 257), but the gradual and moderate transformation of the democratic institutions came to an abrupt end in 322/1 when the Macedonians after their victory in the *Lamian War abolished the democracy and had it replaced by a 'Solonian' oligarchy (Diod. Sic. 18. 18. 4–5). During the Hellenistic age democracy in some form

was restored several times i.e. in 318/7, 307–298(?), 287–103, and 88–85.

4. *Tradition* Between 322 BC and c. AD 1850 Athenian democracy was almost forgotten, and, if mentioned, the focus was on the mythical 'Solonian democracy' known from *Plutarch's *Life of Solon* and *Aristotle's *Politics* (1273ᵇ35–1274ᵃ21). It was not until c.1800, when history began to emerge as a scholarly discipline, that the Athenian democratic institutions were studied seriously and reconstructed, e.g. by August Böckh, from sources such as *Thucydides (2), Demosthenes, and inscriptions. And it was only from c.1850 that the new understanding of Classical Athenian democracy was connected, principally by George Grote, with a budding interest in democracy as a form of government, though now in the form of a 'representative' or 'parliamentary' democracy and no longer as an 'assembly' democracy in which power was exercised directly by the people.

Systematic account: M. H. Hansen, *The Athenian Democracy in the Age of Demosthenes* (1991). Historical account: C. Hignett, *A History of the Athenian Constitution to the End of the Fifth Century BC* (1952). Historical and systematic account combined: G. Busolt and H. Swoboda, *Griechische Staatskunde 2* (1926), 758–1239. Socio-political approach: J. Ober, *Mass and Élite in Democratic Athens* (1989). Political Organization of Attica: J. S. Traill, *Demos and Trittys: Epigraphical and Topographical Studies in the Organization of Attica* (1986). Demes: D. Whitehead, *The Demes of Attica 508/7–ca. 250 BC* (1986). Assembly: M. H. Hansen, *The Athenian Assembly* (1987). Council of five hundred: P. J. Rhodes, *The Athenian Boule* (1972). Lawcourts: S. C. Todd, *The Shape of Athenian Law* (1993). Magistrates: R. Develin, *Athenian Officials 684–21 BC* (1989). Council of the Areopagus: R. W. Wallace, *The Areopagos Council, to 307 BC* (1989). Ideology: K. Raaflaub and M. H. Hansen, in J. Rufus Fears (ed.), *Aspects of Athenian Democracy* (1990), 33–99. Tradition: M. H. Hansen, *G&R* 1992, 14–30; J. T. Roberts, *Athens on Trial* (1995). State of research: J. Bleicken, *Die athenische Demokratie*, 2nd edn. (1994), 437–584. Democracy personified (female) in art: *LIMC* 3/1 (1986), 372–4.

M. H. H.

democracy, non-Athenian and post-Classical Democracy or people's power (see DEMOS) was not an Athenian monopoly or even invention. (See DEMOCRACY, ATHENIAN.) The Archaic Spartan constitutional document (*rhētra*) preserved in Plut. *Lyc.* 6 explicitly says that 'the people shall have the power', but Sparta soon ossified. Sixth-cent. BC *Chios, as an inscription (ML 8) reveals, had a constitution with some popular features, though Classical Chios, like Classical Sparta, was no longer democratic: Thuc. 8. 24 (late 5th cent.) brackets Sparta and Chios and implies that both were oligarchies; for Chios see also *Syll.*³ 986. Classical Greek states other than Athens, such as *Argos (2), were or were perceived as democracies (Thuc. 5. 31. 6 and other evidence) but Athenian influence can usually be postulated (see DEMOCRACY, ATHENIAN). Thus assembly pay, a feature of the developed Athenian democracy (it was introduced only after the main *Peloponnesian War) is also attested at Hellenistic *Iasus and *Rhodes, no doubt exported there originally from Athens. But imperial Athens, despite sweeping remarks in some ancient literary texts, was not doctrinaire about insisting on democracies in the subject states (*Old Oligarch* 3. 11; LACTOR 1³. 101 ff.). It was more important to install or support favourably minded personnel. In any case, to impose 'democracy' on a tiny place like *Erythrae in Ionia did not mean much, given the demographic facts on the ground: thus ML 40, the mid 5th-cent. 'Erythrae decree', shows that the rules for the council established there by Athens were much less rigidly democratic than those at Athens itself (120 members not 500; repeated membership allowed after only four years as opposed to twice in a lifetime; see BOULE).

Democritus

Even in the Hellenistic period, i.e. after 322 BC when Athenian democracy in its classical form was suppressed by Macedon, there was, despite modern Marxist gloom on this topic, more democratic life in Greece (Athens included) than is often realized. Decrees preserved on stone show extensive participation 'from the floor', though intensive modern study of the whole corpus of such decrees has shown that some areas (Italy and Sicily; and fringe territories newly brought under Greek influence by *Alexander (3) the Great and the Hellenistic rulers) were more backward in this respect than others. Even under Rome the city-assemblies of subject Greeks, although despised by the Roman élite (Cic. *Flac.* 16), demonstrably mattered in local politics at least until Trajan (Dio Chrys. *Or.* 34; Plut. *Praecepta gerendae reipublicae*), although some, certainly, were now oligarchic (e.g. Roman *Delphi: C. Vatin, *BCH* 1961, 248–50), and all were increasingly dependent on 'benefactor-politicians' (see EUERGETISM). Public statues personifying the *dēmos* suggest the continued Greek idealization of people-power under the Principate: e.g. K. Erim, *Aphrodisias* (1986), 85; *SEG* 9. 492.

*Polybius (1) (bk. 6) treated some aspects of the Roman constitution in the middle republic as if they were fully democratic, and this perception is shrewder than has sometimes been acknowledged. M. *Porcius Cato (1), for instance, can plausibly be seen as an essentially popular politician. More generally, views widely held in the earlier part of this century, about the importance of clientship or *clientela* (see CLIENS) and about the completeness of aristocratic control of politics, are now less in fashion. For instance, it has been asked, why do we hear so much about mass bribery at election-time if the assemblies were oligarchic and (as the usual view holds) dominated by the better-off? But there were always big differences from Classical Athens: at Rome, popular meetings (COMITIA; CONTIONES) could be summoned only by a magistrate; and at the end of the republic the sheer power, both military and financial, of the military dynasts undermined even such democracy as there was. In any case the evidence of bribery cuts both ways: the prevalence of electoral bribery or *ambitus* always, and especially in the late republic when the stakes were higher, meant that elections expressed the popular will only approximately. (But in both republic and Principate there were other, cruder, outlets for popular feeling, such as demonstrations at the theatre or games, Cic. *Sest.* 106; see ACCLAMATION). It is also relevant that city assemblies tended to be dominated by the city population. Rome was not unique in this, but the size of Italy meant that the problem was specially acute. The puzzle of apparently popular elections within an essentially oligarchic framework can be solved by seeing instances of genuinely contested elections as occasional submissions to popular will—a kind of agreed form of *arbitration. Finally we should remember that the analyses of Greeks like Polybius could themselves have had influence on e.g. the *Gracchi: if you translate 'tribunus' as δήμαρχος (a compound of 'people' and 'rule' first found in Greek at *Syll*³. 601, 190s BC) you import an idea not previously there. That is, the truth about 2nd cent. BC Rome may not be that Greek observers discovered hitherto unnoticed democratic features in the Roman constitution, but that Rome became more (but never fully) democratic precisely as a result of Greek influence exercised by those observers. (See also OPTIMATES; POLITICS *At Rome*.)

P. J. Rhodes, *The Greek City-States: A Source-Book* (1986); D. M. Lewis, 'Democratic Institutions and their Diffusion', *Proc. 8th Epig. Congress* (1984), 55 ff.; G. de Ste. Croix, *CQ* 1975, and *The Class Struggle in the Ancient Greek World* (1981), ch. 5; P. J. Rhodes with D. M. Lewis, *The Decrees of the Greek States* (1996); F. Millar, *JRS* 1984, 1 ff., and 1986, 1 ff.; A. W. Lintott, *ZSS* 1987, 34 ff.; J. A. North, *Past and Present*, 1990, 3 ff.; J. Dunn, in J. Dunn (ed.), *Democracy, the Unfinished Journey* (1992), 244 f.; A. Yakobson, *JRS* 1992, 32 ff.; I. Malkin and Z. Rubinsohn, *Leaders and Masses in the Roman World* (1995). S. H., A. J. S. S.

Democritus, of *Abdera in *Thrace, b. 460–57 BC (Apollod. in Diog. Laert. 9. 41), 40 years after *Anaxagoras according to his own statement quoted by *Diogenes (6). He travelled widely, according to various later accounts, and lived to a great age. In later times he became known as 'the laughing philosopher', probably because he held that 'cheerfulness' (*euthymiē*) was a goal to be pursued in life. There is a story that he visited Athens—'but no one knew me' (Diog. Laert. 9. 36); this may be a reflection of the undoubted fact that *Plato (1), although he must have known his work, never mentioned him by name.

Works Diog. Laert. 9. 46–9 mentions 70 titles, arranged in tetralogies by *Thrasyllus like the works of Plato, and classified as follows: Ethics, Physics, Unclassified, Mathematics, Music (which includes philological and literary criticism), Technical, and Notes. None of these works survives. Of his physical theories, on which his fame rests, only meagre quotations and summaries remain; the majority of texts that have come down to us under his name are brief and undistinguished moral maxims.

From the time of *Aristotle, Democritus and *Leucippus (3) are jointly credited with the creation of the atomic theory of the universe (see ATOMISM); it is now impossible to distinguish the contribution of each. Aristotle's account of the origin of the theory (*Gen. corr.* 1. 8) rightly relates it to the Eleatics (see ELEATIC SCHOOL). *Parmenides argued that what is real is one and motionless, since empty space is not a real existent; motion is impossible without empty space, and plurality is impossible without something to separate the units. Division of what is real into units in contact, i.e. with no separating spaces, is ruled out because (*a*) infinite divisibility would mean there are no real units at all, and (*b*) finite divisibility is physically inexplicable. Against these arguments, says Aristotle, Leucippus proposed to rescue the sensible world of plurality and motion by asserting that empty space, 'the non-existent', may nevertheless serve to separate parts of what exists from each other. So the universe has two ingredients: Being, which satisfies the Eleatic criteria by being 'full', unchanging, and homogeneous, and Non-being or empty space. The pieces of real Being, since it is their characteristic to be absolutely indivisible units, are called 'atoms' (i.e. 'uncuttables'). They are said to be solid, invisibly small, and undifferentiated in material; they differ from each other in shape and size only (perhaps also in weight), and the only change they undergo is in their relative and absolute position, through movement in space.

By their changes of position the atoms produce the compounds of the changing sensible world. Compounds differ in quality according to the shape and arrangement of the component atoms, their congruence or otherwise (i.e. their tendency to latch together because of their shape), and the amount of space between them. It is a matter of controversy whether the atoms have a natural downward motion due to weight (as later in Epicurean theory: see EPICURUS, *Doctrines*)) or move randomly in the void until their motion is somehow directed by collisions with other atoms. In the course of time, groups of atoms form 'whirls' or vortexes, which have the effect of sorting out the atoms by size and shape, like to like. Some of these are sorted in such a way as to produce distinct masses having the appearance of earth, water, air, and fire: thus worlds are formed—not one single world, as in most Greek cosmologies, but an indeterminate number scattered throughout the infinite void, each liable to perish through random atomic motions, as they were originally formed. Leucippus and Democritus produced an account of the evolution within worlds of progressively more complex stages of organization, including human cultures (traces in Diod. Sic. 1. 7–8 and see Lucr. bk. 5).

The *soul, which is the cause of life and sensation, is made of fine round atoms, and is a compound as perishable as the body. Perception takes place through the impact of *eidōla* (thin atomic films shed from the surfaces of sensible objects) upon the soul-atoms through the sense organs. Perceptible qualities are the product of the atoms of the sensible object and those of the perceiving soul. (A relatively full account is preserved in Theophr. *Sens.* 49–82.) They therefore have a different mode of existence from atoms and void—'by convention' as opposed to 'in reality'. See ATOMISM.

Little is known about Democritus' mathematics, although mathematical writings appear in the lists of his works; he must have been a diligent biologist, for Aristotle quotes him often.

Many surviving fragments deal with ethics, but they are mostly short maxims, hard to fit together into a consistent and comprehensive doctrine (see Havelock (in bibliog. below), ch. 6 for a bold effort). His positions, as reported, are close to those of Epicurus, and it is hard to know whether this is historically genuine or a prejudice of the doxographers. His ethical ideal seems to include the idea that the soul-atoms should be protected from violent upheavals; well-being which leads to 'cheerfulness' (*euthymiē*) is a matter of moderation and wisdom (B 191). It is important not to let the fear of death spoil life, and to recognize the limits to which man is necessarily confined (B 199, 203). Pleasure is in some sense the criterion of right action, but there must be moderation in choosing pleasures (B 189, 207, 224, 231). In social ethics, Democritus was apparently prepared to link his view of contemporary society with his theory of the evolution of human communities; he saw that a system of law is by nature necessary for the preservation of society.

Democritus is a figure of great importance who has suffered intolerably from the triumph of his opponents, Plato, Aristotle, and the Stoics (see STOICISM). He defended the infinite universe, plural and perishable worlds, efficient, non-teleological causes, and the atomic theory of matter, as opposed to the single, finite, and eternal cosmos of Aristotle, teleology, and the continuous theory of matter. The best brains preferred his opponents' arguments, and Epicurus and *Lucretius were his only influential followers until the post-Renaissance scientific revolution—by which time his books were lost. See ALCHEMY.

ANCIENT SOURCES DK no. 68; S. Luria, *Democritea* (1970).

MODERN LITERATURE (1) General: K. Lasswitz, *Geschichte der Atomistik* (1890); H. Cherniss, *Aristotle's Criticism of Presocratic Philosophy* (1935); S. Samburedy, *The Physical World of the Greeks* (1956); Guthrie, *Hist. Gk. Phil.* 2; J. Barnes, *The Presocratic Philosophers* (1979); D. Furley, *The Greek Cosmologists* 1 (1987).

(2) Collections: F. Romano (ed.), *Democrito e l'atomismo antico* (1980); L. G. Benakis (ed.), *Proceedings of the First International Congress on Democritus* (1984).

(3) Special: C. Bailey, *The Greek Atomists and Epicurus* (1928; repr. 1964); S. Luria, 'Die infinitesimallehre der antiken Atomisten,' *Quellen und Studien zur Geschichte der Mathematik* B 2 (1933); K. von Fritz, *Philosophie und sprachlicher Ausdruck bei Demokrit, Platon, und Aristoteles* (1938); G. Vlastos, *Philosophical Review* 1945 and 1946; V. E. Alfieri, *Atomos Idea* (1953); E. Havelock, *The Liberal Temper in Greek Politics* (1957); D. J. Furley, *Two Studies in the Greek Atomists* (1967); T. Cole,

Democritus and the Sources of Greek Anthropology (1967); R. Löbl, *Demokrits Atome* (1976); A. Stuckelberger, *Antike Atomphysik* (1979); D. O'Brien, *Theories of Weight in the Ancient World* 1: *Democritus on Weight and Size* (1981); D. Sedley, *Phronesis* 1982; E. L. Hussey, in P. Cartledge and F. D. Harvey (eds.), *CRUX* (1985), 118 ff.; H. Baltussen, *Theophrastus on Theories of Perception* (1993), with extensive bibliogs.

D. J. F.

Demodocus, in *Homer's *Odyssey* (8. 44–5, 62–4), a blind and respected first-class bard at *Alcinous (1)'s court—an image which Homer offers of his own trade. He sings the adultery of *Ares and *Aphrodite (8. 266–366), a comic pendant to the contrasts in *Iliad* 5, and sings the (tragic) Trojan War so realistically that Odysseus weeps (8. 521–35). He was depicted on Bathycles' throne at *Amyclae (c.530 BC; Paus. 3. 18. 11). K. D.

demography See POPULATION, GREEK and ROMAN.

Demon (fl. c.300 BC), author of an *Atthis in at least four books. The fragments all belong to the period of the kings and suggest an antiquarian rather than historical interest, perhaps influenced by the *Peripatetics and comparable with *Ister of Cyrene. The work was criticized by Philochorus.

FGrH 327, L. Pearson, *The Local Historians of Attica* (1942), 89 ff., and see under ATTHIS. G. L. B.; S. H.

Demonax, of Cyprus (2nd cent. AD), Cynic philosopher, known mainly by the life of him ascribed to Lucian. He was from a wealthy family but renounced his inheritance; among his teachers was *Epictetus. Partly itinerant, with a period of residence in Athens, he dispensed advice to individuals and to cities. He starved himself to death when nearly 100 years old; Athens gave him a public burial.

C. P. Jones, *Culture and Society in Lucian* (1986), ch. 9.

W. D. R.; A. J. S. S.

Demophanes and Ecdelus, sometimes named Megalophanes and Ecdemus (Plut. *Phil.* 1), Megalopolitans (see MEGALOPOLIS). While exiled in Athens after c.265 BC they were followers of the *Academic *Arcesilaus (1). Politically active and hostile to tyrants, they helped *Aratus (2) liberate *Sicyon (251) and organized the putsch in which Aristodemus of *Megalopolis was murdered (about the same time). They also acted as constitutional advisers in *Cyrene (perhaps c.250). *Polybius (1) makes *Philopoemen's early association with them responsible for qualities which he admired in him (10. 22). R. M. E.

Demophon (1) Son of *Theseus, often found paired with his brother *Acamas. Both were sent to *Euboea for safety, and from there (in the *Epic Cycle) went to Troy, where they freed their grandmother *Aethra from captivity. Each is named as lover of *Laodice (1) in Troy and Phyllis in *Thrace, and each, on his return to Athens, was linked with an involuntary homicide centring on the *Palladium. Where their myths diverge, Acamas tends to act as colonizer while Demophon succeeds Theseus as king of Athens. It was in his reign that the *Palladium (in various versions) came to Athens, and it may be that the important sanctuary of Demophon (IG 1³. 383. 159, etc.) was part of the Palladium cult complex (cf. his trial ἐπὶ Παλλαδίῳ).

(2) Eleusinian hero, identified in the *Homeric *Hymn to Demeter with the infant son of *Celeus and *Metanira, nursling of *Demeter, who attempted to make him immortal by placing him in the fire. The attempt failed when interrupted by Metanira, and instead Demeter decreed the institution of a mock battle in

his honour—a not uncommon heroic rite. Later, Demophon's role as young boy favoured by the goddesses is taken over by *Triptolemus.

(1) U. Kron, *LIMC* 1. 435–46.; (2) N. J. Richardson, *The Homeric Hymn to Demeter* (1974), 231–6, 245–6. R. Parker, *G&R* 1991, 1–17.   E. Ke.

dēmos See DEMES; DEMOCRACY, ATHENIAN. The Greek word means originally 'district, land', hence particularly (in *Attica and elsewhere) the villages or *demes (*dēmoi*, plural of *dēmos*) which were the main units of country settlement. From 'the place where the people live' the word comes to mean 'the people', as in compounds like *dēmo-kratia*, 'people-power' or '*democracy'; *dēmos* sometimes means 'the sovereign people', sometimes 'the common people'. *Dēmos* personified was glorified with a cult (Athens) and frequently depicted (male, youthful, or bearded) in Athens and other *poleis*: *LIMC* 3 / 1 (1986), 375–82.

D. M. Lewis, in O. Murray and S. Price (eds.), *The Greek City* (1990), 260–3.   S. H.

Demosthenes (1) (d. 413 BC), son of Alcisthenes, Athenian general. After an unsuccessful invasion of *Aetolia in 426 he won two brilliant victories against a Peloponnesian and Ambraciot army invading Amphilochia (see AMPHILOCHI). In 425 his occupation of *Pylos led to a most valuable success, the capture of a body of Spartan hoplites on the adjacent island of Sphacteria. He surprised Nisaea in 424, but failed to take Megara, and in a triple attack on Boeotia, for which he was perhaps responsible, he was unable to land troops at Siphae, since the enemy was forewarned. He was not again entrusted with a major command until 413 when he was sent to reinforce *Nicias (1) at *Syracuse. After failing to regain Epipolae by a night attack, he urged withdrawal from Syracuse, which was delayed until the Athenians lost control of the sea and were driven to attempt escape by land. The rearguard, led by Demosthenes, surrendered on the sixth day, and he was subsequently executed.

Demosthenes apparently had no political ambitions and enjoyed no political influence. He showed inventiveness in trying to break the military stalemate produced by Periclean strategy (see PERICLES (1)), but his plans tended to be too elaborate. He was a skilful tactician and an inspiring leader.

Thuc. bks. 3, 4, 7. M. Treu, *Hist*. 1956, 420 ff.; H. D. Westlake, *Individuals in Thucydides* (1968), chs. 7, 13; V. Hunter, *Thucydides the Artful Reporter* (1973), chs. 4, 6; *CAH* 5² (1992), ch. 9 (D. M. Lewis), and ch. 10 (A. Andrewes); J. Roisman, *The General Demosthenes and his Use of Military Surprise* (1993).   H. D. W.; S. H.

Demosthenes (2) (384–322 BC), the greatest Athenian orator. When Demosthenes was 7 years old his father died, leaving the management of his estate to his brothers, Aphobus and Demophon, and a friend, Therippides. The trustees mismanaged the business, and Demosthenes at the age of 18 found himself almost without resources. He claimed his patrimony from his guardians, who spent three years in attempts to compromise. In the mean time, he was studying rhetoric and legal procedure under *Isaeus (1) and at 21 he brought a successful action against his guardians, but two more years elapsed before he received the remnants of the property. By now he was engaged in the profession of *logographos* (speech-writer) and the reputation gained in private cases led to his being employed as an assistant to prosecutors in public trials.

From 355/4 onwards he came more and more to devote himself to public business. It is not clear how far Demosthenes'

sympathies were engaged in his first public trials, the prosecutions of *Androtion and Leptines in 355 and of Androtion's associate, Timocrates, in 353: *Against Androtion* and *Against Timocrates* he wrote for a Diodorus, and in any case the political tendency of the trials is unsure; *Against Leptines* Demosthenes did deliver himself, and, since Leptines' law was defended by *Aristophon, it is possible that all three trials centred on his policy and that Demosthenes was one of his opponents. This would be consistent with the policy he supported in *On the Symmories* in 354/3: a rumour came that the king of Persia was preparing to attack Greece, as he had threatened to do in 356/5, and Demosthenes, arguing that the city was not properly prepared, opposed the advocates of war, certainly not the *Eubulus (1) group, possibly that of Aristophon. In 353/2 he turned on Eubulus: *On the Syntaxis* seems directed partly against the allocation of surpluses to the *theōrika—at § 30 he sneers about the public works of Eubulus—and partly against the policy of abstaining from all but essential military enterprises.

For the next few years Demosthenes was regularly on the losing side and of minor importance. Early in 352 in *For the Megalopolitans* he argued in favour of promising to support *Arcadia, if Sparta carried out her plan of exploiting *Thebes (1)'s preoccupation with the Third *Sacred War: since Athens based her policy on concord with *Phocis and Sparta, the decision to do no more than give a guarantee to *Messenia was probably right. A few months later Demosthenes wrote *Against Aristocrates* for use in the attack on a proposal to honour *Charidemus in gratitude for his offices in the cession of the *Chersonesus (1) by *Cersobleptes: the speech is notable both as a source of information about the law of homicide and also for the manner in which it regards Cersobleptes, not *Philip (1) II of *Macedonia, as the real enemy in the north. Demosthenes did not yet see what was plain to those he opposed. In late 352 Philip's attack on Cersobleptes carried him very near the Chersonesus, and Demosthenes' eyes were opened. In 351 he delivered the *First Philippic* which pleaded for more vigorous prosecution of the war for Amphipolis: his proposals were not accepted; deeper involvement in the long fruitless struggle may have seemed to endanger the power to defend the vital areas of Thermopylae and Chersonesus. Late in 351 in *On the Liberty of the Rhodians* he urged support of the Rhodian *dēmos* against the oligarchs supported by the Carian dynasty (see RHODES; ARTEMISIA (2)): but the Persian attack on Egypt prompted caution, and Demosthenes' arguments were far from strong. In mid-349 *Olynthus, which had by then lapsed from Philip's alliance, was attacked by Philip and appealed to Athens for help: in the three *Olynthiacs*, delivered in quick succession, Demosthenes demanded the fullest support and, in the last, an end to the law assigning surpluses to the *theōrika*; again he scathingly alluded to the works of Eubulus. There is, however, no reason to suppose that the three expeditions voted were not supported by Eubulus or indeed that they satisfied Demosthenes, and the implementation of his proposals might have brought even greater disaster than the loss of Olynthus. Early in 348 the party of Eubulus involved the city in a costly and inconclusive intervention in Euboea to prevent the island falling into the control of those hostile to Athens: Demosthenes later claimed to have been alone in opposing the expedition; either he was not truthful or he had taken a curious view of Athens' interests. One consequence of his opposition to Eubulus was that he became embroiled in an absurd wrangle with Midias, a prominent supporter of Eubulus, who had slapped his face at the *Dionysia of 348: the case was settled out of court and the speech *Against Midias* was never delivered.

In mid-348, before the fall of Olynthus, Demosthenes successfully defended *Philocrates when he was indicted under the *graphē paranomōn* for his proposal to open negotiations with Philip, and in 347/6, when Demosthenes like *Aeschines (1) was a member of the *boulē, the partnership continued and Demosthenes played a leading part in securing acceptance of the Peace of Philocrates. On the two embassies to Macedon he cut a poor figure before Philip and got on badly with his fellow ambassadors, but the decisive moment came after the second embassy's return when in the assembly on 16 Scirophorion, it was known that Philip had occupied the Gates of *Thermopylae and that Phocis could not be saved. Demosthenes was shouted down and Aeschines made the speech to which Demosthenes constantly recurred. What Demosthenes wanted that day is not clear: if he did want the city to denounce the new Peace, to march out to support Phocis attacked by the Macedonians and *Thessalians from the north and the Thebans from the south, his judgement was seriously awry. From that day Demosthenes determined to undo the Peace. Shortly after, however, in *On the Peace* he counselled caution, and for the moment contented himself with the attack on Aeschines from which he was forced to desist by the successful countercharge against his own associate, Timarchus.

The year 344 brought Demosthenes his opportunity to attack the Peace. Rumours reached Athens that Philip was preparing to intervene in the Peloponnese in support of *Argos (2) and Messene, and Demosthenes went on an embassy to those cities to warn them of the dangers of consorting with Philip: Philip protested, and shortly after Demosthenes' return the embassy of Python and all Philip's allies protested against his misrepresentations, and offered to turn the Peace into a *Common Peace; first reactions were favourable, but in the assembly *Hegesippus (1) succeeded in having the status of *Amphipolis referred to Philip—an oblique way of sabotaging the whole affair—while Demosthenes' contribution was the *Second Philippic* in which he denounced Philip as not worth an attempt at negotiation. (The alternative reconstruction would deny this conjunction and put Python's embassy in early 343.) In mid-343, after the success of *Hyperides' prosecution of Philocrates, Demosthenes judged the moment suitable to resume his attack on Aeschines; *On the False Embassy* sought to exploit the support of Eubulus' party for continuing the Peace and to suggest that Aeschines was really responsible for Philip's use of the peace negotiations to intervene in Phocis in 346. With the support of Eubulus and *Phocion, Aeschines was acquitted by a narrow margin.

With the final collapse in early 342 of proposals to amend the Peace, Philip either began to intervene directly in Greece or was represented by Demosthenes as so doing, and amidst mounting hostility to Macedon Demosthenes went on an embassy to the Peloponnese to set about the organization of an Hellenic alliance for the war he was determined to have. For the moment his efforts came to little, but in 341 in *On the Chersonese* and shortly after, in the *Third Philippic*, he defended the aggressive actions of Diopeithes against *Cardia by arguing that, since Philip's actions already amounted to war, it was absurd to heed the letter of the Peace. Not long after, he delivered the *Fourth Philippic* (of which the authenticity was long doubted but is now widely accepted); in it Demosthenes appears so confident of his control that he dismissed the notion of harm being done by the theoric distributions in words inconceivable in 349, and he successfully

demanded an appeal to Persia to join in attacking Philip. In 341/0 he also formed an alliance with *Byzantium, and by autumn 340, when Philip finally declared war and seized the Athenian cornfleet, Demosthenes was in full charge of the war he had sought, though he was unable to restrain Aeschines from his unwise intrusion at Delphi into the rivalries of central Greece (see AESCHINES I). In mid-339 he moved the suspension of the allocation of surpluses to the *theōrika*, and with Thebes unlikely to side with Philip after having expelled the Macedonian garrison from the Gates, Demosthenes could expect not to have to face Philip in Greece. The sudden seizure of Elatea in Phocis threw Athens into horrified perplexity, but Demosthenes proposed and effected alliance with Thebes, which he later pretended always to have wanted, and Athens and Thebes fought side by side at *Chaeronea in autumn 338.

Demosthenes was present at the battle, and returned so quickly to organize the city's defences that Aeschines could accuse him of running away. He provided corn, repaired the walls, and was so much the man of the hour that he was chosen to deliver the Funeral Oration (see EPITAPHIOS) for 338. With Philip in Greece, the people looked to Demosthenes and he successfully met the frequent attacks on him in the courts. In 337/6 he was theoric commissioner, and Ctesiphon proposed that he be *crowned at the Dionysia for his constant service to the city's best interests: perhaps encouraged by the opening of the Macedonian attack on Persia, Aeschines indicted Ctesiphon, but with the changing events of the next few months he preferred for the moment to let the case lapse. Demosthenes, hoping that the death of Philip was the end of Macedonian domination in Greece, sought to foment troubles for his successor, but *Alexander (3) the Great quickly marched south and Demosthenes had to accept the new monarch. In 335 Demosthenes actively aided the Thebans in their revolt and narrowly escaped being surrendered to Alexander. From then on he seems to have looked to Persia to accomplish the liberation of Greece: such at any rate seems to be the meaning of the many charges of receiving money from the Persians. Demosthenes gave no support to *Agis III at any stage and, when Persia was crushed at *Gaugamela and the revolt of Agis collapsed, Athens was left in disastrous isolation. Aeschines seized the opportunity to renew his attack on Demosthenes through Ctesiphon. The case was heard in mid-330, and Demosthenes defended his acts in *On the Crown*, which is his masterpiece. He declined to fall into the trap of discussing recent events and with supreme art interspersed his discussion of events long past with lofty assertions of principle. Fewer than one-fifth of the jury voted for Aeschines, and he retired to Rhodes. Demosthenes was left in triumph, and the city settled down to acceptance of Macedonian rule, until in 324 word reached Greece that at the coming Olympian Games *Nicanor (1) was to make public a rescript ordering the restoration of exiles. Since this would affect the *cleruchy on *Samos, an agitation began which was to end in the *Lamian War. Demosthenes led a deputation as *architheōros* to protest. Subsequently he engaged in the discussion at Athens about divine honours (see RULER CULT) for Alexander, having also taken the lead in dealing with the sudden appearance of *Harpalus by proposing first that Harpalus be kept prisoner and his money stored on the Acropolis, and later that the *Areopagus investigate the losses. It is difficult to assess Demosthenes' policy in this year: he may have foreseen the new uprising under *Leosthenes and planned to involve Athens, but, since the especial ally of Leosthenes was Hyperides, who led the attack on Demosthenes in the prosecution of early 323,

Demosthenes

Demosthenes appears to have been at odds with the war-party. Equally unsure is his guilt in the Harpalus trial: the Areopagus declared him guilty of appropriating 20 talents, and he was found guilty and fined 50 talents, but, even if he did take the money, he may have intended to use it in service of the state; the whole affair is most obscure. He retired into exile, and lent his support to Hyperides in the creation of the alliance for the Lamian War. He was then recalled to Athens, but after the Macedonian victory at Crannon in 322 he left the city again, and was condemned to death by the decree of *Demades. Pursued by the agents of *Antipater (1), he committed suicide in *Calauria (322).

Modern opinions of Demosthenes' political importance have varied greatly, often in discernible relation to contemporary events. He has been lauded as a solitary champion of liberty and censured as the absurd opponent of progress. With the latter view English scholars have, happily, had little sympathy, but the high esteem in which the works of Demosthenes have been rightly held as works of art has tended to obscure the possibility that, while his devotion to liberty is one of the supreme monuments of liberty, his methods and his policies were not the best suited to attain their end, and that those of his opponents, which we must largely infer from his attacks, were no less directed to maintaining the city's power and independence, and perhaps more apt.

Demosthenes has much to say about Philip's success being due to bribery and was convinced that his own opponents had been corrupted, but in his obsession with this dubitable view he seems blind to the real problem of his day, which was how Greece could be united to counter effectively the military power of the new national state so far greater than the power of any single city-state. There was much to be said against Demosthenes' determination to involve the full military resources of Athens in a war in the north, in particular that in such a war Athens stood to gain most and the other Greeks would not unite for that result. For the defence of Greece itself against invasion there was a real hope of uniting the cities in a *Common Peace, and this appears to have been the policy of Demosthenes' opponents. There was perhaps more enthusiasm than judgement in his military assessments, and since the defeat of Chaeronea appears to have produced a Greece that could never wholeheartedly unite in a war of liberation, it is possible that, if such a decisive battle was inevitable, his opponents might have united Greece for it more effectively. But the situation of Greece was tragic, and Demosthenes was certainly of heroic stature.

Private lawcourt speeches (δίκαι). The series of private speeches begins with those against Aphobus and Onetor (363–362), in which Demosthenes claimed recovery of his property from his guardians, and continues throughout his life (*Against Dionysodorus*, 323–322). Several private speeches attributed (perhaps wrongly) to Demosthenes were delivered on behalf of the *Apollodorus (2) who was his opponent in the *For Phormion*. The speech *For Phormion* (350) and the first *Against Stephanus* (349; the second *Stephanus* is undoubtedly spurious) raise a question of professional morality. Pasion, the banker, appointed his chief clerk *Phormion (2) trustee for his sons; the elder son, Apollodorus, subsequently claimed a sum of money allegedly due to him, but Phormion proved that the claim had been settled some years previously. Apollodorus then prosecuted Stephanus, one of Phormion's witnesses, for perjury. If, as *Plutarch states, Demosthenes wrote *Stephanus A* as well as *For Phormion*, he was guilty of a serious breach of faith, for while the earlier speech extols Phormion's character, the later one contains insinuations against him. The evidence for the authenticity of *Stephanus A* is, however, inconclusive (cf. L. Pearson, *Antichthon* 1969, 18–26). Aeschines asserts that Demosthenes showed to Apollodorus a speech composed for Phormion, but this may be a misrepresentation of some attempt by Demosthenes to act as mediator.

The subjects of the private speeches include guardianship, inheritance, claims for payment, *maritime loans, mining rights, forgery, trespass, assault, etc. In the *Callicles* (which has flashes of humour, seldom found in Demosthenes) the plaintiff alleges that the defendant has flooded his land by blocking a watercourse; in the *Conon*, a brilliant piece of writing, combining Lysianic grace (see LYSIAS) and Demosthenic force, some dissolute young rowdies and their father are summoned for assault.

Demosthenes had many rivals in his lifetime; but later critics considered him the greatest of the orators. His claim to greatness rests on his singleness of purpose, his sincerity, and his lucid and convincing exposition of his argument. In many instances he produces a great effect by the use of a few ordinary words. In his most solemn moments his style is at its plainest and his language most moderate. A master of metaphor, he uses it sparingly, and hardly at all in his most impressive passages. His style varies infinitely according to circumstances; sometimes as simple as *Lysias, now polished like *Isocrates, again almost as involved as *Thucydides (2), he follows no scholastic rule; long and short periods follow each other, or are mingled with passages in the running style not according to any regular system. Thus his carefully prepared utterances give an impression of spontaneity. Such was his control of language that he was generally able to avoid *hiatus without any dislocation of the order of words. He had an instinctive aversion to a succession of short syllables, and even tribrachs are of comparatively rare occurrence. (See PROSE-RHYTHM, GREEK.)

For general bibliography see ATTIC ORATORS.

TEXTS Teubner, *ed. maior*, Fuhr–Sykutris, 3 vols. (1914–27), *ed. minor*, Blass–Fuhr, vols. 1–2 (1928–33), Blass, vol. 3 (1923); OCT, S. Butcher, W. Rennie 3 vols. (1907–55). Text with translation: Loeb (1926–49), 7 vols. (J. H. Vince, A. T. Murray, N. W. and N. J. de Witt); Budé, L. Gernet, M. Croiset, R. Clavaud, and G. Mathieu, 10 vols. (1954–87).

TRANSLATIONS C. R. Kennedy, *Orations*, 5 vols. (Bohn Classical Library) (1880); A. W. Pickard-Cambridge, *Public Orations of Demosthenes*, 2 vols. (1912).

COMMENTARIES H. Weil, *Plaidoyers politiques de Démosthène*, 2 vols. (1883–6); J. E. Sandys and F. A. Paley, *Demosthenes: Select Private Orations*, 2 vols. (1898, 1910); L. Pearson, *Demosthenes: Six Private Speeches* (1972); J. E. Sandys, *Philippics, Olynthiacs, Peace, Chersonese*, 2 vols. (1897, 1900); W. W. Goodwin, *De Corona* (1901); H. Wankel, *Rede für Ktesiphon über den Kranz*, 2 vols. (1976); H. Yunis, *On the Crown* (2000); J. E. Sandys, *Leptines* (1890); D. M. MacDowell, *Against Meidias* (1990) and *On the False Embassy* (2000); W. Wayte, *Demosthenes Against Androtion and Against Timocrates* (1882); J. A. Goldstein, *The Letters of Demosthenes* (1968).

INDEX S. Preuss (1892).

GENERAL A. W. Pickard-Cambridge, *Demosthenes and the Last Days of Greek Freedom* (1914); A. Schaefer, *Demosthenes und seine Zeit*, 2nd edn., 3 vols. (1885–7); F. R. Wüst, *Philipp II von Makedonien und Griechenland* (1938); There are many debatable questions of fact about the career of Demosthenes and very various judgements; the account given here is based on views developed in a series of articles by G. L. Cawkwell (*Rev. Ét. Grec.* 1960, 1962; *CQ* 1962, 1963, 1969, 1978; *JHS* 1963; *Phoenix* 1978) and in *Philip of Macedon* (1978). The fullest modern discussion is in *HM* 2 (1979); see also R. Sealey, *Demosthenes and his Time* (1993). For D. as orator, L. Pearson, *The Art of Demosthenes* (1976).

G. L. C.

Demosthenes (3), of *Bithynia, epic poet of unknown date; composed a *Bithyniaca* in at least ten books.

FRAGMENTS *FGrH.* 699; Powell, *Coll. Alex.* 25–7.　　R. L. Hu.

dentistry in antiquity was part of general *medicine; diseases of the teeth were explained and treated in accordance with the theories on other diseases. The operative technique was excellent (the Hippocratic treatment of the fracture of the mandible is famous; see HIPPOCRATES (2)); extractions were performed at an early date. The methods of preserving the teeth, however, consisted mainly of medicinal and dietetic means; fillings for that purpose were unknown. Loose teeth were fastened with gold wire (Hippoc. Περὶ ἄρθρων 32; Twelve Tables 10. 8). Toothache being considered a chronic disease and one of the greatest torments (Cels. *Med.* 6. 9), hygienic prescriptions were extensively advocated. Cleansing of the teeth with tooth-powder, the tooth-pick (*dentiscalpium*), chewing (σχινίζειν τοὺς ὀδόντας) were recommended in addition to innumerable remedies against bad breath, a favourite topic of Latin epigrammatists. False teeth were set, but only by technicians, the artificial teeth being carved from ivory or other animal teeth. Such prostheses, used by the *Etruscans and Romans, served primarily to hide physical defects and to correct deficiencies of speech, but had probably to be removed before meals. Physicians and dentists refrained from making prostheses, either on account of their technical insufficiency, or because their importance for the process of digestion was not appreciated.

W. Hoffmann-Axthelm, *History of Dentistry* (1981); K. Sudhoff, *Gesch. d. Zahnheilkunde*, 2nd edn. (1926), dissertations on ancient authors enumerated, 75, 97, 102; W. Artelt, *Janus* 1929. Instruments, J. S. Milne, *Surgical Instruments in Greek and Roman Times* (1907); E. Künzl, *Medizinische Instrumenten aus Sepulkralfunden der römischen Kaiserzeit* (1982).　　L. E.; V. N.

Dercylidas, Spartan commander. In 411 BC he became Sparta's first commander in the *Hellespont during the Ionian War (see PELOPONNESIAN WAR), procuring the revolt of *Abydos and (temporarily) *Lampsacus. While (still) *harmost at Abydos during *Lysander's admiralship *c.*407, he was punished for indiscipline following criticism by *Pharnabazus. In 399 he replaced *Thibron (1) as area harmost in Asia Minor. Despite inheriting orders to attack *Caria, he made truce with *Tissaphernes and campaigned against his enemy Pharnabazus, rapidly securing nine cities in Aeolis. During two separate truces with Pharnabazus he plundered Bithynian Thrace (winter 399/8) and secured the Thracian *Chersonese (1) (summer 398) for the Greek cities and prospective Laconian settlers. Ordered in 397 to attack Caria, he was confronted by the joint forces of Tissaphernes and Pharnabazus, but obtained a further truce and an (abortive) offer of peace terms. Although selected for his cunning (being nicknamed 'Sisyphus') and superficially successful, his repeated truces gave Pharnabazus additional time to assemble a Persian fleet.

After serving as one of *Agesilaus II's advisers in 396/5 Dercylidas returned to Sparta, but in 394 was dispatched again to the Hellespont. During the expulsion of *harmosts following Sparta's defeat at *Cnidus, he held on to Abydos and *Sestus against Pharnabazus and *Conon (1), remaining there until replaced in 389. Noted for his liking for foreign service, he was absent from Sparta for over half the period between 411 and 389. He remained a bachelor, thereby risking the indignities imposed on Spartiates who neglected the traditional duty to sire offspring. His career reflects in microcosm the disruptive effects produced by Sparta's prolonged engagement

in foreign warfare in the late 5th and early 4th cents.

RE 5. 240–2, 'Derkylidas' 1; PB no. 228.　　S. J. Ho.

Derveni See DIONYSUS (Derveni crater); ORPHIC LITERATURE; ORPHISM; PALAEOGRAPHY, Introduction (Derveni papyrus); PAPYROLOGY, GREEK.

Despoina, 'The Mistress', an *Arcadian goddess worshipped at *Lycosura together with her mother *Demeter, her foster-father Anytus, and *Artemis (Paus. 8. 37. 3–9); there was an altar to her father, Poseidon Hippios, near the temple. The cult group inside the temple of Despoina was the work of *Damophon of Messene, early 2nd cent. BC. Important fragments remain. We do not know Despoina's actual name, since it was kept secret from those who were not initiates of her mysteries. Her character is related to that of Kore (*Persephone) in Attica; she and Demeter were a paired mother and daughter, and her iconography shows the Eleusinian features (see ELEUSIS) of *kistē* (basket) and sceptre. But the figures of dancers with animal masks on her clothing, and the brutal nature of the *sacrifice made to her in the megaron at Lycosura place her in a fully Arcadian context and bring out her links with the animal world. See ARCADIAN CULTS AND MYTHS.

M. Jost, *Sanctuaires et cultes d'Arcadie* (1985), see index.　　M. J.

destinatio, an electoral term derived from the verb *destinare*. The use of the verb in Livy 39. 32. 9 shows that the 'marking out' or 'fixing on' a candidate at any stage of the electoral process did not guarantee his ultimate election. *Destinatio* is first met in the *tabula Hebana, where a *lex Valeria Cornelia* of AD 5 assigned a preliminary role in the election of consuls and praetors to ten voting centuries named after C. *Iulius Caesar (2) and L. *Iulius Caesar (4) (increased to fifteen in AD 19 and to twenty in AD 23 in honour of *Germanicus and Drusus *Iulius Caesar (1) respectively) and comprising senators and all *equites enrolled in the judicial decuries. The decision of this body was its *destinatio*; its chosen candidates were *destinati*. Their number never exceeded the number of places to be filled, and the vote of the select assembly was succeeded by a vote of the full *comitia centuriata*; Tibiletti was probably right to think of the centuries as *centuriae praerogativae*: *destinati* went forward with the votes of all, and the centuries of the *comitia centuriata*, knowing what their betters had thought, followed suit. *Destinatio* thus did not in theory guarantee election, but it may frequently have done so in practice. In AD 15 elections were effectively transferred to the senate (Tac. *Ann.* 1. 15. 1); it follows that the procedure was reduced to ceremonial. What purpose, if any, the innovation of AD 5 had beyond those of honouring the dead and gratifying the united upper class, is disputed; Holladay's view that it was intended to secure orderly elections is most convincing.

G. Tibiletti, *Principe e magistrati repubblicani* (1953) (bibliog. 283 ff.); Sherk, *Hadrian*, 63 ff. (trans. and bibliog.); A. J. Holladay, *Latomus* 1978, 874 ff. (bibliog.).　　E. S. S.; B. M. L.

detestatio sacrorum, renunciation of family rites. A Roman head of household (*sui iuris*) performed religious rites (*sacra*). These rites were peculiar to each family group. If such a person agreed to be transferred by comitial *adoption (*adrogatio*) into another's family, he had to submit to a pontifical examination prior to proceedings in the *comitia calata* (the 'summoned assembly'). On the pontiffs' being satisfied that, so far as possible, other members of the family existed to continue that family's rites, the individual concerned proceeded to make formal renunciation of his existing family rites.

Gell. *NA* 5. 19. 5–10; 15. 27. 3; Gai. *Inst.* 1. 99; Cic. *Dom.* 34 ff.

A. D. E. L.

Deucalion

Deucalion, in mythology, the Greek Noah, son of *Prometheus, married to Pyrrha daughter of Epimetheus. When *Zeus floods the earth in anger at the sins of the age of bronze (in particular, of *Lycaon (3), Ov. *Met.* 1. 125, 165), Deucalion and Pyrrha, on the advice of Prometheus, build a chest (*larnax*) and live there for nine days and nine nights (Apollod. 1. 7. 2; Ov. *Met.* 1. 163– 413). When they come to land, they repopulate the earth by casting stones over their shoulders, from which people spring (Stith Thompson A 1245, A 1254.1). Greek *genealogy begins with Deucalion's son *Hellen ('Greek'). Deucalion is held to have founded the temple of Olympian Zeus in Athens (see OLYMPIEUM) and there was an annual sacrifice commemorating the final ebbing away of the waters down the crevice there (Paus. 1. 18. 7; Deubner, *Attische Feste* 113). Deucalion and Pyrrha first came to land at sites such as: Othrys in Phthiotis (*Thessaly) where Deucalion is king, Opus in *Locris or its port Cynus (site of Pyrrha's grave—Deucalion's is in Athens, Strab. 9. 4. 2). The purpose of the flood is to create a new beginning for a new world-order. It is scarcely accidental that a son of Prometheus the fire-bearer stars in the flood, or that both are so involved with the creation of mankind. For a unique image of him in Roman art see *LIMC* 3 / 1 (1986), 384–5.

G. Piccaluga, *Lykaon: Un tema mitico* (1968). H. J. R.; K. D.

deus, divus These two words, deriving from the same form (†*deiwo-*), designate two different types of Roman divinity. A *deus* (fem. *dea*, plural *divi* under the republic) was immortal and had never experienced mortal existence; but a *divus*—from the beginning of the Principate at least—was a divinity who obtained this status posthumously and by human agency. Although deification is above all a public phenomenon relating to dead emperors and empresses (see RULER-CULT), apotheosis existed equally in a private context (Cic. *Att.* 12. 36. 1; Frei Stolba, *JSGU* 1990, 125 ff.). The Romans believed that the world was full of divinities, living in the skies, on earth, in water, or underground. Some were known and entered into permanent relations with humans, while others did not manifest themselves, although this does not mean that the Romans neglected them: when they needed to invoke all the divinities present in a locality, e.g. for an expiation, these anonymous deities were designated by the title 'God-or-goddess' (*Sive deus sive dea*). Sometimes these anonymous deities emerged from the shadows and appeared to the Romans, who then conferred on them a name and a cult, just as they attributed a cult and the name *divus* to deceased persons whose deeds and exceptional powers had revealed their divine nature.

As regards the mode of action of the gods, modern opinions differ. According to one, going back to 19th-cent. ethnology, divinities overlap and can be mutually assimilated since they preside over fields as vast and indeterminate as fecundity and fertility. In opposition to this view is the more rigorous conception of the divine function developed by G. Dumézil, according to which a divinity possesses, in a given religious sysem, a precise divine function which he or she exercises in different contexts (e.g. for *Mars, *ARR* 205 ff.); in conformity with the principles of polytheism, a divinity often collaborates with others, without becoming confused with them, even if they are very closely associated. This approach thinks in terms of power and divine functions rather than the 'sacred' and the 'sacred force'.

W. Fowler, *The Religious Experience of the Roman People from the Earliest Times to the Age of Augustus* (1911; repr. 1971); K. Vahlert, *Praedeismus und römische Religion* (1935); H. Wagenvoort, *Roman Dynamism* (1947); Dumézil, *ARR* 21 ff.; Radke, *Entwicklung.* J. Sch.

Deva, the river Dee, whence the name was applied to the legionary fortress at its mouth, modern Chester. Some early occupation *c.* AD 50 can be inferred, but the legionary fortress with earth bank and timber buildings dates from 74–8 and was used first by *legion II Adiutrix and subsequently by XX Valeria Victrix. Timber was replaced by stone, with stone wall, *c.*100. Chester was partially rebuilt in the 200s, but was only occupied at a reduced level by the 360s. Excavation has revealed only fragments of the fortress. An extramural amphitheatre and civil settlement are known.

S. Ward, *Excavations at Chester: 12 Watergate Street, 1985* (1988); S. S. Frere, *Britannia*, 3rd edn. (1987). C. E. S.; M. J. M.

devotio Ritual to devote either enemies or oneself (or both) to gods of the Underworld and death. *Macrobius (*Sat.* 3. 9. 9 ff.) records that in ancient times enemy cities were devoted (*devoveri*) to gods of the Underworld (Dis pater, *Ve(d)iovis, *manes*), after the *evocatio (calling out) of their protective deities. The prayer (*carmen devotionis*) he quotes on the occasion of the *devotio* of *Carthage calls the enemies substitutes (*vicarios*) for the Roman commander and his army, who are thus saved. A better-known variant of this genuine *votum* is the type of *devotio* only attested for P. *Decius Mus (1) (and less unequivocally for his son and grandson, around 300 BC). Here, the Roman commander linked the sacrifice of his own life, through an act of self-*consecratio, with the *devotio* of the enemies. Livy (8. 9. 4 ff.) records the prayer by which Decius devoted the enemy army and himself to the *di manes* and *Tellus. After various ritual preparations, the Roman general, on horseback and wearing the *cinctus Gabinus* (see GABII), rode into the midst of the enemy to seek a voluntary death. Despite a number of ritual prescriptions (possibility of substitution by an ordinary soldier, regulations if this soldier or the general were not killed), it is doubtful whether this type of *devotio* ever belonged to the fixed body of Roman ritual institutions.

H. S. Versnel, *Mnemos.* 1976, 365–410. H. S. V.

di penates See PENATES, DI.

diadem (διάδημα), royal headband, with sceptre and purple an attribute of Hellenistic kingship; a flat strip of white cloth, knotted behind, with the ends left free-hanging. It originated with *Alexander (3) the Great, who probably assumed it to mark his conquest of Asia. Late sources (Diod. Sic. 17. 77. 6; Q. *Curtius Rufus 6. 6. 4) saw it as part of his adoption of Persian royal dress; but archaeology suggests that Persian kings did not wear diadems. A likelier source is the range of headbands already known to the Greeks. The ancient tale of its discovery by the god *Dionysus (Diod. Sic. 4. 4. 4), who wore it to mark his eastern conquests, no doubt reflects some of the symbolism attached to it by *Alexander (3) the Great and his successors. A silver-gilt headband found in Tomb II at Vergina (see AEGAE) may have served as a Macedonian royal diadem. Refused by *Caesar in 44 BC and avoided by earlier Roman emperors, under *Constantine I it became (as a purple band fitted with jewels and pearls) a regular part of the insignia of the reigning Augustus and Augusta (see AUGUSTUS AND AUGUSTA AS TITLES).

R. Smith, *Hellenistic Royal Portraits* (1988), 34 ff. L. A. M.; A. J. S. S.

Diadochi (Διάδοχοι, 'Successors'). This term was applied in a special sense to the more important of *Alexander (3) the Great's officers who ultimately partitioned his empire: *Antigonus (1) I, *Antipater (1), *Cassander, *Lysimachus, *Ptolemy (1) I, *Seleucus (1) I. The 'age of the Diadochi' represents a period extending from Alexander's death (323 BC) at least to the battle of *Ipsus (301), which ended the efforts of Antigonus I to reassemble the whole empire under his own rule, and perhaps to the battle of Corupedium (281), which fixed the main political boundaries of the Hellenistic world for the next century.

See *CAH* 7² 1 (1984).   G. T. G.; S. H.

diagnosis (διάγνωσις, Lat. *cognitio*), lit. 'the means of distinguishing, or recognizing'. The concept of diagnosis is important in ancient forensic oratory and law, but the most extended accounts of its importance are found in the medical writers. Much ancient medical literature is concerned with the way in which the doctor should discern the nature, history, and future course of the patient's illness. Each case dealt with by the doctor involved the recognition of a number of signs which needed to be distinguished and ordered so that the correct treatment could be prescribed, and the progress of the disease anticipated. Prognosis (πρόγνωσις) is effectively a part of diagnosis, and many ancient diagnoses result not so much in naming the affection as in predicting its outcome. Effective prognosis not only increased the patient's confidence in the doctor, but could also encourage the doctor to avoid hopeless cases.

A group of Hippocratic treatises, including *Prognostic*, *Prorrhetic*, and *Critical Days*, deal with the nature of the signs presented to the doctor by the patient. (See HIPPOCRATES (2).) Against the bluff which characterizes much physiological speculation, Hippocratic diagnosis is marked by caution. Treatises such as *Prognostic* (cf. *Epidemics* 1. 10) stress the importance of studying *all* the factors relating to a patient's illness, including habits, environment, age, sex, climate, and so on, before proceeding to diagnosis. The case histories in *Epidemics* 1 and 3 preserve the results of many such initial investigations; the affection is not generally named unless it is a particularly unusual one.

The author of the Hippocratic treatise *On the Art* (ch. 11) notes that some diseases cannot be diagnosed by sight alone without the aid of reasoning. In post-Hippocratic medicine, the cognitive mechanisms of diagnostic practice—and in particular the validity of inferential forms of diagnosis—came under scrutiny. How should signs be interpreted? How far can interpretation go without the aid of theory? Can diagnosis proceed transparently without the interposition of an interpretative framework? The medical Empiricists held that the doctor should build up collections of similar kinds of cases as a basis for the atheoretical determination of the proper indication (ἔνδειξις) for treatment; the Methodists believed that the diseased body presented signs which pointed to the presence of two or three basic morbid states in the body whose diagnosis led directly to the indication for treatment. Following authorities such as *Herophilus, *Galen attached great diagnostic and prognostic significance to the behaviour of the pulse, in addition to the factors stressed by the Hippocratics.

See also MEDICINE; ANATOMY AND PHYSIOLOGY.   J. T. V.

Diagoras, of *Melos, lyric poet active in Athens in the last decades of the 5th cent. BC (Hermippus fr. 43 K–A; Ar. *Av.* 1071 ff., *Nub.* 828 ff.). Renowned for his '*atheism' (Cic. *Nat. D.* 1. 2, 63), he mocked the *mysteries of Eleusis—perhaps in reaction to the capture of *Melos by the Athenians. He was condemned to death, and fled (Diod. Sic. 13. 6, 7). Fragments of his poem survive, but they contain no trace of 'atheism'. In the Arabic tradition Diagoras was notorious for his atheism.

F. Jacoby, *Diagoras ho atheos* (1959); M. Winiarczyk, *Diagorae Melii et Theodori Cyrenaei reliquiae* (1981); L. Woodbury, *Collected Writings* (1991), 118–50.   J. N. B.

dialectic, διαλεκτική (sc. ἐπιστήμη or τέχνη): the science of conducting a philosophical dialogue (διαλέγεσθαι, 'to converse') by exploring the consequences of premises asserted or conceded by an interlocutor. Aristotle considered *Zeno (1) of Elea its founder (Diog. Laert 9. 25), no doubt for his antinomies which derived contradictory consequences from a disputed hypothesis. *Socrates' method of cross-examination, the *elenchos*, was a further landmark in the history of dialectic. But it was his pupil *Plato (1) who formally developed the idea of a dialectical science, and who probably coined the term 'dialectic' itself. While Socrates' arguments had regularly taken the form of refutations, Plato (*Meno* 75c–d) presented dialectic as co-operative investigation based on agreed premises, in contrast to the essentially obstructive method of 'eristic'. In his middle and late periods Plato virtually equated dialectic with correct philosophical method, especially for securing definitions (*Resp.* 531–9; *Soph.* 253). This for him normally means conceptual inquiry into the hierarchy of forms, and can involve the twin analytic methods of collection (into a genus) and division (into species). In the *Republic* dialectic is the supreme science, uniting the first principles of all individual disciplines under a single unhypothetical principle, the Good. Even here it is still viewed as taking the form of oral debate, and as including *elenchos* as one component.

*Aristotle's *Topics*, whose origins lie largely in Plato's *Academy, is his handbook on dialectical method. For him dialectic, while still integral to investigative method and the proper route to knowledge of first principles, differs from scientific 'demonstration' because of the less secure status of its premises, operating as it does from *endoxa*, 'reputable' opinions held 'either by all or most people, or by the wise'. In so operating, dialectic applies Aristotle's standard method of proceeding from 'what appears' (*ta phainomena*) or from 'that which is better known to us' (*gnōrimōteron hēmin*). Training in dialectic includes mastery of debating skills, of complex definitional theory, of rules of inference, and (as covered in his *On Sophistical Refutations*) of the solution of fallacies.

The Dialectical school (see MEGARIAN SCHOOL), influential in the later 4th and early 3rd cents. BC, was a Socratic movement which made dialectical virtuosity its focal concern, perhaps influenced by Socrates' description of dialectical activity as the greatest human good (Pl. *Ap.* 38a). In the Hellenistic age the Stoics (see STOICISM) treated dialectic as a broad division of philosophy, embracing logic, grammar, definition and division, and the study of sophisms, but excluding rhetoric (Diog. Laert. 7. 41–83). The Stoic sage is said to be the only true dialectician, and to possess 'dialectical virtue'. The Epicureans rejected the whole of dialectic as superfluous. The Academics, as critics of all doctrinal stances, were leading practitioners of dialectic, yet also sought to undermine it by attacking its foundational axioms, such as the law of bivalence (Cic. *Acad.* 2. 91–8).

R. Robinson, *Plato's Earlier Dialectic* (1953); G. E. L. Owen (ed.), *Aristotle on Dialectic* (1968); A. A. Long, in J. M. Rist (ed.), *The Stoics* (1978), 101–24.   D. N. S.

dialects, Greek (prehistory) In the first half of the first millennium BC each Greek region and indeed each Greek city spoke and sometimes wrote its own dialect (see GREEK LANGUAGE). The Greeks themselves mentioned four ethnic groups, Athenians,

461

dialects, Italic

*Ionians, *Dorians, and Aeolians (see AEOLIS), characterized by different dialects, though other classifications were also in use. On the basis of shared linguistic features modern scholars classify the dialects into five groups: Attic-Ionic (in Attica, the Ionic islands of the Aegean, and Asia Minor), Doric (in the Peloponnese, the Doric islands of the Aegean, and Asia Minor), north-west Greek (in the northern part of mainland Greece), Aeolic (in *Boeotia, *Thessaly, and part of Asia Minor including *Lesbos) and Arcado-Cyprian (in *Arcadia and *Cyprus, with possible links to *Pamphylia). It is disputed whether the *Mycenaean language, attested in the second millennium BC, belongs to any of these groups, though it has close links with Arcado-Cyprian. Further spreading of the dialects into the west Mediterranean area was caused by later colonization. The geographic separation of closely related dialects requires historical explanation and attempts have been made to reconstruct the original distribution of the dialects and their speakers in the second millennium BC. It is normally accepted, for instance, that in the last part of the second millennium BC the ancestors of the Arcadians and the Cyprians lived in the Peloponnese until some of them took refuge in the central part of the Peloponnese and others migrated to Cyprus. Similarly an early colonization from mainland Greece brought the various dialects to Asia Minor. But we must also account for the differences between the original groups. Until relatively recently it was widely accepted that the future Greeks arrived in Greece in at least three waves: first the ancestors of the Ionians and the Athenians, then those of the Aeolians and perhaps of the Arcado-Cyprians. The last to arrive would have been the ancestors of the Dorians and north-west Greeks, who pushed their way into Peloponnese and Crete dispersing the previous populations; the classical tradition spoke of the return of the *Heraclidae. However, the linguistic evidence by itself is not sufficient to support the three-wave theory and no other reliable evidence is available. More recently it has been argued that the dialect distinctions arose in Greece itself in the second millennium BC, though the details are not clear and we do not know, for instance, how many groups we must postulate for the Mycenaean period. The Mycenaean places of the second millennium like *Pylos, *Mycenae, and *Cnossus were later inhabited by Dorians, but the language of the Mycenaean tablets shows no specifically Doric features and is linguistically more innovative than that of the Dorians. This supports the view that the Dorians moved into the *Peloponnese and *Crete (probably from northern Greece) after the end of the Mycenaean period. Yet it has also been suggested (by John Chadwick) that the Dorians represent the continuation of a class of Mycenaean servants who spoke a dialect that was different from, and more conservative than, that of their masters.

J. Chadwick, *CAH* 2²/1 (1963), ch. 39; L. R. Palmer, *The Greek Language* (1980), 53 ff.; E. Risch, *Kl. Schr.* (1981), 269–89; J. Chadwick, in D. Musti (ed.), *Le origini dei Greci* (1985), 3–12. A. M. Da.

dialects, Italic See ITALY, LANGUAGES OF.

dialogue

Greek As a special literary–philosophical form of writing, dialogue has its origin in *Socrates' philosophical activity; *Aristotle's description of written philosophical dialogues as 'Socratic logoi' (*Poet.* 1447ᵇ11) reflects the association of the form with representations of Socratic conversations, often written by members of Socrates' circle (like *Plato (1)), in which he is himself often the, or a, main speaker. A typical 'Socratic' conver-

sation, or *dialogos*, will be one in which question-and-answer plays a leading role. As the genre develops in antiquity, this element gradually declines in importance, being replaced by long speeches either exclusively by the main speaker with short interjections by others, or more often by different speakers. The beginnings of such developments are already visible in the Platonic corpus, although there they are partly the result of experimentation with the genre.

*Diogenes (6) Laertius (3. 48) says that some people claimed that *Zeno (1) of Elea was the first writer of dialogues, and that Aristotle (fr. 72 Rose) gave this role to one Alexamenus (otherwise unknown); but it is Diogenes' view that in any case it was Plato who closely defined the form, and that it was his dialogues which 'would justly win first prize for their beauty and invention'. Plato is supposed to have been much influenced by the (now lost) prose 'mimes' of *Sophron (which he is said, probably unreliably, to have kept under his pillow); other more obvious influences would have been dramatic dialogue, and debates between speakers in *Herodotus (e.g. 3. 80–2) and *Thucydides (2) (5. 85–113).

*Aristotle's own early works, now lost except for fragments, included some dialogues. According to Cic. *Att.* 13. 19. 4, he appeared as a character in (? some of) them, as Plato never did, but as *Cicero does in his dialogues; Aristotle also apparently subordinated other roles to his own. The same letter (which refers to 'many' dialogues by another pupil of Plato's, *Heraclides (1) Ponticus) gives some general insight into the thinking behind, and the models for, Cicero's dialogues. The writing of dialogues in Greek was revived by *Plutarch in the 1st and 2nd cents. AD, and a little later by *Lucian. *Plutarch's dialogues (e.g. *De genio Socratis*) are modelled especially on Plato's, but are lighter in content, while *Lucian's stance is more usually that of satirist than of philosopher; his range is greater even than Plato's, and shows the influence not only of *Sōkratikoi logoi* but, rather more obviously, of New *Comedy and other later literary developments.

R. Hirzel, *Der Dialog* (1895; repr. 1963); *Oxford Studies in Ancient Philosophy*, suppl. vol. 1992. C. J. R.

Latin Dialogue in the general sense occurs in Latin literature not only in drama but also occasionally in the written versions of speeches, where a passage of dialogue between an orator and his opponent is called an *altercatio*, and notably in Roman *satire. The first Roman known to have written in the specific genre of the literary prose dialogue, in the manner of *Plato (1) and his successors, was M. *Iunius Brutus (1) (father of the tyrannicide or killer of *Caesar), who composed three books on civil law, evidently in the form of a dialogue with his son (Cicero, *De or.* 2. 223–4). *Cicero adopted the dialogue as the medium for most of his philosophical and rhetorical writing, employing Roman characters and settings.

Cicero's first dialogues, *De oratore* (55 BC), *De republica* (54–51 BC) and *De legibus* (perhaps 52–51 BC), were explicitly modelled on Plato and contain a number of Platonic allusions. In the later period of his writing on philosophy and rhetoric (46–44 BC), Cicero experimented with a range of dialogue forms; his use of dialogue is both more varied and more sophisticated than has sometimes been thought. *Brutus*, on rhetoric, follows the manner of *De oratore*. In the *Academica*, *De finibus*, *De natura deorum*, and *De divinatione* the differing philosophical viewpoints are set out in opposing speeches; this adversarial method owed something to Academic techniques of arguing on both sides of a question (*in utramque partem*), and perhaps also to forensic habits. The *Tusculan Disputations*, the first of Cicero's dialogues to be set out

462

in dramatic rather than narrative form, comprises a discussion between an anonymous main speaker (who shares certain characteristics with the author himself) and his pupil or auditor, and there is some use of dialectic in the Socratic mode in addition to Cicero's preferred style of continuous exposition. In *De senectute* and *De amicitia*, short essays on everyday ethical themes, Cicero reverted to a 2nd-cent. historical setting, as in *De republica*.

The importance of literary models other than Plato for Cicero's dialogue technique has been variously assessed. He knew the dialogues of *Xenophon (1) and sometimes alluded to them. Aristotle was invoked as a precedent for dialogues in which the author himself appeared as the most important speaker (e.g. *De finibus*), while *Heraclides (1) Ponticus similarly provided inspiration for the use of characters from the more distant past (*QFr*. 3. 5. 1; *Att*. 13. 19. 4). Cicero's *Hortensius*, a defence of philosophy of which only fragments survive, was probably modelled on Aristotle's *Protrepticus*.

Cicero's contemporary *Varro employed the dialogue form in the extant *De re rustica*, a treatise on farming, and also in the lost series of books entitled *Logistorici*, each of which was named after one of its speakers, while the subject was specified in the subtitle (e.g. *Catus on educating children*); the form may have been similar to that of Cicero's *De senectute* and *De amicitia*, but the priority of one author or the other cannot be established.

Some of the younger Seneca's works (*De providentia*, etc.; see *ANNAEUS SENECA (2), L.) appear in the manuscripts under the title *Dialogi*, but there is no element of actual dialogue in their composition; they would be more appropriately classified as philosophical essays. The Ciceronian form and style clearly suggested itself to *Tacitus (1) as appropriate for his dialogue on rhetoric and literature, the *Dialogus de oratoribus*, in which the claims of older oratory, 'modern' oratory, and poetry are debated. Later Latin dialogues include the *Octavius* of *Minucius Felix, and the *Saturnalia* of *Macrobius. The *De consolatione philosophiae* of *Boethius is in the form of a dialogue between the author and Philosophy. The form continued to be used in the Middle Ages and Renaissance.

R. Hirzel, *Der Dialog* (1895; repr. 1963); E. Becker, *Technik und Szenerie des ciceronischen Dialogs* (1938); R. E. Jones, *AJPhil*. 1939, 307 ff.

J. G. F. P.

Diana (root †*dyw*-'the bright one' (cf. *Jupiter), originally a moon goddess, *contra* Altheim, *Griechische Götter im alten Rom* (1930), 93 ff.), an Italian goddess anciently identified with *Artemis, from whom she took over the patronage of margins and savageness. But the modalities of this evolution remain puzzling (moonlight as the contrary of daylight, and so of civilized life?). Her cult was widespread; see Birt in Roscher, *Lex*. 1. 1003–4 for details. One of her most famous shrines was on Mt. Tifata near *Capua (Vell. Pat. 2. 25. 4 and elsewhere in literature, supported by much inscriptional evidence); the name Tifata means 'holm-oak grove' (Festus 503. 14 Lindsay), which suits Diana's character as a goddess of the wilderness. Most famous of all was her ancient cult near *Aricia (on the shore of the volcanic lake known as the Mirror of Diana, *Speculum Dianae*, below the modern Nemi, i.e. *nemus*, 'grove'). Her temple stood in a grove, which was recorded as dedicated to her by Egerius Baebius (?) of Tusculum, *dictator Latinus* (Cato, *Orig*. 2, fr. 21 Jordan). It was therefore an old religious centre of the Latin League and it is probable, though direct proof is lacking, that the foundation of her temple (probably preceded by an altar) on the *Aventine, traditionally by Servius *Tullius (Livy 1. 45. 2 ff.), was an attempt

to transfer the headquarters of this cult to Rome, along with, what Livy mentions (ibid. 3), the headship of the league. See further REX NEMORENSIS, and for the Massiliote and Ephesian connections of the Aventine temple, see ARTEMIS.

That she was later largely a goddess of women is shown by the processions of women bearing torches (symbols of her name and original function) in her honour at Aricia (Prop. 2. 32. 9–10; Ov. *Fast*. 3. 268–9), also by the character of many of the votive offerings there, which have clear reference to children and childbirth (Wissowa, *RK* 248). Her links with women, along with slaves (Festus 460. 33 ff. Lindsay) and *asylum (Dion. Hal. *Ant. Rom*. 4. 26. 3), seem to inscribe her within the frame of her real field of action—namely, margins.

At Aricia she was associated with *Egeria, and Virbius, an obscure male deity (Ov. *Met*. 15. 544; Servius on *Aen*. 7. 84 and 761; see HIPPOLYTUS 1). Identifications with foreign deities are common all over the west.

In general see Latte, *RR* 169 ff.; Dumézil, *ARR* 407 ff.; R. Schilling, *Rites, cultes, dieux de Rome* (1971), 371 ff.; Radke, *Entwicklung* 160 ff. Aventine temple: L. Venditelli and others, *BArch*. 1990, 163 ff.; for its date and political significance: A. Momigliano, *Terzo contributo* (1966), 641 ff.; M. Gras, *Rev. Ét. Anc*. 1987, 47 ff. Grove at Nemi: A. E. Gordon, in *Calif. Public. in Class. Arch*. 1934; T. F. Blagg, in M. Henig (ed.), *Pagan Gods and Shrines of the Roman Empire* (1986), 211 ff.; C. Ampolo, in *Les Bois sacrés* (1993), 159 ff. Temple at Mt. Tifata: A. de Franciscis, *Archivio Storico di Terra di Lavoro* 1956, 301 ff.; *LIMC* 2/1 (1984), 793 ff.

H. J. R.; J. Sch.

Diasia, an ancient and 'very great' (Thuc. 1. 126. 6) Athenian festival of Zeus *Meilichios, held at Agrae just outside the city on 23 Anthesterion (roughly, late February). According to *Thucydides (2), Athenians attended *en masse*, and sacrificed 'not animal victims, but local kinds of offerings' (*cakes?); animals were, however, offered too, as some are listed in calendars to be sent up for the festival from outlying *demes. It was celebrated 'with a certain grimness' (schol. Lucian 107. 15, 110. 27 f. Rabe), appropriate no doubt to Zeus Meilichios; and it lacked the publicly provided spectacle characteristic of many later-founded Attic festivals. But we hear of relatives dining together, and it was also an occasion to buy *toys for children.

M. H. Jameson, *BCH* 1965, 159–72; Hornblower, *Comm. on Thuc*. 1 (1991), 207–9.

R. C. T. P.

diatribe, term given by modern scholars to works of Greek or Roman popular philosophy and generally implying the following: that they are direct transcriptions or literary developments of addresses given by *Cynic or Stoic (see STOICISM) philosophers on the streets, before large audiences or (in the case of philosophers concerned with moral exhortation rather than systematic argument) to pupils; that they focus on a single theme; that their main aim is to attack vices (hence the modern usage); that they employ a vigorous, hectoring, colloquial (sometimes vulgar) style, with colourful, everyday imagery; that they sometimes have an anonymous interlocutor, thereby providing a dramatic illusion, a degree of argument and (usually) a butt. Such works are regarded as the pagan equivalent of the Christian sermon, which they are supposed to have influenced (from Paul onwards). Alleged examples include the remains of *Bion (1) (often considered the form's inventor) and *Teles, *Arrian's versions of Epictetus' teachings, and various works of the younger *Seneca, *Dio Cocceianus, and *Plutarch. It is also claimed that, while diatribe is a separate form, it had a wide influence upon other types of literature and could sometimes constitute a fairly

Dicaearchus

discrete element within them (thus e.g. *Lucretius' 'diatribe against the fear of death' (3. 830–1094)).

This model has been challenged: some accept the existence of such a tradition but demur at the term; others reject both the term and the notion that there is a sufficiently distinct tradition.

In ancient usage the word's basic meaning ('spending of time') spawns a wide range of applications. The following are potentially germane: 'recreation', 'study' (leisure can be used both seriously and unseriously), 'conversation'/'speech'/'discussion' (including philosophical), 'philosophical school', 'philosophical venue'. (Irrelevant is the specialized rhetorical usage ('dwelling on the point'), as in [Hermog.] περὶ μεθόδου δεινότητος 5.)

Several factors render the implications of the term as a book-title of philosophical works elusive: the general uncertainties surrounding attribution of ancient book-titles, an apparent elasticity of usage, and the loss of almost all the works thus entitled. 'Diatribes' in the title of Arrian's versions of Epictetus' teachings seems to refer to Epictetus' oral 'lectures', which are also described by other terms (*logos, dialexis*, etc.). 'Diatribes' is used of all Bion's works (Diog. Laert. 2. 77); and in *Horace's allusion to *Bioneis sermonibus et sale nigro* (*Epist.* 2. 2. 60), *sermonibus* ('conversations') is a possible gloss on 'diatribes'. But Bion's works are also called *hypomnēmata* (Diog. Laert. 4. 47), a term which sometimes means 'notes' but can cover practically any type of prose writing, and two specific titles are attested ('On Slavery' and 'On Anger'). Elsewhere 'diatribes' are sometimes distinguished from dialogues, protreptics, etc., in which cases the distinction must be one of literary form. The same must be true when the title specifies the subject-matter (e.g. 'Diatribes on Wisdom'). Such cases imply a lecture format corresponding (at some level) to an oral 'lecture'.

Certain conclusions emerge: (*a*) the term 'diatribe' can be used of practically any oral philosophical exposition; (*b*) written works so described must bear some relationship to oral performances, a relationship ranging from more or less direct transcription to quite elaborate literary development; (*c*) in reference to written works, the term 'diatribes' can be used both as a general description and as a specific title; (*d*) as a specific title it implies a literary form: the lecture, a recognizable but inevitably fluid and flexible form; (*e*) almost all the works thus entitled concern ethics; (*f*) the surviving fragments from *Zeno (2)'s and Bion (1)'s 'diatribes' show the sermonizing qualities of the modern model of 'diatribe'; (*g*) the *restriction* of the term 'diatribe' to works of popular philosophy is technically inaccurate, but in the ancient world such works could be so described and seem indeed to have become the dominant 'diatribe'-tradition; (*h*) given the general characteristics of the Cynics, they are likely to have been major contributors to that tradition (whether or not they originated the *written* diatribe), a hypothesis supported by the examples of the Cynic-influenced Zeno and Bion. See also CYNICS.

S. K. Stowers, *The Diatribe and Paul's Letter to the Romans* (1981); H. D. Jocelyn, *LCM* 1982, 3–7; 1983, 89–91; H. B. Gottschalk, *LCM* 1982, 91–2; 1983, 91–2 (sharp theoretical debate); T. Schmeller, *Paulus und die 'Diatribe': Eine vergleichende Stilinterpretation* (1987); P. P. Fuentes González, *Las Diatribas de Teles*, diss. Granada 1990, 101.   J. L. Mo.

Dicaearchus (*RE* 3), of *Messana, Greek polymath and prolific writer, pupil of *Aristotle and contemporary of *Theophrastus and *Aristoxenus: fl. *c.*320–300 BC. He spent some of his life in the *Peloponnese. Fragments only survive of his works, but they show a remarkable range:

Literary and Cultural History (1) The *Life of Greece*, a pioneering history of culture in three books: it began with an idealized worldwide golden age and went on to trace the evolution of contemporary Greek culture, pointing the contribution of Chaldaeans and Egyptians as well as Greeks. (2) *On Lives*, in several books, treating *Plato (1), *Pythagoras (1), and other philosophers: he found 'juvenile' and 'vulgar' elements in the *Phaedrus*. The title suggests a discussion of different lifestyles rather than straightforward biographies, and he presented his subjects as men of action as well as of reflection. (3) *On Alcaeus*, perhaps including a commentary; this again treated wider aspects of cultural history. (4) Works on *Homer, form and titles unknown. (5) *Hypotheseis of the Plots of *Sophocles (1) and *Euripides*, tracing the authors' reworkings of the myths. (6) *On Cultural Contests*, treating musical and poetic competitions. The last three works were important sources for later scholars of literature.

Political (1) *Tripoliticus*, apparently advocating a 'mixed' constitution with elements of monarchy, aristocracy, and democracy. (2) *Constitutions* of Pellene in *Achaea, *Corinth, Athens, and perhaps Sparta, though this last may have been part of (1), with Sparta exemplifying the mixed ideal. (3) *Olympicus* and *Panathenaicus*, more likely political dialogues named after their settings than public orations. (4) *On the Sacrifice at Troy*, i.e. *Alexander (3) the Great's sacrifice before the battle of the Granicus.

Philosophical (1) *On the Soul*, a dialogue on the corporeal nature and mortality of the *soul (this is one of the ways in which he departed from Aristotelian teaching), apparently consisting of two three-book parts named after their settings *At Lesbos* and *At Corinth*. (2) *On the Destruction of Man*, arguing that man is destroyed more by man than by natural disasters. (3) *On Prophecy*, accepting the possibility of the soul's prophetic power in dreams and in frenzy, but doubting its moral value and advisability. (4) *Descent into the *Trophonian Cave*, including immoralities of its priests. See TROPHONIUS. (5) A work on future things, perhaps identical with (3) or (4). (6) *Letter*, probably philosophical, to Aristoxenus.

Geographical Tour of the World (Περίοδος γῆς: the title may not be Dicaearchus' own), apparently including *maps. This established with some accuracy a main parallel of latitude from the straits of Gibraltar to the Himalayas and the assumed eastern Ocean. It included perhaps 'Measurements of Mountains in Greece', whose heights he overestimated. See GEOGRAPHY.

Dicaearchus' learning was as remarkable as his range and originality. He influenced many subsequent writers, including *Eratosthenes, *Panaetius, *Posidonius (2), *Varro, *Josephus, and *Plutarch. *Cicero admired him greatly, taking him as the model advocate of the 'practical' life and Theophrastus as that of the 'theoretical' (*Att.* 2. 16. 3).

FHG 2. 225–53; *GGM* 1. 97–110, 238–43. *RE* Suppl. 11. 526–34; G. B. Giglioni, *Riv. Stor. Ital.* 1986, 629–52; Thomson, *Hist. Anc. Geog.* see index. Fragments in F. Wehrli, *Die Schule des Aristoteles* vol. 1, *Dikaiarchos* 2nd edn. (1967).   C. B. R. P.

Dicaeogenes, a tragic and *dithyrambic poet, probably of the 4th cent. BC, wrote a *Medea* and a *Cyprians* (Arist. *Poet.* 16, mentions the recognition scene).

TrGF 1². 190–2.   A. L. B.

dicing with six-sided dice (κύβοι, *tesserae*) or four-sided knucklebones (ἀστράγαλοι, *tali*; natural or manufactured from e.g. ivory) was a popular amusement in both Greece and Rome, either by itself or in association with board-games. In Rome, where even emperors (esp. *Claudius) were keen players, high sums were often staked; and dicing was officially illegal except at the Saturnalia (see SATURNUS). *Tesserae* may have been used in varying numbers, but *tali* were normally used in fours, the best (though statistically not the rarest) of the 35 possible throws being when each showed a different face (probably = *Venus*). *Canis* ('dog') was the worst throw with both *tali* and *tesserae*, but its precise nature is uncertain. Cheating, sometimes with loaded dice (μεμολυβδωμένοι), was not unknown, and to help prevent it the dice-box or 'tower' was soon introduced. Finds of ancient dice, which include an Etruscan pair, are not uncommon.

RE 13. 1900 ff., 'Lusoria tabula', esp. 1933 ff.   L. A. M.

Dicta Catonis, the title given to a versified handbook of morality, partly pagan, partly Christian, dating in its original form probably from the 3rd cent. AD, which was widely studied in the Middle Ages and translated into many European languages. The maxims are mostly concerned with aspects of private life, and represent, as proverbs do, the experience of the past, traceable sometimes to Greece, sometimes to Roman authors such as *Horace, *Ovid, or Seneca the Younger (L. *Annaeus Seneca (2)). The title 'Cato' was perhaps an unknown author's or compiler's acknowledgement of M. *Porcius Cato (1) (the Censor) as the first moralist of Rome. The attribution to 'Dionysius Cato', a Renaissance invention, survived from Scaliger's edition (1598) until the 19th cent. (Boas).

The collection consists of (*a*) a prefatory epistle in prose; (*b*) 57 *breves sententiae* in prose; (*c*), its most important part, four books of hexameter *Disticha* (288 lines), bks. 2–4 with prefatory epistles in hexameters; (*d*) sixteen additional lines from the Zurich and Verona MSS of Cato; (*e*) 78 single lines (*Monosticha*), as well as a considerable number of lines of Catonian origin (Baehrens thought 52) in a *carmen monostichon* constituting rules for life, *Praecepta vivendi*, and two short poems, possibly Catonian, *De Musis* and *Epitaphium Vitalis mimi*. Baehrens accepted the ascription of the *Praecepta* to Columbanus, but its affiliation is rather with a poem ascribed by Dümmler to Alcuin (*MGH: Poet. lat. aevi Carolini* 1 (1880), 275). This ascription is supported by Boas (1937). Alcuin, Boas believes, did not use the medieval vulgate of 'Cato', but a fragment of the same family as the Veronese fragment. Debate continues concerning the relative chronology of various parts of the collection, the existence of a larger *Corpus Catonianum*, and how much of it was pre-Christian.

TEXT Baehrens, *PLM* 3. 205 ff.; Duff, *Minor Lat. Poets* (with trans.); P. Constant (1938); M. Boas (1952).
RE 5. 1; cf. M. Boas, *Rh. Mus.* (1917–18), *Die Epistola Catonis* (1934), and *Alcuin und Cato* (1937); O. Arngart, *Bull. Soc. Lettres Lund* (1951/2); L. Bieler, *Lustrum* 1957; B. Munk Olsen, *L'Étude des auteurs classiques latins . . .* (1982).   A. Schi.

dictator, an extraordinary supreme magistracy at Rome, used first in military, later in domestic crises.

In Latin cities we find the name 'dictator' given to a regular magistracy, but there is no evidence that this was ever Roman practice. As an emergency magistracy the dictatorship is found frequently in the annals of the Roman republic down to the end of the 3rd cent. BC; it was not used during the 2nd cent. but reappeared in a more powerful form, when granted to *Sulla and then *Caesar. Possible parallels are the *Oscan *meddix tuticus* and the *Etruscan *zilath* or *purth*, but there is no reason to derive the Roman office from them. Although Q. *Fabius Maximus Verrucosus is said to have been elected dictator in the *comitia centuriata* (Livy 22. 8), normally dictators were simply nominated in public by a magistrate with *imperium* (*consul, *praetor, or

interrex) after authorization by the senate—for Sulla and Caesar the authorization was provided by a law. The dictator's function was either to command the army or to perform a specific task, such as holding elections or dealing with a sedition. His 24 *lictores* indicated not so much a revival of the kingship, as *Appian *BCiv.* 1. 98–9 suggests, as a concentration of the powers of the consuls. The dictator (who was also known as *magister populi*, master of the infantry, and had to get permission to mount a horse while in office) immediately appointed a cavalry commander (*magister equitum*) as his subordinate. Existing magistrates remained in office but were generally subordinate to him. Originally dictators resigned as soon as their task was completed, being permitted at most to remain in office for six months. They were therefore not appropriate for emergency overseas commands, and specially chosen proconsuls were used instead (see PRO CONSULE). Contrary to the antiquarian tradition about the origin of the dictatorship, in the middle and later republic the dictator's actions were in theory exempt neither from veto (see INTERCESSIO) by the tribunes (Livy 27. 6. 5) nor from *provocatio (Livy 8. 33. 8). Nor was he himself free from prosecution after leaving office (*CIL* 1². 583. 8–9). Although after 202 BC no short-term dictators were appointed, it appears that this was contemplated in 54/3 BC, and in 52, on the senate's advice, *Pompey was created sole consul instead (senators apparently feared he might abuse dictatorial power). Both Sulla and Caesar, when they were appointed to this office in order to lend constitutional form to their *de facto* supremacy, were given the task of restoring the constitution. Cicero portrays L. *Cornelius Scipio Aemilianus dreaming that he would be appointed to a dictatorship with this function (*Rep.* 6. 12), and the anachronistic fiction suggests that in the 50s BC such a wide-ranging office was now acceptable to many of Cicero's readers. However, when Caesar was eventually appointed *dictator perpetuus*, this completely subverted the original notion of the dictatorship as an emergency office: it became a quasi-monarchy.

Mommsen, *Röm. Staatsr.* 2. 141 ff.; E. S. Staveley, *Hist.* 1956, 101 ff.   A. N. S.-W.; A. W. L.

Dictys Cretensis, supposed companion of *Idomeneus (1) at Troy and alleged author of an account of the Trojan War; fragments survive from a Greek version of the 2nd/3rd cent. AD (*PTeb.* 2. 268). The extant *Ephemeris belli Troiani* (*c.*4th cent. AD), relating the Troy-saga from *Cypria* to *Telegony* (see EPIC CYCLE), is a translation of this work, by one L. Septimius, and like *Dares of Phrygia was much read in the Greekless Middle Ages.

TEXT W. Eisenhut (Teubner, 2nd edn. 1973); S. Merkle, *Die Ephemeris Belli Troiani des Diktys von Kreta* (1989).   S. J. Ha.

didactic poetry, which was not regarded as a separate genre by either Greek or Roman theorists, embraces a number of poetic works (usually in hexameters) which aim to instruct the reader in a particular subject-matter, be it science, philosophy, hunting, farming, love, or some other art or craft. Didactic poems are normally addressed to a particular individual who is seen as the primary object of instruction and acts as a model for the reader. The text generally encourages the reader to identify with the addressee, though exceptions exist (e.g. Perses in *Hesiod's *Works and Days*). The boundaries and internal evolution of the genre are not always easy to determine. A rather clear distinction can be suggested between an older stage of didactic poetry, from *Hesiod (*Works and Days*, *Theogony*) down through the 5th cent. BC (*Parmenides, *Empedocles), which displays a strong concern for overall moral and philosophical instruction, and a later stage, prevalent in Hellenistic times, when didactic poetry preferably deals with specialized and at times obscure topics and appears to become a showcase of poetic dexterity (cf. e.g. *Nicander's *Theriaka*, on snakes; *Aratus (1)'s *Phaenomena*, on astronomy). A similar distinction can be observed in Latin, where *Lucretius—who boasts that he is the first didactic writer in Latin, though limited examples precede him (*Ennius' *Hedyphagetica*, *Accius' *Didascalica*)—emphatically connects his *De rerum natura* with 5th-cent. models, while some of his successors focus on more specialised topics (Germanicus *Iulius Caesar, M. *Manilius, *Grattius, *Columella). *Virgil's *Georgics*, apparently focusing on farming techniques, aspire in fact to the larger didactic purposes of Hesiod and *Lucretius. Didactic elements—which include specific forms of address, transition, and argumentation, often crystallized in quasi-formulaic expressions—are often present in works which are not primarily didactic, such as epistles or satires. In other cases, for instance *Ovid's *Ars amatoria*, the structure and style of didactic poetry is used with a quasi-parodic bent.

In addition to the authors mentioned above, see: DIONYSIUS (9) PERIEGETES; MANETHO; MARCELLUS; MENECRATES (2); OPPIAN; also AEMILIUS MACER; AVIENUS; CARMEN DE FIGURIS; CARMEN DE PONDERIBUS; NEMESIANUS; OVID; SERENUS, Q.; TERENTIANUS MAURUS; TULLIUS CICERO (1), M.; VARRO.

> R. Mynors, *OCD*[1], 277 ff.; W. Kroll, *RE* 12/2, 'Lehrgedicht'; B. Fabian, in H. R. Jauss (ed.), *Die nicht mehr schönen Künste* (1968); B. Effe, *Dichtung und Lehre* (1969); E. Pohlmann, *ANRW* 1. 3 (1973) (on Roman didactic poetry); R. M. Schuler and J. G. Fitch, *Florilegium* 1983 (history of theory); J. Clay and others (eds.), *Mega nepios*, *MP* 31 (on the addressee).   A. Schi.

Didascalia Apostolorum (*The Catholic Teaching of the Twelve Apostles of the Redeemer*), a Church order originally written in Greek, but completely preserved only in Syriac translation. It claims apostolic authorship, but was, in fact, written probably by a bishop in northern Syria in the first half of the 3rd cent. AD for a Gentile Christian community. Its principal aim is moral instruction and canonical regulation for the maintenance of the constitution and order of the Church. In addition, it is a valuable source for the history of Christian penance.

> Ed. A. Vööbus, in *Corpus Scriptorum Christianorum Orientalium*, Scriptores Syri vols. 175, 176, 179, 180 (Syriac text with Eng. trans.). P. Nautin in *EEC* 1 (1992), 235.   W. K.

didascaliae at Rome: production notices, preserved (sometimes incomplete) for *Plautus' *Stichus* and *Pseudolus* (in manuscript A) and for *Terence's plays (in the manuscripts and *Donatus (2)'s commentary). They give brief details of first performance, games at which performed, presiding magistrates, director, composer, type of musical accompaniment, Greek original, order of play in the author's works, and *consuls of the year; some details of later revivals seem to have been included. They were probably compiled in the 1st cent. BC.

> D. Klose, *Die Didaskalien und Prologe des Terenz* (Diss. Freiburg, 1966); H. D. Jocelyn, *CQ* 1980, 387 ff.   P. G. M. B.

didaskalia, lit. 'teaching', came to be used in ancient Greece as the standard term for the production of a performance at a dramatic festival. *Dithyrambs, *tragedies, satyr-plays (see SATYRIC DRAMA), and *comedies were all performances that entailed the 'teaching' (*didaskein*) of choruses; *didaskalia* denoted both the training of the chorus and actors and the production itself, whether of a single play or of a group, and eventually was applied to a poet's entire output. The plural *didaskaliai* was used

of the official list of productions staged at a particular festival; this is the sense in which modern scholars use the word. The keeping of such records by the *archontes* in charge of the festivals is probably as old as the institution of *chorēgia*.

The earliest sample of dramatic records inscribed on stone is *IG* 2[2]. 2318, dating from the 340s BC, which for each year's City *Dionysia gives the names of the archon, the winning tribe and *chorēgos* in the boys' and mens' dithyrambic chorus, and the victorious *chorēgos* and poet in comedy and tragedy, with the name of the victorious leading actor added after the introduction of the contest for the best actor in 449. The beginning of this inscription is missing: the earliest year listed is 473/2 BC, but the record probably went back to the late 6th cent.

*Aristotle, whose scholarly interest in chronology is well known, probably composed his lost books *Victories at the Dionysia* (or *Victories at the City Dionysia and the *Lenaea* according to Hesychius), *Didaskaliai*, and *On Tragedies* at Athens in the period 334–322 BC. He too must have drawn on the *archontes'* records, and his work must have been a source for the Alexandrian scholars who worked on drama and the festivals, particularly *Alexander (8) Aetolus, *Lycophron (2), *Callimachus (3), *Eratosthenes and *Aristophanes (2) of Byzantium. Some traces of this research are evident in the *hypotheseis* (see HYPOTHESIS, LITERARY) to some of the surviving plays. It is possible that Aristotle's work was also used as a source for some of the later inscriptions from Athens. The most important of these is *IG* 2[2]. 2319–23, from a building which may have been erected by an *agōnothetēs* (festival president) in 279/8 BC. It is a list, going back to the 5th cent., of tragedies and comedies at the City Dionysia and the Lenaea, which gives the name of the archon, the poets in order of success, and the title of each play with the name of the leading actor who took part in it. Fragments of *didaskaliai* from other cities and festivals have survived, and there are other types of list, e.g. giving names of poets or of actors; the evidence of all these, combined with information about *chorēgoi* and performers (including the *aulos*-players in the case of the dithyramb), offers valuable perspectives on the sociology and organization of the festivals.

> A. W. Pickard-Cambridge, *DFA*[3]; R. Pfeiffer, *History of Classical Scholarship* (1968); P. Ghiron-Bistagne, *Recherches sur les acteurs dans la Grèce Antique* (1976); H. J. Mette, *Urkunden Dramatischer Aufführungen in Griechenland* (1977); B. Snell and R. Kannicht, *TrGF* 1[2].
> A. W. P.-C.; P. E. E.

Didius (*RE* 5), **Titus**, probably a *novus homo* (see E. Badian, *Chiron* 1990, 404 f.), as tribune 103 BC vainly tried to veto his colleague C. *Norbanus' prosecution of Q. *Servilius Caepio (1). As praetor in Macedonia he conquered the Caeni in eastern Thrace (see M. Hassall and others, *JRS* 1974, 213) and triumphed 100 or 99. As consul 98 with Q. *Caecilius Metellus Nepos, he helped to pass the *lex Caecilia Didia* which, after the troubles of 100–98, consolidated the rules for valid legislation and gave the senate power to decide on validity. Among other provisions, an interval of three *nundinae* (market-days) had to pass between promulgation and the vote, and unrelated measures were not to be proposed in a single bill. Didius then commanded in Spain against the Celtiberians, and with the help of treacherous massacres gained the rare honour of a second triumph (93). A legate in the *Social War (3), he was killed in 89.   E. B.

Didius (*RE* 6; Suppl. 12 and 14) **Gallus, Aulus**, quaestor AD 19 and suffect consul 39, had a slow career that picked up under *Claudius, whom he may have accompanied to Britain. Legate (see LEGATI) of *Moesia c. AD 46, he conducted an expedition to the Tauric *Chersonesus (2), replacing Mithradates with Cotys as king of *Bosporus (2), for which he received *ornamenta triumphalia*. He was also *curator aquarum* and proconsul of Asia 49–50. Legate of *Britain 52–7/8, Didius made no noteworthy advance, though interfering with the *Brigantes, but maintained his predecessors' conquests against the *Silures, founding a fortress of Legio (*legion) XX at Usk. He was the adoptive parent of A. Didius Gallus *Fabricius Veiento.

> ILS 970 f.; AE 1947, 76; 1949, 11 (Smallwood, *Docs. . . . Gaius* 226, 310); U. Vogel-Weidemann, *Die Statthalter v. Africa u. Asia in den Jahren 14–68* (1982), 348 ff.; S. Frere, *Britannia*, 3rd edn. (1987), 66 ff.
>
> R. S.; B. M. L.

Didius (*RE* 8) **Severus Iulianus, Marcus,** Roman emperor in AD 193. Born in 133 to a Milan family, related through his mother to the jurist Salvius *Iulianus, he began a senatorial career with the patronage of M. *Aurelius' mother, rose to the consulate in 175, governing three imperial consular provinces and being proconsul of Africa. After the murder of *Helvius Pertinax on 28 March 193, he outbid the latter's father-in-law Sulpicianus in the 'auction' at the praetorian camp. His position as emperor was challenged at once by *Septimius Severus in Pannonia and *Pescennius Niger in Syria, and he was unpopular with the *plebs*. As Severus' army neared Rome, he was deserted on all sides and murdered in the palace on 2 June.

> Cass. Dio 73; Hdn. 2; SHA *Pertinax, Did. Iul., Sev., Pescennius Niger*. BM *Coins, Rom. Emp.* 5; A. R. Birley, *The African Emperor Septimius Severus*, 2nd edn. (1988).
>
> A. R. Bi.

Dido, legendary queen of *Carthage, daughter of a Phoenician king of Tyre, called Belus by *Virgil. According to *Timaeus (2), the earliest extant source for her story, her *Phoenician name was Elissa, and the name Dido ('wanderer') was given to her by the Libyans. Her husband, called Sychaeus by Virgil, was murdered by her brother *Pygmalion (2), now king of Tyre, and Dido escaped with some followers to Libya where she founded Carthage. In the earlier tradition, in order to escape marriage with a Libyan king (Iarbas in Virgil) Dido built a pyre as though for an offering and leapt into the flames. The story of the encounter of *Aeneas and Dido (chronologically difficult given the traditional dating of Carthage's foundation four centuries after the destruction of Troy) probably appeared in *Naevius' epic *Bellum Poenicum*. According to *Varro it was Dido's sister Anna who killed herself for love of Aeneas. In the classic version in the first and fourth books of Virgil's *Aeneid* Aeneas lands on the coast of Carthage after a storm and is led by Venus to Dido's new city; Dido's infatuated love for the stranger is consummated in a cave during a storm while they are hunting. Mercury (see MERCURIUS) descends to remind Aeneas of his mission to travel to Italy; as Aeneas departs obedient to the call of fate, Dido kills herself on top of a pyre that she has built. Her curse on the Trojans will eventually be fulfilled in the historical wars between Carthage and Rome. Many readers also detect a more recent historical allusion to the charms of *Cleopatra VII in the Virgilian Dido. She has enjoyed a vigorous after-life, in art, in literary reworkings from *Ovid, *Heroides* 7 through to Chaucer and Marlowe, and in numerous operas including Purcell's *Dido and Aeneas* and Berlioz's *Les Troyennes*. Her chastity has also been defended against Virgil by partisans including *Tertullian and Petrarch.

> For the sources see A. S. Pease, *Virgil: Aeneid* 4 (1935), 14 ff.; on the afterlife ibid. 60 ff. See also the articles by La Penna, Canciani, Graziosi, Piccirillo, and Sala in *Enc. Virg.* 2 (1985), 'Didone'.
>
> C. B.; P. R. H.

Didyma, oracular shrine of *Apollo (see ORACLES), located about 16 km. (10 mi.) south of *Miletus. In the Archaic period, it was administered by a priestly clan, the Branchidae, and rose to great prominence in the 6th cent. BC. Three prose oracular responses survive from this period, as does one dedication. In 494 the shrine was destroyed by *Darius I and the Branchidae themselves were exiled to Sogdiana.

The oracle was refounded in the time of *Alexander (3) the Great (probably in 331 BC), and rapidly re-emerged as an extremely important site. It made significant contact with the Seleucids, and, during the brief Ptolemaic control of Miletus, with the Ptolemies as well. (See PTOLEMY (1).) In the imperial period, it ranked with *Claros as one of the great oracular centres of Asia Minor.

Excavations have revealed a massive structure begun when the oracle was refounded. The total building measures 118×60 m. (129×66 yds.) at the *krēpidōma* (platform). A dipteral (double) Ionic colonnade contains 108 columns and a further 12 in the pronaos (forecourt). The western wall of the pronaos is broken by an 8-m. (26-ft.)-wide entrance raised 1.5 m. (5 ft.) above the floor of the pronaos. The cella (roofed chamber) contains two Ionic columns to support the roof, and opens on the north and south sides to small chambers containing staircases, which may have given access to a terrace at the level of the cella roof. The western end of the cella is pierced by three doors leading to a great staircase giving access to the adytum or innermost sanctuary (never roofed). Within the adytum there is a small *naiskos* (chapel) surrounding the sacred spring. The priestess gave her oracles here.

Oracles could be given on only a limited number of days. The maximum was once every four days, and the interval was probably far greater—possibly some months (Men. Rhet. 336). The session itself began with a three-day fast by the prophetess, during which time she apparently resided in the adytum (Iambl. *Myst.* 3. 11). On the appointed day, the prophetess would take a ritual bath and enter the *naiskos*, while those who wished to put questions to her sacrificed outside and choruses sang hymns to the gods. Within the *naiskos*, the prophetess sat on an axle suspended over the sacred spring and, when a question was put to her, she would dip her foot (or her dress) into the spring, but not drink from it, before giving her answer. These answers would probably have been in prose and would then have been turned into verse by the priests. The priests were appointed by the city of Miletus.

Didyma's fate seems to have been sealed by an oracle given in AD 303, advising *Diocletian to initiate his empire-wide persecution of the Christian church (Lactant. *De mortibus persecutorum* 11; Euseb. *Vita Constantini* 2.50). *Constantine I closed the oracle, and executed the priests; it appears not to have functioned thereafter. A number of responses from the imperial period have, however, been discovered on inscriptions and in literary sources (of which the most important is the *Tübingen Theosophy* ed. H. Erbse, *Fragmente griechischer Theosophien* (1941), 167–85).

> H. Erbse, *Fragmente griechischer Theosophien* (1941); A. Rehm and R. Harder, *Didyma 2: Die Inschriften* (1958); W. Günther, *Das Orakel von Didyma in hellenistischer Zeit* (1971); L. Robert, *OMS 5*, (1989), 584–616; H. Parke, *The Oracles of Apollo in Asia Minor* (1985); J. Fontenrose, *Didyma: Apollo's Oracle, Cult and Companions* (1988); P. Athanasiadi, Δελτίον τῆς Χριστιανικῆς Ἀρχαιολοκικῆς Ἑταιρείας 1989–90; C. Morgan, *Hermathena* 1989. The inscriptions of Didyma are available on the *TLG*.
>
> D. S. P.

Didymus (1) (1st cent. BC) belonged to the school founded at *Alexandria (1) by *Aristarchus (2) and himself taught there. A scholar of immense learning and industry (cf. his nicknames Χαλκέντερος ('Brazen-bowels') and Βιβλιολάθας ('Book-forgetting'), the latter because of occasional self-contradictions due to his having forgotten what he had said in earlier books), he is said to have written 3,500 or 4,000 works. His importance for literary history consists primarily in his compilation of the critical and exegetical work of earlier scholars. He was not an original researcher, but rather a variorum editor and a transmitter of learning that might otherwise have been lost. He was criticized by some later scholars, e.g. *Harpocration.

Works 1. He discussed Aristarchus' recension of the Homeric text by comparing copies and by examining Aristarchus' commentaries and special treatises. His results were much used by the scholiasts. 2. Commentaries, with abundant mythological, geographical, historical, and biographical information, on *Homer, *Hesiod, *Pindar, *Bacchylides, *Choerilus(1), *Aeschylus, *Sophocles (1), *Ion (2), *Euripides, *Achaeus (3), *Cratinus, *Aristophanes (1), *Phrynichus (1), *Eupolis, *Menander (1), *Thucydides (2), *Antiphon (1), *Isaeus (1), *Isocrates, *Aeschines (1), *Demosthenes (2), *Hyperides, *Dinarchus. Much of the oldest material in the scholia to Pindar, Sophocles, Euripides, and Aristophanes is ultimately derived from Didymus. A papyrus fragment of his commentary on Demosthenes' *Philippics* illustrates his compilatory method; the quality of the discussion leaves a great deal to be desired. 3. Lexicography: Λέξεις τραγικαί and Λέξεις κωμικαί ('tragic expressions', 'comic expressions'). These collections formed a valuable source for scholiasts and lexicographers, e.g. Hesychius. *On Corrupt Expressions, On Expressions of Doubtful Meaning, Metaphorical Expressions, On Proverbs,* a chief source of the extant works of the *paroemiographers. 4. Grammar: *On Orthography, On Analogy among the Romans, On Inflexions.* 5. Literature and antiquities: *On Lyric Poets,* Ξένη ἱστορία (on myths and legends), *Sympotic Miscellany* (Σύμμικτα συμποσιακά), *On the Axones of *Solon,* works on the death of *Aeneas, the birthplace of Homer, etc., and a polemic against *Cicero, *Rep.,* which was answered by *Suetonius; but this last may be by his namesake *Claudius Didymus (2).

M. Schmidt, *Didymi Chalcenteri grammatici Alexandrini fragmenta* (1854); A. Ludwich, *Aristarchs homerische Textkritik* (1884–5); H. Diels and W. Schubart, *Didymus' Kommentar zu Demosthenes* (1904) (new edition by L. Pearson and S. Stephens (Teubner, 1983)); R. Pfeiffer, *History of Classical Scholarship: From the Beginnings to the End of the Hellenistic Age* (1968), 274–9; S. West, *CQ* 1970, 288–96.   J. F. L.; R. B.; N. G. W.

Didymus (2), **Claudius,** the Younger (1st cent. AD), an Atticist lexicographer, wrote on the incorrect diction of *Thucydides (2) (Περὶ τῶν ἡμαρτημένων παρὰ τὴν ἀναλογίαν Θουκυδίδῃ), abridged the *Attic Lexicon* of Heracleon of Ephesus, and wrote a monograph comparing Latin with Greek.   P. B. R. F.

Didymus (3) (*RE* 11), 'the musician', author of significant writings on harmonics. (See MUSIC § 5.) His novel techniques on the monochord and his original, rather straightforward tetrachordal divisions are closely criticized by Ptolemy (*Harm.* 2. 13–14). *Porphyry quotes extensive passages (*On Ptolemy's Harmonics* 26. 6–29, 27. 17–28. 26) on distinctions between schools of harmonic theory, developed elaborately from the female musician *Ptolemaïs, and cites Didymus as authority for a report known to Ptolemy (*Harm.* 1. 6), originating with *Archytas, about early Pythagorean procedures. He may be responsible for much of Ptolemy's Archytan material. He is perhaps the *Suda*'s Didymus

son of Heraclides, a grammarian and eminent musician of Neronian times.   A. D. B.

diekplous (διέκπλους), a Greek naval term meaning 'a sailing through and out', is used by ancient authors to describe a common manœuvre in which individual ships, sailing together in line abreast, would attempt to break through a line of enemy ships in similar formation. The purpose was to achieve a better position from which to attack the vulnerable flanks of opposing warships. It could be counteracted by forming circles (Thuc. 2. 83), by deepening the formation with extra lines of ships (Xen. *Hell.* 1. 6. 29–31), or by inserting smaller vessels in the gaps between the main warships (Polyb. 16. 4. 8–10). See NAVIES; SHIPS; TRIREME.

H. T. Wallinga, *The Boarding-Bridge of the Romans* (1956); J. F. Lazenby, *G&R* 1987.   P. de S.

dietetics Many ancient medical authorities believed that therapeutic medicine had its origins in the gradual discovery of connections between health and the regulation of one's day-to-day life (δίαιτα). A group of treatises in the Hippocratic corpus (see HIPPOCRATES (2)) is concerned specifically with the study of the living-patterns of both sick and healthy. By the time *Celsus wrote the preface to his treatise *On Medicine,* dietetics had long been established as one of the three main branches of therapeutics, along with *surgery and *pharmacology. Traditionally, Herodicus of Selymbria, a gymnastic trainer, was credited with recognizing the connections between regimen and both health and illness; dietetics was originally thought to have developed in the context of the regulation of life for those training for the games (see Pl. *Resp.* 406a).

Hippocratic dietetic strategy involved the doctor with the healthy as much as the sick. Certain activities were known to be risky, and were thus to be discouraged—too much sex, drinking, reading, inactivity, massage, and so on. Doctors were encouraged to observe with great care all the factors, both internal and external, which might influence the body for good or ill.

This empirical model, however, was not taken by all at face value. Dietetic analysis of disease often meant investigating more or less theoretically the qualities of different types of *food. One dominant medical theory had it that health was a balance of certain factors in the body; an imbalance could be rectified by administering food with the opposite quality. Certain foods were thought to have certain qualities—*honey, for example, is hot and dry according to the author of the Hippocratic treatise *On Regimen,* and can therefore be used to counter the opposite conditions. Theoretical ideas about the pathogenic consequences of imbalance, repletion and depletion, hot, cold, and so on, were widely understood against the background of the idea that 'opposites cure opposites'. Such thinking led to the elaboration of taxonomies of therapeutically important foodstuffs.

The Hippocratic foundations of dietetics—both empirical and theoretical—were important throughout antiquity, even if dietetic ideals appealed in different ways to different societies. Many doctors and writers on gymnastic training continued to develop the subject, including *Galen (*On the Preservation of Health*) and Philostratus (*On Gymnastics*) (see PHILOSTRATI). Several dozen brief *Precepts of Health* survive.

L. Edelstein, *Die Antike* 1931, 255–70 (trans. in L. Edelstein, *Ancient Medicine* (1967)); I. M. Lonie, *Medical History* 1977, 235–60.   J. T. V.

Dieuchidas, of Megara (4th cent. BC) wrote a history of *Megara in at least five books, in which he credits *Solon more than *Pisistratus with establishing the text of *Homer (F 6).

FGrH 485; L. Piccirilli, Μεγαρικά: Testimonianze e Frammenti (1975).
K. S. S.

differentiae, distinctions between words of similar meaning (e.g. *metus, pavor*) formulated by rhetoricians and grammarians to foster precise diction. The drawing of such distinctions can be traced back through the Stoics (see STOICISM) to the early *sophists; Roman interest in the practice appears already in the fragments of *Accius and *Lucilius (1), the *Rhetorica ad Herennium, and *Varro's De lingua latina. Many *differentiae* were discussed by miscellanists (e.g. Aulus *Gellius), by lexicographers (*Verrius Flaccus, *Nonius Marcellus), and by grammarians. Anonymous compilations were sometimes attributed to great names (*Differentiae Suetonii, Diff. Palaemonis*, etc.), and many items were incorporated in glossaries. Alleged *differentiae*, however, often do not correspond to the actual usage of Latin authors.

M. Uhlfelder, De proprietate sermonum vel rerum (1954); G. Brugnoli, Studie sulle differentiae verborum (1955); G. Moretti, Studi Noniani 1984, 179–203.
R. A. K.

digesta See JUSTINIAN'S CODIFICATION.

Diipolieia See DIPOLIEIA.

dikastēria See DEMOCRACY, ATHENIAN; LAW AND PROCEDURE, ATHENIAN, § 2.

Dike (1), personification of Justice, daughter of *Zeus and *Themis, and one of the *Horae, with *Eunomia and *Eirene (Hes. *Theog.* 901–3). She reports men's wrongdoing to Zeus (Hes. *Op.* 256–62), and sits beside him (Aesch. fr. 281a Radt; Soph. *OC* 1381–2, Orph. fr. 23 Kern). In *Aratus (1) (*Phaen.* 96–136) and Roman poets she is the *constellation Virgo or Astraea, who left the earth when the bronze age began (cf. Verg. *Ecl.* 4. 6, *G.* 2. 473–4; Ov. *Met.* 1. 149–50). In Archaic art she punishes Injustice (e.g. chest of *Cypselus, Paus. 5. 18. 2), and later she is shown with a sword in Underworld scenes.

Waser, RE 5. 574–8; H. A. Shapiro, LIMC 3/1. 388–91; R. Hirzel, Themis, Dike und Verwandtes (1907), 58 ff.; H. A. Shapiro, 'Personification of Abstract Concepts in Greek Art and Literature to the End of the Fifth Century BC' (Diss. Princeton, 1976).
N. J. R.

dike (2) (= Case at Law). See LAW AND PROCEDURE, ATHENIAN, § 3.

Dillius (*RE* 2) **Vocula, Gaius,** from *Corduba in Spain, was legate of Legio (*legion) XXII Primigenia in Upper Germany in AD 69. Entrusted by the governor, Hordeonius Flaccus, with the operations against C. *Iulius Civilis, he relieved *Vetera (Xanten) in Lower Germany but had to retreat to defend his own camp at *Mogontiacum (Mainz). He faced dissension among his depleted forces, who were unwilling to accept *Vespasian as emperor, and in spring 70 was murdered at Novaesium (Neuss) by a Roman deserter suborned by *Iulius Classicus. His wife, Helvia Procula, honoured him with a dedication in Rome recording his career (ILS 983).
J. B. C.

Dinarchus (Δείναρχος) (c.360–c.290 BC), the last of the Ten *Attic Orators (for the formation of the *canon, see CAECILIUS (1)). For the outline of his life we largely depend on *Dionysius (7) of Halicarnassus On Dinarchus, chs. 2, 3, and 9. He was born at *Corinth but went to Athens to study rhetoric under *Theophrastus and from 336/5 on constantly and successfully practised the profession of speech-writer (logographos). As a *metic, he was barred from a political career nor was he able

himself to speak in court, but when after the *Lamian War the leading orators of the age, *Demosthenes (2) and *Hyperides, had met their deaths, Dinarchus was left in unchallenged and lucrative supremacy and the period of rule by *Demetrius (3) of Phalerum, his friend and patron, was his heyday. When Demetrius had to retire from Athens at the coming of *Demetrius (4) Poliorcetes in 307/6, Dinarchus, suspect for his wealth and perhaps even more his friendship with 'those who dissolved the democracy' (FGrH 328 F 66), deemed it expedient to remove to Chalcis and stayed there awaiting the opportunity to return. This was negotiated for him by Theophrastus in 292. With his eyesight failing, he stayed with his friend Proxenus, against whom he shortly filed a suit for the recovery of money lost in the house, the only time in Dinarchus' life that he appeared in court. That is the last we hear of him.

Dionysius knew of 87 speeches ascribed to Dinarchus of which he pronounced 60 genuine. We possess only three which scholars agree in assigning to him—*Against Demosthenes, Against Aristogiton,* and *Against Philocles,* all concerned with the investigations into the disappearance of the money deposited in Athens by *Harpalus (324/3). Three of Dionysius' list are to be found in the Demosthenic Corpus (*Orationes* 45, 46, 58; cf. DEMOSTHENES (2)), but scholars have been disinclined to ascribe them to Dinarchus.

Dinarchus marks the beginning of the decline in Attic oratory. He had little originality, except some skill in the use of new metaphors; he imitated his predecessors, especially Demosthenes (Hermogenes, *Id.* 2. 11 calls him κριθινὸς Δημοσθένης, 'a small-beer Demosthenes'), but developed no characteristic style of his own. He knew the technique of prose composition and had command of all the tricks of the orator's trade. He was competent up to a point, but his work is careless and lacking in taste. Thus, the arrangement of his speeches is incoherent; his sentences are long and formless, certain figures of speech, e.g. epanalepsis and asyndeton, are ridden to death, and his invective is so exaggerated as to become meaningless. Numerous minor *plagiarisms are collected by Blass (*Att. Ber.*² 3. 2. 318–21); in particular, a passage about *Thebes (1) in *Demos.* 24 is based on Aeschin. 1. 133, and *Aristog.* 24 is suggested by Dem. 9. 41.

For general bibliography see ATTIC ORATORS.

TEXT Conomis (Teubner, 1975); with trans.: J. O. Burtt, Minor Attic Orators 2 (Loeb, 1954); L. Dors-Méary (Budé, 1990).
COMMENT I. Worthington, A Historical Commentary on Dinarchus: Rhetoric and Conspiracy in later Fourth-Century Athens (1992).
G. L. C.

dining-rooms Reclining on couches while dining was introduced in Greece from the near east, probably around 700 BC. Special rooms were built to accommodate the couches along the lengths of the wall, often on a slightly raised plinth. Floors are durable (cement or mosaic), presumably to allow for swabbing down. Each couch had a low table alongside. Such rooms are referred to by the number of couches they held. Eleven is a frequent number, the resulting dimensions (c.6.3 m. (21 ft.) square) thus giving a reasonable size for general conversation across the room. Dining-rooms in private houses are generally small, those for ritual feasting in *sanctuaries may be larger or very large halls for over 100 couches.

In later Hellenistic times the arrangement called *triclinium* developed. Three large couches in a *pi* (Π) arrangement, each for three diners with head to centre, feet to the outside, making conversation easier. This system was adopted by the Romans. Each couch had its significance: the left couch was the lowest in rank where the family would dine, the host at the top (i.e. on the left); the guests would recline on the other two, the middle one (next to the host) being more honourable: the place on the right was the position of chief honour (*locus consularis*, see Plut. *Mor.* 619 a and f). See CONVIVIUM; MEALS; PALACES; SYMPOSIUM; THOLOS.

J. M. Dentzer, *Le Motif de banquet couché dans le proche-orient et le monde grec du VII au IV siècle avant J-C* (1982); C. Borker, *Festbankett und griechische Architektur* (1983); O. Murray (ed.), *Sympotica* (1990).

R. A. T.

Dinon (or **Deinon**), of Colophon, Greek historian who lived in the 4th cent. BC, father of the Alexander-historian *Cleitarchus (*FGrH* 690 T 2; see ALEXANDER (3) THE GREAT); author of a *Persica* in at least three *syntaxeis* (= parts), each of which contained several books and covered the history of *Persia down to the reconquest of Egypt by *Artaxerxes (3) III Ochos in 343/2 (F 2). The narrative's emphasis is on the romantic, and is sensational in the manner of *Ctesias (cf. e.g. F 10, 17, 22). It was used by *Plutarch in his *Artaxerxes* and by other writers.

FGrH 690. R. Stevenson in H. Sancisi–Weerdenburg and A. Kuhrt (eds.), *Achaemenid History* 2 (1987), 27 ff.; O. Lendle, *Einführung in die griechische Geschichtsschreibung* (1992) 271.

K. M.

Dio (Cassius), historian. See CASSIUS DIO.

Dio Cocceianus, later called Chrysostom (*c.*AD 40/50–after 110), Greek orator and popular philosopher. Born of a wealthy family in Prusa in Bithynia, Dio began a career as a rhetorician at Rome, but soon fell under the spell of the Stoic philosopher C. *Musonius Rufus (see STOICISM). Involved in a political intrigue early in the reign of *Domitian, he was banished (*relegatus*) both from Rome and from his native province, and spent many years travelling through Greece, the Balkans, and Asia Minor as a wandering preacher of Stoic-*Cynic philosophy. Rehabilitated by *Nerva, he became a friend of *Trajan, but continued to travel widely as an epideictic orator. He later retired to his family estates in *Bithynia and became a notable in the province (he figures in the *Letters* of *Pliny (2) as the defendant in a prosecution arising out of a public building contract).

Of the 80 speeches attributed to him, two are actually the work of his pupil *Favorinus. Many are display-speeches, but others, e.g. those delivered before the assembly and council at Prusa, deal with real situations. His themes are varied: mythology, the Stoic-Cynic ideal monarch, literary criticism, popular morality, funeral orations, rhetorical descriptions, addresses to cities, etc. He sees himself as a teacher of his fellow men, and his stock ideas are the Stoic concepts of φύσις ('nature'), ἀρετή ('virtue'), and φιλανθρωπία ('philanthropy'). His language and style are Atticist (see ASIANISM AND ATTICISM), though he avoids the extreme archaism of some representatives of the *Second Sophistic, and often aims at an easy, almost conversational style, suggestive of improvisation. *Plato (1) and *Xenophon (1) are his main models. Dio idealizes the Hellenic past, and feels himself the heir to a long classical tradition, which he seeks to revive and preserve. His Stoic-Cynic philosophy has lost its erstwhile revolutionary *élan*, and become essentially conservative, though he still insists on the philosopher's right to free speech and criticism. His Greek patriotism is in no way anti-Roman. Like his contemporary *Plutarch, he reflects the attitudes and culture of the upper classes of the eastern half of the empire, who were beginning to reach out to a share in political power. He gives a vivid and detailed picture of the life of his times.

TEXT H. von Arnim (1893–6); G. de Budé (1915–19); with trans. J. W. Cohoon, H. L. Crosby, 5 vols., (Loeb, 1932–51).
CONCORDANCE R. Koolmeister and T. Tallmeister (1981).

STUDIES C. P. Jones, *The Roman World of Dio Chrysostom* (1978); P. Desideri, *Dione di Prusa, un intellettuale greco nell'impero romano* (1978).

R. B.; N. G. W.

Diocles (1) (*RE* 33), *Syracusan popular leader, *c.*413–408 BC; apparently confused in antiquity with an Archaic lawgiver of the same name. He revised the constitution (412), replacing *politeia* (restricted democracy) by radical democracy. As general in 409 he failed to assist *Selinus (mod. Selinunte) against the Carthaginians; he was defeated at *Himera, which he abandoned to Hannibal. Probably responsible for the banishment of *Hermocrates, he opposed his recall and was himself banished (408).

B. Caven, *Dionysius I* (1990), 24–43.

B. M. C.

Diocles (2), Athenian comic poet, 'contemporary of *Sannyrion and *Philyllius' according to the *Suda*, i.e. *c.*400 BC. We have six titles and seventeen citations. He was also credited with the invention of a percussion instrument.

Kassel–Austin, *PCG* 5. 18 ff. (*CAF* 1. 766 ff.).

K. J. D.

Diocles (3) (*RE* 53), physician from Carystus on *Euboea; in several ancient medical canons (e.g. Vindicianus, *De med.* 2, fr. 2 Wellmann) he is placed second in fame only to *Hippocrates (2). His writings survive only in quotations, and there are serious problems of attribution in the case of certain fragments. Diocles was perhaps a contemporary of *Aristotle (*c.*384–322 BC) but his dates are highly controversial and the nature of his intellectual relationship to Aristotle and the Lyceum even more so. *Galen claims that he wrote the first anatomical handbook (2. 282 Kühn, fr. 23 W); he also wrote influential works on physiology, aetiology, medical semiotics and prognostics, *dietetics, and *botany (see also ANATOMY AND PHYSIOLOGY). His practice was no less famous than his theory; a type of bandage for the head was named after him, as was a cunning spoon-like device for the removal of arrowheads. The relative sophistication of Diocles' method is evident in an unusual fragment preserved by Galen (6. 455 Kühn, fr. 112 W), where he seems to be arguing for more flexibility in the assignment of pathological effects to given causes on the ground that the mere presence of a certain smell, substance, or other quality does not necessitate uniform reactions in all parts of the body or in all patients. Galen praises him for his appreciation of the importance of practical experience, even in the light of his commitment to theory—a theory which advocated a cardiocentric view of intelligence, and attributed the management of the body to the interactions of the four qualities hot, cold, dry, and moist (fr. 8 W).

TEXTS M. Wellmann, *Die Fragmente der sikelischen Ärtze* (1901); W. Jaeger, *Abh. der preussischen Akademie der Wissenschaften*, phil.-hist. Kl. 1938. 3, 1–46. See also G. A. Gerhard, *Sitz. der Heidelberger Akademie der Wissenschaften*, phil.-hist. Kl. 1913, 13. New edition in preparation by P. van der Eijk.
LITERATURE W. Jaeger, *Diokles von Karystos* (1938; repr. 1963). Recent speculation about Diocles' date is reviewed, with references to earlier work, by H. von Staden, *Herophilus: The Art of Medicine in Early Alexandria* (1989), 44–6. The nature of Diocles' relation to the Lyceum is examined by H. von Staden, in W. M. Calder III (ed.), *Werner Jaeger Reconsidered* (1992).

J. T. V.

Diocles (4) (*RE* 55) mathematician (*c.*200 BC), wrote Περὶ πυρείων ('On Burning-Mirrors'), preserved in Arabic translation. This treats both spherical and parabolic mirrors (giving the first proof of the focal property of the parabola). The second part of the work is concerned with (*a*) solving a problem of *Archimedes by means of intersecting conics; (*b*) solving the problem of finding two mean proportionals ('doubling the cube') by intersecting conics; (*c*) the same by means of a special curve (misnamed 'cissoid' in modern times). Paraphrases of the last three are given by Eutocius (*In Arch. circ. dim.* 160 ff., 82 ff., 66 ff.).

Text (including Eutocius' versions), transl., and comm., with the evidence for Diocles' date, G. J. Toomer, *Diocles On Burning Mirrors* (1976).

G. J. T.

Diocles (5) (*RE* 50), of *Magnesia (1 or 2), mid to late 1st cent. BC, historian of philosophy. Diocles' two attested works, the doxographical *Survey of the Philosophers* (᾿Επιδρομὴ τῶν φιλοσόφων) and the biographical *Lives of the Philosophers* (Βίοι τῶν φιλοσόφων) were a major source for *Diogenes Laertius, whose entire account of Stoic dialectic (7. 49–82) has been thought to derive from the former.

U. Egli, *Das Diokles-Fragment bei Diogenes Laertios* (1981); J. Mansfeld, *Elenchos* 1986, 295 ff.

D. N. S.

Diocles (6), Greek rhetor (orator) of the *Augustan age, whose declamations betrayed moderate Asianist tendencies (see ASIANISM AND ATTICISM).

Sen. *Controv.* 7. 1. 26, 8. 15 f., 10. 5. 26, etc. H. Borneque, *Les Déclamations* (1902), 165.

M. B. T.

Diocles (7), of Peparethos, historian, probably of the 3rd cent. BC and a source for Q. *Fabius Pictor, who followed Diocles in his account of the foundation of Rome.

FGrH 820; A. Momigliano, *Secondo contributo*, 403, and *CAH* 7^2/2 (1989), 89; Fraser, *Ptol. Alex.* 2. 1076 n. 373.

S. H.

Diocletian (Gaius Aurelius Valerius (*RE* 142) **Diocletianus)**, originally named Diocles. Of obscure origins, born in Dalmatia perhaps in the early 240s AD, he rose to command the *domestici* (bodyguard) of the emperor *Numerianus on the Persian campaign of 283–4. When Numerianus was killed by his praetorian prefect Aper, the army proclaimed Diocles Augustus at *Nicomedia (20 November 284); he killed Aper. He campaigned (285) against Numerianus' brother Carinus, who was killed at Margus. A usurper Iulianus was also removed, and Diocletian was sole emperor. Visiting Italy, he proclaimed his comrade-in-arms *Maximian as Caesar and sent him to suppress the *Bacaudae. Maximian was made Augustus (286) and spent the next years defending Gaul. Diocletian spent most of his reign on the Danube or in the east. In 287 he installed Tiridates III as king of Armenia and reorganized the Syrian frontier. He campaigned on the Raetian frontier (288); he fought the Sarmatians (285 or 289), and the Saracens (290).

But the problems of the empire remained serious. On 1 March 293 he established the '*tetrarchy'. To the two Augusti, now known as Iovius and Herculius respectively to emphasize their quasi-divine authority, were added Caesars, *Constantius (1) and *Galerius; these were adopted into the Jovian or Herculian houses by the marriage of Galerius to Diocletian's daughter Valeria and of Constantius to Maximian's (?step-)daughter Theodora. The arrangement would provide an imperial presence in different areas; it might deter usurpers; and the Caesars might become acceptable to the armies and live to succeed as Augusti (but it is most unlikely that the Augusti had yet planned to abdicate). To raise the dignity of the imperial office Diocletian adopted an oriental court ceremonial (*adoratio*) and seclusion. Each tetrarch had his own staff (*comitatus*), and was often on the move in his territory, though *Nicomedia, Trier (*Augusta Treverorum), and *Sirmium often provided an imperial residence; Rome was of lesser importance. In practice the empire was

divided into two; Maximian and Constantius ruled the west, Diocletian and Galerius the east. Diocletian employed Galerius in Oriens until 299, thereafter on the Danube (see DANUVIUS). Diocletian defeated the Sarmatians (294, see SARMATAE) and campaigned against the Carpi (296); many *Bastarnae and Carpi were settled on Roman soil. In Egypt a revolt broke out (297) under Domitianus and Aurelius Achilleus; present in person, Diocletian suppressed this after a long siege of *Alexandria (1), reorganized the administration of *Egypt, and negotiated with the Nobatae on the extreme southern frontier (298). Meanwhile he had sent Galerius to deal with the situation on the Syrian frontier: the Persian king *Narses had expelled Tiridates from *Armenia. Though defeated in his first campaign, Galerius won a total victory (298) and added significant territories to the empire. Campaigning by Constantius continued on the Rhine, but from 298 there was a general lull in rebellions and wars; tetrarchic authority was secure.

Diocletian pursued systematically a long-established policy of dividing provinces into smaller units; by 314 there were about 100, twice the number of a century earlier (see PROVINCIA). The purpose was to ensure a closer supervision, particularly over law and finance, by governors and their numerous staffs; critics saw it as leading to never-ending condemnations and confiscations. All provinces were governed by equestrian *praesides* except Asia and Africa (by senatorial proconsuls) and the divisions of Italy (by *correctores*). To oversee the *praesides*, Diocletian grouped the provinces into twelve new 'dioceses' (see DIOECESIS), each under a new equestrian official, the *vicarius* or 'deputy' of the praetorian prefects. In the later part of his reign, Diocletian began an important reform, separating military from civil power in frontier provinces; groups of provincial armies were put under the command of *duces* (see DUX), so that *praesides* were left with civilian duties only. Senators remained excluded from military commands. His conception of defence was conservative; he made little or no effort to increase the size of the élite field army (*comitatus*), which had been formed in the late 3rd cent. But a huge programme of building and reconstruction of defensive works was undertaken on all frontiers, and these were to be held by sheer force of numbers; the size of the Roman army was perhaps nearly doubled.

The army and the increase of administrative personnel were a heavy financial burden. Diocletian reformed the system of taxation to take inflation into account and to regularize exactions in kind. Taxation was now based on the *iugum*, a new concept, a unit of land calculated from its productivity as much as by its area, and on the *caput*, the unit of human resource. Most revenue and expenditure was now in kind; every year an assessment of all levies payable on each fiscal unit was declared (*indictio) by the praetorian prefects. By the Currency Edict (301) Diocletian attempted to create a unified currency, doubling the value of at least some coins and decreeing that the retariffed currency be used both for paying debts to the *fiscus* and in private contracts. But he could not establish confidence in this revaluation. Late in 301 he tried to halt inflation by the Price Edict. In great detail this fixed maximum prices and wages; despite savage penalties it became a dead letter, as goods disappeared from the market.

Many legal decisions show Diocletian's concern to maintain or resuscitate Roman law in the provinces. He was an enthusiast for what he understood of Roman tradition and discipline, to reinforce imperial unity: hence he decreed the suppression of the Manichees (see MANICHAEISM). This policy forms the backdrop to the persecution of Christians, undertaken possibly on the insistence of Galerius. (See CHRISTIANITY.) Earlier attempts had been made to purge the court and the army, but the first persecuting edict, issued at Nicomedia (23 February 303), was designed to prevent the Church from functioning, by requiring the burning of Scriptures and the demolition of churches, and the banning of meetings for worship; recusants were deprived of any rank, and thus made liable to torture and summary execution and prevented from taking action in court; imperial freedmen were re-enslaved. In Gaul and Britain Constantius contented himself with demolishing churches, and the later edicts were not promulgated outside the areas controlled by Diocletian and Galerius. The second edict imprisoned all clergy; the third released them, but they were to sacrifice first. The fourth edict ordered a universal sacrifice, but implementation was patchy, most severe it seems in Palestine and Egypt.

Late in 303 Diocletian visited Rome for the only time, to celebrate with Maximian his *vicennalia* (the 20th anniversary of his accession). A collapse in health caused him to return to Nicomedia, where on 1 May 305 he abdicated (Maximian reluctantly did the same at Milan), leaving Constantius and Galerius as Augusti, with Flavius Valerius *Severus and C. Galerius Valerius *Maximinus as Caesars. He attended Galerius' conference at Carnuntum (308) but refused to reassume the purple and spent his last years at *Salonae; remains of the palace he built survive. He died about 312. His wife Prisca and only child Valeria were exiled by Maximinus and beheaded by Valerius Licinianus *Licinius. Diocletian's genius was as an organizer; his measures did much to preserve the empire in the 4th cent., and many lasted much longer in the east. The tetrarchy as such broke down when Diocletian's personality was removed, but for most of the 4th cent. more than one emperor was the rule. His reforms were completed by *Constantine (1) I, who introduced further innovations, most notably in the army and in religion.

Jones, *Later Rom. Emp.*; T. D. Barnes, *The New Empire of Diocletian and Constantine* (1982); S. Williams, *Diocletian and the Roman Recovery* (1985); F. Kolb, *Diocletian und die erste Tetrarchie* (1987).   R. P. D.

Diodorus (1) (*RE* 'Diodoros' 36), of *Sinope, New Comedy poet (see COMEDY (GREEK), NEW), brother of *Diphilus; a family monument (*IG* 2². 10321) suggests that he became an Athenian citizen. He had two plays produced at the *Lenaea of 284 BC (*IG* 2². 2319. 61, 63 = 3 C 2 14, 16 Mette), and may have been a comic actor at Delos in 284 and 280 (*IG* 11. 105. 21, 107. 20 = 2 D 1a 21, 1c 20 Mette). Fr. 2: the *parasite's divine rites.

FRAGMENTS Kassel–Austin, PCG 5. 25–30.
INTERPRETATION Meineke, *FCG* 1 418 f.; G. Kaibel, *RE* 5/1 (1903), 661 f.; G. M. Sifakis, *Studies in the History of Hellenistic Drama* (1967), 26; T. B. L. Webster, *Studies in Later Greek Comedy*, 2nd edn. (1970), 152.   W. G. A.

Diodorus (2) (*RE* 'Diodoros' 42) **Cronus**, of *Iasus (died *c.*284 BC), virtuoso dialectician and leading member of the Dialectical school (see MEGARIAN SCHOOL). His pupils included the logician *Philon (6), the founder of Stoicism *Zeno (2), and his own five daughters. His work combined the dialectical traditions founded by *Zeno (1) of Elea and by *Socrates. He was active in both Athens and *Alexandria (1), and profoundly influenced Hellenistic philosophy. His nickname 'Cronus', inherited from his teacher Apollonius Cronus, meant 'Old Fogey'.

His 'master argument' (κυριεύων λόγος), which established his definition of 'possible' as 'what is or will be true', set the terms of the Hellenistic debate about modality (see Cic. *Fat.*).

He gave his own account of a valid conditional, as one which neither was nor is able to have a true antecedent and a false consequent.

In the tradition of Zeno of Elea, he offered four arguments against motion. Two of them exploited his own hypothesis that space and time consist of discrete 'minimal and partless' units. His conclusion was that nothing 'is moving', although things can be said to 'have moved'.

He defended a theory of word-meaning as purely conventional, which he illustrated by changing a slave's name to Ἀλλὰ μήν, 'However'. He also elaborated, and perhaps tried to solve, logical paradoxes like the Sorites and the Liar.

FRAGMENTS G. Giannantoni, *Socratis et Socraticorum Reliquiae* (1990), 1. 413 ff.
COMMENT D. Sedley *PCPS* 1977, 74 ff.   D. N. S.

Diodorus (3) of Agyrium, Sicily (hence **Diodorus Siculus**), is the author of the *Bibliothēkē* ('Library'), a universal history from mythological times to 60 BC. Only 15 of the original 40 books survive fully (bks. 1–5; 11–20); the others are preserved in fragments. Despite his claim to cover all of known history, Diodorus concentrates on Greece and his homeland of Sicily, until the First *Punic War, when his sources for Rome become fuller. But even in its fragmentary state, the *Bibliothēkē* is the most extensively preserved history by a Greek author from antiquity. For the period from the accession of *Philip (1) II of Macedon to the battle of *Ipsus, when the text becomes fragmentary, it is fundamental; and it is the essential source for classical Sicilian history and the Sicilian slave rebellions of the 2nd cent. BC. For many individual events throughout Graeco-Roman history, the *Bibliothēkē* also sheds important light.

Diodorus probably visited *Egypt *c.*60–56 BC, where he began researching his history. By 56, he may have settled in Rome, completing the *Bibliothēkē* there around 30. He read Latin and had access to written materials in Rome, but, despite his admiration for *Caesar, there is no evidence that he personally knew Romans of prominence. Diodorus originally intended to cover events to 46; perhaps the dangers of writing contemporary history of a turbulent period influenced his decision to conclude with the year 60.

Books 1–6 include the geography and ethnography of the *oikoumenē* ('inhabited world') and its mythology and paradoxology (see PARADOXOGRAPHERS) prior to the Trojan War; bks. 1–3 cover the east, bks. 4–6 the west. Of special significance are the description of Egypt in bk. 1, drawn from *Hecataeus (2) of Abdera; the discussion of India in bk. 2, drawn from *Megasthenes; passages from the works of *Agatharchides in bk. 3; and the highly fragmentary Euhemeran material in bk. 6 (see EUHEMERUS).

The fully preserved historical books cover 480–302 and are organized annalistically, with Olympian, Athenian archon, and Roman consular years synchronized—often erroneously. The fragmentary final books, which draw on *Posidonius (2), are probably organized episodically. Occasionally including the same incidents from different authorities or failing to understand the organizational habits of an individual author, Diodorus created numerous, sometimes serious doublets.

The main source for most of the narrative of the Greek mainland is *Ephorus; *Hieronymus (1) of Cardia is the prime authority for the outstanding narrative of the *Diadochi. Sicily receives important independent attention, in which Diodorus employs *Timaeus (2) extensively. For much of the later Roman period,

Diodorus follows *Polybius (1) closely, as the preserved Polybian text shows; he employs Posidonius for many events after 146. But the 19th-cent. belief that all of Diodorus' sources could be identified proved over-confident and attempts to make such identifications continue to provoke great controversy. Further, because few of his sources survive outside his own work, precisely what Diodorus has taken verbatim, what he has confused and entered in error, and what he has consciously interpolated are matters of great dispute. It appears at least that certain themes recur throughout the Bibliothēkē independently of Diodorus' current source. Character assessments, with a strong insistence on personal and collective morality, and an emphasis on the civilizing power of individual benefactors suggest late Hellenistic influence and therefore Diodorus' own philosophy.

TEXTS F. Vogel and C. T. Fischer (Teubner, 1888–1906); with Eng. trans.: C. H. Oldfather and others (Loeb, 1933–67); with Fr. trans.: F. Chamoux and others (Budé, 1972–).
LITERATURE E. Schwartz, *RE* 5. 663–704; J. Palm, *Über Sprache und Stil des Diodoros von Sizilien* (1955); K. Meister, *Die sizilische Geschichte bei Diodor* (Diss. Munich, 1967); F. Walbank, *Kokalos* 1968/9, 476 ff.; J. Hornblower, *Hieronymus of Cardia* (1981); M. Pavan, M. Sordi and others, *Aevum* 1987, 20 ff.; K. Sacks, *Diodorus Siculus and the First Century* (1990).   K. S. S.

Diodorus (4) (*RE* 53), of *Alexandria (1), mathematician and astronomer (1st cent. BC), wrote a work, *Analemma*, on the construction of plane sundials by methods of descriptive geometry. Only the section on the determination of the meridian from three shadow-lengths survives, in Latin and Arabic versions, but later treatments of the subject are found in *Vitruvius, *Heron, and *Ptolemy (4)'s *Analemma* (see MATHEMATICS). The work was important enough for *Pappus (see *Collection* 4. 246) to write a commentary on it. The Diodorus who commented on *Aratus (1)'s *Phaenomena* (see ARATEA) may be the same man.

Fragments and testimonia (for all works of Diodorus) in D. Edwards, *Ptolemy's Περὶ ἀναλήμματος* (Diss. Brown University, 1984), 152–82. *HAMA* 2. 840 ff.   G. J. T.

Diodotus (1) **I,** founder of the Graeco-*Bactrian monarchy. Formerly the *Seleucid *satrap of Bactria-Sogdiana, the date and circumstance of his independence remain uncertain. Some place his rebellion as early as 256 BC, while others prefer a lower chronology falling in the reign of *Seleucus (2) II. He probably issued coins bearing his own portrait and type, 'Thundering Zeus', in *c.*246 BC. His autonomy was assured by the dynastic feuding of the Seleucids, but he was hostile towards the rise of *Parthia and struck few if any coins in his own name. He died *c.*235 BC.

CAH 8² (1989), see index.   F. L. H.

Diodotus (2) **II,** son and successor of *Diodotus (1) I. During his reign (*c.*235–226 BC), he allied with the *Parthians and abandoned the use of the *Seleucid name Antiochus on his coinage. He was overthrown by *Euthydemus (2) I.

CAH 8² (1989), see index.   F. L. H.

Diodotus (3) (*RE* 11), Stoic (see STOICISM), teacher of *Cicero *c.*85 BC, lived later in Cicero's house (Cic. *Brut.* 309; *Acad. pr.* 115; *Tusc.* 5. 113). He died blind *c.*60 and made Cicero his heir (*Att.* 2. 20. 6).   M. T. G.

dioecesis *Diocletian divided Italy and most of the existing provinces into smaller provinces, which he grouped into twelve 'dioceses', each administered by a *vicarius*. These 'vicars' were officially deputies of the praetorian prefects, and facilitated the central bureaucracy's control of provincial governors. The Dio-

cletianic dioceses were Britain, Gaul, Viennensis (see VIENNA), Spain, Africa, Pannonia, Moesia, Thrace, Asiana, Pontica, and Oriens. Italy was in practice divided between the *vicarius Italiae* in the north and the *vicarius* of Rome in the south. The proconsuls of Asia, Achaia, and Africa were not subject to vicarial authority. The number of dioceses increased when *Constantine I divided Moesia into Dacia and Macedonia, and *Valens detached Egypt from Oriens; the latter were administered by a prefect and a *comes* respectively. After Constantine, the prefects ruled directly the diocese in which their seats were located.

Jones, *Later Rom. Emp.* 47, 373–4.   B. H. W.; R. S. O. T.

Diogenes (1), of Apollonia (on the Black or *Euxine Sea), is generally reckoned the last of the Presocratic philosophers (cf. *Theophrastus, *Phys. op.* fr. 2). The best evidence of his date is *Aristophanes (1)'s *Clouds* (423 BC), where his views are parodied. Fragments of *On Nature* are preserved by *Simplicius, whose mention of other works by Diogenes perhaps rests on a misunderstanding.

Probably with his theory of infinite worlds and infinite void and his account of the heavenly bodies in mind, Theophrastus (*Phys. op.* fr. 2) complains that Diogenes' doctrines were mostly a medley derived from *Leucippus (3) and *Anaxagoras. Diogenes' central argument, however, defended an Anaximenean form of material monism (see ANAXIMENES (1)). The first move established the truth of monism as such: interaction between bodies would be impossible if they were essentially different (fr. 2). Next came proofs reminiscent of Anaxagoras that there is much intelligence in the world, as witness its orderly structure and the life of men and other animals (frs. 3 and 4). From this Diogenes inferred his principal thesis: the basic body must be air, since air is what pervades and disposes all things and supports life and intelligence. Differentiation (e.g. of temperature) in air explains differences between species (fr. 5). The causal connection between air and life and intelligence was substantiated in a detailed account of the blood channels, preserved by Aristotle (fr. 6), and appropriated like Diogenes' connected theory of the brain in the Hippocratic treatise *On the Sacred Disease* (see HIPPOCRATES (2)). Diogenes evidently applied his causal scheme systematically. Theophrastus has an extensive passage (*De sensu* 39–45) on the senses, and many physical phenomena were explained on the analogy of sweating and absorption of ἰκμάς, moisture (e.g. magnetism, the flooding of the *Nile).

TEXT DK no. 64.
DISCUSSION/TRANSLATION A. Laks, *Diogène d'Apollonie* (1983); Kirk–Raven–Schofield.   M. Sch.

Diogenes (2) the *Cynic (*c.*412/403–*c.*324/321 BC). The general distortions in the ancient traditions about Cynicism ('doggishness') multiply in the case of Diogenes, who provoked extremes of admiration, hostility, and imaginative invention. All accounts are controversial, but the ancient traditions show certain constants and *Diogenes (6) Laertius 6. 70–3 preserves Diogenes' essential thought.

Accused with his father, moneyer at *Sinope, of 'defacing the currency' (a phrase which was to yield a potent metaphor), Diogenes was exiled some time after 362 and spent the rest of his life in Athens and Corinth. (His capture by pirates, consultation of Delphi, and discipleship of *Socrates' follower *Antisthenes (1) are fictitious.) He evolved a distinctive and original way of life from diverse, mainly Greek, elements: the belief (espoused by certain types of holy men and wise men) that wisdom was a matter of action rather than thought; the principle (advanced by various *sophists, 5th-cent. primitivists, and Antisthenes) of living in accordance with nature rather than law/convention; the tradition, perhaps sharpened by contemporary disillusionment with the *polis, of promulgating ideal societies or constitutions; a tradition of 'shamelessness' (reflected by the symbol of the dog in literature and by the supposed customs of certain foreign peoples); Socratic rejection of all elements of philosophy except practical ethics; Socrates' pursuit of philosophy in the agora rather than in a school; an anti-intellectual tradition; the tradition (variously represented by *Odysseus, *Heracles, the Spartans, and to some extent by Socrates) of physical toughness as a requirement of virtue; the image of the suffering hero and the wanderer (Odysseus, Heracles, various tragic figures); the tradition of mendicancy (represented both in literature and in life); the life of *asceticism and poverty (as represented by various wise men and holy men and labourers); the tradition of the wise or holy man who promises converts happiness or salvation; and various humorous traditions (the jester's practical and verbal humour; Old Comedy's outspokenness and crudity (see COMEDY (GREEK), OLD); Socrates' serio-comic wit).

Diogenes pursued a life as close as possible to the 'natural' life of primitive man, of animals, and of the gods. This entailed the minimum of material possessions (coarse cloak, staff for physical support and protection, purse for food) and of sustenance (obtained by living off the land and by begging); performance in public of all natural functions; training in physical endurance, and a wandering existence in harmony with natural conditions. Freedom, self-sufficiency, happiness, and virtue supposedly followed. It also entailed not merely indifference to civilized life but complete rejection of it and of all forms of education and culture as being not simply irrelevant but inimical to the ideal life. Hence Diogenes' attacks on convention, marriage, family, politics, the city, all social, sexual, and racial distinctions, worldly reputation, wealth, power and authority, literature, music, and all forms of intellectual speculation. Such attacks are imposed by the Cynic's duty metaphorically to 'deface the currency'. Hence the modern implications of the word 'cynic' are misleading. Indeed, humane attitudes came easily to Diogenes (e.g. his advocacy of sexual freedom and equality stemmed naturally from rejection of the family).

Although proclaiming self-sufficiency, Diogenes tried to convert others by his own outrageous behaviour (which went beyond the requirements of the natural life), by direct exhortation employing all the resources of his formidable wit and rhetorical skills, and by various written works. Notwithstanding ancient and modern doubts, it is certain that Diogenes expounded his views in a *Politeia* ('Republic', reconstructable from Diog. Laert. 6. 72 and *Philodemus' On the Stoics) and several tragedies. Such writings, which compromise the ideal of the practical demonstration of philosophical truth and the formal rejection of literature, did not imply real debate with conventional philosophers. Diogenes sparred verbally with *Plato (1) but dismissed his philosophy as absurd; his *Politeia*, while a serious statement of Cynic positions, parodied 'serious' philosophers' pretensions.

Diogenes' missionary activity entailed what his aggressiveness sometimes obscured: recognition of the common humanity of Cynics and non-Cynics. 'Philanthropy' (concern for one's fellow human beings) is integral to Cynicism and essential to Diogenes' celebrated concept of 'cosmopolitanism' (the belief that the universe is the ultimate unity, of which the natural and animal worlds, human beings, and the gods are all intrinsic parts, with the Cynic representing the human condition at its best, at once human, animal, and divine).

Ancient and modern reactions to Diogenes range from appreciation of his wit to admiration for his integrity, denial of his philosophical significance, revulsion at his shamelessness, dislike of the threat he posed to conventional social and political values, and misguided attempts to make him respectable. Yet, whatever the detailed distortions in the Stoic history of philosophy, it was right to locate Diogenes within the great tradition, as even Plato half-conceded when he dubbed him a 'mad Socrates' (Diog. Laert. 6. 54).

See also CRATES (2); CYNICS.

For bibliography see under CYNICS.   J. L. Mo.

Diogenes (3), of *Babylon (c.240–152 BC), succeeded *Zeno (3) of Tarsus as head of the Stoa (see STOICISM). His visit to Rome in 156–155 stimulated interest in Stoicism. *Panaetius was his pupil. He developed distinctive positions in some areas, notably philosophy of language and ethics, where he wrote on such topics as the morality of sale. His significance as a figure in the debates of the period and the development of Stoic positions is only now emerging from renewed study of the *Herculaneum papyri, in which his views are frequently discussed.

Testimonia in von Arnim, SVF 3. 210–43.   J. A.

Diogenes (4), of Tarsus, Epicurean (see EPICURUS) of uncertain date, but probably identical with the author of a book on ποιητικὰ ζητήματα or 'poetical inquiries' (who fl. c.150–100 BC): Strabo 14. 5. 15; Diog. Laert. 6. 81.

Diogenes (5) (*RE* 47a, Suppl. 5 (1931)), of *Oenoanda in Lycia (near mod. Incealiler in Turkey), author of a massive Greek inscription presenting basic doctrines of Epicureanism. The inscription was carved in a *stoa, probably in the 2nd cent. AD. Between 1884 and 1895, 88 fragments were discovered, and were the basis of successive editions until the publication by M. F. Smith of 124 new fragments (1970–84).

The inscription occupied several courses of a wall c.80 m. (87 yds.) long. In the lowest inscribed course was a treatise on ethics dealing (*inter alia*) with pleasure, pain, fear, desire, dreams, necessity, and free will; beneath its columns was inscribed a selection of Epicurus' *Primary Tenets* and other maxims. Immediately above was a treatise on physics, the surviving sections of which include criticisms of rival schools and discussions of epistemology, the origins of civilization and language, astronomy, and theology. Above these main treatises were more maxims, letters of Epicurus (one, addressed to his mother, concerns her anxious dreams), at least three letters written by Diogenes to Epicurean friends, and Diogenes' defence of old age. Fragments survive also of Diogenes' instructions to his friends.

Diogenes records that he was ailing and aged when he set up the inscription, and that he was moved by a desire to benefit his fellows at home and abroad as well as future generations. Although most of the inscription remains buried, the recovered fragments illuminate Epicurean theory and the activity of the school under the Roman empire. See EPICURUS.

TEXT M. F. Smith (1993), with comm. and trans.
STUDY D. Clay, *ANRW* 2. 36. 4 (1990).   D. K.

Diogenes (6) **Laertius,** also called Laërtius Diogenes (*RE* 40), author of an extant compendium on the lives and doctrines of the ancient philosophers from *Thales to *Epicurus. Since he omits *Neoplatonism and mentions no philosopher after

Saturninus (a Pyrrhonian sceptic of the 2nd cent. AD), he probably lived in the first half of the 3rd cent. AD. Nothing whatever is known of his life, not even where and with whom he studied philosophy.

After an introduction on some non-Greek 'thinkers' such as the magi (see MAGUS), and some of the early Greek sages, he divides the philosophers into two 'successions', an Ionian or eastern (bk. 1. 22 to bk. 7) and an Italian or western (bk. 8), and ends with the 'sporadics', important philosophers who did not found successions (bks. 9–10). This arrangement disperses the Presocratics in books 1, 2, 8, and 9. Book 10 is devoted entirely to Epicurus and preserves the texts of several of his works.

In 10. 138 Diogenes speaks of giving the finishing touch to his entire work; but the book is such a tissue of quotations industriously compiled, mostly from secondary sources, that it could have been expanded indefinitely. Diogenes usually drew his material on any one philosopher from more than one earlier compilation, depending by preference on such writers as *Antigonus (4) of Carystus, *Hermippus (2), *Sotion (1), *Apollodorus (6) of Athens, *Sosicrates of Rhodes, *Demetrius (16) and *Diocles (5) of Magnesia, *Pamphila, and *Favorinus, all of whom were themselves industrious compilers. Thus Diogenes' material often comes to us at several removes from the original. Fortunately, he usually names his sources, mentioning over 200 authors and over 300 works by name. As a rule he changes sources continually. Hence his reliability and value also change from passage to passage. For example, his account of Stoic doctrine (8. 39–160; see STOICISM) is reliable and his long quotations from *Epicurus are invaluable when separated from the inserted marginalia that sometimes interrupt the sense. But some Lives, as *Heraclitus', are mere caricatures, and some summaries of doctrine are vitiated by philosophic distortion: for instance, *Aristotle's doctrines are viewed through Stoic, perhaps also Epicurean, eyes.

Diogenes also wrote some wretched poetry, which he quotes more than 40 times and of which he published a separate edition, not extant (1. 39). It has been suggested that Diogenes was himself an Epicurean, or alternatively a *Sceptic; but most probably he was an adherent of no school (cf. Barnes in ANRW 2. 36. 6. 4243–4.) See BIOGRAPHY, GREEK.

TEXTS H. S. Long (OCT, 1964); M. Marcovich (Teubner, forthcoming).

COMMENTARY M. Gigante (1983).

STUDIES J. Meijer, Diogenes Laertius and his Hellenistic Background, Hermes Einzelschr. 40 (1978). Numerous studies collected in Elenchos 1986; also in ANRW 2. 36. 5 (1992), 3556–792, and 2. 36. 6 (1992), 3793–4307. H. S. L.; R. W. S.

Diogenianus (1), *Epicurean. *Eusebius quotes many passages from his polemic against *Chrysippus' doctrine of fate. His date is unknown, but he probably belongs to the 2nd cent. AD, when the polemic of the New *Academy against Chrysippus was at its height.

Ed. A. Gercke, Jahrb. f. cl. Phil. Suppl. 14. 748. W. D. R.

Diogenianus (2), of *Heraclea (3), of the age of *Hadrian. Besides geographical indexes, a collection of proverbs, an *anthology of (Greek) *epigrams, and other works, he compiled in five books an alphabetically arranged epitome of the Lexicon of *Pamphilus (2) as abridged by Vestinus. This epitome was used by *Hesychius, who refers to it under the title of Περίεργω πένητες ('poor scholars'), by *Photius and other Byzantine lexicographers, and by the scholiasts on *Plato (1), *Callimachus (3),

and Nicander up to the 12th cent. A recension of the Corpus Paroemiographorum is probably falsely attributed to him.

E. Norden, Hermes 1892, 625; R. Reitzenstein, Geschichte d. griech. Etymologika (1897), 417 ff.; K. Latte, Hesychii Alexandrini lexicon (1953), pp. xlii–xliv. P. B. R. F.; R. B.

diolkos, stone trackway across the isthmus of *Corinth, for transporting ships and / or cargoes between the Saronic and the Corinthian gulfs. Archaeology suggests a date under *Periander; there is literary evidence that he considered a canal. Wheeled wagons (see TRANSPORT, WHEELED) ran in carved grooves c.1.5 m. (5 ft.) apart; traffic probably moved in one direction at a time. *Triremes used it during the *Peloponnesian War, perhaps after modifications; but it was probably constructed for merchant vessels. It may quickly have become incapable of transporting most vessels fully laden, so that cargoes alone were carried. It was used by a fleet as late as AD 883.

G. Raepsaet and M. Tolley, BCH 1993; J. B. Salmon, Wealthy Corinth (1984). J. B. S.

Diomedes, in mythology (1), son of *Ares and Cyrene, barbarous king of the Thracian Cicones or Bistones; owner of a team of man-eating mares which were kept supplied with human victims by their groom. *Heracles fed the stable-lad, and in some versions the king himself, to the animals and drove them back to Greece as his eighth labour (Pindar, fr. 169 Snell–Maehler), though not before the horses had killed Abderus, one of the hero's companions; the story provided a foundation-myth for the city of *Abdera. The king's punishment was depicted on the Archaic 'throne' at *Amyclae (Paus. 3. 18. 12) and on vases, including a fine cup by Psiax in St Petersburg.

K. Schefold, Gods and Heroes in Late Archaic Greek Art 111 f.; J. Boardman, LIMC 5. 67–71, 'Herakles'.

(2), son of *Tydeus and Deipyle the daughter of *Adrastus (1); one of the chief Achaean warriors in the Trojan War and leader of a contingent of 80 ships from *Argos (2) and *Tiryns. In books 5 and 6 of the Iliad, the so-called Διομήδους ἀριστεία (a title used by Herodotus, 2. 116), his great charge leads to the death of *Pandarus, the removal of *Aeneas from looming defeat by his mother *Aphrodite, and the wounding of the goddess herself and of Ares the war-god; later we are shown a more restrained side of his character as he declines to fight with his hereditary xenos ('guest-friend') *Glaucus (1) of Lycia (6. 119 ff.; see GUEST-FRIENDSHIP). Throughout the poem, but especially in the second half, he offers shrewd and bold advice to the Greek war-council. In the funeral games for *Patroclus he wins both the chariot-race and (against *Aias (1)) the spear-fight. He is particularly associated with *Odysseus in various actions, killing Dolon and *Rhesus in the Doloneia (Book 10), and in the poems of the *Epic Cycle sharing in the murder of *Palamedes (Paus. 10. 31. 2, citing the Cypria), bringing *Philoctetes back from Lemnos, and stealing Athena's talismanic statuette, the *Palladium, from the Trojan citadel.

Other traditions assign him a part in the expedition of the *Epigoni against *Thebes (1), where his father had fought (Il. 4. 405 ff.), and in the restoration of the kingship of Calydon to its rightful line (Apollod. 1. 8. 6). But on his safe return from Troy he had found his wife Aegialea unfaithful; emigrating to Italy, he ended his days with King Daunus in Apulia (see DAUNIANS).

Ø. Andersen, Die Diomedesgestalt in der Ilias (1978); J. Boardman and C. E. Vafopoulou-Richardson, LIMC 'Diomedes' 1. A. H. G.

Diomedes (3) (late 4th or early 5th cent. AD), grammarian, who wrote an *Ars grammatica* in three books (ed. Keil, *Gramm. Lat.* 1. 299–529). His work is of value because, though he rarely mentions his sources, he clearly relied upon earlier grammarians who discussed and illustrated the usages of republican authors. Parallels between his work and that of *Charisius seem to indicate that he borrowed from the latter.

Schanz–Hosius, § 834; R. Kaster, *Guardians of Language* (1988), 270 ff.
J. F. Mo.

Dion (*RE* 2) (c.408–353). Son of Hipparinus, *Dionysius (1) I's father-in-law. A disciple of *Plato (1) from 388/7, married Dionysius' daughter Arete and became his most trusted minister and diplomatist. His vast wealth and notorious Platonism, together with his austerity and ambition for his nephews, aroused the suspicion of *Dionysius (2) II and of the 'old guard' monarchists. Hoping to convert Dionysius, he brought Plato to *Syracuse (367/6), but the disclosure of an indiscreet letter to the Carthaginians led to his banishment. At Athens he associated with the Academy, and he was honoured at Sparta; but Plato failed to reconcile Dionysius with him, and he was dispossessed of his wife and property. Landing in western Sicily (357), and greatly augmenting his small force on the march, he seized Syracuse, less the citadel, in the absence of Dionysius, and was elected general plenipotentiary (with his brother). Dion soon quarrelled with the radical leader Heraclides and was forced to retire to Leontini. Recalled (355) to eject Dionysius' general Nypsius from Syracuse, he became master of the whole city; but his imperiousness, his exactions, his employment of Corinthian advisers, and his intention of establishing some form of Platonist aristo-monarchy, again alienated the *dēmos*. He had Heraclides murdered, but his supporters fell away and he was himself assassinated at the instigation of his Athenian friend Callippus, who (briefly) became the ruler of Syracuse. Austere, haughty, aloof, contemptuous of democracy, tainted by his long connection with tyranny; he was probably sincere in his own interpretation of Platonism; but he lacked the domestic support, the resources, and the devoted military force needed to establish a stable non-democratic regime; and his 'liberation' of Sicily brought only political and social chaos to the island, for nearly twenty years.

H. Berve, *Dion* (1956); B. Caven, *Dionysius I* (1990); H. D. Westlake, *CAH* 6² (1994), ch. 13.
B. M. C.

Dione (Διώνη), consort of *Zeus at *Dodona, where she had a cult as Naïa beside Zeus Naïos. Her name is the feminine equivalent of Zeus and recalls *diwija/diuja* in Linear B, although *Hera already appears beside Zeus on PY Tn 316. Dione is the mother of Aphrodite in Homer (*Il.* 5. 370), a fresh-water *nymph, daughter of *Oceanus and *Tethys, in Hesiod (*Theog.* 353; cf. Pherec. *FGrH* 3 F 90), or first generation *Titan (Apollod. 1. 13). But outside Dodona her influence was limited.

Dione appears on Epirote coins of the 3rd and 2nd cents. BC. On the reverse of a tetradrachm of *Pyrrhus, king of Epirus (c.297 BC), she is shown with sceptre and wearing a headdress (*polos*) (*SNG* Copenhagen 91). Attic vase-painters of the 5th cent. sometimes added her to the circle of *Dionysus' followers, showing Athenian interest in the northern sanctuary of Zeus during the *Peloponnesian War.

E. Simon, *LIMC* (1986), 3/1. 412 f. 'Dione'. H. J. R.; B. C. D.

Dionysia Many festivals of *Dionysus had special names, e.g. the *Anthesteria, the *Lenaea, etc. This article concerns those Attic festivals known as (*a*) τὰ κατ' ἀγροὺς Διονύσια, the Rural Dionysia, and (*b*) τὰ ἐν ἄστει or τὰ μεγάλα Διονύσια, the City or Great Dionysia. Festivals of Dionysus were widespread throughout the Greek world, but we know most about the *Attic ones, for which almost all surviving Greek drama was written.

(*a*) The Rural Dionysia were celebrated, on various days by the different *demes, in the month of Posideon (roughly December). They provided an opportunity for the locality to reproduce elements of the City Dionysia, and we hear of performances of *tragedy, *comedy, and *dithyramb. There survive various inscriptions concerning the proceedings, notably from the *Piraeus, *Eleusis, Icarion, and Aixone. In *Aristophanes (1)'s *Acharnians* Dicaeopolis goes home to celebrate the festival: he draws up a little sacrificial procession in which his daughter is *kanephoros* ('basket-bearer'), two slaves carry the *phallus, Dicaeopolis himself sings an obscene song to Phales, and his wife watches from the roof (241–79; cf. Plut. *Mor.* 527d, 1098b). The song may be of the kind from which, according to Aristotle, *comedy originated (*Poetics* 1449ᵃ11).

(*b*) The City Dionysia belonged to Dionysus Eleuthereus, who was said to have been introduced into Athens from the village of Eleutherae, on the borders of Attica and *Boeotia. At Eleutherae there was a cult of Dionysus μελαναιγίς ('of the black goatskin'), who was said to have driven the daughters of Eleuther mad, and to have appeared at a duel between Xanthus and Melanthus. The festival is generally regarded as having been founded, or at least amplified, during the *tyranny of *Pisistratus. But in fact the archaeological, epigraphic, and literary evidence is so uncertain as to be no less consistent with a date for its foundation right at the end of the 6th cent., just after the establishment of *democracy, in which case the title Eleuthereus would perhaps have been taken to connote political liberty.

The festival was celebrated at the end of March, when the city was again full of visitors after the winter. A preliminary procession brought the image of Dionysus to the theatre (on the south slope of the Acropolis), in commemoration of his original arrival from Eleutherae (our evidence for this does not predate the late 2nd cent. BC). Then, on 10 Elaphebolion, a splendid procession followed an unknown route to the sacred precinct (adjacent to the theatre), where animals were sacrificed and bloodless offerings made. In the procession were carried phalli, loaves, bowls, etc., and the metics were dressed in red. The theatrical performances took place from the 11th to the 14th. Their precise arrangement is unknown, but normal practice in the Classical period was as follows. Three tragedians competed, each with three tragedies and a satyr-play (see SATYRIC DRAMA). There were five comic poets, each competing with a single play. And each of the ten tribes provided one dithyrambic chorus for the men's contest and one for the boys'. At some point before the performance of the tragedies the sons of citizens killed in battle were paraded in full armour in the theatre, and so was the tribute brought by Athens' allies. Various fragmentary inscriptions survive with the remains of lists of the annual performances (or victors). See also CHOREGIA; DIDASKALIA; PROAGON; TRAGEDY.

A. W. Pickard-Cambridge, *The Dramatic Festivals of Athens*, 2nd edn. (1968); H. J. Mette, *Urkunden Dramatischen Aufführungen in Griechenland* (1977); W. R. Connor, *Class. et Med.* 1989, 7–32; D. Whitehead, *The Demes of Attica* (1986), 212–22; S. Goldhill, in J. Winkler and F. Zeitlin (eds.), *Nothing to do with Dionysos* (1990); C. Sourvinou–Inwood, in R. Osborne and S. Hornblower (eds.), *Ritual, Finance, Politics* (1994), 269 ff.
R. A. S. S.

Dionysius (1) (*RE* 1) **I**, born c.430 BC, son of Hermocritus, a well-to-do *Syracusan; wounded (408) in *Hermocrates' attempted coup; secretary to the generals (406), he distinguished himself in the *Acragas campaign (see HIMILCO (2)). By unscrupulous *demagogy he secured the dismissal of the generals and his own election as general plenipotentiary (a title he may have used until 392), obtained a bodyguard, occupied and fortified the citadel (Ortygia), and assumed control of the state. With a large allied army, he failed to raise the siege of *Gela (405), but crushed a revolt of the aristocracy (confiscating their properties), and concluded the Peace of Himilco, which stripped Syracuse of her possessions. Besieged in Ortygia by the rebellious Syracusans (404–3), he came to terms with them (less the exiled aristocracy), giving them, although disarmed, a measure of autonomy. After subjugating eastern Sicily (south of *Messana (mod. Messina)) with a mercenary army (402–399), he prepared for war with *Carthage, fortifying Epipolae, amassing war-material, building a huge fleet, rearming the Syracusans, hiring mercenaries, and forming matrimonial alliances with Syracuse (Andromache, sister of *Dion) and *Locri Epizephyrii (Doris). He invaded the Carthaginian province (397) and stormed *Motya (Mozia), but (396) retired before Himilco to Syracuse; here, following the defeat of his navy off *Catana (Catania), he was besieged until 395, when, with some Corinthian and Spartan aid, he overthrew Himilco's plague-stricken forces. He restored his east Sicilian empire (incorporating Messana), attacked *Rhegium (Reggio) and countered a new Carthaginian threat (395–2); but when the Syracusan army mutinied, he concluded a peace with Carthage (392) that recognized his suzerainty of eastern Sicily. He again attacked Rhegium (390) and starved it into surrender (387), allied himself with the *Lucanians, crushed the forces of the Italiot League on the Eleporus (Galliparo) (389), and incorporated *Iapygia (southern Calabria) in his empire. The year 388 witnessed the fiasco of Dionysius' *Delphic embassy. In 387 he helped Sparta to impose the *King's Peace on Greece; and in 386 a palace conspiracy (probably) led to the banishment of some of his courtiers, including his brother Leptines (later recalled) and the historian *Philistus. To improve his supply of silver, timber, horses, and mercenaries, he extended his power into the Adriatic, founding colonies and establishing friendly relations with the *Senones. He raided *Pyrgi (384), the port of *Caere. The chronology and details of his greatest war (383–probably 375), against the Italiots and allied Carthage, are unclear, owing to a failure in the transmission of *Diodorus (3) Siculus' text (15. 15–17, 24). Attacking *Thurii, he lost his fleet in a storm, but he gained *Croton. In Sicily he routed the Carthaginians at Cabala but was totally defeated at Cronium (Leptines was killed), and made a peace that established the Halycus (Platani) as the common frontier. He sent expeditions to Greece (369, 368), to assist Sparta against the *Boeotians; and Athens, hitherto hostile, voted him a crown and (368) conferred her citizenship on him and his sons. He again invaded western Sicily (368) and besieged *Lilybaeum (Marsala), but his fleet was captured at Drepana (Trapani) and he concluded an armistice. At the *Lenaea at Athens in 367 his play, The Ransom of Hector, won the prize, and a mutual defence treaty was negotiated, whose ratification was perhaps prevented by his death.

Dionysius, who probably styled himself archōn (ruler) of Sicily, was a born leader of men, in peace and war; orator and diplomat, planner and administrator, patron of religion, of his native city, of literature and the arts, a dramatist perhaps no worse than the generality in an age of decline—above all, the greatest soldier that, apart from the Macedonians, ancient Greece produced. He applied mind to warfare, introducing *artillery, Phoenician siege-technique, and the *quinquereme. He could handle large *mer-

cenary armies and small light-infantry detachments; he appreciated the importance of reconnaissance. If his subordinates had not constantly let him down, he might have achieved his life's ambition, to drive the Carthaginians from Sicily. Dionysius represents the irruption onto the historical scene of the new individualism of his age. Portrayed by the anecdotal tradition, above all by the *Academy, as the archetypal tyrant—paranoid, oppressive, obsessed with power—he looms through the historical tradition (*Diodorus (3) (and *Polyaenus (2)), going back through *Ephorus and *Timaeus (2) to Philistus) rather as the first of the Romantic 'great men'; the precursor of *Alexander (3) the Great, *Hannibal, and Napoleon: obsessed not with power but with glory.

B. Caven, Dionysius I (1990); K. F. Stroheker, Dionysios I (1958); H. Berve, Die Tyrannis bei den Griechen (1967); 221–260; D. M. Lewis, CAH 6² (1994), ch. 5.   B. M. C.

Dionysius (2) (RE 2) **II,** tyrant of *Syracuse (367–357 BC); born c.396, eldest son of *Dionysios (1) I and Doris; married half-sister Sophrosyne. Unwarlike and short-sighted, he was estranged from his father, who is said (perhaps falsely) to have excluded him from public life and encouraged his debauchery. Inheriting an empire 'secured with bonds of adamant', he ruled successfully for ten years; making peace with *Carthage (Halycus frontier), assisting Sparta (365), resisting the *Lucanians, combating piracy in the Adriatic, and restoring *Rhegium (mod. Reggio), renaming it Phoebia (honouring his suppositious father, *Apollo). Encouraged by *Dion and *Plato (1) himself, he conceived a passion for philosophy, which split his court between the 'reformers' and the 'old guard', led by the historian *Philistus, and led to a rupture with Dion and eventually (360) with Plato. During his absence in Italy (357), Dion liberated Syracuse and dissolved his empire. Dionysius was confined to the citadel (Ortygia), which, after the death of Philistus (356), he entrusted to his son, and withdrew to *Locri Epizephyrii. In 346 he recovered Syracuse from his half-brother Hipparinus. The Locrians then revolted and massacred his family. Dionysius was again confined to Ortygia by Hicetas, and surrendered it to *Timoleon (344), retiring into private life in Corinth. Denigrated by the Academic tradition (see ACADEMY), Dionysius was neither an ineffectual ruler nor a despot (unless, perhaps, in Locri); but the abandonment of his father's crusade against Carthage deprived the regime of its purpose and its glamour, and it was weakened internally by division and by Dionysius' ill-advised attempt to reduce his soldiers' pay.

H. Berve, Dion (1956), and Die Tyrannis bei den Griechen (1967), 1. 260–78; B. Caven, Dionysius I (1990); H. D. Westlake, CAH 6² (1994), ch. 13.   B. M. C.

Dionysius (3), **Aelius,** an important Atticist lexicographer, of the age of *Hadrian. (See ASIANISM AND ATTICISM.) He compiled ten books of Attikai lexeis. See PAUSANIAS (4).   J. S. R.

Dionysius (4) **the Areopagite,** an Athenian converted at Athens by St *Paul (Acts 17: 34). Four treatises—The Celestial Hierarchy, The Ecclesiastical Hierarchy, The Divine Names, and The Mystical Theology—and ten letters are ascribed to him. These works, the product of a single mind, belong almost certainly to the early 6th cent. AD and were first cited (and ascribed to Paul's convert) in 532. They display an enthusiasm for the *Neoplatonism of *Proclus, while theologically they belong to a Syrian milieu, mistrustful of Chalcedonian Christology. Their

Dionysius of Miletus

heady brew of Neoplatonic philosophy and biblical and liturgical symbolism became immensely popular in the Middle Ages: they exercised a powerful influence both in the east and the west. The author sees the cosmos as a vast theophany in which divine revelation draws all rational creatures back through love into harmony with the unknowable God by a process of purification, illumination, and union: this harmony is displayed in the celestial hierarchy of angelic powers, whose order reflects the threefold nature of the Trinity, and achieved through the similarly triadic sacramental structure of the Church. Scholars are divided as to whether Dionysius' allegiance is fundamentally pagan and Neoplatonic or authentically Christian.

Ed. B. Suchla and others, 2 vols. (Patristische Texte und Studien 33, 36, 1990 f.); Eng. trans., C. Luibheid (1987). A. Louth, *Denys the Areopagite* (1989); P. Rorem, *Pseudo-Dionysius: A Commentary on the Texts and an Introduction to their Influence* (1993); R. Roques, *RAC* 3 (1957), 1075–121.

A. W. L.

Dionysius (5), **of Miletus,** ethnographer and historian, according to the *Suda* (*FGrH* 687 T 2) contemporary of *Hecataeus (1), author of *Troica* in three books, *Description of the Inhabited World, History of Persia* (*Persica*) in Ionic Greek (see GREEK LANGUAGE, §§ 3, 4), *The Events after Darius* in five books, *Historical Cycle* in seven books.

With the possible exception of the *Persica* and *The Events after Darius*, which may be genuine, the historicity of his works has been contested: Jacoby accepts them as historical, von Fritz is probably justified in not doing so, since there are no allusions in Herodotus nor any important quotations in the rest of the tradition. Under no circumstances may one take Dionysius to be an important source for Herodotus (cf. M. Moggi) or even call him the 'father of history'.

FGrH. 687. F. Jacoby, *Abhandlungen zur griechischen Geschichtsschreibung* (1956), see index; K. von Fritz, *Die griechische Geschichtsschreibung*, 2 vols. (1967); M. Moggi, *ASNP* 1972, 433 ff.

K. M.

Dionysius (6) (*RE* 97) **Chalcus** (ὁ Χαλκοῦς, so called after recommending bronze currency to Athens), Athenian orator and poet who led the colonizing expedition to *Thurii (443 BC). His highly-wrought sympotic elegy (see SYMPOSIUM LITERATURE) was rich in riddling metaphors. According to Athenaeus (602b–c) he (once? often?) started a poem with the pentameter.

TEXT B. Gentili and C. Prato, *Poetae Elegiaci* 2 (Teubner, 1985); West, *IE*² 2.

M. L. W.

Dionysius (7), of *Halicarnassus, Greek critic and historian, lived and taught *rhetoric at Rome, arriving 'at the time *Augustus put an end to the civil war', and publishing the first part of his *Roman Antiquities* (Ῥωμαϊκὴ ἀρχαιολογία) 22 years later (*Ant. Rom.* 1. 7). This great work was in twenty books, going down to the outbreak of the First *Punic War; we have the first eleven (to 441 BC), with excerpts from the others. Dionysius used the legends of Rome's origins to demonstrate that it was really a Greek city, and his whole history is an erudite panegyric of Roman virtues. It is also very rhetorical, abounding in long speeches. He doubtless thought of it as exemplifying his literary teaching, which was directed towards restoring Classical prose after what he saw as the aberrations of the Hellenistic period. The treatises in which he developed this programme seem mostly to have been written before the *Antiquities*, though their chronology is much disputed. These are: (1) *On imitation* (Περὶ μιμήσεως), in three books, of which only fragments survive; the judgements on individual authors coincide largely with those in Quintilian *Inst.* 10. 1; (2) a series of discussions of individual

orators (*Lysias, *Isocrates, *Isaeus (1), *Demosthenes (2)), prefaced by a programmatic statement of distaste for 'Asianic' rhetoric (see ASIANISM AND ATTICISM), hope for an 'Attic' revival, and the writer's consciousness that this happy change is due to the good taste of the Roman governing class; (3) a group of occasional works: *On Dinarchus, On *Thucydides* (2) (important), two letters to Ammaeus (one on Demosthenes' alleged indebtedness to Aristotle, the other on *Thucydides (2)), and a letter to Cn. Pompeius on *Plato (1), of whose 'dithyrambic' style Dionysius was very critical; (4) *On Arrangement of Words* (*De compositione verborum*, Περὶ συνθέσεως ὀνομάτων), the only surviving ancient treatise on this subject, full of interesting observations on euphony and onomatopoeic effects (note especially ch. 20, on *Odyssey* 11. 593–6); this was a fairly late work, but the second part of *Demosthenes* (35 ff.) presupposes it.

For all the traditional terminology and character of Dionysius' criticism—he frequently gives the impression of 'awarding marks' for good qualities narrowly and unimaginatively defined—he is an acute and sensitive stylistic critic, whose insights deserve attention; and he understood the importance of linking historical study (e.g. on questions of authenticity) with the purely rhetorical and aesthetic.

TEXTS AND TRANSLATIONS *Roman Antiquities*: ed. C. Jacoby (1885–1925); E. Cary (Loeb, 1937–50). Critical works (*Opuscula*): ed. H. Usener and L. Radermacher, 2 vols. (1899–1929); S. Usher, 2 vols. (Loeb, 1974–85); G. Aujac, 4 vols. (Budé, 1978–91). W. Rhys Roberts, *Three Literary Letters* (1901), and *On Literary Composition* (1910); *On Thucydides* (trans.), W. K. Pritchett (1975).

STUDIES General study of history: E. Schwartz, *RE* 5/1. 934–61; E. Gabba, *Dionysius and the History of Archaic Rome* (1991). On critical works: S. F. Bonner, *The Literary Treatises of Dionysius* (1939); K. Goudriaan, *Over Classicisme* (1989: Dutch, but with Eng. summary); A. Hurst, *ANRW* 2. 30. 1 (1982), 839–65; D. C. Innes, *CHCL* 1. 267–72.

D. A. R.

Dionysius (8) of *Heraclea (3) on the Pontus (*c*.328–248 BC), pupil of *Zeno (2) and others, including *Heraclides (1) of Pontus. As a Stoic (see STOICISM) he wrote philosophical works, and also poetry. An attack of illness in old age led him to abandon the Stoic position that pain, because not morally bad, is not an evil. Subsequently he went over to the *Cyrenaic position that pleasure is our final end; hence his nickname 'the Renegade'. At the age of 80 he committed suicide.

Testimonia in von Arnim, *SVF* 1. 93–6.

J. A.

Dionysius (9) 'Periegetes' ('the Guide'), Greek author, in *Hadrian's time (?), of Περιήγησις τῆς οἰκουμένης ('Geographical Description of the Inhabited World') in 1,185 hexameters (for schoolboys?), describing in pseudo-epic style the known world chiefly after *Eratosthenes, taking little account of subsequent discoveries: land, elliptic (east–west), three continents; ocean, with inlets; Mediterranean; Libya; Europe; islands; Asia. Lost works attributed to Dionysius: Βασσαρικά = Διονυσιακά (legends of Dionysus); Λιθικά (on gems); Ὀρνιθιακά (a history of birds); Γιγαντιάς.

GGM vol. 2, pp. xv ff., 103 ff.; A. Garzya, *Dionysii Ixeuticon* (Teubner, 1963): prose-paraphrase of the Ὀρνιθιακά; Heitsch, *Griech. Dichterfr.* 1; E. H. Bunbury, *A History of Ancient Geography* (1879), 2. 480 ff.; Thomson, *Hist. Anc. Geog.* 228 f., 302, 304, 329 f.

E. H. W.; J. S. R.

Dionysius (10), of Philadelphia, reputed author of an extant poem, Ὀρνιθιακά (a history of birds), which may, however, be by *Dionysius (9) Periegetes.

A. Garzya, *Byzantion* 1957, 195 ff.

J. S. R.

Dionysius (11), of *Samos, Hellenistic 'cyclographer', published a *Kuklos historikos* in seven books, a mythographical romance or, perhaps more probably, a mythological handbook.

FGrH 15.   J. S. R.

Dionysius (12) **Scytobrachion** ('leather-arm': the unexplained nickname was doubtless meant to differentiate him from homonymous authors, but did not succeed) wrote (1) a series of stories set in Libya which, in the manner of *Euhemerus, 'rationalized' the Olympian gods as mortals from the distant past—the *Amazons are prominent, and *Dionysus is assimilated to *Alexander (3) the Great; (2) an equally rationalistic account of the *Argonauts, making *Heracles their leader and explaining away all fabulous elements as misunderstandings (e.g. the fire-breathing bulls were actually 'Taurians' ($T\alpha\tilde{\upsilon}\rho o\iota$)). A new fragment of the latter work (*PHib.* 2. 186, late 3rd cent. BC) suggests a date *c.*250 BC at the latest. His writings were cited by *Apollodorus (6) of Athens and served as mythological sources for *Diodorus (3) Siculus 3–4.

FGrH 32. J. S. Rusten, *Dionysius Scytobrachion*, Papyrologica coloniensia 10 (1982).   J. S. R.

Dionysius (13), of Sinope, Middle (?) Comedy poet (see COMEDY (GREEK), MIDDLE). The learned cook provides humour in one piece (fr. 2).

Kassel–Austin, *PCG* 5 (1986), 32 ff.

Dionysius (14), of *Thebes (1), poet, teacher of *Epaminondas (Nep. *Epam.* 2), regarded by *Aristoxenus (fr. 76 Wehrli, in ps.-Plut. *De mus.* 31) as a practitioner of the old style of *music and listed together with *Pindar, Lamprus, and *Pratinas.   E. Kr.

Dionysius (15) surnamed **Thrax,** 'the Thracian' (*c.*170–*c.*90 BC), son of Teres, of *Alexandria (1), was a pupil of *Aristarchus (2) and later a teacher of grammar and literature at *Rhodes, where his pupils provided him with the silver for a model to illustrate his lectures on *Nestor's cup (Ath. 489, 492, 501). His only surviving work is the $T\acute{\epsilon}\chi\nu\eta$ $\gamma\rho\alpha\mu\mu\alpha\tau\iota\kappa\acute{\eta}$, an epitome of pure grammar as developed by the Stoics and Alexandrians (see GRAMMAR, GRAMMARIANS, GREEK). The work is essentially Alexandrian, but there are traces of Stoic influence. It defines grammar as an $\grave{\epsilon}\mu\pi\epsilon\iota\rho\acute{\iota}\alpha$ (*empeiria* or empiricist craft), but includes $\grave{\alpha}\nu\alpha\lambda o\gamma\acute{\iota}\alpha$ (*analogia*) (see CRATES (3)) among its parts; classifies accents, stops, letters, and syllables; defines the parts of speech, with lists of their qualifications (cases, moods, etc.), and subdivisions, if any, giving examples; and concludes with some paradigms of inflexion. The ultimate aim of the grammarian is stated to be $\kappa\rho\acute{\iota}\sigma\iota\varsigma$ $\pi o\iota\eta\mu\acute{\alpha}\tau\omega\nu$, which has generally been interpreted as meaning 'criticism of poetry'. There is no treatment of syntax in the work. It had, however, an immediate vogue which lasted until the Renaissance, and its authority was continued in the catechisms derived from it which then took its place. Latin grammar early fell under its influence (see e.g. REMMIUS PALAEMON, Q.), and through Latin most of the modern grammars of Europe are indebted to it. Through Syriac and Armenian adaptations its influence spread far beyond Europe. An immense corpus of commentary grew up in Hellenistic, Roman, and Byzantine times around Dionysius' brief text. In recent year there has been controversy about its authenticity.

EDITION Uhlig, in Teubner's *Grammat. Gr.*, eds. G. Uhlig and others (1883).

SCHOLIA Hilgard, same series (1901). R. H. Robins, *Ancient and Mediaeval Grammatical Theory in Europe* (1951), 36 ff.; V. Di Benedetto,

ASNP 1958, 169 ff.; 1959, 87 ff.; R. Pfeiffer, *History of Classical Scholarship: From the Beginnings to the End of the Hellenistic Age* (1968), 266–72.
                                        P. B. R. F.; R. B.; N. G. W.

Dionysius (16) (? 2nd cent. AD), a Greek, son of Calliphron, author of *Description of Hellas* (for schoolboys?); 150 feeble iambics survive: preface (*acrostics); *Ambracia–*Peloponnese; [gap]; *Cretan cities; *Cyclades and Sporades islands.

GGM vol. 1, pp. lxxx, 238–43.   J. S. R.

Dionysus (Linear B *Diwonusos*, Homeric $\Delta\iota\acute{o}\nu\upsilon\sigma o\varsigma$, Aeolic $Z\acute{o}\nu\nu\upsilon\sigma o\varsigma$, Attic $\Delta\iota\acute{o}\nu\upsilon\sigma o\varsigma$) is the twice-born son of *Zeus and *Semele. His birth alone sets him apart. Snatched prematurely from the womb of his dying mother and carried to term by his father, he was born from the thigh of Zeus. Perceived as both man and animal, male and effeminate, young and old, he is the most versatile and elusive of all Greek gods. His myths and cults are often violent and bizarre, a challenge to the established social order. He represents an enchanted world and an extraordinary experience. Always on the move, he is the most epiphanic god, riding felines, sailing the sea, and even wearing wings. His most common cult name was *Bakch(e)ios* or *Bakchos*, after which his ecstatic followers were called *bakchoi* and *bakchai*. Adopted by the Romans as *Bacchus*, he was identified with the Italian *Liber Pater. Most importantly, while modern scholars regard Dionysus inevitably as a construct of the Greek imagination, in the eyes of his ancient worshippers he was a god—immortal, powerful, and self-revelatory.

Throughout antiquity, he was first and foremost the god of *wine and intoxication. His other provinces include ritual madness or *ecstasy (*mania*); the *mask, impersonation, and the fictional world of the theatre; and, almost antonymically, the mysterious realm of the dead and the expectation of an after-life blessed with the joys of Dionysus. If these four provinces share anything in common that illuminates the nature of this god, it is his capacity to transcend existential boundaries. Exceptionally among Greek gods, Dionysus often merges with the various functions he stands for and thus serves as a role model for his human worshippers. In the Greek imagination, the god whose myths and rituals subvert the normal identities of his followers himself adopts a fluid persona based on illusion, transformation, and the simultaneous presence of opposite traits. Both 'most terrible and most sweet to mortals' in Attic tragedy (Eur. *Bacch.* 861), he was called 'Eater of Raw Flesh' ($'\Omega\mu\eta\sigma\tau\acute{\eta}\varsigma$, on *Lesbos, Alcaeus fr. 129. 9 L–P, *POxy.* 53. 3711) as well as 'Mild' ($M\epsilon\iota\lambda\acute{\iota}\chi\iota o\varsigma$, on *Naxos (1), *FGrH* 499 F 4) in actual cult.

The name Dionysus appears for the first time on three fragmentary Linear B tablets from *Pylos and Khania (*Crete) dated to *c.*1250 BC. The tablets confirm his status as a divinity, but beyond that they reveal little about his identity and function in Mycenaean religion. One of the Pylos tablets may point to a tenuous connection between Dionysus and wine; on the Khania tablet, Zeus and Dionysus are mentioned in consecutive lines as joint recipients of libations of honey. But, thus far no physical remains of his cult have been identified with absolute certainty. A Dionysiac connection has been claimed for several archaeological discoveries; none convinces. The most spectacular is the discovery in the early 1960s of a large number of terracotta statues in a late Cycladic shrine at Ayia Irini on *Ceos. Tentatively dated to 1500–1300 BC, these fragmentary, nearly life-sized figures represent mature women who stand or, perhaps, dance. A much later deposit of Attic drinking-vessels was found in the same room; among them is a scyphus of *c.*500 BC inscribed with a dedication to Dionysus by Anthippus of Iulis (*SEG* 25. 960). According to the excavators, the temple was in continuous use from the 15th to the 4th cent. BC. This remarkable find does not prove, however, that Dionysus was worshipped on the site before the Archaic period, let alone continuously from the bronze age to the Classical period. Given the prominence of women in *Minoan religion generally, it is equally far-fetched to identify these figures as Dionysus' female attendants, whether *nymphs, nurses, or *maenads. Yet typical features of Dionysus and his religion—including wine and ivy; divine epiphanies and ecstatic forms of worship; women dancing, handling snakes, or holding flowers; the divine child and nurturing females; and bulls with and without anthropomorphic features—are all prominent in Aegean, especially Cretan religion and art. The earliest Dionysus may indeed be sought in the culture of Minoan Crete (see RELIGION, MINOAN AND MYCENAEAN).

If we had more information on the bronze age Dionysus, he would probably turn out to be a complex figure with a substantial non-Greek or Mediterranean component. Absolute 'Greekness' is a quality that few, if any, Greek gods can claim. This is especially true of their names. If Dionysus signifies '†nysos (son?) of Zeus', as some linguists believe, the god's name would be half Greek and half non-Greek (not *Thracian, however, as its occurrence in Linear B demonstrates). But such etymological neatness is just as improbable as a divine name derived from the god's genealogy. Hardly more plausible is the derivation from *nysai*, the dubious designation for three nymph-like figures on a vase fragment by Sophilus (Beazley, *ABV* 39. 15). Attempts to derive the name Semele from *Phrygian, *bakchos* from *Lydian or *Phoenician, and *thyrsos*—the leafy branch or wand carried by the god and his followers—from *Hittite, though highly speculative, reflect the wide spectrum of potential cross-cultural contacts that may have influenced the early formation of Dionysus and his cult.

In Archaic epic, Dionysus is referred to as a 'joy for mortals' (*Il.* 14. 325) and 'he of many delights' (Hes. *Theog.* 941). The source of all this pleasure is wine, the god's ambivalent 'gift' (Hes. *Op.* 614) which brings both 'joy and burden' (Hes. fr. 239. 1). Dionysus 'invented' wine, just as *Demeter discovered *agriculture (Eur. *Bacch.* 274–83; see CULTURE-BRINGERS). By a common metonymy, the wine-god is also synonymous with his drink and is himself 'poured out' to the other gods as a ritual liquid (*Bacch.* 284). *Libations of mixed or, occasionally, unmixed wine accompanied every animal *sacrifice; wineless libations were the exception. In vase-painting, Dionysus is never far from the wine. Surrounded by cavorting *satyrs and silens, nymphs or maenads he presides over the vintage and the successive stages of wine-making on numerous black-figure vases. Holding in one hand a grapevine and in the other one of his favourite drinking-vessels, either a cantharus or a rhyton, he is often depicted receiving wine from a male or female cupbearer such as Oenopion, his son by *Ariadne, or pouring it on an altar as a libation, or lying on a couch in typical symposiast posture (see SYMPOSIUM). Yet he is never shown in the act of consuming his own gift. His female followers, too, keep their distance from the wine, at least in maenadic iconography. While maenads may carry drinking-vessels, ladle wine, or pour it, they are never shown drinking it.

*Longus' Dionysiac love story of *Daphnis and Chloe culminates in the celebration of the vintage on the Lesbian estate of Dionysophanes, whose name evokes the divine *epiphanies of Dionysus. Wine festivals were celebrated in many regions of the Greek world; in *Elis as well as on *Andros, *Chios, and Naxos, they were accompanied by wine miracles. The oldest festival of

Dionysus, the Ionian-Attic *Anthesteria, was held each spring. In Athens, the highlight consisted of the broaching of the new wine followed by a drinking-contest. On this occasion, as on others, citizen women were excluded from the ceremonial drinking of wine. The admixture of wine and water was allegorized as the nurturing of Dionysus by his mythical nurses (*FGrH* 325 F 12, 328 F 5), or more ominously, as the 'mixing of the blood of Bakchios with fresh-flowing tears of the nymphs' (Timotheus, *PMG* fr. 780). In Attica, myths were told which connected the arrival of Dionysus and the invention of wine with the murder of *Icarius (schol. D *Il.* 22. 29; *LIMC* Dionysos/Bacchus no. 257). Here and elsewhere, Dionysiac myths emphasize the darker aspects of the god, and the perversion of his gifts.

Of Dionysus' four provinces, wine is the most dominant; it often spills over into the other three. Drunkenness can cause violence and dementia (Pl. *Leg.* 2. 672d, 6. 773d, μαινόμενος οἶνος). Yet the ritual madness associated with Dionysus in myth and cult had nothing to do with alcohol or drugs. Seized by the god, initiates into Bacchic rites acted much like participants in other possession cults. Their wild dancing and ecstatic behaviour were interpreted as 'madness' only by the uninitiated. As numerous cultic inscriptions show, the actual worshippers did not employ the vocabulary of madness (*mania, mainesthai, mainades*) to describe their ritual ecstasy; rather, they used the technical but neutral language of *bakcheia* and *bakcheuein*. The practitioners of *bakcheia* were usually women; the exception is Scyles, the 'mad' Scythian king who danced through the streets of *Olbia— an early centre of the Dionysus cult—as a *bakchos* (Hdt. 4. 79). While men, too, could 'go mad' for Dionysus, they could not join the bands (*thiasoi*) of maenadic women who went 'to the mountain' (*eis oros*) every other year in many Greek cities to celebrate their rites. Their notional leader was always the god himself (Eur. *Bacch.* 115 f., 135 ff.; Diod. Sic. 4. 3. 2–3), who appears already in the Homeric version of the *Lycurgus (1) myth—the earliest reference to maenadic ritual—as Dionysus *mainomenos*, 'the maddened god' (*Il.* 6. 132). Known mainly from post-classical inscriptions and prose authors like *Plutarch and *Pausanias (3), ritual maenadism was never practised within the borders of Attica. Athenian maenads went to *Delphi to join the Delphic Thyiads on the slopes of Mt. *Parnassus (Soph. *Ant.* 1126–52; Plut. *De mul. vir.* 13. 249e–f; Paus. 10. 4. 3). Halfway between Athens and Delphi lies *Thebes (1), the home town of Dionysus and 'mother city (*mētropolis*) of the Bacchants' (Soph. *Ant.* 1122), from where professional maenads were imported by other cities (*IMagn.* 215). Erwin Rohde and E. R. Dodds were the first scholars to take a comparative approach to the psychological and anthropological aspects of maenadic ritual and behaviour, but they ignored the fundamental distinction between myth and ritual.

In poetry and vase-painting, Dionysus and his mythical maenads tear apart live animals with their bare hands (*sparagmos*) and eat them raw (*ōmophagia*). But the divinely inflicted madness of myth was not a blueprint for actual rites, and the notion that maenadism 'swept over Greece like wildfire' (Rohde, Nilsson, Dodds) is a Romantic construct that has to be abandoned along with the suggestion that the maenads sacramentally consumed Dionysus in the shape of his sacred animal. The 'delight of eating raw flesh' (Eur. *Bacch.* 139, ὠμοφάγον χάριν) appears in maenadic myth, where it can escalate into *cannibalism. In the entire cultic record, however, omophagy is mentioned only once. In a maenadic inscription from *Miletus, the following directive occurs: 'Whenever the priestess performs the rites of sacrifice on behalf of the [entire] city, no one is permitted to "throw in" (deposit?) the ōmophagion (ὠμοφάγιον ἐμβαλεῖν) before the priestess has done so on behalf of the city' (*LSAM* 48, 276/5 BC). Although the ritual details escape us, a piece of raw meat was apparently deposited somewhere for divine or human consumption. The mere reference to eating raw flesh is significant, given that sacrificial meat was normally roasted or cooked. In this instance, the perverted sacrifice, a mainstay of Dionysiac myth, has left its mark also on Dionysiac cult.

Dionysiac festivals were ubiquitous throughout the Greek world; in Athens alone there were seven such festivals in any given year, five of which were dedicated chiefly to Dionysus—*Oschophoria, Rural *Dionysia, *Lenaea, Anthesteria, and City *Dionysia. The name Oschophoria commemorates the ritual carrying of vine branches hung with bunches of grapes. The Lenaea and both Dionysia featured performances of *tragedy and *comedy. Apart from the new wine, the Anthesteria celebrated the springtime arrival of Dionysus from across the sea. Less is known about two other Dionysiac festivals at Athens, the *Theoinia* and the *Iobakcheia* ([Dem.] 59. 78). Festivals of Dionysus were often characterized by ritual licence and revelry, including reversal of social roles, cross-dressing by boys and men (see TRANSVESTISM, RITUAL), drunken comasts in the streets, as well as widespread boisterousness and obscenity. In Athens as throughout Ionian territory, monumental *phalli stood on public display, and phallophoric processions paraded through the streets (*Semos of Delos, *FGrH* 396 F 24). But, unlike *Pan or the *Hermes of the *herms, Dionysus himself is never depicted with an erection. The god's dark side emerged in rituals and aetiological myths concerned with murder and bloodshed, madness and violence, flight and persecution, and gender hostility (as during the Agrionia). Throughout the Athenian Anthesteria festival, merrymaking predominated, but it was punctuated by ritual reminders of a temporary suspension of the normal structures of daily life—the invasion of the city by spirits of evil, or by the dead, or by strangers called 'Carians'; the silent drinking at separate tables, explained by the myth of the matricide *Orestes' arrival in Athens and the fear of pollution it provoked; the 'sacred marriage' (*hieros gamos*) of the wife of the *basileus* to Dionysus (see MARRIAGE, SACRED); and the cereal meal prepared on the festival's last day for the dead or for Hermes Chthonios (see CHTHONIAN GODS) and the survivors of the Great Flood.

Tragedy and comedy incorporate transgressive aspects of Dionysus, but they do so in opposite ways. While comedy re-enacts the periods of ritual licence associated with many Dionysiac festivals, tragedy dramatizes the negative, destructive traits of the god and his myths. *Aristotle connected the origins of tragedy and comedy with two types of Dionysiac performance—the *dithyramb and the phallic song respectively. Yet, in his own analysis of the tragic genre, he ignored not only Dionysus but also the central role of the gods in the drama. In addition to the mask worn by the actors in character, including the disguised god himself in both *Bacchae* and *Frogs* (see ARISTOPHANES (1)), the choral dance is the most palpable link between Attic drama and Dionysiac ritual. Tragic and comic choruses who refer to their own dancing invariably associate their choral performance with Dionysus, *Pan, or the maenads. Despite Aristotle's silence, tragedy in particular has a lot to do with Dionysus. The tragedians set individual characters, entire plays, and indeed the tragic genre as a whole in a distinct Dionysiac ambience (see COMEDY (GREEK); TRAGEDY, GREEK).

The god so closely associated with exuberant life is also connected with death, a nexus expressed as 'life–death–life' in one of the Dionysiac-*Orphic bone inscriptions from *Olbia. '*Hades and Dionysus are the same' according to *Heraclitus (fr. 15 DK). On an Apulian funerary crater by the Darius painter, Dionysus and Hades are shown in the Underworld each grasping the other's right hand while figures from Dionysiac myth surround them (Toledo 1994.19). A sacred tale ascribed to *Orpheus and modelled on the *Osiris myth describes the dismemberment of Dionysus Zagreus by the *Titans and his restoration to new life; his tomb was shown at Delphi (Orph. fr. 35 Kern; Callim. fr. 643 Pf.). According to another myth, Dionysus descends to the Underworld to rescue Semele from Hades (Iophon, *TrGF* 22 F 3); Aristophanes' comic parody of the god's catabasis (descent) has Dionysus retrieve *Aeschylus (Ar. *Frogs*). In a related ritual, the Argives (see ARGOS (2)) summoned Dionysus ceremonially 'from the water' with the call of a trumpet hidden in thyrsi 'after throwing a lamb into the abyss for the gatekeeper', i.e. for Hades (Plut. *De Is. et Os.* 35. 364f). Dionysus loomed large in the funerary art and after-life beliefs of Greeks and Romans alike. In many regions of the ancient world, tombs were decorated with Dionysiac figures and emblems like the maenad, the cantharus, and the ivy, or bore inscriptions with a Dionysiac message. The tombstone of Alcmeionis, chief maenad in Miletus around 200 BC, announces that 'she knows her share of the blessings' (καλῶν μοῖραν ἐπισταμένη)—a veiled reference to her eschatological hopes (*GVI* 1344). Found in tombs from southern Italy to *Thessaly, the so-called Orphic gold tablets contain ritual instructions and Underworld descriptions for the benefit of the deceased. Two ivy-shaped specimens refer to a ritual rebirth under the aegis of Dionysus, and to wine-drinking in the after-life; a third identifies the dead person as a Bacchic initiate (*mystēs*) (see DEATH, ATTITUDES TO; ORPHIC LITERATURE; ORPHISM).

No other deity is more frequently represented in ancient art than Dionysus. Until about 430 BC, Dionysus is almost invariably shown as a mature, bearded, and ivy-wreathed adult wearing a long chiton often draped with the skin of fawn or feline, and occasionally presenting a frontal face like his satyrs; later he usually appears youthful and beardless, effeminate, and partially or entirely nude. From his earliest depictions on Attic vases by Sophilus and Clitias (*c.*580–570 BC) to the proliferating images of the god and his entourage in Hellenistic and Roman imperial times, Dionysiac iconography becomes more varied while remaining remarkably consistent in its use of certain themes and motifs. Major mythical subjects comprise the Return of *Hephaestus and the Gigantomachy (see GIANTS); Dionysus' birth and childhood; his punishments of *Lycurgus (1), *Pentheus, and the impious sailors whom he turns into dolphins; and his union with Ariadne (as on the Derveni crater of *c.*350 BC from Macedonia). Cult scenes in vase-painting include those on the so-called Lenaea vases, which show a makeshift image of Dionysus—fashioned from a mask attached to a pillar—surrounded by women carrying or ladling wine. It is unclear whether these settings refer to a single festival or represent an artistic montage of authentic ritual elements. The Hellenistic friezes of his temples at *Teos and *Cnidus displayed the *thiasos of satyrs, maenads, and *centaurs; in the theatre at *Perge, we find scenes from the god's mythical life. Most conspicuously, *sarcophagi of the imperial period abound with scenes from Dionysiac mythology such as the god's birth and his Indian triumph—the theme of *Nonnus' monumental epic.

The very existence of Dionysus in the Mycenaean pantheon came as a complete surprise when it was first revealed by Michael

Dionysus, artists of

Ventris in 1953 (see RELIGION, MINOAN AND MYCENAEAN). Already in antiquity Dionysus was considered a foreign god whose original home was Thrace or *Phrygia and who did not arrive on the Greek scene until the 8th cent. BC. The Thracian origin of Dionysus achieved the status of scholarly dogma with the second volume of Rohde's *Psyche* (1894). In Rohde's view, the Thracian Dionysus invaded Greece, where his wild nature was ultimately civilized and sublimated with the help of the Delphic *Apollo, a process commemorated in the myth of Dionysus' exile abroad, the resistance with which his cult was met upon its arrival in Greece, and his ultimate triumph over his opponents. Rohde's Dionysus—*barbarian but happily Hellenized, occasionally wild but mostly mild—appealed to successive generations of scholars from Jane Harrison to Dodds. Wilamowitz derived Dionysus from Phrygia and Lydia rather than Thrace, while Nilsson adopted a theory of multiple foreign origins. As early as 1933, however, Walter F. Otto dissented, emphasizing instead the Greek nature of Dionysus as the epiphanic god who comes and disappears. According to Otto, the myths of Dionysus' arrival—with their dual emphasis on resistance to his otherness as well as on acceptance of his gifts—articulate the essential aspects of the god's divinity rather than the historical vicissitudes of the propagation of his cult. Otto's version of a polar and paradoxical Dionysus categorizes the diversity of Dionysiac phenomena, thus making them more intelligible. It has been argued, after Otto, that the 'foreign' Dionysus is a psychological rather than a historical entity which has more to do with Greek self-definition and the 'Dionysus in us' than with the god's actual arrival from abroad. More recently, Dionysus has emerged as the archetypal 'Other'—in a culturally normative sense—whose alterity is an inherent function of his selfhood as a Greek divinity. However, if such abstractions are pushed too far, Dionysus ceases to be the god he was to the Greeks—present in his concrete manifestations, and in the perplexing diversity of his myths, cults, and images—and becomes a modern concept.

GENERAL O. Kern, *RE* 5 (1903), 1010–46, 'Dionysos', and *RE* 16 (1935), 1210–1314, 'Mysterien'; W. F. Otto, *Dionysus: Myth and Cult* (1965; Ger. orig. 1933); H. Jeanmaire, *Dionysos* (1951); *GGR* 1³ (1967), 564–601; A. Henrichs, "Changing Dionysiac Identities", in B. F. Meyer and E. P. Sanders (eds.), *Self-Definition in the Graeco-Roman World* (1982), 137–60, 213–36; W. Burkert, *Greek Religion* (1985), 161–7, 222–5, 293–5; M. Daraki, *Dionysos* (1985); E. Simon, *Die Götter der Griechen*, 3rd edn. (1985), 269–94; M. Detienne, *Dionysos at Large* (1989; Fr. orig. 1986); H. S. Versnel, *Ter Unus* (1990), 96–205; T. H. Carpenter and C. A. Faraone (eds.), *Masks of Dionysus* (1993); J. N. Bremmer, *Greek Religion, G & R* New Survey 24 (1994).
BRONZE AGE M. E. Caskey, *Keos* 2 (1986), esp. 39–42 (Ayia Irini); M. S. Ruipérez, 'The Mycenaean Name of Dionysos', *Opuscula selecta* (1989), 293–97; Khania tablet: L. Godart and Y. Tzedakis, *RFIC* 1991, 129–49, E. Hallager and others, *Kadmos* 1992, 61–87.
DIONYSUS IN LITERATURE G. A. Privitera, *Dioniso in Omero e nella poesia greca arcaica* (1970); A. Henrichs, 'Greek and Roman Glimpses of Dionysos', in C. Houser (ed.), *Dionysos and his Circle: Ancient Through Modern* (1979), 1–11; L. Käppel, *Paian* (1992), 207–84 (Philodamus, *Paean to Dionysus* = Powell, *Coll. Alex.* pp. 165–71).
TRAGEDY/COMEDY *DFA*³; W. Burkert, 'Greek Tragedy and Sacrificial Ritual', *GRBS* 1966, 87–121; J. J. Winkler and F. I. Zeitlin (eds.), *Nothing to do with Dionysos?* (1990); K. Dover, *Aristophanes: Frogs* (1993); A. Bierl, *Dionysos und die griechische Tragödie* (1991); R. Seaford, *Reciprocity and Ritual* (1994); C. Sourvinou-Inwood, 'Something to do with Athens: Tragedy and Ritual', in R. Osborne and S. Hornblower (eds.), *Ritual, Finance, Politics* (1994), 269–90; A. Henrichs, '"Why Should I Dance?" Choral Self-Referentiality in Greek Tragedy', *Arion* 1995.
ARRIVAL AND RESISTANCE MYTHS K. Kerényi, *Dionysos*

(1976), 129–88; D. Flückiger-Guggenheim, *Göttliche Gäste* (1983); T. Gantz, *Early Greek Myth* (1993).
REGIONAL CULTS AND FESTIVALS Farnell, *Cults* 5 (1909); Nilsson, *Feste*; Deubner, *Attische Feste*; W. Burkert, *Homo Necans* (1983; Ger. orig. 1972); A. Schachter, *Cults of Boiotia* 1 (1981); E. Simon, *Festivals of Attica* (1983); F. Graf, *Nordionische Kulte* (1985); *L'Association dionysiaque dans les sociétés anciennes. Colloque 1984* (1986); A. Henrichs, in M. Griffith and D. J. Mastronarde (eds.), *Cabinet of the Muses* (1990), 257–77 (Dionysus in Attica); S. G. Cole, in R. Scodel (ed.), *Theater and Society in the Classical World* (1993), 25–38 (phallic processions); G. Casadio, *Storia del culto di Dioniso in Argolide* (1994).
PERIODS OF LICENCE F. Graf, *Nordionische Kulte* (1985), 81–96; R. J. Hoffman, *Athenaeum* 1989, 91–115; C. Auffarth, *Der drohende Untergang*, *RGVV* 39 (1991), 15–34, 249–65.
MAENADISM E. R. Dodds, *Euripides: Bacchae*, 2nd edn. (1960); J. Bremmer, *ZPE* 55 (1984), 267–86; M.-C. Villanueva Puig, *Rev. Ét. Anc.* 1988, 35–53 (wine), 1992, 125–54 (iconography); A. Henrichs, *Harv. Stud.* 1978, 121–60, in H. D. Evjen (ed.), *Mnemai: Classical Studies in Memory of Karl K. Hulley* (1984), 69–91, and *Antike u. Abendland* 1994, 31–58; R. Osborne, in C. Pelling (ed.), *Greek Tragedy and the Historian* (1997).
MYSTERY CULTS AND AFTER-LIFE M. P. Nilsson, *The Dionysiac Mysteries of the Hellenistic and Roman Age* (1957), and *GGR* 2². 358–67; M. L. West, *The Orphic Poems* (1983); R. Merkelbach, *Die Hirten des Dionysos* (1988); W. Burkert, *Ancient Mystery Cults* (1987), and 'Bacchic Teletai in the Hellenistic Age', in T. H. Carpenter and C. A. Faraone, *Masks of Dionysus* (1993), 259–75; P. Borgeaud (ed.), *Orphisme et Orphée* (1991); S. G. Cole, 'Dionysus and the Dead', in *Masks of Dionysus*, 276–95; gold tablets: C. Segal, *GRBS* 1990, 411–19, F. Graf, in *Masks of Dionysus*, 239–58; Dionysus in the Underworld: J.-M. Moret, *Rev. Arch.* 1993, 293–318.
ICONOGRAPHY C. Gasparri and others, 'Dionysos, Fufluns, Bacchus', *LIMC* 3 (1986), 1. 414–566, 2. 296–456 (plates), S. Boucher, 'Dionysos Bacchus (In Periph. Occid.)', *LIMC* 4 (1988), 1. 908–23, 2. 612–31 (plates); F. Matz, *Die dionysischen Sarkophage*, 4 vols. (1968–75); T. H. Carpenter, *Dionysian Imagery in Archaic Greek Art* (1986); A. Henrichs, in *Papers on the Amasis Painter and his World* (1987), 92–124; A. Schöne, *Der Thiasos* (1987); C. Bérard and others, *A City of Images* (1989; Fr. orig. 1984), 121–65; F. Berti and C. Gasparri (eds.), *Dionysos, mito e mistero* (1989); F. Lissarague, *The Aesthetics of the Greek Banquet* (1990; Fr. orig. 1987); F. Frontisi-Ducroux, *Le Dieu-masque* (1991); R. Hamilton, *Choes and Anthesteria* (1992); G. M. Hedreen, *Silens in Attic Black-figure Vase-painting* (1992).
MODERN RECEPTION P. McGinty, *Interpretation and Dionysos: Method in the Study of a God* (1978); A. Henrichs, *Harv. Stud.* 1984, 205–40, and in *Masks of Dionysus*, 13–43; G. Maurach, 'Dionysos von Homer bis heute', *Abh. Braunschweigische Wissenschaftliche Gesellschaft* 1993, 131–86; *Oxford Guide to Classical Mythology in the Arts, 1300–1990s* (1993).
A. H.

Dionysus, artists of (οἱ περὶ τὸν Διόνυσον τεχνῖται), generic name for the powerful guilds into which itinerant Greek actors and musicians formed themselves from the 3rd cent. BC, chiefly those (a) 'in *Isthmus and *Nemea', by 112 BC based on *Argos (2) and *Thebes (1); (b) 'in Athens', first attested in 279/8 BC; (c) of Egypt, based in *Alexandria (1); and (d) 'in Ionia and the *Hellespont', at first centred on *Teos. Their formation reflects the demand for Attic-style drama from the 4th cent. on in both Greece and the Hellenistic kingdoms, where they came under royal *patronage. On occasion organizing dramatic performances on a city's behalf, they chiefly served to secure benefits for members, notably personal inviolability in their travels and exemption from military service and local taxes. Like independent *poleis* (see POLIS) they had their own assemblies, magistrates, and ambassadors; a cultic community (sacred, of course, to *Dionysus), each had its own *temenos, priest, and festivities. Roman emperors, notably *Hadrian, took over as patrons and may have encouraged amalgamation into the 'world-wide' guild attested from AD 43 until the reign of *Diocletian and probably surviving much longer. See CLUBS, GREEK.

*DFA*³, ch. 7; *CAH* 7²/1 (1984), 319 f.; *L'Association dionysiaque dans les sociétés anciennes*. Colloque 1984 (1986); I. Stephanis, Διονυσιακοὶ τεχνῖται (1988), with prosopography; C. Roueché, *Performers and Partisans at Aphrodisias* (1993). A. J. S. S.

Diopeithes, decree of (c.432 BC), provided an impeachment procedure against impiety. *Plutarch (*Per.* 32), our only source, says it attacked 'those who fail to respect (*nomizein*) things divine or teach theories about the heavens'. Its object was the philosopher *Anaxagoras, and ultimately his friend *Pericles (1).

M. Ostwald, *Popular Sovereignty*, 528–36. M. Ga.

Diophantus (*RE* 18), of *Alexandria (1) (date uncertain, between 150 BC and AD 280), mathematician, wrote an algebraic work on indeterminate equations, Ἀριθμητικά, in thirteen books, of which six survive in Greek and four more in Arabic. The latter are numbered 4–7, and certainly represent Diophantus' original books 4–7. The Greek books are numbered 1–6 in the MSS, but of these only 1–3 represent Diophantus' original numbering, while '4–6' must be made up of extracts from the original 8–13. In the Greek (but not the Arabic) MSS the words for the unknown (ἀριθμός) and its powers up to the sixth degree are represented by symbols, as is the operation for minus, so that the equations appear in a primitive algebraical notation, but it is likely that this was introduced in Byzantine times rather than by the author. Diophantus' method is to propose a problem, e.g. 'to find three numbers such that the product of any two of them plus their sum is a square' (2. 34), and then to go through every step of finding a single solution, in rational but not necessarily integer numbers. The method for finding more solutions is only implied by the example given. This procedure, using specific numbers, puts Diophantus in a tradition going back ultimately to Babylonian mathematics (see HERON), and is in stark contrast to the abstract methods of classical Greek geometry (see MATHEMATICS). He does not recognize negative or irrational numbers as solutions. Books 1–3 contain linear or quadratic indeterminate equations, many of them simultaneous. Beginning with book 4 cubes and higher powers are found. The solutions often demonstrate great ingenuity. A small treatise by Diophantus on polygonal numbers is preserved, but a work on porisms to which he refers and which may be his own is lost.

TEXT Books preserved in Greek: critical text with Lat. trans. and scholia, P. Tannery (Teubner, 1893, 1895); Eng. trans., T. L. Heath, *Diophantus of Alexandria*, 2nd edn. (1910), adapted, good commentary; Fr. trans., P. ver Eecke (1926).; Preserved in Arabic: J. Sesiano, *Books IV to VII of Diophantus' Arithmetica* (1982), with Eng. trans., comm., and useful conspectus of all extant problems; R. Rashed, ed., *Diophante: Les Arithmétiques 3–4* (Budé, 1984), with Fr. trans.

COMMENT Heath, *Hist. of Greek Maths*. 440 ff. On Diophantus' date see J. Klein, in *Quellen und Studien zur Gesch. d. Math.* 3 (1936), 133 n. 23. G. J. T.

Dios wrote in Greek a Phoenician history whose only remnant is a citation, appearing twice in identical form in Josephus (*AJ* 8. 147–9; *Ap.* 1. 112–15), concerning King Hiram's reconstruction of *Tyre and his triumph in an exchange of riddles with King Solomon.

FGrH 3. 785. T. R.

Dioscorides (1), author of 40 epigrams in the Greek *Anthology, from the *Garland* of *Meleager (2). He imitates *Asclepiades (2)

and *Callimachus (3) and so is not earlier than the late 3rd cent. BC. He wrote a number of epigrams on earlier poets, especially dramatists, the latest being *Machon and *Sositheus; also some elegant and sensuous erotic poems.

Gow–Page, *HE*; T. B. L. Webster, *Hellenistic Poetry and Art* (1964), 141 f. A. D. E. C.

Dioscorides (2) **(Pedanius Dioscorides)** (1st cent. AD), of Cilician Anazarbus, wrote an extensive, five-book work on the drugs employed in medicine. Dioscorides studied under Areius of Tarsus and travelled extensively collecting information about the medicinal uses of herbs, minerals, and animal products. His travels took him to the Greek mainland, Crete, Egypt, and Petra, but he mentions plants from much further afield. In the Preface he describes his travels as leading to a 'soldier-like life', a statement that led later writers to conclude, probably falsely, that he was once a physician in the Roman army.

Dioscorides' Περὶ ὕλης ἰατρικῆς (*Materia medica*, 'Materials of Medicine'), bks. 1–5, lists approximately 700 plants and slightly more than 1,000 drugs, and includes a letter to Areius that serves as an introduction. His method was to observe plants in their native habitats and to research previous authorities on these subjects. Finally he related the written and oral data to his clinical observations on the effects the drugs had on and in the body. He also provided data on preparations, adulterations, and veterinary and household usages. Dioscorides boasted that his method of organization was superior to that of previous works. His scheme was first to organize by categories, such as whole animals, animal parts and products, minerals, and plants—the last subdivided into roots, pot-herbs, fruits, trees, and shrubs. Within each category he arranged drugs according to their physiological reaction on the body. This arrangement by drug affinities was not explained and, as a consequence, many later copyists of his text rearranged his system according to the alphabet thereby obscuring the genius of his contributions. Dioscorides' information aims at medical precision, and his account is relatively free of supernatural elements, reflecting keen, critical observation of how drugs react. His medical judgements were well regarded until the 16th cent. Manuscripts of the *Materia medica* in Greek, Latin, and Arabic are often beautifully illuminated and indicate that Dioscorides' original text was accompanied by illustrations. See BOTANY; PHARMACOLOGY.

TEXT *Materia medica*, ed. M. Wellmann, 3 vols. (1906–14; repr. 1958).

SPURIOUS WORKS Wellmann's edn. also contains a spurious work on poisons (2 bks.), Περὶ ἁπλῶν φαρμάκων, 'On Simple Drugs' (or Εὐπόρυστα, 'Household Remedies'). There are two (sometimes divided into four) additional spurious books on animal poisons, Περὶ δηλητηρίων φαρμάκων ('On Noxious Poisons') and Περὶ ἰοβόλων ('On Venomous Animals'). The tracts on poisons were frequently printed as bks. 6–9 of Dioscorides' works (e.g. ed. C. Sprengel, in vols. 25–6 of *Medicorum Graecorum*, 1829–30. On authenticity, see A. Touwaide, *Janus* 1983, 1–53. Wellmann published as an alternate reading to the *Materials of Medicine* a list of synonyms called *Notha*. These synonyms are in a number of languages and they appear in some manuscripts as glosses. Among the many spurious works is a Latin text called *Ex herbis femininis* ('Female Herbs') that was very popular in the early Middle Ages with lavish illuminated manuscripts. See Latin edn. by H. Kästner, *Hermes* 1896, 578–636; discussion, J. M. Riddle, *Journ. Hist. Biol.* 1981, 43–81.

TRANSLATIONS Old Latin (approx. 6th cent.), K. Hoffmann and others *Romanische Forschungen* 1 (1882–); H. Mihăescu, Bk. 1 (1938); German, J. Berendes (1902; repr. 1983); English, J. Goodyer, 1652–5 (1934; repr. 1959): archaic, faulty text; Eng. trans. of Dioscorides' Letter to Areius, J. Scarborough and V. Nutton, *Transactions of the College of Physicians of Philadelphia* 1982, 187–227.

LITERATURE M. Wellmann, *RE* 5. 1131; J. Riddle, *Dioscorides on Pharmacy and Medicine* (1985), and *Catalogus Translationum et Commentariorum* 4 (1980), 1–143; C. Dubler and E. Terés, 6 vols. (1953–9).

J. M. Ri.

Dioscuri, 'sons of Zeus', a regular title (already found in 6th-cent. BC inscriptions, *CEG* 373, 391, 427, cf. *IG* 12. 3. 359), of Castor and Polydeuces (Pollux), who on the human plane are also Tyndaridae, sons of *Tyndareos. They are the brothers of *Helen, Tyndareos' daughter, in *Homer's *Iliad* 3. 237–244, where they are treated as being dead; but in *Odyssey* 11. 300–4 they are 'alive' even though 'the corn-bearing earth holds them', and the author explains that they are honoured by *Zeus and live on alternate days, 'having honour equal to gods'. Here and in *Hesiod they are sons of Tyndareus and *Leda; later, as in *Pindar (*Nem.* 10. 80–2), Polydeuces is son of Zeus, his twin Castor of Tyndareos, and at Polydeuces' request they share his immortality between them, living half their time below the earth at *Therapne near Sparta, the other half on *Olympus. Very probably the same conception of their double nature as sons both of Zeus and of Tyndareos underlies all these passages, different though the particular emphases are. Similarly ambiguous parentage characterizes another great god/hero, *Heracles (as also *Theseus). Sometimes they are Dioscuri and Tyndaridae in successive lines (*CEG* 373; *Hymn Hom.* 33. 1–2).

Other Greeks recognized Sparta as the centre of their cult. But they were also immensely popular in Attica, for instance, and in effect throughout Greece and Greek Italy (where the Spartan colony of *Tarentum was another centre of the cult). At *Thebes (1), however, the oath 'by the two gods' (e.g. Ar. *Ach.* 905) evoked a local pair of twins, *Amphion and Zethus.

Very broadly, they were gods friendly to men, 'saviours', in a variety of spheres. Their characteristic mode of action is the *epiphany at a moment of crisis. Such interventions are regularly also an expression of their trustworthiness, their eagerness to help those who help or put their trust in them. The poet *Simonides was denied his fee by the *Thessalian prince Scopas, on the grounds that his poem had paid more honour to the Dioscuri than to the mortal patron. A little later, two youths summoned Simonides outside during a banquet in Scopas' palace; the roof collapsed, killing all within (see *PMG*, 510). The Locrians (see LOCRI EPIZEPHYRII), at war with the Crotoniates (see CROTON), appealed to Sparta for help, and were offered and accepted the assistance of the Dioscuri. This showed faith; in the battle that ensued at the river Sagra, two gigantic youths in strange dress were seen fighting on the Locrian side, and the Locrians achieved total victory (W. K. Pritchett, *The Greek State at War* 3 (1979), 21; the same work lists other battle *epiphanies of the Dioscuri, of which that at Lake *Regillus is the most celebrated, Cic. *Nat. D.* 2. 6). The Dioscuri were closely associated with athletic competitions, and here too it is their reliability as helpers that Pindar stresses (*Nem.* 10. 54). Above all (*Hymn Hom.* 33, *passim*) they brought aid at sea, where their saving presence in storms was visible in the electric discharge known as St Elmo's fire.

A characteristic rite was performed in their honour, that of *theoxenia*, 'god-entertaining' (Nilsson, *GGR* 1. 409). Individuals in their own houses, states at their public hearths or equivalent places, set a 'table' to which they then summoned the Dioscuri; votive reliefs sometimes show them arriving at the gallop over a table laid with food. Such 'table-offerings' were quite common in Greek cult, but normally they were made in the shrine of the god or hero concerned. The domestic setting in the case of the Dioscuri creates an added intimacy.

The Dioscuri are distinctive also in the extent to which they are associated with characteristic sacred symbols (about most of which we can say little more than they stress the idea of twinness). Both in art and literature they are constantly associated with horses; and on votive reliefs they appear with some or all of: the *dokana*, two upright pieces of wood connected by two crossbeams (cf. Plut. *De frat. amor.* 478a–b); a pair of amphorae of characteristic shape; a pair of bossed shields; a pair of snakes. They also often wear felt caps, above which stars may appear. (The association of the Dioscuri with stars already appears in Eur. *Hel.* 140.)

In myth, they had three main exploits. When Theseus kidnapped Helen, they made an expedition to Attica, recovered her, and carried off Theseus' mother *Aethra. They took part in the Argonautic expedition (see ARGONAUTS), and on it Polydeuces distinguished himself in the fight against *Amycus. Their final exploit on earth was the carrying off of the two daughters of Leucippus ('white horse'!), the *Leucippides, Phoebe and Hilaeira. Thereupon the nephews of Leucippus, *Idas and Lynceus, pursued them (Pindar, *Nem.* 10, who however makes the provocation a cattle-raid; Theoc. 22. 137 ff.). In the resulting fight Castor and both his pursuers were killed; the sequel of the shared immortality has already been mentioned. On the basis of these adventures the Dioscuri can be seen as ideal types of the young male; but a consistent connection between them and a particular age group cannot be observed in cult.

In art they appear before the middle of the 6th cent. BC on metopes of the *Sicyonian building at *Delphi, with the Argo (ship of the Argonauts), and rustling cattle with Idas. In Attic black-figure they are shown with Tyndareos and Leda. Later the most popular subjects are: the rape of the Leucippides; the Dioscuri as Argonauts; at the *theoxenia*; at the delivery to Leda of Nemesis' egg containing Helen.

Similarities have often been noted between the Dioscuri and the divine twins of other mythologies, above all the Vedic Aśvins, who like them are closely associated with horses.

Nilsson, *GGR* 1². 406–11; Burkert, *GR* 212–13; L. P. B. Stefanelli, *Arch. Class.* 1977; A. Hermary, *LIMC* 'Dioskouroi'.

R. C. T. P.

Dioscurides (1) or **Dioscorides** (1st cent. BC or AD) is reputed to have written *On Customs in Homer*, in which he is said to have interpolated the Homeric text, *On the Life of Homer's Heroes*, *Recollections* of sayings of famous men, *The Spartan Constitution*, *On Institutions*. But these may not be the work of one Dioscurides. Lengthy fragments survive in Athenaeus, Plutarch, and others.

FGrH 594.

J. F. L.; R. B.; J. S. R.

Dioscurides (2), nicknamed '*Phakas*', possibly because of the moles or marks (φακοί) on his face (as *Suda* δ 1206 claims), practised medicine in *Alexandria (1) in the 1st cent. BC as a member of the 'school' of *Herophilus. He perhaps served as *Cleopatra VII's physician, and possibly as an ambassador both of her father (*Ptolemy (1) XII Auletes) and brother, Ptolemy XIII (cf. *Suda* δ 1206; Caes. *BCiv* 3. 109. 3–6). Like many Herophileans, Dioscurides engaged in Hippocratic exegesis (see HIPPOCRATES (2)), writing a polemical work in seven books against all previous Hippocratic lexicographers (Erotianus, pref., and ο 5; Gal. 19. 63, 105 Kühn; cf. Paul of Aegina 4. 24). According to the problematic evidence of the *Suda*, he also wrote 24 renowned medical books, one of which may have been a work on a plague that occurred in Libya during his lifetime (cf. *Posidonius (2) of Apamea, T 113 Edelstein–Kidd).

Ed., trans., and comm.: H. von Staden, *From Andreas to Demosthenes Philalethes* (1995), ch. 9; cf. von Staden, *Herophilus* (1989), 519–22.

H. v. S.

Dioskouroi See DIOSCURI.

Diotima, actual or fictitious priestess of *Mantinea, (*c.*440 BC), from whom *Socrates pretends to have learnt his theory of love, defining its goal as generative in *Plato (1)'s *Symposium.* Other references derive from this.

A. W. P.

Diotimus, author of eleven epideictic and funerary epigrams included in the *Garland* of *Meleager (2), perhaps the Adramyttian attacked by *Aratus (1).

Gow–Page, *HE* 2. 106–7, 270–80.

A. D. E. C.

Diotogenes, the nominal author (otherwise unknown) of a *Neopythagorean work *On Piety* and one *On *Kingship* which defines the qualities of the ideal king as imitator of God and embodiment of law. These works have been variously dated between the 3rd cent. BC and the 2nd cent. AD.

Ed. H. Thesleff, *The Pythagorean Texts of the Hellenistic Period* (1965), 71–7. See ECPHANTUS.

D. O'M.

Diphilus, of *Sinope, brother of *Diodorus (1), New Comedy poet (see COMEDY (GREEK), NEW), born *c.*360–350 BC, lived most of his life at Athens, but died in *Smyrna probably at the beginning of the 3rd cent. (the reference to him in Plaut. *Mostell.* 1149 is useless for establishing his death date: see M. Knorr, *Das griechische Vorbild der Mostellaria des Plautus* (1934), 7 f.). He wrote about 100 plays, winning three *Lenaean victories (*IG* 2². 2325. 163 = 5 C 1 col. 4, 12 Mette). Some 60 titles are known, mostly typical of New Comedy; the nine or so with a mythical connection (e.g. *Danaides, Theseus*) need not all have been mythological burlesques: some could have taken their titles from a man aping a hero of myth (cf. Ath. 10. 421e on *Heracles*), others from a divine prologue (e.g. *Heros*). An unusual title is Αἱρησιτείχης ('Wall-capturer'), which was altered to Στρατιώτης ('Soldier') when the play was rewritten, presumably for a second production (Ath. 11. 496f: the two titles appear as separate entries in the *Piraeus book catalogue, *IG* 2². 2363 = test. 6 KA). Diphilus' reference to 'gilded *Euripides' (fr. 60 KA and Kock: cf. the parody in fr. 74 KA = 73 K) suggests gentle ridicule mingled with admiration. There are many interesting frs.: 17 KA and K, the nationality of the guests is important to a cook (cf. 42 KA = 43 K); 37 KA = 38 K, the unfilial conduct of Ctesippus, son of Chaereas; 70 and 71 KA = 69 and 70 K, *Archilochus and *Hipponax anachronistically *Sappho's lovers; 91 KA and K, a lively description of an unattractive woman.

A play by Diphilus was the original of *Plautus' *Rudens;* his Κληρούμενοι ('Men Casting Lots') of Plautus' *Casina, Συναποθνῄσκοντες* ('Men Dying Together') of Plautus' lost *Commorientes* (*Terence, in the *Adelphoe,* used a scene omitted by Plautus: cf. *Ad.* 6); and possibly Σχεδία ('Raft') of Plautus' *Vidularia.* Although Diphilus' originals may have been completely remodelled by Plautus, certain characteristics common to all the Roman adaptations can doubtless be attributed to the Greek poet: a delight in lively theatrical effects, with clearly contrasted scenes and characterization (see CHARACTER) perhaps less sensitive than that of *Menander (1).

FRAGMENTS Kassel–Austin, *PCG* 5. 47–123, although earlier scholars use the numbering in Kock, *CAF* 2. 541–80.

INTERPRETATION Meineke, *FCG* 1. 446 ff.; G. Kaibel, *RE* 5/1 (1903), 1153 ff. 'Diphilos' 12; A. Marigo, *Stud. Ital.* 1907, 375 ff.; G. Coppola, *Atene e Roma* 1924, 185 ff., and *RFIC* 1929, 161 ff.; U. von Wilamowitz, *Menander: Das Schiedsgericht* (1925), 166 f.; G. Jachmann, *Plautinisches und Attisches* (1931), 3 ff.; W. Friedrich, *Euripides und Diphilos* (1953), 171 ff.; T. B. L. Webster, *Studies in Later Greek Comedy,* 2nd edn. (1970), 152 ff.

W. G. A.

diploma, a modern term describing a pair of small folding bronze tablets copied from the record of soldiers' privileges inscribed in Rome, and first issued by *Claudius to individual auxiliaries and sailors. Since soldiers received their privileges after a number of years' service, even if they had not been discharged, diplomas were not discharge certificates. Auxiliaries and sailors were granted *citizenship for themselves and their children, and marriage rights (*conubium;* see COMMERCIUM), which ensured citizenship for their posterity. At least from *Vespasian's reign diplomas were issued to the praetorian and urban cohorts, conferring *conubium.* From *Trajan's reign diplomas were granted exclusively to veterans (though possibly only to those who specifically requested them), and informally could serve as proof of honourable discharge. The last known example dates to AD 306. Around December 140 the formula on auxiliary diplomas was changed so that soldiers received citizenship for themselves, if required, and for their posterity, but not for existing children. Perhaps as more citizens enlisted in them, the *auxilia* were increasingly assimilated to the condition of citizen troops. Legionaries were probably treated like the urban troops, although they did not receive diplomas, unless in exceptional circumstances, e.g. diplomas of 68 and 70 recording privileges of *legion I and II Adiutrix, recruited largely from the fleet at *Misenum and later constituted as legions.

CIL 16 (ed. H. Nesselhauf); J. C. Mann, *Epig. Stud.* 1972, 233; M. Roxan, *Roman Military Diplomas 1954–77* (1978); *Roman Military Diplomas 1978–84* (1985); W. Eck and H. Wolff, *Heer und Integrationspolitik* (1986).

J. B. C.

diplomacy See ALLIANCE; LAW, INTERNATIONAL.

Dipolieia See ATTIC CULTS AND MYTHS; BOUPHONIA; SACRIFICE, GREEK; ZEUS.

Dipylon, the name used to refer to the double gateway in Athens' city wall leading into the *Ceramicus and to the cemetery immediately outside the wall in that area. The gateway comprised a rectangular courtyard open on the land side, closed by two double doors on the city side; each corner was enlarged to form a tower; a fountain-house adjoined the gateway on the city side. The complex dates from immediately after the *Persian Wars, but was rebuilt in the 3rd cent. BC. The road from the *Agora to the *Academy passed through this gate. Some 75 m. (82 yds.) south-west a similar smaller gateway protected the passage of the Sacred Way to *Eleusis. Between the two gates stood the Pompeion, the marshalling-place for the Panathenaic procession (see PANATHENAEA). From the 11th cent. BC onwards the area was the principal burial-ground of Athens, and the whole area has been well excavated by German archaeologists. The best impression of the cemetery is given by *Pausanias (3) (1. 29), who observed here the tombs of those who fell in war and individual monuments to Harmodius and *Aristogiton, *Cleisthenes (2), *Pericles (1), and other prominent politicians.

J. Travlos, *Pictorial Dictionary of Ancient Athens* (1971), 299–322.

R. G. O.

Dirae

Dirae See ERINYES; APPENDIX VERGILIANA (poem).

Dirce, eponym of the spring/river at *Thebes (1). She was done to death by *Amphion and Zethus, sons of Antiope whom she had mistreated (ultimately Eur. *Antiope*). A Theban rite, where the outgoing hipparch swore in his successor at Dirce's tomb, reflects local tradition (Plut. *De gen.* 5. 578b–c).

F. Heger, *LIMC* 3/1 (1986), 634–44.; H. J. Mette, *Lustrum* 1982, 66–80.
A. Sch.

dirge, in Greek literature a song of lamentation sung antiphonally by a company of mourners and one or more soloists, either actually over the dead body (called the ἐπικήδειον, 'funeral song', by the ancient critics, Procl. quoted in Phot. *Bibl.* 321a30), or on subsequent commemorative days (called a *thrēnos*, Ammon. *Diff.* 54). The earliest evidence for such (amoebaean) dirges is in *Il.* 18. 50–96, 314–55, 24. 718–76; *Od.* 24. 43–64. The form continued and was elaborated in the *kommos* of tragedy (Arist. *Poet.* 12. 1452ᵇ). *Simonides (frs. 520–31 *PMG* Page) and *Pindar (frs. 128a–138 Snell–Maehler) composed poems which were given the title '*thrēnoi*' by the Alexandrians. They were stately, consolatory, and gnomic. Nothing is known of the circumstances of their performance. In Hellenistic times the genre persisted (e.g. *Bion (2), the *Lament for Adonis*).

For the dirge in Latin literature see EPICEDION; NENIA

M. Herfort-Koch, *Tod, Totenfürsorge und Jenseitsvorstellungen in der griechischen Antike: Eine Bibliographie* (1992), 25 f.; M. Alexiou, *The Ritual Lament in Greek Tradition* (1974); E. Reiner, *Die rituelle Totenklage der Griechen* (1938); H. Färber, *Die Lyrik in der Kunsttheorie der Antike* (1936).
C. M. B.; E. Kr.

'Discord' (Discordia) personified. See ERIS.

discus Throwing the discus developed from throwing the *solos* or weight (cf. *Il.* 23. 826–49), and resembled a combination of modern discus-throwing and shot-put. Surviving examples of ancient discuses vary in weight from 1.245 kg. to about 8.5 kg. (2¾–18¾ lb.). (the men's shot is nowadays 7.26 kg (16 lb.); the men's discus is 2 kg. (4.4 lb.)) and in diameter from 16.5 cm. to 34 cm. (6½–13¼ in.), though some of these were perhaps intended as dedicatory offerings or for training purposes only. The throwing action differed from modern discus technique, showing a resemblance to that now used in the shot-put: instead of making two or three complete turns before throwing, the athlete simply swung his arm back and then forwards while rotating his upper body. The throw was made from a *balbis*, a space defined by lines in front and at the sides but not at the back (suggesting that the athlete might move forwards before releasing the discus). The method of throwing is illustrated in vase-paintings and by statues, notably the Discobolus statue by *Myron (1). At the games the discus event was part of the *pentathlon. See AGONES; ATHLETICS.

ANCIENT EVIDENCE *Od.* 8. 186–94; Philostr. *Imag.* 1. 21. S. Miller, *Hesp.* 1983, 79–80, and H. Catling *Arch. Rep.* 1983, 24: description and photo of the 8.5-kg. discus.

MODERN LITERATURE E. N. Gardiner, *Greek Athletic Sports and Festivals* (1910), 310–37; O. Tzachou–Alexandri (ed.), *Mind and Body: Athletic Contests in Ancient Greece* (1989), 99–100, 257–65.
R. L. H.; S. J. I.

disease, the main cause of death in antiquity, is a topic for which there are more sources than for most aspects of life in the ancient world, thanks principally to the Hippocratic corpus (see HIPPOCRATES (2)), *Aretaeus, and the numerous works of *Galen. Additional information may be obtained from palaeopathology, the study of diseases found in human skeletal remains. Ancient medical literature concentrates on chronic and endemic diseases, rather than the major epidemic diseases. In fact the Greek word ἐπιδήμιος, in a medical context, means 'endemic' rather than 'epidemic'.

Malaria and tuberculosis are the most prominent diseases in ancient literature. Malaria occurred in antiquity in three forms, vivax, the commonest, falciparum, the most dangerous, and quartan. All three produce fevers recurring every two or three days which were noticed easily, if not understood, by ancient doctors. The epidemiology of malaria in antiquity resembled that of recent times. In the highly seasonal Mediterranean climate malaria occurs mainly in the summer and autumn and affects adults at least as much as children, helping to explain its importance for ancient doctors. It depends for its transmission on certain species of mosquitoes, and was probably absent from some regions where these vectors did not occur. It is not necessarily associated with marshy environments. The chronology of the spread of malaria in the Mediterranean is disputed. All three types existed in Greece in the 4th cent. BC, but it is uncertain how long before that falciparum malaria had been present. The disease which struck the Athenian forces outside *Syracuse during the *Peloponnesian War may have been falciparum malaria, which was not yet present in Attica, but this interpretation is controversial. W. H. S. Jones argued that the spread of malaria caused the decline of ancient Greek civilization, but this hypothesis is an exaggeration. Similar theories have been advanced to explain the decline of the *Etruscans, and it has also been argued that malaria did not exist in *Sardinia before Phoenician and Roman colonization.

Tuberculosis mostly affected young adults. One Hippocratic text describes it as invariably fatal, probably an exaggeration, but *Aretaeus gives the best ancient description of tuberculosis. Both human pulmonary and bovine tuberculosis were present in antiquity. It was probably common in crowded urban centres.

Ancient authors say hardly anything about childhood diseases, but enteric diseases such as infantile viral diarrhoea and amoebic dysentery probably accounted for most of the high infant mortality observed in cemeteries. Chickenpox, diphtheria, mumps, and whooping cough are all described in connection with attacks on adults, but there is no definite evidence for measles or rubella in antiquity. Cholera was absent. The presence of influenza is uncertain, but the common cold certainly existed. Leprosy was probably endemic in the near east in the bronze age and spread slowly westwards in the Hellenistic period. It probably only occurred sporadically. There is no conclusive evidence for gonorrhoea or syphilis, but some sexually transmitted diseases certainly existed, such as genital herpes and trachoma. The latter was also the main infectious cause of blindness. Heart disease is not prominent in ancient literature, but palaeopathology suggests that underlying conditions such as atherosclerosis were common. Some cancers were well known. Galen states that breast cancer was common.

Some chronic malnutrition diseases were quite common, especially in childhood, e.g. iron-deficiency anaemia, rickets, bladder-stone disease, and night blindness. The Greeks and Romans also took an interest in diseases of plants and animals because of their importance in agriculture. See PLAGUE.

W. H. S. Jones, *Malaria: A Neglected Factor in the History of Greece and Rome* (1907); M. D. Grmek, *Diseases in the Ancient Greek World* (1989; Fr. orig. 1983); J. R. Sallares, *The Ecology of the Ancient Greek World* (1991).
J. R. S.

dissection See ANATOMY AND PHYSIOLOGY, § 4; ANIMALS, KNOWLEDGE ABOUT; VIVISECTION.

Dissoi logoi (lit. 'Double Arguments', i.e. 'Arguments For and Against'), a short sophistic work of unknown authorship, written in Doric dialect (see GREEK LANGUAGE, §§ 3, 4) some time after 400 BC. It consists mainly of arguments for and against various evaluative theses, with frequent appeals to relativity, and also discusses the teachability of virtue.

> EDITIONS DK 2. 405–16; T. M. Robinson, in *Contrasting Arguments* (1984); Eng. trans. in R. K. Sprague (ed.), *The Older Sophists* (1972).
> COMMENT Guthrie, *Hist. Gk. Phil.* 3, ch. 11; J. Barnes, *The Presocratic Philosophers* (1982), ch. 23 (b). C. C. W. T.

dithyramb, choral song in honour of *Dionysus; the origins of dithyramb, and the meaning of the word itself, have been the subject of speculation since antiquity. There are three phases in the history of the genre: (1) pre-literary dithyramb; (2) the institutionalization of dithyramb in the 6th cent. BC; and (3) the latest phase, which began in the mid-5th cent.

Already in phase (1) dithyramb was a cult song with Dionysiac content. It was sung by a group of singers under the leadership of an *exarchōn*, as shown by the oldest piece of literary evidence, Archilochus fr. 120 West. Phase (2) has its roots in the cultural and religious policies of the tyrants (see TYRANNY; PISISTRATUS) and the young Athenian democracy (see DEMOCRACY, ATHENIAN; TRAGEDY, GREEK). *Herodotus (1) (1. 23) says that *Arion in late 7th-cent. *Corinth was the first to compose a choral song, rehearse it with a choir, and produce it in performance, and that he finally gave the name 'dithyramb' to this new kind of choral song. (Some scholars take *ōnomasanta* to mean 'he gave it a title', but titles are not associated with dithyrambs before the 5th cent.) *Lasus of Hermione is connected with dithyramb at Athens: he organized a dithyrambic contest in the first years of the democracy. Each of the ten Athenian tribes (see PHYLAI) entered the competition with one chorus of men and one of boys, each consisting of 50 singers. The financing of the enterprise (payment for the poet, the trainer of the chorus (*chorodidaskalos*), and the pipe-player; and the cost of equipping the chorus) was the responsibility of the *chorēgos* (see CHOREGIA). The winning *chorēgos* could put up a tripod with a dedicatory inscription in the Street of the Tripods. The dithyrambic contest was a competition between the tribes, not the poets, who are never mentioned on the victory inscriptions. Dithyrambs were performed at the following Athenian festivals: the City or Great *Dionysia, the *Thargelia, the (Lesser) *Panathenaea, the Prometheia, the Hephaestia; cf. Lys. 21. 1–4; ps.-Xen. *Constitution of the Athenians* (*Old Oligarch) 3. 4; Antiphon 6. 11. The first victor at the Dionysia at Athens was the otherwise unknown Hypodicus of *Chalcis (509/8 BC). In the first part of the 5th cent. *Simonides (with 56 victories), *Pindar, and *Bacchylides were the dominant dithyrambic poets. Pindar's dithyrambs (frs. 70–88 Maehler) are recognizable as such by their Dionysiac character. The standard content of a Pindaric dithyramb included some mention of the occasion which had given rise to the song, and of the commissioning *polis; praise of the poet; narration of a myth; and some treatment of Dionysiac theology. By contrast, Bacchylides' dithyrambs, with the exception of *Io, lacked these topical allusions. Hence the difficulties of classification which have been felt since Alexandrian times (see ALEXANDRIA (1)): there was a discussion between *Aristarchus (2) and *Callimachus (3) over whether the *Cassandra* of Bacchylides (fr. 23 Snell–Maehler) was a dithyramb or a *paean: *POxy.* 2368. From the mid-5th cent. (phase 3), dithyramb became the playground of the musical avant-garde, as we see from the criticisms of *Pherecrates (fr. 155 K–A) and the reaction of *Pratinas (fr.

708 Page). *Melanippides (2), *Cinesias, *Timotheus (1), and *Philoxenus (1) are the best-known exponents of phase (3): they introduced astrophic form (i.e. their poems were not arranged according to strophe and antistrophe, see METRE, GREEK § 3), instrumental and vocal solos, and 'mimetic' music. In the course of the 4th cent., a recognizably dithyrambic manner and idiom developed, and penetrated other lyric genres also. Songs with dithyrambic content were composed, like Philoxenus' *Banquet*; and in Middle *Comedy (see COMEDY, GREEK (MIDDLE)) we find fairly long passages in dithyrambic style. In the Hellenistic period dithyrambs were performed at the festivals of the Delia and Apollonia on Delos; and at the City Dionysia in Athens until the 2nd cent. AD. But post-Classical fragments (citations) allow no confident judgement about these compositions.

Our knowledge of dithyrambic poetry, esp. Pindar and Bacchylides, is based chiefly on papyrus finds (see PAPYROLOGY GREEK). For phase (3) we are chiefly dependent on citations by *Athenaeus (1) and on the criticisms of the comic poets and *Plato (1).

> TEXTS Page, *PMG.*
> MODERN LITERATURE H. Froning, *Dithyrambos und Vasenmalerei in Athen* (1971); A. W. Pickard-Cambridge, revised T. B. L. Webster, *Dithyramb Tragedy and Comedy* (1962); B. Zimmermann, *Dithyrambos* (1992). B. Z.

Divalia (Angeronalia), Roman festival on 21 December to the goddess *Angerona. The *Fasti Praenestini* describe her statue's mouth as bandaged and connect this with Rome's 'secret name'.

> A. Brelich, *Die geheime Schutzgottheit vom Rom* (1949); Latte, *RR* 134.
> C. R. P.

diverbium, dialogue in a comedy as distinct from *cantica.

divination

Greek Divination is at the heart of Greek religion: *Sophocles in a famous ode can represent a challenge to *oracles as a challenge to religion itself (*OT* 897–910), and the pious *Xenophon (1) in listing the benefits conferred on man by the gods regularly gives special prominence to guidance through 'sayings and dreams and omens' and sacrifices (*Symp.* 4. 48; *Mem.* 1. 4. 15–16, 4. 3. 12; *Cyr.* 8. 7. 3; *Eq.* 9. 8). His *Anabasis* presents in fact much the best panorama of the place of divination in an individual's experience. Before joining *Cyrus (2)'s expedition, which he realized might lead him into political difficulties, Xenophon had, on Socrates' advice, consulted the *Delphic oracle (3. 1. 5–8). At a moment of crisis, he received a dream from, as he thought, Zeus the King, containing both a threat and a promise (*An.* 3. 1. 11–13): 'what it means to see such a dream one can judge from the consequences' (i.e. the rest of the *Anabasis*). A bird-omen which he had witnessed on leaving *Ephesus had been interpreted by a seer as being of similarly mixed significance (6. 1. 23). During the campaign, the army regularly took omens from sacrifice, before marching off or joining battle for instance (see, above all, the account of a four-day delay caused by bad omens in 6. 4–5), and Xenophon also records the consultative sacrifices that he performed whenever an important decision, personal or collective, had to be made (e.g. 6. 1. 22–4, 2. 15). Through divinatory sacrifice Xenophon could, as it were, consult an oracle wherever he found himself, posing the question in exactly the form in which he might have put it to an oracle: 'is it more beneficial and advantageous to stay with King Seuthes or to depart?', for instance (7. 6. 44). He also mentions an omen from a sneeze (3. 2. 8–9). See DREAMS.

divisio

Xenophon thus presents at least five ways in which the will of the gods was revealed (whether spontaneously or in response to a mortal inquiry): at fixed oracular shrines, through dream-interpretation, observation of birds, sacrifice, and 'chance' omens such as a sneeze or an encounter or something said casually at a significant moment (cf. LSJ at σύμβολον III. 2). Lesser methods can easily be added, such as the form of inspired prophecy known as 'belly-talking' (LSJ at ἐγγαστρίμυθοι) or the 'sieve-divination' that *Theocritus introduces to characterize a rustic (*Id*. 3. 31). All Xenophon's five forms are already found in Homer, except the very important technique of divination by sacrifice, which probably entered Greece from the near east in the early Archaic period (with the consequence that bird divination dropped somewhat in significance). Also influential were the collections of verse oracles deployed by χρησμολόγοι, 'oracle-mongers'; these were commonly ascribed to mythical seers such as *Bacis, *Musaeus (1), and the *Sibyl, but 'ancient oracles of *Apollo' could also be among them. As well as such χρησμολόγοι and the staff at oracular shrines, professional diviners included dream-interpreters and above all seers, μάντεις, who specialized in sacrificial divination but no doubt claimed a broader competence. *Isocrates mentions 'books on divination' bequeathed by a seer to a friend who then took up the art and grew rich (19. 5), and the literature on *dream interpretation, of which *Artemidorus (3)'s *Onirocritica* is a late example, is said to go back to a work by the sophist *Antiphon (2). See PROPHECIES.

Professional seers were always exposed to ridicule and accusations of charlatanism, but anthropology teaches that societies which depend on seers also regularly deride them; attacks on individual seers are to be sharply distinguished from a more general scepticism (of which Eur. *Hel.* 744 ff. is a rare instance, and even this concerns only 'seers', not oracular shrines). The philosophical debate on the subject is splendidly presented in *Cicero's *De divinatione*. *Xenophanes, the *Epicureans, *Carneades and others denied the possibility of divination. Some Peripatetics defended 'inspired' prophecy such as the Pythia's (see DELPHIC ORACLE) or that through *dreams, while rejecting inductive divination from signs (*Div.* 1. 5, 113; 2. 100); most Stoics (notably Posidonius (2)) vigorously defended both types, basing their justification upon the powers of gods, fate, and nature (ibid. 1. 125) or the doctrine of συμπάθεια, 'sympathy' between the different parts of the world. See STOICISM.

R. Flacelière, *Greek Oracles* (1965); N. D. Smith, *Cl. Ant.* 1989, 140–58. On sacrificial divination: F. van Straten, in R. Hägg, *Early Greek Cult Practice* (1988), 51–68; M. H. Jameson, in *Greek Tragedy and its Legacy: Studies presented to D. J. Conacher* 1986, 59–66; and (on its origins) W. Burkert, *The Orientalizing Revolution* (1992), 41–53. On military divination: W. K. Pritchett, *The Greek State at War* 3 (1979), 47–90; M. H. Jameson, in V. D. Hanson (ed.), *Hoplites* (1991), 197–228.
R. C. T. P.

Roman All divination stems from the belief that gods send meaningful messages. These messages were classified in a variety of intersecting ways: according to the character of signs through which the message was conveyed, and whether these signs were sent unasked or were actively sought; the time-frame to which a sign was taken to refer (future, present, past) and the content of the message itself (prediction, warning, prohibition, displeasure, approval); and, most importantly, whether the message pertained to the private or public sphere, the observation and interpretation of the latter category of signs forming part of Roman state religion.

The divine message was either intuitively conveyed or required interpretation. *Cicero (*Div.* 1. 12) adopts the division of divination (elaborated by the Stoics, see STOICISM) into two classes, artificial (external) and natural (internal). The latter relied upon divine inspiration (*instinctus, adflatus divinus*), and was characteristic of prophets (*vaticinantes*) and dreamers (*somniantes*). The former was based on art (*ars*) and knowledge (*scientia*). To this category belonged the observation of birds, celestial signs, entrails, unusual phenomena, also astrology and divination from lots. But inspired utterances (see SIBYL) and dreams also required interpretation.

The Roman state employed three groups of divinatory experts: the *augures (augurs), the board of priests for the performance of sacred rites (see QUINDECIMVIRI SACRIS FACIUNDIS), who were in charge of the Sibylline books (see SIBYL), and the *haruspices. The first two were the official state priests; the haruspices were summoned as needed. Their special province was the observation of the entrails of sacrificial victims (haruspicy or extispicy), especially the liver (hepatoscopy). Both the augurs and haruspices observed and interpreted the avian and celestial signs (particularly *fulmina* and *tonitrua*, lightning and thunder), but they treated them differently. For the augurs they were the auspices expressing divine permission or prohibition concerning a specific act; they were indicative of the future only in so far as faulty auspices, and especially wilful disregard of auspices, might cause divine anger (which, however, could manifest itself in a variety of unpredictable ways). But for the haruspices (and also for the non-Roman augurs) the very same signs could be indications of specific future happenings.

All signs were either solicited or unsolicited. The latter could function either as unsolicited *auspicia oblativa* or as prodigies. The former referred solely to a concrete undertaking, the prodigies on the other hand to the state of the republic. They were indications that the normal relationship with the deity, the 'peace of the gods' (*pax deum*), was disturbed. Particularly potent were unusual occurrences (*monstra, ostenta*, Cic. *Div.* 1. 93). In the case of adverse auspices the action in question was to be abandoned; in the case of prodigies it was imperative to find out the cause of divine displeasure (this task often fell to the haruspices) and to perform various ceremonies of appeasement (*procuratio*). See PORTENTS.

The Roman state did not officially employ astrologers (occasionally they were even banned from Rome) or dream-interpreters (*coniectores somniorum*), but their services were sought by many, including the emperors (see ASTROLOGY). Predictions were made also from involuntary motions, sneezing, and from lifeless objects, particularly from (inscribed) lots (*sortes*) drawn from a receptacle and interpreted by the *sortilegi*, with centres at *Praeneste, *Tibur, *Antium, and the fountains of Aponus near *Patavium and of *Clitumnus in Umbria. Also poets were so used, particularly *Virgil (*sortes Vergilianae*).

Popular divination was often scorned as charlatanry (by *Ennius, Cicero, and the elder Cato (M. *Porcius Cato (1): a haruspex could not but laugh on meeting another haruspex), and the government was particularly suspicious of astrologers and inspired prophets. In the Christian empire all forms of divination were prohibited and persecuted, though never eradicated.

A. Bouché-Leclerq, *Histoire de la divination dans l'antiquité* 1–4 (1879–82); A. S. Pease, comm. on Cic. *Div.* (1920–3; repr. 1963); *La Divination dans le monde Etrusco-Italique* = *Caesarodunum*, Suppl. 52, 54, 56 (1985–6); J. Champeaux, *MÉFRA* 1990, 271 ff, 801 ff. (*sortes*); L. Desanti, *Sileat omnibus perpetuo divinandi curiositas* (1990).
J. L.

divisio, Gk. *diairesis*, was, in declamation, the teacher's separation of a case into its constituent arguments. The process could be very intricate, as we see in the *Diairesis zētēmatōn* ('Division of Questions') of *Sopater (2) (4th cent. AD?), who for each type of case identifies a variety of subheadings according to a system not unlike that of *Hermogenes (2). In Latin, the *sermones* of the *Declamationes pseudo-Quintilianeae* are far less formal and detailed; and L. *Annaeus Seneca (1) normally gives the simplest of headings (especially *ius* and *aequitas*, the letter and spirit of the law) when he analyses the speeches of his declaimers. Declaimers would not necessarily insert a formal division in their speeches (though they might sketch one in advance: Sen. *Controv.* 1 pref. 21); if they did, it would naturally follow the narration, as did the *partitio* in judicial oratory (Quint. *Inst.* 4. 5). See DECLAMATION.

S. F. Bonner, *Roman Declamation* (1949), 56–7; D. A. Russell, *Greek Declamation* (1983), ch. 3; D. C. Innes and M. Winterbottom, *Sopatros the Rhetor* (1988), 2–3. M. W.

Divitiacus (1) (1st cent. BC), an Aeduan Druid, whose career typifies the political division that exposed Gaul to conquest. His policy of inviting Roman aid against aggressors (unsuccessfully in 61 BC against *Ariovistus alone, successfully in 58 against both the Helvetii and Ariovistus) enabled him to emerge victorious over his bitter rival, his brother *Dumnorix. *Cicero and *Caesar used their personal contacts with him to form the Roman view of Druidism. See RELIGION, CELTIC.

Caes. *BGall.* 1. 16–20, 31–2; 2. 5.–15; Cic. *Div.* 1. 41. 90. J. F. Dr.

Divitiacus (2), king of the Suessiones *c.*100 BC, and overlord of other tribes of *Celts in both Gaul and Britain.

Caes. *BGall.* 2. 4. 7. C. E. S.

divorce See MARRIAGE LAW.

Diyllus, of Athens (early 3rd cent. BC), son of the atthidographer (see ATTHIS) *Phanodemus and author of a universal history, in 26 books, including that of *Sicily for the period 357–297 BC. The first part began with the Third *Sacred War and overlapped and enlarged *Ephorus' narrative down to 341, and the second and third parts continued with increasing detail until the death of *Cassander, 297. Cited by *Plutarch and *Diodorus (3) Siculus, Diyllus is frequently, though without certainty, considered a major source for *Diodorus (3) books 16 and 17.

FGrH 73. J. Seibert, *Das Zeitalter der Diadochen* (1983), 19–21. G. L. B.; K. S. S.

Dobunni, a British tribe (see BRITAIN) which occupied the modern county of Gloucestershire together with adjacent parts of Somerset, Oxfordshire, and Wiltshire. The coins, at first uninscribed, show affinity with those of *Commius of the Atrebates; later, inscribed coins record the following rulers: Anted, Eisu, Catti, Corio, and Boduoc. Their iron age centre was perhaps Bagendon. By emending Cassius Dio's βοδούννων, otherwise unknown (60. 20), to Δοβούννων, it can be suggested that part of the tribe (under Boduocus) made its peace with *Claudius. An auxiliary fort was placed at Cirencester, and at Kingsholm near Gloucester a fortress for Legio XX was established (*c.* AD 55–8). The *civitas*-capital was created at Cirencester (Corinium) on the evacuation of the military in early Flavian times and a very large forum and basilica were built. A *colonia* was established at *Glevum (Gloucester) in 96–8 on the site of the legionary fortress previously occupied by Legio II Augusta. Two inscriptions (*RIB* 114, (Cirencester) and 2250 (Kenchester)) attest local government.

Corinium became the second largest city in Britain in size (97 hectares (240 acres) within its early 3rd-cent. walls), and in the 4th cent. was very probably promoted capital of Britannia Prima (*RIB* 103). The *civitas* included the iron-working district of the Forest of Dean; its wealthy villas, including some of the largest in Britain (Woodchester, Chedworth, etc.), attest the prosperity of its agriculture.

A. D. McWhirr (ed.), *Roman Gloucestershire* (1981), and in G. Webster (ed.), *Fortress into City* (1988). S. S. F.; M. J. M.

Docimium was a city in *Phrygia, about 25 km. (15½ mi.) northeast of modern Afyon. It was named after a Macedonian founder, Docimus, and was one of the rare Hellenistic settlements of central Phrygia. Under the Roman empire it was known principally for its marble *quarries, which were under imperial control from the time of Tiberius, and which produced enormous quantities of white and polychrome (*pavonazetto*) *marble. This was used for large-scale imperial building projects, for instance in *Trajan's forum at Rome, and widely for prestige civic building in Asia Minor, for instance for the theatre at Hierapolis. Sculpture workshops attached to the quarries were also responsible for making elaborate, decorated *sarcophagi, which were sold both inside and outside Asia Minor, and for producing free-standing sculpture during the 2nd and 3rd cents. AD.

M. Waelkens, *Dokimeion* (1982), and *AJArch.* 1985, 641–53; J. C. Fant, *Cavum Antrum Phrygiae: The Organisation and Operations of the Roman Imperial Marble Quarries in Phrygia* (1989); S. Mitchell, *Arch. Rep.* 1989/90, 88–89 (bibliography). S. M.

Dodona (Δωδώνη), the sanctuary of *Zeus Naïos in *Epirus, and reputedly the oldest Greek oracle. The god's temple-sharer is *Dione Naïa, and both are shown together on coins. Settlement on the site probably began in early Helladic, but there is no evidence of an early Earth (or any other) oracle. Also stories of a mantic gong or oracular spring rising from the roots of Zeus' sacred oak are later inventions (Plin. *HN* 2. 228; Serv. on *Aen.* 3. 466). Traditionally oracular responses emanated from the rustling leaves of the sacred oak or from doves sitting in the tree (Hdt. 2. 55; Hes. frs. 240, 319 M–W). Oracular doves are shown on two Epirote coins (P. R. Franke, *MDAI (A)* 1956, 60 f.). *Odysseus claimed to have gone to Dodona in order to 'hear Zeus' will from the lofty oak' (*Od.* 14. 327 f. = 19. 296 f.). Achilles prayed to the Pelasgian Zeus at Dodona whose prophets the Selli (or Helli, schol. Soph. *Trach.* 1167) 'sleep on the ground with unwashed feet' (*Il.* 16. 233–5). These mysterious male prophets may have been identical with the Tomari (after Mt. Tomaros) of *Strabo (7. 328), but by the mid-5th cent. BC the oracle was operated by three priestesses who later on themselves were called 'the Doves' (Paus. 10. 12. 10; Strabo 7. 329; Hdt. 2. 55). Their method of issuing responses in a trance was borrowed from *Apollo's inspirational oracle at *Delphi (Aristid. *Or.* 45. 11 (ed. Dindorf); cf. Pl. *Phdr.* 244b). Rarely consulted officially by states, the Dodonian oracle generally offered advice on private problems. The enquirer scratched his question on a lead tablet and was answered with a simple 'yes' or 'no'. A number of tablets survive and can be seen in the museum at Ioannina. In the reign of *Pyrrhus, Dodona was made the religious centre of his kingdom and the festival of the Naïa was instituted. The sack by the *Aetolians in 219 BC was followed by a restoration, but the sanctuary never really recovered from the Roman ravaging of Epirus in 167 BC. The festival of the Naïa was revived and lasted till the 3rd cent. AD. A simple tree-sanctuary remains on the site, and the ruins of a small 4th-cent. temple stand beside the recently restored large theatre (17,000 seats) of the 3rd cent. BC. See DELPHIC ORACLE; AETOLIA.

dogs

Nilsson, *GGR* 1³; Hammond, *Epirus*; H. W. Parke, *The Oracles of Zeus* (1967); S. I. Dakaris, *Dodona* (1986).   H. W. P.; B. C. D.

dogs were used by the Greeks and Romans as watchdogs; to guard livestock (but not to herd sheep or cattle); for hunting; and as *pets. *Odysseus, who, attacked by the dogs of *Eumaeus, sits immobile until rescued by the animals' master, is pointed out as an example to the modern traveller in Greece; later in the *Odyssey* the king's own hound *Argos (1*d*) provides one of the most moving moments in the poem, when he greets his disguised master and dies (*Od.* 14. 29–36, 17. 290–307). Among breeds mentioned by classical authors, the Laconian was particularly valued by *Xenophon (1) for hunting; he distinguishes (*Cyn.* 3. 1–4. 9) between a larger Castorian and smaller vulpine, supposedly the result of crossing hounds with foxes. These may have approximated to the modern greyhound and whippet; for boar-hunting Indian, Cretan, and Locrian hounds were also necessary (*Cyn.* 10. 1). Indian hounds were probably mastiffs; better remembered today is the *Molossian mastiff, first mentioned by *Aristotle (*HA* 608ª) and celebrated by *Lucretius (5. 1062–71) who contrasts its behaviour when baying in an empty house, playing with its puppies, or flinching under the lash. *Horace (*Epod.* 6. 5) undertakes to pursue his literary opponents 'like a Molossian or tawny Laconian'. A small breed, like the Maltese terrier, appears on Attic vases; its ancient name is unknown. The Romans knew Italian breeds, like the Umbrian, described by Virgil (*Aen.* 12. 749–55) in close pursuit of a stag, and from early imperial times were familiar with Celtic hounds, including those of Britain, the Agassaeans: small and ugly but strong, swift, and brave. *Arrian (*Cyn.* 2–3) contrasts the slow and ugly Segusians, good only for tracking, with the swift and beautiful *vertragi* and adds a delightful account of his own favourite bitch Horme ('Impulse'). *Martial (14. 200) also praises the *vertragus*, as a soft-mouthed retriever. To Arrian (*Cyn.* 6. 1) no good hound is of a bad colour; in this he disagrees with Xenophon (*Cynegeticus* 4. 1–8) who holds that an unbroken colour indicates a savage strain and favours an admixture of tan. *Columella (*Rust.* 7. 12. 3) considers an unbroken colour advantageous for guard dogs; the shepherd will not mistake an all-white dog for a wolf in the twilight, while round the steading an all-black dog will seem formidable by day, and by night will be seen with difficulty. In fiction, the gigantic watchdog Scylax contributes notably to the confusion at Trimalchio's banquet (Petron. *Sat.* 64, 72).

J. M. C. Toynbee, *Animals in Roman Life and Art* (1973).   J. K. A.

dokimasia, the examination of candidates for office at Athens, before the *thesmothetai (except candidates for the *boulē, who were examined by the outgoing *boulē*). Men already chosen, whether by lot or by vote, but primarily the former, were formally interrogated to ascertain whether they were eligible: e.g. whether they were 30 years old; whether (in the case of certain offices at certain periods, e.g. the archonship: see ARCHONTES) they belonged to a particular census-class; and whether they were not precluded from one office, because they had held it before, or were holding another, or through being under some form of *atimia.

M. H. Hansen, *The Athenian Democracy in the Age of Demosthenes* (1991), 218 ff.; F. S. Borowski, *Dokimasia* (Diss. Cincinnati, 1976).
          A. W. G.; S. H.

Dolabella See CORNELIUS DOLABELLA.

domains In the Homeric poems the *basileis* (lords) have special lots, or *temenē* (see TEMENOS), like those set aside for *Glaucus (1)

and *Sarpedon in *Lycia, the gardens of *Alcinous (1), or the carefully tended orchards of Laertes. These were all prime tracts of the potentially most productive land, yielding high quality produce useful for exchange. The title of others to the land they worked or to a share of other productive rights within the environment is not clear. A theory of property based on delimiting surface area is neither complete nor universal: many other rights continued to exist and to shape the relationship between people, labour, and place of production in the ancient Mediterranean. But the idea of extensive private ownership of land was to spread, and become under the Roman law of property the dominant mode, and that which antiquity bequeathed to European culture (see OWNERSHIP, GREEK IDEAS ABOUT; POSSESSION, LEGAL).

Certain special types of property remained important throughout antiquity, and it is with these that this article is concerned. The common land of early Greek *poleis* (see POLIS) was sometimes really common to the collectivity of citizens, and could, as in many new foundations, be assigned in shares equal by surface area, another step towards the regime of private property. The gods were also proprietors on a large scale, owning *temenē* not unlike those of the Homeric heroes, administered for the running of the cult and sanctuary. Under the Roman empire the legacy of these practices was the wide dispersal of civic holdings (*Arpinum for instance owned land in *Gaul (Cisalpine), *Cos on *Cyprus, *Capua on *Crete, see CNOSSUS) the revenues from which were vital to the survival of urban institutions. But cities were not always good at managing such estates, and the land was vulnerable to private encroachment and a source of financial weakness for many communities. Both benefactors, through gifts and legacies, and the state, through various initiatives in financial overseeing, attempted to remedy the problem. Temple estates also continued to be important, especially in Anatolia, where the enormous fiefs of temples like that of Ma in *Pontus were like separate states (they tended to be assimilated to local cities during the imperial period); in Egypt there was much sacred land which had been administered by the kings, and which continued to be managed by the Roman government of the province. Italian temples and priesthoods like the Vestal virgins also owned estates. The Roman state had started with public land like any *polis*, but for whatever reason the Roman theory of *ager publicus developed in a very special and important way, fuelled by the Struggle of the Orders; it was constantly controversial because of the growing size of revenues from it and its potential importance for the settlement of veterans or plebeians.

The royal lands of the Hellenistic kingdoms represent a quite different tradition, based on the theory of the total ownership of the land by the king. *Egypt was the strongest instance: here outside the *chōra* of Alexandria (1) *gē basilikē* (royal land) was for the most part leased to small producers, and even when it was granted on leases of various kinds to their friends, or their soldiers, remained in a category of *gē en aphesei* (land on release) which suggested the maintenance of royal title. The same practice was extended to Cyrenaica, see CYRENE. The *Seleucids went much further in alienating royal land through similar practices, but especially through their more developed urban policy. Elsewhere royal estates were less ubiquitous, though the kings of *Cappadocia and *Bithynia had substantial domains.

The Roman emperors were the heirs of all these traditions. Forming huge portfolios of landed interests like their senatorial predecessors and contemporaries, they acquired a privileged share of the best productive assets, such as forests (see TIMBER), *quarries, or *mines. Even outside areas that had once experienced Hellenistic royal government, their land-holdings were increasingly run as distinctively imperial estates, with special rules and supervision. At the same time, the imperial domain continued to acquire many characteristics of *ager publicus*, though that always survived as a distinct category.

D. P. Kehoe, *The Economics of Agriculture on Roman Imperial Estates in North Africa* (1988); Rostovtzeff, *Hellenistic World*; D. M. Lewis, in O. Murray and S. R. F. Price (eds.), *The Greek City* (1990).

N. P.

dominium See OWNERSHIP.

Domitian (Titus Flavius (*RE* 77) **Domitianus),** son of the emperor *Vespasian, was born on 24 October AD 51, and remained in Rome during his father's campaign against A. *Vitellius. Surrounded on the Capitol with his uncle, *Flavius Sabinus, he managed to escape and on Vitellius' death was saluted as Caesar by the Flavian army, though the real power lay in the hands of C. *Licinius Mucianus until Vespasian's arrival. In 71 he participated in the triumph of Vespasian and *Titus, and between 70 and 80 held seven consulships, being twice ordinary consul (73 and 80). Although Domitian exercised no formal power, he was clearly part of the dynastic plan, and there is no convincing evidence that he was kept in the background or consumed by jealousy of his brother, whom he succeeded smoothly in 81.

The literary sources, especially *Tacitus (1) and *Pliny (2) the Younger, represent a senatorial tradition hostile to Domitian. But this is a legitimate and important viewpoint, illustrating the tension between aristocratic officials and autocrat. *Suetonius' account, though basically hostile, is more balanced and suggests that a more favourable view did exist, apart from the flattery of poets like *Statius and *Martial.

Domitian was conscientious in the performance of his duties, adopting a stance of moral rectitude, maintaining public decency at shows, and showing respect for religious ritual; three Vestal virgins (see VESTA) suffered capital punishment for breaking their vows of chastity; later, Cornelia, the chief Vestal, was buried alive. He promoted festivals and religious celebrations, showing particular devotion to *Jupiter and *Minerva, and performed the *Secular Games; many public buildings were erected, completed, or restored, including the *Capitol, the *Colosseum, and a great palace on the *Palatine. For the people there were frequent spectacles and banquets, though his cash grants were restrained. He raised military pay by a third, and bestowed by edict additional privileges on veterans and their families; he remained popular with the army and praetorians.

Domitian administered legal affairs diligently and tried to suppress corruption. Suetonius' contention that he achieved equitable provincial administration through careful supervision of officials and governors (*Dom.* 8. 2) has been challenged, but other evidence indicates that Domitian, although authoritarian in his attitude to the provinces (e.g. his abortive order to cut down at least half the provincial vineyards), tried to impress probity and fairness on his appointees; he sensibly granted rights of ownership to those who had appropriated tracts of unused land (*subseciva*); Pliny (2) the Younger's letters to *Trajan show that Domitian's administrative decisions were generally endorsed. The role and influence of equestrians in the administration increased in his reign, but as part of a continuing trend rather than deliberate policy. The effectiveness of his management of imperial finances is disputed, but he probably left a surplus in the treasury; his confiscation of the property of his opponents was for political rather than financial reasons.

Domitian was the first reigning emperor since *Claudius in 43 to campaign in person, visiting the Rhine once, and the Danube three times. *Frontinus in his *Strategemata* reports favourably on Domitian's personal control of strategy and tactics. In 82/3 he fought a successful war against the *Chatti on the middle Rhine, brought the Taunus area under Roman control, and accepted a triumph and the name 'Germanicus'. But the military balance was shifting towards the Danube, and in 85 the Dacians, under king *Decebalus, invaded *Moesia killing its governor, Oppius Sabinus. Domitian came in person in 85 and 86; and after the defeat and death of *Cornelius Fuscus (praetorian prefect), Tettius Iulianus, governor of Upper Moesia, won a victory at Tapae in 88. Since Domitian was facing trouble from the *Marcomanni and *Quadi in *Pannonia, he made peace with Decebalus before launching a campaign against them (spring 89); at the end of 89 he celebrated another triumph. Then early in 92 a legion was destroyed in Pannonia by an incursion of the Sarmatian *Iazyges and the *Suebi, which was eventually contained under Domitian's personal direction. There was also considerable military activity in Britain, where Cn. *Iulius Agricola continued the invasion of northern Scotland; his recall in 84 after an unusually long governorship of seven years, probably reflects military needs elsewhere rather than imperial jealousy.

Domitian failed to find a working relationship with the *senate. He was sometimes tactless and did not conceal the reality of his autocracy, holding ten consulships as emperor, wearing triumphal dress in the senate, having 24 lictors, and becoming *censor perpetuus* in 85, symbolically in charge of the senate; his manner was arrogant, and he allegedly began an official letter: 'Our lord god orders that this be done'. There was a conspiracy in 87, and a rebellion in 89 by L. *Antonius Saturninus, governor of Upper Germany. He apparently had little support among his troops and was easily crushed, but Domitian thereafter forbade two legions to be quartered in one camp. He became more ruthless against presumed opponents, and factions in the aristocracy produced many senators willing to act as accusers. The executions of at least twelve ex-consuls are recorded in the reign, mainly for dissent or alleged conspiracy, and not because they were Stoics (see STOICISM), although Domitian did expel philosophers. The emperor himself observed: 'no one believes in a conspiracy against an emperor until it has succeeded'. The execution in 95 of *Flavius Clemens, his cousin, whose sons he had adopted as heirs, was a mistake since it seemed that no one now was safe. A plot was formed by intimates of his entourage possibly including his wife, Domitia, and he was murdered on 18 September 96; his memory was condemned by the senate.

ANCIENT SOURCES Suet. *Dom.* (ed. F. Galli (1991)); Tac. *Agr.*; Cass. Dio 67; Plin. *Pan.*; Statius, *Silv.*; Martial; M. McCrum and A. G. Woodhead, *Select Documents of the Principates of the Flavian Emperors* (1961).

MODERN WORKS K. H. Waters, *Phoenix* 1964, 49; B. W. Jones, *Domitian and the Senatorial Order* (1979), and *The Emperor Domitian* (1992); B. Levick, *Latomus* 1982, 50; J. C. Anderson, *Hist.* 1983, 93; R. Syme, *Chiron* 1983, 121 (= *RP* 4. 252); P. M. Rogers, *Hist.* 1984, 60.

J. B. C.

Domitius (*RE* 14) **Afer, Gnaeus,** of *Nemausus (mod. Nîmes), wit and orator, who enjoyed a sinister reputation under *Tiberius

Domitius Ahenobarbus, Gnaeus

(Tac. *Ann.* 4. 52), especially as a prosecutor. After crossing swords with Gaius (1), he was made consul in September 39. Later he was *curator aquarum* (see CURA(TIO)), dying in AD 59. *Quintilian knew and admired him.

PIR² D 126; Schanz–Hosius, § 450. 3. M. W.

Domitius (*RE* 18) **Ahenobarbus** (1), **Gnaeus,** was praetor 194 BC and consul 192, when he fought the *Boii. It was probably in this campaign that a contingent of Achaeans served under a Domitius Ahenobarbus against Gauls: L. Moretti, *Iscrizioni storiche ellenistiche* 1 (1967), no. 60. He took part in the battle of *Magnesia, but the statements in *Plutarch and *Appian that he was in effective control of the Roman forces should be rejected.

J. Br.

Domitius (*RE* 20) **Ahenobarbus** (2), **Gnaeus,** as *consul (122 BC) and proconsul (see PRO CONSULE) in *Gaul (Transalpine) defeated the *Allobroges and *Arverni in two major battles, once with the help of Q. *Fabius Maximus Allobrogicus. He treacherously seized the Arvernian king Bituitus and led him in his *triumph (*c.*120). He built stone *trophies in Gaul to commemorate his victories and began the *via Domitia, perhaps establishing a garrison at *Narbo to guard it; and he probably made treaties with the defeated tribes. His censorship (115, probably with L. *Caecilius Metellus Delmaticus) was marked by unusual severity (see CENSOR). He died *c.*104. E. B.

Domitius (*RE* 21) **Ahenobarbus** (3), **Gnaeus,** son of (2), with L. *Licinius Crassus concerned in founding the colony of *Narbo (cf. *RRC* no. 282), kept up his inherited Gallic connections. Tribune 104 BC, he was not co-opted to a priesthood in his father's place. Blaming M. *Aemilius Scaurus (1) for this, he unsuccessfully prosecuted him and passed a law transferring the election of priests of the four major colleges (see COLLEGIUM) from the colleges to an assembly of seventeen tribes drawn by lot. (There were religious objections to election by the whole people.) He was elected pontifex maximus and consul 96, and was censor with Crassus (92). Although they quarrelled violently, they agreed in passing an edict forbidding rhetorical teaching in Latin. E. B.

Domitius (*RE* 23) **Ahenobarbus** (4), **Gnaeus,** was with his father, L. *Domitius Ahenobarbus (1), at Corfinium in 49 BC and like him was dismissed unhurt by Caesar. In 44 he accompanied *Brutus to Macedonia, and in 43 was condemned for participation in the murder of Caesar. From 44 to 42 he commanded a fleet in the Adriatic against the *triumvirs (for his coins see *RRC* 519, one of them perhaps with his father's portrait), but he joined Antony before the treaty of Brundisium (see ANTONIUS (2), M., para. 4), was formally reinstated in his civic rights, and governed Bithynia from 40 to 35 or later. In 36 he took part in Antony's Parthian expedition and in 35 supported C. Furnius, governor of Asia, against Sextus *Pompeius. He was consul in 32; early in the year he and C. *Sosius fled to Antony, and coined for him (*RRC* 521). He opposed the personal participation of Cleopatra (VII) in Antony's war with Octavian, and went over to the latter before Actium, already suffering from a fever which proved fatal. He left only one son (L. *Domitius Ahenobarbus (2)).

G. W. R.; T. J. C.; E. B.

Domitius (*RE* 27) **Ahenobarbus** (1), **Lucius,** called *princeps iuventutis*, 'outstandingly excellent young man', by *Cicero in 70 BC (*Verr.* 2. 1. 139), forcibly resisted C. *Manilius. In 65 Cicero counted on his support in his canvass for the consulship (*Att.* 1.

1. 4). In 58, as praetor, he threatened to prosecute *Caesar for his actions in 59, but had to desist. In 56 he felt sure of becoming consul 55 and announced that he would recall Caesar from Gaul, where he had connections inherited from Cn. *Domitius Ahenobarbus (3). As a result of the conference of *Luca, he had to postpone his consulship to 54 and give up his intention. As consuls he and his colleague Ap. *Claudius Pulcher (3) were involved in a disgraceful election scandal. He became pontifex about 50. In 49 he was appointed to succeed Caesar in Gaul, but after Caesar's invasion collected forces, including tenants from his vast estates in central Italy, at *Corfinium, asking Pompey to relieve him. Owing to a misunderstanding, or a difference on strategy, Pompey did not join him and he surrendered to Caesar, who dismissed him unharmed. He next defended *Massilia against Caesar, but escaped to Greece before its capture, where he fought at *Pharsalus and died trying to escape after the defeat. He was said to be pretentious and brutal, but personally a coward. He was married to Porcia and was the father of Cn. *Domitius Ahenobarbus (4).

Gruen, *LGRR*, see index. For Corfinium see Shackleton-Bailey, *CLA* 4. 448 ff. E. B.

Domitius (*RE* 28) **Ahenobarbus** (2), **Lucius** (*consul 16 BC), the husband of *Antonia (2), elder daughter of M. *Antonius (2) (Mark Antony) and *Octavia (2), the Princeps' sister. Alleged to have been proud, bloodthirsty, and in his youth addicted to chariot-racing, he was *aedile in 22, when he behaved arrogantly to the censor L. *Munatius Plancus; proconsul of Africa (12); legate of Illyricum between 7 and 2, when he marched from the Danube to the Elbe, setting up an altar to Augustus on the further bank of the latter river. The starting-point of his march is uncertain. Next, in command of the army of Germany, he constructed the causeway across the marshes between the Rhine and the Ems known as the *pontes longi*, after which nothing more is heard of him until his death in AD 25 (with obituary notice, Tac. *Ann.* 4. 44).

Syme, *AA*, see index and table 3. R. S.; E. B.

Domitius (*RE* 43; cf. 11) **Calvinus, Gnaeus,** served in Asia in 62 BC, supported M. *Calpurnius Bibulus when he (Calvinus) was tribune in 59, and was praetor in 56. To secure election as consul he made a scandalous deal with the consuls of 54 (Cic. *Att.* 4. 17. 2, etc.); disturbances followed revelation of the plot, but he was finally elected in July 53 for the rest of that year. He may have been exiled in 51 (R. Syme, *Sallust* (1964), 217). In the Civil War he was Caesarian: he fought against Q. *Caecilius Metellus Pius Scipio in Thessaly, commanded the centre at *Pharsalus, was defeated by *Pharnaces II at Nicopolis, and helped Caesar in Africa. In 42, while bringing reinforcements to the triumvirs, he was trapped on the Adriatic by Cn. *Domitius Ahenobarbus (4), and lost his whole force. Consul again in 40, he afterwards governed Spain, with notorious severity to his troops; in 36 he triumphed, and from his spoils decorated the *Regia.

G. E. F. C.; R. J. S.

Domitius (*RE* 50; Suppl. 3) **Corbulo, Gnaeus,** through the six marriages of his mother Vistilia (Plin. *HN* 7. 162) was connected with many prominent families: one of his stepsisters married the emperor *Gaius (1). Probably suffect consul AD 39, in 47 he was legate of Lower Germany when he successfully fought against the Chauci led by Gannascus, but was not allowed by *Claudius to go further. A strict disciplinarian, he made his troops dig a canal between the Meuse and Rhine. Proconsul of Asia under

Claudius, he was soon after *Nero's accession made *legatus Augusti pro praetore* (see LEGATI) of *Cappadocia and *Galatia with the command against Parthia in the war about the control of *Armenia. This started in earnest only in 58, when Corbulo had reorganized the Roman army in the east. He captured Artaxata and *Tigranocerta, installed *Tigranes (4) V as king of Armenia, and received the governorship of *Syria. But Tigranes was driven out of Armenia, the war was renewed in 62, and at Corbulo's request a separate general, L. *Caesennius Paetus was sent to Armenia. After Paetus' defeat, Corbulo obtained in 63 a *maius* *imperium* and was again put in charge of Cappadocia–Galatia, as well as Syria. He restored Roman prestige, and concluded a durable agreement with Parthia: *Tiridates (4), the Parthian nominee to the throne of Armenia, admitted a Roman protectorate. Corbulo probably did not abuse his popularity, but his son-in-law *Annius Vinicianus conspired. In October 66 Nero invited Corbulo to Greece and compelled him to commit suicide. His daughter Domitia Longina became wife of *Domitian in 70. It was the homage of the new dynasty to the name and influence of the greatest general of his time. The account of his achievements in Tacitus (*Ann.* bks. 12–15) and *Cassius Dio (bks. 60–3) derives ultimately to a great extent from Corbulo's own memoirs.

M. Hammond, *Harv. Stud.* 1934, 81 ff.; R. Syme, *Tacitus*, see index, and *JRS* 60, 27 ff. = *RP* 2. 805 ff. Portrait: F. Poulsen, *Rev. Arch.* 1932, 48 ff.
A. M.; G. E. F. C.; M. T. G.

Domitius (*RE* 66) **Marsus,** an Augustan poet, often acknowledged as one of his models by *Martial (who indicates that *Maecenas patronized him, 7. 29. 7–8, 8. 55. 21–4); his work *Cicuta* comprised a collection of satirical epigrams (of which one on Bavius survives) as venomous as hemlock. He also wrote an epic *Amazonis* (Mart. 4. 29. 8), which was not admired, and a prose *De urbanitate* (Quint. *Inst.* 6. 3. 102 ff.). Among his fragments are an epigram on the death of *Tibullus and two on *Atia (1), the mother of Augustus.

D. Fogazza, *Domiti Marsi: Testimonia et Fragmenta* (1981); Courtney, *FLP* 300. E. S. Ramage, *Urbanitas* (1973), 102. *PIR*² D 153. E. C.

Domitius Tullus, Gnaeus, adopted, with his brother Lucanus, by the wealthy Gallic orator Cn. *Domitius Afer. Tullus enjoyed rapid promotion under *Vespasian, who made him a *patrician. He was proconsul of Africa under Domitian and suffect consul for the second time in AD 98. His death in 108 and testament are described in detail by *Pliny (2) and he may be the testator formerly labelled 'Dasumius', known from an inscription at Rome. His niece and adopted daughter Domitia Lucilla the Elder was grandmother of M. *Aurelius.

Plin. *Ep.* 8, 18; *CIL* 6 10229 + *AE* 1976, 77; Syme, *RP* 5. 521 ff.
A. R. Bi.

Domitius (*RE* 88) **Ulpianus,** came from *Tyre where an inscription honouring him has recently been found. He followed an equestrian career in Rome, drafting rescripts (replies to petitions; see CONSTITUTIONS; MAGISTER LIBELLORUM) for *Septimius Severus, to judge from their style, from AD 202 to 209, and at least from 205 onwards did so as secretary for petitions (*a libellis*). In contrast with *Papinianus, on Severus' death at York in 211 he sided with Caracalla, who in 212 by the *constitutio Antoniniana* (see CONSTITUTION, ANTONINE) extended Roman citizenship to all free inhabitants of the empire. Presumably in response to this extension, which suited his outlook, Ulpianus was galvanized into activity in the following years (213–17), systematically composing more than two hundred books (*libri*) in which he expounded Roman law for the benefit, among others, of the new citizenry, emphasized its rational and universal character and appealed to its basis in natural law. Probably under *Elagabalus he became *praefectus annonae* (responsible for the corn supply), in which capacity he is attested in March 222, early in the reign of *Severus Alexander, who in the same year made him praetorian prefect and set him over the two existing prefects. The resulting clashes allowed the praetorian troops, with whom he lacked authority, to mutiny and murder him in 223.

His commentaries on the praetor's edict (*Ad edictum praetoris*) and the civil law (*Ad Sabinum*), in 81 and 51 books respectively, were on an even greater scale than *Paulus'. He also wrote important works *De officio proconsulis* ('On the Duties of the Provincial Governor') and on other officials, besides monographs and manuals for students both elementary and advanced. He had an exalted idea of a lawyer's calling: lawyers were 'priests of justice' devoted to 'the true philosophy'. His fame was immediate and lasting, his works more widely used than those of any other lawyer. A number of spurious works, such as the six books of *Opiniones* ('Opinions'), some of which may have been composed by authors of the same name, were credited to him. One of five jurists whose works were endorsed by the Law of Citations in 426, he was a principal source for Justinian's *Digesta*, of which he provided more than two-fifths (see JUSTINIAN'S CODIFICATION). His clarity and forthright self-confidence make him an attractive writer, inspired by cosmopolitan tendencies, a search for consensus, and a regard for private rights. His work, both comprehensive and closely documented, foreshadows Justinian's *Digesta* which incorporated so much of it. For these reasons he has proved the most influential of Roman lawyers, having done more than anyone to present the law in a form in which it could be adapted to the very different needs of medieval and Renaissance Europe.

Lenel, *Pal.* 2 379–1200; *PIR*² D 169; *HLL* 4, § 424; T. Honoré, *Ulpian* (1982); Syme, *RP* 3. 863–8; D. Liebs, *BHAC* 1984/5 (1987) 175–83; P. Frezza, *Stud. Doc. Hist. Iur.* 1968, 363–75; D. Nörr, *Xenion Zepos* (1973) 555–72; G. Crifo, *ANRW* 2. 15 (1976), 708–89. T. Hon.

Domus Aurea (Golden House), *Nero's residence created after the fire of AD 64, and notorious for its novelties and extravagance (Suet. *Ner.* 31; Tac. *Ann.* 15. 42). Nero was particularly castigated for turning a vast area (*c*.50.5 ha.: 125 acres) of the centre of Rome into a regal park, with residential nuclei dispersed within landscaped *gardens extending from the Palatine to the Oppian and Caelian around an artificial lake. The main entrance was from the Forum along the new *via Sacra through a porticoed vestibule housing a colossal bronze statue of Nero. New palatial buildings were added to existing imperial properties on the Palatine and Esquiline, the best preserved of which is the Oppian wing incorporated into the substructures of the *baths of Trajan. The long porticoed structure, developed on at least two levels with symmetrical five-sided courts either side of a remarkable domed octagonal hall, borrows much from Hellenistic palaces and Roman *villa architecture but uses vaulted concrete construction in an unprecedented fashion (see BUILDING MATERIALS).

D. Hemsoll, in M. Henig (ed.), *Roman Architecture and Architectural Sculpture* (1990), 10 ff.; A. Boethius, *The Golden House of Nero* (1960), 94 ff.; W. L. MacDonald, *Architecture of the Roman Empire* 1, 2nd edn. (1982), 31 ff.; L. Fabbrini, *Analecta Romana Instituti Danici*, Suppl. 10 (1983), 167 ff. J. D.

Donatists The Donatists were members of a puritanical church of the martyrs in 4th- and early 5th-cent. Roman Africa. Their schism from the African Catholics derived from the events of the Great Persecution under *Diocletian and *Maximian (303–5). African clergy who complied with imperial demands to surrender Christian scriptures were dubbed *traditores* or 'surrenderers'. Moderates and rigorists clashed over the procedure for readmitting *traditores* to communion, arguing over how far the Church on earth must be a 'mixed body' containing both righteous and sinners. The death of Mensurius, bishop of *Carthage, accentuated divisions. When Carthaginian Christians elected the archdeacon Caecilian bishop in Mensurius' stead, a strong party of dissenters, backed by Numidian bishops, countered by electing Majorinus as rival bishop (probably 307, but perhaps 311/12). At his death, Majorinus was succeeded by the cleric Donatus, possibly of Casae Nigrae in Numidia.

In the winter of 312/3, *Constantine I ordered the return to Caecilian of confiscated Church property and exempted Caecilian's clergy from a number of fiscal burdens. The opposition appealed to Constantine for arbitration by Gallic bishops as to who was rightful bishop of Carthage. Constantine commissioned Miltiades, bishop of Rome, himself an African, to convoke an episcopal tribunal which decided for Caecilian and condemned Donatus (October 313). The Donatists now asserted that one of Caecilian's consecrators, Felix of Abthugni, had been a *traditor* and therefore incapable of performing a valid consecration. While their complaints were again rejected at the council of Arles (August 314), it was not until February 315 that Felix was cleared, and only in November 316 did Constantine declare Caecilian lawful bishop. By then Donatus' church had won wide acceptance throughout Africa, but apart from a precarious foothold in Rome the movement did not spread outside Africa. For the remainder of the century, the Donatists incurred only intermittent persecution and, despite the exile of Donatus by *Constans (347), apparently remained the majority church until *c*.400.

By the 340s there emerged in southern *Numidia Donatist extremists who became known as Circumcellions, probably through their association with the shrines of martyrs (*cellae*). The Circumcellions, whose social origins remain opaque, perpetrated violent attacks against creditors and landlords. Beneath these seemingly social and economic grievances, however, lay a fundamental religious fanaticism manifested clearly in the Circumcellions' vigorous pursuit of martyrdom by any means, including suicide. Donatist bishops alternately disavowed the Circumcellions and employed them against their Catholic enemies, prompting intervention by imperial forces.

The Donatists' support of the revolt of Firmus (372–5) left them virtually unscathed, but an internal schism involving Maxentius (392–3) and their backing of *Gildo's failed revolt (398) laid the Donatists open to counter-attack by African Catholics and imperial officials. St *Augustine devoted considerable energies to overcoming the schism. A series of imperial rescripts banned the movement (405), and in 411 a conference of more than 500 bishops, presided over by the imperial commissioner Marcellinus, went against them. Years of persecution followed, ended only by the arrival of the *Vandals in 429. Thereafter, Donatists and Catholics seem to have reconciled themselves to a peaceful coexistence of divergent traditions within a single ecclesiastical (Catholic) structure.

Theologically the Donatists were rigorists, following the tradition of *Tertullian and *Cyprian, holding that the Church of the saints must remain holy. They insisted on rebaptizing converts and held that sacraments dispensed by a *traditor* were not only invalid but infected the recipients. Donatist theologians included

Macrobius, Donatist bishop of Rome, and Tyconius, whose work influenced St *Augustine. Despite their appeals to Constantine (313) and Julian (361), the Donatists also accepted a theory of worldly government which practically equated the Roman empire with the apocalyptic image of Babylon. Cultural and economic divisions seem to have contributed to the ecclesiastical controversy, with the Catholics drawing support from the more urbanized and Latinized Proconsular Africa and the Donatists from the more rural and native Numidia and Mauretania.

Donatism produced its own art forms, but not, so far as is known, a Bible in a language other than Latin. With the Coptic and Syrian Churches, it is an example of cultural and religious groupings by regions which characterized both halves of the empire from the late 3rd cent. onwards.

SOURCES Chief are: Optatus, *De schismate Donatistarum* (*CSEL* 26; Eng. trans. 1917); Augustine, anti-Donatist works (*CSEL* 51–3; *Bibliothèque augustinienne* 28–32), some translated in *NPNF* 4, first series; Donatist *Acta Martyrum* (*PL* 8); J.-L. Maier, *Le Dossier du donatisme* 1–2 (1987–9), with bibliog.; S. Lancel, *Actes de la conférence de Carthage en 411* 1–4 (1972–91).

MODERN LITERATURE P. Monceaux, *Histoire littéraire de l'Afrique chrétienne* 4–7 (1912–23); G. G. Willis, *St. Augustine and the Donatist Controversy* (1950); W. H. C. Frend, *The Donatist Church* (1952; with rev. bibliog. 1985); E. Tengström, *Donatisten und Katholiken* (1964).

W. H. C. F.; T. R. B.

donativum, in the imperial period an irregular monetary payment to soldiers, perhaps originally associated with distributions of booty. Donatives celebrated important events linked to the emperor—imperial birthdays, dynastic policy, the defeat of conspiracies, military victories, and especially accession to power. Augustus in his will had bequeathed 1,000 sesterces each to the praetorians, 500 each to the urban soldiers, and 300 each to legionaries, sums which *Tiberius doubled in his own name. But in AD 41 *Claudius paid 15,000 sesterces per man to ensure the crucial support of the praetorians, confirming the importance of a substantial donative in the emperor's own name at his accession and linking the army more closely to his person. Claudius probably made a proportionate payment to other citizen troops, and thereafter a donative accompanied every accession, though it is unclear if auxiliaries (*auxilia*) continued to be excluded from this bounty. Donatives depended on circumstances and were not directly related to regular pay rates; the largest known donative, 25,000 sesterces (more than six times praetorian pay), was paid by *Didius (Severus) Iulianus in 193 at the notorious 'auction' of the empire.

A. Passerini, *Le coorti pretorie* (1939), 114; J. B. Campbell, *The Emperor and the Roman Army* (1984), 165. J. B. C.

Donatus (1) (*RE* 8), **Aelius,** the most influential grammarian of the 4th cent. AD, whose pupils included the future St *Jerome. His two *artes* ('treatises') (ed. L. Holtz (1981), superseding Keil, *Gramm. Lat.* 4. 355–402) attracted many commentators (e.g. *Servius, *Cledonius, *Pompeius) and dominated grammatical learning in Europe until the reemergence of *Priscianus in the 12th cent. The *Ars minor*, intended for beginners, deals with the eight parts of speech in question-and-answer format; the *Ars maior* is more comprehensive and includes sections on the 'flaws' and 'virtues' of speech. Donatus also wrote commentaries on *Terence and *Virgil. The extant Terence commentary is only a much abridged version (lacking *Heautontimoroumenos*) compiled at an unknown date from (probably) two sets of marginal scholia in manuscripts of Terence (ed. P. Wessner, 2 vols. (1902–5): a new edition is needed, see M. D. Reeve, *CPhil.* 1979, 310 ff.); the original commentary cannot be reconstructed. From the Virgil commentary there survive only the dedicatory epistle, the 'Life' of Virgil (drawn from *Suetonius), and the introduction to the *Eclogues* (ed. J. Brummer, *Vit. Verg.* (1912); G. Brugnoli and F. Stok, *Enc. Virg.* 5/2, 437–40; epistle and 'Life' ed. C. G. Hardie (1954)). But the 'vulgate' commentary of *Servius contains much material from Donatus, and the augmented version of Servius ('Servius Danielis') contains still more (G. P. Goold, *Harv. Stud.* 1970, 101 ff.). Some of the doctrine found in commentaries to Donatus' *artes* (U. Schindel, *Die lateinischen Figurenlehren* (1975)), and some of the more learned notes in glossaries (e.g. *Liber glossarum*; see GLOSSA, GLOSSARY, LATIN), may also derive from the commentary on Virgil.

PLRE 1. 268. Herzog–Schmidt, § 527.　　　　　　　R. A. K.

Donatus (2) (*RE* 9), **Tiberius Claudius** (late 4th–early 5th cent. AD?), wrote a long, line-by-line 'interpretation' of the *Aeneid*, dedicated to his son (*Interpretationes Vergilianae*, ed. H. Georgii, 2 vols. (1905–6)). Virtually nothing is known of Donatus himself save that he disapproved of the methods of the schools (see EDUCATION, ROMAN, § 3), and his work in fact is largely independent of the scholastic tradition of commentary on Virgil. Devoted to appreciative paraphrase of the narrative and to judgements (sometimes striking) on the characters' 'psychology', Donatus knew little of the poem's historical background yet was quite certain that its every element was designed to praise *Aeneas and *Augustus: contentedly reductive and reflexively traditionalist, his work embodies the sensibility of an ancient reader 'cut adrift from history'.

PLRE 1. 268 f. Herzog–Schmidt, § 614; M. Squillante Saccone, *Le 'Interpretationes Vergilianae' di Tiberio Claudio Donato* (1985); R. J. Starr, *Cl. Ant.* 1992, 159–74.　　　　　　　R. A. K.

Dorian festivals In contrast to the abundance of *Ionian festivals, only one has a claim to be a marker of Dorian identity, the *Carnea (Karneia). A festival of that name is attested in Sparta, *Thera, *Cyrene, *Argos (2), *Cos, and *Cnidus, a month name *Karneios* much more widely; according to Thucydides, *Karneios* was a 'sacred month' for Dorians (5. 54. 2), and Pausanias speaks of worship of Apollo Karneios as common to all Dorians (3. 13. 3). The month *Hyakinthios* is also often found in Dorian communities, but the corresponding festival Hyacinthia is attested only for Sparta (see HYACINTHUS; SPARTAN CULTS). Other festivals or associated month names such as Agrionia and *Apellai (1–2) that are common in Dorian states also appear in Aeolian regions. Negatively, Herodotus claims (2. 171) that *Thesmophoria were not celebrated by Dorians of the *Peloponnese; see TRIOPAS.

Nilsson, *Feste*; A. E. Samuel, *Greek and Roman Chronology* (1972): for month names.　　　　　　　R. C. T. P.

Dorians can be approached in two ways, structural and narrative. Structurally, Dorian was the name given by Greeks to one of their own linguistic and religious subgroups, the other main group being the *Ionians (but there were also Aeolians from *Aeolis, and the people of *Achaea whom the Dorians conquered, see below). For 'Dorian' as a separate Greek dialect see Thuc. 3. 112. 4 and DIALECTS, GREEK; GREEK LANGUAGE. *Heracles was the warlike ancestor of the Dorians, and there was (see DORIAN FESTIVALS) at least one specifically Dorian festival, the *Carnea. (But Heracles was prominent in the Ionian Athens of *Pisistratus, and Dorian Sparta made a point of recovering the

bones of Achaean *Orestes in the 6th cent. as a way of playing down Dorianism, Hdt. 1. 65 ff. Things polarized later, see below.) Dorians were divided into three *phylai (Hylleis, Dymanes, Pamphili), first attested in *Tyrtaeus 19. 8 West.

There was also a narrative story about Dorians. Standard tradition, e.g. Thuc. 1. 12, held that the Dorians were newcomers who subjected the Achaeans (see ACHAEA) when they arrived in Greece and especially the Peloponnese *c.*80 years after Troy fell, an event put not long before 1200 BC at Thuc. 5. 112 (a speech). *Ephorus put the Dorians' arrival rather later, in 1069. For the romantic story of their arrival, which Greeks called the 'Return of the Heraclidae', see HERACLIDAE. Archaeological evidence is hard to reconcile with all this, especially because in Sparta the break in the pottery record comes *c.*900 BC, and this is too late for the legends, which may therefore not be chronologically usable. A compromise position (Desborough) puts the main Dorian invasion *c.*1200 but the (secondary) occupation of the Peloponnese by newcomers in the late 11th cent.

Dorian–Ionian tensions became acute in the 5th cent.; thus at the new Spartan colony of *Heraclea (4) Trachinia, Ionians and Achaeans were not welcome; Athens' reply was to reinaugurate the Ionian festival of Delian Apollo (Thuc. 3. 92, 104).

H. T. Wade Gery, *CAH* 3[1] (1924), 518 ff.; V. Desborough, *Last Mycenaeans* (1964), 250 ff., and (with N. Hammond) *CAH* 2[2]/2 (1975), 658 ff.; P. Cartledge, *Sparta and Lakonia* (1979), ch. 7; J. Alty, *JHS* 1982, 1 ff.; A. M. Davies, *Verbum* 1987, 8 ff.; I. Malkin, *Myth and Territory in the Spartan Mediterranean* (1994), 38.　　　　　　　S. H.

Dorieus, 'the Dorian', royal Spartan, a younger half-brother of *Cleomenes (1) I by their polygamous father's first wife. Jealousy, ambition, and disaffection prompted him to lead a colonizing expedition (only the second undertaken from Sparta) to Cinyps on the *Libyan coast; but after three years he was expelled by the Carthaginians. His alleged participation in Croton's destruction of *Sybaris (510 BC) is probably legendary, but he did found a settlement near Heraclea Minoa in west Sicily, where he and most of his followers were shortly killed by the joint forces of *Segesta and the Phoenicians.

Hdt. 5. 40 ff. PB no. 252; T. J. Dunbabin, *The Western Greeks* (1948), 348 ff.; P. Cartledge, *Sparta and Lakonia* (1979).　　　　　　　P. A. C.

Dorieus of Rhodes See IALYSUS; RHODES.

Doris, a small area in central Greece enclosing the headwaters of the Cephissus. Its small plain, containing the Tetrapolis of Pindus, Erineus, Boeum, and *Cytinium, is traversed by the route from Malis to Phocis which turns the defences of *Thermopylae and was used by the Persians and Galatians. The *Dorians of Peloponnese, and the Spartans particularly, claimed Doris as their *mētropolis* (Tyrtaeus, fr. 2 West); possibly during the invasion period a section of Dorian invaders halted there. Represented on the amphictionic council, Doris was championed by Sparta (Thuc. 1. 107 with Hornblower, *Comm. on Thuc.*). In the 4th cent. BC it fell into the power of Onomarchus and later of *Philip (1) II. Fourth-cent. walls are extant at Cytinium.

P-K, *GL* 1. 2. 657 ff.; E. Kase and others (eds.), *The Great Isthmus Corridor Route* 1 (1991).　　　　　　　N. G. L. H.

Dorotheus, of Sidon (1st or beginning of 2nd cent. AD), astrological poet who had great vogue with the Arabian astrologers.

Ed. (along with Manetho) H. Koechly (1858); V. Stegemann, *Die Fragmente des Dorotheus* (1939–43).　　　　　　　J. S. R.

Dosiadas, author of a short poem in iambic rhythms called Βωμός ('The Altar') whose shape, as a *technopaignion*, it imitates. In language of Lycophronic obscurity (which may give a guide

Dositheus

to the composer's era, see LYCOPHRON (2)) the altar claims to be a dedication by Jason.

TEXT *Anth. Pal.* 15. 26; Powell, *Coll. Alex.* 175 f.; *Bucolici Graeci*, ed. A. S. F. Gow (1952, repr. 1969), 182 f. A. H. G.

Dositheus (1), of Pelusium (fl. *c*.230 BC), pupil of the astronomer *Conon (2). He continued a connection between the Alexandrian astronomers and *Archimedes which had begun with the latter's studies in *Alexandria (1); Archimedes dedicated several of his books to Dositheus. Observations by him on the time of appearance of the fixed stars (some of them made at places further north than Alexandria) and on weather-signs are recorded in the *Parapegma* of *Geminus and elsewhere. He wrote a work Πρὸς Διόδωρον ('To Diodorus') in which he discussed the *Phaenomena* of *Aratus (1) and *Eudoxus (1)'s researches, and a work on the calendar, Περὶ τῆς Εὐδόξου ὀκταετηρίδος ('on the Eight-year Cycle of Eudoxus'). W. D. R.

Dositheus (2), author of a brief Latin grammar (ed. Keil, *Gramm. Lat.* 7. 376–436; J. Tolkiehn (1913)). His name is Greek, and one of the three manuscripts gives him the unadorned title *magister* ('master'); no more is known of him. Yet the grammar is interesting because most of it survives with a literal Greek translation, not necessarily by Dositheus, but fitting other indications that the grammar was designed and used for teaching Latin as a foreign language, to Greek-speakers. Close parallels with others of this type (*Charisius, Anonymus Bobiensis) imply a common source (*Cominianus ?), and probably a date in the later 4th cent. AD.

Kaster, *Guardians* 278. A. C. D.

Dossen(n)us, a stock character of *Atellana, a glutton, thought by some to have been a hunchback because of a supposed derivation of his name from *dorsum*, 'back'. P. G. M. B.

doxographers See PHILOSOPHY, HISTORY OF.

Draco, according to Athenian tradition, was a lawgiver who introduced new laws in the year when Aristaechmus was archon (see ARCHONTES), probably 621/0 BC. This was the first time that Athenian laws were put in writing. According to one account (*Ath. pol.* 4) he established a constitution based on the franchise of *hoplites, but elsewhere he is only said to have made laws against particular crimes. The penalties were very severe: when asked why he specified death as the penalty for most offences, he replied that small offences deserved death and he knew of no severer penalty for great ones; and the 4th-cent. orator *Demades remarked that Draco wrote his laws in blood instead of ink (Plut. *Sol.* 17). *Solon repealed all his laws except those dealing with homicide.

Such was the tradition current in Athens in the 5th and 4th cents. BC. At that period no one doubted that the homicide laws then in force were due to Draco; this is shown by references in Athenian speeches, and also by an inscription of 409/8 which contains part of the current law and describes it as 'the law of Draco about homicide' (*IG* 1³. 104).

Modern scholars have treated the tradition with varying degrees of scepticism. Some have doubted whether Draco existed at all. The hoplite constitution is generally regarded as spurious (being perhaps an invention of 5th-cent. *oligarchic propagandists). Most accept that Draco introduced laws about homicide and other offences, and some accept that the surviving inscription reproduces his homicide laws with little or no alteration; but details of his other laws cannot now be known.

R. S. Stroud, *Drakon's Law on Homicide* (1968); M. Gagarin, *Drakon and Early Athenian Homicide Law* (1981). D. M. M.

Dracon, of *Stratonicea, in *Caria (3rd–2nd cent. BC), predecessor or contemporary of *Dionysius (15) Thrax; author of a number of works on grammar, metric, and particular lyric poets (*Sappho, *Alcaeus (1), and *Pindar), cited in the *Suda*. The extant Περὶ μέτρων ποιητικῶν ('On Poetical Metres') ascribed to him (ed. G. Hermann (1812)) has been shown to be a 16th-cent. forgery. J. D. D.

Dracontius, Blossius Aemilius, a Christian, a lawyer and *vir clarissimus* (Roman of senatorial rank), well trained in rhetoric, lived in *Carthage towards the end of the 5th cent. AD. For eulogizing in verse the Roman emperor he was imprisoned by Gunthamund, the *Vandal king, but subsequently released. His secular works, marked by unrestrained rhetoric, consist of a collection of short hexameter poems entitled *Romulea*, including rhetorical exercises, epithalamia, and mythological epyllia (*Hylas*, *De raptu Helenae* (*On the Abduction of Helen*), *Medea*); the anonymous *Orestis tragoedia* (*Tragedy of Orestes*), now proved Dracontian, probably belongs to this collection. The Christian poems, written in prison, comprise (*a*) a short elegiac poem of repentance addressed to the king (*Satisfactio*), (*b*) *De laudibus Dei* in three books of hexameters; this, his chief work, shows some poetic imagination, appeals by its personal interest, but is marked by digressions, repetitions, and lack of unity. Dracontius displays a considerable knowledge both of Scripture and of classical Roman literature. Though he is well versed in the poetic diction, exhibiting numerous echoes of the classical poets, his language is often harsh and obscure, the syntax audacious, and the prosody faulty. That the anonymous *Aegritudo Perdicae* is Dracontian cannot be proved.

EDITIONS F. Vollmer, *MGH* 14 (1905), *PLM* 5² (1914). Introd., text, trans., and comm. of *Satisfactio*, by Sister M. St Margaret (1936); *De laudibus Dei*, by J. F. Irwin (1942); *De laudibus Dei* and *Satisfactio*, by C. Moussy and C. Camus (Budé, 1985–8); *Satisfactio* (text only), by F. Speranza (Testi e Studi 9, 1978). *Orestis tragoedia* (concordance), by R. Marino (1981).
LITERATURE Teuffel–Kroll 3⁶. 466 ff.; F. J. E. Raby, *Christian Latin Poetry* (1953), and *Secular Latin Poetry* (1957), with bibliog.; D. Romano, *Studi Draconziani* (1959). *PLRE* 2, 'Dracontius' 2.
A. H.-W.; F. J. E. R.

drainage, drain See CLOACA MAXIMA; SANITATION.

drama, Greek See COMEDY (GREEK); TRAGEDY, GREEK.

drama, Roman See COMEDY, LATIN; TRAGEDY, LATIN.

dreams fascinated the ancients as much as they do us, though it is illegitimate to employ Freudian categories in interpreting ancient dreams: their categories must not be subverted by our own culturally relative theories. Most ancients accepted that there were both significant and non-significant dreams (e.g. Hom. *Od.* 19. 562–7: true dreams come from gates of horn, delusory dreams from gates of ivory; cf. Verg. *Aen.* 6. 893–6). This basic division might itself be subdivided, most elaborately into a fivefold classification: non-predictive dreams, subdivided into *enhypnia* caused by the day's residues and *phantasmata* or distorted visions that come between sleeping and waking states; predictive dreams subdivided into: *oneiroi* that need symbolic interpretation, *horamata* or prophetic visions, and *chrēmatismata* or advice from a god (e.g. Macrob. *in Somn.* 1. 3). The last category is well attested epigraphically by votives put up by people as the result of successful advice or instructions from a god received in a dream, and in the remarkable diary kept by Aelius *Aristides which included numerous visions of *Asclepius and other gods. Dreams were indeed an important aspect of diagnosis in sanctuaries of Asclepius (see INCUBATION).

The idea that dreams could be significant, but might need professional interpreters, is found from Homer onwards (*Il.* 1. 62–7, 5. 148–51; Hdt. 5. 55–6; Theophr. *Char.* 16. 11). Dreambooks were written from the 5th cent. BC onwards; the only surviving example from antiquity is that by *Artemidorus (3).

Philosophers and others discussed whether dreams had a divine origin. The Hippocratic author (see HIPPOCRATES (2)) of the treatise *On the Sacred Disease* urged that dreams were caused merely by disturbances in the brain, and the author of *On Regimen* 4 explained how to use dreams for medical diagnosis. *Plato (1) argued that some dreams came from the gods and were reliable sources of knowledge, *Aristotle that physiological explanations applied, while *Epicurus and *Lucretius located dreams in a theory about the nature of sense perceptions. For *Cicero the possibility of prophetic dreams was an example of *divination that worked in practice, but which was impossible to justify theoretically (*Div.* 1. 39–65, 2. 119–48, with Pease's comm.). Cicero also used a dream narrative (the Dream of Scipio) as part of his *Republic*, the part to which *Macrobius devoted his commentary.

Christian texts also developed the importance of dream visions, in a variety of styles: the Book of Revelation or the *Shepherd* of Hermas both stand as reports of visions; the *Martyrdom of St Perpetua* includes a vivid firsthand report of a dream vision she had of her martyrdom; *Synesius, *On Dreams* (AD 405–6) offered an allegorical interpretation of dreams. Eight handbooks of dream interpretation survive from the Byzantine period.

E. Asmis, *Epicurus' Scientific Method* (1984); C. A. Behr, *Aelius Aristides and the Sacred Tales* (1968); Bouché–Leclercq, *Hist. div.* 1. 277–329; D. Del Corno, *Graecorum de re onirocritica scriptorum reliquiae* (1969); G. Devereux, *Dreams in Greek Tragedy* (1976); E. R. Dodds, *The Greeks and the Irrational* (1951), ch. 4; D. Gallop, *Aristotle on Sleep and Dreams* (1991); J. S. Hanson, ANRW 2. 23. 2 (1980); A. H. M. Kessels, *Mnemos.* 1969; N. Lewis, *The Interpretation of Dreams and Portents* (1976), a sourcebook; R. G. A. van Lieshout, *Greeks on Dreams* (1980); A. D. Nock, *Harv. Theol. Rev.* 1934 = *Essays* 1; *Oxford Dictionary of Byzantium* 1. 661, 3. 1526–7; A. L. Oppenheim, *TAPhS* 46. 3 (1956), on near east; F. T. van Straten, *Bulletin Antieke Beschaving* 1976; A. Volten, *Demotische Traumdeutung* (1942). S. R. F. P.

dress In classical antiquity, items of clothing and jewellery were major personal possessions. The prominence of drapery, i.e. clothing, in Greek and Roman art reflects the importance of dress in daily life.

Most garments were made of *wool, though *linen was used for some tunics and underclothing and *silk was worn by richer women; most frequently, the fibre was left undyed, though women's clothes were more colourful than men's; the clothing of both sexes commonly had areas of decoration in wool dyed either with 'real purple' from sea snails or in imitation of *purple; such decoration was generally very simple, consisting of woven bands and geometric motifs; figurative decoration, where it occurred, was usually tapestry-woven and only rarely embroidered. Clothes were made of large pieces of cloth with simple outlines which had been woven to shape on traditional looms; though certain garments were characteristic of the Greeks and others of the Romans there was no real difference between Greek and Roman clothes in techniques or materials; most classical garments belonged either to the category of mantles and cloaks

that were 'thrown around' and for which the general terms were *periblēma* and *amictus*, or to those items, including tunics, that were 'entered into', *endyma* and *indumentum*; the former often served at night as blankets; all clothes were cleaned by washing and were stored folded-up in chests.

Draped mantles were the characteristic garment of freeborn citizens. The mantle worn by Greek men, and eventually by men and women throughout the eastern Mediterranean and by Roman women, was the *himation*, in Latin *pallium* or *palla*. This was a rectangle, measuring approximately 2.8 × 1.75 m. (9 × 6 ft.), which could be draped in various ways but which was usually supported on the left arm, leaving the right arm free. The mantle worn by Roman men, the Etruscans, and, originally, Roman women too was the *toga, a semicircular piece of cloth which over time became extremely large.

Cloaks were worn by men, either pinned on the right shoulder or joined at the front of the body. Pinned cloaks, used especially by horsemen, could be rectangular or semicircular: two Roman military cloaks, the *paludamentum* and the *sagum* (of Celtic origin), were rectangular; *chlamys*, the old Greek term for a pinned cloak, had by the 1st cent. AD come to mean specifically a semicircular cloak. The closed cloaks, in Latin *birrus* and *paenula*, were also based on semicircles and, being hooded, were suitable for travellers.

The traditional Greek woman's garment, the *peplos*, somewhere between a mantle and a tunic, was an approximately square piece of cloth worn with the top third or so folded over and pinned on both shoulders. By the 4th cent. BC the *peplos* had been largely replaced in the cities by the *himation* but was still worn in the country and by all women during cold weather.

According to tradition, the *peplos*, *himation*, and toga had all at first been worn without a tunic. However, the tunic, *chiton* or *tunica*, had an early history as an independent garment and by the 4th cent. the combination of draped mantle and tunic was the normal form of civilian dress for both men and women. Most tunics were sleeveless, made of two rectangular pieces joined at the sides and on the shoulders or of a single piece folded lengthways or widthways. An alternative to sewing, used to fasten women's tunics on the shoulders, was a series of button-like discs around which fabric from both front and back was wrapped and tied. Sleeved tunics only became common in the late Roman period, when two clearly defined varieties emerged, the narrowsleeved tunic known in Latin as *strictoria*, and the wide-sleeved *dalmatica*. While the dalmatic was worn ungirt, tunics generally were worn with a belt, *zōnē* or *cingulum*, as had been the *peplos*.

Underclothes, like tunics, were probably worn more widely than ancient art or literature suggests. A tunic of linen was often worn under a tunic of wool and men probably mostly wore a triangular loincloth (*perizōma*, and perhaps also *zōnē*; Lat. *subligar* or *licium*), as did women in *menstruation. A number of cloth bands were also used as underclothes, notably the *strophion* or *mamillare*, with which women bound their breasts.

Garments used on the extremities of the bodies illustrate a number of non-woven techniques: the Greek woman's *sakkos* or hairnet was made by a method now known as sprang; stretchy socks, *sokkoi*, employed a looping technique resembling knitting; certain men's hats and some foot-coverings were made of felt, *pilos* or *pilleus*. Leather was the usual material for shoes and sandals but, except in the army, was not employed for clothing. Fur, characteristic of barbarian dress, was not used at all.

The simplicity and conservatism of classical dress was set off, in the case of women, by elaborate coiffures, jewellery, and make-up. For both men and women, hairstyles and footwear shapes changed more rapidly than those of clothing and are consequently a better guide when dating works of art. See COSMETICS; TEXTILE PRODUCTION.

L. M. Wilson, *The Clothing of the Ancient Romans* (1938); M. M. Evans and E. B. Abrahams, *Ancient Greek Dress* (1964); H. Granger–Taylor, *Textile History* 1982, 3–25. H. G.-T.

Druids See MONA; RELIGION, CELTIC.

Drusus See CLAUDIUS DRUSUS, NERO (38–9 BC) and IULIUS CAESAR (1), DRUSUS (*c.*13 BC–AD 23), brother and son respectively of the emperor Tiberius.

Dryope, daughter of *Dryops or of Eurytus, was mother by *Apollo of Amphissus, eponym of *Amphissa. She was transformed either into a *nymph associated with a spring (Nicander in Ant. Lib. *Met.* 32) or a lotus-tree—*Celtis australis* (Ov. *Met.* 9. 330–93). E. Ke.

Dryops, eponym of the Dryopes; his parentage is variously given, and the history of his people, allegedly *Pelasgian, i.e. pre-Hellenic, obscure, but they are stated to have emigrated widely (from the Spercheius valley to *Parnassus, the Argolid (see ARGOS (2)), *Arcadia, etc.); hence perhaps the differing stories which make him the son of gods or men belonging to several of these regions. See also DRYOPE.

C. Arnold–Biucchi, *LIMC* 3/1 (1986), 670. H. J. R.

ducenarii *Augustus, probably in AD 4 (Cass. Dio 55. 13) added to the three existing jury panels (*decuriae*) consisting of equestrians (see EQUITES), a fourth *decuria* recruited from *ducenarii*, i.e. inhabitants of Italy the value of whose property was at least 200,000 sesterces, half the property qualification of an equestrian. The new jury panel dealt with cases involving small sums of money, and subsequently *Gaius (1) (Caligula) added a fifth panel (Suet. *Aug.* 32; *Calig.* 16).

In the imperial period equestrian officials in the service of the state eventually acquired definitions depending on the status of the post they held, as expressed in terms of its salary: *sexagenarii* (60,000 sesterces), *centenarii* (100,000), *ducenarii* (200,000), and later *trecenarii* (300,000).

In the later empire, *ducenarius* remained as one of the ranks depending on the office held by equestrian officials: *egregii, centenarii, ducenarii, perfectissimi,* and *eminentissimi* (the praetorian prefects; see PRAEFECTUS PRAETORIO)). Past holders of these offices retained their rank and privileges, which could also be conferred as an honour by the emperor without tenure of the post. Eventually therefore as the number of men holding these ranks increased, so their status declined.

The title *ducenarius* was subsequently employed to describe a non-commissioned officer in the field army who received three and a half units of rations (*annonae*), which now served as military pay. In the civil service, which was constituted on a military basis (*militia*), many ranks were survivals from the army of the Principate, but some ranks from the field army, including *ducenarius*, were also employed, e.g. by the *agentes in rebus* (imperial couriers).

H. G. Pflaum, *Les Procurateurs équestres sous le haut-empire romain* (1950), and *Les Carrières procuratoriennes équestres sous le haut-empire romain* (1960–1), with Suppl. (1982); A. H. M. Jones, *Studies in Roman Government and Law* (1960), 40, and *Later Rom. Emp.* 525, 578, 583, 599. G. R. W.; J. B. C.

Ducetius, Hellenized *Sicel (see HELLENISM), emerged as a Sicel leader following the appeal of the *Syracusans for Sicel support against the tyrant Thrasydaeus (466 BC). In concert with the Syracusans, he expelled *Hieron (1)'s colonists from *Catana (mod. Catania) to Inessa (461; see AETNA (2)), and (459) took *Morgantina and refounded Menae as Menaenum (Mineo). By 453 (foundation of Palice) he had created the Sicel League (*koinon tōn Sikelōn*), from which only Hybla (Ragusa) held aloof. In 451 he captured Inessa and attacked Motyum (near *Acragas). The growth of his power alarmed Syracuse and Acragas, but he defeated their joint forces (451). Next year he was decisively defeated, his support fell away, and he surrendered to the Syracusans, who sent him into honourable exile at *Corinth. He returned, probably with Syracusan approval (448/7) and founded a Graeco-Sicel colony at Caleacte (on the north coast): this precipitated war between Syracuse and Acragas. Ducetius died *c.*440. It is impossible, on the scanty evidence, to say whether he aimed at creating a true Sicel national confederation or simply a personal empire, on the ruins of Hieron's: whichever it was, it did not long survive his defeat in 450.

B. Niese, *RE* 5 (1903), 1782–3; D. Asheri, *CAH* 5² (1992), ch. 7. B. M. C.

Duilius (*RE* 1), **Gaius,** consul 260 BC, appointed to command in western *Sicily; took over command of Rome's first battle-fleet, following the capture of Cn. *Cornelius Scipio at Lipara. Using the *corvus* (a rotatable boarding-bridge), he defeated the Carthaginians under Hannibal (not the famous Hannibal) off Mylae (mod. Milazzo), rejoined his army, raised the siege of *Segesta, and captured Macella. After returning to Italy (259), he celebrated Rome's first naval triumph, commemorated by the *columna rostrata* (a column decorated with the beaks of captured ships: for its inscription see *ILLRP* 319) in the Forum. From the booty of Mylae, Duilius built a temple to Janus in the forum Holitorium. He was censor in 258 and dictator to hold elections in 231, but never held another command.

B. Caven, *The Punic Wars* (1980), 28–30. B. M. C.

Dumnonii, a tribe in SW Britain (Devon, Cornwall, part of Somerset), apparently formed from diverse iron age groups. The tribe is probably amongst those defeated by *Vespasian soon after AD 43. After the initial military occupation a self-governing *civitas* was created in Flavian times with its capital at *Isca (1) (Exeter) built on the site of the fortress of Legio II Augusta. Villas are few and *Romanization concentrated in Isca. Although not Romanized, there was a substantial population, much of which continued to live in enclosed farmsteads ('rounds'). From the mid-3rd cent. the *tin of Cornwall, known in pre-Roman times, was re-exploited; milestones attest road construction from Gordian III down to Constantine I. Two inscriptions (*RIB* 1843–4) attest work on the *wall of Hadrian by a corvée of the Dumnonii.

M. Todd, *The South-West to AD 1000* (1987). S. S. F.; M. J. M.

Dumnorix, brother of *Diviciacus (1) and, according to his enemies, a man of overweening ambition. Eclipsed by his brother, in 58 BC he struck at the pro-Roman *Aedui by aiding the *Helvetii, and was spared only at Diviciacus' request. Ordered in 54 to accompany Caesar to Britain, he refused and was cut down attempting to escape.

Caes. *BGall.* 1. 3. 9, 18–20; 5. 6–7. C. E. S.; J. F. Dr.

Dura-Europus See EUROPUS.

Duris (*c.*340–*c.*260 BC) tyrant of *Samos and historian. His father probably preceded him as tyrant and his brother, Lynceus, was a renowned comic poet. His history, perhaps entitled *Macedonian History* (Μακεδονικά), was of at least 23 books and covered from 370 to after the battle of Corupedium (281). Because most surviving fragments derive from *Athenaeus (1), they concern examples of excess, and reflect the sensational and perverse. The relations between Duris and the Antigonid family (*Antigonus (1), *Demetrius (4), *Antigonus (2))), and how that may have coloured his history, are unclear. His other historical works are a local history of Samos (Σαμίων ὧροι), in at least two books, and a biography of the Sicilian tyrant *Agathocles (1), in at least four books. The historical works are quoted by several later writers; *Plutarch probably employed them extensively for the *Demetrius*, but whether *Diodorus (3) Siculus did also remains undetermined. So few of his fragments are preserved that no firm assessment of his place within the historiographic tradition is possible. He also wrote several lesser works on tragedy, *Euripides and *Sophocles (1), painting, engraving, contests, customs, and Homeric problems.

FGrH 76. F. W. Walbank, *Hist.* 1960, 216 ff.; R. B. Kebric, *In the Shadow of Macedon: Duris of Samos* (1977); A. Mastrocinque, *Athenaeum* 1979, 260–79; P. Pédech, *Trois historiens méconnus* (1989), 257–389.   K. S. S.

Durotriges, a British tribe (see BRITAIN) in Dorset and surrounding areas. They offered heavy resistance to the Roman advance by Legio II Augusta, commanded by *Vespasian. These campaigns suggest a decentralized social organization during the iron age. The *civitas*-capital was Durnovaria (Dorchester), but the area was later divided, the Durotriges Lindinienses being centred on Ilchester (Lindinis). *RIB* 1672–3 record work by a corvée of the latter on the *wall of Hadrian. Archaeological evidence from Dorchester is fragmentary: within the 32-ha. (79-acre) defences of the later 2nd cent., town houses have been examined; outside, the amphitheatre reused a neolithic henge. The *civitas* was largely agricultural but important stone quarries were exploited at Ham Hill and Purbeck, whilst shale from Kimmeridge was widely used. Christian *mosaics are known from the villas at Frampton and Hinton St Mary, and a large cemetery at Poundbury on the edge of Dorchester may also have been Christian.

RCHM, *Dorset 2: South-East* (1970); J. S. Wacher *The Towns of Roman Britain* (1974).   S. S. F.; M. J. M.

duumviri navales, two officers elected by the Roman people to 'repair and equip the fleet', were first established by a tribunician *lex Decia* in 311 BC (Livy 9. 30. 4). The measure is probably to be connected with the colonization of the Pontine islands (313, modern Ponza, off the Campanian coast), the construction of the *via Appia (312), and the extension of Roman control in *Campania. The primary function of the *duumviri*, who each commanded ten warships, was coastal defence. Their first operation was probably the raid on the Campanian coast in 310 (Livy 9. 38. 2–3), but they are rarely mentioned in the sources, and it seems they were appointed only at irregular intervals, down to the 2nd cent. BC.

J. H. Thiel, *Roman Sea-Power before the Second Punic War* (1954), 9 ff.; C. G. Starr, *Beginnings of Imperial Rome* (1980), 63.   T. J. Co.

dux, 'general', a title informally applied to republican commanders-in-chief and some emperors, but used more precisely from the Severan period of officers who commanded a 'task force' of detachments. *Diocletian made it the formal title ('duke') of the commander-in-chief of certain frontier sectors, a professional soldier who absorbed the military duties of the provincial

governor(s). This separation of civil and military authority was completed by *Constantine I. Henceforth the frontier armies were all commanded by *duces*, although occasionally civil and military authority were combined in difficult provinces like *Tripolitania.

Jones, *Later Rom. Emp.* 44, 608–10.   R. S. O. T.

dyeing was a well-established urban professional craft in the classical world and a branch of empirical chemistry, as the surviving Graeco-Roman dye recipe-books (*PLeid.* 10; *PHolm.*) reveal. *Wool was dyed 'in the fleece' before spinning; flax (see LINEN) was dyed (if at all) as yarn, as was *silk. Dyestuffs were drawn from many sources: plants (e.g. woad, madder), insects (kermes), and shellfish (the muricids). Most plant dyes would not 'take' unless the textile fibres had been pretreated with a mordant like alum or iron; mordants also affect the shade. The vat-dyes from woad and the muricid whelks bonded without a mordant, but had to be fermented first, and the colour developed only after dyed fibre was exposed to light. Red was won from madder root, the scale-bug kermes, and Polish cochineal, whilst blue came mostly from woad. Weld, saffron, dyer's broom, and safflower gave yellow, and oak galls combined with ferrous sulphate black. *Purple was extracted most expensively from the Mediterranean whelks *Murex brandaris*, *Murex trunculus*, and *Purpura haemostoma*, which were crushed to release the dye fluid for the vat. But lichens and bedstraws also gave purple, and a cheap version was commonly achieved by overdyeing woad (blue) with madder (red). Green, too, was a mixture, such as dyer's broom on woad. For browns natural pigmented wools were used. Ancient dyeworks are characterized by cauldrons set in boilers; purple dyers left mounds of spent murex shells outside. See ALCHEMY; TEXTILE PRODUCTION.

R. Pfister, *Seminarium Kondakovianum* 1935, 1–59; Forbes, *Stud. Anc. Technol.* 4², 98 ff.   J. P. W.

Dyme (mod. Kato Achaia), city of the *Achaean ethnos, located on the Elean border (see ELIS). The region was settled from early Helladic times; an extensive late Helladic fortification and settlement has been excavated at Teichos Dymaion (mod. Kalogria). Dyme's Archaic and Classical history remains obscure (the city survives chiefly in its Hellenistic and early Roman form). The Peloponnesian fleet took refuge there after its defeat in 429 BC, and the city was liberated from its Peloponnesian League garrison by *Epaminondas in 367.

In c.280 Dyme joined *Patrae in reviving the *Achaean Confederacy after its dissolution by Macedon. In 208 it was sacked by P. *Sulpicius Galba Maximus as punishment for its allegiance to Macedon, but was resettled by *Philip (3) V. After 146 BC an outbreak of *stasis* was suppressed by the proconsul Q. Fabius Maximus (*RDGE* no. 43; J.-L. Ferrary, *Philhellénisme et impérialisme* (1988), 186 ff.). In 67 a settlement for reformed pirates was established by *Pompey, and a veteran colony was founded in 44 perhaps by *Caesar. Dyme declined during imperial times.

A. D. Rizakis, *Paysages d'Achaie* 1 (1992).   C. A. M.

Dyrrhachium (mod. Durazzo), originally the name of the headland under which the city of *Epidamnus was situated, became the name of the town itself c.300 BC (it first appears on coins of the 5th cent.). The city passed successively through the hands of *Cassander and *Pyrrhus. In 229 it was besieged by the Illyrians, but was delivered and occupied by a Roman force. It served, together with *Apollonia, as a base for the Roman armies in Greece and the Balkan lands, and in 148 became the terminal

Dyrrhachium

point of the northern fork of the *via Egnatia. In 48 *Pompey made Dyrrhachium into his main base on the Adriatic, and he beat off an attack by *Caesar on his entrenched camp nearby (Caes. *BCiv.* 3. 41–72). After the battle of Actium *Octavian drafted evicted partisans of Antony (M. *Antonius (2)) from Italy to Dyrrhachium. (See also EPIDAMNUS.)

R. L. Beaumont, *JHS* 1936, 166 ff.; excavation reports in *Studia Albanica* 1966 and in *Iliria*.   M. C.; N. G. L. H.

earthquakes The Mediterranean is a zone of intense earthquake activity because the plates carrying Africa and Europe are slowly moving together, according to the theory of plate tectonics. Notable earthquakes in antiquity include: *Sparta *c.*464 BC, where an age class perished; Helice in *Achaea 373 BC, where the city was submerged under the sea; *Rhodes 227/6 BC, when the Colossus statue collapsed; *Pompeii AD 62, which suffered severe damage. Some destructions of Mycenaean and Minoan palaces are also attributed to earthquakes. Earthquakes were associated with *Poseidon in mythology: Poseidon the Homeric 'earth-shaker' (*ennosigaios*) was fervently worshipped also as 'earth-holder' (*gaiaochos*) and 'stabilizer' (*asphalios*), in Sparta and elsewhere. King Agesipolis of Sparta was as distinctly unusual in his pragmatic approach to an earthquake in the Argolis in 388 BC (Xen. *Hell.* 4. 7. 4–5) as Herodotus (7. 129. 4) was in his rationalist, seismological explanation of Thessalian geomorphology (see THESSALY). Ancient philosophers and 'scientists', however, frequently speculated about the causes of earthquakes (Sen. *QNat.* bk. 6). Thales thought that the earth moved upon the primeval waters. Anaximenes (1) reckoned that variations in wetness and aridity caused cracks in the earth. Several philosophers, including *Anaxagoras, *Democritus, *Aristotle, and *Posidonius (2), produced theories which involved water or air entering the earth and causing explosions.

RE 22. 480 and Suppl. 4. 344–74; J. Ducat, 'Le tremblement de terre de 464 et l'histoire de Sparte', in *Tremblements de terre, histoire et archéologie* (IVᵉ Rencontres Internationales d'archéologie et d'histoire d'Antibes, 1984), 73–85; P. Autino, *Memorie dell'Istituto Lombardo* 1987, 355–446; J. Andreau, *Annales ESC* 1973, 369–95.   P. A. C., J. R. S.

Ebla (mod. Tell Mardikh in Syria), *c.*55 km. (34 mi.) south of Aleppo, occupied from *c.*3500 BC to the Byzantine period. Italian excavations from 1964 under P. Matthiae uncovered monumental building and vast archives dating from the second half of the third millennium BC. The texts are administrative, historical, lexical, and literary, written with ambiguous brevity in a dialect of Old *Akkadian using Sumerograms and showing West Semitic and Hurrian influence. Industry and trade in metals, textiles, timber, and stone made the city rich. Closely connected with *Mari and Emar on the Euphrates, with *Byblos on the Mediterranean coast, and with Hamazi in Iran, conquered by kings of Agade, *c.*2300 BC, it was later eclipsed by Halam, ancient Aleppo.

P. Matthiae, *Ebla: An Empire Rediscovered* (1980).   S. M. D.

Eburacum (also **Eboracum),** modern York on the Ouse. The legionary fortress lay on the east bank; founded during the campaigns of *Petillius Cerialis in AD 71–4, it was rebuilt by *Agricola *c.*79 and under Trajan, 107/8 (*RIB* 665). Legio IX Hispana replaced VI Victrix (see LEGION) perhaps in the 120s. Excavations within the fortress have been limited, although the headquarters-complex (*principia*) has been explored beneath the Minster. York was the seat of the northern command; *Septimius Severus and *Constantius I died there whilst using it as a campaign base. The *canabae* lay east of the Ouse; the mercantile settlement west of the river became a *colonia* before AD 237, with trade connections extending to Bordeaux (Burdigala; *RIB* 674). The city became the capital of Lower Britain under Severus and Secunda in the time of *Diocletian, and had a bishopric before 314. Recent excavations have located several public buildings (including baths and a possible *collegium* or 'clubhouse'), and identified a phase of monumental replanning during the early 3rd cent.

RCHM, *York* 1: *Eboracum* (1962); P. Ottaway, *Roman York* (1993).
I. A. R.; M. J. M.

Ecbatana, old capital of the *Median kingdom captured by *Cyrus (1) in 550; it became the capital of the Median satrapy and one of the *Achaemenid Persian royal residences. The royal inscriptions show that the Great Kings (especially *Artaxerxes (2) II) built extensively here. It is mainly known from Polybius' glowing description (10. 27–8), since the site has never been excavated, owing to the superimposition of the modern town (Hamadan). Because of its excellent strategic position, it always played a prominent role in the interaction between western Iran and central Asia conducted along the Khorasan route.   P. B.

ecclesia See EKKLESIA.

Echecrates, of Phlius (4th cent. BC), is the person to whom *Phaedo describes the last day of *Socrates' life in *Plato (1)'s *Phaedo.* Late sources describe him as one of several Phliasians attached to the Pythagorean movement in *Magna Graecia (cf. e.g. Cic. *Fin.* 5. 87); in the *Phaedo* he (open-mindedly?) admits to leaning towards a materialist, non-Pythagorean view of the soul (see PYTHAGORAS (1)).

DK 53.   C. J. R.

Echidna, one of many female monsters in Greek mythology. She was daughter of *Phorcys and Ceto (this is the probable interpretation of Hesiod, *Theog.* 295: see West's comm.), was half-woman, half-snake, and was mother by *Typhon of several of the monsters killed by *Heracles and others. The name may also be generic: Herodotus (9. 4) traces the descent of the Scythians to the union of an *echidna* ('serpent') with Heracles.

M. L. West (ed.), *Hesiod: Theogony* (1966), 243–4, 249–56; R. Hošek, *LIMC* 3. 678–9; J. Fontenrose, *Python* (1959), 94–7.   E. Ke.

Echion (᾿Εχίων, 'snake-man'), (1) one of the surviving *Spartoi, see CADMUS; he married Agave and was father of *Pentheus. (2) Son of Hermes and Antianeira, daughter of Menetus. He and his

Echo

twin brother Erytus joined the *Argonauts (Ap. Rhod. 1. 51 ff.). Their home was Pangaeus (Pind. *Pyth.* 4. 180) or Alope (Apollonius). They joined the Calydonian boar-hunt (Ov. *Met.* 8. 311), see MELEAGER (1).

H. J. R.

Echo (᾽Ηχώ). There are two mythological explanations of echoes, neither very early. (*a*) Echo was a *nymph vainly loved by *Pan, who finally sent the shepherds mad and they tore her in pieces; but Earth hid the fragments, which still can sing and imitate other sounds (Longus 3. 23). (*b*) See NARCISSUS (1).

In art: *LIMC* 3 / 1 (1986), 680–3.

H. J. R.

eclecticism, an approach to philosophy which consists in the selection and amalgamation of elements of different systems of thought. The term has been much misused in relation to ancient philosophy, however, little account being taken of the historical perspectives of the individuals concerned. Traditionally it is seen as beginning in the 2nd cent. BC, coinciding with a general decline in the originality of Greek thought. Opposition between the major schools of philosophy tended to give way, in the minds of certain leading figures, to a recognition of the real similarities between them. The Academic *Antiochus (11) of Ascalon, for example, held that the doctrines of the Old *Academy, the Peripatos, and the Stoa (see PERIPATETIC SCHOOL; STOICISM) were in essence indistinguishable, while, on the Stoic side, *Panaetius and *Posidonius (2) incorporate elements of both Platonism and Aristotelianism into their teaching. *Cicero and the younger Seneca (see ANNAEUS SENECA (2), L.) follow a similar trend, in abstracting ideas from various schools, and attempting to fit them into a Roman context. In the writings of *Plotinus and his *Neoplatonic successors, many elements of Aristotelianism and Stoicism are taken over and adapted into a new synthesis. But all these men considered themselves faithful adherents of one school or another, and as merely utilizing formulations developed in another school for the elucidation of their own positions. The only ancient philosopher who called himself an eclectic was *Potamon (2) of Alexandria, of the late 1st cent. BC.

J. M. Dillon and A. A. Long (eds.), *The Question of 'Eclecticism': Studies in Later Greek Philosophy* (1988).

J. M. D.

eclipses Solar and lunar eclipses rank with the most impressive celestial phenomena. They were widely considered ominous—as the story of *Nicias (1)'s final defeat in Sicily shows—and some 250 reports of them occur in ancient sources. The Babylonian records of lunar eclipses to which *Ptolemy (4) had access apparently began in the 8th cent. BC. By the 5th cent., well-informed Greeks like *Thucydides (2) understood (2.28) that solar eclipses can take place only at new, and lunar ones at full moon. *Hipparchus (3), in the 2nd cent., supposedly predicted the motions of the sun and moon, including their syzygies, for 600 years; and Ptolemy, 300 years later, provided precise methods for predicting the time not only of lunar, but also of solar eclipses (a much harder task). Recorded eclipses in Greek and Roman literature provide the only absolute dates for historical phenomena (like the *Peloponnesian War): the dated eclipses recorded by historians of the later Roman republic make it possible to trace the deviation of the months of the republican calendar from their proper positions. It became customary to associate the occurrence of eclipses, retrospectively, with major historical events, and their prediction, anachronistically, with great past thinkers. Hence the legends that an eclipse accompanied *Xerxes' crossing into Greece and that *Thales predicted the solar eclipse of 28 May 585 BC, not to mention the theory that *Odysseus' killing of

*Penelope's suitors took place during a datable eclipse. Though indispensable to the historian, in short, the use of eclipse records calls for discrimination. See PORTENTS.

F. K. Ginzel, *Spezieller Kanon* (1899); A. Demandt, *Abh. Akad. Mainz* 1970; A. T. Grafton, *Joseph Scaliger: A Study in the History of Classical Scholarship* 2: *Historical Commentary* (1993), see index.

A. T. G.

ecloga (ἐκλογή), 'selection', used for a choice extract from a work (Varro, cited by Charisius, *Gramm.* 120. 28 Keil; Cic. *Att.* 16. 2. 6), or (by extension) for any short poem or poem within a poetry-book (Stat. *Silv.* 3 pref. 20, 4 pref. 18; Plin. *Ep.* 4. 14. 9; Suet. *Vita Horatii*, Auson. *Griph.* pref. 10, *Cup.* pref. 10; *schol. Cruq.* Hor. *Sat.* 2. 1). *Ausonius' *Eclogae* (14 Green) is a brief collection of short poems in hexameters and elegiacs. The term is commonly used to refer to *Virgil's *Bucolics*; ancient evidence calls the individual poems of Virgil's collection *eclogae* (Donat. *Vit. Verg.* 9, 43), but entitles the whole collection *Bucolica* (so all the capital MSS and Macrob. 5. 17. 20); this is likely to have been the author's title (matching *Georgica*). The use of *Eclogae* for the later pastorals of *Calpurnius Siculus and *Nemesianus ensured its continued application to Latin pastorals in Carolingian and Renaissance poetry.

K.-E. Henriksson, *Griechische Buchtitel in der römischen Literatur* (1956); A. Traina, *Enc. Virg.* 'Ecloga'.

S. J. Ha.

ecology (Greek and Roman) A modern concept with numerous antecedents in antiquity, when attitudes towards nature (φύσις) varied greatly. *Empedocles devised the theory of the four *elements, leading to the idea of opposites and the theory of the four *humours (Hippoc. *Nature of Man* 4–8), in which an imbalance of the humours causes disease. Different climates cause different humours to prevail in different peoples, producing the theory of environmental determinism in *Hippocrates (2) (*Aer.*). The observed regularities in nature led to a belief in purpose in nature. *Herodotus (3. 107–9) thought that different types of animal had different rates of reproduction appropriate to their natures, an argument for purposeful creation. Other arguments invoked in favour of purposeful creation included the unity and harmony of the universe; the apparent design of human organs, e.g. the eye (*Socrates (1) in Xen. *Mem.* 1. 4. 4–15); the regularities in astronomical phenomena, which led to *astrology and *Ptolemy (4)'s theory (*Tetr.*) of cosmic environmentalism in which the stars influence life on earth; and the idea that the creator acted like an artisan, a theory—very important for *Plato (1) (*Ti.* 27–33), *Cicero, and the younger Seneca (see ANNAEUS SENECA (2), L.)—that was adopted by the early Christian Fathers and laid the foundations for natural theology in later ages. *Aristotle (e.g. *Pol.* 1256$^{a–b}$) turned the concept of purpose in nature into an all-embracing teleology, but rejected Plato's artisan deity. Possibly Aristotle thought that nature advances unconsciously towards ends. *Theophrastus expressed doubts about teleology in biology, invented plant biogeography, and considered climatic change caused by human modification of the environment. The Epicureans (see EPICURUS) rejected design in nature. The Stoics (see STOICISM) fused the aesthetic attitude towards nature, evident in Hellenistic bucolic poetry, with utilitarian attitudes. The earth is beautiful and useful.

J. R. Sallares, *Ecology of the Ancient Greek World* (1991); C. J. Glacken, *Traces on the Rhodian Shore* (1967), pt. 1.

J. R. S.

economic theory (Greek) It is a commonplace that the Greek philosophers had no economic theory. Three reasons are advanced for this absence: (1) the merely embryonic existence of

502

the relevant institutions, especially the market; (2) aristocratic disdain for *trade and exchange; (3) the priority assigned to ethical concerns over technical considerations of exchange and accumulation. While each of these claims contains some truth, the third assumes a modern conception of the autonomy of economics against which ancient theory may make a pertinent challenge.

*Plato (1)'s discussion of the market is sketchy. The *Republic* describes the creation of a market in the 'first city'; *money will be used for internal exchange, and barter for foreign trade. In the Ideal City the lowest class, ruled by bodily appetites, is also called the moneymaking class. The ideal city of *Laws* 5 will have no money, and strict lower and upper limits on amount of ownership. The market legislation of bks. 8 and 11 permits money, but most transacting is done by aliens; again, the state fixes strict limits to acquisition and ownership.

Economic analysis proper begins in *Aristotle's *Politics*. Fundamental to the entire discussion is the idea that material goods are tools of human functioning. Their proper use has a limit set by those requirements. Poverty placing one beneath this limit is a problem for public planning; accumulation above this limit is 'unnatural' and morally problematic. Thus Aristotle criticizes the saying of *Solon, 'Of wealth no boundary stands fixed for men'. The accumulation of goods began as a way of ensuring the presence of needed resources. Because some of these had to be imported from a distance, barter arose; barter led, in turn, to the temporary accumulation of surpluses useful for trade. Eventually coin money was introduced to facilitate deferred exchanges. This, however, gave rise to the idea of accumulating a surplus without reference to need or limit, as if wealth were an end in itself.

Aristotle's analysis is pertinent to recent criticisms of welfare and development economics which appeal to notions of human functioning in interpreting economic notions such as 'the standard of living' and 'the quality of life'.

Elsewhere, Aristotle analyses the relationship between level of wealth and political behaviour, arguing that the essential difference between *democracy and *oligarchy lies in whether rule is by the poor or the rich; it happens that in every city the poor are many and the rich are few.

Hellenistic thought about money focuses on limiting the desire for possessions. Stoic teleology (see STOICISM) is the background for Adam Smith's conception of the 'invisible hand', which should not be understood apart from Stoic ideas of providence and justice. See ECONOMY, GREEK and HELLENISTIC; WEALTH, ATTITUDES TO.

G. E. M. de Ste Croix, *The Class Struggle in the Ancient Greek World* (1981), 69–80; K. Polanyi, in K. Polanyi (ed.), *Trade and Market in the Early Empires* (1957); A. Shulsky, in C. Lord (ed.), *Essays on the Foundations of Aristotelian Political Science* (1991); M. Finley, *P&P* 1970 (= M. Finley (ed.), *Studies in Ancient Society* (1974), 26 ff.); M. Nussbaum and A. Sen (eds.), *The Quality of Life* (1993). M. C. N.

economy, Greek Even if there was 'an economy' in ancient Greece (see CAPITALISM), Greece itself was not a single entity, but a congeries of more than a thousand separate communities. One should therefore speak of Greek economies rather than the Greek economy, and for simplicity's sake it is convenient to divide them into three groups, types, or models. First, there is the 'Archaic' group of which *Sparta can stand as the representative instance. At the opposite extreme is Athens, distinguished both by the exceptional size and number of its economic transactions, and by the exceptional sophistication of its economic institutions. In

between fall the vast range of 'normal' Greek cities or communities, differentiated from the latter chiefly in the scale, and from the former principally in the nature, of their economic arrangements.

Consider the last group first. Our 'economy' is derived from the ancient Greek word *oikonomia*, but this meant originally and usually the management of a private household (*oikos*) rather than that of a 'national' economy (see HOUSEHOLD, GREEK). Ideally, for sound prudential reasons as well as ideological, moral, or political ones, each 'normal' Greek household (comprising a two-generation nuclear family, free and unfree dependants, slaves, animals, land, and other property) aimed to be as self-sufficient as possible, making all due allowance for the basic constants of the changing domestic life-cycle, and the amount and nature of available land and labour. Household economy in Greece was overwhelmingly rural economy, the number of genuine cities or even genuinely urban residential centres being countable on the fingers of a single hand. See URBANISM, GREEK.

Most Greeks living in 'normal' communities were *peasants of one description or another, farming a couple of hectares (say, 5 acres) planted to a mix of *cereals (mainly barley, some wheat) and xerophytic crops (*olives, grapevines (see WINE), *figs above all). Small stock animals, especially sheep and goats (see PASTORALISM, GREEK), constituted a necessary, not a purely optional, complement to agriculture and herbiculture in the absence of artificial fertilizers. In some areas local conditions favoured specialization in one or other crop, or an exceptional amount of stockraising. In coastal settlements there were always some specialist fishermen (see FISHING), but, apart from the Black Sea, Greek waters were not especially favourable to sizeable and predictable shoals of easily catchable fish. Fish remained something of a luxury food by comparison with the staple 'Mediterranean triad' (grain, wine, olive oil) of the Greek peasant diet.

In practice, of course, self-sufficiency remained for most an ideal rather than a lived actuality, so that economic exchange of various kinds was obligatory (see TRADE, GREEK). But such exchanges were typically conducted between individuals—neighbours or at any rate members of the same community—either directly and by barter in kind or through the use of some monetary medium in the local village or town market. The economy of Athens was wholly exceptional in the degree to which the very viability of the civic community depended on the exchange through long-distance trade of a staple commodity, grain (see FOOD SUPPLY). Fortunately, and not incidentally, Athens was exceptionally blessed with a near-unique means of paying for such imports in the shape of the silver (strictly, argentiferous lead) deposits in the *Laurium district of SE Attica. The mines were worked almost entirely by chattel-slave labour (see SLAVERY). To ensure that the silver bullion was channelled productively into the grain trade the Athenian community instituted a wide range of preferential measures backed by severe and enforceable legal sanctions against both citizen and non-citizen miscreants. Athens was also fortunate, and unusual, in that much of *Attica's soil and climate was peculiarly well suited to olive cultivation; the export of olive oil was officially encouraged from as early as 600 BC.

These factors permitted the development in the course of the 5th cent. BC of a genuinely urban sector of the Athenian citizen population, concentrated in what was almost a second city around the port of *Piraeus. But most of those directly and exclusively engaged in Piraeus commerce, as in the other non-agricultural sectors of Athenian economy, were non-Athenian and often non-Greek foreigners, resident (free *metics and slaves) and transient. Both absolutely and as a proportion of the total population (which itself was hypertrophied by 'normal' Greek standards) the foreign element was sensibly greater in Athens than in any other Greek community.

Sparta in its economy as in some other respects represented the opposite pole from Athens. So far from being encouraged as economically desirable or even necessary, foreigners—Greek as well as non-Greek—were periodically expelled from Sparta (*xenēlasiai*). The Spartans did regularly practise economic exchange, but within rather than outside their territory, and with a politically subordinate free population known as *perioikoi, on whom they depended, not least, for supplies of iron. Agriculture and stockraising were left to, or rather forced upon, a subjugated local population of *helots, Greek in speech and culture but servile in status. By dint of exploiting the helots, the Spartans themselves contrived to do no economically productive work whatsoever (except in the sense that war, 'the business of Ares', was itself a means of production). Some other Greek communities exploited workforces of a similar collective character and servile status, but none combined that exploitation with the Spartans' peculiar disdain of all non-military forms of economic activity. The Spartans were not unique in refusing to coin silver or bronze for economic or political purposes, but their retention of a non-convertible domestic 'currency' of iron spits nicely symbolizes their economic eccentricity. See COINAGE, GREEK.

M. I. Finley, *The Ancient Economy* (1973; 2nd edn 1985); M. M. Austin and P. Vidal-Naquet, *Economic and Social History of Ancient Greece: An Introduction* (1977); H.-J. Gehrke, *Jenseits von Athen und Sparta: Die griechische Dritten Welt* (1988); R. G. Osborne, *Classical Landscape with Figures* (1987); T. W. Gallant, *A Fisherman's Tale: An Analysis of the Potential Productivity of Fishing in the Ancient World* (1985), and *Risk and Survival in Ancient Greece* (1991); R. Sallares, *Ecology of the Ancient Greek World* (1991); R. Garland, *The Piraeus from the Fifth to the First Century BC* (1987); S. Hodkinson, 'Explorations in Classical Spartan Property and Society' (Cambridge Ph.D. thesis, 1992). P. A. C.

economy, Hellenistic The regions brought under the control of the Hellenistic kingdoms showed little economic unity or uniformity. Land-use systems ranged from *irrigation regimes in Egypt, Mesopotamia, and parts of Iran (Polyb. 10. 28) through widespread dry farming to the nomad or transhumant *pastoralism of the deserts and the mountains. Land tenure arrangements included, besides private beneficial ownership at all levels of magnitude, land owned by cities, cantons, or temples but rented out to individuals or worked by 'slaves of the shrine' (*hierodouloi), and above all land owned by the kings. Such land might be held in direct tenure and worked by serfs, or alienated to large-scale proprietors (e.g. Austin nos. 180 and 185), or bestowed as allotments (*klēroi*) in various ways on individuals in return for military service, or have its use and revenues assigned to individuals (*dōrea*). Such lands mostly had arable and arboricultural use in producing the basic Mediterranean triad (*cereals, vines (see WINE), *olives) and other supplementary foodstuffs, while other land uses included pasturage, ornamental ground such as the ex-Persian *paradeisoi*, *quarries, *mines, and forests.

Most foodstuff production will have been consumed locally, but some established long-distance flows continued, such as corn from Egypt to the Aegean, cattle and slaves (see SLAVERY) from the Black Sea (Polyb. 4. 38), or *spices and precious stones from India to the Mediterranean. They may well have grown in importance in the Hellenistic period, thereby assisting the growth and enrichment of entrepôt and trading cities such as

*Rhodes, *Alexandria (1), and *Petra. Such cities seem also to have become the main centres of both the production and the consumption of fine decorative goods such as silverware (see PLATE), *glass, and jewellery, while the creation and use of more basic artefacts remained local unless used, as *amphorae universally were, as containers for transport and storage. The growth in the numbers of coin-hoards and of *shipwrecks during the period, together with the development of institutions (e.g. public and private *banks) and installations (*harbours, *lighthouses, etc.), suggest an increase both in the volume of trade and in the monetization of some transactions: the activities of Cretan and other pirates (see PIRACY) increased accordingly.

Rulers and polities affected all such economic activities by their needs, exactions, and benefactions. Old and new Greek cities levied taxes and rents on transactions, statuses, properties, and commodities, but rarely covered expenses comfortably. They tended instead to elicit loans, donations, or endowments from wealthy and benevolent citizens or outsiders, whose services prompted honorary decrees (e.g. Austin nos. 98 and 113) and shifted power relationships in their favour (see EUERGETISM). On a larger scale kings and rulers did the same, redistributing resources via systematic taxation to pay for armies and wars, courts and *bureaucracy, gifts and benefactions, disaster relief and city foundations. For fiscal reasons all royal governments showed some interest in increasing the productive capacity of their territories, e.g. by opening mines, extending the agrarian base or transplanting species, but the older picture of a managed 'royal economy' is not now accepted, even for Egypt. The political act with the biggest impact on the Hellenistic economy was probably Rome's creation of a free port at *Delos in 166 BC, which moved some trade routes and badly damaged Rhodes (Polyb. 30. 31).

C. Préaux, *Le Monde hellénistique* 1–2 (1978), esp. 358–88, 474–524; R. M. Berthold, *Rhodes in the Hellenistic Age* (1984); *CAH* 7²/1 (1984), ch. 5 (E. G. Turner: Egypt), ch. 8 (J. K. Davies: general survey); F. G. B. Millar, in A. Kuhrt and S. Sherwin-White (eds.), *Hellenism in the East* (1987), ch. 5. J. K. D.

economy, Roman The economic history of Rome from the first, like all ancient Mediterranean economies, involved the interaction of the circumstances of local *agriculture with the available *labour supply in the context of opportunities for interregional redistribution in which the exchange of other commodities was involved. It is now certain that from the 7th cent BC. Rome was privileged among other *Tiber valley communities as a centre for the movement of people and materials from peninsular Italy out into the world of Mediterranean contacts. The Romans believed that they had imported cereals from *Campania from at least the early 5th cent., and that they had freed their citizens from the risk of debt-bondage (*nexum*; see DEBT) at the end of the 4th. It was important to their self-image that they considered the area around their city to be of only moderate productivity, and that it had been assigned in lots from an early period to citizens who worked them independently. Historically, this enthusiasm for the lot was of more significance in the concept of public ownership of land, and the practice of dividing and assigning it (see AGER PUBLICUS). This was attested in the formation of new *tribus in the 4th cent. and widely practised in the establishment of *coloniae* in the 3rd and 2nd cents., especially on land which had belonged to defeated opponents of Rome (see COLONIZATION, ROMAN). But the exploitation of allotted land was perhaps never intended to be in theory, and was certainly not in practice, a matter of basic household subsistence. It rapidly became linked with the formation of estate centres (see LATIFUNDIA) for the production of cash crops for mass-marketing, the *villas of the late republican landscape, which were also central to the cultural life of the wealthy families which owned them. The cities grew as *markets and centres of processing, administration, and consumption of the products of this agriculture, and as centres for the control and management of a mutable labour force which included, as a result in part of the victories of the 2nd cent. BC, significant numbers of slaves (see SLAVERY), though their large-scale use in agriculture was generally perceived by the Roman tradition as undesirable. From the beginnings of the large-scale export of *wine from Italy in the mid 2nd cent. the network of economic exchanges involved entrepreneurs, Roman military forces in the field, more or less dependent consumers inside and outside Roman territory, and the city of Rome itself in an increasingly complicated web, in which the non-agricultural resources of the growing imperial state, especially metals (see MINES AND MINING), were an important ingredient. The development over the next centuries of this state of affairs saw frequent changes in the specifics of the geography of the centres of exchange, and the favoured places of investment in production: *olive oil and wine remained important, though we should recall that they are particularly visible archaeologically, and the production of *Baetica, *Africa, and *Tripolitania transformed these regions, with concomitant gain to their market centres and port outlets (see AMPHORAE, ROMAN). The economy of the empire included significant connections with networks of exchange reaching across northern Europe, central Asia, and the Sahara, but most importantly via the *Red Sea with the increasingly complex economy of the Indian Ocean area, to which *Alexandria (1) was central. Rome itself was a consumer on an enormous scale, and therefore exerted a considerable influence on Mediterranean production and exchange, which were also promoted by the need to pay state exactions in cash. But the complexity of the network, the continued local interdependence of the regions of the empire, and the existence of very many smaller centres of consumption, management, and marketing, ensured that the economic life of the Roman world was not wholly oriented on Rome. The social and political forms of economic life were sophisticated and various, though they did not much resemble the practices of early modern Europe: the role of ex-slaves (see FREEDMEN) and the public contract may be singled out, while the availability of credit and the nature of accounting deserve further investigation. See ARTISANS AND CRAFTSMEN; COINAGE (ROMAN); INDUSTRY; TRADE, ROMAN.

K. Greene, *The Archaeology of the Roman Economy* (1986); P. Garnsey and R. Saller, *The Roman Empire, Economy, Society and Culture* (1987), 43–103; A. H. M. Jones, *The Roman Economy*, ed. P. A. Brunt (1974); R. Duncan-Jones, *The Economy of the Roman Empire, Quantitative Studies*, 2nd edn. (1982), and *Structure and Scale in the Roman Economy* (1990). N. P.

Ecphantides, Athenian comic poet and contemporary of *Cratinus, won four victories at the City *Dionysia (*IG* 2^2. 2325. 49), but we have only two titles and six citations.

Kassel-Austin, *PCG* 5. 126 ff. (*CAF* 1. 9 ff.). K. J. D.

Ecphantus, a 4th-cent. BC Pythagorean from Syracuse (or Croton; Iambl. *VP* 267), held that indivisible bodies (monads), moved by a divine power referred to as 'mind' and 'soul', constitute the world, which is spherical and governed by providence. A Neopythagorean treatise *On Kingship* is falsely attributed to him; it exalts *kingship as naturally superior, the mediator

between the gods and man, an essential link in a divinely organized universe. This work, variously dated between the 3rd cent. BC and the early 3rd cent. AD, shows Jewish and/or Gnostic influence (see GNOSTICISM, PYTHAGORAS).

DK 51. *On Kingship*, ed. H. Thesleff, in *The Pythagorean Texts of the Hellenistic Period* (1965), 79–84; W. Burkert and H. Thesleff, in *Pseudepigrapha* 1, Entretiens Hardt 18 (1972), 25 ff.; G. Chesnut, *ANRW* 2. 16. 2 (1979), 1310 ff. D. O'M.

ecstasy In classical Greek the term ἔκστασις may refer to any situation in which (part of) the mind or body is removed from its normal place or function. It is used for bodily displacements, but also for abnormal conditions of the mind such as madness, unconsciousness, or 'being beside oneself'. In the Hellenistic and later periods the notion is influenced by the Platonic concept of 'divine madness', a state of inspired possession distinct from lower forms of madness and as such providing insights into objective truth. *Ekstasis* now acquires the notion of a state of trance in which the soul, leaving the body, sees visions (Acts 10: 10; 22: 17). In later, especially Neoplatonist theory (Plotinus, Porphyry), *ekstasis* is the central condition for escape from restraints of either a bodily or a rational-intellectual nature and thus becomes the gateway to the union with the god (*unio mystica*); see DIONYSUS.

Fr. Pfister, *RAC* 4 (1959), 944–87; I. P. Culianu (Coulianu), *Psychanodia* 1: *A Survey of the Evidence concerning the Ascension of the Soul and its Relevance* (1983), and *Expériences de l'extase* (1984). H. S. V.

Edessa (mod. Urfa, from the indigenous *Urhai*, whence also Gk. Ὀρροηνή, Lat. *Orr(h)ei*), old centre of the moon-god cult attested in neo-Assyrian and neo-Babylonian sources and later the capital of *Osroëne. It was favourably situated in a ring of hills open to the south and surrounded by a fertile plain. It was refounded as a military settlement by *Seleucus (1) I; later its official name was Antioch-Fairflowing (*Kallirhoē*). When Osroëne asserted its independence, traditionally in 132 BC, Edessa became the royal residence. From the time of Pompey, who made a treaty with Abgar II and allowed him an enlarged Osroëne to rule over, Edessa played an ambiguous role in the wars and tensions between Rome and *Parthia. Its sympathies were often with the *Arsacids when prudence dictated compliance with Rome. Captured and sacked in AD 116 and again by L. *Verus, it eventually became a Roman colony (Cass. Dio 77. 12), and thereafter issued a copious coinage. Christianity reached Edessa early, and the town became the most important bishopric in *Syria. At the court of Abgar IX was Bardesanes (Bar Daisān), who was converted to Christianity (*c.*180) but later was regarded as a heretic; he was not an adherent of *Gnosticism but taught an astrological fatalism. Edessa was several times besieged and more than once captured by the *Sasanids; the emperor Heraclius recovered it, but it fell to the Islamic Arabs in 638. It had long been a centre of literary productivity in the Syriac language, the local form of *Aramaic. The population of Edessa was mixed (Semitic and Greek); it had close Iranian affinities. *Mosaics in the tombs of local notables vividly reflect their social habits.

J. Teixidor, *The Pagan God* (1977); F. Millar, *The Roman Near East* (1993), esp. 456 ff., 553 ff. (with bibliog.). E. W. G.; A. T. L. K.

edict The higher Roman magistrates (praetors, aediles, quaestors, censors, the governors of provinces) proclaimed by edicts the steps which they intended to take in the discharge of their office. Formally an edict was valid only for the term of office of the magistrate issuing it, but the new magistrate customarily took over his predecessor's edict, with only such deletions or additions as he thought desirable. The content of the greater part of the edict therefore remained constant (*edictum tralaticium*). The edict of the *praetor urbanus* (see PRAETOR) was of particular importance for the development of the private law. The province of this praetor was in form merely to apply the existing *ius civile*, but in his edict he was able to promise new actions and other remedies and thus in substance to create a mass of new rules (*ius honorarium*). In the formulation of his edict and in its administration during his year of office, the praetor would rely on the advice of jurists. It was no doubt this indirect professional control which enabled the edict to play its vital formative function in the private law. Hadrian commissioned the jurist Salvius *Iulianus to compose a revised version of the edict (*c.* AD 130), which was confirmed by a *senatus consultum*. It thus acquired a permanent form and the praetors lost the power to change it. Iulianus' revision probably extended also to the edict of the *praetor peregrinus* (of which little is known) and of the curule aediles (concerning principally market sales of slaves and animals). The later classical jurists wrote extensive commentaries on Hadrian's edict. Its text has been largely reconstructed on the basis of the many excerpts from these commentaries preserved in Justinian's *Digest* (O. Lenel, *Edictum perpetuum*, 3rd edn. (1927).

> H. F. Jolowicz and B. Nicholas, *Historical Introduction to Roman Law*, 3rd edn. (1972). B. N.

education, Greek

1. Early Period Greek ideas of education (*paideia*), whether theoretical or practical, encompassed upbringing and cultural training in the widest sense, not merely schooling and formal education. The poets were regarded as the educators of their society, particularly in the Archaic period, but also well into the classical, when *Plato (1) could attack *Homer's status as educator of Greece (e.g. *Resp.* 606e, and generally, bks. 2, 3, 10; cf. Xen. *Symp.* 4. 6 for the conventional view). Much education would have taken place in an aristocratic milieu informally through institutions like the *symposium (as in the poetry of *Theognis (1)) or *festivals (cf. the children reciting *Solon's poetry at the *Apaturia, Pl. *Ti.* 21b), backed up by the old assumption that the *aristocracy possessed inherited, not instructed, excellence. Important educational functions were seen by some in the relationship of a boy and an older lover (see HOMOSEXUALITY); or in the very institutions of the city-state (*polis), the city festivals and rituals (e.g. Aeschin. 3. 246; see Loraux (in bibliog. below)). Even in the 4th cent. BC, Plato (*Laws*), for instance, saw the laws as performing educational functions, *Lycurgus (3) of Athens the democratic processes (see Humphreys); cf. DEMOCRACY, ATHENIAN.

There is a tendency in modern work to overformalize Greek education. Before the 5th cent. BC, there must have been some sort of training for any specialized skills (cf. the scribal skills needed by the Mycenaeans), but most of this was probably on an ad hoc and quite individual basis (more like an apprenticeship, as was surely the case with oral epic bards). The evidence for early schooling (i.e. formal group teaching) is remarkably slight: the school laws attributed to Solon (594 BC) by Aeschines (1. 9 ff.) may be later and are in any case primarily about morality; the traditions about Chiron (see CENTAURS) and *Phoenix (2) (cf. *Il.* 9. 443) as ideal educators, teaching their charges all the known skills may reflect some form of early aristocratic instruction. The earliest school mentioned is at *Chios, in 494 BC (Hdt. 6. 27); we also hear of schools at Astypalaea (an Aegean island between *Amorgos and Nisyros) in 492 BC (Paus. 6. 9. 6), at *Troezen in

480 (Plut. *Them.* 10), at Mycalessus in *Boeotia in 413 (Thuc. 7. 29), and less reliably, among allies of the Mytilenaeans in *c.*600 (Ael. *VH* 7. 15). Fifth-cent. Attic vase-paintings show scenes of schooling. But it is likely that at least before the mid-5th cent., education was elementary in our terms, probably confined to the aristocratic strata, and organized simply for individuals (the figure of the later *paidagōgos* may have retained something of an earlier individual tutor; cf. Xen. *Mem.* 2. 2. 6 on home education). That education would also be non-technical, and, as indicated by discussions of the 'old' and the 'new' education in the 5th cent. (cf. Ar. *Clouds*), would be primarily concerned with music and gymnastics. This type of education, or at least its higher levels, was transformed by the *sophists and their successors in to one involving the techniques of prose rhetoric, which then came to form the most typical part of ancient education at the higher level.

2. Sparta Certain Dorian states like *Crete and Classical *Sparta practised a totalitarian and militaristic form of education controlled by the state; see AGŌGĒ. By Classical times, Sparta had adapted its educational system entirely for the purposes of maintaining military strength. From the age of 7 the child was entirely under the control of the state, living in barracks away from parents. The aim of education was to produce efficient soldiers, and though their training included *music and how to read and write, physical education received first priority (see Xen. *Respublica Lacedaemoniorum*; Plut. *Lyc.*). Girls, too, were also educated in the interests of the state, to be the future mothers of warriors (Xen. *Respublica Lacedaemoniorum* 1. 3–4): gymnastics and sport were emphasized, as well as music and *dancing.

3. Classical Athens **Elementary education**
It is unclear how early elementary schooling began in Athens (from which most evidence comes): explicit evidence for schools (see above) is much later than the introduction of the alphabet to Greece in the mid-8th cent. BC, and though it has been thought that the alphabet implies schools to teach it, instruction at this low level could have been carried out without formal institutions. However, *ostracism at Athens may presuppose widespread basic *literacy in the time of *Cleisthenes (2), and schooling is definitely attested for early 5th-cent. Greece.

There were three main elements to elementary education, normally taught in different establishments. The *paidotribēs* dealt with gymnastics, games, and general athletic fitness, mainly in the *palaestra (e.g. Pl. *Grg.* 452b, *Prt.* 313a). The *kitharistēs* taught music and the works of the lyric poets, the lyre school inheriting the musical education of the Archaic period. The *grammatistēs* taught reading, writing, and arithmetic, as well as literature, which consisted of learning by heart the work of poets, especially Homer, who were regarded as giving moral training (see Protagoras on the moral function of music and poetry, *Prt.* 326a). Thus after learning the alphabet (see Pl. *Resp.* 402a–b; *Polit.* 227e–278b, for the methods of learning to read), pupils would progress to learning the poets by heart (*Prt.* 325e). Gymnastics and music (including poetry), then, were the fundamentals. The 'Old Education' parodied in *Aristophanes (1)'s *Clouds* (961–1023) gives most emphasis to physical education and music, saying nothing about letters, either because it was a minor element or too basic to mention. But the predominance of music—which included poetry and dance, and emphasized actual performance—and physical training in the basic Greek education is attested elsewhere (e.g. Pl. *Resp.* 376e); the conservative Plato sees lack of musical training (*achoreutos*) as synonymous with lack of education (*apaideutos*) (*Leg.* 654a–b).

In a single day, the pupil might start with gymnastics, then proceed to the lyre school, and end with letters. But the system was private and fee-paying, far from rigid, and parents might not want their children to participate in all three. Girls as we see from vase-painting, might be educated in all three elements, as well as dancing, though not normally in the same schools as boys or to the same extent. The teacher was normally a free man enjoying the same social status (and remuneration) as a doctor—though in fact often not so highly regarded (cf. *Demosthenes (2) on *Aeschines (1), *De cor.* 265). Assistants might be slaves or free men. Boys were always accompanied to school by a *paidagōgos*, a slave and highly trusted part of the family (cf. Themistocles', Hdt. 8. 75), who helped to bring up the child and at school must have been a helpful overseer. Discipline at school was strict: the symbol of the *paidotribēs'* power to punish was the forked stick, of other teachers the *narthex* (cane). Pupils regularly had to recite what they had learned, and the regular public competitions (all illustrated in vase-scenes), whether literary, musical, or athletic, were an important forum for proving their skill.

The development of group schooling, in which the education previously reserved for the aristocracy is spread to other citizens, may be related, at least in Athens, to the development of the *democracy, but cannot have originated with it. The balance between the physical and intellectual aspects may not have been as harmonious as some modern observers have suggested; it was certainly disputed by Greek thinkers, and the military uses of physical education may have given that side ascendancy (cf. *Prt.* 326 b–c, on gymnastics as useful training for war; see also EPHĒBOI). *Xenophanes (*c.*500) (DK 21 B 2) and *Euripides scoffed at the *athletic (and aristocratic) ideal, while *Pindar, perhaps Aristophanes, and *Xenophon (1) (*Cyn.* 13) supported it. Plato, *Isocrates, and Aristotle (*Pol.* 8) subordinated the physical side to the intellectual.

Higher education

From the late 5th cent. it was possible to pursue further and more specialist education by joining one of the courses offered by the sophists, or listening to their lectures and disputations. Or there were the specialized schools of *rhetoric or philosophy or of *medicine (possible early 'schools' (e.g. of medicine, Hdt. 3. 129, 131), may have been more like loose semi-religious foundations). The most famous were Isocrates' school of rhetoric, founded about 390 BC, Plato's *Academy with its scientific, mathematical, and philosophical curriculum founded soon after, and Aristotle's Lyceum (see ARISTOTLE, para. 5), founded in 335 BC. Some of these higher schools prescribed propaedeutic courses (e.g. geometry for Plato's Academy), which have been seen as the origin of 'secondary education'.

The great educators and theorists

The *sophists were itinerant teachers, who offered education for a fee on a variety of specialized and technical subjects. In general, they claimed to teach political virtue (*aretē*), and most laid great stress on skills useful for political life, especially rhetoric (e.g. *Prt.* 318e–319a). In that sense they rivalled the poets' claim as educators; they offered techniques useful in the Athenian democracy (and open to anyone who could pay), and in charging for their services, aroused much distrust. They were progressive and pragmatic in their views and methods, and belonged to the liberal, democratic tradition of Greek education. They were effectively the first to create a standard teaching system at an advanced level, and the first to include the basic sciences in their

schema (note especially the polymath *Hippias (2), *Prt.* 318e). But they were part of the mainstream of Greek cultural heritage, which they accepted, taught, and enhanced, and against which *Socrates and *Plato (1) reacted so violently. Their ideas initiated and propelled the ferment of discussion about education—including the 'nature versus nurture' debate—that continued so intensely in the 4th cent.

Socrates, on the other hand, distrusted the sophists' claim to be able to teach everything, or indeed even to know anything. Socrates sought not to impart a body of knowledge, but to progress, with his followers, in seeking it. In the educational sphere, he seems to have had a rather conservative reliance on innate gifts; his great influence lies in the famous 'Socratic' method of teaching (below), and in his equation of virtue with knowledge. Plato, however, gives us the most extensive theory of education, in the *Republic* and, in a less extreme form, the *Laws*, where he sets forth the ideal state of a totalitarian mould, influenced by Sparta, and a corresponding system of education in which everything, including most forms of literature and art, which does not serve the interests of the state, is rigidly excluded: his elementary education, for all citizens to the age of 17 or 18, was otherwise rather conservative. Plato's *Timaeus* provided the Middle Ages with the rationale for their quadrivium: though this in fact derived ultimately from Hippias' insistence (*Prt.* 318e) on the four sciences, namely arithmetic, geometry, astronomy, and music. In his early works he strongly opposed the teaching of rhetoric, but later allowed it to be taught in the Academy alongside the more important scientific, mathematical, and philosophical studies. His concept of an educational establishment with permanent buildings, specialist teachers, and an integrated curriculum, may be seen as a precursor of the secondary school (see *Resp.* 536–41 for the appropriate age-range for each stage in Plato's scheme), his founding of the Academy, an association of scholars, as the first university. It was, however, the Lyceum (see ARISTOTLE, para. 5), which became the greatest research institute of antiquity. In *Isocrates' educational innovations, one sees the further development of the rhetorical side of late 5th-cent. culture, as opposed to the philosophical emphasized by Plato and left by Isocrates as marginal to the ultimate rhetorical focus. He owed much to the sophists in subject-matter and teaching methods; his educational aims were to train (a few) students in morality and political skill, hence rhetoric (e.g. *Panathenaicus* 30–2; *Antidosis* 231; *Contra Sophistas* 21), and ultimately to produce political leaders. Other subjects were subservient to the pursuit of rhetorical skill: among these was knowledge of the past, and he distinguished between useful, or cultural, and purely disciplinary subjects like eristic and mathematics (*Antidosis* 261–9). His teaching methods also laid immense stress on the literary composition of prose, seeking to oust the dominant position of the poets in education. It was this primarily rhetorical basis of further education that became the dominant characteristic of ancient education.

Teaching methods

Private tuition, individual tuition, and teaching in small groups are all attested, even for gymnastics (Pl. *Polit.* 294d–e). Learning by heart, for the purposes of recitation, was standard. Even Plato accepted the usefulness of games in elementary education (arithmetic), though he was generally hostile to any experimentation in scientific teaching. At a higher level, pedagogic techniques were most developed in rhetorical teaching. Students memorized commonplaces, stock situations, and stock phrases, along with sample passages like *Gorgias (1)'s *Funeral Oration* (see

EPITAPHIOS) as material for later improvisation (on which much store was set). Psychology, techniques of persuasion, and the art of arguing both sides of a case were also taught. In addition, the sophists, and in particular, Isocrates, supplemented this with further general knowledge (see RHETORIC, GREEK).

The sophists developed both the dialectical method and the lecture, which might take the form of the display *epideixis* or the full technical lecture, which even Plato frequently used though he preferred *dialectic. The dialectic method involves question and answer, in which the respondent makes a real contribution to discussion (as opposed to the Socratic technique). This method was developed by Isocrates into a seminar technique of group discussion and criticism. The Socratic method proceeds by reducing the pupil to a state of *aporia* (or puzzlement) and admission of complete ignorance (not to mention irritation), and then drawing out knowledge by a process of questioning, a process of intellectual 'midwifery' (Pl. *Tht.* 150c). It is well illustrated in the geometry lesson of Plato's *Meno* (see *Meno* 85d–86b for the Socratic explanation given there). *Xenophon (1) advocated the 'activity' method in the *Cyropaedia* where pupils learn justice by practising it in real-life group situations.

4. Hellenistic Education For the Hellenistic period, there is a wealth of inscriptions (see EPIGRAPHY, GREEK) which illuminate the public side of education, and rich *papyrological evidence for school activity (e.g. school exercises). The pattern of education established in Classical Athens was brought in the early years of the Hellenistic era to a definitive form which endured with only slight changes to the end of the ancient world. Greater attention was paid to the education of the ordinary citizen, as reflected in the many separate philosophical treatises on education by thinkers such as *Aristippus (1), *Theophrastus, *Aristoxenus, *Cleanthes, *Zeno (2), *Chrysippus, *Clearchus (3), and Cleomenes. There is definitely an extension of elementary education, with generous foundations set up in some cities to fund teachers: at *Teos (*Syll.*[3] 578 = Austin no. 120) all free boys were to receive education; *Rhodes, funded by *Eumenes (2) II (Polyb. 31. 31), probably came nearest to universal public education (for boys) in antiquity (cf. also at *Delphi, *Syll.*[3] 672 (= Austin no. 206), and *Miletus, *Syll.*[3] 577 (= Austin no. 119)). Girls also received more education than before (e.g. Teos, *Pergamum), but cannot have been educated everywhere as fully as boys. But how far one can really claim universal education among Greek children in the period (as Marrou) is controversial (see Harris for a less optimistic view), and formal education was surely mostly confined to the cities. Greek *paideia* was now regarded as the essential badge of Greekness, and educational institutions—particularly the *gymnasium—were thought necessary to maintain, or assert, Greek identity.

Organization

Education was still mostly paid for by parents, but generous private benefactions in some cities provided for teachers' salaries (esp. Teos, Miletus, Delphi, Rhodes, above), and the cities seem to have taken more formal interest in education, organizing ephebic institutions (see EPHĒBOI) and regulating private benefactions themselves. Most had one gymnasium, some more (see Delorme for evidence). This would be the focus for physical training, which became transformed into an educational centre with schooling for *paides* (12–17) and ephebes: some space was devoted to schooling and lectures, with teachers of literature, philosophy, music (though the evidence suggests that this was not universal: the law from Beroea (*BÉ* 1978, 274 = Austin no.

118) implies the activity was overwhelmingly athletic). Thus it was a centre for Greek culture in the widest sense. The *gymnasiarch (*kosmētēs* in Athens), a state official, was elected for a year to run the gymnasium, and to supervise all aspects of the education (public or private) of the *epheboi* or *neoi* (ex-ephebes, i.e. in their twenties). He might be expected to contribute financially, buying oil or providing extra oil for athletic activity (very widely attested), and paying for one or more teachers' salaries. The increasing financial burdens of the office led to its decay in imperial times to a mere *liturgy with wealth the only qualification. The *paidonomos* had similar duties for elementary education. Girls also sometimes had special officials (e.g. *Smyrna, Pergamum). These officials organized numerous public competitions and awards, sometimes paid for by the gymnasiarch: preserved lists of prizewinners mention (among others) those successful in reading, writing, painting, recitation, verse and song-writing, running, *boxing. Class loads tended to be high, as the recorded complaints of teachers indicate, and the social standing of teachers rather low.

Other innovations of this period were the concentration of all educational activity into a single building; examinations; and the formal division of pupils into educational age groups, though these seem to vary from place to place: *paides* (boys), aged 12–17, *ephēboi*, aged 18–20 in Athens (younger elsewhere), and *neoi*, ex-ephebes, in their twenties. The ephebate, which began as a predominantly military training organized for young men by the state, and in Athens was reinvigorated in the 330s as a two-year training, spread over the Greek world with enormous vitality, and became a kind of cultural-athletic institution for the leisured classes. This came (in Athens from the late 2nd cent. BC) to include intellectual studies in its make-up, though as sport took first place, it is questionable how intellectual any of this education really was.

Elementary and secondary education

Elementary education was dominated by learning to read and write, and learning by heart, by what seem from the papyri to be unnecessarily tedious methods (sport, of course, was also important). At secondary level, adolescents progressed to an overwhelmingly literary curriculum that still involved learning by rote and recitation, and was dominated by the reading and exposition of texts under the care of the *grammaticus*. The canonization of classical literature progressed rapidly, and anthologies used for teaching crystallized certain authors and passages in the educational curriculum. Physical education and music continued; the ancient idea of the *enkyklios paideia*, or general education, was evolved to include the four main sciences, following Hippias, and looking forward to the Seven Liberal Arts of the Middle Ages (grammar, rhetoric, dialectic, geometry, arithmetic, astronomy, music; see MARTIANUS MINNAEUS FELIX CAPELLA). But it is unclear how keenly the scientific subjects were really pursued, and literary studies seem to oust the others. The Classics, particularly Homer, were studied in minute detail and according to rigidly formal rules. The study of grammar (in the modern sense) was added later (1st cent. BC), also composition, and preliminary rhetorical material.

Higher education

After secondary level there were several options of varying levels. The *ephēbeia* did include further cultural studies (literature, rhetoric, philosophy) accompanied by lectures and *libraries; similarly with the older *neoi*. But for really serious 'higher education' in the recognizably modern sense, there were the great centres of learning—Athens, Pergamum, and Rhodes for philosophy and rhetoric; *Cos, Pergamum, or Ephesus for medicine; *Alexandria

(1) for the whole range of higher studies (see MUSEUM).

The teachers

Teachers were elected by the cities for a year at a time and supervised by the *gymnasiarch and *paidonomos*. There were three grades of literary teacher: the *grammatistēs* (elementary level), *grammaticus* (secondary), and rhetor or sophist (higher). The *paidonomos* and ephebes might engage skilled itinerant teachers for short periods. Ordinary teachers received little more pay than a skilled workman, private ones less than those provided with a salary by the city: music teachers received most, then the literary teacher, then the *paidotribēs*. A good teacher would receive gifts, prizes, and sometimes tax-exemption (teachers were exempt from the salt tax in Ptolemaic Egypt).

See also LITERACY; ORALITY.

H. I. Marrou, *History of Education in Antiquity* (1956; 7th. Fr. edn. 1977); W. V. Harris, *Ancient Literacy* (1989); F. A. G. Beck, *Greek Education, 450–350 BC* (1964), and *Album of Greek Education* (1975), for vase evidence; W. Jaeger, *Paideia*, 3 vols. (1944–6); N. Loraux, *Invention of Athens* (1986; Fr. orig. 1981); M. P. Nilsson, *Die hellenistische Schule* (1955); E. Ziebarth, *Aus dem griechischen Schulwesen*, 2nd. edn. (1914); J. Delorme, *Gymnasion* (1960); C. A. Forbes, *Neoi* (1933); S. Humphreys, in *The Craft of the Ancient Historian: Essays in Honour of C. G. Starr* (1985), 199 ff.; N. M. Kennell, *The Gymnasium of Virtue* (1995). F. A. G. B.; R. T.

education, Roman

1. Early Italy and the republic There is very little reliable evidence bearing upon formal education in the early period. Education was then certainly centred on the family and was probably based upon apprenticeship supervised by the father—in poorer homes an apprenticeship to agriculture or trade, in more aristocratic circles to military service and public life (what later became known as the *tirocinium militiae* and the *tirocinium fori*). The authority of the father, legalized as *patria potestas*, was absolute and could only in theory be questioned by the censors. The Roman mother had a more restricted, domestic role but she too was traditionally expected to take a personal, central responsibility and to set a strong moral example (see MOTHERHOOD, Roman). It is not certain when reading and writing became a serious part of Roman education: the 7th-cent. BC ivory writing-tablet with inscribed alphabet found at Marsiliana d'Albegna and 6th-cent. bucchero (pottery) models of wooden writing-tablets (*tabulae ansatae*) from Etruria may imply that *literacy was then already becoming a part of everyday life. Institutions like the religious calendars, the census, and the codification of the *Twelve Tables point in this direction and by the end of the 4th cent. BC it would certainly have been hard for a Roman senator to do without reading and writing. It is not known how such elementary instruction was given though it was often reckoned to be a parental responsibility; references to schools in the 5th and 4th cents. BC are probably anachronistic.

2. The later republic and the empire As Rome's contacts with the Greek-speaking world grew in the 3rd and 2nd cent. BC, a predominantly Greek pattern of education evolved (see EDUCATION, GREEK), omitting however the *gymnasium and emphasis on competitive physical education. Aristocratic Roman families often employed Greek-speaking tutors for their children (*Livius Andronicus and *Ennius were early and conspicuous examples) and these tutors—often slaves or freedmen—commonly taught both Greek and Latin; competence in both languages remained a feature of an upper-class education until the western and eastern empires parted company. This tradition of tutors in wealthy families continued alongside the growth of schools. A freedman,

Spurius *Carvilius, is credited with opening the first fee-paying school for elementary reading and writing in the second half of the 3rd cent. BC and thereafter the elementary teacher (*ludi magister* or *litterator*) running a small school became a lowly, noisy, and familiar part of Roman life. The Greek custom of a family *paedagogus* who took the children to and from school and supervised their life and habits was also adopted; the custom burgeoned especially after the Third Macedonian War when cheap, well-qualified Greek slaves became easily available. The second stage of education was in the hands of the *grammaticus who taught language and poetry and who might be either a private tutor with a family or a teacher with his own school. He could be a person of some learning and consequence. Teachers of *rhetoric, the third stage of Greek and Roman education, first appear in the 2nd cent. BC at Rome—*Crates (3) of Mallus was said to have been influential—and, in the absence of Latin instructional material, taught Greek theory and practice. Latin materials corresponding to the Greek rhetorical manuals appeared in the 1st cent. BC (e.g. the *Rhetorica ad Herennium*) and Plotius Gallus is said to have opened the first school for teaching rhetoric in Latin about 94 BC. Cicero's works on oratory were a major contribution to teaching rhetoric in Latin and *Quintilian's *Institutio Oratoria* published about AD 95 includes a developed and humane picture of Roman rhetorical training at its best. From the middle of the 2nd cent. BC, when three visiting Greek philosophers made a great impression with their lectures in Rome, philosophy could play a significant part in the education of some wealthier young Romans. Teachers were soon available in Italy, though no philosophical schools were founded in Rome until *Plotinus and *Porphyry attracted pupils in the 3rd cent. AD: the young were glad to travel and to visit one of the four famous schools in *Athens or other centres where philosophers taught. From the 1st cent. AD there were law schools at Rome which founded an important tradition of legal education culminating in the great law school at *Berytus (mod. Beirut) in the eastern empire. Augustus attempted with some success to use Roman and Italian traditions to create a Roman counterpart to the Greek *ephebeia* (see EPHĒBOI) in the revival of the *lusus Troiae* at Rome and the *collegia iuvenum* in the Italian cities; in this there was more than a hint of political education. Later emperors, local communities, and benefactors like *Pliny (2) the Younger sometimes subsidized charitable and educational activity from personal interest, generosity, public duty, or political expediency but there was nothing like national or regional provision for education.

3. Levels and subjects of study The three levels of Roman education represented by the *ludi magister*, the *grammaticus*, and the rhetor were probably never rigidly differentiated. Although formal education usually began when children were about 7 years old and transfers to the *grammaticus* and rhetor frequently happened at about the ages of 12 and 15 respectively, progress between the levels was often more a matter of achievement than age group; the roles of teachers sometimes overlapped considerably. All three levels followed a Greek pattern: the elementary teacher, for instance, taught reading by the familiar progression—letters, syllables, words—with much use of the gnomic example sentence (*sententia*). Writing and some basic mathematics were also his province. Echoes of the ancient schoolroom can be heard in the *colloquia* ('discourses') which occur in the bilingual school-books known as the *Hermeneumata*. The *grammaticus* advanced the study of both language and poetry (rarely prose). As Roman grammarians like *Varro and *Remmius Palaemon adapted Alexandrian grammatical theory to Latin (especially that of *Dionysius (15) Thrax), some systematic morphology was taught; syntax was rather diffusely approached via correctness of speech and the avoidance of solecism. In teaching poetry, attention was paid to expressive reading (lectio) followed by the teacher's explanation (enarratio) and, where appropriate, analysis (partitio). Homer's pre-eminent place in Greek schools was originally taken by poets like Livius Andronicus (who supplied the Odyssey in Saturnian verse translation), Naevius, and Ennius. Q. *Caecilius Epirota is credited with the introduction of contemporary poetry to Roman schools in 26 BC and later Virgil supplanted most earlier poets (Terence becoming the Roman counterpart to *Menander (1)). The teaching of rhetoric followed the Greek model closely with a series of preliminary exercises (*progymnasmata—sometimes taught by the grammaticus) leading on to the theory and practice of *declamation with the two major groupings of suasoriae (advice offered in historical or imaginary situations) and controversiae (court-room cases). The five traditional parts of rhetoric were the basis of instruction: inventio, dispositio, elocutio, memoria, and actio (see RHETORIC, LATIN). The teaching of philosophy which young Romans encountered seems to have been based very much upon studying the works of the founder of a philosophical school and the commentaries of his successors.

4. Schools and teachers Elementary teachers usually seem to have worked in suitable spaces in public porticoes or squares, in hired accommodation off the street, or in their own rooms; the idea of the school as a dedicated building is misleading. The grammaticus and the rhetor probably commanded better but not institutional accommodation. It is likely that most schools were small and though the monthly fees doubtless varied, such evidence as there is suggests that elementary teachers of some kind were affordable by all but the poor. Towns but not villages under the empire might be expected to have teachers and schools. Boys were almost certainly in a majority but some girls did attend too. The regular equipment for pupils consisted of waxed or whitened wooden writing-tablets, pen, and ink (though exercises were certainly written on papyrus when it could be afforded). In the elementary school lessons began at dawn and discipline was strict and unashamedly physical. There is some evidence for the education of slaves in paedagogia or training-schools attached to wealthy houses; the training sometimes included reading and writing as well as the household tasks required of them.

The status of elementary teachers was low; many were ex-slaves and had only a small and hazardous income. The grammaticus was better respected and *Suetonius' De grammaticis gives sketches of a poor but not ill-regarded profession. The rhetor could charge higher fees and the most famous could become men of some consequence under the empire. The ratio of maximum fees payable to the ludi magister, the grammaticus, and the rhetor in *Diocletian's Price Edict was 1 : 4 : 5. The rhetor was at first an object of some suspicion in Rome; in 161 BC rhetors were expelled from the city and Latin rhetoricians suffered the same fate in 92 BC. However, from the time of *Caesar teachers were more favoured; now and then they received various immunities, exemptions, and privileges by imperial edict, though imperial patronage was largely reserved for the highest levels. *Vespasian for instance endowed imperial chairs in Greek and Latin rhetoric at Rome, *Quintilian being the first holder of the Latin chair; Marcus *Aurelius endowed four chairs of philosophy and a chair of rhetoric at Athens. Emperors and politicians looked for visibility and prestige in exchange for their generosity.

S. F. Bonner, Education in Ancient Rome (1977); H. I. Marrou, History of Education in Antiquity (1956; 7th Fr. edn. 1977); J. Bowen, A History of Western Education 1: The Ancient World (1972); M. L. Clarke, Higher Education in the Ancient World (1971); W. V. Harris, Ancient Literacy (1989).
J. V. M.

Eëtion ('Ηετίων), king of the city of Thebe in the *Troad, and father of *Andromache. *Achilles sacked the town and killed him along with his seven sons, but gave him a warrior's burial (Il. 6. 395 ff.).
A. H. G.

Egeria, water goddess, worshipped with *Diana at Aricia (Verg. Aen. 7. 762–4, 775), apparently with the *Camenae outside the porta Capena in Rome (see the entry in Richardson, Topog. Dict. Ancient Rome; cf. Juv. 3. 17). Her name may be connected with egerere ('to deliver': Festus 67 Lindsay) or with the gens Egeria (Livy 1. 21. 3, 38. 1, with Ogilvie's notes; Cato, fr. 58 Peter; Festus 128 Lindsay). Pregnant women sacrificed to Egeria for easy delivery (Wissowa, RK 219–21, 248–9; cf. F. Altheim, Griechische Götter (1930), 127–9; A. Gordon, Univ. California Publ. Class. Arch. 2 (1934), 13–14). She was allegedly *Numa's consort and adviser (Livy 1. 21. 3), appropriate for the connection between prophecy and Egeria and the Camenae as water divinities.

Latte, RR 170.
C. R. P.

Egesta See SEGESTA.

Egnatius (RE 9), **Gellius,** Samnite general who organized the coalition of Samnites, Gauls, Etruscans, and Umbrians that was defeated at *Sentinum in 295 BC. Egnatius, like the Roman consul P. *Decius Mus (2), died in the battle (Livy 10. 21–9).
E. T. S.; T. J. Co.

Egnatius, Gnaeus, as *praetor in the mid-140s BC and one of the earliest regular governors of the Roman province of Macedonia (perhaps the first) built the *via Egnatia. His full name ('son of Gaius') and proconsular rank are known from a bilingual *milestone found near Thessaloniki, first published in 1974; he must be the same man as Cn. Egnatius C.f. of the tribe Stellatina who appears as the senior witness to a *senatus consultum sent to Corcyra (RDGE 4), plausibly dated on independent grounds to the late 140s.

C. Romiopoulou, BCH 1974, 813–16; cf. H. Mattingly, NC 1969, 103–4.
T. C. B.

Egnatius (RE 36) **Rufus, Marcus,** son of an equestrian friend of *Cicero's, won popularity as an aedile (c.26 BC) by organizing a private fire brigade, which inspired *Augustus to form the *vigiles. He became praetor and in 19 tried to win a consulship refused by the absent Augustus, but the consul C. *Sentius Saturninus rejected his candidacy. After rioting by his supporters he was accused of conspiring against Augustus and executed.
E. B.

Egypt

Pre-Ptolemaic Egypt began its historic period c.3200 BC. By a convention derived from *Manetho this era is divided into 31 dynasties which are currently grouped into several phases: the Thinite or Archaic period (Dynasties 1–2, c.3200–2700) is the formative stage of pharaonic civilization. The Old Kingdom (Dynasties 3–4, c.2700–2159) sees the establishment of a highly centralized state which peaked in the Fourth Dynasty with the builders of the Giza pyramids. Foreign relations, peaceful and otherwise, were maintained with Nubia to the south, Libya, and Asia, but there was no attempt to establish an empire. Culturally, this age is distinguished by work of the highest quality in architecture, sculpture, and painting. The fabric of government collapsed at the end of the Sixth Dynasty to create the First Intermediate period (Dynasties 7–mid-11, *c*.2159–2040), an age of political dissolution and cultural decline. The country was reunited by Montuhotep II *c*.2040 to create the Middle Kingdom (mid-Dynasty 11–12, *c*.2040–1786). The major new initiative of this period was the integration into the Egyptian state of Lower *Nubia as far as the Second Cataract. This development was paralleled by significant involvement in Asia, but this stopped short of imperial control. As in the Old Kingdom, there is ample evidence of high-quality work in the visual arts, but this epoch is distinguished culturally above all as the classic age of Egyptian language and literature. The Middle Kingdom disintegrated in the Thirteenth Dynasty to inaugurate the Second Intermediate period, the most important event of which was the establishment of Asiatic control by the Hyksos over most of Egypt, an episode which conferred major military and cultural benefits as well as providing the impetus for expansion into Asia during the New Kingdom (Dynasties 18–20, *c*.1575–1087). This great age of Egyptian militarism created in the Eighteenth Dynasty an empire which stretched from the Euphrates to beyond the Fourth Cataract in Nubia, and the resources generated made possible a great flowering of achievement in the visual arts, in particular great temples such as those of Karnak and Luxor and the mortuary temples of Western *Thebes (2) as well as the brilliantly decorated tombs in the Valleys of the Kings and Queens. The decline in Egypt's imperial position at the end of the dynasty was reversed by Seti I and Ramesses II in the early Nineteenth Dynasty, but they never succeeded in recovering all the lost territory in Asia. The later New Kingdom is largely characterized by gradual decline generated by internal divisions, economic difficulties, and foreign aggression. The Late Dynastic period (Dynasties 21–31, *c*.1087–332) is marked by long periods of foreign occupation by Libyans, Nubians, and Persians punctuated by short, if sometimes brilliant, periods of national resurgence. It terminates with the occupation by *Alexander (3) the Great in 332.   A. B. L.

Ptolemaic In the period from the death of *Alexander (3) the Great in 323 BC until the defeat of *Cleopatra VII with Antony at Actium in 31 BC the Egyptian throne was held by Macedonians, and from 304 by the one family (for which see PTOLEMY (1)) descended from Alexander's general Ptolemy son of Lagus. Externally the main problem remained the extent of the kingdom, while internally the nature of administrative control and relations with the native Egyptians formed the major concerns of this new resident dynasty of foreign pharaohs. For the modern observer it is the incomplete nature of the historical record which presents problems. Contemporary historical analysis is limited in period (*Polybius (1), *Diodorus (3) Siculus), much of it concentrating on the scandalous and sensational (*Pompeius Trogus, *Justin), and while numerous papyri and ostraca, preserved through the dry desert conditions, join with inscriptions to make Egypt better documented than other Hellenistic kingdoms, these illustrate the details of administration and everyday life without its wider context.

Territorially the Nile valley formed a natural unit. Ptolemy I added *Cyrene and *Cyprus to the kingdom, both significant territories in Ptolemaic history. Under *Ptolemy II control was extended over much of the Aegean (see CYCLADES) and the coast

of Asia Minor organized as the Island League; this was later lost. But the territory most fought over with the Seleucid rulers of Syria was Coele ('Hollow') Syria: Palestine and the Gaza strip. This strategic area was Ptolemaic until the battle of Panion in 200, when it passed to Seleucid control. The final episode in the struggles of these two kingdoms came in 168 when *Antiochus (4) IV's successful invasion of Egypt was halted at Eleusis (a suburb of *Alexandria (1)) by Roman intervention. To the south the doubtful loyalty of the Thebaid proved an ongoing threat to the traditional unity of Upper and Lower Egypt. The area was in revolt from 206 to 186, under the control of rebel kings Haronnophris and Chaonnophris and again for three years from 88. The destruction of *Thebes (2) by *Ptolemy IX brought relative peace to the south for 75 years. See NATIONALISM (Hellenistic and Roman).

Internally the Ptolemies used local expertise as they set up their royal administration based on the traditional divisions or nomes of Egypt. Self-governing cities were few: *Alexandria (1), which served as capital from 312 BC, the Greek Delta port of *Naucratis and *Ptolemais (2) (mod. El-Menshā) founded by Ptolemy I as a Greek city in the south. Through a hierarchical bureaucracy, taxation of rich agricultural land and of the population and their livestock was based on a thorough census and land-survey. Greek was gradually introduced as the language of the administration and Greeks were privileged, both socially and in the tax-structure. The categorization however of Greek was now not an ethnic one, but rather one acquired, through employment and education. The wealth of the country (from its irrigation-agriculture and from taxes) was employed both for further development in the countryside (with agricultural initiatives and land-reclamation, especially in the *Fayūm) and, in Alexandria, for royal patronage and display. The cultural life of the capital, with the *Museum and *Library strongly supported under the early Ptolemies, played an important role in the definition of contemporary Hellenism.

Like other Hellenistic monarchs, the Ptolemies depended for security on their army, and Ptolemaic troops were tied in loyalty to their new homes by land-grants in the countryside. From the reign of Ptolemy VI local *politeumata* were also founded as settlements for both soldiers and attached civilians. As the flow of immigrant recruits grew less, Egyptian troops were increasingly used, a development Polybius noted (5. 107. 3) as dangerous to the country. These troops too might become settlers (cleruchs) in the countryside (with smaller plots), as might the native police and other security forces. Land was further used in gift-estates to reward high-ranking officials; the *dioikētēs* ('finance minister') *Apollonius (3) under Ptolemy II was one of these.

In a soft approach to Egyptian ways, the Ptolemies early recognized the importance of native temples, granting privileges, and supporting native cults. For the Ptolemies were both Egyptian pharaohs and Greek monarchs. The new god *Sarapis with his human aspect, an extension of the native Osiris-Apis bull, typifies this dual aspect of the period. Royal co-operation—for mutual ends—with the high priests of *Memphis, central city of Lower Egypt where from the reign at least of Ptolemy V the king was crowned Egyptian-style, contrasts with the problems posed by the breakaway tendencies of Thebes and Upper Egypt. General tolerance and even financial support for native temples characterize the religious policy of the regime. In the important field of law two separate legal systems continued in use.

The sister-marrying Ptolemaic dynasty is, from the late 3rd cent., consistently represented as in decline. (Details of palace

Egyptian deities

feuds and struggles may be found under PTOLEMY (1) I–XIV.) From the mid-2nd cent. the shadow of Rome loomed large, yet Egypt was the last Hellenistic kingdom to fall under Roman sway.   D. J. T.

Roman After two centuries of diplomatic contacts, Egypt was annexed as a province of the Roman people in 30 BC by Octavian (Augustus) after his defeat of Mark Antony (see ANTONIUS (2), M.) and *Cleopatra VII. Although the Romans adapted many individual elements of the centralized bureaucracy of the Ptolemaic kingdom, and although the emperor could be represented as a pharaoh, the institutions of the Ptolemaic monarchy were dismantled, and the administrative and social structure of Egypt underwent fundamental changes. The governor (prefect) and other major officials were Roman *equites* appointed, like the administrators of other 'imperial' provinces, by the emperor for a few years. Egypt was garrisoned with three, later two, legions and a number of auxiliary units. For private business pre-existing Egyptian and Greek legal forms and traditions were generally respected, but under the umbrella of the principles and procedures of Roman law. A closed monetary system based on the Alexandrian silver tetradrachm was maintained, but the tetradrachm was made equivalent to the Roman denarius. The Egyptian temples and priesthood were allowed to keep most of their privileges, but in tacit return for the ubiquitous spread of the Roman imperial cult (see RULER-CULT). Local administration, previously entrusted to salaried officials and private contractors, was gradually converted to a liturgic system (see LITURGY (ROMAN)), in which ownership of property brought an obligation to serve. This was enabled by Augustus' revolutionary conversion of the category of 'cleruchic' land (see CLERUCHY), allotments held in theory at royal discretion in return for military service, into fully private property, of which there had been very little in Ptolemaic Egypt. The Romans also increased the status of the towns and their inhabitants. Alexandria enjoyed the greatest privileges, but the *mētropolis* ('mother-city', i.e. chief town) of each regional administrative unit (nome, see NOMOS (1)), was under Augustus given some self-administration through liturgic magistrates, then encouraged to erect public buildings and to behave like cities elsewhere, until in AD 200/1 *Septimius Severus granted *boulai* (councils) to Alexandria and all the *mētropoleis*. See METROPOLIS (c). As part of this urbanization the Romans introduced a strict social hierarchy with ethno-cultural overtones: Roman and Alexandrian citizens were legally marked off, mainly by their exemption from the poll-tax, from the other inhabitants, who were called 'Egyptians'. Within the category of 'Egyptians' the metropolites (original residents of the *mētropoleis*) enjoyed some privileges, principally a reduced rate of poll-tax, and within them a theoretically hereditary group of 'Hellenic' descent, defined by membership of the *gymnasium, formed the socio-political élite of each *mētropolis*. Large private estates developed in the 2nd cent. and flourished in the 3rd, so that Egypt, like other eastern provinces, was dominated and run by a local 'Greek', urban-based landowning aristocracy. Despite urbanization, the bulk of the population remained peasants, many of them tenant-farmers of 'public' (previously 'royal') and 'sacred' land for the traditional, variable, but quite high, rents in kind. The imperial government exported some of this tax-wheat to feed Rome, but it was equally if not more interested in the cash revenues of Egypt. Roman tax-rates often followed Ptolemaic precedent, though the annual poll-tax in cash was a striking novelty; the chronic fiscal problems uniquely documented in

the papyri were probably typical of much of the ancient world. Whether economic conditions were better or worse than in previous periods is difficult to judge. The single greatest disaster of the Roman period was the Antonine *plague of the mid-160s to 170s, but the country seems to have recovered fully by the early 3rd cent. Generally Roman Egypt had a vigorous and increasingly monetized economy. The main cultural division was between the 'Hellenic' life of the metropolites and the village life of the Egyptian-speaking majority, even after the universal grant of Roman citizenship in 212. But most peasants were involved in the money economy, many acquired some literacy in Greek, and the scale of urbanization implies considerable social mobility. The political and fiscal reforms of *Diocletian at the end of the 3rd cent., capping longer-term developments such as the growth of *Christianity—which led to the re-emergence of Egyptian as a literary language (Coptic)—brought about another social, administrative, and cultural revolution which marked the end of 'Roman' Egypt. Egypt remained a province of the Byzantine empire until it came under Arab rule in AD 642. (See RACE; FOOD SUPPLY, ROMAN; PEASANTS.)

PRE-PTOLEMAIC *CAH*[2] vols. 1–6 (1970–94); E. Drioton and J. Vandier, *L'Égypte*, 4th edn. (1962); A. H. Gardiner, *Egypt of the Pharaohs* (1961); B. J. Kemp, *Ancient Egypt: Anatomy of a Civilisation* (1989); L. Schofield and W. W. Davies, *Egypt, the Aegean and the Levant* (1995); W. S. Smith, *The Art and Architecture of Ancient Egypt* (1981); B. Trigger and others, *Ancient Egypt: A Social History* (1992).

PTOLEMAIC PERIOD M. Rostovtzeff, *Hellenistic World*; C. Préaux, *L'Économie royale des Lagides* (1939), and *Les Grecs en Égypte* (1947); N. Lewis, *Greeks in Ptolemaic Egypt* (1986); E. Will, *Histoire politique du monde hellénistique* (1979, 1982); J. Baines and J. Málek, *Atlas of Ancient Egypt* (1980); R. S. Bianchi, *Cleopatra's Egypt* (1988); P. M. Fraser, *Ptolemaic Alexandria* (1972); D. J. Thompson, *Memphis under the Ptolemies* (1988); R. S. Bagnall, *The Administration of the Ptolemaic Possessions* (1976); H. Maehler and V. M. Strocka, *Das ptolemäische Ägypten* (1978); L. Criscuolo and G. Geraci, *Egitto e storia antica* (1989); J. H. Johnson, *Life in a Multi-cultural Society* (1992); R. S. Bagnall and P. Derow, *Greek Historical Documents* (1981); M. M. Austin, *The Hellenistic World* (1981).

ROMAN General surveys: A. K. Bowman, *Egypt after the Pharaohs* (1986); N. Lewis, *Life in Egypt under Roman Rule* (1983).

Documents (papyri): O. Montevecchi, *La papirologia*, 2nd edn. (1988).

Topics: Augustan settlement: G. Geraci, *Genesi della provincia romana d'Egitto* (1983). Administration and cities: Jones, *Cities E. Rom. Prov.*[2] (1971), ch. 11; A. K. Bowman, *The Town Councils of Roman Egypt* (1971). Society: H. Braunert, *Die Binnenwanderung* (1964). Economy: A. C. Johnson, *Roman Egypt*, vol. 2 of T. Frank (ed.), *An Economic Survey of Ancient Rome* (1936); S. L. Wallace, *Taxation in Egypt from Augustus to Diocletian* (1938). Law: R. Taubenschlag, *The Law of Greco-Roman Egypt in the Light of the Papyri*, 2nd edn. (1955). Transition: R. S. Bagnall, *Egypt in Late Antiquity* (1993).   D. W. R.

Egyptian deities the Graeco-Roman view of Egyptian religion is sharply fissured. Despite Hdt. 2. 50. 1 (comm. A. B. Lloyd, 1975–88), many writers of all periods, and probably most individuals, found in the Egyptians' worship of animals a polemical contrast to their own norms (though cf. Cic. *Nat. D.* 1. 29. 81 f.), just as, conversely, the Egyptians turned animal-worship into a symbol of national identity (cf. Diod. Sic. 1. 86–90). The first Egyptian divinity to be recognized by the Greek world was the oracular *Ammon of the *Siwa oasis (Hdt. 2. 54–7); but *oracles have a special status. The only form of Late-period Egyptian religion to be assimilated into the Graeco-Roman world was to a degree untypical, centred on anthropomorphic deities—*Isis, *Sarapis, and Harpocrates—and grounded in Egyptian vernacular enthusiasm quite as much as in temple ritual. The other gods which became known in the Graeco-Roman world, *Osiris, *Anubis, *Apis, *Horus, *Bubastis, Agathodaemon (see AGATHOS DAIMON), Bes, etc., spread solely in their train. Moreover, especially in the Hellenistic period, a nice balance was maintained between acknowledgement of their strangeness (Isis *Taposirias, Memphitis, Aigyptia*, etc.) and selection of their universal, 'hearkening', 'aiding', 'saving' roles.

From the late 4th cent. BC, these cults were most commonly introduced into the Greek world, primarily to port- and tourist-towns, by (Hellenized) Egyptians, i.e. immigrant metics: cf. *IG* 11. 4. 1299, comm. H. Engelmann (1975²). Sometimes they were introduced by Greeks who had served or lived in Egypt (e.g. *SEG* 38. 1571, 217 BC). There is a growing consensus that they were often indirect beneficiaries of Ptolemaic political suzerainty. Within a generation or two they became sufficiently attractive to Greeks of some social standing to be able to press for recognition as thiasoi (see THIASOS): it was when they proselytized among the citizen body that they were regulated by city governments and incorporated as civic deities. Full-time Egyptian priests were then obtained for larger temples, and subordinate *synodoi* (associations) formed, e.g. *melanephoroi* (lit. 'the black-clad'), *pastophoroi* ('shrine-carriers'), analogous to a development widespread in Late-period Egypt. In many smaller communities the Greek model of annual priesthoods was adopted. (See PRIESTS.) In the west, Isis reached *Campania from *Delos in the late 2nd cent. BC. At Rome the situation was initially volatile: the private *Isium Metellinum* (75–50 BC) and an illegal shrine on the Capitol were pulled down in 53 BC (Dio Cass. 40. 47. 3, cf. 42. 26. 2). The first public temple was the *Iseum Campense* (43 BC). The cults became attractive to members of the decurial class in the 1st cent. AD, spreading from Italy unevenly into the western empire. Neither slaves nor the poor are anywhere much in evidence.

Animal-worship: K. A. D. Smelik and E. A. Hemelrijk, *ANRW* 2. 17. 4 (1984), 1852–2000, 2337 ff.; F. Dunand, in *Les Grandes Figures religieuses* (1986), 59–84. Spread: L. Vidman, *Isis und Sarapis bei den Griechen und Römern* (1970); F. Dunand, *Le Culte d'Isis dans le bassin orientale de la Méditerranée*, 3 vols. (1973), and in *Religions, pouvoir, rapports sociaux* (1980), 71–148; M. Malaise, *ANRW* 2. 17. 3 (1984), 1615–91; F. Mora, *Prosopografia isiaca* (1990), 2. 72–112; among slaves: F. Bömer, *Gymnasium* 1989, 97–109.

R. L. G.

Eileithyia (Εἰλείθυια, Cretan Ἐλεύθια), Minoan goddess of birth. She had numerous cults throughout Greece and the *Cycladic islands but mainly in *Laconia (two temples at Sparta, Paus. 3. 14. 6, 17. 1), and in *Crete where she was chief goddess of Lato (Jessen, *RE* 5 'Eileuthyia'). Her name is obscure, probably non-Greek, so that etymologies, including the tempting connection with (*Demeter) Eleusinia (Nilsson, *MMR*² 521; F. R. Willetts, *CQ* 1958, 221 ff.), remain conjectural. Eileithyia occurs beside the place-name Amnisos on tablet KN Gg 705 (*ereutija*). She had a cave sanctuary there which Odysseus claims to have seen on his visit to king *Idomeneus (1) of *Cnossus (*Od.* 19. 188). Inside the goddess was worshipped in the form of a stalagmite during middle Minoan (palace period), and her cult was remembered until Roman times. Eileithyia Inatia had another cave-cult at Tsoutsouros (Inatos) with votive figurines of pregnant and parturient women. In Greek myth Eileithyia is the daughter of Hera (Hes. *Theog.* 922; Hom. *Il.* 11. 271) and often Eileithyiae (in the plural) are associates of *Artemis (Artemis Eileithyia) in their function as goddesses of *childbirth. Eileithyia helps or hinders a birth in epic (*Il.* 16. 187; 19. 103; *Hymn Hom. Ap.* 97). At *Il.* 19. 119 the Eileithyiae are synonymous with *Alcmene's birth pangs.

The winged figure seen assisting at the birth of Athena depicted on a 7th-cent. BC Tenean relief pithos (Tenos Museum; Simon (1980), fig. 165) may be Eileithyia, but the scene has been variously interpreted. The goddess is often shown in scenes of divine births from Archaic times, although her iconographic form and attributes were never clearly defined. See CRETAN CULTS AND MYTHS.

Nilsson, *MMR*² 518–23; *GGR* 1³ 312–14; E. Tyree, *Cretan Sacred Caves* (1974), 24–7; E. Simon, *Die Götter der Griechen*, 2nd edn. (1980), 187; R. Olmos, *LIMC* 3/1 (1986), 686–99 'Eileithyia'.

H. J. R.; H. W. P.; B. C. D.

Einsiedeln Eclogues, two incomplete Latin pastorals (see PASTORAL POETRY, LATIN) comprising 87 hexameters, first published in 1869, and named after the Swiss monastery where they were discovered. They are the work of an unidentified author writing under *Nero: just possibly the two poems are by different hands. In the first, dating probably to AD 64 or 65, two competing shepherds praise the emperor—whose *Troica* is said to eclipse *Virgil's *Aeneid*—in terms so extravagant that critics are undecided whether to regard the poem as botched panegyric, or as ironic and derisive. In the second, the shepherd Mystes celebrates the return of the *golden age, but, paradoxically, asserts that 'satiety' and 'cares' corrode his enjoyment of it. He also rebuts indignantly the denial by the 'doltish herd' that the Neronian era is a new golden age, thereby conceding implicitly the existence of opposition to the emperor. Again it is difficult to determine the author's attitude towards Nero: the difficulty is compounded by the corrupt state of the text, and by the incompetence and obscurity of the writing.

TEXT Korzeniewski, *Hirtengedichte aus neronischer Zeit* (1971); C. Giarratano (with Calpurnius and Nemesianus) (1924).
TRANSLATION Duff *Minor Lat. Poets* 1.
STUDIES W. Schmid, *Bonner Jahrb.* 1953; W. Theiler, *Stud. Ital.* 1956; Fuchs, *Harv. Stud.* 1958; G. Scheda, *Studien zur bukolischen Dichtung der neronischen Epoche* (Diss. Bonn, 1969); Verdière, *ANRW* 2. 32. 3.

L. C. W.

Eirenaeus (Lat., Minucius Pacatus), a grammarian of the Augustan age, pupil of *Heliodorus (2) the metrist, and cited by *Erotian. See also GLOSSA, GLOSSARY, GREEK.

J. S. R.

Eirene, peace personified. In poetry *Hesiod (*Op.* 901–3) has her and her sisters ('Observance of the Laws' and 'Justice'), daughters of Zeus and Themis, watch over the field crops of men. She receives a lyric prayer in Euripides' *Cresphontes* (fr. 453 Nauck) and appears often elsewhere (e.g. Bacchyl. fr. 4. 61 ff. Snell–Maehler). She is the title (but silent) character of *Aristophanes (1)'s *Peace*, produced in 422/1 BC, just days before the Peace of *Nicias (1). Her cult is known only for Athens. Plutarch (*Cim.* 13. 6) has the Athenians build an altar for her about 465 to commemorate peace with the Persians (see CALLIAS, PEACE OF), probably mistakenly (see Jacoby, *FGrH* 3b Suppl. 1. 523–6). The *Common Peace of 371 was commemorated by an annual state sacrifice to her (Isoc. 15. 109–10; Nepos, *Timotheus* 2. 2; *IG* 2². 1496. 94–5) and by a statue, by *Cephisodotus (1), of her carrying the child *Plutus ('Wealth') (Paus. 1. 8. 2).

RE 5 (1905), 2128–34, 'Eirene'; *LIMC* 3/1 (1986), 700–5.

J. D. M.

eiresiōnē, an olive branch carried by singing boys at the *Pyanopsia and (?) *Thargelia at Athens, and at an unknown festival of *Apollo on *Samos. At the Pyanopsia, a public *eiresiōnē* was deposited at a temple of Apollo, others at house doors (where they remained, probably, till the next year). The branch was hung with figs, fruits, and other symbols of agricultural abundance,

513

and according to the song brought 'figs and fat loaves' and other good things with it; householders were expected to give the boys a present in return.

Nilsson, *GGR*, 1³. 122–5; C. Calame, *Thésée et l'imaginaire athénien* (1991), 296–301. R. C. T. P.

eisangelia (εἰσαγγελία) in Athenian law was the name of four distinct types of prosecution.

1. The accuser denounced someone to the *ekklēsia or the *boulē for treason. In the 4th cent. BC a law (quoted in *Hyperides, *For Euxenippus* 7–8, 29; cf. Dem. 49. 67) specified offences for which this procedure could be used: subversion of the *democracy, betrayal of Athenian forces or possessions to an enemy, and corrupt deception of the Athenian people by an orator. In the 5th cent. it had been possible to use *eisangelia* for serious offences not specified in any law; the best known cases are the prosecutions for profanation of the *mysteries (see ELEUSIS) and mutilation of the *herms in 415. But in the 4th cent. this seems to have been no longer permitted, and prosecutors sometimes made tortuous efforts to bring various charges under one or other of the headings specified in the law. A case might be either referred to a jury or tried by the *ekklēsia* itself, but after the middle of the 4th cent. no instances of trial by the *ekklēsia* are known.

2. The accuser denounced an official to the *boulē for maladministration. The *boulē could impose a fine up to 500 drachmas. If it considered a heavier penalty was required, it referred the case to a jury.

3. The accuser denounced a public arbitrator for misconduct of an arbitration. The case was heard by the whole body of public arbitrators. If the accused arbitrator was found guilty, he was disfranchised, but could appeal to a jury.

4. The accuser denounced a guardian for maltreatment of an orphan, and prosecuted him before a jury.

A common feature was that in *eisangelia*, unlike other public actions, the prosecutor suffered no penalty if he obtained less than one-fifth of the jury's votes.

M. H. Hansen, *Eisangelia* (1975); P. J. Rhodes, *JHS* 1979, 103–14; M. H. Hansen, *JHS* 1980, 89–95. D. M. M.

eisphora ('paying-in'), a general word for payments made for a common cause by a plurality of contributors; and in particular the name of a property tax known in a number of Greek states and in the Ptolemaic empire.

In Athens *eisphora* is attested in *IG* 1³. 52 = ML 58 (probably 434/3 BC) as an extraordinary tax which can be levied after a vote of immunity in the assembly, and *Thucydides (2) mentions a levy in 428/7 (3. 19), but we have no details about the 5th-cent. tax. In the 4th cent. *eisphora* was a proportional levy, imposed when the assembly chose and at a rate which the assembly chose, on all whose declared property exceeded a certain value; probably the class of *eisphora*-payers was larger than the class of *liturgy-performers; *metics were liable, on disadvantageous terms. The *timēma*, the total assessment of all men or of all liable for *eisphora*, is said to have been 5,750 or 6,000 talents (Polyb. 2. 62. 7; Dem. 14. 19). In 378/7 those liable were organized in 100 *symmoriai ('partnerships'); and shortly afterwards the richest three members of each *symmoria* were given the duty of advancing the whole sum due from their *symmoria* as a *proeisphora*, and left to reimburse themselves from the other members.

In Boeotia (see BOEOTIA; FEDERAL STATES) *eisphora* was a regular tax in the federation of the late 5th and early 4th cent. BC (*Hell. Oxy.* 19. 4 Chambers), an extraordinary levy in at any rate some of

the cities in the Hellenistic period. In the *Achaean Confederacy *eisphora* was a levy imposed on the sometimes reluctant member states by the confederacy (e.g. Polyb. 4. 60. 4). About 280 the League of Islanders (see CYCLADES) thanked *Ptolemy (1) II for lightening or removing the burden of *eisphora* imposed by *Ptolemy (1) I (*IG* 12. 7. 506 = *Syll.*³ 390). Within Ptolemaic Egypt *eisphora* was an extraordinary tax on land.

Athens: G. E. M. de Ste. Croix, *Class. et Med.* 1953, 30–70; R. Thomsen, *Eisphora* (1964); P. Brun, *Eisphora, syntaxis, stratiotika* (1983), 3–73. Boeotia: P. Roesch, *Études béotiennes* (1982), 297–301. Achaean Confederacy: J. A. O. Larsen, *Greek Federal States* (1968), 232–4. Egypt: *PTeb.* 1, p. 431. F. M. H.; P. J. R.

ekklēsia (in some states *(h)ēliaia* or its dialect equivalent, or *agora*), the assembly of adult male citizens which had the ultimate decision-making power in a Greek state. There was room for variation, according to the complexion of the regime, in the membership of the assembly (an *oligarchy might use a property qualification to exclude the poor), the frequency of its meetings, and the extent to which the business it could discuss and its freedom in discussing it were limited by the prerogatives of the magistrates and/or a council.

In the Homeric world (see HOMER) assemblies met occasionally, to deal with the business of the king or noble who summoned them. Active participation was limited to the leading men and the religious experts, while the ordinary men would shout their approval or remain ominously silent. In *Iliad* 2. 211–77 the commoner *Thersites presumes to make a speech, but *Odysseus' rebuke to him meets with general applause.

In *Sparta the assembly of full citizens was guaranteed regular meetings and a final right of decision by the Great Rhetra attributed to *Lycurgus (2) (see APELLAI (1)). The assembly appears more powerful, and the *gerousia (council of elders) less powerful, in the narratives of *Thucydides (2) and *Xenophon (1) than in the Rhetra with its rider and in *Aristotle's *Politics*: ordinary members could not speak or make proposals, and the assembly was perhaps most powerful when the *gerousia* was divided. Voting was by acclamation.

At Athens, as elsewhere, the character of the assembly developed with progress towards *democracy. Probably the poorest citizens were never formally excluded, but at first were not expected to play an active part. Originally the assembly perhaps decided only questions of peace and war, and formally elected the magistrates; it was probably involved in the special appointments of *Draco and *Solon; Solon's creation of a second council to prepare business for the assembly was probably coupled with regular meetings for the assembly, and his *(h)*ēliaia* may have been a meeting of the assembly for judicial purposes. *Cleisthenes (2)'s new organization of the citizen body had no direct effect on the assembly, but the high level of participation which his system required will have had an indirect effect. The assembly gained further powers from *Ephialtes (4)'s reform of the *Areopagus, including perhaps the right to try *eisangeliai ('impeachments'). By the second half of the 5th cent. BC all major and many minor decisions of the Athenians were taken by the assembly.

The regular meeting-place of the assembly was the *Pnyx, in the south-west of the city; the theatre of Dionysus was increasingly used from the late 4th cent. Eventually there were four regular meetings in each of the ten prytanies of the year, and probably extraordinary meetings could be summoned in addition when necessary: the increase from one regular meeting per prytany, which survived as the Principal Assembly (*kyria ekklēsia*), may have been made in the second half of the 5th cent. Meetings were summoned by the *prytaneis on behalf of the council; the presidents were at first perhaps the *archontes, in the second half of the 5th cent. the prytaneis, and from the early 4th cent. the *proedroi (these both being committees of the council). The requirement of a quorum of 6,000 for some categories of business suggests that an attendance of that size could be, but was not always, attained. In the 5th cent. citizens were not paid to attend the assembly, as they were paid to hold office or serve on juries, but payment for attending the assembly was introduced by *Agyrrhius shortly after the democratic restoration of 403. Voting was by ballot when it was necessary to check that a quorum had been achieved, but otherwise by show of hands, when there was not a precise count but the presiding officers adjudged the majority.

Some items of business were prescribed by law for particular occasions in the year; every item on which the assembly was to make a decision had to be the subject of a probouleuma (prior resolution by the council), which could but did not have to incorporate a specific proposal, but in the assembly any citizen could speak and could propose a motion or an amendment. In the 5th and 4th cents. the assembly took its duties seriously, but in the Hellenistic period it became more of a rubber stamp to the council. From the early 6th cent. to the late 5th laws could be enacted only by a decree of the assembly; the 4th cent. attempted to distinguish between decrees (psēphismata), which were particular and/or ephemeral but included all decisions in the field of foreign affairs, and laws (nomoi), which were general and permanent, and for which a more elaborate procedure was devised. Various precautions were taken against improper and overhasty decisions in the assembly, but they did not always prove effective in a crisis.

In bodies larger than the single city, assemblies were less practicable but were sometimes used. In the Delphic *amphictiony the main deciding body was the council, but there could also be an assembly of all who were present at the time of a meeting. The federal state of Boeotia (see BOEOTIA; FEDERAL STATES) did not have an assembly in the constitution which was in force to 386, but the revived federation of the 370s did have an assembly, and the *Arcadian League formed after the battle of *Leuctra had an assembly of the Ten Thousand. The *Aetolian and *Achaean Confederacies of the Hellenistic period both had assemblies as well as councils. In such bodies, even when voting was by cities rather than by individuals, inhabitants of the city where the assembly met might exercise undue influence: for that reason in 188 *Philopoemen proposed that the Achaean Confederacy should abandon the rule by which regular meetings were always held at Aegium (Livy 38. 30).

In general: G. Busolt, Griechische Staatskunde, 3rd edn. (1920–6). Sparta: A. Andrewes, Ancient Society and Institutions . . . V. Ehrenberg (1966), 1–20. Athens: M. H. Hansen, The Athenian Assembly in the Age of Demosthenes (1987); R. K. Sinclair, Democracy and Participation in Athens (1988), chs. 3–5. Larger units: J. A. O. Larsen, Representative Government in Greek and Roman History (1955), and Greek Federal States (1968).

A. W. G.; T. J. C.; P. J. R.

ekphrasis, an extended and detailed literary description of any object, real or imaginary. 'There are ekphraseis of faces and objects and places and ages and many other things' (Hermog. Prog. 10; cf. Dion. Hal. Rhet. 10. 17, Lucian, Hist. conscr. 20, Apthonius, Progymnasmata 12). The rhetoricians thus systematized into a rhetorical exercise (*progymnasma) a poetic technique stretching from the description of the shield of Achilles in the Iliad to that

of Hagia Sophia by *Paulus Silentiarius. Most were of works of art. Ekphraseis was a work by *Callistratus (5), and Eikones was the title of works by Philostratus (see PHILOSTRATI), *Lucian, and others.

P. Friedländer, Johannes von Gaza und Paulus Silentiarius (1912); D. Fowler, JRS 1991, 25 ff.; J. A. W. Heffernan, The Museum of Words: The Poetics of Ekphrasis from Homer to Ashbery (1993). J. S. R.

Elagabalus, Roman emperor. See AURELIUS ANTONINUS (2), M.

Elagabalus, deus Sol invictus ('Invincible Sun-god Elagabalus'), oracular deity of *Emesa, his sacred symbol a conical black stone. His cult was established in Rome from the later 2nd cent. AD. In 218 his hereditary priest at Emesa became emperor as *Elagabalus and made the god the supreme official deity of the empire with precedence over Jupiter. This short-lived promotion (including translation of the sacred stone to the Palatine) was ended by the emperor's assassination, although the cult survived to enjoy the patronage of *Aurelian. See ORIENTAL CULTS; SOL.

G. Halsberghe, ANRW 2. 17. 4 (1984), 2181 ff.; Y. Hajjar, ANRW 2. 18. 4 (1990), 2257 ff. (oracle; bibliog.). A. J. S. S.

Elam, ancient kingdom in SW Iran centred on two main cities, *Susa and Anshan (near *Persepolis), whose rulers were members of the same family at some periods. Connected with *Mesopotamia by raids, by the intermittent vassaldom of Susa, and by the use of *cuneiform script, its written records began c.3200 BC with proto-Elamite, still undeciphered, continued in *Akkadian, and ended in Elamite, a non-Indo-Iranian language still in the process of decipherment. It controlled the supply of minerals and timber to Mesopotamia, with which it shared many features of material culture. Famous for a special kind of bow, its archers were prized mercenaries in the 7th cent. The earliest known dynasties belong to the mid-third millennium, its latest to the early 6th cent., despite the sack of Susa by *Assyria in 646 BC. It was absorbed into the Achaemenid empire.

E. Carter and M. W. Stolper, Elam (1984). S. M. D.

Elatea, large city in NE *Phocis, strategically important because of its position along a vital road running through the Cephissus valley between *Macedonia and *Boeotia. *Xerxes destroyed it in 480 BC; *Philip (1) II unexpectedly occupied it in 339 BC in his *Chaeronean campaign. The Elateans repulsed Cassander in 305 BC. *Philip (3) V reduced Elatea in 207 BC, after which it remained loyal to Macedonia until T. *Quinctius Flamininus conquered it in 198 BC. It successfully resisted *Mithradates VI's attack in 86 BC, for which Rome rewarded it with a grant of freedom (see FREE CITIES). In Pausanias (3)'s day (10. 34. 2) Elatea resisted the Costobocs, a band of barbarian invaders.

J. G. Frazer, Pausanias's Description of Greece 5 (1898); F. Schober, Phokis (1924). J. Bu.

Elatus ("Ἔλατος), 'Driver', the name of (1) a Trojan ally killed by *Agamemnon (Il. 6. 33); (2) one of *Penelope's wooers (Od. 22. 267); (3) the eponym of *Elatea (Paus. 8. 4. 2–4); (4) a Centaur (Apollod. 2. 85); (5) a Lapith, father of Polyphemus the *Argonaut (schol. Ap. Rhod. 1. 40); father of Taenarus eponym of *Taenarum (ibid. 102).

LIMC 3/1 (1986), 708–9. H. J. R.

Elea

Elea (or **Velia;** mod. Castellamare), *Phocaean colony, founded *c.*540 BC, 60 km. (37 mi.) south of *Paestum. Economically reliant on agriculture and fishing, it was noted for the *Eleatic school of philosophers. In 290 BC, it was conquered by Rome and later became a *municipium (89 BC). It became fashionable as a resort in the Augustan period and retained its Greek culture until the 1st cent. AD. Statues from that period now attest an interesting medical society which looked back to *Parmenides; see ELEATIC SCHOOL.

Various authors in 'Velia e Focei in Occidente', *PP* 1966, and 'Nuovi Studi su Velia', *PP* 1970. K. L.

Eleatic school ('Ελεατικὸν ἔθνος, Pl. *Soph.* 242d), a philosophical school represented by Aristotle and the doxographic tradition as having been founded at *Elea in Lucania by *Xenophanes, and by *Plato (1) (perhaps jokingly) as having begun earlier still, but now agreed to have started with *Parmenides of Elea at the end of the 6th cent. BC. There is no close connection between Xenophanes' monotheism, reached by a critique of Homeric theology, and Parmenides' closely argued proof that what exists is single and indivisible and unchanging. It is Parmenides whose theories are defended by the other major representatives of the 'school', *Zeno (1) and *Melissus; Zeno shows paradoxes in the ideas of plurality, divisibility, and change, and Melissus maintains a modified version of Parmenides' conclusions against the pluralism of Empedocles and the atomists (see ATOMISM). Unlike Zeno, Melissus was not from Elea nor apparently a pupil of Parmenides, and with him the 'school' ended, though *Gorgias (1) tried his hand at an essay in the Eleatic style.

There was also an Eleatic medical society which looked back to Parmenides under his cult name Ouliades; the healing god was Apollo Oulios. (Refs. in E. Rawson, *Intellectual Life in the Late Roman Republic* (1985), 30 f.). G. E. L. O.; S. H.

elections and voting

Greek In the Greek states voting was used in councils, assemblies, and lawcourts; appointments were made by election or by allotment (see SORTITION) or sometimes by a combination of the two. In Athens and elsewhere *psēphisma* (from *psēphos,* 'voting-stone') became the standard word for a decree of the council (*boulē) or assembly (*ekklēsia), and *cheirotonia* ('raising hands') was used for elections; but in *Athens voting was normally by show of hands (not precisely counted) in the council and assembly both for decrees and for elections, but by ballot in the lawcourts. Ballots seem first to have been used on occasions when a count was necessary to ensure that a quorum was achieved, but by the end of the 5th cent. BC it had been realized that voting by ballot could be secret voting. In *Sparta voting by acclamation survived to the Classical period for elections and for decrees of the assembly. In the Hellenistic and Roman periods some decrees of some states report numbers of votes cast for and against.

J. A. O. Larsen, *CPhil.* 1949, 164–81; M. Piérart, *BCH* 1974, 125 ff.; P. J. Rhodes, *GRBS* (1981), 125–32. P. J. R.

Roman At Rome adult male citizens had the right to vote to elect the annual magistrates, to make laws, to declare war and peace, and, until the development of the public courts in the late republic, to try citizens on serious charges. But the remarkable feature of the Roman system was that matters were never decided by a simple majority. Votes were always cast in assigned groups, so that a majority of individual votes decided the vote of each group, and a majority of groups decided the vote of the assembly as a whole. The three groupings of the *curiae* (*curia (1)), centuries

(*centuria), and tribes (*tribus) made up the different types of *comitia.

In the two important *comitia* the overall procedures for voting were similar. Cicero (*Flac.* 15) noted that Romans considered matters and voted standing up, whereas the Greeks sat down. The vote was preceded by a *contio, a public meeting, to present the issues or the candidates involved. The presiding magistrate dissolved this by the command to the citizens to disperse (*discedere*) into the areas roped off for each group. From their enclosures the groups of citizens proceeded, when called, across raised gangways (*pontes*), erected at the site of the assembly. Originally each voter was asked orally for his vote by one of the officials (*rogatores*), who put a mark (*punctum*) against the appropriate name or decision on his official tablet. From 139 to 107 BC a series of four laws introduced the secret ballot. Now the voter was handed a small boxwood tablet covered in wax on which he recorded his vote with a stylus. In most cases a single letter was sufficient: in legislation, V for assent (*uti rogas*) and A for dissent (*antiquo*); in judicial cases L for acquittal (*libero*) and C for condemnation (*condemno*); in elections the voter was expected to write the names for himself (M. *Porcius Cato (2) is supposed to have rejected many votes clearly written in the same hand, Plut. *Cat. Min.* 46). The completed tablet was then dropped into a tall wickerwork voting-urn (*cista*) under the control of guardians (*custodes*), who forwarded it to the tellers (*diribitores*). The process of casting the vote is illustrated on a coin of P. Licinius Nerva of the late 2nd cent. BC. In the *comitia centuriata* people voted successively, class by class, and the results were announced as they went along. In the *comitia tributa* successive voting was used in legislative and judicial assemblies, but simultaneous voting probably in elections. This may explain why legislative assemblies regularly took place at a variety of places, some quite restricted, such as the *forum Romanum, *Capitol, and Circus Flaminius (see CIRCUS), while the large spaces of the *Campus Martius were needed for elections. It was here that Caesar planned a huge building, the Julian Enclosures (*Saepta Iulia), to house the electoral process. The project was continued by the triumvir M. *Aemilius Lepidus (3) and completed in 26 BC under Augustus by M. *Vipsanius Agrippa, who was also responsible for beginning a connected building to house the tellers (the Diribitorium).

The lot played a vital role in the electoral process. It was used to pick the tribe (designated as the *principium*) or the century (*centuria praerogativa*) which voted first and provided a lead for the other voters. The lot also determined the order of voting by the tribes or the order in which the votes were announced. This was important, because the first candidates to achieve a simple majority of the groups were declared elected up to the number of posts available, even though they might not have polled the largest number of votes, if all the votes of all the groups had been counted.

The significance for Roman politics of this elaborate and time-consuming voting process has often been played down by historians. However, the great lengths to which members of the élite went to win votes (see COMMENTARIOLUM PETITIONIS) is testimony to the fact that the voting assemblies represent a truly democratic element in republican Rome. (See DEMOCRACY, NON-ATHENIAN.) In typical Roman fashion the voting procedures, in a modified form, remained under the Principate, even when the substantive decision-making had passed to the emperor and the senate.

Important details of the electoral procedures can be found from two inscriptions of the imperial period: the *tabula Hebana and the Charter of Malaga (*ILS* 6089). See also L. R. Taylor, *Roman Voting Assemblies* (1966); E. S. Staveley, *Greek and Roman Voting and Elections* (1972); A. Yakobson, *JRS* 1992.   J. J. P.

Electra (᾽Ηλέκτρα, Dor. ᾽Αλέκτρα), in mythology: (1) daughter of *Oceanus and *Tethys, wife of Thaumas, mother of *Iris and the Harpies (*Harpyiae; Hes. *Theog.* 265 ff.).

(2) Daughter of *Atlas and Pleione, and one of the Pleiades (Apollod. 3. 10. 1); mother by Zeus of *Dardanus and *Iasion (ibid. 3. 12. 1).

(3) Daughter of *Agamemnon and *Clytemnestra, and sister of *Orestes. She does not appear in epic, the first certain mention of her being in the *Oresteia* of *Stesichorus (fr. 217 Davies, *PMGF*), although she was said to be Homer's Laodice, renamed because of her long unwedded state (*Il.* 9. 145, cf. Xanthus fr. 700 *PMG* Page). Our major source for her story is Athenian tragedy, where she plays a central role in Orestes' vengeance on Clytemnestra and her lover *Aegisthus for the murder of Agamemnon. Her first appearance is in the *Choephoroe* of *Aeschylus, where she is unalterably hostile to her mother and Aegisthus, welcoming her brother, joining with him in an invocation to Agamemnon's ghost, but not actively involved in the killings. In fact here the focus is still mainly on Orestes, with Electra disappearing from view once the vengeance begins. But her role is very much developed in *Sophocles (1) and *Euripides.

In Sophocles' *Electra*, the main focus of the play is Electra herself, a steadfast, enduring figure, passionately grieving over her father's murder and passionately set on revenge. She rescued Orestes, then a young child, from his father's murderers (12, 296–7, 1132–3), and now longs for his return. The move from despair to joy in the scene where she laments over the urn, believing it to hold the ashes of her dead brother, then learns that the man beside her is in fact the living Orestes himself, gives us perhaps the most moving recognition scene in extant tragedy. She is a strong and determined character who, when she believes Orestes dead, is willing to kill Aegisthus entirely unaided (947 ff., 1019 ff.); then, when it comes to the murder of Clytemnestra, she urges Orestes on, shouting out to him at the first death-cry of her mother, 'Strike, if you have the strength, a second blow' (1415).

In Euripides' *Electra* she is even more active in the murder: Orestes is weak and indecisive, and it is Electra who is the dominant figure, driving him to kill Clytemnestra and even grasping the sword with him at the moment of murder (1225), although afterwards she is as full of remorse as before she was full of lust for revenge. In Euripides' *Orestes* she appears as a desperately faithful nurse and helper to her mad brother, abetting him and his comrade Pylades in their attacks on *Helen and *Hermione. In some accounts she later marries Pylades (Eur. *El.* 1249; *Or.* 1658 f.; Hyg. *Fab.* 122, where she also meets Orestes and Iphigenia at Delphi and nearly murders the latter, who she thinks has murdered him).

There is no certain representation of Electra in art before the beginning of the 5th cent. BC, where she is present at the murder of Aegisthus; later her meeting with Orestes at the tomb of Agamemnon became popular: see I. McPhee, *LIMC* 3 / 1. 709–19.
                                                                H. J. R.; J. R. M.

elegiac poetry, Greek This may be initially defined as poetry in elegiac couplets (see METRE, GREEK), one of the most popular metres throughout antiquity. The term ἐλεγεῖον, normally meaning 'elegiac couplet', is derived from ἔλεγος, a sung lament that must have been characteristic in this metre, but the metre was always used for many other purposes. We also find the feminine ἐλεγεία, 'elegy', i.e. a poem or poetry in elegiacs.

A stricter definition distinguishes between elegiac poetry (elegy) and *epigram (which was often but not necessarily in elegiac metre). Elegy, in the early period, was composed for oral delivery in a social setting, as a communication from the poet to others; an epigram was information written on an object (a tombstone, a dedication, etc.). The distinction was not always so clear after the 4th cent. BC, when the epigram came to be cultivated as a literary genre, but on the whole it can be sustained. As *epigram has its own entry in this volume, we shall concentrate here on elegy.

All archaic elegy is in (epic-) Ionic dialect (see GREEK LANGUAGE, § 4), whatever the author's provenance, and the form must have evolved among *Ionians side by side with hexameter poetry. It is already established on both sides of the Aegean by *c.*650 BC when the first recorded elegists appear: *Archilochus, *Callinus, and *Tyrtaeus. From then till the end of the 5th cent. BC elegy was a popular medium; some poets used no other. Extant poems vary in length between two lines and 76 (*Solon fr. 13 West); Solon's *Salamis* was of 100 (Plut. *Sol.* 8. 2), while such poems as *Mimnermus' *Smyrneis* and *Simonides' *Battle of Plataea* may have been longer still.

Many pieces presuppose the *symposium as the setting in which they were designed to be heard (e.g. Thgn. 467, 503, 825, 837, 1047, 1129; *Xenophanes 1; Simon. eleg. 25 W; Dionysius Chalcus 1–5; Ion 26–7). *Theognis (1) (239–43) anticipates that (his elegies addressed to) Cyrnus will often be sung by young men at banquets in a fine, clear voice to the accompaniment of *auloi* (flutes, oboes). There are other mentions of an aulete accompanying the singing of elegy in the symposium (Thgn. 533, 825, 941, 943, 1056), and an early 5th-cent. vase-painting (Munich 2646) shows a reclining symposiast with words of an elegiac verse issuing from his mouth while an aulete plays. Presumably there were conventional melodies that the aulete could repeat or vary for as long as required, without his having to know what verses were to be sung, as he would need to in the case of lyric. Certain elegists (Tyrtaeus, Mimnermus) are said to have been auletes themselves. Other settings are occasionally suggested: carousal through the streets after the party (Thgn. 1045, cf. 1065, 1207, 1351); a military encampment (Archil. 4; Thgn. 887, 1043); a public square in the evening (? Thgn. 263). Elegiac laments may sometimes have been sung at funerals, and these or other elegiac compositions at certain festivals where prizes were awarded for aulody, i.e. singing to *aulos* accompaniment, as happened at the *Pythian festival in 586 BC (Paus. 10. 7. 4–6) and at the *Panathenaea from about 566.

A common use of elegy in the 7th cent. was in exhorting the poet's fellow citizens to fight bravely for their country (Callinus 1, Tyrt. 10–12 W, as well as Mimnermus 14 W, Solon 1–3 W); Callinus' opening 'How long will you lie there?' may imply the symposium setting. In other poems of Tyrtaeus and Solon the exhortation is political, presumably not delivered before a mob but to a social gathering from which participants might pass the message on to other gatherings. Solon, at least, also wrote elegies of a more personal, convivial character. Mimnermus was famous for elegies celebrating the pleasures of love and youth. He also used the versatile elegiac for his *Smyrneis*, a quasi-epic (for the symposium?), complete with invocation of the Muses, on the Smyrnaeans' heroic repulse of the Lydians around the time of the poet's birth.

The largest surviving body of archaic elegy is the collection of poems and excerpts, some 1,400 lines in all, transmitted under the name of Theognis. He is actually only one among many poets represented, ranging in date from the 7th to the early 5th cent. BC. Here we find a wide cross-section: political and moralizing verse, social comment, personal complaint, convivial pieces, witty banter, love poems to nameless boys. Other items are reflective or philosophic, and develop an argument on some ethical or practical question. This *dialectic element was a feature of elegy from the start, but became more prominent later, for example in Xenophanes and *Euenus.

With the publication of *POxy.* 3965, Simonides now appears as the major 5th-cent. elegist. He used the medium to celebrate the great battles of 480/79 BC; his grandiose poem on Plataea (eleg. 10–17 W) recalls Mimnermus' *Smyrneis* (see PLATAEA, BATTLE OF). His more personal poetry is now also represented by some fine fragments. Lesser 5th-cent. elegists include Euenus, *Dionysius (6) Chalcus, *Ion (2) of Chios, and *Critias. They are all symposium-oriented, and this is still the situation in what looks like an early 4th-cent. piece, Adesp. eleg. 27 W. But the symposium was fast losing its songfulness, and elegy in the classical style was drying up. Isolated poems are quoted from Philiscus of Miletus and *Aristotle, containing posthumous tributes to *Lysias and *Plato (1) respectively. Meanwhile, *Antimachus' use of elegiac metre for a long mythological poem, his *Lyde*, set a new pattern. (The existence of long antiquarian elegiac poems by *Semonides, Xenophanes, and *Panyassis is doubtful.) Antimachus and (nominally) Mimnermus were the two principal models for Hellenistic elegists such as *Philitas, *Hermesianax, *Phanocles, *Alexander (8) Aetolus, *Callimachus (3) (*Aetia*), *Eratosthenes (*Erigone*), who combined romantic subject-matter with mythological learning, sometimes on a large scale. But the metre was now taken up again by many poets for diverse purposes; witness its use for a hymn (Callim. *Hymn.* 5), a bucolic singing-contest (Theoc. *Id.* 8. 33 ff.), medicinal didactic (Nic. frs. 31–2 Gow–Scholfield, Eudemus in *Suppl. Hell.* 412A). This last application continued into the 1st cent. AD (Aglaias, Philon of Tarsus, Andromachus). Otherwise the elegiac metre rather fell out of favour under the empire except for epigrams. *Gregory (2) of Nazianzus made some use of it, and it appears in a 4th-cent. encomium of a Beirut professor (*PBerol.* 10558).

TEXTS, COLLECTIONS Pre-Alexandrian: B. Gentili and C. Prato, *Poetae Elegiaci* 1–2 (Teubner, 1979–85); West, *IE*[2]. Hellenistic: Powell, *Coll. Alex.*; *Suppl. Hell.*

TRANSLATIONS J. M. Edmonds, *Elegy and Iambus* 1–2 (Loeb, 1931); West, *GLP.*

GENERAL C. M. Bowra, *Early Greek Elegists* (1938); M. L. West, *Studies in Greek Elegy and Iambus* (1974); A. W. H. Adkins, *Poetic Craft in the Early Greek Elegists* (1985); E. L. Bowie, *JHS* 1986, 13–35.

M. L. W.

elegiac poetry, Latin *Ennius introduced the elegiac couplet into Latin (Isid. 1. 39. 15); four epigrams, epitaphic in form, survive under his name (*var.* 15–24 Vahlen; 43–6 Courtney). *Lucilius (1) (bks. 22–5) used the metre for epitaphs and other short poems descriptive of slaves. An anecdote in Aulus *Gellius (19. 9) offers an early glimpse of elegiac epigram on erotic themes, Hellenistic in flavour (*Valerius Aedituus, *Porcius Licinus, and Q. *Lutatius Catulus (1), *c.*150–100 BC); a Pompeian wall bears witness to the popular diffusion of such work in the second quarter of the 1st century BC (Ross (see bibliog. below), 147–9). The careers of *Catullus (1) and *Ovid bound the elegiac genre's most concentrated and distinctive period of Roman development. In particular, by early Augustan times elegy emerges as the medium for cycles of first-person ('subjective') poems describ-ing the tribulations, mostly erotic, of a male poet who figuratively enslaves himself to a single (pseudonymous) mistress, distances himself from the duties associated with public life, and varies his urban *mise en scène* with escapist appeals to other worlds, mythological (*Propertius, Ovid) or rural (*Tibullus). 'Love-elegy', though the term is widely used by modern critics, was not for the Romans a formal poetic category. However a canonical sequence of *Cornelius Gallus (as originator), Tibullus, Propertius, and Ovid is explicitly offered by Ovid (*Tr.* 4. 10. 53–4; cf. *Ars Am.* 3. 536–8); and *Quintilian's later adoption of this same canon to represent Latin elegy at large arguably reflects the central role of Augustan 'love-elegy' in defining the genre. Among elegiac works by other hands in the *Corpus Tibullianum* especially noteworthy is the group associated with the female poet *Sulpicia (1).

The question of Greek precedent for the format of Latin 'love-elegy' has long been disputed. Propertius repeatedly pairs *Callimachus (3) and *Philitas as literary models. The latter is among a number of late Classical and Hellenistic elegists who wrote extended poems in which (this is controversial) mythological narratives may have been framed or unified by 'subjective' discussion of the poet's own beloved (cf. esp. *Antimachus, test. 7 Wyss, *POxy.* 3723); Catullus 68 has been adduced as a possible link to such a tradition. This search for origins remains inconclusive, and is further hampered by a lack of reliable knowledge concerning Gallus; the new fragment published in 1979 only adds to the uncertainty concerning the format and development of Gallan elegy. More accessible are continuities in Augustan 'love-elegy' with the erotic conceits of short Hellenistic epigram, and with the situations and characters of New Comedy. Most immediately important is the influence of Catullus' portrait of Lesbia as developed piecemeal in the elegiac epigrams, in 68, and in the polymetrics.

Even in the heyday of 'love-elegy', the associations of the genre were never exclusively amatory. *versibus impariter iunctis querimonia primum,* | *post etiam inclusa est voti sententia compos,* 'Verses unequally joined framed lamentation first, then votive epigram': Horace's interest (*Ars P.* 75–6) in defining the genre in terms of its traditional origins finds some reflection in the practice of his own elegiac contemporaries (cf. Ovid's poem of mourning for Tibullus at *Am.* 3. 9. 3–4). With its stress upon separation and loss, and its morbid flights of fancy (especially in Propertius), Roman elegiac love may be implicated from the outset in funereal lament. The association with votive *epigram is no less available for reclamation: allusions to fictional inscriptional contexts, funereal or otherwise dedicatory, abound in literary elegy. To some extent, as in Greek, the elegiac couplet is an all-purpose metre, save that its sphere of operation can often be defined negatively as 'not epic'. The paired contrasts between public and private, martial and peaceful, hard and soft, weighty and slight which dominate the aesthetic and moral vocabulary of late republican and early imperial poetry are associated above all with an opposition between epic and elegy, deriving ultimately from Callimachus' *Aetia* prologue. *Epic is constantly immanent within elegy as the term against which it defines itself—even in those long narrative elegies which come near to closing the gap between the two genres. Ovid's career as an elegist, from 'subjective' *Amores* to epistolary *Heroides*, didactic *Ars Amatoria*, aetiological *Fasti*, funereal *Tristia*, and vituperative *Ibis*, is the pre-eminent demonstration of the ability of a classical Roman genre to expand its range without losing its identity.

After Ovid the metre was used chiefly for epigrams and short occasional poems (many examples in *Anthologia Latina*). The use of elegy for epigram reached a peak in the work of *Martial, whose couplets can excel Ovid's in wit and technical virtuosity. The elegiac couplet is favoured by many late antique poets, including *Ausonius and *Claudian, but generally with no strong sense of linkage between metre and subject-matter.

Metre The elegiac hexameter differs little from the heroic. The special effects appropriate to epic were not often required in elegiac writing, and the general character of the line is smooth and fluent. Of five pentameters by Ennius which survive four end in disyllables, and it may be that this rhythm was the most satisfactory to the Roman ear: certainly, though the epigrammatists mentioned above, para. 1, and Catullus freely admitted words of from three to five syllables to the end of the line, following Greek practice, the disyllabic ending became the rule in Propertius' later poems and in Ovid (however, in *Her.* 16–21, the *Fasti*, and the poems of exile he reverts occasionally to the looser usage). After Catullus elision became both rarer and, when used, less harsh. These developments were undoubtedly dictated by artistic preferences, but Catullus' 'un-Augustan' usages must not be interpreted as evidence of technical incapacity: the occasionally harsh rhythms of e.g. poem 76 are part of the designed effect of the poem (cf. E. Harrison, *CR* 1943, 97 ff.; Ross, 115 ff.). From the very beginning the Latin couplet, unlike the Greek, tended to be self-contained: genuine enjambment between couplets is extremely rare. For modern Latin verse-writing, from the Renaissance onwards, the strict Ovidian form of the couplet has generally been the preferred model. It is above all ideally suited to pointed expression, conveyed through variation and antithesis: half-line responding to half-line, pentameter to hexameter, couplet to couplet. See HELLENISTIC POETRY AT ROME; METRE, LATIN.

STUDIES A. A. Day, *The Origins of Latin Love-Elegy* (1938), discussed in F. Cairns, *Tibullus* (1979), 214 ff.; G. Luck, *The Latin Love Elegy* (1959; 2nd edn. 1969); R. O. A. M. Lyne, *The Latin Love Poets* (1980); D. F. Kennedy, *The Arts of Love* (1993); R. Heinze, *Ovids elegische Erzählung* (1919), repr. in *Vom Geist des Römertums* (1960), discussed in S. E. Hinds, *The Metamorphosis of Persephone* (1987), 99 ff.
METRE M. Platnauer, *Latin Elegiac Verse* (1951); D. O. Ross, jr., *Style and Tradition in Catullus* (1969). Cf. also E. Lissberger, *Das Fortleben der römischen Elegiker in den Carmina Epigraphica* (Diss. Tübingen, 1934).
E. J. K.; S. E. H.

Elegiae in Maecenatem Tradition ascribes to *Virgil two such elegies (wrongly combined in the MSS and divided by Scaliger). As they were written after *Maecenas' death (8 BC), Virgil (d. 19) cannot be the author. In the former elegy the unknown poet tells us that Lollius (either M. *Lollius, consul 21 BC, cf. Hor. *Carm.* 4. 9. 33, or another Lollius) made him write this poem. This elegy defends Maecenas against the charge of weakness and love of ease. The second elegy contains the farewell words of the dying Maecenas, who expresses gratitude to his friend Augustus.

Their date is disputed. By some they are dated shortly after Maecenas' death; on the strength of eleg. 1. 1–2 many ascribe to the same poet the anonymous *Consolatio ad Liviam*. Others rightly reject this on account of metre and diction, though the Maecenas elegies follow the *Consolatio* in places. As both *Consolatio* and Maecenas elegies borrow from Ovid's *Metamorphoses*, *Tristia*, and *Ex Ponto* (1–3), it is probable that the Maecenas elegies were written after AD 13; Schoonhoven suggests AD 50–75.

TEXTS Teubner (*PLM* 1, Vollmer); OCT *Appendix Vergiliana* (1965); Duff *Minor Lat. Poets*, with Eng. trans.; H. Schoonhoven, with Eng. trans. and comm. (1980).
H. Schoonhoven, *ANRW* 2. 30. 3 (1983), 1789 ff.
P. J. E.

elements (στοιχεῖα, Lat. elementa). στοιχεῖα gradually became the standard Greek word for 'elements', and it was used with a range of senses similar to the English term used to translate it. Etymologically it means 'one of a series' (στοῖχος). Eudemus, quoted in the 6th cent. AD by *Simplicius in his *Commentary on Aristotle's Physics* (7. 13), says that the word was first used in this sense by *Plato (1) (see e.g. *Ti.* 56b, 61a6).

The term has important connotations in logic, mathematics, and discussions of scientific method as well as natural philosophy. *Aristotle (*Metaph.* 1014ᵃ26) defined an element as the primary constituent in something—be it object, speech, or a geometrical proof—which is indivisible into any other kind of thing. In the case of an object the elements might be the four Empedoclean roots, in that of speech the letters which make up a word, or in that of a geometrical proof the basic axioms and indemonstrables upon which the proof depends. In general, the concept of elements is fundamental to the widely held Greek—not just Aristotelian—conceptions of science as axiomatic-deductive in character. Basic mathematical works are often called *Elements*; best-known examples include the *Elements* of *Euclid, and the *Elements of Harmonics* by *Aristoxenus.

Aristotle is the most important source for early attempts at discovering the elements of the physical world. Most of the first philosophers, he says, supposed that the only origins of all things were material. 'That out of which everything is made, that from which things first came, that into which they finally resolve, and that which persists even though modified by actions performed upon it—this they called an element, an origin of things which exist' (*Metaph.* 983ᵇ7). Aristotle reports that *Thales, for instance, gave water this status, *Anaximenes (1) air, *Anaximander 'the boundless', while *Empedocles named earth, air, fire, and water. It is far from clear that these early thinkers were really seeking to answer precisely those questions which *Aristotle attributes to them. In fact, it is likely that Empedocles' four 'roots' were the first clearly stated elemental substances into which everything in the world could be resolved. Empedocles' theory, in various forms, remained the dominant element theory for the rest of antiquity.

The early atomists *Leucippus (3) and *Democritus are credited with a different kind of theory which sought to explain the qualitative variety in the physical world by appeals to the interaction of indivisible, impassive particles moving in a void (see ATOMISM). Plato, on the other hand, took on the four Empedoclean elements, but traced them further back to their origins in two types of elementary triangle. Throughout antiquity, there was a keen debate over the relative importance of the Empedoclean elements, and fire's status was especially problematic. (See FIRE.)

Among the Stoics (see STOICISM), *Chrysippus and *Zeno defined the elements of the material world—earth, air, fire, and water—as substances out of which everything else is initially composed through alteration, and into which everything is dissolved, without suffering either of these fates themselves during the lifetime of a particular world.

See G. E. R. Lloyd, *The Revolutions of Wisdom* (1987), 226–30, with references to earlier work.
J. T. V.

Elephantine (mod. Gesiret Assuan), capital of the Ombite nome (see NOMOS (1)) in Upper *Egypt, on an island off Aswan below the first Nile cataract, occupied till the Arab period as a military and customs-post on the frontier with *Nubia. Jewish mercenaries formed a garrison here from the 26th Dynasty onwards and established a temple of Yahweh. Their papyri and ostraca allow detailed insights into Persian administration in Egypt and the daily life of the community. Many Ptolemaic ostraca survive. There were temples (with nilometers) of Chnum and Satet, the latter partly rebuilt by Ptolemy II Philadelphus. Under the Romans Philae and *Syene became more important.

E. Jomard, *Description d'Égypte: Antiquités*, ch. 3.; W. Kaiser and others, *MDAI(K)* 1990, 185–249; O. Rubensohn, *Elephantine—Papyri* (1911); A. Calderini, *Dizionario dei nomi geografici dell'Egitto* 2. 138–40 (1975). Inscriptions: ML 7; OGI 168; IGRom. 1289–91; A. Cowley, *Aramaic Papyri of the Fifth Century* BC (1923), cf. P. Grelot, *Documents araméens d'Égypte* (1972); U. Wilcken, *Griechische Ostraka aus Aegypten* (1899); B. Porten, *Archives from Elephantine* (1968). W. E. H. C.

elephants Although *ivory was known to the prehistoric Greeks and is mentioned in *Homer, they first encountered war-elephants at *Gaugamela in 331 BC. The ivory probably came originally from Africa, but the first war-elephants were Indian (*Elephas maximus*). Although not used by *Alexander (3) the Great, war-elephants were used by his successors, particularly the *Seleucids and Ptolemies (see PTOLEMY (1)).

When the Seleucids gained control of the Indian sources, the Ptolemies managed to capture and train African 'forest' elephants (*Loxodonta africana cyclotis*), then found in the hinterland of the Red Sea. Smaller than Indian elephants, they are not to be confused with East African 'bush' elephants (*Loxodonta africana*), the latter being larger than the Indian and unknown to the ancients. The 'forest' elephant is now almost extinct, but until comparatively recently was still found in the Gambia. The main difference between the two types was that the Indian was large enough to carry a howdah containing one or more missile-armed soldiers in addition to the mahout, whereas the African carried a single mahout, and although he could carry javelins, the elephant itself was the main weapon. When the two types met at *Raphia, the Africans were defeated, but they were heavily outnumbered.

The Romans first encountered elephants when *Pyrrhus used Indians in his invasion of Italy, hence the term 'Lucanian cows'. Both at *Heraclea (1) in 280 BC and at *A(u)sculum Satrianum in 279, they had considerable success, in the first routing the Roman cavalry—untrained horses will not face elephants—in the second actually breaching the Roman infantry line after it had been driven back by Pyrrhus' phalanx.

By this time the Carthaginians were also using African elephants, drawn from the forests of the Atlas region. They fought against the Romans in the First *Punic War, in Sicily and in the defeat of M. *Atilius Regulus in Africa. Their appearance is clearly shown on Carthaginian coins minted in Spain. *Hannibal, famously, took elephants across the Alps in 218 BC. They helped win his first victory at the *Trebia, but all save one died during the winter of 218/7. This carried Hannibal through the marshes of the Arno in 217, and may be the one called 'Surus', mentioned by M. *Porcius Cato (1) (in Plin. *HN* 8. 5. 11). But although Hannibal received more in 215, and used them in an attempt to break the siege of *Capua in 211, it was only at the battle of *Zama that he used them again in quantity, and there P. *Cornelius Scipio Africanus nullified their effectiveness by opening lanes through his ranks.

The Seleucids continued until their downfall to make use of elephants, but although the Romans also sometimes used them in war (e.g. at *Cynoscephalae, *Numantia, and Thapsus), they were mainly kept for the arena or ceremonial. During the empire there was an imperial herd in *Latium. It is strange that they were never used as pack-animals or for road-building, as they

were by the British army as late as the Second World War.

H. H. Scullard, *The Elephant in the Greek and Roman World* (1974). J. F. La.

Eleusinia, a festival of games, celebrated at *Eleusis, never (in Attic sources) the Eleusinian mysteries. The games were celebrated on a grand scale every fourth year (the third of the Olympiad), on a lesser scale two years later (the first of the Olympiad). There was a procession, and the prize was a certain quantity of grain from the Rarian field (the part of the plain of Eleusis on which allegedly grain was first cultivated). The Eleusinia and *Panathenaea were, together with the City *Dionysia, the most important agonistic festivals (see AGŌNES) at Athens.

K. Clinton, *AJPhil.* 1979, 1–12; J. Morgan, *AJArch.* 1996; Deubner, *Attische Feste* 91–2. K. C.

Eleusis, the most famous *deme in Athens after *Piraeus, on a land-locked bay with a rich plain, was a strong prehistoric settlement but merged with Athens sometime before the 7th cent. BC. Its hill (called Akris) and sanctuary were enclosed by fortification walls in the late 6th century, and it became one of the three main fortresses for the defence of western *Attica (with Panakton and *Phyle). There was an important theatre of *Dionysus there, and the sanctuary of *Demeter and Kore (see PERSEPHONE) was the site of many festivals of local or national importance (*Eleusinia, *Thesmophoria, Proerosia, *Haloa, Kalamaia), but the fame of Eleusis was due primarily to the annual festival of the *Mysteries, which attracted initiates from the entire Greek-speaking world. Within the sanctuary of the Two Goddesses the earliest building that may be identified as a temple is geometric. Its replacement by increasingly larger buildings (two in the Archaic period, two attempted but not completed in the 5th cent.), culminating in the square hall with rock-cut stands built under *Pericles (1), the largest public building of its time in Greece, bears eloquent witness to the ever increasing popularity of the cult. The unusual shape of this temple reflected its function as hall of initiation (usually called Anaktoron, sometimes Telesterion). Destroyed by the Costobocs in AD 170, it was rebuilt under Marcus *Aurelius, who also brought to completion the splendid propylaea, a copy of the *Propylaea on the Athenian Acropolis. In this he followed the initiative of *Hadrian, who was primarily responsible for the physical renewal of the sanctuary in the 2nd cent. The sanctuary evidently ceased to exist after AD 395.

J. Travlos, Eleusis, *Bildlexikon zur Topographie des antiken Attika*; G. E. Mylonas, *Eleusis and the Eleusinian Mysteries* (1961); P. Darque, *BCH* 1981, 593–605 (Mycenaean period); Clinton, *Iconography*, app. 7. K. C.

Eleven (οἱ ἕνδεκα), Athenian officials, appointed by lot, who had charge of the prison and executions. They took into custody persons accused of serious theft or certain other crimes. If the thief was caught red-handed (ἐπ' αὐτοφώρῳ) and admitted his guilt, they had him executed without trial; otherwise they presided over the court which tried him. They also had charge of cases of *apographē*, in which property was forfeited to the state. (See LAW AND PROCEDURE, ATHENIAN.)

J. H. Lipsius, *Das attische Recht und Rechtsverfahren* (1905–15), 74–81; U. E. Paoli, *Altri studi di diritto greco e romano* (1976), 221–32; M. H. Hansen, *Apagoge, Endeixis and Ephegesis against Kakourgoi, Atimoi and Pheugontes* (1976). D. M. M.

ēliaia (ἡλιαία), often but less correctly spelled *hēliaia*, was a meeting of Athenian citizens to try a legal case, or a building in which such meetings were held. It has generally been thought that, when *Solon introduced trials by the people in the early 6th cent. BC, the *ēliaia* was simply the *ekklēsia*, called by this different name when it was performing a judicial function. An alternative view is that Solon established it as a separate body, consisting of citizens selected by lot, and able to be subdivided to try two or more cases at once. This view is based primarily on passages in which *Aristotle attributes to Solon establishment of 'the law-court' or 'the lawcourts' (*Pol.* 1273^b35–1274^a5; *Ath. pol.* 7. 3, 9. 1); on the usual view, these passages are regarded as meaning merely that Solon's innovation led eventually to the lawcourts of the 4th cent.

After the middle of the 5th cent., when a plurality of jury courts certainly existed, the name *eliaia* was used either for all these courts collectively or for any one of them. It was also the name of a particular large court building, used for trials over which the *thesmothetai* presided; its location remains uncertain.

D. M. MacDowell, *The Law in Classical Athens* (1978), 29–35; M. H. Hansen, *Class. et Med.* (1981–2), 9–47, repr. with addenda in M. H. Hansen, *The Athenian Ecclesia 2* (1989), 219–62; M. Ostwald, *Popular Sovereignty*, 9–12; R. Sealey, *The Athenian Republic* (1987), 60–70.
D. M. M.

Elis, the plain of NW *Peloponnese, famed for horse-breeding. In Classical times it was occupied by a people related by race and language to the Aetolians, arriving from the north.

Prehistory There are fairly extensive remains of Mycenaean occupation, with a concentration near and at *Olympia. Notable too is the evidence for Mycenaean cult and habitation at the 'Dymaean wall' on the Araxus promontory and the Mycenaean tumulus at Samikon (*PECS* 'Elis'; see PYLOS). In the Catalogue of the Ships (*Il.* 2. 592) the boundaries of *Nestor's kingdom extend to the *Alpheus (for the problem thus presented and that of the cattle-raid at *Il.* 11. 670 ff., see Hainsworth, *Iliad. comm.*). Dark Age (sub-Mycenaean and protogeometric) burials are attested on the site of the later city of Elis; there is a large geometric cemetery near Killini.

History The Eleans' small neighbours of *Pisa (1), Lepreum, and Triphylia long kept an uneasy independence. Their boundaries with the *Arcadians of Heraea were established by treaty (ML 27 of *c.*500 BC). The Eleans presided over the *Olympian Games, traditionally founded in 776 BC; but they may not have had effective control until two centuries later. They lived a rural life away from the political mainstream; a council of 90 life members formed a closed circle within the oligarchy (Arist. *Pol.* 1306^a12 ff.). There was a *synoecism in the 470s (Strabo 8. 3. 2; Diod. Sic. 11. 54), but the political implications of this are not clear. The Eleans were early and loyal allies of Sparta, until in 420 Sparta championed the independence of Lepreum, whereupon Elis joined Athens and *Argos (2); she was punished in 399 with the loss of Triphylia, which after 369 was united with Arcadia. Elis was now for a brief period a moderate democracy. In the 3rd cent. the Eleans were allies of the *Aetolian Confederacy and fought frequent wars with the Arcadians. Under the Principate Elis flourished along with the Olympian Games, to Roman respect for which the city owed its (free and) immune status (see A. Spawforth, *Hesp.* 1994). Its wealthy élite, including an Italian element (S. Zoumbaki, *ZPE* 99 (1993), 227 ff.) is detailed in Olympia's epigraphy.

The town of Elis on the Peneus was built *c.*471 BC, and replaced Olympia as a political centre. It was open and extensive; considerable remains have been excavated, including the theatre.

P–K, *GL* 3. 2. 2. 323 ff.; R. Baladié, *Le Péloponnèse de Strabon* (1980), see index; A. Rizakis (ed.), *Achaia und Elis in der Antike* (1991). Archaeology: N. Yalouris, *PECS* 'Elis'; excavation reports in Ἔργον 1973, 1975–7, 1980–3, 1990. History: D. Lewis, *CAH* 5² (1992), 103 ff.; J. Roy, *CAH* 6² (1994), ch. 7; R. Flacelière, *Les Aetoliens à Delphes* (1937), see index.
T. J. D.; R. J. H.; A. J. S. S.

Elis, school of, philosophical school reportedly founded by *Phaedon, is said shortly to have become, or merged with, the school of *Eretria (Diog. Laert. 1. 18–19; 2. 85, 105, 126). (Not the same as the *Eleatic school.)
C. J. R.

elocutio novella, modern name for the style of *Cornelius Fronto, Aulus *Gellius, and *Apuleius extracted from Fronto's comment on a speech by Marcus *Aurelius, *nonnihil interdum elocutione novella parum signatum* (151. 3–4 van den Hout²), through the misinterpretation 'occasional passages were insufficiently stamped with the New Style': the true sense is 'insufficiently clear by reason of extravagant expression', a vice the emperor was prone to (Fronto 159–60: Cass. Dio 71. 5. 3).

L. A. Holford-Strevens, *CQ* 1976, 140–1; P. Soverini, *Tra retorica e politica in età imperiale* (1988), 201–20.
L. A. H.-S.

Elogius, Quintus (the name is very uncertain), Augustan writer of memoirs cited as an authority on the Vitellian family by *Suetonius (*Vit.* 1).
C. B. R. P.

Elymais, Greek term for western part of ancient *Elam, i.e. mod. Khuzistan in SW Iran. The main city is *Susa, lying in a well-irrigated plain, hence another term (broadly) for the region is 'Susiana'. Elymais / Susiana constituted an important administrative and economic region under the *Achaemenids and *Seleucids, although it is possible that central control of the mountainous territory beyond the Susa plain was never tight. In the mid-2nd cent. BC, local dynasts claimed a measure of autonomy, declared by their issue of coins; throughout the *Parthian period, they exercised some authority. Some of their names show that, despite the marked Hellenization (see HELLENISM) of Susa, elements of Elamite culture survived, as is further attested by features of the local religion (Nannaia). The art of Arsacid Elymais has links with that of *Hatra. Elymais' autonomy came to an end under the first *Sasanid rulers.

G. Le Rider, *Suse sous les Séleucides et les Parthes* (1965); R. N. Frye, *A History of Ancient Iran* (1984), 273–5.
A. T. L. K.

Elysium (Elysian Fields or Plain), a paradise inhabited by the distinguished or (later) the good after their death. The name appears first in *Odyssey* 4. 563 ff., where it is the destination of Menelaus (1) as husband of Helen. It is situated at the ends of the earth and is the home of *Rhadamanthys; a gentle breeze always blows there, and humans can enjoy an easy life like that of the gods. Such a destiny is unique in Homer, and, as in the case of the clearly comparable *Islands of the Blest, Elysium tends to be reserved for the privileged few, although the base broadens with time. A typical later description of such a place is at Verg. *Aen.* 6. 637 ff. The name Elysium perhaps derives from ἐνηλύσιος, 'struck by lightning', death by lightning being regarded as a kind of apotheosis.

W. Burkert, *Glotta* 1960–1, 208–13; Hainsworth, *Odyssey* 1–8 comm. 227.
E. Ke.

emancipation in the modern sense means freeing from slavery; for this sense see SLAVERY. The present article is concerned with the technical term of Roman law. Emancipation of this sort is the release of a son or daughter from *patria potestas* by a voluntary renunciation by the *pater familias*. The emancipated person became legally independent (*sui iuris*) and, if a male, a *pater familias*, even if he had as yet no family of his own. Since emancipation removed him from his original family, he lost his rights in that family, and in particular his rights to succession to property on death (see DETESTATIO SACRORUM; INHERITANCE ROMAN). It was therefore not necessarily a benefit. It was first made possible by taking advantage of a rule of the *Twelve Tables that a father who sold his son three times was deprived of his *potestas*. Three collusive sales (by *mancipatio*) were made to a friend, who made two intervening releases by manumission (which restored the son to the father) and after the third sale either made a third manumission or mancipated the son back to the father for him to make the manumission. The advantage of the latter procedure was that it vested in the father the rights of succession etc. to the son. The *Twelve Tables referred only to sons and this was construed strictly so that for daughters or grandchildren one *mancipatio* was held to suffice. *Justinian finally abolished these formalities and substituted a simple declaration before a magistrate. The emperor Anastasius had earlier (AD 502) introduced emancipation by imperial rescript (see CONSTITUTIONS; MAGISTER LIBELLORUM) where the son was absent. Justinian preserved this as an alternative in all cases.   B. N.

embatērion The ἐμβατήριον was properly a marching-tune (Polyb. 4. 20. 12). Hence it was also a marching-song, such as the Spartans sang when under arms (Ath. 630f; schol. Dion. Thrax 450. 27), like the anapaests (see METRE, GREEK) attributed to *Tyrtaeus (*Carm. pop.* 18–19; cf. Dio Chrys. 2. 59).

embryology Several barely intelligible accounts of animal reproduction (and in particular of the origins and development of the human embryo) are preserved amongst the fragments of the Presocratic philosophers. It is debatable whether or not these accounts—amongst which one should include zoogonies and anthropogonies such as that of *Anaximander who argued that the first living creatures had their origin in a kind of earthy moisture (DK 12 A 30)—should be described as 'embryological' in a modern scientific sense. (Anaximander seems mainly to have been concerned with explaining the ultimate origin of man, given that he is unusual in requiring intensive nursing after birth. He ended up by positing a first generation of humans born at puberty.) It should also be remembered that the word *embryon* in Greek does not always correspond to the modern 'embryo', but can often refer even to newly born infants. Ancient 'embryology', then, covers a whole range of problems, from generation to the nutrition of neonates. The three Hippocratic treatises (see HIPPOCRATES (2)) concerned with generation, heredity and sex differentiation, and paediatric physiology—*Diseases* 4, *On Generation*, and *On the Nature of the Child* together with the later medical works spawned by them, including *Soranus' *Gynaecology*, and *Galen's *On the Seed*—could all be described as wholly or partly 'embryological'.

Certain basic problems occupied investigators throughout antiquity. In general terms the physiology of conception was central, but much effort was expended on accounting for the sex of the unborn child, the way in which it ultimately assumes the characteristics of its parents, how long all this takes to happen, and whether or not this gestation-period is the same for male and female. There was also a fierce debate, both moral and

scientific, over whether the embryo is alive or not, and if so, what kind of life it possesses. *Abortion was a controversial practice, as the very word *embryosphaktēs*, 'embryo-slaughterer', used to describe an instrument employed by *Soranus of Ephesus, suggests.

*Parmenides of Elea seems to have held that sex is dependent on the position of the foetus in the womb—'on the right, boys; on the left, girls' (DK 29 B 17, a one-line fragment preserved by Galen); *Anaxagoras argued that the side from which the male seed is secreted is important (males on the right, females on the left (DK 59 A 107)). Other theories of sex-determination appealed to the role of heat. *Empedocles linked male to hot, female to cold conditions in the womb at the time of conception (DK 31 B 65), or the relative strength of the male and female seed secreted by the parents. Some theories appeal to other types of causal factor—the 5th-cent. BC Pythagorean, *Philolaus of Croton, seems to have argued (more judiciously perhaps) that *all* living bodies are composed of the hot (DK 44 A 27).

Adherents of what is often (but anachronistically) called the 'pangenesis' doctrine held that the seed comes from the whole of the body; hence disabled or mutilated parents should be expected to have disabled offspring (see DEFORMITY). A father with a mark on his arm will have children similarly marked. This view is generally traced back to *Democritus of Abdera, but similar views are expressed in the Hippocratic corpus, notably at *Diseases* 4. 32 and *On Generation* 3. *Aristotle attacked this type of theory, especially at *GA* 721^{b}11 ff. He pointed out—amongst many other objections—that it is simply not true that deformed parents necessarily have deformed offspring. He also argued by analogy with plants that new growth can be produced from cuttings. His own view was that the man's seed provides the form, and the efficient cause of the generation of the embryo, with the woman providing the material. For Aristotle, the heart develops first; the embryo then progressively actualizes its higher and higher potentialities (*Parts of Animals* 666^{a}18 ff). (Much ancient work in this area is coloured by the assumed inferiority of the female sex, although some authorities, including *Alcmaeon (2), Anaxagoras, and Parmenides, argue that the female secretes a seed which has its own role in reproduction.)

The nature of embryonic development within the womb also attracted attention. How does it grow? (Perhaps the earliest practical and systematic examination of the phenomenon survives in the Hippocratic work *On the Nature of the Child* 29; here, by drawing an analogy with what he has seen to be the case with developing hens' eggs, the author seeks to demonstrate that the human embryo grows gradually in the womb, surrounded by membranes with an umbilicus at the centre. In the 2nd cent. AD, *Galen investigated the *anatomy of the human embryo, drawing important conclusions about the difference between the structure of the heart in the unborn and post-natal child.) Or is the embryo 'concocted'? The doxographers ask: Is the newly conceived embryo a miniature animal, fully formed from the start? Or are new parts added to it as it grows? If the latter, how long does it take for articulations to develop? It is far from clear exactly when the Greeks decided how long the human embryo takes to gestate. Several Hippocratic (and later, Galenic) works deal with the viability of premature babies (*On the Seven-Months Child, On the Eight-Months Child*). The Hippocratic treatise *On Fleshes* deals with the problems of the gestation-period in man by assigning special status to the number seven. Whatever parts the body needs, it has them within seven days of the seed entering the womb, argued its author [*Fleshes* 19]. Numerological speculation remains characteristic of this area of study; its most extreme expression can perhaps be seen in the Hippocratic treatise *On Sevens*, and ultimately in works with much more general application like the *Tetr.* of *Ptolemy (4). See GYNAECOLOGY.

J. Needham, *A History of Embryology,* 2nd edn. (1959); I. M. Lonie, *The Hippocratic Treatises 'On Generation', 'On the Nature of the Child', 'Diseases IV',* (1981). G. E. R. Lloyd, *Science, Folklore and Ideology,* (1983) (with full references to other works, both ancient and modern.). J. T. V.

Emerita Augusta (mod. Mérida), a colony on the Anas (Guadiana) founded by Augustus in 25 BC for *veterans of *legions V and X. It was approached from the south by a 64-arch bridge. Many monuments partly survive, including an amphitheatre, circus, and temple: *Agrippa presented it with a great theatre. It also had colonial and provincial fora. Its aqueducts were fed from a large reservoir constructed near by. The colony was reinforced by *Otho. It was capital of *Lusitania and in the 4th cent. became diocesan capital (see DIOECESIS) of the Spains; it remained important under the Visigoths (see GOTHS).

M. Almagro, *Guía de Mérida* (1983); J. Arce, *Homenaje a Saenz Buruaga* (1983), 209 ff. S. J. K.

Emesa, on the Syrian *Orontes (mod. Ḥomṣ), was long the centre of an Arab kingdom. King Sampsigeramus I in the 1st cent. BC, having failed to gain control of former Seleucid territories, became a Roman ally. In the early 1st cent. AD Sampsigeramus II and Azizus continued this policy, though for the end of the century the history of Emesa is obscure. At the end of the 2nd cent. AD it re-emerged as the native city of *Iulia Domna, *Iulia Avita Mammaea, *Elagabalus, and *Severus Alexander. It was famed for the temple of its sun-god, *Elagabalus.

R. D. Sullivan, *ANRW* 2. 8. 198–219; *Anchor Bible Dictionary* 2. 496–7; I. Shahīd, *Rome and the Arabs* (1984). J. F. H.

Emona (mod. Ljubljana in Slovenia), was a city in SW *Pannonia on the main route between NE Italy and the Danube. Under Augustus it had been a legionary base occupied by Legio XV Apollinaris: on its transfer to *Carnuntum, *c.* AD 15, Emona was settled with a *colonia* of legionary *veterans.

J. Šašel, *RE Suppl.* 11. 540 ff. J. J. W.

Empedocles (*c.*492–432 BC), a philosopher from *Acragas in Sicily. Most details of his life are uncertain. Book 8 of *Diogenes (6) Laertius provides the largest selection of legends. Much of our biographical information (especially the manner of his death and claims that he was a doctor and prophet and considered himself a god) may have been extrapolated from his poetry. There is no reason to doubt his aristocratic background, that his family participated in the *Olympian Games, that he was involved in political life, or that he was active in both the religious and the philosophical spheres. He apparently travelled to mainland Greece to recite at the Olympian Games and visited *Thurii soon after its foundation in 443 BC. Pythagoreanism was clearly a philosophical inspiration. Equally important was *Parmenides, whose thought shaped the basic ideas underlying Empedocles' philosophy. There is no evidence that he was familiar with the work of *Zeno (1), *Melissus, or the atomists; he probably knew the work of *Anaxagoras, certainly that of *Xenophanes.

According to Diogenes Laertius (8. 77), he was the author of two poems, *On Nature* and *Purifications.* (The *Suda* entry for Empedocles mentions only an *On Nature,* though it is often emended to agree with Diog. Laert.) Other authors refer to one poem or the other, not both. The relationship between these two poems is problematic, with no consensus about the distribution of the fragments. Hence the suspicion that *On Nature* and *Purifications* are alternative titles for a single work. Our sources also mention works of dubious authenticity: medical writings in prose and verse, tragedies, a hymn to *Apollo, an *Expedition of *Xerxes.* But the surviving fragments can be fairly well accommodated in the work(s) on natural philosophy and religion.

Empedocles is especially important for:

1. *His response to Parmenides,* who argued that no real thing could change or move and that the world was static. Empedocles accepted that *real* objects did not change; but against Parmenides he claimed that there could be several such things, his four 'roots' or elements, which moved under the influence of Love and Strife. All six of Empedocles' realities were often personified as gods. The events of the world's history result from the interaction of these entities.

2. *Introducing the notion of repeated world cycles.* The influence of Love and Strife alternated; hence the history of the cosmos was cyclical. The principal controversy about the details of the cosmic cycle centres on whether or not there is a recognizable 'world' during each half (under the increasing power of Love and under that of Strife). When Love is supreme, the world is a homogeneous whole; when Strife has conquered, the elements are completely separated.

3. *The claim that there are only four basic forms of perceptible matter:* earth, water, fire, and air. Unlike *Aristotle, who adopted his view, Empedocles thought that these forms of matter were unchangeable. Empedoclean matter is often treated as particulate; hence, despite his denial of void, there is reason to suspect that he influenced *atomism.

4. *The effluence theory.* A simple mechanism of pores and effluences was used to explain perception (effluences from sense-objects entering into the pores of sense organs), mixture, and many other natural processes. This notion had a major influence, especially on atomism.

5. *A theory of reincarnation and the transmigration of the soul.* Despite the claim that *transmigration occurs, there is no clear indication of whether the *daimones* (spirits) which move from body to body survive for ever or only until the end of the current world cycle. His claim that even human thought is identifiable with the blood around the heart points to the physical nature of the transmigrating *daimōn.* Orphic and Pythagorean views are also relevant (see ORPHISM; PYTHAGORAS (1)).

DK 31; J. Bollack, *Empédocle,* 4 vols. (1965–9); R. Wright, *Empedocles: The Extant Fragments* (1981); B. Inwood, *The Poem of Empedocles* (1992). B. I.

emphyteusis, in late Roman law a lease in perpetuity or for a long term. It was more akin to ownership than to an ordinary lease, and the emperor Zeno (*c.* AD 480) resolved a controversy by ruling that it was *sui generis.* As regulated by *Justinian (*Cod. Iust.* 4. 66. 2–4), it was alienable (but the owner could pre-empt or claim a fine) and inheritable; it was protected by a variant of the *vindicatio* (see OWNERSHIP); and it was terminable only for non-payment of rent for three years. It derived from earlier institutions, developed (from Greek models) in the 3rd and 4th cents. AD, originally for grants of imperial lands, especially *ius perpetuum,* a perpetual lease of land belonging to the *fiscus, and *ius emphyteuticarium* (ἐμφύτευσις), a long-term lease applicable to lands of the *patrimonium Caesaris.* Justinian merged in it the similar institution of the Principate by which state or municipal land was granted in perpetuity or for a long term at a small rent (*vectigal—hence the land was called *ager vectigalis*). The tenant had *possession (*possessio*), and at least in some circumstances a variant of the *vindicatio*, but to what extent it had the other characteristics of *emphyteusis* is disputed.

L. Mitteis, *Zur Gesch. der Erbpacht im Altertum* (1901); F. Lanfranchi, *Studi sull'ager vectigalis* 1 (1938); 2 (= *Ann. Univ. Camerino, sez. giur.* 1939); 3 (= *Ann. Triestini* 1940); M. Kaser, *Sav. Zeitschr.* 1942, 34 ff.; L. Bove, *Ricerche sugli agri vectigales* (1960); E. Levy, *West Roman Vulgar Law: The Law of Property* (1951), 43 ff., 77 ff. B. N.

emporion, general term for 'a trading-place' (LSJ), as in *Strabo's reference (4. 4. 1) to the anonymous British entrepôt (presumably Hengistbury Head) used by traders from Gallia Belgica. In essence, an *emporion* was an ad hoc community where a mixed and possibly shifting population of traders engaged in activities that would be well understood in the quarter of Athens of the same name. Outside Greece, a trading-post did not need to be established with the official acts deemed appropriate to the foundation of a true *apoikia*: an *emporion* could be the result of nothing more solemn than temporary or more long-lasting market forces. Such was clearly the case at *Pithecusae, inhabited by Chalcidians, Eretrians, and a certain number of Levantines. This centre, however, supported a population that seems to have been numbered in thousands rather than hundreds from the earliest 'pre-colonial' times so far attested archaeologically, with all that this required—and had demonstrably received long before the end of the 8th cent. BC—in the way of precisely the kind of social, indeed urban, organization that is commonly attributed to the *polis. It might be concluded that at Pithecusae an *emporion* effectively evolved into an overseas Euboean *polis*, i.e. an *apoikia*, whether officially recognized as such at home or not, and that accordingly the Pithecusan experience accelerated the development of the *polis*-concept for future use—at home no less than abroad. Herodotus applied the term *emporion* to a group of places on the Black Sea (see EUXINE), where knowledge of seven languages was needed to do business with the Scythians (Hdt. 4. 24). If any of these unnamed centres were in fact officially colonies, it would appear that some *apoikiai* could function, or be seen to function, essentially as *emporia*. Given the strong trading interests of the main colonizing cities, this would hardly be surprising. See TRADE, GREEK.

A. Mele, *Il commercio greco arcaico* (1979). D. W. W. R.

Emporion (mod. Empùries), place-name, a Massiliote colony (see MASSALIA) to the north-east of Barcelona. Excavations have distinguished the original Massiliote port (Palaeopolis) from the later Greek Neapolis. There was an indigenous settlement near by. It was the landing-port of Roman expeditions in 218, 211, and 195 BC. Towards 100 BC a Roman town was built on the western side of the Neapolis and in 45 BC *Caesar added legionary veterans. All three settlements were combined and became the *municipium of Emporiae under *Augustus: the coinages represented all three in turn. Its patrons included *Agrippa and members of the Julio-Claudian family. Decline began under the Flavians and it had become a small walled centre by the early Christian period.

X. Aquilué and others, *El Forum Romà d'Empùries* (1984); E. Sanmartí and J. M. Nolla, *Empùries: Guía Itineraria* (1988). S. J. K.

Empusa, a Greek bogey-woman who, in *Aristophanes (1) *Ran.* 285–95 (see scholia) takes the form of, in succession, a cow, mule, beautiful woman, and dog. The shaman *Apollonius (12) of Tyana rescued a young philosopher from her amorous and deadly clutches (Philostr. *VA* 4. 25). She is often identified with *Hecate or the *Lamia (1).

RE 5 (1905), 2540–3, 'Empusa'. J. D. M.

endeixis See LAW AND PROCEDURE, ATHENIAN.

Endelechius, (?)Severus Sanctus, friend of *Paulinus of Nola and Sulpicius *Severus (so probably Gallic in origin), professor of rhetoric at Rome. The only work preserved is a poem *De motibus boum* (A. Riese, *Anthologia* (1894), no. 893), 33 Asclepiadic stanzas, naïve in content but elegant (though not Horatian: several unrelated rhymes) in form. A dialogue between cowherds, it recommends Christianity as a protection from cattle-plague, but whether the plague is actual or fictional is unknown. Endelechius participated at Rome with one Crispus Salustius in a revision of the text of *Apuleius' *Metamorphoses* in 395, and at about the same time received from Paulinus of Nola the text of the latter's panegyric on *Theodosius (2), in which the emperor was praised for his piety.

W. Schmid, *RAC* 5 (1960); *PLRE* 2. 975–6, 'Sanctus' 2. O. S.; J. F. Ma.

Endius, Spartan ambassador and *ephor. He was one of the unsuccessful envoys to Athens in 420 BC deceived by *Alcibiades into denying their full negotiating powers. Nevertheless, as ephor in 413/2, he co-operated with Alcibiades in rivalry with *Agis II to ensure that a fleet was sent to *Chios. Relevant here is the hereditary guest-friendship (see FRIENDSHIP, RITUALIZED) between their families dating back to at least *c.*550. In 410 Endius conveyed the Spartan peace offer after *Cyzicus, and probably negotiated the prisoner exchange of 408/7.

RE 5. 2253; *PB* no. 264. Thuc. 5. 44–6; 8. 6–12; Diod. Sic. 13. 52–3; Androtion, *FGrH* 324 F 44. S. J. Ho.

endogamy, marrying within (1) the citizen body or (2) the kin group. 1. Colonists and others on the margins of the Greek world often intermarried with native populations, and the Archaic élite regularly made marriage alliances with their peers in other Greek cities; prominent Athenian sons of such unions include *Themistocles and *Cimon. *Pericles (1)'s law (451/0) requiring Athenian citizens to have two citizen parents effectively precluded marriages with foreigners (except for those given the privilege of *epigamia*). Other cities may have had similar restrictions on citizenship in the Classical and Hellenistic periods (*Byzantium, *Rhodes, Oreus (see HISTIAEA), Arcadian *Orchomenus (2)—*Siphnos and *Gortyn are known exceptions). Within communities, *Hesiod recommended taking a wife who lived nearby (*Op.* 700–1), and in Athens at least there was some propensity outside the élite to marry within the *deme (and so presumably the neighbourhood). At Rome, *conubium*, legal capacity to marry, ordinarily characterized citizens only, but cities and individuals could be granted this right (*ius conubii*) as a mark of special status. Otherwise marriages were invalid. Yet they certainly occurred, especially among soldiers debarred from marriage during service. Both Greeks and Romans tended to marry within the same social and economic class.

2. The *Bacchiadae of *Corinth were reportedly endogamous (Hdt. 5. 92β), a tendency widespread in the Greek world, though generally less extreme: the *Gortyn law code, contrary to some earlier interpretations, does not envisage compulsory cross-cousin marriage, still less represent a survival of such a practice in early Greece as a whole. At both Gortyn and *Athens, however, the rules concerning the marriage of an heiress favoured kin, the father's brothers and their sons, and unions between uncles and

nieces, first cousins, and other kin (especially on the father's side) were regular at Athens. There is also evidence for endogamy in the royal houses of *Sparta. At Rome, however, marriages between uncle and niece were long illegal, and those between first cousins apparently less common than at Athens. One attested motive for contracting such marriages as did occur was to provide for a woman with little or no dowry; avoiding them might prevent family quarrels and ensure that a wife had allies against her husband and his kin (Plut. *Quaest. Rom.* 289d–e).

W. K. Lacey, *The Family in Classical Greece* (1968); I. Morris, *GRBS* 1990, 233–54; R. Osborne, *Demos: The Discovery of Classical Attika* (1985); S. Treggiari, *Roman Marriage* (1991).   M. G.

endowments The ancient world was unfamiliar with the modern notion of a foundation whose funds are vested in itself. Endowments in antiquity were set up by vesting property in a public or private body, and stipulating how the income should be used. Some endowments served private purposes, such as performing commemorative rites at a tomb. In Greece, as in Rome, these were set up by bequeathing property to a family group (in Rome usually the settlor's freedmen). Public endowments mostly had religious or social purposes: in Hellenistic Greece religious endowments predominated; in Rome under the Principate social ones. Property was bequeathed (or gifted) to an eligible public corporation to be used for a certain purpose. Under Roman law not all public bodies were eligible beneficiaries: by the end of the 1st cent. AD all towns were; under Marcus *Aurelius *collegia* (guilds, see CLUBS, ROMAN) became so; and *Justinian included numerous charities. Typical purposes were games and alms (*alimenta*), as well as public buildings or baths. Since these were intended to be perpetual or else required maintenance, donors were much concerned with ensuring compliance with their intentions. Provisions for forfeiture of the endowment in the event of non-compliance are well attested epigraphically. Attempts at supervision both from the imperial centre and by imperial officials such as the *curator rei publicae* (city commissioner) were—as with other municipal administration—not wholly effective. Matters improved greatly only under Justinian, when an effective private-law remedy was provided by which compliance could be compelled.

B. Laum, *Stiftungen in der griechischen und römischen Antike* 1, 2 (1914); P. Veyne, *Le Pain et le cirque* (1976; abr. Eng. trans. 1990); E. F. Bruck, *Über römisches Recht im Rahmen der Kulturgeschichte* (1954), ch. 2; J. Andreau, *Ktema* 1977, 157; D. Johnston *JRS* 1985, 105.   D. E. L. J.

Endymion (᾿Ενδυμίων), a handsome mortal with whom the moon-goddess, *Selene, fell in love; according to the scholiast on Ap. Rhod. 4. 57 f. (who adds much other detail), the story was already alluded to in Sappho. He now sleeps eternally in a cave on Mt. Latmus in Caria (see HERACLEA (2)), where his lover visits him periodically—no doubt during the dark phase of the lunar month. Other versions (e.g. Apollod. 1. 7. 5; Paus. 5. 1. 3 ff.) located him in *Elis, and linked him with the *Olympian Games; another (Hesiod, fr. 260 M–W) even claimed he had tried to rape *Hera, like *Ixion.

H. Gabelmann, *LIMC.*   A. H. G.

Enipeus (᾿Ενιπεύς), god of a river (in *Thessaly, or Elis, schol. *Od.* 11. 238, cf. Strabo 8. 3. 32), loved by *Tyro, daughter of *Salmoneus. As she wandered beside it, *Poseidon took the form of the river-god and possessed her, making a wave curve over them to hide them. She was mother of *Pelias and *Neleus.

H. J. R.

enktēsis, 'possession in', and related words, commonly defined by the addition of γῆς καὶ οἰκίας ('of land and house'), are used to define the right to own real property within a state. Since this right was normally limited to citizens, it became the practice to make special grants of *enktēsis* to privileged foreigners, together with other rights and honours such as proxeny (see PROXENOS).

For examples see *Syll.*[3], index; Tod 2, index. Athens: J. Pečírka, *The Formula for the Grant of Enktesis in Attic Inscriptions* (1966).
J. A. O. L.; P. J. R.

Ennianista, self-description of entertainer who gave a well-received public reading of *Ennius at Puteoli (Gell. *NA* 18. 5); if modelled on performances by *Homeristae,* it included action. The story attests Ennius' widespread popularity in the 2nd cent. AD.

R. J. Starr, *Rh. Mus.* 1989, 411–12; L. Gamberale, *Riv. Fil.* 1989, 49–56.
L. A. H.-S.

Ennius, Quintus (239–169 BC), an immigrant of upper-class Messapian origin (see MESSAPII) brought to Rome in 204 by M. *Porcius Cato (1) (consul 195) and given the *citizenship in 184 by Q. Fulvius Nobilior (consul 153). Cato found him serving in a Calabrian regiment of the Roman army in Sardinia. At Rome he made himself acceptable to the Cornelii, the Sulpicii, and the Caecilii as well as to the Fulvii. He lived in a modest house on the Aventine and taught Greek and Latin grammar to the young men of the great families. He composed plays for the public festivals down to the year of his death, although never, like *Livius Andronicus, acting roles in them. He also composed a large amount of non-dramatic verse and at least one work in prose. M. *Fulvius Nobilior took him on his staff to Aetolia in 189. Biographers noted a fondness for alcohol and declared him to have died of gout.

Three titles (*Caupunculus, Pancratiastes, Telestis* (?)) have the smell of the (Greek) New Comedy (see COMEDY (GREEK), NEW). To some of the twenty recorded tragic titles (*Achilles, Aiax, Alcmeo, Alexander, Andromacha, Andromeda, Athamas, Cresphontes, Erechtheus, Eumenides, Hectoris Lytra, Hecuba, Iphigenia, Medea, Melanippa, Nemea, Phoenix, Telamo, Telephus, Thyestes*) are attached fragments sufficiently extensive to indicate that Ennius had a particular liking for *Euripides and that he translated his tragedies in the free manner Latin poets had been using for half a century. Compared with Euripides, he seems to us to have written rather grandly. To Cicero's contemporaries, comparing him with *Pacuvius and *Accius, he seems to have made his personages use the everyday language (*Orat.* 36). He also wrote a play in the tragic style on an incident of early Roman history (*Sabinae*) and another on Nobilior's deeds in Aetolia (*Ambracia*). The character of the *Scipio is disputed.

A narrative poem in fifteen units on the history of the Roman people from the fall of Troy to the seizure of Ambracia and the triumphal return of the elder Nobilior was intended by Ennius to do better what *Naevius had attempted in his *Carmen belli Poenici.* Its title, the (libri) *Annales,* appropriated that of the record which the *pontifices kept in notoriously simple prose of religiously significant events. Instead of the ancient *Camenae, Ennius invoked the *Musae* (*Muses), newly imported and given a home by Nobilior in a new temple on the *Campus Martius. He represented himself as a reincarnation of Homer and replaced the *Saturnian verse with a Latin version of the dactylic hexameter rather closer to the Homeric pattern than, say, the verses of the stage were to those of the Classical Athenian tragedians and comedians. The archaic vocabulary used by Livius and Naevius was pruned but some items survived, and many novelties appropriate to dactylic metrical patterns of an openly Greek origin were introduced. Books 1–3 took Ennius' story down to the expulsion of the last king and the foundation of the republic; 4–6 dealt with the reduction of Etruria and Samnium and the seeing off of the Epirote king *Pyrrhus; 7–9 with the driving of the Carthaginians back to North Africa and the incorporation within the Roman state of the old Greek cities of southern Italy and Sicily; 10–12 with the campaigns of the first decade of the 2nd cent. on the Greek mainland and in Spain; 12–15 with the defeats inflicted on *Philip (3) V, *Antiochus III, and the *Aetolian Confederacy. The poem emphasized the constant expansion of the Roman empire and the eclipse suffered by the Greek states which had sacked Troy and by their descendants. The gods of Olympus were made to support and assist the expansion. There was little on the other hand about the internal politics of the city of Rome. A number of Ennius' themes were foreign to the old Greek epic tradition. e.g. autobiography, literary polemic, grammatical erudition, and philosophical speculation.

Ennius added a further three books to the *Annales* in the last years of his life. These books featured the deeds of junior officers, rather than those of the generals, in the wars of the 180s and 170s against the Istrians, Ligurians, and other minor tribes.

Whereas it had been the custom to write epitaphs for leading men in Saturnian verses and even in senarii, Ennius composed pieces on P. *Cornelius Scipio Africanus (d. 184) and on himself in a Latin version of the elegiac couplet. The notion that Scipio's soul may have been assumed into heaven went against conventional Roman doctrine on the after-life, as did the deification of Romulus narrated in the first or second book of the *Annales*.

The *Epicharmus* presented, in trochaic septenarii of the theatrical type, an account of the gods and the physical operations of the universe. The poet dreamed he had been transported after death to some place of heavenly enlightenment.

The *Euhemerus* presented a theological doctrine of a very different type in a kind of mock-simple prose modelled on the Greek of *Euhemerus of Messene and earlier theological writers. According to this doctrine the gods of Olympus were not supernatural powers still actively intervening in the affairs of men, but great generals, statesmen, and inventors of olden times commemorated after death in extraordinary ways. The relationship of such a view to what Ennius expounded in the *Annales*, the epigrams, and the *Epicharmus* can only be guessed at.

The *Hedyphagetica* must have seemed to move from yet another philosophical position. It took much of its substance from the gastronomical epic of *Archestratus of Gela, a work commonly associated with Epicureanism. A reference to Ambracia suggests Ennius' own mature experience. The eleven extant hexameters have prosodical features avoided in the more serious *Annales*.

The *Sota* employed a metrical form associated with *Sotades (2) and probably presented similar themes in a similar tone.

The remains of six books of *Saturae* show a considerable variety of metres. There are signs that Ennius sometimes varied the metre within a single composition. A frequent theme was the social life of Ennius himself and his upper-class Roman friends and their intellectual conversation. Some scholars have detected the influence of *Callimachus (3)'s *Iambi*. The character of the *Protrepticus / Praecepta* is obscure.

Ennius stands out among Latin writers for the variety of the works he produced. Some of his tragedies were still performed in the theatre during the late republic. The *Annales* was carefully studied by *Cicero, *Lucretius, *Catullus (1), *Virgil, *Ovid, and Lucan (see ANNAEUS LUCANUS, M.), and its text was still available

in the Flavian period. Recitations were given during the time of *Hadrian. Copies had become rare by the 5th cent., but a reader of *Orosius' *Histories* obtained access to one. Commentators on Virgil's *Aeneid* liked to point out borrowings from the older poem. *Nonius Marcellus is the only late writer who can be shown to have read any of the tragedies. *Apuleius was able to find in a library a copy of the *Hedyphagetica* and *Lactantius one of the *Euhemerus*. See TRAGEDY, LATIN.

E. H. Warmington, *Remains of Old Latin* 1 (rev. 1956), 2 ff. (with trans.); J. Vahlen, *Ennianae Poesis Reliquiae*, 2nd edn. (1903); H. D. Jocelyn, *The Tragedies of Ennius* (1967); O. Skutsch, *The 'Annales' of Q. Ennius* (1985); F. Skutsch, *RE* 5 (1905), 2589 ff.; H. D. Jocelyn, *ANRW* 1. 2 (1972), 987 ff.; O. Skutsch and others, *Ennius*, Entretiens Hardt (1972); S. Timpanaro, *Stud. Ital.* 1946, 41 ff.; 1947, 33 ff., 179 ff.; 1948, 5 ff.; S. Mariotti, *Lezioni su Ennio* (1951; rev. 1991). H. D. J.

Ennodius, Magnus Felix (AD 473/4–521), from Provence, cleric of Milan, bishop of Pavia (513–21). Author of works supporting Pope Symmachus in the Laurentian schism, a biography of his predecessor Epiphanius of Pavia, a panegyric of *Theoderic (1), letters, model speeches, and secular and sacred poems. In form and in their blend of classical and Christian elements these works continue the epistolary and poetic traditions of the 4th and 5th cents. They cast significant light on literary education in Rome and Milan, on aristocratic society in northern Italy and southern Gaul, and on both secular and ecclesiastical politics in the Ostrogothic kingdom of Theoderic.

TEXT F. Vogel, *MGH, AA* 7.
J. Fontaine, *RAC* 'Ennodius'. I. N. W.

Entella See SICILY.

Enyalius See ARES.

Eos ('Ἠώς, Ἔως), the personified goddess of the dawn, daughter of Theia and the sun-god *Hyperion (Hes. *Theog.* 372). In Homer her formulaic epithets are 'rosy-fingered' and 'saffron-robed', reflecting the pale shades of the dawn sky; and while the Sun himself has a four-horse chariot, Eos, to mark her subsidiary status, is content with a chariot and pair (*Od.* 23. 246, where the team are named as Lampus, 'Shiner', and Phaethon, 'Blazer').

Her mythology centres on her role as a predatory lover: she carries off the handsome hunters *Cephalus (Ov. *Met.* 7. 690 ff.) or *Orion (*Od.* 5. 121 ff.) as they stalk their own prey in the morning twilight, or seizes the Trojan prince Tithonus to be her heavenly gigolo. It is the latter whose bed she leaves when day breaks at *Od.* 5. 1, and by whom she became the mother of *Memnon (1), the eastern warrior-prince and Trojan ally. She begged immortality for Tithonus from *Zeus, but forgot to ask for eternal youth to go with it, so that he shrivelled away until nothing was left but a wizened, piping husk (hence the origin of the cicadas, Hellanicus, *FGrH* 4 F 140); she locked him into a room and threw away the key (*Hymn. Hom. Ven.* 218 ff.). The explanation of these stories, in which a goddess's love is used as a metaphor for death, is to be found in the Greek practice of conducting funerals at night, with the *soul departing at daybreak (Vermeule).

In art she is usually winged, first appearing in the 6th cent. BC in scenes concerning the death of her son: she balances *Thetis in the *psychostasia* ('weighing') of the fates of *Achilles and Memnon or at the fight itself, or (on Duris' fine cup in the Louvre) she weeps over his corpse in a moving *pietà*. For the 5th cent. the favoured theme is the pursuit and abduction of Cephalus and Tithonus, not always clearly distinguished; see Caskey–

Beazley, *Attic Vase Paintings in the Museum of Fine Arts, Boston* 2 (1954), 37 f.

C. Weiss, *LIMC* 'Eos'; E. Vermeule, *Aspects of Death in Early Greek Art and Poetry* (1979), 18–21, 162–5.   A. H. G.

Epaminondas (d. 362 BC), Theban general, famous for his victories at the battles of *Leuctra and *Mantinea. Of his early career little is known. He is said to have been a pupil of *Lysis (1) of Tarentum, and to have saved the life of *Pelopidas at Mantinea, presumably during the Spartan siege in 385, but played a minor role in the liberation of Thebes in 379, and in the subsequent rebuilding of the *Boeotian Confederacy. However, by 371 he was one of the boeotarchs (Boeotian federal officials), and, as such, represented Thebes at the peace conference in Sparta, walking out when *Agesilaus refused to allow him to take the oath on behalf of the Boeotians as a whole.

Although all seven boeotarchs were at Leuctra, Epaminondas was clearly regarded as the architect of victory, and was re-elected for 370. Late in the year he went to the aid of the *Arcadians, and was largely responsible for the crucial decision to press on with the invasion of the Spartan homeland—the first in historical times—and, above all, to free *Messenia. In the summer of 369 he led a second invasion of the Peloponnese, which succeeded in further eroding Spartan influence, without quite matching previous triumphs. But his successes and, possibly, high-handed behaviour, aroused jealousy, and he was not re-elected boeotarch for 368, though legend has it that while serving as an ordinary *hoplite he was called upon to to rescue the Boeotian army when it got into difficulties in *Thessaly. Re-elected for 367, his third invasion of the Peloponnese finally put an end to Sparta's 300-year-old Peloponnesian League. The removal of the fear of Sparta, however, aroused old antagonisms, and by 362 Thebes found herself fighting many of her erstwhile allies in alliance with Sparta. At the battle of Mantinea, Epaminondas was killed in the moment of victory.

Though an innovative tactician, Epaminondas' strategic and political sense may be questioned. His attempt to challenge Athenian supremacy at sea in 364 had little lasting effect, and some of his dealings in the Peloponnese were questionable. But his traditional nobility of character presumably reflects how he appeared to contemporaries, and he possibly lacked the ruthlessness necessary to impose Thebes' will on her quarrelsome allies, once they ceased to fear Sparta. He may honestly have wanted to create an alliance of independent states in which Thebes would be no more than first among equals.

RE 5/2, 'Epameinondas' 1; G. L. Cawkwell, *CQ* 1972, 254 ff.; J. Buckler, *The Theban Hegemony 371–362 BC* (1980); J. Roy, *CAH* 6^2 (1994), ch. 7.   J. F. La.

Epaphroditus (1) (*RE* 4), *Nero's freedman and secretary, received military honours for helping him unmask the Pisonian conspiracy (*ILS* 9505; cf. Tac. *Ann.* 15. 55, 72; see CALPURNIUS PISO (2), c.) and accompanied him in his final flight (Suet. *Ner.* 49). He was again secretary (*a libellis*) of *Domitian, by whom he was killed (AD 95), apparently because he had helped Nero to commit suicide (Suet. *Dom.* 14). *Epictetus was his slave. He is probably not the man to whom Flavius *Josephus dedicated his *Contra Apionem* and *Jewish Antiquities*.

W. Eck, *Hist.* 1976, 381 ff.; T. Rajak, *Josephus* (1983), 223–4.   A. M.; M. T. G.

Epaphroditus (2), of Chaeronea (1st cent. AD), in his youth was a slave of the Alexandrian scholar Archias, who became his teacher. After obtaining his freedom from the governor of Egypt, M. Mettius, he taught at Rome and acquired an enormous library. He died in the reign of *Nerva at the age of 75. His works included: commentaries on *Homer's *Iliad* and *Odyssey* (Steph. Byz., entry under Λαπίθη, etc.; *Etym. magn.* 165. 3, etc.), which dealt with etymology, grammar, and interpretation; commentaries on *Hesiod's *Scutum* (*Etym. Gudianum*, ed. A. de Stefani, 1919–20 repr. 1965. 36. 13) and *Callimachus (3)'s *Aetia* (schol. Aesch. *Eum.* 2); Λέξεις, probably an etymological work (schol. Ar. *Vesp.* 352); Περὶ στοιχείων (schol. Theoc. 1. 117).

L. Cohn, *RE* 5.   J. F. L.; N. G. W.

Epeius, in mythology, (1) son and successor as king of *Elis of *Endymion (Paus. 5. 1. 4). (2) Son of Panopeus, and builder, with Athena's help, of the Wooden Horse (*Od.* 8. 493). In the *Iliad* he is a poor warrior, but an excellent boxer and winner of the *boxing match at Patroclus' funeral games (23. 664–99); later he casts the weight very badly (ibid. 839–40). In Stesichorus (*Iliu Persis*, 200 Davies, *PMGF*) he is a water-carrier to *Agamemnon and *Menelaus (1), and *Athena pities his hard toil.

LIMC 3/1 (1986), 798–9.   H. J. R.; J. R. M.

ephēboi originally meant boys who had reached the age of puberty, and was one of several terms for age classes; but in 4th-cent. BC Athens it came to have a special paramilitary sense, boys who in their eighteenth year had entered a two-year period of military training. In the first year they underwent, in barracks in Piraeus, training by *paidotribai* (physical trainers) and technical weaponry instructors, all under the general supervision of a *kosmētēs* and of ten (later twelve) *sōphronistai*, one from each of the tribes (*phylai). In the second year they served at the frontier posts of Attica as *peripoloi*. They may have had ritual duties.

Despite the military amateurism of which Thucydides (2) makes Pericles (1) boast in the surprising ch. 2. 39, it is unlikely that there was no system of training before the 4th cent., and traces of the later 'oath of the ephebes' (Tod 204 = Harding 109, 4th cent.) have been detected in e.g. *Thucydides (2) and *Sophocles (1). And structuralist accounts of the ephebate bring out its (ancient?) function as a rite of passage; they point to the marginal character of service on the frontiers and to the civic exemptions and exclusions to which ephebes were subject, i.e. ephebes were made non-hoplites in preparation for being real *hoplites. But it is agreed that there is no hard evidence for a formal ephebic system before the mid-330s when Epicrates introduced a law about it (Harpocration, entry under 'Epikrates'). Certainly no ephebic inscription has yet been found dated securely to before 334.

From the 3rd cent. BC the *ephēbeia*, based on the *gymnasium, was a universal feature of the *polis; the usual assumption, that Athens provided the model, is probably exaggerated. The institution flourished for as long as the polis: in *Paphlagonia it was still being introduced under *Commodus (*IGRom*. 3. 1446). Attested at *Oxyrhynchus as late as AD 323 (*POxy.* 42), its final disappearance in the 4th cent. reflects the depleted finances of the late Roman city and the eventual devaluation of physical education.

The Athenian *ephēbeia* ceased to be compulsory in 305 BC and from 282 BC service was reduced to one year; thereafter, there and elsewhere, it increasingly resembled an association for young 'gentlemen', with a (superficial) intellectual training (notably classes in philosophy, letters, rhetoric, and music are attested) coming to supplement athletics and arms-drill. This tendency towards pacifism (a function of the decreased importance of civic militia), although widely found, was not universal: in Macedonia, where a 'national' army underpinned the monarchy, ephebes performed only military exercises down to 168 BC; at *Sparta archaism explains the unusually long-lived emphasis on rough team-sports. See AGOGE.

The post-Classical *ephēbeia* was a civic instrument for relaying a basic and, on the whole, surprisingly uniform cultural Hellenism to the rising generation; it functioned too as a definer of social status (a role institutionalized in Roman *Egypt, where 'those from the gymnasium' enjoyed tax-perks) and as a transmitter of civic tradition and identity through ephebic participation in local *festivals, *agōnes, and cults (as shown by G. Rogers for Roman *Ephesus). And, not least, it was a means of containing the potential rowdiness of youth (see Ἔργον 1984, 23 for an ephebic law of 24/3 BC requiring ephebes in the theatre 'not to clap, nor hiss, but to watch silently and decorously'). See EDUCATION, GREEK and ROMAN; GYMNASIARCH.

Ath. pol. 42, with Rhodes, *CAAP.* C. Pélékidis, *Histoire de l'éphébie attique* (1962); O. Reinmuth, *The Ephebic Inscriptions of the Fourth Century BC* (1971), with the important review of D. Lewis, *CR* 1973, 254; P. Siewert, *JHS* 1977, 102 ff.; S. Humphreys, in J. Eadie and J. Ober (eds.), *The Craft of the Ancient Historian* (1985) 206 ff.; P. Vidal-Naquet, *The Black Hunter* (1986), ch. 5; A. H. M. Jones, *The Greek City* (1940), ch. 14; H. I. Marrou, *History of Education in Antiquity* (1956; 7th Fr. edn. 1977), pt. 2, chs. 1, 9; Parker, *ARH* 253 f..   S. H., A. J. S. S.

ephēgēsis See LAW AND PROCEDURE, ATHENIAN.

ephēmerides, 'diaries', a term applied particularly to the Royal Diaries of *Alexander (3) the Great, which were supposedly compiled by his chief secretary, *Eumenes (3), and are sporadically cited by *Plutarch, *Arrian, *Aelian, and *Athenaeus (1). It is traditionally held that the extant fragments derive from a court journal kept by Eumenes and exploited extensively in *Ptolemy (1) I's history. But the preserved quotations are tendentious, focusing on Alexander's last illness and his intemperate drinking habits. An anachronistic reference to *Sarapis has suggested forgery; but it is more likely that the work was a genuine memoir by Eumenes, composed close to the events in diary form. If so, it has a political purpose, to rebut contemporary rumours that Alexander had been poisoned. Instead it documents a series of drinking bouts culminating in a gradually intensifying fever. Eumenes no doubt used his name and position to inspire credence, but there is no evidence that he represented the diaries as archival material. Their content is personal and their influence was probably small.

FGrH 117. L. Pearson, *Hist.* 1954, 429 ff.; N. G. L. Hammond, *Historia* 1988, 129 ff.; A. B. Bosworth, *From Arrian to Alexander* (1988), ch. 7.
A. B. B.

Ephesus, city at the mouth of the river Caÿster on the west coast of *Asia Minor, which rivalled and finally displaced *Miletus, and owing to the silting up of both harbours since antiquity has itself been displaced by Izmir (*Smyrna) as the seaport of the *Maeander valley. Ephesus was founded by Ionian colonists led by Androclus son of *Codrus. It had little maritime activity before Hellenistic times, was oligarchic in temper, and open to indigenous influences. The city maintained itself against the *Cimmerians and also *Lydia until its capture by *Croesus, who contributed to the construction of the great temple of Artemis. Under *Persia it shared the fortunes of the other coastal cities; it was a member of the *Delian League, but revolted *c.*412 BC and sided with Sparta. The Archaic Artemisium, burnt down in 356 BC, was rebuilt in the 4th cent. BC, the Ephesians refusing *Alexan-

der (3) the Great's offer to fund the cost (Strabo 14. 1. 22). The city was replanned by *Lysimachus, considered one of their *city-founders by later Ephesians, and passed with the kingdom of *Attalus III to Rome in 133 BC. An enthusiastic supporter of *Mithradates VI (88–85 BC), it was deprived by Sulla of its free status. Under the Principate it eclipsed *Pergamum as the economic and administrative hub of provincial *Asia (see PORTORIA). Seat of Roman officialdom and one of the province's original *conventus centres, it was also its chief centre for the (Roman) *ruler-cult and thrice *neōkoros by the early 3rd cent. AD. Acts of the Apostles ch. 19 gives a vivid picture of the Artemisium's religious and economic importance for the Roman city. As seen today Ephesus is the product of the prosperous centuries of late antiquity, when it was the seat of the governor of *Diocletian's reduced province of Asia and a metropolitan archbishopric. Among urban developments was the creation of the Arcadiane, a major colonnaded thoroughfare with street lighting, dominated by statues of the four evangelists. Several important Christian shrines include the tomb of St John, where *Justinian built a major *basilica, round which the Byzantine town grew after Arab attacks in the 7th cent. Ephesus again became an administrative centre in the 8th cent., and remained important until captured by the Turks in 1304.

Excavations: *Ephesus* 1– (1906–). Inscriptions: H. Wankel and others, *Die Inschriften von Ephesos* 1–8 (1979–84). Roman customs-law: *SEG* 29. 1180 (see LEX (1); PORTORIA). *PECS* 306 ff.; C. Foss, *Ephesus after Antiquity* (1979); D. Knibbe and W. Alzinger, *ANRW* 2. 7. 2 (1980), 748 ff.; A. Bammer, *Das Heiligtum der Artemis von Ephesos* (1984), and *Ephesos* (1988); R. Oster, *Bibliography of Ancient Ephesos* (1987); G. Rogers, *The Sacred Identity of Ephesos* (1989).
W. M. C.; J. M. C.; C. R., A. J. S. S.

ephetai (ἐφέται) were an Athenian jury, 51 in number. Their origin and early history are obscure, but by the 5th cent. BC they seem to have been selected by lot from the members of the *Areopagus and to have been concerned with homicide cases only. Under the presidency of the *basileus* (see ARCHONTES) they sat at the Palladion to try persons accused of unintentional killing, of complicity (βούλευσις) in killing, or of the killing of a slave, a metic, or a foreigner; at the Delphinion to try persons accused of killing who defended themselves by claiming that the act was committed lawfully; and at Phreatto to try persons accused of a second killing when already exiled for the first. Thus they tried almost all kinds of homicide not considered important enough for trial by the Areopagus itself. A likely exception is the formal trial of unknown killers and of homicidal animals and inanimate objects; these cases were heard at the *Prytaneion, possibly by the *ephetai* but more probably without any jury. The *ephetai* also took part in the procedure for pardoning a man exiled for unintentional homicide if there were no surviving relatives of the victim. It has been argued that by the end of the 5th cent. the 51 *ephetai* were replaced by ordinary juries under the same name, but this view should probably be rejected.

D. M. MacDowell, *Athenian Homicide Law* (1963); M. Gagarin, *Drakon and Early Athenian Homicide Law* (1981); R. Sealey, *CPhil.* 1983, 275–96; E. M. Carawan, *CPhil.* 1991, 1–16.
D. M. M.

Ep(h)ialtes (Ἐφιάλτης, Ἐπ-), in mythology, (1) a giant; (2) one of the *Aloadae; also (3) a demon of nightmare. See Rose, *Handb. Gk. Myth.*; *LIMC* 3/1 (1986), 801–03.

Ephialtes (4), Athenian politician, about whom little is known. About 465 BC he led a naval expedition beyond *Phaselis. In the late 460s he became the leading opponent of *Cimon. He resisted the sending of help to the *Spartans in 462 during the *helot revolt, on the ground that Sparta was Athens' rival for power. Supported by *Pericles (1), he took advantage of Cimon's absence or less probably of the feeling of anger on his dismissal from Sparta to pass measures taking from the *Areopagus its judicial powers of political importance. This aroused such strong feelings that Cimon was ostracized (see OSTRACISM), but later Ephialtes was murdered.

PA 6157. R. Sealey, CPhil. 1964, 11–22; R. W. Wallace, GRBS 1974, 259–69; J. Martin, Chiron 1974, 29–42; M. Ostwald, Popular Sovereignty 28–40; P. J. Rhodes, CAH 5² (1992), ch. 4. A. W. G.; T. J. C.; P. J. R.

Ephialtes (5), or **Epialtes** of Trachis, is said to have shown to *Xerxes the path by which the Persians outflanked *Leonidas (1) at Thermopylae. The Delphic amphictiony set a price on his head (479 or 478 BC), and the Spartans honoured as a hero another Trachinian who assassinated Ephialtes from personal motives (some ten years later, on his return from Thessaly, where he had taken refuge).

Hdt. 7. 213 ff. P. T.

Ephippus (1), Middle *Comedy poet, named in the *Lenaean list immediately before *Antiphanes with between one and four victories (IG 2². 2325. 145 = 5 C 1 col. 3. 6 Mette). Of the twelve known titles, six may indicate mythological burlesque: in Busiris, *Heracles fought when drunk (fr. 2). Ridicule is frequent: fr. 14, a full-length portrait of an elegant student of *Plato (1). Fr. 5 (how a fish larger than *Crete is prepared for the table) has an early reference to *Celts.

FRAGMENTS Kassel–Austin, PCG 5. 131–52.
INTERPRETATION Meineke, FCG 1. 351 ff.; G. Kaibel, RE 5/2 (1905), 2858, 'Ephippos' 3; T. B. L. Webster, Studies in Later Greek Comedy, 2nd edn. (1970), 40 ff., 51 f. W. G. A.

Ephippus (2), of *Olynthus, contemporary of Alexander, wrote a work on the deaths of *Alexander (3) the Great and *Hephaestion (1) (FGrH 126), which is quoted by *Athenaeus (1) for its lurid but circumstantial detail. A. B. B.

ephors, probably 'overseers' (but possibly connected with ouros, 'a guardian'), civil magistrates attested in several Dorian states (*Thera, *Cyrene, Euesperides, *Heraclea (1) in Lucania) besides *Sparta. The board of five were elected annually by the citizens (by an 'excessively childish' procedure, according to *Aristotle), and the senior ephor gave his name to the year. Combining executive, judicial, and disciplinary powers, and unconstrained by written laws, they dominated the everyday running of affairs, subject only to the requirement of majority agreement and the knowledge that their office was held for one year only and was unrepeatable. Their origin is uncertain; most ancient authors ascribed the creation of the office to *Lycurgus (2), but they are not explicitly mentioned in the Lycurgan 'Great Rhetra', and a rival ascription was to King *Theopompus (1), though there was no genuine ephor list extending back to the assumed period of his reign (c. 720–675 BC). The eligibility of all Spartans for the office and their relationship with the kingship suggest that the ephors were created in some sense as popular, anti-aristocratic officials.

Each month they exchanged oaths with the kings, the king swearing to rule according to the city's established laws, the ephors swearing on behalf of the city to keep the king's position unshaken so long as he abided by his oath. The balance of obligation is clear. The ephors had a general control over the kings'

conduct, could prosecute them before the Spartan supreme court (*gerousia plus ephors), settle disputes between them, and enforce their appearance before their own board at the third summons. Two ephors accompanied the kings on campaign. It would nevertheless be wrong to interpret Spartan political history as a straightforward contest between kings on the one hand and ephors on the other.

In administration they negotiated with representatives of other states, convoked and presided over the assembly, supervised the state educational regime, and gave orders for the mobilization and dispatch of the army. They could depose and prosecute other officials. In major political trials they both presided and executed the sentences. They dealt more summarily with the *perioikoi, and most summarily of all with the *helots, over whom they exercised an arbitrary power of life and death through the *krypteia. Briefly abolished between 227 and 222 BC by *Cleomenes (2) III, who also ended the traditional dyarchy and reformed the gerousia, the ephorate survived until at least the 3rd cent. AD.

Xen. Respublica Lacedaemoniorum. 8, 15. G. Gilbert The Constitutional Antiquities of Sparta and Athens (1895); W. den Boer Laconian Studies (1954); G. E. M. de Ste. Croix, The Origins of the Peloponnesian War (1972); H. D. Westlake, GRBS 1976, 343–52; P. Cartledge, JHS 1978, 25–37; P. A. Rahe Hist. 1980, 385–401; P. J. Rhodes Hist. 1981, 498–502; P. Cartledge, Agesilaos and the Crisis of Sparta (1987). P. A. C.

Ephorus, of Cyme (c.405–330 BC), a historian whose now lost work is of great importance because *Diodorus (3) Siculus followed it extensively. In antiquity, he was thought to have been a student of *Isocrates; there are in fact clear echoes of Isocratean sentiments in the Ephoran parts of Diodorus, and some of the character assessments found in Diodorus are in the Isocratean style. His pro-Athenian bias might also have come from Isocrates.

The 30-book History ('Ιστορίαι) avoided the mythological period—although it included individual myths—beginning with the Return of the *Heraclidae and reaching the siege of *Perinthus, in 340. His son, Demophilus, completed the work with an account of the Third *Sacred War. His work was grand in scope and far longer than 5th-cent. histories. According to *Polybius (1), he was the first universal historian, combining a focus on Greek history with events in the barbarian east. Ephorus may have been the first historian to divide his work by books, and he provided each with a separate proem. Individual books were apparently devoted exclusively to a particular area (southern and central Greece, Macedonia, Sicily, Persia), but within each book events were sometimes retold episodically, sometimes synchronistically.

Ephorus drew on a diversity of sources, historical and literary, at times using good judgement (he preferred the *Oxyrhynchus historian to *Xenophon (1)), at other times making unfortunate choices (he coloured *Thucydides (2)'s account with material from 4th-cent. pamphleteers). Of special interest to Ephorus were migrations, the founding of cities, and family histories (see GENEALOGY).

The History was widely quoted in antiquity and was generally complimented for its accuracy (except in military descriptions). It was known to Polybius and was extensively used by *Strabo, *Nicolaus of Damascus, *Polyaenus (2), *Plutarch, and possibly *Pompeius Trogus. But its greatest significance lies in the probability that Diodorus followed it closely for much of Archaic and practically all of Classical Greek history. In paraphrasing

Ephraem Syrus

Ephorus, Diodorus supplies critical information, especially about 4th-cent. mainland history.

His other works include a history of *Cyme (᾽Επιχώριος λόγος), a treatise on style (Περὶ λέξεως), and two books (Περὶ εὑρημάτων) which aimed at satisfying the demand for popular information on diverse topics characteristic of the period.

FGrH 70. G. L. Barber, *The Historian Ephorus* (1935); R. Drews, *AJPhil.* 1962, 383–92, and 1963, 244–55; C. Rubincam, *Phoenix* 1976, 357–661; G. Schepens, *Historiographica Antiqua* (1977), 95–118.   K. S. S.

Ephraem Syrus, *c.* AD 307–73, was born at *Nisibis where he lived until Jovian's surrender of the city to the Persians (363) forced him to move to *Edessa. He wrote (mainly verse) in Syriac; he could read Greek and was influenced by Hellenistic rhetoric. His 'hymns' contain many historical references, e.g. to the death of *Julian the Apostate and the surrender of Nisibis, to the sufferings of the Church under Julian and the restoration of Church life under the Persians, and to the Arian controversy (see ARIANISM). Greek adaptations of his verses were current during his lifetime, and the fame he enjoyed is attested by *Jerome. A small but increasing proportion of his works has been critically edited.

D. Hemmerdinger-Iliadou and J. Kirchmeyer, in *Dictionnaire de Spiritualité* 4 (1959), 800 ff.; E. Beck, *RAC* 5 (1961), 520 ff.; S. P. Brock, *The Harp of the Spirit: Eighteen Poems of Saint Ephrem* (1975); J. and S. N. C. Lieu, in S. N. C. Lieu (ed.), *The Emperor Julian: Panegyric and Polemic*, 2nd edn. (1989), 89 ff.   H. C.; J. F. Ma.

Ephyra (also **Cichyrus**: Strabo 7. 7. 5), a city in western Epirus near the mouth of the *Acheron river. Here *Neoptolemus (1) landed on his return from Troy (Pind. *Nem.* 7. 37–9) and *Odysseus came to gather poison for his arrows (*Od.* 1. 259–62). The ancient city is marked by a circuit-wall of three phases at modern Xylokastro. Some 600 m. (650 yds.) to the south, at Agios Ioannis, excavations have confirmed the heavily built remains of a death oracle (*nekyomanteion*), whose importance was mentioned by Herodotus (5. 92). The structure, which included an underground chamber, dates to the Hellenistic period and was apparently destroyed by the Romans in 167 BC. See CAVES, SACRED; ORACLES.

PECS 310–11.   W. M. M.

epic The purely metrical ancient definition of epic, or ἔπος, ἔπη (lit. 'word', 'words'), as verse in successive hexameters includes such works as *Hesiod's didactic poems and the philosophical poems of the Presocratics. In its narrower, and now usual, acceptance 'epic' refers to hexameter narrative poems on the deeds of gods, heroes, and men, a kind of poetry at the summit of the ancient hierarchy of genres. The cultural authority of epic throughout antiquity is inseparable from the name of *Homer, generally held to be the earliest and greatest of Greek poets; the *Iliad* and the *Odyssey* establish norms for the presentation of the heroes and their relation with the gods, and for the omniscience of the inspired epic narrator. According to Herodotus (2. 53), Homer and Hesiod established the names, functions, and forms of the Greek gods; a typical specimen of the biographical and critical idolatry of Homer in later antiquity is found in the pseudo-Plutarchan *On the Life and Poetry of Homer*.

Post-Cyclic Greek epics on mythical or legendary subjects included *Panyassis' *Heraclea* (5th cent. BC) and *Antimachus' *Thebais* (late 5th cent. BC); Antimachus' scholarly and self-conscious reworking of the epic traditions anticipated the Alexandrian scholar-poets such as *Apollonius (1) Rhodius, the author

of the surviving *Argonautica* (mid-3rd cent. BC). Historical epic began with *Choerilus (2) of Samos' *Persica* (late 5th cent. BC), and flourished in the panegyrical epics written to heroize the achievements of *Alexander (3) the Great and his successors, as well as in nationalistic epics like *Rhianus' *Messeniaca*; but such works did not enjoy a long life (fragments in *Suppl. Hell.*).

The history of epic in Rome begins with *Livius Andronicus' translation in the native *Saturnian verse of the *Odyssey* (3rd cent. BC). This was followed by *Naevius' historical epic in Saturnians, the *Bellum Poenicum*. The commemorative and panegyrical functions of epic particularly appealed to the Romans; for a century and a half the classic Roman epic was *Ennius' *Annals*, the hexameter narrative of Roman history (finished before 169 BC). Republican generals and statesmen had themselves commemorated in both Greek and Latin epics; *Cicero gives a portrait of a typical Greek epic panegyrist in his speech in defence of A. *Licinius Archias, and himself composed autobiographical epics on his own successes. *Virgil revolutionized the genre by combining the legendary and the historical strands of epic in the *Aeneid*, which immediately established itself as the central classic of Roman literature. Later Latin epics, both legendary (*Ovid's *Metamorphoses*, *Statius' *Thebaid*, *Valerius Flaccus' *Argonautica*) and historical (*Lucan's *Bellum civile*, *Silius Italicus' *Punica*), are composed through a continuous dialogue with the *Aeneid*.

In later antiquity panegyrical (*Claudian in Latin; for the Greek fragments see E. Heitsch (ed.) *Die griechischen Dichterfragmente der römischen Kaiserzeit: 1. Abh. der Akademie der Wissenschaften in Göttingen, ph.-hist. Kl. 3. Folge no. 49/1961* (²1963); II. no. 58/1964 1) and mythological (*Quintus Smyrnaeus, *Nonnus) epic continued in abundance. Virgil and his Latin successors were the main models for the epics of the Latin Middle Ages and the Renaissance.

S. Koster, *Antike Epostheorien* (1970); G. L. Huxley, *Greek Epic Poetry, from Eumelos to Panyassis* (1969); K. Ziegler, *Das hellenistische Epos*, 2nd edn. (1966; It. trans. 1988, with additions by M. Fantuzzi); R. Häussler, *Das historische Epos der Griechen und Römer bis Vergil* (1976).   P. R. H.

epic, biblical, a late antique genre in which material from the Bible is versified in hexameters. Six major texts survive, the earliest being (1) the *Evangeliorum libri IV* of *Iuvencus. (2) The *Heptateuchos* of 'Cyprianus Gallus' versifies the first seven books of the Old Testament, and may originally have extended further. (3) The *Carmen Paschale* of Caelius *Sedulius consists of four books which synthesize the Gospel narratives, preceded by a résumé of Old Testament miracles. A prose version of the same material was written to accompany the poem. Provenance is uncertain, but the works are usually dated to AD 425–50. (4) The *Alethia* of Claudius Marius Victorius, a teacher of Marseilles, is a three-book paraphrase of the earliest portion of Genesis, written *c.*430. (5) Alcimus Avitus, born of a noble family *c.*450 and appointed bishop of Vienne *c.*490, wrote a five-book epic *De spiritalis historiae gestis*, treating Genesis 1–3, the Flood, and the Crossing of the Red Sea. (6) The *De actibus Apostolorum* of the Italian subdeacon Arator treats the material of Acts in two books, devoted respectively to Sts Peter and Paul. It received public readings in Rome in 544.

It is sometimes argued that these texts were produced in order to make Christian material stylistically acceptable to educated pagans, and hence to aid conversion, but this is never explicit in the poems themselves, and hard to believe for the later works. Moreover, it is difficult to draw the generic boundaries between these poems and other contemporary texts which involve much

biblical narrative while clearly having a theological orientation—
*Dracontius' *Laudes Dei* and *Prudentius' *Apotheosis* and *Hamartigenia*.

TEXTS Arator: A. P. McKinley, *CSEL* 72 (1951); Avitus: R. Peiper, *MGH AA* 6/2 (1883); Victorius: P. Hovingh, *CCSL* 128 (1960); 'Cyprianus Gallus': R. Peiper, *CSEL* 23 (1891); Sedulius: J. Huemer, *CSEL* 10 (1885).

LITERATURE R. Herzog, *Bibelepik* 1 (1975); J. Fontaine, *Naissance de la poésie dans l'occident chrétien* (1981); M. Roberts, *Biblical Epic and Rhetorical Paraphrase in Late Antiquity* (1985). M. J. B.

Epic Cycle, ἐπικὸς κύκλος, a collection of early Greek epics, artificially arranged in a series so as to make a narrative extending from the beginning of the world to the end of the heroic age. Apart from the *Iliad* and *Odyssey* (see HOMER), we possess only meagre fragments of the poems involved, and our knowledge of what poems were involved is itself incomplete. We are best informed about those that dealt with the Trojan War and related events: there were six besides the *Iliad* and *Odyssey*, and summaries of their contents are preserved in some Homer manuscripts as an extract from the *Chrestomathia* of *Proclus (see NEOPLATONISM; but some think an earlier Proclus). *Apollodorus (6) and *Hyginus (3) (see MYTHOGRAPHERS) draw on a related source for their accounts of the Trojan War. Among monumental sources, the 'Tabula Iliaca' (*IG* 14. 1284) is of particular interest.

2. The poems were composed by various men, mainly or wholly in the 7th and 6th cents. BC. (Earlier dates given by chroniclers are valueless.) The Cycle is not mentioned as a whole before the 2nd cent. AD. But a Trojan Cycle, at least, seems to have been drawn up not later than the 4th cent. BC, since *Aristoxenus (*Vitae Homeri*, p. 32 Wilamowitz) knew an alternative beginning to the *Iliad* evidently meant to link it to a preceding poem. Indeed, some of the Trojan epics seem designed merely to cover an allotted span of events; Arist. *Poet.* 1459ᵃᵇ criticizes the *Cypria* and *Little Iliad* for their lack of a unifying theme.

3. The cyclic poems (this term by convention excludes the *Iliad* and *Odyssey*) were sometimes loosely attributed to Homer; but *Herodotus rejects this for the *Cypria* (2. 117) and queries it for the *Epigoni* (4. 32), and later writers generally use the names of obscurer poets or the expression ὁ (τὰ Κύπρια, etc.) ποιήσας, 'the author of (the *Cypria*, etc.)'. The poems seem to have been well known in the 5th and 4th cents., but little read later; no papyrus fragment of them has been identified. *Proclus' knowledge of them is demonstrably indirect.

4. The poems known or presumed to have been included in the Cycle, and the poets to whom they were ascribed, were as follows.

(1) In first place stood a theogony (*OCT Homeri Opera* 5. 96–8). Comparison with Apollodorus and *Orphica* indicates that an Orphic theogony was chosen, but doctored.

(2) *Titanomachia*: *Eumelus or *Arctinus of Miletus.

(3) *Oidipodeia* (6,600 lines): *Cinaethon of Lacedaemon.

(4) *Thebais* (7,000 lines): Homer (but more often anonymous). Highly esteemed by Pausanias (9. 9. 5), who says that even *Callinus knew the poem as Homer's; but if the name is correct, Callinus may only have alluded to the legend and to 'earlier singers'. On the subject of this and the following poem, see ADRASTUS (1).

(5) *Epigoni* (7,000 lines): Homer. ('Antimachus' in schol. Ar. *Pax* 1270 might mean Antimachus of Teos, but may be a confusion with the *Thebais* of *Antimachus of Colophon). Cited by Herodotus and parodied by *Aristophanes (1). The first line survives, and implies another poem preceding. See EPIGONI.

(6) *Cypria* (11 books): Homer, *Stasinus of Cyprus, or Hegesias of (Cyprian) Salamis. The poem dealt with the preliminaries of the Trojan War (wedding of Peleus and Thetis, judgement of Paris, rape of Helen) and all the earlier part of the war down to the point where the *Iliad* begins. Fr. 1 implies no poem preceding. It was familiar to Herodotus, *Euripides, *Plato (1), and *Aristotle. The title seems to refer to the poem's place of origin.

(7) *Iliad*. There were alternative versions of the beginning and end which linked it with the adjacent poems (above, § 2; schol. *Il.* 24. 804a).

(8) *Aethiopis* (5 books): Homer or Arctinus. The main events were the deaths of *Penthesilea, *Thersites, *Memnon (1), and Achilles. The title refers to Memnon's Ethiopians; there was an alternative title *Amazonia*.

(9) *Little Iliad* (4 books): Homer, *Lesches of Mytilene or Pyrrha, Thestorides of Phocaea, Cinaethon, or Diodorus of Erythrae. The suicide of *Aias (1), the fetching of *Philoctetes and *Neoptolemus (1), the Wooden Horse, *Sinon, the entry into Troy. (The last part, which overlaps the *Iliu Persis*, is omitted by Proclus, and may have been omitted from the poem when it formed part of the Cycle.) The poem must have acquired the name Ἰλιάς independently of the *Iliad*, and then been called 'little' (μικρά) to distinguish it.

(10) *Iliu Persis* (Ἰλίου πέρσις, gen. -ιδος) (2 books): Arctinus or Lesches. The Trojan debate about the horse, *Laocoön, the sack of Troy, and departure of the Greeks. Aeneas left the city before the sack, not as in Virgil. The same title was given to a poem of Stesichorus.

(11) *Nostoi* (5 books): Homer, Agias (or Hegias) of Troezen, or Eumelus. The returns of various Greek heroes, ending with the murder of Agamemnon, Orestes' revenge, and Menelaus' homecoming. The *Odyssey* alludes to these events—so much that it cannot have been intended to accompany the *Nostoi*—and its poet knew Ἀχαιῶν νόστος, 'the Return of the Achaeans', as a theme of song (1. 326, cf. 10. 15). Stesichorus also wrote *Nostoi*.

(12) *Odyssey*. *Aristophanes (2) of Byzantium and *Aristarchus (2) put the end of the poem at 23. 296, and so perhaps counted what followed as part of the *Telegonia*.

(13) *Telegonia* (2 books): Eugammon of Cyrene or Cinaethon. An element of romantic fiction was conspicuous here (see ODYSSEUS). The appearance in a Cyrenean poet of Arcesilaus as a son of Odysseus suggests a 6th-cent. date (cf. ARCESILAS), and *Eusebius dates Eugammon to 566.

5. Various other early epics were current in antiquity, and some of them may have been included in the Cycle.

TEXTS Davies, *EGF*; Bernabé, *PEG* 1.

DISCUSSION F. G. Welcker, *Der epische Cyclus*, 2nd edn. (1865–82); D. B. Monro, *Homer's Odyssey, Books XIII–XXIV* (1901), 340 ff.; A. Severyns, *Le Cycle épique dans l' école d' Aristarque* (1928); A. Rzach, *RE* 11. 2347 ff.; W. Kullmann, *Die Quellen der Ilias* (1960); G. L. Huxley, *Greek Epic Poetry* (1969); J. Griffin, *JHS* 1977, 39 ff.; M. Davies, *The Epic Cycle* (1989). M. L. W.

epicedion (ἐπικήδειον, sc. μέλος) is a term applied to poems (or speeches) honouring the dead. Theoretically distinct from the *dirge (θρῆνος), *epitaphios, or *consolation, as being delivered or performed over the corpse and before the funeral, it nevertheless is barely distinguishable from these in content ([Dion. Hal.] *Rhet.* 6. 1), and its common themes (irrevocable fate, cruel destiny, sorrow of survivors, hopes of immortality) are naturally also those of funerary *epigrams. The word itself is not very common. *Plutarch (*Pel.* 1) uses it of an elegiac poem commemorating some heroic Spartans; *Statius (*Silv.* 2 praef.) applies it

Epicharmus

to his poem on the death of Glaucias (*Silv.* 2. 1), and it is included in the titles of *Silvae* 5. 1, 5. 3, 5. 5. *Ausonius applies it to a poem in honour of his dead father, which is in fact an address put in his father's mouth (as often in grave epigrams), and says it is a title taken from the Greek, dedicated to the honour of the deceased, and is an expression of affection rather than praise. Poems lamenting the deaths of animals (e.g. *Anth. Pal.* 7. 189–216; Catull. 3; Ov. *Am.* 2. 6; Stat. *Silv.* 2. 4 and 5) naturally use modifications of the same topics.

R. Lattimore, *Themes in Greek and Latin Epitaphs* (1962); commentaries on Statius' *Silvae*: F. Vollmer (1898), H. Frère–H. J. Izaac (1944); W. Kese, *Untersuchungen zu Epikedion und Consolatio in der römischen Dichtung* (1950); F. Cairns, *Generic Composition in Greek and Roman Poetry* (1972), 90–1; G. Herrlinger, *Totenklage um Tiere in der antiken Dichtung* (1930). D. A. R.

Epicharmus, a Sicilian writer of comedy, was active during the first quarter of the 5th cent. BC, as is clear from his reference to *Anaxilas (1) of Rhegium (fr. 98) and possibly to *Aeschylus (fr. 214). He was probably a native of *Syracuse (our earliest evidence for this is Theoc. *Epigr.* 18 and *Marm. Par.* 71), but other cities laid claim to him; Arist. *Poet.* 1448ᵃ32 is ambiguous, but may mean that the Sicilian Megarians (see MEGARA HYBLAEA) regarded him as their own. Aristotle surprisingly says that he was 'much earlier than *Chionides and *Magnes', and if this is true he must have been an established poet during the last part of the 6th cent.

The titles, citations, and fragments of his plays (now significantly augmented by papyri) indicate that he was particularly fond of mythological burlesque; *Heracles and *Odysseus were the 'heroes' of some of these burlesques. *Logos and Logina* is shown by fr. 87 to have been mythological in character, a fact which could hardly have been guessed from its title. Some titles, like those of Attic comedies, are plurals, e.g. *Islands, Persians, Sirens.* No fragment enables us to decide beyond doubt how many actors these plays required or whether they required a chorus. The abundance of plural titles constitutes a prima facie case for a chorus. Certain fragments (6, 34) suggest that there *may* have been three actors on stage simultaneously, but this evidence is far from decisive. The scale of his plays is also uncertain. His language is Sicilian Doric, and is as colourful and sophisticated as that of Old Comedy; he uses a variety of metres κατὰ στίχον ('according to the line'), but there are no lyrics among the extant fragments.

A considerable number of philosophical and quasi-scientific works were attributed to Epicharmus in antiquity. The hard core of these may have been a collection of maxims made from his plays (cf. Theoc. *Epigr.* 18), but as early as the 4th cent. BC the *Pseudepicharmeia* were regarded as forged (Aristox. fr. 45 Wehrli), and continued to be so regarded by critical historians, though the less critical treated them without scruple as genuine works of Epicharmus. A certain Alcimus argued that *Plato (1) derived much of his doctrine from Epicharmus (Diog. Laert. 3. 9 ff.), but it is hardly credible that the passages cited in support of this allegation were composed early in the 5th cent.; one of them (fr. 171) appears to parody the technique (πάνυ μὲν οὖν, 'yes, no doubt') of Platonic dialogue. The tradition that Epicharmus was a Pythagorean (see PYTHAGORAS (1)) first appears in Plutarch (*Num.* 8).

Kaibel, *CGF* 88 ff.; Olivieri, *FCGM* 1. 3 ff.; C. Austin, *Comicorum Graecorum Fragmenta in papyris reperta* (1973), 52 ff.; Pickard-Cambridge–Webster, *Dithyramb²* 230 ff. K. J. D.

Epicrates, Middle Comedy poet (see COMEDY (GREEK), MIDDLE)

from *Ambracia. In a wittily amusing fr. (10 KA = 11 K, written before 347 BC) he attributes to *Plato (1) and his pupils research into the taxonomy of gourds.

FRAGMENTS Kassel–Austin, *PCG* 5. 153–63, although earlier scholars use the numbering in Kock, *CAF* 2. 282–8.
INTERPRETATION Meineke, *FCG* 1. 414 f.; G. Kaibel, *RE* 6/1 (1907), 120 f. 'Epikrates' 21. W. G. A.

Epictetus (mid-1st to 2nd cent. AD), Stoic philosopher from Hierapolis in Phrygia; in early life a slave of *Epaphroditus (1) in Rome. Eventually freed by his master, he studied with *Musonius Rufus. Epictetus taught in Rome until *Domitian banished the philosophers in AD 89. He set up a school at *Nicopolis (3) in Epirus, where his reputation attracted a following which included many upper-class Romans. *Arrian published the oral teachings (*Discourses*, Διατριβαί) of Epictetus. Four books of these survive, along with a summary of key teachings known as the *Manual* (Ἐγχειρίδιον). These writings and his personal reputation made an impact on the emperor Marcus *Aurelius; the *Manual* has been an important inspirational book in both ancient and modern times.

Epictetus' teaching took two forms. He taught basic works of *Stoicism, especially those of *Chrysippus, and shows considerable familiarity with technical matters. In the *Discourses*, however, great emphasis is placed on the need to put philosophical sophistication to work in reforming moral character; learning is of little value for its own sake.

Epictetus' philosophy was largely consistent with earlier Stoicism, although its idiom differs markedly. A major doctrinal innovation was his commitment to the innate character of moral beliefs; for earlier Stoics, such ideas were natural but not innate. Another novelty is in the organization of his teaching: Epictetus divided it into three 'themes' (τόποι), concerning (1) the control of desires and passions, (2) actions, and (3) assent. Other leading ideas include: (*a*) a contrast between what is in the power of the agent and what is not; beliefs, desires, plans, reactions, and interpretations of experience are 'up to us', while events which happen to us are not. This leads him to emphasize the *use* we make of our presentations in contrast to their mere reception. (*b*) An intense focus on προαίρεσις, the power of individual moral choice. (*c*) The Socratic claim that all men act according to what they believe to be good for them; hence, the proper response to moral error is an effort at education and not anger. (*d*) A powerful belief in divine providence. He interprets the rational, cosmic deity of Stoicism in a more personal sense with an emphasis on the need to harmonize one's will with that of the deity.

TEXT H. Schenkl *Epicteti Dissertationes* (Teubner 1894).
See also A. Bonhöffer, *Epictet und die Stoa* (1890), and *Die Ethik des Stoikers Epictet* (1894). B. I.

Epicurus (b. *Samos, 341 BC; d. Athens, 270 BC), moral and natural philosopher. His father Neocles and mother Chaerestrate, Athenians of the *deme Gargettus, emigrated to the Athenian *cleruchy in Samos. As a boy he was taught by a Platonist, Pamphilus (1). He served as an *ephebe in Athens, when *Xenocrates (1) was head of the *Academy and *Aristotle was in *Chalcis; the playwright *Menander (1) was in the same class of the ephebate as Epicurus. He rejoined his family, who had then settled on the Asian mainland at Colophon. At this time or earlier he studied under *Nausiphanes, from whom he learnt about the *atomist philosophy of *Democritus. At 32 he moved to *Mytilene in Lesbos, then to *Lampsacus on the Hellespont; at both places he set up a school and began to acquire pupils and loyal friends.

About 306/7 he bought a house in Athens, with a garden that became the eponymous headquarters of his school of philosophy. Apart from occasional visits to Asia Minor, he remained in Athens until his death in 270, when he bequeathed his garden and school to *Hermarchus of Mytilene (his will survives, in Diog. Laert. 10, the main source for his biography).

The Epicurean school (The Garden). He and his followers lived together, secluding themselves from the affairs of the city and maintaining a modest and even austere standard of living, in accordance with the Master's teaching. They included slaves and women. Contemporary Epicureans mentioned in the literature were his most devoted companion, *Metrodorus (2) of Lampsacus, who died before Epicurus; Leontius and his wife Themista, also of Lampsacus; Hermarchus, his successor; and a slave called Mys.

The school was much libelled in antiquity and later, perhaps because of its determined privacy, and because of Epicurus' professed hedonism. The qualifications that brought this hedonism close to *asceticism were ignored, and members of rival schools accused the Epicureans of many kinds of profligacy. In Christian times, Epicureanism was anathema because it taught that man is mortal, that the cosmos is the result of accident, that there is no providential god, and that the criterion of the good life is pleasure. Hence such caricatures as Sir Epicure Mammon, in Ben Jonson's *Alchemist*, and the modern use of the word 'epicure'.

Writings Diog. Laert. 10. 26 reports that Epicurus wrote more than any of the other philosophers—about 300 rolls. Most of these are now lost. Fragments of his 37 books *On Nature* survive in the volcanic ash at *Herculaneum, and efforts to restore and interpret them, begun around 1800, are now in progress with renewed vigour. The following three letters and two collections of maxims have been preserved intact, the first four all in Diog. Laert. 10: (1) Letter to Herodotus (*Hdt.*): a summary of his philosophy of nature; (2) Letter to Pythocles (*Pyth.*): a summary of astronomy and meteorology; (3) Letter to Menoeceus (*Men.*): a less technical summary of Epicurean morality; (4) *Kyriai doxai* (*KD*), *Ratae sententiae*, or *Principal Doctrines*: 40 moral maxims; (5) *Sent. Vat.* (*VS*): 81 similar short sayings identified in a Vatican manuscript by C. Wotke in 1888.

Present-day knowledge and appreciation of Epicurean philosophy depends very largely on the great Latin epic poem of his later follower, *Lucretius' *De rerum natura*.

Doctrines The purpose of philosophy is practical: to secure a happy life. Hence moral philosophy is the most important branch, and physics and epistemology are subsidiary. (For this tripartition, see Sext. Emp. *Math.* 11. 169, and for the comparative evaluation *KD* 11 and Diog. Laert. 10. 30).

1. Epistemology

The main sources are *Hdt.*, Lucr. 4, and critical comments in Sext. Emp. *Math.* Epicurus held that sense perception is the origin of knowledge, and defended its reliability with a physical account of it. Physical objects, being made of atoms, give off from their surface thin films of atoms, called *eidōla*, which retain the shape and some other characteristics of their parent body and implant its appearance on the sense organs of the perceiver. This appearance is somehow transmitted to the soul-atoms which constitute the mind. The appearance itself is never false: falsehood occurs only in the opinion (*doxa*) the mind forms about it. If appearances conflict, a closer look or a sound argument or experience of the

context may serve to 'counter-witness' all but one consistent set of opinions: in some cases (especially in astronomy, where no closer look is possible) we must accept that all beliefs not counter-witnessed are somehow true.

Epicurus was apparently not able to articulate an explanation of concept-formation and theorizing by minds made of atoms and void. The extant texts show frequent use of analogical reasoning, from phenomena to theoretical entities.

2. Physics

Epicurus adopted the atomist theories (see ATOMISM) of Democritus, with some changes that can often be seen as attempts to answer Aristotle's criticisms.

The original atomist theory was a response to the *Eleatic school of *Parmenides, *Zeno (1), and *Melissus. Arguments about Being and Not-being show that there must be permanent elements—atoms of matter. Arguments about divisibility show that there must be indivisibles—construed by Epicurus as inseparable parts of atoms. The observed fact of motion proves that there must be empty space in which atoms can move.

Change is explained as the rearrangement of unchangeable atoms. The universe is infinite, both in the number of atoms and in the extent of space. Our cosmos, bounded by the region of the heavenly bodies, came into being through random collisions of suitable atoms, and it will some day dissolve again into its component atoms. It is one of an indefinite number of cosmoi, past, present, and future.

Atoms move naturally downwards at constant and equal speed because of their weight, unless they collide with others. But they would never collide unless some of them sometimes swerved from the straight downward path. (This postulate, which also accounts for the self-motions of animals (see below), is not mentioned in any surviving text of Epicurus, but is set out at some length by Lucretius, 2. 62–332, mentioned by other classical writers, and generally agreed to have been advanced by Epicurus himself.)

Gods exist, atomic compounds like everything else, but take no thought for this cosmos or any other, living an ideal life of eternal, undisturbed happiness—the Epicurean ideal. It is good for men to respect and admire them, without expecting favours or punishments from them.

Both creation, as in *Plato (1)'s *Timaeus*, and the eternity of the cosmic order, as in Aristotle's world picture, are rejected: natural movements of atoms are enough to explain the origin and growth of everything in the world. A theory of the survival of the fittest explains the apparently purposeful structure of living things.

Epicurus was a thoroughgoing physicalist in his philosophy of mind. The soul is composed of atoms, all extremely small but distinguished by shape into four kinds: fire, air, and breath (but all somehow different from their ordinary namesakes), and a fourth, unnamed kind. At death the component atoms are dispersed.

The swerve of atoms somehow accounts for the possibility of actions performed by choice, by humans and some other animals: without the swerve, apparently, all actions would be as fully determined as the fall of a stone dropped from a height. How this works is a matter of continuing controversy.

3. Moral philosophy

'We say that pleasure is the beginning and end of living happily' (*Men.* 128). It is a datum of experience that pleasure is naturally and congenitally the object of human life. Since it is a fact, however, that some pleasures are temporary and partial, and involve pain as well, it is necessary to distinguish between pleasures, and to take only those which are not outweighed by pains. Pain is caused by unsatisfied desire; so one must recognize that those desires that are natural and necessary are easily satisfied; others are unnecessary. The limit of pleasure is the removal of pain; to seek always for more pleasure is simply to spoil one's present pleasure with the pain of unsatisfied desire. Pleasure is not so much the process of satisfying desires (*kinetic* pleasure) but rather the state of having desires satisfied (*katastematic* pleasure).

Pleasure of the *soul, consisting mainly of contemplation or expectation of bodily pleasure, is more valuable than bodily pleasure. The ideal is *ataraxia*, freedom from disturbance. The study of philosophy is the best way to achieve the ideal. By teaching that the soul, made of atoms as the body is, dies with the body, it persuades us that after death there is no feeling: what happens after our death, like what happened before our birth, is 'nothing to us'. By teaching that the gods do not interfere and that the physical world is explained by natural causes, it frees us from the fear of the supernatural. By teaching that the competitive life is to be avoided, it removes the distress of jealousy and failure; by teaching one how to avoid intense emotional commitments, it frees us from the pain of emotional turmoil. (The main sources are Epicurus *Men.*, *KD*, and *VS*, and Lucretius 3 and 4.)

Epicurean moral philosophy thus finds room for most of the conventional Greek virtues of the soul; its main difficulty is to justify the virtues that are concerned with the well-being of other people—especially justice. Those who are wise will avoid injustice, Epicurus argues, because one can never be certain of remaining undetected. But Epicurean morality was less selfish than such statements made it appear. The Epicurean communities were famous even among their enemies for the friendship which bound members to each other and to the founder. See also DIOGENES (5) OF OENOANDA.

BIBLIOGRAPHIES In A. A. Long and D. Sedley, *The Hellenistic Philosophers* (1987); also P. DeLacy 'Some Recent Publications on Epicurus and Epicureanism', *Classical Weekly* (1955); H. J. Mette, 'Epikuros 1963–78', *Lustrum* 1979; *Suzetesis* 2 (1983).

TEXTS AND TRANSLATIONS H. Usener, *Epicurea* (1887), text of extant works and fragments, excluding papyri; C. Bailey, *Epicurus* (1926), text (excluding fragments), Eng. trans., and comm.; J. Bollack and others, *La Lettre d'Épicure* (1971), *Hdt.* with Fr. trans. and comm.; G. Arrighetti, *Epicuro*, 2nd edn. (1973), text, including papyrus fragments of *On Nature*, It. trans., and comm.; J. Bollack and others, *La Pensée du plaisir* (1975), *Men.* and *KD* with Fr. trans. and comm.; A. Laks, 'La Vie d'Épicure dans Diog. Laerce. 10. 1–34', *Cahier de philologie, Univ. Lille* 1976; A. A. Long and D. Sedley, *The Hellenistic Philosophers* (1987), selected texts, trans., and comm.

COLLECTIONS OF ESSAYS M. Schofield and others (eds.), *Doubt and Dogmatism* (1980); J. Brunschwig and others (eds.), *Science and Speculation* (1982); *Suzetesis* (1983); M. Schofield and others (eds.), *The Norms of Nature* (1986); J. Barnes and M. Mignucci (eds.), *Matter and Metaphysics* (1989); J. Brunschwig and M. Nussbaum, *Passions and Perceptions* (1992).

MODERN STUDIES C. Bailey, *The Greek Atomists and Epicurus* (1928).; W. Schmid, in *RAC* 'Epikur'; K. Kleve, *Gnōsis Theōn, Symbolae Osloenses* Suppl. 19 (1963); R. H. Kargon, *Atomism in England from Heriot to Newton* (1966); D. J. Furley, *Two Studies in the Greek Atomists* (1967); B. Farrington, *The Faith of Epicurus* (1967); H. Steckel, *RE* Suppl. 11 (1968) 'Epikur'; P. Boyancé, *Épicure* (1969); H. J. Krämer, *Platonismus und hellenistische Philosophie* (1971); J. M. Rist, *Epicurus: An Introduction* (1972); C. Diano, *Scritti epicurei* (1974); D. Sedley, *Cahier de philologie, Univ. Lille* 1976; V. Goldschmidt, *La Doctrine d'Épicure et le droit* (1977); D. Konstan, *Some Aspects of Epicurean Psychology* (1973); M. Gigante, *Scetticismo e epicureismo* (1981); J. Gosling and C. C. W. Taylor, *The Greeks on Pleasure* (1982). D. Sedley, *Phronesis* 1982; D. Clay, *Epicurus*

and Lucretius (1983); E. Asmis, *Epicurus' Scientific Method* (1984); P. Mitsis, *Epicurus' Ethical Theory* (1988); J. Annas, *Hellenistic Philosophy of Mind* (1992).   D. J. F.

Epidamnus, a joint colony of *Corcyra and *Corinth, founded *c.*625 BC as a port of call on the Adriatic coast and a focus of trade from Illyria. This trade was at first constituted as a monopoly for the benefit of the ruling oligarchy, which further strengthened its ascendancy by restricting industrial pursuits to public slaves. By 435 the commons had nevertheless gained control and expelled the oligarchs; when put under siege by the latter, they invoked the aid of Corcyra, and when this was refused they applied to Corinth. The Corinthians reinforced the democracy with new settlers, but shortly afterwards the city was recaptured by the Corcyraeans. This scramble of Corinthians and Corcyraeans for Epidamnus was a contributory cause of the *Peloponnesian War. For the later history of Epidamnus, see DYRRACHIUM.

Excavation reports in *Iliria*.   M. C.; N. G. L. H.

Epidaurus, one of the small states of the Argolic Acte, on a peninsula of the Saronic Gulf with evidence of occupation in the late bronze age. By the Classical period it was recognized as a *Dorian community, at times probably subject to *Argos (2); grazing dues payable to the Argive-controlled temple of *Apollo Pythaeus, non-payment of which in 419 BC led to war between Argos and Epidaurus, are not to be regarded as evidence of political dependence.

There are remains of walls on the site of Epidaurus: the best-preserved monument is its theatre. More significant is the sanctuary of Asclepius some 7 km. (4½ mi.) inland, towards Argos, near a small sanctuary of Apollo Maleatas, with a small Doric temple: the small sanctuary of Apollo was enlarged *c.*330 BC with a massive terrace wall. The healing-cult of Apollo's son *Asclepius, elevated to divine status, seems to have been given particular impetus by the effects of the *plague at the time of the Peloponnesian War, developing considerably in the 4th cent. The temple, peripteral but not large, was built *c.*370 BC. Adjacent to it was the *abaton*, where the sick spent the night in hope of a healing visitation from the god (see INCUBATION), and the circular *thymelē* or tholos, probably to be regarded as the cenotaph of Asclepius as a hero. Other buildings include the well-preserved theatre, attributed by Pausanias (3) in error to *Polyclitus (2) the sculptor; whoever this Polyclitus was, he also designed the *thymelē* (see THOLOS). Later structures include a large colonnaded courtyard building with a projecting, ramped ceremonial approach often described as a gymnasium; with rooms laid out with feasting couches, a more specialized banqueting function is more likely. A propylon, at the entrance to the sanctuary from Epidaurus town, creates no physical barrier (there are no doors in it) but clearly demarcates the entrance into sacred territory. After a decline in the later Hellenistic period, and spoliation in the 1st cent. BC, the sanctuary revived in the 2nd cent. AD, when many buildings were reconstructed or replaced. The sanctuary ceased to function in the 4th cent. See also ISYLLUS.

Fouilles d'Épidaure, vol. 1 only (1893); P. Kavvadias, *Tò Ἱερὸν τοῦ Ἀσκληπιοῦ ἐν Ἐπιδαύρῳ* (1900); E. J. Edelstein and L. Edelstein, *Asclepius* (1945); A. Burford, *The Greek Temple Builders at Epidaurus* (1969); R. A. Tomlinson, *Epidauros* (1983).   R. A. T.

Epigenes (1), of Sicyon, is recorded in the *Suda* as the first tragic poet (entry under Θέσπις), and as having with his tragedies given rise to the proverb, 'Nothing to do with Dionysus' (entry under οὐδὲν πρὸς τὸν Διόνυσον). Among the indications of a Peloponnesian origin for tragedy there is another which concerns *Sicyon: Herodotus (5. 67) mentions 'tragic choruses' there, which were transferred by the tyrant *Cleisthenes (1) from hero-cult to the cult of *Dionysus.

R. A. S. S.

Epigenes (2), Middle *Comedy poet. Fr. 6 refers to *Pixodarus, satrap of Caria from 340/39 to 335/4 BC.

FRAGMENTS Kassel–Austin, PCG 5. 165–9.
INTERPRETATION Meineke, FCG 1. 354 f.; G. Kaibel, RE 6/1 (1907), 64, 'Epigenes' 13; C. A. P. Ruck, IG 2². 2323. 50 f. W. G. A.

Epigoni, sons of the '*Seven against Thebes': as with the latter, the names and number vary (Homer names *Diomedes (2), Sthenelus, Euryalus, *Alcmaeon (1), and *Amphilochus). The sons succeeded where their fathers had failed, drove the Cadmeans out of Thebes, and restored *Thersander to the throne sought by his father Polynices. All of the Epigoni but one (Aegialeus, son of *Adrastus (1), sole survivor of the first expedition) survived. This happened in the same generation as, but before, the Trojan War (e.g. Homer, Il. 4. 406–10). The word epigoni is also sometimes used of the generation after the *Diadochi (the immediate successors of *Alexander (3) the Great).

Bernabé, PEG 1. 29–32; Davies, EGF 26–7; Apollod. The Library, trans. J. G. Frazer (Loeb; 1921), 1. 377–9. A. Sch.

Epigonus, Pergamene sculptor, active c.240–220 BC. Epigonus signed eight dedications at *Pergamum; Plin. HN 34. 88 mentions him as the author of numerous bronzes, including a Trumpeter and a Weeping Child caressing its murdered mother. A dying Celtic trumpeter (a copy) in the Capitoline Museum is usually connected with the former. Its original is attributed to Epigonus' long statue-base in the sanctuary of Athena Polias Nicephorus, dedicated by *Attalus I for his victories over the *Celts and *Seleucids in 237–223. This base, in turn, has prompted the substitution of Epigonus' name for the otherwise unknown Isigonus in Pliny's list of those who 'did the battles of Attalus and Eumenes against the Gauls' (HN 34. 84; see also ANTIGONUS (4); PHYROMACHUS). The Trumpeter is a virtuoso study in ethnic realism, evoking the pathos of the situation through his posture and stoic expression, as blood seeps from a chest wound.

M. Mattei, Il Galata Capitolino (1987); A. F. Stewart, Greek Sculpture (1990), 205 ff., 301 ff., figs. 667 ff. A. F. S.

epigram, Greek

Archaic An epigram was originally nothing more than an inscription on an object or monument to say whose it is or who made it, who dedicated it to which god, or who is buried beneath it. The earliest known are in hexameters (CEG 1. 432 and 454, the Dipylon oenochoe and Pithecusae scyphus, both c.720 BC), but by c.500 they were predominantly in what was to be the classic metre of epigram, the elegiac couplet. The earliest consist largely of formulae (e.g. τύμβος ὅδ' ἐστί, στῆθι καὶ οἴκτιρον, . . . ἐπέθηκε θανόντι, . . . μ' ἀνέθηκε 'this is tomb (of so-and-so), stand and take pity . . . (so-and-so) set up (this) for the deceased . . . (so-and-so) dedicated me') plus the appropriate proper names in stereotyped epicizing phraseology. The material in Peek, GVI 1 (limited to epitaphs) is arranged by such formulae.

Classical Epigrams written for monuments are normally anonymous; the earliest signed by the author date from c.350 (CEG 2. 819, 888. ii). The first poet credited with writing epigrams is *Simonides, though only one of the many ascribed to him (Page, FGE 119–23, 186–302) can be accepted, the simple and dignified epitaph on the seer Megistias (Hdt. 7. 228; FGE 195–6).

Many others are attributed in Hellenistic and later times to famous poets (Page, FGE), but even if authentic present generic problems. For example, the couplet πολλὰ πιὼν καὶ πολλὰ φαγὼν καὶ πολλὰ κακ' εἰπὼν | ἀνθρώπους κεῖμαι Τιμοκρέων Ῥόδιος, 'I, Timocreon the Rhodian, lie here after drinking and eating a lot and uttering a lot of abuse' (FGE 252) is certainly a 5th cent. parody of funerary epigram, but at the time it would have been called a *scolium and sung at the *symposium. It is hard to believe *Euripides wrote the undistinguished distich that *Plutarch read on a monument to the Athenians who died in Sicily (FGE 155–6), but there seems no reason to doubt *Aristotle's authorship of the epigram on a statue of his friend *Hermias (1) at Delphi (FGE 31–2). On the other hand, the love epigrams attributed to *Plato (1) are 'plainly *Alexandrian in tone, contents and style' (Page, FGE 125–7). Down to c.400 BC study of the epigram is in effect limited to anonyma: P. Friedländer and H. Hoffleit, Epigrammata (1948) remains a useful companion to CEG 1–2.

Hellenistic With the 3rd cent. we find an enormous expansion of non-inscriptional epigram. Reitzenstein distinguished two schools: the Dorian-Peloponnesian and Ionian-Alexandrian. The first represents a natural development from inscriptional poetry: literary embellishments of epitaphs and *dedications. Fictitious dedications were a neat way to treat the lives of humble folk rather than kings and generals, through the different objects vowed by rustics, hunters, and fishermen—or even hetairai. *Anyte of Tegea wrote on women and children and pastoral themes, epitaphs on animals rather than humans. *Leonidas (2) of Tarentum was the most influential writer of this school, influential too in establishing an ornate style and dithyrambic vocabulary as its medium. *Asclepiades (2) and *Callimachus (3) wrote about wine, women, boys, and song, renewing the themes of Classical sympotic elegy and lyric, though they were selective in the motifs they treated, investing them with that combination of allusiveness, conciseness, and wit that were ever after to be the hallmarks of the genre (Giangrande, in L'Épigramme grecque). The simple exchange between passer-by and tomb we find in Classical epitaphs is expanded into witty dialogue under the influence of *mime. The epitaph is developed into poems on those long as well as recently dead, and epigrams on writers are especially common (M. Gabathuler, Hell. Ep. auf Dichter, 1937). The dedication also evolved into the *ekphrasis on a work of art, another form with a long future. In addition to more conventional themes, *Alcaeus (3) of Messene wrote political lampoons. Poets would vie with each other in treating the same themes.

Early Hellenistic epigrams were often quite long and in metres other than elegiacs. Most of the major poets published books of Ἐπιγράμματα. The first known to consist entirely of elegiacs (on the evidence of the Milan roll) is *Posidippus (2). It has sometimes been argued that epigrams were now 'book-poetry', but they continued to be written for their original function as well as for the symposium. Callimachus and Posidippus in particular wrote a number of epigrams for Alexandrian monuments. Hellenistic epigrams on victors in the games became less factual and more literary, characterized by mythological allusion and motifs from Classical epinicion (J. Ebert, Epp. auf Sieger (1972), 19–22, 191–2, 205–8). The Milan roll has revealed that Posidippus wrote almost twenty epigrams on equestrian victors.

Graeco-Roman Epigrammatists of the late republic and early empire, most now writing for Roman patrons, represent a striking change of direction, away from the erotic and sympotic (with the exception of *Philodemus and Marcus *Argentarius) to the ecphrastic (see ECPHRASIS) and epideictic: jokes, paradoxa, witty anecdotes, invitations to dinner, epigrams to accompany presents or congratulate on birthdays or the cutting of a son's first beard. The late 1st cent. AD saw the development of the satiric epigram, best represented by the Neronian *Lucillius: attacks on the faults, not of individuals, but of entire classes and professions (doctors, athletes, thin men). There was also a short-lived revival of the erotic with Rufinus (under Nero) and the pederastic with *Straton (3) (under Hadrian).

Not the least interesting development of the 3rd and 4th cent. is the re-emergence of the anonymous inscriptional epigram. Honorific inscriptions that in the early empire would have been in prose are increasingly in verse, often verse of some distinction and elegance. There is unfortunately no modern corpus, but many are quoted and discussed in L. Robert's *Épigrammes du Bas-Empire* (1948).

Byzantine Towards the end of the 4th cent. the Alexandrian schoolmaster *Palladas wrote satiric epigrams with a difference, powerful, pessimistic tirades against his profession, and rueful laments on the impotence of a declining paganism. At the same time *Gregory (2) of Nazianzus (*Anth. Pal.* bk. 8) was writing epigram after epigram on his family (12 on his father, 52 on his mother), conventional in every respect (vocabulary, imagery, variation, point) except their Christianity and their disregard of Classical prosody. The age of *Justinian saw a remarkable renaissance of the classicizing epigram. *Agathias, Paul the Silentiary (see PAULUS (2)), Macedonius the consul, Julian the Egyptian, and many other professional men and civil servants returned to Hellenistic models, writing erotic, sympotic and dedicatory poems in a remarkably homogeneous style, a fusion of the traditional conventions and motifs with the bombast and metrical refinement of *Nonnus. Their literary paganism is so thoroughgoing that we are astonished by the occasional use of the same style and vocabulary to describe a Christian icon (R. C. McCail, *Byzantion* 1971, 205–67). This was the end of creative writing in the genre.

See too ANTHOLOGY and individual epigrammatists, especially MELEAGER (2) and PHILIPPUS (2).

R. Reitzenstein, *Epigramm und Skolion* (1893), and *RE* (1907), 'Epigramm'; R. Keydell, *RAC* (1962), 'Epigramm'; *L'Épigramme grecque*, Entretiens Hardt (1968); S. Tarán, *The Art of Variation in the Hellenistic Epigram* (1979); E. Degani, *La cultura ellenistica* (Storia e civiltà dei Greci 9), (1977), 266–99; Gow-Page, *HE* and *GP*; D. L. Page, *Further Greek Epigrams* (1981); W. Seelbach, *Kleines Wörterbuch des Hellenismus* (1988), 157–84; A. Cameron, *The Greek Anthology* (1993), and *Callimachus and his Critics* (1995), ch. 3. A. D. E. C.

epigram, Latin The use of metrical inscriptions in Latin is attested from the second half of the 3rd cent. BC. The two most ancient *elogia* in the tomb of the Scipios (*CIL* 1^2. 9, probably from around 230 BC, and *CIL* 1^2. 7 cut around 200 BC) are in *Saturnians, and limit themselves to a sober indication of the name, career, achievements, and civic virtues of the subject, in accordance with traditional Roman models for the praise of the great (cf. also the inscription in Saturnians from the 3rd cent. BC quoted in Cic. *Fin.* 2. 116). There is greater elaboration in the two Scipionic inscriptions in Saturnians datable to around the middle of the 2nd cent. BC which lament figures whose early deaths prevented their attaining glory (*CIL* 1^2. 10 and 11). There is little trace of Greek culture or stylistic sensibility in these early epitaphs or in the rare dedicatory inscriptions from the same period, but the

Latin taste for verbal effects such as alliteration, tricola, and antithesis is much in evidence. Saturnians continued to be used for commemorative inscriptions, in homage to Roman tradition, up to at least 133 BC (*Schol. Bob. ad Cic.*, p. 179 Stangl, on an epigram commissioned from *Accius), long after the form had been abandoned in literature.

*Ennius introduced into Latin not only the hexameter but also the elegiac couplet, the usual metre of Greek epigram. All the extant epigrams of Ennius preserve the norms of Roman honorific inscriptions and could have been inscribed, though *Cicero, who quotes them, did not know of any actual inscriptions. Two refer to the tomb of Scipio Africanus (and are thus to be dated after his death in 183 BC), and another two, of uncertain authenticity, refer to a portrait (on a tomb ?) and to the poet's own grave. The sober, monumental solemnity, the recall to communal values (Ennius celebrates his role as poet of Roman glory), and the usual verbal effects of archaic Latin style recall the Scipionic *elogia*, but the metre, the density of expression (three of the epigrams consist of a single couplet), the motif of the dead man speaking in the first-person from his tomb and declining lament, the elevated conception of the poet's role, and the very fact that he dedicates an epigram to himself as poet—all these are to be explained by Ennius' grafting of Hellenistic Greek culture onto the Roman tradition. Also in evidence is a clear articulation of the logical divisions of the poem, something which remains a feature of the Latin elegiac epigram (*Alcaeus (3) Mess. *Anth. Pal.* 9. 518), but these austere and elevated epigrams of Ennius still remain far from the light charm of Hellenistic Greek epigram.

*Gellius (*NA* 1. 24) quotes the epigrams that *Naevius (in Saturnians), *Plautus (in hexameters), and *Pacuvius (in senarii) supposedly wrote for their tombs. The authenticity of Pacuvius' epitaph, of a studied simplicity and modesty and recalling formulae of 2nd-cent. BC inscriptions (*CLE* 848, and cf. 53) is not impossible: but the other two are typical celebrations of dead poets, with clever elaboration in archaic style of commonplaces of Hellenistic epigram (the genre practised by the dead poet is orphaned or ceases all together, the deities of poetry are in mourning). Gellius found the Plautus epigram, and perhaps the other two, in *Varro: all three may have been written by a 2nd-cent. BC grammarian, perhaps to be included in biographies of the poets, in accordance with a Hellenistic custom continued also at Rome. One may compare *Virgil's famous epitaph, *Mantua me genuit . . .*, 'Mantua bore me', cited in Aelius *Donatus (1)'s Life: Varro himself in his *Imagines* provided epigrams to accompany a series of portraits of famous men, and we know of similar series of epigrams by T. *Pomponius Atticus (Nep. *Att.* 18. 5 ff.) and *Octavius Titinius Capito (Plin. *Ep.* 1. 17. 3, 1st cent. AD). In the same tradition is the self-presentation in a single distich of the obscure poet Pompilius, who claims to be a pupil of Pacuvius, and is thus datable to the 2nd cent. BC. We also have the epitaph, certainly fictitious, written by *Lucilius (1) for one of his slaves (frs. 579 f. Marx), a couplet in which the formality of epigraphic convention is lightened by familiar language and a tone of ironic and affectionate condescension. This is from book 22 of the *Satires*: there are other fragments in couplet form on Lucilius' slaves in the same book, which some think was a collection of epigrams.

The latest epitaph in the tomb of the Scipios (from a little after 139 BC) is in elegiacs: the Greek metre introduced by Ennius became the commonest form used in both literary and inscribed epigrams, though the hexameter became popular in inscriptions after the Augustan period, and from the 2nd to the 1st cent. BC senarii were also common. Inscriptional verse, especially epitaphs for the dead, from which the Latin epigram had developed in the first place continued with its own development. There is clear evidence for a degree of professional composition, using a repertory of formulae and motifs dealing with the dead, their virtues, their survival through renown or the affection of their loved ones, and the loss felt at their departure: a repertory which for all its conventionality provides insight into the mentality and beliefs prevalent in the Roman world. Many of these motifs continued, albeit transformed, into Christian epitaphs, which are extremely common from the 4th cent. AD. Throughout, the influence of high-style poetry, especially Virgil and *Ovid, is strong.

From the end of the 2nd cent. BC, the band of Greek intellectuals attached to the great Roman families began to include epigrammatists, whose poems served as a cultured accompaniment and ornament for the lives of their patrons. From the hand of one of these patrons, Q. *Lutatius Catulus (2) (consul 102 BC), an important member of the Roman nobility and a passionate admirer of Greek culture, who was the patron of the Greek epigrammatists *Antipater (3) of Sidon and A. *Licinius Archias, we have two homoerotic epigrams. One of the two (clearly inspired by Callim. *Epigr.* 41) is cited by Gellius, *NA* 19. 9, together with two epigrams of *Valerius Aedituus and one by *Porcius Licinus. We do not know what if any connection there was between these three 'pre-neoteric' figures, but the poems are the earliest Latin epigrams of the Hellenistic type, on sentimental themes and independent of the epigraphic tradition. They share a manneristic treatment of the commonplaces of Greek love poetry, with an obvious striving for conceptual and pathetic effects and emphatic figures (questions, apostrophe, antithesis): a concentration of devices that perhaps shows the traces of the expressionism of the archaic Roman tradition. The slightly later epigrams of Tiburtinus, of which we have graffiti fragments from the smaller theatre at Pompeii (*CLE* 934 f.), show that these tendencies were widely diffused. With Catulus the epigram becomes for the first time at Rome the ideal genre for the leisure hours of the refined and recherché upper-class amateur. From the time of Cicero we have many references to (and a few fragments of) short poems written for pleasure and cultural display by leading Romans, or composed by more important authors as a marginal addition to their more serious productions. As well as elegiacs, we find poems in hexameters, phalaecian hendecasyllables, and iambics, together forming a Roman genre of short poetry in various metres on erotic, polemical, or humorous themes. In this genre, Greek traditions of epigram and iambus interact with Roman traditions (influenced themselves by Greek iambus) of personal and political polemic, attested from the time of Naevius and then common from the time of Caesar, and of humorous or satirical verse of popular origin, found, for example, in the scurrilous verses sung by soldiers at Roman triumphs. This varied genre had no fixed name, but 'epigram' was certainly one of the terms used (cf. Plin. *Ep.* 4. 14. 9), and *Martial's usage gave it currency. The first two modest examples of polemic or humorous epigram known to us are quoted by Varro and ascribed to one Manilius (in senarii) and Papinius (elegiacs): they are full of the verbal play used for humorous polemic, but, like a similar couplet attributed to Cicero, they show no significant contact with Greek Hellenistic epigram. They are perhaps related to the *epigrammata* ascribed to the comic poet *Quinctius Atta (d. 77 BC).

This production of everyday minor verse at Rome, the product

of leisure and an ingredient in social relations, increased in the time of Caesar and Augustus. It was still practised by Greek epigrammatists living in Roman high society (e.g. *Philodemus, and later *Crinagoras and *Antipater (5) of Thessalonica), and it was an important element in the work of *Catullus (1) and the other 'new poets', who wrote short poems to accompany gifts, to console or thank, invite or congratulate, to celebrate (seriously or humorously) the most diverse events of the society in which they lived, and to engage in polemic and invective on public or private matters. Collections of *epigrammata* are attested for *Helvius Cinna, C. *Licinius Calvus, and Cornificia, but other terms (*poemata* etc.) were used to refer to the same sort of poems. Amongst the meagre remains may be noted the poems written by *Furius Bibaculus for his friend Valerius Cato (two friendly jests in senarii, one inspired by *Leonidas (2), *Anth. Pal.* 6. 226, and two more complimentary poems in hendecasyllables), the poems of Calvus mocking Caesar (senarii) and *Pompey (an elegiac couplet), and the refined elegiacs in which Cinna (echoing Callimachus, *Epigr.* 27) presented a de luxe edition of Aratus (1). The verses of these poets, with those of Catullus, signal the birth of a new literary language for the description of everyday life, at times delicate, at times realistic and incisive, even crude and obscene, but always artistically light and elegant. The Catullan or neoteric 'revolution' was the use of this genre and language to express an intensely personal emotional world and to affirm a system of values in which even the smallest day-to-day event, rather than being merely the subject of amateur versifying, became the occasion for poetry of the highest level which could absorb all the energies of a poet of the greatest ambition. In this way, Catullus gave pride and full literary dignity to Roman minor verse, and became its classic practitioner. In the Catullan collection as we have it the 'epigrams' in elegiacs (poems 69–116) are separate from the 'polymetrics' in iambics, hendecasyllables, and lyric metres (1–60), but it is uncertain to what extent this represents Catullus' own distinction. The two groups share themes to an extent, but the epigrams show a neater composition and a more rational analysis of emotion, with extensive use of antithesis and parallelism but a less unusual and innovative language. This may be due, as Ross suggests (see bibliog. below), to the greater influence of the native Roman tradition on the elegiacs: the presence of Hellenistic epigram is more marked in the polymetrics. At any rate, already in the pseudo-Virgilian *Catalepton*, and later in the *Priapea* and Martial, elegiacs are freely mixed with poems in the other Catullan metres within a single collection, which suggests that Catullus' short poems were viewed collectively as a distinct genre. Catullus never uses epigraphic forms: they are avoided even in the poems for the death of his brother (101) and the sparrow (3) and on the dedication of the boat (4), even though these draw on elements of the funerary and votive epigram. In Catullus, the short poem expresses a vivid subjectivity which is nourished not only by Hellenistic epigram but also by the traditions of Greek lyric, archaic elegy, and iambus, with the latter's harshness and obscenity, and it accordingly has no place for the 'objectivity' proper to the epigraphic form.

Martial considers Catullus the canonical model of Latin epigram, placing alongside him as second in importance *Domitius Marsus, of whom we possess a few fragments, all in elegiacs. His collection entitled *Cicuta*, 'Hemlock', seems to have consisted largely of invectives, and includes an epigram very much in Catullus' manner against Virgil's adversary the poet Bavius: an interest in literary polemic is confirmed by attacks on two famous grammarians. Other epigrams by Domitius Marsus attempt a recuperation of the epigraphic form, with a lament for *Tibullus (and Virgil) which shows a Hellenistic delicacy and one for *Atia (1), Octavian's mother, which in its single couplet recalls the solemn and concise monumentality of Ennius. Like another epigram for Atia it involves itself in the contemporary political debate not, as was usual in epigram, through insulting the enemy but through the celebratory function that epigram had had in early Rome and to which it returned in the Augustan and imperial periods, as can be seen also in Greek epigrams such as those of Crinagoras. We do not know if Domitius' collection, like Catullus', included love poetry (cf. Mart. 7. 29. 8). The treatise on wit (*De urbanitate*) ascribed to him suggests that Domitius' poetry had a systematic interest in comic effects that could have interested Martial. Martial's other named models were *Albinovanus Pedo (an epic poet, friend of Ovid) and *Cornelius Lentulus Gaetulicus (consul AD 26): all we know of their epigrams is that Martial cited them as precedents for his own obscenity. We do not know if Gaetulicus sang of his love for Cesennia in his epigrams, and it is also uncertain whether he is to be identified with the Gaetulicus who is the author of several epigrams in the Greek Anthology.

We have only scant remains of the epigrams written by the Augustan elegist *Valgius Rufus and Ovid. The epigrams of the pseudo-Virgilian *Catalepton*, some of which go back to the Augustan period and may even be by Virgil, show clear Catullan influence in metre, in various echoes and parodies, and in general in the concept of the short poem: a space for jokes, polemic, and wordplay, but also for expressions of friendship and affection or for autobiographical meditations. There is also an 'epideictic' poem of moralizing content, a type of composition that reappears in Martial and which must have been practised also as a school or occasional exercise. This form predominates, along with poems on friendship, love, and polemic, in a series of 70 epigrams (*Anth. Lat.* 232, 236–9, 396–463 Riese, almost all in elegiac couplets) that have been attributed to the younger Seneca (see ANNAEUS SENECA (2), L.). Two are so ascribed in two manuscripts, while the others follow on from them in a third: some refer to the Corsican exile or Cordoban birth of Seneca, or to people of his circle, and the moral themes dealt with have affinities with Seneca's philosophical works. They may be by Seneca (especially from the time of his exile: there are links with Ovid's exile poetry) or from his circle, but they may also be school exercises of a later date. One noteworthy cycle (419–26 R) deals with the British triumph of Claudius, which took place during Seneca's exile: the celebratory epigram thus begins to encompass official events connected with the imperial (*ruler-)cult, as it will do frequently in Martial.

In contrast to these serious epigrams, the anonymous collection of *Priapea* offers licentious entertainment with more than a hint of pornography. It consists of about 80 poems in Catullan metres, often dedicatory, in which the heavily obscene content contrasts with the elegance of the form and the admirably varied treatment of a single theme (with its own literary tradition, from Greek epigram—there are around 40 Priapea in the Greek Anthology—to Catullus (fr. 1), *Horace (*Sat.* 1. 8), and Tibullus (1. 4)). The collection is often dated to the Augustan period, but must be later than book 1 of Martial, since Priapea 1. 1 f. recalls Martial 1. 4. 1 (the reverse process is unlikely, since Martial would hardly defend himself against charges of obscenity by citing the opening of a pornographic collection).

Martial's own epigrams, though drawing extensively on Greek epigram, reflect above all the varied and lively nature of the preceding Roman tradition: they offer homage and celebrate events public and private, accompany the events of everyday social life and turn them into elegant expressions of culture, offer space for moral reflection and for literary and personal polemic, and entertain with pungent wit, jokes, and pornography. On the other hand the erotic or sentimental element and the affirmation of personal individuality which play so large a part in Catullus' claim to fame are more marginal in Martial. He develops rather the satiric epigram and the epigram as a part of social relationships: that is, precisely those aspects which seem to a modern most 'epigrammatic'. To this minor genre, developed in its apparently most superficial aspects, Martial attributes the full dignity of an artistic instrument adapted to offer a realistic interpretation of the world. Like Catullus, but on different grounds, he is bold in contrasting it with the more prestigious and elevated genres, which are seen as divorced from the real-life experience of the reader. It is with good reason that he became for modern writers the classic epigrammatist, and helped to fix the form. Developing tendencies seen in Greek Hellenistic and imperial epigram and in Catullus (and even Ennius), he offers at the end of many of his epigrams that incisive, and often unexpected, 'pointed' formulation of the essential meaning of the poem which is seen as the essence of modern epigram.

Martial's original attempt to give importance to the genre was not taken entirely seriously by contemporary authors: *Pliny (2) (*Ep.* 3. 21) considers Martial's aspiration to immortality little more than a naïve illusion. Pliny himself and their mutual friends composed for entertainment, and with a certain condescension, elegant and trifling verses of which Pliny quotes a few examples (*Ep.* 4. 27, 7. 4, 7. 9). This type of amateur production assured continued success for the epigram as a minor genre, though it tended to lose its identity, never in any case very clear, within a more general generic framework of minor poetry. This can be seen in the experimental lyric/epigrammatic works of the so-called *poetae novelli* (*Florus (3), the emperor Hadrian, and *Annianus at the beginning of the 2nd cent. AD, then later *Septimius Serenus and *Alfius Avitus). In an archaizing and 'decadent' style they recall the formal experimentation of *Laevius, writing in rare lyric or dramatic metres on sentimental, erotic, didactic, or pastoral themes in a light, affected manner which at times is subtly melancholic. Amongst the few fragments that we have, it is the work of Florus, with its prevailing gnomic element, which has the most epigrammatic character, but as a whole the remains do not show any influence from Martial nor relevant affinities with Greek epigram. In the 4th cent. AD, however, the epigram is again popular, with its more frivolous aspects still to the fore. *Ausonius composed a short collection of varied epigrams, some translated or adapted from extant Greek epigram (by authors of the 1st and 2nd cents. AD). They also show little influence from Martial, and even though they are frequently satirical and sometimes obscene, they lack real aggression. In contrast to Catullus and Martial, hendecasyllables and choliambics are avoided. We find similar characteristics (except for the absence of obscenity) in the *Epigrammata Bobiensia* collected and in large part written on the model of Ausonius by the senator Naucellius around AD 400. As in Ausonius and the late antique epigram in general, there are frequent descriptions of objects, buildings, and works of art (*ekphraseis*), versified maxims, and elegant and leisurely variations on the same theme. A novelty in the tradition on the other hand is Ausonius' collections of epigrams on a single theme, either of some poetic weight (*Parentalia*, *Commemoratio professorum*), or with a slighter didactic or rhetorical character.

Their brevity and occasional nature bring many of Ausonius' other poems close to the epigram, and in Claudian's minor poetry we find a number of true and proper epigrams (satirical, erotic, on objects, etc.). The Christian poets of the 4th and 5th cents. used the genre essentially for their own practical purposes, didactic or commemorative. Thus we find sepulchral epigrams in praise of martyrs and others (only later collected in books), such as those written for inscription by *Damasus I; epigrams for sacred edifices (churches, baptisteries), usually with citation of the dedicator, the architect, and the occasion, and praise of the saint to whom they are dedicated (we have examples by Damasus, *Ambrose, and *Paulinus of Nola); and epigrams on themes from Scripture, supposedly to accompany visual representations, though whether this was actually true is uncertain. We have examples of this last group by Ambrose (21 hexameter couplets), *Prudentius (the *Dittochaeon* in groups of four hexameters), and about a century later the hexameter triplets of Rusticus Elpidius. *Augustine's follower *Prosper Tiro of Aquitaine wrote a series of epigrams to illustrate maxims taken from Augustine's works. In the 5th cent., the pagan tradition was continued by two bishops well trained in classical rhetoric, *Sidonius Apollinaris and *Ennodius. The former wrote on objects, gifts, and secular buildings, and short verse letters, at times with elegant concluding points; although he was well-acquainted with Martial, he did not develop the satiric or comic aspects, which prevail, on the other hand, in Ennodius, even with a certain amount of obscenity. But Ennodius' 150 or so epigrams are far from the spirit of Martial, with the rhetorical and recherché nature of their fictitious themes, their general absence of liveliness, and the recurrence of descriptive poems on objects, places, animals, works of art, etc. (as in Ausonius, *Claudian, and Sidonius). Both Sidonius and Ennodius also give space to the values and motifs of the pagan tradition even in their poems on the dead and on sacred places. At the beginning of the 6th cent. the Carthaginian *Luxorius composed a book of 89 epigrams modelled on Martial in both tone and metre, with a prevalence of satiric poems, including some on contemporary persons, and some notable obscenities. Luxorius' vivacity and energy is considerable, even if theme and treatment also show the artificiality that late antique epigram derived from rhetoric. Luxorius' book was included in a large collection put together in Africa in the Vandal period, around 534, preserved in the Codex Salmasianus (Par. Lat. 10318) and sometimes called the *Anthologia Latina*, though that term is usually used for the whole of the Codex Salmasianus collection, with the other collections included in Riese's Teubner edition. Most of the poems are anonymous and late, though some are attributed to classical poets, and they are mainly rhetorical in character (on mythological and historical themes, on objects, etc.), with a few satirical epigrams. They included a series of 100 *riddles by *Symphosius in hexameter triplets, with ingenious and entertaining descriptions of everyday objects, the prototype of many similar medieval collections. In the second half of the 6th cent. *Venantius Fortunatus returned to the epigram and related forms to describe his own experiences, personal relationships, and journeys: poetic epistles for friends and patrons, convivial poems, and poems for gifts are joined by numerous epitaphs and poems on sacred buildings. Finally, from the 6th and 7th cents. we may note the epigrams of *Isidorus (2) of Seville on authors and books both Christian and pagan, and those of Eugenius of Toledo, who took up again many of the themes of the late antique epigram (epitaphs, poems for churches and everyday objects) with a variety of moralizing, didactic, and

autobiographical elements, but without any satirical touches and showing a strong Christian spirit. In one sense, the epigram had come a long way from its origins: in another, the sternly serious early Romans who had begun the tradition could not but have approved.

TEXTS Buecheler, *Carm. Epigr.* 1–2, with Suppl., ed. E. Lommatzsch (1894–1930); *Anth. Lat.* ed. Riese (1, 1894²; 2, 1906²), and Shackleton Bailey (1, 1982); Morel, *FPL* (1927²), and Morel–Büchner (1982), Courtney *FLP*, with comm.; *Gli epigrammi attribuiti a Seneca*, ed. C. Prato (1964), with comm.; *I frammenti dei 'Poetae Novelli'*, ed. S. Mattiaci (1982), with comm.; *Epigrammata Bobiensia*, ed. F. Munari (1955), W. Speyer (1963); *Priapea*, ed. F. Vollmer (1923), comm. by C. Goldberg (1992); *Aenigmata Symphosii*, ed. F. Glorie, *CSEL* 133 A (1968).

STUDIES E. Galletier, *Études sur la poésie funéraire d'après les inscriptions* (1922); R. Lattimore, *Themes in Greek and Latin Epitaphs* (1942); R. Reitzenstein, *RE* 6 (1907) 'Epigramm'; R. Keydell, *RAC* 5 (1962), 'Epigramm'; M. Citroni, *L'epigramma*, in F. Montanari (ed.), *La poesia latina* (1991), 171 ff.; D. O. Ross, *Style and Tradition in Catullus* (1969); V. Buchheit, *Studien zum Corpus Priapeorum* (1962); S. Mariotti, *RE* Suppl. 9 (1962), 'Epigrammata Bobiensia'; G. Bernt, *Das lateinische Epigramm im Übergang von der Spätantike zum frühen Mittelalter* (1968); P. Laurens, *L'Abeille dans l'ambre* (1989); M. Lausberg, *Das Einzeldistichon* (1982).   M. Ci.

epigraphy, Greek, the study of inscriptions engraved on stone or metal in Greek letters. Coin-legends (see COINAGE, GREEK) are for the numismatist, whereas painted mummy-labels and ink-written texts on *ostraca, especially popular in Egypt, are the realm of the papyrologist; inscriptions painted or incised on vases and pottery (see POTTERY (GREEK), INSCRIPTIONS ON) are the combined prey of vase-experts and epigraphists.[1] (Superscript figures refer to the bibliographical notes at the end of the article.) Interest in inscriptions is not a modern phenomenon; already in antiquity people studied specific inscriptions. In the early 3rd cent. BC *Craterus (2) published a collection of decrees (Ψηφισμάτων συναγωγή); a hundred years later *Polemon (3) of Ilium received the nickname στηλοκόπας ('tablet-glutton') for his fanatical attention to inscriptions. With the Renaissance, interest in antiquities went hand in hand with admiration for the ancient literary inheritance. With Cyriacus of Ancona there began a long series of travelling scholars, who in their notebooks produced beautiful descriptions and drawings of ancient sites and the inscriptions on them. Initially, inscriptions tended to be disregarded or even despised by the champions of the revered literary sources; but when the latter came under the attack of Cartesian rationalism and Pyrrhonian scepticism, epigraphical shares increased in value on the historical stock exchange:[2] inscriptions were authentic and direct and could not be disqualified as forgeries or highly biased accounts. Since then, inscriptions have increasingly become part of the standard menu of scholars interested in any aspect of Greek civilization and society, though due largely to the somewhat chaotic organization of epigraphic publications (which means that the material is often less than perfectly accessible) that same menu could do with a somewhat higher shot of epigraphical calcium.

In two respects epigraphy is an auxiliary science: there is a rather complicated and occasionally even abstruse, technical aspect, as well as an organizational aspect, already briefly alluded to above. Once these aspects are under control, epigraphy is just one of the disciplines which together claim to study Graeco-Roman society and civilization, and nearly always it is the problem and/or the region which decide whether or not inscriptions play an auxiliary role in relation to the literary sources.

The technical part of our discussion begins with finding

inscriptions: excavations and *Forschungsreise* (research-motivated travel) are the two main sources. Modern construction-work hitting on ancient substructures, the demolition of an old house, a peasant ploughing his land: these all can often produce inscriptions which the modern traveller may (or may not) be lucky enough to find on his path. Some finds may get to the local museums;[3] others find their way illegally to the European and American antiquities market; still more end up as building material in new peasant dwellings or are simply smashed up. Systematic excavations of urban centres and temple complexes yield(ed) large numbers of texts: *Delphi, *Delos, the Athenian agora (see ATHENS, TOPOGRAPHY), *Olympia, *Thasos, *Ephesus, *Priene, *Claros are just a few random examples of sites which were highly productive. Once an inscription has been found, the next stage is that of cleaning and deciphering it. The human eye may be helped by a photo[4] or a paper or latex squeeze. Inscriptions are engraved in uninterrupted lines of capitals; punctuation is virtually non-existent, though in Roman times dots are occasionally used to separate words, but never systematically. The Greeks began to write in the early Archaic period (8th/7th cent. BC): initially brief texts on ceramics and on stone, betraying the Semitic origin of the script: simple names, tombstones, dedications, signatures of manufacturers, abecedaria. Some scholars argue that these short texts were abridged versions of longer ones and thus presuppose the existence of longer hexametric poetry; others, with greater common sense and less uncontrolled fantasy, deny any literary pretension. Where and when exactly the borrowing from the Semites took place is still one of the most hotly debated questions among specialists. It probably happened in a north-west Semitic setting shortly after 800 BC.[5] In the course of a long process of borrowing and adaptation, the Greek communities all developed their own peculiar set of letters: it is the period of *The Local Scripts of Archaic Greece*, to quote the title of L. H. Jeffery's standard work on the subject.[6] The so-called boustrophedon style, in which lines, like ploughing oxen, move from right to left, from left to right, and so on until the end, is an adaptation of the Semitic habit of writing from right to left. In due course a sort of general koinē-alphabet (SEE KOINE; ALPHABET) came into existence, whose letter-forms, needless to say, slowly evolved between the Classical and the Roman imperial period. For decipherment a clear eye and knowledge of the Greek capital script as given in any grammar for beginners will suffice; for further judgement on the style of lettering and the ensuing date of the text, certain general principles have to be applied in combination with the most intricate technical expertise. As to the former, one may point, for example, to the pi with two equal *hastae* (Π) following upon the Classical and early Hellenistic pi with two unequal *hastae* (Γ'), the alpha with broken cross-bar (Λ) versus the classical A, and the habit of adorning the ends of letters first with slight thickening and later on with heavy horizontal and vertical strokes (*apices*)—the more apices and the thicker, the later the text. As to technical expertise, in recent years fundamental research has begun on the existence of so-called cutters' hands:[7] on the basis of a reasonable corpus of texts from one city or temple and an equally reasonable number of internally dated specimens within that corpus, close study of the lettering leads to the discovery of hands of cutters. Here enormous potential for new research opens up: an area where true scholarly devotion and a sharp, unbiased eye are more in demand than the passion of a historian. So far S. V. Tracy's work has resulted in a firm reshuffling of dates of important and long-known texts.[8] The search for cutters' workshops is paralleled by

a search, especially in *Asia Minor,[9] for workshops which produce funerary reliefs, inscribed or otherwise. Here the focus is iconographical but heavily indebted to epigraphically dated specimens. Cutters' hands become stone-carvers' hands here. One is reminded of a similar development in the realm of painters' workshops in early modern Europe. The great individual artist recedes in favour of a group of masters and apprentices united in several workshops.

Inscriptions often come to us in a mutilated form: either the format of the entire text is preserved but the wear and tear of time has obscured various letters of lines; or part of the stone is missing. In both cases the noble art of restoring illegible passages or half-preserved lines has to be applied. Restorations can be offered only on the basis of parallels. One must be able to recognize certain key terms or expressions which are characteristic of a specific category of texts (e.g. a dedication, an honorary decree for a specific category of people). After having collected a fair sample of unrestored parallel-texts one might be able to offer some suggestions. In other words, restoration of mutilated inscriptions enlarges our dossier of related texts; it does not enlarge our knowledge of ancient phenomena. The great masters of Greek epigraphy—M. Holleaux, A. Wilhelm and L. Robert[10]—have, in their innumerable articles, shaped this *ars restorandi*.[11] Finally, the interpretation of the deciphered and, if possible, restored text must be attempted, i.e. the application of up-to-date knowledge of the larger context of our text. This presupposes a detailed knowledge of the main categories of inscriptions and their local varieties (epitaphs, epigrams, dedications, decrees, royal/imperial letters) and a decent command of what is already known from other sources about specific persons or topics recorded in our text.

The organization of Greek epigraphy is complex and still rather unsatisfactory: apart from isolated attempts at collection in the early modern period, it was under the auspices of the Academy in Berlin that the first efforts were made to present Greek inscriptions systematically. Between 1828 and 1877 A. Boeckh, J. Franz, E. Curtius and A. Kirchhoff published the four big volumes of the *Corpus Inscriptionum Graecarum*, which covered the entire ancient world. The texts were arranged geographically and within each area according to broad general categories: public inscriptions (viz. decrees, catalogues, lists), dedications, and epitaphs; vol. 4 contained the *incerta*, Jewish and Christian texts and the 'small fry' on *instrumenta domestica* (pots, pans, perfume-bottles etc.). Comments were in Latin and majuscle copies of all texts were added to the transcriptions in ordinary Greek. The age of photography was still to come. Elaborate indices facilitated historical research. *CIG* did not escape the fate of all corpora planned over a long period: by the time of its completion it was no longer the complete collection of known Greek texts. A never-ending flow of casual new finds and of impressive excavations (e.g. at Olympia, Delphi, *Epidaurus and Priene) produced inscriptions which remained outside *CIG*. *CIG* remains the only corpus aiming at coverage of the entire Greek-speaking ancient world; after 1877 fragmentation was the rule.

In 1903, on the initiative of U. von Wilamowitz Moellendorff, the Berlin Academy launched a new, and geographically much more limited, corpus: *Inscriptiones Graecae*, which focused on Greece (including the areas on the west and north coasts of the Black Sea (see EUXINE)) and the Aegean islands (with *Crete and *Cyprus). Fifteen volumes were planned; some never appeared; those that did suffered from the same tragic deficiency as noted above for *CIG*. After the Second World War the rhythm of publication slowed down considerably. It was not until 1972 that there appeared a fascicle of *IG* 10 (*Macedonia), devoted to the inscriptions from *Thessalonica. In 1981 and 1993 there appeared a third edition of *IG* 1: an attempt to bring up to date the collection of Archaic and Classical decrees and lists of magistrates from Athens/Attica up to *c*.400 BC. In the mean time 'national' corpora were published by organizations in countries which had engaged on important excavations abroad, or which assumed responsibility for the inscriptions found within their borders. The French school at Athens, responsible for the excavations at Delphi, published in *Fouilles de Delphes* 3 a volume specially devoted to the inscriptions from Delphi; in 1977 an official *Corpus des Inscriptions de Delphes* was launched. It seems doubtful whether *IG* 8, planned to cover Delphi, will ever appear. A similar story can be told for Crete, where the Italians published *Inscriptiones Creticae* in four volumes, so that *IG* 13 will probably remain no more than a mere number. Bulgarian, Romanian, and Russian academies or institutes started their own national corpora: *Inscriptiones Graecae in Bulgaria repertae*, *Inscriptiones Scythiae Minores* in Romania; the Russians after their early *IOSPE* volumes[12] continued with *Corpus Inscriptionum regni Bosporani* (1965). Greek scholars from the Athens Centre de Recherches de l'Antiquité grecque et romaine, under the direction of M. B. Hatzopoulos, are busy preparing a corpus of inscriptions from Macedonia and *Thrace. Preparatory results appear in the Centre's series *Meletemata*. In addition A. Rizakis and G. Touratsoglou have independently published the first volume of inscriptions of Upper Macedonia.[13]

As the above survey suggests, for the Greek Orient (i.e. Turkey, the Levant, Egypt and Cyrenaica (see CYRENE; PENTAPOLIS)) the situation is disastrous: *CIG* is still the only basic corpus! Attempts to provide complete corpora for specific regions are rare. *T(ituli) A(siae) M(inoris)*—a project of the Vienna Academy aiming to cover the whole of Asia Minor—has so far published volumes on parts of *Lycia, *Pisidia, *Bithynia, and *Lydia only.[14] The ten volumes of *MAMA* are not corpora but 'rapports d'exploration' for parts of *Phrygia, *Lycaonia, *Caria, and *Cilicia.[15] In the mean time corpora of a large number of important and epigraphically rich cities have appeared in the impressive series of *Inschriften griechischer Städte aus Kleinasien* (1972–   ).[16] It is doubtful whether in future it will be worth making comprehensive regional corpora including these cities; what remains as suitable subject-matter for corpora are the areas not included in these cities. In the Levant the French series of *Inscriptions grecques et latines de la Syrie* (1929–86) proceeds slowly.[17]

For those who want to have a collection of texts as complete as possible for a specific area or city, there are two indispensable 'instruments de travail' which enable scholars to fill up the gap in the existing corpora. The first is the *Bulletin Épigraphique*, an annual survey in the *Revue des Études grecques* since 1888, and from 1938 to 1984 written by J. and L. Robert.[18] Following a series of specific rubrics (corpus; alphabet; institutions; to name just a few) the epigraphical harvest of a year is presented geographically. The material is briefly discussed; some important words or phrases may be quoted from new texts, but the texts are not presented *in toto*. The basic corpus available for a certain region can be relatively simply updated by going through that region in *BE*. Separate indexes for 1938–77 ('mots grecs'; 'mots français'; a concordance of publications) enormously facilitate the use of this stupendous mass of material; though the indexes by definition only record the words and phenomena which the Roberts saw fit to mention in their summaries.[19] From 1987 onwards a team under the direction of P. Gauthier has continued the *BE*

on the same principles, though perhaps with a less convenient arrangement and with slightly less complete coverage.

Secondly, there is *Supplementum Epigraphicum Graecum*, founded in 1923 by J. J. E. Hondius (vols. 1–10), taken over by A. G. Woodhead in 1951 (vols. 11–25), and continued by H. W. Pleket and R. S. Stroud from 1978 (vols. 26 ff.; vol. 41 appeared in 1994). Up to vol. 20 the number of regions represented in each volume varies; but in the end these twenty volumes together offer fair coverage of all the regions of *CIG*. Vol. 21 is solely dedicated to Attica; vols. 22–5 offer coverage of a limited number of areas up to the year 1969 only. *SEG* presents the complete texts of all new finds, with app. crit. and brief explanatory remarks, but without translation. Between the appearance of vol. 25 (1971) and vol. 26 (1979) there is a gap. Vol. 25 includes material up to 1969, whereas vol. 26 covers the harvest of 1976. With *SEG redivivum* the language changed from Latin to English; the principle remains the same: the presentation of all new texts of a given year, of all new readings and restorations suggested for known texts in that same year, and bibliographical summaries of such articles and books as are heavily concerned with epigraphical material. In addition to the traditional indexes of *SEG* 1–25 (proper names; names of kings and Roman emperors; geographical names; religious words, including names of months), new ones were devised, comprising military terms, important Greek words (a new version of the old *CIG*-rubric *verba notabilia*) and selected topics. Elaborate concordances at the end of each volume enable scholars quickly to update the *status quaestionis* of an inscription. A consolidated index, with concordance, has been published for vols. 26–35.[20] All in all *SEG* 26–41 may be said to cover all the relevant material from 1976 (vol. 26) to 1991 (volume 41). For the 'gap' the *Bulletin Épigraphique* is the sole remedy. In the future, electronic media, above all CD-Rom, will undoubtedly join *BE* and *SEG* for the dissemination of all new evidence; whether these media in the long run will oust the printed material remains to be seen. So far various initiatives have been undertaken in isolation and without much visible impact on historico-epigraphical scholarship.[21]

All the corpora and auxiliary instruments are arranged geographically and within each region according to broad categories of inscriptions: public inscriptions (decrees, catalogues, honorary inscriptions, edicts, and letters), dedications, and the ubiquitous epitaphs. For thematic studies other than regional or urban history, such an arrangement is hardly productive. Thematic corpora do exist but they are rare. 'Thematic' means collections not only of Jewish[22] and Christian[23] inscriptions but above all of texts all pertaining to one smaller or larger historical theme. F. Sokolowski's collection of sacred laws is a case in point: taken together these texts provide magnificent insights into the workings of sanctuaries—their financial operations, the functions and emoluments of priests and other sacred officials, and the prescribed behaviour of the worshippers both in and outside the temple.[24] Robert's corpus of gladiator-inscriptions, by now heavily out of date but easily updated by going through the rubric 'gladiateurs' in *BE*, is another relevant example: by their mere numbers and distribution over time and space, these texts provide the fundamental material for a chapter in the social and cultural history of the Greek cities of the empire, which became wildly enthusiastic about these bloodiest of games.[25]

The content of inscriptions is extremely variable. L. Robert's dictum, that in almost every inscription there is history,[26] is somewhat exaggerated. Thousands of small epitaphs contain nothing more than a few names; and most names are common and trite.

The method of the 'mise en série' is necessary if one's aims are general description and theory-building. Funerary *epigrams and epitaphs with curse- and fine-formulas, when collected and studied as a group, provide valuable insights into views on after-life, popular ethics, and the degree of monetarization of urban and rural areas.[27] Confrontation with the literary sources enables us to identify possibly eccentric views of literary authors. Dedications (the second largest category), temple laws, oracles, prayers, and regulations concerning religious and agonistic festivals (the latter always having a religious component) offer us a wealth of detailed knowledge about the Greek religious mentality, the organization and function of cults, the status of priests and, in general, the place of religion in civic life. Confession inscriptions, typical of Lydia/Phrygia in Asia Minor, inform us about ancient ideas about *sin and the types of human behaviour eliciting divine punishment (often in the form of disease), and ultimately leading to confession of guilt and the erection of a stele (stēlographia).[28]

Outstanding documents, of course, get most publicity and tend to monopolize the attention of the non-initiated. The Attic tribute quota-lists (see TRIBUTE LISTS), the *Gortyn law code, the official autobiography of Augustus in the bilingual *Res gestae, the recent customs law from Ephesus (see PORTORIA), a large dossier of texts concerning *Antiochus (3) III and the city of *Teos, two spectacular long honorary decrees for local politicians and benefactors from *Claros, the very detailed gymnasium law from Macedonian Beroea (see GYMNASIARCH; EDUCATION, GREEK), the philosophical 'catechism' of Epicureanism (see EPICURUS) by *Diogenes (5) of *Oenoanda, *Diocletian's bilingual Price Edict, the dossier concerning the foundation and financing of the Demostheneia in Oenoanda and the preceding negotiations between the founder (C. Iulius Demosthenes) and the local council and assembly:[29] all those texts provide unique information either on periods and topics for which literary sources are relatively abundant, or for more obscure regions for which inscriptions are often the only source, given the fact that nearly all local historiography is lost.

But it is through the 'mise en série' of the smaller texts on a large variety of themes that epigraphy sheds most light on subjects for which the literary sources often provide no more than a general framework. This is true for subjects as unrelated to each other as the thousands of *amphora stamps,[30] which are highly relevant for the organization of amphora production, the involvement of the city, and the vicissitudes of export of oil and wine; the hundreds of artists' signatures (sculptors, vase-painters, with recent emphasis on workshops rather than on one outstanding artist);[31] manumission records (especially those from Delphi and *Buthrotum);[32] texts concerning associations (see CLUBS), professional, cultic and otherwise[33] (highly relevant for the vexed question of whether or not there were 'guilds' in ancient cities and, if so, what was their nature); texts about schools and *gymnasia[34] and thus the *education of Greek youngsters, with its strong emphasis on physical exercise; and texts illuminating the enormous circuit of agonistic *festivals, athletic and musical, and the rise of the professional athlete, his social background and mentality (see AGŌNES; ATHLETICS).[35]

Inscriptions were ubiquitous in ancient cities: in the *agora, in *sanctuaries and in *cemeteries. They were so numerous—and sometimes painted in colours!—that L. Robert once wrote about the Graeco-Roman world as 'a civilization of epigraphy'. In recent times there has been lively study of the relation between the omnipresence of inscribed stones (plus graffiti) and *liter-acy;[36] in addition attention has been drawn to the symbolic value of inscriptions, often so long and occasionally put up so high on a wall that nobody actually could, or probably wanted to, read them. Studies of 'the epigraphic habit' and the reasons for both the growth and decline of inscribed stones under the empire will undoubtedly shed further light on the formation of the political culture and mentality of late antiquity.[37]

Inscriptions function as a sort of '*archive' for the historian. They are not archival documents. In fact they are a selection of the papyrus documents stored in city archives. It is in the Hellenistic-Roman period that city archives became important: not only public documents but also private records were stored (and thereby ratified) in archives.[38] A stock phrase in epitaphs mentioning a monetary fine for offenders is that a copy of the text is kept in the archive of the city. Not all texts stored in archives were inscribed on stone; nor did all the inscribed ones survive the wear and tear of time.[39] So all in all, surviving inscriptions have undergone a double process of selection; through their mere number and the enormous variety in their subject-matter, for the ancient historian they are the equivalent of the more systematically preserved paper archives studied by the medievalist and the early modern historian.

An excellent bibliography can be found in F. Bérard, D. Feissel, P. Petitmengin, and M. Sève, Guide de l'épigraphiste: Bibliographie choisie des épigraphies antiques et médiévales (1986) (abbreviation: Guide).

1. Introductions: A. G. Woodhead, The Study of Greek inscriptions, 2nd edn. (1981); G. Klaffenbach, Griechische Epigraphik, 2nd edn. (1966); L. Robert, 'Épigraphie', in L'Histoire et ses méthodes (Encyclopédie de la Pléiade) (1961), 453–497 (Ger. trans. by H. Engelmann, Die Epigraphik der klassischen Welt (1970)); B. F. Cook, Greek inscriptions (1987). Cf. also Guide 19–20.

2. E. W. Bodnar, Cyriacus of Ancona and Athens (1960); H. J. Erasmus, The Origin of Rome in Historiography from Petrarch to Perizonius (1962), 67 ff. (for Pyrrhonism and Descartes); A. D. Momigliano, 'Ancient history and the antiquarian', in Studies in Historiography (1966), 1 ff.

3. Museum collections: The Collection of Ancient Greek Inscriptions in the British Museum 1–4 (1874–1916); L. Robert, Collection Froehner 1: Inscriptions grecques (1936); E. Breccia, Iscrizioni greche e latine (Alexandria Museum) (1911); J. G. Milne, Greek inscriptions (Cairo Museum) (1905); A. Dain, Inscriptions grecques du Musée du Louvre: Les Textes inédits (1933); H. W. Pleket, The Greek Inscriptions in the 'Rijksmuseum van Oudheden' at Leyden (1958); H. Malay, Greek and Latin Inscriptions in the Manisa Museum (Denkschr. Österr. Akad. Wiss., phil.-hist. Kl. 237; 1994); cf. Guide 128–9.

4. For photographs cf. H. Roehl, Inscriptiones Graecae antiquissimae (1882); Imagines inscr. Graec. antiquiss., 3rd edn. (1907); O. Kern, Inscriptiones Graecae (1913); J. Kirchner, Imagines inscr. Atticarum, 2nd edn. (1948).

5. For the nature of Archaic inscriptions and the problem of Semitic origin cf. SEG 39. 1764; more in general, cf. the rubric 'Alphabet' in the Varia-section of SEG volumes.

6. L. H. Jeffery, The Local Scripts of Archaic Greece, 2nd edn. (1990), with a detailed Suppl. by A. W. Johnston, 423–81.

7. S. V. Tracy, Attic Letter-cutters of 229–86 BC (1990); cf. SEG 40. 295.

8. S. V. Tracy Chiron 1990, 59–96 (on inscriptions from Samos).

9. M. Cremer, Hellenistisch-römische Grabstelen im nordwestlichen Kleinasien 1 (Mysia) and 2 (Bithynia) (1991–2); for workshops in Phrygia cf. SEG 40. 1186 and T. Lochmann, Bulletin du Musée Hongrois des Beaux-Arts 1991, 17–21; for workshops of Rhodian sculptors cf. V. C. Goodlett AJArch. 1991, 669–81.

10. M. Holleaux, Études d'épigraphie et d'histoire grecques 1–4 (1938–68); A. Wilhelm, Kl. Schr. 1–2 (1974–84); cf. Guide 281; L. Robert, Opera Minora Selecta 1–7 (1969–90); for Robert's entire œuvre cf. Guide, Index des auteurs, entry under Robert, Louis.

11. A handsome, short introduction for editors of inscriptions is S. Dow, Conventions in Editing (1969).

12. B. Latyshev, *Inscriptiones antiquae orae septentrionalis Ponti Euxini Graecae et Latinae* 1², 2, 4 (1885–1916).

13. So far 18 volumes have appeared in the *Meletemata* series (1985–94); A. Rizakis and G. Touratsoglou, Ἐπιγραφὲς Ἄνω Μακεδονίας (1985). For an exhaustive list, with full titles, of all the volumes of *CIG*, *IG*, the various national corpora, and sundry smaller additions to specific areas cf. *Guide* 33–74. *Guide* now fully supersedes J. J. F. Hondius, *Saxa Loquuntur* (1938).

14. *Tituli Asiae Minoris* 1–3 (E. Kalinka and R. Heberdey: Lycia, Pisidia, 1901–41); 4. 1 (F. K. Dörner: Nicomedia and the Bithynian peninsula, 1978); 5. 1–2 (P. Herrmann: NE and NW Lydia, 1981–9).

15. *MAMA* 1–10 (1928–93).

16. So far 31 cities have been covered, some in more than one volume.

17. So far appeared *IGLS* 1–2, 3. 1, 3. 2, and 4–5 (by L. Jalabert and R. Mouterde); 6–7 (by J.-P. Rey-Coquais); 8. 3 (by J. F. Breton); 13. 1 (Bostra, by M. Sartre) and 21 (*Inscriptions de la Jordanie 2*, by P.-L. Gatier).

18. The *Bulletins* of 1939–84 have been published together in ten volumes (1972–87).

19. *Index du Bulletin Épigraphique (1938–68)*, pt. 1: *Les mots grecs*; pt. 2: *Les publications*; pt. 3: *Les mots français* (L'Institut Fernand Courby, 1972–5); J. Marcillet-Jaubert and A.-M. Vérilhac, *Index du Bulletin Épigraphique (1966–73)* (1979); J. Marcillet-Jaubert and A.-M. Vérilhac, *Index du Bulletin Épigraphique (1974–77)* (1983). Indexes for the remaining *Bulletins* (1978–84) have been announced but have not appeared so far.

20. H. Roozenbeek, *Supplementum Epigraphicum Graecum: Consolidated Index for volumes 26–35* (= 1976–85) (1990).

21. Cf. *Actes du colloque 'Épigraphie et Informatique, 26–27 Mai 1989, Lausanne'* (1989), for a survey of current computerized programmes.

22. J. B. Frey, *Corpus Inscriptionum Judaicarum*, 2 vols. (1936–52); P. W. van der Horst, *Ancient Jewish Epitaphs* (1991); J. W. van Henten and P. W. van der Horst, *Studies in Early Jewish Epigraphy* (1994); W. Horbury and D. Noy, *Jewish Inscriptions of Graeco-Roman Egypt (with an Index of the Jewish Inscriptions of Egypt and Cyrenaica)* (1992); G. Lüderitz, *Corpus jüdischer Zeugnisse aus der Cyrenaika* (1983); B. Lifshitz, *Donateurs et fondateurs dans les synagogues grecques: Répertoire des dédicaces grecques relatives à la construction et à la réfection des synagogues* (1967). Consultation of the rubric 'inscriptions gréco-juives' in the *Bulletin Épigraphique* provides a quick update.

23. H. Grégoire, *Recueil des inscriptions grecques-chrétiennes d'Asie Mineure* (1922); E. Gibson, *The 'Christians for Christians' inscriptions of Phrygia* (1978); G. Lefebvre, *Recueil des inscriptions grecques-chrétiennes d'Égypte* (1907); N. A. Bees, *Corpus der griechisch-christlichen Inschriften von Hellas* 1. 1 (1941); A. C. Bandy, *The Greek Christian inscriptions of Crete* (1970); V. Besevliev, *Spätgriechische und spätlateinische Inschriften aus Bulgarien* (1964); S. L. Agnello, *Silloge di iscrizioni paleocristiane della Sicilia* (1953); E. Popescu, *Inscriptiile grece ti i latine din secolele IV–XIII discoperite în România* (1976); D. Feissel, *Recueil des inscriptions chrétiennes de Macédoine du III⁰ au VI⁰ siècle*, BCH Suppl. 8 (1983); for a quick update cf. the rubric 'Inscriptions chrétiennes et byzantines' in the *Bulletin Épigraphique*.

24. F. Sokolowski, *LSAM*; *LSCG*; *LSS*.

25. L. Robert, *Les Gladiateurs dans l'Orient grec* (1940). Other thematic corpora include: F. G. Maier, *Griechische Mauerbauinschriften*, 2 vols. (1959–60); A.-M. Vérilhac, ΠΑΙΔΕΣ ΑΩΡΟΙ: *Poésie funéraire*, 2 vols. (1978–82); *Def. tab.* Audollent.

26. L. Robert, *Opera Minora Selecta* 6 (1989), 591 n. 5.

27. On curses cf. J. H. M. Strubbe, in C. Faraone and D. Obbink (eds.), *Magika Hiera: Ancient Greek Magic and Religion* (1991), 33–59; cf. also his article on curses in Jewish epitaphs in J. W. van Henten and P. W. van der Horst, *Studies in Early Jewish Epigraphy* (1994), 70–127.

28. G. Petzl, *Die Beichtinschriften Westkleinasiens* (1994).

29. B. D. Meritt, H. T. Wade-Gery, and M. F. McGregor, *The Athenian Tribute Lists* (*ATL*) 1–4 (1939–53); B. D. Meritt and A. B. West, *The Athenian Assessment of 425 BC* (1934); R. F. Willetts, *The Law Code of Gortyn* (1967); E. G. Hardy, *The Monumentum Ancyranum* (1923); for the Ephesian customs law cf. *SEG* 39 (1992), 1180; for Antiochus III and Teos cf. *SEG* 41 (1994), 'Teos'; J. and L. Robert, *Claros* 1: *Décrets hellén-*istiques (1989; cf. *SEG* 39. 1243–4); P. Gauthier and M. B. Hatzopoulos, *La loi gymnasiarchique de Beroia* (1993); Diogenes-inscription: ed. M. F. Smith (1993), with comm. and trans.; S. Lauffer, *Diokletians Preisedikt* (1971); M. Wörrle, *Stadt und Fest im kaiserzeitlichen Kleinasien: Studien zu einer agonistischen Stiftung aus Oinoanda* (1988).

30. J.-Y. Empereur and Y. Garlan (eds.), *Recherches sur les amphores grecques. Actes du Coll. internationale, Athènes 10–12 Septembre 1984*, BCH Suppl. 13 (1986); cf. also J.-Y. Empereur and Y. Garlan, 'Bulletin archéologique: Amphores et timbres amphoriques', *Rev. Ét. Grec.* 1987, 58–109.

31. J. Marcadé, *Recueil des signatures de sculpteurs grecs* (1953); D. Viviers, *Recherches sur les ateliers de sculpteurs et la cité d'Athènes à l'époque archaïque: Endoios, Philergos, Aristoclès* (Acad. Royale de Belgique, Cl. des Beaux-Arts; 1992).

32. K. Hopkins, 'Between Slavery and Freedom: On Freeing Slaves at Delphi', in *Conquerors and Slaves* (1978); P. Cabanes, 'Les Inscriptions du théâtre de Bouthrôtos', in *Actes Colloque 1972 sur l'esclavage* (1974), 105–209.

33. J. P. Waltzing, *Étude historique sur les corporations professionelles chez les Romains depuis les origines jusqu'à la chute de l'empire occident* 3: *Recueil des inscriptions* (1899); F. Poland, *Geschichte des griechischen Vereinswesens* (1909).

34. M. P. Nilsson, *Die Hellenistische Schule* (1955); C. Pélékidis, *Histoire de l'éphébie attique des origines à 31 avant J.-C.* (1962).

35. For Greek agonistic inscriptions cf. L. Moretti, *Iscrizioni agonistiche greche* (1953).

36. W. V. Harris, *Ancient Literacy* (1989); J. H. Humphrey (ed.), *Literacy in the Roman World*, JRA Suppl. 3 (1991).

37. R. MacMullen, 'The Epigraphic Habit in the Roman Empire', *AJPhil.* 1982, 233–46.

38. For the increasing importance of city archives in the Hellenistic period cf. M. Wörrle, *Chiron* 1983, 283–368.

39. Cf. G. Klaffenbach, *Bemerkungen zur griechischen Urkundenwesen* (*Sitz. Akad. Berlin*, Kl. f. Sprachen, 1960. 6). H. W. Pl.

epigraphy, Latin, the study of Latin texts inscribed on durable objects, usually of stone or bronze. It is concerned both with the form of the inscriptions and with their content, and so impinges on many other fields, e.g. art history, palaeography, philology, history, law, religion. It excludes, but cannot ignore, texts on coins and gems; it has a strong interest in Greek inscriptions of the Roman period; it includes some texts written with paint or pen and ink (see e.g. AMPHORAE AND AMPHORA STAMPS, ROMAN).

2. The epigraphist must first decipher all that can be read on the inscribed object, however much damaged it is and then, where possible, propose restorations of what is illegible or lost: processes for which modern techniques, such as computer-enhanced photographs and computerized indices of formulae, are currently supplementing long-standing aids, such as photographs taken in raking lights and squeezes (impressions made with absorbent paper or latex). The resulting text can then be interpreted as a historical document.

3. The first-known collection of transcribed Latin inscriptions was made c. AD 800 and preserved in MS at Einsiedeln. On this, as on subsequent collections made by early antiquaries, and on artists' drawings of ancient monuments, we rely for knowledge of many lost texts. Serious study began in the 18th cent., among its outstanding early exponents being Bartolommeo Borghesi; a great advance was made in the 19th, with the plan for a complete corpus of Latin inscriptions, undertaken in Germany, chiefly, on the intiative of Th. Mommsen. That is still in progress but current collections are commonly compiled and published on a national basis.

4. The reputed oldest of all Latin inscriptions, a maker's label on a gold fibula from Praeneste of the late 7th cent. BC (*ILS* 8561), is now thought by some scholars to be a 19th-cent. forgery; the

oldest on stone is a religious regulation on a stone marker from the forum Romanum, probably of the mid-6th cent. (*ILS* 4913). Examples are scarce before the 3rd cent., not common before the 2nd; the majority are early imperial, but they continue to the end of the ancient world, and after. They come from all parts of the Roman empire and occasionally beyond it, and are particularly valuable in providing evidence from the provinces as well as from Rome and Italy; although the yield from the eastern provinces is small, that from the west, especially Africa, is large. New examples are constantly accruing, but what we have is an accidentally-found fraction of the original total, which itself was the product of restricted sections of the population of the Roman world; it is not to be taken as representative of Roman society as a whole.

5. The texts may be formal documents such as laws, treaties, legal contracts, wills (*acta*), or records of individuals and their activities (*tituli*), whether inscribed in their honour, at their commission, or, quite casually, by themselves (*graffiti*); epitaphs form the largest single group (see EPIGRAM, LATIN). The earliest show the *Latin language at a date well before any surviving literature, the later its development in everyday usage. They can give information on governmental policy and administration, on persons and events, and on many aspects of life and thought on which the literary sources are silent or inadequate. The cumulative evidence even of trivial examples may be enlightening; and any text may prove more informative than it appears, if it is considered in its archaeological context. Something of the range may be summarily indicated as follows.

(*a*) Public *acta*, a comparatively small category, since important documents were often inscribed on bronze which was later melted down (but some bronzes have survived, particularly in Italy and Spain), include a series of laws of the republic and early empire, e.g. a judiciary law which may be that of C. *Sempronius Gracchus and the *Lex de imperio Vespasiani* (*FIRA* 1. 84 f.; 154 f.); some *senatus consulta*, e.g. much of the *s.c. de Bacchanalibus* of 186 BC (*ILS* 18), and several recently discovered senatorial proposals for *post mortem* honours to *Germanicus (*AE* 1984. 508); and many magisterial documents, especially edicts, letters, rescripts, and public speeches of emperors (cf. *ILS* 206, 423, 705, 212). Also noteworthy are the *fasti* of consuls, local magistrates, and triumphing generals (*Inscr. Ital.* 13. 1) which clarify the chronological framework of Roman history, and the calendars (*Inscr. Ital.* 13. 2), essential to the study of official Roman religion. For the inscribed autobiography of Augustus, see RES GESTAE.

(*b*) The *tituli* of men in public life (*ILS* 1 f., 862 f.) present members of the administrative personnel of Rome, provide lists of the offices and achievements of individuals, often otherwise unknown, and tell something of the official in action, his social and personal background, his overt ideals and ambitions (cf. the Scipionic epitaphs, *ILS* 1–7). Taken as a whole, they show developments in the administrative system: for example, from the simple career of a republican senator to its complex imperial counterpart in which the magistracies may be a minor element in a string of appointments created by emperors (see CAREERS, ROMAN); they illustrate the creation of new provinces, the emergence of the equestrian civil service and that of the imperial slaves and freedmen; they contain details indicative, for instance, of increasing recruitment of officials from the provinces, or of significant connections between families in public life. Laudatory inscriptions also indicate the honours and titles accorded to, and the qualities admired in, public men at different periods. Imperial

inscriptions provide evidence for the titles of emperors and for their policies and propaganda.

(*c*) Local government is illustrated by inscriptions containing municipal charters like the recently discovered *lex Irnitana* (*AE* 1986. 333), careers of municipal officials, decrees of local authorities, records of public works and services, with some details of their finances (often supplied by private generosity), occasionally, as at *Pompeii, election notices (*ILS* 6044 f.).

(*d*) Military affairs appear in the inscriptions of units and individual soldiers (*ILS* 1986 f.) which throw light on the organization and deployment of all branches of the armed forces. They reflect in general on foreign policy, and in detail on sources of recruitment, terms of service, lines of promotion, the religious and other interests of the men, relations with civilians, and prospects on demobilization, especially the prospect of Roman citizenship for men in auxiliary units, for which virtually all our information derives from military *diplomata* (*CIL* 16); see DIPLOMA. Two series of handwritten texts, (1) the *Vindolanda tablets, on wooden leaves, (2) on ostraka from Gholaia (Bu Ngem) in Tripolitania, are currently adding remarkable insights into camp life in these forts for the short periods to which they refer.

(*e*) Religion is the subject of some formal documents of type (*a*) above, e.g. regulations for sanctuaries and temples (*ILS* 4906 f.), Calendars of festivals, accounts of official ceremonies such as the Augustan and Severan Secular Games (*ILS* 5050, 5050*a*) and the *acta* of the *fratres arvales (*ILS* 5026 f.). There are also many dedications to many deities, a striking demonstration of the effort and expenditure continuously invested in Roman religion. Something can be seen from them, for instance, of the character of particular cults, the survival of some older cults, the introduction of new ones like ruler-cult or Mithraism, and the interaction of Roman with local cults. Recent large finds of lead curse-tablets (R. Tomlin and D. Walker, *The Temple of Sulis Minerva at Bath* 2, 1988) have stimulated interest in these widespread devices for harnessing divine power to the dedicators' interests in recovery of property, success in love, victory in the races, etc. (*ILS* 8746).

(*f*) Social institutions can sometimes be vividly illustrated: for example, the numbers of specialized servants in the house of a Roman noble (S. Treggiari, *PBSR* 1975, 48 f.), the activities of *clubs (*collegia*), especially those whose members included tradesmen (*ILS* 7212 f.), the delights of public baths (*ILS* 5664 f.), the popular types of entertainment, with their performers and fans (*ILS* 5051 f.), the lives and relationships of ordinary families (*ILS* 7366 f.), including those of slaves and freedmen, social gradings, social mobility, and ages at marriage and death (unfortunately not productive of valid statistics). More generally the spread of urbanization and *Romanization is reflected in the use of inscriptions itself, the use of Latin, the presence or absence of inscriptions in local languages, inscribed public buildings, references to local government, and changing styles of nomenclature; indeed the whole history of nomenclature, with its ethnic, social, and political implications, is heavily dependent on epigraphy (see NAMES, PERSONAL, ROMAN). Currently inscriptions are being used in debate on the extent of *literacy in the Roman world; but it is not easy to assess how many people actually read them, how many illiterates heard them read by others (cf. *Supplementa Italica* 1988, 78–84), and, in either case, on how many occasions.

(*g*) Economic life is casually, but quite frequently, indicated by references to crafts and trades, for example, occasionally to such matters as taxation, rents, costs of buildings, and, in Diocletian's Price Edict, of a wide range of goods and services; with that a Diocletianic edict concerned with currency revaluation must now be associated (C. M. Roueché, *Aphrodisias in Late Antiquity*, ch. 12). In some areas, tablets, like those of a banker/auctioneer at Pompeii, *Caecilius Iucundus, briefly illuminate a particular activity in some detail. More clues to the operations of industries and commerce seem to be offered by the texts classed in collections of inscriptions as *instrumentum*—stamps (see e.g. BRICKSTAMPS (ROMAN)), signatures, marks, and other messages on many manufactured goods, on metal ingots or blocks of marble, and painted or penned texts relating for instance to the contents of amphorae or to kiln-loads (cf. W. V. Harris (ed.), *The Inscribed Economy*, 1993); their interpretation, however, is not always straightforward.

(*h*) Christian inscriptions begin as a group hardly, if at all, differentiated from the pagan texts of their time, but develop formulas and other features of their own, especially after the Peace of the Church. The earlier texts are often ordinary tombstones or pilgrims' *graffiti* (cf. Kaufmann, *Handbuch* (see bibliog. below), 303 f.). Later they include more ambitious items, such as building inscriptions for churches. The set of verse *elogia* on popes and martyrs, written by Pope *Damasus (366–84) and finely cut by *Filocalus in letters which may have been especially designed for the purpose, form a landmark in this development of a specifically Christian epigraphic tradition (Kaufmann, *Handbuch* 327 f.). They show something of early Christian society, the organization of the Church, the survival of pagan features, and the emergence of new ideas, including heresies.

6. Most inscriptions were incised. The more important were cut with care, and, from the late republic onwards, often with art; lines and letters were painted onto the surface (sometimes lightly chiselled), in the more formal cases with mechanical aids, otherwise free-hand; the width and depth of strokes, occasionally also the height, were varied with a view both to legibility and to aesthetics; there was careful attention to the layout and proportions of the text in relation to the context. Incised letters on stone might be picked out in red, on bronze in white. Other methods were, for example, to fix metal letters to stone by pegs (such letters rarely survive, but see *ILS* 4921*b* for a reference to them in a temple inventory; texts may be deducible from the positions of the peg-holes), to insert letters formed of strips of metal, coloured marble, or mosaic tesserae, to paint them, or to write them with pen and ink.

7. The letters (see ALPHABETS OF ITALY) were originally very like those of the archaic Greek alphabet in Italy. By the early imperial period, cutters had developed (*a*) the formal Latin capital (*scriptura monumentalis, litterae lapidariae, litterae quadratae*), a carefully designed lettering, beautifully adapted to a monumental context and well illustrated on the base of *Trajan's Column; (*b*) a less formal alphabet based on the brush-painted letters of ephemeral public notices (best-known from Pompeian walls), used mainly for private but also for some minor public texts (Rustic capitals); (*c*) a small neat capital (*scriptura actuaria*) presumably derived from a formal pen-hand, and suited for recording long documents, e.g. laws. Rounded letters (*scriptura uncialis*), borrowed from the forms used on papyri and parchments, appear on stone from the 3rd cent. AD, and the cursive hand in common use is frequent at all dates in *graffiti*, in waxed tablets such as those found at Pompeii (*CIL* 4. 3340 f.), and occasionally on stone-cut texts of a crude type.

8. In addition the cutters used signs: (*a*) stops between words and phrases (occasionally syllables), in the form of round dots, squares, triangles, and, later, more elaborate shapes like ivy-leaves (*hederae distinguentes*); (*b*) from the Sullan age to the mid-

3rd cent. AD, the *apex*, recalling an acute accent, to mark vowels long by nature; (*c*) from the end of the republic, the superscript bar to mark abbreviations. There was no uniformity of practice in the use of such signs and cutters often misplaced them, being more interested in their decorative value than their significance. For figures, see NUMBERS, ROMAN.

9. Of the cutters we know little, but there are workshop advertisements from Panormus (*ILS* 7680) and Rome (*ILS* 7679); a few signatures, like those of Aemilius Celer who painted notices at Pompeii (ILS 5145) or *Filocalus (*ILCV* 963); and some references to the craft on tombstones.

10. The drafts from which the cutters worked were no doubt sometimes written in cursive letters and difficult to read, which may account for some nonsensical letter-groups in inscriptions. The existence of virtually identical, but quite elaborate funerary texts at widely distant places (cf. *ILS* 2082 from Rome and 2257 from Burnum) may suggest the existence of handbooks from which an unimaginative client might choose a text. In addition there was heavy use of conventional formulas in all inscriptions and this often makes it possible to restore damaged texts with reasonable probability. Restored letters are conventionally printed within square brackets [   ].

11. Most texts were composed with great brevity, though a trend to verbosity is apparent in the 4th cent. AD. Space was also saved by abbreviating words, often drastically, by ligaturing letters and, sometimes, by using *sigla* (e.g. 7 = centurion), all of which present difficulties to the modern reader (most handbooks list those in common use). The resolutions of abbreviations and *sigla* are conventionally printed within round brackets (   ).

12. Some inscriptions are precisely dated by the consular year or an emperor's tribunician year, and even by the day of the month; others can be assigned within more or less exact chronological *termini* on grounds of content, for instance prosopography, the use of a particular title, formula, or spelling, and occasionally of the material on which they appear; thus, *marble is rare in Rome before the end of the republic. Letter-forms may be an approximate guide, but are inevitably a subjective one, and liable to mislead because of the idiosyncrasies or gaucheries of the cutters.

On all aspects and for up to date listing of new corpora and selections of inscriptions, see now F. Bérard and others, *Guide de l'épigraphiste*, 2nd edn. (1989), with supplement published 1990. The list given below is very limited in scope.

INTRODUCTORY F. Millar, in M. Crawford (ed.), *The Sources of History* (1983), ch. 2; A. E. Gordon, *Illustrated Introduction to Latin Epigraphy* (1983); G. Susini, *The Roman Stonecutter* (1973), *Epigrafia romana* (1982); L. Keppie, *Understanding Latin Inscriptions* (1991); H. P. V. Nunn, *Christian Inscriptions* (1952).

HANDBOOKS R. Cagnat, *Cours d'épigraphie latine*, 4th edn. (1914); J. E. Sandys, *Latin Epigraphy*, 2nd edn. (rev. S. G. Campbell, 1927); I. Calabi Limentani, *Epigrafia latina* (1968); O. Marucchi, *Christian Epigraphy* (1912); C. M. Kaufmann, *Handbuch der altchristlichen Epigraphik* (1917).

REFERENCE E. de Ruggiero and others, *Dizionario epigrafico di antichità romane* (1886–   ); O. Gradenwitz, *Laterculi Vocum Latinarum* (1904; repr. 1966), includes a reverse index of Latin words which gives invaluable help with damaged texts.

ILLUSTRATION F. Ritschl, *Priscae latinitatis monumenta epigraphica ad archetyporum fidem . . . repraesentata* (1862); E. Hübner, *Exempla scripturae epigraphicae latinae e Caesaris morte ad aetatem Iustiniani* (1885); A. E. and J. S. Gordon, *Album of Dated Latin Inscriptions, Rome and the Neighbourhood* 1: *Augustus to Nerva* (1958), 2: *AD 100–199* (1964), 3: *AD 200–525* (1965); A. Degrassi, *ILLRP, Imagines* (1965).

PALAEOGRAPHY J. Mallon, *Paléographie romaine* (1952), and

CRAcad. Inscr. 1955, 126 f.; L. Robert, ibid. 195 f.; J. S. and A. E. Gordon, *Contributions to the Palaeography of Latin Inscriptions* (1957).

CORPORA *Corpus Inscriptionum Latinarum* (*CIL*) (1863–) is basic, but often now incomplete and in serious need of revision: vol. 1, which has been reissued in revised form (*CIL* 1², 2), contains all republican inscriptions; vol. 16 all military *diplomata*; vol. 17 milestones; vol. 18 (in preparation) verse texts, regardless of provenance; the rest are arranged geographically—2 Spain; 3 provinces of Asia and the Levant, Greek-speaking provinces of Africa and Europe, Illyricum; 4 Pompeii, Herculaneum, Stabiae; 5 Cisalpine Gaul; 6 City of Rome; 7 Britain; 8 Africa; 9 Calabria, Apulia, Samnium, Sabini, Picenum; 10 Bruttium, Lucania, Campania, Sicily, Sardinia; 11 Aemilia, Etruria, Umbria; 12 Narbonese Gaul; 13 the Three Gauls and Germany; 14 Latium; 15 City of Rome (*instrumentum domesticum*); volumes are brought up to date by supplements from time to time; but for most volumes it is now necessary to look for subsequent and separate publications (see *Guide de l'épigraphiste* cited above); thus for vol. 6 it is essential to consult the series *Tituli*, for all other Italian volumes the two series *Inscriptiones Italiae* (1931–) and *Supplementa Italica* (1981–); while vol. 7 is completely superseded by R. G. Collingwood, R. P. Wright, and others, *The Roman Inscriptions of Britain* (*RIB*) 1 (1965), 2. 1 (1990), 2. 2 (1991), 2. 3 (1991), 2. 4 (1992).

RUNNING RECORDS (newly published inscriptions and epigraphic work). *L'Année Épigraphique* (*AE*), published separately and, from 1888 to 1961, in *Rev. Arch.*; for Roman Britain only in *JRS* from 1921 to 1969 and subsequently in *Britannia*; cf. also an approximately quinquennial survey of inscriptions relevant to Roman Studies by J. M. Reynolds and others in *JRS* (1960–).

SELECTIONS The basic ones are H. Dessau, *Inscriptiones Latinae Selectae* (*ILS*) (1892–1916); A. Degrassi, *Inscriptiones latinae liberae reipublicae* (*ILLRP*) (1957–63); E. Diehl, *Inscriptiones latinae Christianae veteres* (*ILCV*) (1925–31), with supplements ed. J. Moreau (1961), H. I. Marrou (1967), and A. Ferrua (1981). There are also very many shorter selections by theme, some of them with the texts in translation, for which see *Guide de l'épigraphiste* ch. 6. J. M. R.

Epilycus, a Greek comic poet of uncertain date. His Κωραλίσκος (a Cretan word for 'Youth') contained an anapaestic (see METRE, GREEK) passage in Doric (fr. 4).

FRAGMENTS Kassel–Austin, *PCG* 5. 170–3, although earlier scholars use the numbering in Kock, *CAF* 1 803 f. INTERPRETATION Meineke, *FCG* 1. 269; G. Kaibel, *RE* 6/1 (1907), 158 f. 'Epilykos' 3. W. G. A.

epimelētēs, 'one who takes care' (Greek). In Greek cities this title was given either to regular magistrates who managed special departments, such as the water supply (ἐπιμελητὴς τῶν κρηνῶν, 'of fountains', in Athens), the docks, or festivals, or to special commissioners appointed for some temporary purpose, such as the erection of a public building. A. H. M. J.; P. J. R.

Epimenides, of Crete, holy man of the late 7th cent. BC, supposed to have been called in to purify Athens after the sacrilege of the *Cylon affair (*Ath. pol.* 1); Plato, however, puts him a century later (*Leg.* 642d). As in the case of *Aristeas, any genuine traditions were quickly obscured by legends and miraculous tales, such as those of his great age (157 or 299 years), his out-of-the-body experiences, the boyhood nap from which he awoke to discover that 57 years had elapsed (Diog. Laert. 1. 109) or the *asceticism which enabled him to survive on an appetite-suppressant of his own devising (Plut. *Mor.* 157d). Many early epic works were attached to his name, including oracles, a *Theogony*, and an Argonautic poem.

DK 3; *FGrH* 457. E. R. Dodds, *The Greeks and the Irrational* (1951), ch. 7; J. Svenbro, *Phrasikleia* (1988), ch. 7. A. H. G.

epinician poetry, victory odes for athletes and equestrian victors; see AGONES; BACCHYLIDES; PINDAR; SIMONIDES.

Epiphanius, *c.* AD 315–403, born in Eleutheropolis, Palestine. He became a monk, and in 367 bishop of *Salamis (2) (Constantia) in Cyprus. Regarding *Origen (1) as the source of *Arianism, he attacked both in his *Ancoratus* (373) and *Panarion* (374–6), which includes the chief Greek philosophies among its 80 heresies. Ignorant and suspicious of Greek culture, he feared that *allegory would deny the historicity of Scripture and the resurrection of the body. Nevertheless his *De gemmis* and *De mensuris et ponderibus* allow typology, the latter being also an important source on Greek versions of the Old Testament.

Ed. K. Holl, 3 vols. (1915–33; completed 1980); R. P. Blake and H. de Vis, *Epiphanius, De Gemmis* (1934). W. Schneemelcher, *RAC* 5 (1961), 909 f; A. Pourkier, *L'Hérésiologie chez Épiphanie de Salamine* (1992). H. C.; M. J. E.

epiphany occurs in both myth and cult when a god reveals his presence or manifests his power to a mortal or group of mortals, who 'see' or 'recognize' the god. Gods may appear in anthropomorphic form (as extraordinarily beautiful or larger than life; in the likeness of their cult statue; or disguised as ordinary mortals), as a disembodied voice, or as animals. Divine epiphanies take the form of waking or *dream visions; they may be accompanied by miracles or other displays of power (ἀρεταί), be protective or punitive; they may be sudden and spontaneous, or occur in response to a prayer. The concept is much older than the term (Hdt. 3. 27. 3; *SIG*³ 398. 17, 278 BC). As early as the Minoan period, scenes of divine epiphany in cultic settings appear on seal rings. From Homer onwards, epiphany scenes constitute an essential element of epic narrative (Athena in *Il.* 1, *Od.*, and *Meropis* fr. 3 Bernabé) and hymnic poetry (self-revelation of *Demeter, *Aphrodite, and *Dionysus in their respective *Hymn. Hom.*; Callim. *Hymns* 2, 5, 6). Stage epiphanies are more frequent in tragedy (Athena in Aesch. *Eum.* and Soph. *Aj.*; *deus ex machina* in Eur.; Dionysus in *Bacch.*) than comedy (Ar. *Ran.*, cf. *Plut.*; divine prologues in *Menander (1) and *Plautus). From the 4th cent. onwards, epiphany emerges increasingly as a function of cult: an example is *SIG*³ 1151/*IG* 2². 4326, a dedication to *Athena consequent on an epiphany. Throughout the Hellenistic period, collections of divine epiphanies promoted faith and served religious propaganda in the cults of such gods as *Asclepius (*Iamata* of *Epidaurus, *IG* 4. 1². 121–4; Aelius *Aristides' *Hieroi Logoi*, based on his diary of the god's visitations), *Apollo (Istrus, *FGrH* 334 F 50–52), Athena (Lindian temple chronicle, *FGrH* 532 D), as well as Isis and *Sarapis (Totti nos. 11 and 19). In contrast to the importance of omens (see PORTENTS), epiphany is not a feature of Roman state religion. But Roman poets and historians freely adapted Greek epiphanic conventions. Separate trajectories lead from divine epiphany to *ruler-cult, from the ἐποπτεία ('watching') of the Eleusinian *mysteries to the sublimation of epiphany in *Neoplatonism, and from the pagan concept of divine self-manifestation to Christian and *Gnostic forms of revelation.

F. Pfister, *RE* Suppl. 4 (1924), 277–323, 'Epiphanie'; Burkert, *GR* 40–4, 186–8; R. Lane Fox, *Pagans and Christians* (1986), 102–67, 700–11; H. S. Versnel, *Ter Unus* (1990), 190–6. Cf. A. D. Nock, *Essays* (1972), 1. 152–6 (ἐπιφανής as applied to deified kings); A. Henrichs, *Harv. Stud.* 1978, 203 ff. (on Hor. *Carm.* 2. 19 Bacchum ... vidi); M. Totti, *Ausgewählte Texte der Isis- und Sarapis-Religion* (1985). A. H.

Epirus ("Ηπειρος, 'Mainland'), north-west area of Greece, from Acroceraunian point to *Nicopolis (3), with harbours at *Buthrotum and Glycys Limen (at *Acheron's mouth); bordered on south by gulf of Ambracia, and on east by Pindus range with pass via Metsovo to Thessaly. Three limestone ranges parallel to the coast and the Pindus range enclose narrow valleys and plateaux with good pasture and extensive woods; alluvial plains were formed near Buthrotum, Glycys Limen, and Ambracia. Epirus had a humid climate and cold winters. In terrain and in history it resembled Upper Macedonia. Known in the *Iliad* (see HOMER) only for the oracle at *Dodona, and to *Herodotus (1) for the oracle of the dead at *Ephyra, Epirus received Hellenic influence from the Elean colonies in Cassopaea and the Corinthian colonies at *Ambracia and *Corcyra, and the oracle at Dodona drew pilgrims from northern and central Greece especially. *Theopompus (3) knew fourteen Epirote tribes, speakers of a strong west-Greek dialect, of which the Chaones held the plain of Buthrotum, the Thesproti the plain of Acheron, and the Molossi the plain near Dodona, which forms the highland centre of Epirus with an outlet southwards to Ambracia. A strong Molossian state, which included some Thesprotian tribes, existed in the reign of Neoptolemus c.370–368 BC (Ἀρχ. Ἐφ. 1956, 1 ff.). The unification of Epirus in a symmachy led by the Molossian king was finally achieved by *Alexander (6), brother-in-law of *Philip (1) II of Macedon. His conquests in southern Italy and his alliance with Rome showed the potentialities of the Epirote Confederacy, but he was killed in 330 BC. Dynastic troubles weakened the Molossian state, until *Pyrrhus removed his fellow king and embarked on his adventurous career. The most lasting of his achievements were the conquest of southern Illyria, the development of Ambracia as his capital, and the building of fortifications and theatres, especially the large one at Dodona. His successors suffered from wars with Aetolia, Macedon, and Illyria, until in c.232 BC the Molossian monarchy fell. An Epirote League with a federal citizenship was then created, and the meetings of its council were held probably by rotation at Dodona or Passaron in Molossis, at Gitana in Thesprotis, and at Phoenice in Chaonia. It was soon involved in the wars between Rome and Macedon, and it split apart when the Molossian state alone supported Macedon and was sacked by the Romans in 167 BC, when 150,000 captives were deported (see CHAROPS). Central Epirus never recovered; but northern Epirus prospered during the late republican period, and Augustus celebrated his victory at *Actium by founding a Roman colony at Nicopolis. Under the empire a coastal road and a road through the interior were built from north to south, and Buthrotum was a Roman colony. Ancient remains testify to the great prosperity of Epirus in Hellenistic times. See CHAONES; MOLOSSI; THESPROTI.

C. Carapanos, *Dodone et ses ruines* (1878); S. I. Dakaris, *Archaeological Guide to Dodona* (1971; Gk. 1986); P. R. Franke, *Die antiken Munzen von Epirus* (1961); Hammond, *Epirus*; P. Cabanes, *L'Épire de la mort de Pyrrhos à la conquête romaine* (1976); excavation reports in ΠΑΕ Ἔργον, *Studia Albanica*, and *Iliria*; P. Cabanes (ed.), *L'Illyrie méridionale et l'Épire dans l'antiquité* (1993). N. G. L. H.

epistatēs, 'chairman' (Greek). At Athens the *epistatēs* of the *prytaneis, chosen daily by lot from the *prytaneis*, held the state seal and keys and in the 5th cent. BC with his colleagues presided in the council (*boulē) and assembly (*ekklēsia). The *proedroi who early in the 4th cent. took over the duty of presiding likewise had their *epistatēs*. Other Greek states sometimes have an *epistatēs* like the Athenian, sometimes use *epistatai* as the title of a board like the *prytaneis*. In the Hellenistic kingdoms the title *epistatēs* is given to an agent of the king within a subject city, who exercises considerable power. A. H. M. J.; P. J. R.

Epistle to Diognetus, Greek Christian apology of uncertain authorship, date (perhaps 3rd cent. AD), and provenance (perhaps

*Alexandria (1)). It contains an exposition of the Christian doctrine of God, of the Christian life in the world, and of the reasons for and the time of the salvation of the sinner brought about by the coming of the Son of God. The ending (chs. 11–12) is perhaps secondary.

Ed. (with Ger. trans.) K. Wengst, *Schriften des Urchristentums 2: Didache (Apostellehre), Barnabasbrief, Zweiter Klemensbrief, Schrift an Diognet* (1984); Eng. trans. A. Roberts, J. Donaldson, and A. Cleveland Coxe, *The Ante-Nicene Fathers: Translations of the Writings of the Fathers down to AD 325* 1 (1886; repr. 1979), 25–30. S. Zincone, *EEC* 1 (1992), 237.
W. K.

Epitadeus, putative Spartan *ephor. According to Plutarch, *Agis* 5, he introduced, some time after the *Peloponnesian War, a law authorizing the gift or bequest of *property, thereby undermining the equality of Spartan landholding. The law's context has been subject to various interpretations, including attempts to identify Epitadeus with the lawgiver to whom *Aristotle (*Pol. 2. 1270ᵃ) ascribes the rules concerning all forms of alienation, and even (rather implausibly) with an officer (Epitadas) killed in 425 BC. An increasingly common view is that Epitadeus and his law were invented, perhaps following a Platonic model (see PLATO (1)), by supporters of the late 3rd-cent. reforming kings to 'explain' the corruption of the similarly fictional 'Lycurgan equality' (see LYCURGUS (2)) which they claimed to be restoring. Gift and bequest were probably traditional rights; the latter is attested historically c.400 BC, before Plutarch's dating for Epitadeus.

E. Schütrumpf, *GRBS* 1987, 441–57; S. Hodkinson, *CQ* 1986, 378–406; D. Asheri, *Athenaeum* 1961, 45–68; J. Christien, *RHDFE* 1974, 197–221.
S. J. Ho.

epitaphios (logos), a funeral speech, delivered, according to Athenian custom, by a citizen chosen on grounds of intellect and distinction (Thuc. 2. 34, perhaps just a way of introducing *Pericles (1)), at a public funeral of those who had fallen in battle. This practice, said to have been unique to Athens (Dem. 20. 141) and arguably introduced 464 BC, was continued into Roman times and was clearly a solemn and important occasion. But before *Hyperides the only certain names of speakers chosen are those of Pericles in 440 (Plut. *Per.* 8) and 431, *Demosthenes (2) after the battle of *Chaeronea (338), and Archinus at some date in between.

The conventional form comprised: tribute to the virtues of the dead, sometimes with particular reference to their youth; summary of their country's glorious achievements in the past (especially in the *Persian Wars); *consolation to relatives; and exhortation to the survivors to imitate their virtues. *Thucydides (2) (2. 35–46) purports to give in full the Funeral Speech delivered by Pericles at the end of the first year of the *Peloponnesian War, but this speech may have been idiosyncratic in its concentration on the Athens of the present and its silence on the after-life (contrast Hyp. 6. 35 ff. and [Dem]. 60. 33 f.; Lys. 2. 80 is closer to Thuc. in merely speaking vaguely about immortality).

As a contrast to the impersonal austerity of Pericles we have the speech of Hyperides on the general *Leosthenes (a personal friend) and the other dead of the *Lamian War (322 BC). *Lycurgus (3) *Leoc.* 39–40 is in effect a condensed *epitaphios* to the *Chaeronea dead. In addition we have a florid fragment by *Gorgias (1) (DK 82 B 5–6); *Lysias 2, which may be genuinely Lysianic (differences from other Lysianic speeches may be due to differences of genre); and Demosthenes 60 (not genuinely Demosthenic). Finally *Socrates in [Plato] *Menexenus* recites a funeral speech implausibly said to have been composed by

epithalamium

*Aspasia for delivery by Pericles. See LAUDATIO FUNEBRIS.

G. Kennedy, *The Art of Persuasion in Greece* (1963), 154 ff.; F. Jacoby, *JHS* 1944, 37 ff. (= *Abhandlungen* 260 ff.); K. Dover, *Lysias* (1968), 61–7 and *Greek Popular Morality* (1974), 266; J. Ziolkowski, *Thucydides and the Tradition of Funeral Orations at Athens* (1981), and other refs. at Hornblower *Comm. on Thuc.*, notes on 2. 35–46; N. Loraux, *Anc. Soc.* 1975, 1 ff. and *The Invention of Athens* (1986); W. K. Pritchett, *The Greek State at War* 4 (1985), 106–24; L. Coventry, *JHS* 1989, 1 ff.

J. F. D.; S. H.

epithalamium, a song (or speech) given 'at the bridal chamber (θάλαμος)' ([Dion. Hal.] *Rhet.* 4. 1); a regular feature of marriages (see MARRIAGE CEREMONIES). Strictly speaking, it is distinct from the general 'wedding song' (γαμήλιος), cf. Eust. 1541. 49, and from the *'hymenaeus', the processional song which accompanied the newly-married couple to their house (Hom. *Il.* 18. 491–6; ps.-Hes. *Sc.* 272–85; Eur. *Tro.* 308–41; Ar. *Peace* 1316–57; Ap. Rhod. 4. 1160). In literature, however, the title 'epithalamium' predominates. *Menander (4) Rhetor (399–405 Spengel) actually uses the term as a synonym for 'wedding speech' (γαμήλιος), preferring the more explicit 'bedding-down speech' (κατευναστικός) for the ceremony at the bedroom door.

The tradition is of course old. *Sappho's wedding songs were famous. Comedy (*Aristophanes (1)'s *Peace*, *Birds*) and tragedy (*Euripides' *Troades*, *Iphigenia at Aulis*, *Phaethon*) provide examples. Among Hellenistic poems *Theocritus 18 (Helen and Menelaus) stands out. But Latin poetry offers more: e.g. *Catullus 61, 62, and 64 (Peleus and Thetis), *Statius *Silvae* 1. 2, *Claudian (Honorius and Maria, Palladius and Celerina). Catullus 61 and Claudian's poems for Honorius preserve something of the *'Fescennine' element of suggestive or bawdy humour which is natural to the tradition. In *Ausonius' *Cento nuptialis* (*Idyll* 13), lines of Virgil are strung together (see CENTO) to provide a whole narrative of the wedding, from the banquet to the consummation, explicitly described. Some later authors (see [Dion. Hal.] *Rhet.* 2, Himerius, *Oration* 9 (Colonna)) rejected this in the interests of respectability, and made the speech essentially a formal encomium on bride and bridegroom, with the inevitable topics of the luckiness of the day and the hope of offspring. Christian writers (the Latin poets *Sidonius, *Dracontius, and *Venantius; the Greek orator Choricius of Gaza) generally continued to use the imagery and mythology of their pagan predecessors, as indeed Renaissance poets have done. The literary epithalamium has had little connection with the religious aspect of marriage rites.

Besides commentaries on relevant texts (e.g. Menander Rhetor, Catullus), see P. Maas, *RE* 9 / 1 (1914), 130–134, *Hymenaios*; D. L. Page, *Sappho and Alcaeus* (1955), 71–4, 119–26; A. L. Wheeler, *AJPhil.* 1930, 205 ff.; H. Färber, *Die Lyrik in der Kunsttheorie der Antike* (1936) 1. 37 f., 2. 49 ff.; R. Muth, *Wien. Stud.* 1954, 5–45; D. A. Russell, *PCPS* 1979, 104–17; E. Contiades-Tsitsoni, *Hymenaios und Epithalamion* (1990).

E. Kr., D. A. R.

epithets, divine

Greek In considering the very numerous surnames or epithets of gods it is necessary first to distinguish between those appearing only as literary (especially epic) ornaments and those known to have been used in cult. Thus we have no proof that *Athena was ever addressed in ritual as γλαυκῶπις ('grey-eyed'); it is her stock epithet in *Homer, *Zeus' pet-name for her (*Il.* 8. 373). It seems unlikely that *Ares was prayed to as βροτολοιγός ('ruinous to mortals'); he is so addressed by Athena (*Il.* 5. 31), which is a very different thing, and it is his stock epithet (as ibid. 846). But there are many borderline cases, hard to decide. We have no instance

of *Athena being called Pallas in cult, yet it is not easy to suppose that so familiar a name was never used for her by worshippers; Zeus' stock epithet, 'cloud-gatherer', appears in the vocative, νεφεληγερέτα, in epic in many places where it is syntactically a nominative, strongly suggesting that its form had become fixed by some ancient liturgical phrase, which, however, is quite lost to us. The immediate function of the epithet in epic is often to form with the proper name a convenient metrical unit. Now and then an epithet is used to avoid mentioning an ill-omened name; *Hades in Sophocles, *OC* 1606, is Zeus χθόνιος ('of the earth'), and in Aesch. *Supp.* 231 he is even Zeus ἄλλος ('other', 'another').

But coming to those epithets which are guaranteed by their occurrence in liturgical formulas, dedications, and the official names of temples, we may distinguish the following classes. (1) Purely local, meaning that the deity in question is worshipped, or has a temple or altar, at such-and-such a place. Thus *Apollo Δήλιος is simply Apollo who is worshipped in *Delos, and differs from the Pythian (see DELPHI), or any other similarly named Apollo, not otherwise than as Our Lady of Lourdes does from Our Lady of Loreto. *Dionysus Κυδαθηναιεύς (*Syll.*³ 109. 16 and elsewhere) is nothing but the Dionysus who has a cult in the Attic deme Κυδαθήναιον (Kydathenaion). Such titles may tell us something of the history of the cult, if the title does not fit the immediate locality; a *Demeter Ἐλευσία worshipped at Pheneos in *Arcadia (Paus. 8. 15. 1) manifestly has something to do with the famous cult at *Eleusis, and the local legend said as much. (2) Titles indicating association with another god. These are often of some historical importance, and at times puzzling. Apollo Carneius (*Syll.*³ 736. 34 and 69) has behind him a history of identification; 'Hephaestian' Athena (ibid. 227. 20) need surprise no one, in view of the resemblance of some functions of the two deities (see HEPHAESTUS); but it is less easy to see why she had a temple at *Megara (1) under the title Αἰαντίς (Paus. 1. 42. 4). (3) Undoubtedly the largest and most important class of epithets, however, have reference to the functions of the god or goddess, either in general or with reference to some particular occasion on which his or her power was manifest. Thus, Zeus has a great number of titles denoting his control of the weather and all that depends on it; he is Βροντῶν, Thunderer, Κεραύνιος, God of the thunderbolt, Ὄμβριος, Sender of rainstorms, Ὑέτιος, Rainer, and as a natural consequence Γεωργός, Farmer; also Οὔριος, God of favourable winds, and so forth. Examples may be found in Farnell, *Cults* (index under 'Zeus'), and references there; also the corresponding entry in the index to A. B. Cook, *Zeus*. *Aphrodite has epithets denoting her power over the sexual life of mankind, as Ἀμβολογήρα, 'Delayer of old age'; her connection with love whether licit or illicit, for example Πάνδημος 'Goddess of the whole people', in her Athenian worship as a deity of marriage (Farnell, 2. 658); and on the other hand Ἑταίρα (see HETAIRAI) and even Πόρνη (see PROSTITUTION, SECULAR) (ibid. 667). These last belong to an extremely curious subclass in which the characteristics of the worshipper are transferred to the deity; both signify the goddess who is worshipped by harlots. *Hera is similarly called Παῖς, Τελεία, and Χήρα at her three shrines in Stymphalus, in other words Maid, Wife, and Widow (Paus. 8. 22. 2); she naturally received the worship of women of all ages and conditions. The local legend was somewhat at a loss to explain the third title, since Zeus cannot die, and invented a quarrel between the two leading to a separation; clearly the sense of such epithets was no longer remembered when *Pausanias (3) wrote.

Epithets referring to the higher (moral or civic) qualities of a deity are not uncommon, though less so than those which are due to his or her natural functions. It is to be noted that there is a tendency in later ages to read such qualities into an old title; thus Athena Προναία at Delphi, so named from the fact that her shrine was in front of the temple of Apollo, had so decided an inclination to become Πρόνοια that some manuscripts of Herodotus 8. 37. 2 have been infected by it. As genuine examples may be instanced Apollo Ἀρχηγέτης ('Founder') (see APOLLO), Athena βουλαία (of the *boulē).

Late hymns, for instance those of the *Orphic collection, have a strong tendency to heap up epithets, including the most unheard-of and fanciful, e.g. no. 28 (Abel), to *Hermes.

Burkert, GR 184.

H. J. R.; S. H.

Roman Each deity had its name, but this name could be hidden (cf. Brelich) or unknown (hence the formula in addresses 'whether god or goddess', *sive deus, sive dea*, cf. Alvar). If it was known, and could be uttered (as the hidden name could not), it was often accompanied by epithets and surnames (*cognomina*). They are either descriptions used informally or true names occurring in actual cult (attested in formulas, dedications, and names of temples), although strict distinction is not always possible. We can distinguish several classes of epithets and surnames: (1) Purely literary descriptions, e.g. of *Mars by *Virgil as harsh, wicked, untamed, savage, or powerful in arms, *durus, impius, indomitus, saevus, armipotens* (*Ecl.* 10. 40; *G.* 1. 511; *Aen.* 2. 440, 11. 153, 9. 717). (2) Popular descriptions derived either from a special feature (often iconographic) of a deity, e.g. *Hercules Bullatus, 'Wearing a bulla' (an amulet worn by young boys), Puerinus, 'Youthful', Pusillus, 'Small' (*CIL* 6. 302, 126; Mart. 3. 47. 4) (also Monolithus ('Made of a single stone') Silvanus (*CIL* 6. 675)), or from a story concerning a deity, e.g. *Minerva Capta, 'Captured', because she was transported to Rome after the capture of Falerii Veteres in 241 BC (Ov. *Fast.* 3. 835–48). (3) Geographical and local descriptions, e.g. *Bona Dea Subsaxana (*Curiosum* and *Notitia Urbis Romae*, 92, A. Nordh, *Libellus de regionibus urbis Romae*, 1949) because she had her shrine *sub Saxo*, 'under the Rock' (of the Aventine: Cic. *Dom.* 136–7; Ov. *Fast.* 5. 147–58), *Diana Aventinensis, Tifatina, *Fortuna Praenestina, or *Venus Erycina, after their temples on the *Aventine, in *Tifata, *Praeneste, and *Eryx (Erice in Sicily), such descriptions often functioning (especially in dedications) as regular surnames, as was the case e.g. with *Jupiter Dolichenus ('of Doliche' in Syria). (4) Descriptions indicating association with another deity attested in archaic prayers (*comprecationes*, Gell. *NA* 13. 23), e.g. *Lua Saturni, Herie Iunonis*, the second name standing in the genitive, thus indicating that the first deity was an emanation of the second or was acting in its sphere, cf. *Moles Martis*, 'Oppressions' of Mars. (5) Epithets referring to the civic standing of a deity: Jupiter Optimus Maximus, 'the Best (and) the Greatest, *Juno Regina, 'the Queen'. (6) Most numerous are epithets describing the function of a deity or its particular manifestation: *Apollo Medicus, 'Healer', Bona Dea Nutrix, 'Nurse', Jupiter Tonans, 'Thunderer', Stator, 'Stayer' (he stopped the advance of the enemy, Livy 1. 12. 3), Mars Ultor, 'Avenger' (he helped *Augustus to avenge the murder of *Caesar), Venus Verticordia, 'Changer of Hearts' (she averted women's minds from lust to chastity, Val. Max. 8. 15. 12). Deities for whom the most epithets are attested are Jupiter (over 100), Fortuna, Juno (over 40), Hercules, Mars, Venus (over 30), *Lares, *Mercurius, *Silvanus (over 20). A complete list of Roman divine epithets is yet to be compiled.

C. F. H. Bruchmann, *Epitheta deorum quae apud poetas Graecos leguntur* (Teubner, 1893); J. B. Carter, *De Deorum Romanorum cognominibus*

(1898), and *Epitheta deorum quae apud poetas Latinos leguntur* (1902); A. Brelich, *Die geheime Schutzgottheit von Rom* (1949); B. Gladigow, *RAC* 11 (1985), 1202 ff.; J. Alvar, *Numen* (1985) 236 ff.

J. L.

epitome (ἐπιτομή)

Greek The Hellenistic age was the first to feel the growth of recorded literature as a burden; and the age which cast doubt on the propriety of a 'big book' (Callim. fr. 465 Pf.) also pioneered the abridgement of long works, especially technical treatises. The practice became a common, even an obsessive, feature of post-Classical Greece. *Aristophanes (2) of Byzantium epitomized *Aristotle's *Historia animalium*, and his epitome was later epitomized by Sopater. *Pamphilus (2)'s glossary was reduced from 95 books to 30, then from 30 to 5. *Oribasius twice epitomized his own *Collectiones Medicae*. Various significant works now survive only in epitome, from the epic *Cypria* (abridged in prose) to the opening of *Athenaeus (1)'s *Deipnosophistae*. See also THEOPOMPUS (3).

M. S. Si.

Latin Convenient and informative compendia based on the writings of others were being produced at Rome by the end of the republic, especially in history: M. *Iunius Brutus (1), for example, epitomized *Polybius (1) and (perhaps) one or two of the Latin annalists, and *Ateius Philologus composed a brief summary (*breviarium*) of all Roman history for *Sallust; by the late 1st cent. AD *Martial knew an epitome of *Livy. Short histories, however derivative, could be stylish (see FLORUS (1)), but schematic summaries predominated: thus Livy's *Periochae*, and *Justin's epitome of *Pompeius Trogus. There was no loss while the original works remained, on papyrus, but the taste for epitome limited their chances of survival during the change to the parchment codex: though senatorial traditionalism in the 4th cent. AD helped to save some of Livy, Trogus was lost. Concise writing set its fashion. Late historians used the epitome to introduce their accounts of contemporary events (see EUTROPIUS (1); FESTUS; cf. AURELIUS VICTOR), or to give Roman background to the Christian interpretation of history (see OROSIUS).

Meanwhile practical 'digests' continued: for example, Sex. *Pompeius Festus epitomized the great antiquarian dictionary of *Verrius Flaccus, and *Priscian in effect epitomized his own massive *Institutio* of grammar (eighteen books) by producing an abbreviated *Institutio de nomine et pronomine et verbo* (Keil, *Gramm. Lat.* 3. 443–56) more suited for school use. *Cassiodorus proves the value of this modest form of transmitting knowledge that would otherwise have been lost.

M. Galdi, *L'epitome nella letteratura latina* (1922).

R. A. K.

Epona, a Celtic goddess known from dedications that spread from Spain to the Balkans, and northern Britain to Italy. Her name derives from the Celtic word for 'horse', and the most common iconography of the goddess shows her seated sidesaddle on a horse; Latin writers mention her as the goddess of the stable (Juv. 9. 157; Apul. *Met.* 3. 27). She is also at times depicted with fruits or a cornucopia, attributes that link her with the mother goddesses. Her original cult area was in NE Gaul, and monuments are very frequent in the regions of the *Aedui (near Dijon), the *Treveri (around the Mosel), and east of the Rhine to the border. The wider dispersal is due largely to devotees in the army, often members of the cavalry, but she also has a festival in a civic calendar of 27 BC from northern Italy. See RELIGION, CELTIC.

S. Boucher, *LIMC* 5 (1990), 985–99.

J. B. R.

eponymoi are those, usually gods or heroes, after whom something is named or thought to be named. Most frequently place-names—regions or cities—are considered to be named from an eponymous hero, such as Arcas for Arcadia, or the heroine Sparte/Sparta for the city of the same name. Historical characters also gave their names to cities (Antioch, Alexandria). The phenomenon was common all over the Greek world and also in Roman Italy.

Divisions of the populace also had heroic eponyms. In Athens, the *eponymoi* (with no further qualification) were the ten heroes who gave their names to the ten Cleisthenic tribes created in 508/7 BC (see CLEISTHENES (2); PHYLAI). These heroes, who were said to have been picked by *Delphi from a list of a hundred submitted, all had separate, presumably pre-existing cults, to which members of the new tribes gradually became in some measure attached; they had also, apparently, a collective cult in the Agora (see ATHENS, TOPOGRAPHY), where statues of the ten were situated and tribal notices posted.

A completely different case is the 'eponymous magistrate' who gives his name to his year of office, like the Athenian archon (see ARCHONTES; PATRONOMOS).

Kron, *Phylenheroen*; T. L. Shear, *Hesp.* 1970, 145–222; S. Rotroff, *Hesp.* 1978, 196–209.   E. Ke.

Epopeus/Epops, an old mythical figure, whose name suggests a relationship with *Zeus Epopetes. According to the *Cypria* (see EPIC CYCLE) he was king of *Sicyon and seduced the Boeotian *Antiope; the result, *Amphion and Zethus, is mentioned by the 6th-cent. poet Asius (fr. 1 Davies). Eumelus (Paus. 2. 1. 1 = fr. 5 Davies) said that he was son of Aloeus, son of *Helios, and father of Marathon, the eponym of the Attic region of that name (see MARATHON).

Burkert, *HN* 185–90.   H. J. R.; J. N. B.

Eporedia (mod. Ivrea), founded *c*.100 BC as a Roman colony at the foot of the Alps, to guard over the *Salassi. A theatre, amphitheatre, and aqueduct are known. Under the late empire it was a garrison town and the seat of a bishopric.

L. B. Taborelli, *Quad. della Sop. Arch. del Piemonte* 1987, 97–157.
                                                                                   E. T. S.; T. W. P.

Eprius Marcellus, Titus Clodius, born of humble parentage at *Capua, was praetor AD 48, legate of *Lycia and proconsul of *Cyprus, and suffect consul in 62. After his Lycian legateship in 57 he was prosecuted for extortion, but secured acquittal by bribery and had his accuser exiled. In 66 he was one of the accusers of *Thrasea Paetus, and received 5 million sesterces after the condemnation. *Columella dedicated his *De cultura vinearum et arborum* to him. After the Flavian entry into Rome in 70 he became a champion of the new government, and engaged in fierce controversies with *Helvidius Priscus (Tac. *Hist.* 4. 6–8, 43). He was rewarded with the proconsulate of Asia, perhaps with special powers, for three years (70–3), and obtained a second consulate (suff.) in May 74. He also held three priesthoods, and was regarded not only as one of the most powerful orators of the age but as an intimate counsellor of *Vespasian (Tac. *Dial.* 8, *Hist.* 2. 95). But just before Vespasian's death he was accused by *Titus of conspiracy with A. *Caecina Alienus, was condemned by the senate, and committed suicide.

ILS 992; *SEG* 18. 587; G. Wissowa, *RE* 6/1 (1907), 261–5; J. A. Crook, *AJPhil.* 1951, 162 ff.; A. R. Birley, *Fasti of Roman Britain* (1981), 228–30.
                                                                                   G. E. F. C.; M. T. G.

epulones See SEPTEMVIRI EPULONES.

epyllion (*ἐπύλλιον*, diminutive of *ἔπος*) is the term applied in modern (not ancient) times to 'miniature epic', a narrative poem of up to *c*.600 hexameters, usually about an episode from the life of a mythological hero or heroine. This was a favourite form from *Theocritus and *Callimachus (3) until the 'new' poets contemporary with *Catullus (1), with the *Ciris* as a belated revival. The topic is preferably unfamiliar, the love motif (often pathological love) becomes prominent in the later specimens, and often a second theme or a description of an object is enclosed within the main narrative; the style tends to be more subjective and emotional than in formal *epic, and the scale of the narrative is uneven, with some events elaborated (especially emotional speeches) and others quickly passed over. The term is also used of more or less self-contained sections of longer poems, such as the *Aristaeus episode in Virgil's *Georgics* and the individual stories in *Ovid's *Metamorphoses*.

See M. M. Crump, *The Epyllion from Theocritus to Ovid* (1931); W. Allen, *TAPA* 1940, 1; R. O. A. M. Lyne, *Ciris* (1978), 32; K. J. Gutzwiller, *Studies in the Hellenistic Epyllion* (1981).   E. C.

Equirria, two Roman festivals of horse-racing on 27 February and 14 March (Ov. *Fast.* 2. 857 ff., 3. 517 ff.). The first was founded by *Romulus (Varro, *Ling.* 6. 13) and the second was connected with the martial festival of the October Horse: U. Scholz, *Studien zum altitalischen und altrömischen Marskult und Marsmythos* (1970), 115 ff. (see MARS).

G. Dumézil, *Fêtes romaines d'été et d'automne* (1975), 161 ff; H. Wagenvoort, *Studies in Roman Literature, Culture and Religion* (1956), 224 ff.
                                                                                   C. R. P.

equites

Origins and republic The early history of the cavalry at Rome is overlaid with legend and speculation. The kings are said to have enrolled 300 *celeres* or *trossuli* (later doubled) for the *legion. They wore loincloths, tunics with the *clavus, *trabeae* (short embroidered cloaks), and *mullei* (strapped red shoes); they were armed with lances and their horses were adorned with *phalerae* (silver disks). Their insignia, in various adapted forms, later became the distinctive attire of patricians, magistrates, and senators. Twelve hundred *equites* were allegedly added by Servius *Tullius. These 1,800 had their horses supplied and maintained by the state (hence *equites equo publico*), out of the property taxes paid by widows and orphans. They were to serve ten campaigns. In the centuriate assembly they formed eighteen *centuriae*, later including (it seems) those too old for service. This voting privilege survived in essence as long as the assembly. In the classical republic these *equites* were enrolled by the *censors, after financial, physical, and moral scrutiny (*recognitio*). At least since 304 BC (see Q. *Fabius Maximus Rullianus), though rarely in the late republic, they paraded to the Capitol in the *transvectio* on 15 July. Men of aristocratic birth always had preference for enrolment.

About 400 BC, men on their own horses (*equites equo privato*) were added to the cavalry. They did not share the voting privilege, but were given at least some of the status marks, of the others. In the 3rd cent. Roman cavalry proved increasingly ineffective in war and by 200 was largely replaced by *auxilia. But *equites* retained their social eminence and became a corps from which officers and the staffs of governors and commanders were drawn. This new 'equestrian' service was within the reach of any wealthy and well-connected family and the old exclusiveness was undermined. In 129 senators (but not their non-senatorial relatives) were excluded from the equestrian centuries (Cic. *Rep.* 4. 2).

Whatever the motive, this marks the beginnings of the later *ordo equester* as a distinct body. C. *Sempronius Gracchus excluded senators from service on the *repetundae court. Although the positive qualifications for service are largely lost, various considerations, especially the need to exclude senators (*FIRA* 7 ll. 13 and 16), make it certain that the jurors were not defined as registered *equites equo publico*, i.e. the qualification must have been by wealth. The law on the Asian taxes is therefore also unlikely to have defined bidders as belonging to that class. Gracchus' prescription was followed in other *quaestiones, permanent or special; as a result, the composition of juries became, for a generation (106–70), an object of bitter contention between the senatorial and the equestrian *ordo*, firmly establishing their distinctness.

Another result was the transformation of the *ordo* itself. Pliny (*HN* 33. 34) derives the later *ordo equester* from the Gracchan jurors, and what evidence we have supports him. The wealthy *publicani gradually became the dominant element on juries and within the *ordo*: Cicero could rhetorically identify them with it. The 'public horse' and the annual parade are nowhere mentioned in our ample record of the age of Cicero, except for one political demonstration by *Pompey in 70. Between 70 and at least 50, there were no censorships culminating in a *lustrum*, so the list of strictly defined *equites* could not be kept up. By 50 (even), the influx of Italians, to whose leading men the jury courts had been opened since 70, made a return to the old restriction politically impossible. The law of L. *Roscius Otho allocating special rows of seats to *equites* probably confirmed the definition by wealth: we cannot be certain, but Cicero (quoted by Asc. p. 78 C) links it with the judiciary law of L. *Aurelius Cotta, which certainly did. The attested objection of the *plebs* was no doubt precisely to that definition: the Roman *plebs* never objected to traditional status distinctions.

The new *ordo* was a disparate body. Round an aristocratic Roman core (men like T. *Pomponius Atticus) were grouped leading men from colonies and *municipia, publicani*, and even *negotiatores—many of similar background, but some self-made men. Free birth and a landed interest were prerequisites for social recognition (cf. Cic. *Off.* 1. 51). Senators and *equites* in the late republic thus formed a plutocracy sharing both landed and business interests, in a continuous range of proportions.

In social standing, *equites* were almost equal to senators, freely intermarrying even with patrician nobles and gaining entry to the senate (though not the consulate—see NOBILITAS) if they wanted it (see Cic. *Sest.* 97). But as a class they preferred the pursuit of money and pleasure to political responsibility, and they thus formed the non-political section of the upper class rather than (as in the empire) an intermediate class. Their history is an important part of that of the late republic, particularly in view of their control of the *quaestiones* during most of that time. Various *populares tried to mould them into a political force opposed to the senate and the *nobilitas*; but their social and economic interests, especially after the enfranchisement of Italy, were basically too similar to permit this. *Sulla, after decimating them in the proscriptions, followed the example of M. *Livius Drusus (2) and deprived them of leadership by adlecting the most prominent survivors to the senate, and of power by taking the courts from them. But strengthened by the influx of Italians and by increasing financial power, wooed by Pompey, and largely restored to the courts by the law of Cotta, they rose to unprecedented influence in the 60s, when Cicero and the senate—aware of the basic community of interests of the two classes—tried to unite them behind the *principes in a *concordia ordinum*. Yet, though often united on a single issue (e.g. against threats to financial stability by demagogues or threats to freedom of profiteering by statesmen), sometimes even for a lengthy period, they were too disparate in composition and too non-political to form a stable grouping. Preventing necessary reform (especially in the provinces), they remained a disruptive and irresponsible element with no programme or allegiance, until the Civil War substituted military for economic power. Caesar deprived them of the Asian tithe, but opened a new avenue for them by making prominent *equites* like C. *Oppius (2) and L. *Cornelius Balbus (1)—a splendid example of a non-traditional *eques*—his political and financial agents. The support of these men, as well as the precedent, proved important to Augustus.

Plin. *HN* 33. 8–36. A. Alföldi, *Der frührömische Reiteradel und seine Ehren-abzeichen* (1952); A. Momigliano, *JRS* 1966, 16 ff. (these items put forward two sets of opposing speculations on origins); H. Hill, *The Roman Middle Class in the Republican Period* (1952): see review by T. R. S. Broughton, *CPhil.* 1955, 275 ff.; C. Nicolet, *L'Ordre équestre à l'époque républicaine* 1 (1966), 2 (1974: prosopography and index)—the standard work; T. P. Wiseman, *Hist.* 1970, 67 ff.; P. A. Brunt, *The Fall of the Roman Republic* (1988), 144 ff.   E. B.

Imperial period Under the emperors the *equites* constituted a second aristocratic order which ranked only below the senatorial order in status. *Equites* in the wider sense (see below) provided the officer corps of the Roman army and held a wide range of posts in the civil administration (see PROCURATOR) as it developed from its limited beginnings under Augustus.

The precise criteria for membership of the order remain disputed. On a wider definition, which will be accepted here, all Roman citizens of free birth who possessed the minimum census qualification of 400,000 sesterces automatically qualified as members of the order. Thus when the younger Pliny (*Ep.* 1. 19) offered a friend from Comum a gift of 300,000 sesterces 'to make up the wealth required of an *eques*', he implies that this gift of itself would be sufficient to make his friend an *eques*. However, it remains possible that these were necessary but not sufficient criteria and that, in addition, some formal act of authorization, perhaps even the grant of the public horse (see below), by the emperor was necessary.

The equestrian order, widely defined, was much more numerous than the senatorial order and socially and politically (in terms of the range of its public roles) more heterogeneous. Although the total number of *equites* at any time cannot be determined, already under Augustus they were relatively numerous. Strabo records that recent censuses had revealed 500 men of equestrian census at both Gades and Patavium (Strabo 169, 213C). During the course of the first two centuries the possession of equestrian rank spread widely through the provinces. This diffusion mirrored the extension of Roman *citizenship. From the beginning of the Principate Baetica and Narbonensis are well represented, in the 1st cent. AD and after Africa and the Greek east. Far fewer *equites* are attested in the Danubian provinces, Germany, Gaul, and Britain. The vast majority of the order came to be constituted by the landed gentry of the municipalities of Italy and of the cities of the most urbanized provinces. Although these men were eligible to take up the military and civilian posts reserved for *equites*, the majority of them continued rather to play a local political role as senior local magistrates and councillors or as high priests of the imperial cult.

Within the order three specific subsets of unequal importance can be identified, namely the holders of the public horse (*equus *publicus*), the jurors at Rome, and the military and civilian office-holders. The re-emergence of the category of *equites equo publico* under Augustus formed part of his traditionalist social policies. He restored the long disused parade (*transvectio*) of July 15, while allowing men handicapped by age or ill health to parade on foot, and those over 35 to have the choice of retaining or giving up the (notional) *equus publicus*; the occasion was also combined with an examination by Augustus of the physical and moral fitness of these *equites*. On one occasion more than 5,000 men are recorded as taking part in this ceremony (Dion. Hal. *Ant. Rom.* 6. 13). This subset of *equites* formed a distinct corporation which might dedicate statues or play a role in the funeral of an emperor. The grant of this status was at the discretion of the emperor who could also withdraw it.

Augustus also established four boards (*decuriae*) of jurors (*iudices*), each of 1,000 men, who were of equestrian rank but, according to the elder Pliny (*HN* 33. 30–3), were not as such called *equites* until AD 23. Owing to the pressure for places Gaius (1) added a fifth *decuria*. Like the public horse the status of juror was solely in the gift of the emperor. For example a Q. Voltedius Optatus Aurelianus, from Carthage, was granted the public horse by *Trajan and entry to the *decuriae* by *Hadrian; another local notable from Africa received both statuses from *Antoninus Pius (*ILS* 9406–7). Both statuses, as dignities conferred by the emperors, came to some extent to be honorific privileges which did not necessarily involve the expectation of the exercise of actual duties at Rome. Both statuses cease to be attested after the first part of the 3rd cent.

Within the political system of the Principate the most significant, if a minority, subset of equestrians was constituted by those who served as equestrian officers in the army and as senior civil administrators. Each year there were about 360 posts available for senior officers of equestrian rank: prefectures of cohorts, military tribunates, and prefectures of cavalry units. A minority of these officers were not typical equestrian landed gentry but instead ranking soldiers who had attained the rank of senior centurion (*primipilus) in a legion and thereby acquired equestrian status. Tenure of these officer-posts was normally the necessary precursor for advancement to the senior civil administrative posts, reserved for *equites*, though from the early 2nd cent. tenure of the post of *advocatus fisci* (see FISCUS) became an alternative precursor. In the provinces emperors appointed *equites* as procurators who had prime responsibility for fiscal administration; at Rome from the reign of Augustus key posts, such as the praetorian prefecture or the prefecture of the corn supply, were reserved for equestrians. From the late 1st cent. the posts of the palatine officials, for example, control of the imperial correspondence, were transferred from freedmen to equestrians. Senior equestrian administrators formed with senior senators the political élite of the empire. They intermingled socially with senators; they married into senatorial families; like senators they could be summoned to serve on the emperor's *consilium. Sons of leading equestrian officials were the prime source of recruitment of new senatorial families. On occasion, especially under *Vespasian and Marcus *Aurelius, senior equestrians might be adlected by the emperor into the senate.

From the latter part of the 2nd cent. equestrian officials began to acquire regular appellations of rank—*vir eminentissimus* ('most renowned') for the praetorian prefects, *vir perfectissimus* ('most accomplished') for the other prefects and higher procurators, *vir egregius* ('excellent') for the rest. In the course of the 3rd-cent. crisis equestrian officers, often men who had risen to equestrian

status via the chief centurionate, began to replace senators as army commanders and provincial governors. This process culminated in the reforms of *Diocletian under whom the higher military posts and almost all administrative posts passed into the hands of *equites*. During the first half of the 4th cent. repeated attempts were made to confine equestrian rank to office-holders and to exclude *curiales*. In the same period the title *perfectissimus* (*egregius* disappears under *Constantine I) was extended downwards to officials of minor rank, eventually being awarded in three grades. By the end of the century this process had been overtaken by a similar diffusion of senatorial honours among officials, and at this point the equestrian order ceases to be a recognizable element in the Roman state.

A. Stein, *Der römische Ritterstand* (1927); G. Alföldy, *The Social History of Rome* (1985), ch. 5; P. A. Brunt, *JRS* 1983, 42 ff.; S. Demougin, *L'Ordre équestre sous les Julio-Claudiens* (1988); Jones, *Later Rom. Emp.* 525 ff; Millar, *ERW* 279 ff.   F. G. B. M.; G. P. B.

equites singulares Augusti were mounted imperial bodyguards, probably established by the Flavians with a strength of 500, later rising to 1,000. They were recruited from auxiliary cavalry *alae*, predominantly Germans and Pannonians, and acted as the *praetorians' cavalry arm. They had a camp near the Lateran and in the 2nd cent. were commanded by a tribune.

M. Speidel, *Die Equites Singulares Augusti* (1965).   H. M. D. P.; J. B. C.

eranos was essentially concerned with *reciprocity: at first of food, and later of money. In *Homer, *eranos* refers to a meal for which each diner contributed a share (*Od.* 1. 226); alternatively, the venue might be rotated. This earlier meaning was never lost (Xen. *Mem.* 3. 14. 1); but, by the later 5th cent. BC, the concept had evolved to include a *credit system, common in Athens, whereby contributors lent small sums to help out a common acquaintance in need (Lys. 20. 12; cf. Pl. *Ap.* 38b). The strong obligation to lend was matched by a reciprocal obligation to repay as soon as possible. The reciprocity inherent in the *eranos*-idea is reflected in metaphorical usage: to die in battle for the *polis* was to offer one's *kallistos eranos* ('finest contribution'), receiving in return 'immortal praise' (Thuc. 2. 43. 1). Readiness to contribute towards *eranos* loans could be cited in Athenian courts as an aspect of civic virtue (Antiphon 2. 2. 12); failure to repay as indicative of general degradation (Lys. fr. 38 Gernet–Bizos). Disputed is the extent to which eranists in Athens were ad hoc groupings, or fixed associations (see CLUBS, GREEK), somewhat resembling friendly societies. The terminology of *eranos* credit appears in Hellenistic papyri from Egypt, but in contexts where interest was apparently paid.

J. Vondeling, *Eranos* (1961); G. Maier, *Eranos als Kreditinstitut* (1969); M. I. Finley, *Land and Credit in Ancient Athens* (1952; repr. 1985); P. C. Millett, *Lending and Borrowing in Ancient Athens* (1991); E. M. Harris, *Phoenix* 1992, 309 ff.; E. Leider, *Der Handel von Alexandria* (1933).
                                                                                    P. C. M.

Erasistratus of Iulis on Ceos (about 315–240 BC ?) is the only scientist other than *Herophilus to whom ancient sources attribute systematic scientific dissections of human cadavers. *Cornelius Celsus claims that Erasistratus, like Herophilus, also vivisected convicted criminals (see VIVISECTION). The extant evidence leaves little doubt that he performed vivisectory experiments on animals. Often taking a functional approach to his anatomical discoveries, he combined detailed descriptions of parts with explanations of their physiological roles. Thus he not only gave the first reasonably accurate description of the heart valves but also demonstrated that their function is to ensure the irreversibility of the flow through the valves.

Three consistent features of Erasistratus' approach are his use of mechanistic principles to explain bodily processes, an Aristotelian teleological perspective, and the verification of an *hypothesis by means of *experiment. His major mechanistic principle is that matter naturally moves by means of 'following toward what is being emptied' (πρὸς τὸ κενούμενον ἀκολουθία), i.e. if matter is removed from any contained space, other matter will enter to take its place, since a natural massed void (or 'vacuum') is impossible.

Using this principle, he united respiration, the vascular system, the nervous system, muscular activity, appetite, and digestion in a single, comprehensive physiological model, which he probably presented in his *General Principles* (Οἱ καθόλου λόγοι). External air moves into the lungs through the windpipe and bronchial ducts as the thorax expands after exhalation. Some of the breath (pneuma) in the lungs then moves through the 'vein-like artery' (i.e. the pulmonary vein) into the left ventricle of the heart, when this ventricle expands after contraction. The pneuma in the left cardiac ventricle in turn is refined into 'vital' (ζωτικόν) pneuma before being pushed into the arteries when the heart contracts. Excess air in the lungs, having absorbed some of the superfluous body heat produced by the heart, is exhaled as the thorax contracts, but, in accordance with his principle that matter 'follows towards what is being emptied', fresh breath rushes into the thorax again as it expands. The pulmonary breathing cycle thus both cools the body and provides the arteries with life-sustaining *pneuma.

The nerves, too, carry pneuma: some of the 'vital' pneuma is pumped through arteries from the left cardiac ventricle to the brain, where it becomes further refined into 'psychic' (ψυχικόν) pneuma, which in turn is distributed to the body through the sensory and motor nerves. Appetite and digestion—both of which he also explains partly in terms of the principle that matter 'follows toward that which is being emptied'—provide the liver with liquid nutriment to process into blood, which then flows from the liver into the veins by the same mechanical principle. The arteries and the nerves, then, contain only pneuma, whereas the veins distribute only blood (as nutriment). The muscles, like other organic structures, consist of 'triple-braided' strands (τριπλοκίαι) of veins, arteries, and nerves. The pneuma carried to the muscles by arteries and nerves allows the muscles to contract or relax, thereby rendering voluntary motion possible.

In his *pathology Erasistratus introduced several causes of diseases, all ultimately instances of different forms of matter (blood, pneuma, various liquids) that normally are rigorously separated, somehow not remaining separated. 'Plethora', a condition typically marked by excessive blood-nutriment in the veins, can cause inflammation, which can lead to fever, swollen limbs, diseases of the liver or stomach, epilepsy, and other ailments, in part because excessive blood in the veins can cause a dangerous spillover (παρέμπτωσις) of blood into the arteries through inosculations (συναναστομώσεις) between veins and arteries, thus impeding the arterial flow of vital pneuma.

Like Herophilus, he argued that there are no diseases peculiar to women. In treating patients, his guiding principles (in part presented in *Hygieina* 1–2) were, first, to prevent plethoric conditions by means of regimen; secondly, to ensure, by relatively mild measures, the return to its proper place of matter that has gone astray. He emphasized the stochastic nature of symptomatology and therapeutics, opposed drastic measures, and rejected tradi-

tional uses of bloodletting, thereby provoking the notorious ire of *Galen. Other attested treatises include *On Fevers*, *On Expectoration of Blood*, *On Paralysis*, *On Dropsy*, *On Podagra*, *On the Abdominal Cavity*, and *On Divisions*. See MEDICINE, § 5. 2.

I. Garofalo (ed.), *Erasistrati fragmenta* (1988). P. Brain, *Galen on Bloodletting* (1986); G. E. R. Lloyd, *JHS* 1975, 172–5. H. v. S.

Eratocles (probably late 5th cent. BC), musical theorist discussed by *Aristoxenus, empiricist rather than Pythagorean in approach (Aristox. *Harm.* 5. 9–6. 31, cf. Pl. *Resp.* 531a–b). He distinguished conjunct from disjunct systems, analysed scales quantitatively, probably using diagrams and measuring intervals as multiples of the quarter-tone, and developed representations of ἁρμονίαι (attunements) as octave-species, orderly transformations of one another. Though clearly a pioneer in systematic musical analysis, he was criticized by Aristoxenus for perceptual errors, and for failing to demonstrate conclusions scientifically. A. D. B.

Eratosthenes, of *Cyrene (*c*.285–194 BC), pupil of *Callimachus (3) and *Lysanias (2). After spending several years at Athens, where he came under the influence of *Arcesilaus (1) and *Ariston (1) of Chios, he accepted the invitation of *Ptolemy (1) III Euergetes to become royal tutor and to succeed *Apollonius (1) Rhodius as head of the Alexandrian Library. He thus became a member of the Cyrenaean intelligentsia in Alexandria, of which the central figure was Callimachus. His versatility was renowned and criticized, and the eventual Alexandrian verdict was to describe him as βῆτα, 'B-class' (that is to say, not 'second rate' but 'next after the best specialist in each subject'), and πένταθλος, an 'all-rounder'. Others, more kindly, called him 'a second Plato' (see PLATO (1)). In more than one field, however, and particularly in chronology and mathematical and descriptive *geography, of which, thanks to *Strabo, we know most, his work long retained much of its authority.

Works (almost entirely lost in direct quotation).

1. Literary criticism. Eratosthenes evidently attached considerable importance to his researches in this field, for we are told by *Suetonius that he was the first scholar to call himself by the proud title of φιλόλογος. His most important work seems to have been the treatise *On Ancient Comedy*, in at least twelve books; this dealt with literary, lexical, historical, and antiquarian matters, and problems of the authorship and production of plays.

2. Chronology. His Χρονογραφίαι represented the first scientific attempt to fix the dates of political and literary history. He also compiled a list of Olympian victors (see OLYMPIAN GAMES). In this field his most significant achievement (later abandoned) was to replace a partly mythical pre-historic chronology by one based on supposedly assured data (the fall of Troy).

3. Mathematics. He investigated a wide range of mathematical and geometrical problems and was accepted as an equal by *Archimedes, who addressed his *Methodus* to him, after the death of his earlier disciple *Conon (2) of Samos. In his *Platonicus* (perhaps a dialogue) he apparently discussed mathematical definitions and the principles of music. Among his geometrical works were the *On Geometrical Means* and *On the Duplication of the Cube*. The latter included his poem on that well-worn theme, addressed to Ptolemy III. In his *On the Measurement of the Earth* (probably a preliminary work to his *Geographica*) he treated mathematical geography, calculating with a higher degree of accuracy than his predecessors the circumference of the earth. He was the first systematic geographer, and the *Geographica* (Γεωγραφικά, three books) dealt with mathematical, physical, and ethnograph-

ical geography, being based on a division of continents on a geometrical basis into 'seals' (σφραγιδες), a term perhaps borrowed from contemporary Ptolemaic terminology of land-measurement. The work opened with a sketch of the history of the subject, with especial reference to the Homeric poems, and this, along with the mathematically more exact work of *Hipparchus (3), formed the main source of Strabo's theoretical geography in books 1–2. For the Asiatic section his work was based to a considerable extent on the data provided by the *bematists of *Alexander (3) the Great and the early *Seleucids.

4. Philosophy. His works in this field, the *Platonicus*, mentioned above, and the *Ariston* (named after the Chian philosopher *Ariston (1) whom Eratosthenes had heard with some scepticism in Athens) were severely criticized by Strabo for their dilettanteism, but we know virtually nothing of their contents, and Strabo, as a good Stoic, was nettled by Eratosthenes' disenchantment with his Stoic teachers. (See STOICISM.) Archimedes, in sending to Eratosthenes the text of his *Methodus*, called him 'a leader of philosophy' (φιλοσοφίας προεστώς), and there is no reason to regard this as polite condescension. It seems likely that these philosophical writings belong to the pre-Alexandrian phase of Eratosthenes' career.

5. Poetry. As a poet Eratosthenes for the most part eludes us, though his 'Alexandrian' characteristics are evident in theme and occasional quotation. His statement that the aim of poetry is to entertain, not to instruct, reflects a coherent *ars poetica*. His short epic *Hermes* described the birth of the god *Hermes, his youthful exploits, and his ascent to the planets. The short epic *Anterinys* or *Hesiod* dealt with the death of *Hesiod and the punishment of his murderers. [Longinus] (*Subl.* 33. 5) praises the elegy *Erigone*, which told the myth of Icarius and his daughter, as 'a faultless little poem' (διὰ πάντων ἀμώμητον ποιημάτιον). These, however, have vanished, and the longest surviving fragments of his versatile muse are the delightful poem on the Duplication of the Cube (see above), and the short piece on the youth of Hermes.

Eratosthenes' intellectual calibre is seen both in chance utterances which reveal him as a man of insight and conviction (perhaps also of prejudice) and also in an occasional glimpse of a wide moral and political understanding, notably in his comment in his *Geographica* (Strab. 66) that Greek and 'barbarian' (the Indians and the Arians, the Romans and the Carthaginians, 'with their wonderful political systems') should be judged by the unique criterion of morality and not of race (see BARBARIAN). His candour and independence of judgement may go some way towards explaining that, although the names of some of his direct pupils are known, he seems to have established no lasting following associated with his name; we hear of no Ἐρατοσθένειοι, as there were 'Callimacheioi', 'Aristarcheioi', and others.

See GEOGRAPHY; MAPS.

GENERAL The ancient biographical tradition is fullest (perhaps too full) in the *Suda* ε 2898 = FGrH 241 T 1. Modern works: G. Bernhardy, *Eratosthenica* (1822), a pioneer work, now mainly of historical interest; Susemihl, *Gesch. gr. Lit. Alex.* 1. 409–28; E. Schwartz, *Charakterköpfe aus der Antike*, 4th edn. by J. Stroux (1956): the section on Eratosthenes was first published in 1909; Knaack, *RE* 6/1 (1907), 'Eratosthenes' 4; Fraser, *Ptol. Alex.*, index vol., 34, 100 (= Fraser (1)), and 'Eratosthenes of Cyrene', *Proc. Brit. Acad.* 1970, 176–207 (with brief bibliog. 206–7) (= Fraser (2)); R. Pfeiffer, *History of Classical Scholarship* (1968), 152–70 (esp. for literary works).

LITERARY CRITICISM AND SCHOLARSHIP C. Strecker, *De Lycophrone Euphronio Eratosthene comicorum interpretibus* (1884): fragments, with some omissions; Pfeiffer, *Hist. Class. Scholarship*.

CHRONOLOGY FGrH 241; Fraser (1), 456–7, (2), 198–200; Pfeiffer, *Hist. Class. Scholarship*, i, 163–4.

MATHEMATICS I. Thomas, *History of Greek Mathematics* (1939, 1941), 1. 100, 290 ff., 2. 260 ff.; Heath, *Hist. of Greek Math.* 2. 104 ff.; Fraser (1), 400 ff., (2), 186–7 (for Archimedes and Eratosthenes).

GEOGRAPHY H. Berger, *Die geographischen Fragmente des Eratosthenes* (1880; repr. 1964), and *Geschichte der wissenschaftliche Erdkunde der Griechen*, 2nd edn. (1903), 406 ff., 441 ff.; J. O. Thomson, *Hist. Anc. Geog.* see index, and esp. 158 ff.; D. R. Dicks, *The Geographical Fragments of Hipparchus* (1960), *passim* and index; Fraser (1), 1. 525 ff.

PHILOSOPHY Schwartz, *Charakterköpfe* (see General section above); F. Solmsen, *TAPA* 1942, 192–3; E. P. Wolfer, *Eratosthenes von Kyrene als Mathematiker und Philosoph* (1954)

POETRY Texts: Powell, *Coll. Alex.* 58 ff.; *Suppl. Hell.* 397–9. Discussions: Pfeiffer, *Hist. Class. Scholarship*, 168–170; Fraser (1), 623–4. (For the *Catasterismi* see Fraser (1), 2. 303 n. 303, and the bibliog. in Fraser (2), 206 (g); for the text of the pseudo-Eratosthenic *Catasterismi* see *Mythographi Graeci* 3 (1), ed. A. Olivieri, for whose edition see Knaack, *RE* 6. 303–4). P. M. F.

Erechtheum, the third outstanding building on the Athenian Acropolis, begun in 421 BC and finished, after a lapse, in 407 BC; built of Pentelic marble (see PENTELICON), with friezes of black *Eleusis stone to take applied white marble relief sculpture. Exact details of its construction are known from a contemporary inscription (*IG* 1³. 474). The main structure is divided into four compartments: the largest (east cella) has a prostyle-hexastyle Ionic portico; the west end is closed by a wall with engaged columns and corner piers. At this end is a unique and boldly projecting (though small) south feature—the 'porch of the maidens', with draped female figures (*caryatides) serving as supports—and, nearly opposite on the north side, a still more boldly projecting porch with Ionic columns (partly reassembled in early 20th cent.) standing on a lower level and having the tallest order of the whole composition.

The temple replaced to some extent the large 6th-cent. temple of *Athena whose foundations can be seen between it and the *Parthenon. We know from Pausanias (1. 26. 5–27. 3) that the Erechtheum housed a number of ancient cults (this may partly account for its complicated form) and many sacred spots and objects—the venerable image of Athena Polias, a golden lamp made by *Callimachus (2), a salt well and the mark of *Poseidon's trident, an altar of Poseidon and *Erechtheus, and altars of *Butes (1) and *Hephaestus. Near the west end of the building were shrines of *Cecrops and *Pandrosus, and the original sacred olive of Athena. A minority view (Jeppesen) denies the usual identification of the famous 5th-cent. building with the Erechtheum of Pausanias.

The Erechtheum was much admired in antiquity: the caryatids were copied for the *forum Augustum and Hadrian's villa at *Tibur; the Athenians faithfully replicated its details in their temple to Roma and Augustus.

G. P. Stevens and J. M. Paton, *The Erechtheum* (1927); J. Travlos, *Pictorial Dictionary of Ancient Athens* (1971); K. Jeppesen, *The Theory of the Alternative Erechtheion* (1987). T. F.; R. E. W.; A. J. S. S.

Erechtheus, a cult figure worshipped on the Athenian Acropolis, formally identified with *Poseidon but often regarded as an early king of Athens. The confusion surrounding his identity and status is compounded by his closeness to *Erichthonius, from whom he may not have been consistently distinguished much before the 4th cent. BC. The Iliadic Catalogue (Hom. *Il.* 2. 546–51) knows an Erechtheus who was born from Earth, brought up by Athena and installed in her sanctuary, and who is worshipped with sacrifice of bulls and rams; this gives the kernel of his myth and cult. His cult title (at least in the earlier period) 'Poseidon Erechtheus' may result from a character like that of *Poseidon the earthshaker (ἐρέχθω = tear, smash). About Erechtheus the king, the most consistently told tradition was that of the war against *Eleusis. This he won by killing the enemy leader *Eumolpus, son of Poseidon, but was thereupon himself killed by a blow of Poseidon's trident. (See HYACINTHIDES.) With *Cecrops, Erechtheus is seen as the prototype ancestor of all Athenians, who are poetically named *Erechtheidai*; but he was also one of the tribal *eponymoi, in which capacity he was probably conceptualized more as a typical hero than as the quasi-divine figure of the original cult.

> Kron, LIMC 4. 923–51, and Phylenheroen 32–83, 249–59; N. Loraux, The Children of Athena (1993; Fr. orig. 1981), 37–57; R. Parker, in J. Bremmer (ed.), Interpretations of Greek Mythology (1987), 193–202; E. Kearns, Heroes of Attica 113–15, 160, 210–11.   E. Ke.

Eresus (now Skála Eresoú), a small coastal *polis* in SW *Lesbos; birthplace of Theophrastus and probably Sappho. The earliest finds are Archaic. Its small *harbour had an artificial mole. In 428 BC the defences were strengthened by the Mytileneans. Eresus was soon recaptured by Athens, but the Classical–Hellenistic walls partly survive. Like the rest of Lesbos the city revolted in 412; after *Thrasybulus retook it c.390 the Athenians reinstated a democracy. Later Eresus joined the *Second Athenian Confederacy. After the *Social War (1) it had a pro-Macedonian tyranny until *Alexander (3) the Great's reign. It was Ptolemaic in the 3rd cent. Roman and early Christian inscriptions and buildings (bath complex, churches, etc.) attest a degree of prosperity. The medieval settlement was 4 km. (2½ mi.) inland.

> IG 12. 2. 526–76, 12 Suppl. 120–33; N. Spencer, BSA 1995; RE 6/1 (1907), 420–1; Arch. Rep. 1989–90.   D. G. J. S.

Eretria, a city of *Euboea. It joined its neighbour *Chalcis in trade in Syria, and colonizing in Italy, Sicily, and the north Aegean. In the late 8th cent. they fought over the Lelantine plain. Swiss excavations have revealed an important cemetery near the west gate, which included a remarkable hero-shrinè; also an interesting temple of *Apollo Daphnephoros. *Aristagoras (1) of Miletus sought its help for the *Ionian Revolt against Persia and in the avenging expedition sent by Darius the city was besieged and burnt. Eretria was in the *Delian League, revolted in 446, but was recovered (IG 1³. 39 for the settlement). Athens probably installed a colony. In 411 it revolted again, with the rest of Euboea (cf. ML 82). A member of the *Second Athenian Confederacy (378–377), it again revolted (349), and subsequently was the victim of Athenian and Macedonian intrigues. In the Second Macedonian War T. *Quinctius Flamininus sacked the city, which after the Roman victory was nominally free. Eretria took little part in the struggle of the Greek leagues against Rome, and in the time of Augustus still ranked as the second city of Euboea. Like Athens, Eretria had a system of *demes: Wallace, Hesp. 1947; N. Jones, Public Organization in Ancient Greece (1987); D. Knoepfler, in Acts of the Copenhagen Polis Centre 4 (1997) 75 f. See also LEFKANDI; LYSANIAS (1).

> Strabo 10. 1. 8 ff.; IG 12 (9), 11 ff.; J. R. Green and R. K. Sinclair, Historia 1970, 515–27; J. Boardman, CAH 3²/1 (1982), ch. 18b; W. G. Forrest, CAH 3²/3 (1982), ch. 39d; D. M. Lewis, CAH 5² (1992), 135 f. Fuller account than the above in PECS (T. W. Jacobsen).   W. A. L.; S. H.

Eretria, school of, (philosophy) founded by *Menedemus (1) as a continuation of the school of Elis (see ELIS, SCHOOL OF), is mentioned by Diog. Laert. 1. 17–19, 2. 105, 126; Strabo 9. 393;

Cic. Acad. 2. 129. Menedemus had a large following, but only one follower, Ctesibius, is known by name. The last trace of the school is in the title of a work of the Stoic *Sphaerus against it.   W. D. R.

Ergitium, a minor Daunian settlement in northern Apulia, between *Teanum Apulum and *Sipontum. It was a station on the *via Traiana, and has been tentatively identified with Il Cassone, a site 6 km. (3¾ mi.) south-east of S. Severo, which had a *centuriation system based on 16-actus squares.   K. L.

Erichthonius, an Athenian hero connected with the Acropolis and its cults. It is possible that he was originally identical with *Erechtheus, the older attested name, a hypothesis strengthened by the lack of clear evidence for a separate cult. He is distinguished from his near homonym by the emphasis placed on his birth and infancy. *Hephaestus attempted to rape *Athena, but succeeded only in spilling his seed on her thigh; she wiped it off with a piece of wool (ἔριον), and dropped it on the ground, whereupon the Earth conceived Erichthonius, after his birth handing him over to Athena—the last episode being a popular subject on red-figure vases. Athena shut the child in a chest or basket and in turn entrusted him to the daughters of Cecrops, who with disastrous results disobeyed her instructions not to look inside (see AGLAURUS; PANDROSUS). Almost certainly the myth relates to rituals performed on the Acropolis, in particular the *Arrhephoria. By the late 5th cent. BC historical tradition clearly distinguished Erichthonius the *autochthon from his grandson Erechtheus, and attributed the institution of various religious practices, notably the celebration of the *Panathenaea, to him.

> U. Kron, LIMC 4. 923–51; J. Mikalson, AJPhil. 1976, 141–53 (contra, N. Robertson, Rh. Mus. 1985, 231–95); E. H. Loeb, Die Geburt der Götter in der griechischen Kunst (1979), 165–81, 334–44; C. Bérard, Anodoi (1974), 34–8; J. Peradotto, Arethusa 1977, 92–101; N. Loraux, The Children of Athena (1993; Fr. orig. 1981), 37–71.   E. Ke.

Eridanus (᾽Ηριδανός), mythical river (see PHAETHON), having Electrides (Amber-) Islands at its mouth. Named by *Hesiod (Theog. 338) as a real river, the Eridanus was placed first in unknown northernmost Europe, or in western Europe, flowing into the northern Ocean. *Herodotus (3. 115) and *Strabo (5. 215) doubted its existence. *Aeschylus called it 'Spanish', meaning the Rhône (see Plin. HN 37. 32). Greek authors from the time of *Pherecydes (1), see FGrH 3 F 74, agreed to identify the Eridanus with the Po (see PADUS), and Roman writers followed suit (since there are no islands at the mouth of the Po, some authors sought these in the east Adriatic). The description of the Eridanus as an amber-river may embody the memory of an early amber-route from Jutland up the Elbe and Rhine (Rhenus) and down the Rhône (Rhodanus) or across the Alps to north Italy (see AMBER).

> E. Simon, LIMC 'Eridanos' 1.   E. H. W.; A. J. S. S.

Erigone, name of two figures in Attic mythology, both associated with the aiōra ('swing') rite of the *Anthesteria. In the first story, subject of the poetic narrative of *Eratosthenes, she is daughter of *Dionysus' host *Icarius (2), who hanged herself on finding her father's body. When other girls began to follow suit, her curse was appeased by the institution of the aiōra, swinging representing a modified form of hanging. The second version makes her daughter of *Aegisthus and *Clytemnestra, who brought *Orestes to trial for their murder and on his acquittal hanged herself. In other tellings, she was the mother of Orestes' illegitimate son Penthilus (Cinaethon fr. 4 Davies), or she was nearly killed by him but rescued by Artemis, who made her a

Erinna

priestess in Attica (Hyg. *Fab.* 122). Myth and cult combine to place Erigone in a group of heroines and goddesses associated with hanging; see King and Cantarella below.

F. Solmsen, *TAPA* 1947, 242 ff; R. Merkelbach, in *Studi . . . A. Rostagni* (1963), 469–519; E. Pochmarski and R. M. Gais, *LIMC* 3. 823–5; H. King, in A. Cameron and A. Kuhrt (eds.), *Images of Women in Antiquity* (1983), 108–25; E. Cantarella, in S. R. Suleiman (ed.), *The Female Body in Western Culture* (1986), 57–67. E. Ke.

Erinna, poet, 4th cent. BC (Eusebius gives a floruit of 352; the *Suda* erroneously makes her 'a companion and contemporary of *Sappho'). The *Suda* offers four places for her birth and domicile, *Teos, *Lesbos, *Rhodes, and Telos. The statement that she died unmarried at the age of 19 (*Suda*; cf. *Anth. Pal.* 7. 11. 13) may rest on conjecture derived from her poetry. Three epigrams in the Anthology are ascribed to her (6. 352, 7. 710, 712), perhaps falsely, but her reputation was based on a poem of 300 hexameters called *The Distaff* ('Ἠλακάτη), which presented her as spinning and weaving at her mother's insistence (*Anth. Pal.* 9. 190). The largest surviving fragment laments her friend Baucis, who died shortly after marrying, and sets the games, tasks, and terrors of childhood against Erinna's grief; she gives her age as 19. Whether the poem is autobiographical is uncertain. Some doubted its authenticity (Ath. 283d). In the innovative blend of content, dialect (a mixture of Doric and Aeolic), and metre, and the concern for bourgeois themes, Erinna reflects contemporary and prefigures Hellenistic poetry. Her reputation in the Hellenistic period was high (she is compared with *Homer and Sappho *Anth. Pal.* 9. 190).

TEXT *Suppl. Hell.* 186 ff.
CRITICISM M. L. West, *ZPE* 25 (1977), 95–119; J. M. Snyder, *The Woman and the Lyre* (1989), 86–97. C. C.

Erinyes, chthonian powers (see CHTHONIAN GODS) of retribution for wrongs and blood-guilt especially in the family. Individually or collectively they carry out the curses of a mother or father (*Il.* 9. 571; cf. *Il.* 9. 454, 11. 280; Hes. *Theog.* 472; Aesch. *Sept.* 70; *Eum.* 417), or they are personified curses without moral significance (*Od.* 2. 135; *Il.* 21. 412). Outside the family, the Erinys blinds a man's reason (*Il.* 19. 87; *Od.* 15. 234); and, as *daimōn beneath the earth, she protects a solemn oath (*Il.* 19. 259; cf. 3. 279). She also looks after beggars (*Od.* 17. 475) and generally ensures the natural order of things, like guarding the rights of an elder brother (*Zeus, *Il.* 15. 204) or silencing *Achilles' horse Xanthus, given a voice by *Hera (*Il.* 19. 409). Heraclitus extends the Erinyes' control over the cosmic order (DK 22 B 94). Also the concept of Erinyes as the souls of the dead (Rohde, *Psyche* (4th Ger. edn.), 270; Nilsson, *GGR* 1³. 100) is a moral development from their primary chthonian nature. Their negative function as powers of death predominates in popular imagination (Hes. *Theog.* 217–22; Aesch. *Eum.* 125), and is reflected in epitaphs (*Anth. Pal.* 7. 188). Aeschylus calls them daughters of Night (*Eum.* 321 f., 416, see NYX) and introduces them to the stage repulsively dressed in black, with snakes for hair but wingless (*Cho.* 1048–50; *Eum.* 48 f.; Paus. 1. 28. 6). According to Hesiod's genealogy, which is closer to their divine chthonian origins, they spring from Earth, made pregnant by Uranus' blood (*Theog.* 185).

In *Arcadian cult Erinys was identified with Demeter (Paus. 8. 25, 42). Together with Poseidon she produced the horse Arion (1) (Hesych.; Apollod. 3. 6. 8). Her background and nature resembled that of Medusa, loved by Poseidon and mother of Pegasus (1) (Hes. *Theog.* 281). The connection with horse and water illustrates Erinys' dual nature as chthonian goddess of vegetation and death. The latter allied her with other agents of death like the Harpies (*Od.* 20. 77 f.; Quint. Smyrn. 8, 243), Keres, Moirai, and Melainai (Black Ones).

Erinys' name occurs in Linear B (*erinu* KN Fp 1). Her link with Potnia (Potniai) in Boeotia also hints at a prehistoric past, as does the Gorgoneion on a late Minoan vase from Cnossus (*Arch. Rep.* 1980/1, fig. 34). On the other hand, their cult as Semnai ('August') at Athens (Paus. 1. 28. 6), Eumenides ('Kindly') in Sicyon (Paus. 2. 11. 4), and their identification with the Ablabiai ('Harmless') (Erythrae, *Syll.*³ 1014b 67), reveal attempts at neutralizing the Erinyes' dark powers through euphemisms.

The Eumenides occur on a number of votive steles from the Argolid. Three Erinyes together with Hecate and an *eidōlion* in the Underworld on an Attic black-figure *lekythos* (470 BC, Athens Nat. Mus. inv. no. 19765) seem to belong to the same iconographic tradition that relates to the chthonian function of these figures. In the vast majority of instances, however, representations of the Erinyes were based on the theatre of Aeschylus and remained popular in this form in Greek, Etruscan, and Roman art. In later writers there are only three of them and their names are Tisiphone, Allecto, and Megaera (schol. on Lycophr. *Alex.* 406). See CURSES.

E. Wüst, *RE* Suppl. 8 'Erinys'; B. Dietrich, *Hermes* 1962, 129–48; S. Karouzou, *JHS* 1972, 64–73, pl. 18; H. Sarian, *LIMC* 3/1 (1986) 826–43 'Erinys'. H. J. R.; B. C. D.

Eriphus, Middle Comedy poet (see COMEDY (GREEK), MIDDLE), as the two mythological titles, *Aeolus* and *Meliboea*, suggest.

FRAGMENTS Kassel and Austin, *PCG* 5. 178–82.
INTERPRETATION Meineke, *FCG* 1 420 f.; G. Kaibel, *RE* 6/1 (1907), 460, 'Eriphos' 3. W. G. A.

Eris, 'Strife' (Discordia in Latin), often personified as a goddess in poetry. She appears in several Homeric battle scenes, e.g. *Il.* 4. 440–5 (where she is the sister of *Ares), 11. 3–14. *Hesiod at *Theogony* 225–32 makes her the daughter of Night (*Nyx) and mother of Toil, Pain, Battles, Bloodshed, Lies, Ruin, and the like. At *Works and Days* 11–26, however, he declares that there is not just one Eris but two, a bad Eris who fosters war and a good Eris who stimulates men to work through a spirit of competition.

Eris is given a mythical role by the *Cypria* (see EPIC CYCLE; para. 4 (6)): at the instigation of Zeus she attended the wedding of *Peleus and *Thetis and there created rivalry between *Athena, *Hera, and *Aphrodite, which led to the Judgement of *Paris and thus to the Trojan War. Much later sources (first *Hyginus (3), *Fab.* 92) say that she was angry at not being invited to the wedding and created the rivalry by tossing the 'Apple of Discord' among the guests as a prize for the most beautiful.

H. Giroux, *LIMC* 3/1 (1986), 846–50, 'Eris'. A. L. B.

Eros, god of love. Eros personified does not occur in Homer, but the Homeric passages in which the word *erōs* is used give a clear idea of the original significance. It is the violent physical desire that drives Paris to Helen, Zeus to Hera, and shakes the limbs of the suitors of Penelope (*Il.* 3. 442, 14. 294; *Od.* 18. 212). A more refined conception of this Eros who affects mind and body appears in the Archaic lyric poets. Because his power brings peril he is cunning, unmanageable, cruel (Alcman 36; Ibycus 6; Sappho 136; Thgn. 1231); in Anacreon he smites the lovestruck one with an axe or a whip. He comes suddenly like a wind and shakes his victims (Sappho, Ibycus). Eros is playful, but plays with frenzies and confusion. He symbolizes all attractions which provoke love. He is young and beautiful, he walks over flowers, and the roses are 'a plant of Eros' of which he makes his crown (*Anacreonta* 53. 42). He is sweet and warms the heart (Alcman 101).

With Himeros ('Desire') and Pothos ('Longing'), Eros is a constant companion of *Aphrodite, although he can appear with any god, whenever a love story is involved. Hesiod seems to have transformed the Homeric conception of Eros. Although he describes Eros in terms almost identical with Homer as the god who 'loosens the limbs and damages the mind', he also makes him, together with Earth and Tartarus, the oldest of all gods, all-powerful over gods and men. With Eros as a cosmic principle, *Parmenides found a place for him, perhaps as the power which reconciles opposites. This philosophic conception contributed to the Epicurean picture of omnipotent Eros (Ath. 13. 561), took abstruse mythological shape in Orphic cosmogonies (Ar. *Av.* 696) (see ORPHIC LITERATURE; ORPHISM), and formed the background for Plato's discussions of Eros in *Symposium* and *Phaedrus*.

Hellenistic poets continue the more playful conception of Anacreon, the tricks Eros plays on mortals, the tribulations of those who try to resist him, and the punishments he receives for his misdeeds. His bow and arrows, first mentioned by Euripides (*IA* 548–9), play a great part in these accounts. Frequently a plurality of Erotes is introduced (*Anacreonta*; *Anth. Pal.*; Ap. Rhod. 3. 452, 687, 765, 937) because both love and the god who symbolized it could multiply.

Eros had some ancient cults and much individual worship. He was always the god of love directed towards male as well as female beauty. Hence his images in the gymnasia, his cult among the *Sacred Band in Thebes (Ath. 13. 561 f, 602a), and the altar in Athens erected by Hippias' (1) lover (Ath. 13. 609d). As a god of fertility Eros is celebrated in the very old cult in *Thespiae (Paus. 9. 27. 1–5), and in the joint cult with Aphrodite on the north slope of the Athenian Acropolis. In Thespiae Eros was represented by an aniconic image; in Athens phallic symbols have been found in the sanctuary. In both cults festivals were celebrated; that in Thespiae, called Erotidia, incorporated art, athletics, and equestrianism. Altars to Eros at the *Academy in Athens and the gymnasium at *Elis were matched by ones to Anteros (Paus. 1. 30. 1, 6. 23. 3), whom Eros sometimes wrestles. In Philadelphia, worshippers called themselves Erotes; other cult centres include Leuctra, *Velia, and *Parium in Mysia.

Eros in Archaic art is hard to differentiate from other winged males. An Attic plaque shows him wingless. On vases, he appears alone, carrying lyre or hare, or in myth, especially accompanying Aphrodite, winged, boyish, sometimes with bow and arrows. During the Classical period he increasingly associates with women, in domestic scenes or weddings. He appears in military and athletic scenes, and was painted by Zeuxis (1) and Pausias. The Erotostasia occurs occasionally. Scopas' group of Eros, Pothos, and Himeros at Megara is an early sculpture. In the Hellenistic period, he is a putto, common in terracottas and with Psyche. See SEXUALITY.

RE 6, 'Eros'; *LIMC* 3/1. 850–942; 4/1. 1–12; *Eros Grec*, exhib. cat. (Athens, 1990). G. M. A. H.; J. R. T. P.; K. W. A.

Erotian, grammarian and author of the most famous Hippocratic lexicon of antiquity. Lived in the 1st cent. AD.

TEXT E. Nachmanson, *Vocum Hippocraticarum collectio cum fragmentis* (1918); cf. HIPPOCRATES (2). J. T. V.

Erucius, of Cyzicus (fl. 50 BC), author of fourteen epigrams in the Greek Anthology. *Anth. Pal.* 7. 368 commemorates a woman captured in the sack of Athens by Sulla (86 BC); 7. 377 is a mysterious attack on *Parthenius; 6. 96 arguably imitates Virgil, *Ecl.* 7. 2–4 (G. Williams, *Change and Decline* (1978), 126).

Gow–Page, *GP* 2. 278–87; A. Seth-Smith, *Mnemos.* 34 (1981), 63–71. A. D. E. C.

Erucius Clarus, Sextus, protégé and friend of *Pliny (2) the Younger, was the nephew of Septicius Clarus, Praetorian prefect early in Hadrian's reign. After a slow start, Erucius won distinction as legionary legate in *Trajan's Parthian War, capturing *Nisibis. He became city prefect under Antoninus Pius and was consul for the second time (as ordinarius) in AD 146, but died in the same year.

Plin. *Ep.* 1.16, 2.9; Cass. Dio 68. *PIR*² E 96; Syme, *RP* 2. 482 ff. A. R. Bi.

Erysichthon, a mythological figure usually located in Thessaly, whose story is best known from *Callimachus (3)'s Sixth Hymn. Despite warnings, he cut down a grove sacred to *Demeter, and was punished by insatiable hunger, to satisfy which he was forced to ruin himself and his household. In some versions (e.g. Ov. *Met.* 8. 846–74) he had a daughter Mestra who had received from her lover *Poseidon the power of changing into whatever shape she chose; she therefore supported her father by being sold in various animal forms and escaping to be resold.

The Attic hero Erysichthon was son of *Cecrops, who was associated with *Delos and died young. The two may sometimes have been identified (Robertson).

N. Hopkinson, *Callimachus: Hymn to Demeter* (1984), 18–30; N. Robertson, *AJPhil.* 1984, 369–408; U. Kron, *LIMC* 4. 14–21; W. Burkert, *Structure and History in Greek Mythology and Ritual* (1979), 134–6. E. Ke.

Erytheia, 'the red, or blushing, one', i.e. sunset-coloured. Name of (1) one of the *Hesperides (Apollod. 2. 114); (2) the daughter of Geryon, and also his island (Steph. Byz., entry under the name; Paus. 10. 17. 5).

Erythrae, one of the twelve cities of the Ionian League (see PANIONIUM), on the coast opposite the island of Chios. Allegedly founded by a party from Crete, and later by *Ionians under Cnopus son of *Codrus, the city was prosperous from the start. Falling in turn, with the rest of Ionia, under *Lydia and then *Persia, Erythrae was later a member of the *Delian League; an important inscription (*IG* 1³. 14, probably late 450s) shows Athens brazenly regulating her affairs to suit Athenian interests, apparently after a revolt; her later assessment of seven talents was among the highest in Ionia. In the fourth century Erythrae was in the Hecatomnid i.e. Persian satrapal sphere of influence (see Tod 155 and *SEG* 31. 969, honours to *Mausolus and *Idrieus). It also made a treaty with *Hermias (1), see Tod 165. Erythrae enjoyed free and immune status under *Alexander (3) the Great and the *Seleucids. Under the Principate it probably belonged to the *conventus of *Smyrna. It is listed as a bishopric in the diocese of Asia, but little archaeological evidence is known from the later period, although the Classical city wall, over 3 km. (2 mi.) long, is well preserved in part, and the theatre has been excavated.

*CAH*² 5 (1992), 56 ff.; *PECS* 317; H. Engelmann and R. Merkelbach, *Die Inschriften von Erythrai und Klazomenai* 1–2 (1972–3).
G. E. B.; C. R., A. J. S. S.

Eryx, an Elymian settlement and a mountain (Monte San Giuliano: 751 m. (2,460 ft.) above sea-level) above Drepana (mod. Trapani) in western Sicily. An attempt by *Dorieus to establish a settlement (Heraclea) in the neighbourhood failed. Dependent on *Segesta in the 5th cent. BC, Eryx was occupied later by the

Carthaginians, though temporarily seized by *Pyrrhus (278 or 277). Phoenician masons' marks are found on the defensive walls, and Punic legends appear on the coinage from the 4th cent. Phoenician associations are also indicated by the rite of sacred *prostitution in the cult of Astarte-*Aphrodite-Venus on the acropolis rock. The Elymian settlement was evacuated in 259 during the First Punic War, and the inhabitants were transferred to Drepana. L. Iunius seized Eryx and established a fort on the lower slopes to isolate Drepana (249). *Hamilcar (2) Barca captured the town but not the temple or the lower fort (244); thus he failed to relieve Drepana, although maintaining his position until 241. The Romans stressed the Elymian–Trojan associations of the cult: Virgil (*Aen.* 5. 759 f.) makes *Aeneas visit Eryx and found the temple. The cult enjoyed great popularity during the republic (cf. Diod. Sic. 4. 83. 4) and widespread diffusion (sanctuaries of Venus Erycina were established at Rome in 217 and 184 BC, as well as elsewhere), but it declined in the early empire, despite *Claudius' repair of the temple (Suet. *Claud.* 25. 5; cf. Tac. *Ann.* 4. 43). Today nothing survives of the sanctuary, which underlies a 12th-cent. castle. (See SICILY.)

PECS 317–18; BTCGI 7 (1989), 349–78. Diffusion of the cult: S. Moscati, *Oriens antiquus* 1968, 91–4. Temple: *Not. Scav.* 1935, 294–328. Cult: R. J. A. Wilson, *Sicily under the Roman Empire* (1990), 283–5.

H. H. S.; A. G. W.; R. J. A. W.

Esquiline The name, in the form Esquiliae, denoted the eastern plateau formed in Rome by *montes Oppius* and *Cispius*, the *regio Esquilina* being the second of the republican Four Regions (Varro, *Ling.* 5. 49–50 (see REGIO)). In the iron age and much later it was used as a cemetery, in particular for paupers (Hor. *Sat.* 1. 8. 8–13). It was included within the republican wall (*Wall of Servius) and provided later sites for *Nero's *Domus Aurea and the Thermae (see BATHS) of *Titus and *Trajan. Under Augustus the name was applied to Regio V, outside the republican wall, which contained *gardens belonging to wealthy aristocrats, notably the Horti Maecenatis (see MAECENAS); many of these subsequently came into the possession of the emperors. Beyond lay the Sessorium, an imperial residence. The arch of *Gallienus (*CIL* 6. 1106) recalls the porta Esquilina of the republican wall.

M. Cima and E. La Rocca, *Le tranquille dimore degli dei* (1986); Coarelli, *Roma* 208 ff; Richardson, *Topog. Dict. Ancient Rome* 146.

I. A. R.; J. R. P.

Essenes, Jewish religious group known to have flourished in Judaea in the 1st cent. AD. The doctrines and customs of the Essenes were described in detail by *Josephus and *Philon (4), and in a short notice by Pliny the Elder. References in Christian literature were mostly derived from Josephus. The Essenes lived in regimented communities dedicated to pious *asceticism. They were to be found above the Dead Sea (*Pliny (1)) or in all the towns of *Judaea (Josephus). Josephus mentions two kinds of Essene, one group which was celibate, and others who married. Some relationship between the Essenes and the sectarians at Qumran by the Dead Sea who produced some of the *Dead Sea Scrolls is plausible but impossible to prove. If the Qumran sectarians were indeed Essenes, there must have existed even more varieties of Essenism and doctrines must have changed over time. According to Josephus and Philon, the Essenes were noted for their communal solidarity and discipline, their strict interpretation of the Law of Moses, and their devotion to their beliefs to the point of martyrdom, but the descriptions in these writers may have been over-idealized in order to impress a non-Jewish audience. See RELIGION, JEWISH.

Texts referring to Essenes are collected in A. Adam and C. Burchard, *Antike Berichte über die Essener*, 2nd edn. (1972), and in G. Vermes and M. Goodman, *The Essenes According to the Classical Sources* (1989) (texts and trans.). Discussion in Schürer, *History* 2. 562–90; T. S. Beall, *Josephus' Description of the Essenes Illustrated by the Dead Sea Scrolls* (1988).

M. D. G.

Eteocles, the older son of *Oedipus. After the blinding and retirement of their father, he and his brother Polynices twice insulted him, once by setting before him certain vessels which had belonged to Laius, and then by giving him a portion of meat less honourable than a king deserved (Cyclic *Thebais*, frs. 2–3 Davies/Bernabé/Kinkel, see EPIC CYCLE). Oedipus therefore cursed them. The two brothers agreed to reign in alternate years, Eteocles taking the first year, Polynices leaving *Thebes (1) for *Argos (2). At the end of his year Eteocles refused to give up the throne; Polynices returned with his father-in-law *Adrastus (1) and the 'Seven'; in the ensuing battle, the two brothers met and killed each other (see SEVEN AGAINST THEBES).

In art: *LIMC* 4 / 1 (1988), 26–37.

A. Sch.

Eteoclus, son of Iphis, Argive hero (see ARGOS (2)). At a fairly early stage of the tradition he seems to have replaced *Parthenopaeus as one of the *Seven against Thebes, cf. ADRASTUS (1) (see Paus. 10. 10. 3). Then *Aeschylus (*Sept.* 458) or his authority included both him and Parthenopaeus, apparently so as to be able to leave Adrastus out of the actual assault; hence later writers (as Soph. *OC* 1316 and Eur. *Supp.* 872) use the same list.

See U. von Wilamowitz-Moellendorff, *Aischylos, Interpretationen* (1914), 100.

H. J. R.

Ethiopia was a name usually applied by the Greeks to any region in the far south (but north of the equator). Perhaps originally designating radiance reflected by dwellers in the east from the morning star, it soon came to mean the land of the 'Burnt-faced People'. An ethnic connotation is found already in *Homer (*Od.* 1. 22 etc.), and as geographical knowledge increased a distinction was made between western and eastern Ethiopians. Early Greek interest in Ethiopia was largely concerned with the source of the *Nile. Ethiopia was favoured by the gods, and hence has an important place in utopian literature. From Herodotus onwards Ethiopia designated especially the lands south of Egypt comprising most of the modern states of Sudan and Ethiopia, the ancient Kush, *Meroe, and Aksum. Ethiopians formed contingents in the Persian army during *Xerxes' invasion of Greece (Hdt. 7. 70) and Greeks visited Ethiopia from the 6th. BC onwards. The early Ptolemaic period saw increased economic contact with Meroe, but also fleets charting the African coast of the *Red Sea, activity eventually opening the routes to *India. Contacts between Meroe and Rome continued throughout the 1st cent. AD, but the emergence of a powerful state centred upon Aksum contributed to the eventual fragmentation of Meroe, and during the later Roman period Aksum was the major Ethiopian state. In later Classical literature (e.g. *Heliodorus (4), *Aithiopica*) Ethiopia is again a quasi-mythical land, but with the addition of ethnographic details culled from the encyclopaedists. See RACE.

F. M. Snowden, *Blacks in Antiquity* (1970).

R. G. M.

ethnicity (see RACE). In social science usage, a term coined (in 1953) to describe that condition 'wherein certain members of a society in a given social context choose to emphasize as their most meaningful basis of primary extrafamilial identity certain assumed cultural, national or somatic traits' (O. Patterson in Glazer and Moynihan, 308); a socio-political strategy of selective advantage enacted within a dominant political organization, which rests on insistence upon the significance of group distinctiveness and identity, and the rights that derive from it. Ethnic identity is not a 'natural' condition, but rather a self-conscious statement using selected cultural traits as diacritical marks. Ethnic groups are thus mutually exclusive, and are more usually constituted with reference to kinship than to territory. Dynamic and strongly contextualized, ethnic expression is characteristic of complex societies.

In the ancient Greek world, ethnicity is of importance in two principal areas. First, in the context of the *ethnos*, a category of state which existed alongside the **polis*, but which is only rarely treated by ancient sources. *Ethnē* are diverse, with no single form of constitution. They are characterized by the fact that by contrast with *poleis* (which retained total autonomy), individual communities surrendered some political powers (usually control of warfare and foreign relations) to a common assembly. Their inhabitants were thus required to express a range of local and regional loyalties of varying degrees of complexity and strength. By contrast with *poleis*, the role of urban centres in *ethnē* varied greatly; settlement structures range from a high degree of urbanization and local autonomy (e.g. **Boeotia*, which was tantamount to a collection of small *poleis*) to scattered small villages with little urban development (e.g. **Aetolia*). According to **Aristotle (Pol.* 1326[b]*), ethnē* are characterized by their large populations. Although the *ethnos* is sometimes equated with primitive tribalism, social and political developments from the 8th cent. BC onwards (in religion and **colonization*, for example) often bear comparison with evidence from *poleis*, and the *ethnos* was a varied and long-lived phenomenon. Equally, *ethnē* have been seen as the origin or precursors of the federal states created from the 4th cent. onwards (e.g. the **Achaean* and **Aetolian* Confederacies). These, however, incorporated many former *poleis*, and relations between citizen groups were thus more formally constituted, often drawing on earlier concepts of **sympoliteia* and **isopoliteia*.

In Hellenistic and Roman times, the concept of ethnicity may be applied to a variety of 'outsider' groups (e.g. Jews) who sought or were accorded particular status or rights within a broader imperial context. Hence the status and political role of these groups varied over time, and ancient sources are often imprecise in distinguishing between ethnic groups, the *natio* (or nation, usually the dominant ethnic group in a region), and the tribe (which in the case of the Roman division of state, may originally have been constituted on an ethnic basis). See NATIONALISM; RACE.

N. Glazer and P. Moynihan (eds.), *Ethnicity* (1975); J. A. O. Larsen, *Greek Federal States* (1967); C. Morgan, *PCPS* 1991, 131–63. C. A. M.

ethnics See NAMES, PERSONAL, GREEK; STEPHANUS OF BYZANTIUM.

Etna See AETNA.

Etruscan discipline, Etruscan religion See HARUSPICES; RELIGION, ETRUSCAN.

Etruscan language The Etruscan language was long held to be obscure and mysterious. This it no longer remains, even if there are still large gaps in our knowledge of its grammar and lexicon and in our understanding of the texts—larger than is the case with other languages of comparable attestation. For access to Etruscan is made more difficult by its genealogical isolation, which was already recognized by **Dionysius (7) of Halicarnassus (Ant. Rom.* 1. 30. 2). The only language that has so far been shown to be 'related' to Etruscan, i.e. to be descended from a common

source, is the pre-Greek idiom of **Lemnos*, and the evidence even for this is limited to just a few texts. It may at best provide an argument in favour of the view championed by Herodotus (1. 94) that the Etruscans originated in the region of the Aegean and Asia Minor. See ETRUSCANS, § 2.

Our sources for Etruscan are: (*a*) *c*.9,000 epigraphic texts—mostly from Etruria, several from **Latium, *Campania, *Umbria, *Corsica*, and the Po valley (see PADUS), and one or two from further afield (Narbonensis and Tunisia)—dated *c*.700–10 BC; (*b*) a *liber linteus* (linen book), two-thirds of which (*c*.1,500 words) is preserved in the binding of an Egyptian mummy in Zagreb; (*c*) 40–50 glosses, i.e. meanings given for Etruscan words in Latin or Greek texts (*aisar* 'deos', Suet. *Aug.* 97); (*d*) a series of Etruscan loanwords in Latin (*satelles* 'bodyguard', from Etr. *zatlaθ*, originally 'axe-bearer') and of Latin or Greek loanwords in Etruscan (*culiχna*, from Gk. κυλίχνη 'goblet').

Since no well-known language has yet been discovered to be related to Etruscan, the procedure of linguistic comparison that has proved its worth elsewhere, by which one would infer from the formal similarity of an Etruscan word with one in a known language that the meaning too is similar (the 'etymological' method), affords no general access to Etruscan and can be applied only in the case of loanwords. The number and usefulness of the glosses is limited. The Etruscan–Latin bilingual inscriptions contain almost nothing but personal names. Beyond this, only an indirect approach to Etruscan is possible, consisting of three steps: (1) deducing the 'message' of the text from the archaeological context—possible only with context-bound texts such as captions to images, signatures, or epitaphs; (2) breaking down the 'message' into its parts, to be correlated with parts of the text—possible only with short texts, and made easier by comparing similar texts in better-known languages from the same cultural milieu (the 'bilinguistic' method: *mini muluvanece* = Venetic *mego donasto*, 'me gave', at the beginning of dedicatory inscriptions); (3) checking the hypotheses thus produced by applying the values to all instances of a word or form (the 'combinatory' method); by this means access may also be gained to parts of longer context-independent texts. Naturally this procedure does not provide an explanation of every detail.

The Etruscan script is an **alphabet*, taken over (before 700 BC) from a (West) Greek school-alphabet (in the earliest texts $X = ks$, not *kh* as in the East Greek alphabet), and in its turn the source of the Latin script. It can therefore be read, i.e. we know in general terms how the letters were pronounced. Of the 26 signs of the model alphabet, *b, d, o,* and *ś* were never used (but they were learned, and some were passed on to Latin), then in the 6th–5th cents. BC, *k, q,* and *x* were given up, while on the other hand 8 for *f* was introduced. The values of the letters may be established from (*a*) the sound-values of the corresponding Latin and Greek signs, (*b*) Latin transcriptions of Etruscan words and names, and (*c*) orthographical variants within Etruscan itself. From which it appears that Etruscan had only four vowels: *a, e, i, u* (later pronounced *o*); no voiced obstruents but only voiceless ones: *k* (mostly written *c*), *p, t,* and with additional features, *z* = *t^s, φ, θ*; and a large number of fricatives: *χ, h, f, s, š*, perhaps *θ* = Eng. *th*. In the early 5th cent. BC, short internal vowels were lost, which accounts for the accumulations of consonants in late forms (the gentile name *Vestrcna* from *Vestricina*).

Etruscan is an agglutinating language. So in the noun, for instance, number and case are each marked by an individual affix: *clan* 'son', genitive *clen-s*, pl. *clen-ar*, gen. pl. *clen-ar-as*. Apart from the genitive, an ablative (*clen*) and a locative (*spure* < *spura-i* 'in

Etruscans

the community') have so far been recognized; the latter can be formed from the genitive (*Pultuce-s-i* 'in the (workshop) of Pultuce') and be combined with postpositions (*spure-ri* 'for the community'). Nominative and accusative are distinguished only in pronouns (*mi* 'I', acc. *mi-ni* 'me'; *ca* 'this', acc. *cn*). There is a long misunderstood feature of articulation, whereby an inflected demonstrative pronoun is attached as an enclitic to an adjective or a genitive: *sacni+ca* 'the pure (pl.)' (?), gen. *sacni+cla*; *Tin-s+ta* 'the (son) of Jupiter', *Arnθ-al+iσa* 'the (son) of Arnth', gen. *Arnθ-al+iσla* 'of the (son) of Arnth' (double genitive). In the verb, far fewer details have been explained than in the noun and pronoun. Distinctions of person and number have not so far been demonstrated, but there is evidence for distinctions of tense (*ame* 'is, am', preterite. *am-ce*), mood (imperative *tur* 'bring', jussive *tur-a*), and diathesis (*mene-ce* 'set up', passive *mena-χe*). There has been little investigation of Etruscan syntax. The normal order of constituents seems to have been Subject–(Direct) Object–Verb–other elements: *Vl. Afuna Vl. Pesnaliσa cn σuθi ceriχunce* (Ru 5. 1, CIE), 'Vel Afuna, (son) of Vel (and) of Pesnei this grave has built'. A pronominal object, however, stands in first position and attracts the verb: *itun turuce Venel Atelinas Tinas cliniiaras* (Ta 3. 2 CIE), 'this offered Venel Atelinas to the sons of Zeus'.

The most noticeable gaps in our knowledge of Etruscan concern the lexicon. Yet the meaning is plain for a number of words, particularly those with clearly definable referents: kinship terms such as *clan* 'son', *seχ* 'daughter', *puia* 'wife', *ati* 'mother', *apa* 'father'; numerals such as *θu* 'one', *zal* 'two', *ci* 'three', *maχ* 'five', including compounded forms like *θun-em ce-alχ-* 'un-de-triginta (= 29)'; finally legal terms: *lautni* 'libertus', *zilaθ* 'praetor', *spur(a)* 'state'. Far more numerous are the words whose meaning can be only approximately or incompletely determined: *turuce/turce* 'dedicated', *nunθen* 'invoke', *zinace/zince* 'set up'; *zusle* is a sacrificial animal, *fase* some sacrificial offering that cannot be counted, etc. Knowledge of the lexicon is closely connected with the nature of the surviving material. The majority of the Etruscan texts are funerary inscriptions, which mostly contain only personal names, but sometimes also biographical data. They are broadly intelligible, as are the inscriptions (mainly from the Archaic period) recording ownership, manufacture, and dedications. Some measure of comprehension, finally, has been achieved for certain sections (some quite lengthy) of the longest Etruscan text, the description of rituals, arranged according to the calendar, in the *liber linteus*, as well as for the beginning of the second longest (and likewise ritual) text on the clay tablet from Capua. On the other hand, the long agreement (129 words) on the *cippus* (stone marker) from Perugia (Pe 8. 4 CIE) and the detailed account of the career of *Laris Pulena* (Ta 1. 17 CIE) are still largely obscure, while in the case of the quasi-bilingual inscription from *Pyrgi (Cr 4. 4 CIE), found in 1964, the Phoenician parallel text has not provided the elucidation of the Etruscan text that was at first expected because it presents the same content in a different fashion.

TEXTS Of the *Corpus Inscriptionum Etruscarum* (CIE) there have so far appeared the volumes with the monumental inscriptions of Etruria proper (1 (1883–1902), 2 (1907–70)), also the *instrumentum* inscriptions from Tarquinii and Volsinii (3. 1 (1982), 2 (1987)), and the *Supplementum* with the *liber linteus* (1911). A very useful selection of texts is provided by M. Pallottino, *Testimonia Linguae Etruscae*, 2nd edn. (1968), while the collection *Etruskische Texte: Editio minor*, ed. H. Rix and others (1991), aspires to completeness; both editions contain detailed indexes. An index giving words in their context is supplied by M. Pallottino, M. Pandolfini Angeletti, and others, *Thesaurus Linguae Etruscae 1: Indice lessicale* (1978), with supplements 1984, 1985 (reverse

index), 1991. Newly discovered inscriptions are regularly published in the periodical *Studi Etruschi*.

GENERAL PRESENTATIONS M. Pallottino, *Etruscologia*, 7th edn. (1984), pt 3 (Eng. version, *The Etruscans* (1978)); H. Rix, in M. Cristofani (ed.), *Gli Etruschi: Una nuova immagine* (1984), 210–38; L. Agostiniani, LALIES (1992) 37–74.

INTRODUCTION M. Cristofani, *Introduzione allo studio dell'etrusco*, new edn. (1991).

PARTICULAR TOPICS M. Cristofani, 'L'alfabeto etrusco', in *Popoli e Civiltà dell'Italia Antica*, 6 (1978), 403–28; C. de Simone, *Die griechischen Entlehnungen im Etruskischen* 2 vols. (1968–70); G. Colonna, 'Nomi etruschi di vasi', *Arch. Class.* 1973–4, 132–50; H. Rix, 'Etr. *un, une, unuχ* "te, tibi, vos" e le preghiere dei rituali paralleli nel *liber linteus*', *Arch. Class.* 1991, 665–91.   H. R.

Etruscans (Tyrsenoi, Tyrrheni, Etrusci), historically and artistically the most important of the indigenous peoples of pre-Roman Italy, and according to M. *Porcius Cato (1) the masters of nearly all of it (Serv. *on Aen.* 11. 567)—a claim confirmed by archaeology for the area between the Tridentine Alps and the gulf of Salerno. Modern research has raised the status of Etruscan civilization to a level that is demonstrably superior to the traditional picture of a poor relation of Greece and a mysterious prelude to Rome.

The conflict in the sources between the Etruscans' alleged eastern (Hdt. 1. 94) and autochthonous (Dion. Hal. *Ant. Rom.* 1. 25–30) origins has been resolved by D. Briquel's convincing demonstration that the famous story of an exodus, led by *Tyrrhenus from Lydia to Italy, was a deliberate political fabrication created in the Hellenized milieu of the court at Sardis in the early 6th cent. BC. Herodotus' authority is not diminished by this: his account is indeed prefaced by the words 'The Lydians say . . .'. Archaeologically, M. Pallottino's hypothesis of ethnic formation in Etruria itself has long provided the best explanation of the facts (but for the linguistic viewpoint see ETRUSCAN LANGUAGE, § 1): the possessors of the indigenous *Villanovan culture between the Arno and the Tiber were iron age Etruscans, who gained much in the 9th and 8th cents. from the interest shown by the outside world in their mineral resources, and in the 7th were able to acquire and commission luxury goods and adornments of east Mediterranean ('*orientalizing') types for the tombs of their 'princes'. Foremost among the early bearers of outside influences were the Euboean traders who had established themselves at *Pithecusae by the mid-8th cent.: their alphabet was modified to accommodate the pre-existing phonetic systems already characteristic of different Etruscan-speaking zones, and there can be little doubt that it is the first western Greeks who are ultimately responsible for the exaggerated perception of ethnic unity ('Tyrsenoi') in an area that had in fact inherited a significant degree of regional individuality from its final bronze age.

The continuity in settlement and in the basic culture of the 8th and 7th cents. at the mainstream Villanovan–Etruscan centres was accompanied by major developments both in society and in artistic production. The *praenomen–nomen* combination, a clear sign of proto-urban organization, is attested epigraphically from the beginning of the 7th cent., as are recognizably local schools of fine painted pottery, soon joined by bucchero (the only exclusively Etruscan product), bronze-work, and jewellery—categories in which the contributions of native Etruscan and expatriate Greek and Levantine specialists and entrepreneurs are inextricably linked. Oil and wine were also produced and exported on a large scale by the mid-6th cent. By then, too, the social class represented by the early orientalizing princely tombs had given way to a broader, *polis*-based, category of prosperous merchants

560

and landowners. Their last resting-places take the form of single-family chamber-tombs, ranged along streets in well-planned cemeteries which have yielded a rich harvest of imported vases from all the best Attic black-figure and red-figure workshops. The chambers at *Tarquinii and a few other centres have preserved the largest extant complex of pre-Roman painting in the classical world: prior to the 4th cent., its naturalistic and frequently cheerful depiction of banquets, games, and hunting affords a welcome glimpse of the 'real' Etruscan character underneath the veneer of Hellenization (see HELLENISM) constituted by the mass of prestige goods imported (and made locally) not only for deposition in tombs but also—and increasingly—to supply the votive requirements of major sanctuaries like that at *Pyrgi.

The expansion of some Etruscan centres beyond the relatively narrow confines of Etruria proper began at an early stage with the foundation of the Tarquin dynasty at Rome by Lucius *Tarquinius Priscus (reigned traditionally 616–578). The presence of the Tarquins, who turned Rome into a city, doubtless facilitated control of the land route to Campania, where Volturnus (*Capua) became the chief Etruscan city. To the north, *Felsina (Bologna) enjoyed a similar status in the Po valley from the late 6th cent., when growing Greek activity on land and at sea to the south made it imperative to cultivate new markets—not least with the mysterious Celtic communities north of the Alps, who had acquired a taste for the contents of the fine bronze flagons made in *Vulci when *Arruns of *Clusium (Chiusi) set off to entice them into Italy for his own purposes at the end of the 5th cent. (Livy 5. 33). In the event, the *Celts added their own not inconsiderable weight to the pressure on the Etruscans that was already building up from Rome (whence the Tarquins were expelled in 509), from the Greek south (where the battle of *Cumae was lost in 474) and from other quarters as well (the Carthaginians and the Italic peoples). Of these, the inexorable advance of Rome into Etruria and Umbria was by far the most serious threat to the survival of what was still an essentially cantonal phenomenon as distinct from a nation: city-states, loosely organized in a League of Twelve Peoples, capable of meeting in council at the federal sanctuary of Voltumna near *Volsinii—and of denying federal assistance to *Veii, threatened by Rome since the end of the 5th cent., for primarily religious reasons. Livy's comment (5. 1. 6) on this episode, to the effect that the Etruscans paid more attention than any other people to religious considerations, is one of the relatively few positive statements about the Etruscans in the ancient sources: no Etruscan literature has survived, and Greek and Roman authors were far from objective observers of such matters as commercial rivalry (which they defined as piracy) and social customs (notably those concerning the position of women) that were not those of Greece and Rome. See ETRUSCAN LANGUAGE; RELIGION, ETRUSCAN.

HISTORY AND GENERAL G. Dennis, *Cities and Cemeteries of Etruria*, 3rd edn. (1883); H. H. Scullard, *The Etruscan Cities and Rome* (1967); W. V. Harris, *Rome in Etruria and Umbria* (1971); M. Pallottino, *The Etruscans*, 2nd edn. (1975; *Etruscologia*, 7th edn. 1984), and *A History of Earliest Italy* (1991; It. orig. 1984); L. Bonfante, *Out of Etruria* (1981), and (ed.), *Etruscan Life and Afterlife* (1986); M. Sprenger and others, *The Etruscans: Their History, Art and Architecture* (1983; Ger. orig. 1977); M. Gras, *Trafics tyrrhéniens archaïques* (1985); D. Ridgway, *CAH* 4² (1988), 634 ff.; A. Rallo (ed.), *Le donne in Etruria* (1989); *Atti II Congresso Internazionale Etrusco, Firenze 1985* (1990); D. Briquel, *L'origine lydienne des Etrusques* (1991).

ART AND ARTEFACTS J. D. Beazley, *Etruscan Vase-painting* (1947); W. Ll. Brown, *The Etruscan Lion* (1960); I. Strøm, *Problems Concerning . . . the Etruscan Orientalizing Style* (1971); L. Bonfante, *Etrus-*

can Dress (1975); A. Boëthius, *Etruscan and Early Roman architecture*, 2nd edn. (1978); O. J. Brendel, *Etruscan Art* (1978; with survey of subsequent bibliography by F. R. Serra Ridgway, *JRA* 1991, 5 ff.); T. B. Rasmussen, *Bucchero Pottery from Southern Etruria* (1979); N. T. de Grummond (ed.), *A Guide to Etruscan Mirrors* (1982); E. Richardson, *Etruscan Votive Bronzes* (1983); S. Haynes, *Etruscan Bronzes* (1985); F.-H. Massa Pairault, *Recherches sur l'art et l'artisanat étrusques hellénistiques* (1985); S. Steingräber, *Etruscan Painting* (1986; Ger. orig. 1984); S. S. Leach, *Subgeometric pottery from Southern Etruria* (1987); E. Macnamara, *The Etruscans* (1990): a companion to the Etruscan gallery in the British Museum.
D. W. R. R.

etymologica The etymologies in *Plato (1)'s *Cratylus* influenced Hellenistic thinkers, especially Stoics (see STOICISM), and writings 'On Etymologies' or the like are attested for *Chrysippus, *Heraclides (1) Ponticus, *Apollodorus (6) of Athens, *Demetrius (13) Ixion and *Philoxenus (4).

After Hellenistic times, etymological and lexicographic publications were intertwined, and the researches of Hellenistic scholars formed the basis of all later writings (whose source-relationships are accordingly intricate). They were alphabetically arranged, and had two purposes: (1) to aid the reading of ancient authors, and (2) to collect suitable vocabulary for use in pure 'Atticist' prose. In the early Roman empire there were massive word-collections (now lost) by Dorotheus of Ascalon (at least 108 books) and *Pamphilus (2) (95 books), which were in turn condensed and excerpted by others. From the later empire, fragments remain of specialist lexica by Aelius *Dionysius (3), *Pausanias (4), *Phrynichus (3), and others, which were still read by *Photius and *Eustathius.

Byzantine lexicography begins with several compilations (Orion of Thebes, Methodius, the so-called 'Cyril-lexicon') now lost but used extensively in later works. The *Lexicon* of Photius and the lexical entries of the *Suda* are still preserved. Several subsequent important lexica are preserved anonymously: from the 12th cent., there is the misnamed '*Etymologicum magnum*' (ed. T. Gaisford, 1841), which is actually partly *based* on a work called Ἐτυμολογικὸν μέγα. Manuscripts of this source have now been discovered as well, and it is known as the *Etymologicum (magnum) genuinum* (9th–10th cent.; not yet fully edited). This *Et. Gen.* (which lists the source of each entry) is based on Methodius, with additions from a wide variety of lexica, grammarians, and scholia. Other works derived in part from *Et. Gen.* are the so-called *Etymologicum Gudianum* (11th cent.) and the *Etymologicum* of the grammarian Symeon (12th cent., not yet fully edited).

The value of these *etymologica* lies in their information on ancient scholarship, and citations of ancient works otherwise lost.

In addition to authors mentioned above, see APOLLONIUS (11) SOPHISTA; DIOGENIANUS (2); GLOSSA, GLOSSARY, GREEK; HARPOCRATION, VALERIUS; HESYCHIUS; PHILOXENUS (4); POLLUX, IULIUS; SELEUCUS (6) HOMERICUS.

On the Byzantine period see especially R. Reitzenstein, *Geschichte der griechischen Etymologica* (1897); K. Alpers, *Bericht über Stand und Methode der Ausgabe des Etymologicum Genuinum* (1969). For the whole topic, L. Cohn, 'Griechische Lexicographie,' appendix to K. Brugmann and A. Thumb, *Griechische Grammatik (Handbuch der Altertumswissenchaft* 2. 1) (1913), 577–99.
J. S. R.

Etymologicum magnum See ETYMOLOGICA

etymology in the ancient world was always closely connected with questions concerning the ultimate origin of language. Was the sound of a word merely a matter of convention (the theory of *nomos*), or was there some natural relationship between the sign and the thing signified (the theory of *physis*)? In general the latter view prevailed. The popular assumption that the study of a name could reveal τὸ ἔτυμον, 'the truth', about the thing accounts for the importance attached to etymology in ancient thought and literature. But as the ancients had little understanding of comparative philology, in practice their etymologies never attained any degree of accuracy.

Etymology based on the belief in the significance of names begins with the poets. So *Homer associates the name of *Odysseus with ὀδύρομαι, 'to grieve' (*Od.* 1. 55), and ὀδύσσομαι, 'to hate' (*Od.* 1. 62), and plays on the literal meanings of such compound names as *Astyanax and *Telemachus. *Aeschylus connects the name of *Zeus with ζῆν, 'to live' (*Supp.* 584), and the name of *Helen of Troy with a long series of dire compounds from the verb ἑλεῖν, 'to destroy' (*Ag.* 681–90). Similar examples abound in *Hesiod, *Pindar, *Sophocles (1), and *Euripides. Historians such as *Hecataeus (1) of Miletus and *Herodotus (1) used etymology as a means of deriving historical facts from the 'true meanings' of personal and place names, while philosophers from *Heraclitus (cf. DK 22 B 5, B 26, B 48, B 114) onwards looked to etymology to provide information about the true nature of things.

By the late 5th cent. BC the question of the relationship between words and the things they named had become a matter of debate amongst the *sophists. The main statement of this controversy occurs in Plato's *Cratylus*, where Cratylus, a follower of Heraclitus, argues for *physis* against Hermogenes, who supports the theory of *nomos*. *Socrates himself, perhaps with some irony, takes up an intermediate position, suggesting that some words may originally have been significant, but that their form had been so corrupted over time that this significance was no longer recognizable. Socrates' conclusion (438d) is that names are of little value in establishing reality. The dialogue is our main source for the practice of etymology in Greek and raises a number of ideas which play a significant role in subsequent etymological theory. Language is derived from a few basic roots, στοιχεῖα (422a–b), whose individual sound-elements are associated with particular ideas (426c ff.), as *rho* with motion, *lambda* with smoothness, *iota* with subtlety, etc. Sound changes may be brought about by a desire for euphony, εὐστομία (cf. 404d, 407b, 414c–d), a modern phonetic principle. Finally comparison of Greek with foreign words (409d ff.) hints at a notion of the comparative study of languages.

After the *Cratylus* evidence for Greek etymological theory is thin. Alexandrian literary critics, such as *Aristophanes (2) of Byzantium, used etymology as an aid to elucidating rare words in earlier poetic texts. The scholarly interests of this period were reflected in the works of contemporary poets who introduced deliberate etymological wordplay into their verse. Although Aristotle (*Int.* 16ᵃ4–7) rejected the natural theory of language, seeing words as a conventional set of signs, he still had derivations such as δικαστής, 'judge', from δίχα, 'apart' (*Eth. Nic.* 1132ᵃ31). But the main emphasis in the later philosophical schools was on *physis*, with Stoic teaching emphasizing the importance of etymology as a guide to the true nature of things and developing further the ideas of 'sound symbolism' found in the *Cratylus*. The Stoic etymological works of *Chrysippus and *Cleanthes greatly influenced the Roman tradition, particularly through the grammarian *Crates (3) of Mallus and L. *Aelius, the teacher of *Cicero and *Varro. Stoic etymologizing is apparent in Cicero's account of the gods' names in *De natura deorum* book 2, while

*Varro mentions a debt to Cleanthes (5. 9) and Chrysippus (6. 2) in his etymological work *De lingua Latina*. The Epicurean view of naturally arising sounds being later formed into words by convention (Epicurus, *Letter to Herodotus* 1. 75), is reflected in *Lucretius (5. 1028–90) and accounts for his fondness for the analogy between letters and atoms, by which, for example, *ignis*, 'fire', is found in *lignum*, 'wood' (1. 911–14).

The most important surviving Latin work on etymology is Varro's *De lingua Latina*. Although books 2–4 on the theory of etymology have not survived, it is possible from remarks scattered in books 5–9, which deal with etymological practice, to build up some idea of his views. A small initial stock of words (6. 36) was thought up by a number of original name-givers (8. 7) and applied to things in accordance with their nature (6. 3). This original stock was then increased by *declinatio*, by which he meant the human process of deriving one word from another and the natural process of morphological inflexion (9. 4). In practice Varro's methods differ little from those found in the *Cratylus* or later Stoic sources. Chapter 6 of *Augustine's *De dialectica*, which itself may have been based on the lost books of Varro's *De lingua Latina*, lists the following Stoic methods of derivation: (1) through similarity (*a similitudine*) with the sound of the word (onomatopoeia), as in the case of *balatus* the 'bleating' of sheep, or with its impression on the senses, as with the harsh-sounding *vepres*, 'brambles'; (2) through similarity between one thing and another: so *crura*, 'legs', are named from *crux*, 'cross', because legs are long and hard like a wooden cross; (3) through various types of proximity (*a vicinitate*), as for example with *horreum*, 'granary', which is named from the thing it contains, *hordeum*, 'barley'; (4) from contrariety (*e contrario*), as with *lucus*, 'a grove', because *minime luceat*, 'it has little light', and *bellum*, 'war', because it is not a *res bella*, 'pretty thing'. Examples of all these types can be found in Varro, though there is some evidence that he avoided the more outlandish Stoic explanations of his teacher L. *Aelius in favour of etymologies based on sound changes that were a familiar part of the Latin morphological system (Pfaffel, see bibliog. below).

Etymologizing in Latin poetry is found from Ennius on, but was given added impetus in the Augustan period because of the increased importance of Alexandrian literary principles and perhaps because of the higher profile given to such speculation by the theoretical works of Varro and his contemporaries *Nigidius Figulus and *Verrius Flaccus. The Atticist movement of this period, which saw etymology as the touchstone of purity of diction in both Greek and Latin, would also have contributed to its growing importance (see ASIANISM AND ATTICISM). In Rome as in Greece the main function of etymology continued to be the elucidation of archaic or unusual words in poetic texts. The numerous examples which occur from the 3rd cent. on in commentators such as *Porphyrio, *Donatus (1), and *Servius can give useful clues to etymologizing in the texts on which they are commenting. Etymology also abounds in technical writing on law, medicine, astronomy, and botany, where its function is the precise definition of terms. At the close of the classical period much of this material was collected and passed on to us in the *Etymologiae* of *Isidorus (2) of Seville (*c.* AD 570–636). Despite the importance of etymology in ancient thought and literature, there was little development in the actual practice of derivation over the whole period from the *Cratylus* to Isidore.

K. Barwick, *Probleme der stoischen Sprachlehre und Rhetorik* (1957); F. Cavazza, *Studio su Varrone etimologo e grammatico* (1981); J. Collart, *Varron, Grammairien latin* (1954), ch. 4; H. Dahlmann, *Varro und die hellenistische Sprachtheorie* (1932); F. Della Corte, *La filologia latina dalle origini a Varrone* (1937); O. Keller, *Lateinische Volksetymologie und Verwandtes* (1891); L. Lersch, *Die Sprachphilosophie der Alten* (1838–41), 3. 3 ff.; R. Maltby, *A Lexicon of Ancient Latin Etymologies* (1991); F. Müller, *De veterum, imprimis Romanorum, studiis etymologicis* (1910); W. Pfaffel, *Quartus gradus etymologiae: Untersuchungen zur Etymologie Varros in De lingua Latina* (1981); R. Pfeiffer, *History of Classical Scholarship* i (1968), entry under 'etymology'; V. Pisani, *Etimologia* (1967); R. Schröter, *Studien zur varronischen Etymologie* (1959); H. Steinthal, *Geschichte der Sprachwissenschaft bei den Griechen und Römern* 1 (1890), 331 ff.; E. Wölfflin, *Archiv für lateinische Lexikographie* 1893, 421–40, 563–85.

R. Ma.

Euangelus, a New (?) Comedy poet (see COMEDY (GREEK), NEW). One fragment (ten trochaic tetrameters) is preserved in which a host discusses with a cook the preparations for a wedding banquet.

FRAGMENT Kassel–Austin, *PCG* 5. 184–5.
INTERPRETATION Meineke, *FCG* 1. 492; G. Kaibel, *RE* 6/1 (1907), 844, 'Euangelos' 8.

W. G. A.

Euanthius (*RE* 2) (4th cent. AD), author of a commentary on *Terence. The only parts remaining are some sections of the treatise on drama (*De fabula*) which is now prefixed to the commentary of Aelius *Donatus (1).

Ed. G. Cupaiuolo (1979). Herzog–Schmidt, § 526. 2. *PLRE* 1. 287.

P. G. M. B.

Euboea, also (Call. *h. Delos* 20; Strabo 10. 1. 2) called Long Island, Μάκρις, because it stretched from the gulf of *Pagasae to *Andros, shared the culture of the *Cyclades in the bronze age. The chief cities in antiquity were *Chalcis and *Eretria; in between was *Lefkandi, where remarkable 10th-cent. BC finds have revised notions of the so-called Dark Age of Greece. Other cities were *Histiaea, Geraestus, and marble-rich Carystus. In the 8th cent. Chalcis and Eretria were active mercantile centres which led the islanders to involvement in an *emporion at *Al Mina in Syria by 800. They established colonies on the NW shores of the Aegean and in Italy and Sicily (see COLONIZATION, GREEK; PITHECUSAE) and fought over the Lelantine plain, which lay between them, in the 8th cent. Eretrian control of some of the Cyclades passed to Athens, which in 506 compelled Chalcis to surrender part of the plain and installed a *cleruchy (Hdt. 5. 77). In 490 the Persian *Datis attacked Euboea, capturing Eretria and Carystus. Euboean contingents fought Persia at the battles of *Salamis (1) and *Plataea. Owing to Boeotian intrigues, Euboea revolted from Athens in 446, but was reconquered by *Pericles (1), who planted more cleruchies (see HISTIAEA), though probably not on Chalcis. The cities remained tributary allies of Athens in the *Delian League and in the *Peloponnesian War Euboea was 'more valuable to Athens than Attica itself' (Thuc. 8. 96, cf. 2. 14 for Euboea as Athens' larder); it revolted in 411. Some sort of Euboean league may have been formed at this time, but the cities individually joined the *Second Athenian Confederacy and the Euboean league was re-formed only in 341 and fought *Philip (1) II of Macedon at *Chaeronea, falling under Macedonian control thereafter. (The extent of Macedonian influence in Euboea in the 340s is disputed.) In 308–304 Euboea belonged to the *Boeotian Confederacy (*Syll.*³ 323), but was otherwise mostly in the Macedonian sphere until declared free by T. *Quinctius Flamininus in 196.

In 146 BC Chalcis at least supported the *Achaean Confederacy and was punished by L. *Mummius; 'all Euboea' is said to have gone over to *Mithradates VI in 88 BC; by 78 BC at the latest the island paid Roman taxes (*RDGE* 22). Under the Principate Euboea enjoyed a somewhat muted existence, although the actuality of the rhetorical picture of economic decline painted by Dio *Chrysostom (Or. 7), apparently with reference to Carystus, site of imperial marble-quarries, needs cautious assessment. *Aedepsus by contrast boomed. Chalcis, in the 1st cent. BC home to numerous *negotiatores, remained the chief city. A Euboean *koinon* (league) is attested under Nero.

IG 12 (9); F. Geyer, *Topographie und Geschichte der Insel Euboia* (1903), and *RE* Suppl. 4. 431 ff.; M. Holleaux, *Études d'épigraphie et d'histoire grecques* (1938–68), 1. 41 ff.; W. Wallace, *The Euboean League and its Coinage* (1956); G. Cawkwell, *Phoenix* 1978, 42 ff.; O. Picard, *Chalcis et la confédération eubéenne: Étude numismatique et d'histoire* (1979); J. Boardman, *CAH* 3²/1 (1982), 754 ff.; W. G. Forrest, *CAH* 3²/3 (1982), 249 ff.

W. A. L.; J. B.; S. H., A. J. S. S.

Eubouleus (Εὐβουλεύς), 'the good counsellor', was a major god in the Eleusinian *mysteries, and played an important role in the myth presented in the secret rite: he brought *Kore back from the Underworld. In art he is a torch-bearer and usually stands next to Kore (see PERSEPHONE) after her return, or between Theos and Thea (as *Hades and *Persephone were called in the mysteries) before her return. In related myth (not dramatized in the cult) he is a swineherd (Kern, *Orph. frag.* 51), son of Dysaules and brother of *Triptolemus, who gave *Demeter news of the rape of Kore; in one version his swine were swallowed up with Kore, which is why piglets are thrown into pits at the *Thesmophoria (Kern, *fr.* 50). But he evidently was not worshipped at the Attic Thesmophoria. Outside Attica Eubouleus appears as (1) an epithet of *Zeus as god of earth and fertility, worshipped at local Thesmophoria; (2) a euphemistic title of Hades; and (3) the name of one of a group of 'Orphic' Underworld deities (see ORPHISM).

Graf, *Eleusis*, 171–4; Clinton, *Iconography*, chs. 2–3.

K. C.

Eubulides (*RE* 8), of Miletus, mid-4th cent. BC, dialectician associated with the *Megarian school. He was an outspoken critic of *Aristotle, a teacher of *Demosthenes (2), and the reputed author of several classic puzzles. Some of these—the Sorites ('How many grains make a heap?'), the Liar Paradox ('Is "I am lying" simultaneously true and false?'), and the Horned Argument ('Have you lost your horns?')—raise problems for the simple true/false dichotomy. Others, such as the Veiled Man, seem epistemological.

K. Döring, *Die Megariker* (1972).

D. N. S.

Eubulus (1) (*c.*405–*c.*335 BC), probably the most important Athenian statesman of the period 355–342. In 355, after thirteen years' struggle to regain *Amphipolis and the *Chersonese (1) and the brief but disastrous *Social War (1), the imperialistic advocates of war were discredited and the state near bankruptcy. Rising under the aegis of Diophantus of the *deme of Sphettus, Eubulus by means of his position as a theoric commissioner gradually assumed control of the whole of Athens' finances, and raised public and private prosperity to a level probably not attained since the 5th cent. An extravagant version of the sort of methods he probably followed is to be found in *Xenophon (1)'s *De vectigalibus*, but the most important guarantee of economic recovery was a law which made it difficult for the assembly to draw on the routine revenues of the state for inessential military operations. Thus he was able to employ the annual surpluses on a programme of public works: the distribution of money to the people, τὸ θεωρικόν, probably instituted in this period, engaged only a small part of the moneys controlled by the theoric commission. See THEŌRIKA. In the wider spheres of policy, to judge from the allusions of *Demosthenes (2), he sought to concentrate Athens' military resources on the defence of the essential interests of Athens and of Greece, and to exclude *Philip (1) II from Greek affairs by uniting the Greeks in a *Common Peace, his chief associates being Midias, *Aeschines (1), and *Phocion. The expedition to *Thermopylae in 352, the intervention in *Euboea in 348, and the attempt to unite the Greeks against *Philip (1) II in 347/6 (or 348/7) are the chief fruits of this policy. Like almost all Athenian statesmen, he felt himself forced to accept the peace negotiated in 346 by *Philocrates and Demosthenes. After Philip used the peace to intervene in Phocis, Demosthenes determined to renew the war, but Eubulus and his supporters sought to maintain and extend the peace. By mid-344 the opposition of Demosthenes and *Hegesippus (1) was beginning to weaken Eubulus' influence; in 343 the parties were fairly evenly balanced; but in 342 Demosthenes and the war-party were in full control. No more is heard of Eubulus after the battle of *Chaeronea, and he may, like Aeschines, have retired from active politics. By 330 he was dead.

J. J. Buchanan, *Theorika* (1962), 53–66; G. L. Cawkwell, *JHS* 1963, 47 f.; P. J. Rhodes, *CAH* 6² (1994), 569 f.; E. Badian in W. Eder (ed.) *Die athenische Demokratie* (1995), 100 ff. G. L. C.

Eubulus (2), Middle (see COMEDY (GREEK), MIDDLE) Comedy poet, active *c*.380–*c*.335 BC. Won six victories at the *Lenaea (*IG* 2². 2325); said to have composed 104 plays, and 57 titles are extant. About one half of the extant titles suggest mythological or tragic (particularly Euripidean) burlesque; thus, fr. 9 K–A (the *Antiope*) rewrites the *deus ex machina* speech from *Euripides' *Antiope* in comic mode, and frs. 36–7 do the same to the messenger-speech of the *Ion*. In the *Semele* or *Dionysus* we see the new god establishing his regime (i.e. the rules for symposia). The *Dionysius*, however, seems in part to have been an attack on the Syracusan tyrant's literary pretensions (see DIONYSIUS (1) I), a form of political comedy which shows how the fragments point both forwards and back in literary history. Noteworthy is the metrical variety of the fragments: hexameters (frs. 106–7) for *riddles; lyric dactyls (frs. 102–3), very likely from the *parodos* of *Stephanopolides* ('The Garland-Sellers'); dactyls and ithyphallics (frs. 34, 137, probably monodic); cretic-paeonic tetrameters, narrative of a dinner party (fr. 111).

R. L. Hunter, *Eubulus: The Fragments* (1983); Kassel–Austin, *PCG* 5; H.-G. Nesselrath, *Die attische mittlere Komödie* (1990). R. L. Hu.

Euclid (Εὐκλείδης) (RE 7), mathematician (date uncertain, between 325 and 250 BC). Nothing is known of Euclid's life: the biographical data linking him with *Alexandria (1) and *Ptolemy (1) I are worthless inferences by late authors (*Pappus and *Proclus) who seem to have had no more information about him than we do. His fame rests on the Στοιχεῖα or *Elements* which goes under his name. It is in thirteen books (bks. 1–6 on plane geometry, 7–9 on the theory of numbers, 10 on irrationals, 11–13 on solid geometry). The work as it stands is the classical textbook of elementary *mathematics. which remained the standard (in many languages and versions) for 2,000 years. It incorporates (and eliminated) many works on the '*elements' by writers predating Euclid, notably *Eudoxus (1), and it seems impossible to define precisely Euclid's own contribution, or to determine how much the extant version was changed after him (the recension by *Theon (4) of Alexandria was the basis of all printed editions before Peyrard's of 1814–18). Commentaries, of which fragments are preserved in the Arabic of an-Nayrīzī, were

written by *Heron, Pappus, and *Simplicius. The extant commentary of Proclus on book 1 is valuable chiefly for its citations from earlier lost writers. 'Book 14' of the *Elements* is by *Hypsicles, 'book 15' a compilation from late antiquity.

Other geometrical works by Euclid are (1) *Data*, which defines 'given' for geometrical entities and proves what parts of a figure must be 'given' to determine the whole; it was an important part of the 'Domain of Analysis' (Ἀναλυόμενος τόπος) outlined by Pappus (bk. 7); (2) *On Divisions* [*of Figures*], extant only in Arabic. Lost works are (1) Ψευδάρια ('Fallacies'); (2) Τόποι πρὸς ἐπιφανείᾳ ('Surface-loci'), of uncertain content; (3) a work on the four-line locus, important in the theory of conics; (4) *Porisms*, perhaps also auxiliary to conics. The 'four books on conics' attributed to him by Pappus (7. 30) is probably the latter's conjecture.

Other extant works by or attributed to Euclid are the following. (1) *Phaenomena*, on elementary spherical geometry as applied to astronomy. It has much in common with *On the Moving Sphere* by *Autolycus (2). (2) *Optics*, an elementary but influential treatise on geometrical *optics. (3) *Catoptrics*, a work on the optics of reflection which in its present form is a late compilation, but may contain 'Euclidean' material (see CATOPTRICS). (4) Two treatises on music, *Section of the Canon* and *Harmonic*. The Euclidean authorship of these is disputed.

EDITIONS *Euclidis Opera Omnia*, ed. J. L. Heiberg and H. Menge (with Lat. trans.), 8 vols. (Teubner, 1883–1916): 1–5 (rev. E. S. Stamatis, 1969–77), *Elements* (with scholia); 6, *Data* (with Marinus' commentary); 7. optical works; 8, *Phaenomena*, musical works, and fragments; a supplement by M. Curtze (1899) contains the medieval Latin translation of an-Nayrīzī (Anaritius). For the musical works see also *Musici Scriptores Graeci*, ed. C. von Jan (1895). Arabic text of *On Divisions*, with Fr. trans., by F. Woepcke, *Journal Asiatique* 1851, 233 ff.; Eng. trans. from Woepcke's French, with additions, by R. C. Archibald, *Euclid's Book on Division of Figures* (1915).

TRANSLATIONS *Elements*: T. L. Heath, 3 vols., 2nd edn. (1926), with historical introduction and comm.; Books 7–9, J. Itard, *Les Livres arithmétiques d'Euclide* (1961), with comm. *Data*: C. Thaer (Ger., 1962). *Optics* and *Catoptrics*: Ver Eecke (Fr., 1938).

COMMENT *Proclus, Comm. on Elem. I*, ed. Friedlein (Teubner, 1873); trans., G. R. Morrow (1970); for history of text and editions, J. L. Heiberg, *Litterargeschichtliche Studien über Euklid* (1882), and T. L. Heath's trans. 1, introd.; W. R. Knorr, *The Evolution of the Euclidean Elements* (1975); Heath, *Hist. of Greek Maths.* 1. 354 ff. *Optics*: A. Lejeune, *Euclide et Ptolémée* (1948). *Catoptrics*: A. Lejeune, *Recherches sur le catoptrique grecque* (1954). The attempts to restore the *Porisms* by Simson, *Opera Quaedam Reliqua* (1776), 315 ff., and by Chasles, *Les Trois Livres des Porismes d'Euclide rétablis* (1860) are futile. For the works of Euclid falling under the 'Domain of Analysis' see *Pappus, Book 7*, ed. A. Jones (1986), with Jones's notes on the alleged *Conics*, 399–400, and Euclid's 'biography', 402–3. *Phaenomena*: *HAMA* 2. 748 ff. G. J. T.

Euclides (1), of Megara (*c*.450–380 BC), associate of *Socrates and founder of the *Megarian school. He was present at the death of Socrates and thereafter housed Plato and other members of the circle. Among his pupils were the logicians *Eubulides and *Stilpon (or Stilpon's teacher). Cicero puts him in the tradition of *Eleatic monism, and this may be connected with the report that he held the good to be one thing, having no opposite but named in many ways—e.g. as God, wisdom (φρόνησις), intelligence (νοῦς). His positive doctrines are otherwise unknown; his practice of attacking the conclusion and not the premisses of an opponent's argument is attested and puts him in the 'eristic' tradition which dates from late in the 5th cent., rather than in that of the Eleatics or (at his best) Socrates. Hence his leadership of a school of logicians whose contribution to philosophy was minimal but whose interest in logical paradoxes was taken over by the Stoic logicians.

Diog. Laert. 2. 106–12.   G. E. L. O.

Euclides (2), Athenian archon (see ARCHONTES) in 403/2 BC, the year in which the democracy officially made a fresh start after the oligarchy of the *Thirty Tyrants. From that year Athens officially adopted the *Ionian instead of the Attic *alphabet, though some earlier inscriptions have Ionian spellings and some later have Attic.

PA 5674.; Develin, AO 199   V. E.; P. J. R.

Eucratides I ('the Great'), Graeco-Bactrian king c.170–145 BC. His brilliant but warlike reign marked the climax of Greek rule in *Bactria(-Sogdiana). Just. Epit. 61. 6. 1–5 compares him to Mithradates the Great of *Parthia, while Apollodorus of Artemita (quoted at Strabo 15. 1. 3) calls him 'ruler of a thousand cities'. His parents Heliocles and Laodice, commemorated on a special series of his coins, are otherwise unknown; however, Laodice is portrayed wearing a *diadem and was therefore from a royal family. Some believe her to be a sister of *Antiochus (3) III the Great, but most scholars reject this view and associate her with either the family of *Diodotus (2) II or *Euthydemus (2) I. Eucratides apparently seized power in Bactria, and then waged wars in Sogdiana, Arachosia, Drangiana, Aria, and finally NW India. His principal adversary was probably King *Demetrius (8) I (son of Euthydemus I), though some argue for *Demetrius (9) II. After enduring a long siege, Eucratides overcame Demetrius and claimed the territories of Parapamisadae and *Gandhara. It is likely that he also defeated the relatives of Demetrius I, including the ephemeral kings *Euthydemus (3) II, Agathocles, and Pantaleon. A campaign against *Menander (2) I is also possible.

The career of Eucratides may be traced in his voluminous coinage, which is among the finest and most innovative from antiquity. Besides commemorating his parents, he portrayed himself in heroic pose and added the epithet 'Great' to his royal title. His standard coin-type, the charging *Dioscuri, seems to celebrate the famous cavalry of Bactria. South of the Hindu Kush mountains, he issued rectangular and bilingual coins (Greek/Prakrit) on an Indian standard for local commerce. He also struck the largest known gold coin from the ancient world, a numismatic masterpiece weighing 20 staters (169 g.: almost 6 oz.).

Eucratides was brutally assassinated c.145 BC by one of his sons, probably Plato. Another son, Heliocles 'the Just', avenged the crime, but Bactria-Sogdiana soon fell victim to nomadic invaders from the north and Parthian encroachment from the west.

A. K. Narain, CAH 8² (1989), 399 ff.   F. L. H.

Euctemon, astronomer, observed the summer solstice at Athens, together with *Meton, in 432 BC (Ptol. Alm. 3. 1). He is also associated with the Metonic nineteen-year luni-solar cycle. He composed a παράπηγμα, an astronomical calendar listing the dates of rising and setting of stars and associated weather phenomena, which is excerpted by later extant calendars.

A. Rehm, Sitz. Heidelberg 1913. 3, Abh. Bayerisch. Akad. 1941, 122–40, RE Suppl. 7. 175–98, 'Episemasiai', and RE 18. 1295–1366, 'Parapegma'; HAMA 2. 623, 627–8.   G. J. T.

Eudemus (RE 11), of Rhodes (later 4th cent. BC), pupil and friend of *Aristotle. No account of his life survives, though Simplicius (in Phys. 924. 13) mentions a biography by a certain Damas.

Eudemus had a strong claim to succeed Aristotle as head of the Lyceum (see ARISTOTLE, para. 5), but *Theophrastus was preferred. Later, Eudemus may have returned to Rhodes to set up his own school; but he remained faithful to Aristotle's teaching, and continued in close contact with Theophrastus, for a fragment of a letter to the latter concerning the interpretation of a passage in Aristotle's Physics survives (Simpl. in Phys. 923. 11).

Eudemus compiled histories of arithmetic and geometry, astronomy, and theology. His name is coupled with Theophrastus' in important innovations in modal logic; he also wrote on rhetoric, and possibly on zoology. Numerous passages from his work on physics are preserved by *Simplicius; for the most part it is a paraphrase of Aristotle's Physics, though occasionally Eudemus attempts to reduce Aristotle's treatment to a more rigid scheme. The attribution of the Eudemian Ethics to Eudemus, rather than to Aristotle himself, is generally rejected.

TEXTS F. Wehrli, Die Schule des Aristoteles 8, 2nd edn. (1969).
STUDIES F. Wehrli in Überweg–Flashar 530–3; U. Schoebe, Quaestiones Eudemeae (1931): on the first book of the Physics; E. Meyer, RE Suppl. 11 (1968), 652–8.   R. W. S.

Eudorus (1), in mythology, a Myrmidon captain, son of *Hermes and Polymele (Il. 16. 179 ff.).

Eudorus (2), of *Alexandria (1) (fl. c.25 BC), Platonist philosopher. Chief works (lost): Diairesis tou kata philosophian logou, a summary of the ethical section of which is preserved by Stobaeus; commentaries on the Timaeus, Categories, and Metaphysics. He seems to have turned the very Stoicized Platonism of *Antiochus (11) of Ascalon in a more transcendental direction, under the influence of *Neopythagoreanism.

H. Dörrie, Hermes 1944, 25 ff.; J. M. Dillon, The Middle Platonists (1977), ch. 3; P. Moraux, Aristotelismus, 2. 509–27 (1984).   J. M. D.

Eudoxus (1) (RE 8), of *Cnidus, (c.390–c.340 BC) was an outstanding mathematician and did important work in *astronomy and geography; he was versatile in 'philosophy' in general. According to the not entirely trustworthy ancient biographical tradition (see especially Diog. Laert. 8. 86 ff.), he was a pupil of *Archytas in geometry and of *Philistion in medicine; he came to Athens to hear the Socratics when about 23, later spent time in Egypt studying astronomy with the priests, then lectured in *Cyzicus and the Propontis, visited the court of *Mausolus, and finally returned to teach at Athens, where he was acquainted with Plato; he drew up laws for Cnidus, and died aged 52.

In geometry he invented the general theory of proportion, applicable to incommensurable as well as commensurable magnitudes, found in Euclid bk. 5 (scholion in Heiberg, Euclidis Opera 5. 280). This greatly helped to assure the primacy of geometry in Greek *mathematics. He also developed the method of approach to the limit (misnamed 'method of exhaustion' in modern works) which became the standard way of avoiding infinitesimals in ancient mathematics, He was thus able to prove that cone and pyramid are one-third of the cylinder and prism respectively with the same base and height (Archim. Method pref.). Of his solution to the problem of doubling the cube nothing certain is known.

In astronomy he was the first Greek to construct a mathematical system to explain the apparent motions of the heavenly bodies: that of the 'homocentric spheres'. *Simplicius' account of this (in Cael. 492. 31 ff.), which gives its title as Περὶ ταχῶν ('On Speeds'), reveals both the high level of mathematics and

565

the low level of observational astronomy of the time: Eudoxus combined uniform motions of concentric spheres about different axes with great ingenuity to produce, for instance, a qualitatively correct representation of the retrogradations of some planets; but the underlying observational data are few and crude, and the discrepancies of the results with the actual phenomena often gross (for later corrections see CALLIPPUS and ASTRONOMY). Its adoption in a modified form by Aristotle was responsible for its resurrection in later ages. More practical (and very influential) was Eudoxus' description of the *constellations, with calendaric notices of risings and settings, which appeared in two versions, named Ἔνοπτρον and Φαινόμενα. The latter is known through its adaptation by *Aratus (1) in his immensely popular poem of the same name; the commentary of *Hipparchus (3) on both Eudoxus and Aratus is extant (see the edn. of Manitius (Teubner, 1894), p. 376 for refs. to Eudoxus). Another calendaric work was the Ὀκταετηρίς ('Eight-year [luni-solar] Cycle'). The papyrus treatise named Εὐδόξου τέχνη, though composed much later, contains some elementary calendaric and astronomical information which may derive from Eudoxus. There is some evidence for Babylonian influence in Eudoxus' astronomical work.

The Γῆς περίοδος ('Circuit of the Earth'), in several books, was a work of mathematical and descriptive geography.

FRAGMENTS AND TESTIMONIA F. Lasserre, *Die Fragmente des Eudoxos von Knidos* (1966).

MATHEMATICS Heath, *Hist. of Greek Maths.* 1. 320 ff.; O. Becker, 'Eudoxosstudien' 1–5, in *Quellen u. Studien z. Gesch. d. Math.* B2 and B3 (1933–6).

HOMOCENTRIC SPHERES G. Schiaparelli, 'Le sfere omocentriche di Eudosso, di Callippo e di Aristotele' (1875), repr. in his *Scritti sulla storia della astronomia antica* 2, Ger. trans. in *Abh. zur Gesch. d. Math.* 1 (1877), 101 ff.; HAMA 2. 674–83.

CALENDAR Geminus, ed. M. Manitius (1898), 108 ff., 210 ff.; A. Böckh, *Über die vierjährigen Sonnenkreise der Alten* (1863). *Εὐδόξου τέχνη*. Editio princeps, with the interesting illustrations, ed. Letronne and Brunet de Presle, *Notices et Extraits des Manuscrits* 18. 2 (1865); F. Blass, *Eudoxi Ars Astronomica* (Kiel Festschrift, 1887).

GEOGRAPHY Fragments in Lasserre, 96 ff; see further F. Gisinger, *Die Erdbeschreibung des Eudoxos von Knidos* (1921).   G. J. T.

Eudoxus (2), of Rhodes (fl. 225–200 BC?), historian, perhaps identical with the author of *Periploi* (GGM 1. 565), which may have formed a part of Eudoxus' histories.

FGrH 79.

Eudoxus (3), of Cyzicus (2nd cent. BC), Greek navigator. After 146 BC he was sent by *Ptolemy (1) VIII Euergetes of Egypt with a stranded Indian guide to find the sea-route to India; sent again later, he was on his return blown some way down east Africa, consorted with indigenes, returned to *Alexandria (1) with some wreckage allegedly said to be part of a ship of *Gades (mod. Cadiz), decided that Africa could be circumnavigated, and determined to go round it to India, avoiding Ptolemaic dues. Having collected cargoes at various ports, he set out from Gades, with music-girls, doctors, and carpenters on board, but was driven aground south of Morocco. Returning, he saw perhaps Madeira, failed to persuade *Bocchus I of Mauretania to help him, cut across land to the Mediterranean, and, with much greater equipment, sailed again down west Africa, and disappeared.

Strabo 2. 98–102. J. Thiel, *Eudoxus van Cyzicus* (1939, in Dutch); Cary–Warmington, *Explorers* 98 ff.; (Pelican edn.) 123 ff.; Hyde, *Greek Mariners* 200 ff., 245 ff.; Fraser, *Ptol. Alex.* 1. 182–4.   E. H. W.; A. J. S. S.

Euenus, of Paros (5th cent. BC), rhetorician and sophist, wrote some elegiac and other verse, of which fragments survive; to be distinguished from two (?) homonymous later epigrammatists.

West, *IE²* 2. 63–7; Gow–Page, *GP* 2. 289.   M. L. W.

euergetism, neologism of French scholarship (*évergétisme*, from εὐεργέτης, 'benefactor') to describe the socio-political phenomenon of voluntary gift-giving to the ancient community. Embracing the beneficence of Hellenistic kings and Roman emperors, whose subjects saw such philanthropy as a cardinal virtue of rulers (see KINGSHIP), it has been studied in recent years above all in relation to the *polis, of which benefaction by wealthy citizens (including women) becomes a defining characteristic from the 3rd cent. BC until late antiquity, as is attested by thousands of honorific inscriptions memorializing donors; it is also a feature of republican Rome, where the liberalities of senators in kind at least (public building, spectacle) resemble that of their humbler Greek contemporaries, and of the (Mediterranean) Roman city in general. In Greece the origins of euergetism go back to the aristocratic ideal of liberality found in Homer and echoed by Aristotle, who included acts of 'magnificence' (*megaloprepeia*) such as feasting the city among the virtues of the well-born man (*Eth. Nic.* 1119ᵇ19–1122ᵃ17). In Classical Athens beneficence in this tradition, while lingering into the 5th cent., was essentially inimical to the ideal equality of Athenian *democracy, which preferred instead to impose on rich citizens the compulsory duty of the *liturgy. Although 4th-cent. Athens conferred the title 'benefactor' on foreigners, only in the 3rd cent. does the type of the 'benefactor politician' emerge clearly in the Greek city, as with one Boulagoras of Samos (*c*.245 BC), who combined office-holding with gifts from his own purse to his city, in return receiving a crown and inscription (*Syll.*³ 366 = Austin no. 113). *Aristotle saw munificence in office as a cynical device of rich oligarchs (*Pol.* 1321ᵃ31–42); Veyne (see bibliog. below) sees Hellenistic 'benefactor politicians' as symptomatic of a weakening of democracy (see DEMOCRACY, NON-ATHENIAN) in favour of increasing dependence on the rich few. Others (following Gauthier) postpone this 'decline' until the advent of Roman domination, when (largely unaccountable) regimes of gift-giving notables in effect became the system of government in the Greek city; it is to this phase (from *c*.150 BC) that the extreme forms of honours for local benefactors, including cult (see THEOPHANES), belong (as well as the hailing of the Romans by some Greek cities as 'common benefactors', *koinoi euergetai*). Civic euergetism was a mixture of social display, patriotism, and political self-interest. It was not charity, since its main beneficiary was the citizen-group, although its increasing embrace under Roman rule of the whole city (i.e. slaves and foreigners) prepared the way for the emergence of bishops and wealthy lay Christians as local benefactors, whose protection and material assistance, however, now specifically included the *humiliores* (see HONESTIORES). Probably at no time was the economic significance of euergetism as great as the vast number of honorific inscriptions might suggest.

P. Veyne, *Le Pain et le cirque* (1976), abr. Eng. trans., *Bread and Circuses* (1990); P. Gauthier, *Les Cités grecques et leurs bienfaiteurs*, BCH Suppl. 12 (1985); J.-L. Ferrary, *Philhellénisme et impérialisme* (1988), 124 ff. (Romans as 'common benefactors'); *10th International Congress of Greek and Latin Epigraphy: Rapports préliminaires* (1992); F. Quass, *Die Honoratiorenschicht in den Städten des griechischen Ostens* (1993). Kings as benefactors: K. Bringmann, in A. Bulloch and others (eds.), *Images and Ideologies* (1993), 7 ff.   A. J. S. S.

Euetes The *Suda* (ε 2766) implies that he was an Athenian writer of comedy contemporary with *Epicharmus, but there may here be confusion with the like-named tragedian of the same period.

Kassel–Austin, *PCG* 5. 276; Snell, *TrGF* 1². 84, 345 (6 T 1).   W. G. A.

Eugammon, epic poet. See EPIC CYCLE, para. 4 (13).

Eugenius, Flavius, western usurper AD 392–4. A teacher of Latin grammar and rhetoric, he was known to *Symmachus (2) and became *magister scrinii* (see MAGISTER MEMORIAE) at the court of *Valentinian II. After the suicide of Valentinian (15 May 392), his Frankish *magister militum* Arbogast proclaimed Eugenius as Augustus (22 August), but he failed to secure recognition from *Theodosius (2) I. Nominally a Christian, Eugenius sympathized with the pagan revival conducted by his praetorian prefect *Nicomachus (4) Flavianus, and restored the altar of Victory in the senate-house. On 6 September Theodosius defeated him and Arbogast at the river Frigidus and Eugenius was executed.

J. Straub, *RAC* 6. 860–77; *PLRE* 1. 293, 'Eugenius' 6; J. Matthews, *Western Aristocracies and Imperial Court*, AD 364–425 (1975), 238 ff. Coinage: Mattingly–Sydenham, *RIC* 9.   J. F. Ma.

Eugraphius (early 6th cent. AD), author of a commentary on *Terence (ed. P. Wessner in *Donati Commentum*, 3. 1). His interest is chiefly in the rhetorical qualities and characterization of the plays, and often he does little more than paraphrase the text of Terence. He probably knew the commentary of *Donatus (1) on Terence and that of *Servius on Virgil. The work is found in two versions, one of which contains interpolations.

PLRE 2. 417; Schanz–Hosius, § 1117.   P. G. M. B.

Euhemerus (Εὐήμερος), of Messene, perhaps wrote while in the service of *Cassander (311–298 BC), but was perhaps active as late as 280 BC. He wrote a *novel of travel which was influential in the Hellenistic world. The substance of the novel is known from fragments, especially in *Diodorus (3) Siculus, see below, and from an epitome by *Eusebius. Euhemerus described an imaginary voyage to a group of *islands in the uncharted waters of the Indian Ocean and the way of life on its chief island, Panchaea. The central monument of the island, a golden column on which the deeds of *Uranus, *Cronus, and *Zeus were recorded, gave the novel its title Ἱερὰ ἀναγραφή, 'Sacred Scripture'. From this monument Euhemerus learnt that Uranus, Cronus, and Zeus had been great kings in their day and that they were worshipped as gods by the grateful people. Earlier authors had written of imaginary utopias but the utopia of Euhemerus was particularly relevant to the position of those Hellenistic rulers who claimed to serve their subjects and on that account to receive worship for their services (see RULER-CULT, GREEK). Euhemerism could be interpreted according to taste as supporting the traditional belief of Greek epic and lyric poetry which drew no clear line between gods and great men; as advancing a justification for contemporary ruler-cults; or as a work of rationalizing *atheism. At the same time Euhemerus was influenced by the beliefs of the wider world which had been opened up by the conquests of *Alexander (3) the Great, and his novel reflected the awareness of new ideas in an exciting situation.

The theory of god and man which was advanced by Euhemerus seems to have made little impression on the Greeks, but Diodorus, apparently taking the romance for fact, embodied it in his sixth book, which survives in fragments. In Latin it had more success after the publication of the *Euhemerus* of *Ennius, and euhemerizing accounts of such mythological figures as *Faunus exist. The Christian writers, especially *Lactantius, liked

to use it as evidence of the real nature of the Greek gods. Euhemerus' name survives in the modern term 'euhemeristic', applied to mythological interpretation which supposes certain gods (e.g. *Asclepius) to be originally heroes. See also CULTURE-BRINGERS; DIONYSIUS (12) SCYTOBRACHION; HECATAEUS (2); IAMBULUS; ISLANDS; LEON (2); PHILON (5); PRODICUS.

FRAGMENTS Ed. G. Nemethy (1889), G. Vallauri (1956), M. Winiarczyk (BT, 1991), and Jacoby, *FGrH* 63 (no comm., but see *RE* 6. 952 ff. = *Griechische Historiker* (1956), 175 ff.); see also J. Vahlen, *Ennianae poes. reliquiae*, 2nd edn. (1903), 120 f.; 223 f.

STUDIES R. von Pöhlmann, *Gesch. der sozialen Frage*, 3rd edn. (1925), 293 ff.; P. van Gils, *Quaestiones Euemereae* (Thesis, Kerkrade–Heerlen, 1902); Nilsson, *GGR* 2², 286 ff.; H. F. van der Meer, *Euhemerus of Messene* (Diss. Amsterdam, 1948); T. S. Brown, *Harv. Theol. Rev.* (1946), 259 ff.; H. Dörrie, *Abh. Akad. Gött.* 1964, 218 f.; H. Braunert, *Rh. Mus.* 1965, 255 ff.; Fraser, *Ptol. Alex.* 1. 289 ff.; E. Gabba, *JRS* 1981, 58; S. Price, *Rituals and Power* (1984), 38 f.; K. Sacks, *Diodorus Siculus and the First Century* (1990), 70 f.   H. J. R.; S. H.

Euhesperides See BERENICE (a); PENTAPOLIS.

Eumaeus, *Odysseus' faithful swineherd, a man of royal birth but carried off as a child by Phoenician sailors and sold to Laertes (*Od.* 15. 403 ff.). He gives Odysseus refuge on his return to Ithaca disguised as a beggar (*Od.* 14), and later helps him kill the suitors (see PENELOPE).   J. R. M.

Eumelus (fl. *c.*730 BC), Corinthian poet, of the Bacchiad family (see BACCHIADAE; CORINTH). The works ascribed to him are as follows (only fragments survive; all except the first were epics):

1. A *Prosodion* written for the Messenians. 2. *Corinthiaca*: a history of the Corinthian kingship from Helios at least as far as Glaucus (2). A prose version was known to *Aristobulus (2) and *Pausanias (3). 3. *Bougonia*: subject uncertain. 4. *Europia*: apparently various legends connected with Thebes. 5. The *Titanomachia* was ascribed to Eumelus or to Arctinus. 6. The *Nostoi* (see EPIC CYCLE para. 4 (11)) seems to be ascribed to Eumelus in schol. Pind. *Ol.* 13. 31.

The authenticity and antiquity of these works is a matter of considerable doubt.

Davies, *EGF* 95 ff.; Bernabé, *PEG* 1. 106 ff.; G. L. Huxley, *Greek Epic Poetry* (1969), 60 ff.   M. L. W.

Eumenes (1) **I** (d. 241 BC), ruler of *Pergamum, nephew and successor of *Philetaerus (2) (263). Eumenes extended Pergamene control in Mysia and Aeolis and defeated *Antiochus (1) I near Sardis (262). Although he paid protection money to the *Galatians he maintained a mercenary army, garrisoning i. a. the forts Philetaireia and Attaleia and controlling the port cities Elaia and Pitane. Pergamum enjoyed a constitution of democratic structure, though Eumenes, who as dynast stood outside the constitution, appointed the *strategoi* (chief magistrates) and so controlled the finances.

R. E. Allen, *The Attalid Kingdom* (1983).   R. M. E.

Eumenes (2) **II** (d. 158 BC), king of *Pergamum (197–158), eldest son and successor of *Attalus I. Characteristic is the family solidarity of Eumenes, his mother Apollonis, and his three brothers, which gave unusual inner strength to the dynasty. Eumenes, immediately threatened by *Antiochus (3) III, was Rome's major ally in the war against him, culminating in the battle of *Magnesia (189), and he made the greatest gains from the ensuing Peace of Apamea (188) which divided Seleucid territory north of the Taurus between Pergamum and *Rhodes. Pergamum became immediately rich but also a guarantor of stability in the Roman interest. A new coinage, the cistophori ('basket-bearers'), introduced sometime after 188, marked Pergamum's new economic role. Roman support did not mean peace: wars with *Prusias (1) I of Bithynia (187–183) and *Pharnaces I of Pontus (183–179) were ended by Roman intervention. A major victory against *Galatians (184) made the grateful Greeks call him Soter ('Saviour'); he celebrated it at home by extending the Pergamene temple of Athena Nikephoros ('Victory-Bringer') and making her festival pan-Hellenic. In the 170s Eumenes' building programme transformed Pergamum into a splendidly equipped capital city and produced the apogee of Pergamene plastic art (e.g. the Great Altar of Zeus); contacts with major Greek centres—*Athens, *Miletus, *Delphi, *Cos—were marked by massive gifts; diplomacy produced a successful coup, when he helped *Antiochus (4) IV to succeed his murdered brother *Seleucus (4) IV in Syria (175). Instrumental in influencing Rome to annihilate the Macedonian monarchy (The Third Macedonian War: 170–168), Rome's victory ironically rendered Eumenes' strength superfluous and suspicious, and the senate began to dismantle it. It courted his brother Attalus, refused to receive Eumenes, while encouraging Prusias, and declared the rebellious Galatians free, after Eumenes had just defeated them. In 160/59 *Attalus II became co-ruler, but the peak of Pergamene power was past.

C. Habicht, *CAH* 8² (1989), 324–34; R. E. Allen, *The Attalid Kingdom* (1983).
R. M. E.

Eumenes (3), of Cardia (*c.*361–316 BC), secretary to *Philip (1) II and *Alexander (3) the Great of Macedon. A royal favourite, bitterly resented by many native Macedonians, he received the prestigious command of a hipparchy of *Companions during Alexander's last year, and after the king's death he attached himself to *Perdiccas (3), in whose interest he probably composed the Royal Diaries (see EPHEMERIDES). Thanks to Perdiccas he was appointed *satrap of *Cappadocia and installed in office by the royal army (322). As head of the Perdiccan forces in Asia Minor he had successive victories over Neoptolemus and *Craterus (1) (321) but was isolated after Perdiccas' death and condemned to death at Triparadeisus. Brought to bay in Cappadocia and besieged at Nora (319/18), he came to terms with *Antigonus (1), but immediately sided with *Polyperchon and accepted command of the 'Silver Shields', veterans of Alexander's hypaspists. These he controlled adroitly by representing himself simply as a medium for their deceased king and won the leadership of the coalition of satraps which resisted the expansionist ambitions of Peithon and Antigonus (1). In an epic campaign in the Iranian highlands the inconclusive battle of Paraetacene (317) was followed by Gabiene (early 316), where his Macedonians lost their baggage (and families) to Antigonus. Consequently Eumenes was surrendered to his death. Despite his political brilliance he had no lasting impact.

Berve, *Alexanderreich* 2. no. 317; J. Hornblower, *Hieronymus of Cardia* (1981); R. A. Billows, *Antigonus the One-Eyed* (1990); Heckel, *Marshals* 346 f.
A. B. B.

Eumenides See ERINYES.

Eumenius (*RE* 1) is known to us only from the extant speech (*Paneg. Lat.* 9) which he delivered in *Augustodunum (Autun) in AD 297 or 298 before the governor of the province of Lugdunensis Prima, advocating the rebuilding of the war-damaged school and promising his own generous financial support. We learn that he was of Greek descent, and that before being appointed *to the school he had been *Constantius I's *magister memoriae. Whether

he delivered any other of the *XII Panegyrici Latini* is uncertain.
PLRE 1. 294–5.
A. H.-W.; M. W.

Eumolpus, the 'fair singer', was the mythical ancestor of the Eleusinian clan (see GENOS) of the Eumolpidae, as Keryx was of the Kerykes. He appears first in the *Homeric Hymn to Demeter* (184, 475) as one of the rulers of *Eleusis instructed by the goddess in the *mysteries. According to the Eumolpidae he was the son of *Poseidon and the first *hierophantēs. In art he holds a sceptre, like the *hierophantēs*, who with his melodious voice, saw himself as re-enacting the role of Eumolpus. According to Apollod. 3. 201 ff. he was son of Poseidon and Chione daughter of *Boreas. The story of her throwing him into the sea, in shame, may perhaps be an *aition* of hieronymy, a ritual in which the hierophant consigned his former name to the sea. The various ancient genealogies of Eumolpus and his adventures in Ethiopia and Thrace reflect in large part attempts to reconcile the Eleusinian *hierophantēs* with the homonymous Thracian king who led the Eleusinians against the Athenians; but the latter story evidently is no older than the 5th cent. BC, perhaps invented by Euripides.

O. Kern, *RE* 6/1, 'Eumolpos'; Graf, *Eleusis*, 17–18; Clinton, *Iconography,* 75–8.
K. C.

Eunapius, Greek sophist and historian, was born at Sardis *c.* AD 345 and studied there under Chrysanthius, and later in Athens under *Prohaeresius. When he returned to Sardis he entered the circle of local *Neoplatonists, learned *theurgy and medicine (he is sometimes described as an 'iatrosophist'), and mainly taught rhetoric. A fervent admirer of the emperor *Julian and a convinced opponent of Christianity, he wrote to defend his old faith. His History is now lost except for fragments, though much of its character can be recovered from later writers who used it (see below). It continued the work of *Herennius Dexippus, and went in fourteen books from AD 270 to 404; it was finally concluded in about 414. A first edition had however appeared many years earlier, since the work is referred to in the *Lives of the Sophists* of *c.*396, and since traces of its influence can be detected in *Ammianus Marcellinus' account of Julian's Persian campaign; some scholars however ascribe the resemblances to Ammianus' direct use of one of Eunapius' sources, Julian's doctor *Oribasius. According to *Photius (*Bibl.* 77), who had seen both versions, the second edition of the History appeared in a toned-down form because of the very anti-Christian attitude of the first version, though it is not agreed whether the new edition was prepared by Eunapius himself, or what form the revisions took, since the surviving version of the History still seems very outspoken. Apart from his use of Oribasius' memoir on Julian's Persian campaign we know little about Eunapius' sources; he himself complained about the lack of reliable information on contemporary events in the western part of the empire (in which he contrasts sharply with his successor *Olympiodorus (3)). He was himself an important source, not only to the pagan *Zosimus, but also to Christian historians, notably *Philostorgius and *Sozomen; the latter opens his History with an attack on the view of the conversion of Constantine I propounded by Eunapius (whom he does not name). Eunapius' *Lives of the Sophists* are extant in full. They follow *Philostratus' model and on the basis of first-hand information deal mainly with 4th-cent. Neoplatonists, of whom Eunapius gives an idealized picture in order to compete with the biographies of Christian saints. In particular, they trace a line of Neoplatonic descent from *Iamblichus (2), to which the emperor Julian also adhered.

TEXTS Fragments of the Histories in *FHG* 4. 7 ff.; and with full introd., trans. and comm. in R. C. Blockley, *The Fragmentary Classicising Historians of the Later Roman Empire*, 2 vols. (1981–3); see also the edn. of Zosimus by F. Paschoud (Budé, 1971–89). *Lives of the Sophists*, ed. G. Giangrande (1956), and W. C. Wright (Loeb, 1922).

See also E. A. Thompson, *The Historical Work of Ammianus Marcellinus* (1947), 28 ff., 134 ff.; *A History of Attila and the Huns* (1948), 16 ff.; W. R. Chalmers, *CQ* 1953, 165 ff.; A. F. Norman, *CQ* 1957, 129 ff.; A. D. E. Cameron, *CQ* 1963, 232 ff.; J. F. Matthews, *The Roman Empire of Ammianus* (1989), ch. 8. 3, and pp. 182 f.; R. J. Penella, *Greek Philosophers and Sophists in the Fourth Century AD* (1990).   J. F. Ma.

Euneos and **Thoas** (Εὔνεως, Θόας), sons of *Jason (1) and *Hypsipyle, whose best-known exploit was to free their mother from captivity at Nemea. The fact that their great-grandfather was *Dionysus appears to be significant: they brought wine to the Achaeans at Troy (*Il.* 7. 468–71), and the Attic *genos* Euneidai was closely associated with the cult of Dionysus Melpomenos.

G. W. Bond (ed.), *Hypsipyle* (1963), ll. 17–20; G. Berger-Doer, *LIMC* 4. 59–62.   E. Ke.

eunomia ('good order'). See LYCURGUS (2); POLIS; TYRTAEUS; SPARTA, § 2. In mythology, Eunomia is sister of *Dike (1).

eunuchs

Religious In the Classical period, religious eunuchs are a feature of several Anatolian cults of female deities, extending across to Scythia (Hdt. 4. 67: not shamans) and to the southern foothills of the Taurus mountains, but independent of Babylonian and Phoenician (Euseb. *Vit. Const.* 3. 55. 2 f.) practices (See ANATOLIAN DEITIES). As a whole the institution created a class of pure servants of a god (Matt. 19: 12). Its significance derives from a double contrast, with the involuntary castration of children for court use and the normal obligation to marry. The adult self-castrate expressed in his body both world-rejection and -superiority.

Two forms may be distinguished. (1) A senior, or even high, priest in a temple, e.g. the eunuchs of *Hecate at Lagina in *Caria (Sokolowski, *LSAM* no. 69. 19, etc.); the Megabyz(x)us of *Artemis at *Ephesus (Strabo 14. 1. 23; Vett. Val., 2. 21. 47); the *Attis and Battaces, the high priests of Cybele at *Pessinus. (2) A member of an itinerant (at Rome restricted) group of servants of the goddess (μητραγύρται), not priests, who might or might not be eunuchs. The best known are the galli (also βάκηλοι) of the cults of *Cybele and *Atargatis (the fanatici of Ma-Bellona were not castrated). Catullus' *Attis* (poem 63) has led to excessive emphasis upon subjective meaning (cf. Plut. *Nic.* 13). Self-castration was a (decisive) step into a status 'between worlds', parallel to poverty (but cf. Val. Max. 7. 7. 6), homelessness, self-laceration, ecstatic dancing. Cross-dressing (esp. earrings) and face-whitening advertised the anomalous state (see TRANSVESTISM, RITUAL). The value of eunuchism probably shifted over time, e.g. from the 2nd cent. AD towards negative *asceticism (cf. Justin Martyr, *Apologia* 29. 2). Some Phrygian *Montanists picked up the theme in a radical Christian idiom.

A. D. Nock, *Essays* 1 (1972), 7–15 (orig. in *ARW* 1925); G. M. Sanders, *RAC* 8 (1972), 984–1034; P. Bilde, in *Religion and Religious Practice in the Seleucid Kingdom* (1990), 151–87; H. Herter, *RAC* 4 (1959), 620–50.   R. L. G.

Secular To the classical world eunuchs were despised figures who haunted the courts of oriental monarchs. The Persian king employed them prominently as guardians of his harem and loyal protectors of his throne, even exacting boys for castration as tribute from some subject peoples (Hdt. 3. 92). The disgust expressed by Classical authors at the alien customs of Persia was tempered by an acknowledgement of the trustworthiness which the eunuchs displayed to their royal masters (Hdt. 8. 105; Xen. *Cyr.* 7. 5. 58 ff.).

By the time of Augustus eunuchs had begun to enter the households of some leading Romans, notably imperial associates like *Maecenas (Sen. *Ep.* 114. 6) and *Sejanus (Plin. *HN* 7. 129). Later the praetorian prefect of *Septimius Severus had a hundred Roman citizens castrated to provide eunuch attendants for his daughter (Cass. Dio 75. 14). The presence of eunuchs around prominent courtiers reflected the trend set by emperors themselves: *Claudius already had a favourite eunuch (Posides) among his freedmen (Suet. *Claud.* 28), while the licentious behaviour attributed to *Nero and others involved eunuchs as accomplices (e.g. Suet. *Ner.* 28). In AD 62 Nero even placed a eunuch in command of a detachment of troops (Tac. *Ann.* 14. 59).

Eunuchs belonged to the private world of their masters (in the 4th cent. AD a Roman senator's retinue might include a 'throng of eunuchs': Amm. Marc. 14. 6. 17). By late antiquity, however, imperial eunuchs were more than mere domestic servants. In the time of *Diocletian they could be described as those 'on whom the whole palace and the emperor himself depended' (Lactant. *De mortibus persecutorum* 15), and they came to occupy a central place in the late Roman court. Usually freed slaves from Armenia or Persia, they formed a close corps of palace attendants headed by the imperial chamberlain, *praepositus sacri cubiculi*, who as a *vir illustris* (i.e. in the most senior class of senators) had parity of rank with the leading functionaries of the empire. Under Constantius II the chamberlain Eusebius was accused of running the government (e.g. Amm. Marc. 18. 4. 3); *Arcadius (2)'s eunuch *Eutropius (2) rose to be consul in the east in AD 399, and led a military expedition against the Huns; in AD 550 *Justinian made his *praepositus* *Narses supreme commander in Italy. Their permanent presence made these eunuch-courtiers influential channels of access to the emperor, and greatly enriched them in the process, thus adding resentment to the general distaste which they continued to attract. For late Roman rulers, however, this same social exclusion was a guarantee of unlimited loyalty.

RE Suppl. 3. 449–55; Jones, *Later Rom. Emp.* 566–70; K. Hopkins, *Conquerors and Slaves* (1978), 172–96.   E. D. H.

Eunus (RE 1), a Syrian slave in Enna, led a slave revolt in Sicily. Adopting the royal name of Antiochus and issuing coins (in bronze), he collected a large force, chiefly of slaves, gained control of much of Sicily and defeated several Roman armies. L. *Calpurnius Piso Frugi won the first major successes against him (133 BC) and P. *Rupilius finally captured Enna and Eunus, who died in prison at *Morgantina.

Diod. Sic. 34 (surviving in fragments), from Posidonius, is the main source.   E. B.

eupatridai The term, meaning literally 'the well-fathered ones', came to be used exclusively in Athens, initially to denote an aristocracy of birth. Its earliest attested uses are on a mid-6th-cent. gravestone (*IG* 12. 9. 296) and in the drinking-song which commemorated the *Alcmaeonid seizure of Leipsydrion in 513 BC (*Ath. pol.* 19. 3). Such uses are compatible with its having been initially an informal term (perhaps analogous to the *Corinthian *Bacchiadae) for the set of families which monopolized the magistracies of state 'by birth and wealth' before the creation of the *Solonian classes (*Ath. pol.* 3). However, *Ath. pol.* 13. 2 preserves a tradition that on the expulsion of the archon (see ARCHONTES) Damasias in September 580 the archonship was held in commission by five *eupatridai*, three *agroikoi* ('farmers'), and two *demiourgoi* ('public workers'): if reliably transmitted, the term had official standing to denote a class whose creation later tradition, probably stemming from the lost beginning of *Ath. pol.*, attributed to *Theseus (Plut. *Thes.* 25. 2). Later usage, already changing in *Isocrates' disingenuous description of the ancestry of Alcibiades, son of the famous *Alcibiades (Isoc. 16. 25), assimilated the *eupatridai* to a *genos*. Members of a *genos* so named appear in late Hellenistic documents from *Delphi and Athens, and in the Roman period filled the office of 'sacred expounder from *eupatridai*' (*IG* 2². 5049 and 7447).

> H. T. Wade-Gery, *CQ* 1931, 1–11, 77–89 (= *Essays in Greek History* (1958), 86–115); *APF* 10–15; D. Roussel, *Tribu et cité* (1976), 55 ff.; P. J. Rhodes, *CAAP* 74 ff., 182 ff.; T. Figueira, *Hesp.* 53 (1984), 447–74.
>
> J. K. D.

Euphantus, of Olynthus, tutor of *Antigonus (2) Gonatas, to whom he dedicated a treatise Περὶ βασιλείας ('On *Kingship'). He also wrote contemporary history (Ἱστορίαι) and several tragedies.

> *FGrH* 74.

Euphemus, an *Argonaut, son of *Poseidon, connected with the foundation legend of *Cyrene. According to *Pindar (*Pyth.* 4, cf. Ap. Rhod. 4. 1730–64) he was given a clod of earth with instructions to drop it into the sea at *Taenarum; his descendants in the fourth generation would then rule over *Libya. But the clod was washed overboard at *Thera, and instead Libya was colonized from that island in the seventeenth generation.

> R. Vollkommer, *LIMC* 4/1. 67–8; G. Huxley, *Pindar's Vision of the Past* (1975), 37–8.
>
> E. Ke.

Euphorbus, in mythology, a Dardanian, son of *Panthous, who wounded *Patroclus (*Il.* 16. 806 ff.), and was afterwards killed by *Menelaus (1) (17. 45 ff.). *Pythagoras (1) claimed to have been Euphorbus in a former incarnation and to recognize his shield (Hor. *Carm.* 1. 28. 9 ff., and commentators there).

> *LIMC* 4/1 (1988), 68–9.
>
> H. J. R.

Euphorion (1), son of *Aeschylus, is said by the *Suda to have won four victories with plays written by his father but not produced in his lifetime (more probably one victory with four plays?), as well as writing plays of his own. In 431 BC he defeated both *Sophocles (1) and *Euripides.

> *TrGF* 1². 88.
>
> A. L. B.

Euphorion (2), of Chalcis, Greek poet; b. 275 BC (*Suda*), pupil of the philosophers Prytanis and *Lacydes and the poet Archebulus of Thera; he profited from the patronage of the wife of *Alexander (9), ruler of Euboea, and was appointed librarian at *Antioch (1) by *Antiochus III (who ruled 223–187). He was possibly given Athenian citizenship.

Euphorion was a scholar-poet in the tradition of *Callimachus (3): monographs on the *Isthmian Games and other historical and mythological subjects are attested; he is also credited with a lexicon to *Hippocrates (2), and two of his epigrams appear in *Meleager (2)'s anthology. He was best known though for his hexameter poetry, of which only tantalizingly small fragments have been preserved; even the more extensive papyrus fragments discovered this century do not permit confident judgements on the nature or merits of his poems, which ancient readers found difficult (cf. Cic. *Div.* 2. 133, Clem. Al. *Strom.* 5. 8. 51). The *Suda*

mentions only three works, *Hesiod*, *Mopsopia*, and *Chiliades*, but other sources yield over twenty titles, which however cast little light on the content of the poems. At least three (*Thrax*, *Curses* or *The Goblet-thief*, *Chiliades*) were curse-poems, recounting obscure mythological stories in abstruse terms (cf. Ovid's *Ibis*): *Chiliades* apparently predicted the certain punishment of Euphorion's adversaries by citing oracles which had been fulfilled after a lapse of a thousand years. His interest in recondite lore and aetiology is reminiscent of *Callimachus (3), whose style he closely imitated; his diction is basically Homeric, with learned elaborations.

Euphorion was imitated by later poets, e.g. *Nicander and *Nonnus; probably through Parthenius he influenced *Catullus (1), *Cornelius Gallus, *Virgil, and the author of the *Ciris (but the reference to *cantores Euphorionis* in Cicero, *Tusc.* 3. 45, is hard to interpret).

> TEXTS Powell, *Coll. Alex.* 28–177; *Suppl. Hell.* 413–53; L. A. de Cuenca (1976), with Sp. trans.
>
> COMMENT F. Scheidweiler, *Euphorionis fragmenta* (1908); B. A. van Groningen, *Euphorion* (1977): inadequate—note the important review by H. J. Lloyd-Jones, *CR* 1979, 14–17; on the curse-poems: L. Watson, *Arae: The Curse Poetry of Antiquity* (1991); epigrams: Gow–Page, *HE* 2. 284–6.
>
> F. W.

Euphranor, Greek sculptor and painter, active *c.*370–330 BC. Only his colossal marble *Apollo Patrous has survived. A virtuoso all-rounder, he also made personifications (Aretē, Hellas, i.e. Virtue and Greece), heroes (*Achilles, *Paris) and portraits (*Philip (1) II, *Alexander (3) the Great), wrote on proportion and colours, and painted the Battle of *Mantinea (362), the Twelve Gods, and *Theseus with *Democracy and *Demos in the Stoa Basileios. Attributions include the Piraeus Athena, the Lansdowne Paris, and the Rondanini Alexander.

> O. Palagia, *Euphranor* (1980); A. F. Stewart, *Greek Sculpture* (1990), 179, 287 f., figs. 311 f.
>
> A. F. S.

Euphrates, the longest river of western Asia, and the more westerly of the Two Rivers of *Mesopotamia. Originating in the Armenian highlands from its two headstreams Kara Su (Pyxurates) and Murad Su (Arsanias), which join above Melitene (Malatya), it flows south-west to the Taurus, then south-east. In the alluvial plain of Babylonia it was connected, in antiquity, with the *Tigris by numerous navigation and irrigation canals. In classical times it was crossed by a number of bridges, for instance at *Zeugma and *Babylon. It served as a political boundary between Armenia and Cappadocia, Sophene and Commagene, and Upper Mesopotamia and Syria (Strabo 16. 746–9; Plin. *HN* 5. 83; Ptol. *Geog.* 5. 12). The Parthian empire reached the permanent limit of its expansion westwards at the Euphrates in 53 BC. After the Romans in AD 66 recognized the rule of an Arsacid king over Armenia they began the construction of a military *limes along the upper and middle course of the river; forts along its right bank guarded for more than 500 years the imperial frontier against first the Parthian, later the Sasanid kings.

> R. McC. Adams, *Heartland of Cities* (1981), *Defence of the Roman and Byzantine East*, 2 pts. (1986), and *The Eastern Frontier of the Roman Empire*, 2 pts. (1989). M. S. D.; E. W. G.; J. Wi.

Euphron New Comedy poet (see COMEDY (GREEK), NEW), dated to the middle of the 3rd cent. BC by his allusion to *Nicomedes I of Bithynia (fr. 11. 2). Nine titles are known. Fr. 1, the great discoveries of cooks (see H. Dohm, *Mageiros* (1964), 131 ff.).

> Kassel–Austin, *PCG* 5. 282–92 (*CAF* 3. 317 ff.). W. G. A.

Euphron, of Sicyon. See SICYON.

Eupolemus (fl. *c*.150 BC), a Hellenized Jewish historian from Palestine, wrote (in Greek) *On the Kings in Judaea*, a popular history of the Jews in a rhetorical style; fragments are quoted by Clement of Alexandria and Eusebius.

FGrH 723; Schürer, *History* 3. 517 ff.   A. J. S. S.

Eupolis was regarded as one of the greatest poets of the Old Comedy (e.g. Hor. *Sat.* 1. 4. 1). His first play was produced in 429 BC (Anon. *De com.* 9 p. 7); he won three victories at the *Lenaea and at least one at the City *Dionysia (IG 2². 2325. 59, 126). The datable plays are: *Numeniae* at the Lenaea in 425 (hyp. 1 Ar. *Ach.*), *Maricas* at the Lenaea in 421 (schol. Ar. *Nub.* 551), *Flatterers* at the City Dionysia in 421 (hyp. 1 Ar. *Pax*), *Autolycus* in 420 (Ath. 216d), and *Baptae* after 424 (fr. 89 refers to Ar. *Eq.*) but before 415 (Aristid. *Or.* 3. 444 D relates a story which, though untrue, presupposes 415 as the last possible date for *Baptae*). *Cities* is probably to be dated *c.*420 BC; it has many personal references in common with Ar. *Nub.*, *Vesp.*, and *Pax*. *Demes* must be later than 418 (fr. 99. 30 ff. refers to the Mantinea campaign of that year; see MANTINEA, BATTLES OF) and earlier than 406 (fr. 110 shows that the younger Pericles is still alive); 412 is the most probable date. Eupolis died 'in the Hellespont, during the *Peloponnesian War' (*Suda*), sometime after 415 (Eratosth. quoted in Cic. *Att.* 6. 1. 18). We have nineteen titles and nearly 500 citations, with substantial papyrus fragments of, and commentaries on, *Maricas*, *Prospaltii*, and *Taxiarchi*.

Flatterers ridiculed *Callias (1), son of Hipponicus, for cultivating the company of *sophists—a comic poet's view of the kind of scene portrayed in Pl. *Prt.* 314 ff. *Maricas* was an attack on *Hyperbolus, comparable with *Aristophanes (1)'s attack on *Cleon in *Knights*; like Aristophanes' *Lysistrata*, it had two opposed choruses. In *Demes* great Athenians of the past were brought up from the Underworld to give advice to the present. In *Taxiarchi* the soft-living *Dionysus is subjected to hard military and naval training by *Phormion (1). Eupolis' style seemed 'abusive and coarse' to the author of Anon. *De com.* 33 p. 9, but 'highly imaginative and attractive' to Platonius, *Diff. com.* 1 p. 6).

Kassel–Austin, PCG 5. 294 ff. (CAF 1. 258 ff.).   K. J. D.

Euripides, Athenian tragic playwright.

Career Euripides was born probably in the 480s. He first took part in the dramatic competitions of the City *Dionysia at Athens in 455 BC, the year after the death of *Aeschylus (Life 32: he came third; the plays included *Daughters of Pelias*, his first treatment of the story of *Medea); he died in 407–6, leaving, like *Sophocles (1) later in the same year, plays still unperformed (*Iphigenia at Aulis, Alcmaeon in Corinth, Bacchae*: schol. Ar. *Frogs* 67), with which he won a last, posthumous victory (*Suda*, entry under the name). His first victory came only in 441 (*Marm. Par.* 60; plays unknown). He won again in 428 (hyp. *Hippolytus*), but in his lifetime won only four victories at the Dionysia (*Suda*): he was thus far less successful in the competition than Aeschylus (thirteen victories) or Sophocles (eighteen victories). In 438 he was defeated by Sophocles (hypothesis (see HYPOTHESIS, LITERARY) to *Alc.*; Euripides' plays were *Cretan Women, Alcmaeon in Psophis, Telephus, Alcestis*); in 431 he was third to Aeschylus' son, *Euphorion (1), and Sophocles (hyp. *Med.*: his plays were *Medea, Philoctetes, Dictys, Theristae*); in 415 second to Xenocles (Ael. *VH* 2. 8; Euripides' plays were *Alexander, Palamedes, Trojan Women, Sisyphus*); in 409 second, perhaps to Sophocles (hyp. *Phoen.*; his plays included

Phoenissae and perhaps *Oenomaus* and *Chrysippus*). In 408 he probably competed at the Dionysia for the last time with plays that included *Orestes* (schol. *Or.* 371). Soon afterwards he left Athens on a visit to Macedon, as guest of the Hellenizing king *Archelaus (2), and wrote a play there about an eponymous ancestor of the king (much as Aeschylus had written a play about the foundation of the city of Aetna while in Syracuse as guest of the tyrant, *Hieron (1)). He never returned to Athens but died in Macedon. There is no good reason to accept the ancient tradition that he had left Athens an embittered man, finally despairing after a series of defeats by almost unknown playwrights (Satyrus, Life of Eur. fr. 39; Philodemus *de vitiis*, col. 13: Satyrus' Life is largely a work of fiction).

Plays Euripides wrote some ninety plays (*Suda*, entry under the name). By chance we have more than twice as many of them as we have plays by either Aeschylus or Sophocles. They fall into two categories: the first, a group of ten plays which have been transmitted to us in our medieval manuscripts complete with the accumulation of ancient notes and comments that we call *scholia. They represent the same kind of volume of 'selected plays' as we have for the other two playwrights. They are: *Alcestis, Medea, Hippolytus, Andromache, Hecuba, Trojan Women, Phoenissae, Orestes, Bacchae*, and *Rhesus*. The last is probably not by Euripides; the plays are in their likely chronological order; *Bacchae* has lost its scholia and the end of the play is partly missing. The other nine plays are: *Helen, Electra, Heraclidae, Heracles, Suppliant Women, Iphigenia at Aulis, Iphigenia among the Taurians, Ion, Cyclops*. They have been transmitted in only a pair of closely related 14th-cent. manuscripts (known as L and P); they have no scholia and they are in a rough (Greek) alphabetical order. There is little doubt that they represent the chance survival of one volume (perhaps two) of the 'complete plays' of Euripides, which circulated in alphabetical order, as we know from ancient lists of plays and collections of 'hypotheseis' (prefaces) to the plays (see Barrett, ed. *Hippolytos*, 45–61): they therefore represent a random sample of Euripides' work. Nine of the surviving plays are dated: *Alcestis* (438), *Medea* (431), *Hippolytus* (428), *Trojan Women* (415); *Helen* (412); *Phoenissae* (409); *Orestes* (probably 408); *Bacchae* and *Iphigenia at Aulis* (between 408 and 406). The remaining plays can be dated more roughly but with some confidence on the evidence of Euripides' writing of the verse of spoken dialogue in his plays. Statistical studies have shown that the tendency he clearly displays to write an ever freer, looser iambic verse line, by replacing 'long' syllables with pairs of 'short', is steadily progressive and not subject to sudden fluctuations (Dale, ed., *Helen*, with references to earlier work). The likely sequence (with approximate dates) is: *Heraclidae* (430), *Andromache* (426), *Hecuba* (424), *Suppliant Women* (422), *Electra* (416), *Heracles* (414), *Iphigenia among the Taurians* (413), *Ion* (410). The satyr-play *Cyclops* is late, probably around 408. We also have, mostly from papyrus texts, sizeable fragments of several other plays: *Telephus, Cretans, Cresphontes, Erechtheus, Phaethon, Alexander, Oedipus, Hypsipyle, Archelaus* (in their probable chronological order).

'Realism', fragmentation, formalism Ever since *Aristophanes (1)'s portrayal of Euripides, in his play *Frogs*, as an intellectual iconoclast who insisted on confronting the darker and more disturbing aspects of everyday reality (*Frogs* 959), and Aristotle's quotation of an opaque remark attributed to Sophocles, to the effect that he (Sophocles) presented men 'as they ought to be', while Euripides presented them 'as they are' (*Poet.* 1460ᵇ33 ff.), Euripides has tended to be read as a 'realist'. Plays such as *Trojan

Euripides

Women (which sharply focuses on the savage brutality of war, in the middle of war); *Aeolus* (which takes incest as its theme: we know of it only from its 'hypothesis') and *Cretans* (whose action turns on sexual intercourse between a woman and a bull) have been cited in evidence. Moreover it has seemed obvious to many critics (already in antiquity: [*Longinus], *Subl.* 15. 4–5) that a naturalistic treatment of human psychology, particularly female psychology, is another hallmark of Euripidean theatre: witness Medea, Phaedra, Hecuba, Electra, Creusa but also Ion, Orestes (in *Orestes*), and Pentheus. It is undoubtedly true that there are strands of 'realism' in Euripides' writing for the theatre: for example, Medea's presentation of herself as mistrusted 'foreigner' and oppressed and exploited 'woman' (*Med.* 214–58) and her subsequent slow, tortured progress to infanticide; Orestes sickened and eventually driven mad by the corrosive effects of guilt (*Or.* 34–45; 208–315, including the only 'mad scene' in extant Greek tragedy); or the voyeurism of Pentheus in *Bacchae*. But these are strands only in an extremely fragmented whole. For it is arguable that a vision of human experience as inherently fragmented and as defined by the co-existence of disparate, even contradictory, strands forms the very heart of Euripidean sensibility.

If we go back to *Medea* and read it attentively, we shall find that the Medea we have encountered in the passage already referred to exists, within the world of the play, alongside other Medeas: before the passage mentioned, she has been heard offstage, giving incoherent voice only to pain and articulate only in universal cursing and damnation, of herself and her own children as well as of her enemies; immediately after it, she is transformed into a subtle adversary who patently and easily outwits her most powerful enemy. Subsequently she becomes successively brilliant orator, pathetic victim, devious manipulator, exultant (and uncanny) avenger, tormented mother until her final metamorphosis (involving a stunning *coup de théâtre*) into the demonic figure who, in an aerial chariot drawn by snakes, closes the play with prophecies and taunts sent down from beyond his reach upon the husband who deserted and humiliated her.

Hippolytus too introduces us to a similarly fragmented world: the play is framed by the appearance of two human-like divinities, cool, articulate, and frighteningly rational in their revenges; in between it is given over to humans, in three very disparate and distinct 'movements'. The first of these movements comprises the uncanny and disturbing passage across the stage of Hippolytus, who, it is clear, lives apart in a world of his own making and companioned by his own, personal, chorus; as he leaves, we are confronted, first, by a world of women, characterized by an intimacy which is warm and close but also painful, and by a Phaedra, who is successively delirious with hunger and unspoken sexual desire and then, immediately, rational, articulate, and analytical in presenting her decision to take her own life. That world is shattered by its own intimacies, which lead by slow degrees but with a sense of psychologically convincing inevitability first to deadly revelation and then to misguided intervention. The intervention goes terrifyingly astray. Phaedra dies and the world of women in which she has lived is replaced by a world of men, that of her husband and Hippolytus, the stepson with whom she had, by Aphrodite's will, fallen obsessively in love. This male world is characterized no longer by intimacy and warm relationship but by distance and cold rhetoric: in this world there is no communication, only speech-making and the cut-and-thrust of distichomythia (the formal exchange of pairs of lines). The scene ends in Theseus' invocation of a male divinity, his own father, to

destroy his son and it is followed at once by the messenger's description of that destruction: the description demonstrates that divinity is not human, but bestial and capable of tearing men literally apart and of bringing about the annihilation of all that they have made.

Moreover, Euripidean 'realism' is conveyed to the reader/spectator through the medium of a marked, if equally fragmented, formalism. It has been a stumbling-block for many critics that Euripidean theatricality is expressed in stiffly formal, often detached, 'set pieces'. Euripides characteristically opens his plays with a markedly non-naturalistic 'prologue', in the form of a monologue, which acts as a kind of separate overture. Almost as characteristically he closes them with a detached tailpiece: the shape of the action is broken and brought to a halt by the intervention, sometimes (as in *Medea*) of a character from that action, now transformed, but more often a divinity (as in *Hippolytus*, *Andromache*, *Suppliant Women*, *Electra*, *Iphigenia among the Taurians*, *Ion*, *Helen*, *Orestes*, *Bacchae*). The divinity often apparently makes a highly theatrical apparition off the ground in mid-air, the so-called 'deus ex machina' (already a problem for Aristotle: *Poet.* $1454^{b}2$ ff.). Confrontation between dramatic persons frequently takes the form of an exchange of symmetrical and brilliantly rhetorical speeches, transparently forensic in tone, a special kind of bravura set-piece which modern scholars have called an *agōn*.

Innovation and recurrence In *Frogs* Aristophanes presents Euripides (comically) as a compulsive innovator and subverter of tradition. In his handling of the traditional stories which he (like the other 5th-cent. playwrights) took as the material out of which to make his plays, he clearly innovates: Medea's infanticide; Heracles' killing of his wife and children after, not before, the labours; Electra's marriage to a peasant farmer; the trial of Orestes before the Argive assembly; Thebes, years after Oedipus' discovery of the truth, still inhabited by Iocasta, Oedipus, and Antigone (and by a transient chorus of Phoenician girls!)—all these seem to be Euripidean innovations. There is a kind of restlessness to Euripidean experimentation (*Phoenissae* provides a good example) that many critics have taken to be definitive of his theatrical imagination. But innovation is not in itself a peculiarly Euripidean trait: Aeschylus (especially in *Suppliant Women* and *Oresteia*) and Sophocles (especially in *Philoctetes*) both gave themselves the freedom to reshape traditional stories in order to create new fictional worlds for the tragic theatre.

At least as characteristic of Euripides is the tendency to create theatre, almost obsessively, out of recurring dramatic situations which echo and resonate with each other. Very often these situations have women at their centre, women as victims and/or deadly avengers: examples are *Medea*, *Hippolytus*, *Andromache*, *Hecuba*, *Electra*, *Trojan Women*, *Ion*, *Helen*, *Iphigenia at Aulis*. Sometimes structural echoing (as between *Medea* and *Hippolytus*), situational parallels (as between *Electra* and *Orestes* or between *Hecuba* and *Trojan Women*), or emotional resonances (as between *Medea* and *Ion*) almost give the impression that the later play is a reworking of the earlier. Similarly *Bacchae* recurs to the theme of divine revenge through the subjugation and perversion of human will that he had treated in *Hippolytus*. But these are not 'revivals' under another name. Each reworking offers a different vision of the human condition and these disparate visions are enacted in very different structural forms: the ending of *Hecuba*, for example, is quite other than, and carries a very different sense of '*closure' from, that of *Trojan Women*.

Speech and song: the late plays The late plays of Euripides (roughly those of the last decade of his life, the plays that come after *Trojan Women* and *Heracles*) have thrown up major problems of interpretation and have led to strong critical disagreement. In so far as there has been a consensus, plays such as *Iphigenia among the Taurians*, *Ion*, and *Helen* have been characterized as 'escapist' or as 'tragicomedies', while others such as *Phoenissae*, *Orestes* and *Iphigenia at Aulis* (*Bacchae*, it is agreed, is somehow 'different') have been called 'epic theatre' or 'melodrama'. The underlying assumption has been that Euripides has turned away from the painful realities of tragic experience to offer his audiences less demanding, more 'entertaining' forms of theatre: the very real sufferings caused by the *Peloponnesian War between Athens and the Spartan alliance have often been invoked in explanation.

The late plays are also often seen as the moment in Athenian theatre history when the chorus goes into terminal decline: its songs become fewer, more 'irrelevant' to the action and more purely decorative in function. (The charge of 'irrelevance' has indeed been laid against Euripides' use of the chorus even in his earliest surviving plays, for example in the third *stasimon* of *Medea*, ll. 824–65.) The two issues (of the changing nature of late Euripidean theatre and the 'decline of the chorus') need to be taken together.

Sung and spoken text together form the 'script' of the Greek tragic theatre from the earliest surviving play, Aeschylus' *Persians* of 472 BC, to the last, Euripides' *Bacchae* and *Iphigenia at Aulis* and Sophocles' *Oedipus at Colonus*, and in almost all the plays that we have actors and chorus both sing and speak (it is generally assumed that the spoken lines marked 'Chorus' in our manuscripts were in fact spoken only by the chorus-leader). But song is the characteristic mode of choral utterance and speech that of actors. In the late plays of Euripides this distinction becomes very much less clear as actors are increasingly given arias and duets to sing and moments of great emotional intensity in these plays are marked by such songs. Thus, for example, Creusa's anguished and distracted aria of self-revelation at *Ion* 859–922; the recognition duet of Menelaus and Helen at *Helen* 625–97; the murder scene of *Orestes* 1246–1310; and the final encounter and last farewells of Antigone and Oedipus at *Phoenissae* 1539–81, 1710–57. Sung text is also used to convey young innocence at *Ion* 82–183 and *Phoenissae* 103–92. At the same time choral songs are becoming more infrequent, though the stanzas that form them are getting longer.

Moreover, Euripides increasingly uses 'astrophic' song, that is song not composed of the responding, metrically 'rhymed' stanzas that throughout the history of tragedy had characterized the song of both chorus and actors. We have external evidence that connects these changes to new developments in musical composition, developments that were seemingly designed to make possible freer, aurally less predictable vocal lines. The key figure in these developments appears to have been Euripides' younger contemporary, *Timotheus (1), who is plausibly associated with Euripides in a number of ancient anecdotes. Such music and the writing that goes with it, composed of long sentences, free in syntax, that seem to float without ultimate closure (they are brilliantly parodied by Aristophanes in *Frogs*), are clearly the medium for a different perception of human experience than that of the earlier plays. It is not that Euripides' perception is no longer 'tragic' (though a number of the late plays, such as *Ion*, *Iphigenia among the Taurians*, and *Helen*, do end with apparent 'happiness'); rather Euripides now seems to see human beings not just as articulately analytical in confronting suffering but

simultaneously as living in a world of shifting, unstable, and often contradictory emotions. It is through song, and the associative juxtaposition of sensations, thoughts, and experiences that have always characterized Greek song, that such fleeting and unstable forms of consciousness are conveyed in the late plays.

Alongside this almost operatic use of song, Euripides also employs in the late plays other new formal devices to create new versions of the tragic. They include vastly extended passages of stichomythia (exchanges of single lines, dialogue at its most tensely formal) and the use of metres taken from much older forms of tragedy, such as the trochaic tetrameter (*Or.* 729–806, which includes 25 successive lines divided between two speakers, shows both formal devices together). The result is a series of plays whose emotional atmosphere is much more difficult to seize and characterize. Their themes still include human isolation and inexplicable suffering, failures of communication, the victimization of women, and the drive to revenge, even the terrors of madness, themes that have marked earlier Euripidean theatre but in a bewildering variety of new dramatic modes.

The last two plays that we have, *Bacchae* and *Iphigenia at Aulis*, point up the paradoxical and disconcerting multiplicity of Euripides' theatrical imagination. *Bacchae* eschews almost all the formal innovations of the other late plays (though not the freer iambic verse nor the extended stichomythia scenes) and offers a vision of human experience that combines a stark and shocking view of the power of divinity with a luxuriant but ambiguous emotionalism which veers from joyful calm to exultant savagery: men and women are crushed and overwhelmed by collision with a divine power which they cannot comprehend. *Iphigenia at Aulis* takes us into another world. It makes much use of actor arias and duets (including an extended passage of sung text given to Agamemnon, as well as long arias for Iphigenia); it deploys greatly extended passages of stichomythia, much of it in trochaic tetrameters and involving free use of broken lines. The choral songs are more numerous than in other late plays and the first of them (the entry-song of the chorus) is very long. Above all it creates an emotionally charged but unstable world marked by botched deception and exciting disclosure, by an anti-hero, Agamemnon, who is tormented by indecision, and by a young Iphigenia, who combines a childlike innocence with heroic self-determination. The worlds of *Iphigenia* and of *Bacchae* barely touch and yet, in the theatre, they were juxtaposed, played one after the other before the same audience. They attest not merely the variety of Euripides' theatrical imagination (to the very end of his life) but also a fact that we should always remember: that his audiences, like those of Aeschylus and Sophocles, were accustomed to the experience of tragedy not in the form of a single play but as a sequence of three disparate tragic fictions, rounded off by anti-tragic burlesque. The disparateness of Euripides' theatrical imagination plays to that expectation.

TEXT J. Diggle (OCT, 1981–94); with Fr. trans., L. Meridier, H. Grégoire, L. Parmentier, and F. Chapouthier (Budé, 1923–); fragments in *TGF*, rev. edn., with Suppl. by B. Snell (1964), pp. 361–716, Suppl. pp. 3–20; H. von Arnim, *Supplementum Euripideum* (1913), with Satyrus' Life; C. Austin, *Nova Fragmenta Euripidea* (1968); Page, *Gk. Lit. Pap.* 1. 54–134, with Eng. trans.; *Hypsipyle*, ed. G. W. Bond (1963); *Phaethon*, ed. J. Diggle (1970). See *CHCL* 1. 769 for further edns. of fragmentary plays; note esp. A. Harder, *Euripides' Cresphontes and Archelaus* (1985).

TRANSLATION R. Lattimore and D. Grene (eds.), 2nd edn., 2 vols. (1992); D. Kovacs (Loeb, 1994–).

CONCORDANCE J. T. Allen and G. Italie (1954); Suppl., ed. C. Collard (1971).

Europa

SCHOLIA Ed. E. Schwartz (1887–91).

COMMENTARIES Most plays have now been edited in the OUP or Aris and Phillips series of Euripides' commentaries; note especially *Medea*, ed. D. L. Page (1938); *Ion*, ed. A. S. Owen (1939); *Bacchae*, ed. E. R. Dodds, 2nd edn. (1960); *Alcestis*, ed. A. M. Dale (1954); *Heracles*, ed. G. W. Bond (1981); *Orestes*, ed. C. W. Willink (1986); *Hippolytus*, ed. W. S. Barrett (1964); *Helen*, ed. A. M. Dale (1967); *Orestes*, ed. M. L. West (1987); *Trojan Women*, ed. S. Barlow (1986); *Electra*, ed. M. J. Cropp (1988); *Alcestis*, ed. D. Conacher (1988); *Hecuba*, ed. C. Collard (1991); *Cyclops*, ed. R. Seaford (1984); *Heraclidae*, ed. J. Wilkins (1993); *Phoenissae*, ed. D. Mastronarde (1994).

CRITICISM G. Murray, *Euripides and his Age*, 2nd edn. (1946); R. P. Winnington-Ingram, *Euripides and Dionysus* (1948); A. Rivier, *Essai sur le Tragique d'Euripide*, 2nd edn. (1975); W. Zürcher, *Darstellung des Menschen im Drama des Euripides* (1947); G. M. A. Grube, *The Drama of Euripides* (1961); G. Zuntz, *The Political Plays of Euripides*, 2nd edn., 1963); *Entretiens Hardt* 6 (1960); A. Lesky, *Die tragische Dichtung der Hellenen*, 3rd edn. (1972); Eng. trans. (1983); R. Lattimore, *Story Patterns in Greek Tragedy* (1964); T. C. W. Stinton, *Euripides and the Judgment of Paris* (Hell. Soc. London, Suppl. Paper, 1965); N. C. Hourmouziades, *Production and Imagination in Euripides* (1965); T. B. L. Webster, *The Tragedies of Euripides* (1967); D. J. Conacher, *Euripidean Drama* (1967); S. Barlow, *The Imagery of Euripides* (1971); A. P. Burnett, *Catastrophe Survived* (1971), and *YClS* 1977; B. Knox, *Word and Action* (1979); P. Pucci, *The Violence of Pity in Euripides' 'Medea'* (1980); E. Segal (ed.), *Oxford Readings in Greek Tragedy* (1984); H. Foley, *Ritual Irony* (1985); S. Goldhill, *Reading Greek Tragedy* (1986); N. Loraux, *Tragic Ways of Killing a Woman* (1987); C. Segal, *Interpreting Greek Tragedy* (1986); E. Hall, *Inventing the Barbarian* (1989); A. N. Michelini, *Euripides and the Tragic Tradition* (1987); J. Gregory, *Euripides and the Instruction of the Athenians* (1991); M. R. Halleran, *Stagecraft in Euripides* (1985); C. Segal, *Euripides and the Poetics of Sorrow* (1993); M. Lloyd, *The Agon in Euripides* (1992); I. F. de Jong, *Narrative in Drama: the Art of the Euripidean Messenger-Speech* (1991).   J. P. A. G.

Europa, in mythology, is usually said to be the daughter of the Phoenician king *Agenor, though Homer (*Il.* 14. 321) makes her the daughter of *Phoenix (1). *Zeus saw her when she was playing with her companions on the seashore and was filled with desire for her. So he turned himself into, or sent, a beautiful bull, which approached her and enticed her by its mildness to climb on its back. At once it made off with her and plunged into the sea, then swam to *Crete. There Zeus made love to her, and she bore him two or three children, *Minos, *Rhadamanthys, and, in post-Homeric accounts, *Sarpedon. She was then married to Asterius, king of Crete, who adopted her sons as his own. Zeus gave her three presents: the bronze man *Talos (1) (Ap. Rhod. 4. 1643) to guard the island, a hound which never missed its quarry ([Eratosth.] 33), and a javelin which never missed its mark (ibid., cf. Ov. *Met.* 7. 681 ff.). These last passed afterwards to Minos, thence to *Procris and so to her husband *Cephalus. Agenor, anxious about Europa, sent his sons *Cadmus, *Phoenix (1), and Cilix to find her, and their mother Telephassa went too. But when they failed to find Europa they all chose to settle elsewhere, and Agenor never saw them again (Apollod. 3. 1. 1). The bull whose form Zeus had taken became the *constellation Taurus ([Eratosth.] 14).

Europa with the bull was a favourite theme in art from the 6th cent. BC: see M. Robertson, *LIMC* 4/1. 76–92. For the *Europa* of *Moschus see W. Bühler, *Die Europa des Moschos* (1960).

H. J. R.; J. R. M.

Europe The name Εὐρώπη originally stood for central Greece (*Hymn. Hom. Ap.* 250, 290). It was soon extended to the whole Greek mainland and by 500 BC to the entire land mass behind it. The boundary between the European continent and Asia was usually fixed at the river Don. *Homer vaguely knew dark regions of the west and north, but his range of information hardly extended north of Greece or west of Sicily.

The Mediterranean seaboard of Europe was chiefly opened up by the Greeks between 800 and 500 BC (see COLONIZATION, GREEK). The Atlantic coasts and 'Tin Islands' were discovered by the Phoenicians (see CASSITERIDES); *Pytheas circumnavigated Britain and followed the mainland coast at least to Heligoland. The Baltic Sea was probably not entered by Greek or Roman ships; Scandinavia was almost wholly unknown until quite late during the Roman empire after the invasions by the Goths; and *Thule remained a land of mystery.

The prehistoric *amber routes across Europe from Jutland and the Baltic were unknown to later explorers. The Greeks penetrated by way of the Russian rivers as far as Kiev or perhaps Smolensk; central and north Russia remained to them a land of mythical peoples and of the fabulous *Rhipaean mountains; north of the Balkans they located the equally mythical *Hyperboreans. Greek pioneers ascended the Danube to the Iron Gates, and the Rhône perhaps to Lake Léman. But Herodotus had only a hazy notion of central Europe, and the Hellenistic Greeks knew little more (see ALPS; HERCYNIAN FOREST).

The land exploration of Europe was chiefly accomplished by the Roman armies. These completed the Carthaginian discovery of Spain; under Caesar they made Gaul known; under Augustus' generals, M. *Licinius Crassus (2), *Tiberius, and Drusus (see CLAUDIUS DRUSUS, NERO), they opened up the Balkan lands, the Alpine massif, and the Danube basin (see DANUVIUS). Roman traders rediscovered the amber route from Vienna to the Baltic, and Trajan revealed the Carpathian lands by conquest (see DACIA). Tiberius and Drusus also overran west Germany to the Elbe, but central Germany remained outside known Europe.

The Europe–Asia polarity was important in Greek ideology (Diod. Sic. 11. 62; ML 93); the two together were taken to represent the whole inhabited space. (Africa/Libya being sometimes added as a third constituent). A Eurocentric chauvinism is evident in Roman thought (cf. Plin. *HN* 3. 1. 5: Europe is 'by far the finest of all lands').

Cary–Warmington, *Explorers* 12 ff., 108 ff., 229 ff.; (Pelican edn., 21 ff., 132 ff.); Cary, *Geographic Background* 231 ff.; M. Ninck, *Die Entdeckung von Europa durch die Griechen* (1945); A. Schoening, *Germanien in d. Geog. des Ptolemaeus* (1962); G. Schuette, *Classica et Mediaevalia* 1951, 236 ff.; O. Brogan, *JRS* 1935, 195 ff.; H. J. Eggers, 'Der römische Import im freien Germanien', *Atlas der Urgeschichte* 1 (1951); R. E. M. Wheeler, *Rome beyond the Imperial Frontiers* (1955), 21 ff.

On ancient conceptions of 'Europe' (as opposed to 'Asia') see Momigliano, *Terzo Contributo* 489 ff., and P. Hardie, *Virgil's Aeneid: Cosmos and Imperium* (1986), 311 ff..   E. H. W.; S. H.

Europus (also **Dura**), on the middle *Euphrates, founded by the *Seleucids as a military colony c.300 BC, and a *polis in the 2nd cent. BC. Its importance is chiefly archaeological: excavations in the 1920s and 1930s provide detailed information about a Graeco-Macedonian settlement in the near east under the Seleucids, Parthians, and Romans. The new site was laid out on a grid-plan (see HIPPODAMUS) within heavy fortifications; a 2nd.-cent. BC parchment (*PDura* 15) shows that the territory was divided into hereditary farm-plots (*klēroi*). The *Seleucid phase is marked by an *agora, Greek-style *houses, a temple of *Zeus Megistos with mixed Greek and Mesopotamian elements, and a 'palace' in Graeco-Achaemenid style recalling that at *Ai-Khanoum. Occupied by *Parthia c.100 BC, it served for the next 250 years as a Parthian frontier-town; the survival of Greek as the official language and (probably) that most in daily use suggests continuing Greekness. Taken by Rome in AD 165, it became a garrison-town on the eastern *limes*; a Roman camp, military equipment, and important Roman military archives belong to this phase. Captured by the *Sasanids *c.*257, it was then abandoned.

F. Cumont, *Les Fouilles de Doura-Europos 1922–3* (1926); J. Johnson, *Dura Studies* (1932); M. Rostovtzeff and others, *Excavations at Dura-Europos, Preliminary Reports* (from 1929), and *Final Reports*; M. Rostovtzeff, *Dura-Europus and its Art* (1938); *PECS* 286 f.; *Doura-Europos Études* (1986); W. Hoepfner and E.-L. Schwander, *Haus und Stadt* (1986), 141 ff.; S. Downey, *Mesopotamian Religious Architecture* (1988); F. Millar, *The Roman Near East* (1993), 445 ff. M. S. D.; E. W. G.; A. J. S. S.

Eurybiades, presumably one of 'the first in birth and wealth' (Hdt. 7. 134. 2) among the Spartans, commanded the 'Hellenic League' fleet at the battles of *Artemisium and *Salamis (480 BC). The chief glory for the latter went to *Themistocles, with whose spirit of adventure Eurybiades may not have seen eye-to-eye, but a statue seems to have been erected in his honour at Sparta.

PB no. 317. P. A. C.

Eurycleia, *Odysseus' nurse, who recognizes Odysseus on his return to Ithaca by the boar's scar on his leg (*Od.* 19. 392 ff.), abets his killing of the suitors (21. 380 ff., see PENELOPE), and exults at their deaths (22. 407 ff.). Subject of ancient, esp. Roman, art: *LIMC* 4/1 (1988), 101–3. J. R. M.

Euryclides and Miccion See ATHENS, HISTORY.

Eurydice (1), 'broad-judging'. The best-known bearer of this name was the wife whom *Orpheus either brought back from the Underworld or (Verg. *G.* 4) lost again in the process. The story is first referred to by *Euripides (*Alc.* 357–62) and *Plato (1) (*Symp.* 179d), but the name Eurydice first occurs on 4th-cent. BC pottery and in literature not until [Moschus], *Epitaphios Bionis* 124; it may have stood on a late 5th-cent. relief of which Roman copies survive. Hermesianax calls Orpheus' wife Agriope (fr. 7. 2 Powell). It is uncertain whether Virgil's version, in which Eurydice was killed by a snake as she was fleeing from *Aristaeus, was original to him. As early as the *Epic Cycle *Aeneas' wife was called Eurydice (*Cypria* fr. 23 Davies), and there are clear similarities between the hero's loss of Creusa in *Aeneid* 2 and Orpheus' loss in *Georgic* 4.

J. Heurgon, *Mélanges d'archéologie* 1932, 6–60; C. M. Bowra, *CQ* 1952, 113–26; G. Schwarz, *LIMC* 4. *Epitaphios Bionis* in A. S. F. Gow, *Bucolici Graeci* (1952), 120. R. L. Hu.

Eurydice (2), born Adea (*c.*337–317 BC), granddaughter of two Macedonian kings, *Perdiccas (3) III and *Philip (1) II, was educated by her mother, the Illyrian princess Cynane, after her father was executed by *Alexander (3) the Great. In 322 she escaped with her mother from *Antipater (1)'s custody and won Perdiccas' protection. With his support she married the nominal king, *Philip (2) Arrhidaeus and assumed the regnal name Eurydice. Ambitious and dissatisfied with a ceremonial role, she opposed Antipater at Triparadeisus (321); and in 317 she used her husband's name to depose the regent *Polyperchon and aligned herself with *Cassander. Her army melted away before an invasion led by Polyperchon and the queen mother, *Olympias, and she was driven to suicide alongside her murdered husband. She was rehabilitated by Cassander, and her remains were buried in state with those of Philip.

HM 3. 119 ff., 138 ff. A. B. B.

Eurymedon (now *Köprüçayi* or *Pazarçavi*), one of the principal rivers of the south coast of Asia Minor. Rising in the Pisidian mountains it flows southwards for something over 160 km. (100 mi.) into the mare Lycium (Gulf of Antalya). Some 13 km. (8 mi.) from its mouth is the city of *Aspendus, and further up the ruins of Selge stand high above its right bank. It was reckoned navigable in antiquity at least as far as Aspendus. At the mouth of the Eurymedon in or about 466 BC the Athenian *Cimon gained a double victory over the Persian forces by sea and then by land (Thuc. 1. 100; Plut. *Cim.* 12); a well-known epigram attributed to *Simonides has been connected with this victory (Page, *FGE* 'Simonides' 45). On the problems about the epigram (for which see also Diod. Sic. 11. 62; Peek, *GVI* 16) see Page, *FGE* 266 ff., denying the Eurymedon connection; he gives extensive earlier literature. An Attic red-figure vase may refer humorously to the Persian defeat: G. Ferrari Pinney, *JHS* 1984, 181 ff. (sceptical). G. E. B.; S. H.

Eurypontids, or Euryphontids, was the name of the junior of the two Spartan royal houses (the senior being *Agiads). The most notable Eurypontid kings were *Agesilaus II, *Agis II and IV, *Archidamus II, and *Leotychidas II. P. A. C.

Eurypylus, a minor Iliadic figure sometimes identified with an important hero of *Patrae, having connections with both *Artemis and *Dionysus. At the fall of Troy Eurypylus received a chest containing an image of Dionysus, and on opening it went mad. He was told at *Delphi to establish the worship of the god in the chest wherever he found a 'strange/foreign sacrifice'; the condition was fulfilled by the human sacrifice given to Artemis Triclaria at Patrae, and on the establishment of the cult of Dionysus Eurypylus was cured. At the same time human sacrifice in the Artemis cult was abolished, another oracle having declared that it would cease when a foreign king arrived with a foreign god. In cult as well as myth Eurypylus links both deities: his tomb was in the sanctuary of Artemis Laphria, but he was worshipped at the festival of Dionysus Aesymnetes.

Paus. 7. 19. 1–20. 2. M.-A. Zagdoun and D. Gondicas, *LIMC* 4. 109–11; J. Mattes, *Der Wahnsinn im griechischen Mythos* (1970), 44–5, 51–2; J. Herbillon, *Les Cultes de Patras* (1929), 38–48, 123–9. E. Ke.

Eurystheus, in mythology, son of Sthenelus and Nicippe, and granted rule of the Argolid by *Zeus through *Hera's trickery (*Il.* 19. 95–125). *Heracles was enslaved to him while he performed his twelve Labours, on the orders of the *Delphic oracle and as a punishment for killing his wife and children in a fit of madness. In art Eurystheus is depicted as a coward, hiding fearfully in a great jar when Heracles delivers e.g. the Erymanthian boar (see *LIMC* 5/1. 45–6). Even after Heracles' death, Eurystheus persecuted his descendants (Eur. *Heraclidae*). J. R. M.

Eurytion, in mythology, (1) Geryon's herdsman, see HERACLES, *LIMC* 4/1 (1988), 112–17 (in art). (2) A *Centaur (*Od.* 21. 295 ff.); getting drunk and misbehaving at *Pirithous' wedding-feast, he began the quarrel between Centaurs and men. (3) Brother of *Pandarus (Verg. *Aen.* 5. 495 ff.). (4) See PELEUS.

Eusebius, of Caesarea (*c.* AD 260–339), prolific writer, biblical scholar and apologist, effective founder of the Christian genres of Church history and chronicle, and the most important contemporary source for the reign of *Constantine I. His intellectual formation at *Caesarea (2) in Palestine owed much to the influence of Pamphilus (martyred 310), by whom he was apparently adopted, and to their joint use of the library of *Origen (1). From his election as bishop of Caesarea *c.*313 until his death in 339,

Eustathius

Eusebius played a significant role in ecclesiastical politics in the eastern empire. He attended and assented to the decisions of the council of Nicaea in 325, having been readmitted to communion after recanting his earlier views; but though he delivered a speech at the dedication of Constantine's church of the Holy Sepulchre in Jerusalem (335) and encomia for the emperor's *decennalia* (315–16) and *tricennalia* (335–36), he was probably not such a confidant of Constantine as has commonly been supposed. He was present at the council of Tyre in 335 as an opponent of *Athanasius, and shortly afterwards at Jerusalem when *Arius was readmitted to the church. His *Life of Constantine*, left unfinished at his death, sought to create the impression of a harmonious and consistent imperial religious policy from the accession of Constantine (306) to the reign of his three sons, beginning in September 337.

Eusebius wrote biblical commentaries, in which the profound influence exerted on him by Origen is tempered by his own historical perspective; his *Onomasticon*, 'a biblical gazetteer', is an important source for the historical geography of Palestine. The two editions (? before 303 and 325–6) of his lost *Chronicle*, represented by *Jerome's Latin version and by an Armenian translation, synthesized Old Testament, near eastern, and Graeco-Roman history into a continuous chronological sequence accompanied by chronological tables. The object, as in his *Ecclesiastical History*, was to demonstrate that God's plan for salvation subsumed the whole of history. The same thinking lay behind his *Preparation for the Gospel* and *Proof of the Gospel* (after 313), apologetic works in which pagan philosophy is refuted and the Roman empire seen as the necessary background for the coming of Christ and the establishment of Christianity. The *Preparation* reveals Eusebius's immense debt to the library of Origen, with its many citations from Greek historians, *Philon, and especially Middle Platonist philosophy. An early work, *Against Hierocles*, attacks the comparison of the pagan *Apollonius (12) of Tyana with Christ; in the *Preparation* the main target is *Porphyry, whose anti-Christian arguments Eusebius systematically set out to refute. The later *Theophany* (325–6 or later), extant in Syriac translation, and his last works repeat many of the same apologetic themes.

Eusebius's integrity as a historian has often been challenged, and indeed the later part of his ten-book *Ecclesiastical History* (which may have been begun in the 290s but only reached its final form in 324–5) was successively extended and clumsily revised as immediate circumstances changed. The *Life of Constantine*, in four books, has seemed so suspect on the grounds of bias and inconsistencies that Eusebian authorship has been denied. But the authenticity of the many documents cited or mentioned has been vindicated in one major case by the identification of the same text on papyrus, and modern scholarship is more willing than before to recognize the complexity of Eusebius's methods. The citation of documentary evidence marks both works off from secular historiography. However, Eusebius' aim was not so much objectivity as persuasion: close study of the reworking of parts of the *Ecclesiastical History* in the *Life of Constantine* shows that he deliberately developed and enhanced his own earlier argument in the light of later reflection. Both works reflect the powerful impact of Christian persecution on Eusebius' thought but unlike the *Ecclesiastical History*, which took its main shape before or during the persecution of 303–13, and went on to cover only the part of Constantine's reign up to the defeat of Licinius in 324, the much later *Life of Constantine* reflects Eusebius' mature, if one-sided, understanding of the implications of a Christian imperial system.

TEXTS AND TRANSLATIONS Migne, *PG* 19–24, or (better) *GCS* (note esp. the edn. of the *Life of Constantine* by F. Winkelmann (1975); rev. edn. 1992). *Ecclesiastical History*, trans. G. Williamson; see also *NPNF* 1: *Preparation for the Gospel*, trans. E. H. Gifford (1903); *Life of Constantine*, trans. and comm. A. Cameron and S. G. Hall (forthcoming); Tricennalian Oration: *In Praise of Constantine*, trans. H. A. Drake (1976).

STUDIES D. S. Wallace-Hadrill, *Eusebius of Caesarea* (1960); T. D. Barnes, *Constantine and Eusebius* (1981); R. M. Grant, *Eusebius as Church Historian* (1980); G. Chesnut, *The First Christian Histories: Eusebius, Socrates, Sosomen, Theodoret and Evagrius* (1977); R. Farina, *L'impero e l'imperatore cristiano in Eusebio di Cesarea* (1966); J. Sirinelli, *Les Vues historiques d'Eusèbe de Césarée durant la période prénicéenne* (1961); A. Louth, *JTS* 1990, 111–23.   A. M. C.

Eustathius (12th cent. AD) born and educated in *Constantinople, was deacon at St Sophia and taught rhetoric (and probably grammar) in the patriarchal school until 1178, when he became metropolitan of *Thessalonica, in which position he continued till his death (*c.*1194). His works of classical scholarship were written before 1178. Henceforward he devoted himself to the practical duties of his spiritual office and to combating the prevailing corruption of monastic life.

Works (1) Classical: *Commentary on Pindar*, of which only the introduction survives; this gives information on lyric poetry (especially *Pindar's) and Pindar's life, and shorter notes on the *Olympian Games and the *pentathlon. The *Commentary on Dionysius Periegetes* contains discursive scholia, valuable for citations from earlier geographers, historians, the unabridged *Stephanus of Byzantium, and the lost works of *Arrian. The *Commentaries on Homer's Iliad and Odyssey* (Παρεκβολαὶ εἰς τὴν Ὁμήρου Ἰλιάδα (Ὀδύσσεια)) are a vast compilation, in which the Iliad commentary is twice as long as that on the Odyssey. They are evidently based on Eustathius' lectures. Prefaces deal with the differences between the poems and with the cultural importance of Homer. The notes discuss chiefly questions of language, mythology (sometimes interpreted allegorically), history, and geography. Their value consists particularly in the assemblage of material drawn from the old *scholia and the lost works of earlier scholars and lexicographers. His quotations from classical authors are taken mostly at second hand. He often illustrates a point by reference to the customs and observances of his own time and to contemporary vernacular Greek.

(2) His other works include an account of the conquest of Thessalonica by the Normans (1185), in which he was personally involved. It is a perceptive account of life in an occupied city, in which victors and vanquished alike are corrupted and demoralized. He also wrote polemics e.g. the famous *Inquiry into Monastic Life*; letters to the emperor, church dignitaries, and others; speeches and addresses, homilies and tracts, some of which have historical value. Eustathius was the outstanding scholar of his time, enthusiastic for traditional learning, for the preservation of books, for sound principles of education, and for the moral reawakening of monasticism. He is regarded as a saint by the Orthodox Church, and portrayed in a fresco in the church of the Virgin in the Serbian royal monastery of Gračanica (*c.*1321); see DIONYSIUS (9); STEPHANUS OF BYZANTIUM; ARRIAN.

TEXTS G. Stallbaum, *Commentarii ad Iliadem et Odysseam* (1825–30); M. van der Valk, *Eustathii archiepiscopi Thessalonicensis commentarii ad Homeri Iliadem pertinentes* (1971–87); A. Kambylis, *Eustathios von Thessalonike: Prooimion zum Pindarkommentar* (1991); G. Bernhardy, *Dionysius Periegetes* (1828), 67–310; T. L. F. Tafel, *Eustathii Metropolitae Thessalonicensis opuscula* (1832); S. Kyriakides, *Eustazio di Tessalonica: La espugnazione di Tessalonica* (1968); J. R. Melville Jones, *Eustathios of*

Thessaloniki: The Capture of Thessaloniki (1988) (text and Eng. trans.); Migne, *PG* 135–6.

STUDIES A. Kazhdan and S. Franklin, *Studies in Byzantine Literature of the Eleventh and Twelfth Centuries* (1984), 115–195; R. Browning, in R. Lamberton and J. J. Keaney (eds.), *Homer's Ancient Readers* (1992), 141–4; A. Kambylis, *Eustathios über Pindars Epinikiendichtung: Ein Kapitel der klassischen Philologie in Byzanz* (1991).   J. F. L.; R. B.

Eustochius, of *Alexandria (1), physician, became a pupil of *Plotinus in Plotinus' old age (Porph. *Plot.* 7) (prob. *c.* AD 270), and is said to have edited his master's works.

PLRE 1. 'Eustochius' 1.

Euthycles, a writer of Old or Middle Comedy (see COMEDY (GREEK), OLD and MIDDLE), with two titles preserved.

FRAGMENTS Kassel–Austin, *PCG* 5. 541–2.
INTERPRETATION Meineke, *FCG* 1. 269 f.; G. Kaibel, *RE* 6/1 (1907), 1507, 'Euthykles' 6.   W. G. A.

Euthydemus (1), of Chios, *sophist, an older contemporary of *Socrates. In the *Euthydemus* *Plato (1) presents him as a ridiculous figure. He has sometimes been thought to be unhistorical and merely a mask for Plato's criticism of *Antisthenes (1). His historicity is proved by independent references by *Aristotle; but Plato may have used him quite freely for the purpose of pillorying eristic views and arguments.

CAH 5² (1992), 348.   W. D. R.

Euthydemus (2) **I,** Graeco-Bactrian king (*c.*226–186 BC). Belonging to a family from Magnesia (on the Maeander?), he rose to power in *Bactria-Sogdiana by overthrowing *Diodotus (2) II. His independence was challenged by *Antiochus (3) III, who defeated Euthydemus' cavalry and besieged his capital, Bactra-Zariaspa (mod. Balkh), for two years (208–206 BC). The resilience of Euthydemus, and the common danger of a nomad invasion from the north, compelled Antiochus to acknowledge Bactria's autonomy. The masterful portraiture on Euthydemus' abundant coinage attests a long reign during which his kingdom was made secure and prosperous. At his death, *c.*186 BC, his son *Demetrius (8) I became king.

CAH 7²/1 (1984) and 8² (1989), see indexes.   F. L. H.

Euthydemus (3) **II,** probably the son of *Demetrius (8) I and grandson of *Euthydemus (2) I, briefly ruled *Bactria *c.*170–160 BC. He, along with his relatives Agathocles and Pantaleon, issued the world's first nickel coinages. It is likely that all were eventually defeated and killed by the usurper *Eucratides I.

CAH 8² (1989), esp. 398 ff.; coin-portrait: N. Davis and C. Kraay, *The Hellenistic Kingdoms* (1973), 142.   F. L. H.

Euthymus, an early 5th-cent. *boxer and Olympian victor, best known for the story of his victory over the malevolent hero of Temesa (Callim. *Aet.* frs. 98–9; Ael. *VH* 8. 18; Paus. 6. 6. 4–11). In Pausanias' account this hero, one of *Odysseus' companions, had been lynched after raping a local girl, but continued to demand a virgin as wife each year; Euthymus, coming to Temesa, fell in love with that year's victim, fought and banished the hero, and married the girl. The story combines several familiar motifs, in particular that of the ending of human sacrifice. Euthymus himself, like several contemporary athletes, became the object of heroic or even divine cult; see HERO-CULT.

J. Fontenrose, *Cal. St. Class. Ant.* (1968), 73–104; P. E. Arias, *ASNP* 1987, 1–8.   E. Ke.

euthyna, euthynai ('straightening'), the examination of accounts which every public official underwent on expiry of his office. At Athens the examination fell into two parts, the *logos* ('account'), concerned with his handling of public money and dealt with by a board of ten *logistai* ('accountants'), and the *euthynai* proper, an opportunity to raise any other objection to his conduct in office, dealt with by a board of ten *euthynoi* ('straighteners') appointed by the council (*boulē*). These officials could dismiss accusations or pass them on to the courts. Comparable accounting procedures are attested epigraphically in several other Greek states.

Ath. pol. 48. 3–4, 54. 2. M. Piérart, *Ant. Class.* 1971, 526–73; J. Davies in R. Osborne and S. Hornblower (eds.), *Ritual Finance Politics* (1994), 201 ff.   A. W. G.; P. J. R.

Eutropius (1), the historian, probably from Gaul, who took part in Julian's Persian campaign (AD 363) and was *magister memoriae of Valens, published a survey of Roman history (*Breviarium ab urbe condita*) in ten books. Beginning with Romulus, he reached the Sullan Civil War in book 5, Caesar's death in book 6 and covered the empire to *Jovian's death (AD 364) in books 7–10. The subject-matter for the republic is based in the main upon the *Epitome* of Livy, for the empire upon the end of the *Epitome*, and upon an 'Imperial History' (see also AMMIANUS MARCELLINUS; HISTORIA AUGUSTA), closing with personal knowledge of events. The work is short, but well balanced, showing good judgement and impartiality. It was translated into Greek by Paeanius about 380, adapted by Capito of Lycia, and used by *Jerome, *Orosius, *Isidorus (2), and Paulus Diaconus. It seems certain that Eutropius was the same as the correspondent of *Symmachus (2) who became praetorian prefect of Illyricum of *Theodosius (2) I in 381 and consul (with *Valentinian II) in 387.

TEXTS AND TRANSLATION H. Droysen (ed. minor, 1878; ed. maior, 1879); C. Wagener (1884); F. Rühl (1887). Trans., introd. and comm., H. W. Bird, *Eutropius: Breviarium* (1993).
LITERATURE M. Galdi, *L'epitome nella lett. latina* (1922); A. Momigliano, in A. Momigliano (ed.), *The Conflict between Paganism and Christianity in the Fourth Century* (1963), ch. 4; W. den Boer, *Some Minor Roman Historians* (1972). Career, *PLRE* 1. 317 'Eutropius' 2.
A. H. McD.; J. F. Ma.

Eutropius (2), minister of the emperor *Arcadius (2) and a *eunuch, was the most influential man in the east from AD 395 to 399, when he became consul, the first eunuch to hold the office. See EUNUCHS (secular). To maintain the independence of the east against *Stilicho, effectively ruler of the west, he allied with *Alaric the Goth. In 399 he was overthrown by the general Gainas and the senator Aurelian and executed. The poet *Claudian wrote vigorously against him.

A. D. Cameron, *Claudian* (1970).   E. A. T.; W. L.

Eutyches (*RE* 6) (6th cent. AD), pupil of *Priscian and a grammarian (probably) at Constantinople, wrote a handbook (*ars*) on the verb in two books (Keil, *Gramm. Lat.* 5. 447–88) and a work on aspiration excerpted by *Cassiodorus (ibid. 7. 199–202).

PLRE 2. 445 f.; Herzog–Schmidt, § 704.   R. A. K.

Eutychides, Sicyonian sculptor, pupil of *Lysippus (2), active *c.*330–290 BC. Famed for his *Tyche for *Antioch (1) (founded in 300), known in many copies and widely imitated by other cities; wearing a mural crown and holding a sheaf of wheat, she was seated on a rock symbolizing Mt. Silpius, with the river *Orontes swimming at her feet. Personifications were his speciality; Pliny (*HN* 34. 78) describes his Eurotas as 'wetter than water'.

A. F. Stewart, *Greek Sculpture* (1990), 200 ff., 298 f., figs. 626 ff.   A. F. S.

Euxenides, mentioned by the *Suda* (ε 2766) as an Athenian writer of comedy contemporary with *Epicharmus.

Kassel–Austin, *PCG* 5. 544.　　　　　　　　　　　W. G. A.

Euxine Sea (*Eὔξεινos*, lit. 'the hospitable'), the Greek name for the Black Sea, evidently a euphemism. From a Mediterranean perspective, it was cold, very deep, not very saline, and prone to storms. It carried extensive trade both between its shores and with the Mediterranean world (e.g. Polyb. 4. 38).

The once-popular notion that Greek penetration of the Black Sea was impossible before *c.*700 BC, is no longer tenable, though Greek settlement there seems to have been minimal before that date. Most Greek settlements around the Black Sea were established during the 6th cent. BC and regarded themselves as Milesian foundations.

The Black Sea and its region became a favourite subject of geographical disquisition throughout antiquity (e.g. ps.-Scylax, *Polybius (1), ps.-Scymnus, *Arrian, *Ammianus Marcellinus, ps.-Arrian, and *Procopius). It was a convenient locus of 'otherness', notably of *Amazons. The earliest extant treatment of the Black Sea is that of Herodotus (esp. 4. 85–6), whose errors and misconceptions are such that it has even been claimed that he did not visit the Black Sea. In the Byzantine period the Black Sea enjoyed a new significance through its proximity to the centre of power; see TRADE; COLONIZATION, GREEK; MILETUS.

D. C. Braund, *Georgia in Antiquity* (1994); R. Drews, *JHS* 1976, 18–31; A. J. Graham, *BICS* 1958, 25–42; F. Hartog, *The Mirror of Herodotus* (trans. 1988).　　　　　　　　　　　D. C. B.

Evadne (*Eὐάδνη*), in mythology, (1) a daughter of *Poseidon, who became by *Apollo mother of *Iamus, ancestor of the prophetic clan of the Iamidae in *Olympia (Pind. *Ol.* 6. 29 ff., see U. von Wilamowitz–Moellendorff, *Isyllos* (1886), 178). (2) Daughter of Iphis and wife of *Capaneus, one of the *Seven against Thebes. She burned herself on his funeral pyre (Eur. *Supp.* 980 ff.).

H. J. R.

Evagoras (*Eὐαγόρας*, *c.*435–374/3 BC), an interesting and important figure in Greek, Persian, and Cypriot history. He was a member of the Teucrid house (cf. Tod 194), the traditional rulers of *Salamis (2). Exiled during his youth, which fell in a period of Phoenician domination, he gathered some 50 followers at Soli in Cilicia, and with their help established himself as ruler of Salamis in 411. His subsequent policy aimed at strengthening *Hellenism in *Cyprus by co-operation with Athens (which honoured him *c.*407, perhaps for shipping corn there); and his court became a centre for Athenian *émigrés*, of whom *Conon (1) was the most distinguished. A clash with Persia was ultimately inevitable, but in his early years he was not out of line with Persia, and he postponed the confrontation by assisting in the revival of Persian sea-power culminating in the triumph of *Cnidus (394, see ATHENS (history)). Athens now honoured him for his services as a 'Greek on behalf of Greece'. War finally came *c.*391 and dragged on for ten years. In alliance with Acoris of Egypt, Evagoras at first more than held his own. He not only extended his rule over the central cities of Cilicia, but also captured Tyre and dominated Phoenicia. In 382 Persia mobilized an overwhelming force against him, Evagoras lost control of the sea at Citium in 381, and was forced to sue for peace, obtaining reasonably favourable terms, through dissensions among the Persian commanders. In 374 he was assassinated in a palace intrigue.

The most detailed source for his life, *Isocrates, *Evagoras*, is not altogether reliable factually; but it, together with Isocrates'

other 'Cyprian orations' the *To Nicocles* (Evagoras' son) and the *Nicocles*, is an important document of early Greek kingship theory (see KINGSHIP).

Xen. *Hell.* 4. 8. 24, 5. 1. 10; Diod. Sic. 14–15; Isoc. 9, cf. 2 and 3 (all ed. E. Forster (1912)); *IG* 1³. 113; Tod 109 + *SEG* 29. 86; K. Spyridakis, *Evagoras I von Salamis* (1935); G. F. Hill, *History of Cyprus* 1 (1940), 125–43; E. Costa, *Hist.* 1974, 40 ff.; D. M. Lewis, *Sparta and Persia* (1977), 129 f.; F. G. Maier, *CAH* 6² (1994), ch. 8d, and M. Ostwald and J. P. Lynch, ibid. 600.　　　　　　　　　　　D. E. W. W.; S. H.

Evagrius Scholasticus (*c.* AD 535–*c.*600), legal adviser to *Gregory (1) I, Chalcedonian patriarch of Antioch (1). Last of its genre, his *Church History* (431–594) merges with secular historiography in form and contents; despite weak chronology, it is a major source for the 6th-cent. east.

Ed. J. Bidez and L. Parmentier (1898); Eng. trans. E. Walford (1846); P. Allen, *Evagrius Scholasticus* (1981).　　　　　　　　　　　S. J. B. B.

Evander was in origin probably a minor hero or divinity of *Arcadia. Some attributed him human parents (Echemus of Tegea, and Timandra, daughter of Tyndareos) but he was more commonly regarded as a son of *Hermes by a nymph (Themis or Nicostrate). Through Hermes he was descended from Atlas and hence could be credited with kinship with *Aeneas through *Dardanus (Verg. *Aen.* 8. 134–7) and also with *Atreus (so in Accius' *Atreus*).

Independent Greek evidence for Evander or his cult is (at best) scanty. He appears predominantly in Roman (or Rome-orientated) sources as fleeing Arcadia, landing at the site of Rome on the advice of his mother (identified with *Carmentis) and (usually) being allowed to settle on the Palatine by Faunus. The legend was probably based on, and explained, the name of the Palatine (supposedly derived from Pallanteum in Arcadia, or from Pallas, variously described as Evander's grandfather, son, or grandson, or from Pallantia, Evander's daughter) and the sanctuary and ritual of the Lupercal (identified as the cult of the Arcadian 'wolf-god', Lycaean *Pan; see LUPERCALIA). An etymological association of Evander and *Faunus (both names being interpreted as 'beneficent') may also be involved but is not directly attested.

The legend has no historical foundation but served to emphasize Rome's Greek cultural credentials. Q. *Fabius Pictor attributed to Evander the introduction of the alphabet to Rome (fr. 1 P) and as he brought *Hercules to Italy (G. Manganaro, *PP* 1974, 389 ff.), he may, like later sources, have placed the Hercules-Cacus episode and consequent foundation of the Ara Maxima under Evander. Some later authors elaborated this civilizing Greek input (*Varro (and perhaps *Cato (Censorius)) even made Evander responsible for an Aeolic substrate in Latin and Ateius Philologus traced to him the (Greek) name of Rome itself; cf. also Dion. Hal. *Ant. Rom.* 1. 31 ff.). Others, however, such as Livy and Virgil, limit severely its significance for Rome's future cultural identity.

Ogilvie, *Comm. Livy 1–5*, 51 ff.; J. Poucet, *Les Origines de Rome* (1985), 74 ff., 128 ff.　　　　　　　　　　　A. D.

evidence, ancient attitudes to (Greek and Roman). There are various contexts in which Greeks and Romans sought to demonstrate things. Problems of knowledge were raised by philosophers at least as early as *Plato (1) (this is one function of the theory of forms), even though epistemology did not become an independent issue until the rise of Pyrrhonian scepticism (see PYRRHON). In history, however, the question particularly interested the founders of the genre. *Herodotus repeatedly identifies his informants, even when he explicitly rejects their accounts (e.g. 1. 182. 1). *Thucydides (2) too uses oral testimony, but realizes the dangers of oral tradition (see ORALITY): this presumably is why he sticks to contemporary history, where he combines an explicit theory of cross-examination (1. 22–3) with a steadfast refusal to acknowledge his sources. One later Greek historian, *Polybius (1) (e.g. 4. 2. 3), pays at least lip-service to Thucydides' views on evidence, but the question did not apparently worry Roman writers: *Livy's Preface displays an explicit commitment to the truth, but he makes no use of primary sources; and even this commitment seems to be undermined by the half-heartedness with which *Cicero acknowledges the historian's duty not to lie (De or. 2. 62 with Brut. 42).

The principal arena for evidence is the lawcourt. Witnesses in Classical Athens took precedence over documents (see LITERACY; ORALITY), but they could not be cross-examined (indeed, after c.380 BC their evidence was submitted in writing), and although they are cited over 400 times in the surviving orations, they serve mainly to confirm the version of events given by the litigant as speaker. Only a free adult male could witness in an Athenian court: a woman could swear an evidentiary *oath, and a slave could be required to give evidence under torture, but in each case this required the consent of both litigants, and none of the 42 attested challenges to torture was ever carried through. Greek rhetorical theorists distinguish various categories of persuasive arguments (pisteis, traditionally 'proofs'). *Aristotle (Rh. 1375ᵃ 24–5) notably classifies laws as forms of evidence alongside witnesses, agreements, oaths, and torture, but this reflects a system where to cite the law is the litigant's privilege, not the judge's duty.

Rules of evidence in the Hellenistic papyri are more elaborate (e.g. PHal. 1. 24–78, 222–33, from *Alexandria (1)), and in Roman law still more so. Witnesses play an essential role in a range of early transactions (e.g. *mancipatio) as well as in court proceedings, and by *Justinian's time detailed rules govern their number, reliability and social status (Dig. 22. 5. 1–3). There is a general trend for documentary evidence to become more important at the expense of witnesses (Cod. Iust. 4. 20. 18). As at Athens, slaves could give evidence only under torture, but the opportunities for using such testimony were progressively restricted by successive emperors (Dig. 48. 18. 1). It is striking that despite a number of relevant titles in the Digest, and although the topic interested the rhetorical theorists (*Quintilian, Inst. 5. 1–7, influenced by *Aristotle but adapted to Roman law), evidence does not appear as a subject in Roman legal textbooks (Gaius' or Justinian's Institutes) or in their modern counterparts. S. C. T.

evidence, Roman Evidence, in the sense of the methods by which the facts at issue in a legal proceeding are established, was of little interest to the Roman jurists. For them the proof of facts was the concern of the advocates. We are told that the jurist *Aquilius Gallus, when consulted about such a matter, would declare that it had nothing to do with the law, but was something for Cicero ('non hoc ad ius, ad Ciceronem': Cic. Top. 12. 51). This division between law and fact was embodied in the division, in both the legis actio procedure and the formulary system, between the proceedings before the magistrate (in iure) and before the lay judge (apud iudicem). It is commonly assumed, in reliance on the example of other primitive systems, that there had been a stage when the verdict was arrived at by recourse to the irrational or supernatural. Thus, since the word *sacramentum has the primary meaning of *oath, it is assumed that originally the legis actio sacramento remitted the verdict to the outcome of an oath. In historic times, however, the use of oaths (with the exception of the iusiurandum in litem) was confined to the stage in iure. The establishment of facts was within the free discretion of the lay judge.

Witnesses play a prominent part in Roman law, but there was no legal preference for their evidence, as opposed to proof by other means. Witnesses might have at least two functions: to ensure the publicity of a legal act or to provide proof that it had occurred. Thus a number of formal acts required for their validity the presence of a particular number of witnesses, e.g. confarreatio (the oldest and most solemn form of Roman marriage; ten witnesses), *mancipatio and other transactions per aes et libram (five), and there were similar requirements for the mancipatory will and its derivative, the praetorian will (see INHERITANCE, ROMAN). The large number of witnesses required suggest that their primary purpose was to ensure that the act was public and seriously intended. The witnesses could indeed be required to give evidence in any dispute about the act, but that the act had taken place could be proved in any other way acceptable to the judge.

The witnesses were an essential part of the formality of the act. The absence of the requisite number would invalidate the act, even if it could be proved to have taken place. Conversely the formal contract of *stipulatio did not require witnesses. Since only the parties to a contract could be affected by it, there was no need for publicity and the assembling of a number of witnesses for a rapidly concluded transaction might well be cumbersome. By the end of the republic therefore recourse to documentary proof was evidently so common that Cicero could class stipulatio as a written act (Cic. Top. 26. 96). Up to Diocletian however the texts emphasize that written evidence is not required and that written documents cannot affect the truth about status, property, or contracts.

In the later empire there is a change. The freedom of the judge to evaluate the evidence is restricted by many rules. Oral testimony is distrusted as against the evidence of documents. The evidence of a single witness is allowed no weight at all. Many legal presumptions are introduced, in the sense that if certain facts are proved, the judge, whatever his own view of the probabilities may be, is required to infer certain other facts. This presumption may operate either regardless of evidence to the contrary (conclusive presumption) or in the absence of such evidence, or of a certain quantity or quality of such evidence (rebuttable presumption). For example, stipulatio required in strict principle that the requisite words should have been spoken by the parties in the presence of each other, though in practice, as has been said above, the stipulatio came quite early to be regarded as a written act and the parties might in fact never speak the words or even meet. This difference between principle and practice meant that it was possible for a party to escape from such a written undertaking by pleading that the parties never met at the relevant time. Justinian, regarding such a plea as dishonest, provided that a stipulatory document recording that the parties had been present was not to be challenged except by the clearest proof, preferably documentary, that both parties had been absent from the locality in question for the whole of the relevant day (Cod. Iust. 8. 37 (38). 14).

M. Kaser, Das röm. Zivilprozessrecht (1966); G. Pugliese, Jus 1960, 386 ff. (= Rec. Soc. Jean Bodin 1964, 277 ff.). B. N.

evocatio A ritual by which, in the course of a war, a Roman general would attempt to deprive the enemy of divine protection, by formally offering their protecting deity a new home and cult at Rome. The clearest recorded case is the evocation of *Juno Regina from the Etruscan city of *Veii in 396 BC (Livy, 5. 21 ff.)—a process which led to the establishing of her cult on the *Aventine hill in Rome. There has been some debate over how long this ritual continued to be practised, and (in particular) whether the record of the evocation of Juno from Carthage in 146 BC (Serv. on *Aen.* 12. 841) is anything more than antiquarian invention. The discovery of an inscription at Isaura Vetus (in modern Turkey), apparently recording an *evocatio* in c.75 BC, suggests that the ritual survived at least to the late republic. There are, however, changes from earlier practice: in 75 BC the deity seems to have been offered a home not in Rome, but in provincial territory.

V. Basanoff, *Evocatio* (1947); J. LeGall, *Mélanges Heurgon* 1 (1976), 519–24; M. Beard, J. North, and S. Price, *Religions of Rome* (forthcoming).
M. B.

exchange See FINANCE; GIFT; MONEY; RECIPROCITY.

exēgētēs (ἐξηγητής), an interpreter or expounder, usually of sacred lore. The Athenians traditionally considered *Apollo Pythios (i.e. Apollo of *Delphi) their *exēgētēs*. At Athens exegesis of the *patria*, sacred and ancestral law, was an old custom, but from c.400 BC they entrusted it to officials specifically appointed for the task: (1) one *exēgētēs* elected by the dēmos from the *eupatridai; (2) one *exēgētēs* chosen by the Pythia (see DELPHIC ORACLE), called *exēgētēs Pythochrēstos*; (3) three *exēgētai* of the Eumolpidae (see EUMOLPUS), who expounded the *sacra* of the *mysteries. The Athenian *exēgētai* were generally concerned with the unwritten sacred law, but they often pronounced on secular and domestic questions (e.g. duties and obligations) untouched by statutes and of possible religious implications. Other cities too had *exēgētai*, official or unofficial.

J. H. Oliver, *The Athenian Expounders of the Sacred and Ancestral Law* (1950); F. Jacoby, *Atthis* (1949), ch. 1; Clinton, *Sacred Officials*.
J. E. F.; K. C.

exile

Greek Exile (φυγή, literally 'flight') is permanent (*aeiphygia*) or long-term removal from one's native place, usually as a punishment imposed by government or other superior power. In Greece it was from earliest times a standard consequence of homicide, and was as much a religious way of getting rid of a source of *pollution as a punishment. Thus *Zeus in *Homer's *Iliad* is said to make men exiles, driving them like a gadfly over the face of the earth (24. 532 f.).

In Classical Greece exile was a punishment for various offences, such as professional failure by a general or ambassador (for Athens see e.g. Thuc. 4. 65, 5. 26. 5). Sometimes, however, the ambiguity of the word 'to flee'—'be exiled' or 'flee'—means we do not know if an individual was formally exiled or simply fled voluntarily to escape worse. In addition, we often hear of political exiles, as individuals or groups; where the latter feature in the sources, it is usually because they are intriguing against their home government (see e.g. Thuc. 1. 115. 4 or 6. 7. 1 and 3). Again, it is sometimes unclear whether such exiles were driven out by actual decree or because life was for whatever reason intolerable. Occasionally whole communities were displaced; these and other *émigré* groups in ancient Greece, as in other periods and places, tended to keep their sense of identity, see e.g. Thuc. 5. 32 and Lys. 23 for the Plataeans (see PLATAEA) at Athens:

their aim was naturally to recover their lost homeland, and this sometimes happened, also (like the original exile) by fiat of a superior power or syndicate of powers, or by diplomatic or other upheaval. For instance, the *King's Peace of 386 BC and its successors (see COMMON PEACE) led to restoration of exiles (Xen. *Hell.* 5. 1. 34, etc.), but it is disputed whether the agreements contained actual clauses to this effect. Again, as a result of *Alexander (3) the Great's 'Exiles' Decree', exiles returned to their origins (Tod 201, 202). This led in effect to a 'redistribution of land' of the kind ironically forbidden by Alexander's father *Philip (1) II, and by Alexander himself, by the terms of the League of Corinth (Dem. 17). As beneficiaries of this general policy, Samians returned to *Samos in 322 BC, 44 years after their expulsion by Athens, which therefore found itself with an influx of refugees of its own; the *Lamian War between Athens and Macedon was the result.

The 5th-cent. Athenian institution of *ostracism was an unusual sort of exile in that it was for ten years only and involved no loss of property. Other states such as *Argos (2) and *Syracuse had or borrowed similar practices.

E. Balogh, *Political Refugees in Ancient Greece* (1943); J. Seibert, *Die politischen Flüchtlinge und Verbannten in der griechischen Geschichte* (1979); P. McKechnie, *Outsiders in the Greek Cities in the Fourth Century BC* (1989); J. Roisman, *Anc. Soc.* 1986, 23 ff. On the King's Peace, G. L. Cawkwell, *CQ* 1981.
S. H.

Roman Exile, either undertaken voluntarily to escape a penalty (usually death), or imposed as a punishment, was common in the ancient world. In Rome it was originally voluntary. A person threatened by criminal proceedings for a capital offence could, even after the proceedings had begun, but before sentence, remove himself from Roman jurisdiction. This self-banishment was tolerated by the magistrates, provided that the person did not return from exile. In the late republic this *exsilium* was institutionalized as, in effect, a substitute for the death penalty. The magistrates were required to allow a condemned person time to escape before a capital sentence was executed. After his departure a decree of *aqua et igni interdictio* (denial of water and fire) excluded him from all legal protection and threatened him with death if he returned illicitly.

This kind of exile was replaced under the principate by a formal sentence of *deportatio* or of the milder penalty of *relegatio* (*relegation).

G. Crifò, *Ricerche sull' 'exilium' nel periodo repubblicano* (1961); E. L. Grasmück, *Exilium—Untersuchungen zur Verbannung in der Antike* (1978).
B. N.

experiment Greek and Roman scientists did not refer directly to the experimental method. However, in a variety of contexts they described testing procedures that were clearly deliberate investigations designed to throw light on problems or to support theories. Examples can be found in the Presocratic philosophers, the Hippocratic writers (see HIPPOCRATES (2)), *Aristotle, *Erasistratus, *Ptolemy (4), and *Galen.

We should distinguish first the areas where experimental investigation is possible from those where it is not. Direct experiments in astronomy are out of the question. This was also true, in antiquity, in relation to most problems in meteorology (thunder and lightning) and in geology (*earthquakes). In such cases ancient scientists often conjectured analogies with other more accessible phenomena that were directly investigable. Thus *Anaximenes (1) may have tried to support *Anaximander's theory of lightning as caused by wind splitting the clouds by suggesting that it is like the flash of an oar in water. Similarly some of the experimental interventions described in the Hippocratic writers incorporate an element of analogy. The writer of *Diseases* 4, for instance, describes a system of intercommunicating vessels which can be filled or emptied by filling or emptying one of them. He uses this to explain the movements of the humours between the main sources in the body (stomach, heart, head, spleen, liver). What this shares with an experiment is the careful construction of an artificial set-up. Where it differs from experiment in the strict sense is that its relevance to the physiological problem discussed depends entirely on the strength of the analogy suggested (in this case a mere conjecture).

Sometimes, however, direct interventions are proposed. Examples can be given from *physics, harmonics, optics, physiology, and *anatomy. Thus Aristotle states that he has proved by testing ($\pi\epsilon\pi\epsilon\iota\rho\alpha\mu\acute{\epsilon}\nu o\iota$) that sea water on evaporation becomes fresh (*Meteor.* 358^b 16 ff): however he then goes on to claim that the same is true of other flavoured liquids including wine—a typical risky extension of an experimental result. In harmonics, testing procedures were used by pre-Platonic Pythagoreans (see PYTHAGORAS (1)) in their investigations of the numerical relations expressed by the concords of octave, fifth, and fourth, although later writers who report that those relations were discovered by Pythagoras himself are generally untrustworthy. Some such reports claimed, for example, that he made that discovery by weighing hammers that gave certain notes: yet that would not yield the result described.

*Optics provides one of our fullest examples of a series of careful experiments, though the results have been adjusted to suit the general theory proposed. In his *Optics* (5. 8 ff.) Ptolemy describes his investigations of refraction between three pairs of media (from air to water, air to glass, and water to glass). He describes the apparatus used and records the results to within a half degree for angles of incidence at 10-degree intervals. However, the results all exactly confirm the general 'law' that takes the form $r = ai - bi^2$, where r is the angle of refraction, i the angle of incidence, and a and b constants for the media concerned. Elsewhere he provides convincing experimental proof of the elementary laws of reflection (3. 3), to establish, for instance, that the angle of incidence equals the angle of reflection.

Experiments in the strict sense were attempted also in the life sciences. Erasistratus described one in which a bird is kept in a vessel without food for a given period of time, after which he weighed the animal together with the visible excreta and compared this with the original weight. This he took to show that there are invisible effluvia from animals—again an overinterpretation of a correct result. Galen used experimental *vivisections on animals to investigate a variety of problems. He showed the peristalsis of the stomach in one, and produced a detailed account of the courses of the nerves in systematic experiments on the spinal cords of pigs. In the latter case no general theory is at stake: what the experiments reveal is the precise connection between vital functions and particular nerves.

Ancient scientists thus showed considerable ingenuity in devising testing procedures. However what this exemplifies is not so much the idea of a crucial experiment, an ideally neutral means of adjudicating between theories antecedently deemed to be of equal plausibility, as the appeal to tests specifically to support or to falsify a theory. In this way, experiments in antiquity are an extension, though an important one, of the use of evidence. See EVIDENCE, ANCIENT ATTITUDES TO.

H. von Staden, *BICS* 1975, 178–99; I. M. Lonie, *The Hippocratic Treatises 'On Generation', 'On the Nature of the Child', 'Diseases IV'* (1981); G. E. R. Lloyd, *Methods and Problems in Greek Science* (1991). G. E. R. L.

Ex(s)uperantius (*RE* 2), **Iulius**, 4th (?) cent. AD Latin historical writer. His 'little book' (*opusculum*) describes the Civil War of C. *Marius (1) and *Sulla to the death of *Sertorius. It clearly depends on *Sallust (*Jugurthine War* and *Histories*), imitating his style as well as reproducing his content. Errors and garblings abound.

Ed. N. Zorzetti (1982). C. B. R. P.

Ezechiel, author of the *Exagoge*, a tragedy in Greek about Moses and the escape of the Israelites from Egypt. Nothing is known of his life, but he must have been a Hellenized Jew active between the late 3rd and early 1st cent. BC, probably at *Alexandria (1). He is credited with 'Jewish tragedies' in the plural, but we know only the *Exagoge*, of which 269 lines are preserved. It is based on the *Septuagint version of Exodus 1–15, but includes some free invention and aspires, with mixed success, to Euripidean style (see EURIPIDES). Though obviously untypical, it provides valuable evidence for Hellenistic tragedy. See JEWISH GREEK LITERATURE.

TrGF 1². 288–301; *Musa Tragica* 216–35, 298–300; B. Snell, *Szenen aus griechischen Dramen* (1971), 170–93; H. Jacobson, *The Exagoge of Ezekiel* (1983). A. L. B.

Fabius (*RE* 44) **Ambustus, Marcus,** consul 360, 356, 354 BC. In 360 he reputedly earned an *ovatio* for successes against the *Hernici. His victories against the Faliscans and Tarquinians in 356 may be invented since C. *Marcius Rutilus was subsequently appointed *dictator to confront a major Etruscan threat. In 354 a triumph over Tibur is recorded (*Diodorus (3) Siculus speaks of a truce with *Praeneste); he may also have participated in successful campaigning against *Tarquinii and in the first Samnite treaty (if genuine). As *interrex in 355(?) and 351 (and unsuccessfully as dictator in 351) he sanctioned the election of two patricians as consuls, breaking the pattern of patrician–plebeian colleges established in 366.

K.-J. Hölkeskamp, *Die Entstehung der Nobilität* (1987).   A. D.

Fabius (*RE* 48) **Ambustus, Quintus** In Livy (5. 35. 4 ff.) and related sources he and two brothers were sent as envoys in 391 BC at the request of *Clusium to negotiate the withdrawal of the Gauls but violated protocol by fighting against them. The Gauls demanded their surrender but the people responded by electing them consular tribunes for 390, when their military failings contributed to the Gallic sack of Rome. Fabius was supposedly prosecuted by a tribune in 389 for his actions at Clusium but died before the trial. However, the Clusine episode (of which *Diodorus (3) Siculus has a different and possibly earlier account (14. 113. 4 ff.)) is itself probably fiction: Clusium had no reason to appeal to Rome nor did the Gauls need a specific *casus belli*. The story serves to explain the Gallic attack on Rome, and in its Livian form to regularize and justify Gallic conduct according to Roman conceptions and portray Rome as the protector of Italy against the Gauls.

J. Wolski, *Hist.* 1956, 24 ff.; *CAH* 7²/2 (1989), 302 ff.   A. D.

Fabius (*RE* 53) **Buteo, Marcus,** was consul 245 BC (*Florus' story of a naval victory over Carthage and subsequent shipwreck is fictitious) and *censor 241. About 220 he put to death his own son, accused of theft. It was probably he, and not Q. *Fabius Maximus Verrucosus who headed the embassy delivering the Roman ultimatum to Carthage in 218. In 216, after *Cannae, as senior ex-censor he was appointed *dictator to fill the gaps in the senate caused by losses in the war.

Scullard, *Rom. Pol.* 274.   J. Br.

Fabius Cilo, Lucius, from Baetica. Consul designate at the time of Commodus' murder, he quickly joined L. *Septimius Severus in the Civil War, taking a force to Perinthus in AD 193, then governing Pontus-Bithynia (193–4) and Upper Moesia (195–6); he commanded another task force in 196, and was governor of Upper Pannonia 197–202. Soon after returning to Rome he became urban prefect and held his second consulship (as *ordinarius*) in 204. Severus enriched him and his Rome mansion, the *domus Cilonis*, became a landmark. After P. *Septimius Geta (2)'s murder at the end of 211 he narrowly escaped death, being saved by popular outcry. *Amphorae from Baetica show that he was a producer of olive oil.

A. Caballos Rufino, *Los senadores hispanorromanos* 1 (1990), 132 ff.
A. R. Bi.

Fabius (*RE* 6) **Gallus, Marcus,** Epicurean (see EPICURUS) friend of Cicero, who addresses to him *Fam.* 7. 23–7. In 45 BC he was among those who wrote anti-Caesarian eulogies of M. *Porcius Cato (1). See IULIUS CAESAR (1), C.; ANTICĂTO.

D. R. Shackleton Bailey, *CR* 1962, 195 f., and *CLA* 4. 347 (correcting Fadius to Fabius); cf. also *Ep. ad Fam.* 1 (1977), 417.   M. T. G.

Fabius (*RE* 90) **Iustus, Lucius,** was a friend of *Pliny (2) the Younger and received the dedication of *Tacitus (1)'s *Dialogus*; he believed that the age of great orators had gone. Possibly a legionary legate *c.* AD 97, he was *suffect consul in 102, taking the place of L. *Licinius Sura. Governor of Lower Moesia (105–8), he was governing Syria by 109.

R. Syme, *JRS* 1957, 131, *JRS* 1959, 26 (= *Danubian Papers* (1971), 122), and *AE* 1981, 746.   J. B. C.

Fabius (*RE* 102) **Maximus, Paullus,** son of Q. Fabius Maximus (suffect consul 45 BC) was given as praenomen the cognomen of his ancestor L. *Aemilius Paullus (2). An intimate friend of *Augustus, he was consul 11 BC, proconsul of Asia (10–9) and *legatus Augusti* in Hither Spain (3–2). As proconsul of Asia he introduced a calendar reform, imposing on all cities a uniform year that began on Augustus' birthday (EJ 98). Rumour said (implausibly: see R. Syme, *Some Arval Brethren* (1982) 70 f.) that he accompanied Augustus on a secret visit to Agrippa *Iulius Caesar (Agrippa Postumus) in AD 14, and that his death, which followed shortly, was suicide, occasioned by the betrayal of the secret to *Livia Drusilla by his wife Marcia, daughter of L. *Marcius Philippus (3). He was a pontifex and *frater arvalis*. Africanus Fabius Maximus (consul 10 BC), named after P. *Cornelius Scipio Aemilianus Africanus, was probably his brother, and Paullus Fabius Persicus (consul AD 34) probably his son.

Syme, *RR* and *AA*, see indexes. For coin-portraits, M. Grant, *From Imperium to Auctoritas* (1946), 387. For the calendar reform, U. Laffi, *Studi classici e orientali* 1967, 5–98.   T. J. C.; R. J. S.

Fabius (*RE* 109) **Maximus Aemilianus, Quintus,** son of L. *Aemilius Paullus (2) and elder brother of P. *Cornelius Scipio Aemilianus, was adopted by a son or grandson of Q. *Fabius Maximus Verrucosus. Both he and Scipio served with distinction under Paullus during his campaign against *Perseus (2) in 168 BC. He was praetor 149, governing Sicily, and consul 145, when he took entirely new troops to face *Viriatus in Further Spain, and was forced to spend the year training them. Proconsul 144, he inflicted two defeats on Viriatus. He served under Scipio at *Numantia in 134–3, and died shortly afterwards, before Scipio.

A. E. Astin, *Scipio Aemilianus* (1967), 13–15, 102–5.   J. Br.

Fabius (*RE* 110) **Maximus (Allobrogicus), Quintus,** son of the preceding and nephew of P. *Cornelius Scipio Aemilianus, under whom he perhaps served as quaestor in Spain and whose funeral eulogy he delivered. He was praetor (*c*.124 BC) in Spain, and consul (121) and proconsul in Transalpine Gaul (with Cn. *Domitius Ahenobarbus (2)). He triumphed *c*.120 and built the first *triumphal arch (*fornix Fabianus*) in Rome; see FORUM ROMANUM. He may have become censor 108. The Fabii remained patrons of the *Allobroges (see FABIUS SANGA, Q.).   E. B.

Fabius (*RE* 114) **Maximus Rullianus, Quintus,** consul 322, 310, 308, 297, 295 BC. Surviving accounts of his career are obscured by factual uncertainties; patriotic and family fictions; supposed clashes with L. *Papirius Cursor (1), Ap. *Claudius Caecus, and even P. *Decius Mus (2) (his colleague in his last three consulships); and apparent duplicates of incidents from the career of Q. *Fabius Maximus Verrucosus (Cunctator). Thus his supposed clash with L. Papirius Cursor in 325 (Fabius Pictor fr. 18 P) apparently owes much to Cunctator's quarrel with M. *Minucius Rufus (1) in 217 and his role as his son's legate in 292 is modelled on actions of both Cunctator and *Scipio Africanus. In 322 some sources attributed him major successes in Samnium and Apulia, and a triumph. As *dictator in 315 he captured Satic- ula but was defeated by the Samnites at Lautulae. *Diodorus (3) Siculus (19. 101. 3) alone attributes him a second dictatorship in 313 and the capture of *Fregellae, Calatia, and *Nola. In 310 he reputedly relieved *Sutrium and forced *Arretium, *Cortona, and *Perusia to a truce. The allocation of operations in Samnium and Etruria in 308 is uncertain and the prorogation of his command (and victory at *Allifae) in 307 is difficult to accept. As censors in 304 he and Decius Mus reputedly reversed the tribal reforms of Ap. Claudius Caecus and instituted the formal cavalry parade (*transvectio equitum*; see EQUITES). In 297 and perhaps 296 he campaigned in Samnium, but in 295 he and Decius won a crucial victory over the alliance of Samnites, Etruscans, and Celts at *Sentinum. He may be the Q. Fabios depicted in a military scene on an Esquiline tomb frieze.

E. T. Salmon, *Samnium and the Samnites* (1967); W. V. Harris, *Rome in Etruria and Umbria* (1971); E. La Rocca, *Dialoghi di Archeologia* 1984, 31 ff.   A. D.

Fabius (*RE* 116) **Maximus Verrucosus, Quintus,** grandson or great-grandson of Q. *Fabius Maximus Rullianus, as consul 233 BC celebrated a *triumph over the Ligurians and unsuccessfully opposed the agrarian bill of C. *Flaminius (1). He was *censor 230, consul for the second time 228, and *dictator (probably) 221. In 218 he perhaps opposed an immediate declaration of war on Carthage. Dictator again in 217, after the Roman defeat at Lake *Trasimene, he began his famous policy of attrition, believing that Hannibal could not be defeated in a pitched battle; this earned him the name 'Cunctator' (the Delayer). He allowed Hannibal to ravage the Campanian plain, but then blocked his exits; Hannibal, however, escaped by a stratagem. Opposition to Fabius' policy at Rome led to his *magister equitum, M. *Minucius Rufus (1), receiving *imperium equal to his. When Minucius was enticed into a rash venture, Fabius rescued him. The traditional policy of fighting fixed battles was resumed in 216, but after the

disaster at *Cannae there was no alternative to Fabius' policy. With the help of his position as the senior member of the college of *augures—he is said to have been an augur since 265—he became suffect consul for the third time for 215, operating in Campania. He was re-elected for 214, helped to recapture *Casili- num and had a number of successes in Samnium. In 213 he perhaps served as legate to his son. Direct control of affairs now passed to other men, but Fabius reached his final consulship in 209, when he recaptured *Tarentum and was made *princeps senatus. In 205, together with Q. *Fulvius Flaccus (1), he strongly opposed P. *Cornelius Scipio Africanus' plan to invade Africa. He was no doubt alarmed by Scipio's growing prestige, but genuinely believed that taking the war to Africa posed unneces- sary dangers. It was Scipio who brought the war to an end, but Fabius' cautious strategy which made victory possible. Fabius died in 203. He had been *pontifex since 216 as well as augur (see AUGURES), a distinction unique until *Sulla and *Caesar.

J. Briscoe, *CAH* 8² (1989), ch. 3, *passim*; Sumner, *Orators* 230 ff. (stemma and career).   J. Br.

Fabius (*RE* 126) **Pictor, Quintus,** the first Roman historian. He wrote in Greek; the Latin annals ascribed to a Fabius Pictor are probably a later translation of Pictor's work. A member of the senate and perhaps of the *decemviri sacris faciundis* (see QUINDECIMVIRI), he went on an embassy to *Delphi in 216 BC, but is not recorded in any other magistracy. His reasons for writing in Greek were both literary—the possibility of writing in Latin did not occur to him—and political, the need to defend Roman policy to the Greek world. Like other early historians of Rome, he appears to have dealt at length with the foundation legend (following *Diocles (7) of Peparethos) and then passed rapidly to recent history. His historical approach owed much to *Timaeus (2). *Polybius (1), though aware of Fabius' pro-Roman bias, used him for his account of the First and Second *Punic Wars. Fabius wrongly embraced the view that the Barcids alone (see HAMILCAR (2); HANNIBAL) were responsible for the second war. He is quoted by *Livy in the first and second decades (ten-book sections), but it is disputed whether Livy knew his work at first hand. He appears (called Pictorinus) in a list of Greek historians and their works inscribed on the walls of the gymnasium at *Tauromen- ium (*SEG* 26. 1122).

FRAGMENTS Peter, *HRRel.* 1². 5–39, *FGrH* no. 809.

STUDIES E. Badian, *Latin Historians* (1966), 2–6, and *LCM* 1976, 97– 8; Momigliano, *Terzo Contributo* 55–68, and *The Classical Foundations of Modern Historiography* (1990), ch. 4; Manganaro, *PP* 1974, 388–409.   J. Br.

Fabius (*RE* 140) **Rusticus,** from Spain, was perhaps not a Roman senator. He wrote a History, whose eloquent style led *Tacitus (1) (*Agr.* 10. 3) to compare him to *Livy. His work had won recognition before the end of *Domitian's reign (Quint. *Inst.* 10. 1. 104), but it is uncertain whether his unawareness of the correct shape of Britain, which was demonstrated by Cn. *Iulius Agricola's fleet in AD 84, indicates composition before 84. His work is cited by Tacitus for *Nero's reign (*Ann.* 13. 20. 2; 15. 61), but its limits are not known. Whether or not it was used by Tacitus for the *Histories* or by Plutarch for his 'Emperors' of 69 is disputed. He was hostile to Nero and praised his friend and patron *Seneca the Younger. He may have survived until AD 108 (*CIL* 6. 10229. 24), unless the person mentioned there is his son.

Syme, *Tacitus*, see index and app. 29.   M. T. G.

Fabius Sanga, Quintus

Fabius (*RE* 143) **Sanga, Quintus,** senator in 63 BC. Hereditary patron of the *Allobroges (a Gallic tribe), hence descended from Q. *Fabius Maximus (Allobrogicus). When envoys from the tribe were approached by the 'Catilinarian' conspirators (see SERGIUS CATILINA, L.), they duly reported the fact to Sanga as their patron; he in turn informed Cicero, who was able to use the Gauls as double agents. (Sall. *Cat.* 41. 4–5). Sanga is not heard of again.

R. J. S.

Fabius (*RE* 151) **Valens,** suffect consul AD 69, born at Anagnia of equestrian stock, was 'undisciplined in character though not deficient in talent' (Tac. *Hist.* 3. 62). A legionary commander in 68 in Lower Germany, he supported *Galba, was instrumental in disposing of the governor Fonteius Capito, and instigated the proclamation of A. *Vitellius as emperor. An army commander at the battle of *Bedriacum, he was highly honoured by Vitellius, but was prevented by illness from reaching northern Italy in time to oppose the Flavian forces. After the capture of *Cremona, he slipped away to Gallia Narbonensis but was captured and executed.

J. B. C.

fable, a short story in the popular tradition of Greece and other ancient cultures. Fables found their way into literature as illustrative examples; later they were compiled into collections.

They usually deal with a conflict in which animals speak and intervene, but the characters may also be plants, sundry objects, men, or gods, Fable normally deals with the triumph of the strong, but also portrays the cunning of the weak and their mockery of, or triumph over, the powerful. Fables also stress the impossibility of changing nature; some give aetiological explanations. Most often there is a comic element; sometimes the 'situation' of a protagonist is depicted, from which the audience may draw analogies.

It is therefore impossible to offer a fixed definition. The boundaries of fable intermesh with those of myth, animal proverbs, anecdotes, tales, and *chreiai*. Fable is normally fiction, but does at times use anecdotes about real characters. It reflects popular literature and may satirize the values and abuses of the dominant social classes.

Greek fable undoubtedly originated in Greece, but clearly absorbed foreign traditions, particularly Mesopotamian fable (itself based on Sumerian fable); compare, for instance, the fable of the eagle and the serpent in the Akkadian *Etana*. The Greeks themselves attributed the origin of certain fables to Libya or Egypt. In its turn, Greek fable influenced Indian fable. From the time of *Lucilius (1) through to the Middle Ages Greek fable gave rise to numerous fables in Latin.

In Greek literature fable appears as an example, used *pari passu* with myth and the historical or fictitious anecdote, from the time of *Hesiod, *Op.* 42 ff. ('The Hawk and the Nightingale'). Thereafter it is found above all in the writers of iambics (*Archilochus, *Semonides), and was used by elegists (*Theognis (1)), lyric poets (*Simonides) and playwrights. It appears in prose in *Herodotus (1) and is a favourite medium of the Socratic writers. It was associated with *Socrates (cf. Pl. *Phd.* 60b) and is used in *Plato (1), *Xenophon (1), *Antisthenes (1), and *Aristotle.

From the end of the 5th cent. BC, the authority of fable was often attributed to *Aesop, whom a dubious historical tradition identifies as a Phrygian slave in Samos (Hdt. 2. 134). Yet it is clear that from the 5th century onwards there was a legend, seemingly influenced by the Assyrian story of Ahikar, of a person named Aesop who was connected with *Delphi. Aesop emerges as a popular character who tells anecdotes, jokes, and fables, and gives lessons in wisdom.

From the Hellenistic era on, classical fable produced new versions, and new fables were constantly being created. Fable spread through four channels. (1) Authors such as *Cercidas, *Callimachus (3), *Ovid, Seneca the younger (see ANNAEUS SENECA (2), L.), *Lucian, *Plutarch, Aulus *Gellius, *Libanius, *Aelian, *Basil, and *Gregory (2) of Nazianzus continued to use fable as an example. (2) Fables narrated by Aesop appeared in the Life of Aesop, which has come down to us in different versions. The prototype is variously dated to the Hellenistic period or the 1st cent. AD. (3) Fables were sometimes enlarged upon to create a burlesque animal epic, such as the *Batrachomyomachia* ('The Battle of the Frogs and Mice') (perhaps Hellenistic). (4) The chief means of diffusion was that of the collections of fables, the first of which was compiled by *Demetrius (3) of Phaleron around 300 BC (Diog. Laert. 5. 80). From this collection derived various others, some anonymous, others 'signed' by authors like *Phaedrus (4), *Babrius, and *Avianus (below), who attempted to turn fable into a poetic genre; others were 'signed' by rhetors such as Aphthonius, whose fables were basically designed for study in schools (as various *programmata* (proclamations) point out).

The oldest preserved collection of fables (fragmentary) is PRyl. 493, written during the 1st cent. AD; like the others known to us it derives from lost collections of Hellenistic date. The subsequent history of these is controversial, but two stages may be noted. (1) Demetrius' brief collection gave rise to others, which in turn added new fables, either old or newly created. Influenced by the *Cynics, the main targets of these fables are power, wealth, beauty, covetousness, sloth, and breaches of natural law. They also satirize women, doctors, and athletes, and make Aesop into a quasi-Cynic. The fables are put into choliambic or iambic verse of a popular kind, but rarely into elegiac couplets. (2) From the 2nd cent. BC these Cynic collections were put into prose. From the diverse prose versions there emerged the 'signed' collections, either poetical or rhetorical, which naturally in turn introduced changes. The Cynic character of fable was only partially preserved.

The chief surviving collections of fables from antiquity are as follows. (*a*) The Augustana Collection, reflecting the stage of evolution which mainstream fable, derived from the prose versions, had reached by late antiquity. The date of this collection is controversial, but it probably dates from the 4th or 5th cents. (*b*) Phaedrus (4). (*c*) Babrius. (*d*) Avianus. (*e*) Rhetorical collections. These are of imperial date and always brief; the most important are those by pseudo-Dositheus, from the 2nd cent. AD, a Greek collection with a Latin version; a Greek collection of the 4th cent. by Aphthonius; and the Greek collection in the Brancacciano Codex (probably 5th cent.). (*f*) The Syriac collections from the 4th and 5th cents. Although these fables are preserved only in Syriac (and in related Arabic versions) or in Greek translations from the Syriac (the so-called Fables of Syntipas, by the 11th-cent. Andreopoulos), they derive from the ancient Greek tradition.

EDITIONS Anonymous Greek collections and Bodleian paraphrase: E. Chambry, 2 vols. (1925–6); anonymous Greek collections, ps.-Dositheus, Aphthonius, Theophylactus, Syntipas: A. Hausrath, 2 vols. (1950, 1956, and reprs.); Augustana, *Vita Aesopi*: B. E. Perry, *Aesopica* (1952); *Vita Aesopi*, with mod. Gk. trans.: M. Papathomopoulos (1989); Babrius and Phaedrus, with Eng. trans.: B. E. Perry (Loeb, 1965); Babrius: M. J. Luzzato and A. La Penna (1986); Avianus:

A. Guaglianone (1958); F. Gaide, with Fr. trans. (1980); Syriac fables, Fr. trans.: B. Lefèvre (1951); Brancacciano Codex: F. Sbordone (1932).
STUDIES A. Hausrath, *RE* 6/2. 1704 ff.; S. Josefovic, *RE* Suppl. 14. 15 ff.; F. R. Adrados, *Estudios sobre el léxico de las fábulas esópicas* (1948), *Historia de la Fábula Greco-Latina* (1979–87), *Spektrum der Wissenschaft* 1981, 23–36, and *Prometheus* 1992, 139–49; M. Nøjgaard, *La Fable antique* (1964–7); various authors, *La Fable*, in *Entretiens Hardt* 30 (1984); M. J. Luzzato, *JÖB* 1983, 137–87; S. Jadrkiewitz, *Sapere e paradosso nella Antichità: Esopo e la favola* (1989).   F. R. A.

fabri in the early Roman army were armourers, organized in two centuries and commanded by prefects. Probably at an early date these centuries lost their separate existence, and in *Caesar's day the technical work of *fabri* was done by skilled legionaries. Although the prefect of engineers (*praefectus fabrum*) had lost his original function, the title remained, now denoting an aide-de-camp of a commander.

J. Suolahti, *The Junior Officers of the Roman Army in the Republican Period* (1955), 205.   J. B. C.

Fabricius (*RE* 9) **Luscinus, Gaius,** consul in 282, 278 BC, censor in 275, on each occasion with Q. Aemilius Papus. In 282 he rescued *Thurii from *Sabellian besiegers and triumphed for successes against the *Bruttii, *Lucani, and Samnites (see SAMNIUM). He took a leading role in the embassy to *Pyrrhus after *Heraclea (1) or *Ausculum Satrianum and in 278 triumphed again for victories over Bruttii, Lucani, Samnites, and Tarentines. As *censor he sensationally excluded a patrician ex-consul, P. Cornelius Rufinus, from the senate for possessing 4½ kg. (10 lb.) of silver tableware, one of the first attested censorial expulsions. The later stories of his poverty, austerity, and incorruptibility (such as his rejection of Pyrrhus' gifts or of offers to poison Pyrrhus) endowed him with a heroic nobility matching that of Pyrrhus himself and associated him with other contemporary 'new men' (notably M'. *Curius Dentatus) as idealized exemplars of antique frugality.

O. Skutsch, *The Annals of Quintus Ennius* (1985), 347 ff.; *CAH* 7²/2 (1989), see Index; E. Baltrusch, *Regimen Morum* (1989), 18.   A. D.

Fabricius (*RE* 15) **Veiento, Aulus Didius Gallus,** had been *exiled in AD 62 for libelling senators and priests and using his influence with *Nero to sell offices. However he enjoyed great prestige under the Flavians, being consul under *Vespasian, suffect consul for the second time in 80 as replacement for *Titus, and consul for the third time under *Domitian (AD 83?). He appears among the advisers of Domitian (Juv. *Sat.* 4. 113—'sagacious Veiento') and retained his influence under *Nerva, sitting beside him at a dinner party (Plin. *Ep.* 4. 22). Subsequently his position was weakened and he was shouted down in a senate meeting (ibid. 9. 13). His career shows that influence in imperial councils did not necessarily depend on holding governorships and administrative posts.   J. B. C.

fabula (besides meaning 'story', 'talk', '*fable') was the general Latin term for 'play' or 'drama'. Ancient terminology is not entirely consistent, but the following types of Latin *fabulae* are mentioned: *fabula *Atellana*; *crepidata*, almost certainly adaptations of Greek tragedy (*crepida* was a type of Greek shoe); *palliata*, sometimes used of all drama with a Greek setting, but normally restricted to comedy (*pallium* = Greek cloak); *planipedia* (= *mime, also called *mimus* or *mimica*; *planipes*, 'flatfoot', was a term for a mime-actor); *praetexta(ta)*, serious drama on Roman historical subjects (the *toga praetexta* was worn by magistrates); *Rhinthonica*, plays in the style of *Rhinthon's *phlyakes* (perhaps

a term for *Atellanae* with mythological subjects); *togata* ('drama in a toga'), sometimes used of all drama set in Rome or Italy, but normally restricted to a type of comedy set there (also apparently known as *tabernaria*, 'private-house drama'); *trabeata* (see MAECENAS MELISSUS, C.). The Life of Lucan (see ANNAEUS LUCANUS, M.) says that he wrote *salticae fabulae*, 'dancing plays', evidently libretti for the *pantomime. A distinction is also found between comedies that are *motoriae* ('full of movement'), *statariae* ('static'), and *mixtae* ('mixed'). Some modern (but no ancient) authorities use the terms *fabula cothurnata* for adaptations of Greek tragedy (the *cothurnus* was the thick-soled boot worn by Italian tragic actors) and *fabula riciniata* for mime (the *ricinium* was a hood worn as part of the costume in mimes). See COMEDY, LATIN; TRAGEDY, LATIN.

W. Beare, *The Roman Stage*, 3rd edn. (1964), 264–6; A. Lesky, *Gesammelte Schriften* (1966), 583 ff; C. O. Brink, *Horace on Poetry*, 2. *The Ars Poetica* (1971), on l. 288.   P. G. M. B.

Faesulae, (mod. Fiesole), an *Etruscan town in the hills above Florence, probably on the site of an iron age sanctuary. The orientalizing period is represented nearby by the Montagnola tomb at Quinto Fiorentino, which is similar to the Pietrera tumulus at *Vetulonia. The parallels at *Populonia, *Volaterrae, and *Felsina for the carved stone funerary steles (*c*.520–470 BC) of Faesulae draw attention to the importance of its position as a point of contact with Etruria Padana. The best archaeological evidence for the town itself dates from the early 3rd cent. BC, the date of the town wall, the cemetery, and the temple. Extensive remains of the Roman baths are also visible. Faesulae favoured Rome in the Second *Punic War but in the *Social War (3) was defeated by L. Porcius (*RE* 7) Cato. It subsequently became a *colonia* for *Sulla's veterans; this led to unrest among the expropriated landowners as demonstrated in the course of the Catilinarian conspiracy (see SERGIUS CATILINA, L.).

M. Lombardi, *Faesulae* (1941); A. de Agostino, *Fiesole* (1949); F. Boitani and others, *Etruscan Cities* (1975) 31 ff.   D. W. R. R.

fairs See MARKETS.

Falernus ager Fertile tract of north *Campania, Roman from 338 BC and distributed to citizens of *tribus Falerna*. Near the sea and on the *via Appia, it became one of the foremost Italian centres of investment agriculture, and its famous *wine contributed greatly to the export trade of the late republic. It supported many *villas, several villages, and towns of which the most important was Forum Popillii (near mod. Carinola).

P. Arthur, *Romans in North Campania* (1991).   N. P.

Faliscans, the iron age inhabitants of the Treia basin, and the northern neighbours of *Veii. They spoke a 'distinct and special language' (Strabo 5. 2. 9), akin to Latin, but were culturally and politically under strong *Etruscan influence. There were a number of townlike settlements within the territory, some occupied from the late bronze age; the principal city was Falerii Veteres (mod. Città Castellana). In 241 BC, the Romans captured Falerii, transplanting its inhabitants to a new site, Falerii Novi, 5 km. (3 mi.) to the west. They migrated back to their old centre in early medieval times. In the Villa Giulia Museum in Rome are finds from Faliscan cemeteries, and fine architectural *terracottas from the temples of Falerii Veteres. The latter include the famous shrine of Juno Curitis, described by *Ovid (*Am.* 3. 13. 1 ff.), one of whose wives was of Faliscan origin. See ITALY, LANGUAGES OF.

M. W. Frederiksen and J. B. Ward-Perkins, *PBSR* 1957, 67 ff.; T. W.

family, Greek

Potter, *A Faliscan Town in South Etruria* (1976), and *The Changing Landscape of South Etruria* (1979); *La civiltà dei Falisci* (exhib. cat., 1990).

J. B. W.-P.; T. W. P.

family, Greek See HOUSEHOLD, GREEK.

family, Roman English 'family' has connotations which have changed during its long history and vary according to context. Biologically, an individual human being is related to parents, through them to ascendants, aunts, uncles, siblings, and cousins, and may, by sexual intercourse with someone of the opposite sex, in turn become a parent, linked by blood to descendants. Blood relations for Romans were *cognati*, the strongest ties normally being with parents and children and the siblings with whom an individual grew up. Relationship established through the sexual tie of marriage was *adfinitas*; kin by marriage were *adfines* (in strict usage from engagement until dissolution of the marriage). Law initially stressed blood relationship through males: *agnati* (father's other children, father's siblings, father's brothers' children, a man's own children, etc.) inherited on intestacy. By entering **manus* (marital power), a married woman came into the same agnate group as husband and children; if she did not, her legal ties and rights were with her natal family.

The group under the power of a *paterfamilias* (see PATRIA POTESTAS), whether or not they lived under the same roof, was sharply distinguished; there might be other living agnates outside this group. Agnatic forebears were present in family consciousness as recipients of ritual, as **imagines* (portraits) in an aristocratic house, and as links between the living. For the Romans, *familia* could originally mean the patrimony; its more normal usages were to describe (1) those in the power of a *paterfamilias*, kin, or slaves, or (2) all the agnates who had been in such power, or (3) a lineage, like the Julian house, or (4) a group or household of slaves (Ulpian, *Dig.* 50. 16. 195. 1–4). A lineage in the broadest possible sense, a group allegedly descended from a common mythical ancestor, was **gens*; its members shared a middle name (*nomen gentilicium*), e.g. Tullius/a, as members of an agnatic *familia* might share a last name (*cognomen*), e.g. Cicero. (The class of those sharing a *gentilicium* extended to newly enfranchised citizens, slaves, and their descendants: see NAMES, PERSONAL, ROMAN.) *Domus*, besides meaning the building in which someone lived (home or residence: see HOUSES, ITALIAN), covers (1) the **household of free, slave, and freed persons and (2) a broader kinship group including cognates (e.g. the imperial 'family' or dynasty, *domus Caesarum*). Increasingly, descent in the female line (*maternum genus*) came to be valued in sentiment, appraisal of status, and inheritance practices.

The nuclear family is described, in relation to its male head, as consisting of wife and children (*uxor liberique*). Similarly a list of those closest to a particular individual would be drawn up to suit various contexts: Cicero for instance in writing to his brother Quintus at an emotional moment might stress his brother, his daughter, his own son, his nephew (his only surviving close kin), his wife (*QFr.* 1. 3. 3). In relation to an individual, the kin or affines who count change with the phases of life and accidents of survival. The evidence of epitaphs illustrates close family ties as they existed at the time of commemoration: the person(s) who pay for a monument may do so out of love, duty as kin, or duty as beneficiary/ies. Where the commemorator is specified we get a glimpse of how the family operated, as we do from juristic sources, e.g. on dowry or succession, or literary sources, which chiefly reflect the expectations and practice of the upper classes. Although ties with remoter relations by blood or marriage are acknowledged when they exist, emphasis is normally on the nuclear family (one's wife/husband and children, or parents and siblings). In the absence of these, as for soldiers debarred from legal marriage or ex-slaves who theoretically had no parents and in practice might have been prevented from forming a family, comrades or fellow freedmen/women (*conliberti/ae*) might form a substitute family.

R. P. Saller, *Phoenix* 38 (1984), 336–55; B. Rawson, *The Family in Ancient Rome* (1986), and *Marriage, Divorce and Children in Ancient Rome* (1991); K. Bradley, *Discovering the Roman Family: Studies in Roman Social History* (1991); D. I. Kertzer and R. P. Saller, *The Family in Italy from Antiquity to the Present* (1991); S. Dixon, *The Roman Family* (1992). S. M. T.

famine Catastrophic breakdowns in the production and distribution of essential foodstuffs, resulting in exceptionally high mortality from attendant epidemic **diseases, were rare in the ancient world. The typical natural and man-made causes of famine were omnipresent: crop failure caused by the unreliable Mediterranean rainfall (see CLIMATE) or pests and diseases, destruction in war, state oppression and incompetence, poor arrangements for transport, storage, and distribution, and profiteering by the élite. Specific food-shortages of varying intensity and chronic malnutrition of the poor were common, but most of the population were subsistence farmers whose primary strategy of production was to minimize risk, and the political culture helped towndwellers to pressure their leaders to resolve food crises before they became critical. The exaggerated references to 'famine' in the ancient sources echo the political rhetoric of an urban society where famine was a frequent threat but a very infrequent experience. Local climatic variation meant that relief supplies were normally available within the region, given the political will to obtain them. The severe food-shortages over extensive areas of the eastern Mediterranean world attested in 328 BC, AD 45–7 (the 'universal famine' of Acts 11: 28), and AD 500 were quite exceptional. Most famines were local, brief, and primarily man-made, such as the three best-attested famines in Athens of 405/4, 295/4, and 87/6 BC, all the result of siege, or the food-shortages at Rome in 67 BC and AD 5–9, the former apparently intensified, if not caused, by Pompey's manipulation of the supply network, the latter by the diversion of supplies to emergency military operations in Dalmatia and Germany. See FOOD SUPPLY.

P. Garnsey, *Famine and Food Supply in the Graeco-Roman World* (1988); C. Virlouvet, *Famines et émeutes à Rome des origines à la mort de Néron* (1985); H. P. Kohns, *Versorgungskrisen und Hungerrevolten in spätantiken Rom* (1961); P. Garnsey and C. R. Whittaker (eds.), *Trade and Famine in Classical Antiquity* (1983). D. W. R.

Fannius (*RE* 7), **Gaius,** Roman politician. Son-in-law of C. **Laelius (2) and pupil of **Panaetius, he became tribune (?130s BC), praetor (?126), and was then elected consul for 122 with the backing of C. **Sempronius Gracchus. As consul he broke with Gracchus, opposing his Italian legislation in a celebrated speech (Cic. *Brut.* 99–100). His identification with the historian of the same name was a puzzle for **Cicero (*Att.* 12. 5b), and remains uncertain. The History concentrated on contemporary events, was anti-Gracchan, included speeches, and was only moderately stylish (Cic. *Brut.* 81, 101; *Leg.* 1. 6). **Sallust praised its truthfulness (*Hist.* 1. 4 Maurenbrecher).

Fragments in Malcovati, *ORF*[4] no. 32; Peter, *HRRel.* 1[2]. cxciii–cxcix, 139–41. Shackleton Bailey, *CLA* 5. 400–3; G. V. Sumner, *The Orators in Cicero's Brutus* (1973), 53–5, 170–4; F. Càssola, *Vichiana* 1983, 82–96.

C. B. R. P.

Fannius (*RE* 16) **Caepio,** headed a conspiracy against **Augustus in 23 or 22 (see TERENTIUS VARRO MURENA, A.). When prosecuted by *Tiberius before the *quaestio maiestatis* (**maiestas* court) he attempted to escape but was betrayed and executed.

H. H. S.; R. J. S.

fantastic literature, or fiction of the unreal, took two forms in antiquity: (*a*) fantasies of travel beyond the known world; (*b*) stories of the supernatural. Both look back to the Phaeacian tales in the *Odyssey*, which became a byword for the unbelievable (cf. [Longinus] *Subl.* 9. 14).

From the Hellenistic period we know of a series of descriptions of imaginary lands, such as those by *Euhemerus, *Hecataeus (2) of Abdera, and *Iambulus. Their primary purpose was social and moral comment, but they often seem to have been authenticated by an adventure story, which provided entertainment but also drew attention to the question of how literally they were to be believed. Antiphanes of Berge's account of the far north was so transparently fictitious that 'Bergaean' became synonymous with 'fantasist'. Although these works were criticized as falsehoods, some recognized that undisguised fiction represented an area of licence for the imagination (e.g. Strabo 2. 3. 5). Fantasies of this kind are parodied in the space-travel of *Lucian's *True History*, but, despite his satirical programme, Lucian's invention acquires its own fantastic momentum.

Tales of the supernatural also make doubt and belief their central theme. Lucian's *Philopseudes* tells stories of ghosts and magic, including the Sorcerer's Apprentice, while mocking those who believe them. Fantastic episodes occur in the novels, notably of *Iamblichus (1) and *Apuleius, whose characters share the reader's hesitation as to the nature of the phenomena (see NOVEL). The fragments of *Phlegon of Tralles contain the story of an amorous revenant, while Philostratus (*VA* 4. 25) narrates the detection of a vampire. Photius (*Bibl.* cod. 130) knew the collection of ghost stories of the neoplatonist Damascius (d. *c*. AD 458), but most literature of this kind has been lost. Papyrus fragments include two ghosts (*POxy.* 1368, from the *Phoenicica* of *Lollianus; *PMich.* inv. 3378) and a wizard (*PMich.* inv. 5 + *PPal. Rib.* 152).

The two strands of fantasy united in the *Wonders beyond Thule* of *Antonius Diogenes, which combined travel beyond real geography with witchcraft, Pythagorean philosophy, and self-conscious authentication, all arguably intended to subvert the reality of the perceptible world. See PARADOXOGRAPHERS.

T. Todorov, *The Fantastic: A Structural Approach to a Literary Genre*, trans. R. Howard (1973), which, however, uses the term in a more restricted sense.

J. R. Mo.

Fanum Fortunae (mod. Fano), near the mouth of the *Metaurus in Umbria: important highway junction, where the *via Flaminia reached the Adriatic. Named after a temple of Fortune, it also contained *Vitruvius' celebrated *basilica (Vitr. 5. 1. 6). Neither has survived, but the arch of Augustus (who made Fanum a *colonia*; see COLONIZATION, ROMAN) is intact.

E. T. S.; T. W. P.

farm buildings

Greek There are no distinct agricultural buildings in Archaic and Classical Greece: those who exploited the land lived in and worked from houses indistinguishable from those inhabited by others who gained their livelihood in other ways. A number of rural buildings, both isolated buildings and buildings which are part of larger complexes, have been excavated, and many more are known from archaeological surface survey. (See ARCHAEOLOGY, CLASSICAL.) Many of these buildings, and the prime example

is the *house near the cave of *Pan at Vari in Attica, have no features that directly associate them with agriculture, and even permanent, as opposed to seasonal, residence is difficult to demonstrate archaeologically. Two particular types of sites have been supposed to be particularly likely to be farms: buildings closely associated with regular land divisions in a colonial landscape, such as those found in the territory of ancient *Metapontum in south Italy or in the Crimea (see CHERSONESUS (2)); and tower buildings. Of the agricultural function of the former there can be little doubt, although the material has yet to be published in sufficient detail to enable any deductions to be made about the precise nature of the residential group or of their agricultural enterprises. Tower buildings, which are found in some Aegean islands and some parts of the Greek mainland, seem, on the other hand, to have been multifunctional, and there is clear evidence for some towers changing their role during a long history: the building of towers may be more a product of pressures created by insecurity or by the need for display than of any particular agricultural demand. See AGRICULTURE, GREEK.

S. Isager and J. E. Skydsgaard, *Ancient Greek Agriculture* (1992), 67–82; *BSA* 1973, 355–452; 1985, 119–28.

R. G. O.

Roman Archaeological field-survey has focused attention on the existence of very large numbers of structures in the Roman countryside (seemingly far more densely populated and economically productive than was once believed). Some of these buildings were components of villas, others isolated structures. Regional surveys provide a framework for the interpretation of these different categories of site with major repercussions for our understanding of the historical sources. In some regions of Italy, for instance, the continued existence of numerous small sites (farmsteads?) alongside the major villas would seem to suggest that either free *peasants or tenants survived alongside the large slave-run estates (**latifundia*). In areas of optimal site preservation (such as parts of North Africa), survey has revealed a remarkable degree of detail about entire tracts of ancient rural landscapes.

Particular importance attaches to detailed survey or excavation of productive facilities (for example, olive and wine presses, kilns) and storage buildings (barns, *granaries, wine/oil cellars) in that these can provide evidence for the nature and scale of rural exploitation. For example, the specialization in *olive cultivation of parts of Africa and southern Spain can be demonstrated by the archaeological evidence of numerous, large-scale processing facilities. Capital investment in such oileries would have been high, with the most sophisticated mills and presses perhaps being supplied by specialist contractors. Examination of the presses, of settling-vats, and of storage facilities allows important estimates of maximum production to be made. See AGRICULTURE, ROMAN; VILLA.

J. Rossiter, *Roman Farm Buildings in Italy* (1978); K. D. White, *Roman Farming* (1970); G. Barker and J. Lloyd, *Roman Landscapes* (1991); J.-P. Brun, *L'Oléiculture antique en Provence: Les Huileries du départment du Var* (1986); B. Hitchner and others, *Ant. af.* 1990, 231 ff; D. J. Mattingly, *JRA* 1988, 33 ff.; R. Hingley, *The Romano-British Countryside* (1990).

D. J. Ma.

fasces comprised bundles of rods, approximately 1.5 m. (5 ft.) long and of elm- or birchwood, and a single-headed axe; they were held together by red thongs and carried by *lictores. A miniature iron set from a late 7th-cent. tomb at *Vetulonia supports the later tradition of their Etruscan origin. They were the primary visible expression of magisterial authority and hence the focus of a complex symbolism of the magistrates' legitimacy and of their powers *vis-à-vis* citizens, subjects, and each other. They were regularly regarded (and in the republican period used) as instruments of execution and by common consent the absence of the axe from the fasces of magistrates (other than *dictators and triumphing generals) within Rome symbolized citizen rights of appeal (*provocatio) against capital *coercitio*. The alternation of precedence between the two *consuls was manifested in alternate 'tenure' of the fasces, and the number of a magistrate's fasces depended on his rank: consuls (and in the republic proconsuls) had twelve and hence also reputedly their predecessors, the kings); dictators probably had twenty-four, *praetors and *magistri equitum* (see MAGISTER EQUITUM) probably six. In the Principate, senatorial governors had the number appropriate to their previous magistracy, imperial legates had five. In 19 BC Augustus was given the right to twelve fasces 'everywhere in perpetuity' (Cass. Dio 54. 10. 5), though some suppose he had twenty-four outside Rome (cf. also Cass. Dio 67. 4. 3 (*Domitian)); as *imperatores* emperors always had their fasces laurelled. Curule aediles and quaestors (but not censors) may also have had fasces and lictors were progressively assigned to those giving games, envoys, certain priests, and others. In the late republic, at least, the staves (*bacilli*) carried before municipal magistrates were carefully distinguished from the fasces.

E. S. Staveley, *Hist.* 1963, 458 ff.; A. J. Marshall, *Phoenix* 1984, 120 ff.
A. D.

fasti, the calendar of *dies fasti*, *dies comitiales*, and *dies nefasti*, which indicated when a specific legal process organized by the urban praetor (the *legis actio*) and assemblies might or might not take place; it received definitive publication by Cn. *Flavius in 304 BC. Vulgarly, *dies nefasti* came to be thought of as ill-omened days. We know of the sacral calendars of M. *Fulvius Nobilior (consul 189 BC) and *Verrius Flaccus (at *Praeneste), and have fragments of the pre-Julian calendar of *Antium (84–55 BC) and twenty calendars mainly of the Augustan and Tiberian periods; also two 'rustic' almanacs, and in book form the calendar of AD 354 and the calendar of Polemius Silvius (AD 448–9). The *Fasti* of Hydatius (covering 510 BC–AD 478), and the *Chronicon Paschale (7th cent. AD) are chronicles of events.

The word *fasti* also includes other listings: *fasti consulares* (of eponymous magistrates), *fasti triumphales* (of triumphs), and *fasti sacerdotales* (of priests), including the *fasti* of the *feriae Latinae* (festival of *Jupiter celebrated by the Latini). Of *fasti consulares* we have the exemplar from Antium (84/55 BC) and the so-called *fasti Capitolini*, which were inscribed on an arch in the forum Romanum 18/17 BC; the *ludi saeculares* (*Secular Games) were added, until AD 88. *Fasti triumphales* were also inscribed on the same arch, from Romulus down to the last 'republican' triumph, that of L. *Cornelius Balbus (2) in 19 BC, and were also inscribed elsewhere.

The authenticity of the *fasti consulares* and *triumphales* has been much debated. The reconstruction for the 5th cent. BC was necessarily speculative, perhaps politically tendentious, and has both omissions and interpolations; it was sounder in its main lines for the 4th cent., and from *c.*300 BC appears consistently accurate, presumably using full regular records. This suggests that the inclusion of magistrates' names and cult notices may have followed directly on the publication by Cn. Flavius. See TABULA PONTIFICUM.

Inscr. Ital. 13. 1 (1947), 13. 2 (1963). Beloch, *Röm. Gesch.* 1–62; De Sanctis, *Stor. Rom.* 1. 1; E. Pais, *Fasti triumphales pop. Rom.* (1920); *I fasti trionfali del popolo Romano* (1930); A. Drummond, *CAH² 7/2 (1989), 17–

21, 173–8, 627–44; Steinby, *Lexicon* 81–5; see also CALENDAR, ROMAN.
A. H. McD.; S. R. F. P.

fasting (νηστεία, *ieiunium*) is the temporary abstinence from all food (ἀποχὴ τροφῆς) for ritual, ascetic, and medicinal purposes. Alien to Roman practice except for the *ieiunium Cereris* (Livy 36. 37. 4), which was considered a Greek import, it was infrequent in Greek cult, where feasting was more central than fasting. The Greeks, who used the meat of sacrificial animals, amongst other foodstuffs, as offerings to the gods and as meals for human worshippers (see SACRIFICE, GREEK), did not recognize extended periods of ritual fasting on the scale of the Muslim Ramadan or Christian Lent. In the few cults that made fasting a ritual requirement, its observance was always brief, lasting up to an entire day, and in exceptional circumstances up to three days.

According to *Clement of Alexandria, those initiated into the Eleusinian *mysteries declared that they had performed the required rites preliminary to initiation by reciting the following 'password' (*synthēma*): 'I fasted (ἐνήστευσα), I drank the ritual drink (*kykeōn*), I took from the chest (*kistē*), and having worked [with the sacred implements] I removed [them] into the basket and from the basket into the chest' (*Protr.* 2. 21. 2). In fact, the initiation proper was preceded by a whole day of fasting, which ended at nightfall with the drinking of the *kykeōn*. The initiates' fast, like their breaking of it, had an aetiological precedent in the fasting of Demeter herself, who roamed the earth for nine days abstaining from *ambrosia and nectar, and even from bathing (*Hymn. Hom. Cer.* 49 f.). Later, at Eleusis, 'wasting away with longing for her deep-bosomed daughter, she sat unsmiling, tasting neither food nor drink' (200 f.), until the jests of *Iambe prompted her to laugh and to drink the *kykeōn*. Similarly, Achilles refused food after the death of *Patroclus (*Il.* 19. 303–56). In Greek culture, as in many others, self-neglect was an outward sign of extreme grief and mourning (Meuli: see bibliog. below). Fasting was equally integral to another women's festival of Demeter, the *Thesmophoria. On its second day, called 'the Fast' (*Nēsteia*) by the Athenians, the participating women 'fasted like mullets', a fish known for its empty stomach (Athen. 307f). On this day, the 'gloomiest day' of the festival (Plut. *Dem.* 30. 5), the subversive women in *Aristophanes (1)'s *Thesmophoriazusae* hold their assembly while keeping a strict fast (984 νηστεύομεν δὲ πάντως, cf. Ar. *Av.* 1519). In addition to fasting, the celebrants at the Thesmophoria had to be sexually abstinent for several days. Fasting and sexual abstinence often went hand in hand as techniques designed to promote ritual purity (see PURIFICATION) and, conceivably, to heighten spiritual awareness. More importantly, for the Greeks they signal a ritual departure from the social conventions of normal life.

A short fast may have been observed by male initiates in the cult of the Thracian goddess Cotys (*Eupolis fr. 77 K–A 'without breakfast and having eaten nothing at all'). Fasting was also practised as a preparatory rite in mystery religions of the oriental type (especially those of *Isis and Magna Mater; see CYBELE), as well as in *magic (e.g. PGM IV 52 ff.). Abstention from certain kinds of food—all or some meats; particular fish, such as the red mullet; or vegetables like mint and beans—is related to fasting. According to Callimachus (fr. 191. 61 f. Pf.), *Pythagoras (1) taught men 'to abstain from eating (νηστεύειν) animate creatures'. *Porphyry's *On Abstinence from Living Things* (Περὶ ἀποχῆς ἐμψύχων), a treatise on vegetarianism inspired by Theophrastus' *De Pietate*, refers to similar food taboos from various parts of the Mediterranean world. (See ANIMALS, ATTITUDES TO.) Esoteric groups like the 'Orphics' (see ORPHISM) and Pythagoreans were vegetarians and surrounded their daily lives with other dietary prohibitions, many of which corresponded to the rules of conduct imposed on members of some private cults (e.g. G. Petzl (ed.) *Die Inschriften von Smyrna*, 728). Christian ascetics abstained from wine and meat, and often kept prolonged fasts more rigorous than any observed by pagan holy men. See ASCETICISM.

L. Ziehen, *RE* 17 (1936), 88–107 Νηστεία; R. Arbesmann, *RAC* 7 (1969), 447–524, 'Fasten, Fastenspeisen, Fasttage'; W. Burkert, *Lore and Science in Ancient Pythagoreanism* (1972), 177 f.; K. Meuli, *Gesammelte Schriften* (1975), 1. 342 f., 409–33. Eleusis: N. J. Richardson, *The Homeric Hymn to Demeter* (1974), 165–7, 218–26; Burkert, *HN* 269 f. (the *synthēma*). Thesmophoria: Deubner, *Attische Feste* 55 f.; N. Hopkinson, *Callimachus: Hymn to Demeter* (1984), comm. on ll. 5–16.   A. H.

fate The common Greek words for fate mean 'share', 'portion': *moira, aisa, moros, morsimos, heimartai*. One's share is appointed or falls to one (*potmos, peprōmenon*) at birth (*Il.* 20. 128, 24. 209–10; *Od.* 7. 198). The most important share is man's universal fate of death. *Moira, aisa, potmos*, etc. either expressly or by implication primarily refer to death from which even the gods cannot protect man (*Od.* 3. 236–8). In *Homer's *Iliad* *Zeus considers saving his son *Sarpedon and *favourite Hector from imminent death (*Il.* 16. 435–8, 22. 174–6), but *Hera and *Athena dissuade him from upsetting the natural order of things. Exceptions to this predominantly negative idea of fate are rare: *Agamemnon is *moirēgenēs* ('favoured by fate') and *olbiodaimōn* ('of blessed lot') in *Il.* 3. 182 (cf. Pind. *Pyth.* 3. 84), or Zeus knows the good and evil *moira* of mortal men (*moiran / ammorien, Od.* 20. 76).

The workings of fate can appear irrational. At one moment the Pythia (see DELPHIC ORACLE) tells Lydian enquirers that 'no one not even the god can escape his appointed *moira*', at the next *Apollo postpones the sack of *Sardis for three years to help *Croesus (Hdt. 1. 91). Nevertheless a governing principle of proper order attaches to the basic meaning of 'share' in *moira, aisa*, and their derivatives, even when they do not obviously refer to fate. They can describe a section of land (*Il.* 16. 68), share of booty (*Il.* 9. 318), a part of the night (*Il.* 10. 253), or portions of meat (*Od.* 3. 40, 66, etc.). *Moira* already occurs in Linear B in the sense of 'share' (*moroqa*, KN C 954; PY An 519; Ventris–Chadwick, *Docs.*² (1973), 562). The developed notion of due order determined all shares, including that of fate and death, which fitted into a kind of prescribed order of the world.

In Homer the decisive factors were tradition, social hierarchy (cf. Agamemnon's epithet of *moirēgenēs*), and seniority (the *Erinyes support the elder brother, *Il.* 15, 204). Any action or speech that followed such carefully defined criteria was said to be *kata moiran, en moirei* (in accordance with *moira*; e.g. *Il.* 1. 286, 19. 186, 256). The impersonally appointed fate often meant little more than the orderly sequence of the plot. It was, for example, fated for *Odysseus to return to Ithaca eventually (*Od.* 5. 41 f., 9. 532 f.). Consequently this fate can be transgressed by any infringement of the rules of society. So the Cyclops Polyphemus (see CYCLOPES) did not act *kata moiran*, 'in accordance with fate', when he ate his guests (*Od.* 9. 352). Examples are legion in both Homeric epics. Of interest is an added moral dimension in e.g. *Od.* 22. 413 where not only the *moira* of the plot brought the suitors down but also their wicked deeds. In *Od.* 1. 32–41 Zeus explains that *Aegisthus caused his own suffering by acting *hyper moron* (beyond *moros/moira*) in marrying *Clytemnestra and killing Agamemnon. This sense of order extended to the entire cosmos whose proper running was guaranteed by fate, generally with the gods' co-operation (H. Erbse, *Funktion d. Götter* (1986),

287). *Heraclitus said that 'if the sun should overstep his bounds, the Erinyes will find him out' (DK 22 B 94).

The impersonal *moira* and *aisa* were not natural agents of fate. That role normally fell to the *daimōn*, an often malign 'Augenblicksgott' (god of impulse) who could be blamed for sudden unexpected happenings. Etymologically *daimōn* means 'giver of share', yet neither his status or nature is clearly defined in epic. He tends to occur in the plural and is all but synonymous with the general *theos, theoi* who give good and bad fortune to men (Hes. *Op.* 122–6). In later literature and philosophy the *daimōn* stands for a man's personal fate (*daimōn genethlios*, Pind. *Ol.* 13. 105; cf. *potmos syngenēs*, *Nem.* 5. 40) from birth (Menander in Clem. Al. *Strom.* 5. 14. 13). In *Plato (1)'s myth of Er man chooses his own *daimōn* (*Resp.* 10. 617e; cf. *Phdr.* 249b), but more usually it is allotted to him (Soph. *OC* 1337; Pl. *Phd.* 107d; Theoc. *Id.* 4. 40). However, the distinction between individual fate and character virtually disappears (ἦθος ἀνθρώπῳ δαίμων, Heraclitus DK 22 B 119; cf. Epicharmus DK 23 B 17).

The Moirai, like the related *Horae, Erinyes, and possibly the goddess *Nemesis, possessed more colourful identities in popular belief and as *chthonian cult figures. It is difficult to know which preceded the other: deity or concept. Both existed from early times. Certainly the idea of a personal Moira or Aisa (who lacked cult) was already familiar to Homer and *Hesiod as an agent that binds its victim, overcomes him, or leads him to his death (*Od.* 11. 292; *Il.* 18. 119, 13. 602). The imagery reflects funeral inscriptions, as does the concept of Moira, Aisa, or the Klothes as spinners of fate (*Il.* 24. 209–11, 20. 127 f.; *Od.* 7. 196–8; cf. the related popular notions of the weaving and singing of fate). The Moira that, together with Zeus and Erinys, cast confusion into Agamemnon's mind also suggests a cultic origin (*Il.* 19. 87 f.; cf. 410; Aesch. *PV* 516). The Moirai appear on the François vase (6th cent. BC) and on the still earlier Cypselus chest (see CYPSELUS, CHEST OF). However, their genealogy as daughters of Zeus and *Themis and personification in the trinity of Clotho, Lachesis, and Atropos were the fruit of Hesiodic theology (*Theog.* 904 f.; daughters of Night, *Theog.* 217; see NYX).

There is no conflict between this concept of fate and the gods. When Zeus weighs two 'dooms' (*kēres*) against each other (*Il.* 8. 69, 22. 209), the image does not imply his dependence on a superior agency of fate. The golden scales are a *façon de parler*, a poetic device, to raise the tension at a critical moment in the narrative by appearing to create a momentary doubt regarding the outcome of an event which always firmly remains in the control of Zeus. On the contrary, Zeus and the other Olympians ensure the orderly sequence of events like Odysseus' return (*Od.* 18, 353), or they may influence the moment of a hero's death (*Od.* 16. 447), and in that respect they can be said to be masters of human fate (*moira theou, theōn, Od.* 3. 269; cf. Zeus' epithet *Moiragetēs* ('guide of fate'), Paus. 5. 15. 5). Fate gradually assumed a wider significance (Pind. *Pyth.* 12. 30; *Nem.* 6. 13 f.), until the Presocratics, Heraclitus, and the Stoics elevated Heimarmene to an absolute power, the *ordinem seriemque causarum* ('orderly succession of causes') (Cic. *Div.* 1. 125, with a Stoic etymology from εἴρομαι, 'speak, tell') and the same as *anankē* ('necessity'). Neoplatonists equated *heimarmenē* with *physis* ('nature'), in order to exempt man's soul from the stranglehold of fate (Iambl. in Stob. 1. 5. 18 W). The problematic relationship of *heimarmenē* with *pronoia* or providence and free will could only be resolved through faith. In fact the cults of *Mithras and *Isis promised their followers release from the malevolent power of *heimarmenē*.

The notion of a universal power of fate was less evident in

Faunus

Roman thought. The Parcae became goddesses of fate through assimilation with the Moirai. Originally a goddess of birth (from *parere*, †*Parica*) Parca appeared under three different guises as Nona, Decima, and Morta, presumably in relation to the month of a birth (Varro in Gell. *NA* 3. 16. 10), or in the case of Morta with a stillbirth (Latte, *RR* 53), although the juxtaposition of a birth goddess and death is strange. Neither does *Morta* < *mors* suit the context in Livius Andronicus who identified it with Moira (*Odyssia*; Gell. 3. 16. 11), a more attractive linguistic cognate (†*mor-ia*; †*mor-ta*, Radke, *Götter*, 223 f.).

The etymology of *fatum* (*fari*) suggests a primary connection with *oraculum*—the spoken word of the gods—but that is historically misleading. In literature *fatum* was a frequent euphemism for *mors* or *calamitas*, but it merely echoed Greek concepts. The personified plural Fata were modelled on the three Moirai who appear on coins of Diocletian and Maximian but with the legend, *Fatis victricibus*. Parcae and Fata were also virtually indistinguishable in Roman literature and art (cf. the Parcae as *tria Fata* in Gell. *NA* 3. 16. 9 f.). The 'writing' Fata Scribunda, who were invoked at the birth of a child (Tert. *De anim.* 39. 2), ignore the etymology of *fatum* and may be a later invention. A masculine form *fatus* probably arose from a common misuse of gender in vernacular Latin (Petron. *Sat.* 42, 71, 77). But the Fatae in dedicatory inscriptions (*CIL* 2. 89) seem to be Romanized foreign (Celtic) figures. See also FORTUNA / FORS; STOICISM; TYCHE.

U. Bianchi, *Dios Aisa* (1953); P. C. B. Pistorio, *Fato e Divinità* (1954); B. C. Dietrich, *Death, Fate and the Gods* (1967).   N. R.; B. C. D.

Faunus (apparently from the root of *favere*, 'kindly one', a euphemism, although this is debated: cf. Radke, *Götter* 119 ff., *contra* K. Latte, *Gnomon* 1954, 18), a god of the forests, was especially connected with the mysterious sounds heard in them, hence his titles (or identification with) Fatuus and Fatuclus (Serv. on *Aen.* 6. 775), both meaning 'the speaker'. His dwelling-place, wild forests (*silvicola*, Verg. *Aen.* 10. 551), made him a protector of transhumant flocks. His first temple, dedicated on the Tiber island in 193 BC, was built with money from a fine imposed on the *pecuarii* ('drovers') (Liv. 33. 42. 10; 34. 53. 3; anniversary on 13 February, *Fast. Viae Principe Amedeo, Inscr. Ital.* 13. 2, no. 32). From this time on he was identified with *Pan, to the point that his original traits can no longer be separated from those of the Greek god. 'Wild', *agrestis* (Ov. *Fast.* 2. 193 etc.), he is endowed in ritual (see LUPERCALIA) and myth with a lubricity earning him the surname Inuus (Serv. on *Aen.* 6. 775) and recalling the adventures of Pan and his power to excite irrepressible desire. Like him, Faunus also pursues women in their dreams (Incubus, Isid. *Orig.* 8. 11. 103). Finally, his opposition to civilized society allowed him to be claimed as one of the mythical kings of early Latium, son of *Picus or *Mars, or one of the gods of Arcadian *Evander. He had female counterparts, Fauna (of whom we know practically nothing; see BONA DEA) and Fatua (Cornelius Labeo in Macrob. *Sat.* 1. 12. 21). He was on occasion oracular (*Aen.* 7. 81 ff.; Dion. Hal. *Ant. Rom.* 5. 16. 2–3 and elsewhere). For his alleged connection with the Lupercalia, see H. J. Rose, *Mnemos.* 1933, 386 ff.

Wissowa, *RK* 208 ff.; Latte, *RR* 83 ff.; Dumézil, *ARR* 344 ff.
H. J. R.; J. Sch.

Faustina, aunt and wife respectively of M. Aurelius. See ANNIA GALERIA FAUSTINA (1) and (2).

Faustulus, a mythical figure, shepherd of King Amulius, husband of *Acca Larentia, who found *Romulus and Remus

being suckled by the she-wolf. In a further rationalization his wife was the she-wolf herself (*lupa*, loose woman, prostitute). He reared the twins, and when Remus was brought before Numitor for an act of brigandage, told Romulus the whole story, whereupon the twins and their grandfather killed Amulius.

Livy 1. 4. 6 ff. Mommsen, *Röm. Forsch.* 2. 1 ff.; D. Briquel, in *Hommages R. Schilling*, (1983), 53 ff.; J. Scheid, *Romulus et ses frères* (1990), 590 ff.; *LIMC* 4 / 1 (1988), 130 ff.   H. J. R.; J. Sch.

Faventinus See CETIUS.

Favonius (*RE* 1), **Marcus,** of municipal birth (see MUNICIPIUM), admirer and excessive imitator of *Cato (Uticensis), especially in rude forthrightness. He attacked P. *Clodius Pulcher in 61 BC, and vehemently (but ineffectually) opposed *Caesar, *Pompey, and *Crassus in the 50s. Aedile 53, praetor (after a failure) in 49 and active on Pompey's side, he was pardoned after Pompey's death. Tired of civil war, he kept out of the plot against Caesar, but later joined the Liberators, was captured at Philippi, and executed.   E. B.

Favonius (*RE* 2) **Eulogius,** rhetor from Carthage and pupil of *Augustine, who wrote a *Disputatio* commenting on two aspects of Cicero's *Somnium Scipionis*.

Ed. A. Holder (1901), R.-E. van Weddingen (1957); Schanz–Hosius, § 1123; *PLRE* 1. 294.   M. W.

Favorinus (Φαβωρῖνος) (*c.* AD 85–155), sophist, philosopher, and man of letters. Born in Arelate (mod. Arles), he learned Greek in (?) Marseilles (see MASSALIA), and worked exclusively in that language for the whole of his professional career; he may also have studied with Dio Chrysostom (see DIO COCCEIANUS) in Rome. His speaking tours took him to Athens, Corinth, and Ionia, where he contracted a bitter feud with his fellow sophist *Polemon (4). He was a friend of *Plutarch, and the teacher and associate of *Herodes Atticus, *Fronto, and Aulus *Gellius (who quotes and refers to him frequently in the *Noctes Atticae*). At Rome he moved in the circle of the emperor *Hadrian, was advanced to the rank of an *eques*, and held the office of a provincial high priest. About AD 130 he fell into disfavour, although it is disputed whether or not he was exiled. Under Antoninus Pius he recovered his status and influence. Though ancient sources speak of him as a *eunuch, he is more likely to have been a sufferer from cryptorchism.

His extensive works (nearly 30 titles are attested) may be divided into three categories: (*a*) Miscellanies, principally the *Memoirs* and the *Miscellaneous History*, of which the first was devoted to stories about philosophers. These are the earliest known examples of the type of work later produced by Aelian and Athenaeus (1). (*b*) Declamations, comprising the *Corinthian* ('Dio', *Or.* 37), *Fortune* ('Dio', *Or.* 64), and *Exile* (PVat. II). (*c*) Philosophical works, ranging from *The Philosophy of Homer* and *Socrates and his Erotic Art* to *Plutarch, or the Academic Disposition*, *Cataleptic Phantasy*, and *The Pyrrhonian Modes*. The last three at least seem to have been substantial contributions to serious philosophical debate, in which Favorinus presented himself as an adherent of the 'old' scepticism of the *Academy, as opposed to the 'new' scepticism of the Pyrrhonists (see PYRRHON).

Philostr. *VS* 1. 8 (489–92). R. Förster, *Scriptores Physiognomici* 1 (1893), 161; A. Barigazzi, *Favorino, Opere* (1966). W. Schmid, *RE* 6 (1909), 2078; L. Holford-Strevens, *Aulus Gellius* (1988), ch. 6.   M. B. T.

Fayūm, a natural depression in west-central Egypt in whose centre is the Birket Qārūn, remnant of Lake *Moeris, fed by the

Bahr Yusuf. Far more extensive in Herodotus' day, Ptolemy II instigated its drainage. The area formed the Arsinoite (ex-Crocodilopolite) nome (see ARSINOË (1); NOMOS (1)), divided into the *merides* ('sectors') of Heraclides, Themistus, and Polemon. Many papyri and inscriptions survive from its towns and villages. The lake is now saline.

Hdt. 2. 148–9 (comm. A. B. Lloyd); Strab. 17. 1. 4, 35, 37–8. J. Ball, *Contributions to the Geography of Egypt* (1939), 178–229. *PTeb.* 2, pp. 343–424; É. Bernand, *Recueil des inscriptions grecques du Fayoum* 1–3 (1975–81). W. E. H. C.

Febris, patron goddess of fever (malaria, without doubt; see DISEASE), belonging to a group of baleful divinities invoked by the Romans to stop them from exercising their powers. She possessed three cult places in Rome: on the *Palatine, the *Esquiline, and the *Quirinal (Cic. *Leg.* 2. 28; Val. Max. 2. 5. 6; Plin. *HN* 2. 16). We know almost nothing about her cult. According to *Valerius Maximus, cured persons deposited in her sanctuary charms (*remedia*) which had been in contact with their bodies, perhaps because they passed for representations of the power of the goddess. In the 2nd–3rd cents. AD, the sick invoked as well the goddesses Tertiana or Quartana (*CIL* 7. 99; 12. 3129); in Cicero's day they were not yet deified (*Nat. D.* 3. 24).

Wissowa, *RK* 246; Latte, *RR* 52; Eisenhut, *RE* 24. 829 ff. J. Sch.

federal states are found in the Greek world from the late 6th cent. BC. The term is used of those organizations in which the separate city states (see POLIS) of a geographical and ethnic region were combined to form a single entity at any rate for purposes of foreign policy, while for local purposes retaining their separate identity as city states and their separate citizenship. Thus *Boeotia was a federal state in which the individual communities were still regarded as cities, whereas *Attica formed the city-state of Athens and the *demes did not have the degree of *autonomy appropriate to cities. Tribal states in the less urbanized parts of Greece were like federal states in that the tribal organization comprised units with a considerable degree of local autonomy. There is no ancient Greek term which precisely denotes a federal state: the words most often used are *koinon* ('commonwealth') and *ethnos* ('nation'; see ETHNICITY). An account follows of some of the more important federations.

The earliest evidence of a federal state is in (probably) 519 BC, when *Plataea resisted incorporation in a Boeotian federal state dominated by *Thebes (1) and gained the protection of Athens (Hdt. 6. 108); there are references to the boeotarchs, the chief magistrates of the federation, in 480–479 (Paus. 10. 20. 3; Hdt. 9. 15. 1). The federation may have broken up after the Persian Wars, and for a time Boeotia was controlled by Athens, but it was revived after 446 and we have evidence for its basic mechanisms (Thuc. 5. 38. 2; *Hell. Oxy.* 19 Chambers). The individual cities had similar constitutions, with one quarter at a time of the full citizens who satisfied a property qualification acting as a probouleutic council. The federation was based on electoral units, eleven after 427 and perhaps nine before; the largest cities with their dependencies accounted for more than one unit, while the smallest were grouped together to form a unit; each unit provided one boeotarch and 60 members of a council of 660, and within the council one quarter at a time acted as the probouleutic body. In 386 *Sparta regarded the federation as infringing the principle of autonomy enshrined in the Peace of Antalcidas (see KING'S PEACE), and insisted on its dissolution. The federation as revived in the 370s again had electoral units and boeotarchs, but its decision-making body was an assembly, and it was dominated

to a greater extent by Thebes. Thebes was destroyed after revolting against *Alexander (3) the Great in 335, and was refounded *c*.316; the federation survived in the Hellenistic period, based now not on electoral units but on cities. (See BOEOTIA).

*Thessaly was divided regionally into four tetrads, each of which came to be headed by a tetrarch; the tetrads could combine to elect a single leader, the *tagos*, but there seem to have been substantial periods when there was no *tagos*, either because the need for one was not felt or because dissension made the appointment of an agreed leader impossible. The peoples of the surrounding mountains were *perioikoi* ('dwellers around'), whom the Thessalians controlled when they were strong enough to do so. During the 5th cent. cities developed, and became more important than the tetrads. At the end of the century a dynasty of tyrants came to power in Pherae; *c*.375 *Jason (2) of Pherae obtained the title of *tagos*; in the 360s the opponents of Pherae, led by the *Aleuadae family of *Larissa, organized themselves in a *koinon* with an *archōn* ('ruler') and four polemarchs ('war-rulers'); appeals for support to Macedon and to Thebes culminated in the overthrow of the tyrants by *Philip (1) II of Macdeon in 352 and his being made *archōn* of Thessaly. In the course of his later interventions Philip revived the old tetrarchies. Thessaly survived into the Hellenistic period as a federation of cities under the control of the Macedonian king, and a new federation was created by the Romans in 194.

In *Arcadia moves towards unity in the 5th cent. seem not to have gone very far, but a federal state (see ARCADIAN LEAGUE) was founded after the battle of *Leuctra and a new capital was created for it at *Megalopolis. There was an assembly of the Ten Thousand, probably all citizens, and also a council; the chief magistrates were 50 *damiorgoi* ('public workers'), representing the cities in proportion to their size, and a single *stratēgos* ('general'). Before long the federation split: one of the two divisions certainly claimed to be the Arcadian *koinon* and the other may have done so. No more is heard of an Arcadian League after the 320s.

The *Aetolian Confederacy (like the Achaean, see below) began as a tribal state in the Classical period, and in the Hellenistic period developed into organizations with members from outside their original *ethnos*. The Aetolians in the 5th and 4th cents. had both tribal units and city units, and some kind of federal organization. When the confederacy expanded, in the 3rd cent., neighbouring peoples were designated *telē* and perhaps given a status equivalent to that of one of the three Aetolian tribes, while more distant recruits were given *isopoliteia* ('equality of citizenship') either with an Aetolian city or with the whole confederacy. The confederacy had an assembly which held two regular meetings a year, with voting by individuals, a large representative council, and a smaller executive committee, the *apoklētoi* ('those called away'); the principal magistrates were the *stratēgos* and the hipparch ('cavalry commander').

The *Achaean Confederacy already had outside members in the fourth cent. It broke up at the end of the century but was revived in 281/0 and began to acquire outside members in 251/0. There were four regular *synodoi* ('meetings') a year, attended by both a representative council and an assembly, in both of which voting was by cities; later in the 3rd cent. major questions of foreign policy were transferred to extraordinary *synklētoi* ('summoned meetings'), which involved usually both council and assembly but sometimes only the council. The confederacy had two *stratēgoi* until 255, one thereafter. The individual cities of the confederacy continued to have an active political life of their own. See CONCILIUM.

Felicitas

E. A. Freeman, *History of Federal government in Greece and Italy*, 2nd edn. by J. B. Bury (1893); G. Busolt, *Griechische Staatskunde*, 3rd edn., 2 (1926), 1395–1575; J. A. O. Larsen, *Representative Government in Greek and Roman History* (1955), and *Greek Federal States* (1968); V. Ehrenberg, *The Greek State*, 2nd edn. (1969), 120–31; A. Giovannini, *Untersuchungen über die Natur und die Anfänge der bundesstaatlichen Sympolitie in Griechenland* (1971); F. W. Walbank, *Selected Papers* (1985), 20 ff.; P. J. Rhodes, *CAH* 6² (1994), 579 ff. and in M. H. Hansen (ed.), *The Ancient Greek City-State* (1993), 161 ff.   J. A. O. L.; P. J. R.

Felicitas, a goddess of good luck, not heard of till the middle of the 2nd cent. BC, when L. *Licinius Lucullus (1) dedicated her temple on the *Velabrum (see Platner-Ashby, 207); another was planned by Caesar and erected after his death by M. *Aemilius Lepidus (3) where the Curia Hostilia had stood (ibid.). She is associated with *Venus Victrix, *Honos, and Virtus at Pompey's theatre (*fast. Amiternini* on 12 August); with the *Genius Publicus and Venus Victrix on the Capitol (ibid., 9 October). The supposed association with the Numen Augusti on the *fasti Praenestini* (on 17 January) results from a wrong reading (Degrassi, *Inscr. Ital.* 13. 2. 115). Thereafter she is important in official cult under the emperors, appearing frequently on coins (*Felicitas saeculi* with figure of the goddess) and in addresses to the gods in dedications, etc., immediately after the Capitoline triad.

Wissowa, *RK* 266–7; E. Wistrand, *Felicitas imperatoria* (1987).
H. J. R.; J. Sch.

Felix, perhaps **Claudius Felix**, brother of *Antonius Pallas, was appointed *procurator of *Judaea by *Claudius in AD 52, although an imperial freedman (cf. Suet. *Claud.* 52; Tac. *Hist.* 5. 9). One of his three wives was a daughter of Antony (see ANTONIUS (2), M.) and *Cleopatra VII, another—Drusilla—sister of M. *Iulius Agrippa (2) II. He captured and crucified bandits, and massacred the followers of an Egyptian prophet, but was suspected of conniving with *sicarii* (assassins) in the murder of the high priest Jonathan. He was sermonized by the apostle *Paul, whom he kept in prison in *Caesarea (2) for two years. The quarrel over control of Caesarea between Jews and 'Greeks' led to his recall by the emperor (date uncertain).

Joseph. *AJ* 20. 137–44, 160–81; *BJ* 2. 252–70; Acts 21: 38; 23–4. Schürer, *History* 1. 460–6.   T. R.

Felix, Flavius, Latin poet of senatorial rank. His verses, often unclassical in quantity, include a poem on baths built by Thrasamond, *Vandal king in Africa (AD 496–523).

Anth. Lat. 210–14. O. Skutsch, *RE* 6/2 (1909), 2597–8.   A. J. S. S.

Felsina (mod. Bologna) was the most important of the twelve *Etruscan cities traditionally founded north of the Apennines in the mid-6th cent. BC. By then, the preceding late bronze–iron age centre that gives its name to the *Villanovan culture was already a flourishing and well-connected entrepôt for trade with Europe north of the Alps: to all intents and purposes, Bologna was a city by the end of the 7th cent. The Certosa cemetery has produced the finest of a number of 6th/5th-cent. bronze situlae decorated with repoussé figures, quantities of Greek pottery imported presumably via Spina and Atria, and a number of 5th-cent. funerary steles, some of which bear the earliest representations of Gauls to be found in the Mediterranean world. The Roman colony of *Bononia (1) was founded in 189 BC.

BTCGI 4 (1985), 'Bologna'; C. Morigi Govi and D. Vitali (eds.), *Il Museo Civico archeologico di Bologna* (1982); D. Vitali (ed.), *Celti ed Etruschi nell'Italia centro-settentrionale* (1987); G. Bermond Montanari and others, *La formazione della città in Emilia Romagna*, exhib. cat. (Bologna, 1987): conference proceedings and essays.   D. W. R. R.

feminism See WOMEN and entries listed at the end of that entry.

Fenestella (52 BC–AD 19 or, possibly, 35 BC–AD 36), the antiquarian annalist (see ANNALS, ANNALISTS), wrote a Roman history in at least 22 books, perhaps from the origins, certainly to 57 BC; the citations of *Asconius Pedianus reflect his special authority for the Ciceronian period. The fragments, which, however, may come also from works on constitutional and social antiquities, show his wide antiquarian interests and critical ability, in the Varronian tradition. The Elder *Pliny (1) used him, and an *epitome was made. See SCHOLARSHIP, ANCIENT (Roman).

Peter, *HRRel.* 2. cix. 79; L. Mercklin, *De Fenestella* (1844); J. Poeth, *De Fenestella* (1849); *PIR²* F 144.   A. H. McD.

Feralia, Roman festival on 21 February which concluded the ancestors' festival (*Parentalia) which had begun on 13 February. Each household made offerings at the graves of its dead: Ov. *Fast.* 2. 533 ff. with F. Bömer's comm. (1957–8), Varro, *Ling.* 6. 13, Festus 75 Lindsay; cf. Cic. *Att.* 8. 14. 1. It is marked *NP* (i.e. probably *nefas feriae publicae*, a time when legal business should not be done) in imperial calendars but *F* (i.e. *fas* or *fastus*, a time when the courts were open) in the *fasti Antiates* (cf. *Inscr. Ital.* 13. 2. 334 ff.). There is no evidence for a public ritual.

J. Gager, *Curse Tablets and Binding Spells From the Ancient World* (1992), 251 f.   C. R. P.

Ferentinum (mod. Ferentino), town of the *Hernici, whose loyalty to Rome in 306 BC secured a measure of independence for it until 90 BC. Its well-preserved walls, with polygonal lower and squared upper courses, are singularly interesting: the two styles may be coeval (1st cent. BC for the citadel fortifications).

G. Lugli, *La tecnica edilizia romana* (1957), 127 ff.   E. T. S.; T. W. P.

feriae See FESTIVALS, ROMAN.

Feronia (Fē-, Verg. *Aen.* 7. 800; Hor. *Sat.* 1. 5. 24; and elsewhere), an Italian goddess, of presumably Sabine origin. She was officially received in Rome during the 3rd cent. BC (272 according to Castagnoli and Coarelli; around 225 according to Ziolkowski: see bibliog. below) and given a temple in the Campus Martius (*fasti arvales*) on 13 November (temple C of the Largo Argentina, according to Castagnoli and Coarelli; temple A according to Ziolkowski). At any rate, in 217 BC this temple already existed (Livy 22. 1. 18). Her principal place of worship was the grove of Capena, later *Lucus Feroniae, near Mt. Soracte (Cato, *Orig.* 1, fr. 26 Jordan; Verg. *Aen.* 7. 697; Strabo 5. 2. 9; Plin. *HN* 3. 51). Her cult, however, is shown by inscriptional and other evidence to have been widespread in central Italy (see Wissowa, *RK* 285 f.; Latte, *RR* 189). The etymology of her name is problematic (cf. Radke, *Entwicklung* 103; Dumézil *ARR* 419 f.). Of her cult and function almost nothing is known. Strabo (5. 2. 9) says that a ceremony of fire-walking was performed in her precinct, but this seems to be a confusion with the so-called Apollo of *Soracte (see Verg. *Aen.* 11. 785 ff. and commentators there). Near Tarracina slaves were set free in her shrine (Serv. on *Aen.* 8. 564). Weighing all the evidence, Dumézil proposed that the function of Feronia was to convert the savage forces of nature for human use.

Latte, *RR* 189 f.; Dumézil *ARR* 414 ff.; F. Castagnoli, in *Mem. dei Lincei* 1948, 93 ff.; F. Coarelli, *L'area sacra di Largo Argentina* 1: *Topografia e storia* (1981), 9 ff.; Ziolkowski, *Temples* 25 ff.; *LIMC* 4/1 (1988), 132 f.   H. J. R.; J. Sch.

Fescennini (versus), songs of ribald abuse at weddings (literary representation: Catull. 61. 119–48), so called from the Etruscan town of Fescennia near Falerii, presumably for excellence in such entertainments; the alternative etymology (Paul. Fest. 76) from the *fascinum* ('witchcraft') they averted, though linguistically untenable, points to an apotropaic function as of soldiers' songs at *triumphs (Plin. *HN* 28. 39). The word is also applied to *amoebean ribaldry at harvest-festivals (Hor. *Epist.* 2. 1. 145–6) conjecturally linked with the origins of Roman drama, *Augustus' satirical verses attacking *Asinius Pollio (Macrob. *Sat.* 2. 4. 21), *Annianus' erotica (Auson. *Cent. nupt.* 139. 9–10 Green), and *Claudian's very decorous wedding-poems for *Honorius and Maria (11–14); *Fescenninus*, used of the wedding-singer at Sen. *Med.* 113, denotes a slanderer at Cato, *ORF* 113 = fr. 86 Sblendorio Cugusi. L. A. H.-S.

festivals

Greek Greek festivals were religious rituals recurring, usually every year, two years, or four years, at fixed times in the calendar. Unlike *sacrifices and other *rituals performed for specific occasions (e.g. marriage) or in times of crisis, they were intended, in general terms, to maintain or renew the desired relationship with supernatural powers. In the Classical period it was believed that this relationship was maintained by rendering honour, at the appropriate time and in the appropriate manner, to the deity.

Festivals proper (*heortai*) should be distinguished from annual sacrifices (*thysiai*), however large, and the many other rituals that together formed the religious calendar. *Heortai* are described as pleasant and joyful religious experiences with an abundance of good food, good company, and good entertainment, a combination seen in many Mediterranean religious festivals today. The atmosphere and characteristics of *thysiai* and other rituals varied greatly, sometimes being very sombre, depending on the deity, purpose, and cult personnel involved. But heortology has traditionally investigated the dating and description of all calendrically recurring rituals, and that is the sense in which 'festival' is usually understood in Classical scholarship.

The festivals of Athens are best known, and their origins, like those of all Greek festivals, are multifarious, with, for example, some going back to pre-Greek neolithic times (e.g. *Bouphonia), some instituted to honour contemporary Hellenistic kings (e.g. Ptolemaieia). Over the centuries new elements were added to old festivals (e.g. the *Panathenaea) and separate festivals on consecutive days may have coalesced into one (e.g. *Anthesteria). Many were of one day only (e.g. *Thargelia); some, like the City *Dionysia in Athens, ran five or six days. Athens had at least 60 days a year devoted to annual festivals.

The religious concerns of the Greeks were many, and the variety of the festivals and rituals reflects this. Rarely, furthermore, does a single festival address only one concern. Despite the risk of great oversimplification, we may isolate some major types of developed festivals. Agonistic festivals, each eventually assigned to an Olympian deity, consisted initially of a *pompē* (procession), a *thysia* (sacrifice), an *agōn* (contest, see AGŌNES), and a banquet, in that order. The contests might be 'gymnastic' (human and animal races of various types, boxing, wrestling, etc.) or of the Muses (lyre- and pipe-playing, recitations, dancing, and drama), or both. The original *agōn* at *Olympia was, according to myth, simply a 200-m. (*c.*220-yd.) foot-race. As contests were added, some were placed before the procession, and by the 5th cent. BC the programmes had become very large. Such

festivals were the model for those established by monarchs in the Hellenic period.

Periodic fertility rituals, many going back to the neolithic period, were often performed by women, often in secret. Some were genuine *mysteries (as at Eleusis). Those centred on agriculture naturally occurred at critical times in the farming cycle, e.g. at ploughing (Proerosia), at seeding (*Thesmophoria), and at harvest (Anthesteria), with rituals appropriate to the deity and crop in question. Because concepts of human, animal, and crop fertility were intertwined, sympathetic *magic played a role. For this reason, and because of their secrecy and the combining of two or more festivals, the rituals of fertility festivals are particularly complex and opaque.

Through certain annual rituals, again of great antiquity, the Greeks initiated young people into adult society, in Athens particularly at the *Apaturia for young men and at the Brauronia (see BRAURON) for young women. The rituals differed significantly from city to city, but generally followed the pattern of separation, liminal experience, and reintegration characteristic of such *rites of passage.

A festival presumes a group, in the Greek context the smallest being a village (a deme in Athens: see DEMES), the usual the *polis, a few confederations (see FEDERAL STATES), and the largest (rare) all the Greeks. By the Classical period the *polis* had absorbed many village festivals and now financed and administered them. Through festivals a *polis* like Athens might celebrate its own origins (the Synoecia, see SYNOECISM), its national identity and accomplishments (Panathenaea), or, even, in later times, its military victories. The festivals could be integrated, mythologically, into the legendary history of the city, as, at Athens, the *Oschophoria and Deipnophoria were tied to Theseus' expedition to Crete. In all festivals the roles and often even dress of the participants maintained traditional divisions of citizen status, gender, age, and office; and thus a festival could provide cohesion to the group but simultaneously reassert traditional social orders. But, on the other hand, a few festivals, the Cronia in Athens (Philochorus, *FGrH* 328 F 97) and the Hybristica in *Argos (2) (Plut. *Mor.* 245e–f) provided a temporary reversal of the social order, with slaves acting as masters or women as men. Confederations of states with both tribal and geographical ties had cult centres with their own festivals, e.g. the Panionia (see PANIONIUM) for *Poseidon at Mycale (Hdt. 1. 148). It was not until the 4th cent. that philosophers such as *Isocrates used the pan-Hellenic festivals at Olympia, *Isthmia, and *Delphi as examples and occasions for promoting a sense of shared identity among all Greeks.

Deubner, *Attische Feste*; H. W. Parke, *Festivals of the Athenians* (1977); Nilsson, *Feste*; Burkert, *GR* 99–109, 225–46, 254–64. J. D. M.

Roman (Lat. *feriae*). The basic notion included not only the honouring of the gods, but also restrictions on public life: the courts were closed, some agricultural work was restricted, and in some cases holidays given to other workers. Festivals were of various kinds: some fixed by the regular calendar of the *fasti* (*stativae*) (see CALENDAR, ROMAN); movable festivals (*conceptivae*), such as the *feriae sementivae* dedicated to *Tellus and *Ceres, were held annually on days appointed by priests or magistrates; special festivals (*imperativae*) were ordered, again by magistrates or priests, because of a specific event, a prodigy, a disaster, or a victory. A major element in many public festivals was the accompanying games (see LUDI). Besides public festivals, the period assigned to private ceremonial might be classed as *feriae*—e.g. birthdays or the ten days of mourning (*denicales*).

Festus

C. Jullian, Dar.-Sag. 2. 1042–66; Wissowa, *RK* 432–49; G. Dumézil, *ARR* 559–65, and *Fêtes romaines d'été et d'automne* (1975); T. Klauser, *RAC* 7 (1969), 747–66; H. H. Scullard, *Festivals and Ceremonies of the Roman Republic* (1981).   H. W. P.; S. R. F. P.

Festus See POMPEIUS FESTUS, SEX. (scholar); PORCIUS FESTUS (procurator of Judaea).

Festus ('Rufus' or 'Ruffus' Festus only in poor MSS), historian and senator from Tridentum, 'of the lowest birth' (Amm. Marc. 29. 2. 22). He was *magister memoriae* under Valens (*c.* AD 369) and proconsul of Asia (372–8), when he won notoriety for his execution of the Neoplatonist *Maximus (3) and persecution of intellectuals generally. He wrote the extant *Summary of Roman History* (*Breviarium rerum gestarum populi Romani*) from the origins to the accession of Valens, to whom it was dedicated, appearing after the Gothic peace (369). The first part described the conquest of the Roman provinces, the second the eastern wars from Sulla, especially the Parthian Wars. It represents ultimately the epitomized Livian tradition and a compendious imperial History.

Ed. W. Förster (1874); C. Wagener (1886); J. W. Eadie, *The Breviarium of Festus* (1967); B. Baldwin, *Hist.* 1978, 192 ff.; *PLRE* 1, 'Festus' 3.
                                        A. H. McD.; A. J. S. S.

fetiales, priests of the Latin states, concerned with the procedures and laws of declaring wars and making treaties. Our information comes from Rome, where they formed a college (*collegium) of twenty members, who advised the senate on issues of peace and war, and had their own legal tradition (the *ius fetiale*). The institution presupposes that similar priests, with whom Roman *fetiales* interacted, existed in the other Latin states.

*Livy gives an account of their ritual (1. 24) in the form of a narrative, no doubt an antiquarian reconstruction, but perhaps based on priestly sources. In making a treaty (*foedus), two *fetiales* were sent out, who met with *fetiales* from the other side; one carried herbs (the *verbenarius*), the other (the *pater patratus*), having heard the new treaty read out, pronounced a curse that would operate against the Romans, should they be first to break the treaty. The other side did the same. The sacrifice of a pig with a special stone knife (*lapis silex*) confirmed the transaction.

In the case of a declaration of war, the *pater patratus* entered the territory of the state against whom the Romans claimed a grievance and made a public declaration of the claim (*clarigatio*), calling on *Jupiter to witness the justice of the Roman case. If satisfaction had not been offered within 33 days, the Roman senate and people proceeded to declare war and this was conveyed by the *fetialis* again travelling to the boundary, making the declaration, and throwing a symbolic spear into enemy territory. The consequence of these proceedings was that the war was a just war (*bellum iustum*).

Whether or not this ritual was literally followed in the archaic period, we meet it in the later republic completely transformed by the distances to be travelled, the lack of enemy *fetiales*, the requirements of diplomacy, and so on. For instance, the symbolic spear-throwing took place inside Rome, on ground near the temple of *Bellona ritually regarded as non-Roman. But the *fetiales* were still being consulted prominently in the 2nd cent. BC; there is no reason to believe they had ceased to exist in the late republic and no evidence as to what if anything their Augustan 'revival' revived.

There has been much debate as to whether the fetial doctrine of the 'just war' inhibited aggressive war-declarations by Rome, and led to defensive attitudes and a consequent lack of consciously imperialist policies. (See IMPERIALISM, ROMAN.) The theory seems to rest on a confusion of ritual propriety (which was what the *fetiales* looked for) with power politics (which were not their concern). But undoubtedly Roman historians, and therefore surviving accounts, were influenced by the expectation, implicit in fetial doctrine, that Rome's wars derived from enemy misbehaviour and Roman piety.

Wissowa, *RK* 550–4; Brunt, *RIT* 288–323; J. Rupke, *Domi Militiae: die religiöse Konstruktion des Krieges in Rom* (1990), 97–117.   J. A. N.

fibula ($\pi\epsilon\rho\acute{o}\nu\eta$, $\pi\acute{o}\rho\pi\eta$). The primitive brooch or fibula, of violin-bow form resembling the modern safety-pin, is found in late bronze age contexts in Greece, northern Italy, and central Europe. The fibula was probably an Aegean invention, developed in the 13 cent. out of a Minoan pin which had the end bent to prevent slipping. By further bending until the end, flattened into a catch, could engage the point, the fibula was produced, and the addition of a spiral coil at the angle to increase tension was also of early date. Later improvements enlarged the bow so as to grip more cloth. Large fibulae from mainland Greece, of late geometric times, have broad catchplates with incised decoration; the Cypriot type has a double-arched bow, the Asiatic a stilted one. The 'spectacle' type, in which the bow is replaced by spiral coils of wire, may have been of Danubian origin. Fibulae were made in *gold, *silver, and *bronze and might have *amber, *ivory, or bone attachments. After the 6th cent. the fibula falls into comparative disuse in Greece, and no new types appear until Roman times. In Italy the development was unbroken and the types more varied: the bow looped, bent, threaded with discs, or thickened into the 'leech' or 'boat' form; the catchplate set transversely or fantastically prolonged. In the 5th cent. BC a simpler type became universal and gave rise to the La Tène forms, in which the spiral spring is bilateral, and ultimately to the Roman in which, under the early empire, a hinge replaces the spiral.

C. Blinkenberg, *Fibules grecques et orientales* (1926); K. Kilian, *Fibeln in Thessalien* (1975); R. Hattatt, *Ancient Brooches and Other Artefacts* (1989).
                                        F. N. P.; M. V.

fideicommissa A Roman testator could choose, in disposing of his estate, between the formal methods of the *ius civile* (civil law), will and legacy, and the informal device of *fideicommissum* (roughly 'trust'); or he could combine the two. Originally the *fideicommissum* was simply a request by the testator to a person who benefited from his estate to transfer part of it or even the whole estate to another person; and any force which that request had was purely moral. *Augustus, however, charged the consuls with enforcing certain *fideicommissa*; two standing praetors for trusts (later reduced to one) came into being under *Claudius. The procedure employed was the new extraordinary one (*cognitio extra ordinem*). One of the initial attractions of *fideicommissa* was that they could benefit those (such as foreigners and the proscribed (see PROSCRIPTION)) unable to become heirs or legatees. But this possibility was progressively restricted; and the consuls are in any event unlikely to have allowed the proscribed to claim their *fideicommissa*. The lasting attraction of *fideicommissa* lay instead in part with the procedural advantages of *cognitio*; and principally in their lack of legal formality. While a will required that the first provision of all be the appointment of the heir in set words, and that any legacies be charged on him in set forms, no formal constraints affected *fideicommissa*. This led to the development of a practice of asking that a will, if it turned out to be formally invalid, should be upheld in fideicommissary form.

Indeed, there was no need to make a will at all, since a *fideicommissum* could simply be charged on the heir who would succeed on intestacy. This role appears to have become paramount in post-Classical times, when the term *fideicommissum* was often used in contrast to testamentary succession. Although in principle the *fideicommissum* might also have been employed to set up family settlements for a number of generations, there is little evidence that this was ever done. Under Justinian the two institutions of legacy and *fideicommissum* were fused. The unitary system which resulted was much closer to the *fideicommissum* than to the legacy: the informal nature of the *fideicommissum* was extended to the legacy; and where the rules of the two institutions conflicted, Justinian, who regarded the *fideicommissum* as the *humanior* ('more humane') of the two, decreed that its rules should prevail. See INHERITANCE, ROMAN.

D. Johnston, *The Roman Law of Trusts* (1988).   D. E. L. J.

Fidenae (mod. Castel Giubileo), the first station on the *via Salaria. First settled in the bronze age, it grew to 45.5 ha. (112 acres) and frequently fought Rome, which controlled a rival *Tiber-crossing 8 km. (5 mi.) downstream. Conquered by Rome in 498 BC, Fidenae dwindled to unimportance. Its quarries supplied stone for the *wall of Servius at Rome. In AD 27 a wooden amphitheatre burnt down there causing great loss of life.

L. Quilici and S. Quilici Gigli, *Fidenae*, Latium Vetus 5 (1986); *Bull. Com. Arch.* 92 (1987–8), 459 ff.   E. T. S.; T. W. P.

Fides, the Roman personification of good faith. Although her temple (on the *Capitol, near that of *Jupiter, with whom she is closely connected) is no older than 254 BC (see Ziolkowski, *Temples* 28 ff.), her cult is traditionally very old, said to have been founded by *Numa (Livy 1. 21. 4) although it should be noted that Jupiter himself once discharged her function (Wissowa, Freyburger). Livy also gives details of her ritual; the *flamines, meaning probably the *flamines maiores* (see Dumézil, *ARR* 198 f.), drove to her shrine in a covered carriage drawn by two beasts, and the sacrificer must have his hand covered with a white cloth. A pair of covered hands is indeed her symbol, as often on coins commemorating the *fides* of the Augusti, the legions, etc., in imperial times. Since giving the hand is a common gesture of solemn agreement, the symbolism is natural.

Wissowa, *RK* 133 f.; Latte, *RR* 237; G. Freyburger, *Fides: Étude sémantique et religieuse depuis les origines jusqu'à l'époque d'Auguste* (1986); *LIMC* 4/1 (1988) 133 ff.   H. J. R.; J. Sch.

fig The fig-tree is an underrated food source in antiquity, producing more calories per unit area than any other crop: 15,000,000 kilocalories per hectare. Though vigorous, the trees are sensitive to severe frost and need long, hot summers for the fruit to ripen. Normally they were propagated by cuttings. Fig fertilization fascinated ancient writers, and was accurately described by *Theophrastus (*Caus. pl.* 2. 9; *Hist. pl.* 2. 8). Figs flower internally, within the embryo fruit, on male and female trees. For pollination they depend on the fig wasp which crawls out of the male and into the female fruits.

Figs were an important sweetener: few forms of sugar were available (Ath. 3. 74d–f). Choice fresh figs were valued, and many early and late varieties bred to extend the season are mentioned by Theophrastus and the Roman agronomists. Dried figs (Gk. *ischades*) were food for slaves or poor rustics (Columella, *Rust.* 12. 14; Ath. 2. 54f–55a, 2. 60b–c), or 'emergency rations' (Ar. *Pax* 634, 636, 1215–23; *Ach.* 799–810). They feature in the diet of slaves in the Linear B tablets from *Pylos. Because of their high sugar content, tightly packed figs keep for several years.

The irritant, latex-like sap of fig trees was thought to have medicinal qualities. They also featured in religious ceremonies, for example the rites of Artemis Orthia in Sparta (see SPARTAN CULTS) where boys were beaten with their branches or the Attic *Thargelia, celebrated in May at fig fertilization time, when the *pharmakoi*, 'scapegoats' (see PHARMAKOS), wore 'black' and 'white' (male and female) figs.

Theophr. *Caus. pl.*, *Hist. pl. passim*; Columella, *Rust.* 5. 9–11, 10. 414–18, 12. 14–15, *De arboribus* 21; Ath. 3. 74c–80e; F. Olck, *RE* 6/2 (1909), 2100 ff.   L. F.

Filocalus, Furius Dionysius, calligrapher of Pope *Damasus I (AD 366–84), produced many of Damasus' inscriptions in the Roman *catacombs. (See EPIGRAPHY, LATIN, § 9.) He is perhaps also the author of the *Chronicle of 354* (ed. T. Mommsen, *Chronica minora* 1 (*MGH AA* 9, 1892), 13–196; *Inscr. Ital.* 13. 2. 237–62) which contains various tables, lists, and chronicles relating to the history and geography of the city of Rome and the Roman empire, a world chronicle, a calendar of traditional festivals, a list of Roman bishops and martyrs, and a list of the popes until Liberius.

M. R. Selzman, *On Roman Time* (1990), 202 ff.; U. Dionisi in *EEC* 2 (1992), 682.   W. K.

Fimbria See FLAVIUS FIMBRIA, C.

finance, Greek and Hellenistic The collective deployment of resources by the community inevitably has socio-political implications (who pays? who benefits?). But public finance in Greek states rarely had economic aims beyond the broad balancing of incomings and outgoings: demand-management through running a budget deficit or surplus was unknown. *Oikonomia* ('economics') as applied to state finance preserved autarkic attitudes appropriate to its original meaning of 'household management' (Xen. *Mem.* 3. 4). Recurring expenditure (primarily on administration, cult, ambassadors, defence, maintenance of fortifications, gymnasia, and public buildings) would be met from a variety of revenues (rents and royalties from state property, including mines and quarries, court fees and fines, taxes on non-citizens, sales taxes, excise duties and customs dues). Collection of taxes was regularly farmed out by auction to private individuals (*Ath. pol.* 47. 2 ff.). Extraordinary expenditure (typically through warfare or food shortage; occasionally, on public building) was met through ad hoc measures: property and poll taxes, public loans, creation of monopolies, *epidoseis* (contributions), or confiscations ([Arist.] *Oec.* 2). Warfare itself was seen as potentially productive (Arist. *Pol.* 1256^b), and might occasionally prove so. Systems of Greek public finance may be assessed in so far as they conform to or deviate from these norms.

Minoan and Mycenaean communities seem to have been unique in the Greek world in their degree of direct, central control over resources. The testimony of the Linear B tablets, in conjunction with extensive storage facilities within the palaces, suggests a 'redistributive' system of economic exchange, rigidly controlled from the centre (there are parallels in temple-based economies of the near east; see MINOAN and MYCENAEAN CIVILIZATION). All this ended with the onset of the so-called Dark Age (c.1100 BC). The well-stocked storerooms of the *Odyssey* (2. 337 ff.) may dimly recall Mycenaean palaces, but redistribution was replaced in the world of Homer by *reciprocity between and within aristocratic *oikoi* (households). Resources were deployed by the giving of gift and counter-gift (see GIFT, GREECE): in return

595

for their contributions to the élite, the people received protection (*Il.* 12. 310 ff.; *Od.* 13. 13 ff.). Arrangements in Archaic and even Classical *Sparta resembled Homeric organization in the near absence of any centralized system of finance. The mainstay of the regime was the agricultural produce appropriated from the *helots by individual Spartiates, who passed on a portion to their *sussition* (public mess). Details are obscure (the *perioikoi* may have made contributions in cash or kind), but the small scale of resources under central control helps to account for the poor showing of late 5th-cent. Sparta as a city (Thuc. 1. 10). Much the same might be said of the rudimentary systems of finance (e.g. the *naukrariai* and *kōlakretai* in Athens) deployed by the aristocracies dominating early Archaic *poleis*. Archaic tyrants provide a stark contrast: their characteristically heavy expenditure on public buildings and central, civic institutions gave the *polis* a new, urban emphasis. Necessary resources were raised by a combination of personal taxes and other, extraordinary measures: in Athens, a tax on agricultural produce (Thuc. 6. 54). Also characteristic of Archaic tyranny was the effective merging of the tyrant's own resources with those of the state (*Ath. pol.* 16. 1). The ending of *tyranny caused an immediate reaction against the tyrants' financial methods: taxes on the person became a symbol of oppression, restricted to non-citizens and those of low status.

Archaic Athens broadly conformed to this pattern; as late as the 480s, it was proposed that a windfall gain of 100 talents from the silver mines at *Laurium be parcelled out among the citizen body (*Ath. Pol* 22. 7). Shortly after, Athenian finances were transformed by the acquisition of a tribute-paying empire (see DELIAN LEAGUE). Figures from the eve of the Peloponnesian War give a crude impression of scale: from a total annual revenue (internal and external) of approximately 1,000 talents (Xen. *An.* 7. 1. 27) some 600 talents derived from the empire (Thuc. 2. 13). This made possible the maintenance of a massive navy, an extended programme of public building, provision of public pay, and the accumulation on the Acropolis of a strategic reserve of at least 6,000 talents (Thuc. 2. 13). Against this, expenses of war were heavy: one talent in pay to keep one trireme at sea for one month. As the Peloponnesian War progressed, there was (in addition to an upward reassessment of the tribute in 425: ML 69) increasing reliance on payments of *eisphora*—an extraordinary property tax falling on the wealthy. By contrast, the Spartan system was poorly placed to generate the resources needed for extended warfare. Appeals for contributions from sympathetic individuals proved inadequate (ML 67), and only massive subventions of Persian gold made possible the eventual Spartan victory. The importance of imperial revenues for Athens' *democracy became apparent in the 4th cent., when the range of public payments was actually extended to include assembly pay and payments from the theoric fund (see THEŌRIKA). Collective aspirations may be read into the explicit aim behind the proposals in *Xenophon (1)'s *Poroi* ('Revenues'): maintenance of the citizen body at public expense. Attempts to revive the tribute-paying empire failed and heavier burdens therefore fell on the wealthy (Xen. *Oec.* 2. 5 ff.). The degree to which increasing demands disrupted and alienated the Athenian élite is disputed. There emerged in the course of the 4th cent. a group of financial experts (including *Eubulus (1) and culminating in *Lycurgus (3)), who occupied tailor-made offices and made the most of Athens' internal resources.

Characteristic of finance in Classical Athens was the *liturgy system, placing the élite under an obligation to perform public services (notably the *trierarchy and *chorēgia). Liturgies were

an integral part of the democratic system: in return for public services, liturgists might (or might not) receive popular consideration in politics and the courts. Significantly, Aristotle (*Pol.* 1321ᵃ) recommends that oligarchies attach expensive duties to high public office, so excluding all but the wealthy. The citizens of 4th-cent. *Pharsalus handed over their acropolis and control of their finances to their wealthiest citizen; in return he used his fortune as a revolving loan-fund, smoothing out imbalances in income and expenditure (Xen. *Hell.* 6. 1. 2) This privileging of wealth ties in with the broadly post-democratic practice of *euergetism, common in Hellenistic cities. The *euergetēs* ('benefactor') earned enhanced status, and possibly material rewards, by making donations in cash or kind to the advantage of the citizen body.

Amongst the Hellenistic monarchies, Ptolemaic *Egypt had a system of public finance of exceptional complexity. Revenues from farmland were assessed in painstaking detail and collected directly; collection of dues from vineyards, orchards, and gardens was farmed out. Additionally, the *apomoira* (a tax on wine, fruit, and vegetables) was assessed by royal officials, but the right to collect was sold to contractors. Customs dues were graduated from 20 to 59 per cent, according to the goods involved (contrast the flat 5 per cent tax from Classical Athens). There were varying rates of tax on sale and gift of property and privileges (e.g. tax concessions) and, apart from sundry minor taxes (including a poll tax), intricately organized *monopolies on an extended range of goods and services. Other Hellenistic kings raised revenue from their subject cities partly by imposing specific taxes, partly by levying contributions (*phoros*), which were creamed off internal revenues, raised in the usual ways.

A. Andreades, *A History of Greek Public Finance* (1933); Ventris–Chadwick, *Docs*²; M. I. Finley, *The World of Odysseus* (1977); and *Economy and Society in Ancient Greece* (1981), 41 ff, 199 ff.; G. E. M. de Ste. Croix, in A. C. Littleton and B. S. Yamey (eds.), *Studies in the History of Accounting* (1956), 14 ff., and *Classica et Mediaevalia*, 1953, 30 ff.; P. Millett, *Lending and Borrowing in Ancient Athens* (1991), and in J. Rich and G. Shipley (eds.), *War and Society in the Greek World* (1993), 177 ff.; L. Migeotte (ed.), *L'emprunt public dans les cités grecques* (1984), and *Les Souscriptions publiques dans les cités grecques* (1992); P. Brun, *Eisphora, Syntaxis, Stratiotika* (1983); S. Humphreys, in J. W. Eadie and J. Ober (eds.), *The Craft of the Ancient Historian* (1985), 199 ff.; P. Garnsey, *Famine and Food Supply in the Graeco-Roman World* (1988); P. Veyne, *Bread and Circuses* (1990; Fr. orig. 1976); Rostovtzeff, *Hellenistic World*; C. Préaux, *L'Économie royale des Lagides* (1939); A. H. M. Jones, *The Roman Economy* (1974), 151 ff.; S. von Reden, *Exchange in Ancient Greece* (1995).

P. C. M.

finance, Roman 'Taxes are the sinews of the state'. So claimed both Cicero and the great jurist Ulpian. Despite this recognition of the central importance of taxation no systematic ancient treatment of Roman public finance survives. Extended financial documents are also rare (though see now the elaborate schedule of the *portoria of Asia, *AE* 1989, 681). Therefore many details about (e.g.) the allocation and collection of taxes or about the character of fiscal institutions (such as the *fiscus, the *patrimonium*, and the *res privata* (for both the latter see PATRIMONIUM)) remain obscure and disputed. Despite the serious deficiencies in our evidence the broad features of the history and development of Roman public finance through the republic and the Principate to the later empire can be delineated with some confidence.

In the republic there were, traditionally, two major types of revenue namely the regular *vectigalia and the *tributum*, an extraordinary (in principle) levy on the property of Roman citizens. The total size of this levy was decided by the senate and varied from year to year. The earliest detailed account of republican public finance survives in the sketch of the Roman constitution in the sixth book of *Polybius (1), reflecting conditions in the mid-2nd cent. BC. The *aerarium*, the central depository of the state for both cash and documents, was managed by two urban quaestors; but all decisions as to payments from it were made by the senate. On setting out on campaign a consul could draw funds on his own responsibility. But further payments, for the supplies, clothes, or pay of the army, had again to be authorized by the senate. The senate also made a quinquennial grant to the censors, on the basis of which they let out contracts for building and repairs of public buildings in Rome and the *municipia* and *coloniae* of Italy and for the exploitation of public properties— rivers, harbours, gardens, *mines, and land. Ultimate control of the contracts, for instance in altering the terms, again lay with the senate.

The most important development, not reflected in Polybius' account of the last two centuries of the republic, was the acquisition of a territorial empire overseas. At first resources were extracted from the conquered via *booty and war indemnities, in the medium term by the imposition of regular taxation (tribute) in cash or kind. Provincial governors (and their quaestors) were responsible for the supervision of the collection of tribute and for expenditure in their province. After 123 BC in Asia certainly (and perhaps elsewhere) the process of collection of tribute was contracted out to *publicani*. Two prime consequences ensued from this development. First, the levying of tribute on Roman citizens in Italy was abandoned from 167 BC onwards. Secondly, the revenues of the state were greatly increased. On one speculative estimate (Frank, *Econ. Survey* 1. 141) annual revenues in the early 2nd cent. BC were 12.5 to 15 million denarii. By the late 60s BC they had increased to 50 million; and according to a difficult passage of Plutarch (*Pomp.* 45), Pompey's great conquests in the 60s further increased revenues to either 85 or 135 million. The continuing access of new revenues both meant that Rome's continuous wars were in the long term self-financing and allowed the creation of novel forms of public expenditure such as the distribution of subsidized, later free, corn to Roman citizens. (See FOOD SUPPLY.) Even so, as in many pre-industrial societies, public revenues remained modest in relation to the private wealth of the élite. So the fortune of *Crassus alone amounted to 48 million denarii.

The establishment of imperial rule entailed far-reaching changes in public finance and the creation of an elaborate fiscal state. First, although the senate retained the function of making routine votes of funds, effective control over the state's finances came to lie with the emperor and his agents. Under Augustus we meet for the first time the publication of general accounts (*rationes*) of the public funds. At his death full details of the state's finances were in the hands of his personal slaves and freedmen. The public post of *a rationibus* (first held by imperial freedmen, later by senior equestrians) soon emerged. By the late 1st cent. AD this official was responsible for estimating the revenues and expenditure of the state. Secondly, direct taxation in the provinces, in the form of the poll tax and the land tax, was placed on a new footing through the introduction by *Augustus and *Agrippa of periodic provincial censuses. These mapped out the human and physical resources of the provinces and formed the basis for the assessments of tribute for each city and its territory. Whenever a new province was annexed, a census was taken. Provincial governors and imperial procurators supervised the collection of tribute; the process of collection devolved on the

individual civic authorities. (See DECAPROTI; DECEMPRIMI). Thirdly, Rome's revenues were vastly increased, although no secure figures survive. The annexation of new provinces (that of Egypt in 30 BC was especially important) of itself increased revenues. A new array of indirect taxes were introduced. The most important were, probably, the *vicesima hereditatum* (5% tax on inheritances) of AD 6 (hypothecated to the discharge payment for veterans) and the *quinta et vicesima venalium mancipiorum* (4% tax on the sale of slaves) of AD 7 (hypothecated to the pay of the *vigiles). The first three centuries AD also saw the steady accretion of landed property (via legacies, gifts, and confiscations) in the hands of the emperor. The importance of revenue from such crown property was considerable, if unquantifiable, and is already manifest in Augustus' own account, in his *Res gestae*, of his expenditure on public needs. By the late 2nd cent. there were two departments of crown property, the *patrimonium* and the *res privata*, though the distinction between them remains obscure. This formidable array of revenues (tribute in cash and kind, indirect taxes, revenues from crown property) enabled the imperial state to carry out, on a *routine* basis, key political functions such as the distribution of the corn-dole at Rome, the upkeep of the imperial court, the construction and maintenance of an elaborate road network (see ROADS) across the empire, the payment of salaries to senatorial and equestrian officials, and, above all, the funding of the vast standing armed forces of *c*.350,000 men. This fiscal system was predicated, in its mature form in the 2nd cent., on a basic predictability of expenditure and revenue and on the state's ability to exercise uncontested authority over the territory of the empire. However, potential problems in the form of sudden emergencies or increases in expenditure were already apparent in the later 2nd cent. The great northern wars under Marcus *Aurelius rapidly depleted the reserves of the treasury. In turn the major pay rises for the army of *Severus and *Caracalla were funded in part by significant debasements of the silver coinage. (See COINAGE, ROMAN.) The generalized political and military crisis, which enveloped the empire from the 230s onwards, was to shatter the fiscal apparatus and its preconditions. The state's ability to raise revenues was undermined by its failure to maintain routine central authority over the empire; the census-system collapsed, invasion and civil war destroyed accumulated capital and crops. To meet its needs the state resorted to irregular and arbitrary requisitions in kind and to runaway debasement of the coinage. By the 260s the precious-metal content of the silver coinage had been reduced to about 5 per cent. Hyper-inflation wrecked the whole monetary system.

A measure of stability was only restored to the public finances with the reassertion of central authority over the empire. *Diocletian, in a striking repetition of the measures of Augustus, re-established censuses throughout the empire. Payments of tax (predominantly in kind) were assessed by units of population (*capitatio*) and of land (*iugatio*), although the principles and workings of this system, which certainly varied from area to area, are still subject to debate. The finances of the empire were now managed through three departments. The *res privata* dealt primarily with imperial property. The *sacrae largitiones* controlled mines, mints, and state factories, collected taxes and levies in cash, and paid donatives to the troops. (See DONATIVUM.) The office of the praetorian prefects, the most important of the three, was responsible for the rations of soldiers and officials, for the maintenance of the *cursus publicus* (see POSTAL SERVICE) and of most public buildings, and for calculating annually the required rate of the indiction to produce the supplies in kind.

Frank, *Econ. Survey* 1 and 5; Jones, *Later Rom. Emp.* 411 ff.; E. Badian, *Publicans and Sinners* (1972); R. MacMullen, *Roman Government's Responses to Crisis, AD 235–337* (1986); P. A. Brunt, *Roman Imperial Themes* (1990).   G. P. B.

fire (πῦρ, *ignis*) has special status in ancient myth, religion, cosmology, physics, and physiology. According to Greek myth, *Prometheus stole it from the gods for mortals with dire consequences, and the name of the god *Hephaestus is often synonymous with it. Fire figures prominently in the cosmologies of *Heraclitus, *Parmenides, the Pythagoreans (see PYTHAGORAS (1)), and *Empedocles, to name only a few.

The status of fire as an element presented problems throughout antiquity. *Theophrastus noted at the beginning of his treatise *De igne* ('On Fire') that 'of the simple substances fire has the most special powers'; much of the rest of the work is concerned with describing its various manifestations, and coming to terms with the problem of how such an element can only exist in the company of a material substrate, and how it can generate itself and be generated in such a variety of ways. Heat, flame, and light are different species of fire in many theories including that of *Aristotle. Fire's dynamic properties, and its natural tendency to move upwards in space, figure in all kinds of physiological and cognitive theories. In many biological theories, fire's special status is linked to breath, and life itself. In Stoic physics (see STOICISM), fire is the one element which remains constant even when one particular world-order comes to an end. The Stoic *Cleanthes insisted that fire, as heat, gave the whole world its coherence.

In purely practical terms, fire was not easy to kindle, and the easiest way to ensure its availability was to keep a flame or glowing embers (ζώπυρα) burning. If a fire went out, and could not be relit from a neighbour's hearth, it could be restarted by rubbing together two pieces of wood surrounded by tinder. The fire-drill (πυρεῖον, *igniarium*, *ignitabulum*) consisted of a drill and a base made of hardwood. The drill was rotated with the aid of a bow-like contrivance. Fire could also be kindled from sparks struck from flint or pyrite, or with the help of a burning-glass. Burning-glasses are mentioned by *Aristophanes (1) (*Clouds* 766 ff.), but this method of fire-lighting seems to have been quite rare; it may be the case that *Archimedes knew that fire could be kindled by suitably arranged mirrors, although the story that he set fire to the Roman fleet besieging Syracuse in this way must be apocryphal.

Fire is also normally essential to animal sacrifice, see SACRIFICE, GREEK. See also: PNEUMA; ELEMENTS.

TEXT Theophrastus, *De igne*, ed. and trans. V. Coutant (1971). C. H. Whitman, *Homer and the Homeric Tradition* (1967), ch. 7; W. D. Furley, *Studies in the Use of Fire in Ancient Religion* (1981).   J. T. V.

Firmicus Maternus, Iulius, of *Syracuse, wrote (AD 334–7) an astrological treatise, *Mathesis*, in eight books, the first containing an apologia for *astrology. In this book he promised to provide a Latin summary of the wisdom of Babylonian and Egyptian astrologers. In doing so he reveals considerable ignorance of the technical aspects of the subject; the panegyric on *Constantine (1) in book 1 is however of considerable interest, as is the discourse on the lingering death of *Plotinus (*Math.* 1. 10. 13–14, 1. 7. 14–22). He later converted to *Christianity and wrote *Concerning the Error of Profane Religions*, a blistering attack upon traditional cult in which he urged *Constantius II and *Constans to eradicate paganism (343–50). The most interesting

features of this work are his effort to contrast pagan symbolism with Christian, his accounts of the origins of some ancient cults, and the insight that he offers into the impact of Constantinian legislation against traditional cults in the western empire.

TEXTS *Mathesis*, P. Monat (1992–   ), with trans.; *De errore*, R. Turcan (1982), with trans. English translations: *Mathesis*, J. R. Bram (1975); *De errore*, C. Forbes (1970).   D. S. P.

first-fruits (ἀπαρχαί, see also APARCHĒ). The custom of offering firstlings to the gods from the produce of agriculture, hunting, or fishing was widespread in ancient Greece, ranging in scale from simple gifts in humble agrarian settings to organized donations made in the context of the Eleusinian *mysteries. One common form is known as *panspermia*, the bringing of a mixture of fruits at various festivals, sometimes cooked in a pot (at the *Thargelia and *Pyanopsia). *Thalusia* are, according to the lexicographers, the *aparchai* of the fruits and the first loaf baked after the threshing. Firstlings of animal sacrifice are offered by *Eumaeus in *Od.* 14. 414–53. At the mysteries *aparchai* of wheat and barley are requested of all Athenians, allies, and even other Greeks, to be delivered after the spring harvest, and were sold to provide sacrifices and a dedication (*IG* 1³. 78). In the opinion of the Greeks first-fruits were brought in order to ensure fertility. They survive in ecclesiastical usage today under the ancient name κόλλυβα.

Nilsson, *GGR* 1³. 127–30; Burkert, *GR* 66–8.   K. C.

fiscus originally meant 'basket' or 'money-bag' and thence came to denote the private funds of an individual or, in an administrative context, to mean the public funds held by a provincial governor. In the Principate it came to denote both the private funds of the emperor and the whole financial administration controlled by the emperor.

The questions of the origins, legal nature, and revenues of the imperial *fiscus*, of its relationship to the *aerarium, and of the normal meaning of the term remain hotly disputed. Three principal, if overlapping, views exist.

1. The *fiscus* was the property of the emperor, its income was formed principally by the revenues of the imperial provinces (Mommsen, *Röm. Staatsr.* 2³. 998 ff.). On this view the distinction between *fiscus* and *aerarium* was a product of the 'dyarchy' of emperor and senate and of the division of the provinces.

2. *Fiscus* was used originally only of the private funds of the emperor (e.g. Sen. *Ben.* 7. 6. 3.), by extension from the usage relating to private persons. Its revenues came at first from properties, gifts, and inheritances, plus probably *aurum coronarium* and *manubiae. Its steady acquisition of wider sources of income represents an encroachment of the emperor on the public domain.

3. The *fiscus* came to operate as the central imperial treasury. Its officials were responsible for the administration and oversight of the revenues of the imperial state (both public taxes and the crown property and revenues of the emperor) and for their disbursement.

Although our sources are confused and confusing, it is probable that the third meaning became the dominant usage, a usage which reflected the centralization of control over the financial resources of the imperial state under the authority of the emperor and his agents. It is clear that by the end of the 1st cent., if not before, the *fiscus* was a recognized legal entity. *Nero appointed a praetor to hear cases between the *fiscus* and private persons (*Dig.* 1. 2. 2. 32), while *Hadrian instituted the post of *advocatus* *fisci* to represent the *fiscus* in such cases. The legal writers of the late 2nd and 3rd cents. indicate that the *fiscus* had a number of important privileges in litigation; in this period such cases were normally judged by imperial procurators (see PROCURATOR). Indeed fiscal jurisdiction became a major sphere of administrative law which could be contrasted with both public and private law (*Dig.* 3. 6. 13).

A number of other specific *fisci* (e.g. *fiscus Asiaticus, fiscus Alexandrinus, fiscus castrensis*) are attested, but little is known of their relationship to the *fiscus*. Only the *fiscus Judaicus* is relatively well understood. It received the special poll tax of two denarii a year paid by all Jews after the revolt of 66–70. See FINANCE, ROMAN.

O. Hirschfeld, *Die kaiserlichen Verwaltungsbeamten* (1905), 29 ff., 48 ff.; H. Last, *JRS* 1944, 51 ff.; A. H. M. Jones, *Studies in Roman Government and Law*, ch. 6; F. Millar, *JRS* 1963, 29 ff.; P. A. Brunt, *Roman Imperial Themes* (1990), ch. 7; M. Goodman, *JRS* 1989, 40 ff.

F. G. B. M.; G. P. B.

fish, sacred Fish, hard to classify biologically and inhabitants of the alien world of water, had a considerable role in ancient religion: in diet, they were sometimes taboo (various species to Pythagoreans, see PYTHAGORAS (1), and in Egypt), and sometimes ingredients in ritual meals (as in Samothrace). They were kept in *sanctuaries, and sometimes used to provide *oracles (as at Sura in *Lycia). The most famous fish observances were connected with the Syrian cult of *Atargatis (Xen. *An.* 1. 4. 9; Lucian, *Syr. D.*), which spread to other areas (*Syll.*[3] 997 is a set of regulations for the care of the fish of this cult at Smyrna): the priests ate the fish, which were prohibited to other worshippers. Fish became important in early Christianity, perhaps in a Syrian tradition, but also because of the acrostic ICHTHYS (Ἰ(ησοῦς) Χ(ριστὸς) θ(εοῦ) υ(ἱὸς) σ(ωτήρ): Jesus Christ, Son of God, Saviour).

F. J. Dölger, *ΙΧΘΥΣ* (1910, 1928–43).　　　N. P.

fishing Fish populations of the *Mediterranean are less abundant than those of the oceans. Gradients of temperature and salinity resulting from the depth and the closure of the ecosystem, however, promote the life cycle of several important species on the continental shelves (but see FOOD AND DRINK). The migratory habits of many important species bring them into contact with many Mediterranean islands and coastlands.

Since the routes of the shoals are far from predictable, places where their movements are topographically constrained (such as straits like Messina (see MESSANA), the *Bosporus (1), or *Hellespont, or lagoons and their entries) are of obvious importance. Numbers are very variable from year to year: gluts occur, but dearth is so frequent as to make it unwise to make fish protein more than a supplement (if a locally and occasionally important one) to a subsistence diet. The nutritional usefulness is greatly increased by processing to make the resource sustainable in times of general dearth, and movable inland or by sea: drying and salting are the principal techniques, and the evaporite salt of pans on the fringes of lagoons used for fishery anyway constituted an important symbiotic resource. The salt in salt fish (with the minerals in the fish) was probably of as much dietary importance as the protein.

Even in conditions of glut, and assuming very favourable conditions for fishing, total yields cannot have constituted an important aggregate contribution to the protein needs of even small ancient populations, compared with *cereal or legume staples (see FOOD AND DRINK). They did, however, play a significant role in diversifying a diet based on those staples, which was important both nutritionally and culturally in the classic Mediterranean pairing of staple and 'relish'—in Greek *opson*. Salted or pickled fish was the *opson par excellence* (the mod. Greek *psari*, 'fish', is derived from *opsarion*), and widely available for use in small quantities.

To the producer, this demand gave the catch the economic status of a cash crop, and enabled the secondary purchase of more protein than could easily have been acquired through consuming the fish. On this base of widely disseminated eating of fish-pickle, the fisherman could rely on a still more lucrative market in fresh fish which could fetch high prices in luxury provision markets. This combination of an urbane—and urban—ready availability of fish *opsa* with the opulent associations of fresh fish prized by the connoisseur underlies the great prominence of fish in the Athenian comic tradition. What had been characteristic of Athens became a feature of most towns in the Hellenistic and Roman periods; study of the *amphorae reveals the scale and complexity of the trade in *garum* (as the pickle came to be known), while the competitive consumption of the exquisites of high society provided a continuing stock of anecdote about colossal prices and singular specimens. The fisherman became a type of opportunism and poverty, proverbially wild, but a familiar and parasitical accompaniment to all that was best about stylish living.

Fishing in the open sea was chancy and hazardous, but essential for the most prized fish. Many local markets were supplied from the rocky shores. The fisheries of the formerly extensive wetland lagoons of the Mediterranean coasts were the easiest to develop artificially, because they were sheltered, shallow, and had controllable inlets and outlets, and systematic pisciculture grew from their management. Both archaeological and literary evidence shows the extent to which Roman pisciculture developed, and the elaboration of fishponds for both fresh and salt-water fish. Processing plants for making pickle were also built on a grand scale, from the early Hellenistic period in the Black Sea area, and in the Roman period on the coasts of southern Spain and Mauretania. This economy depended on, and is an interesting indicator of, a developed interdependence of markets in the Mediterranean. See COSA; MEALS; OPPIAN.

T. Gallant, *A Fisherman's Tale* (1985); R. I. Curtis, *Garum and Salsamenta* (1991).　　　N. P.

flamines, Roman priests within the college of the *pontifices. There were three major, twelve minor *flamines*, each of them assigned to the worship of a single deity, though this did not preclude their taking part in the worship of other deities, as when the *flamen Quirinalis* conducted the ritual for *Robigus on April 25. The three major ones were the *flamen Dialis, Martialis*, and *Quirinalis*—of *Jupiter, *Mars, and *Quirinus; according to the system of Georges Dumézil, these three gods formed the most ancient and senior triad of Roman gods, representing the three Indo-European functions of law, warfare, and production. Of the twelve deities served by a minor *flamen*, we know ten, including *Ceres, *Flora, and *Volcanus; but next to nothing is known of their priests' duties.

The three major *flamines* were always patricians and chosen by the members of the pontifical college, never elected. The *Dialis* in historic times was bound by an elaborate system of ritual rules, marking the holiness of his person and protecting it from pollution (Gell. *NA* 10. 15). They meant that he and his wife (the *flaminica*) had perpetual religious obligations. If these rules

599

originally applied to other *flamines* as well, they had been much relaxed by the later republic, for they could hold high office, even up to the consulate; successive *pontifices maximi* did, however, dispute the right of the *flamines* to abandon priestly duty, leave Rome, and so hold provincial commands, like other politician-priests; in the case of the *Dialis*, this right was still disputed when the priesthood lapsed, for unknown reasons, between 87 and *c*.12 BC. In this gap, we know that the rituals were maintained by the pontifices. Since the flaminate was the only priesthood devoted to a specific deity, it was the natural model for the new priesthood devised first for Caesar and for successive emperors after their deaths. Specific rules and privileges were borrowed from old to new *flamines*, but not the full set of restrictions. See CONCILIUM; RULER-CULT.

Wissowa, *RK* 504–7; G. Dumézil, *Jupiter, Mars, Quirinus* (1941); S. Weinstock, *Divus Julius* (1971), 305–8, 401–10; J. H. Vanggaard, *The Flamen: A Study in the History and Sociology of Roman Religion* (1988).

J. A. N.

Flamininus See QUINCTIUS FLAMININUS, T.

Flaminius (1) (*RE* 2), **Gaius,** was the only politician before the Gracchi to mount a serious challenge to the senatorial establishment on behalf of the *populares* (see OPTIMATES, POPULARES). The tradition, initially influenced by Q. *Fabius Pictor, presents a hostile picture of him, particularly so *Polybius (1), *Livy, and sources dependent on Livy, and it is hard to separate fact from fiction. A *novus homo*, he was tribune of the *plebs* 232 BC, and, against opposition led by Q. *Fabius Maximus Verrucosus, carried a law distributing the *ager Gallicus*—land between Ravenna and Sena Gallica, confiscated from the *Senones 50 years earlier—in individual lots to needy Roman citizens. Polybius describes the law as the beginning of the perversion of the people, and claims that it caused the Gallic invasion of 225. Praetor in 227, Flaminius was the first annual governor of Sicily. As consul in 223 he led the first Roman army to cross the river Po (*Padus), and won a victory over the *Insubres. Polybius is critical of his generalship. Later sources say that prodigies (see PORTENTS) caused the senate to annul the results of the elections, and they sent a letter to the consuls ordering them to abdicate, but Flaminius refused to open it until after the battle. It is said that his triumph was voted by the people, and according to Plutarch the consuls were eventually forced to abdicate. He may have been appointed *magister equitum* by the dictator Q. Fabius Maximus Verrucosus, probably in 221, but they had to abdicate because of a portent during the procedure. As censor in 220 he built the *via Flaminia and the Circus Flaminius. He is said to have been the only senator to support the law of Q. *Claudius in 218. Livy portrays him as being opposed by virtually the whole senate; in fact he may have had the support of the Scipios and their allies. He was elected consul for the second time for 217, is said to have neglected to take the *auspicia at Rome, to have entered office at *Ariminum, and to have ignored unfavourable omens. He took up position at *Arretium, but *Hannibal marched past him towards the heart of Etruria. Flaminius followed, and because of morning fog was caught in ambush at Lake *Trasimene. He was killed and 15,000 men with him. The defeat was ascribed to his neglect of religious observances.

Scullard, *Rom. Pol.* 44–55; Walbank, *HCP* 1. 192–3, 207–10, 410–20; Z. Yavetz, *Athenaeum* 1962, 325–44; R. Develin, *Ant. Class.* 1976, 638–43, and *Rh. Mus.* 1979, 268–77; A. M. Eckstein, *Senate and General* (1987), 10–18.

J. Br.

Flaminius (2) (*RE* 3), **Gaius,** son of the preceding, was praetor

in 193 BC, when he was governor of Hither Spain; the senate rejected his attempt to have one of the urban legions assigned to him. He remained in Spain until 190, and was elected consul for 187. He defended M. *Fulvius Nobilior against the attacks of his colleague M. *Aemilius Lepidus (1). Both consuls were assigned to Liguria; Flaminius defeated the Friniates and the Apuani, and built a road (not to be confused with the *via Flaminia built by his father) from *Bononia (1) (Bologna) to *Arretium (Arezzo).

J. Briscoe, *ANRW* 2. 30. 2. 1101.

J. Br.

Flavia (*RE* 227) **Domitilla,** *Domitian's niece, was exiled and her husband, the consul *Flavius Clemens, executed in AD 95 on a charge of atheism, or disrespect for the Roman gods. Domitilla perhaps espoused Judaism, though *Eusebius (*Hist. Eccl.* 3. 18) believed that she favoured *Christianity (his reference to her as niece of Clemens is probably a simple error). The Christian 'Coemeterium Domitillae' on the via Ardeatina may be connected with her.

E. M. Smallwood, *CPhil.* 1956, 8; M. Sordi, *Atti Congr. Inter. Std. Vespasiani* (1981), 150.

J. B. C.

Flavia Iulia, daughter of *Titus by his second wife, was born *c*. AD 65 just before her parents' divorce. She married her cousin T. *Flavius Sabinus, and after his execution (*c*.84) lived with her uncle Domitian as his mistress. She died in 91, and was deified.

PIR[2] F 426; B. Jones, *The Emperor Domitian* (1992), 38 ff. G. E. F. C.

Flavian emperors and period See ROME, HISTORY § 2.2.

Flavius (*RE* 15), **Gnaeus,** who lived around 300 BC, was the son of a freedman of Appius *Claudius Caecus, whose secretary he became. Sextus *Pomponius says that he purloined and published a manuscript compiled by Appius containing formulas used in litigation or 'actions in law' (*legis actiones*: see LAW AND PROCEDURE, ROMAN, § 2. 2). Other writers assume that Flavius compiled the book himself or had Appius' consent. This book (Flavius' civil law, *Ius civile Flavianum*) was supposedly the first to publicize the *legis actiones*, previously a monopoly of the pontiffs; and in his term as aedile (304) Flavius is said to have published a calendar of court-days on which *legis actiones* were permitted, again revealing a secret (see FASTI). As a result of these services he became, despite his humble origin, a tribune of the people, senator, and curule aedile. Discounting the democratic colouring, we may accept that Flavius published the *legis actiones*, certainly no secret, in a convenient form and that he gave out an improved version of the calendar, hitherto difficult of access.

J. G. Wolf, *Gött. Nachr.* 1980, no. 2; Wieacker, *RRG* 1, 524–7; F. Schulz, *History of Roman Legal Science* (1946), 9–10.

T. Hon.

Flavius Caper (2nd cent. AD), grammarian whose lost treatises *On Latinity* (concerning orthography, morphology, and semantics) and *On Nouns of Ambiguous Gender* (drawing on the elder Pliny) were much used by later writers. Two extant treatises attributed to a Caper, on orthography and on words of ambiguous or disputed form (Keil, *Gramm. Lat.* 7. 92–107, 107–12), are not his.

PIR[2] F 271; Herzog–Schmidt, § 438. R. A. K.

Flavius (*RE* 62 and Suppl. 12) **Clemens** (consul AD 95), grandson of *Vespasian's brother *Flavius Sabinus (the *praefectus urbi*) and husband of *Flavia Domitilla (the niece of *Domitian); an ineffectual person ('contemptissimae inertiae', Suet. *Dom.* 15. 1), he was put to death and his wife exiled soon after his consulate. They are said to have been guilty of ἀθεότης (impiety), by implication of practising Judaism (Cass. Dio 67. 14. 1 f.); later tradition alleges that they were Christians. Domitian intended two of the seven children (*ILS* 1839) of Clemens—Vespasian and Domitian as they were to be called, see FLAVIUS DOMITIANUS, T.—to succeed him; they are not heard of after 96. According to Suetonius, Clemens' death hastened that of Domitian: want of an adult heir probably encouraged assassins.

B. Jones, *The Emperor Domitian* (1992), see index.　　R. S.; B. M. L.

Flavius (*RE* 78) **Domitianus, Titus,** son of *Flavius Clemens, *Domitian's cousin, and *Flavia Domitilla. He and his brother were named by Domitian as his successors, receiving respectively the names Domitian and Vespasian. *Quintilian tutored them.

J. B. C.

Flavius (*RE* 88) **Fimbria, Gaius,** son of a *novus homo* (consul 104 BC as colleague of C. *Marius (1)), supported L. *Cornelius Cinna (1), killed some eminent men after Cinna's capture of Rome, and tried to assassinate or prosecute Q. *Mucius Scaevola (2) after the death of Marius (86). Sent to Asia as legate of the consul L. *Valerius Flaccus (3), he killed Flaccus and took over his army (85). Ruthless but successful, he nearly captured *Mithradates VI, but L. *Licinius Lucullus (2) allowed him to escape, to negotiate with *Sulla. After they had made peace, Sulla attacked Fimbria with overwhelming superiority and forced him to commit suicide. The two legions of *Fimbriani* were not allowed to return: their remnants still fought under Lucullus until released by A. *Gabinius (2).　　E. B.

Flavius (*RE* 166; Suppl. 12) **Sabinus** (suffect consul ?47), born AD 8 at latest, elder brother of the emperor *Vespasian. Like him he took part in the invasion of *Britain (AD 43). He was legate (see LEGATI) of *Moesia for seven years (*c*.53–60) and *praefectus urbi* for twelve according to Tac. *Hist.* 3. 75, necessitating an additional tenure before the governorship (?56–60; 61–8; 69); many suspect the text, or the historian. When the Flavian forces approached Rome in December 69 he had all but completed negotiations for the abdication of A. *Vitellius, but was set upon by auxiliary troops of the German armies. After a siege on the *Capitol, where he and his son and grandsons had taken refuge, he was taken to Vitellius and killed. In Tacitus' judgement 'there was no question of his integrity and sense of justice; he talked too much'.

G. Townend, *JRS* 1961, 54 ff.; K. Wallace, *Hist.* 1987, 343 ff.; M. Griffin, *Seneca* (1976), 456 f.; B. Levick, *The Emperor Vespasian* (1996), see indexes.　　R. S.; B. M. L.

Flavius (*RE* 169) **Sabinus, Titus,** grandson of *Flavius Sabinus, son of the Flavius Sabinus who commanded Othonian troops (see OTHO); held his first suffect consulship in AD 69 (Tac. *Hist.* 1. 77; 2. 36). He was married to the emperor *Titus' daughter *Flavia Iulia, who allegedly was *Domitian's mistress. Sabinus was consul in 82 with Domitian, and was executed on the ground that the herald had declared him elected not consul but emperor, probably in 82–3, when the *Chronicle* of *Eusebius mentions punitive measures by the emperor (cf. Cass. Dio 67. 3. 3), although a later election to a second consulship (87) has been canvassed. His disgrace perhaps involved the banishment of *Dio Cocceianus (*Or.* 13. 1).

See bibliog. to FLAVIUS SABINUS. B. Jones, *The Emperor Domitian* (1992), see index.　　G. E. F. C.; B. M. L.

Flevo lacus, the modern Ijsselmeer, originally an estuarine lake opening to the North Sea. It became accessible from the Rhine after *Drusus' canalization (*c*.12 BC) of the Vecht (*Fossa Drusiana*,

see CANALS), and thus provided the commanders of the early Julio-Claudian German campaigns with a handy sea-route to the Ems, Weser, and Elbe. In the 3rd cent. AD it appears to have joined with the North Sea as the result of the submerging of land to its north and west.

C. M. Wells, *The German Policy of Augustus* (1972), 101 ff.　　J. F. Dr.

flight of the mind In *Pindar (fr. 292 Snell–Maehler) and *Bacchylides (5. 16 ff) flight is a metaphor for elevation of poetic style. The philosopher *Parmenides (DK 28 B 1) spoke of his own ascent to knowledge as a journey in a heavenly chariot, and the mind's capacity to explore the universe was adduced by later thinkers as a proof of its innate divinity (Pl. *Tht.* 173; Xen. *Mem.* 1. 4. 17, etc.). When the *soul was conceived as separable, the image could be taken literally: in *Plato (1)'s *Phaedrus* (246c–248c) a pageant of celestial chariots is an allegory for the initial state of souls, and in such works as Cicero's *Somnium Scipionis* ascent to the stars is the destiny of the good soul after death. Cicero depends on Plato's *Timaeus* (41d–e), perhaps through *Posidonius (2); but *Maximus (1) of Tyre appeals to the legend of *Aristeas as evidence that the soul is immortal and capable of flight (10. 2; cf. 11. 9–10). The motif is found in popular theosophy (e.g. *Hermetica*, ed. W. Scott (1924), 1. 24–7), while parody in Hermias (*Irrisio* 17), *Lucretius (1. 66 ff), Horace (*Carm.* 1. 28. 4), and even perhaps *Aristophanes (1) (*Clouds* 225, 1503) suggests that it was frequent in Pythagoreanism (see PYTHAGORAS (1)). In the pseudo-Platonic *Axiochus* (370d–e) a discourse on immortality is said to have translated the hearer's mind to the upper regions, the metaphorical flight being made to anticipate the soul's ascent to heaven; and once again a parody in Lucretius (3. 14 ff) may imply that the thought is common.

R. M. Jones, *CPhil.* 1926.　　M. J. E.

Flora (Oscan *Flusia*: Conway, *Ital. Dial.* nos. 46; 175 a; L 24), an Italian goddess of flowering or blossoming plants, mainly cereals (also found in Agnone, Vittorino, and Furfo, as well as Rome). The antiquity of her cult in Rome is proved by the existence of a *flamen Floralis* (see FLAMINES), but her festival is not in the 'calendar of Numa' and therefore was movable (*feriae conceptivae*) Flora had an old temple on the *Quirinal, dedicated on 3 May, but, shortly after the foundation of the Floralia in 240–1 BC, and on the advice of the Sibylline books, she was given a second temple in 238 close to the Circus Maximus (Plin. *HN* 18. 286; cf. Ziolkowski, *Temples*, 31 ff.). Its dedication day was 28 April (*fasti Praenestini*; rededication by *Tiberius on 13 August, *fasti Allifani*). The games (*ludi Florales*) were celebrated annually from 173 BC (Ov. *Fast.* 5. 329 f., from 28 April to 3 May). These included farces (*mimi* (see MIME)) of a highly indecent character (Ov. ibid. 331 with Frazer's comm.). She is often considered a foreign, heavily Hellenized, goddess (see HELLENISM). Some think that her Hellenization took place in Italy (Wissowa *RK* 197; F. Altheim, *Terra mater* (1931), 132; Radke, *Götter*, 129 ff.). A middle way is taken by Le Bonniec (195 ff.), who thinks that only the obscene part of the Floralia are of Hellenic origin. But there is no decisive reason for seeing Flora as a foreign goddess.

Latte, *RR* 73; H. Le Bonniec, *Le Culte de Cérès à Rome des origines à la fin de la République* (1958), 195 ff.; *LIMC* 4 / 1 (1988), 137 ff.

H. J. R.; J. Sch.

Florentia (mod. Firenze, Florence) may have been in existence by the mid-first cent. BC (Florus 2. 8: text doubtful), but this, and the date of the *colonia* there, is disputed. It was laid out as a rectangular walled *castrum* (fort), and expanded rapidly. The forum, baths, theatre, and amphitheatre are known, as are two early Christian basilicas. It was the seat of a bishopric and a considerable fortress (Procop. *Goth. 3. 5. 6*), under the late empire, and by *Lombard times the capital of a duchy.

C. Hardie, *JRS* 1965, 122 ff.; M. L. Pegna, *Firenze, delle origini al medievo* (1974); L. J. F. Keppie, *Colonisation and veteran settlement in Italy* (1983), 175 ff.   E. T. S.; T. W. P.

Florianus, Marcus Annius (*RE* 46), praetorian prefect, and perhaps half-brother, of the emperor *Tacitus (2). On the death of Tacitus at Tyana (summer AD 276) he was recognized as emperor everywhere except Syria and Egypt, where he was challenged by *Probus. The two met for battle at Tarsus but Florianus, a mediocre general facing a more experienced rival, was killed by his own men (autumn 276).

PLRE 1. 37; R. Syme, *Emperors and Biography* (1971).   J. F. Dr.

Florus (*RE* 9), name of three Latin authors, usually, but not unanimously, identified as the same man.

(1) Lucius Annaeus (Iulius in Cod. Bamberg) Florus, Roman historian, author of the *Epitome bellorum omnium annorum DCC* ('Abridgement of all the Wars over 700 Years'); wrote no earlier than *Antoninus Pius to judge from pref. 8 and 1. 5. 5–8. His work is an outline of Roman history with special reference to the wars waged up to the reign of Augustus, with the suggestion that the latter had brought peace to the world. Some manuscripts describe it as an *epitome of *Livy; but it is sometimes at variance with Livy. The author also made use of *Sallust, *Caesar, and in one passage (pref. 4–8) probably the elder Seneca (see ANNAEUS SENECA (1), L.); and there are reminiscences of *Virgil and Lucan (see ANNAEUS LUCANUS, M.). It is planned as a panegyric of the Roman people. 'The tone is pious and ecstatic, condensed Livy' (Syme, *Tacitus* 2. 503).

(2) Publius Annius Florus, poet and rhetorician, author of the imperfectly preserved dialogue *Vergilius orator an poeta* ('Was Virgil an Orator or Poet?'); born in Africa, he took part as a youth in the Capitoline Games (see AGŌNES) under *Domitian, afterwards residing at Tarraco. Of the dialogue only a fragment of the introduction remains. It was probably written about AD 122; its diction closely resembles that of the *Epitome*.

(3) Annius Florus, poet-friend of *Hadrian, whose risky lines on the emperor beginning 'Ego nolo Caesar esse' ('I don't want to be a Caesar') had the honour of a retort from him (SHA *Hadr.* 16. 3). Other fragments are preserved (Riese, *Anth. Lat.* 1. 1, nos. 87–9 and 245–52). They are not sufficient to enable judgement to be passed on the author's poetry and hardly justify the theory that the famous *Pervigilium Veneris* is his work.

TEXTS O. Jahn (1852); E. Forster (Loeb, 1929); E. Malcovati (with *Dialogue*), 2nd. edn. (1972); P. Jal (Budé, 1967).

STUDIES F. Goodyear, *CHCL* 2. 664 ff., 898 ff. (with bibliog.); L. Bessone, *ANRW* 2. 34. 1 (1993), 80 ff. *PIR*² A 650.

E. S. F.; G. B. T.; A. J. S. S.

focalization See LITERARY THEORY AND THE CLASSICS; NARRATIVE, NARRATION.

foedus means a treaty, solemnly enacted, which established friendship, peace and alliance between Rome and another state in perpetuity. A *foedus* was distinct from *indutiae* ('truce'), which ended a state of war and lasted for an agreed number of years (up to a century). Treaties of alliance (*foedera*—hence 'federation' etc.) were either equal or unequal. An equal treaty (*foedus aequum*) set both parties on an equal footing, and enjoined each to give military assistance to the other in the event of a hostile attack. The earliest known example is the treaty of Spurius

*Cassius Vecellinus of 493 BC, the terms of which are given in Dion. Hal. *Ant. Rom.* 6. 95. In an unequal treaty (the term *foedus iniquum*, though attested in literature, was probably not an official formula) the second party was required to acknowledge and respect the *maiestas* (lit. 'greatness') of the Roman people, and was effectively compelled to provide Rome with military forces on demand. Treaties were often negotiated by Roman military commanders, but they needed ratification at Rome by a vote of the *comitia centuriata*. The religious formalities, which included oaths and sacrifices, were supervised by the *fetiales. Treaties were engraved on bronze tablets and either displayed in public, like the treaty of Spurius Cassius (Cic. *Balb.* 53), or kept in temples or other public buildings (Roman practice seems to have varied in this respect). The first two Carthaginian treaties (Polyb. 3. 22–3) are exceptional, and seem to have followed a non-Roman model different from the standard *foedus*.

For bibliography see SOCII.   A. N. S.-W.; T. J. Co.

folk-songs (Greek) The Greeks, like other peoples, had their folk-songs, often rooted in ancient popular and ritual traditions. However, it is impossible to give dates to the songs or to construct a history. They may be roughly classified as follows: (*a*) to gods (*Carm. pop.* 5, 8, 14, 25, 26); (*b*) ritual songs (ibid. 2); (*c*) occupational (ibid. 3, 23, 28); (*d*) apotropaic songs (ibid. 13); (*e*) love-songs (ibid. 7, 27).

TEXT Page, *PMG* 847–83; G. Lambin, *La Chanson grecque dans l'antiquité* (1992); D. A. Campbell (ed.), *Greek Lyric 5* (1993), 233–69.

C. M. B.; E. Kr.

folk-tale As an identifiable and critically useful category of prose narrative the folk-tale owes its broad characterization to a generalized abstraction of the typical themes, plots, structures, and characters of the popular stories collected by the Grimm brothers in Germany in the early 19th cent. and by A. N. Afanasiev in Russia 50 years later. These orally transmitted *Märchen*, polished and perfected over centuries by generations of peasant storytellers, tap into deep strata of psychological and social wisdom, and are badly served by their relegation to the nursery, as 'Fairy Tales', in modern societies. As a general rule, the stories engage protreptically and optimistically with the problems faced by the powerless (poor, young, unregarded) male hero in his attempts to assert himself in a world of hostile forces, aided by animal or supernatural helpers; the goal and climax consists in maturity and marriage. Encouraging or consolatory templates for female behaviour make a natural complement. But the range is wide, and the invention fertile. Aarne and Thompson attempted to gain an overview by laboriously classifying themes and motifs ('K1111.0.1. Learning to play fiddle: finger caught in cleft'), but an altogether more acute and sophisticated analytical approach was carved out by Vladimir Propp, who brilliantly showed how the apparently random proliferation of narrative possibilities could be reduced to an elegant algebra of permitted moves and structural sequences. Greek (and to a smaller extent Roman) tales offer a cornucopia of such themes, whose extent can only be hinted at here. The careers of *Perseus (1) and *Bellerophon are perfect exemplifications of the basic type (which can be traced even further back, to 13th-cent. Egypt, as with *The Tale of Two Brothers*). The Odyssean episode of the hero trapped in the giant's cave (see CYCLOPES; ODYSSEUS) finds parallels from Finland to Mongolia (see J. G. Frazer's appendix 13 to his Loeb edition of Apollodorus, and D. L. Page, *The Homeric Odyssey*, (1955, repr. 1976), ch. 1), and though some of these may be secondary refractions of the famous Homeric account (Fehling, see bibliog. below) it beggars belief that *all* other versions fall into this category; early oral diffusion of the powerfully attractive theme, from some undetermined source, seems probable. Herodotus too adapts many *Märchen* to the purposes of his Histories, notably the pranks of the unnamed trickster-thief who pitted his wits against the Pharaoh Rhampsinitus (2. 121), and who survives as the *Meisterdieb* of the Grimms' collection (no. 192); cf. also e.g. the tales of *Perdiccas (1) (8. 137), Euenius (9. 93), *Arion (2) (1. 24), or *Democedes (3. 135). Even 5th-century drama draws up plots from the folk-tale reservoir (*Sophocles (1)'s lost *Polyidus*, *Euripides' *Alcestis*), and the same is true of Hellenistic poetry (*Erysichthon, and Acontius and Cydippe, in *Callimachus (3)). There is at least a prima facie case for supposing that some ancient Greek tales have managed to retain their core structure intact through constant retellings right down to modern times (see esp. Dawkins 1950, no. 33, 'Myrmidonia and Pharaonia', as a version of the Erysichthon story). In Latin, the classical example is the Cinderella-like story of Cupid and Psyche, recounted in a much elaborated version by Apuleius in *Met.* books 4–6; see the separate edition by E. J. Kenney (1990). Even this brief sketch should make it clear that while this is a rich and underexploited field of research at least two obstacles stand in the way of any attempt to focus the subject more precisely: first, the impossibility of marking off Greek 'folk-tale' from myth, legend, saga, popular history, and biography, etc.; secondly, the fact that since our knowledge of the form in Graeco-Roman culture is by definition confined to preserved *literary* texts the relevant material is necessarily contaminated with features determined by its generic context. And it should be noted that D. Fehling has issued abrasive challenges both to the assumption that authors like Herodotus and Apuleius drew heavily on sub-literary popular narratives (1971, 1977) and to the hypothesis of continuity from antiquity to modern times (1972).

GENERAL S. Thompson, *The Folktale* (1946); V. Propp, *The Morphology of the Folktale* (Eng. trans. 1968); B. Bettelheim, *The Uses of Enchantment* (1975).

GREECE AND ROME W. Aly, *Volksmärchen, Sage und Novelle bei Herodot und seinen Zeitgenossen* (1921; rev. edn. 1969); W. R. Halliday, *Indo-European Folk-tales and Greek Legend* (1933); S. Trenkner, *The Greek Novella in the Classical Period* (1958); D. Fehling, *Herodotus and his 'Sources'* (1971; rev. Eng. trans. 1989), and *Amor und Psyche: Die Schöpfung des Apuleius und ihre Wirkung auf das Märchen* (1977).

MODERN GREECE R. M. Dawkins, *Forty-five Stories from the Dodekanese* (1950), and *Modern Greek Folktales* (1953); D. Fehling, *Rh. Mus.* 1972, 173–96. A. H. G.

follis A bag for coins, then—by the late 3rd or early 4th cent. AD—a bag containing a fixed number of coins, then a unit of account; the value of this unit of account varied over the centuries from the Tetrarchic period onwards. There is no clear evidence in practice that the term applied to an individual coin before the reforms of Anastasius (AD 491–518), though the metrological writers contain some confused statements which may be interpreted in this way.

A. Cameron, *Num. Chron.* 1964, 135–8; M. F. Hendy, *Studies in the Byzantine Monetary Economy* (1985), 338–42, 475–92. M. H. C.

Fonteius (*RE* 12), **Marcus**, began his career under L. *Cornelius Cinna (1), but joined *Sulla. He served in Spain and Macedonia and after his praetorship governed Transalpine Gaul (probably 74–72 BC), enthusiastically exacting men, money, and grain for the wars in Spain and elsewhere. Accused *repetundarum* (see REPETUNDAE), he was defended by Cicero in a speech partly extant and was probably acquitted. E. B.

Fontinalia, Roman festival on 13 October to Fons, god of *springs (Varro, *Ling.* 6. 22), outside the porta Fontinalis (Festus 75 Lindsay), perhaps at a shrine dedicated by C. Papirius Maso (consul 231 BC): Platner–Ashby 210. Fontus is dubious (Latte, *RR* 77 n. 1); some made *Janus father of Fons by Juturna: Arn. *Adv. nat.* 3. 29. C. R. P.

food and drink The ancient diet was based on cereals, legumes, oil, and wine. *Cereals, especially wheat and barley, were the staple food and the principal source of carbohydrates. They were eaten in many different ways, e.g. as porridge and bread. The rich could afford a more diversified diet and ate less cereal than the poor. *Athenaeus (1) describes many types of bread and *cakes. Probably only the rich could afford 'white' bread, but even the best bread available in antiquity was much coarser than modern bread.

Legumes (field beans, peas, chick-peas, lentils, lupins, etc.), a common find in archaeological excavations at *Pompeii, were an important part of the diet. They were incorporated into bread and complemented cereals because they are a rich source of protein.

The Greeks used the generic term *opson* for 'food eaten with bread or other cereal products' (*sitos* and *frumentum*). Fish, which might be fresh, dried, or pickled, occupied a prominent place in *opson*, especially at Athens. It was important as a source of protein and oils. Many species were known. However, fish are scarce in the Mediterranean because of the absence of large stretches of continental shelf off the coast (see FISHING). They probably did not make a major contribution to the diet. Shellfish were also eaten.

*Olive oil was the main source of fats, which are necessary to make a cereal-based diet palatable. Fats, which have a very high calorific value, were also obtained from other sources, e.g. sesame oil. The use of butter was a mark of *barbarians; so was the drinking of beer and to some extent that of *milk. Milk was generally used for making cheese. The most important beverage was *wine, usually diluted and often artificially flavoured. It was even consumed by young children. *Honey was used for sweetening.

Meat was a luxury for most people. In classical Athens it was generally eaten only at feasts accompanying religious festivals. (See SACRIFICE.) Poultry, game, and eggs played a large part in Roman cookery, but there was comparatively little butcher's meat, apart from pork and sometimes veal. Peasants generally kept pigs. Wild birds (partridges, quails, pheasants) were also eaten. The soldiers of the Roman army had a higher standard of living and a more varied diet than the bulk of the population of the Roman empire.

For ordinary people vegetables (e.g. onion, garlic, turnip, radish, lettuce, artichoke, cabbage, leek, celery, cucumber) provided the most important addition to the basic diet. Wild plants were also gathered for eating. Among fruit, *figs, grapes, apples, and pears played a leading part. (Potato, tomato, most citrus fruits, and banana were not available in antiquity.) Sauces, such as the Roman fish-sauce *garum* (see FISHING), and condiments and herbs were very popular. The Romans disliked the natural tastes of most cooked foods. This partiality for flavourings is an important thread of continuity from past to present in Mediterranean cookery. See COOKERY.

J. André, *L'Alimentation et la cuisine à Rome* (1981); L. Foxhall and H. Forbes, *Chiron* 1982, 41–89; T. W. Gallant, *A Fisherman's Tale* (1985); J. I. Miller, *The Spice Trade of the Roman Empire* (1969); J. Wilkins, D. Harvey and M. Dobson (eds.) *Food in Antiquity* (1995). J. R. S.

food supply

Greek For Greek city-states of the Archaic and Hellenistic periods the ethos of self-sufficiency (*autarkeia*) dominated the ideology of food supply. In reality few Greek cities ever outgrew the food production capacities of their territory and the small number which did responded by intensifying agricultural production. This is well documented in the case of Athens. However, most Greek states operated in politically and environmentally unstable conditions. Weather (see CLIMATE) and warfare posed constant, but unpredictably timed, hazards. Consequently, some degree of shortfall in food supply could be expected perhaps as often as once in five years.

By 'food' (*sitos*) is meant *cereals. Though other crops were grown and important in the ancient Greek diet, grain was the preferred staple, especially wheat and barley. Hence shortfalls in these crops proved the most problematic at all levels. Grain was at the heart of the political discourses which evolved around the problem of food supply in most city-states.

Grain was grown not by cities but by individual households, on private land. Therefore shortages had to be met with ad hoc measures on the part of government, city-states virtually never having either central grain production or storage facilities. General shortfalls in the cereal harvest enhanced class tensions, since wealthy landowners would not have suffered to the same degree as small-scale cultivators. Shortfalls also provided opportunities for the rich to gain political capital and to manipulate grain supplies. From the 4th cent. BC onwards, benefactions of grain by wealthy individuals are regularly documented in inscriptions, and become part of the political strategies employed in élite competition for power (see EUERGETISM).

City-states were empowered to do little in the likely event of grain shortage. Only one free, state-sponsored, grain distribution is known (Samos: *SEG* 1. 366). Generally states behaved as middlemen, aiming to encourage imports, or donations and subsidized sales by the rich (e.g. *IG* 5. 1. 1379; J. Pouilloux, *Choix d'inscriptions grecques* (1960), no. 34, p. 126; *IDélos* 442A 101; 399A 69–73). Incentives might be offered to private traders, but many were not citizens, and the profits they made were greatly resented (Lys. 22).

It is sometimes difficult to ascertain how 'genuine' food shortages were. It is perhaps significant that with one possible exception, barley, which was considered inferior for food, was not imported. Wheat, the preferred cereal (and most of the time probably the prerogative of the rich) was the usual grain from overseas. It is difficult to know how much of this imported wheat the poor ever ate. However, ensuring the supply of wheat itself became a political issue, as is shown by the careful diplomacy with which the Bosporan kingdom (a major supplier of wheat to Athens) was treated (see SPARTOCIDS). See AGRICULTURE, GREEK; FAMINE.

L. F.

Roman The growth of Rome to a city of perhaps 250,000 inhabitants in the time of the *Gracchi and of up to one million under *Augustus, far outstripping the productive capacity of her hinterland, created an unprecedented demand for imported foodstuffs. The supplying of Rome was always left mainly to private enterprise, and the main source was always Italy (including Sicily and Sardinia), but the political pressure on the Roman government to deal with actual or feared shortages led to some institutionalized public underpinning of the mechanisms of supply, which were enabled by exploitation of Rome's imperial revenues. In the early and middle republic individual magistrates competed either to

win popular favour by securing extra supplies from subject or allied states where they had some personal influence, or to win noble approval by quashing popular complaints. C. *Sempronius Gracchus took the momentous step of establishing a regular public distribution of a set monthly ration of grain (*frumentatio*) at a set price to adult male citizen residents, which P. *Clodius Pulcher made free in 58 BC. Other legislation alternately cut and increased the number of entitled recipients, called the *plebs frumentaria*, until in 2 BC Augustus stabilized it at or below 200,000. Augustus also reorganized the system of storage and distribution under an imperial appointee of equestrian status called the *praefectus annonae*, who also had a more general remit to watch over food supplies. This public supply (*annona*), drawing on the grain paid to the state as rent or tax in Sicily, Africa, and (from 30 BC) Egypt, helped the privileged minority who held tickets of entitlement (see TESSERA), which could be inherited or sold. But the monthly ration did not meet a family's need for grain, and the tickets did not necessarily go to the poor. All residents will still have relied on the private market to some extent (or, if they had them, on produce from their farms), and the majority will have used it for most of their supplies. Shortages could and did occur, especially in the supply of wheat (see CEREALS), leading emperors to make ad hoc interventions to hold down prices, or stimulating long-term improvements such as the successive new ports at *Ostia. Wealthy private individuals often gave free meals or tokens for food to their clients (see CLIENS), but this generosity was unreliable and also not particularly directed at the poor. At the end of the 2nd cent. AD *Septimius Severus added free *olive oil to the rations received by the *plebs frumentaria*, and in the 270s Aurelian added free pork and cheap *wine, and the monthly wheat ration was replaced with a daily issue of bread. As Rome ceased to be the empire's capital in the 4th cent., the responsibility for maintaining supplies to the decreasing population fell first on the senatorial nobility and then on the Church. See FAMINE; GRANARIES; NAVICULARII.

P. Garnsey, *Famine and Food Supply in the Graeco-Roman World: Responses to Risk and Crisis* (1988); G. Rickman, *The Corn Supply of Ancient Rome* (1980); P. Veyne, *Bread and Circuses* (partial Eng. trans. 1990); A. B. J. Sirks, *Food for Rome* (1991); E. Tengstrom, *Bread for the People: Studies of the Corn-Supply of Rome during the Later Empire* (1974). D. W. R.

Fordicidia (Sabine *Hordicidia*: Conway *Ital. Dial.* 1. 385; Varro, *Rust.* 2. 5. 6; Festus 91 Lindsay), Roman festival on 15 April, when a *forda* (pregnant cow) was sacrificed to *Tellus (Ov. *Fast.* 4. 630 ff. with F. Bömer's comm.; Tellus may not have featured in earlier times). It and the *Fornacalia were the only festivals which in historic times were organized on the basis of the *curiae* (1).

RE 5 A 794 ff.; Latte, *RR* 68 ff. C. R. P.

forgeries, literary

Greek The idea of literary property had already evolved by the 5th cent. BC, when *Herodotus (1) doubted the Homeric authorship of *Epigoni* and *Cypria* (2. 117, 4. 32); see EPIC CYCLE, para. 4. 5, 6. Even then, and even when bibliographic scholarship developed in the 3rd cent. BC, *pseudepigraphic literature continued to circulate. Forgeries form a subclass: works written, or at least attributed (it is often unclear which), with intent to deceive. Various overlapping motives can be distinguished. (1) Authority. *Solon and *Pisistratus allegedly interpolated the Homeric text in Athens' interest (Strabo 9. 1. 10 etc); Onomacritus inserted an oracle of his own among those of *Musaeus (1) (Hdt. 7. 6. 3). Gaps in the record invited filling: Musaeus and

*Orpheus (Pl. *Resp.* 364e), many Pythagorea and Epicharmea (see PYTHAGORAS (1); EPICHARMUS), the last paean of *Socrates (Diog. Laert. 2. 42), letters of *Euripides (*Vit. Arati.* 1, p. 10. 18 Martin). A Lycian temple displayed a letter (on papyrus) written by *Sarpedon from Troy (Plin. *HN* 13. 88). (2) Profit. Famous names fetched higher prices. *Aristotle found on sale bundles of forensic speeches 'by' *Isocrates' (fr. 140 R); *Lucian's 'False Critic' had sold a rhetorical *technē* of his own as the work of *Tisias (*Pseudol.* 30); *Galen came across a book passed off under his own name (*Scr. min.* 2, p. 91 Mueller). Antique copies fetched more than new ones: so *Juba (2) II of Mauretania bought manuscripts of Pythagoras that had been artificially yellowed (*FGrH* 275 T 11). (3) Malice. To embarrass *Theopompus (3), *Anaximenes (2) of Lampsacus forged the *Trikaranos* in his style (*FGrH* 72 T 6); *Heraclides (5) Ponticus (himself accused of forging tragedies of Thespis) was caught validating a fake tragedy of *Sophocles (1) (Diog. Laert. 5. 92 f). No doubt vexatious accusations were as common as actual forgeries.   P. J. P.

Latin The seven books on pontifical law by King Numa *Pompilius found in 187 BC must have been a forgery, i.e. a work written by someone other than Numa and deliberately passed off as the king's. During at least two periods, at the end of the 2nd cent. BC and at the beginning of the 2nd of our era, scholars raised doubts about items held in Roman libraries under famous names. It is not, however, at all clear how many of the 130 comedies attributed to *Plautus were composed with the precise purpose of cheating the public. Similarly unclear are the origins of the pieces cheerfully added to *Virgil's three famous works by *Suetonius and others. *Libraries, then as now, abhorred anonymous volumes. The rhetorical exercise of composing utterances appropriate to historical personages in particular situations of their known careers produced many works not originally designed to deceive anyone. Here may belong such things as *Cicero's letter to *Octavian, Sallust's letter to Caesar and his invectives against Cicero. The works of famous authors often acquired extra verses from nameless persons whose motives can only be guessed at. To be distinguished from forgery is the invention of a set of non-existent authors, as has been suggested in regard to the biographies of the *Historia Augusta*.   H. D. J.

W. Speyer, *Die literarische Fälschung im heidnischen und christlichen Altertum* (1971); A. Grafton, *Forgers and Critics* (1990).

Forma urbis, a plan showing the city of Rome after AD 203 at a scale of roughly 1:240, engraved on 151 slabs of marble decorating a wall of the temple of Peace, perhaps in the office of the *praefectus urbi* (urban prefect). About 10 per cent of the total remains, some fragments being known only from Renaissance drawings. A few pieces appear to belong to an earlier version presumably from the Flavian complex.

G. Carettoni, *Forma Urbis Romae* (1960); E. Rodriguez Almeida, *Forma Urbis Marmorea: Aggiornamento generale* (1981).   J. D.

Formiae (mod. Formia), on the *via Appia above Gaeta. A Volscian settlement, it was given part-citizen rights (*sine suffragio*) in 338 BC, and the full franchise in 188 BC (see CITIZENSHIP, ROMAN). It was a Hadrianic *colonia*, and its fine climate and surroundings made it a fashionable resort, with coastal *villas all the way from Formiae to Gaeta. Cicero was murdered at his villa in 43 BC, but the villa itself is not certainly identified. The town was destroyed by the Saracens in the 9th century.

S. Aurigemma and A. De Santis, *Gaeta, Formia, Minturno* (1955).
                E. T. S.; T. W. P.

Fornacalia, one of the movable *festivals (*feriae conceptivae*; cf. L. Delatte, *Ant. Class.* 1936, 391 ff.), tied to the Quirinalia (17 February) and celebrated then (*Fasti Praenestini*). It was called *stultorum feriae* (fools' festival) according to Ovid (*Fast.* 2. 531–2 with F. Bömer's comm. on 513; cf. Festus 304, 418, 419 Lindsay) because those too stupid to know their *curiae* celebrated then instead of on the proper day, proclaimed by the *curio maximus* (Ov. ibid. 527–8). This makes it a festival of the *curiae (1), not the people. It consisted of ritual either to benefit the ovens (*fornaces*) which parched grain, or to propitiate the obscure goddess Fornax (Ov. ibid. 525, 6. 314; Lactant. *Div. inst.* 1. 20. 35; Latte, *RR* 143).

A. Momigliano, *JRS* 1963, 110.   C. R. P.

fortifications

Greek In the Aegean area small towns with perimeter walls appear early in the bronze age (Khalandriani). More usual is the fortified acropolis, increasingly developed in the troubled times of the late bronze age (*Tiryns, *Mycenae, Athens (see ATHENS, TOPOGRAPHY). These are built with large irregular blocks of stone in Cyclopean style. With repairs, they survive as the principal defences of their location into the Classical period.

The simple yet robust brick walls of Old Smyrna (900–600 BC, J. M. Cook, *BSA* 1958/9, 35 ff.) illuminate the somewhat obscure position in the Dark Age and Archaic period. Extensive town walls began to develop in the 6th and, especially, 5th cents. BC. These are usually of mud-brick on a stone footing. The Athenian walls at *Pylos were built with stone facings, with rubble and clay packing, an increasingly common form of construction, while the system of *Long Walls shows how large-scale fortifications were used for strategic ends. Fourth-century improvements in *siegecraft and the introduction of *artillery created increasing problems. Fortification designers steadily responded to the challenge. Experiments were made to improve the structure of the walls, dividing their lengths into compartments and using binding courses through the entire thickness of the wall. Other methods saw variations to the fill, using mud-brick instead of clay packing, but these and the usual clay fills tended to dry out and crumble, leaving the wall vulnerable to a battering. Techniques employed by the Phoenicians at *Tyre, blocks of outsize dimensions and mortared together with gypsum were tried at Dura-*Europus, but the technique was not adapted in the Aegean area. A system apparently employed at Rhodes, buttressing the walls internally with arcading, may have helped defeat the siege-engines of *Demetrius (4) Poliorcetes, but again was not generally adapted. Towers increased in number and, from *Messene (369 BC) onwards, in height, leading to the tall towers equipped with artillery of the Hellenistic period (e.g. tall towers at *Aegosthena, *Perge). Their upper chambers were embrasured for defensive catapults. Walls, occasionally casemated for artillery (Perge, *Side, *Rhodes), became thicker and higher. A ditch (Posidonia, i.e. *Paestum) or ditches combined with outworks (*proteichisma*) (*Syracuse, *Selinus) attempted to hamper the approach of powerful Hellenistic siege-engines. The final defences of Syracuse, designed by *Archimedes, present the acme of Hellenistic fortification. Though the advantage was always with the attacker, defences sometimes included numerous sally-ports to facilitate active resistance. *Philon (2) of Byzantium (*c.*200 BC; cf. Vitr. *De arch.* 1. 5) admirably summarizes the full, relatively sophisticated Hellenistic defensive technique.
                I. A. R.; E. W. M.; R. A. T.

Fortuna/Fors

Roman Early Roman fortifications derived from Etruscan and Greek antecedents, which were both a defence and a civic monument. For the early wall of Rome attributed to Servius Tullius (6th cent. BC), see WALL OF SERVIUS. A free-standing stone wall of 4th-cent. date bounds the early *castrum* (fort) at *Ostia. The fortifications of Roman republican colonies in Italy usually took advantage of naturally defensible sites, with walls in ashlar or polygonal masonry and powerful gateways (e.g. *Cosa). The Punic and Greek wars familiarized the Romans with the methods of and defences against Hellenistic siege warfare, and the Civil Wars of the late republic promoted more advanced defensive ideas at some Italian sites such as modifications to the Servian wall at Rome and new walls at Ostia.

During the relative peace of the Principate urban fortifications were largely a matter of civic pride, requiring authorization from Rome. In the east, existing city walls were maintained and sometimes embellished by refacing and the provision of elaborate gates. Few new circuits were initiated. In the west, provision of fortifications was closely linked to status. Augustan veteran colonies generally received defences of carefully laid walls, towers of various shapes, and monumental gateways. At some the walls reflected the planning of military *camps (e.g. Aosta (*Augusta Praetoria)), at others the walls were impractically long, enclosing large, open areas (e.g. Nîmes (*Nemausus)); a monument more than a defence. A few other important western towns acquired walls before AD 200 (e.g. Trier (*Augusta Treverorum)), as did several in Africa. Britain had a tradition of 1st- and 2nd-cent. earthwork defences. Military defences (earth, timber, and turf to *c.* AD 100, stone thereafter) were more functional, but elaborate gateways suggest motives of display.

From the 3rd cent. AD the revival of Persia, barbarian invasions in Europe, and chronic civil war caused more general fortification. Late Roman defences, military and civilian, usually consisted of thick, high walls, regularly-spaced projecting towers (sometimes for artillery), small gateways, and large ditches. In the west, Rome was provided with an elaborate new circuit of defences (see WALL OF AURELIAN) in the later 3rd cent. Otherwise, urban defences tended to enclose relatively small areas (often less than 20 ha.: 50 acres), though care over facing and gates suggests a degree of monumentality. Some *villas (in the Balkans) and hilltop sites (in Gaul) were fortified. European barbarians were not equipped for siege warfare but in the east the Persians were (cf. Amm. Marc. 19; 31. 6. 4). There cities were strongly fortified, culminating in the monumental triple walls and moat of the land walls of *Constantinople under Theodosius II (408–50).

A. S. E. C.

GREEK F. G. Maier, *Griechische Mauerbauinschriften*, 2 vols. (1959, 1961); F. Krischen, *Die Stadtmauern von Pompeii und griechische Festungsbaukunst in Unteritalien und Sizilien* (1941); F. E. Winter, *Greek Fortifications* (1971); A. W. Lawrence, *Greek Aims in Fortification* (1979); J.-P. Adam, *L'Architecture militaire Grecque* (1982).

ROMAN I. A. Richmond, *The City Walls of Imperial Rome* (1930); T. W. Potter, *Roman Italy* (1987); J. Maloney and B. Hobley (eds.), *Roman Urban Defences in the West* (1983); S. Johnson, *Late Roman Fortifications* (1983).

Fortuna/Fors the goddess of Chance or Luck, Greek *Tyche, of great importance in Italian and Roman religion, but not thought by the Romans to be part of the oldest stratum of their religious system (no feast-day in the oldest calendar, and no *flamen*; see FLAMINES). Instead, her introduction was importantly attributed to the rather anomalous figure of King Servius

*Tullius, who was associated with several of the more important of her numerous cults at Rome (Plut. *Quaest. Rom.* 74). Oracles of Fortuna existed at *Antium (Macrob. *Sat.* 1. 23. 13) and at *Praeneste, where the important cult of Fortuna Primigenia (the First-born: Plut. *Quaest. Rom.* 106) was much embellished during the age of Roman and Italian success in Mediterranean conquest and its economic rewards. The combination of political achievement and a patronage of procreation is common in Fortuna-cults (for the latter, see e.g. *ILLRP* 101, dedication by a local woman to Praenestine Fortuna as daughter of *Jupiter, to secure procreation, and note the existence of an important cult of Fortuna Muliebris, Women's Luck).

At Rome the most important 'Servian' cults of Fortuna were that of Fors Fortuna on the right bank of the Tiber (e.g. Tac. *Ann.* 2. 41), and that of the *forum Boarium. Here Fortuna was twinned with the cult of *Matuta Mater (the goddesses shared a festival on 11 June), and the paired temples have been revealed in the excavations beside the church of S. Omobono: the cults are indeed archaic in date. The cult statue was draped in two togas, which rendered it practically invisible (Plin. *HN* 8. 197). Praenestine Fortuna Primigenia was adopted at the end of the 3rd cent. BC in an important cult of Fortuna Publica Populi Romani (the 'Official Good Luck of the Roman People') on the *Quirinal outside the porta Collina. No temple at Rome, however, rivalled the magnificence of the Praenestine sanctuary. The Fortune that won battles or wars was also the object of a number of cults, and the goddess in various guises was important to the presentation of late-republican leaders and the emperors (Augustus' cult of the 'Fortune of Return' (from duty in the provinces), Fortuna Redux, is an example).

J. Champeaux, *Fortuna: Recherches sur le culte de la Fortune à Rome et dans le monde romain des origines à la mort de César* 1 (1982); 2 (1987). N. P.

Fortunatae insulae See ISLANDS OF THE BLEST.

forum, an open square or market-place in a Roman town, hence the name of several Roman market towns such as Forum Appii, Iulii, etc. In contrast to the *forum Boarium (cattle market) and Holitorium (vegetable market) at Rome, the *forum Romanum was also a place of public business, a role later shared with the imperial fora. Public fora of this kind, combining political, judicial, and commercial functions, formed the focal point of most Roman towns particularly in the western empire. A typical forum, as at *Pompeii, was a long, rectangular open space flanked by a variety of public buildings, including variously temples, basilicas, speakers' platforms, senate-house, and other public offices, as well as *tabernae* (see INNS AND RESTAURANTS), often in an informal arrangement with colonnades on two or more sides (cf. Vitr. *De arch.* 5. 1. 1–4, 5. 2); the open space was adorned with honorific statues and other minor monuments. The imperial fora at Rome provided models for more monumental complexes, most common in the European provinces (e.g. *Tarraco, Spain; *Augusta Raurica, Switzerland) but also found in North Africa (e.g. *Lepcis Magna). These were symmetrical colonnaded squares, dominated by either a major temple (usually either a *capitolium* (temple of the Capitoline triad *Jupiter, *Juno, and *Minerva) or dedicated to the imperial (*ruler) cult) or a transverse *basilica across one short end, or both. See AGORA; MARKETS AND FAIRS; URBANISM (Roman).

R. Martin, *MÉFRA* 1972, 903 ff.; J. B. Ward-Perkins, *JRS* 1970, 1 ff.; M. Todd, in F. Grew and B. Hobley (eds.), *Roman Urban Topography in the Western Empire* (1985), 56 ff.; *Los foros romanos de las provincias occidentales* (1987). J. D.

forum Augustum or **Augusti,** dedicated in 2 BC, the vast precinct (110 × 83 m.: 120 × 90 yds.) of *Mars Ultor in Rome, vowed by Octavian at *Philippi. The octastyle marble Corinthian temple stood on a lofty podium at the north end; the interior of the cella, flanked by columns, terminated in an apse housing colossal statues of Mars, *Venus, and Divus Julius. Caesar's sword and many works of art were kept there. The temple was set against a high precinct wall of fire-resistant peperino, irregular in plan, which cut off the populous *Subura. Broad flights of steps flanking the temple led from the Subura into the forum through *triumphal arches, dedicated to Drusus (see CLAUDIUS DRUSUS, NERO) and *Germanicus in AD 19. The forum area was flanked by Corinthian porticoes enriched with coloured marble, and crowned by a tall attic decorated with *caryatides copied from the *Erechtheum at Athens; behind these were large semicircular exedrae. Statues of *Romulus and of *Aeneas adorned the exedrae, while others representing the Julian family and Roman state heroes decorated the porticoes; laudatory inscriptions from the bases of the statues survive. Here youths assumed the *toga virilis* (the symbol of manhood) and provincial governors ceremoniously departed or returned.

P. Zanker, *Forum Augustum* (1968); J. Ganzert and V. Kockel, in *Kaiser Augustus und die verlorene Republik* (1988), 149 ff.; Nash, *Pict. Dict. Rome* 1. 401 ff.   I. A. R.; D. E. S.; J. D.

forum Boarium, the area of ancient Rome bounded by the *Capitol, *Palatine, and *Aventine hills, adjacent to the *Tiber island, named (according to Varro, *Ling.* 5. 146) after the city's cattle market (see MARKETS AND FAIRS). Its importance as a commercial and port area from an early date is reflected both by the 8th-cent. BC Greek pottery found here, and the presence of cults with Greek (and Phoenician) associations such as that of *Hercules at the Ara Maxima; here too were the temples of *Fortuna and *Matuta Mater, and *Portunus.

F. Coarelli, *Il Foro Boario* (1988); Richardson, *Topog. Dict. Ancient Rome* 163–4.   J. R. P.

forum Caesaris or **Iulium,** dedicated by *Caesar in 46 BC, on land bought eight years earlier for 60 million sesterces (Cic. *Att.* 4. 16. 8), and completed by Octavian (*Augustus). The forum (approximately 160 × 75 m.: 175 × 82 yds.) had long colonnades on the east and west sides and a series of shops behind the western colonnade. The main entrance was at the southern end and by the SW corner lay the new Curia Iulia. (See CURIA.) The focal point of the forum was the octastyle temple of *Venus Genetrix, mythical foundress of the Julian *gens,* which was completely rebuilt after a fire and rededicated in AD 113 by *Trajan.

C. Morselli and E. Tortorici, *Curia, Forum Iulium, Forum Transitorium* 1 (1989); C. M. Amici, *Il foro di Cesare* (1991); Richardson, *Topog. Dict. Ancient Rome* 165–7.   I. A. R.; D. E. S.; J. R. P.

Forum Iulii (mod. Fréjus), presumably founded by *Caesar as a market town (*forum*). It owed its joint role of colony (for *veterans of Legio VIII Hispana; see LEGION) and of naval base (for warships captured at Actium)—hence its hybrid title: *Colonia Octavanorum Pacensis Classica*—to Augustus. Fréjus' harbour was, however, subject to silting (it is now dry) and, though still of strategic importance in AD 69, it had probably already lost its fleet; it certainly declined during the late empire. Extensive remains survive. It was the birthplace of Cn. *Iulius Agricola and probably of C. *Cornelius Gallus.

A. L. F. Rivet, *Gallia Narbonensis* (1988), 226 ff.   C. E. S.; J. F. Dr.

forum Nervae or **Transitorium** in Rome, built by *Domitian, was dedicated by *Nerva in AD 97. It converted the Argiletum, which approached the *forum Romanum between the *forum Augustum and the temple of Peace, into a monumental avenue (120 × 45 m.: 131 × 49 yds.). At the east, against the south exedra of the forum Augustum, stood a temple to *Minerva, Domitian's patron goddess; reliefs illustrating her cult and legends decorated the marble frieze and attic of the peperino precinct wall, divided into shallow bays by detached marble columns. Traffic from the *Subura to the east entered through a curved monumental portico, south of the temple; at the west end was a monumental arch. Severus Alexander (see AURELIUS SEVERUS ALEXANDER, M.) placed colossal statues of his deified predecessors here.

P. H. von Blanckenhagen, *Flavische Architektur und ihre Dekoration* (1940); C. Morselli and E. Tortorici, *Curia, Forum Iulium, Forum Transitorium* 1 (1989), 53 ff., 237 ff.; Nash, *Pict. Dict. Rome* 1. 433 ff.   I. A. R.; J. D.

forum Romanum, the chief public square of Rome, surrounded by monumental buildings, occupied a swampy trough between the *Palatine, *Velia, *Quirinal, and *Capitol. The edges of the marsh were covered with cemeteries of early iron age settlements on the surrounding hills, until the area was made suitable for building in the late 7th cent. BC by the canalizing of the *Cloaca Maxima, and the deposition of considerable quantities of fill. The *Regia and temple of *Vesta were traditionally associated with this period, while the earliest dated monuments are the temples of *Saturnus (497 BC: Livy 2. 21) and *Castor (484 BC: Livy 2. 20, 42). The forum became the centre of Roman religious, ceremonial, and commercial life, as well as the political activities which took place in the adjacent *Comitium; balconies (*maeniana*) were in 338 BC built above the shops surrounding the forum, to allow for the viewing of the gladiatorial shows which took place there. Butchers and fishmongers were, however, soon relegated to the *macellum* (see MARKETS AND FAIRS) and *forum piscarium,* as more monumental buildings were constructed around the forum. *Basilicas were introduced in 184 BC by M. *Porcius Cato (1) (Livy 39. 44); his work was soon imitated by the basilica Aemilia et Fulvia (179 BC) on the north side of the square, and basilica Sempronia (170 BC) on the south.

The growing population of Rome and the increasing importance of popular politics were reflected by the transfer from the Comitium to the forum of the *comitia tributa* in 145 BC; in 121 L. Opimius restored the temple of Concord, following the death of C. *Sempronius Gracchus and his supporters, and built a new adjacent basilica. In the same year the first *triumphal arch, to Q. *Fabius Maximus (Allobrogicus), was set up over the *via Sacra beside the Regia. The temple of Castor was rebuilt in 117 (Cic. *Scaur.* 46).

Much of the present setting, however, is due to *Sulla, *Caesar, and *Augustus. Sulla rebuilt the *Curia (2) on a larger scale to accommodate the senate of 600 members, obliterating much of the Comitium in the process; Caesar planned a new basilica Iulia, to replace the old basilica Sempronia, which, like his Curia Iulia, was finished by Augustus. After Caesar's assassination a column was erected to mark the site of his pyre and later (29 BC) replaced by the temple of Divus Iulius; this, and the adjacent Parthian arch of Augustus (19 BC), had the effect of monumentalizing the east end of the forum. New *Rostra in front of the temple of Divus Iulius faced the 'old' Rostra, rebuilt by Caesar and then Augustus. Many ancient monuments were restored: the Regia

(36 BC), the basilica Aemilia (14 BC), and the temples of Saturnus (42 BC), Castor (AD 6), and *Concordia (AD 10).

Comparatively few changes were made to the topography of the forum under the empire; the imperial fora, the Campus Martius, and the Palatine provided more scope for emperors keen to make their mark on the city. New temples were, however, dedicated to deified emperors and empresses (Augustus, *Vespasian, *Antoninus Pius, and *Annia Galeria Faustina (1)) while Domitian set up an equestrian statue of himself in AD 91; and the arch of Septimius Severus was built in AD 203. A major fire in AD 283, however, provided an opportunity for a major reconstruction under Diocletian, with a row of monumental columns set up in front of the basilica Iulia, and the Curia rebuilt. Later structures included a statue of *Stilicho and the column of Phocas (AD 608).

F. Coarelli, *Il foro romano* 1 (1983); 2 (1985); C. F. Giuliani and P. Verduchi, *L'area centrale del foro romano* (1987); Richardson, *Topog. Dict. Ancient Rome* 170–4.   I. A. R.; D. E. S.; J. R. P.

forum Traiani or **Ulpium**, the greatest of the imperial fora in Rome, paid for by Dacian spoils, was built for *Trajan by the architect *Apollodorus (7) and dedicated in AD 112. The colonnaded court, 310 × 185 m. (339 × 202 yds.), lay between the *Capitol and *Quirinal, impinging on the slopes of both by immense semicircular exedrae. A single portico closed the south, where its main entrance, adorned by a *triumphal arch in 117, faced the *forum Augustum; the lateral porticoes were double. The basilica Ulpia, with broad nave, double aisles, and two very large apsidal tribunals, occupied the forum's north side. Behind it lay Greek and Latin *libraries, flanking a colonnaded court framing *Trajan's Column, 38 m. (125 ft.) high. The inscription on the base states that its purpose was to show the depth of the cutting required for the forum: this refers to the scarping of the *Quirinal, where an elaborate complex of shops on six levels, linked by streets and staircases and with an interesting market-hall, screens a terraced rock-face separated from the forum by a fire wall and street. The libraries and column originally marked the end of the complex, but Hadrian added the temple of Deified Trajan beyond them.

P. Pensabene, *Arch. Class.* 1989, 27 ff.; J. Packer, *AJArch.* 1992, 151 ff.; Nash, *Pict. Dict. Rome* 1. 450 ff.   I. A. R.; J. D.

founders, city Founders were chiefly important before *Alexander (3) the Great in the case of colonies (see APOIKIA), founded under the leadership of an oikist (οἰκιστής), whose achievements frequently led to his posthumous worship as a hero (see HERO-CULT). In 5th-cent. BC Athens oikists were state officials who returned home after completing their task, as with Hagnon at *Amphipolis. Among Hellenistic founders of cities (*ktistēs* was now the preferred term) kings naturally loomed largest, although not all attended in person the founding rituals like Alexander the Great (Arr. *Anab.* 3. 1. 5). As a device for asserting a Hellenic ancestry compatible with the cultural and ethnic preferences of the ruling power, city-founders acquired a new significance in the Hellenistic and Roman empires: thus Cilician Mallus gained tax-exemption from Alexander (Arr. *Anab.* 2. 5. 9) on the strength of mutual kinship through *Argos (2). Precisely because such claims had a political value, their 'truthfulness' must be assessed cautiously, especially when they were set in the mythic past and demand belief in otherwise unattested mainland Greek colonization of Asia. In the Roman east, stimulated by the *Panhellenion, city-founders were celebrated in local coinages and monuments

as important sources of civic prestige; rhetors were advised to measure their praise according to the order 'god, hero, or man' (Menander Rhetor 1. 353, ed. Russell and Wilson). 'Ktistēs' by now was also an honorific title applied to civic benefactors, especially patrons of building. See also ARCHĒGETĒS.

W. Leschhorn, '*Gründer der Stadt*' (1984); J. Strubbe, *Anc. Soc.* 1984–6, 275–304; I. Malkin, *Religion and Colonization in Ancient Greece* (1987).   A. J. S. S.

fountains See NYMPHAEUM; WATER.

Four Hundred, the, a revolutionary *oligarchic council set up to rule Athens in 411 BC. The movement started in the fleet at *Samos in summer 412, when *Alcibiades offered to win Persian help for Athens if an oligarchy were established. *Pisander (2) was sent to Athens to prepare the way, and secured an embassy to negotiate with Persia. Though the Persian negotiation failed and the oligarchs discarded Alcibiades, it was then too late to stop. In spring 411 the oligarchic clubs (*hetaireiai*) murdered prominent democrats and intimidated the council (*boulē*) and assembly (*ekklēsia*). So far the published programme was 'moderate': abolition of civilian stipends (see DEMOCRACY, ATHENIAN for such political pay) and the restriction of the franchise to 5,000, those 'able to serve the state in person or with their wealth'. But after Pisander's return to Athens in May a meeting of the assembly, summoned to hear the proposals of a constitutional commission, was persuaded or terrorized into electing five men who, indirectly, selected 400 to act as a council with full powers to govern. The supporters of the original 'moderate' programme were overwhelmed by the extremists of the 400, who never summoned the 5,000, and who attempted unsuccessfully to negotiate with Sparta. But the democrats regained the upper hand in the fleet at Samos; and when the Peloponnesians attacked *Euboea, the squadron hastily sent by the 400 was defeated. *Theramenes, who had been one of the men behind the oligarchy, now came out for the moderates, the 400 were overthrown, and the 5,000 were instituted (September); but after the victory at *Cyzicus (410) full democracy was restored.

Thuc. bk. 8, with *HCT* 5; *Ath. pol.* 29–33, with Rhodes, *CAAP*. G. E. M. de Ste. Croix, *Hist.* 1956, 1–23; P. J. Rhodes, *JHS* 1972, 115–27; Ostwald, *Popular Sovereignty*; A. Andrewes, *CAH* 5² (1992), ch. 11.   A. A.; P. J. R.

Franks (Franci), a Germanic people who conquered Gallia (*Gaul), and made it Francia (France). Their adoption of Gallo-Roman Catholic culture was the seed of French civilization and, hence, that of medieval and modern western Europe. Despite their great importance, their first appearance is late (*c.* AD 260), their name ('the bold', 'the fierce') suggesting a coalition of *German tribes on the middle and lower Rhine. From then to the end of the 4th cent. they caused the empire frequent trouble, though they also gave it loyal generals and soldiers. Indeed, 4th-cent. emperors allowed some Frankish settlement on Roman soil in return for military service. However, during the early 5th cent., when the Rhine frontier weakened and the German occupation of Gaul began in earnest, the Franks, like the *Alamanni, seemed destined to be eclipsed by relative newcomers. There was some movement across the Rhine into Belgica Secunda, but it was not until the late 5th and early 6th cents. that the various Frankish groups were united by the Salians Childeric and Clovis, and moved south to break the *Visigoths and *Burgundians.

E. James, *The Franks* (1988).   J. F. Dr.

fratres arvales (arval brothers), a priestly college in Rome. Our detailed knowledge of the brotherhood comes from their inscribed records (now known as the *Acta fratrum arvalium*), found mostly on the site of their sacred grove 8 km. (5 mi.) outside Rome on the *via Campana* (mod. La Magliana). The earliest surviving inscription dates from 21–20 BC, while the only republican reference to the arvals is found in Varro (*Ling.* 5. 85). It is a reasonable conjecture that the brotherhood was an ancient priesthood of the city, which had ceased to function by the end of the republic and was revived under Augustus.

The college consisted of twelve members chosen from senatorial families by co-optation; the reigning emperor was always a member. The president (*magister*) and the other main official (*flamen*) were elected annually. Their main ritual obligation was the festival of the goddess *Dea Dia, to whom their grove was dedicated. In the course of this festival the brothers sang the famous 'song' of the arval brethren, the *Carmen arvale. Their other rituals mainly concerned the imperial house: annual vows 'for the safety of' the reigning emperor, sacrifices on his birthday, on his recovery from illness, etc.

Their grove has been partly excavated; it housed not only a temple of Dea Dia, but a variety of other cult buildings (a 'tetrastyle' dining-room; a shrine of the imperial cult; a bath-building; even a circus). These buildings appear not to have been dismantled until the very end of the 4th cent. AD, even though the inscribed texts cease some time before (a fragment survives from 304; but the main series stops in the mid-3rd cent.).

HISTORY J. Scheid, *Les Frères arvales* (1975); R. Syme, *Some Arval Brethren* (1982); M. Beard, *PBSR* 1985, 114–62; J. Scheid, *Romulus et ses frères* (1990).

TEXTS OF ACTA W. Henzen, *Acta fratrum arvalium* (1874); *CIL* 6. 2023–119, 32338–98, 37164 f. For new fragments, see references in Scheid (1990); J. Scheid is preparing a new edition of the *Acta*.

EXCAVATIONS OF GROVE H. Broise and J. Scheid, *Recherches archéologiques à La Magliana* (1987); H. Broise and J. Scheid, in U. de Cazanove and Scheid (eds.), *Les Bois sacrés* (1993), 145–57.   M. B.

free cities (*civitates liberae, eleutherai poleis*) formed a privileged category in Rome's system of provincial government. In the east the status ultimately derived from the blanket declaration of Greek freedom by T. *Quinctius Flamininus (196 BC); by the late republic a free city was one with a special agreement with Rome allowing it local autonomy (*suis legibus uti*) and sometimes tax-immunity (*immunitas*), although whether these two privileges were routinely coupled (Bernhardt) is debated (Ferrary). With dependence implicit, the status was liable to Roman encroachment and sudden cancellation, although emperors respected its outward forms, as the *Aphrodisias 'archive' shows, until well into the 3rd cent.

R. Bernhardt, *Hist.* 1980, 190–207; J.-L. Ferrary, *Philhellénisme et impérialisme* (1988), 7 n. 7; A. Lintott, *Imperium Romanum* (1993), 36–41.   A. J. S. S.

freedmen, freedwomen Emancipated slaves were more prominent in Roman society (little is known of other Italian societies before their enfranchisement) than in Greek city-states or Hellenistic kingdoms (see SLAVERY). In Greek the words *apeleutheros/a* and *exeleutheros/a* are used; in Latin *libertus/a* designates the ex-slave in relation to former owner (*patronus/a*), *libertinus/a* in relation to the rest of society. In Greek communities, freed slaves usually merged with other free non-citizens. In Rome, the slave freed by a citizen was normally admitted to citizenship (see CITIZENSHIP, ROMAN). A slave might be released from the owner's control by a fictitious claim before a magistrate with executive power (*imperium*) that he/she was free (manumission *vindicta*), by being ordered to present himself to the censors for registration as a citizen (manumission *censu*: in these forms public authority attested citizen status and made it impossible for the slave to be a slave), or by will (manumission *testamento*, where implementation of the owner's command was postponed until he/she died and depended on acceptance of the inheritance and public validation). A slave freed informally lacked citizenship and other rights, but was protected by the praetor, until Augustus introduced Latin rights, with the possibility (expanded by later emperors) of promotion to full citizenship. Augustus also, by the Fufio-Caninian law of 2 BC (introducing a sliding scale to limit the number of slaves who could be freed by will) and the Aelio-Sentian law of AD 4 (a comprehensive law, which included minimum ages for slave and manumitter and barred from citizenship slaves deemed criminal), regulated the previously untrammelled right to manumit.

In Greece, the ex-slave might be bound to perform services while the ex-owner lived; in Rome, continuing dependency took the form of part-time services (*operae*; *libertae* married with patron's consent were exempt from paying these to a male patron), possible remunerated work, the obligation of dutifulness, and some inheritance rights for the patron and descendants against the freed slave's heirs other than non-adopted children. Freedmen were usually registered in the four urban voting tribes (*tribus), excluded from major public offices and military service, but given a role in local elective office and cult. Children born after their mother's manumission were free-born and under no legal disabilities, though servile descent might be remembered (especially by the upper classes) for several generations. Freed slaves document their activity in urban trades and crafts; the most prominent, wealthy, and envied were usually freed by the upper classes: literature emphasizes the exceptions—writers such as *Terence, the fictitious millionaire Trimalchio (see PETRONIUS ARBITER) or the bureau-chiefs of the early emperors such as *Narcissus (2) and M. *Antonius Pallas. See NAMES, PERSONAL ROMAN.

M. K. Hopkins and P. J. Roscoe, in M. K. Hopkins (ed.), *Conquerors and Slaves* (1978), 133–71; S. Treggiari, *Roman Freedmen during the Late Republic* (1969); A. M. Duff, *Freedmen in the Early Roman Empire* (1928; repr. 1958); K. R. Bradley, *Slaves and Masters in the Roman Empire* (1984), ch. 3; P. R. C. Weaver, *Familia Caesaris* (1972).   M. I. F.; S. M. T.

freedom in the ancient world On the individual and social levels, the distinction between free and unfree is as old as slavery, and individual or collective freedom from dues, taxes, and other obligations as old as communities with centralized government. These concepts are attested in Egyptian and Mesopotamian documents and the Hebrew Bible. Nevertheless to these civilizations—as to ancient China—the concepts of free citizens or of political freedom were unknown. Typically, near-eastern societies were characterized by a plurality of statuses 'between slavery and freedom' (Pollux) and ruled by autocratic and divinely sanctioned monarchs or an absolute divine law. Obedience and integration into a given order were the prime virtues; the rise and fall of empires and cities, protection from foreign enemies, or, individually, status change or protection from domestic exploitation were seen as results of divine will. Such conditions were not conducive to recognizing freedom as a political value. Despite their charter myth of liberation from Egyptian slavery, even the Hebrews (see JEWS) began to use freedom politically only under

Hellenistic influence. About Phoenician city-states we know too little to judge.

Eleutheros and *liber* probably both derive from IE †*leudh-* (perhaps initially 'grow'), designating the legitimate member of a descent group or community. The distinction free–unfree is attested in the earliest Greek and Roman texts (Linear B, Homer (e.g. *Il.* 6. 455, 463), *Twelve Tables). As 'chattel *slavery' became predominant, earlier status plurality was often replaced by a sharp contrast: slave–free. *Freedmen were enfranchised in Rome but not in Greece (see CITIZENSHIP, GREEK and ROMAN).

Current evidence indicates that freedom was first given *polit-ical* value by the Greeks, in a world of small *poleis* (see POLIS) which were not subject to imperial control, where power was not centralized, autocratic, or divinely sanctioned but broadly distributed, and communal well-being depended on many citizens, so that early forms of equality survived and gained importance over time. Loss of freedom was frequent, both for individuals (war, piracy, debt bondage), and communities (tyranny).

Nevertheless, freedom was articulated politically only when *Lydian and especially *Persian expansion to the Aegean for the first time subjected Greek *poleis* to foreign rule, often supporting local tyrants (see TYRANNY). This danger of double 'enslavement' and the confrontation with the autocratic Persian state made the Greeks aware of the free character of their societies. Earliest allusions to political freedom and the emergence of an abstract noun (*eleutheria*) date to the Persian Wars of 480/79 and their aftermath (e.g. *Aeschylus, *Persae* 403).

Vowing the continued defence of Greek liberty against Persia. Athens assumed leadership in the *Delian League (478) which was soon converted into a naval empire; allies became subjects who could hope only to preserve self-administration (*autonomia*; see AUTONOMY). Freedom quickly deteriorated into a political slogan. In the *Peloponnesian War, *Sparta propagated the liberation of Hellas from Athens as *polis tyrannos*, though primarily protecting its own interests and soon turning oppressor itself.

Domestically, freedom initially meant 'absence of tyranny'. Constitutional development was dominated first by 'order' (*eunomia* (see LYCURGUS (2))), then by equality (*isonomia*), which, in democracy, eventually included all citizens, thus approximating *isonomia* to *demokratia* (Hdt. 3. 80. 6.). *Eleutheria* was claimed by democracy when democracy and oligarchy were perceived as mutually exclusive, partisan forms of rule, so that the *dēmos* could be free only by controlling power itself (ps.-Xen. *Ath. pol.* 1. 6. 9). Similarly, a new term for 'freedom of speech' (*parrhēsia*) supplemented 'equality of speech' (*isēgoria*). Rejecting the extension of full rights to all citizens, *oligarchs accepted as 'free citizens' only those wealthy enough to engage in liberal arts and occupations (*eleutherios paideia*, *eleutherioi technai*) and communal service. When *eleutherios* was set against *eleutheros* the concept of the 'free citizen' was divided ideologically, as proportional equality was opposed to numerical equality. Aristotle later included liberality (*eleutheriotēs*) in his analysis of virtues (*Eth. Nic.* 4. 1).

In the 4th cent. BC Sparta, Athens, and *Thebes (1) claimed to promote the liberty of those subjected by others. The liberty of the Greeks in Asia, sacrificed by Sparta in 412, was definitively yielded in the *King's Peace (386). The charter of the *Second Athenian Confederacy guaranteed the members' *eleutheria* and *autonomia*. The Messenian *helots were freed by Thebes after *Leuctra (371). To end continuous internecine warfare, *Isocrates called for a pan-Hellenic crusade against Persia to liberate

the Hellenes—a programme realized by *Alexander (3) the Great only after Greek liberty was crushed at the battle of *Chaeronea (338).

In the Hellenistic period, politics were controlled by the great powers; local autonomy was the best that could be attained. Yet the kings, competing for political and material support, presented themselves as protectors of Hellenic civilization and liberty. Declarations of freedom for the Hellenes were thus an old tradition when, after his victory over *Philip (3) V, *Flamininus in 196 pronounced that the king's Greek subjects 'shall be free, exempt from tribute, and subject to their own laws' (Livy 33. 32. 5–6).

The use of freedom in philosophy was more complex. Fifth-century *sophists emphasized the strong individual's right to erupt from enslavement by the conventions of *nomos* and rule over the weaker in accordance with nature (*Antiphon (2), Callicles in *Plato (1)'s *Gorgias*). Others contested the validity of traditional social distinctions; *Alcidamas declared slavery as contrary to nature. Despite *Aristotle's elaborate refutation (*Politics* 1), this view was echoed by the Stoics (see STOICISM) and discussed thoroughly by Roman jurists. Yet other sophists propagated cosmopolitanism, individualism, and 'freedom from the state' (*Aristippus).

One aspect of democratic *eleutheria* was 'to live as you like' (Arist. *Pol.* 1317^b 11). Plato caricatured such 'excessive' freedom in *Republic* 8–9; Isocrates denounced it when advocating *patrios politeia* (*Areop.* 20). Generally, *Socrates and his pupils avoided *eleutheria*. Originating in popular morality (echoed in *Euripides), the notion of freedom from all kinds of dependencies (especially on material goods and passions) induced generations of thinkers (*Antisthenes (1), *Diogenes (2), *Bion (1)) to stress self-control (*sōphrosynē*, *enkrateia*) as decisive means to achieve inner freedom.

Loss of political freedom and the need for new orientations gave philosophy broad appeal as a means to achieve happiness (*eudaimonia*: see DAIMŌN). Despite fundamental differences, both Epicureans (*Sent. Vat.* 77) and Stoics (Epictetus 4. 1) believed in freedom as the goal and principle of life. (See EPICURUS; STOICISM.)

Lack of contemporary sources allows no certainty about the process by which *libertas* was politicized in Rome. The expulsion of the kings or the struggle for abolition of debt bondage are possible contexts. The late republican élite developed an aristocratic concept of *libertas*, supporting equality and opposing *regnum* ('kingship') and extraordinary power of individuals and factions. By contrast, the *libertas populi* was not egalitarian and did not aim at political participation. It was primarily defensive, focusing on equality before the law and the protection of individual citizens from abuse of power by magistrates. *Libertas* rested on institutions, *ius*, and *lex (1); it was embodied by the *tribuni plebis* and their rights of *provocatio* and *auxilium* (*duae arces libertatis tuendae* ('twin poles of the defence of liberty') Livy 3. 45. 8). In late republican conflicts *libertas* was claimed by *populares* against oppression by *optimates (thus connected with the secret ballot) or a *factio paucorum* ('party of the few') (Caes. *BCiv.* 1. 22. 5; Augustus, *RG* 1).

During the empire, power was concentrated in one man's hands. Although *libertas* remained a favoured slogan of imperial ideology, nevertheless, according to *Tacitus (1) (*Agr.* 3. 1), *principatus ac libertas* were not reconciled before *Nerva. Even so, liberty was increasingly reduced to the elementary meaning of security and protection under the law.

While freedom lost political significance, *eleutheria*/*libertas* became an important element in Christian teaching, emphasized especially by *Paul. Through God's gift and Christ's sacrifice his followers are liberated from sin, the finality of death, and the old law. Such freedom, however, involves subjection to the will of God: Christ's followers are God's 'slaves.' The freedom promised to Christians is available to all humans, including the lowly and slaves, but it is not of this world and does not militate against existing social dependencies and political or ethical obligations. Accordingly, Christians did not oppose slavery as an institution, but in accepting slaves into their community they anticipated the universal brotherhood of the free expected in another world.

D. Nestle, *RAC* 8 (1972), 269–306, 'Freiheit'; W. Warnach, *Hist. Wörterb. der Philos.* 2 (1972), 1064 ff., 'Freiheit' 1; M. Pohlenz, *Griechische Freiheit* (1955); K. Raaflaub, *Die Entdeckung der Freiheit* (1985); C. Wirszubski, *Libertas as a Political Idea at Rome* (1950); J. Bleicken, *Staatliche Ordnung und Freiheit in der römischen Republik* (1972); M. I. Finley, *Economy and Society in Ancient Greece* (1982), chs. 7–9.   K. R.

Fregellae, in the Liris valley near mod. Ceprano, was a Latin colony (see IUS LATII) established in 328 BC; this provoked the Second Samnite War (see SAMNIUM). Staunchly loyal to Rome against Pyrrhus and Hannibal (when, *c*.211 BC, the city walls may have been built), it revolted against Rome in 125 BC, and was largely destroyed. A new foundation, Fabrateria Nova, some kilometres away, replaced it, although Strabo (5. 3. 10) reports the existence of a village and festivals. An important sanctuary of *Asclepius, built in the second quarter of the 2nd cent. BC, has been excavated, and was apparently destroyed in 125 BC. There are signs that some occupation continued down to the 4th cent. AD.

F. Coarelli, *Fregellae 2: Il santuario di Esculapio* (1986); M. H. Crawford and others, *PBSR* 1984, 21 ff; 1986, 40 ff.   E. T. S.; T. W. P.

Frentani, *Oscan-speaking people between the Marrucini and the peoples of Apulia, on Italy's Adriatic coast. Chief settlements: Ordona, Histonium, Buca, Anxanum, *Larinum. Tribally organized, they sided with Rome, after initial hostility in the Second Samnite War (see SAMNIUM), and remained her loyal allies until the *Social War (3), when they joined the insurgents. They were rapidly Romanized after that.

E. T. Salmon, *Samnium and the Samnites* (1967); A. La Regina and others, *Sannio, Pentri e Frentani* (1980).   E. T. S.; T. W. P.

friendship, Greek The principal Greek terms customarily translated as 'friendship' have a semantic range wider than this translation suggests. *Philia* and *oikeiotēs* could both be used of *kinship ties, while *hetaireia* could also designate confraternities and political associations. The relative scarcity in the Greek world of institutions for the provision of vital services may partly explain this semantic difference. Friends provided, as Hands puts it (see bibliog. below), 'services analogous to those provided by bankers, lawyers, hotel owners, insurers and others today'.

Hence the great importance that the Greeks attached to their most intimate circles of friends. Friends, like kin, could be called upon in any emergency; they could be expected to display solidarity, lend general support, and procure co-operation (e.g. Lys. 19. 59). The obligations of friendship were less rigidly defined than those of kinship or ritualized *friendship. One's circle of friends, however, probably exerted an even more pervasive influence on one's behaviour and outlook than one's kin or ritualized friends. Friends were therefore supposed to be alike: a friend was ideally conceived of as one's 'other self' (Arist. *Eth. Nic.* 1169^{b}6).

The sources reveal a marked tendency towards the forging of new friendships and the intensifying of existing ones. One device

employed to achieve the latter end was multiplication of the ties of interdependence between friends by means such as marriage, homosexual relationships (see HOMOSEXUALITY), or partnership in various enterprises. Another was the exchange of favours (*euergesiai, charites*): Cleobulus of Lindus is reported to have said that 'we should do a favour to a friend to bind him closer to us and to an enemy in order to make a friend of him' (Diog. Laert. 1. 91). While a favour rendered created a moral obligation to reciprocate (see RECIPROCITY), often by returning a favour not merely equal to but more valuable than the favour received, friends were also supposed to cherish, or at least to feign, sentiments which impelled them to altruistic action. 'Where a loan is involved', writes the author of the *Problems* attributed to *Aristotle, 'there is no friend; for if a man is a friend he does not lend but gives'. Millett has shown that a surprisingly high percentage of loans in Athens were made by kin and friends without demanding securities or charging interest. See CREDIT, ERANOS.

Logically and historically, friendship preceded the city. In the world reflected in the Homeric poems, most friendships were personal attachments. In the small, compact world of the city-state, personal ties were supplemented by rights and obligations arising from participation in formal institutions and in a multiplicity of informal groups and connections. Among friends whose interdependence derived from several spheres of activity, the sanctions available through interdependence in one sphere could be used to enforce the fulfilment of obligations incurred in another. This dense involvement could lead to the disruption of friendships. According to the Aristotelian *Magna Moralia*, friends who were also fellow citizens competed for superiority and engaged in violent dispute so that in the end they ceased to be friends (2. 1211^{a}46). From the communal point of view, strong friendship ties and the informal groupings to which they gave rise appear often to have constituted a threat to political stability (see CLUBS, GREEK; HETAIREIAI).

Ideally, friendship ties were supposed to bind together status equals. In some cases, however, there was a striking lack of agreement between image and reality. Friendship ties between men from different age groups were not uncommon, nor were friendships between men of unequal status, verging in reality upon dependence. The Greek language, however, offered no appropriate pair of hierarchical status designations: *Polybius (1), trying to interpret for his Greek public what the Romans called *patronus and *cliens, found in his repertoire of Greek terms nothing more suitable than *philoi*.

The lyric poetry of *Sappho allows us a rare glimpse of friendship between women, and reinforces the conclusion which emerges from a general consideration of Greek society: because respectable women lived secluded from contact with men, women tended to form intense emotional relationships with one another.

A. W. H. Adkins, *CQ* 1963, 30 ff; P. Cartledge, *PCPS* 1981, 17 ff.; K. J. Dover, *Greek Popular Morality* (1974); P. Easterling, in R. Porter and S. Tomaselli (eds.), *The Dialectics of Friendship* (1989); A. R. Hands, *Charities and Social Aid in Greece and Rome* (1968); G. Herman, *Ritualised Friendship and the Greek City* (1978), ch. 2; P. Millett, *Lending and Borrowing in Ancient Athens* (1992).   G. He.

friendship, philosophical See LOVE AND FRIENDSHIP.

friendship, ritualized (or guest-friendship), a bond of trust, imitating kinship and reinforced by rituals, generating affection and obligations between individuals belonging to separate social units. In Greek sources this bond is called *xenia, xeiniē*, and

friendship, ritualized

xeineiē; in Latin, *hospitium*. The individuals joined by the bond (usually men of approximately equal social status) are said to be each other's *xenos* or *hospes*. As the same terms designated guest-host relationships, *xenia* and *hospitium* have sometimes been interpreted in modern research as a form of hospitality. *Xenia*, *hospitium*, and hospitality do overlap to some extent but the former relationships display a series of additional features which assimilate them into the wider category called in social studies ritualized personal relationships, or pseudo-kinship. The analogy with kinship did not escape the notice of the ancients themselves. According to the *Aristotelian Magna Moralia*, *xenia* was the strongest of all the relationships involving affection (*philia*) (2. 1381ᵇ29). Aulus *Gellius wrote that a relationship with a *hospes* should take precedence over kinship and marriage in matters of affection and obligation (*NA* 5. 13. 5).

The lexicographer *Hesychius defined *xenos* as 'a friend (*philos*) from abroad', and this definition holds good for the Roman *hospitium*: a ritualized friendship dyad could consist, for example, of an Athenian and a Spartan, a Thessalian and a Persian, a Carthaginian and a Syracusan, or a Roman and an Epirote, but very rarely consisted of two Athenians or two Romans. From its first appearance in *Homer (e.g. *Il*. 6. 224–5) onwards, ritualized friendship has been abundantly attested in both Greek and Latin sources from all periods and areas of classical antiquity. In late antiquity, it disappears from view. There are good reasons to assume, however, that it was gradually annexed by the Christian Church, since it reappears in a new guise in the early medieval variants of godparenthood: Latin *compaternitas*, and Byzantine *synteknia*.

One feature that ritualized friendship shared with kinship was the assumption of perpetuity: once the relationship had been established, the bond was believed to persist in latent form even if the partners did not interact with one another. This assumption had two practical consequences. First, the bond could be renewed or reactivated after years had elapsed, a variety of symbolic objects signalling that it once existed (*symbolon*, *pista*, *tessera hospitalis*). Secondly, the bond did not expire with the death of the partners themselves, but outlived them, passing on in the male line to their descendants.

If ritualized friends belonged to separate social units, how did their paths come to cross? Random encounters were made possible by the extraordinary geographic mobility of the Greeks and Romans, as well as by circumstances such as wars, festivals, and *colonization. Stories of how two eminent people first met and developed a liking for each other, and how they (or their descendants) recognized each other after many years of separation, undoubtedly exercised a special fascination over the ancients (e.g. Hdt. 3. 139 ff.).

The beginning of the relationship had to be marked with a ceremony, as did the reactivation of a relationship after many years. The rites of initiation into *xenia* and *hospitium* consisted of a diversity of symbolic elements enacted in sequence: a solemn declaration ('I make you my *xenos*', and 'I accept you'), an exchange of symbolic gifts (see GIFT, GREECE), a handshake, and finally feasting (Xen. *Hell*. 4. 1. 39; Curt. 6. 5. 1 ff; Cic. *Deiot*. 8; Livy 23. 9. 3–4; Aeschin. 3. 224. See SYMPOSIUM). The rites were obviously intended to lend the bond an aura of sacrosanctity, rendering it indissoluble. In practice, the bond could fade away through disuse. Its moral context was, however, such that only exceptionally was it interrupted by means of a formal ceremony (e.g. Hdt. 4. 154. 4, 3. 43. 2).

Ritualized friends were, by virtue of their prescribed duties,

veritable co-parents. A *xenos* or *hospes* was supposed to show a measure of protective concern for his partner's son, to help him in any emergency, and to save his life (Hom. *Il*. 21. 42; Dem. 50. 56; Hdt. 9. 76; Lys. 18. 10; Plaut. *Mil*. 133–45). A father's partner in relation to the former's son was designated by a technical term: *patrikos* (or *patroos*) *xenos* in Greek, and *paternus hospes* in Latin. If the natural father was absent, ill, or dead, this paternal friend was expected to act as a substitute father. According to *Euripides' *Electra* and *Orestes*, for instance, *Orestes was brought up, following the murder of *Agamemnon, in the household of Agamemnon's *xenoi*. Similarly, in real life, Aratus, following the murder of his father, was brought up in the household of his father's *xenoi* at *Argos (2) (Plut. *Arat*. 2–3). Cicero relates that on sensing danger he sent his children to the court of his *hospes* *Deiotarus, king of Galatia (*Att*. 5. 17, cf. 18. 4). Neglect of coparental duties was strongly disapproved of, often evoking violent emotions (Eur. *Hec*. 689–714; Aeschin. 3. 225). Betrayal of ritualized friendship in general sometimes appears as a sin against the gods (Diod. Sic. 20. 70. 3–4).

In conformity with the co-parental obligations, a father was supposed to name a son after his partner. The custom is more often found in Greek than in Roman sources (Thuc. 8. 6. 3; Diod. Sic. 14. 13. 5; Hdt. 3. 55). No explanation of its rationale survives, but a belief that some of the paternal friend's character traits will be passed on to the child with his name can be inferred from the paternal friend's obligation to take a share in the child's education (Hom. *Il*. 9. 483 ff., with Plut. *Phil*. 1; Livy 9. 36. 3, 42. 19. 3).

Ritualized friendship was an overwhelmingly upper-class institution in both Greece and Rome. The people involved in it belonged to a small minority, renowned for their wealth and identified by lofty titles such as 'hero', 'tyrant', '*satrap', 'nobleman', 'consul', 'governor', and 'emperor'. Throughout antiquity, such people lent each other powerful support, often at the expense of their inferiors, so frequently that ritualized friendship may justly be regarded as a tool for perpetuating class distinctions. The forms of mutual support practised included the exchange of valuable resources (e.g. money, troops, or grain), usually designated gifts, and the performance of important services (e.g. opportune intervention, saving life, catering for every need) usually designated benefactions (Greek *euergesiai*, Latin *beneficia*: see EUERGETISM). The circulation of these goods and services created what may be described as networks of ritualized friendship. The Greek and Roman worlds differed markedly in how these informal networks were integrated into their wider political systems.

In the world reflected in the Homeric poems, *xenia* and the networks to which it gave rise were of paramount importance to the hero. The hero abroad found in a *xenos* an effective substitute for kinsmen, a protector, representative, and ally, supplying in case of need shelter, protection, men, and arms; the community was not sufficiently organized to interfere with this sort of co-operation. The relationship being largely personal, ritualized friendship was, together with marriage, the Homeric forerunner of political and military alliances. The emergence of the *polis* during the 8th and 7th cents. BC was accompanied by significant interactions between its nascent systems and this pre-existing network of personal alliances. Nor did the fully-fledged *polis* lead to the abolition of this network: throughout the Classical age, dense webs of ritualized friendship still stretched beyond its bounds, at times facilitating, at times obstructing the conduct of foreign affairs (e.g. Andoc. 2. 11; Thuc. 2. 13). For the upper classes of the Classical age, these networks offered an alternative means to the civic system of pursuing their own interests. In the Hellenistic age, the circles of 'friends' (*philoi*) came to be recruited from among the personal or paternal *xenoi* of the kings; having turned royal officials, these members of governing élites are often found to be acting as mediators between the kings and their own communities of origin, deriving substantial benefits from both systems. The impact of *xenia* upon the Greek civic system is most evident in the creation by the *polis* of *proxenia*, a bond of trust, clearly modelled upon *xenia*, between a *polis* and a prominent individual outside it (see PROXENOS).

Under the republic, prominent Romans maintained extensive ties of *hospitium* with prominent non-Romans both elsewhere in Italy and overseas. In the lawcourts, for instance, both *Cicero and *Caesar defended members of the aristocracy from various Italian communities. Pompey had hereditary ties of *hospitium* with the Numidian king *Juba (1) (Caes. *BCiv.* 2. 25), while Mark Antony (M. *Antonius (2)) was an ancestral *xenos* of the Herods of Judaea (Joseph. *AJ* 14. 320). *Livy was probably attributing contemporary customs to an earlier age when he assigned to the Etruscan king *Tarquinius Superbus motives epitomizing the role of ritualized friendship in a country of separate communities: 'the Latin race he strove particularly to make his friends, so that his strength abroad might contribute to his security at home. He contracted with their nobles not only ties of *hospitium* but also matrimonial connections' (Livy 1. 49. 9). The sort of upper-class coalitions reflected in this example could, however, easily be overpowered by the state, and therefore posed less of a threat to the Roman community than such coalitions previously had to any single Greek city-state. Rome followed in Greece's footsteps by devising *hospitium publicum*, a public institution analogous to *proxenia*, modelled on *hospitium*.

Hospitium, like *patronage, was instrumental in the *Romanization of local élites (Livy 9. 36. 3, 42. 19. 3–6), in their upward social mobility, and in their integration into the Roman ruling class (e.g. Cic. *Clu.* 25. 165, with *Vir. ill.* 80. 1). Within the Roman empire, the communities in which ritualized friends lived gradually became part of a larger-scale political system, and this change tended to relax the principle that ritualized friends must belong to separate communities. Fronto saw nothing unusual in characterizing as a *hospes* a friend who originated from the same African city as himself, and a 2nd-cent. AD inscription from Spain sees *hospitium* as compatible with kinship ties (*Ad amicos* 1. 3; *CIL* 2. 2633).

M. I. Finley, *The World of Odysseus*, 2nd edn. (1972); G. Herman, *Ritualised Friendship and the Greek City* (1987), *CQ*, 1990, 349 ff., and 'Godparenthood, Coparenthood and "Guest-friendship" ', forthcoming; Mommsen, *Röm Forsch.* 1864, 321 ff.; T. P. Wiseman, *New Men in the Roman Senate* (1971), ch. 3. G. He.

friendship, Roman See AMICITIA; FRIENDSHIP, RITUALIZED.

Frisii, a Germanic people, who lived on the North Sea coast from west of the Ijsselmeer eastwards to the Ems. Like the Bructeri and Chauci, they were divided into two sections, *maiores* and *minores*, but the significance is unknown. Overrun by *Drusus in 12 BC, they paid their tribute in oxhides. They revolted in AD 28 following extortionate tax demands and maintained their freedom until 47. They were again hostile in 68–9, and thenceforth remained generally independent, though they provided troops for the Roman army. It seems likely that from the mid-3rd cent. they co-operated with the Frankish confederation (see FRANKS).

Tac. *Ann.* 4. 72. R. Brandt and J. Slofstra, *Roman and Native in the Low Countries* (1983); E. James, *The Franks* (1988). J. F. Dr.

Fritigern, leader of the *Gothic Tervingi, who seized power *c.* AD 376 in the crisis provoked by the arrival of the *Huns; championed a policy of seeking asylum inside the Roman empire, and seems to have wanted a negotiated peace. He nevertheless fought and won the battle of Hadrianople (378). Still in power *c.*380, he was ousted, in unknown circumstances, before the peace of 382.

P. J. Heather, *Goths and Romans 332–489* (1991). P. J. H.

Frontinus See IULIUS FRONTINUS, SEX.

Fronto See CORNELIUS FRONTO, M.

Frontoniani, Sidonius' term (*Epist.* 1. 1. 2) for orators in M. *Cornelius Fronto's style. They need not have regarded themselves in that light, or as a school, nor were they necessarily his contemporaries, but from *Sidonius Apollinaris' 5th-cent. AD perspective archaizing mannerists were followers of their most eminent representative. Only *Iulius Titianus is named, mocked by the others for imitating the 'worn-out style' (*veternosum dicendi genus*) of Cicero's letters (which Fronto himself admired: 104. 12–14 van den Hout[2]). See ARCHAISM IN LATIN. L. A. H.-S.

Frusino (mod. Frosinone), on the *via Latina. It participated in, and indeed instigated, the revolt of some *Hernici against Rome in 306 BC and lost much territory in consequence. Although reduced to a *praefectura*, it remained reasonably prosperous. Today it is a large town with negligible traces of antiquity. E. T. S.; T. W. P.

Fucinus Lacus, a large lake at the centre of Italy. It lacked a visible outlet, but legend stated that the river Pitonius from the Paeligni country traversed it without their waters mingling, the Pitonius reappearing near Sublaqueum to supply the aqua Marcia (Pliny, *HN* 2. 224, 31. 41; Lycoph. *Alex.* 1275), see AQUEDUCTS. The lake sometimes overflowed (Strab. 5. 240; exaggerated). Claudius, employing 30,000 men for eleven years, executed Caesar's plan to drain the lake: an *emissarium* was excavated 5.6 km. (3½ mi.) through a mountain ridge to carry the lake waters to the *Liris (Suet. *Iul.* 44; *Claud.* 20 f., 32). But Claudius' efforts were not entirely successful. Even repairs to his *emissarium* by Trajan and Hadrian proved in vain (Cass. Dio 60. 11. 33; Dessau, *ILS* 302; SHA *Hadr.* 22). Drainage attempts recommenced in AD 1240, but were unsuccessful until the 19th cent., when practically the whole lake-bed was reclaimed.

E. Agostinoni, *Il Fucino* (1908); C. Letha, *I Marsi e il Fucino nell'antichità* (1972). E. T. S.; T. W. P.

Fufius (*RE* 10) **Calenus, Quintus,** assisted P. *Clodius Pulcher as tribune in 61 BC, supported *Caesar as praetor (59), and some years later served under him in Gaul and in the Civil War (especially in Greece), becoming consul in 47 (not elected till September) with P. *Vatinius. After Caesar's death he supported his friend M. *Antonius (2) against his enemy Cicero. He held part of Italy during the Philippi campaign, and then governed Gaul for Antonius with eleven legions, which, on his death (40), his son handed over to Octavian.

Syme, *Rom. Rev.*, see index. E. B.

Fulgentius (*RE* 3), **Fabius Planciades,** a late 5th-cent. writer of Christian persuasion from somewhere outside Rome, possibly Carthage, to whom are attributed the *Mythologiae*, a set of allegorical interpretations of various pagan myths, the *Expositio Vergili-*

anae continentiae secundum philosophos moralis, an allegorical interpretation of the *Aeneid*, and the *Expositio sermonum antiquorum*, an explanation of 62 obsolete words illustrated by citations of authors ranging from *Naevius to *Martianus Capella. The three works, which share a single tradition, are marked by considerable foolishness of thought and by an extremely mannered style. *Petronius Arbiter, *Apuleius, and Martianus Capella exercised a strong influence. Many of the citations Fulgentius makes of earlier Greek and Latin authors have been thought bogus. The *De aetatibus mundi et hominis*, a summary of world history, sacred and profane, is attributed by its tradition to a 'Fabius Claudius Gordianus Fulgentius'. It resembles in quality of thought and style the mythological and lexicological works attributed to Fabius Planciades Fulgentius. All four works, and in particular the *Mythologiae*, were much read in the Middle Ages. They were then attributed to a Fulgentius, bishop of Ruspe (AD 467–532), the author of a number of sermons and rhetorically but soberly expressed refutations of *Arianism and Pelagianism (see PELAGIUS). Some scholars still accept this attribution. An allegorical account of the story of *Statius' *Thebaid* attributed to a 'Fulgentius episcopus' appears to have been composed in the 12th or 13th cent.

TEXT R. Helm (1898), rev. J. Préaux (1970); Eng. trans. L. G. Whitehead (1971).

PLRE 2. 488 F. Skutsch, *RE* 7/1 (1910), 215–27 'Fulgentius' 3; P. Langlois, *Jahrb. f. Ant. u. Christ.* 1964, 94–105; B. Bischoff, *Mittelalt. Stud.* 2 (1967), 271 n. 138; F. Bertini, *Studi Noniani* 1972, 33–60.

H. D. J.

fulling See TEXTILE PRODUCTION.

Fulvia (*RE* 'Fulvius' 113), offspring of two noble families, became the best-known of late republican ladies active in politics and a prototype of empresses. Born in the late 70s BC, she married P. *Clodius Pulcher, supported his policies and called for vengeance after his assassination. Briefly married to C. *Scribonius Curio (2), she married M. *Antonius (2) after Curio's death, took an active part in his management of politics after Caesar's death and later in the *proscriptions, greatly enriching herself. When Antonius took charge of the east, she supported his cause in Italy, ultimately combining with his brother L. *Antonius (Pietas) in opposing Octavian. Besieged with him at *Perusia, where her presence was exploited by hostile propaganda, she was allowed to join her husband after its fall, but was badly received by him and soon died. Her daughter by Clodius was briefly Octavian's first wife; for her sons by Antonius see ANTONIUS ANTYLLUS, M. and ANTONIUS, IULLUS. In later literature (especially Cass. Dio) she became the type of the wicked matron, contrasted with the virtuous *Octavia (2).

ILLRP 1106, 1112 (derisive sling-bullets; cf. SLINGERS; see J. Hallett, *AJAH* 1977); Martial 11. 20 (quoting Augustus). Modern (often feminist) treatments are numerous; but see D. Delia, in S. B. Pomeroy (ed.), *Women's History and Ancient History* (1991), 197 ff., with critical bibliog. See also B. Kreck, *Untersuchungen zur politischen und sozialen Rolle der Frau in der späten römischen Republik* (1975), R. A. Bauman, *WPAR* 83 ff. There are no identified portraits. Attempts to discern her features on various coins and busts are romantic fiction.

E. B.

Fulvia Plautilla Augusta, Publia, daughter of the praetorian prefect C. *Fulvius Plautianus, married M. *Aurelius Antoninus (1) (Caracalla) in AD 202, when she received the title Augusta. On the fall of her father (205) she was banished to Lipara and was put to death by Caracalla in 212.

RIC 4/1. 267 ff., 309; *PIR*² F 564.

A. R. Bi.

Fulvius (*RE* 58) **Flaccus, Marcus,** supporter of Ti. *Sempronius Gracchus (3) and agrarian commissioner from 130 BC. When the commission was prevented from dealing with public land held by Italians (see CORNELIUS SCIPIO AEMILIANUS, P.), he proposed to offer the citizenship (or, if they preferred it, *provocatio*) to individual Italians to obtain the land, thus introducing the 'Italian problem' into Roman politics. Elected consul (125) on this programme, he was circumvented by the senate, which ordered him to assist *Massilia against the *Salluvii. Returning to triumph (123), he stooped to a tribunate (122) to aid C. *Sempronius Gracchus in carrying an amended version of his policy, and shared in his defeat and death. Cicero (*Brut*. 108) describes him as scholarly, thus correcting the hostile picture in Plutarch as a violent drunkard initiating Gracchus' rebellion.

The main sources are App. *BCiv*. 1 and Plut. *C. Gracch*. See E. Badian, *Foreign Clientelae* (1958), index, and *Dialoghi di archeologia* 4–5 (1970–1), 385–92; D. Stockton, *The Gracchi* (1979), index.

E. B.

Fulvius (*RE* 59) **Flaccus (1), Quintus,** was consul in 237 BC, when he fought Gauls and *Ligurians. He was elected censor in 231, but forced to abdicate because of a fault in the election. Consul again in 224, he and his colleague forced the *Boii to submit. He was urban praetor in both 215 and 214, in the latter year being appointed without lot in order to guard the city. Consul for the third time in 212, he captured the camp of *Hanno (2) near Beneventum (mod. Benevento), and he and his colleague Ap. Claudius Pulcher began the siege of *Capua (S. Maria Capua Vetere), which they captured as proconsuls in 211; Fulvius ordered the execution of the leaders of the revolt. He stayed in Campania in 210, and was appointed dictator to hold the elections for 209, presiding over his own election to a fourth consulship, during which he received the surrender of several towns in southern Italy. His command was prorogued both in 208, when he was again at Capua, and in 207, when he commanded in Bruttium. In 205, together with Q. *Fabius Maximus Verrucosus, he opposed P. *Cornelius Scipio Africanus' plan to invade Africa, and probably died soon afterwards.

J. Briscoe, *CAH* 8² (1989), 54–71.

J. Br.

Fulvius (*RE* 61) **Flaccus (2), Quintus,** son of the preceding, was curule aedile in 184 BC, when he tried unsuccessfully to stand at a praetorian by-election. Praetor eventually in 182, he spent that and the following two years in Spain fighting the *Celtiberians, and celebrated a triumph. He was consul in 179 with his own brother L. Manlius Acidinus Fulvianus; both consuls commanded in *Liguria, and Fulvius was awarded a second triumph. *Censor in 174–3, he was responsible for an extensive building programme in Rome and Italy. But he stripped the temple of Juno Lacinia, in southern Italy, of its marble tiles in order to roof his own temple of Fortuna Equestris in Rome; the senate ordered their restitution. In 172 news of the death of one son and the serious illness of another in Illyria caused him to commit suicide. It was believed that the anger of Juno Lacinia had driven him mad.

J. Briscoe, *JRS* 1964, 73–4.

J. Br.

Fulvius (*RE* 73) **Iunius Macrianus, Titus,** emperor AD 260–1, son of Fulvius Macrianus, a staff officer of *Valerian. After Valerian's capture, the elder Macrianus recognized *Gallienus and then, himself disqualified from imperial office by his lameness, elevated his two sons, Macrianus and Quietus. The former and his father were destroyed by Gallienus' troops in Thrace;

Quietus was killed at Emesa by *Septimius Odaenathus of Palmyra.

PLRE 1. 528; J. Šašel, Situla 1961, 3 ff.; J. F. Drinkwater, RSA 1989, 123 ff.
B. H. W.; J. F. Dr.

Fulvius (*RE* 91) **Nobilior, Marcus,** as praetor 193 and proconsul 192 BC in Further Spain, won a number of victories. Consul in 189, he conducted the siege of *Ambracia, eventually forcing the Aetolian Confederacy to accept peace terms. He was accompanied by the poet *Ennius, who celebrated Fulvius' exploits in both the *Annales* and the play *Ambracia*. He accepted the surrender of *Cephallenia, but the city of Same on the island immediately revolted, forcing Fulvius to undertake another long siege. He also intervened in a dispute between the Achaean Confederacy and Sparta. In 187 his conduct at Ambracia was attacked by the consul M. *Aemilius Lepidus (1), a bitter political opponent, who blamed Fulvius for his failure to secure the consulship on two previous occasions. An attempt by Lepidus to block Fulvius' triumph was unsuccessful. In 179 he and Lepidus were elected censors, and publicly reconciled. It may have been now, rather than in 187, that he dedicated a temple to *Hercules and the *Muses; it contained statues of the Muses (which, together with other works of art, Fulvius had removed from Ambracia), and a commentary by Fulvius on the *fasti.

E. Badian, Entretiens Hardt 1972, 183–99; Scullard, Rom. Pol. 180–1; O. Skutsch, The Annals of Ennius (1985), 144–6, 553–9; V. M. Warrior, Chiron 1988, 325–6 (chronology); J.-M. Pailler, Bacchanalia (1988), 682–703.
J. Br.

Fulvius (*RE* 101) **Plautianus, Gaius,** a native of *Lepcis Magna and kinsman of L. *Septimius Severus, was rapidly given important responsibilities. Probably prefect of the *vigiles in AD 195 (CIL 14 Suppl. 4380), he was praetorian prefect at latest on 1 January 197, was soon an honorary senator (clarissimus vir), and was comes (see COMITES) of Severus on all his expeditions from 193–202. In 202 his daughter *Fulvia Plautilla married *Caracalla with the title Augusta, he himself became ordinary *consul in 203, and in spite of at least one major quarrel with Severus, he appeared virtually all-powerful when Caracalla suddenly engineered his murder (205).

A. R. Birley, The African Emperor Septimius Severus, 2nd edn. (1988), esp. 220 f.
A. R. Bi.

Fundanius, Gaius, author of *fabulae *palliatae praised by Horace, *Sat.* 1. 10. 40–2. Belonging to *Maecenas' circle, he is imagined to describe Nasidienus' dinner (*Sat.* 2. 8. 19). Perhaps he was the *eques who joined Caesar in Spain in 45 BC (Bellum Hispaniense 11. 3; RE 'Fundanius' 2).
P. G. M. B.

Fundanus, Minicius or **Minucius** See MINICIUS.

Fundi (mod. Fondi), a Volscian town on the *via Appia. It obtained Roman *citizenship early (sine suffragio, 338 BC); full franchise, 188 BC), and became a prosperous *municipium. It has fine walls (originally 3rd-cent. BC, rebuilt 1st cent. BC), laid out in a square, and a street plan fossilized in the modern layout (see URBANISM). Its territory produced the choice Caecuban *wine; kilns for manufacturing the transport *amphorae have been found.

Not. Scav. 1971, 330 ff.
E. T. S.; T. W. P.

funerals See DEAD, DISPOSAL OF; DEATH, ATTITUDES TO.

Furies See ERINYES.

Furius (*RE* 34) **Antias** (i.e. of Antium), **Aulus** (fl. 100 BC), friend of Q. *Lutatius Catulus (1) (Cic. *Brut.* 132), epic poet influenced by Ennius and in turn influencing Virgil. From his *Annales*, a historical poem in at least eleven books, A. *Gellius (*NA* 18. 11) quotes six hexameters.

Courtney, FLP 97–8.
J. W. D.

Furius (*RE* 37) **Bibaculus, Marcus,** Latin poet, is said by *Jerome to have been born at Cremona in 103 BC. *Suetonius makes him a pupil of *Valerius Cato, another Cisalpine, and quotes two hendecasyllabic epigrams on Cato by him (*Gram.* 11); *Tacitus (1) mentions him and Catullus together (*Ann.* 4. 34. 5: cf. Quint. *Inst.* 10. 1. 26) as the authors of lampoons on 'the Caesars' which *Caesar and *Octavian ignored. These data seem to connect him with the circle of the *novi poetae* or 'new poets' (and he may be the Furius of Catullus 11, 16, 23, and 26); but in that case Jerome's date must be some twenty years too early. A contemporary poet whom *Horace accuses of bombast (*Sat.* 2. 5. 40) is identified by the scholia with Furius Bibaculus, author of a poem on 'the Gallic War', which may be the hexameter *Annales* (in at least eleven books) of one Furius from which *Macrobius (*Sat.* 6. 1) quotes some lines. The difficulty of ascribing a historical poem to the Bibaculus of Suetonius and Tacitus has suggested that there were two poets of the same name and that Jerome's date belongs to the epic poet—a precarious suggestion in view of the incompleteness of our knowledge of the literary currents of the time. See HELLENISTIC POETRY AT ROME.

Fragments in Courtney, FLP 192–200. G. B. Conte, Latin Literature (1994), 141.
C. J. F.; A. J. S. S.

Furius (*RE* 41) **Camillus (1), Lucius** According to Livy (7. 24. 11, 25. 10 ff.), as dictator in 350 BC he supervised the election to the consulship of 349 of himself and a fellow patrician (Diod. Sic. 16. 59. 1 has different consuls in 349) and as consul repulsed the Gauls, aided by the heroism of M. *Valerius Corvus. He or the consul of 338 (L. *Furius Camillus (2)) was reputedly dictator in 345, defeating the *Aurunci and vowing the temple of *Juno Moneta.

K.-J. Hölkeskamp, Die Entstehung der Nobilität (1987); A. Ziolkowski, AJPhil. 1993, 206 ff.
A. D.

Furius (*RE* 42) **Camillus (2), Lucius** As consul in 338 BC he triumphed (see TRIUMPH) over Pedum and *Tibur, allegedly received (with C. *Maenius) an equestrian statue in the Forum, and took a leading role in the Latin settlement (Livy 8. 13. 10 ff.). Re-elected consul for 325, he was forced by illness to appoint L. *Papirius Cursor (1) dictator to take command in *Samnium. (See also FURIUS CAMILLUS (1), L.).
A. D.

Furius (*RE* 44) **Camillus, Marcus,** consular tribune 401, 398, 394, 386, 384, 381, supposedly censor 403, and dictator 396, 390, 389, 368, 367 BC. His alleged campaigns against the Falisci and Capenates (see FALISCANS; CAPENA) in 401 and 398 hardly account for his appointment as dictator in 396 to complete the seizure of *Veii. After the victory he built a temple to the Veientan *Juno Regina on the *Aventine. He also reputedly restored the temple of *Matuta Mater in the *forum Boarium, but whether this can be reconciled with the archaeological evidence from the S. Omobono sanctuary is contentious.

In 394 he supposedly secured the surrender of Falerii, after refusing the offer of a *Faliscan schoolmaster to hand over his charges as hostages. Against this are set suggestions that his success at Veii attracted divine envy or (particularly in Livy (5. 23. 5 f.)) that by using the white horses of Jupiter and Sol in his triumph he set himself above his fellow citizens. These attempts to explain his subsequent fall are supplemented by stories of growing political tensions between Camillus and the *plebs*, culminating in his trial and exile in 391 (though *Diodorus (3) Siculus (14. 117. 6) records a tradition dating it after the Gallic sack of Rome in 390 (see BRENNUS (1)). However, the different accounts of Camillus' prosecutors and the charges against him (misappropriation or inequitable distribution of the Veientan booty or the triumph with white horses) support the view that this entire narrative was invented as an explanation for Camillus' apparent inability to prevent the Gallic sack and is partly modelled on the fate of Achilles and Scipio Africanus.

Similarly, the varying accounts of the departure of the Gauls in 390 and recovery (or non-recovery) of the gold paid as ransom suggest that the story of Camillus' recall, appointment as dictator, and dramatic intervention at the moment the ransom was weighed out is patriotic fiction, perhaps of late date (the Lucius who saved Rome according to *Aristotle (Plut. *Cam.* 22) can hardly be Marcus Camillus). Also fictitious will be the story of his decisive opposition to a renewed proposal of settlement at Veii, though this may go back to *Ennius (*Ann.* 154 f. Skutsch with comm.). Accounts of his actions in 390 may be influenced by parallels with *Sulla; they enable Livy to depict him in Ciceronian term as a 'second founder' of Rome and 'father of his country' (*parens patriae*), who articulates a highly traditionalist conception of the Roman identity, particularly in its religious dimension (5. 51 ff.).

Though Camillus' campaigns against the *Volsci and recovery of *Sutrium under 389 and 386 may be duplicates and the rapidity of Rome's recovery after the Gallic sack exaggerated, these advances and the absorption of *Tusculum in 381 may plausibly symbolize Roman resurgence, whatever Camillus' own role in them. However, his (apparently late) introduction into the trial of M. *Manlius Capitolinus is a dramatizing invention, as may be the dictatorships of 368 (reputedly to obstruct the Licinio-Sextian rogations: see LICINIUS STOLO) and 367 (when he supposedly defeated the Gauls and restored domestic harmony): his alleged creation of a temple of *Concordia (367) is almost certainly anachronistic.

Ogilvie, *Comm. Livy 1–5*; Drummond, *CAH* 7²/2 (1989), 298 ff.; Momigliano, *Secondo contributo*, 89 ff.; F. Coarelli, *Il foro boario* (1988), 216 ff.
A. D.

Furius (*RE* 78) **Philus, Lucius,** friend of P. *Cornelius Scipio Aemilianus, shared his cultural interests and was one of the patrons of *Terence. (See SCIPIONIC CIRCLE.) On this account he is introduced by Cicero as one of the interlocutors in *De republica*. As consul in 136 BC he, with Scipio and C. *Laelius (2) as assessors, was in charge of the inquiry into the treaty made by C. *Hostilius Mancinus with the Numantines (Cic. *Rep.* 3. 28) and, assigned Hither Spain as his province, of the surrender of Mancinus to the enemy. On this mission he took Q. *Caecilius Metellus Macedonicus and Q. *Pompeius, enemies of his and of each other, as *legati* to witness his action. He spoke good Latin, but without distinction (Cic. *Brut.* 108). The Furius said by Macrobius (*Sat.* 3. 9. 6 ff.) to have recorded one or both of two formulae of *evocatio* he quotes is probably Philus.

Astin, *Scipio*, see index; Sumner, *Orators* 61 (stemma). A. E. A.; E. B.

Furius (*RE* 89) **Sabinius Aquila Timesitheus, Gaius,** a brilliant equestrian administrator of humble origins. Having held a remarkable number of vicarial procuratorships (see VICARIUS) under *Severus Alexander, *Maximinus, and *Gordian III, in AD

241 he was appointed *Gordian III's praetorian prefect, and soon became his father-in-law. Till his death, on campaign in the east late in 243, he virtually ran the empire, restoring the monarchy to what it had been under Severus Alexander.

ILS 1330, and see under GORDIAN III. H. M. D. P.; J. F. Dr.

Furius Victorinus, Titus, began as an equestrian officer in the *tres militiae* (see TRIBUNI MILITUM) and, after holding various procuratorships, the prefecture of both Italian fleets (see NAVIES), of the *vigiles, and the *annona, was prefect of Egypt in AD 159–60, becoming praetorian prefect in 160. He held this post until his death, probably from the plague, in 168, at the beginning of the Marcomannic War.

SHA *Ant. Pius, M. Ant.*; *PIR*² F 584; H.-G. Pflaum, *Les Carrières procuratoriennes équestres* (1960–1), no. 139. A. R. Bi.

furniture The table, chair, and couch are the central canon of ancient furnishings. Their principal characteristic (by contrast with early modern and modern furnishings) is portability, essential in the circumstances of ancient domestic life, with use of space, and even choice of house, at least among the élite, varying with season and occasion. Heavy desks and armoires, immovable dressers and cabinets had no place in a theory of habitation which revolved round the current location of the principal persons of the family; their environment had to be speedily arranged for them, if not around them, with screens, curtains, and equipment for the current activity, be it eating, drinking, sleeping, writing—and portable furniture to support small utensils, *lamps, containers. Furniture was also a form of capital accumulation (as its place in inventories from the Mycenaean period already shows), deriving value from rare materials, ebony in Greek usage, *citrus* (Gk. *thyon*, *Callitris quadrivalvis*, a North African tree) in Roman, see TIMBER; or workmanship (lathe-turning is known in Assyria; fine figured representations, as on the chest of *Cypselus, were common, and best known to us from the wooden sarcophagi of the Crimea). The very wealthy needed large quantities to equip communal dining: the case of the younger Seneca's 500 *citrus*-wood tables with *ivory legs illustrates the pursuit of both quality and quantity. Oak and beech were used for cheaper furniture; cypress, cedar, and maple had a good reputation. Fine bronze, gold, silver, and enamel became widespread, as the finds of *Pompeii and *Herculaneum testify; luxury furniture of this kind was held to have arrived in Rome from Anatolia with the triumph of Cn. *Manlius Vulso in 187 BC. Representations in Greek vase-painting and Roman wall-paintings attest a very great variety of styles. See HOUSES, GREEK and ITALIAN.

G. M. A. Richter, *The Furniture of the Greeks, Etruscans and Romans* (1966); W. Deonna, *Le mobilier délien* (1938); R. Meiggs, *Trees and Timber in the Ancient Mediterranean World* (1983), 279–99. N. P.

Furrina, Roman goddess whose relatively early importance is reflected in the festival of the Furrinalia (25 July) and the existence of a *flamen Furrinalis* (see FLAMINES). Her cult at Rome was located in a sacred grove on the slopes of the *Janiculum in Transtiberim: here C. *Sempronius Gracchus died in 121 BC (Plutarch, *C. Gracch.* 17, Hellenizing the cult interestingly in calling the place *also Eumenidōn*, 'the grove of the Furies', from the analogy Furrina-Furiae: later dedications refer to 'Furrinian nymphs' rather than to a single goddess). The site, in a well-watered cleft in the hillside, became an important cult place in the Syrian tradition in the later empire (see SYRIAN DEITIES), and its well-preserved remains offer an interesting case history of the constant process of reinterpretation of the forms of cult in the religious tradition of the city.

N. Goodhue, *The Syrian Sanctuary of the Janiculum* (1975). H. Scullard, *Festivals and Ceremonies of the Roman Republic* (1981), 168–9.   N. P.

furtum See THEFT.

Fuscus See ARELLIUS FUSCUS; ARISTIUS FUSCUS; CORNELIUS FUSCUS; PEDANIUS FUSCUS.

Gabii, an ancient Latin city (see LATINI) 19 km. (12 mi.) to the east of Rome, and situated in a geographically critical position on both east–west and north routes. Occupied from the middle bronze age, it developed rapidly from the 9th cent. BC; *c.*350 tombs of the Latian culture have been excavated at Osteria dell'Osa. According to tradition it was founded by *Alba Longa (Verg. *Aen.* 6. 773). Its resistance to *Tarquinius Superbus, separate treaty with Rome, and special role in augural practices (see AUGURES) prove its early importance (Livy 1. 53 f.; Dion. Hal. *Ant. Rom.* 4. 53; Varro, *Ling.* 5. 33). After 493 BC Gabii appears as Rome's ally. Under the empire Gabii was a prosperous *municipium with celebrated baths and ornate Hadrianic buildings (*ILS* 272). Although still a bishopric in the 9th cent. AD, there are few standing remains, most notably the temple of *Juno (early 5th cent. BC, rebuilt in the 2nd cent. BC). There was also an archaic temple (6th cent. BC) possibly of *Apollo (cf. Livy 41. 16). The Romans reputedly derived from Gabii the *cinctus Gabinus*, a particular mode of wearing the *toga which was used in certain ceremonial rites (Serv. on *Aen.* 7. 612; Livy 5. 46).

L. Quilici, *Collatia* (1974), 439; M. Almagro Gorbea, *El santuario de Juno en Gabii* (1982); A. M. Bietti Sestieri, *Preistoria e protostoria nel territorio di Roma* (1984), 160 ff. T. W. P.

Gabinius (1) (*RE* 6), **Aulus,** allegedly grandson of a slave, served under Q. *Caecilius Metellus Macedonicus in Macedonia (148 BC) and in 146 was sent to warn the Achaeans against war. As tribune 139, he introduced vote by ballot in elections.

A. H. McD.; E. B.

Gabinius (2) (*RE* 10–11), **Aulus,** probably grandson of A. *Gabinius (1), was military tribune under *Sulla and later his envoy to L. *Licinius Murena and *Mithradates VI. As tribune 67 BC, he transferred Bithynia-Pontus and part of the army from L. *Licinius Lucullus (2) to the consul M'. *Acilius Glabrio (3), discharging the *Fimbriani* (cf. FLAVIUS FIMBRIA, C.). He then passed a law setting up a command with wide powers against the pirates, intended for *Pompey. (To overcome a veto, he initiated a process of deposition against his colleague Trebellius.) He served under Pompey in the east and was made consul 58 by the three dynasts, with L. *Calpurnius Piso Caesoninus. The consuls supported P. *Clodius Pulcher against Cicero, and Gabinius ultimately received the rich province of Syria as his reward. There he alienated the *publicani by largely taking over the tax collection for his own benefit. He restored *Ptolemy (1) XII (Auletes) (who reportedly paid him 10,000 talents), left Roman legionaries to support him, and intervened in Judaea, imposing a settlement acceptable to *Antipater (6). Guilty of contravening several laws, and having made important enemies, he was prosecuted on his return and finally convicted *repetundarum*, even though his

enemy Cicero had been forced by Pompey to defend him. He went into exile (54), was recalled by *Caesar and fought for him in Illyria, dying of illness at *Salonae (47).

E. Badian, *Philol.* 1959, 87 ff.; C. F. Konrad, *Klio* 1984, 151 ff. (stemma). For the *lex Gabinia Calpurnia* on Delos (58), see C. Nicolet and others, *Insula Sacra* (1980). E. B.

Gades (Phoenician Gadir; now Cádiz), north-west of Gibraltar. The traditional foundation by *Phoenicians of *Tyre *c.*1100 BC is lowered by archaeologists to the 8th cent. BC. The port lay on the island of Erytheia. The sanctuaries to Baal Hammon and Heracles-Melqart and the cemetery lay on Cotinussa island immediately to the south. A third island (Antipolis) lay to the east. Gadir originally traded for metals with *Tartessus. It issued coins with Phoenician lettering down to the early 1st cent. BC. It had been *Hamilcar (2) Barca's first Spanish base and, after going over to Rome in 206 BC, enjoyed favoured status. After various acts of patronage *Caesar granted municipal status (see MUNICIPIUM) to Gades after 49 BC (*Urbs Iulia Gaditana*), reaffirmed by *Augustus. Construction of Roman Gades (Didyma) on Cotinussa was begun by 46 BC, aided by the patronage of the Cornelii Balbi. (See CORNELIUS BALBUS (1–2), L.) The theatre, amphitheatre, circus, and cemetery have been located. *Columella and *Hadrian's mother came from the city. Production of fish sauce (see FISHING) was important to its economy. Little is known about its fate in the middle or late empire.

J. Ramirez Delgado, *Los primitivos nucleos de asentamiento en la ciudad de Cádiz* (1982); J. F. Rodríguez Neila, *El municipio romano de Gades* (1980). S. J. K.

Gaia, Gē, the Earth, a primordial goddess. In Hes. *Theog.* (116 ff.) the original entity was *Chaos, then came Gaia and other beings like *Eros. Gaia had many children from her son *Uranus, including the *Titans. In the Titanomachy she assists *Zeus by telling him what he needs to do to win (Hes. *Theog.* 626–8). But after the defeat of the Titans (820–2) she produces, from her union with *Tartarus, the monster *Typhon who was a threat to the order of the Olympians, but was defeated by Zeus. The Olympians chose Zeus as their ruler on Gaia's advice. She is generally ambivalent: she can be deceitful and threatening, dangerous, and gives birth to creatures that pester gods and men. But she is also a positive nurturing figure. In Athens there was an important cult of Gē Kourotrophos; the sanctuary of Gē Kourotrophos and *Demeter Chloe was near the entrance to the Acropolis (Paus. 1. 22. 3). Besides offerings to Gē and to Gē Kourotrophos (and other mentions of the latter (cf. e.g. Ar. *Thesm.* 300)), there also appears in sacrificial *calendars, a figure called simply Kourotrophos, who may have been identical to Gē Kourotrophos, though we cannot be certain. A popular episode in Attic art is the representation of the birth of *Erichthonius, where Gaia is shown as a woman emerging from the ground, handing the baby Erichthonius to Athena. The story that Gaia was the original owner of the *Delphic oracle is not a reflection of cult history, but a myth. The earliest evidence for a cult of Gaia at Delphi is early 5th cent. BC. At *Olympia, *Pausanias (3) tells us (5. 14. 10) the sanctuary of Gaia (Gaion) had an ash altar of Gaia and it was said that in earlier times there had been an oracle of Gē there.

M. B. Moore, *LIMC* 4 (1988), 171–7, 'Ge'; T. Hadzisteliou Price, *Kourotrophos: Cults and Representations of the Greek Nursing Deities* (1978); C. Bérard, *Anodoi: Essai sur l'imagerie des passages chthoniens* (1974), 26–9, 34–8; Nilsson, *GGR* 1³. 456–61; Farnell, *Cults* 3. 1–28, 307–11; Deubner, *Attische Feste* 26–7; C. Sourvinou-Inwood, *'Reading' Greek Culture* (1991), 217–43. C. S.-I.

Gaiseric, king of the *Vandals and *Alans AD 428 to 477. In 429 he transported his followers from Spain to North Africa, and by 439 had conquered *Carthage. In the 430s, 441–2, and the late 460s he survived major Roman attempts to overthrow him. His most famous exploit was the sack of Rome in June 455, when the city was stripped of many treasures, but the sack was part of a broader bid to a role in imperial politics, including support for Olybrius' claims to the throne and marrying his son Huneric to Eudocia, a daughter of *Valentinian III. These plans came to nothing, but Constantinople was forced to treat with him in c.474.

C. Courtois, *Les Vandales et l'Afrique* (1955); F. Clover, *The Late Roman West and the Vandals* (1993). P. J. H.

Gaius (1), the emperor, 'Caligula' (Gaius Iulius (*RE* 133) Caesar Germanicus, AD 12–41), son of *Germanicus and *Agrippina the Elder, born at *Antium (31 August). In 14–16 he was on the Rhine with his parents and, dressed in miniature uniform, was nicknamed 'Caligula' ('Bootee') by the soldiers. He went with his parents to the east in 17 and, after Germanicus' death in 19, lived in Rome with his mother until her arrest in 29, then successively with *Livia Drusilla and *Antonia (3) until he joined *Tiberius on Capreae. The downfall of Tiberius' favourite *Sejanus in 31 was to Gaius' advantage, and it was probably engineered by him and associates such as the prefect of the watch (*vigiles) *Macro, who also benefited. After the death of his brother Drusus *Iulius Caesar (2) in 33 Gaius was the only surviving son of Germanicus and, with Tiberius *Iulius Caesar Nero 'Gemellus'—*Claudius' claim not being considered—next in succession. He became pontifex in 31 and was quaestor two years later, but received no other training in public life. Tiberius made Gaius and Gemellus joint heirs to his property, but, supported by Macro, now prefect of the praetorian guard (see PRAEFECTUS PRAETORIO), Gaius was proclaimed emperor (16 March 37); Tiberius' will being declared invalid by the senate, although his acts as a whole were not invalidated; Gaius made an appropriately perfunctory effort to have him deified.

Gaius' accession was greeted with widespread joy and relief, and his civility promised well. One symbolic gesture was the restoration of electoral choice to the popular assemblies, taken from them in 14 (it failed and Gaius had to revert to Tiberian procedure). Gaius needed to enhance his authority and held the consulship four times, in 37 (suffect, so that the men in office in March were not disturbed), 39, 40 (sole consul), and 41; he became *Pater Patriae (father of his country), a title refused by Tiberius, on 21 September, 37. In the early months of his rule he honoured the memory of his mother, father, and brothers and spoke abusively of Tiberius. Antonia, a restraining influence, died

on 1 May 37. In October Gaius was seriously ill; Philon (4)'s view (*Leg.* 14, 22) that this unhinged him has been given too much attention. But the illness may have brought the succession question into prominence: some time before 24 May 38, Gaius executed both Macro and his rival Gemellus. In 39 Gaius quarrelled with the senate, revised his attitude towards Tiberius' memory, announcing the return of slandering the emperor as a treasonable offence. The same year he married his fourth wife, Milonia Caesonia, who had already borne him a daughter, proving her fertility. The autumn and winter of 39–40 Gaius spent in Gaul and on the Rhine; a conspiracy was revealed whose leader, Cn. *Cornelius Lentulus Gaetulicus, commander of the Upper Rhine army, was executed. This conspiracy may be connected with the simultaneous disgrace of his brother-in-law (and possible successor) M. *Aemilius Lepidus (6) and of Gaius' surviving sisters *Iulia Agrippina and *Iulia (5) Livilla. After his return to Rome (in ovation, on 31 August 40) Gaius was in constant danger of assassination, having no successor to avenge him, displayed increasing brutality, and was murdered in the palace on 22 or 24 January 41. His wife and daughter were also murdered.

The government of Gaius was autocratic and capricious, and he accepted extravagant honours which came close to deification. His reign has been interpreted as a departure from the Augustan Principate to a Hellenistic monarchy. Rather, Gaius seems to have been engaged in discovering the limits of his power ('for me anything is licit', Suet. *Calig.* 29). He was a person of the highest descent (he once banished *Agrippa from his ancestry by postulating incest between Augustus and his daughter *Iulia (3)), which helps to account for the unprecedented attention paid to his sisters, *Iulia Drusilla, whose death in 38 was followed by a public funeral and consecration, Livilla, and Agrippina; he possessed an exceptional intellect and a cruel and cynical wit; and he demanded exceptional homage and was savage if his superiority was not recognized. A gifted orator, who delivered Livia's *laudatio funebris at the age of 17, he enjoyed writing rebuttals of successful speeches. By insisting on primacy in everything Gaius left even courtiers no role of their own. He had terrified the senators, humiliated officers of the praetorian guard (who carried out the assassination), and only the masses seem to have regretted his passing.

Gaius was a keen builder, interested in the state of Italy's roads and in Rome's water supply (he began the aqua Claudia (see AQUEDUCTS) and *Anio Novus). For the sake of the grain supply he began to improve the harbour at *Rhegium. He also completed the reconstruction of the theatre of Pompey and created a circus in the Vatican; other constructions were for his own pleasure, for instance the bridge of boats from *Puteoli to Bauli (39), an ephemeral extravagance to outdo *Xerxes or overawe a Parthian hostage.

Gaius' high expenditures were economically advantageous, ending the sluggishness of Tiberius' regime. His achievements abroad, with the exception of his deployment of client rulers, were negative. He probably raised two new *legions (XV and XXII Primigeniae) for an invasion of Germany or Britain. However, his forays into Germany in the autumn of 39 may have been exercises intended to restore discipline after the fall of Gaetulicus and to commemorate the campaigns of Germanicus in 13–16 (the famous collection of sea shells, 'spoils of Ocean', probably alludes to the North Sea storms that Germanicus had encountered; here the *Chauci and *Chatti were still causing trouble in 41. The conquest of Britain was only mooted, and was considered achieved when *Cunobelinus' son Adminius came to render homage (Gaius could not afford to leave the centres of empire in 39–40). By deposing and executing *Ptolemy (2) of Mauretania he provoked a war that was brought to an end only in the next reign. For the Jews under Gaius see below.

Suet. *Calig.* (comm. by J. A. Marner, 1949); Cass. Dio 59; Joseph. *AJ* 18. 6. 8. 205–19. 2. 5. 111; Philo, *In Flacc.*, ed. H. Box (1939); *Leg.*, ed. and trans. E. M. Smallwood, 1961; *The Acts of the Pagan Martyrs: Acta Alexandrinorum*, ed. and comm. H. A. Musurillo (1954). J. P. V. D. Balsdon, *The Emperor Gaius (Caligula)* (1934); A. Barrett, *Caligula—The Corruption of Power* (1990); D. Boschung, *Die Bildnisse des Caligula* (1989). J. P. B.; B. M. L.

Gaius and the Jews Soon after his accession, Gaius conferred a kingship in Palestine upon his friend, the Herodian *Agrippa I. However, their understanding did not prevent discord between the inconsistent emperor and his Jewish subjects. A savage conflict between Jews and Greeks in *Alexandria (1) stood unresolved when Gaius died. The prefect, A. *Avillius Flaccus, seemingly abandoning any pretence at even-handedness when Gaius succeeded, had backed the Greek side in the long-standing dispute with the Jews over citizen rights. Agrippa I, visiting *en route* for his kingdom, was mocked by the Greek crowd and a pogrom thereby unleashed. It was on the emperor's birthday that Jews who had survived the assaults on the Jewish quarter were rounded up in the theatre and made to eat pork. While Gaius did have Flaccus arrested and replaced in late 38, he disdainfully ignored the delegations sent to Rome by both groups, leaving his successor to investigate and settle the matter.

Among the Jews of Palestine, Gaius' policy was heading for disaster when he died. A statue of the emperor was to be placed in the Jerusalem Temple and worshipped: this was perhaps Gaius' reaction to the Alexandrian Jewish delegation (Josephus), perhaps a response to the destruction by Jews at Jamnia, of their pagan neighbours' altar to the emperor (Philon). Stalling by P. *Petronius, governor of Syria, apparently sympathetic to Jewish pleas, delayed developments; and the intervention of Agrippa, whose long and perhaps genuine letter to Gaius is quoted by *Philon (4), is alleged to have effected the abandonment of the plan. Philon claims that it was then reinstated by secret orders; but this he could scarcely have known. In general lines, however, the events are well documented: Philon was a participant, heading the Alexandrian Jews' delegation to Gaius, while *Josephus offers two distinct accounts of the events in Palestine.

Philo, *Leg.*, ed. and trans. E. M. Smallwood (1961); *In Flacc.*; Joseph. *BJ* 2. 184–203; *AJ* 18. 257–309. T. R.

Gaius (2) (*RE* 2), the famous 2nd-cent. AD law teacher, was lecturing in 160/1 and still alive in 178. Though a Roman citizen, he was known, and apparently chose to be known, by the single undistinctive name 'Gaius'. Some phrases in his work read as if written in Rome; others point to an eastern province. The key to the puzzle may be that Gaius, who speaks of the school of *Masurius Sabinus and C. *Cassius Longinus (2) as his teachers (*nostri praeceptores*), had his legal education in Rome but taught and wrote mainly in the east, *Berytus (mod. Beirut), since Augustus a Roman colony with Italian status (*ius Italicum*), being a possible location. He is best known for his *Institutes* ('Teaching Course'), elementary lectures for students delivered in 160–1 but probably not published by himself. A 5th-cent. manuscript of these lectures, the most substantial legal work of the Principate to survive, was discovered in Verona in 1816 overwritten by later writing. Despite scribal errors most modern scholars regard the text as largely genuine. It is marked by clarity of style, attention

to history, concern for classification, and a critical attitude to legal rules, for example the lifelong tutelage of women (*Inst.* 1. 190). It employs a 'Socratic' method of teaching (see SOCRATES) which often leaves unanswered the problem raised. A later work called *Res cottidianae* ('Everyday Matters'), at one time said to be of the 3rd cent. or later but now thought to be a genuine work of Gaius, refines and develops the sometimes loosely expressed text of the *Institutes*. Gaius was a prolific writer, the author of 30 books (*libri*) *Ad edictum provinciale* ('On the Provincial Edict'), a treatise *Ad legem XII tabularum* ('On the Law of the Twelve Tables'), and numerous other monographs. Justinian's compilers (see JUSTINIAN'S CODIFICATION) excerpted 521 passages from his works.

Opinions differ as to his merits. He was no casuist; but his classifications are at least in part original. He invented or carried forward new types of legal literature, with an emphasis, natural if he was writing in the provinces, on imperial law. Gaius' *Institutes* were known in Egypt early in the 3rd cent. but, again perhaps because he was a provincial writer, none of his works are cited by later authors such as *Ulpian who would be likely to have known of them. In the 4th cent. his work spread to the west, and in 426 was officially recognized by the Law of Citations, which put him on a level with *Papinianus, *Paulus, Ulpianus, and *Modestinus as a writer whose work as a whole possessed authority. In Justinian's time he is affectionately called *Gaius noster* ('our Gaius') and Justinian's *Institutes* ('Teaching Course') are in effect a second edition of his work of that name. Through Justinian his has proved to be the most influential teaching manual for lawyers; and his classifications formed the basis of civil law systems in Europe up to the time of the French and German codes.

INSTITUTES See G. Studemund, *Apographum* (1874); editions by E. Seckel and B. Kuebler (Teubner, 1935); F. de Zulueta, with trans. and comm. (1946, 1953); W. M. Gordon and O. F. Robinson, with trans. (1988); M. David and H. L. W. Nelson, *Studia Gaiana* 2–3, with comm. (1954–68, incomplete), cf. H. L. W. Nelson, *Überlieferung, Aufbau und Stil von Gai Institutiones* (1981).
LITERATURE Lenel, *Pal.* 1. 182–266; 2. 1261; *PIR*² G 22; *HLL* 4, § 426; W. Kunkel, *Kleinere Schriften* (1974), 186–213; Honoré (1962); F. Casavola, *Giuristi Adrianei* (1980), 145–62; D. Liebs, *ANRW* 2. 5 (1976), 294–356; O. Stanojevic, *Gaius noster* (1989). T. Hon.

Gaius Caesar See IULIUS CAESAR (2), C.

Galatea (Γαλάτεια, perhaps 'milk-white'), name of a sea-nymph, first in *Homer (*Il.* 18. 45); her legend was apparently first told by *Philoxenus (1) (see *PLG*⁴ 3. 609 ff.). Polyphemus (see CYCLOPES) loved her, and wooed her uncouthly; the story is a favourite especially with pastoral writers (Theoc. *Id.* 6, 11; Bion, fr. 16 Gow OCT *Buc. Gr.*; Moschus, Ἐπιτάφιος Βίωνος (*Lament for *Bion* (2), in Gow, as above, 140 ff., lines 58 ff.; Verg. *Ecl.* 9. 39 ff.; cf. 2. 19 ff.; 7. 37 ff.; but particularly Ov. *Met.* 13. 738 ff.). In this, the earliest surviving passage which adds anything important to the story, Galatea loved a youth, Acis, son of *Faunus (Pan ?) and a river-nymph. Together they listened in hiding to Polyphemus' love-song, but when he had finished he rose to go and caught sight of them. Galatea dived into the sea, but Polyphemus pursued Acis and hurled a huge rock at him. As it fell on him and crushed him, Galatea turned him into a river, which bore his name ever after. The whole may well be a local Sicilian tale. The resemblance between Galatea's name and Γαλάτης, a Gaul, seems to underlie a less-known version in which she finally accepted Polyphemus' attentions and had by him a son, Galas or Galates, ancestor of the Gauls (see App. *Ill.* 2)—

mere pseudo-historical or pseudo-mythical aetiology. The love-story appears in Roman art, especially wall-painting (*LIMC* 5. 1 (1990), 1000–5). H. J. R.

Galatia is used, when applied to territory in the east, in two senses.

(1) The name of a region in central *Asia Minor stretching east and west of modern Ankara, comprising parts of what was formerly *Phrygia and *Cappadocia; this was occupied and settled by migrating Celtic tribes, who had crossed the Helles-pont in 278 BC and reached the area in the following decade after much raiding and plundering in western Anatolia. These Galatians were defeated in two battles by *Attalus (1) I of Perga-mum around 230 BC and by a Roman army under Cn. *Manlius Vulso in 189 BC. In the 1st cent. BC they became firm allies of Rome, acting as a bulwark against *Mithradates VI, and in the generation before the Augustan settlement Galatian tribal leaders controlled territory in Asia Minor from the Pamphylian coast to *Trapezus. Their central territory was divided between three tribes, the Tolistobogii in the west (who controlled the former temple state of *Pessinus), the Tectosages around *Ancyra, and the Trocmi in the east around Tavium. According to *Strabo 12. 5. 1, each tribe was subdivided into four sections and ruled by a tetrarch (see TETRARCHY). A common council of the three tribes met at a place called Drynemeton (the word means 'sacred oak-grove') and tried cases of murder. The Galat-ians maintained their Celtic character throughout the imperial period and Celtic was still spoken in the rural districts as late as the 6th cent. AD (see CELTIC LANGUAGES; CELTS).

(2) The name of a Roman province, formed in 25 BC from the former kingdom of the Galatian tetrarch *Amyntas (2), which comprised Galatia in the narrow sense, much of eastern Phrygia, *Lycaonia, *Isauria, *Pisidia, and *Pamphylia. Other territories in *Paphlagonia and *Pontus were added to the province between 6 BC and AD 64. Under Augustus until AD 6 a Roman force, Legio VII, was stationed in the south, and the province was usually governed by consular legates; thereafter until the Flavian period the governors were more often of praetorian status. Under *Ves-pasian Galatia was combined with Cappadocia to form a huge provincial complex covering all of central and eastern Anatolia as far as the river Euphrates, which was now defended by legions stationed at Satala in Armenia Minor and at *Melitene in eastern Cappadocia. Galatia/Cappadocia thus became one of the most important military command areas in the empire. After AD 112 the Pontic regions and Cappadocia were given their own consular legate, and Galatia reverted to praetorian governors; the province was further reduced in size when Lycaonia and Isauria were removed to form the triple province with Cilicia under *Antoni-nus Pius. The provincial arrangements of the later empire saw further reductions and divisions.

It is disputed whether the Galatians addressed in St *Paul's epistle were the inhabitants of Galatia in the narrow sense (the so-called 'North Galatian' theory) or the inhabitants of the southern part of the Galatian province, citizens of Pisidian *Antioch (2), Iconium, Lystra, and Derbe, which Paul is known to have visited (the 'South Galatian' theory). The latter is more likely.

F. Stähelin, *Geschichte der kleinasiatischen Galater*, 2nd edn. (1907); W. M. Ramsay, *A Historical Commentary on St Paul's Epistle to the Gal-atians* (1899); R. K. Sherk and S. Mitchell, *ANRW* 2. 7. 2 (1980), 954–1052, 1053–81; S. Mitchell, *Anatolia*, 2 vols. (1993). W. M. C.; S. M.

Galba, the emperor (Servius Sulpicius (*RE* 63) Galba, 3 BC–AD 69), from an ancient patrician family, son of C. Sulpicius Galba

and Mummia Achaica, through the empress *Livia's favour moved in the most elevated social circles of the Julio-Claudian era. He was governor of *Aquitania, consul (33), governor of Upper Germany (40–2), and proconsul of Africa (44–5); his stand-ing was recognized by the award of triumphal insignia and three priesthoods. Governor of Hispania *Tarraconensis from 60, he was approached in 68 by C. *Iulius Vindex, who was instigating revolt against *Nero. Galba had his troops proclaim him as repre-sentative of the senate and people of Rome, and enrolled a new *legion (eventually VII Gemina) in addition to the one in his province. Although Vindex was defeated, Nero's suicide and the support of C. *Nymphidius Sabinus and the praetorians encour-aged Galba to march on Rome, accompanied by *Otho, governor of *Lusitania. Once in power, Galba tried to recover Nero's extravagant largess, but the execution of several opponents including L. *Clodius Macer who had raised revolt in Africa, and the brutal killing of soldiers recruited by Nero from the fleet, cast a shadow. His avarice was notorious. He declined to pay the praetorians the donative (see DONATIVUM) promised by Nymphidius, saying that it was his practice to levy his troops not to buy them. He compounded this misjudgement by failing to control his own supporters, and by sending his newly recruited legion to *Pannonia. 'In everyone's opinion he was capable of being emperor had he never ruled' (Tac. *Hist.* 1. 49). When on 1 January the legions of Upper Germany, who felt that they had been cheated of their reward for defeating Vindex, renounced their allegiance, Galba decided to adopt a successor, choosing L. *Calpurnius Piso Frugi Licinianus. Otho, coveting this role for himself, fomented revolt among the praetorians, who murdered Galba on 15 January 69.

SOURCES Tac. *Hist.* 1. 1–49; Suet. *Galb.*; Plut. *Galb.* (for the common source of these three authors, see Syme, *Tacitus*, app. 29; G. B. Townend, *AJPhil.* 1964, 337); Cass. Dio 63. 22–64. 7.

MODERN DISCUSSION G. E. F. Chilver, *JRS* 1957, 29; R. Syme, *Tacitus*, 152, and *Hist.* 1982, 460 (= *RP* 4. 115); P. A. Brunt, *Latomus* 1959, 531 (= id., *Roman Imperial Themes* (1990), 9); K. Wellesley, *The Long Year, AD 69* (1975); G. E. F. Chilver, *A Historical Commentary on Tacitus' 'Histories' I and II* (1979). J. B. C.

Galen, of *Pergamum (AD 129–?199/216) in a spectacular career rose from gladiator physician in Asia Minor to court physician in the Rome of Marcus *Aurelius. The son of a wealthy architect, he enjoyed an excellent education in rhetoric and philosophy in his native town before turning to medicine. After studying medicine further in *Smyrna and *Alexandria (1), he began prac-tising in Pergamum in 157, and went to Rome in 162. Driven out by hostile competitors, or fear of the *plague, in 166, he returned in 169, and remained in imperial service until his death. A prodi-gious polymath, he wrote on subjects as varied as grammar and gout, ethics and eczema, and was highly regarded in his lifetime as a philosopher as well as a doctor.

Although *Plato (1) and *Hippocrates (2) were his gods, and *Aristotle ranked only slightly below them, he was anxious to form his own independent judgements, and his assertive person-ality pervades all his actions and writings. His knowledge was equally great in theory and practice, and based in part on his own considerable library. Much of our information on earlier medicine derives from his reports alone, and his scholarly delinea-tion of the historical Hippocrates and the writings associated with him formed the basis for subsequent interpretation down to the 20th cent.

He made ambitious efforts to encompass the entirety of medi-cine, deriding those who were mere specialists or who rejected any engagement with theory. The best physician was, whether or not he knew it, also a philosopher, as well as a man good with his hands. Galen reports some spectacular surgical successes, like his removal of a suppurating breastbone, and he expected even moderate healers to be able to perform minor *surgery. Although he rarely refrained from laying down the law on how to *diagnose and treat patients, he equally stressed the inadequacy of general rules in an individual case. Although contemporaries credited him with almost miraculous skills in prognosis (which incorporated diagnosis), especially in what might be termed stress-related diseases, he replied that they were easily derived from Hippocratic first principles and that a sound diagnosis depended on close observation of every detail. His authoritative bedside manner would also have contributed to his success with patients.

Galen was particularly productive as anatomist and physiologist (see ANATOMY AND PHYSIOLOGY). Dissecting animals, especially monkeys, pigs, sheep, and goats, carefully and often, he collected and corrected the results of earlier generations by experiment, superior factual information, and logic. His physiological research was at times masterly, particularly in his series of experiments ligating or cutting the spinal cord. At others, his reliance largely on non-human anatomy, coupled with his belief that the basic structures of the human body had been described by Hippocrates, led him to 'see' things that were not there, e.g. the *rete mirabile* at the base of the human skull, cotyledons in the womb, and a connection between spleen and stomach.

His *pathology, founded on the doctrines of the four *humours and of three organic systems, heart, brain, and liver, explained disease mainly as an imbalance, detectable particularly through qualitative changes in the body. His *pharmacology and *dietetics were largely codifications of earlier learning, enlivened by personal observations and occasional novel ideas, as with his (unfulfilled and later influential) attempt to classify drugs according to twelve grades of activity.

His philosophy was equally eclectic. His major enterprise to create a logic of scientific demonstration, surviving only in fragments, went beyond Aristotle and the Stoics (see STOICISM) in both the range and precision of its arguments. Later authors credited him with innovations in syllogistic logic, and with powerful critiques of *Peripatetic and Stoic ideas on motion. In his psychology, he favoured a Platonic tripartite *soul over the Stoic unity, bringing the evidence of anatomy to support his case, in the same way as he used Aristotelian ideas on mixture to explain changes in the physical humours. His 'philosophical autobiography', *On My Own Opinions*, reveals the interactions between his medicine and his philosophy, as well as the limits he placed on certitude.

Galen's monotheistic views, his ardent belief in teleology, and his religious attitude—even anatomy was a veneration of God, and he was convinced of the personal protection of *Asclepius—foreshadow the Middle Ages. His dominant influence on later generations, comparable only to that of Aristotle, is based on his achievements as scientist, logician, and universal scholar, and on his own self-proclaimed insistence on establishing a medicine that was beyond all sectarianism. The dissension of earlier science could be conquered by an eclectic rationality based ultimately on notions in which all shared, and be turned into a stable system of Galenic medical and practical philosophy. See MEDICINE, § 6. 1.

TEXTS *Opera omnia*, C. G. Kühn (1821–33), largely complete for the Greek, but text often unreliable; repr. 1964–5, with extensive bibliography. A few texts in Teubner: *Scripta Minora* 1–3 (1884–93); *Institutes of Logic* (1896); *On Dieting* (1898); *On Temperaments* (1904); *On the Use of*

Parts (1879); Loeb has *On the Natural Faculties* (1916). The *CMG* series (1909– 	) has published much improved texts, since 1963 with trans. and comm. (lists in bibliographies below). Works in *CMG* but not in Kühn are: *Commentary on Plato's Timaeus* (1934) (new fragments edited by C. Larrain (1992)); *On Procatarctic Causes* (1937); *On Habits* (1941); *On the Parts of Medicine; On Cohesive Causes; Regimen in Acute Diseases according to Hippocrates* (1969); *On the Differences between Homoeomerous Parts* (1970); *On Examining the Physician* (1988); and substantial sections from the *Commentaries on Epidemics I, II, III and VI* (1932–40). Other published treatises preserved only in the oriental tradition include: *Anatomical Procedures IX–XV*, M. Lyons, Eng. trans. (1962); *Commentary on Airs, Waters, Places* (sections), A. Wasserstein (1988; full edition forthcoming); *Commentary on the Hippocratic Oath*, F. Rosenthal, *Bull. Hist. Med.* 1956; *Compendium of the Timaeus*, R. Walzer (1941); *On Demonstration* (fragments), I. von Müller, *Abh. Akad. Wiss. Münch.* 1895; *On Medical Experience*, R. Walzer (1944); *On Medical Terminology*, M. Meyerhof, *Abh. Berl. Akad.* 1931; *On Morals*, J. Mattock, *Festschrift R. Walzer* (1972); *On My Own Opinions*, V. Nutton, *Festschrift P. Moraux*, 2 (1987).

ENGLISH TRANSLATIONS include: *Hygiene*, R. M. Green (1951); *Anatomical Procedures I–IX*, C. Singer (1956); *On the Passions and Errors of the Soul*, P. Harkins (1964); *On the Use of Parts*, M. T. May (1968); *On the Opinions of Hippocrates and Plato*, P. DeLacy (*CMG* 1978–84); *On Prognosis*, V. Nutton (*CMG* 1979); *On Respiration and the Arteries*, D. Furley and J. Wilkie (1983); *On Sects; Outline of Empiricism; On Medical Experience*, M. Frede and R. Walzer (1985); *On Bloodletting*, P. Brain (1986); *On Examining the Physician*, A. Z. Iskandar (*CMG* 1988); *On the Therapeutic Method I–II*, R. J. Hankinson (1991); *On the Seed*, P. DeLacy (*CMG* 1993). The selection of passages in A. J. Brock, *Greek Medicine* (1929), remains valuable.

WORKS Titles and editions: G. Fichtner, *Corpus Galenicum* (1990), includes also spuria. Arabic tradition: M. Meyerhof, *Isis* 1926; M. Ullmann, *Die Medizin im Islam* (1970); F. Sezgin, *Geschichte des arabischen Schrifttums* 3 (1970). Chronology: J. Ilberg, *Rh. Mus.* 1889, 1892, 1896, 1897; K. Bardong, *Nachr. Akad. Wiss. Göttingen* 1941; D. Peterson, *Bulletin of the History of Medicine* 1977.

LITERATURE Bibliography: K. Schubring, repr. of Kühn, vol. 20 (1965); V. Nutton, *Karl Gottlob Kühn and his Edition of Galen* (1976); G. Fichtner (1990). General surveys: J. Mewaldt, *RE* 7. 578; W. A. Greenhill, *Smith's Dictionary of Greek and Roman Biography* (1846), 'Galen'; L. G. Wilson, *Dictionary of Scientific Biography* 5 (1972), 272. Biography: G. Sarton, *Galen of Pergamon* (1954), but weak; G. W. Bowersock, *Greek Sophists in the Roman Empire* (1969); B. P. Reardon, *Courants littéraraires grecs* (1971); G. E. R. Lloyd, *Greek Science after Aristotle* (1973); V. Nutton, *From Democedes to Harvey* (1988), and *CAH* 11² (forthcoming). Medical ideas: C. Singer, *A Short History of Biology* (1931); C. R. S. Harris, *The Heart and the Vascular System* (1973). Philosophy: P. Moraux, *Der Aristotelismus bei den Griechen* 2 (1984). Subsequent influence: O. Temkin, *Galenism* (1973). Collections of papers on Galen: V. Nutton (ed.), *Galen: Problems and Prospects* (1981); P. Manuli and M. Vegetti, *Le Opere Psicologiche di Galeno* (1988); F. Kudlien and R. J. Durling, *Galen's Method of Healing* (1991); J. A. Lopez Férez, *Galeno: Obra, Pensamiento, e Influencia* (1991); J. Kollesch, *Galen und das hellenistische Erbe* (1993).   L. E.; V. N.

Galerius (Gaius Galerius Valerius Maximianus (*RE* 2); originally named Maximinus), of peasant stock, was born in the 250s AD on the Danube at a place he later renamed Romulianum after his mother Romula. A herdsman, tough and uneducated, he rose high in the army and (perhaps) became praetorian prefect of *Diocletian, to whom his loyalty was unswerving. On the establishment of the *tetrarchy Diocletian proclaimed him Caesar (293); he divorced his wife and married Diocletian's daughter Valeria. He appears to have been in Egypt from 293–5. Defending the frontier with Persia against an attack by Narses, he was severely defeated between Carrhae and Callinicum (297), but raising reinforcements from the Balkans he attacked through *Armenia, marched down the Tigris, advanced to *Ctesiphon and returned up the Euphrates, gaining total victory (298). The peace treaty was entirely favourable to Rome: substantial territory was annexed. Thereafter he moved to the Danube provinces. Various campaigns against the Marcomanni, Carpi, and Sarmatians followed; he settled many Sarmatians within the empire. His religious views coincided with those of Diocletian. Prompted, it is said, by his mother, he urged Diocletian to begin the persecution of Christians (see CHRISTIANITY) at Nicomedia (303). On Diocletian's abdication, Galerius became Augustus (1 May 305); his subordination to *Constantius I meant little, as both Caesars, Flavius Valerius *Severus and C. Galerius Valerius *Maximinus, were his men (the latter son of his sister). Along with the Danubian provinces he now took on responsibility for Asia Minor. Senior Augustus from Constantius' death (306), he reluctantly accepted Constantine I as Caesar. The census conducted on Galerius' orders included city populations; at Rome this provoked the rebellion of *Maxentius, whom Galerius refused to recognize, sending the Augustus Severus against him. When Severus was defeated, Galerius invaded Italy but was forced to retreat (307). Summoning Diocletian, he attempted a new settlement of the empire at Carnuntum (11 November 308). Diocletian refused to resume the throne; Galerius appointed *Licinius Augustus, and declared Maxentius a public enemy. Constantine (see CONSTANTINE I) and Maximinus spurned the title *filii Augustorum* (sons of the Augusti), and Galerius recognized them as Augusti (309/10). Suffering from an agonizing illness, he issued an edict ending the Christian persecution (30 April 311) but died very shortly afterwards.

T. D. Barnes, *Constantine and Eusebius* (1981). R. P. D.

Galerius (*RE* 8) **Trachalus, Publius** (consul AD 68), Neronian orator, perhaps from *Ariminum (Rimini). *Quintilian especially praises his voice and delivery (*Inst.* 10. 1. 119; 12. 5. 5). *Tacitus (1) says (*Hist.* 1. 90) that it was believed that *Otho made use of him as a speech-writer. He may have gone on to be proconsul of Africa (*CIL* 5. 5812).

*PIR*² G 30; Schanz–Hosius, § 450. 6. J. W. D.; G. B. A. F.; M. W.

Galilee first appears as the name of the northern part of Palestine, east of the Jordan, in 1 Maccabees (see MACCABEES). When it was still largely Gentile territory, Simon the Hasmonean (see HASMONEANS) took armed assistance to the Jews there. It was occupied by Aristobulus I, rapidly becoming predominantly Jewish. From Herod (1), it passed to Herod (2) Antipas, who founded there the Jewish city of *Tiberias, and then to Agrippa I, to the Roman procurators, and to Agrippa II, in succession. 'The two Galilees' (upper and lower) were controlled by *Josephus in the Jewish Revolt, and rapidly subdued by Vespasian. After the *Bar Kokhba Revolt, Galilee became a stronghold of Judaism: the patriarchate was located in various of its towns at different times. Excavation reveals Sepphoris, prominent already before the revolt, to have become a major centre. The remains of many scattered *synagogues of the 2nd–4th cents. survive in the countryside, but those from the time of Jesus have largely perished. T. R.

Galinthias, friend or servant of *Alcmene. When, at *Hera's command, *Eileithyia and the Moirai (see FATE) were delaying the birth of *Heracles, she broke their spell by shouting that Alcmene had given birth. Galinthias was punished by being turned into a weasel. Earliest source: Nicander in Ant. Lib. 29 (as *aition* for a Theban ritual; also told by Ovid, *Met.* 9. 281–323 (of Galanthis), Pausanias 9. 11. 3 (of Historis). Ister (*FGrH* 334 F 72) and Aelian (*NA* 12. 5) tell of the weasel, not the person. A. Sch.

Gallic Wars, the name given to the campaigns by which *Caesar

completed the Roman conquest of *Gaul (58–51 BC). The survival of Caesar's own account of this conquest (his *Commentaries*) makes us uniquely well informed about it. However, modern research has demonstrated the dangers of unquestioning acceptance of Caesar's story: his attitudes to, dealings with, and description of Gauls and Germans were always determined by deep-rooted cultural prejudices and immediate political needs, and often by an expedient combination of the two. The Gallic conquest was probably unpremeditated; and is certainly incomprehensible if considered in isolation from the late republican power-struggle. According to Caesar, appeals for his intervention on behalf of one Gallic tribe against another, or against German intruders, involved him in campaigns beyond the existing Roman province in southern Gaul, and drew him as far as the Rhine (see AEDUI; ARIOVISTUS; HELVETII). At the end of 58 Caesar took up winter quarters in the north-east, an act threatening permanent occupation of all Gaul. In 57, accordingly, he had to meet preventive attacks by the peoples of northern Gaul (see BELGAE; NERVII); by his victories over these he brought northern France and Belgium under Roman control. In 56 Caesar had evidently resolved on the complete subjugation of Gaul, for in this year he forced the submission of the peoples of the Atlantic seaboard (see VENETI (1)). It is uncertain whether the peoples of central Gaul at this time came to terms with him; but these were now ringed off within the Roman area of occupation, and Caesar at this stage considered the pacification of Gaul as complete.

In this belief Caesar spent the campaigning seasons of 55 and 54 in Germany and Britain. But sporadic revolts in northern Gaul kept him occupied throughout the winter of 54/3 and the following summer, and in 52 he was confronted by a formidable coalition of peoples in central Gaul under the leadership of *Vercingetorix. The decisive duel between Caesar and Vercingetorix, the most critical event in the Roman conquest of Gaul, culminated in the siege of *Alesia. The reduction of Alesia by famine and the capture of Vercingetorix broke Gallic resistance, and the local rebellions which flared up here and there in 51 were easily dealt with. For the results of the conquest, see GAUL (TRANSALPINE).

M. Rambaud, *L'Art de la déformation dans les Commentaires de César* (1953); A. King, *Roman Gaul and Germany* (1990), 42 ff. M. C.; J. F. Dr.

Gallienus, emperor. See LICINIUS EGNATIUS GALLIENUS, P.

Gallio See ANNAEUS NOVATUS.

Gallus (poet) See CORNELIUS GALLUS, C.

Gallus Caesar, Flavius Claudius Constantius Along with his half-brother *Julian, he survived the massacre of most of his kinsmen in AD 337, to be appointed Caesar in the east by *Constantius II in 351. Based at *Antioch (1), he successfully resisted the incursions of Persian satraps and a local Jewish rebellion, but his civilian government was seen as harsh and repressive. He clashed with the councillors of Antioch and with imperial officials, and was eventually (354) recalled to Constantius' court in Milan. On the way he was deposed and executed near Pola (Amm. Marc. 14. 11). E. D. H.

games (i.e. ritual contests) See AGŌNES; ATHLETICS; LUDI.

games One of the earliest games played in Greece, if we may believe *Athenaeus (1), was marbles: the suitors of *Penelope shot their alleys in turn against another marble, representing the queen; the first one to hit had another turn, and if he were

Gandhara

successful again he was considered to be the presumptive bride-groom. A favourite game at Athens was draughts (πεσσοί). The board was divided into 36 squares, and on them the oval pieces were moved; the centre line was called ἱερὰ γραμμή ('sacred line'), perhaps because when you crossed it you were on the enemy's ground. More popular still was the 'Wine-throw' (κότταβος), especially at the end of dinner (see SYMPOSIUM). The players, reclining on their left elbow, had to throw with their right hand the last drops of wine from their cups at a target; this might be saucers floating in water or an object that might fall when hit.

At Rome the two favourite games were 'Twelve Lines' (*duodecim scripta*) and 'Robbers' (*ludus latrunculorum*). The first resembled our backgammon or race-game. The other, also played on a board, had pieces of different value, *calculi, latrones, mandrae*, and the object was either to take or check—*ad incitas redigere*—your opponent's pieces. There were also two games, common to Greeks and Romans, whose names explain themselves, 'Odd and Even' and 'How many fingers do I hold up?' See BALL GAMES.

W. B. Becker, *Charicles*, 7th edn. (1886), 348–55, and *Gallus*, 2nd edn. (1880), 455–80; B. A. Sparkes, 'Kottabos', *Archaeology* 1960, 202–7; British Museum, *Guide to . . . Greek and Roman Life*, 3rd edn. (1929), entry under 'Games'; A. Rieche, *Römische Kinder- und Gesellschaftsspiele* (1984). F. A. W.; M. V.

Gandhara was the name of the region around Peshawar and included the Swat valley with its capital at Taxila (*Takshashila*; see TAXILES). References to it are made in early Indian texts, in Achaemenid inscriptions where it is listed as a satrapy, in accounts of *Alexander (3) the Great's campaign, and later in Chinese sources. Its central location in relation to Indo-Bactrian trade and its access to central and western Asia made it economically prosperous. Sculpture at Buddhist monastic sites, reflecting north Indian, Bactrian, Parthian, and Roman features has come to be referred to as the Gandhara style. See BACTRIA.

B. C. Law, *Historical Geography of Ancient India* (1954); L. Nehru, *Origins of the Gandhara Style* (1989). R. Th.

Ganymedes (Γανυμήδης; suggesting γάνος, 'sheen' (esp. of wine) + μήδεα, ambiguously 'cunning', and 'genitals'); handsome young Trojan prince (son of Tros at *Il.* 20. 231–5; *Laomedon, Little Iliad* fr. 6 Davies, and in *Euripides) carried off to *Olympus (1) by *Zeus, as his compatriot Tithonus was by *Eos the dawn-goddess. His kidnapping is usually said to have been effected by Zeus himself, either in person (as on the fine 5th-cent. BC terracotta from Olympia), or in the shape of his eagle-avatar. As reparation, his father received a marvellous breed of horses (*Il.* 5. 265–7; *Hymn. Hom. Ven.* 202–17) or a golden vine (*Little Iliad*). Though early versions emphasize the boy's beauty, Zeus' motivation is given as the need for a noble and presentable wine-steward; a homoerotic interest on the god's part does not become explicit until later (Thgn. 1345–8), but Attic vase-painting and Hellenistic art stress this aspect (hence 'catamite', from *catmite* in (unvoiced) *Etruscan via Latin *catamitus*). See HOMOSEXUALITY.

H. Sichtermann, *LIMC* 4/1 (1988), 154–69; P. Bruneau, *BCH* 1962, 193–228; E. Vermeule, *Aspects of Death in Early Greek Art and Poetry* (1979), 164–7; J. Bremmer, *Arethusa* 1980, 279–88, at 286. A. H. G.

Garamantes See AFRICA, EXPLORATION.

gardens Two strands of landscape management coalesce in ancient Mediterranean garden culture: the intensification of agricultural production in fertile places where a high input of *labour can achieve very high yield per unit area; and the local improvement of the amenity of the natural environment for human activities of all kinds, like building a house but relying much more on what nature provides. Both, above all else, depend on use of *water, and are inextricably linked.

Culturally, the main traditions (including the amenity of plants and trees in Minoan art) all go back to the gardens of the Fertile Crescent. The Persian combination of preserve and pleasaunce known as *paradeisos* has a special place. Early Greek intensive horticulture created places whose amenity, for abundance of shade or the presence of water, was esteemed (already in Homer, esp. *Od.* 7. 112 ff.), and this was the style of the famous Garden of the philosopher *Epicurus. Trees were planted in *sanctuaries for their cultic significance or for shade, and by extension, in public places such as the *agora. But a high aesthetic tradition dates only from the domestication of the *paradeisos* in the 4th cent. BC and especially the Hellenistic and Roman periods.

This garden-art aimed particularly at reshaping place, and gave rise to the Roman name of formal gardening, *ars topiaria* (which went far beyond 'topiary', though this was one of its techniques). Use of slopes, views of different scenery, the deployment of architectural adjuncts and numerous sculptures, and the evocation of specific literary or traditional landscapes or stories were among the themes (as in Hadrian's villa at *Tibur); natural features such as springs, streams, hills, caves, and woods, were improved or created *ex novo*. In all this plants were important, but not central; specimen exotics (*viridia*, whence *viridiarium*) evoked alien worlds (as birds and animals, which might also be ultimately destined for the table, did too) or pleased through scent, foliage contrast, or shade. Flowers were prized, but in Mediterranean conditions and before much improvement of the strain, were very limited in their season (hence the value of twice-blooming roses) and grown more for their use in garlands than for their effect in a bed.

Remembering the days when a *hortus* was the lot of a citizen, the whimsical Roman élite labelled its suburban garden-palaces 'vegetable gardens', *horti*, and these often achieved remarkable levels of costly and allusive complexity. On a humbler scale, the features of *ars topiaria* were very widely disseminated across the Roman world. For our understanding, the town gardens of *Pompeii are especially important, with the garden-paintings which complemented them, but good examples come also from Fishbourne in Britain and Conimbriga in Portugal, Thuburbo Maius in Africa and several cities of southern France.

P. Grimal, *Les Jardins romains*, 2nd edn. (1969); W. F. Jashemski, *The Gardens of Pompeii* (1979 and 1994); E. MacDougall (ed.), *Ancient Roman Gardens* (1981), and (ed.), *Ancient Roman Villa-gardens* (1987). N. P.

Garganus mons, promontory projecting from *Apulia into the Adriatic to form the 'spur' on the Italian boot. Its forested mountain rises over 1,500 m. It is the Matinus celebrated by Horace (*Odes* 1. 28. 3; 4. 2. 27; *Epod.* 16. 28), but otherwise seldom appears in ancient literature. E. T. S.; D. W. R. R.

Gargilius Martialis, Quintus (early to mid-3rd cent. AD) was famed for his work on *gardens (Serv. on *G.* 4. 147; Cassiod. *Inst.* 1. 28. 5). Part of the *De hortis* is extant, while two other fragments, on the medical properties of fruits and on remedies for oxen (*Curae boum*), are usually attributed to him. Both *Palladius (1) and the Arab writer Ib'n-al-Awam cite him extensively. Whether the extant writings belonged to a comprehensive manual or to separate monographs is unknown. That the fragment on gardens concerns *arboriculture is due not to manuscript confusion but to the importance (proven by recent archaeological investigation) of fruit-trees in gardens. Although Gargilius merely lists the views of his sources on controversial points, his occasional criticism of earlier writers (at 4. 1 he accuses *Columella of negligence), his autopsy, and his practical experience help to explain the esteem of antiquity. His discussion of the peach, a tree barely mentioned by Columella, shows that arboriculture had continued to develop. A citation (4. 1) from *Virgil's *Eclogues* and the attention to prose rhythm throughout place Gargilius among those technical writers who, like *Columella, aimed to delight as well as to instruct their literary readers. See AGRICULTURAL WRITERS.

TEXTS S. Condorelli (all fragments) (1978); I. Mazzini, *De hortis* (1978).
LITERATURE I. Mazzini, *Atti e Memorie dell'Arcadia* 1977, 99–121; J. M. Riddle, *Journal of the History of Medicine and Allied Sciences* 1984, 408–29; W. F. Jashemski, *The Gardens of Pompeii* (1979).   M. S. Sp.

Gaudentius (*RE* 1) (perhaps 4th cent. AD). His *Introduction to Harmonics* contains an intriguing preface, a series of Aristoxenian propositions (1–9, 17–19; see ARISTOXENUS) arranged around and qualified by Pythagorean doctrine about ratios (10–16; see PYTHAGORAS (1)), and three chapters (20–3) on notation: 23, giving tables, is incomplete. Certain details are unparalleled elsewhere, but intellectual originality is not the work's main objective. It is a sane and practical guide for beginners.

Ed. C. von Jan, *Musici Scriptores Graeci* (1895), repr. with It. trans. in L. Zanoncelli, *La Manualistica musicale greca* (1990).   A. D. B.

Gaugamela, village in Iraq (now Tell Gomel?), scene of *Alexander (3) the Great's decisive victory over *Darius III of Persia in 331 BC. The battle appears to have opened with a Persian attempt to outflank Alexander's right, which was defeated, while a charge of scythed chariots in the centre was also routed by Macedonian light troops. Then Alexander led his Companions (see HETAIROI), and the right and centre of his *phalanx, to attack a developing gap in the centre of the Persian line, whereupon Darius fled with Alexander in pursuit. Meanwhile, a force of Persian cavalry may have exploited a gap in the centre of the Greek line to attack their camp, and although it was driven off by allied Greek infantry, the Macedonian left also came under extreme pressure. However, this attack, too, was eventually contained, and turned into a rout on news of the flight of the rest of the Persian army.

M. Streck, *RE* 7/1 (1910), 861–5; Diod. Sic. 17. 56–61; Arr. *Anab.* 3. 11–15; Curt. 4. 13. 26–16; Plut. *Alex.* 31–3. A. B. Bosworth, *Conquest and Empire* (1988).   J. F. La.

Gaul (Cisalpine) The prosperous northern region of modern Italy, comprising the Po (*Padus) plain and its mountain fringes from the Apennines to the Alps, was known to the Romans as Cisalpine Gaul. In the middle republic it was not even considered part of Italy, which extended only to the foothills of the Apennines along a line roughly from Pisa (see PISAE) to Rimini (*Ariminum). Beyond the Apennines lay Gaul, a land inhabited by Celtic peoples whom the Romans looked upon with fear and wonder. (See GAUL (TRANSALPINE).)

The background to this situation is difficult to reconstruct in detail. Archaeological evidence broadly confirms literary reports of *Etruscan settlement in Emilia-Romagna during the 6th cent. BC, and of the infiltration of Celtic peoples (see CELTS) from beyond the Alps during the 5th and 4th cents. Rich warrior graves of the iron age Golasecca culture in Piedmont and Lombardy point to a warrior aristocracy similar to that of the Hallstatt

culture of central Europe; and these same Golasecca sites during the 5th and 4th cents. contain increasing amounts of La Tène material. Further south there is evidence of a growing Celtic presence in Emilia-Romagna, where Etruscan and La Tène graves are found side by side in the same cemeteries.

The most detailed literary account of the Gallic occupation of the Po valley is that of *Livy (5. 34–5), who describes a succession of migrations by different tribes, beginning with the *Insubres, who moved into the region around Milan (*Mediolanum) in the 6th cent. BC. They were followed, in the course of the next two centuries, by the *Cenomani, Libui, Salui, *Boii, and Lingones. The last group to arrive were the *Senones, who by the start of the 4th cent. had occupied the strip of land along the Adriatic known as the *ager Gallicus*. This account, which can be supplemented by other sources, is compatible with the archaeological evidence, although the latter implies a process of gradual infiltration rather than violent invasions. By the early 4th cent. the Gauls had completely displaced the Etruscans in the Po valley, and had begun to make occasional raids across the Apennines into peninsular Italy (in one of which, in c.386 BC, they sacked Rome). Further Gallic invasions occurred sporadically throughout the 4th and 3rd cents. (Polyb. 2. 18–31), culminating in the great invasion of 225 BC, which the Romans and their Italian allies defeated at *Telamon (2).

The Romans responded by invading Cisalpine Gaul, which they overran in a three-year campaign of conquest ending with the capture of Mediolanum (Milan) in 222. Their efforts to consolidate the conquest, which included the foundation of colonies at *Placentia (Piacenza) and *Cremona, were however interrupted by *Hannibal's invasion, which prompted the Gauls to rebel. After defeating Hannibal, the Romans resumed their plan of conquest, which they completed in 191 with a victory over the Boii, the most powerful of the Cisalpine Gallic tribes. The colonies at Placentia and Cremona were refounded (190 BC), and further colonies were settled at *Bononia (1) (= Bologna, 189 BC), *Parma, and *Mutina (both 183). In 187 the *via Aemilia (from which the modern region of Emilia takes its name) was constructed from Ariminum to Placentia. As a result of this great programme of colonization (still evident in aerial photographs which show traces of *centuriation throughout the region), virtually all of the land south of the Po was occupied by settlers from peninsular Italy, while the northern part of the plain remained largely in the hands of its Celtic inhabitants, who were henceforth known to the Romans as Transpadani. (See TRANSPADANA.)

After the *Social War (3) Cisalpine Gaul was formally separated from Italy and became a province, with its southern border at the Rubicon; but all the colonial settlers who were not already Roman citizens were enfranchised. The rest of the free population, which effectively meant the Transpadani, were given Latin rights (see LATINI), a decision that they greatly resented; the demand for full citizen rights became a hot political issue in the following decades, until the Transpadani were finally enfranchised by Caesar in 49. In 42 Cisalpine Gaul was fully integrated within Italy, and under Augustus was divided into four of the eleven administrative regions of Italy (VIII–XI).

In the centuries after 200 BC Cisalpine Gaul was rapidly and thoroughly Romanized, and few traces of Celtic language and culture remained by the time of the empire. An area of rich agricultural land, much of which was reclaimed by Roman drainage schemes in the lower Po valley, Cisalpine Gaul achieved great prosperity; by the time of *Strabo, who gives an eloquent

Gaul (Transalpine)

description of it (5. 1. 12, 218 C), it had become what it still is today, one of the most wealthy and prosperous parts of Europe.

D. Foraboschi, *Lineamenti di storia della Cisalpina romana* (1992); G. E. F. Chilver, *Cisalpine Gaul: Social and Economic History from 49 BC to the Death of Trajan* (1941); G. A. Mansuelli and R. Scarani, *L'Emilia prima dei Romani* (1961); A. J. Toynbee, *Hannibal's Legacy* (1965), 2. 252 ff.; L. Barfield, *Northern Italy before Rome* (1971); P. Tozzi, *Storia padana antica* (1972); *I Galli e l'Italia*, exhib. cat. (Rome, 1978); D. and F. R. Ridgway (eds.), *Italy before the Romans* (1979), 415 ff.; C. Peyre, *La Cisalpine gauloise de IIIe au Ier siècle av. J.C.* (1979); R. Chevallier, *La Romanisation de la celtique du Pô* (1983); D. Vitali (ed.), *Celti e Etruschi nell'Italia centro-settentrionale dal V. sec. a.C. alla romanizzazione* (1987); W. V. Harris, *CAH* 8² (1989), 107 ff.; M. T. Grassi, *I Celti in Italia* (1991); *I Celti*, exhib. cat. (Milan, 1991).   T. J. Co.

Gaul (Transalpine) comprised the area from the Pyrenees and the Mediterranean coast of modern France to the English Channel, and the Atlantic to the Rhine and the western Alps. As a geopolitical entity, it emerged in the 1st cent. BC and lasted into the 5th cent. AD. Augustus divided Gaul into four provinces: Narbonensis, Lugdunensis, Aquitania, and Belgica. The Flavians annexed the *Agri Decumates and attached them to Upper Germany—carved, like Lower Germany, out of Belgica (see GERMANIA). *Diocletian subdivided all six Gallic provinces, making a total of thirteen.

Gaul was predominantly Celtic in culture (see CELTS), but it did not include the Celts of the Danube and northern Italy; and it contained Ligurians and Iberians in the south, and Germanic immigrants in the north-east. The south had also been heavily influenced by Greek *colonization. Hence 'Gaul' was not a natural unit, but a Roman artefact. In order to protect the route to Spain, Rome helped *Massalia against bordering tribes. The result was, in 121 BC, the formation of 'the Province' (*Provincia*), from the Mediterranean to Lake Geneva, with its capital at *Narbo. In 58–51 BC, Caesar seized the remainder of Gaul, justifying his conquest by playing on Roman memories of savage attacks over the Alps by Celts and Germans. Italy was now to be defended from the Rhine (*Rhenus).

Initially, indeed, the Romans treated the Gauls as *barbarians. They disparaged Gaul beyond the Province as *Gallia Comata*—'Long-haired Gaul', and generally mismanaged the Province itself. However, Gaul was not far behind Rome. Ligurian communities had long emulated Massilia; and, in the Celtic core, Caesar found nations (*civitates*) establishing urban centres (*oppida*) which, though hardly classical cities, had significant socio-economic functions. Under the more prudent rule of the emperors, the Province, now Narbonensis, was seeded with military colonies, and became a land of city-states, comparable with Italy. In the other 'Three Gauls', colonies were few and the *civitates* were retained, but their leaders vied with each other in acquiring the conquerors' culture.

The *Romanization of northern Gaul is illustrated by the dominance of Latin, and the emergence of the Graeco-Roman city. The *civitates* were too large to be city-states, but they contained towns that could be designated as their administrative centres and developed, under local magnates, in accordance with classical criteria. Most were unwalled. On the land, Romanization took the form of *villas—at this time working farms as much as country residences.

The population of Gaul was large: *c*.10,000,000. Agriculture flourished. One of the great engines of its success was the Rhine army, which stimulated trade by purchasing supplies from the interior. Commerce was facilitated by an extensive road- and river-network. The metropolis of high imperial Gaul was *Lugdunum (1) (Lyons), at a main junction of these networks. There was little resistance to Roman rule. Localized revolts in AD 21 and 69–70 were easily suppressed; they probably accelerated the demise of the pre-Roman aristocracy. Few Gauls subsequently involved themselves in Roman imperial careers.

Early Roman Gaul came to an end late in the 3rd cent. External pressures exacerbated internal weaknesses, and neglect of the Rhine frontier resulted in barbarian invasions and civil war. For a while Gaul was governed by a separate line of emperors (beginning with *Postumus). Though order was restored, much had changed: the Agri Decumates were abandoned; and cities began to be fortified. However, there had still been no move to gain independence; and, after the restructuring of the empire by Diocletian and Constantine I, Gaul enjoyed stability and enhanced prestige.

For Rome renewed its commitment to defend Italy from the Rhine. A praetorian prefect was based in northern Gaul, usually in *Augusta Treverorum (Trier), and rulers frequently sojourned there. Though the frontier was occasionally broken, it was always restored. There was a recovery of economic prosperity, though uneven. Trier was endowed with magnificent buildings, but most cities never recovered their former grandeur. The upper classes now eagerly sought posts in the imperial administration, making much of their rhetorical skills (the 4th cent. saw the blossoming of Gallic education). When not at court, influential Gauls, such as *Ausonius, favoured the country life and built themselves palatial villas. Christianity spread; an episcopal hierarchy developed, and monasticism was introduced.

From 395, the division of the empire between eastern and western rulers again caused the neglect of the Rhine frontier, reflected in the transfer of the Gallic prefect to *Arelate (Arles). By 418, the consequence of Germanic invasion and civil war, *Franks and *Burgundians were established over the Rhine, and the *Visigoths in *Aquitania. These were kept in check, until the death of Flavius *Aetius and the growing debility of the western government created a power-vacuum. The 460s and 470s saw Visigothic encroachment on Roman territory to the east, while the Burgundians expanded westwards from Savoy. In 476, the last imperial possessions in the south were ceded to the Visigoths.

Gaul suffered badly. Refugees fled southwards, only to find high taxation and corruption. Yet, as is evident from the writings of *Sidonius Apollinaris, the aristocracy remained remarkably resilient. Down to the mid-5th cent., its members tolerated the Germans while still looking to Rome for status and protection. Thereafter, they increasingly worked for the barbarian kings. Thus, at least in the centre and south of the country, the Gallo-Roman cultural legacy was bequeathed intact to the successor-kingdoms.

Roman Gaul seemed destined to become Visigothic Gaul until, late in the 5th cent., Clovis led the Salian Franks south, and eventually drove the Visigoths into Spain.

C. Jullian, *Histoire de la Gaule* (1908–26); Grenier, *Manuel*; C. E. Stevens, *Sidonius Apollinaris* (1933); O. Brogan, *Roman Gaul* (1953); P.-M. Duval, *Paris antique* (1961), and *Les sources de l'histoire de France* 1 (1971); R. Étienne, *Bordeaux antique* (1962); J.-J. Hatt, *Histoire de la Gaule romaine*, 2nd edn. (1970); E. M. Wightman, *Roman Trier and the Treveri* (1970), and *Gallia Belgica* (1985); C. Ebel, *Transalpine Gaul* (1976); J. F. Drinkwater, *Roman Gaul* (1983); R. van Dam, *Leadership and Community in Late Antique Gaul* (1985); A. L. F. Rivet, *Gallia Narbonensis* (1988); A. King, *Roman Gaul and Germany* (1990); J. F. Drinkwater and H. Elton (eds.), *Fifth-Century Gaul* (1992).   J. F. Dr.

Gavius (*RE* 11) **Bassus,** late republican scholar whose (lost) works on *etymology (*De origine vocabulorum*) and religious antiquities (*De dis*) are quoted by *Quintilian, A. *Gellius, and *Macrobius.

Herzog-Schmidt, § 283. R. A. K.

Gavius Maximus, Marcus, was son of Gavius Bassus, prefect of the Pontic fleet while *Pliny (2) was governing *Pontus-*Bithynia; the family was from Rome but domiciled at *Ephesus. Maximus was procurator of Mauretania Tingitana under Hadrian and became praetorian prefect (**praefectus praetorio*) early in *Antoninus Pius' reign; he retained office for nearly twenty years (*c.* AD 139–59), being described as 'very severe' by the Augustan History.

PIR[2] G 104; Fronto, *Ad Antoninum Pium*; SHA *Ant. Pius*. W. Eck, in W. Eck (ed.), *Prosopographie und Sozialgeschichte* (1993), 368 ff. A. R. Bi.

Gavius (*RE* 22) **Silo,** a Spanish declaimer occasionally cited by L. *Annaeus Seneca (1). Augustus heard him in court at *Tarraco (Tarragona) in 26/5 BC.

PIR[2] G 112; Schanz–Hosius, § 336. 9. 7. M. W.

Gaza, an ancient city of the Philistines and one-time stronghold of the pharaohs (late bronze age). Located in a fertile region and in a key position on the *via maris*, the route from Egypt to Asia, it was the Mediterranean outlet of the Arabian *trade. For long an ally of the Assyrians, it was later a Babylonian, then a Persian, garrison town. In the Persian period its 'Philisto-Arab' coins were based on the Attic standard and reflect connections with Greece, although its main economic links remained with *Arabia and the Minaeans of the south. In 448 BC Herodotus considered the city as one of the largest *markets in the east (3. 5); its wealth came from Nabataean trade. Stormed by *Alexander (3) the Great after a lengthy siege in 332 BC, it became an important city of the Ptolemies (see PTOLEMY (1)) until 198 BC, when *Antiochus III made it Seleucid. It was destroyed by the Jewish ruler, Alexander Jannaeus (see HASMONAEANS), in 96 BC; *Pompey declared it a *free city (hence its era, dated from autumn 61 BC), and A. *Gabinius (2) rebuilt it on a new site, like its predecessor some 21 km. (13 mi.) inland from the harbour. It was granted to *Herod (1) in 30 BC, then reverted to the province of Syria. Its coins cease with *Gordian III, who, like *Hadrian, was honoured by the city as a benefactor. Later it acquired the status of a Roman colony. It was for long a flourishing centre of Hellenistic culture, with a famous school of rhetors. In 635 it was conquered by the Arabs under Omar.

DCPP, 'Gaza'; U. Rappaport, *IEJ* (1970), 75 ff.; Jones, *Cities E. Rom. Prov.* ch. 10; H. J. Katzenstein, *Transeuphratène* 1 (1989). E. W. G.; J.-F. S.

Gela (*Γέλα,* mod. Gela), on the south coast of Sicily, was founded in 688 BC by Cretans and Rhodians, itself colonizing *Acragas a century later. Commanding the fertile plain of the river Gelas, it spread its influence inland to native settlements such as Butera (Omphace?) and Monte Bubbonia (Mactorion?). Its tyrants Cleander and *Hippocrates (1) made it temporarily Sicily's strongest state; but on *Gelon's transfer of the seat of power to Syracuse many Geloans were forced to accompany him, and *Hieron (1) exiled many others. Repopulated after 466, Gela prospered again, refounding *Camarina in 461 and supporting Syracuse in 427–424 and 415–413. *Aeschylus died in Gela in 456. Abandoned by *Dionysius (1) I in 405 and in consequence completely destroyed by the Carthaginians, it never fully recovered. A revival under *Timoleon after 338 was frustrated

by *Agathocles (1), who slaughtered 4,000 Geloans in 311. In 282 Phintias of Acragas removed Gela's inhabitants to his new foundation Phintias (Licata); the *Mamertines subsequently destroyed the empty city. The acropolis (two major temples and some smaller ones), partly occupied by housing in the Hellenistic period, has been extensively excavated at the eastern end of the city. The surviving stretch of Timoleontic fortifications at the west end of the city, constructed of mud-brick and stonework and still standing up to 8 m. (26 ft.) high, is one of Sicily's most remarkable ancient monuments, as is a well-preserved, early Hellenistic bath-house nearby.

PECS 346–7; *BTCGI* 8 (1990), 5–65; Gabba–Vallet, *Sicilia antica* 1. 561–71; Dunbabin, *Western Greeks, passim*; P. Griffo and L. von Matt, *Gela* (1963); E. De Miro and G. Fiorentini, *Kokalos* 1976–7, 430–47 (acropolis). A. G. W.; R. J. A. W.

Gelimer, the last *Vandal king of Africa (AD 530–4), was the great-grandson of *Gaiseric. He deposed his pro-Roman cousin Hilderic in 530, but in 533 an east Roman army led by *Belisarius landed in Africa and occupied *Carthage. Gelimer was defeated and taken prisoner, having failed in a bid to escape to Spain, and was sent to *Constantinople (534). He was given an estate in Galatia despite refusing to abandon his Arian Christianity (see ARIANISM). P. J. H.

Gellius (*RE* 2), **Aulus,** Roman miscellanist, born between AD 125 and 128, author of *Noctes Atticae* ('Attic Nights') in twenty books. Internal evidence suggests publication *c.*180; an apparent echo in *Apuleius' *Apology,* sometimes used to support an earlier date, can be otherwise explained. A probable reference in M. *Cornelius Fronto apart, all knowledge of Gellius comes from his work: reconstruction of his life depends on the assumption, so far unfalsified, that his anecdotes, even if fictitious, are not anachronistic. There are slight but uncertain indications that he came from a *colonia* in Africa: however, most of his life was spent at Rome. He studied with *Sulpicius Apollinaris, and knew Fronto; but the deepest impression was made on him by *Favorinus. He spent at least a year in Athens completing his education as a pupil of Calvenus Taurus; he visited Ti. *Claudius Atticus Herodes (2) in his summer retreat at *Cephisia, attended the Pythian Games of (probably) August 147, and enjoyed the life of a student and a tourist. After his return he was appointed a judge to try private cases (14. 2. 1); but his interest in the law is essentially antiquarian.

The *Noctes Atticae* (of which we lack the start of the preface, the end of bk. 20, and all bk. 8 except the chapter-headings) is a collection of mainly short chapters, based on notes or excerpts he had made in reading, on a great variety of topics in philosophy, history, law, but above all grammar in its ancient sense, including literary and textual criticism. According to his preface, Gellius conceived the notion of giving literary form to his notes during the long winter's nights in Attica (whence the title), but completed the project (some 30 years later) as an instructive entertainment for his children. Variety and charm are imparted by the constant changes of topic, purportedly reproducing the chance order of Gellius' notes (a cliché of such works), and by the use of *dialogue and reminiscence as literary forms for conveying information; the dramatizations are generally fictitious, though in settings based on Gellius' own experience. The characters of Gellius' friends and teachers are finely drawn; the fictitious persons are less individual.

Gellius is well read in Latin, less so in Greek (though he shows some knowledge of Homeric scholarship); his judgement is sens-

ible rather than incisive. His style blends the archaic (see ARCHA-
ISM IN LATIN), the self-consciously classical, and the new: he lifts
words from early authors but also invents new ones, he construes
plenus only with the genitive but occasionally admits *quod* clauses
instead of accusative and infinitive. He shares the age's preference
for Early Latin and *Sallust over Augustan and Silver writers, but
admires *Virgil and will hear no ill of *Cicero (10. 3; 17. 5); most
striking, however, is his liking for *Claudius Quadrigarius, of
whom he supplies almost half the extant fragments.

In later antiquity Gellius was diligently read by *Nonius Marcellus, *Ammianus, and *Macrobius; in the Middle Ages he was
excerpted in several florilegia. For the Renaissance he was a well-
spring of learning and a model for humanistic writing; though
displaced from his central position and disparaged along with
his age, he has never lacked readers who relish not only the
information he conveys, the quotations he preserves, and the
reflections he arouses, but also the charm of his style and his
infectious love of books.

TEXTS M. J. Hertz (1883–5); C. Hosius (Teubner, 1903); P. K. Mar-
shall (OCT 1968; repr. 1990); R. Marache, bks. 1–15 in 3 vols. (Budé,
1967–89); F. Cavazza (1985–   ).
TRANSLATION J. C. Rolfe (Loeb, 1927).
STUDIES L. A. Holford-Strevens, *Aulus Gellius* (1988); R. Marache,
*La Critique littéraire de langue latine et le développement du goût archaïsant
au IIe siècle de notre ère* (1952); S. M. Beall, '*Civilis Eruditio*: Style and
Content in the "Attic Nights" of Aulus Gellius' (Ph.D. Diss. Univ. of
California at Berkeley, 1988); M. L. Astarita, *La cultura nelle 'Noctes
Atticae'* (1993); G. Anderson, *ANRW* 2. 34. 2 (1994), 1834 ff.

L. A. H.-S.

Gellius (*RE* 4), **Gnaeus,** a Roman historian of the later 2nd
cent. BC, perhaps identical with a moneyer of 138 BC (*RRC* no.
232). His *Annals,* which may date from many years later, covered
the history of Rome from its origins to at least 146 BC (fr. 28
Peter), but now survive only in fragments. Even if a reference to
a book 97 is unreliable, it is certain that the period to the Second
*Punic War filled at least 30 books. The scale of the work was
therefore similar to that of *Dionysius (7) of Halicarnassus, by
whom it was consulted. The fragments suggest that Gellius had
wide-ranging antiquarian interests and Hellenistic erudition, but
the true character of the work remains largely unknown.

Peter, *HRRel.* 1². cciv, 148; E. Badian, in T. A. Dorey (ed.), *Latin Historians* (1966), 11 ff.; E. Rawson, *Latomus* 1976, 689–717 (= *Roman Culture
and Society* (1991), 245–71); T. P. Wiseman, *Clio's Cosmetics* (1979), 20 ff.

T. J. Co.

Gellius (*RE* 17), **Lucius,** born *c*.136 BC, studied oratory under
C. *Papirius Carbo (1) (Cic. *Brut.* 105), becoming a competent but
undistinguished orator (ibid. 174). After being peregrine praetor
(94), he went to either Asia or Cilicia *pro consule*. Stopping off at
Athens, he offered to reconcile the rival philosophical schools,
perhaps noticing their dangerous involvement with rival politicians. In the *Social War (3) he served under Cn. *Pompeius
Strabo. Not heard of until 72, he became consul, was defeated
by *Spartacus, and with his colleague Cn. *Cornelius Lentulus
Clodianus passed a law enabling commanders to confer citizenship for valour. As *censors 70, he and Lentulus purged the
corrupt senate. He served under *Pompey against the pirates,
opposed *Catiline and *Caesar, and lived on, amid troubles with
his son (adopted from the Valerii Messallae), until the late 50s.

The *cognomen* Publicola commonly conferred on him is erroneous: see *BICS* Suppl. 51 (1988), 8 n. 11.

E. B.

Gello, vicious female spirit (like *Empusa, *Lamia (1), and

*Mormo) that steals children, in ancient, medieval, and modern
Greek belief, first attested in *Sappho (fr. 178 Lobel-Page).
Supposedly (*Suda*) a woman from *Lesbos who died untimely.
Associated with *Gallū*, Sumerian/Akkadian term for a demon,
e.g. by Burkert. See FOLK-TALE.

P. Perdrizet, *Negotium Perambulans in Tenebris* (1922); P. Maas, *RE* 7
(1912), 1005–6; J. C. Lawson, *Modern Greek Folktale and Ancient Greek
Religion* (1910), 176–9; W. Burkert, *Die orientalisierende Epoche* (1984),
80–1; Rohde, *Psyche*, app. 6.

H. J. R.; K. D.

Gelon (*RE* 3), son of Deinomenes, greatest of Sicilian tyrants
before *Dionysius (1) I; he was *Hippocrates (1)'s master-of-
horse, and on his death (*c*.491 BC), seized the tyranny of *Gela.
He formed an alliance with *Theron of Acragas, married his
daughter Damarete, and with him fought the Phoenicians of
western Sicily. He restored the exiled aristocracy (*gamoroi*) of
Syracuse (485), but seized the city, which became the seat of his
power; his brother *Hieron (1) became ruler of Gela. He enlarged
his empire by alliance (*Leontini) and conquest (*Camarina, a
town called Euboea, and *Megara Hyblaea were incorporated in
the Syracusan state). He transferred half the population of Gela
to Syracuse. In these ways he built up the strongest single military
power in Hellas. The growth of his power, allied to Theron's,
alarmed *Anaxilas (1) of Messana (Messina), Terillus of Himera,
and the Phoenicians; and from 483, Carthage prepared for war.
Gelon was prevented from helping the metropolitan Greeks
against *Xerxes by *Hamilcar (1)'s arrival in NW Sicily; and he
probably deposited a large sum at Delphi, to buy off Xerxes, if
victorious. The victory of Himera (480) left Gelon, by alliances
and the submission of his enemies, virtually the overlord of Sicily,
and gave two generations of peace with Carthage. Gelon was
now the accepted ruler of Syracuse (the story that he was
acclaimed general plenipotentiary is much later, perhaps
invented by *Philistus). He enfranchised 10,000 mercenaries, and
built temples at Himera and *Syracuse, where his public works,
and peace, gave great prosperity, and his reign was looked back
on as a golden age. He died in 478/7, and was succeeded by
Hieron.

A. G. Woodhead, *The Greeks in the West* (1962), 76 ff.; H. Berve, *Die
Tyrannis bei den Griechen* (1967), 140–7; D. Asheri, *CAH* 4² (1988), ch.
16.

B. M. C.

Geminus (*RE* 1), writer of elementary textbooks on mathematical subjects (*c*. AD 50); see MATHEMATICS. His only extant work is
Εἰσαγωγὴ εἰς τὰ φαινόμενα ('Introduction to Astronomy'),
which gives a factual account of basic concepts in *astronomy,
mathematical geography, and the calendar. Although the mathematics in this hardly goes beyond listing numerical parameters,
it is important as a source for Greek knowledge of Babylonian
astronomy, which appears particularly in the sections on the
moon, and for the account of Greek luni-solar calendaric schemes
(see ASTRONOMY). The *parapēgma* (astronomical calendar)
appended to this treatise is not by Geminus, but considerably
older. Geminus also wrote a treatise on the scope of the mathematical sciences entitled Περὶ τῆς τῶν μαθημάτων τάξεως or
θεωρίας, in at least six books, which is cited by various writers,
especially *Proclus and the scholiasts on *Euclid book 1. This
included a classification of the mathematical sciences, arithmetic,
geometry, *mechanics, *astronomy, *optics, geodesy, *music,
and *logistic* (practical calculation), an examination of the first
principles, definitions, postulates, axioms, and the structure
based on them. It also included a classification of the various

kinds of 'lines' (*curves* in modern mathematics) and surfaces. *Simplicius (*in Phys.* 291–2 D) quotes from an epitome by Geminus of the *Meteorologica* of *Posidonius (2).

EDITIONS Εἰσαγωγή: best by Manitius (Teubner, 1898), with Ger. trans., some fragments of other works, and excerpts from the medieval Lat. trans. (important for the text); Budé ed. (1975), with Fr. trans.

COMMENT *HAMA* 2. 578–89 (for Geminus' date see 579–80); K. Tittel, *De Gemini Stoici studiis mathematicis* (1895), with index of references to his lost work; Heath, *Hist. of Greek Maths.* 2. 222 ff. On the optical part of the work see R. Schoene, *Damianos' Schrift über Optik, mit Auszügen aus Geminos* (1897). G. J. T.

gems Precious stones were valued in antiquity as possessing magical and medicinal virtues, as ornaments, and as seals when engraved with a device. Such engravings (intaglios) in soft media like steatite or *ivory are found in early Minoan days; the use of hard stones dates from the middle Minoan age. Late Minoan and Mycenaean gems have a rich repertory of human and animal designs; the favoured shapes are the lenticular (round) and amygdaloid (sling-stone) (see MINOAN and MYCENAEAN CIVILIZATION). In sub-Mycenaean and geometric times the art of working hard stones was largely lost. A revival in the 7th cent. BC is usually associated with the island of *Melos, and the commencement of Classical gem-engraving in the 6th cent. is marked by the introduction of the scarab (beetle) form of seal from Egypt. This was soon abandoned in Greece for the scaraboid, which omits the beetle-back. The late 5th and 4th cents. mark the high point of Greek gem engraving. In Hellenistic times the choice of subjects grows restricted, but excellent work was done in portraiture. In Italy the Etruscans used the scarab until the 3rd cent.; gems of the later Roman republic show a wide range of subjects, combined with clumsiness of execution. With Augustus begins the large series of 'Graeco-Roman' gems. A period of indifferent work in the middle empire is succeeded by a revival under Constantine I.

Several gem-engravers are recorded in literature, e.g. Pyrgoteles, who worked for *Alexander (3) the Great; others are known from their signatures on extant stones, though many signatures are false. Engravers of gems used the drill and the wheel. These had to be coated with powdered emery (of which *Naxos (1) was and is an important source), except for working softer stones such as steatite, which was consequently often used in the earlier periods. The stones most favoured for engraving in view of their durability, moderate hardness, and absence of grain were quartzes, especially those of the crypto-crystalline variety such as agate, plasma, jasper, carnelian, and most popular of all, sard. Red garnet, amethyst, lapis lazuli were much prized in jewellery. *Cameos in which design and background were in contrasted colours were made of layered stones such as onyx and sardonyx. Of the hardest stones, emeralds, aquamarines, and sapphires were rarely engraved, while the diamond, probably unknown before the 1st cent. AD, was not even cut. The diamond-point, however, was sometimes used for engraving other stones. Imitations of gems in glass paste were apparently much in demand; in the British Museum collection they even outnumber sards. Glass imitations of rock crystal and red garnet were considered particularly convincing.

F. Matz, H. Biesantz, and I. Pini (eds.), *Corpus der minoischen und mykenischen Siegel* (1964–); J. Boardman, *Greek Gems and Finger Rings* (1970); P. Zazoff, *Die antiken Gemmen* (1983); M. Henig, *Classical Gems* (1994). F. N. P.; D. E. E.; M. V.

genealogy, the enumeration of descent from an ancestor. Legendary pedigree was particularly important in Greece. Before fighting, *Homeric heroes boast of their ancestry, citing between two and eight generations of ancestors (e.g. *Il.* 6. 145–211, Glaucus (3)). *Hesiod's poetry is preoccupied with legendary ancestry (*Theogony, Catalogue of Women*); even aristocrats in Classical Athens (which put more stress on recent achievements) claimed descent from important local and Homeric heroes, and thence from the gods: cf. the Philaid genealogy (Marcellin. *Life of Thucydides* 3; see CIMON; MILTIADES); *Andocides was descended from *Odysseus and therefore *Hermes (Hellanicus, FGrH 323a F 24), *Alcibiades from Eurysaces (and *Zeus) (Pl. *Alc.* 1. 121a), *Plato (1) from *Solon and *Codrus (Plut. *Sol.* 1. 2). Other groups, cities, colonies, or tribes (see ETHNICITY), might trace descent from a single legendary figure (see FOUNDERS, CITY), and genealogies were sometimes akin to king-lists (e.g. *Sparta), or assimilated with lists of office-holders. Some of the first prose writers recorded (or worked out) genealogies, mostly legendary, as well as their chronological implications: *Hecataeus (1) (*c.*500 BC), *Acusilaus, *Pherecydes (2), *Hellanicus (1). Genealogies and their enumeration were evidently popular (Polyb. 9. 1. 4), especially in Sparta, as *Hippias (2) found (Pl. *Hp. mai.* 285d), despite Plato's criticisms (*Tht.* 174e ff.). They reflect the enormous significance attributed by the Greeks to origins and the original ancestor in determining the character of future generations. Prestige, status, even moral character, might be derived from the original progenitor, preferably legendary, heroic, or divine. (The Romans, more interested in their recent ancestors (Polyb. 6. 53 f.) only adopted the Greek penchant for legendary ancestry in the course of Hellenization (see HELLENISM) from the 2nd cent. BC (Wiseman: see bibliog. below).) Political and tribal affiliations might, similarly, be seen in genealogical terms. Given the value of the original ancestor, it is therefore unsurprising that the intervening links were sometimes vague or forgotten, and it may be the professional genealogists who did much to create continuous and coherent stemmata (Thomas). However, intermediate ancestors would also, obviously, carry prestige or opprobrium, and unsuitable ancestors would drop from view. Such is the moral or political importance of ancestry, that genealogy tends to reflect the current position or claims of a family, and thus it is usually the least reliable of historical traditions. Numerous inconsistencies would arise from the symbolic reflection of current status in past genealogy, and it is these contradictions which the genealogists were in part trying to resolve.

R. Thomas, *Oral Tradition and Written Record in Classical Athens* (1989); M. L. West, *The Hesiodic Catalogue of Women* (1985); F. Jacoby, *Abhandlungen zur griechischen Geschichtsschreibung* (1956), 100 ff.; E. Gabba, *JRS* 1981, 50 ff. (on true and false history); T. P. Wiseman, *G&R* 1974, 153 ff. R. T.

gender See GYNAECOLOGY; HETEROSEXUALITY; HOMOSEXUALITY; MARRIAGE; SEXUALITY; WOMEN.

generals See DUX; IMPERATOR; IMPERIUM; PRO CONSULE, PRO PRAETORE; STRATĒGOI; and names of individual generals.

genethliacon Both Greeks and Romans celebrated *birthdays (γενέθλιος ἡμέρα, *dies natalis*), and there was a religious aspect to the celebration, especially in Rome, where each person's *genius natalis* was an object of worship. Evidence for the composition of appropriate poems and speeches, whether for individual birthdays or for the anniversaries of famous men of the past, begins in Augustan times with the Greek birthday-present poems of *Crinagoras (*Anth. Pal.* 6. 227, 6. 261, 6. 345) and a number of Latin poems (Tib. 1. 7, 2. 2, 4. 5; Prop. 4. 10; Ov. *Tr.* 3. 13, 5. 5).

genius

Prescriptions for birthday speeches are found in Greek treatises on epideictic rhetoric (*Menander (4) Rhetor 412–13 Spengel; [Dion. Hal.] *Rhet.* 3), and there are several actual examples ([Aristid.], *Or.* 30 Keil, Himer. *Or.* 45 Colonna). Menander's rules represent the piece as a specialized form of encomium; [Dionysius] is more detailed, and advises beginning with the lucky features of the day. Later Latin poetry also has notable examples: e.g. Statius, *Silvae* 2. 7, to Lucan's widow (see ANNAEUS LUCANUS, M.) on the anniversary of Lucan's birth (cf. Mart. 7. 21–3), Auson. *Idyll* 5 (to a grandson on reaching the age of 16).

T. C. Burgess, *Epideictic Literature* (1902), 142–6; F. Cairns, *Generic Composition in Greek and Roman Poetry* (1972).   D. A. R.

genius, lit. 'that which is just born'. The *genius*, for a long time understood as the deification of the power of generation (Wissowa, *RK* 175; Latte, *RR* 103; H. Le Bonniec, *Rev. Ét. Lat.* 1976, 110 ff.), was defined by Dumézil (see bibliog. below) following the criticisms of W. Otto (*RE* 7 (1912), 1157 ff.) as 'the entirety of the traits united in a begotten being'. It is a deified concept, its seat in the forehead (Serv. on *Aen.* 3. 607), and is not far from the notion of the self. The *genius* forms the 'double' of the male, and is both born and dies with him. (Hor. *Epist.* 2. 2. 183 ff.). At an unknown date the same idea was developed for the 'double' of a woman (the *iuno*). This divine being, distinct from its human 'double', was the object of a cult. Although in common parlance every male, slave or free, seems to have a *genius*, in family-cult only one *genius* was honoured in each *household, that of the *paterfamilias*, particularly on the occasion of marriage (Festus 83. 23 Lindsay), but also in the ordinary worship at the shrine of the *Lares: see the 'priest of our *genius* Lucius' (*AE* 1983, 23); also G. Boyce, *Memoirs of the American Academy at Rome* 1937, pls. 17.1 (a large serpent, bearded and therefore male—a well-known convention in Roman art—beneath a scene of sacrifice) and 18.1 (two such serpents, one beardless—i.e. female, presumably the *iuno* of the *materfamilias*). The *genius* of the *paterfamilias* was also invoked as a witness during oath-taking by family members.

The *genius* was not limited to individual humans. Divinities equally, at least ones with an official 'birth' or entry into the body of communal cults, possessed a *genius* or a *iuno* (*genius*: first in 58 BC, *ILLRP* 508. 16; *iuno*: *CIL* 6. 2099. 2. 1). By extension every locality and establishment where the Romans exercised an activity had a *genius* which expressed the totality of its traits at the moment of constitution (e.g. *genius Romae*, Serv. on *Aen.* 2. 351; *genius coloniae, oppidi, ILLRP* 116 f.). The cult of the *genius* of the *paterfamilias*, a pillar of domestic and client relationships, was used by *Augustus to link Roman citizens closely to his person: associated with the *Lares Augusti* in crossroads-shrines, invoked with the *genius* of the *paterfamilias* at private banquets, the *genius Augusti*, double of the living emperor, rapidly became an important element in Roman *ruler-cult. It was generally represented (like the *iuno* of the empresses) by a togate male with the features of the ruler, carrying a cornucopia and often a patera. In the speculations of grammarians and philosophers the *genius* was assimilated to the Greek *daimōn.

W. Otto, *RE* 7. 1155 ff.; G. Dumézil, *ARR* 357 ff., and in *Hommages R. Schilling* (1983), 85 ff.; L. Chioffi, *MGR* 1990, 165 ff.; H. Kienckel, *Der römische Genius* (1974); D. Fishwick, *Harv. Theol. Rev.* (1969), 356 ff. (= *ICLW* 2/1 (1991), 375 ff.).   J. Sch.

genos The word *genos* was widely and variously used in Greek of all periods to denote 'species', 'genus', 'sort', 'category', 'birth', 'kin', 'race', 'lineage', 'family', 'generation', 'posterity', etc. Probably from its use to denote '(noble) lineage' (already in Theognis

894, Pindar, *Ol.* 6 and 8, and frequently in Herodotus), it came to be used in 4th-cent. BC Athenian orators and inscriptions in a quasi-precise sense to denote a set of families or individuals who identified themselves as a group by the use of a collective plural name. Some such names were geographical (e.g. Salaminioi; see SALAMIS (1); SUNIUM) or occupational (e.g. Bouzygai, 'ox-yokers'), but most were patronymic in form (e.g. Amynandridai, Titakidai), implying the descent of their members—the *gennētai*—from a fictive or real common male ancestor. About 60 such groups are known, some attested only in the lexicographers, who typically define them as '(name): *genos* of true-born (*ithageneis*) at Athens'.

The size, composition, and functions of such *genē* have been much debated. Though some *genos* names are said to be also *phratry names, *genē* were not identical with phratries. Some 4th-cent. evidence suggests that a *genos* could be a constituent part of a phratry, perhaps as its most prominent *oikos* ('house'), a suggestion which is supported by the (5th-cent.?) law providing that *phrateres* were obliged to enrol as members 'both the *orgeōnes* and the *homogalaktes* ['foster-brothers'], whom we call *gennētai*' (Philochorus, *FGrH* 328 F 35). Since certain 5th-cent. inscriptions define the responsibilities and privileges of various *genē* in matters of cult (e.g. *IG* 1³. 6 C: Eumolpidai and Kerykes, see EUMOLPUS; *IG* 1³. 7: Praxiergidai), *genē* may primarily have been the groups or lineages which provided the holders of certain major hereditary priesthoods. However, not all *genē* are known to have 'possessed' priesthoods or other cultic privileges, and though some late Hellenistic inscriptions from Athens and *Delphi show the members of sacred delegations being selected from various named *genē*, they reflect an antiquarian revival in the interests of a *de facto* oligarchy as much as any real cultic tradition. Again, while some small *genē* such as the Eteoboutadai were genuinely priestly, others such as the Brytidai ([Dem.] 59. 61) or the Salaminioi show a larger and more widely scattered membership, preoccupied with the proprieties of admission, with common property, and with the internal distribution of the perquisites of *sacrifices. More puzzling is the assertion in *Ath. pol.* F 3 that at some early stage of Athenian society each of the four old *Ionian tribes (see PHYLAI) was divided into three 'trittyes or phratries', each phratry comprising 30 *genē* and each *genos* comprising 30 men. The implication, that all citizens were *gennētai*, is contrary to the run of the extant evidence and is more likely to reflect 4th-cent. antiquarian theorizing than the historical reality of any period.

Aristotle's reference (*Pol.* 1272ᵃ34) to the Cretan *kosmoi* being chosen 'not from all but from certain *genē*' illustrates the non-Athenian use of the term.

J. Toepffer, *Attische Genealogie* (1889): still the only systematic collection of material; W. S. Ferguson, *Hesp.* 1938, 1–74; B. D. Meritt, *Hesp.* 1940, 86–96; A. Andrewes, *JHS* 1961, 1–15; P. MacKendrick, *The Athenian Aristocracy, 399 to 31 B.C.* (1969); F. Bourriot, *Recherches sur la nature du genos* 1–2 (1976); D. Roussel, *Tribu et cité* (1976), 17–88; J. K. Davies, *Wealth and the Power of Wealth* (1981), 105 ff.; Rhodes, *CAAP* 66 ff.   J. K. D.

genre, a grouping of texts related within the system of literature by their sharing recognizably functionalized features of form and content. Theory of genre as such is quite lacking in antiquity (its place is taken by theories of *imitatio) and ancient theoretical discussions of specific literary genres are few and for the most part unsatisfactory. They operate according to criteria which are one-sidedly formal (generally metrical), thematic (the characters' moral or social quality, the general subject-matter), or pragmatic (the situation of performance), but scarcely attempt to correlate or justify them; they are more interested in classifying existing works than in understanding the mechanisms of literary production and reception and are directed to the needs of the school and the library, not to the critic's; they bungle some genres (lyric) and ignore others (the novel). Rhetorical handbooks sometimes distinguish among oratorical genres, but the precise relation between their (often pedantic) prescriptions and the literary works remains uncertain.

*Plato (1) (*Resp.* 3. 392d–394c) differentiates a number of existing poetic genres in terms of their constitutive modes of presentation: mimetic (tragedy, comedy), diegetic (dithyramb), or mixed (epic). But among the theoreticians it is only *Aristotle who provides *in nuce* a genuinely complex theory, combining considerations of form, content, the author's and audience's psychology, metre, language, performance, traditionality, and evolution. Yet his surviving *Poetics* focuses mostly upon a single genre and is often elliptical and tentative: it furnishes many of the elements of a useful theory but does not fully work them out. Later theories tend restrictively to prescribe appropriate contents or style (*Horace, *Ars poetica*), to speculate about historical origins (Hellenistic theories of tragedy and pastoral), or to list the multiplicity of transmitted forms (*Proclus' *Chrestomathia*).

Modern attempts to found genre theories upon these ancient discussions have usually been sterile. Instead, more progress can be made by concentrating upon the actual practice of ancient poets, which reflects a much more sophisticated and supple sense of how genres really function. In Archaic Greece, poetic genres seem to have been defined not only by immanent characteristics of form and content but also by communally recognized, often ritually sanctioned situations of performance. The gradual emancipation of literature from such performative contexts facilitated the poets' awareness of and artistic experimentation with genres. Even before the Hellenistic period, poets designated genres by the names of their 'inventors' (*Homer for epic, *Archilochus for iambic invective) and *Euripides and *Aristophanes (1) ironically juxtaposed elements from disparate genres. But the Hellenistic philologists' classification of earlier literature into catalogues and *canons made it easier for poets definitively to isolate formal and thematic constants as specifiable rules for determining generic identity: already *Accius wrote, *nam quam varia sint genera poematorum, Baebi, quamque longe distincta alia ab aliis, nosce* ('Learn, Baebius, how various the genres of poems are and how much they differ from one another': Charisius, *Gramm.* 141. 34 = Accius fr. 8 Funaioli); and a strong interest in genres is obvious among the Augustan poets, manifested for example in *Virgil's exploration of the boundary separating elegy from pastoral (*Ecl.* 10), in Horace's discussion of the 'empty slot' of Augustan tragedy (*Epist.* 2. 1), and in *Ovid's witty experimentation with new and paradoxical genres (*Heroides, Remedia amoris*).

Much confusion has been caused in modern times both by attempts to hypostasize genres, attributing to them an existence independent of the particular literary works, and by the opposed overreaction, denying the very existence of genres. But even without handbooks, genres function within texts as a way of reducing complexity and thereby not only enriching, but even enabling literary communication: for, by guiding *imitatio* and identifying as pertinent the strategic deployment of topoi (see TOPOS) and of conspicuous stylistic and thematic features, they select only certain contexts out of the potentially infinite horizon of possible ones. Hence genre is not only a descriptive grid devised by philological research, but also a system of literary projection inscribed within the texts, serving to communicate certain expectations to readers and to guide their understanding. See REGISTER.

G. B. Conte *Genres and Readers* (1994). G. B. C., G. W. M.

gens ('lineage') derives from a root denoting procreation and the *gens* was frequently conceived as comprising the free-born descendants of a common ancestor in the male line. That distant ancestor (*princeps gentis*) was commonly a fiction and a real or supposed kinship link between those claiming membership of the same *gens* became increasingly difficult to demonstrate. Since all members of a *gens* bore the same *nomen* (e.g. Mucius), by the late republic alternative definitions based membership of a *gens* on tenure of the same *nomen*, not kinship (cf. especially Q. *Mucius Scaevola (2) quoted in Cic. *Top.* 29 (with further conditions, particularly non-servile extraction)). Such definitions may have been created as a practical means of identifying those legally entitled to lineage inheritance rights, but the basis on which, and consistency with which, such cases were determined remains unknown.

In the *Twelve Tables members of a *gens* (*gentiles*) shared an intestate inheritance in default of immediate heirs or agnates (relatives in the male line up to the sixth degree). They probably also enjoyed comparable parallel rights of guardianship (in case of intestacy) and supervision of the profligate (as certainly of the insane). Potentially these rights could be exercised by any Roman citizen. The alleged patrician claim that they alone 'had a *gens*' (*gentem habere*: Livy 10. 8. 9) is probably a learned canard, based on the claim that the *patricians were originally those that could invoke their father (*patrem ciere*) and hence alone were free-born. In the late republic plebeian *gentes* were certainly recognized (e.g. Cic. *Verr.* 2. 1. 115).

As a collective social or political phenomenon, however, the lineage appears only at the aristocratic level. Individual lineages might have a common cult or ritual, distinctive customs, or communal burial-places. In the mid–late republic, at least, these served primarily to reinforce the prestige and sense of common identity of the lineage (cf. Cic. *Off.* 1. 55), but there is no evidence that they were universal; the cohesion of individual lineages will have varied (particularly according to size and number of branches) and specific branches of a lineage may reinforce their own identity by employing a distinguishing *cognomen*, adopting distinctive practices, and using a separate sepulchre. Not surprisingly, there is little evidence for concerted social or political action by a lineage (or an individual branch) in this period. At best, perhaps, lineage links created the basis of an appeal for assistance from and to individuals, but in general only close relatives might feel obliged to respond. Lineage inheritance rights were correspondingly eroded by the growth of testamentary succession and the increasing rights of near cognates at intestate succession: the last recorded attempt to exercise them is attested in the late 1st cent. BC (Riccobono, *FIRA* 3. 69 (*'Laudatio Turiae')), and by the mid-2nd cent. AD they were obsolete (Gai. *Inst.* 3. 17).

In the early republic lineages may have been a more potent social and political force. Membership of the patriciate appears to have been determined by lineage (although later at least individual lineages were sometimes deemed to include both patricians and plebeians) and some lineages may have assumed responsibility for particular public cults. However, collective lineage action, such as that of the Fabii which culminated in the disaster at the *Cremera (477), may be exceptional, and modern theories that the lineage was the primary socio-political unit or that it predated the formation of the Roman community remain unsubstantiated. There is no evidence for an organizational structure to the lineage, common land-ownership, communal clients, systematic endogamy, or even common feasting (other presumably than after lineage sacrifices). Laelius Felix's implication that individuals were assigned to the ancient *curiae* 'ex generibus hominum' (Gell. *NA* 15. 27. 5) need mean only that membership of a *curia* was hereditary, not that a *curia* was an assemblage of lineages. The clear emergence of a wealthy élite from the 8th cent., the creation of the *nomen* in the 7th and the evidence of (Etruscan) funerary practice all support the hypothesis that the notion of the lineage developed progressively from the 8th–7th cent., perhaps primarily as an instrument of élite self-protection and advancement. Even so, its potential role was increasingly (though not necessarily consistently) restricted by the communal interests of the citizen body and the patriciate, by growing central political control, by the developing complexity of individual socio-political networks, and by the rival attractions of charismatic individuals. See NAMES, PERSONAL, ROMAN.

G. W. Botsford, *Political Science Quarterly* 1907, 663 ff.; *CAH*² 7/2 (1989), 98 ff. (A. Momigliano), 146 ff. (A. Drummond), 711 ff. (bibliog.); P. A. Brunt, *The Fall of the Roman Republic and Related Essays* (1988).   A. D.

Genua (mod. Genoa) was settled from at least the 5th cent. BC, and was an important harbour town of Liguria (see LIGURIANS), with *Etruscans in the population. By 218 BC it was in Roman control, and was destroyed by *Hannibal. Once restored, it was used as a base against the Ligurians (Livy 30. 1, 32. 29; Val. Max. 1. 6. 7). Ancient writers seldom mention Genua, however, although *Strabo (4. 202) lists its exports and imports.

E. T. S.; T. W. P.

Genucius (*RE* 5), **Lucius,** tribune of the *plebs* (see TRIBUNI PLEBIS) in 342 BC and, according to some writers consulted by Livy (7. 42. 1), author of a number of reforming plebiscites (see PLEBISCITUM). One prohibited the loaning of money at interest, while the others enacted that no one should hold the same magistracy twice within ten years, nor two offices at the same time, and that it should be permissible for both consuls to be plebeian (see PLEBS). The first of these laws was long remembered but rarely enforced (Tac. *Ann.* 6. 16; App. *BCiv.* 1. 54), and the second was observed for barely twenty years. The last is problematic and may have been incorrectly reported. The first time both consuls were plebeian was in 172 BC; on the other hand, from 342 onwards one of the two consuls was always a plebeian, and this may have been the main provision of Genucius' law. See CONSULS.

J.-C. Richard, *Hist.* 1979, 65–75; K.-J. Hölkeskamp, *Die Entstehung der Nobilität* (1987), 105 ff.; T. J. Cornell, *CAH* 7²/2. (1989), 333, 337, 345.

T. J. Co.

geocentricity The theory that the earth lies at the centre of the universe belongs to Greek scientific astronomy and should not be attributed to earlier thinkers such as Anaximander or Pythagoras in the 6th cent. BC. The first to whom the notion that the earth is spherical and lies at the centre of a spherical universe is credibly attributed is *Parmenides (early 5th cent.). By the time of *Eudoxus (1) (*c*.360) the standard view was that the stationary spherical earth lies at the centre, around which rotates the outermost sphere of the fixed stars, once daily about the poles of the equator, carrying with it the intermediate spheres of the other heavenly bodies (also centred on the earth, but rotating in the opposite sense about different poles). That is the basis of *Aris-

totle's picture of the world, which dominated the cosmology of antiquity and the Middle Ages. According to this the sublunar region is composed of the four mutable *elements, earth, air, fire, and water, whose natural motion is in a straight line, i.e. 'down' towards the central earth, or 'up' away from its centre. Everything above that region (including the visible heavenly bodies) is composed of an immutable 'fifth element' whose natural motion is circular.

Alternative hypotheses are occasionally found. In the 5th cent. *Philolaus proposed that the earth, like all other heavenly bodies, rotated about a central fire. Later *Heraclides (1) Ponticus suggested that the central earth rotates on its axis while the sphere of the fixed stars is stationary. The Epicureans (see EPICURUS), following earlier atomists (see ATOMISM), maintained that the natural motion of all matter was 'down' (in an absolute sense), and that the apparently circular motions in the visible universe were temporary aberrations. In the 3rd cent. *Aristarchus (1) of Samos advanced a heliocentric hypothesis, in which the earth revolved together with the other planets about the central stationary sun, while the sphere of the fixed stars is stationary at an enormous distance. This was generally rejected, on physical rather than astronomical grounds.

The geocentric system is justified by Ptolemy, *Alm.* 1. 1–8. For theories up to Aristarchus see T. L. Heath, *Aristarchus of Samos* (1913; repr. 1959), pt. 1.

G. J. T.

geography The Homeric poems (see HOMER) display a quite complex sense of place, and of the ordering of the world, in which there is already a notable sense of theory. The *Iliad*'s *Catalogue of Ships* systematically evoked the Greek homeland, and its names remained recognizable for the most part (though in some cases perhaps by learned re-creation); the wider world was much less precisely docketed (making later authorities such as *Eratosthenes believe—the theory of *exōkeanismos*—that Homer had deliberately relegated *Odysseus' wanderings to a vague outer darkness), and there was therefore much less onomastic continuity. The listing of such places begins more recognizably in *Hesiod, and some quite elaborate conception of the layout of the *Mediterranean was clearly associated with the complex movements of people and materials in the Archaic periods, and indeed already present in the Phoenician, Euboean, and Corinthian ambits of the 8th cent. BC; the choice of name for the later *apoikiai* reflects a geographical sophistication in which the toponyms of the homeland are replicable in an alien world, a habit of thought which remained common in Macedonian and Roman practice (see COLONIZATION, GREEK). From the relatively undocumented practice of the Archaic period the practical literature of coastwise description or *periploi* developed, to be given a *prōtos heuretēs* (discoverer) in *Scylax of Caryanda, and first represented for us by the 4th-cent. text known as [Scylax] or pseudo-Scylax. The first notion of geographical description as a discipline is connected conceptually: the *periodos gēs* ('circuit of the earth') that goes back to the Hesiodic corpus.

Geography by the 5th cent. had three distinct strands: this small-scale documentation of the actualities, as of particular sea routes; wider theories about the layout of land and sea on a global scale; and ideas about the place of the *oikoumenē* (inhabited world) in the order of the cosmos. Both of the more theoretical approaches are apparent in *Hecataeus (1) of Miletus and Herodotus (who combined a geographical and ethnographical perspective): it is plausible to suggest an origin in 6th-cent. Ionia, in which new approaches to the physical nature of the universe, inspired in part by contacts with the Fertile Crescent and Egypt, combined with the active seafaring experience of states like Miletus and Samos. The role of *Pythagoras (1) (who postulated a spherical earth) and his followers should also be noted. The invention of the map was attributed to *Anaximander.

Learned geography, in tandem with *astronomy, came during the 4th cent. to an advanced understanding of the nature of the earth as a rotating sphere of a realistic size (the role of *Aristotle and *Dicaearchus should be noted); and the theory of the latitudinal zones or *klimata* was refined. A mathematical geography emerged (limited in the end by the available instruments), advanced in the work of Eratosthenes of Cyrene and *Hipparchus (3) of Nicaea, which culminated in the 2nd cent. AD in the work of Claudius *Ptolemy (4), the most detailed attempt made in antiquity to project the layout of the physical and human world on the surface of the globe. By 300 BC it was known to the informed that the *oikoumenē* of which detailed information was available could only occupy a small portion of the northern hemisphere. It was also at this time, by coincidence or not, that the idea of accumulating information systematically on the edges of received knowledge began, in a way that suggests comparison with the 'voyages of discovery' in the first age of European colonialism. The work of the companions and followers of *Alexander (3) the Great, above all, established a link between formal geography and political dominion which was to be of great importance to the Roman experience. (See BEMATISTS.) It also offered, through the development of the ethnographic tradition, an analytical content for the genre which went beyond description and cataloguing, though it continued to use these techniques.

Eratosthenes, whose contribution, in late 3rd-cent. *Alexandria (1), to *geōgraphia* as a separable discipline was enormous, needs separate consideration. He set new standards of verification by rejecting the Homeric tradition and insisting on a clear distinction between fictitious wonder-descriptions and the recording of fact, established a blend of descriptive and mathematical geography as a new genre, made the mapping of the *oikoumenē* its centre, systematized the deployment of a system of co-ordinates of latitude and longitude in order to do so, and applied the benefits of Ptolemaic statecraft: for instance his accurate estimate of the earth's circumference depended on the measurement of *Egypt in the interests of land management, and his theory of the *sphragides*, conceptual units for the subdivision of space, was also indebted to agrimensorial practice. (See GROMATICI.)

Geographical ordering became central to the formation of administrative units. Borrowing perhaps from the geographically defined satrapies of the *Achaemenid dominion, the Athenians had subdivided their *archē* ('empire') in a practical way into five units. Geographical organization of a sometimes complex kind was also a feature of the states of Alexander and his Successors (*Diadochi), and the usefulness of correct topographical information for coercion and exaction was established. In this way geographical work in the Hellenistic period, by *Timaeus (2), Eratosthenes, *Artemidorus (2), *Polybius (1), *Posidonius (2), and eventually *Strabo, had a practical relationship to history, and came to be a major ingredient in the self-definition of the nascent Roman, Mediterranean-wide state. Roman contributions were of a practical kind: the *commentarii* of commanders and governors; C. *Iulius Caesar (1) has a place of honour here, blending the claim to practical personal observation with Herodotean ethnographical themes; later exemplars, such as *Licinius

Mucianus, consul AD 70 and 72, were more given to the thaumatological: Strabo was not complimentary about the Roman contribution to geography (3. 4. 19 (166 C)). The Augustan epoch, with its spectacular universal claims to rule in time and space, made very full use of the geographical tradition in its construction of images, while putting it to practical use too. Thereafter geography as such became an ingredient in the encyclopaedic tradition, and the later authors who survive are mainly excerptors or epitomizers of the earlier tradition (like the elder *Pliny (1)'s geographical excursus in *Natural History* 2–6). The exceptions are *Pomponius Mela, who represents an attempt at a Latin geography, and *Arrian's rather self-conscious *periplous* of the *Euxine, deliberately mixing the *genres, as was common at the time.

GENERAL Earlier bibliography is shaped by different notions of what geography is as a modern discipline: but see J. O. Thomson, *A History of Ancient Geography* (1948); C. Van Paassen, *The Classical Tradition of Geography* (1957). More attention has been given to the question in Italy and France recently: F. Prontera, *Geografia e geografi nel mondo antico: Guida storica e critica* (1983); M. Sordi, *Geografia e storiografia nel mondo classico* (1988); C. Jacob, *Géographie et ethnographie en Grèce ancienne* (1991); F. Cordano, *La geografia degli antichi* (1993).
EARLY GREEK GEOGRAPHY D. R. Dicks, *Early Greek Astronomy to Aristotle* (1970); P. Pédech, *La Géographie des grecs* (1976).
ALEXANDRIAN GEOGRAPHY Fraser, *Ptol. Alex.* 520–53. See too AGATHARCHIDES.
ROMAN GEOGRAPHY E. Rawson, *Intellectual Life in the Late Roman Republic* (1985), 250–66; C. Nicolet, *L'Inventaire du monde* (1988), Eng. trans., *Space, Geography and Politics in the Early Roman Empire* (1991). N. P.

geometry See MATHEMATICS.

Gerasa, later Antioch on the Chrysorhoas and modern Jerash in Jordan, was probably a Seleucid foundation under *Antiochus (4) IV. Captured by Alexander Jannaeus (103–76 BC, see HASMONAEANS), it remained in Jewish hands until in 63 BC it became part of Roman *Syria and of the Decapolis. Its prosperity, dependent on caravan trade, increased later when Trajan annexed Nabataea (see ARABIA). Gerasa, having become part of the Arabian province, enjoyed a 'golden age' under the Antonines. In the 3rd cent. AD the city and its trade declined until a revival under *Justinian; then followed capture by Persians (614; see SASANIDS) and Arabs (635). Extensive ruins survive: triumphal arch, colonnaded street and forum, temples of *Zeus (built AD 22–43) and *Artemis (c. AD 150), theatres, and several Christian churches (5th/6th cents.).

C. H. Kraeling, *Gerasa: City of the Decapolis* (1938); Schürer, *History* 2. 149–55; *Jerash Archaeological Project* 1 (1986), 2 (1989). J. F. H.

Gergovia, an *oppidum* of the *Arverni, held by *Vercingetorix against Caesar in 52 BC. The identification of Gergovia with the hill-fort on the Plateau de Merdogne, renamed Gergovie by Napoleon III, has become less certain following excavations which suggest that it was permanently occupied from only c.30 BC. It lasted into the 1st cent. AD, when it was superseded by Augustonemetum (mod. Clermont) to the north-west (cf. BIBRACTE). An alternative site for Gergovia is on the Côtes de Clermont plateau, north of Clermont.

Caes. BGall. 7. 4. 2, 34–53. C. Jullian, *Histoire de la Gaule* 3 (1909), 465 ff.; J. Moreau, *Dictionnaire de géographie historique* (1972); R. Périchon, *Les Découvertes archéologiques sur l'oppidum de Gergovie* (1975); J. Collis, *Oppida* (1984), 17, 216. J. F. Dr.

Germania, a name applied by the Romans both to lands east of the Rhine (*Rhenus), occupied by 'free' Germans, and to imperial

Germanic languages

provinces for the most part to the west of this river, carved out of *Gaul. This confusion arose out of Augustus' plans to create the province of Germania Magna, with its eastern border on the Elbe but with its capital in Cologne (*Colonia Agrippinensis). Following the failure of this project the Rhineland became a military zone, garrisoned by two armies of four legions, each under a senatorial legate. However (perhaps to obscure defeat and maintain a claim to Free Germany—cf. the 3rd-cent. treatment of *Dacia), that on the northern Rhine was still called the army of 'Lower' and that on the southern the army of 'Upper Germany'. The areas they controlled were effectively provinces, with their capitals at Cologne and Mainz (*Mogontiacum) respectively, but their formal designation as such (as *Germania Inferior* and *Germania Superior*) did not come until *c.* AD 90, as part of the Flavian reorganization of the Rhine frontier (see LIMES). During the high empire the German provinces flourished, thanks to imperial military spending (though the legionary garrison was halved) and trade with the empire and free Germany, and greatly stimulated the general Gallic economy. Under *Diocletian, Germania Inferior was renamed *Germania Secunda*, while Superior became *Prima* and *Maxima Sequanorum*, all three belonging to the diocese (*dioecesis*) of the Gauls. During the 4th cent., though an increased imperial presence ensured continued protection and patronage, the German provinces were badly affected by Frankish and Alamannic attacks. They disappeared during the first half of the 5th cent.

J. F. Drinkwater, *Roman Gaul* (1983), 54 ff.; W. Eck, *Die Statthalter der germanischen Provinzen* (1985); A. King, *Roman Gaul and Germany* (1990).

J. F. Dr.

Germanic languages The Germanic (Gmc.) languages constitute one of the ten major branches of the *Indo-European (IE) family. Proto-Germanic (PGmc.), the inferred common parent of the group, was a sister language to Proto-Greek, Proto-Italic, Proto-Indo-Iranian, and other descendants of Proto-Indo-European (PIE), which is presumed to have been spoken around 4000 BC. PGmc. probably remained a fairly homogeneous speech community until the last few centuries before the beginning of the Christian era, when it split into East Gmc., North Gmc., and West Gmc. dialects. The early Germanic peoples were illiterate at this time, so that our knowledge of PGmc. is based entirely on comparative reconstruction. Since all the early Gmc. languages are still fairly close, however, the sounds and forms of PGmc. are recoverable with reasonable accuracy.

The earliest and most archaic Gmc. language of which we have extensive remains is *Gothic*, the only attested representative of the EGmc. dialect group. Our knowledge of Gothic is almost entirely based on the Bible translation made around the middle of the 4th cent. by the heretical (Arian) Gothic bishop Wulfila. Of this translation substantial fragments survive, amounting to slightly more than half of the New Testament. Written in a Greek-based alphabet of Wulfila's invention, they are preserved in Italian manuscripts dating from the 6th cent. Likewise of Italian provenance is the so-called *Skeireins*, a fragmentary commentary on the Gospel of St John. Gothic early became extinct in Italy and Spain, the two major areas of Gothic settlement; Gothic-speaking minorities, however, probably survived longer north of the Alps and in the Crimea, where a short word-list was compiled in the 16th cent. Of the closely related EGmc. languages spoken by the *Vandals, Gepids, Burgundians, and other tribes nothing survives except the evidence of personal names.

Still older than the Gothic Bible, and reflecting an even more

conservative linguistic stage, are the earliest inscriptions in the runic alphabet. This writing system, ultimately derived from a North Italian prototype, was apparently common to all the pagan Germanic peoples; in a modified form it continued in use in parts of Scandinavia until modern times. The oldest runic inscriptions, few in number and very brief, come from southern Scandinavia and go back to the 3rd cent. AD. The language of these meagre texts is called *Runic* (or *Primitive*) *Norse*; though reckoned as NGmc., it shows few divergences from PGmc. before *c.* AD 500. After the 5th cent. the Scandinavian inscriptions grow longer and take on a more pronouncedly dialectal character, gradually approaching the literary Norse of the high Middle Ages. Significant records in *Old Norse* proper, written in the Roman alphabet, begin in the 12th cent. In its *Old Icelandic* variety, this language is the vehicle of an important medieval literature, the older part of which was written down in the 13th cent. Modern Icelandic has changed remarkably little from its medieval ancestor. Modern Norwegian, Danish, and Swedish (from *c.*1500), far less conservative, are descended from the corresponding Old Norse dialects of the Scandinavian mainland.

The WGmc. languages are only vestigially attested before the 8th cent. They present a more diverse picture than the Scandinavian dialects—so much so that many scholars have doubted the utility of WGmc. as a basis of classification. *Old English*, generally written in the Roman alphabet (there are also a few early runic sources), is represented by a substantial and varied literature. Most of our texts are in the West Saxon dialect and date from the 9th–11th cents., although some works, such as the epic *Beowulf*, incorporate a great deal of archaic and dialectal material. Middle and Modern English are conventionally dated from *c.*1100 and 1450, respectively. The closest relative of Old English is *Old Frisian*, attested in laws from the 13th cent. and continued in the modern dialects of the Frisian islands. The early continental WGmc. languages are *Old Low Franconian*, *Old Saxon*, and the assemblage of dialects traditionally grouped together as *Old High German*. Old Low Franconian, the ancestor of Middle and Modern Dutch, is chiefly known from the fragments of a 10th-cent. translation of the Book of Psalms. Old Saxon, spoken in north-western Germany, is best attested in the *Heliand*, a long poem on the life of Christ from the first half of the 9th cent. Its immediate descendant, Middle Low German, was widely employed for literary purposes in the late Middle Ages, but the modern Low German dialects are mere patois. Old High German, distinguished from the neighboring WGmc. languages by the High German Consonant Shift, is documented in glosses and literary texts from the Carolingian and Ottonian periods. The bulk of Old High German literature is of ecclesiatical inspiration, but the succeeding Middle High German period (from *c.*1050) is rich in texts of every description. Early Modern (or New) High German is dated from *c.*1350.

J. H. J.

Germanicus See IULIUS CAESAR, GERMANICUS.

Germans (*Germani*), after the *Celts the second major linguistic and cultural grouping encountered by the Graeco-Roman world in northern Europe. It was the Romans' failure, between 12 BC and AD 9, to absorb the Germanic peoples west of the Elbe that compelled them to centre the defence of their western empire on the Rhine (*Rhenus) and upper Danube (*Danuvius). Sporadic German raiding in the 1st and 2nd cent. AD developed into prolonged trouble in the 3rd cent. with the emergence of the Frankish and Alamannic threat to Gaul and Italy, and with the application of Gothic pressure on the lower and middle Danube. The relative pacification of the *Goths in the 260s and 270s (see HERULI) left the *Franks and the *Alamanni as Rome's most important Germanic enemies down to the last quarter of the 4th cent., after which large-scale Gothic settlement south of the Danube unbalanced imperial foreign and domestic politics. The early 5th cent. saw the Goths sweep from Thrace through the Balkans into Italy, thence to Spain and back to Gaul. *Vandals, Sueves, and *Burgundians also crossed the Rhine in force. The Alamanni were less adventurous, but from the 480s the Franks began to move south.

The early development of the Germanic peoples is notoriously difficult to establish. Modern research has demonstrated how much our two best informants, *Caesar and *Tacitus, were influenced by their cultural prejudices and their literary strategies. (For example, Caesar's emphasis on the Rhine as a distinct boundary between Celts and Germans is now recognized as political, not ethnographic, in origin.) The views of the Celtic Gauls no doubt also confused the picture (the ethnic, 'German', appears to have been Gallic, picked up and exploited by Caesar, and never applied by Germans to themselves). The chroniclers of the post-Roman Germanic successor-kingdoms were equally capable of inventing significant elements of their early history; and modern studies have been bedevilled by nationalism and ideology. The conventional view is that German language and culture originated in northern Germany and lands about the western Baltic from about 500 BC. Movement of peoples, leading to the reversal of Celtic expansion and Germanic contact with the Mediterranean world, took place from c.300 BC. In the west, this included the *Cimbric migration of the 2nd cent. BC—probably also the date of German settlement across the lower Rhine. The early 1st cent. saw the arrival of the *Suebi on the upper Rhine. In the east, the Germanic *Bastarnae appeared on the borders of Thrace as early as c.200 BC; and the same period probably saw the establishment of the distant ancestors of, amongst others, Burgundians, Goths, and Vandals, between the Oder and the Vistula.

The reconstruction of Germanic society faces similar problems, and must also take into account the wide geographical spread of Germanic settlement and cultural differences between its many peoples. However, careful combination of our best literary information (above all, Tacitus' *Germania*) with modern archaeological research produces a picture of a simple (by comparison with the Celtic) but developing iron age society, with permanent farms and villages. Agriculture was both arable and pastoral, and produced raw materials which could be traded for the finished goods of the Roman empire. Though there could be nominal kings, real political power was diffused among local clan chiefs: unlike the Celtic, the Germanic peoples produced no proto-urban settlements which might accommodate central administrations. They were effectively unified only in time of war, under a battle-leader—the final decision on whom, as with all matters of importance, was taken by the warriors in a tribal assembly. It was this absence of a clearly defined state-structure that afforded the Germans a highly flexible response to Roman aggression, and protected them from conquest.

See also GERMANIC LANGUAGES.

Tac. *Germ.*, ed. Anderson (1938), ed. Much (3rd edn., 1967). Much, *RE* Suppl. 3. 546 ff.; L. Schmidt, *Geschichte der deutschen Stämme*, 2nd edn. (1934–41); E. A. Thompson, *The Early Germans* (1965); M. Todd, *The Northern Barbarians* (1975); P. Heather, *Goths and Romans* (1991).
J. F. Dr.

gerousia, the council of elders in Greek cities, notably at *Sparta. The Archaic and Classical Spartan *gerousia* comprised 28 men aged over 60, drawn *de facto* (if not *de iure*) from the leading families, together with the two kings. Membership was for life; vacancies were filled through competitive acclamation by the citizens. Its functions included control over resolutions introduced before the assembly (*probouleusis*), although its application to matters of foreign policy is debated; trial of important criminal cases (although there is dispute over royal trials); and supervision of laws and customs. Sparta's Hellenistic and Roman *gerousia* underwent various changes. Membership was reduced to 23, the minimum age to perhaps 40, and the office became annual. Its supervisory role was taken by the *nomophylakes*, who with the *ephors assumed much of the probouleutic function. The council of Roman Sparta was a composite of all three sets of officials.

Councils of elders, varying in size and criteria for membership, are attested in certain other Classical *poleis*. The character of Hellenistic and Roman *gerousiai*, and sometimes styled *hiera*, 'sacred', especially common in Asia Minor, is disputed; but they probably functioned primarily as select social or religious societies of rich and well-born citizens, frequently centred on the gymnasium.

RE 7. 1264–8; G. E. M. de Ste. Croix, *The Origins of the Peloponnesian War* (1972), 124–38, 349–54; P. Cartledge and A. Spawforth, *Hellenistic and Roman Sparta* (1989), esp. 51–2, 198–9; A. H. M. Jones, *The Greek City* (1940), 225–6; J. H. Oliver, *The Sacred Gerousia* (1941).   S. J. Ho.

Gerrha, a city in what is today NE Saudi Arabia, possibly Thaj or Hofuf. The name may derive from †*han-Hagar*, in the local Hasaitic dialect attested epigraphically in the region, via Aramaic *Hagarā* (W. W. Müller in von Wissmann, 29 n. 21a). *Nicander speaks of the 'nomads of Gerrha' (*Alex.* 244), but *Aristobulus (1), *Eratosthenes (Strabo 16. 3. 3), *Agatharchides, and *Pliny (1) (*HN* 6. 32. 147) concentrate on their role as merchants in Arabian aromatics (see SPICES). In 205 BC *Antiochus (3) III visited Gerrha and was given large quantities of silver, frankincense, and stacte for not interfering with the Gerrhaeans 'perpetual peace and freedom' (Polyb. 13. 9. 4–5). See ARABIA.

J. Tkač, *RE* 7 (1912), 1270–2; H. von Wissmann, *Die Geschichte von Saba '* 2 (1982); D. T. Potts, *The Arabian Gulf in Antiquity* 2 (1990), 85–97.
D. T. P.

Gesoriacum (Bononia under the later empire; mod. Boulogne-sur-Mer), a town of the Morini and almost certainly the Portus Itius (i.e. 'channel harbour') of Caesar; under the empire the normal port of embarkation for Britain and station of the *classis Britannica*. Its *lighthouse was constructed by Caligula (see GAIUS (1)). *Carausius' fleet was blockaded here in AD 293.

Tabula Imperii Romani: M31 (1975), 52 f.; S. Johnson, *Roman Forts*, 2nd edn. (1979), 84 ff.; E. M. Wightman, *Gallia Belgica* (1985).
C. E. S.; J. F. Dr.

Gessius Florus, Roman knight from Clazomenae, married Cleopatra, a friend of *Poppaea Sabina, and thus gained the favour of *Nero who in AD 64 appointed him *procurator of *Judaea which Gessius proceeded to govern ruthlessly. Although Josephus' account of his villainies may be exaggerated, he certainly inflamed Jewish feeling (e.g. a demand for 17 talents from the Temple treasury led to rioting and bloodshed) and helped to precipitate the great insurrection of 66.

PIR[2] 170; Schürer, *History* 1. 470, 485 f.   H. H. S.

gestures (Gk. *schēmata, cheironomia, hypokrisis*; Lat. *gestus, actio*) convey attitude, intention, and status. Greeks and Romans moved trunk and limbs to precede, accompany, intensify, undercut, and replace words. Posture, orientation (Soph. *OT* 728), separating social-distance (proximity in supplication), facial expression (frowns, arched brows), and paralinguistic cues (pauses, pitch-changes, silences, hissing) also express emotion and modulate speech. Social meaning is divulged through ritualized acts (saluting, drink-pledges) and informal behaviour (pursed lips, nodding, nail-biting: Ar. *Lys.* 126, *Vesp.* 1315; Prop. 2. 4. 3). Behaviour may be intended (handclasp, embrace, kiss) or unintended (shriek, hiccough, horripilation, odour), sometimes even unconscious (sweat, lip-biting, eye-tics). The latter two categories of psychophysical reactions 'leak' hidden feelings. Apparel, tokens, and unalterable 'badges' of identity (guest-gifts (see GIFT, GREECE), dowry, winding-sheet, shields, scars, limps) assert gender, age, and status. Some behaviours exhibit ethological constants (tears, grins, cowering, shrinking); others are culture-specific (Hellenic ethnogests: thigh-slapping, negative upward head-nod: *Il.* 15. 113, 16. 125 (*Achilles), 6. 311; *Od.* 21. 129; angry cheek-scratching: Heliod. *Aeth.* 2. 8).

Minute or sweeping gestures regularly enhance or preclude verbal communication. Like words, gestures may be subtle, bombastic, or ambiguous. Turned thumbs meant life or death in *amphitheatre ritual. Informally, *Cicero jumped for joy (*Fam.* 16. 16. 1). Some gestures are magically symbolic. Evil-eye apotropisms, earth-stomping demonic conjurations, and head and hand orientation during *prayer (*Il.* 9. 568, 1. 450) convey hopes and demands, like curse, entreaty, and invocation. Surreptitious and private erotic sign-languages (Ov. *Am.* 1. 4. 15–38) coexist with public signs of respect or mockery—hand motions, catcalls, and rhythmic clapping (Dem. 18. 265; Pers. 1. 58–60; Cic. *Pis.* 65). Emblematic sign-languages appear between strangers employing different tongues (Ov. *Tr.* 5. 10. 36; *Met.* 6. 579). Diplomatic negotiation employs formal emblems of homage and contempt (*proskynēsis*: Hdt. 1. 134; Achilles hurling the sceptre: *Il.* 1. 245).

Greek art depends on gesture and bearing to encode narrative nuance. Besides instrumental actions depicted (partying, killing, mourning), gestures *per se* carry symbolic messages and artists' meaning along with the iconology of mythical attributes, gender, class, and culture. Facial expression is curiously ignored until the Hellenistic age. Roman public and private art (funeral portraits) formalize the comportment of authority, rank, and beneficence. Imperial coins and sculpture (*Trajan's Column) impart ideology through 'body-language'. Later Roman and Byzantine gesture, especially in court and official art, transmitted messages that had previously been written or spoken.

Greek literature reveals mental and emotional states and status-manipulation through mien and deportment: Chryses brandishes sceptre and ransom, Achilles glowers, Dolon's teeth chatter, abased *Priam kisses enemy hands, boorish Polyphemus whistles, *Odysseus extends his empty beggar's hand, and *Penelope's suitors violate turf-boundaries and table-etiquette. In lyric, *Sappho 'leaks' symptoms of despair. Tragedy presents ceremonious movement, dramatic starts, altered body 'badges', and delayed contact (Eur. *Alc.* 1113–18; Soph. *OC* 1607–11). Significant objects (dildos, royal robes, and birth-tokens) 'speak' in comedy, as do obscene hand-motions and thrashing movements (Ar. *Ach.* 765, *Thesm.* 636, *Av.* 1460–9, Aeschin. 1. 25 for oratory). *Herodotus (1) and later historians provide dramatic gestures: Thrasybulus of *Miletus' wordless harvest of pre-eminent grain-stalks (Hdt. 5. 92). *Plato (1) and the novelists (see NOVEL) include 'quiet' gestures and personal peculiarities (idiogests): gait, facial

demeanour, heroic motionlessness. Note too *Socrates' piercing glances, the blushes of flustered Chariclea, or Calasiris' smiles (Heliod. *Aeth.* 3. 5, 5. 2).

In Latin literature, the range is similar. *Plautus' Demipho complains of those who leer, nod, wink, or whistle at pretty women (*Merc.* 403–8). *Virgil emphasizes spontaneous gestures of confusion and despair (blush, sob). He teases readers with gestures withheld, a proffered hand not reciprocated or extended (*Aen.* 1. 408–9, 12. 930–1). *Ovid prefers gestures of etiquette, conscious manipulation, or coercive bodily rhetoric (*Met.*: polite *Vertumnus, Iphis' gifts, barrister Odysseus). Literature, art, rhetorical handbooks, and theatrical descriptions of *pantomime (Dion. Hal. *Dem.*; Cic. *Or.*; Quint. *Inst.* 11. 3 ff.; Lucian, *Salt.*) offer rewarding examples of the wordless languages of antiquity.

C. Sittl, *Die Gebaerden der Griechen und Roemer* (1890); R. Brilliant, *Gesture and Rank in Roman Art* (1963); G. Neumann, *Gesten und Gebärden in der gr. Kunst* (1965); D. Arnould, *Le Rire et les larmes* (1990); D. Lateiner, *Sardonic Smile: Nonverbal Behavior in Homeric Epic* (1995).

D. G. L.

Geta, Roman emperor. See SEPTIMIUS GETA (2), P.

Getae, a Thracian tribe who had settled by the 4th cent. BC on the lower Danube to the south and east of the Carpathians (see THRACE). Greek writers tended to confuse them with the Dacians (see DACIA) while later writers applied their name to the *Goths, with whom they had nothing in common. J. J. W.

Giants, a mythological race of monstrous appearance and great strength. According to *Hesiod they were sons of Ge (Earth) from the blood of *Gaia/*Uranus which fell upon earth; he describes them as valiant warriors (*Theog.* 185). *Homer considers them a savage race of men who perished with their king Eurymedon (*Od.* 7. 59). The prevailing legend of the fight of the gods and the Giants was formulated in Archaic epics and was embroidered by many later writers. A substantial account is given by *Apollodorus (6) (1. 6. 1.). When the gods were attacked by the Giants they learned that they could win only if they were assisted by a mortal. They called in *Heracles, who killed the giant Alcyoneus and many others with his arrows. *Zeus, who led the gods, smote with his thunderbolt Porphyrion who attempted to ravish *Hera; *Athena killed Pallas or Enceladus; *Poseidon crushed Polybotes under the rock that became the island of *Nisyros (Strabo 489); *Apollo shot Ephialtes; *Hermes slew Hippolytus; *Dionysus killed Eurytus and many other Giants besides who were caught in his vine; and Hephaestus aided the gods, throwing red-hot iron as missiles. The Giants were defeated and were believed to be buried under the volcanoes in various parts of Greece and Italy, e.g. Enceladus under *Aetna (1). Bones of prehistoric animals were occasionally believed to be bones of giants.

The Gigantomachy was one of the most popular myths in Greece and accordingly the names of participants and the episodes of the battle vary from writer to writer and from representation to representation. Zeus, Heracles, Poseidon, and later Athena, are the usual protagonists. In its early stage the myth seems to represent a variation of the popular motif of the tribe that attempted to dethrone the gods; in a more advanced stage of culture the myth was interpreted as the fight of civilization against barbarism.

In art the Giants are first shown as warriors or wild men, later as snake-legged monsters. The most famous sculptural renderings are found on the Archaic treasury of the Siphnians at *Delphi and on the Hellenistic altar of *Pergamum.

F. Vian, *La Guerre des Géants* (1952); A. van Windekens, *BN* 1956, 59; W. Havers, *Sprache* 1958, 23; M. Delcourt, *History of Religions* (1965), 209 ff.; P. Hardie, *Virgil's Aeneid: Cosmos and Imperium* (1986), chs. 3, 4; F. Vian with the collaboration of M. B. Moore, *LIMC* 4/1 (1988), 191–270.   G. M. A. H.

gift, Greece In the Homeric poems, gift-giving perhaps receives more attention than any other peaceful heroic activity. It has three outstanding features. First, gifts have an extremely wide range of functions. The word 'gift' (*dōron*) was, as Finley (see bibliog. below) puts it, 'a cover-all for a great variety of actions and transactions which later became differentiated and acquired their own appellations … payments for services rendered, desired or anticipated; what we would call fees, rewards, prizes and sometimes bribes' (and, we should perhaps add, taxes, loans, and diplomatic relationships). Secondly, gifts are often extremely valuable; those referred to include cattle, armour, women, and even entire cities. Thirdly, gifts are frequently given within contexts such as *marriage, *funerals, friendship, and ritualized friendship (see FRIENDSHIP, GREECE and FRIENDSHIP, RITUALIZED), either to initiate or to perpetuate amiable relationships. The claim sometimes made in modern research (by Hooker, for example) that these features of gift-giving existed in poetical fantasy rather than in social reality is contradicted by the recurrence of these features in later non-poetical descriptions of gift-giving.

At all periods of Greek history, gift exchange differed sharply from exchanges, such as trade, conducted outside the context of amiable relationships. In trade, the exchange was a short-term, self-liquidating transaction, generating neither binding relationships nor moral involvement. Within the context of amiable relationships, a gift was not merely meant to 'pay off' a past gift or service, but to render the recipient indebted, and thus set going a *reciprocity mechanism. Gifts served a multiplicity of purposes: they repaid past services, created new obligations, and acted as continual reminders of the validity of a bond. Gift-exchange differed from trade in that the exchange of goods was not the primary object of the transaction. It must be stressed, however, that commodities of high use value (metal objects, *timber, and grain, for example) circulated as gifts, and that at least some of these commodities could not always be obtained by means of trade.

The *polis made a half-hearted attempt to curb the prevalence of gift-giving. By opening alternative channels of commodity supply, it presumably reduced the volume of vital resources circulating as gifts. Inside the *polis*-framework, the sort of gift-giving which could have hindered the impersonal functioning of political institutions ('gifts' made to individual citizens in return for their votes, for example) seems effectively to have been checked. Outside the *polis*, however, reality remained very much like the one reflected in the Homeric poems; élite members integrated into politically separated communities went on circulating substantial resources amongst themselves as gifts. The channels through which these resources moved coincided to a great extent with networks of ritualized *friendship.

This external involvement had important consequences both for the *polis'* social structure and for its political life: citizens involved in this sort of network could significantly improve their standing within the community by means of resources obtained from outside. In general, the community looked favourably upon donations made to it by such citizens. Receiving gifts from an

outsider could also be seen as *bribery, however: the *dōron*-gift became a *dōron*-bribe if there was some suspicion that the countergift might involve trading with communal interests. See also CORRUPTION.

The expression 'Greek gifts' is an allusion to Verg. *Aen.* 2. 49, *timeo Danaos et dona ferentes* ('I fear the Greeks even when they bring gifts'), said about the Trojan Horse. For the story see SINON.

M. I. Finley, *RIDA* 1955, 167 ff., and *The World of Odysseus* 2nd edn. (1977); G. Herman, *Ritualised Friendship and the Greek City* (1987); J. T. Hooker, *BICS* 1989, 79 ff.; I. Morris, *Man* 1986, 1 ff.; S. von Reden, *Exchange in Ancient Greece* (1995).   G. He.

gift, Rome See AMBITUS; EUERGETISM; FRIENDSHIP, RITUALIZED.

Gildas, British author of *The Ruin and Conquest of Britain* (*De excidio et conquestu Britanniae*), a moralizing work attacking the local leaders held responsible for *Britain's troubles following the Roman withdrawal and the coming of the *Saxons. Apart from his *Christianity, very little is known about the author, and the date of composition is controversial, most scholars placing it *c.* AD 540, although a higher dating (*c.*479–84) has been championed (Higham). For all its errors, the work is an invaluable source for the Saxon settlement, as well as containing a history (4–26) of Britain down to the author's own day, the only ancient account of its kind.

Ed. M. Winterbottom (1978), with Eng. trans. N. Higham, *The English Conquest* (1994).   A. J. S. S.

Gildo, son of King Nubel of *Mauretania, served as a Roman officer, and AD 386–98 held the extraordinary and very powerful command of *comes et magister militum utriusque militiae per Africam* (see COMITES; MAGISTER MILITUM), supplementing the authority of a Roman commander with that of a native prince. His daughter Salvina married a nephew of the empress Flacilla. In 397 he revolted from the western government, and declared his allegiance to the east. He was defeated and killed in 398 by an army under his brother Mascezel.

PLRE. 1. 395–6.   W. L.

Gla (ancient name unknown), a rocky outcrop at the NE end of Lake *Copais in *Boeotia, was surrounded by a massive fortification in the 14th cent. BC, plausibly as part of a building programme that included large-scale drainage, to control the resulting fertile land. The fortress contained only a few structures (administrative and storage?) in an inner compound. It was abandoned in the later 13th cent. BC.

GAC G 9; *LH Citadels*, 91 ff.   O. T. P. K. D.

gladiators, combatants at games Gladiatorial combats, held at the funerals of dead warriors in Etruria (see ETRUSCANS), were introduced to Rome (perhaps by way of Samnium and Campania) in 264 BC, when three pairs fought at the funeral games given in honour of D. Iunius Pera. Down to *Caesar's Games in 46 BC the justification (or pretext) was always the death of a male relative, but these were in part commemorative of Caesar's daughter *Iulia (2), in part not commemorative at all. These contests, like beast-fights (see VENATIONES), became increasingly important as a route to popular favour for their promoter, forming an important, though normally brief (because highly expensive) item in games held at Rome and in other towns (see AEDILES). However, five thousand pairs fought in eight different games given by *Augustus (*RG* 22. 1) and the same number in a single series of games given by *Trajan to celebrate the conclusion of the Dacian War in AD 107. At Rome the original

Glanum

venue was the *forum Romanum. The first stone amphitheatre was built by *Statilius Taurus under Augustus, but it was only with the building of the Flavian amphitheatre (*Colosseum) that Rome had a specialized venue larger than those in quite small Italian towns (the fine amphitheatre to be seen at Pompeii goes back to the early years of the Sullan colony). *Antiochus (4) IV Epiphanes introduced these games to the Syrian capital, Antioch (1), *c.*170 BC and later they spread to all parts of the Roman empire. Gladiators were of four types: the *murmillo*, with a fish for the crest on his helmet, and the Samnite, both heavily armed with oblong shield, visored helmet, and short sword; the *retiarius*, lightly clad, fighting with net and trident; and the Thracian with round shield and curved scimitar. Prisoners of war and condemned criminals were compelled to fight as gladiators. Those who fought on a professional basis were either slaves, bought for the purpose, or free volunteers who for a fee bound themselves to their owner by an oath (*auctoramentum gladiatorium*) which permitted him to kill or maim them (in practice a gladiator was too valuable an investment to be wasted outside the games and the life of a defeated combatant was often spared by the audience's wish). They were trained in schools under a *lanista* (who was sometimes a retired gladiator) and might be acquired as an investment, to be hired or sold to games-promoters. In the late republic they were frequently used as the core of a gang or armed entourage. It appears that even members of the senatorial and equestrian orders were attracted to a gladiatorial career, which had a macabre glamour deriving from courage, physical strength, and sexual potency. In consequence there was legislation under Augustus and *Tiberius to prevent members of these orders becoming gladiators (Levick, below), which remained an infamous profession (*Dig.* 28. 2. 3 pref.). After *Domitian gladiatorial games could only be given at Rome by emperors; outside Rome they required official sanction. Restrictions on games in the towns of the empire seem to be related more to the expenditure involved for the promoters than to any distaste. Opposition to the idea of such games centred on their being bloodshed for fun, but for *Cicero (*Tusc.* 2. 41) and the younger *Pliny (2) (*Pan.* 33. 1) this did not apply if those fighting were condemned criminals. Gladiatorial combats were first prohibited in AD 325, when *Constantine I decided that they were too bloodthirsty a peacetime activity (*Cod. Theod.* 15. 12. 1; *Cod. Iust.* 11. 44).

L. Robert, *Les gladiateurs dans l'Orient grec* (1940); K. Hopkins, *Death and Renewal* (1983) ch. 1; T. Wiedemann, *Emperors and Gladiators* (1992); B. M. Levick, *JRS* 1983, 97 ff. J. P. B.; A. W. L.

Glanum (Γλανόν), a Greek and Roman town south of St-Rémy-de-Provence. The earliest element was a *Ligurian shrine, but in the 2nd cent. BC a Massiliote settlement grew up (see MASSALIA), owing its prosperity to its location on a major route between Italy and the Rhône (Rhodanus). Structures uncovered include several Hellenistic houses and a possible *bouleutērion*, and the town struck its own coins.

*Romanization was under way in the 1st cent. BC, but swiftly accelerated under Augustus, with the construction of extensive public buildings, and the acquisition of Latin rights (*ius Latii*: Pliny, *HN* 3. 37). To the north stand 'Les Antiques', a monumental arch and a mausoleum; the latter has been claimed as a cenotaph for Gaius *Iulius Caesar (2) and his brother Lucius *Iulius Caesar (4). After the destruction of Glanum by barbarians (*c.* AD 275) the site was abandoned and a new walled town built at St-Rémy itself.

H. Rolland, *Le Mausolée de Glanum* (1969); P. A. Février and others,

Histoire de la France urbaine 1 (1980), 198 ff.; A. L. F. Rivet, *Gallia Narbonensis* (1988), 198 ff. A. L. F. R.; J. F. Dr.

glass (ὕαλος (also 'rock crystal'), *vitrum*). The art of producing a vitreous surface on stone, powdered quartz (faience), or clay was known in pre-dynastic Egypt and passed to Crete during the second millennium BC. Glazed objects are common on Greek sites of the Archaic period, some of them Egyptian imports, others probably made locally. In Hellenistic and Roman times Egypt and Asia Minor were centres of fabrication of glazed wares, which often imitated bronze.

Objects composed entirely of glass paste begin to appear in Egypt about 1500 BC, when two allied processes seem to have been in use: modelling molten glass about a core of sand, and pressing it into an open mould. The chief Mycenaean glass is dark blue imitating lapis lazuli, used for beads, inlays, and architectural ornaments. In the 6th cent. small vases made by the sand-core process became known in Greece; they have opaque blue, brown, or white bodies and a marbled effect was produced on their surface by means of a comb or spike. In the Hellenistic period mould-made bowls come into fashion; these were produced mainly in Egypt. Here the tradition of opaque polychrome glass was continued into Roman times with *millefiori* bowls, in which marbled and other polychrome patterns were formed by fusing glass canes of various colours and pressing them into moulds. In the same tradition are the vessels in two layers carved in imitation of hard-stone *cameos: the Portland vase in London is the best-known example.

The invention of glass-blowing in the 1st cent. BC (probably in Syria) wrought great changes in the glass industry, which, hitherto limited to relatively expensive surrogates for luxury goods, now became capable of cheap mass-production, but even then the most highly valued glass was 'colourless and transparent, as closely as possible resembling rock crystal' (Plin. *HN* 36. 198). Glass was used in the home and for funerary *furniture. Glassworks have been located in many provinces, but in the later western empire, Belgic Gaul and Germany had taken the place of Italy and southern Gaul. Even Britain had some glass-works. The vessels, even when plain, show much variety of form, and there are several styles of decoration—tooling or applying relief ornament to the surface when warm, cutting or engraving or painting when cold. Window glass, made by a primitive process of rolling, was known at *Pompeii, and later became common; in the later empire also begins the use of glass for *mirrors. Gemstones were imitated in glass paste at all periods from the 7th cent. BC onwards (see GEMS). Burning-glasses were used, and these may conceivably have been used as magnifying glasses by gem engravers; spectacles were unknown.

Faience: V. Webb, *Archaic Greek Faience* (1978); Glazed pottery: H. Gabelmann, *JDAI* 1974, 89; Glass: P. Fossing, *Glass Before Glass-blowing* (1940); D. F. Grose, in W. D. Kingery (ed.), *High Technology Ceramics* (1986); M. Newby and K. S. Painter, *Roman Glass: Two Centuries of Art and Invention* (1991); M. Vickers *JRA* 1996. F. N. P.; M. V.

Glauce, feminine of the adjective γλαυκός ('grey'), the colour of the sea, hence applied to water divinities. A spring Glauce at *Corinth (Paus. 2. 3. 6) is named, as often, after a mythic maiden who committed suicide there. She develops into the daughter of the king 'Creon' ('ruler') whose marriage to *Jason (1) in *Euripides' *Medea* sets the plot in motion. (See also CREUSA (3).) K. D.

Glaucus (1–4), a name given to several, apparently unrelated, characters, of whom the following stand out:

(1) (= *LIMC* 'Glaukos' 5) Glaucus son of Hippolochus, with his cousin *Sarpedon led the Lycians at Troy (*Il.* 2. 876). He subsequently fell fighting over the body of *Achilles. Glaucus claimed descent through his grandfather *Bellerophon from Glaucus (2) (*Il.* 6. 152–211). The Lycian connection would be in harmony with other Corinthian links with the east.

(2) (= *LIMC* 'Glaukos' 3) Glaucus son of *Sisyphus, of Ephyre (in this case, *Corinth: see G. S. Kirk on *Il.* 6. 152–3). Identified by *Asclepiades (1) of Tragilus (*FGrH* 12 F 1) as the Glaucus of Potniae who was eaten by his horses at the funeral games for *Pelias (Paus. 6. 20. 19 identifies him as the Taraxippus, 'Horse-scarer', at Isthmia). The story may go back to *Aeschylus' *Glaucus Potnieus* (*TrGF* 3. 148–58). Most sources locate the horses' (usually mares') stables at Potniae south of *Thebes (1), but why this should be so is not clear.

(3) (= *LIMC* 'Glaukos' 2) Glaucus infant son of *Minos and Pasiphae, who fell into a jar of honey and was drowned. His body was recovered by the seer *Polyeidus (1), who revived him, gave him the gift of prophecy but later revoked it.

(4) (= *LIMC* 'Glaukos' 1) Glaucus Pontius or Thalassius, a sea-*daimōn* with prophetic powers (e.g. Eur. *Or.* 362–5; Arist. fr. 490 R). Located, at least since Aeschylus' *Glaucus Pontius* (*TrGF* 3. 142–8) in the vicinity of the Euboean strait. He was a mortal deified, usually by eating a magical herb. Possible cult in the Marathonian tetrapolis (*IG* 1³. 255; see MARATHON). The people of Boeotian *Anthedon claimed him as one of their own (Heraclides Creticus 1. 24 Pf.; Theolytus, *Coll. Alex.* p. 9 F 1; Ov. *Met.* 13. 903–6; Paus. 9. 22. 6–7).

LIMC 4/1 (1988) (various authors); M. Corsano, *Glaukos* (1992).
A. Sch.

Glaucus (5) of *Rhegium (*c*.410 BC) wrote an important work *On the Ancient Poets and Musicians* (used by ps.-Plut. *De mus.*), which inaugurated the ancient study of the history of lyric poetry. It dealt with the chronological and musical relation between the poets (e.g. Olympus, *Terpander, *Archilochus. Glaucus is sometimes identified with Glaucon the rhapsode (Pl. *Ion* 530d) and commentator on Homer's *Iliad*. In later antiquity Antiphon (probably *not* *Antiphon (1) but *Antiphon (2) the sophist) came to be considered the author of Glaucus' work.

FHG 2. 23 f.; E. Hiller, *Rh. Mus.* 1886, 398–436.
J. F. L.; E. Kr.

Glevum, Roman Gloucester, was founded as a military base for the conquest of Wales. A vexillation fortress of Legio XX Valeria (see LEGION) was constructed at Kingsholm in *c*. AD 49 when P. *Ostorius Scapula was moving against the Silures. A tombstone of Cohors VI Thracum may imply an auxiliary fort also. Legio XX moved to Usk in *c*.58. The fortress beneath modern Gloucester was then constructed for Legio II Augusta in *c*.65/6. It was occupied until *c*.74/5. In 96–8 the vacant fortress was settled as a *colonia* (*ILS* 2365), but was perhaps overshadowed by the prosperity of Corinium (Cirencester). Colonial tile-works are attested by stamps reading *R(ei) P(ublicae) G(levensium)* and sometimes mentioning magistrates.

H. R. Hurst, in G. Webster (ed.), *Fortress into City* (1988).
S. S. F.; M. J. M.

Glitius (*RE* Suppl. 3. 786 ff.; Suppl. 12. 381), **Atilius Agricola, Quintus,** from *Augusta (3) Taurinorum (Turin), perhaps of senatorial family, *Trajan's general, known from inscriptions (*ILS* 1021, 1021a (= E. M. Smallwood, *Documents Illustrating the Principates of Nerva, Trajan and Hadrian* (1966), 205): CIL 5. 6974–81); Atilius (his gentile name) was military tribune in *Moesia and

quaestor to *Vespasian (AD 78 at latest); praetor, *iuridicus* in Hither Spain, commander of Legio VI Ferrata in Syria, legate (see LEGATI) of Belgica (95?–96/97), suffect consul 97, decorated as governor of *Pannonia in Trajan's first Dacian War (101–2, see DACIA), suffect consul again (103), and *praefectus urbi*.

Syme, *RP* 7, see index.
H. H. S.; B. M. L.

glossa, glossary

Greek In Greek literary criticism *glōssai* (lit. 'tongues', γλῶσσαι) meant any words or expressions (not being mere neologisms or metaphors) ἃ οὐδεὶς ἂν εἴποι ἐν τῇ διαλέκτῳ ('which no one would utter in conversation', Arist. *Poet.* 1458ᵇ32), i.e. belonging not to the spoken language familiar to the critic (1458ᵇ6), but to a dialect, literary or vernacular, of another region or period (1457ᵇ4). The interpretation of Homeric *glōssai*, misunderstood already by Hesiod, fell, no doubt, from the first, to schoolmasters (cf. Ar. *Daitaleis*) and rhapsodes, and it appealed to sophistic interest in language: cf. *Democritus, Περὶ Ὁμήρου ἢ ὀρθοεπείης καὶ γλωσσέων ('On Homer or on correct speech and *glōssai*'). The living dialects were early used for the purpose (cf. Arist. *Poet.* 1461ᵃ12), but, apart from *Aristarchus (2), Alexandrian commentators, no less than the Pergamenes, usually preferred to explain by etymology, as did *Neoptolemus (2) of Parium in Περὶ γλωσσῶν Ὁμήρου ('On the *glōssai* of Homer'). Interest in dialects was fostered by 5th-cent. linguistic speculations, and in the next two centuries by Peripatetic studies, not least in natural history and its vocabulary, and by monographs based on personal knowledge of local dialects before the levelling operation of the *koinē*. The spirit of Alexandrianism in literature further encouraged search for linguistic oddities. Sometimes literary glosses were collected with only sporadic dialectal illustration, as the Homeric Glosses of *Philitas and *Simmias (2). Some specifically dialectal collections were devoted to Homer, Alcman, the Old Comedy, etc.; others were not so related to particular authors or styles, e.g. the Φρύγιαι φωναί ('Phrygian dialects') of Neoptolemus, the Ἐθνικαὶ λέξεις ('Foreign words') of Zenodotus (perhaps not the Alexandrian), and the Αἰολικαὶ γλῶσσαι ('Aeolic *glōssai*') of *Antigonus (4) of Carystus. The Ὀνομαστικόν (Onomasticon), often with dialectal variants, also became common: e.g. *Callimachus (3) compiled names of winds, fishes, and months; Dionysius Iambus had a chapter on fishermen's terms, and *Eratosthenes other vocational vocabularies. *Aristophanes (2) of Byzantium excelled all in the scope and diversity of his lexicographical labours (cf. Ael. *NA* 7. 47). In his footsteps followed his pupil Artemidorus (on Doric, and cookery), Philistides (on names of family relationships), and many others, notably, in the 1st cent. BC, Cleitarchus of Aegina, who proved a fertile source of dialect glosses under the empire. The Περὶ τῶν ὑποπτευομένων μὴ εἰρῆσθαι τοῖς παλαιοῖς ('On words suspected of not having been used by the ancients') of Aristophanes (see above) is a prototype of the 'Atticist' lexica which were common in the 1st cent. AD and still more in the following centuries. The first professed Atticist lexicographer was Eirenaeus of Alexandria (end of 1st cent. AD), and the ultimate sources of most later Atticists are also Alexandrian. As to glosses of all kinds, in the 1st cent. BC compilation largely displaces independent research, and almost exclusively prevails under the empire; to the latter period, down to Constantine I, the extant scholiasts and lexicographers are directly or indirectly indebted; but the sources thus absorbed have generally perished. The many glossaries and word-lists surviving in papyri show the importance of such aids to reading in an age when the literary and spoken languages diverged considerably. Some of these are mere jejune lists; others are works of scholarship in which entries are supported by quotations. Some are general alphabetical lists, others limited to the vocabulary of a particular dialect or a particular craft.

K. Latte, *Philol.* 1925, 136; R. Reitzenstein, *Geschichte d. gr. Etymologika* (1897); R. A. Pack, *The Greek and Latin Literary Texts from Greco-Roman Egypt*, 2nd edn. (1965), 1658 ff.; see also under GRAMMAR, GRAMMARIANS, GREEK ETYMOLOGY.　　　　　　　　　　　　　　P. B. R. F.; R. B.

Latin The need for interpretations of rare or obsolete words (γλῶσσαι) arose with the serious study of literature and antiquities; the earliest reference to Latin glosses is in *Varro (*Ling.* 7. 10). Some of the work of republican scholars like *Aurelius *Opillus and *Ateius Philologus was of a glossographical kind, and *Verrius Flaccus exploited collections of glosses on *Plautus, *Ennius, *Lucilius (1), etc.

The extant Latin glossaries (generally named from their first item, e.g. Abstrusa, Abavus, or from the home of their chief MS, e.g. St Gall, Erfurt) cannot be traced back farther than the 5th or 6th cent. AD. They arose largely from the needs of monastery teachers who gathered together and arranged in a roughly alphabetical order the marginalia from copies of the Bible, *Terence, *Virgil, *Orosius, etc., in their own or neighbouring libraries; only rarely did such marginalia contain any scholarly comment, and few glossary compilers had e.g. Sex. *Pompeius Festus' abridgement of Verrius Flaccus or *Isidorus (2)'s *Etymologiae* from which to borrow. Copies of a glossary thus constructed sometimes had a wide circulation and formed the basis for larger, derivative compilations; for example, Abstrusa (which contained material from a good Virgil commentary) and Abolita (which contained Festus items and Terence and Apuleius glosses) form the foundation for Abavus, Affatim, etc., and above all for the huge (early 9th-cent.?) encyclopaedic *Liber Glossarum* (= *Glossarium Ansileubi*), which also includes long passages from *Jerome, *Ambrose, *Gregory (1), *Isidorus (2), etc. The value of such glossaries is fourfold: their interpretations sometimes provide evidence for Late Latin or Early Romance linguistic developments; they sometimes contain evidence useful for establishing the text of an author; they occasionally transmit some fragment of ancient learning; and they illuminate the intellectual needs and horizons of the milieux in which they were compiled.

Among later collections of glosses the best known are those of Salomon (10th cent.) and Papias (11th cent.), both of which rely on the *Liber Glossarum*. Of Latin–Greek or Greek–Latin glossaries may be mentioned: the Cyril-glossary (6th cent.?) falsely attributed to the 5th-cent. patriarch of Alexandria (see CYRIL OF ALEXANDRIA) and not yet fully published; the Philoxenus-glossary falsely attributed to the consul of AD 535; and the *Hermeneumata* falsely attributed to Dositheus. Glossaries with Old English, Celtic, or Germanic interpretations also survive.

J. Tolkiehn, *RE* 12/2 (1925), 2432–82, 'Lexikographie'; G. Goetz, *RE* 7/1 (1910), 1433–66, 'Glossographie'. W. M. Lindsay and H. J. Thomson, *Ancient Lore in Medieval Latin Glossaries* (1921); J. F. Mountford, *Quotations from Classical Authors in Medieval Latin Glossaries* (1925). Vol. 1 (1923) of the *Corpus Glossariorum Latinorum* (ed. G. Goetz) comprises an introductory study, *De origine et fatis glossariorum Latinorum* (fundamental); vols. 2–5 transcribe the oldest MSS of the chief early medieval glossaries (with readings of other MSS in the app. crit.): 2 (1888) contains Latin–Greek (= Philoxenus) and Greek–Latin glossaries; 3 (1892) contains the ps.-Dositheus *Hermeneumata*; 4 (1889) contains Abstrusa + Abolita (= *Glossae codicis Vaticani 3321*) and short derivative glossaries; 5 (1894) contains the Placidus-glossary, excerpts from the *Liber Glossarum*, etc.; vols. 6 and 7 (1899–1901) present the

items of vols. 2–5 in alphabetical and corrected form. The series *Glossaria Latina* (ed. W. M. Lindsay and others) provides editions of the chief glossaries, with indications (where possible) of the source of each item: vol. 1 (1926) contains all the glossary material of the *Lib. Gloss.*; 2 (1926), the Arma, Abavus, and Philoxenus-glossaries; 3 (1926), Abstrusa and Abolita; 4 (1930), Placidus (and an edn. of Festus based on glossary material); 5 (1931), the Abba and AA glossaries. Fragments of ancient bilingual glossaries have been edited by J. Kramer (1983). On the Cyril-glossary see M. Naoumides, *ICS* 1979, 94 ff. Of Latin–Old English glossaries, the Leyden has been edited by J. H. Hessels (1906), the Corpus by W. M. Lindsay (1921), and the Harley by R. T. Oliphant (1966). Latin–Celtic glossaries have been edited by W. Stokes and J. Strachan, *Thesaurus Palaeohibernicus*, 2 vols. (1901–3), with Supplement (1910) (cf. R. Thurneysen, 'Irische Glossen', *Zeitschrift für Celtische Philologie* 21); Latin–Germanic, by E. Steinmeyer and E. Sievers, *Die Althochdeutschen Glossen*, 4 vols. (1879–98).　　　R. A. K.

Glycon (1), poet of unknown date and place to whom the glyconic metre is attributed by *Hephaestion (2) (33. 12). Nothing else is known about him. The epigram in *Anth. Pal.* 10. 124 is thought to be a different poet of later date, since it appears with other late poems.

RE 7/1. 1469; M. L. West, *Greek Metre* (1982), 29 ff.　　　C. M. B.; B. Z.

Glycon (2), Athenian sculptor (early 3rd cent. AD), known from his signature on the Farnese Hercules in Naples, found in the baths of Caracalla. The statue is a version of a late 4th-cent. type often attributed to *Lysippus (2).

D. E. E. Kleiner, *Roman Sculpture* (1992), 338 f., fig. 305; cf. A. F. Stewart, *Greek Sculpture* (1990), 190, fig. 566.　　　A. F. S.

Gnathia (mod. Fasano), a Messapian port, 58 km. (36 mi.) south of *Barium, which dominated land and sea communications, handling trade with Greece. It prospered in the Hellenistic period, a phase characterized by proliferation of rich burials and Greek-influenced monumental architecture, and flourished until late antiquity. See POTTERY, GREEK (end) for 'Gnathian Ware'.

O. Parlangeli, *Studi Messapici* (1960); E. Greco, *Magna Grecia* (1981).　　　K. L.

gnōmē, a maxim or aphorism: an important facet of Greek literary expression from the earliest period. Hes. *Op.* 694 is representative: μέτρα φυλάσσεσθαι· καιρὸς δ' ἐπὶ πᾶσιν ἄριστος ('keep the rules: proportion is best in all things'). The subject is usually human life or the terms of human existence, articulated as a succinct general truth or instruction. The word γνώμη is attested in this sense from the late 5th cent. BC (e.g. Ar. *Eq.* 1379; Democr. 35), soon after which *gnōmologia* is a recognized category of rhetorical analysis (e.g. Arist. *Rh.* 2. 21).

Gnomes are used: (*a*) in argument, to relate or distinguish particular and general: 'the Athenian war-dead will never be forgotten—heroes have the whole world for their tombstone' (Thuc. 2. 43. 3); 'women (they say) live safe at home while men go to war . . . I would rather take up arms three times than give birth once' (Eur. *Med.* 248–51); (*b*) singly, as self-sufficient maxims, like the Delphic γνῶθι σεαυτόν ('know thyself') and μηδὲν ἄγαν ('nothing in excess'). Instances of both kinds are often aggregated in clusters or simple lists, from the Hesiodic *Precepts of Chiron* to the so-called *Monostichi* ('One-liners') *of Menander*, from Democritus' prose aphorisms (apparently entitled *Gnomae*, DK 68 B 35) and *Isocrates' To Nicocles* to the late paroemiographical collections (see PAROEMIOGRAPHERS). Such aggregations have a broadly educational rationale, and some (such as the 'Menandrian') are specifically identifiable as school texts.

Horna and von Fritz, *RE* Suppl. 6 (1935), 74 ff.; P. Huart, *ΓΝΩΜΗ chez Thucydide et ses contemporains* (1973).　　　M. S. Si.

Gnosticism is a generic term primarily used of theosophical groups which broke with the 2nd-cent. Christian Church; see CHRISTIANITY. A wider, more imprecise use of the term describes a syncretistic religiosity diffused in the near east, contemporaneous with and independent of Christianity. In recent years (especially following the full publication of the Coptic Gnostic texts discovered at Nag Hammadi in Upper Egypt in 1946), the diversity of beliefs in the various 'Gnostic' sects has been increasingly emphasized, with some scholars unwilling any longer to use 'Gnosticism' as a collective term at all, or even the broad grouping into 'Valentinian' and 'Sethian' traditions, but no new consensus has yet emerged. Many ingredients of 2nd-cent. Gnosticism are pre-Christian, but there is no evidence of a pre-Christian religion or cultic myth resembling Christianity as closely as the systems of Basilides, Valentinus, and *Manichaeism, all of which owed the essentials of their beliefs to Christianity, or even as the doctrine of Simon Magus, which provided a rival religion of redemption with a redeemer replacing Christ.

The principal characteristics of the 2nd-cent. sects are (1) a radical rejection of the visible world as being alien to the supreme God and as incompatible with truth as darkness with light; (2) the assertion that elect souls are divine sparks temporarily imprisoned in matter as a result of a precosmic catastrophe, but saved by a redeemer, sent from the transcendent God, whose teachings awake the sleepwalking soul to a consciousness of its origins and destiny, and also include instructions how to pass the blind planetary powers which bar the *soul's ascent to its celestial home. The first proposition has close affinities with late Jewish apocalyptic; for the second the Gnostics claimed, with some reason, large support in the dialogues of *Plato (1).

To explain how humanity came to need such drastic redemption, many Gnostics expounded Genesis 1–3 as an allegory of the fall of a female cosmic power, normally termed Sophia, a primal 'sin' (arising from restlessness or inquisitiveness) which led to the making of this visible world by an incompetent or malevolent demiurge. So the natural world betrays nothing of a beneficent creative intention. This cosmogony provided the ground for an ethic which in most sects was rabidly ascetic, but in a few groups (especially Carpocrates') produced a religion of eroticism, supported by an antinomian interpretation of St *Paul's antithesis of law and grace and by an extreme predestinarianism.

The principal sources of Gnosticism are the Platonist dualism of the intelligible and sense-perceptible (material) realms, in which matter is invested with quasi-demonic properties by what was seen by later Platonists as an evil world-soul (cf. *Leg.* 896e; *Tht.* 176e), Hellenized forms of Zoroastrianism (chiefly attested in *Plutarch's interpretation of *Isis and *Osiris), Mithraism (see MITHRAS) with its theme of the soul's ascent through the seven planets (modified to form part of the Ophite Gnostic system as described in Origen, *C. Cels.* 6), Judaism which, besides the Book of Genesis, contributed the apocalyptic themes of the conflict between angelic powers and of the deliverance of the elect from this evil world, Hermeticism (Hermetic tracts feature in the Nag Hammadi corpus), and above all *Christianity, to which Gnosticism appears like a diabolical *Doppelgänger*. The evidence of the Pauline Epistles (esp. Galatians, 1 Corinthians, Colossians) shows the author (who may not always be Paul) using language often close to that of Gnosticism, and at the same time strenuously resisting Gnostic tendencies in the churches. The fact that some of the proto-Gnostic elements in the Epistles can also be found in *Philon (4) suggests that extreme liberalizing Judaism was a material cause of Gnostic origins. Nevertheless, the Jewish element is not strong in all the systems, and in many there is an anti-Semitic spirit. From the 2nd cent., attitudes resembling Gnosticism appear in pagan texts, especially in *Plutarch's theosophical tracts, the Hermetic corpus, *Numenius of Apamea, the *Chaldaean Oracles*, and alchemists like Zosimus (see ALCHEMY). It is entirely possible that some Gnostic influence passed from Numenius to *Plotinus and *Porphyry. Plotinus' passionate attack on the Gnostics (*Enn.* 2. 9) is the work of a man who not only had to purge his own circle but felt within himself the power of Gnostic attitudes; and the *theurgy of later *Neoplatonism is near to some of the grosser forms of 2nd-cent. Gnosticism combated by the Church. See HERMES TRISMEGISTUS; ZOROASTER.

In Christianity Gnosticism produced a sharp reaction against its rejection of the doctrines of the goodness of the creation and the freedom of man. The capacity of individual sects for survival was also weakened by the syncretistic acceptance of all religious myths as valid and true (see SYNCRETISM). Nevertheless, Gnosticism had a strikingly successful future in Manicheism, one form of which still survives in the Mandaeans of Iraq.

SOURCES Coptic Gnostic documents are now available in English in J. M. Robinson (ed.), *The Nag Hammadi Library* (1977), and in Coptic in the definitive edition of the Nag Hammadi codices being published by Brill of Leiden. Earlier discoveries: C. Schmidt, *Koptisch-gnostische Schriften* (1905). Fragments of Heracleon, Marcion, and Valentinus are preserved in quotations made by orthodox critics (esp. Irenaeus, Tertullian, Clement of Alexandria, Hippolytus (2), Origen (1)).

LITERATURE H. Jonas, *The Gnostic Religion* (1958); R. M. Grant, *Gnosticism and Early Christianity* (1959); K. Rudolph, *Gnosis* (1977): Eng. trans., R. McL. Wilson (1983); E. Pagels, *The Gnostic Gospels* (1979); B. Layton (ed.), *The Rediscovery of Gnosticism*, 2 vols. (1980); R. T. Wallis and J. Bregman (eds.), *Neoplatonism and Gnosticism* (1992).   J. M. D.

goats See MENDES; PAN; PASTORALISM.

gods, Olympian See OLYMPIAN GODS, OLYMPIANS; RELIGION, GREEK; THEOS.

gold (χρυσός, *aurum*) is rare in Greece, and the source of the rich treasures found in bronze age tombs (*Mycenae, etc.) is unknown. The island of *Siphnos prospered in the 6th cent. BC by its gold productions; later the mines were flooded. Mines on *Thasos, opened by the *Phoenicians, were working in *Thucydides (2)'s day, but have not been found. *Macedonia and *Thrace had a large auriferous area, where the mines of Mt. *Pangaeus were working before 500 BC. In Asia Minor, gold came from Mysia, *Phrygia, and *Lydia; their wealth is attested by the stories of *Midas (1), *Croesus, and the river Pactolus. Electrum (ἤλεκτρον), a natural alloy of gold and silver, was panned in the rivers of Asia Minor, and was used for the earliest coins (see COINAGE, GREEK) and for jewellery. *Colchis also furnished gold, Scythians brought supplies from central Asia, and *Carthage received gold from West Africa. Yet there was a relative scarcity of gold in Greece until the conquests of *Alexander (3) the Great made available the hoards of Persia.

Early *Etruscan tombs show a wealth of gold furniture comparable to that of bronze age Greece. Traces of early mining are found in several districts of Italy, in particular the Apennines. At Rome the metal long remained rare; it probably first became common through war indemnities. Under the late republic and early empire the main source of supply (apart from *booty from the Hellenistic east) was Spain, where the north-west and *Baetica yielded immense quantities. Gold was also mined in southern France and dredged from rivers in other parts of Gaul; there are also workings in south Wales. After the 1st cent. AD the western goldfields were largely superseded by those of the Balkans, *Noricum, and *Dacia. The supply from these fell off during the 3rd cent. AD.

M. Rosenberg, *Geschichte der Goldschmiedekunst* (1910–25); H. Quiring, *Geschichte des Goldes* (1948); O. Davies, *Roman Mines in Europe* (1935); R. A. Higgins, *Greek and Roman Jewellery*, 2nd edn. (1980); M. Vickers, *AJArch.* 1994.   F. N. P.; M. V.

golden age, an imagined period in early human history when human beings lived a life of ease, far from toil and sin. The most important text is *Hesiod *Op.* 109–26 (see West's comm.), which talks of a 'golden *genos*', i.e. species or generation, as the first in a series: reference to a golden *age* occurs first in Latin (*aurea saecula, aurea aetas*: cf. H. C. Baldry *CQ* 1952, 83; Gatz 65, 228). Other well-known passages include Aratus, *Phaen.* 100–14 and Ovid, *Met.* 1. 89–112 (where see Bömer) but the motif was widespread in ancient literature (cf. *Aetna* 9–16 on the theme as hackneyed) and parodied in comedy from the 5th cent. BC (Athen. 6. 267e–270a). The golden age is associated especially with Cronus or *Saturnus and is marked by communal living and the spontaneous supply of food: its end comes with a series of inventions that lead to the modern condition of humanity (first plough, first ship, first walls, and first sword: cf. Smith on Tibullus 1. 3. 35 ff.). Rationalist thinkers tended to reject the model in favour of 'hard' primitivism or a belief in progress, but the function of the myth was always to hold up a mirror to present malaises or to presage a future return to the idyll (cf. Verg. *Ecl.* 4).

A. O. Lovejoy and G. Boas, *Primitivism and Related Ideas in Antiquity* (1935); W. K. C. Guthrie, *In the Beginning* (1957); A. Kurfess, *RAC* 1 (1950), 144–50, 'Aetas Aurea'; B. Gatz, *Weltalter, goldene Zeit und Sinnverwandte Vorstellungen* (1967); K. Kubusch, *Aurea Saecula, Mythos und Geschichte: Untersuchung eines Motivs in der antiken Literatur bis Ovid* (1986).   P. G. F., D. P. F.

Golden Fleece See ARGONAUTS; JASON (1); MEDEA; PELIAS.

Golden House See DOMUS AUREA.

Gordian I (Marcus Antonius (*RE* 61) **Gordianus Sempronianus Romanus),** Roman emperor, AD 238. An elderly proconsul of Africa, he intervened in a riot against *Maximinus, only to find himself proclaimed emperor. He made his son, Gordian II, his colleague. The senate, also hostile to Maximinus, quickly acknowledged them. However, the rebels were militarily weak, and when Capelianus, governor of Numidia, moved against them with his legionary army, Gordian II was killed and Gordian I committed suicide after a reign of only a few weeks (early 238). The senate, compromised, continued the insurrection, under *Balbinus and Pupienus.

See GORDIAN III.   J. F. Dr.

Gordian III (Marcus Antonius (*RE* 60) **Gordianus),** grandson of *Gordian I by a daughter, was forced on *Balbinus and Pupienus as their Caesar and, after their murder (mid AD 238), saluted emperor by the praetorians at the age of 13. The conduct of affairs was at first in the hands of his backers but, as fiscal and military difficulties increased, it passed to the praetorian prefect C. *Furius Sabinius Aquila Timesitheus (241). Timesitheus prepared a major campaign against Persia which, beginning in 242, achieved substantial success before his death, by illness, in 243. Gordian replaced Timesitheus with one of the latter's protégés, M. *Iulius Philippus, who continued the war. However, the Roman army suffered defeat near *Ctesiphon, and shortly afterwards Gordian died of his wounds (early 244). He was succeeded by Philippus.

Though the period of the Gordians shows some of the characteristics of the 3rd-cent. 'crisis', it is best interpreted as a reversion to the Severan monarchy after the aberrance of *Maximinus.

X. Loriot, *ANRW* 2. 2 (1975), 657 ff.; K. Dietz, *Senatus contra Principem* (1980); E. Kettenhofen, *Die römisch-persischen Kriege des 3. Jhdts n. Chr.* (1982).   J. F. Dr.

Gordium (mod. Yassıhüyük), capital of ancient *Phrygia, situated at the point where the river *Sangarius is crossed by the main route westward from the Anatolian plateau to the sea (the Persian 'Royal Road'). The site was occupied in the early bronze age and the Hittite period, and Phrygian settlement probably began in the 10th cent. BC. Gordium became the main Phrygian centre in the 8th cent., at the end of which it reached its greatest prosperity under King *Midas (2). The site had massive fortifications and impressive palace buildings, and many richly furnished tumuli were built around it in the 8th to 6th cents., including one which has been identified as the tomb of Midas himself. Gordium was destroyed by the invading *Cimmerians in the early 7th cent. but recovered, only to lose importance under Persian domination. It was visited by *Alexander (3) the Great (333), who cut the famous 'Gordian Knot'. The Hellenistic settlement was destroyed during the Roman expedition against the Galatians of 189 BC, led by Cn. *Manlius Vulso. In Strabo's day there was a village at the site. See ASIA MINOR (pre-Classical).

G. and A. Körte, *Gordion*, *JDAI* 1904; R. S. Young, *PECS* 360; *Arch. Rep.* 1989/90, 129; O. W. Muscarella (ed.), *Phrygian Art and Archaeology*, nos. 3–4 (1988); A. J. N. W. Prag, *Anat. St.* 1989, 159–65 (Midas' skull).   D. J. B.; S. M.

Gordyene, a small Hellenistic kingdom (remnant of the *Seleucid empire), originally the land of the Kardouchoi, east of sources of Tigris, bordering Armenia (Strabo 16. 1. 8 and 24). It was a vassal kingdom of *Tigranes II (1) the Great, who enlarged it at the expense of Parthian *Adiabene. Its last king, Zarbienus, was executed for plotting with L. *Licinius Lucullus (2) (Plut. *Luc.* 29), who later looted its treasures. Pompey resisted Parthian claims, sent L. *Afranius (2) to overrun it, and restored most of it to Tigranes (Cass. Dio 37. 5. 4). Occupied by *Trajan but regularly part of the Parthian and *Sasanid empires, it was finally ceded to Persia by *Jovian (Amm. Marc. 25. 7. 8 f.).

Baumgartner, *RE* 7 Γορδυηνή; U. Kahrstedt, *Artabanos III* (1950), 59 ff.   E. W. G.

Gorgias (1), of *Leontini (*c.*485–*c.*380 BC), one of the most influential of the *sophists, important both as a thinker and as a stylist. He is said to have been a pupil of *Empedocles; his visit to Athens as an ambassador in 427 is traditionally seen as a landmark in the history of rhetoric, introducing Sicilian techniques into the Athenian tradition of oratory (see RHETORIC, GREEK). However this may be, his stylistic influence was enormous. The extant *Encomium of Helen* and *Defence of Palamedes*, as well as the fragment of his *Epitaphius* (DK 82 B 6; see EPITAPHIOS), illustrate clearly the seductions of his antithetical manner, with its balancing clauses, rhymes, and assonances: antithesis, homoeoteleuton, and parisosis became known as the 'Gorgianic figures'. There is a wonderful *parody of the style in Agathon's speech in *Plato (1)'s *Symposium* (194e–197e). At the same time, these speeches also contain serious reflection on the power of words (λόγος) and on moral responsibility. We also possess summaries of a philosophical work (Sext. Emp. *Math.* 7. 65 ff. = DK 82 B 3), and *On Melissus, Xenophanes and Gorgias* (preserved among the works of *Aristotle, 974ᵃ–980ᵇ Bekker). From these, it is apparent that

Gorgias argued that 'nothing is', and even if anything is, it cannot be known, or indicated by one person to another. How serious these sceptical arguments were has been much debated.

FRAGMENTS DK 82; L. Radermacher, *Artium Scriptores* (1951). Translation by G. A. Kennedy, in R. K. Sprague, *The Older Sophists* (1972). Separate edn. of *Helen* by D. MacDowell (1982).

See in general: E. R. Dodds, edn. of Plato, *Gorgias* (1959), 6 ff.; Norden, *Ant. Kunstpr.*³ 63 ff. (with important updating by G. Calboli in the Italian translation (*La prosa d'arte antica*), by B. H. Campana, 1986); Guthrie, *Hist. Gk. Phil.* 3. 269–74; G. B. Kerferd, *The Sophistic Movement* (1981), 44–5, 78–82, 93–9. D. A. R.

Gorgias (2), a rhetor, who was teaching at Athens in 44 BC (Cic. *Fam.* 16. 21. 6), and was the author of four books on figures, abridged as one book in Latin by his contemporary *Rutilius Lupus (Quint. *Inst.* 9. 2. 102). This abridgement, or what purports to be it, survives. Cicero's son (*Fam.* 16. 21. 6) speaks of his father's disapproval of Gorgias as a teacher; and since the Latin abridgement includes (with approval) examples from 'Asianist' orators like *Hegesias (2), there is some ground for labelling Gorgias an 'Asianist' (see ASIANISM AND ATTICISM).

Edition of Rutilius Lupus by E. Brooks (1970); text also in Halm, *Rhet. Lat. Min.* 3–21. G. A. Kennedy, *The Art of Rhetoric in the Roman World* (1972), 337. D. A. R.

Gorgo/Medusa, female monsters in Greek mythology. According to the canonical version of the myth (Apollod. 2. 4. 1–2) *Perseus (1) was ordered to fetch the head of Medusa, the mortal sister of Sthenno and Euryale; through their horrific appearance these Gorgons turned to stone anyone who looked at them. With the help of *Athena, *Hermes, and *nymphs, who had supplied him with winged sandals, *Hades' cap of invisibility, and a sickle (*harpē*) Perseus managed to behead Medusa in her sleep; from her head sprang Chrysaor and the horse *Pegasus. Although pursued by Medusa's sisters, Perseus escaped and, eventually, turned his enemy Polydectes to stone by means of Medusa's head.

*Hesiod (*Theog.* 270–82) already knows the myth which shows oriental influence: the Gorgons' iconography has been borrowed from that of Mesopotamian Lamashtu; Perseus saved *Androm-eda in Ioppe-Jaffa, and an oriental seal shows a young hero seizing a demonic creature whilst holding a *harpē*. Gorgons were very popular—often with an apotropaic function, as on temple-pediments—in Archaic art, which represented them as women with open mouth and dangerous teeth, but in the 5th cent. they lost their frightening appearance and became beautiful women; consequently, the myth is hardly found in art after the 4th cent. BC.

Perseus' adventure was already popular in Etruria in the 5th cent. Roman authors, such as Ovid (*Met.* 4. 604–5. 249) and Lucan (9. 624–733), concentrated especially on Medusa's frightening head.

Perseus was connected with *initiation in Mycenae, and his slaying of Medusa probably has an initiatory background: the reflection of the young warrior's test. Actually, descriptions of the Gorgo's head relate features of the Archaic warrior's fury: fearful looks, gaping grin, gnashing of teeth, violent war cry. The popularity of the Gorgo's head, the Gorgoneion, on warriors' shields also points to its terrifying effects. The myth of Perseus and Medusa, then, is an important example of the complex inter-relations in the Archaic age between narrative and iconographical motifs, between Greece and the orient. See ORIENTALISM.

I. Krauskopf, *LIMC* 4/1 (1988), 285–344; M. Jameson, in R. Hägg and

G. Nordquist (eds.), *Celebrations of Death and Divinity in the Bronze Age Argolid* (1990), 213–23 (Perseus in Mycene); J.-P. Vernant, *Mortals and Immortals* (1991), 111–49; W. Burkert, *The Orientalizing Revolution* (1992), 83–7. J. N. B.

Gortyn, Gortyn law code Gortyn was a city in central *Crete. From the 7th cent. BC are known a temple to *Athena on the acropolis, and one to *Apollo Pythios on the plain; an agora lies at the foot of the acropolis. By the 3rd cent. BC Gortyn was one of the most important cities on the island. It had conquered Phaestus, gaining an extensive territory and a good harbour at Matala in addition to the one at Lebena, and had entered into long-term hostilities with *Cnossus. After Cnossus had been captured by Q. *Caecilius Metellus (Creticus), Gortyn, which had sided with the Romans, was made the capital of the new province of Crete-*Cyrene. The well-preserved Roman-period city was extremely extensive (c.150 ha.: 370 acres), and includes a large governor's residence (*praetorium*), baths, a circus, a theatre and amphitheatre, and seven Christian basilicas including one to Agios Titos (late 6th/early 7th cent. AD). There are Hellenistic, Roman, and Byzantine cemeteries. The city was destroyed by the Arabs.

Of Gortyn's various early inscribed laws the most extensive is the Gortyn law code. This consists of a variety of laws probably enacted since at least the 6th cent. BC, and only slightly reorgan-ized when they were inscribed c.450 BC. The inscription is built into an odeum restored in AD 100 on one side of the agora, but had probably always been displayed in this area. The laws deal with the family and family property, with slaves (see SLAVERY), surety, donations, mortgage, procedure in trials, and other items. Slaves had certain rights for their protection; they were also allowed to have their own property and even to marry free women. There was also a clear distinction, especially in matters of hereditary right, between family and private property. There were detailed regulations on *adoption, and the property rights of heiresses and of the divorced wives of citizens. The modern distinction between criminal and family law does not apply, nor does the modern expectation that laws are egalitarian. For example, rape was not a criminal offence, but led to a fine, the level of which varied widely in accord with the status of the victim (whether male or female) and of the rapist. Witnesses, some on oath, and the oath of the party, served to establish a case; but the judge decided at his own discretion. The laws of Gortyn are probably the most important source for Archaic–Classical Greek law, and reveal a high level of juristic conceptions. See INHERITANCE, GREEK; LAW IN GREECE.

Strabo 10. 476–7; *IC* 4, with testimonia. I. F. Sanders, *Roman Crete* (1982); *Creta Antica* (1984); A. Di Vita, *Gortina* 1 (1988); G. F. La Torre, *ASAA* 1988–9. Law Code: *IC* 4. 72; J. Kohler and E. Ziebarth, *Das Stadtrecht von Gortyn* (1912); R. F. Willetts, *The Law Code of Gortyn* (1967); ML 41; M. Gagarin, *GRBS* 1982. V. E.; L. F. N., S. R. F. P.

Goths, a Germanic people, who, according to *Jordanes' *Getica*, originated in Scandinavia. The Cernjachov culture of the later 3rd and 4th cents. AD beside the Black Sea, and the Polish and Byelorussian Wielbark cultures of the 1st–3rd cents. AD, provide evidence of a Gothic migration down the Vistula to the Black Sea, but no clear trail leads to Scandinavia. In the mid-3rd cent. AD, Goths from the Black Sea region (see HERULI) launched heavy attacks upon Asia Minor and the Roman Balkans. These were eventually halted by the victories of *Gallienus, *Claudius II (Gothicus), and *Aurelian. The Goths have usually been viewed as from this date divided into two—Visigoths and Ostrogoths—

but the Gothic world of the 4th cent. probably comprised a number of chieftainships; how many is unknowable. Visigoths and Ostrogoths were actually the product of a later convulsion occasioned by the inroads of the *Huns. As a direct result, two separate Gothic groups crossed the Danube in 376, their victory at Hadrianople in 378 paving the way for a more ordered coexistence with Roman power after 382. These two groups were definitively united by *Alaric (395–411) to create the Visigoths, but only after being joined by a third large contingent: the survivors of Radagaisus' attack on Italy in 405–6. This force was settled in the Garonne in 418, and, as Roman power waned, created a Gothic kingdom in Gaul and Spain, especially under Euric (466–84). Further east, various (but not all the other) Gothic groups who had either fled to the Romans after *c.*400 or survived Hunnic hegemony, were united in various stages between *c.*450 and 484 behind the family of *Theoderic (1) to create the Ostrogoths, who then carved out a kingdom in Italy after 489. Theoderic further united both Gothic kingdoms in 511, but this did not survive his death (526). The Ostrogothic kingdom was destroyed by the Byzantines in twenty years of warfare after 536; Visigothic Spain was eventually conquered by Muslim forces in the early 8th cent.

E. A. Thompson, *The Goths in Spain* (1969); H. Wolfram, *History of the Goths* (1988); M. Kazanski, *Les Goths* (1991); P. J. Heather, *Goths and Romans 332–489* (1991). P. J. H.

government/administration (Greek) The Greek states involved their citizens, as far as possible, in carrying out decisions as well as in making decisions, and did little to develop a professional *bureaucracy. The need for regular administrators was reduced by such practices as tax-farming, the system of *liturgies, through which rich citizens were made directly responsible for spending their money for public purposes, and reliance on individuals to prosecute offenders not only for private wrongs but also for wrongs against the state.

Democratic Athens, with its large number of citizens, its extensive overseas interests, and money with which to pay stipends, developed a particularly large number of administrative posts—700 internal and 700 external in the 5th cent. BC, according to the text of *Ath. pol.* 24. 3, though the second 700 is probably corrupt. The work of administration, where it could not be devolved, was divided into a large number of separate, small jobs, and most of those were entrusted to boards of ten men, one from each tribe, appointed by lot for one year and not eligible for reappointment to the same board: it was assumed that the work required loyalty rather than ability. The council of five hundred, itself appointed by lot for a year, acted as overseer of the various boards. (See BOULĒ.) Thus when a partnership of citizens made a successful bid for the collection of a particular tax in a particular year, the contract would be made by the *pōlētai ('sellers') in the presence of the council. If they paid the money on time they would pay it to the *apodektai ('receivers') in the presence of the council, and if they defaulted the council would use the *praktores* ('exacters') to pursue them (*Ath. pol.* 47. 2–48. 1). See generally DEMOCRACY, ATHENIAN. Smaller states probably subdivided the work less and used smaller boards or single officials. P. J. R.

Gracchan means 'to do with the GRACCHI' (see below).

Gracchi (the tribunes). See SEMPRONIUS GRACCHUS (3), TI., and SEMPRONIUS GRACCHUS, C.

Graces See CHARITES.

Graeae (Γραιαί, 'Crones'), supporting actors in the cast of the

*Perseus (1) *folk-tale. Hesiod (*Theog.* 270 ff.) makes them daughters of the monstrous pair *Phorcys and Ceto, like the Gorgons; and their role is to be pale precursors and minimally equipped counterparts of that powerful trio (see GORGO). While their sisters are characterized by their writhing snaky locks, gnashing fangs, and deadly glare, these feeble hags are grey-haired from birth and can muster only a lone tooth and a single eye between them, which they must use in turn; Perseus intercepts the eye as it is handed from one to another, thus forcing them to reveal the next stage of his quest. Hesiod knows two names, Pemphredo and Enyo; Aeschylus (*PV* 794 ff.) has the more usual three-sister pattern (*Fates, *Charites; cf. *Harpyiae), and the third name is later given as Deino (Apollod. 2. 4. 2).

C. Kanellopoulou, *LIMC* 4/1 (1988), 362–4. A. H. G.

Graeco-Persian style An amalgam of Greek and *Achaemenid Persian stylistic traits. The Persian conquest of Lydia and Ionia in the 6th cent. BC led to craftsmen from the west working for Persian patrons. A foundation tablet from the palace of *Darius I at *Susa attests the activities of Ionian and Carian masons and carpenters. *Theodorus (1) of Samos was commissioned to make a gold wine-mixing bowl for Darius' bedroom (Ath. 12. 515a), and a golden vine encrusted with emeralds and rubies that 'grew' over the Great King's bed is also attributed to him (Ath. 12. 514f; Himer. *Ecl.* 31. 8). Nothing on this scale survives in precious metal: some silver-gilt *phialai*, 'libation bowls' (one from *Rogozen), indicate the ways in which Persian motifs might be rendered by Greek or Ionian craftsmen. The degree to which monumental Achaemenid sculpture depended on Greek stylistic norms is uncertain; there may well have been a two-way traffic between the Greek and Persian worlds, and matters will be clearer when chronological issues are resolved. By the later 5th cent., there is a genre of Persian gem-engraving that is distinctively Greek in both form and content. In contrast with the formality of Achaemenid court art, 'Graeco-Persian' *gems display a range of motifs showing the home life of Persian aristocrats, their hunting activities, and their prey. They provide visual analogues to *Xenophon (1)'s accounts of Persian life in the *Cyropaedia*. These gems appear to have been made in the western part of the Persian empire, in Asia Minor and Syria. Persian motifs were adopted by Greek sculptors, judging by e.g. a throne bearing a relief based on *Ahuramazda (in Berlin), and the griffins on the pedestal of a candelabrum probably from Hadrian's *Tibur villa (at Newby Hall, Yorkshire).

J. Boardman, *Intaglios and Rings* (1975), 28–34; E. Porada, *Cambridge History of Iran* (1985), 811–19; M. C. Root, in H. Sancisi–Weerdenburg and A. Kuhrt (eds.), *Achaemenid History* 6 (1991), 1 ff. M. V.

grain supply See FOOD SUPPLY (Greek and Roman).

grammar, grammarians, Greek (see LINGUISTICS, ANCIENT) Linguistic analysis and classification begin, in Greece, with the 5th-cent. sophists. Their phonetic studies are reflected in the title of a lost work of *Democritus, *On Euphonious and Cacophonous Letters*, and in a fragment of Euripides' *Palamedes* ἄφωνα καὶ φωνοῦντα συλλαβὰς τιθείς.... *Plato (1) (*Cra.* 424c; cf. *Tht.* 203b) mentions a classification of the alphabetic sounds as (*a*) voiced (the vowels), (*b*) ἄφωνα but not ἄφθογγα (the ἡμίφωνα of *Aristotle), and (*c*) ἄφωνα καὶ ἄφθογγα (the largest class): the last are the ἄφωνα of the Alexandrians, who followed *Aristotle in dividing them into δασέα, ψιλά, and μέσα (χ θ φ, κ τ π, and γ δ β), and used σύμφωνα (consonants) to include both second and third classes, (*b*) and (*c*) above.

Plato notices two distinctions of accentual intonation, 'acute' and 'grave' (*Cra.* 399 b), Aristotle also a third, intermediate, our circumflex (*Poet.* 1456^{b}33). In ps.-Arcadius at p. 186—probably a 16th-cent. interpolation—*Aristophanes (2) of Byzantium is said to have invented signs for the accents (and other marks); but earlier work in this subject was eclipsed by that of *Aristarchus (2).

Grammatical classification of words begins with *Protagoras, who first distinguished γένη ὀνομάτων as ἀρρένα, θήλεα, and σκεύη. Aristotle has the same terms, but sometimes uses μεταξύ for σκεύη, and notes that many σκεύη are ἀρρένα or θήλεα. By the 1st cent. BC οὐδέτερον (neuter) came into use, and κοινόν (common) was added, and ἐπίκοινον (i.e. of one gender but used of both sexes).

Plato (*Soph.* 261d) makes a practical discrimination between examples of two classes of words, ῥήματα and ὀνόματα, distinguished by their potential functions as predications and designations respectively, in a sentence. Aristotle (*Poet.* 20) names and defines ὄνομα, ῥῆμα, σύνδεσμος, and ἄρθρον; but as to the two last the text is disputed as to both definitions and examples. These four, however, with στοιχεῖον, συλλαβή, πτῶσις, and λόγος (composite statement—possibly without verbs) Aristotle calls parts of speech. He includes under πτώσεις all forms of the noun (which comprises also our pronoun, adjective, and adverb) other than the κλῆσις, our nominative, and all verb-forms except the present indicative (ῥῆμα in the narrowest sense). These flexions, whether nominal or verbal, have no separate names. Subject and predicate are distinguished as ὑποκείμενον and κατηγορημένον.

The stages leading up to Stoic grammar (see STOICISM) are obscure. There is evidence that *Chrysippus discriminated τὰ προσηγορικά, perhaps as a class of noun. *Diogenes (3) of Babylon recognized five parts of speech—Aristotle's with the addition of προσηγορία (common noun). His pupil, *Antipater (2) of Tarsus, added a sixth, named by him μεσότης (as allied to noun and verb), by others πανδέκτης, but excluded from the final Stoic classification, which was the same as that of Diogenes. The terminology of inflexion—as of most phenomena—was greatly developed by the Stoics. In Chrysippus, *On the Five Cases*, the fifth was almost certainly the adverb (cf. Aristotle); for the Stoics did not reckon the vocative a case. The nominative they called ὀρθή or εὐθεῖα; the others (πλάγιαι, oblique) were γενική, indicating a γένος, δοτική, used after verbs of giving, and αἰτιατική, denoting the αἰτιατόν, the result caused. A tense (χρόνος), present (ἐνεστώς) or past (παρῳχημένος), might be ἀτελής (sometimes called παρατατικός), imperfect, or τέλειος (or συντελικός), perfect; a past tense might be described as ἀόριστος, undefined in respect of this distinction. The future tense was named ὁ μέλλων (χρόνος). Predications by finite verbs (κατηγορήματα or συμβάματα, while ῥῆμα is, in contrast, restricted to the infinitive) were classified as active (ἐνεργητικά), passive (παθητικά, including reflexives, ἀντιπεπονθότα), and οὐδέτερα (neuter, e.g. ζῶ); or, on another basis, as complete (our intransitive) and incomplete (our transitive—requiring an object), with other refinements as to παρασυμβάματα (e.g. μέλει μοι).

From their predecessors the *Alexandrians adopted ὄνομα (but not, as an independent part of speech, προσηγορία), ῥῆμα, σύνδεσμος, and ἄρθρον; also the adverb (including our interjections), under a name, ἐπίρρημα, the history of which is obscure. To these they added ἀντωνυμία (personal and possessive pronouns only) and πρόθεσις—a term which Chrysippus used, but in what sense is not clear; the later Stoics had a class of προθετικοὶ σύνδεσμοι. The eighth part was created by separating the μετοχή (participle) from the verb; and some proposed, in vain, to give

the infinitive and possessive adjective a like status. These eight were known to Aristarchus, and were standardized by the textbook of his pupil, *Dionysius (15) Thrax. Thus far Greek grammar was descriptive. With the Atticist movement we find prescriptive grammar coming to the fore. One of the results of this change is the growth of false forms, known only to grammarians and those who followed them.

Systematic syntax made little progress until the 1st cent. AD (see HABRON; THEON (1)): the next century saw, however, the great and original work of *Apollonius (13) Dyscolus.

For the history of kindred studies, see GLOSSA; GLOSSARY, Greek and ETYMOLOGY. It should be noted that γραμματική is much wider in meaning than 'grammar'. Of the six elements in Dionysius Thrax's definition of γραμματική only two belong to 'grammar'; the rest fall under lexicography or literary criticism.

P. B. R. F.; R. B.

grammar, grammarians, Latin (see LINGUISTICS, ANCIENT) The Romans came to study their own language only late, under the impulse of Hellenistic philosophy; the Greek influence was permanent and is clearly indicated by the calques that constitute much of Latin grammatical terminology (e.g. *casus*~πτῶσις, *coniugatio*~συζυγία). It was the doctrine of the Stoics—represented by the τέχνη περὶ φωνῆς, as part of the theory of 'dialectic'—that provided the most important model for Roman handbooks. The surviving examples, which include short 'school grammars' and massive treatises, generally have three main sections: (*a*) introductory definitions of essential concepts (e.g. *vox*, *littera*, *syllaba*); (*b*) an analysis of the parts of speech; and (*c*) a survey of 'flaws' and 'virtues' (*vitia et virtutes orationis*: probably not part of the Stoic legacy). When fully expanded, section (*b*) treated each part of speech according to its attributes: *nomina* (nouns *and* adjectives) according to *qualitas* ('proper' or 'appellative'), *genus* (= gender), *figura* (simple or compound, e.g. *felix* vs. *infelix*), *numerus*, and *casus*; verbs according to *qualitas* (*perfecta*, *inchoativa*, etc.), *genus* (*activum*, *passivum*, *neutrum*, *deponens*), *figura* (again, simple or compound), *persona*, *numerus*, *modus*, *tempus*, and *coniugatio*. Section (*c*) included discussions of 'barbarisms' (errors in the morphology of individual words), 'solecisms' (faults in the co-ordination of two or more words), and other 'flaws' (e.g. pleonasm), as well as 'tropes' (e.g. metaphor), 'metaplasms' (intentional 'reshapings' of words), 'figures of speech' (e.g. anaphora), and 'figures of thought' (e.g. *allegory—though these last were sometimes thought more properly the rhetor's concern). Syntax was for the most part treated obliquely (e.g. in discussion of 'solecism'), though Priscian addressed the subject directly. Late grammars also sometimes included other sections, on (e.g.) orthography, 'idioms' (= differences between Greek and Latin usage), prose rhythm, and metre, but these topics were often the subjects of separate treatises.

Interest in grammatical matters at Rome is first attested in the works of *Lucilius (1) and *Accius (2nd cent. BC). From the end of the 2nd cent. to the middle of the 1st a number of writers on language are known—for example, L. *Aelius, *Antonius Gnipho, *Ateius Philologus, *Nigidius Figulus, and *Santra—but *Varro's linguistic thought, developed in at least ten different works and most fully accessible in the surviving books *De lingua Latina*, is the earliest we can reconstruct in any detail. Drawing a basic distinction between words of invariable and variable form, and (for the latter) between derivational morphology (the realm of *etymology and semantics) and inflexional morphology (the realm of grammar strictly so called), Varro came to identify only four parts of speech: words with case (nouns, pronouns, adjectives), words with tense (verbs), words with both (participles), and words with neither (adverbs, etc.). Though his terminology often differs from that of the later handbooks, Varro does recognize five inflexionally similar sets of nouns (grouped according to the ablative singular) and three distinct sets of verbs: his analysis therefore anticipates, in principle if not in word, all subsequent analysis of Latin inflexional morphology.

No complete grammatical work survives from the 1st cent. AD, but *Quintilian offers a detailed sketch (*Inst.* 1. 4–8) and portions of the influential *ars* of *Remmius Palaemon (mid-1st cent.) are quoted by later authors. These fragments show that with Palaemon (if not earlier) the eight parts of speech were distinguished in the form familiar today, the ending of the genitive singular was the basis for classification into declensions, and the four conjugations were distinguished by the final syllable of the second person singular present indicative active. The practice of illustrating and validating doctrine by quoting from authoritative authors (Cicero, Terence, Virgil, Horace) was also firmly established.

From the 2nd cent. AD there survive tracts on orthography by *Velius Longus and *Terentius Scaurus and—quite possibly—an abbreviated version of Scaurus' *ars*: if this is indeed a 2nd-cent. work, it is the earliest Latin grammatical handbook to survive in anything like its original form; otherwise that distinction must go to the *ars* of *Sacerdos, written (probably) in the late 3rd cent. In the 4th to the 6th cents. the grammatical tradition continued along the lines laid down by scholars of the early empire: refinements in doctrine were offered here and there, but the main conceptual categories remained intact. Specially noteworthy texts from late antiquity include *Dositheus (2)'s bilingual *ars*, designed to teach Latin to speakers of Greek; the two versions of Aelius *Donatus (1)'s *ars* (*minor* and *maior*), which together gave Europe its most influential linguistic guide down to the 12th cent.; the dense compilations of *Charisius and *Diomedes (3), who gathered substantial excerpts from earlier treatises and arranged them in 'mosaics' of grammatical lore; and the eighteen-book *Institutio* of *Priscian, the most impressive work of linguistic analysis to survive intact from Latin antiquity.

Beyond the articles for the individuals named above, see also ALBINUS (2); ASMONIUS; AURELIUS OPILLUS; CLEDONIUS; COMINIANUS; CONSENTIUS; FLAVIUS CAPER; IULIUS ROMANUS; MARIUS VICTORINUS; PHOCAS; POMPEIUS; RUFINUS (3); SERVIUS.

The extant treatises of the 3rd–6th cents. are collected in Keil, *Gramm. Lat.*; the standard edn. of Charisius is now that of K. Barwick (1922); of Dositheus, J. Tolkiehn (1913); of Donatus, L. Holtz (1981); the *ars* of Scaurus(?) is discussed by V. Law, *Rh. Mus.* 1987, 67–89; some early Latin fragments are included in A. Wouters, *The Grammatical Papyri from Graeco-Roman Egypt* (1979). Funaioli, *Gramm. Rom. Frag.* and A. Mazzarino, *Grammaticae Romanae Fragmenta Aetatis Caesareae* (1955), give the remains of republican and early imperial grammarians. See also K. Barwick, *Remmius Palaemon und die römische Ars Grammatica* (1922); L. Holtz, *Donat et la tradition de l'enseignement grammatical* (1981); E. Hovdhaugen, *Foundations of Western Linguistics* (1982); E. Rawson, *Intellectual Life in the Late Roman Republic* (1985), ch. 8; D. J. Taylor (ed.), *The History of Linguistics in the Classical Period* (1987); R. A. Kaster, *Guardians of Language* (1988).   R. A. K.

grammateis, secretaries, of various kinds; generally not responsible magistrates, though like them appointed for a year only, by election or by lot. In Athens the principal secretary, responsible for publishing documents which emanated from the council or assembly, was until the 360s a member of the council (*boulē*), elected to serve for one prytany (see PRYTANEIS) only, thereafter a citizen appointed by lot for the whole year. Other secretaries included one, appointed by election, whose duty was to read documents aloud at meetings of the assembly (see ANAGNOSTES). Various boards of officials had secretaries of their own. In the 4th cent. BC there was a secretary to the *thesmothetai, appointed by lot from the tribe (see PHYLAI) which had not supplied any of the nine *archontes, who functioned as a tenth archon in matters such as the organization of the lawcourts where each tribe needed to be represented.

In the *Achaean Confederacy (perhaps only until 255) the principal secretary was an important official; in the *Aetolian Confederacy the principal secretary was joined by a second, the secretary of the council, before the end of the 3rd cent.

Athens: *Ath. pol.* 54. 3–5. P. J. Rhodes, *The Athenian Boule* (1972), 134–41. Achaea and Aetolia: A. Aymard, *Mélanges Iorga* (1933), 71–108 (but the second Aetolian secretary is now attested in 207).

A. W. G.; P. J. R.

grammaticus is the Latin term (from γραμματικός = 'literate/educated', hence 'scholar of literature') denoting the professional teacher of language and literature, especially poetry (Quint. *Inst.* 1. 4. 2); 'grammarian' is a convenient, not an adequate, translation. After their initial appearance at Rome (late 2nd–early 1st cent. BC) Latin *grammatici* came to serve as instructors of upper-class boys at the first stage of formal education, responsible for teaching correct Latinity via the grammatical handbook (*ars grammatica*), for giving line-by-line explication of poetic texts, and (often) for providing preliminary exercises in composition, before their pupils advanced to the rhetor. Commonly slaves and freedmen in the earliest period (Suet. *Gram.* 5–24), *grammatici* later more often belonged to the 'respectable' classes (*honestiores*), like the children they taught. See EDUCATION, ROMAN; LINGUISTICS, ANCIENT.

S. F. Bonner, *Education in Ancient Rome* (1977), chs. 5, 14–17; R. A. Kaster, *Guardians of Language* (1988).   R. A. K.

granaries

Greek In late bronze age Assiros in Macedonia corn was kept in wicker or similar containers, in storerooms within the houses. Otherwise large terracotta storage jars (pithoi) were used, especially in the centralized palace economies. Similar individual storage continued into the Classical period. An unusual terracotta pyxis found in a burial of *c*.850 BC from the Athenian agora excavations has represented on its lid a series of up-ended miniature pithoi, probably a model of the storage-systems employed for grain. Large storerooms would have been required for the corn imported in quantities by Classical Athens, and would have been adjacent to the great harbour of *Piraeus, where the corn market (Alphitopolis Stoa) was built in the time of *Pericles (1). Similarly, storerooms adjacent to the harbour at *Delos may have served in part for the storage of grain, though there is no evidence to determine what goods were kept in them.   R. A. T.

Roman Purpose-built structures (*horrea*) for storing grain and other commodities developed in the late republic for the alimentation of Rome, and later at forts for military provisions. At Rome and *Ostia *horrea* were brick or masonry courtyard-structures surrounded by storerooms (sometimes on dwarf walls for ventilation). Similar structures are known from other port cities. Military granaries were large sheds of timber or stone raised on posts or dwarf walls, the grain being kept in bins. Some small, private granaries imitating *horrea* have been excavated. *Hadrian's masonry granaries in *Lycia (*Patara, Andriace) are the best-preserved in the east.

GREEK R. Garland, *The Piraeus* (1987); J. Camp, *The Athenian Agora* (1986), fig. 16; P. Bruneau, *Guide de Délos*, 3rd edn. (1983), 257.
ROMAN G. Rickman, *Roman Granaries and Store Buildings* (1971).
A. S. E. C.

Granicus, river in NW Asia Minor (now Kocabaş), scene of *Alexander (3) the Great's first victory over the Persians (334 BC). Of the sources *Arrian's version is probably preferable. Alexander began the battle on the right, launching an attack on the Persian cavalry lining the river-bank with the left squadron of Companions (see HETAIROI) and other cavalry between them and the phalanx to their left. The attack was driven back, but when the Persians pursued into the river-bed, Alexander led his remaining Companions obliquely to the left into their disordered ranks. After a short fight, the Persian cavalry fled, leaving their Greek mercenaries, stationed in the plain beyond the river, to be surrounded and annihilated. Assessment of Alexander's tactics depends on whether his first attack was a feint, and whether his second, oblique advance was deliberate or dictated by the terrain.

RE 7/2, 'Granikos' 3; Diod. Sic. 17. 19–21; Arr. *Anab.* 1. 13–16; Plut. *Alex.* 16. A. B. Bosworth, *Conquest and Empire* (1988). J. F. La.

Granius (*RE* 13) **Licinianus,** author of a compendium of Roman history. The arrangement is annalistic (see ANNALS), with digressions; most of the material seems to come ultimately from *Livy, but he knows other authors too, notably *Sallust. The remains, preserved in a now largely illegible London palimpsest, come from books 26(?), 28, 33(?), 35, 36, referring to events of 165–162, 105, and 86–77 BC. Post-Hadrianic in date, the work shows an interest in curiosities, prodigies, anecdotes, and antiquarian explanations of institutions. Servius also quotes his *Cena* ('Dinner') for a detail of ancient drinking practice.

Ed. N. Criniti (1981); comm. by B. Scardigli (1983). N. Criniti, *ANRW* 2. 34. 1 (1993), 119–205. C. B. R. P.

graphē (γραφή) in Athenian law was a type of prosecution, the commonest public action. The name seems to imply that when this procedure was instituted its distinctive feature was that the charge was made in writing, whereas in other actions the charge was made orally. Any Athenian with full citizen-rights who wished (ὁ βουλόμενος) could prosecute; and since prosecution by anyone who wished was introduced by *Solon, it is probable, though not attested, that it was Solon who introduced *graphē*. By the 4th cent. BC charges in other actions also were put in writing, but the name *graphē* continued to be used for an ordinary public action, excluding special types like *apagōgē* or *phasis* (see LAW AND PROCEDURE, ATHENIAN, § 3). Sometimes it was used more loosely to refer to any public action, or to the written charge in any case.

J. H. Lipsius, *Das attische Recht und Rechtsverfahren* (1905–15), 237–62; G. M. Calhoun, *The Growth of Criminal Law in Ancient Greece* (1927).
D. M. M.

graphē paranomōn (γραφὴ παρανόμων) in Athens was a prosecution for the offence of proposing a law or decree which was contrary to an existing law in form or content. As soon as the accuser made a sworn statement (ὑπωμοσία) that he intended to bring a *graphē paranomōn* against the proposer, the proposal, whether already voted on or not, was suspended until the trial had been held. If the jury convicted the proposer, his proposal was annulled and he was punished, usually by a fine; if a man

was convicted three times of this type of offence, he suffered disfranchisement.

It is not known when this type of action was instituted, but the earliest known cases are the prosecution of Speusippus by Leogoras in 415 BC (Andoc. 1. 17) and a case involving *Antiphon (1) and *Demosthenes (1), the general, around the same time (Plut. *Mor.* 833d). At that period *ostracism had recently fallen out of use, and in its place a *graphē paranomōn* became a popular method of attacking prominent politicians; *Aristophon is said to have boasted that he had been acquitted on this type of charge 75 times. The most famous example is the prosecution of Ctesiphon by *Aeschines (1) for his proposal to confer a crown on *Demosthenes (2), the orator; the surviving speeches of Aeschines, *Against Ctesiphon*, and Demosthenes, *On the Crown*, were written for this trial.

In the 4th cent. it was also possible to prosecute by *graphē* for 'making an unsuitable law' (νόμον μὴ ἐπιτήδειον θεῖναι). If more than a year had elapsed since a law was passed, its proposer could no longer be punished, but the law was annulled if the prosecution was successful; this was the situation in the case for which the orator Demosthenes wrote his speech *Against Leptines*.

H. J. Wolff, 'Normenkontrolle' und Gesetzesbegriff in der attischen Demokratie, Sitz. Heidelberg. Akad. (1970); M. H. Hansen, *The Sovereignty of the People's Court in Athens in the Fourth Century B.C. and the Public Action against Unconstitutional Proposals* (1974). D. M. M.

Gratian (Flavius Gratianus (*RE* 3)**),** son of *Valentinian I who made him Augustus when aged 8 (AD 367). Ruling the west from 375 he made his tutor *Ausonius praetorian prefect, and (379) appointed *Theodosius (2) I emperor in the east. Based at Milan (Mediolanum), he was much influenced by St *Ambrose, dropped the title pontifex maximus and had the statue of Victory removed from the Roman senate-house, despite protests from *Symmachus (2). Unable to concentrate on defending Gaul as well as the Upper Danube, he was overthrown by *Magnus Maximus and murdered at Lyons (Lugdunum (1), 383).

J. Matthews, *Western Aristocracies and Imperial Court A.D. 364–425* (1975). R. P. D.

Grattius 'Faliscus' (less correct 'Gratius', Buecheler, *Rh. Mus.* 1880, 407: CIL 6. 19117 ff.: his connection with Falerii (see FALISCANS), based on l. 40, and the epithet 'Faliscus' reported from a lost MS, are not universally accepted), Augustan poet contemporary with Ovid before AD 8 (*Pont.* 4. 16. 34), has one extant work in about 540 hexameters, the *Cynegetica*. In it he treats of the chase and especially the management of *dogs for *hunting. It is difficult to decide whether he owes anything to *Xenophon (1) (or pseudo-Xenophon) and the tradition of hunting literature; for his list of breeds of dogs he may have used an Alexandrian source. The Latin influence most operative upon him is that of *Virgil's *Georgics*; but he also borrowed from the *Aeneid* and *Ovid, much less from *Lucretius. Authorities differ as to his influence on the similar poem by *Nemesianus.

The earlier part of his work, after a proem, deals with equipment for capturing game (nets, snares, spears, and arrows); the remaining part (150–541) deals with huntsmen, dogs, and *horses. Here, the allotment of nearly 300 lines to dogs (their breeding, points, and ailments) justifies his title. Grattius diversifies his theme by the introduction of episodes, a eulogy on the chase, the accounts of two clever huntsmen (Dercylus (95 ff.) and Hagnon (213 ff.)), the homily on the deleterious effects of luxurious fare on human beings (somewhat amusingly juxtaposed with plain feeding for dogs), and two descriptive passages, a Sicilian grotto (430 ff.) and a sacrifice to the huntress Diana (483 ff.). The concluding portion on horses is mutilated. Grattius' diction—which includes numerous technical terms and *hapax legomena*—and versification are Augustan, but he does not always express himself lucidly. How far his inadequacies are to be ascribed to his exiguous MS tradition (Vindob. 277 (8th–9th cent.) is the sole independent witness) is uncertain.

TEXTS M. Haupt, *Ovidii, Gratii et Nemesiani Cynegetica* (1838); E. Baehrens, *PLM* 1 (1879); F. Vollmer, *PLM* 2/1 (1911).

COMMENTARIES P. J. Enk (1918); R. Verdière (1964); C. Formicola (1988), with concordances.

BIBLIOGRAPHY R. Helm, *Lustrum* 1956.; *RE* 7/2 (1912), 1841–6.

A. Schi.

Gravisca See TARQUINII.

Greece (geography) Greece with the Aegean basin is part of the great mountain zone running from the Alps to the Himalayas. For 70 million years the land mass of Africa has been burrowing irresistibly under Europe. This mighty force has displaced, shattered, crumpled, and stretched the rocks, creating mountain ranges, ocean trenches, gorges, and upland basins. The Cretan island arc displays one of Europe's most dramatic changes of level, from the Hellenic trench, 4,335 m. (14,222 ft.) deep, immediately to the south, to peaks up to 2,456 m. (8,058 ft.) high on *Crete itself. Northward lies the Cycladic chain of volcanoes (see CYCLADES), from *Nisyros through Santorini (see THERA) and *Melos to *Methana, the volcano within sight of Athens. Mainland mountains range from Taygetus (2,407 m.: 7,897 ft.) in the south through *Parnassus (2,457 m.: 8,061 ft.) to *Olympus (1) in the north, at 2,917 m. (9,570 ft.) the highest peak in modern Greece. Mountain-building continues, as shown by frequent *earthquakes in ancient and modern Greece.

The geology is very varied. Most of the higher mountains are of hard limestone, but there are also phyllites, gneisses, granites, serpentines, and volcanic rocks. Softer marls, sandstones, and clays, occurring at lower altitudes, were laid down during periods of submergence later in geological history.

Erosion has gone on since the mountains began to form: whole mountain ranges have been carried away and their remains deposited to form new rocks. It was particularly active during the ice ages, 2 million to 12,000 years ago, when there were violent changes of climate (although little development of glaciers). Erosion has created cultivable land in the plains, into which sediments were washed off the hillsides. It continues conspicuously in the Pindus mountains, the northern *Peloponnese, and *Rhodes; elsewhere, as in Crete, most deposits are strongly consolidated and hold together despite very steep slopes. Erosion has been increased by human activity, but by how much is controversial.

Greece is rather poor in minerals. Clay for pottery comes from particular local sources. Sometimes limestone has been turned into a crystalline form under great pressure; hence the marbles of *Paros, *Naxos (1), *Thasos, and of *Pentelicon in Attica. Small deposits of iron ore are frequent, but tin and most of the copper for making bronze had to be imported. The silver-mines of *Laurium were essential to the economy of Athens.

Greece has a sharply seasonal Mediterranean *climate. The winter rainy season (typically October–May) is warm, seldom frosty, and the time of activity and growth. The dry season of summer is hot, rainless, relentlessly sunny, and is the dead season. The mountains intercept rain-bearing depressions, producing a disparity between the wet west of Greece (e.g. Ioannina, 1,195

mm. (47 in.) of rain in an average year) and the dry east (Athens, 384 mm.: 15 in.). The west coast of Asia Minor is again well watered in winter (Smyrna, 719 mm.: 28 in.). Summer temperatures sometimes reach 40°C (104°F), especially inland, but are tolerable because of north winds and dry air. Mountain areas, as in Pindus and *Arcadia, are difficult to live in all the year, because there are cold winters as well as dry summers: the growing season is very short, and frost-sensitive crops, especially olives, cannot be grown.

The prehistoric climate, as inferred from pollen cores, had been less arid than today's. How far climate differed in classical times is uncertain. Known fluctuations such as the Little Ice Age (AD 1550–1750) forbid us to assume it as constant. Ancient accounts suggest that it may have been slightly less strongly seasonal than today, with rivers more dependable and snow less rare. The deadly heat of the *kávsoma* (heatwave) in the modern Athenian summer is aggravated by the urban microclimate and air pollution.

Traditional Greek *agriculture, now much in decline, was based on cereals, olives, vines, and herding animals. (New World crops—potato, tomato, tobacco, maize—were unknown in antiquity.) It involved seasonal hard work, ploughing, sowing, picking olives, and tending vines; an unhurried harvest; and long periods of relative leisure.

Inland transport is relatively easy for a mountainous country; it was seldom difficult to make *roads between the fertile basins. Seafaring called for great skill: the coasts are wild and terrible with cliff-bound promontories, razor-edged reefs, and surf-pounded beaches. There were few good harbours, and no tide to help in getting in or out. Sailors feared the sea in winter, and land travel was then difficult because of flooded fords. See LANDSCAPES (ANCIENT GREEK).

P–K, *GL*; O. Rackham and J. A. Moody, *The Making of the Cretan Landscape* (1994). O. R.

Greece (prehistory and history)

Stone Age The stone age is divided into the palaeolithic (to *c.*9000 BC), mesolithic (*c.*9000–7000 BC) and neolithic (7th–4th millennia BC); *metallurgy began during the neolithic, before the conventional neolithic–bronze age transition.

Classical Greece was an essentially agricultural society and as such can trace its origins back to the first farming communities in Greece in the early neolithic (7th millennium BC). Some at least of the domestic livestock and crop species were introduced from the near east, but Greece had long been occupied by palaeolithic and mesolithic gatherer-hunters (e.g. at Franchthi cave, Argolid). It is unclear whether the first farmers were of indigenous, immigrant or mixed stock. Known early farming settlements (e.g. Argissa) are heavily concentrated in the fertile lowlands of the eastern mainland, particularly in *Thessaly. The southern mainland and smaller Aegean islands, the heartland of both bronze age palatial civilization and the Classical *polis*, were not widely colonized by farmers until the later neolithic and early bronze age (5th–3rd millennia BC). The earliest farmers laid the biological foundations of Classical agriculture, growing a range of *cereal and pulse crops and keeping sheep, goats, cattle and pigs. The vine was a significant resource (possibly cultivated) by *c.*5000 BC, but systematic use of the *olive and the introduction of the horse and donkey are not attested until the bronze age. There is no evidence for the plough in neolithic Greece, and early farming may have resembled the intensive 'horticulture' and small-scale stock-rearing still practised in some hill-villages, rather than the extensive agriculture and specialized *pastoralism which dominate the present landscape and, to some extent, the ancient sources. Neolithic subsistence was probably based on grain crops, with livestock most important as an alternative food source after crop failure. Farmers introduced fallow deer to many islands, making hunting a viable option, but the principal mechanisms for coping with the risk of crop failure in the arid southeast of Greece were social. Field surveys indicate that early farmers lived in small village communities. Excavations at sites such as Sesklo and Nea Nikomedeia have shown that the basic residential and economic unit was a family household, but houses were crowded close together and cooking facilities were located outdoors, ensuring social pressure to share cooked food. In the colonization of agriculturally marginal regions, sharing with close neighbours will have been less effective as a defence against local crop failure. Here a dispersed pattern of 'hamlet' settlements developed, with greater emphasis on distant social ties. Distant social contacts are more difficult to cultivate than close neighbours but are potentially more effective as a source of hospitality in the event of local crop failure. Early neolithic communities were probably egalitarian in the sense that there was no inequality independent of age, gender, and ability. Villages rarely grew to a size demanding institutionalized authority to maintain order. In some late neolithic (6th-millennium BC) villages (e.g. Dimini), however, a central house was segregated within a large courtyard and probably housed some sort of community leader. From the final neolithic (5th millennium BC) onwards, settlements frequently exceeded the organizational limits of egalitarian society. The economic isolation of the family household was now reinforced by moving cooking facilities into an internal 'kitchen' (as at Sitagroi) or walled yard (as at Pevkakia), suggesting that sharing between neighbours had given way to centrally controlled redistribution. By the end of the neolithic, with consolidation of the domestic mode of production and the attendant struggle between household self-sufficiency and indebted dependence on a wider community, the most basic elements of Classical rural society may already have been in place.

D. R. Theochares, *Neolithic Greece* (1973). P. H.

Bronze age Viewed at its broadest, the history of bronze age Greece seems a cyclical alternation between periods of expansion, fuelled by increasingly intensive exploitation of the land and involvement in overseas exchange, and contraction to a more nearly self-sufficient 'village' level. While warfare and population movement may have been additional contributory factors in periods of decline, they are unlikely to have played a very significant role; in particular, there is no good evidence that a 'coming of the Greeks' (at whatever date this is placed) had a very marked impact. Rather, the most significant development was the establishment of the *Minoan civilization of Crete, which evidently did not use the Greek language, but had an essential formative influence on the *Mycenaean civilization, which evidently did, at least in its core region, the southern mainland. The effective domination of the Aegean by Mycenaean civilization from the 14th cent. BC onwards marks a step towards the creation of 'Greece'; but the development of many characteristic features of later Greek civilization was a very complex process, much of which took place after the bronze age (cf., for the most typical form of religious *sacrifice, N. Marinatos and B. Bergquist, in R. Hägg, N. Marinatos, and G. Nordquist, *Early Greek Cult Practice* (1988)).

Obviously this is very different from the picture of early Greece that *Thucydides (2) built up (1. 1–20) from analysis of his only available source, the legendary traditions; these gave no suggestion of the length of that past, the long-term stability of the agricultural economy, the importance of exchange, the high level of social organization in the palace societies, or the very existence of 'pre-Greek' civilizations. This is hardly surprising, for to judge from other cultures the primary purpose of such traditions is not the transmission of factual information but the validation of claims to territory and status (see ORALITY), and they can only too readily be tampered with, as in the historical period in Greece. The most vivid elements in the traditional material, the Homeric epics, belong to a genre that cannot be expected to offer a wholly realistic picture of life; but where their setting is realistic, it is becoming increasingly apparent that, while incorporating late bronze age details, it has much more to do with the Dark Age.

E. Vermeule, *Greece in the Bronze Age*, 2nd edn. (1972); C. Renfrew, *The Emergence of Civilisation* (1972); P. M. Warren, *The Aegean Civilisations*, 2nd edn. (1989); R. Treuil, P. Darcque, J.-C. Poursat, and G. Touchais, *Les Civilisations Égéennes* (1989); O. Dickinson, *The Aegean Bronze Age* (1994). On the Homeric tradition see most recently O. Dickinson, *G & R* 1986, 20 ff., E. S. Sherratt, *Antiquity* 1990, 807 ff., and J. Whitley, *BSA* 1991, 341 ff.; E. J. Forsdyke, *Greece Before Homer* (1956) is a usefully critical analysis of other 'traditional' material. O. T. P. K. D.

Archaic, Classical, Hellenistic
'Dark Ages'
(*c*.1100–776 BC). The period after the Mycenaean collapse and before the 8th-cent. BC renaissance is traditionally regarded and described as the Dark Age of Greece. For several centuries after the disappearance of Linear B, writing ceases to be a category of evidence, and the only other source of information, archaeology, shows that contact even between closely neighbouring communities sank (e.g. in Attica) to low levels. But this picture has been modified by brilliant 10th-cent. finds at *Lefkandi on *Euboea, attesting eastern connections and memories of a Mycenaean past. The Dark Age of Greece should not, in fact, be seen entirely negatively, but as an exploratory period in which Greece itself was gradually resettled by pioneers (the prime instance is Attica, see ATHENS, history), and in which Greeks settled areas like Ionia (see IONIANS) for the first time. But the word colonization, which implies a central organizing authority, is not yet appropriate for this sort of tentative internal expansion and haphazard overseas movement. And the absence of writing had its positive side, the creation in an originally oral mode of the great epics of *Homer, the *Iliad* and *Odyssey*.

Archaic age
(776–479 BC). The conventional date for the beginning of the historical period of Greece is 776 BC, the date of the first *Olympian Games on the reckoning of *Hippias (2) of Elis. This is probably not too far out for the event in question; but the early 8th cent. was a turning of the page in several other ways as well. Iron began to be worked with new sophistication; the alphabet was taken over from the east; and colonies began to be sent out in a more organized way (see COLONIZATION, GREEK), above all from *Euboea, which between 750 and 730 colonized *Cumae and *Pithecusae in the west and was involved in *Al Mina in the east. The 8th cent. was also the age of *polis* formation and political *synoecism, perhaps themselves a result, in part, of the colonizing movement, but also of the rise of religious leagues or *amphictionies. (Religious factors have certainly been urged in recent years by students of the emergent *polis*: it has been remarked

that *polis* formation was marked by the placing of *sanctuaries, often and for no obvious reason dedicated to *Hera, at the edge of *polis* territory.) Some of all this, not just writing, but perhaps even the idea of the self-determining *polis* community, may actually be Phoenician not Greek in inspiration, and there was a famous and perhaps influential early first-millennium amphictiony of Israel. But whatever the truth about Semitic primacy, early Greek society soon acquired distinctive features and institutions, most of which continued to be important in Classical times and later. Among these were athletics and religiously based athletic events like the Olympian Games, already mentioned; the *gymnasium which provided training for both athletics and its elder brother, warfare; the *symposium, at which aristocratic values were inculcated; and *homosexuality, which was related to all the other phenomena just mentioned. Some other characteristic features of Greek society are more easily paralleled elsewhere, e.g. ritualized *friendship; but institutionalized *proxeny, which developed out of this, was specifically Greek.

All this contributed to such shared Greek consciousness as there was (see ETHNICITY; NATIONALISM), but the chief way in which early Greek states interacted was through warfare, a paradoxical activity in that in Greece at most periods it was a ritualized, i.e. shared, activity (see WAR, RULES OF) but at the same time war is, obviously, an assertion of separateness. Equally the four great Panhellenic ('all-Greek', see PANHELLENISM) sanctuaries, *Olympia, *Delphi, *Isthmia, *Nemea (1), were a symbol of what Greeks had in common, but they were also a focus for interstate competition exercised in various ways (see DELPHI), and constituting an alternative to war; indeed struggles for influence at sanctuaries sometimes developed into wars proper, see SACRED WARS. And sanctuaries were the repositories of tithes or tenth-fractions of the *booty which was a reason for and result of warfare; this booty was often turned into dedications, producing a connection between great art and great suffering which was noticed by Jacob Burckhardt.

The first war which can be called in any sense general was the Lelantine War fought by *Chalcis and *Eretria for control of the plain between them; but each side had allies from further away and links with rival colonial networks have been suspected. But exaggeration on the part of ancient, and anachronism on the part of modern, writers make the truth about this early conflict hard to establish. If there were networks at this time they are less likely to have been firm interstate groupings for purposes of trade or politics than informal systems of aristocratic friendships between entrepreneurial individuals like *Sostratus (1) of Aegina, whose prosperous commercial activities in Italy were interestingly illuminated by archaeology and epigraphy in the 1970s (see AEGINA).

Commercial and economic prosperity on the one hand, and individual dynamism on the other, combined on *Thucydides' view to produce *tyranny. There is much to be said for this: colonization and trade were connected, and the combination meant that Greece was exposed to luxuries on a new scale. But the chief modern explanation for tyranny is military, in terms of *hoplite warfare, a partial repudiation of individual aristocratic fighting methods, corresponding to that political repudiation of control by hereditary aristocracies which was the essence of tyranny. A main attraction of this theory is coincidence of time: the first tyrannies, of *Pheidon at Argos and *Cypselus at Corinth, are best put at mid-7th cent., when hoplites appear.

Two states which did not have tyrannies in this first phase are *Sparta and *Athens, indeed Sparta famously avoided tyranny

until Hellenistic times (see NABIS). Sparta was remarkable in other ways also, for instance by not sending out many colonies in the historical period (with the important exception of *Tarentum, Greek Taras, in south Italy) but above all in having annexed its next-door neighbour *Messenia in the later 8th cent. The inhabitants were turned into state slaves or *helots. Other neighbours of Sparta became *perioikoi, a subordinate status to which some communities of *Laconia also belonged. Sparta later became a tight and repressive place, but Archaic Sparta guaranteed political power to the *damos* or people—meaning perhaps only the class of hoplite fighters—at an impressively early date (?7th cent.) when *democracy elsewhere was still in the future. But the political momentum at Sparta was lost, partly through the need to hold down Messenia and the helots; this in turn called for the strict *agōgē. Simple infantry strength enabled Sparta to coerce much of the *Peloponnese by the later 6th cent., though propaganda also helped, the deliberate muting of Sparta's unpopular *Dorian aspect.

Athens was also unusual among Greek states, above all in the size of its directly controlled territory, *Attica, its natural assets (including a supply of silver) and its physical suitability for a naval role (see ATHENS, history). Athens, like Sparta, avoided tyranny in the 7th cent., but unlike Sparta, Athens did experience an attempt at one at this time, the failed coup of *Cylon *c*.630. But a generation later *Solon's reforms (594) both resembled and circumvented—for the moment—tyrannical, anti-aristocratic solutions carried out elsewhere. His creation of a new *boulē* of 400 members was an important move towards democracy, as was the opening of high political office on criteria of wealth not birth; but even more crucial was abolition of the demeaning if not always economically crippling status of hectemorage (see HEKTĒMOROI). Indirect but important consequences of this abolition were the development of a self-conscious citizen élite (see CITIZENSHIP, GREEK) and the related rise of chattel-*slavery. Solon also permitted appeal to the *dikastērion* (see DEMOCRACY, ATHENIAN; LAW AND PROCEDURE, ATHENIAN), and legislated in the social sphere; but some of the detailed traditions about his economic reforms are suspect because they imply the existence of *coinage, which in fact begins in the middle of the 6th cent., too late to be relevant to developments at the beginning of it (though accumulation of gold and silver may well be relevant, cf. above on the effects of colonization).

Solon's reforms were critical for the longer-term development of Athens and indeed Greece, but in the short term they were a failure because Athens did after all succumb, for much of the second half of the 6th cent., to a tyranny, that of *Pisistratus and his sons *Hippias (1) and *Hipparchus (1). Under these rulers, Athenian naval power was built up, a vigorous foreign policy pursued, splendid buildings erected, and roads built. But the tyrants were driven out in 510 and *Cleisthenes (2) reformed the Athenian constitution in a democratic direction in 508/7.

Meanwhile Achaemenid *Persia had been expanding since *Cyrus (1) overthrew *Croesus in 546, and the new power had begun to encroach on the freedom of the East Greeks in Ionia (see IONIANS) and even islands like *Samos. The Athenians, like other mainland Greeks, were insulated from immediate danger by their distance from geographical Ionia, but they were in the racial and religious senses Ionians too, and when in 499 the *Ionian Revolt broke out, itself perhaps the result of restlessness induced by awareness of Cleisthenes' democratic reforms, Athens sent help to the rebels, who, however, were defeated at Lade (494).

How far this help provoked the *Persian Wars, by drawing *Darius I's vengeful attention to Athens, and how far they were simply an inevitable consequence of Persian dynamism, is not clear from the account of our main source *Herodotus (1). A first expedition led by *Datis and *Artaphernes failed at the battle of *Marathon, in Attica (490); then at the battles of *Thermopylae, *Artemisium, *Salamis (all 480), and *Plataea (479) a far larger Persian invasion by *Xerxes was beaten back. The Greek successes of the Persian Wars were of enormous importance in conditioning Greek attitudes to themselves, to each other (see MEDISM; THEBES (1)), and to the '*barbarian' (as Persians were now more aggressively defined), for centuries to come: see PERSIAN-WARS TRADITION. The victories were immediately commemorated by state dedications in the great sanctuaries (see DELPHI; OLYMPIA), except that Nemea got no big dedication. Poetry by *Aeschylus and *Simonides, and the prose of Herodotus, signalled the Great Event in literature, as did buildings on the Athenian acropolis; only *Thucydides (2) and his speakers show some impatience with the theme (see EPITAPHIOS).

The pentekontaetia

(c.50-year period 480–430 BC). In the west (Italy and Sicily), the Greek states shared the culture of their *mētropoleis in Greece itself (see esp. OLYMPIA), but there were differences. Here Greeks (like North African *Cyrene with its Berber neighbours) always had to live alongside non-Greeks, both relatively small-scale but vigorous indigenous groups like Messapians (see MESSAPII) in the hinterland of Taras (*Tarentum), and great powers like *Etruscans in central Italy, or *Carthage whose base was in North Africa but which had outposts in Sicily. Herodotus reports a huge massacre of Tarentines by Messapians c.475 and this threat conditioned much of Tarentine history for centuries. And at Himera and Cumae the western Greeks under their tyrants *Gelon and *Hieron (1) defeated Carthage and the Etruscans in battles which contemporaries compared to the high points of the Persian Wars. But inter-Greek tensions were no less acute: *Croton and Locri (Epizephyrii) fought a great Archaic battle at the Sagra river, and when *Thurii in the mid-5th cent. replaced Archaic *Sybaris, destroyed in 508, it soon found itself at war with neighbouring Taras. But more peaceful developments were possible, as at *Elea, where a medical school connected with the cult of *Apollo 'Ouliades' flourished from the 5th cent. BC to Roman times; *Parmenides was involved with it. Athenian and Peloponnesian interest in the west was always lively, partly for grain and partly for shipbuilding *timber from south Italy; but partly also because ties of kinship (συγγένεια) between colonies and mētropoleis were taken seriously.

The great struggle of the 5th cent. was between Athenians and the Peloponnesians led by Sparta. The germs of this are detectable even in the Persian Wars, and when the Athenians took over the leadership of Greece in 487 (see DELIAN LEAGUE), Sparta's response was mixed. But Sparta, despite having crushed for the moment the perennially ambitious rival *Argos (2) in 494, had internal problems in the Peloponnese and, for several years from the mid-460s, difficulties with the helots to cope with. So stretched were the Spartans that they invited the Athenians in to help them against the helots, but the Athenian democracy moved on a step in just this period (see EPHIALTES (4)) and the Athenians under *Cimon were dismissed from Sparta. Sparta's troubles meant that the Athenian empire was able to expand without check from the Greek side until the end of the 460s and the outbreak of the First *Peloponnesian War (460–446), when Sparta did, as often in its history, take some action to protect or further

its interests (including religious) in central Greece. So far from curbing Athenian expansion, that war saw Athenian influence rise to its maximum extent: for over ten years after the battle of Tanagra Athens even controlled *Boeotia (457–446). It may be that the take-over was possible because Athens capitalized on *stasis inside the cities of Boeotia. (Throughout Classical Greek history there was a risk that stasis would open the door to outside interference. But Thucydides may be right to link it particularly with the period introduced by the main Peloponnesian War: in the pentekontaetia a degree of stability was guaranteed by the existence of two power blocs: contrast the post-431 period and the 4th cent.) Democratic Athens did not however insist on democracy in Boeotia, allegedly permitting oligarchies instead; nor is it certain that the *Boeotian Confederacy ceased to exist in the Athenian period, although Athens' departure in 446 may have led to a federal reorganization.

Despite preoccupations in Greece, Athens in this period continued the struggle against Persia which was the ostensible purpose of the Delian League; but after the Eurymedon victory of 466 a preliminary peace may have been made, see CALLIAS, PEACE OF. A great Athenian expedition against Persia in Egypt in the 450s failed utterly, and in 450 the main Callias peace was made, though this is controversial. Thereafter, until 413, Athens and Persia were in a state of uneasy peace.

The Peloponnesian War

The First Peloponnesian War ended with the *Thirty Years Peace of 446, and this instrument regulated Athenian–Spartan relations until the great *Peloponnesian War of 431–404. The *Archidamian War, ended by the Peace of *Nicias (1), failed to achieve the Peloponnesian objective of 'liberating' Greece, i.e. breaking up the Athenian empire. *Propaganda, such as the exploiting of sanctuaries like Delphi and Ionian *Delos, was as much a weapon as open fighting. Athenian exuberance climbed to its highest level in 415, when the Sicilian expedition was launched, to end in catastrophe two years later. Persia re-entered the picture in 413, an important moment because it introduced a long phase of Greek history, ending only with *Alexander (3) the Great, in which Persia's voice would often be decisive. As Athens and Sparta wore each other down, other emergent powers like *Macedonia, itself destined to overthrow Persia eventually, grew in resources and self-confidence, especially under the strong rule of *Archelaus (2); and *Thebes (1), another 4th-cent. giant, profited from the war, notably by annexing *Plataea in 427. Small states tried to protect their territorial integrity by aligning with the strongest and closest power of the moment.

The Fourth Century

The end of the war in 404 coincided with another equally momentous event, the establishment in power of *Dionysius (1) I in Sicily, the prototype for many a 4th-cent. and Hellenistic strong man: tyranny, in fact, revives. Even in conservative Sparta there are traces of personality cult, detectable in *Lysander's victory monument at Delphi for the final victory at *Aegospotami. And he got cult at *Samos. See RULER-CULT (1), GREEK.

Lysander's methods were harsh, and Spartan aggression in this period led, startlingly soon after the end of the Peloponnesian War, to the outbreak of the anti-Spartan *Corinthian War, ended by the *King's Peace. This curtailed Sparta's activities in Asia Minor (of which the most famous episode was the Anabasis or Persian expedition of *Xenophon (1) and the Ten Thousand, in its initial phase a covertly Spartan operation to replace Artaxerxes II by his brother *Cyrus (2)). But the price of eliminating Sparta was surrender of the region to Persia, and a general Greek political retreat east of the Aegean. However over the next 50 years cultural *Hellenism advanced, alongside Persian and indigenous culture, through activity by e.g. *Mausolus.

Much strengthened in Greece by the King's Peace, Sparta proceeded to fresh aggressions in north and central Greece, always a tendency when domestic or other preoccupations permitted. Sparta's coercion of *Olynthus aroused no general protest but the occupation of the Cadmea (acropolis) of Thebes in 382 shocked and alarmed Greek opinion, and in 379 Thebes was liberated with Athenian help. Thebes and other places now joined a *Second Athenian Confederacy (378). But as Thebes' power itself grew, especially after it defeated Sparta at *Leuctra (371), Athens and Sparta found themselves driven together in the 360s when Thebes tried to usurp Athens' position at sea and (with more success) to weaken Sparta in the Peloponnese by founding Arcadian *Megalopolis and reconstituting *Messenia after centuries and equipping it with a new physical centre, the city of *Messene.

*Philip (1) II of Macedon succeeded to a politically weak but economically strong Macedon in 359, which he rapidly strengthened further at the expense of all his neighbours, Greeks included. The story of Athens' diplomatic relations with him is intricate (see DEMOSTHENES (2)); features of the Peace of *Philocrates may indicate that he planned a Persian invasion as early as 346, but he was obliged to defeat the Greeks at the battle of *Chaeronea in 338 before the expedition could start. In the event he was assassinated in 336. Alexander, his son, carried the project through (334–323) in a whirlwind campaign which took him to Egypt, Persia, Afghanistan, India, and the Persian Gulf. For the campaigns see ALEXANDER (3). The city-foundations of Alexander (see ALEXANDRIA (1–7)) are the most important part of his legacy but hard to estimate in detail: archaeological evidence is spectacular (see AI KHANOUM) but patchy, and the literary record is contaminated by rivalries between Seleucids and Ptolemies (see below).

Hellenistic period

(323–31 BC). After Alexander died aged 32 there was never much chance that the unity ($\tau\grave{\alpha}\ \mathring{o}\lambda\alpha$) of his improvised empire would be perpetuated by any one of his Successors—the name given not to an orderly sequence of post-Alexander rulers (they adopted the title 'king' in a rush in 306) but to a whole clutch of his former marshals, controlling different areas but at overlapping times. (See DIADOCHI.) The 'satrapies' were distributed at Babylon in 323 and again at Triparadeisus in 320; another arrangement was reached in 311. The generation after Alexander's death is full of complex military and political history, recorded by *Hieronymus (1) of Cardia, who described the Successors' attempts to acquire as much 'spear-won territory' as possible, while mouthing slogans about the 'freedom of the Greeks' (see FREEDOM IN THE ANCIENT WORLD); the closest any of them got to a dominant position was *Antigonus (1) the One-Eyed (helped by his son *Demetrius (4) the Besieger), but his desire to reconstruct Alexander's empire is not certain and anyway he was killed at *Ipsus in 301. This battle and Corupedion (281), where Seleucus defeated *Lysimachus of Thrace, determined that Asia would be Seleucid, though Lysimachus' defeat also led indirectly to the emergence of an important minor kingdom, that of the Pergamene Attalids. See PERGAMUM.

The first and longest-lasting Successor empire to establish itself was that of the Ptolemies (see PTOLEMY (1)) in Egypt, partly because its physical base was self-contained and hard to strike at. But Ptolemaic foreign policy was not insular or pacific; the dynasty had overseas possessions such as *Cyprus and *Crete,

exercised hegemonical policies in Greece (see CHREMONIDES) and the Aegean, and fought six Syrian wars in the Hellenistic age against the *Seleucids, the most spectacularly successful of all the Successor rulers.

Seleucid methods (see SELEUCUS (1–4); ANTIOCHUS (1–8)) owe much to Achaemenid Persia (cf. e.g. IDRIEUS), but were innovative too; but as with Alexander, the difficulty of assessing Seleucid urbanization is particularly tantalizing (the Ptolemies founded only one Greek city in Egypt, *Ptolemais (2) Hermiou). Recent writers urge that Mesopotamia as opposed to Anatolia or Syria was the engine-room of Seleucid power, and claim that Babylonian and other non-Greek elements in Seleucid culture played a prime role. Evidence from *epigraphy continues to emerge about these topics; Seleucid history is at the time of writing in a state of exciting flux: new finds, work, and insights can be expected, making confident generalization unusually precarious.

Macedon itself was much fought over and partitioned: at different times it was subject not only to Demetrius (4), but to *Cassander, Lysimachus, and *Pyrrhus of Epirus. Not until after 276 did Demetrius' son *Antigonus (2) Gonatas consolidate the kingdom properly. Thereafter under the Antigonid rulers (see ANTIGONUS (3) DOSON; DEMETRIUS (6) II; PHILIP (3) V) Macedon reverted to something like its historical role as it had been before it ballooned under Alexander, though older conceptions of an essentially Macedonian kingdom, supporting its supporters in Greece, have had to be modified in the light of new evidence from *Labraunda in Caria for 3rd-cent. Antigonid activity in the area.

In Greece itself a major development of the age (already adumbrated in the 4th cent.) was the further development of federations or leagues (see FEDERAL STATES), not just the old-established *Boeotian Confederacy, but the *Arcadian (with its centre at Megalopolis), the *Achaean (see also ARATUS (2)), and the *Aetolian, which controlled Delphi for much of the 3rd cent. Sparta's history continues to be distinctive: it stayed out of the Achaean Confederacy until the 190s. Social problems were more acute here than elsewhere, but not different in kind.

Rome made its first decisive eastern intervention in 229, the first Illyrian War; but significant contacts, e.g. with Egypt, antedate this. Philip V's alliance with *Hannibal meant that there would certainly be an eventual Roman reckoning with Macedon, and Philip was defeated in 197 at *Cynoscephalae and his son *Perseus (2) at Pydna in 168, after which Macedon was divided into four republics. Meanwhile the Seleucid *Antiochus III had been defeated at the battle of *Magnesia in 190, though the resulting Peace of Apamea was an amputation not a death: Seleucid power in the east was unaffected, nor should the rise of new splinter kingdoms and states in *Bactria and *Judaea, for example, be straightforwardly taken as indicating terminal Seleucid decline.

The Achaean Confederacy rose against Rome in 146 and was smashingly defeated; Corinth was destroyed.

Detailed bibliography is not here attempted in view of the completion in 1994 of the second (actually entirely new) edn. of the Greek volumes of the *Cambridge Ancient History*, where up-to-date treatments of Greek history to Hellenistic times, and full modern bibliographies, can be found; see vols. $2^2/2$ (1975); $3^2/1$ and 3 (1982); 4^2 (1988); 5^2 (1992); 6^2 (1994); $7^2/1$ (1984); 8^2 (1989).

S. H.

Roman After 146 BC Rome supervised Greece through the governors of Macedonia; a separate province called *Achaia was first created in 46 BC. Parts of Greece supported *Mithradates VI in

88 BC, *Athens with enthusiasm, and suffered accordingly in Sulla's campaigns; the earliest evidence for regular Roman taxation follows. Until Actium Greece remained a theatre for Roman warfare, piratical and civil, imposing heavy demands on her cities, sometimes met with difficulty, as at Gytheum in 71 BC (*Syll.*³ 748 = Sherk, *Augustus* 74). In the early Principate, with Roman *philhellenism conferring few tangible benefits, the mainland Greeks at first remained—with the notable exception of *Sparta—reluctant subjects; there was unrest at Augustan Athens, and the imperial cult in Greece shows a retarded development, with no supra-city collaboration on record before *Nero. Reconciliation was hardly advanced by the colonial foundations of Caesar at *Corinth and Augustus at *Patrae and *Nicopolis (3), the last two accompanied by enforced movements of local populations and cults, or by Rome's proprietary attitude to Greece's heritage, evinced by imperial projects to translate works of art and even a whole cult (*Eleusis) to Rome (Suet. *Calig.* 22; *Claud.* 25). Nero's short-lived restoration of Greece's autonomy in AD 66 (date: T. Barnes, *JRA* 1989, 252–3), in spite of causing local hardship (*IG* 4². 80–1 = Sherk, *Hadrian* 73), won him some Greek approval. Under Trajan the recruitment of Roman senators from Athens and Sparta advanced Greek political integration; writing at the time, *Plutarch (*Praec. ger. reip.*) counselled resigned acceptance of Roman dominion. *Hadrian conferred benefaction throughout the province; his foundation of the *Panhellenion (131/2) promoted an influx of easterners to Greece, among them the travel-writer *Pausanias (3). In the later 2nd and early 3rd cents. Greece flourished as a cultural centre (see AGŌNES; SECOND SOPHISTIC). Levels of prosperity varied regionally; ancient writers stress depopulation in Roman Greece, but the archaeological evidence for an emptied countryside down to 200 (Alcock, see bibliog. below), rather than merely confirming this picture, may point as well to greater nucleation (i.e. rural villages and migration to urban centres); certainly some cities now prospered, as could a small place like *Aedepsus; *tourism was probably a significant source of wealth. The *Heruli (267) damaged Athens, prompting Athenian self-defence (see HERENNIUS DEXIPPUS, P.). In the 4th cent. gradual Christianization wound down traditional cults, although the *Panathenaea were still being celebrated c.410 (*IG* 2². 3818 with *PLRE* 2 'Plutarchus' 2). In 396 *Alaric sacked Corinth, Argos (2), and Sparta, prompting a wave of defensive building throughout the province. Recent archaeology shows a previously unsuspected prosperity in the 5th–6th cents., down to the Slav invasions (from 582); many basilical *churches were built, and the countryside was densely populated.

S. Alcock, *Graecia Capta* (1993); R. Kallet-Marx, *Hegemony to Empire* (1995). A. J. S. S.

Greek language

1. Introduction In the Classical period Greek was spoken in mainland Greece (including the Peloponnese), in the islands of the Aegean (including Crete, Rhodes, and Cyprus), and in the Greek colonies in Asia, Africa, and Italy. It is the European (and Indo-European) language with the longest attested history; the first documents belong to the second half of the second millennium BC and there is no real break between ancient Greek and the modern language of Greece. Most of the evidence from the 8th cent. BC until now is written in the Greek *alphabet, but at an early stage two syllabic scripts were also in use: Linear B in the second half of the second millennium rendered the Greek spoken by the exponents of Mycenaean civilization (see MYCENAEAN LANGUAGE; PRE-ALPHABETIC SCRIPTS (GREECE)) while a distantly related script, syllabic Cyprian, was used for the local dialect of Cyprus from the end of the second millennium to the 3rd cent. BC. The language changed in time: conventionally we distinguish an ancient period which goes from the first attestation of Mycenaean Greek (in Linear B) to the end of Hellenistic Greek (roughly in AD 300), a Byzantine and medieval period (until c.1650), and a modern period. Here we concentrate on the central period of ancient Greek in the 5th and 4th cents. BC. After a general account of its development we give a very brief discussion of the main features of the language.

2. Origins Greek is related to language groups such as Italic, Germanic, Indo-Iranian, Celtic, Slavic, Anatolian, Armenian, Albanian, etc., all of which descend from an unattested parent language (conventionally called Indo-European or IE), which we partially reconstruct through comparison (see LINGUISTICS, HISTORICAL AND COMPARATIVE). It is not possible to establish whether Greek belongs to a specific subgroup of IE; the old theory that it was closely related to Latin or Italic has long since been exploded. It shares a number of features with Armenian and Indo-Iranian, but they are not sufficient to define specific subgroups. The ancient belief that the language was autochthonous cannot be accepted; Indo-European speakers must have reached Greece from elsewhere, though the language may have acquired its main characteristics in Greece itself. Some specific features which distinguish ancient Greek from the Indo-European parent language are listed below.

3. Dialects When we speak of Greek we often mean Attic, i.e. the dialect of Athens. Yet from the Mycenaean period until the late Hellenistic period there was no standard Greek language and all cities or regions had different forms of speech, which they transmitted to their colonies. Even Mycenaean is only one of the varieties of second-millennium Greek. These local 'dialects' had equal or similar status and presumably most of them were mutually intelligible. Until the late 4th cent. BC (and often much later) they were used in normal oral intercourse and for written documents, laws, letters, etc. The contemporary inscriptions provide the best evidence for the differences, which encompass phonology, morphology, syntax, and lexicon (e.g. Lesbian παίσας 'of all' (fem.), Attic πάσης; Lesbian ἔμμεναι 'to be', Attic εἶναι; Thessalian αἰ μά κε κις, Arcadian εἴ δ' ἂν τις, Ionic-Attic ἐὰν δέ τις 'but if anyone' with a different order of the indefinite pronoun and the potential particle κε / ἄν from e.g. Phocian αἰ δέ τις κα; West Greek λέ(ι)ω 'I want', Attic θέλω). On the basis of shared features modern scholars classify the various forms of Greek (partly on the model of the ancient grammarians, see GRAMMAR, GREEK) into groups: Ionic-Attic, Arcado-Cyprian, Aeolic (which includes Lesbian, Boeotian, and Thessalian), Doric (which includes dialects like Laconian, Argolic, etc.), and North-West Greek (see DIALECTS, GREEK (PREHISTORY)).

In spite of the absence of a standard language, from the 5th cent. BC at the latest—but probably much earlier—the Greeks thought of themselves as speaking a common language; for Herodotus (8. 144) τὸ Ἑλληνικόν ('Hellenism') was based on shared blood, language, customs, and religion. See HELLENISM AND HELLENIZATION. Greek was not identified with any of the dialects, but by the early 3rd cent. the Athenians were reproached for behaving as if Greek and Attic were the same thing (*Posidippus (1), fr. 30 KA). In the same period we begin to find that in the local inscriptions the dialect is sometimes replaced by a form of language which is very close to Attic though not identical with it; it is the beginning of the so-called Ionic-Attic κοινὴ διάλεκτος (common language), which eventually prevailed and provided Greece with a standard language from which the later dialects developed. By the end of the 2nd cent. BC most local inscriptions were no longer in dialect; in contrast with the many dialects of the earlier colonies, the language brought to Asia and Africa by *Alexander (3) the Great and his Successors was a form of *koinē*. For a brief period other forms of common language, such as the so-called Doric *koina* of Peloponnese, prevailed in certain areas of mainland Greece, but in the end they were all replaced by the *koinē* (in the inscriptions at least).

4. Literary Greek Literary texts too were composed in different dialects but the dialect was mostly determined by the literary genre and its origin rather than by the author's origin. *Hesiod, who spoke Boeotian (an Aeolic dialect), composed hexameters in the same mixed dialect (based on Ionic) as Homer, while *Pindar, also a Boeotian, wrote choral poetry in a very different mixed dialect which included some Doric features. The iambic trimeters of Attic tragedy are written in a very literary Attic heavily influenced by Homer and by Ionic, but the choruses are written in Doric or rather in a literary form of Attic with superimposed Doric features (μάτηρ for Attic μήτηρ 'mother', etc.). Notice that for the literary dialects we tend to speak, as the grammarians did, of Aeolic, Ionic, and Doric rather than of Thessalian, Euboean, Cretan, and the like (Attic and Lesbian are exceptions), since the dialect used does not normally show features specific to a town or locality: it is more a generic colouring.

The history of literary Greek starts with *Homer, i.e. with a poetic language which, because of the various stages of its formulaic development, is remote from the language of normal conversation and under an Ionic patina includes both late and early features as well as features of different dialects: Mycenaean, Aeolic, Ionic. Because of its cultural importance and its wide diffusion epic poetry provided a common linguistic ground for a linguistically divided culture; in spite of its Ionic colouring the epic language is used for *Tyrtaeus' elegiac poetry which exhorted the Doric Spartans to war and for the verses of the oracle at Delphi, a North-West Greek city. The risk was that the prestige and all-pervading influence of the epic language might have led to the fossilization of all literary language. Yet the dialects—and the way in which they were tied to different literary genres—provided a source for linguistic renewal. Elegiac poetry was composed in epic language but some forms of it were in a more or less purified form of Ionic. We have melic poetry in Lesbian (*Sappho and *Alcaeus (1)), Ionic (*Anacreon) and even Boeotian (*Corinna, though we are uncertain about the date); in these texts we observe not only the phonology and morphology of the various dialects but presumably also some new lexicon and the characteristics of a simpler style. Iambic and trochaic verses favoured Ionic and we find in *Hipponax' poetry, for instance, a rich vocabulary full of colloquialisms and of foreign words; *Archilochus too comes much closer to the language of conversation than Homer. Comedy, which can be in Attic but also in Doric, allows colloquialisms not tolerated in tragedy. Yet the multiplicity of literary dialects also leads to new forms of artificiality. The language of choral poetry is a mixed language which is characterized by a 'Doric' (i.e. non-Attic-Ionic) patina, but in fact exploits elements of all forms of poetry. The result of so much mixture may be magnificent as in Pindar but may also

sound baroque: *Aristophanes (1)'s parody of Pindar (*Av.* 941 ff.) makes this clear. Literary prose can, though need not, be closer to conversational language. Its first forms came from Ionia; even a Doric doctor like *Hippocrates (2) wrote of medicine in Ionic. Attic literary prose, which started in the 5th cent., shows clear signs of Ionic influence but eventually acquires linguistic forms and a style of its own. We have limited evidence for Doric prose.

In Hellenistic times the use of the literary dialects becomes more artificial; *Theocritus wrote his *Idylls* in epic language, in Doric, and in Aeolic (i.e. Lesbian), a *tour de force* which reflects the learned style of Alexandrian poetry. At a later stage we find deliberate attempts to spurn the *koinē* and to prefer an accurate imitation of Attic. At the same time a prose text like the New Testament shows both Semitic influences and a higher level of colloquial simplicity.

5. Development The presence of dialects effectively prevents us from treating the development of Ancient Greek as a continuous process from Homer (or Mycenaean) to the *koinē*. Yet some changes seem to be widely attested in the Greek-speaking area either because of similar structural forces or because of mutual influences between dialects. In the official or literary language the complexity of sentences increases and the simpler patterns are reserved for the colloquial style or specific rhetorical effects. The article, which is absent from Mycenaean and still vestigial in Homer, is generalized in all dialects and is used to nominalize adjectives, participles, infinitives, and whole sentences. A new abstract and technical vocabulary is created through the use of suffixation (-ικος, -ισμος, -μα, etc.) or of composition. Greek is the one European language in which we can follow the independent creation of an abstract or technical vocabulary; the other languages, Latin included, directly or indirectly exploited Greek as a model or as a source of loan words.

6. Linguistic Features We list here some of the main features of ancient Greek, with special reference to classical Attic.

Phonology

The phonological system of Classical Attic is relatively well known (see PRONUNCIATION, GREEK). In the Classical period the vocalic system had five short vowels ([a, e, o, i, y]) written α, ε, ο, ι, υ and seven long vowels ([a:, ε:, e:, ɔ:, o:, i:, y:]), written α, η, ει, ω, ου, ι, υ (the letters in square brackets [ ] are phonetic symbols, with the colon indicating length). Four diphthongs were relatively frequent: [ai, au, eu, oi], written αι, οι, αυ, ευ. The so-called long diphthongs ([a:i, ε:i, ɔ:i], i.e. αι (or ᾳ), ηι (or ῃ), ωι (or ῳ), were rarer and tended either to merge with the short diphthongs or to lose the second element.

The consonantal system included the dental fricative [s], the glottal fricative [h] (the rough breathing) which had a very limited distribution, and four sonorants: the two liquids [l, r] and the two nasals [n, m]. The nine stops were organized according to three modes of articulation (voiceless, voiceless aspirate, and voiced) and three places of articulation: labial ([p, pʰ, b]), dental ([t, tʰ, d]), velar ([k, kʰ, g]). Unlike the modern language Ancient Greek had geminate consonants such as [pp, ll, mm] etc.

Some dialects have five long vowels (a:, e:, o:, u:, i:), instead of seven, and in most dialects we find a [u, u:] pronunciation of υ. The distribution of vowels also differs. Attic and Ionic changed the inherited [a:], which is preserved in all other dialects, into [ε:], written η, though in Attic this change was never completed and after [e], [i], [r] the sound reverted to [a:]. Hence Doric and Aeolic μάτηρ vs. Attic-Ionic μήτηρ and Attic χώρᾱ vs. Ionic χώρη. The tendency to monophthongize dipthhongs, which is typical of later Greek, is implemented earlier in dialects like Boeotian.

The consonantal system is relatively stable in all varieties of Greek, but some dialects still preserve [w] (written with Ϝ, the so-called digamma), which was lost in Attic. Other dialects tend to change the aspirated stops into fricatives at an early stage or to lose the (secondary) intervocalic [s] which is found elsewhere. Hence Laconian σιός 'god' for Attic θεός, where σ- may well indicate a dental fricative [θ] (cf. English *th*) and Laconian Μῶhα 'Muse' corresponding to Attic Μοῦσα.

For the accentual system of Greek and the major phonological changes which mark the shift from classical to Byzantine Greek, see PRONUNCIATION, GREEK.

The system just described contrasts with that reconstructed for Indo-European (see LINGUISTICS, HISTORICAL AND COMPARATIVE). The Indo-European 'laryngeal' consonants were lost; the voiced aspirate stops (†b^h, etc.) yielded voiceless aspirates; the vocalic resonants †r̥, †l̥, †m̥, †n̥ were replaced by vowels or combinations of consonant and vowel, while the consonantal variants [j, w] of *i* and *u* tended to disappear; the inherited labiovelar stops (†k^w, g^w, g^{wh}) merged with velars, dentals, or labials, depending on the environment. Indo-European *s* changed to *h* word-initially before a vowel and internally between vowels, where it was eventually lost; all word-final stops were lost and final *-m* changed to *-n*. Not all of these changes are pre-Mycenaean, but those concerning the aspirates, the vocalic resonants, †s, probably final †-m, and the final stops are. Other changes involved sound clusters and differed in the various dialects; in Mycenaean, Arcado-Cyprian, Ionic-Attic, and Lesbian, but not in Doric and North-West Greek, *-ti* became *-si* (cf. Att. δίδωσι 'gives' and Dor. δίδωτι); in most dialects (including Ionic) *[kj, tj] became [ss], but in Attic and Boeotian we find [tt] (cf. Ion. θάλασσα, Att. θάλαττα).

Morphology and Syntax

Greek is a heavily inflected fusional language where the different grammatical categories are mostly marked by suffixes (nominal and verbal endings) or, far less frequently, by prefixes (e.g. the verbal augment or the reduplication). Infixation in verbs like λαμβ-άνω 'I take' vs. ἔ-λαβ-ον 'I took') is at best marginal. Note that one unsegmentable morpheme fulfils various functions: [o:], written -ου in πολίτου 'of the citizen' marks genitive, singular, and masculine. Suffixation and composition are the two most productive means of word-formation.

Nouns and adjectives are classified into inflexional classes (declensions) according to their phonological shape (o-stems, a-stems, consonantal stems). In the Classical period the nominal inflexion distinguished five cases (nominative, vocative, accusative, genitive, dative), three numbers (singular, dual, plural) and three genders (masculine, feminine, and neuter). Later developments led to the loss of the dual (which in some dialects is absent from the earliest attestations) and even later ones to that of the dative. Gender was determined by agreement patterns rather than by semantic factors or the phonological shape of the word (ἵππος 'horse/mare' can be masculine or feminine without any difference in inflexion). It was normal (though not compulsory) to use masculine and feminine for males and females but words for inanimate objects could be masculine, feminine, or neuter. In progress of time inflexional classes came to be tied to gender as is the case in Modern Greek. At the same time in Hellenistic Greek we witness a drastic simplification of the earlier inflexional variety.

Verbal morphology is highly complicated. A first distinction is between finite and non-finite forms; the former are characterized by personal endings for the singular, dual, and plural (there is not a full complement of dual endings and they too tend to disappear). The latter include participles, verbal adjectives, and infinitives, which are marked by special suffixes and share some of the syntactical, and in some instances morphological, properties of the noun.

In the finite verb the main grammatical categories are aspect, which indicates the way in which action etc. is envisaged (durative or imperfective, punctual or aoristic, stative or perfective), time (present, past, future), mood (indicative, subjunctive, optative, and imperative), voice (active, middle, passive), person (first, second, and third singular, dual or plural). Most verbs have three main stems (distinguished by vocalic alternation or affixation or more rarely by different roots) which indicate different aspects: durative/imperfective (e.g. πειθ- with the present πείθω 'I persuade, am persuading' and the imperfect ἔπειθον 'I was persuading'), or punctual/aoristic (e.g. πεισ- with the aorist ἔ-πεισα 'I persuaded'), or stative/perfective (e.g. πεποιθ- with the perfect πέποιθα 'I am persuaded' and the pluperfect ἐπεπείθειν 'I was persuaded'). Except for the future the so-called tenses (present, imperfect, aorist, perfect, pluperfect, future, future perfect) in the non-indicative moods and the non-finite forms mark primarily contrasts of aspect, while the indicative forms indicate both time and aspect distinctions: Xen. *Cyr.* 5. 5. 22 ἐλθὼν οὖν ἔπειθον αὐτοὺς καὶ οὓς ἔπεισα τούτους ἔχων ἐπορευόμην σοῦ ἐπιτρέψαντος, 'I went (part. aorist) and I tried to persuade them (imperfect) and keeping (part. present) with me those whom I persuaded (ind. aorist) I continued on my expedition (imperfect), since you allowed it (part. aorist).' The perfect is a special case; it starts indicating a state (πέποιθα 'I am convinced') and then develops a resultative use often accompanied by new forms (5th cent.: πέπεικα 'I have persuaded'), which makes it very similar to the aorist. Eventually it is lost and replaced by periphrastic forms. Contrasts of voice and person are marked by the endings. The middle voice emphasizes the participation or the involvement of the subject: active δικάζω 'I sit/am sitting in judgement', middle δικάζομαι 'I go/am going to law (on my own behalf)'. There are a few forms marked by suffixes which are exclusively passive, but otherwise the middle has also passive value, a pattern which will eventually prevail.

Word order is relatively free. The verb may precede or follow the object; similarly the subject may precede or follow the verb. Clitic particles tend in the early stages to occupy the second position in the clause (Xen. *Hell.* 3. 1. 11 ὁ ἀνήρ σοι ὁ ἐμὸς καὶ τἆλλα φίλος ἦν ..., 'my husband was devoted to you in other things too ...'), but they often gravitate towards the word with which they have the closest semantic links. In Homer we still find preverbs separated from verbs in so-called tmesis (ἐπὶ ... ἔτελλε), but there too and in Classical prose 'preverbs' are either compounded with verbs (cf. ἐπέτελλε 'enjoined') or serve as prepositions which 'govern' an inflected noun. The simple sentence may be limited to a verb without expressed subject (ὕει 'it rains'). In longer sentences grammatical agreement is regular: the verb normally agrees in number with the subject; the adjective agrees in number, gender, and case with the noun to which it refers. Attic, however, preserves the inherited rule by which a subject in the neuter plural can agree with a verb in the singular: τὰ ζῷα τρέχει, 'animals run'. Nominal sentences composed of subject and predicate without any finite verb are frequent: Thuc. 2. 43. 3 ἀνδρῶν γὰρ ἐπιφανῶν πᾶσα γῆ τάφος, 'for of famous men the whole earth [is] a memorial'. Attic prose develops complex forms of subordination; dependent clauses with finite verbs are normally introduced by conjunctions or relative pronouns, while verbs of saying and other verbs may be followed by 'accusative with infinitive' constructions: Xen. *Hell.* 2. 2. 10 ἐνόμιζον δὲ οὐδεμίαν εἶναι σωτηρίαν ..., 'they believed that there was no escape'.

Dialects show considerable morphological differences, partly determined by their different phonological development, partly by separate analogical processes (cf. e.g. the Aeol. dat. plur. of the type πόδεσσι 'to the feet', with a new ending -εσσι, vs. Att. -σι in ποσί). They do not, however, differ substantially in their morphosyntactic categories. Some syntactic differences are well known (e.g. Arcadian and Cyprian construe prepositions like ἐς (Att. ἐκ) and ἀπύ (Att. ἀπό) with the dative instead of the genitive found in Attic; Elean uses the optative in commands, etc.); others may not have been detected. Even so, there is remarkable similarity in the whole of the Greek-speaking area. If contrasted with IE, Greek has lost some case distinctions: the IE ablative and genitive have merged into the Greek genitive, and similarly the instrumental, locative, and dative into the Greek dative. The extensive use of prepositions is new. The complex arrangement of the verbal system is largely inherited and shows remarkable similarities with that of Indo-Iranian (Vedic and Greek are the only languages to preserve the distinction between optative and subjunctive). Greek has introduced new regularities—the creation of a contrast between middle and active perfect and of a resultative perfect; the pluperfect (to match the imperfect), the future, a separate passive, etc. Later developments show a preference for analytic rather than synthetic forms. It is still disputed how far IE allowed subordination, but the complex patterns found in Greek prose are certainly due to innovation. Perhaps the most important development is the creation of the article. In Homer ὁ, ἡ, τό still largely function as demonstrative or relative pronouns but in Classical prose they are used as articles. The article allows the creation of nominal forms which would be impossible otherwise (e.g. τὸ κακόν, τὸ εὖ, τὸ εἶναι, lit. 'the bad', 'the well', 'the be') and also marks the distinction between attributive and predicative function as in ὁ καλὸς παῖς or ὁ παῖς ὁ καλός 'the handsome boy' as contrasted with καλὸς ὁ παῖς 'the boy (is) handsome'. The development of intellectual language owes more to the article than to any other syntactical feature of Greek.

Lexicon

Though lexical differences between dialects are commonplace, if we allow for phonological differences, most of the basic vocabulary of Greek is shared by all dialects. The bulk of the early Greek lexicon is built on inherited Indo-European roots but numerous words cannot be etymologized and presumably belonged to pre-Greek populations. They include nouns and place names ending in -ινθος and -σσος / -ττος and a number of words for flora, fauna, etc. of Mediterranean origin (σῦκον 'fig', μίνθη 'mint', etc.). In addition even by Mycenaean times we find words of Semitic origin like σήσαμον 'sesame', κύμινον 'cummin', χρυσός 'gold', χιτών 'tunic', etc. In the Classical period it is noticeable that the cultural insularity of the Greeks and their reluctance to learn foreign languages led to very few borrowings from the outside; by contrast the later contacts with the Romans produced a large crop of loanwords or calques. New vocabulary is normally built via suffixation and composition; both processes are productive all through the history of the language. Compounds are characteristic of literary language (where they may be new creations or may be taken from the epitheta of the religious language and the formulae of oral poetry), but also occur in everyday language: the flavour of Pindar's μελησίμβροτος 'which is an object of care to men' or of the comic σαρκασμο-πιτυο-κάμπτης 'sneering pine-bender' (Aristophanes) is different from that of the innumerable -πωλης compounds of Attic inscriptions (κριθοπώλης 'barley seller', ἀρτοπώλης 'bread seller', etc.) which have only practical overtones.

HISTORY OF THE LANGUAGE A. Meillet, *Aperçu d'une histoire de la langue grecque*, 8th edn. (1975); O. Hoffmann and A. Debrunner, *Geschichte der griechischen Sprache* rev. A. Scherer (1969); L. R. Palmer, *The Greek Language* (1980); R. Browning, *Medieval and Modern Greek*, 2nd edn. (1983).

DIALECTS F. Bechtel, *Die griechischen Dialekte*, 1–3 (1921–4); C. D. Buck, *The Greek Dialects*, 2nd edn. (1955); A. Thumb, *Handbuch der griechischen Dialekte*, pt. 1, ed. E. Kiekers (1932), pt. 2, ed. A. Scherer (1959); R. Schmitt, *Einführung in die griechischen Dialekte* (1977); V. Bubeník, *Hellenistic and Roman Greece as a Sociolinguistic Area* (1989); C. Brixhe (ed.), *La Koiné grecque antique: Une langue introuvable?* (1993).

(HISTORICAL) GRAMMAR, GENERAL R. Kühner, *Ausführliche Grammatik der griechischen Sprache*. 1: *Elementar- und Formenlehre*, 3rd edn. by F. Blass, 2 vols. (1890–2), 2: *Satzlehre*, 3rd edn. by B. Gerth (1898–1904); E. Schwyzer and A. Debrunner, *Griechische Grammatik*, 2nd edn., 4 vols. (1959–71); F. Blass and A. Debrunner, *Grammatik des neutestamentlichen Griechisch*, 11th edn. (1961; Eng. trans. 1961); H. Rix, *Historische Grammatik des Griechischen* (1976); M. Meier-Brügger, *Griechische Sprachwissenschaft*, 2 vols. (1992); A. L. Sihler, *New Comparative Grammar of Greek and Latin* (1995).

PHONOLOGY L. Lupaş, *Phonologie du grec attique* (1982); W. S. Allen, *Vox Graeca*, 3rd edn. (1987); M. Lejeune, *Phonétique historique du mycénien et du grec ancien* (1972); S.-T. Teodorsson, *The Phonemic System of the Attic Dialect 400–340 B.C.* (1974), *The Phonology of Ptolemaic Koine* (1977), and *The Phonology of Attic in the Hellenistic Period* (1978); L. Threatte, *The Grammar of Attic Inscriptions*, 1: *Phonology* (1980).

MORPHOLOGY AND SYNTAX P. Chantraine, *La Formation des noms en grec ancien* (1933), and *Morphologie historique du grec*, 2nd edn. (1961); E. Risch, *Wortbildung der homerischen Sprache* (1973); H. Rix, *Historische Grammatik des Griechischen*, 2nd edn. (1992); Y. Duhoux, *Le Verbe grec ancien* (1992); B. L. Gildersleeve, *Syntax of Classical Greek from Homer to Demosthenes* (1900–11); W. W. Goodwin, *Syntax of the Moods and Tenses of the Greek Verb* (1912); J. Wackernagel, *Vorlesungen über Syntax*, 2 vols. (1926); M. S. Ruipérez, *Estructura del sistema de aspectos y tiempos del verbo griego antiguo* (1954); A. C. Moorhouse, *The Syntax of Sophocles* (1982); J. D. Denniston, *The Greek Particles*, 2nd edn. (1959); K. J. Dover, *Greek Word Order* (1960).

DICTIONARIES H. G. Liddell, R. Scott, and H. Stuart Jones, *Greek-English Lexicon*, 9th edn. (1968) with supplement (1996); *Diccionario griego–español* (1980–   ).

ETYMOLOGICAL DICTIONARIES H. Frisk, *Griechisches Etymologisches Wörterbuch* (1954–72); P. Chantraine, *Dictionnaire Étymologique de la langue grecque: histoire des mots* (1968–80). A. M. Da.

Gregory (1) I, the Great, pope AD 590–604, of senatorial and papal family; probable prefect of Rome *c.*573; subsequently monk; deacon, 578; *apocrisiarius* (lit. 'delegate', a church official) at Constantinople, 579–585/6 (despite his poor Greek); then adviser to Pope Pelagius II. When pope, despite ill-health, he valiantly administered a Rome stricken by flood, plague, and famine, shrunken in population and isolated and threatened by Arian (see ARIANISM) and pagan *Lombards. He reorganized papal estates for Rome's supply, centralizing their administration through appointments, paid imperial troops, appointed officers, and negotiated with the Lombards. He devotedly served the Byzantine empire as the 'holy commonwealth', but sometimes acted independently of emperor and exarchs. Warfare and political fragmentation limited his powers, but expectation of the Day of Judgement sharpened his sense of spiritual responsibility for the world. As churchman, he upheld ecclesiastical discipline in Italy and Dalmatia, maintained authority in the vicariate of Illyricum, restructured the dioceses of his dwindling patriarchate, and laboured to convert Jews and *pagan rustics. He urged Church reform on the Merovingians, reviving the vicariate of Arles at their request. He struggled (against imperial opposition) to end the Three Chapters schism in Venetia and Istria, and (with small success, and perhaps small need) to suppress African *Donatism. He worked to convert the Lombards through queen Theodelinda, and organized a mission to the Anglo-Saxons (596). In the east, he maintained papal appellate jurisdiction, and was friendly with the patriarchs of *Alexandria (1) and *Antioch (1). With Constantinople, he quarrelled over its patriarch's title Oecumenical, wrongly seen as challenging Rome's primacy. Generally, though, he was sensitive to local religious traditions.

A contemplative at heart, he saw episcopal duties as a necessary, but uncongenial extension of his monastic vocation into the secular world. His diaconal appointments favoured monks, alienating Rome's secular clergy. No original theologian, he was an eloquent moralizer and mystic, striving to make sense of his beleaguered world, and transmitting much patristic thought to the Middle Ages. His *Moralia in Iob* proved enormously popular; his *Cura pastoralis* remains a mirror for priest and bishop. His *Dialogues* (whose authenticity has been challenged) inspiringly portrayed the Italian Church as ascetic, preaching, thaumaturgic, but episcopally controlled. His *Homiliae in Ezechielem*, preached to the besieged city, movingly lament Rome's decay. He defended sacred art, reformed the Roman liturgy, and perhaps established a choir school. He conventionally condemned bishop Desiderius of Vienne for inappropriately teaching classical culture, and suspected its influence on potential monks, but conventionally acknowledged its utility in biblical studies; his straightforward, rhythmically skilful prose shows rhetorical training. (Many letters, though, are chancery-drafted.) A chief founder of the papal states, and of papal prestige in the post-Roman west, his leadership, and vigorous sense of Rome's political and Christian traditions, justified his epitaph as 'God's consul'.

EDITIONS Migne, *PL* 75–9, including principal life by Johannes Diaconus; *Registrum Epistolarum*, ed. P. Ewald and L. M. Hartmann, *MGH* (1891–9), and D. Norberg, *CCSL* 140A (1982); (with comm.), *Hom. in Ezech.* and *Moralia* ed. P. Verbraken and M. Adriaen, *CCSL* 142–4 (1963–79).

TEXTS AND TRANSLATIONS SC with Fr. trans. (various editors): *Moralia* (1952–74); *Dialogues* (1978–80); *Comm. in Canticum Canticorum* (1984); *Hom. in Ezech.* (1986–90); *Comm. in Reg. I* (1989); *Reg. Epp.* (1991); *Cura* (1992). Eng. trans.: *Moralia*, J. Bliss (1844–50); *Cura and Selected Letters*, J. Barmby (1894); *Cura*, H. Davis (1950); *Dialogues*, O. J. Zimmermann (1959).

LITERATURE J. Richards, *Consul of God* (1980); J. Fontaine and others, *Grégoire le Grand* (1986); C. Straw, *Gregory the Great* (1988); R. Godding, *Bibliografia di Gregorio Magno, 1890–1989* (1990).   S. J. B. B.

Gregory (2) **of Nazianzus** (AD 329–89) was educated at Athens in the company of *Basil of Caesarea, of whom he composed a crucial portrait in his *Oration 43*. He shared for a short period Basil's enthusiasm for practical *asceticism but did much to encourage his friend to take up controversial writing and pastoral office.

His own career was marred by indecisiveness: he was never able to define an acceptable balance between the 'philosophic life' and engagement in ecclesiastical affairs. He was probably inhibited by his father's hopes (the elder Gregory was a bishop also) and by Basil's success, which he could not help admiring in spite of differences between them.

That inadequacy was highlighted by his brief tenure of the see of *Constantinople, upon which he was suddenly thrust in 381

and which he almost as suddenly abandoned. Events allowed him, however, to influence the ecumenical council of that year and contribute to the resulting defeat of *Arianism. His historical significance springs from his detailed, honest, and lively letters, a series of polished and thoughtful orations (some of theological importance), and relatively uninspired poetry that nevertheless contains valuable autobiographical information.

TEXTS AND TRANSLATIONS Migne, *PG* 35–8; continuing editions of *Orationes*, ed. P. Gallay and others in SC (1978–); *Grégoire de Nazianze, Discours 4–5, Contre Julien*, ed. and trans. J. Bernardi, SC 309 (1983); F. L. Norris, *Faith Gives Fullness to Reasoning: The Five Theological Orations of Gregory Nazianzen*, trans. L. Wickham and F. Williams (1991); *Funeral Orations by St. Gregory Nazianzen and St. Ambrose*, trans. L. P. McCauley (1953) (includes *Oration 43*); *Letters*, ed. P. Gallay, GCS 53 (1969); *Gregory of Nazianzus, Three Poems*, trans. D. M. Meehan (1987); *Saint Gregory of Nazianzus, Selected Poems*, trans. J. McGuckin (1986).

STUDIES P. Gallay, *La Vie de saint Grégoire de Nazianze* (1943); M.-M. Hauser-Meury, *Prosopographie zu den Schriften Gregors von Nazianz* (1960); R. Radford Ruether, *Gregory of Nazianzus, Rhetor and Philosopher* (1969); T. Spidlík, *Grégoire de Nazianze: Introduction à l'étude de sa doctrine spirituelle* (1971).   P. R.

Gregory (3) **of Nyssa** (c. AD 330–95) was the master figure of Greek Christian theology. Deeply learned in Platonism and in the thought of *Origen (1), he imparted to that tradition a strong mystical flavour of his own, while safeguarding its orthodoxy. He was unable to engage in controversy without elevating the debate to timeless significance (and his criticism of Eunomius added much to the work of his brother *Basil of Caesarea).

It would be wrong, however, to regard him as a remote seer. He was married, and capable of pursuing secular interests for a number of years. Even in Church affairs, in spite of misgivings on Basil's part, he had practical interests and pastoral skills. His theology, therefore, was more than academic. He saw world and divinity associated dynamically, allowing human beings to develop the 'image of God' within them and to become in the process 'like unto God' (such were his key notions). His view of the relation between freedom and grace was correspondingly integrated and helped to save the eastern Church from the polarities that afflicted *Augustine.

His works were representative and influential, Christianizing further almost every traditional genre. Particular value may be attached to his Life of his sister Macrina, which propounded a doctrine of 'philosophy', offered useful illustration of the ascetic life, and prompts reflection on virginity and the place of women in the early Church.

TEXTS AND TRANSLATIONS *Gregorii Nysseni opera*, ed. W. Jaeger (1952–90); *Grégoire de Nysse, Traité de la virginité*, ed. and trans. M. Aubineau, SC 119 (1966); *Grégoire de Nysse, Vie de sainte Macrine*, ed. and trans. P. Maraval, SC 178 (1971); *Saint Gregory of Nyssa, Ascetical Works*, trans. V. W. Callahan (1967); *Encomium of Saint Gregory Bishop of Nyssa on his Brother Saint Basil Archbishop of Caesarea*, ed. and trans. J. A. Stein (1928).

STUDIES J. Daniélou, *Platonisme et théologie mystique: Doctrine spirituelle de saint Grégoire de Nysse* (1953), and *L'Être et le temps chez Grégoire de Nysse* (1970); W. Völker, *Gregor von Nyssa als Mystiker* (1955); M. Harl (ed.), *Écriture et culture philosophique dans la pensée de Grégoire de Nysse* (1971); A. Spira (ed.), *The Biographical Works of Gregory of Nyssa* (1984).   P. R.

Gregory (4) **Thaumaturgus** (c. AD 213–c.275) was born of a prominent family of Neocaesarea, Pontus (formerly Cabeira; mod. Niksar). He studied law at *Berytus (Beirut), but when visiting *Caesarea (2) (Palestine) was converted to Christianity by

Grillius

*Origen (1). His parting panegyric of gratitude describes Origen's methods of instruction. On returning to Pontus he successfully preached Christianity as bishop of Neocaesarea. His memory was venerated a century later by *Basil of Caesarea and *Gregory (3) of Nyssa, the latter of whom wrote a Life on the basis of Pontic folk-traditions which ascribed to him extraordinary prodigies as 'the wonder-worker'. Of particular interest, both for contemporary historical conditions and for the liturgical development of the 3rd-cent. Church, is the 'Canonical Letter' written in the aftermath of the Gothic invasions of Pontus in the mid-250s, in which various grades of penance were laid down for Christians who had exploited the invasions for their own advantage.

Panegyric, ed. P. Koetschau (1894). J. Quasten, Patrology 2 (1953), 123 ff; R. van Dam, Cl. Ant. 1982, 272 ff.; P. Heather and J. Matthews, The Goths in the Fourth Century (1991), ch. 1.   J. F. Ma.

Grillius (5th cent. AD), a rhetorician cited by *Priscian (Keil, Gramm. Lat. 2. 35. 24 ff.) and author of a commentary on Cicero's De inventione (excerpts survive: ed. Halm, Rhet. Lat. Min. 596–606).

PLRE 1. 404; Herzog–Schmidt, § 617.   R. A. K.

gromatici, Roman land-surveyors. They were more commonly called mensores or agrimensores, gromatici being a late term derived from the groma, which was the most important of the surveyor's instruments, used to survey straight lines, squares, and rectangles. It consisted of a wooden pole, on top of which was attached a cross; plumb-lines hung from each arm of the cross. Recent analysis suggests that the traditional reconstruction of a curved angle-bracket to connect the pole to the cross does not tally with the remains found in a surveyor's workshop in Pompeii in 1912, and may be unnecessary.

The primary objective of the land surveyor was to establish limites, roadways or baulks intersecting at right angles and dividing the land into squares or rectangles (centuriae, hence limitatio, centuriatio (see CENTURIATION)). He first plotted the two basic limites (decumanus maximus and cardo maximus), and then more limites were established parallel to these and designated 'first limes to the right or left of the decumanus maximus', and 'first limes on the near or far side of the cardo maximus', and so on.

Civilian surveyors were often *freedmen and constituted a professional group whose activities were well known in Roman life (e.g. Plaut. Poen. 49; Ov. Met. 1. 135); they were in great demand at the end of the republic and in the early Principate when vast amounts of land were distributed to soldiers (see VETERANS). In the later empire they were absorbed into the imperial bureaucracy. They established boundaries on private estates, assessed land for the census and land-tax, and most importantly measured and divided public land (*ager publicus) for the establishment of colonies; when they had taken the colonists to their allocations and completed a map of the settlement and a register of each holding, the founder signed the records, copies of which were kept in the colony and in Rome. Surveyors also advised in all kinds of land dispute. They were expected to master not only practical implementation, but also law and jurisdiction relating to land-holding. Under the empire, army *camps and forts were laid out by military surveyors attached to each legion, who could also advise on land disputes in the provinces or construction projects (e.g. ILS 5795). The work of surveyors is strikingly illustrated by fragments of a stone record of the land survey instituted at *Arausio (mod. Orange) in AD 77. Part of a plan (forma) of the territory round the river Ana in *Lusitania has also been discovered.

Many technical treatises on land surveying were collected in an edition of the 6th cent. AD, including works ascribed to *Frontinus, *Hyginus (2), cf. (4), *Siculus Flaccus, *Iunius Nipsus, *Innocentius, and the anonymous *Libri coloniarum. Furthermore, the Arcerianus and Palatine manuscripts of the texts contain many colour illustrations, dating from the 6th–7th and 9th cents., of surveying techniques and settlements mentioned by the authors. The works in the collection, although badly corrupted in transmission and sometimes obscurely expressed, are of unique historical importance for their detailed description of the nature and practice of land settlement, and the role of emperors, especially Augustus, in regulating urban centres in a rural environment.

TEXTS F. Blume, K. Lachmann, and A. Rudorff, Die Schriften der römischen Feldmesser, 2 vols. (1848–52; repr. 1962); C. Thulin, Corpus Agrimensorum Romanorum 1/1 (Teubner, 1913; repr. 1971); J. Bouma, Marcus Iunius Nipsus–Fluminis Varatio, Limitis Repositio (1993).
GENERAL :
J. Bradford, Ancient Landscapes (1957); F. Castagnoli, Le ricerche sui resti della centuriazione (1958); A. Piganiol, Les Documents cadastraux de la colonie romaine d'Orange, Gallia, Suppl. 16 (1962); O. A. W. Dilke, Imago Mundi 1967, 9; The Roman Land Surveyors (1971); F. T. Hinrichs, Die Geschichte der gromatischen Institutionen (1974); M. Clavel-Lévêque and others, Cadastres et espace rural: Approches et réalités antiques (1983); G. Chouquer and others, Structures agraires en Italie centro-méridionale (1987); P. Sáez Fernández, Habis 1990, 205; O. Behrends and L. Capogrossi Colognesi (eds.), Die römische Feldmesskunst (1992); D. J. Gargola, Land, Laws and Gods (1995).   J. B. C.

Grumentum (mod. Grumento Nova), founded c.600 BC, but not prominent before the Roman conquest. It entered into alliance with Rome in 327/6 BC, when Rome negotiated a treaty with the Lucanians, but may have revolted after 216. In 122 a Gracchan colony was founded on confiscated *ager publicus. It was sacked by *Spartacus, but subsequently recovered. There are Roman public buildings and it was noted for its wine. It was abandoned in the 6th cent. AD.

C. Turano, La Calabria antica (1977).   K. L.

guardianship

Greece The development of the law of guardianship in Greece and Rome was influenced by the change in the conception of guardianship itself, which began as a right of preserving and protecting the ward's property in the interest of the whole kin (as contingent heir of the ward), but became gradually a duty of the guardian in the interest of the ward. This explains the restrictions imposed upon the guardian with regard to his control over the child's property, and the increasing supervision of public authorities over his activity as guardian. The Greek guardian was either epitropos (lit. 'trustee', 'steward') of boys and girls until their majority—18 years in the case of boys—and registration in the citizen list, or kyrios (lit. 'master', 'lord') of women for lifetime or until marriage. Guardians were appointed by the father's will; failing testamentary appointment the next relatives (brother or uncle), being the most likely successors, were entitled to claim the guardianship; in the absence of these an official (the chief archon in Athens) appointed the guardian. The guardian had to provide for the ward's education, attend to all his interests, and represent him in legal transactions: in general he was required—as Plato, Laws 11. 928 recommends—to act on his behalf with the same solicitude as for a child of his own. The administration of property by the guardian, especially of landed property, was submitted to the control of magistrates. Action for damages caused by the guardian might be brought against him by the ward within five years of the end of the guardianship. The principles of guardianship of women were analogous; but a woman could dispose freely of objects of lesser importance, without the help of her *kyrios*. See INHERITANCE.

O. Schulthess, *Vormundschaft nach griechischem Recht* (1886); Beasley, *CR* 1906, 249 ff.; J. H. Lipsius, *Attisches Recht und Rechtsverfahren* 2. 2 (1912); L. Mitteis, *Grundzüge der Papyruskunde* (1913), 248 ff.; A. R. W. Harrison, *Law of Athens, Family and Property* (1968), 97 ff.; D. M. MacDowell, *The Law in Classical Athens* (1978), 93–5; S. C. Todd, *The Shape of Athenian Law* (1993), see index under *epitropos, kyrios*.

A. B.; B. N.

Rome Roman law distinguished *tutela* and *cura* as types of guardianship of persons *sui iuris*, i.e. those not subject to father or husband (by *patria potestas* or *manus* (see MARRIAGE LAW)). *Tutela* concerned children below the age of puberty (*impuberes*, eventually boys under 14, girls under 12) and women, *cura* those above these ages but under 25 (minors), lunatics, and spendthrifts.

The original purpose of guardianship, conservation of property, is clear in the rule which gave *tutela* of an *impubes* on the death of the *paterfamilias* (see PATRIA POTESTAS) to the nearest male agnate (relation through males) as *tutor legitimus* (guardian indicated by statute; a male ex-owner was also statutory guardian to his freedwoman), the person who would inherit if the ward (*pupillus/a*) died. But already in the *Twelve Tables the father could appoint someone else by will. Later, failing these, a magistrate would appoint one. *Tutela* of males ended with puberty, when the ward could beget an heir who would exclude the agnate from the inheritance. But a female's children did not fit this definition, so *tutela* of women was for life. In classical law it became attenuated because of changing attitudes to family. The grant of choice of guardian by the will of a husband to a wife in *manus* (attested for 186 BC), Augustus' introduction of the parents' right *ius liberorum*, Claudius' abolition of agnatic *tutela* mark stages towards disappearance. By Cicero's day, many upper-class women could treat the guardian's authorization (*auctoritas tutoris*) as a 'rubber-stamp', necessary but easily obtained.

Tutela's shift from privilege to burden appears in the evolution of the *tutor*'s liability for misconduct. In early law he was liable only for fraudulent misappropriation, but in the later republic he could be required to account for his conduct according to the principles of good faith. Rules accrued, as did grounds (*excusationes*: office, ill health, etc.) which exempted from service as guardian one appointed by a will or an official.

The *tutor*'s concern was with property, not a child's custody or upbringing or a woman's personal life. He might administer it directly (but the ward might repudiate his acts when he came of age) or validate the ward's acts. A woman's *tutor* did not (in classical law) administer, but his *auctoritas* was needed for important transactions such as purchase of slaves or land, *manus*, and dowry (but not marriage itself).

Cura minorum grew out of the *lex Laetoria* or *Plaetoria* (*c*.200 BC) and the praetorian remedy of *in integrum restitutio*, the cancellation of exploitative transactions with an independent minor. So, to protect transactions with a minor, an adult was called in to approve them, a practice which in the Principate led to the institution of a *curator* appointed by a magistrate at the minor's request. Justinianic law (see JUSTINIAN'S CODIFICATION) largely assimilates *tutela* and *cura* of minors.

Gai. *Inst.* 1. 142–99; S. Dixon, *Tijdschrift voor Rechtsgeschiedenis* 1984, 343–71.

A. B.; B. N.; S. M. T.

guest-friendship See FRIENDSHIP, RITUALIZED.

Gyges, king of *Lydia (*c*.680–645 BC), founded the Mermnad dynasty by murdering King Candaules and marrying his widow (Hdt. 1. 8–14; cf. Pl. *Resp.* 2. 359d). The word tyrant (see TYRANNY) first appears in Greek applied to Gyges (Archil. fr. 19 West). He started the exploitation of *gold from the Pactolus; attacked *Miletus and *Smyrna, captured Colophon and sent sumptuous offerings to *Delphi. He gained Assyrian protection against the *Cimmerians, but lost it later by helping *Psammetichus I of Egypt. He was killed in a new Cimmerian invasion; his tomb was famous (Hipponax fr. 42 West) and has been identified in the royal tumulus cemetery at Bin Tepe. His son Ardys succeeded him.

Hdt. 1. 8–14. G. M. A. Hanfmann, *Sardis from Prehistoric to Roman Times* (1983), chs. 4–5; M. Mellink, *CAH* 3²/2 (1991), 643 ff.; A. Andrewes, *Greek Tyrants* (1956), 20 ff.; C. Ratté, *JHS* 1994, 157.

R. T.

Gylippus, Spartan officer, was sent in 414 BC to command the Syracusans against Athenian attack. His arrival restored confidence and an early victory safeguarded the construction of the counter-wall which prevented a land blockade, thereby regaining the initiative for Syracuse. *Lysander's subordinate in 405, he brought home the booty and Persian money after Sparta's defeat of Athens at Aegospotami, but stole 300 talents and on detection fled into exile.

RE 7. 1967–9, 'Gylippos' 1; PB no. 196; H. D. Westlake, *Individuals in Thucydides* (1968), ch. 14.

S. J. Ho.

gymnasiarch (γυμνασίαρχος). In Classical Athens gymnasiarchs were appointed annually from the ten tribes (*phylai*) to organize *torch-races; the post was an (especially burdensome) *liturgy. The gymnasiarch of the Hellenistic and Roman *polis was general supervisor of the civic *gymnasium (or gymnasia), responsible (helped by a staff of assistants and specialists) for its practical administration and the moral supervision (e.g. the policing of *homosexuality) of its youthful users (see EPHEBOI), for whom he was a fearsome authority-figure (e.g. Plut. *Amat.* 755a) empowered to fine and flog. The heavy costs of physical training, mainly oil (see OLIVE) for *athletics and fuel for hot *baths, made the office a target for the *euergetism of rich citizens. The numerous inscriptions honouring generous incumbents naturally stress this aspect; the sole surviving 'gymnasiarchic law' (from 2nd-cent. BC Beroea in Macedonia: Austin 118) paints a picture of burdensome responsibilities and liability to both physical assault in office and, out of it, prosecution for malfeasance. The centrality of the gymnasium to civic life ensured the gymnasiarch local prominence; in the *Acts of the Pagan Martyrs* Alexandrian gymnasiarchs led anti-Roman demonstrations; the Athenian gymnasiarchy was prestigious enough for Mark Antony (see ANTONIUS (2), M.) to don its insignia with relish (Plut. *Ant.* 33. 10). In Egypt gymnasiarchs are attested as late as 370 (*POxy.* 2110).

A. H. M. Jones, *The Greek City from Alexander to Justinian* (1940), 221–6; P. Gauthier and M. Hatzopoulos, *La Loi gymnasiarchique de Beroia*, Meletemata 16 (1993).

A. J. S. S.

gymnasium In Greek cities, the gymnasium originated as a place of exercise for the citizens, specifically to fit the *epheboi for the rigours of service as *hoplites. At first no more than an open space, with a water supply, often sited in conjunction with a sanctuary or shrine, as late as the 5th cent. BC gymnasia seem not to have needed architectural development, shade and shelter being provided rather by groves of trees. Descriptions of the

gynaecology

Athenian gymnasia, the Lyceum, Cynosarges, and above all the Academy conform with this (see ATHENS, TOPOGRAPHY).

Frequented also by older citizens, and particularly from the connection with the 4th-cent. philosophers, they became more intellectual centres. Though the element of exercise was never lost, the concept of education became more important. Some—those at Athens in particular—through the interests of the philosophical schools became in effect universities. More usually in the cities of the Hellenistic age they functioned as secondary schools. More specialized architecture was required, and the gymnasia became enclosed areas, their buildings arranged largely on the courtyard principle. The *Academy at Athens acquired such a courtyard, with shrine-building and fountain-house, but is badly preserved and not fully understood. Better-preserved examples are found in the Asia Minor cities. The lower gymnasium at *Priene is adjacent to the stadium which provides *athletic facilities. The gymnasium itself is wholly a school building, comprising a small courtyard with rooms opening off. One, its walls liberally inscribed by the pupils, is the classroom; another provides tubs and running cold water for washing. The gymnasium at *Pergamum is larger and more complex (the details partly obscured by the later intrusion of a Roman bath-building) but included its own running-track. A similar running-track, roofed but with ample ventilation, has been identified next to the so-called forum of Caesar at *Cyrene, indicating that this was originally a colonnaded exercise ground of a Hellenistic gymnasium.

Gymnasia were generally provided by the city. That at *Alexandria (1) was situated at the centre of the city, close to the agora. As a centre of education it became a focus for the maintenance of Greek identity in the face of non-Greek settlement and Roman political control.

In their function as schools gymnasia continued to flourish in the Greek cities during the Roman period. In the west the exercise facilities were more usually developed in the context of the bath-buildings, especially at Rome in the imperial thermae (see BATHS). See EDUCATION, GREEK; GYMNASIARCH; PALAESTRA.

J. Delorme, *Gymnasion* (1960); M. I. Finley and H. W. Pleket, *The Olympic Games: The First Thousand Years* (1976); S. L. Glass, in W. J. Raschke (ed.), *The Archaeology of the Olympics* (1988).   R. A. T.

gynaecology existed in the ancient world as a medical specialism, but its separate identity was not always permitted by wider medical theories. The significant question was this: do women have diseases peculiar to their sex, or are they subject to the same conditions as men, only requiring a separate branch of medicine to the extent that they have different organs to be affected? In other words, is gynaecology necessary?

The majority of the surviving gynaecological treatises come from the Hippocratic corpus (see HIPPOCRATES (2)) and probably date to the late 5th and early 4th cents. BC. These treatises include three volumes of *Gynaecia* (*Mul.*), usually translated as 'Diseases of Women', but which can also mean women's sexual organs, *menstruation, or therapies for women's diseases. In contrast to the rest of the Hippocratic corpus, these texts include long lists of remedies using plant and animal ingredients. The third volume concerns the treatment of barren women. A separate short treatise discusses the medical problems of unmarried girls at puberty (*Virg.*) while others focus on the process of generation. A large number of the case histories in *Epidemics* trace the progress of disease in women patients.

In keeping with a culture in which women could be seen to constitute a separate 'race', *Mul.* 1. 62 criticizes those doctors who make the mistake of treating the diseases of women as if they were men. For the Hippocratics of the *Gynaecia*, women require a separate branch of medicine because they are seen as fundamentally different from men, not merely in their reproductive organs, but in the texture of their flesh, seen as 'wet' and 'spongey', like wool. Because of this texture, women are thought to absorb more fluid from their diet, menstruation being necessary to remove the surplus. There was, however, no uniformity on female difference, other Hippocratic texts applying identical principles—such as the theory of 'critical days', in which certain numbered days were seen as those on which the crisis in a disease occurred—to diseases of both men and women.

The debate on the status of gynaecology continued. Alexandrian anatomy, associated in particular with *Herophilus, moved from fluids to organs, and women came to be seen more as reverse males than as a separate race. Whereas men's reproductive organs are outside, women were seen as having the same organs inside. Papyri show that Hippocratic recipes for women's diseases continued to be transmitted. *Soranus summarizes the position before his own time; writers such as the early 4th-cent. BC *Diocles (3) of Carystus and the Empiricist sect believed there were conditions specific to women, while the 3rd-cent. *Erasistratus and Herophilus, together with writers of the Methodist persuasion (see MEDICINE, § 5. 3), believed there were not. Instead, Methodists thought that the same principles governed all diseases, men and women being made of the same materials behaving according to the same rules. Soranus himself claimed that although some conditions, such as pregnancy and lactation, were specific to women, their diseases were not generically different. *Galen (*Parts of Medicine* 1. 2–3 and 5. 8) lists as legitimate medical specialisms pediatrics and geriatrics, but not gynaecology.

Despite these changes from Hippocratic beliefs, some forms of therapy for women's diseases continued to be used more readily than in the treatment of men with analogous conditions. Foremost among these was the fumigation, in which vapours were passed into the womb through its mouth. These were believed to open the womb, thus permitting retained matter to be expelled and semen to enter. Ancient gynaecological recipes, like purificatory ritual, made use of sulphur, asphalt, squill, and laurel, as well as animal excrement.

Beliefs about the interior of the female body were also remarkably persistent, despite evidence to the contrary. For example, although Herophilus discovered the ovaries and the uterine ligaments, the function of the former was not understood—women continued to be seen as containers for male seed—and the presence of the latter was not widely seen as contradicting the Hippocratic notion that the womb was capable of some degree of movement within the body. Instead, the 'wandering womb' theory was merely rephrased, for example being seen in terms of 'sympathy' between upper and lower parts of the body permitting the latter to cause symptoms in the former. See ANATOMY AND PHYSIOLOGY; BOTANY; CHILDBIRTH; EMBRYOLOGY; PHARMACOLOGY.

L. Dean-Jones, *Women's Bodies in Classical Greek Science* (1994); P. Diepgen, *Der Frauenheilkunde der alten Welt* (1937); G. Gourevitch, *Le Mal d'être femme* (1984); H. Grensemann, *Hippokratische Gynäkologie* (1982); A. E. Hanson, in J. Scarborough (ed.), *Ancient Medicine* (1995); P. Manuli, in S. Campese and others (eds.), *Madre Materia* (1983), 142–92; H. von Staden, *Helios* 1992, 7–30.   H. K.

Habron, of Phrygia and Rhodes (1st cent. AD), a Greek grammarian at Rome. His Περὶ ἀντωνυμίας ('On the pronoun') is cited, sometimes with approval, by Apollonius (13) Dyscolus.

FRAGMENTS R. Berndt, *Berliner philologische Wochenschrift* 1915.
N. G. W.

Hades (Homeric Ἀΐδης, Ἀΐς, also Ἀϊδωνεύς; aspirated Ἅιδης in Attic only; cf. E. Schwyzer, *Dialectorum Graecorum Exempla Epigraphica Potiora* (1923), 1. 48), son of *Cronus and Rhea (Hes. *Theog.* 453–56) and husband of *Persephone (*Od.* 10. 491), is 'Lord of the dead' (*Il.* 20. 61) and king of the Underworld, the 'house of Hades' (Hom., Hes.), where he rules supreme and, exceptionally, administers justice (Aesch. *Supp.* 228–31, *Eum.* 273–5). After Homer, Hades is not only the god of the dead, but also the god of death, even death personified (Semon. 1. 14; Pind. *Pyth.* 5. 96, *Nem.* 10. 67, *Isthm.* 6. 15; Soph. *Ant.* 581; Eur. *Alc.* 262; R. Seaford on Eur. *Cyc.* 397). Hades refers normally to the person; in non-Attic literature, the word can also designate the Underworld (*Il.* 23. 244; *Od.* 11. 635; Heraclitus DK 22 B 98; Anac. 50. 9 f. Page, Luke 16. 23). Cold, mouldering, and dingy, Hades is a 'mirthless place' (*Od.* 11. 94; Hes. *Op.* 152–5). The proverbial 'road to Hades' (Lucian *Catapl.* 14) is 'the same for all' (*Anth. Pal.* 7. 477. 3 f., 11. 23. 3). *Aeacus, son of *Zeus, 'keeps the keys to Hades' (Apollod. *Bibl.* 3. 12. 6; cf. *GVI* 1906. 4, *PGM* IV 1464 f.); the same is said of Pluton (Πλούτων) (Paus. 5. 20. 3), *Anubis (love charms from Roman Egypt: *PGM* IV 341 f., 1466 f.; *Supp. Mag.* 2. 299, entry under κλείς), and Christ (Rev. 1. 18). The 'gates of Hades' (*Il.* 5. 646) are guarded by 'the terrible hound', *Cerberus, who wags his tail for the new arrivals, but devours those attempting to leave (Hes. *Theog.* 311 f., 767–73). Hades, too, was sometimes perceived as an eater of corpses (Soph. *El.* 542 f.). Without burial, the dead cannot pass through Hades' gates (*Il.* 23. 71–4; Eur. *Hec.* 28–54). Once inside, they are shrouded in 'the darkness of pernicious Hades' (*SEG* 26. 1139. 9).

Like the *Erinyes/Eumenides ('Angry/Kindly Ones') and *Demeter ('Earth-mother', cf. Eur. *Bacch.* 275 f., Derveni papyrus col. 18 (*ZPE* 47 (1982) after p. 300)), Hades lacked a proper name; as in the case of other nameless *chthonians, his anonymity was a precaution (Pl. *Cra.* 403a7). He was referred to by descriptive circumlocutions as 'chthonian Zeus' (*Il.* 9. 457; M. L. West on Hes. *Op.* 465), 'the chthonian god' (Hes. *Theog.* 767), 'king of those below' (Aesch. *Pers.* 629), 'Zeus of the departed' and 'the other Zeus' (Aesch. *Supp.* 156 f., 231), 'the god below' (Soph. *Aj.* 571; Eur. *Alc.* 424), or simply 'lord' (Eur. *Alc.* 852). As the Lord of the Dead, he was dark and sinister, a god to be feared and kept at a distance. Paradoxically, he was also believed to 'send up' good things for mortals from his wealth below (West on Hes.

Theog. 969; Ar. fr. 504 K–A; Pl. *Cra.* 403a3–5); he is a 'good and prudent god' (Pl. *Phd.* 80d7).

The two opposite but complementary aspects of his divinity are reflected in a host of positive and negative epithets. Of the latter, Hades, 'the invisible one' according to ancient etymology (E. R. Dodds on Pl. *Grg.* 493b4, cf. Soph. *Aj.* 607 ἀΐδηλος Ἀΐδας, but modern linguists are divided on this), recalls the darkness of his realm. The 'wolf's cap of Hades' (Ἄϊδος κυνέη), worn by *Athena in the *Iliad* (5. 844 f.) and by Aita/Hades in Etruscan art (*LIMC* 'Hades/Aita' nos. 5–6, 10–12, 21), makes its wearers invisible (Ar. *Ach.* 390; Pl. *Resp.* 612b). Other negative epithets are 'hateful' (*Il.* 8. 368 στυγερός, like the *Styx), 'implacable and adamant' (*Il.* 9. 158 ἀμείλιχος ἠδ᾽ ἀδάμαστος), 'tearless' (Hor. *Carm.* 2. 14. 6) and 'malignant' (βάσκανος, cf. M. W. Dickie, *ZPE* 100 (1994), 111–14). Epithets which euphemistically address his benign and hospitable aspects include *Clymenus ('Renowned'), *Eubouleus ('Good Counsellor': Nic. *Alex.* 14; *GVI* 2030. 9), Euchaites ('the Beautiful-haired One': Clarian oracle *ISestos* 11. 24, *c.* AD 166), Eukles ('Of Good Repute': Orph. fr. 32 c–e 2 Kern; Hsch. ε 6926), Hagesilaos ('Leader of the People': Aesch. fr. 406 Radt; A. W. Bulloch on Callim. *Hymn* 5. 130; *GVI* 1370. 2), Pasianax ('Lord over All': *Def. tab.* Audollent, nos. 43–4), Polydektes or Polydegmon ('Receiver of Many': *Hymn. Hom. Cer.* 9, 17), Polyxeinos ('Host to Many': Aesch. fr. 228 Radt; Callim. fr. 285 Pf.), and Pluton ('Wealth', πλοῦτος, personified; cf. Soph. fr. 273 Radt). Originally a divinity in his own right, during the 5th cent. BC Pluton became Hades' most common name in myth as well as in cult (first attested on a phiale by Douris, *LIMC* 'Hades' no. 28, *c.*490 BC; Soph. *Ant.* 1200, Pl. *Grg.* 523a4, Isoc. 9. 15; *IG* 1³. 5. 5, 386. 156, 2². 1363. 21 'priestess of Pluton', 1672. 169, 1933. 2; *Hymn. Orph.* 18).

Hades was not a recipient of cult (Soph. *Ant.* 777–80). Like *Thanatos, he was indifferent to prayer or offerings (Aesch. fr. 161 Radt; Eur. *Alc.* 424). The abnormal cult of Hades at Elis, with a temple open once a year, then only to the priest (Paus. 6. 25. 2 f.), and his *temenos* at Mt. Minthe near Pylos (Strabo 8. 344) are the exceptions that prove the rule. But throughout the Greek world—at *Eleusis, *Sparta, *Ephesus, *Cnidus, and *Mytilene, among numerous other places—he received cult in his beneficial aspect as Pluton, often alongside his consort Persephone. The couple were widely worshipped as Pluton and Kore (*IG* 2². 1672. 182, 4751; *CEG* 2. 571); at Eleusis, they were also known as Theos and Thea. Pluton is related to the Eleusinian cult figures *Plutus and Eubouleus as well as to other friendly chthonians such as Zeus Meilichios and Zeus Eubouleus (see CHTHONIAN GODS). In various curse tablets, however, he is invoked along with *Demeter and Kore or, more menacingly, with the Erinyes, *Hecate, *Hermes, Moirai, and Persephone (Gager (see bibliog.

Hadrian (Publius Aelius Hadrianus)

below), nos. 53, 84, 89, 110, 134); *curses in the name of Hades and Persephone are less common (*Def. tab.* R. Wünsch, no. 102b13–16; W. Peek, *Kerameikos* 3 (1941), 98 no. 9. 18). So-called Plutonia marked entrances to the Underworld (Strab. 5. 244).

Apart from the story of Persephone's abduction by him, few myths attach to Hades. By giving her the forbidden food of the dead to eat—the pomegranate—he bound Demeter's daughter to return periodically to his realm (*Hymn. Hom. Cer.* 370 ff.). Their union was without issue; its infertility mirrors that of the nether world (*Apollodorus (6) of Athens, *FGrH* 244 F 102a2). When the sons of Cronus divided the universe amongst themselves, Hades was allotted the world of the dead, Zeus obtained the sky, and Poseidon the sea (R. Janko on *Il.* 15. 185–93; Richardson on *Hymn. Hom. Cer.* 86). As ruler of the dead, Hades was always more ready to receive than to let go (Aesch. *Pers.* 688–90). Two kindred gods, Demeter and *Dionysus, as well as heroes like *Heracles, *Theseus, and *Orpheus descended alive to Hades and returned to earth. Ordinary mortals went there to stay; *Alcestis, *Eurydice (1), and *Protesilaus were among the few allowed to leave (cf. Plat. *Symp.* 179c). Heracles wrestled with Thanatos (Eur. *Alc.* 843–9) and wounded Hades with his arrows (*Il.* 5. 395–7; Paus. 6. 25. 2 f.). Hades' mistress Minthe (see MENTHE) was changed into the mint plant by Persephone (Strabo 8. 344, Ov. *Met.* 10. 728–30; cf. Oppian, *Halieutica* 3. 486 ff.).

Alcestis' death vision of Hades, who comes to get her, is dim but frightening (Eur. *Alc.* 259–62 Diggle: 'Someone is leading me, leading me away—don't you see?—to the hall of the dead. He stares at me from under his dark-eyed brow. He has wings—it's Hades!'). In Greek art, Hades and Pluton—differentiating between the two is not always possible—are wingless human figures lacking any terrifying aspects. Zeus-like and bearded, Hades-Pluton is a majestic, elderly man holding a sceptre, twig, cornucopia, pomegranate, or cantharus. On some vases, Hades is shown averting his gaze from the other gods (*LIMC* nos. 14, 22, 148). Unlike Hades, Thanatos is represented with wings (Eur. *Alc.* 843; often in vase-painting, e.g. Euphronius, calyx-crater, New York, Met. Mus. 1972.11.10; Thanatos Painter, lecythus, London, BM D 58). Conceptually and iconographically, Dionysus (Heraclitus fr. 15 DK) and *Sarapis (H. Heubner on Tac. *Hist.* 4. 83 f.) in their chthonian aspects have affinities to Hades-Pluton.

Hades was the universal destination of the dead until the second half of the 5th cent. BC, when we first hear of the souls of some special dead ascending to the upper air (*aithēr*), while their bodies are said to be received by the earth (Athenian epitaph, c.432 BC, *IG* 1³. 1179. 6 f. = *CEG* 1. 10. 6 f.; Eur. *Supp.* 533 f.; *CEG* 2. 535, 558). Notably, the souls of the heroized daughters of *Erechtheus 'do not go to Hades', but reside in heaven (Eur. *Erech.* fr. 65. 71 f. Austin). The various Underworld topographies found in Homer (*Od.* 11) and Virgil (*Aen.* 6), in the esoteric gold leaves containing descriptions of Hades, and in the apocryphal *Apocalypse of Peter* reflect changing constructs of the afterlife. See DEATH, ATTITUDES TO, GREEK; TARTARUS.

LITERATURE Preller–Robert, *Griechische Mythologie* (1894) 1. 798–846; R. Lattimore, *Themes in Greek and Latin Epitaphs* (1942); N. J. Richardson, *The Homeric Hymn to Demeter* (1974); E. Vermeule, *Aspects of Death in Early Greek Art and Poetry* (1979); Burkert, *GR* 194–9; J. G. Gager, *Curse Tablets and Binding Spells from the Ancient World* (1992); T. Gantz, *Early Greek Myth* (1993), 70–3, 123–8.

ETYMOLOGY P. Thieme, in R. Schmitt (ed.), *Indogermanische Dichtersprache* (1968), 133–53.

CULTS AND EPITHETS Farnell, *Cults* 3. 280–8, 376–8; B. Prehn, *RE* Suppl. 3 (1918), 867–78 'Hades'; E. Wüst, *RE* 21 (1951), 990–1027 'Pluton'.

POLARITY/ANONYMITY A. Henrichs, in H. Hofmann and A. Harder (eds.), *Fragmenta Dramatica* (1991) 161–201; S. Scullion, *CL. Ant.* 1994, 75–119.

KEYS TO HADES K. J. Dover, *Aristophanes: Frogs* (1993), 52 f.; S. Morenz, *Religion und Geschichte des alten Ägypten* (1975), 510–20.

ICONOGRAPHY R. Lindner, S.-C. Dahlinger, N. Yalouris, and I. Krauskopf, 'Hades', 'Aita', 'Pluto', *LIMC* 4 (1988), 1. 367–406, 2. 210–36 (plates); C. Sourvinou-Inwood, *'Reading' Greek Culture* (1991), 147–88; Clinton, *Iconography*, esp. 105–13.   A. H.

Hadrian (Publius Aelius (*RE* 64) Hadrianus), emperor AD 117–38. The Aelii of *Italica were among the earliest provincial senators; his mother Domitia Paullina was from *Gades (mod. Cádiz). When his father died, Hadrian became the ward of *Trajan, his father's cousin, and of P. *Acilius Attianus (85). Early devotion to Greek studies earned the nickname, *Graeculus* ('little Greek'); a passion for hunting was apparent when he visited Italica (90). After the vigintivirate (see VIGINTISEXVIRI, VIGINTIVIRI), he was tribune in Legio II Adiutrix (95) and V Macedonica (96). Sent to congratulate Trajan on his adoption in 97, he remained in Upper Germany as tribune of XXII Primigenia, under L. *Iulius Ursus Servianus, husband of his sister Paulina. In 100 he married Trajan's great-niece *Sabina Augusta, a match arranged by *Pompeia Plotina, a devoted supporter. As Trajan's quaestor (101) he had to polish his Latin (his 'rustic accent' was mocked). He joined Trajan for the First Dacian War (101–2); was tribune of the *plebs*; then legate of I Minervia in the Second Dacian War (105–6), perhaps being praetor *in absentia*. He governed Lower Pannonia and was suffect consul (108). When Trajan's closest ally L. *Licinius Sura died, Hadrian took over as imperial speech-writer. In 112 he was archon at Athens, where he was honoured with a statue; its inscription (*ILS* 308 = Smallwood 109) confirms the career in the SHA. When the Parthian expedition began (October 113), he joined Trajan's staff, becoming governor of Syria at latest in 117; and was designated to a second consulship for 118. His position was thus very strong when Trajan died at Selinus in Cilicia on 8 August 117. The next day his adoption by Trajan was announced. A single aureus with the reverse HADRIANO TRAIANO CAESARI (*BM Coins, Rom. Emp.* 3. lxxxvi, 124) cannot dispel the rumours that Plotina had staged an adoption after Trajan died. Hadrian was disliked by his peers and had rivals, but the army recognized him; the senate had to follow suit. Plotina and the guard prefect Attianus took Trajan's body to Rome, while Hadrian faced the crisis in the east. He abandoned the new provinces (Armenia, Mesopotamia, and Assyria), dismissed Trajan's favourite *Lusius Quietus from his command in Judaea, and probably wintered at Nicomedia, leaving Catilius Severus as governor of Syria. A rising in Mauretania, no doubt provoked by the dismissal of Quietus, a Moor, was suppressed by Hadrian's friend Q. *Marcius Turbo. Britain was also disturbed; Q. *Pompeius Falco, governor of Lower Moesia, was probably sent to Britain to restore control when Hadrian reached the Danube in spring 118. He negotiated with the Roxolani and evidently evacuated the Transdanubian part of Lower Moesia annexed by Trajan. C. *Iulius Quadratus Bassus, governor of Dacia, had died campaigning; Hadrian summoned Turbo to govern part of Dacia, with Lower Pannonia. Dacia was divided into three provinces. Turbo, an equestrian, was given the same rank as a prefect of Egypt.

Meanwhile Attianus was active. Four ex-consuls, C. *Avidius Nigrinus, *Cornelius Palma Frontonianus, Publilius Celsus, and Lusius Quietus, were killed for plotting treason. When Hadrian reached Rome (9 July 118), the senate was hostile. He claimed not to have ordered the executions but took steps to win popularity. First came a posthumous triumph for Trajan's Parthian 'victory'. Crown-gold (*aurum coronarium*) was remitted for Italy and reduced for the provinces; a new, more generous, largess was disbursed to the *plebs*; overdue tax was cancelled on a vast scale; children supported by the *alimenta* received a bounty, bankrupt senators a subsidy; lavish gladiatorial games were held.

Hadrian, consul for the second time for 118, took as colleague *Pedanius Fuscus, husband of his niece Iulia: Fuscus was a likely heir. In 119 he was consul for the third and last time, and changed guard prefects. One new prefect was Septicius Clarus, to whom the younger Pliny had dedicated his Letters; C. *Suetonius Tranquillus, protégé of Pliny and Septicius' friend, became *ab epistulis*. The second prefect was Turbo: he was to take charge during Hadrian's absences, together with M. *Annius Verus, a senator of Spanish origin, linked by kinship to Hadrian. Verus, consul for the second time in 121 and urban prefect, was rewarded by a third consulship in 126. On 21 April 121, the birthday of the city, Hadrian inaugurated a vast temple of *Venus and Roma in the forum Romanum, designed by himself: one of many fields in which he dabbled and claimed expertise (see APOLLODORUS (7)). A poet, he boasted of his cithara-playing and singing, was expert in mathematics—and in military science. A favourite occupation was debating with sophists (see SECOND SOPHISTIC). *Favorinus yielded: 'who could contradict the Lord of Thirty Legions?' To the legions Hadrian now turned, leaving in 121 for the Rhineland. In Upper Germany and Raetia he erected a continuous palisade, Rome's first artificial *limes*, symbolizing his policy of peace within fixed frontiers. Legions and *auxilia*—with a few exceptions—were to remain in the same bases, local recruiting became prevalent. Hadrian set out to improve discipline and training— *Arrian was to dedicate his *Tactica* to Hadrian, registering the emperor's innovations. In 122 he crossed to Britain, taking his friend *Platorius Nepos, promoted from Lower Germany to Britain, and VI Victrix. The empress Sabina, the prefect Septicius, and Suetonius also went. An obscure imbroglio involving these three led to the men's dismissal. The main business was 'the wall to separate Romans and barbarians', as the SHA *vita* tersely puts it. The *wall of Hadrian was far more elaborate than any other *limes*: the bridge at the eastern end of the wall bore his name, Pons Aelius (Newcastle upon Tyne)—perhaps he designed it. From Britain he made for Spain, via southern Gaul, where he commemorated his horse in verse and Plotina with a basilica (she died early in 123). He wintered at Tarragona, calling a meeting of delegates from the peninsula: military service was on the agenda. Italica was not favoured with a visit, although— showing disdain—he granted it the status of *colonia*. Conscious perhaps of the coming 150th anniversary of 27 BC, Hadrian now shortened his names to Hadrianus Augustus: a claim to be a new founder of the empire.

A Moorish uprising was dealt with at this time, perhaps without his personal involvement. News from the east determined his next move. Perhaps visiting Cyrenaica *en route*—he resettled refugees from the Jewish uprising in a new city (Hadrianopolis)—his goal was the Euphrates, to confirm peace with Parthia. After an extensive tour of Asia Minor, he sailed (autumn 124) to Athens. There he was initiated in the Eleusinian *mysteries, visiting many other cities before his return to Rome, via Sicily, in summer 125. He stayed in Italy for three years, touring the Po valley for six months in 127; during this period he created four 'provinces' in Italy, each with a consular governor. The senate was displeased—Antoninus abolished them (see

ANTONINUS PIUS). In 128 he accepted the title *pater patriae*; then began his last tour with a visit to Africa and Mauretania, creating another *limes*; he lectured the troops at *Lambaesis, displaying his knowledge of manœuvres (Smallwood 328). Briefly at Rome in late summer, he crossed to Athens, where he wintered again, dedicated the *Olympieum and assumed the name Olympius. After participating in the mysteries (spring 129), he went via Ephesus to Syria, wintering at Antioch (1), visiting Palmyra in spring 130, and going through Arabia and Judaea to Egypt. In Judaea he founded a *colonia* at Jerusalem, Aelia Capitolina; and banned circumcision: measures to Hellenize the Jews—a fatal provocation. Hadrian was accompanied not only by Sabina but by a young Bithynian, *Antinous (2): his passion for the youth, embarrassing to many Romans, was a manifestation of his *Hellenism. After inspections of *Pompey's and *Alexander (3) the Great's tombs, debates in the Museum, and hunting in the desert, a voyage on the Nile ended in tragedy: Antinous was drowned. Hadrian's extreme grief was only assuaged by declaring his beloved a god (duly worshipped all over the empire) and naming a new city on the Nile (perhaps already planned) *Antinoöpolis. Hadrian went from Egypt to Lycia; by the winter of 131–2 he was back at Athens, to inaugurate the Olympieum and found the *Panhellenion, the culmination of his philhellenism.

In 132 the Jews rebelled under *Bar Kokhba, rapidly gaining control of considerable territory. Hadrian was briefly in Judaea, summoning his foremost general, Sex. *Iulius Severus, from Britain to crush the revolt. It lasted until 135; by then Hadrian had been back at Rome for a year, worn out and ill, staying mostly at his *Tibur villa. In 136 he turned his mind to the succession. The aged Servianus and his grandson Fuscus had aspirations; but Hadrian hated both and forced them to suicide. To universal surprise, he adopted one of the consuls of 136, as L. *Aelius Caesar. It may have been remorse for the killing of Nigrinus, Aelius' stepfather, in 118. But Aelius died suddenly on 1 January 138. Hadrian now chose Aurelius *Antoninus (Pius) and ensured the succession far ahead by causing him to adopt in turn his nephew Marcus (= Marcus *Aurelius) and Aelius' young son Lucius (= Lucius *Verus). Marcus, a favourite of Hadrian and grandson of Annius Verus, had been betrothed to Aelius' daughter. Hadrian died (10 July 138) with a quizzical verse address to his restless soul. He was buried in his new mausoleum (Castel Sant'Angelo) and deified by a reluctant senate. An intellectual and reformer (the Perpetual Edict, codified by Salvius *Iulianus, and the extension of Latin rights were major measures (see EDICT; IUS LATII)), by his provincial tours, amply commemorated on the coins, by his frontier policy, and promotion of Hellenism, he made a deep impact on the empire.

ANCIENT SOURCES Literary: Cass. Dio 69 (in epitome and excerpts) and SHA *Hadr.* (full but garbled), both mainly hostile, are the most important; Philostr. *VS*. Coins: *BM Coins, Rom. Emp.* 3. Inscriptions: Smallwood, *Docs. . . . Nerva*.
MODERN LITERATURE *PIR*[2] A 184; Syme, *Tacitus*, and *RP* 1–6; G. W. Bowersock, *Greek Sophists in the Roman Empire* (1969); H. Halfmann, *Itinera Principum* (1986); A. Birley, *Hadrian* (1997); M. Boatwright, *Hadrian and the Cities of the Roman Empire* (2000).   A. R. Bi.

Hadrian of Tyre See ADRIANUS.

Hadrian's Wall See WALL OF HADRIAN.

Hadrumetum (mod. Sousse), a seaport 96 km. (60 mi.) south of *Carthage founded by *Phoenicians probably in the 7th cent. BC. In 310 BC it was besieged by the army of *Agathocles of Syracuse, to whom it surrendered (Diod. Sic. 20. 17. 1–5). *Hannibal made Hadrumetum his base for the *Zama campaign. It joined the Romans in 146 BC, and was made a *civitas libera et immunis*. In 46 BC it opposed *Caesar; his plans for a colony there were probably carried out in 42–40. Under *Trajan it became the *Colonia Concordia Ulpia Traiana Frugifera*. Numerous figured mosaic floors from private houses testify to its prosperity in the middle and late empire, based on agriculture, horse-breeding, and shipping. Under *Diocletian's reorganization it became capital of the province of Byzacena. It was an important Christian centre; part of its extensive *catacombs is still accessible.

PECS 372; L. Foucher, *Hadrumetum* (1964), and *La Maison des masques à Sousse*, Notes et Documents NS 6 (1965). Mosaics: L. Foucher, *Inventaire des mosaïques: Sousse* (1960). Sculpture: N. de Chaisemartin, *Les sculptures romaines de Sousse et des sites environnants* (1987).
W. N. W.; B. H. W.; R. J. A. W.

Haemon (*Αἵμων*), (1) eponym of Haemonia, i.e. *Thessaly, and father of Thessalus (Rhianus fr. 25 Powell).

(2) Grandson of *Cadmus: leaving *Thebes (1) on account of homicide, he came to Athens, and his descendants went successively to *Rhodes and *Acragas.

(3) Son of the Theban *Creon (1): early epic seems to place him in the generation of *Oedipus: he was apparently killed by the *Sphinx (*Oedipodeia* fr. 1), and his son Maeon was one of the Thebans who ambushed *Tydeus (*Il.* 4. 394). The tragedians place him later, as the fiancé or lover of *Antigone (1).

(4) The same name is given to other minor figures in the *Iliad* (4. 296, 17. 467).
A. L. B.

Hagesander, Athenodorus, and **Polydorus,** Rhodian sculptors, active between 50 BC and AD 25. Pliny, *HN*. 36. 37 f. mentions them as the authors of the *Laocoön, found in Rome in 1516 and immensely influential thereafter. In 1959 more groups signed by them were discovered at *Spelunca. The groups all probably feature Odysseus: dragging Ajax's body, trying to steal the *Palladium, fighting *Scylla (1), and blinding Polyphemus. Other replicas show that the trio were essentially high-class copyists, adapting Hellenistic baroque compositions for Roman patrons. Yet while most scholars accept a late republican or early imperial date for them, opinion remains divided as to whether they are the men known from Rhodian inscriptions of *c*.50 and 42 BC or homonymous descendants.

G. E. Lessing, *Laokoon* (1766); A. F. Stewart, *Greek Sculpture* (1990), 96 ff., 309 ff., figs. 732 ff.
A. F. S.

Hagnon See AMPHIPOLIS; FOUNDERS, CITY; THERAMENES.

Haliartus, Boeotian city on the southern littoral of Lake *Copais below Mt. *Helicon. Mentioned in the *Iliad* for its meadows, it was inhabited from the early Helladic period until the Byzantine. In 395 BC it formed, together with Lebadea and *Coronea, one unit of the Boeotian Confederacy (see BOEOTIA; FEDERAL STATES). The Spartan *Lysander lost the first major battle of the *Corinthian War there in 395 BC. Haliartus later supported *Thebes (1) during its hegemony. C. Lucretius Gallus destroyed the city in 171 BC during the Third Macedonian War; Athens received its territory. It was uninhabited in *Strabo's day; *Pausanias (3) none the less saw a rustic village.

J. Fossey, *Topography and Population of Ancient Boeotia* (1988), 301 ff.; J. Bintliff and A. Snodgrass, *Antiquity* 1988, 61 ff.; J. Bintliff, in G. Barker and J. Lloyd (eds.), *Roman Landscapes* (1991).
J. Bu.

Halicarnassus, Greek city of *Caria commanding the sea-route between *Cos and the Asiatic mainland. Founded *c*.900 BC from *Troezen in the Argolid, it is said by the Halicarnassian *Herodotus to have been one of the cities participating in the *Dorian festival at Triopion (see TRIOPAS); but in Classical times its culture was Ionic, and a high proportion of its citizens had Carian names. It was the capital of a minor dynasty which included *Artemisia (1). It joined the *Delian League and served as an Athenian naval station after the allies revolted in 412. *Mausolus, dynast and *satrap of the Persian province of Caria, made his capital at Halicarnassus *c*.370 and incorporated into it a number of non-Greek ('Lelegian') villages by *synoecism; intensive field survey (Radt, see bibliog. below) has revealed the density of settlement at these Lelegian hilltop sites. Thereafter, with its great wall circuit, closed harbour, dockyard, public buildings, and the funerary temple of the dynasty (the *Mausoleum), Halicarnassus was one of the spectacular cities of the ancient world. Captured by *Alexander (3) the Great after an arduous siege in 334, it was in turn subject to Mausolus' sister *Ada (who 'adopted' Alexander), Philoxenus, Asander, *Antigonus (1), *Lysimachus, and the Ptolemies (see PTOLEMY (1)) (until 197), then in 129 came under Roman rule.

Strabo 14. 2. 16–17. C. T. Newton, *Halicarnassus, Cnidus and Branchidae* (1863); G. E. Bean and J. M. Cook, *BSA* 1955, 85 ff.; W. Radt, *MDAI(I)* Beiheft 3 (1970); G. E. Bean, *Turkey Beyond the Maeander*, 2nd edn. (1980), chs. 9–11; Cook, *CAH* 3²/1 (1982), 751 f.; M. Mellink, *CAH* 4² (1988), 223 f.; S. Hornblower, *Mausolus* (1982), and *CAH* 6² (1994), 223.
J. M. C.; S. H.

Halieis A small town (inhabited 7th to 4th cent. BC, and then abandoned) on Porto Kheli Bay near the tip of the Argolic peninsula. Excavations show city walls, an acropolis, an orthogonal plan (from the 6th cent. BC), private houses and a submerged extramural sanctuary of *Apollo. At times at least independent and led by Tirynthian refugees (see TIRYNS), it was occupied by Athens in the *Peloponnesian War.

M. Jameson, *Hesp.* 1969, and *Scientific American* 1974; T. Boyd and W. Rudolph, *Hesp.* 1978; M. Jameson, C. N. Runnels, and T. H. van Andel, *A Greek Countryside: The Southern Argolid from Prehistory to the Present Day* (1994), see index under 'Halieis'.
M. H. J.

Halimous, a small Attic *deme on the coast south of *Phaleron. The City *Thesmophoria included a procession to the sanctuary of *Demeter at Halimous, which also had sanctuaries of *Aphrodite, *Dionysus, and *Heracles. Deme affairs are thrown into lurid light by Demosthenes 57, the appeal of a former demarch against being expelled from the deme and hence disenfranchised. The historian *Thucydides (2) was a member of this deme.
R. G. O.

Halirrhothius, an Attic hero, son of *Poseidon. He raped *Aglaurus' daughter Alcippe and was therefore killed by her father Ares, thus precipitating the latter's trial by the *Areopagus court. A less well-known tradition brings him into the context of the rivalry between *Athena and *Poseidon: sent by Poseidon to chop down Athena's olive-trees, he accidentally lopped off his own leg and died.

Kearns, *Heroes of Attica* 144–5.
E. Ke.

Haloa An Attic, perhaps exclusively Eleusinian (see ELEUSIS), festival of *Demeter and *Dionysus (and perhaps *Poseidon) conducted largely by women on the 26th day of the winter month of Posideon. *Haloia* probably derives from *halōs*, in the sense of 'worked land, garden plot' rather than the unseasonal 'threshing-floor'. Records at Eleusis of the purchase of a large quantity of firewood for the Haloa suggest that a bonfire, as well as manipulation of sexual symbols, ribaldry, drinking and feasting, encouraged revivification at a dead time of year.

A. Brumfield, *The Attic Cults of Demeter* (1981), 104–31. M. H. J.

haltēres (ἁλτῆρες) were pieces of iron or stone used by Greek long jumpers. Shaped and gripped like modern dumb-bells, they normally weighed between 1.4 and 2.3 kilos (3–5 lb.). The long jump was a standing jump without a run-up: while holding the *haltēres*, the athlete would probably throw his arms forwards and upwards on take-off, and then downwards and backwards when in mid-air, hoping thereby to increase the distance of the jump (cf. Arist. *IA* 705ᵃ). See ATHLETICS. F. A. W; R. L. H.; S. J. I.

Halys (the 'Salt river', so called from the salt springs in its upper course), the longest river in *Asia Minor (about 1,050 km. (650 miles) in length), now called Kızılırmak, the 'Red river'. It rises near the Armenian border and flows in a great loop from south-west to north-east to join the *Euxine west of Amisus. In the time of *Croesus it divided the Lydian kingdom from the Persian empire; hence 'Croesus by crossing the Halys destroyed a great empire'. There was a bridge across it in the 5th cent. (Hdt. 1. 75), the position of which has not been conclusively determined. Herodotus (5. 52), probably in error, made the Royal Road from *Sardis to the Cilician Gates cross the Halys.

W. M. C.; G. E. B.

Hama, an ancient city of north Syria, which became the centre of one of the Aramaean kingdoms of the early first millennium BC. Destroyed by Sargon II of Assyria at the end of the 8th cent., it revived as Epiphaneia in the Hellenistic period, but never rivalled its neighbour *Apamaea-Orontes.

J. D. Hamkins, *Reallexikon der Assyriologie* 4 (1972), 67–70, 'Hamath'. J. and J. C. Balty, *Apamée antique* (1979). J.-F. S.

Hamilcar (1) (*RE* 1), Carthaginian *basileus*—uncertain whether king or suffete (see CARTHAGE (history), § 3). A Magonid, whose mother, according to Herodotus, was Greek. He leagued with Terillus of Himera and *Anaxilas (1), and probably with *Xerxes (Diod. Sic. 11. 1. 4), landed in Sicily (480) to crush *Theron and *Gelon, but was defeated by them at *Himera (near Termini Imerese) and killed. According to Carthaginian tradition, he immolated himself to the gods at the moment of defeat.

D. Asheri, *CAH* 4² (1988), ch. 16. B. M. C.

Hamilcar (2) (*RE* 7) **Barca** (probably = Semitic *Baraq*, lightning), father of *Hannibal, took over the command of the Carthaginian fleet in 247 BC and ravaged the coast of Bruttium (see BRUTTII). Landing in Sicily, he seized Heircte, near Palermo, where he held the Romans at bay by frequent skirmishes, and raided the Italian coast as far as *Cumae. In 244 he seized *Eryx but was unable to raise the siege of Drepanum. After the Carthaginian defeat at the battle of the Aegates isles in 241 he negotiated the peace terms and then resigned his command. When attempts to suppress the subsequent revolt of the mercenaries in the service of Carthage failed, he was appointed to replace his enemy *Hanno (2) as commander (240). A bitter struggle, with appalling atrocities on both sides, ended in 238 or 237, when Hamilcar and Hanno were eventually persuaded to co-operate. After the end of the mercenary war he was sent to *Spain, taking his 9-year-old son Hannibal with him. Starting from *Gades, he conquered southern and south-eastern Spain and founded a city at Acra Leuce (?Alicante). In 231 Rome sent an embassy to investigate

the situation; Hamilcar replied that the aim of his conquests was to secure money with which to pay the indemnity for the First Punic War. He died in 229, drowned while retreating from the siege of Helice (?Elche). Although the story that he made Hannibal swear an oath never to be a friend of Rome is not incredible, it does not follow that Hamilcar was himself planning war with Rome. But after the loss of Sicily and *Sardinia he wanted to add Spain's mineral wealth and manpower to Carthage's resources, thus enabling it to fight a new war effectively when war came.

H. H. Scullard, *CAH* 7²/2 (1989), 563–8, 8² (1989), 21–5; Walbank, *HCP* 1. 119–23, 140–52; R. M. Errington, *Latomus* 1972, 25 ff.

H. H. S; J. Br.

Hannibal (*RE* 8), Carthaginian general. He was born in 247 BC, the eldest son of *Hamilcar (2) Barca. After making Hannibal swear an oath never to be a friend of Rome, Hamilcar took him to Spain in 237, where he stayed during the commands of both his father and his brother-in-law *Hasdrubal (1), marrying a Spaniard from Castulo. In 221 he assumed the supreme command in Spain on the death of Hasdrubal (confirmed by the popular assembly at Carthage) and reverted to his father's policy by attacking the Olcades, who lived on the upper Anas (Guadiana). In 220 he advanced beyond the Tagus (Tajo) as far as the Durius (Duero), defeating the Vaccaei and the Carpetani. Regarding Rome's alliance with *Saguntum (Sagunto) as a threat to Carthage's position in Spain, he decided to defy her, and put pressure on Saguntum. He rejected a Roman protest, and after consulting Carthage began the siege of Saguntum in spring 219, knowing that war with Rome would result, and took the city eight months later.

Hannibal had decided, without waiting for a Roman declaration of war, to take the initiative by invading Italy; probably less with the object of destroying Rome than of detaching her allies (an expectation warranted by Carthage's experience in her wars with the Greeks) and so weakening her that she would give up Sicily, Sardinia, and Corsica, and undertake not to molest Carthage's North African and Spanish empire. He left his capital, *Carthago Nova (mod. Cartagena) in May 218, with a professional army of 90,000 infantry and 12,000 cavalry (Iberians, Libyans, and Numidians) and *elephants, leaving his brother Hasdrubal to hold Spain; and subdued, regardless of cost, the area between the Ebro and the Pyrenees. He remained there until September, presumably in the expectation of meeting and destroying the army of the consul P. *Cornelius Scipio (1) before invading Italy. Then, with 50,000 infantry, 9,000 cavalry, and 37 elephants, he marched to the Rhône, avoided battle with Scipio (belatedly *en route* to Spain), and continued towards the Alps, which he crossed in about fifteen days, with great difficulty and enormous loss of life. The route he took remains a matter for conjecture: he seems to have marched up the valley of the Isère, past Grenoble, and then perhaps took the difficult Col du Clapier pass, having missed the easier Mt. Cenis pass. He arrived in the area of Turin about the end of October, defeated P. Cornelius Scipio (who had returned to Italy) in a cavalry skirmish at the Ticinus (Ticino) near Pavia, and then, having been joined by many Gauls, won the first major battle of the war at the *Treb(b)ia, a little to the west of Placentia (Piacenza), against the combined forces of Scipio and Ti. Sempronius Longus (end of December). In May 217 Hannibal crossed the Apennines (losing an eye in the passage of the Arno), ravaged Etruria, and with the help of early-morning fog, trapped the consul C. *Flaminius (1) in an ambush at Lake *Trasimene. Flaminius and 15,000 men

Hanno

were killed and 10,000 captured. Hannibal proceeded to Apulia, and thence to Samnium and Campania, while the dictator Q. *Fabius Maximus Verrucosus embarked on his strategy of following Hannibal but avoiding a pitched battle. Hannibal returned to Apulia (eluding Fabius) for the winter. In 216 he inflicted a devastating defeat on both consuls, who commanded over-strength armies, at *Cannae; only 14,500 Romans and allies escaped death or captivity. After each battle he dismissed the Italian prisoners to their homes while holding the Romans (see e.g. Livy 22. 58).

Cannae led to the defection of southern Italy, including Capua (S. Maria Capua Vetere), the second city in Italy, and part of Samnium; but central Italy and all the Latin colonies remained loyal to Rome, and with Roman commanders avoiding another pitched battle, Hannibal achieved little in the following three years (215–213), although he concluded an alliance with *Philip (3) V of Macedon (215), and helped to bring about the revolt of *Syracuse (214). He received no assistance from Spain, where Hasdrubal was on the defensive, and little from Carthage. He failed to gain control of a port, despite attacks on *Cumae, *Neapolis (Naples), *Puteoli (Pozzuoli) and *Tarentum (Taranto), and his persistent assaults on *Nola were repulsed; several towns were recaptured by Rome, notably *Casilinum (Capua) and *Arpi (near Foggia). In 212, however, he captured Tarentum by stealth, although the citadel remained in Roman control, and this was followed by the defection of three neighbouring Greek cities. In 211, in an attempt to relieve the siege of Capua (begun the previous year), Hannibal marched on Rome itself but failed to force the Romans to withdraw troops from Capua, and returned to the south; soon afterwards Capua fell, its fall being preceded by that of Syracuse. Hannibal was now being pressed ever further south—from 212–11 onwards, with one possible exception, he spent every winter in the extreme south of Italy—and suffered a further blow in 209 when Fabius recaptured Tarentum. In 208, however, he caught both consuls in an ambush in Lucania; one, M. *Claudius Marcellus (1), was killed immediately, his colleague fatally wounded. In Spain, P. *Cornelius Scipio Africanus had captured Carthago Nova (209) and defeated Hasdrubal at Baecula (Bailen) (208). Hasdrubal slipped out of Spain, but in 207 his defeat and death on the *Metaurus (Metauro) dashed Hannibal's hopes of receiving reinforcements. Hannibal was now confined to Bruttium, where he stayed until 203—in 205 he could not prevent Scipio recapturing *Locri Epizephyrii—when he was recalled to Africa to defend Carthage. After abortive peace negotiations with Scipio, he was decisively defeated at *Zama (202), and successfully urged his countrymen to make peace on Rome's terms.

Hannibal now involved himself in domestic affairs; as suffete (chief magistrate) in 196 he introduced constitutional reforms to weaken the power of the oligarchs, and reorganized the state's finances so that the war indemnity could be paid to Rome without levying additional taxes. His enemies reacted by alleging to Rome that Hannibal was intriguing with *Antiochus (3) III of Syria. When a Roman commission of enquiry arrived, Hannibal fled, ultimately reaching Antiochus (195). He urged Antiochus to go to war with Rome; he asked for a fleet and an army with which to stir Carthage to revolt, or, failing that, to land in Italy. He accompanied Antiochus to Greece in 192, and advised him to bring Philip V into the war and invade Italy. In 190, bringing a fleet from Syria to the Aegean, he was defeated by the Rhodians off Side. The peace agreed between Rome and Antiochus provided for his surrender; he fled to Crete and then to *Prusias (1)

I of Bithynia, whom he supported in his war with *Eumenes (2) II of Pergamum. In 183 or 182 T. *Quinctius Flamininus persuaded Prusias to surrender Hannibal, a fate which he preempted by taking poison.

Hannibal has been widely acknowledged, in both antiquity and modern times, as one of the greatest generals in history. He brought to perfection the art of combining infantry and cavalry, he understood the importance of military intelligence and reconnaissance and he commanded the unflagging loyalty of his troops. But he failed against Rome because all the assumptions upon which his policy and his strategy were based—that huge numbers of Gauls would follow him to Italy, that Carthage would recover the command of the sea and reinforce him from Africa and that Hasdrubal would bring him reinforcements from Spain, and, above all, that Rome's confederation would break up following Rome's defeat in the field—proved fallacious. Roman propaganda accused Hannibal of perfidy and cruelty; as far as the latter charge is concerned, although he could be chivalrous at times, his attitude to those who resisted him was uncompromising. But the record of Rome's treatment of defectors makes far grimmer reading.

H. H. Scullard and J. Briscoe, *CAH* 8² (1989), 32–79; Walbank, *HCP* 1–3; Briscoe, *Comm.* 31–33, 34–37, see indexes; G. Charles-Picard, *Hannibal* (1967); J. F. Lazenby, *Hannibal's War* (1978); Caven, *Punic Wars*, chs. 8–20; J. Seibert, *Hannibal* (1993): exhaustive German survey of problems and bibliography.   B. M. C.

Hanno (1) One of the Greek *periploi, a wonder-journey purporting to be a translation of a Punic inscription, recounts the adventures of a large expedition southwards along the Atlantic coast of Morocco, under the leadership of this Carthaginian, in about 480 BC. It records the foundation of settlements such as Mogador and Agadir, but the topographical detail becomes obscure after Lixus, and there is controversy over how far the continuing voyage is based on real and discoverable detail. Older accounts had Hanno reach Senegal and Sierra Leone, and the colourful detail includes a high volcanic peak, the 'Chariot of the Gods', and an encounter with gorillas.

TEXTS *GGM* 1. 1–14; text and trans. ed. J. Blomqvist (1979).
COMMENT J. Ramin, *Le Périple d'Hannon/The Periplus of Hanno* (1976).   N. P.

Hanno (2) (*RE* 14), called 'the Great' in later sources, led the anti-Barcid faction at Carthage. He was the Carthaginian commander in Africa during the latter years of the First Punic War; for his part in the Mercenary War (see HAMILCAR (2)). Livy's assertion that he opposed Hasdrubal's request that *Hannibal should join him in Spain is unhistorical (Hannibal had not left Spain), but Livy's claim that Hanno proposed that Hannibal should be ordered to withdraw from *Saguntum and be surrendered to Rome may contain a germ of truth. He urged the making of peace with Rome after the battle of *Cannae. He reappears at the end of the war when he took part in the peace negotiations after *Zama. Some see him as the representative of the landed nobility who stood for a policy of expansion in Africa rather than foreign conquests in the interests of the merchant class.

Walbank, *HCP* 1. 118.   J. Br.

harbours The earliest man-made harbour facilities in the Mediterranean region were the riverside quays of Mesopotamia and Egypt, for which records go back to at least the second millennium BC. Maritime installations probably began to appear around the Levantine coast in the early iron age, but the earliest securely datable harbour-works are the late 6th-cent. breakwater and ship-sheds of *Polycrates (1), tyrant of *Samos (Hdt. 3. 60). The development of specialized naval and merchant vessels, and a gradual increase in overseas trade, meant that quays and docks of increasing size and complexity were required in the Classical and Hellenistic periods.

Early construction techniques made the most of natural features such as sheltered bays and headlands, as at *Cnidus. Exposed shores were protected with breakwaters and moles, like that at Samos. The development in Roman times of concrete which could set underwater enabled ambitious offshore constructions to be attempted, notably *Caesarea (2) in Palestine. *Lighthouses, warehouses, and colonnades (see STOA) of some magnificence were common features in Hellenistic and Roman times.

Military harbours often featured fortifications. Narrow entrances, towers, and booms or chains were used to control access from the sea, with walls to guard against attack from the land. In the Classical period Athens, *Megara, and *Corinth were joined to their respective harbours by *long walls. The ship-sheds at *Carthage seem to have been placed on an island in the middle of the inner harbour, providing excellent security.

Ancient harbours were often very cosmopolitan places, attracting travellers and traders from far afield and having a high proportion of foreign residents. The *Piraeus was renowned for its large metic population (see METICS), *Alexandria (1) had its Jewish quarter, and the epigraphic evidence from *Delos attests the presence of numerous Italian and eastern merchants. Their working populations would have included stevedores, lightermen, fishermen, pilots, and clerks. They might also be the haunts of prostitutes and thieves. Large harbours were important sources of revenue (see PORTORIA) for ancient states, directly from harbour fees and customs duties, as well as indirectly from sales taxes and the profits of merchants. See ARCHAEOLOGY, UNDERWATER; NAVIES; SHIPS.

D. J. Blackman, *International Journal of Nautical Archaeology* 1982; A. M. McCann, *The Roman Port and Fishery of Cosa* (1987); R. L. Vann (ed.), *Caesarea Papers, JRA* Suppl. 5 (1992). P. de S.

Harmodius See ARISTOGITON.

harmost (ἁρμοστής) the title of a Spartan military governor or commander abroad, first attested in 412 BC (Thuc. 8. 5. 2) but probably already used at *Heraclea (4) Trachinia in 426 (Thuc. 3. 92). Harmosts became common in occupied cities after the fall of Athens in 404, occasionally with wider commands, e.g. *Thibron (1) and Euxenos in Asia Minor (Xen. *Hell.* 3. 1. 4, 4. 2. 5), Teleutias in Chalcidice (ibid. 5. 2. 18 and 37). One is attested in *Cythera (*IG* 5. 1. 937, ? 4th cent. BC); but it is unlikely that such officials regularly governed the towns of the *perioikoi.

H. W. Parke, *JHS* 1930, 37 ff.; P. Cartledge, *Agesilaos* (1987), 92 ff.
W. G. F.

Harpalus (d. 324 BC), Macedonian noble and boyhood friend of *Alexander (3) the Great, was exiled during the dynastic troubles of 337/6 and enjoyed high favour after Alexander's accession. He deserted the expedition shortly before *Issus (333) but was reinstated in 331 and placed over the central treasuries of the empire. Based at *Babylon, he controlled the finances of the central satrapies and lived in regal style. On Alexander's return to the west he fled first to Cilicia and then to mainland Greece, where his presence was a formidably disruptive factor. Admitted into Athens in summer 324 he was arrested and his monies

sequestered on the Acropolis. He escaped amidst accusations of bribery (which eventually ruined *Demosthenes (2) and *Demades) and took his mercenary army to Crete, where he was murdered by his lieutenant, *Thibron (2).

Berve, *Alexanderreich* 2, no. 143; Heckel, *Marshals* 213 ff.; E. Badian, *JHS* 1961, 16 ff.; A. B. Bosworth, *Conquest and Empire* (1988). A. B. B.

Harpalyce (1), a mythical Thracian princess brought up by her father as a warrior. On one occasion she saved his life in battle, but when finally he died she became a brigand, and was eventually caught and killed. She received heroic honours in the form of a mock battle at her tomb (Hyg. *Fab.* 193).

(2) daughter of *Clymenus (2a) of Argos, given in marriage to Neleus' son Alastor but raped by her father, to whom in revenge she served up her younger brother at a feast. She was thereupon transformed into a bird (Parth. 13, from *Euphorion (2)).
E. Ke.

Harpocrates See HORUS.

Harpocration, Valerius, of *Alexandria (1), lexicographer. He is perhaps to be identified among the tutors of the emperor *Verus (SHA *Verus* 2. 5), and his date is established by the mention of him in a papyrus letter (*POxy.* 2192) of the 2nd cent. AD, which also shows that he was in touch with an intellectual circle in *Oxyrhynchus. His *Collection of Fine Passages* (Συλλογὴ ἀνθηρῶν) is not extant; the title suggests a similarity to *Apuleius' *Florida*. His *Lexicon of the Ten Orators* is preserved in an abridgement and a longer form. It is designed mainly as an aid to reading, not to composition in Atticist Greek. The contents are words (including proper names) and phrases, mainly from the orators, in alphabetical order, generally assigned to their sources, with explanations of points of interest or difficulty. Some entries deal with non-oratorical literature, and Harpocration quotes nearly every important Greek writer, from Homer onwards. He gives valuable information on many topics, mainly religious, legal, constitutional, and social. His sources include scholarly works of the imperial age, e.g. some by *Didymus (1), and earlier writings by historians and antiquarians, e.g. *Hecataeus (1), *Hellanicus, *Theopompus (3), and *Ister, as well as Hellenistic monographs by *Aristophanes of *Byzantium and *Aristarchus (2). The Aristotelian *Athenian Constitution* (see ATHENAION POLITEIA) is also regularly cited.

EDITIONS I. Bekker (1833); W. Dindorf (1853); J. J. Keaney (1991).
N. G. W.

Harpyiae, Harpies, 'snatchers', personify the demonic force of storms and are always represented as winged women. They serve to explain the traceless disappearance of *Odysseus (*Od.* 1. 241, 14. 371) or the sudden death of the daughters of *Pandareos (20. 66–78). Their names—Podarge (*Il.* 16. 149–51) or Aello and Okypete (Hes. *Theog.* 267)—reflect their speed. Usually, as in Hesiod, there are only two, but later sources—perhaps under influence of the theatre—sometimes mention three Harpies or leave their number unspecified. The fast messenger of the gods, *Iris, is their sister. The main role of the Harpies in myth occurs in the context of the *Argonauts: they plague the Thracian king *Phineus by snatching away his food before being chased off by the sons of *Boreas. The episode already occurs in *Hesiod (fr. 150–6 M–W) and becomes very popular in Hellenistic times: *Apollonius (1) of Rhodes (2. 234–434) relates it in detail.

L. Kahil, *LIMC* 4. 1 (1988), 444–50; 4.2, 266–71. J. N. B.

haruspices, *Etruscan diviners. The term is composed of *haru-*

Hasdrubal

(*hari-*, *aru-*), etymology uncertain, and the suffix *-spex*, 'one who inspects'; in the bilingual inscription *CIL* 11. 6363 from Pisaurum (Pesaro) Etruscan *netśvis* seems to correspond to Latin *haruspex*. The Etruscan word for the general concept of 'priest' is unknown; the haruspices are represented as wearing the conical cap, similar to the *pilleus* (*apex*), in Rome the headgear of *flamines* (see FLAMEN). In Roman sources the haruspices appear as interpreters of *fulgura* (thunderbolts), *ostenta* (unusual happenings), and above all *exta* (entrails, especially liver). They were members of the Etruscan aristocracy (to be distinguished from private itinerant diviners, *vicani haruspices*, Cic. *Div.* 1. 132). When need arose they were on the senate's orders called from Etruria to explain prodigies and *portents, especially when thunderbolts struck public places; they would give a formal reply, *responsum*, and propose a remedy (Cic. *Leg.* 2. 21; *Har. Resp.*; *Nat. D.* 2. 11, where the characterization of the haruspices as barbarous should not be pressed). They always appear as a group, and this presupposes some sort of organization. The inscription *CIL* 6. 32439 (end of the republic or beginning of the empire) is the first document attesting the college of 60 haruspices; it may go back to the mid-2nd cent. when the senate decreed that sons of Etruscan nobles (*principes*) should be trained in the *disciplina* (Cic. *Div.* 1. 42; Val. Max. 1. 1. 1). The college or *ordo* (presided over by an official called *magister haruspicum*, *haruspex maximus*, or *primarius*) was reorganized under *Claudius; the haruspices and their doctrine were placed under the supervision of the pontiffs (Tac. *Ann.* 11. 15). Individual haruspices were often attached to Roman magistrates and, later, emperors; and there also existed public haruspices in various Roman cities. With *Constantine I began the persecution of the haruspices; after a short revival under *Julian they were banned by *Theodosius (2) I (*Cod. Theod.* 16. 10. 12; AD 392), though their art lingered for a long time. See also RELIGION, ETRUSCAN; TAGES.

C. O. Thulin, *Die etruskische Disciplin* (1905–6, 1909; repr. 1968); L. Bonfante, *Etruscan Dress* (1975); A. J. Pfiffig, *Religio Etrusca* (1975); M. Torelli, *Elogia Tarquiniensia* (1975); G. Cresci Marrone and G. Mennella, *Pisaurum 1* (1984); L. B. Van der Meer, *The Bronze Liver of Piacenza* (1987); A. Maggiani, in *Secondo Congresso Internazionale Etrusco* (1989); S. Montero, *Política y adivinación en el bajo imperio romano: Emperadores y harúspices* (1991). J. L.

Hasdrubal (1) (*RE* 5), a popular leader in *Carthage and son-in-law of *Hamilcar (2) Barca, whom he accompanied to Spain in 237 BC. At some point he returned to Africa to suppress a Numidian uprising. He succeeded to the command in *Spain on Hamilcar's death in 229 and achieved more by diplomacy than by force of arms. He married a Spanish princess and founded *Carthago Nova. In 226–5 he concluded the 'Ebro Treaty' with Rome, which specified that Carthaginian armed forces were not to cross the river Ebro. He was assassinated in 221. The statements of Q. *Fabius Pictor that he tried to overthrow the Carthaginian constitution and acted in Spain as a ruler independent of the Carthaginian government are improbable.

H. H. Scullard, *CAH* 8² (1989), 25–32; Walbank, *HCP* 1. 167–72, 310–11; R. M. Errington, *Latomus* 1972, 34 ff. H. H. S.; J. Br.

Hasdrubal (2) (*RE* 7), son of *Hamilcar (2) Barca and younger brother of *Hannibal, who left him in command in Spain in 218 BC. He crossed the Ebro and inflicted losses on the Roman troops who had defeated *Hanno (2), but retreated south again. In 217 he launched a combined land and sea attack north of the Ebro which led to his defeat at the mouth of that river. Uncertainty surrounds the years that followed, but it seems that in 214 Has-

drubal was recalled to Africa to deal with a revolt by *Syphax. Back in Spain, he led one of the three armies whose pursuit of Cn. *Cornelius Scipio Calvus led to the latter's death in 211. In 208 he was defeated by the young *Scipio Africanus at Baecula (Bailen), north of the Baetis, but he escaped with most of his army, crossed the Pyrenees, and reached Gaul and the route to Italy. Unexpectedly faced by the armies of both C. *Claudius Nero and M. *Livius Salinator he decided to avoid a battle and instead to attempt to march down the *via Flaminia to meet Hannibal. He was pursued, and in 207 at the battle of the *Metaurus he was defeated and killed.

J. Briscoe, *CAH* 8² (1989), 55–60; Walbank, *HCP* 2. 267–74. J. Br.

Hasdrubal (3) (*RE* 10), son of Gisgo, commanded a Carthaginian army in Spain from 214 until 206 BC. In 211 he and *Mago (2) brought about the defeat and death of P. *Cornelius Scipio (1) and then joined *Hasdrubal (2) in pursuit of Cn. *Cornelius Scipio Calvus. In 207 he was forced to retreat from his base at Orongis (mod. Jaen) to *Gades, and in 206 he and Mago were decisively defeated by P. *Cornelius Scipio Africanus at Ilipa, north of Seville. He fled to *Syphax in Africa, where they met Scipio Africanus. Scipio's hope of securing Syphax's support was thwarted when Syphax married Hasdrubal's daughter *Sophonisba. In 204 Hasdrubal was commander-in-chief in Africa and forced Scipio to raise the siege of *Utica. In spring 203 Scipio burnt the camps of Hasdrubal and Syphax, and though Hasdrubal raised new forces and persuaded Syphax to rejoin the conflict, Scipio defeated them at the battle of the Great Plains. Shortly before the battle of *Zama Hasdrubal committed suicide, having, it seems, been convicted of treason.

J. Briscoe, *CAH* 8² (1989), 59–60, 63; Walbank, *HCP* 2. 296–304, 426–33. J. Br.

Hasdrubal (4) (*RE* 13) commanded the Carthaginian forces defeated by *Masinissa in 151/0 BC. Although condemned to death at Carthage, he assembled a rebel army. After the Roman declaration of war he was recalled to assume command. He held out against the Romans in the countryside (149/8) and then moved to Carthage (147). He executed Roman prisoners and prominent Carthaginians who opposed him. When the situation became hopeless he tried unsuccessfully to persuade P. *Cornelius Scipio Aemilianus to spare Carthage, but eventually surrendered to him, and spent the rest of his life in unchained captivity in Italy. His wife, however, killed herself and their children. Polybius (38. 7–8) presents a hostile portrait of him.

Astin, *Scipio*, see index; Walbank, *HCP* 3. 695–8. J. Br.

Hasmoneans A family of Jewish high priests and kings, descended from Mattathias, the father of Judas Maccabeus (see MACCABEES). Prominent between 165 and 37 BC, they ruled *Judaea between 142 and 63, creating a Jewish state of dimensions comparable to David's kingdom and anticipating Herod's. Josephus derives the family name (absent in 1 and 2 Maccabees) from the great-grandfather of Mattathias. They belonged to the priestly house of J(eh)oarib, and regarded Modein, near Lydda, as their ancestral home.

Hasmonean ascendancy was based first on military success against *Seleucid armies and then on effective diplomacy with monarchs and pretenders. Jonathan, the youngest of the five sons of Mattathias, came to terms with the general Bacchides, raised an army in support of *Demetrius (10) I, and thus recovered Jerusalem, leaving only the Akra fortress in the hands of Jewish 'Hellenizers' (see HELLENISM). When ambassadors to *Sparta brought back letters attesting Jewish kinship with the Spartans, this was a statement that Hasmonean Judaea was part of the Greek world. Jonathan was formally installed as high priest, and so, with the approval of *Alexander (10) Balas, was his brother and successor, Simon (142–135 BC). Judaea was now offered remission from tribute by *Demetrius (11) II, claiming an independent chronological era, and the right of coinage (probably not exercised). The Akra surrendered and Jerusalem was triumphantly reunited; the city was enlarged within a now complete circumvallation. Simon's third son, John Hyrcanus (135–104 BC), succeeding after his father's murder, was challenged on his accession by *Antiochus (7) VII (Sidetes), who besieged Jerusalem. The two soon came to terms, however, and Hyrcanus joined the Parthian expedition of Sidetes. Hyrcanus also renewed the treaties which his predecessors had made between the Hasmonean state and Rome. His bronze coinage (now securely attributed) appears to be the dynasty's first issue. Hyrcanus' son Aristobulus I (104–103 BC) abandoned the traditionalist reluctance to combine kingship with high priesthood and assumed the kingly diadem. The coins of Aristobulus' brother Alexander Jannaeus (104/3–76) carry open monarchic symbols, and inscriptions in Greek and *Aramaic as well as Hebrew.

The reign of Jannaeus' chosen successor, his widow, queen Salome Alexandra (76–67), marked the end of Hasmonean power. Her two sons, Hyrcanus II (assisted by the Idumaean *Antipater (6)) and Aristobulus fell out over the succession, but in 63 BC *Pompey made Hyrcanus ethnarch, though the former Hasmonean kingdom was stripped of its extensions and administered by Rome. Aristobulus was imprisoned after appearing in Pompey's triumph. A succession of failed revolts during the 50s and 40s on behalf of Aristobulus or of one or other of his sons culminated in Caesar's liberation from captivity of Aristobulus who died shortly afterwards. In the Parthian invasion of 40 BC Hyrcanus was captured and, after mutilation to disqualify him for the priesthood, he was replaced by a son of Aristobulus, who issued the last Hasmonean coins under the Hebrew-Greek name Mattathias Antigonus. He was beheaded on Antony's orders when Jerusalem fell to *Herod (1) in 37. Finally, by marrying Mariamme, granddaughter of both Hyrcanus and Aristobulus, Herod united the two warring branches of the Hasmoneans and continued a line which was remembered with pride in Palestine. The historian *Josephus was later to boast matrilineal Hasmonean descent (Vita 2).

Notwithstanding the dynasty's auspicious beginnings, its rulers met with opposition from important groups in Jewry. Josephus insists that John Hyrcanus was supremely favoured by God; but the Babylonian *Talmud represents the influential *Pharisees as chiding him bitterly for combining the high priesthood with temporal power. His son Jannaeus was pelted with the ritual citrons at Tabernacles and personally witnessed the crucifixion of 800 of his dissident subjects. The Wicked Priest of the *Dead Sea Scrolls is understood by many modern interpreters as a Hasmonean, either Jonathan or Jannaeus (or both). Queen Salome Alexandra, by contrast, is said to have succeeded in healing a serious breach and winning the approval of the pious.

The Hasmoneans fought constantly, and expansion began early. Jonathan acquired southern Judaea, the Philistine city of Ekron and parts of *Samaria. Simon targeted the coastal strip, replacing some of the inhabitants of Joppa with Jews, and controlling Joppa's access to Jerusalem by taking Gezer (Gazara). Hyrcanus hired foreign mercenaries and his main conquests lay in Moab, in *Idumaea, where he Judaized the population, and in

Samaria, where, after several campaigns, he utterly destroyed the city. Aristobulus I annexed Ituraea in Lebanon. Jannaeus took what remained of Palestine and of Moab, and also, across the Jordan, the Peraea and the Golan. He encouraged *Cleopatra III's invasion of Palestine, in opposition to her son Ptolemy IX ('Lathyrus'; see PTOLEMY (1)). Tradition, influenced by Pompeian propaganda, casts him as a destroyer of Greek cities; in fact, his image was as much Hellenistic as Jewish.

Maccabees 1 and 2; Joseph. AJ 13. 1–15. 13; BJ 1. 48–357. Schürer, History 1. 164–242; V. Tcherikover, Hellenistic Civilization and the Jews (1969); Cambridge History of Judaism (1989), 292–351; CAH 9^2 (1994), ch. 8b.
T. R.

Haterius (RE [Suppl. 3] 3a), **Quintus** (suffect consul 5 BC), Augustan orator and declaimer (see DECLAMATION), who may have married a daughter of M. *Vipsanius Agrippa. *Tacitus portrays his obsequiousness under *Tiberius, and his obituary (Ann. 4. 61, AD 26) is not complimentary to his eloquence. Augustus quipped that his headlong delivery needed a brake. L. *Annaeus Seneca (1) cites him not infrequently, and discusses his style at length in Controv. 4 pref. 6–11.

PIR^2 H 24; Schanz–Hosius, § 336.7; Syme, AA 145–6.
M. W.

Hatra (mod. al-Ḥaḍr) in semi-desert northern *Mesopotamia, c.80 km. (50 mi.) south of Mosul, flourished greatly as a semi-independent city with water resources and territory between Rome and *Parthia c. AD 90–241, as impressive ruins show. Nearly 400 inscriptions occur, mostly in (widespread) *Aramaic, often with Seleucid-era dating. German, then (1950s–1980s) British, French, American, and Iraqi explorations have illuminated its predominantly (Semitic) Arab version of hybrid Semitic, Greek, Roman, and Iranian 'Parthian' culture.

Iraqi soundings showed nomad encampment beginnings, then slow development through mud-brick phases into stone-using grandeur. Remote, with effective military, tribal, and religious organizations, it controlled and profited from (rather than traded with) the surrounding territory it called 'Arabia', and resisted Rome (e.g. *Trajan). Its earliest text (AD 97/8) recorded one of thirteen temple buildings. In the period c. AD 90–176 six 'Lords' (MRY, maria) ruled: NŠR-YHB, WRWD, NṢRW (mentioned AD 128/9, 133, and 138, with priesthoods), M'NW (149; ŠMŠ-BRK was elected 'Steward' by all Hatra citizens, 151), WLGŠ, and SNṬRWQ. Hatra and its environs blossomed: notable are a circular layout (c.200 ha.: 495 acres); a contour-following earlier earth wall and later double wall, 6 km. (3.7 mi.) long with a ditch and approximately 90 large and 163 small towers (130s ?); streets and houses; 78 rectangular tombs (earliest, 108); a vast, central, walled, rectangular 'House of the God' with two Romanized temples and oriental open-fronted vaulted halls (iwans, one dated 112, others of WRWD and NṢRW), statuary and frontal reliefs of deities and notables, and wall-paintings. Kings 'of the Arabs' followed: SNṬRWQ I (mentioned 176/7), his son 'BD-SMY' (192/3)—probably *Herodian (2)'s 'Barsamia', who resisted *Septimius Severus (198, 200)—and SNṬRWQ II, with further architecture, art, and coin commissions. Around 233–41 the Roman Gordian Cohort was present. In April 241 the *Sasanid *Sapor I destroyed both city and kingdom. *Ammianus Marcellinus found Hatra deserted in 363.

W. Andrae, Hatra 1–2 (1908–12); H. Ingholt, Parthian Sculptures from Hatra (1954); E. E. D. M. Oates, Sumer 1955, 39–43 (Roman presence); A. Maricq, Syria 1955, 273 ff.; ibid. 1957, 288 ff.; J. Walker, Num. Chron. 1958, 167 ff. (on coinage); D. Homès-Fredericq, Hatra et ses sculptures parthes (1963); J. Teixidor, Syria 1966, 93 ff.; S. B. Downey, Berytus 1966,

97–109, and *Sumer* 1970, 227–30; J. M. C. Toynbee, *Sumer* 1970, 231–5, and *JRS* 1972, 106–10; S. B. Downey, *Sumer* 1974, 175–81; F. Safar and M. A. Mustafa, *Al-Hadhr: Madinat Al-Shams* ('Hatra, City of the Sun God', in Arabic) (1974); M. A. R. Colledge, *Parthian Art* (1977), see index, *Sumer* 1977, 135–40, and *Iconography of Religions* 14. 3: *The Parthian Period* (1986); J. K. Ibrahim, *Pre-Islamic settlement in Jazirah* (1986), good on Hatra and Khirbet Jaddalah history, culture, architecture, art, and pottery, with valuable catalogue of inscriptions in translation; S. B. Downey, *Mesopotamian Religious Architecture: Alexander through the Parthians* (1988), see index.   M. A. R. C.

Hattuša Capital city of the *Hittites, *c.*1650–1200 BC, near the modern village of Boğazköy (Boğazkale), 150 km. (93 mi.) east of Ankara in Turkey. The site has been under excavation by German archaeologists since 1906, and besides the massive Hittite occupation has produced pre- and post-Hittite levels. Among the principal finds has been the royal archives of thousands of *cuneiform clay tablets.

K. Bittel, *Hattusha* (1970).   J. D. Ha.

healing gods In all times, illness has been a major crisis both in the lives of individuals and communities; to overcome such a crisis has been a major task of religion. Specific divinities became patrons of human healers or were renowned for their special ability to help individuals, some presiding over healing springs; a frequent strategy was to regard illness as the result of *pollution and then to try to cure it with cathartic rituals; see PURIFICATION.

In Greece, the main divinity responsible for healing was *Apollo who already in the *Iliad* sent the *plague and took it away again; behind this function, there lie ancient near-eastern conceptions. Apollo remained a healer throughout the Archaic and Classical ages; in Ionian cities (and their colonies), he often bore the *epiclesis* ἰητρός, 'physician' (N. Ehrhardt, *MDAI(I)* 1989, 115–22); as Apollo Medicus, his cult was introduced to Rome in 433 BC. In the course of the 5th cent., Apollo's role as a healer was contested and slowly replaced by the much more personal and specialized hero *Asclepius, whom myth made Apollo's son and whose fame radiated chiefly from his Epidaurian sanctuary; in his main sanctuaries (*Epidaurus, *Cos, *Pergamum), Asclepius succeeded Apollo who, however, still retained a presence in spite of the fame of his son. The ritual of Asclepius developed *incubation as a specific means to obtain healing in *dreams.

Other divinities could, under given circumstances, heal as well. When a specific illness was understood as possession, as in the case of epilepsy (the 'sacred disease', see Hippoc. *Morb. sacr.*), the god or hero who had caused the possession held also the key to its healing. For some diseases *Demeter was thought useful as well, as was the mighty 'averter of evil' (ἀλεξίκακος) Heracles. Besides, many places had local heroes whom people could ask for healing, like the Oropian seer *Amphiaraus (with incubation) or the Athenian 'Hero Physician', Ἥρως Ἰατρός. Among the functions of local *nymphs, there was also help with female sterility and birth.

Rome followed the course set by Greece, introducing first Apollo Medicus, then, in 204 BC, Asclepius from Epidaurus; later, as in Greece, nymphs and Hercules were thanked for help, as were the Egyptian gods *Isis and *Sarapis; Rome also venerated the goddess *Febris, 'Fever'. Besides, and from time immemorial, Italy had a large number of local shrines, often of female, motherly divinities who were supposed to heal; one of their main concerns, to judge from the large number of anatomic *votive offerings, was with female fertility. Chiefly in the ancient Celtic provinces of Gaul and Britain, cults at healing springs were

important (see RELIGION, CELTIC); their divinities kept their Celtic names or were identified with Roman gods, like Apollo or, in Roman Bath, Minerva (Sulis); see AQUAE SULIS.

See APOLLO; ASCLEPIUS; DISEASE; INCUBATION.

There is no full treatment. Greece: F. Kutsch, *Attische Heilgötter und Heilheroen* (1913); G. Lanata, *Medicina magica e religione popolare in Grecia fino all'età di Ippocrate* (1967); Italian ex-votos: M. Tabanelli, *Gli ex-voto poliviscerali etruschi e romani: Storia, ritrovamento, interpretazione* (1962). The Celtic healers have provoked a lively discussion, see A. Rousselle, *Croire et guérir: la foi en Gaule dans l'antiquité tardive* (1990) and the catalogue *Dieux guérisseurs en Gaule romaine* (1992).   F. G.

heating for cooking and warmth was primarily supplied in the classical world by charcoal stoves: hence the importance of charcoal-burning. The stoves took the form of chafing-dishes, gridirons, or braziers, elaborated in the Hellenistic world into double-walled vessels heated by fire or boiling water, of which examples for table use have been discovered at *Pompeii. Equally old is the oven, without a flue and heated by blazing wood that was withdrawn upon exhaustion of the air within, like the modern pizza-oven. The use of hot *water for bathing is as old as *Homer (*Od.* 8. 249, 253) and precedes him at Minoan Cnossus, while Herodotus (4. 75) mentions sweat-baths, traditionally assigned to Sparta (Strabo 3. 154; Mart. 6. 42. 16) and warmed with heated stones. In the Roman empire, heating was revolutionized by the introduction of the heated floor or *hypocaust, at first only in public and private *baths, but later also in living areas.

RE 7 (1912), 'Heizung'.   J. D.

Heaven See URANUS; ZEUS; and entries listed under AFTER-LIFE.

Hebe, a personification of ἥβη, the standard Greek word for 'adolescence, puberty' (hence too *epheboi). Hebe is normally a daughter of *Hera and *Zeus, and thus a sister of *Ares and *Eileithyia (Hesiod, *Theog.* 922); only in a late-attested tradition of uncertain origin (*Myth. Vat.* 1. 204) is she born of Hera alone, made fertile by a lettuce. She is often mentioned and depicted as cupbearer of the gods (e.g. Hom. *Il.* 4. 2) and as bride of *Heracles (e.g. Hes. *Theog.* 950–5); this marriage is always viewed from the perspective of the groom, to whom it brought reconciliation with Hebe's mother Hera, a home on *Olympus (1), and eternal youth (i.e. godhead). She occasionally appears in cult, normally in association with the circle of Heracles, as in the *deme Aixone in *Attica where a temple of Hebe seems to have been the centre of a cult complex in which *Alcmene and the *Heraclidae were also honoured (*IG* 2². 1199, 2492); at Phlius and *Sicyon she was identified with figures also known as Ganymeda and Dia (Paus. 2. 13. 3–4; Strabo 8. 6. 24, 382 C).

A.-F. Laurens, *LIMC* 'Hebe' 1.   R. C. T. P.

Hecale, eponymous heroine and object of cult in the Attic *deme of Hecale. In her honour *Theseus founded a cult of Zeus Hekaleios, because she had entertained him kindly on his way to fight the bull of *Marathon; by the time he returned she had died. *Callimachus (3) wrote a very influential hexameter narrative poem about her, of which significant fragments survive; his main source was the Atthidographer (see ATTHIS) *Philochorus (*FGrH* 328 F 109, from Plut. *Thes.* 14).

A. S. Hollis, *Callimachus, Hecale* (1990); E. Simon, *LIMC* 4, 'Hekale'.   R. L. Hu.

Hecataeus (1) (*RE* 3), son of Hegesander, of *Miletus, the most important of the early Ionian prose-writers (see LOGOGRAPHERS). For his date we depend on Herodotus' account (5. 36, 124–6) of his role in the planning of the *Ionian Revolt (500–494 BC); his prudent opposition, based on geopolitical considerations, suggests a relatively senior figure.

Besides improving *Anaximander's map of the world, which he envisaged as a disc encircled by the river Oceanus, he wrote a pioneering work of systematic *geography, the *Periēgēsis* or *Periodos gēs* ('Journey round the World'), divided into two books, *Europe* and *Asia* (which included Africa). (We do not know why *Callimachus (3) regarded as spurious the text of the latter known to him.) This offered information about the places and peoples to be encountered on a clockwise coastal voyage round the Mediterranean and the Black Sea, starting at the Straits of Gibraltar and finishing on the Atlantic coast of Morocco, with diversions to the islands of the Mediterranean and inland to Scythia, Persia, India, Egypt, and Nubia. It is uncertain how far his information rested on his own observations, as is the extent of Herodotus' debt to his work. We have over 300 fragments, but many are merely citations in *Stephanus of Byzantium recording the occurrence of a place-name in the *Periēgēsis*.

His *mythographic work, the *Genealogies* (or *Histories* or *Heroologia*) occupied at least four books (see GENEALOGY). We have fewer than 40 fragments; they reveal a rationalizing approach to the legends of families claiming a divine origin (including, apparently, his own (Hdt. 2. 143)). As is shown by his treatment of the stories of Geryon and Cerberus (frs. 26, 27), he evidently believed that behind the fabulous elaborations of tradition lay historical facts distorted by exaggeration or by literal interpretation of metaphors. His opening proclaims his intellectual independence (fr. 1): 'Hecataeus of Miletus speaks thus. I write what seems to me to be true; for the Greeks have many tales which, as it appears to me, are absurd.'

The fragments are too short to give a fair idea of his style; ancient critics regarded as clear but much less varied and attractive than that of Herodotus.

TEXT *FGrH* 1 (in 2nd edn.); *Lustrum* 1978, 1 f., and 1985, 33; G. Nenci, *Hecataei Milesii Fragmenta* (1954).

LITERATURE H. Diels, *Hermes* 1887, 411 ff.; F. Jacoby, *RE* 7. 2666 ff. (= *Griechische Historiker* (1956), 185 ff.); L. Pearson, *Early Ionian Historians* (1939), ch. 2; K. von Fritz, *Die griechische Geschichtsschreibung* 1 (1967), ch. 3; R. Drews, *The Greek Accounts of Eastern History* (1973), ch. 1; S. West, *JHS* 1991, 144 ff.   S. R. W.

Hecataeus (2), of *Abdera, *c*.360–290 BC, author of philosophical ethnographies, pupil of *Pyrrhon the sceptic (*FGrH* 264 T 3), visited Egyptian *Thebes (2) (T 4) under *Ptolemy (1) I (305–283).

Works (1) *On the Hyperboreans* (*FGrH* 264 F 7–14), fictitious travelogue on a northern people dwelling on an island on the utmost borders of the world (cf. esp. F 7): model for *Euhemerus of Messene. (2) *Aegyptiaca* (F 1–6), idealizing account of the country and people, the exemplary nature of the Egyptian way of life and form of government. Hecataeus' enthusiasm bordered on 'Egyptomania' (Jacoby). He was the chief source for Diod. Sic. 1. 10–98 on Egypt. The digression on the Jews in Diod. Sic. 40. 3. 8 = Hecataeus F 6 is the first mention of Jews in a Greek author—the work *On Jews* referred to in Flavius Josephus (*Ap.* 1. 186 ff. or rather 2. 42 ff.) is not genuine. (3) *On the Poetry of Homer and Hesiod* (T 1): lost.

FGrH 264. O. Murray, *JEA* 1970, 141 ff.; K. Meister, *Die griechische Geschichtsschreibung* (1990); O. Lendle, *Einführung in die griechische Geschichtsschreibung* (1992).   K. M.

Hecate was a popular and ubiquitous goddess from the time of *Hesiod until late antiquity. Unknown in *Homer and harmless in Hesiod, she emerges by the 5th cent. as a more sinister divine figure associated with magic and witchcraft, lunar lore and creatures of the night, dog sacrifices and illuminated cakes, as well as doorways and crossroads. Her name is the feminine equivalent of Hekatos, an obscure epithet of *Apollo (Chantraine, *Dictionnaire étymologique de la langue grecque* (Paris 1968–80) 1. 328 on ἕκατος, ἑκατηβόλος), but the Greek etymology is no guarantee that her name or cult originated in Greece. Possibly of Carian origin (see CARIA), and certainly outlandish in her infernal aspects, she is more at home on the fringes than in the centre of Greek polytheism. Intrinsically ambivalent and polymorphous, she straddles conventional boundaries and eludes definition.

In Hesiod's *Theogony*, she is the granddaughter of the *Titans *Phoebe and Coeus, daughter of Perses and *Asteria, and first cousin of Apollo and *Artemis (for other genealogies see schol. Ap. Rhod. *Argon.* 3. 467). In a remarkable digression (411–52), the authenticity of which has been unduly doubted, Hecate is praised as a powerful goddess who 'has a share' of earth, sea, and sky—but not the Underworld—and who gives protection to warriors, athletes, hunters, herders, and fishermen. As with all gods, she may choose to withhold her gifts. But, because her functions overlap with those of other divinities, she lacks individuating features. Furthermore, the Hesiodic Hecate contrasts sharply with the goddess' later manifestations, which tend to be much more menacing. Where and how this differentiation occurred remains uncertain.

Throughout her long history, Hecate received public as well as private cult, the latter often taking forms that were anything but normal. She was worshipped in liminal places, and sacrifices to her were as anomalous as the goddess herself. The earliest archaeological evidence is a dedication to Hecate on a circular altar in the precinct of Apollo Delphinios at *Miletus (A. Rehm, *Milet.* 1. 3 (Berlin, 1914), no. 129, before 500 BC); she had her own shrine 'outside the gates'—as opposed to the Coan cult (see cos) of Hecate 'in the city' (*LSCG* 169 A 5)—where she received libations of unmixed wine (*LSAM* 50. 25–9, 450 BC). In Athens *Hermes Propylaios and Hecate Epipyrgidia ('On the Ramparts') watched the entrance to the Acropolis (Paus. 1. 22. 8, 2. 30. 2). Similarly, altars and cult images of the trimorphic Hecate (*hekataia*) stood in front of private homes (Aesch. fr. 388 Radt, Ar. *Vesp.* 804) and especially at forks in the road (Apollodorus of Athens, *FGrH* 244 F 110), after which she was named τριοδῖτις and Trivia.

The documentation for the Hecate cult in Classical Athens is particularly rich and varied. Her favourite food offerings consisted of a scavenging fish (see FISH, SACRED) tabooed in other cults—the red mullet (τρίγλα, Apollodorus 244 F 109; Antiphanes fr. 69. 14 f. K–A)—of sacrificial *cakes decorated with lit miniature torches (Soph. fr. 734 Radt; Diphilus fr. 27 K–A; *LIMC* 'Hekate', no. 47), and, most notoriously, of puppies. The illuminated cakes were offered at the time of the full moon (Philochorus, *FGrH* 328 F 86). So-called 'suppers of Hecate' (Ἑκαταῖα sc. δεῖπνα)—consisting of various breadstuffs, eggs, cheese, and dog-meat—were put out for her at the crossroads each month to mark the rising of the new moon (Ar. *Plut.* 594 ff. with schol., fr. 209 K–A). On an Attic lecythus, a woman deposits a puppy and a basket with sacrificial cakes in front of burning torches (Beazley, *ARV*² 1204. 2). Attested for Athens, Colophon, *Samothrace, and *Thrace, dog sacrifices to Hecate were alimentary as well as cathartic (Sophron in Page, *GLP* 73. 7; Plut. *Quaest. Rom.* 280c, 290d). During Hellenistic and Roman times, she was worshipped as the regional mother-goddess at her main Carian sanctuary at Lagina near *Stratonicea. There, the ritual carrying of a sacred key (κλειδαγωγία) was part of her cult, of which the clergy included a priest and priestess as well as eunuchs. On the temple frieze, she carries to *Cronus the stone that represents the newborn *Zeus; in another scene, she participates in the Gigantomachy (LIMC nos. 98–100; see GIANTS). No dogs were sacrificed in the Lagina cult, but the puppy sacrifices, prominent in *Hittite and Carian purification rituals, point to an early Anatolian connection. See ANATOLIAN DEITIES.

Hecate was identified with other divine figures such as Ereschigal, the Babylonian goddess of the Underworld (PGM LXX); the Thessalian Enodia (Soph. fr. 535. 2 Radt; Eur. Hel. 569 f.) and *Brimo (Ap. Rhod. Argon. 3. 861 f., 1211; LIMC nos. 303, 305); the Sicilian Angelos (schol. Theoc. 2. 11/12b; cf. R. Arena, Iscrizioni greche arcaiche di Sicilia e Magna Grecia 1 (1989), no. 38 = L. Dubois, Inscriptions grecques dialectales de Sicilie (1989), no. 55, c.450 BC); *Persephone (Soph. Ant. 1199 f., Eur. Ion 1048 f.); *Iphigenia (Stesichorus fr. 215 Davies, EGF; Paus. 1. 43. 1, cf. Hesiod fr. 23a. 26 M–W); and especially Artemis (IG 12. 8. 359, Thasos, c.450 BC; IG 4². 499, Epidaurus, imperial period). In Athens, too, she was worshipped as Artemis Hecate (IG 1³. 383. 125–7, 429/8 BC) and as Kalliste, another of Artemis' cult titles (Hsch. κ 489; cf. IG 2². 4665–8). Sacrifices to Artemis Hecate and to Kourotrophos were performed in Hecate's shrine at Erchia in Attica (LSCG 18 B 6–13, 375/50 BC). Hecate was also associated with various male gods, including Apollo Delphinios, *Asclepius, Hermes, *Pan, Zeus Meilichios, and Zeus Panamaros.

Like all *chthonian divinities, Hecate was perceived as simultaneously terrible and benign. Her 'good' side is addressed by her Hesiodic epithet 'nurturer of the young' (Hes. Theog. 450 κουροτρόφος, echoed in later sources). In Aeschylus, the title 'Hekata' refers to Artemis in her association with childbirth (H. F. Johansen and E. W. Whittle, Aeschylus: The Suppliants (1980) on Supp. 676) and young animals (Ag. 140 West). The Hecate seen in Eleusinian myth and cult is propitious and caring. She assists *Demeter in her search for Persephone (Kore), and after the reunion of mother and daughter becomes Kore's 'minister and attendant' (Richardson on Hymn. Hom. Cer. 24 f. and 440). Attic vase-painters included Hecate in their depictions of the return of Kore and the mission of *Triptolemus (LIMC nos. 10–23); in the Attic *deme of Paiania, Hecate's cult and priestess were attached to the local Eleusinion (IG 1³. 250 = LSS 18, 450/30 BC). In later versions of the myth, Hecate is another daughter of Demeter and retrieves Persephone from the Underworld (Callim. fr. 466 Pf., Orph. frs. 41–2 Kern). Mystery cults (see MYSTERIES) of Hecate also existed, as on *Aegina and Samothrace; a woman initiate claims on her tombstone to have been immortalized in death as the 'goddess Hecate' (GVI 438a, Thrace, imperial period).

Although Hecate lacked a mythology of her own, her nocturnal apparitions, packs of barking hell-hounds, and hosts of ghostlike revenants occupied a special place in the Greek religious imagination. As 'the one of the roadways' (ἐνοδία), she protected the crossroads as well as the graves by the roadside. She also guarded the gates to Hades. According to one of the hymns to *Selene-Hecate embedded in the Paris magical papyrus, Hecate keeps the keys that 'open the bars of Cerberus' and wears 'the bronze sandal of her who holds *Tartarus' (PGM IV 2291–5, 2334 f.; cf. Suppl. Mag. 49. 57–61). A permanent fixture of the Greek and Roman Underworld, she gives Virgil's *Sibyl, a priestess of Apollo and Hecate, a guided tour of Tartarus (Aen. 6. 35,

564 f.). Because of her association with the chthonian realm and the ghosts of the dead, Hecate looms large in ancient *magic. Sorceresses of all periods and every provenance, such as Medea, Simaetha, and Canidia, invoke her name as one who makes powerful spells more potent (Soph. frs. 534–5 Radt; Eur. Med. 397; Ap. Rhod. Argon. 3. 1035 ff.; Theoc. Id. 2. 12–16; Hor. Sat. 1. 8. 33). On curse tablets (see CURSES) dating from the Classical to the imperial period, Hecate is conjured in conjunction with *Hermes Chthonios, Gē (see GAIA) Chthonia, Persephone, or Pluton (see HADES) (Def. tab. Audollent, nos. 38, 41, Wünsch, nos. 104–7). In a specimen from Hellenistic Athens, Hecate Chthonia is invoked 'along with the maddening *Erinyes' (no. 108b 2 Wünsch = Gager no. 69). In the *theurgy of the Chaldaean Oracles adopted by the Neoplatonists, Hecate, though still linked to demons, has become an epiphanic celestial deity (see EPIPHANY) and cosmological principle—the Cosmic *Soul—accessible through ritual as well as contemplation.

Representations of Hecate in art fall into two broad categories—her images are either single-faced or three-faced. The earliest example of the former type may be an inscribed terracotta figurine of a woman seated on a throne, dedicated by 'Aigon to Hecate' (Athens, late 6th cent. BC; IG 1². 836; LIMC no. 105). After c.430 BC, the goddess of the crossroads is often represented as a standing female figure with three faces or bodies, each corresponding to one of the crossing roads. The trimorphous Hecate is said to be the creation of *Alcamenes (LIMC no. 112). She is often shown wearing the polos (divine head-dress) and holding torches in her hands (Hymn. Hom. Cer. 52; LIMC nos. 1–94), and occasionally with a phiale, a sword, snakes, boughs, flowers, or a pomegranate. Central to her cult, the three-faced image of Hecate is depicted on two Attic vases from the Classical period (LIMC nos. 48, 206). On the Altar of Zeus at *Pergamum, Hecate and her dog attack a serpentine giant; her single body supports three heads and three pairs of arms (LIMC no. 191). Exceptionally, on a calyx crater with the death of *Actaeon, a winged Hecate urges on his maddened dogs while Artemis looks on (LIMC no. 96). On an equally unique vase, Hecate has man-eating dogs for feet and is accompanied by three *Erinyes (LIMC no. 95).

Greek wordsmiths went to great lengths in their efforts to verbalize the triple aspects of the trimorphic goddess. In one of the comedies of Chariclides, she is humorously invoked as 'lady Hecate of the triple roads, of the triple form, of the triple face, enchanted by triple-fish [mullets]' (fr. 1 K–A δέσποιν᾽ Ἑκάτη τριοδῖτι, τρίμορφε, τριπρόσωπε τρίγλαις κηλευμένη). A curse tablet from the imperial period addresses her similarly as 'Lady Hecate of the heavens, Hecate of the Underworld, Hecate of the three roads, Hecate of the triple face, Hecate of the single face' (SEG 30. 326 = Gager no. 84; cf. PGM IV 2525–30, 2820–6). Playing with sacred *numbers added to her mystery.

J. Heckenbach, RE 7 (1912), 2769–82, 'Hekate'; U. von Wilamowitz-Moellendorff, Der Glaube der Hellenen (1931–2), 169–77; T. Kraus, Hekate (1960); M. L. West, Hesiod, Theogony (1966), 276–80; A. Kehl, RAC 14 (1988), 310–38, 'Hekate'; S. I. Johnston, ZPE 88 (1991), 217–24. Local cults: Nilsson, Feste 394–401; Farnell, Cults 2. 501–19, 549–57, 596–602; A. Laumonier, Les Cultes indigènes en Carie (1958), 344–425; F. Graf, Nordionische Kulte (1985), 229 f., 257–9; A. Henrichs, in H. Hofmann and A. Harder (eds.), Fragmenta dramatica (1991), 180–7 (Athens); Clinton, Iconography, esp. 116–20. 'Hecate's suppers': K. Meuli, Gesammelte Schriften (1975), 2. 923 f.; C. H. Greenewalt, Ritual Dinners in Early Historic Sardis, Univ. Calif. Publ. Class. Stud. 1978, esp. 42–5; W. Burkert, in Le Sacrifice dans l'antiquité, Entretiens Hardt 27 (1981), 117 f.; R. Parker, Miasma (1983), 222–4, 357 f., 362 f. Hecate in magic and theurgy: H. D. Betz (ed.), The Greek Magical Papyri in Translation 1

(1986; 2nd edn. 1992), esp. 78–92; S. I. Johnston, *Hekate Soteira* (1990); J. G. Gager, *Curse Tablets and Binding Spells from the Ancient World* (1992). Iconography: E. Simon, *MDAI(A)* 1985, 271–84; H. Sarian, *LIMC* 6 (1992), 1. 985–1018, 2. 654–73 (plates).　　　　　A. H.

Hecatomnus of *Mylasa, son and successor of Hyssaldomus, was *satrap (see MAUSOLUS) of the Persian province of *Caria after the fall of *Tissaphernes, and commanded the fleet in the Persian operations against *Cyprus in 390 BC (Diod. Sic. 14. 98). He made Greek dedications at *Labraunda and *Sinuri and was honoured at *Caunus (*SEG* 12. 470). After his death his children (*Mausolus and *Artemisia (2), *Idrieus and *Ada, *Pixodarus) ruled in succession as satraps and despots in SW Asia Minor.

Strabo 14. 2. 17. L. Robert, *Le Sanctuaire de Sinuri* 1 (1945), 98 ff.; *ILabraunda* 2, no. 27; S. Hornblower, *Mausolus* (1982), chs. 2, 11; S. Ruzicka, *Politics of a Persian Dynasty: The Hecatomnids in the Fourth Century BC* (1992).　　　　　J. M. C.; S. H.

Hecatompylus (mod. Shahr-i Qumis) near Damghan, NE Iran, a site 8 km. (5 mi.) long identified by British excavators (1960s) as capital (also, Comis ?) of the Seleucid and Parthian province Comisene, created an imperial capital allegedly by the second king of *Parthia, Tiridates. Excavation has revealed Parthian cultural activity, particularly *c*.217–50 BC, as signalled by finds of a stone bowl, pottery, amphora-rhyton, potsherds with a heterographic Parthian (*Aramaic) text; clay seals with un-Hellenic imprints; burials; a rectangular, six-tower, fortified courtyard-residence; and tall, squarish, mud-brick, vaulted 'shrines' with projections (recalling a Median fire-temple), filled in *c*.50 BC. *Isidorus (1) (1st cent. AD), *Parthian Stations* 9, reported Comisene had (only) 'villages'.

J. Hansman and D. Stronach, articles in *Journal of the Royal Asiatic Society* 1968, 1970, 1974; M. A. R. Colledge, *Parthian Art* (1977), see index entry under Shahr-i Qumis, and *Iconography of Religions* 14. 3: *The Parthian Period* (1986), 10, 15, pl. 11a.　　　　　M. A. R. C.

Hecaton, of Rhodes, Stoic (see STOICISM), pupil of *Panaetius, wrote mainly on ethics and was, after Panaetius and *Posidonius (2), the most influential Stoic of the 'middle Stoic' period. His works were on such topics as goods, the virtues, the emotions, final ends, and right actions. Cicero preserves some of his arguments, which deal with problem cases in ethics, including conflicts of duties; from these he appears to have been interested in casuistry and applications of ethical theory.

H. Gomoll, *Der stoische Philosoph Hekaton* (1933).　　　　　J. A.

Hecatoncheires, hundred-handed monsters, Cottus, Briareos, and Gyes, sons of Heaven and Earth (Hes. *Theog.* 147 ff.); aided *Zeus against the *Titans (713 ff.). Briareos (called Aegaeon by men) was brought by *Thetis to protect Zeus against *Hera, *Poseidon, and *Athena (*Il.* 1. 396 ff.).

LIMC 4. 1 (1988), 481–2.

Hector, in mythology son of *Priam and *Hecuba, husband of *Andromache and father of *Astyanax (*Il.* 6. 394 ff.), and the greatest of the Trojan champions. In *Homer's *Iliad* he first appears leading the Trojans out to battle (2. 807 ff.); he reproaches *Paris for avoiding *Menelaus (1) (3. 38 ff.), and arranges the truce and the single combat between the two (85 ff.). He takes a prominent part in the fighting of books 5 and 6, but in the latter goes back to the city for a while to arrange for offerings to be made to the gods. He thus meets Andromache and Astyanax on the city walls in one of the best-known scenes of the *Iliad*, then returns with Paris to the battle. In book 7 he challenges any Greek hero to single combat, and is met by the greater *Aias (1), who has rather

the better of the encounter; they part with an exchange of gifts. In book 8 he drives the Greeks back to their camp and bivouacs on the plain. In the long battle of books 11–17 he takes a prominent part, leading the main attack on the fortifications of the Greek camp which nearly succeeds in burning the Greek ships. During the battle he is struck down with a stone thrown by Aias (14. 409 ff.), but restored to strength by *Apollo at the command of Zeus (15. 239 ff.). He kills *Patroclus (16. 818 ff.), and strips him of his arms despite the efforts of the Greeks. After the appearance of *Achilles at the trench, full of rage at Patroclus' death, Hector again bivouacs on the plain, against the advice of *Polydamas (18. 249 ff.). After the Trojan rout on the following day, he alone refuses to enter Troy, but stands his ground and waits for Achilles despite the entreaties of his parents (22. 35 ff.). At Achilles' approach he flees, but after a long chase halts, deceived by Athena into thinking that *Deiphobus has come to his aid. In the subsequent fight he is killed, and with his dying words begs Achilles to return his body to Priam, then predicts Achilles' own death (22. 337 ff.). But Achilles, still overcome with rage and hatred, drags Hector's body behind his chariot, though the gods keep it safe from harm. Finally, when Priam comes by night to the Greek camp to beg for the return of his son (24. 189 ff.), Achilles' anger is eased and replaced by pity. The body is ransomed, an eleven-day truce is agreed, and the *Iliad* ends with Hector's funeral. Later poets add nothing of importance to Homer's account.

Hector is depicted in art from the 7th cent. on, setting out for battle, fighting Aias or some other hero, meeting his death at Achilles' hands, and his body being dragged and ransomed: see O. Touchefeu, *LIMC* 4. 1 (1988), 482–98.　　　　　H. J. R.; J. R. M.

Hecuba (Ἑκάβη), wife of *Priam, and daughter of Dymas king of Phrygia (*Iliad* 16. 718), or of Cisseus (Eur. *Hec.* 3). The name of her mother was one of the problems posed by *Tiberius (Suet. *Tib.* 70). She was the mother of nineteen of Priam's fifty sons (*Il.* 24. 496), including *Hector and *Paris.

In *Homer she is a stately and pathetic figure, coming only occasionally into the foreground (*Il.* 6. 251–311, 22. 79–92, 24. 193–227, 283–301, 747–60). In Euripides she is more prominent. The first half of his *Hecuba* deals with the sacrifice of her daughter *Polyxena, the second with her revenge on the Thracian king Polymestor, who has murdered her youngest son Polydorus. Turning from victim to savage avenger she blinds Polymestor and kills his sons, and he makes a curious prophecy of her end (1259–73): on the ship transporting her to Greece she will be transformed into a bitch and then plunge into the sea (Ovid, *Met.* 13. 567–71, more intelligibly makes the transformation occur as she is stoned by Polymestor's countrymen). In *Trojan Women* she is again the central character, battered by a succession of woes, and incidents include her moral victory in a debate with Helen (860–1059) and her allotment as a prize to *Odysseus (1260–86). For her role in *Alexandros* see PARIS.

A.-F. Laurens, *LIMC* 4. 1 (1988), entry under 'Hekabe', 473–81; 4.2, 280–3.　　　　　A. L. B.

Hedylus, of Samos, author of twelve epigrams quoted in the *Anthology and *Athenaeus (1), mainly on food and drink. According to Athen. 297e his mother (Hedyle) and grandmother (Moschine) were also poets. He worked in *Alexandria (1) and may have compiled a collection of epigrams by himself and *Asclepiades (2) and *Posidippus (2), both of whom he admired and imitated (A. D. E. Cameron, *Greek Anthology* (1993), 369–76).

Gow–Page, *HE*; Fraser, *Ptol. Alex.* 571–5.　　　　　A. D. E. C.

Hegemon, of *Thasos, identified by *Aristotle (*Poet.* 1448ᵃ12) as the first Greek parodist (see PARODY, GREEK); this presumably means that he raised parody into an independent genre with a separate place in competitions. According to *Polemon (3) (cited by Ath. 15. 699a) he won victories at Athens with several such compositions, and a long fragment mentions a prize of 50 drachmas. Hegemon also wrote a play 'in the style of Old Comedy' (Ath. ibid., cf. 1. 5a–b), which may imply 5th-cent. BC dating (see COMEDY (GREEK), OLD).

FRAGMENTS Parody: P. Brandt, *Corpusculum poesis epicae graecae ludibundae* 1 (1888), 37–49. Comedy: Kassel–Austin, *PCG* 5. 546–7.

INTERPRETATION Meineke, *FCG* 1. 214 f.; Wilamowitz, *Hermes* 1905, 173 f. (= *Kl. Schr.* 4 (1962), 220 f.; A. Körte, *RE* 7/2 (1912), 2595 f. 'Hegemon' 3.
W. G. A.

Hegesander (*RE* 4), of *Delphi (2nd cent. BC), Greek writer. He compiled at least six books of *Memoirs,* an ordered collection of unreliable anecdotes concerning Hellenistic kings, courtiers, philosophers, courtesans, etc.; references mainly in *Athenaeus (1) (*FHG* 4. 412–22).
C. B. R. P.

Hegesias (1), philosopher of the *Cyrenaic school (*c.*290 BC). He was nicknamed Πεισιθάνατος ('Death-persuader') because his emphasis on the ills of human life was thought to encourage *suicide. He maintained that happiness was unattainable and that the wise agent should therefore seek, not happiness, but the avoidance of distress.

For bibliog. see CYRENAICS.
C. C. W. T.

Hegesias (2), of Magnesia (3rd cent. BC), historian and orator. Some fragments of his *History of Alexander* survive (*FGrH* 142). See ALEXANDER (3) THE GREAT. All ancient judgements of his style are hostile; as the typical 'Asianist' (see RHETORIC, GREEK), he was the *bête noire* of classicizing writers from the time of Cicero onwards (see, e.g., Cic. *Brut.* 286; Dion. Hal. *Comp.* 4. 28; 'Longinus' 3. 2). His fragments show strongly rhythmical short cola, eccentric expression, and 'Gorgianic' figures: see GORGIAS (1).

Norden, *Ant. Kunstpr.* 134 ff.
D. A. R.

Hegesippus (1) (*c.*390–*c.*325 BC), Athenian statesman, contemporary with *Demosthenes (2), nicknamed Κρωβύλος ('Topknot') from his old-fashioned hairstyle, an obscure but not unimportant figure. He was already a man of note in the 350s, and in 355 proposed the decree of alliance with *Phocis. In the 340s he became prominent as a vigorous opponent of *Philip (1) II, and appears to have been one of the very few Athenian statesmen who opposed the making of the Peace of *Philocrates (schol. to Dem. 19. 72). In 344/3 he played a decisive part in obstructing the offer of Philip, brought by Python of Byzantium, to turn the Peace into a *Common Peace of all the Greeks. With Demosthenes' support, Hegesippus persuaded the Athenians to send him on an embassy to renew their claim on *Amphipolis, which they had renounced in 346; as was to be expected, he was unceremoniously received by Philip, and, when in early 342 Philip made the offer again, Hegesippus exerted himself to secure its final rejection. The speech *De Halonneso* ([Dem.] 7) is now generally agreed to be his contribution to the debate on that occasion (*Dionysius (7) of Halicarnassus, who accepted it as Demosthenic despite strong contrary indications of style, was not followed by Libanius). The speech is misleadingly titled from the first topic with which it deals; it is really concerned to answer a letter from Philip περὶ τῆς ἐπανορθώσεως τῆς εἰρήνης ('on the amendment of the peace') (§ 18 ff.) and manifests a complete refusal to assent to the decisions of 346. His policy was, in short,

like that of Demosthenes, to seek a renewal of the war (cf. Plut. *Mor.* 187e and Aeschin. 2. 137). He was still active in politics after the battle of *Chaeronea, but was not one of the *demagogues whose surrender *Alexander (3) the Great demanded in 335.
G. L. C.

Hegesippus (2), New Comedy poet (see COMEDY (GREEK), NEW). In fr. 1 a vainglorious cook talks about his art, in 2 a parasite praises *Epicurus.

FRAGMENTS Kassel–Austin, *PCG* 5. 548–51.

INTERPRETATION Meineke, *FCG* 1. 475 ff.; A. Körte, *RE* 7/2 (1912), 2610, 'Hegesippos' 3; A. Giannini, *Acme* 1960, 172 f.; H. Dohm, *Mageiros* (1964), 148 ff.
W. G. A.

Hegesippus (3) (fl. *c.*250 BC), author of a handful of funerary and dedicatory epigrams in the Greek *Anthology, from the *Garland* of *Meleager (2). *Anth. Pal.* 6. 266 now appears in *PKöln* 204 with poems of Mnasalces.

Gow–Page, *HE*.
A. D. E. C.

Hegetor, a physician of the 'school' of *Herophilus. The criticisms of Hegetor by *Apollonius (8) of Citium (*c.*90–15 BC?) provide a *terminus ante quem.* Hegetor shared other Herophileans' keen interest in pulse theory, as Galen (8. 955 Kühn) and Marcellinus (*On Pulses,* ch. 3) confirm, but among later Herophileans he stands virtually alone in sharing Herophilus' emphasis on the importance of *anatomy. There is, however, no explicit evidence that Hegetor followed Herophilus' example of conducting systematic human dissection. In a fragment from his treatise *On Causes* (Περὶ αἰτιῶν), preserved by Apollonius of Citium, Hegetor criticizes the Empiricists' use of analogy; he suggests that an exact knowledge of the anatomy of the thigh and of its attachment to the socket of the hip-joint, rather than analogies provided by the successful surgical treatment of other kinds of joints, would lead to a clear distinction between treatable and incurable cases of dislocated thigh bones.

H. von Staden, *From Andreas to Demosthenes Philalethes* (1995), ch. 7. Cf. von Staden, *Herophilus* (1989), 512–14.
H. v. S.

Heircte (Εἴρκτη, Ἑρκταί, Ἑρκτή), a mountain near *Panormus (mod. Palermo) in Sicily, seized and held by *Hamilcar (2) Barca (247–244 BC) in order to strike at the rear of the Roman armies besieging Drepana and Lilybaeum and to threaten Panormus. Its identification with Monte Pellegrino, Monte Castellaccio, and, most recently, Monte Pecorato have been advanced.

Polyb. 1. 56 (cf. Walbank, *HCP* on the passage); *CAH* 7²/2 (1989), 164 n. 72.
H. H. S.; A. J. S. S.

hektēmoroi (ἑκτήμοροι), 'sixth-parters', a class of peasants in Attica before *Solon. Exactly what they were and what Solon did for them was not clearly remembered and is much disputed. They had to hand over to the rich one-sixth of the produce of the land they worked for them, on penalty of enslavement for themselves and their families, and this obligation was signalled by markers (ὅροι) of wood or stone; Solon abolished the status and uprooted the markers, thus 'freeing the black earth' as he put it.

The nature of the original obligation is the most controversial feature of all this. It was surely no ordinary debt, certainly not one in monetary form (*coinage was still in the future). Nor is it easy to understand the jump straight from indebtedness to slavery: loss of the land would have been an obvious intermediate stage, if the land had originally belonged (in some rudimentary sense of that word) to the *hektēmoroi.* The jump, to make it intelligible, would require the further hypothesis of inalienability of land, and there is no good evidence for this. So recent scholars suggest that hectemorage was a voluntary servitude, entered into by the weak for protection by the powerful; or else that land was allotted to pioneers during the Dark Age resettlement of Attica (see ATHENS (history)), on condition of permanent payment of one-sixth of the produce.

Rhodes, *CAAP* 89 ff.; A. Andrewes, *CAH* 3²/3 (1982), 377 ff.
A. W. G.; T. J. C.; S. H.

Helen (Ἑλένη), daughter of *Zeus and *Leda (or Zeus and *Nemesis, according to an early variant); wife of *Menelaus (1) of Sparta; the beautiful woman whose abduction by Paris was the cause of the Trojan War.

Helen was also worshipped (at *Sparta and on *Rhodes) as a goddess associated with trees (see TREES, SACRED). It is generally agreed that she must have been a goddess before she was a mortal heroine, but the connection between these two different incarnations is obscure. It has been suggested that the repeated seductions of the mortal Helen are derived from temporary absences of the goddess in the cult myths.

In *Homer she is entirely human. As we see her in the *Iliad* (3. 121–244, 383–447, 6. 343–69, 24. 761–76), she is deeply conscious of the shame of her position at Troy, though it is unclear how far she is responsible for this. *Hector and *Priam treat her kindly; the Trojan elders marvel at her beauty (3. 146–60); and she is in general a sympathetic character. In the *Odyssey* (4. 120–305), after her return to Sparta, she is seen as a respectable wife and queen, though Menelaus' curious story of her role in the episode of the Trojan Horse (271–89) presents a less complimentary picture.

Later writers supply further mythical details: how she was born from an egg (Zeus having visited *Leda in the form of a swan); how she was abducted by Theseus but rescued by her brothers, Castor and Polydeuces (see DIOSCURI); how she was wooed by all the greatest heroes of Greece before her marriage to Menelaus. She now generally stands condemned for having willingly accompanied Paris to Troy. A story often illustrated on vases is that Menelaus, after the capture of Troy, intended to kill her, but dropped his sword on seeing her breasts (*Little Iliad* fr. 19 Davies, *EGF*). In a much-debated episode of *Virgil (*Aen.* 2. 567–88), it is *Aeneas who thinks of killing her.

The 6th-cent. poet *Stesichorus wrote a poem in which he held Helen to blame, but then, we are told, was punished with blindness for having slandered a goddess. His sight returned when he wrote a palinode (two palinodes by one account) saying that she never went to Troy at all: the gods lodged her in Egypt for the duration of the war and put a phantom Helen in her place. This version is then rationalized at *Herodotus (1) 2. 112–20.

The tragedians, especially *Euripides, often condemn Helen for her adultery. An attempt at self-defence is refuted by *Hecuba in a debate at *Trojan Women* 860–1059, and she is presented as vain and shallow at *Orestes* 71–131. In his *Helen*, however, Euripides follows the version of Stesichorus' palinode: Menelaus, returning from Troy with the phantom Helen, is astonished to find the real Helen in Egypt, and the pair then escape by trickery from the wicked king Theoclymenus, son of *Proteus.

The sophist *Gorgias (1) composed a *Defence of Helen* as a light-hearted rhetorical exercise, and this is carried further in an encomium by *Isocrates (Isoc. 10).

LIMC 'Helene'; M. L. West, *Immortal Helen* (1975); L. L. Clader, *Helen: the Evolution from Divine to Heroic in Greek Epic Tradition*, Mnemos. Suppl. 42 (1976). A. L. B.

Helenius Acro (2nd cent. AD) wrote (lost) commentaries on *Terence (*Adelphi* and *Eunuchus* at least) and *Horace; evidence for a commentary on *Persius is very slight. The extant *scholia on Horace referred to as 'pseudo-Acro' comprise a complex blend of two traditions, 'A' (probably derived from a 5th-cent. commentary) and '§' (represented by three medieval recensions). These scholia may contain material from Acro (alongside material from *Pomponius Porphyrio and *Servius), but their attribution to Acro does not antedate the Renaissance. See SCHOLARSHIP, ANCIENT (Roman).

Ed. Keller (1902–4), with important discussion by G. Noske, *Quaestiones Pseudacroneae* (1969); a new edition is needed. Herzog–Schmidt, § 444. *PIR²* H 48. R. A. K.

Helenus, in mythology, son of *Priam, warrior and prophet. In the *Iliad* he gives prophetic advice to *Hector (6. 76, 7. 44), and is wounded by *Menelaus (1) at the battle of the ships (book 13). Captured by *Odysseus, he prophesied the fall of Troy if *Philoctetes was brought there with his bow (Soph. *Phil.* 604–13). After the fall of Troy he was carried off by *Neoptolemus (1), who gave him *Andromache as his wife (Eur. *Andr.* 1243). They settled in Epirus and made 'a little Troy'; there they were visited by *Aeneas, to whom Helenus prophesied his future wanderings (Virg. *Aen.* 3. 294–505). C. B.

heliaea See ELIAEA.

Helicon, mountain in SW *Boeotia sacred to the *Muses. Running from Phocis to *Thisbe in Boeotia, it stretched northwards to Lake Copais and southwards to the Corinthian Gulf. Its most famous feature is the Valley of the Muses, the site of *Ascra, the unbeloved home of Hesiod. *Thespiae celebrated a festival of the Muses, and the oldest tripod dedicated was reputedly that of Hesiod. The Thespians also established a festival of Love there. Above the Grove of the Muses was Hippocrene, a fountain supposedly created when *Bellerophon's horse struck the ground with his hoof.

A. R. Burn, *BSA* 1949, 313 ff. J. Bu.

Heliodorus (1), of Athens, wrote (c.150 BC?) a 15-book work on artistic works on the Athenian Acropolis, with historical and other digressions.

FGrH 373. F. W. W.; K. S. S.

Heliodorus (2), a metrist who flourished in the middle of the 1st cent. AD. He gave *Aristophanes (1)'s comedies a colometry (division of the text into cola), adding metrical signs (σημεῖα) and a continuous metrical analysis. Many of the results of his labours are preserved in the scholia to Aristophanes. He was the principal authority used by *Juba (3). See METRE, GREEK.

D. Holwerda, *Mnemos.* 1964, 113 ff., and 1967, 247 ff. K. J. D.

Heliodorus (3), a popular surgeon of the time of *Juvenal (who lived c. AD 60–140; cf. Juv. 6. 373), probably from Egypt. He belonged to the Pneumatic school (see PNEUMATISTS).

Works (1) Χειρουργούμενα ('On Surgery'; principal work, chiefly known from Oribasius and in fragments preserved in late Latin translations); (2) ? Περὶ ἄρθρων πραγματεία or Ἐπιμήχανος ('Treatise on Joints'); (3) Περὶ ὀλισθημάτων πραγματεία ('On Dislocation'); (4) Περὶ ἐπιδέσμων ('On Bandages'); (5) Περὶ μέτρων καὶ σταθμῶν ('On Weights and Measures'); (6) *Epistula phlebotomiae* ('On Blood-letting'; Lat. trans.). See SURGERY.

TEXTS H. E. Sigerist, *AGM* 1920, 1–9, and 1921, 145–56; M.-H. Marganne, *Études de Lettres de Lausanne* 1 (1986), 65–73.
W. D. R.; V. N.

Heliodorus

Heliodorus (4), Greek novelist. His ten-book *Ethiopian Story of Theagenes and Charicleia* (Αἰθιοπικὰ τὰ περὶ Θεαγένην καὶ Χαρίκλειαν) closes with a signature naming his father as Theodosius 'of the race of the Sun' and their city as Phoenician *Emesa. A 4th-cent. date can be argued, not from *Socrates Scholasticus' (*Hist. eccl.* 5. 22) implausible identification of him with a bishop of Tricca, but from the possible use, in Heliodorus' account of the siege of Syene (9. 3 f.), of *Julian's description of the siege of *Nisibis in *Orations* 1 and 3 (of AD 357). But more probably Julian used Heliodorus (see Szepessy and Maróth in bibliog. below), allowing the date nearer 230 which is suggested by similarities to *Philostratus' *Apollonius* and *Achilles (1) Tatius.

The central figure is Charicleia, born white and hence exposed by her mother the Ethiopian queen. Conveyed by a travelling Greek, Charicles, from Ethiopia to Delphi and there given a good Greek education, she became priestess of *Artemis, at whose festival she and a Thessalian aristocrat, Theagenes, fall in love. Aided by a priest from Memphis, Calasiris, searching for Charicleia at her mother's request, they elope, and after many novelistic adventures—pirates, brigands, lustful suitors, false deaths—they at last reach Ethiopian *Meroe, where they escape being sacrificed, and Charicleia, recognized by her parents, marries Theagenes.

Heliodorus masterfully launches his reader into mid-story, with a bizarre scene of blood, bodies, and booty on an Egyptian beach viewed through the eyes of mystified brigands. When the couple, seized by other brigands, seem about to reveal their story to readers and to Cnemon, an Athenian assigned to tend them, instead Cnemon tells his own tale, flowing from his stepmother's lust for him, a tale further entwined with theirs in the person of a slave Thisbe, whose murder is for some time thought to be Charicleia's. We only learn how Charicleia and (much later) Calasiris reached Delphi, and left it, with Theagenes, for Egypt from Calasiris' long narrative (2. 24. 5 to 5. 1) to the naïve listener Cnemon in Egyptian Chemmis, and further vital action—the discovery that Charicleia is in Chemmis too (bought by their host Nausicles as Thisbe) delays its completion to 5. 17–32. Thereafter the linear narrative exploits surprise more than suspense, save that we always wonder if the couple will 'really' be reunited.

Recurrent *metaphors from the tragic stage and assessments, by characters and author, of the gods' and Fate's role in the universe, invite us to read the work as elevated and deeply serious; Charicleia's outstanding beauty is idealistically conveyed, and just as Theagenes abhors the advances of others so Charicleia persistently defers sex with him until their goal of Ethiopia and marriage. Yet in some scenes Grand Guignol trespasses on the comic, recalling that Calasiris, in a sense a symbol for the author, and the work's only interesting character, combines true piety with mendacious trickery. The novel becomes a *tour de force* in which one literary trick succeeds another. Most are conventional—*dreams, *oracles, and examples of *ekphrasis (the beach-scene, a carved jewel, siege-works, an oasis, a giraffe)—but Heliodorus' exploitation of them is unusually complex and subtle. His Atticism (see ASIANISM AND ATTICISM) is careful, and his long periods, with much especially participial subordination, are a better vehicle for extended narrative than the short sentences of Achilles and *Longus. Since Amyot's French translation (1547) there have been numerous others into modern languages, and Heliodorus has influenced both literature (e.g. Sidney's *New Arcadia*, Tasso's *Gerusalemme liberata*, Cervantes' *Persiles*)

and painting (e.g. Dubois's Fontainebleau cycle). See NOVEL, GREEK.

EDITIO PRINCEPS Basel, 1534 (Opsopoeus).

STANDARD EDITIONS R. M. Rattenbury, T. W. Lumb, and J. Maillon (Budé, 1935–43; 2nd edn. 1960); A. Colonna (1938), but see Budé vol. 3 pref. No commentary since Coraes (1804), in modern Greek.

TRANSLATIONS J. R. Morgan, in B. P. Reardon (ed.), *Collected Ancient Greek Novels* (1989); M. Hadas (1957); W. Lamb (1961).

CRITICISM T. R. Goethals, *The Aethiopica of Heliodorus* (Diss. Columbia 1959); G. N. Sandy, *Heliodorus* (1982); V. Hefti, *Zur Erzählungstechnik in Heliodors Aethiopika* (1950); E. Feuillâtre, *Études sur les Éthiopiques d'Héliodore* (1966); Rohde, *Griech. Roman*, 453 ff.; K. Münscher, *RE* 8 (1913), 20–8, 'Heliodorus' 15; Christ–Schmid–Stählin 2 / 2⁶. 820 ff.; A. Lesky, *A History of Greek Literature* (1966), 866–7; E. L. Bowie, *CHCL* 1. 694–6 (= paperback 1 / 4 (1989), 134–6); H. Rommel, *Die naturwissenschaftlich-paradoxographischen Exkurse …* (1923); T. Hägg, *The Novel in Antiquity* (1983), 54–73; G. Anderson, *Eros Sophistes* (1982), 33–40, and *Ancient Fiction* (1984); W. Bühler, *Wien. Stud.* 1976; G. N. Sandy, *TAPA* 1982, 141–67; J. J. Winkler, *YClS* 1982; J. R. Morgan, *Cl. Ant.* 1982, *JHS* 1989, *TAPA* 1989, and *Groningen Colloquia*, ed. H. Hofmann, 4 (1992); M. Pulquério Futre Pinheiro, *Estruturas técnico-narrativas nas Etiópicas de Heliodoro* (1987); S. Bartsch, *Decoding the Ancient Novel* (1989); J. Fritsch, *Der Sprachgebrauch des griechischen Romanschriftsteller Heliodor und sein Verhältnis zum Atticismus*, 2 vols. (1901–2).

DATE M. van der Valk, *Mnemos.* 1941; A. Colonna, *Athenaeum* 1950; T. Szepessy, *Acta Antiquae Academiae Scientiarum Hungaricae* 1957; R. Keydell, in *Polychronion: Festschrift Dölger* (1966); C. Lacombrade, *Rev. Ét. Grec.* 1970; T. Szepessy, *Acta Antiquae Academiae Scientiarum Hungaricae* 1976; M. Maróth, *Acta Antiquae Academiae Scientiarum Hungaricae* 1979; C. S. Lightfoot, *Hist.* 1988.   E. L. B.

Heliopolis (mod. Baalbek) was the religious centre of the *Ituraean *tetrarchy, after whose dissolution it became a Roman colony (15 BC). The cult of the Heliopolitan triad, *Jupiter, *Venus, and *Mercury, became widespread in the Roman world. The huge 1st-cent. AD temple of Jupiter-Hadad (Ba'al-Hadad having been worshipped here earlier), its two courtyards (completed AD 244–9), the adjacent Antonine-period temple of Mercury-Bacchus (see DIONYSUS), and another small circular temple are among the most impressive monuments of the Syrian school of Hellenistic architecture.

T. Wiegand, *Baalbek* (1921–5); Y. Hajjar, *La Triade d'Héliopolis-Baalbek* (1977–85).   J. F. H.

Helios, the sun. In early Greece Helios was always treated with reverence but received little actual cult. *Anaxagoras' announcement that the 'sun was a red-hot mass' caused outrage (DL 2. 12, etc.) and it was not uncommon to salute and even pray to the sun at its rising and setting (Pl. *Symp.* 220d, *Leg.* 887e, cf. Hes. *Op.* 339, and for respect Pl. *Ap.* 26c), but *Aristophanes (1) can treat the practice of sacrificing to sun and moon as one that distinguishes *barbarians from Greeks (*Pax* 406). Hence evidence for actual cults is scarce and usually cannot be shown to be ancient (Farnell, *Cults* 5. 419 f.; but for Athens in the 3rd cent. BC see now *SEG* 33. 115. 12). The exception was *Rhodes, where Helios—subject in fact of the original 'colossus of Rhodes'—was the leading god and had an important festival, the Halieia (Nilsson, *Feste*, 427); the myth explaining this prominence is told in Pindar, *Ol.* 7. 54 ff. In Homer he is invoked and receives an offering as witness to an oath (*Il.* 3. 277), and his all-seeing, all-nurturing power is often stressed in poetry (see Aesch. *Cho.* 984–6 with A. F. Garvie's note).

For his most important myth see PHAETHON. He is regularly conceived as a charioteer, who drives daily from east to west across the sky (a conception with both Indo-European and near-eastern parallels). His journey back each night in a cup is already attested in *Mimnermus fr. 12 West (for many further early poetic references see Ath. 469 c ff.).

The identification of the Sun with *Apollo was familiar in the 5th cent. BC but did not become canonical until much later (doubts still in Callim. *Hecale* fr. 103 Hollis): *Aeschylus in *Bassarides* probably associated it with *Orpheus, the religious innovator (M. L. West, *Studies in Aeschylus*, (1990), 38–42), and a passage in *Euripides (*Phaethon* 225 Diggle) where it appears unambiguously for the first time also mentions (whether for this reason or another is unclear) 'those who know the secret names of the gods'. (The identification is also attested for the scientists *Parmenides and *Empedocles: DK 28 A 20, 31 A 23). The 'visible gods' of heaven acquired new prominence in the astral religion of *Plato (1), and *Cleanthes the Stoic named the sun the 'leading principle' (ἡγεμονικόν) of the world (SVF 1. 499). Through indirect influence from philosophy, worship of Helios probably became more common in the late Hellenistic period and after. But it was not until the later Roman empire that Helios/*Sol grew into a figure of central importance in actual cult.

Farnell, *Cults*, 5. 417–20; Nilsson, *GGR* 2. 332, 508–19; A. J. Festugière, *La Révélation d'Hermès Trismégiste* 2 (1949), chs. 5–7; N. Yalouris, *LIMC* 5. 1005–34.   R. C. T. P.

Hell See DEATH, ATTITUDES TO; HADES; TARTARUS.

Hellanicus (1) of Lesbos (*c*.480–395 BC) was a *mythographer, ethnographer, and chronicler of major significance. Though his background was in the tradition of Ionian *historiē* begun by Hecataeus (1), he deserves to be ranked with *Herodotus (1) and *Thucydides (2) (Gell. *NA* 15. 23) in the effect he had on the development of Greek *historiography. He wrote extensively, but only some 200 fragments have survived.

His five works of mythography (the study of myth as history)—*Phoronis, Deukalioneia, Atlantis, Asopis,* and *Troika*—brought together in a form that was definitive for later scholarship the efforts of earlier mythographers to collate and integrate the disparate corpora of *mythoi* into a coherent and chronologically consistent narrative. The effect of this creative activity upon the whole classical tradition is incalculable.

His ethnographic works (studies of peoples and places) were even more extensive, ranging from areas in Greece (Thessaly, Boeotia, Arcadia, and Lesbos) to foreign countries (Egypt, Cyprus, Scythia, and Persia). They were, however, less influential, partly because they were largely unoriginal, partly because they were overshadowed by the great work of Herodotus.

His other area of interest was the Universal Chronicle. Hellanicus pioneered the use of victor lists (Carnean Games; see CARNEA) and of magistrates (priestesses of *Hera at *Argos (2)) to establish a common chronology for Greek history (see TIME-RECKONING).

He combined all his talents late in life in Athens to create the first local history of *Attica (*Atthis), based upon his ordering of the succession of mythical kings and the list of eponymous archons. His *Atthis* (called *Attike Syngraphe* by Thucydides, 1. 97) covered in two books all Athenian history to the end of the *Peloponnesian War. Its tone was influenced by Athenian national *propaganda. Thucydides criticized Hellanicus but used his *Priestesses* (2. 2. 1, 4. 133. 2).

FGrH 4, 323a and 608a.   P. E. H.

Hellanicus (2), grammarian, a pupil of *Agathocles (2) of

Cyzicus, *c*.230/20–160/50 BC. He was interested in Homer and Herodotus, but titles of his works do not survive.

Ed. F. Montanari (1988).   N. G. W.

hellanodikai ('Greek judges'), the title of the chief judges at the *Olympian Games, the *Nemean Games, and the Asclepian Games (see ASCLEPIUS) at *Epidaurus. The Olympic *hellanodikai* were appointed for a single festival from the leading families of *Elis: they presided over the games, exercising disciplinary authority over the athletes, and over the banquet which ended the festival. The title was also used for a magistracy in *Sparta (Xen. *Lac.* 13. 11).   F. A. W.; P. J. R.

Helle, daughter of *Athamas and sister of Phrixus, who, while escaping with her brother from their stepmother Ino, fell into the sea from the flying ram with the Golden Fleece which was carrying them to *Colchis; the sea was thereafter known as Helle's sea or *Hellespont.   E. Ke.

Hellen, eponymous ancestor of the *Hellenes, son or brother of *Deucalion (Thuc. 1. 3. 2; schol. Pind. *Ol.* 9. 68). His sons were Dorus, *Xuthus (father of *Ion (1)), and *Aeolus (2), the ancestors of the *Dorians, *Ionians, and Aeolians (Hes. fr. 9 M–W).   E. Ke.

Hellenes (Ἕλληνες), the name by which the Greeks called, and still call, themselves. Originally it and the territorial name 'Hellas' appear to have been confined to an area south of the river Spercheios, in the vicinity of *Thermopylae. In Homer the Greeks are called 'Achaeans', 'Argives', or 'Danai', but 'Panhellenes' (see PANHELLENISM) appear under *Aias (2), son of Oeleus, the Locrian hero (*Il.* 2. 530), and 'Hellenes' under *Achilles (*Il.* 2. 684), whose home was the Spercheios valley. Similarly, 'Hellas' is a district in Achilles' kingdom (*Il.* 2. 683), though it apparently extended southwards, perhaps to Eleon in *Boeotia (*Il.* 9. 447 ff.).

How and why the name came to be applied to all Greeks and the whole of Greece is uncertain, but the original centre of the *amphictiony which later came to control *Delphi was at Anthela in the area where the original Hellenes lived (Hdt. 7. 200. 2), and it is possible that the name came to have a wider connotation as the influence of Delphi spread, perhaps in connection with western colonization. On the other hand, the title of the umpires at the Olympian Games, *hellanodikai*, if early, may indicate that the spread of the name had something to do with those games. See also HELLEN.

H. T. Wade-Gery, *JHS* 1924, appendix; W. G. Forrest, *Hist.* 1957; R. Hope Simpson and J. F. Lazenby, *The Catalogue of the Ships in Homer's Iliad* (1970).   J. F. La.

Hellenica Oxyrhynchia See OXYRHYNCHUS, THE HISTORIAN FROM.

Hellenism, Hellenization, Greek culture (cf. HELLEN; HELLENES) and the diffusion of that culture, a process usually seen as active. The relation between the two modern words is controversial: should the longer word be avoided (see ORIENTALISM) because of its suggestion of cultural imperialism? (Cf. Bowersock (see bibliog. below): 'Hellenization is . . . a modern idea, reflecting modern forms of cultural domination'.)

The ancient terminology is interesting but treacherous. The earliest use of the verb 'Hellenize' (Gk. ἑλληνίζειν) is in a linguistic context: Thucydides 2. 68 says the Amphilochian Argives were 'Hellenized as to their present language' by the Ambraciots. But the extra words 'as to . . . language' perhaps (though see *CR* 1984, 246) indicate that the word normally had a wider, cultural sense.

Hellenism, Hellenization

Nevertheless, 'Hellenism' in the Classical period is not quite on all fours with *Medism, which has a political tinge. The asymmetry is interesting because it underlines the absence, in the evidence which has come down to us, of a non-Greek point of view from which political sympathy with Greece could be expressed (see PERSIAN WARS: THE PERSIAN VIEWPOINT).

But the most famous use of 'Hellenism', Ἑλληνισμός, is at 2 Maccabees 4: 13, cf. Acts of the Apostles 6: 1; 9: 29 for 'Hellenists', Ἑλληνισταί. Here too it seems that more is meant than just speaking Greek. *How* much more, is disputed.

In modern times the 19th-cent. historian J. G. Droysen, taking his cue above all from the Maccabees and Acts passages, gave 'Hellenismus' (the German is best not translated) a powerful and extended sense, not just 'correct Greek' but 'fusion of Greek and non-Greek'. Droysen associated the word with a particular period, that between *Alexander (3) the Great and the victory of Octavian (later *Augustus) at *Actium. It was in this period, the 'Hellenistic Age', that Greek culture was most intensely diffused; this diffusion was seen as a success story, not least because it made possible the eventual rise and spread of *Christianity.

The post-colonial, late 20th cent. has reacted against such a simple picture. In the Droysenian and post-Droysen view of the ancient world there was arguably (cf. Bernal) some neglect of the non-Greek, especially the Semitic, contribution to Greek achievements. Even in the study of the religion and art of the Archaic period (see GREECE (HISTORY)) the near-eastern element has recently (Burkert) been stressed, though this too is a controversial topic.

'Hellenization or Hellenism?' is a question best approached by considering the main alleged agents of the process of Hellenization (alternatively phrased, 'the main vehicles of Hellenism').

Conventionally, Hellenization has in modern times been associated with the post-Alexander period, so that as we have seen the word 'Hellenistic' was (and is) regularly confined to the centuries 323–31 BC. But epigraphic evidence (see EPIGRAPHY, GREEK), above all that collected and edited by Louis Robert, has shown that in the Persian Empire of the *Achaemenids (5th and 4th cents. BC), Greek language and even constitutional forms were adopted by dynasts in *Lycia like *Pericles (2) of Limyra and by *Mausolus and his family. Such adoption was perfectly compatible with anti-Greek political behaviour, as the career of Mausolus himself demonstrates. (There is a parallel here with the ambiguities of *philhellenism in the Roman period.) And rulers like Mausolus did strange things with the Greek governmental apparatus they copied: Greek eyebrows would lift at the sight of a decree like that (*ILabraunda* no. 40) by which Mausolus and *Artemisia (2) conferred block proxeny (essentially an individual honour, see PROXENOS) on the citizens of *Cnossus, in a decree which opens 'it seemed good to Mausolus and Artemisia', just like a two-person *polis. And Mausolus avoided the great Panhellenic sanctuaries, preferring the local Carian shrines like *Sinuri and *Labraunda: this is a sort of 'Carianization' alongside the more obvious, *and surely real*, Hellenization. See ASIA MINOR.

Such patriotic retention or reinvention of local culture goes right through the history of post-Classical Asia Minor. It is true that places like *Aspendus or *Side 'discovered' their Greek origins in the early Hellenistic period when it was convenient to do so (see e.g. *SEG* 34. 282, *Argos (2)/Aspendus link); Greeks expressed this sort of thing in terms of '*kinship', συγγένεια; that is, the relation between *mētropolis and daughter-city. (The idea is not just Hellenistic, note already Thuc. 1. 95. 1, the justification for the *Delian League in terms of kinship between *Ionians.)

Fictitious descents and *genealogies were popular, especially Argive (*Philip (1) II and Alexander the Great themselves claimed Argive descent, cf. Hdt. 5. 22 and Thuc. 5. 80; see FOUNDERS, CITY; KINSHIP). But against such assertions of Greekness, real, exaggerated, or imagined, must be set the survival (or artificial resurrection?) of Iranian and other indigenous proper names into the Roman imperial period, and ambiguous cultural behaviour like that of Mausolus, already considered.

Alexander's own aims in this department have not escaped the re-examination to which the rest of his behaviour and career have been exposed in the years since the Second World War. *Plutarch's enthusiastic view of Alexander the Hellenizer was always suspect, and the opposite, modern, view—Hellenization as an instrument of oppression—was never wholly convincing. P. Briant (see his entry COLONIZATION, HELLENISTIC in this dictionary) now offers a subtler conception: the indigenous populations were neither marginalized on the one hand, nor subjected to enforced Hellenization on the other. Whatever Alexander's intentions, exciting new evidence like that from Kandahar in Afghanistan (see ALEXANDRIA (3)) shows that the Greek culture introduced by him flourished thousands of miles from the old Greek centres (see too AI KHANOUM; CLEARCHUS (3); and note *SEG* 20. 326, a bilingual (Greek and Aramaic) Buddhist text from 3rd-cent. BC Kandahar).

Similar, though worse, problems of understanding arise with the *Seleucids. Their foundation of enduring Greek *poleis* (see POLIS) has long been reckoned as an impressive Hellenizing achievement, and here too (see ICAROS (2), mod. Failaka) epigraphic evidence speaks eloquently about geographical areas on which the literary sources are silent. But recent work (Sherwin-White and Kuhrt) has tended to emphasize the continuity between Achaemenid *Persian and Babylonian structures (see SELEUCIDS in this dictionary). Traditionalists will however still wish (see esp. F. Walbank, *LCM* 13 (1988), 108 ff.) to protest that the Seleucids never forgot that they were a Graeco-Macedonian dynasty; and we still await a full re-examination of C. Habicht's striking statistics (*Vierteljahrschr. für Soziologie* 1958, 1 ff.) about the small number of indigenous personnel employed by the Seleucids. At present his case has not been overthrown.

In one troubled area of policy, Seleucid treatment of the *Jews, the modern debate has been specially lively (Hengel; Millar 1978). How far are early 2nd-cent. developments (see MACCABEES) to be attributed to a 'Hellenizing party' in Judaea itself and how much to Seleucid insistence?

At Rome too, the acceptance or rejection of cultural Hellenism remained an issue (see PHILHELLENISM; PORCIUS CATO (1), M.) even after the possibility of Greek or Macedonian military or political victories over Rome had evaporated.

The Greek *polis* and its culture not only survived into the Roman period; the introduction of the *polis* was the normal method by which Romans imposed their own authority in the Greek east (though '*polis*' by that time did not quite mean the same as in the days of the Delian League; see further ROMANIZATION (the east), and Millar in Hansen). There is plenty of evidence, especially epigraphic, for élite acceptance of this long-lasting blend of Greek and Roman values. But inscriptions and literary texts are never the whole story; and in Asia Minor, in particular, the attachment to cultural systems other than those of Hellenism continues to be traceable until very late dates. Large allowance must, then, be made both for the tastes of groups other than the élites whom alone our evidence allows us to see, and for the assertive awareness, by the élites themselves, of the non-Greek dimension to their own past. This is particularly true of Asia Minor. Nevertheless it is remarkable that highly traditional Greek forms of discourse should have been used to negotiate a relationship with non-Greek culture in the Hellenistic period proper (Parsons). It is also remarkable that these same traditional literary forms (including and especially *rhetoric and *epigram), and also that traditional pagan Greek *religion (including and especially oracles, see Lane Fox (below, bibliog.) and ORACLES (late antiquity)), should have propelled Hellenism as far into late antiquity as they did. Even in Byzantine antiquity, Christian epigrammatists catch perfectly the idioms of pagan Hellenism. See also GREEK LANGUAGE; JULIAN.

ANCIENT SOURCES Hdt. 8. 144; ML 7, 93 with *Fouilles de Xanthos 9* (1992); Tod 138, 139, 161, 194; *SEG* 28. 942 and other texts in S. Hornblower, *Mausolus* 364–9; OGI 90 and 233 (= Austin no. 190); *BSA* 1982, 79 ff. (*Romulus and Remus at Chios); Diod. Sic. 18. 7. 1.

LITERATURE Rostovtzeff, *Hellenistic World* 472–502; 1032–1134; A. Momigliano, *Alien Wisdom* (1975); R. Bichler, *Hellenismus* (1983): Droysen etc.; S. Said (ed.) *Ἑλληνισμός* (1991); E. Hall, *Inventing the Barbarian* (1989); M. Bernal, *Black Athena* (1987–); W. Burkert, *The Orientalizing Revolution* (1992), with R. Osborne, *Journal of Mediterranean Archaeology* 1993, 231 ff.; F. Walbank, *The Hellenistic World*, 2nd edn. (1993), ch. 4; C. Préaux, *Le Monde hellénistique*, 1978, 545 ff.; S. K. Eddy, *The King is Dead: Near Eastern Resistance to Hellenism* (1961); P. Briant, *Rois, tributs et paysans* (1982), 227 ff.; P. Fraser, *Afghan Studies* 1979, 9 ff.; J. D. Grainger, *The Cities of Seleucid Syria* (1990); A. Kuhrt and S. M. Sherwin-White, *Hellenism in the East* (1987); S. M. Sherwin-White and A. Kuhrt, *From Samarkhand to Sardis* (1993); S. Hornblower, *Mausolus* (1982), esp. ch. 12, and *CAH* 6² (1994), ch. 8a; F. Millar, *PCPS* 1983, 55 ff., *The Roman Near East* (1993), *Journal of Jewish Studies* 1987, 143 f., and in M. H. Hansen, *The Ancient Greek City-State* (1993); S. Mitchell, *Anatolia*, 2 vols. (1993); Fraser, *Ptol. Alex.* 786 ff. (Cyrene); P. J. Parsons, in A. W. Bulloch, E. S. Gruen, and others (eds.), *Images and Ideologies: Self-Definition in the Hellenistic World* (1993), 152 ff. (literary treatments); M. Hengel, *Judaism and Hellenism* (1974), and F. Millar, *Journal of Jewish Studies* 1978, 1 ff.; J. Boardman, *The Diffusion of Classical Art in Antiquity* (1995). On Rome: A. Toynbee, *Hannibal's Legacy* (1965), 2, chs. 13–14; E. Rawson, *CAH* 8² (1989), ch. 12; E. S. Gruen, *Studies in Greek Culture and Roman Policy* (1990) and *Culture and National Identity in Republican Rome* (1992). Later antiquity: R. Lane Fox, *Pagans and Christians* (1986); G. Bowersock, *Hellenism in Late Antiquity* (1990).

S. H.

Hellenistic age See HELLENISM, HELLENIZATION.

Hellenistic poetry at Rome The influence of Hellenistic Greek poetry on Roman poetry can hardly be overestimated. Latin poetry is from its beginnings based on scholarly appreciation of the literary production of the Greeks and it was from the perspective of the literary and scholarly activity of the Hellenistic period that the Romans viewed Greek literature as a whole. The fragmentary nature of early Latin poetry means that the first stages of the *reception of Hellenistic poetry at Rome remain obscure. It is possible that *Livius Andronicus employed the work of Hellenistic commentators on Homer in translating the *Odyssey* and that *Naevius and *Accius knew and imitated the *Argonautica* of Apollonius. The *Annales* of *Ennius provides better evidence. When he proclaims his originality, presents himself as *dicti studiosus* (a student of language) proud of his stylistic superiority over his predecessors, and describes his poetic initiation, he has in mind *Callimachus (3)'s *Aetia*, although the exact nature and extent of his debt remain unclear. Poets of the late 2nd and early 1st cent. BC such as Q. *Lutatius Catulus (1), *Laevius, Cn. *Matius, *Sueius and *Lucilius (1) are more or less obscure figures but clearly influenced by Hellenistic poetry and so important forerunners of later trends.

For *Catullus and a few like-minded contemporaries, perhaps under the guidance of *Parthenius, the ideal of Hellenistic elegance and style was represented by Callimachus. Catullus' 95th poem represents a Callimachean manifesto evoking the generic and stylistic grounds on which the new poets establish their literary credo. They cultivate a studied elegance in vocabulary, word order, metre, and narrative form with the aim of bringing Callimachean refinement to Latin poetry. *Epic and drama give way to polymetric experiments in lyric and iambic poetry, to *epigram and narrative elegy, and to the *epyllion. Cicero uses the terms οἱ νεώτεροι (*Att.* 7. 2. 1, hence the modern word 'neoterics') and *poetae novi* (*Orat.* 161) to refer critically to these 'modern' poets and when he refers to the *cantores Euphorionis* (singers after the manner of *Euphorion (2), *Tusc.* 3. 45) he probably has the same people in mind. But although the ageing *Cicero considered their verse too affected, the poetry of his youthful years shows that even he did not escape Hellenistic influence.

Some scholars stress the continuity between the New Poets and the Augustans and emphasize the Hellenistic element in Augustan poetry. Others argue that Augustan classicism represents an essentially 'post-modernist' movement which moves beyond the 'modernist' Hellenistic aesthetic. All agree, however, that Hellenistic poetry plays a fundamental role, and *Virgil, *Horace, *Propertius, *Tibullus, and *Ovid all owe much to Hellenistic models and the Callimachean aesthetic. But there is more to Hellenistic poetry at Rome than Callimachus. *Philitas, *Euphorion (2), *Theocritus, *Aratus (1), *Apollonius (1) Rhodius, the epigrammatists collected in the *Garland* of Meleager (see MELEAGER (2)), and many others were all read and imitated. Hellenistic influence may also be seen more generally in the presence, in a more or less concentrated way, of certain features which may be found in poetry of any genre. Hellenistic *doctrina* (learning) may be displayed by the use of obscure myths or less-well-known versions of better-known stories, of recondite epithets and learned etymologies. The Latin poets also follow Hellenistic precedent in cultivating sophisticated techniques of allusion to one or more literary models and self-consciously drawing attention to their literary tradition. Similarly, the art of imitating a model by making use of commentaries is typically Hellenistic. Hellenistic too is the writing of carefully structured poetic books (see BOOKS, POETIC).

The poets of the post-Augustan period continue to read Hellenistic poetry but do so with one eye on its *reception in 1st-cent. BC Latin poetry and it is against the latter that they measure themselves. It is now the Augustan poets rather than the Hellenistic Greeks who represent the ideal of elegance and style. Nevertheless, in works such as the *Silvae* of *Statius and in the poems of *Ausonius, *Claudian, and the *Anthologia Latina* the spirit of Hellenistic poetry lives on at Rome. See ELEGIAC POETRY, LATIN.

From a vast bibliography see W. Kroll, *Studien zum Verständnis der römischen Literatur* (1924); M. Puelma Piwonka, *Lucilius und Kallimachos* (1949); W. Wimmel, *Kallimachos in Rom* (1960); J. K. Newman, *Augustus and the New Poetry* (1967), and *Roman Catullus and the Modification of the Alexandrian Sensibility* (1990); D. O. Ross Jr., *Style and Tradition in Catullus* (1969); J. Granarolo, *D'Ennius à Catulle* (1971); A. Traglia, *Poetae Novi* (1974); F. Cairns, *Tibullus: A Hellenistic Poet at Rome* (1979); W. V. Clausen, *Virgil's Aeneid and the Tradition of Hellenistic Poetry* (1987); G. O. Hutchinson, *Hellenistic Poetry* (1988), ch. 6. D. P. N.

hellēnotamiai ('treasurers of the Greeks'), were the chief financial officials of the *Delian League. Their office was in *Delos until 454/3 BC, in Athens after that; but from the first they were

Hellespont

Athenians appointed by Athens (one from each tribe, probably by election). They received the tribute from the allies, and from 453 paid the *aparchē* (first-fruits) to the treasury of Athena; and they made payments on the instructions of the assembly, chiefly to generals for their campaigns but sometimes for other purposes (such as the Acropolis buildings). In or shortly before 411 an enlarged board of twenty *hellēnotamiai* was given responsibility for both the league and the state treasuries; with the fall of the Athenian empire in 404 the office was abolished.

A. G. Woodhead, *JHS* 1959, 149–52.   A. W. G.; P. J. R.

Hellespont, the narrow strait dividing Europe from Asia at the final exit of the waters of the Black Sea (see EUXINE) and Marmara into the Aegean—the modern Dardanelles. It was crossed by the Persian army under *Xerxes between *Sestos and *Abydos, at the narrowest part near the modern Nagara Point. It was again crossed by *Alexander (3) the Great in 334 BC. A strong current runs out from the Hellespont into the *Aegean. Callipolis (mod. Gallipoli), Lampsacus, Sestos, and Abydos are on its shores, with the sites of Troy and Dardanus on the Asiatic side. All cities alike derived much of their wealth from the fisheries (see FISHING), and from the passage of people and armies from Europe to Asia and vice versa. The name Hellespont is connected with the legend of Phrixus and *Helle.

J. Boardman, *The Greeks Overseas*, 3rd edn. (1980), 264 ff.   S. C.

Hellespontine Phrygia the district of *Asia Minor closest to the *Hellespont. See DASCYLIUM; PHARNABAZUS.

helots Some Greek states had servile populations which were not privately owned chattel-slaves or *douloi* (see SLAVERY), but, because their status seemed superior in important respects, came to be categorized as 'between free men and (chattel) *douloi*' (Pollux 3. 83). Unlike the latter, they were not imported individually from outside but enslaved collectively as a national group. Very little is known about any of them except the helots of *Sparta, but the evidence even for the helots is such that scholars have come to diametrically opposite conclusions both as to the timing of their enslavement and as to the nature of their servitude.

The name helots (*heilōtai*) is probably derived from a root meaning 'capture', and according to the usual view first the Laconian and then the Messenian helots (see LACONIA; MESSENIA) were reduced to servitude by conquest between about the 10th and the 7th cents. BC; it was at any rate as a conquered people that the Spartans treated the helots in the historical period, actually declaring war on them annually by proclamation of the *ephors. Greek writers stressed Spartan brutality towards the helots (e.g. Thuc. 4. 80), and the *krypteia* system of helot control, which also served as a manhood *initiation ritual for would-be Spartiates, was nothing if not brutal. But not all helots wanted to eat their Spartan masters, even raw, as one disaffected Spartan agitator claimed (Xen. *Hell.* 3. 3. 6); indeed, some of them established close working relationships with them, and it was these—mainly Laconians, presumably—who were employed on a large scale in the army and, especially during and after the *Peloponnesian War, liberated in substantial numbers (thereby becoming known as *neodamōdeis*). By contrast, the helots of Messenia seem to have nursed a permanent hostility born of 'national' cohesion, and the great helot revolts of the 7th, 5th, and 4th cents. were largely if not wholly Messenian affairs. See NATIONALISM.

Actual figures for helots are unavailable. Herodotus (9. 10, 29) implies an unacceptably high 7:1 ratio, and Xenophon (*Hell.* 3. 3.

4–11) confirms that they outnumbered their masters by some way. Perhaps they even outnumbered the total free population of Laconia and Messenia, a balance unknown in communities with a chattel-slave population. Unlike such slaves, too, the helots reproduced themselves through family relations, albeit under threat of dissolution by murder, and were granted some property rights. But they were like slaves in being also themselves property—of the Spartan community rather than individual Spartan men and women. The Spartan assembly alone had the power to manumit them, which it exercised exceptionally—and duplicitously—in particular to compensate for the dearth of citizen manpower (*oliganthrōpia*) that became ever more apparent from about 450 on. They survived as a self-perpetuating body until *Epaminondas freed the Messenians in 369, and *Nabis the remaining Laconian helots early in the 2nd cent. BC.

Apart from their military obligations to the community as a whole, the main responsibility of the helots was to provide their individual Spartan masters and mistresses with a fixed quota of natural produce (either a percentage or an absolute amount, depending on which sources are followed). From that contribution—or tribute—the Spartan citizen paid over to his mess (*sussition*) the amount required to maintain his citizen standing. The helots thus 'enjoyed' the ambivalent position of being both the bedrock of the entire Spartan polity, and the enemy within.

D. Lotze, *ΜΕΤΑΞΥ ΕΛΕΥΘΕΡΩΝ ΚΑΙ ΔΟΥΛΩΝ* (1959); P. Cartledge, in P. Cartledge and D. Harvey (eds.), *Crux: Essays in Greek History presented to G. E. M. de Ste Croix* (1985), 16–46; Y. Garlan, *Slavery in Ancient Greece* (1988); P. Cartledge and A. J. S. Spawforth, *Hellenistic and Roman Sparta* (1989); R. Talbert, *Hist.* 1989, 22–40; P. Cartledge, *Hist.* 1991, 391–3; J. Ducat, *Les Hilotes, BCH* Suppl. 20 (1989); A. Paradiso, *Forme di dipendenza nel mondo greco: Ricerche sul VI. libro di Ateneo* (1991); S. J. Hodkinson, 'Explorations in Classical Spartan Property and Society' (Cambridge Ph.D. thesis, 1992), ch. 3.   P. A. C.

Helvetii, a Celtic people (see CELTS) originally located in southern Germany, which c.100 BC migrated to an area between lakes Constance and Geneva, and the Jura and the Alps. In 58 a second migration was defeated by *Caesar, who sent the survivors home and later planted a veteran colony at Noviodunum Equestrium (Nyon): a secure central Swiss Plateau blocked barbarian invasion of Gaul and allowed easy communication with the Rhine. Under *Augustus the Helvetii became part of Gallia Belgica, from *Domitian of Germania Superior. They were organized like other Gallic *civitates*, with their capital at Aventicum, and several *pagi*. They paid dearly for their opposition to *Vitellius (AD 69), but were favoured by the Flavians, and subsequently enjoyed significant prosperity. However, when the *limes* was abandoned c.260, their region was exposed to the attacks of the Alamanni and was heavily fortified. By 460 it was under the control of the Burgundians and Alamanni.

F. Stähelin, *Die Schweiz in römischer Zeit*, 3rd edn. (1948); D. van Berchem, *Les Routes et l'histoire* (1982).   C. E. S.; J. F. Dr.

Helvidius Priscus, son of a *primipilaris* (see PRIMIPILUS) from *Samnium was tribune of the *plebs* in AD 56, praetor in 70. In early youth he studied philosophy seriously, and about 55 married (as his second wife) Fannia, daughter of *Thrasea Paetus, whose political doctrines he shared. Exiled after his father-in-law's condemnation in 66, he returned under *Galba, and though earlier a friend of *Vespasian, he took a critical attitude towards the Flavian regime from the start (Tac. *Hist.* 4. 6–8, 43). Later his attacks on the emperor became vehement, and he was exiled by 75 and subsequently executed. Though he had clearly refrained from holding office in the later tyrannical phase of Nero's reign, his Stoic principles (Tac. *Hist.* 4. 5) were compatible with acceptance of the Principate as a political system (see STOICISM), and *Cassius Dio (66. 12) probably reflects the deliberate misrepresentations of C. *Licinius Mucianus when he says that Helvidius advocated δημοκρατία, 'democracy', i.e. the republican system. He did insist on senatorial independence and freedom of expression (Epictetus 1. 2. 19–24; Tac. *Hist.* 4. 5). His criticism of Vespasian's son or sons probably related to their conduct and not to the idea of hereditary succession in itself.

Helvidius' son by his first marriage, a friend of *Tacitus (1) and *Pliny (2) the Younger, became consul under *Domitian but was executed *c.*93.

D. R. Dudley, *A History of Cynicism* (1937), 132 ff.; Rostovtzeff, *Roman Empire*² 114 ff.; C. Wirszubski, *Libertas as a Political Idea at Rome* (1950), 124–9, 148; Syme, *Tacitus*; P. A. Brunt, *PBSR* 1975, 7 ff.
G. E. F. C.; M. T. G.

Helvius (*RE* 12, cf. 11) **Cinna, Gaius,** a native apparently of Brescia and a friend of *Catullus (1), with whom he was probably in *Bithynia in 57/6 BC (Catull. 10); he seems to have been there also in 66 BC at the end of the Mithradatic War and to have brought back the poet *Parthenius to Rome. Cinna was a *doctus poeta,* 'learned poet', of the 'Alexandrian' school; Parthenius probably instilled in him the love of the exceedingly obscure *Euphorion (2), and he is the likely target of Cicero's barb at *cantores Euphorionis,* 'singers in the manner of Euphorion' (*Tusc.* 3. 45, July 45). His miniature epic *Zmyrna*, the work of nine years (Quint. *Inst.* 10. 4. 4; Catull. 95) was a masterpiece of the 'new' poetry and was much admired (Catull. 95; cf. Virg. *Ecl.* 9. 35). Its subject, the Cyprian legend of the incestuous love of Zmyrna (or *Myrrha) for her father, gave opportunity for developing the Alexandrian interest in the psychology of passion, and its allusive learning was such that in Augustan times it already needed a commentary, which was provided by L. Crassicius (Suet. *Gram.* 19). Cinna sent off the young *Asinius Pollio on a visit to Greece with a *propemptikon*; it too needed a commentary (supplied by Iulius Hyginus; see HYGINUS (1)) in Augustan times. He also wrote light verse in a variety of metres. He was tribune in 44 BC and was lynched at Caesar's funeral because he was mistaken for the anti-Caesarian L. *Cornelius Cinna (2). See HELLENISTIC POETRY AT ROME.

T. P. Wiseman, *Cinna the Poet* (1974); H. Dahlmann *AAWM* 1977. 8; L. C. Watson *Stud. Ital.* 1982, 93; J. Morgan *CQ* 1990, 558; Courtney, *FLP* 212.
E. C.

Helvius (*RE* Suppl. 3. 895) **Pertinax, Publius,** born in Liguria AD 126, the son of a freedman; he abandoned a career as a schoolteacher and sought a commission as a centurion; rejected, he gained appointment as an equestrian officer in Syria *c.*160. The wars of the 160s brought further posts, in Britain and Moesia, followed by a procuratorship and (*c.*169) command of the *classis Germanica*. An inscription near Cologne (*AE* 1963. 52) records his career to that point and a further procuratorship in Dacia. He was soon assisting *Claudius Pompeianus in clearing the Marcomannic invaders out of Italy (170–1); he was made a senator by M. *Aurelius and after further success became consul (175); he then governed both Moesias, Dacia, and Syria. Dismissed in 182 by *Tigidius Perennis, he was in retirement until 185, when he governed Britain, suppressing a major mutiny; he became prefect of the *alimenta in Italy, proconsul of Africa, and, in 192, prefect of Rome and consul for the second time. Apprised in advance of the plot against *Commodus, he was hailed

emperor by an enraptured senate in the night of 31 December 192. In spite of his humble origin, his phenomenal career had won him unrivalled respect. His attempts to redress the financial crisis and restore discipline soon aroused hostility from the guard. Two coups, on 3 January and in early March, failed, but on 28 March he was killed by mutinous soldiers. *Septimius Severus assumed the name Pertinax shortly afterwards and deified him.

SHA *Pert.*; Cass. Dio 73; Hdn. 2. *BM Coins, Rom. Emp.* 5; A. R. Birley, *The Fasti of Roman Britain* (1981), 142 ff., and *The African Emperor Septimius Severus*, 2nd edn. (1988).
A. R. Bi.

Hemithea, in mythology a daughter of Staphylus, was established by *Apollo as a healing deity at Kastabos in southern *Caria (Diod. Sic. 5. 62–3). Her sanctuary has been identified on a spur of the Eren Dağ. The temple, in the Ionic order with 6 by 12 columns, was built in the late 4th cent. BC, and the cult was at its height in the following period of Rhodian domination.

J. M. Cook and W. H. Plommer, *Sanctuary of Hemithea at Kastabos* (1966).
J. M. C.

Hendeka See ELEVEN.

Heniochus, Middle Comedy poet (see COMEDY (GREEK), MIDDLE). One of his plays was named Πολύευκτος ('Polyeuctus'), not necessarily after the well-known supporter of *Demosthenes (2); it was a common name. From the prologue of another comedy, perhaps titled Πόλεις ('Cities'), eighteen verses (fr. 5) are spoken by a deity or abstraction who introduces the assembled cities (did they form the chorus ?); they have come to *Olympia to make thank-offerings for freedom, but the disturbing influences of *Democracy and *Aristocracy thwart their purpose. This has been interpreted as a reference to either the naval confederacy of 377 BC (see SECOND ATHENIAN CONFEDERACY) or the situation after the battle of *Chaeronea in 338.

FRAGMENTS Kassel–Austin, *PCG* 5. 552–7.
INTERPRETATION Meineke, *FCG* 1. 421 f.; A. Körte, *RE* 8/1 (1912), 283 ff. 'Heniochos' 2; U. von Wilamowitz-Moellendorff, *Menander, Das Schiedsgericht* (1925), 145 n. 1; H. Breitenbach, *De genere quodam titulorum comoediae atticae* (Diss. Basel, 1908), 40.
W. G. A.

Hephaestion (1) (d. 324 BC), Macedonian noble. Arguably the most intimate friend of *Alexander (3) the Great, he came to prominence after the death of *Philotas (330), when he shared command of the Companion cavalry with *Cleitus (1) the Black. Subsequently he had numerous independent commands, notably the commission to advance down the Kabul valley and bridge the Indus (327). One of the élite bodyguards, he was further distinguished by his elevation to the chiliarchy, the principal ceremonial role at court, and at the mass marriage of Susa (324) his bride (like Alexander's) was a daughter of *Darius III. His sudden death at Ecbatana (autumn 324) plunged Alexander into a paroxysm of grief, and a colossally extravagant pyre was planned (but never executed) for his obsequies. His importance is measured by Alexander's affection. Nothing suggests that his abilities were outstanding.

Berve, *Alexanderreich* 2, no. 357; Heckel, *Marshals* 65 ff.
A. B. B.

Hephaestion (2), metrist, probably to be identified with the tutor of *Verus (AD 130–69). His treatise Περὶ μέτρων ('On Metres'), originally written in 48 books, was reduced by successive abridgements to an ἐγχειρίδιον ('handbook') in one book, in which form it is extant. Ancient commentaries on Hephaestion sometimes enable us to reconstruct the earlier, fuller, versions; and parts of the extant treatise appear to belong to one of these versions, not to the final abridgement (Π. σημείων and Π. παραβάσεως), while others may not come from Hephaestion at all (Π. ποιήματος, Π. ποιημάτων). The work is divided into the following parts: (1) on long and short syllables; (2) on συνεκφώνησις (synizesis); (3) on feet, in general; (4) on catalexis; (5)–(13) on the various feet, including the antispast (∪ – – ∪); (14) on cola composed of heterogeneous feet; (15) on ἀσυνάρτητα (combinations of two cola separated by diaeresis, e.g. the Archilochean dicolon); (16) on πολυσχημάτιστα (cola which assume varying forms). There follow appendices dealing with the building of a poetic structure out of lines and cola (Π. ποιήματος, Π. ποιημάτων) and with notation for elucidating that structure (Π. σημείων). Besides the *Encheiridion* various other works on metre are ascribed to Hephaestion in the *Suda*.

Hephaestion belonged to the school of metrists who sought to explain metre by analysing it into its primary elements (μέτρα πρωτότυπα), that is, the feet, as opposed to others who derived all metres from the Homeric hexameter and the iambic trimeter. His treatment of lyric metre is almost confined to solo lyric and comedy, and he rarely tries his hand on the more difficult measures of choral poetry and tragedy. His procedure is extremely mechanistic, and we learn little from him directly of the true nature of Greek metric. But he has preserved many fragments of lost poems which are of great value to metrical science. See also METRE, GREEK.

TEXT M. Consbruch (Teubner, 1906).   J. D. D.; K. J. D.

Hephaestus (Ἥφαιστος), Greek god of *fire, of blacksmiths, and of artisans (see ARTISTS). The name, of uncertain etymology, has no certain attestation in Linear B, though there is the possibility of reading a theophoric name in Minoan Cnossus. See MINOAN CIVILIZATION; PRE-ALPHABETIC SCRIPTS (GREECE).

In *Homer, Hephaestus is so closely connected with fire that earlier scholars felt tempted to derive the god from the element: he owns the fire (e.g. *Il.* 9. 468) and helps fight Scamander with it (*Il.* 21. 328–82); in a formula, his name is metonymically used for fire (*Il.* 2. 426 etc.). On the other hand, he is the divine master-artisan who fabricates *Achilles' shield and miraculous automata, self-moving tripods (*Il.* 18. 373–9), golden servant maidens (ibid. 417–21), or watchdogs for king *Alcinous (1) (*Od.* 7. 91–4, after oriental models). In the divine society of Homer, he is an outsider: he works, even sweats (*Il.* 18. 372); he is laughed at when he tries to replace *Ganymedes (*Il.* 1. 571–600); he is married to *Aphrodite but cuckolded (*Od.* 8. 267–366); his feet are crippled (in Archaic iconography they are turned backwards): the outsider even lacks divine bodily perfection. His mother *Hera had conceived him without a male partner (Hes. *Theog.* 927; *Zeus as father *Il.* 1. 578, 14. 338; *Od.* 8. 312), as Gaia had done with some monsters; seeing the crippled offspring, she cast him out of *Olympus (1), and he grew up with the sea goddesses Eurynome and *Thetis (*Il.* 18. 395–405); or Zeus had thrown him out because he had sided with Hera, and he had landed on Lemnos where the indigenous Sinties tended him (*Il.* 1. 590–4). But he is not to be underestimated: his works evoke wonder; when serving the gods he intentionally provokes laughter; and he takes his cunning revenge on *Ares and Aphrodite and on Hera, and is brought back into Olympus (Alc. 349 LP). Thus, the Homeric picture preserves among an aristocratic society the physiognomy of a cunning blacksmith whose professional skills are highly admired and secretly feared, and whose social skills should not be underrated. It is very much the position blacksmiths have in Archaic societies. With the exception of Athens (see below), later

mythology continues without fundamentally new concepts. His workshop was located beneath active volcanoes, especially *Aetna (1), and the *Cyclopes were assigned to him as his workmen; he was also connected with natural fires, like the one on Lycian Olympus (Sen. *Ep.* 79. 3). That he had created mankind (Lucian, *Hermot.* 20) is but a witty extrapolation from his role in the creation of *Pandora (Hes. *Op.* 70 f.).

Foremost among his cult places is the island of Lemnos where he landed when thrown out from Olympus. One of its two towns is called Hephaestia, with a sanctuary whose priest was eponymous. He is connected with the mysteries of the *Cabiri whose father he was (Hdt. 3. 37; Samothracian mythology according to Strabo 10. 3. 20 f., 472 C) and whose ritual structure may derive from secret societies of blacksmiths. The Homeric Sinties were regarded as pre-Greek Thracians (Stephanus of Byzantium entry under Λῆμνος) or *Etruscans (Τυρσηνοί, schol. Ap. Rhod. 1. 608), and the cult in the Lemnian sanctuary of the Cabiri begins before the Greek settlement; thus, non-Greek elements play a role in this cult, reinforcing the marginality of Hephaestus.

Better known is the Athenian cult where he is connected with Athena, the goddess of cunning intelligence. In his sanctuary above the Agora ('Theseion'), which was built after 450 BC, there stood a group of Hephaestus and Athena Hephaestia, set up in 421/0 by Alcamenes (Cic. *Nat. D.* 1. 83). At the same time, the festival Hephaestia in honour of Hephaestus and Athena was reorganized as a *penteteris* (festival celebrated every fifth year) with a splendid torch-race and lavish sacrifices (*LSCG* 13): the splendour of the festival reflects the position of artisans in the Athenian state. The same holds true for the Chalkeia on the last day of Pyanopsion, a festival dedicated to Athena and Hephaestus when the artisans went in procession through the town (Soph. fr. 844 Radt). The god was also important in the *Apaturia when the participants in their best robes and with torch in hand offered a hymn and a sacrifice to the god (Harp. entry under λαμπάς). Here and in the Hephaestia, the torch alludes to the theme of new fire (which is also present in the Lemnian cult). Athenian mythology tells of Hephaestus' abortive attempt to rape *Athena; from his spilled semen grew *Erichthonius, the ancestor of the autochthonous Athenians—the myth explains Hephaestus' role in the Apaturia and the theme of (new) beginnings.

He was very early identified with Roman *Volcanus (F. Coarelli, *Il foro romano: periodo arcaico* (1983), 177) and with Etruscan Sethlans (see RELIGION, ETRUSCAN).

In Archaic iconography, Hephaestus appears especially in the scene of his return to Olympus under the guidance of *Dionysus. He is also shown helping Zeus to give birth to Athena (east pediment of the *Parthenon) and in the assembly of the gods. The statue of a standing Hephaestus by *Alcamenes with a discreet indication of his limp was famous (Cic. *Nat. D.* 1. 83).

In general see Farnell, *Cults* 5. 374–95, and Burkert, *GR* 167–8; for blacksmiths, M. Eliade, *Forgerons et alchimistes* (1977); for the automata C. A. Faraone, *GRBS* 1987, 257–80; A. Hermary and A. Jacquemin, *LIMC* 4 (1988), 627–54; M. Delcourt, *Héphaistos ou la légende du magicien* (1957).   F. G.

Hera (Ἥρα or Ἥρη; Mycenaean *Era*). This major figure in the pantheon, daughter of *Cronus and wife of *Zeus, is already attested by name on two Mycenaean tablets, one from *Thebes (1) (TH Of 28), the other from *Pylos (PY Tn 316), where she appears together with Zeus. *Boeotia and especially the *Peloponnese are precisely the two regions of Greece where the cult of Hera is most prevalent. According to Homer (*Il.* 4. 51–2),

Hera's favourite cities were *Argos (2), *Sparta, and *Mycenae; several cults are actually attested at Sparta, and her most famous sanctuary was on the hill dominating the Argive plain, where there was a temple perhaps from the 8th cent. BC. Sanctuaries with buildings at least as ancient are known at *Perachora, *Tiryns (on the site of the megaron of the Mycenaean palace), and *Olympia. Of island sites, the best known is the sanctuary on *Samos, where the main building, rebuilt in the 6th cent. BC, was mentioned by Herodotus, who comments on its magnificence (3. 60). Thus, as Burkert observes, the most ancient and important temples were those of Hera. Her cults also spread at an early date to the colonies of the west, where later she became identified with the Roman *Juno. Her sanctuaries (see HERAION) on the Lacinian promontory and at the mouth of the Sele were much frequented: see CROTON; PAESTUM.

In the Classical period, Hera's distinguishing feature compared with other goddesses is her double connection with royalty and marriage. In this way she is closely associated with Zeus, who made her 'last of all, his flourishing wife' (Hes. Theog. 921). Her queenliness and noble beauty are abundantly stressed in her epithets and in artistic representations. The ancient formula potnia Herē is succeeded by that of basileia, 'queen'. She is described as 'golden-throned', and is often thus represented, sometimes seeming to surpass her husband in importance: at Olympia, an Archaic statue showed Zeus standing beside Hera enthroned, while in the Argive Heraion the famous chryselephantine statue by *Polyclitus represented the god in the form of a cuckoo perched on the sceptre held by the goddess—in her other hand she held a pomegranate; and on her head-dress were figures of the Charites and the Horae (Paus. 2. 17. 3–4). One of Plato's myths (Phdr. 253b) clearly underlines her royal qualities: according to this the followers of Hera are those who seek in love a 'kingly nature'.

Marriage is stressed constantly in Hera's myths and cults. It is attested by epithets such as Gamelia, Gamostolos, Syzygia, Zeuxidia, and especially Teleia, sometimes in connection with Zeus Teleios. Rituals in her honour connected with a sacred *marriage are recorded in various places, notably in Athens, where this marriage served as a social and institutional paradigm: at the festival of Theogamia, celebrated in Gamelion, the divine couple were given the title of πρυτάνεις τῶν γάμων, 'magistrates of marriages' (schol. on Ar. Thesm. 973–6). In Crete, the marriage was re-enacted annually by the river Theren 'in imitation of weddings' (Diod. Sic. 5. 72. 4). But Hera was not only the patron of marriages; she was often given the title of Parthenos, 'girl', and associated with prenuptial rites, including sometimes the lying together of the two sexes (Callim. fr 75 Pf.; cf. Homer, Il. 14. 295 with scholia). Marital separation, suggested by Hera's mythology, is also evoked in cult, particularly at *Plataea (Paus. 9. 3. 3; Euseb. Praep. evang. 3. 1. 6) and at *Stymphalus, where Hera was called simultaneously Pais 'child', Teleia 'wife', and Chēra 'widow' or 'separated', thus covering the whole life of women, with its turning-points. An Argive ritual, whereby every year the statue of Hera was bathed in a spring at Nauplia to restore the goddess's virginity (Paus. 2. 38. 2) indicates the recurrent nature of these separations.

*Motherhood, though part of Hera's personality, is little stressed, particularly in cult. Her children are *Ares, *Hebe, and *Eileithyia, goddess of childbirth, whose name she bears at Argos; in her sanctuary at Paestum, she is sometimes shown as a *kourotrophos. She suckled *Heracles, a scene often shown on Etruscan mirrors, but her relationship with the hero, whose name could be taken to mean 'glory of Hera', is ambivalent. She acted as nurse to monsters born to Earth, the Lernaean Hydra and the Nemean lion; in addition she was the sole parent of the monster *Typhon and also, according to Hesiod (Theog. 927–8), *Hephaestus, whom she produced in anger, to defy her husband. But these episodes by their exceptional nature in fact illustrate Hera's close links with the marriage bond, which she herself protects and guarantees.

The marriage of Zeus and Hera is part of a complex symbolism including the natural world of plants and animals. This is shown by Hera's oldest sanctuaries, which are often situated in fertile plains away from urban settlements. The statue of Polyclitus mentioned above is relevant here. The sacred marriage described by Homer (Il. 14. 346–51), despite the alterations due to epic, still bears traces of this natural symbolism, and we also find mentioned the flourishing garden at the edge of the Ocean, which served as marriage-bed for the two deities (e.g. Eur. Hipp. 748–51). We can see a relationship between the goddess called Boöpis ('ox-eyed') and herds of cows, and also with horses, especially in connection with a sacred marriage. Io, changed into a heifer by Zeus in bull form, was the priestess of Hera at Argos, where Hera's rule extended over the animal herds of the plain (see CLEOBIS AND BITON). At *Olympia, where Hera Hippia ('of horses') was worshipped alongside *Poseidon Hippios, contests among girls had been established in honour of the goddess by *Hippodamia in thanks for her marriage to Pelops. These facts may be linked with two other chthonian features, isolated as they are: the oracles of Hera, at Perachora and *Cumae, and the funerary cult given to *Medea's children in one of Hera's sanctuaries at *Corinth.

Hera was also worshipped as protector of cities and other social groups, especially at Argos and on Samos; Alcaeus calls her πάντων γενέθλα, 'mother of all' (fr. 129 LP), in a hymn of invocation where she appears between Zeus and Dionysus. It is in this context that she is sometimes shown armed. At Argos the prize at the games held during the Heraia festival was a shield. Despite this protecting function, it is noteworthy that literary presentations, from the Iliad onwards, tend to stress the destructive and capricious side of Hera's nature.

As with most of the Greek pantheon, Hera's origins are unclear. There is no certain etymology for her name; if the modern consensus sees Linear B Era as the feminine of hērōs (ἥρως), this itself has given rise to differing interpretations. The supporters of an Indo-European origin from the root †yer explain the name variously as meaning 'heifer' (van Windekens), 'the goddess of the year' (Haudry), or 'a girl of marriageable age' (Pötscher). Chantraine, on the other hand, inclines towards a pre-Greek origin for both Mycenaean words. But a solution to the problem of the name would not explain the whole issue of Hera's origin. Associated as she is with Zeus from the Mycenaean period onwards, it is clear that Hera preserves certain characteristics of an Indo-European divine couple; but in her sovereign power, tending towards the universal, it is difficult not to see traces of an Aegean great goddess.

S. Eitrem, RE 8. 369–403, and RE Suppl. 3. 906–9; A. Kossatz-Deissmann, LIMC 4. 659–719; K. Kerényi, Zeus und Hera (1972); A. Motte, Prairies et jardins de la Grèce antique (1973), 104–14, 214–32; Burkert, GR 131–5; W. Pötscher, Hera: Eine Strukturanalyse im Vergleich mit Athena (1987). A. Mot., V. P.-D.

Heraclea (1) (mod. Policoro), Tarentine colony (see TARENTUM), founded in 433 BC, close to the site of *Siris. The headquarters of the Italiote League was moved there after 387 BC. Heraclea became a Roman ally in 278 BC but revolted during the Hannibalic War (see PUNIC WARS). It reluctantly became a *municipium in 89 BC (Cic. *Balb.* 21; *Arch.* 6). A Roman municipal law was found here, inscribed on the reverse of a Greek *centuriation scheme.

E. Greco, *Magna Grecia* (1981).   K. L.

Heraclea (2) by Latmus, a city of *Caria allegedly founded by *Endymion, on the slope of Mt. Latmus, c.25 km. (15½ mi.) east of Miletus; in antiquity it stood at the head of an Aegean gulf gradually silted up by the *Maeander to become (not before Roman times) a lake. The present city, laid out on a grid, is a refoundation, superseding Classical Latmus, the site of the last lying outside and east of the superb Hellenistic circuit-wall, which (on grounds of style) is unlikely to be pre-*Alexander (3) the Great; the move may have been the work of *Mausolus. A Delphic inscription of c.260 BC, when the city belonged to *Ptolemy (1) II, shows its diplomatic exploitation of a mythical kinship through *Aetolus, Endymion's son, to win favour with the *Aetolian Confederacy (L. Robert, *BCH* 1978, 477 ff.; cf. CYTINIUM). Captured by *Antiochus (3) III, the city was given free status (190) by the Scipio brothers (P. *Cornelius Scipio Africanus and L. *Cornelius Scipio Asiagenes) in a letter still extant (*RDGE* 35; Eng. trans. Sherk, *Augustus* no. 14). The city survived into late antiquity; there are extensive remains.

PECS 384 f.; S. Hornblower, *Mausolus* (1982), esp. 320 ff.   A. J. S. S.

Heraclea (3) Pontica, a Megarian and Boeotian colony (see MEGARA (1); BOEOTIA) founded c.560 BC in the land of the Mariandyni, who were reduced by the colonists to serfdom but could not be sold outside the city's territory. Heraclea was the most important settlement on the south shore of the Black Sea (see EUXINE) between *Byzantium and *Sinope; it founded colonies at Callatis and *Chersonesus (3) and plied an active trade, its people being among the chief Euxine navigators in the time of *Xenophon (1). Civil discord led to *tyranny which lasted 84 years until 280 BC, a period which is said to have seen the town at its most prosperous. Clearchus, a pupil of *Plato (1) and *Isocrates who seized power in 364/3, was murdered in 353/2. He was succeeded by his brother Satyrus and then by his two sons Timotheus and Dionysius. The latter, who ruled 337/6–305, extended his dominions in 334, supported *Antigonus (1) I Monophthalmus and finally took the title king. He was succeeded by his widow Amastris, of Persian stock, who briefly married *Lysimachus of Thrace (302), before he abandoned her for Arsinoë II, daughter of *Ptolemy (1) I. Amastris returned to Heraclea and founded a city which bore her name, but was murdered by her sons. Lysimachus then took control until his death in 280, when a democracy was established. With the rise of the Bithynian and Pontic kingdoms, and of Galatian power in the interior, Heraclea lost influence and territory. Although an ally of Rome after 188 BC, it was forced to join *Mithradates VI in 74 and was taken and sacked by the Romans in the Third Mithradatic War. A colony founded by *Caesar failed to restore Heraclea to its former prosperity, and the colonists were massacred by a Galatian dynast who had been installed by M. *Antonius (2). The city was overshadowed by its neighbours Prusias and Amastris under the Roman empire. Heraclea's history in the Hellenistic period is unusually well known, thanks to the partial survival of the works of local historians, including *Nymphis and *Memnon (3).

FGrH 430–4; Strabo 12. 3. 4 ff. Magie, *Rom. Rule Asia Min.* 307 ff. and index; W. Hoepfner, *Herakleia Pontike* (1966); D. R. Wilson, *PECS* 383; S. Burstein, *Outpost of Hellenism: The Emergence of Heraclea* (1974); H.

Lund, *Lysimachus* (1992), see index; *CAH* 6² (1994), 222 (Hornblower) and 489, 498 (Hind); also 9² (1994), 244–5 (A. N. Sherwin-White).
                                                       T. R. S. B.; S. M.

Heraclea (4) Trachinia, Spartan colony founded in 426 BC on a spur of Mt. Oeta's eastern slopes, about 8 km. (5 mi.) from *Thermopylae, to serve as a Spartan military and naval stronghold. Under the strict authority of a *harmost and exposed to attacks from neighbours, the city was denied an easy development. Taken by the Boeotians and Argives (see BOEOTIA; ARGOS (2)) during the *Corinthian War, it later reverted to Spartan control. *Jason (2) of Pherae dismantled its walls and returned it to the people of Oeta, who made it the capital of their federation, which was first under the control of the Aetolians, then the Romans, who took the city in 191 BC.

Y. Béquignon, *La Vallée du Spercheios* (1937); S. Hornblower, *Harv. Stud.* 1992, 169 ff., and *Comm. on Thuc.* 1 on 3. 92; I. Malkin, *Myth and Territory in the Spartan Mediterranean* (1994), ch. 8.   B. H.

Heracles, the greatest of Greek heroes. His name is that of a mortal (compare Diocles), and has been interpreted as 'Glorious through *Hera' (Burkert 210, Chantraine 416, Kretschmer 121–9 (see bibliog. below)). In this case, the bearer is taken as being—or so his parents would hope—within the protection of the goddess. This is at odds with the predominant tradition (see below), wherein Heracles was harassed rather than protected by the goddess: perhaps the hostility was against worshippers of Heracles who rejected allegiance to the worshippers of Hera on whom the hero depended. This could have happened when *Argos (2) had established control over the *Heraion and *Tiryns (possibly reflected in an apparent falling-off of settlement at *Tiryns late in the 9th cent. BC: Foley 40–2). Some of the inhabitants of Tiryns might have emigrated to *Thebes (1), taking their hero with him. Traditionally Heracles' mother and her husband (*Alcmene and *Amphitryon) were obliged to move from Tiryns to *Thebes (1), where Heracles was conceived and born (*LIMC* 1/1. 735). However, there is no agreement over the etymology of the name, an alternative version deriving its first element from 'Hero'.

Heracles shared the characteristics of, on the one hand, a hero (both cultic and epic), on the other, a god. As a hero, he was mortal, and like many other heroes, born to a human mother and a god (Alcmene and *Zeus; Amphitryon was father of *Iphicles, Heracles' twin: the bare bones of the story already in Homer, *Il.* 14. 323–4). Legends arose early of his epic feats, and they were added to constantly throughout antiquity. These stories may have played a part in the transformation of Heracles from hero (i.e. a deity of mortal origin, who, after death, exercised power over a limited geographical area, his influence residing in his mortal remains) to god (a deity, immortal, whose power is not limited geographically). See HERO-CULT.

Outside the cycle of the Labours (see below), the chief events of Heracles' life were as follows: Hera pursued him with implacable enmity from before his birth, which she managed to delay until after that of *Eurystheus. She then sent serpents to Thebes to attack Heracles in his cradle, but the infant strangled them. Later, she drove him mad and caused him to murder his Theban wife, Megara, and their children (there are different versions). In his youth, Heracles led the Thebans in their successful revolt against *Minyan *Orchomenus (1). He also took part in an expedition against Troy and sacked Oechalia (*LIMC* 5/1. 111–13), accompanied the *Argonauts (113–14), founded the *Olympian games, and ultimately died by burning on Mt. Oeta (128–9: death came as a relief from the poison given him inadvertently by his wife *Deianira, who had hoped to regain his love thereby: the dying *Centaur Nessus, from whom Heracles rescued his wife, had given her the poison as a love potion. She used it when Heracles took Iole home).

The Labours themselves (twelve is the canonical number, but there is little agreement on the full complement) support, by their geographical distribution, the contention that, however popular Heracles became in other parts of the ancient world, his origins were in the *Peloponnese, and more specifically in the Argolid. He was sent to perform them by Eurystheus of Argos, to whom he was bound in vassalage. Six belong to the northern part of the Peloponnese, and might be taken to represent either a gradual spread of Argive ambitions in that region, or, with equal likelihood, the growing popularity of Heracles over a steadily widening area. These tasks were to deal with (1) the Nemean lion (northern border of the Argolid; see NEMEA); (2) the Lernaean Hydra (SW Argolid); (3) the Erymanthian boar (NW *Arcadia); (4) the hind of Ceryneia (*Achaea); (5) the Stymphalian birds (NE Arcadia; see STYMPHALUS); (6) the stables of Augeas (*Elis). The other Labours are situated at the ends of the habitable world or beyond: the Cretan bull to the south, the horses of the Thracian *Diomedes (1) to the north, the quest for the belt of the *Amazon queen to the east, the search for the cattle of Geryon to the west, the apples of the *Hesperides at the edge of the world, and *Cerberus in the world of the dead. Many but not all of the Labours are already depicted in Greek art of the geometric and early Archaic periods (LIMC 5/1. 5–111 and 187). Also early to appear are two feats outside the canon, a fight against Centaurs (187), and a struggle with *Apollo for the Delphic tripod (133–43 and 187; see OMPHALE). The encounters with Centaurs take place in Arcadia and Thessaly; the fight with Apollo might reflect a struggle for political control over *Delphi between its inhabitants and those of Malis (Trachis and Mt. Oeta). A good survey of Heracles' Labours (Praxeis) and Parerga (incidental labours) in art is given by Carpenter 117–34.

The iconography of Heracles was firmly established by the Archaic period, but even before then it is possible to identify him from the subject-matter. The major identifying symbols were the lion-skin cape and hood (flayed from the Nemean lion), his club, and his bow and arrows (LIMC 5/1. 183–6).

Throughout his life and many adventures, Heracles was guided closely by *Athena (LIMC 5/1. 143–54), by whom he was introduced to *Olympus (1) after his death (122–8). The apotheosis of Heracles was represented in literature and art by giving him—after his death—a wife in the person of *Hebe, i.e. 'youth', or rather the embodiment of the prime of life, for it is the permanent possession of this boon which most distinguishes gods from men. The story is attested definitely by the 6th cent. BC (121–2 and 160–5). In popular cult, Heracles was recognized and invoked as a god from at least late in the 6th cent. (for example, the inscription CEG 1. 309 = IG I². 825 from *Phaleron). *Herodotus (1) (2. 44. 5) writes approvingly of those Hellenes who worshipped Heracles both as an immortal Olympian and as a hero. The practice must have been common, if not widespread (cf. Pind. Nem. 3. 22: Heracles a 'hero god').

As in the case of Apollo, his divine rival for the Delphic tripod, the cult of Heracles spread at least partly through the absorption of local cult figures—in Heracles' case, mostly heroic—of similar nature. Individuals adopted Heracles as a more or less personal patron (Rusten 296); at the communal level, he presided over ephebes (see EPHĒBOI) as their ideal in warfare and their patron

in military training (Burkert 211; Graf 99), whence his patronage of the *gymnasium (a role often shared with *Hermes), and over the young in general (Kearns 35–6). He was primarily associated with the activities of men rather than women, which may explain the regulations barring women from his rites or even his sanctuaries, e.g. LSS 63 (*Thasos), LSAM 42 (*Miletus). Occasionally, however, the character of the local hero whom Heracles had deposed might override the general practice, as in the case of the western Boeotian Charops Heracles, who was served by a priestess (Schachter 3–9).

The geographical distribution of his cults is, as one might expect, as wide as that of his legends. Interestingly, evidence from Tiryns and Argos, although early in the former, is sparse (Tiryns: SEG 30. 380. 15a, first half of the 6th cent.; Argos: his name scratched on two fragments of an Attic crater of the fourth quarter of the 5th cent., BCH 1989, 721). That he was established at Thebes by the Homeric period cannot be doubted, although the earliest contemporary evidence for cult occurs in the 5th cent. (Schachter 14–30). He was worshipped fairly widely throughout Boeotia, and neighbouring *Attica (Woodford 211–25).

One of the earliest places to produce archaeological evidence for a cult of Heracles is the sanctuary on Mt. Oeta, site of his immolation (Béquignon 206–15). Another important early site is at *Thasos, where evidence extends from soon after the foundation of the colony (Des Courtils and Pariente). The Thasian cult exemplifies several features of the worship of Heracles: first, his treatment as a god; second, his function as promachos, champion or protector, of the community (particularly its urban centre); third, the tendency to syncretize (see SYNCRETISM) Heracles with other deities, local or otherwise, in the case of Thasos, the other being Melqart of *Tyre (Bonnet 346–71).

The sanctuary at Thasos, which may be typical, included not only a sacrificial area, but also a temple and extensive dining-facilities (the last often illustrated in vase-painting and so probably typical: Woodford 213–14); descriptions of other Herakleia (e.g. at Thebes: Paus. 9. 11. 4–7) would lead us to expect the existence of extensive athletic facilities as part of the complex. All of this public devotion to bodily well-being would have helped to produce the impression of Heracles as a boisterous glutton.

As noted above, Heracles was adopted by individuals or states as a symbol or protecting deity, to which numerous towns named after him bear eloquent testimony. Boeotian Thebes used Heracles as its symbol from at least the second half of the 5th cent. BC, if not earlier. In the preceding century *Pisistratus of Athens made Heracles his personal divine protector and legitimator of his actions (Boardman 1988 and 1989; but see IMAGERY; PROPAGANDA). The Macedonian royal family ('Argeads') claimed lineal descent from Heracles for similar motives (Hammond and Griffith 164–5; see HELLENISM; KINSHIP). Most notoriously, however, the *Dorian rulers of the *Peloponnese sought to legitimate their claims to sovereignty by tracing their descent to Heracles through his sons, the *Heraclidae, who, as the tale was told, 'returned' to the Peloponnese from the north to claim their inheritance (Hooker 41–5).

Y. Béquignon, La Vallée du Spercheios (1937); J. Boardman, CAH 4² (1988), 421–2, and JHS (1989), 158–9; J. Boardman and others, LIMC 4. 1 (1988), 5/1 (1990); C. Bonnet, Melqart (1988); Burkert, GR; T. H. Carpenter, Art and Myth in Ancient Greece (1991); P. Chantraine, Dictionnaire étymologique de la langue grecque 2 (1970); J. Des Courtils and M. Pariente, in R. Etienne and M.-T. Le Dinahet (eds.), L'Espace sacrificiel (1991), 67–73; A. Foley, The Argolid 800–600 BC (1988); F. Graf, Nordionische Kulte (1985); Hammond and Griffith, HM 2; J. T. Hooker,

Heraclidae

The Ancient Spartans (1980); Kearns, *Heroes of Attica*; P. Kretschmer, *Glotta* 1917; J. S. Rusten, *Harv. Stud.* 1983; A. Schachter, *Cults of Boiotia* 2 (1986); A. D. Trendall, *LIMC* 1/1 (1981); S. Woodford, in *Studies Presented to George M. A. Hanfmann* (1971); K. Galinsky, *The Herakles Theme* (1972).
A. Sch.

Heraclidae ('Ηρακλεῖδαι). The myth of the return of the descendants of *Heracles to the *Peloponnese functioned, above all, as a charter myth for the division of the Peloponnese between different *Dorian states. The fullest accounts are in Diod. Sic. 4. 57–8 and Apollod. 2. 8 (167 ff.), but there is no doubt that the myth was already familiar in all essentials in the 5th cent. BC; *Tyrtaeus in the 7th cent. had already told how *Zeus had granted *Sparta to the Heraclidae who left 'windy Erineos' in the Dorian heartland of north Greece (fr. 2 West).

*Eurystheus, persecutor of Heracles, continued to persecute the exiled sons of Heracles after their father's death; the Athenians in particular gave them aid. After various adventures, the Heraclidae enquired of Delphi (see DELPHIC ORACLE) when they could return, and were told to do so at the third harvest. *Hyllus supposed this to mean the third year, but failed and was killed in single combat against a Peloponnesian champion at the Isthmus (cf. already Hdt. 9. 26. 3–5). A hundred years later his descendant *Temenus again inquired, and got the same reply, which was now interpreted for him as meaning the third generation. The Dorians therefore tried again, in three companies, led by Temenus, Cresphontes, and the sons of Aristodemus, Eurysthenes and Procles. They entered by Elis, taking, again by oracular advice, the 'three-eyed man' for their guide; he turned out to be Oxylus of *Aetolia, whose mule, or horse, had only one eye. Conquering the *Peloponnese, they divided it into three parts, of which Cresphontes took *Messenia, Temenus *Argos (1), and the sons of Aristodemus Lacedaemon, thus founding the dual kingship of *Sparta (see AGIADS; EURYPONTIDS). In the fighting Tisamenus, son of *Orestes and grandson of *Agamemnon, was killed, thus ending the line of the Pelopidae.

Several incidents of the myth had a life independent of the aetiological function of the whole. Athenian writers in particular made much of the support given to the Heraclidae in *Attica (Eur. *Heraclidae*; doubtless Aeschylus' lost *Heraclidae*; public funeral orations; see EPITAPHIOS), and several Athenian *demes even paid *hero-cult to them and the companions of their wanderings, *Iolaus and *Alcmene.

F. Prinz, *Gründungsmythen und Sagenchronologie* (1979); M. Schmidt, *LIMC* 'Herakleidai'.
R. C. T. P.

Heraclides (1) **Ponticus,** 4th cent. BC philosopher of the *Academy. Born of a wealthy and aristocratic family in *Heraclea (3) Pontica, he came to *Plato (1)'s Academy in Athens as a pupil of *Speusippus. Like other Academics, he wrote a version of Plato's lectures *On the Good*; he also studied with *Aristotle, probably while Aristotle was still in the Academic school (he does not really belong to *Die Schule des Aristoteles*, the 'school of Aristotle'). He was placed in temporary charge of the Academy during Plato's third visit to Sicily (361/0) and after the death of Plato's successor *Speusippus (338) he was runner-up for the headship of the school. He returned to Heraclea. He was still alive at the time of Aristotle's death in 322.

The fragments of his writings, mostly dialogues, reveal the wide variety of his interests—ethical, political, physical, historical, and literary. Diog. Laert. 5. 86–8 gives a list of his writings; more are mentioned in other sources.

Heraclides' significance for posterity lies in four directions: in the distinctive form of his dialogues; in physics, particularly astronomy; in his eschatology; and in his contribution to the Pythagorean legend (see PYTHAGORAS (1)). His dialogues were famous for their elaborate proems, their colourful use of historical personages, and the seductive quality of their anecdotes and myths. They influenced *Cicero, whose *De republica* may give some indication of their characteristics, and *Plutarch.

On *astronomy, although the evidence is confused and even contradictory, it seems probable that Heraclides held (1) that the universe is infinite; (2) that the earth rotates on its axis once daily from west to east at the centre of the cosmos; (3) that the sun circles around the earth from east to west in the ecliptic once a year; and (4) that the planets Venus and Mercury move in circular orbits with the sun as centre. One repeated testimonium (113 Wehrli) says that he claimed along with certain Pythagoreans that each of the stars is a separate cosmos.

In *physics he had a theory of 'seamless masses' (*anarmoi onkoi*), a term also found in testimonia about the physiology of *Asclepiades (3) of Prusias in Bithynia (1st cent. BC). Whatever significance they had for Asclepiades, it seems probable that for Heraclides they represented the elementary particles of Plato's *Timaeus*, which unlike atoms can somehow dissolve into fragments and regroup so as to form a different element. See ATOMISM.

In a way typical of 4th-cent. philosophy, Heraclides combined this interest in science with an interest in eschatology and in such shamanistic figures, real or invented, as Empedotimus, *Abaris, Pythagoras, and *Empedocles. In the vision of Empedotimus (frs. 96 and 98 Wehrli) the *soul is described as substantial light, having its origin in the Milky Way.

The list of his works in Diog. Laert. 5. 86 includes several ethical books: *On Justice*, *On Sōphrosynē*, *On Piety*, *On Virtue*, *On Happiness*, etc. There are also many books on music and poetry. Few fragments of these survive.

Fragments with German commentary in F. Wehrli (ed.), *Die Schule des Aristoteles* 7, 2nd edn. (1969). The best monograph is H. Gottschalk, *Heracleides of Pontus* (1980), with bibliog., especially full on astronomy. Also R. Daebritz, *RE* 8; I. M. Lonie, *Phronesis* 1964, and *Mnemos.* 1965; F. Wehrli, *RE* Suppl. 11 (1968), 675–86; Guthrie, *Hist. Gk. Phil.* 5; J. Vallance, *The Lost Theory of Asclepiades of Bithynia* (1990); M. Ostwald and J. P. Lynch, *CAH* 6² (1994), 608 ff.; A. B. Bosworth, in I. Worthington (ed.), *Ventures into Greek History* (1994), 15 ff.
D. J. F.

Heraclides (2), of Cyme, *c.*350 BC, author of a history of *Persia (*Persica*) in five books; books 1–2 entitled *Paraskeuastika* ('Introduction', *FGrH* 689 T 2) contained information on the country and its people. Fragments 1, 2 and 4, preserved verbatim in *Athenaeus (1), afford valuable insight into the life and atmosphere of the court of the Great King. Used in *Plutarch's *Artaxerxes*.

FGrH 689. D. M. Lewis, *Sparta and Persia* (1977), 4, 17 n. 88; O. Lendle, *Einführung in die griechische Geschichtsschreibung* (1992).
K. M.

Heraclides (3) **Lembus** (2nd cent. BC), statesman, historian, and amateur scholar living in *Alexandria (1), excerpter and epitomizer of earlier works. We have 76 fragments from his excerpts of *Aristotle's *Politeiai* (histories of Greek constitutions, now lost except for the *Athenian Constitution*; see ATHENAION POLITEIA); these primarily recount trivial anecdotes. He also wrote epitomes of *Sotion (1)'s Διαδοχαί ('Successive [heads]' of philosophical schools), and 'Lives' by *Satyrus (1) and *Hermippus (2); all three epitomes were heavily used by *Diogenes (6) Laertius. Other works: a History in 37 books, a *Lembeutikos Logos*, and perhaps a life of *Archimedes.

FRAGMENTS *FHG* 3. 167; *Politeiai*: Dilts, *GRBS* Monogr. 5.

M. Ga.

Heraclides (4), of Tarentum (fl. 85–65 BC), a pupil of *Mantias and a renegade Herophilean (see HEROPHILUS), became one of the more influential, versatile, and theoretically nuanced physicians of the Empiricist school. He advocated experience as the foundation of medicine but freely accommodated causal explanation (e.g. correlating divergent causes of the same disorder with different treatments). His large treatise on external and internal therapy was used extensively by *Galen and Caelius Aurelianus, his dietetic *Symposium* by *Athenaeus (1) of Naucratis, his pharmacological works (including *Theriaca*) by Galen and Galen's sources (see PHARMACOLOGY), and his extensive Hippocratic exegeses (including his influential polemics against Bacchius) by *Erotian and Galen; see HIPPOCRATES (2). Heraclides' pulse theory is known through Galen. About 90 fragments and testimonia survive.

Ed. and comm., K. Deichgräber, *Die griechische Empirikerschule* (1930; 2nd edn. 1965).

H. v. S.

Heraclides (5) **Ponticus the Younger**, grammarian, from *Heraclea (3) Pontica, pupil of *Didymus (1), later taught at Rome under *Claudius and *Nero, and wrote three books in Sapphic hendecasyllables (Ath. 649c), which may have influenced *Statius' *Silvae*. These were erudite and obscure (*Etymologicum Gudianum* 297, 50; Artem. 4. 63) in the style of *Lycophron (2). He also wrote epic poems and *Pyrrichae* of which nothing is known.

Susemihl, *Gesch. gr. Litt. Alex.* 2. 196.

C. M. B.

Heraclitus (fl. *c*.500 BC), son of Bloson of Ephesus. Of aristocratic birth, he may have surrendered the (honorific) *kingship voluntarily to his brother. He is said to have compiled a book and deposited it in the temple of *Artemis. The surviving fragments are aphorisms, dense and cryptic. With implicit self-description, Heraclitus writes that the Delphic god (see DELPHIC ORACLE) 'neither says nor conceals, but gives a sign'. The fragments form a cross-referring network rather than a linear argument.

Heraclitus' central concept is that of *logos*, by which he apparently means at once his own discourse, connected discourse and thought in general, and the connected order in things that we apprehend. Most people, he holds, go through life like sleepers, experiencing the world with little understanding, each lost in a private vision. Waking up to the shared public order requires inquiry, sense-experience, and self-examination: 'I went in search of myself.'

The order we experience is a constant process of change; thus, stepping into the same river, we find different waters constantly flowing by us. Change, indeed, is necessary to the maintenance of cosmic order: 'the barley drink separates if it is not stirred.' Criticizing *Anaximander, who had contrasted the strife of the elements with their due order or *Dikē, Heraclitus insists that *Dikē* is strife, and that nature is comparable to a taut bow, with tensions in opposite directions. Developing his dynamic conception of periodic orderly change, he selects *fire as a basic element, in terms of which all things are measured, and whose measures are preserved over time. Stoic thinkers (see STOICISM) understood him to predict the periodic conflagration of the entire cosmos; they may have been right.

*Aristotle charged Heraclitus with denial of the Principle of Non-Contradiction because he asserts that certain opposites (the

way up and the way down, day and night, etc.) are 'one'. Very likely, however, Heraclitus was charting the many ways in which opposites figure in our discourse. Sometimes one and the same thing will be seen to have opposite properties in relation to different observers; sometimes a thing will have opposite properties when viewed from different perspectives; sometimes one opposite cannot be understood or defined without reference to the other opposite. This excavation of the logical structure of language is part of inquiry into nature.

Heraclitus is the first Greek thinker to have a theory of *psychē or '*soul' as it functions in the living person. He connects *psychē* with both *logos* and *fire, and appears to think of it as a dynamic connectedness that can be overwhelmed by a 'watery' condition, which spells death. He connects this idea with praise of temperate living and of those who pursue 'ever-flowing fame' rather than bestial satiety. He attacks the Dionysian cult (see DIONYSUS) and shows disdain for a central aspect of popular religion, saying 'corpses are more to be thrown away than dung'.

In politics he shows aristocratic sympathies, but insists on the importance of public law. All human laws, he insists, are nourished by one divine law—presumably speaking of the unitary divinity that he identifies with the changing order of nature.

DK 22. 1; C. H. Kahn, *The Art and Thought of Heraclitus* (1979); G. Kirk, *Heraclitus: The Cosmic Fragments* (1954); M. Marcovich, *Heraclitus* (1967); B. Snell, *Hermes* 1926, 353 f.; M. Nussbaum, *Phronesis* 1972, 1 ff., 153 ff.; G. Vlastos, *AJPhil.* 1955, 337 ff.; D. Wiggins, in M. Schofield and M. Nussbaum (eds.), *Language and Logos* (1982).

M. C. N.

Heraion, sanctuary of *Hera. The most important are the Heraion of *Argos (2), and the Heraion of *Samos. Both are situated at some distance from the cities which controlled or dominated them. The Argive Heraion is at an important but abandoned late bronze age site, which may have influenced its selection; the Samian Heraion also may have had earlier significance. Both developed early, having peripteral temples by at latest the first half of the 7th cent. BC. These had stone footings, with wooden columns. Both sanctuaries include structures designed for the crowds of worshippers, particularly stoas from which to view the religious activities, and processional ways linking them physically and symbolically with the *polis*-centre. See SANCTUARIES.

Argos: C. Waldstein, *The Argive Heraeum* (1902–5); R. A. Tomlinson, *Argos and the Argolid* (1972). Samos: German excavations published in the series *Samos* 1– (1961–); H. Kyrieleis, *Führer durch das Heraion von Samos* (1981) and in N. Marinatos and R. Hägg (eds.) *Greek Sanctuaries* (1993), 125 ff. On both Argos and Samos (and other Heraia) see F. de Polignac, *Cults, Territory, and the Origins of the Greek City-State* (1995).

R. A. T.

heralds (*kērykes*) in *Homer were important aides of the kings, used for such tasks as maintaining order in meetings, making proclamations, and bearing messages. They were under the protection of *Hermes, were inviolable, and carried a herald's staff as a symbol of authority. In later Greece they retained much of their importance, assisting magistrates in assemblies and law-courts and bearing messages to other states. In this capacity they are to be distinguished from ambassadors (*presbeis*), who were not similarly inviolable but who might be authorized not only to transmit formal messages but also to negotiate. Heralds could circulate freely even during wars, and so were sometimes sent to open negotiations by requesting permission to send ambassadors. The Roman public crier (*praeco*) was a more humble attendant of magistrates. See APPARITORES.

J. A. O. L.; P. J. R.

Herculaneum

Herculaneum Roman *municipium* on a spur of Vesuvius commanding the coast-road, 8 km. (5 mi.) south-east of Naples (Strabo 5. 4. 8; see NEAPOLIS). An independent member of the Samnite league centred on Nuceria in the 4th cent. BC and subsequently allied to Rome, it joined the allied cause in the *Social War (3): Oscan civic institutions (see OSCANS) were replaced by Roman ones in 89 BC. Its origins are still obscure, though the regular street-plan and the name suggest that it may have been a dependency of the Greek *apoikia at Naples (perhaps of the 6th or 5th cent.).

Recent discoveries have made its municipal life seem comparably vigorous with its neighbours', but restricted hinterland, limited communications, and a small harbour denied it much economic opportunity. On present evidence, the streets (whose plan is more regular than that of *Pompeii) show little sign of heavy traffic (nor are there stepping-stones for pedestrians); shops and workshops are unobtrusive. As the centre of a resort-coast, however, renowned for its beauty and salubrious climate, and close enough to Naples to be a kind of luxury suburb, the town benefited from the wealth of local proprietors (including Roman senators). The grandest property (known from its rifling in 1750–61), the Villa of the Papyri, north-west of the town, on terraces overlooking the sea, was embellished with gardens, waterworks, and statues and inspired the mod. Getty Museum, Malibu (USA). The name derives from the 1785 papyrus scrolls found there. Though carbonized, these can be painstakingly unrolled: Epicurean in taste (see EPICURUS), they include many of the works of *Philodemus of Gadara. Many of the town houses were also expensively equipped. See HOUSES, ITALIAN.

The town was damaged by the *earthquake of AD 63 and obliterated by the eruption of AD 79. Deeply buried by ash which solidified to form a tufaceous rock, the remains (especially organic material such as wood or papyrus) are better preserved, but much more difficult to excavate, than those of Pompeii. The first explorations, using tunnels, date from the early 18th cent.; some 5 ha. (12 acres) have since been completely uncovered (representing only about a quarter of the urban core and inner suburbs). The houses appear less atrium-centred and generally more varied in plan than those of Pompeii; they preserve considerable evidence of the upper stories (e.g. the Casa a Graticcio, built of rubble in a timber frame). Public buildings, mostly dating from the Julio-Claudian period, are much less well attested (a theatre and basilica were recorded by the first excavators: a modest forum, essentially the widening of the Decumanus Maximus, and a large palaestra lie on the edge of the existing site). On the ancient coast are important baths (the 'Terme Suburbane'), and recent work has uncovered the skeletal remains of many dozens of the inhabitants killed at the harbour while attempting to escape the eruption.

A. Maiuri, *I nuovi scavi di Ercolano*, 2 vols. (1958); J. J. Deiss, *Herculaneum, Italy's Buried Treasure* (1985); A. and M. De Vos, *Pompei, Ercolano, Stabia* (1982), 259–306. N. P.

Hercules, from *Hercles*, Italic pronunciation of the name *Heracles. His is perhaps the earliest foreign cult to be received in Rome (perhaps from *Tibur), the Ara Maxima (Coarelli, *Il Foro boario* 60 ff. (see bibliog. below)), which was his most ancient place of worship, being within the *pomerium of the *Palatine settlement. It was probably desired to make the *forum Boarium, in which it stood, a market-place under the protection of a god better known than the local deities. The theory of some ancients (as Propertius 4. 9. 71 ff.) that he is identical with *Semo Sancus

Dius Fidius, although revived in modern times by Preller (Preller–Jordan, *Römische Mythologie*[3] (1881–3) 2. 272 ff.) is untenable, and seems ultimately to rest on nothing better than the interpretation of *Dius Fidius* as *Iovis filius*. His cult had become very popular with merchants, no doubt because of his supposed ability to avert evil of all kinds (see HERACLES) and the long journeys involved in his Labours and other exploits. It was common to pay him a *tithe of the profits of an enterprise (see e.g. Macr. *Sat.* 3. 6. 11; *ILLRP* 136, 149, 155); this was not confined to commercial dealings but included spoils of warfare.

His worship at the Ara Maxima had some interesting features. No other god was mentioned (Plut. *Quaest. Rom.* 90, citing Varro); no women were admitted (Propert. ibid. 21 ff.); dogs were excluded (Plut. *Quaest. Rom.* 90). The sacrificial meat had to be eaten or burnt daily (Varro, *Ling.* 6. 54; Serv. on *Aen.* 8. 183): hence the popularity of the sanctuary. The ritual was originally in the hands not of the pontiffs but of two *gentes*, the Potitii and Pinarii, of whom the former were senior (Plut. ibid. 60, Veranius in Macrob. *Sat.* 3. 6. 14); in the censorship of Appius *Claudius Caecus, 312 BC, it passed to the state (Asper in Macrob. ibid. 13); thereafter an annual sacrifice was celebrated on 12 August by the urban praetor (Varro, *Ling.* 6. 54; attested in inscriptions from the reign of *Commodus: cf. *ILS* 3402 ff.). It was performed in Greek fashion (Varro in Macrob. ibid. 17). The exclusion of women is found also in his cult at *Lanuvium (Tert. *Ad nat.* 2, 7).

For his numerous other places of worship at Rome, see P. Gros, *Aurea Templa: Recherches sur l'architecture religieuse de Rome à l'époque d'Auguste* (1976); Coarelli 60 ff., 164 ff.; Ziolkowski, *Temples* 45 ff. The most important, after the Ara Maxima, are a sanctuary of Hercules Cubans within Caesar's Gardens, temples of Hercules Custos near the Circus Flaminius (probably *c.*220 BC), of Hercules Victor (or Invictus) near the porta Trigemina (the surviving round temple, anniversary on 13 August, Coarelli 92 ff.), of Hercules Musarum near the Circus Flaminius (erected by M. *Fulvius Nobilior *c.*187 BC; see J.-L. Ferrary, *Philhellénisme et impérialisme* (1988), 566 ff.), of Hercules Pompeianus near the Circus Maximus, of Hercules Victor (dedicated on the Caelian by L. *Mummius in 142 BC), and of Hercules, a round temple in the forum Boarium, called *aedes Aemiliana Herculis* decorated with frescoes by M. *Pacuvius.

Identification or comparison with Hercules was common among the later emperors, as *Commodus (SHA *Comm.* 1. 8. 5), C. *Iulius Verus Maximinus (*Max.* 18. 4. 9; 6. 9); see Nock, *JRS* 1947, 102 ff.

Wissowa, *RK* 271 ff.; J. Bayet, *Les Origines de l'Hercule romain* (1926); Latte, *RR* 213 ff.; D. van Berchem, *Rend. Pont.* 32 (1959/60), 61 ff.; F. Coarelli, *Il Foro boario dalle origini alla fine della Repubblica* (1988); M. Verzar, *MÉFRA* 1985, 295. For Hercules as a moral figure: J. Liebeschuetz, *Continuity and Change in Roman Religion* (1979), 170 ff.
H. J. R.; J. Sch.

Hercynian Forest, properly the wooded heights of Thuringia and Bohemia. Originally put near the Pyrenees (schol. on Dionys. Per. 286) or among the Celts (schol. Ap. Rhod. 4. 640) near the Northern Ocean (Diod. Sic. 5. 21, etc.), *Aristotle (*Mete.* 1. 13) placed it in north Europe, and *Timaeus (2) found the Danube's sources in it ([Arist.] *Mir. Ausc.* 105). The name came to be used for all wooded mountains extending from the Rhine to the Carpathians. *Caesar (*BGall.* 6. 25) heard that it was more than nine days' journey wide, sixty days' travel long from the Black Forest along the Danube's northern bank (see DANUVIUS), and thence turned north. Strabo extends it from Lake Constance and the Danube sources to the north frontier of Bohemia and

Moravia. After the exploratory conquests of *Tiberius and Drusus (see CLAUDIUS DRUSUS, NERO) the Hercynian Forest was clearly distinguished from the Alps and was identified with the heights extending round Bohemia and through Moravia to Hungary (Plin. *HN* 4. 80, 99–100; Tac. *Germ.* 28, 30). In *Ptolemy (4) (*Geog.* 2. 11. 7) the name is restricted to a range between the Sudetes and the Carpathians.

L. Rübekeil, *Suebica* (1992).   E. H. W.; J. F. Dr.

Herdonia (mod. Ordona), *Messapian city, 25 km. (15½ mi.) south of Foggia. It was powerful in the 4th cent. BC, becoming a Roman ally during the Second Samnite War. In 214, it seceded to *Hannibal, and was destroyed in 212. Although Herdonia recovered enough to be recognized as a *municipium*, the Roman city was much smaller than the Messapian one. After AD 109, it became a station of the *via Traiana. Extensive excavation has revealed a walled area of 20 ha. (50 acres) containing burials, a street network, and monumental buildings dating to the 4th cent. BC and the Roman period.

D. Mertens, *Ordona*, 7 vols. (1965–83); M. Marin, *Topografia storica della Daunia antica* (1970).   K. L.

Herennius Dexippus, Publius, Athenian notable and historian (3rd cent. AD), author of (1) an account of the Successor-period (Τὰ μετὰ Ἀλέξανδρον), lost; (2) a History from mythical times to AD 269/70 in twelve books (fragments survive); and (3) a *Scythian History* (Σκυθικά) covering the Gothic Wars from AD 238 to Aurelian; preserved largely in *Zosimus, it has many Thucydidean echoes (see THUCYDIDES (2)). The ancient tradition (SHA *Gall.* 13. 8) that he personally led Athenian resistance to the *Heruli in AD 267 has been doubted.

FGrH 100; *IG* 2². 3669 (= E. Sironen, in P. Castren (ed.), *Post-Herulian Athens* (1994), 17 ff.); F. Millar, *JRS* 1969, 20 ff.; G. Fowden, *JHS* 1988, 51 n. 13. *PIR*² H 104.   A. H. McD.; A. J. S. S.

Herennius (*RE* 31) **Modestinus,** a lawyer of the first half of the 3rd cent. AD and a pupil of *Ulpian, had connections in *Pontus (northern Turkey). In *Caracalla's reign he consulted Ulpian from Dalmatia, where he evidently held some junior office. From late 223 to early 226 he perhaps composed rescripts (replies to petitions, here of a sympathetic and helpful sort) as Alexander Severus' *a libellis* (secretary for petitions); see AURELIUS SEVERUS ALEXANDER, M. He became *praefectus vigilum* (chief of police; see VIGILES) in Rome soon after this and was still giving *responsa* (consultative opinions) in 239. Probably as a teaching aid he composed nine books (*libri*) of *Differentiae* ('Distinctions'), ten of *Regulae* ('Guidelines'), and twelve of *Pandectae* ('Encyclopedia'). From his consultative practice came nineteen books of *Responsa*. Among his monographs six books on exemption from guardianship, written for a lawyer friend in Pontus, are of special interest as the most substantial legal work known to have been composed in Greek; in general Modestinus made an effort to come to terms with provincial practice and Greek notions of law. Though in some ways a transitional figure, who foreshadows the more limited legal culture of the late 3rd cent. AD, his opinions were highly regarded and he was included among the five jurists of authority listed by the Law of Citations of 426. Justinian's compilers (see JUSTINIAN'S CODIFICATION) used over 300 passages from his work.

Lenel, *Pal.* 1. 701–56; *PIR*² H 112; *HLL* 4, § 427; Kunkel 1967, 259–61; Honoré 1981, 76–80; T. Masiello, *I libri excusationum di Erennio Modestino* (1983).   T. Hon.

Herennius (*RE* 44) **Senecio,** a native of Hispania *Baetica, was

its quaestor and afterwards in AD 93 supported *Pliny (2) the Younger in the prosecution of Baebius Massa, an oppressive governor of Baetica. He refused to stand for higher office under *Domitian, wrote the Life of *Helvidius Priscus, and was prosecuted by Mettius Carus and put to death by Domitian in the latter part of 93. His memory was attacked by M. *Aquilius Regulus and celebrated by Pliny in his *Letters*.   A. M.; M. T. G.

Herillus, of Carthage, pupil of *Zeno (2), who developed Stoic ideas (see STOICISM) in a distinctive way which lost currency and came to seem unorthodox after *Chrysippus' writings established Stoic orthodoxy. Like *Ariston (1), he refused significance to general distinctions of non-moral value. He emphasized knowledge rather than virtuous action, in a way tending to separate them, and declaring the former to be our proper final end in life (*telos*). Those who fall short of knowledge aim at a *hupotelis* or subordinate end.

Testimonia in von Arnim, *SVF* 1. 91–3.   J. A.

Hermagoras, of Temnos (fl. *c.*150 BC), the most influential teacher of rhetoric of his time, author of an elaborate system which we know in fair detail from later writers, especially *Cicero, *Quintilian, and *Hermogenes (2). His most important work was on 'invention' (εὕρεσις); he did little for the theory of style. By discussing not only themes involving particular situations (ὑποθέσεις), but also general *theses* (θέσεις e.g. Should a man marry?) he helped to extend the scope of rhetorical education to cover moral and philosophical subjects. His complex and subtle classification of 'types of issue' (στάσεις, *status*) was decisive for later theory, and it is for this which he was chiefly remembered (see RHETORIC, GREEK).

There seem to have been at least two other rhetors called Hermagoras, one a disciple of *Theodorus (3) of Gadara, and one of the 2nd cent. AD.

D. Matthes, *Hermagorae Temnitae Testimonia et Fragmenta* (1962), and *Lustrum* 1958, 58–214; G. A. Kennedy, *The Art of Persuasion in Greece* (1963), 303 ff., and *CHCL* 1. 198–9.   D. A. R.

Hermaphroditus, half-male, half-female divinity, his cult first attested in the 4th cent. BC at Athens, where he provided *Posidippus (2) with the title of a comic play (lost) in the early 3rd. *Diodorus (3) (4. 6. 5) makes him the offspring of *Hermes and *Aphrodite; Ovid (*Met.* 4. 285 ff.) provides a lengthy aetiology (the prayers of the nymph Salmacis that she and her beloved might never be parted are dramatically granted). A favourite subject of Hellenistic and Roman artists, he is invariably depicted with developed breasts and male genitals, his physique soft and boyish. At republican Rome natural hermaphrodites (*androgyni*) were considered ill-omened prodigies (see PORTENTS) and were liable to ritual drowning at birth. See DEFORMITY.

In art: *LIMC* 'Hermaphroditos' (with full bibliog.).   A. J. S. S.

Hermarchus (*RE* 1), **of Mytilene,** Epicurean, studied under *Epicurus in *Mytilene before the school was moved to *Lampsacus in 306 BC, and in 271 he succeeded Epicurus as head of the school. Epicurus' will enjoins his heirs to put part of the revenues of his estate at Hermarchus' disposal for the maintenance of the school, and bequeaths to him the whole of Epicurus' library. With Epicurus, *Metrodorus (2), and Polyaenus, *Hermarchus (1) was treated as representing the authoritative form of the Epicurean doctrine. *Porphyry in *Abst.* 1 preserves an important extract from Hermarchus on natural rights and the origin of homicide law in the development of civilization.

Hermeneumata

Works Hermarchus is especially known for his polemical works, Πρὸς Πλάτωνα, Πρὸς Ἀριστοτέλην, Πρὸς Ἐμπεδοκλέα ('Against *Plato (1)', 'Against *Aristotle', 'Against *Empedocles', the last in 22 books!), Περὶ τῶν μαθημάτων ('Against the Professors'); he also wrote Ἐπιστολικά ('Letters').

FRAGMENTS F. Longo Auricchio, *Ermarco, Frammenti: edizione, traduzione e commento*, La scuola di Epicuro 6 (1988).   W. D. R.; D. O.

Hermeneumata 'Translations' (the addition 'Pseudo-Dositheana' only preserves a 17th-cent. misattribution). A title found in manuscripts for various gloss-collections, but nowadays mostly applied to Greek–Latin school-books designed to teach children vocabulary and idiom in both languages. Nine versions survive, varying in content but similar in structure: an alphabetical verb-list, noun-lists by topics (e.g. the theatre, foods, kinship, trees), and vivid scenes from everyday life ('*colloquia*'). Bilingual texts sporadically accompany these (e.g. *Aesop, *Hyginus (3a), a legal fragment). The tradition had developed in the west by the 4th cent. AD, though elements of it are older. Much of the material remains unexplored by social or linguistic historians. See GLOSSA, GLOSSARY (Latin).

Ed. G. Goetz, *Corpus glossariorum latinorum* 3; HLL 6, § 611. 6. Cf. A. C. Dionisotti, JRS 1982, 83–125 at 85–92.   A. C. D.

Hermes (Ἑρμῆς). Already attested among the Mycenaean pantheon (tablets from Cnossus in *Crete, *Pylos, and *Thebes (1); see RELIGION, MINOAN AND MYCENAEAN), the god has no original connection with the ἕρμα or cairn of stones, as was once thought. Myths about Hermes are mostly concerned with his childhood, told in the *Homeric Hymn to Hermes* (last third of the 6th cent. BC; see HYMNS). He was the son of *Zeus and the *nymph *Maia, born on Mt. Cyllene in *Arcadia. On the day of his birth, he left his cradle, found a tortoise which he made into a lyre, then went to Pieria where he stole 50 cows belonging to *Apollo, which he led backwards to a cave where he sacrificed two and hid the others, before returning to Cyllene; finally he made up the quarrel with Apollo. Later, he invented the syrinx (pipe; but see SYRINX) and was taught *divination by Apollo. Apart from these stories of his childhood, Hermes plays only a secondary part in other myths. He has no recognized wife, but two sons, Eudorus and *Pan, are attributed to him. He is characterized by a great variety of functions. Above all, he is a messenger god, who carries out the orders of Zeus with due respect. In this capacity, he appears as a subordinate deity, giving the ultimatum of Zeus to *Prometheus, for instance, or acting as his go-between when he is enamoured of *Ganymedes. He is generally well-disposed, and negotiates the ransom of Hector with pleasantness and good humour. His titles stress his speed and beneficence. He is also the god who guides: he shows transhumant shepherds the way and leads teams of animals; he guides people, especially travellers, for whom he marks out the route in the form of a pillar or herm (see below). He takes divine children to safety (thus he gives *Dionysus to the Nymphs of Nysa, as depicted in the famous statue by *Praxiteles, and *Arcas to Maia), and is generally a patron of children (*Heracles, *Achilles); he also helps heroes such as *Perseus (1), for whom he obtains the bronze sickle used by the hero to decapitate Medusa (see GORGO), and Heracles. He leads *Hera, *Aphrodite, and *Athena to *Paris, the judge in their beauty contest. As god of movement, he is leader of the Nymphs and the *Charites. Finally as *psychopompos* (one who escorts *souls), he leads the dead to *Hades, summoning them to the journey beyond, taking them by the hand and accompanying them on to *Charon (1)'s boat.

Another aspect of Hermes is that of a god of abundance, fertility and prosperity (*Hymn. Hom. Merc.* 529). He is the patron of herdsmen and of the fruitfulness of herds and flocks; he is himself a cowherd and shepherd (ibid. 491–4). This form of Hermes is called Nomios, 'pastoral' and Epimelios, 'presiding over sheep', and is often shown in art as Hermes *kriophoros* ('ram-bearing'), especially in Arcadia and *Boeotia. He is also sometimes a 'lord of animals', of horses in particular. More generally, he is the god of every kind of prosperity. The herm, a quadrangular pillar topped with a head, with tenons on its sides and a phallus on the front, was very popular from the end of the 6th cent. onwards, and not only recalls Hermes' powers of fertility but, as an apotropaic talisman, also guarantees the success of all sorts of undertakings. (See HERMS.) It is found in towns both at the threshold of houses and inside them, and became a sort of mascot bringing luck both to cities and to individuals (the mutilation of the herms at Athens was perceived as a bad omen on the eve of the Sicilian expedition: Thuc. 6. 27. 3). In the same context, Hermes is also the god of trade (on Delian seals of the Hellenistic age he appears holding a purse).

Hermes is an ingenious god, expert in both technology and magic. From his birth onwards, he was skilled in trickery and deception, and in the *Homeric Hymn* (292) he is 'prince of thieves'. Even in cult, he is attested as trickster and thief (Hermes Dolios at Pellene in *Achaea and Hermes Kleptes in *Chios). But most often he uses his power in mischief, illusion, and mystery. He creates a lyre out of the shell of a tortoise, he puts on his feet sandals which erase footprints. He is an expert in knots and chains. Like a magician he knows how to put the enemy camp to sleep (*Iliad* 24) and to call up the dead. As a corollary, this god of *mētis* (prudence, cunning) and of mediation (see Kahn in bibliog. below)), has no part in violence. He is the least warlike of the gods; he is dragged into the battle with the *Giants, and linked with murder only in the story of *Argos (1). He prefers persuasion to weapons, and appears frequently as patron of orators. He can also be a musician: he is the inventor of the syrinx, and accompanies the dances of the Nymphs and the Charites. Only in a late period, as Trismegistus ('thrice-greatest'), does he come to preside over mystical revelations, as the successor to the Egyptian god Thoth and god of the 'hermetic' (see HERMES TRISMEGISTUS). A final function of Hermes, attested above all from the 4th cent. BC, is that of god of athletes—one linked, no doubt, to the youthful appearance and charm which the god assumed for seduction (*Il.* 24. 376–7, 433). See ATHLETICS. In this role he is frequently associated, particularly in the *gymnasium, with *Heracles. He even became, at a late date, the god of the school and of *education.

Hermes' main aspects are shown in his physical appearance and iconography. His attributes are the caduceus (κηρύκειον), the herald's sign which he almost always carries, the traveller's hat (*petasos* or *pilos*), with or without wings, and the winged sandals which evoke his quality of speed. He is generally bearded in the earlier period, but an unbearded type develops from the 4th cent. onwards. He is clothed in a *chlamys* or a *chlaina*, with sometimes a furry leopard-skin. Side by side with this very frequent representation of the god of herds and flocks, the god of music, the messenger and guide, or the *chthonian god, we find the herm (see above), whose identity as Hermes is sometimes stressed by a caduceus painted on the shaft. This form, attested in sculpture as well as on vases, was very popular and could symbolize most of the functions of the god. In some cases, especially to indicate Hermes as god of the gymnasium, the pillar wears a cloak.

The cult of Hermes is particularly widely diffused in the Peloponnese, where Pausanias mentions numerous myths, rituals, cults, and herms. Passing over the more ordinary examples (Pellene, Pheneos, and Mt. Cyllene, *Megalopolis, *Tegea, *Corinth, *Argos (2)), we may point out the oracular ritual in front of a pillar of Hermes at Pharae in Achaea (Paus. 7. 22. 2). In Athens, Hermes had a very ancient cult (cf. the *xoanon* or ancient statue dedicated on the Acropolis by *Cecrops), and in the form of the herm he was present everywhere in the city. The Hermaia, a young boys' festival, were celebrated in his honour. His cult is also attested in Boeotia (*Tanagra) and in the *Cyclades: at *Delos he is the god of the gymnasium. At Cydonia in Crete, the Hermaia were a popular festival where slaves took the part of their masters. Hermes was not a major divinity, but because he was essentially kindly, he was one of the most familiar gods in the daily lives of the Greeks.

L. Kahn, *Hermès passe ou les ambiguïtés de la communication* (1978); M. Jost, *Sanctuaires et cultes d'Arcadie* (1985), see index; G. Siebert, *LIMC* 5. 285–387, with bibliog. 289–90. M. J.

Hermes Trismegistus, the Hellenistic *Hermes, Egyptianized through contact with the Egyptian Thoth. 'Trismegistos' derives from the Egyptian superlative obtained through repetition (Hermes appears as 'Great, Great, Great' on the Rosetta stone), which is later simplified through the substitution of the prefix *tris* in the Roman period (Festugière, *La Révélation* (see below), 1. 73–4). According to *Clement of Alexandria he was the author of 42 'fundamental books' of Egyptian religion, including astrological, cosmological, geographical, medical, and pedagogic books as well as hymns to the gods and instructions on how to worship. The extant corpus of Hermetic writings (in Greek, Latin, and Coptic) includes astrological, alchemical, iatromathematical, and philosophic works. Some elements in some of the philosophical books (especially the *Asclepius* and *Corpus Hermeticum* 16) are overtly anti-Greek in sentiment, but the basic content of the works is thoroughly Hellenic and offers an insight into 'popular Platonism' (see PLATO (1)) in the Roman world as spread through small groups of literate people who gathered around a teacher for instruction (Fowden 193). Hermes also appears frequently in *PGM*, a reflection of Thoth's role as the god of *magic, and may be connected with late antique *theurgy.

TEXTS Philosophical works, A. D. Nock and A. J. Festugière, 1–4 (1945–54); B. Copenhaver, *Hermetica* (1992), Eng. trans. with notes. STUDIES A. J. Festugière, *La Révélation d'Hermès Trismégiste*, 1–4 (1944–54), fundamental for all aspects of the corpus; G. Fowden, *The Egyptian Hermes*, 2nd edn. (1993). D. S. P.

Hermesianax, of Colophon, Greek poet of the early 3rd cent. BC, pupil and friend of *Philitas, author of *Leontion* and possibly also of *Persica* (fr. 12 Powell). *Leontion* (the title was apparently the name of his mistress) was in elegiacs, and in three books; it may have been modelled on the *Lyde* of *Antimachus. It exemplifies several of the typical features of Hellenistic poetry: a fondness for linguistic rarities, interest in love (esp. if unhappy), and stress on aetiology. Fr. 1 (from bk. 1) describes Polyphemus gazing out to sea, which suggests a reworking of the Polyphemus–*Galatea story from Philoxenus (himself mentioned in fr. 7. 69–74); frs. 2 and 3 (Daphnis and Menalcas) may belong to the same book, possibly devoted to the love affairs of herdsmen. Book 2 included the tale of Arceophon's rejection by Arsinoë, and her subsequent metamorphosis into stone (fr. 4 = Ant. Lib. *Met.* 39) and possibly

also the story of Leucippus' incest (fr. 5 = Parth. *Amat. narr.* 5). The longest fragment (7), 98 lines long, is preserved, in a corrupt form, by Athenaeus (13. 597b); it consists of a fanciful catalogue of love affairs of poets from *Orpheus to *Philitas, and of philosophers (*Pythagoras (1), *Socrates, *Aristippus). Typically, the poets' subject-matter is presented as biographical evidence, and some of the pairings can hardly be meant to be taken seriously (e.g. *Homer and *Penelope, *Hesiod and 'Ehoea'; *Alcaeus and *Anacreon are, anachronistically, rivals for the love of *Sappho; Socrates courts *Aspasia). Fr. 8 mentions an elegy for the *Centaur *Eurytion (2), which strongly supports the ascription to Hermesianax of the newly recovered poem preserved in *PBrux.* 8934 and *PSorbonn.* 2254 (= *Suppl. Hell.* 970).

TEXTS Powell, *Coll. Alex.* 96–106; Diehl, *Anth. Lyr. Graec.* 56–64; trans. of fr. 7 in Gulick (ed.), Athenaeus vol. 6 (Loeb, 1937); M. Huys, *Le Poème élégiaque hellénistique P.Brux. Inv. E. 8934 et P.Sorbonne Inv. 2254* (1991). F. W.

Hermetic writings See HERMES TRISMEGISTUS.

Hermias (1), tyrant of Atarneus (in Mysia, opposite *Lesbos) *c.*355 BC. A former student of the *Academy (though he never met *Plato (1)), he introduced a more moderate regime, admitting the Platonists Erastus and Coriscus of Scepsis to a share in his power and encouraging them to found a new philosophical school at Assos. There they were joined on Plato's death (348) by *Aristotle, *Xenocrates (1), and *Callisthenes, and later by *Theophrastus. Aristotle became an intimate friend of Hermias and married his niece and adopted daughter Pythias. Hermias possessed a formidable naval, military, and financial power, and was virtually independent of the Persian empire. An interesting inscription (Tod 165) records honours to Hermias by *Erythrae. He negotiated, with Aristotle's assistance, an understanding with Macedonia. In 341, however, he was treacherously arrested at a conference with *Mentor (2), and sent captive to the Great King, who vainly tried to coerce him into revealing the plans of *Philip (1) II and executed him. He was a recipient of Plato's sixth epistle and is said to have written on the immortality of the soul. Callisthenes wrote an encomium of him (*FGrH* 124 F 2).

W. Jaeger, *Aristotle* (1934), 105; D. E. W. Wormell, *Yale Studies in Classical Philology* 5 (1935); R. Lane Fox, in J. Boardman and C. Vaphopoulou–Richardson (eds.), *Chios* (1986), 111 f.; *CAH* 6² (1994), 94 f., 220, 224 (S. Hornblower), 620 ff. (M. Ostwald and J. Lynch). D. E. W. W.

Hermias (2), of Cypriot *Curium, choliambic poet. One fragment, attacking the Stoics for hypocrisy, survives; manner and metre point to the 3rd cent. BC, and verse 1 resembles the opening choliambic verse of *Callimachus (3)'s *Iambi.

Powell, *Coll. Alex.* 237; cf. *Suppl. Hell.* no 484. R. L. Hu.

Hermias (3), otherwise unknown Christian author of the *Satire on the Profane Philosophers*. This small Greek treatise of uncertain date (perhaps *c.* AD 200) aims at exposing the contradictions of the teachings of the major philosophical schools as regards the nature of the soul and the universe. The author relies heavily on doxographical sources.

Ed. R. P. C. Hanson and D. Joussot, *Hermias—Satire des philosophes païens*, SC 388 (1993), with Fr. trans. and comm.; P. Siniscalco, *EEC* 1. 378. W. K.

Hermione, in mythology daughter of *Menelaus (1) and *Helen (*Od.* 4. 14). According to Homer, Menelaus betrothed her to *Neoptolemus (1) while he was away at Troy, and the wedding took place after the war (ibid. 3–9). The marriage, however,

Hermippus

was childless; according to *Euripides' *Andromache*, Hermione blamed this on spells cast by *Andromache, Neoptolemus' concubine won at Troy, and would have had both Andromache and Molossus, her son by Neoptolemus, put to death if old *Peleus, Neoptolemus' grandfather, had not intervened to save them. Neoptolemus was then murdered by *Orestes while at *Delphi enquiring why Hermione was childless, and she was carried off by Orestes, to whom in this version she had originally been promised (*Andr.* 966–81). According to Eur. *Or.* 1655, however, she was never married to Neoptolemus. All authors (except for schol. Pind. *Nem.* 10. 12, citing Ibycus, who says she married Diomedes) agree that she became Orestes' wife, and mother of his son Tisamenus (Paus. 2. 18. 6).

LIMC 5. 1 (1990), 388–90.   J. R. M.

Hermippus (1), Athenian comic poet and brother of *Myrtilus, won at least one victory (435 BC) at the City *Dionysia and four at the *Lenaea, the first *c.*430 BC (*IG* 2². 2325. 57, 123). We have ten titles and 94 citations. Ἀρτοπώλιδες ('The Women Sellers of Bread'), in which *Hyperbolus and his mother were ridiculed (cf. Ar. *Nub.* 551 ff. with schol.), must belong to the period 421–416. Fr. 47 (from an unnamed play) refers to *Cleon's attack on *Pericles (1) in 431 or 430; fr. 63 (from Φορμοφόροι ('The Porters')) is of interest because it names (with jokes interspersed) the characteristic imports to Athens from various Mediterranean countries *c.*430–420 BC, and fr. 77 (play unnamed) represents *Dionysus giving his opinions on different wines. Several of Hermippus' titles indicate mythological burlesque.

Kassel–Austin, *PCG* 5. 561 ff. (*CAF* 1. 224 ff.).   K. J. D.

Hermippus (2) (*RE* 6), of Smyrna (fl. 3rd cent. BC), follower of *Callimachus (3), biographer of philosophers, writers, and lawgivers. *Plutarch and *Diogenes (6) Laertius used him as a source; his role in the tradition of *Aristotle's bibliography is controversial. He revelled in falsified sensationalism, particularly in death scenes. See BIOGRAPHY, GREEK.

TEXT F. Wehrli, *Die Schule des Aristoteles*, Suppl. 1 (1974).
STUDIES F. Wehrli in Überweg–Flashar 583–6; I. Düring, *Aristotle in the Ancient Biographical Tradition* (1957); C. Lord, *AJPhil.* 1986.
                                                                        R. W. S.

Hermippus (3), grammarian of the time of *Trajan and *Hadrian, from Berytus (a village of the interior, not the harbour-town, according to the *Suda*). By birth a slave, he became a pupil of *Philon (5) of Byblos. His works include *Interpreting Dreams* in five books; *On the Number Seven*; and *About Slaves Eminent in Learning*.

FHG 3. 35; Christ–Schmid–Stählin 2/2⁶. 868.

Hermocrates (*RE* 1), Syracusan statesman and general; see SYRACUSE. At the peace conference at *Gela (424 BC) he alerted the Siceliots, and at Syracuse (418–416) his fellow citizens, to the threat posed to their liberty by Athens. He played a prominent part in the defeat of the Athenian expedition as adviser (415), general plenipotentiary (414), and as adviser to *Gylippus (413). Sent as admiral to Asia (412), he was exiled *in absentia* by the radical democracy, after the battle of Cyzicus (410). Provided with funds by *Pharnabazus, he returned to Sicily (409), and with a private army seized *Selinus and ravaged the Carthaginian province. Refused an amnesty in 408, he attempted to seize Syracuse with the aid of partisans inside the city (including *Dionysius (1) I) and was killed. He was praised as a patriot by *Thucydides (2) (and as a man by *Xenophon (1)); an opponent

of radical democracy, he may in the end have contemplated the establishment of a tyranny.

D. Asheri, *CAH* 5² (1992), ch. 7; B. Caven, *Dionysius I* (1990), 21–45.
                                                                        B. M. C.

Hermogenes (1), a Greek architect from *Alabanda in Caria (Vitr. *De arch.* 3. 2. 6). His date is a matter of debate, though a floruit *c.*170 BC seems probable. His chief works are the temple of *Dionysus at *Teos and the temple of *Artemis Leucophryene at *Magnesia (1) ad *Maeandrum, both in the Ionic order. From these, and from his books about them, *Vitruvius derived some of the principles of proportion included in his own book, even though the remains of the two temples do not exactly agree with the precepts he attributes to Hermogenes; nor was the octastyle pseudodipteral type of temple invented by Hermogenes as he states, though he revived its use. He also includes Hermogenes among those architects who objected to the use of the Doric order in sacred buildings because of the complications arising from the spacing of the triglyphs. This may result from the reconstruction of the Doric temple of *Asclepius at *Pergamum as an Ionic building after its destruction by *Prusias II in 156 BC. Strabo praised the Magnesian temple, and it is probable that Hermogenes' influence on Roman architecture of the Augustan period was considerable. See ARCHITECTS.

Vitr. *De arch.* 3. 3, 4. 3, 7 pref.; Strabo 14. 1. 40 (647C). W. Hoepfner and E.-L. Schwandner (eds.), *Hermogenes und die hochhellenistische Architektur* (1990).   R. A. T.

Hermogenes (2) (*RE* 22), of Tarsus (2nd cent. AD), rhetor. A child prodigy, admired by Marcus *Aurelius, he failed to fulfil his promise as a speaker (hostile account in *Philostratus, *VS* 2. 577), but wrote a comprehensive set of textbooks on rhetoric which were much used in Byzantine and Renaissance times. We have two works which are certainly genuine: one on *staseis* (types of issue, see RHETORIC, GREEK), and one on *ideai* (types of style). Other works in the corpus are spurious ('On the Method of Forcefulness', Περὶ μεθόδου δεινότητος, and 'On Invention', Περὶ εὑρέσεως) or of doubtful authenticity (a set of *progymnasmata). The most significant is the book on types of style, which deals with seven types, all to be seen as ingredients in the perfection of *Demosthenes (2) but, identifiable, in various proportions, in other authors: they are clarity (σαφήνεια), grandeur (μέγεθος), beauty (κάλλος), rapidity (γοργότης), character (ἦθος, covering qualities like simplicity, subtlety, and sweetness), sincerity (ἀλήθεια), and forcefulness (δεινότης). A somewhat similar scheme is to be found in the 'Art of Rhetoric' falsely ascribed to P. Aelius *Aristides, and dating from much the same period. It is a refinement of the doctrine of 'virtues of speech' (ἀρεταὶ λέξεως) found in *Dionysius (7) of Halicarnassus and ultimately traceable to *Theophrastus.

TEXT AND COMMENTARIES H. Rabe (1913) supersedes L. Spengel (*Rhetores Graeci* 2 (1853)). Syrianus' commentaries on Περὶ ἰδεῶν and Περὶ στάσεων were also edited by Rabe (1892–3); these and other Byzantine commentaries are in C. Walz, *Rhetores Graeci* (1832–6), vols. 4–6. English translation of 'Types of Style' by C. W. Wooten (1987); of 'On Stases' by R. Nadeau (*Speech Monographs* 31 (1964), 361–424); see also M. Heath, *Hermogenes On Issues* (1995).
See also: D. Hagedorn, *Zur Ideenlehre des Hermogenes* (1964); G. A. Kennedy, *Art of Rhetoric in the Roman World* (1972), 619–33; D. A. Russell, *CHCL* 1. 314–17.   D. A. R.

Hermogenianus, Aurelius (?), a Roman lawyer of the late 3rd and early 4th cent. AD; of a systematic cast of mind, he came from the eastern empire and, to judge from evidence both of style and access to material, was *Diocletian's *magister libellorum (master of petitions) from the beginning of AD 293 to the end of 294, after which he probably served *Maximian in the west in the same capacity. He used the spare and uncompromising rescripts (replies to petitions; see CONSTITUTIONS; MAGISTER LIBELLORUM) which he drafted in that capacity, along with some western material, as the basis for his compilation of imperial laws (Codex Hermogenianus), probably completed in Milan in 295. Two further editions were published in the author's lifetime, at least one more after his death. His Codex remained in use until superseded by Justinian's Codex of 528, which incorporated many of its laws (see JUSTINIAN'S CODIFICATION). Around 300 Hermogenianus wrote six books (libri) of Iuris epitomae ('Summaries of the Law'), a synopsis of classical legal writing, in which the sources are not identified. An inscription uncovered in Brescia in 1983 shows that an Aurelius Hermogenianus, probably the same man, became praetorian prefect under Constantius Caesar (see CONSTANTIUS I) not later than 305. He is important as the first lawyer who made an effort to reduce the law to a small number of basic principles, such as respect for the individual will, from which solutions to concrete problems could be deduced. This effort was further developed by the natural law and historical schools of jurisprudence from the 17th cent. onwards.

Lenel, Pal. 1. 265–78; HLL 5, § 505; D. Liebs, Hermogenians Iuris Epitomae (1964), and Liebs 1987, 36–51, 137–44; ZRG 1990, 385; Honoré 1981, 119–32; A. Cenderelli, Ricerche sul Codex Hermogenianus (1965).

T. Hon.

Hermopolis Magna (mod. El-Ashmunein), a nome-capital (see NOMOS (1)) on the west bank of the Nile and Graeco-Roman customs-post between Middle and Upper *Egypt. Buildings described by Jomard have largely disappeared. The temple of Thoth, completed by the Ptolemies, the Komasterion (assembly-hall for the priests called komastai), and Dromos (ceremonial entrance-way) of Hermes can be identified. Damage after the Jewish Revolt in Trajan's reign was repaired. In the 5th–7th cents. a cathedral was built. Many literary and documentary papyri survive, the latter detailing the administration.

E. Jomard, Description d'Égypte 4 (1809), ch. 14. Papyri: BKT 1, 2, 4, 6, 7; PAmh. 2 (1901); Corpus Papyrorum Hermopolitanarum (1905); PFlor. 1 (1906), 3 (1915); PLips. (1906); PLondon 3 (1907), 5 (1917); PStras. 1 (1912), 5 (1973); PRyl. 2 (1915), 4 (1952); PBrem. (1936); BGU 12 (1974); PHerm. Landl. (1978); PCharite (1980); PHeid. 4 (1986). On Rubensohn's excavations (1903–6) see BGU 12, xiv–xix. G. Roeder, Hermopolis 1929–39 (1959); A. J. Spencer and D. M. Bailey, Excavations at El-Ashmunein 1, 2, 4 (1983–92); G. Méautis, Hermoupolis-la-Grande (1918).

W. E. H. C.

herms were marble or bronze four-cornered pillars surmounted by a bust. Male herms were given genitals. Herms originated in piles of stones (ἔρματα) used as road- and boundary-markers, but early on developed into the god *Hermes (but see that entry). As representations of Hermes they were viewed also as protectors of houses and cities. The Athenians claimed credit for the developed sculptural form (Paus. 1. 24. 3), and herms were particularly common in Athens, at crossroads, in the countryside, in the Agora, at the entrance of the Acropolis, in sanctuaries, and at private doorways. The sacrilegious mutilation of the herms in 415 BC led to the exile of *Alcibiades (Thuc. 6. 27 ff.). Other deities, e.g. *Aphrodite (Paus. 1. 19. 2), were also occasionally represented as herms, and the Romans in copying Greek portrait statues converted some into herm form.

W. Burkert, Structure and History in Greek Mythology and Ritual (1979), 39–41; R. G. Osborne, PCPhS 1985, 47 ff.

J. D. M.

Hermus (now Gediz Çayı), the largest river on the west coast of Asia Minor after the *Maeander, is mentioned by Homer (Il. 20. 392). Herodotus (1. 80, cf. Strabo 626, Plin. HN 5. 119) says it rises on the holy mountain of the Dindymene Mother in *Phrygia (now Murat Dağı) and enters the sea by *Phocaea. This is also its present course; but at some unknown time it left its bed and turned to the south after passing the gorge west of *Magnesia (2) ad Sipylum and ran into the gulf of *Smyrna. In 1886, to save the gulf from becoming silted up, the river was diverted back into its ancient bed. Among its tributaries are the Hyllus and the gold-bearing Pactolus.

G. E. B.

Hernici inhabited the Trerus valley and hills north of it in Italy (Strabo. 5. 231: inaccurate). Their treaty with Rome in regal times is possibly apocryphal (Dion. Hal. Ant. Rom. 4. 49; Festus 476 Lindsay). But they certainly signed a defensive alliance with Rome c.486 BC, and in the subsequent wars against *Aequi and *Volsci fought staunchly (Dion. Hal. 8. 64 f.; Livy 2. 41, etc.: untrustworthy). Later, in 387 and 362, the Hernici opposed Rome but renewed the old alliance in 358 (Livy 6. 2 f., 7. 6 f.). After remaining loyal in the Latin War the Hernican cities, except Ferentinum, Aletrium, and Verulae, were led into war against Rome in 306 by *Anagnia, but were easily conquered and granted partial, later full, citizenship (Livy 9. 42 f.; Festus 262 Lindsay). Hernican territory became part of Latium and the Hernici were so completely Latinized that their own language cannot be discovered. Possibly it was a Latinian dialect, but their name meaning 'men of the rocks' (Festus 89 Lindsay) looks *Oscan. See LANGUAGES OF ITALY.

G. Devoto, Gli antichi Italici (1951), 127 f.

E. T. S.; T. W. P.

Hero (Ἡρώ) **and Leander** (Λέανδρος), mythological lovers. Hero was priestess of *Aphrodite at *Sestus; Leander lived at *Abydos, saw her at a festival, fell in love with her, and used to swim the *Hellespont at night to see her until a storm put out the light by which she guided him, and he was drowned; Hero leapt from her seaside tower onto his corpse.

Originally perhaps a local Hellespontine tale, the story was probably popularized by one or more Hellenistic poets (Suppl. Hell. 901 ?) and later was well known to Roman writers (Verg. G. 3. 258–63; Ov. Her. 18–19). The most detailed extant treatment is that of Musaeus (5th/6th cent. AD), a learned Christian and/or *Neoplatonist. His 343-line hexameter *epyllion, which owes much in diction to the Nonnian school (see NONNUS), contains many contextual and linguistic allusions to Homer, and employs to fine effect the motifs of light and darkness: Hero's lamp is equated with the life of her lover in an ingenious variety of ways. The poem inspired Marlowe's Hero and Leander and many other later works.

Text of Musaeus: K. Kost (1971), with comm.; P. Orsini (Budé, 1968); T. Gelzer and C. H. Whitman (Loeb, 1975; with C. A. Trypanis, Callimachus, Fragments); E. Livrea and P. Eleuteri (Teubner, 1982); N. Hopkinson, An Imperial Anthology, comm. (1994), 42–54, 136–85. Language: T. Gelzer, MH 1967, 129–48, and 1968, 11–47.

N. H.

hero-cult Heroes (ἥρωες, fem. ἡρωῖναι, ἡρώισσαι) were a class of beings worshipped by the Greeks, generally conceived as the powerful dead, and often as forming a class intermediate between gods and men. Hero-cult was apparently unknown to the Mycenaeans; features suggestive of the fully developed phenomenon have been found in 10th-cent. BC contexts, but it is not until the 8th cent. that such cults become widespread and normal. The reasons for its rise have been much debated, but seem likely to be somehow connected with more general social changes at that date.

Although Greek authors expect the phrase 'heroic honours' to convey something definite, there was in practice much variation in the type of cult given to heroes. At one end of the spectrum it could have a strong resemblance to the offerings given to a dead relative; at the other, it might be barely distinguishable from worship paid to a god. Many features cited by ancient and modern authorities as typical of heroic *sacrifice occur also in divine cults with a '*chthonian' aspect: holocaust sacrifice on a low altar, using dark animals, performed at night. Such rites, characteristic of the form of sacrifice known as *enagismos*, certainly seem designed to contrast with 'normal' sacrifice, *thusia*, in the strict sense, but there are too many examples of heroic sacrifices which do not conform to this pattern to be dismissed as anomalies (see SACRIFICE, GREEK). Epigraphic evidence, in particular the Attic sacrifice calendars, shows that very often the hero's offering was distinguished from the god's simply by its lesser value, but even this is not universal, especially where the hero represents an old divinity or forms the focal point of a festival. Again, while heroes' sanctuaries tended to be smaller and less splendid than those of gods, often indeed occupying a small space within a divine precinct, a few heroes, such as *Hippolytus (1) at *Troezen, had sanctuary complexes as impressive as those of any god. Hero-shrines were often—not always—constructed around tombs, real or supposed, and the hero had a very close connection with that particular place, being far more localized than a god. The only real exception to this is *Heracles, who is in any case as much god as hero.

Concepts of heroes were as variable as their cult, if not more so. There is some evidence that heroes as a class were viewed as at least potentially malign, to be placated with apotropaic ritual rather than worshipped in the normal sense, but this is true only rarely of individual heroes, who more often appear as patrons or saviours of their city, as helpers in sickness or personal danger, and generally as benefactors. The traditions of their lives, deaths, and actions after death, however, usually contain some element of singularity or paradox. Many cult heroes were identified with the characters of heroic *epic, but bronze age credentials were not necessary: the newly dead might be given heroic honours, generally by oracular command, if they conformed to one of the heroic patterns, for instance by instituting a divine cult or founding a city. Still other heroes were probably never very clearly identified by their worshippers, but went by appellations such as 'the hero in the salt-pan' or 'the reed-man'. Heroines in particular might appear in groups named only for their place of cult, and in such cases seem closer to *nymphs than to the powerful dead. In other instances a heroine or heroines, often nameless, may be associated with a hero and receive sacrifice with him, generally an offering of lesser value; but there was no shortage of named heroines such as *Aglaurus or *Iphigenia who were independent of male heroes.

From the 4th cent. onwards there was a tendency in many parts of the Greek world for mourners to depict the ordinary dead in heroic forms, to call them 'hero', and even on occasion to establish regular heroic cult and a priesthood. The exceptional nature of the older heroes was thus undermined, and the changed political circumstance of the Hellenistic and Roman periods further reduced the relevance of the many heroic cults which were closely connected with a sense of civic identity. A number of old cults flourished still in the time of *Pausanias (3), but perhaps the majority had fallen into disuse.

A. Brelich, *Gli eroi greci* (1958); Farnell, *Hero-Cults*; A. D. Nock, *Harv. Theol. Rev.* 1944, 141–74 (= *Essays* (1972), 2. 575–602); I. Morris, *Antiquity* 1988, 758–61; Kearns, *Heroes of Attica*.   E. Ke.

Herod (1) **the Great** (*c*.73–4 BC), son of the Idumaean *Antipater (6), was through him made governor of Galilee in 47 BC and then, with his brother, designated tetrarch (see TETRARCHY) by *M. Antonius (2) (Mark Antony). Herod escaped the Parthian invasion of 40, and, while the Parthian nominee, the *Hasmonean Antigonus, occupied the throne, Herod was declared king of *Judaea by Antony and the senate. In 37, having married Mariamme, granddaughter to both of the feuding Hasmoneans, Hyrcanus and Aristobulus, Herod took *Jerusalem, with the assistance of C. *Sosius. *Octavian, whom Herod supported at *Actium, confirmed his rule, adding a number of cities. In 23, Herod received territories north-east of the Sea of Galilee—Trachonitis, Batanea, and Auranitis. Herod's rule meant that the kingship and high priesthood were now again separate in Judaea, though the latter was in the king's gift: he promoted a new high-priestly class, centred on a handful of diaspora families, who thus acquired great wealth and standing. The palace élite, of mixed ethnic affiliation, also grew. Herod was an able administrator and a skilful financier. He taxed the country heavily, but also developed its resources, to which end his artificial harbour at *Caesarea (2) contributed. Spectacular building projects were a hallmark of his reign, including the rebuilding of Samaria as Sebaste, a characteristic string of fortress-palaces, most notably *Masada, and Herodium, also his burial place. *Jerusalem acquired an amphitheatre as well as a theatre, whose decorations aroused the suspicion of some Jews. But his greatest undertaking, the rebuilding of the Temple, was left entirely to priests, to preserve purity. There, offence was given by a golden eagle put over the gate at the very end of his reign, a time when tensions with the *Pharisees, earlier his friends, were running high. Lavish donations outside Palestine established Herod as a benefactor on an empire-wide scale, as well as a flamboyant *philhellene; the *Olympian games and the city of Athens were among the beneficiaries. Through his personal good offices, his visits to Rome, and the mediation of *Nicolaus of Damascus and of M. *Vipsanius Agrippa, Herod long retained Augustus' confidence. He may have been exempt from tribute. But, in 9 BC, an unauthorized war against the *Nabataeans incurred imperial displeasure. Also increasingly unacceptable was his savagery towards the large family produced by his ten wives: intrigues led him to execute his favourite, Mariamme I, in 29, her two sons in 7, and his eldest son and expected heir a few days before his death. Serious disturbances then allowed Roman intervention, and the division of his kingdom between his remaining sons, *Herod (2) Antipas, *Archelaus (4), and *Philip (4), was formalized.

Joseph. *AJ* 14. 158–17. 208; *BJ* 1. 203–673. A. Schalit, *König Herodes: Der Mann und sein Werk* (1969); A. H. M. Jones, *The Herods of Judaea* (rev. impression, 1967), 28–155; M. Stern, in S. Safrai and M. Stern (eds.), *The Jewish People in the First Century* 1 (1974), 216–307; Schürer, *History* 1. 287–329.   T. R.

Herod (2) **Antipas,** following the will left by his father *Herod (1), was appointed by Augustus tetrarch of Galilee (where he rebuilt the city of Sepphoris and founded *Tiberias) and of Peraea, a non-adjacent territory across the Jordan. Both John the Baptist and Jesus were active in Antipas' territory. John was imprisoned as a troublemaker in the fortress of Machaerus and then executed (perhaps at the instigation of Salome). Luke has *Pontius Pilatus trying unsuccessfully to transfer to Antipas, in

Jerusalem, the responsibility for trying Jesus. Probably in AD 35/6, Antipas was involved in bringing together L. *Vitellius, governor of Syria, and *Artabanus II of Parthia. Antipas had divorced his wife, a daughter of *Aretas IV of Nabataea, in favour of his niece Herodias (mother of Salome); in 36/7, Aretas took revenge by successfully invading Peraea. In 39 Antipas asked *Gaius (1) for the title of king, but he was instead deposed and exiled, on evidence offered by his nephew and brother-in-law, *Agrippa I, who inherited his *tetrarchy.

Josephus, *AJ* 18. 27, 36–8, 101–5, 109–25, 147–50, 240–55; *BJ* 2. 94–5, 167–8, 181–3. Schürer, *History* 1. 340–53; H. W. Hoehner, *Herod Antipas* (1972). A. H. M. Jones, *The Herods of Judaea* (rev. impression, 1967), 176–83, 195–6.   T. R.

Herod (so called in Acts of the Apostles) See IULIUS AGRIPPA (1–2), M.

Herodas, or perhaps **Herondas,** composer of *mimiamboi* in choliambics (iambic trimeters in which the penultimate syllable is long). Seven poems survive more or less complete on a papyrus published in 1891, an eighth (*The Dream*) is partially legible, and there are scraps of others; they range in length from 79 to 129 verses and are transmitted with individual titles. Herodas was probably active in the middle of the 3rd cent. BC. Poem 2 and probably 4 are set on *Cos; poem 1 is set outside Egypt but refers to the glories of *Alexandria (1), and poem 8 very likely refers to the literary squabbles of the Alexandrian Museum; the younger *Pliny (2) names Herodas in the same context as Callimachus (*Ep.* 4. 3. 4). Herodas, like *Callimachus (3) in his *Iamboi*, claims *Hipponax as his authorizing model for the use of choliambics (poem 8), and the *mimiamboi* are written in a creative, literary approximation to the Ionic of Hipponax. In style and theme, however, Herodas is more indebted to comedy and the *mime tradition of *Sophron; there is as yet no passage of Herodas that approaches the sexual and scatological explicitness of the Archaic iambus.

Each *mimiambus*, except poem 8, has more than one speaking 'part', even if minimally so (poem 2); each poem assumes the presence of mute extras. It has been hotly debated whether they were originally composed only to be read, to be performed by a single mime, or by a troupe. Their learned character suggests that Herodas envisaged the possibility of a reading audience—he may even have arranged them into a collection—but it is not possible to decide on internal grounds how they were originally performed; the onus of proof, however, falls on those who deny that some at least were acted by a small troupe of players.

(1) *The Procuress.* An old woman seeks to persuade a younger one to take a new lover while her current man (? husband) is away in Egypt. The theme is familiar from comedy and Roman elegy (Prop. 4. 5; Ov. *Am.* 1. 8). (2) *The Brothel-keeper.* A brothel-keeper prosecutes a client before a Coan court for stealing one of his girls and damaging his house. The speech is a masterpiece of shameless rhetoric and inversion of the topoi of legal oratory. (3) *The Schoolteacher.* A mother brings her truant son to school to be flogged for neglecting his studies in favour of gambling. (4) *Women Making a Dedication and Sacrifice to Asclepius.* Two women bring a thank-offering to the healing god and admire the artworks in his (probably Coan) temple, cf. Theoc. 15. (5) *The Jealous Woman.* A mistress threatens terrible punishment upon the slave who has been her lover because he has slept with another woman; he is begged off by the intercession of a young female slave. (6) *Women Visiting for a Chat.* A woman called Metro visits a friend (cf. Theoc. 15) to enquire where she got a wonderful leather

dildo; after receiving the information she goes off in pursuit of the maker, Kerdon. (7) *The Shoemaker.* Metro brings some friends to visit Kerdon in his shoe-shop; he shows them his wares. Our memory of poem 6 allows us to sense that more than shoes is involved here. (8) *The Dream.* A master (who turns out to be the poet) relates a dream in which his goat is killed by (?) 'goatherds' who then use its skin in the rustic game of *askoliasmos*, in which the dreamer himself wins the prize; *Dionysus and Hipponax also seem to appear in the dream. He interprets the dream to mean that 'amidst the *Muses [i.e. probably, 'in the *Museum'] many men will tear at my songs, the products of my labour' (cf. Callim. fr. 1 Pf.), and he forecasts a position of honour for himself after Hipponax in the history of choliambic verse.

The very diverse background of the *mimiamboi* shows them to be typical of their age—both modern and archaizing, learned and 'low'. They are 'realistic' in the sense that the characters and what they say have 'real life' analogues, but they depend upon an audience which knows how stylized is the view of life presented—that it derives its particular flavour from the transference of comic themes to a mimic mode—and can appreciate the productive clash between versification and language on one side and subject-matter on the other. The *mimiamboi* were perhaps more widely read and appreciated in later antiquity than the very scanty external evidence suggests. See MIME, GREEK.

TEXT I. C. Cunningham (Teubner, 1987), with full bibliog.
COMMENTARIES W. Headlam and A. D. Knox (1922); P. Groeneboom, Poems 1–6 (1922); G. Puccioni (1950); L. Massa Positano, Poems 1–4 (1970–3); I. C. Cunningham (1971).
GENERAL G. O. Hutchinson, *Hellenistic Poetry* (1988), 236–57; G. Mastromarco, *The Public of Herondas* (1979, 1984); V. Schmidt, *Sprachliche Untersuchungen zu Herondas* (1968); R. G. Ussher, *Quaderni urbinati di cultura classica* 1985, 45 ff.; F.-J. Simon, *Tὰ κύλλ' ἀείδειν: Interpretationen zu den Mimiamben des Herodas* (1991).   R. L. Hu.

Herodes Atticus See CLAUDIUS ATTICUS HERODES, TI. (1–2).

Herodian (1) **(Aelius Herodianus),** son of *Apollonius (13) Dyscolus, of *Alexandria (1), grammarian at Rome under M. *Aurelius. He wrote works on the accentuation of the *Iliad* and *Odyssey,* and of Attic. These he afterwards included in his *Katholikē prosōdia,* reviewing the accentuation of (it is said) some 60,000 words. It was in twenty books plus an appendix: 1–19 contained rules of accentuation, the 20th dealt with quantities and breathings, and the appendix with enclitics, synaloepha, and some other points concerning words in combination. Apart from some later quotations, this immense work survives only in epitomes by Theodosius and ps.-Arcadius. It was largely based on *Aristarchus (2) and his successors in this field. Only one of Herodian's works is transmitted in its original form, *Περὶ μονήρους λέξεως* ('On Anomalous Words'). The *Φιλέταιρος*, a short Atticist lexicon, is not generally regarded as authentic. Herodian disagrees with his father's extreme doctrines of *analogy, expressly repudiating such forms as *ἶμι* (see APOLLONIUS (13) DYSCOLUS). Of his many other works the titles of about 30 survive, together with extracts and quotations by later scholars: they cover many departments of grammar, including e.g. treatises on various parts of speech, figures, declensions, conjugations, defective verbs, and some anomalous words such as *ὕδωρ*. Herodian ranks with his father as one of the greatest, as he is the last, of original Greek grammarians. A number of later compilatory works are falsely attributed to him.

EDITIONS *Φιλέταιρος*: A. Dain, 1954; *Π. μον. λέξ.*: Dindorf, 1823; *Π. μον. λέξ., Π. Ἰλιακῆς προσῳδίας, Π. διχρόνων*, Lehrs, 1848;

Herodian

Herodiani Reliquiae (much conjectural reconstruction), Lentz in Teubner's *Gramm. Gr.*

Cf. also H. Erbse, *Beitr. zur Überlieferung d. Iliasscholien* (1960), 311 ff.; A. R. Dyck, *ANRW* 2. 34. 1 (1993), 772–94.   P. B. R. F.; R. B.; N. G. W.

Herodian (2), of eastern origin, perhaps from *Antioch (1), a subordinate official in Rome early in the 3rd cent. AD and probably an imperial freedman (see *PIR*² H 160), wrote a *History of the Empire after Marcus* in eight books from M. *Aurelius to *Gordian III (AD 180–238). Moralizing and rhetorical, his work is often unreliable, although his value increases with his contemporary knowledge.

TEXTS L. Mendelssohn (1883); K. Stavenhagen (1922); F. Cassola, *Erodiano* (1968), text with Italian trans.; C. Whittaker (Loeb, 1969).

G. Bowersock, *CHCL* 1. 710 ff., 892 (bibliog.).

A. H. McD.; A. J. S. S.

Herodicus, of Babylon (perhaps late 2nd cent. BC), pupil of *Crates (3), author of Κωμῳδούμενοι ('Persons Satirized in Comedy', see AMMONIUS (1)), Σύμμικτα ὑπομνήματα ('Miscellaneous treatises'), and Πρὸς τὸν φιλοσωκράτην ('Against the admirer of *Socrates').

M. Müller, *De Seleuco Homerico* (1891), 10 ff.; J. Steinhausen, Κωμῳδούμενοι (1910); A. Dittmar, *Aischines von Sphettos* (1912), 56 f.; H.-G. Nesselrath, *Die attische mittlere Komödie* (1990), 75–6.   J. D. D.; J. S. R.

Herodotus (1), of *Halicarnassus (now Bodrum on the Aegean coast of Turkey), historian. 'Herodotus of Halicarnassus' are (in Greek) the first two words of a long historical narrative, the earliest we possess. It looks back to the fall of the *Lydian kingdom in western Turkey in 545 BC and forwards to events in the early 420s, during the great war between Athens and Sparta (see PELOPONNESIAN WAR), but it has as its focus and *raison d'être* (1. 1) the 'war between Greeks and non-Greeks', which we call the *Persian Wars. We do not know exactly when it was written but it was already familiar in Athens in 425 BC, when *Aristophanes (1) parodied its opening chapters in one of his plays (*Ach.* 515 ff.). We know very little about the life of its author: he nowhere claims to have been an eyewitness or participant in any of the major events or battles that he describes (unlike *Aeschylus), but records conversations with those who were (8. 65, 9. 16) and with the grandsons of those involved in events of the late 6th cent. (3. 54; cf. 3. 160, 4. 43 where Herodotus' informant may well be the exiled grandson of the Persian Zopyrus, referred to in 3. 160). This fits with the dating of his birth traditional in antiquity ('a little before the Persian Wars', Dion. Hal. *Thuc.* 5; '484 BC', Gell. *NA* 15. 23). But the latter date is suspicious: it is 40 years before the foundation of the Athenian colony at *Thurii in southern Italy in which Herodotus is said to have taken part and where he is said to have spent the rest of his life and died (Steph. Byz., entry under *Thourioi*: his grave was shown there; Aristotle, *Rh.* 3. 9, already refers to him as 'Herodotus of Thurii'); 40 years is an ancient biographer's formula for his subject's age at a turning-point in his life and the whole chronology may be imaginary. His birthplace, Halicarnassus in *Caria, was a Greek city, founded some 500 years earlier, but by Herodotus' time it was subject to *Persian control; it lay on the extreme western edge of the great empire that had its administrative centre three months' journey (5. 50) to the east, in Iran. Intermarriage with the neighbouring non-Greek population, who were Carians, was widespread (ML 32) and Herodotus was a cousin of the Halicarnassian epic poet *Panyassis, who had a Carian name. He seems to have taken part in political struggles against the Persian-nominated tyrant Lygdamis, grandson of the

*Artemisia (1) who figures prominently in his narrative (7. 99; 8. 68–9, 87–8, 93, 101–3); these struggles ended in Panyassis' death and Herodotus' exile. Most of what he tells us about himself concerns his travels and enquiries (see (3) below). He is likely to have died where his allusions to later events themselves end, in the 420s; he may well have been less than 60 when he died.

2. Herodotus' narrative is built from smaller narratives and from summaries of events that are peripheral to his main concern. These smaller narratives, often told in rich detail and equipped with verbatim reports of many conversations, are sometimes told in Herodotus' own person; sometimes in the special syntax which ancient Greek reserves for things reported on another's authority. They are generally linked by chronological succession (particularly, at the beginning, the succession of eastern kings), and as cause and effect; but sometimes they go temporarily backwards (effect is followed by its explanatory cause in another story) or move sideways, to take in events elsewhere which throw light on something in the main line of the story. Their starting-point is in answer to the question with which Herodotus ends his first sentence: 'What caused Greeks and non-Greeks to go to war?'. After surveying traditions (Persian and Phoenician, according to Herodotus) which traced the origin of the conflict to the reciprocal abduction of legendary princesses (*Io, *Europa, *Medea, *Helen: 1. 1–5), Herodotus declares his own view that the story cannot reliably be taken back beyond the reign of the Lydian king *Croesus (1. 5), who began the process of absorbing the Greek communities of the Aegean coast into his kingdom and whose fall brought the power of Persia into contact with these communities, which were promptly forced into submission. The first book explains how these events occurred, deals with the Persian conquest of the Median kingdom which embroiled Lydia and led to its annexation by Persia, and continues the expansionist reign of the Persian king *Cyrus (1) the Great to his death in battle in 530 BC. Book 2 takes the form of a massive excursus on the geography, customs, and history of *Egypt, which was the next target of Persian expansionism, under Cyrus' son and successor, *Cambyses. Book 3 continues the reign of Cambyses down to his death in 522 BC, after a failed attempt to invade Ethiopia; it goes on to describe the turmoil that followed and the eventual emergence of *Darius I as the new king of Persia, and deals with his administrative settlement of the empire (3. 88–97). Book 4 covers Darius' abortive attempt to subdue the nomadic Scythian tribes who lived to the north and east of the Danube and across southern Russia, and deals also with Persian expansion along the North African coast. Book 5 traces further Persian expansion, into northern Greece and the southern Balkans, and narrates the unsuccessful attempt of the Aegean Greek communities to free themselves from Persian control (the so-called *Ionian Revolt: 5. 28–38, 98–6. 42): Herodotus signals, ominously, the fatal support that Athens gave to that revolt (5. 97). Book 6 begins the story that runs continuously to the end of Herodotus' narrative in book 9: the Persian determination to have revenge for Athenian interference in the affairs of its empire and the first seaborne attack on mainland Greece, which was defeated at Marathon in 490 BC. Books 7–9 embrace the huge expedition mounted in 480–479 by Darius' son and successor, *Xerxes, and the Greek response to that threat; the opening engagements, at sea off *Artemisium and on land at *Thermopylae; the climactic battles of *Salamis and *Plataea, which forced the Persian army and navy to withdraw to the north; and the carrying of the war back across the Aegean, ending in the battle of Mycale, on the Turkish coast

opposite *Samos. At various points, episodes in the history of Greek communities not at first directly in contact with Persian power, such as *Sparta, *Athens, *Corinth, and Samos, are inter-leaved, often at length, with the main narrative of Persian expansion as they explain how these communities became involved or failed for a time to be involved, until all are seamlessly joined together in books 7–9.

3. The stories from which Herodotus' narrative is built derive sometimes (as we have seen) from distinguished individuals, sometimes from 'collective' informants ('the Corinthians say . . .'; 'we Spartans have a story . . .'; 'I heard the story in Proconessus and Cyzicus . . .'). Occasionally his source may have been a document (for example, his description of the satrapy system set up by Darius to administer the Persian empire). But the overwhelming mass of his material must derive from oral tradition and that tradition will always have been local, even familial. Thus the overall conception of a narrative that would draw on these local traditions but would connect them so as to span more than 70 years and take in much of the known world was Herodotus' own, and it is his most brilliant and original achievement. Herodotus did not speak any language other than Greek but he writes of interpreters in Egypt (2. 154) and at the Persian court (3. 38, 140), where also there were Greek officials in high places. He writes repeatedly of what was told to him in an astonishing range of places: where he could, he preferred to trust what he could see for himself (2. 99; cf. 2. 147, 4. 81, 5. 59) and could enquire into (Herodotus' word for 'enquiry' is *historiē*, which brought the word 'history' into the languages of Europe). Where he could not, he listened (see ORALITY). He writes of enquiries made in the northern Aegean, in southern Italy, round the shores of the Black Sea (see EUXINE), in Egypt (where he travelled as far up the *Nile as *Elephantine: 2. 29), at *Dodona in NW Greece, and at *Cyrene in Libya; of things seen on the Dnieper in southern Russia; in *Babylon on the Euphrates; at *Tyre in Lebanon; of talking to Carthaginians (see CARTHAGE) and to the inhabitants of *Delphi. He is familiar with the geography of Samos, of *Attica, and of the Nile delta, which he compares to the mouth of the *Acheloüs river in NW Greece, as well as to the coast of Turkey from Troy south to the Maeander. He takes for granted a detailed knowledge of the topography of *Delos, of the Athenian Acropolis, and of Delphi. Everywhere he writes of what was said to him by 'the locals'. It is of the essence of Herodotus' method of *historiē* that he builds the process of enquiry into his narrative: he writes not only of his sources, their agreements and disagreements, but also of his own belief and disbelief at what he is told (he is, he writes, under an obligation to report what was said to him, but under no obligation to believe it: 7. 152. 3); sometimes too he records his inability to decide, or the impossibility of arriving at an answer to some question he is enquiring into (sometimes because it is beyond the reach of human memory; sometimes because it lies too far away, too far beyond the limits of his travels). Unlike *Thucydides (2), he does not present his account of the past as smoothly authoritative, the result of work not to be done again (Thuc. 1. 23) but as one man's struggle, not always successful, to discover and record what heroic men, non-Greek as well as Greek, have achieved, before those achievements are obliterated by time (1. 1).

4. It is not merely Herodotus' travels that cover an astonishing range but also his understanding of the variety of human experience. He does not disguise the fact that the Greek-speaking world was the cultural as well as the geographical centre of his perceptions. But he writes, almost always open-mindedly, of the

differences that distinguish Persians from Scythians, Babylonians, Indians, and Egyptians, as well as from Greeks. For Egypt, he has a model to help him understand the way their world works: it is simply the world of other men upside down; the Egyptians do the opposite of what is universal elsewhere, just as the Nile behaves in a way that inverts the behaviour of all other rivers by flooding in high summer (2. 35). He is less sure of what makes Persian culture cohere but describes what seem to him its distinctive features (the features, that is, that make the Persians un-Greek: 1. 131–40). He is relatively unsuccessful too in grasping the 'ideologies' that made one religion different from another. That is hardly surprising: he records religious practice everywhere with precision, but he has nothing to teach him the 'meaning' of *ritual, as he has for Greek religion in the epic poems of *Homer and *Hesiod (2. 53). He is sure that for all men, however much they know of other cultures, their own culture is superior (3. 38). But when he is faced with something totally alien to his experience and to Greek experience generally, such as the culture of the Scythian nomads, who have no aspect of permanence to their lives (no statues, altars, or temples, except to Ares, the god of war; no agriculture, no buildings, no walls or settlements even), though he can admire their ability to escape Persian domination by never staying to confront the enemy, 'for the rest', he writes, 'I do not like them' (4. 46). They offer him no point of resemblance and they do not fit. None the less, he describes their culture also dispassionately. For Herodotus it is important that things should fit: he is at home with symmetries. He is persuaded of the truth of a story of young Nasamonian tribesmen wandering across the Sahara and finding a great river flowing west–east, because the river they found must have been the Nile. Its identity is guaranteed by the symmetry of its course with that of the Danube (see DANUVIUS), which flows west–east from the Pyrenees and then turns south, as the Nile turns north, to flow out 'opposite the Nile' (2. 32–3)! But such a priori geography exists alongside acute empirical observation of the world around him, as in his defence of the proposition that the land of Lower Egypt is the product of the Nile's silting over ten or twenty thousand years (2. 11–12).

5. Herodotus' vast narrative coheres because it is strung on two lines of connection which pass through time. The first is kinship; the second *reciprocity. Reciprocity is the demand that all men respond to what is done to them with like for like ('equals for equals', in Herodotus' own phrase: 1. 2): with good for good and with hurt for hurt. The demands of reciprocity are absolute, admit of no exceptions and, Herodotus believes, are common to all men. They also outlive time, since they are inherited. The principle of reciprocity is essential to Herodotus' writing: to answer the question 'why did this happen?' it is necessary to ask the further question: 'to what previous act was this act a response?'. The chain of reciprocity may reach far back and encompass many people. Thus the search for a 'beginning' is common to all narrative and it is no surprise that, faced with the question 'why did non-Greeks and Greeks go to war (in the 5th cent. BC)?', Herodotus finds an answer in events far distant in space and more than three generations in the past, with Croesus of Lydia and his 'beginning of wrongful acts against Greeks' (1. 5). It is the logic of reciprocity that explains not only the two Persian invasions of Greece but also, for example, the bitter hostility between Athens and *Aegina, which lasted from the mid-6th cent. until the Athenians expelled the Aeginetans from their island in 431 BC (5. 82–7: Herodotus describes it as 'owed from before') and the complex of obligations which tied Persia,

Sparta, Corinth, and *Corcyra together in their several relationships with Samos over more than a generation (3. 44–53, 139–40). For the most part, the question 'why?' is not a problem for Herodotus. Events that are too uncanny, shocking, or momentous for merely human explanation call into play the actions of divinity which are assumed also to be determined by the logic of reciprocity (1. 90–1, 6. 75, 82, 7. 133–7). He seems too to be at ease with the question of the 'meaning' of events. Both in his own person and also in the person of various 'warners' who appear in his narrative (men such as *Solon; the Egyptian pharaoh *Amasis' uncle, the Persian Artabanus, and Croesus, after his downfall), the thread of events seems to be illuminated by general statements: 'human success stays nowhere in the same place', Herodotus (1. 5); 'divinity is jealous and disruptive', 'man is the creature of chance', and 'in everything one must look to the end', 'Solon' (1. 32); 'there is a cycle of human experience: as it revolves, it does not allow the same men always to succeed', 'Croesus' (1. 207). These look to add up to what Lateiner (see bibliog. below) has called Herodotus' 'historical philosophy'. But they do not in reality fit together; rather they are what ancient Greeks called *gnōmai* (see GNOME) and their function is closer to that of the proverb than to any 'law' of historical process: they are not discountenanced by contradiction. Nor do references to 'what was going to be', to notions of a man's 'portion', or 'what is assigned' make Herodotus a historical determinist. Rather they represent the storyteller's sense of the shape of his story. Closer perhaps to the heart of Herodotus' sense of things are 'wonder' (a very Herodotean word) at human achievement, the 'great and wonderful deeds of men' (1. 1) and the emotional undercurrent to events that so often gives his narrative a tragic colour: two compelling and haunting examples are the story of the deadly quarrel between *Periander, the tyrant of Corinth, and his own son (3. 49–53: characteristically, the story is introduced to explain another event, Corinthian and Corcyrean involvement in the affairs of Samos), and the astonishing moment at *Abydos when Xerxes, in the act of mounting his great invasion of Greece and engaged in reviewing his vast invasion force, bursts into tears on reflecting that in a hundred years not one of these splendid warriors would be living (7. 45–7: his uncle, Darius' brother Artabanus, replies that more painful still is the fact that in so short a life there was not one who would not, again and again, wish himself dead to escape the distress of living).

6. The singularity of Herodotus' methods and achievement has always meant that he was problematic to his readers. He has been read with most enthusiasm and greatest understanding in periods of the rapid expansion of men's horizons, such as the Hellenistic period of *Alexander (3) the Great's eastern conquests and in the Age of Discovery. But two adverse responses constantly recur: the first that he is a mere storyteller, charming perhaps but not a serious historian (that view, without the acknowledgment of charm, goes back to Thucydides (1. 21–2; cf. Aristotle, *Gen. an.* 3. 5)); the other view is that he is a liar. This view also has ancient supporters (especially *Plutarch in his bizarre essay, *On the Malice of Herodotus*: Plutarch's beloved *Thebes (1) does not emerge very well from Herodotus' account of events). But it was revived at the end of the last century by Sayce and is currently championed by Fehling and Armayor: Fehling's view would make the untravelled Herodotus the inventor of plausible-sounding encounters with 'those who should know' about the fantastic events he wishes to pass off as veracious. There are problems, certainly, about believing everything that Herodotus says he saw or was told but they are not so great as the problem of recognizing Fehling's Herodotus in the text that we have.

TEXT *Herodoti Historiae*, ed. K. Hude, 2 vols. (OCT, 1926–7).

TRANSLATIONS *Herodotus: The Histories*, trans. A. de Selincourt, 2nd edn. (Penguin, 1972); *The History: Herodotus*, trans. D. Grene (1987); R. Waterfield (1998).

COMMENTARIES There is no up-to-date commentary on Herodotus: How and Wells (1912) is still useful, but very antiquated. A commentary in several volumes in Italian by D. Asheri and others is in progress and will be translated into English. For book 2, A. B. Lloyd (1975–88) is valuable.

LEXICON J. E. Powell's *Lexicon to Herodotus* (1938) is index as well as lexicon and indispensable for any serious work on Herodotus.

CRITICISM J. A. S. Evans, *Herodotus* (1982), and *Herodotus, Explorer of the Past* (1991); D. Fehling, *Herodotus and his 'Sources'* (Eng. trans. 1989); C. W. Fornara, *Herodotus: An Interpretative Essay* (1971); J. Gould, *Herodotus* (1989), and in S. Hornblower (ed.), *Greek Historiography* (1994), 91 ff.; E. Hall, *Inventing the Barbarian* (1989); F. Hartog, *The Mirror of Herodotus* (Engl. trans. 1988; Fr. orig. 1980); *Herodotus and the Invention of History, Arethusa* 20, special number (1987); V. Hunter, *Past and Process in Herodotus and Thucydides* (1982); H. R. Immerwahr, *Form and Thought in Herodotus* (1966); F. Jacoby, 'Herodot', in *Griechische Historiker* (1956; repr. from *RE* Suppl. 2 (1913)); M. Lang, *Herodotean Narrative and Discourse* (1984); D. Lateiner, *The Historical Method of Herodotus* (1989); W. Marg (ed.), *Herodot WdF* 26, 2nd edn. (1981); J. L. Myres, *Herodotus, Father of History* (1953); W. K. Pritchett, *The Liar School of Herodotus* (1993); R. Thomas, *Herodotus in Context* (2000). Reception: O. Murray, *CQ* 1972, 200 ff. For further bibliography, see Gould (1989), 150–5.   J. P. A. G.

Herodotus (2), pupil of *Agathinus and adherent of the Pneumatic school of medicine (see PNEUMATISTS), wrote, in the Flavian period (AD 70–96), *Physician* and *On remedies* (lost); an extant *Diagnosis of severe and chronic illnesses* has been attributed to him on no secure grounds.   V. N.

Heron (*RE* 5), of Alexandria (1), (fl. AD 62) mathematician and inventor, was known as ὁ μηχανικός. The following works are associated with his name. (1) *Metrica*, three books, on the measurement of surfaces and bodies, and their division in a given ratio. (2) *Definitions* (Ὅροι), defining geometrical terms and concepts. (3) *Geometrica*, (4) *Stereometrica*, and (5) *On Measures* (Περὶ μέτρων), all works of practical mensuration. (6) *Pneumatica*, on the construction of devices worked by compressed air, steam, and water. (7) *On Automata-making* (Περὶ αὐτοματοποιϊκῆς), mostly on the construction of θαύματα ('miracle-working' devices used especially in temples). (8) *Mechanica*, three books (extant only in Arabic, but extensively excerpted by *Pappus book 8), on how to move weights with the least effort, containing (book 1) the foundations of *statics and dynamics, (book 2) the five simple machines, (book 3) the building of lifting-machines and presses. (9) *Dioptra*, on the construction and use of a sighting-instrument for measurement at a distance (with additions describing unrelated instruments, e.g. a hodometer). (10) *Catoptrica* (extant only in Latin translation), on the theory and construction of plane and curved mirrors (see CATOPTRICS). (11) *Belopoeica*, on the construction of war-catapults. Some of these, notably (3), (4) and (5), can hardly be by Heron in their present form, but all may well be based on treatises by him.

Other works by Heron no longer extant include a commentary on *Euclid's *Elements* (substantial remains in an-Nayrīzī's commentary on Euclid); Βαρουλκός, describing a machine for lifting huge weights by means of a combination of gear-wheels (parts are incorporated into *Mechanica* 1. 1 and *Dioptra* 37); *On Water-clocks* (Proclus, *Hypotyp.* 120); and *Cheiroballistra*, another type of artillery weapon (fragmentarily preserved). The *Geodaesia* and

Liber geoponicus are later compilations, largely extracts from the *Geometrica* and other mensurational works.

Heron, although very adept at both mathematics and applied mechanics, was probably not very original in either. But his mensurational works are of great importance as our main source for practical mathematics in Graeco-Roman antiquity. While classical 'Euclidean' mathematics aimed at constructing and proving theorems, 'Heronic' mathematics was directed towards solving practical problems, if necessary by approximation. Thus, Heron gives examples of approximations to irrational square- and cube-roots. He solves quadratic equations arithmetically, and gives the formula for the area of a triangle, $\triangle = \sqrt{\{s(s-a)(s-b)(s-c)\}}$. The origins of this type of mathematics lie in Mesopotamia. In *pneumatics, *mechanics, and the other sciences too, though Heron often discusses theoretical matters, his purpose is utility and amusement; hence we get detailed descriptions, with figures, of devices such as siphons, a self-regulating lamp, a water-organ, pulley-systems, and a variety of mechanical toys. Although the discovery of the principles behind these, and perhaps many of the devices too, were due to Heron's predecessors, such as Ctesibius, here too he is of major importance as a source (see PHYSICS).

EDITIONS (1) to (10) in *Heronis Opera*, 5 vols. and suppl., ed. W. Schmidt and others (Teubner, 1899–1914), with Ger. trans. and fragments. See also Hultsch, *Heronis Alexandrini geometricorum et stereometricorum reliquiae* (1864). *Belopoeica*, ed. with trans. in E. W. Marsden, *Greek and Roman Artillery, Technical Treatises* (1971), 17 ff. For the *Cheiroballistra*, ibid. 206 ff.

COMMENT Heron's mathematics: Heath, *Hist. of Greek Maths*. 2. 298 ff. etc. *Pneumatica*: A. G. Drachmann, *Ktesibios, Philon and Heron* (1948). *Mechanica*: A. G. Drachmann, *The Mechanical Technology of Greek and Roman Antiquity* (1963). *Belopoeica*: E. W. Marsden, *Greek and Roman Artillery, Historical Development* (1969). *Dioptra*: A. G. Drachmann, in C. Singer (ed.), *A History of Technology* 3 (1957), 609 ff.; *HAMA* 2. 845–8 (including Heron's date). *Catoptrics*: A. Lejeune, *Recherches sur la catoptrique grecque* (1957). G. J. T.

Herophilus, of Chalcedon (*c*.330–260 BC), Alexandrian physician, pupil of *Praxagoras of Cos. He and *Erasistratus were the only ancient scientists to perform systematic scientific dissections of human cadavers. If the controversial but unequivocal evidence of several ancient authors is to be trusted, Herophilus also performed systematic vivisectory experiments on convicted criminals—experiments made possible, according to A. *Cornelius Celsus, only by royal intervention (see VIVISECTION). Herophilus' numerous anatomical achievements included the discovery of the nerves. He distinguished between sensory and 'voluntary' (motor) nerves, described the paths of at least seven pairs of cranial nerves, and recognized the unique characteristics of the optic nerve. The first to observe and name the *calamus scriptorius* (a cavity in the floor of the fourth cerebral ventricle), he called it κάλαμος ('reed pen') because it resembles the carved out groove of a writing pen. His dissection of the eye yielded the distinction between cornea, retina, iris, and chorioid coat.

From his *Anatomica* 1 the first reasonably accurate description of the human liver is preserved. He also identified and named the duodenum (δωδεκαδάκτυλον). From *Anatomica* 3 fragments concerning the reproductive parts are extant. Using the analogy of the male parts, he discovered the ovaries, which he called the female 'twins' or testicles (δίδυμοι, 'twins', being a traditional term for the male testicles). He likewise discovered the Fallopian tubes, but without determining their true course and function. In the male, he meticulously identified previously unknown parts of the spermatic duct system. *Anatomica* 4 seems to have dealt with the anatomy of the vascular system. Adopting Praxagoras' distinction between veins and arteries, he added basic observations on the heart valves, on the chambers of the heart, and on various vascular structures. The *torcular Herophili*, a confluence of several great venous cavities (sinuses) in the skull, was first identified and named (ληνός, 'wine vat') by Herophilus.

In his physiopathology, he appears to have accepted the traditional notion that an imbalance between *humours or moistures in the body is a principal cause of disease, but he insisted that all causal explanation is provisional or hypothetical. The 'command centre' of the body is in the fourth cerebral ventricle (or in the cerebellum, which is indeed the region responsible for all muscular co-ordination and for the maintenance of equilibrium). From the brain, sensory and motor nerves proceed like offshoots. Neural transmissions, at least in the case of the optic nerve, are said to take place by means of *pneuma, which is ultimately derived from the air through respiration. Respiration is attributed to the natural tendency of the lungs to dilate and contract through a four-part cycle.

His *On Pulses* (Περὶ σφυγμῶν), became the foundation of most ancient pulse theories. A faculty (δύναμις) flowing from the heart through the coats of the arteries causes the regular dilation (διαστολή) and contraction (συστολή) of the arteries, which thus 'pull', transport, and distribute a mixture of blood and *pneuma* from the heart throughout the body (the veins, by contrast, contain only blood). Using metrical analogies, he described the relations between diastole and systole as successively assuming pyrrhic, trochaic, spondaic, and iambic rhythms, viz. in infancy, childhood, adulthood, and old age. He had sufficient faith in the diagnostic value of the pulse to construct a portable clepsydra, adjustable for the patient's age, to measure the frequency of his patient's pulses.

Reproductive physiology and pathology are well represented in his extant fragments. His *Midwifery* (Μαιευτικόν) apparently tried to demystify the uterus by claiming that it is constituted of the same material elements as the rest of the body and is governed by the same faculties. Although certain 'affections' (πάθη) are experienced only by women (conception, parturition, lactation), there is no disease peculiar to women. He also discussed the normal duration of pregnancy, causes of difficult *childbirth, and whether the foetus is a living being. *Tertullian charges him with possession of an instrument known as 'foetus-slayer' (ἐμβρυοσφακτής) and implies that he performed abortions. Gynaecological issues are also addressed in his *Against Common Opinions* (Πρὸς τὰς κοινὰς δόξας): *menstruation is helpful to some women, harmful to others (see ABORTION; GYNAECOLOGY; MIDWIVES).

His semiotic system, known as a 'triple-timed inference from signs' (τρίχρονος σημείωσις), his descriptions of causes and symptoms of many physical and mental disorders, and his threefold classification of *dreams are among many further achievements that provoked both acclaim and polemical responses throughout antiquity. See ANATOMY AND PHYSIOLOGY; MEDICINE, § 5. 1.

Ed., trans., and comm.: H. von Staden, *Herophilus: The Art of Medicine in Early Alexandria* (1989; repr. 1994). H. v. S.

Heruli, a Germanic people, who participated in the 3rd-cent. AD invasions of Roman territory from the Black Sea region, particularly the expedition of 268–70 through the Dardanelles. Not attested again until the mid-5th cent., when they were subject to Hunnic hegemony; they had probably been subject to the Goths in between. They re-established independence after

Hesiod

*Attila's death, and fought wars to maintain it against Lombards, Gepids, and Romans. See HERENNIUS DEXIPPUS, P.   P. J. H.

Hesiod, one of the oldest known Greek poets, often coupled or contrasted with *Homer as the other main representative of early epic. Which was the older of the two was much disputed from the 5th cent. BC on (*Xenophanes in Gell. *NA* 3. 11. 2; Hdt. 2. 53; *Ephorus, *FGrH* 70 F 101, etc.): Homer's priority was carefully argued by *Aristarchus (2), and generally accepted in later antiquity. Hesiod's absolute date is now agreed to fall not far before or after 700 BC. Of his life he tells us something himself: that his father had given up a life of unprofitable sea-trading and moved from Aeolian *Cyme to *Ascra in Boeotia (*Op.* 633–40); that he, as he tended sheep on Mt. *Helicon, had heard the *Muses calling him to sing of the gods (*Theog.* 22–35, a celebrated passage); and that he once won a tripod for a song at a funeral contest at *Chalcis (*Op.* 650–60). For his dispute with Perses see below (2). He is said to have died in Hesperian (Ozolian) *Locris (Thuc. 3. 96, etc.), but his tomb was shown at *Orchomenus (1) (Arist. fr. 565 Rose, *Certamen* 14, Paus. 9. 38. 3). For the story of his meeting and contest with Homer see *Certamen Homeri et Hesiodi* (A. Rzach, Teubner ed. *Hesiod*³ (1913), 237 ff.). The poems anciently attributed to him are as follows (only the first three have survived complete, and only the first two have a good claim to be authentic):

1. The *Theogony* (Θεογονία). The main part of the poem, which is prefaced by a hymn to the Muses (1–104; cf. the *Homeric Hymns*), deals with the origin and genealogies of the gods (including the divine world-masses Earth, Sea, Sky, etc.), and the events that led to the kingship of *Zeus: the castration of *Uranus by *Cronus, and the overthrow of Cronus and the *Titans, the 'former gods' (424), by the Olympians. This 'Succession Myth' has striking parallels in Akkadian and Hittite texts, and seems originally to have come from the near east. Hesiod's version shows some stylistic awkwardness and inconcinnity, but is not without power. Interlaced with it are the genealogies, which run smoother. The first powers born are *Chaos, Earth (see GAIA), and (significantly) *Eros (116–22). From Chaos and Earth, in two separate lines, some 300 gods descend; they include personified abstracts, whose family relationships are clearly meaningful. There is an interesting passage in praise of the un-Homeric goddess *Hecate (411–52), further myths, notably the aetiological tale of *Prometheus (521–616), and a detailed description of Tartarus (720–819). The poem ends with the marriages of Zeus and the other Olympians, and a list of goddesses who lay with mortal men. This last section, which refers to *Latinus (1013) and led on to the *Catalogue* (below, 4), is agreed to be post-Hesiodic, though opinions vary as to where the authentic part ends.

2. The *Works and Days* (Ἔργα καὶ Ἡμέραι, abbr. '*Op.*'). This poem, apparently composed after the *Theogony* (cf. 11–24 with *Theog.* 225), would be more aptly entitled 'the Wisdom of Hesiod'. It gives advice for living a life of honest work. Hesiod inveighs against dishonesty and idleness by turns, using myths (Prometheus again, with the famous story of *Pandora, 42–105; the five World Ages, 106–201), parable (202–12), *allegory (286–92), proverbial maxims, direct exhortation, and threats of divine anger. The sermon is ostensibly directed at a brother Perses, who has bribed the 'kings' and taken more than his share of his inheritance (37–9); but Perses' failings seem to change with the context (cf. 28 ff., 275, 396), and it is impossible to reconstruct a single basic situation. Besides moral advice, Hesiod gives much

practical instruction, especially on agriculture (381–617, the year's 'Works'), seafaring (618–94), and social and religious conduct (336–80, 695–764). There is a fine descriptive passage on the rigours of winter (504–35). The final section, sometimes regarded as a later addition, is the 'Days' (765–828), an almanac of days in the month that are favourable or unfavourable for different operations. Some ancient copies continued with an *Ornithomanteia*, a section on bird omens. The poem as a whole is a unique source for social conditions in early Archaic Greece. It has closer parallels in near eastern literatures than in Greek, and seems to represent an old traditional type. (*Virgil's *Georgics*, though much influenced by Hesiod, are shaped by the Hellenistic tradition of systematic treatment of a single theme (see DIDACTIC POETRY).)

It has always been the most read of Hesiodic poems. There was even a 'tradition' that it was Hesiod's only genuine work (Paus. 9. 31. 4); but he names himself in *Theog.* 22, and links of style and thought between the two poems confirm identity of authorship. Both bear the marks of a distinct personality: a surly, conservative countryman, given to reflection, no lover of women or of life, who felt the gods' presence heavy about him.

3. The *Shield* (Ἀσπίς), abbr. '*Sc.*', is a short narrative poem on Heracles' fight with Cycnus, prefaced by an excerpt from the fourth book of the *Catalogue* giving the story of Heracles' birth (1–56). It takes its title from the disproportionately long description of Heracles' shield (139–320), which is based partly on the shield of Achilles (*Il.* 18. 478–609), partly on the art of the period c.580–570 (R. M. Cook, *CQ* 1937, 204 ff.); this proves that *Aristophanes (2) of Byzantium was right in denying the poem to Hesiod). Disproportion is characteristic of the work; the Homeric apparatus of arming, divine machination, brave speeches, and long similes is lavished on an encounter in which two blows are struck in all. Parts of the description of the shield betray a taste for the macabre.

4. The *Catalogue of Women* (Γυναικῶν Κατάλογος) or *Ehoiai* (Ἠοῖαι) was a continuation of the *Theogony* in five books, containing comprehensive heroic *genealogies with many narrative annotations. Numerous citations and extensive papyrus fragments survive. The poem was accepted as Hesiod's in antiquity, but various indications point to the period 580–520 BC.

5. Other lost poems. (*a*) Narrative: *Greater Ehoiai* (genealogical); *Melampodia* (at least three books; stories of famous seers); *Wedding of *Ceyx, *Idaean Dactyls, *Aegimius (at least two books; alternatively ascribed to *Cercops of Miletus or Clinias of Carystus). (*b*) Didactic: *Precepts of Chiron* (addressed to *Achilles; see CENTAURS); *Astronomy* (risings and settings—and myths?—of principal stars); *Greater Works*. A few fragments of most of these poems survive.

TEXTS AND COMMENTARIES F. Solmsen, R. Merkelbach, and M. L. West, *Hesiodi Opera* (OCT, 3rd edn. 1990). *Theog.*: West, 1966. *Op.*: West, 1978; W. J. Verdenius, 1985 (lines 1–382 only). *Sc.*: J. Russo, 2nd edn., 1965.

TRANSLATIONS H. G. Evelyn-White, 2nd edn. (Loeb, 1936); R. Lattimore (1959); M. L. West (1988), *Theog.* and *Op.* only.

GENERAL H. Schwabl, *RE* Suppl. 12. 434–86; H. Fränkel, *Early Greek Poetry and Philosophy* (1975; Ger. orig. 1962), ch. 3; G. P. Edwards, *The Language of Hesiod* (1971); W. W. Minton, *Concordance to the Hesiodic Corpus* (1976); M. Hofinger, *Lexicon Hesiodeum* (1978), *Supplementum* (1985), *Index Inversus* (1973). Lost works: J. Schwartz, *Pseudo-Hesiodeia* (1960); M. L. West, *The Hesiodic Catalogue of Women* (1985).   M. L. W.

Hesione (Ἡσιόνη), in mythology, (1) an Oceanid (see NYMPHS), wife of *Prometheus (Aesch. *PV* 560). (2) Wife of *Nauplius (1) and mother of *Palamedes, Oeax, and Nausimedon (Apollod. 2. 23). (3) Daughter of *Laomedon (ibid. 3. 146). After her rescue from the sea-monster by *Heracles, she was taken prisoner by him when he captured Troy, given as the prize of valour to *Telamon (1), and granted leave to save any prisoner she chose; she therefore bought (ἐπρίατο) her brother Podarces for a nominal price, and he was henceforth called Πρίαμος (*Priam). By Telamon she became mother of *Teucer (2) (Apollod. 2. 136; 3. 162).

H. J. R.

Hesperides, the daughters of Night (*Nyx) and Erebus (Hes. Theog. 215) or, in later versions, of Hesperis and *Atlas (Diod. Sic. 4. 27. 2) or of Ceto and Phorcys (schol. on Ap. Rhod. 4. 1399), were guardians of a tree of golden apples given by Earth to Hera at her marriage. From the same tree came the apples thrown down by Hippomenes (or Melanion) in his race against *Atalanta. The garden of the Hesperides was popularly located beyond the *Atlas mountains at the western border of the Ocean. The number of the sisters, renowned for their sweet singing, varies from three to seven. Names attributed to them include Aigle, Erytheia, Arethusa, Hespere, and Hesperethusa. In some accounts they were associated with the *Hyperboreans. *Heracles succeeded in taking the apples after slaying Ladon, the dragon who guarded the tree. The subject was popular in Greek art, especially on painted pottery.

I. McPhee, LIMC 'Hesperides'.

A. J. S. S.

Hesperus (Ἕσπερος; Lat. Vesper, Vesperugo), the Evening Star; shown in art as a boy carrying a torch. Early tradition makes him the son of Astraeus (or *Cephalus) and *Eos (see Hyg. Poet. Astr. 2. 42) but later he was associated with *Atlas as his son or brother (Diod. Sic. 3. 60; Serv. on Verg. Aen. 1. 530, 4. 484). He disappeared from Mt. Atlas in a whirlwind after climbing up to observe the stars. As father of Hesperis, he was grandfather of the *Hesperides.

LIMC 2. 1 (1984), 918–19 nos. 74–84.

Hestia, the goddess of the hearth, closely related to *Vesta. Respect for and worship of the hearth are characteristic of the Greeks from earliest times. In the Mycenean age the king's throne-room, in megaron form, was the architectural centre of the palace, and in the very centre of that room was a low, round hearth, c.4 m. (13 ft.) in diameter. After the fall of monarchies, the kings' hearths as political centres and sites for asylum and the entertainment of foreign visitors were succeeded by official state hearths housed in public buildings called prytaneia. There, at least in some cities, the fire was kept continuously burning (Plut. Num. 9. 5–6). To unify Attica Theseus eliminated the various local prytaneia in favour of a single *prytaneion in Athens (Thuc. 2. 15. 2; Plut. Thes. 24. 3). As a token of continuity a *metropolis sent to a newly founded colony fire from its own hearth. Similarly each family had its own hearth where small offerings were placed at meal times. Newborns, brides, and new slaves were initiated into the family by various rituals at or around the hearth. In *Argos (2) the death of the head of the family required the extinguishing of the hearth fire and the fetching of new, unpolluted fire (Plut. Mor. 296f–297a). Analogously, after the *Persian occupation of much of Greece in 480 BC, *Delphi ordered the Greek states to extinguish their fires, because they had been polluted by the Persians (see POLLUTION), and take new fire from the prytaneion at Delphi (Plut. Arist. 20. 4–5).

Although one of the twelve Olympians, Hestia has little mythology, unable as she was to leave the house. She is not mentioned by *Homer, for whom ἱστίη is simply 'fireplace'. *Hesiod and authors after him make her a daughter of *Cronus and Rhea (Theog. 453–4). She 'liked not the works of *Aphrodite', rejected *Apollo and *Poseidon as suitors, and swore herself to lifelong virginity. Zeus accordingly granted her 'to sit in the middle of the house, receiving the "fat" of offerings', to be honoured in all temples, and to be a goddess 'senior and respected among all men' (Hymn. Hom. Ven. 21–32; cf. Homeric Hymn to Hestia (29)). The *hymns reflect cult realities. It may well have been the duty of the maiden daughters of the family to tend the hearth. Even at sanctuaries and sacrifices of other gods Hestia regularly received a preliminary offering; in *prayers and *oaths she was usually named first (Pind. Nem. 11. 1–7, Ar. Av. 865–88 (parody)). 'To begin from Hestia' became a proverb (Pl. Cra. 401b and d). But Hestia's extremely close tie to one physical object, the hearth, is uncharacteristic of Greek gods and probably limited her development in both myth and cult. In art she appears as a veiled young woman, heavily draped: LIMC 5. 1. (1990), 407–12.

RE 8 (1912), 1257–1304; I. Malkin, Religion and Colonization in Ancient Greece (1987), 114–34.

J. D. M.

Hestiaea See HISTIAEA.

Hestiaeotis, the most westerly of the four tetrades (districts) of *Thessaly. Its extent was defined by Aleuas the Red c.550–500 BC (see ALEUADAE): it incorporated the four cities of Tricca, Pharcadum, Pelinna, and Gomphi. Later it came to include the cities gradually occupied by the 'Thessalians who live below Mt. Pindus' (Strabo): Phaeca, Ligynae, and Aeginium (mod. Kalambaka), the capital of Tymphaea.

In the 4th cent. BC a new city, Metropolis, appeared in the SW part of the eastern plain, created by the *synoecism of various minor settlements, the names of which are not preserved. This newcomer rapidly developed into a rival to Gomphi and enlarged itself at the latter's expense, gradually absorbing other cities in the region: Thamiae-Ithome (known from Homer) c.200 BC, Onthyrium, Polichna, and, finally (before the beginning of the 1st cent. AD), very probably Methylium in *Thessaliotis as well.

F. Gschnitzer, Hermes 1954, 451 ff.; B. Helly in Topographie antique et géographie historique en pays grec (1992), 85 f. and L'état Thessalien (1995).

B. H.

Hesychius, of Alexandria (1), author of a lexicon of rare words found in poetry or in Greek dialects; probably to be dated to the 5th cent. AD, if the Eulogius whom he addresses in his introductory epistle is to be identified with Eulogius the scholastikos. The comprehensive scope of his design is indicated both in that epistle and in the title, Alphabetical Collection of all Words. The work, Hesychius says, was based on the specialist lexica (see GLOSSA, GLOSSARY, GREEK) of *Aristarchus (2), Heliodorus (1st cent. BC), *Apion, and Apollonius, son of Archibius (pupil of Apion), and on *Diogenianus and *Herodian (1); Hesychius seems to have added the interpretations of a number of proverbs which are included. The lexicon is known only from a 15th-cent. MS, badly preserved, and in many places interpolated (even obliterated) by expansions and other notes made by the first editor, Marcus Musurus (1514). Bentley showed that the biblical glosses in Hesychius are interpolations; less successful attacks have been made on the Latin and Atticist items. The original, as Hesychius says, included the sources of the rare words listed. The sources, however, have disappeared in the severe abridgement which has reduced the lexicon to a glossary, copious though that remains.

hetairai

Hesychius often preserves correct readings for which easier synonyms have been substituted in our extant MSS of Greek literature. His dialectal items are sometimes imperfect: he writes Ϝ either as *B* (less often *Y*) or as Γ (less often *T*), as e.g. Γοιδα· οὐκ οἶδα [sic cod.], Γιογόν [sic cod.]· ἴσον. Nevertheless, he is of the greatest value for the study of Greek dialects, the interpretation of inscriptions, and the criticism of poetic texts.

EDITIONS Alberti, 1746–66; Schmidt, 1858–68; ed. minor, 1867; K. Latte, *A–O* (1954–6).

A. von Blumenthal, *Hesychiosstudien* (1930).   P. B. R. F.; R. B.

hetairai ('companions', sing. *hetaira*) is an Attic euphemism for those women, slave, freed, or foreign, who were paid for sexual favours (see PROSTITUTION, SECULAR). The term first appears with modifiers (Herodotus 2. 134. 1 *hetairēs gynaikos*, 2. 135. 5 *epaphroditoi hetairai* i.e. 'charming' (a word derived from *Aphrodite) *hetairai*; Metagenes, *Aurai* fr. 4 K–A, 411 BC, *orchēstridas hetairas*); *Aristophanes (1) is the first to use the word without a modifier (*Pax* 439–40, produced 421 BC; *Thesm.* 346, produced 411 BC; but cf. *Hymn. Hom. Merc.* 31–2).

There was a class and semantic distinction, but not a legal one, between the hetaira and the *pornē* ('buyable woman'), at least in later sources (see the argument in Athenaeus 13. 571–2). A *pornē*, even a lowly brothel slave, could gain her freedom, become an independent contractor, become the lover (hetaira) of some wealthy man or men, and thereby exert her own influence and obtain her own great wealth; the literary *bioi* of *Aspasia, Lais, Neaira, Phryne, Rhodopis/Doricha, and Thais indicate as much. Membership of the category hetaira implied beauty, education, and the ability to inspire ruinous infatuation in both foolish young men and those older and presumably wiser.

Greek literature about hetairai cannot yield concrete historical evidence for the realities of their lives, but instead constructs, from a male viewpoint, those women whose function it was to provide pleasure within a social ideology which defined women as wives, concubines, or prostitutes and allotted to each her separate place ([Dem.] 59. 122). Because the category 'prostitute' was the most fluid and the most exotic of the three, it was the most dangerous for men and the most productive of literary comment, ranging from the cynical to the romantic. The most important sources are Greek New *Comedy and derivative literature such as Hellenistic *chroniques scandaleuses*, *Machon, *Athenaeus (1), and *Lucian and *Alciphron. The last three sources offer convincing and amusing sketches of the psychology and methods employed by hetairai. A few male sources offer a counterbalance to the generally glamorized picture: *Menander (1)'s *Samia* (esp. ll. 377–9 and 390–6) and *Phoenicides (fr. 4 K–A) limn the hardships and perils. The Hellenistic woman poet *Nossis (*thēlyglossos*, 'with woman's tongue') wrote epigrams which may suggest the sensibility hetairai cultivated for themselves as well as the impressions they may have wished the public to hold of them (see Nossis no. 4 in D. L. Page, *Epigrammata Graeca* (1975)).

K. Schneider, *RE* 8 (1912), 1331–72; H. Herter, *Jahrbuch für Antike und Christentum* 1960, 70 ff.; M. Henry, in A. S. Richlin (ed.), *Pornography and Representation in Greece and Rome* (1992), 250–68.   M. M. H.

hetaireiai, associations of *hetairoi* ('comrades'). In some, perhaps most, *Cretan cities the citizens were grouped in *hetaireiai* as part of the military system; each had its table in the city's *andreion* ('men's mess': cf. the messes, *syssitia*, at *Sparta). There is some evidence for the use of the words *hetairos* and *hetaireia* by associations of a wholly private character, as professional guilds. However, the *hetaireiai* best known to us are associations in Athens, particularly of young, upper-class men, which combined a social function with a political: the furtherance of the ambitions of their leading members, and mutual assistance in the lawcourts and at elections. They are sometimes called *synōmosiai*, 'sworn groups', from the oaths of loyalty which might be required. The mutilation of the *herms in 415 BC was said to be the work of a *hetaireia* to which *Andocides belonged; and the informal political activity which led to the oligarchic regimes of the *Four Hundred in 411 and the *Thirty Tyrants in 404 was conducted in part through the *hetaireiai*. In reaction against that, the revised law code of the 4th cent. included provisions against subversive *hetaireiai*. See also CLUBS, GREEK.

Crete: R. F. Willetts, *Aristocratic Society in Ancient Crete* (1955), 22–7. Athens: G. M. Calhoun, *Athenian Clubs in Politics and Litigation* (1913); F. Sartori, *Le eterie nella vita politica ateniese del VI e V secolo a.C.* (1957); F. Ghinatti, *I gruppi politici ateniesi fino alle guerre persiane* (1970); C. Pecorella Longo, 'Eterie' e gruppi politici nell'Atene del IV sec. a.C. (1971); Andrewes, *HCT* 5 (1981), 128 ff.   T. J. C.; P. J. R.

hetairoi, the 'Companions' of early *Macedonian kings. The loose structure of the Macedonian court meant that personal status was principally defined by relationship to the king; *hetairoi* were at first an élite because they were the king's friends, his retinue (cf. the epic use of the term), who equally functioned as senior officers of state and militarily as the king's own cavalry, among them his bodyguards. As the state grew and its royal structures became firmer, so the number of *hetairoi* also grew. Under *Philip (1) II, after the major expansion and consolidation phase (*c*.340 BC), according to *Theopompus (3) (*FGrH* 115 F 225b) there were 800 of them, some from Macedonia, some from *Thessaly, some from Greece, who participated in Philip's distribution of newly conquered lands. These men were, even now, personally selected by the king, but within them different circles of status developed—not all could be daily advisers, and those who were, the particularly close personal companions, formed an informal council of state. From Philip's time, adolescent sons of *hetairoi* were recruited to be royal pages.

Militarily *hetairoi* were cavalry—perhaps at first the only cavalry. As numbers of cavalry available grew, the *hetairoi* became an élite unit serving closely with the king, until *Alexander (3) the Great called all Macedonian cavalry 'Companion Cavalry'. The same development occurred with the heavy infantry, whom Alexander named *Pezetairoi* ('Infantry Companions'), a name which may have been first used by Alexander II for an élite unit.

Hammond and Griffith, *HM* 2; R. M. Errington, *A History of Macedonia* (1990; Ger. orig. 1986).   R. M. E.

heterosexuality and *homosexuality are not strictly applicable to the Graeco-Roman world (this remains controversial). Discussions of sex could focus on either pleasure or procreation. Pleasures were categorized and valued on the distinction between active (penetrating an orifice with a penis) and passive. Heterosexual acts (not people) were distinguished from homosexual not as radically differing pleasures but primarily on the basis of social consequence: only the former produce children.

What was most important in heterosexual acts was the status of the woman and the man's degree of responsibility towards her and her offspring: wife, concubine, hetaira, prostitute, slave ([Dem.] 59. 112, 122). The purpose of wives was to produce legitimate children (Xen. *Mem.* 2. 2. 4; Men. *Dys.* 842; *FIRA* 3. 17). Marriage was primarily a nexus of social and economic exchange (see MARRIAGE LAW). Love between husband and wife was neither necessary nor expected (Lucr. 4. 1278–87; but contrast Cimon and Isodice, Sulla and Valeria). However, mutual respect, affection, and love could and did arise (IG 2². 12067, Dem. 40. 27, Plin. Ep. 7. 5). Expressions of wives' love for husbands are common, seldom the reverse (ILS 7472). Wives were expected to be modest even during sex (Plaut. Amph. 839–42; Lucr. 4. 1268–77; Plut. Praec. coniug. 16–18). Later marriage contracts specify sexual responsibilities for both partners (PEleph. 1; cf. Plut. Sol. 20). A strict double standard was enforced. Men had recourse to *hetairai for love affairs and sophisticated entertainment, or to prostitutes for quick relief (see PROSTITUTION, SECULAR). Slaves, male or female, could be routinely used for sex (Muson. 12). Concubinage offered a stable, legal (sometimes contractual) status to those for whom marriage was impossible or undesirable; see CONTUBERNIUM.

Control of wives' sexuality (virginity, *adultery) was important to assure the legitimacy of the children (Lys. 1. 33–5; [Dem.] 59. 112–13) and so social stability. Athenian fathers could sell their corrupted unmarried daughters into slavery (Hyp. Lyc. 1. 12–13; Plut. Sol. 23: no known cases). Tests (if ever applied) for virginity were mostly magical: the hymen was not fully recognized even by anatomists.

Adultery meant intercourse with a married woman; she was the object of adulteration. The offence was against her husband and a matter of 'self-help' justice until the lex Iulia. A man caught in the act (seduction or rape) with another's wife, mother, sister, daughter, or concubine, could be killed, sexually abused, or fined. Cuckoldry, however, was less of an obsession than in later 'Mediterranean' societies. Adulterous wives must be divorced ([Dem.] 59. 85–8; Dig. 48. 5. 2. 2) and were barred from public ceremonies. Roman law permitted fathers to kill adulterous daughters (Dig. 48. 5. 23–4). Rape of a free male or female was subject to monetary fine; half for a slave (Lys. 1. 32; Plut. Sol. 23).

Female orgasm is acknowledged (Hippoc. De genitura 4; Ar. Lys. 163–6; Lucr. 4. 1192–1207; Ov. Ars am. 2. 682–4) but largely ignored by the (male) sources. At the same time women were thought to be sexually voracious ([Hes.] fr. 275M–W). Roman (and to a lesser extent Greek) sources illustrate a marked scale of pleasure for the actor and humiliation for the object: vagina, anus, mouth. Anal intercourse, considered a Spartan proclivity (Ath. 13. 602a; Ar. Lys. 1148–74), was also practised as a form of birth control (Hdt. 1. 61) and perhaps as a substitute for defloration early in marriage (for Rome, Priapea ed. A. Baehrens, PLM 3. 7–8; Sen. Controv. 1. 2. 22; Mart. 11. 78). Receiving fellatio was especially prized. Cunnilingus was most vile and degrading to the giver (Ar. Eq. 1280–9, Vesp. 1280–3; Gal. 12. 249 Kühn; Mart. 11. 61).

Reproduction was controlled through infant exposure, contraception, and *abortion. Most forms of *contraception were useless but some barriers (wool and wax pessaries) or mild spermatocides (e.g. cedar oil) may have been intermittently successful. Coitus interruptus is almost never attested (Archil. 196a West ?). Surgical abortion was dangerous and avoided by the doctors (Sor. Gyn. 1. 65; Ov. Am. 2. 13–14); oral or vaginal drugs were largely ineffective.

Vase-painting (c.575–450 BC) and other artistic (e.g. *mirrors) and literary sources illustrate a wide variety of postures for intercourse. Black-figure favours standing rear-entry; red-figure shows greater use of couches. Intercrural sex with women seems unknown. Though the man is always the dominant partner, the positions seem to have few symbolic overtones. Sexual violence, group-sex, as well as occasional scenes of tenderness (kisses, caresses, eye-contact) are shown. Sex reappears in Hellenistic and Roman decorative arts, depicting primarily heterosexual intercourse of individual couples in domestic rather than symposiastic settings (see SYMPOSIUM).

Love as a theme in literature shows a marked periodicity. The personal celebrations of the lyric poets largely disappeared in the Classical age. Love re-emerged in New Comedy (see COMEDY (GREEK), NEW) and the *novel (adumbrated in *Aristophanes (1)'s Lysistrata) in a predominantly social, domestic, and hence heterosexual form. Hellenistic poetry focused on forbidden and pathological love (Ap. Rhod. 3; Theoc. 2). *Epigram worked conceits on pleasure and pain with both women and boys. Roman comedy transmitted some of this to Latin poetry. *Catullus made romantic love in our sense central to his life and poetry. The theme of erotic passion was continued by the elegists, parodied by *Ovid, and largely disappeared from the western tradition until its rediscovery in Courtly Love. See EROS; LOVE AND FRIENDSHIP; PORNOGRAPHY; SEXUALITY.

D. Cohen, Law, Sexuality, and Society (1991); L. Dean-Jones, Women's Bodies in Classical Greek Science (1993); S. Dixon, Roman Mother (1988); K. J. Dover, Greek Popular Morality (1975), and Greek Homosexuality (1978); P. Dubois, Sowing the Body (1988); M. Foucault, History of Sexuality, 1–3, (1978–86; Fr. orig. 1976–84); J. Hallett and M. Skinner, Roman Sexualities (1995); D. Halperin, One Hundred Years of Homosexuality (1990); D. Halperin and others (eds.), Before Sexuality (1990); M. Kilmer, Greek Erotica (1993); D. Konstan, Sexual Symmetry (1994); W. Lacey, Family in Classical Greece; R. O. A. M. Lyne, Latin Love Poets (1980); B. Rawson (ed.), Marriage, Divorce and Children in Ancient Rome (1991); A. Richlin, Garden of Priapus (1992 (1983)), and (ed.), Pornography and Representation (1992); S. Treggiari, Roman Marriage (1991); J. Winkler, Constraints of Desire (1990).
H. N. P.

hiatus

Greek In Greek hiatus is the relation between a vowel at the end of a word and a vowel at the beginning of the immediately following word when the first of those two vowels is not elided (short α, ε, and ο can always be elided, except in the definite articles τό and τά), when the two are not reduced to one syllable by 'crasis' (e.g. ἀνήρ = ὁ ἀνήρ) or 'prodelision' (e.g. ὅ γ' ἔχω 'γώ = ∪ ∪ – –), and the first is not a long vowel or diphthong scanned short by 'correption' (e.g. Sappho fr. 105 Lobel-Page ἐρεύθεται ἄκρῳ ἐπ' ὕσδῳ = ∪ – ∪ ∪ – ∪ ∪ – –).

1. Hiatus in poetry

(For hiatus at verse-end see METRE, GREEK, § 2.)

(a) Hiatus within a verse is common in epic, and many types of epic hiatus persist in lyric, including the lyric of drama, above all before words which originally began with digamma (e.g. ἄναξ, ἔπος and the dative singular pronoun οἱ).

(b) In tragedy it is found with exclamations, e.g. Eur. Supp. 805 ἰώ ἰώ responding to 818 ἔχεις ἔχεις, and with utterances of an exclamatory character, e.g. Aesch. Pers. 1018 ὁρῶ ὁρῶ responding to παπαῖˉπαπαῖˑ

(c) Often in comedy, occasionally in tragedy, we find hiatus after τί and ὅτι and in certain phrases, e.g. εὖ οἶδα, εὖ ἴσθι. After περί hiatus may occur in comedy, and in 4th-cent. comedy the scansion of οὐδέ (or μηδέ) εἷς (or ἕν) as three syllables is normal.

It is noteworthy that hiatus in post-Homeric poetry does not coincide with pause, but just the opposite: it occurs most conspicuously within a closely-knit phrase.

J. Descroix, Le Trimètre iambique (1931), 26 ff.

2. Hiatus in prose

Hiatus was of considerable interest to literary critics, who observed (Demetr. *Eloc.* 68–73, 299; Dion. Hal. *Comp.* 23) that *Isocrates studiously avoided it. We can see for ourselves that *Thucydides (2) and *Xenophon (1) did not. We can speak of tendencies to avoidance in the later works of *Plato (1) and in some (not all) oratorical texts in the latter part of the 4th cent., especially in *Demosthenes (2), but it is impossible for us to know the extent to which what is presented as hiatus in manuscript texts was avoided in utterance by elision of elidable vowels, crasis with καί or the definite article, prodelision, or even on occasion correction. There is, however, a certain correlation in the manuscripts of Demosthenes between hiatus and phrasal pause. No prose text, of course, could be wholly free of hiatus—e.g. before ἄν and οὖν or after εἰ or ἤ—without bizarre choices of words or distortion of word order which would be unacceptable to an orator's audience.

Blass, *Att. Ber.* 2. 139 ff., 458 ff.

K. J. D.

Latin The term hiatus (Lat. *hiare*, to gape), in regard to Latin, covers all cases in which a final vowel or diphthong, or vowel + *m*, fails to undergo elision before a vowel at the beginning of the following word (or before *h* + vowel). Since there is no device for recording elision or its absence in normal written Latin, the presence of hiatus must be deduced from metre or other evidence. We may distinguish (1) hiatus in the spoken language, (2) hiatus in formal prose, (3) hiatus in verse.

On (1), *Cicero implies (*Orat.* 150–2) that hiatus was unnatural in spoken Latin. On (2), the same passage notes that the Greek avoidance of hiatus was unnecessary in Latin because of the natural tendency to run vowels together in speaking. Nevertheless certain conjunctions of vowels, especially similar ones, were avoided (see esp. Quint. *Inst.* 9. 4. 33). Study of *prose-rhythm has indicated that hiatus was possible at colon-end (where there would be a natural break in speaking) and that vowel + *m*, if treated as a short syllable, may produce a better clausula in some instances (Quint. *Inst.* 9. 4. 40 implies that vowel + *m* was not fully elided).

In verse (3), hiatus was permissible under various circumstances:

(*a*) In the older dramatic metres, hiatus was resorted to relatively frequently, as is confirmed by Cicero (cited above). In Plautus, therefore, the presence of hiatus should not be taken as proof of textual corruption. The circumstances under which hiatus was allowed in dramatic verse, other than at an obvious sense-break, have not been precisely defined. Hiatus apparently occurs with some frequency at the main caesura of a line (e.g. Plaut. *Men.* 67 *illi divitiae*ǀ*evenerunt maxumae*), between the fourth and fifth foot of an iambic senarius (e.g. Plaut. *Rud.* 7 *ambulo* ǀ *interdius*) and after the first cretic of a trochaic septenarius. It is also to be suspected that hiatus is sometimes employed for the sake of clarity of enunciation, e.g. the proper name at Plaut. *Capt.* 31 or the case-ending of *patri*, ibid. 10.

(*b*) Hiatus is regular after monosyllabic interjections such as *o*, *heu* (e.g. Hor. *Carm.* 1. 1. 2 *o et praesidium et dulce decus meum*); cf. also the hiatus of *mehercule* in Catullus 38. 2.

(*c*) 'Epic correction' (i.e. the shortening, rather than elision, of a long final vowel or diphthong before a following vowel), an imitation of Greek poetic practice, is found firstly in contexts with a particular Greek flavour, secondly as a means of admitting words otherwise excluded from dactylic verse (and often for both of these reasons together: Cic. *Aratea* fr. 24 and Lucr. 6. 716 *etesiae*, Verg. *G.* 1. 281 *Pelio Ossam*; before a Greek word, Verg. *Aen.* 3. 211 *insulae Ionio*), and thirdly for special poetic effect as in

Verg. *Ecl.* 3. 79 *vale vale inquit* (cf. Ov. *Met.* 3. 501).

(*d*) In earlier poets, final vowel + *m* is sometimes left unelided and treated as a short syllable, e.g. *flagitium hominis* attested several times in Plautus; Ennius *Ann.* 332 *milia militum octo*, ibid. 494.

(*e*) Correption or 'prosodic hiatus' of monosyllables is a special case, not confined to Graecizing contexts. It probably reflects actual *pronunciation. It is regular in drama, e.g. Plaut. *Merc.* 744 *nam qui amat, quod amat si habet, id habet pro cibo*. It occurs occasionally in Lucretius, Catullus, Virgil, and Horace's *Satires*. The non-elision of monosyllables ending in -*m* occurs with a similar distribution and should probably be counted in this category rather than the preceding.

(*f*) Hiatus at a caesura or strong sense-break in the dactylic hexameter is relatively common in Virgil (e.g. *G.* 1. 4 *sit pecori, apibus* . . ., *Aen.* 1. 405) and occurs occasionally in Ovid and later poets, presumably in imitation of Virgilian style.

(*g*) Hiatus (with neither correption nor sense-break) can add to the peculiar effect of a spondaic hexameter-ending in the so-called 'neoteric' style, e.g. Verg. *Ecl.* 7. 53 *castaneae hirsutae*, or to that of a recital of Greek names as in *G.* 1. 437 *Glauco et Panopeae*.

The avoidance of hiatus across line-end is called synaphaea and is regular in Horace's *Odes*. In general hiatus is largely avoided by poets from Ovid onwards.

M. Leumann, J. B. Hofmann, and A. Szantyr, *Lateinische Grammatik* (1977), 1. 122–3; H. Drexler, *Einführung in die römische Metrik* (1967); W. Lindsay, *Early Latin Verse* (1922), ch. 3; D. S. Raven, *Latin Metre* (1965).

J. G. F. P.

Hibernia ('Ἰέρνη), Ireland, first known to the Greeks through Massiliote (see MASSALIA) mariners (*c.*525 BC) as being 'five days' sail from Brittany, near the Albiones' island'; see ALBION. *Eratosthenes (*c.*235 BC), probably through *Pytheas' circumnavigation of *Britain (*c.*310–306), placed Ireland correctly on his map. *Strabo (4. 201) says that, oblong in shape, it lay near and north of Britain and contained greedy incestuous cannibals. *Mela (3. 6. 53) makes Ireland nearly as large as Britain, oblong, with pastures that caused the cattle to burst, and savage untrustworthy husbandmen. The elder *Pliny (1) gives as its area 1290 × 160 km. (800 × 100 mi.). Cn. *Iulius Agricola may have reconnoitred Ireland. *Ptolemy (4) (*Geog.* 2. 2) shows fair knowledge of the whole coast, giving sixteen peoples of the counties Wicklow, Kildare, Waterford, Wexford, Kerry, Dublin (Eblana, south of the mouth of the river Bubinda—the Boyne), and Connacht province; also the rivers Shannon, Barrow, Lagan, Avoca, Boyne, Liffey. *Iulius Solinus added the detail that Ireland has no snakes; the older tendency to place Ireland between Britain and *Spain was due probably to early direct voyages from Spain.

E. H. W.; M. J. M.

Hicetas (*RE* 4), of *Syracuse (5th cent. BC), Pythagorean (see PYTHAGORAS (1)). Two inconsistent views are attributed to him: that the earth rotates on its axis while the rest of the heavenly bodies are motionless; and the theory associated with *Philolaus that the earth rotates about a central fire. See GEOCENTRICITY.

DK 50. See T. L. Heath, *Aristarchus of Samos* (1913), 187–9. G. J. T.

Hierocles, Stoic (see STOICISM) of the time of *Hadrian (AD 117–38) wrote (1) an *Elements of Ethics*, of which we have the beginning on papyrus; this may have been an introduction to (2) a work on ethics, passages from which are preserved in *Stobaeus. The former deals with familiarization (*oikeiōsis*) as the starting-point of Stoic ethics, and with self-perception as what starts it. The latter deals with duties, introducing the image of concentric circles to illustrate expansion of concern for others. Hierocles is orthodox and his work seems to be a textbook, but it is lively and makes striking use of examples.

Ed. H. von Arnim, *BKT* 4 (1906). J. A.

Hierocles' *Synekdemos*, a list of cities in the eastern Roman empire, recorded by province, in geographical (not administrative) order. The date, which depends on the inclusion or exclusion of dynastic names for particular cities, is debated: it was probably based on an official list of the mid-5th cent. AD, partly revised in *Justinian's reign. Although its information is incomplete, this can be supplemented by the register of George of Cyprus (c.600) and other sources to permit a reconstruction of urban distribution in eastern provinces.

Ed. E. Honigmann (1939); Jones, *Cities E. Rom. Prov.* 514–21. L. M. W.

hierodouloi The term *hierodoulos* is variously used to describe slaves who are technically the property of a god and live on land owned by temples, slaves who are attached to the service of a god through a gift or civic decree, and slaves who were manumitted through a fictitious sale to a god; occasionally, it is applied to devotees of a cult who refer to themselves as 'slaves of the god'.

Hierodouloi of the first sort are better described as 'serfs of a divinity', rather than as 'slaves' in the classical sense. They are attached to villages belonging to a divinity. This status, in Anatolia, can be traced to the Hittite period, and seems to be analogous to that of the Sirkirtu in Mesopotamia (see ANATOLIAN DEITIES; ASIA MINOR (pre-classical)). This ancient Anatolian system survived well into the Roman imperial period, and conferred immunity from imperial taxation in so far as the temples to which they were attached were immune. According to the jurists of the Severan period, such *hierodouloi* appear to have been characterized as 'freedmen'. It is possible that sacred slaves of this sort also existed during Mycenaean times; they are attested in Egypt into the imperial period (Debord 83–90 (see bibliog. below)).

In the Greek world, slaves, like other property, could be given to a divinity. Although such slaves could be called *hierodouloi*, their status was categorically different from that of the *hierodouloi* previously discussed since they acquired their condition through attribution rather than birth. Such slaves passed under the control of the city controlling the sanctuary, and their condition was determined by the civic authorities. They may best be regarded as 'public slaves of the god' (Debord 88).

Manumission through consecration to a divinity should not be confused with either status described above; it took two forms: unconditional freedom and conditional freedom. A slave who was manumitted on terms of conditional freedom was bound to continue in the service of a former master for a set period of time (usually until a master's death). Under both systems, the god acted as a guarantor of the former slave's new status (Hopkins 133–71).

The final usage of the term has nothing to do with status at all, being merely a rhetorical form used to express devotion to a god. See FREEDMEN; SLAVERY.

P. Debord, *Aspects sociaux et économiques de la vie religieuse dans l'Anatolie gréco-romaine* (1982); K. Hopkins, *Conquerors and Slaves* (1978). D. S. P.

***hieromnēmones*,** religious officials, found in many Greek states. *Aristotle (*Pol.* 1321ᵇ) classifies them with the civil registrars of public and private documents, and temples frequently served as record offices. Their functions varied widely: some appear as archivists, others as financial officers, some managed the festivals or controlled temple properties, and in several cities, e.g. Issa and *Byzantium, they were the eponymous magistrates. They usually formed a college, and the position was one of responsibility and honour. Best known are the *hieromnēmones* who represented their states in the Delphic-Pylaean amphictiony (see AMPHICTIONY; DELPHI). Their number was normally 24, but varied considerably under the Aetolian domination (c.278–178 BC). Their exact relationship to the other delegates, the *pylagorai* (in the Aetolian period called *agoratroi*), is not clear. The duties of the *hieromnēmones* are set forth in a law of 380 (*IG* 2². 1126). Their tenure of office varied from state to state: in the 4th cent. the Thessalian *hieromnēmones* served for several years, the Athenians one year, while the Malians sent different *hieromnēmones* for each of the semi-annual meetings; a Chian decree of 258–254 (*Syll.*³ 443) stipulates that their delegate should serve one year and be ineligible for reappointment. For *hieromnēmones* in charge of 'the (?) treasury' and 'the grain' (ἐπὶ θησαυρῷ and ἐπὶ τῷ σίτῳ) at *Locri Epizephyrii see *Klearchos* 1961–2; for *hieromnēmōn* as a functionary of a private cult association see *AJArch.* 1933, 254. The term was sometimes used to translate the Latin *pontifex*.

G. Roux, *L'amphictionie, Delphes et le temple d'Apollon au ivᵉ siècle* (1979), 20 ff. F. R. W.; A. J. S. S.

Hieron (1) **I** (*RE* 11), regent at *Gela for his brother *Gelon (485–478 BC), and tyrant (see TYRANNY) of *Syracuse (478–466); fought at *Himera (480), and married the daughter of *Anaxilas (1). Having narrowly avoided war with *Theron, over Himera and domestic issues, he married (thirdly) Theron's niece. He intervened in Italiot affairs, protecting *Locri Epizephyrii against Anaxilas, offering aid to *Sybaris against *Croton, defeating the *Etruscans at sea in alliance with *Cumae (474), colonizing *Pithecusae (mod. Ischia), and strengthening his influence in *Rhegium and *Messana. He completed the subjugation of the Ionian cities of the east coast of Sicily, destroying *Naxos (2) and *Catana (Catania) and resettling their inhabitants in *Leontini. He refounded Catana, adding territory taken from the Sicels, renaming it *Aetna (2), and establishing his son Deinomenes as regent. Thrasydaeus, Theron's successor at *Acragas, fought him for the hegemony of Greek Sicily (c.472) and was defeated. Acragas and Himera now recovered their liberty. Hieron died in 466 at Aetna, and was buried there, being accorded, as founder, the heroic honours he craved. By nature suspicious and more despotic than Gelon, he envied the glamour and heroic status of his brother, and sought to emulate his reputation by pursuing an energetic foreign policy and by his patronage both of the great Greek *festivals and their centres and of poets such as *Bacchylides, *Pindar, *Simonides, *Xenophanes, and *Aeschylus.

H. Berve, *Die Tyrannis bei den Griechen* (1967), 148–52; D. Asheri, *CAH* 5² (1992), ch. 7. B. M. C.

Hieron (2) **II** (*RE* 13), tyrant (see TYRANNY), later king, of *Syracuse (c.271–216 BC); claimed, without grounds, descent from *Gelon. Between 275 and 271, Hieron was elected general, seized power as the result of a military coup, allied himself with the popular faction, and was perhaps elected general plenipotentiary. He attacked the *Mamertines, and after a severe defeat and further preparation, routed them on the Longanus river (west of *Messana) (265). He was then acclaimed king. Alarmed by the Mamertines' alliance with Rome, Hieron joined the Carthaginians (see CARTHAGE) in besieging Messana (264); but forced by the Romans to withdraw, and besieged in Syracuse, he came to terms (263), preserving much of his kingdom, but becoming in effect a subordinate of Rome. His loyalty to Rome in the First *Punic War earned him the revision of his treaty (248): it became a *foedus aequum* (a treaty as between equals), he received additions to his kingdom and the indemnity still outstanding was remitted. Hieron maintained an efficient navy and policed the sea, enjoyed friendly relations with Carthage (after 241), *Rhodes, and *Egypt, improved (with the help of his friend *Archimedes) the defences of Syracuse, and enriched Syracuse and his kingdom by his building. He supplied Rome with grain, both before and during the Second *Punic War, and co-operated with her at sea (218, 216) and sent troops and money (217, 216). He died shortly after *Cannae (216); his son (and colleague) Gelon having predeceased him, he was succeeded by his grandson Hieronymus, and Syracuse abandoned her Roman allegiance. 'Naturally regal and statesmanlike' (*Polybius (1)), Hieron was sufficiently realistic to jettison his early imperial aspirations in favour of loyalty to Rome and the prosperity and well-being of his people. His system of taxation, adopted by Rome after her annexation of Sicily (241)—the *lex Hieronica*—was regarded as both efficient and equitable.

H. Berve, *Die Tyrannis bei den Griechen* (1967), 462–71, and *König Hieron II* (1956); H. Scullard, *CAH* 7²/2 (1989), 539–65; J. Briscoe, *CAH* 8² (1989), ch. 3; E. Rawson, ibid. ch. 12. B. M. C.

Hieronymus (1), of Cardia, historian and statesman, was in the entourage of his fellow Cardian (and relative?) *Eumenes (3), acting as his emissary at the siege of Nora (319/8 BC) and passing to the court of *Antigonus (1) the One-eyed (Monophthalmus) after Eumenes' death at Gabiene (316). He served with Antigonus in Syria (312/1) and at *Ipsus (301), and under *Demetrius (4) Poliorcetes governed Thebes (1) after its revolt in 293. He ended his days with *Antigonus (2) Gonatas. His great history spanned the period from *Alexander (3) the Great's death (323) to at least the death of *Pyrrhus (272). It was *Diodorus (3) Siculus' authority for Greek affairs in bks. 18–20, and was used extensively by *Plutarch, *Arrian, and *Justin. The extant fragments only hint at its dimensions and content. The main evidence is Diodorus' digest of his work, which in bks. 18–20 abruptly rises to a quality not found elsewhere in the *Bibliothēkē*. Excellently informed (see, for instance, the description of the battle lines at Paraetacene and Gabiene, which Hieronymus witnessed), he supplied documentation such as the texts of Alexander's Exiles' Decree and *Polyperchon's *diagramma* of 319/8, and carefully explained the motives of the various protagonists (particularly Eumenes and Antigonus Monophthalmus). The lively and lucid narrative was varied by pertinent digressions like the descriptions of Alexander's funeral car and the Indian practice of suttee. He was not without bias, understandably favourable to Eumenes and Antigonus Gonatas, and markedly unsympathetic to Athenian democracy, but there is nothing to equal the sustained prejudice of *Polybius (1), his only Hellenistic rival in 'pragmatic history'. (For this term see POLYBIUS (1).)

FGrH 154; J. Hornblower, *Hieronymus of Cardia* (1981). A. B. B.

Hieronymus (2) (*RE* 12), of *Rhodes, philosopher and historian of literature, lived at Athens c.290–230 BC, under the protection of *Antigonus (2) Gonatas. He left the *Peripatetic school when it was declining under *Lyco's headship, and founded an eclectic school, defining the goal of life as freedom from pain and trouble.

Works *On Suspension of Judgement*; *On Drink*; *Symposium*; a work on ethics; *On Not Being Angry*; *On Poets*; *Historical Memoranda*; *Miscellaneous Memoranda*; *On Isocrates*; *Letters*. The fragments illustrate his love of literary gossip.

Texts in F. Wehrli, *Die Schule des Aristoteles* 10 (1959), 1–44. Wehrli in Überweg–Flashar 575–7. R. W. S.

hierophantēs, chief priest of the Eleusinian *mysteries, was chosen for life from the hieratic clan of the Eumolpidae (see EUMOLPUS). He was distinguished by a head-band (στρόφιον), myrtle wreath, and a robe probably of purple, and like many priests he carried a sceptre. Among Athenian priests he was the most revered. An impressive, melodious voice was an important requirement for appointment. Before the celebration he sent forth *spondophoroi* to proclaim truce for the period of the mysteries. He opened the ceremonies with a proclamation that *barbarians, murderers, and those defiled must keep away. In presenting the mysteries to the initiates he was assisted by the *dadouchos* and two *hierophantides*; at a climactic moment in the rite he emerged from the hall of initiation (the Anaktoron, or Telesterion) amidst a brilliant flood of light. He also took part in other state festivals and had some minor public duties. Starting in the 2nd cent. BC he practised hieronymy, i.e. he suppressed his own name (upon entering office he threw it into the sea in a special ceremony) and replaced it with 'Hierophantes'.

Hierophantai also occur in cults of *Demeter and *Dionysus elsewhere (e.g. at *Gela, Lerna, Phlius, Andania in *Messenia), some of which were modelled to a certain extent on the Eleusinian mysteries.

Clinton, *Sacred Officials*, and *Iconography*; F. Cumont, *AJArch*. 1933, 243–4 (cults of Dionysus). K. C.

hieros gamos See MARRIAGE, SACRED.

hiketeia See SUPPLICATION, GREEK.

Hilaria Roman festival on 25 March, one of a series of five festivals to the Magna Mater or *Cybele (15–26 March), when she rejoiced in *Attis' resurrection (Macrob. *Sat.* 1. 21. 7–10). It apparently belongs to the later empire (Julian, *Or.* 5. 168, 169, 175; cf. G. Thomas, *ANRW* 2. 17. 3 (1984), 1518–21). *Filocalus' calendar gives a 3 November Hilaria associated with an Isis festival (28 October–1 November).

Inscr. Ital. 13. 2. 431, 526–7; M. Salzman, *On Roman Time* (1990), 172–3; Wissowa, *RK* 321–7. C. R. P.

Hilary of Arles Succeeding his hero Honoratus in AD 430, Hilary presided over the most prestigious see of southern Gaul until his death in 449. Its aggrandizement was based on possession of a mint, a splendid circus, the residence of the praetorian prefect and, from 418, the meetings of the new council of the Seven Provinces. Competition with neighbouring Vienne intensified ambitions in the city and took a specifically ecclesiastical form from the time of Patroclus (d. 426), persisting long enough to benefit Caesarius at the end of the century (c.470–542).

Hilary's career and writings illustrate the growing importance of the monastery of Lérins (of which he had been a member) and its impact on the pastoral life of the Gallic Church; a carefully preserved network of aristocratic families in Gaul, who deliberately extended their influence into the hierarchy of the Church, still in collaboration with secular peers; and the shifting tensions between the Church in Gaul and the bishop of Rome, especially during the pontificate of *Leo I (d. 461). His panegyric on Honoratus carried the genre to a new level of Christianization and influenced subsequent hagiographical practice.

TEXTS *Vitae sanctorum Honorati et Hilarii episcoporum Arelatensium*, ed. S. Cavallin (1952); *Hilaire d'Arles: Vie de S. Honorat*, ed. M.-D. Valentin, SC 235 (1977); *Collectio Arelatense*, ed. W. Gundlach, *MGH Ep.* 3/1 (1892), *Ep.* 9–21. Refs. also in Gregory of Tours, *Historiae* 4. 26, 30; *Liber in gloria martyrorum* 67–8. *CIL* 12. 949.

STUDIES R. Mathisen, *Ecclesiastical Factionalism and Religious Controversy in Fifth-Century Gaul* (1987); J. F. Drinkwater and H. Elton (eds.), *Fifth-Century Gaul: A Crisis of Identity?* (1992). P. R.

Hildesheim treasure, the largest hoard of Roman silver *plate from outside the empire's frontiers; found in 1868 at Hildesheim in south Hanover and now in Berlin; assigned to the Augustan age and possibly booty from a Germanic success against a Roman army. The principal piece is a mixing-bowl covered with floral relief resembling that of the *Ara Pacis; there is also a series of drinking-bowls with embossed designs of *Minerva, *Hercules and the snakes, reliefs of *Cybele and *Men-*Attis, and Bacchic emblems (see DIONYSUS).

E. Pernice and F. Winter, *Der Hildesheimer Silberfund* (1901). F. N. P.

Himera ('Ιμέρα), on the north coast of *Sicily, was founded *c.*649 BC by the Zanclaeans (see MESSANA), helped by the clan of the Myletidae, exiled from *Syracuse. *Stesichorus was its most famous citizen. In the early 5th cent. it was controlled by a tyrant Terillus who, on his expulsion by *Theron of *Acragas, appealed to Carthage. The Carthaginian expedition was decisively defeated at Himera (480 BC), where a fine Doric temple in the lower town celebrated the triumph of *Gelon and Theron. On the plateau above, a sanctuary area with three temples has been excavated, as well as extensive areas of 5th-cent. BC housing. Independent of *Acragas after 461, Himera was obliterated by Carthage in 409 as an act of revenge, and the site abandoned.

In 408/7 the Carthaginians founded Thermae Himeraeae (mod. Termini Imerese) 11 km. (7 mi.) to the west, where the Himeraean refugees settled. Although in Carthaginian territory, it was completely Greek (it was sometimes even referred to as Himera), and was the birthplace of *Agathocles (1). Within the Roman province of Sicilia after 241 BC, it became a *colonia* under *Augustus and flourished in the early empire. An amphitheatre and a fine aqueduct are the principal surviving monuments of this period.

PECS 393; *BTCGI* 8 (1990), 248–73; Gabba–Vallet, *Sicilia antica* 1. 573–9; Dunbabin, *Western Greeks, passim*; *Himera* 1 (1970), 2 (1976), 3/1 (1988); N. Allegro and others, *Quaderno Imerese* (1972), and *Secondo Quaderno Imerese* (1982); N. Bonacasa (ed.), *Himera: Zona archeologica e antiquarium* (1986). Recent work: C. A. Di Stefano (ed.), *Da Terra in Terra* (1991) (pub. 1993), 63–112. Thermae Himeraeae: O. Belvedere, *Kokalos* 1982–3, 71–86, and *L'acquedotto Cornelio di Termini Imerese* (1986); R. J. A. Wilson, *ANRW* 2. 11. 1 (1988), 144–53, and *Sicily under the Roman Empire* (1990), *passim*. A. G. W.; R. J. A. W.

Himerius (*c.* AD 310–*c.*390), Greek rhetorician. Born in Prusias in *Bithynia, he studied in Athens, where he spent most of his life as a successful teacher of rhetoric. He was a younger contemporary and rival of *Proaeresius. He visited *Constantinople, *Thessalonica, *Nicomedia, and *Antioch (1), among other places. Of his 80 speeches *Photius read 72, but there survive now only 24, with excerpts from ten others. Six are declamations on themes from Athenian history, the rest deal with contemporary subjects, and include addresses to high Roman officials, inaugural lectures and other ceremonial orations in connection with his school, and a funeral oration on his son. Unlike *Themistius and *Libanius Himerius has no interest in politics; he is equally untouched by philosophy. His eloquence is an end

in itself, like poetry. His style is marked by wealth of imagery, care for euphony, avoidance of the concrete, and frequent quotations from classical poetry. Though the school orations are of some interest, Himerius in the main displays a talent for saying nothing gracefully and at length. Among his pupils were *Gregory (2) of Nazianzus and *Basil of Caesarea. He is still cited as a model in the 14th cent. by Joseph Rhakendytes.

SOURCE Eunapius, *VS* 95 Boiss.; Photius, *Bibl.* cod. 165.
EDITION A. Colonna (1951).
G. Kennedy, *Greek Rhetoric under Christian Emperors* (1983), 138 ff.; *PLRE* 1. 731. R. B.

Himilco (1), of Carthage, cited in later antiquity as a pioneering Atlantic navigator, (Plin. *HN* 2. 169; Avienus 114–35, 380–9, 406–15, cf. *Pytheas); his voyage, like that of *Hanno (1), was very early in the 5th cent. BC. Four months' journey north from *Gades took him into an area of calms, shoals, and tangled seaweed: it is more likely that these hazards are embroideries of what he experienced on a coasting voyage to the Brittany area than that he inadvertently reached the Sargasso Sea, as has sometimes been maintained.

Cary–Warmington, *Explorers* 31–3. N. P.

Himilco (2) (*RE* 1), colleague (probably cousin) of Hannibal, commander of the Carthaginian expedition against the Sicilians (407/6 BC); succeeded to the command on Hannibal's death. He sacked *Acragas after a long siege and a defeat in the field. He defeated *Dionysius (1) I before *Gela (406), and took Gela and Camarina. He concluded peace with Dionysius, making Carthage overlord of much of Greek Sicily. But war began again in 397. As commander-in-chief in 397/6, Himilco failed to relieve *Motya (Mozia)—his ships were driven off by catapults—but (396) he drove Dionysius back to *Syracuse, founded *Lilybaeum (Marsala), replacing Motya, advanced along the north coast, and took *Messana (Messina); and after Mago (admiral) had defeated Dionysius' navy off *Catana (Catania), he invested Syracuse. Plague (as in 406) weakened his army, Dionysius' sortie overran his positions, and he made terms (395), surrendering his war-chest and evacuating his Carthaginian citizen-troops. On his return to Carthage, he committed suicide. A pertinaceous soldier only, he owed most of his successes to his enemies' mistakes.

L. Maurin, *Semitica* 12 (1962); B. Caven, *Dionysius I* (1990). B. M. C.

Hippalus, the merchant discoverer, in the Augustan or Tiberian age, of new ways of navigating the Arabian Sea: specifically the possibility of using the (very violent: his ships must have been substantial) SW *monsoon to make deep-sea voyages from the south coast of *Arabia to the NW coast of India, and the SE monsoon (a gentler wind) for the journey back to the mouth of the *Red Sea (his name was given to an African cape, part of the Arabian Sea, and to the wind itself). Regular contacts archaeologically attested from the 1st cent. BC onwards at e.g. Arikamedu (see INDIA) suggest that Hippalus was not unique, but the increasing importance of this region and its communications in the economic history of the old world in the first half of the first millennium AD is indubitable.

Plin. *HN* 6. 100–6, 172; Ptol. *Geog.* 4. 7. 12; *It. Alex.* 110; *Peripl. M. Rubr.* 57. V. Begley and R. D. De Puma (eds.), *Rome and India: The ancient Sea Trade* (1991). N. P.

Hipparchus (1), younger son of *Pisistratus of Athens (6th cent. BC). Closely associated with his elder brother *Hippias (1), he was known particularly as patron and lover of the arts (*Ath. pol.* 18). He invited *Anacreon and *Simonides to Athens, and set up

Hipparchus

*herms around *Attica with words of gnomic wisdom ([Pl.] *Hipparch.* 228d–e); see GNOME. The same source (228b) credits him, improbably, with bringing the text of *Homer to Athens, and more plausibly, with adding Homeric recitals to the *Panathenaea. It is unclear how much of the artistic momentum of Pisistratid Athens (esp. the temple of Olympian *Zeus) should be associated specifically with him. He was murdered by Harmodius and *Aristogiton in 514 BC, partly prompted by amorous intrigue.

See bibliog. under HIPPIAS (1); PISISTRATUS. J. A. Davison, *TAPA* 1955 ff. for Homer. R. T.

Hipparchus (2) (fl. *c*.260 BC), New Comedy poet (see COMEDY (GREEK), NEW) and (probably) actor. In frs. 1 and 3 foreign drinking-cups (κόνδυ, λαβρώνιος) are mentioned, and in Ζωγράφος ('The painter'), fr. 2, the painter praises professional skill.

Kassel–Austin, *PCG* 5. 605 ff.

Hipparchus (3) (*RE* 18), astronomer, (fl. second half of 2nd cent. BC). Born at *Nicaea (1) in Bithynia, he spent much of his life in Rhodes; his recorded observations range from 147 to 127. His only extant work, the *Commentary on the Φαινόμενα of Eudoxus and Aratus*, in three books, contains criticisms of the descriptions and placings of the *constellations and stars by those two (see ARATUS (1); EUDOXUS (1)), and a list of simultaneous risings and settings. Valuable information on Hipparchus' own star coordinates has been extracted from it. Most of our knowledge of Hipparchus' other astronomical work comes from *Ptolemy (4)'s *Almagest* (see index under 'Hipparchus' in Toomer's trans.).

Hipparchus transformed Greek astronomy from a theoretical to a practical science, by applying to the geometrical models (notably the eccentric/epicyclic hypothesis) that had been developed by his predecessors (see ASTRONOMY) numerical parameters derived from observations, thus making possible the prediction of celestial positions for any given time. In order to do this he also founded *trigonometry, by computing the first trigonometric function, a chord table. He constructed viable theories for the sun and moon, and, using several ingenious methods for determining the lunar distance (which he was the first to estimate accurately), developed a theory of parallax. He was thus able to compute both lunar and solar eclipses. For the planets, however, he refused to construct a theory, contenting himself with compiling a list of observations from which he showed the insufficiency of previous planetary models. He is famous for his discovery of the precession of the equinoxes, which is connected both with his investigations of the length of the year and his observations of star-positions.

Hipparchus was a systematic and careful observer, who invented several instruments, possibly including the plane astrolabe (see ASTRONOMICAL INSTRUMENTS). He had a critical and original mind and a fertile mathematical invention. But he could not have achieved what he did without the aid of Babylonian astronomy, of which he displays a knowledge far deeper than any Greek before or after him, and the success of which in predicting phenomena he evidently wished to emulate. Not only did he have access to the wealth of Babylonian observational records (which he seems to have been instrumental in transmitting to the Greek world), but he also adopted many numerical parameters directly from Babylonian astronomy (e.g. the very accurate length of the mean synodic month, together with all the other mean motions in his lunar theory), and used a number of Babylonian arithmetical procedures, which were only later (by

*Ptolemy (4)) replaced with strictly geometrical methods. Hipparchus' skill in combining the Babylonian and Greek traditions in astronomy was crucial to the successful propagation of the science in that form for over a thousand years.

Hipparchus' geographical treatise, which we know mainly from Strabo, was a polemic against the *Geography* of *Eratosthenes, criticizing descriptive and especially mathematical details. Other works by him include an astronomical calendar of the traditional type, treatises on *optics and combinatorial arithmetic, *On Objects Carried Down by their Weight*, and a catalogue of his own writings. He also wrote on *astrology, and his establishment of methods for computation of celestial positions undoubtedly contributed to the enormous expansion of that 'science' in the Graeco-Roman world soon after his time.

EDITIONS *Comm. in Arat.*, ed. Manitius (Teubner, 1894), with Ger. trans.; *Geographical Fragments*, ed. D. R. Dicks (1960), with trans.

COMMENT Most up-to-date detailed treatment (with bibliog.), G. J. Toomer, *Dict. Sci. Biogr.* Suppl. 1 (1978), 207–24, 'Hipparchus'. Essential: *HAMA* 1. 274–343. On the vexed question of Hipparchus' 'star catalogue' and its relationship to Ptolemy's: G. Grasshoff, *The History of Ptolemy's Star Catalogue* (1990). On Babylonian elements in Hipparchus' work: G. J. Toomer in *Studies in Memory of Abraham Sachs* (1988), 353–62; A. Jones, *Journal for the History of Astronomy* 1991, 101–25. G. J. T.

Hippasus, of *Metapontum, an early Pythagorean later regarded as having founded the branch of the school called μαθηματικοί or 'mathematicians' (see PYTHAGORAS (1)), and as having been punished for revealing a mathematical secret: later sources disagree both on the punishment (expulsion, shipwreck) and on the secret (irrational magnitudes, construction of the dodecahedron). *Aristotle couples him with *Heraclitus as having identified the source of the world with *fire.

DK 18. M. T. Cardini, *I Pitagorici* 1 (1958); W. Burkert, *Weisheit und Wissenschaft* (1962); Guthrie, *Hist. Gk. Phil.* 1. 320 ff. G. E. L. O.

hippeis

1. Aristocracies In a number of Greek states the aristocracy was known as the 'hippeis' (e.g. *Eretria and Boeotian *Orchomenus (1); and cf. the 'hippobotai', of *Chalcis and, below, the Spartan élite (§ 3) and Athenian property class (§ 4)). Aristotle (*Pol.* 1297[b]17 ff., cf. 1289[b]36 ff. and 1321[a]8 ff.), while drawing attention to the fact that only the wealthy possessed *horses, seems to have thought that this was the basis of their political power, since their states depended upon cavalry in war. But although there is some evidence for cavalry in early wars, for example the 8th-cent. BC Lelantine War, it is doubtful whether many Greek states south of Boeotia really had powerful forces of cavalry in early times. No cavalry is mentioned in *Tyrtaeus, for example, and the Athenians notoriously had no cavalry at the battle of *Marathon, despite the existence of a class of *hippeis*. The term may rather reflect a time, real or imagined, when heroes rode to battle in chariots, as they do in *Homer, where *hippeis* means charioteers. Even when the war-chariot was abandoned, it may have continued in use among the wealthy for ceremonial purposes— at funerals or in funeral games—and those who used it have continued to be called 'charioteers'. Thus, as late as 424 BC, there was allegedly an élite force of Theban infantry made up of pairs of 'charioteers' and 'warriors' (Diod. Sic. 12. 70. 1), perhaps the 'Sacred Band'. Alternatively, aristocrats may have ridden their horses to the battlefield, where they dismounted to fight on foot.

P. A. L. Greenhalgh, *Early Greek Warfare* (1973); M. T. W. Arnheim, *Aristocracy in Greek Society* (1977). J. F. La.

2. Cavalry Archaeological evidence shows that *horses were originally used in Greece to pull chariots, not for riding, and if the Homeric poems reflect real, contemporary warfare, this was still true in the 8th cent. BC. Even after men had started to ride *horses, it is possible that in most places they originally simply rode them to the battlefield, and then dismounted to fight on foot, at least once *hoplites had become the dominant force. The use of cavalry was, in any case, never on a large scale except in areas suited to the breeding of horses, such as *Macedonia, *Thessaly, and *Boeotia. Only the wealthy could afford horses, and in most areas this meant that any cavalry force was bound to be small. Thus the Athenians only instituted a proper cavalry force after the *Persian Wars, drawn from the second of *Solon's property classes (see § 4 below), and even by 431 BC it was only 1,000 strong. Sometimes it was very effective (e.g. against the Spartan invading forces and at both the first and second battle of Mantinea), but it was never a battle-winner. Similarly, the Spartans did not even raise a proper cavalry force until 424 BC, and then although the rich provided the horses, they did not themselves form the cavalry, and *Xenophon (1) is strongly critical of its effectiveness. Thessalian cavalry, on the other hand, was famous from the time of the 8th-cent. BC Lelantine War, and Theban cavalry performed excellently at the battles of *Plataea and *Leuctra. All these cavalry forces, however, were missile-armed and incapable of defeating infantry unless the latter was caught in the wrong terrain or not properly formed.

Cavalry came into its own in the Macedonian army and in those of *Alexander (3) the Great's successors, and it was his 'Companions' (see HETAIROI) who gave Alexander victory in all three of his great battles. The key to the success of Macedonian cavalry was its use of a lance made of cornel wood, as opposed to javelins. This at last gave cavalry the capability of breaking enemy infantry, though it was still mostly used to exploit gaps already forming in infantry lines, as probably at the battle of *Chaeronea, and certainly at *Gaugamela.

> E. Lammert, *RE* 8 (1913), entry under Ἱππεῖς, 1689–1700; J. K. Anderson, *Ancient Greek Horsemanship* (1961); P. A. L. Greenhalgh, *Early Greek Warfare* (1973); G. R. Bugh, *The Horsemen of Athens* (1988); I. G. Spence, *The Cavalry of Classical Greece* (1993); L. J. Worley, *Hippeis: The Cavalry of Ancient Greece* (1994). J. F. La.

3. Spartan élite A force of probably young, aristocratic Spartans, 300-strong, chosen by officers called *hippagretai*. Despite the name ('horsemen'), there is no evidence that they ever fought on horseback. Certainly by 418 BC they fought on foot (Thuc. 5. 72. 4), and there is reason to believe that the Spartans had no cavalry before 424. The name may have something to do with their ownership of horses, or even, originally, chariots. In Homer the term means 'charioteers', and in one of the earliest reference to the Spartan *hippeis* (Hdt. 8. 124. 2–3), they escort *Themistocles to the border after he has been presented with a chariot.

> J. F. Lazenby, *The Spartan Army* (1985). J. F. La.

4. Athenian property class At Athens *hippeis* may originally have been used of all the richest citizens, but in his constitution *Solon gave the name to the second of his four property classes, comprising men whose land yielded between 300 and 500 *medimnoi* of corn or the equivalent in other produce (*Ath. pol.* 7. 3–8. 1). (For the other classes see PENTAKOSIOMEDIMNOI; THĒTES; ZEUGITAI.) The archonship (see ARCHONTES) was open to members of this class by the beginning of the 5th cent. BC if not originally; in 457/6 eligibility was extended to the third class, the *zeugitai* (the class of *hoplites). P. J. R.

Hippias (1), tyrant (see TYRANNY) of Athens 527–510 BC, son and successor of *Pisistratus, in close association with his brother *Hipparchus (1) (*Thucydides (2)'s insistence on constitutional primacy (6. 53 ff.) may be over-legalistic). His rule was at first mild. Leading aristocrats held the eponymous archonship (see ARCHONTES), *Cleisthenes (2) in 525/4, *Miltiades in 524/3; Hipparchus patronized the arts. The famous Attic owl coinage probably begins in his reign (see COINAGE, GREEK), as does the building of the temple of Olympian Zeus (*Olympieum), the largest in contemporary Greece (Arist. *Pol.* 1313ᵇ; though perhaps planned earlier); extensive work on the temple to Athena on the Acropolis (*c.*520); and the altar of the Twelve Gods in the Agora. His rule became harsher after Hipparchus' assassination. The *Alcmaeonids based at Leipsydrion, tried but failed to oust him; the Spartans under *Cleomenes (1) I, spurred on by *Delphi and Cleisthenes, invaded Attica and finally succeeded. He and his family escaped to *Sigeum and later to *Darius I's court. He was with the Persian forces at the battle of *Marathon.

> D. M. Lewis, *CAH* 4² (1988), ch. 4. See also bibliog. under PISISTRATUS.
> R. T.

Hippias (2), of *Elis, *sophist, a younger contemporary of *Protagoras. He acquired great fame and wealth as a teacher and orator, claiming competence in mathematics, astronomy, grammar, poetry, music, and history, as well as in various handicrafts and in mnemonic techniques. He is perhaps (but see following entry) to be identified with the *Hippias (3) reported by Proclus as having discovered the *quadratrix*, a curve used in attempts to square the circle. His voluminous works included an elegy on the drowning of a chorus of boys from *Messenia, a collection of historical material, a list of Olympian victors (see OLYMPIAN GAMES), and a work on the nomenclature of various peoples.

> DK 86; Eng. trans. in R. K. Sprague (ed.), *The Older Sophists* (1972); Guthrie, *Hist. Gk. Phil.* 3, ch. 11. C. C. W. T.

Hippias (3) (fl. late 3rd cent. BC or later), geometer, wrote on curves called *quadratrices* (*tetragōnizousai*) for constructing the rectification of the circle and circular arcs (equivalent to the circle quadrature). The curve, earlier applied to this end by *Nicomedes (5) (late 3rd cent. BC), is also applicable for trisecting any angle, as may have been discovered by Dinostratus (mid-4th cent. BC). The frequent identification of this Hippias with the sophist, *Hippias (2), results from misinterpretation of the two passages where the geometer is mentioned by *Proclus (*In Euclidem*, ed. Friedlein, 272. 7, 356. 11).

> W. R. Knorr, *Ancient Tradition of Geometric Problems* (1986), 80–6, 226–33. W. R. K.

hippiatrici See VETERINARY MEDICINE.

Hippo Regius (just south of mod. Annaba in Algeria: the coastline has changed since antiquity), a seaport first used by the Carthaginians, probably from the 6th cent. BC (although no finds earlier than the 5th cent. have yet been made). Its first historical mention is in the last decade of the 4th cent. BC, if the Hippo of Diod. Sic. 20. 57. 6 is this one. As its name implies it was later the residence of Numidian princes, although nothing is known of this phase. In 205 BC Scipio's legate C. *Laelius landed here during the Second *Punic War (Livy 29. 3. 7), and in its harbour *Sittius captured the Pompeians' fleet in 46 BC (*BAfr.* 96). It became a *municipium* under *Augustus, and by the mid-2nd cent. AD had acquired colonial status. Later in the 2nd cent. it became the base of one of the three *legati* of the proconsul of Africa. It controlled a vast territory (*ILAlg.* 1. 134 shows that this extended at least 40 km. (25 mi.) from Hippo in the south-westerly direction; cf. also 1. 109), and the rural folk were still speaking Punic in Augustine's day (*Ep.* 209). *Augustine was bishop from 395 to 430, and died while the city was being besieged by the *Vandals. The forum, market, baths, theatre, and a large church, together with a domestic quarter, are the principal excavated monuments.

PECS 394–6; H. van M. Dennis, *Hippo Regius* (1924); E. Marec, *Hippone La Royale*, 2nd edn. (1954); J.-P. Morel, *Bulletin d'archéologie algérienne* 1968, 35–84; S. Dahmani, *Hippo Regius* (1973).   B. H. W.; R. J. A. W.

Hippobotus (late 3rd–early 2nd cent. BC), philosophical historian. His *On Sects* and *Catalogue of Philosophers* were sources for *Diogenes (6) Laertius.

H. von Arnim, *RE* 8 (1913), 1722–3; J. Mejer, *Diogenes Laertius and his Hellenistic Background* (1978).   D. N. S.

Hippocoön, a hero evidently important in Spartan tradition, son of Oebalus and elder brother of *Tyndareos, whom he forced into exile. He quarrelled with Heracles on the arrival of the latter in *Sparta and together with his numerous sons was killed by him. Many of the cult heroes of Sparta were identified with his sons (Paus. 3. 14. 6–15. 2).

C. Calame, in J. Bremmer (ed.), *Interpretations of Greek Mythology* (1987), 153–86.   E. Ke.

Hippocrates (1) (*RE* 7) succeeded his brother Cleander (assassinated *c*.498 BC) as tyrant (see TYRANNY) of *Gela. He formed a strong mercenary army (*Gelon was his master-of-horse) and, by subjugating his Greek and *Sicel neighbours, built up a territorial empire stretching in a broad band across Sicily, from Gela and *Camarina (acquired by treaty from *Syracuse) on the south coast to Callipolis, *Naxos (2), and *Leontini (mod. Lentini) on the east. Zancle (*Messana) was his ally, but in 493 he helped Samian refugees to seize the city. Unable to take Syracuse after defeating the citizens on the Helorus river (492/1), he accepted the mediation of *Corinth and *Corcyra. He was killed (491) near Hybla by the Sicels.

D. Asheri, *CAH* 4² (1988), ch. 16; H. Berve, *Die Tyrannis bei den Griechen*, 2 vols. (1967), 1. 137–40.   B. M. C.

Hippocrates (2) (*RE* 16, and Suppls. 3, 6, 13), of *Cos, probably a contemporary of Socrates (469–399 BC), was the most famous physician of antiquity and one of the least known. The important early corpus of medical writings bears his name (see MEDICINE, § 4), but many scholars insist that he cannot be confidently connected with any individual treatise, let alone with any specific doctrines. He remains for many a 'name without a work', in the words of Wilamowitz; and even in antiquity the nature of his personal contributions to medicine were the subject of speculation.

All kinds of anecdotes and medical doctrines have been connected at different times to the name of Hippocrates. One influential ancient biographical tradition, represented by a *Life of Hippocrates* (attributed to *Soranus of Ephesus and probably a source for several much later commentators including the Byzantine scholar Johannes *Tzetzes), maintains that he was taught medicine by his father and by the gymnastic trainer Herodicus of Selymbria (see DIETETICS), and that he sat at the feet of the sophist *Gorgias (1) of Leontini, the eponym of *Plato (1)'s dialogue. Hippocrates on this account worked throughout Greece, and is supposed to have died at *Larissa in Thessaly. The evidence for his acquaintance with certain 5th-cent. *sophists is supported

by A. *Cornelius Celsus, who claims that the historical Hippocrates was the first to separate medicine from philosophy, and much more strongly by *Plato (1), who mentions Hippocrates several times. Plato suggests that he taught medicine for a fee (*Prt.* 311b) and offers a cryptic glimpse into his medical thought, reporting that he claimed that one could not understand the nature of the body without understanding the nature of the whole (*Phdr.* 270c). This difficult passage in the *Phaedrus* attracted much comment in antiquity, and has continued to do so, since it represents the only early independent reference to Hippocrates' method.

The Anonymus Londinensis papyrus (see MENO) points to an ancient confusion about the historical Hippocrates' pathological doctrines. On one view, which is ascribed to *Aristotle (and which seems to be rejected as historically incorrect by the author of the papyrus), Hippocrates held that disease is caused by vapours given off by the residues of undigested food. The 'real' Hippocrates, claims the author of the papyrus, related disease to regimen, to one's way of life. And indeed, one influential modern scholar, W. D. Smith, has argued that the Hippocratic treatise *On Regimen* can be ascribed to Hippocrates himself, but his thesis has not found widespread support. Many scholars have sought to align parts of these characterizations of Hippocratic theory with particular Hippocratic treatises, but with limited success. Others, following other ancient witnesses, have seen the hands of Hippocrates' sons *Thessalus (1), Dracon, and *Polybus (3) in other Hippocratic treatises.

To a large degree, modern ideas about Hippocrates' theory and practice have been shaped by those who wrote commentaries on him in antiquity. *Herophilus of Chalcedon is traditionally regarded as the first Hippocratic commentator, and the earliest surviving work of Hippocratic exegesis is the commentary on *Joints* by *Apollonius (8) of Citium. The best-known ancient commentator is *Galen, who presents us with an Hippocrates as the head of a medical school based in Cos and set against a rival school centred on *Cnidus. Galen's Hippocrates is credited with profound philosophical as well as medical talents, in many cases anticipating Plato and Aristotle. He advocates a four-*humour theory, based on an underlying four-*element and four-quality theory similar to that associated with *Empedocles. Galen's reasons for presenting the kind of Hippocrates he did are very complex, and they are coloured by his own philosophical sympathies with Plato, Aristotle, and *Stoicism.

There is also an ancient pseudepigraphic tradition which contains spurious anecdotal material about Hippocrates' life. The stories that he diagnosed lovesickness in King *Perdiccas (2) II of Macedon, halted the great Athenian *plague of 430 BC by burning fires throughout the city before discovering an antidote, and that he was called by the insensitive people of *Abdera to treat the supposed mad hilarity of the philosopher *Democritus, are very likely to be fictitious. In the Middle Ages, wildly anachronistic tales of his exploits in Rome were in circulation. There are many Hippocratic myths, then, and the Hippocratic 'question' remains unanswered because it is probably unanswerable.

See also ANATOMY AND PHYSIOLOGY; DIETETICS; MEDICINE.

TESTIMONIES Pl., *Prt.* 311b–c, *Phdr.* 270c–d (discussed by Galen, esp. at *De methodo medendi* 1. 2. 7 (10. 13 Kühn); Arist. *Pol.* 1326ᵃ14 ff.; Anonymus Londinensis 5 ff.; [Soranus?], *Vita Hippocratis*, ed. J. Ilberg *CMG* 4. (1927).

TEXTS The most extensive edition of the Hippocratic corpus remains E. Littré, *Œuvres complètes d'Hippocrate*, 10 vols. (1839–61). Modern critical editions of some individual works can be found in the

CMG, and in the Budé and Loeb collections. For the pseudepigrapha, see W. D. Smith, *Pseudepigraphic Writings: Hippocrates* (1990).

LITERATURE K. Deichgräber, *Die Patienten des Hippokrates* (1982); R. Joly, in M. Ruse (ed.), *Nature Animated* (1983), 29–49 (favouring Hippocratic authorship of *Epidemics* 1, 2, *Fractures*, and *Joints*); G. E. R. Lloyd, 'The Hippocratic Question', *CQ* 1975, 171–92 (repr. with additions in *Methods and Problems in Greek Science* (1991), 194–223 (a general, sceptical overview)); J. Mansfeld, *GRBS* 1980, 341–62. On the development of ancient characterizations of Hippocrates, see W. D. Smith, *The Hippocratic Tradition* (1979); O. Temkin, *Hippocrates in a World of Pagans and Christians* (1990); J. R. Pinault, *Hippocratic Lives and Legends* (1992).

J. T. V.

Hippocrates (3) (fl. end of the 5th cent. BC), of Chios, mathematician and astronomer. In geometry he was first to show that the cube duplication is equivalent to finding two mean proportionals between lines in the given ratio. He also constructed rectilinear figures equal to three forms of 'lunules' (*mēniskoi*), figures bounded by two circular arcs, and showed how a certain fourth case, if known, would solve the circle quadrature. A long fragment from *Eudemus on these quadratures is reported by Simplicius (*in Phys.* 1. 2, ed. Diels, 60–9). According to Proclus, Hippocrates was first to compile an 'Elements' of geometry, which would appear to have anticipated substantial parts of *Euclid's books 1, 3, and 6. In *astronomy, Hippocrates was known for a theory of comets, reported by Aristotle (*Mete.* 1. 6).

W. R. Knorr, *Ancient Tradition of Geometric Problems* (1986), 22–39; G. E. R. Lloyd, *Apeiron* 1987, 103–28. W. R. K.

Hippodamia (1), daughter of King Oenomaus of *Pisa (later *Olympia) in the Peloponnese. Her suitors were forced to engage in a chariot-race with her father, second prize being decapitation; eventually *Pelops cheated his way to victory and won her. (2) Bride of the Lapith *Pirithous, whom the drunken *Centaurs tried to seize at the marriage feast.

LIMC 5. 1 (1990), 439–40. A. H. G.

Hippodamus, of *Miletus, was the most famous Greek town-planner. He was born probably about 500 BC. Ancient authorities speak of his *nemēsis* or allocation of sites. Towards the middle of the 5th cent. he planned *Piraeus for the Athenians, and boundary stones found there are probably evidence of his work (cf. R. Garland, *The Piraeus* (1987)). The agora there was known as the Hippodamian. In 443 he went with the colony to *Thurii and he may well have been responsible for its rectangular plan. *Strabo (14. 2. 9) records a tradition that the 'architect of Piraeus' planned Rhodes which was founded in 408 BC. Most modern authorities reject this on the ground that the date is too late for Hippodamus. Aristotle (*Pol.* 2. 5) speaks of Hippodamus' foppish appearance, and his political theories, and notes that he thought that the ideal size for a city was 10,000 (i.e. probably citizens).

His name is often attached to the rectangular or gridiron type of layout for the streets of planned cities, which he certainly knew but clearly did not invent. It is likely that he theorized about the proper arrangement of towns, and the location of the various elements in them. Hoepfner and Schwandner argue interestingly (but on slender evidence) that at Piraeus and elsewhere he designed a uniform type of citizen-house for the residential area. See URBANISM.

R. Martin *L'Urbanisme dans la Grèce Antique*, 2nd edn. (1974); W. Hoepfner and E.-L. Schwandner, *Haus und Stadt in klassischem Griechenland* (1986). R. A. T., A. J. S. S.

Hippolytus (1), son of *Theseus and an *Amazon (Antiope or Hippolyte), was devoted to the hunt and to the virgin *Artemis, ignoring Aphrodite, who responded by afflicting Hippolytus' stepmother Phaedra with a passion for him. When he rejected her, she accused Hippolytus to *Theseus (just returned from the Underworld) of making advances to her, and killed herself. *Poseidon, responding to the prayer of Theseus, sent a bull from the sea which caused the death of Hippolytus in a chariot crash as he left *Troezen for exile.

The story was a famous one (Paus. 1. 22. 1). It was dramatized in lost tragedies by *Sophocles (1) (*Phaedra*) and *Euripides (*Hippolytus Calyptomenus*), in both of which it seems that Phaedra is, as in the much later play by the younger *Seneca (*Phaedra*), lustful and unscrupulous. In a second, surviving version by Euripides (*Hippolytus Stephanephorus*) on the other hand, Phaedra has a strong sense of modesty which struggles with her passion, and it is the nurse rather than Phaedra herself who approaches Hippolytus. The myth was also handled by *Ovid (*Her.* 4). In one version Hippolytus is restored to life by *Asclepius (as early as the epic *Naupactica*, fr. 10c Davies, *EGF*) and taken to *Diana's sanctuary at *Aricia in southern Italy, where he is identified with her attendant Virbius (Callim. fr. 190 Pf.; Verg. *Aen.* 7. 765–82).

In cult Hippolytus is also associated with *Aphrodite. At Athens she had a shrine ἐφ᾽ Ἱππολύτῳ ('at Hippolytus') on the Acropolis (Eur. *Hipp.* 31–3). At Troezen, the place of his death, he had a precinct containing a temple of *Aphrodite and a hero-cult in which girls about to marry lamented for him and offered him their hair (Eur. *Hipp.* 1423–30; Paus. 2. 32. 1). Hippolytus embodies the persistence of virginal resistance to marriage, a resistance which the girls themselves must abandon. In *Pausanias (3)' time the Troezenians refused to show his tomb, and maintained that he had become the constellation Auriga. The name Ἱππόλυτος may derive from the unharnessing of horses in a sacrificial context in the Troezenian cult of Poseidon. The first of the myth's many depictions in classical art (on 4th-cent. Apulian vase-painting) were probably prompted by Attic drama: *LIMC* 5. 1 (1990), 445–64.

W. S. Barrett (ed.) *Euripides, Hippolytos* (1964), introd.; W. Fauth, *Hippolytos und Phaidra* (1958–9); W. Burkert, *Structure and History in Greek Mythology and Ritual* (1979), 111–18. R. A. S. S.

Hippolytus (2), *c.* AD 170–*c.*236, styled bishop of Portus and (probably) rival to Callistus of Rome (217–22), whom he reckoned a heretic because of his denial of the hypostatic identity of the Logos. (See further his *Contra Noetum* and *Refutation* bk. 9.) He died in exile in Sardinia under Maximinus' persecution. Though allegedly reconciled, he is more often named than quoted in later writing. A statue of him in Rome gives a list of his works, but the attribution of almost every work that goes under his name has been disputed. Book 1 of the *Refutation of all Heresies* (the *Philosophumena*) was once ascribed to Origen (1); books 4–10 were found in the last century, and, along with the *De Universo* and the *Chronicle*, are assigned by Nautin to one Josippus. The work yields valuable fragments of the Presocratic philosophers, but he assimilates them blatantly to the Christian heresies which he attempts to trace to them. The *Chronicle* extends to 234, and, like the massive *Commentary on Daniel*, was written to quench apocalyptic expectation.

TEXTS Commentaries, ed. Bonwetsch (1897); *Elenchos*, ed. Wendland (1916), Marcovich (1966); *Chronicle*, ed. Bauer (1929).

STUDIES P. Nautin, *Hippolyte et Josipe* (1947); J. Mansfeld, *Heresiography in Context* (1992). H. C.; M. J. E.

Hippon, also called **Hipponax,** natural philosopher of the

Hipponax

Periclean age (5th cent. BC), probably came from *Samos. He treated water or the moist as the principle of all things, reasoning chiefly from observation on the semen of animals. He considered the *soul (seated in the brain) to be derived from the semen and to be itself moist, and devoted special attention to the development of the human body from the embryonic state to maturity. See EMBRYOLOGY. Aristotle describes him as a second-rate thinker, probably because of his materialistic bias. He was lampooned as an *atheist by *Cratinus and this became his stock epithet in later writers. See also *Aristophanes (1) *Clouds* 96 with Dover's and Sommerstein's notes.

DK 38. W. D. R.; S. H.

Hipponax ('Ἱππῶναξ), poet of *Ephesus and *Clazomenae (late 6th cent. BC), composed entertaining monologues and songs, probably for a popular festival (see IAMBIC POETRY, GREEK). His favourite metre was the scazon (choliambus) with its deliberate 'wrong' ending. He uses colourful, vulgar language, and portrays himself as a disreputable character whose life is full of brawling, burglary, poverty, cheap drink, and sexual episodes of a farcical and scatological nature. He pours abuse and imprecations on his enemies, chief among whom is the sculptor Bupalus. One glutton is made the object of an epic parody (frs. 128–9a W). Hipponax' work was much admired and imitated in the Hellenistic period. At least part of it survived as late as the 12th cent., but we know it now from papyrus and quotation fragments.

TEXT E. Degani (Teubner, 2nd edn. 1991); West, *IE²* 1.
COMMENTARY O. Masson (1962).
TRANSLATION West, *GLP.*
GENERAL E. Degani, *Studi su Ipponatte* (1984); B. M. W. Knox, *CHCL* 1. 158 ff. M. L. W.

Hipponium (mod. Monteleone), a Locrian colony (see LOCRI EPIZEPHYRII) founded *c.*600 BC, about which little is known. It fought against *Dionysius (1) I in 388 and was sacked, but later rebelled against *Syracuse. It fell to the *Bruttii *c.*356–4. In 192 Rome founded the (much better documented) Latin colony of Vibo Valentia on the site. Its municipal status, abundant epigraphy, and monumental architecture suggest that it flourished. For an Orphic text (*c.*400 BC) from Hipponium see *SEG* 26 (1976), 1139; see ORPHISM.

E. Greco, *Magna Grecia* (1981); Hornblower, *Comm. on Thuc.* 2 (1996), n. on 5. 5. 3. K. L.

Hippothoon or **Hippothon**, a hero located at *Eleusis, son of *Poseidon and Alope the daughter of Cercyon. His mother was the subject of several tragedies, including one by Euripides (frs. 105–13 Nauck). He was one of the ten Attic tribal *eponymoi.

Kron, *Phylenheroen* 180–2, and *LIMC* 5. 468–71; Kearns, *Heroes of Attica* 80–91, 173. E. Ke.

Hirtius (*RE* 2), **Aulus** (consul 43 BC), since *c.*54 BC an officer of *Caesar, who sent him as envoy to *Pompey in December 50. In the Civil Wars he served in Spain, was possibly *tribunus plebis* in 48, and was at *Antioch (1) in spring 47; in 46 he was praetor and next year governed Transalpine Gaul (see GAUL (TRANSALPINE)). After Caesar's murder he was consul designate, and Cicero induced him to take arms against Antony (M. *Antonius (2)) (43). With Octavian he raised the siege of *Mutina, but was killed in the victory, receiving with his colleague C. *Vibius Pansa Caetronianus a public funeral. Hirtius added to Caesar's *De Bello Gallico* an eighth book, and probably also wrote the *Bellum Alexandrinum*; his correspondence with Cicero, published in nine books, and the draft for Caesar's *Anticato* have not survived.

A notorious epicure, Hirtius was also a fluent and reasonably painstaking writer: his military competence was probably not as low as Quintus *Tullius Cicero (1) later pretended (Cic. *Fam.* 16. 27. 2). G. E. F. C.

Hispalis (mod. Sevilla), on the lower Baetis (Guadalquívir), was a native settlement founded in the 8th cent. BC. First mentioned in *Caesar's *Civil War* (see BELLUM CIVILE), it was a shipbuilding and trading port. It received a modest *deductio* of veterans from Caesar as the *Colonia Hispalis Romula*, which was reinforced by *Otho. Hispalis soon grew in size and importance. Excavations have revealed a temple, public baths, and houses and it has been suggested that it had two fora. It was the principal port for the export of oil and metals from the richest province of the west. Imperial procurators and agents of the *praefectus annonae* operated there. It had a bishop from the early 4th cent., and later became the metropolitan see, occupied in the 7th cent. by *Isidorus (2).

J. Campos, *Excavaciones arqueológicas en la ciudad de Sevilla* (1986). S. J. K.

Histiaea, a city on the NW coast of *Euboea, with a rich plain facing Thessaly. It was said to have been founded from Thessaly by Ellopians, and in the Catalogue of Ships is characterized as rich in vines (*Iliad* 2. 537). It was sacked by the Persians after their defeat at *Artemisium and subsequently joined the *Delian League. For their part in the Euboean revolt the Histiaeans were expelled by Athens in 447/6, and 2,000 cleruchs (see CLERUCHY) were established in the new colony, Oreioi, a deme of Histiaea (*IG* 1³. 41); but the city with the new name was not demonstrably on a different site. The Histiaeans returned after the *Peloponnesian War. They remained suspicious of Athens and were slow to join the *Second Athenian Confederacy (Diod. 15. 30; Tod 123, line 114) in the 370s; see Tod 153 and comm. for the 350s. The Macedonians took an early interest in this part of the island. The city was taken by *Attalus II and the Romans in 199 and sacked. It later served Roman fleets. There are scanty bronze age finds from the acropolis by the sea, slight Classical remains, and a Byzantine circuit wall. The commercial importance of Hellenistic Histiaea is demonstrated by the wide circulation of its coins and the number of *proxeny decrees it passed. See AEDEPSUS.

L. H. Sackett and others, *BSA* 1966, 39 f.; M. McGregor, *Hesp.* Suppl. 19 (1982), 101 ff. Fuller account than the above in *PECS* (T. W. Jacobsen). Coins, etc.: L. Robert, *Études de numismatique grecque* (1951), ch. 7, *Hellenica* 11–12 (1960), ch. 5, *Monnaies grecques* (1967), 37. See also EUBOEA. J. B.; S. H.

Histiaeus, Milesian tyrant (see MILETUS), loyal Persian functionary and ambitious empire-builder (*c.*515–493 BC), saved *Darius I's expedition beyond the Danube (see DANUVIUS) when fellow Greek autocrats pondered betraying their overlord (*c.*513). He protected Darius' interests in the undermanned western provinces of Anatolia, suitably rephrasing for Hellenic sensibilities oriental monarchy's commands, and gained Darius' gift of Edonian Myrcinus on the river Strymon, a hub for Ionian penetration and economic exploitation of the *Thracian-*Macedonian coastlands (Hdt. 5. 11, cf. 8. 85).

Suspected of potential rebellion or excessive power by rival Persian grandees, he was summoned to *Susa, long detained, and honoured by Darius as his Aegean expert. Histiaeus overboldly promised (499) to regain the allegiance of Miletus and other Ionian cities that *Aristagoras (1), his appointed deputy and relative, had led into rebellion. Like *Hecataeus (1) (Hdt. 5. 36), he appreciated Persian power and Hellenic inadequacies. Sent to pacify Ionia, after several Ionian repulses (6. 1–5), he dared not return to Susa and so departed for his Thracian project. Unlikely ever to have encouraged Aristagoras' premature mainland revolt, his absence from the defeat at Lade suggests realistic evaluation of the coalition's chances. He subsequently launched shipping-raids from *Byzantium and descents on *Chios, *Thasos, and Lesbos that less resemble self-interested marauding than independent operations. He intended either to curry renewed favour with Darius or support faltering rebels. As he foraged near Atarneus, Persian units captured and impaled him (6. 26–30, 493).

Herodotus unsurprisingly found only hostile Greek and Persian sources. This first Greek *biography supplies sinister motives for Histiaeus' every mysterious move, but the biased narrative invites doubts about parochial malice. Herodotus acknowledges Histiaeus' steady services to Darius that led Harpagus and *Artaphernes to execute him. Largely irrelevant to the Ionian Revolt, Histiaeus was none the less vilified both for starting it and for avoiding martyrdom in it. See IONIAN REVOLT.

Hdt. bks. 4–6. G. Grundy, *The Great Persian War* (1901); A. Blamire, *CQ* 1959, 142; O. Murray, *CAH* 4² (1988), 486 ff. D. G. L.

Historia Augusta Title given by I. Casaubon (1603) to a collection of biographies (see BIOGRAPHY, ROMAN) of Roman emperors, Caesars, and usurpers from AD 117 to 284 (*Hadrian to *Carinus and *Numerianus). The present text is not complete, as there is a lacuna for the years 244–59. Though the work is modelled on *Suetonius' 'Lives of the Twelve Caesars' (*De vita Caesarum*) there is no cogent reason to believe that it was a direct continuation of Suetonius and that it therefore originally included the Lives of *Nerva and *Trajan. According to the complex manuscript tradition the biographies were written by six different authors who lived in the time of *Diocletian and *Constantine I. Some of the biographies are dedicated to Diocletian or Constantine, others to private persons. Yet, unless one is to postulate multiple series of biographies, there is an inherent contradiction in the claims of authorship, because four of the supposed 'authors'—Aelius Spartianus, Iulius Capitolinus, Vulcacius Gallicanus, Aelius Lampridius—say that they have written more biographies than appear in our present compilation. Only two 'authors'—Trebellius Pollio and Flavius Vopiscus—do not profess to have written more than the extant biographies. The *Scriptores Historiae Augustae* (as the six 'authors' are usually called) claim to have used many literary sources, only a few of which, such as *Herodian, are extant, although others, such as the senatorial biographer of the Severan period, *Marius Maximus, and the Athenian *Herennius Dexippus, of whom fragments survive, are well attested as historical authors. Furthermore, they quote numerous documents (letters of emperors, *senatus consulta*, inscriptions, etc.) which are unevenly distributed among the biographies. Lives of little-known emperors and usurpers are filled with documents, whereas there is no document in the Lives (which appear altogether more reliable) of Hadrian, *Antoninus Pius, Marcus *Aurelius, and *Septimius Severus. This would in itself be enough to raise suspicion as to the authenticity of the supposed documents and as to the integrity of the texts which contain them, as well as to the true identity and character of the six 'authors'. Indeed, the *Historia Augusta* has never enjoyed great authority among scholars, although it is our only continuous account of the history of the emperors of the 2nd and 3rd cent. (it is so used, for example, by Gibbon). More radical criticism was expressed for the first time by H. Dessau in *Hermes* 1887, 337 ff., and his

paper opened up a new era in the study of the *Historia Augusta*. Dessau contended that the *HA* was not written in the time of Diocletian and Constantine, but in the time of *Theodosius (2) I, and that there was only one author behind the six names of the alleged biographers. One of his many impressive arguments was that the Life of Septimius Severus, chs. 17–19, copies *Aurelius Victor, *De Caesaribus* (written *c*. AD 360) and the Life of Marcus Aurelius 16. 3–18. 2 depends on *Eutropius (1) 8. 11–14 (written AD 369). Many other arguments advanced since the time of Dessau, relating to Roman imperial institutions (for example *eunuchs), the nomenclature of characters mentioned in the Lives, apparent allusions in the text to events of a later period, and affinities of style and temperament with other authors such as *Ammianus Marcellinus and St *Jerome, have strengthened the case for thinking that the text is anachronistic for the early 4th cent. but fits comfortably into its last decades (or later). Research on the style of the work has also emphasized the uniformity of style between the Lives, supporting the conclusion that the author was a single person and not the six alleged. There is general agreement that the documents, letters, and other such evidence adduced in the Lives are largely inauthentic, with a concentration of these in the later Lives, and in the largely derivative Lives of the usurpers and lesser emperors, the so-called *Nebenviten*, of the earlier period.

If this is its nature, opinions vary widely as to the purpose of the collection. Responding to Dessau and raising the question of motive for literary fraudulence on such a scale, Mommsen suggested that an original text written under Diocletian and Constantine was substantially revised under Theodosius. Other scholars, following Dessau in the notion of a total forgery, have proposed different dates of composition: under *Constantius II (H. Stern), under Julian (N. H. Baynes), in AD 394 (W. Hartke), in the early 5th cent. (O. Seeck, J. Straub), as late as the early 6th cent. (A. von Domaszewski). This last date is made very improbable by the fact that the *HA* seems to have been used by Q. Aurelius Memmius *Symmachus (2) (quoted in Jordanes, *Getica* 15. 85) towards the end of the 5th cent. The question of date goes along with that of the aims of the writer of the *HA*. The work shows senatorial sympathies and does not approve of hereditary monarchy, nor of interference by the army in politics. In some passages a tolerant view of religious diversity is implied, which has led to the opinion that the author concealed his identity and time of writing to attack Christianity and to present paganism as more tolerant. Unfortunately none of these views is expressed with sufficient consistency to make them convincing as explanations of the entire text. More recently, R. Syme has set aside the question of motive, seeing the author as a 'rogue grammarian' who warmed to his task, becoming more inventive and humorous as he proceeded; and Tony Honoré has seen a sufficiently precise legal expertise to identify the author as a lawyer working in the imperial service. Research on the sources of the *HA* and on the character of individual Lives is leading to a better understanding of how the text can be used as a historical source, and it is this more pragmatic approach that is gaining ground over the quest for the author's motives. There is, however, general agreement that the author is a single person working in or very close to the last decade of the 4th cent.

TEXT E. Hohl (1927, repr.); D. Magie, 2 vols. (Loeb, 1922–32); trans. A. R. Birley, *Lives of the Later Caesars* (Penguin, 1976, repr.): the earlier lives to Heliogabalus.
STUDIES Momigliano, *Secondo Contributo* 105 ff. (= *Studies in Historiography* (1966), ch. 9); P. White, *JRS* 1967, 115 ff.; R. Syme, *Ammianus*

historiography, Greek

and the *Historia Augusta* (1968), and *Emperors and Biography* (1971); T. D. Barnes, *The Sources of the Historia Augusta* (1978); T. Honoré, *JRS* 1987, 156 ff.   J. F. Ma.

historiography, Greek That Greeks invented history-writing is not certain: the Jewish 'Succession Narrative' in the books of Samuel and Kings antedates every Greek claimant to be the first historian. But direct Jewish influence on Greece is unlikely, and much biblical narration is a tram not a bus—driven by divine not humanly contingent causal forces.

*Homer is not historiography and is slippery ground for the historian. But his characters show awareness of the past and are impelled by an urge to leave glory to posterity; thus *Achilles sings of the famous deeds of men and *Helen weaves into a web the story of the sufferings she has herself brought about. The poet himself speaks of 'men who exist nowadays' by contrast with inhabitants of the world he describes. *Genealogies, of the sort that feature in Homeric battle-challenges, are essential to a historical perspective on human events, and they form the link between Homer and *Hecataeus (1) of Miletus, the first true Greek historian: he wrote a prose work on genealogy, as well as a description of the world known to him, and a work on mythology. His younger critic and improver was *Herodotus (1): the urge to correct and improve on a predecessor is one of the main dynamics of Greek historiography. But the prose of Hecataeus was not Herodotus' only stimulus: Herodotus' nine-book work may owe at least as much to poets who (unlike Homer) did treat historical events in verse: it is now known that *Simonides handled the Persian War in detail and compared it explicitly to the Trojan War (*POxy.* 3965). The implications of this for the understanding of the beginnings of Greek historiography have yet to be properly drawn.

Herodotus' repudiation of myth was less explicit and famous than that of *Thucydides (2), but equally or (because earlier) more important: Herodotus restricts himself to historical time and to information he can check. How far he did check that information has been controversial since antiquity, but the sceptical case has not been made out. On the contrary Herodotus' work shows many authentic traces of the oral tradition (see ORALITY) on which its author drew.

Thucydides knew and reacted against Herodotus' work and there are obvious differences, above all a more linear narrative which concerned itself more narrowly with male activities like war and politics. But there are similarities too; thus Homeric influence is detectable in detail not just on Herodotus but on Thucydides also, who has a rhetoric of his own and should not be crudely opposed to Herodotus as *literacy is opposed to orality: Thucydides' famous preface declares his work to be *not so much* a prize composition (a word which hints at the displays of the *sophists) as a possession for ever. This formulation does not exclude recitation of sections in high finish, or even performance of debates and dialogue. By including (i.e. inventing) speeches at all, both historians were copying Homer, and Thucydides' very difficult speeches resemble Homer's in that their style is different from the narrative.

Western Greece, i.e. Italy and Sicily, developed its own historiography, which however borrowed from and interacted with that of old Greece. Thus *Antiochus (10) of Syracuse may have written his account to supplement Herodotus' gappy treatment of the west; but Antiochus was in his turn drawn on by Thucydides; who was then a close model for *Philistus, who straddles the 5th and 4th cents.

Antiochus and Philistus were in effect local historians, though

Sicily is a big place and they were hardly parochial figures. Similarly local historians studied the great states of old Greece, producing above all the *Atthides* or histories of Athens (see ATTHIS). The first Atthidographer was, however, not an Athenian at all, *Hellanicus (1) of Mytilene on Lesbos. But the great 4th- and 3rd-cent. Atthidographers, *Androtion and *Philochorus, were Athenians who used their literary works to express definite political viewpoints; theirs was not directionless antiquarianism.

The main stream of historiography after Thucydides was, however, navigated, as so often in the ancient world, by more cosmopolitan and restless writers, like the exiled Athenian *Xenophon (1). His preoccupation in the *Hellenica* with the Peloponnese is marked but his perspective is just too wide for this work to be called local history. He takes his chronological starting-point and some other obvious external features from Thucydides, but his religious values and his use of the illuminating digression are more reminiscent of Herodotus. His *Anabasis* is a snapshot of Persian Anatolia which reveals his gifts as a social historian and is a prime source for modern students of religion and warfare.

Thucydides never ceased to have influence even in the 4th cent. when to find him cited by name is rare, though another and more hard-headed continuator of Thucydides than Xenophon, the Oxyrhynchus historian (see OXYRHYNCHUS, THE HISTORIAN FROM), does mention him. *Aeneas Tacticus, not an intellectual, shows knowledge both of Thucydides' narrative and his speeches, and Thucydides' remarks on speeches were discussed by *Callisthenes, whose *Hellenica* (used by *Ephorus later in the 4th cent. and thus at one remove by *Diodorus (3) Siculus) faintly transmits an important alternative tradition to that of Xenophon. 'Faintly', because Callisthenes resembles other big names of 4th-cent. Greek historiography in that it survives only in 'fragments' or quotations. The same is true of Ephorus, whose universal history, enormously popular in antiquity, drew on Thucydides for the 5th cent., then on the Oxyrhynchus historian (late 5th and early 4th), then on Callisthenes (? *King's Peace onwards). But Ephorus also comes down to us mediated by Diodorus. The sources of Diodorus' Persian material for the 4th cent. (*Ctesias? *Dinon?) are disputed, even more so his Sicilian material. Ephorus was one 'Sicilian' source but it is hard to know how much to attribute to *Timaeus (2), a major figure in Greek understanding of the west.

Another Thucydidean continuator and partial imitator (he echoes the Thucydidean Funeral Speech) was *Theopompus (3), who wrote about *Philip (1) II of Macedon in a way which may owe something to Thucydides' fascination with the individual *Alcibiades. But the great individual of the age was *Alexander (3) the Great, whose 'Deeds' were reported by Callisthenes, by Dinon's son *Cleitarchus (the source of Diodorus book 17 and of the vulgate tradition about Alexander generally), and by *Arrian's sources *Ptolemy (1) I and *Aristobulus (1). Alexander, the new *Achilles as his historians presented him or as he presented himself, and his glorious Deeds take us back to Homer where this survey began.

'Fragmentary' historians are collected in F. Jacoby's *Fragmente der griechischen Historiker* (FGrH), 15 vols. (1923–). For individual historians see the particular entries in this dictionary. On Thucydides' 4th-century and Hellenistic *reception see S. Hornblower, *JHS* 1995, 47 ff. E. Schwartz *Griechische Geschichtsschreiber* (1959) and Jacoby, *Griechische Historiker* (1956), are two major collections of reprinted *RE* articles from earlier in this century. A great recent authority was A. Momigliano, see his *Classical Foundations of Greek Historiography* (1990), but more inspiring are his *Studies in Historiography* (1966) and *Essays in*

Ancient and Modern Historiography (1977). General surveys: J. B. Bury, *The Greek Historians* (1909) is still valuable; of more modern works see T. S. Brown, *The Greek Historians* (1973); H. R. Immerwahr and W. R. Connor in *CHCL* 1; O. Murray, 'The Greek Historians', in J. Boardman and others (eds.), *Oxford History of the Classical World* (1986); K. Meister, *Griechische Geschichtsschreibung* (1990); H. Verdin, G. Schepens, and E. de Keyser (eds.), *Purposes of History: Studies in Greek Historiography from the 4th to the 2nd Cents.* BC (1990); J. M. Alonso-Nuñez (ed.), *Geschichtsbild und Geschichtsdenken im Altertum* (1991); O. Lendle, *Einführung in die griechische Geschichtsschreibung* (1992); S. Hornblower (ed.), *Greek Historiography* (1994), ch. 1.   S. H.

historiography, Hellenistic In an age that witnessed the conquests by *Alexander (3) the Great and his Successors and then the Roman succession to virtually all that had been theirs, Greeks substantially expanded history-writing to include new themes, styles, and genres. In the 1st cent., BC *Dionysius (7) of Halicarnassus claimed that the day was not long enough for him to recite the names of all the historians (*Comp.* 4. 30). The increase in history-writing was due to the necessity to explain new events, lands, and peoples. It was nurtured by the patronage of Hellenistic monarchs and Roman aristocrats and by the growth of *libraries and centres of scholarship, most notably in *Alexandria (1) and *Pergamum, and finally in Rome.

Most of that rich and diverse writing is lost. Substantial parts of *Polybius (1), *Diodorus (3) Siculus, and Dionysius of Halicarnassus survive, as do some of the works of *Appian, *Arrian, *Cassius Dio, *Herodian (2), and *Plutarch from the Roman period. Fragments from the lost works of nearly a thousand historians, preserved by later authors as quotations or paraphrases, are collected in F. Jacoby's *Die Fragmente der griechischen Historiker* (*FGrH*). Although still incomplete, it is a treasure trove of information and, arranged by genre, presents an organizational scheme which helps make sense of the complex subject. Work on it has now (1994) been resumed by an international team.

Spanning centuries and continents, Hellenistic historiography, however, defies categorization. The ancients themselves did not submit history to the same rigours or canons as they did philosophy, rhetoric, and science; nor was history part of the educational curriculum. Rhetoricians, apparently far more often than historians themselves, commented on the principles of history writing, usually by evaluating historical narrative for style. Hellenistic history never developed acknowledged classics. Egyptian papyri, as well as literary references, suggest that *Herodotus (1), *Thucydides (2), and *Xenophon (1) (followed by *Theopompus (3) and *Ephorus) continued throughout antiquity to be the best-known historians. Polybius, the most renowned Hellenistic historian, was not read closely a century after he wrote (so Dionysius of Halicarnassus). The Attic revival made these Classical writers better objects of rhetorical imitation.

Rhetoric played an important role in the development of narrative. Historians had, since Thucydides, added speeches for variety, colour, and dramatic tension. *Isocrates, a practitioner of the epideictic style of oratory, influenced Theopompus and Ephorus to include also character assessments in passing moral and practical judgements on their subjects. Perhaps related is the development of so-called tragic history. The invocation of highly emotive scenes lent drama to the narrative and entertained the reader. Although Polybius, in choosing a more utilitarian approach, inveighed against the use of tragic history as counterfactual (he attacked especially *Phylarchus), a few episodes in his surviving narrative also bear its influence.

Local chronicles—important in the development of Classical historiography—continued to be produced in abundance in the Hellenistic period. But other genres emerged. Biography developed fully, with its Hellenistic emphasis on individual characterization and character type. *Satyrus (1) and *Cornelius Nepos were precursors of *Plutarch, *Suetonius, *Philostratus, *Eunapius, and other pagan and Christian hagiographers. Ethnographies became important for explaining the new lands under Greek and then Roman control, and even traditional narratives contained much ethnographic material, leading to amalgams such as the works of *Strabo and *Pausanias (3). Indeed, the novel emerged from the same spirit of discovery, with many of the romances situated in exotic lands and the main characters 'historical' figures, such as Alexander the Great, Ninus, and *Semiramis. Despite their interest in ethnography, Hellenistic historians rarely learned local languages and frequently forced their interpretations of foreign cultures into categories familiar to Greek audiences. *Megasthenes idealized the social structure of India in Greek philosophical constructions, as did *Hecataeus (2) in his analysis of Egypt; Polybius, who spent two decades in Italy, presented a description of Roman political institutions (book 6) based on an Aristotelian model of government (see ARISTOTLE) and marred by an inability to understand Romans on their own terms.

The most significant historical genre that developed in the Hellenistic period was universal history. The Roman conquest made the study of the *oikoumenē* ('inhabited world') a compelling topic, a subject initially treated by Polybius (although *Timaeus (2) had been the first to cover Rome at length). The growth of universalistic philosophies, especially *Stoicism, brought another unifying theme: the power of the common good. Diodorus Siculus used the theme of individual benefactors and civilizing agents haphazardly, but *Posidonius (2) could suggest, with some ambivalence, that Roman might represented a unifying force for the common benefit of all. This notion, reinterpreted, became influential with Christian writers such as St *Augustine. But few practitioners of universal history were broadly inclusive of other ethnic groups except as they came into contact with Graeco-Roman civilization. Universalistic historiography became truly ecumenical only when it abandoned time-bound narrative in the form of Judaeo-Christian apocalyptic and prophecy.

Just as Thucydides implicitly acknowledged and followed Herodotus, a series of later historians built their narratives on previous ones. This succession of historical works helped develop the notion of historical tradition, with historians increasingly quoting from and drawing on past works (no more evident than in the case of Plutarch). It also spawned the belief that historical narrative could be created without primary research: Diodorus Siculus and Arrian (to choose extremes in quality) compiled narratives based on accepted earlier traditions. New interpretations of past events were generally derived from rationalizing or from new perspectives, rarely from new research. The very diversity and abundance of Hellenistic history-writing assured a widespread acceptance of the principle that the past, as well as the present, needed to be recalled and reinterpreted—if not also reinvestigated. It encouraged the invocation of history for justification of present policy or for *propaganda, such as occurred in the generally anti-Roman Sibylline oracles (see SIBYL). In the Greek revival of the 2nd cent. AD (see SECOND SOPHISTIC), Arrian consciously modelled his works after Xenophon's, as if an echo of Classical form and style would bestow legitimacy.

Greek historiography profoundly influenced its Roman counterpart (beginning with Q. *Fabius Pictor who wrote in Greek) and created the paradigms of historical investigation in other Mediterranean lands. *Maccabees II, an epitome of *Jason (3) of Cyrene's larger work in Greek, contains episodes in the style of tragic history, and *Josephus' *Jewish Antiquities* reflects the work of Dionysius of Halicarnassus. See JEWISH GREEK LITERATURE. *Manetho's study of Egypt and *Berossus' history of Babylonia are based on Hellenistic examples of history-writing. Although early Christian historiography departs conceptually by identifying a pre-existing spirit that was to outlast all history, some books of the New Testament, especially Luke and *Acts of the Apostles, bear the influence of Hellenistic historiography and rhetorical devices. Christian hagiography develops from the Greek biographical tradition, and *Eusebius, who initiated ecclesiastical history, drew heavily on documents in a manner similar to his Greek predecessors.

See the articles on individual historical writers and LOGOGRAPHERS.

The texts of and commentaries to the fragments are provided by F. Jacoby, *Die Fragmente der griechischen Historiker*, (*FGrH*) 15 vols. (1923–). C. Müller, *Fragmenta Historicorum Graecorum*, 5 vols. (1841–70), contains some authors not yet covered by Jacoby but is otherwise superseded. A. Momigliano, in hundreds of essays now included in *Contributo alla storia degli studi classici e del mondo antico* (1955–92 = 9 *Contributi* in 12 vols.), has done fundamental interpretative work, as has F. Walbank, *Historical Commentary on Polybius*, 3 vols. (1957–79) and *Selected Papers* (1985).

The annotated bibliography in Momigliano's remarkable 'Greek Historiography', *History and Theory* 17 (1978), 1–28, replaces all previous ones. Momigliano produced subsequently: *Sui fondamenti della storia antica* (1984), *The Classical Foundations of Modern Historiography* (1990), and *The Development of Greek Biography*, 2nd edn. (1993). Other works of note include: P. M. Fraser, *Ptolemaic Alexandria*, 3 vols. (1972); T. P. Wiseman, *Clio's Cosmetics* (1979); A. B. Bosworth, *A Historical Commentary on Arrian's History of Alexander* 1 (1980) and 2 (1995), with a (final) vol. 3 to come, covering bks. 6 and 7 and the *Indike*; P. Stadter, *Arrian of Nicomedia* (1980); J. Hornblower, *Hieronymus of Cardia* (1981); C. Fornara, *The Nature of History in Ancient Greece and Rome* (1983); P. Pédech, *Historiens compagnes d'Alexandre* (1984), and *Trois historiens méconnus* (1989); C. Habicht, *Pausanias's Guide to Ancient Greece* (1985); L. Pearson, *The Greek Historians of the West* (1987); K. Sacks, *Diodorus and the First Century* (1990); E. Gabba, *Dionysius and the History of Archaic Rome* (1991).

K. S. S.

historiography, Roman

historiography, Roman Presentation of the Roman past was firmly rooted in the Roman present. Historians proclaimed a desire to help and inspire contemporary readers in their public life (e.g. Sall. *Iug.* 4; Livy, pref. 10; Tac. *Ann.* 4. 32–3), and the past was often moulded to provide antecedents for contemporary events or rephrased in contemporary terms, sometimes for tendentious reasons, sometimes just to make the story more excitingly familiar. Roman writers were also more often public men than their Greek counterparts (e.g. *Cato (Censorius), *Sallust, C. *Asinius Pollio, *Tacitus (1)), and their contemporary narrative told of events in which they had played a part: the result was an emphasis on this recent history, which usually comprised the bulk even of those works which covered Rome's history from its foundation (*ab urbe condita*).

Still, historiography was not simply a masked version of the memoir. It aspired to tell the story of the Roman state, not just of an individual's experiences. At first this usually involved an outline of Rome's history from its beginnings, with special emphasis on the inspiring foundation stories. The result was an hourglass structure, with most space given to the beginnings and the present, and a sketchier account of the period in between: that is already visible in Q. *Fabius Pictor, traditionally the earliest

Roman historian, and survives in most of his *ab urbe condita* successors (including *Ennius, who did much to shape the Roman view of history). Another aspect, as Cicero (*De or.* 2. 51–3) ruefully observed, was the evocation of traditional Roman *annales* (see ANNALS). Writers may only rarely have consulted the *annales maximi* themselves, but the texture of such material—bare lists of omens, magistrates, triumphs, etc.—was still familiar; Cato fr. 77 and *Sempronius Asellio frs. 1–2 (both ed. Peter) protested at the historical inadequacy of such catalogues, but versions of these lists figured even in the developed genre, usually conferring an aura of tradition and antiquity. The annalistic structure, organizing material in a year-by-year fashion, also became regular.

Rome took her past seriously; it became part of that seriousness to insist that its history was told with suitable literary and rhetorical art (cf. Cic. *Leg.* 1. 5, *De or.* 2. 36). For Fabius Pictor and his early successors—L. *Cincius Alimentus, A. *Postumius Albinus, C. *Acilius—this meant writing in Greek, thus fitting Roman history into the mainstream of Hellenistic historical literature, which greatly influenced its Roman equivalent; the use of Greek also promoted the presentation of Rome to a cultured Greek audience as Rome advanced eastwards. The Latin prose genre was pioneered by M. *Porcius Cato (1), whose *Origines* extended the focus to the Italian cities, and L. *Cassius Hemina; but the change of languages did not end the influence of Greece, nor reduce the literary pretensions. From an early stage history drew a great deal from rhetoric, including many clear boons: an eye for evidence, a nose for bias, an alertness to arguments from probability, the capacity to impose structure on recalcitrant material. But rhetorical virtuosity also promoted the imaginative expansion of the past. Second- and first-cent. BC writers filled out the bare annalistic record with circumstantial narrative, sometimes creatively reconstructing what 'must have' happened, sometimes glorifying a family or providing a precedent, sometimes simply for artistic effect. The voluminous works of Cn. *Gellius in the 2nd cent. and *Valerius Antias in the 1st seem to have been particularly rich in such elaboration.

This should not obscure the commitment to discovering the truth, however much it might then be embellished and strengthened with supporting detail. Writers do discuss the reliability of questionable material, with varying critical acumen (e.g. Livy 2. 21, 6. 1, 38. 56–7; Tac. *Ann.* 4. 10–11, 13. 20); Livy's predecessors aspired to find out new facts as well as provide a new artistic veneer (pref. 2). There was no clear distinction between antiquarianism and historiography at least in the 2nd cent. BC, and even later writers show some respect for documentary sources, e.g. C. *Licinius Macer and Q. *Aelius Tubero with the 'linen books', and perhaps Tacitus with the senatorial *acta. Still, Roman writers doubtless underestimated the sheer difficulty of discovering distant truth. Cicero (*De or.* 2. 62–3) insists on truthfulness as the first law of history, but gives most emphasis and thought to the rhetorical 'superstructure' (*exaedificatio*) built on this acknowledged 'foundation' (*fundamentum*); when *Pliny (2), *Ep.* 5. 8, considered writing ancient history, he considered it 'easy to find out about, but burdensome to bring together'. Writers might identify their sources' political bias; they rarely asked more searching questions about the texture and origin of their material.

Partisan bias was intensified by the struggles of the *Gracchan age, and these accentuated the concentration on the present. One aspect was a stepping up of the reinterpretation of the past in contemporary terms: this seems to have typified the work of

L. *Calpurnius Piso Frugi, then in the 1st cent. C. Licinius Macer. The more straightforward development was the tendency to omit earlier history altogether. Asellio combined this with a Polybian determination (see POLYBIUS (1)) to emphasize important interpretative strands; he apparently began in 146 BC, perhaps deliberately beginning where Polybius stopped. A number of writers carried on this practice of continuation, self-consciously producing a serial canon of Roman history: thus, it seems, *Sisenna continued Asellio, and Sallust's *Histories* continued Sisenna. A middle position, less exclusively contemporary but still eschewing the distant past, was occupied by Q. *Claudius Quadrigarius, who apparently began with the Gallic sack (387 BC), and earlier by L. *Coelius Antipater, whose work on the Second *Punic War introduced the historical monograph to Rome. Cicero (*Leg.* 1. 6–7) stresses the stylistic advances made by Coelius and Sisenna, but he felt that Rome was still waiting for her great national historian. Cicero never wrote the work himself.

*Sallust's *Bellum Catilinae* and *Bellum Iugurthinum* abandoned annalistic form and developed the monograph, using these two episodes to illustrate themes of wider significance, especially that of moral decline. The analysis is schematic, but is carried through with concentration and structural deftness; and Sallust moulded an appropriate style, concise, epigrammatic, rugged, and abrupt. Meanwhile *Caesar had written a different sort of monograph in his commentaries; their form (see COMMENTARII) leaves them outside the mainstream, but he still adapted techniques from historiographic rhetoric to fit his insidiously persuasive plainness of manner. C. Asinius Pollio wrote of the Civil War (between Caesar and *Pompey) and its antecedents, beginning with 60 BC. His incisive and independent analysis influenced the later Greek versions of *Appian and *Plutarch.

Pollio was less influential in Rome itself, largely because *Livy's 142-book *ab urbe condita* came to dominate the field. The great Roman history had been written at last. Livy offered something new, with a more even treatment of past and present: the great bulk of his history was pre-contemporary, partly, as he explains in the preface, because decline was relatively recent, and the best ethical examples were to be found in the earlier centuries. His moralizing is, however, more than Roman bias; it is also a form of explanation, isolating the strengths which carried Rome to its success, and might yet prove her salvation. The preface suggests that his contemporary books may have projected a less rosy view of Rome's morality, with degeneration explaining the less happy developments of the last century.

As in other genres, an Augustan classic had a stifling effect, and Livy's bulky eminence deterred rivals. History too changed, and the early Principate shows writers balancing traditional forms with a new world where the achievements of the Roman people, with the annual rhythm of changing magistracies, no longer captured the central themes of imperial reality. *Velleius Paterculus controlled his recent narrative around leading individuals, Caesar, *Augustus, and *Tiberius, and treated his material with rhetorical exuberance. His enthusiasm for the new world contrasted with A. *Cremutius Cordus' nostalgia for the old, and Cremutius paid with his life; the elder Seneca (see ANNAEUS SENECA (1), L.) dealt more safely with the transition from republic to Principate. *Trogus had earlier set Roman history in its universal context; *Hyginus (1) and *Valerius Maximus collected *exempla*; at some point Quintus *Curtius Rufus turned to Greece, and wrote in Roman style about *Alexander (3) the Great's heroics. A more traditional style was followed by *Aufidius Bassus and his continuator *Pliny (1) the Elder, though their general histories were complemented by detailed studies of particular wars. M. *Servilius Nonianus, *Cluvius Rufus, and *Fabius Rusticus also wrote substantial works.

*Tacitus (1)'s achievement is accentuated by this background. In many ways he was highly traditional. He kept the annalistic form; he chose relatively recent events; he wrote of senate and generals, not just emperors and courts. Yet the old forms are at odds with their content, so often pointing the contrast with the republic. The annual rhythms are overridden by the impact of emperors and their changing characters; further themes cut across the years and reigns—the power of advisers and the great ladies of the court, the regrettable necessity of one-man rule in a world unfit to rule itself, the inert senators who exchange hypocrisies with their prince. Brilliant rhetorical sharpness and devastating analysis serve each other well. Livy, at least in his surviving books, was the historian of a romanticized past; Tacitus exposed dispiriting reality.

Tacitus defied imitation as much as did Livy. Imperial historiography was always in danger of collapsing into imperial biography; that had been clear since Velleius, and from the 2nd cent. AD biography dominated the field (see BIOGRAPHY, ROMAN; HISTORIA AUGUSTA). The classical historians stimulated epitomes (*Ampelius, *Justin, *Eutropius (1), *Festus, *Obsequens) or at most rhetorical reformulation (*Florus, *Granius Licinianus, *Exsuperantius); they were not imitated until the last flowering of the genre with *Ammianus Marcellinus, who finally addressed a great theme, and was adequate to the task. See also LATIN, MEDIEVAL.

The standard edition of the fragments is still, remarkably, H. Peter, *HRRel.*; the early writers also figure in *FGrH* nos. 809–15. E. Badian, in T. A. Dorey (ed.), *Latin Historians* (1966), and E. Rawson, *Intellectual Life in the late Roman Republic* (1985), ch. 15, provide the best surveys of the republican tradition. See also B. W. Frier, *Libri Annales Pontificum Maximorum: The Origins of the Annalistic Tradition* (1979); T. P. Wiseman, *Clio's Cosmetics* (1979); and several papers of E. Rawson collected in *Roman Culture and Society* (1991). On style see A. D. Leeman, *Orationis Ratio* (1963). A. J. Woodman, *Rhetoric in Classical Historiography* (1988) is a subtle treatment of artistic embellishment; P. A. Brunt, in *Studies in Greek History and Thought* (1993), 181 ff., insists on the commitment to truth. E. Noè, *Storiografia imperiale pretacitiana* (1984), traces developments in the early empire. C. Fornara, *The Nature of History in Ancient Greece and Rome* (1988), brings together the two cultures. V. Pöschl, *Römische Geschichtsschreibung*, Wege der Forschung 90 (1969), collects important articles. See also works cited under the individual authors mentioned.   C. B. R. P.

history of classical scholarship See SCHOLARSHIP, ANCIENT and SCHOLARSHIP, CLASSICAL, HISTORY OF.

Hittites People of ancient Anatolia, known principally from excavations at *Hattuša, where their royal archives of thousands of *cuneiform clay tablets were discovered. The term 'Hittite', adapted from the OT ḥtym, derives ultimately from the central Anatolian land of *Hatti*. As the chief language of the Hattuša archives, Hittite was deciphered in 1915 and recognized as Indo-European, forming with Luwian and Palaic, which are also known from Hattuša, the Anatolian group of Indo-European, its oldest known branch. Besides the cuneiform script, Hittite kings also used an epichoric hieroglyphic for writing monumental inscriptions in Luwian. See ANATOLIAN LANGUAGES.

Hittite history divides into the Old Kingdom (*c.*1650–1500 BC), Middle Kingdom (*c.*1500–1400), and Empire (*c.*1400–1200). Following the establishment of the authority of Hattuša in central Anatolia, the Hittite kings conquered and dominated *Syria. At the fall of the Hittite empire, Hattuša was destroyed and the Hittite tradition of cuneiform literacy discontinued.

'Neo-Hittite' states survived in SE Anatolia and north Syria, continuing the traditions of Hittite culture and writing monumental inscriptions in hieroglyphic Luwian. These states flourished from the 10th to the 8th cent. BC, but were ultimately destroyed and colonized by the Assyrian empire, at which point the Hittites disappear from history. See ASIA MINOR, pre-classical.

O. R. Gurney, *The Hittites*, rev. edn. (1990). J. D. Ha.

Homer The ancient world attributed the two *epics, the *Iliad* and the *Odyssey*, the earliest and greatest works of Greek literature, to the poet Homer. Against this general consensus a few scholars at *Alexandria (1) argued for different authorship of the two poems; and modern critics, in the 150 years after Wolf (1795), went further and questioned the unity of authorship of each poem. However, the difficulties on which these 'analysts' based their discussions have been resolved through a greater understanding of oral poetry, and now most scholars see each as the work of one author. Whether he was the same for both remains uncertain. They have a great deal of common phraseology, but the *Odyssey* is less archaic in language and more repetitive in content, it views the gods rather differently, and for a few common things it uses different words. Such changes might occur in the lifetime of one person. As nothing reliable is known about Homer, perhaps the question is not important.

There is some agreement to date the poems in the second half of the 8th cent. BC, with the *Iliad* the earlier, about 750, the *Odyssey* about 725. This was the age of colonization in the Greek world (see COLONIZATION, GREEK), and it may be no accident that the *Iliad* shows an interest in the north-east, towards the Black (*Euxine) Sea, while much of the *Odyssey* looks towards the west. In *Od*. 6. 7–10 many have seen an echo of the founding of a Greek colony. As to Homer himself, the *Iliad* at least suggests a home on the east side of the *Aegean Sea, for storm winds in a simile blow over the sea from *Thrace, from the north and west (9. 5), and the poet seems familiar with the area near *Miletus (2. 461) as well as that round *Troy (12. 10–33). Moreover, the predominantly Ionic flavour of the mixed dialect of the poems suits the cities of the *Ionian migration on the other side of the Aegean. *Chios and *Smyrna have the strongest claims to have been his birthplace.

2. The *Iliad* is the longer of the two by a third, consisting of over 15,600 lines, divided into 24 books. The book division seems to have been later than the original composition, although the books do in many cases represent distinct episodes in the plot (e.g. books 1, 9, 12, 16, 22, 24). There is now broad agreement that we have the poem virtually as it was composed, with the exception of book 10, where the evidence for later addition is strong. For the rest, an individual intelligence is shown by the theme of the anger of *Achilles, begun in the quarrel with *Agamemnon in 1, kept before us in the Embassy of 9, transferred from Agamemnon to *Hector in 18, and resolved in the consolation of *Priam, Hector's father, in 24; also by the tight time-scale of the epic, for, in place of a historical treatment of the Trojan War (see TROY), the *Iliad*, from book 2 to 22, records merely four days of fighting from the tenth year, separated by two days of truce. Even the beginning and end add only a few weeks to the total.

Thus the action is concentrated, but the composition subtly expands to include the whole war, with echoes from the beginning in books 2 to 4, and the final books repeatedly looking forward to the death of Achilles and the fall of Troy. The centre is occupied by a single day of battle between 11 and 18, with the Trojans temporarily superior, Greek leaders wounded, their strongest and most mobile fighter (Achilles) disaffected, only Ajax (see AIAS (1)) and some warriors of the second rank holding the defence. The turning-point is in 16, when *Patroclus, acting on a suggestion from *Nestor in 11, persuades Achilles to let him go to the rescue of their comrades, and thus starts the sequence that leads to his own death (16), Achilles' return (18), Hector's death (22), and the conclusion of the epic (24).

3. High among the qualities of the *Iliad* is a vast humanity, which justifies comparison with Shakespeare. The poet understands human behaviour and reactions. There are numerous well-differentiated portraits of leading figures, introduced on the Greek side in the first four books, whose successes in action reinforce their heroic status, and whose personal feelings and relationships are expressed in the very frequent speeches. Figures of the second rank (e.g. Meriones, *Antilochus) support the leaders; and a large number of minor characters, who appear only to be killed, add a sense of the pathos and waste of war, through background details, particularly reference to families at home. The Trojans have their leaders too, but their efforts are essentially defensive, and the desperate situation of their city, and the threat to the women and children, contrast with the more straightforward heroics of the Greeks. Three women of Troy, *Hecuba, *Andromache, and *Helen, appear at key moments in books 6 and 24, the first two also in 22.

There is also what Pope called 'invention', a constant brilliance of imagination infusing the reports of action, speeches of the characters, and descriptions of the natural world. The language has a kind of perfection, due to a combination of phrases worn smooth by traditional use and the taste and judgement of the poet; and features which had been technical aids to the oral bard seem to have assumed the form of art in the *Iliad*—the use of formulae and repeated story patterns, ring-composition in the construction of speeches, the pictorial effects of extended similes.

4. The *Odyssey*, about 12,000 lines long, was probably composed in its present form in imitation of the already existing *Iliad*. Its 24 books show exact construction. Four books set the scene in *Ithaca ten years after the end of the war, and send Odysseus' son *Telemachus to two of the most distinguished survivors, Nestor at *Pylos and *Menelaus at *Sparta, in search of news of his father. The next four show Odysseus himself released from the island of *Calypso and arriving at the land of the Phaeacians (see SCHERIA), a half-way house between the fairy-tale world of his adventures and the real world of Ithaca which awaits him. There, in 9 to 12, he recounts his adventures to the Phaeacians. That completes the first half; the second is devoted to Odysseus' return home, the dangers he faces, and his eventual slaughter of the suitors of his wife *Penelope. In book 15, the two strands of the first half are brought together, when Telemachus returns from Sparta and joins his father.

For reasons difficult to guess, the quality of composition fades at the end, from 23. 296, which the Alexandrian scholars *Aristophanes (2) and *Aristarchus (2) confusingly describe as the 'end' of the *Odyssey*. However, at least two parts of the 'continuation' (i.e. what follows 23. 296) are indispensable for the completion of the story—the recognition of Odysseus by his old father Laertes, and the avoidance of a blood feud with the relatives of the dead suitors.

5. The *Odyssey* is a romance, enjoyable at a more superficial level than the heroic/tragic *Iliad*. We can take sides, for the good

people are on one side, the bad on the other. Even the massacre of the suitors and the vengeance on the servants who had supported them are acceptable in a story of this kind. The epic depends very much more than the *Iliad* on a single character; and Odysseus has become a seminal figure in European literature, with eternal human qualities of resolution, intellectual curiosity, and love of home. Apart from books 9 to 12, the settings are domestic, Ithaca, Pylos, Sparta, and Scheria (the land of the Phaeacians). The effect of this is that the gentler qualities of politeness, sensitivity, and tact come into play, as in the delicate interchanges between Odysseus and *Nausicaa (the princess on Scheria) and her parents. On the other hand, the boorish behaviour of the suitors shows a break-down of the social order.

For many readers the adventures are the high point. The *Lotus-eaters, Cyclops (see CYCLOPES), king of the winds, cannibal giants, witch *Circe, *Sirens, *Scylla (1), and Charybdis are part of the *folk-tale element in western consciousness. They are prefaced by a piratical attack on a people in *Thrace, near Troy, and concluded on the island of the Sun, an episode which results in the elimination of Odysseus' surviving companions, leaving him alone to face the return home. In the middle, in book 11, comes the visit to the Underworld, where he sees figures from the past and receives a prophecy of the future.

The combination of precision of observation and descriptive imagination is on a par with the *Iliad*; examples are Odysseus in the Cyclops' cave, Odysseus in his own house among the suitors of his wife, the recognition by his old dog *Argos (1*d*). One gets the impression, however, more strongly with the *Odyssey* than the *Iliad*, that the tale has been told many times before, and some superficial inconsistencies may be the effect of variant versions (e.g. the abortive plans for the removal of the arms in 16. 281–98).

6. The dactylic hexameter has a complex structure, with from twelve to seventeen syllables in the lines, and some precise metrical requirements. Milman Parry demonstrated that features of composition, notably pervasive repetition in the phraseology, derive from the practice of illiterate oral bards, who would learn the traditional phrases (formulae) in their years of apprenticeship; see ORALITY. This explains many aspects that worried analytical critics since the days of the *Alexandrians; for repetition of a half-line, line, or sequence of lines had been taken by readers used to the practice of later poets as evidence for corruption in the text, and an adjective used inappropriately had seemed to be a fault, instead of the inevitable consequence of the use of formulae.

Of equal significance to the repetition of formulaic phrases in the composition of oral poetry is the repetitive, though flexible, use of what are called typical scenes, patterns in the story, sometimes described as 'themes'. These range from the four arming-scenes in the *Iliad* (in books 3, 11, 16, 19), scenes of arrival and departure, performance of sacrifices, descriptions of fighting, to the repeated abuse directed at Odysseus in the second half of the *Odyssey*. Such 'themes' performed a parallel function to the formulae, giving the experienced bard material for the construction of his songs in front of an audience.

Virtually all scholars now accept that oral poetry theory has added to our understanding. Difference remains about whether Homer himself was an illiterate bard, or whether his position at the end of a long tradition shows a bard using the possibilities of literacy while still retaining the oral techniques. The ultimate problem of the survival of the two epics is inextricably bound up with this question. Three possibilities divide the field. Either the poet composed with the help of writing, the Greek alphabet having become available at just the right time; or the poems were recorded by scribes, the poet himself being illiterate; or they were memorized by a guild of public reciters (*rhapsodes) for anything up to 200 years (there being evidence for a written text in Athens in the 6th cent.).

7. The language in which the poems are composed contains a mixture of forms found in different areas of the Greek world. The overall flavour is Ionic, the dialect spoken on *Euboea, other islands of the eastern Aegean such as Chios, and on the mainland of Asia Minor opposite them. Attic Greek was a subdivision of Ionic, but Atticisms in the epic dialect are rare and superficial. Second in importance to Ionic in the amalgam is Aeolic, the dialect of north Greece (*Boeotia and *Thessaly) and the northern islands such as *Lesbos. Where Aeolic had a different form from Ionic, the Aeolic form mostly appears as an alternative to the Ionic in the epic language when it has a different metrical value. More deeply embedded are certain words and forms which belonged to the dialect of southern Greece in the Mycenaean age, sometimes described as Arcado-Cypriot, because it survived into historical times in those two widely separated areas of the Greek world. See DIALECTS, GREEK; GREEK LANGUAGE.

The historical implications of all this are obscure. The geographical location during the Mycenaean age of the speakers of what later became Ionic and Aeolic was necessarily different from that in historical times; and the dialects themselves obviously developed differently in different areas. What is clear, however, is that the linguistic picture is consistent with that presented by oral theory. Some features are very ancient (often preserved in the formulaic phrases), some quite recent. An important conclusion is that late linguistic forms are not to be seen as post-Homeric interpolations, but more probably come from the language of the poet himself, while earlier ones had reached him through the tradition. It is noted that the similes in the *Iliad* contain a high proportion of 'late' forms.

8. The assumed date of the Trojan war falls in the 13th cent. BC, towards the end of the Mycenaean age; for the Mycenaean palaces on the mainland were destroyed from about 1200. There is thus a gap of some four and a half centuries between the date of composition of the *Iliad* (about 750) and the legendary past which is its setting. The 8th cent. is essentially more important for the epics than the 13th; but the history of the Mycenaean age and of the shadowy times that lay between is naturally of the greatest interest. Here archaeologist and historian combine. We have the extraordinary discoveries of Schliemann at *Mycenae, and the excavations at Troy itself by Schliemann (1870–90), Blegen (1932–8), and Korfmann (1981–   ). Historical evidence from the 13th cent. has come to the surface. It is, however, unsafe to assume too close a connection with Homer. For the passage of time, and a retrospective view of a heroic age, have moved the picture nearer to fiction than reality. Only fossilized memories of the Mycenaean age survive in his work.

After the destruction of the palaces a long Dark Age intervened, lightened to some extent recently by the discovery at *Lefkandi in Euboea of a city with important trade connections in the 10th and 9th cents. It must have been during the Dark Age that heroic poetry developed and spread, even if (as seems probable) it originated in the Mycenaean age. Historians see in the epics reflections of the society and political aspirations of this period, even of the 8th cent. See GREECE, PREHISTORY AND HISTORY.

9. Hexameter poetry continued after Homer, with Hesiod and the *Homeric Hymns*, and the poems of the *Epic Cycle, which

described the two legendary wars of the heroic age, those against Thebes and Troy. The Theban epics are lost, but for the Trojan we have summaries of the contents of six poems (*Cypria*, *Aethiopis*, *Little Iliad*, *Sack of Troy* (*Iliu Persis*), *Returns* (*Nostoi*), *Telegony* (*Telegonia*), which had been fitted round the *Iliad* and *Odyssey* to create a complete sequence from the marriage of *Peleus and *Thetis to the death of Odysseus. The summaries, attributed to 'Proclus' (perhaps a grammarian of the 2nd cent. AD), are found in some manuscripts of the *Iliad*. These cyclic epics were obviously later than the Homeric poems, and from a time when oral composition had ceased and public performance was by rhapsodes, not traditional bards. Their significance for us is that they represent the subject-matter of heroic poetry as it was before Homer; for the *Iliad* itself, being the individual creation of a poet of genius, was not typical. Thus, by a time reversal, the partially known later material can make some claim to priority over the earlier. A school of 'neoanalysts' argues that episodes in books 8 (rescue of Nestor), 17 (recovery of the body of Patroclus), 18 (mourning of Thetis), and 23 (funeral games) echo situations connected with Achilles in the repertoire of the oral bards, which later appeared in the cyclic *Aethiopis*. The importance of this is that it seems to give us an insight into the creativity of the *Iliad* poet. See EPIC.

TEXT *Iliad*: ed. T. W. Allen (1931). *Odyssey*: ed. P. Von der Mühll (3rd edn. 1961); T. W. Allen (2nd edn. 1917–19).

COMMENTARY *Iliad*: G. S. Kirk and others (1985–93). *Odyssey*: A. Heubeck and others (It. edn. 1981–6; Eng. edn. 1988–92).

TRANSLATION *Iliad*: R. Lattimore (1951; M. M. Willcock, *A Companion to the Iliad* (1976)), M. Hammond (1987). *Odyssey*: R. Lattimore (1965; P. V. Jones, *Homer's Odyssey: A Companion to the English Translation of R. Lattimore* (1988)); W. Shewring (1980); E. V. Rieu (2nd edn. 1991).

GRAMMAR P. Chantraine, *Grammaire homérique*, 2 vols.: 1 (3rd edn. 1958), 2 (2nd edn. 1963).

CRITICISM U. von Wilamowitz-Moellendorff, *Die Ilias und Homer* (1916); W. Schadewaldt, *Iliasstudien* (1938; 3rd edn. 1966); J. T. Kakridis, *Homeric Researches* (1949); G. Strasburger, *Die kleinen Kämpfer der Ilias* (1954); D. L. Page, *History and the Homeric Iliad* (1959); W. Kullmann, *Die Quellen der Ilias* (1960); A. B. Lord, *The Singer of Tales* (1960); G. S. Kirk, *The Songs of Homer* (1962); W. Schadewaldt, *Von Homers Welt und Werk*, 4th edn. (1965); F. Matz and H.-G. Buchholz, *Archaeologia Homerica* (1967–); D. Lohmann, *Die Komposition der Reden in der Ilias* (1970); Milman Parry, *The Making of Homeric Verse* (writings from 1928 to 1937 collected by A. Parry (1971)); B. Fenik, *Studies in the Odyssey* (1974); A. Heubeck, *Die homerische Frage* (1974); N. Austin, *Archery at the Dark of the Moon* (1975); M. I. Finley, *The World of Odysseus*, 2nd edn. (1977); J. Griffin, *Homer on Life and Death* (1980); R. Janko, *Homer, Hesiod and the Hymns* (1982); I. J. F. de Jong, *Narrators and Focalizers* (1987); M. W. Edwards, *Homer, Poet of the Iliad* (1987).   M. M. W.

Homeridae, a guild devoted to reciting *Homer's poetry (Pind. *Nem.* 2. 1; Pl. *Phdr.* 252b) and telling stories about his life (Pl. *Resp.* 599e; Isoc. 10. 65; the extant 'Lives of Homer' must ultimately derive from this source). Ordinary *rhapsodes looked up to them as authorities and arbiters. They flourished in *Chios, and it is said that they were originally Homer's descendants (Harpocration, entry under Ὁμηρίδαι, quoting *Acusilaus and *Hellanicus), but later admitted others, who foisted much of their own work on Homer (schol. Pind. *Nem.* 2. 1; see CYNAETHUS). It was on them that Chios based its claim to Homer (Strab. 14. 1. 35; *Certamen* 13–15).

T. W. Allen, *Homer, the Origins and the Transmission* (1924), 42 ff.
                                                                M. L. W.

homicide See AREOPAGUS; LAW AND PROCEDURE, ATHENIAN and ROMAN (§ 3).

homonoia (ὁμόνοια), lit. 'oneness of mind', a political ideal first met in Greek writers of the later 5th cent. BC, essentially signifying either (1) concord or unanimity within the *polis and especially the avoidance of *stasis or (2) the achievement of *Panhellenic unity against the *barbarian (i.e. *Persia or *Macedonia). The ideal was sufficiently powerful (because so rarely attainable) to attract theoretical praise, as perhaps in the lost speech *On Concord* by *Gorgias (1) (408 BC?), and, from the 4th cent. BC on, personification (a woman) and worship, as with the Panhellenic cult of the 'Homonoia of the *Hellenes' at *Plataea (*BCH* 1975, 51 ff. = Austin no. 51 (trans.); see PERSIAN-WARS TRADITION). The restoration of internal *homonoia* is a constant theme of Hellenistic decrees for foreign *judges (see ARBITRATION, GREEK). In imperial times a mass of local coin-issues celebrated *homonoia* between pairs of cities, above all in Asia Minor, in some cases probably marking the resolution of neighbourly quarrels (see Dio Chrys. *Or.* 38. 22, 26–31). Internal *homonoia* remained a persistent theme of local Greek politics, preoccupying writers like *Plutarch, *Dio Cocceianus, and P. Aelius *Aristides. See CONCORDIA.

P. Funke, *Homonoia und Arche* (1980); R. Pera, *Homonoia sulle monete da Augusto agli Antonini* (1984); A. Sheppard, *Anc. Soc.* 1984–6, 229 ff.; H. Shapiro, *LIMC* 5. 1 (1990), 476–9: 'Homonoia' (iconography).
                                                                A. J. S. S.

homosexuality No Greek or Latin word corresponds to the modern term *homosexuality*, and ancient Mediterranean societies did not in practice treat homosexuality as a socially operative category of personal or public life. Sexual relations between persons of the same sex certainly did occur (they are widely attested in ancient sources), but they were not systematically distinguished or conceptualized as such, much less were they thought to represent a single, homogeneous phenomenon in contradistinction to sexual relations between persons of different sexes. That is because the ancients did not classify kinds of sexual desire or behaviour according to the sameness or difference of the sexes of the persons who engaged in a sexual act; rather, they evaluated sexual acts according to the degree to which such acts either violated or conformed to norms of conduct deemed appropriate to individual sexual actors by reason of their gender, age, and social status. It is therefore impossible to speak in general terms about ancient attitudes to 'homosexuality', or about the degree of its acceptance or toleration by particular communities, because any such statement would, in effect, lump together various behaviours which the ancients themselves kept rigorously distinct and to which they attached radically divergent meanings and values. (Exactly the same things could be said, of course, and with equal justification, about *heterosexuality.)

It is not illegitimate to employ modern sexual terms and concepts when interrogating the ancient record, but particular caution must be exercised in order not to import modern, western sexual categories and ideologies into the interpretation of the ancient evidence. Hence, students of classical antiquity need to be clear about when they intend the term 'homosexual' descriptively—i.e. to denote nothing more than same-sex sexual relations—and when they intend it substantively or normatively—i.e. to denominate a discrete kind of sexual psychology or behaviour, a positive species of sexual being, or a basic component of 'human sexuality'. The application of 'homosexuality' (and 'heterosexuality') in a substantive or normative sense to sexual expression in classical antiquity is not advised.

Greek and Roman men (whose sexual subjectivity receives

vastly greater attention in the extant sources than does women's) generally understood sex to be defined in terms of sexual penetration and phallic pleasure, whether the sexual partners were two males, two females, or one male and one female. The physical act of sex itself required, in their eyes, a polarization of the sexual partners into the categories of penetrator and penetrated as well as a corresponding polarization of sexual roles into 'active' and 'passive'. Those roles in turn were correlated with superordinate and subordinate social status, with masculine and feminine gender styles, and (in the case of males, at least) with adulthood and adolescence. Phallic insertion functioned as a marker of male precedence; it also expressed social domination and seniority. The isomorphism of sexual, social, gender, and age roles made the distinction between 'activity' and 'passivity' paramount for categorizing sexual acts and actors of either gender; the distinction between homosexual and heterosexual contacts could still be invoked for certain purposes (e.g. Ov. *Ars am.* 2. 682–4; Achilles Tatius 2. 33–8), but it remained of comparatively minor taxonomic and ethical significance.

Any sexual relation that involved the penetration of a social inferior (whether inferior in age, gender, or status) qualified as sexually normal for a male, irrespective of the penetrated person's anatomical sex, whereas to *be* sexually penetrated was always potentially shaming, especially for a free male of citizen status (e.g. Tac. *Ann.* 11. 36). Roman custom accordingly placed the sons of Roman citizens off limits to men. In Classical Athens, by contrast, free boys could be openly courted, but a series of elaborate protocols served to shield them from the shame associated with bodily penetration, thereby enabling them to gratify their male suitors without compromising their future status as adult men.

Pederasty Paiderastia is the word that the Greeks themselves employed to refer to the sexual pursuit of 'boys' (*paides* or *paidika*; Lat. *pueri*) by 'men' (*andres*; *viri*). The conventional use of the term 'boy' to designate a male in his capacity as an object of male desire is somewhat misleading, because males were customarily supposed to be sexually desirable to other males mostly in the period of life that extended from around the time of puberty (which probably began quite late in the ancient Mediterranean) to the arrival of the full beard (see AGE); the first appearance of down on a boy's cheeks represented to some the peak of his sexual attractiveness, whereas the presence of more fully developed hair on the male face, buttocks, and thighs typically aroused in men intense sexual distaste. By 'boy', then, the ancients designated what we would call an adolescent rather than a child. Moreover, 'man' and 'boy' can refer in both Greek and Latin to the senior and junior partners in a pederastic relationship, or to those who play the respective sexual roles appropriate to each, regardless of their actual ages. A boy on the threshold of manhood might assume the sexual role of a boy in relation to a man as well as the sexual role of a man in relation to another boy (e.g. Xen. *Symp.* 8. 2), but he might not play both roles in relation to the same person. Although some Athenian men may have entertained high-minded intentions towards the boys they courted, it would be hazardous to infer from their occasional efforts at self-promotion (Pl. *Symp.* 184c–185b; Aeschin. *In Tim.* 132–40) that Greek pederasty aimed chiefly at the education and moral improvement of boys instead of at adult sexual pleasure.

Sexual relationships between women are occasionally described by male authors in the vocabulary used to articulate distinctions of age and sexual role in pederasty (e.g. Plut. *Lyc.* 18.

4, *Amat.* 763a), but solid evidence for a comparable polarization of sexual roles in female same-sex sexual relations is lacking.

Periodization The most remarkable feature of ancient same-sex sexual relations is the longevity of the age-structured, role-specific, hierarchical pattern that governed all respectable and virtually all recorded sexual relationships between males in classical antiquity. There is evidence for the existence of such a pattern as early as Minoan times and as late as the end of the Roman empire in the west. *Homer, to be sure, did not portray *Achilles and *Patroclus as lovers (although some Classical Athenians thought he implied as much (Aesch. frs. 135, 136 Radt; Pl. *Symp.* 179e–180b; Aeschin. *In Tim.* 133, 141–50)), but he also did little to rule out such an interpretation, and he was perhaps less ignorant of pederasty than is sometimes alleged: he remarks that *Ganymedes was carried off to be the gods' cupbearer because of his beauty (*Il.* 20. 232–5) and he singles out for special mention the man who was—with the exception of Achilles—the most beautiful man in the Greek host (*Il.* 2. 673–4). (Male beauty contests are well documented in the Greek world from Hellenistic times; they may have been institutionalized earlier.)

Sexual relations between males at Rome conformed closely to the age-differentiated, role-specific pattern documented for Greece. The traditional belief that Roman men regarded 'homosexuality' with repugnance and that its presence at Rome was the result of Greek influence is mistaken. To be sure, sexually receptive or effeminate males were harshly ridiculed, and the public courtship of free boys (which the Romans thought of as 'Greek love') was discountenanced as severely as was the seduction of free girls; however, the sexual penetration of male prostitutes or slaves by conventionally masculine élite men, who might purchase slaves expressly for that purpose, was not considered morally problematic. We do hear a good deal more from Roman sources about adult pathics (Sen. *QNat.* 1. 16. 1–3; Petron. *Sat.* 92. 7–9, 105. 9; Juv. *Sat.* 9) and about the sexual pursuit by adult males of male beloveds who had passed beyond the stage of boyhood (Suet. *Galb.* 22). None the less, as in Greece so in Rome did masculinity consist not in the refusal of all sexual contact with males but in the retention of an insertive sexual role and in the preservation of bodily (particularly anal) inviolability.

'Greek Love' The fullest testimony for Greek pederastic norms and practices derives from Classical Athens, but surviving evidence from elsewhere in the Greek world largely accords with the Athenian model. Greek custom carefully differentiated the sexual roles assigned to men and to boys in their erotic relations with one another. Good-looking boys supposedly exerted a powerful sexual appeal that men, even when good-looking, did not. Accordingly, men were assumed to be motivated in their pursuit of boys by a passionate sexual desire (*erōs*) which the boys who were the targets of that desire did not conventionally share, whence the Greek habit of referring to the senior partner in a pederastic relationship as a *subject* of desire, or 'lover' (*erastēs*), and the junior partner as an *object* of desire, or 'beloved' (*erōmenos*). A boy who chose to 'gratify' (*charizesthai*) the passion of his lover might be actuated by a variety of motives, including (on the baser end of the scale) material gain or social climbing and (on the higher end) affection, esteem, respect, and non-passionate love (*philia*), but—although a man might stimulate a boy sexually—neither sexual desire nor sexual pleasure represented an acceptable motive for a boy's compliance with the sexual demands of his lover. Even pederastic relationships characterized by mutual love and tenderness retained an irreducible element of emotional

and erotic asymmetry, as is indicated by the consistent distinction which the Greeks drew in such contexts between the lover's *erōs* and the beloved's *philia*. By contrast, women were believed capable of returning their male lovers' sexual passion, and so could be spoken of as exhibiting *anterōs* ('counter-desire')—a term never applied in an erotic sense in the Classical period to boys, except by *Plato (1) in a highly tendentious philosophical context (*Phdr.* 255c–e).

The asymmetries structuring pederastic relationships reflected the underlying division of sexual labour. Whereas a boy, lacking his lover's erotic motivation, was not expected to play what the Greeks considered an 'active' sexual role—he was not expected, that is, to seek a sexual climax by inserting his penis into an orifice in his lover's body—a man was expected to do just that, either by thrusting his penis between the boy's thighs (which was considered the most respectful method, because it did not violate the boy's bodily integrity) or by inserting it into his rectum. Respectable erotic relations between men and boys preserved the social fiction, to which some honourable lovers may even have adhered in actual practice, that sexual penetration of the boy took place only between the legs (the so-called intercrural position), never in the anus or—what was even worse—in the mouth. It was not a question of what people actually did in bed (the boy was conventionally assumed to be anally receptive to his older lover) so much as how they behaved and talked when they were out of bed. Hence the story about Periander, the 6th-cent. BC tyrant of *Ambracia, who asked his boy, 'Aren't you pregnant yet?': the boy, who had apparently raised no objection to being anally penetrated on repeated occasions, was sufficiently outraged by this question when it was put to him aloud—and doubtless in the presence of others—that he responded by killing the tyrant in order to recover his masculine honour (Plut. *Amat.* 768f).

The Greek insistence on drawing a clear distinction between the beloved's *philia* and the lover's *erōs* reveals its purpose in this context. Whatever a boy might do in bed, it was crucial that he not seem to be motivated by passionate sexual desire for his lover, because sexual desire for an adult man signified the desire to be penetrated, to be subordinate—to be like a woman, whose pleasure in sexual submissiveness disqualified her from assuming a position of social and political mastery. A boy who indicated that he derived any enjoyment from being anally receptive risked identifying himself as a *kinaidos*, a pathic, a catamite: no modern English word can convey the full force of the ancient stigma attached to this now-defunct identity. Similarly, a man who retained as his beloved a boy on the threshold of manhood thereby cast doubt on his own masculinity, for if the grown boy was not himself a *kinaidos*, then the man who continued to love him must be. And since both Greek men and Greek women (if we credit the desires imputed to the latter by male authors) liked males who looked young, any man who either did look or who tried to look younger than his years exposed himself to the suspicion of harbouring pathic desires or adulterous intentions.

Origins and Causes Scholars have speculated about the factors responsible for the visibility and cultural prestige accorded to pederasty in Greek culture. Among the explanations commonly advanced are: (1) Greek males were driven to seek romance and sexual gratification with other males, *faute de mieux*, by the seclusion and enforced intellectual impoverishment of *women; (2) pederasty was a vestige of earlier male *initiation rituals which featured sexual contact between men and boys. Against the first

explanation it may be objected that the seclusion of women was less an actual social practice than an occasional social ideal, that the plentiful availability of both male and female prostitutes (see PROSTITUTION, SECULAR) argues for the existence in some men of specifically pederastic preferences, and that many societies rigorously separate male and female social spheres without also promoting pederasty. In assessing the limited explanatory value of the initiatory model, it is important to notice, first of all, that pederastic *rites of passage are more fully (though still scantily) attested in Crete and the Peloponnese than in Attica; next, that Classical Athenian pederasty proceeded by means of elective pair-bonding, not by the compulsory induction of entire *age classes (individual boys had to be courted, unless they were prostitutes, and they could always withhold their consent); and, finally, that pederastic sex was not a prerequisite for admission to any rank or group membership in Athenian society, and it could in fact lead to the forfeiture of certain privileges, if a boy conducted himself disreputably. Moreover, recent comparative work in ethnography has shifted the burden of explanation by establishing that age-structured and role-specific patterns of same-sex sexual contact are relatively common in pre-industrial cultures, whereas the homosexual/heterosexual pattern is rare, and tends to be limited to the modern, western, industrialized world.

Lesbianism Evidence for sexual relations among women in antiquity is sparse, although ancient writers did on occasion represent women as erotically attracted to one another (e.g. Pl. *Symp.* 191e; Ov. *Met.* 9. 666–797). In an irony all too typical of the state of preservation of ancient sources, the earliest attestation of female homoerotic desire occurs in the work of a male author—namely, in the *partheneia* of the late-7th-cent. Spartan poet *Alcman, who wrote choral odes to be performed by a cohort of unmarried girls in which individual maidens extol the beauty and allure of named favourites among their leaders and age-mates (frs. 1, 3 Page, *PMG*). Further expressions of homoerotic desire can be found a few decades later in the fragmentary poetry of *Sappho, who came from *Mytilene on the island of Lesbos, whence the 19th cent. derived its euphemism for female homosexuality, 'lesbianism'. In antiquity, by contrast, at least from the 5th cent. BC, 'Lesbian' sex referred to fellatio and Sappho figured as a prostitute; the earliest association of Lesbos with female homoeroticism dates to the 2nd cent. AD (Lucian, *Dial. meret.* 5. 2; cf., however, Anac. fr. 358 Page, *PMG*). The interpretation of Sappho's poems is complicated by the fact that no writer of the Classical period found their homoeroticism sufficiently remarkable to warrant mention (although a red-figure Attic hydria, attributed to the *Polygnotus group, from about 440 BC portrays Sappho in what may be a female homoerotic setting (Beazley, *ARV*² 1060, no. 145)); the earliest to touch on it were the Augustan poets of the late 1st cent. BC (Hor. *Carm.* 2. 13. 24–5; Ov. *Her.* 15. 15–19, *Tr.* 2. 365). So either Sappho's earlier readers and auditors saw nothing homoerotic in her poems or they saw nothing remarkable in Sappho's homoeroticism. The Sapphic tradition may have been revived by the Hellenistic poet *Nossis of Locri.

Perhaps the cultural predominance of the penetration model of sex obscured non-penetrative eroticism among conventionally feminine women, for which in any case there seems to have been no established terminology. The female same-sex sexual practice that imperial Greek and Roman writers alike singled out for comment was 'tribadism', the sexual penetration of women (and men) by other women, by means of either a dildo or a fantastically large clitoris. Although the word *tribas* is attested for the first time in Greek in the 2nd cent. AD, an equivalent Latin loan word crops up in the previous century (Phaedrus 4. 15(16). 1; Sen. *Controv.* 1. 2. 23) and the figure of the hypermasculine phallic woman may be considerably older. The tribade makes memorable appearances, though not always under that name, in imperial literature (Sen. *Ep.* 95. 21; Mart. 1. 90, 7. 67, 7. 70; Lucian *Dial. meret.* 5): she is represented as a shaven-headed butch, adept at wrestling, able to subjugate men and to satisfy women.

Deviance and Toleration Ancient sources are informed by the routine presumption that most free adult males, whatever their particular tastes, are at least capable of being sexually attracted by both good-looking boys and good-looking women; such attraction was deemed normal and natural. No specifically sexual stigma attached to the act of sexual penetration of a woman, boy, foreigner, or slave by a man, although certain kinds of sexual licence incurred disfavour (the expenditure of extravagant sums of money on prostitutes of either sex, the corruption of free boys, and the adulterous pursuit of citizen women were regarded as signs of bad character in a man and even as actionable offences at Athens; the seduction of free youth of either sex was criminalized as *stuprum* at Rome). Thus, it would not have been unexpected to ask of a man who confessed to being in love whether his object was a boy or a woman, and at least one surviving marriage-contract from Hellenistic *Egypt (PTeb. 1. 104) commits the prospective husband not to maintain either a female concubine or a male beloved. The most glamorous and boastworthy same-sex liaison in Greece was that between a free man and a free boy of good family, unaffected by considerations of material gain and untainted by suggestions of sexual degradation; a respectable citizen could brag about such a relationship in the lawcourts. And the song of Harmodius and *Aristogiton, which celebrated the pederastic couple who killed one of the Pisistratids and thereby supposedly freed Athens from tyranny, functioned in the democratic period as something like the Athenian national anthem.

Not all expressions of same-sex eroticism were approved by the ancients. They did not have a concept of sexual perversion, but they did stigmatize forms of sexual behaviour which they considered shameful, unconventional, or unnatural. Plato is exceptional in treating pederasty (along with female homosexuality) as unnatural in the *Laws* (636b–c, 838–41), although some later moralizing writers do so treat it (along with other civilized luxuries such as warm baths and potted plants: Sen. *Ep.* 122. 7–8). Women who prefer women over men incur male disapproval from Hellenistic times (Asclepiades 7 (Gow–Page, *HE* 1. 46, no. 7)). But what principally seemed deviant to the ancients was sexual behaviour at odds with a person's gender identity and social status—that is, sexual receptivity in men and sexual insertivity in women, both interpreted as signs of gender inversion. Ancient writers occasionally speculated about the causes of inversion: their explanations range from ingenious physiological hypotheses (Arist. [*Pr.*] 4. 26; Phaedrus 4. 15(16)) to observations about the tyranny of pleasure (Pl. *Grg.* 494c–e) and imputations of pathology (Arist. *Eth. Nic.* 7. 5. 3–4 = 1148^{b}26–35; Caelius Aurelianus, *On chronic diseases* (ed. I. Drabkin), 4. 9). See EDUCATION; GYMNASIARCH; LOVE AND FRIENDSHIP; SEXUALITY.

K. J. Dover, *Greek Homosexuality* (1978), and *The Greeks & their Legacy* (1988), 115–34; H. Patzer, *Die griechische Knabenliebe* (1982); B. Sergent, *Homosexuality in Greek Myth* (1986; Fr. orig. 1982); M. Foucault, *The Use of Pleasure* (1985; Fr. orig. 1984), & *The Care of the Self* (1986; Fr. orig. 1984); M. Golden, *Phoenix* 1984, 308–24; J. Henderson, in M.

Grant & R. Kitzinger (eds.), *Civilization of the Ancient Mediterranean* (1988), 1249–63; M. B. Skinner, *Arethusa* 1989, 5–18; J. Hallett, *Yale Journal of Criticism* (1989); D. M. Halperin, *One Hundred Years of Homosexuality* (1990); J. J. Winkler, *The Constraints of Desire* (1990); C. A. Williams, 'Homosexuality and the Roman Man' (Diss. Yale, 1992); M. W. Gleason, *Making Men* (1995); P. F. Dorcey, *Before Lesbianism* (forthcoming); B. J. Brooten, *Love Between Women* (1996); K. De Vries, *Homosexuality & the Athenian Democracy* (forthcoming).   D. M. H.

honestiores The Romans made a broad distinction, which was at first social but acquired in the Principate and thereafter an increasing number of legal consequences, between an upper class usually termed *honestiores* and a lower class of *humiliores*. No legal definition of the two classes is found, and the allocation of an individual to one or the other was probably at the discretion of the court. The legal consequences lay in part in the private law, but were most marked in the criminal law, *honestiores* being subject to milder penalties than *humiliores* (rarely the death penalty, never death by crucifixion or *bestiis obicere*; *relegatio in insulam* in place of forced labour in the mines, etc.). The distinction is not the same as that drawn in the later empire between *potentiores* and *tenuiores*. The legal relevance of the latter distinction lies not in privileges conferred on the *potentiores*, but on the contrary in the restrictions which the legislator attempted to impose on their abuse of their wealth or position.

G. Cardascia, *Rev. Hist. de Droit* 1950, 305 ff., 461 ff.; P. Garnsey, *Social Status and Legal Privilege in the Roman Empire* (1970). See also STATUS, LEGAL AND SOCIAL, ROMAN.   B. N.

Honestus, of *Corinth, author of ten *epigrams in the Greek *Anthology and another dozen inscribed at *Thespiae, nine on statues of the *Muses, one on Livia *Drusilla.

Gow–Page, *GP* 2. 301–7; W. Peek, Γέρας Α. Κεραμοπούλλου (1953), 609–34; C. P. Jones, *Harv. Stud.* 1968, 249–55.   A. D. E. C.

honey (μέλι; *mel*), the chief sweetener known to the ancients, who understood apiculture (Arist. *Hist. an.* 623^{b}5–627^{b}22; Verg. *G.* bk. 4) and appreciated the different honey-producing qualities of flowers and localities. Thyme honey from *Hymettus in Attica was very famous, both for its pale colour and sweet flavour; Corsican, harsh and bitter; Pontic, poisonous and inducing madness (Dioscorides, *Materia medica* 2. 101–3). Honey was used in cooking, confectionery, and as a preservative. It was used in medicines, e.g. for coughs, ulcers, and intestinal parasites (Theophr. *Hist. pl.* 9. 11. 3, 18. 8). It had a very important role in religion, cult, and mythology. Its religious associations derive from the idea that it was a *ros caelestis* ('heavenly dew'), which fell on to flowers from the upper air for bees to gather (Arist. *Hist. an.* 553^{b}29–30). According to poets it dripped from trees in the *golden age (Ov. *Met.* 1. 111–12). It was used in *libations to the dead (Hom. *Il.* 23. 170), in rites for *Persephone and *Hades, for *Hestia, and in the cult of *Mithras. In literature honey was given to infants to impart qualities such as wisdom or eloquence. The infant *Plato (1) was fed with honey by bees (Cic. *Div.* 1. 78). *Zeus was called Melissaios from a similar legend of his Cretan birth. See also BEE-KEEPING.

RE 15. 364–84; W. Robert-Tornow, *De apium mellisque apud veteres significatione et symbolica et mythologica* (1893); H. M. Ransome, *The Sacred Bee in Ancient Times and Folklore* (1937); J. H. Waszink, *Biene und Honig als Symbol des Dichters in der griechisch-römischen Antike* (1974).   J. R. S.

Honorius (*RE* 3), b. AD 384, younger son of *Theodosius (2) I, who made him Augustus (393). From 395 he ruled the west but was dominated by *Stilicho and then, after an interlude of civilian rule under Olympius and Jovius, by *Constantius III whom

Honos and Virtus

Honorius made Augustus (421). While Honorius lived safely in *Ravenna, failure to pay *Alaric for his services led to three sieges of Rome (408–10), its sack (410), and the capture of Honorius's half-sister *Placidia, whom Athaulf, who led the Visigoths (see GOTHS) to Gaul (412), forced to marry him. Chaos in Gaul had followed the crossing of the Rhine by the *Vandals and others, who occupied Spain (409), to which the Visigoths withdrew (415); *Constantine III's usurpation led to loss of control in Britain. Other usurpers included Priscus Attalus, whom the Visigoths made emperor twice. Married in turn to both of Stilicho's daughters, Honorius died childless (423), his few political interventions having been generally disastrous.

> A. D. E. Cameron, *Claudian, Poetry and Propaganda at the Court of Honorius* (1970); J. Matthews, *Western Aristocracies and Imperial Court A.D. 364–425* (1975).   R. P. D.

Honos and **Virtus**, deities at Rome personifying military courage and its reward; their cult was selected for two major commemorative temples by successful generals: M. *Claudius Marcellus (1) after his conquest of *Syracuse (dedicated after some controversy by his son in 205 BC), and C. *Marius (1) after the Cimbric War. We know little of the latter (though it was large enough to hold the senate-meeting at which *Cicero was recalled from exile, Cic. *Sest.* 116), but Marcellus' temple outside the porta Capena was of some importance: richly equipped with his spoils, it survived well into the imperial period.

> H. H. Scullard, *Festivals and Ceremonies of the Roman Republic* (1981), 165–6.   N. P.

honour See HONOS; PHILOTIMIA.

hoplites (ὁπλῖται), Greek heavy infantry. Equipment included bronze helmet of varying shape, corslet, originally of bronze, but later of leather or linen, and bronze greaves; sometimes extras such as arm-guards. Most important was a circular shield of wood or stiffened leather, faced with bronze, about 80 cm. (*c.*30 in.) in diameter, held by inserting the left arm through a central band (*porpax*, πόρπαξ), and gripping a cord or strap at the rim (*antilabē*, ἀντιλαβή). Offensive weapons were a thrusting-spear, 2.5–3 m. (8–10 ft.) long, with iron point and butt, and short iron swords, sometimes straight, sometimes curved. The equipment was expensive and since hoplites were normally expected to provide their own, they had to be relatively wealthy.

They deployed for battle shoulder to shoulder, usually eight or more deep, each man relying on his right neighbour's shield for the protection of his right side, since the shield-grip meant that half the shield projected to the left. At a signal the *phalanx advanced at the double or at a walk, and when within spear-thrust, the front ranks stabbed at their opponents, usually overarm. But with the rear ranks possibly literally pushing against the backs of those in front, sooner or later the opposing lines crashed together and the frequently mentioned 'shoving' (ōthismos, ὠθισμός) began. When one or other side gave way, pursuit was not carried far, since once ranks broke, hoplites became much more vulnerable. Though the hoplite phalanx was unwieldy, it was formidable when driving forward, as the Persians found at the battles of *Marathon and *Plataea. It could be defeated by other troops if attacked in flank or rear, or if caught in broken terrain, but they had to be in overwhelming numbers and skilfully handled.

> V. Hanson, *The Western Way of War* (1989), *The Other Greeks* (1995), and (ed.), *Hoplites: The Ancient Greek Battle Experience* (1991).   J. F. La.

Horace (Quintus Horatius Flaccus) was born on 8 December 65 BC in *Venusia in *Apulia (mod. Venosa) and died on 27 November 8 BC (*Epist.* 1. 20. 26–7; Life). Thanks to the almost complete preservation of *Suetonius' Life and numerous biographical allusions in the poetry, we are relatively well informed about his life. His father was a *freedman (*Sat.* 1. 6. 6, 45–6), though this need not mean, as some have supposed, that he had come as a slave from the east. Even an Italian could have been enslaved as a result of the *Social War (3), in which Venusia was captured by Rome. Horace presents himself as brought up in the old Italian style (cf. *Sat.* 1. 4. 105–29 with Ter. *Ad.* 414–19) and his father may well have come from Italy itself. The father had a fairly small landholding in Venusia (*Sat.* 1. 6. 71) but in his role as *coactor* (public auctioneer) obtained what was clearly not an inconsiderable amount of money (*Sat.* 1. 6. 86, Life); otherwise he could not have afforded to send his son to Rome and then Athens for an education that was the equal of that of a typical upper-class Roman of the time (*Sat.* 1. 6. 76–80, *Epist.* 2. 1. 70 f.; Life). This ambitious education was clearly intended to help Horace to rise in society, and at first this plan met with success. While in Athens, Horace joined the army of *Brutus as a *tribunus militum* (*Sat.* 1. 6. 47 f.; Life), a post usually held by *equites (see TRIBUNI MILITUM). But all these high hopes were brought to nothing by the fall of Brutus and the loss of the family's property (*Epist.* 2. 2. 46–51). Horace counted himself lucky to be able to return to Italy, unlike many of his comrades-in-arms, and to obtain the reasonably respectable position of *scriba quaestorius* (*Sat.* 2. 6. 36 f.; Life; see APPARITORES). It was in this period that he wrote his first poems (*Epist.* 2. 2. 51 f.), which brought him into contact with *Virgil and *Varius Rufus. They recommended him to *Maecenas, then gathering around him a circle of writers; and when Maecenas accepted him into this circle in 38 BC (*Sat.* 1. 6. 52–62, 2. 6. 40–2), and later gave him the famous Sabine farm, his financial position was secure. His property put him in the higher reaches of the *equites* census (cf. *Sat.* 2. 7. 53) and he now possessed the leisure to devote himself to poetry. He was acquainted with many leading Romans, and on friendly terms with a considerable number of them, most notably his patron Maecenas. In his later years *Augustus also sought to be on close terms, as several letters written in a warm and candid tone attest (Life). But Horace knew well how to preserve his personal freedom. Augustus offered him an influential post on his personal staff (*officium epistularum*) but Horace turned this down (Life) and as *Epistle* 1. 7 demonstrates he showed a similar independence towards Maecenas.

Works
Epodes
The *Epodes* or *Iambi* (cf. *Epod.* 14. 7; *Epist.* 1. 19. 23) form a slender book of 17 poems. They include some of Horace's earliest poems, written before the encounter with Maecenas, but work on them continued throughout the 30s BC and poems 1 and 9 allude to the battle of *Actium: the collection as a whole seems to have been published around 30 BC. Horace's formal model was *Archilochus, the founder of *iambus*, to whom he joins *Hipponax (*Epod.* 6. 13 f.; *Epist.* 1. 19. 23–5). He thus introduced for the first time into Rome not only the metrical form of early Greek iambus, but also some of the matter (cf. *Epod.* 10, which is closely related to the disputed papyrus fragment Archilochus 79a Diels = Hipponax 115 West). See IAMBIC POETRY, GREEK and LATIN. Horace's adoption of this early form may be compared with the incorporation of classical and pre-classical motifs in the visual art of the day, but it did not represent a rejection of the

Callimachean principle (see CALLIMACHUS (3)) that every detail of a poem should be artistically controlled and contribute to the overall effect. Even the 'archaic' epodes are written in a style of painstaking elegance. The central theme of iambic poetry was traditionally invective, that is personal attack, mockery, and satire (*Epist*. 1. 19. 25, 30 f.; cf. Arist. *Poet*. 1448^b 26 ff.), and Horace may have taken up the genre in his affliction after the battle of *Philippi as a way of preserving his self-respect in hard times. But only some of the *Epodes* are *invectives (4, 5, 6, 8, 10, 12, 17), and even in these the targets are either anonymous or figures about whom we know next to nothing. Horace clearly avoids the sort of personal attacks on important contemporary figures that we find in *Catullus. A different aspect of early Greek poetry is taken up in *Epodes* 7 and 16. Just as the early Greek poets (including Archilochus: cf. fr. 109 West with *Epod*. 16. 17 ff.) on occasions addressed themselves to the general public, so in these poems Horace represents himself as warning and exhorting the Roman people. There are no iambic elements in the poems to Maecenas: *Epod*. 3 is a joke, *Epod*. 14 an excuse, and in *Epod*. 1 and 9 one friend talks to another in the context of the decisive struggles of 31 BC. Other epodes take up motifs from other contemporary genres (elegy in 11 and 15, pastoral in 2) but with significant alterations of tone: Horace ironically breaks the high emotional level of the models with a detached and distant *closure. *Epode* 13 anticipates a theme of the *Odes* (cf. *Carm*. 1. 7).

Satires

Contemporaneously with the *Epodes*, Horace composed his two books of *satires (*Satira*: 2. 1. 1, 2. 6. 17). He also calls them *Sermones*, 'conversations' (2. 3. 4, *Epist*. 1. 4. 1, 2. 1. 250, 2. 2. 60), which suits their loose colloquial tone that seems to slide from one subject to another almost at random. The first book contains ten satires, the second eight. The earliest datable reference is to the 'journey to *Brundisium' undertaken with Maecenas and his circle in 38 or 37 BC and described at length in *Sat*. 1. 5, the latest is to the settlement of veterans after the civil war in 30 BC (*Sat*. 2. 6. 55 f.). Some of the poems may have been written before 38, but there is no evidence that any are later than 30. Horace's model is *Lucilius (1), but he represents himself as determined to write with greater care and attention to form (*Sat*. 1. 4, 1. 10, 2. 1), and thus, again, as a follower of Callimachus (cf. especially *Sat*. 1. 10. 9–15, 67–74). Another difference from Lucilius is that Horace's satires are less aggressive. While the pugnacious poet of the 2nd cent. took sides in the political struggles of his time, Horace chooses a purely private set of themes. In *Sat*. 1. 4 and 2. 1 he represents personal abuse as a typical element in satire, but declares that he himself does not attack any contemporary public figures. When he names people as possessed of particular vices, as in the *Epodes* they are either unknown or no longer alive, and it is clear that the names represent types rather than individual targets. The criticism of vice occurs less for its own sake than to show the way to a correct way of life through an apprehension of error. In these passages Horace comes close to the doctrines and argument-forms of popular philosophy (so-called *diatribe), even if he rejects the sometimes fanciful tone of the Cynic-Stoic wandering preachers; see CYNICS; STOICISM. His style is rather to tell the truth through laughter (*ridentem dicere verum*), and not only to show others the way but also to work at improving himself and making himself more acceptable to his fellow human beings (*Sat*. 1. 4. 133–8). The autobiographical aspect of many satires is another Lucilian element. Just like Lucilius, he makes his own life a subject for his poetry, and his personal situation is a central theme of poems like *Sat*. 1. 4, 1. 6, 1. 9, and 2. 6, and a

partial concern in many others. Both books are arranged according to theme. In the first book, related poems are grouped together in three groups of three: 1–3 are diatribes, 4–6 are autobiographical, and 7–9 relate anecdotes, while in the last poem of the book Horace offers a retrospective look at the individuality of his satiric production. In contrast to the first book, the poems of the second book are mostly *dialogues. They are arranged so that poems from the second half of the book parallel poems of the first in motif: in the dialogues of *Sat*. 1 and 5 an expert is asked for advice, the theme of 2 and 6 is the value of a simple life on the land, in 3 and 7 Horace faces some decidedly dubious representatives of popular philosophy who inflict long sermons on him, and the theme of 4 and 8 is the luxuriousness of contemporary Roman banqueting.

Odes (Carmina)

After the publication of the *Epodes* and *Satires* around 30 BC, Horace turned to lyric poetry. The earliest datable reference is in *Odes* 1. 37, which celebrates Augustus' defeat of *Cleopatra VII at Actium in 31 BC, though it is not impossible that some odes were written earlier than this: 1. 14, for instance, on the 'ship of state', whose situation fits best the time before Actium (though the poem is open to different interpretations, and it has even been doubted whether it is in fact a political allegory at all). At any rate, the first three books of the *Odes*, 88 poems in all, seem to have been published as a collection in 23 BC. The concluding poem, 3. 30, looks back on the work as a completed unit, and does not envisage a sequel. After the composition, at Augustus' bidding, of the *Carmen saeculare* in 17, however, a fourth book of 15 poems was added, which also seems to have been inspired by Augustus (Life).

Horace declares that his main literary model in the *Odes* was the early Greek *lyric poetry from *Lesbos, especially that of *Alcaeus (1) (*Carm*. 1. 1. 33 f., 1. 32, 3. 30. 13 f.; *Epist*. 1. 19. 32 f.). He is indebted to this model for the metrical form of the *Odes* but he also begins a series of poems with an almost literal translation of lines by Alcaeus (the so-called 'mottoes'), which serve as a springboard for his own developments (e.g. 1. 9, 1. 18, 1. 37, 3. 12). He also takes over motifs from other early lyric poets, such as *Sappho (1. 13), *Anacreon (1. 23), and *Pindar (1. 12, 3. 4, and some of the higher-style poems in book 4). His view of this early poetry, however, is that of a poet trained in the modern contemporary Hellenistic style: the *Odes* are not written in the simple language of the archaic models but are full of the dense and sophisticated allusivity that was the inevitable result of the complex literary world of Augustan Rome. He also takes over a number of themes from Hellenistic poetry, especially from Greek epigram (cf. 1. 5, 1. 28, 1. 30, 3. 22, 3. 26). See HELLENISTIC POETRY AT ROME.

Although the major themes of the *Odes* are the usual ones of ancient poetry, Horace's treatment of them is, as far as we can tell, markedly different. The hymns to the gods, for instance, are not meant for cult performance but encounter the world of Greek divinity more with aesthetic pleasure than in an act of pious worship. His love poetry takes a different line from that of his contemporaries. While Catullus and the elegists (see ELEGIAC POETRY, LATIN) had tended to make a single beloved the focus of their life and poetry, Horace's poems are concerned with a variety of women (and boys; see HOMOSEXUALITY). Although passionate obsession is not entirely alien to the *Odes*, typically Horace tries to free himself from extreme emotion and move himself and his beloved towards a calm and cheerful enjoyment of the moment. The *sympotic poetry diverges distinctively from that of Alcaeus.

Horace (Quintus Horatius Flaccus)

Horace does not set out to drown his sorrows, but to give himself and his friends at the drinking-party (see CONVIVIUM) a brief moment of freedom from care, in poems which, as earlier in the *Satires*, lead often to reflection on the right way to live one's life. Friendship is an important theme throughout the *Odes*: they are hardly ever soliloquies, but poems addressed to a friend offering help and advice. The political themes begun in the *Epodes* are taken further. Although Horace declines to celebrate Augustus or Agrippa in the traditional Roman form of panegyric epic (1. 6, 1. 12), from the time of the poem celebrating the defeat of Cleopatra (1. 37) on he offers explicit praise of the new ruler as one who had brought peace and through his policies maintained it. He also declares his support for the attempt by Augustus to restore 'ancient Roman' customs and morality (3. 1–6 and 3. 24). In the later *Ode* 3. 14, in the *Carmen saeculare*, and in the poems of book 4 the panegyric of the Augustan epoch comes even more to the fore, and it is celebrated as an epoch of peace, a second *golden age.

Horace's *Odes* differ in one essential respect from the norms of modern, especially post-Romantic, lyric poetry. Modern lyric strives as far as possible for a unity of atmosphere within one poem, but this is found in Horace only in his shortest poems. More commonly, as F. Klingner (see bibliog. below) noted, within a single poem there are significant movements and changes in content, expression, and stylistic level. Poems written in high style with important content often conclude with a personal and apparently insignificant final turn. In other odes, the whole poem moves considerably from the content or atmosphere of the opening, most often from a distressed or agitated emotional level to a dissipation of tension. In other odes again, a concrete situation gives rise to thoughts which move far away from it, with the result that the meaning of the poem seems to rest on these general reflections rather than in the poem's situation. And a fourth possibility is a form of ring-composition: an opening section is followed by a second part very different in content and tone, and the final section then returns to the mood of the opening. A harmonious balance is also aimed at in the order of poems within the books. Poems of important content and accordingly a high stylistic register tend to be placed at the beginning and end of books, with lighter poems placed next to them for contrast (cf. 1. 4, 1. 5, 2. 4, 2. 5, 3. 7–3. 10 towards the beginning of books, 3. 26, 3. 28, 4. 12 towards the end). In contrast, the first book ends with the light, cheerful short sympotic poem 1. 38, preceded by the weighty victory poem 1. 37. See BOOKS, POETIC.

Epistles *book 1*

After the publication of the *Odes*, Horace returned to hexameter poetry and the conversational style of his earlier *Sermones*, but this time in the form of letters addressed to a variety of recipients. Although Lucilius had written satires in the form of letters, the notion of a complete book of verse epistles was comparatively novel. The poems are naturally not real letters actually sent to their addressees, but the choice of the letter-form was a literary device which gave Horace a concrete starting-point and a unified speech-situation. The dating of the collection is uncertain: the last line of *Epistles* 1. 20 refers to the consuls of 21 BC, and many would place the publication in that year, but 1. 12. 26 seems to refer to the defeat of the *Cantabri in 19 BC (Cass. Dio 54. 11). In the programmatic *Epistle* 1. 1 Horace grounds his choice of the new form in his advancing old age: philosophical reflection and a concentration on questions of how to lead one's life now suit him better than the usual themes of lyric. The philosophical

meditation that this declaration places at the centre of his work is an essential theme of the book, but not its only concern. Horace writes also more generally of the circumstances of his own life, and offers his friends various forms of counsel. Many elements recall the *Satires*, but the choice of the letter-form brings a more unified tone to the varied content. The last epistle (1. 20) is an address to the book itself, portrayed as a young slave eager to be free of its master.

Epistles *book 2*, Ars poetica

From *Satires* 1. 4 and 1. 10 on, poetry itself had been a constant concern of Horace's poetry, and this becomes the central theme of the two long poems of *Epistles* book 2 (2. 1. to Augustus and 2. 2 to Florus) and the *Ars poetica*. These poems are again hard to date: but *Epist.* 2. 2. 141 ff. contrasts a philosophical concern for the right way of life with the themes of lyric in similar terms to *Epist.* 1. 1 and the two poems are unlikely to be far apart chronologically. *Epist.* 2. 2 is thus probably written before Horace's resumption of lyric poetry in book 4 of the *Odes* (17 BC). On the other hand *Epist.* 2. 1. 132–7 probably alludes to the *Carmen saeculare*, and 2. 1. 252 seems to recall *Odes* 4. 14. 11 f. from the year 15. Thus the letter to Augustus (2. 1) seems to be later than the letter to Florus (2. 2). The dating of the *Ars poetica* is particularly controversial: in 301–9 Horace says that he is not currently writing (lyric) poetry, but this ironic remark can be situated either before or after *Odes* book 4. The interpretation of all three letters is difficult, because their logical articulation is deliberately obscured by the colloquial tone of a *sermo* or conversation and their various themes are interwoven without clearly marked transitions between them. The great commentary of C. O. Brink has however made many points clearer. In the letter to Augustus (2. 1), Horace complains that the taste of the contemporary public turns more to the cheap theatrical effects of earlier Latin writers than the authors of his own generation. He sees this as unfair, and accuses the older writers of being careless and deficient in taste. The letter to Florus (2. 2.) is more personal. In it, Horace explains to his friend why he no longer writes poetry but has turned to philosophy, and offers a candid picture of the restrictions and difficulties of a poet's life at Rome. The *Ars poetica* begins with the proposition that every poem must be a unified whole (1–41), and after a few verses on the necessary ordering of material (42–4) turns to poetic language and the correspondingly appropriate style (45–118). Lines 119–52 then move via a sliding transition to the choice of material and its treatment, with examples taken both from epic and from drama. Lines 153–294 concentrate on the various genres of dramatic poetry, and in the final section (295–476), after another sliding transition, the reader is offered general rules for the poet's craft. This varied subject-matter is given unity by the recurring insistence on values such as appropriateness, clarity, and artistic composition. Horace's teaching lies in the tradition of *Aristotle's school, the *Peripatetic, though the *Ars* does not draw directly on the extant *Poetics* and *Rhetoric* but on later versions of the school's doctrine, particularly (according to the ancient commentator *Pomponius Porphyrio) the early Hellenistic philosopher *Neoptolemus (2) of Parium. There are striking parallels between the *Ars* and the meagre fragments we possess of Neoptolemus, but it is not impossible that other works also lie behind the *Ars*. At any rate, Horace's own contribution lies less in offering a new view of the existing tradition than in his poetic transformation of it through images and vignettes.

BIBLIOGRAPHIES E. Burck in Kiessling–Heinze (see Commentaries section below); W. Kissel, *ANRW* 2. 31. 3 (1981), 1405–558;

E. Doblhofer, *Horaz in der Forschung nach 1957* (1992).

TEXTS D. Lambinus (2nd edn. 1568); R. Bentley (1711); O. Keller and A. Holder (1864–9; 2nd edn. 1909–25); F. Klingner (3rd edn. 1959); I. Borzsák (1984); D. R. Shackleton Bailey (1985).

SCHOLIA Porphyrio, ed. A. Holder (1894); ps.-Acron, ed. O. Keller (1902–4).

COMMENTARIES I. G. Orelli, I. G. Baiter, G. Hirschfelder, and W. Mewes (4th edn. 1886–92); E. C. Wickham (3rd edn. 1881–96); F. P. Lejay, *Satires* (1911); A. Kiessling and R. Heinze, pt. 1 (14th edn. 1984), pt. 2 (11th edn. 1977), pt. 3 (11th edn. 1984); R. G. M. Nisbet and M. E. Hubbard, *Odes Book 1* (1970), *Odes Book 2* (1978); C. O. Brink, *Horace on Poetry*, vols. 1–2 (2nd edn. 1985), vol. 3 (1982); H. P. Syndikus, *Die Lyrik des Horaz*, vol. 1 (2nd edn. 1989), vol. 2 (2nd edn. 1990).

STUDIES O. Keller, *Epilegomena zu Horaz* (1878–80); W. Y. Sellar, *Horace and the Elegiac Poets* (1891); G. Pasquali, *Orazio lirico* (1920); L. P. Wilkinson, *Horace and his Lyric Poetry*, 2nd edn. (1951); S. Commager, *The Odes of Horace* (1962); A. La Penna, *Orazio e l'ideologia del principato* (1963); F. Klingner, *Studien zur römischen und griechischen Literatur* (1964), 305–518; D. West, *Reading Horace* (1967); G. Williams, *Tradition and Originality in Roman Poetry* (1968); V. Pöschl, *Horazische Lyrik* (1970); R. O. A. M. Lyne, *The Latin Love Poets* (1980), 201–38; N. Rudd, *The Satires of Horace*, 2nd edn. (1982); G. Davis, *Polyhymnia: The Rhetoric of Horatian Lyric Discourse* (1991).

LEXICA L. Cooper, *A Concordance to the Works of Horace* (1916); D. Bo, *Lexicon Horatianum* (1965–6). H. P. S.

Horae, goddesses of the seasons (Ὧραι). *Hesiod makes them daughters of *Zeus and of *Themis ('Divine Law') and names them *Eunomia ('Good Order'), *Dike ('Justice'), and *Eirene ('Peace') (Hes. *Theog.* 901, followed e.g. by Pind. fr. 30 Snell–Maehler). But according to *Pausanias (3) (9. 35. 2) in *Attica they bore names relating to growth and the effects of the seasons: Thallo ('Blooming') and Karpo (from καρπός, 'crop, fruit'), and *Philochorus says that offerings to them were boiled, not roasted, to encourage the goddesses to avert excessive heat (*FGrH* 328 F 173). Often they remain anonymous. They guard the gates of *Olympus (1) (Hom. *Il.* 5. 749–81), and are regularly linked with the birth, upbringing, and marriages of gods and heroes (Hes. *Op.* 75; *Hymn Hom. Ven.* 5; Pind. *Pyth.* 9. 60; Moschus 2. 164, etc.); common associates are the Graces or *Charites (Paus. 9. 35. 2 and Ar. *Pax* 456), *Demeter 'bringer of the Seasons' (*Hymn Hom. Cer.* 54, etc.), *Helios and *Apollo (*SEG* 33. 115. 12), *Aphrodite (Ar. *Pax* 456; *Hymn Hom. Ven.* 5 ff.), and *Dionysus (Philochorus, *FGrH* 328 F 5b).

In the great procession of *Ptolemy (1) II Philadelphus in the 3rd cent. BC marched four Horae, each bearing their appropriate fruits (Ath. 198b). Such differentiated 'season Horae' were a favourite theme of Graeco-Roman art thenceforth. The new motif remained potentially in relation with religion, because the orderly procession of the seasons was a signal proof of the divine order of the world (see e.g. Cic. *Nat. D.* 2. 49, with A. S. Pease's note).

Farnell, *Cults* 5. 426; C. Habicht, *Studien zur Geschichte Athens in der hellenistischen Zeit* (1982), 87–90 (on the Attic Horae); E. E. Rice, *The Grand Procession of Ptolemy Philadelphus* (1983), 49 ff.; V. Machaira, *LIMC* 5. 1 (1990), 502–10, 'Horai'; L. A. Casal, ibid. 510–38, 'Horai/Horae'. R. C. T. P.

Horatii The Horatii were triplets who, in an ancient Roman legend, fought as champions against the Curiatii, also triplets, in order to decide the outcome of a war between their respective cities, Rome and *Alba Longa. The view of the surviving sources is that the Horatii were Roman, but *Livy, most interestingly, tells us that earlier historians had disagreed about which brothers belonged to which city. Two of the Horatii, and all three Curiatii,

were killed; on returning home the surviving Horatius killed his sister, when she wept for one of the Curiatii to whom she had been betrothed. Horatius was convicted of murder, but was allowed by King Tullus *Hostilius to appeal to the people, who acquitted him. The story thus offered a precedent for the right of appeal (*provocatio), and was also associated with many ancient monuments and relics in and around Rome. For the 'oath of the Horatii' see next entry.

G. Dumézil, *Horace et les Curiaces* (1942); Ogilvie, *Comm. Livy 1–5*, 109 ff. T. J. Co.

Horatii, oath of the, subject of a painting exhibited in 1785 by J.-L. David, who however appears to have made up the idea of the oath, though the men depicted are certainly the famous legendary *Horatii.

A. Brookner, *Jacques-Louis David* (1980), ch. 5. S. H.

Horatius (*RE* 9) **Cocles** In one of the most famous of all Roman legends, Horatius and two companions held the Sublician bridge against the invading army of Lars *Porsenna until it could be demolished, whereupon he swam back to safety across the Tiber. An archaic statue of a one-eyed man, which stood in the Volcanal in the *Comitium, was thought by the Romans to represent Horatius (his surname, Cocles, means 'one-eyed'). The earliest reference to the legend occurs in *Polybius (1) (6. 55. 1–4).

Walbank, *HCP* 1. 740; Ogilvie, *Comm. Livy 1–5*, 258; F. Coarelli, *Il Foro Romano* (1983), 161 ff. T. J. Co.

Horatius Flaccus See HORACE.

horologium Augusti See SOLARIUM.

horse- and chariot-races In the funeral games for *Patroclus the chariot-race is the premier event (Hom. *Il.* 23. 262–538). The heroes drive two-horse chariots normally used in battle over an improvised cross-country course, round a distant mark and home again. Similar funeral games for other heroes are recorded; and heroes as well as gods were remembered at the Panhellenic festivals. Malicious ghosts (*Taraxippoi*, 'horse-frighteners') sometimes panicked the horses. But, despite the story of the race by which *Pelops won his bride and kingdom (see HIPPODAMIA), equestrian events were not the oldest in the historic Olympia festival (see OLYMPIAN GAMES). *Pausanias (5. 8. 7–8) records the introduction of four-horse chariots in the 25th Olympiad (680 BC); of ridden horses in the 33rd; and of other equestrian events at irregular intervals thereafter. Regular hippodromes were now used. No material remains survive; but literary evidence (e.g. Soph. *El.* 681–763) shows that competitors raced to a marker about 550 m. (c.600 yds.) distant, round which they made a 180° left-hand turn before galloping back to round another marker. The number of laps varied (twelve for the four-horse chariots). Over 40 teams might take part, and the sport was dangerous, though elaborate arrangements (at least at Olympia; Paus. 6. 20. 10–14) were made to ensure a fair start. Owners, not drivers or riders, received the glory, and equestrian events were supported by tyrants, and commemorated by epinician poets (e.g. Pind. *Ol.* 1, 2).

At Rome, a horse-race preceded the sacrifice to *Mars (whether considered as a war- or fertility-god is disputed) of the *equus October*. The chariots that drew vast crowds to the Circus Maximus (see CIRCUS) and its provincial equivalents were managed by factions, whose distinguishing colours—white, red, blue, and green—were thought by *Tertullian (*De spect.* 9. 5) to represent the seasons. The date at which the factions were formed is uncertain. Blue and green eventually predominated. Horses (supplied by large stud-farms) and drivers became famous, many names being preserved in inscriptions, including leaden curse-tablets; see CURSES. Races resembled the Greek ones but with no more than twelve entries. A raised barrier (*spina*) connected the turning-points. For emperors—*Gaius (1)'s support of the Greens is notorious; Suet. *Calig.* 55—the races provided occasions for public display; for men-about-town opportunities to impress girlfriends (Ov. *Ars Am.* 1. 135).

J. H. Humphrey, *Roman Circuses and Chariot Racing* (1986).   J. K. A.

horses The present state of the evidence indicates that the horse was domesticated on the Ukrainian steppe during the neolithic period. It was known in *Mesopotamia during the third millennium BC and early bronze age horse-bones have been found in *Macedonia. Shortly before the middle of the second millennium horse-drawn war-chariots were widely used in the near east, including Eighteenth-Dynasty *Egypt. Chariots are represented in the art of Grave Circle A at *Mycenae, and horse-bones were found in abundance at Troy VI. In the *Cnossus Linear B tablets (see MYCENAEAN LANGUAGE) horses and chariots are associated with armour; the vocabulary (*i-qo*, horse; *po-ro*, foal) is *Indo-European. See MINOAN and MYCENAEAN CIVILIZATION. Mounted men are rarely shown in Egyptian and Mycenaean art; it is at least clear that bronze age horses were capable of bearing riders, and the reasons why chariotry precedes cavalry are disputed. In the Old Testament, kings continue to ride in chariots long after the appearance of 'horsemen riding upon horses', and the art of the Assyrian New Kingdom shows the gradual development of cavalry during the early iron age, with Scythian influence becoming evident in the 7th cent. BC. See ASSYRIA. In Greece, the Homeric epics and geometric art suggest that chariots were used until the 8th cent. BC as transports for armoured men who fought on foot; thereafter Greek and Roman literature and art show the widespread use of ridden horses for warfare, racing, and hunting. Well-to-do Romans, including women, also travelled on horseback (Hor. *Epist.* 1. 15. 10–13; Plut. *Quaest. Rom.* 83; Apul. *Met.* 1. 2). Mules were used to plough, and to pull carts; but both Greeks and Romans used horses mainly for riding and light draught, including under the empire not only chariot-racing but the *postal service and (Prop. 4. 8. 15; Ov. *Am.* 2. 16. 49–50) the pleasure-vehicles of courtesans. The unsuitability of ancient harness to equines has frequently been remarked in modern times, but the most recent experiments indicate that this has been exaggerated. The horse remained a 'status symbol' long after cavalry service ceased to be the privilege of the rich (see HIPPEIS); and the broken-down horse in the mill or carrying manure was pitied or despised as an example of fallen pride (Apul. *Met.* 9. 11–13; Juv. 8. 66–7; [Aesop] *Fab.* 17). Many different breeds are named in ancient literature, from the Nisaeans of *Media (Hdt. 7. 40)—solidly built but, to judge by the *Persepolis reliefs, not much over fourteen hands high—to the smooth-gaited pacing horses of Spain (Plin. *HN* 8. 166). It is now generally supposed that all these were derived from a single wild stock. Breeding was generally unscientific, chosen stallions (desirable qualities listed by Virgil: *G.* 3. 72–94) being admitted to herds of free-ranging mares. Descriptions of ancient veterinary practice are found in the Roman *agricultural writers and in the *Corpus Hippiatricorum Graecorum*. (See VETERINARY MEDICINE.) Of more general interest is *Xenophon (1)'s *Art of Horsemanship*, which is today required reading for candidates for the examinations

administered by the British Horse Society. See HORSE- AND CHARIOT-RACES.   J. K. A.

Hortensius (*RE* 7), **Quintus,** a plebeian who was appointed *dictator to reconcile the orders after a debt crisis had sparked the final secession of the *plebs to the *Janiculum in *c.*287 BC (the precise date is uncertain, but it was between 289 and 285). He carried a *lex Hortensia* by which plebiscites (see PLEBISCITUM) were to be binding on the whole people, and thus became indistinguishable from laws (*leges*, see LEX (1)). This important measure gave the plebeian assembly the same unfettered legislative competence as the other assemblies (see COMITIA), and marked a decisive stage in the conflict of the orders. Another *lex Hortensia* mentioned by Macrobius (*Sat.* 1. 16. 30), which allowed lawsuits to take place on regular market days (*nundinae*), may also have been proposed by this Hortensius. But he remains a shadowy figure (though our meagre sources preserve the detail that he was the only dictator to die in office), and the historical significance of his dictatorship is hard to understand, if only because the content of his legislation bears little obvious relation to the crisis that brought him to power.

Mommsen, *Röm. Staatsr.* 3. 153, 372 ff.; G. W. Botsford, *The Roman Assemblies* (1909), 313 ff.; F. De Martino, *Storia della costituzione romana* 2, 2nd edn. (1960), 149 ff.; A. K. Michels, *The Calendar of the Roman Republic* (1967), 103 ff.; G. Maddox, *Latomus* 1983, 277–86, and in *Sodalitas: Scritti in onore A. Guarino* 2 (1984), 85–95; K.-J. Hölkeskamp, *Archiv für Kulturgeschichte* 1988, 271–312.   P. T.; T. J. Co.

Hortensius (*RE* 13) **Hortalus, Quintus,** descendant of the preceding and grandson of C. *Sempronius Tuditanus, was one of the foremost Roman orators. Born 114 BC, he served in the *Social War (3), became prominent during *Sulla's absence from Rome, joined him in time, and dominated the courts in the seventies, using a florid 'Asianic' style even though he had never studied in the east, and resorting to shameless bribery. Defeated by *Cicero in the *Verres case, despite his best efforts at legal trickery and intimidation, he was consul 69 and remained an eminent speaker and defender of the *optimates. He opposed *Pompey's special commands, but joined Cicero in several *causes célèbres*, with Cicero always speaking last. Like his friend L. *Licinius Lucullus (2), he gradually withdrew from politics into cultivated luxury and was famous for his gourmet cuisine and his affection for his lampreys. (Cicero puts him among the *piscinarii*, aristocrats solely concerned about their fishponds.) He died in 49. Cicero always distrusted him, but incurred a heavy moral obligation when Hortensius sponsored him for the augurate (see *Brut.* 1). After Hortensius' death he amply repaid it in his rhetorical and philosophical works, especially in the *Brutus* and even more in the *Hortensius* where, with Cicero, he is the chief speaker.   E. B.

Horus (Egyptian *Ḥrw*, 'he is far off'), one of the most important Egyptian gods, soon equated, like other falcon-headed deities, with the sun-god Re. His main centre was Edfu in Upper *Egypt, where the fullest (Ptolemaic) version of the myth is found. Horus was very early a royal god, and played with *Set ('the two brothers') a key role in the mythic establishment of an ideal pharaonic order based on the resolution of their conflict. In the first Edfu myth, Horus as the Winged Disk harpoons his enemies from Upper to Lower Egypt. But in the Osiris-cycle, Horus became *Isis' son, and heir of the dead *Osiris, whom he avenged. In this form, as Harsiësis, he may be contrasted with the older or 'great' Horus. A Horus child 'with the finger in his mouth' occurs already in the Pyramid Texts, but no official cult can be traced until the late New Kingdom, when, perhaps at *Thebes (2), Harsiēsis became, or was ousted by, Harpocrates (Egyptian Ḥr-p3-ḥrd, 'Horus the child'). Motifs from two minor divinities, Šed and Neper, were combined with Harsiēsis to create a deity with three manifestations: the sun in its first two hours above the horizon (Harpocrates as demiurge on the lotus), a god of fertility, and the infant of the divine pair Isis and Osiris. Harpocrates' main cults in the Hellenistic, but chiefly Roman, period were at *Pelusium in the Delta, and in the *Fayūm. The 'great' Horus appears in the Graeco-Roman period mainly as a rider, recalling the Isiac festival of his victory over Set. Outside Egypt, Harpocrates, as nursling of Isis, predominates overwhelmingly.

J. G. Griffiths, *The Conflict of Horus and Seth* (1960); W. Brashear, *RAC* 16 (1992), 574–97; F. Dunand, *Religion populaire en Égypte romaine* (1979); B. Jaeger and others, *LIMC* 4. 1 (1988), 415–45.　　　　R. L. G.

Hosidius Geta (2nd cent. AD), author of a *cento tragedy *Medea* composed entirely of hexameters from *Virgil, according to his contemporary *Tertullian (*De praescr. haeret.* 39). Such a tragedy, based on *Euripides, is found in the *Anthologia Latina*, with dialogue in hexameters and choral lyrics in final half-hexameters, and most identify it with that mentioned by Tertullian.

TEXT Ed. G. Salanitro (1981); R. Lamacchia (Teubner, 1981).
CRITICISM G. Salanitro, *Enc. Virg.* 'Osidio Geta'.
*PIR*² H 214.　　　　S. J. Ha.

Hosidius (*RE* 6; Suppl. 12) **Geta, Gnaeus,** perhaps the subject of an acephalous inscription from Histonium (*ILS* 971), in AD 42 as propraetorian legate (see LEGATI) in *Mauretania fought against the Moor Salabus. Afterwards he (if Γναιός is read for Γάιος in Cass. Dio 60. 20. 4), or his brother, served as legionary legate on Aulus *Plautius' staff during the invasion of Britain and distinguished himself at the 'Medway' battle. As suffect consul (AD 47?) he promoted the *SC Hosidianum* on urban conservation (*ILS* 6043 = Smallwood, *Docs. . . . Gaius* 365).

R. Syme, *AJPhil.* 1956, 270 (= *RP* 1. 297).　　　　H. H. S.; B. M. L.

hospitium See FRIENDSHIP, RITUALIZED.

Hostilius, Tullus, the sixth king of Rome (conventionally 672–641 BC). The supposed derivation of Hostilius from *hostis* ('enemy') prompted his depiction as a martial figure. He reputedly campaigned against *Fidenae, *Veii, and the Sabines (see SABINI), but as early as *Ennius (*Ann.* 120–6 Skutsch), accounts of his reign were dominated by the conflict with *Alba Longa (determined by the duel of the *Horatii and Curiatii), the destruction of Alba itself, and the incorporation of its citizens in the Roman state. This sequence is probably a fiction based on later Roman legitimation of her hegemony in *Latium as Alba's supposed successor, her supervision of Alban cults, the claims of certain Roman lineages to be of Alban origin, and the later absence of a 'city' of Alba Longa; its historicity is not demonstrated by changes in settlement patterns in the Alban hills from the later 9th cent. BC on. The ascription to Hostilius of the first senate-house, *Curia (2) Hostilia, and the associated *Comitium will be an aetiological fiction, although the first floor of the Comitium area goes back at least to the late 7th cent. and architectural terracottas imply an important structure (an early *curia*?) here by *c.*600 BC.

Ogilvie, *Comm. Livy 1–5*, 105 ff.; J. Poucet, *Les Origines de Rome* (1985).　　　　A. D.

Hostilius (*RE* 18) **Mancinus, Gaius,** *praetor urbanus c.*140 BC.

As consul in 137 he was defeated by the Numantines. His quaestor Ti. *Sempronius Gracchus (3) secured a peace that saved the army; but it was disowned by the senate at the suggestion of P. *Cornelius Scipio Aemilianus, and Mancinus, with his own consent, was surrendered in expiation. When the Numantines refused to accept him, he returned, was readmitted to citizenship and again became praetor.　　　　E. B.

Hostius wrote an epic entitled *Bellum Histricum* in at least two books, of which scanty fragments survive. This was presumably about the war of 129 BC conducted by C. *Sempronius Tuditanus, to whom Hostius was probably related as *Ennius to M. *Fulvius Nobilior.

M. A. Vinchesi, in V. Tandoi (ed.), *Disiecti Membra Poetae* 1 (1984), 35; Courtney *FLP* 52.　　　　E. C.

household

Greek The household (*oikos*) was the fundamental social, political, and economic unit of ancient Greece (Arist. *Pol.* 1. 2), though its precise links to larger political and economic structures changed regionally and over time. At one level it was a co-resident group, many (though not all) of whose members were kin or affines (related by marriage). Patrilateral kinship was probably more common than matrilateral in household settings, since marriage was patrilocal, i.e. women tended to move into their husband's house and household on marriage (see MATRILOCALITY). Though a nuclear family (parents and children) might form the household's core, there is considerable evidence for the regular appearance of stem families (nuclear family plus a grandparent) and various kinds of extended families, especially incorporating unmarried female relatives (aunts, sisters, nieces, cousins, etc.). The senior man in the household usually took charge of 'official' relations with the outside world and acted as the head of household (*kyrios*). None the less, women never relinquished membership of the household into which they were born and might move back into it if the marriage were dissolved. Women, then, usually lived out their lives in two households, men in only one.

Households also included many non-kin members, of lower, non-citizen status. Most notable were slaves, who belonged to most of the well-off households mentioned in the sources; see SLAVERY. But other dependants such as freedmen or women might also be present (the household in Demosthenes 47 included an old, ex-slave nurse who must have been of metic status; see METICS). Lodgers (*Antiphon 1) might also have been considered household members during their sojourn. Households, especially wealthy ones, must often have been quite large. Given the relatively small size of even rich Greek *houses (e.g. at 4th-cent. BC *Olynthus the size-range of houses was 150–300 m.²: 1600–3200 ft.²), living conditions must have been crowded by modern standards. See HOUSES, GREEK.

The concept of the household rose above its physical reality and covered not only people but property, land, and animals as well. At this level the households of the élite frequently expanded in scope beyond the co-resident unit to include other estates, farms, and businesses. The household formed the most significant structure of economic management in ancient Greece. (See ECONOMY, GREEK.) Transmission of property to the succeeding households of the next generation was via partible inheritance (see INHERITANCE, GREEK). Because the household conceptually constituted the limits of trust and loyalty, businesses and long-term financial arrangements rarely expanded beyond it. Even on the death of the head of household, male heirs (normally brothers) did not necessarily divide all the economic resources and construct two new households (Lys. 32).

S. B. Pomeroy (trans. and comm.), *Xenophon, Oeconomicus: A Social and Historical Commentary* (1994); L. Foxhall, *CQ* 1989, 22–44; L. Nevitt, 'Variation in the Form and Use of Domestic Space in the Greek World in the Classical and Hellenistic Period' (Ph.D. thesis, Cambridge, 1992). L. F.

Roman 'Household' is the usual English translation of Latin *familia*, a term to which the jurist Ulpian (*Dig.* 50. 16. 195. 1–5), understanding its application to both property and persons, assigned several meanings: the physical household; the persons comprising a household (e.g. patron and freedman); a body of persons united by a common legal tie such as all kin subject to a living *paterfamilias*, or a body more loosely connected such as all agnatically related kin; a body of slaves, or slaves and sons; and all blood descendants of an original family founder. (To some degree *familia* overlapped with the term *domus*.) Accordingly, study of the Roman household can range from archaeological investigation of the physical structures in which Romans lived (see HOUSES, ITALIAN) to the exclusive history of *slavery. But it is now primarily associated with the field of family history, the principal constituents of which are the composition, organization and evolution of the family through its life-course. Understood ideally to comprise a married couple, their children, the house in which they lived, and their common property (which could include human property), the household in *Cicero's view (*Off.* 1. 54) was the very foundation of society. The special case of Roman *Egypt apart, it is about the household at the social level Cicero represents that most is known.

The orientation of the household was strictly patriarchal, with its head (*paterfamilias*) wielding enormous power (*patria potestas*) over his dependants, including the power of life and death over his children and slaves. In reality the implicit harshness of the regime towards adult children who, unless emancipated, could not become legally independent and own property until their fathers died, was probably tempered by demographic factors that released many from its constricting effects as they reached their early and mature adult years. The role of the *materfamilias*, stereotypically conceived, was subordinate and, beyond reproduction in marriage, largely confined to matters of domestic management in a context where ideas of economic self-sufficiency were all-important (see MOTHERHOOD). It does not follow, however, that Roman wives and mothers were devoid of all social and economic power, as the example of Cicero's wife *Terentia indicates. The ideal was propagated that marriage (see MARRIAGE LAW) was a union for life, but because of early spousal death and divorce both men and women might anticipate a succession of marriages through their adult lives. This frequently produced family and household reconstitution, with principals commonly finding themselves aligned in complex familial arrangements, involving both kin and non-kin members. Accordingly the composition of the Roman household was far from simple, its membership constantly in flux, and, especially because of the presence of servants (to whom the day-to-day care of children was often entrusted), not at all confined to immediate nuclear attachments.

SOURCES J. F. Gardner and T. Wiedemann, *The Roman Household* (1991).

BIBLIOGRAPHY J.-U. Krause, *Die Familie und weitere anthropologische Grundlagen* (1992).

STUDIES K. R. Bradley, *Discovering the Roman Family* (1991); S. Dixon, *The Roman Family* (1992); R. P. Saller, *Patriarchy, Property, and Death in the Roman Family* (1994); R. S. Bagnall and B. Frier, *The Demography of Roman Egypt* (1994). K. R. B.

houses, Greek Private houses of the Classical and Hellenistic periods were basically the same throughout the Greek world. Most rooms opened onto one or more sides of a small, rectangular courtyard, as did a doorway to the street, often preceded by a short passage. Windows were few and small and living areas were not visible from the street. An upper storey, reached by a ladder or, more rarely, a built stairway, was common but is often hard to detect. Construction was in mud-brick or rubble on stone socles. Interior walls were plastered and often painted simply, mostly in red and white. Floors were of beaten earth. In most houses, on the ground floor, one or two rooms with heavier floors and provisions for bathing, heating water, and cooking can be identified, but cooking could take place on simple hearths or portable braziers in any room or in the courtyard. The concept of the hearth and its goddess, *Hestia, symbolized the identity and cohesion of the *household (*oikos*) but formal, fixed hearths were not common, nor were *altars for domestic ritual.

A larger room, facing south for winter sunshine, and shaded by a shallow porch, may often have served as the principal living-room in the type of house that has been termed *prostas* (it is especially clear at *Priene). A type with a long porch or room fronting more than one other room has been called the *pastas* type (favoured at *Olynthus, *Thasos, and *Eretria). Roofs were either pitched and covered with brush and *terracotta tiles (or only by brush) or flat, depending on regional climate and traditions.

Frequently a more elaborately decorated room with a distinctive floor-plan served to receive guests, predominantly men (it was usually called the *andron*, 'men's room'). The floor, in cement, was raised slightly around all four sides for the placement of dining-couches, usually five, seven, or eleven in number, which resulted in the room's doorway being off-centre (see DINING-ROOMS; SYMPOSIUM). The lower rectangle in the middle of the room was sometimes decorated with pebble *mosaics. The *andron* has been found in modest as well as large houses, in country as well as town, all over Greece, but is lacking at Thasos.

Women's quarters are mentioned in literary sources but cannot be securely identified in the surviving architecture and are not simply to be equated with the second storey. Rather, certain rooms or areas of the house, depending on the composition and needs of the inhabitants, were assigned primarily to women. The house as a whole may have been regarded as women's domain (see WOMEN), apart from the *andron* and wherever unmarried men, slave or free, slept. No distinct quarters for slaves are distinguishable architecturally, although female slaves might be separated by a locked door from the male.

The household was an economic as well as social unit. Much of the processing and storage of the products of the family's land took place in the house. Stone parts of oil-presses have been found in the houses of towns inhabited mostly by farmers. Wells, cisterns for rainwater, and pits for collecting waste for manure are found in courtyards; see WATER-SUPPLY. If a craft was practised that too took place in the house; distinctive workshops are rare. One room, opening onto the street, was sometimes separated to serve as a shop, not necessarily occupied by the residents of the house. Houses could be home to several persons or families, especially in cities like Athens with large transient, foreign, and slave populations (see METICS; SLAVERY).

The same general concept and design of the private house was used in city, village, and countryside. In the last the courtyard might be larger to accommodate animals and equipment and commonly a tower of two or three storeys, round or square, and more heavily built than the rest, was entered from the courtyard. Such towers, often the only conspicuous remains of houses in the countryside, have been identified in towns as well. They appear to have been used primarily for the safe keeping of goods and persons, slave and free, especially, but not only, in more isolated locations.

The development of the Greek house is inseparable from that of the settlement. Houses were contiguous, sharing party-walls. The privacy of each adjacent unit and the concomitant independence of each *oikos* were vital. When new settlements were established, streets were laid out orthogonally (see URBANISM); initially house plots were probably of uniform size, though in the course of time changes occurred. The modesty of the Classical houses of all classes is striking. Large houses with two courtyards are first found in Eretria in the 4th cent. BC and in towns of the Hellenistic period. Courtyards may have a peristyle on four sides. Only in the Hellenistic and Roman periods do some Greek houses approximate to the descriptions of the Roman author *Vitruvius (De arch. 6. 7). The *palaces of monarchs and tyrants (see TYRANNY) took the form of elaborations of the larger private houses.

J. Graham, in D. Robinson and J. Graham, *Excavations at Olynthus* 8: *The Hellenic House* (1938); Y. Grandjean, *Recherches sur l'habitat Thasien à l'époque grecque* (1988); W. Hoepfner and E.-L. Schwandner (eds.), *Haus und Stadt im klassischen Griechenland* (1986); M. Jameson, in O. Murray and S. Price (eds.), *The Greek City* (1990) and in S. Kent (ed.), *Domestic Architecture and the Use of Space* (1990). M. H. J.

houses, Italian The social structures which underlay the Greek house, a *household unit (in Greek, *oikos*), which was capable of representing both a citizen lot in the space of the town, and the symbolic abode of the head of a lineage, were shared by Italy in the period of its first *urbanism. Where there was an idea of equality among a limited group of ruling families the two ideas coalesced comfortably. *Etruscan urbanism shows signs of both ends of this spectrum; fine aristocratic houses are known, which tally with the power and pretensions of what we know of some of the city élites, while the urban texture of places like *Marzabotto resembles the topography of wider citizen franchise as seen at *Olynthus or *Priene. The discoveries of the 1980s on the slopes of the *Palatine hill at Rome showed how already in the 6th cent. BC the Roman élite was living along the *via Sacra, beside the Forum, in a series of roughly equal *oikopeda* (house-plots) of considerable size which formed the base of the topography of the area until the great fire of AD 64. The Roman aristocracy thus identified itself with a historic home in the city centre as much as any early modern or modern aristocrat with a feudal estate in the countryside. Something similar may be guessed for other Italian aristocracies of tenacious traditions like that of *Tarquinii.

This is the background to the first really copious evidence, the 3rd–2nd-cent. BC houses of *Pompeii, which show a regular plan and a systematic division of urban space, but a very considerable variety of size and levels of wealth, the House of the Faun being absolutely outstanding by the standards of anywhere in the Mediterranean world. In these houses it is relatively easy to identify the features which *Vitruvius, our principal literary source, regarded as canonical, but their evolution in different parts of Italy should not be taken for granted. The traditional houses of the centre of Rome seem also to have adhered to the basic pattern of atrium with rooms round it; where more space was available, this traditional arrangement could be combined with peristyles and gardens, offering scope for planned suites of rooms, interesting light effects, and amenities such as ornamental plantings or fountains, and providing more flexible spaces for living, entertaining, politics, and the cultural activities which were integral to upper-class life. The politicians of the late republic were credited with various changes to the use of houses; and luxury in domestic appointments was thought to have taken off dramatically in the 1st cent. BC; but the setting for both processes seems to have been the traditional 'Pompeian/Vitruvian' house.

The salient feature of this traditional plan was the atrium—a rectangular space open to the sky at the centre, columned in the more elaborate forms, with wide covered spaces on each of the four sides, one of which gave onto the outside world through a vestibule. Originally the site of the family hearth, whose smoke caused the blackening (*ater*) which gave the place its name, this was also the abode of the household deities, and housed the copies of the funerary masks which were the sign of the family's continuity and identity (see IMAGINES; LARES). The adjacent rooms, including a *tablinum* and *cubicula*, were in fact flexible in their use, and this flexibility is the key to the understanding of all Roman domestic space, even in very much more elaborate dwellings. A *triclinium* for convivial dining was an early and frequent adjunct, but *meals could be taken in a variety of different rooms, if they were available, according to season and weather (see CONVIVIUM; DINING-ROOMS).

*Augustus' house on the Palatine, reached by passing along the street of venerable aristocratic addresses (the houses had been rebuilt many times) from the Forum, consisted of an amalgamation of several *domus* of the traditional sort, so that he could enjoy the advantages of considerable space while claiming moderation in his domestic circumstances. The building of very large complexes nearby under *Gaius (1) (for example, the platform of the 'Domus Tiberiana', which supported a country villa in the heart of Rome) and *Nero, whose Golden House (*Domus Aurea) spread over a large section of the city centre and took playful manipulation of Roman domestic tradition to the limit, took a different line, but *Domitian's enormous palace, overpowering and monarchic in its axiality though it was, is recognizably an ancient *domus* on a hugely inflated scale (see PALACES).

For most inhabitants of the Roman city, however, this spacious life was impossible; it was normal to live in someone else's property, and in much less space. The wealthy had long accommodated slaves, dependants, and visitors around the principal spaces of their houses—on the street frontages, from which the principal rooms were averted, on upper floors, or even under the floors of the main premises, in warrens of small rooms. Parts of the *domus* accessible from outside could be let profitably for accommodation or for a variety of economic activities. Purpose-built rental accommodation, in the form of whole blocks in the city or its environs given over to the sort of unit that fringed a normal *domus*, goes back at least to the middle republic. The demand for such premises grew so fast that those who could afford to build them saw a valuable source of rental income, and a style of architecture developed which had this type of dwelling-space in mind. By the imperial period, multi-storey tenement blocks, which are usually known as *insulae*, housed all but a tiny fraction of the population of Rome and other big cities. Not all this accommodation was of low quality; some was sited in attractive areas, some *cenacula* (apartments) were sufficiently large, those on the lower floors were not inconvenient (the 'Garden Houses' at *Ostia for instance), and many people of quite high status could afford no better. The introduction of kiln-fired brick almost certainly made these developments safer and more salubrious than had been the case in the republic (see BUILDING MATERIALS, ROMAN). Estimates of the living conditions in the *insulae* we know best, those of Ostia—where we cannot tell if we are looking at privileged or marginal housing—illustrate a more general difficulty in the study of the Roman house, that of understanding the density of occupation and the pattern of human interaction represented by the layout of rooms. Scholarship has concentrated on typology rather than function, and has been given to making facile assumptions about standards of comfort, convenience, and cleanliness based on modern cultural stereotypes. Despite the enormous quantity of archaeological explanation, ancient domestic society still needs investigation.

The atrium proved remarkably tenacious. But by late antiquity the houses of even the topmost élite had adopted in preference the looser arrangements of porticoes and reception rooms which had been developed in suburban villas (*horti*, see GARDENS) and the country *villa.

A. Wallace-Hadrill, *Houses and Society in Pompeii and Herculaneum* (1994); J. R. Clarke, *The Houses of Roman Italy* (1991); A. Boethius, *The Golden House of Nero* (1960). See also under ARCHITECTURE, ROMAN.

N. P.

housework, a specifically female task, was evidently not of interest to male authors, and there are no surviving household accounts or instructions. 'Women's work' meant weaving and the other tasks required in fabric-making: cleaning and carding wool, spinning and dyeing thread. *Xenophon (1), in the *Oeconomicus*, envisages a young wife whose only domestic training is in fabric-making: he suggests that she can train slaves to make fabric, supervise household supplies, equipment, and labour, and, for exercise, fold clothes and bedding and knead dough. *Columella (*Rust.* 12. 1–3) says that the bailiff's wife on a Roman estate should supervise wool-working and preparation of meals, and should ensure that the kitchens, the shelters for animals, and especially the sickroom are clean. But there is silence on the details of ordinary daily tasks: providing meals and washing up; washing and drying clothes and household textiles; cleaning the house and its equipment, including fireplaces, braziers, and *lamps; and, in many households, tending plants, poultry, and domestic animals. There are inscriptions recording the jobs of slaves in great Roman households, but they specify the more prestigious tasks of the dining-room staff and personal attendants.

The most informative sources on everyday housework are Christian texts on virginity, which (if addressed to women) emphasize the burdens of the harassed housewife or (if addressed to men) minimize the tasks for which a man might want a female partner: washing clothes, making beds, lighting fires, and cooking (see COOKERY). Some household equipment has survived relatively well, especially pottery, metal furniture and tableware, and stone tables and benches, but there are few examples of wooden furniture or textiles. See HOUSEHOLD; HOUSES, GREEK and ITALIAN; TEXTILE PRODUCTION.

S. Treggiari, *PBSR* 1975, 48–77; G. Clark, *Women in Late Antiquity* (1993). E. G. C.

hubris, intentionally dishonouring behaviour, was a powerful term of moral condemnation in ancient Greece; and in Athens, and perhaps elsewhere, it was also treated as a serious crime. The common use of *hubris* in English to suggest pride, over-

confidence, or any behaviour which may offend divine powers, rests, it is now generally held, on misunderstanding of ancient texts, and concomitant and over-simplified views of Greek attitudes to the gods have lent support to many doubtful, and often over-Christianizing, interpretations, above all of Greek tragedy.

The best ancient discussion of *hubris* is found in *Aristotle's *Rhetoric*: his definition is that *hubris* is 'doing and saying things at which the victim incurs shame, not in order that one may achieve anything other than what is done, but simply to get pleasure from it. For those who act in return for something do not commit *hubris*, they avenge themselves. The cause of the pleasure for those committing *hubris* is that by harming people, they think themselves superior; that is why the young and the rich are hubristic, as they think they are superior when they commit *hubris*' (*Rh.* 1378^{b}23–30). This account, locating *hubris* within a framework of ideas concerned with the honour and shame of the individual, which took a central place in the value-systems of the ancient Greeks, fits very well the vast majority of texts exploiting the notion, from *Homer till well after Aristotle's own time (with the notable exception of some philosophically significant developments in some of *Plato (1)'s later works). While it primarily denotes gratuitous dishonouring by those who are, or think they are, powerful and superior, it can also at times denote the insolence of accepted 'inferiors', such as women, children, or slaves, who disobey or claim independence; or it may be used to emphasize the degree of humiliation actually inflicted on a victim, regardless of the agent's intention; some cases, especially applied to verbal insults, may be humorously exaggerated; and revenge taken to excessive or brutal lengths can be condemned as constituting fresh *hubris*.

Hubris is most often the insulting infliction of physical force or violence: classic cases are Meidias' punch on *Demosthenes (2)'s face in the theatre (see Demosthenes 21), and the assaults by Conon and sons on the speaker of Demosthenes 54, when the middle-aged Conon allegedly gloated over the body of their battered victim in the manner of a triumphant fighting-cock. Further common forms of hubristic acts are sexual assaults (rape, seduction, or deviant practices), where emphasis is thereby placed on the dishonour inflicted on the victims or on the male householders responsible for them. Since states too seek to protect their honour, *hubris* is commonly applied to invasions, imperialist 'enslavement', or military savagery, often, but not exclusively, when committed by '*barbarian' powers. In consequence, Greek cities took *hubris* very seriously as a political danger, both to their collective freedom and status, and as communities functioning internally through respect for law and the well-being of their members. Unchecked *hubris* was held to be characteristic of *tyrannies, or of *oligarchies or *democracies serving their own class (depending on one's viewpoint), and to be a major cause of *stasis or civil wars. In Athens, probably from *Solon's laws of the early 6th cent. BC, a legal action for *hubris* existed, and its public significance was signalled by the possibility of the heaviest penalties, and by the fact that the action was (as a *graphē) open to any Athenian with full citizen rights, not restricted to the victim of the dishonour. While our limited evidence suggests that the action was infrequently used, its ideological importance as a safeguard for poorer citizens in the democracy was none the less considerable.

Hubris is not essentially a religious term; yet the gods naturally were often supposed to punish instances of it, either because they might feel themselves directly dishonoured, or, more frequently, because they were held to uphold general Greek moral and social values. Nor is it helpful to see Greek tragedy centrally concerned to display the divine punishment of hubristic heroes; tragedy focuses rather on unjust or problematic suffering, whereas full-scale acts of *hubris* by the powerful tend to deprive them of the human sympathy necessary for tragic victims.

For the views summarized here, see N. R. E. Fisher, *Hybris* (1992) and in A. Powell (ed.), *The Greek World* (1995), 44 ff.; good treatments also in D. M. MacDowell, *G&R* 1976, 14 ff.; K. J. Dover, *Greek Popular Morality* (1974), and *Greek Homosexuality* (1978); D. Cohen, *G&R* 1991, 171–88, and *Law, Society and Sexuality: The Enforcement of Morals in Classical Athens* (1991) (largely on Athenian society and law); R. Lattimore, *Story Patterns in Greek Tragedy* (1964), 22 ff.; M. Dirat, *L'Hybris dans la tragédie grecque* (1972); B. Vickers, *Towards Greek Tragedy* (1973); S. Said, *La Faute tragique* (1977); A. N. Michelini, *Harv. Stud.* 1978, 35 ff.; E. Cantarella, in *Symposion 1979* (1981), 85 ff. (largely on Homer and tragedy). N. R. E. F.

humiliores See HONESTIORES; STATUS, LEGAL AND SOCIAL, ROMAN.

humours (χυμοί = 'juices'; Lat. *(h)umores*). The words strictly suggest some kind of fluid substance and can be used of the sap in plants, but they are most commonly found in medical contexts. The explanation of disease—and even human behaviour—in terms of the interactions and relative proportions of fluids in the body is a very ancient one. In some Hippocratic treatises (see HIPPOCRATES (2)) the more general term ὑγρά ('moistures') is used as an alternative. At this level of generality there is little to distinguish many different pathological theories, but in practice there was little agreement as to which fluids counted as humours, and which were the most important. Many different kinds of humoral theory were in circulation. Most influential were those which related the qualities of the humours to qualities which had been associated with the Empedoclean *elements, where earth, water, *fire, and air were sometimes analysed in terms of hot, cold, wet, dry. This in turn enabled a correlation to be made with the four seasons. *Galen gives the four humours of the Hippocratic treatise *On the Nature of Man*—blood, phlegm, yellow bile, and black bile—a special status which they continued to enjoy. But the Hippocratic author of *Affections* proposes that bile and phlegm are the principal fluids involved in disease; *On Generation* advocates a four-humour system of blood, water, bile, and phlegm. *Praxagoras of Cos is credited with an extremely complex humoral pathology, involving as many as a dozen different types of humour. Humoral pathologies remained important throughout antiquity, but they were by no means the only models employed in the explanation of diseases. Doctors like *Erasistratus, *Asclepiades (3), and the Methodists (see MEDICINE, § 5. 3) were at pains to develop alternative pathological models.

E. Schöner, *Das Viererschema in der antiken Humoralpathologie*, Sudhoff's Archiv, Beiheft 4 (1964); H. von Staden, *Herophilus: The Art of Medicine in Early Alexandria* (1989), 244–7. J. T. V.

Huns, a Mongolian nomadic people who appeared in SE Europe *c*. AD 370, destroyed the Gothic communities (see GOTHS) on the Black (*Euxine) Sea, and drove large numbers of refugees into the Roman empire (376). Early in the 5th cent. they advanced into central Europe, displacing other barbarians into Italy and Gaul, and laying the foundations of their own empire, mostly north of the Danube. This achieved its greatest extent (from the Ukraine to the Rhine) under *Attila (434–53). After Attila's death, his realm was divided between his sons, who were defeated in 454 by a coalition of their subjects. The Huns' society and culture remains elusive and, despite their demonization by Rome, their

historical significance requires prudent assessment. Their prowess as cavalrymen was as much exploited by Roman generalissimos (in particular, Flavius *Aetius) as it was turned against the empire; and, though they exacted large quantities of gold from the eastern empire, they failed to win any of its territory.

E. A. Thompson, *A History of Attila and the Huns* (1948); O. J. Maenchen-Helfen, *The World of the Huns* (1973). E. A. T.; J. F. Dr.

hunting Epic heroes (see HOMER) hunt to fill their bellies or to rid the land of dangerous beasts (Hom. *Od.* 9. 154–48, 10. 157–63; *Il.* 9. 533–49). The boar is the most formidable antagonist; venison is highly valued; mentions of lions are problematic. Hunters go on foot, armed with spear or bow. In Greek Classical literature the educational value of hunting is emphasized (Pl. *Leg.* 822d; Xen. *Cyn.* 1), but hunting is still for the pot and the methods described in *Xenophon (1)'s *Cynegeticus* (*Hunting Man*) are often unsporting. These include the use of snares and foot-clogs and the beating of fawns so that their cries will draw their mothers within range. Hare-hunting receives special attention; the hunters, on foot, drive the hares into nets with the help of hounds. Hounds and nets are also used for boar-hunting; but the beast must ultimately be faced by men on foot armed with boar-spears. Opportunities for hunting on horseback are rare and generally to be found in the east (compare Xen. *An.* 1. 5. 1–3 and, for the 'paradises' or game-parks of the Persian *satraps, *An.* 1. 2. 7). *Alexander (3) the Great's conquests enabled the Macedonian nobles to hunt on a gigantic scale and established the hunt as a paradigm of manly (especially kingly) virtue, which is reflected in funerary art (notably the 'Tomb of *Philip (1) II' at Vergina (see AEGAE), and the 'Alexander Sarcophagus'; see SIDON). The Roman conquerors took over the apparatus of the Macedonian kings (Polyb. 31. 29. 1–12) though enthusiasm for hunting was not universal—a 'slavish' occupation according to *Sallust (*Cat.* 4. 1). The distinction between amateur sportsmen and 'slavish' professionals (already found in *Plato (1) and Xenophon) becomes marked in the Roman period. Professionals (including wildfowlers using nets and lime-twigs) hunt for the market, or to supply their masters. Sportsmen follow Greek methods; but often hunt on horseback. *Dido's hunt (Verg. *Aen.* 4. 129–70) may be based on the actual practice of driving game from the hills to be ridden down on level ground. *Hadrian (AD 117–38) particularly distinguished himself as a big-game hunter—lion, bear, and boar (Cass. Dio 69. 10. 2–3); but his friend *Arrian, whose *Cynegeticus* was professedly written to supplement Xenophon's work, coursed hares on horseback, taking more pleasure in the chase than in the kill. Didactic poems on hunting from the imperial period include the works of *Grattius 'Faliscus' (fl. AD 8), *Oppian (fl. 211), and *Nemesianus (fl. 283). Country sports, including boar-, stag-, fox-, and hare-hunting, and the hunt breakfast, are depicted in the mosaic of the 'Little Hunt' at *Piazza Armerina (*c*. AD 300). Hunting (including exploits of *Heracles, *Meleager (1), and other mythical figures) continues to be used as a paradigm, in domestic as well as funerary art. The slaughter of captured beasts in the *amphitheatre forms a separate subject; see VENATIO.

J. K. Anderson, *Hunting in the Ancient World* (1985). J. K. A.

Hyacinthides or **Parthenoi** ('Maidens'), cult titles of a group of heroines in Athens identified as daughters of *Hyacinthus or daughters of *Erechtheus, sacrificed for the safety of the city and in some versions metamorphosed into the star-group *Hyades. The 'Daughters of Erechtheus' story occurs in *Euripides' *Erech-*

theus; it is unclear how much is Euripidean invention, but the details given about their cult (fr. 65 Austin, *Nova Fragmenta Euripidea*: dances by young girls in their honour, restrictions on entry into the sanctuary, a ban on wine) are presumably accurate, and it is likely to have been concerned with the city's escape from crisis.

Kearns, *Heroes of Attica* 59–63, 201–2.   E. Ke.

Hyacinthus, Dorian god or hero at *Amyclae near Sparta. His festival Hyacinthia (see DORIAN FESTIVALS) and month Hyakinthios recur in many other Dorian locations. A pre-Greek figure (cf. the suffix *-nth-* of his name), he merged with Apollo probably before the end of the bronze age. Hence the popular myth in which Apollo kills his young favourite with an unlucky throw of the discus (Eur. *Hel.* 1469 ff.; Apollod. 3. 116). In Alexandrian tradition (also in Attic vase-painting) *Zephyrus caused Hyacinthus' death by blowing the discus off course. A flower (iris) sprang from the boy's blood with the letters *AI AI* ('alas, alas') inscribed on its leaves (Ov. *Met.* 10. 215; cf. the etymology of Aias by Ovid, *Met.* 13. 396). Hyacinthus' death was an important element of the three-day Amyclaean Hyacinthia (Athen. 139d ff.). The hero received a preliminary sacrifice on the first day at his tomb which formed the base of Apollo's 6th-cent. BC altar / throne with relief sculptures by Bathycles including Hyacinthus' translation to heaven with his sister *Polyboea (2). See SPARTAN CULTS.

Originally Hyacinthus may have been a dying nature-god like *Adonis. As the youthful male associate of a goddess of nature, he symbolized the annual cycle of vegetation. Memories of his past function are preserved in the Cnidian cult of Artemis Hyakinthotrophos. Though bearded at Amyclae (Paus. 3. 19. 3 f.), Hyacinthus, like other Divine Children, is more frequently portrayed as a beautiful youth. As the *erōmenos* of Apollo and Zephyrus, who is often shown in lively pursuit of his loved one, Hyacinthus became a popular subject for Attic vase-painters of the early 5th cent. BC.

Nilsson, *GGR* 1³. 316 f.; M. J. Mellink, *Hyakinthos* (1943); B. C. Dietrich, *Kadmos* 1975, 133–42; L. and F. Villard, *LIMC* 5/1 (1990), 546–50, 'Hyakinthos'; M. Petterson, *Cults of Apollo at Sparta: The Hyakinthia, the Gymnopaidiai and the Karneia* (1992).   H. J. R.; B. C. D.

Hyades ('Yάδες, 'the Rainers'), a group of five stars in Taurus, so named because their acronychal rising and setting (respectively 17 October and 12 April according to *Eudoxus (1)) are at rainy times of the year; called Suculae in Latin, as if from ὗς. Mythologically they were nurses of *Dionysus (see Hyg. *Fab.* 182. 2 and Rose's note); but the story, which seems to go back to *Pherecydes, is very confused in the forms which we have. Another account (Hyg. *Poet. astr.* 2. 21; schol. *Il.* 18. 486; Eust. 1155. 45 ff.) is that they are sisters who cried themselves to death when their brother Hyas was killed hunting. See CONSTELLATIONS; HYACINTHIDES.

LIMC 5. 1 (1990), 543–6.   H. J. R.

hybris See HUBRIS.

Hydaspes, river of the Punjab (probably the Jhelum), where *Alexander (3) the Great defeated *Porus in 326 BC. After continually stretching the enemy by marching and countermarching along the river, Alexander crossed it before dawn under cover of a thunderstorm, probably with only 6,000 foot and 5,000 horse. Porus sent forward an advance force of Indian cavalry and chariots which was routed by Alexander's cavalry screen, and interspersed his infantry with *elephants, placing cavalry and chariots

on the wings. But under attack by Alexander's cavalry, the Indian horse took refuge amongst the infantry, causing confusion, and uncovering its flanks and rear. In the centre the Macedonian infantry were able to open gaps in their line to accommodate elephants where necessary, and to use their *sarisae* ('pikes') to drive others back on their own infantry, after dislodging their mahouts. Virtually surrounded, the Indian army was all but annihilated, and Porus himself captured.

Arr. *Anab.* 5. 9 ff.; Curt. 8. 13–14. A. B. Bosworth, *Conquest and Empire* (1988).   J. F. La.

hydrostatics, a special field of *statics, within the geometric theory of *mechanics, deals with the properties of weights in fluid media, and in particular with the conditions for stability of floating bodies. The basic principles and their application are from *Archimedes in the two books *On Floating Bodies* (Περὶ ὀχουμένων). Archimedes here demonstrates that a floating body displaces a volume of fluid equal to its own weight (book 1, prop. 5) and proves the stability of floating spherical segments (props. 8–9) and the conditions of density and shape entailing the stability of floating paraboloidal segments (book 2). The analogue for bodies denser than the medium, that is, that their weight when immersed in the fluid is reduced by an amount equal to the weight of the displaced fluid (book 1, prop. 7), can be extended into a procedure for determining specific weights, as in the hydrostatic balance attributed to Archimedes in the *Carmen de ponderibus*.

E. J. Dijksterhuis, *Archimedes* (1956; corr. edn. 1987), ch. 14; W. R. Knorr, *Ancient Sources of the Medieval Tradition of Mechanics* (1982).   W. R. K.

Hydruntum (mod. Otranto), in southern Italy, *Messapian city, 46 km. (29 mi.) south-east of Lecce. It was an important port for trade and communications with Greece and *Epirus, and may have been the terminus of the *via Appia. It remained important throughout antiquity.

G. Susini, *Fonti per la storia greca e romana del Salento* (1962); F. D'Andria, *Archeologia dei Messapi* (1990).   K. L.

Hyettus (mod. Dendra), small *polis in NW *Boeotia, named supposedly after Hyettus of *Argos (2), who came to the region in the heroic period. In Classical times it was dependent upon its stronger neighbour *Orchomenus (1), but became autonomous after the reduction of the latter in 371 BC. Situated on a strong point, it existed from the 6th cent. BC into the Byzantine period. The acropolis was walled, but little is known of the lower city. Excavations have revealed numerous Hellenistic and Roman inscriptions, the most prominent being two that honour *Septimius Severus and *Caracalla respectively.

R. Étienne and D. Knoepfler, *Hyettos de Béotie*, *BCH* Suppl. 3 (1976).   J. Bu.

Hygieia ('Yγίεια), personified Health, said to be daughter of *Asclepius and associated with him in cult; in the Hippocratic oath (see HIPPOCRATES (2)), her name follows immediately on his, and they share many later dedications. Her first attestation is a statue set up in *Olympia, together with an image of Asclepius, by Micythus of *Rhegium who lived in *Tegea after 467 BC (Paus. 5. 26. 2); still earlier is the *epiclesis* (name) 'Yγίεια of Athena in Athens, attested from the late 6th to the late 5th cent. BC. Here, Hygieia was introduced by Telemachus together with Asclepius in 429/19—without entirely ousting the cult of *Athena Hygieia (Paus. 1. 23. 4). Ordinarily, her cult is subordinated to that of Asclepius, with the one exception of Titane near *Sicyon where she had an Archaic image hidden by women's dedicated hair and garments (Paus. 2. 11. 6), reminiscent of the cult of Iphigenia in *Brauron. The *hymn of *Licymnius (2) of Chios which addresses her as 'Mother most high' (*PMG* 769) and connects her directly with *Apollo underlines this unusual independence. See also ASCLEPIUS.

U. Hausmann, *Kunst und Heiltum: Untersuchungen zu den griechischen Asklepiosreliefs* (1948); H. Sobel, *Hygieia: Die Göttin der Gesundheit* (1990); F. Croissant, *LIMC* 5 (1991), 554–72, 'Hygieia'; H. A. Shapiro, *Personifications in Greek Art: The Representation of Abstract Concepts 600–400 B.C.* (1993), 125–31.
F. G.

Hyginus (1), **Gaius Iulius**, a Spaniard (according to another account, an *Alexandrian brought to Rome by *Caesar), a *freedman of *Augustus, appointed by him librarian of the Palatine Library (Suet. *Gram.* 20). A pupil of *Alexander (11) 'Polyhistor', he was himself a teacher and was a friend of *Ovid, who addresses him in *Tr.* 3. 14. His writings, now lost, covered a wide range of scholarship: (*a*) a treatise *On Agriculture*, perhaps including the work *On Bees* cited by *Columella; (*b*) a commentary on *Virgil, cited by A. *Gellius and *Servius, apparently both exegetical and critical; (*c*) historical and archaeological works— *On Trojan Families*; *On the Origin and Site of Italian Cities*; *On the Life and Histories of Illustrious Men*; *Examples*; (*d*) works on religion—*On the Qualities of the Gods*; *On the Di Penates*.

See Peter, *HRRel.*; Funaioli, *Gramm. Rom. Frag.*; J. Christes, *Sklaven und Freigelassene als Grammatiker und Philologen im antiken Rom* (1979). *PIR*² I 357.
C. J. F.; A. J. S. S.

Hyginus (2) wrote *c.* AD 100 on the establishment of boundaries, categories of land, including their designation on maps, and land disputes. He also mentions a collection (no longer extant) of imperial decisions on land-holding. A treatise on land division and allocation should perhaps be assigned to another author, conventionally designated *Hyginus (4) Gromaticus. See GROMATICI.
J. B. C.

Hyginus (3) Two extant Latin works are attributed to a Hyginus who cannot be identified with Augustus' freedman (Hyginus (1)) or with the *gromaticus* (Hyginus (4)).

(*a*) *Genealogiae*, a handbook of mythology, compiled from Greek sources, probably in the 2nd cent. AD. The work was abbreviated, perhaps for school use, and has suffered later accretions; its absurdities are partly due to the compiler's ignorance of Greek. The usual title *Fabulae* is due to the *editio princeps* of Micyllus (Basel, 1535), now the only authority for the text; the manuscript which he used is lost. See MYTHOGRAPHERS.

Critical edn.: H. J. Rose (1934). A. Henrichs, in J. Bremmer (ed.), *Interpretations of Greek Mythology* (1987), 252, 272 n. 47.
C. J. F.

(*b*) A manual of astronomy, based on Greek sources, possibly by the same author.

Hyginus (4). To Hyginus Gromaticus has been mistakenly ascribed an incomplete treatise *On Camp Fortifications* (so named in the 16th cent.), which discusses the methods for siting military camps, measuring the internal areas (*castrametatio*) for a hypothetical army, and establishing fortifications. Its date is uncertain and has been placed in the late 2nd cent. AD, or the 3rd century AD, or most persuasively, the reign of *Trajan. See GROMATICI.

M. Lenoir, *Pseudo-Hygin: Des fortifications du camp* (1979).
J. B. C.

Hylas, son of the Dryopian Theiodamas, after whose murder by *Heracles he became Heracles' protégé. He accompanied the *Argonauts but disappeared during a stop at Cius in Mysia: he went to fetch water and the *Nymph (e.g. Ap. Rhod. 1229 ff.) or Nymphs (e.g. Theoc. 13. 43 ff.) of the spring fell in love with him and dragged him into the water. His companions searched for him in vain, and Heracles forced the locals to go on searching and, to ensure their compliance, took as hostages boys from noble families whom he settled at *Trachis. This is the *aition* for a Cian ritual involving a sacrifice and ritual search in which the priest called 'Hylas' three times and was answered by the echo. In most versions Hylas was Heracles' *erōmenos* (see HOMOSEXUALITY), in some (cf. e.g. Euphorion fr. 81 Groningen) he was Polyphemus' (see CYCLOPES).

ANCIENT SOURCES Ap. Rhod. *Argon.* 1. 1207–1357; schol. Ap. Rhod. *Argon.* 1. 1355–7a (cf. Davies, *EGF* p. 142); Theoc. 13; Nicander in Ant. Lib. 26; Apollod. 1. 9. 19; Strab. 12. 4. 3; Photius and *Suda*, entry under *Hylan kraugazein*; Hsch., entry under *epiboa to[n] Mysion*; Zen. 6. 21. The myth of Hylas was popular in Hellenistic and Roman poetry and art.
MODERN LITERATURE G. Türk, *De Hyla* (1895); Preller–Robert 836–42; B. Sergent, *Homosexuality in Greek Myth* (1987), 155–62; C. Segal, *Hermes* 1974, 27–34; G. L. Huxley, *JHS* 1989, 185–6; J. H. Oakley, *LIMC* 5 (1990), 574–9; R. Hunter, *The Argonautica of Apollonius* (1993).
C. S.-I.

Hyllus, in mythology, eldest son of *Heracles by *Deianira (Soph. *Trach.* 55, etc.) or Melite (schol. ibid. 54). See HERACLIDAE.

LIMC 5. 1 (1990), 579–82.

Hymenaeus The cry *hymēn ō hymenaie* (with variants) was traditional in Greek wedding songs (e.g. Ar. *Pax* 1332–56). It presumably arose as a mock lament for the bride's hymen in the anatomical sense (though this has been disputed), but it was soon taken as an invocation to a marriage-god (e.g. Eur. *Tro.* 310–25). *Pindar, fr. 128c. 7–8 Snell–Maehler, relates that Hymenaeus died on his wedding night and was lamented, like *Linus and Ialemus, by a goddess; cf. Eur. *Phaethon* 233–5, where Hymen is a son of *Aphrodite. These conceptions are later elaborated, and Hymenaeus or Hymen is often found as god of marriage in Roman literature (e.g. Catull. 61). See also EPITHALAMIUM.

P. Linant de Bellefonds, *LIMC* 5. 1 (1990), 583–5; 5.2. 401.
A. L. B.

Hymettus, mountain south-east of Athens reaching 1,026 m. (3,366 ft.). An important source of high-quality *marble in both Classical and Roman periods. *Pausanias (3) (1. 32. 2) tells of a statue and altar to Zeus on Hymettus, and dedications from the 8th cent. BC to Roman times, including many with early inscriptions, have been excavated just north of the summit. In Latin literature it evokes the famous Attic *honey.

M. K. Langdon, *A Sanctuary of Zeus on Mount Hymettos* (1976).
R. G. O.

hymns (Greek) 'Hymn' is a simple transliteration of a Greek word; but the relation of Greek to English hymns is not at all simple. *hýmnos* has at least three meanings: (1) a song of any kind; (2) any song in honour of a god; (3) a particular type of song in honour of a god. Use (1), the first attested, is standard in Archaic poetry; (2) would perhaps have been judged normal by a Greek of the Classical period; (3) distinguishes the hymn from other forms of song in honour of gods, such as the paean, the *prosodion* (processional), and the 'proem' (below), which would all count as *hýmnoi* by use (2). Hymns in this narrow sense may have been principally what the rhetorician *Menander (4) was to call 'cletic' or summoning hymns. As a working definition, (2) is the most useful, because the various forms differentiated in (3) probably shared numerous features of style and content (see below: but about some of these forms we know very little). They are, then, best seen as species within a genus which it is convenient to call 'hymn'.

Modern hymns are written to be performed, communally, on a potentially unlimited number of occasions. The ancient hymn proves less easy to define by reference to the circumstances of performance. The only complete specimens that survive from before the year 400 BC are the *Homeric Hymns*, hexameter compositions ranging from a handful of lines to several hundred. In early sources they are described as προοίμια, 'preludes', because originally at least they were sung as introductions to other hexameter compositions (such no doubt as heroic epic). It is commonly supposed that the longer *Homeric Hymns* had grown into works that stood on their own; the further supposition is often added that they were recited at a festival of the god whom they honour (a possibility that, however, has internal support only in the case of the *Hymn to Delian Apollo*); but, being hexameter works, they were of course not performed chorally. (Other composers of supposedly Archaic hymns known to *Pausanias (3)— *Olen, Pampho, *Orpheus, *Musaeus (1)—also used hexameters.) Similarly, the fragmentary hymns of *Alcaeus (1), if they were presented at festivals at all, were surely, like the rest of his work, sung by a single voice. Another possible context of performance for a short hymn was the *symposium (Pl. *Symp.* 176a).

The hymns of the early choral lyric poets are lost, a few scraps aside, with the important exception of substantial fragments of *Pindar (*Paeans* in particular) and to a lesser extent of *Bacchylides. For Pindar, the *paean is an occasional poem, written to be performed on a particular occasion by a particular chorus; and to a remarkable extent it is given over to glorification, sometimes through mythological exempla, of the country from which the chorus derives. Thus in Pindar's hands it comes to resemble the epinician ode unexpectedly closely. The early ὕμνοι that most recall our hymns are in fact the imitations of the form embedded in drama, above all in the parabases of Old Comedy (see COMEDY (GREEK), OLD).

The picture changes after 400, because the character of our evidence changes: from the 4th cent. and the Hellenistic and Roman periods there survive more than ten hymns that were piously inscribed on stone in sanctuaries (Powell, *Coll. Alex.* 136–73; Page, *PMG* 933–7). Most have a clear relation to cult practice: two have musical notation, one is preceded by instructions for use, another is known in four copies of varying date and provenance. All are comparatively restricted in length, simple in structure, and devoted to praise of the god; not all, however, were necessarily intended for choral rather than solo performance. Guilds of ὑμνῳδοί are also widely attested epigraphically in the Roman period. Conversely, many hymns were also composed that were not, in all seeming, intended for performance: instances are as diverse as the *Hymns* of *Callimachus (3), *Cleanthes' *Hymn to Zeus*, hymns to Fortune and to Nature and to Rome, and in due course epideictic compositions such as the prose hymns of Aelius *Aristides. A special place belongs to the *Orphic Hymns*, a collection of 87 short hexameter poems composed for use, it is generally supposed, by an Orphic society in Asia Minor in or near the 2nd cent. AD: the one surviving ancient Greek hymn-book; see ORPHIC LITERATURE.

Typical features of hymns include: lists of the god's powers and interests and tastes and favourite places (often showing distinctive stylistic features); accumulations of the god's *epithets; portrayals of the god engaged in characteristic activities; greetings, summonses, and *prayers to the god; and, most important of all,

accounts of how the god was born and acquired his or her 'honours' and functions. For the hymn, the fundamental form of 'theology' is 'theogony'.

R. Wünsch, *RE* 9 (1916), 140–83: 'Hymnos'; E. Norden, *Agnostos Theos* (1913); L. Ziehen, *RE* Suppl. 7 (1940), 279–81: 'Hymnodoi'; A. E. Harvey, *CQ* 1955; J. Rudhardt, in P. Borgeaud (ed.), *Orphisme et Orphée* (1991); L. Käppel, *Paian* (1992); M. L. West, *Ancient Greek Music* (1992); W. D. Furley, *JHS* 1995.   R. C. T. P.

hymns (Roman) See CARMEN, and the various particular entries beginning CARMEN, e.g. CARMEN ARVALE.

Hypatia, woman learned in mathematics, astronomy, and philosophy (d. AD 415). Daughter of the mathematician *Theon (4) of *Alexandria (1), she revised the third book of his *Commentary on the Almagest*. Commentaries by her on *Diophantus and *Apollonius (2) are lost. Influential in Alexandria as a teacher of Neoplatonist philosophy, she was torn to pieces by a mob of Christians at the instigation of their bishop (later Saint) Cyril (but see CYRIL OF ALEXANDRIA).

Edition of the *Commentary on the Almagest* by A. Rome, Studi e Testi 106 (1943): see introd. pp. cxvi–cxxi. Socrates Scholasticus 7. 15. See also the letters of *Synesius, her pupil; Gibbon, *Decline and Fall*, ch. 47; R. Hoche, *Philol.* 1860, 435 ff.; J. Sesiano, *Books IV to VII of Diophantus' Arithmetica* (1982), 71 ff.; M. Dzielska, *Hypatia of Alexandria*, trans. F. Lyra (1995).   G. J. T.

Hyperbolus (d. 411 BC), 5th-cent. Athenian *demagogue during and after the *Archidamian War, specially prominent after the death of *Cleon. He is sneered at in comedy for his doubtful paternity and foreign (?slave) origin, but ostraca (see OSTRACISM) show his father had the perfectly normal and reputable Greek name Antiphanes. In 417, 416, or 415 (the date is disputed) an ostracism was held by which Hyperbolus expected to secure the removal of *Alcibiades or *Nicias (1), but they secretly allied against him, and he was himself ostracized. He went to *Samos, where he was murdered by oligarchical revolutionaries. He is condemned by *Thucydides (2) in unusually violent terms (8. 73); but, since he was the constant butt of comic poets, his influence must have been considerable. To some extent he can be rehabilitated by sensible-looking decrees which he proposed or amended (*IG* 1³. 82 and 85). See also DEMAGOGUES.

E. Vanderpool, *Semple Lectures*, 2nd series (1973), 217 ff. (ostraca, with illustrations); W. R. Connor, *The New Politicians of Fifth-Century Athens* (1971), see index; A. Andrewes, *CAH* 5² (1992), 440 ff.; P. J. Rhodes, in R. Osborne and S. Hornblower (eds.), *Ritual, Finance, Politics* (1994).   H. D. W.; S. H.

Hyperboreans, legendary race of *Apollo-worshippers living in the far north, 'beyond the North Wind'; first mentioned in *Hesiod's *Catalogue* (fr. 150. 21 ff. M–W). For *Pindar (*Pyth.* 10. 30 ff.) their land is an earthly paradise presided over by the god, who overwinters there (Alcaeus fr. 307 LP); only heroes like *Perseus (1) or (Pind. *Ol.* 3. 16 ff.) *Heracles might reach it. Elsewhere it functions as a magical place to which things may conveniently disappear (Apollo's first Delphic temple, Paus. 10. 5. 9, see DELPHI; *Croesus from his pyre, Bacchyl. 3. 57 ff.) or from which they may mysteriously materialize (the straw-wrapped offerings to Apollo which were passed down a long chain of real-world intermediaries before eventually reaching *Delos, Hdt. 4. 33–5; cf. Callim. *Hymn* 4. 281–99, Paus. 1. 31. 2). The Delian cult has attracted much speculation; it may perhaps have been a local attempt to trump the Delphic Daphnephoria.

D. L. Page, *Sappho and Alcaeus* (1955), 244 ff.; J. D. P. Bolton, *Aristeas of*

Proconnesus (1962); J. Romm, *The Ends of the Earth in Ancient Tradition* (1992); W. H. Mineur on Callim. *Hymn* 4. 281–99. A. H. G.

Hyperides (Ὑπερείδης), (389–322 BC), prominent Athenian statesman, rated by the ancients second only to *Demosthenes (2) amongst the Ten Orators (see ATTIC ORATORS). He studied rhetoric under *Isocrates and began his career by writing speeches for others (i.e. he was a *logographos*). His political career opened with an attack on *Aristophon in 363/2. There were other, perhaps numerous, such prosecutions of leading figures, the most notable being his successful prosecution of *Philocrates in 343 which heralded his future bitter opposition to Macedon (see PHILIP (1) II), and after the battle of *Chaeronea he assumed a leading role. Immediately after the action in which 1,000 Athenians had died and 2,000 were captured, he sought to provide replacements by making *metics citizens and freeing slaves; he was himself duly indicted for this unconstitutional measure but it showed his determination to resist, as did indeed his prosecution of *Demades and other collaborationists and his vigorous plea to the Athenians not to accede to *Alexander (3) the Great's demand in 335 for Demosthenes and others (amongst whom Hyperides was counted by *Arrian, but *Plutarch *Dem.* 23 makes it clear enough that he was not one). In 324/3 he led the attack on Demosthenes and others who were accused of appropriating the money deposited by *Harpalus. Presumably he wanted it for the coming revolt against Macedon. Indeed Hyperides was the chief supporter of *Leosthenes and of Athenian action in the *Lamian War. Fittingly he was chosen to deliver the Funeral Oration (see EPITAPHIOS) of late 323, a speech of which much survives. With the collapse of the Greek resistance, Hyperides had to flee. He was captured and put to death, *Antipater (1), in one version, first ordering the cutting out of the tongue which had so bitterly assailed him and Macedon, a not ignoble end for one of the heroes of Greek liberty.

Works Although in antiquity of the 77 speeches preserved under the name of Hyperides over 50 were regarded as genuine, except for a few fragments his work was unknown to moderns until 1847. Between that year and 1892 papyri were discovered containing several of his speeches, in whole or in part, most notably the all too fragmentary attack on Demosthenes of 324/3.

In general tone he is akin to *Lysias. He borrowed words and phrases from comedy, thus bringing his language into touch with the speech of everyday life. *'Longinus' *On the Sublime* draws attention to his wit, his suavity and persuasiveness, his tact and good taste. He can be sarcastic and severe without becoming offensive; his reproof often takes the form of humorous banter. He speaks with respect of his adversaries and avoids scurrilous abuse.

For general bibliog. see ATTIC ORATORS.
TEXT F. G. Kenyon (OCT, 1906); C. Jensen (Teubner, 1917), with index; with Fr. trans., G. Colin (Budé, 1946); with Eng. trans., J. O. Burtt, *Minor Attic Orators* 2 (Loeb, 1954).
COMMENTARY D. Whitehead (2000)
SPECIAL STUDIES D. Gromska, *De Sermone Hyperidis* (1927); U. Pohle, *Die Sprache des H. in ihren Beziehung zur Koine* (1928); G. Bartolini, *Iperide: Rassegna di problemi e di studi (1912–1972)* (1977); J. Engels, *Studien zur politischen Biographie des Hypereides: Athen in der Epoche der lykurgischen Reformen und des makedonischen Universalreiches* (1989). G. L. C.

Hyperion, a *Titan, husband of his sister Theia and father by her of the Sun, Moon, and Dawn (Hes. *Theog.* 371 ff., cf. 134 f.). Often the name is used as an epithet of the Sun himself, as *Od.* 12. 133.

Hypnos, the god of sleep in Greek mythology. Hypnos is fatherless, son of *Nyx and brother of *Thanatos (Hes. *Theog.* 211, 756). According to *Hesiod he lives in the Underworld and never sees the sun, but in contrast to his brother he comes softly and is sweet for men. In *Homer, however, Hypnos lives on *Lemnos and gets from *Hera the Charis (see CHARITES) Pasithea as wife. He is human at first, but changes into a bird of the night before he makes Zeus fall asleep (*Il.* 14. 231 ff.). Throughout antiquity Hypnos was usually thought of as a winged youth who touches the foreheads of the tired with a branch (Verg. *Aen.* 5. 854) or pours sleep-inducing liquid from a horn. Myths about Hypnos are few: he helps to bury *Sarpedon (*Il.* 16. 672) and is said to have fallen in love with *Endymion whom he made to sleep with open eyes (Ath. 13. 564c). He had a cult in *Troezen (Paus. 2. 31. 3). In art, Hypnos carried by Nyx was shown on the chest of *Cypselus; on vases, he and Thanatos carry *Memnon (1), Sarpedon, and human warriors to the grave. A beautiful Hellenistic statue known through several copies shows Hypnos gliding over the ground and pouring sleep-bringing liquid from his horn.

B. Sauer in Roscher, *Lex.* 'Hypnos'; Paus. ed. Frazer, 3. 600; H. Schrader, *Winckelmannsprogramm Berlin* 1926; E. Pottier, 'Étude sur les lécythes blancs', *Bibl. Éc. Franç.* 1883; D. Jones, *CR* 1949, 83; Y. Jeannin, *Revue archéologique de l'Est et du Centre-Est* 1963, 118 ff.; G. Wöhrle, *Hypnos der Allbezwinger* (1995). G. M. A. H.

hypocaust (ὑπόκαυστον; *hypocaustum*), a raised floor heated from below by a furnace (ὑπόκαυσις; *praefurnium*). Elementary types are found in some Hellenistic baths (Gortys in *Arcadia; *Gela in Sicily) but the fully developed system originated in central Italy and is already found in *baths *c*.100 BC (Stabian baths, *Pompeii; cf. Val. Max. 9. 1. 1, Plin. *HN* 9. 168) and in private *houses by the later 1st cent. *Vitruvius (*De arch.* 5. 10) describes the *suspensurae* (raised floors) as carried on narrow brick piers (*pilae*) set at regular intervals and supporting 60-cm. (24-in.) square tiles (*bipedales*); the piers are commonly square, but round or polygonal bricks, hollow terracotta cylinders, and solid stone are also found. Heating was effected by radiation. From the later 1st cent. BC cavity-wall and sometimes vault heating was added, achieved in various ways but most commonly in the empire with rectangular wall-tubes (*tubuli*). Wood was the usual fuel. Hypocausts, often consisting of masses of masonry intersected by channels, were also used for domestic heating particularly in colder lands and increasingly in the late empire (*Dig.* 32. 1. 55).

I. Nielsen, *Thermae et Balnea* (1990), 14 ff.; D. Krencker and E. Krüger, *Die Trierer Kaiserthermen* (1929), 332 ff.; H. Hüser, *Saalburg Jahrbuch* (1979), 12 ff. J. D.

hypothesis, literary (Greek). (1) Prefixed to plays. Nearly all Greek dramas have an introductory note giving an outline of the plot and often other information; a number of them are in verse. They are of three main types, though they have become much confused in the course of transmission. Far the most important are those which are based on the introductions which *Aristophanes (2) of Byzantium seems to have prefixed to each play in his edition. These consist of a terse note on the subject-matter and of information on the production, etc., of the play assembled from Alexandrian reference books, especially the *Pinakes* of *Callimachus (3), and so ultimately from *Aristotle's *Didascaliae*. No complete hypothesis of this type survives, but it can be seen that the following information was given in the case of tragedy: treatment of subject, if any, by other poets; the scene of action; the identity of the chorus and first speaker; the number of the play in chronological order; the date of production, success in the competition, and names of competing plays; name of *chorēgos* (see CHORĒGIA). Sometimes critical judgements are added. The second type is of Byzantine origin and mainly for school use; they are verbose, full of elementary information, and many of those belonging to comedies contain garbled history. The third type is associated especially with *Euripides. Each contains a competent summary of the plot keeping to the past tense throughout and supplying names for characters who are nameless in the play. These seem to have been intended as substitutes for the plays rather than as introductions and form a sort of mythological compendium. In addition to those which occur in the MSS of the plays many fragments of the collection have been recovered on papyrus (POxy. 27. 2455, 2457, and 52. 3653; PSI 1286) grouped by initial letters in the same sort of quasi-alphabetical order as is found in the list of plays on the Piraeus stone IG 2. 2. 992 and as is indicated by the numerals attached to plays in the Laurentian MS of *Euripides. They are a valuable source of information on lost plays. Since their date is probably of the 1st cent. BC they cannot be the same as those allegedly produced by *Dicaearchus for *Sophocles (1) and Euripides (Sext. Emp. Math. 3. 3), which appear to have contained also investigations into the origin of the poet's subject-matter.

The hypotheses of comedies are on the whole better supplied with didascalic information. (See DIDASKALIA.) A number of them are the work of an Atticizing writer, perhaps Symmachus, of early imperial times and they are similar to the hypothesis of *Cratinus' *Dionysalexandros* (POxy. 4. 663). The portions of the hypotheses of *Menander (1)'s *Hieraiai* and *Imbrioi* (POxy. 10. 1235) seem to be part of a complete set comparable to the Euripides hypotheses, but in the case of Menander in addition to the opening line of the play didascalic information is supplied.

Verse hypotheses, rare for tragedy, seem to have been regularly prefixed to comedies. Those of *Aristophanes (1) are all of ten lines, the two that survive for Menander, *Dyscolus* and *Heros*, are of twelve. The date of the papyri shows they are not Byzantine, but whether their language is Hellenistic is doubtful. The frequent ascription to the other Aristophanes (of Byzantium; see above) carries no weight.

L. Cohn, RE 2. 998 f.; A. Körte, Hermes 1904, 481 ff. (on the Cratinus hyp.); T. O. H. Achelis, Philol. 1913–14; L. Radermacher, Aristophanes: Ranae (1954), 74 ff.; G. Zuntz, Political Plays of Euripides (1963), ch. 6; W. Michel, De fabularum Graecarum argumentis metricis (1908).

D. W. L.; N. G. W.

(2) Hypotheses to the speeches of *Demosthenes (2) written by *Libanius for the proconsul Montius, an enthusiastic admirer of Demosthenes.

(3) A particular case propounded for discussion in rhetorical schools, contrasted with a general question (θέσις) discussed in dialectical schools. The distinction is, however, not always observed.

H. Thom, Die Thesis (1932), 61 f.

J. D. D.

hypothesis, scientific

The English transliteration of the Greek word ὑπόθεσις can conceal something of the variety of senses this term has in ancient contexts. Etymologically it suggests 'the basis upon which something else is grounded'. In Greek the term may be applied to the summary of the plot of a play (see HYPOTHESIS, LITERARY), a political or legal proposal, a topic to be discussed, a proposition to be proved, an unprovable assumption which is the basis for deduction, an acceptable supposition which its author may or may not choose to prove, or a fully fledged

model or system of explanation which permits further work. *Ptolemy (4) can describe his model of the wandering heavenly bodies, for example, as his 'hypotheses' of the planets. Strict logical senses of the term can be traced back at least to *Plato (1) and *Aristotle; Aristotle defines a hypothesis as a thesis which assumes either part of a contradiction as a basis for further deduction (An. post. 72ᵃ20–4.). Hypotheses are one of the three starting-points (with axioms and definitions) of Aristotelian 'scientific demonstration'.

Two early occurrences of the term are often used to illustrate the beginnings of two distinctive methodological positions which dominated much ancient investigation into nature. Probably the earliest use of the term to describe a postulate or assumption—something which has not, or cannot be proven but which forms the basis for further theoretical investigation—occurs in the first chapter of the Hippocratic treatise (see HIPPOCRATES (2)) On Ancient Medicine, where the use of such hypotheses in medicine is condemned. Medicine has no need of them, claims the author, in the way that inquiries into the 'things above and below the earth' do. These are subjects where we cannot know if we are being presented with the truth or not, where reasoning is based on principles whose reliability is not readily testable. Medicine for the author, by contrast, proceeds as it always has done, through the empirical study of *dietetics.

The other important early discussions of the term are in Plato's *Phaedo* (99d–101e) and *Meno* (86e). To take just the second example, Socrates remarks that a hypothesis is 'the sort of thing that geometers often make use of in their inquiries'. He offers the cryptic case of a geometer asked if a given area can be inscribed as a triangle within a given circle. The geometer replies by describing a 'hypothetical' method which would lead him to the correct solution; he makes the problem depend on another proposition, the hypothesis, whose validity and consequences should then be tested to throw light on the original problem.

The relative dates of these Hippocratic and Platonic passages have given rise to some debate, but most scholars now agree that On Ancient Medicine was written before the Meno passage. Whatever the case, On Ancient Medicine and the hypothetical method outlined in the Meno represent two opposing methodological models, each of which continued to be developed in a variety of contexts for many centuries. On Ancient Medicine, with its own argument that medicine arose out of empirical dietetic investigation—'traditional', or 'ancient' medicine—stands opposed to the hypothetical methods which are attributed by its author to other unnamed, but probably non-mathematical, philosophers and to the geometer by Plato, and which are examined in most detail by Aristotle in the Organon. The dispute between the two models can be seen continuing in later Greek sectarian medicine, where empiricist 'anti-theoretical' doctors engaged in lively debate with those who believed that theory and the logical apparatus needed to test it were indispensable. *Galen's faith in the medical relevance of proof through deduction is consistently stressed throughout his surviving œuvre, even if in practice his tolerance of the hypothetical is flexible.

A. Wasserstein, Revue philosophique de la France et de l'Étranger 1972, 3–14; G. E. R. Lloyd, Aristotle, the Growth and Structure of his Thought (1963; new edn. 1991). On Galen's logic, see J. Barnes in F. Kudlien and R. Durling (eds.), Galen's Method of Healing (1991); G. E. R. Lloyd, in Methods and Problems in Greek Science (1991), 49–69.

J. T. V.

Hypsicles (RE 2), of *Alexandria (1), mathematician and astronomer (fl. c.150 BC), wrote: (1) 'Book 14' added to *Euclid's *Elements*. This contains interesting propositions and historical information about relationships between the regular dodecahedron and eicosahedron inscribed in the same sphere. (2) *On Rising-times* (Άναφορικός), which adapts to the latitude of Alexandria a Babylonian arithmetical scheme for computing the times taken by individual signs of the zodiac to rise. It is the earliest Greek work to use the 360-degree division of the circle. *Diophantus (ed. Tannery 1. 470) quotes a definition of a polygonal number from a lost work of Hypsicles. Also lost is a work on the harmony of the spheres (*Achilles Tatius (2), ed. Maass, *Comm. in Arat.* 43).

EDITIONS *Elements 14*, in *Euclidis Opera Omnia 5* (Teubner, 1888; repr. 1977). Άναφορικός, ed. De Falco and Krause (1966), with Ger. trans.

COMMENT *Elements 14*, Heath, *Hist. of Greek Maths.* 1. 419 ff.; best: G. Loria, *Le scienze esatte nell'antica Grecia* (1914), 270 ff. Άναφορικός, *HAMA* 2. 715 ff. Evidence for date in Fraser, *Ptol. Alex.* 2. 612 n. 381.
G. J. T.

Hypsicrates (probably 1st cent. BC), historian, may be identified with the grammarian Hypsicrates of *Amisus; he may have served *Caesar, who freed Amisus in 47 BC, as *Theophanes served *Pompey. His work was perhaps rather a history of the times than a local chronicle of *Pontus, and was possibly *Strabo's source for Bosporan affairs (see BOSPORUS (1)).

FGrH 190; R. Syme, *Anatolica* (1995), 292.   A. H. McD.; S. H.

Hypsipyle (a) Because the women of *Lemnos neglected the rites of *Aphrodite, she made them stink, and their husbands left them to take concubines from *Thrace. They then murdered all the males on the island, except that Hypsipyle hid her father King Thoas, son of *Dionysus, and got him out of the country (cf. Hypermestra amongst the *Danaids). She now governed Lemnos and received the *Argonauts when they came. The women mated with them, and Hypsipyle had two sons (see EUNEOS) by *Jason (1). The myth is interpreted as the counterpart of a new year ritual where women form a temporary separate society (as in the *Thesmophoria) and a ship (represented by the Argonauts) bears new fire from *Delos, allowing households to be re-formed. (b) 'Later', Hypsipyle as a slave is sold to Lycurgus king of *Nemea (1), whose wife employed her as nurse to her child Opheltes or Archemorus. While she shows a watering-place to the passing army of the *Seven against Thebes, a snake kills Opheltes. Amphiaraus secures her pardon and the *Nemean Games are founded in the child's honour.

(a) and (b) are clearly in origin two different Hypsipyles, one from Lemnos and one from Nemea.

(a) Ap. Rhod. 1. 609 ff. and schol.; Apollod. 1. 9. 17; Hyg. *Fab.* 15. W. Burkert, *CQ* 1970, 1–16. (b) Eur. *Hyps.* (with G. W. Bond's edn. 1963); Stat. *Theb.* 4. 715 ff.; Apollod. 3. 6. 4; Hyg. *Fab.* 74.   H. J. R.; K. D.

Hypsistos (Ύψιστος), 'Most High', one of the commonest divine *epithets in late antiquity. The most important application was one familiar from a wide range of literary and epigraphic texts, beginning in the Hellenistic period, whereby 'highest god', θεὸς ὕψιστος, was the standard way of referring in Greek to the god of Judaism. Dedications to θεὸς ὕψιστος are, however, found in places where no Jewish or Christian presence is yet attested, and a broader disposition to exalt a particular god, temporarily at least, as 'highest' is doubtless to be recognized. The widespread cult of 'Highest God' in Anatolia perhaps represents a compromise or synthesis between Jewish, Christian, and pagan tendencies, of the kind continued by the 'Hypsistarian' sect of *Cappadocia in the 4th cent. AD (*Gregory (2) of Nazianzus, *Or.* 18. 5).

In many cults, as in one established on the deserted *Pnyx in Athens in the 2nd cent. AD, dedications to 'Highest God' or plain 'Highest' alternate with others to 'Highest *Zeus'; in such cases there is usually still less reason to suspect Jewish worshippers. This Athenian 'Highest Zeus' is a healer, while in a flourishing Macedonian cult first attested in the 1st cent. BC (S. Drougou, *Egnatia* 1990, 45–71) dedications are regularly made 'on behalf of' members of the dedicant's family. The functions implied are not those of the classical *Zeus, associated with high places and even termed 'highest' though he was (occasionally ὕψιστος in poetry, e.g. Aesch. *Eum.* 28, and often Hypatos in cult), and it looks as if this 'Highest Zeus' of post-Classical worship is normally a product of *syncretism (in *Macedonia the influence of *Sabazius has been suggested). How many distinct figures underlie the various 'Highest Zeus'es of late antiquity remains to be clarified.

A. D. Nock, *Harv. Theol. Rev.* 1936, 55–69 (= *Essays on Religion and the Ancient World* (1972), 1. 416–27), still fundamental; for various regions see L. Robert, *Opera Minora Selecta* (1969–90), 1. 411–17, 5. 594; M. Tačeva-Hitava, *Balkan Studies* 1978, 59–75; S. Sanie, in *Hommages à M. J. Vermaseren* 3 (1978), 1092–1115; T. Drew-Bear and C. Naour, *ANRW* 2. 18. 3 (1990), 2032–43; B. Forssen, *Hesp.* 1993, 507–21; S. Mitchell, *Anatolia*, 2 vols. (1993), 2. 49–51.   R. C. T. P.

Hyrcanus See HASMONEANS.

Hyrnetho/Hyrnatho, Eponym of the Argive (see ARGOS (2)) tribe Hyrnathioi (who were the non-*Dorian, or not fully Dorian, tribe of Argos), *Temenus' daughter and Deiphontes' wife. After her brothers had had their father killed for favouring her and *Deiphontes, in some versions of the myth Hyrnetho and Deiphontes succeeded Temenus; in others, the kingdom was split between them and Hyrnetho's brothers, who tried to persuade her to leave Deiphontes and abducted her when she refused. Deiphontes came to her rescue but one of her brothers killed her while dragging her away. Deiphontes buried her in a *heroon* (see HERO-CULT) at *Epidaurus and established a cult. (Nicolaus of Damascus, *FGrH* 90 F 30; Apollod. 2. 8. 5; Paus. 2. 19. 1–2, 26. 2, 28. 3–7; cf. *POxy.* 2455 frs. 9–13 on Euripides' *Temenidae* and *Temenus*). She also had a grave at Argos (Paus. 2. 23. 3).

P. Friedländer, *RE* 11. 535–6; L. H. Jeffery, *Archaic Greece* (1976), 140, 150.   C. S.-I.

Hysiae (SW of *Argos (2)), **battle of** See PHEIDON; SPARTA.

Hysiae, small city in SE *Boeotia situated on the foothills of Mt. Cithaeron above the Asopus river along the road between *Plataea and *Attica. *Thebes (1) seized it either in 519 or 509 BC, but Athens regained it shortly thereafter. *Mardonius occupied it before the battle of *Plataea, and afterwards it again became a dependency of Plataea. By 395 BC Hysiae and *Orchomenus (1) constituted two units of the Boeotian Confederacy (see BOEOTIA; FEDERAL STATES), a Theban design to weaken the position of Orchomenus. *Pausanias (3) mentions only the remains of an unfinished temple of *Apollo and a sacred well still to be seen.

F. Bölte, *RE* 9. 1 (1914), cols. 1171–5; J. M. Fossey, *Topography and Population of Ancient Boiotia* (1988), 112 ff.   J. Bu.

hysteria, contrary to popular belief, was not so named by the Greeks. In Hippocratic *gynaecology (see HIPPOCRATES (2)) the womb (Gk. *hystera*) was indeed believed to 'wander' around the body, as a result of menstrual suppression, exhaustion, insufficient food, sexual abstinence, or because it is abnormally dry or light (e.g. Hippoc. *Mul.* 1. 7). However, neither the classic picture of symptoms familiar from 19th-cent. literature, nor the disease label, existed. Hysteria derives not so much from Hippocratic medicine, in which a number of different disorders were distinguished according to the part of the body to which the errant womb moved (e.g. *Mul.* 2. 123–31), as from the category of 'suffocation of/by the womb' dating to the Hellenistic period. The discovery by *Herophilus of the ligaments anchoring the womb to the abdominal cavity led to new explanations of how the womb could cause disturbances of breathing. *Galen (*De loc. aff.* 6. 5) drew a distinction between suffocation caused by retained menstrual blood and that caused by retained female 'seed', the latter being more severe. *Aretaeus suggested that 'sympathy'

exists between the womb and the higher organs, allowing the breathing to be affected by the womb (*On the Causes and Symptoms of Acute and Chronic Diseases* 4. 11). In an attack of hysterical suffocation, the patient was generally thought to lie as if dead, with no perceptible pulse. Therapies included sneezing, the application of foul smells to the nostrils to drive the womb down, venesection at the ankle, and marriage and pregnancy. See MEN-STRUATION.

H. King, in S. Gilman and others, *Hysteria Beyond Freud* (1993), 3–90; B. Simon, *Mind and Madness in Ancient Greece* (1978); I. Veith, *Hysteria: The History of a Disease* (1965); H. von Staden, *Herophilus* (1989).

H. K.

Iacchus (Ἴακχος), patron god of the initiates in their procession to *Eleusis in the *mysteries. In origin he was probably a personification of the ritual cry ἴακχ᾽ ὦ ἴακχε (Ar. *Ran.* 316) sung by the initiates as they marched; cf. HYMENAEUS. In art he is a torchbearer, seen conducting (or in the company of) initiates, usually divine initiates (*Heracles, *Dionysus, *Dioscuri). In the mysteries the procession of initiates, led by a priest called Iacchagogus (i.e. bearer of Iacchus), was given a day of its own (Boedromion 20; the escort (πομπή) of the sacred objects by priestesses, priests, and magistrats of Athens took place on the preceding day). Late traditions made Iacchus the son of *Demeter, of *Persephone, and of Dionysus, or the consort of Demeter, but evidently none of this was derived from the mysteries.

The name Iacchus, like Bacchus, was also used of *Dionysus, frequently in literature, but in cult there was never confusion between the Eleusinian god of initiates and Dionysus, who was not worshipped in the mysteries. The important sanctuary of Dionysus at Eleusis caused some confusion between him and Iacchus among non-Athenian writers in antiquity and even more among modern scholars.

Clinton, *Iconography*, chs. 2–3; Graf, *Eleusis*, 40–59.   K. C.

Ialmenus, in mythology, son of *Ares and *Astyoche; leader, with his brother *Ascalaphus, of the contingent from Aspledon and *Orchomenus (1) at Troy (*Il.* 2. 511 ff.).

Ialysus was one of three independent Dorian cities on *Rhodes until the *synoecism with *Lindus and Camirus created the federal Rhodian state in 408/7 BC. The city lay near Mt. Filerimos, the ancient acropolis with remains of the temple of *Athena Polias and *Zeus Polieus (over older remains) and a fountain-house. The civic area below is unexcavated, but the extensive necropolis revealed tombs of Mycenaean to Classical date. The north-eastern third of Rhodes was Ialysian territory, and included the sanctuary of Apollo Erethimios at Theologos.

The Diagoridae were a noble family of Ialysus whose members included several *Olympian victors (the boxer Diagoras is celebrated in Pind. *Ol.* 7) and Dorieus, an oligarch exiled by Athens during the Peloponnesian War. He joined Sparta in 412 BC, and the Diagoridai were restored in 411 (Thuc. 8. 35 ff.). Their oligarchic rule continued after the synoecism until the democratic revolution in 395–4.

Inscriptions in *IG* 12. 1 (1895). *Clara Rhodos* 1928, 56 ff.; *RE* Suppl. 5. 748–9; G. Konstantinopoulos, *Arhaia Rodos* (1986) (in Greek).
          E. E. R.

Iambe, eponym of the iambic rhythm, made the mourning *Demeter laugh at *Eleusis by her jesting in the *Homeric Hymn to Demeter* (198–205). She comes from *Halimous on the coast near Athens in *Philicus' *Hymn to Demeter* (*Suppl. Hell.* 676–80), and is connected with jesting by women at the *Thesmophoria (Apollod. 1. 5. 1). She was also said to be the daughter of *Echo and *Pan (Philochorus, *FGrH* 328 F 103 etc.), and a Thracian (Nic. *Alex.* 130).

P. Maas, *RE* 9. 633; N. J. Richardson, *The Homeric Hymn to Demeter* (1974), 213–18.   N. J. R.

iambic poetry, Greek 'Iambic' metre got its name from *iambos* (ἴαμβος), a term associated in various parts of Greece with traditional jesting and ribaldries in certain festivals of *Demeter and *Dionysus. This and similar words (διθύραμβος ('*dithyramb'), θρίαμβος, ἴθυμβος) seem to be pre-Hellenic. At *Eleusis the ribaldry was traced back to the mythical *Iambe (*Hymn. Hom. Cer.* 192–205). At *Syracuse the *iambistai* were dancers (Ath. 181c). *Epicharmus (fr. 88 Kaibel, *CGF*) associates *iamboi* with Aristoxenus of Selinus, an Archaic poet from whom one anapaestic verse attacking seers is quoted. In Ionia in the 7th and 6th cent. BC the *iambos* achieved literary status when *Archilochus and others published monologues and songs composed for *festival entertainment and characterized by satirical denunciation of individuals or types, amusing narrations, and lubriciousness. The term 'iambic poetry' applies primarily to this material and to later literature inspired by it.

A recurrent feature in the Ionian texts is the first-person account of extravagant sexual adventures that the speaker claims to have had. In some cases he perhaps adopted a character role such as a cook (Semon. 24 West), a peasant farmer (*Hipponax 26 W), or a burglar (Hipponax fr. 32 W); there are possible suggestions of a phallus being worn (Archil. 66–7; Hipponax 78. 14 W), as later by some comic actors. The characteristic metres are the iambic trimeter and trochaic tetrameter, the paradoxical 'scazon' forms of these (with penultimate long), and simple epodic strophes of various sorts. The three principal iambographers of the Archaic period are *Archilochus, *Semonides of Amorgos, and Hipponax; but Archilochus, at least, wrote much that does not belong under the heading of *iambos*. The important Demeter cult on *Paros probably provided the setting for his *iamboi*. The word ἴαμβοι first occurs in a fragment of his (215), as something associated with festivity and fun. Semonides' and Hipponax' *iamboi* reflect other local Ionian traditions, in Hipponax' case perhaps that of the Ephesian (see EPHESUS) Thargelia (cf. frs. 5–10 + 104. 49 W). Some pieces by one Ananius, similar to Hipponax', circulated with his. The 'Homeric' *Margites* and the anti-women monologue of Susarion may also be counted as *iamboi*, and one of *Anacreon's poems is cited under this designation (Page, *PMG* 432). In the 5th cent. BC the Athenian comic poet *Hermippus (1) produced some *iamboi*, perhaps as a temporary substitute for comedy. Old Comedy (see COMEDY (GREEK), ORIGINS OF) had in fact much in common with the *iambos*, and probably developed out of something analogous.

In the Hellenistic period the distinctive style of Hipponax in particular attracted imitators. His choliambic metre was taken up by Aeschrion and *Asclepiades (2), both of Samos, then by *Phoenix (3) of Colophon, *Callimachus (3), *Herodas, *Apollonius (1) Rhodius (*Canobus*), and others. Callimachus in his book of *Iamboi* presented himself as a Hipponax *redivivus* (fr. 191 Pf.), while taking some of his metres from Archilochus. He retained Hipponax' dialect and some of his diction. Herodas did likewise (with less restraint), but created a new genre, the *mimiambos*, by writing character *mimes (dialogue or monologue) in the Hipponactean language and metre, appropriately for the low-class urban life portrayed. Cercidas, besides writing some choliambics, forged another new combination with his *Meliamboi*, which were 'iambic' in their satirical content and racy language but lyric in form.

Iambic metre, though named after the Ionian *iambos*, was always available for more serious purposes. The trimeter was used in inscribed and literary epigrams at all periods besides the hexameter and elegiac. Archilochus, Semonides, and *Solon sometimes used it for serious reflective, personal, or political poems. It was adopted as the natural metre for monologue and dialogue in Attic drama. In the later 4th and 3rd cents. BC it was employed by various philosophers, moralists, and satirists (*Chares (3), *Crantor, *Crates (2), *Zeno (2), *Cleanthes), and by *Machon for his *Chreiai*. In the 2nd cent. BC *Apollodorus (6)'s iambic *Chronica* started a tradition of didactic poems in this metre (pseudo-*Scymnus, Servilius Damocrates, *Philemon (7), and others yet obscurer). From the 4th cent. AD the trimeter came into more general use for hymns, encomia, narrative poems, etc., and for prologues to hexameter poems. The choliambic too was put to some use in the Roman period, in particular by *Babrius for his Aesopic fables (see AESOP) and in parts of the Alexander Romance (see PSEUDO-CALLISTHENES).

TEXTS West, *IE*[2]; Powell, *Coll. Alex.*; A. D. Knox, *Herodes, Cercidas and the Greek Choliambic poets* (Loeb, 1929); Lloyd-Jones and Parsons, *Suppl. Hell.*; see also under individual authors.

DISCUSSION M. L. West, *Studies in Greek Elegy and Iambus* (1974), ch. 2.

M. L. W.

iambic poetry, Latin The Roman grammarian *Diomedes (3) (Keil, *Gramm. Lat.* 1. 485. 11 ff.) defines an *iambus* as follows: 'an abusive poem, usually composed in ⟨iambic⟩ trimeters followed by epodic dimeters … it derives its name from τὸ ἰαμβίζειν, which means "to abuse". The main Greek exponents of this kind of poetry are *Archilochus and *Hipponax; the main Roman exponents are *Lucilius (1), *Catullus (1), *Horace, and ⟨*Furius⟩ Bibaculus.' Diomedes here makes, either explicitly or by implication, three points about Latin iambic.

(*a*) It is verse in the manner of the old Ionian iambographers Archilochus and Hipponax (see IAMBIC POETRY, GREEK). Thus Horace's *Epodes*—the main Latin representative of iambic poetry—specifically invoke the precedent of these two poets (6. 13–14). Elsewhere, Horace claims to have been the first to introduce 'Parian' (i.e. Archilochean) iambics to Rome, and to have imitated in his *Epodes* 'the metres and spirit' of Archilochus, though not his subject-matter (*Epist.* 1. 19. 23 ff., a deeply contentious passage). Similarly Catullus, Horace's predecessor in the genre, more than once echoes Archilochus in such a way as to advertise his debt to him: see especially 40. 1 ff.

(*b*) The main characteristic of the genre was its abusiveness.

Hence Horace, in *Odes* 1. 16. 2, speaks of *iambi* as *criminosi* ('insulting'), while *Pomponius Porphyrio, in commenting upon this poem, remarks 'iambic verse is reckoned the most suitable for abuse'. Elsewhere, *iambus* is glossed as 'pugnacious' (Ov. *Ib.* 521), as 'vengeful' (Stat. *Silv.* 2. 2. 115), and as the product of rage (Hor. *Ars P.* 79).

(*c*) It was, by and large, the presence of such abuse, rather than metrical criteria, which classified a poem as iambic. This is why Diomedes, and Apuleius too (*Apol.* 10), describe Lucilius as an iambographer, though the bulk of his work is in hexameters, and he actually wrote very little in iambics. The same reasoning underlies Catullus' application of the term *iambi* to insulting verses written in the hendecasyllabic metre.

Leaving aside for the moment Horace's *Epodes*, Latin iambic may be said to comprise several pieces in the *Catalepton* (see APPENDIX VERGILIANA) (notably the ferocious no. 13), various *Priapea* which exhibit a witty line in sexual insults (an important topic in *iambus*), the lost work of Ovid's contemporary Bassus, some of Ausonius, and, most importantly, the brief sceptic (i.e. mocking, satirical) poems of Catullus and the Neoterics (see HELLENISTIC POETRY AT ROME). A favourite target was politicians and their henchmen; cf. Tac. *Ann.* 4. 34, 'one may read poems of Catullus and Bibaculus which are replete with abuse of the Caesars.' In view of Catullus' propensity for 'savage *iambi*', some have treated as disingenuous Horace's claim to have been the first to transplant Archilochean iambic to Rome. But it is better to regard the *Epodes* as deploying for the first time at Rome the *full* range of Archilochean (and Hipponactean) iambic, rather than iambic in the narrower Diomedean and Catullan sense of poetry of personal abuse.

What in fact sets the *Epodes* apart from the bulk of Latin iambic is precisely this breadth of theme, allied to a muting of the genre's pugnaciousness. The latter development is signalled when Horace describes the *Epodes* (*Epist.* 1. 19. 23 ff.) in terms which echo *Callimachus (3)'s programmatic disclaimer, in his *Iambi*, of Hipponactean bellicosity. Thus the poems are concerned with subjects as diverse as friendship, food, social hygiene, contemporary politics, amatory misfortunes, erotic débâcles, moral hypocrisy, and witchcraft, as well as traditional targets of *iambus* such as lecherous crones and social upstarts. See also under individual authors.

J. Newman, *Catullus and the Modification of the Alexandrian Sensibility* (1990), 43 ff.; G. Gerhard, *RE* 9. 1 (1914), cols. 651–80: 'Iambographen'; A. Cavarzere, *Orazio: Il libro degli Epodi* (1992), 9 ff.; V. Grassmann, *Die erotischen Epoden des Horaz* (1966), E. Fraenkel, *Horace* (1957); W. Fitzgerald, *Ramus* 1988; C. Macleod *CQ* 1977 (= *Collected Essays* (1983), 262 ff.).

L. C. W.

Iamblichus (1) (fl. *c.* AD 165–180), Greek novelist (see NOVEL, GREEK) who alleged Syrian birth and mother-tongue, author of *The Babylonian History* (Βαβυλωνιακά) or *The Story of Sinonis and Rhodanes* (Τὰ κατὰ Σινωνίδα καὶ Ῥοδάνην) which he claims to have got from his tutor, a 'Babylonian' captured in *Trajan's Parthian war. The *Suda* says there were 39 books (subdivisions) and preserves some fragments. These, with *Photius' *epitome (*Bibl.* cod. 94) of a text that he says had 16 books (p. 68. 15 Habrich)—an abridgement or a different edition?—attest many typical novelistic elements. The separated lovers, surviving many hazards in a near-eastern setting, including rivals' lust and sorcery, were at last reunited. Mistaken identity and false deaths contributed to melodrama, but plot and characterization, sometimes criticized, are hard to assess on our scanty remains. Rhetoric marks speeches and *ekphraseis*.

EDITION E. Habrich (Teubner, 1960); S. A. Stephens and J. J. Winkler, *Ancient Greek Novels: The Fragments* (1993).

ENGLISH TRANSLATION G. N. Sandy, in B. P. Reardon (ed.), *Collected Ancient Greek Novels* (1989).

CRITICISM Rohde, *Griech. Roman*, 388 ff.; W. Kroll, *RE* 17 (1914), 640–5, 'Iamblichos' 2; Christ–Schmid–Stählin 2/2⁶. 817 ff.; A. Lesky, *A History of Greek Literature* (1966), 864; E. L. Bowie, *CHCL* 1. 692 (= paperback 1/4 (1989), 132); T. Hägg, *The Novel in Antiquity* (1983), 32–4; G. Anderson, *Eros Sophistes* (1982), 51–4; A. Borgogno, *Hermes* 1975.
E. L. B.

Iamblichus (2) (*c.* AD 245–*c.*325), *Neoplatonist philosopher, born at Chalcis in Coele Syria (mod. Qinnesrin), probably studied with *Porphyry in Rome or Sicily; later he founded his own school in Syria (? at Apamea). Extant writings: (1) A compendium of Pythagorean philosophy (largely compiled from extracts derived from earlier writers, Platonic, Aristotelian, and Pythagorean, see PLATO (1), ARISTOTLE, PYTHAGORAS (1)), of which the first four books survive: On the Life of Pythagoras (*VP*), *Protrepticus* (believed to contain material from Aristotle's lost *Protrepticus*), *On General Mathematical Science* (*Dcms*), *On Nicomachus' Arithmetical Introduction* (*In Nic.*); (2) The 'Reply of Abammon to Porphyry's Letter to Anebo', known as *De mysteriis* (*Myst.*). Iamblichus' lost writings (of which fragments survive) include a work *On the Soul* (excerpts preserved in *Stobaeus); one *On the Gods*, probably used by *Macrobius and *Julian; an extensive exposition of Chaldaean theology; letters (excerpted by Stobaeus); and commentaries on Plato and Aristotle which were fundamental sources for later Greek Neoplatonist commentators.

Iamblichus' successors (in particular Syrianus and Proclus) credit him with determining the direction taken by later Neoplatonic philosophy. He established a standard school curriculum; imposed a systematic method of interpreting Plato; extended the use of mathematical ideas in philosophy; refined Neoplatonic metaphysics; and incorporated in Neoplatonic philosophy what he took to be the 'theologies' of the ancients (Egyptians, Persians, Chaldaeans, Orphics (see ORPHISM), Pythagoreans), their demonology and their rites, in particular Chaldaean *theurgy. See NEOPLATONISM.

TEXTS *VP*, L. Deubner (2nd edn. 1975), trans. G. Clark (1989), J. Dillon and J. Hershbell (1991); *Protrepticus*, H. Pistelli (1888), text and Fr. trans. E. des Places (1989); *Dcms*, H. Pistelli (2nd edn. 1975); *In Nic.*, H. Pistelli (2nd edn. 1975); *Myst.*, text and Fr. trans. E. des Places (1966).

FRAGMENTS Commentaries on Plato, text and trans. J. Dillon (1973); on Aristotle, text in Larsen (below) vol. 2. The attribution to Iamblichus of the *Theology of Arithmetic*, ed. V. de Falco (2nd edn. 1975), trans. R. Waterfield (1988), is doubtful.

IDEAS AND INFLUENCE J. Dillon, *ANRW* 2. 36. 2 (1987), 862 ff.; B. Larsen, *Jamblique de Chalcis* (1972); J. Finamore, *Iamblichus and the Theory of the Vehicle of the Soul* (1985); D. O'Meara, *Pythagoras Revived* (1989); H. Blumenthal (ed.), *The Divine Iamblichus* (1993). See also bibliog. under NEOPLATONISM.
D. O'M.

Iambulus (3rd cent. BC?), Hellenistic author of a utopian travel narrative, now lost, a summary of which is preserved by *Diodorus (3) Siculus (2. 55–60). Nothing is known about him except that his name is Scythian. His work may have been a forerunner of the *novel but apparently contained no romantic element. It is a fantastic description of the author's journey to an Island of the Sun (located in the ocean south of Arabia—perhaps Sri Lanka), where people live idyllically for 150 years and then lie down and die peacefully. The people have double tongues, and so can carry on two conversations at once! After seven years there Iambulus is expelled and returns home via India. The description of the

island, its inhabitants, and their customs, seems partly inspired by utopian social theories then current (perhaps of Stoic (see STOICISM), Euhemerist (see EUHEMERUS), or *Cynic origin). The men hold women and children in common; they worship heavenly bodies; and the eldest male serves as king. The writing of utopian literature was undoubtedly stimulated by increased contacts with the east after *Alexander (3) the Great's conquest; and Iambulus' work may in turn have influenced the Attalid Pergamene pretender *Aristonicus (1) (who led a rebellion against Rome, which had recently acquired *Pergamum) to establish Heliopolis ('Sun City') in Asia Minor in 131 BC.

See also ISLANDS.

Tarn, *Alexander* 411–14; J. Ferguson, *Utopias of the Classical World* (1975); E. Gabba, *JRS* 1981, 58 f.; W. W. Ehlers, *Würzburger Jahrbücher für die Altertumswissenschaft* 1985.
M. Ga.

Iamus, legendary ancestor of the prophetic clan of the Iamidae at *Olympia (see DIVINATION, GREEK). *Pindar (*Ol.* 6. 28–73) makes him son of *Apollo and *Evadne (1), daughter of *Poseidon and *Spartan Pitane. At his birth Evadne left him in a bed of pansies (ἴα), and he was fed on honey (ἰῷ μελισσᾶν) by snakes. As a young man he prayed to Poseidon and Apollo, and Apollo told him to go to Olympia where he received the gift of divination. The most famous Iamid of Pindar's time was Tisamenus of Elis, who was given Spartan citizenship (Hdt. 9. 33–6; Paus. 3. 11. 6–8): this is probably what led to the link between Iamus and Pitane. The clan continued at Olympia well into the 3rd cent. AD.

H. Hepding, *RE* 9. 685–9; U. von Wilamowitz-Moellendorff, *Isyllos von Epidauros* (1886), 162–85; L. Weniger, *ARW* 1915, 53 f.; E. Simon, *LIMC* 5. 614–15; H. W. Parke, *The Oracles of Zeus* (1967), 174–85.
N. J. R.

Ianuarius Nepotianus, author of a loose and imperfect epitome of *Valerius Maximus before the 6th cent. AD. Identification with the Severan procurator . . . Nepotianus (*PIR*² N 47) has been wrongly suggested.

H.-G. Pflaum, *Carrières procuratoriennes* 2 (1960), 651 ff.
A. J. S. S.

Iapetus, a *Titan cast by Zeus into the depths of Tartarus (*Iliad* 8. 479). In Hesiod (*Theog.* 134, 507 ff.), son of Earth (see GAIA) and Heaven (see URANUS), father of *Prometheus, Epimetheus, *Atlas, and *Menoetius—by an Oceanid Clymene or Asia (Apollod. 1. 2. 3; Lycoph. 1283), or by Themis (Aesch. *PV* 18). His name appears not to be Greek, and may derive from the near east, a version of Japheth son of Noah (Genesis 9–10) (see West on *Theog.* 134).
K. D.

Iapygia, the Greek name for the Sallentine peninsula, sometimes also used to denote the whole of *Apulia. The inhabitants (Iapyges) were Messapii in language (see MESSAPIC LANGUAGE) and culture, but many settlements had close connections with the Greeks and show signs of Hellenization (see HELLENISM).

E. De Iuliis, *Gli Iapygi* (1988).
K. L.

Iasion (or **Iasius**) was loved by *Demeter, slept with her 'in a thrice-ploughed field', and was killed by *Zeus' thunderbolt (Hom. *Od.* 5. 125–8). In *Hesiod's *Theogony* this happened in *Crete, and their child was *Plutus, the earth's wealth (969–74). This suggests the agricultural symbolism of the myth.

His birth was recorded in the Hesiodic *Catalogue* (fr. 185. 6 M–W). Later he was son of Zeus and *Electra (2), and brother of *Dardanus and Harmonia, and played a part in the Samothracian mysteries (see MYSTERIES; SAMOTHRACE), as husband of *Cybele and father of Corybas and Plutus (cf. Hellanicus, *FGrH* 4 F 23;

Iason

Diod. Sic. 5. 48–9). Italian legend made him son of *Corythus (1), and a migrant from Italy to Samothrace (Verg. *Aen.* 3. 167 f. and *Servius on the passage). See also IASUS, IASIUS.

W. Gundel, *RE* 9. 752–8; P. Müller, *LIMC* 5/1. 627–8.   N. J. R.

Iason See JASON.

Iasus, city of *Caria, on an inlet north of Bargylia and opposite modern Küllük; a self-styled colony of *Argos (2) and *Miletus (Polyb. 16. 12. 1 ff.). Its peninsula-site (called by Strabo 14. 2. 21 an island) was already occupied in the Mycenaean and geometric periods; when revealed in the 4th cent. BC by inscriptions, its civic and tribal organization is fully Greek, although the population contained Carian elements. A member of the *Delian League, it was sacked by the Peloponnesians in 412 BC and 'destroyed' by *Lysander in 405 (Thuc. 8. 28. 2–4, 25). Subordinate to *Mausolus, against whom a local plot is attested (Blümel (see bibliog. below), no. 1), it was favoured by *Alexander (3) the Great, persuaded by Iasians in his service to return to it the 'little sea' (A. Heisserer, *Alexander the Great and the Greeks* (1980), 169 ff.), part of the rich fishing-ground from which Iasus famously earned its living (Strabo 14. 2. 21). Later *Seleucid, it received an unusual gift from *Laodice (3), *Antiochus III's queen, in the form of dowries for needy girls (Blümel no. 4 = Austin no. 156). Attached to the *conventus of *Alabanda under the Principate, it later became a bishopric in the diocese of Caria. Italian excavations since 1960 have revealed cemeteries, a theatre, *bouleutērion*, agora, and a Byzantine church, rebuilt on a lavish scale in the 5th cent.

W. Blümel, *Die Inschriften von Iasos* 1–2 (1985), including testimonia and coins; *PECS* 410 f.; F. Berti, in *Arslantepe, Hierapolis* etc. (1993), 189 ff.   A. J. S. S., C. R.

Iasus, Iasius, names of various legendary figures, including Arcadian Iasus, son of *Lycurgus (1) and father of *Atalanta (Apollod. 3. 9. 2 etc.), perhaps the same as Arcadian Iasius who won the first horse-race at *Olympia (Paus. 5. 8. 4, 8. 48. 1); Iasius or Iasus, king of *Minyan *Orchomenus (1) and father of Amphion whose daughter Chloris married *Neleus (Hom. *Od.* 11. 281–6, Pherecydes, *FGrH* 3 F 117; Paus. 9. 36. 8, etc.); one of the *Idaean Dactyls (Paus. 5. 14. 7); and various early kings of *Argos (2). Sometimes equated with *Iasion, *Demeter's lover.

G. Weicker, *RE* 9. 783–5.   N. J. R.

Iavolenus Priscus See OCTAVIUS TIDIUS TOSSIANUS IAVOLENUS PRISCUS, C. (or L.).

Iazyges, a Sarmatian nomadic people (see SARMATAE), originally lived near the Lower Danube (Ov. *Pont.* 1. 2. 7 f.), but during the first half of the 1st cent. AD they migrated westwards to occupy the Hungarian plain between the Danube (see DANUVIUS) and the Theiss (Plin. *HN* 4. 80), threatening both *Pannonia and *Dacia. *Domitian campaigned at least once against them (AD 89); under *Trajan they became Roman allies, but later joined in the Marcomannic Wars against Rome (see MARCOMANNI). Wars also occurred in 283, 284, and 358.

A. Mócsy, *Pannonia and Upper Moesia* (1974).   J. J. W.

Iberia (1), one of the ancient names for *Spain.

(2) The ancient name for the eastern half of Georgia, between *Colchis and Transcaucasian *Albania and north of *Armenia. Its chief river was the Cyrus (Georgian Mtkvari). The expeditions of *Pompey in 65 BC and of P. *Canidius Crassus for Antony (see ANTONIUS (2), M.) in 37/6 BC took Roman forces into Iberia, though Roman knowledge remained vague (see CAUCASUS). From *Augustus onwards, Roman emperors engaged in active diplomacy in Iberia: some diplomatic gifts, esp. silver plate, have survived in burials at the Iberian capital (mod. Mtskheta). Under *Antoninus Pius, King Pharasmanes II of Iberia made a grand visit to Rome. Through the 3rd and 4th cents. AD Iberia was claimed by both Rome and *Sasanid Persia. From the end of the 4th cent., Iberia (Christian since *c*.337) was largely under Persian control.

D. C. Braund, *Georgia in Antiquity* (1994).   D. C. B.

Ibycus, 6th-cent. BC lyric poet, native of *Rhegium in southern Italy. His date is controversial. The *Suda* states that he went to *Samos in Ol. 54 (564–560 BC), while *Eusebius gives his floruit as Ol. 60 (540–536), which would link his stay in Samos to *Polycrates (1)'s reign. Little is known of his life. He was said to have left Rhegium when he might have become tyrant (see TYRANNY), whence the proverb 'more antiquated/more foolish than Ibycus' (Diogenian. 2. 71). Tradition maintained that he was murdered by robbers, who were brought to justice through birds which witnessed the murder (e.g. Plut. *Mor.* 509f; *Anth. Pal.* 7. 745); 'Ibycus' cranes' became proverbial (Zen. 1. 37).

On the strength of Ath. 4. 172d–f (which suggests that Ibycus was sometimes credited with authorship of the *Funeral Games for Pelias* composed by Stesichorus) it is widely believed that Ibycus' work divides into two categories: extended heroic narratives in the Stesichorean manner (see STESICHORUS), and homoerotic/encomiastic poetry (though no certain trace of the former survives). The longest surviving fragment from the second category (282) is an encomium consisting of an elaborate dismissal of martial mythic themes in favour of the beauty of Polycrates. The few substantial erotic fragments show a penchant for elaborate imagery (286, an extended contrast between a fertile grove in the spring and the poet's destructive desire; 287, on love in old age, which presents love as a hunter and the poet as a retired racehorse called back to the contest). The same visual imagination is seen in other fragments (317, 321). The myths with possible or probable erotic content (284, 285, 289(a), 291, 294, 295, 309, 324) probably come from this category. The poems are all composed in the choral lyric dialect, in a variety of metres.

TEXT Davies, *PMGF* 1. 242–305; with trans., D. A. Campbell, *Greek Lyric 3* (Loeb, 1991), 208 ff.
CRITICISM C. M. Bowra, *Greek Lyric Poetry*, 2nd edn. (1962), 241 ff.; D. E. Gerber, *Euterpe* (1970) 207 ff.; D. A. Campbell, *Greek Lyric Poetry* (1967), 305 ff.   C. C.

Icarius (1), father of *Penelope. Though the name is well established in *Homer's *Odyssey*, little is said about the person. Later tradition (e.g. Apollod. 3. 10. 5–6) places him in *Sparta, as son of *Oebalus or Perieres. Unwilling to allow Penelope to depart with her new husband, he followed her on the journey until *Odysseus told Penelope to choose between them; for reply, she veiled her face to indicate embarrassment and modesty, and Icarius abandoned his attempt, realizing that she preferred to go with Odysseus (Paus. 3. 20. 11).

(2) Attic hero probably worshipped in the *deme Icaria, evidently the possessor of a rich sanctuary (*IG* 1³. 253. 6, 9). In a common story-type, he gave hospitality to *Dionysus, who taught him how to make wine. However, when he gave some to his neighbours they thought he had poisoned them and so killed

him. (For the sequel, see ERIGONE.) The story is not attested before *Eratosthenes.

For both, D. Gondicas, *LIMC* 5. 645–7.   E. Ke.

Icaros (1) (also Ikaria, the modern name), an eastern Aegean island (255 sq. km.: 98 sq. mi.); long, narrow, lacking good harbours, and dominated by its neighbour *Samos. The precipitous south side rises to *c*.1,000 m. (3,300 ft.); the greener north probably produced the wine mentioned by ancient writers. The legendary Icarus, *Daedalus' son, fell into the sea hereabouts.

At Nas in the north-west is an Archaic temple of *Artemis Tauropolos. The two Classical towns, Oinoe on the north coast and Therma (near hot springs) in the south-east, paid tribute separately to the *Delian League. Therma has a Classical cemetery, fortifications, and Hellenistic-Roman baths; it was renamed Asklepieis *c*.200 BC but apparently superseded by Drakanon, a fortified settlement further east. Strabo describes Icaros as nearly uninhabited and used by Samian pastoralists; but Oinoe, at least, flourished under the Principate, when an odeum and baths were built.

A. J. Papalas, *Ancient Icaria* (1992); [British Admiralty] Naval Intelligence Division, *Greece* 3 (1945), 546–54; *RE* 9/1 (1914), 978–85.
          D. G. J. S.

Icaros (2) (mod. Failaka), an island off Kuwait, at the mouth of an ancient course of the Euphrates river. It was settled from the third millennium BC, and visited by an expedition sent by *Alexander (3) the Great to the Persian Gulf (Strabo 16. 3. 2): *Ikaros* might be the Hellenization (i.e. Greek version) of a local name. The *Seleucids built a fortress on Failaka, in use from the early 3rd to the mid-2nd cent. BC: it is 60 m. (200 ft.) square, and two temples were excavated inside the walls; two other sanctuaries were found outside. Greek material and inscriptions attest a Macedonian settlement which probably served as a military—and naval—outpost on the maritime route to *India. After the fall of the Seleucid empire, the island temporarily came under Characenian domination in the 1st cent. AD. A Christian church of the 6th cent. has recently been excavated.

C. Roueché and S. Sherwin-White, *Chiron* 1985, 1 ff. (see *SEG* 35. 1476 ff.); J.-F. Salles in A. Kuhrt and S. Sherwin-White (eds.), *Hellenism in the East* (1987), 84–6; D. T. Potts, *The Arabian Gulf in Antiquity* 2 (1990), 154–96.   J.-F. S.

Icarus See DAEDALUS.

Iceni, a British tribe in Norfolk and Suffolk; see BRITAIN. The Gallows' Hill, Thetford, settlement may have been the iron age centre. The following pre-Roman rulers are attested on coinage: Anted, Ecen, and Prasto. The tribe voluntarily made a treaty with *Claudius, but in AD 47 rebelled against forcible disarmament. *Prasutagus was established as *client king until his death in AD 60/1, when the attempted suppression of independence by Roman officials caused the rebellion of the tribe under his wife *Boudicca. After the harsh suppression of this outbreak (from which economic recovery was slow) a self-governing *civitas* was created with its capital at Venta (Caistor-by-Norwich). The town remained small (within its undated 14-ha. (35-acre) walls). There has been little excavation within the town, although later 2nd-cent. public baths, two temples, and the forum basilica have been explored. Apart from a considerable local pottery industry, the *civitas* was agricultural with some evidence for wool production in the 4th cent., but few villas. The area was none the less wealthy and has produced a series of silver and gold hoards (e.g. Mildenhall and Thetford). In the 3rd cent. the coast was protected

by *Saxon Shore forts, and there is evidence for Germanic settlements from early in the 5th.

S. S. Frere, *Britannia*, 3rd edn. (1987).   S. S. F.; M. J. M.

Icilius (*RE* 2), **Lucius,** a plebeian hero, though probably of patrician descent, betrothed to *Verginia and leader of the second secession (see SECESSIO), has little claim to historical existence, but the *lex Icilia de Aventino publicando* (traditionally dated 456 BC), the text of which was still preserved in Augustus' time in the *Aventine temple of *Diana (Dion. Hal. *Ant. Rom.* 10. 32. 4), is indisputably a genuine document of *c*.450. The law provided allotments on the Aventine to the *plebs* either as agricultural or (very probably) as building land. It was later attributed to Icilius merely because of his renown as a popular hero.

Ogilvie, *Comm. Livy 1–5*, 446 f.; A. Drummond, *CAH* 7²/2 (1989), 139, 237.   P. T.

iconography See IMAGERY.

Ictinus was one of a number of fine *architects who worked at Athens in the time of *Pericles (1). In conjunction with *Callicrates (1) he designed the *Parthenon and with a certain Carpion, otherwise unknown, as co-author, wrote an account of it (Vitr. *De arch.* pref. 7). He was also one of a series of architects—Coroebus, Ictinus, Metagenes—who worked at *Eleusis on the Telesterion, the great hall in which the performance of the *mysteries took place; the plan of the hall, with its rows of columns supporting the roof, was repeatedly modified.

From the design of the *Parthenon it is clear that Ictinus was very interested in the ideal mathematical relationships between the different elements of temple architecture; his imposition of the ratio $2^2 : 3^2$ demonstrates an ability to go beyond the traditional evolutionary approach to proportions. No doubt his book explained his theorizing, though nothing of this survives. This may be responsible for the attribution to him (by Pausanias 8. 41. 7–9) of the temple at *Bassae, which, however, hardly measures up to the Parthenon in its detail.

R. Carpenter, *The Architects of the Parthenon* (1970), 167, 182.   R. A. T.

Ictis See VECTIS.

Idaean Dactyls (Δάκτυλοι Ἰδαῖοι), the Fingers of Mt. Ida in *Phrygia or, according to some, *Crete (Ap. Rhod. *Argon.* 1. 1129; Pliny *HN* 7. 197). First mentioned in the *Phoronis* epic (fr. 2 Davies, *EGF*) as attendants of the Mother Goddess Adrasteia, they are small (Paus. 8. 31. 3) fabulous beings who discovered the working of iron. Their name is explained in various *aitia* through their size (cf. Ger. 'Däumling', Tom Thumb), or number: five or ten (five brothers and five sisters, Soph. fr. 364–6 Radt). According to *Apollonius (1) Rhodius (1. 1129 ff.), the *Nymph Anchiale bore them in the Dictaean cave clutching the earth with her fingers in her birth-pains (further versions in Lobeck, *Aglaoph.* 1156 ff.). In an Elean tradition (see ELIS) they are *Heracles (not Alcmene's son), Paeonaeus, Epimedes, *Iasius, and Idas (or Acesidas) (Paus. 5. 7. 6).

Identified with the *Curetes, they guard the infant *Zeus in the Dictaean cave (Paus 5. 7. 6); but they are also related to the *Corybantes (offspring of the Dactyls in Phrygia, Strabo 10. 3. 22), *Cabiri, *Telchines (H. Herter, *RE* 5 A(1) (1934), 223), and other dwarfish sprites. Their history began in prehistoric times in the sphere of a Mother Goddess connected with the early working of metal, an eastern invention that travelled west via *Cyprus, *Rhodes, and Crete. The novel skill was invested with magic powers in popular imagination, which also credited the

Idaeus

Dactyls with inventing the mysteries, organizing the first *Olympian Games, and teaching *Paris music. See also HESIOD.

B. Hemberg, *Eranos* 1952, 41–59; R. J. Forbes in F. Matz and H.-G. Buchholz, *Archaeologia Homerica* 1, part K (1967).   H. J. R.; B. C. D.

Idaeus, 'connected with Ida', and so (*a*) a title of *Zeus (*Il.* 16. 605 (Trojan) and on Cretan coins and (usually in a dialect form) inscriptions); (*b*) a stock name for sundry little-known Trojans or Cretans (list in Stoll in Roscher's *Lexikon* 2. 95). (*c*) Magic name for a finger, perhaps the index (*PGM* v. 455).

LIMC 5. 1 (1990), 639–42.   H. J. R.

Idalium (mod. Dhali), a small inland city of *Cyprus, in a long-populated area (perhaps the 'Edi'al' of the Esarhaddon prism), was 16 km. (10 mi.) SSE of Nicosia, on the south side of the Yalias valley, where in the 11th cent. BC it replaced a complex of bronze age sites further east at Ayios Sozomenos. It stood on the twin acropolis hills of Ambelleri and Moutti tou Arvili, with the lower town between; it had sanctuaries of Athena, Aphrodite, and Apollo-Reshef. The longest known syllabic inscription (the de Luynes tablet), and the bilingual lapidary inscription which allowed the syllabary's decipherment, were found here. Its kings (who may have shared power with a '*dēmos*') struck coins from *c.*500 BC; *c.*470 it was overwhelmed and permanently absorbed by Citium, its Phoenician neighbour to the south.

E. Gjerstad, *SCE* 2 (1935), 460 ff.; O. Masson, *Les Inscriptions chypriotes syllabiques*, rev. edn. (1983), 233 ff.; H. W. Catling, *RDAC* 1982, 227 ff.; L. E. Stager and others, *American Expedition to Idalion* (1974).   H. W. C.

Idas and Lynceus, prominent figures in early Peloponnesian legend, sons of Aphareus, king of *Messenia (though *Poseidon is sometimes credited with the paternity of Idas). As the 'Apharetidae' they form a Messenian heroic pair to rival their Spartan cousins, the *Dioscuri; when the latter tried to steal their brides, the daughters of *Leucippus (1) (see LEUCIPPIDES), a fight led to the death of all but Polydeuces (Theoc. 22. 137 ff.). *Pindar's version (*Nem.* 10. 60 ff.) is more respectful to the sons of *Zeus, loading the blame onto the Apharetidae and making cattle, not women, the cause of the violence. Earlier Idas, the dominant brother, had competed with *Apollo for Marpessa, daughter of the river Euenus, daring to draw his bow against the god (*Iliad* 9. 558 ff., where he is called 'mightiest of men'; cf. Bacchyl. 20); when Apollo carried her off (Paus. 5. 18. 2 on the chest of Cypselus, see CYPSELUS, CHEST OF; contrast Apollod. 1. 7. 8 where Idas is the kidnapper, using a winged chariot lent by Poseidon), Zeus arbitrated the dispute and allowed Marpessa to decide between her suitors; she preferred security to glamour, and chose Idas.

The brothers participated together in both the great ventures of their epoch, the Argonautic expedition (in which *Apollonius (1) presents Idas as a hot-tempered braggart; see ARGONAUTS) and the Calydonian boar-hunt (see MELEAGER (1)). Lynceus' contribution to the partnership is his 'lynx-eyed', even X-ray (Apollod. 3. 10. 3) vision.

C. Schwanzar, *LIMC* 1. 1 (1981): 'Apharetidae'; H. Fränkel, *MH* 1960, 1–20.   A. H. G.

Idmon, 'the knowing one', name of several skilful persons, especially a seer, son of *Apollo or Abas (Ap. Rhod. 1. 139 ff. and schol.), who accompanied the *Argonauts although he foreknew he would not return alive (ibid. and 2. 815 ff.); he was killed by a boar in the country of the Mariandyni.   H. J. R.

Idomeneus (1), in mythology son of *Deucalion and grandson

of *Minos. He was one of the suitors of *Helen (Hes. fr. 204. 56 ff. M–W), and later led the Cretan contingent to Troy with 80 ships (*Il.* 2. 645–52). He is a major figure in the *Iliad*, older than most of the other Greek leaders (13. 361), but a great warrior (see e.g. 13. 210–515), and one of the nine who volunteered to stand against *Hector in single combat (7. 161 ff.). Meeting with a great storm on his journey home after the war, he vowed that if he returned safely he would sacrifice to *Poseidon the first living creature which met him when he landed in *Crete. This turned out to be his own son (Serv. on *Aen.* 3. 121). When he fulfilled, or tried to fulfil, the vow, a plague broke out, and to appease the gods he was forced to leave Crete for Italy.

LIMC 5. 1 (1990), 643–5.   J. R. M.

Idomeneus (2) (*c.*325–*c.*270 BC), biographer and politician of *Lampsacus. Friend of *Epicurus, but perhaps more *Peripatetic than Epicurean. Wrote *On the Followers of *Socrates*: there are surviving fragments on the Socratic *Aeschines (2); *On Popular Leaders* (Περὶ δημαγωγῶν, see DEMAGOGUES) in at least two books: fragments in *Plutarch and *Athenaeus (1) concern leading Athenian politicians; and *History of *Samothrace*. Following the Peripatetic, anecdotal method, Idomeneus reproduced unreliable scandal, perhaps attacking his political opponents.

FGrH 338; complete edition and revised Life: A. Angeli, *Chron. Erc.* (*BCPE*), 1981, 41–101.   F. W. W.; K. S. S.

Idrieus (or **Hidrieus),** son of *Hecatomnus and younger brother of *Mausolus, was *satrap (see MAUSOLUS) of the Persian province of *Caria 351–344 BC with his sister-wife *Ada. Idrieus helped *Phocion of Athens to suppress the revolt from Persia of *Cyprus (Diod. Sic. 16. 42: mid-340s). He was honoured at Ionian *Erythrae (*SEG* 31. 969) and made remarkably assertive Greek dedications at *Labraunda, including a temple with his own name prominent on the architrave (*ILabraunda* no. 16); there is another elegant Idrieus dedication from *Amyzon (*OGI* 235), and Idrieus and Ada were active at *Sinuri.

Strabo 14. 2. 17; Tod 161; Michel 804. L. Robert, *Le Sanctuaire de Sinuri* 1 (1945), 94 ff.; *ILabraunda* 2; S. Hornblower, *Mausolus* (1982), chs. 2, 11, inscriptions at 364 ff.; L. Robert, *Fouilles d'Amyzon* (1983), 93 ff.; S. Ruzicka, *Politics of a Persian Dynasty: The Hecatomnids in the Fourth Century BC* (1992); F. G. Maier, *CAH* 6² (1994), 329 f. (Cypriot affair).   S. H.

Idumaea, the lowland hill-country of southern *Judaea, was settled by the Edomites between the 8th and 6th cents. BC as a result of the *Nabataean Arab occupation of biblical Edom. Idumaea was annexed by John Hyrcanus (see HASMONEANS) soon after 129 BC and the inhabitants Judaized. In 63 *Pompey detached its chief towns, Adora and Marisa, from Judaea. In 40 Idumaea became a toparchy in the kingdom of *Herod (1), whose father *Antipater (6) had been a leading Idumaean. Another such, Herod's governor of the region, Costobar, schemed unsuccessfully against Herod to establish an independent power there, with the help of *Cleopatra VII. It became part of the ethnarchy of Herod's successor *Archelaus (4) and, in AD 6, of the Roman province of *Judaea. The Idumaeans, though apparently not regarded as full Jews, played a major role in the First Jewish Revolt and were involved in the faction fighting within Jerusalem. The *Bar Kokhba Revolt was focused in the area. Eusebius testifies to significant Jewish villages there in late antiquity.

A. Kasher, *Jews, Idumaeans and Ancient Arabs* (1988).   T. R.

Iguvium, modern Gubbio in Umbria (see UMBRIANS). First settled in the bronze age, it was an important iron age centre, which minted its own coins. The *tabulae Iguvinae were found here in 1444. There is a fine Roman theatre.

J. W. Poultney, *Bronze Tables of Iguvium* (1959). E. T. S.; T. W. P.

Ilerda (mod. Lleida), Iberian city of the Ilergetes in Catalonia, on the banks of the Segre. Founded in the late 3rd cent. BC, it issued coins as Iltirta during the republic. Here in 49 BC *Caesar defeated *Pompey's legates L. *Afranius (2) and M. *Petreius. It developed under Rome, was an Augustan (?) *municipium and was still a regional economic and religious centre in the 5th cent. AD.

A. Perez, *La ciutat romana d'Ilerda* (1984). S. J. K.

Iliad See ACHILLES; HOMER.

Ilias Latina (*Homerus Latinus*), an *epitome in Latin of *Homer's *Iliad* in 1,070 hexameters, attributed in the manuscripts simply to 'Homerus' or (strangely) 'Pindarus'; initial and final *acrostics (with emendation) yield 'ITALICUS SCRIPSIT'; a Baebius Italicus is suggested by many. Praise of the Julian house at 899–902 suggests a date earlier than AD 68. The epitome is uneven and decreases progressively in fullness (lines 1–685 cover *Il.* 1–9, 686–1062 *Il.* 10–24), concentrating on the great duels and some of the famous set pieces, and its epilogue addresses the *Muses, *Athena, and *Apollo in the poet's own person. Poetic style and the use of the hexameter are competent, echoing *Virgil and *Ovid, but monotonous and undistinguished. Its chief importance lies in preserving the events of the *Iliad* for centuries ignorant of Greek.

TEXT PLM Vollmer/Morel, 2. 3; M. Scaffai (1982), with It. trans. and comm.
Cf. further M. Scaffai, *Enc. Virg.* 'Ilias Latina'; P. K. Marshall in *Texts and Transmission* 191–4. S. J. Ha.

Iliona ('Ιλιόνη), in mythology, eldest daughter of *Priam and *Hecuba (Verg. *Aen.* 1. 653–4). Wife of Polymestor (see HECUBA), she saved the life of Polydorus by passing him off as her son, Polymestor thus murdering his own child (Hyg. *Fab.* 109, cf. Pacuvius, frs. of *Iliona*). H. J. R.

Ilium, an Aeolian foundation of the 7th cent. BC on the site of ancient *Troy, which became a successful Hellenistic and Roman city. It possessed a famous temple of Athena (visited by *Xerxes and *Alexander (3) the Great) which was the centre from the 4th cent. BC onwards of a religious synedrion. The landing of C. Livius Salinator in 190 BC inaugurated cordial relations with Rome, although the city was sacked by *Flavius Fimbria's unruly troops in 85 BC. The emperors followed *Caesar's example in patronizing Ilium and its temple, because of the legend that the founders of Rome were of Trojan origin (see AENEAS; KINSHIP).

C. Boulter, *PECS* 406–7 (with bibliog.); P. Frisch, *Die Inschriften von Ilion* (1975) (with testimonia). D. E. W. W.; S. M.

Illyrian language At present it is not possible to give a linguistic definition of 'Illyrian', a term which has often been used to indicate the language(s) anciently spoken in the Balkan peninsula (excluding Greek). There are no inscriptions written in 'Illyrian'. Consequently the features of the 'Illyrian' language have been puzzled out (and genetically defined) merely on the basis of personal names and place names from the Balkans; on this basis *Messapic has also been derived from 'Illyrian'. Yet it is impossible to reconstruct a historical language, with all its complex phonological and morphological structure, merely from onomastic data. The main exponent of 'Illyrianism' was the German scholar H. Krahe, who defined as 'Illyrian' a vast onomastic complex spread through the whole Balkan peninsula. Krahe himself, however, explicitly recognized (in 1956) that this position was not tenable, thus opening the way to further work. Later scholars (J. Untermann, R. Katičič, C. de Simone) introduced a concept of an 'onomastic region' (*Namengebiet*) which is not based on etymological assumptions. The most important result is the identification of a south-eastern onomastic region, which has its epicentre in modern Albania (where the real Illyrians of the ancient tradition must also be localized). See ILLYRII.

R. Katičič, *The Ancient Languages of the Balkans* (1976). C. de S.

Illyricum, the Roman name for the territory of the *Indo-European Illyrians beyond the *Adriatic sea. Their attacks on shipping brought Roman intervention in the First and Second Illyrian Wars (229/8, 219 BC): see DEMETRIUS (6); TEUTA. During the Second Punic War the Illyrian kingdom acted as a buffer state between Rome and Macedon, and at the peace after *Cynoscephalae (197 BC) the Illyrians under Pleuratus II (206–180) were awarded some Macedonian territories. Under his successor Gentius (c.180–168), however, *piracy was revived and as an ally of *Perseus (2) of Macedon they were defeated by the praetor L. Anicius Gallus in 168 (Livy 44. 30–2). The settlement, by which the kingdom was divided into three parts, did not lead to a permanent Roman administration in Illyricum, and only sporadic campaigns by consuls or proconsuls are attested, chiefly against the Delmatae (see DALMATIA). In 59 BC Illyricum was allotted to *Caesar along with Cisalpine Gaul (see GAUL (CISALPINE)) and during the winters between his campaigns in Gaul he administered his province from *Aquileia (Caes. *BGall.* 2. 35, 5. 1–2). During the Civil War the Illyrians sided with the Pompeians while the established coastal settlements of Roman citizens (*conventus civium Romanorum*) supported Caesar. His legates were defeated more than once, but during Caesar's dictatorship P. *Vatinius made headway against the Delmatae. Later *Octavian undertook limited campaigns in the area, mainly for propaganda and military reasons, against the Iapudes and Pannonians (see PANNONIA) in 35 BC, and against the Delmatae in 34/3. After 27 Illyricum remained a 'public' province (i.e. one not directly controlled by the emperor) until Roman control was advanced along the Sava valley to the Danube (see DANUVIUS) during the Bellum Pannonicum of 13–9 by *Tiberius. The institution of Illyricum as an imperial province took place in 11 BC, if not earlier (Cass. Dio 54. 34. 4). Illyricum was subsequently divided into two provinces, known by the Flavian period as *Dalmatia and *Pannonia. This division perhaps followed the Pannonian uprising of AD 9. Illyricum appears on a military diploma of AD 60 (*CIL* 16. 4) to denote the province of Pannonia alone. A monument of the early Tiberian period from Epidaurum in Dalmatia (*CIL* 3. 1741) erected by the *civitates superioris provinciae Hillyrici* has been taken as evidence that before the Flavian period Dalmatia was known as *Illyricum superius* and Pannonia as *Illyricum inferius*, but this reading rests on a single 16th-cent. MS record of the now fragmentary text. Under the empire the Danubian provinces (*Noricum, Pannonia, Dalmatia, *Moesia Superior, and *Dacia) were grouped in a single customs-area, *portorium Illyricum* (see PORTORIA). Later *Illyriciani* denoted the groups of officers who controlled the Danube armies during the crises of the 3rd cent. From *Diocletian onwards Illyricum denoted two dioceses (see DIOECESIS), *Illyricum orientale* or *dioecesis Moesiarum*, *Illyricum occidentale* or *dioecesis Pannoniarum*.

N. G. L. Hammond, *JRS* 1968, 1 ff. (Roman campaigns to 168 BC); J. Wilkes, *The Illyrians* (1992), 183 ff. J. J. W.

Illyrii

Illyrii, a large group of related *Indo-European tribes, who occupied in classical times the western side of the Balkan range from the head of the *Adriatic Sea to the hinterland of the gulf of Valona and extended northwards as far as the eastern *Alps and the Danube (see DANUVIUS) and eastwards into some districts beyond the Balkan range. The name was properly that of a small people between Scodra and the Mati river, and it was applied by the Greeks and later by the Romans to the other tribes with which they had regular contact. Thus Illyris meant to the Greeks the southern part of the area, that neighbouring *Macedonia, *Epirus, and the Greek cities on the Adriatic coast and islands, and *Illyricum meant to the Romans the whole area from the eastern Alps to the gulf of Valona. The earliest signs of Indo-European penetration into Illyris have been found at Pazhok in central Albania, where chieftains of a 'Kurgan' culture were buried in mortuary chambers in large tumuli in the latter part of the third millennium, and there is ample evidence of seafaring and traffic in the southern Adriatic Sea in the second millennium, when piratical groups made settlements in *Corcyra and in *Leucas. The southwards expansion of Illyrian peoples into what is now central Albania occurred probably in the 10th cent. BC. Later, people of a similar culture reached Vergina (see AEGAE) in the Haliacmon valley. Greek colonies were planted on the Albanian coast at Epidamnus (later called *Dyrrhachium) in the late 7th cent., at *Apollonia in the early 6th, and on the Dalmatian islands Corcyra Nigra (now Korčula), Issa (Vis), and Pharos (Hvar). Enlivened by Greek trade and ideas the Illyrian tribes, which were always warlike on land and sea, exerted continual pressure on Macedonia and Epirus and raided far into the Mediterranean Sea. Individual tribes became very powerful—in particular the *Liburni, *Dardani, Ardiaei, and Autariatae—but they enslaved their neighbours and never created an effective combination of tribal states against a common enemy. When Macedonia became strong under *Philip (1) II and Epirus under *Pyrrhus, they occupied the southern part of Illyris. When the power of Macedonia and of Epirus declined, the Illyrians pressed southwards by land and by sea, and in particular the Ardiaean kingdom, based on the southern Dalmatian coast, expanded southwards to Scodra and Lissus under Pleuratus I (*c.*260 BC) and under his son Agron. On the death of the latter his widow *Teuta was acting as regent for Pinnes when the first clash with Rome occurred. See ILLYRIAN LANGUAGE; ILLYRICUM; PIRACY.

H. Krahe, *Die Sprache der Illyrier* (1955); A. Mayer, *Die Sprache der alten Illyrier* 1–2 (1957–9); Hammond, *Epirus*; BSA 1967, 239 ff.; JRS 1968, 1 ff.; J. Wilkes, *The Illyrians* (1992). N. G. L. H.; J. J. W.

Ilus, in mythology, (1) son of *Dardanus (Apollod. 3. 140). (2) His grand-nephew, son of Tros and father of *Laomedon. He founded *Ilium, being guided to the site by a cow (cf. CADMUS) and received the *Palladium from heaven (ibid. 141–3).

LIMC 5. 1 (1990), 650.

imagery The identification of scenes in sculpture, painting and the minor arts has long been a major activity of classical *archaeology, although it has traditionally been accorded less emphasis than the identification of artists' hands. In all the figurative arts conventional schemes were developed, sometimes under the influence of near-eastern iconography, for portraying particular mythological figures and episodes, and the use and development of these schemes can now conveniently be studied through the *Lexicon Iconographicum Mythologiae Classicae* (= *LIMC*, 1981–). Individual artists exploited conventional imagery not simply by replicating it, but by playing variations on a theme or by echoing the conventional scheme for one episode when portraying a different one. An extreme form of this is iconographic parody.

The origins of particular iconographic schemes, and the reasons why the popularity of scenes changes over time, are rarely clear. Ceramic vessels may owe some of their imagery to lost gold or silver *plate, and some vases can reasonably be held to take over the imagery of lost wall-paintings or of famous sculptures, such as the Tyrannicides group (see ARISTOGITON), although it is also possible in some cases that vase-painting influenced subsequent sculptural imagery. Influence from drama (see TRAGEDY, GREEK and COMEDY, GREEK) has also frequently been alleged: few images in Attic vase-painting represent scenes from tragedies on stage in any straightforward way, but direct representation of scenes from comic drama is popular in 4th-cent. BC south Italian pottery. In the Greek world, public sculpture often carried broadly political meaning, using the otherness of more or less fantastic figures, *Centaurs or *Amazons, to define the behaviour of the good citizen. Whether particular mythical images on pottery also carry political significance, and the popularity of particular scenes at particular times is a result of their value as political *propaganda, is more hotly debated. At Rome, sculptural style as well as imagery were used to convey political points, particularly during the empire, and the Classical and Hellenistic Greek and republican Roman heritage was manipulated to political ends.

Recently, much work has been devoted to the non-mythological imagery on painted pottery, and has exploited this to excavate the ideology of the Greek city, stressing the way in which imagery can create ways of seeing as well as reflect them. Changes in the popularity of particular scenes or types of scene over time, at least when those changes extend over the work of several different painters, may indicate changing social agendas. There is no doubt that the imagery on pots has a close relationship with the use to which those pots are put, and this can be seen particularly clearly with both vessels deposited in graves and vessels used at the *symposium, many of which are, in one way or another, self-referential. One of the most valuable sources of information here lies in the way in which painters restrict scenes of certain types of activity to imaginary characters, such as *satyrs. But it is obviously problematic to assume that the attitudes displayed at the symposium were shared by society as a whole. The chance preservation of extensive areas of private housing at *Pompeii and *Herculaneum, enables us to see programmes of imagery with which some rich individuals surrounded themselves, and the care and originality with which they constructed visual narratives out of linked imagery.

Images were an extremely important part of religious cult. Cult statues sometimes incorporated whole programmes of mythical imagery, as in the *Athena Parthenos; see PHIDIAS. In the Roman world religious imagery became increasingly complex, and more or less arcane symbolic programmes are associated with mystery cults. Christianity, with its use of types and antitypes drawn from pagan mythology as well as from both Old and New Testaments, further enriched the interpretative range of familiar imagery. See ART, ANCIENT ATTITUDES TO; ART, FUNERARY; MYTHOLOGY; PAINTING; PISISTRATUS; POTTERY; PROPAGANDA; SCULPTURE.

J. Henle, *Greek Myths: A Vase Painter's Notebook* (1973); C. Bérard and others, *A City of Images* (1989; Fr. orig. 1984); J. Blok, *Bulletin Antieke Beschaving* 1990, 17–28; R. L. Gordon, *Journal of Mithraic Studies* 1976,

119–65; P. Zanker, *The Power of Images in the Age of Augustus* 1988; M. Thompson, *Marsyas* 1960–1, 36–77. R. G. O.

imagines, wax portrait-masks of Romans who had held the higher magistracies (see MAGISTRACY, ROMAN), were prominently displayed in shrines in the family mansion, with lines of descent and distinctions indicated. They were worn by actors impersonating the deceased in full ceremonial dress at public sacrifices and family funerals (see Polyb. 6. 53), at first only of male descendants, after *c*.100 BC gradually of female descendants as well (see Q. *Lutatius Catulus (2), C. *Iulius Caesar). The right to this, and to having one's own *imago* preserved, was forfeited by criminal conviction (see Cic. *Sull.* 8), by *proscription, and, under the empire, by *damnatio memoriae*. The families 'known' (Latin '*nobiles'*) to the public through these processions formed the *nobilitas*, though the term was later restricted in application. By the early empire, and probably even in the late republic, the *imagines* of all qualified men to whom the deceased was related by birth or marriage seem to have been displayed at his funeral, and the right to keep the deceased's *imago* was assumed by his family, perhaps even his *gens*. The custom lasted, no doubt with further changes, into the late empire. These *imagines* played a part in the development of Roman *portraiture.

Polyb. 6. 53; Plin. *HN* 35. 6 ff. (partly rhetorical). H. Meyer, *RE* 9 (1914), 1097–1104, 'Imagines maiorum'. E. B.

Imbros (now İmroz in Turkey), a hilly island (225 sq. km.: 87 sq. mi.) in the NE *Aegean, rarely explored by archaeologists. With good water but little arable and few harbours, it was important mainly as an Athenian stepping-stone to the *Hellespont. The town, in the north-east, had a harbour mole, theatre, cemetery, piped water-system, and fortification walls; inscriptions name the Great Gods of *Samothrace and other cults, mainly Attic.

Like *Lemnos, Imbros may have been inhabited by non-Greeks until relatively late. *Miltiades captured both islands from the Persians. Inscriptions reveal Athenians on Imbros before 490 BC, but they may have been a minority, or later suspected of *Medism, for 'Imbrians' appear in the Athenian tribute lists. An Athenian *cleruchy was sent *c*.447. Imbrians fought for Athens in the *Peloponnesian War; they retained Attic demotics and tribal names (see DEMES; PHYLAI), and the city had Athenian institutions even during several brief periods of independence between 403 and the 2nd cent. Rome confirmed Athenian rule in 166 BC. Imbros was still Athenian in the 2nd cent. AD, but Septimius Severus may have freed it. The Roman town expanded but is not mentioned again until after 500.

E. and G. Andreiou, Ἀρχαιολογία, 1991; C. Fredrich, *MDAI(A)* 1908; *IG* 12. 8. 46–149; 12 Suppl. p. 148; *RE* 9 / 1 (1914), 1106–7; R. Parker, in R. Osborne and S. Hornblower (eds.), *Ritual, Finance, Politics* (1994), 344–6. D. G. J. S.

imitatio (μίμησις), the study and conspicuous deployment of features recognizably characteristic of a canonical author's style or content, so as to define one's own generic affiliation (see GENRE).

Although Plato (*Resp.* 10) and Aristotle (*Poet.*) often apply μίμησις philosophically to the semantic relation by which language or art represent their objects, the more widespread ancient usage of the term is rhetorical, to designate a later writer's relation of acknowledged dependence upon an earlier one. The Muse is the daughter of memory: poets have always learned from other poets (ἕτερος ἐξ ἑτέρου σοφὸς τό τε πάλαι τό τε νῦν, 'one

learns his skill from another, both long ago and now': Bacchyl. *Paean* fr. 5 Snell–Maehler) and are listeners or readers before they become singers or writers. But starting already with the *sophists, the careful study and imitation of (usually written) models of discourse became an established educational technique. Throughout antiquity, a strong continuity in method and attitude linked school exercises on canonical texts (memorization, excerpting, paraphrase, translation, commentary, variation of theme or style, comparison) with a poetic practice which drew attention to its skilled use of models, 'not so as to filch but to borrow openly, in the hope of being recognized' (Seneca the Elder, *Suas.* 3. 7 on Ovid).

Ancient rhetoricians and pedagogues discuss the methods and dangers of *imitatio* in detail and with considerable psychological acumen; the most interesting surviving treatments are by *Dionysius (7) of Halicarnassus, Seneca the Elder (L. *Annaeus Seneca (1)) (*Controversiae*) and the Younger (L. *Annaeus Seneca (2)) (*Ep.* 114), '*Longinus' (*Subl.* 13–14), and *Quintilian (*Inst.* esp. 10. 2). The ancient discussions cover many of the textual relations described by modern theories of intertextuality, including prominent use of allusion—so that a later author can demonstrate that he belongs to the same genre as an earlier one or acquire by reflection some of his prestige—and covert use to create an élite community of those readers cultured enough to recognize it; but *parody is neglected (ancient imitation always implies admiration), *plagiarism is despised (as κλοπαί or *furta*), and global intertextuality within the linguistic or literary system is ignored (ancient imitation is always directed to individual authors grouped together by genre).

Typically, ancient literary theory, which never entirely abandoned a model of oral communication, tends to view systematic issues like tradition and genre in interpersonal, binary, and hence moralistic terms. Ancient discussions of imitation urge emulation and rivalry (ζῆλος), not servile dependence, recommend critical study and a plurality of models, and establish as the highest goal a melding of the student's personality with his model's. Reverence for the great men of the past as heroes to be imitated is a fundamental feature of ancient culture which, specified in literary terms as *imitatio* of the canonical authors, contributed importantly to the later notion of the pedagogical value of antiquity as a whole and decisively shaped the classical tradition. See EDUCATION, ROMAN; LITERARY CRITICISM IN ANTIQUITY; LITERARY THEORY AND CLASSICAL STUDIES; RHETORIC, LATIN.

A. Reiff, *Interpretatio, imitatio, aemulatio: Begriff und Vorstellung literarischer Abhängigkeit bei den Römern* (1959); A. Thill, *Alter ab illo: Recherches sur l'imitation dans la poésie personnelle à l'époque augustéenne* (1979); D. A. Russell, in D. West and A. J. Woodman, *Creative Imitation and Latin Literature* (1979); G.-B. Conte, *The Rhetoric of Imitation* (1986); P. J. Parsons in A. Bulloch and others (eds.), *Images and Ideologies* (1993), 162 ff. G. B. C., G. W. M.

immunitas was the exemption of a community or an individual from obligations to the Roman state or of an individual from obligations to a local community. As regards Roman taxation cities acquired immunity by *lex (1) or *senatus consultum or imperial decree. Immune status was in theory permanent but in practice, especially under the empire, revocable as in the case of Vespasian's revocation of Nero's grant of *libertas* and *immunitas* to Greece (see GREECE, HISTORY). Temporary grants of immunity from taxation, in special circumstances (e.g. natural disasters) are also attested; they might be made either by the emperor or by the senate. See FREE CITIES.

imperator

Immunity for life from Roman taxation could also be granted to individuals by *lex, senatus consultum,* or imperial decree. Immunity from other state services (military service, forced labour, the provision of supplies to officials or soldiers) was also granted, as by the edict of Octavian as triumvir on the privileges of veterans (*FIRA* 1². 56).

Equally important was the question of immunity from local *munera* (see CYRENE, EDICTS OF; LITURGY; MUNUS) to which all adult male citizens and *incolae* ('resident aliens') of communities were normally liable. Immunity might be granted either by Rome or by the community. Besides personal grants there was general exemption under the empire for such groups as shippers supplying corn to Rome, *conductores* and *coloni* of imperial estates, and local philosophers, rhetors, and doctors. By the late 2nd cent. AD an elaborate set of rulings about such local immunities had evolved. In general the hearing of petitions and disputes about all forms of immunity became a central feature of the imperial role.

In the Roman army *immunes* were soldiers promoted from the ranks and released from ordinary duties to perform certain skilled tasks (*Dig.* 50. 6. 7).

Millar, *ERW* chs. 7–8 and *JRS* 1983, 76 ff.   G. P. B.

imperator (αὐτοκράτωρ), a generic title for Roman commanders, became a special title of honour. After a victory the general was saluted *imperator* by his soldiers. He assumed the title after his name until the end of his magistracy or until his triumph. Sometimes the *senate seems to have given or confirmed the title. The origin of this form of honour is unknown, but some religious meaning is possible (cf. the formula *Iuppiter imperator*). The first certainly attested *imperator* is L. *Aemilius Paullus (2) in 189 BC, as the evidence about P. *Cornelius Scipio Africanus is uncertain. The title was assumed especially by proconsuls (see PRO CONSULE) and gained new importance through *Sulla before he was appointed dictator. The increasing influence of the army in the late republic made *imperator* the symbol of military authority. Sulla occasionally stated (and *Pompey emphasized) that he was saluted *imperator* more than once. *Caesar first used the title permanently, but it is doubtful whether in 45 BC he received from the senate a hereditary title of *imperator* (as Cass. Dio 43. 44. 2 states). *Agrippa in 38 BC refused a triumph for victories won under *Octavian's superior command and established the rule that the *princeps* should assume the salutations and the triumphs of his legates. Henceforth, apparently, Octavian used *imperator* as praenomen (*imperator Caesar*, not *Caesar imperator*), perhaps intending to emphasize the personal and family value of the title. Thus the title came to denote the supreme power and was commonly used in this sense. But, officially, *Otho was the first to imitate Augustus, and only with *Vespasian did *Imperator* ('emperor') become a title by which the ruler was known. The formula *imperator Caesar* was sometimes extended to members of the family of the *princeps* who were associated with him in power. On the death of a *princeps*, or during a rebellion, the *salutatio* of a general as an *imperator* by an army indicated that he was the candidate of that body for the imperial dignity.

The use of the praenomen did not suppress the old usage of *imperator* after the name. After a victory the emperor registered the *salutatio imperatoria* after his name (e.g.: Imp. Caesar ... Traianus ... imp. VI). From the second half of the 3rd cent. the emperor was deemed to receive a *salutatio* every year. The number of the salutations became practically identical with the number of the years of the reign.

Theoretically, governors of senatorial provinces, having their own *auspicia* (see AUSPICIUM), could assume the title of *imperator*. But the last instance of such a *salutatio* is that of Q. *Iunius Blaesus, proconsul of Africa in AD 22 (Tac. *Ann.* 3. 74).

D. McFayden, *The History of the Title Imperator under the Roman Empire* (1920); A. von Premerstein, *Vom Werden und Wesen des Prinzipats* (1937), 245 ff.; M. Grant, *From Imperium to Auctoritas* (1946); R. Syme, *Hist.* 1958, 172–88 (= *RP* 1. 361–77); R. Combès, *Imperator* (1966); J. Deininger, *ANRW* 1. 1. (1972), 982–97; F. De Martino, *Storia della costituzione romana* 4, 2nd edn. (1974); J. S. Richardson, *JRS* 1991, 1.

A. M.; T. J. Co.

imperialism

Carthaginian See CARTHAGE.

Greek and Hellenistic One Greek definition of *freedom included the ability of a state to exercise rule over others (cf. Hdt. 1. 210; Thuc. 8. 68. 4; Arist. *Pol.* 1333ᵇ38–1334ᵃ2; Polyb. 5. 106. 4–5). The 5th-cent. BC Athenians justified their rule over other Greeks by appealing to the motives of fear, honour, and interest: 'it has always been the law that the weaker should be subject to the stronger' (Thuc. 1. 76. 2). *Thucydides (2) himself interpreted the early history of Greece as the gradual emergence of greater powers with the ability to control superior resources (1. 1–19). It was common for the major states to seek to dominate weaker ones, as *Syracuse in Sicily, especially under the tyrants (see TYRANNY), and Sparta and Athens on the mainland of Greece and in the Aegean (see PELOPONNESIAN LEAGUE; DELIAN LEAGUE). Smaller states did the same: for example *Elis in the NW Peloponnese claimed to hold neighbouring cities through the right of conquest (Xen. *Hell.* 3. 2. 23), and *Sinope extracted tribute from her colonies on the Black Sea (Xen. *An.* 5. 5. 7–10). But the fragmentation of the Greek world into hundreds of states, the consequent dispersion of resources, and the strong Greek attachment to independence and its symbols, all militated against the emergence of lasting empires in the Greek world, and even inhibited the formation of durable alliance systems except in special circumstances. The territorial empires of the near east, based on deliberate military conquest and the imposition of regular tribute on subjects, were long familiar to the Greeks (cf. Hdt. 1. 6 on the Lydians, 1. 95–6 and 130 on the succession of empires from the Assyrians to the Persians, 3. 89–97 on the tribute of the Persian empire; see LYDIA; ASSYRIA (1); PERSIA; ACHAEMENIDS). But this eastern model did not transfer easily to Greek conditions. Athens' exceptional success in the 5th cent. encouraged emulation by others, but also stimulated the resistance of smaller states to encroachments on their independence and the imposition of regular tribute (cf. the manifesto of the *Second Athenian Confederacy in 377, Tod no. 123). Hence the numerous failures of Greek interstate relations in the 4th cent.: the Greeks never successfully bridged the gap between *alliance or league (see FEDERAL STATES) on the one hand, and empire on the other. The future lay rather with military monarchies that could command greater resources and work on a scale that would eventually transcend the Greek world itself. *Dionysius (1) I of Syracuse, *Jason (2) of Pherae, and *Mausolus of Caria may variously be seen as precursors to *Philip (1) II of Macedon. His transformation of Macedonian power provided the basis for *Alexander (3) the Great's conquest of the Persian empire and the subsequent emergence of the kingdoms of the Successors (or *Diadochi). The new Macedonian monarchies in Asia, culturally part of the

Greek world, became heirs to the former eastern empires and their methods. But the Antigonid rulers of Macedon (see ANTIGONUS (1–3); DEMETRIUS (4) and (6); PHILIP (3); PERSEUS (2)) never succeeded in devising a formula that would permanently reconcile the Greek mainland to their domination. This failure facilitated Roman intervention, hence eventually the absorption of much of the Hellenistic world into the Roman empire.

P. D. A. Garnsey and C. R. Whittaker (eds.), *Imperialism in the Ancient World* (1978); J. A. O. Larsen, *CPhil.* 1962, 230–4; M. I. Finley, *Ancient History: Evidence and Models* (1985), 67–87; F. Gschnitzer, *Abhängige Orte im griechischen Altertum* (1958); M. M. Austin, *CQ* 1986, 450–66; P. Briant, *Rois, tributs et paysans* (1982). M. M. A.

Persian See PERSIA.

Roman Although 'imperialism' was first used to describe the growth of the colonial empires of the European powers in the late 19th and early 20th cents., it is now frequently used in the context of the expansion of Roman power in Italy and particularly of the creation of its Mediterranean and European empire from the 3rd cent. BC to the 1st cent. AD.

Rome in the early and middle republican periods (5th to 2nd cents. BC) was a profoundly military society, as can be seen for instance from the military nature of the political power of the city's magistrates (*imperium), the need of any aspiring magistrate to have performed ten years of military service (Polyb. 6. 19. 4), and the religious and political importance attached to the *triumph. By the end of the war with *Pyrrhus in 272 BC, Rome controlled the greater part of Italy south of the river Po by a network of relationships which had grown out of the fighting against the *Aequi, *Volsci, and *Etruscans in the 5th and early 4th cents., the Latins (see LATINI) and the Campanians (see CAMPANIA) in the mid-4th cent. (leading to the dissolution of the Latin federation in 338), and the Samnites (see SAMNIUM) and other south Italians, of which the final stage was the Pyrrhic wars (see PYRRHUS). Some communities (mostly former Latin and Campanian allies) were incorporated into the Roman people (though geographically distinct from it, and often without full political rights), and the remainder were classified as allies (*socii), either as part of a reconstituted 'Latin' alliance or with a separate treaty of their own. Of these, only the Roman communities were properly speaking part of the expanded city of Rome, while the allies were under an obligation to provide military assistance and (especially in the case of the Latins) held certain rights from the Romans.

In the period of the two great wars against the Carthaginians (264–241 and 218–202 BC; see PUNIC WARS), the Romans, backed by this military alliance, became involved in wars in *Sicily, *Sardinia, *Corsica, *Spain, *Greece, and North Africa (see AFRICA, ROMAN). From this grew the beginnings of the Roman empire outside Italy. Roman commanders were assigned commands by the senate by the allocation of a *provincia or area of responsibility. Such *provinciae were not essentially territorial, nor were they permanent; but in areas in which the Romans wished to exercise a long-term military control through the presence of armed forces it became necessary to allocate a *provincia on a regular basis. Sometimes this seems to have occurred considerably later than the conflict that initially brought Roman soldiers to the area. The Carthaginians were defeated in Sicily by 241 and Sardinia was seized in 238, but Roman *praetors were sent to these islands on a regular basis only from 227 BC (Livy, *Per.* 20; Pomponius, *Dig.* 1. 2. 2. 32). Similarly in Spain, although it was a *provincia from the beginning of the Second Punic War in 218, praetors were only sent on a regular basis from 196 (Livy 32. 27–

8). Within this essentially military pattern, other elements of imperial control developed, particularly taxation of the local communities and jurisdiction exercised by Roman commanders over non-Romans.

In the first half of the 2nd cent. BC, and especially in the context of the wars with the Hellenistic powers of the eastern Mediterranean, Roman imperialism took a different form. Roman armies were sent to Greece during the Macedonian wars and to Asia Minor to fight against the Seleucid king, *Antiochus (3) III. Here long-term *provinciae were not established when the fighting ended, and control of the regions was exercised in a more remote fashion, through treaties and diplomacy. For *Polybius (1) however, writing in the second half of the century, this represented an extension of Roman control as real as that exercised directly in the western Mediterranean (Polyb. 1. 1); and although Macedonia became a long-term province after the failure of *Andriscus' attempt to seize the throne there (149/8 BC), Polybius seems to regard this as no more than a different and more direct form of the domination which the Romans already held.

Further large-scale additions were made as a result of the organization of the east by *Pompey, following the defeat of *Mithradates VI of Pontus (66–62 BC), and of the campaigns of *Caesar in Gaul (58–49 BC). The largest expansion, however, came under *Augustus, who not only completed the conquest of the Iberian peninsula but also added the new provinces of *Raetia, *Noricum, *Pannonia, and *Moesia along the line of the river Danube (see DANUVIUS). It appears that he was only prevented from a further expansion into that part of Germany (see GERMANIA) between the Rhine and the Elbe by the disastrous defeat of P. *Quinctilius Varus in AD 9, which led to the loss of three legions. Thereafter, apart from *Claudius' conquest of southern Britain in 43, *Trajan alone (97–117) made further large-scale additions, of which only Dacia and *Arabia survived the retrenchment of his successor, *Hadrian.

Although the mechanisms of Roman imperialism are fairly clear, the motivation of the Romans has been the subject of much debate. It was long believed, following Mommsen, that their intentions were essentially defensive, and only incidentally expansionist. Modern scholars have rejected this view, and have suggested alternative motives, including economic benefits (which undoubtedly resulted from the growth of the empire) and a desire for territorial annexation. Whatever else was the case, it is clear that throughout the period of expansion, the political classes at Rome were determined that other states should do what Rome required of them, and, although it is dangerous to attempt to provide a single explanation of so complex a phenomenon as Roman imperialism, it would appear that it was changes in the Roman understanding of what were the most effective means of achieving this control that shaped the way the empire grew.

W. V. Harris, *War and Imperialism in Republican Rome, 327–70 BC* (1979); J. S. Richardson, *PBSR* 1979, 1 ff. and *Hispaniae* (1986); A. W. Lintott, *Imperium Romanum: Politics and Administration* (1993). J. S. Ri.

imperium was the supreme power, involving command in war and the interpretation and execution of law (including the infliction of the death penalty), which belonged at Rome to the kings (see REX) and, after their expulsion, to *consuls, military tribunes (see TRIBUNI MILITUM) with consular power (from 445 to 367 BC), *praetors, *dictators, and masters of the horse (see MAGISTER EQUITUM). Viewed generally, *imperium* represents the supreme authority of the community in its dealings with the individual, and the magistrate in whom *imperium* is vested represents the community in all its dealings. In practical terms, *imperium* may be seen as the power to give orders and to exact obedience to them (cf. *imperare*, to command). It was symbolized by the *fasces borne by the *lictors, of which the dictator had 24, the consul 12, and the praetor 6, to which was added the axe when the magistrate left the precincts of the city. Later in the republic *imperium* was held also by proconsuls and propraetors (see PRO CONSULE, PRO PRAETORE), who were either ex-magistrates or private individuals upon whom a special command had been conferred (*privati cum imperio*), and by members of certain commissions (e.g. boards for the distribution of land, Cic. *Leg. agr.* 2. 28). Its application was increasingly restricted: first, when two consuls (originally two 'praetors') replaced the king, by the principle of collegiality and tenure of office limited to one year; the dictator, who had no colleague, held office for a maximum of six months. Secondly, by the *leges Valeriae* (traditionally of 509, 449, and 300 BC, see LEX (2)) and the *leges Porciae* (probably of the early 2nd cent. BC, see LEX (2)), magistrates were not allowed to execute citizens at Rome without trial owing to the citizen's right of *provocatio* to the people. This right of appeal was extended, whether by a *lex Porcia* or, possibly, by convention, to citizens abroad. Thirdly, the *imperium* of promagistrates was generally restricted to the bounds of their *provinciae*. *Imperium* needed ratification by a *lex curiata, a convention which persisted at least to the end of the republic (Cic. *Leg. Agr.* 2. 26; *Fam.* 1. 9. 25). To a promagistrate (whether ex-magistrate or *privatus cum imperio*), *imperium* was granted for a year at a time, or until his commission was achieved. Grants of *imperium* for a specified term of several years occur only towards the end of the republic, the earliest being the grant of *imperium* to *Pompey for three years by the *lex Gabinia* of 67 BC (see LEX (2), *leges Gabiniae*); this *imperium* was further distinguished by being *infinitum*, i.e. not subject to the usual territorial limits of a *provincia*.

Under the republic, in case of conflict, the *imperium* of a consul, with twelve fasces, could probably override that of a praetor, who held six. As between consuls and proconsuls, each with twelve fasces, the consul could override the proconsul by virtue of the *auctoritas* of his office. Conflict in the same area between proconsuls arose first in 67 between Pompey (pursuing pirates with proconsular *imperium*; see PIRACY) and Q. *Caecilius Metellus (Creticus), proconsul of *Crete. So, in 57, the question of allowing Pompey, in virtue of his corn commission, *imperium* greater than that of other proconsuls was mooted, and *Brutus and *Cassius were granted *imperium maius* in the east by the senate in 43.

*Octavian held *imperium*, first *pro praetore* and later as consul, in 43, as *triumvir from 42 to 33, and as consul in 31–23 (and, from 27, as proconsul of a large number of provinces). When in 23 he resigned the consulship, his proconsular *imperium* was made *maius*, and it was provided that it could be exercised from within the city. By this same enactment (or by another in 19 BC according to Cass. Dio 54. 10. 5) Italy was included within the field of his *imperium*. *Imperium* was granted to him for ten-year periods in 27 and 8 BC and AD 3 and 13, and for five-year periods in 18 and 13 BC. It was voted to succeeding emperors at their accession by the senate (cf. *ILS* 229, with Tac. *Ann.* 12. 69, referring to *Nero's accession), though ratification of the senate's decree by a *lex curiata* probably remained a formal requirement (Gai. *Inst.* 1. 5, and cf. *FIRA* 1². 15, the *lex 'de imperio Vespasiani'*, where the *imperium* is defined; see VESPASIAN).

Imperium maius was sometimes granted to others besides the emperor for the creation of a single military command, as to *Germanicus in the east in AD 17 (Tac. *Ann.* 2. 43) and to *Corbulo in AD 63 (Tac. *Ann.* 15. 25). It might also be conferred as a way of associating an individual with the *imperium* of the emperor and thereby signalling him as a suitable successor, as with *Tiberius (Tac. *Ann.* 1. 3; Vell. Pat. 2. 121).

As Rome's dominion came to extend overseas in the 3rd and 2nd cents. BC (see IMPERIALISM, ROMAN), it was conceived of in terms of the power to issue orders and to exact obedience to them (so Polyb. 3. 4. 2–3 and elsewhere), in terms, that is, of *imperium* (cf. Cato (Censorius) fr. 164 Malcovati). The first official expression of this is found in Greek. The treaty between Rome and Thracian Maroneia from the 160s BC (*SEG* 35. 823) refers to 'the Roman people and those under them' (ὁ δῆμος ὁ ʽΡωμαίων καὶ οἱ ὑπ᾽ αὐτοὺς τασσόμενοι), and this standard phrase appears in Latin in Rome's treaty with Callatis on the Black Sea (*ILLRP* 516, from the early 1st cent. BC) as 'the Roman people and those under their *imperium*' ([. . . *poplo Rom]ano quei*[*ve*] *sub inperio* [*eius erunt* . . .]). It was with reference to the principle and nature of supreme authority within the state that the authority of Rome itself over others was perceived and defined, and so it was to the *imperium Romanum* of the republic that the Roman empire succeeded.

Mommsen, *Röm. Staatsr.*; A. H. J. Greenidge, *Roman Public Life and Legal Procedure in Cicero's Time* (1901), 410 ff.; F. F. Abbott, *A History and Description of Roman Political Institutions*, 3rd edn. (1911); E. Täubler, *Imperium Romanum* (1913); M. Grant, *From Imperium to Auctoritas* (1946); H. M. Last, *JRS* 1947, 157 ff.; E. S. Staveley, *Hist.* 1956, 74 ff.; H. F. Jolowicz and B. Nicholas, *Historical Introduction to the Study of Roman Law* (1972); P. A. Brunt, *JRS* 1977, 95 ff.; P. S. Derow, *JRS* 1979, 4 ff.; A. Giovannini, *Consulare imperium* (1983); J. S. Richardson, *JRS* 1991, 1 ff.; C. Nicolet and others, *Cahiers du Centre G. Glotz* 1992, 163 ff.; A. W. Lintott, *Imperium Romanum: Politics and Administration* (1993), 22 ff.
P. S. D.

impiety, official action against See INTOLERANCE, INTELLECTUAL AND RELIGIOUS.

Inachus, an Argive river and river-god, father of *Io. He was made judge between *Poseidon and *Hera when both claimed *Argos (2), and decided in favour of Hera, whose cult he introduced (Apollod. 2. 13; Paus. 2. 15. 4–5); Poseidon therefore dried up his waters. He is often represented as a mortal, ancestor of the Argive kings, and therefore the earliest figure in Greek legend.

In art he appears rarely: *LIMC* 5. 1 (1990), 653–4. H. J. R.

incense is the general name given to a variety of aromatic gum-resins which, when heated, produce a fragrant odour. Often used interchangeably with frankincense (Gk. λίβανος (probably a direct loan from South Arabian *libān*, from the Semitic root *lbn*, meaning 'white, milky'; cf. Plin. *HN* 12. 60, who says that the best frankincense was the white variety harvested in the autumn), Lat. *tus/thus*), it is the oleo-gum-resin extracted chiefly from the species *Boswellia sacra* Flückiger and *Boswellia carterii* Birdwood, of the family Burseracea. Incense was widely burnt as a religious offering in the ancient world, as an accompaniment to acts of divination, on the occasion of a burial, and as a gesture of homage (e.g. on the occasion of *Alexander (3) the Great's entry into Babylon, Curt. 5. 1. 20). See below, INCENSE IN RELIGION. The natural distribution of frankincense-producing *Boswellia* is restricted to Dhofar and eastern Hadhramaut, in southern *Arabia; the island of Socotra (Dioscurides); the Coromandel coast of *India; and northern Somalia. *Sappho (44. 30 L–P) preserves the earliest Greek reference to λίβανος, while *Herodotus (1) (3. 107) contains the earliest Greek reference to specifically Arabian frankincense, and *Theophrastus (*Hist. pl.* 9. 4) obviously had firsthand accounts of the frankincense-producing area of southern *Arabia to draw on in drafting his detailed treatment of it. *Eratosthenes (in Strabo 16. 4. 2), *Agatharchides of Cnidos (fr. 97 *FGrH* no. 86), Pliny (1) (*HN* 12. 30. 54), and the *Periplous Maris Erythraei* (§§ 27, 29; see PERIPLOI) provide further testimony. Arabian frankincense was always the most important variety in the ancient world, and given the large quantities of frankincense consumed it is natural that a lively trade should have developed in this commodity. In the earlier periods it was transported overland by, among others, Sabaean, Minaean, and Gerrhaean merchants (see GERRHA), to *Gaza, and thence on to the cities of the eastern Mediterranean. In the Roman era, maritime trade seems to have been more important. The *Periplous Maris Erythraei* identifies the port of Qana as the principal point of frankincense export by sea in ancient south Arabia.

F. N. Hepper, *JEg. Arch.* 1969, 66–72, and *Bulletin on Sumerian Agriculture* 1987, 107–14; J. P. Mandaville, Jr., in *The Scientific Results of the Oman Flora and Fauna Survey 1977 (Dhofar)* (1980), 87–9; W. W. Müller, *Theologische Quartalschrift* 1969, 350–68, and *RE* Suppl. 15 (1978), 699–777; K. Nielsen, *Suppl. Vetus Testamentum* 1986, 16–24. D. T. P.

Incense in religion Fragrance of burning wood, herbs, spices, and resins fulfilled ritual functions on three levels: first, to neutralize odours of burning sacrificial flesh, hair, hoofs and horns, etc. (see SACRIFICE); secondly, to generate appropriate mood and ambience; thirdly, metaphorically, incense was an expression of the intangible yet distinctly felt presence of the divine as well as the 'rising' to heaven of either prayers or souls of the dead. *Myrrh and frankincense were most common in Greek religion, probably imported from southern Arabia since the 8th cent. BC via Phoenicia (see PHOENICIANS) and *Cyprus and retaining their Semitic names. The more expensive and finer incense gradually came to replace fragrant wood (cf. Ov. *Fast.* 1. 337 ff.). In Greece incense-burning was particularly associated with *Aphrodite (cf. Sappho fr. 2; 44. 30 L–P). Granules of incense were thrown directly onto the altar or burnt separately in special braziers.

M. Detienne, *The Gardens of Adonis: Spices in Greek Mythology*, trans. J. Lloyd (1977; Fr. orig. 1972); Burkert, *GR* 62. I. M.

incest, sexual intercourse or marriage with close kin, was restricted throughout classical antiquity. However, terminology and the particular relations prohibited varied with place and time. Though μητροκοίτης, 'mother's bedmate', occurs in *Hipponax, most of the Greek words referring to specific close-kin unions are much later in date and no general word for incest is found before the Byzantine period. *Incestum*, attested as a Latin technical term from the late republic, carries connotations of impurity absent from the Greek vocabulary. Sexual relations involving parent and child were forbidden everywhere we have evidence; their occurrence in Greek myth generally evokes horror, yet the participants are sometimes marked as numinous by their transgression of the usual limits of human conduct. Siblings of the same father could marry at *Athens, of the same mother at *Sparta. Even marriages between full siblings were recognized among the Greeks of Hellenistic and Roman *Egypt, an unusual practice perhaps intended to preserve the ethnic identity of a small and isolated settler élite and the privileges to which it provided access. Siblings by adoption might marry under Roman law if one of them was first emancipated from *patria potestas. But marriages between nieces and paternal uncles—encouraged

in the Athenian epiclerate, see INHERITANCE, GREEK—were made legal only in the time (and the marital interests) of *Claudius, and were outlawed again by *Constantius II and *Constans (*Cod. Theod.* 3. 12. 1). Marriages between men and their sisters' daughters, granddaughters, and great-granddaughters, or between men and their aunts, were forbidden throughout. Despite a tradition that marriages between first cousins were once unknown, they are attested for the 3rd cent. BC and unremarkable until banned by *Theodosius (2) I in about AD 384 or 385. (The ban was lifted in 409, *Cod. Theod.* 3. 10. 1.) Allegations of incest were aimed at political opponents at both Athens (*Cimon, *Alcibiades) and Rome (P. *Clodius Pulcher). Public legal sanctions at Athens, if any, are unknown. In republican Rome, offenders are said to have been thrown from the *Tarpeian Rock, though the penalty in classical law was deportation, and that only in the cases of closest kin. Women involved in incestuous marriages with collateral kin might escape punishment entirely, though extramarital incest risked the usual penalties for adultery. But the Christian emperors imposed harsher provisions.

K. Hopkins, *Comparative Studies in Society and History* 1980, 303 ff. (Roman Egypt); J. Rudhardt, *Revue française de psychanalyse* 1982, 731–63; E. Karabélias, in G. Thür (ed.), *Symposion 1985* (1989), 233–51; B. D. Shaw, *Man* 1992, 267–99; P. E. Corbett, *The Roman Law of Marriage* (1930). M. G.

incubation, *ritual sleep in a sanctuary (see SANCTUARIES) in order to obtain a dream, mostly for healing.

Incubation is known from sanctuaries of *Asclepius, but also from other healing sanctuaries like the Amphiaraion at *Oropus or oracular shrines like the *Daunian ones of *Calchas (Strabo 6. 3. 9 (284 C)) and Podalirius (Lycoph. *Alex.* 1050). Such sanctuaries mostly had specific halls where patients slept during the night (ἐγκοιμητήριον or ἄδυτον), with high walls to prevent casual (or intentional) prying. *Aristophanes (1) (*Plut.* 653–747) gives a detailed description of a night in the Asclepieum in the *Piraeus, a Pergamene inscription (see bibliog. below) adds details, while the healing inscriptions from *Epidaurus, Lebena, Rome, and Pergamum although directly aimed at promoting the cult, allow some insights into the nature of the *dreams, as does the diary of Aelius *Aristides.

Incubation is possible only in a culture which believes that at least some dreams can always open communication with a superhuman world; thus, the experience of incubation is always formulated as a real meeting with the god (or his divine assistants), and the sanctuary is a place where the god 'reveals himself in person to man' (Philostr. *VA.* 1. 7). The structure of the ritual concurs: the ritual setting takes care that all dreams allow this meeting. Preliminary cathartic rites and offerings in the evening are a preparation for entering the doubly sacred space (a consecrated space inside the sacred space of the sanctuary) where man and god converse: these preliminaries comprise cathartic ablutions (see PURIFICATION) before entering the precinct (in Athens a bathe in the sea, Ar. *Plut.* 656–8), sacrifices when entering the sleeping-hall—bloodless cakes for Asclepius, a ram for *Amphiaraus, Podalirius, or Calchas; in Pergamum, Mnemosyne ('memory' in order to remember the dream) was among the recipients. In the sleeping-hall, one slept on a στιβάς (a makeshift bed of twigs), or on the hide of the sacrificial animal, not on a bed; one donned a white robe, an olive wreath, having previously removed all rings, girdles, and belts. The *stibas*, a 'natural' bed, belongs also to Bacchic mystery cults (see DIONYSUS; MYSTERIES) where similar experiences took place (J.-M. Ver-

India

poorten, *Rev. Hist. Rel.* 1962, 147–60); the white robe, wreath, and absence of all bonds express the new, non-human sphere; the animal hide belongs to the god, not to the sacrificer. During the night, the god and his helpers appeared, gave advice, and performed cures (even Ar. *Plut.* 698–747 takes this to be evidence of the personal presence of the gods). When leaving the hall in the morning, one had to pay a fee to the temple treasury.

Incubation survived the advent of *Christianity, and was absorbed into the cult of Byzantine saints as a means of obtaining healing—a phenomenon which survived up to modern times.

See ASCLEPIUS; HEALING GODS; MACHAON AND PODALIRIUS.

L. Deubner, *De incubatione capita quattuor* (1900); F. Graf, in O. Reverdin and B. Grange (eds.), *Le Sanctuaire grec* (1992), 186–93; for Aristophanes, E. Roos, *Op. Ath.* 1960, 55–93; for Pergamum, M. Wörrle, *Altertümer von Pergamon* 8. 3 (1969), no. 161 (*LSAM* 14); the healing inscriptions, M. Guarducci, *Epigrafia greca* 4 (1978), 143–66, with the addition of H. Müller, *Chiron* 1987, 193–233. For a text from *Amphipolis see C. Véligianni, *ZPE* 100 (1994), 391 ff. F. G.

India This country had early trade connections with the *Persian Gulf, but it remained unknown to Mediterranean peoples until the extension of the Persian empire to the Indus and the voyage of Darius' admiral *Scylax down the Kabul and Indus rivers and perhaps round Arabia to Suez (Hecataeus, *FGrH* 214 F–294–9; Hdt. 3. 98 ff., 4. 44). Even so, India remained a land of fable and wonders (as in the *Indica* of *Ctesias, *c*.400 BC); it was believed to lie in the farthest east, yet Indians were confused with Ethiopians, and in popular belief India and *Ethiopia formed one country. The conquests of *Alexander (3) the Great (327–325) brought more accurate knowledge of NW India as far as the river Hyphasis (Beas) and vague information about the Ganges valley and Sri Lanka; and the voyage of *Nearchus reopened a sea connection with the Persian Gulf. *Seleucus (1) I controlled the north-west but *c*.302 conceded the control to the Mauryan king Chandragupta (see SANDRACOTTUS). He kept a resident named *Megasthenes at Chandragupta's court at Pataliputra (see PALIBOTHRA), who published much detail about India (see ARRIAN; DIODORUS (3); STRABO); and King *Ashoka in the 3rd cent. sent embassies to the Hellenistic kings. In the 2nd cent. NW India was occupied by the Graeco-Bactrian rulers (see BACTRIA; DEMETRIUS (9) II; EUTHYDEMUS (2–3) I-II; INDO-GREEKS; MENANDER (2)); but the rise of the Parthian empire (see PARTHIA) separated India from the Greek lands, and invaders from central Asia (*c*.80–30 BC) obliterated the Greek principalities in the Indus valley; see GANDHARA. In the 1st cent. AD Chinese *silk reached the Roman dominions through India, but land communications with India remained irregular. The chief routes to India were (1) via Meshed and the Bolan and Mula passes, (2) via Merv (*Antioch (3)), Balkh, Kabul, and Peshawar. Roman connections with this area, although not direct, are evident from the excavations at sites such as Sirkap (Taxila) and Begram.

Sea communications between India and the Persian Gulf were maintained by the *Seleucids, but were interrupted under Parthian rule. Direct travel from Egypt to India was impeded for long by the *Arabs of Yemen, whose monopoly of trade was not seriously challenged by the Ptolemies (see PTOLEMY (1)), and the voyages of *Eudoxus (3) to India were not too successful. The Arab obstruction was removed by the great appetite of Rome for eastern luxuries in the prosperous days of *Augustus, and by the discovery of open-sea routes from Aden to India. In the 1st cent. BC, or soon after, observation of the *monsoon encouraged mid-ocean routes leading to various points on the western coast where settlements were subsequently established (Plin. *HN* 6.

96–100). Augustus received Indian envoys (Cass. Dio 54. 9), and Greek and Levantine merchants organized a regular trade from Egypt. In Augustus' day 120 ships sailed to India every year, and under his early successors the drain on Roman money to pay for Indian imports caused occasional anxiety (Plin. *HN* 6. 101, 12. 84). But recent studies suggest that this drain was illusory. The main goals of visitors from the Roman world were western India and the Chera, Chola, and Pandya kingdoms of south India. The principal imports to Rome were perfumes, *spices (especially pepper), *gems, *ivory, pearls, Indian textiles, and Chinese silk. The Romans exported linen, coral, *glass, base metals, 'Arretine' tableware (see POTTERY, ROMAN), wine in *amphorae, etc., and also sent quantities of *gold and *silver (and later copper) coins, of which large hoards have been found in south India and the eastern Deccan as well as some clay *bullae* ('amulets') of Roman coins. Roman artefacts occur in western India, the Deccan, and southern India at sites such as Nasik, Nevasa, Kolhapur, Akota, and Karvan; at Ter, Bhokardan, Brahmagiri, Chandravalli, Maski, Kondapur; and at Amaravati and Sisupalagarh.

The chief markets on the west coast were Barbaricon and *Barygaza (mod. Broach) and the southern towns of Muziris (? Cranganore) and Nelcynda (? Kottayam). Beyond Cape Comorin the Greeks visited Colchoi (Kolkai), Camara (perhaps Kaveripattinam), a trading-station now called Arikamedu near Pondicherry (? Poduce), and Sopatma (? Madras); a few reached the Ganges mouth and brought news of Burma, Malaya, and the Thinae or Sinae (in south China, see SERES). Greek traders figure in Tamil literature as residents in ports and some inland centres (AD 70–140). The Maldives and Laccadives came into this circuit, Sri Lanka was circumnavigated (see TAPROBANE); and one Alexander, taking advantage of the bay of Bengal monsoon, is said to have sailed past Burma and Malaya to Vietnam and even to China proper (Ptol. *Geog.* 7. 1–2). A few Roman artefacts of the 2nd cent. AD were found at Oc-eo in Cambodia and on the Mekong river. These could have come in the course of the Roman trade with India being extended eastwards by Indian traders (see ASIA, SOUTH-EAST). Nevertheless, Greek geographers always underrated the extent of India's southward projection and exaggerated the size of Sri Lanka. From *c*. AD 200 direct Graeco-Roman trade declined, communications with India passed into the hands of intermediaries (Arabians, Axumites (see AXUMIS), Sasanid Persians), and India again became a land of fable to the Mediterranean world. The founders of Christian settlements in India came largely from Persia.

E. H. Warmington, *The Commerce between the Roman Empire and India*, 2nd edn. (1974); A. K. Narain, *The Indo-Greeks*, 2nd edn. (1962); W. W. Tarn, *The Greeks in Bactria and India*, 2nd edn. (1951); R. E. M. Wheeler, *Rome beyond the Imperial Frontiers* (1955), *Ancient India*, 2 July 1946, and in W. Grimes (ed.), *Aspects of Archaeology* (1951); J. Vogel, in G. C. Miles (ed.), *Archaeologica Orientalia in Memory of E. Herzfeld* (1952); J. I. Miller, *The Spice Trade of the Roman Empire* (1969); M. G. Raschke, *ANRW* 2. 9. 2 (1978); L. Casson, *The Periplus Maris Erythraei* (1989); V. Begley and R. de Puma (eds.), *Rome and India* (1992). E. H. W.; R. Th.

indictio under the Principate meant the compulsory purchase of food, clothing, and other goods for the army and the court. Owing to the inflation of the mid-3rd cent. AD the payments made for such purchases became derisory and were finally abandoned. From the time of *Diocletian the term *indictio* was applied to the annual assessment of all levies in kind made by the praetorian prefects: the *indictio* declared the amount of each item (wheat, barley, wine, oil, clothing, etc.) payable on each fiscal unit (*caput*, *iugum*, etc.). From 287, indictions were numbered serially in cycles of five years, from 312 in cycles of fifteen years. The number of the indiction was regularly used for dating financial years (which began on 1 September) and sometimes for dating other documents. See FINANCE, ROMAN.

Jones, *Later Rom. Emp.* 448 ff.

A. H. M. J.

indigetes or ***-ites, indigitamenta,*** 'invoked deities'. Both words, as well as the corresponding verb *indigitare*, are fairly common and there is no doubt that they mean respectively a class of Roman gods and a list of gods. The lists of *indigitamenta* known from the fragments of *Varro, *Antiquitates divinae* 14 (ed. Cardauns, 1. 64 ff.), for the most part are antiquarian compilations without cultic value (Wissowa, *Ges. Abh.* 304 ff.), with the exception of the deities invoked during the sacrifice to *Ceres (J. Bayet, *Croyances et rites dans la Rome antique* (1971), 177 ff.) and during some expiations of the *fratres arvales* (Dumézil, *ARR* 35). These lists of minor deities whose name is reduced to their function are subordinated to the major divinities whose activity they second. Nowadays there is agreement that the *indigitamenta* do not represent a primitive stage in formation of personalized deities.

The meaning of *indiges* has prompted a debate. Wissowa contrasted the *di indigetes*, understood as *indigenae*, 'autochthonous', with the *di novensides*, 'newly installed', and classed all Roman deities in these two categories. But today this view has been abandoned after the criticisms of Koch, Latte, and Weinstock, even though the etymology of *indigenes* is not definitively established. Preferable to the pre-deist interpretation, 'active within' (H. Wagenvoort, *Roman Dynamism* (1947), 99 ff.), is the hypothesis of R. Schilling (*Rev. Ét. Lat.* (1979)) according to which *indiges* (†*inag-et-*), its sense passive, means 'invoked'. From this adjective would then derive *indigitare* and *indigitamenta*, 'invoked deities'.

The epithet *indiges* was applied to the god *Sol and to Jupiter who, at *Lavinium, was gradually assimilated to Aeneas.

Altheim, *Hist. Rom. Rel.* 1. 106 ff.; C. Koch, *Gestirnverehrung im alten Italien* (1933), 78 ff.; Latte, *RR* 43; S. Weinstock, *RE* 17. 1 (1936), cols. 1185–9.

J. Sch.

Indo-European and Indo-Europeans For the last 200 years it has been recognized that languages such as Greek, Latin, and Sanskrit share regularities which indicate a close historical relationship (see LINGUISTICS, COMPARATIVE AND HISTORICAL). This grouping, termed Indo-European (IE) to indicate its geographical extent in historical times, includes some nine major living language-groups and also extinct ones known only through inscriptions. The earliest recorded examples belong to the second millennium BC, and include extinct *Anatolian languages such as *Hittite and Luwian (*c.*17th cent. BC); as well as the bronze age form of Greek written in Linear B (e.g. at *Cnossus, 14th cent. BC); but many unrecorded languages and language-groups of this family must once have existed, only some of which gave rise to successors which have left evidence in written or spoken form. The peoples who spoke any of this family of related languages might be termed—in a purely linguistic sense—Indo-Europeans.

The present distribution of IE languages reflects processes known to have taken place in historical times, such as the spread of Latin and the diversification and consolidation (particularly in relation to political boundaries) of its Romance derivatives; or the rupture of a once continuous distribution of IE languages across the Eurasian steppes, by the westward movement of Turkic speakers in the first millennium AD and early Middle Ages. In addition, the relatively close relationship of certain language-groups such as Celtic and Italic (see ITALY, LANGUAGES OF) can most plausibly be explained by processes of expansion and diversification taking place in later prehistoric times on the edges of the ancient world, during the later second and early first millennia BC. More problematic, however, are reconstructions of earlier prehistoric conditions on the basis of the IE distribution as a whole, including the postulated existence of a people or set of peoples who have been termed 'proto-Indo-Europeans'. The development of comparative IE linguistics (philology) in the 19th cent. gave rise to a particular historical model of language change which reflected both the procedures of the comparative method and the expectations of national history and prehistory. The procedure of reconstructing a common ancestral language whose regular transformation would have produced the variety of known IE languages placed an emphasis on processes of linguistic divergence; the migrationist paradigm of contemporary prehistory provided a convenient method of geographical dispersal. The outcome was a search for a plausible homeland where the speakers of a common ancestral language, '†proto-Indo-European' (†PIE), once lived, and a series of attempts to identify a particular culture which would correspond to it in the archaeological record.

While both the Caucasus and northern Germany were once leading contenders for this role, the demonstration by archaeologists that the horse was first domesticated on the Pontic steppes has encouraged a belief in the expansion of †PIE-speakers (often identified with a group of bronze age cultures using tumulus—*kurgan*—burial) from this area. Although a connection with early pastoralism may help to explain why the main eastern branch of IE (Indo-Iranian) covers such a wide geographical area around the steppes, the solution of the question of IE 'origins' is unlikely to be quite so simple. In the area between central Europe and the Caucasus (on both sides of the Black Sea), socio-linguistic processes less easy to reconstruct by classical methods (including convergence, perhaps initially among specific social or occupational groups) are likely to have had as important a role in the progressive formation and dissemination of early IE languages as did steady divergence from a single common ancestor. While archaeology can demonstrate some of the underlying processes of economic, social, and cultural change, therefore, it offers no easy correlations with entities like †PIE which have been postulated on linguistic grounds.

For a good summary of the conventional view, J. P. Mallory, *In Search of the Indo-Europeans: Language, Archaeology and Myth* (1989); for a radical attempt to identify †PIE with earlier farming groups, A. C. Renfrew, *Archaeology and Language: The Puzzle of Indo-European Origins* (1987); both models compared and criticized in A. and S. Sherratt, *Antiquity* 1988, 584–95, and J. Robb, *Antiquity* 1993, 747–60.

A. Sh., S. Sh.

Indo-Greeks were the Hellenistic kings of *Bactria and of the north-west of the Indo-Pakistan subcontinent (see INDIA), including *Gandhara, ruling from the mid-2nd cent. BC to the Christian era. They are known primarily from extensive numismatic evidence. The coins carry the bust of the king, usually characterized by fine portraiture, legends either in Greek or bilingually in Greek and Brahmi, a monogram, and symbols often with Hellenistic themes. Among their kings the best-remembered in *India was *Menander (2), whose power extended to the western Ganges valley, but only for a limited period. They were also patrons of Buddhism and of Hindu Bhagavatism. Some, such as Heliodorus, identified with a Vaishnava sect. Rich finds at urban centres such as Begram and Sirkap (Taxila) point to active commerce.

J. Marshall, *Taxila* (1951); W. W. Tarn, *The Greeks in Bactria and India,*

2nd edn. (1951); A. K. Narain, *The Indo-Greeks*, 2nd edn. (1962); O. Guillaume, *Analysis of Reasonings in Archaeology* (1990); N. Davis and C. Kraay, *The Hellenistic Kingdoms* (1973), ch. 5 (coin-portraits).

R. Th.

industry (Greek and Roman). Industry in the sense of hard labour (Gk. *ponos*; Lat. *labor*) the Greeks and Romans knew all too much about; total freedom from productive labour (*scholē, otium*) remained a governing ideal from one end of pagan antiquity to the other. But industry in the modern sense of large-scale manufacturing businesses they knew hardly at all, let alone as the characteristic form of manufacturing unit. That role was always filled by the individual workshop (*ergastērion*), and it is no accident that the largest Greek or Roman industrial labour force on record barely tipped over into three figures. Nor did élite Greeks and Romans value labourers any more highly than *labour as such; this was partly because manual labour, even when not actually conducted by slaves (see SLAVERY), was nevertheless always apt to attract the opprobrium of slavishness. As Herodotus (2. 167) put it, the Corinthians (see CORINTH) despised manual craftsmen (*cheirotechnai*) the least, the *Spartans the most—but all élite Greeks despised them. On the other hand, they always felt boundless admiration for skill (*technē, ars*), and some forms of ancient pre-industrial craftsmanship demanded that quality in the highest degree. See ART, ANCIENT ATTITUDES TO; ARTISANS AND CRAFTSMEN.

Craftsmanship in stone, wood, bone, earth, and leather, as well as the use of colour for painting and of fire for cooking, were palaeolithic inventions; textiles, fired pottery, architecture, and shipbuilding were neolithic discoveries. Metalwork and glass-making began with the bronze age, as did the oversight of craftsmanship by written prescription and the imposition of exact measures and weights in the Minoan and Mycenaean palace-economies. Besides smiths and glaziers the Linear B tablets present an array of specialist craftsmen including potters, brewers, jewellers, leather-workers, and perfumiers. See MINOAN and MYCENAEAN CIVILIZATION.

*Homer and *Hesiod mention a considerable variety of craftsmen, some of the more expert and specialized being non-Greek. But only the metalworkers had their own workshops, and this is in accord with the florescence of bronze-working associated with the great Panhellenic sanctuaries of *Olympia (from the 10th cent. BC), *Delphi (9th), and *Delos (8th) in particular. Their standards were eventually matched by the potters and (if they were separate) vase-painters, above all those of *Athens, *Argos (2), and Corinth; the latter too could boast at least one shipbuilder of distinction by 700 BC (Thuc. 1. 13. 3). In the course of the 7th and 6th cents. workshops and studios proliferated, no longer tied principally to sanctuaries. Depictions of potters, leather-workers, and smiths occur on Attic black- and red-figure vases, themselves often products of the highest craft and finish. As is revealed both by the workers' names (Lydus = 'the Lydian', Amasis (Egyptian), Epictetus = 'the purchased') and by an isolated painted text (Lydus 'the slave'), many of the craftsmen were not only not Athenian citizens but non-Greek slaves.

The concomitant development of the Athenian empire and the *Piraeus in the 5th cent. BC provided a further stimulus to Greek craftsmanship, both quantitative and qualitative. No one, according to *Plutarch, would wish actually to be Phidias, but the products of *Phidias' extraordinary craft skill were universally admired. The anonymous labours of an army of stone-carvers have left us a legacy of accomplished dressed masonry and decorative sculptural detail carved in the hardest material (marble).

Gem-cutters like Dexamenes of Chios and die-engravers (see COINAGE, GREEK) like those who produced the decadrachms of *Syracuse were hardly less accomplished. At Athens craftsmanship interacted with high culture and politics in interesting ways. Plato's *Socrates was fond of analogies from craftsmanship, and the real Socrates was reputedly the son of a stonemason. The fathers of *Cleon, *Isocrates, and *Demosthenes (2) made their piles through employing skilled slave craftsmen—tanners, flute-makers, and cutlers respectively. But the biggest 'industrialists' on record in Classical Athens were the metic brothers (see METICS) Polemarchus and *Lysias (the latter a noted speech-writer), even if it is not absolutely certain that their 120 slaves all worked full time in the family shield-making business (exceptionally lucrative, thanks to the *Peloponnesian War). A more usual size of workshop was the one staffed by ten slaves owned by *Aeschines (1)'s opponent Timarchus. Some such skilled slaves were privileged to be set up in business on their own account by their masters. The craftsmen of Athens were sedentary—indeed, in the case of the mine-slaves who extracted and processed the argentiferous lead ores of *Laurium, possibly shackled. But itinerant Greek craftsmen operated as far afield as south Russia (within the Scythian sphere) and the Alps, working on the spot under commission from local potentates. There may also have been a few wandering craftsmen in rural districts of Greece during the Classical period.

The Hellenistic age produced a growth of the Greek *ergastērion* system but also to some degree marked a return to the Mycenaean pattern of palace-centred industries. Textile and food production were affected. Several glass-producers of the 1st cent. BC and a potter, Aristion, of *c.*200 BC seem to have had workshops in more than one town. Glass-blowing was invented in the second half of the 1st cent. BC. The Ptolemies (see PTOLEMY (1); EGYPT (Ptolemaic)) 'nationalized' several Egyptian crafts: the production of papyrus scrolls, oil, perfumes, textiles (other than woollen), and beer became government monopolies. Craftsmen in these trades became government employees, who were controlled by tax-farmers and government officials, received salaries, and, in the production of oil, a share of the profits. A government production-schedule was issued annually, and the workers received their tools and raw materials from central stores. Large enterprises for fish-curing, metalworking, and brick-making were also properties of the Ptolemies.

In Rome of the kings (*c.*750–500 BC), according to tradition, specialized crafts of metal- and leather-workers, potters, dyers, musicians, and *fabri* (all-purpose handymen) were organized in societies known as *collegia* (see COLLEGIUM). In later republican times (coeval with the Hellenistic age) Roman craftsmanship developed on Greek lines. This was a period of enormous expansion of the Roman empire and intense specialization of all kinds of economic activity (see ECONOMY, ROMAN), and among the many imports to Rome and Italy from the Greek east were not only staple foodstuffs and luxury finished goods but skilled Greek craftsmen, not a few of whom had been reduced to servitude by their slave-hungry imperial masters. These worked generally on a larger scale, though not usually according to radically different legal or economic conditions, than their free and slave counterparts in the old country. As in old Greece, an attempt was made to erect social barriers between the political élite and the sordid business of production and commerce, but even the Roman senate was not entirely devoid of manufacturing entrepreneurs; the big names of C. *Rabirius Postumus with his large *terra sigillata* workshops, C. Sestius and his stamped wine-amphorae, and L. *Domitius Ahenobarbus (1) and his stamped bricks are examples. The large and assured demand provided by Roman armies outside Italy was often a vital factor stimulating the production and distribution of consumable commodities. The politicization of the *collegia* (see CLUBS, ROMAN) at Rome was another late republican phenomenon, prompting official measures to dissolve or curb them.

Under the Principate craftsmanship of the Greek and Roman workshop type spread throughout the provinces of the empire. Remnants of administered economy persisted, especially in mining districts, temples, and public domains; but even the Ptolemaic monopolies were broken up or changed into monopolistic concessions for small districts farmed out to independent craftsmen. The local markets of provincial districts were furnished with bricks, coarse pottery, cheap leather goods and metalwork, *terra sigillata*, cheap textiles, and so on by craftsmen working from public and private estates. There were, however, local exceptions to the general pattern both in scale and in management; an apparently huge private-enterprise development of olive-growing and *olive oil distribution in Cyrenaica (see CYRENE), traceable physically through the surviving containers (see AMPHORAE, ROMAN), and an imperially inspired development of stone *quarries in the *mons Claudianus area of Egypt, are just two conspicuous instances.

During what appears to have been the general crisis of the 3rd cent. AD control of industry and craftsmanship began to revert to centralized, imperial direction. *Diocletian's reforms aimed at rendering the compulsory organization of labour final. The number of independent workshops decreased everywhere, and the state provided for its own requirements by establishing manufactories in all provinces and by regulating the more important *collegia* of craftsmen throughout the empire. Sons had to follow their father's trade, and large taxes were levied on the corporations collectively. Gradually, and especially during the reign of *Justinian I, they received privileges that enabled them to influence prices, to buy raw materials cheaply for all members, to regulate production and sale, workshop capacity, and size of membership. See also TECHNOLOGY; TRADE; TRADERS.

H. Blümner, *Technologie und Terminologie der Griechen und Römer* 1², 2–4 (1879–1912); H. Francotte, *L'Industrie dans la Grèce ancienne*, 2 vols. (1900–1); H. Bolkestein, *Economic Life in Greece's Golden Age*, 2nd edn. (1958), ch. 3; F. M. Heichelheim, *An Ancient Economic History* 1 (1958), 261 ff., 510 ff., 2 (1964), 93 ff., 207 ff.; Jones, *Later Rom. Emp.* ch. 21; C. Mossé, *The Ancient World at Work* (1969; Fr. orig. 1966); P. Garnsey (ed.), *Non-slave Labour in the Greco-Roman World*, PCPS Suppl. 6 (1980); H. Schneider, in H. Schneider (ed.), *Geschichte der Arbeit: Vom alten Ägypten bis zur Gegenwart* (1980), 95–154; M. Henig (ed.), *A Handbook of Roman Art* (1983); C. Nicolet, *CAH* 9² (1994), 623 ff. P. A. C.

infamia as a legal term embraces a variable number of disabilities (the common one being an incapacity to act or appear for another at law—*postulare pro aliis*) imposed in a variety of circumstances. It is at root social, involving loss of *fama* ('reputation') or *existimatio* ('good name'), but is given legal content by *leges*, *senatus consulta*, imperial constitutions, or by the praetor's edict in specific situations, such as condemnation in ordinary criminal prosecutions, condemnation in civil actions for delict and in other civil actions in which the defendant was guilty of a breach of faith (partnership, guardianship, mandate, etc.), engaging in certain disreputable occupations. In classical law there is no single concept of *infamia* (or *ignominia*—the earlier word: see Gai. *Inst.* 4. 182), but in the law of Justinian (see JUSTINIAN'S CODIFICATION) there appears to be an attempt to generalize.

A. H. J. Greenidge, *Infamia in Roman Law* (1894) (out of date but still useful); M. Kaser, ZRG 1956, 220. B. N.

infanticide, killing of infants ($\H{\epsilon}\kappa\theta\epsilon\sigma\iota\varsigma$, *expositio*, 'putting outside', probably a euphemism), a method of family limitation. The term as generally used by historians also covers exposure of infants, because it is seldom possible to ascertain what actually happened in specific cases. Infanticide is commonly mentioned in myths and legends, e.g. *Oedipus, *Cyrus (1) the Great, *Romulus and Remus. Its frequency probably varied temporally and regionally. For example, *Polybius (1) (36. 17) attributed population decline in Hellenistic Greece (see POPULATION, GREEK) to family limitation, but there is little evidence for it in earlier periods, especially in Athens. The Egyptians and the Jews were said to rear all their children, while the Carthaginians sacrificed children to Moloch (see CARTHAGE). *Soranus (*Gyn.* 2. 10: Eng. trans., O. Temkin, 1956) discussed reasons for not bringing up infants. Infants might have been exposed if they were deformed (see DEFORMITY), as in Sparta and Rome, or if they were the product of rape or *incest. Poverty is another possible motive, although the poor often have more children than the rich. There is little evidence for selective female infanticide. The *Gortyn law code permitted infanticide in certain circumstances, while in *Thebes (1) a law outlawed infanticide but allowed poor parents to sell children. In *Ephesus children could also be sold in cases of extreme poverty. In Rome *patria potestas* in principle allowed a father to execute his own children, but Roman law until the time of *Constantine I prohibited foster-parents from enslaving exposed infants whom they had brought up (*alumni*), if free-born. The rise of *Christianity to become the official religion of the Roman empire caused considerable changes. The Christian Apostolic traditions rejected infanticide. A law of 374 AD treated infanticide as equivalent to parricide.

J. R. Sallares, *The Ecology of the Ancient Greek World* (1991); E. Eyben, *Ancient Society* 1981/2, 5–82; J. Boswell, *The Kindness of Strangers* (1988). J. R. S.

inheritance

Greek In Athens, if a deceased man left legitimate sons, they shared the property equally; if a son predeceased his father leaving sons of his own, those sons inherited their father's share. If the deceased man left a daughter but no son, the daughter's sons inherited. If she did not yet have a son, she was *epiklēros* (imprecisely translated 'heiress') and could be claimed in marriage by the nearest male relative, who took charge of the property until their son was old enough to take it over. If there were no legitimate children, relatives within the *ankhisteia* could claim. A man without sons could in effect choose an heir by adoption: the adoptee became legally the son of the adopter and so inherited the property, but could not oust an *epiklēros*; he might marry her himself, but anyway her son inherited eventually. A law introduced by *Solon permitted adoption by will, taking effect only on the testator's death. Another possibility was posthumous *adoption, by which the relatives arranged for one of themselves to become legally the deceased man's son. But a will or adoption could not be used to disinherit legitimate children.

The only other Classical Greek city from which detailed inheritance laws survive is *Gortyn. There sons and daughters shared the property, but a son's share was double a daughter's. A daughter without brothers was called *patroiokos*; her rights generally resembled those of the Athenian *epiklēros*, but differed in details. In *Sparta there are said to have been 9,000 lots of land which, until the late 5th cent. BC, were passed down from father to son and could not be divided; but details of this system are obscure, and some scholars disbelieve in it entirely (see J. F. Lazenby, *CQ* 1995, 87 ff.).

A. R. W. Harrison, *The Law of Athens* 1 (1968), 122–62; D. M. MacDowell, *The Law in Classical Athens* (1978), 92–108, and *Spartan Law* (1986), 89–110; R. Lane Fox, in P. Cartledge and F. D. Harvey (eds.), *Crux* (1985), 208–32; S. Hodkinson, *CQ* 36 1986, 378–406; S. Todd, *The Shape of Athenian Law* (1993), see index under 'inheritance'.　　D. M. M.

Roman Among the propertied classes of Rome testation was regarded as a duty (*officium*). But where there was no will or it was invalid, the first claimants were the *sui heredes* (those in the paternal power (*patria potestas*) of the deceased who by his death became independent); in their absence, second came the nearest agnates; and last—only in early law—members of the *gens* (clan). The praetor, however, innovated by allowing cognates and emancipated children to claim.

Roman law recognized wills by the time of the *Twelve Tables (c.450 BC). The essential feature of a Roman will was the appointment of an heir or heirs. The whole estate of the deceased including debts devolved on the heir, whose liability was unlimited. Strictly, *sui heredes* could not refuse even an insolvent estate, but in practice the praetor allowed them to abstain; only under Justinian was the liability of heirs limited, provided they completed an inventory of the estate within 90 days. In his will a typical testator might appoint tutors to his children, manumit slaves, and charge his heir to pay legacies. These were payable provided the estate was solvent, but were cut back if they exceeded three-quarters of the estate (*lex Falcidia* of 40 BC). Particularly important was the legacy *per vindicationem*, so called since it made the legatee owner of the object and entitled him to bring a *vindicatio* (action asserting his ownership) and the more versatile legacy *per damnationem*, which merely imposed an obligation (*damnatio*) on the heir to make payment. The *fideicommissum* ('trust'), an important alternative to the legacy, evolved during the Principate.

The earliest wills could be made only at a twice-yearly assembly (*comitia calata*) or when war was imminent (*in procinctu*). For more mundane use the *testamentum per aes et libram* ('will by bronze and scales') was developed, and had suppressed the other types by the end of the republic. In the presence of a *libripens* ('scale-bearer') and five witnesses the testator made a formal conveyance of his estate (*mancipatio*) to a trustee, and declared his intentions regarding his estate. That declaration, for reasons of secrecy, soon came to be made in writing: thus the will came into being, and the conveyance became a mere formality. The praetor actually abandoned it and would grant possession of the estate (*bonorum possessio*) to a person named heir in a will sealed by seven witnesses. *Bonorum possessio* (see POSSESSIO) was one of the praetor's most fertile creations, and was later granted to persons he regarded as entitled in preference, or in addition, to those entitled under civil law. Of other types of will, the military will was the most important. It had no need to comply with legal formalities, but was valid for only a year after the soldier left military service. There was much to be said for avoiding the formal demands of the civil law: the urge to do so was the driving force behind the development of *fideicommissa*.

By the end of the republic certain relatives of the testator were regarded as having a legitimate expectation of sharing in his estate: if without good reason they were left less than a quarter of their prospective intestate share, they could bring the *querela inofficiosi testamenti* ('complaint of an undutiful will') to upset

the will. Earlier law had insisted only that *sui heredes* be either appointed heirs or formally disinherited, so that it was clear that they had not been forgotten. The *querela* was a modest but important first step in recognizing a fixed entitlement, and marked a further refinement of the conception of the *officium* owed by the Roman testator in composing his will.

P. Voci, *Diritto ereditario romano* 1², 2 (1967, 1963); M. Amelotti, *Il testamento romano* (1966); G. Grosso, *I legati in diritto romano* (1962); F. von Woess, *Das römische Erbrecht und die Erbanwärter* (1911); E. Champlin, *Final Judgments* (1991).　　D. E. L. J.

inhumation See DEAD, DISPOSAL OF.

initiation is the set of rituals which transforms girls and boys into adults. In Greece, these rituals were the combined product of the *Indo-European heritage and indigenous traditions, as the Minoan frescos show (see MINOAN CIVILIZATION). In historical times full rituals can be found only in Sparta and Crete, but scattered notices from other cities and the mythological tradition about the 'career' of heroes, such as *Achilles and *Theseus, suggest that puberty rites once existed all over Greece. *Apollo and *Artemis were the most important gods connected with these rites.

The Greeks had no term for initiation, but various cities used the term *agōgē, literally 'the leading of a horse by one's hand', and related words. This view reflects itself not only in Archaic poetry, where boys and girls are often addressed as foals and fillies, but also in mythological onomastics: youths connected with initiation regularly have names with the element *hippos* ('horse'): *Leucippus (1–2), *Leucippides, Melanippe, etc. Clearly, youths were seen as wild animals, who had to be domesticated before entering adult society.

Regarding girls, our best information comes from Sparta, where their 'education' prepared them for *motherhood through physical exercises and dancing in choruses. Aristocratic girls had to pass through a lesbian relationship (see HOMOSEXUALITY) to mark the contrast with their final destination, *marriage; a similar custom existed on Lesbos where *Sappho instructed aristocratic girls. Special stress was laid on the enhancing of the girls' physical beauty: not unusually, a beauty contest concluded the girls' initiation. See BRAURON.

Male puberty rites survived into the 4th cent. BC on *Crete, where at the age of 17, after an informal training, sons of aristocrats together with boys of lower classes were gathered into bands, *agelai* or 'herds of horses', which were supervised by their fathers. Here they received a training in dancing, singing, hunting, fighting, and letters. The rites were concluded with a brief stay in the countryside, where the aristocratic youth passed through a homosexual affair (see HOMOSEXUALITY). The festivals in which the new adults showed off to the community belong to the most important ones of Crete.

Similar rites existed in Sparta, but their character changed after the Messenian Wars. The *agōgē* was extended by the introduction of *age classes and training became increasingly harsher when Sparta's position started to depend on a decreasing number of citizens. In Athens the original initiatory structures had disintegrated in the course of the Archaic age, but its 'military service', the *ephēbeia* (see EPHĒBOI), still displays various initiatory features.

In Rome, boys' initiation did not survive into the republic, but the traditions about *Romulus and Remus with their band of youths and run-away criminals strongly suggest its one-time existence, as does the myth of Caeculus of *Praeneste. See also RITES OF PASSAGE.

Greece: A. Brelich, *Paides e partenoi* (1969); C. Calame, *Les Chœurs de jeunes filles en Grèce archaïque*, 2 vols. (1977); K. Dowden, *Death and the Maiden* (1989); J. Bremmer and A. Lardinois, in J. Bremmer (ed.), *From Sappho to De Sade*, 2nd edn. (1991), 1–14, 15–35 (pederasty and Sappho, respectively). Rome: J. N. Bremmer and N. M. Horsfall, *Roman Myth and Mythography* (1987), chs. 3, 4.　　　　　　　　　　J. N. B.

iniuria and defamation Many disputes surround the meaning of the term *iniuria* in 8. 4 of the *Twelve Tables: 'If he has committed an *iniuria* the penalty is 25' (*Si iniuriam faxsit, XXV poenae sunto*). It is not even clear whether there was a delict called *iniuria*, for according to A. *Gellius the text of 8. 4 was 'If he has done something to another by *iniuria* . . .' (*Si iniuria alteri faxsit, . . .*), *iniuria* merely being a qualification. But whatever the answer, it is most likely that 8. 4 dealt with physical assaults of a rather trifling nature, as opposed to *membrum ruptum* ('mutilation of a limb') of 8. 2 and *os fractum* ('breaking of a bone') of 8. 3. An important element inherent in the delict was the humiliation suffered by its victim. This aspect was to attain an ever greater significance until, in the course of the later republic, the specific manner in which the insult had been inflicted mattered so little that the requirement of a physical assault was dropped and protection thus extended to the non-physical aspects of personality. This change of perception found its expression in four specific edictal promises. (*a*) The oldest one (with forerunners in the Twelve Tables) dealt with *convicium*. This was a kind of stylized defamation where several people assembled at somebody's house in order to raise an insulting and abusive clamour. (*b*) The edict *de adtemptata pudicitia* was designed to protect the moral reputation of honest women and of children under age wearing the *toga praetexta*. It covered three closely related situations: *abducere comitem* ('abduction of companion'), *adsectari* ('following about'), and *appellare* ('accosting'). (*c*) The most generally worded edict dealt with any act which was apt to bring another person into disrepute (*infamandi causa quid facere*) like malicious use of mourning-dress or publication of lampoons. (*d*) The fourth edict concerned beating another person's slave (*servum alienum verberare*), which was regarded as an insult to the master.

Claims arising under these edicts (plus some residual cases) came to be referred to in classical Roman law by the collective name *actio iniuriarum*; whether there existed a further general edict dealing with *iniuria* is very doubtful. Common to all of the situations covered was that the offender had acted (1) in disregard of another person's personality (*contumelia*), (2) contrary to sound morals (*contra bonos mores*) and (3), typically, with the intention to insult (*animus iniuriandi*). However, the *actio iniuriarum* probably continued to be granted also in cases of physical injury. It was a purely penal remedy; the penalty was 'as much money as may appear equitable' (*quantam pecuniam . . . bonum aequum videbitur*) and involved disgrace (*infamia*). The flexible manner of assessing the penalty had already been introduced by an *edictum de iniuriis aestumandis* (late 3rd/early 2nd cent. BC), since the 25 asses of the Twelve Tables had become derisory owing to inflation (cf. the amusing anecdote told by Gellius, *NA* 20. 1. 12). Certain violent forms of contumelious *iniuria* became the object of criminal proceedings in 81 BC (*lex Cornelia de iniuriis*).

D. Daube, *Atti Verona 1951*, 413 ff.; F. Raber, *Grundlagen klassischer Injurienansprüche* (1969); R. Wittmann, *Sav. Zeitschr.* 1974, 285 ff.; A. Manfredini, *Contributi allo studio dell' 'iniuria'* (1977), and *Diffamazione verbale* (1979); A. Völkl, *Verfolgung der Körperverletzung* (1984); E. Pólay, *Iniuria Types in Roman Law* (1986); R. Zimmermann, *The Law of Obligations* (1990), 1050 ff.　　　　　　　　　　R. Z.

Innocentius, land-surveyor. An *agrimensor* (see GROMATICI) of this name is known in AD 359 (Amm. Marc. 19. 11. 8), but the treatise said to be extracted from the work *De litteris et notis iuris* by Innocentius is of later date (probably 5th–6th cent.). Commonly known as *casae litterarum*, it differentiates between 39 types of estate (*casa* = villa or farm); each is given a letter of the Latin or Greek alphabet, and the diagrams incorporate these letters together with distinguishing features of each estate. The language is of interest for the development of vulgar Latin.

Å. Josephson, *Casae Litterarum: Studien zum Corpus agrimensorum Romanorum* (1950); *Casae Litterarum*, ed. Å. Josephson (1951). Each contains text, apparatus criticus, and German tr.　　　O. A. W. D.

inns, restaurants In primitive times hospitality towards strangers was universal. It remained common throughout antiquity, and for men of social standing was provided by the networks of guest-friendship (see FRIENDSHIP, RITUALIZED). In the Hellenistic and Roman world, with greatly increased *travel, these relations were very widespread. But as early as the 5th cent. BC there is evidence of the common existence of inns in cities and by the roadside (κατάλυσις, 'resting place'). Standards varied enormously: in the cheapest, travellers had to provide their own food and bedding, and even physical safety could not be taken for granted. Though hotels for higher-status people existed—ambassadors might have to use them for purposes of state (Dem. 19. 158)—inns in general had a reputation for bedbugs, discomfort, rough-houses, and prostitution (see PROSTITUTION, SECULAR). Famous shrines in due course provided public accommodation, run either by the host city or by other cities for their own citizens—not always to their satisfaction; *Thucydides (2) (3. 68) gives the earliest example, at *Plataea (427 BC); for another, recently excavated at *Nemea, see D. Birge and others, *Nemea 1* (1992), ch. 2.

In the Roman world conditions were similar. Men of standing tried to avoid using inns and were never seen in taverns or restaurants. They had their own 'halts' (*deversoria*) along roads which they travelled frequently (e.g. to their country estates), or could use those of their friends. When they travelled further, they could expect hospitality (private or public) and, under the empire, sometimes used the facilities of the *postal service. Yet—as in Greece—anyone might have to stop at an inn on a long journey (e.g. *Horace's to *Brundisium); and though innkeeping was classed among disgraceful trades, good and even luxurious establishments existed. Taverns (*popinae*) were universally popular among the lower classes, many of whom had no adequate cooking facilities at home (see COOKERY), and became centres of their social life, often noisy and dangerous to public order. Various emperors passed legislation restricting the sale of prepared food and wine and, by building baths, provided alternative attractions.

In *Pompeii taverns, restaurants, and inns (some with accommodation for animals) were common. The inns (*cauponae*) clustered near the gates and the town centre and were mostly kept by easterners. In better-class places conditions would be pleasant, with dining-areas perhaps set out in a garden and musical entertainment and good food provided. The best hotels in *Pompeii were converted upper-class mansions. In lesser places, a colourful inn-sign might go with two or three dingy rooms, and customers had to eat sitting on stools and sleep on hard and bug-infested beds. Female company—no doubt of varying kinds—was universally provided if required. This accounts for the fact that innkeepers are classed with *lenones* (pimps).

A. Hug, *RE* 10. 2 (1919), cols. 2459–61: 'Katagogion'; in *RE* 18. 3 (1949), cols. 520–9: 'Pandokeion'; T. Kleberg, *Hotels, restaurants et cabarets dans l'antiquité romaine* (1957); J.-M. André and M.-F. Baslez, *Voyager dans l'antiquité* (1993), 449 ff.; R. Laurence, *Roman Pompeii* (1994), esp. 78 ff.

E. B.; A. J. S. S.

Ino-Leucothea is a goddess connected with *initiation and rites of reversal. The names are already combined by *Homer (*Od.* 5. 333 f.), but Ino appears independently in myth, as do Leucothea and her festival Leucathea in cult. Leucothea was worshipped in 'the whole of Greece' (Cic. *Nat. D.* 3. 39), but it is difficult to get a clear idea of her festivals, which often seem to have contained features of dissolutions of the social order: her sanctuary at *Delos was connected with a phallagogy (see PHALLUS), and in *Chaeronea slaves and Aetolians (see AETOLIA) were excluded. In *Teos the ephebes (see EPHĒBOI) became adult during the Leucathea, here the first month of the year. This initiatory aspect of Leucothea may well have led to her identification with Ino, who is also connected with initiation: she founds a contest for boys in *Miletus and raises *Dionysus, in a typical initiatory way, 'as a girl' in *Euboea (Apollod. 3. 28). It is probably also this connection with growing up which made Aristotle assign the famous temple at *Pyrgi to Leucothea, but *Strabo to *Eileithyia. The story of Ino's raising of Dionysus and *Hera's subsequent anger, which caused her death, sometimes together with her son *Melicertes, was a favourite theme in tragedy and comedy.

Burkert, *HN* 178 f.; F. Graf, *Nordionische Kulte* (1985), 405 f.; A. Nercessian, *LIMC* 5 (1990), 657–61: 'Ino-Leukothea'.

J. N. B.

inscriptions See EPIGRAPHY, GREEK and LATIN; POTTERY, GREEK, INSCRIPTIONS ON.

instauratio When a religious ceremony was interrupted or wrongly performed (*vitium*) it had to be repeated from the beginning. We hear particularly of *instauratio* of games (*ludi*) and the Latin Festival (*feriae Latinae*; e.g. Livy 2. 36. 1, 32. 1. 9, 41. 16. 1; Cic. *Div.* 1. 55, with Pease's comm.). To pontifical *instauratio sacrorum* ('of rites') corresponded augural repetition and renewal of vitiated auspices (Livy 5. 52. 9); *repetitio auspiciorum* ('repetition of auspices') concerned primarily military auspices of a commander (see AUSPICIUM); *renovatio* ('renewal') was accomplished through abdication of all curule magistrates (see MAGISTRACY, ROMAN).

J. L.

institutes (*institutiones*). This was one of the titles given to elementary textbooks of Roman law. The best-known work of this kind is the *Institutes* of *Gaius (2). This was taken by *Justinian as the basis of his own *Institutes*. Though intended, like its model, as a students' manual, this work was given legislative validity. It was compiled by *Tribonianus and the professors Theophilus and Dorotheus, who had also been among Tribonianus' collaborators in the compilation of the *Digest* (see JUSTINIAN'S CODIFICATION). It is essentially a cento or patchwork. The structure and a substantial part of the content come from the *Institutes* of Gaius, but the rest is taken from other classical elementary works, together with matter supplied by the compilers themselves to deal with post-classical changes in the law (mainly those made by Justinian himself). The principal classical sources (apart from Gaius' *Institutes*) are the *Res cottidianae*, another elementary work attributed to Gaius, and the *Institutes* of other jurists (Florentinus, *Ulpian, *Marcianus). The identification of these sources is usually made possible by the fact that the passages also appear, with attributions, in the *Digest*.

A contemporary Greek paraphrase of Justinian's *Institutes* survives, attributed, probably correctly, to Theophilus.

F. Schulz, *History of Roman Legal Science* (1946); C. Ferrini, *Opere* (1929), vols. 1–2; A. Zocco-Rosa, *Justiniani Institutionum Palingenesia*, 2 vols. (1908); T. Honoré, *Tribonian* (1978).

B. N.

Insubres lived north of the Po (see PADUS). The most powerful people in Cisalpine Gaul (see GAUL (CISALPINE)), they frequently exercised dominion of the neighbouring Taurini, Salassi, etc. Their capital was *Mediolanum (Milan; Strab. 213 C). Livy (5. 34) represents them as *Aedui who entered Italy via the Mont Genèvre pass; but the archaeological evidence suggests that they may be correlated with the Golasecca culture, and thus arrived in Italy before 400 BC. Indeed, the name Insubres is thought to be pre-Celtic. About 232 BC they clashed with Rome. At *Clastidium (222) M. *Claudius Marcellus (1) stripped the *spolia opima* from their king. In 218 the new Latin colony at *Cremona and *Hannibal's arrival incited them to fresh efforts, until finally they were subjugated in 194 (Polyb. 2. 17 f.; Livy, bks. 21–34). Subsequently they disappeared as a separate nation. Insubrian districts obtained Latin rights (see IUS LATII) in 89, full citizenship in 49 BC.

For bibliog. see CISALPINE GAUL.

E. T. S.; T. W. P.

Interamna Lirenas, mod. Pignataro, in *Latium near the confluence of the *Liris and Rapido. A Latin colony here (312 BC) helped contain the Samnites (see SAMNIUM).

E. T. S.

Interamna Nahars (mod. Terni), in Umbria, near the confluence of the Velinus and the Nar, in fertile terrain. An important iron age centre, it became a prosperous *municipium*, with an amphitheatre of Tiberian date.

E. T. S.; T. W. P.

Interamnia (mod. Teramo), in southern *Picenum at the confluence of the Vezzola and the Tordino, town of the Praetuttii, whose name survives in *Abruzzi*.

E. T. S.

intercessio, 'interposition', was the right of one Roman magistrate (see MAGISTRACY, ROMAN) to veto the activity of another magistrate of equal or lesser authority. The possibility arose because magistrates were conceived as exercising collegiate power; only a magistrate with no peer, as the dictator was, could act free of this possible interference. The tribunes of the people (*tribuni plebis*) shared with the regular magistrates the normal right of interposition against each other's acts but in addition, at some point in the republic, they obtained a veto over all other, superior, magistrates and enactments of bodies presided over by magistrates such as the comitial assemblies and the senate. They were able to exercise this extraordinary power, more revolutionary than constitutional in tendency, by virtue of their personal inviolability, even against magistrates, which was ultimately guaranteed by the people.

Mommsen, *Röm. Staatsr.* 1³. 258 ff., 2³. 290 ff.

A. D. E. L.

interest, rates of As in modern, industrial society, the ancient world had a complex of rates of interest, varying across time and space. There, however, the similarity ends: ancient interest rates are more social than economic indicators and cannot be read to reveal trends over time. Underlying rates of interest were fixed by custom and stayed stable over long periods: from the 5th to the 2nd cent. BC the temple of *Apollo on *Delos lent money at 10% p.a. (akin to a tithe?). In 4th-cent. Athens, the 'prevailing' rate of interest seems to have been 12% p.a. (literally, 'one drachma interest on each mina lent per month'). The major distinction in loan transactions lay between charging interest and lending interest-free: a pre-existing personal relationship between lender and borrower was thought to preclude the taking of interest (see

CREDIT). A rate of 1% per month was apparently seen in Athens as reasonable for an 'impersonal' loan transaction (Dem. 27. 17; *Ath. pol.* 52). Particular circumstances could result in higher rates: high risk of default (3% per month: Lys. fr. 38 Gernet–Bizos), unsecured, short-term lending of small sums (25% per day: Theophr. *Char.* 6. 9). As the great majority of loans was raised to cover unforeseen, often emergency expenditure, the charging of interest could be seen as exploitation of the borrower's misfortune (Dem. 45. 69); hence a part of the opposition to lending at interest from *Plato (1) (*Leg.* 742c) and [*Aristotle] (*Pr.* 950ᵃ28 ff.). Compound interest (*anatokismos*) was seen as particularly exploitative (Ar. *Nub.* 1155 f.; Pl. *Leg.* 842d). The major exception was *maritime loans, from which the borrower could hope to make a profit, justifying the charging of anything between 12½ and 30% (possibly more) on the sum lent for the duration of the voyage. From the Roman world, Tacitus (*Ann.* 6. 16) singled out lending at interest as a long-standing social problem. The *fenus unciarium* of the *Twelve Tables may well refer to an annual interest maximum of 100%. Throughout Roman history, attempts were made to fix maximum rates of interest: the *lex Genucia* of 342 BC apparently banned all lending at interest. This and less extreme measures were undermined by the practical needs of borrowers (App. *BCiv.* 1. 54) and the power of creditors. *Brutus avoided the official interest maximum of 12% in the province of Cilicia (and possibly the whole empire) by virtue of a special decree from the senate (Cic. *Att.* 6. 1, 2). *Justinian I attempted to match annual interest maxima to specific circumstances: *c.*5% for cash loans, 12½% for loans in kind, and 4% for loans made by senators. With greater realism, Athenian law forbade any restriction on the charging of interest (Lys. 10. 18).

G. Billeter, *Geschichte des Zinsfusses im griechischen-romischen Altertum bis auf Justinian* (1898; repr. 1970); P. C. Millett, *Lending and Borrowing in Ancient Athens* (1991); R. Bogaert, *Banques et banquiers dans les cités grecques* (1968); R. Parker, *Miasma* (1983), 173; T. Frank, *An Economic Survey of Ancient Rome* 1–5 (1933–40); C. Appleton, *Nouvelle revue historique de droit français et étranger* (1919), 467 ff.; H. E. Finck, *Das Zinsrecht der graeco-aegyptischen Papyri* (1962); J. A. Crook, *Law and Life of Rome* (1967); Jones, *Later Rom. Emp.* 775, 868 f.   P. C. M.

interpolation is the name given to retrospective changes in (legal) texts, especially those made by the compilers of Justinian's 6th-cent. AD codification (see JUSTINIAN'S CODIFICATION) in texts dating from before AD 300 (see LEGAL LITERATURE). Justinian, following the example of Theodosius II (see THEODOSIAN CODE), gave his commissioners both for the *Codex* and the *Digesta* power to shorten and alter the texts they edited to make them concise, clear, and elegant; but he went beyond Theodosius in instructing them to ensure that the texts were consistent with one another. The law promulgating the *Digesta* says that the compilers made many important changes for reasons of utility. This suggests that they went even further, and amended the texts in order to improve the law and not merely to ensure consistency. From about 1500 scholars began to search for these changes, and up to the Second World War the hunt gathered speed. It was argued that many passages had been radically rewritten or even composed from scratch. Words and phrases were picked out as 'unclassical' and hence reliable signs of interpolation.

On the other hand Justinian's Greek-speaking compilers had to edit the Latin texts rapidly if they were to finish on time and they could not go beyond the powers Justinian conferred on them. Moreover the old writers did not compose in a uniform style. Not all that seems odd in Justinian's codification can in any event be put down to his compilers. Some changes must have taken place when works were copied and (perhaps) re-edited between their original composition and the 6th cent.; sometimes at least mistakes in copying and marginal comments crept into the texts. Hence from about 1950 a reaction against the hunt for Justinianic interpolations set in, and in recent years the tendency may have been to underestimate their extent and importance.

A balance is called for. The changes made by the 6th-cent. compilers, apart from shortening and improving the style, were in practice confined to (1) bringing out what they thought was the real meaning of the old texts; (2) adapting texts about obsolete institutions such as mortgage by conveyance (*fiducia*) to analogous institutions e.g. mortgage by agreement (*hypotheca*); (3) more generally, shifting passages from one context to another, often without changing the wording, for example to give them a wider scope; and (4) cautiously extending rules and classifications on lines for which there was some precedent in the older writers or which could plausibly be seen as necessary to secure consistency in the law. In general they avoided innovation except on the authority of one of Justinian's reforming laws, of which more than 170 survive in the *Codex* of 534. A complication is that they sometimes made changes, perhaps through haste, in only one or two of several possible texts, contrary to the avowed aim of ensuring consistency. For example, when the compilers on good ancient authority changed a *Codex* text to allow a third party to sue on a contract, they left unchanged several other texts which deny the third party a right to sue.

O. Gradenwitz, *Interpolationen in den Pandekten* (1887); D. Daube, *Sav. Zeitschr.* 1959, 149 ff.; F. Wieacker, *Textstufen klassicher Juristen* (1960); Wieacker, *RRG* 1, 154 ff.; M. Kaser, *Zur Methodologie der römischen Rechtsquellenforschung* (1972); T. Honoré, in *Studies A. A. Schiller* (1986) 97 ff.; D. Johnston, *Oxford Journal of Legal Studies* 1989, 149 ff.   T. Hon.

interpolation, literary See TEXTUAL CRITICISM.

interpretatio Graeca See INTERPRETATIO ROMANA; RELIGION, THRACIAN; SYNCRETISM.

interpretatio Romana, lit. 'Latin translation' (Tac. *Germ.* 43. 3); a phrase used to describe the Roman habit of replacing the name of a foreign deity with that of a Roman deity considered somehow comparable. At times this process involved extensive identification of the actual deities, while in other cases, the deities, though sharing a name, continued to be sharply distinguished. Different Latin names could sometimes be substituted for the same foreign name, depending on which characteristic of the god was chosen as the basis for comparison. The earliest of these 'translations' were from Greek: thus 'Zeus' was translated by 'Iuppiter' (see ZEUS; JUPITER). The process continued as the Romans came into contact with other cultures, so that the German 'Wodan' was called '*Mercurius' by Roman writers. Only in a few cases were foreign divine names adopted directly into Latin, e.g. '*Apollo' and '*Isis'. See SYNCRETISM.

G. Wissowa, *ARW* 1916–19, 1–49.   J. B. R.

interpreters See BILINGUALISM; EXĒGĒTĒS.

interrex Under the Roman republic, if both *consuls died or left office without successors appointed, the 'auspices reverted to the patrician senators' who selected one of their number as *interrex*. *Interreges*, who were of *patrician birth and usually ex-consuls, held office in succession, each for five days, with consular powers. Their principal duty was to supervise the election of one or both new consuls: the theory that they simply presented one or two names to the assembly for acceptance or rejection has not been substantiated. The name *interrex* supports Roman assumptions

intertextuality

that the institution derived from the regal period (see REX) and was used to effect the choice of a new king, although some scholars dispute its regal origins or think it had a sacral function originally.

J. Jahn, *Interregnum und Wahldiktatur* (1970); R. Rilinger, *Der Einfluss des Wahlleiters bei den römischen Konsulwahlen von 366 bis 50 v. Chr.* (1976); E. Ferenczy in *Festgabe für U. von Lübtow* (1980), 45 ff.; *CAH* 7²/2 (1989), see index.　　　　A. D.

intertextuality See IMITATION; LITERARY THEORY AND CLASSICAL STUDIES; MIMESIS; PLAGIARISM.

intolerance, intellectual and religious For most Greek states our evidence is too poor and patchy for us to be able to say much. We know a little about 5th-cent. BC Athens. Sir K. Popper famously praised it as an 'open society' but the tolerance of that society had limits. There is some evidence for literary censorship, though of a haphazard and perhaps ineffective sort. *Phrynichus (1) got into trouble near the beginning of the century for putting on a *tragedy dealing with a sensitive political topic (Hdt. 6.21). Between 440 and 437 BC there were formal restrictions on ridicule in theatrical comedy (Fornara no. 111 with the important discussion of 'political censorship' at *DFA*³ 364; cf. COMEDY (GREEK), OLD, § 4). On the other hand there were (Dover and Stone) no 'witch-hunts' against intellectuals, though *Anaxagoras and other associates of *Pericles (1) were prosecuted in the courts. Anaxagoras' ostensible offence was impiety, and the decree of *Diopeithes, if historical, would provide hard evidence for public control of religious teaching. (See also ATHEISM; DIAGORAS; THEODICY.) *Alcibiades and others were punished severely for profaning the Eleusinian *mysteries (see ANDOCIDES), but Dover is right that the offending action was not necessarily 'the product of earnest intellectual inquiry'. The reasons for *Socrates' execution in 399 are still disputed by scholars, but political considerations were surely at least as relevant as religious: Socrates was critical of the working of *democracy, and had taught prominent oligarchs (see OLIGARCHY). *Aeschines (1) (1.173) in the mid 4th cent. explicitly makes the latter point, which could not be made openly in 399 because of the *amnesty granted to oligarchs compromised by involvement with the *Thirty Tyrants.

In the Hellenistic period the poet *Sotades (2) incurred severe, perhaps capital, punishment for his outspokenness, but he went quite far in his criticism of the *incest of *Ptolemy (1) II. The historian *Philochorus was put to death by *Antigonus (2) Gonatas for being too partial to the same Ptolemy. The most notable (actually unique) instance of Hellenistic religious persecution was *Antiochus (4) IV's treatment of the *Jews. In Rome, *censors, despite their name, were not responsible for literary or artistic censorship in the modern meaning of the word. Book-burning, 'that Roman peculiarity' (Thomas), is however attested in authoritarian periods of Roman history (see e.g. Cassius Dio 56. 27. 1). Roman attitudes to foreign religions were generally cosmopolitan; see RELIGION, ROMAN. The suppression of the *Bacchanalia in 186 BC was exceptional. For Roman treatment of Jews see JEWS and GAIUS (1): *Gaius and the Jews*; for persecution of Christians see CHRISTIANITY. See also PHILOSOPHERS AND POLITICS; PROTAGORAS; SEMITISM, ANTI-.

K. J. Dover, *The Greeks and their Legacy* (1988), 135 ff.; I. F. Stone, *The Trial of Socrates*, 231 ff. For book-burning see R. Thomas, *Literacy and Orality in Ancient Greece* (1992), 169 and n. 31.　　　　S. H.

invective may be defined as a form of literature which, having regard to the *mores* and ethical preconceptions of a given society, sets out publicly to denigrate a named individual. Its concrete manifestations are λοιδορία, ὄνειδος, κακηγορία, ψόγος, and *vituperatio*, all terms signifying abuse. Such abuse follows well-articulated rhetorical guidelines. The target is attacked on the grounds of birth, upbringing, 'banausic' occupation (see ARTISANS AND CRAFTSMEN; LABOUR), moral defects such as avarice or drunkenness, physical shortcomings (lameness, warts, and the like), eccentricities of dress, ill fortune, and so on. These same categories of abuse are found irrespective of the form in which the invective is couched. This might be a senatorial or forensic speech, iambic poem, political pamphlet, curse-poem, epigram, or full-blown essay in the genre such as the pseudo-Sallustian *Invectives* (see SALLUST) or *Claudian's *In Rufinum* ('Against Rufinus'). Outstanding examples of invectives delivered in the public arena are *Demosthenes (2)'s speech *On The Crown* and *Cicero's *In Pisonem* ('Against Piso') and second *Philippic*.

The primary object of invective was to *persuade* the audience that one's accusations were true. Plausibility was thus more important than veracity. At the same time, invective aimed to give pleasure to the listeners. Cicero and Demosthenes both attest the enjoyment which derived from seeing others abused. The same factor underlies the personal attacks of Old Comedy (see COMEDY (GREEK), OLD), the insulting *Fescennini of the Romans, political lampoons, and the very existence of the iambic genre, which was grounded in vituperation (see IAMBIC POETRY). Despite the existence of legislation against ψόγος in Greece and Rome, invective flourished in both cultures.

S. Koster, *Die Invektive in der griechischen und römischen Literatur* (1980); W. Süss, *Ethos* (1910), 245 ff.; Fr. Brecht, *Motiv- und Typengeschichte des griechischen Spottepigrams* (1930); U. Paoli, *Rome, its People, Life and Customs* (1963), 267 ff.; R. G. M. Nisbet (ed.), *Cicero: In Pisonem* (1961), app. 6; I. Opelt, *Die lateinischen Schimpfwörter und verwandte sprachliche Erscheinungen* (1965).　　　　L. C. W.

invulnerability was commonly ascribed to the legendary heroes in the 'cyclic' epic tradition (see EPIC CYCLE), but is rigorously excluded from the Homeric poems (see HOMER) as quite incompatible with the principle that the great warriors are genuinely fighting for their lives. However, most examples have an 'escape clause'; there is one vulnerable spot, or one weapon which can wound. *Achilles, famously, had been dipped in the Styx by his mother Thetis, and his skin could only be pierced where she had suspended him by the heel. *Aias (1) was wrapped as a baby in the skin of the Nemean lion (itself invulnerable, until *Heracles had the idea of strangling it, and skinning it with its own claws), and could only be wounded in his armpit, where the hide had failed to make contact. The Lapith hero *Caeneus fights with two swords because, as Beazley saw, the invulnerability granted to him (né her) by *Apollo meant he could dispense with a shield; the *Centaurs eventually neutralize him by battering him into the ground. Early artistic representations of the Centauromachy and the deaths of Aias and Achilles show that these cyclic versions were widely popular. Cities, similarly, may be impregnable until their talisman can be captured (*Troy's '*Palladium'); and a country may be invincible if it can guard the secret grave of an enemy hero buried on its territory (*Sparta and *Arcadia, Hdt. 1. 67 f.; Athens and *Thebes (1), Soph. *OC*). See CEPHALUS.

J. D. Beazley, *BaBesch.* 1939, 4–14; J. Griffin, *JHS* 1977, 39–53. A. H. G.

Io, in mythology, priestess of *Hera at the Argive *Heraion, daughter of Iasus (Apollod. 2. 1. 3; see IASUS, IASIUS) or the river *Inachus (tragedy). *Zeus seduces her but when Hera discovers, she is transformed into a white cow by Zeus or by Hera, and tethered to an olive-tree in the Heraion grove with the monster *Argos (1*b*) 'All-seeing' as guard. Hermes kills Argos, but Hera inflicts a gadfly upon the bovine Io, who now wanders distraught around the world (in Aesch. *PV* past the remote Caucasus to receive a lecture from the enchained *Prometheus) until finally she comes to Egypt, where with a touch (*ephaptein*) of his hand Zeus restores her and presently Epaphus is born to her, the ancestor of *Danaus who will return to *Argos (2) with the Danaids, his daughters. Because of her bovine shape, Io was identified with the Egyptian *Isis (who had assumed the bovine characteristics of Hathor). In rationalized versions, she was kidnapped by *Phoenician traders (Hdt. 1. 1. 4–5), and the Egyptians sent Inachus a bull in compensation (Ephorus *FGrH* 70 F 156).

Her *metamorphosis belongs to a pattern of association of girls reaching maturity with animals (cf. the *Proetides at nearby *Tiryns) and has been argued to reflect rites of transition into adulthood (see INITIATION; RITES OF PASSAGE). But it is also a story of the priesthood at the Heraion, of *genealogy (Danaus), and of growing awareness of the non-Greek world. Sociologically, the story is interesting for its projection of frenzy and marginalization onto the girl reaching maturity.

In art the monster Argos covered in eyes and the bovine Io provided unusual subjects, popular in Greek colonies too. The influential 4th-cent. BC painting by *Nicias (2) (Plin. *HN* 35. 132) was perhaps imitated by murals at *Pompeii.

ANCIENT SOURCES Hesiod's account (*Cat.* frs. 124–7 M–W) is partly visible through Apollod. 2. 1. 3–4; Aesch. *PV* 561–886; Ov. *Met.* 1. 583–750; Plin. *HN* 16. 239.

LITERATURE K. Dowden, *Death and the Maiden* (1989), ch. 6; S. Eitrem, *RE* 9 (1916), 1732–43; J. M. Davidson, in D. C. Pozzi and J. M. Wickersham (eds.), *Myth and the Polis* (1991), 49–63; N. Yalouris, *LIMC* 5/1 (1990), 661–76.
K. D.

Iocasta See OEDIPUS.

Iolaus, younger companion and helper of *Heracles, was identified as the son of his half-brother *Iphicles and often appeared with Heracles in cult. He was worshipped notably at *Thebes (1) and in *Sicily and *Sardinia, where he was said to have led a colonizing expedition (see COLONIZATION, GREEK). His distinguishing feature in myth and cult is his connection with youth; even as an old man he was rejuvenated for one day in order to defeat *Eurystheus, according to *Euripides (*Heracl.* 843–63).

Diod. Sic. 4. 24. 4–6, 29–31, 38; A. Schachter, *Cults of Boiotia* (1981–), 2. 17–18, 64–5; M. Pipili, *LIMC* 5. 686–96.
E. Ke.

Iolcus (mod. Volos) is situated on the northern shore of the bay of Volos, sheltered by Mt. *Pelion. A high mound at the west end of the modern town was first occupied in the early bronze age, and Pefkakia (ancient Neleia?), on a nearby coastal promontory, from the late neolithic period; the material from these sites is still largely unpublished, but demonstrates contacts with *Macedonia and southern Greece from the early bronze age onwards. Iolcus was evidently a significant Mycenaean settlement, probably the leading settlement in *Thessaly, though its history remains obscure; a tholos-tomb and cemetery of pit-graves, some wealthy, dating *c.*1450–1350 BC are associated with the coastal site, but the main area of settlement for much of the Mycenaean period may have been at Dhimini inland, where there are two good tholostombs. After *c.*1200 BC the centre of settlement was again close to the coast, and the site continued to be locally important until Archaic times, but subsequently became an insignificant village, overshadowed by *Pagasae.

GAC H 1; V. R. d'A. Desborough, *The Greek Dark Ages* (1972), 208 ff.
O. T. P. K. D.

Ion (1), a heroic name, especially that of the ancestor of the *Ionians. The early tradition appears to agree in making him son of *Xuthus and grandson of *Hellen; Athenian claims to primacy among the *Ionians are expressed in the tradition that his mother was *Creusa (1), daughter of the Athenian king *Erechtheus. The more familiar story that his true father was *Apollo is not certainly attested before *Euripides' *Ion*; this version not only eliminates all non-Athenian ancestry, but also indicates Ionians as superior to *Dorians by making Dorus, along with Achaeus (1) (already Xuthus' son in Hesiod fr. 10a M–W[2] line 23) son of Creusa and Xuthus (1589–94).

In *Attica, Ion has connections both with the Gargettus area, where there is a *deme Ionidai, and with the east coast (e.g. Paus. 1. 31. 3), but he eventually became a central figure in both cult (e.g. *IG* 1[3]. 383. 147–9) and myth; as well as his parentage, Athenian writers record the help given by him to Erechtheus in the Eleusinian War, and the contribution made by him to the *synoecism (Philochorus, *FGrH* 328 F 13; *Ath. pol.* 41. 1). He was also invoked in connection with the Ionians of the *Peloponnese (Paus. 6. 22. 7).

N. Loraux, *The Children of Athena* (1993; Fr. orig. 1981), 184–236.
E. Ke.

Ion (2), of Chios, an unusually versatile poet and prose author, seems to have been born in the 480s BC and to have come to Athens about 466. He was dead by 421, when *Aristophanes (1) paid a graceful tribute to him at *Peace* 834–7.

Works included the following. (1) *Tragedies and satyr-plays (*TrGF* 1[2]. 95–114); see SATYRIC DRAMA. The *Suda* says that Ion wrote 12 or 30 or 40 plays, the first in 451–448. He was defeated by *Euripides in 438, but on another occasion he is said to have won first prize in both tragedy and *dithyramb and to have made a present of Chian wine to every Athenian citizen. He was admitted by later critics into a canon of five great tragedians. *'Longinus' (*Subl.* 33) found his plays faultless and elegant but sadly lacking in the inspired boldness of *Sophocles (1). We have eleven titles and some brief fragments, notably from the satyric *Omphale*. (2) Lyric poetry (Page, *PMG* 383–6). This included *dithyrambs, encomia, *paeans, and *hymns. (3) *Elegiac poetry (West, *IE*[2] 2. 79–82). This mainly consisted of drinking-songs, to judge from the surviving fragments. One song (fr. 27) was apparently written for a *symposium given by *Archidamus II king of Sparta. (4) Perhaps comedies, but these rest only on one doubtful source. (5) The *Triagmos* (DK1.377–1), a philosophical work, in prose, of *Pythagorean tendencies, in which Ion ascribed a threefold principle to all things. (6) A *Foundation of Chios* (*FGrH* no. 392), probably in prose. (7) *Epidemiai* or *Visits*, a book of reminiscences, in prose. This recounted Ion's meetings with, and impressions of, great men of his day, and was perhaps his most original work, and the most interesting to us. Surviving fragments describe meetings with *Cimon, *Aeschylus, and Sophocles, all of whom Ion admired (the conversation of Sophocles at a symposium on Chios is the subject of a long extract). Also mentioned, but not necessarily known to him in person, were *Themistocles, *Pericles (1) (whom Ion disliked), *Archelaus (1), and *Socrates.

A. von Blumenthal, *Ion von Chios* (1939); M. L. West, *BICS* 1985, 71–8; J. Barron, in J. Boardman and C. E. Vaphopoulou-Richardson (eds.), *Chios* (1986), 89 ff.; K. J. Dover, *The Greeks and their Legacy* (1988), 1–12 (= Boardman, etc., as above, 27 ff.); H. Strasburger, *Studien zur alten*

Ionian festivals

Geschichte 3 (1990), 341–51; O. Lendle, *Einführung in die griechische Geschichtsschreibung* (1992), 28–32.   A. L. B.

Ionian festivals Festivals constitutive of the *Ionians on several levels of identity.

Festivals which were specific to the Athenian and Ionian festival-calendars were already in antiquity used as an argument for a common origin (see Hdt. 1. 147 for the *Apaturia, or Thuc. 2. 15. 4 for Anthesteria); they date back to before the Ionian migration (10th cent. BC). They include *Anthesteria, Apaturia, *Boedromia, *Lenaea, *Plynteria, *Pyanopsia (or Pyanepsia or Κυανόψια), and *Thargelia. Some festivals are only marginally important, as Boedromia (attested only through the month-name) or Pya-/Kyanepsia. The Anthesteria attest a cult of *Dionysus already before the emigration, the Apaturia point to the social importance of gentilicial rites. Exceptionally, common rituals confirm the connection, such as the expulsion of the *pharmakos* at the Thargelia or the ship-cart procession attested for the *Dionysia in Athens, in Archaic *Clazomenae (?), and in Roman *Smyrna.

The Ionians themselves articulated their identity in two festivals. In the Archaic age, first the Cycladic (see CYCLADES), then later all Ionians met at the festival of Delian Apollo (see *Homeric Hymn to Apollo*, 147–64; mid-7th cent?). See DELOS. The (mainly Asia Minor) Ionian cities held their common festival, the Panionia, in the *Panionium, a sanctuary of Poseidon Heliconios in the territory of Melie or, after the destruction of Melie c.700 BC, of *Priene (Vitr. *De arch*. 4. 1. 4). During the Persian occupation, the cult was continued by *Ephesus, to be reactivated in the Panionium in the 4th cent; a sacred law from this period attests the primacy of Zeus Βουλαῖος, i.e. the prime function of political meeting. During the Hellenistic and imperial epochs, ruler-cult became important for the Panionia; the imperial Panionia were again held in the major towns.

M. B. Sakellariou, *La Migration grecque en Ionie* (1958); F. Graf, *Nordion-ische Kulte* (1985). For the Panionium: G. Kleiner, *Panionion und Melie* (1967) and see PANIONIUM.   F. G.

Ionian Revolt The eastern Greeks, prosperous and compliant subjects of *Persia from c.546/5 BC, remained uniquely quiet at *Darius I's irregular accession. Further Persian expansion in *Egypt, the Black Sea (see PONTUS), and *Thrace, however, increased imperial tax-exactions and reduced Hellenic market-share and attractive mercenary opportunities. Resenting *barbarian overlords, autocratic regimes (see TYRANNY), and conscript service for Persian power, most Ionian cities (see IONIANS) followed Milesian *Aristagoras (1) in deposing local tyrants (499; Hdt. 5. 37). Significant Athenian and Eretrian assistance arrived to raze *Sardis, a satrapal capital (see SATRAP). Ethnic religious assembly (*Panionium), political organization (*probouloi, koinon*, league coinage), and intercity operations proved eastern Greek capacities for unified action. *Hellespontines, *Carians, and many Cypriots consequently joined the rebels. Samian and Lesbian interests (see LESBOS; SAMOS), however, diverged from Milesian and Carian. Inadequate revenues and budgetary mechanisms and disputed military hierarchies further crippled determination.

Persia mobilized and defeated Hellenes and allies at *Ephesus, *Cyprus, and *Labraunda, then reconquered Anatolian territories by amphibious, triple-pronged, city-by-city advances. Both commands welcomed a decisive naval battle near crucial *Miletus (at Lade, 494; Hdt. 6. 6–17). Approximately 70,000 allied Greeks in 353 ships, capable Dionysius of *Phocaea command-ing, faced 600 largely Phoenician vessels. Co-operation among the predominantly Chian, Samian, Milesian, and Lesbian contingents—rivals to begin with—collapsed when battle commenced. Persian 'politics' and bribery succeeded where sheer force had not. Many fought bravely, but most Samians had agreed to defect. Miletus was sacked, the inhabitants killed, enslaved, or expatriated. The coastal and island mop-up was easy and ruthless (6. 18–20, 31–3).

*Herodotus (1)'s account, based on surviving losers' biased reconstructions, replays and exasperatedly explains the defeat. Like the westerners' later edifying victory, the eastern Greeks' edifying defeat demanded heroes and villains. Short-sighted tyrants, Ionian disorganization, and military disinclination are blamed throughout. Ionian achievements are trivialized or negated, as each *polis* castigated the others' motives (6. 14; see IONIANS). Herodotus condemned the liberation as doomed from birth (5. 28, 97, 6. 3, 27), but his facts allow alternative reconstructions. Initial successes and co-ordination suggest that liberation was possible.

Revolt produced four positive results. *Mardonius replaced the unpopular Hellenic tyrants on Persia's western borders with more democratic regimes. *Artaphernes renegotiated tribute collections (6. 42–3). Persian westward expansion was delayed. The autonomous Balkan Greeks, observing the risks of capitulation and resistance to Persia, realized that independence could be preserved. See also LYSANIAS (1).

Hdt. bks. 5–6. A. Burn, *Persia and the Greeks* (1962); P. Tozzi, *La Rivolta Ionica* (1978); D. Lateiner, *Hist*. 1982, 129; O. Murray, *CAH* 4² (1988), ch. 8.   D. G. L.

Ionian Sea ('Ιόνιος, 'Ιώνιος κόλπος), used as an alternative to '*Adriatic Sea' for the waters between the Balkan peninsula and Italy, and like 'Adriatic', sometimes extended to include the sea east of Sicily. No clear line of demarcation exists between the two seas. Unknown to Homer and occurring for the first time in Aeschylus (*PV* 840), the name would seem to originate from early Ionian seafaring to the west.   W. M. M.

Ionian War see PELOPONNESIAN WAR.

Ionians ('Ίωνες, 'ΙάΓονες), a section of the Greek people mentioned only once by Homer (*Il*. 13. 685, 'Ιάονες ἑλκεχίτωνες ('tunic-trailing Ionians')), but important later, after the central part of the west coast of *Asia Minor (still non-Greek in Homer) had become known as Ionia.

Ionia was colonized, according to early traditions, by refugees from the Greek mainland, flying before the *Dorians and other tribes from NW Greece (Mimnermus in Strabo, 634 C; Hdt. 1. 145–8; Thuc. 1. 12). Herodotus (1. 146–7) speaks of the mixed blood of the colonists, and adds that some of them took the women of the conquered *Carians. All were, however, reckoned as Ionians 'who trace their descent from Athens and keep the *Apaturia'.

The claim of Athens to be the mother-city of all Ionians will not hold, as Herodotus himself says; and the eponymous ancestor *Ion (1) could only artificially be worked into the Athenian *genealogies, themselves extremely artificial. But the Athenian claim to be the 'eldest land of Ionia' was as old as *Solon, and long preceded any Attic claims to political predominance (*Ath. pol*. ch. 5); and it receives confirmation from the appearance of some of the four ancient 'tribes' (see PHYLAI) of Attica—the Aigikoreis, Hopletes, Geleontes, and Argadeis—in inscriptions of *Delos, *Teos, *Ephesus, *Perinthus (a colony of *Samos),

*Cyzicus and *Tomis (Milesian colonies). There may be some truth in the Athenian claim to have organized expeditions to Ionia, but this was inflated in the time of the *Delian League (see below).

For the Ionic dialect see GREEK LANGUAGE, §§ 3, 4.

The Ionians, from about 750 BC, developed precociously (see the brilliant picture in the *Hymn to Delian Apollo*; see HYMNS (GREEK)). Throughout the east 'Yawani' (Javan: Genesis 10: 2) became the generic term for 'Greek'. They were, however, exposed to attack from the Lydian and Persian monarchies, and the effort to throw off Persian rule, exercised through Greek 'tyrants', ended in ruin after a struggle of six years (494), see IONIAN REVOLT. Then came Athenian overlordship and the devaluing of Ionians as unmanly (Hdt. 1. 143, 5. 69; Thuc. 5. 9, 6. 77, 8. 25). The generalization that credited Dorians with more steadfastness, Ionians with more intelligence, is in each case open to numerous exceptions: contrast the sobriety of Ionian *Olbia or *Massalia (Strabo 179–80; Dio Chrys. *Borysthenite Discourse*) with the unstable brilliance of Dorian *Syracuse and *Tarentum in *Thucydides (2) and *Livy. The Dorian–Ionian polarity was exaggerated (though not invented) by 5th-cent. Athenian *propaganda.

See also ALPHABET, GREEK; AUTOCHTHONS; CHIOS; DORIANS; EPHESUS; IONIAN FESTIVALS; IONIAN REVOLT; MAGNESIA; MILETUS; PANIONIUM; PHOCAEA; PRIENE; SAMOS.

E. Will, *Doriens et Ioniens* (1956); J. M. Cook, *The Greeks in Ionia and the East* (1962); G. L. Huxley, *The Early Ionians* (1966); J. Alty, *JHS* 1982, 1 ff.; R. Parker, in J. Bremmer (ed.), *Interpretations of Greek Mythology* (1987), 187 ff.; S. Hornblower, *Harv. Stud.* 1992, 169 ff.; J. M. Cook, *CAH* 2²/2 (1975), 773 ff., 3²/1 (1982), 745 ff., and 3²/3 (1982), 196 ff.; O. Murray, *CAH* 4² (1988), 461 ff.; S. Hornblower, *CAH* 6² (1994), 209 ff.; N. F. Jones, *Public Organisation in Ancient Greece* (1987).

A. R. B.; S. H.

Iophon, son of *Sophocles (1), was himself a successful tragic poet. The *Suda* credits him with 50 plays. He won first prize in 435 BC, second in 428, when *Euripides came first and *Ion (2) third. *Aristophanes (1), *Frogs* 73–9, implies that Iophon is the best surviving tragic poet now that Euripides and Sophocles are dead, but also that the merits of his work may have been due to help from his father. The story in the *Life of Sophocles* and elsewhere that he tried to obtain control of his father's property by accusing him of senility, and that Sophocles disproved the charge by reading from *Oedipus at Colonus*, is doubtless an invention.

TrGF 1². 132–5; *Musa Tragica* 89–93, 280–1.   A. L. B.

Iphicles, in mythology, twin brother of *Heracles, also called Iphiclus. He was Heracles' companion on some exploits and father of Heracles' better-known companion *Iolaus. Two other children of his were killed by Heracles in his madness (Apollod. 2. 61 ff.; schol. on Lycoph. 38 and *Od.* 11. 269; Nic. Dam. *FGrH* 90 F 13 Jacoby).

LIMC 5. 1 (1990), 734–6.   H. J. R.

Iphicrates, Athenian general who achieved fame commanding *peltasts at *Corinth (393–389 BC), when he mauled a Spartan *mora* ('brigade') (390). Redeployed to the *Hellespont following conflict about the Corinth–*Argos (2) union (see CORINTH; SYMPOLITEIA) he eliminated Anaxibius (389) and undertook naval operations. After the *King's Peace he married Cotys' sister and spent a decade in Thrace before joining an unsuccessful Persian invasion of Egypt (373). Having quarrelled with *Pharnabazus he fled to Athens and supported *Callistratus (2) against *Timo-

theus (2). His Corcyran campaign drove Sparta to peace negotiations (371). Proposed honours incensed a descendant of Harmodius (see ARISTOGITON): Iphicrates contemptuously rehearsed his achievements as a self-made cobbler's son and won. Having assisted Sparta (369) he went north, where he preserved the Macedonian throne for his adoptive brothers—including *Philip (1) II—but failed at *Amphipolis. Callistratus' eclipse caused his replacement by Timotheus (365). They were later reconciled (their children married) but the Embata débâcle (356) (see SOCIAL WAR (1)) finished both their careers, though a robust *apologia* secured Iphicrates' acquittal. No 4th-cent. commander had greater repute among *cognoscenti* (cf. copious treatment in *Polyaenus (2)), but the equipment reforms (small shield, enlarged spear and sword, special boots, linen corslets) ascribed to him—and their bearing on Macedonian developments—are controversial.

RE 9 (1916), 'Iphikrates' 1; W. K. Pritchett, *The Greek State at War* 2 (1974) esp. 117 ff.; J. G. P. Best, *Thracian Peltasts* (1969); AO and *CAH* 6² (1994), see indexes.   C. J. T.

Iphigenia, the daughter of *Agamemnon and *Clytemnestra (or, according to the less common version, of *Theseus and *Helen (cf. e.g. Duris, *FGrH* 76 F 92; Stesichorus fr. 191 Davies, *PMGF*; Nicander in Ant. Lib. 27)). *Artemis demanded her sacrifice as the price for sending a fair wind to the Greeks waiting at *Aulis to sail for Troy. In some versions (cf. *Cypria, argumentum* Bernabé, *PEG* p. 41; Kinkel, *EGF* p. 19) Artemis was angry because Agamemnon had killed a deer—and boasted that he was a better hunter than Artemis. In another version he had killed a sacred goat kept in Artemis' grove and made the same boast (*Cypria* fr. 23 Bernabé, *PEG*; cf. Soph. *El.* 566–9). In a less common version it is the non-fulfilment of a vow that caused Artemis' wrath; in *Apollodorus (6) (*Epit.* 3. 21) it was caused both by Agamemnon's boasting and by the fact that *Atreus had not sacrificed the golden lamb to her, though he had vowed to sacrifice to her the most beautiful animal in his flocks (*Epit.* 2. 10). According to one version Agamemnon sent for Iphigenia on the pretext of marriage to *Achilles. In Aesch. *Ag.* 218–49 it is suggested that she died at the altar—or at least that the spectators thought she did. In most versions Artemis snatched her away and saved her; a hind replaced her and was sacrificed in her place (*Cypria argumentum* Bernabé, *PEG* p. 41; Kinkel, *EGF* p. 19). Alternatively she was replaced by a bear, and in one of this version's variants the sacrifice took place at *Brauron not Aulis (Phanodemus, *FGrH* 325 F 14; schol. Ar. *Lys.* 645). In *Nicander cited in Ant. Lib. 27 she was replaced by a calf. In *Hesiod (*Cat.* fr. 23a. 15–26 + b M–W) Artemis replaced Iphimede (as she is called there) by an *eidōlon*; Iphimede becomes Artemis *einodia*, which is understood by Pausanias (1. 43. 1) to mean that she became *Hecate (cf. Stesichorus fr. 215 Page, *PMG* = 215 Davies, *PMGF*). In the *Cypria* (*argumentum*, Bernabé, *PEG* p. 41; Kinkel, *EGF* p. 19; see EPIC CYCLE) Iphigenia is carried off to Tauris (see CHERSONESUS (2)) and made immortal by Artemis. In the Hesiodic *Catalogue*, the *Cypria*, Stesichorus fr. 215 Davies, *PMGF*, and the stories underlying Hdt. 4. 103 (cf. Paus. 1. 43. 1), she then becomes divine. In the version in Euripides' *IT* she becomes a priestess of Artemis, first in the Taurid and then at Brauron (*IT* 1462–6). In the Taurid she was forced to preside over human sacrifices; on recognizing her brother (*Orestes) in one of the prospective victims she fled with him and Artemis' statue, which Athena instructed them to take to Attica. At *Brauron she was associated with the rite of the *arkteia*, had a heroon, and received *hero-cult; the clothes of women who died in *childbirth were dedicated to her. Her relationship to Artemis varies in the different cults. In some, as at Brauron and at Aegira (Paus. 7. 26. 5), she is distinct from Artemis; in others she is identified with Artemis (cf. Paus. 2. 3. 1; Hsch., entry under Iphigeneia). She had a heroon also at *Megara (1), where, in the local version of the myth, she was alleged to have died (Paus. 1. 43. 1). Nicander in Ant. Lib. 27 combines the priesthood in the Taurid with immortality conferred by Artemis at Leuce, where Iphigenia married Achilles. According to Herodotus (4. 103) the Taurians sacrifice shipwrecked men and any Greeks they capture to a goddess Parthenos whom they identify with Agamemnon's daughter Iphigenia.

L. Kahil and others, *LIMC* 5 (1990), 706–34; A. Henrichs, in *Le Sacrifice dans l'antiquité*, Entretiens Hardt 27 (1981), 198–208; Kearns, *Heroes of Attica* 27–33, 57–8, 174; P. Brulé, *La Fille d'Athènes* (1987), 180–7 and passim; H. Lloyd-Jones, *JHS* 1983, 87–102; A. J. N. W. Prag, *The Oresteia: Iconographic and Narrative Tradition* (1985), 61–7, 73; J.-M. Croisillé, *Latomus* 1963, 209–25; K. Dowden, *Death and the Maiden* (1989), 43–7, 129–30 and passim.

C. S.-I.

Iphis, in mythology, (1) father of *Eteoclus, one of the *Seven against Thebes, and of *Evadne (2), wife of *Capaneus. (2) A young Cypriot, who loved Anaxarete, a noblewoman of that island. She would have none of him, and he finally hanged himself at her door; she looked, unmoved, from her window, and was turned by Aphrodite into stone. The resulting image was called Aphrodite *prospiciens* (ἐκκύπτουσα ?).

See Ovid, *Met.* 14. 698 ff., cf. Ant. Lib. 39 (from Hermesianax).

H. J. R.

Ipsus, small town in central *Phrygia, precise location unknown, where *Antigonus (1) the One-eyed was defeated and killed by *Lysimachus and *Seleucus (1) I in 301 BC, in a battle in which over 150,000 men are alleged to have taken part. Few details are known, but it appears that Antigonus' son, *Demetrius (4), after a successful cavalry charge against Seleucus' son, the future *Antiochus (1) I, pursued too far, thus exposing his father's flank to Seleucus' *elephants, which had been given to him by the Indian king, Chandragupta (*Sandracottus), in return for the cession of Seleucus' Indian territories. Antigonus, hoping that his son would return, waited too long and was killed. The battle finally put paid to any practical possibility of the reunification of *Alexander's (3) the Great empire. Seleucus' elephants frequently figure on his later coinage.

Plut. *Demetr.* 28–9. *RE* 9/2, 'Ipsos'; W. W. Tarn, *JHS* 1940.

J. F. La.

Ireland See HIBERNIA.

Irenaeus (c. AD 130–c.202), sometimes called the first systematic Christian theologian, was born in Asia Minor, had contacts in youth with *Polycarp of Smyrna, but spent most of his active life in Gaul, becoming bishop of Lyons (*Lugdunum (1)) c.178. He was thus an important link between east and west, and intervened at Rome on behalf of the Montanists (see MONTANISM) at Lyons (177/8) and the Quartodecimans of Asia (190), who observed Easter on 14 Nisan, the day of the Passover, rather than the following Sunday. Only two of his numerous works survive, the vast anti-Gnostic (see GNOSTICISM) *Adversus haereses* (mainly in a Latin translation) and the short *Proof of the Apostolic Preaching* (in an Armenian translation). His constructive exposition of Christian theology developed out of his critique of Gnostic systems, and was characterized by stress on traditional elements in Christianity.

TEXTS *Adv. haer.*: Migne, *PG* 7; W. W. Harvey (1857). *Proof*: *PO* 12 (with Eng. trans.).

J. N. D. K.

Iris, goddess of the rainbow and messenger of the gods. She is usually employed by *Zeus in *Homer's *Iliad*, once by *Hera (18. 165 ff.), whose officious minister she later becomes (Eur. *HF* 822 ff.; Callim. *Hymn* 4. 66 f., 215 ff., etc.). At *Il.* 23. 198 ff. she summons *Boreas and *Zephyrus on her own initiative to help *Achilles, and resists their boisterous advances, but *Alcaeus (1) makes her mother of *Eros by Zephyrus (fr. 327 L–P; cf. Plut. *Mor.* 765e ff.). She is 'wind-footed' and 'storm-footed' in the *Iliad*, where the rainbow portends war or storm (17. 547–52), and *Hesiod (*Theog.* 265 ff.) makes her daughter of Thaumas and *Electra (1), and sister to the *Harpyiae or Harpies (storm-winds). She is sometimes described as amorous (schol. *Il.* 5. 353 etc.), but *Theocritus calls her 'still virgin' as bedmaker to Zeus and Hera (17. 133 f.).

In Archaic art (François vase, etc.) she has winged boots and short chiton like *Hermes, but later is winged, with long or short dress, and carries a herald's staff. She appears in many divine or heroic scenes as messenger, as servant of Hera (*Parthenon frieze, etc.), and sometimes as a lone traveller beset by *satyrs or *Centaurs.

G. Weicker, *RE* 9 (1916), 2037–45; A. Kossatz-Deissmann, *LIMC* 5/1. 741–60.

N. J. R.

iron The new technical processes which introduced the widespread use of iron to the Mediterranean seem to have originated between the 13th and the 9th cent. BC. Although its introduction has been linked to the downfall of the palatial societies of the eastern Mediterranean (c.1200 BC), this now seems unlikely. Iron was used for Mycenaean jewellery, and is mentioned in Homer (*Od.* 9. 391–3). An iron crater-stand was one of the votives dedicated by *Alyattes at *Delphi (Hdt. 1. 25).

Greece possesses small iron-deposits, but the main sources in Classical times were Elba and the *Chalybes country behind *Trapezus. Elba was a major source of iron, and the slag-heaps from *Populonia in Etruria seem to represent an annual iron output of 1,600 to 2,000 tons from that city alone. Other ancient sources used include *Thrace and, under the Roman republic, *Spain. The iron mines were one of the prizes of the Third Macedonian War (Livy 45. 29). From about 40 BC Rome drew on the deposits of *Noricum. The mines of inner *Dalmatia are of later date. In many parts of *Gaul there are enormous slag-heaps, and British iron (see BRITAIN) was used locally. Indian ore is mentioned (see INDIA).

The furnaces of the ancients could not normally produce cast iron. Statues were made by chasing pure wrought iron. Weapons were made of mild steel. Quenching to harden is known as early as *Homer, and certain waters were thought (without reason) to be particularly suitable. The Romans understood intentional carburization and annealing, and by complicated damascening they produced blades which would not snap. They did not use water-power, and all iron-working was by hand. Semi-nomadic indigenes often reduced the ore in the mountains, and sold the blooms at cities or at military forts, where they were forged into tools. See METALLURGY; MINES AND MINING.

O. Davies, *Roman Mines in Europe* (1935); Forbes, *Stud. Anc. Technol.* 9; T. A. Wertime and J. D. Muhly, *The Coming of the Age of Iron* (1980); J. D. Muhly and others, *Anat. St.* 1985, 67 ff.; R. Drews, *The End of the Bronze Age* (1993), 73–6; G. Camporeale, *L'Etruria mineraria* (1985).

O. D.; D. W. J. G.

irrigation *Mesopotamia (*Babylonia) and *Egypt were the main areas of the ancient world where agriculture depended on irrigation from a river rather than rainfall. In Mesopotamia the powerful *Euphrates and *Tigris rivers permitted irrigation of extensive plains through a radial network of descending *canals. The more gentle gradient of the Nile and its very narrow valley meant that local basin irrigation was predominant in Egypt. Both these 'natural' systems required heavy communal work to clear canals and repair dykes, and careful drainage to avoid salination, but only the former, being an integrated system, demanded a single centralized control. 'Artificial' irrigation was necessary for land which lay above the flood-level and for additional watering of other land outside the period of inundation. The pole-mounted scoop (Arabic *shaduf*) was always the cheapest and commonest mechanical aid; the Persian/Hellenistic periods saw the appearance of the far more efficient and expensive man-powered Archimedean screw (see ARCHIMEDES) and animal-powered wheel with pot-garland (Arabic *saqiyah*), but they were rare, only achieving significant diffusion on the large private estates of Roman Egypt and elsewhere (also in Roman *mines, to extract water). In general 'artificial' irrigation was so laborious or costly in the ancient world that it remained confined to small plots of horticultural cultivation for the market. See AGRICULTURE, GREEK and ROMAN; WATER.

M. G. Ionides, *The Régime of the Rivers Euphrates and Tigris* (1937); K. W. Butzer, *Early Hydraulic Civilisation in Egypt* (1976); M. Schnebel, *Die Landwirtschaft im hellenistischen Ägypten* (1925), ch. 2; J. P. Oleson, *Greek and Roman Mechanical Water-Lifting Devices* (1984); T. Schiøler, *Roman and Islamic Water-Lifting Wheels* (1973). D. W. R.

Isaeus (1), Athenian speech-writer (*c*.420–340s BC)

Life The skimpy ancient biographical tradition ([Plut.] *Mor.* 839e–f, *Dionysius (7) of Halicarnassus' critical essay *Isaeus*, and a Life preceding the speeches in the main MSS) preserves his father's name, Diagoras, but was uncertain whether he was Athenian or from *Chalcis in Euboea. *Isocrates reportedly taught him, but he plainly also studied *Lysias' speeches and was himself a teacher of *Demosthenes (2) and author of a *technē*, a speech-writer's manual. His working life extended from *c*.389 to the 350s, perhaps to 344/3 if a lengthy quotation by Dionysius traditionally printed as speech 12 was by him and is correctly dated. The ancient tradition had his activity extend down to the reign of *Philip (1) II of Macedon.

Works As a professional speech-writer (*logographos*) in Athens, he specialized in inheritance cases. Some 64 speech-titles were known in antiquity, 50 of which were reckoned genuine. Eleven survive complete, of which four can be internally dated (speech 5 in 390 or 389, 6 in 364 or 363, 7 in 355 or 354, and 2 in the 350s), while stylometric criteria have been plausibly used by Wevers (see bibliog. below) to date the remainder. The subject-matter of his speeches is fundamental for Athenian social history, lying as it does where the study of Athenian legal practice converges with those of oratorical professionalism, property acquisition strategies (see INHERITANCE), and private familial behaviour.

Style Dionysius chose him, with Lysias and Isocrates, to illustrate the older style of Attic oratory, and devoted a shrewd and sympathetic essay to him, comparing his style to that of Lysias. As he rightly said, though each speech is superficially lucid, he so 'uses insinuations and preliminary expositions and contrived divisions of material . . . and embroiders his speeches by alternating argument with emotional appeal' that he gained 'a reputation for wizardry and deceit' (*Isaeus* 3 and 4). The accuracy of Dionys-

ius' judgement can be confirmed by following the analyses in Wyse's classic edition, a masterpiece of sceptical deconstruction.

TEXT T. Thalheim (Teubner, 1903 and reprints); with trans.: P. Roussel (Budé, 1922); E. S. Forster (Loeb, 1927).

STUDIES W. Wyse (1904), text and commentary; R. F. Wevers, *Isaeus: Chronology, prosopography and social history* (1969).

INDEX W. A. Goligher and W. S. Maguinness (1964); J. M. Denommé (1968). J. K. D.

Isaeus (2), Syrian rhetorician, famous in Rome *c*. AD 100 for his extempore speeches and vigorous, epigrammatic style (Plin. *Ep.* 2. 3; Philostr. *VS* 513). J. B. C.

isagogic literature, works offering an introduction (εἰσαγωγή, though other words are also used) to an art or science (cf. ps.-Soranus, *Quaestiones medicinales* 21; V. Rose, *Anecdota Graeca et Graecolatina* 2 (1870), 244–5). It seems to be a form of writing first used by the Stoics (C. O. Brink, *Horace on Poetry* 1 (1983), 22; see STOICISM). The word is used in Latin under the Greek form or Latinized as *isagoga* (Gell. *NA* 1. 2. 6, 14. 7. 2, 16. 8. 1; *TLL* 7/2. 489. 39 ff.) but more commonly is rendered by *institutio* or *introductio*. Although attempts have been made to see elements such as a division of the subject into *ars and *artifex (e.g. Quint. *Inst.* books 2–11, *Ars oratoria*, book 12, *Orator*) as specific to introductory works, modern scholars tend to be more sceptical, and there is in any case no clear distinction between εἰσαγωγαί and actual handbooks, τεχναί, *artes*. Works that have been seen as possessing isagogic elements include the treatises on agriculture of M. *Porcius Cato (1), *Varro, and *Columella; *Cicero, *Partitiones oratoriae*; [Q. Tullius *Cicero (1)], *Commentariolum petitionis*; *Horace, *Ars Poetica*; *Vitruvius, *De architectura*; A. *Cornelius Celsus, *De medicina*; Sex. *Iulius Frontinus, *De aquis*; *Quintilian, *Institutio oratoria*; and *Vegetius, *Epitoma res militaris*.

K. T. Schäfer, *RAC* entry under 'Eisagoge'; M. Fuhrmann, *Kl. Pauly* entry under 'Isagogische Literatur'; L. Mercklin, *Philol.* 1849, 413–29; E. Norden, *Hermes* 1905, 481–528; J. Börner, *De Quintiliani institutionibus oratoriae dispositione* (1911); H. Dahlmann, *Varros Schrift De poematibus und die hellenist.-röm. Poetik* (*Abhandlungen der Akademie der Wissenschaften und der Literatur Mainz* 1953. 3); C. O. Brink, *Horace on Poetry* 1 (1983); M. Fuhrmann, *Das systematische Lehrbuch* (1960); E. Rawson, *Roman Culture and Society* (1991), 324–51.

C. F.; G. W. W.; D. P. F., P. G. F.

Isauria, an ill-defined region of the *Taurus mountains sandwiched between *Pisidia to the west, *Lycaonia to the north, and Rugged *Cilicia. The towns of old and new Isaura have been localized on the north-facing slopes of the Taurus, south-east of lake Trogitis (Suğla Göl). Both were reduced by P. *Servilius Vatia in a campaign of 76–74 BC which brought him the cognomen Isauricus; new Isaura was subsequently chosen to be one of his southern capitals by the Galatian *Amyntas (2), and the extensive surviving fortifications at the site (now Zengibar Kalesi) were largely his work. Later sources, confirmed by onomastic evidence, reckon much of the mountainous country which extended from here south-east towards Seleuceia on the Calycadnus to have been Isaurian territory. Isauria's inhabitants were tough *montagnards* who resisted outside control at all periods of their history. Isaurian claims to self-determination were invariably regarded by outsiders as examples of banditry, and the terms Isaurian and brigand became virtually synonymous. See BRIGANDAGE. Under the Roman empire they supplied numerous recruits for the legions and for auxiliary forces, but in the 4th cent. AD they asserted their independence to such effect that the mountain fringes had to be garrisoned with a virtual *limes*

Isauricus to contain them (see LIMES). At the end of the 5th cent. an Isaurian military family placed its own candidate, Zeno, on the imperial throne in Constantinople. Although the cities of Isaura were mostly small and unsophisticated, the region produced a distinctive regional art and was an important centre of early *Christianity.

R. Syme, *RP* 5.661 ff. and 6.287 ff.; J. F. Matthews, *The Roman World of Ammianus Marcellinus* (1989), 355–67; B. D. Shaw, *Journal of the Social and Economic History of the Orient* 1989.   S. M.

Isca, British river-name (see BRITAIN), hence applied to sites on rivers so called: (1) Modern Exeter on the Exe, established as a fortress of Legio II Augusta (see LEGION) *c.* AD 55, used for auxiliary units in the period *c.*65–85, becoming the *civitas*-capital of the *Dumnonii during the Flavian period. The barracks, the legionary baths, and part of the *principia* (headquarters) have been excavated. The civil town was built directly on top of the fortress, with the forum basilica constructed *c.*80/5. (2) Modern Caerleon on the Usk was from *c.* AD 74/5 the fortress of Legio II Augusta, although it was not initially fully occupied. In the 140s–150s it was largely rebuilt in stone. Despite a reduction in garrison during the 3rd cent. it remained in active occupation down to about 260, before being turned over to civilian occupation by the end of the century. Christian martyrs Aaron and Julius may be realities (Gildas 10), but an archbishopric is uncertain. Buildings including baths, barrack-blocks, and an amphitheatre have been excavated.

A. L. F. Rivet and C. Smith, *The Place-names of Roman Britain* (1979). (1) P. Bidwell, *Roman Exeter: Fortress and Town* (1980). (2) G. C. Boon, *Isca* (1972); J. D. Zienkiewicz, *The Legionary Fortress Baths at Caerleon* (1986).
C. E. S.; M. J. M.

Ischia See PITHECUSAE.

Ishtar, Mesopotamian goddess of love and war, variously described as daughter of Sin (moon-god) or of Anu (sky-god), with various attributes according to different city traditions. At *Uruk she was identical with Sumerian Inanna, lover of Dumuzi (Tammuz); at Dilbat she was the planet Venus; at Kish she was warlike; at Arbela (see GAUGAMELA) her oracle was famous in the 7th cent. BC and her temple there organized loans far abroad; at *Nineveh (1) her Hurrian-influenced entourage included demons of disease. Probably all her temples were centres for cult prostitution of various kinds; see PROSTITUTION, SACRED. Her name was used as a generic term for goddess, sometimes in the plural, facilitating *syncretism with other goddesses in the pantheon. She is often depicted as naked, or with a lion, with weapons, or with the rod-and-ring of kingship. She plays major roles in literary texts, such as the Epic of Gilgamesh and in Ishtar's Descent to the Underworld.

C. Wilcke, *Reallexikon der Assyriologie* 5 (1976–80), 'Inanna/Ishtar'.
S. M. D.

Isidorus (1), of Charax, a Parthian Greek ((Spasinou) Charax is near the mouth of the *Tigris at the head of the Persian Gulf), of the early 1st cent. AD, whose works on the pearl-fisheries of the *Persian Gulf and on the way-stations of the routes across the desert to *Syria were quoted by the elder *Pliny (1).

GGM 1. lxx f.; *FGrH* 781; W. Schoff, *The Parthian Stations of Isidore of Charax* (1914); D. Potts, *The Arabian Gulf in Antiquity* (1990); O. A. W. Dilke, *Greek and Roman Maps* (1985), 124.   N. P.

Isidorus (2) **Hispalensis,** Isidore, bishop of Seville (*c.*600–36), came from a Roman family of considerable influence in Visi-

gothic *Spain (see GOTHS): his brother Leander was his predecessor at Seville (*c.*577–*c.*600). He is the author of numerous theological and historical works including a *Chronica maiora*, continuing the *Chronicle* of *Jerome, a *Historia Gothorum*, written in 624 and subsequently revised with additions on the *Vandals and Sueves, *De natura rerum*, and *Quaestiones in Vetus Testamentum*. He was also concerned greatly with linguistic issues, as in the *Differentiae* and the *Synonyma*, and above all in his final work, the incomplete *Etymologiae*, which was edited into twenty books by Braulio, bishop of Saragossa (631–51). This last encyclopaedic text dealt with the liberal arts, medicine, law, religion, language, human geography, nature, etc. It drew extensively on earlier writers, and, having an enormous circulation, was one of the main routes by which classical learning was transmitted to the Middle Ages.

TEXTS Migne, *PL* 81–4; *Etymologiae*, ed. W. M. Lindsay, 2 vols. (1911); J. Fontaine, *Isidore de Séville* (1959); F. Brunhölzl, *Histoire de la littérature latine du Moyen Âge* 1, pt. 1 (1990), 78–93, 257–60.   I. N. W.

Isigonus, of Nicaea (1st cent. BC or 1st cent. AD), a writer of *paradoxa* (see PARADOXOGRAPHERS), who probably drew to some extent on Varro, and was himself drawn upon by Pliny the Elder.

A. Westermann, *Paradoxographi* (1839), 162 f.; *FGrH* 674; A. Giannini, *Paradoxographorum graecorum reliquiae* (1966), 146–8.   J. S. R.

Isis (Egyptian *3s* or *3st*, Gk. Ἶσις, Εἶσις), 'mistress of the house of life', whose creative and nurturing functions made her the most popular divinity of the Late period in the Egyptian *Fayûm and delta. As such she absorbed, or was equated with, many other divinities, acquiring a universal character expressed in Gk. as μυριώνυμος, 'invoked by innumerable names' (Plut. *De Is. et Os.* 53, 372f; cf. Apul. *Met.* 11. 5, comm. J. G. Griffiths (1975)). The hieroglyphic form of her name, whose meaning is disputed, connects her with the royal throne and with *Osiris: his centre at Busiris was close to hers in the twelfth nome (see NOMOS (1)). A connected narrative of her myth appears late, doubtless under Greek influence (Diod. Sic. 1. 13–27; Plut. *De Is. et Os.* 12–19, 355d–358d). In the Egyptian versions, the myth generally begins with Set's murder of her brother and husband, Osiris, whom she and her sister Nephthys revive by mourning. Impregnated by Osiris after his resurrection, Isis gives birth to *Horus, who, after 'redeeming his father', ascends his throne, and later attacks and rapes, even beheads, Isis. In return, Isis chops off his hands. In the theology of the New Kingdom she has several linked roles: as a goddess who protects the coffin, she is 'mother', 'wet-nurse', of the dead, and brings about rebirth; as midwife, she protects women in giving birth and suckling—she is often the 'king's wet-nurse'; equated with Sothis (Sirius), she brings the Nile flood and the new year; equated with the snake-goddess Renenutet, the goddess of harvest, she is 'mistress of life'; as magician and protector, as in the Graeco-Egyptian magical papyri, she is 'mistress of heaven'. See MAGIC.

In Egyptian popular religion of the Hellenistic and Roman periods, these roles are simplified to three: protector of women and marriage; goddess of maternity and the new-born (Isis suckling Harpocrates (see HORUS) or *Apis); guarantor of the fertility of fields and the abundance of harvests. Herodotus' identification of Isis with *Demeter (2. 59, 156. 5), and the later view of Isis and Osiris as inventors of arable farming (Diod. Sic. 1. 14. 1–3), reproduce only the last of these motifs. The version of Isis that was attractive in the Graeco-Roman world universalized this popular representation: dispenser of life, protector (especially of the family), healer, deliverer, and so mistress of the universe. A more complex account of Isis was available through the aretalogies. Six versions are known (esp. *IG* 12. 5. 739, and Diod. Sic. 1. 27, both late 1st cent. BC). They are now generally regarded as variants of a first-person praise-scheme produced (in the 2nd cent. BC) at *Memphis by Hellenized priests, deliberately excluding many features of Egyptian Isis. But the earliest surviving example, from Maroneia near *Abdera (*SEG* 26. 821, *c.*100 BC, comm. Y. Grandjean (1975)), merely alludes to the scheme, and is thus a bridge to the more numerous '*hymns' (ten known, including Apul. *Met.* 11. 5. 1–5, 25. 1–6). Isidorus, the author of the three earliest surviving hymns (1st cent. BC), from the Egyptian temple at Medīnet Mādī, speaks expressly of 'interpreting' Egyptian texts for Greek use (comm. V. Vanderlip, *American Studies in Papyrology* 1972). No credence is now given to the old view that the Egyptian cults offered a deeper spirituality through personal salvation: the mysteries of Isis, whatever their origin, were always secondary. Discussion of Isis' success has centred on two themes, both vaguely Weberian. A 'political' view comes in two forms. (1) The world-affirmation inherent in Egyptian Isiac religion made it attractive as a personal religion both to successful *metics (Egyptian emigrants) and to a 'broad church', including local élites; even if often incorporated into the civic calendar, it remained sufficiently marginal to retain authority through the god's personal demand on the worshipper (Dunand). (2) The motif of personal subjection to and dependence upon Isis is combined with that of freedom from fate. This paradox reproduces the negotiation between free cities and absolute Hellenistic kings / Roman emperors; the Egyptian cults validated this uneasy relation for individuals (Versnel). The second theme is that of *women: though not dominant, women were important, as suggested by Augustan poetry (Prop. 2. 33a; Tib. 1. 3; Ov. *Am.* 2. 13, etc.). Isis may have given a religious overtone to a positive view of female sexuality. See EGYPTIAN DEITIES.

F. Solmsen, *Isis among the Greeks and Romans* (1979). Egypt: M. Münster, *Untersuchungen zur Göttin Isis* (1968); F. Dunand, *Le Culte d'Isis dans le bassin oriental de la Méditerranée* 1 (1973). Aretalogies: J. Bergman, *Ich bin Isis* (1968); J. Leclant, *ANRW* 2. 17. 3 (1984), 1692–1709. Texts: M. Totti, *Ausgewählte Texte der Isis- und Sarapis-Religion* (1985). Epigraphy: L. Vidman, *Sylloge inscriptionum religionis Isiacae et Sarapiacae* (1969). Temples: R. A. Wild, *ANRW* 2. 17. 3 (1984), 1739–1847, and *Water in the Cultic Worship of Isis and Sarapis* (1981). Success: F. Dunand, in *Religions, pouvoir, rapports sociaux* (1980), 71–148; H. S. Versnel, *Inconsistencies in Greek and Roman Religion*, i. *Ter Unus* (1990), 39–95. Women: S. K. Heyob, *The Cult of Isis among Women* (1975); C. Veligianni-Terzi, *Rh. Mus.* 1986, 63–76; E. J. Walters, *Attic Grave-Reliefs that Represent Women in the Dress of Isis* (1988).
R. L. G.

islands were and are one of the most obvious features of Greek life. 'The islands', as a geographical collective, formed one of the tribute districts of the 5th-cent. BC Athenian empire (see DELIAN LEAGUE), and 'islanders' is almost a synonym for Athens' subjects (Thuc. 7. 5, 30, 82, and often in *Aristophanes (1), see Sommerstein on *Peace* 298); but more often island status implies separateness. Islands in *Homer can symbolize remoteness and even magical strangeness (*Od.* 6, *Scheria; later utopias also tend to be situated on islands). Although in the real world 'islanders' could be a synonym for people in an exposed and defenceless situation (*Brasidas in Thuc. 4. 120. 3; see also Eur. *Heracl.* 84 with Wilkins's note for contempt for islanders), nevertheless island status was also seen as desirable because it meant security (*Old Oligarch* ch. 2). Literary works on 'Islands' by e.g. *Callimachus (3) (fr. 580 Pf. and vol. 1. p. 339) formed a recognizable Greek literary genre of writing by *paradoxographers; thus *Diodorus (3)'s book 5 was 'On Islands' (title: 5. 2). Poets cele-

brated particular islands (*Pindar, *Ol.* 7 for *Rhodes and several of his *Nemean Odes* for *Aegina; Callim., *Hymn to Delos*). *Relegation to islands was a punishment for members of the Roman élite in the imperial period. See also EUHEMERUS; IAMBULUS; ISLANDS OF THE BLEST; PERAEA; SEA POWER; SEMOS; XENAGORAS.

E. Gabba, *JRS* 1981, 55–60; J. P. V. D. Balsdon, *Romans and Aliens* (1979), ch. 8 (relegation); P. Vidal-Naquet, *The Black Hunter* (1986), and (ed.), *La démocratie grecque vue d'ailleurs* (1990), 139–59, 353–61; N. Purcell in O. Murray and S. Price (eds.) *The Greek City* (1990), for a different view (islands facilitating mobility); I. Malkin, *Myth and Territory in the Spartan Mediterranean* (1994), 97.
S. H.

Islands of the Blest (Fortunatae insulae) were originally, like the 'Gardens of the *Hesperides', the mythical winterless home of the happy dead, far west on Ocean shores or islands (Hom. *Od.* 4. 563 ff.; Hes. *Op.* 171; Pind. *Ol.* 2. 68 ff.). Comparable is *Homer's description of *Elysium (*Od.* 4. 563–9); in both cases entry is reserved for a privileged few. The islands were later identified with Madeira (Diod. Sic. 5. 19–20; Plut. *Sert.* 8) or more commonly with the Canaries, after their discovery (probably by the Carthaginians). The Canaries were properly explored by King *Juba (2) II (*c.*25 BC–*c.* AD 23), who described apparently six out of the seven. From the meridian line of this group *Ptolemy (4) (*Geog. passim*) established his longitudes eastwards.

Cary–Warmington, *Explorers* 52 ff. (Pelican, 69 ff.); Thomson, *Hist. Anc. Geog.* 184, 262; Hyde, *Greek Mariners* 150 ff.; J. Delgado, *Archivo español de Arqueología* 1950, 164 ff.
E. H. W.; E. Ke., S. J. K.

Ismene See ANTIGONE (1); OEDIPUS.

Isocrates (436–338 BC), Athenian orator of central importance. Although he lacked the voice and the confidence ever to address a large audience and so played no direct part in the affairs of the state, his written speeches, which presumably were of some influence on public opinion, provide us with a most valuable commentary on the great political issues of the 4th cent. His system of education in rhetoric exercised a profound effect on both the written and the spoken word: his many pupils included the historians *Ephorus and *Theopompus (3), the atthidographer *Androtion, and the orators *Hyperides and *Isaeus (1). Judgements of his importance have variously treated him as the prophet of the Hellenistic world, and as the specious adulator of personal rulers, but, admired or despised, he cannot be neglected in the study of his age.

Life As son of a rich man, he studied under *Prodicus, *Gorgias (1) in Thessaly, *Tisias, and the moderate oligarch, *Theramenes. He was also a follower of *Socrates. Thus, while the *Peloponnesian War was destroying both his father's fortune and his city's, he was receiving his education from teachers who included the critics of democracy and empire, and the effect was lasting.

In the 390s he turned his theoretical training to account and wrote speeches for others to use in the courts. Orations 16–21 belong to this early phase. Soon discontented with the profession of *logographos* (speech-writer), he began to train others in rhetoric. In *Against the Sophists* he advertised his principles, and of the early writings the *Helen* and *Busiris* displayed his skill on themes already treated by others. It was perhaps in this period before the *King's Peace that he opened a school on *Chios. The *Panegyricus*, published in 380 after ten years of composition, was his version of a conventional subject celebrated by Gorgias and Lysias; its demand that the Greeks unite under the shared hegemony of Athens and Sparta was familiar (see PANHELLENISM), and the long period of composition suggests that it was intended to be an

Isocrates

enduring masterpiece of its kind, not, as some have supposed, a topical plea for the establishment of the *Second Athenian Confederacy. One of Isocrates' most distinguished pupils was *Timotheus (2) whom at some stage Isocrates had accompanied on campaign and served by writing his dispatches to the Athenian people, and as a result of Timotheus' successes Athens was able in 375 to make the peace which embodied the principle of the shared hegemony. Despite the fact that Persia's position in the peace was unchanged, Isocrates lauded it, perhaps partly on personal grounds, and began to address pleas, very similar in form to the *Philippus* of 346, to eminent individuals begging them to assume the lead against Persia, first *Agesilaus, then *Dionysius (1) I, then *Alexander (5) of Pherae (cf. Speusippus' *Letter to Philip* 13) and later perhaps *Archidamus III (cf. *Epistle* 9, of doubtful authenticity). Their reaction is not recorded, nor that of other Greeks, but the ambitious proposals of *Jason (2) of Pherae suggest that Isocrates' pleas were to some not wholly impracticable.

In 373 when *Thebes (1) seized *Plataea, he composed the *Plataïcus* purporting to be a speech to the Athenian assembly urging reprisals, and this may have been a sincere manifestation of antipathy to Thebes as a disruptive rival to Athens and Sparta. Likewise the *Archidamus* (366), the imagined speech of the future Spartan king about the Peace of 366/5, may reflect Isocrates' own inclinations. But other writings in this period can hardly be much more than rhetorical exercises, viz. the orations *To Nicocles* (c.372), *Nicocles* (c.368), and *Evagoras* (c.365); see EVAGORAS.

The failure of Athens in the *Social War (1) and the perilous financial position of the state in 355 stirred Isocrates to denounce in the *De pace* the war policy of the imperialists as the way to bankruptcy, and to demand, in place of the limited peace being made with the allies, a *Common Peace and the solution of economic difficulties by the foundation of colonies in *Thrace: on the question of a Panhellenic crusade the speech is strikingly silent; the Persian ultimatum of 355 had ruled it out for the moment. The speech is a companion piece to the *Poroi* of *Xenophon (1); both writings illuminate the financial and foreign policy of *Eubulus (1). Shortly after, in the *Areopagiticus*, Isocrates advocated return to a sober constitution under which the *Areopagus would exercise its ancient general supervision of all aspects of life: although some would ascribe the speech to the period before the Social War, it probably belongs to 354 when the supporters of *Chares (1) were beginning to raise their heads again, and in view of the impending prosecution of Timotheus Isocrates may have been in a gloomy mood about the future of Athens under its existing constitution. The treatise must have made a curious impression on his countrymen. Certainly by 353 Isocrates was very much on the defensive. By then he had amassed wealth unprecedented for his profession, and by the law of Periander (? 357) he had become liable to frequent *trierarchies; challenged in 354/3 to an *antidosis, Isocrates had emerged from the court unsuccessful and, imagining himself as a second Socrates, felt moved to write his apologia in the *Antidosis* of 353, in which he criticized his rivals and gave some account of what he himself professed. This is the chief source of our knowledge of his system of education.

In 346 he published his most important treatise, the *Philippus*. Written between the voting of the Peace of *Philocrates and *Philip (1) II of Macedon's intervention in *Phocis, it expounded afresh the programme of the *Panegyricus* and called on Philip 'to take the lead of both the concord (see HOMONOIA) of the *Hellenes and the campaign against the *barbarians' (προστῆναι τῆς τε

τῶν Ἑλλήνων ὁμονοίας καὶ τῆς ἐπὶ τοὺς βαρβάρους στρατείας) (§ 16) and to relieve the misery of Greece by planting colonies in the western satrapies of the Persian empire (§ 120). In the following year, when Philip instead of beginning the crusade had got himself wounded in war against northern barbarians, Isocrates sent a further letter (*Epistle* 2) urging Philip to begin the campaign against Persia and so acquit himself of slanderous accusations about his real intentions; there is no suggestion here that Isocrates thought of a League of Corinth (see CORINTH, LEAGUE OF) as the necessary instrument for Philip's leadership of 'the concord of the Hellenes'. We do not know how Isocrates reacted to Philip's proposal to extend the peace brought in 344 by his old pupil Python, but shortly after the collapse of this diplomatic initiative in early 342, he began the last of his great treatises, the *Panathenaicus*, the completion of which was delayed by illness until 339. It was in part personal apologia, in part a comprehensive comparison of Athens and Sparta greatly to the glory of the former. Nowhere did he manifest any further interest in the great theme of the *Panegyricus* and the *Philippus*. Events had disappointed him and the epistles *To Alexander* (? 342) and *To Antipater* (? 340) were purely personal. One last effort remained. After discussion with *Antipater (1), when after *Chaeronea he came to negotiate, Isocrates wrote an appeal to Philip (*Epistle* 3) to set about the programme of the *Philippus*. The Peace of *Demades was the answer, and at the time of the annual burial of the dead in autumn 338 Isocrates starved himself to death.

Significance In the realm of political ideas large claims have been made for Isocrates as the man who inspired Philip with the idea of attacking Persia, who envisaged not only the form of Hellenic league that established concord and defined the relation of Greece and the Macedonian kings but also the flowering of Greek culture in the Hellenistic world. These claims cannot be substantiated. The various writings addressed to Philip probably helped Philip to form a clearer idea of the nature and strength of the Panhellenist movement the support of which he needed, but that they did more is a conjecture against which Isocrates' own words in *Epistle* 3 (§ 3) contend. His ideas about the partnership of Philip and the Greeks appear from the treatises to have been very imprecise, and the fact that he was said to have sent substantially the same epistle to Philip as to *Agesilaus suggests that he sought little more than a good general for the campaign. As to the role of the new colonies, he appears not to have thought of a dispersion of Greeks beyond Asia Minor, and far from the leavening of barbary he spoke as if Greek cities would form separate free entities surrounded by barbarians, ruled as barbarians had to be ruled. For the colonies were to effect merely the removal from Greece of the impoverished, and he had no vision of the prosperity that could and did flow from the creation of new trading areas. On the other hand, Isocrates did provide answers to the two great problems of his age, viz. the discord (*stasis) within cities due to poverty, and the discord between cities due to petty ambitions and rivalries, and one has only to compare the views of *Plato (1) and *Aristotle to see that, naïve as Isocrates seems, he was by far the most practical; neither of the philosophers explained how cities were to be kept from destroying each other, and their plans for ensuring concord within the city by controlling the growth of population contrast unfavourably with Isocrates' proposals to settle in prosperity those whose poverty was the source of revolutionary violence.

Much has been made of the somewhat imprecise proposals for curing the ills of *democracy in the *Areopagiticus. It is to be noted that these proposals are part of a long tradition deriving from his early master, Theramenes, and found fulfilment in the arrangements of *Demetrius (3) of Phalerum: Isocrates was not alone. In his other writings the tone is very different, and this outburst may have been occasioned largely by the serious condition of Athens after the Social War.

In the history of education Isocrates has an important place. See EDUCATION, GREEK. The details of his system remain somewhat obscure, but it would seem that his pupils received under his personal supervision a course of instruction which was neither purely speculative nor a mere training in rhetoric. He disdained the business of the lawcourts as well as 'astrology, geometry, and the like' which at best, he held, did no harm but were of no use 'either in personal matters or in public affairs', and he eschewed the logic-chopping of *dialectic, 'the so-called eristic dialogues'. For him the true concern of higher education was 'discussion of general and practical matters', the training of men for discussion and action in the sphere of the practical. What exactly such 'great affairs' were he did not specify, but it would seem that the sort of matters discussed in his own speeches provided the themes for his pupils' speeches which were to be well, that is persuasively argued.

In all this he was in contrast to *Plato (1) whose teaching was at once highly theoretical and essentially dogmatic. Plato aimed to teach men what to think, Isocrates how to argue. There was, not surprisingly, tension between the two and (though many have denied it) with delicate irony Plato in the *Phaedrus* (279a) sneered at Isocrates, who defended himself and his system in the *Antidosis*.

Writings Of the 60 orations extant under his name in Roman times, 25 were considered genuine by *Dionysius (7), and 28 by *Caecilius (1). Twenty-one survive today; six are court speeches. Of the nine letters extant the authenticity of 1, 3, 4, and 9 has been questioned but never disproved.

The works of Isocrates represent Attic prose in its most elaborate form. Dionysius (*Comp.* 23) compared it to 'closely woven material', or 'a picture in which the lights melt imperceptibly into shadows'. He seems, in fact, to have paid more attention to mere expression than any other Greek writer. He was so careful to avoid *hiatus that Dionysius could find no single instance in the whole of the *Areopagiticus*; he was very sparing even in the elision of short vowels, and crasis, except of καί and ἄν, occurs rarely. Dissonance of consonants, due to the repetition of similar syllables in successive words, and the combination of letters which are hard to pronounce together, is similarly avoided. These objects are attained without any perceptible dislocation of the natural order of words. Another characteristic of the style is the author's attention to rhythm; though avoiding poetical metres, he considered that prose should have rhythms of its own, and approved of certain combinations of trochee and iambus (see PROSE-RHYTHM, GREEK). His periods are artistic and elaborate; the structure of some of the longer sentences is so complex that he overreaches himself; he sacrifices lucidity to form, and becomes monotonous. His vocabulary is almost as pure as that of *Lysias, but while the simplicity of Lysias appears natural, the smoothness of Isocrates is studied.

For general bibliog. see ATTIC ORATORS.

TEXTS Benseler–Blass (Teubner, 1879), and E. Drerup, vol. 1 (1906); with trans.: Norlin and van Hook, 3 vols. (Loeb); Mathieu and Brémond, 4 vols. (Budé).

INDEX S. Preuss (1904).

SPECIAL STUDIES G. Mathieu, *Les Idées politiques d'Isocrate* (1923); N. H. Baynes, *Byzantine Studies and other Essays* (1955), 144–67; K. Bringmann, *Studien zu den politischen Ideen des Isokrates* (1970); F. Seck (ed.), *Isokrates*, WdF no. 351 (1976); G. L. Cawkwell, in T. J. Luce (ed.), *Ancient Writers* 1 (1982), 313–30; Y. L. Too, *The Rhetoric of Identity in Isocrates* (1995). For Isocrates' place in the history of education see W. Jaeger, *Paideia* 3 (Eng. trans. 1945), and H. I. Marrou, *Histoire de l'éducation dans l'antiquité*, 7th edn. (1977; Eng. trans. 1956); and for his relation to Plato, C. Eucken, *Isokrates: Seine Positionen in der Auseinandersetzung mit den zeitgenössischen Philosophen* (1983).
G. L. C.

isonomia ('equality of law') seems, along with other compounds of *iso*-, to have been a prominent term in Greek political discourse in the late 6th and early 5th cents. BC. *Herodotus (1) uses *isonomia* in his Persian debate to refer to *democracy (3. 80. 6, 83. 1), and elsewhere to refer to constitutional government as opposed to *tyranny (3. 142. 3, 5. 37. 2); in the second sense he also uses *isegoria* ('equality of speech') and *isokratia* ('equality of power') (5. 78, 92. α 1). For *Thucydides (2) *isonomia* is a term which can be applied to a respectable and broadly based *oligarchy (3. 62. 3, 4. 78. 3) as well as to a democracy. The *scolia* ('drinking-songs') celebrating Harmodius and *Aristogiton praise them both for killing a tyrant and for giving Athens *isonomia* (Page, *PMG* 893–6): the word was probably used at first to advertise Athens' freedom from *tyranny, but may have been taken over by *Cleisthenes (2) as a slogan for his reforms.

M. Ostwald, *Nomos and the Beginnings of the Athenian Democracy* (1969).
P. J. R.

isopoliteia ('equal citizenship') is a term used from the 3rd cent. BC, either instead of *politeia* ('citizenship') for grants of *citizenship by a Greek state to individuals (e.g. *IG* 5. 2. 11 = *Syll.*³ 501) or, particularly, for grants to whole communities (e.g. *IG* 5. 2. 419 = *Syll.*³ 472). Modern scholars distinguish between *isopoliteia*, by which states which were to remain independent exchanged rights, and *sympoliteia*, by which two or more states combined to form a single state, but the language of ancient texts is more varied. The citizens of *Plataea may have been given a form of actual or potential Athenian citizenship when they became allies of *Athens in 519 (Thuc. 3. 55. 3), and after the destruction of their city in 427 they were given Athenian citizenship with certain limitations ([Dem.] 59. 104–6); in 405 the Samians (see SAMOS) were given the right to act as Athenian citizens in Athens, though Samos was to remain an independent state (*IG* 2². 1 = ML 94 + Tod 97); the arrangements between *Argos (2) and *Corinth in the 390s may have involved mutual grants by which citizens of one state could act as citizens of the other. In the Hellenistic period treaties of *isopoliteia* are common, weakening the principle that one could only exceptionally acquire citizenship by migration. The *Aetolian Confederacy used the device of *isopoliteia*, with the whole confederacy or with an individual Aetolian city, as a means of attaching distant states to the confederacy.

G. Busolt, *Griechische Staatskunde*, 3rd edn. (1920–6); J. A. O. Larsen, *Greek Federal States* (1968), 202–7; W. Gawantka, *Isopolitie* (1975).
J. A. O. L.; P. J. R.

Issus, town in SE Cilicia, giving its name to the battle in which *Alexander (3) the Great defeated *Darius III of Persia in 333 BC. The battle was fought alongside a river called 'Pinarus', which is either the Deli Çay or the Payas, 30 or 20 km. (19 or 12 mi.) north of Iskenderun. Much is uncertain, but possibly a Persian cavalry attack on their right, near the sea, was defeated by Alexander's Thessalians, moved from his right, while Alexander himself managed to cross the Pinarus on his right, break through the weak Persian left, and wheel to threaten the Persian centre. The right of the Macedonian *phalanx also managed to cross the river, and break through, whereupon Darius fled, pursued by Alexander, but the left of the phalanx suffered severely, and much of the Persian army managed to retreat in good order, when the Macedonians turned to plundering its camp.

RE 9/2, 'Issos'. Diod. Sic. 17. 33 ff.; Arr. *Anab.* 2. 6 ff.; Curt. 3. 10. 1 ff.; Plut. *Alex.* 20. A. B. Bosworth, *Conquest and Empire* (1988).   J. F. La.

Ister (Ἴστρος), river, was the name (of Thracian origin) given by the Greeks to the lower Danube (see DANUVIUS). From a knowledge of its estuary, where they established a colony before 600 BC (see ISTRIA (1)), the Greeks drew conclusions as to the size of the Danube. *Hesiod mentioned it as one of the four great streams of the world (*Theog.* 337). *Herodotus (1) regarded it as the largest river of Europe and a northern counterpart to the *Nile (4. 47–51). He correctly stated that it had a constant volume of water, but mistakenly assumed that its last bend was to the south and was quite in the dark as to its source. In the 3rd and 2nd cents. BC the Greeks probably ascended as far as the Iron Gates, but they remained ignorant as to the river's upper course; perhaps misled by a vague inkling of the river Save, and by the name of the Histri in the hinterland of Trieste, they imagined that the Ister threw off an arm into the Adriatic. This error was corrected by the Roman advance from Italy into the Danube basin after 200 BC; the identity of the Ister with the Danuvius was probably established during *Octavian's Illyrian campaign in 35 BC (Sall. *Hist.* fr. 79 Maurenbrecher). Personified as the son of *Oceanus, the river-god is represented on the coinages of *Nicopolis (2) ad Istrum and *Istria (2).

M. Bărbulescu, *LIMC* 5. 1 (1990), 804–6: 'Istros'.   M. C.

Ister (c.250–200 BC), author, probably from *Paphos. He studied under *Callimachus (3) of Cyrene at *Alexandria (1). He was a contemporary of the biographer *Hermippus (2). His work was in the grammatical tradition of his teacher. He wrote on a number of subjects, though only 77 fragments remain. Of these the great majority are from his *Attica* in four books. This was not an *Atthis*, but a digest of statements (largely but not only from the *Atthides*) on matters related to cult, religion, and institutions of Attica in the mythical period (i.e. the time of the kings). By excluding the historical period he surely helped create the idea that the *Atthis* was an antiquarian rather than an historical genre. His other major work, also on Athenian affairs, was called *Atacta*.

FGrH 334.   P. E. H.

Isthmia (sanctuary of *Poseidon), a Corinthian *Panhellenic shrine 16 km. (10 mi.) east of *Corinth, beside the modern Athens–Corinth road. A hippodrome and hero shrine (West Foundation) lie 2 km. (1¼ mi.) south-west, with additional cults in the Sacred Glen.

The sanctuary was established c.1050 BC in an area of Mycenaean settlement. The first temple (a peripteral i.e. colonnaded building with wall-paintings), c.690–650, had a 30-metre (100-foot) altar and *temenos* wall. It was rebuilt after fires in c.470–460 and 390. The first stadium (early 6th cent. BC) accords with C. *Iulius Solinus' (7. 14) foundation date for the *Isthmian Games; a larger stadium (further south-east) was built c.300 BC. A bath (originating c.4th cent.) survives in Roman form. A theatre (established by 390) probably held musical rather than dramatic contests. Isthmia was a major assembly place; it was at the games in 196 BC that T. *Quinctius Flamininus announced the *freedom of the Greeks.

After L. *Mummius sacked Corinth in 146 BC, Isthmia was abandoned and the games transferred to *Sicyon; returned to the Roman colony c.2 BC, they were resumed at Isthmia c. AD 50–60, when the theatre was renovated, followed, by 100, by the temple and *temenos* wall. A heroon of Palaemon (see MELICERTES) dates from the mid-1st cent. AD; the first, Hadrianic, temple of Palaemon was transferred during the reign of Marcus *Aurelius. Cult activity ceased during the 3rd cent.

On the Rachi ridge to the south is a small, mainly Hellenistic, settlement (abandoned c.200 BC).

See the continuing *Isthmia* series (cf. bibliog. to next entry); E. Gebhard and F. Hemans, *Hesp.* 1992, 1–77.   C. A. M.

Isthmian Games The Isthmian Games (see ISTHMIA) were held near *Corinth in honour of *Poseidon, the prize being originally a crown of pine, but during the Classical period one of dry celery. They were said to have been founded to commemorate the death of *Melicertes (or Palaemon), *Ino's son, or (according to Athens) by *Theseus after he had killed the robber *Sinis. They were reorganized as a *Panhellenic festival c.582 BC, held biennially in April or May, and administered by Corinth, whose position as a commercial centre made them popular. Chariot- and horse-races were prominent (see HORSE- AND CHARIOT-RACES), and there was a special four-lap foot race called the *hippios* ('equestrian'). Musical contests are attested from the 3rd cent. BC. The Archaic temple of Poseidon was rebuilt in the mid-5th cent. BC. The Archaic stadium lay near the temple and precinct of Palaemon, but was later replaced by one outside the stadium.

K. Schneider, *RE* 9 (1916), 2248–55; O. Broneer, *Isthmia*, 3 vols. (1971–3); M. C. Sturgeon, *Isthmia* 4 (1987); the series continues.   N. J. R.

Istria (1) (Istros, Histropolis), a coastal city some 50 km. (30 mi.) north of *Tomis, with its territory stretching to the Danube estuary: hence its name (Danube = *Ister). Its modern site has been greatly affected by the movements of the Black (*Euxine) Sea, partly submerged and partly silted-up. A meagre literary tradition makes it a Milesian (see MILETUS) foundation (e.g. Hdt. 2. 33; in 657/6 BC (Eusebius) or c.770 (ps.-Scymnus)): Milesian influence is later discernible in its institutions.

Istria has been the subject of intensive archaeology for decades, not only in its urbanized centre, but also in its civic territory. The earliest pottery which reached Istria from the Aegean world came c.650 BC (notably, middle Wild Goat Style I). Archaeology has also indicated substantial cultural interaction and osmosis between Greek and non-Greek there. Imported *amphorae include the products of *Thasos, *Rhodes, *Cnidus, *Chersonesus (3), *Cos, *Paros and, especially, *Sinope: the latter probably brought not *wine but olive oil to Istria. See OLIVE.

Istria grew swiftly through the 6th cent. BC and continued to enjoy prosperity through the Hellenistic age, when imported amphorae were particularly numerous. However, the construction of a large defensive wall in the Hellenistic period, together with the explicit evidence of inscriptions, shows that there were problems too. In particular, there were recurrent difficulties between the city and the tribal groupings of the hinterland: it seems that the forces of *Burebistas inflicted substantial damage on the city.

The earliest direct contact with Rome came with the campaign of M. *Terentius Varro Lucullus in 72/1 BC. Despite its problems, Istria continued to flourish into the 7th cent. AD.

P. Alexandrescu and W. Schuller (eds.), *Histria: Eine Griechenstadt an der rumänischen Schwarzmeerküste* (1990); N. Ehrhardt, *Milet und seine Kolonien*, 2nd edn. (1988).   D. C. B.

Istria (2) or **Histria,** a peninsula at the NE extremity of the *Adriatic sea, lying between Venetia (see VENETI (2)) and *Illyricum and extending inland towards the Julian *Alps. The Illyrian Istri inhabited the peninsula, eastward to the plateau of the Cicceria and Monte Maggiore, and to the river Arsia; the western strip of the Istrian peninsula was inhabited by the *Liburni. The Istri were known as pirates (Livy 10. 2. 4; see PIRACY), but Rome did not interfere before 221 BC, when the Istri seized a ship carrying corn. How far they were subdued then is not known, since the Second *Punic War must have hindered the Romans from establishing their power in Istria. As the Istri showed a hostile attitude when *Aquileia was founded, the Romans conquered them after capturing their chief settlement (178/7); however, they did not cease to threaten Aquileia thereafter, e.g. in 171 (Livy 43. 1. 5). In 129 BC the Istri were among a number of tribes in the north-east of Italy who surrendered to C. *Sempronius Tuditanus (*Inscr. Ital.* 13. 3. 90; cf. *AE* 1953, 95). In 52 the Istri attacked *Tergeste (Trieste), to whose aid *Caesar sent troops (Caes. *BGall.* 8. 24); this was probably their reason for siding with *Pompey in the Civil War. In the west their territory must once have reached the Timavus (Strabo 5. 9, 215 C), but the Formio was made the frontier in the 1st cent. BC, no doubt because the Celtic Carni occupied the territory round Tergeste. Istria, which was part of *Illyricum during the republic, became part of Italy under *Augustus and with Venetia formed Regio X. The boundary with Illyricum was the river Arsia.

H. Nissen, *Italische Landeskunde* 2/1 (1902), 237 ff.; A. Gnirs, *JÖAI* 1915, 99 ff., and *Istria praeromana* (1925); archaeological reports in *Not. Scav.*; A. Degrassi, *Aevum* 1933, 279 ff., 'Notiziario archeologico' in *Atti e Mem. d. Soc. Istriana d. Arch. e Stor. patria* 1928 ff., and *Il confine nord-orientale dell'Italia romana* (1954); for inscriptions, *Inscr. Ital.* 4, fasc. 1–4 (1934–51). F. A. W. S.; J. J. W.

Isyllus (late 4th cent. BC), of *Epidaurus, author of six poems found in inscriptions at Epidaurus. Poems 1 (in trochaic tetrameters) and 3 (in an elegiac couplet followed by three dactylic hexameters) are dedications. In poem 2 (in dactylic hexameters) the poet praises himself for the introduction of a procession to Phoebus (i.e. *Apollo) and *Asclepius at Epidaurus. Poem 4 (in ionics) is a *paean to Apollo and Asclepius, poem 5 (in dactylic hexameters) a *hymn to Asclepius. Style and language show the influence of the New *Dithyramb.

TEXT Powell, *Coll. Alex.* 132 ff.; L. Käppel, *Paian* (1992), 380 ff.
LITERATURE J. Sitzler, *RE* 9/2. 2283; U. von Wilamowitz-Moellendorff, *Isyllos von Epidauros* (1886); West, *GM* 142 f.; L. Käppel, *Paian* (1992), 200 ff. B. Z.

Italica (mod. Santiponce, near Seville), a strategic foundation by P. *Cornelius Scipio Africanus in 206 BC at the site of a native Turdetanian town. Under *Augustus (?) it received municipal status (see MUNICIPIUM), was walled, and provided with a theatre. It was the ancestral home of the emperors *Trajan and *Hadrian. The latter granted it colonial status and was probably responsible for the construction of a new walled extension to the town, comprising a temple (Traianeum), baths, amphitheatre, other public buildings, colonnaded streets, and houses with mosaics. It began to decline by the 3rd cent. but was still an important walled centre under the Visigoths (see GOTHS).

A. García y Bellido, *Colonia Aelia Augusta Italica* (1960). S. J. K.

Italy (see also ITALY, LANGUAGES OF; RELIGION, ITALIC). The name *Italia,* probably a Graecized form of Italic *Vitelia* (= 'calf-land'), was originally restricted to the southern half of the 'toe' but was gradually extended. By 450 BC it meant the region subsequently inhabited by the *Bruttii (Theophr. *Hist. pl.* 5. 8); by 400 it embraced *Lucania as well (Thuc. 6. 4, 7. 33); *Campania was included after 325, and by *Pyrrhus' day (early 3rd cent. BC) Italia as a geographical expression meant everything south of Liguria and Cisalpine Gaul (Zonar. 8. 17; see LIGURIANS; GAUL (CISALPINE)); this area, however, only acquired political unity after the *Social War (3). Cisalpine Gaul was not officially incorporated until *Augustus' time when, accordingly, Italy reached its natural Alpine frontiers. Unofficially, however, whatever the administrative divisions, the whole country south of the Alps had been called Italy from *Polybius (1)'s time onwards. The Augustan poets also call Italy *Hesperia* (= 'the western land'), *Saturnia* (= strictly *Latium), *Oenotria* (= strictly SW Italy), *Ausonia* (= 'the land of the Ausones', *Opica* to the Greeks; strictly Campania).

Italy's greatest length is roughly 1,100 km. (680 mi.); the greatest breadth of the peninsula proper is some 240 km. (150 miles). Its long coastline possesses comparatively few, mostly indifferent ports, Genoa (see GENUA), Spezia, Naples (see NEAPOLIS), *Tarentum, *Brundisium, *Ancona, and *Pola being noteworthy exceptions. In compensation, however, Italy could exploit its central position to build a Mediterranean empire. Mountains, valleys, and plains in juxtaposition feature the Italian landscape. On the north are the *Alps, a natural but not impossible frontier: the Carnic Alps pass is not formidable and the Brenner from time immemorial has been used by invaders attracted by Italy's pleasant climate, fertility, and beauty; the Alps actually are steeper on the Italian side. Between Alps and *Apennines lies the indefensible north Italian plain watered by the Po (see PADUS). The Apennines traverse peninsular Italy, impeding but not actually preventing communications; the ancients' belief that they abounded in minerals was erroneous, since Italy only possessed some alluvial *gold, copper (Etruria), *iron (Elba), and *marble (Liguria).

Despite fertile upland valleys the mountain districts usually permitted only a relatively frugal existence. The plains, however, were amazingly productive, being enriched partly by volcanic activity (Euganean district in the north, Alban hills in Latium, mons Vultur in *Apulia, the still-active *Vesuvius in Campania), partly by fertilizing silt carried down by numerous rivers which in winter contained adequate amounts of water. (Northern Italy also possessed important lakes, but not central and southern Italy apart from *Trasimene, *Fucinus, and water-filled craters like *Albanus and *Avernus.) Italy's natural products were consequently abundant and varied: *olives, various fruits, *cereals, *timber, etc., even though some typically Italian products of today e.g. oranges and tomatoes, were unknown in antiquity. The variety is explained chiefly by the varied climate, which is temperate if not cold in the mountains and northern Italy and warm if not hot in southern Italy. Possibly the ancient climate was slightly more equable; malaria (see DISEASE) was certainly less prevalent. Italy contains excellent pasturage; in many districts ranching supplanted agriculture (see TRANSHUMANCE). Also its seas abound in fish (see FISHING).

Italy was thus well adapted to support human life, and did so from palaeolithic times. Agriculturally based neolithic settlements first appear in some parts of the peninsula around 5000 BC, and metal technology in the third millennium BC. During the bronze age (the so-called *Apennine culture of the second millennium BC), the first settlements in naturally-defended positions are found, especially in western central Italy. There was some trade with, and perhaps colonization by, the Mycenaeans in SW coastal areas from about 1400. In the flatlands of Emilia, around Modena (see MUTINA), *Parma and Piacenza (see PLACENTIA), there emerged in the middle to late bronze age the *terramara culture, with low-lying villages built on piles; a mould for casting a terramara-type axe has been found at *Mycenae. From the late second millennium BC, there began to develop the 'proto-Villanovan' and then the *Villanovan cultures. Iron came into limited use, and during the 8th cent. BC, contact was established between Etruria, Latium, and the early Greek colonies in southern Italy (see COLONIZATION, GREEK). This was a stimulus to, and a profound influence upon, the emergence of the *Etruscan cities, which grew out of Villanovan settlements in Etruria. The cities of Latium, including Rome, likewise expanded. Elsewhere in Italy an immensely diverse mosaic of peoples began to achieve cultural and political identities. Down the east coast were *Veneti (2), Picenes (see PICENUM), *Daunians, Peucetians, and *Messapians. In the mountainous backbone of Italy were Ligurians, *Umbrians, Sabines (see SABINI), Samnites (see SAMNIUM), Volsci, Lucanians, and the Bruttii of Calabria; the Samnites in particular expanded out of their homelands in the 5th cent. BC. The coastal fringes of SW and southern Italy, together with *Sicily, comprised *Magna Graecia. In the north, Gauls settled from c.400 or before. In the west, apart from the Etruscans, there were the Latins of Latium, the related *Faliscans and *Hernici, *Aurunci-Ausones, and Oenotri (= *Sicels?). Some 40 languages were spoken altogether, and the peoples varied greatly in culture and level of civilization. Italy's mountainous topography accentuated and perpetuated such divergences.

Ultimately, the peoples of Italy were for the first time united under the hegemony of Rome. This was a protracted task, occupying the half-millennium between the 5th cent. BC and the reign of Augustus. *Romanization was slow and uneven, but was aided by the gradual creation of a new road network; by the founding of citizen, Latin and, later, veteran, colonies; and by the diffusion of the Latin language, mass-produced Roman goods, new concepts of town planning, and the spread of Romanized villas and farms. It was also fuelled by the profits brought in through the wars of conquest, which encouraged public and private patronage, as a means of social and political advantage.

With Italy finally unified, Augustus divided it into eleven administrative districts (regiones):

I. Latium, Campania, Picentini district
II. Apulia, Calabria, Hirpini district
III. Lucania, ager Bruttius
IV. Region inhabited by Samnites, Frentani, Marrucini, Marsi, Paeligni, Aequiculi, Vestini, Sabini
V. Picenum, Praetuttii district
VI. Umbria, ager Gallicus
VII. Etruria
VIII. Gallia Cispadana
IX. Liguria
X. Venetia, Istria, Cenomani district
XI. Gallia Transpadana

From the late 1st cent. AD, Italy's political and commercial pre-eminence began to wane. The process accelerated under the African and Syrian Severan dynasty (193–235), and, under *Diocletian, the imperial court moved to *Mediolanum (Milan), 300. Diocletian also initiated administrative changes, so that by *Constantine I's time, Italy was divided into sixteen provinces which now included Sicily, *Sardinia, *Corsica, and *Raetia. *Christian-

ity made relatively gradual progress in Italy after the edict of Milan (313) until the later 4th cent., a major period of church building in Rome, Milan, and elsewhere. In 404 the imperial court moved to the well-protected town of *Ravenna, and when the Ostrogoths (see GOTHS) under *Odoacer deposed the last western Roman emperor, *Romulus Augustulus, in 476, Ravenna was retained as a capital, and further embellished. The Byzantine reconquest (535–54) was soon checked by the *Lombard invasions of 568.

ANCIENT SOURCES *Strabo's detailed description (bks. 5 and 6) is good; among other things it corrects Polybius' assertion (2. 14) that Italy is triangular. *Pliny (1)'s account (HN 3. 38–132) is based on Augustus' Commentaries. *Pomponius Mela (2. 58–73), *Ptolemy (4) (bk. 3), and the Liber coloniarum are less important. Amongst others *Varro (Rust. 1. 2. 1 f.), Virgil (G. 2. 136 f.), *Dionysius (7) of Halicarnassus (1. 36 f.), *Propertius (3. 22. 17 f.), Pliny (HN 37. 201 f.), and *Rutilius Claudius Namatianus (2. 17 f.) extol Italy's beauty and fertility. Roads are described in the *itineraries, especially the Antonine Itinerary (4th-cent. copy of a work of c. AD 212) and *Peutinger Table, which is probably based on Castorius' world-map of AD 366. See, too, the separate articles on VIA APPIA, etc.

For epigraphic finds see CIL 11, Inscr. Ital. (1932–), and Supplementa italica, new series. Archaeological journals and series include: Arch. Anz., Archeologia Medievale, Collection and Mélanges École française de Rome (MÉFRA), Dial. di Arch., Forma Italiae, JRA, JRS, Memoirs of the American Academy at Rome, Mon. Ant., Opus, PBSR.

MODERN LITERATURE (mainly for Roman Italy): Schiavi in Italia (1988); R. P. Duncan-Jones, The Economy of the Roman Empire (1982); S. Dyson, Community and Society in Roman Italy (1991); A. Giardina (ed.), Società romana e impero tardoantico, 3 vols. (1986); A. Giardina and A. Schiavone (eds.), Società romana e produzione schiavistica, 3 vols. (1981); P. Gros, Architecture et société à Rome et en Italie centrale et méridionale (1978); A. Keaveney, Rome and the Unification of Italy (1987); L. J. F. Keppie, Colonisation and Veteran Settlement in Italy (1983); C. Nicolet, Les Structures de l'Italie romaine (1977); T. W. Potter, Roman Italy (1987); E. T. Salmon, The Making of Roman Italy (1982); P. Sommella, Italia antica: l'urbanistica romana (1988); M. S. Spurr, Arable Cultivation in Roman Italy (1986); A. Tchernia, Le Vin de l'Italie romaine (1986); R. Thomsen, The Italic Regions from Augustus to the Lombard Invasions (1947); B. Ward-Perkins, From Classical Antiquity to the Middle Ages (1984); J. B. Ward-Perkins, Cities of Ancient Greece and Italy (1974), and Roman Imperial Architecture (1981); P. Zanker (ed.), Hellenismus in Mittelitalien (1976), and The Power of Images in the Age of Augustus (1988).

E. T. S.; T. W. P.

Italy, languages of After the introduction of the *alphabet by the Greeks in the 8th cent. BC and its adoption by the native peoples, *literacy gradually spread throughout Italy. Epigraphic remains (see EPIGRAPHY) then provide evidence for a variety of languages down to the 1st cent. BC, when the spread of Latin that accompanied the extension of Roman power throughout the peninsula led to the disappearance of all other tongues (except only Greek), at least in their written form, by the Augustan period.

There are a number of languages of *Indo-European descent. Many of these can be grouped together and classified as an Italic branch of *Indo-European, with two major subgroups in central and southern Italy consisting of Latin (see LATIN LANGUAGE) and *Faliscan on the one hand and the Osco-Umbrian (or Sabellic) languages on the other (see OSCAN AND UMBRIAN; SABELLI), and perhaps also including geographically remote *Venetic. The term 'Italic', however, is also used by some (mainly Italian) scholars to refer only to the Osco-Umbrian group; this usage generally accompanies a belief that Osco-Umbrian was a quite separate branch of Indo-European and that the notable innovatory features shared with Latin and Faliscan are the result of contact and borrowing. The Osco-Umbrian subgroup consists of Oscan, Umbrian, South Picene (the first of these languages to be attested, with inscriptions dated to the 6th and 5th cents.; see PICENUM), and a number of scantily recorded languages such as Paelignian, Volscian, and Marrucinian. See PAELIGNI; VOLSCI; MARRUCINI.

There are other Indo-European languages that do not belong to the Italic branch. *Messapic, attested in the Sallentine peninsula from the 6th cent. BC on, has been held to show links with the language of *Illyria across the *Adriatic sea, but present knowledge is not sufficient to substantiate this. Various dialects of Greek were spoken in the numerous colonies established in coastal regions from *Cumae round to *Tarentum, and also in *Sicily, from the 8th cent. BC onwards. Greek loan-words appear in many of the languages of Italy, including Latin; suggestions that some of these may date to the Mycenaean period are not convincing. A form of *Celtic known as Lepontic, very similar to Gaulish, is found in inscriptions from NW Italy, from the mid-6th to the 1st cent. BC. Further advances of Celtic-speakers into the Po valley (see PADUS) and even further south took place in the republican period; there are a few Gaulish inscriptions from the last two cents. BC.

The classification of some linguistic remains from Sicily is dubious. Sicel, the language of some inscriptions from the eastern part, seems to be of Indo-European origin, but claims that it belongs to Italic are over-confident. See SICELS. The mainly fragmentary inscriptions from *Segesta that have been labelled Elymian show too few characteristics to be securely assigned to any linguistic group.

Among the non-Indo-European languages of ancient Italy, the most important is undoubtedly *Etruscan. Attested from c.700 to the late 1st cent. BC, this was spoken not only in Etruria proper but also in areas of Etruscan expansion, particularly *Campania, before the Samnite take-over in the later 5th cent. (see SAMNIUM), and the Po valley, and in the area around Bologna (see BONONIA (1)), which later became Celtic-speaking. The only generally accepted connections for Etruscan are with a language found (essentially in one important inscription) on *Lemnos in the northern Aegean, which may provide some clue as to its origins. Less certain is any relationship between Etruscan and Raetic, a poorly attested language from the Alpine region north of *Verona; see RAETIA. From Novilara on the Adriatic coast comes an unintelligible inscription (c.500 BC), together with a few fragments, in an otherwise unknown language. Punic, by contrast, which is found in texts from Carthaginian colonies in Sicily, is a Semitic language, and the only one of these non-Indo-European languages to have well-established antecedents.

See also ALPHABETS OF ITALY; CELTIC LANGUAGES; ETRUSCAN LANGUAGE; LATIN LANGUAGE; MESSAPIC LANGUAGE; OSCAN AND UMBRIAN; VENETIC LANGUAGE.   J. H. W. P.

Ithaca (᾿Ιθάκη), in *Homer's poetry the island homeland of *Odysseus and the capital of his kingdom. Judging from the suitors who tried to win this realm by marrying *Penelope, it also included Dulichium, Same, and *Zacynthus (Od. 1. 245–8). From ancient times, the Homeric island was identified with modern Ithaca, a small narrow island between *Cephallenia and *Leucas off the *Acarnanian coast. Because Homer's descriptions and modern topography do not always match, some scholars still debate the 'Ithaka-Frage' or 'Ithaca question', although most would accept the verdict of the ancients and reject W. Dörpfeld's argument (see bibliog. below) that modern Leucas was Homeric

Ithaca. The recent excavation of a large tholos-tomb on Cephallenia may now shift the debate to that island.

Although excavations at Aetos (at the narrow strip of land in the island's middle) and Pelikata (near Stavros by Polis Bay) have not produced a clear Mycenaean palace-complex like that at *Pylos, they have revealed two bronze age settlements, both inhabited during the Mycenaean period. Finds of *Corinthian, *Cretan, and *Rhodian pottery (from a sanctuary on the slopes of Mt. Aetos and from the cave near Polis Bay) reveal the island as a staging-post for Greek *trade to Italy, up to, and perhaps even after, the foundation of Corinthian colonies (see COLONIZATION, GREEK). The cave at Polis Bay was the site of cult activity from the bronze age to Roman times: inscriptions reveal the worship of *Athena, *Hera, the *Nymphs, and Odysseus and bits of twelve splendid geometric tripods recall the ones brought home by Odysseus from Phaeacia i.e. *Scheria (Od. 13. 13, 217, 363 ff.). Curiously, Ithaca played no major role in the events of Classical Greece.

RE 9 (1916), 2289–93 with Kl. Pauly 2 (1967), 1486–7; PECS 421; P–K GL 2. 491–502; Lexikon der historischen Stätten 282–3; W. Dörpfeld, Alt–Ithaka (1927).   W. M. M.

Ithome, a prominent and easily fortified mountain rising isolated in the *Messenian plain (806 m.: 2,646 ft.), was the natural rallying point of the Messenians in their struggles for independence against *Sparta and, in 369 BC, site of the new city of *Messene. In the first Messenian War (late 8th cent. BC) they held it for twenty years; on its fall they lost their freedom. In the rising of the *helots against Sparta in the 5th cent. it was fortified and became a chief centre of resistance. A sanctuary and cult of *Zeus Ithomatas crowned the summit.

Tyrtaeus; Thuc. 1. 101–3.   T. J. D.; R. J. H.; A. J. S. S.

itineraries, the terrestrial equivalent of *periploi, sequential lists of settlements, way-marks, or posting-stations, often with distances between them. As a genre, they originated with the Roman practice of making an iter, the military expedition into or through hostile territory which underlay the Roman theory of road-building. Thus the area of operation of Roman power could be marked out as a series of measured routes, and these were recorded and evoked very variously, from official monuments (like the Golden Milestone of the Forum in Rome) to souvenir ex voto dedications like the Vicarello cups. The best-preserved written version (in a MS which has also an Itinerarium maritimum) is that usually known as the Antonine Itinerary (Itinerarium provinciarum Antonini Augusti), a probably military document of the late 3rd cent. AD (it has tetrarchic names) which has been of the highest value in the reconstruction of the topography of the Roman road-network; the *Peutinger Table presents similar information in a different form. The late Ravenna Cosmography (c.700) adapts the form for geographical description; the tradition continued in the Jerusalem pilgrim literature, such as the Bordeaux Itinerary (AD 333). See PILGRIMAGE; ROADS.

O. Cuntz (ed.), Itineraria Romana 1 (1929); A. and M. Levi, Itineraria picta: Contributo allo studio della Tabula Peutingeriana (1967); O. A. W. Dilke, Greek and Roman Maps (1985), 112–29, 174–6.   N. P.

Itinerarium Egeriae, an account of a pilgrimage to the Holy Land in AD 381–4 (including visits to Egypt, Sinai, and Mesopotamia), written from Constantinople for a western audience described as 'sorores', probably a circle of pious Christian laywomen in Spain or Gaul to which Egeria belonged. Although the text displays admiration for eastern monks, it is only later tradition which makes Egeria herself a nun. The sole MS, apart from fragments, was discovered at Arezzo in 1884. The text is incomplete, but provides detailed information about the Church liturgy of Jerusalem and the holy places, as well as a record of the pilgrim's journey to biblical sites in the Sinai peninsula and elsewhere in the Holy Land, and to the monks and martyr-shrines of Edessa. Egeria's 'late' Latin makes her text of interest to philologists. See PILGRIMAGE.

Ed. P. Maraval, SC 296 (1982); J. Wilkinson, *Egeria's Travels*, rev. edn. (1981).
E. D. H.

Ituraea The Ituraeans, a bedouin Arab people, occupied the Beqa' valley in Lebanon, where Chalcis their capital and *Helio-polis their religious centre were located, from the 2nd cent. BC. In the early 1st cent. BC, under their ruler (called *tetrarch) and high priest Ptolemy (85–40), they almost captured *Damascus. Ptolemy was confirmed by *Pompey; his son Lysanias (40–36) made an alliance with the Parthians and was killed by Antony (M. *Antonius (2)), who granted his dominions to Cleopatra VII. The tetrarchy was restored by *Octavian (30) to Zenodorus, who was, however, soon deprived of most of it, accused of profiting from the predatory activities of his own countrymen. Parts were granted to *Berytus, *Sidon, and Damascus; part became the tetrarchy of Abilene; Batanaea, Trachonitis, and Auranitis went to *Herod (1) the Great, who on Zenodorus' death in 20 received Paneas and Gaulanitis also. Herod's Ituraean dominions passed to his son *Philip (4), M. *Iulius Agrippa (1) I, who also came to rule Abilene, and M. *Iulius Agrippa (2) II, who ruled in addition Arcene in northern Lebanon. Chalcis, according to Josephus, formed a kingdom for Agrippa I's brother, Herod, and then for Agrippa II (though doubt has been cast on the identification of this Chalcis with Ituraean Chalcis). Famed as archers, the Ituraeans contributed several cohorts and an *ala* to the imperial army.

Jones, *Cities E. Rom. Prov.*; G. Schmitt, *ZDPV* 1982, 110–24; W. Schottroff, *ZDPV* 1982, 125–52.
J. F. H.

iudex In the Roman civil process, with its division into two stages, before the magistrate (*in iure*) and before the judge (*apud iudicem*), the *iudex* was a private person taken from the higher social classes (the qualifications varied in the course of time), who was appointed to conduct the hearing in the second stage. No special legal knowledge was required. The choice of the judge lay with the parties and was normally, but not necessarily, made from a panel of qualified persons (*album iudicum*). The parties' choice was approved by the magistrate before whom the proceedings *in iure* were conducted. The *iudex* could not refuse the commission conferred on him by the magistrate's order to hear the case (*iussum iudicandi*), except on recognized grounds. For the proceedings at the trial see LAW AND PROCEDURE, ROMAN, § 2.

The *Twelve Tables are said (Gell. *NA* 20. 1. 7) to have punished by death the judge convicted of bribery; and the praetorian edict introduced a special civil remedy against a judge who 'made the case his own' (*qui litem suam fecit*), but the scope and nature of the judge's liability is much debated.

There are references to an *arbiter* as well as a *iudex*, but in historical times there is no discernible distinction.

In some cases the trial might not take place before a single *iudex*, but before several *recuperatores*, or before the courts of the *centumviri* or the *decemviri stlitibus iudicandis*.

In the *cognitio extraordinaria* the judge was appointed, independently of the parties, by the official before whom the case

first came. He was now called *iudex datus*, *pedaneus*, or *specialis* and his competence (final decision or partial investigation) depended on his commission. Under the late empire the use of the term *iudex* became much wider: any official with jurisdictional or administrative power was so called. Justinian's constitution *Cod. Iust.* 3. 1. 14. 1 demonstrates the wide application of the term.

For bibliog. see LAW AND PROCEDURE, ROMAN, § 2. J. Mazeaud, *La Nomination du iudex unus* (1933); G. Broggini, *Iudex arbiterve* (1957); P. Birks, *Cambridge Law Journal* 1988, 36 ff.
B. N.

iudicium populi is the term used by *Cicero for a trial before an assembly. Before the growth of *quaestiones such trials may have simply been classed as *iudicia publica*. According to Cicero (*Dom.* 45) such a trial normally comprised three separate investigations (*anquisitiones*) before a *contio, in which the prosecuting magistrate both presided and prosecuted, and then, after a *trinundinum, a final vote. However, the *lex Osca tabulae Bantinae* (see LEX (2)) decrees that such trials should have five parts. The *Twelve Tables (Cic. *Leg.* 3. 11) laid down that votes on a citizen's *caput* (i.e. his life or citizen status) could only take place in the greatest assembly, the *comitia centuriata*. But votes in trials for a financial penalty could take place before the tribes, in the *comitia tributa* or *concilium plebis* (see COMITIA). In the early republic we are told that *duumviri perduellionis* and *quaestores parricidii* prosecuted in these trials; in the middle and late republic they were a matter for tribunes, aediles, and perhaps quaestors. If one of these was prosecuting on a capital charge, he needed the assistance of a magistrate with the auspices appropriate to summon the *comitia centuriata*, i.e. a consul or praetor. On the relation of *provocatio* to assembly trials see under PROVOCATIO, and on the nature of ordinary criminal justice see under LAW AND PROCEDURE, ROMAN, § 3, and QUAESTIONES.

C. H. Brecht, *Sav. Zeitschr.* 1939; W. Kunkel, *Untersuchungen zur Entwicklung des römischen Kriminalverfahrens*; A. W. Lintott, *ANRW* 1. 2 (1972).
A. B.; B. N.; A. W. L.

Iulia (1) (*RE* 'Iulius' 541), daughter of two *patrician parents, a Caesar and a Marcia related to a consul of 118 BC, married C. *Marius (1) after his successful Spanish command (114–13), to the mutual advantage of the wealthy and ambitious *novus homo and the Caesares—descended from *Venus, but with only one recent consulship and several young men embarking on public careers. She became the mother of C. *Marius (2), whose consulship (82), a hopeless position bringing mortal danger, she deplored. Her nephew *Caesar turned her funeral *laudatio* (69) into a glorification of their family and a public revival of the Marian cause.
E. B.

Iulia (2) (*RE* 'Iulius' 547), daughter of *Caesar and Cornelia (daughter of L. *Cornelius Cinna (1)), born *c.*73 BC, was betrothed to Q. Servilius Caepio, but married in April 59 to *Pompey; their mutual affection bound Pompey more strongly to her father Caesar. In 55 the sight of Pompey returning from the *comitia* bespattered with blood allegedly caused a miscarriage; and next year she died in childbirth, the child dying a few days later. On the people's insistence, she was buried in the *Campus Martius, and in 46 Caesar held magnificent shows near her tomb.

On the possibility that Caepio was *Brutus the tyrannicide, see F. Münzer, *RE* 13. 497 f.
G. E. F. C.; R. J. S.

Iulia (3) (*RE* 'Iulius' 550), only daughter of *Augustus (by *Scribonia), was born in 39 BC and betrothed in 37 to M.

*Antonius Antyllus. She was brought up strictly by her father and stepmother *Livia Drusilla. In 25 she married her cousin M. *Claudius Marcellus (5) and in 21 *Agrippa, to whom she bore Gaius *Iulius Caesar (2) and Lucius *Iulius Caesar (4), *Iulia (4), *Vipsania Agrippina (2), and Agrippa *Iulius Caesar (Agrippa Postumus). Her third marriage, to *Tiberius (in 11) is said to have been happy at first, but estrangement followed, and her behaviour may have contributed to Tiberius' decision to retire from Rome in 6. In 2 BC Augustus learned of her alleged adulteries (e.g. with Iullus *Antonius) and banished her to Pandateria; in AD 4 she was allowed to move to *Rhegium. Scribonia voluntarily shared her exile. Augustus forbade her burial in his mausoleum, and Tiberius kept her closely confined and stopped her allowance, so that she died of malnutrition before the end of AD 14. *Macrobius (*Sat.* 2. 5) speaks of her gentle disposition and learning, and gives anecdotes attesting her wit.

Syme, *Rom. Rev.* and *AA*, see indexes; E. F. Leon, *TAPA* 1951, 168 ff.; P. Sattler, *Studien aus dem Gebiet der alten Geschichte* (1962), 1 ff.; R. A. Bauman, *The Crimen Maiestatis* (1967), 198 ff.; E. Meise, *Untersuchungen zur Geschichte der Julisch-Claudischen Dynastie* (1969), 5 ff.
T. J. C.; R. J. S.

Iulia (4) (*RE* 'Iulius' 511), daughter of *Agrippa and *Iulia (3), was born *c*.19 BC and married (*c*.4 BC) L. *Aemilius Paullus (4). After her husband's fall *Augustus relegated her for adultery, then recalled her, and finally (AD 8) banished her permanently to the island of Trimerus off the Apulian coast, where she died in 28.

Syme, *Rom. Rev.* and *AA*, see indexes; E. Meise, *Untersuchungen zur Geschichte der Julisch-Claudischen Dynastie* (1969), 40 ff.
T. J. C.; R. J. S.

Iulia (5) (*RE* 'Iulius' 575), sometimes called Livilla, youngest daughter of *Germanicus and *Vipsania Agrippina (2), born in AD 18. In 33 she married M. Vinicius (grandson of M. *Vinicius and consul in 30 and 45). After the accession of her brother *Gaius (1) she received special honours like her sisters *Iulia Agrippina and *Iulia Drusilla, but in 39 was relegated to the Pontian islands for adultery with her brother-in-law, M. *Aemilius Lepidus (6). *Claudius restored her, but *Messallina accused her of adultery with the younger Seneca (see ANNAEUS SENECA (2), L.) and she was again banished and then killed (42?).

Syme, *AA*, see index.
T. J. C.; R. J. S.

Iulia Agrippina, 'the Younger Agrippina' (AD 15–59), eldest daughter of *Germanicus and *Vipsania Agrippina (2), was born on 6 November AD 15 at Ara Ubiorum. In 28 she was betrothed to Cn. Domitius Ahenobarbus, to whom she bore one son, the later emperor *Nero, in 37. During the principate of her brother *Gaius (1) (37–41) her name, like those of her sisters, was coupled with the emperor's in vows and oaths; but when she was discovered at *Mogontiacum late in 39 to be involved in the conspiracy of Cn. *Cornelius Lentulus Gaetulicus, she was sent into banishment. She was recalled by her uncle *Claudius, who married her in 49. Aided by M. *Antonius Pallas, the younger Seneca (see ANNAEUS SENECA (2), L.), and Sex. *Afranius Burrus, she quickly achieved her ambitious purpose. Receiving for herself the title Augusta (see AUGUSTUS, AUGUSTA AS TITLES), she persuaded Claudius to adopt Nero as guardian of his own son Britannicus (see CLAUDIUS CAESAR BRITANNICUS, TI.). She was generally believed to have poisoned Claudius, to make room for Nero (54). In the first years of Nero's rule she was almost co-regent with him but, after Pallas had fallen in 55 and Burrus and Seneca turned against her,

she lost her power. In March 59 she was murdered at *Baiae by a freedman, *Anicetus, acting on Nero's instructions. She wrote an autobiography.

PIR[2] I 641. R. Scott, *Latomus* 1974, 105 ff.; V. Rudich, *Political Dissidence under Nero* (1993), see index. Portraits: Fittschen and Zanker 3, no. 5, with refs.
J. P. B.; A. J. S. S.

Iulia Avita Mamaea, younger daughter of *Iulia Maesa, wife of Gessius Marcianus, was mother of M. *Aurelius Severus Alexander and became Augusta (see AUGUSTUS, AUGUSTA AS TITLES) on his accession (AD 222). She enjoyed unusual prominence for an empress throughout her son's reign, sharing his popularity until military pressures turned the army against the dynasty; she was murdered with him in March 235.

Hdn. 6; SHA *Alex. Sev.* (largely fiction). *PIR*[2] J 649; E. Kettenhofen, *Die syrischen Augustae* (1979).
A. R. Bi.

Iulia Balbilla, granddaughter of Ti. *Claudius Balbillus and Antiochus IV, king of *Commagene (see under ANTIOCHUS (9)), sister of C. *Iulius Antiochus Epiphanes Philopappus, visited the Colossi of *Memnon with *Hadrian and *Sabina on 19–21 November AD 130. In commemoration she composed four elegiac poems in superficial Aeolic dialect, still inscribed on one of the colossi.

TEXT A. and É. Bernand, *Les Inscriptions du colosse de Memnon* (1960).
DISCUSSION *PIR*[2] I 650. M. L. West, in H. G. Beck (ed.), *Kuklos: Festschrift Keydell* (1978); E. L. Bowie, in D. A. Russell (ed.), *Antonine Literature* (1990), 61–3.
E. L. B.

Iulia (*RE* 'Iulius' 566) **Domna,** daughter of Iulius Bassianus, priest of *Elagabalus at the Arab city of *Emesa in Syria, married L. *Septimius Severus in AD 187; her sons M. *Aurelius Antoninus (1) (Caracalla) and P. *Septimius Geta (2) were born in 188 and 189. She became Augusta (see AUGUSTUS, AUGUSTA AS TITLES) in 193 and 'mother of the camp' in 195; out of favour with Severus during the predominance of C. *Fulvius Plautianus, she devoted herself to patronage of literature, inspiring Philostratus' *Life of Apollonius* (see PHILOSTRATI). She was in *Britain during the expedition of 208–11. Although trying in vain to save Geta, she was given a prominent role under Caracalla, becoming 'mother of the senate and of the fatherland' and managing his correspondence; she took her own life in 217, after Caracalla's murder. Her sister was *Iulia Maesa.

Cass. Dio 73–9; SHA *Sev.*, *M. Ant.* M. T. Raepsaet-Charlier, *Prosopographie des femmes de l'ordre sénatorial* (1987), no. 436; A. R. Birley, *The African Emperor Septimius Severus*, 2nd edn. (1988).
A. R. Bi.

Iulia (*RE* 'Iulius' 567) **Drusilla,** born probably in AD 16, the second daughter of *Germanicus and *Vipsania Agrippina (2). She was married in 33 to L. Cassius Longinus (consul 30) and afterwards to M. *Aemilius Lepidus (6). Her name, like her sisters', was compulsorily included in vows and oaths after the accession of her brother *Gaius (1) (Caligula). She was his favourite sister, and it was rumoured that their relations were incestuous. She was named as Gaius' heir during his illness (late 37), but died in 38. Public mourning was enforced throughout the empire and, though there was no precedent in Roman history for the consecration of a woman, she was consecrated as Panthea, probably on the anniversary of Augustus' birthday.
J. P. B.; R. J. S.

Iulia (*RE* 'Iulius' 579) **Maesa,** sister of *Iulia Domna, had two daughters by her marriage to C. *Iulius Avitus Alexianus, *Iulia Soaemias Bassiana and *Iulia Avita Mamaea. She took part in the coup which led to her grandson Elagabalus (M. *Aurelius

Iulia Soaemias Bassiana

Antoninus (2)) becoming emperor, and was made Augusta (see AUGUSTUS, AUGUSTA AS TITLES) and given other honours in AD 218; she switched her support to her other grandson, M. *Aurelius Severus Alexander, in 221/2 and retained a respected position until her death in 224; but her political influence is exaggerated by *Herodian (2).

Cass. Dio 78–9; Hdn. 5. E. Kettenhofen, *Die syrischen Augustae* (1979); M. T. Raepsaet-Charlier, *Prosopographie des femmes de l'ordre sénatorial* (1987), no. 445. A. R. Bi.

Iulia (*RE* 'Iulius' 596) **Soaemias Bassiana,** daughter of *Iulia Maesa, wife of Sex. *Varius Marcellus and mother of M. *Aurelius Antoninus (2) (Elagabalus), whose elevation she helped to secure in AD 218. Closely associated with her son, she was murdered with him in 222. A. R. Bi.

Iulianus (emperor) See JULIAN.

Iulianus (Lucius Octavius Cornelius Publius Salvius (*RE* 14) **Iulianus Aemilianus),** an important Roman lawyer of the 2nd cent. AD, came from Hadrumetum (Hammamet) in Africa (Tunisia) and was a pupil of *Javolenus Priscus. *Hadrian appreciated his legal expertise and made him quaestor at double the normal salary with responsibility for editing the praetor's edict, which was then enacted in permanent form by a decree of the senate in 131. He was a member of Hadrian's *consilium* (council; see CONSILIUM PRINCIPIS) and one of the heads of the Sabinian school (see MASURIUS SABINUS) in succession to Javolenus. He was consul in 148, then governor of Lower Germany, followed by a period out of office which fits the likely date of composition of the *Digesta* ('Ordered Abstracts'), then governor of Nearer Spain about 161–4, and in 167/8 of Africa (Carthage). The future emperor M. *Didius Severus Iulianus was perhaps his nephew.

Beginning with excerpts from and comments on lesser writers (*Ex Minicio, Ad Urseium Ferocem*) his best-known work, the *Digesta* in 90 books (*libri*), follows the same order as *Iuventius Celsus' similar work, that of the edict followed by a section on separate laws and senatorial decrees. It is notable for its rich casuistry, based mainly on the discussion of cases taken from practice and teaching. Self-confident and original in his views, Iulianus seldom cites other lawyers, even when he adopts their views, and his criticisms, more moderate than those of Celsus, are apt tactfully to omit the name of the victim. He was a typical Sabinian (see MASURIUS SABINUS) in his search for workable solutions and his acceptance of anomalies. No one is more often cited by his fellow lawyers and his work was annotated by, among others, *Ulpius Marcellus, *Cervidius Scaevola and *Iulius Paulus. For a time overshadowed by the late classics such as *Aemilius Papinianus, he is named only as a secondary authority in the Law of Citations of 426, but Justinian honoured him as the most eminent of Roman lawyers and the precursor of his own codification.

Lenel, *Pal.* 1. 317–500; *PIR*[1] S 102; *HLL* 4, § 414; Kunkel 1967, 157–66; A. Guarino, *Labeo* 1964, 364–426; T. Honoré, *RHDFE* 1964, 1–44; D. Nörr, in A. Watson (ed.), *Daube Noster* (1974), 233–52; E. Bund, *ANRW* 2. 15 (1976), 408–54; F. Casavola, *Giuristi adrianei* (1980), 163–84; V. Scarano Ussani, *L'utilità e la certezza: Compiti e modelli del sapere giuridico in Salvio Giuliano* (1987). T. Hon.

Iulius (*RE* 45) **Africanus,** an orator of the 1st cent. AD from Gaul. He was highly regarded, notably by *Quintilian (*Inst.* 10. 1. 118), who preserves (8. 5. 15) a nauseating fragment from his loyal address to *Nero after the murder of *Iulia Agrippina (AD 59).

PIR[2] I 120; Schanz–Hosius, § 450. 4. M. W.

Iulius Africanus, Sextus, Christian philosopher of Aelia Capitolina (see JERUSALEM), who went *c*. AD 220 on an embassy to *Elagabalus which secured city rank and the title of Nicopolis for Emmaus, and under M. *Aurelius Severus Alexander established a library in the *Pantheon at Rome. His principal works were the *Chronographies* (Χρονογραφίαι) in five books, a synchronization of sacred and profane history from the Creation to AD 221, which was the basis of *Eusebius' *Chronicle*, and the Κέστοι, or 'Charmed Girdles' in 24 books, a miscellany of information, chiefly relating to magic, on various topics ranging from medicine to tactics. He also wrote a letter to Origen (1), in which he questioned the authenticity of the story of Susannah, and a letter to a certain Aristides, in which he harmonized the two genealogies of Christ.

Ed. Migne, *PG* 10. 63–94. H. Gelzer, *Sextus Julius Africanus und die byzantinische Chronographie* (1880–98); W. Reichardt, *Die Briefe des Sextus Julius Africanus an Aristides und Origenes* (1909); *ODCC*[2] 768. J. F. Ma.

Iulius (*RE* 49) **Agricola, Gnaeus** (AD 40–93), son of L. Iulius Graecinus, a senator from *Forum Iulii (mod. *Fréjus*), was brought up by his mother after his father's execution by *Gaius (1) (Caligula). After study at *Massalia, he was *tribunus laticlavius* in *Britain during the *Boudiccan revolt (60–1). He then married Domitia Decidiana, was *quaestor of Asia (63–4), tribune of the *plebs* (66; see TRIBUNI PLEBIS), and *praetor (68). Appointed by *Galba to recover temple property, after joining the Flavian side he recruited troops in Italy. Commanding Legio XX (see LEGION) in Britain, he saw action under Q. *Petillius Cerialis (71–3). He was made a *patrician, served as legate (see LEGATI) of *Aquitania for 'less than three years' (73–6), became *consul (76?) and *pontifex, then legate of Britain for seven years (77–84), winning *ornamenta triumphalia.

Apart from mentions by *Cassius Dio, a lapidary inscription at *Verulamium (St Albans), and inscribed lead pipes from Chester, Agricola is known entirely from the biography by his son-in-law *Tacitus (1). See BIOGRAPHY, ROMAN. He was certainly exceptional: the only senator known to have served three times in one province; unusually young as governor of Britain; the longest known tenure there. Favour from *Vespasian and *Titus may be surmised. In his first season (77) he conquered Anglesey; in the second he was in northern England and southern Scotland. Measures to promote *Romanization in his second winter are stressed by Tacitus. In his third season (79) he advanced to the Tay, leading to (following Cass. Dio) Titus' fifteenth imperatorial acclamation; in the fourth (80) he consolidated along the Forth–Clyde. His fifth season (81) was in the west of Scotland: he drew up his forces facing *Ireland, which he told Tacitus could easily have been conquered. He then tackled the Caledonians, victory narrowly eluding him in the sixth season (82) but being won at a great battle late in the seventh, mons Graupius, probably September 83. He ordered the fleet to circumnavigate Britain, finally proving that it was an island. Recalled, presumably in spring 84, he was denied further appointments because of *Domitian's jealousy, according to Tacitus. See BRITAIN, ROMAN.

Tacitus, *Agricola*, ed. R. M. Ogilvie and I. A. Richmond (1967). A. R. Birley, *The Fasti of Roman Britain* (1981), 73 ff.; W. S. Hanson, *Agricola and the Conquest of the North* (1987), and *ANRW* 2. 33. 3 (1991), 1741 ff.; M. T. Raepsaet-Charlier, ibid. 1807 ff. A. R. Bi.

Iulius Agrippa (1) **I, Marcus** (10 BC–AD 44), called 'Herod' in the Acts of the Apostles but 'Agrippa' on his coins. A grandson of *Herod (1) the Great and eventually ruler of his former kingdom. He lived in Rome from childhood, under the patronage of *Antonia (3) (minor), until the death of the elder Drusus (Drusus *Iulius Caesar (1)) in AD 23. Josephus narrates Agrippa's subsequent attempts to raise funds in Palestine and Italy. He was imprisoned by *Tiberius in 36 for a treasonable remark, but, when his friend *Gaius (1) acceded, appointed *tetrarch of those territories north-east of the Sea of Galilee which were previously ruled by his uncle *Philip (4), and those of Lysanias. In 39 the substantially Jewish areas of *Galilee and Peraea, until then under *Herod (2) Antipas, were added. Agrippa's appearance, when he passed through *Alexandria (1), sparked off the anti-Jewish riots there. Shortly before Gaius' assassination, he dissuaded the emperor from desecrating the Temple. In 41 *Claudius, in whose accession Agrippa had been involved, added *Judaea and *Samaria, to complete his kingdom. But the emperor was later displeased by Agrippa's extension of the city wall in north *Jerusalem and by his inviting client kings to Tiberias. Agrippa's dramatic death in the Caesarea amphitheatre is embroidered in tradition. His respect for Judaism was remembered longer than his benefactions to *Caesarea (2), Sebaste, *Berytus, and *Heliopolis. *Acts of the Apostles makes him responsible for the execution of James brother of John and Peter's imprisonment.

Joseph. *AJ* 18. 143–301, 19. 236–359; *BJ* 2. 178–82; Philon, *Leg.* 261–330; *In Flacc.* 25–40; Acts 12: 1–23. Schürer *History* 1. 442–54; D. R. Schwartz, *Agrippa I: The Last King of Judaea* (1990); A. H. M. Jones, *The Herods of Judaea* (corr. imp. 1967), 184–216.   T. R.

Iulius Agrippa (2) II, Marcus (b. AD 27/8), did not succeed his father *Agrippa I in 44, but lived in Rome. There he supported the Jews before the emperor Claudius against the Samaritans and the procurator Cumanus. In 50 Agrippa was appointed king of Chalcis in the southern Beqa' valley, succeeding to the position of his uncle *Herod (1) the Great. As controller of the Temple, he also received the right to appoint and depose high priests. In 53 his territory was exchanged for the area in the Lebanon and anti-Lebanon region once ruled by *Philip (4) and then by his own father. Nero added parts of *Galilee and of Peraea. Agrippa's coins carry the imperial portrait. He lavished attention on the Temple and had his *Jerusalem palace close by. But in 66 he and his sister *Berenice (4) were expelled from the city by the Jewish leadership, having failed to persuade the Jews to tolerate *Gessius Florus' conduct as procurator. Unable to prevent revolt, Agrippa supplied cavalry and archers to the Romans throughout the war, and accompanied Titus during its latter stages. He was rewarded by an enlargement of his territory. In 75, when Berenice went to live with Titus in Rome, Agrippa received praetorian status there. He supplied *Josephus with information for the *Jewish War* and commended the work on publication. Indications in Josephus that Agrippa was dead before the publication of the *Antiquities* and the *Life* (93/4) are compatible with the epigraphic evidence from his kingdom, and they discredit Photius' statement (*Bibl.* 33) that Agrippa died in 100.

St. *Paul appeared before him.

Joseph. *BJ* 2. 335–421 and throughout; *AJ* 19. 360–3, 20. 104, 135–223; *Vit.* 340–67, etc.. Schürer, *History* 1. 471–83; F. Millar, *The Roman Near East, 31 B.C. to A.D. 337* (1993), 61–79, 91–2; A. H. M. Jones, *The Herods of Judaea* (corr. imp. 1967), 217–61.   T. R.

Iulius Alexander, Tiberius, of an opulent Alexandrian Jewish family, was the son of Alexander the Alabarch, who gilded the Temple gates, and nephew of *Philon (4). A renegade from Judaism, he rose high in the service of Rome. He was *procurator governing *Judaea (c. AD 46–8), when he crucified the two sons

of Judas the Galilean; Cn. *Domitius Corbulo's general staff officer in *Armenia (63), he was soon prefect of Egypt (see PRAEFECTUS). His long edict, published after *Galba's accession, survives (*OGI* 669). During the Jewish–Greek conflict at *Alexandria (1) associated with the Jewish Revolt, Alexander employed the army in the Jewish quarter. His troops took the oath for *Vespasian on 1 July 69, adopted as the *dies imperii* ('accession date'). Close also to *Titus, Alexander became his chief of staff (*praefectus praetorio*) for the end of the Jewish War (*PHib.* 2. 215).

E. G. Turner, *JRS* 1954, 54–64; V. Burr, *Tiberius Julius Alexander* (1955); G. Chalon, *L'Édit de Tiberius Julius Alexander* (1964).   R. S.; T. R.

Iulius Antiochus Epiphanes Philopappus, Gaius, Commagenian prince (see COMMAGENE), *suffect consul AD 109, and Athenian archon (see ARCHONTES) and benefactor; hardly other than 'King' Philopappus of *Plutarch's *Table-Talk* (*Quaest. conv.* 1. 10). Chiefly famous for his lavish mausoleum astride the Museum hill at Athens, where he lived and was a citizen. A descendant of *Seleucus (1) I, he was the grandson of Antiochus IV of Commagene (see ANTIOCHUS (9)).

*PIR*² I 155; D. Kleiner, *The Monument of Philopappos in Athens* (1983).   A. J. S. S.

Iulius Atticus, probably of Gallic origin, wrote, in *Tiberius' time, the first specialized monograph on viticulture (*Columella, *Rust.* 1. 1. 14). He apparently aimed to produce *wine in bulk while cutting costs (ibid. 4. 1–2).

K. D. White, *Roman Farming* (1970); A. Tchernia, *Le Vin de l'Italie romaine* (1986).   M. S. Sp.

Iulius Aurelius Uranius Antoninus, Lucius, head of the priestly house of *Emesa who, following the capture of *Antioch (1) by *Sapor I (AD 253), proclaimed himself Roman emperor and successfully resisted a Persian assault on his city. He apparently disappeared from the scene before *Valerian I arrived to repair the eastern frontier (254). His reign is typical of the way in which threatened communities were driven to self-help in the worst period of the 3rd-cent. 'crisis', but expressed and justified their independence of action in imperial, not nationalistic, terms.

H. R. Baldus, *Uranius Antoninus: Münzprägung und Geschichte* (1971).   J. F. Dr.

Iulius Avitus Alexianus, Gaius, husband of *Iulia Maesa and grandfather of the emperor Elagabalus (M. *Aurelius Antoninus (2)), began an equestrian career in the *tres militiae*, and after a single procuratorship was adlected to the senate by L. *Septimius Severus, his wife's brother-in-law. He commanded a legion and was governor of *Raetia, where he dedicated an altar to the god *Elagabalus (*AE* 1962, 229), and consul. He later accompanied Severus to *Britain as *comes*, was prefect of the *alimenta*, legate (see LEGATI) of *Dalmatia, and proconsul of *Asia under *Caracalla, whom he predeceased (early in AD 217).

Cass. Dio 78; *AE* 1962, 229, and 1979, 450. H. Halfmann, *Chiron* 1982, 217 ff.; A. R. Birley, *The African Emperor Septimius Severus* (1988), 223, no. 45.   A. R. Bi.

Iulius (*RE* 128) **Caesar, Agrippa (Marcus Vipsanius Agrippa Postumus),** third son of M. *Vipsanius Agrippa and *Iulia (3), born in 12 BC after his father's death, was adopted by *Augustus with *Tiberius in AD 4, becoming Agrippa Iulius Caesar. He is agreed to have had a fine physique but, perhaps because he fell foul of Augustus, reports of his personality were unfavourable: *ferocia* is alleged ('intractability' is the mildest translation). In AD 6 Augustus 'abdicated' him, removing him from the Julian family, took over his property, and relegated him to *Surrentum; in 7 the senate exiled him to Planasia. See ISLANDS; RELEGATION; EXILE (ROMAN). Probably a defeat in the struggle for the succession caused his disgrace rather than simple personality defects: the settlement of AD 4 gave more power to Tiberius than Agrippa, his sister *Iulia (4), and their associates could accept. Attempts to rescue him and put him at the head of a military insurrection are alleged. The story of Augustus visiting him on Planasia is generally rejected. He was killed immediately after the death of Augustus in AD 14, it is not clear on whose instructions. A slave called Clemens impersonated him in 16 and was executed.

B. Levick, *Tiberius the Politician* (1972), see index; S. Jameson, *Hist.* 1975, 287 ff.; Syme, *AA*, see index.   G. W. R.; T. J. C.; B. M. L.

Iulius (*RE* 136) **Caesar** (1), **Drusus** (*c*.13 BC–AD 23), only surviving son of the later emperor *Tiberius, by Vipsania. Originally Nero Claudius Drusus, he became a Caesar in AD 4, on Tiberius' adoption by *Augustus. He married *Germanicus' sister *Livia Iulia (Livilla). He succeeded in suppressing the mutiny of the Pannonian legions after Augustus' death in AD 14, was consul in 15, and did well in *Illyricum 17–20, celebrating an ovation. His relations with Germanicus were friendly, despite mischief-makers. Germanicus' death (19) made him Tiberius' sole prospective successor: after his second consulship (21) he received tribunician power (22); his death in the next year opened the succession question. His taste for the games made him popular, though he is reported dissolute and violent. He had quarrelled with *Sejanus, and when Sejanus fell (31) it was alleged that Livilla, who was Sejanus' mistress, had poisoned him. His surviving twin son Tiberius *Iulius Caesar Nero 'Gemellus' was set aside by *Gaius (1) as *princeps iuventutis, then put to death; his last known male descendant (through his daughter Iulia) was *Rubellius Plautus, killed on *Nero's orders in 62.

R. S. Rogers, *Studies in the Reign of Tiberius* (1943), 89 ff.
J. P. B.; B. M. L.

Iulius (*RE* 137) **Caesar** (2), **Drusus** (AD 7–33), second surviving son of *Germanicus and *Vipsania Agrippina (2), married to Aemilia Lepida, was regarded after the death of Drusus *Iulius Caesar (1) in 23 as second only to his elder brother Nero *Iulius Caesar as successor to *Tiberius. He backed *Sejanus' attack on household informers brought about his own denunciation (30); in 33 he died, imprisoned in the palace, allegedly of starvation. An impostor, appearing in the east, attests his popularity.   J. P. B.; B. M. L.

Iulius (*RE* 131) **Caesar** (1), **Gaius,** born 100 BC (Suet. *Iul.* 88. 1), of a *patrician family without social equals, as descendants of *Venus and *Aeneas, but with little recent political success. His father's sister *Iulia (1) married C. *Marius (1), and her cousins L. *Iulius Caesar (1) and C. *Iulius Caesar Strabo Vopiscus profited by his unforeseen success, but Caesar's father never became consul. L. *Cornelius Cinna (1) while in power, gave Caesar his daughter Cornelia in marriage and made him *flamen Dialis* as successor to L. *Cornelius Merula—a post of supreme honour but normally precluding a consulship (no doubt thought unattainable). *Sulla, after his victory, annulled his enemies' measures, including this appointment, but as a fellow patrician spared Caesar's life, even though he refused to divorce Cornelia and voluntarily resign his priesthood.

Most of the next decade Caesar spent in Asia, studying and winning military distinction, including a victory over an advance force of *Mithradates VI and a *corona civica* (the Roman Victoria

Cross); but two prosecutions of ex-Sullani (Cn. *Cornelius Dolabella (1) and C. *Antonius), although unsuccessful, established his fame as an orator. In 73 he was co-opted a *pontifex, largely through family connections, and returned to Rome. Elected *tribunus militum*, he supported amnesty for the associates of M. *Aemilius Lepidus (2). As quaestor 69, before going to his province of Further Spain, he lost both his aunt Iulia and his wife. He conducted their funerals in the grand aristocratic manner (see NOBILITAS), stressing his aunt's (and thus partly his own) descent from kings and gods (Suet. *Iul.* 6. 1) and, for the first time since Sulla, displaying Marius' *imago* (see IMAGINES) and distinctions in public. (He no doubt similarly displayed Cinna's at Cornelia's funeral.) On his return from Spain he found the Latin colonies beyond the Po (*Padus) vigorously demanding Roman citizenship and supported their agitation, but did nothing to further their cause in Rome. He supported the laws of A. *Gabinius (2) and C. *Manilius, conferring extraordinary commands on *Pompey (clearly a most useful patron), and he married Pompeia, a granddaughter of Sulla. With Pompey overseas, he courted another powerful ex-Sullan, M. *Licinius Crassus (1), Pompey's enemy, joining him in various political schemes in return for financial support, which enabled Caesar to spend large sums as curator of the *via Appia and as aedile (65). In 64, in charge of the murder court, he resumed his vendetta against Sulla by offering to receive prosecutions of men who had killed citizens in Sulla's proscription.

In 63 Q. *Caecilius Metellus Pius' death left the chief pontificate vacant, a post normally held by eminent ex-consuls. Although two (P. *Servilius Isauricus, to whom Caesar was bound in loyalty as to his old commander in Cilicia, and Q. *Lutatius Catulus (2)) sought the office, Caesar announced his candidacy and through lavish bribery won the election. This and his election to a *praetorship for 62 established him as a man of power and importance. He supported L. *Sergius Catilina, who advocated a welcome cancellation of debts, but covered his tracks when Catiline turned to conspiracy. The consul *Cicero, who to the end of his days was convinced of Caesar's involvement, had to proclaim his innocence. In his prosecution of C. *Rabirius (1) he left the legality of the so-called *senatus consultum ultimum* in doubt, and when Cicero wanted the death penalty under that decree for the conspirators betrayed by the Allobrogan envoys (see ALLOBROGES), Caesar persuaded most senators to vote against it, until a speech by M. *Porcius Cato (2) changed their minds.

As praetor he joined the tribune Q. *Caecilius Metellus Nepos in agitating for the recall of Pompey against Catiline's forces. Suspended from office, he demonstratively submitted, and the senate, eager to avoid alienating him, reinstated and thanked him. In December, when Pompeia was *ex officio* in charge of the rites of the *Bona Dea, from which men were strictly excluded, P. *Clodius Pulcher gained access disguised as a woman—it was said, in order to approach Pompeia in her husband's absence—and was ejected. Caesar, while asserting the innocence of Clodius (a man congenial to him and worth cultivating) and of Pompeia, divorced her, proclaiming that his household must be free even from suspicion. With his consulship approaching, he could now seek a more advantageous marriage.

But first he had to go to his province of Further Spain. His creditors applied for an injunction to stop him from leaving, and he was saved from this unprecedented indignity by Crassus' standing surety for part of his debts: his provincial spoils would cover the rest. He now 'had to make a bigger profit in one year than *Verres had in three' (Will, see bibliog. below) and, largely neglecting his routine duties, he concentrated on attacking independent tribes. The booty enabled him to clear his debts and pay large sums into the treasury, all without incurring a risk of prosecution. About mid-60 he returned to Rome, was voted a *triumph by a co-operative senate, and prepared to claim his consulship. There was a technical obstacle: to announce his candidacy for the consulship he had to enter Rome long before the triumph could be arranged, but that would forfeit his *imperium and right to triumph. The senate was ready to give him a dispensation, but his enemy Cato, although only an ex-tribune, arranged to be asked to speak and talked the proposal out. Caesar decided to put power before glory and entered the city.

He now could not afford to lose, so he needed allies and a massive infusion of money. A brilliant stroke secured both. In his absence Pompey and Crassus had failed—partly because each had opposed the other—to obtain what they respectively wanted from the senate: ratification of Pompey's eastern settlement and land for his veterans, and a remission of part of the price offered for the tithe of Asia by the *publicani. Caesar, on good terms with both, persuaded them to support his candidacy: he promised to give each what he wanted without harm to the other, provided they refrained from mutual opposition. Pompey now persuaded his wealthy friend L. *Lucceius to join Caesar in his canvass: in return for paying the expenses for bribery (no doubt with Crassus' help), he could expect to succeed through Caesar's popularity. But Caesar's enemies, led by the upright Cato, collected a huge bribery fund for Cato's son-in-law M. *Calpurnius Bibulus, who secured second place after Caesar.

As consul Caesar appealed to the senate for co-operation in formulating the laws to satisfy his allies. Frustrated by his enemies, he passed them in the assembly by open violence, aided by friendly tribunes (see VATINIUS, P.). Bibulus withdrew to his house, announcing that he was stopping all future meetings of the assemblies by watching the sky for omens. This unprecedented step, of doubtful legality, was ignored by Caesar, who satisfied Pompey and Crassus and went on to pass further legislation, i.a. on *repetundae and on the publication of senate debates. Pompey and Crassus, satisfied (especially) with his assuming the onus for his methods, now joined him in an open alliance (sometimes erroneously called the 'First Triumvirate'). Pompey married *Iulia (2) and Caesar married *Calpurnia (1), whose father, L. *Calpurnius Piso Caesoninus, was made consul 58, with Pompey's aide Gabinius as colleague. For further insurance, Clodius was allowed to become a plebeian and tribune 58. Caesar's reward was a law of Vatinius, giving him Illyricum and Cisalpine Gaul for five years. The senate obligingly added Transalpine Gaul. Early in 58 attempts to prosecute Caesar were averted, and moderates in the senate attempted conciliation by offering to have his legislation re-enacted in proper form. But Caesar refused, since this would admit guilt and impair his dignitas. The breach between him and the senate majority thus became irreparable.

A movement by the *Helvetii gave him an unforeseen chance of starting a major war, which after nearly a decade and many vicissitudes led to the conquest of the whole of Gaul (see GALLIC WARS). It was in Gaul that he acquired the taste and the resources for monarchy and trained the legions that could 'storm the heavens' (BHisp. 42. 7). Young Roman aristocrats flocked to him to make their fortunes, vast sums (sometimes made palatable as loans) flowed into the pockets of upper-class Romans and, as gifts, to cities and princes, to support Caesar's ambitions. The depleted treasury received none of the profits and was forced to pay for his legions. In his triumphs of 46 (see below) he displayed 63,000 talents of silver and spent about 20,000 of his own money (together enough to create the fortunes of 5,000 *equites), much of it booty from Gaul. Plutarch, on the basis of Caesar's figures, reports that a million Gauls were killed and another million enslaved. Requisitions of food and punitive devastations completed human, economic, and ecological disaster probably unequalled until the conquest of the Americas.

In Rome Caesar's position remained secure until 56, when his bitter enemy L. *Domitius Ahenobarbus (1), confident of becoming consul 55, promised to recall and prosecute him, and Cicero, back from exile, hoped to detach Pompey from him. Crassus informed him of what was going on, and they summoned Pompey to *Luca, where he was persuaded to renew the compact. Pompey and Crassus became consuls 55, receiving Spain and Syria respectively for five years, while Caesar's command was renewed for five years in Gaul; Pompey was to stay near Rome to look after their interests, governing Spain through legati. But the alliance soon disintegrated. Iulia died (54) and Crassus, attacking *Parthia, was killed at *Carrhae (53). In 52 Pompey married a daughter of Caesar's enemy Q. *Caecilius Metellus Pius Scipio and made him his colleague as consul. Caesar now secured legal authorization to stand for a consulship in absence in 49; but the legality of this became doubtful, and his claim that it included the right to retain imperium (hence immunity from prosecution) was denied by his enemies. (The legal position is obscured by partisan distortion.) Pompey was gradually (perhaps reluctantly) forced to co-operate with them, to avoid a consulship by Caesar in 48, which would have left him irreversibly at Caesar's mercy. In 49 Caesar invaded Italy and started a civil war, nominally to defend the rights of tribunes who had been forced to flee to him for protection, but in fact, as he later admitted (Suet. Iul. 30. 4), to escape conviction and exile.

He rapidly overran Italy, where there were no reliable veteran legions to oppose him. As he moved down the peninsula, he kept making specious peace offers, retailed with considerable distortion in book 1 of his Civil War. Ahenobarbus was forced to surrender at Corfinium, and Pompey, knowing that Italy was untenable, to the chagrin of his aristocratic supporters crossed to Greece, hoping to strangle Italy by encirclement. Caesar broke it by defeating Pompey's legati in a brilliant campaign in Spain and then taking *Massalia. In 48 he crossed to Greece, though Pompey controlled the seas, and besieged him at *Dyrrhachium. A tactical defeat there turned into de facto strategic victory when Pompey withdrew to Thessaly, where both sides received reinforcements. Persuaded, against his better judgement, to offer battle at *Pharsalus, Pompey was decisively defeated, escaped to Egypt and was killed. Caesar, arriving there in pursuit, intervened in a domestic conflict over the kingship and was cut off for months in Alexandria, until extricated by troops from Asia Minor and a Jewish force under *Antipater (6). He spent three more months in Egypt, chiefly with *Cleopatra VII, whom he established on the throne and who after his departure bore a son whom she named *Ptolemy (1) Caesar. Then, moving rapidly through Syria and Asia Minor, he reorganized the eastern provinces, easily defeated *Pharnaces II at Zela, and in September 47 returned to Italy. There he had to settle an army mutiny and serious social unrest, fanned during his absence by M. *Caelius Rufus and T. *Annius Milo and after their death by P. *Cornelius Dolabella (1).

Meanwhile the republican forces had had time to entrench

themselves in Africa, where Metellus Scipio assumed command, aided by *Juba (1) I. Caesar landed in December. After an inauspicious beginning he gained the support of *Bocchus II and P. *Sittius and, deliberately inviting blockade at Thapsus, won a decisive victory that led to the death of most of the republican leaders (including Scipio and Cato). On his return he was voted unprecedented honours and celebrated four splendid triumphs (20 September–1 October 46), nominally over foreign enemies, to mark the end of the wars and the beginning of reconstruction. But Cn. *Pompeius Magnus (2), soon joined by his brother Sextus *Pompeius and T. *Labienus (1), consul for the second time, raised thirteen legions in Spain and secured much native support. In November Caesar hurriedly left Rome to meet the threat. The Pompeians were forced to offer battle at Munda (near *Urso) and were annihilated with the loss of 30,000 men in Caesar's hardest-fought battle. After reorganizing Spain, with massive *colonization, he returned to Rome and celebrated a triumph over 'Spain'.

Caesar had been *dictator (briefly), nominally for holding elections, in 49, consul for the second time 48, and dictator for the second time after Pharsalus; he was consul for the third time and *curator morum* in 46 and dictator for the third time (designated for ten years ahead, we are told: Cass. Dio 43. 14. 3) after Thapsus; he held his fourth, sole, consulship for nine months and his fourth dictatorship in 45, and was consul for the fifth time and (from about February) *dictator perpetuo* (see RRC 480/6 ff.) in 44. The specification of his dictatorships after the first is lost in the *fasti*, but at least the third and fourth were probably, like Sulla's, *rei publicae constituendae* ('for settling the republic'). Apart from epigraphic evidence (see Broughton, MRR 3. 108), this is suggested by Cicero's references and by the fact that the work of reform began after Thapsus. The specification (if any) of the perpetual dictatorship is beyond conjecture. In addition to introducing the Julian calendar (see CALENDAR, ROMAN), his most lasting achievement, he considerably increased the numbers of senators, priests, and magistrates, for the first time since *c*.500 created new patrician families, founded numerous colonies, especially for veterans and the city *plebs*, and passed various administrative reforms. His great-nephew Octavian, adopted by Caesar in his testament in 45, was made a pontifex aged about 16 and, although he had no military experience, was designated *magister equitum* in 44, aged 18. Caesar, although he adopted the dress and ornaments of the old Roman kings, refused the invidious title of *rex* (king), but, thinking gods superior to kings (Suet. *Iul.* 6. 1), aimed at deification (see RULER-CULT), which after gradual approaches he finally achieved shortly before his death (Cic. *Phil.* 2. 110: M. *Antonius (2) was designated his *flamen*; see FLAMINES). It was the culmination of increasingly unprecedented honours voted by the senate (Cass. Dio lists them at various points), perhaps in part to see how far he would go, and he accepted most of them.

He had no plans for basic social, economic, or constitutional reforms, except to graft his divine and hereditary rule onto the republic. The abyss this opened between him and his fellow *nobiles* made him uncomfortable, and he planned to escape from Rome to wage a major Parthian war. As all remembered the disruption caused by his temporary absences during the Civil Wars, the prospect of being ruled by an absent divine monarch for years ahead proved intolerable even to his friends. He was assassinated in Pompey's theatre, in a widespread conspiracy hastily stitched together to anticipate his departure, on 15 March 44.

Caesar was a distinguished orator in the 'Attic' manner, believing in '*analogy' (on which he wrote a treatise; see ANALOGIA,

DE) and in the use of ordinary words (Gell. *NA* 1. 10. 4). His speeches, at least some of which were published, and his pamphlet attacking Cato's memory, are lost. Seven books on the Gallic War (an eighth was added by A. *Hirtius) and three on the Civil War survive, written to provide raw material for history and ensure that his point of view would prevail with posterity. Distortion at various points in the *Civil War* is demonstrated by evidence surviving in Cicero's correspondence. For praise of Caesar's style, see Cic. *Brut.* 262 (strongly tinged by flattery).

The only contemporary literary sources apart from his own works that survive are Cicero and *Sallust's *Catiline*. Important inscriptions will be found in *ILLRP* and coins in *RRC*. For the contemporary picture of Caesar the basic study is by H. Strasburger: an expanded edition is reprinted in his *Studien zur Alten Geschichte*, ed. Schmitthenner and Zoepffel (1982), 343 ff. All later historians of the republic naturally deal with Caesar. *Appian's *Civil Wars* and *Cassius Dio's *History*, largely based on contemporary sources not clearly identifiable, are the most important. Plutarch's *Caesar* and references in his Lives of Caesar's contemporaries show wide reading of both friendly and hostile sources. *Suetonius (*Divus Iulius*: the first of his biographies of the first twelve emperors) draws on archival as well as literary material.

Caesar's name was used as the title of emperors and princes from *Augustus down to the 20th cent. (It supplied, *i.a.*, the Russian 'Tsar' and the German 'Kaiser'.) Criticism of him, as a symbol of contemporary rulers, was discouraged throughout European history by monarchs and their censors. In the 19th cent., Th. Mommsen's passionate portrait of Caesar conceived under the influence of the failure of German liberal aspirations in 1848, saw him as the liberator of Rome from oppression by the aristocracy (identified with the Prussian *Junker*). His long eulogy, in vol. 3 of his *Römische Geschichte*, concludes: 'The secret [of Caesar's character] lies in its perfection.' His history stops before the assassination, which he could not bear to relate. Mommsen's Caesar could not want titular honours as king and god. That view was challenged by Eduard Meyer (*Caesars Monarchie und das Prinzipat des Pompeius* (1918)), who, contrasting Caesar with Pompey, whom he regards as foreshadowing Augustus' 'constitutional monarchy', sees Caesar—improbably, in view of the contemporary state of Ptolemaic Egypt—as introducing a Ptolemaic divine monarchy (see PTOLEMY (1); EGYPT, Ptolemaic) over a 'world empire' no longer centred in Rome. Developed by J. Carcopino in France, this was vigorously rejected by the British tradition (e.g. Adcock in the *CAH* and Syme in *Rom. Rev.*), which tended to see Caesar as an English gentleman. Assessments of all studies of Caesar both general and in detail, from about 1914 to 1974, will be found in H. Gesche's excellent volume *Caesar* in the series Erträge der Forschung (1976). The most comprehensive biography, listing nearly all the sources and many modern views, is by M. Gelzer (translated from the corrected 6th edn. as *Caesar: Politician and Statesman* (1968)). The most ambitious recent treatment is C. Meier's romantic German biography (see *Gnomon* 1990, 22 ff.); against this, see W. Will, *Julius Caesar: Eine Bilanz* (1992), with recent biblg., to which add E. Wistrand, *Caesar and Contemporary Society* (1979).   E. B.

Iulius (*RE* 134) **Caesar** (2), **Gaius,** eldest son of *Agrippa and *Iulia (3), was born in 20 BC and adopted by *Augustus in 17. Augustus evidently hoped that he or his brother L. *Iulius Caesar (4) would succeed him, and the favour he showed them probably caused *Tiberius' retirement in 6. In 5, when Gaius assumed the *toga virilis*, he was designated consul for AD 1, admitted to the senate, and saluted by the *equites as *princeps iuventutis*. From now on he was virtually heir apparent. In 1 BC he married *Livia Iulia and was sent with proconsular authority to the east. In AD 2 he had a conference with the Parthian king on the Euphrates and appointed a Roman nominee king of Armenia. This led to a revolt, which Gaius suppressed. Seriously wounded at the siege of Artagira, he died eighteen months later in *Lycia on his way back to Italy (21 February AD 4) greatly to Augustus' sorrow and dismay. He and Lucius were honoured in the following year by the naming after them of ten electoral centuries (see TABULA HEBANA).

Syme, *Rom. Rev.*, see index; M. L. Paladini, *Nuova rivista storica* 1957, 1 ff.; P. Sattler, *Studien aus dem Gebiet der alten Geschichte* (1962), 1 ff.; P. Zanker, *The Power of Images in the Age of Augustus* (1988), esp. 215–23.

G. W. R.; T. J. C.; E. B.

Iulius (*RE* 138) **Caesar, Germanicus** (before adoption Nero Claudius Drusus Germanicus), elder son of Nero *Claudius Drusus and *Antonia (3), was born 24 May 15 or 16 BC and adopted in AD 4 by his uncle *Tiberius. As Tiberius was immediately adopted by *Augustus, Germanicus became a member of the Julian *gens in the direct line of succession; and his career was accelerated by special dispensations. He served under Tiberius in Pannonia (7–9), and Germany (11). In 12 he was consul, and in 13, as commander-in-chief in Gaul and Germany, he won his first salutation as *imperator* (EJ 368) in a campaign against the Germans, clearing them out of Gaul and re-establishing order there. By now he was a popular figure, held like his father to entertain 'republican' sentiments, and his affability contrasted with Tiberius' dour reserve. But, though by no means incapable, he was over-emotional, and his judgement was unsteady. When, on the death of Augustus, the lower Rhine legions mutinied, his loyalty was proof against the (perhaps malicious) suggestion that he should supplant Tiberius, but his handling of the situation lacked firmness: he resorted to theatrical appeals and committed the emperor to accepting the mutineers' demands. On dynastic matters the two were at one, but their political style was different, and there was soon a marked difference of view as to how Germany (see GERMANIA) should be handled, Tiberius adhering to the precept of the dying Augustus that rejected immediate territorial advance.

In the autumn of 14 Germanicus led the repentant legions briefly against the *Marsi. But he was eager to emulate his father and reconquer parts of Germany lost after the defeat of P. *Quinctilius Varus. He campaigned in the spring of 15 against the *Chatti, *Cherusci, and Marsi, and rescued the pro-Roman Cheruscan Segestes from *Arminius. In the summer he attacked the *Bructeri, reached the saltus *Teutoburgiensis, paid the last honours to Varus, and recovered legionary standards: after an indecisive battle with the Cherusci under Arminius, his forces suffered heavy losses on their way back. For the main campaign of 16 a great fleet was prepared and the troops were transported via his father's canal and the lakes of Holland to the Ems, whence they proceeded to the Weser and defeated Arminius in two battles at Idistaviso (near Minden) and somewhat to the north; the fleet suffered considerable damage from a storm on its homeward journey.

Although Germanicus claimed that one more campaign would bring the Germans to their knees, Tiberius judged that results did not justify the drain on Roman resources, and recalled him to a *triumph (26 May 17) and a command to reorder the 'overseas' provinces as proconsul with *maius* *imperium* (subordinate to that of Tiberius). Germanicus entered on his second consulship (18) at *Nicopolis (3), crowned Zeno, son of *Polemon (1), king of Armenia (so winning an *ovatio*), and reduced *Cappadocia and *Commagene to provincial status. In 19 he offended Tiberius by entering Egypt, which Augustus had barred to senators without permission, and by the informal dress he wore there; his reception was tumultuous (EJ 320(b), 379; Smallwood, *Docs. . . . Gaius* 370, lines 24–7). On his return to Syria

the enmity between him and Cn. *Calpurnius Piso (3), whom Tiberius had appointed governor as a check on Germanicus, led to his ordering Piso to leave the province. He fell mysteriously ill, and on 10 October died near *Antioch (1), convinced that Piso had poisoned him. His death—compared by some with that of *Alexander (3) the Great—provoked widespread demonstrations of grief and in Rome suspicion and resentment; many honours were paid to his memory (see TABULA HEBANA); his ashes were deposited in the mausoleum of Augustus at Rome. His reputation remained as an overwhelming political advantage to his brother and descendants.

Germanicus married *Agrippina the Elder, the daughter of *Agrippa and *Iulia (3). She bore him nine children, among whom were Nero *Iulius Caesar (d. 31), Drusus *Iulius Caesar (2) (d. 33), *Gaius (1) (later emperor), *Agrippina the Younger, *Iulia Drusilla, and *Iulia (5). Eloquent and studious, he wrote comedies in Greek (all lost) and Greek and Latin epigrams; he also translated into Latin the *Phaenomena* of *Aratus (1), bringing it up to date and adding further matter on the planets and the weather.

K. Christ, *Drusus und Germanicus* (1956); E. Koestermann, *Hist.* 1957, 429 ff., and 1958, 332 ff.; W. Akveld, *Germanicus* (1961); G. Sumner, *Latomus* 1967, 413 ff.; D. Timpe, *Der Triumph des Germanicus: Untersuchungen zu den Feldzügen der Jahre 14–16 in Germanien* (1968); J. González, *ZPE* 55 (1984), 55 ff. (*tabula Siarensis*); B. Gallotta, *Germanico* (1987); W. Eck and others, *SC de Cn. Pisone patre* (forthcoming). Compositions: Schanz–Hosius 2. 437 ff. Iconography: V. Poulsen, *Claudische Prinzen* (1960); H. Jucker, *JDAI* 1977, 211 ff. (bibliog.).

A. M.; T. J. C.; B. M. L.

Iulius (*RE* 142) **Caesar** (1), **Lucius**, brother of C. *Iulius Caesar Strabo Vopiscus (below) and half-brother of Q. *Lutatius Catulus (1), probably governed *Macedonia *c.*94 BC, was *consul 90 and in charge of the southern front in the *Social War (3), winning a major battle against *Papius Mutilus after several defeats. He passed the basic law offering Roman *citizenship to Italian communities that accepted it (Cic. *Balb.* 21) and, as censor 89 with P. *Licinius Crassus (1), intended to start enrolling them, but could not compile a citizen register. With his brother he opposed C. *Marius (1), whom he had previously supported, over the Mithradatic command (see MITHRADATES VI), and was killed after Marius' capture of Rome (87/6). His daughter married M. *Antonius (Creticus), becoming the mother of M. *Antonius (2).

E. B.

Iulius (*RE* 143) **Caesar** (2), **Lucius**, son of (1) and father of (3), hence uncle of M. *Antonius (2). *Quaestor in Asia 77 BC, he was *consul 64 and *censor, with C. *Scribonius Curio (1), in 61. In 63 he and C. *Iulius Caesar (1) were appointed *duoviri* to try C. *Rabirius (1) for *perduellio*. He served under Caesar in Gaul, but took no part in the Civil War. As *praefectus urbi*, illegally appointed by Antonius, he was unable to check tribunician disturbances. After Caesar's death he opposed Antonius and was proscribed, but saved by the intercession of his sister Iulia, Antonius' mother. He wrote books on augural law.

T. J. C.; E. B.

Iulius (*RE* 144) **Caesar** (3), **Lucius,** son of (2), played a part, obscure in detail, in negotiations between *Caesar and *Pompey, under whom he was serving, in 49 BC. After failing to prevent the crossing of C. *Scribonius Curio (2) to Africa, he served there under M. *Porcius Cato (2), was pardoned after Cato's death, but mysteriously killed soon after.

On the negotiations see D. R. Shackleton Bailey, *JRS* 1960, 88 ff. For a stemma of the Caesares of the republic (unreliable for the last generation), see G. V. Sumner, *Phoenix* 1971, 264.

E. B.

Iulius Caesar, Lucius

Iulius (*RE* 145) **Caesar (4), Lucius,** second son of *Agrippa and *Iulia (3), was born in 17 BC and at once adopted, with his elder brother Gaius *Iulius Caesar (2), by *Augustus. In 2 BC, when he assumed the *toga virilis, he received the honours previously conferred on Gaius. He died at *Massalia, on his way to Spain, on 20 August AD 2.

> Syme, *Rom. Rev.*, see index; P. Zanker, *The Power of Images in the Age of Augustus* (1987), esp. 215–23.   G. W. R.; E. B.

Iulius (*RE* 146) **Caesar, Nero,** eldest of the three surviving sons of *Germanicus and *Vipsania Agrippina (2), was, after the death of *Tiberius' son Drusus *Iulius Caesar (1) in AD 23, at the age of 17 next in succession to the Principate, along with his younger brother Drusus *Iulius Caesar (2). Twice commended to the senate by Tiberius, he held the quaestorship, probably in 26, but in 29 Tiberius, believing the accusations of *Sejanus against him and his mother, denounced him in a dispatch to the senate. He was deported to Pontia and put to death there in 31.

> B. Levick, *Tiberius the Politician* (1976), see index.   J. P. B.; B. M. L.

Iulius (*RE* 156) **Caesar Nero 'Gemellus', Tiberius,** one of the twin sons born in AD 19 to Drusus *Iulius Caesar (1), son of Tiberius, and Livilla (*Livia Iulia). Tiberius made him heir to his property jointly with *Gaius (1) (Caligula). The senate annulled the will and Gaius adopted Tiberius Gemellus and allowed him to be hailed as *princeps iuventutis. He was put to death, however, during the first year of Gaius' principate.

> B. Levick, *Tiberius the Politician* (1976), and A. Barrett, *Caligula: The Corruption of Power* (1990), see indexes.   J. P. B.; B. M. L.

Iulius (*RE* 135) **Caesar Strabo Vopiscus, Gaius,** brother of Lucius *Iulius Caesar (1) and half-brother of Q. *Lutatius Catulus (1), supported C. *Marius (1), who married *Iulia (1), and was land commissioner under a law of L. *Appuleius Saturninus passed for Marius. He was aedile 90 BC and, without having been praetor, wanted a special dispensation to stand for the consulship of 88, hoping for the Mithradatic command (see MITHRADATES VI). Opposed by Marius and by P. *Sulpicius Rufus, he made them into allies. He was killed after Marius' capture of Rome (87/6). Famous as an orator and wit, he is the main speaker on wit and humour in Cicero's *De oratore*. He was a model for *Caesar.

> E. B.

Iulius (*RE* 306) **Callistus, Gaius,** an influential *freedman of the emperor *Gaius (1), who took part in the conspiracy leading to Gaius' murder in AD 41. Under *Claudius, he increased his wealth and power in the post of *a libellis* ('in charge of petitions'). Between 44 and 48 the medical writer *Scribonius Largus thanked him for bringing his work to Claudius' attention. He prudently refused help to *Narcissus (2) in accomplishing the downfall of *Valeria Messalina, but later was unsuccessful in championing the claims of *Lollia Paulina to be Claudius' (fourth) wife. He died c.52.   J. P. B.; M. T. G.

Iulius (*RE* 167) **Canus** or **Kanus,** a Stoic martyr (see STOICISM), executed by *Gaius (1) after a long dispute with him. The younger Seneca (L. *Annaeus Seneca (2)) (*Tranq.* 14. 4–10) celebrates his calm courage and his determination to observe his *soul as it left the body and report his findings (see also Plut. *Mor.* fr. 211 Sandbach (Loeb edn., vol. 15)).   M. T. G.

Iulius Celsus Polemaeanus, Tiberius See LIBRARIES.

Iulius (*RE* 184) **Cerialis,** poet and friend of *Martial (10. 48, 11. 52) and *Arruntius Stella, author of a *Gigantomachy* and of *Georgics*

on the model of *Virgil. The grandiose epic theme on the one hand, and the imitation of Virgil on the other, are both typically Flavian features. It has been suggested that he is identical with the Kerealios who is the author of the Greek epigrams *Anth. Pal.* 11. 129 and 144, and with the addressee of Pliny, *Ep.* 4. 21 (and 2. 19 ?).

> *PIR*[2] I 261.   M. Ci.

Iulius (*RE* 186) **Civilis, Gaius,** a Batavian prince (see BATAVI) and Roman citizen disaffected because of his treatment by *Nero, was suborned by M. *Antonius Primus to disrupt the despatch of reinforcements to the Vitellians (see VITELLIUS, A.) in Italy. By pretending to support *Vespasian he concealed his plans for a nationalist revolt. Helped by unconquered German tribes and eight cohorts of Batavians serving in the army, he unsuccessfully attacked the legionary camp at *Vetera (Xanten). Nevertheless in AD 69–70, Gallic tribes, especially the *Treviri and Lingones, offered support, and the depleted legionary garrisons including Vetera were forced to surrender, the men at Novaesium (Neuss) taking an oath to the 'Gallic empire'. Q. *Petillius Cerialis, despatched in 70 to suppress the rebellion, defeated Civilis at Rigodulum and occupied Trier (*Augusta Treverorum). Despite some minor successes, Civilis suffered another defeat near Vetera and was forced to surrender, though his ultimate fate is unknown.

> P. A. Brunt, *Latomus* 1960, 494 (= *RIT* (1990), 33).   J. B. C.

Iulius (*RE* 188) **Classicianus Alpinus, Gaius,** perhaps originated from the *Treveri. As *procurator of *Britain (AD 61) he favoured a policy of conciliation, and begged Nero to recall the harsher C. *Suetonius Paulinus. His tombstone was found in London (*AE* 1936, 3; *RIB* 12).

> Syme, *Tacitus* 456; Frere, *Britannia*[3] 74.   A. M.; M. T. G.

Iulius (*RE* 189), **Classicus,** from Trier (*Augusta Treverorum), belonged to a wealthy family which boasted regal ancestry. He was a Roman citizen, commanding a cavalry *ala of his own tribe, but in AD 70 defected to the rebel C. *Iulius Civilis and attempted to rouse the Gallic tribes. He procured the murder of the Roman commander C. *Dillius Vocula and with his associates Iulius Tutor, also from Trier, and the Lingonian, Iulius Sabinus, forced the Roman soldiers on the Rhine to swear loyalty to a 'Gallic empire'. Remaining loyal to Civilis, he fought resolutely and vigorously against the Roman counter-offensive. His fate is unknown.   J. B. C.

Iulius (*RE* 196) **Cornutus Tertullus, Gaius,** from *Attaleia in Pamphylia. Already a senator, he was promoted to praetorian rank by *Vespasian (AD 73/4), but in the next 24 years held only two posts, as legate in *Crete and *Cyrene and proconsul of Narbonensis (see PRO CONSULE; GAUL (TRANSALPINE)). He was a friend of *Pliny (2) the Younger, with whom he held the prefecture of the public treasury (98–100) and a suffect consulship (100) although he was at least twenty years older. He was the guardian of the daughter of the younger Helvidius Priscus (see HELVIDIUS PRISCUS). Pliny spoke of him as a man of exceptional merit and integrity, an exemplar of antique virtues, and far removed from ambitious feelings (*Ep.* 5. 14). Notably, he held no military posts in his career, but proceeded to be curator of the *via Aemilia (c.105), commissioner for the census in *Aquitania (c.109–10), legate (see LEGATI) with propraetorian power of *Pontus-*Bithynia (c.112–14/115) in succession to Pliny, and proconsul of Africa (probably in 116–17; see AFRICA, ROMAN). The retardation of his career under *Domitian may indicate his own lack of interest in advancement, for political or personal reasons, rather than imperial doubts about his reliability or competence.

ILS 1024; S. Jameson, *JRS* 1965, 54; W. Eck, *Senatoren von Vespasian bis Hadrian* (1970), 182; *Chiron* 1983, 147; H. Halfmann, *Die Senatoren aus dem östlichen Teil des Imperium Romanum* (1979), 117.   J. B. C.

Iulius (*RE* 197) **Cottius, Marcus,** son of an enfranchised native king, Donnus, offered no opposition to *Augustus' pacification of the Alpine region (see ALPS) and continued ruling a number of native tribes as *praefectus civitatium* (ILS 94 = EJ 166, cf. Plin. *HN* 3. 138). He erected an arch in honour of Augustus at Segusio (Susa) in 7–6 BC and improved the road over the Mt. Genèvre (Amm. Marc. 15. 10. 2). The territory, annexed by *Nero after the death of his homonymous son, is still known as the Cottian Alps.

D. Braund, *Rome and the Friendly King* (1984), see index.
                                                      R. S.; B. M. L.

Iulius Eurycles, Gaius, son of Lachares of *Sparta, who was executed by Antony (M. *Antonius (2)) for *piracy, fought at *Actium on the side of *Octavian, who rewarded him with the Roman *citizenship and allowed him to become ruler of Sparta. He exercised a sort of tyranny, and his influence extended over the Eleutherolaconian towns (see LACONIA) and elsewhere. *Cythera, which *Augustus handed over to Sparta in 21, became his personal possession. Towards 7 BC he visited the court of *Herod (1) and *Archelaus (5), making mischief at the former; on his return to Greece he was the cause of widespread disturbances which led to his being accused twice before Augustus and banished, perhaps before 2 BC. He seems to have died soon after this. Under the more discreet rule of his son Laco his memory was rehabilitated; a Trajanic descendant was the first Spartan senator.

PIR² I 301; P. Cartledge and A. Spawforth, *Hellenistic and Roman Sparta* (1989), ch. 7.   A. M.; T. J. C.; A. J. S. S.

Iulius Florus See IULIUS SACROVIR.

Iulius (*RE* 243) **Frontinus, Sextus,** perhaps from southern Gaul, served as urban *praetor in AD 70 and then assisted in suppressing the revolt of *Iulius Civilis, receiving the surrender of 70,000 Lingones. Consul in 72 or 73, he served as governor of Britain (73/4–77) where he crushed the *Silures in south Wales, establishing a fortress for Legio II Augusta (see LEGION) at Caerleon (*Isca (2)), and then attacked the Ordovices. He may have accompanied *Domitian during his German campaign in 82/3, was proconsul of Asia in 86, and was subsequently appointed by *Nerva in 97 as *curator aquarum* (superintendent of aqueducts). He held his second, *suffect, consulship in 98, and his third, ordinary, consulship in 100, both times with *Trajan. Pliny described him as one of the two most distinguished men of his day (*Ep.* 5. 1). He died in 103/4.

Works Frontinus wrote in an uncluttered, direct style about several technical subjects: the history, administration, and maintenance of the *aqueducts of Rome (*De aquis urbis Romae*); he cites engineers' reports, official documents, plans, and senatorial decrees, with details of quantity, supply, and abuses of the system. The book is a source of the highest value for the study of the working of the Roman water-supply, and the history and administration of the city of Rome in general. It combines a rhetorical pride in the Roman achievement in this field with a willingness to list very technical statistics. In the *Strategemata* Frontinus discusses techniques of military command, using stratagems drawn mainly from past commanders, though including several recent examples, particularly from Domitian's campaigns in Germany;

the work is divided into three books by categories: before battle, during and after battle, sieges; a fourth book contains maxims on the art of generalship. Doubts about its authenticity are probably unjustified. Frontinus claims to provide practical guidance for contemporary commanders, and the *Strategemata* may have served as a textbook in a society with no formal means of training men for public office. Another treatise on Greek and Roman military science is now lost. Frontinus was probably the author of several works on land-surveying, partly preserved in the *Corpus Agrimensorum* (see GROMATICI), covering categories of land, land measurement and division, boundary marking, and types of dispute.

CAREER *PIR²* I 322; A. R. Birley, *The Fasti of Roman Britain* (1981), 69.

TEXTS *Aqueducts*: P. Grimal, *Les Aqueducs de la ville de Rome* (Budé, 1944). *Stratagems* and *Aqueducts*: C. E. Bennet and M. B. McElwain (Loeb, 1925); authenticity of fourth book, G. Bendz, *Die Echtheitsfrage des vierten Buches der frontinschen Strategemata* (1938). Surveying: C. Thulin, *Corpus Agrimensorum Romanorum* 1/1 (1913). General: J. Costas Rodríguez, *Frontini Index* (1985).

STUDIES Water supply: H. Evans, *Water Distribution in Ancient Rome* (1994); A. T. Hodge, *Roman Aqueducts and Water Supply* (1992). *Stratagems*: B. Campbell, *JRS* 1987, 13. Surveying: O. A. W. Dilke, *The Roman Land Surveyors* (1971).   J. B. C., N. P.

Iulius (*RE* 254) **Gabinianus, Sextus,** taught rhetoric in Gaul c. AD 76 according to Jerome, and is mentioned by Tacitus (*Dial.* 26).

PIR² I 331; Schanz–Hosius, § 480. 5.   M. W.

Iulius (*RE* 363) **Modestus,** learned freedman of C. Iulius *Hyginus (1) (Suet. *Gram.* 20), whose interests in grammar and antiquarian lore he shared.

PIR² I 432; Mazzarino, *Gramm. Rom. Frag.* 9–23.   R. A. K.

Iulius (*RE* 382) **Paulus,** a celebrated Roman lawyer whose origin is unknown. Taught by *Cervidius Scaevola, he was active in Rome as advocate, teacher, and writer. Under *Septimius Severus he was assessor to *Aemilius Papinianus as praetorian prefect and became a member of the emperor's council (see CONSILIUM PRINCIPIS) and perhaps head of the records office (*a memoria*). He was thus able to publish reports of cases decided by Severus (*Imperiales sententiae, Decreta*), in which he shows his sturdy independence. Though the matter is disputed, he was possibly made praetorian prefect by *Elegabalus in AD 219, when the emperor married Iulia Cornelia Paula, whose name suggests that she was the lawyer's daughter. The marriage was dissolved in 220. Paulus was banished but was recalled by M. *Aurelius Severus Alexander (222–35), whom he served as counsellor while continuing to write.

His output in some five decades came to over 300 books (*libri*), including 16 on the civil law (*Ad Sabinum*) and 78 on the praetor's edict (*Ad edictum praetoris*), besides notes on earlier writers and dozens of monographs on particular topics. The big commentaries came early in his career, and the monographs often develop themes touched on in them. There are also 26 books of *Quaestiones* ('Problems') and 23 of *Responsa* ('Opinions') derived mainly from Paulus' extensive consultative practice. His fame attracted several spurious works, including the so-called *Pauli sententiae* ('Paul's Views'), compiled in the late 3rd cent. but endorsed by Constantine I as genuine. The Law of Citations of 426 named him as one of five lawyers whose corpus of work had authority, and Justinian's compilers (see JUSTINIAN'S CODIFICATION) selected over 2,000 passages from him, some 17 per cent of the *Digesta*,

Iulius Phaedrus, Gaius

often to supplement the account given by *Ulpian. His bent as a writer was academic, even doctrinaire, his tone sharp, his outlook basically cautious; but his remarkable range of interests ensured that his ideas were continually evolving. Influenced by Aristotelian natural law and Stoic philosophy (see ARISTOTLE; LAW OF NATURE; STOICISM), he along with Ulpian helped to ensure the adaptation of Roman law to a cosmopolitan society.

Lenel, *Pal.* 1. 951–1308; *PIR²* I 453; *HLL* 4, § 423; D. Liebs, *Kl. Pauly* 2. 1550 f.; C. A. Maschi, *ANRW* 2. 15 (1976), 667–707; Syme, *RP* 2. 790–804, and ibid. 3. 1393–1414. T. Hon.

Iulius Phaedrus (or Phaeder), Gaius See PHAEDRUS (4).

Iulius (*RE* 386) **Philippus, Marcus,** Roman emperor AD 244–9. An Arabian from Shahbā (SE of *Damascus), he became praetorian prefect of *Gordian III and, early in 244, succeeded him as emperor. After making peace with Persia, he immediately went to Rome. His reign saw the thousandth anniversary of the city (247–8), and the beginning of the 3rd-cent. 'crisis' proper, characterized by invasion over the Danube (see DANUVIUS) and Roman civil war. Philippus repelled the Carpi (245/7), but left Pacatian's rebellion and a major Gothic incursion (see GOTHS) to *Decius (248/9). Decius' troops proclaimed him emperor in summer 249, and in the autumn he defeated and killed Philippus at Verona.

Stories that Philippus engineered the death of Gordian III, and was a Christian (see CHRISTIANITY), are unconvincing. More significant is his typical—as a gifted provincial administrator—late-Severan ascent through the equestrian hierarchy to become a careful and conscientious ruler, only to discover that military skills now counted for more than bureaucratic ones.

X. Loriot, *ANRW* 2. 2 (1975), 788 ff.; L. de Blois, *Talanta* 1978/9, 11 ff.; H. A. Pohlsander, *Hist.* 1980, 463 ff., and 1982, 214 ff.; G. W. Bowersock, *Roman Arabia* (1983, corrected repr. 1994), 121–8; D. Potter, *Prophecy and History . . .* (1990). J. F. D.

Iulius (*RE* Suppl. 14. 425a) **Quadratus Bassus, Gaius,** from *Pergamum, of regal ancestry, legate (see LEGATI) of *Judaea *c.* AD 102/3–5, *suffect consul 105, commander and companion of *Trajan in the Second Dacian War, winning triumphal ornaments (see DACIA; ORNAMENTA). Governor of *Cappadocia–*Galatia (*c.*107–10), he probably held a command in the Parthian War (see PARTHIA), governed *Syria (*c.*115–17), and was appointed to Dacia in 117, where he died (winter 117/8). On *Hadrian's instructions, he received a public funeral at Pergamum. Bassus was related to a nexus of aristocratic Pergamene families, but his kinship with C. Antius A. Iulius Quadratus (consul for the second time, as *ordinarius,* 105), is unclear.

C. Habicht, *Pergamon* 8/3 (1969), no. 21; H. Halfmann, *Die Senatoren aus dem östlichen Teil des Imperium Romanum* (1979), 119. J. B. C.

Iulius (*RE* 434) **Romanus** (3rd cent. AD) wrote an extensive grammatical work entitled Ἀφορμαί ('Origins'), of which considerable fragments are preserved by *Charisius.

Schanz–Hosius, § 603. J. F. M.

Iulius (*RE* 452) **Sacrovir,** a noble of the *Aedui, whose family had received Roman *citizenship, perhaps from *Caesar. In AD 21 he and Iulius Florus of the *Treveri led a rebellion against Rome of which the basic cause was indebtedness of some Gauls due to taxation and private borrowing at high *interest rates. Sacrovir collected a large army of his countrymen and occupied *Augustodunum (mod. Autun), but was easily defeated by C. Silius, legate (see LEGATI) of the Upper Rhine army, and immolated himself with his followers in Gallic style.

Tac. *Ann.* 3. 40–6. C. Jullian, *Histoire de la Gaule* 4 (1913), 153 ff.; J. Drinkwater, *Roman Gaul* (1983), see index. A. M.; T. J. C.; B. M. L.

Iulius Secundus, among recent orators specially mentioned by *Quintilian (*Inst.* 10. 1. 120, 3. 12). Like M. *Aper, another of the characters in Tacitus' *Dialogus,* he came from Gaul. A quiet and elegant speaker, he also wrote a biography of *Iulius Africanus. He was secretary to *Otho.

PIR² I 559; G. W. Bowersock, *Greek Sophists in the Roman Empire* (1969), app. 1. J. W. D.

Iulius Severus, Sextus, who, possibly through *adoption, also bore the names Gnaeus Minicius (*RE* 11) Faustinus, from the colony of Aequum in *Dalmatia, was described as foremost among *Hadrian's outstanding commanders (Cass. Dio 69. 13), unusually holding four consular governorships. After commanding Legio XIV Gemina (see LEGION) in *Pannonia, he was governor of the one-legion province of Upper *Dacia (AD 119–26/7), *suffect consul 127, governor of Lower *Moesia (*c.*128–30/1), and of *Britain (*c.*131–3), from which he was transferred to *Judaea to suppress the Jewish Revolt. He accomplished this efficiently and brutally, systematically destroying Jewish forts and settlements. He won *ornamenta triumphalia, remaining as governor of the province (now called Syria Palaestina), before proceeding to *Syria itself (*c.*135).

A. R. Birley, *The Fasti of Roman Britain* (1981), 106. J. B. C.

Iulius Solinus, Gaius, wrote (probably soon after AD 200) *Collectanea rerum memorabilium,* a geographical summary of parts of the known world, with remarks on origins, history, customs of nations, and products of countries. Almost the whole is taken from *Pliny (1)'s *Natural History* and *Pomponius Mela without acknowledgement. There is a meagre addition about the British Isles (see BRITAIN) which gives us Tanatus (Thanet); the stone jet, found abundantly in Britain; and the absence of snakes in Ireland (see HIBERNIA). He introduced the name 'mare Mediterraneum' ('*Mediterranean sea').

EDITIONS Mommsen, 1895², repr. 1958; that of Saumaise, prefixed to his *Plinianae exercitationes* (1689), is still useful. Trans. A. Golding, 1587, repr. in facsimile 1955. H. Walter *Die Coll. R. M. des C. Iul. Solinus* (1968).
PIR² I 583. E. H. W.

Iulius Tiro comes next after *Quintilian in *Suetonius' list of rhetors or orators (*Gram. Rhet.* 41 Brugnoli). He perhaps is the senator C. Iulius (*PIR²* I 603) Tiro Gaetulicus and the person (*RE* 510) whose forged will is mentioned by Pliny (*Ep.* 6. 31).

Schanz–Hosius, § 480. 6; Syme, *RP* 2. 718. M. W.

Iulius Titianus, rhetor (3rd cent. AD), nicknamed 'the ape of the age' for his versatility of imitation; derided by other so-called *Frontoniani for his Ciceronianizing *Letters of Famous Women* (see TULLIUS CICERO (1), M.). He also wrote declamations on Virgilian themes (see VIRGIL), a *Chorographia* (or *Libri provinciarum*), and prose fables versified by *Ausonius and possibly *Avianus: from honoured imperial tutor he declined to itinerant provincial schoolmaster. Some identify fabulist and schoolmaster with a son said to have taught *Iulius Verus Maximinus Thrax' son (SHA *Max.* 27. 5) but by others regarded as fictitious.

PIR² I 604; K. Thraede, *Hermes* 1968, 608–13. L. A. H.-S.

Iulius Ursus Servianus, Lucius, born *c.* AD 47, husband of *Hadrian's sister, Aelia Domitia Paullina, he held his first, *suffect, consulship in 90, if he may be identified with the Servius Iulius Servianus of the *fasti Potentini* (Syme, *Tacitus* 636). In winter

97/8 he succeeded *Trajan as governor of Upper Germany (see GERMANIA), soon moving to Upper *Pannonia (Plin. *Ep.* 8. 23), and accompanied the emperor in the First Dacian War, becoming consul for the second time (as *ordinarius*) with L. *Licinius Sura in 102. He was a friend of *Pliny (2) the Younger, to whom he persuaded the emperor to grant the rights of fathers of three children. According to Xiphilinus, Trajan mentioned Servianus as a suitable successor, though in Zonaras the comment is attributed to Hadrian (Cass. Dio 69. 17; Syme, *Tacitus* 486). His relations with Hadrian perhaps deteriorated and the emperor gave no special honour to his sister Paullina on her death (*c.*132). Although Servianus achieved the signal distinction of a third consulship in 134, he was very elderly and apparently resented Hadrian's choice in 136 of L. Aelius as his successor, perhaps expecting that the 18-year-old son of his son-in-law *Pedanius Fuscus Salinator (ordinary consul with Hadrian in 118) would be selected (Cass. Dio 69. 17). Hadrian, already ill himself, ordered both their deaths although Servianus, now a nonagenarian, protested his innocence, cursing his brother-in-law. The emperor was determined to ensure that his chosen successor faced no opposition.

PIR² I 569 = 631; R. Syme, *Tacitus* (1958), see index.   J. B. C.

Iulius (*RE* 520) **Valerius Alexander Polemius,** author in the mid-4th cent. AD of an extant Latin version of the Greek Alexander Romance of *Pseudo-Callisthenes. Its style shows some colourful and archaic features, imitating earlier poets and Apuleius.

Ed. B. Kühler (1888); Herzog–Schmidt 5. 212–14. *PLRE* 1. 709–10.
S. J. Ha.

Iulius Verus, Gnaeus, a senator from Aequum in *Dalmatia, evidently the son of Sex. *Iulius Severus (suffect consul AD 127), had a long and distinguished career beginning with a tribunate (see TRIBUNI MILITUM) in the Jewish War under *Hadrian. *Suffect consul probably in 151, he then governed Lower Germany (see GERMANIA) and *Britain, being attested in the latter province in 158. Legate (see LEGATI) of *Syria during the Parthian War, he then supervised the raising of the new *legions II and III *Italicae*, was *comes* (see COMITES) of the emperors in the Marcomannic Wars (see MARCOMANNI), and was designated to a second consulship, but died in 179 before taking office.

PIR² I 618; A. R. Birley, *The Fasti of Roman Britain* (1981), 118 ff.
A. R. Bi.

Iulius (*RE* 526) **Verus Maximinus, Gaius** (Roman emperor AD 235–8), also known as Maximinus Thrax ('the Thracian'), a Danubian of relatively humble stock, exploited the opportunities of the Severan army to gain numerous senior appointments. He became emperor by chance at Mainz (*Mogontiacum, March 235), in the mutiny against M. *Aurelius Severus Alexander. An equestrian outside the ruling clique, he was unsure of his position. He attempted to conciliate the senate from afar, remaining on the frontier with his troops and attempting to act the successful warrior-emperor: he campaigned vigorously over the Rhine and Danube. However, his overtures were unwelcome, his absence from Rome politically unwise, and his wars expensive. The revolt of *Gordian I recalled him to Italy, where he then faced *Balbinus and Pupienus. The stubborn resistance of *Aquileia caused Maximinus to lose his judgement, and the military initiative. His troops became disheartened with the lack of progress and finally murdered him and his son (spring 238).

A. Bellezza, *Massimino il Trace* (1964); R. Syme, *Emperors and Biography*

(1971); X. Loriot, *ANRW* 2. 2 (1975), 657 ff.; K. Dietz, *Senatus contra principem* (1980).   J. F. Dr.

Iulius (*RE* 532) **Victor, Gaius** (4th cent. AD ?), author of an *ars rhetorica* of little originality, owing much to *Cicero and *Quintilian. The final chapters, on conversation and letters, are of interest.

Ed. R. Giomini and M. S. Celentano (1980); Schanz–Hosius, § 842. *PLRE* 1. 961.   M. W.

Iulius (*RE* 534) **Vindex, Gaius,** descended from the kings of *Aquitania and son of a Roman senator who had possibly been adlected by Claudius, was governor of Gallia Lugdunensis (see GAUL (TRANSALPINE)) when he revolted from *Nero (spring AD 68). Vindex had no Roman troops under his command and although he received support from many Gauls and the native noblemen in his province, he probably intended the overthrow of Nero, not nationalist secession. His appeal to other governors for assistance was answered only by *Galba in Spain, and although *Vienna (mod. Vienne) in Narbonensis supported him, *Lugdunum (1) (Lyons) rejected his approaches. The army of Upper Germany under L. *Verginius Rufus defeated the rebels at *Vesontio (Besançon), though the circumstances remain obscure, since Rufus had apparently been intriguing with Vindex before the battle, and his troops may have forced him to fight.

P. A. Brunt, *Latomus* 1959, 531 (= *RIT* (1990), 9); J. B. Hainsworth, *Hist.* 1962, 86.   J. B. C.

Iunia (*RE* 'Iunius' 198) **Calvina,** daughter of M. *Iunius Silanus Torquatus, a young woman of exceptional charm, married a son of the censor L. *Vitellius, who (AD 48) accused her of incest with her brother L. *Iunius Silanus (to help *Agrippina the Younger). She was banished from Italy (49), but recalled by Nero after Agrippina's death; she survived until the late 70s.

H. H. S.; B. M. L.

Iunius (*RE* 149) **Arulenus Rusticus, Quintus** (suffect consul AD 92), a Stoic philosopher (see STOICISM), friend of *Thrasea Paetus, whose defence of senatorial rights he supported. As tribune in 66 Rusticus was dissuaded by Thrasea from vetoing the senatorial decree condemning him to death. Praetor in 69, he was wounded during a senatorial delegation sent by *Vitellius to the advancing Flavians (i.e. *Vespasian's troops). After writing laudatory accounts of Thrasea and *Helvidius Priscus he was executed by Domitian *c.*93.   J. B. C.

Iunius (*RE* 41) **Blaesus, Quintus,** probably a *novus homo* of municipal origin, *suffect consul AD 10. As legate (see LEGATI) of *Pannonia he failed to quell the mutiny which *Tiberius' son Drusus *Iulius Caesar (1) finally reduced (September AD 14). One of Tiberius' preferred candidates for the proconsulship of Africa and the war against *Tacfarinas (AD 21), he was prorogued in the command and broke the rebellion. He was awarded triumphal ornaments (see ORNAMENTA), and was hailed *imperator* and allowed to accept the designation, the last time it was taken by a private citizen. This was a compliment from Tiberius to Blaesus' sister's son *Sejanus; Sejanus' fall in 31 involved his own death.

Syme, *AA*, see index.   H. H. S.; B. M. L.

Iunius (*RE* 46a in Suppl. 5. 356 ff.) **Brutus, Lucius,** was reputedly responsible for the expulsion of *Tarquinius Superbus after the suicide of *Lucretia and was one of the first two *consuls in 509 BC until he met a heroic death in battle against the Tarquins. His role as liberator was embellished with stories of his feigning idiocy to survive the tyranny of Superbus (based on his *cognomen*

Iunius Brutus, Marcus

Brutus (= 'stupid') and may itself be fiction (some scholars argue that *Porsenna overthrew the Tarquins). The plebeian status of the later Iunii has raised doubts about the authenticity of his consulship or the alleged early patrician monopoly of the office. As Superbus' cousin, whose own future power was portended by his fulfilment of a *Delphic oracle, Brutus symbolized the tensions inherent in the transition to the republic: his statue, with sword unsheathed, stood alongside those of the kings on the *Capitol, he reputedly engineered the abdication of his fellow consul L. *Tarquinius Collatinus, and executed (two of) his sons for plotting the restoration of the Tarquins. This exemplary story allowed enemies of Caesar's murderers to dispute the claim of later Iunii Bruti, especially *Brutus, to descend from the architect of republican liberty (claims probably already propagated in *Accius' play *Brutus*).

CAH 7²/2 (1989), 178, 258 f.; A. Mastrocinque, *Lucio Iunio Bruto* (1988).
A. D.

Iunius (*RE* 52) **Brutus** (1), **Marcus**, as tribune 83 BC established a colony at *Capua. In 77, as a legate of M. *Aemilius Lepidus (2), he commanded in Cisalpine Gaul (see GAUL (CISALPINE)), surrendered to *Pompey at *Mutina and, after a promise of safe conduct, was executed. He was the father of the tyrannicide M. *Iunius Brutus (2).
E. B.

Iunius (*RE* 53) **Brutus** (2), **Marcus**, son of (1) and of *Servilia, born (probably) 85 BC, was adopted by his uncle (?) Q. Servilius Caepio by 59 and was henceforth called Q. Caepio Brutus. Brought up by M. *Porcius Cato (2), he was educated in oratory and philosophy and long retained a fierce hatred for his father's murderer *Pompey. In 58 he accompanied Cato to *Cyprus and in 56 lent a large sum to *Salamis (2) at 48 per cent interest p.a., contrary to the *lex Gabinia* (see LEX (2) under *leges Gabiniae*), procuring a senate decree to validate the loan. As moneyer (perhaps 55) he issued coins showing *Libertas and portraits of his ancestors L. *Iunius Brutus (who overthrew *Tarquinius Superbus) and C. *Servilius Ahala, the tyrannicide (*RRC* 433). As quaestor 53 he went to Cilicia with Ap. *Claudius Pulcher (3), whose daughter he had married, and there lent *Ariobarzanes I a large sum, probably to enable him to pay interest on his huge debt to Pompey. When *Cicero succeeded Appius, he found that an agent of Brutus had been made prefect of cavalry to extort money from Salamis and that five Salaminian senators had been killed. He cancelled the appointment, but to avoid offence to Brutus gave a similar post to Brutus' agent in Cappadocia and recognized the validity of the loan to Salamis (Cic. *Att.* 5. 21–6. 1). In 52 Brutus defended T. *Annius Milo and in a pamphlet attacked Pompey's wish for a dictatorship, but in 50 they both defended Appius against P. *Cornelius Dolabella (1), and in 49 he joined the Republican cause, having been formally reconciled with Pompey. After *Pharsalus he successfully begged Caesar for pardon and, no doubt through Servilia's influence, became one of his protégés. He was made a pontifex and in 47 sent to govern Cisalpine Gaul, while Caesar went to Africa to fight Cato and the republicans. During this time he developed relations with Cicero, who dedicated various philosophical and rhetorical works to him and, at his request, wrote a eulogy of Cato after Cato's death. (Finding it unsatisfactory, Brutus wrote one himself.) Although he now divorced Claudia and married Cato's daughter *Porcia, widow of M. *Calpurnius Bibulus, he remained on good terms with Caesar, met him on his return from Munda, assured Cicero of Caesar's laudable optimate intentions, and was made *praetor*

urbanus for 44 and designated consul for 41. But when Caesar became *dictator perpetuo* (February 44), Brutus, reminded of his heritage, joined, and *ex officio* took the lead in, the widespread conspiracy that led to Caesar's assassination before his departure for his Parthian War. Outmanœuvred by M. *Antonius (2), whose life he had spared on the Ides of March, he and C. *Cassius Longinus (1) had to leave Rome and, failing to win popular approval, left Italy for Greece (August 44). With Antonius now openly against them, Brutus collected close to 400 million sesterces from the treasuries of Asia and Syria and confiscated the supplies Caesar had prepared for his campaign. He and Cassius gradually seized all the eastern provinces, building up large armies, partly of veterans. When Cicero, in his *Philippics*, swung the senate behind them, they received *imperium maius* in the east. Brutus captured, and later executed, Antony's brother C. *Antonius; after P. Cornelius Dolabella's death he acquired Asia and completed its conquest, and during 43 and 42 squeezed it dry for his armies. The money was turned into a large coinage (*RRC* 500–8) and Brutus, alone among the republicans, put his own head on one of the gold coins. He also won the title of *imperator* in Thrace. In 42 he and Cassius, with about 80,000 legionaries plus auxiliaries, twice met Antony and *Octavian at *Philippi. In the first battle Cassius, defeated by Antony, committed suicide, while Brutus impressively defeated Octavian. In a second battle, forced on Brutus, he was defeated, deserted by his soldiers, and also committed suicide. His body was honourably treated by Antony.

Arrogant, rapacious, calculatingly ambitious, Brutus yet professed a deep attachment to philosophy. Cicero admired but never liked him, and ignored his warnings not to trust Octavian. A renowned orator, with an austere and dignified style, he despised Cicero's as 'effeminate and spineless' (Tac. *Dial.* 18. 5). His literary works (philosophy, historical epitomes, poetry) are lost, as are his letters, except for a few surviving among Cicero's. With Cassius, he was officially condemned under the empire, but revered by many as the last defender of Roman freedom.

Cicero is the only contemporary source. Plutarch wrote a eulogistic biography and the later historians (especially Appian and Cassius Dio) treat him at length. Syme, *Rom. Rev.*, see index; M. L. Clarke, *The Noblest Roman* (1981) (useful on Brutus' fame); E. Wistrand, *The Policy of Brutus the Tyrannicide* (1981); M. H. Dettenhofer, *Perdita Iuventus* (1992), 99 ff., 192 ff. (in German).
E. B.

Iunius (*RE* 55a in Suppl. 5) **Brutus Albinus, Decimus,** probably son of Decimus Brutus (consul 77 BC) and Sempronia, the associate of L. *Sergius Catilina (Catiline): from the name Albinus given to him by Greek writers and on coins it is clear that he was adopted by a Postumius Albinus. As a young man he served under *Caesar in Gaul and distinguished himself by a naval victory over the *Veneti (1) in 56. He successfully commanded a Caesarian fleet at *Massalia in 49, and was appointed governor of Transalpine Gaul (see GAUL (TRANSALPINE)), where he suppressed a rebellion of the Bellovaci (46). He took part in the conspiracy against Caesar, in spite of the marked favour shown him by the dictator, who had given him another provincial command in Cisalpine Gaul and designated him consul for 42. In April 44 he went to his province, and in December refused to surrender it to M. *Antonius (2) (Mark Antony), who claimed it in virtue of the law he had passed in June. Besieged by Antony in *Mutina, he was released by the victory of A. *Hirtius and *Octavian in April 43. With Hirtius dead and the other consul C. *Vibius Pansa Caetronianus dying, the senate placed Brutus in command of their troops, but their two veteran legions preferred to resume service under Octavian, who, moreover, failed to help Brutus with the pursuit of Antony. Brutus followed Antony into Transalpine Gaul and joined L. *Munatius Plancus in June, but was then deserted by him. He now planned to join *Brutus in Macedonia, but was abandoned by his army, captured by a Gallic chief, and put to death by Antony's order.

Tyrrell and Purser, *Correspondence of Cicero* 6². lxxxiv ff.; Syme, *Rom. Rev.*, see index. For his coins see *RRC* nos. 450–1; on his name, D. R. Shackleton Bailey, *Two Studies in Roman Nomenclature* (1976), 86 ff.

T. J. C.; R. J. S.

Iunius (*RE* 57) **Brutus Callaicus, Decimus,** as consul 138 BC and proconsul fought successfully in *Iberia (1). After triumphing over the Lusitani (see LUSITANIA) and Callaeci he commissioned a temple to *Mars adorned with statues by *Scopas. He accompanied C. *Sempronius Tuditanus to *Illyricum and participated in the suppression of C. *Sempronius Gracchus. He was an orator, philhellene, and a patron of *Accius.

Astin, *Scipio*, see index.

E. B.

Iunius (*RE* 58) **Brutus Damasippus, Lucius,** fought for the government in the *bellum Sullanum* (see CORNELIUS SULLA FELIX, L.) and was defeated by *Pompey (83 BC). As praetor (? *urbanus*) 82 he had four unreliable senators killed, including Q. *Mucius Scaevola (2). He tried to relieve C. *Marius (2) at *Praeneste, but was defeated by Sulla at the Colline gate (see PONTIUS TELESINUS), captured, and executed.

E. B.

Iunius (*RE* 68) **Congus** is mentioned by C. *Lucilius (1) in book 26 of his satires (595 f. Marx) as their most desirable reader, neither excessively learned nor ill-informed. He was possibly the youthful dedicatee of a satire in that book. Later he became a distinguished antiquarian and jurist. He was dead by 54 BC. An identification with Iunius Gracchanus who wrote on Roman magistracies is likely but not certain.

C. Cichorius, *Untersuchungen zu Lucilius* (1908).

M. C.

Iunius (*RE* 108) **Nipsus, Marcus** (perhaps 2nd cent. AD), *gromaticus*; author of treatises on mensuration, replacement of boundaries, and surveying of rivers.

Ed. K. Lachmann, *Die Schriften der röm. Feldmesser* 1 (1848), 285 ff.

Iunius (*RE* 113) **Otho,** declaimer (see DECLAMATION). Formerly an elementary schoolmaster, he owed his advancement (*praetor AD 22) to L. *Aelius Seianus (Tac. *Ann.* 3. 66). He published four books of *colores*; his technique is illustrated by L. *Annaeus Seneca (1) (esp. *Controv.* 2. 1. 33–5, 37–9).

*PIR*² I 788; Schanz–Hosius, § 336. 9. 8.

M. W.

Iunius Pennus See LEX (2), Lex Iunia, 126 BC.

Iunius Rusticus, Quintus, Stoic senator (see STOICISM), son of *Domitian's victim of the same names, was consul suffect in AD 133. A mentor of Marcus *Aurelius, he was appointed city prefect when the latter became emperor and was consul for the second time (as *ordinarius*) in 162. As prefect he sentenced *Justin Martyr to death c.166.

M. Aurelius, *Med.*; Cass. Dio 71; SHA *M. Ant. PIR*² I 814.

A. R. Bi.

Iunius (*RE* 163) **Silanus** (1), **Decimus,** second husband of *Servilia, hence brother-in-law of M. *Porcius Cato (2), failed to gain the consulship of 64 BC, but succeeded in 63 for 62 as colleague of L. *Licinius Murena, through extensive bribery, for which Cato, who prosecuted Murena, refused to prosecute him. In the senate discussion on the fate of the followers of L. *Sergius

Catilina he proposed the 'extreme penalty', but after *Caesar's speech weakly explained he had meant imprisonment. Towards the end of the year he and Murena passed the *lex Iunia Licinia* requiring publicity for bills promulgated. He was dead by 57. His three daughters respectively married P. *Servilius Isauricus, C. *Cassius Longinus (1) (the tyrannicide) and M. *Aemilius Lepidus (3), the triumvir.

E. B.

Iunius (*RE* 164) **Silanus** (2), **Decimus** Son of C. *Iunius Silanus (1). When his affair with *Iulia (4), the granddaughter of *Augustus, became known, he voluntarily went into exile (AD 8). Thanks to the influence of his brother M. *Iunius Silanus (2), *Tiberius allowed him to return (20), but not to hold office.

H. H. S.; B. M. L.

Iunius (*RE* 158) **Silanus** (1), **Gaius** represents a collateral branch of the family of the Silani (the other main branch was represented by M. *Iunius Silanus (1) and his descendants). His three sons C. *Iunius Silanus (2), M. *Iunius Silanus (2), and D. *Iunius Silanus (2) were all prominent.

H. H. S.; B. M. L.

Iunius (*RE* 159) **Silanus** (2), **Gaius** (consul AD 10), son of C. *Iunius Silanus (1), moved the *SC Silanianum* on the torture of slaves, and governed Asia (20/1). Accused of extortion and *maiestas*, he was exiled (22): Tac. *Ann.* 3. 66 ff.

H. H. S.; B. M. L.

Iunius (*RE* 155) **Silanus, Gaius Appius** (consul AD 28), son of C. *Iunius Silanus (2), was acquitted on a charge of *maiestas* (32). The emperor *Claudius recalled him from the governorship of *Tarraconensis (40/1) to marry Domitia Lepida, mother of *Valeria Messallina; this was in 41. Allegedly having refused her advances, Silanus was accused by her and *Narcissus (2) of planning to murder Claudius and killed (42).

Syme, *Rom. Rev.*, see index, and *AA* ch. 14 and index; B. Levick, *Claudius* (1990), 58 f.

H. H. S.; B. M. L.

Iunius (*RE* 180) **Silanus, Lucius** (praetor AD 48), son of M. *Iunius Silanus Torquatus, was betrothed to *Claudia Octavia daughter of the emperor *Claudius. He went as a youth with Claudius to Britain and received the *ornamenta triumphalia*. Through *Iulia Agrippina ('Agrippina the Younger') he was deprived of his praetorship and expelled from the senate (for alleged incest with his sister *Iunia Calvina). He committed suicide on the day that Claudius married Agrippina (49).

H. H. S.; B. M. L.

Iunius (*RE* 172) **Silanus** (1), **Marcus** (consul 25 BC), of varied political allegiance. He supported his brother-in-law M. *Aemilius Lepidus (3) in 44, went over to M. *Antonius (2) (Mark Antony) at *Mutina (43), fell out of favour with the *triumvirs, fled to Sextus *Pompeius and returned to Rome after the pact of Misenum (39), served under Antony in Greece (34–32), but before Actium went over to *Octavian. He was made *patrician and was consul with Augustus. (For the suggestion that the consul of 25 is not the legate of 43, see Broughton, *MRR* 3. 32).

H. H. S.; B. M. L.

Iunius (*RE* 174) **Silanus** (2), **Marcus,** suffect consul AD 15, son of C. *Iunius Silanus (1), was influential with *Tiberius and the senate. In 33 his daughter Iunia Claudia married *Gaius (1) (Caligula), who killed Silanus in 38 (Cass. Dio 59. 8. 5 wrongly calls him the 'golden sheep'; see IUNIUS SILANUS (3), M., about whom this was really said).

H. H. S.; B. M. L.

Iunius Silanus Marcus

Iunius (*RE* 176) **Silanus** (3), **Marcus** (consul AD 46, for the whole year), son of M. *Iunius Silanus Torquatus. Born in AD 14, a great-great-grandson of *Augustus, he was proconsul of Asia in 54. Although he lacked ambition (the emperor *Gaius (1) called him a 'golden sheep'), *Iulia Agrippina 'the Younger' thought his descent dangerous to her son *Nero and that Silanus might try to avenge the death of his brother L. *Iunius Silanus. He was poisoned while proconsul of Asia in 54, his son exiled and killed in 65.   H. H. S.; B. M. L.

Iunius (*RE* 182) **Silanus Torquatus, Decimus** (consul AD 53), son of M. *Iunius Silanus Torquatus, was forced to suicide (64) because he could boast descent from *Augustus. He was charged with excessive largess, leaving no way out but that of revolution: some of his freedmen had titles appropriate to the imperial household.   H. H. S.; B. M. L.

Iunius (*RE* 183) **Silanus Torquatus, Lucius,** son of M. *Iunius Silanus (3) and nephew of Iunia Lepida, the consul's sister. She had married the jurist C. Cassius Longinus (2). Silanus was brought up in their home. In 65 Nero accused him of treason and incest with his aunt. He was exiled and murdered before he left Italy (cf. L. Petersen, *Hist.* 1966, 328 ff.).   H. H. S.; B. M. L.

Iunius (*RE* 175) **Silanus Torquatus, Marcus** (consul AD 19, for the whole year), grandson of M. *Iunius Silanus (1). With Norbanus he passed the *lex Iunia Norbana* (see LATINI IUNIANI). He was proconsul of Africa (36–9; 29–35 is canvassed on the basis of *ILS* 6236). He married Aemilia Lepida, a great-granddaughter of *Augustus, and all his four children suffered from that descent. They were M. *Iunius Silanus (3), D. *Iunius Silanus Torquatus, L. *Iunius Silanus, and *Iunia Calvina.   H. H. S.; B. M. L.

iuridicus was the title given to certain officials of praetorian rank (see PRAETOR, Caesar and imperial period) who performed judicial functions in civil cases in Italy (outside Rome and its environs). They were appointed by the emperor and assigned to particular districts. The first known appointment was by Marcus *Aurelius in AD 163, but *Hadrian had created similar offices of consular rank (abolished by *Antoninus Pius). The *iuridici* disappear under the Dominate (the name sometimes given to the period after AD 284). Later uses of the title (as in the *Digest*) are to be referred to the *iuridicus Alexandreae*, a high judicial officer in Egypt, known also from papyri as δικαιοδότης. In other imperial provinces *legati iuridici* with limited jurisdiction (called in some inscriptions simply *iuridici*), also appointed by the emperor, are found from Vespasian on.   B. N.

ius civile This term derives its meaning from its context. By contrast with **ius gentium* in the 'theoretical' sense it is the law of a particular state and usually, unless otherwise qualified, the law of Rome. By contrast with *ius gentium* in the 'practical' sense it is that part of the law of Rome which is applicable only to Roman citizens. By contrast with the law deriving from the edicts of magistrates (*ius honorarium*) it is law deriving from statute and from the unwritten 'common law' as interpreted by the jurists. The term is also used in a still narrower sense to denote only the product of the jurists' interpretation.   B. N.

ius gentium, or law of nations, has three main senses. (1) In a 'practical' sense it denotes that part of Roman private law which was open to citizens and non-citizens alike. The institutions of the old **ius civile* were accessible only to Romans, but the growth of international trade made it necessary to recognize some insti-

tutions which could be applied by Roman courts to relations between foreigners and between foreigners and citizens. The course of the development of this *ius gentium* is conjectural. No doubt the establishment c.242 BC of the office of *praetor peregrinus* (see PRAETOR) played a part, but there must have been other factors, since in classical law *ius gentium* was not regarded as a praetorian creation and it was applicable also to relations purely between citizens. It included even some institutions which were part of the old *ius civile* (notably **stipulatio*, except in the form using '*spondeo*'). It embraced in fact the most flexible and commercially significant parts of Roman law. After the *constitutio Antoniniana* (see CONSTITUTION, ANTONINE), when the same law was applied to Romans and foreigners, *ius gentium* in this sense was only an historical reminiscence.

(2) In a more 'theoretical' sense *ius gentium* is equated with the philosophical *law of nature (*ius naturale*). Thus for *Gaius (2) (*Inst.* 1. 1) *ius gentium* is 'the law observed by all nations', by contrast with the *ius civile* of each individual state; and this universal law is that which 'natural reason establishes among all mankind'. *Ius naturale* therefore looks to the origin of this law in natural reason, while *ius gentium* looks to its universal application.

(3) *Ius gentium* also sometimes denotes legal rules governing relations between states, corresponding to modern 'public international law'.

H. F. Jolowicz and B. Nicholas, *Historical Introduction to Roman Law,* 3rd edn. (1972); G. Lombardi, *Ricerche in tema di ius gentium* (1946), and *Il concetto di ius gentium* (1947); and see bibliog. under LAW OF NATURE.   B. N.

ius Italicum was a privilege granted to certain communities in the Roman provinces whereby their land was treated in law as if it were in Italy. It was thus exempted from the rule that land in the provinces belonged to the state and could not be fully owned by private individuals; and the land and its inhabitants were free from taxes (*tributum soli* and *tributum capitis*). Under the empire this was the highest privilege obtainable by a provincial municipality (see MUNICIPIUM). *Augustus gave it only to genuine citizen colonies, mostly his eastern foundations. Later it was granted along with colonial rights to Roman municipalities, but, for fiscal reasons, sparingly. *Septimius Severus, however, gave it not only to three municipalities of Africa, his native province, but, after their co-operation in the civil war, to several Greek cities. This development typified the assimilation of east and west, which the *constitutio Antoniniana* (see CONSTITUTION, ANTONINE) completed.

A. N. Sherwin-White, *The Roman Citizenship*, 2nd edn. (1973).   B. N.

ius Latii, the Latin right, refers primarily to the legal status of those Latins (see LATINI) who after 338 BC shared the right of marriage (*conubium*) and commerce (**commercium*) with Romans. Latins settling in Rome acquired Roman *citizenship and vice versa. Those, whether from Rome or Latium, who settled in Latin colonies acquired coloniary Latin status, which, at least by the empire, differed from the wider Latin right in not permitting intermarriage. An entirely separate status of Junian Latinity (see LATINI IUNIANI) was created for certain categories of freed slave by a Junian law under *Augustus. Latin rights were conferred on many communities in Italy, Gaul, Spain and Africa in the late republican period. It is clear that such communities were known as Latin *municipia* (towns) into the imperial period but the practical consequences of Latin status remain obscure. Those who served as magistrates of Latin *municipia* acquired Roman citizenship from about 150 BC onwards. Under *Hadrian, if not before, in colonies possessing greater Latinity (*Latium maius*) decurions (*decuriones*) as well as magistrates received Roman citizenship.

Asc. *Pis.* 3 Clark; Gai. *Inst.* 1. 22 ff., 96. H. Galsterer, *Herrschaft und Verwaltung im republikanischen Italien* (1976); Millar, *ERW* app. 4.

A. D. E. L.

ius liberorum **Augustus' marriage laws (the Julian law of 18 BC and Papio-Poppaean of AD 9) rewarded parents. For example, precedence in public office was offered to married men and fathers. Three children (in Rome), four (for freed slaves and residents in Italy), or five (in the provinces) qualified parents for full exemptions, including, for women, exemption from being in guardianship and, for men, from acting as guardians. The fictitious status of parent, especially of three children (conferred e.g. on *Livia Drusilla), came to be granted as a privilege and favour by the emperors. See MARRIAGE, LAW OF, ROMAN; PATRONAGE, NON-LITERARY.

S. M. T.

ius primae relationis, the right of prior proposal. When in 23 BC *Augustus ceased to hold the consulship, certain rights and powers were voted him by the senate by way of compensation. Among these was the right of putting a single proposal at any point during senate meetings (Cass. Dio 53. 32. 5). Since Augustus retained, by virtue of the tribunician power (see TRIBUNI PLEBIS), a capacity to introduce business into the senate, this additional right must have in some way privileged his business; the term *ius primae relationis* is, however, an invention of modern scholarship. The reference in the Law concerning *Vespasian's Authority to putting a proposal (*relationem facere*) is probably connected with this right. An inscription and less secure references in the SHA (e.g. *Alex. Sev.* 1) indicate that later emperors came to be allowed the privilege for up to five items of business.

R. J. A. Talbert, *The Senate of Imperial Rome* (1984), 165–6; C. Nicolet, *MÉFRA* 1988, 827–66.

A. D. E. L.

Iustinianus; Iustinus See JUSTINIAN; JUSTIN.

Iustitia, Roman equivalent of *Dike (1); mostly in poetry, but had a temple from 8 January AD 13 (Ov. *Pont.* 3. 6. 25; *fasti Praenestini* under 8 January; see further Wissowa, *RK* 333; Latte, *RR* 300 ff.) and was among the virtues celebrated by Augustus' famous *clipeus virtutis* (the golden shield set up in the Senate-house and inscribed with the emperor's virtues, 27 BC). In inscriptions she sometimes has the title Augusta.

J. Hellegouarc'h, *Le Vocabulaire latin des relations et des partis politiques sous la République* (1972), 256 ff.; B. Lichocka, *Iustitia sur les monnaies impériales romaines* (1974).

H. J. R.; J. Sch.

iustitium (derived from *ius sistere*, 'stopping legal business'), was the temporary suspension of jurisdiction and judicial operations by magistrates and judges in civil and criminal matters. It was proclaimed by a magistrate in an edict, usually on the senate's authority. It was originally used in a military crisis, especially a *tumultus*, to enable the people to concentrate on raising an army. Its use as a mark of mourning survived into the Principate. In the late republic we find it employed as a form of political pressure (Plut. *Ti. Gracch.* 10, *Sull.* 8; App. *BCiv.* 1. 56).

A. B.; A. W. L.

Iustus, a leading citizen of *Tiberias, of moderate political persuasion, was an opponent of *Josephus' command in Galilee in AD 66/7, during the First Jewish Revolt. After being implicated, with members of his family, in the revolt of Tiberias, he fled to *Agrippa II, who protected him and later made him his secretary. After Agrippa's death, he published an account of the war. A chronicle of the Jewish kings, attested by Photius (*Bibl.* 33) was probably a separate work. Josephus' *Life* gives prominence to a vigorous polemic against his personality and his writing.

T. Rajak, *CQ* 1973, 345–68.

E. M. S.; T. R.

Iuvenalis See JUVENAL.

Iuvencus, Gaius Vettius Aquilinus, a Spanish priest of noble family, born at Eliberri in *Baetica, the first exponent of *biblical epic, and arguably the earliest poet to use an established classical genre to treat explicitly Christian subject-matter. His *Evangeliorum libri IV* was written somewhat before AD 330, and narrates the contents of the Gospels, particularly St Matthew's, in 3,311 hexameter verses. *Jerome praised the boldness of the undertaking and its fidelity to its source.

Ed. J. Huemer, *CSEL* 24. N. Hansson, *Textcritisches zu Juvencus mit vollständigem Index verborum* (1950); J. Fontaine, *Naissance de la poésie dans l'occident chrétien* (1981).

M. J. B.

iuvenes (or **iuventus**), 'youths', 'youth', of military age. When a Roman boy adopted the *toga virilis, usually at 14, he became a *iuvenis*. At 17 those intending to follow an equestrian or senatorial career started the military service which was a normal preliminary. *Iuvenes* of 14–17 years of age who were *equites (including the sons of senators) served at Rome their *tirocinium*, a preparation for military service. This institution originated in the Roman republic (Cic. *Cael.* 11) but was reorganized by *Augustus, to invigorate the youth of the upper classes at Rome (cf. *Maecenas' speech, Cass. Dio 52. 26), an important part of the imperial ideology (*tabula Siarensis, fr. IIb, 1. 17). Two factors interested Augustus in the youth: concern, general among his contemporaries, to educate future generations in traditional Roman ways and offer them a model, and in particular his desire to recall military aspects of the equestrian order. The *iuventus* filled the rows of the *cuneus iuniorum* (wedge-shaped division of seats for *iuniores*, or younger men) in the theatre and took part in the Circensian Games. They practised physical exercises (*exercitatio campestris*) and riding, paraded at great festivals, and held their own games, the Ludi Sevirales, games presided over by the *seviri* (see below). (The Lusus Troiae ('Troy Game') was celebrated by those who were still *pueri*, 'boys'.) *Nero held games called Iuvenalia to accompany the first shaving of his beard (AD 59) and organized a body of picked youths, perhaps known as *iuvenes Augustiani*. A *collegium iuvenum Augustianorum* was established, perhaps by *Domitian.

Institutions for freeborn youths in the Italian towns also came into existence, instilling *esprit de corps* and the ideal of service. By the 2nd cent. AD, they had spread through the western provinces (cf. *Dig.* 48. 19. 28. 3).

Iuventus was also used in a wider sense to indicate at Rome the whole body of *equites equo publico* (i.e. *equites under the age of 35 who were still *iuniores* technically, and sons of senators under the age of 25). Augustus also reintroduced the annual parade (*travectio*), the riders grouped in six *turmae* ('squadrons') of three centuries, commanded by noble *seviri* ('six men': i.e. six presidents or commanders). Augustus inspected (*recognovit*, Suet. *Aug.* 38. 3) the force; a board of three was sometimes appointed for the purpose (*ILS* 9483 = EJ 209). This is the sense of *iuventus* in the courtesy title '*princeps iuventutis'; coins significantly show *Titus and *Domitian on horseback.

M. Rostovtzeff, *Klio*, Beiheft 3 (1905), 59 ff.; L. R. Taylor, *JRS* 1924, 158 ff.; M. Della Corte, *Iuventus* (1924); S. L. Mohler, *TAPA* 1937, 442 ff.; P. Veyne, *Rev. Ét. Anc.* 1960, 100 ff.; Y. Le Bohec, ibid. 1975, 108 ff.; G. Pfister, *Die Erneuerung der röm. Iuventus durch Augustus* (1977); M.

Jaczynowska, *Les Associations de la jeunesse romaine sous le Haut-Empire* (1978); Z. Yavetz, in E. Segal and F. Millar, (eds.), *Caesar Augustus: Seven aspects* (1984), 1–36; S. Demougin, *L'Ordre équestre sous les Julio-Claudiens* (1988), 135 ff.
J. P. B.; B. M. L.

Iuventas, goddess, not of youth or youthful beauty in general, but of the *iuvenes*, the *novi togati*, or men of military age (contrast HEBE). She controlled the admission of males into the community and protected them as *iuvenes. She had a shrine in the vestibule of Minerva's cella in the Capitoline temple (Dion. Hal. *Ant. Rom.* 3. 69. 5), and is said to have been there before the temple was built, she and *Terminus refusing to leave (ibid. and Livy 5. 54. 7; but see Latte, *RR* 256). When any young man took the *toga virilis*, it seems that a contribution was made to her temple chest (Dion. Hal. *Ant. Rom.* 4. 15. 5). A sacrifice to *Spes and Iuventas commemorated the day of Octavian's assumption of the *toga virilis* (*Feriale Cumanum* on 18 October).

Wissowa, *RK* 135 f.; G. Dumézil, *Dieux souverains des indo-européens* (1977), 172 ff.; Radke, *Entwicklung*, 18 ff.
H. J. R.; J. Sch.

Iuventius (*RE* 13) **Celsus Titus Aufidius Hoenius Severianus, Publius,** of a family with *Umbrian connections, was the son of a lawyer and himself a bold and creative legal writer. He was praetor in AD 106 or 107, governor of *Thrace and later Asia (Minor), and a member of *Hadrian's council (*consilium principis*). Hadrian accorded him the honour of a second consulship in 129. Both father and son were leaders of the Proculian school (see PROCULUS). Much of his extensive writing was collected in 39 books (*libri*) of *Digesta*, from which some 144 excerpts survive in *Justinian's work of the same name, along with many citations of his views, especially by *Ulpian. His *Digesta* set the pattern that such works should collect the author's writings and arrange them in the order of the praetor's edict as settled by *Iulianus in AD 131, followed by an appendix dealing with special laws. A man of independent mind but vehement in controversy (Plin. *Ep.* 6. 5), he replied to one enquirer 'either I misunderstand your point, or your enquiry is extremely stupid'. Ingenious in the search for principle, we owe to him such pithy maxims as that 'law is the art of the good and just' (*ius est ars boni et aequi*), and that to know laws is to know their force and effect, not their wording.

Lenel, *Pal.* 1. 127–70; Bremer 2/2. 494–504; *PIR*² I 882; *HLL* 3, § 396. 4; Kunkel 1967, 146–7; H. Hausmaninger, *ANRW* 2. 15 (1976), 382–407; F. Casavola, *Giuristi adrianei* (1980), 107–25, 197–226; Honoré 1962, 138–40.
T. Hon.

Iuventius (*RE* 16) **Laterensis, Marcus,** descended from a 2nd-cent. consul of ultimate Tusculan origin, served in *Bithynia and after his quaestorship (*c.*63 BC) in *Cyrene and *Crete. In 59 he abandoned his tribunician candidacy to avoid an oath to preserve *Caesar's *agrarian law, and in 58/7 he worked on behalf of the exiled *Cicero. Defeated for the curule aedileship (see AEDILES) by Cn. *Plancius, he unsuccessfully prosecuted Plancius (who was defended by Cicero), alleging that an *eques* by origin could not defeat a *nobilis* without bribery. Praetor 51, he is not heard of during the Civil War. In 43, as a legate under M. *Aemilius Lepidus (3), he committed suicide when Lepidus

joined M. *Antonius (2), and was posthumously honoured by the senate.
E. B.

ivory (ἐλέφας, *ebur*), a material derived from the tusk of the Asiatic or African *elephant or the tooth of the hippopotamus. Capable of being carved in the round, or in relief, used as inlay, as a veneer, turned on a lathe, or even moulded, ivory was a multi-purpose commodity that was imported into the Mediterranean from North Africa and the Levant. The Old Persian for the Nile delta meant 'The Tusks'. There were flourishing schools of ivory-working in bronze age Crete (see MINOAN CIVILIZATION), but many 'Minoan' statuettes in museums outside Greece are suspected forgeries. Rich finds of ivory inlays at *Nimrud, Arslan Tash, and other near-eastern sites have echoes in ivory objects found at *Ephesus, *Samos, *Delphi, and in *Laconia. At all periods, *furniture was decorated with ivory plaques. Ivory was used for the flesh parts of cult statues (e.g. *Phidias' chryselephantine *Athena Parthenos and his *Zeus at *Olympia), and for temple doors.

R. D. Barnett, *Ancient Ivories in the Middle East* (1982); J. L. Fitton (ed.), *Ivory in Greece and the Eastern Mediterranean* (1992).
J. B.; M. V.

Ixion ('Ιξίων), legendary king of *Thessaly, was a primal offender against divine order. *Pindar (*Pyth.* 2. 21 ff.) records two crimes: not only was he the world's first parricide (victim unspecified; Pherecydes, according to the scholiast on Ap. Rhod. 3. 62 (*FGrH* F 51), named him as his father-in-law Eïoneus), but after *Zeus had purified him (Aesch. *Eum.* 717 f., 441; see PURIFICATION) he reoffended by attempting to rape his benefactor's wife *Hera. For his intended victim Zeus substituted a cloud-image, which conceived Centaurus ('Pokewind', named as usual after the father), sire of the *Centaurs. His punishment was to be crucified on a fiery wheel which revolves throughout eternity—i.e. presumably the sun; Ixion is condemned to become part of the operating mechanism of Zeus' universe, as *Sisyphus heaves the sun-disc up to the zenith only to see it roll back down, and as *Atlas and *Prometheus support the weight of the sky at its western and eastern limits.

C. Lochin, *LIMC* 5. 1 (1990), 857–62; E. Simon, *JÖAI* 1955, 5–26, and *JDAI* 1967, 275–95.
A. H. G.

iynx, a bird (ἴυγξ 'wryneck'—so named for its mating-gesture) eponymous with a mythological figure and with the wheel to which it was affixed as an implement of erotic magic. Iynx, the daughter of *Peitho or *Echo, employed magic to seduce *Zeus either for *Io or for herself. Offended, *Hera turned her into a bird (Callim. fr. 685 Pf.). As early as the Archaic period, a love-charm in the form of a spoked wheel with a spread-eagled iynx fastened to it was suspended and spun to attract a love-object. *Pindar (*Pyth.* 4. 214) attributes the iynx-wheel's invention to *Aphrodite and its first use to *Jason (1), who secures *Medea's love with its magic. By Theoc. *Id.* 2, the bird has vanished from the wheel, but has left its name behind: Simaitha spins a birdless ἴυγξ to beguile Delphis.

A. S. F. Gow, *JHS* 1934, 1–13, and *Theocritus*, 2nd edn. (1952), 2. 41; J. de la Genière, *Rev. Ét. Anc.* 1958, 27–35; C. A. Faraone, *CJ* 1993, 1–19.
A. H.

Janiculum, the prominent ridge on the west bank of the *Tiber at Rome, some 6 km. (3½ mi.) long; the name was anciently connected with *Janus. The place was an early defensive outpost (Livy 1. 33); a red flag was flown from the hill when the *comitia centuriata* was meeting on the *Campus Martius (Cass. Dio 37. 28). It was later enclosed in a great salient of Aurelian's wall (see WALL OF AURELIAN). Here lay the tomb of King *Numa; also the Lucus Furrinae, scene of the death of C. *Sempronius Gracchus and later occupied by the temple of the Syrian deity *Jupiter Heliopolitanus (see HELIOPOLIS). Otherwise the district was primarily industrial and residential.

N. Goodhue, *The Lucus Furrinae and the Syrian Sanctuary on the Janiculum* (1975); Coarelli, *Roma* 338–42; Richardson, *Topog. Dict. Ancient Rome* 205.   I. A. R.; J. R. P.

Janus, god of door and gate (*ianua*) at Rome (the term also for the type of honorific gateway that we misleadingly call '*triumphal arch'). Like a door, he looked both ways, and is therefore depicted as a double-headed and bearded man (the image chosen for many early Roman coins). More generally he controlled beginnings, most notably as the eponym of the month January (he was named first in prayer, e.g. Livy 8. 9. 6, the *devotio* of P. *Decius Mus (1)), and was linked with the symbolism of the gate at the beginning and end of military campaigns (the bad omen of the departure of the Fabii (see GENS) from Rome before their destruction at the battle of the *Cremera involved going through the right-hand *ianus* or arch of the city-gate instead of the left, Livy 2. 49. 8). This was most famously expressed in the ritual of the closing of the temple of Janus Geminus in the Forum in times of complete peace: under Numa, in 235 BC, three times under *Augustus, and more frequently in the imperial period. *Domitian transferred the cult to a new shrine in the forum 'Transitorium' (see FORUM NERVAE).

This shrine (as depicted on coins) was little more than a gateway itself. It was probably *geminus*—'twin'—in being a four-way arch, like the 'arch of Janus' which survives in the *forum Boarium (the porta Triumphalis through which victorious generals crossed the *pomerium into the city probably had this shape). There are serious topographical problems about the nature and relationship of the other ancient shrines of Janus along the *via Sacra, which may have been related to crossings of the early watercourses in the area. A sanctuary in the forum Holitorium was C. *Duilius' monument for his victory at Mylae (260 BC).

Janus was a god of considerable importance (*divom deus*, god of gods, in the *Hymn of the Salii*, Varro, *Ling.* 7. 27; for cosmic significance, Ov. *Fast.* 1. 101 f.). The *rex sacrorum* sacrificed to him in the *Regia on the *dies Agonalis* of 9 January.

L. Holland, *Janus and the Bridge* (1961); H. Scullard, *Festivals and Ceremonies of the Roman Republic* (1981), 60–1.   N. P.

Jason (1), in mythology, son of Aeson and Alcimede, and leader of the *Argonauts in their quest for the golden fleece; Ἰάσων was sometimes etymologized in antiquity as 'the healer'. In the most common version, Jason was brought up in the Thessalian countryside by the *Centaur Chiron after *Pelias took the throne of *Iolcus in place of Aeson. When Jason returned to Iolcus to claim his inheritance, Pelias, forewarned by an oracle to beware of a man wearing only one sandal, recognized the danger and devised the expedition to recover the golden fleece from the kingdom of Aia in the extreme east (cf. Pind. *Pyth.* 4; Ap. Rhod. *Argonautica*). The expedition itself follows a familiar pattern of *rite-of-passage stories in which young men must undergo terrible ordeals before claiming their rightful inheritance; *Apollonius' Jason, in particular, resembles the tragic *Orestes in the hesitation he feels in the face of what he must do. The expedition is successfully completed with the assistance of *Hera, who wishes to punish Pelias for neglecting to honour her, and Aphrodite who makes the Colchian princess *Medea fall in love with Jason. Already in the *Odyssey* (12. 72) Jason is 'dear to Hera', and Apollonius explains that he once carried her across a torrent when she was disguised as an old woman; later sources combine this incident with the fateful loss of a sandal (cf. Hunter on *Argon.* 3. 66–75). After Jason and Medea had taken revenge upon Pelias, they fled to *Corinth where they lived until Jason decided to marry Creon's daughter; in the version made famous by *Euripides' *Medea*, Medea then killed their two sons and his new bride. There are various accounts of Jason's death, of which the most colourful are that he killed himself in despair (Diod. Sic. 4. 55. 1), that he was killed when a plank from the rotting *Argo* fell on him as he slept, and that the stern-piece which he had dedicated to Hera fell on him when he entered her temple (Eur. *Med.* 1386–7 with schol.). Along with many other Argonauts, he was said to have taken part in the Calydonian boar-hunt (Apollod. 1. 8. 2; Ov. *Met.* 8. 302; see MELEAGER (1)).

O. Jessen, *RE* 9. 759–71; C. Segal, *Pindar's Mythmaking: The Fourth Pythian Ode* (1986); B. K. Braswell, *A Commentary on the Fourth Pythian Ode of Pindar* (1988); J. Neils, *LIMC* 5 (1990), 629–38.   R. L. Hu.

Jason (2), 4th-cent. BC tyrant (see TYRANNY) of *Pherae in *Thessaly. Poor documentation conceals connections between his career and the ambitions of *Lycophron (1) (Jason's father?). Jason initially ruled Pherae jointly with Polyalces and abandoned paternal Spartan associations for Theban ones (see THEBES (1)) by 385 BC (formal alliance postdates 375/4; he never joined the *Second Athenian Confederacy), but the power which (Spartan intervention being refused) forced *Pharsalus' capitulation (375/4) and made him *tagos remains a surprise, though one component was Jason's mercenary army, led by someone who

Jason

(*Xenophon (1) thought) understood effective military leadership. During the period 373–371 Thessaly's unification provoked the hostility of *Phocis—and Jason supported *Timotheus (2) in an Athenian court (winter 373/2). After *Leuctra (371) Thebes asked him to exterminate the defeated Spartans. Jason arranged disengagement, believing uneasy balance of power suited him better. In 371/0 he secured Perrhaebia (see PERRHAEBI) and adjacent regions, concluded an alliance with *Amyntas (1), argued for Thessalian hegemony, and planned to supervise the Pythian festival (370; see DELPHI; PYTHIAN GAMES)—as hieromnēmōn, but with an army. He perhaps intended a Persian crusade (see PANHELLENISM), but assassination by conspirators whose motives remain unclarified, though five survived to receive acclaim, left the point unresolved. Parallels with *Philip (1) II of Macedon have often been drawn.

> H. D. Westlake, *Thessaly in the Fourth Century* (1935); J. K. Davies, *Democracy and Classical Greece*, 2nd edn. (1993), 235 ff.; C. J. Tuplin, *Failings of Empire* (1993); *CAH* 6² (1994), see index; B. Helly, *L'État Thessalien* (1995).   C. J. T.

Jason (3), of *Cyrene, wrote, before 124 BC, a Greek history in five books about Judas Maccabaeus and his brothers. The author of 2 Maccabees describes his own work as an abridgement of Jason (2 Macc. 2: 19–25). Jason's cultural background is presumed to lie in the important Greek-speaking Jewish communities of Cyrenaica. See MACCABEES.

> FGrH 182. Schürer, *History* 3. 531–4; M. Hengel, *Judaism and Hellenism* (Eng. edn. 1974), 1. 95–9.   T. R.

javelin, throwing the The javelin (ἄκων) was a spear about 2.5 m. (8 ft.) long, probably with a metal point. Round the middle was bound a thong with a loop through which the athlete placed his first finger, or first and middle fingers, when throwing. As he let go of the javelin he held onto the loop of the thong which, as it unwound, gave a spinning motion to the javelin thereby increasing distance and accuracy (cf. the motion of a modern rifle bullet). In the *Panathenaea competitors threw their javelins while riding on horseback past a target. See ATHLETICS.

> E. N. Gardiner, *Greek Athletic Sports and Festivals* (1910), 338–58; H. M. Lee, *JHS* 1976, 70–9.   R. L. H.; S. J. I.

Javolenus Priscus See OCTAVIUS TIDIUS TOSSIANUS IAVOLENUS PRISCUS, C. (or L.).

Jaxartes, Asiatic river (mod. Syr Darya, flowing into the Aral Sea). Though known perhaps to *Herodotus (1) by repute, it was discovered by *Alexander (3) the Great, who founded *Alexandria (5) Eschate (Khodzhend) on it. The Greeks thought that it flowed into the Caspian (which perhaps was once true—see CASPIAN SEA), and sometimes confused it with the *Araxes (now the Aras). *Ptolemy (4) gives geographical details of tribes on its banks.

> Strabo 11. 507 ff.; Ptol. *Geog.* 6. 12–14. Thomson, *Hist. Anc. Geog.* 85, 127 f. S. Sherwin-White and A. Kuhrt, *From Samarkhand to Sardis* (1993), 19, 103, 105.   E. H. W.; A. J. S. S.

Jerome (Eusebius Hieronymus) (c. AD 347–420), biblical translator, scholar, and ascetic. Born into a Christian family at Stridon in *Dalmatia, he was educated at Rome at the school of Aelius *Donatus (1), and later studied rhetoric. During a stay at Trier (*Augusta Treverorum), where he had probably intended to enter imperial service, his *Christianity took on greater meaning, and around 372, fired with ascetic zeal (see ASCETICISM), he set out for the east. After two years or more at *Antioch (1), he finally withdrew to the desert of Chalcis to undertake the penitential life of an anchoritic monk. Here he began to learn Hebrew, with

immense consequences for biblical scholarship. But after no more than a year or so he returned to Antioch, where he was ordained priest. Back in Rome in 382, he quickly won the confidence of Pope *Damasus, at whose request he commenced work on what was to become the core of the *Vulgate version of the Bible. There too he formed friendships with several aristocratic women who had dedicated themselves to Christianity and were living austere and simple existences. His association with the widow Paula in particular combined with other factors to put him in a bad light with the generality of Roman Christians, and following Damasus' death he was effectively hounded from the city (385). Paula followed him to Palestine, where, at Bethlehem, they founded a monastery and a convent. Here Jerome remained for the rest of his life, devoting himself to the ascetic way and to Christian learning.

Jerome was a prolific writer. In addition to his translations of Scripture, he produced numerous commentaries on books of the Bible, for which he drew heavily on previous commentators such as *Origen (1). Polemical works on a variety of religious issues reveal a bitter and vitriolic side to his nature. His surviving correspondence, which discloses a network of connections across the whole Mediterranean world and in high places, is of the greatest interest for the study of 4th- and 5th-cent. Christianity. Other works of importance include his translation and expansion of *Eusebius of Caesarea's *Chronicle* of world history, and the *De viris illustribus*, a catalogue of 135 mainly Christian writers.

The famous dream in which Jerome saw himself accused of being not a Christian but a 'Ciceronian' (see TULLIUS CICERO (1), M.), and which seems to have resulted in his giving up reading pagan literature altogether for many years, is a reflection of the tension felt by many Christians of the time between their religious beliefs and their classical heritage. Over a long period Jerome himself succeeded in resolving this conflict, and perhaps more than any other of the Latin Fathers he can be seen as a man of the classical world who happened to be Christian. His classicism is evident not only in his frequent quotations from classical literature, but often in his style. While his scriptural translations and exegetical works tend to be simple and unadorned, other texts display the full fruits of rhetorical training and the verve of a great natural talent steeped in the best writings of an earlier age. If his enduring importance lay most of all in the *Vulgate, in his teaching on celibacy, and in his contribution to western monasticism, he also ranks among the finest writers of Latin prose.

> TEXTS Migne, *PL* 22–30; *CCSL* 72–80 (1958–90; continuing); Letters, I. Hilberg, *CSEL* 54–6 (1910–18); *Chron.*, R. Helm (1956); *De vir. ill.*, E. C. Richardson (1896), A. Ceresa-Gastaldo, with comm. (1988).
> COMMENTARIES *Ep.* 57, G. J. M. Bartelink (1980); *Ep.* 60, J. H. D. Scourfield (1993); *Adversus Rufinum*, P. Lardet (1993); *Commentary on Jonah*, Y.-M. Duval (1985).
> TRANSLATIONS Various works: W. H. Fremantle (1893, repr. 1979). Letters: J. Labourt (1949–63; in French); (selection) F. A. Wright (Loeb, 1933). Dogmatic and polemical works: J. N. Hritzu (1965). Homilies: M. L. Ewald (1964–6).
> STUDIES F. Cavallera, *Saint Jérôme: Sa vie et son œuvre* (1922); H. Hagendahl, *Latin Fathers and the Classics* (1958); P. Antin, *Recueil sur saint Jérôme* (1968); J. N. D. Kelly, *Jerome* (1975); S. Rebenich, *Hieronymus und sein Kreis* (1992).   J. H. D. S.

Jerusalem ('Ιεροσόλυμα and 'Ιερουσαλήμ) was repopulated and the Temple reconstructed with the blessing of *Cyrus (1), some 50 years after the destruction of 587 BC, by Jews returning from the Babylonian exile. In the 440s, the walls were rebuilt and their completion marked by a great celebration of the Tabernacles festival, described in the Book of Nehemiah. Palestine as a whole came into *Alexander (3) the Great's empire after *Issus, and there are traditions that he visited the Temple and paid his respects to the high priest. A schematic sketch of Ptolemaic Jerusalem (see PTOLEMY (1); EGYPT (Ptolemaic)) occurs in the Letter of *Aristeas, where it is dominated by a temple on a hill. Attempts to stamp on Jerusalem the forms of a Greek city, apparently with the added name Antioch, were set in motion by the Hellenizers (see HELLENISM) under *Antiochus (4) IV, who himself established a pagan cult in the Temple in 168/7; but within three years the shrine was rededicated by the *Maccabees. A capacious *Seleucid citadel, whose location is still undetermined, dominated the city, and was occupied by Hellenizing Jews until its demolition by Simon in 142. In 135/4 *Antiochus (7) VII Sidetes besieged Jerusalem, and John Hyrcanus was accused of ransacking the tomb of David on Mount Zion to pay for its defence. Under the *Hasmoneans, the city became a major centre, expanding to the west and north. During *Pompey's siege of 63, to settle the war between the two Hasmonean brothers, Aristobulus held out in the Temple, and in the aftermath Pompey personally inspected the shrine and removed Temple treasures, including the famous golden vine; but little physical damage was inflicted. The capture and pillaging of Jerusalem by the *Parthians in 40 led to C. *Sosius' siege and recapture in 37 and the installation of *Herod (1).

Herod transformed Jerusalem: the city acquired a theatre, hippodrome, and amphitheatre, all now vanished; a palace defended by three massive towers (the lower courses of 'Phasael' are in the present Tower of David); the Antonia fortress, of which the paved courtyard and other installations remain. Above all, starting in 20/19 BC, the Temple was reconstructed, in white stone, with copious gold covering. The biblical prescriptions were still followed, but the height was doubled and the surrounding courts expanded. The Temple mount was erected on a vast retaining platform, of which the 'Western wall' ('Wailing wall') and adjoining extensions are a remnant, as well as the traces of a great course of stairs, 'plaza', and shops exposed by excavation at the SE corner. The valley between this and the élite residential quarter in the upper city was bridged. There the excavated houses, with their copious ablution cisterns, bear witness to the sophisticated but religiously correct lifestyle of the high priestly and lay élite of Second-Temple Jerusalem. The landmark monumental tombs standing in the Kedron valley confirm the impression. Diaspora benefactors (see JEWS) had contributed to the Temple, and Jewish pilgrims converged from far afield during the three 'foot festivals'. The inscription of the Theodotus synagogue, rare evidence of a pre-70 *synagogue in Jerusalem, speaks about the reception of visitors. Some Diaspora Jews had tombs in Jerusalem, including the converted royal family of *Adiabene. For the elder *Pliny (1), Jerusalem was 'by far the most famous city of the east'.

In the revolt of AD 66, after the reduction of other parts of the country, Jerusalem became the centre first of the faction-fighting between the rival rebel leaders and then of unified resistance. The destruction of the city and the Temple by *Titus in 70, after a five-month siege, were a major turning-point in its history. The walls were razed, leaving only the three towers. The priestly class all but disappeared. After the revolt, the camp of Legio X *Fretensis* (see LEGION) was located at Jerusalem. After the *Bar Kokhba Revolt, *Hadrian refounded the city as a military colony, Aelia Capitolina, but there is little conclusive evidence of large-scale

reconstruction. Christian sources claim that Jews were barred. In any event, Jewish religious life perforce ceased to be focused on Jerusalem. The Christian holy places were not developed until Constantine I. The church of the Holy Sepulchre was dedicated in 335, and a second great basilica was built on the Mount of Olives, to mark the supposed site of the Ascension. Again, a pilgrim trade benefited the city; and in the 5th cent. the empress Eudocia included Mount Zion and the original City of David within its walls. See PILGRIMAGE (CHRISTIAN).

E. Stern (ed.), *The New Encyclopaedia of Archaeological Excavations in the Holy Land* (1992); N. Avigad, *Discovering Jerusalem* (1984); *Jerusalem Revealed* (Israel Exploration Society, 1975); J. Jeremias, *Jerusalem in the Time of Jesus* (1969); G. A. Smith, *Jerusalem* (1907–8).   T. R.

Jewish-Greek literature originates with the Greek translation of the Hebrew Pentateuch (Torah; see ARISTEAS, LETTER OF), made in the 3rd cent. BC. A unique, literal style was adopted, Hebraized in syntax and distinctive in vocabulary. The first versions were revised, and the rest of the Hebrew Bible was translated, together with numerous Apocryphal books, over succeeding centuries, to constitute what we know as the *Septuagint. Jews heard and read the Bible in Greek not only in the Diaspora (see JEWS), but also in various contexts in Palestine: a Greek scroll of the Minor Prophets was found at Nahal Hever on the Dead Sea (see DEAD SEA SCROLLS), and Qumran has yielded Greek biblical fragments. Such texts served the many Jews whose primary means of expression was Greek, as well as bilingual groups accommodating to a Greek environment.

In the case of certain, sometimes canonical books, the Greek translation is free enough to have become a creation in its own right. The translation of Ecclesiasticus (the book of Ben Sira) was made in Egypt under *Ptolemy (1) VII Euergetes (i.e. before 116 BC) by the author's grandson, who ruminates in his preface on the problems of turning one language elegantly into another, addressing himself to scholars living 'in a foreign land'. First Esdras is an imaginative version of the Book of Ezra, which survives alongside a literal one. Passages which seem to have been original compositions in Greek were sometimes added to Semitic texts: the Greek Esther has substantial digressions of Hellenistic type, supplementing the story's drama and romance; in a colophon in some manuscripts, the translator says that his work was taken to Egypt and describes himself as Lysimachus son of Ptolemy from *Jerusalem.

A varied literary culture evolved around the Greek Bible, in general dependent upon biblical material for content, style, or both. While this literature was read largely by Jews, and subsequently by Christians, some authors aspired also to a Gentile audience. There is no real evidence to suggest, however, that any of them were aiming at proselytization.

*Alexandria (1) was the first and principal home of this creativity, as emerges from the marked Egyptian orientation of many fragments. But it is clear that Jewish literature in Greek was also written in the cities of Asia Minor, in *Cyrene, and in other major Diaspora centres. Biblical themes were adapted to diverse Greek literary genres. Precise dates for the earliest works are hard to come by, since much of this literature survives only in small fragments, cited by Eusebius in the *Praeparatio evangelica* or by *Clement of Alexandria, from the anthology of the 1st-cent. BC Roman polymath *Alexander (11) Polyhistor.

In prose, history, in the widest sense, was the dominant mode. At the end of the 3rd cent. BC Demetrius ('the Chronographer') offered comparative dates for biblical events. *Eupolemus, sometimes identified with Judas Maccabaeus' ambassador to Rome of the same name (see MACCABEES), gave more picturesque renderings of biblical episodes, with accretions from Jewish oral interpretation (*midrash). Artapanus made Moses the founder of Egyptian religion and identified him with *Musaeus (1) and with *Hermes. *Joseph and Asenath* is a novelistic account (see NOVEL, GREEK) of Joseph's love for Potiphar's daughter and her adoption of the mysteries of Judaism. Cleodemus Malchus, of whom only a short fragment survives, presented the Libyan people as descendants of Abraham as well as of Hercules. Comments on Abraham and on the Egyptians, ascribed by *Josephus to *Hecataeus (2) of Abdera (who did write on the Jews) are believed to derive from a Hellenistic-Jewish work, nowadays known as Pseudo-Hecataeus.

*Aristobulus (2) gave his exegesis a philosophical slant, dedicating to Ptolemy (probably *Ptolemy (1) VI Philometor) a partly allegorical interpretation of the Torah which anticipates *Philon (4). He is sometimes identified as the teacher of Ptolemy who is named as the recipient of a letter from Jerusalem in the preface to 2 Maccabees (1: 10). With copious quotation of Greek poetry, genuine and spurious, he presented Moses as the father of Greek philosophy. The Wisdom of Solomon, of uncertain date and provenance, in form adopts the oriental proverbial mode, but describes in philosophical language, tinged with echoes of the Greek Bible, the rule in the world of a personified wisdom sprung from God.

Among verse writers, Philon the Epic Poet recounted stories of Abraham, Joseph, and Jerusalem in his work, while Theodotus focused on the town of Shechem, and especially the rape of Dinah. *Ezekiel the Tragedian's drama on the Exodus, influenced by *Aeschylus and *Euripides, may well have been designed for performance. Perhaps as late as the 1st cent. AD, a generalized Jewish ethic was put into hexameter by Pseudo-Phocylides, with, however, a marked lack of interest in specific religious practices; see PHOCYLIDES (2). In a quite different mould are the Jewish prophetic texts amongst the heterogeneous collection of Greek Sibyllines (see SIBYL), which derive from a broad geographical and chronological span.

History-writing on contemporary or at any rate post-biblical themes was also practised. First Maccabees is a translation from the Hebrew, in which the influence of the historiography of Samuel and Kings is still dominant. But 2 Maccabees is a paraphrase of an independent Greek historical work on the same subject. (See JASON (3); MACCABEES.) Third Maccabees recounts a fictitious persecution of the Jews in Alexandria supposedly at the hands of *Ptolemy (1) IV Philopator; while 4 Maccabees embeds an account of the fictitious deaths of the seven Maccabean martyrs and their mother in an amalgam of rhetoric and philosophy characteristic of the *Second Sophistic.

*Philon (4), *Josephus, and Josephus' contemporary *Iustus of Tiberias also belong to the tradition of Jewish-Greek literature. Composition did not cease with the destruction of the Temple in AD 70. We must suppose that Jews were still writing in Greek at the same time as Christians were adopting the earlier products of this tradition as their own.

Schürer, *History* 3 / 1. 470–704; *FGrH* 3; C. R. Holladay, *Fragments from Hellenistic Jewish Authors* 1: *Historians* (1983), 2: *Poets* (1989); J. H. Charlesworth, *The Old Testament Pseudepigrapha* 2 (1985); M. Hengel, *Judaism and Hellenism* (Eng. edn. 1974); J. J. Collins, *Between Athens and Jerusalem* (1983).   T. R.

Jews (in Greek and Roman times). The Jews at the beginning of the period were an ethnic group with distinctive religious practices. In the course of the period, the religious definition acquired new emphasis, and significant numbers of Jews became Jews by conversion rather than birth.

Palestine A demographically mixed region, this was understood to be the homeland of the Jews throughout the period, though in fact housing a minority of them. More precisely, the Jews belonged to the small area around *Jerusalem known in Greek as *Ioudaia*, whence the name *Ioudaioi*. However, the two revolts against Roman rule brought about the physical exclusion of the Jews from their centre.

From 538 to 332 BC the Jews of Palestine were a part of the *Persian empire. Coins reveal that their territory was called Yehud and the Persian governor *pekah*. The high priest seems to have been the highest Jewish official. A century of Ptolemaic rule (see PTOLEMY (1); EGYPT (PTOLEMAIC)) followed *Alexander (3) the Great's death. The Zeno papyri (see APOLLONIUS (3)) illuminate in general the administration and economic life of the area, and reveal the high-level dealings of Tobias, a Jewish landowner east of the Jordan, with the Ptolemaic governor Apollonius.

In 200 Palestine passed into *Seleucid hands, and the pressure of Hellenism was manifested, first in dissension within the high priestly families, and then in *Antiochus (4) IV's installation of a pagan cult in the Temple (168 / 7 BC), which was resisted by the *Maccabees. Only in 142 BC was the Seleucid garrison expelled from Jerusalem. For the next 80 years, the Jews were ruled by the hereditary *Hasmonean high priests, attaining complete autonomy after the death of *Antiochus (7) VII in 134 BC. The expansion of Jewish territory involved a phenomenon new to Judaism, the conversion of the neighbouring peoples, Idumaeans and Ituraeans, at least partly by force. See IDUMAEA; ITURAEA.

*Pompey's intervention in 63 BC, occasioned by a quarrel between the two sons of the defunct queen, Alexandra Salome, led to the installation of one of them, Hyrcanus, and to the reduction of the kingdom, with the freeing of the conquered Greek cities. A. *Gabinius (2) organized the ethnarchy in 57 into five self-governing communities, with Hyrcanus remaining as ethnarch until his removal by the *Parthians and the appointment of the Idumaean convert *Herod (1) as ruler.

In AD 6 *Judaea was annexed, together with *Samaria and Idumaea, to form the Roman province of Judaea, administered by equestrian officials (prefects, later procurators). A census in that year crystallized opposition and generated an ideology of resistance. Called by *Josephus the 'fourth philosophy', this tendency was evidently the source of the subsequent, more famous rebel groupings, *sicarii* and *zealots. A pattern of procuratorial misgovernment enlisted the sympathies of the Jewish crowd in Jerusalem and of the poor in *Galilee to the anti-Roman cause. The high-priestly and landowning élites criticized Rome only under extreme provocation, as when the emperor *Gaius (1) attempted to have his statue placed in the Temple (39 / 40). The installation of M. *Iulius Agrippa I (41–4) by Claudius was to prove merely a brief interlude in the regime of the procurators. Famines, banditry, and the breakdown of the working relationship between the Jewish ruling class and Rome marked the years before the outbreak of the First Jewish Revolt in 66. The Temple sacrifices for the emperor's welfare were terminated, and a provisional government in Jerusalem appointed regional leaders (including the historian Josephus), chose a demotic high priest by lot, abolished debt, and issued its own freedom coinage. But the Jews were deeply divided politically. In Galilee the conflict between pro- and anti-war elements made resistance ineffectual. In besieged Jerusalem, three rebel factions conducted a civil war until the last stages of the siege.

In 70 the Judaean victory of *Vespasian and *Titus, confirmed by the burning of Jerusalem and the (perhaps accidental) destruction of the Temple, was crucial in consolidating the Flavian seizure of power. Much was made of '*Judaea capta*' in Flavian *propaganda, culminating in the *triumph over the Jews. Jewish-owned land in Judaea was expropriated.

From 70 the province of Judaea was governed by legates and a *legion (X Fretensis) was stationed in Jerusalem. Jewish religious and cultural life centred for a generation on Jamnia (Jabneh), an enclave on the Judaean coast, where a new definition of Judaism without a Temple was evolved by the first *rabbis.

The revolt in the Diaspora under Trajan, in 115–17, produced disturbances in Palestine, suppressed by *Lusius Quietus. Of greater significance was the second great revolt in Palestine, led by *Bar Kokhba. Its long-term causes are ill-documented, but the immediate triggers were *Hadrian's prohibition of circumcision, and his plan to turn Jerusalem into the Roman *colonia* of Aelia Capitolina. After the costly suppression of this revolt, in 135, the name of the province became *Syria Palaestina, another legion (VI *Ferrata*) was stationed in Galilee, and, according to Christian sources, Jews were altogether excluded from Jerusalem.

A further revolt occurred under *Antoninus Pius, in spite of his exemption of the Jews from Hadrian's ban on circumcision. Later, the Jews are said to have supported *Avidius Cassius; and a rebellion in the time of *Septimius Severus is probably associated with the rising of *Pescennius Niger.

During the 3rd cent. Jewish life flourished in Galilee: *synagogues began to proliferate, in villages as well as towns; rabbinic influence on daily life grew; and Jews played their part in some of the newly refurbished cities, notably *Caesarea (2). The patriarch, located successively in several Galilean towns, operated as the representative of the Jews of Palestine and was closely associated with the rabbis. Greek was widely used by the educated élite, though the first great rabbinic compilation, the *Mishnah, was written in Hebrew, *c.*200. Prosperous Jews from the Syrian and Phoenician Diaspora were buried, alongside rabbis, in heavily figurative *sarcophagi, in the spacious vaults and catacombs of Beth Shearim.

This vigorous community life, and the building of synagogues, continued into the era of Christianization (see CHRISTIANITY) in the Holy Land which followed the conversion of *Constantine I, when sites associated with biblical events became focuses of *pilgrimage. But from then on there were spiritual claims to Jerusalem, Judaea, and Galilee which rivalled those of the Jews.

A destructive Jewish revolt in Palestine, allegedly centred on a supposed Messiah, is ascribed by one source to the reign of *Gallus Caesar (350/1). This may have been a protest against Christian anti-Jewish legislation. But it was left to a pagan emperor, *Julian the Apostate, to plan for the rebuilding of the Jewish Temple and the restoration there of the blood sacrifices. An earthquake, a fire, and various supernatural manifestations put a stop to the construction; and a year later (363) Julian was dead.

The Diaspora The dispersion of the Jews began in 586 BC, when Nebuchadnezzar took the inhabitants of Jerusalem into captivity. Many of them did not return when permitted by *Cyrus (1) of *Persia in 538, but remained voluntarily in *Babylonia, where flourishing communities existed for centuries, producing in late antiquity the greatest monument of rabbinic learning, the Babylonian *Talmud. During the Hellenistic period, many Jews migrated from Palestine and also from Babylonia, settling around the eastern Mediterranean, especially in Syria, Asia Minor, and Egypt. Jewish military colonists had lived at *Elephantine for centuries, and now they were joined by new military and civilian settlers in both countryside and town. The community at *Alexandria (1) became the most important in the Diaspora, the splendour of its synagogue a byword, its mixed Jewish-Greek culture highly creative. Numbers alone made the Jews prominent inhabitants of the city. But by the 1st cent. AD there were sizeable communities in most of the cities of the eastern Mediterranean. The *Acts of the Apostles is important testimony to the local prominence of synagogues.

Expansion to Italy and the west began later, but the community in Rome was established by the mid-2nd cent. BC. Jews taken as slaves after the various wars in Palestine swelled the numbers of the Diaspora, as in due course did the voluntary attachment of pagans to the Jewish synagogues of Rome. Inscriptions from the Jewish *catacombs of Rome reveal the existence of eleven synagogues in the 2nd to 4th cents. AD, whose names suggest an earlier, in some cases an Augustan, foundation.

Diaspora Jews retained their identity and the basic religious practices of Judaism—male circumcision, observance of the sabbath, and other festivals (notably Tabernacles) and the avoidance of non-kosher meat. Until AD 70, their allegiance to the Temple and to Jerusalem as their mother city was signalled by the payment of the Temple tax and by the practice of pilgrimage at the major agricultural festivals.

At the same time, inscriptions concerning Jewish benefactions and commemorations from many cities in the eastern Roman empire make it clear that the Jews adapted to their varied environments. Greek was their native language. In Cyrenaica, at *Berenice (a), there were Jewish town-councillors and Jewish ephebes (see EPHEBOI) as early as the 1st cent. AD. In the 3rd cent. the phenomenon is quite common. Non-Jews expressed attachment to the Jewish synagogue by becoming benefactors, 'God-fearers' (or sympathizers), and proselytes. The great Jewish inscription from *Aphrodisias shows an association of Jews and proselytes subscribing to a memorial together with a separate group of 'God-fearers', including councillors.

The advocacy of Hyrcanus and the Herodians (see HASMONEANS; HEROD (1) and (2); IULIUS AGRIPPA (1–2), M.), together with their own diplomacy, gained for Jewish communities in the Roman provinces the patronage successively of *Caesar, of Antony (M. *Antonius (2)), and of *Augustus. In their disputes with their neighbours, they were assisted by Roman decrees which upheld their right to observe their customary practices; and these decrees were adopted empire-wide as precedents. Synagogues, though classed as *collegia* (associations: see COLLEGIUM), were exempted by Caesar from his general ban. The right to raise, deposit, and transmit the Temple tax was upheld. Sometimes, special food markets were permitted, sometimes exemption granted from court appearances on the sabbath or from military service which rendered sabbath observance impossible. Christian authors were later to describe Judaism as a *religio licita* ('legitimate religion') in the Roman empire on the basis of these arrangements; see RELIGION, ROMAN. Furthermore, after the destruction of the Temple, the two-drachma (half-shekel) tax paid by all adult Jewish males to the Temple was extended to women and children, diverted to *Jupiter Capitolinus, and deposited in the new **fiscus iudaicus*. *Domitian's exactions were notoriously harsh, but *Nerva issued coins announcing his removal of the abuses. Implicit in the taxation was an official acknowledgement of the existence of Jewish communities, and this also contributed to the Christians' sense that the Jews had been 'legalized'.

Periodic expulsions of the Jews from the city of Rome were short-lived and did not undermine their standing elsewhere. Three expulsions of the Jews are recorded: in 139 BC; by *Tiberius in AD 19; and by *Claudius. The authorities' fear of disturbance and of un-Roman practices, rather than overt proselytizing, was the immediate cause of anti-Jewish measures, as of those against other alien cults and practices. The Jews do not appear to have been actively seeking converts during this period. It was not until the reign of *Septimius Severus that conversion to Judaism was forbidden; even then, there was no Jewish 'mission'.

In spite of—or because of—Jewish acculturation, friction between Jews and their neighbours was not uncommon. In Alexandria, anti-Semitic literature was produced in the Hellenistic period; but it was the Roman annexation of Egypt which shook a centuries-long political equilibrium by redefining the privileges accorded to Alexandrian citizens, and excluding the Jews from them. In AD 38, a visit of M. *Iulius Agrippa I to Alexandria sparked the first pogrom in Jewish history, when synagogues were burnt, shops looted, and the Jews herded into a ghetto. Trouble returned in 66, at a time when the outbreak of revolt in Palestine also provoked Greek–Jewish violence in a number of Syrian cities. The failure of the revolt saw further attacks on urban Jews.

In 115 the Jews of Cyrenaica rose against their pagan neighbours and against the Roman authorities, inflicting considerable damage and targeting pagan temples. The uprising, which suggests considerable frustration, spread to Alexandria and other parts of Egypt; and to *Cyprus, where it was furthered by a charismatic leader. The rebellion in 116 in *Trajan's new Mesopotamian province (see MESOPOTAMIA), coinciding with these events, brought in the Jews of Babylonia. The revolts were suppressed by Q. *Marcius Turbo with considerable effort. An era of more peaceful co-existence for the Jewish Diaspora ensued, and the increasingly high profile of Jewish communities in some cities is attested by excavated remains of synagogues. The case of *Sardis is particularly noteworthy, where a massive synagogue adjoined the city's main baths-complex, and was refurbished several times, well into the Christian era. The legal restrictions placed on Jews by the Christian emperors of the 4th and 5th cents. did not in the first instance crush the activities of the synagogues.

Schürer, History 1–3; L. Grabbe, Judaism from Cyrus to Hadrian (1992; Eng. edn. 1995); E. Bickerman, The Jews in the Greek Age (1988); Cambridge History of Judaism 2 (1989); V. A. Tcherikover, Hellenistic Civilization and the Jews (1959); E. M. Smallwood, The Jews under Roman Rule (1976); L. Feldman, Jew and Gentile in the Ancient World (1993); P. Trebilco, Jewish Communities in Asia Minor (1991); M. Avi-Yonah, The Jews of Palestine (1976); L. V. Rutgers, The Jews in Late Ancient Rome (1995); P. Schäfer, A History of the Jews in Antiquity (1995), and Judaeophobia. Attitudes towards the Jews in the Ancient World (1997). T. R.

Jocasta See OEDIPUS.

Jordanes, an historian who worked c. AD 550, almost certainly in *Constantinople. Of Gothic descent (see GOTHS), he had worked as a military secretary before his *conversio* (see CONVERSION), probably to a monastic life. He has left two extant works: a summary of Roman history known as the *Romana*, and the so-called *Getica*, an account of Gothic history which claims to be closely based on the lost Gothic history of *Cassiodorus,

using a MS from the latter's own household. Controversy surrounds both works. Ensslin (see bibliog. below) argued influentially that the *Romana* was in substance the lost Roman history of Aurelius Memmius Symmachus, and Momigliano and Goffart have both argued that the *Getica*'s account of its author and purposes are a deliberate sham hiding the work's important political purposes; they disagree over whether Jordanes was in the employ of respectively Cassiodorus or the eastern imperial court. Consensus now seems to have emerged that the Ensslin thesis is unsustainable and that the *Romana* is precisely what it claims to be. A similar view that the *Getica* should also be taken much more at face value has been argued in some recent work, but consensus has not yet been established.

Ed. Th. Mommsen in MGH AA 5/1 (1882); trans. C. C. Mierow (1915). Romana: W. Ensslin, Sitz. Bayerisch. Akad. 1948, but see esp. B. Croke, Chiron, 1983. Getica: A. Momigliano, Proc. Brit. Acad. 1955; W. Goffart, Narrators of Barbarian History (1988), but see esp. N. Wagner, Getica (1967); J. J. O'Donnell, Hist. 1982; B. Croke, CPhil. 1987; P. J. Heather, Goths and Romans 332–489 (1991). P. J. H.

Josephus (Flavius Iosephus) (b. AD 37/8), was a Greek historian but also a Jewish priest of aristocratic descent and largely Pharisaic education (see PHARISEES), and a political leader in pre-70 *Jerusalem. Though a zealous defender of Jewish religion and culture, his writing is largely hostile to the various revolutionary groups, whom he regarded as responsible for the fall of the Temple: his theology centres on the idea that God was currently on the Romans' side. Participation in a delegation to Rome (c.64) impressed on him the impracticality of resistance. When the Jerusalem leaders put him in charge of *Galilee, he played an ambiguous role. He was besieged at Jotapata, but when captured, evaded a suicide pact and, he claims, was freed when his prophecy of *Vespasian's accession came true. He remained close to *Titus until the fall of Jerusalem, making several attempts to persuade the besieged city to surrender. He was given Roman citizenship, and, after the war, an imperial house to live in in Rome, a pension, and land in Judaea.

He first wrote an account of the war, now lost, in *Aramaic for the Jews of Mesopotamia. Most, if not all, of the seven books of the Greek *Jewish War* appeared between 75 and 79. The first book and a half sketch Jewish history from the Maccabean revolt (see MACCABEES) to AD 66. Much of the rest is based on Josephus' own experience, together with eyewitness reports from others and, probably, the diaries (*commentarii*) of Vespasian and Titus. The triumph at Rome over *Judaea capta* is described in detail. The *Jewish Antiquities*, in twenty books, published in 93/4, is a history of the Jews from the Creation to just before the outbreak of revolt, ostensibly for Greek readers. The biblical history of the first ten books depends not only on the Hebrew and Greek Bibles, but also on current Jewish oral interpretation. For the postbiblical period, works of Jewish-Hellenistic literature such as the Letter of Aristeas (see ARISTEAS, LETTER OF), 2 Esdras, and 1 Maccabees (see MACCABEES) are adapted. In the later part, there is a substantial dependence on the histories of *Nicolaus of Damascus. The famous *testimonium* to Jesus is partly or even wholly an interpolation. Appended to the *Antiquities* was the *Life*—not a full autobiography, but a defence of Josephus' conduct in Galilee, responding to his critics, especially *Iustus of Tiberias. The *Against Apion* was an apologia for Judaism in two books, demonstrating its antiquity in comparison with Greek culture, and attacking anti-Semitic writers, from the 3rd cent. BC to *Apion. Josephus' writings were preserved by the early Church. See JEWISH GREEK LITERATURE; HISTORIOGRAPHY, HELLENISTIC.

TEXTS B. Niese (1887–9; repr. 1955); S. A. Naber (1888–96); with Eng. trans., H. St J. Thackeray, R. Marcus, A. Wikgren, and L. H. Feldman (Loeb, 1926–65).

K. H. Rengstorf, *A Complete Concordance to Flavius Josephus* (1973–83); L. H. Feldman, *Josephus and Modern Scholarship (1937–1980)* (1984), and *Josephus: A Supplementary Bibliography* (1986); H. Schreckenberg, *Bibliographie zu Flavius Josephus* (1968).

STUDIES T. Rajak, *Josephus: The Historian and his Society* (1983); P. Bilde, *Flavius Josephus between Jerusalem and Rome: His Life, his Works and their Importance* (1988); S. J. D. Cohen, *Josephus in Galilee and Rome* (1979); H. St J. Thackeray, *Josephus, the Man and the Historian* (1929).
E. M. S.; T. R.

Jovian became Roman emperor when, as the senior staff officer (*protector domesticus*) serving in the Persian campaign of *Julian, he was proclaimed Augustus (see AUGUSTUS, AUGUSTA AS TITLES) on the latter's death in June AD 363. To secure the army's safe return from enemy territory, he made an unfavourable peace with the Persians, surrendering the Roman lands beyond the *Tigris, which had been won by *Diocletian's treaty of AD 299, and the cities of *Nisibis and *Singara. He died in February 364, aged 33, at Dadastana on the borders of Bithynia and Galatia, overcome (according to one report: Amm. Marc. 25. 10) by fumes from a charcoal stove.
E. D. H.

Juba (1) **I,** son of Hiempsal II of *Numidia. On an embassy to Rome he was insulted by *Caesar, and C. *Scribonius Curio (2) later proposed to annex his kingdom. He inevitably joined *Pompey in 49 BC and defeated and killed Curio. After *Pharsalus he began to aim at annexing Roman Africa, which Q. *Caecilius Metellus Pius Scipio is reported to have promised him. Excluded from Utica by M. *Porcius Cato (2) and attacked by P. *Sittius and *Bocchus II, he none the less fought by Scipio's side at Thapsus (46), but after their defeat could not rally any support and died in a suicide pact with M. *Petreius. Our picture of him is dominated by his Caesarian enemies.

[Caes.] *Bellum Africum*. For the coins see Mazard, pp. 49–52.   E. B.

Juba (2) **II,** king of *Mauretania and son of *Juba (1) of *Numidia, was led in *Caesar's triumph in 46 BC when still an infant, and brought up in Italy; he received the Roman *citizenship, apparently from *Octavian, and accompanied him on campaigns. Perhaps first reinstated in Numidia, in 25 he received from Augustus the kingdom of Mauretania, at which parts of Gaetulia rebelled and were put down with the help of a Roman proconsul, Cossus Lentulus (consul 1 BC); and in 17 Juba seems to have taken part in the defeat of *Tacfarinas. He married first (by 20 BC) Cleopatra Selene, the daughter of Antony (M. *Antonius (2)) and *Cleopatra VII, and secondly Glaphyra. He died *c.* AD 23 and was succeeded by *Ptolemy (2), his son by Cleopatra.

Juba was also a person of deep learning, who sought to introduce Greek and Roman culture into his kingdom. His capital at Iol, refounded as *Caesarea (3), and in the west *Volubilis, where he may have had a second residence, became fine cities. His artistic collections were remarkable. He developed the production of the 'Gaetulian' *purple, perhaps prepared by his invention from orchil (see also DYEING). He wrote many books (now lost) in Greek: works on Libya, Arabia, and Assyria; a history of Rome; researches into language, drama, and painting; a treatise on the plant euphorbia, which he discovered and named after his doctor Euphorbus, brother of *Antonius Musa; and Ὁμοιότητες, a comparative study of antiquities, mainly Greek and Roman. *Pliny (1) the Elder and *Plutarch were among the authors who used his writings. He organized an exploratory mission to the Canary Islands (see ISLANDS OF THE BLEST).

FGrH 275. S. Gsell, *Hist. anc. de l'Afrique du Nord* 8 (1928), 206 ff.; P. Romanelli, *Storia delle prov. rom. dell'Africa* (1959), 156 ff.; K. H. Priese, *Studien zur Topographie des äthiopischen Niltales im Altertum* (1974). Gaetulian territory: J. Desanges, *Rev. Ét. Lat.* 1964, 33 ff. Purple: J. Desjacques and P. Koeberlé, *Hespéris* 1955, 193 ff.; J. Gattefossé, *Hespéris* 1957, 329 ff. Literary works: Christ–Schmid–Stählin 2. 401 ff.; Iconography: G. M. A. Richter, *Portraits of the Greeks* (1965), 280 f.
A. M.; T. J. C.; K. S. S.

Juba (3), of Mauretania, wrote a lost treatise on metric based on *Heliodorus (2) and used by later Latin grammarians.

PIR² I 60; Schanz–Hosius, § 606.   J. F. Mo.

Judaea first appears in the Hellenistic period (see HELLENISM) as the name for the primarily Jewish territory (see JEWS) around *Jerusalem. Acquiring, under the *Hasmoneans, much enlarged borders and a substantial non-Jewish population, especially in the coastal cities, the territory was reduced by *Pompey after 63 BC, and was then reorganized by A. *Gabinius (2), the governor of Syria, into five districts. Growing again under *Herod (1), Judaea became a Roman procuratorial province after the banishment in AD 6 of Herod's successor there, *Archelaus (4). Eleven toparchies are listed by Josephus (*BJ* 3. 54–5), and a slightly different list is given by *Pliny (1) (*HN* 5. 14. 70). The term Judaea might also be used loosely, for in Luke–Acts where it sometimes simply denotes the part of Palestine inhabited by Jews, excluding even *Caesarea (2). After 70 Judaea was put by *Vespasian under an imperial legate (see LEGATI), with a permanent legionary garrison. The Jewish population dwindled after the *Bar Kokhba Revolt of 135. Nevertheless, Judaea figures regularly in the *Mishnah, in connection with rabbinic regulations, often in association with *Galilee and Peraea (trans-Jordan).   T. R.

Judas Maccabaeus See MACCABEES.

judges, Carthaginian (*suffetes*) See CARTHAGE.

judges, foreign, modern coinage to describe a judge or panel of judges (*xenikon dikastērion*) sent by one Greek city to hear lawsuits in another, often on the basis of a shared tie of *kinship (*syngeneia*). Attested mainly from honorific decrees on stone, these judges—commonly between one and five with a secretary—are known from the 4th cent. BC until the Antonines, but above all in Hellenistic times (see HELLENISM), when their dispatch could be orchestrated by kings or royal officials, as well as the Greek leagues (*koina*). They are found hearing both public and private suits, including disputes over written contracts (*sumbolaia*); long backlogs in local courts are a frequently cited reason for their presence. References to foreign judges who restored concord (*homonoia*) among citizens link this demand for impartial jurisdiction with the internal unrest (*stasis*), often based on the indebtedness of the poor to the rich, which marked many Greek cities in Hellenistic times. See ARBITRATION, GREEK.

L. Robert, *Xenion: Festschrift für P. J. Zepos* (1973) (= *OMS* 5 (1989), 137 ff.).   A. J. S. S.

judges, Greek For 'judges' in the world of *Hesiod see LAW IN GREECE, and for Athens up to *c.*462 see ARCHONTES. But thereafter Athens mainly relied on *jurors* instead, see LAW AND PROCEDURE, ATHENIAN, § 2.

judges, Roman See IUDEX; LAW AND PROCEDURE, ROMAN.

Jugurtha, grandson of *Masinissa outside the line of succession, served at *Numantia under P. *Cornelius Scipio Aemilianus, hereditary patron of the Numidian dynasty, and on his recommendation was adopted by King Micipsa and given pre-eminent rank over his brothers. After Micipsa's death (118 BC) the 'legitim-ate' brothers Hiempsal and Adherbal objected to his primacy, but he had Hiempsal assassinated and attacked Adherbal, who fled to Rome to appeal for assistance. A commission under L. *Opimius divided Numidia, giving the more primitive western part to Jugurtha and the more developed eastern part to Adherbal. In 112 Jugurtha attacked Adherbal, besieged him in *Cirta, and despite two Roman embassies (one under the *princeps senatus* M. *Aemilius Scaurus (1)) captured Cirta and killed him. Some Italian businessmen who had helped in the defence were also killed, and this caused outrage in Rome and led to agitation for war by C. *Memmius (1). In 112 the consul L. *Calpurnius Bestia invaded Numidia, but soon gave Jugurtha a tolerable peace, perhaps through the efforts of his Roman friends, but certainly through hesitation over starting a long colonial war. Summoned to Rome under safe-conduct to reveal his protectors, Jugurtha was forbidden to speak by a tribune and, after having a pretender murdered, left hurriedly. In Numidia the war was incompetently waged by S. *Postumius Albinus (consul 110), and his brother and legate Aulus was forced to capitulate in his absence. An outcry over aristocratic 'corruption' in Rome led to the institution of a commission of enquiry (see MAMILIUS LIMET-ANUS, C.) and the election of Q. *Caecilius Metellus Numidicus for 109. Metellus in two campaigns achieved considerable success, but got no nearer ending the war. His legate C. *Marius (1), profiting by this, intrigued to gain the consulship (107), prom-ising quick victory, but he too was unable to deliver it, despite army reforms including the first enrolment of *proletarii* in the legions. The war was finally won when *Sulla persuaded *Bocchus I to surrender Jugurtha to Marius. He was executed after Marius' triumph (104).

As Sallust saw, the Jugurthine War marks an important stage in the decline of the oligarchy and the organization of attacks on it. Above all, Marius' army reform unwittingly prepared the way for the use of armies loyal to their commander in politics and civil war.

Sallust's *Bellum Iugurthinum* is the chief source. See R. Syme, *Sallust* (1964), chs. 10 and 11; G. M. Paul, *A Historical Commentary on Sallust's Bellum Jugurthinum* (1984)—both with ample bibliographies.   E. B.

Julia, Julius, etc. For Roman names in 'J' see under 'I', except for JULIAN, JUSTIN, JUSTINIAN, and JUVENAL.

Julian 'the Apostate' (Iulianus (*RE* 26), Flavius Claudius), emperor AD 361–3, was born at *Constantinople in 331, the son of a half-brother of *Constantine I, Julius Constantius. After his father's murder in dynastic intrigues of 337, Julian was placed by *Constantius II in the care of an Arian bishop (see ARIANISM) and from 342 was confined for six years on an imperial estate in Cappadocia. He impressed his Christian tutors there as a gifted and pious pupil (see CHRISTIANITY), but his reading of the Greek classics was inclining him in private to other gods. In 351, as a student of philosophy, he encountered pagan Neoplatonists (see NEOPLATONISM) and was initiated as a theurgist by *Maximus (3) of Ephesus. For the next ten years Julian's *pagan 'conversion' remained a prudently kept secret. He continued his studies in Asia and later at Athens until summoned to Milan by Constantius to be married to the emperor's sister Helena and proclaimed Caesar with charge over Gaul and Britain (6 November 355). Successful Rhineland campaigns against the *Alamanni and *Franks between 356 and 359 proved Julian a talented general and won him great popularity with his army. When Constantius ordered the transfer of choice detachments to the east the army

mutinied and in February 361, probably with tacit prompting, proclaimed Julian Augustus (see AUGUSTUS, AUGUSTA AS TITLES). Constantius' death late that year averted civil war and Julian, now publicly declaring his paganism, entered Constantinople unopposed in December. A purge of the imperial court quickly followed, drastically reducing its officials and staff. In his brief reign Julian showed remarkable energy in pursuit of highly ambi-tious aims. An immediate declaration of general religious toler-ation foreshadowed a vigorous programme of pagan activism in the interest of '*Hellenism': the temples and finances of the ancestral cults were to be restored and a hierarchy of provincial and civic pagan priesthoods appointed, while the Christian churches and clergy lost the financial subsidies and privileges gained under Constantine and his successors. Though expressly opposed to violent persecution of Christians, Julian overtly dis-criminated in favour of pagan individuals and communities in his appointments and judgements: measures such as his ban on the teaching of classical literature and philosophy by Christian professors and his encouragement of charitable expenditure by pagan priests mark a determination to marginalize Christianity as a social force. His attempts to revive the role of the cities in local administration by restoring their revenues and councils and his remarkable plan to rebuild the Jewish Temple at *Jerusalem are best appraised in the light of this fundamental aim.

Julian's military ambitions centred on an invasion of *Persia intended to settle Rome's long-running war with *Sapor II. To prepare his expedition he moved in June 362 to *Antioch (1), where his relations with the mainly Christian population deteri-orated markedly during his stay. The expedition set out in March 363 but despite some early successes it was already in serious difficulties when Julian was fatally wounded in a mêlée in June 363. He left no heir (Helena died childless in 360, and Julian did not remarry), and after his death the reforms he had initiated quickly came to nothing.

Julian's personal piety and intellectual and cultural interests are reflected in his surviving writings, which show considerable learning and some literary talent. They include panegyrics, polemics, theological and satirical works, and a collection of letters, public and private. Of his anti-Christian critique, *Against the Galileans*, only fragments remain. His own philosophic ideol-ogy was rooted in Iamblichan *Neoplatonism (see IAMBLICHUS (2)) and *theurgy. How forcefully it impinged on his public religious reforms is controversial: on one view, they were directed more to the founding of a Neoplatonist 'pagan Church' than to a restoration of traditional Graeco-Roman polytheism, and their potential appeal to the mass of contemporary pagans was corres-pondingly limited.

WORKS W. C. Wright (Loeb, 1913–23); J. Bidez and others (Budé, 1924–64).

STUDIES J. Bidez, *La Vie de l'empereur Julien* (1930); G. Bowersock, *Julian the Apostate* (1978); R. Braun and J. Richer (eds.), *L'Empereur Julien: De l'histoire à la légende* (1978); P. Athanassiadi-Fowden, *Julian and Hellenism* (1981); J. Bouffartigue, *L'Empereur Julien et la culture de son temps* (1992); H. Bird, *Classical Views* 1982, 281 ff. (survey of research); R. B. E. Smith, *Julian's Gods* (1995).   R. B. E. S.

Julianus, lawyer. See IULIANUS.

Julio-Claudian emperors and period See ROME, HISTORY, § 2.2.

Junian Latins See LATINI IUNIANI.

Juno, an old and important Italian goddess and one of the chief deities of Rome. Her name derives from the same root as *iuventas* (youth), but her original nature remains obscure. Wissowa's argument (see bibliog. below) that she developed from the *iuno* attributed to individual women is probably mistaken, since that concept apparently arose during the republic on the analogy of the **genius*. On the other hand, her roles as a goddess of women and as a civic deity were both ancient and widespread, and it is difficult to give priority to either. Juno was widely worshipped under a number of epithets throughout central Italy. Some of her important civic cults in Rome were in fact imported from this region. Thus in the 5th cent. BC Juno Regina was brought from the **Etruscan town of **Veii and received a temple on the **Aventine. Also apparently Etruscan in origin was the Capitoline Triad of **Jupiter, Juno, and **Minerva; the Capitoline Juno was by the late republic also identified as Regina ('Queen'), and regularly carried that epithet in the imperial period. Another imported cult was that of Juno Sospita, the chief deity of Lanuvium (mod. Lanuvio), which from 338 BC onwards was administered jointly with Rome. The distinctive iconography of this goddess, who wears a goatskin and carries a spear and shield, indicates a martial character; Dumézil believed that her full epithet, Sospita Mater Regina, confirmed his thesis that Juno was originally trivalent, with influence over military prowess, fertility, and political organization. The cult of Juno Lucina, the goddess of childbirth, appears both in Rome and in other parts of **Latium. The foundation-day of her temple on the **Esquiline, March 1, was traditionally celebrated as the Matronalia, when husbands gave presents to their wives. Peculiar to Rome is Juno Moneta, whose cult dates to the 4th cent. BC. The ancient association of her epithet with *monere* (to warn) is usually accepted, but its origins are unknown. The first mint in Rome was later located in or near her temple on the *arx*, hence the derivation of 'money' from Moneta. Other epithets, such as Pronuba, belong more to poetry than cult. The Roman conception of Juno's character was deeply affected by her identification with similar goddesses of other cultures. The most important was the Greek **Hera: her mythology and characteristics were largely adopted for Juno, who was thus firmly established by the time of **Plautus as the wife of Jupiter and the goddess of marriage. The great goddess of **Carthage, Tanit, was also identified at a relatively early date with Juno, but had much less influence on her character. Apart from her part in the Capitoline Triad, Juno played a relatively minor role in the provinces. The exceptions are northern Italy, where the mother goddesses were sometimes called *iunones*, and Africa, where Juno **Caelestis was heir to the cult of Tanit.

Wissowa, *RK*; Dumézil, *ARR*. J. B. R.

Jupiter (*Iuppiter*), sovereign god of the Romans, bears a name referring to the 'luminous sky' (†*Dyew-pater*), the first member of which is etymologically identical with that of **Zeus. He was known to all Italic peoples.

Even if associated with the sky, storms, and lightning, Jupiter was not just a god of natural phenomena. These expressed and articulated, in fact, his function as sovereign divinity. Jupiter was sovereign by virtue of his supreme rank and by the patronage derived from exercise of the supreme power. His supreme rank was signified by the fact that the god or his priest was always mentioned at the head of lists of gods or priests, and that the climactic point of the month, before the waning of the moon, was sacred to him in particular (Macrob. *Sat.* 1. 15. 14). In addition, the Roman symbol of power, the sceptre (*sceptrum*), belonged to him and functioned as his symbol (Festus 81 Lindsay). This privilege was described by the traditional epithets of *optimus maximus*, 'the

best and the greatest', or by the title *rex* given him by the poets (cf. Radke, *Entwicklung* 241 ff.). His patronage of the exercise of sovereign power expressed itself in the fact that no political action could be accomplished without his favourable and prior judgement, expressed through the auspices (see AUSPICIUM) and in the celebration of the **triumph*, representing the fullest exercise of Roman supremacy. Between these two poles the figure of Roman Jupiter must be constructed.

In rituals as well as in mythical narratives (see G. Dumézil, *Les Dieux souverains des Indo-Européens* (1977)), the exercise of sovereignty by Jupiter, which made him into a deity with a political function, is presented under two aspects. On the one hand Jupiter was patron of the violent aspect of supremacy. As well as falling lightning, the Roman triumph, ending at his temple, represented the inexorable side of this power. From this point of view it is understandable that the grape and its product, **wine*, were placed under his patronage (see VINALIA). But Jupiter was also a political god, who agreed to exercise power within the limits imposed by law and good faith. It was he who took part in the institution of *templa* (see TEMPLUM), those inner spaces in which the important activities of the Roman people took place (see AUSPICIUM), and patronized the *nundinae*, traditional days of popular assembly (Macrob. *Sat.* 1. 16. 30). It was he too who, by means of the auspices, conferred legitimacy on the choices and decisions of the Roman people. Finally, he was the patron of **oaths and treaties, and punished perjurers in the terrible manner appropriate.

From the end of the regal period, the most brilliant of Jupiter's seats was his temple on the **Capitol*, which he shared with **Juno Regina (in the cella or chamber to the left) and **Minerva (in the right-hand cella). This triad constituted the group of patron deities of the city of Rome, whose well-being was the subject of an annual vow (Livy 41. 14. 7 ff.); under the empire, vows for the health of the ruler and his family were celebrated on 3 January. The first political action of the new consuls was the acquittal of these vows, formulated the previous year, and their utterance afresh. The anniversary of the Capitoline temple was celebrated during the Ludi Romani (4–19 September) on the Ides of September (13 September). On the Ides of November, during the Ludi Plebei or Plebeian Games (4–17 November; see LUDI; PLEBS), a great banquet was celebrated on the Capitol (*Iovis epulum*: see SEPTEMVIRI EPULONES), reuniting the Roman élite around the supreme god, along with Juno and Minerva. It was to the Capitol as well, and specifically to the *arx*, that the procession concluding the 'rites of the Ides', *sacra idulia*, ascended (Festus 372 Lindsay, entry under 'sacram viam'). Finally, the Ludi Capitolini, celebrated in honour of Jupiter Feretrius (15 October, Plut. *Rom.* 25; *Schol. Bern.* on Verg. *G.* 2. 384), their date of foundation uncertain, point to a third ancient sanctuary of Jupiter on the Capitol. Jupiter Feretrius, whom it is difficult to separate from Jupiter Lapis or 'Stone' (see Gell. *NA* 1. 21. 4; Livy 1. 24. 8 (see FETIALES), 30. 43. 9; Festus 102. 11 Lindsay), was invoked in treaties; the famous flint used in the most solemn oaths was kept there, as well as the *sceptrum* by which oaths were taken (Festus 81. 16 Lindsay). A tradition reactivated by **Augustus attributed to Jupiter the 'first' **spolia opima* (Festus 204. 8 Lindsay; cf. J. Rüpke, *Domi militiae* (1990), 217 ff.).

Jupiter was frequently associated with other deities. From a very early period an association thought by many to reflect **Indo-European ideas linked him with **Mars and **Quirinus. On the Capitol he shared his temple with Juno and Minerva. Near this temple were found deities who fell in some sense within his orbit:

Jupiter Dolichenus

*Fides and the problematic Dius Fidius, patrons of good faith and oaths.

The special priests of Jupiter were the *flamen Dialis* and his wife (see FLAMINES) and, where the auspices were concerned, the *augures (interpretes Iovis optimi maximi,* 'interpreters of Jupiter Best and Greatest', Cic. *Leg.* 2. 20).

Wissowa, *RK* 113 ff.; C. Koch, *Der römische Juppiter* (1937). For the temples of Jupiter: Platner–Ashby 291 ff.; Richardson, *Topog. Dict. Ancient Rome,* 218 ff.; Ziolkowski, *Temples* 79 ff.; G. Dumézil, *Les Dieux souverains des Indo-Européens* (1977), 153 ff.; J. R. Fears, *ANRW* 2. 17. 1 (1981), 56 ff.
J. Sch.

Jupiter Dolichenus (Iupiter Optimus Maximus Dolichenus), high god of Doliche in *Commagene, now Dülük, near Gaziantep, eastern Turkey. The original temple on top of Dülük Baba Tepe has not been excavated, but the god's stance on a bull, holding lightning-bolt and double-axe, indicate clearly his ancestry in the *Hittite storm-god Teshub. All three connote the transcendent but ambivalent power of natural forces. At Rome, he is invoked as *conservator totius poli,* 'he who maintains the whole firmament'. There are no literary texts. No monument from the *Persian occupation or the Hellenistic period (see HELLENISM) is known: the cult first spread in the 2nd cent. AD, well after Rome's absorption of Doliche into Syria (?31 BC or AD 17). Two votive triangles for processions found at Dülük confirm that such cult objects, like most other aspects of the cult in the west, derive directly from Doliche. But the modest western sanctuaries show no common pattern. The counterpart of Iupiter Optimus Maximus Dolichenus is usually named *Juno Sancta/Regina. Two other pairs also occur: Sun and Moon, and the Castores, who appear Hellenized as the *Dioscuri, or as figures emerging from rock or pedestal.

Known adherents in the west almost all bear names suggesting first- or second-generation immigration. Organization is enigmatic. Priesthoods seem to have been numerous but temporary. Worshippers, *fratres* (literally 'brothers'), were admitted to the sacred feasts only after a period of instruction as *candidati* ('candidates'), each group of which had a *patronus* ('patron'). Those outside these groups were termed *colitores.* The function of *scriba/notarius* ('scribe', 'notary') suggests that written records were important. Though women might be *colitores,* none is known to have been priest or full member.

Outside Rome itself, the cult spread mainly in the Rhine–Danube area and *Britain. Up to a point, it was a religion of military loyalty, especially under the Severans (see ROME, HISTORY). Many sanctuaries were plundered by *Maximinus Thrax (AD 235–8) and never rebuilt. Though the *Aventine temple was used into the 4th cent. AD, the sack of Doliche by *Sapor I in 252 evidently undermined the cult.

M. Hörig and E. Schwertheim, *Corpus cultus Iovis Dolicheni* (1987); M. Hörig, *ANRW* 2. 17. 4 (1984), 2136–79; M. P. Speidel, *The Religion of Iuppiter Dolichenus in the Roman Army* (1978).
R. L. G.

juries, jurors See LAW AND PROCEDURE, ATHENIAN and ROMAN (§§ 3. 8 and 10).

jurisprudence, jurists See LAW, ROMAN, SOCIOLOGY OF; LAWYERS; LEGAL LITERATURE.

Justin (Marcus Iunian(i)us Iustinus), dated to the 2nd, 3rd, or even (Syme) 4th cent. AD, important as the author of a Latin *epitome of the otherwise lost 'Philippic Histories' of *Pompeius Trogus, whom he seems to have followed closely, confining his authorial voice to moralizing passages.

Ed. O. Seel (Teubner, 1972); Eng. trans., J. Yardley (1994), including *Prologi;* Italian trans., S. Amantini, *Giustino: Storie Filippiche* (1981). *PIR²* I 713. Date: Syme, *RP* 6. 358 ff.
A. H. McD.; A. J. S. S.

Justin Martyr (c. AD 100–65), a Christian *apologist, flourished under *Antoninus Pius and died a martyr in Rome after his condemnation as a Christian (see CHRISTIANITY) by the *praefectus urbi Q. *Iunius Rusticus. At the beginning of his *First Apology* he tells us that he was born at Flavia Neapolis (the ancient Shechem in Samaria) of *pagan parents. He seems never to have been attracted to Judaism, though he knows seven Jewish sects (*Trypho* 80. 4). His account of his early disappointments in philosophy (*Trypho* 3 ff.) is conventional, but he was certainly a Platonist (see PLATO (1)) when converted to Christianity. The Stoics (see STOICISM) he knew and admired, but more for their lives than for their teachings, and his conversion owed much to the constancy of Christian confessors (*2 Apol.* 12).

After leaving *Samaria, he set up a small school in Rome, and wrote two apologies, nominally directed to Antoninus Pius. One (c.155) defends Christianity in general against popular calumny and intellectual contempt; the second (c.162) is inspired by acts of persecution following denunciations of Christians to the authorities. It reveals that Christians served in the army and that Christian wives sometimes divorced their pagan spouses. Justin's pupil *Tatian attributes his death to information given by Crescens, a Cynic rival (*Oratio* 19).

Justin's work is not so much a synthesis of Christianity, paganism, and Judaism as an attempt to discover an underlying homogeneity. This he effects by his doctrine of the Logos, which, as Christ, was present in many Old Testament epiphanies, and guarantees the unity of scriptural inspiration. (So he maintains in his *Dialogue with Trypho,* the first great work of Christian typology.) In the *Apologies* (esp. *2 Apol.* 13) he anticipates *Clement of Alexandria and the *Alexandrian school by arguing that a 'spermatic *logos', identical with or related to Christ, instructs every man in wisdom, so that even pagan philosophers foreshadowed Christian truth. Like the other apologists, he accepts the civil authorities, and at once explains and enhances the attraction of Christianity for Greek-speaking intellectuals of the period. Because of his reputation, a number of feeble apologies were also attributed to him; of these the *De monarchia* and *Cohortatio ad Graecos,* unusually replete with Christian or Jewish forgeries, are occasionally a useful source of fragments from authentic pagan dramas.

EDITIONS J. C. T. Otto, 3 vols. (1842–8) and 5 vols. (1876–81); J. C. van Winden, *An Early Christian Philosopher: Trypho 1–9* (1971).

STUDIES A. Harnack, *Judentum und Judenchristentum in Justinus' Dialog mit Trypho,* Texte und Untersuchungen 39 (1913); E. R. Goodenough, *The Theology of Justin Martyr* (1923); W. Schmid, *Zeitschrift für N.T. Wissenschaft* 1941; R. Holte, *Stud. Theol.* 1958; H. Chadwick, *Early Christian Thought and Classical Tradition* (1967); L. W. Barnard, *Justin Martyr* (1967), and *Sc. J. Theol.* 1969; J. Daniélou, *Message évangelique et culture hellénistique* (Eng. trans. 1973).
W. H. C. F.; M. J. E.

Justinian (Flavius Petrus Sabbatius Iustinianus), eastern Roman emperor AD 527–65. He was born c.482 at Tauresium, near Bederiana in *Thrace, a place subsequently graced with the city of Justiniana Prima (mod. Caricin Grad). His father Sabbatius married a sister of the future emperor Justin, who adopted his nephew. Under Anastasius he joined the *scholae* or guards, and became a *candidatus,* personal imperial bodyguard. During the succession dispute in 518 Justinian was offered the throne but supported his more senior uncle, whose position he helped secure by eliminating potential rivals, Amantius and Vitalian.

From his residence in the palace of Hormisdas he was now the dominant influence on imperial decisions, as revealed by his correspondence with Pope Hormisdas that healed the Acacian schism. Promotion reflected his power, *comes* ('count') in 519, *magister militum praesentalis* ('general in attendance') in 520, consul in 521 when celebrations were exceptionally lavish, patrician and *nobilissimus* ('most noble') before 527. After 523 he married the former actress Theodora, but only after the empress Lupicina, who strongly opposed the match, had died and Justinian persuaded Justin to repeal the law prohibiting marriages between senators and actresses. Justinian, apparently a staunch Chalcedonian, married a Monophysite.

Justinian was crowned Augustus (see AUGUSTUS, AUGUSTA AS TITLES) on 1 April 527, succeeded as sole emperor on Justin's death on 1 August, and soon began a campaign to enforce legislation against heretics, pagans, and male homosexuals, while in 530/1 permitting Monophysites exiled by Justin to return. Imperial success depended on God's favour, a recurrent concern throughout Justinian's reign, so that deviants must be corrected or eliminated, but Justinian's conception of orthodoxy was sufficiently flexible to encourage him repeatedly to attempt religious reunification. Negotiations with Monophysites were pursued in 531/2, and in March 533 an imperial edict proclaimed the oneness of Christ, underlining this through the Theopaschite formula that the Christ who suffered in the flesh was one of the Trinity. This departure from rigid Chalcedonian doctrine seemed to presage toleration, but Monophysites failed to respond as intended. Further attempts at compromise began in the 540s, with Justinian's decision to secure condemnation of specific writings by three leading 5th-cent. opponents of Monophysites, Theodore of Mopsuestia, *Theodoret of Cyrrhus, and Ibas of Edessa. This culminated in anathema for these so-called Three Chapters at the fifth ecumenical council in *Constantinople in 553, when Pope Vigilius subscribed under extreme compulsion. This compromise, too, failed to reconcile Monophysites who now possessed a separate episcopal hierarchy, and created schism in Italy and Africa for about 50 years. Towards the end of his reign Justinian engaged in discussions with Nestorian bishops from Persia, and in his last year, concerned to achieve unity to the very end, he adopted the extreme Monophysite doctrine of Aphthartodocetism, that Christ's body was incorruptible: this prompted fresh expulsions of bishops, though now the victims were leading Chalcedonians.

After religion Justinian's second great passion was law and administration. In 528 he established a commission to codify all valid imperial constitutions from Hadrian to the present: the *Codex Iustinianus* was first promulgated in 529, with a revised edition in 534. A second commission, appointed to excerpt and codify the works of classical jurists, published the *Digest* in December 533 (see JUSTINIAN'S CODIFICATION). Thereafter Justinian continued to legislate energetically, with about 150 *Novels* (*Novellae*: 'new constitutions') promulgated on a wide variety of administrative, legal, ecclesiastical, and criminal matters in a confident assertion of the efficacy of imperial action. Justinian also imposed his image on Constantinople after the Nika riot (532) necessitated extensive reconstruction, with the architecturally innovative St Sophia as centre-piece.

Warfare occupied much of Justinian's attention: he inherited conflict with *Sasanid Persia which, although briefly interrupted by the Endless Peace in 532, resumed in 540 and dragged on until 561/2. His greatest ambition was to reconquer the provinces of the western empire: Africa was quickly recovered from the *Vandals in 533/4, but Ostrogothic Italy (see GOTHS; ITALY) proved much harder in spite of apparent triumph in 540 and the peninsula was not secured until 561/2; part of Spain was fortuitously recovered in 551. While intending to concentrate aggressive warfare in the west Justinian devoted much money and energy to enhancing the defences of the Balkans and eastern frontier: Armenia, Mesopotamia, and Syria required protection from the Persians, Thrace, and Illyricum from raids by Bulgars, Gepids, and *Slavs which on occasion even threatened the suburbs of Constantinople. Human and natural destruction had to be restored. *Procopius' *Buildings* provides a panegyrical survey of Justinian's efforts: fortifications were improved, but other components of an active defence may have been neglected. Beyond the frontiers diplomacy and money were exploited to maintain peace and dilute threats, with mixed success and adverse reaction from advocates of 'traditional' Roman aggression.

Justinian led an austere life, working hard for long hours and expecting the same of subordinates. He identified and exploited talent, John the Cappadocian and Peter Barsymas as administrators, *Tribonianus the lawyer, the generals *Belisarius and *Narses, the architect Anthemius, and the writers *Procopius and *Paulus the Silentiary. Their various efforts ensured that the long reign presented, in general, a successful façade, though in some areas the reality of the achievement is questionable. Justinian's most trusted assistant, Theodora, died in 548; thereafter the childless Justinian failed to attend to the most pressing concern for every prudent emperor from *Augustus onwards, namely the identification and grooming of a successor.

PLRE 2. 645–8; A. Cameron, *CAH* 14^2 (forthcoming); A. H. M. Jones, *Later Rom. Emp.* ch. 9.   L. M. W.

Justinian's codification is a term loosely used to describe the three volumes (*Codex, Digesta* or *Pandectae, Institutiones*) in which Justinian (AD 527–65) tried to restate the whole of Roman law in a manageable and consistent form, though this restatement, which runs to over a million words, is too bulky and ill-arranged to count as a codification in the modern sense.

Ninety years after the *Theodosian Code of 438 a new *codex was needed to collect the laws enacted in the intervening period. Justinian, with a keen sense of his predecessors' neglect and his own superior dedication, seized the opportunity to carry out part of the programme envisaged by *Theodosius (3) II in 429. This involved including all imperial laws in one volume and ensuring that the laws in it were consistent with one another (C. *Haec* pref.). Within a few months of becoming emperor in 527, he ordered a commission of ten, mostly present or recent holders of public office, to prepare a comprehensive collection of imperial laws including those in the three existing codices (*Gregorianus, Hermogenianus,* and *Theodosianus*), so far as they were still in force, together with more recent laws (*novellae*). The laws were to be edited in a short and clear form, with no repetition or conflict, but attributed to the emperors and dates at which they had originally been issued. The commission contained some lawyers but its head was the politically powerful non-lawyer, John of Cappadocia. Within fourteen months the *Codex Iustinianus* in twelve books (*libri*) was finished and on 7 April 529 was promulgated as the exclusive source of imperial laws, the earlier codes being repealed (C. *Summa*). Its practical aim was to curtail lawsuits; and its compilation was widely regarded as a major achievement. It fitted a vision in which Justinian saw himself as rapidly restoring and extending the empire, in which process military and legal achievements would reinforce one another (C. *Summa* pref.). This 529 *Codex* does not survive, but the second edition of 534 does.

Besides the laws in the *Codex*, C. *Summa* allowed the writings of the old lawyers of authority to be cited in court. Their views not infrequently conflicted, the conflicts being settled by counting heads according to the Law of Citations of 426. In 429 Theodosius II had looked forward to a time when this voluminous material could be arranged under subject-headings and harmonized. Probably, though the matter is controversial, Justinian from the start intended to undertake the further project of collecting, condensing, and amending the rest of Roman law, provided someone could organize it: the incentive to outdo Theodosius still applied. At any rate, Justinian first arranged for the 50 most prominent conflicts between the old writers to be settled (*Quinquaginta decisiones*), then in December 530 (C. *Deo auctore*) ordered that these old works, which ran to over 1,500 books (*libri*), be condensed in 50 books and given the title *Digesta* ('Ordered Abstracts') or *Pandectae* ('Encyclopaedia'). For that purpose he set up a second commission consisting of élite lawyers under the quaestor *Tribonianus, who had shown his mettle as a member of the earlier commission, along with another official, four law professors, and eleven advocates. They were to read the works of authority, none of them written later than about AD 300, and excerpt what was currently valid. As for the *Codex*, the commissioners were to edit the texts in a clear form with no repetition or contradiction. Thirty-nine writers were used for the compilation. The commission was not to count heads but to choose the best view, no matter who held it. In the upshot *Ulpian, who provided two-fifths of the *Digesta*, was their main source; *Paulus provided one-sixth.

The commission worked rapidly and the *Digesta* or *Pandectae* was promulgated on 16 December 533 (C. *Tanta / Dedōken*). The speed of the operation has led some scholars to suppose that the commissioners, instead of reading the original sources, worked from previous collections of material. But nothing on the required scale has been traced, and Tribonianus would have dismissed reliance on secondary sources as disreputable, even supposing it escaped detection. Time was saved in another way. As F. Bluhme discovered in 1820, the works to be read were divided into three groups, extracts from which are generally kept together in the finished *Digesta*. The inference is that three subcommittees were appointed to read the three groups of works; and the operation was perhaps further subdivided within the committees. Justinian, in whose palace the commission was working, could be relied on to see that the timetable was kept to, as he did with the construction of Hagia Sophia.

The compilers had authority not merely to eliminate obsolete or superfluous texts but to alter those they kept. The extent to which they made use of this power is controversial (see INTERPOLATION). In any event, if the new version of a text differed from the old, the new prevailed, on the theory that Justinian was entitled to amend the previous law as he wished. But the amended texts were 'out of respect for antiquity' attributed to the original authors and books. This was a compromise, unsatisfactory from a scholarly point of view, which enabled Justinian to claim that everything in the *Digesta* was his, while in fact often reverting to the law as it was before 300.

The practical aims of the *Digesta* were to shorten lawsuits and provide a revised law syllabus to be used in the schools of *Berytus (mod. Beirut) and *Constantinople (C. *Omnem*). To complete the reform of law-teaching Justinian ordered Tribonianus and two of the professors to prepare an up-to-date edition

of *Gaius (2)'s lectures, the *Institutiones*, making use also of other elementary teaching books by writers of authority. The professors perhaps each drafted two books, while Tribonianus brought the whole up to date by adding an account of recent legislation, especially Justinian's. The *Institutiones* like the *Digesta* was promulgated in December 533. It has survived and was for many centuries a successful students' first-year book. Then in 534 a second edition of the *Codex* of 529 was produced, which included the reforming laws of the intervening five years. This also has survived. The codification was now at an end. To avoid conflicting interpretations, commentaries on it were forbidden. Justinian however continued to legislate without pause, mainly in Greek, and private collections of his later laws (*novellae*) have been preserved.

His codification had a practical and a political aim. Its practical impact, though considerable, was limited by the fact that it was wholly in Latin. Hence in the Greek-speaking Byzantine empire few could make proper use of it until the coming of a Greek collection of laws, the *Basilica*, which in the 9th and 10th cents. at last fused the two main sources of law, *Codex* and *Digesta*. In the west Justinian's laws were in force for two centuries in parts of Italy and in North Africa until the expansion of Islam in the 7th cent.

The political aim of the codification was to renew, reform, and extend the Roman empire in its civil aspect. In this Justinian was in the long run successful, but not in the way he foresaw. He thought that the spread of Roman law depended on military conquest. In the west that proved short-lived; and when from the 11th cent. onwards his codification came to be taken as the basis of legal education and administration throughout Europe, it was not by force of arms but through its prestige and inherent rationality that his version of Roman law was adopted.

TEXTS *Corpus Iuris Civilis* 1: *Institutiones*, ed. P. Krüger (1928), translated as *Justinian's Institutes* by P. Birks and G. McLeod (1987) and *Digesta*, ed. T. Mommsen (1905), translated as *The Digest of Justinian*, 4 vols., ed. A. Watson, (1985); vol. 2: *Codex Iustinianus*, ed. P. Krüger, (1906); vol. 3 *Novellae*, ed. R. Scholl and W. Kroll (1954).

MODERN LITERATURE R. von Mayr and M. San Nicolò, *Vocabularium Codicis Iustiniani*, 2 vols. (1923–5); F. Bluhme, 'Die Ordnung der Fragmente in den Pandektentiteln': *ZGR* 4 (1820), 257; G. Rotondi, *Scritti giuridici* 1 (1922); F. Wieacker, *Vom römischen Recht*, 2nd edn. (1961), 242–87; T. Honoré, *Tribonian* (1978); G. Mantovani, *Digesto e masse Bluhmiane* (1987). T. Hon.

Justus See IUSTUS.

Juvenal (Decimus Iunius Iuvenalis), Roman satirist. Known primarily for the angry tone of his early *Satires*, although in later poems he developed an ironical and detached superiority as his satiric strategy. The highly rhetorical nature of the *Satires* has long been recognized but only recently has the allied concept of the 'mask' (*persona*) been deployed (primarily by Anderson, see bibliog. below) to facilitate assessment of the *Satires* as self-conscious poetic constructs, rather than the reflections of the realities of Roman social life for which they have often been read. This approach is reinforced by rejection of the biographical interpretation, in which Juvenal's 'life' was reconstructed from details in the *Satires*. In fact, virtually nothing is known of his life: he is the addressee of three epigrams of *Martial (themselves highly sophisticated literary constructions) which indicate his skill in oratory. The absence of dedication to a patron in Juvenal's *Satires* may suggest that he was a member of the élite. The few datable references confirm Syme's assessment that the five books were written during the second and third decades of the 2nd cent. AD (or later), at about the same time as *Tacitus (1) was writing his *Annals*. There is no reason to doubt that the *Satires* were written and published in books. Book 1 comprises *Satires* 1–5, book 2 *Satire* 6 alone, book 3 *Satires* 7–9, book 4 *Satires* 10–12, and book 5 *Satires* 13–16 (the last poem is unfinished).

In book 1 Juvenal introduces his indignant speaker who condemns Rome (satire is an urban genre), especially the corruption of the patron–client relationship (*amicitia*) (in *Satires* 1, 3, 4, and 5; see CLIENS; PATRONAGE) and the decadence of the élite (in 1, 2, and 4). *Satire* 1, following predecessors in the genre, provides a justification for satire and a programme of the angry tone and the victims of satirical attack. These include the 'out-groups' (Richlin) who transgress sexual and social boundaries, such as the passive homosexuals of *Satire* 2 (see HOMOSEXUALITY) and the social upstarts, criminals, and foreigners attacked by Umbricius in *Satire* 3 (Umbricius figures himself as the last true Roman, driven from an un-Roman Rome). The Roman élite are portrayed as paradigms of moral corruption: the selfish rich are attacked in *Satires* 1 and 3 and the emperor *Domitian is portrayed as sexual hypocrite and autocrat in 2 and 4. Those dependent on these powerful men are not absolved from blame: the courtiers humiliated by Domitian by being asked to advise on what to do with an enormous fish in *Satire* 4, like the client humiliated by his wealthy patron at a dinner party in 5, are condemned for craven compliance.

The focus upon Roman men in book 1 is complemented by the focus upon Roman women in book 2, which consists of the massive *Satire* 6, comparable in length to a book of epic. The speaker fiercely (but unsuccessfully) attempts to dissuade his addressee from marriage by cataloguing the (alleged) faults of Roman wives. Here Juvenal develops his angry speaker in the ultimate rant which seems to exhaust the possibilities of angry satire; thereafter he adopts a new approach of irony and cynicism. Initially (in book 3) Juvenal's new, calmer persona takes up the same topics as treated in book 1, although his detachment invites a less stark perspective: clients and patrons (*Satires* 7 and 9) and the corruption and worthlessness of the élite (8). He then marks his change of direction explicitly at the start of book 4, where the speaker states his preference for detached laughter over tears as a reaction to the follies of the world; in the remainder of *Satire* 10 he accordingly demolishes first the objects of human prayer, then the act of prayer itself. His programmatic declaration is borne out by the 'Horatian' tone and topics (see HORACE) of *Satire* 11 (where an invitation to dinner conveys a condemnation of decadence and a recommendation of self-sufficiency) and 12 (where true friendship is contrasted with the false friendship of legacy-hunters). The speaker of book 5 becomes still more detached and cynical as he turns his attention to the themes of crime and punishment, money and greed. The opening poem, *Satire* 13, offers a programmatic condemnation of anger in the form of a mock *consolation, which indicates clearly the development from book 1 where anger was apparently approved.

Juvenal claims that his satire replaces *epic (*Sat.* 1) and *tragedy (6. 634–61): his chief contribution to the genre is his appropriation of the 'grand style' from other more elevated forms of hexameter verse, notably epic. This contrasts markedly with the sometimes coarse language of *Lucilius (1) and the tone of refined 'conversation' adopted by Horace in his satirical writings. Juvenal's satiric 'grand style' mingles different lexical levels, ranging from epic and tragedy (e.g. the epic parody in *Satires* 4 and 12) to mundanities, Greek words, and occasional obscenities. His penchant for oxymora, pithy paradoxes, and trenchant questions makes Juvenal a favourite mine for quotations, e.g. *mens sana in corpore sano* (10. 356) and *quis custodiet ipsos custodes?* (6. 347–8): 'a healthy mind in a healthy body' and 'who guards the guards themselves?' The *Satires* also appropriate the themes and structures of other forms of discourse: they are rhetorical performances which develop for satiric ends material drawn from epic (*Homer, *Virgil, *Ovid) and pastoral poetry; situations and characters of comedy and mime; philosophical ideas and texts (including *Plato (1) and the Hellenistic philosophical schools); and rhetorical set-pieces (consolation, persuasion, farewell speech).

Juvenal's *Satires* apparently present reassuring entertainment for the Roman male élite audience. However, inconsistencies written into the texts allow alternative views of Juvenal's speakers as riddled with bigotry (chauvinism, misogyny, homophobia) or as cynically superior. In literary history, Juvenal's significance is in bringing to fullest development the indignant speaker: his 'savage indignation' had a lasting influence on Renaissance and later satire (as Johnson's imitations of *Satires* 3 and 10, *London* and *The Vanity of Human Wishes*, indicate) and remains central to modern definitions of 'satire'. See SATIRE.

TEXT A. E. Housman (2nd edn. 1931), W. V. Clausen (OCT, rev. 1992).

COMMENTARY E. Courtney, *A Commentary on the Satires of Juvenal* (1980).

TRANSLATION N. Rudd, *Juvenal: The Satires* (1991).

INDEX VERBORUM M. Dubrocard (1976).

SCHOLIA VETUSTIORA Ed. P. Wessner (1931).

STUDIES W. S. Anderson, *Essays on Roman Satire* (1982); J. C. Bramble, *CHCL* 2. 597–623; S. H. Braund, *Beyond Anger: A Study of Juvenal's Third Book of Satires* (1988); A. Richlin, *The Garden of Priapus: Sexuality and Aggression in Roman Humor* (1983).

DATE Syme, *Tacitus*, apps. 74 and 75, and *RP* 3. 1135–57.

BIBLIOGRAPHIC SURVEY S. H. Braund, *Roman Verse Satire*, *G&R* New Survey 23 (1992).

PROSOPOGRAPHY J. Ferguson, *A Prosopography to the Poems of Juvenal* (1987).   S. M. B.

Kairos, personified Opportunity. He had an altar at *Olympia (Paus. 5. 14. 9) and *Ion (2) of Chios (cited there) called him the youngest son of *Zeus (i.e. Opportunity is god-sent) in a *hymn possibly composed for this cult. A cult existed at *Velia by the mid-5th cent. BC. In *Antimachus (fr. 32 B. Wyss), Kairos is one of *Adrastus (1)'s horses. He has no mythology, but was a favourite subject in art, especially from the time of *Lysippus (2), whose bronze statue showed him between youth and age, tiptoeing, with a razor and scales, representing the fleeting nature of Opportunity (and the precision of the sculptor). Describing the statue (echoed in imperial reliefs and gems), *Posidippus (2) (*Anth. Plan.* 4. 275) says he had his hair over his eyes but was bald behind, since Opportunity can be grasped as he approaches, but never once he has passed. In literature, Kairos also encompasses time (differentiated from Chronos) and the seasons.

LIMC 5/1. 819–20, 921–6; A. F. Stewart, *AJArch* 1978, 163–71.

H. J. R.; K. W. A.

kanephoroi (κανηφόροι) were usually young women who bore baskets or vessels (κανᾶ) in religious processions. In the Panathenaic procession the young women were chosen from noble houses, and were required to be of good family (Harpocration, Photius, Hesychius, entries under the word), unmarried, and of unsullied reputation; hence 'to be fit to carry the basket' is to live chastely (as Men. *Epit.* 221 Allinson), and to reject a candidate was a grave insult (Thuc. 6. 56. 1). Serving as a *kanephoros*, as with other religious tasks, such as the little bears of Artemis of *Brauron, was thus not a normal *rite of passage for young girls but a mark of special prominence (cf. Ar. *Lys.* 642–7). They were dressed in splendid raiment; hair and garments were decked with gold and jewels; they were powdered with white barley-flour and wore a chain of figs (ἰσχάδων ὁρμαθός). They carried vessels of gold and silver, which contained all things needed in the sacrificial ceremony: *first-fruits, the sacrificial knife, barley-corns (ὀλαί or οὐλαί), and garlands. The sacred utensils were kept in the Pompeion, the 'procession house'. *Erichthonius was said to have introduced *kanephoroi* at the *Panathenaea. Certainly the institution was very old, and its object was doubtless to secure the efficacy of the sacrificial materials by letting them touch nothing that was not virginal and therefore lucky and potent.

Kanephoroi are also found in other Attic cults, e.g. those of *Apollo, *Dionysus, and *Isis, and in the cult of *Zeus Basileus at Boeotian Lebadea (see TROPHONIUS).

E. Pfuhl, *De Atheniensium pompis sacris* (1900), 20 ff.; K. Mittelhaus, *RE* 10. 1865 f.; Deubner, *Attische Feste* 25; and numerous references in Nilsson, *GGR* 2, see index; H. W. Parke, *Festivals of the Athenians* (1977); E. Simon, *Festivals of Attica: An Archaeological Commentary* (1983).

J. E. F.; H. J. R.; I. M.

Kasios (Κάσιος), **Zeus,** an oriental god connected with Mt. Casius (mod. Jabal al-Aqra') near *Antioch (1). In Ugaritic texts this mountain, called ṣapānu, is the abode of Ba'al, a weathergod like *Zeus. Casius/Ḥazzi plays a part in the Hurrian-Hittite Ullikummi myth and figures in Zeus' conflict with the dragon *Typhon (Apollod. *Bibl.* 1. 6. 3). Zeus Kasios is also associated with a mountain near *Pelusium.

RE 10. 2265 ff.; A. Caquot and others, *Textes Ougaritiques* 1: *Mythes et légendes* (1974).

J. F. H.

Kēres, in post-Homeric usage, powers of evil. They pollute and make unclean (Pl. *Leg.* 937d, like the *Harpyiae or Harpies), and are associated with ills of all kinds such as disease (Soph. *Phil.* 42), old age and death (Mimnermus fr. 2. 5–7 West), and troubles in general (Empedocles fr. 121 DK, Semonides fr. 1. 21 W). They are in varying degrees personified, sometimes being treated as the bringers of evil and sometimes as the evil itself. In *Homer, *kēr* and *kēres* seem less like malignant agents, more like impersonal fates; but the fate of which they are the vehicle is always evil, almost invariably in fact that of death. In *Iliad* 22. 210–11, *Zeus weighs the fates of death of *Hector and *Achilles, to decide which hero is to perish; later in the book (365), Achilles counters Hector's prediction of his death with 'I shall suffer my fate [lit. receive *kēr*], when Zeus chooses to bring it to pass'. Even Homer once, in an exceptional context, shows a personified 'dire Kēr' manhandling the dead and dying on the battlefield (*Il.* 18. 535). In art, to judge from literary descriptions (e.g. Paus. 5. 19. 6, on the chest of Cypselus (see CYPSELUS, CHEST OF)), Kēres could be a blend of human and bird of prey, rather like Harpies or *Sirens; they are hard to identify on surviving monuments.

It used to be argued that *kēres* were 'originally' *souls of the dead, largely because souls were supposedly banished at the end of the Athenian festival Anthesteria with the iambic formula θύραζε κῆρες, οὐκετ' Ἀνθεστήρια: 'away, Keres, Anthesteria is over'. But (even if this reading rather than the variant Κᾶρες, 'Carians' (see CARIA), is correct) it does not follow that *kēres* means souls just because in a particular context souls could be addressed as such, perhaps abusively: 'away, hobgoblins'.

Nilsson, *GGR*, 1. 222–5; B. C. Dietrich, *Death, Fate and the Gods* (1965); *DFA*³ 13–15.

R. C. T. P.

keys and locks The primitive Greek door-fastening was a horizontal bolt working in staples behind the door (μοχλὸς θύρας, ὀχεύς; *sera, claustrum*). From the outside the bolt was drawn by a strap passing through a hole in the door; it was withdrawn by inserting through a second hole a bar (κλείς, *clavis*) bent twice at right angles, so that its end engaged in a groove in the bolt. This bar is the 'temple key' of Greek art. Subsequently a slot was cut in the bolt, into which a vertical peg (βάλανος) fell as the bolt moved forward; then a βαλανάγρα had to be employed to hook up the peg before the bolt could move back. It remained long in use, with growing complexity of the slots and correspondingly of the prongs of the key. The modern form of lock in which the key rotates the bolt on a pivot is not found before Roman times, but is then common, as are movable padlocks. The key in art is often a symbol of power, as when *Hecate holds the key of *Hades (κλειδοῦχος, clavigera); to give or take back the household keys was a Roman form of divorce.

R. Vallois, Dar.–Sag., 'sera'; A. Hug, RE 2 A 1 (1921), cols. 565–9 'Schlüssel'; C. J. Singer and others, History of Technology 2 (1956), 415–16.
F. N. P.

King's Peace, of 386 BC, epoch-making arrangement, foreshadowed in negotiations in 392, and imposed by king *Artaxerxes (2) II of Persia, whereby the *Corinthian War was ended. The peace guaranteed the *autonomy of the Greeks, in exchange for recognition that the cities in Asia, also the 'islands' *Clazomenae (not actually an island) and *Cyprus, should belong to Persia (Xen. Hell. 5. 1. 31). Other detailed terms have been posited. The Spartan *Antalcidas was prominent in the negotiations, hence the alternative name Peace of Antalcidas.

G. L. Cawkwell, CQ 1973 and 1981; R. K. Sinclair, Chiron 1978; M. Clark, BSA 1990; R. Urban, Der Königsfrieden von 387/86 (1991); E. Badian, in M. Flower and M. Toher (eds.), Georgica (1991); R. Seager, CAH 6² (1994), ch. 4.
S. H.

kingship (basileia) The Mycenaean political system (see MYCENAEAN CIVILIZATION) was monarchic, with the king (wanax) at the head of a palace-centred economy; the 10th-cent. BC 'hero's tomb' at *Lefkandi may imply some limited continuity into the Dark Age. Kingship appears to have been rare later: *Homer borrows elements from Mycenae and the near east, but seems essentially to be describing an aristocratic world, in which the word basileus is often used in the plural of an office-holding nobility. The earliest true monarchies were the 7th–6th-cent. *tyrannies, which were regarded as aberrations; the Spartan dual 'kingship' (see SPARTA) is a form of hereditary but non-monarchic military leadership. The Classical period knew kingship only from myth and as a *barbarian form of rule, found in tribal areas and in the near east. *Sophists established a theoretical table of constitutions, with kingship and tyranny as the good and bad forms of monarchy, opposed to the rule of the few and the rule of the many (see OLIGARCHY; DEMOCRACY; POLITICAL THEORY). In the 4th cent. BC, developments in *Thessaly (*Jason (2)), *Syracuse (*Dionysius (1) I and (2) II), *Caria (*Mausolus), and *Cyprus (Nicocles and *Evagoras), and especially the rise of Macedon under *Philip (1) II, demonstrated the practical importance of monarchy; and *Plato (1), *Xenophon (1), and *Isocrates elaborated theories justifying kingship.

After *Alexander (3) the Great, monarchy became a dominant form of government in the Greek world. The Hellenistic monarchies (see GREECE, PREHISTORY AND HISTORY; HELLENISM) controlled vast territories by conquest ('land won by the spear'), and often made use of existing local administrative practices, presenting themselves as successors to earlier kings; they encouraged and established indigenous forms of king-worship (see RULER-CULT). In practice monarchies were hereditary, and claims were made to divine descent. In Greek cities the forms of king-worship were based on the idea of the king as saviour and benefactor (see EUERGETISM; SOTER), or new *founder of the city: the king and

sometimes his family were living gods to be worshipped with temples, cult *statues, and festivals. In the free cities such honours were often diplomatic, and reflected the needs of alliances. Roman proconsuls also found themselves honoured; and the emperors accepted and systematized emperor-worship in the Greek provinces of the empire.

A philosophical theory of monarchy developed in the early Hellenistic period: philosophers were often welcomed as advisers at court, and representatives from all major philosophical schools except the *Cynic are known to have written treatises On Kingship. These seem to have rested on a common theoretical basis: kingship was 'rule without accountability'; it was justified by the perfect virtue of the king, which should be exemplified in a series of actions towards his subjects. The main virtue was love of his subjects (philanthrōpia); others were beneficence (euergesia), justice, self-control, wisdom, foresight, courage. Though the king need not be a philosopher, he should listen to their advice. The king's actions would ensure the love of his subjects. The doctrine of the king as 'living law' was not part of the theory, which was singularly weak in legal justification. Apart from some derivative pseudo-Pythagorean fragments of uncertain date (see DIOTOGENES; PYTHAGORAS (1)), no treatise On Kingship survives, but their influence can be detected in contemporary literature (most clearly in the pseudonymous Letter of Aristeas (see ARISTEAS, LETTER OF) to Philocrates on the Greek translation of the Torah), and in the language used in government documents.

It is doubtful whether this theory affected Roman attitudes to the emperor until the mid-1st cent. AD. But thereafter a series of writers describe the duties of the emperor in language derived from Hellenistic kingship theory; the most important of these are *Philon (4), the younger Seneca, De clementia (see ANNAEUS SENECA (2), L.), and *Dio Cocceianus, Or. 1–4. In the high empire a distinction became established between rhetorical speeches addressed 'to a king' and in direct praise of him (see PANEGYRIC (LATIN)), and philosophical treatises of advice 'on kingship', presenting an ideal picture even when addressed to a particular king. Fourth-cent. writers (*Themistius, *Julian, *Libanius, *Claudian, *Synesius) make much of this distinction. Kingship theory also influenced Christian theology (see CHRISTIANITY), and was used by *Eusebius in the portrayal of *Constantine I, the first Christian emperor. It was therefore an important influence on Byzantine political thought. See also REX.

J. Kaerst, Studien zur Entwicklung und theoretischen Begründung der Monarchie im Altertum (1898); F. Dvornik, Early Christian and Byzantine Political Philosophy: Origins and Background (1966); P. Hadot, RAC 8 (1972), 555–632, 'Fürstenspiegel'; R. Drews, Basileus (1983); F. W. Walbank, CAH 7²/1 (1984), ch. 3; E. R. Goodenough, YClS 1928, 53–192; W. Schubart, Arch. Pap. 1937, 1–26; L. Delatte, Les Traités de la royauté de Diotogène, Sthénidas et Ecphante (1942); C. Habicht, Gottmenschentum und griechische Städte, 2nd edn. (1970); P. Beskow, Rex Gloriae (1962); L. Koenen and L. Mooren in E. van 't Dack, P. van Dessel, and W. van Gucht (eds.), Egypt and the Hellenistic World, Studia Hellenistica 27 (1983).
O. Mu.

kinship is not treated separately, at full length, in this dictionary. 'The promise of a unified and general theory of kinship has not been realized; indeed the very definition of the field is in dispute, some scholars arguing that the project of a comparative science of kinship rests on the illusion that in all societies "kinship" systems are ordered on similar principles': so the anthropologist Adam Kuper begins his entry 'Kinship' in A. and J. Kuper (eds.), Social Science Encyclopedia ed. 2 (1996), 441–3; the reader is referred to Kuper's article for an up-to-date discussion of the theoretical position. However he concludes that 'the resemblances between domestic institutions in societies all over the world are so remarkable that it is hard to understand why anthropologists should have lost sight of commonalities'. Certainly some modern criticisms ('the cultural critique') of traditional kinship study seem inappropriate to the study of the ancient Greeks and Romans. For instance it has been said that genealogy, an institution which assumes that blood relationships structure social systems, is simply the imposition of western categories on other peoples (see ORIENTALISM). But Greek interest in *genealogy is securely attested (in other words, perhaps, the ancient Greeks were to that extent 'westerners'). And there is no doubt that Greeks of the Classical and Hellenistic periods were themselves very interested in the idea of kinship (syngeneia) between peoples or cities, and that they based political claims and requests on such real, exaggerated, or imagined kinship-ties. (For a collection of the relevant inscriptions and a good discussion of Greek words for 'kin' and 'kinship' terminology see O. Curty, Les Parentés légendaires entre cités grecques (1995); see also Hornblower, Comm. on Thuc. 2 (1996), Introduction, section 4 on 'Thucydides and ξυγγένεια' and C. P. Jones, Kinship Diplomacy in the Ancient World (1999)). The Romans also defined themselves in terms of such kinship connections; see AENEAS. All this might seem to encourage rather than discourage generalization about kinship in the ancient world.

Nevertheless, many of the theoretical problems about such generalization remain. The problems are scarcely less if we confine ourselves either to the Greeks (among whom it is only the Classical Athenians who are really well attested, through orators and inscriptions, and thus susceptible to detailed analysis) or to the Romans. (On Athens, S. C. Humphreys, Anthropology and the Greeks (1978), 193 ff., and the introductory material in R. J. Littman, Kinship and Politics in Athens 600–400 BC (1990), may be found helpful.) We therefore prefer to direct readers to those particular entries in this dictionary which cover, or have a bearing on, ancient kinship-institutions or ideas about kinship, namely: ADOPTION; FAMILY, ROMAN; FOUNDERS, CITY; GENEALOGY; GENOS; GENS; HOUSEHOLD; INCEST; INHERITANCE; JUDGES, FOREIGN; MARRIAGE CEREMONIES and MARRIAGE LAW; MATRIARCHY; MATRILOCALITY; PHRATRY; PHYLAI; PROSOPOGRAPHY; TRIBUS; WOMEN.

S. H.

koinē (standard Greek; also sometimes used more generally of shared culture) See GREEK LANGUAGE.

Koinē Eirēnē See COMMON PEACE.

kōlakretai (κωλακρέται) were Athenian officials in charge of the state treasury. The date of their institution is not known, but they existed at least as early as the time of *Solon. References in inscriptions and in *Aristophanes (1) show that they still had charge of public money in the 5th cent. BC and disbursed money for various purposes, including the pay of jurors. They are not heard of after 411 BC and were probably abolished in that year. Some, perhaps all, of their functions were taken over by the *hellēnotamiai.

ATL 3. 359–66; FGrH 3b Suppl., comm. on 324 F 5. P. J. Rhodes, The Athenian Boule (1972), 102; P. Harding, Androtion and the Atthis (1994), 91–4, 134–8.
D. M. M.

Korai See SCULPTURE, GREEK.

Kore See PERSEPHONE/KORE.

Kouroi See SCULPTURE, GREEK.

Kourotrophos, 'child-nurturer', appears to be known both as a divine epithet and (despite Hadzisteliou-Price, below) as an independent goddess over much of the Greek world. Although lacking in mythology, she is evidently an important figure of cult, appearing frequently in sacrifice groups connected with fertility and child care.

Th. Hadzisteliou-Price, Kourotrophos (1978); Clinton, Iconography 31–7.
E. Ke.

Knossos See CNOSSUS.

Kronos See CRONUS.

krypteia Part of the Classical Spartan upbringing (see AGŌGĒ) during which (probably, selected) youths traversed the countryside, concealing themselves by day. It represents arguably the transformation of an early *initiation rite. Some sources present it as a lengthy test of individual endurance without equipment or prepared rations, others as a brief exercise by a group provided with supplies and daggers for killing prominent *helots; these may be sequential stages of the institution. Different modern interpretations of the krypteia—military preparation or a transitional period of 'opposition' to adult *hoplite life—are not necessarily incompatible.

E. Levy, Ktema 1988, 245–52; P. Vidal-Naquet, The Black Hunter (1986; Fr. orig. 1981), ch. 5.
S. J. Ho.

Kushans See SERES.

La Tène culture See CELTS.

Laberius, Decimus (*c.*106–43? BC) a Roman knight who, like the younger *Publilius Syrus, formalized the popular south Italian *mime, composing scripts in the metre and language of comedy. His surviving 43 titles and 178 lines (Bonaria) suggest some mythical burlesque but more Italian themes, such as popular festivals, comic trades, impersonation, and sexual escapades, for which he coined new comic language. Forced by a challenge of *Caesar in 46 to act in his own mime in competition with Syrus, he mocked his rival by acting a Syrian slave under the lash, protesting in a prologue his own humiliation and the loss of public liberty (Macrob. *Sat.* 2. 6. 6–7. 5; Suet. *Iul.* 39).

TEXT Duff, *Minor Lat. Poets*; M. Bonaria *Mimorum Romanorum Fragmenta* 1 (1956).

W. Beare, *The Roman Stage* (1964), 149–58.   E. F.

Labienus (*RE* 5), **Quintus**, son of Titus *Labienus (1), was sent to *Parthia by *Cassius in winter 43/2 BC to solicit help against the *triumvirs. *Philippi marooned him in Parthia, but in winter 41/0 he and the king's son Pacorus led Parthian troops into Syria and defeated Antony's governor L. *Decidius Saxa; then, with Saxa's army, which went over to him, Labienus overran part of Asia Minor. On his coins he calls himself 'Q. Labienus Parthicus imp.', claiming that a victory over the Parthians had forced them to become allies. In 39 he was defeated and killed by P. *Ventidius.

The coins: *RRC* 524.   T. J. C.; E. B.

Labienus (1) (*RE* 6), **Titus** (*c.*100–45 BC), served under P. *Servilius Isauricus as military tribune in Cilicia (*c.*78–74). In 63 as tribune of the *plebs* he conducted the prosecution of C. *Rabirius (1) for *perduellio*, obtained the re-enactment of the *lex Domitia* providing for elections to priesthoods (see LEX (2)), and proposed honours for *Pompey. Appointed legate of *Caesar, he acted as his principal subordinate in Gaul (58–51), and he was entrusted with the independent conduct of important operations (e.g. against the *Treveri 54–53 and Parisii (see LUTETIA) 52—the latter a strategical and tactical masterpiece). Caesar may have intended him for consul, perhaps in 48 (a probable inference from *BGall.* 8. 52. 2), but at the beginning of 49 he deserted to Pompey. There is reason to believe that Labienus came from *Picenum, and, like many men from that area, was always a partisan of Pompey. He fought at *Pharsalus and in the African campaign, and died in the campaign of Munda (March 45).

Syme, *RP* 1. 62 ff.; W. B. Tyrrell, *Hist.* 1972, 424 ff.   C. E. S.; R. J. S.

Labienus (2), **Titus,** Augustan orator and declaimer, whose furious *invective earned him the nickname 'Rabienus' (i.e. 'rabid'), and who retained sympathy for the cause of *Pompey.

He wrote a history, and a pamphlet against *Maecenas' favourite Bathyllus. He committed suicide when his books were burned by senatorial decree; *Gaius (1) restored them to circulation (Suet. *Calig.* 16).

Main source, Sen. *Controv.* 10 pref. 4–8; Schanz–Hosius, § 336. 1. *PIR²* L 19.   M. W.

labour, as a factor in the production of wealth, has no equivalent in Greek or Latin. Association of the terms *ponos* and *labor* with drudgery reflects the negative attitudes of ancient élites, for whom 'labour' was the antithesis of *scholē* and *otium* (time available for leisure, politics, education, and culture). Consequently, the labour of theoretically free wage-earners and craftsmen tended to be assimilated to slavery (Arist. *Pol.* 1337ᵇ19 ff.; Cic. *Off.* 1. 159 f.). *Wages were seen as purchasing the person as opposed to labour-power; the supposedly degrading nature of craft-work (*banausia*) led to the downgrading of the individual worker (see ART, ANCIENT ATTITUDES TO; ARTISANS AND CRAFTSMEN). Surviving sources reveal nothing resembling modern conceptions of unions or trade-guilds (see CLUBS), strikes, or common programmes of action; nor, aside from occasional epitaphs, is there any awareness of the 'dignity of labour'. Striking is the absence of any sustained competition or resentment between types of labour. Throughout the Greek and Roman worlds are found instead shifting, complementary relationships between different forms of exploitation. Already in *Hesiod's *Works and Days* (less clearly in the *Odyssey*) there exist crude equivalents of 'free', 'wage', and 'slave' labourer, combined on the peasant farm. In quantitative terms, the dominant form of labour on the land throughout the ancient world may broadly be described as 'compulsory labour', whereby the politically weak performed obligatory labour dues for the powerful. From the Greek world, the *helots are the best known of these unfree agricultural workforces 'between freedom and slavery' (*Pollux). There was a similar pattern in the Roman empire, with Romans in the provinces retaining pre-existing systems of compulsory labour. In cities, the labour of independent artisans and their families would be supplemented by slaves (a permanent workforce) or wage labourers (for casual labour). Large public projects would require extensive hired labour (Plut. *Per.* 12. 5; Suet. *Vesp.* 8. 5). Exceptional were Classical Athens and Roman Italy and Sicily during the late republic, where chattel-*slavery was widespread in the countryside (though supplemented by wage labour at harvest). In both cases, the citizen status of *peasants made problematic their direct exploitation by landowning élites. Italian peasants, however, always remained vulnerable. As the number of chattel-slaves gradually (though never completely) diminished, the later centuries of the empire saw a lowering

809

of peasant status and their progressive re-exploitation: tenant farmers were tied to the land as *coloni* (see COLONUS). The relationship of the colonate and allied forms of compulsory labour to the eventual emergence of feudalism remains obscure. See CLASS STRUGGLE; INDUSTRY.

C. Mossé, *The Ancient World at Work* (1969); J. L. Stocks, *CQ* 1936, 177 ff.; J. M. André, *L'Otium dans la vie morale et intellectuelle romaine* (1966); S. R. Joshell, *Work, Identity and Legal Status at Rome* (1992); M. I. Finley, *The World of Odysseus* (1977), *Economy and Society in Ancient Greece* (1981), 116 ff., *The Ancient Economy* (1973; repr. 1985), and *Ancient Slavery and Modern Ideology* (1980); G. E. M. de Ste Croix, *The Class Struggle* (1981); P. Garnsey (ed.), *Non-slave Labour in the Greco-Roman World* (1980); G. Nussbaum, *CQ* 1960, 186 ff.; P. A. Brunt, *JRS* 1980 81 ff.; M. K. Hopkins, *Conquerors and Slaves* (1978); A. H. M. Jones, *The Roman Economy* (1974), 293 ff.; C. R. Whittaker, in M. I. Finley (ed.), *Classical Slavery* (1987), 88 ff.   P. C. M.

Labraunda, sanctuary of *Zeus Labraundos in *Caria, between *Mylasa (to which it was linked by a sacred way) and *Amyzon, occupying a mountainous and beautiful position. (Hdt. 5. 119 speaks of Zeus Stratios but the inscriptions mostly have Zeus Labraundos, a part-Greek part-indigenous deity; cf. *Sinuri.) The 4th-cent. BC Hecatomnid *satraps built lavishly at the sanctuary, laying it out afresh (see IDRIEUS; MAUSOLUS) and their well-carved dedications can still be seen on the site. (Other inscriptions, *ILabraunda* nos. 40 and 42, illustrate the political activities and policies of *Mausolus and *Pixodarus.) Thereafter there was a gap in building activity until Roman imperial times, but from the Hellenistic period there is an extensive dossier concerning the interesting figure of Olympichus, who was first a general of *Seleucus (2) II and then became in effect an independent operator, like Mausolus before him. But Olympichus had to obey the instructions of, without being formally subordinate to, *Philip (3) V of Macedon. Labraunda inscription no. 5 provides valuable epigraphic evidence for Antigonid Macedonian involvement in Caria, an important development poorly attested in literary sources, which do, however, know of a Carian expedition by *Antigonus (3) Doson. There are also inscriptions from Labraunda in Carian, a reminder of Caria's mixed culture.

Labraunda Swedish Excavations and Researches, multi-author series; see esp. J. Crampa, vols. 3/1 (1969) and 3/2 (1972) for the Greek inscriptions (= *ILabraunda*) (with *SEG* 40. 969 ff.), M. Meier-Brügger, vol. 2/4 (1983) for the Carian. Architecture: vols. 1/1 (K. Jeppesen, 1955) for the Propylaea, and 1/2 (A. Westholm, 1963) for the architecture of the sanctuary (*hieron*). See also G. E. Bean, *Turkey Beyond the Maeander*, 2nd edn. (1980), ch. 4; S. Hornblower, *Mausolus* (1982); T. Linders and P. Hellström (eds.), *Architecture and Society in Hecatomnid Caria* (1989); M. Mellink, *CAH* 3²/2 (1991), 664; S. Le Bohec, *Antigone Doson* (1993), 327–61.   S. H.

Labyrinth (λαβύρινθος), a complex building constructed by *Daedalus for king *Minos of Crete and commonly identified with the Minoan palace of Cnossus (see MINOAN CIVILIZATION). The labyrinth's confusing system of passages, from which no one could escape (Plut. *Thes.* 15), concealed the Minotaur which fed on human victims until destroyed by *Theseus (Paus. 1. 27. 10; Apollod. *Bibl.* 3. 1. 4, *Epit.* 1. 7–11). The hero imitated its twists and turns in a ritual dance on *Delos (Plut. *Thes.* 21). Later the name was applied to a quarry at *Gortyn with many chambers and to other labyrinthine structures at Nauplia (Strabo 8. 6. 2), *Lemnos (Plin. *HN* 36. 86, 90), and in *Egypt (Hdt. 2. 148). The maze-like design occurs on Cretan coins and in Greek vase-painting, and proved popular in Roman mosaics (cf. a Pompeian graffito with inscription: 'Labyrinthus. Hic habitat Minotaurus',

'Labyrinth. Here lives the Minotaur', Dar.-Sag. 3². 883, fig. 4317). Similar designs can already be seen on Minoan seals and frescos of the second palace at Cnossus. A newly discovered Minoan fresco from Tell el-Dab'a (anc. Avaris) in Egypt (Hyksos period, 16th cent. BC) combines the characteristic pattern with a bull and acrobats (see W. V. Davies and L. Schofield, *Egypt, the Aegean and the Levant* (1995)).

A plausible derivation of the non-Greek word from (Lydian) λάβρυς 'double axe' connects the labyrinth with a potent Minoan religious symbol (Plut. *Quaest. Graec.* 45, 301f–302a (weapon of Zeus Labraundos; see LABRAUNDA), A. Heubeck, *Praegraeca* (1961), 25). Linear B (see MYCENAEAN LANGUAGE) mentions a labyrinth (*dapurito-*) of Potnia (KN Gg 702; cf. X 140).

R. Eilmann, *Labyrinthos* (1931); W. Pötscher, *Aspekte und Probleme der Minoischen Religion* (1990), 52–66.   G. M. A. H.; B. C. D.

Lacedaemon See LACONIA; SPARTA (for which Lacedaemon was the official name).

Lachares, Athenian general after *Ipsus (301 BC), used his mercenary troops to crush an attempted usurpation by his colleague, Charias (before 297). Allegedly on *Cassander's instigation he used his troops to make himself tyrant, and stripped the Acropolis of its treasures (including the gold from the cult statue of Athene) to pay his men (296). News of his coup attracted *Demetrius (4) Poliorcetes, who starved the city into submission (? 295). Lachares escaped before the surrender and bought his way to Boeotia. His subsequent fate is variously attested.

The chronology of Lachares' 'tyranny' is disputed; see C. Habicht, *Untersuchungen zur politischen Geschichte Athens* (1979); M. J. Osborne, *Naturalization in Athens 2* (1982), 144 ff.   A. B. B.

Laconia (Λακεδαίμων or ἡ Λακωνικὴ [γῆ]), the SE district of the Peloponnese (see PELOPONNESUS), bordering *Arcadia to the north and *Messenia to the west. Until the 190s BC (see below), Laconia was controlled by *Sparta and was the 'nuclear territory' (Cartledge) of the Spartans. A mountainous region, dominated by limestone formations and its derivatives, Laconia comprises the Parnon range in the east (peak 1,935 m.: 6, 348 ft.) running south to the *Malea peninsula, and the Taygetus range in the west (peak 2,407 m.: 7,897 ft.) which towers over the plain of Sparta and extends south to the Mani peninsula. In between is the valley of the Eurotas, joined by the Oenus above Sparta, which empties into the Laconian Gulf at Helos. Natural resources occur in the south, iron near Neapolis and copper and silver/lead ores around Molaoi; *lapis lacedaemonius* is quarried near Croceae and *rosso antico* in the Mani (see MARBLE). The main areas of cultivable land are the Eurotas valley (especially the plain of Sparta) and the Helos and Molaoi plains.

Palaeolithic occupation occurs at caves in the Mani. The only important neolithic settlement is at Kouphovouno near Sparta but early bronze age sites are widespread. Since c.1600 BC, when a flourishing Mycenaean kingdom (see MYCENAEAN CIVILIZATION) emerged, the centre of political power has always been located in the plain of Sparta. The main site at the *Menelaion and others like Agios Stephanos on the Helos plain were destroyed c.1200 BC. From then until the arrival of *Dorian settlers c.950 BC, Laconia was severely depopulated. By c.700 BC Sparta controlled most of Laconia and had begun its expansion into *Messenia, reducing much of the conquered population to helotry (see HELOTS). Spartiate territory comprised the plain of Sparta and its surrounds, the rest of Laconia being divided among nominally independent perioecic towns (see PERIOIKOI) whose origins are mostly obscure. The northern frontiers were established *c*.540 BC after long disputes with *Argos (2) and *Tegea. Communications with the outside world were through Tegea to the north and Gytheum, Sparta's port and naval station, to the south. Spartan control of Laconia was uninterrupted until 338 BC when *Philip (1) II divided its northern borderlands between Argos, Tegea, and *Megalopolis and awarded land on Taygetus to *Messene. Although some areas were recovered, the forced incorporation of Sparta and its dependencies into the *Achaean Confederacy in 192 BC effectively ended Spartan hegemony of Laconia. A league of Laconian towns excluding Sparta, instituted during the 2nd cent. BC, was transformed into the 'League of the Free Laconians' (κοινὸν τῶν Ἐλευθερολακώνων) under *Augustus, finally freeing the perioecic towns from Spartan domination. Initially twenty-four in number, they were reduced to eighteen by the Antonine period. Their cult centre was at the Hyperteleatum.

F. Bölte and others, *RE* 3 A 2 (1929), 1265–1528, 'Sparta'; *IG* 5. 1; P–K, *GL* 3/2. 412 ff.; *GAC* 107 ff.; P. Cartledge, *Sparta and Lakonia* (1979); P. Cartledge and A. Spawforth, *Hellenistic and Roman Sparta*, 2nd edn. (2002); G. Shipley in J. M. Sanders (ed.), *Philolakon* (1992), 211 ff.; J. B. Rutter, *AJArch* 1993, 745 ff. R. W. V. C.

Lactantius (Lucius Caelius (Caecilius ?) Firmianus also called **Lactantius),** *c.* AD 240–*c*.320, a native of North Africa, pupil of *Arnobius, one of the Christian apologists (see CHRISTIANITY). Under *Diocletian he was officially summoned to teach rhetoric at *Nicomedia; the date of his conversion is uncertain, but is earlier than the persecution of 303, when his Christianity caused him to lose his position at Nicomedia. He remained there until he moved to the west in 305; in extreme old age he was tutor (*c*.317) to Crispus, eldest son of *Constantine I.

Of Lactantius' numerous works on various subjects, only his Christian writings survive. He began these after the outbreak of the persecution. The *De opificio Dei* demonstrates providence from the construction of the human body. The *Divinae institutiones* (303–13), begun as a reply to attacks on *Christianity by the philosopher and official Hierocles, was intended to refute all opponents past, present, and future. The order of composition of the books, like the date of the *Epitome*, is uncertain. The work shows knowledge of the major Latin poets, and above all of Cicero, but little of Greek apart from spurious Orphic and Sibylline poems. The *De ira Dei* (after 313) makes anger, as a disposition rather than a passion, an essential property of God. The *De mortibus persecutorum* (317/8) is designed to show that the fate of persecutors is always evil, and may therefore have exaggerated the role of the unfortunate *Galerius in inspiring the persecution of his own times. One poem by Lactantius, the *Phoenix*, also survives.

At the Renaissance Lactantius, the most classical of all early Christian writers, came to be known as the Christian Cicero. Except in the *Epitome*, he shows little philosophic knowledge or ability, and has little of importance to say on Christian doctrine or institutions. The latter defect, at least, can be explained as the accustomed reserve of the Christian apologist when writing for hostile or unbelieving readers.

EDITIONS S. Brandt and G. Laubmann, *CSEL* 19, 27; *De ira Dei*, H. Kraft and A. Wlosok (1957); *Epitome*, E. H. Blakeney (1950); *De mort. pers.*, J. L. Creed (1984).

STUDIES R. Pichon, *Lactance* (1901); R. M. Ogilvie, *The Library of Lactantius* (1978). Jas. S.; M. J. E.

'Lactantius (*RE* 2) Placidus', the name under which is transmitted a commentary on *Statius' *Thebais* dating (in its original form) to the 5th or 6th cent. AD (ed. Jahnke, 1898: inadequate).

R. D. Sweeney, *Prolegomena to an Edition of the Scholia to Statius* (1969). Herzog–Schmidt, § 614. R. A. K.

Lacydes of Cyrene succeeded *Arcesilaus (1) as head of the Middle *Academy in 241/0, BC, and held the position till at least as late as 224/3, after which the headship was in abeyance till *Carneades became head; Lacydes died in 206/5. He is sometimes described as founder of the New Academy, but in truth he simply emphasized the scepticism (see SCEPTICS) which was already well developed in Arcesilaus. He seems to have made no important contribution to philosophy. W. D. R.

Laelius (1), Gaius (*c*.235–*c*.160 BC), served in Spain (209–206) and then in Africa (205–202) under P. *Cornelius Scipio Africanus, whose close friend and protégé he became. With Scipio's support he became *quaestor (202), plebeian aedile (197; see AEDILES), *praetor (196), and *consul (190; as colleague of Scipio's brother L. *Cornelius Scipio Asiagenes). He later served on embassies to King *Perseus (2) (174–173) and to Transalpine Gaul (170). He met *Polybius (1) during the latter's period of detention in Rome (167–150) and provided him with firsthand information about Scipio (Polyb. 10. 3. 2).

RE 12, 'Laelius' 2; Broughton, *MRR*. P. S. D.

Laelius (2), Gaius (*c*.190–after 129 BC), son of C. *Laelius (1) and, as closest friend of P. *Cornelius Scipio Aemilianus, part of the '*Scipionic Circle'. He became involved with the embassy of Athenian philosophers (155), especially the Stoic *Diogenes (3), and with *Panaetius, whose work he was influential in publicizing at Rome. These connections earned him the nickname *Sapiens* ('wise'). In 147–146 he served with Scipio Aemilianus in Africa, and went on to be *praetor in 145 and *consul in 140. He was augur from before 140 until his death. His reputation as an orator was considerable. As praetor he successfully resisted the proposal of the tribune C. Licinius Crassus that priesthoods be filled by popular election and not co-optation. He mooted (as praetor, or possibly as consul) an agrarian measure but withdrew it in response to senatorial opposition. He assisted the consuls of 132 (P. *Popillius Laenas and P. *Rupilius) in the persecution of the supporters of Ti. Sempronius Gracchus (3), and (in 131 or 130) opposed the measure of the tribune C. *Papirius Carbo (1) allowing re-election to the tribunate. He is the central figure in Cicero's *De amicitia* and appears also in the *De republica*.

RE 12, 'Laelius' 3; H. H. Scullard, *JRS* 1960, 62 ff.; Astin, *Scipio*; A. W. Erskine, *The Hellenistic Stoa* (1990); Broughton, *MRR* (with vol. 3 Suppl. p. 116). P. S. D.

Laelius (*RE* 13) Archelaus, a friend of *Lucilius (1) and (probably) a freedman, with whom the grammarian *Pompeius Lenaeus read Lucilius' satires (Suet. *Gram.* 2: early 1st cent. BC).

Herzog–Schmidt, § 193. R. A. K.

Laertes See HOMER; ODYSSEUS.

Laestrygones, cannibal giants encountered by *Odysseus (*Od.* 10. 80–132). They inhabit 'the lofty city of Lamus', ruled by King Antiphates, who eats one of Odysseus' men. The nights are so short there that one can earn a double wage, which suggests the distant north (Crates in schol. *Od.* 10. 86). Greek tradition located them in *Sicily (Hes. fr. 150. 26 MW, Thuc. 6. 2. 1, etc.), especially *Leontini (Theopompus, *FGrH* 115 F 225, etc.), but the Romans placed them at *Formiae in *Campania (Cic. *Att.* 2. 13. 2, etc.).

Laevius

*Horace playfully connects Lamus with the family of the Aelii Lamiae (*Carm.* 3. 17).

K. Meuli, *RE* Suppl. 5 (1931), 537–40; C. Lochin, *LIMC* 6/1. 187–8; D. Page, *Folktales in Homer's Odyssey* (1973), 23–48.   N. J. R.

Laevius, reasonably identified with a Laevius Melissus mentioned by Suet. *Gram.* 3 = fr. 31 Courtney, wrote at least six books of *Erotopaegnia*, playful lyrics on amatory themes, probably early in the 1st cent. BC. Other titles (*Adonis*, *Helena*, *Alcestis*, *Ino*, *Sirenocirca*, *Protesilaodamia*) probably refer to parts of that collection, as the *Phoenix* certainly does. The fragments show a fanciful, sentimental, and romantic treatment of the love stories of mythology. He experimented with a variety of metres (particularly iambic dimeters in systems with synapheia after the manner of *Anacreon, actual anacreontics, and anapaestic dimeters), even changing metres within poems, and with bizarre and novel diction (compounds, diminutives, Greek loanwords, new forms and uses of words, often based on *analogy or *etymology). In the *Phoenix* he reproduced the Hellenistic conceit of the *technopaegnion*, adjusting the length of the lines to produce the shape of wings, but he has affinities not only with Hellenistic writing but also with Anacreon (see above) and (in his choice of themes) Euripides. *Varro, whom he seems to mention in fr. 3, was influenced by him to employ a wide range of metres in his *Saturae Menippeae*, but otherwise he attracted virtually no attention until the archaizing writers of the 2nd cent. AD, who were interested in his linguistic idiosyncrasies and imitated his unorthodox metres; his influence can be seen particularly in *Septimius Serenus. See ARCHAISM IN LATIN; METRE, GREEK and LATIN.

F. Leo *Hermes* 1914, 180; D. O. Ross, *Style and Tradition in Catullus* (1969), 155; Courtney, *FLP* 118.   E. C.

Laius See OEDIPUS.

Lamachus (d. 414 BC), Athenian general, one of the *stratēgoi* as early as *c.*435 and well known for his military leadership by 425, when he was caricatured as a blustering soldier in the *Acharnians* (572 ff.) of *Aristophanes (1). In 424 he led an unsuccessful expedition into the Black Sea (see EUXINE), using *Heraclea (3) Pontica as his base (Thuc. 4. 75). In 415 he was appointed with *Alcibiades and *Nicias (1) to command the expedition to Sicily. He urged an immediate attack on *Syracuse, but failed to convince his colleagues. The rapid progress of the Athenian blockade in 414 seems to have been largely due to his energetic leadership; it ended abruptly when he was killed in a skirmish. In later plays Aristophanes pays tributes to his heroism.

For the Sicilian command see Thuc. bk. 6. A. Andrewes, *CAH* 5² (1992), ch. 10.   H. D. W.; S. H.

Lambaesis (mod. Tazzoult), a Roman military base and town in *Numidia, north of the Aurès range. It is first attested in AD 81 when a fort was built (*AE* 1954, 137), later to be covered by the civilian town. Another fort, 4 km. (2½ mi.) to the north-west, is known only from aerial photography; it was here on a column that *Hadrian's address to the troops was inscribed, much of it surviving (*ILS* 2487 and 9133–5). Between the two forts lies a third military base, the 20-ha. (50-acre) military fortress for the Legio III Augusta, which was built here by Trajan, probably in 115–17, to guard the route which led north from the Sahara through Vescara (Biskra) and Calceus Herculis (El Kantara). The legion was disbanded by *Gordian III but was restored to its former fortress by *Valerian (253). It is to the 3rd cent. that most of the visible buildings of the legionary fortress belong, the finest extant example anywhere in the Roman empire (see

FORTIFICATIONS). Still standing to room-height at its centre is the tetrapylon, referred to misleadingly by modern scholars as the *praetorium*, but named on its inscription of 267/8 apparently as the *groma* (*AE* 1974, 723), because it was here at the centre of the fortress that the surveyor (see GROMATICI) set up his *groma* during the laying-out of the fortress. The structure served as the vestibule of the headquarters (*principia*); other excavated buildings include offices, storerooms, messrooms, baths, a *fabrica* (workshop), and of course barracks. An amphitheatre was built outside the walls. To the south-east of the fortress a considerable town developed with its own baths, arches, and temples, including a Capitolium and a sanctuary of *Aesculapius: when the separate province of Numidia was created in 197/8, this town became its capital.

PECS 478–9; R. Cagnat, *L'Armée romaine d'Afrique* (1913), 429–519; M. Janon, *Antiquités africaines* 1973, 193–254, and 1985, 35–102; F. Rakob and S. Storz, *MDAI(R)* 1974, 253–80; Y. Le Bohec, *La Troisième Légion Auguste* (1989), esp. 407–24.   R. J. A. W.

Lamia (1), best known as the name of a nursery bogey, like *Empusa, *Mormo, and *Gello, who stole or ate children. In myth she was a beautiful Libyan, daughter of *Belus and Libya, whose children by *Zeus were killed in jealousy by *Hera. She then assumed a monstrous form and began to seize and kill the children of other women.

Schol. Ar. *Pax* 758; J. Boardman, *LIMC* 6. 189; J. Fontenrose, *Python* (1959), 100–4, 115–17.   E. Ke.

Lamia (2), chief city of the Malians, dominating the lower valley of the Spercheios and controlling the route linking *Thessaly with central Greece, along with a port, Phalara, used by the Thessalians. Occupation is attested from the neolithic until today. Fortified *c.*400 BC, Lamia provided a defensive position against both *Heraclea (4) Trachinia and campaigns launched from central Greece against Thessaly. In the *Lamian War (to which it gave its name) *Antipater (1) was besieged there without success (323/2). Under Aetolian control in the 3rd cent., it was taken by the Romans in 190 BC.

Y. Béquignon, *La Vallée du Spercheios* (1937).   B. H.

Lamian War (323–322 BC), fought, after the death of *Alexander (3) the Great, by Macedon under *Antipater (1) against a Greek coalition led by *Athens and *Aetolia. It took its name from *Lamia (2) in *Thessaly, where Antipater was besieged (see LEOSTHENES). The war ended with the Greek defeat at *Crannon.

J. S. Morrison, *JHS* 1987; O. Schmitt, *Der Lamische Krieg* (1992).   S. H.

Lampon 5th-cent. BC Athenian seer, see LYSIPPUS (1), also ML p. 221 and Plut. *Per.* 6 with P. Stadter's n.

Lamprocles (early/mid-5th cent. BC), Athenian musician and poet, teacher of *Damon (2), composer of *dithyrambs (Athen. 491c) and a famous *hymn to Athena quoted by *Aristophanes (1) (*Nub.* 967). He is said to have recognized the real nature of the Mixolydian mode (ps.-Plut. *De mus.* 1136d), see MUSIC, § 6. 2.

TEXT Page, *PMG* 379 f.
LITERATURE H. Abert, *RE* 12/1. 586 f.; A. Barker, *Greek Musical Writings* 1 (1984), 221; M. L. West, *Greek Music* (1992), 223 f.   B. Z.

lamps (λύχνος; *lucerna*) were made of *gold, *silver, *iron, *lead, *bronze, and ceramic. Only the last two kinds survive in any quantity; the epigraphic record is concerned with metal lamps alone. Lamps were not only used for *lighting, but served as votive offerings in sanctuaries and as tomb-furniture. They might be placed on stands, or be suspended on chains or cords. *Olive oil was the usual fuel. Middle and late Minoan (see MINOAN CIVILIZATION) clay and stone lamps are plentiful, usually having unbridged nozzles; otherwise, recognizable lamps of the early iron age only survive in the eastern Mediterranean. *Homer has but a single reference to a lamp (*Od.* 19. 34), of gold, but pottery 'cocked-hat' lamps of Athenian manufacture (akin to examples known in the Levant) are found from the 7th cent. BC. The more efficient bridged nozzle was introduced, probably in Asia Minor or the islands, soon afterwards. Thereafter Greek lamps have a tendency to become less open and shallow. Silver-rich *Athens would appear to be the main innovator of new forms; metal and ceramic versions were exported and copied over much of the Greek world. Moulded pottery lamps were introduced at the beginning of the 3rd cent. BC but were displaced in the 1st cent. AD when Italian lamps, with dished tops bearing relief pictures were introduced, some types, by their wide diffusion, raising important questions about Roman economic organization (Harris, see bibliog. below). Subjects include animals, birds, dramatic masks, vegetal ornaments, and mythological, religious, sporting, and pornographic scenes. The forms of both metal and pottery lamps are extremely varied, and elaborate specimens with many nozzles are not uncommon. In the 2nd and 3rd cents. AD there was a revival of high-quality pottery-lamp manufacture in *Corinth and Athens, while Italian lamps tended to be of poorer quality. From the 4th cent. some of the best quality pottery lamps were produced in North Africa, probably near *Carthage, and some bear Christian symbols. Their red-gloss surface may have been intended to evoke gold. After the 6th cent. few pottery lamps of good workmanship were produced, except in Palestine and Egypt. Several Byzantine bronze lamps survive.

L. Toutain, Dar.–Sag. 'lucerna'; S. Loeschcke, *Lampen aus Vindonissa* (1919); R. H. Howland, *Athenian Agora* 4 (1958); J. Perlzweig, *Athenian Agora* 7 (1961); D. M. Bailey, *A Catalogue of Lamps in the British Museum* (1975–), and *JRA* 1991; W. V. Harris, *JRS* 1980; M. Vickers, *AJArch.* 1994. D. M. B.; M. V.

Lampsacus was a Phocaean colony (see PHOCAEA; COLONIZATION, GREEK) in northern *Troas. Its strategic importance guarding the eastern entrance to the *Hellespont explains its historical significance. Its inhabitants attempted to check the elder Miltiades' domination of Thracian *Chersonesus (1) in the late 6th cent. BC. (See MILTIADES.) The Persian king *Artaxerxes (1) assigned the city to Themistocles, whom it supplied with the wine for which it was famous. The high tribute of twelve talents which it paid to the Athenian empire (see DELIAN LEAGUE) and the gold coinage issued during the 4th cent., when the city enjoyed a long period of self-government, suggest its general prosperity. It was notoriously plundered by *Verres, when he was quaestor of Asia (Cic. 2 *Verr.* 1. 24. 63).

W. Leaf, *Strabo on the Troad* (1923), 92; A. M. Mansel, *Kl. Pauly* 3. 473–4. D. E. W. W.; S. M.

land division (Greek) Traces of regular division of settlement space have been found even in Dark-Age Zagora on *Andros. Some early Greek colonies (see COLONIZATION, GREEK), notably *Megara Hyblaea, show a degree of planning in the organization of urban space in strips along major arterial streets, and in the reservation of an area for a communal *agora. Many Archaic foundations show a grid of rectangular blocks divided by large streets, although in some colonies (e.g. *Selinus, *Himera) the imposition of a regular street plan was subsequent to the initial

settlement. In Greece proper, an Archaic (6th cent.) grid is now attested at *Halieis.

The more or less ordered subdivisions of urban space in colonial foundations probably had a social and political correlate in the approximately equal status of colonial settlers. This is explicit in inscriptions about the setting up of colonies in the Classical period, where equal division is extended to the countryside also (e.g. *Syll.*[3] 141, and cf. Pl. *Leg.* 736–41). Connections between space and society were explored and exploited systematically in the 5th cent. by *Hippodamus of Miletus, with whom our sources connect the planning of *Piraeus, *Thurii, and *Rhodes, and whose ideas are critically discussed by *Aristotle in *Politics* book 2. The plan of Thurii is known only from *Diodorus (3) Siculus (12. 10), but aerial photography and field archaeology have revealed that the plan of Rhodes (408/7 BC) was based on large blocks, apparently 600 feet to a side (on a foot of 0.335 m. or 13.2 in.). In 'Hippodamian' plans the grid is more important than the arteries, and Classical foundations often display smaller blocks and more numerous streets, as in the classic cases of *Olynthus and *Priene. High priority is put on uniform blocks of housing. See HOUSES, GREEK.

Regular subdivision of the countryside can only more rarely be demonstrated. Good examples have been discovered archaeologically at *Metapontum and in the Crimea (*Chersonesus (2)) (4th cent. BC), where the units, which measure 630×420 m. (689×459 yds.), seem each to comprise six 50-*plethra* squares (in this a *plethron*—a measure varying in size—of 882 sq. m. would be involved, and the 50-*plethra* squares were just under 4.5 ha., or 11 acres, in size); and epigraphically at Hellenistic *Heraclea (1)-*Siris and *Larissa in Thessaly, in the latter case once more apparently using 50-*plethra* square units. But regular units may not always indicate regular land-holdings, and the desire to grow a range of crops suitable for different ecological niches (cf. *Syll.*[3] 141) must have rendered the rural picture necessarily more complex than the urban.

T. D. Boyd and M. H. Jameson, *Hesp.* 1981, 327–42; W. Hoepfner and E.-L. Schwandner, *Haus und Stadt* (1986). R. G. O.

land ownership See DOMAINS; LATIFUNDIA; OWNERSHIP, GREEK IDEAS ABOUT and ROMAN; POSSESSION, LEGAL.

landscapes (ancient Greek) The wonderful beauty and diversity of Greece was seldom fully appreciated by ancient Greeks (to whom it was commonplace). Greece has a rich flora and fauna, with many species peculiar to the country, or to one mountain or island (especially *Crete).

The land comprises six ecological zones: (1) plains, now nearly all cultivated; (2) cultivable hillsides on softer rocks; (3) uncultivable hillsides on harder rocks; (4) high mountains; (5) fens; (6) coasts and sea.

In pre-neolithic times Greece was more wooded than now; in the drier east the trees probably formed savannah, with spaces between them. Crete and other islands may have differed from the mainland, owing to their peculiar faunas (nearly all extinct by the Classical period) including dwarf elephants and hippopotamuses. During the neolithic and bronze ages the landscape was increasingly affected by human activity and by a change to a more arid *climate. The date and nature of deforestation are controversial, but there is no good evidence that Classical Greece was more wooded than today.

By Classical times the changes were largely completed. Greece looked not very different from Greece today, leaving aside urbanization, road-making, and bulldozing. An important difference is the disappearance of fens, mostly destroyed in the 19th cent. There have been changes in the coastline, famously at *Thermopylae. In land-use, the Classical Greeks had much more grain and legume cultivation than today (see CEREALS; FOOD AND DRINK), and much less *olive-growing; they kept cattle and pigs, as well as the sheep and goats which are now the remaining livestock.

Terracing extends the cultivated area onto the hills, especially by breaking up softer rocks and allowing roots to penetrate. Stone-walled terraces reached a peak in the 19th century and are now mostly disused. There was some terracing in the Classical period, but how much is still uncertain.

Ancient Greece was not, as today, a land only of cities and big villages in an otherwise uninhabited countryside. There were small towns, small villages, hamlets, and single farms, grading into field-houses lived in only seasonally. Something like this pattern of settlement (lacking the single farms) can still be seen in west Crete.

At least half the land was natural vegetation, consisting as today of *phrygana* (dwarf shrubs), *maquis* (shrubs), savannah (scattered trees), or woodland. The first three were valuable pasture-land (see PASTURAGE). Woodland of oak, pine, fir, beech (in the north), and cypress (in Crete) was mainly in the uncultivable mountains; the woods of lowland Greece today have mostly sprung up in the last 150 years. See TIMBER.

Good and bad land have not always been the same. Some rugged, water-retaining, fertile mountains, such as northern Parnon in *Laconia, have a record of dense population. Some plains, such as that of *Nemea, have had periods of use only as pasture. Undrained fens, now despised, were a precious source of summer pasture for cattle.

Ancient city-states varied hugely in territory and resources. Athens and Sparta, the two giants, had access to all six ecological zones. But even Athens was not self-sufficient in timber and not always in grain. It depended on buying imports with silver from the mines of *Laurium (smelted, presumably, with fuel from the *maquis* of uncultivable hills). Some tiny 'cities' (see POLIS) had only one or two zones, like the three states on the barren mountain-isle of *Amorgos, or the 'city' of Tarrha at the mouth of the Samaria gorge in Crete, with no apparent resources at all except cypress timber. See AGRICULTURE, GREEK; GREECE (GEOGRAPHY).

R. Osborne, *Classical Landscape with Figures* (1987); G. Shipley and J. Salmon (eds.), *Human Landscapes in Classical Antiquity* (1996). O. R.

land surveyors See GROMATICI.

land tenure See COLONUS; EMPHYTEUSIS.

languages See ANATOLIAN; ARAMAIC; CELTIC; DIALECTS, GREEK (PREHISTORY); ETRUSCAN; GERMANIC; GREEK; ILLYRIAN; ITALY, LANGUAGES OF; LATIN; LYCIAN; LYDIAN; MACEDONIAN; MESSAPIC; MYCENAEAN; OSCAN AND UMBRIAN; PERSIAN, OLD; PHRYGIAN; SEMITIC; SPAIN, PRE-ROMAN SCRIPTS AND LANGUAGES; SUMERIAN; VENETIC.

Lanuvium (mod. Lanuvio), an ancient Latin city (see LATIUM) in the Alban hills (Cato fr. 58 Peter; Strabo 5. 239); it has yielded a notable 'tomb of the warrior' of *c.*470 BC. In 338 BC, Rome granted Lanuvium Roman *citizenship, and officially adopted its famous cult of *Juno Sospes (Livy 8. 14; Cic. *Nat. D.* 1. 83). The temple (4th–3rd cent. BC, overlying an earlier one) is known. Although it suffered in the Civil Wars (App. *BCiv.* 5. 24) Lanuvium, unlike many Latian towns, continued to flourish even in imperial times (however, reject *Lib. colon.* 235). T. *Annius Milo, Q.

*Roscius Gallus, and *Antoninus Pius were born there (Cic. *Mil.* 27, *Div.* 36; SHA *Ant. Pius* 1, *Comm.* 1). Lanuvium was often confused with *Lavinium: hence its medieval name Civita Lavinia.

A. E. Gordon, *The Cults of Lanuvium* (1938); G. Chiarucci, *Lanuvium* (1983); F. Coarelli, *Archeologia e Società* 2/2 (1977), 62–70; *Arch. Laz.* 1987, 203 ff. E. T. S.; T. W. P.

Laocoön, a Trojan prince, brother of *Anchises and priest of *Apollo Thymbraeus or *Poseidon. Of his story as told by *Arctinus (*Iliu Persis*; see EPIC CYCLE), *Bacchylides, and *Sophocles (*Laocoön*), we know little. In the standard version (Verg. *Aen.* 2. 40–56, 199–231; Apollod. *Epit.* 5. 17–18), he protested against drawing the Wooden Horse (see EPEIUS (2)) within the walls of *Troy, and two great serpents coming over the sea from the island of *Tenedos killed him and his two sons (so *Euphorion (2); in Arctinus, Laocoön and one son; in Bacchylides, Sophocles, *Apollodorus (6), and *Quintus Smyrnaeus (12. 444–97), only the sons). According to Hyginus (*Fab.* 135. 1) the serpents were sent by Apollo to punish him for having married in spite of his priesthood, in *Quintus Smyrnaeus and *Virgil, by *Athena on account of his hostility to the Horse.

In art, Laocoön is the subject of the famous marble group in the Vatican showing father and sons in their death-agony. It was made by three Rhodian sculptors (see HAGESANDER, ATHENODORUS, AND POLYDORUS). The group was exhibited in the palace of *Titus, and was said by *Pliny (1) (*HN* 36. 37) to have surpassed all other works of painting and sculpture. The death of Laocoön is shown on two wall-paintings from *Pompeii, and late Imperial gems. Two south Italian vases show Laocoön as devotee of *Apollo Thymbraeus.

LIMC 6/1. 196–201. H. J. R.; K. W. A.

Laodice (1), in mythology, a stock name for women of high rank, meaning 'princess' (cf. CREON; CREUSA), e.g. (*a*) a daughter of Priam (see ACAMAS; DEMOPHON (1)), (*b*) a daughter of *Agapenor; she founded the temple of Paphian *Aphrodite (see PAPHOS) in *Tegea (Paus. 8. 53. 7, cf. 5. 3); (*c*) daughter of *Agamemnon (*Il.* 9. 145), later replaced by *Electra (3). H. J. R.

Laodice (2), probably a niece of *Antiochus (1) I, married her cousin *Antiochus (2) II, by whom she had two sons and two or three daughters. Antiochus repudiated her and her children in favour of *Berenice (2) (daughter of *Ptolemy (1) II), whose son (b. 251 BC) became heir apparent. The result, when Antiochus died, was a war of succession, in which Egypt supported Berenice's son ('Third Syrian', or 'Laodicean War', 246–241), though *Ptolemy (1) III's expedition in Syria did not prevent mother and son from being killed by Laodice's supporters. Tradition gives Laodice a share in organizing the resistance (especially in Asia Minor) which enabled her elder son to succeed as *Seleucus (2) II.

W. Otto, *Beiträge zur Seleukidengeschichte des 3. Jahrhunderts v. Chr.* (1928); H. Heinen, *CAH* 7²/1 (1984), 420 f. G. T. G.; S. S.-W.

Laodice (3), daughter of *Mithradates II of *Pontus, married *Antiochus (3) III at *Zeugma (221 BC) at a ceremonial royal wedding (Polyb. 5. 43. 1–4). The marriage was one of several examples (e.g. *Seleucus (1) I) of the *Seleucids' use of marriage alliances with non-Greek dynasties and kingdoms.

From the start of the Seleucid dynasty, the queen had won public honours and recognition from Greek cities in and outside the empire. A rare example of the powers of a Seleucid queen is given in Laodice's letter (*c*.195) to *Iasus in *Caria, after Antiochus' capture of the city, detailing her benefactions (*euergesia*; see EUERGETISM), including the grant for ten years of corn, to be used by its sale (at fixed prices; i.e. no profiteering!) to found dowries 'for the daughters of needy citizens', plus the undertaking of further aid (carefully) in accordance with the king's wishes. This inscription (Austin 156, cf. *SEG* 26. 1226) gives an indication of the queen's power, who can in her own right communicate with cities by letter, like the governors of satrapies, and either from her own resources, or perhaps local crown resources, fund subsidies at a time of crisis.

There is now a growing corpus of inscriptional evidence for civic cults for Laodice (at *Sardis, 213; *Teos, 204–3; Iasus, *c*.195), which not only gives an official picture of a great queen, but may have prefigured and perhaps paved the way for Antiochus' inclusion, by 193, of Laodice in the first Seleucid state *ruler-cult of the living king, his ancestors, and his queen.

Of Laodice's children, *Seleucus (4) IV and *Antiochus (4) IV reigned as kings, while her daughter, Cleopatra I, was married to *Ptolemy (1) V.

P. Gauthier, *Nouvelles Inscriptions de Sardes* 2: *Documents royaux du temps d'Antiochos III* (1989); S. Sherwin-White and A. Kuhrt, *From Samarkhand to Sardis* (1993).   S. S.-W.

Laodicea-Lycus, a city founded by *Antiochus (2) II (261–246 BC) and named after his wife *Laodice (2). It occupied the site of an older settlement on a flat hill overlooking the valley of the river Lycus a few miles east of its junction with the *Maeander. A decree in Greek of 267 BC (Wörrle, *Chiron* 1975, 421 f.) from two villages (Kiddioukome and Neoteichos) attests Hellenization (see HELLENISM) and an example of a 'mixed settlement', from which the later city was founded. It lay on an important trade route; it was head of a *conventus* and one of the 'Seven Churches' of the Apocalypse. *Diocletian made it *mētropolis* (b) of the province of *Phrygia.   W. M. C.; S. S.-W.

Laodicea-Nihavend, inside *Media on the fertile Nisaean plain, *c*.96 km. (60 mi.) from, and on the route to, *Ecbatana, this being the trunk-road from *Babylonia through Media to *Bactria. The site and existence of this Greek *polis* (at modern Nihavend) were revealed by the find of a Greek inscription, a copy of a famous edict of *Antiochus (3) III, dated to 193 BC, which gives the *terminus ante quem* of the foundation. The edict, documenting Antiochus' institution and organization of a state cult for *Laodice (3), throughout the empire, incidentally attests Laodicea as a *polis*, with magistrates and, not surprisingly, a *Seleucid governor.

L. Robert, *Hellenica* 7 (1949), 5–22; S. Sherwin-White and A. Kuhrt, *From Samarkhand to Sardis* (1993).   S. S.-W.

Laomedon, a legendary king of *Troy, son of *Ilus (2) and Eurydice, and father of several children, including *Priam and *Hesione (3). He was renowned for his treachery (Apollod. 2. 5. 9): he had the walls of Troy built for him by *Apollo and *Poseidon, but then refused to pay them the agreed wage. As punishment, Apollo sent a plague and Poseidon a sea-monster which could only be appeased by the sacrifice of Hesione. But *Heracles saved her and killed the sea-monster, at which once again Laomedon refused to pay an agreed reward, this time the divine horses which *Zeus had once given him in exchange for *Ganymedes. In due course Heracles returned to Troy with an army, captured the city with the help of *Telamon (1), and killed Laomedon and all his sons except *Priam, giving Hesione to Telamon

as a concubine and leaving Priam to rule Troy (Apollod. 2. 6. 4). Laomedon was buried at the Scaean gate, and it was said that Troy would be safe while his grave remained undisturbed (Serv. on *Aen*. 2. 241; cf. Plaut. *Bacch*. 955).

J. Boardman, *LIMC* 6. 1 (1992), 201–3.   J. R. M.

Laos (mod. Scalea), founded by *Sybaris in the 7th cent. BC. It offered asylum to the Sybarites after the destruction of Sybaris, but was itself conquered by the Lucanians (see LUCANIA) *c*.450. An attempt to reconquer it with Syracusan assistance (see SYRACUSE) failed. It was finally abandoned during the Hannibalic war (see PUNIC WARS); there was a later villa in the area.

P. Guzzo and E. Greco, *Not. Scav.* 1978.   K. L.

Lapiths See CENTAURS; PIRITHOUS.

Lappius (*RE* 'Appius' 13; Suppl. 1) **Maximus, Aulus Bucius** (name: *AE* 1961, 319), *suffect *consul AD 86, and again in 95 (a rare honour). He was legate (see LEGATI) of Legio VIII Augusta (see LEGION), proconsul (see PRO CONSULE) of *Bithynia (*c*.82). As legate of Lower Germany (see GERMANIA) he crushed the rebellion of L. *Antonius Saturninus in 89, a 'German war' because *Chatti were involved (*ILS* 1006 = MW 60; in *Epit. de Caes.* 11. 10 he is conflated with the *procurator Norbanus). He was governor of *Syria in 91 and obtained a pontificate (see PONTIFEX) with his second consulship, surviving until at least 102. His (later?) claim to have destroyed the conspirators' papers before *Domitian arrived won him credit.

W. Eck, *Die Statthalter der germanischen Provinzen vom 1.–3. Jahrh.* (1985), 149 ff.; B. Jones, *The Emperor Domitian* (1992), see index.
          G. E. F. C.; B. M. L.

Larcius Licinus, first orator to seek fame in the centumviral court (see CENTUMVIRI), wrote *Ciceromastix* attacking *Cicero's style. As *iuridicus* of Hispania *Tarraconensis (AD 73/4), he unsuccessfully offered the elder *Pliny (1), then *procurator, 400,000 sesterces for his notebooks: he died in office.

PIR[2] L 95; Syme, *RP* 2. 755–6.   L. A. H.-S.

Larentalia, Roman festival on 23 December of funeral rites (*Parentalia*: *fasti Praenestini*) at the supposed *Velabrum tomb of the goddess *Acca Larentia (Varro, *Ling*. 6. 23–4; Macrob. *Sat.* 1. 10. 11 ff.), celebrated by the pontifices (Cic. *Brut*. 1. 15. 8). Acca, connected with Greek and Sanskrit roots for 'mother', may be the *Lares' mother (Ogilvie on Livy 1. 4. 7).

Kl. Pauly 1. 23 ff.; Latte, *RR* 92 ff.   C. R. P.

Lares (older *Lases*, Arval hymn: *ILLRP* 4). There are two principal theories of origins; it is impossible to prefer one.

1. E. Samter, *Familienfeste der Griechen und Römer* (1901), considers them ghosts. He starts from the *Lar familiaris*, connecting him with the cult of the dead on two grounds: (*a*) if a bit of food falls on the floor during a meal, it is proper to burn it before the Lares (Plin. *HN* 28. 27). Since ghosts notoriously haunt the floor, the food, therefore, has gone to the ghosts' region and is formally given to them. (*b*) At the Compitalia it was customary to hang up a male or female puppet for each free member of a household, a ball for each slave (Festus 272 Lindsay; cf. 108, 273), that the Lares might spare the living and take these surrogates. This seems a precaution against ghosts and accords with the crossroads as favourite places for ghosts; cf. Frazer on Ov. *Fast*. 2. 615 at pp. 459 ff. This theory had languished until M. Guarducci published the Tor Tignosa dedicatory inscription *Lare Aineia D(onom)*, *Bull. Com. Arch.* 1956–8, 3 ff. and S. Weinstock, *JRS* 1960, 114 ff.;

this supports the Lar as a deified ancestor (cf. C. Phillips, *Hermes* 1976, 247 ff.). Although H.-G. Kolbe, *MDAI(R)* 1970, 1 ff., and others have questioned the reading *Aineia*, the inscription's site (crossroads, cave with sulphur spring) supports the ancestor/ghost theory; cf. T. J. Cornell, *LCM* 1977, 77 ff.

2. Wissowa (*RK* 166 ff.) asserts that the Roman dead are honoured not in the house but at their graves; the hearth is the place of *Vesta and the *di *Penates* and the Lar (*familiaris*) was a later intruder. He reconciles this with the ceremonial at the crossroads by observing that a *compitum* is properly and originally the place where the paths separating four farms meet (schol. Pers. 4. 28; the oft-cited *Gromatici*, 302. 20 ff. (= F. Blume, *Die Schriften der römischer Feldmesser* (1848); see GROMATICI) do not mention *compitum*, but cf. L. Holland, *TAPA* 1937, 428 ff.) This has no ghostly associations, but regularly had a chapel of the Lares; Latte, *RR* 90 ff., would substitute *purification for *sacrifice. Thus the *Lar familiaris* (in origin, Lar of the servants, rather than of the household generally) would have come to the house via farm-slaves.

The Lares, whatever their origins, expand (apart from purely theoretical developments of their name to signify ghost or **daimōn*) into (*a*) guardians of any crossway, including one in a city: hence arose in Rome the *collegia compitalicia*, associations (see COLLEGIUM) of mostly *freedmen, who tended the shrines, and ran the festival; *Augustus restored those colleges which had been banned in the late republic, adding his own *genius*; into (*b*) guardians of roads and wayfarers, *Lares viales*, including travellers by sea, *Lares permarini*; into (*c*) guardians of the state in general, *Lares praestites* (see especially Wissowa, *Ges. Abh.* 277 ff.; Ov. *Fast.* 5. 129 ff. with Bömer's note); into (*d*) a variety of sometimes obscure associations (listing in Roscher, *Lex.* 2. 1885 ff.).

Some later stories feature the Lares. Ovid (*Fast.* 2. 599 ff.) reports their begetting by *Mercurius on Lara—possibly his own invention, but cf. E. Tabeling, *Mater Larum* (1932), 40 ff., 69 ff. In one version of the birth of King Servius *Tullius, from a *phallus arising from ashes and impregnating the servant Ocrisia with a flame, later appearing around his head marking him for the kingship, his father is the *Lar familiaris* (Plin. *HN* 36. 204); cf. Dion. Hal. *Ant. Rom.* 4. 2; Ov. *Fast.* 6. 631 ff.; Ogilvie on Livy 1. 39. 1, 5. Since the cult of the *Lar familiaris* ultimately became universal (D. Orr, *ANRW* 2. 16. 2 (1978), 1575 ff.), *lar* or *lares* is used like *penates*, by metonymy, for 'home'.   C. R. P.

Larinum (mod. Larino), a city on the northern border of Daunia (see DAUNIANS). There was a substantial pre-Roman settlement. Larinum became a Roman ally (see SOCII), then a *municipium* in 89 BC. It was a centre of the wool trade, and its municipal politics are unusually well known (Cic. *Clu.*).

A. Di Niro, *Sannio: Pentri e Frentani dal VI al I secolo a.C.* (1981); E. de Felice, *Larinum*, Forma Italiae 36 (1994).   K. L.

Larissa, chief city of *Thessaly, in the north-east of the east plain, on the right bank of the river Peneus. Founded by *Acrisius, father of Danaë and grandfather of *Perseus (1), it took its name from the nymph Larissa, depicted on civic coins of the 4th cent. BC, mother of Pelasgus, Achaeus, and Phthius, eponymous heroes of the local population.

Its history, little-known for the earliest period, is linked with the *Aleuadae, who ruled the city from the beginning of the 6th to the end of the 4th cent. BC. Developing rapidly, Larissa dominated the cities of *Pelasgiotis, becoming the leading power of Thessaly. Around 400 domestic strife between oligarchic factions weakened it to the profit of *Pherae, which captured the city on two occasions. At Aleuad instigation, *Philip (1) II of Macedon took it in 352 and made it his principal bastion in Thessaly. Macedonian domination ended in 197 BC. Larissa, with Thessaly, came under Roman control, became capital of the Thessalian federation, and continued to develop at the expense of neighbours. Few traces of the ancient city, underneath the modern town, survive.

F. Stählin, *Das hellenische Thessalien* (1924), 94 ff.; B. Helly, *L'état Thessalien* (1995).   B. H.

Larunda, obscure Roman goddess, perhaps Sabine (Varro, *Ling.* 5. 74) and *chthonian (Wissowa, *RK* 234). She was honoured on 23 December on the *Velabrum. The long quantity of the first syllable (Auson. *Technop.* 8. 9 Peiper = p. 179 Green) suggests a connection with *Acca Larentia and not Lar (short *a*), but cf. Ogilvie on Livy 1. 4. 7. Some equated her with Lara, mother of the *Lares (Ov. *Fast.* 2. 599 ff. with Bömer's notes; E. Tabeling, *Mater Larum* (1932)), others (Varro, *Sat. Men.* 463 Buechler, *Ling.* 9. 61) with *Maniae*, (woollen puppets), implying the *Lares compitales* (see LARES). Certainty seems impossible. See LARENTALIA.

Kl. Pauly 3. 502 ff., 956 ff.; Latte, *RR* 92.   C. R. P.

Lasus (Λᾶσος), 6th cent. BC, son of Charminus, of Hermione, lived at the court of *Hipparchus (1), where he disclosed the forgeries of Onomacritus (Hdt. 7. 6. 3; see FORGERIES, LITERARY, GREEK). Rival of *Simonides (schol. Ar. *Vesp.* 1410), he composed *hymns (Ath. 624e) and *dithyrambs excluding the letter 's' (Ath. 455c). He introduced the dithyrambic competitions in Athens (*c*.508), and wrote the first book about *music (*Suda*; schol. Pind. *Ol.* 13. 25; schol. Ar. *Av.* 1403; Clem. Al. *Strom.* 1. 16).

Ed. Page, *PMG* 702–6. C. A. Privitera, *Laso di Ermione nella cultura ateniese e nella tradizione storiografica* (1965).   C. M. B.; E. Kr.

latifundia (large estates) 'have ruined Italy and are now ruining the provinces'. *Pliny (1) the Elder (*HN* 18. 35) put *latifundia* at the centre of debate about the development of the Roman rural economy. But what were *latifundia*? Divergent modern definitions abound and confuse: large pastoral ranches beginning in the 3rd cent. BC; slave-staffed oil- and wine-producing villas (either single properties or the scattered estates of one owner) first described by M. *Porcius Cato (1) *c*.160 BC (see VILLA; SLAVERY); any property above 500 *iugera* (125 ha.: 309 acres) of whatever period: all of which 'ruined' Italy by forcing *peasants from the land. Others dismiss Pliny's remark as generalized nostalgia and refer to archaeological surveys that not only emphasize the diversity of rural settlement but also show that villas and peasant farms often existed side by side. Yet if Pliny is allowed credence, the term *latifundia* applies strictly to extensive unitary estates, resulting in an aggregation of properties, too large to farm according to the labour-intensive methods of cultivation of the slave-staffed villas recommended by the *agricultural writers (*HN* 18. 35; cf. Columella *Rust.* 1. 3. 12). *Latifundia* are thus to be defined not so much by crop or measurement as by management principles. Pliny refers to the reaping-machine and long-handled scythe typical of Gallic *latifundia* (*HN* 18. 261, 296), which saved time and labour but wasted grain and hay. On such large estates tenants were probably increasingly employed alongside or in preference to poorly supervised (and thus uneconomical) slaves (cf. Columella *Rust.* 1. 7. 6). In this interpretation *latifundia* 'ruined' an agriculture previously dominated by the slave-staffed villa. Some such process (modern explanations of it differ) occurred in the 1st cent. AD both in the *ager Cosanus* in Etruria (see COSA), where field-survey and excavation indicate that medium-sized villas gave way to larger estates, and in the *ager Falernus* (see FALERNUS AGER) in *Campania, another heartland of the slave-staffed villa. Analysis of all literary references now suggests that *latifundia* developed in Italy in the Julio-Claudian period. But how widespread did they become? It might be relevant that only a generation later *Pliny (2) the Younger readily contemplated just such an aggregation of two large estates on the upper *Tiber (*Ep.* 3. 19), and that an agglomeration of properties is noticeable in the contemporary alimentary tables (see ALIMENTA) from Veleia in Cisalpine Gaul (see GAUL (CISALPINE)) and Ligures Baebiani in Samnium (see SAMNITES). As for the provinces specifically associated with *latifundia*, fieldwork in *Sicily suggests a similar trend of amalgamation in the late 1st and early 2nd cents. AD; evidence from northern Tunisia (see AFRICA, ROMAN) points to the formation of large estates consisting of a central villa and scattered, probably tenant, farms; while sculptural reliefs of the Gallic reaping-machine have been found at Reims and near Trier (*Augusta Treverorum). See AGRICULTURE, ROMAN; DOMAINS.

Frank, *Econ. Survey*; K. D. White, *BICS* 1967, 62–79, and with A. J. L. van Hoof, *Hist.* 1982, 126–8; J. K. Evans, *AJAH* 1980, 19–47; R. P. Duncan-Jones, *The Economy of the Roman Empire*, 2nd edn. (1982); P. W. de Neeve, *Colonus* (1984); V. I. Kuziscin, *La grande proprietà agraria nell'Italia romana* (1984); K. Greene, *The Archaeology of the Roman Economy* (1986); R. J. A. Wilson, *Sicily Under the Roman Empire* (1990); G. Barker and J. Lloyd (eds.), *Roman Landscapes* (1991).   M. S. Sp.

Latin, medieval, literary In the nine centuries following the fall of the western Roman empire, the *Latin language underwent major changes as it was absorbed by newly-settled immigrant races. Syntax and vocabulary of written Latin differs radically from classical usage, while the gap between the written and spoken language widens gradually to produce vernaculars at varying distances from the parent tongue. Throughout the period, however, in western Europe, Latin remains the main vehicle of written communication.

The contours of literary development during these centuries remain unclear. Some regions and periods are almost barren of evidence, against which the great richness of other milieux (the Carolingian period, or 12th-cent. France, for example) stands out with possibly specious clarity. Uncertainties abound particularly with secular literature, for which the means of preservation were often insecure.

Monasteries, as centres of *education and *literacy, play a key role in the transmission of classical texts, but also in the production and diffusion of both secular and explicitly Christian writing. See CASSIODORUS; CHRISTIANITY. Some genres span the entire period. Hagiography is one ubiquitous example, extant in large quantities from most areas in Europe. In prose or verse, and often associated with a particular cult centre, saints' lives could serve as didactic works, as institutional history, as entertainment, or more often as an encouragement to pilgrimage by recording miracles occurring at a shrine. Other forms centred more explicitly on the Bible—works of exegesis, doctrine, or polemic, and pastoral epistles.

The liturgy too stimulated creativity, resulting in a great diversity of usage across Europe. Standard components of the Mass or the Office were expanded by the addition of new material, the process known as 'troping'. Homilies, prayers, and hymnody are produced and circulated, often anonymously, both for public use and private meditation. New forms also emerge. In the 9th cent. there develops the sequence, a lyrical, often complex elaboration of scriptural themes sung during the Mass, while the practice of

responsorial chanting generates the earliest forms of liturgical drama towards the end of the century.

Historiography takes many forms. In a number of monasteries, annals were kept, recording events of local and national significance, sometimes extending over many decades. More ambitious and coherent projects of national historiography appear early in the period, two prominent examples being the *History of the Franks* by Gregory of Tours, and the *Ecclesiastical History of the English People* by the Anglo-Saxon monk Bede (*c.*729). Secular biography re-emerges later and more sporadically, but works on the Carolingian emperors illustrate the potential diversity of the form, involving political and military narrative, panegyric, and supernatural anecdotage.

Epic in the style of *Virgil and *Statius is sometimes attempted, but the genre also undergoes development in the direction of panegyric, or of narrative romance. More vulnerable and ephemeral was secular lyric. The intended milieux for such collections as the *Cambridge Songs*, Ripoll and Arundel lyrics, and *Carmina Burana* are not always known, but the verse they contain is striking, with pervasive Ovidian influence (see OVID). The 13th-cent. Beuron MS, for example, contains both metrical and rhythmic poetry organized in categories—moral and satirical, erotic and convivial lyric, with admixtures of classical excerpts and vernacular poems.

M. Manitius, *Geschichte der lateinischen Literatur des Mittelalters* (1911–31); F. Brunholzl, *Geschichte der lateinischen Literatur des Mittelalters* 1 (1975); E. R. Curtius, *European Literature and the Latin Middle Ages*, trans. W. Trask (1953); K. Strecker, *Introduction to Medieval Latin*, trans. R. B. Palmer (1957); D. Norberg, *Introduction à l'étude de la versification latine médiévale* (1958); *La Poésie latine rhythmique du moyen age* (1954); B. Bischoff, *Mittelalterliche Studien: Ausgewählte Aufsätze zur Schriftkunde und Literaturgeschichte* (1966–81).   M. J. B.

Latin language

1. Introduction Latin belongs to the Italic group of *Indo-European (IE) languages, which includes Faliscan (see FALISCANS), Umbrian, and Oscan (see OSCAN AND UMBRIAN). It was originally spoken in Latium from 800 BC or earlier and with the spread of Roman power became the common language first of Italy, then of the western Mediterranean and Balkan regions of the Roman empire. The language of the illiterate majority of Latin-speakers, Vulgar Latin (VL), evolved through its regional dialects into the Romance languages. It is known from casual remarks by ancient grammarians, comparative Romance reconstruction, and deviations from classical norms in manuscript and epigraphic texts.

Refined versions of the language were developed early on for specific socio-cultural purposes—legal and ritual texts, public oratory, senatorial and pontifical records, and Saturnian verse. The earliest of these survive in corrupt and fragmentary forms, e.g. the *Twelve Tables and the *Carmen arvale ('Hymn of the Arval Brethren'). Later examples are the senate's decree (*ILLRP* 519) on the cult of Bacchus (186 BC; see BACCHANALIA) and the Scipio Epitaphs (*c.*250–150 BC; *ILLRP* 309–17. See CORNELIUS SCIPIO, various entries). The combination of these native written genres and the influence of Greek models from *c.*240 BC onwards led eventually to the written form of the Roman dialect, *sermo urbanus* 'urban(e) speech', that we know as Classical Latin (CL). In contrast to the dialects of Greek the non-Roman dialects played no part in Latin literary culture or, from the classical period onwards, in local administration.

CL is defined by the characteristics common to literary authors in the period *c.*90 BC–*c.* AD 120. It is a highly artificial construct which must be regarded linguistically as a deviation from the mainstream of the language, namely VL. Nevertheless for centuries a spectrum of usage linked the highest literary compositions through the informal idiom of the letters and conversation of their authors and the plain registers of legal, administrative, and technical writings to the Latin of the masses. The spectrum was ruptured long before the 9th century. The Strasburg Oaths (AD 842), which are in an early form of French, are reported in a contemporary chronicle composed by Nithard in medieval Latin. The regional variants of VL, difficult to infer from the written texts of any period, had now become the Romance languages. The literary tradition, modelled on CL but infiltrated by vulgar elements, was now medieval Latin. Most oral renderings of medieval Latin would have been almost as incomprehensible to *Cicero as the Romance languages.

A spectrum of Latinity did survive however in the various registers of ecclesiastical Latin, which has no linguistic unity apart from its common Christian lexicon—*ecclēsia* 'church', *baptizāre* 'baptize', *presbyter* 'priest', *resurrexiō* 'resurrection', *saluātor* 'saviour', *iūstificāre* 'justify', etc. At one end is the vulgarized idiom of the Scriptures, then the plain technical Latin of the Church bureaucracy and doctrinal pronouncements, finally the language of the early hymns and above all the collects and prayers of the Liturgy.

Sections 2–5 indicate some of the more distinctive characteristics of Latin.

2. Phonology Vowel length was functional in CL, both in the lexicon, e.g. *pŏpulus* 'people', *pōpulus* 'poplar', *lĕuis* 'light', *lēuis* 'smooth', *incĭdere* 'to fall on', *incīdere* 'to incise', and in the grammar, e.g. *rosă* (nom. sing.) 'rose', *rosā* (abl. sing.), *manŭs* 'hand' (nom. sing.), *manūs* (nom. pl.). The rounded front vowel [y], written as *y*, was used to render Greek upsilon, e.g. *tyrannus* 'tyrant'. The relative frequency and distribution of short vowels were affected by raising ('vowel weakening') in non-initial syllables between *c.*450 and *c.*250 BC, e.g. †*obfaciom* > *officium* 'duty', †*abagetes* > *abigitis* 'you drive off', †*exfactos* > *effectus* 'done'. Syncope, the end-point of raising, occurs at all periods, e.g. †*tretetolet* > *rettulit* 'brought back', †*opifacīna* > *officīna* 'workshop', *ualidē* > *ualdē* 'very much', later *dominus* > *domnus* 'master'.

Most of the inherited diphthongs survived into early Latin but were reduced to long vowels by 150 BC, e.g. *indoucere* 'to bring in', *oinos* 'one', *deicere* 'to say' > *indūcere*, *ūnus*, *dīcere*. Only two remain frequent, *ae* and *au*. The former (< *ai*) is replaced by *e* in some dialects before 150 BC and the new pronunciation was general by AD 400, though the digraph continued to be written inconsistently. Most dialects of VL seem to have retained *au*, but some Italian dialects already had *o*, as in Sabine *plostru* for *plaustrum* 'cart'.

The glides [w] and [j] were never graphically distinct from [u] and [i], of which they are often regarded merely as positional variants. Even their consonantal reflexes, [v] and [dʒ] etc., continued to be written as *u* and *i* until the Renaissance. The first secure evidence for a phonetic shift is *baliat*, *iuuente* for *ualeat* 'farewell', *iubente* 'ordering' in early imperial VL and *Gianuaria* for *Ianuaria* in the 6th cent.

Of the inherited stops *p*, *d*, *k*, etc., *qu*, a velar *k* with lip-rounding inherited from Proto-Indo-European (PIE), survives uniquely in Latin. Its original voiced equivalent *gu* may already have been a cluster [gw]. Scattered evidence for palatalization occurs already in the 2nd and 3rd cents. AD, e.g. *oze*, *terciae*, *Vincentzus* for *hodie* 'today', *tertiae* 'third', *Vincentius*. These changes were accepted

by some 5th-cent. grammarians. By this time spellings like *intcitamento*, *dissessit* for *incitāmentō* 'at the instigation', *discessit* 'he left' were appearing in VL.

Aspirated stops, written as *ph*, *th*, *ch* from *c.*150 BC, were introduced for Greek loanwords like *theātrum*, *māchina*.

Of the two nasals *n* had a positional variant [ŋ] before velars, as in *uncus* 'hook', *tangō* 'I touch'. The sequence *Vns* tended to be replaced by *V̄s*, as in *agrōs* (< †*agrons*) 'fields', *cōsul* (< †*consul*), and this became universal in VL, with *mēsa* for *mensa* 'table', *pēsare* for *pensare* 'to weigh'. A weak articulation of *-m*, reflected in metre, is attested in early *uiro*, *omne*, (CL *uirum* 'man', *omnem* 'all'), and in its total disappearance in VL.

The unvoiced sibilant *s* was rhotacized intervocalically before *c.*350 BC, e.g. *āsa*, *Numisios* > *āra* 'altar', *Numerius*. Loss of *-s* in sequences like *omnibu(s) prīnceps* is attested in some dialects and in Ennian epic, but was repaired analogically before the classical period, and *-s* survived in most areas of early Romance. The letter *z*, representing [z:] was imported to render Greek zeta; e.g. *Zephyrus* 'West Wind'. The precarious status of [h] is shown by variants like *nīl*, *mī*, *comprendere* for *nihil*, *mihi*, *comprēhendere* and the grammarians' debates about *(h)erus*, *(h)arēna*, etc.

There were severe restrictions on consonant clusters. Many had been reduced in early Latin, e.g. *iouxmenta*, †*trānsdō* > *iūmenta* 'beasts of burden', *trādō* 'I hand over'. Those that survived were often restricted positionally; thus *gn* occurs medially, e.g. *cognōscō*, but no longer initially, e.g. *nōscō* < *gnōscō*, and never finally; *sp*, *st*, *sk* initially and medially, but in final position only *-st*, as in *est*, *post*; *ps* and *ks* occur initially only in Greek loans, but are often found in medial and final position, e.g. *dīxī*, *ops*; *nt* medially and finally, never initially.

Latin like English and Modern Greek had a stress accent. It originally fell on the initial syllable but before 250 BC had shifted, falling on the penultimate syllable, if heavy, otherwise on the antepenultimate, e.g. *legĕtis* 'you will read', *legéntēs* 'reading', but *légitis* 'you read', *mīlitēs* 'soldiers'. The connection between quantity and stress is seen in early 'iambic' shortening, e.g. *bĕnĕ* (< †*bénē*) 'well', *égŏ* (< †*égō*) 'I', in syncope (see above), and in the tendency in later Latin for vowel length to correlate with stress, e.g. *quándŏ* 'when', *légitis*, *bĕne*.

3. Lexicon A high proportion of the basic lexical stock has widespread IE cognates; e.g. *auris* 'ear', *canis* 'dog', *dare* 'to give', *edere* 'to eat', *nouus* 'new', *plēnus* 'full', *quīnque* 'five', *trēs* 'three', *uīuere* 'to live'. Some have assured cognates only in Greek, e.g. *cinis* 'ash'; others only in West IE, e.g. *annus* 'year', *flōs* 'flower', *manus* 'hand', in Celtic, e.g. *loquor* 'I speak', or in Germanic, e.g. *aqua* 'water'. Finally some have no known cognates, e.g. *arbor* 'tree', *mulier* 'woman', *niger* 'black', *caedere* 'to cut'.

The native resources were extended by composition. Complexes, formed by affixation to lexical roots, are frequent. Thus *pater* 'father', *patrius* 'ancestral'; *legere* 'to choose', *leg-iō* 'legion'; *lec-tor* 'reader', *lec-tiō* 'a reading'; *fingere* 'to fashion', *fig-mentum* 'image', *fig-ūra* 'shape'; *probus* 'honest', *prob-itās* 'honesty'; *fortis* 'brave', *forti-tūdō* 'bravery'. Some of these formants are distinctively Latin. Denominative verbs were assigned to the first conjugation in all periods, e.g. *dōnāre* 'to give' from *dōnum* 'gift', *pācāre* 'to pacify' from *pāx* 'peace'. Compounds, made up of more than one lexical root, were not as frequent as in Greek but were productive in every period, e.g. *agri-cola* 'field-dweller' > 'farmer', *arti-fex* 'maker of craftwork'. Compound-complex forms like *bene-fic-ium* 'benefit', *ad-uen-tus* 'arrival' carry the process even further.

Latin had many loanwords. From Oscan or Sabine (see SABINI) came *bōs* 'cow', *multa* 'fine', *nāsus* 'nose'; from *Etruscan *ātrium* 'hall', *fenestra* 'window', *satelles* 'attendant', perhaps even *populus* 'the people'. Greek was a very prolific source, e.g. *āēr* 'air', *balineum* 'bath', *bracchium* 'arm', *cista* 'chest', *gubernāre* 'to direct', *massa* 'lump', *nauta* 'sailor', *poena* 'punishment'. In the learned vocabulary, beside loans such as *grammaticus* 'philologist', *historia* 'history', *mūsica* 'music', *philosophus* 'philosopher', many calques were modelled on Greek, e.g. *essentia* 'essence', *quālitās* 'quality', as were loan translations like *cāsus* 'grammatical case', *ratiō* 'logical argument'.

VL even replaced basic lexemes by Greek loans, e.g. *colpus* (< *kólaphos*) for *ictus* 'blow', *gamba* (< *kampḗ*) for *crūs* 'leg', *parabolāre* (< *parabolḗ*) for *loquī* 'to speak'. Lexical mortality is illustrated by the replacement of *canō* 'I sing', †*speciō* 'I look at', *pleō* 'I fill', †*fendō* 'I ward off' by *cantō*, *spectō* (and *conspiciō*), *impleō*, *dēfendō*. Again VL has many examples: *bellus* (and *formōsus*) for *pulcher* 'beautiful', *bucca* for *ōs* 'mouth', *caballus* for *equus* 'horse', *iectāre* for *iacere* 'to throw', *portāre* for *ferre* 'to carry', etc.

4. Morphology Nouns were organized into six paradigms, e.g. (1) *mensa* 'table', (2) *seruus* 'slave', (3a) *urbs* 'city', (3b) *turris* 'tower', (4) *manus* 'hand', (5) *diēs* 'day'. All were inherited types except (5), which was formed in Italic. The *i*- stems (3b), which in PIE had been closely parallel to *u*- stems (4), gradually merged in Latin with the consonant stems (3a). Paradigms (4) and (5) had few members. In VL these were either transferred to (2) and (1), as *manus*, *-ūs* to *manus*, *-ī*, and *diēs* to *dia*, or were replaced by other lexemes, as *rēs* 'thing' by *causa* 'cause'.

The three inherited genders are systematically identifiable only in adjectives. Thus *nauta ualidus* (masc.) 'a sturdy sailor', *humus ūda* (fem.) 'moist ground', *animal formōsum* (neut.) 'a well-formed animal'. Of the three PIE numbers the dual was lost already in Italic, traces surviving only in forms like *duo* and perhaps *duae*.

Seven of the eight PIE cases survived, ablative and instrumental having already merged in Italic. Nominative and vocative remained distinct only in the singular of (2), *Marcus* (nom.) *Marce* (voc.). The locative has no distinct morphology at all; thus *Rōmae* (1) 'at Rome' is identical with genitive and dative, and the locative plural is identical with the dative-ablative in all paradigms. Of the eleven possible case forms (nom. voc. acc. gen. dat. loc. abl. sing.; nom.-voc. acc. gen. dat.-loc.-abl. pl.) paradigm (2) has the most, with eight, paradigm (5) has the least, with six. In VL the cases eventually collapsed to two, a nominative and an oblique.

The gen. sing. *-ī* in (2) *serui* 'of the slave' has a unique correspondent in Old Irish *maqi* 'of the son', while the nom.-voc. pl. of (1) *mensae* 'tables' and (2) *serui* 'slaves', in which the Italic forms in *-ās* and *-ōs* have been replaced by the pronominal endings, are uniquely paralleled in Greek. The pronouns, as in other IE languages, share only a few of their case-forms with nouns. The anaphoric and deictic pronouns *is* and *ille* supply third-person pronouns beside *ego* 'I' and *tū* 'thou'.

Adjectives all belong to paradigms (1), (2), or (3). In the comparison of adjectives the formants *-ior-*, *-is-*, and *-mo-* are inherited, but the composite formant in e.g. *alt-is-simus* 'highest' seems unique to Latin.

Verbs were organized into five paradigms; e.g. (1) *stāre* 'to stand', (2) *monēre* 'to warn', (3a) *dīcō*, *dīcere* 'to say', (3b) *capiō*, *capere* 'to take', (4) *audīre* 'to hear'. Inherited athematic verbs such as Gk. *hístēmi* were reshaped and assigned to conjugations (1) and (2). Thematic verbs like Gk. *légō* are reflected in (3).

All the PIE grammatical categories—person, number, tense, mood, and voice—were retained. Number was determined solely by concord with the subject.

The tense system, as in Greek, distinguishes imperfective and perfective aspect, e.g. *scrībēbam* 'I was writing', *scrīpsī* 'I wrote', also used as a perfect 'I have written'; cf. Gk. *égrapsa* 'I wrote', but *gégrapha* 'I have written'. PIE aorist and perfect formants both appear in the Latin perfect, e.g. *dīxī* 'I (have) said' and *tutudī* 'I (have) struck'. Notable innovations are the *-b-* forms in the future (also in Faliscan) and imperfect (also in Oscan), e.g. *stābō* 'I shall stand', *stābam* 'I was standing', which were periphrastic in origin (< †*stāsi bhwō* 'I am to be in the act of standing'); also the *-w-* perfects, which are used mostly in paradigms (1), (2), and (4); and the creation of new relative-time tenses, past-in-the-future *audīuerō* 'I shall have heard', past-in-the-past *audīueram* 'I had heard'. Important for Romance are the reintroduction of the perfect/past definite distinction by the use of *scrīptum habeō* as a perfect 'I have written', which was already emerging in CL, and the use of *scrībere habeō* in rivalry with *scrībam* 'I shall write', not attested before the late 2nd cent. AD.

The optative and subjunctive moods had already merged in Italic and the Latin subjunctive has traces of both formations: optative in *sim* 'I would be', *dīxerim* 'I would say'; subjunctive in *dīcās* 'you would say', and perhaps *stēs* 'you would stand'. The creation of imperfect and pluperfect subjunctives, *dīcerem*, *dīxissem*, is an innovation. The medio-passive formant *-r*, also found in Old Irish and Hittite (see ANATOLIAN LANGUAGES), was already established in Italic. The perfect passive tenses were analytic: *laudāta est* 'she has been praised' beside *laudātur* 'she is being praised'. The middle sense is seen in e.g. *uertor* 'I turn myself' and *indūtus* 'having put on'. It also accounts for 'deponents' like *sequor* 'I follow', *ūtor* 'I use'.

The infinitives reflect PIE verbal nouns. They had however become absorbed into the verb system both in syntax, e.g. *pācem petere* 'to seek peace' beside *pācis petitiō*, and by their marking for tense and voice, e.g. *dīcere* 'to say', pass. *dīcī*, perf. *dīxisse*, etc. The supines in *-tum* and *-tū* are cognate with Sanskrit declined infinitives. The gerund, as in *audiendō* 'by hearing' etc., seems ultimately to be derived from the gerundive *audiendus* 'which is to be heard', a verbal adjective unknown outside Italic. The imperfective participle in *-nt-*, as in *monens* 'warning', and the perfect passive in *-tus*, as in *monitus* 'warned', are both inherited; the future in *-tūrus*, as in *monitūrus*, is peculiar to Latin.

5. Syntax Among distinctively Latin case uses is the extension of the allatival dative of inanimate nouns, e.g. *ūsuī est* 'it is useful', *quindecimuirī sacrīs faciundīs* 'the fifteen commissioners for religious practices'; also the comitative use of the ablative to assign a quality adnominally, e.g. *dux aequō animō* 'a leader with a calm mind'; and to indicate attendant circumstances adverbially, e.g. *dīs fauentibus* 'with the blessing of the gods', *crīnibus dēmissīs* 'with their hair let down', whence the 'absolute' construction, which in Latin acquired, as the Greek genitive absolute also did, fully clausal functions.

As in other IE languages, prepositions had been developed to give precision to 'local' case functions. Thus in the accusative the allatival *ad urbem* 'to the city' and perlatival *per tōtam noctem* 'all through the night' are distinguished from *urbem condidit* 'he founded the city', *proelium pugnābant* 'they were fighting a battle'. In the ablative the instrumental *gladiō pugnābat* 'he fought with a sword' was similarly distinguished from the locatival *in urbe* 'in the city' and the ablatival *ex urbe* 'from the city' and *ab eō condita*

Latin literature

est 'it was founded by him'. Abstract extensions, as in the last example, are widespread; cf. *propter* 'because of' (< 'close to') and *de* 'concerning' (< 'down from') etc. In contrast to Greek most Latin prepositions were confined to one case, thus reducing the semantic importance of the case. Hence VL *cum discentēs suōs* 'with his pupils', with accusative for ablative. In VL these prepositional phrases encroached on simple case uses; as in *dē sagittā percutere* 'to hit with an arrow', for the simple ablative, *uenditiō dē campō* 'sale of the field' for gen. *campī*, and *ad illam dīxit* 'he said to her' for dat. *illī*. All this contributed substantially to the massive case syncretism in late VL (see § 4 above).

Latin shares exclusively with Greek the development of the accusative + infinitive construction to render indirect speech. There were not enough infinitives or subjunctives to represent the distinctions required in principal and subordinate clauses respectively, and the whole inefficient construction gave way to clauses with *quod, quia* (perhaps modelled on Gk. *hōs, hóti* 'that'), to a larger extent in the later written language and totally in VL. The subjunctive as the mood of unreality was used in both members of unreal conditional sentences, e.g. *sī hoc dīcās, errēs* 'If you were to say this, you would be wrong'. But it tended in time also to become the mood of subordination generally (hence the name), as in *cum hoc dīxisset, exiit* 'when he had said this, he left', *sciō quid crēdās* 'I know what you think', *adeō clāmābat ut exīrent* 'he shouted so much that they left'.

Latin shares, again exclusively, with Greek the development of complex sentence structure, most notably the periodic form, which was a major legacy to later European languages. Attention to rhythm, especially at clause-ends, and pragmatic considerations of emphasis, anaphora, etc. led to departures from the normal word order, subject–object–verb (SOV), which was inherited from PIE. In VL, where SVO seems to have become established at an early date, the subsequent collapse of the case system precluded variations of the classical kind.

> J. N. Adams, *The Vulgar Latin of the Letters of Claudius Terentianus* (1977); W. S. Allen, *Vox Latina: A Guide to the Pronunciation of Classical Latin* (1978); R. Coleman, *Transactions of the Philosophical Society 1975*, 101–56; *PCPS* 1990, 1–25; J. Collart, *Histoire de la langue latine* (1967); J. Herman, *Le Latin vulgaire* (1967); M. Leumann, J. B. Hofmann, and A. Szantyr, *Lateinische Grammatik*, 3 vols. (1965–79); D. Norberg, *Manuel pratique de latin médiéval* (1968); L. R. Palmer, *The Latin Language* (1954); F. Stolz and W. Schmid, *Geschichte der lateinischen Sprache* (1966); V. Väänänen, *Introduction au latin vulgaire* (1981). R. G. C.

Latin literature The standard reference works are in German: (1) M. Schanz, C. Hosius, and G. Krüger, *Geschichte der römischen Literatur* (in I. von Müller's *Handbuch der Altertumswissenschaft*): 4th edn., 1: *Die römische Literatur in der Zeit der Republik* (1927), 2: *Die römische Literatur in der Zeit der Monarchie bis auf Hadrian* (1935); 3rd edn., 3: *Die Zeit von Hadrian 117 bis auf Constantin 324* (1922); 2nd edn., 4/1: *Die römische Literatur von Constantin bis zur Gesetzsgebungswerk Justinians*, erste Hälfte: *Die Literatur des vierten Jahrhunderts* (1914), 4/2: ibid., zweite Hälfte: *Die Literatur des fünften und sechsten Jahrhunderts* (1920). This is being replaced under the direction of R. Hertzog and P. L. Schmidt: the first volume to appear is vol. 5, *Restauration und Erneuerung*, dealing with Latin literature from AD 284 to 374 (1989). (2) W. S. Teuffel and L. Schwabe, *Geschichte der römischen Literatur*, 6th–7th edn. by W. Kroll and F. Skutsch, 3 vols. (1913–20). There is an English translation of the 5th edn. by G. G. W. Warr (1891), still useful on details. (3) M. Manitius, *Geschichte der lateinischen Literatur des Mittelalters*, 3 vols. (1911–31), also in the *Handbuch* series (see LATIN, MEDIEVAL).

Many surveys and bibliographies, in various languages and of varying quality, appear in the massive volumes of: *Aufstieg und Niedergang der römischen Welt*, ed. W. Haase and H. Temporini (1972–   ).

As well as the usual sources of bibliographical help, note also the Italian journal *Bollettino di Studi Latini*, which publishes both annual bibliographies and regular surveys.

The most extensive treatments in English are: J. Wight Duff, *Literary History of Rome from the Origins to the Close of the Golden Age*, 3rd edn. (1953; corr. imp. 1960 by A. M. Duff), and *Literary History of Rome in the Silver Age, from Tiberius to Hadrian* (1930). Still useful is: H. J. Rose, *A Handbook of Latin Literature* (1954). There are however a number of more up-to-date treatments, of which the best are: *The Cambridge History of Classical Literature 2: Latin Literature*, ed. E. J. Kenney and W. V. Clausen (1982); G. B. Conte, *Manual of Latin Literature*, trans. J. B. Solodow (1994). Both of these contain bibliographies.

Finally, two Italian works may be mentioned: A. Rostagni, *Storia della Letteratura Latina*, 3rd edn. (1964) is particularly well illustrated; and G. Cavallo, P. Fedeli, and A. Giardina, *Lo Spazio Letterario di Roma Antica*, 4 vols. (1989–91) offers an up-to-date and sophisticated account of the circumstances of literary production and *reception at Rome. R. B.; P. G. F., D. P. F.

Latin right See IUS LATII.

Latini The Latins were the inhabitants of Latium Vetus (see LATIUM). From very early times they formed a unified and self-conscious ethnic group with a common name (the *nomen Latinum*), a common sentiment, and a common language; they worshipped the same gods and had similar political and social institutions. Archaeological evidence shows that a distinctive form of material culture (the so-called 'Latial culture') was diffused throughout all of Latium Vetus from the final bronze age (*c.*1000 BC) onwards. The Latins' shared sense of kinship was expressed in a common myth of origin; they traced their descent back to *Latinus (the father-in-law of *Aeneas) who after his death was transformed into *Jupiter Latiaris and worshipped on the Alban mount (see ALBANUS MONS). Even if this version of the legend is relatively late, the annual festival of Jupiter Latiaris (the *feriae Latinae*) was extremely ancient. The main ritual event was a banquet, at which representatives of the Latin communities each received a share of the meat of a slaughtered bull (see SACRIFICE, ROMAN). Participation in the cult was a badge of membership; it was regularly attended by all the Latin peoples, including the Romans, well into the imperial period. Similar cult centres existed at *Lavinium, *Aricia, and *Tusculum, and these too may have been common to all the Latins from an early date.

There is enough evidence, therefore, to make it probable that the Latins formed a linguistic, cultural, and religious community long before the emergence of organized city-states in the 6th cent. BC. It is probable also that the social and legal rights that the Latin peoples shared in common in historical times were a relic of this pre-urban period. These shared rights, which are unparalleled elsewhere, include *conubium*, the right to contract a legal marriage with a partner from another Latin state; *commercium*, the right to deal with persons from other Latin communities and to make legally binding contracts; and the so-called right of migration (*ius migrationis*), the capacity to acquire the citizenship of another Latin state simply by taking up residence there.

There is no good evidence, however, that the early Latin communities formed any kind of political union. On the contrary, they are presented in the sources as independent states that were frequently at war with one another. According to tradition Rome became dominant under the later kings (see REX; ROME, HISTORY), who established some kind of military hegemony over much of Latium; this is probably an authentic fact, since it is presupposed in the first Carthaginian treaty of 509 BC (Polyb. 3. 22; see CARTHAGE). After the fall of the monarchy, however, the Latins rebelled from Rome, and formed an alliance centred at Aricia. It is this anti-Roman alliance, if anything, that can be termed the 'Latin League', a modern phrase with no equivalent in Latin. The struggle between Rome and the Latin alliance culminated in the battle of Lake *Regillus (499 or 496 BC), and was finally resolved by the treaty of Sp. *Cassius Vecellinus (493), which established peace and a defensive military alliance on equal terms between Rome and the Latin League.

The alliance persisted into the 4th cent., and probably saved Latium from being overwhelmed by the encroachments of the *Aequi and *Volsci. Successful campaigns that resulted in conquest of territory allowed the allies to found colonies, in which Romans and Latins both took part. The newly founded colonies became independent communities, with the same rights and obligations as the existing Latin states; they were therefore known as Latin colonies (coloniae Latinae).

During the 4th cent. BC Roman territorial ambitions (signalled by e.g. the annexation of Tusculum in 381) began to be seen as a threat by the Latins, who in 341 finally took up arms together with their southern neighbours, the Volsci, *Aurunci, *Sidicini, and Campani (see CAMPANIA). The ensuing 'Latin War' ended in disaster for the Latins and their allies, and in 338 the Romans imposed a settlement whereby some Latin and Volscian cities were incorporated in the Roman state with full *citizenship (e.g. Aricia and *Antium). The other Latins remained allies and continued to share mutual privileges with Rome (conubium and commercium), but were forbidden to have any dealings with each other (details in Livy 8. 14). The Latin League was thus finally dissolved. From now on Latin status meant that the city in question had a distinctive relationship with Rome, rather than being part of a wider community. The Romans also embarked on a new programme of colonization after the Latin war (beginning with *Cales in 334), and conferred Latin status on the newly founded colonies, even though they were outside Latium. By 200 BC the few remaining independent communities in Latium were only a small minority of the Latin name; the majority of Latins lived in the colonies, which were spread throughout Italy. After the *Social War (3), when the Latins received full Roman citizenship, 'Latin' ceased to be an ethno-linguistic term and became a purely juridical category (see IUS LATII). See COLONIZATION, ROMAN.

Mommsen, Röm. Staatsr. 3. 607; J. Beloch, Der italische Bund (1880), and Röm. Gesch.; M. Gelzer, RE 12 (1924), 940–63, 'Latium'; A. Alföldi, Early Rome and the Latins (1965), to be used with caution; E. T. Salmon, Roman Colonization under the Republic (1969); A. N. Sherwin-White, The Roman Citizenship, 2nd edn. (1973); A. Bernardi, Nomen Latinum (1973); M. Humbert, Municipium et civitas sine suffragio (1978); T. J. Cornell, CAH 7²/2 (1989), 243 ff., 317 ff., 360 ff.   T. J. Co.

Latini Iuniani were former slaves (see SLAVERY) who had been manumitted (i.e. freed) without the formalities required by law or in breach of the restrictions imposed by Augustus on the freedom of masters to manumit. Until a lex Iunia (Norbana?) of either *Augustus or *Tiberius such slaves enjoyed only a twilight status under praetorian protection. The lex made them, not Roman citizens, but Latini, a status now without any connection with geographical origin. The chief civil disability of a Latinus

Iunianus was that on his death his property reverted to his former master. This would provide a motive for a master to stop short of full manumission, but it is not clear what reasons of policy there were for the establishment of the status in the first place. The master could at any time make the manumission fully effective by repeating it in one of the recognized forms and the Junian Latin could achieve the same end by his own efforts by engaging in various activities in the public interest or by having a 1-year-old legitimate child. *Justinian abolished the status in 531.

A. N. Sherwin-White, The Roman Citizenship, 2nd edn. (1973).   B. N.

Latinus, eponymous hero of the *Latini. *Hesiod (Theog. 1011–16) makes him son of *Circe and *Odysseus and king of the Tyrrhenians (i.e. *Etruscans, see West's comm.); he is later said to be the son of *Faunus (Verg. Aen. 7. 47–9) or even *Hercules (Dion. Hal. Ant. Rom. 1. 43. 1). *Callias (5) in the 4th cent. BC (FGrH 564 F 5) reports that he married Rhome, a Trojan companion of *Aeneas, and was the father of *Romulus; other early versions have him either giving his daughter to Aeneas in marriage or dying in battle against him (cf. Cato, Orig. frs. 9 and 11 Peter (inconsistent); Livy 1. 1. 5–11). *Virgil's Aeneid shows Latinus as honourable but aged and powerless, dominated by his queen Amata and by *Turnus (1), who declare war on Aeneas although Latinus has already given him his daughter Lavinia in marriage (Aen. 7). Latinus survives the war, and his abortive peace treaty with Aeneas (Aen. 12. 161–215) anticipates the future reconciliation between Trojans and Latins.

V. J. Rosivach, Enc. Virg. 'Latino'.   S. J. Ha.

Latium Ancient Latium was a region whose borders only partly coincide with those of modern Lazio. Ancient sources make a useful distinction between Old Latium (Latium Vetus), the land of the ancient *Latini, bounded to the north-west by the rivers *Tiber and *Anio and to the east by the *Apennines and the Monti Lepini, and Greater Latium (Latium Adiectum), which included the territory of the *Hernici, *Volsci, and *Aurunci, and extended south-eastwards as far as the borders of *Campania. Under *Augustus Latium (Adiectum) was combined with Campania to form the first of the fourteen regions of Italy. Physically Latium Vetus consists of a coastal plain (the name is connected etymologically with latus, 'broad') with mountainous spurs extending towards the sea from the Apennines. The defensible hilltop sites provided by these outcrops were occupied by the earliest human habitations, which developed into substantial settlements during the iron age. Latium Vetus is dominated by the volcanic complex of the Alban hills, whose summit, the *Albanus mons, rises to nearly 1,000 m. (3,280 ft.), and was the site of the cult of *Jupiter Latiaris, the patron god of the Latins. To the south lay the Pomptine plain, a low-lying and marshy region, much of which probably remained uninhabited throughout antiquity (see POMPTINE MARSHES); but evidence of drainage, especially around the northern fringes of the plain, is provided by numerous underground tunnels (cuniculi) which are certainly very ancient and probably date from before 500 BC. The evidence suggests that, with the exception of the Pomptine Marshes, Latium Vetus was productive and supported a large population in the Archaic age; by the 6th cent. its chief settlements had become city-states. After the Roman conquest, which was complete by 300 BC, the cities of Latium began to decline, and writers of the imperial period record the disappearance of many once-famous places. This phenomenon was no doubt caused partly by the centripetal pull of the city of Rome and by the effects of warfare, particularly the

Civil Wars of the 1st cent. BC; but there is no reason to think that the area became completely depopulated. Ancient writers who lamented the desolation of the Campagna (see CAMPANIA) were referring principally to the decline of cities and the replacement of free-born *peasants by slaves (who provided the labour on large agricultural estates (*latifundia; see SLAVERY). Malaria seems to have been endemic in the region from the earliest times (see DISEASE), and there is no reason to think that it became more pestilential in the late republic and Principate; that conclusion would hardly be consistent with the fact that Latium contained numerous luxury *villas during the early empire.

T. Ashby, *The Roman Campagna in Classical Times* (1927); A. Bianchini, *Storia e paleografia della regione pontina nell'antichità* (1939). Cuniculi: R. de la Blanchère, *MÉFRA* 1882, 94 ff., 207 ff.; Dar.–Sag. 1/2 (1887), 1591–4, 'cuniculus'; S. Quilici Gigli, *Archeologia Laziale* 1983, 112 ff. On the issues of depopulation and malaria: P. A. Brunt, *Italian Manpower* (1971), 345 ff., 611 ff., and 726 (in the 1987 reprint). T. J. Co.

latrines See SANITATION.

laudatio funebris (cf. *TLL* 7/2. 1040. 40, first in Sen. *Suas.* 6. 21; *laudatio* alone is more common), the funeral oration praising the dead's accomplishments and virtues. Because of the public nature of funerals, the *laudatio funebris* offered an opportunity to display the family's status, to connect the deceased's merits with his or her illustrious ancestors, and to reinforce collective values. Important *gentes* (see GENS) preserved and displayed orations over the years, thus creating a self-flattering if often fictional historical record (Cic. *Brut.* 61). *Laudationes funebres* devoted to women show the same combination of private and public concerns. The first case of a *laudatio funebris* for a woman is that of Q. *Lutatius Catulus (1) for his mother Popilia.

The *laudatio funebris* seems to have incorporated elements drawn from different settings: the public oration *pro rostris* ('in front of the Rostra'), the private graveside *laudatio*, the praises of the dead by the *praefica*, and the choral *nenia, the latter two possibly alternating as in the speech for *Caesar by M. *Antonius (2) (App. *BCiv.* 2. 143 ff.). The *laudatio* underwent significant changes in both style and contents, and acquired a more definite structure, in conjunction with the evolution of a rhetorical style in the 2nd cent. BC. Another major development is marked by the emergence of a specifically Christian brand of *laudatio*, which becomes a form of *consolatio* with strong didactic overtones (consolatory remarks were previously avoided). Neither *Cicero nor *Quintilian devotes a separate treatment to the rhetorical structure of the *laudatio*, which followed the same rules as *encomia*. No *laudatio* survives in its entirety, though the so-called *'Laudatio Turiae', preserved epigraphically, is substantial. The structure and tone of the *laudatio* had considerable impact on the development of Latin *biography. See CONSOLATION; EPITAPHIOS.

F. Vollmer, *RE* 12/1 (1925), 992–4 and *Laudationum funebrium romanorum historia et reliquiarum editio* (1892); W. Kierdorf, *Laudatio Funebris: Interpretation und Untersuchungen zur Entwicklung der römischen Leichenrede* (1980). On the *Laudatio Turiae* see next entry. On *Augustus' laudatio for M. *Vipsanius Agrippa: L. Koenen, *ZPE* 5 (1970), 217 ff. A. Schi.

'Laudatio Turiae', the longest known private Roman inscription (*ILS* 8393 + A. E. Gordon, *AJArch.* 1950, 223 ff.); originally in two long columns, the first of which is lost, but most of the second survives in four fragments. It is in the form of a *laudatio funebris*, almost certainly not actually delivered, addressed by an aristocratic husband to a deceased wife, who had not only been an ideal Roman matron, but who had saved him and secured his

rehabilitation during the *proscriptions. The inscription was set up in various places in Rome. Since the part concerning the proscriptions is vaguely parallel to an account (App. *BCiv.* 4. 44. 189 ff.) of a Turia, wife of a later consul of 19 BC, the inscription, in which the names of the couple are lost, has traditionally been assigned to this Turia, but this is now generally rejected and there are no good arguments for the identification.

RE 7 A (1948), 1389–90, 'Turius' 4. Recent text and comm. by E. Wistrand, *The So-Called Laudatio Turiae* (1976); full discussion of the actual inscription and analysis of contents by N. Horsfall, *BICS* 1983, 85 ff. (Each of these includes clear photographs of the surviving fragments.) E. B.

Laurentum (mod. Tor Paterno), on the Tyrrhenian coast, to the south of *Ostia; an imperial *villa, much developed in the Antonine period, and covering at least 27 ha. (66 acres); *Commodus stayed there (Hdn. 1. 12. 2). Near by was the associated *Vicus Laurentium Augustanorum*, which developed rapidly from Tiberian times (see TIBERIUS), and was replanned with imperial support in the Antonine period. The younger *Pliny (2)'s villa (*Ep.* 2.17) remains to be identified. Laurentum is referred to in the *Peutinger Table.

G. Emiliani and others, *Castelporziano* 1–3 (1985–92). T. W. P.

Lauriacum, mod. Lorsch near Enns on the Danube, was a Celtic and Roman settlement in *Noricum. An earth and timber military station occupied from the 1st cent. AD was superseded before 191 (*CIL* 3. 15208 = *ILS* 9082) by the fortress of the newly raised Legio II Italica (see LEGION), previously stationed nearby at Albing. The civil settlement flourished and achieved city status. Lauriacum was destroyed by the *Huns around the middle of the 5th cent.

M. Kandler and H. Vetters, *Der römische Limes in Oesterreich* (1986), 92 ff. J. J. W.

Laurium, a hilly district in south *Attica near Cape *Sunium, was one of the largest mining districts of Greece, producing *silver from argentiferous lead ores. The geology features overlying strata of schists and marbles/limestones, with the richest ores at the first and third 'contacts'. Some exploitation started in the early bronze age, certainly at *Thoricus. Early operations involved opencast and gallery mining, and later included the sinking of deep shafts. Athens' issue of silver *coinage stimulated production, enhanced by the finding of rich, probably 'third contact' lodes at Maroneia before 483 BC (*Ath. pol.* 22. 7); this financed Themistocles' fleet programme. The mines flourished throughout the 5th cent. till the Decelean War, then declined, revived greatly in the second half of the 4th cent., were dormant in the 3rd but reworked in the 2nd, until the slave revolt of 103 BC. There were spasmodic attempts to reprocess tailings in the 1st cent. AD, and to reopen mines in the 4th. Copious industrial remains throughout the area include shafts, galleries, reservoirs, washing-tables, buildings, and smelteries. Excavations (e.g. at Agia Trias, Soureza, Agrileza) have revealed notable examples of surface 'factories' (*ergastēria*) with cisterns, grinderies, cemented ore-washeries, workrooms and slave-quarters, some arranged in regular compounds. Mines, considered state property, were leased for fixed terms to private citizens by the *pōlētai, and surface installations built by individuals for use or lease. Fragments of *pōlētai*-leases have been found in the Athenian Agora. See METALLURGY; MINES AND MINING, GREEK.

C. E. Conophagos, *Le Laurium antique* (1980); J. E. Jones, *G&R* 1982, 169–82; M. K. Langdon, *The Athenian Agora* 19: *Poletai Records* (1991). J. E. J.

Laus Pisonis, a panegyric in 261 hexameters on a Calpurnius Piso, probably the conspirator of AD 65 (cf. Tac. *Ann.* 15. 48; see CALPURNIUS PISO (2), c.). Efforts to identify the author have been fruitless.

TEXT Duff, *Min. Lat. Poets*; A. Seel (Diss. Erlangen, 1969); R. Verdière, *T. Calpurnii Siculi De Laude Pisonis*, etc. (1954); J. Amat (1991), with Calpurnius Siculus.
Cf. M. D. Reeve, *Illinois Classical Studies*, 1984, 42–8; E. Champlin, *MH* 1989, 101–24.   E. J. K.; A. S.

lavatories See SANITATION.

Lavinia See LATINUS; TURNUS (1).

Lavinium (mod. Pratica di Mare), where *Aeneas landed in *Latium, a large town of the Latin League (see LATINI), whose federal sanctuary it became in the 6th cent. BC: thirteen large archaic altars survive *in situ*, dating between the 6th and 2nd cents. BC. Near by was a 4th-cent. heroon, built over a 7th-cent. tumulus-tomb (cf. Dion. Hal. *Ant. Rom.* 1. 64. 5). Finds attest direct links with the Greek world, and Lavinium may have played an important role in transmitting Greek influence to Rome. The Romans revered Lavinium for its Trojan associations, its Venus temple common to all Latins, its cults of *Vesta and *Penates, and its loyalty in the Latin War. After the 3rd cent. BC, it became, however, of little importance.

F. Castagnoli, *Lavinium 1* (1972); *Enea nel Lazio*, exhib. cat. (1981); M. Torelli, *Lavinio e Roma* (1984); P. Sommella, M. Fenelli, and M. Guaitoli, *Quaderni della ricerca scientifica* 1985, 327 f.   E. T. S.; T. W. P.

law, international Under this heading law must be taken in its widest sense to include customary, religious, and moral law. Some approach to statutory law can be seen in the amphictionic laws (see AMPHICTIONY), the covenant after the battle of *Plataea of 479 BC (Thuc. 2. 71), and the *King's Peace; and the relations of states to each other were regulated by treaties. Nevertheless, international law remained essentially customary and, in contrast to the laws of individual states, which also had once been customary, was never officially recorded or codified. The importance of religion is seen in the amphictionic oath (see AMPHICTIONY), the fetial rites (see FETIALES), and the practice of ratifying treaties by *oaths.

Certain Panhellenic practices were relatively well developed by Homeric times (see HOMER), when *heralds and ambassadors were considered inviolable and the sanctity of sworn agreements was recognized. Similar evidence is supplied for early Italy by the fetial code with its demand that every war be a just war. Greek practice was soon expanded by the amphictionic oath and the truces for the Panhellenic games (see PANHELLENISM; and ISTHMIAN, NEMEAN, OLYMPIAN, and PYTHIAN GAMES).

In both countries treaties were negotiated at an early date. The Greek treaties (σπονδαί, ὅρκοι, συνθῆκαι) obviously were descended directly from the agreements of Homeric times, while the Roman organization of Italy indicates extensive use of treaties relatively early. Omitting armistices, the chief classes were treaties of peace, of alliance, and of friendship. The lack of treaties need not mean hostility. Thus, though Rome had treaties of friendship (*amicitia*) with several states, friendly relations often existed without such a treaty. Though permanent treaties probably were made at an early date, the oldest Greek treaties preserved in detail were made for a limited period, and though there are some 5th-cent. examples (e.g. ML 10 and comm.), treaties 'for all time' did not become the rule before the 4th cent. The short-term treaties of peace probably were not looked upon as interrupting a natural state of war by a temporary rest, but as imposing additional obligations for the period of their duration. Many Greek treaties contained clauses providing for the *arbitration of disputes, and even in their absence arbitration was frequently offered. The system was used with some success and continued to be used under Roman supervision in the 2nd and 1st cents. BC.

Private international law developed more slowly. At first *piracy, private seizure (see SYLE), and enslavement of foreigners were common. In fact, the theory of the complete absence of rights for foreigners not protected by special arrangements was retained by Roman jurists (*Dig.* 49. 15. 5). The foreigners in question are not enemies, but the theory does not involve the doctrine that all strangers are enemies. On the other hand, there was a high regard for the sanctity of suppliants and for hospitality. Out of this grew hereditary exchanges of private hospitality (see FRIENDSHIP, RITUALIZED) and later the institution of *proxenoi, to which the Roman *hospitium publicum* roughly corresponded. Outright piracy soon was widely condemned, and the feeling developed that private seizure should be used only as a reprisal for wrongs suffered. Its use sometimes was further regulated and limited by treaties. Courts, too, began to give protection to foreigners, sometimes when no treaties existed, but probably more frequently on the basis of commercial treaties (see SYMBOLON). These, at least at Athens, were ratified by a jury-court and so probably were regarded as contracts of a less sacred nature—but not less binding—than other treaties. More extensive rights were granted through treaties of *isopoliteia. Related to this for Rome was the frequent grant of *commercium.

The regard for what was customary or morally right applied to many points not so far mentioned, for instance to the rules of war. Such a basis for law meant that the standards varied from time to time and from place to place. According to *Thucydides (2), a lowering of standards resulted from the *Peloponnesian War, while the accusation of *piracy constantly made against the people of *Aetolia implies that their standard was lower than those of other states. Nor were all foreigners treated alike, but *barbarians were shown less consideration than closely related states. Yet there was always a line which could not be overstepped without incurring censure: Thuc. 4. 97–8 with Hornblower, comm.

Roman expansion, at first glance, seems to leave less scope for development of international law in the Roman empire than in Greece (see IMPERIALISM, ROMAN). It must not be forgotten, however, that Rome's early organization of Italy was based on international law and that the existence of free and allied cities also outside Italy and the control of states not formally annexed caused the Roman empire to be governed for long largely by a modified form of international law.

See also ALLIANCE; AMPHICTIONY; ARBITRATION; ASYLIA; FETIALES; FOEDUS; HERALDS; ISOPOLITEIA; LAW IN GREECE; POSTLIMINIUM; PROXENOS; SYMBOLON; WAR, RULES OF.

C. Phillipson, *The International Law and Custom of Ancient Greece and Rome* (1911); E. Täubler, *Imperium Romanum* (1913); A. Heuss, *Die völkerrechtlichen Grundlagen der römischen Aussenpolitik in republikanischer Zeit* (1933), and *Klio* 1934; V. Martin, *La Vie internationale dans la Grèce des cités* (1940); D. J. Mosley, *Envoys and Diplomacy in Ancient Greece* (1973); D. Kienast, *RE* 13 (1973), 629–730, 'Presbeia'; F. Adcock and D. J. Mosley, *Diplomacy in Ancient Greece* (1975); E. Baltrusch, *Symmachie und Spondai: Untersuchungen zum griechischen Völkerrecht der archaischen und klassischen Zeit (8.–5. Jahrhundert v. Chr.)* (1994).   J. A. O. L.; S. H.

law, Roman, sociology of During the later republic and early empire, the Roman jurists developed law, particularly private law, on the basis of what they called the 'art' (*ars*) of law-finding: they subjected existing legal rules and institutions to intense and sustained intellectual scrutiny, with the aim of isolating the basic principles that controlled the rules, and then applying these principles in the creation of new law. The activity of the Roman jurists opens a new chapter in the history of law. From a sociological standpoint, the central task is to evaluate how this new form of thinking contributed to Rome's broader social development.

The jurists' legal authority rested primarily not on their official position, but on their accumulated knowledge of law and experience in manipulating it. In Max Weber's terminology, they were *honoratiores*: independent legal experts who monopolize the study of law, but are available for consultation by litigants and lay judges in particular. However, during the empire the small corps of jurists (probably never more than ten to twenty at any time) was gradually transformed into a legal élite presiding over a much larger legal profession. See LAWYERS, ROMAN. This is particularly true after AD 150, when most jurists were absorbed into the emperor's central bureaucracy.

At first the jurists transmitted their methods and results from generation to generation internally, through writing and informal teaching. Formal elementary legal education is not attested before the mid-2nd cent. AD, as law became a more established and accessible profession.

The jurists' extensive writings were central to the continuity of their law-finding. By and large, their writings were problem-oriented; the jurists did not decide actual cases, but instead developed law through exploring hypothetical fact-situations. In this way the jurists preserved a distance between themselves and the Roman judicial system; questions of law were solved abstractly, as general propositions not closely tied to the disputed facts of particular cases. In many functional respects the jurists thus resembled modern appellate judges.

Socially, the jurists belonged to the empire's élite, usually by birth though some jurists seem to have risen by their legal talent. Their work is closely associated with the capital city, and particularly with the operation of its judicial system, which was, to be sure, widely imitated throughout the empire. Although as individuals the jurists differed somewhat in outlook, their social homogeneity is obvious: wealthy and powerful men drawn increasingly from across the empire, but usually not from the topmost ranks of the senatorial aristocracy.

Their social homogeneity doubtless contributes to a certain narrowness of vision in their writings, a perceptible tendency to concentrate on legal problems of significance mainly to the upper strata of Roman society; such problems also arose more frequently at trials in Rome than in the provinces. Although the jurists evaluate these problems even-handedly, both the framework of their analysis and their understanding of social reality are constricted. For example, they say virtually nothing about ordinary wage labour, tenement housing, or peasant agriculture, but much about the management of large estates, succession to the wealthy, and commerce in staples and luxury items.

The narrowness of the jurists' vision has major implications for modern interpretation of their writings by social historians. More broadly, it raises difficult issues about the social reach of Roman private law: to what extent is it yet another manifestation of a highly stratified society, in which relatively few individuals control not only all common social goods, but also the apparatus of justice?

None the less, within this restricted sphere, the jurists display considerable sensitivity to the conflicting interests and demands of diverse social groups. Where juristic knowledge of social activity can be closely examined, it is accurate and deep, though casually acquired. By and large, the jurists do not develop Roman law through broad statements of public policy, but instead incrementally, decision by decision, frequently after fierce internal debate among themselves. This process lent itself to the tacit accommodation of social interests. As the jurists became more confident in their methods, they increasingly justified decisions through reference to external social values such as fairness (*aequitas*) and practicality (*utilitas*).

This incremental legal growth gradually raised the salience of law as a distinct institution within Roman society. Although lay criticism of the jurists and their law was common, it was also internalized as part of the process whereby new legal rules arise through reaction to existing law. The jurists, furthermore, could create new law without resort to cumbersome legislation; and the emperors left them largely free to do so. As a result law achieved, in the Roman world, substantial independence and social responsiveness; it became more sharply differentiated than in earlier Mediterranean societies.

The differentiation of law ranks among the most historically significant Roman accomplishments, but its immediate consequence for Roman society is equivocal, at any rate in comparison with the role law would later play in the west. The social and economic institutions of the empire do not appear to have altered significantly despite the encouragement of juristic liberalism. Juristic concepts of legality and due process probably did influence the growth of the imperial bureaucracy and judiciary; but except in private law, Roman progress was less than impressive. Roman law thus did not serve as a vehicle to promote the further differentiation of society.

The one obvious exception to this pattern is Roman law's contribution to integrating the empire's upper strata. As Roman *citizenship gradually spread, its élite became both larger and more internally disparate, no longer united by the traditional social values of earlier city-states; Roman aristocrats were forced to rub shoulders with wealthy *freedmen and provincial magnates. (See SENATORS, PATTERNS OF RECRUITMENT.) Law provided Romans with a predictable structure of expectations within their most vital social relationships: marriage, the family, contracts, and succession. It thus served to hold society together, an advantage signalled by Roman authors from *Cicero (*Caecin.* 65–78) to Aelius *Aristides (*On Rome* 60, 102). The advantage was especially marked for those members of the upper strata, such as the municipal nobilities, whose social position was not always well protected against their superiors (see DECURIONES). Most jurists were themselves members of these social groups, at least by birth. See HONESTIORES.

From a sociological perspective, the most historically significant contributions of Roman law probably depended less on the specific content of its rules than on its emergence as a more or less autonomous discipline that was insulated by its professionalism from directly contending social pressures. In this respect, the jurists correctly defined justice, as *Ulpian did (*Dig.* 1. 1. 10. 1), primarily in formal terms: 'according to each person his right'.

Classical Roman private law was only marginally influenced by legislation. However, from the early 2nd cent. AD the rescripts of Roman emperors (see CONSTITUTIONS) played an ever larger role in defining, and soon also in making, law. After the independent juristic movement collapsed in the early 3rd cent., the imperial chancellery emerged as the major source of authoritative legal innovation, a position it retained during the later empire. Legal experts continued, however, to influence law, not only through the chancellery where they often served, but also, in the east, through the great law schools.

These late imperial developments were not necessarily negative; judicial procedure, in particular, assumed a much more modern appearance. But with the disappearance of the jurists, legal thinking lost much of its earlier dynamism and integrity, and law became increasingly indistinguishable from governance; a mood of retrospection prevailed. The independent voice of the jurists, and the view of law they had championed, survived to later ages largely through the extensive excerpts from their writings in Justinian's *Digest* (see JUSTINIAN'S CODIFICATION).

K. M. T. Atkinson, 'The Education of the Lawyer in Ancient Rome', *South African Law Journal* 1970, 31–59; B. W. Frier, *Landlords and Tenants in Imperial Rome* (1980), and *The Rise of the Roman Jurists: Studies in Cicero's Pro Caecina* (1985); W. Kunkel, *Herkunft und Soziale Stellung der Römischen Juristen*[2] (1967); N. Luhmann, *A Sociological Theory of Law* (trans. E. Kung-Utz and M. Albrow, 1985); D. Nörr, *Rechtskritik in der Römischen Antike* (1973); Max Weber, *On Law in Economy and Society* (trans. E. Shils and M. Rheinstein, 1954); Wieacker, *RRG*, 2 vols. (1988 and 1991).   B. W. F.

law and procedure, Athenian

1. Legislation Greeks used the same word (νόμος) for both custom and law, and the beginning of law is hard to define. One reasonable view is that an unwritten rule should be regarded as a law if the community or the ruler approves it and imposes or authorizes punishment for infringement of it. In this sense laws forbidding some offences (e.g. murder, theft, bigamy) must have existed since primitive times. An alternative view is that only rules stated in writing are really laws. The transition from oral to written law began in the 7th cent. BC, but was not completed until the end of the 5th cent. in Athens (and later in other cities). See LITERACY; ORALITY.

The first written laws in any Greek city are said to have been drawn up by *Zaleucus for the city of *Locri Epizephyrii in south Italy. The first written laws in Athens are attributed to *Draco in the year when Aristaechmus was archon (probably 621/0). His laws, except that on homicide, were superseded in 594/3 by those of *Solon. These laws were inscribed on wooden blocks (ἄξονες, see AXONES) for everyone to read. Later these inscriptions were transferred to stone and many additions and alterations were made, but the Athenians continued to refer to their code as the laws of Solon.

After democracy was established, new laws were made by majority vote in the *ekklēsia. For most of the 5th cent. there was no sharp distinction between a law (*nomos*) laying down a permanent rule and a decree (*psēphisma*) for a particular occasion. Legislation was not systematic, and some confusions and contradictions arose. From 410 onwards efforts were made to rectify this situation. Existing laws were revised to remove obscurities or inconsistencies, and were all inscribed on stone; henceforth no uninscribed law was to be enforced, and no decree could override a law. New decrees were still made by the *ekklēsia*, but the making of new laws was handed over to groups of citizens known as *nomothetai.

2. Judicature Until the early 6th cent. BC all verdicts were given by the archons or the *Areopagus or the *ephetai. Solon instituted a system of trial by the *ēliaia, probably for appeals against the archons' verdicts (see ARCHONTES) or for imposition of penalties above certain limits. The next stages of development are obscure, but presumably appeals became so usual that the archons practic-

ally ceased to give verdicts and the *ēliaia* (if it was a single body) did not have time to hear all the cases referred to it. A system of juries was therefore set up, in which each jury consisted of a number of citizens who tried a case on behalf of all the citizens.

For the period after the middle of the 5th cent. we have fuller information. Volunteers for jury service (who had to be citizens over 30 years old) were called for at the beginning of each year, and a list of 6,000 jurors for the year was drawn up. To encourage volunteers, each juror received a small fee for each day on which he sat to try a case. This payment was introduced by *Pericles (1), who probably fixed it at two obols; it was raised to three obols, probably on the proposal of *Cleon, not later than 425. Since the payment was less than an able-bodied man would earn by an ordinary day's work, one of its effects was that many of the volunteers were men who were too old for work. This state of affairs is satirized in *Aristophanes (1)'s *Wasps*.

The number of jurors who formed a jury varied according to the type of case, but was normally several hundred. In one trial it is said to have been 6,000. In the 4th cent. odd numbers (e.g. 501) were used, to avoid a tie in the voting, but there is no evidence for odd numbers in the 5th cent. It is not known what method was used in the 5th cent. for allocating jurors to courts (*dikastēria*, sing. *dikastērion*). By the early 4th cent. a system of lot was used for this purpose, and later in the century a more complicated system of lot (described in detail in *Ath. pol.* 63–6) was introduced. The aim was to prevent *bribery by making it impossible to know beforehand which jurors would try which case.

Each trial was arranged and presided over by a magistrate or group of magistrates. Different magistrates had responsibility for different types of case. The (eponymous) archon had charge of cases concerning family and inheritance rights. The *basileus* had charge of homicide cases and most cases connected with religion. The *polemarchos had charge of cases concerning non-Athenians. The *thesmothetai had charge of a wide variety of cases; in general any type of public case which did not clearly fall within the province of another magistrate came to them. The *Eleven had charge of cases of theft and similar offences. The *stratēgoi had charge of cases concerning military and naval service, and there were several lesser boards of magistrates with responsibility for particular types of case, such as the *apodektai and the *nautodikai. In the 4th cent. most types of private case were handled by four judges selected by lot for each of the ten tribes (see PHYLAI), sometimes known collectively as the Forty.

In the 5th cent. and the first half of the 4th each magistrate sat regularly in the same court. The *ēliaia* was the court of the *thesmothetai*. Other courts, perhaps not all in use at the same time, were the Odeum, the Painted *Stoa (στοὰ ποικίλη), the New Court (τὸ Καινόν), the Inserted Court (τὸ Παράβυστον), the Court at Lykos (τὸ ἐπὶ Λύκῳ), the Kallion, and the Triangular, Greater, and Middle Courts (τὸ Τρίγωνον, τὸ Μεῖζον, τὸ Μέσον). In the later 4th cent. magistrates no longer sat regularly in the same courts, but were allocated to courts by lot each day. Distinct from all these courts were the Areopagus and the other special homicide courts, manned by the *ephetai, in which a different procedure was followed. A few cases were tried by the *boulē or the *ekklēsia.

3. Actions The law on any particular subject generally specified the action to be raised against a transgressor; for some offences the prosecutor had a choice of actions. The principal distinction was between public actions (δίκαι δημόσιαι) and private actions (δίκαι ίδιαι or simply δίκαι). The following were the main differences. (*a*) A private action concerned a wrong or injury done to an individual. A public action concerned an offence which was regarded as affecting the community as a whole. (*b*) A private action could be raised only by the person who claimed that he had suffered wrong or injury. A public action might be raised by a magistrate or official acting on behalf of the state. But the scope of public prosecution was widened by Solon to allow prosecution by 'anyone who wishes' (ὁ βουλόμενος); this meant any free adult male, except that some actions could not be brought by a non-citizen and none could be brought by a disfranchised citizen (see ATIMIA). (*c*) In a private action damages or compensation might be awarded to the prosecutor. In a public action any fine or penalty was paid to the state. However, to encourage public-spirited citizens to prosecute offenders on behalf of the state, financial rewards were given to successful prosecutors in certain public actions, notably *phasis* and *apographē*. This had the unintended effect of encouraging the rise of *sycophants (habitual prosecutors). (*d*) To deter sycophants penalties were imposed, in most public actions, on a prosecutor who dropped a case after starting it or who failed to obtain at least one-fifth of the jury's votes; he had to pay a fine of 1,000 drachmas and forfeited the right to bring a similar action in future. These penalties did not apply in private actions.

The various public actions were named after their method of initiation. (*a*) *Graphē* was the most ordinary public action, so named presumably because it had originally been the only one in which the charge had to be put in writing, though by the 4th cent. written charges had become the rule in other actions too. (*b*) *Apagōgē*. The prosecutor began proceedings by arresting the accused and handing him over to the appropriate magistrates, usually the Eleven. This procedure was used especially against thieves caught in the act and against persons caught exercising rights to which they were not entitled. The speeches of *Antiphon (1) *On the Murder of Herodes* and *Lysias *Against Agoratus* concern cases of *apagōgē*. (*c*) *Endeixis*. The prosecutor made a denunciation to the magistrates, and might go on to arrest the accused. This procedure too was used against persons accused of exercising rights to which they were not entitled. The case of *Andocides *On the Mysteries* is the best known example. (*d*) *Ephēgēsis*. The prosecutor led the magistrates to the accused, and they arrested him—a procedure very similar to *apagōgē* and *endeixis*, and used for the same kind of offence. (*e*) *Phasis*. The prosecutor pointed out goods or property involved in an offence, such as goods smuggled into Athens from abroad without payment of customs duties. If he won the case, he was rewarded with half of the fine exacted or property confiscated. This action is satirized in Aristophanes' *Acharnians*. In the 4th cent. it was extended to some other kinds of offence which we cannot define exactly. (*f*) *Apographē*. The prosecutor listed property which he alleged was due to the state and was being withheld. If he won the case, he was rewarded with three-quarters of the property recovered. Several surviving speeches were written for this type of case, e.g. Lysias *On the Property of Aristophanes* and [*Demosthenes (2)] *Against Nicostratus*. (*g*) *Eisangelia* of the most serious type was initiated by a denunciation to the *boulē* or the *ekklēsia*, which might either decide to try the case itself or refer it to a jury. (*h*) *Probolē*. The prosecutor made a denunciation to the *ekklēsia*. The *ekklēsia* voted on it, but this hearing did not constitute a trial; if the prosecutor proceeded with the case, it was tried subsequently by a jury. This procedure was used against men accused of sycophancy (see above) or of deceiving the Athe-

nian people, and also for offences concerning festivals. The case of Demosthenes, *Against Meidias* is the best-known example. (*i*) In addition, a case arising from an accusation made at a *dokimasia* or a *euthyna* was similar to a public action in some respects.

A special type of private action was *diadikasia*. This was used when a right (e.g. to claim an inheritance) or an obligation (e.g. to perform a *trierarchy) was disputed between two or more persons. Its distinctive feature was that there was no prosecutor or defendant: all the claimants were on equal terms. Another special category of private action was *dikē emmēnos* ('monthly case'), which by the second half of the 4th cent. could be used for most financial cases, including disputes with foreign merchants. It was in some way a faster procedure, probably because it was available every month, but there is doubt about the details.

Homicide cases were treated differently from others. If a person was killed, his relatives were required to prosecute the killer. The prosecution followed a special procedure, including a proclamation to the killer to keep away from sacred and public places, three pre-trials at monthly intervals, and special oaths. The trial, at which the prosecutor and the defendant each made two speeches, was held not in an ordinary court, but at one of several special open-air courts, with the *Areopagus or the *ephetai* as the jury.

4. Procedure When anyone wished to raise either a private or a public action, he gave his charge to the appropriate magistrate. It was the responsibility of the prosecutor to deliver the summons to the defendant. The magistrate held an inquiry (ἀνάκρισις), at which he heard statements and evidence from both parties. Some minor cases could be decided by the magistrate forthwith, but generally the purpose of the inquiry was simply to satisfy him that the case should be taken to court. At this stage a defendant might object by the procedure of *paragraphē* that the wrong form of action had been raised, and then this question had to be decided before the action could proceed further. A private action coming before the tribe judges (the Forty) was referred by them to a public arbitrator, and did not go on to trial by jury unless one or other of the litigants refused to accept the arbitrator's verdict.

At the trial the magistrate presided, but he did not give directions or advice to the jury, and did not perform the functions of a modern judge. The prosecutor spoke first and the defendant afterwards. If either litigant was a woman or child, the speech was made by the nearest adult male relative; but otherwise each litigant had to speak for himself, unless clearly incapable, though he might deliver a speech written for him by a speech-writer (*logographos*), and he might call on friends to speak too in his support. In the course of his speech he could request to have laws or other documents read out to the court. He could also call witnesses. See EVIDENCE, ANCIENT ATTITUDES TO. Until some date in the first half of the 4th cent., witnesses gave their evidence orally, and might be questioned by the speaker who called them (but not cross-examined by his opponent). Later in the 4th cent. witnesses gave evidence beforehand in writing, and at the trial merely signified assent when their statements were read out. Disfranchised citizens, women, children, and slaves could not speak as witnesses, although they could be present in court without speaking; a written record of a slave's statement could be produced as evidence if the statement had been made under *torture. A certain length of time, varying according to the type of case, was allowed for each litigant to make his speech, the time being measured by a water-clock (see CLOCKS).

When the speeches were over, the jury heard no impartial

summing-up and had no opportunity for discussion, but voted at once. In the 5th cent. each juror voted by placing a pebble or shell in an urn; there was one urn for conviction and one for acquittal. In the 4th cent. each juror was given two bronze votes, one with a hole through the middle signifying conviction and one unpierced signifying acquittal, and he placed one in a 'valid' (bronze) urn and the other in an 'invalid' (wooden) urn; this method helped to ensure that the voting was secret and that each juror cast only one valid vote. When all had voted, the votes were counted, and the majority decided the verdict. A tie was treated as acquittal. There was no appeal from the jury's verdict. However, a losing litigant who proved that a witness for his opponent had given false evidence could claim compensation from the witness, or in some instances got a case reopened; and there were a few exceptional occasions when the *ekklēsia* decreed that verdicts should be set aside.

For some offences the penalty was laid down by law, but in other cases the penalty or the amount of damages had to be decided by the jury. In such cases, when the verdict had been given against the defendant, the prosecutor proposed a penalty and the defendant proposed another (naturally more lenient). Each spoke in support of his proposal, and the jury voted again to decide between them. Payment of money was the most usual kind of penalty, but other penalties regularly imposed were partial or total disfranchisement, confiscation of property, confinement in the stocks, *exile, or death. See PUNISHMENT (GREEK AND ROMAN PRACTICE). Long terms of imprisonment were not normally imposed. Cf. PRISON.

The chief fault of the Athenian courts was that a jury could too easily be swayed by a skilful speaker. Most jurors were men of no special intelligence; yet, without impartial advice or guidance, they had to distinguish true from false statements and valid from invalid arguments, and they had to interpret the law as well as decide the facts. It says much for the Athenians' alertness and critical sense that the system worked as well as it did. The advantages were that the large juries were hard to bribe (see BRIBERY) or browbeat, and that the courts and the people were as nearly as possible identical, so that an accused man felt that he was being judged by the Athenian people, not merely by some government official or according to an obscure written rule. Thus the institution of popular juries was one of the Athenians' greatest democratic achievements. See also DEMOCRACY, ATHENIAN.

J. H. Lipsius, *Das attische Recht und Rechtsverfahren* (1905–15); R. J. Bonner and G. Smith, *The Administration of Justice from Homer to Aristotle* (1930–8); A. R. W. Harrison, *The Law of Athens* (1968–71); D. M. MacDowell, *The Law in Classical Athens* (1978); M. Gagarin, *Early Greek Law* (1986); S. C. Todd, *The Shape of Athenian Law* (1993).   D. M. M.

law and procedure, Roman The subject is here dealt with in three sections: civil law; civil procedure; and criminal law and procedure.

1. Civil law (*ius civile*) in its broadest sense was the law of the city of Rome as opposed to that of some other city. In a narrower sense it refers to the secular law of Rome, private and public, to the exclusion of sacred law (*ius sacrum*). This section deals, so far as the sources of law are concerned, with civil law in the first sense, but as regards substantive law is confined to the second.

From the standpoint of sources the beginning and end of Roman civil law are conveniently marked by the *Twelve Tables and Justinian's codification (see JUSTINIAN'S CODIFICATION). Dating from about 450 BC the law of the Twelve Tables was treated by the Romans as the starting-point of their legal history. Though

much of it became obsolete it was never technically superseded until Justinian's legislation of AD 528–34. These two documents, neither of which is systematic enough to be called a code in the modern sense, were of very different bulk, the first consisting of a few score laconic sentences, the second running to well over a million words.

Four periods of legal history are commonly distinguished in the interval between the Twelve Tables and Justinian's codification: (*a*) the early republic, a period of relatively primitive law ending in the 3rd cent. BC; (*b*) the late republic, a formative period in which an independent legal profession took shape, beginning about 200 BC and ending with the victory of *Augustus in 31 BC; (*c*) the classical period, spanning the first three cents. AD and roughly corresponding with the Principate. Its core was an age of relative stability between 68 and 235, which is often subdivided into three: the early classical period of the Flavian dynasty (68 to 96), the high classical age of the adoptive emperors (96 to 180) and the late classical flowering from Commodus to the fall of the Severan dynasty (180 to 235). See ROME, HISTORY. At this time important treatises (see LEGAL LITERATURE) were being written by lawyers who, particularly in the middle period, were free to give expression to their sense of justice without the distraction of political pressures. There followed 60 years of disorder, up to 300, which have been termed epiclassical. In these, private law changed very little but legal writing almost dried up. The period ends with a determined effort by *Diocletian (284–305) to revive classical law in its essential features. Finally follows (*d*) the post-classical period of the later empire, in which *Constantine I and his successors introduced important reforms in public and procedural law and in the religious life of the empire but made only limited changes in private law. In the east this period ends with Justinian's 6th-cent. codification, which introduced some important reforms and simplifications, but often reverted to the law of the classical period. In the west the post-classical period ends with the disintegration of the empire in the 5th cent. AD. It has been seen by some as one of legal decline and vulgarization; but it is doubtful whether this assessment is accurate. Some of the terms mentioned embody a mixture of political, legal, and literary value judgements. They need to be used with caution.

A striking mark of the law of the early Roman republic was its formalism. Both in legal transactions and litigation solemn oral forms were necessary and sufficient. The will of the parties was denied effect unless clothed in these forms. In this respect Roman law resembled primitive systems elsewhere; but it differed from them in the simplicity and economy of the forms used (see ADOPTION, ROMAN; EMANCIPATION; MANCIPATIO; NEXUM; STIPULATIO). A small number of these served a wide variety of purposes; *mancipatio* and *stipulatio* are good examples. As in other early systems Roman private law was confined to citizens. The *ius Quiritium* (right of citizens: see IUS GENTIUM) was all-important and the community excluded foreigners from the use of the formulae it had devised. The Roman *family preserved its traditional, exclusive organization in which its male head occupied a central place as the person in whom legal power was concentrated (see PATRIA POTESTAS). The state hardly interfered in relations between him and those subject to him, free or unfree, over whom indeed he had the power of life and death.

In the last two to three cents. BC, however, the expansion of Rome's commerce and empire over the Mediterranean world (see IMPERIALISM, ROMAN) made it impossible to maintain the exclusiveness of the old civil law. New, informal institutions appeared, which depended on the intention of the parties rather than the observance of external forms. An important example is the class of agreements binding by consent alone (consensual contracts: see CONTRACT), which provided a way of enforcing the principal commercial transactions, such as sale, lease, and partnership. These new institutions were open to foreigners and citizens alike (see IUS GENTIUM). The form of *stipulatio*, which could be used to make any lawful agreement legally binding, was also widened so that it was now open to foreigners. Special boards of assessors (*recuperatores*) had early been set up for disputes with non-citizens, and about 242 BC a special magistrate for matters involving foreigners (*praetor peregrinus*; see PRAETOR (REPUBLIC)) was created with jurisdiction over these cases. In the same period the old rigid procedure for the trial of suits between citizens, called *legis actiones* (actions in law) gave way to the less formal and more flexible 'formulary procedure' (see § 2. 4 below). These developments were made possible by a first flowering of legal thought and writing, stimulated by contact with Greek culture but with an insistence on verbal clarity and precision which is markedly Roman.

Legislation played only a minor part in these changes. Apart from the Twelve Tables, legislation (see COMITIA) did little to develop private law during the republic. Such statutes (see LEX (1); PLEBISCITUM) as were enacted usually touched only the detail of existing institutions. The *lex Aquilia* (see DAMNUM INIURIA DATUM), which provided a broad range of remedies for damage to property, is a notable exception. Decrees of the senate (*senatus consulta*) also played little part in private and criminal law, and their legal force was uncertain. See SENATUS CONSULTUM.

The chief factor in releasing the old civil law from its early rigidity was the development of magisterial law (*ius honorarium*: see EDICT). In the sense explained above this formed part of civil law but in a narrower sense was contrasted with it. The key magistrate in its development was the urban praetor in Rome (see PRAETOR (REPUBLIC)). He like other magistrates published an annual edict setting out how he proposed to exercise his jurisdiction. In the last century of the republic this became an instrument by which, with the help of lawyers whom he consulted, significant innovations were introduced. A concurrent aspect of the development was the gradual introduction of the formulary procedure, by which the issue to be litigated no longer had to be expressed in one of the small number of ritual modes admitted by the old system of *legis actiones*. Instead it was embodied in a formula drawn up before the magistrate and adapted to the alleged facts of the case, though the actual trial was normally conducted by someone else. Thus the magistrate, who controlled the granting of formulae, the most important of which were incorporated in his edict, in effect acquired the power to reform and develop the law. Formally, it is true, he had no such power; his function was to administer the law and not to change it. But with the introduction of the new procedure he was able to grant new remedies by way both of right of action and defence, and thereby, as *Aemilius Papinianus was to put it two centuries later, to 'support, supplement, and correct the civil law' (*Dig*. 1. 1. 7. 1). He supported it by giving more effective remedies to enforce existing rights (see e.g. INIURIA AND DEFAMATION). He supplemented the civil law by recognizing claims which the civil law did not recognize, for example the claims of those legitimate blood relations who were technically not members of the family to the possession of a deceased estate. He corrected the law by barring claims which it recognized, for example because it would be dishonest in the circumstances to allow their enforcement. In some areas this power to supplement and correct produced a

dualism between the old civil and newer magisterial law. There was succession by magisterial law alongside succession by civil law, and magisterial rights of property, regarded by some as amounting to ownership, existed alongside ownership by civil law. Indeed writers in the Principate treat civil law and magisterial law in separate works or successive parts of the same work. Their integration in Justinian's codification is the outcome of the efforts of the law schools and lawyers of the later empire.

Augustus made a serious attempt to adhere to republican forms of legislation (*lex*, *plebiscitum*: see LEX (1) and (2)) but they were little used by his successors and disappeared altogether during the course of the 1st cent. AD. As an instrument of legislation *senatus consulta* took their place. Emperors influenced, and even dictated, the content of such of these decrees as were of general importance, and the emperor's speech (*oratio*) proposing the decree came often to be cited in place of the decree itself. Thus the codification of the praetor's edict was effected by a decree of the senate drafted by *Iulianus on *Hadrian's behalf. See EDICT; PRAETOR (CAESAR AND IMPERIAL PERIOD).

The emperor's powers were at first conceived as modelled on those of republican magistrates. Thus the emperor might issue edicts, give instructions to officials, towns or provincial assemblies (see CONCILIUM), grant charters or citizenship, decide cases as a judge, and reply to petitions from private individuals. By the time of Hadrian these various pronouncements came to be grouped together as *constitutions of the emperor (*constitutiones principis*). In the mid-2nd cent. AD *Gaius (2) treats them as having formally, and not merely in practice, the force of law. Some constitutions, like edicts, could openly innovate, something which with the codification of the praetor's edict in AD 131 other magistrates could no longer do. Thus *Caracalla in 212 employed an edict to grant citizenship to the free inhabitants of the empire (see CONSTITUTION, ANTONINE). But the emperor along with lawyers of authority continued in the Principate to make law indirectly, if interstitially, through rulings made in particular cases. Decisions made by the emperor acting as a judge (*decreta*) and replies or rescripts on his behalf to petitions on points of law (*subscriptiones*, *rescripta*; see CONSTITUTIONS), though in principle merely interpreting existing law, possessed a force which went beyond the case in point and served to fill gaps in the law and resolve ambiguities. Their force was analogous to but greater than that of the opinions (*responsa*) of lawyers of authority (see LAWYERS). By the end of the late classical period this imperial case law, mainly embodied in rescripts, supplanted the case law embodied in practitioners' opinions as an instrument for developing the law without legislating. After *Herennius Modestinus in the early 3rd cent. AD, and Aquila who may have been his pupil, collections of *responsa* cease, though lawyers naturally continued to give opinions as before. The change was not as dramatic as it may sound, since in practice lawyers, often those who are known to us from their writings, such as Modestinus himself, *Arcadius Charisius, and *Hermogenianus, went on drafting the rescripts which issued in the emperor's name. But after Diocletian, though replies on points of law continued to issue from the imperial offices (*scrinia*), they too were no longer collected and published.

The opportunity for lawyers to make an independent contribution to the development of the law therefore disappeared by the end of the 3rd cent. It was the lawyers of the classical period who composed the works which, via Justinian's codification, have proved to be the chief legacy of Roman law to medieval and modern civilization (see LEGAL LITERATURE). Indeed that is the main reason for calling the period 'classical'.

A factor which tended to break the pattern of the earlier law was the development of institutions, for example *fideicommissum* (a provision similar to a trust: see INHERITANCE, ROMAN), which were imperial innovations and so cut across the old lines between civil and magisterial law. To enforce these new institutions 'extraordinary' procedures and jurisdictions were created outside the formulary system. These procedures of extraordinary inquiry (*cognitio extra ordinem* or *cognitio extraordinaria*: see § 2. 13, 14 below) gradually spread to jurisdiction over ordinary civil law cases and by the early 4th cent. entirely supplanted the formulary procedure.

Problems had arisen from the conquest of provinces (see PROVINCIA) to which the Romans conceded from the first the right of organizing their legal life according to their own laws. Only those provincials on whom Roman citizenship was conferred, individually or by groups or regions, had to observe Roman private law in their legal relations. Conflicts between Roman and local law were submitted to the emperor, who not infrequently decided in favour of local law. Caracalla's general grant of Roman citizenship in AD 212 in theory abolished these conflicts, but local law continued to a varying extent to be accommodated in the guise of long-standing custom. This was treated as part of Roman law provided that, unlike *incest or polygamy, it did not outrage Roman susceptibilities.

In the reign of Constantine I independent legal writing came to an end (see LEGAL LITERATURE) and the imperial government, now firmly bureaucratized, assumed a monopoly of legal development. Some scholars, influenced by the mystique of decline and fall, have treated the ensuing centuries as a period of legal degeneration, in which classical law was replaced by 'vulgar law'. The detailed evidence hardly supports this view. The law schools of Rome and *Berytus (mod. Beirut) flourished in the post-classical period, teaching classical law. Many other towns had their law teachers, and the number of lawyers needed to fill posts such as those of assessor to provincial governors increased. A factor which creates an impression of decline is that the constitutions issuing from the imperial legislature (the consistory) in the later empire were drafted by the emperor's *quaestor, who had become his principal spokesman. Quaestors were rhetorically skilled but until about AD 400 were seldom lawyers, though they had access to professional advice in the imperial offices (*scrinia*). The language of legislation was therefore untechnical; indeed there was often a conscious avoidance of technicalities. But though this created some danger of misunderstanding, lawyers were at hand to explain what was meant. Hence classical private law continued in force over a wide area, though with some modifications. In particular, contrary to what has sometimes been asserted, the basic distinctions between ownership and possession, contract and conveyance remained intact. Only when invaders overran the west and captured Rome, disrupting the administration of justice along with the imperial administration as a whole, can one properly speak of vulgarization. The Roman law of the successor states such as those of the Visigoths (see GOTHS) and *Burgundians (*lex Romana Visigothorum*, *lex Romana Burgundionum*) does indeed often present a simplistic version of Roman law.

In the east the invasions were repelled. By the 6th cent. the law school of Berytus had built up a tradition of teaching and analysis of the classical texts over some 300 years; and in 425 *Theodosius (1) II imposed imperial control on law teaching in *Constantinople. This enabled Justinian to draw for his codification on teachers from both centres along with officials and practising lawyers who had been taught in them. It was therefore inevitable that the tendency of the codification would be to move back towards classical private law, in so far as it had been modified in the post-classical period. The same was not of course true of public or religious law. But even in private law Justinian was a reformer to the extent that with *Tribonianus' help he eliminated obsolete institutions and over-subtle distinctions and settled points of dispute among the classical lawyers, developing the received tradition in an incremental way. In general Justinian favoured equitable solutions, though sometimes at the cost of certainty. He not infrequently changed his mind. The influence of Christian thinking, hardly noticeable in the codification apart from legislation on religious matters, is more strongly marked in the *Novellae* (new legislation) enacted from 535 onwards.

SOURCES Wieacker *RRG* 1 and 2, *Vom römischen Recht*, 2nd edn. (1961), 161–86, 222–41, and *Ausgewählte Schriften* 1, ed. D. Simon (1983), 240–54; *HLL* 3, §§ 323, 394; 4, §§ 410–11; 5, § 502; F. Schulz, *Roman Legal Science* (1946), rev. as *Geschichte der römischen Rechtswissenschaft* (1961); H. F. Jolowicz, *Historical Introduction to the Study of Roman Law*, 3rd edn. (1972); W. Kunkel, *An Introduction to Roman Legal and Constitutional History*, 2nd edn. by J. M. Kelly (1973; Ger. orig., 5th edn. 1967); E. Levy, *West Roman Vulgar Law: The Law of Property* (1951); W. E. Voss, *Recht und Rhetorik in den Gesetzen der Spätantiken* (1982); D. Liebs, *ANRW* 2. 15 (1976), 197–286, and *ZRG* 1983, 485–509; Honoré 1981.

SUBSTANTIVE CIVIL LAW M. Kaser, *Römisches Privatrecht* 2. 1, 2 (1971–5); W. W. Buckland, *Textbook of Roman Law*, 3rd edn. by P. G. Stein (1963); J. A. Crook, *Law and Life of Rome* (1967); J. A. C. Thomas, *Textbook of Roman Law* (1976). T. Hon.

2. Civil procedure 1. The Roman civil trial was governed in the course of history by three systems of procedure: that of the *legis actiones*, the formulary system, and the *cognitio extra ordinem* or *cognitio extraordinaria*. The periods during which these systems were in use overlapped to some extent, but, broadly speaking, the *legis actiones* prevailed until, probably in the second half of the 2nd cent. BC, they were largely replaced by the formulary system; the *cognitio extraordinaria* gradually encroached on the formulary system during the Principate and finally superseded it under the Dominate (i.e. after AD 284).

2. The first two systems shared a central feature: the division into two stages. The first took place before a magistrate, *in iure*, and its purpose was to define and formulate the issue (i.e. the limits of the dispute between the parties). This stage culminated in joinder of issue (*litis contestatio*), an acceptance by the parties, under the magistrate's supervision, of the issue thus formulated and the nomination, in the usual case, of the *iudex* authorized by the magistrate. It was the *iudex* who presided in the second stage (*apud iudicem*) when the case was heard and argued. He was a private person empowered by the magistrate's order to give judgement, but he was more than a mere private arbitrator, because that judgement was recognized by the state and gave rise to execution proceedings, though in the last resort it was the successful plaintiff who had to put these into effect. Only in the stage *in iure* were certain formalities observed; the stage *apud iudicem* was entirely informal. The differences between the *legis actio* system and the formulary system lay in the proceedings *in iure*. See IUDEX.

3. The procedure by *legis actio* (which existed in the time of the Twelve Tables: Gai. *Inst*. 4. 17a) required the plaintiff and the defendant ritually to assert their rights in one or other of five sets of exactly prescribed formal words (Gai. *Inst*. 4. 11 ff.). Three of these sets of words served to initiate a claim and the other two

to obtain execution. Of the former the most general, applicable to claims of ownership and to claims originating in obligations, was the *legis actio sacramento*. This involved in historical times a formal wager between the parties as to the validity of their claims, each party depositing as his stake a fixed sum of money (**sacramentum*). The other forms for initiating a claim were (a) the *legis actio per iudicis arbitrive postulationem*, available only for cases for which it had been specifically authorized by statute; the cases of which we know were claims based on a solemn promise (*stipulatio*) and disputes about property owned by more than one person, but there were apparently others; (b) the *legis actio per condictionem*, introduced by a *lex Silia* and a *lex Calpurnia*, probably in the 3rd cent. BC, for claims for specific sums of money or specific things asserted to be owing by the defendant to the plaintiff. The two forms of *legis actio* for obtaining execution were *per manus iniectionem* and *per pignoris capionem*. By the former the creditor proceeded against the person of the condemned debtor and by the latter against his property.

4. The *legis actio* system had the disadvantage that it was inflexible. In particular it seems that the praetor could neither create new forms of action nor extend the existing *legis actiones* to claims not recognized by the law. These defects were removed by the formulary system. The characteristics of this system were that for each cause of action there was an appropriate form of action, expressed in a set of words or *formula*; and that the praetor had the power to create new *formulae* to meet new needs. The *formula* constituted the pleadings. Thus, if there had been a contract of sale (*emptio venditio*) and the seller refused to deliver what he had sold, the buyer had an action on the purchase (*actio empti*), and conversely if the buyer refused to pay the price, the seller had an action on the sale (*actio venditi*); and each action had an appropriate *formula* in which the issue was defined. But while the *formula* varied from action to action, its structure was based on some permanent essential parts: the *intentio* (concise formulation of the plaintiff's claim) and the *condemnatio*, by which the judge was directed to condemn the defendant if he found after hearing the evidence and the arguments that the plaintiff's case was good, otherwise to acquit him. To suit the complexities of each case the *formula* might be extended by additional clauses, e.g. by a *demonstratio*, which served to determine more precisely the matter at issue where the *intentio* was indefinite (*incerta*), i.e. where the claim was not for a specific sum or thing; or by an *exceptio*, a clause on behalf of the defendant excluding his condemnation if he should prove a fact recognized by the praetor as making such condemnation unjust (e.g. that the plaintiff had been guilty of bad faith: *exceptio doli*; or that the plaintiff had agreed not to sue the defendant: *exceptio pacti*); and the plaintiff might reply to the *exceptio* by a *replicatio* expressing a countervailing plea (e.g. that the defendant had subsequently agreed to waive the agreement not to sue: *replicatio pacti*); and so on. The whole *formula* was framed as a succession of conditional clauses governing an order by the magistrate to the judge to condemn or acquit the defendant. Model *formulae* for all recognized actions, defences, etc. were published with the edict. The principle that each cause of action had its appropriate *formula*, coupled with the power of the praetor to create new *formulae* (or new parts of *formulae*) either generally in the edict or on the facts of a particular case, lay at the root of the law deriving from praetors and other magistrates (*ius honorarium*).

5. All actions, except those intended only to settle a preliminary question (*actiones praeiudiciales*), necessarily led to a *condemnatio* for a money sum. There could therefore be no order for specific performance or for the restitution of a thing, though it was open to the defendant to make such restitution before judgment. In some actions the *condemnatio* was made conditional on the defendant's not having made restitution, the plaintiff being allowed to make his own assessment of the value. In the ordinary case it was for the *iudex* to make the assessment of the amount which the defendant must pay (*litis aestimatio*), whether it was the value of a thing or damages.

6. The origins of the formulary system are obscure. Gaius (*Inst.* 4. 30) says only that the *legis actiones* were replaced by the *formula* by a *lex Aebutia* (probably in the latter part of the 2nd cent. BC) and by two *leges Iuliae* (17/6 BC), but the part played by each of these pieces of legislation is conjectural. It is likely that the *formula* originated well before the *lex Aebutia* in proceedings between **peregrini* (aliens, to whom the *legis actiones* were not open) under the jurisdiction of the *praetor peregrinus* (first created 242 BC), or in the provinces. In either case the proceedings would depend entirely on the *imperium* of the magistrate authorizing them and would therefore be free of the restrictions imposed on suits between citizens by *legis actio*. It is also likely that the *formula* was admitted before the *lex Aebutia* in suits between citizens arising out of the newer, flexible institutions open to citizens and peregrines alike. If this is so, the *lex Aebutia* would for the first time have allowed the formulary procedure as an alternative to the *legis actio* in cases involving the old *ius civile*, and the *leges Iuliae* would have abolished the *legis actiones* altogether, except for proceedings before the centumviral court (see CENTUMVIRI).

7. The actions of the formulary system were derived from that part of the functions of the praetor known as *iurisdictio*. There were, however, other remedies which derived from his **imperium*. They are in form orders issued for the purpose of the administration of justice, but since the praetor generally avoided using direct means of enforcing obedience, disputes concerning these orders might lead to an action which would be tried in the ordinary way. From the point of view of the development of the general law the most important of these orders were the interdicts (*interdicta*). Their object was to give immediate protection to threatened or violated interests of the plaintiff. If the defendant ignored the interdict, or disputed the plaintiff's right to it, a procedural wager would, in the usual case, enable the matter to be litigated by an ordinary action. A variety of private interests were protected in this way, but the most important were possession and the praetorian rights of inheritance created by a grant of possession of a deceased estate (*bonorum possessio*). Interdicts also protected rights of a public character, such as public rights of way.

8. In addition to interdicts, praetorian orders included *missiones in possessionem* and *in integrum restitutiones*. A *missio in possessionem* was an authorization to enter into possession either of a particular thing or of the whole of a person's property, with the purpose of putting pressure on that person, e.g. on the owner of a building to give security against the threat of damage caused by the building to a neighbour (*damnum infectum*), or on a losing defendant to an action to comply with the judgment. An *in integrum restitutio* was an order reversing the consequence of a general rule of law which the praetor considered in the particular case to be inequitable. So a minor (i.e. a person under 25 years of age) could seek *in integrum restitutio* if his inexperience had led him to enter into a disadvantageous transaction, even though he could not show that the other party actually took advantage of his youth.

9. The bringing of an action began with an extra-judicial

summons, *in ius vocatio*, by which the plaintiff personally summoned the defendant to follow him before the magistrate. The Twelve Tables contained detailed provisions governing this summons. The only way of avoiding an immediate appearance before the magistrate (which could be secured by force in case of resistance) was for the summoned party to give a guarantor (*vindex*).

10. The proceedings *in iure* might begin with preliminary questions, such as whether the magistrate had jurisdiction in the matter or whether the parties had the capacity to appear in court. A negative result of this inquiry would result in a rejection of the case (*denegatio actionis*) and an end to the proceedings. Normally, however, the stage *in iure* was devoted to defining the issue. There might be discussions about the composition of the *formula*, especially when the case was not provided for in the edict and the plaintiff tried to obtain the grant of a new *formula* (or a new part of a *formula*, such as an *exceptio*) adapted to the particularities of the case. The proceedings ended with *litis contestatio*. This required the co-operation of the parties, but neither of them could prevent the achievement of this act by repeated refusal. The plaintiff would run the risk of *denegatio actionis* and the defendant of *missio in possessionem*. After *litis contestatio* there could not be another trial of the same issue; and it was with reference to the moment of *litis contestatio* that the judge had to decide controverted matters.

11. The trial took place usually before a single *iudex*, but in some cases before several *recuperatores* or before the *centumviri* or the *decemviri stlitibus iudicandis* (see DECEMVIRI). The *iudex* was bound of course to consider the issues as they were presented in the *formula* and in so doing to apply the law, but otherwise he was uncontrolled and could take what advice he chose. Aulus *Gellius (NA 14. 2) records that, when faced, on his first appointment as a *iudex*, with a difficult decision on a matter of fact, he sought the opinion of *Favorinus, a philosopher. At the end of the hearing the *iudex* was bound to announce his verdict to the parties in accordance with the *condemnatio*, unless he was willing (as Aulus Gellius was on that first occasion) to swear an oath that the matter was not clear to him (*rem sibi non liquere*). In that event the case would be remitted to another *iudex* for a retrial.

12. If the unsuccessful defendant did not carry out the terms of the judgment, the plaintiff could not proceed immediately to execution. He must first bring an action on the judgement (*actio iudicati*). In this action the defendant could not dispute the merits of the judgement, but he might plead that it was invalid, e.g. for want of jurisdiction or defect of form, or that he had already satisfied it. In such a case there would be *litis contestatio* and a trial in the usual way. There were, however, two deterrents to frivolous defences: the defendant had to give security; and, if he lost, he would be condemned in double the amount of the original judgement. If the defendant neither satisfied the judgement nor defended the *actio iudicati*, the magistrate would authorize the plaintiff to proceed either to personal or to real execution. In the latter case the magistrate made a decree putting the creditor in possession of all the debtor's property and there followed what was in effect a bankruptcy.

13. The formulary system was the ordinary procedure of the classical period, but from the time of Augustus there developed beside it various other forms of procedure in particular contexts, which are commonly referred to collectively as *cognitio extraordinaria* or *cognitio extra ordinem* (investigation outside the ordinary procedure of the formulary system). The *princeps* (rarely) or a magistrate or (most commonly) a delegated official conducted the entire trial; there was no division into two stages and no private *iudex*. The process was still, however, a judicial one and the development of a system of appeals served to secure uniformity. The trial had the character more of an investigation than of a hearing of a dispute between adversaries. In this respect it was the forerunner of the procedure which is found on the continent of Europe today.

14. In the republic there was no possibility of appeal, except to the very limited extent that a judgment could be called into question by defending the *actio iudicati*. In the early Principate, however, some appeal to the emperor seems to have been allowed, and in cases dealt with by *cognitio extraordinaria* or *cognitio extra ordinem* where the trial would normally be before a delegated judge, it would be natural to allow an appeal to the person who had made the delegation. Certainly it soon became a regular institution, with the higher court not only quashing the original decision, but substituting its own. The appeal was made orally or in writing (*libelli appellatorii*) to the trial judge, who sent the entire dossier to the higher official, with a written report (*litterae dimissoriae* or *apostoli*). There were penalties for frivolous appeals. Justinian made an extensive reform of the system of appeal and his *Novella* 82 settled the rule that all judgements were appealable, except those of the praetorian prefect (**praefectus praetorio*).

H. F. Jolowicz and B. Nicholas, *Historical Introduction to the Study of Roman Law,* 3rd edn. (1972); M. Kaser, *Das römische Zivilprozessrecht* (1966); G. Pugliese, *Processo civile romano* 1 (1961), 2 / 1 (1963); O. Lenel, *Edictum Perpetuum,* 3rd edn. (1927); P. Collinet, *La Procédure par libelle* (1935), and *La Nature des actions, des interdits et des exceptions dans l'œuvre de Justinien* (1947); R. Orestano, *L'appello civile in diritto romano,* 2nd edn. (1953); J. M. Kelly, *Princeps iudex* (1957), *Roman Litigation* (1966), and *Studies in the Civil Judicature of the Roman Republic* (1976). A. H. J. Greenidge, *The Legal Procedure of Cicero's Time* (1901), is out of date, but still useful. B. N.

3. Criminal law and procedure 1. Criminal law was not originally distinguished from civil law at Rome, as it is in modern legal systems, both by procedure and by the fact that in successful actions judgement is given in favour of the public authority rather than those who have been wronged. Moreover, when this distinction regarding procedure and judgement did come to be made, we find a different categorization of criminal and civil wrongs from those which are normally found in modern systems. *Theft for example was originally treated as a private wrong (delict) pursuable by civil action; only much later did it become usual to bring a criminal prosecution. *Adultery was not originally a matter for a civil suit (in Roman society no ground was needed for a divorce), but later became a crime. It is possible to see a progression from private revenge towards a system where public authority and those acting for the public undertake the pursuit of crimes, but this progression was never complete. We can distinguish phases in this development. In the oldest phase of criminal law we find, side by side with private revenge, the practice of settlements between offended and offender, at first voluntary and sporadic, later obligatory. By the end of this phase the beginnings of a new system can be observed: intervention of the community in punishing some crimes, especially those directed against its own structure or existence. Next, the community takes in its hands the repression of offences, not only those which menace the public order or interest directly, but also those affecting private property or interest. The Twelve Tables represent a combination of the first two phases, while in the advanced republic the intervention of public authority, hitherto exceptional, becomes more and more common. Under the Principate it gains dominance, and under the late empire and Justinian it becomes exclusive, having absorbed nearly the whole field of private criminal law. A survival of the idea of vengeance is found in the *noxae deditio*, the surrender of the wrongdoer (slave or son under *patria potestas*) to the person wronged, though by the late empire this practice was limited, when the surrender of sons was abolished.

2. The Romans did not create an organic body of statutes relating to criminal law. The *Twelve Tables are primarily concerned with civil actions and even in the fragmentary provisions of tables 8 and 9 we find a mosaic of varied penal provisions rather than a code. They were restricted to such criminal matters as interested a primitive peasant community, and therefore were inadequate when the republic became more sophisticated and powerful. The copious legislation of the republic did not solve the problem as these *leges* dealt only with single crimes or groups of crimes. In the late republic it is noticeable that some offences were treated by several *leges* voted within a short period of time, e.g. the *crimen repetundarum* (see REPETUNDAE) or *ambitus*. As *Tacitus (1) later noted (*Ann.* 3. 27), when public affairs were at their worst, there were most laws. The emphasis was on crimes by senators and magistrates, people acting in the public sphere, but elaborate laws were also created against homicide and violence by any person. Some attempt was made under *Sulla to revise comprehensively criminal procedures but the result was no more a systematic treatment or a coherent code than the later legislation of *Caesar, Augustus, and subsequent emperors, however creative this was in particular details. Extensive interpretation of earlier statutes to cover new facts (wherein the senate co-operated as long as it remained active), or modification of penalties in the direction of greater or lesser severity, constitutes all the legislative activity of the empire in substantive criminal law. The procedure *cognitio extra ordinem* or *cognitio extraordinaria*, it is true, caused the introduction of new ideas into the general doctrines of penal law; and imperial constitutions applied some novel conceptions; but all these, being sporadic and exceptional, did not give an impulse to systematic elaboration.

3. The jurists of the 2nd cent. AD—the best period of classical *jurisprudence—contributed to the development of criminal law far less than to that of civil law. A compilation analogous to the *edictum perpetuum* (see EDICT) in civil law would certainly have roused their interest in criminal matters; and it is noticeable how fertile was their contribution to doctrines of private delicts, with which the praetorian edict dealt (cf. the excellent elaboration of *iniuria, Dig.* 47. 10), in comparison with their modest part in public criminal law. The effect of the interpretative work of all these more or less authoritative elements (imperial rescripts and edicts, *senatus consulta*, practice of *cognitio extraordinaria* or *cognitio extra ordinem* (see § 2. 13, 14 above), jurisprudence) was that offences quite different from those which were described and made punishable in republican statutes were subjected to the statutory penalties. The exact terms of the original criminal statute might on occasion become obscure. Thus (*a*) Sulla's *lex Cornelia testamentaria* (*nummaria*, called also *de falsis*), which originally dealt with falsification of wills and of coins, was extended not only to the forgery of documents and the assumption of false names, titles, or official rank, but even to corruption in litigation, as when a juror, accuser, witness, or advocate was bribed, in which case both giver and receiver were punishable. Even a juror who neglected the *constitutions of the emperors was punished according to this statute. (*b*) The *lex Iulia de ambitu* was applied

to cases of pressure exercised on a juror by the accuser or the accused, though the original field of the statute was electoral *corruption. See AMBITUS. Interestingly, there appears in some jurists of the 2nd cent. AD a desire to return to the exact provisions of the original statute, even at the cost of discarding some later case law.

4. Under the late empire criminal legislation is directed more to penalties than to the doctrinal treatment of offences. The punishableness of some delicts varied under the influence of political or religious points of view; the creation of new categories of crimes in this long period is restricted to abduction and offences against the Christian religion after its recognition by the state. The profession of *Christianity had at one time been prosecuted as *crimen maiestatis* (see MAIESTAS). Justinian's legislative compilations show the first endeavour to collect the scattered provisions of public and private criminal law into a systematic whole (see JUSTINIAN'S CODIFICATION). The *Digest*, books 47–9, and *Codex*, book 9, give a well-arranged design of criminal law, procedure, and penalties. The compilers, of course, found some help in works of the latest classical jurists, who in just appreciation of the difficulties created by this fluctuating and uncertain state of criminal legislation dealt with these matters in monographs: *De iudiciis publicis* (*Marcianus, Macer, *Paulus), *De poenis* (Paulus, Claudius (or Venuleius) Saturninus, Modestinus), *De cognitionibus* (*Callistratus (4)). But all these and similar works, though doubtless meritorious and useful, aimed rather at collecting material than at creative criticism or presentation of new ideas. Even the terminology distinguishing different categories of offences does not show that stability and precision which is so excellent a feature of Roman legal language. The terms most used are *crimen, delictum, maleficium*; but it can hardly be affirmed that these expressions had a particular exclusive sense, though generally *crimen* indicates more serious offences directed against the state or public order, whilst *delictum* is rather used for delicts against private property or personal integrity and of no great harmfulness. The meaning of *maleficium* as a general term is even less technical, especially as it was used for designating sorcery and magic arts. All endeavours to bring order into classical texts by allotting to these terms an exclusive technical sense and removing all inconvenient texts as interpolated break down because of the indiscriminate use of these terms.

5. For the distinction between public and private offences we likewise lack any precise definition or statement of distinguishing marks; and yet it was of fundamental importance for developed Roman criminal law. This distinction rested upon a practical, rather than a doctrinal, differentiation of offended interests, and found its visible consequences in the fields of procedure and penalties, which differed greatly in the two spheres. The Roman jurists dealt more with the distinction between *iudicia publica* and private *actiones poenales* than with that between the interests violated as public or private, and the post-classical and Justinianic classification into *delicta privata, crimina extraordinaria*, and *iudicia publica* (Rubric to Digest 47. 1, 47. 11, 48. 1) was also made from a procedural point of view.

6. The private delicts form a group apart: the wrongdoer is exposed to an action under the ordinary civil procedure by the person wronged, the effect of which is that he must pay a pecuniary penalty to the plaintiff (to be distinguished from another *actio* by which the restitution of the *res* or compensation is claimed— *rei persecutio*). The state as such did not show any interest in the prosecution of these offences, except where the offender was a magistrate or other official (*repetundae*), but the proceedings had

a punitive character. By contrast with other civil proceedings (i.e. for *rei persecutio*) they did not lie against the heir if the wrongdoer died before he had been sued, and each of several wrongdoers was liable for the whole penalty. The principal forms were theft (*furtum*); robbery (*rapina*, theft combined with violence); damage to property (**damnum iniuria datum*); assault, and in general all affronts to the plaintiff's dignity and personality (**iniuria*). The praetor also made other wrongs actionable, such as threats (*metus*), deceit (*dolus*), malicious corruption of other people's slaves, and the like. Praetorian law also introduced a category of actions for misdemeanours which affected public interest, e.g. damage to the **album* of magistrates, violation of sepulchres, and pouring liquids or throwing things out into the streets. In such cases anyone, *quivis ex populo* (hence the names *actiones populares*), could be plaintiff and claim the penalty. Proceedings for private delicts were in later times greatly restricted in favour of the criminal *cognitio extra ordinem* or *cognitio extraordinaria*.

7. The special domain of criminal law is, however, the second group of crimes prosecuted by public organs in *iudicia publica*. The oldest law knew the intervention of the state, as avenger of offences against its security or against public order, only in exceptional cases such as treason (**perduellio*), desertion to the enemy, or special forms of murder (**parricidium*). For the evolution of this group the series of criminal *leges* of the last two centuries of the republic (especially the *Corneliae* and *Iuliae*, i.e. those of Sulla and Caesar) were of the greatest importance. They instituted special criminal courts for particular crimes, extending in large measure the competence of the state to the prosecution and punishment of criminal acts. A survey of the various kinds of crimes allotted to the **quaestiones perpetuae* shows that they comprehended not only offences against the state, its security, and organization, or public order in the widest sense of the word, but also the more serious offences against life, personal integrity, private interests (falsification of wills and documents, serious injuries), and morality (adultery).

8. However, even with the help of the senate, imperial constitutions, and the jurists, this legislation covered only part of the offences needing repression. Furthermore, the *quaestiones* operated only at Rome and tried Roman citizens only (not women or slaves or *peregrini*). Under Augustus we find in Cyrene trials of **peregrini* by panels of jurors (see CYRENE, EDICTS OF), but we cannot assume that this practice was widespread in the provinces and normally criminal jurisdiction would have been a matter for the provincial governor or his legate. A solution was found for these and other problems with the development of the procedure called *cognitio extra ordinem* or *extraordinaria*, as not being subordinated to the *ordo iudiciorum*. The trials in these *iudicia publica extra ordinem* were always conducted by public officials. Jurisdiction was exercised—apart from political offences and senatorial matters reserved for the senate—chiefly by the emperor and the prefects and in particular provinces by *praesides* and procurators as the emperor's delegates (see PROCURATOR). The sphere of *cognitio extra ordinem* became, thanks to imperial policy, more and more extensive and superseded the *quaestiones*, which are not mentioned after M. **Aurelius Severus Alexander. On the strength of new legislative provisions new forms of offences arose (called later *crimina extraordinaria*), e.g. fraud (*stellionatus*), participation in illicit corporations, displacing of boundary stones, special types of theft (*fures balnearii, nocturni*). Whilst in *quaestiones* only the penalty laid down by the statute could be pronounced, the imperial judges had discretion in grading the penalty according to their appreciation of all the facts of the case. Moreover, penalties might

vary according to the status (free / slave, man / woman) or rank of the convicted person: in particular, by the early 2nd cent. AD poorer citizens and others of low rank came to be punished more severely than those of higher rank. The increase in the discretion of magistrates during the 3rd and 4th cents. AD made the accused more vulnerable to arbitrary severity. See HONESTIORES

9. From the earliest times the intention of the wrongdoer was taken into consideration; even the legendary law of **Numa on parricide required that the murderer had acted knowingly with malice (*sciens dolo*); the analogous expression in republican laws was *sciens dolo malo*. More adequate differentiation between different states of mind was developed in the practice of the *cognitio extra ordinem* or *extraordinaria*, influenced also by imperial constitutions. In appreciating the atrocity of the act and depravity of its author the judge considered the intensity and persistence of the delinquent's will (*dolus*), the question of whether the act had been committed with premeditation or on sudden impulse, whether it had been provoked by a moral offence (e.g. murder of an adulterous wife when caught in the act) or was due to drunkenness ('*per vinum*'). A late classical jurist, Claudius Saturninus, known only by a treatise on penalties, distinguished seven points to be taken into consideration in determining the punishment: reason, person, place, time, quality, quantity, and effect (*Dig.* 48. 19. 16). Judicial liberty, however, gave occasion for arbitrariness: the 3rd cent., with the decline of imperial authority, brought anarchy into criminal jurisdiction. Under the late empire fixed penalties—now more severe than formerly—were restored, the discretion of the judge in the infliction of punishment having been abolished.

10. The magistrates invested with *imperium*, acting personally or by delegates, were in general the organs of criminal justice. From early times their power of punishment was restricted by **provocatio ad populum* (appeal to the people), which on one view required a judgement by an assembly, on another view, encouraged but did not compel a reference to an assembly, and on a third only applied when there had been no formal trial, that is, when the magistrate applied coercive measures against disobedient or recalcitrant citizens, e.g. **prison, castigation, and fines (*multae*). Foreigners, slaves (see SLAVERY), and **women were also subjected to this kind of coercion, but had no redress. There were two fundamentally different forms of procedure under the republic, trial before the assembly (the so-called *iudicium populi*) and *quaestio* (tribunal of inquiry). Both were originally based on the inquisitorial principle: before an assembly the magistrate for the most part acted both as prosecutor and president of the assembly simultaneously; in the early *quaestiones* he, aided by a *consilium* of advisers, decided whether an accusation laid before him required investigation, controlled the investigation and production of evidence, and ultimately delivered a verdict and sentence. However, the latter procedure was modified when *quaestiones perpetuae* were set up by statute in the 2nd and 1st cents. BC. In these the investigation of crimes and production of evidence was a matter for the plaintiff or prosecutor; the selection of a jury was regulated by the relevant statute and both plaintiff and defendant had rights of rejection. At the trial itself, although the presiding magistrate might ask questions, procedure was adversarial, the verdict was determined by the jury, and the sentence was either fixed by the statute or a limited discretion was allowed to the jury, especially with financial penalties (*litis aestimatio*). This accusatory system was, however, abolished in trials *extra ordinem* or *extraordinaria*, where, once information had been laid about a crime, the magistrate had once more full

initiative in prosecution and conducted the trial from beginning to end. The statutes establishing the *quaestiones* had specifically ruled out any appeal to another authority against verdict or sentence. An unsuccessful proposal was made by Mark Antony (M. *Antonius (2)) to introduce appeal to the assembly from certain *quaestiones*, but the situation only changed decisively with the advent of the Principate. Augustus' tribunician power (see TRIBUNI PLEBIS) was associated with the right to hear appeals and a prerogative of mercy (according to Cass. Dio, this grant was made in 30 BC). Moreover, the *lex Iulia de vi publica* incorporated sanctions against the disregard of appeals by those subject to coercion or criminal sentences throughout the empire.

11. The Roman penal system was peculiar in its distinction between public and private penalties, reflecting the division into public and private offences. The private penalty seems originally a substitute for private vengeance and retaliation (*talio* = infliction on the delinquent of the same injury as that done by him), but pecuniary composition between the parties (*pacisci*) was already an option at the time of the Twelve Tables and later became compulsory. A private penalty consisted in payment of a sum of money to the person wronged, and is to be distinguished from *multa*, a fine inflicted by a magistrate and paid to the state. Public penalties originated, as in other primitive systems, in the idea of public revenge, or religious expiation for crimes against the community, or religious conceptions ('sacer esto'), and, for serious offences, entailed the elimination of the guilty person from the community. The death penalty (*poena capitis*) was inflicted in different ways. The Twelve Tables refer to burning, for arson, and suspension (perhaps a form of *crucifixion) for using magic on crops. We later hear of decapitation, precipitation from the *Tarpeian Rock, and drowning in a sack (for parricide). It should not be thought that the more grotesque penalties were all primitive. In republican times the execution (and even the sentence) could be avoided by voluntary *exile of the wrongdoer. Banishment was later applied as an independent penalty in various forms: *aqua et igni interdictio*, *relegation, *deportatio*. Under the empire we find condemnation to heavy work in mines (*metalla*) or public works (*opus publicum*) or to the gladiatorial training-schools (*in ludos*). These penalties were normally combined with loss of citizenship, while *damnatio in metalla* ('condemnation to the mines', considered as the penalty closest to death) normally also involved loss of liberty and flagellation; an accessory penalty was the total or partial confiscation of property. Execution might take the form of exposure to wild beasts in the arena (see VENATIONES). It is noticeable that the Romans applied imprisonment only as a coercive or preventive measure, not as a penalty (see PRISON); the Roman conception of penalty laid more stress upon its vindictive and deterrent nature than on correction of the delinquent (see PUNISHMENT (GREEK AND ROMAN PRACTICE)). The advent of Christianity led to some changes in the modalities of punishments but did not mitigate their severity.

Mommsen, *Röm. Strafr.*; W. Kunkel, *Untersuchungen zur Entwicklung des röm. Kriminalverfahrens in vorsullanischer Zeit* (1962); J. A. Crook, *Law and Life of Rome* (1967).   A. B.; B. N.; A. W. L.

law in Greece Modern work on this subject is conditioned by two important considerations. In the first place, it is Rome and not Greece which dominates European legal history: indeed, because the Greek world produced no jurists, its law is perhaps best studied not as a source of juridical principles but rather as a way of understanding how particular ancient societies perceived

and regulated themselves. The second constraint is the distribution of our sources, which are rich but geographically and temporally very patchy.

Classical Athenian law (see LAW AND PROCEDURE, ATHENIAN) is well documented from the Attic Orators (*c*.420–320 BC): over 100 lawcourt speeches survive, though we rarely hear the result or even the opponent's case, and our manuscripts do not usually preserve the texts of witnesses' statements or legal statutes. Further information, particularly about judicial procedure, can be gleaned from Athenian comedy (especially *Aristophanes (1)'s *Wasps*) and from the Aristotelian *Athenaion Politeia* (esp. §§ 63–9); anecdotes in the philosophers or historians occasionally presuppose points of law; and the Athenian habit of recording public decisions on stone has left large numbers of texts, though few of these are strictly legislative (see EPIGRAPHY, GREEK).

The other significant body of evidence comprises private documents written on papyrus (see PAPYROLOGY, GREEK). Papyrus was widely used throughout classical antiquity, but for climatic reasons virtually none survives except in Egypt, where Greek was the dominant language of administration under Ptolemaic and Roman rule (*c*.320 BC–*c*. AD 630). The range of these texts is vast (wills, letters, agreements, etc.), and though often fragmentary, they give us an unparalleled picture of law operating at ground level.

Otherwise we have only scattered data. Even for such an important *polis as *Sparta we rely on chance remarks in *Aristotle and *Plutarch about inheritance, or incidental details in historians about the trials of particular kings. The loss of *Theophrastus' *Laws* is keenly felt: surviving fragments suggest that this was a comparative study after the manner of *Aristotle's *Politics*, which might have filled many gaps in our knowledge. The study of non-Athenian inscriptions may eventually offer a comparative understanding of judicial procedure throughout the Greek world; but it is an indication of our present ignorance that the Cretan city of *Gortyn has the best-known legal system outside Athens and Egypt because of the chance survival of one extensive inscription, the so-called Gortyn code.

Origins The origins of law in Greece are important but hard to distinguish. There are traces of dispute settlement in the earliest surviving literary works (*c*.725–700 BC), most notably *Homer's depiction of a homicide trial on the Shield of *Achilles (*Iliad* 18. 497–508), while *Hesiod's *Works and Days* involves an inheritance dispute between the poet and his (possibly fictitious) brother. It has been argued that the Shield represents a process of voluntary *arbitration which by Hesiod's time has become compulsory, but this seems unlikely, given that Hesiod's aristocrats-cum-judges appear politically weaker than their Homeric counterparts. Better perhaps is the suggestion that Homer's judges are not arbitrators: rather, what they hear is the killer taking the initiative in claiming the protection of their community against the threat of summary vengeance from his victim's relatives. But such individual literary portrayals cannot be permitted to sustain theories of legal evolution.

The earliest signs of legislation in the Greek world belong around 600 BC. This is the period in which later Greeks located the activity of semi-mythical legislators in widely spread Greek communities (*Zaleucus at *Locri Epizephyrii in southern Italy, *Charondas at *Catana in Sicily, *Draco and *Solon at Athens). It also provides the context for the earliest surviving public inscriptions: fragmentary laws (mostly regulating judicial procedure and the holding of public office) from Dreros in *Crete shortly before 600 (ML 2) and from *Chios, *Eretria, and near *Naupactus over the following century. The joint phenomenon of legislators and inscribed laws invites explanation, but traditional hypotheses appear unsatisfactory: places like Locri and Catana seem remote from near eastern influence, but few of the affected communities were colonies; the needs of *traders do not seem to have concerned the early legislators, while the idea that publication of law is a move towards open government rests on anachronistic assumptions about the nature and spread of writing. See LITERACY; ORALITY. A recent suggestion, indeed, sees writing as a new technology seeking a function, but this may ignore an apparent time-lag between its introduction in private contexts and the subsequent decision to use it for inscribing laws.

Unity Whether it is legitimate to speak of Greek law as a single entity is a long-disputed question. Scholars working on the papyri generally look for unity where those studying the orators perceive diversity; and German and Italian scholars tend to emphasize broad juristic principles held throughout the Greek world, at the cost (in the view of their Anglo-American counterparts) of ignoring real and major differences of detail.

There are underlying problems of *ethnicity, *nationalism, and evolution. What does it mean to be Greek? How far is Greekness a racial, cultural, or linguistic identity, and how strong is its political significance? Herodotus' Athenians (8. 144), admittedly, can appeal to the shared customs which distinguish Greeks from barbarians (non-Greeks). Classical *poleis*, however, were independent communities, each with its own political system and the jealously guarded right to make its own laws (see AUTONOMY; POLIS). Even in the Hellenistic period the Greek world was never a nation-state, and it is anachronistic to assume that the *poleis* were aiming towards a goal of political unity.

The dispute is significant because of its consequences. Evolutionary theories misleadingly imply that Gortyn represents a stage through which every Greek community passed on its road from Homeric dispute settlement to the law of the orators; they also encourage gap-filling, such that regulations attested only at Athens are predicated of the papyri and vice versa. Greek law, if it existed, was not a national legal system, but a family of systems like Islamic law today. See ARBITRATION; JUDGES, FOREIGN.

M. I. Finley, *Use and Abuse of History* (1975), ch. 8; M. Gagarin, *Early Greek Law* (1986); H. J. Wolff, *Enc. Brit.* 8[15]. 398–402; L. Foxhall and A. Lewis (eds.), *Greek Law in its Political Setting* (1996). S. C. T.

law of nature embodies the belief that there are certain principles or institutions which are so rooted in 'nature' that they are of universal validity. *Aristotle divided law into that which was natural and that which was man-made, the former being the same everywhere and equally valid everywhere. This idea became a commonplace, especially among the Stoics (see STOICISM), and is frequently echoed by *Cicero. For him, as for Aristotle, the fact that a principle is found everywhere is a proof of its naturalness and therefore of its validity. This leads to the identification, both by Cicero and by *Gaius (2), of natural law with *ius gentium. This is strictly a confusion of thought, since natural law is law which ought to be universally applied and *ius gentium* is law which is in fact so applied, but the jurists did not concern themselves with this distinction. For them the philosophical natural law is no more than an ornament, carrying no suggestion that an inconsistent man-made law might be invalid. Only in the case of *slavery did Gaius remark that according to natural law all men were born free, but by the *ius gentium* they might be slaves.

*Ulpian seems to have given natural law a different meaning. For he equates it with the instincts which humans share with animals. The prominent position of this text in Justinian's *Institutes* and *Digest* (see JUSTINIAN'S CODIFICATION) gave it an undeserved influence in later thought.

When the jurists invoke the idea of 'nature', as they often do, it is usually in the much more imprecise sense of what seemed to follow from the physical quality of men or things. Thus the 'natural' way of transferring ownership of a physical thing is to hand it over, by contrast with the rule of the *ius civile* that *mancipatio* was necessary for the transfer of ownership of *res mancipi*. Similarly 'natural reason' as the source or justification of an institution is hardly more than common sense or 'what stands to reason'.

E. Levy, *Gesammelte Schriften* (2 vols.; 1963), 1 (= *CPhil.* 1943 = *Studia et documenta historiae et iuris* 1949); C. A. Maschi, *La concezione naturalistica del diritto e degli istituti giuridici romani* (1937); and see bibliog. under IUS GENTIUM. B. N.

lawyers, Roman or jurists (*iuris prudentes, iuris consulti, iuris periti, iuris studiosi*) were a specialized professional group in Roman society (see LAW, ROMAN, SOCIOLOGY OF) distinct from those humble clerks and notaries who copied documents and recorded proceedings. That society was unusual in that in the later republic and empire there emerged for the first time in history a class of secular legal experts who, whether they made a living from their profession or not, were regarded as the repositories of a special type of learning useful to the state and private citizens. Until the 3rd cent. BC knowledge of the law and its procedure was a monopoly of the patrician priesthood, the college of *pontifices, whose advice was sought on the law of the state cult but also on secular forms. From then on (see CORUNCANIUS, TI.; FLAVIUS, CN.) some who were not members of the priestly college began to give advice on law; but until the end of the republic the same people were often expert in sacred, public, and private law. Their functions resembled those of modern lawyers. They gave opinions to people who consulted them (*respondere*), helped them to draft documents or take other measures to avoid legal pitfalls (*cavere*), and advised on litigation and its proper forms (*agere*). They were consulted by magistrates such as the urban praetor on the formulation of his edict and by lay judges (*iudices*) on the law they should apply in the cases before them (see IUDEX). They taught mainly by allowing others to listen to them as they practised, but sometimes actively undertook to instruct pupils. Some lawyers wrote books (see LEGAL LITERATURE), but this was not essential. In principle their services were free, but they were not forbidden to accept gifts from those who consulted or were taught by them, though unlike other professionals such as surveyors and doctors there was even in the empire no procedure by which they could sue for a fee (*honorarium*).

In the republic and early empire the number of lawyers was small. Membership of this élite group of intellectuals depended on being taught by another member and enjoying a sufficient regard from the group as a whole for one's independence of judgement and depth of learning. It continued, even in the empire, to depend on professional opinion and not on official recognition or employment, valuable as the latter might be for the success of the lawyer's career. Legal expertise often ran in families (see ANTISTIUS LABEO, M.; IUVENTIUS CELSUS; MUCIUS SCAEVOLA (2), Q.; NERATIUS PRISCUS, L.). The existence of such a small, intimate body of specialists explains why in their writings lawyers so often cite one another's opinions. They aim to convince other lawyers. *Advocacy was not in the republic and early empire a normal part of a lawyer's career, rhetoric being a separate discipline, but was not ruled out. In the republic and early empire lawyers often came from senatorial families but legal expertise could also be the avenue by which 'new men' (see NOVUS HOMO) rose in the world, as with *Alfenus Varus, *Pegasus, the father of *Celsus, and *Javolenus Priscus. Lawyers often held public office, but C. *Aquillius Gallus and M. *Antistius Labeo set the precedent of preferring practice or scholarship to public life.

As a prestigious non-political group the legal profession presented Augustus with a problem since it comprised, for example, not only his supporter C. *Trebatius Testa but the latter's republican pupil Labeo. He declined to bring the profession directly under his own control (*Res gestae* 6) but devised a system by which certain lawyers were granted the privilege of giving opinions publicly on his authority (*ius respondendi ex auctoritate principis*). *Tiberius gave the first such grant to a non-senator, *Masurius Sabinus. The practical working of this scheme is obscure, since in general neither grants nor refusals of the privilege are recorded. In the middle of the 1st cent. AD another division occurred in the profession, the leading lawyers grouping themselves into two schools. The Cassian school was founded by C. *Cassius Longinus (2) with the help of his teacher Sabinus; a century later its members came to be called Sabinians. Though the matter is controversial, the Proculian school (see PROCULUS) seems to have differed from its rivals in outlook and method, and these differences, though not the organization into schools, went back to C. *Ateius Capito (2) and Antistius Labeo. The Proculians were less tied to tradition and more insistent on logical rigour than their rivals, the Cassians readier to tolerate anomalies and tackle new problems piecemeal. Sextus *Pomponius records the succession of the heads of the two schools well into the 2nd cent. AD, each school at that stage having two or more heads. Around 160 *Gaius (2) still speaks of 'Sabinus and Cassius and our other teachers'.

Early in the 2nd cent. *Hadrian made some important changes. He ruled that the opinions of privileged lawyers, when in agreement, bound judges, and is said to have discouraged applications for the privilege by senators who were not professionally expert. More important, he reorganized the imperial administration in a way which offered a well-paid career structure to Romans of equestrian status (see EQUITES), who henceforth were to replace *freedmen as heads of the imperial offices. Of these the office of petitions (*libelli*) was held by a lawyer at the latest from *Antoninus Pius onwards. Marcus *Aurelius made the holder of this office, the secretary *a libellis* (later *magister libellorum*), registrar of the emperor's court. Equestrian lawyers could now aspire even to the highest imperial post, that of praetorian prefect, as in the case of Taruttienus Paternus in the reign of Marcus Aurelius, *Papinianus, probably *Paulus, and *Ulpian and *Hermogenianus. These opportunities attracted men of talent to the imperial service and, under an emperor committed to government according to law, created an influential group of lawyers holding public office. This in turn increased the demand for formal law teaching; there now emerge prominent teachers and writers such as *Gaius (2) and Sextus Pomponius who did not practice. In the east law teaching in *Berytus (mod. Beirut) goes back to the late 2nd or early 3rd cent. and the city remained an important centre of legal study from then onwards.

Around 200 *Septimius Severus, keenly interested in the administration of justice, created more posts for lawyers, and

the new Roman citizens enfranchised by Caracalla in 212 (see CONSTITUTION, ANTONINE) swelled the demand for legal advice, especially in the provinces. In the later empire the number of lawyers in official posts again increased, as the number of emperors, praetorian prefects, their deputies (vicars), and provincial officials who needed legal advice multiplied. But though *Diocletian attracted able lawyers to his service, *Constantine I kept them at a distance, and for two generations none is known to have risen to high public office. Then in the late 4th and early 5th cent. they again began to do so. The career structure now ran from law school through practice as an advocate or a post as assessor to an official, and service to one or more of the offices of state (*scrinia*) to the quaestorship (see QUAESTOR; also ANTIOCHUS (13) CHUZON; TRIBONIANUS). In some cases such as that of Antiochus it ended with a praetorian prefecture, as with his predecessors two hundred years earlier.

In the west the legal profession along with the administration as a whole was disrupted by the 5th-cent. invasions of the *Goths and others. In the east it was subjected to extensive state control. In 425 *Theodosius (3) II (see THEODOSIAN CODE) reorganized higher education including law teaching in *Constantinople. He divided public from private teaching, allocating public space to only two law professors, who were forbidden to take private pupils. From 460 a candidate wishing to practise before the court of the praetorian prefect of the east needed to produce a certificate from his law teachers. The number of lawyers at the various bars was now fixed, and preference in filling vacancies was given to the sons of existing advocates. Justinian had thus a considerable pool of talent to draw on for his codification (see JUSTINIAN'S CODIFICATION).

That codification was the work of a self-conscious legal élite, inheriting a tradition which, despite the growth of state control, went back in an unbroken line to the republic. Its impact on Roman public life naturally varied from time to time according to the sympathies of different emperors and the felt need to give high priority to civil administration and hence to insist on the legal values of clarity, precision, impartiality, and conformity to rule.

For details of individual lawyers see the special articles under their names. See also LAW, ROMAN, SOCIOLOGY OF.

Wieacker, *RRG* 1. 519–675, *RRG* 2, and *Vom römischen Recht*, 2nd edn. (1961), 128–60; Kunkel 1967; P. Stein, *Cambridge Law Journal* 1972, 8–31, and *Bullettino dell'istituto di diritto romano* 1978, 55–68; D. Nörr, *Rechtskritik in der römischen Antike* (1974); D. Liebs, *ANRW* 2. 15 (1976), 197–286, 288–362, *Jurisprudenz* 1988, and *Sav. Zeitschr.* 1989, 210–47; O. Behrends, *Index* 1983/4, 189–225; B. W. Frier, *The Rise of the Roman Jurists: Studies in Cicero's Pro Caecina* (1985).   T. Hon.

lead is mined in part for the extraction of *silver from its ores. Some of the major sources in the Greek world were located at *Laurium in *Attica, on *Siphnos, and in *Macedonia. There were extensive workings in Anatolia (see ASIA MINOR). In the western Mediterranean, lead was mined on *Sardinia and in Etruria (see ETRUSCANS). Roman extraction took place in *Spain, *Gaul, and *Britain. Stamped lead 'pigs' show that lead was being extracted from the Mendips shortly after the Roman invasion of Britain (*CIL* 7. 1201). In the late empire lead mines were operating in the Balkans. Lead isotope analysis has allowed different sources to be identified. Thus lead from Archaic deposits in Laconia, as well as traces identified in Roman skeletal material from Britain, can be traced back to Laurium.

Buildings associated with the extraction of silver from the argentiferous lead ore have been excavated at Laurium. Litharge (the by-product of this process) has been found in protogeometric and even bronze age contexts. In the Greek world lead was used to form the core of bronze handles, to fix steles to their bases, and for small offerings (such as those found in the sanctuary of *Artemis Orthia at *Sparta). In the Roman period lead was used for water pipes. It was extensively used for desilvering pyritical ores and for alloying with copper to save *tin, both processes being known in pre-Roman times. The addition of lead to the alloy simplifies the cold-working. Lead was combined with tin to make pewter. See METALLURGY; MINES AND MINING.

C. E. Conophagos, *Le Laurium antique* (1980); W. Gowland, *Archaeologia* 1917–18, 121 ff.; M. Besnier, *Rev. Arch.* 1919, 31; 1920, 211; 1921, 40; G. C. Whittick, *JRS* 1931, 256 ff. (for 'pigs'); O. Davies, *Roman Mines in Europe* (1935); Forbes, *Stud. Anc. Technol.* 8^2 193 ff.; W. G. Cavanagh and R. R. Laxton, *BSA* 1984, 23 ff. (for lead figurines). For scientific analysis: R. H. Brill and J. M. Wampler, *AJArch.* 1967, 63 ff.; R. H. Brill, *Phil. Trans. Roy. Soc. Lond.* A 269 (1970), 143 ff. O. D.; D. W. J. G.

leagues See FEDERAL STATES; and under particular leagues.

leases, agricultural Farming of land under some sort of tenancy arrangement goes back to a time before our historical records begin. Problems with private tenancy agreements may underlie the 'Solonian crisis' (see SOLON), and the leasing out of their lots by the cleruchs (see CLERUCHY) sent to *Salamis (1) at the end of the 6th cent. BC was restricted (ML 14). In Classical Athens leasing could be officially arranged by the archon (see ARCHONTES) for orphan estates, and it is likely that this led to quite large areas of private land being leased, but there is not much evidence for details of private land-leasing arrangements, at Athens or elsewhere in Greece. By contrast, there is abundant Classical and Hellenistic evidence for the leasing out of lands owned by corporate bodies, particularly religious groups (see CLUBS). The most interesting Greek leases from the agricultural point of view are the leases, mainly of 4th-cent. date, which prescribe the agricultural regime. They insist on regular ploughing, digging round vines and olives, application of manure, biennial fallow, in some cases with a pulse crop sown in fallow years, and forbid removal of wood, manure, and topsoil (e.g. *Syll.*^{3} 963). See AGRICULTURE, GREEK.

At Rome, M. *Porcius Cato (1) is already familiar with detailed lease agreements, but it seems likely from the evidence of *Columella and *Pliny the Younger that private land leasing became increasingly common. Leasing conditions varied from one part of the empire to another, but short leases (of five years), and leasing of land in small parcels, seems to have been normal, with the landowner often providing tools and even slaves. Share-cropping arrangements are known from Italy and Egypt and seem to have been common in Africa where they were one way of encouraging tenants of imperial estates to bring land into cultivation. The *Digest*, papyrus-archives from Egypt, and inscriptions from North Africa offer a wealth of detailed information. See EMPHYTEUSIS.

R. Osborne, *Chiron* 1988, 279–323; W. Heitland, *Agricola* (1921), 252–7, 342–76; M. I. Finley (ed.), *Studies in Roman Property* (1976), 35–70, 103–22. R. G. O.

Lebadea See TROPHONIUS.

Lechaeum, northern/western port of *Corinth on the Corinthian Gulf, more important than *Cenchreae since Corinthian interests were concentrated in the west. There is no natural harbour: two artificial basins were excavated c.600 BC. Long Walls were built from Corinth c.450 (cf. LONG WALLS (Athens)). During

the *Corinthian War, Spartans were admitted to the Long Walls by treachery; Lechaeum was captured, and Corinthian exiles used it as a base for raids on the rest of Corinthian territory. The establishment of the Roman *colonia* of Corinth in 44 BC triggered further development of the harbour, now linked to Corinth's forum by a paved street (1st cent. AD). The only major excavations on the site have revealed a huge *basilica of the 5th cent. AD.

RE Suppl. 5, 'Lechaion'; J. B. Salmon, *Wealthy Corinth* (1984); J. Wiseman, *The Land of the Ancient Corinthians* (1978). J. B. S.

lectisternium, a Roman version of Greek *klinē* and *theoxenia, a banquet for gods whose images were placed on a cushioned couch or couches (*lectus*, *pulvinar*). The ceremony (supervised by priests but also involving public participation) was meant to propitiate gods and repel pestilence or enemy. It was first celebrated in 399 BC at the behest of the Sibylline books (see SIBYL) for *Apollo, Latona, *Hercules, *Diana, *Mercury, and *Neptune (Livy 5. 13. 4–8; Dion. Hal. *Ant. Rom.* 12. 9), later for *Iuventas, *Juno, *Saturnus, Magna Mater (see CYBELE), and (in 217) the twelve great gods. In private cult *lectisternia* are attested in connection with birth rites (Varro in Serv. on *Aen.* 10. 76).

M. Nouilhan, in A.-F. Laurens (ed.), *Entre hommes et dieux* (1989), 27 ff.; T. Köves-Zulauf, *Römische Geburtsriten* (1990). J. L.

Leda, mother of the *Dioscuri (Castor and Pollux/Polydeuces) and *Helen (as well as *Clytemnestra and the minor figures Timandra and Phylonoe), wife of *Tyndareos, daughter of King Thestius of *Pleuron (Aetolia). She is a mythic not a cult figure. Genealogically, she supports the linking of the Tyndarids with *Aetolia, as found in the earliest genealogical authors (Hes. *Cat.* fr. 23a M–W; *Asius in Paus. 3. 13. 8; see GENEALOGY) and reinforced by the hero-shrine of the eponym Pleuron in *Sparta (Paus. ibid.). Most striking is the myth that *Zeus in the form of a swan copulated with Leda, who subsequently produced an egg containing Helen (Eur. *Hel.* 17 ff., 257–9) and Polydeuces (Apollod. 3. 10. 7), an egg displayed in Sparta (Paus. 3. 16. 1). Castor, thus the mortal twin, was born to Tyndareos on the same night. In a different version, stemming from the cult of *Nemesis at *Rhamnus (*Attica) and its local Helen, Nemesis transforms herself to escape Zeus and finally in the form of a goose is fertilized by Zeus in the form of a swan (in the *Cypria* fr. 7 Davies, *EGF*); Leda only finds the egg, or has it brought to her.

Egg births are not unfamiliar in mythologies, but generally give rise to the world or to mankind (Stith Thompson, A 1222). The Orphic god (see ORPHISM) Phanes emerged from an egg, and in Egypt the earth-god Geb, whose attribute is the goose, laid the cosmic egg. The story is rather out of place in Greek mythology and might seem specially incredible (Eur. *Hel.* 257–9, or *Cratinus in his comedy *Nemesis*, Edmonds, *FAC* 1, frs. 107–10).

For art Leda offered an exotic theme: Leda and the swan, or even Leda discovering the egg. From the Attic vase-painter Exekias on she was available to accompany the Return of the Tyndarids.

S. Eitrem, *RE* 12. 1116–25; L. Kahil and others, *LIMC* 6 (1992), 231–46. K. D.

Lefkandi, a coastal site (ancient name unknown) in *Euboea between *Chalcis and *Eretria. Inhabited from the early bronze age until its desertion c.700 BC, perhaps following the Lelantine War (see GREECE, HISTORY, archaic age), it flourished in the late Helladic IIIC period. During the Dark Ages Lefkandi was an important centre in a region uniting *Euboea, *Thessaly, east central Greece, and *Scyros. Cemeteries spanning the 11th to

9th cents. have revealed significant wealth and, from *c*.950 BC, abundant evidence for contact with *Cyprus and the Levant. A unique, massive apsidal building (almost 50 × 14 m. (164 × 46 ft.); *c*.1000 BC), with external and internal colonnades supporting a steep raking roof, represents a new form of monumental architecture following the end of the bronze age and prefigures Greek temple design. Inside the central hall were buried a man and woman, and four horses: woman and horses had apparently been killed in a chieftain's funeral ceremony. After a short life the building was demolished and covered with a mound. Whether it served as a chieftain's house, destroyed following his burial inside, or as a cult-place erected over a heroic warrior's tomb (see HERO-CULT), is debated.

M. R. Popham and others, *Excavations at Lefkandi, Euboea, 1964–66* (1968); M. R. Popham, *Lefkandi* 1 (1979–   ); *BSA* 1982, 213 ff.; *Arch. Rep.* 1988–9, 117 ff.   R. W. V. C.

legal literature refers to those works of *lawyers which in their treatment of legal matters went beyond mere collections of laws and formulae. Legal literature was the most specifically Roman branch of Latin literature, and until the Byzantine age nearly all works on law were in Latin, which remained the language of legislation in the east until AD 535. But they can only be understood in the light of those Greek genres which were imitated in Rome. They were for the most part written in plain but technically accurate language. They consisted of one or more books (*libri*), generally of 10,000–15,000 words each, divided into titles each with a rubric and often numbered. We depend for their early history mainly on the account given by Sextus *Pomponius. About 300 BC Appius *Claudius Caecus is said to have written a book *De usurpationibus* ('On Interruption of Title'). A century later Sextus *Aelius Paetus besides publishing laws and formulae wrote on the interpretation of the *Twelve Tables. Later in the 2nd cent. BC a number of writers are mentioned, some influenced by Greek philosophy and dialectics. One influential work was M. Iunius Brutus' three books (*libri*) in dialogue form *De iure civili* ('On Civil Law'). In the next century Q. *Mucius Scaevola (2)'s eighteen books on the same topic became the first standard work on law. Though casuistic, it was incisive enough to remain the subject of commentary 200 years later. At the end of the republic *Alfenus Varus' 40 books of *Digesta* ('Ordered Abstracts') remained, despite the title, a bulky collection of opinions (*responsa*) given mainly by himself and his teacher Servius *Sulpicius Rufus in particular cases. A few monographs were written, and some short commentaries on the praetor's *edict. But with M. *Antistius Labeo in the early empire an important new genre appears, that of the large-scale commentary.

Little republican writing has survived. The literature of the empire, of which thanks to Justinian's codification (see JUSTINIAN'S CODIFICATION) we have a great deal, included, apart from these genres, critical editions of and commentaries on earlier works and teaching manuals. Discussion of cases still predominates, since lawyers spent most of their time giving opinions and advice on concrete problems to private clients, magistrates, officials, or the emperor himself. Advanced teaching took the similar form of discussing difficult cases, real or imaginary (*quaestiones, disputationes*), and lawyers carried on correspondence with pupils and friends (*epistulae*). Collections of *responsa, quaestiones*, and *epistulae* were published, at first by the lawyer's pupils, later by himself. Q. *Cervidius Scaevola and *Aemilius Papinianus published little else, and even the *Digesta* of *Iulianus are mainly casuistic.

Large-scale commentaries began as stated with Labeo, who wrote massive treatises on the urban and peregrine praetors' edicts. This genre returned to prominence in the 2nd cent. AD when the climate of opinion set by *Antoninus Pius and Marcus *Aurelius favoured precision in the administration of justice. Sextus Pomponius' edictal commentary of that period ran to about 150 books, a record never surpassed. He and others also wrote large treatises on the *Ius civile* ('Civil Law') of Mucius Scaevola and *Sabinus. Shortly before and after 200 *Paulus and *Ulpian became the last to practise the extended commentary, at about half Pomponius' length. These works, intended for officials and private practitioners, reproduced as much of the basic text as was necessary to understand the commentary.

Monographs were popular and remained so up to *Arcadius Charisius at the end of the 3rd cent. AD. They included works on particular branches of the law, like adultery, and offices, like that of consul. Aspiring lawyers seem often to have written one at the start of their career, to put down a professional marker. Another young man's genre was the edition of an earlier work with *notae* (critical comments). Thus Paulus showed his paces by annotating Labeo's *Pithana* ('Persuasive Propositions'). But some monographs were ambitious and innovative. Both Ulpian and especially Paulus composed many, the first setting guidelines for public officers such as provincial governors, the second exploring and refining many branches of law and procedure.

Teaching manuals were slow in developing. An early example is *Neratius Priscus' *Regulae* ('Guidelines'). They were in demand in the provinces (see GAIUS (2)), but when Roman citizenship was extended in AD 212 leading lawyers in Rome took them up and extended their scale. The textbook (*Institutiones*) of *Marcianus, written around 220, ran to sixteen books (*libri*). Other types of work intended mainly for students were *regulae* ('guidelines'), *differentiae* ('distinctions'), and *pandectae* ('encyclopaedia'), the last two titles innovations of *Herennius Modestinus.

Three monographs of Arcadius Charisius are to be dated to around 290. But the market for large-scale original works was now saturated. We find instead summaries and epitomes in up to six or seven books. Examples are the *Iuris epitomae* ('Summaries of the Law') of *Hermogenianus in six books, *Sententiae receptae* ('Received Views'), attributed to Paulus, in five, and works of *Regulae* ('Guidelines') of similar length attributed to Gaius and Ulpian. There were also of course the semi-official collections of imperial constitutions by Gregorius and Hermogenianus (see CODEX) and an unofficial collection of about 320 of uncertain authorship known as *Fragmenta Vaticana*. It consisted of imperial *constitutions and excerpts from the private writings of lawyers and ran to the equivalent of about twenty books. There was an enlarged edition towards the end of the 4th cent. These were mere compilations, with no element of originality. The last legal treatise was perhaps the *Opiniones* ('Opinions') in six books, falsely attributed to Ulpian, which seems to belong to the reign of *Constantine I. Two generations later a more slanted compilation appeared which is perhaps to be seen as a Christian reply to pagan propaganda. The late 4th- or early 5th-cent. *Lex Dei quam Deus precepit ad Moysen* ('Law which God Gave to Moses') is generally known as the *Collatio* ('Comparison') *legum Romanarum et Mosaicarum* since it sets out parallels between the law of Moses and Roman law in order to demonstrate the priority of the Mosaic law. This was a familiar Christian theme at the time.

Constantine I was hostile to what he saw as the undue complexity of classical law and was concerned that the law should be simple, unchallenged, and subject to his control. He ruled that the spurious and recent, but elementary, *Pauli Sententiae* was a genuine work of authority and invalidated Paulus' and Ulpian's sometimes critical notes on Papinianus. The canon of writings of authority was now closed, and the political and ideological climate under Constantine and his sons was hostile to any further private legal publication.

For individual authors see the entries under their names.

P. Jörs, *RE* 5 (1905), 484–543, 'Digesta'; A. Berger, *RE* 10/1 (1917), 1159–1200, 'Iurisprudentia'; Wieacker *RRG* 1. 563 f.; *HLL* 5, §§ 413, 418, 420, 425; W. Kalb, *Roms Juristen nach ihrer Sprache dargestellt* (1890); H. Fitting, *Alter und Folge der Schriften römischen Juristen*, 2nd edn. (1908); F. Schulz, *Roman Legal Science* (1946), rev. as *Geschichte der römischen Rechtswissenschaft* (1963); T. Honoré, *Studia et documenta historiae et iuris*, 1962, 162–232; P. Frezza, *SDHI* 1977, 202–12; D. Liebs, in M. Fuhrmann (ed.), *Die römische Literatur* (1974).   T. Hon.

legati in the late republic were senators serving on the staff of a military commander or governor, on whose recommendation they were appointed by the senate. *Pompey and *Caesar appointed their own *legati*, who had propraetorian power (see PRO CONSULE, PRO PRAETORE) and often exercised semi-independent command. 'The role of *legati* is distinct from that of commanders; the former must do everything according to orders, the latter must without restriction decide the overall strategy' (Caesar, *BCiv.* 3. 51). *Augustus developed this idea, appointing a *legatus*, a senator of consular rank who later held the title *legatus Augusti propraetore*, to govern each province for which he was responsible, except Egypt, which had equestrian officers. Each legion in a province was commanded by a senator of praetorian rank (*legatus legionis*), subordinate to the governor. In one-legion provinces, the governor also commanded the legion, except in Africa where *Gaius (1) appointed a separate legate, leaving the proconsul responsible for civil administration. *Legati Augusti* rarely held more than two senior commands, generally of about three years' duration. Many recorded their careers on monuments, but the interpretation of these is disputed and it remains doubtful if many were systematically prepared for army command, or had significant military expertise (see CAREERS, ROMAN; CURSUS HONORUM).

Legatus Augusti propraetore also designated a senator appointed by the emperor to a special task, notably, from the 2nd cent. AD, as his adviser and companion (*comes*) on campaign.

G. Iacopi, *Diz. Epigr.* (1949), 'Legatus'; B. Campbell, *JRS* 1975, 11; A. R. Birley, *The Fasti of Roman Britain* (1981), 4.   J. B. C.

legion

1. Early republic There is scant information for the organization of the Roman legion, which perhaps consisted of a levy of 1,000 men from each of the three 'tribes' (see TRIBUS) of the early regal period; see REX; ROME, HISTORY. By the end of the 5th cent. BC the legion numbered about 6,000 men, but *Polybius (1), writing *c*.150 BC, provides the earliest detailed account of its structure, and he probably refers to the army after the war against *Hannibal (see PUNIC WARS). The legion varied in size between 4,200 and 5,000 men subdivided into 30 maniples (see MANIPULUS) arranged in three lines; while light-armed troops (*velites*) formed a screen, the *hastati* (spearmen) and *principes* (chief men), chosen on the basis of age and experience, made up two ranks, followed by the most experienced soldiers (*triarii* or 'third rank men'). The legion was supported by 300 cavalry.

*2. Marius to *Actium* C. *Marius (1) is credited with a change in the tactical structure of the legion from maniple to cohort (see

COHORS), though in practice this may have been a more gradual development; there were ten cohorts, each containing six centuries of 80 men, making the strength of a legion 4,800, although the first cohort may have been larger. Around this time an eagle (*aquila*) was adopted as the symbol of each legion, personifying its permanent existence. The *velites* and legionary cavalry were replaced by specialist auxiliary troops (see AUXILIA) from foreign or conquered peoples.

3. The Principate *Augustus created from the surviving legions of the triumviral period a standing, professional army with which he aimed to meet all military needs. In AD 14 there were 25 legions in service, increasing by the Severan era (see ROME, HISTORY) to 33. Each legion, organized in cohorts, with 120 legionary cavalry, comprised about 5,400 men, had its own number and honorific title, and was commanded by a senatorial *legatus legionis* (see LEGATI), except in *Egypt and later in *Mesopotamia (annexed in 198) where the legions were under equestrian prefects. See PRAEFECTUS.

Legionaries were recruited from Roman citizens and increasingly from the provinces, so that by the time of *Hadrian, few Italians served in the legions. In addition, soldiers tended to be recruited locally as legions acquired permanent provincial bases. From the late 1st cent. legionaries served 25 years and were paid a salary of 1,200 sesterces (see STIPENDIUM). Pay was supplemented by donatives (see DONATIVUM), and legionaries enjoyed superannuation and various legal privileges (see CONTUBERNIUM).

4. Later empire *Diocletian increased the legions to at least 67, though perhaps not retaining their traditional complement. Under *Constantine I most remained and others were established, although those in the field army numbered only 1,000 men, commanded by tribunes. Frontier troops consisted partly of traditional legions, perhaps up to half their usual strength, commanded by prefects.

5. The individual legions Legio I: formed originally by *Caesar or C. *Vibius Pansa Caetronianus; served with *Octavian from 41 BC; perhaps the legion deprived of its title *Augusta* after disgracing itself in Spain in 19 BC. Served on the Rhine, *c*.16 BC–AD 69, based at Ara Ubiorum (Cologne; see COLONIA AGRIPPINENSIS) from AD 9, subsequently at *Bonna (Bonn); some of the legion participated in A. *Vitellius' march on Rome; disbanded in 70 for collusion with the rebel C. *Iulius Civilis; some of its soldiers may have been included in VII Gemina; had title *Germanica* from service on the Rhine (*AE* 1976, 515, possibly Augustan); see GERMANIA.

Legio I Adiutrix ('Helper'): formed by *Nero in AD 68 from sailors at *Misenum; made into a formal legion by *Galba. Fought at *Bedriacum for *Otho, capturing the eagle of XXI Rapax; sent by Vitellius to Spain. In 70 transferred to *Mogontiacum (Mainz) in Upper Germany, and *c*.86 to *Pannonia. Possibly sent to *Moesia during *Domitian's campaigns against *Decebalus, but by 97 stationed at *Brigetio (Pannonia); granted the title *pia fidelis* ('loyal and faithful') by *Trajan, took part in the Dacian Wars and may have remained as part of the garrison of *Dacia; probably accompanied Trajan on the Parthian campaign (see PARTHIA), returning with Hadrian to the Danube (see DANUVIUS); from *c*.120 based at Brigetio (Upper Pannonia).

Legio I Italica: raised by Nero from Italians, probably in AD 66 for the planned Caspian expedition. Sent to Gaul in 68, based at *Lugdunum (Lyons); supported Vitellius at the second battle of *Bedriacum; sent by *Vespasian to Moesia; stationed at Novae.

Legio I Macriana Liberatrix ('Macer's Liberating'): raised in 68 by L. *Clodius Macer, the rebellious governor of Africa; disbanded by *Galba.

Legio I Minervia: formed by Domitian in 83 with title *Flavia Minervia* (he specially favoured Minerva), stationed thereafter at Bonna (Bonn) in Lower Germany. Granted titles *pia fidelis Domitiana* ('Domitian's loyal and faithful') for loyalty in L. *Antonius Saturninus' revolt of 89. Took part in Trajan's Dacian Wars and the Parthian campaign of Lucius *Verus.

Legio I Parthica: formed by *Septimius Severus before 197; named in honour of his Parthian campaign; stationed in Mesopotamia at *Singara.

Legio II Adiutrix ('Helper'): Vespasian had accepted it as a formal legion by 7 March AD 70, when it had the titles *pia fidelis* ('loyal and faithful'); may have largely consisted of sailors originally recruited by Nero from the fleet at Misenum, some of whom were sent by Vitellius to oppose the Flavian advance but surrendered at *Narnia. Fought against Iulius Civilis and accompanied Q. *Petillius Cerialis to *Britain in 71; based at *Lindum (Lincoln) and finally, by Agricola's time, at *Deva (Chester). Transferred to the Danube *c.*87 or later, it is known to have been operating in Moesia by 92 (*ILS* 2719); subsequently stationed at *Aquincum (Budapest) in Lower Pannonia, participating in Trajan's invasion of Dacia; took part in Verus' Parthian campaign.

Legion II Augusta: raised possibly by C. Vibius Pansa in 43 BC; reconstituted by Augustus, from whom it took its name, perhaps for a victory; served in Spain from 30 BC, transferred to Germany after AD 9; from 17 based at *Argentorate (Strasburg); took part in the invasion of Britain in 43; from 74 or 75 permanently based at *Isca (2) (Caerleon).

Legio II Italica: recruited from Italians *c.* AD 165 by Marcus *Aurelius, soon became garrison of *Noricum, stationed at Ločica, then at Albing, and from *Commodus onwards at *Lauriacum. Known as *Italica pia* ('Italian loyal') from its foundation; between 192 and 200 acquired additional title *fidelis* ('faithful').

Legio II Parthica: raised by Septimius Severus before AD 197; named in honour of his Parthian campaign; from about 202 stationed at Albanum (see ALBA LONGA), 21 km. (13 mi.) south of Rome, the first legion in the imperial period to be permanently based in Italy. Travelled to the east for *Caracalla's Parthian War; under *Elagabalus had title *pia fidelis felix aeterna* ('loyal, faithful, fortunate, eternal').

Legio II Traiana Fortis ('Trajanic Brave'): formed by Trajan probably *c.* AD 105 and named after himself; the second legion raised by the emperor. Later stationed in Syria, transferred to Egypt *c.*125, based at *Nicopolis (4) near *Alexandria (1).

Legio III Augusta: possibly raised by C. Vibius Pansa in 43 BC or by Octavian, 41/0 BC; stationed in Africa probably from 30 BC onwards, first at *Ammaedara, then at *Theveste under Vespasian, and finally (*c.* AD 98 at the latest) at *Lambaesis; bore its title from some victory won under Augustus; cashiered by *Gordian III in 238 for supporting its rebellious legate Capellianus; reinstated by *Valerian in 253.

Legio III Cyrenaica: raised before 30 BC probably by M. *Aemilius Lepidus (3) or Mark Antony (M. *Antonius (2)) ; stationed in Egypt early in Augustus' reign; its title came from service in *Cyrene. On the reduction of the Egyptian garrison, it was based at *Nicopolis (4) with XXII Deiotariana; perhaps temporarily constituted the initial garrison of the province of *Arabia annexed in 106, but may have been soon replaced by VI Ferrata; participated in Trajan's Parthian War before returning to Egypt (winter quarters still attested in 119); then moved to Arabia (attested in 140s), permanently stationed at *Bostra.

Legio III Gallica: raised by *Caesar, subsequently fought with Mark Antony in the east; title indicates service in Gaul, 48–42 BC. Stationed in *Syria 30 BC onwards; transferred to Moesia by Nero just before his death; fought for Vespasian at the second battle of Bedriacum. Moved back to Syria in 70; at an uncertain date based at Raphaneae, remaining there throughout the 2nd cent. When Septimius Severus divided Syria, it constituted the garrison of Phoenice; cashiered for sedition against Elagabalus in the winter of 218/9; reconstituted by M. *Aurelius Severus Alexander and transferred to Danaba, near *Damascus.

Legio III Italica: recruited from Italians by Marcus Aurelius *c.* AD 165 and permanently stationed in *Raetia at *Castra Regina (Regensburg); for a time after its formation had the title *concors* ('united').

Legio III Parthica: formed by Septimius Severus before 197; named in honour of his Parthian campaign; based in Mesopotamia, probably at Rhesaena.

Legio IV Flavia Felix ('Flavian Fortunate'): reconstituted by Vespasian in AD 70 from former IV Macedonica and stationed at Burnum in Dalmatia; transferred to Upper Moesia *c.*86, stationed possibly at *Singidunum (Belgrade) from *c.*86 to 101/2. Participated in Trajan's Dacian Wars; formed part of the garrison of Dacia, based for a time at Sarmizegethusa Ulpia, before returning to Moesia, probably early in Hadrian's reign, and its permanent station at Singidunum.

Legio IV Macedonica: raised by Caesar in 48 BC, joined Octavian; title indicates early service in *Macedonia; stationed in Spain, arguably at Herrera de Pisuerga, 30 BC–*c.* AD 43, transferred to Upper Germany, possibly to replace XIV Gemina at Mogontiacum (Mainz). Supported Vitellius, a detachment fighting at Bedriacum; the remainder of the legion surrendered to Iulius Civilis and was subsequently disbanded by Vespasian.

Legio IV Scythica: raised before 30 BC possibly by Antony. From 30 onwards served in Macedonia, and may have acquired its title from campaigns against Scythians in 29–27 BC; by AD 9 was part of the garrison of Moesia; in 56/7 transferred permanently to Syria; based at *Zeugma from Vespasian's reign.

Legio V Alaudae ('Larks'): formed by Caesar in 52 BC from native population of Transalpine Gaul (see GAUL (TRANSALPINE)); its title celebrates the crest of bird feathers on the helmet; reconstituted by Antony in 44 BC and incorporated into Octavian's army after Actium. In Spain, 30–19? BC, then transferred to Rhine frontier; lost its eagle in Gaul, 17 BC (Vell. Pat. 2. 97); by AD 14 stationed at *Vetera (Xanten) in Lower Germany. Supported Vitellius, fighting at both battles of Bedriacum; probably transferred by Vespasian to Moesia, although possibly disbanded at this time; if it survived, it was subsequently annihilated probably under Domitian on the Danube, *c.*85–6.

Legio V Macedonica: raised in 43 BC by C. Vibius Pansa or possibly in 41/0 BC by Octavian; served in Macedonia 30 BC–AD 6, from which it took its title, then transferred to Moesia; subsequently stationed at Oescus; sent to Armenia in 61/2, later served under Vespasian in the Jewish War. Transferred back to Oescus in 71, remaining there as part of the garrison of Lower Moesia on the division of the province in 86. Moved to Troesmis during or after Trajan's Dacian Wars. After participating in the Parthian War of Lucius Verus (162–6), transferred to Potaissa in Dacia in 167 or 168. When Dacia north of the Danube was abandoned in 274/5, returned to Oescus as garrison of the newly created province of Dacia Ripensis.

Legio VI Ferrata ('Ironclad'): raised by Caesar in 52 BC in Cisalpine Gaul; reconstituted by M. *Aemilius Lepidus (3) in 44

BC, taken over by Antony in 43. Incorporated into Octavian's army and stationed thereafter in Syria, perhaps at Raphaneae; was part of the Flavian army that marched on Italy in 69, but soon returned. From 72 probably stationed at *Samosata. Became the garrison of the new province of Arabia for a time, perhaps replacing III Cyrenaica. Subsequently transferred to Caparcotna in *Judaea, becoming part of the garrison of the new province of *Syria Palaestina. Granted titles *fidelis constans* ('faithful and steadfast') for supporting Septimius Severus against C. *Pescennius Niger; perhaps transferred to Syria Phoenice under Severus Alexander.

Legio VI Victrix ('Victorious'): raised 41/0? BC by Octavian; in Spain, 30 BC–AD 69; transferred to Rhine frontier, 69/70, where it rebuilt and occupied the camp at *Novaesium (Neuss) in Lower Germany. For loyalty in revolt of L. Antonius Saturninus in 89, Domitian granted titles *pia fidelis Domitiana* ('Domitian's loyal and faithful'). By 105 stationed in Vetera; transferred to Britain, probably in 122; permanently stationed at *Eburacum (York).

Legio VII: raised in 59 BC or earlier, reconstituted by Octavian in 44 BC; probably served in the Balkans and from AD 9 constituted part of the garrison of *Dalmatia, based at Tilurium. Granted titles *Claudia pia fidelis* ('Claudian loyal and faithful') for loyalty during the revolt of L. *Arruntius Camillus Scribonianus, governor of Dalmatia, AD 42. Transferred to Moesia possibly in 56/7, based at *Viminacium from the time of Vespasian onwards. Supported Vespasian and fought at the second battle of Bedriacum.

Legio VII Hispana ('Spanish', *AE* 1972, 203): raised by Galba in Spain, nicknamed *Galbiana* (Tac. *Hist.* 2. 86). Accompanied Galba to Rome; then sent to *Carnuntum (Pannonia), later fought for Vespasian. Reconstituted in 70, perhaps incorporating soldiers of Legio I, and given name *Gemina* ('Twin'); received title *felix* ('fortunate') possibly for distinguished service in Upper Germany in 72/3. By the end of 74 it had been sent back to Spain, probably to Legio (León) which became its permanent base. Under Septimius Severus, the legion had the titles: *Gemina pia felix* ('Twin, loyal, and fortunate'), possibly for loyalty against *Clodius Septimius Albinus.

Legio VIII Augusta: raised in 59 BC or earlier; reconstituted by Octavian in 44 BC; from 30 onwards served in the Balkans and after AD 9 was stationed at *Poetovio (Ptuj) in Pannonia; bore its title from some victory won under Augustus; transferred c.45 to Moesia, based at Novae. Moved to Upper Germany in 70; stationed at Argentorate (Strasburg).

Legio IX Hispana ('Spanish'): possibly descended from Caesar's ninth legion disbanded in 46/5 BC; or possibly a new foundation by Octavian in 41/0 BC; acquired its name from service in Spain (30–19? BC), transferred to Illyricum, after AD 9 serving in Pannonia, perhaps at *Siscia; known as *Macedonica* in the early empire (*ILS* 928 (Augustan) and *AE* 1919, 1), from this service in the Balkans; temporarily transferred to Africa, AD 20–4, for the war against *Tacfarinas. Participated in the invasion of Britain in 43; later stationed at Lindum (Lincoln); suffered heavy losses in Boudicca's rebellion. Under Vespasian, c.71, moved to Eburacum (York). Last attested in Britain in 108 and later its base at York was taken over by VI Victrix. The legion was probably not lost in Britain but transferred elsewhere, surviving at least into the mid-120s (on the evidence of the careers of senatorial officers, although suggestions that it perished in the Jewish Revolt, 132–5, or in the Parthian War, 161, are pure speculation.

Legio X Fretensis (named after the *fretum* or channel between Italy and Sicily, suggesting participation in naval battles): raised by Octavian, 41/0? BC; served in Macedonia after 30 BC, and by AD 14 at the latest was in Syria; in 17 based at Cyrrhus, later at *Zeugma. Sent in 66 to fight in the Jewish War, took part in the sieges of *Jerusalem and *Masada, thereafter stationed at Jerusalem; moved to Aela on the Red Sea in the second half of 3rd cent.

Legio X Gemina ('Twin'): raised in 59 BC or earlier; reconstituted by M. *Aemilius Lepidus (3) in 44 BC, taken over by Antony in 43; the successor of Caesar's tenth legion, it was added to Octavian's army after Actium, perhaps incorporating troops from another legion; stationed in Spain, probably at Petavonium (Rosinos de Vidriales), from 30 BC; transferred to *Carnuntum in Pannonia in AD 63, sent back to Spain in 68; moved to Lower Germany in 70, stationed at *Noviomagus (Nijmegen). Granted the title *pia fidelis Domitiana* ('Domitian's loyal and faithful') for loyalty in the rebellion of L. Antonius Saturninus in 89. Transferred to Pannonia c.103, firstly at *Aquincum (Budapest), subsequently at *Vindobona (Vienna).

Legio XI: of uncertain origin, possibly descended from Caesar's eleventh, raised in 58 BC, but may have been newly formed by Octavian in 41/0 BC. After service in the Balkans, from AD 9 stationed in Dalmatia at Burnum. Granted title *Claudia pia fidelis* ('Claudian loyal and faithful') for loyalty during the revolt of L. Arruntius Camillus Scribonianus, governor of Dalmatia, AD 42. Supported Vespasian at second battle of Bedriacum. Sent in 70 to Upper Germany to help suppress the rebellion of Iulius Civilis; based at *Vindonissa (Windisch). Moved to Pannonia c.101, stationed at Brigetio; later transferred to Lower Moesia, based at Durostorum.

Legio XII Fulminata ('Thunderbolt-armed'): probably descended from the twelfth legion raised by Caesar in 58 BC. Reconstituted in 44/3 BC, served with Antony in the east; probably sent to Egypt by Augustus; by the end of his reign in Syria; served with L. *Caesennius Paetus in Armenia, but was disgraced by the surrender at Rhandeia and sent back to Syria. Based for a time at Raphaneae, it fought in the Jewish War and may have temporarily lost its eagle in the retreat of *Cestius Gallus from Jerusalem in AD 66; transferred in 70 to Cappadocia, based at *Melitene. The story of an extraordinary rainstorm which supposedly rescued the twelfth legion during Marcus Aurelius' campaign against the *Quadi in 172, may, if true, refer to a legionary detachment; named *certa constans* ('firm and steadfast') by Marcus Aurelius for loyalty in the revolt of *Avidius Cassius in 175.

Legio XIII Gemina ('Twin'): uncertain origin, perhaps descended from Caesar's thirteenth, raised in 57 BC, or formed by Octavian in 41/0 BC and amalgamated with another legion after *Actium; served in *Illyricum in the early empire; after AD 9 moved to the Rhine, eventually at Vindonissa (Windisch) in Upper Germany. Transferred to Pannonia c.45, based at Poetovio (Ptuj); probably moved to Vindobona (Vienna) by Domitian. Took part in Trajan's Second Dacian War and possibly also the First, becoming part of the first garrison of Dacia, permanently based at Apulum. When Dacia across the Danube was abandoned in 274/5, it was transferred to Ratiaria in the new province of Dacia Ripensis.

Legio XIV Gemina ('Twin'): uncertain origin, perhaps descended from Caesar's fourteenth, raised in 53 BC, or possibly newly formed by Octavian in 41/0 BC; perhaps amalgamated with another legion after Actium; served in *Illyricum in the early empire; from AD 9 at Mogontiacum (Mainz) in Upper Germany. Took part in the invasion of Britain in 43; later based at *Viroconium (Wroxeter); won titles *martia victrix* ('martial and victorious') after defeating *Boudicca, 60–1. Recalled in 67 by Nero for his intended eastern campaign; sent back to Britain by Vitellius; transferred to the Rhine in 70 for the campaign against Iulius Civilis, stationed at Mainz. After supporting L. Antonius Saturninus in 89 it was moved to the Danube in 92/3, possibly based near Mursa (then in Upper Moesia); transferred *c.*101 to Vindobona (Vienna) in Pannonia; a detachment took part in the Dacian Wars, and by 114 the legion was based at Carnuntum (Upper Pannonia).

Legio XV Apollinaris ('*Apollo's'): raised by Octavian in 41/0 BC or earlier; served in Illyricum in the early empire; after AD 9 in Pannonia, based possibly at *Emona; probably transferred to Carnuntum early in *Tiberius' reign after the mutiny of AD 14. Moved to the east in 63 for Cn. *Domitius Corbulo's campaigns, fought in the Jewish War (66–70), returning to Carnuntum in 71. A detachment took part in Trajan's Dacian Wars, and the legion was probably transferred to the east for the emperor's Parthian campaigns; after 117 stationed at Satala in Cappadocia.

Legio XV Primigenia ('First-born', i.e. of a new group of legions): raised probably by *Gaius (1) in AD 39 for his intended German campaign. Based at Mogontiacum (Mainz), then moved to *Bonna (Bonn) and finally to *Vetera (Xanten) in Lower Germany. A detachment took part in Vitellius' invasion of Italy, but after a siege at Vetera the remainder surrendered to the rebel Iulius Civilis, and the legion disappeared from the army lists.

Legio XVI: formed by Octavian possibly in 41/0 BC; on the Rhine frontier 30 BC onwards; had name *Gallica* (first attestation, *ILS* 2695, reign of Claudius), from service in Gaul of uncertain date. After AD 9 based at Mogontiacum (Mainz) in Upper Germany. Transferred by Claudius to *Novaesium (Neuss) in Lower Germany. Part of the legion took part in Vitellius' invasion of Italy; the remaining soldiers were disgraced by their surrender to Iulius Civilis and the legion was subsequently disbanded by Vespasian who reconstituted it as XVI Flavia Firma.

Legio XVI Flavia Firma ('Flavian Steadfast'): the reconstituted legion was sent by Vespasian to the east, and was serving in Syria in 75; moved later to Satala in *Cappadocia; after Trajan's Parthian War, permanently stationed in Syria at *Samosata.

Legiones XVII, XVIII, XIX: raised by Octavian possibly in 41/0 BC, although there is no record of their activities during the Civil Wars. Probably stationed on the Rhine from 30 BC onwards, they were all destroyed in AD 9 (although XVII is not specifically mentioned) in a military disaster in the Teutoburg Forest (see TEUTOBURGIENSIS, SALTUS); their commander, P. *Quinctilius Varus, committed suicide. The legions' numbers were not used again, though the eagle of the nineteenth and one of the others were recovered during the campaigns of *Germanicus (AD 15–16), and the remaining one in 42 (Tac. *Ann.* 1. 60, 2. 25; Cass. Dio 60. 8).

Legio XX Valeria Victrix: raised by Octavian in 41/0 BC, or possibly after Actium; in Spain, 30–20? BC, then in Illyricum at Burnum until AD 9; transferred to Ara Ubiorum (Cologne) in Lower Germany. Moved to Novaesium (Neuss) during Tiberius' reign, took part in the invasion of Britain in 43; first based at *Camulodunum (Colchester), then near Gloucester (*Glevum) from 49; played an important part in the campaigns of Cn. *Iulius Agricola and may have constructed the fortress of Inchtuthil *c.*83–7; on the withdrawal of II Adiutrix from Britain, Inchtuthil was evacuated and Valeria Victrix was stationed at *Deva (Chester). The legion's title is perhaps to be translated 'Valiant

Victorious', deriving from its role in Boudicca's defeat, 60–1.

Legio XXI Rapax ('Predatory'): raised by Octavian in 41/0 BC or possibly after Actium; perhaps based in Raetia in the early empire. After AD 9 was transferred to Vetera (Xanten) in Lower Germany, and *c.*46 to Vindonissa (Windisch) in Upper Germany. Took part in the Vitellian invasion of Italy, then fought against Iulius Civilis in 70 before taking up its station at Bonna (Bonn) in Lower Germany. Transferred in 83 to Mogontiacum (Mainz) in Upper Germany; having supported L. Antonius Saturninus in 89, was sent to the Danube; subsequently annihilated, probably in 92 in battle against the Sarmatians.

Legio XXII Deiotariana: raised by King *Deiotarus of Galatia, trained and equipped on the Roman model; incorporated into the Roman army by Augustus probably before 25 BC and stationed in Egypt, at *Nicopolis (4). Its fate is unclear; may have been destroyed in the Jewish Revolt of AD 132–5.

Legio XXII Primigenia ('First-born'): formed along with XV Primigenia and stationed *c.* AD 43 at Mogontiacum (Mainz) in Upper Germany. Accompanied Vitellius on his march to Rome; transferred briefly to Carnuntum; by 71 had returned to a new station at Vetera (Xanten) in Lower Germany. Granted title *pia fidelis Domitiana* ('Domitian's loyal and faithful') for loyalty in 89, and in 92/3, on the transfer of XIV Gemina to the Danube, was moved to Mainz.

Legio XXX Ulpia Victrix ('Ulpian Victorious'): formed by Trajan and named after himself (M. Ulpius Traianus) probably *c.* AD 105; its number shows it was the thirtieth legion in the army. Stationed at Brigetio (Upper Pannonia), participated in the Second Dacian War before being transferred in 122 to Vetera (Xanten) in Lower Germany when VI Victrix was sent to Britain.

W. Kubitschek and E. Ritterling, *RE* 12 (1925), 'Legio'; A. Passerini, *Diz. Epigr.* (1950), 'Legio'; G. Forni, *Il reclutamento delle legioni da Augusto a Diocleziano* (1953), and *ANRW* 2. 1 (1974), 339; J. C. Mann, *Legionary Recruitment and Veteran Settlement during the Principate* (1983); L. Keppie, *The Making of the Roman Army* (1984), 205; Y. Le Bohec, *La IIIᵉ Légion Auguste* (1989); M. A. Speidel, *JRS* 1992, 87. For further bibliog. see under ARMIES, ROMAN.   J. B. C.

Lelantine War See GREECE (HISTORY), Archaic Age; LEFKANDI.

Lelegians See HALICARNASSUS.

Lemnos, an island of the northern *Aegean sea, about halfway between the Chalcidic peninsulas (see CHALCIDICE) and the coast of *Asia Minor. Its volcanic activity lay behind the myth that it was the foundry of *Hephaestus, although recent studies suggest that Lemnos' fumarole fields with their smoke, vapours, and burnt earth, rather than actual volcanic cones and eruptions, have characterized the island's geology during human history. Lemnos had an important bronze age culture, and appears in *Homer's *Iliad* as a provisioning station for the Achaeans at *Troy. The early population was non-Greek. A late 6th-cent. BC inscription in the native Lemnian language (*IG* 12. 8. 1), now partially deciphered, bears affinities to the *Etruscan language. The earliest Greek inscription is dated to *c.*500, by which time Lemnos began to receive Athenian colonists led by the younger *Miltiades acting in his capacity as ruler of the Thracian *Chersonesus (1). Athenian interest in this strategically located island is further evidenced by the establishment of a *cleruchy *c.*450. After a brief period of Spartan rule (404–393) Lemnos again fell within the Athenian orbit. Together with the neighbouring islands of *Imbros and *Scyros it remained an advanced Athenian base in the northern Aegean. Despite occasional raids by *Philip (1) II of

Macedon, and brief periods of rule by early Hellenistic dynasts, Lemnos retained its Athenian affiliation well into the Hellenistic period. In the settlements following the battle of *Pydna (167 BC), Rome confirmed Athenian rule over Lemnos as a reward for Athens' loyalty during the Macedonian wars.

P. Forsyth, *Échos du monde classique*, 1984; L. van der Meer, *Oudheidkundige mededelingen uit het Rijksmuseum van Oudheiden te Leiden*, 1992; R. Parker, in R. Osborne and S. Hornblower (eds.), *Ritual, Finance, Politics* (1994), 339 ff. (the cleruchy). E. N. B.

Lemuria, Roman private *ritual on 9, 11, and 13 May to propitiate apparently anonymous, dangerous, and hungry ghosts (*lemures*), then prowling about houses: Ov. *Fast.* 5. 419 ff. The ritual's midnight time and tossing of black beans have been taken as 'magical' (Frazer on 5. 421) but this view relies on false anthropological assumptions. Sometimes distinguished from the ancestral spirits of the *Parentalia (13–23 February) on the basis of malignancy versus benevolence, but Ov. *Fast.* 2. 547 ff. contradicts this.

F. Cumont, *Lux Perpetua* (1949), 396 ff.; H. J. Rose, *Univ. Calif. Publ. Class. Philol.* 1941, 89 ff.; Latte, *RR* 99. C. R. P.

Lenaea, a Dionysiac festival (see DIONYSUS) celebrated in Athens on the 12th day of the month Gamelion (January–February), which in other Ionian calendars is called Lenaion. The name is derived from λήνη, 'maenad'. The official Athenian name, Διονύσια τὰ ἐπὶ Ληναίῳ ('Dionysia at the Lenaion'), proves that it took place in this sanctuary, which was probably in the agora. Officials of the Eleusinian mysteries (see ELEUSIS; MYSTERIES) joined the *basileus* (see ARCHONTES) in the conduct of the festival. We hear of a procession, and there are various slight indications of mystic ritual. The rituals depicted on the so-called 'Lenaea vases' may have occurred at this festival. Notices in *Hesychius and *Photius indicate that drama was performed in the Lenaion before the Athenians built their theatre; but probably dramatic contests at the Lenaea were formally organized only from about 440 BC. In the 5th cent. it seems that the contests in comedy were arranged much as at the City *Dionysia, but that the tragic contests at the Lenaea were less prestigious, with only two tragedians competing, each with two tragedies. See TRAGEDY, GREEK.

Deubner, *Attische Feste* 123–34; *DFA*³ 25–42; F. Kolb, *Agora und Theater, Volks- und Festversammlung* (1981), ch. 3. R. A. S. S.

Lentulus See CORNELIUS LENTULUS (various entries).

Leo (1) **I,** the Great, pope AD 440–61. As deacon, though an unoriginal theologian, he influenced Popes Celestine I and Sixtus III on doctrine, and served in secular diplomacy. As pope, he purged Manichaeans (see MANICHAEISM) from Rome, in partnership with senate and emperor, and attacked Pelagians (see PELAGIUS) and *Priscillianists. He intervened against Eutychian Monophysitism, opposing the council of Ephesus (449), which had spurned his Christological manifesto; this *Tome* was accepted at Chalcedon (451). He annulled Chalcedon's equation of Rome and Constantinople, but improved contact with Constantinople, establishing an *apocrisiarius* (secretary). Proclaiming the authority of St. Peter, through interventions and administrative restructurings, and despite worsening communications, he strengthened papal power in the Balkans and crumbling western provinces. (However, *Valentinian III's grant of primacy throughout the west (445) implies imperial supremacy.) His buildings, iconography, liturgies, cult of St. Peter, and encouragement of charity and observance of the Christian calendar enhanced Rome's sacred status. Confronting *Attila (451) and *Gaiseric

(454), he helped to turn back the Huns and minimize the *Vandal sack. His surviving letters (many drafted by others) and 96 sermons are lucid and forceful, with imperial and liturgical resonances.

TEXTS Ed. Migne, *PL* 54–6. Letters: ed. C. Silva-Tarrouca, in *Textus et Documenta* (1932–5); ed. E. Schwartz, *Acta Conciliorum Oecumenicorum* 2/4 (1932); Eng. trans. of all, E. Hunt (1957). Sermons, ed. A. Chavasse, *CCSL* 138 (1973); ed. with Fr. trans., R. Dolle (2nd edn., 1964–73); Eng. trans. (with Letters), C. L. Feltoe (1894).

E. Caspar, *Geschichte des Papstums* 1 (1930); P. A. McShane, *La Romanitas et le Pape Léon le Grand* (1979). S. J. B. B.

Leo (2) **I** (emperor), born in *Dacia *c.* AD 400, was a military officer until becoming Augustus (see AUGUSTUS, AUGUSTA AS TITLES) at *Constantinople (457–74) through the influence of the Alan Aspar. A massive expedition against *Vandal Africa failed expensively, but Leo used Isaurians (see ISAURIA) to balance German domination in Roman armies and thwart Aspar's plan to control the eastern empire.

PLRE 2. 663–4, 'Leo' 6. L. M. W.

Leochares, Athenian sculptor, active *c.*370–320 BC; worked mainly in bronze, specializing in gods and portraits. Small bronze replicas of his *Zeus Brontaeus ('Thundering Zeus') survive, and a marble relief from *Messene may copy his group (with *Lysippus (2)) of *Craterus (1) rescuing *Alexander (3) the Great from a lion. He was responsible for the sculptures of the west side of the *Mausoleum at Halicarnassus, to which have been attributed several slabs of the Amazon frieze now in the British Museum (BM 1013–15). Other attributions include the Demeter from *Cnidus, the Acropolis Alexander, and (in copy) the Apollo Belvedere.

A. F. Stewart, *Greek Sculpture* (1990), 180 f., 191 ff., 282 ff., figs. 529 ff., 568, 571 ff.; A. Kozloff and D. G. Mitten, *The Gods' Delight* (1988), no. 29 (Zeus). A. F. S.

Leon (1), of Byzantium. Sharp-tongued *Academy pupil who inspired Byzantine resistance to *Philip (1) II (340/39 BC) and crucially persuaded the city to accept help from *Phocion (another Academy product). He was later executed when a letter from Philip disingenuously mentioned his refusal to pay what Leon had demanded to betray the city. He was perhaps the author of a lost pseudo-Platonic *Alcyon* (see PLATO (1)), but historical and rhetorical works ascribed to him in *Suda* probably belong to others. His fate attracted imperial-period *declamation-writers.

RE 12, 'Leon' 23; *FGrH* 132. C. J. T.

Leon (2), of *Pella (?late 4th cent. BC), wrote a book on the Egyptian gods, in the form of a letter from *Alexander (3) the Great to his mother *Olympias, in which the gods are represented as in origin human kings, the discoverers of agriculture and other means of human subsistence.

FGrH 659; see also EUHEMERUS; CULTURE-BRINGERS. E. Ke.

Leonidas (1), *Agiad king of *Sparta (reigned *c.*490–480 BC), succeeded on the mysterious death of his half-brother *Cleomenes (1) I, whose daughter Gorgo he married. In 480, while the rest of the Spartans were prevented by the obligation to celebrate the annual *Carnea festival, he marched to Thermopylae (see THERMOPYLAE, BATTLE OF) with a hand-picked Spartiate advance guard of 300 (all 'men who had sons living'), some Greek volunteers picked up *en route*, and others brought under compulsion. The pass was apparently secured with some 7,000 hoplites, in

Leonidas

time to enable the concurrent and linked naval operations off *Artemisium. But though Leonidas repelled Persian assaults for two days, he failed to prevent his flank being turned via the Anopaea path. Dismissing the main body, Leonidas remained with 1,100 Boeotians, some *helots and *perioikoi, and his own guard (minus one suffering from ophthalmia). The Spartiates died to a man, counter-attacking fiercely. Leonidas' corpse was mutilated, but some 40 years later what were deemed to be his remains were brought back to Sparta for ceremonial reburial, and a hero-shrine (see HERO-CULT) was later established in his and the regent *Pausanias (1)'s honour. A magnificent marble statue found on the Spartan acropolis and datable to the early 5th cent. was immediately nicknamed 'Leonidas' but in fact represents some other hero—or a god.

Hdt. 7. 204–39; Diod. Sic. 11. 3–11. A. R. Burn, *Persia and the Greeks* (1962; repr. 1984), 273, 378 ff., 403 ff.; P. Cartledge, *Sparta and Lakonia* (1979); W. R. Connor, *TAPA* 1979, 21–7; J. F. Lazenby, *The Defence of Greece* (1993), ch. 6.   P. A. C.

Leonidas (2), of Tarentum, author of about 100 epigrams from *Meleager (2)'s *Garland* in the Greek *Anthology and one of the most influential epigrammatists of the early 3rd cent. BC. He does not (like his contemporaries *Callimachus (3) and *Asclepiades (2)) write of love and the *symposium, but mainly epitaphs and dedications for humble folk, rustics, fishermen, and sailors, though his verse is ornate, full of baroque compounds and odd terms set out in complex sentences. He purports to have led a vagabond life himself (*Anth. Pal.* 7. 715), and his poems do reflect a number of different places in mainland Greece and the eastern Aegean. His autobiographical poems and insistence on his poverty suggest the influence of Cynicism (he wrote an epitaph for *Diogenes (2), *Anth. Pal.* 7. 67). See CYNICS. Many later poets, both Greek and Roman, admired and imitated him (*Anth. Pal.* 10. 2–6 are successive imitations of 10. 1 by Leonidas on spring).

Gow–Page, *HE* 1. 1955 ff.; L. A. Stella, *Cinque poeti dell'Antologia palatina* (1949); T. B. L. Webster, *Hellenistic Poetry and Art* (1964), 217 f.; M. Gigante, *L'edera di Leonida* (1971).   A. D. E. C.

Leonidas (3) or **Leonides**, of *Alexandria (1), epigrammatist working at Rome under *Nero and *Vespasian; claims to have been originally an astrologer (*Anth. Pal.* 9. 344 = 21 Page, *FGE*). 'Invented' isopsephic poems, i.e. distichs in which the numerical value (α = 1 etc.) of each verse, or quatrains in which the numerical value of each distich, is the same; *Anth. Pal.* 9. 356 (33 Page), a poem replete with Callimachean motifs (see CALLIMACHUS (3)), proclaims his novelty.

J. Geffcken, *RE* 12. 2031–3; Page, *FGE* 503–41.   R. L. Hu.

Leonnatus (c.358–322 BC), Macedonian nobleman, related to the Argeads through Eurydice, mother of *Philip (1) II. As bodyguard of Philip II, Leonnatus helped kill his murderer Pausanias; under *Alexander (3) the Great, whom he accompanied to Asia, he fulfilled diplomatic missions, became bodyguard (*sōmatophylax*) in 332 and participated in all further political and military events of Alexander's expedition, distinguishing himself also as independent commander. At *Babylon (323) he was foreseen as protector for *Roxane's unborn child (*tutor*: Curt. 10. 7. 9), but then received *Hellespontine Phrygia as satrapy (see SATRAP). Both *Antipater (1) and *Olympias offered him marriage alliances but before either could be realized he was killed while moving to relieve Antipater in *Lamia (2) (322).

Berve, *Alexanderreich*, no. 466; Heckel, *Marshals* 91 ff.   R. M. E.

Leontini in *Sicily (mod. Lentini, although the excavated

remains of the south gate, walls, and tombs are nearer Carlentini) was founded from *Naxos (2) in 729 BC on a commanding hillside position south of the plain of Catania. Flourishing in the 6th cent. (its ruler Panaetius being the earliest Sicilian tyrant), it was captured by *Hippocrates (1) c.494 BC, and thereafter was usually dominated by *Syracuse, with intervals of precarious freedom. Its alliance with the Athenians (renewed in 433/2 BC: see *IG* 1³. 54) was implemented in 427 when its most famous citizen, the orator *Gorgias (1), led its delegation to Athens. Hieronymus, successor of *Hieron (2) II, was murdered there in 215, and after further provocations Leontini was sacked by the Romans who then besieged Syracuse. A *civitas decumana* under the Roman republic (i.e. it was a city liable to pay a tithe, see DECUMA) suffered in the First Slave War (104–101 BC), and by *Cicero's time it had become a 'wretched and deserted city' (*civitas misera atque inanis*: Cic. *2 Verr.* 2. 66. 160). It was abandoned in the early empire, although the existence of a 6th-cent. bishopric at Leontini indicates late Roman and Byzantine resettlement.

Good description in Polyb. 7. 6. *PECS* 497–8; *BTCGI* 8 (1990), 524–55; Gabba–Vallet, *Sicilia antica* 1. 581–9; Dunbabin, *Western Greeks, passim*; G. Rizza (ed.), *Scavi nelle necropoli di Leontini (1977–1982)* (= *CronASA* 21) (1991).   A. G. W.; R. J. A. W.

Leosthenes, son of Leosthenes, Athenian from the *deme of Kephale (d. 322 BC). *Stratēgos* (general) for the home defence in 324/3, his experience as mercenary captain enabled him to repatriate to *Taenarum (1) those dismissed by *Alexander (3) the Great's 'mercenary decree'. When Alexander died (323) Leosthenes had 8,000 men available, and with *Hyperides he persuaded Athens to fight the Macedonians and negotiated the Hellenic League, whose troops he commanded. He was chiefly responsible for early allied successes which shut up *Antipater (1) in *Lamia (2). His death devastated the Greek cause. In Athens Hyperides delivered the funeral oration (Hyp. 6); in the *Piraeus Arcesilaus decorated a stoa with a picture of Leosthenes and his sons (Paus. 1. 1. 3).

O. Schmitt, *Der Lamische Krieg* (1992).   R. M. E.

Leotychidas II, *Eurypontid king of *Sparta (reigned c.491–469 BC), succeeded his cousin and former marriage-rival, the deposed *Demaratus (2), through the machinations of *Cleomenes (1) I. In 479, as commander-in-chief of the 'Hellenic League' fleet, he fomented the revolt of *Chios and *Samos and decisively defeated the Persians in a land and sea battle off Cape Mycale. In 478 or 477 he led another combined Hellenic force on a punitive expedition against the Medizing aristocracies of *Thessaly, taking *Pagasae and perhaps *Pherae, but failing to capture *Larissa and being recalled to Sparta to face a charge of bribery. He evaded condemnation by retiring to Tegea, where he remained as titular king until his death.

Hdt. 6. 65 ff. P. Cartledge, *Sparta and Lakonia* (1979); J. P. Barron, *CAH* 4² (1988), 611–16.   P. A. C.

Lepcis (on some inscriptions **Leptis**) **Magna** (neo-Punic *Lpqi*). One of the Phoenician *emporia* (cf. Sall. *Iug.* 78; Sil. *Pun.* 3. 257), founded on the coast of *Tripolitania shortly before 600 BC, on the basis of the most recent archaeological evidence. See EMPORION. It was powerful enough c.515 to expel *Dorieus' fledgling Greek colony of Cinyps 18 km. (11 mi.) to the east (Hdt. 5. 42; cf. 4. 175, 198). Little is known of the early town, which lay in the area of the Augustan forum; a 4th/3rd-cent. BC necropolis underlies the theatre. Lepcis' prosperity derived largely from the fertility of its hinterland, where many farms with olive-presses are known: already by 46 BC *oil production was of a scale for *Caesar to levy an annual tribute on Lepcis of three million pounds of oil after *Thapsus (*BAfr.* 97). Lepcis expanded rapidly under the early empire, becoming a *municipium* under the Flavians (AD 69–96), and a *colonia* under *Trajan. *Septimius Severus, a native of the city, adorned it with splendid buildings, including a new forum (Lepcis' third), a basilica, a four-way arch richly decorated with sculpture, and a colonnaded street with *nymphaeum leading to a newly built harbour. It was a bishopric by the 3rd cent. Fresh city walls (late 3rd or early 4th cent.) saved Lepcis from the Austuriani who in 365 devastated its territory (Amm. Marc. 28. 6). Thereafter the city declined: its Byzantine walls enclosed only a fraction of its former size. The exceptionally well-preserved ruins of Lepcis, excavated since 1920, include—apart from the Severan buildings—the Augustan forum, theatre, and market, the amphitheatre and adjacent circus, and the Hadrianic baths. The small but virtually intact 'Hunting Baths', so named from a *venatio* fresco (see VENATIONES) in its *frigidarium*, are of great interest; several rich *villae maritimae* are known in its hinterland.

PECS 499–500; D. E. L. Haynes, *Antiquities of Tripolitania* (1956), 71–106; G. Caputo and E. Caffarelli, *The Buried City* (1966); M. Squarciapino, *Leptis Magna* (1966); J. B. Ward-Perkins, *The Severan Buildings at Lepcis Magna* (1993). Theatre: G. Caputo, *Il teatro augusteo di Leptis Magna* (1987). Harbour: R. Bartoccini, *Il porto romano di Leptis Magna* (1958). Hunting baths: *Archaeologia* 1949, 165–95. Hinterland: D. J. Mattingly, *Libyan Studies* 1988, 21–41. *Villae maritimae*: A. Di Vita, *La villa della 'Gara delle Nereidi' presso Taguira* (1966); O. Al Mahjub, in A. Farioli Campanati (ed.), *III Colloquio Internazionale sul mosaico antico, Ravenna 1980* (1983), 299–306; E. Salza Prina Ricotti, *Rend. Pont.* 1970–1, 135–63.   O. B.; R. J. A. W.

Leptines See DEMOSTHENES (2).

Lerna: the 'House of the Tiles', Greek site south of *Argos (2), a fine example of the early Helladic II 'corridor house' type, now widely identified (J. W. Shaw, *AJArch.* 1987, 59 ff.). It is large (25 × 12 m.: 82 × 39 ft.), two-storeyed, regularly planned with central, axially arranged rooms between corridors, and roofed with clay and schist tiles. Among the finds were groups of clay sealings for jars, boxes, and baskets, suggesting that it had held considerable stores. Such buildings probably had important functions, but their nature is still disputed (most recently, M. H. Wiencke, *AJArch.* 1989, 503 ff.).

See *GAC* A 13 for the prehistoric site.   O. T. P. K. D.

Lesbonax, grammarian of uncertain date and author of a short treatise Περὶ σχημάτων (i.e. grammatical peculiarities) illustrated with examples, many taken from *Homer.

Ed. D. L. Blank (1988).   N. G. W.

Lesbos (now Lesvos or Mytilini), the third largest *Aegean island (1,630 sq. km.: 629 sq. mi.) after *Crete and *Euboea, 10 km. (6 mi.) from NW *Asia Minor. It is divided into three lobes on the south side by the long, narrow-mouthed gulfs of Kalloni and Gera. The volcanic western and northern mountains rise to 968 m. (3,176 ft.); the south-eastern hills are greener and more fertile. Alluvium (partly marshy) occurs around the gulfs and in the east, where Thermi (an important bronze age site) has hot springs.

Lesbos was usually divided between five competing *poleis*: *Mytilene (the most powerful), *Methymna, *Pyrrha, *Antissa, and *Eresus. A sixth, *Arisbe (2) (near Kalloni), was absorbed by Methymna in the Archaic period. Some of the towns had land in Asia Minor. Settlement is relatively dispersed: there are import-

ant rural sanctuaries at Klopedi (temple of *Apollo), Mesa, and elsewhere, and the frequent rural towers and enclosures may be further evidence of inter-*polis* rivalry.

Proximity to Anatolia and the *Hellespont partly explains the distinctive early culture. The earliest Greek settlers (10th cent. BC ?) may have brought to the island its Aeolian dialect (see DIALECTS, GREEK); Mytilene and Pyrrha have protogeometric remains. Lesbian culture retained unusual features, such as the characteristic grey *bucchero* pottery which may imply a continuity of pre-Aeolian population or culture. *Cybele was worshipped in several towns.

The importance of seafaring is indicated by the *harbour moles at several of the towns. Lesbian transport *amphorae are found throughout the Greek world; amphora kilns have been located on the island. As élite wealth increased, a distinctive aristocratic culture grew up: Lesbos was the home of the poets *Sappho, *Alcaeus (1), *Terpander, and *Arion (2), the historian *Hellanicus (1), and the philosopher *Theophrastus. Lesbians founded colonies in the Hellespont and challenged Athens for control of *Sigeum around 600 BC. The island came under *Persian domination during the *Persian Wars. The cities joined the Athenian alliance (see DELIAN LEAGUE), but their rivalries persisted: Methymna did not back Mytilene's revolt in 428, and was alone in not having an Athenian *cleruchy imposed afterwards. Lesbos revolted again in 412.

After the *Peloponnesian War the island increasingly has a single history. It oscillated between Athenian, Spartan, and Persian rule until *Alexander (3) the Great's expedition. In the Hellenistic period it came under Ptolemaic domination (see PTOLEMY (1)); after the Macedonian wars the towns formed a league. Mytilene and Methymna were the seats of bishops from the 5th cent.

H. Williams and N. Spencer, in G. K. Sams (ed.), *The Garland Encyclopedia of Ancient Anatolia* (1994), 'Lesbos'; G. D. Kontis, Λέσβος καὶ ἡ μικρασιατική της περιοχή (1978); M. Paraskevaïdis, *PECS* 'Lesbos'; N. Spencer, *BSA* 1995; [British Admiralty] Naval Intelligence Division, *Greece* 3 (1945), 492–514; W. Lamb, *Thermi* (1936); *RE* 12/2 (1925), 2107–33.   D. G. J. S.

Lesches, of *Mytilene or *Pyrrha (?7th cent. BC), epic poet named as author of the *Little Iliad* or (Paus. 10. 25. 5) *Iliu Persis*. See EPIC CYCLE.   M. L. W.

Leto (Λητώ, Lat. *Latona*), a Titaness (see TITAN), daughter of Coeus and *Phoebe (Hes. *Theog.* 406–8).

In myth, her only role is to be mother of *Apollo and *Artemis (Hes. *Theog.* 918–20). Local legends locate the birth in various places. The main version is the one given in the Delian part of the *Homeric Hymn to Apollo*, where the island of *Delos allows Leto to give birth to her twins on condition that it would become Apollo's main cult place (or that the island, now floating, would become stable, Callim. *Hymn* 4, and Ov. *Met.* 6. 333: a typical motif in foundation legends); grasping the palm-tree (v. 117; others add an olive-tree, Ov. *Met.* 6. 335), Leto is delivered of Apollo (and, in later authors, of Artemis as well). *Aristotle, *Hist. an.* 580ᵃ15, adds that Leto had come as a she-wolf from the *Hyperboreans to Delos: this connects her with Apollo Λύκειος, Apollo 'Of the Wolves'. Another important place was *Ephesus where the birth legend, with emphasis on Artemis, was connected with the local cult of the *Curetes and influenced by the myth of Rhea giving birth to *Zeus (Strabo 14. 1. 20, 639 f., see D. Knibbe, in *Forschungen in Ephesos* 9/1. 1 (1981)). Minor sanctuaries held similar claims, e.g. the oracular shrine of

*Tegyra (Plut. *Pel.* 16. 6), the sanctuary of Zoster (east coast of *Attica; Steph. Byz. 'Zoster') or the Letoon of *Xanthus in *Lycia.

Former scholars, following the lead of Wilamowitz, derived Leto from Lycia. The excavations in the Letoon of Xanthus show that it belonged to an indigenous 'Mother' who in the 5th cent. BC was identified with Greek Leto, as she was identified in other places with other Anatolian goddesses, often as 'Mother Leto'. Her Greek cult is often closely connected with that of Apollo and Artemis, as on Delos, where she had her own sanctuary, or in *Didyma, while she is curiously absent from cult in *Delphi.

In some sanctuaries, her cult is more independent. In certain Greek cities (Delos, Ephesus, or *Chios), she has a priestess, while her Anatolian cults usually have a priest. See PRIESTS. In Roman times, some Anatolian cities celebrated Letoa, festivals and contests for a former local deity. In several places, Leto is connected with the same care for younger members of society that otherwise is characteristic of Apollo and Artemis. In Chios, Leto received the dedications of parents for the victory of their daughter (F. Graf, *Nordionische Kulte* (1985), 60–2); there is evidence from Chios for girls' *athletics (Athen. 13. 20. 566e) which must have their roots in the world of *initiation. For Leto Phytia in Phaestus on *Crete, a myth tells of the transformation of a girl into a young man in order to explain the ritual of Ekdysia whose dependence on initiatory ritual is undisputed (Ant. Lib. 17, see the notes of M. Papathomopoulos, (1968)). The Athenian Demotionidai (see PHRATRIES) put up the list of their new members in the local Letoon (*Syll.*[3] 921. 125); and the strange epithet κυανόπεπλος, 'with a dark cloak' in Hes. *Theog.* 406 might be explained by the usually black or dark cloaks of ephebes (see EPHEBOI).

The Delian Letoon contained a small wooden image (*Semos in Ath. 14. 2. 614a), one of the rare representations of Leto alone. The triad is attested already in the Daedalic (see DAEDALUS) statuettes from 7th-cent. BC Dreros on *Crete and is the common image both in temples and in vase-painting.

See APOLLO; ARTEMIS.

For the evidence from Xanthus see *Fouilles de Xanthos*, esp. vols. 6, H. Metzger and others, *La Stèle trilingue du Létôon* (1979), and 7, A. Balland, *Inscriptions d'époque impériale du Létôon* (1981); see also T. R. Pryce, *Hist.* 1983, 1–13. For Delos see esp. H. Gallet de Santerre, *La Terrasse des Lions, le Létôon et le Monument de granit à Délos*, Exploration archéologique de Délos 24 (1959), and P. Bruneau, *Recherches sur les cultes de Délos à l'époque hellénistique et à l'époque impériale* (1970). Iconography: G. Berger-Doer, *LIMC* 6 (1992), 267–72, 'Leto'.　　　　F. G.

letters, Greek Letters in the Greek world could be written on metal, wax-coated wood, fragments of earthenware, animal skin, and (above all) papyrus (see BOOKS, GREEK AND ROMAN); a very early surviving example (*c*.500 BC) is on *lead (*PCPS* 1973, 35). Literary references begin with the murderous message of *Proetus (*Il.* 6. 168; see BELLEROPHON); the earliest correspondence attested in a historical source is that of *Amasis of Egypt and *Polycrates (1) in the early 520s (Hdt. 3. 40–3). At least until the late 5th cent. BC, and perhaps into the 4th, letter-writing was not a widespread habit.

Surviving letters are of many different kinds. Roughly, one may distinguish:

1. Letters of otherwise unknown private individuals and officials, preserved either by mere chance, or because kept for personal or administrative *archives. The vast majority of these are known from papyrus finds from Graeco-Roman Egypt, and date from the middle of the 3rd cent. BC onwards. Ranging from business reports to soldiers' and students' letters home, they

shed light on the social and economic life of both the Ptolemaic kingdom (see EGYPT, Ptolemaic) and the Roman province, as well as on everyday linguistic usage. See e.g. APOLLONIUS (3).

2. Official letters to and from the cities, senior officials, kings, and emperors of the Hellenistic and Roman periods, preserved and often 'published' because of their public importance to sender or recipient. They survive mainly on inscriptions, though some few are also found on papyrus, or included in literary texts e.g. *Letter of Aristeas* 35 (see ARISTEAS, LETTER OF); Joseph. *AJ* 12. 3; Diog. Laert. 7. 7.

3. Private correspondence of famous individuals, collected and published because of the interest of contents, style, or author. The practice is first attested for *Aristotle's correspondence, published by *Artemon (2) of Cassandreia. The first such set of letters actually preserved is that of the emperor *Julian; those of *Libanius enjoyed the greatest subsequent renown. In most or all of such cases, publication was by someone other than the author; the first individual known to have seen to the publication of his own (in Greek) was *Gregory (2) of Nazianzus (*Ep.* 54).

4. Exploitation of the letter form for various more public kinds of communication. This very broad category includes: (*a*) 'open' letters with apologetic or propagandistic aims, such as those (whether genuine or spurious) of *Isocrates, *Plato (1), and *Demosthenes (2). This application seems to have declined in favour in the imperial era (though note Aristid. *Or.* 19 Keil), and to have been revived by the 2nd-cent. Christian *apologists. (*b*) Letters of personal moral / philosophical advice and instruction, as written most famously by *Epicurus and his disciples. Letters of *consolation (e.g. *Plutarch's to his wife, *Mor.* 608a) belong in this category, as also do the epistles of St *Paul. (*c*) Technical and scholarly treatises in epistolary form, on topics as varied as philology, mathematics, engineering, and medicine, as for instance those of *Dionysius (7) of Halicarnassus to Ammaeus and Cn. Pompeius. (*d*) Dedicatory letters, usually attached to compilations of some kind: e.g. those prefacing *Phrynichus (3)'s *Atticist*, *Parthenius' Love Stories*, and *Arrian's *Discourses of Epictetus*. See DEDICATIONS. (*e*) Magical letters, the form being used both for the issuing of *curses and for the conveying of instruction (cf. (*b*) above) from adept to pupil (e.g. *PGM* 1. I and IV; H. D. Betz, *The Greek Magical Papyri in Translation* (1986), 4 ff., 40 ff.).

5. Fictitious letters. This last category (again a broad one) covers both (*a*) pseudonymous letters of kinds (3) and (4*a*–*c*) above, attributed to great names but in reality the products of a later era, and (*b*) wholly 'literary' sets of letters attributed to entirely fictitious individuals or groups. Examples of (*a*) include some of the letters attributed to Isocrates and Demosthenes, and perhaps all of those attributed to Plato (though the case of *Ep.* 7 in particular is disputed); the moral / philosophical epistles attributed to such figures as *Anacharsis, *Hippocrates (2), *Socrates, and *Diogenes (2); and the more historically slanted letters of *Themistocles and Chion. Many of these belong to the period between the 1st cent. BC and the 1st cent. AD, though some (e.g. those of Phalaris, famously exposed by Bentley) may be as late as the 5th cent. In category (*b*) come the collections of letters by *Aelian, Aristaenetus, *Alciphron, and Philostratus (see PHILOSTRATI). In both categories a narrative line can be sustained through a sequence of separate letters, in the manner of a rudimentary epistolary *novel. See FORGERIES, LITERARY, GREEK.

6. Compared with Latin literature, there is one very striking absence: the verse epistle, present only in the form of a few very brief letters of invitation in the *Palatine Anthology* (6. 227; 11. 44).

As a matter for literary theory and practical instruction, letter-writing attracted the attention of grammarians from at least the 2nd cent. BC onwards. *Artemon (1) included some theoretical remarks in his edition of Aristotle's correspondence; Dionysius of Alexandria (1st cent. BC) wrote on the use of χαίρε in letters; *Theon (3) mentions letter-writing as an exercise in his *Progymnasmata*. Still extant are the discussion of epistolary style in *Demetrius (17) *On Style* (223) and the *Model Letters* attributed to another *Demetrius (15).

GENERAL K. Dziatzko, *RE* 3 (1899), 836; J. Sykutris, *RE* Suppl. 5 (1931), 185; J. Schneider, *RAC* 2 (1954), 568; W. Harris, *Ancient Literacy* (1989), see index under 'letter'; R. Hercher, *Epistolographi graeci* (Greek text with Latin tr., 1873).

PAPYRI S. Witkowski, *Epistulae privatae graecae*, 2nd edn. (1911); A. S. Hunt and C. Edgar, *Select Papyri* 1 (Loeb, 1952).

ROYAL CORRESPONDENCE C. B. Welles, *Royal Correspondence in the Hellenistic Period* (1934).

PSEUDEPIGRAPHA R. Bentley, *Dissertation upon the Epistles of Phalaris* (1699); G. Capelle, *De Cynicorum epistulis* (1896); J. Sykutris, *Die Briefe des Sokrates und der Sokratiker* (1933); I. During, *Chion of Heraclea* (1951); A. Malherbe, *The Cynic Epistles* (1977).

THEORY V. Weichert, *Demetrii et Libanii . . . Τυπ. ἐπ. et Ἐπ. χαρ.* (1910); F. Exler, *The Form of the Ancient Greek Letter* (1923); H. Koskenniemi, *Studien zur Idee und Phraseologie des griechischen Briefes* (1956); A. Malherbe, *Ancient Epistolary Theorists* (1988).   M. B. T.

letters, Latin Letters of all kinds naturally played an even more important role in the vast extent of the Roman empire than in Greece, but we have fewer examples from the archaeological record because Latin was little used in Egypt, where most of the Greek examples have been found. Vindolanda in northern England has considerably increased the corpus, however (see VINDOLANDA TABLETS), and a number of public letters, especially from emperors, have been preserved in inscriptions (Millar, *ERW* 213–28; Oliver (Greek only, with trans.)). See EPIGRAPHY, LATIN, § 5a.

As in Greece, letters were normally written with a reed pen (*calamus*) and ink (*atramentum*) on papyrus (*charta*), which was then rolled up and sealed with a thread. Wooden tablets (as at Vindolanda, cf. A. K. Bowman, *ZPE* 18 (1978), 237–52) and *ostraca might also on occasion be used. Short notes might also be scratched with a *stilus* on wax-covered folding tablets (*codicilli*): these are a prominent feature of love elegy (cf. Fedeli on Prop. 3. 23, McKeown on Ov. *Am.* 1. 11–12). The recipient could erase the message and use the same tablets for his reply (Cic. *Fam.* 6. 18. 1; Plin. *Ep.* 6. 16. 8). *Cicero generally wrote to T. *Pomponius Atticus, his most intimate friend, in his own hand (*suo chirographo*) unless for some special reason (*Att.* 2. 23. 1, 8. 13. 1), but an amanuensis was frequently used (*librarius* or *servus ab epistulis*). Cicero's secretary M. *Tullius Tiro appears to have kept copies of letters dictated to him (*Fam.* 7. 25. 1), and to have pasted together in rolls (*volumina*) those which Cicero thought worth keeping. It is no doubt to this practice that we owe the preservation of Cicero's *Epistulae ad familiares*, though his intention, expressed in 44 BC (*Att.* 16. 5. 5), of revising and publishing a selection remained unfulfilled. His letters to Atticus and to his brother Quintus *Tullius Cicero (1) were preserved by their recipients, and the former probably remained unpublished for a century after his death. There was never a public *postal service for private correspondence, although *Augustus instituted a system of post-couriers for official correspondence along the main routes of the empire: private individuals might have their own slave couriers (*tabellarii*), who could cover 50 Roman miles (*c.* 76 km.) a day, and the companies of tax-farmers (see PUBLICANI)

had their own postal service (*publicanorum tabellarii*).

Cicero's correspondence offers a broad cross-section of the different forms and *registers of letter (see *Fam.* 2. 4 for his own classification: cf. A. J. Malherbe, *Ancient Epistolary Theory* (1988); P. Cugusi, *Evoluzione e forme dell'epistolografia latina* (1983); Iulius Victor, *Ars Rhetorica*, pp. 105–6 Giomini and Celentano): book 13 of the *Ad familiares*, for instance, is entirely devoted to letters of recommendation (*litterae commendaticiae*, cf. Hor. *Epist.* 1. 9); see PATRONAGE (NON-LITERARY). The *Ad familiares* offer in addition nearly 100 letters from other correspondents, including Ser. *Sulpicius Rufus' famous letter of condolence to Cicero on the death of his daughter *Tullia (2) (*Fam.* 4. 5). See CONSOLATION. The letters to Atticus, in contrast, tend to be less formal, and show a marked difference in linguistic register. The Ciceronian collections formed the model for *Pliny (2)'s epistolary self-presentation, and for other collections such as those of Fronto (cf. E. Champlin, *JRS* 1974, 156–7) and Symmachus (2) (cf. J. F. Matthews, in J. W. Binns (ed.), *Latin Literature of the Fourth Century* (1974), 58–99; J. P. Callu (ed.), *Symmaque: Lettres* 1 (1972), 16–22).

A second model was that of the Greek philosophical letter, as represented by those of *Epicurus and the collection ascribed to *Plato (1). This tradition is best represented by the younger Seneca's *Epistulae morales* (see ANNAEUS SENECA (2), L.). As in Greek, individual treatises might be published in letter form, and the introductory prefaces to prose works may take the form of a letter.

The two traditions both influenced the poetic epistle, attested in the 2nd cent. BC (cf. *Lucilius (1) frs. 181–3, 341 Marx; Cic. *Att.* 13. 6. 4 on Sp. Mummius) and later (*Catullus 65, 68a, cf. 35) but represented above all by *Horace's *Epistles* (cf. E. F. Morris *YClS* 1931, 18–114) and *Ovid's collections of exile poetry, the *Tristia* and the *Ex Ponto* (cf. W. Stroh, *ANRW* 2. 31. 4 (1981), 2640–4; H. Rahn *A&A* 1958, 105–20). Horace in particular constantly plays on the conventions of the everyday letter, defamiliarizing or recontextualizing them (cf. e.g. 1. 8 and the formulae of address, 1. 9 and the commonplaces of recommendation). Ovid's *Heroides*, letters of mythological heroines, represent a different tradition again (cf. H. Jacobson, *Ovids Heroides* (1974); H. Dörrie, *Der heroische Brief* (1968); F. Spoth, *Ovids Heroides als Elegien* (1992), 85–106). *Martial and *Statius have epistolary prose prefaces to their verse collections (cf. Coleman on Stat. *Silv.* 4. 1, pp. 53–5): later writers like *Ausonius offer mixed collections of prose and verse (27 Green).

Letter-writing of all kinds was particularly popular amongst Christian writers (see CHRISTIANITY), in part because of the use of the letter form in the New Testament and other early Christian texts (cf. J. W. White, *ANRW* 2. 25. 2 (1984), 1730–56; K. Berger, loc. cit. 1326–63; M. Naldini, in G. Asdrubali Pentiti and M. C. Spadoni Cerroni (eds.), *Epistolari Cristiani 2: Epistolari Latini* (1990), 5–14): the collections of *Ambrose, *Jerome, *Paulinus of Nola, *Augustine, *Sidonius Apollinaris, and *Cassiodorus are notable examples.

The letter in both its 'subliterary' and literary forms combines rhetorical direction and self-presentation in an artful representation of reality: hence its importance in modern theoretical discussions, especially in relation to the epistolary *novel (cf. J. K. Altman, *Epistolarity: Approaches to a Form* (1982); L. S. Kauffman, *Discourses of Desire: Genders, Genre, and Epistolary Fiction* (1986), and *Special Delivery: Epistolary Modes in Modern Fiction* (1992); J.-L. Bonnet and M. Bossis (eds.), *Les Correspondances* (1983)). See FORGERIES, LITERARY, LATIN; also under individual authors.

P. Cugusi (ed.), *Corpus epistularum Latinarum papyris tabulis ostracis servatum*, 2 vols (1992), and *Epistolographi Latini minores*, 2 vols. (1970–9); H. Peter, *Der Brief in d. röm. Lit.* (1901); J. Sykutris, RE Suppl. 5 (1931), 'Epistolographie'; K. Thraede, *Grundzüge griech.-röm. Brieftopik* (1970); P. Cugusi, *Evoluzione e forme dell'epistolografia latina* (1983); Shackleton Bailey *CLA* 1. 59 ff.　　　　R. G. C. L.; P. G. F., D. P. F.

Leucas, an island in the *Ionian Sea, opposite the coast of *Acarnania. It derived its name from the white limestone cliffs on its west coast. Its SW promontory, Cape Leucatas, has a sheer drop of 610 m. (2,000 ft.); suspected criminals were hurled from it, and if they survived the ordeal were rescued in boats (Strabo 10. 452). The shallow waters between its NE coast and the mainland were liable to be closed to navigation by the formation of a sand-bar. The early Corinthian colonists (see CORINTH) cut through this spit (Strabo ibid.), but in the 5th cent. BC ships had to be hauled across it (Thuc. 3. 81, 4. 8).

Leucas took its culture from the mainland in prehistoric times, but it was subject also to occasional influences from the north, which are indicated by the occurrence of 'barbotine' pottery late in the early neolithic period and by interesting groups of tombs under tumuli of early Helladic and middle Helladic date. In the Mycenaean period it was on the fringe of the Greek world and is to be identified with the Homeric Dulichium rather than, as Dörpfeld argued, with the Homeric *Ithaca. See HOMER. The history of the island in Classical times begins with the arrival of Corinthian colonists *c*.625 BC, who soon dominated the native population and remained loyal to their mother-city.

In the *Persian Wars Leucas furnished contingents to the Greek fleet at the battle of *Salamis and to the army at the battle of *Plataea, and gave active assistance to Corinth in the *Peloponnesian War. After a brief alliance with Athens against *Philip (1) II of Macedon it passed into the hands of various Hellenistic rulers (*Cassander, *Agathocles (1), *Pyrrhus), but *c*.250 it joined the Acarnanian Confederacy, of which it became the capital. The Romans besieged and captured it in 197; in 167 they detached it from Acarnania and constituted it a *free city.

P–K, *GL* 2. 2, 460 ff.; *IG* 9. 1; W. Dörpfeld, *Alt-Ithaka* (1927); W. M. Murray, in A. Raban (ed.), *Archaeology and Coastal Changes* (1988).
　　　　M. C.; N. G. L. H.

Leuce Come ('White Village'), probably mod. ʿAynūnah (28°2' N, 35°12' E) on the NW coast of *Arabia. Arab *Nabataeans here received in small ships eastern wares for *Petra and the west. A 25% due was levied there, perhaps by a Roman centurion. *Aelius Gallus in his expedition against southern Arabia landed there in 25 BC. It seems to have declined after Nabataea became a Roman province (AD 106). It may be *Ptolemy (4)'s 'Auara'.

Strabo. 16. 4. 23–4; L. Casson (ed.), *Periplus Maris Erythraei* 19. S. E. Sidebotham, *Roman Economic Policy in the Erythra Thalassa* (1986); M. G. Raschke, *ANRW* 2. 9. 2 (1978).　　　　W. E. H. C.

Leucippides Phoebe and Hilaeira, the daughters of *Leucippus (1), were cousins both of the Spartan *Dioscuri and of the sons of the *Messenian king Aphareus, *Idas and Lynceus; engaged to marry the latter, they were seized at the altar by Castor and Polydeuces (see DIOSCURI) and a violent fight (expressing the enmity between the two neighbouring regions of the Peloponnese; see PELOPONNESUS) ensued. See *Pindar, *Nem.* 10 (glossing over the cause) and *Theocritus 22. 137 ff. (laying it bare).

F. Gury, *LIMC* 6 (1992), 'Dioskouroi', § 11c.　　　　A. H. G.

Leucippus, 'person who keeps white horses', hence 'rich man, noble'. Name of fifteen mythological characters, see Stoll in Roscher's *Lexikon*, entry under the name, but especially (1) father

of Hilaeira and Phoebe, see LEUCIPPIDES; (2) a young Cretan turned from a girl into a boy by a miracle of *Leto (Ant. Lib. 17).

Leucippus (3), originator of the atomic theory in the second half of the 5th cent. BC. His birthplace is reported to be *Elea, *Abdera, or *Miletus (Diog. Laert. 9. 30), but all of these may be inferences from affinities between his work and that of philosophers known to come from these places; Miletus is slightly more probable than the others. He wrote later than *Parmenides, and almost certainly later than *Zeno (1) and *Melissus. *Epicurus is said to have denied his existence (Diog. Laert. 10. 13), but this is not to be taken seriously, in the face of *Aristotle's frequent mentions of him.

Works Of the Democritean works (see DEMOCRITUS) collected by Thrasyllus (Diog. Laert. 9. 45–9), two are sometimes attributed to Leucippus: *The Great World System* and *On Mind*. Both attributions appear to stem from *Theophrastus and may well be right.

For the atomic theory, see ATOMISM; DEMOCRITUS of Abdera. Various attempts have been made to separate Leucippus' contribution from that of his more prolific pupil Democritus, but none is sufficiently convincing.

ANCIENT SOURCES DK 67.
MODERN LITERATURE See bibliog. under DEMOCRITUS.
　　　　D. J. F.

Leucon (1), writer of Old Comedy (see COMEDY (GREEK), OLD) active during the *Peloponnesian War (*Suda* λ 340). Fr. 1 mentions the politician *Hyperbolus.

FRAGMENTS Kassel–Austin, *PCG* 5. 611–14, although earlier scholars use the numbering in Kock, *CAF* 1. 703 f.
INTERPRETATION Meineke, *FCG* 1 217 f.; A. Körte, RE 12/2 (1925), 2283, 'Leukon' 6.　　　　W. G. A.

Leucon (2), 4th-cent. BC king of *Bosporus (2). See SPARTOCIDS.

Leucos Limen, Egyptian *Red Sea port, important in oriental trade, linked with *Coptus on the Nile by a track with stations.

D. S. Whitcomb and J. H. Johnson, *Quseir al-Qadim 1978* (1979); R. S. Bagnall, *BASP* 1986, 1–60; A. Bülow-Jacobsen and others, *BIFAO* 1994, 27–42; S. E. Sidebotham, *Roman Economic Policy in the Erythra Thalassa* (1986).　　　　W. E. H. C.

Leucothea See INO-LEUCOTHEA.

Leuctra, place in SW *Boeotia where the Boeotians defeated the Spartans in 371 BC. *Epaminondas of Thebes massed his Thebans, 50 deep, on his left, opposite the Spartans themselves, with the élite *Sacred Band perhaps forming the front ranks, and the remaining Boeotians, opposite Sparta's allies, echeloned back to the right. The battle opened with a clash between the cavalry, unusually placed in front of the phalanxes (see PHALANX), and the defeated Spartans reeled back into their advancing infantry. The latter's confusion was compounded by an attempt either to increase depth or to extend to the right, or both, and at this point the Sacred Band charged. The Spartan king, Cleombrotus, was mortally wounded, and although his men managed to recover his body, they eventually gave way, with heavy losses, particularly among the Spartiates. The battle ended two centuries of Spartan domination on the battlefield. See also TEGYRA.

RE 12/2, 'Leuktra' 1. Xen. *Hell.* 6. 4. 4 ff.; Diod. Sic. 15. 55–6; Plut. *Pel.* 23. J. Buckler, *The Theban Hegemony 371–362 BC* (1980); J. F. Lazenby, *The Spartan Army* (1985).　　　　J. F. La.

lex (1) (*a*) Statute, passed by one of the assemblies of the Roman people; the *lex Hortensia* of 287 BC conferred the force of statute on *plebis scita*, measures passed by a meeting of the **plebs*, and these came in time to be referred to loosely as *leges*. See PLEBISCI-TUM. The passage of a *lex* involved a magistrate presenting a proposal in the form of a question: 'Would you wish, would you order, Quirites, that . . .? This then, as I have spoken, so I ask you, Quirites.' The measure had normally to be promulgated, publicized, at least three market days, *nundinae*, beforehand (see TRINUNDINUM); and there could then be debate in a series of informal gatherings, *contiones* (see CONTIO); but in the assembly the people could only answer yes or no. Once the measure had been passed, the subjunctives of the dependent clauses of the *rogatio* were converted into the future imperatives which are characteristic of Roman legislative style. The text was then both published and placed in the archives. In the late republic and for the period of the early empire for which legislation survived, there was a tendency not to bother to carry out this process of conversion: only the enforcement clauses of the *sanctio* at the end appeared in the future imperative. For *lex curiata* see IMPER-IUM, and separate entry LEX CURIATA.

In the same period, there was increasing discussion of the sources of law, of which statutes formed only one kind; under the empire, decrees of the senate, which had been marginal under the republic, increased in importance (see SENATUS CONSULTUM); and imperial pronouncements became the principal source of law (see CONSTITUTIONS).

The retrospective juristic classification of *leges* into *leges perfec-tae*, *leges minus quam perfectae*, and *leges imperfectae* is of no rele-vance whatever to republican legislation.

A *lex satura* was a statute which dealt with different subjects in one bill; they were forbidden by the *lex Caecilia Didia* of 98 BC.

(b) Charter, conferred on a community in order to regulate its status and order its affairs, such as the *lex Tarentina* (Crawford *Roman Statutes* (see bibliog. below), no. 15) or the *lex Irnitana* (see TABULA IRNITANA).

Note that although *leges*, as (a), have been *rogatae*, 'proposed', and *leges*, as (b), have been *datae*, 'conferred', *rogatae* and *datae* are participles, not adjectives: it is a mistake to create two categor-ies of *leges rogatae* and *leges datae*; for there is no reason why a *lex* should not be *rogata* and then *data*.

It is of course likely that most charters already under the republic were simply conferred by magistrates or by those responsible for founding a colony (see COLONIZATION, ROMAN) or constituting a *municipium*, basing themselves on existing legisla-tion, but without presenting a *rogatio* to an assembly. The Flavian *leges* such as the *lex Irnitana* were manifestly not *rogatae*.

(c) Set of regulations devised by the censors for the execution of the contracts let by them, whether for the collection of rev-enues or the construction of buildings or the sale or leasing of public property, *lex censoria*. See CENSOR. We are now much better informed about the former from the *lex portorii Asiae* (provisionally published by H. Engelmann and D. Knibbe, *Das Zollgesetz der Provinz Asia = EA* 1989, *SEG* 29. 1180; see PORTORIA); a text modelled on the *lex censoria* for the construction of build-ings is the *lex parieti faciendo* from **Puteoli, *ILLRP* 518.

(d) Set of regulations for a province, *lex provinciae*; the institu-tion of the **edict of a provincial governor probably goes back to the 3rd cent. BC, as do wide-ranging settlements of newly conquered areas. But it is very doubtful if anything which could be called a *lex provinciae* existed before the last generation of the republic. See PROVINCIA.

(e) Set of regulations for an altar, *lex arae*, or other sacred building or place (see e.g. *ILS* 112 (Narbo), 4906–16).

(f) Set of regulations for a contract between individuals, *lex* (e.g. for the sale of olives) *dicta*; the earliest examples are those in the *De agricultura* of **Cato (Censorius).

(g) The *leges regiae* are a set of rules, very disparate in character and from very disparate sources, attributed to the kings of Rome; some may be quite early; see Crawford, *Roman Statutes*, no. 40, introd.

(h) *Leges sacratae* are regarded in the Roman historical tradition as sworn agreements of the *plebs*, offenders against which were then outlawed; they were the mechanism by which the *plebs* was regarded as having protected its tribunes in the early period.

(i) *Leges Romanae barbarorum* is the term assigned by modern scholars to the various 'codes' adopted by the successor king-doms in the west and deriving from Roman law; see P. Vinogra-doff, *Roman Law in Medieval Europe* (1909).

M. H. Crawford (ed.), *Roman Statutes* (1996), and in A. Schiavone (ed.), *Storia di Roma* 2. 1 (1990), 91–121; general introd., A. Watson, *Law-Making in the Later Roman Republic* (1974); P. A. Brunt, *JRS* 1977, 95–116; M. Lemosse, in *Studi A. Biscardi* 1 (1981), 235–44 = *Études romanistiques* (1981), 107–16. M. H. C.

lex (2) It is clear from **Priscian, *Institutes* 2. 49–50 = 2. 75 Keil, that the concept of *leges frumentariae, agrariae, nummariae*, and so on (see below) was familiar to the Romans. We discuss a number of these and then list some important examples of some of the different kinds of *leges* of *lex* (1). We then append a set of miscellaneous regulations and laws. See in general J.-L. Ferrary and P. Moreau, *Les Lois du peuple romain* (forthcoming), and M. H. Crawford (ed.), *Roman Statutes* (1996).

leges agrariae: see AGRARIAN LAWS AND POLICY; FLAMINIUS (1), C.; SEMPRONIUS GRACCHUS (3), TI., and SEMPRONIUS GRACCHUS, C.; also *lex Thoria* (below).

leges annales: statutes regulating minimum ages for and intervals between different magistracies; see CURSUS HONORUM; VILLIUS (ANNALIS), L.; A. E. Astin, *The Lex Annalis before Sulla* (1958).

leges de ciuitate: statutes conferring **citizenship or Latinity on categories of Latin and Italian communities; the most famous is the *lex Julia* of 90 BC, the first year of the **Social War (3); see A. N. Sherwin White, *Roman Citizenship*, 2nd edn. (1973), ch. 6.

leges frumentariae: statutes providing for the subsidized or free distribution of grain to (some of) the Roman people; see FOOD SUPPLY; SEMPRONIUS GRACCHUS, C.; G. E. Rickman, *The Corn Supply of Ancient Rome* (1980); P. Garnsey, *Famine and Food Supply in the Graeco-Roman World* (1988); A. Giovannini (ed.), *Nourrir la plèbe* (1991).

leges iudiciariae: statutes dealing with the establishment and organization of the criminal courts; see QUAESTIONES.

leges repetundarum: see REPETUNDAE.

leges sumptuariae: statutes regulating consumption and display; see D. Daube, *Roman Law: Linguistic, Social and Philosophical Aspects* (1969), 117–28; E. Gabba, *Del buon uso della ricchezza* (1988); also *lex Fannia, Didia, Licinia* (below).

leges tabellariae: statutes which progressively from 137 BC intro-duced the secret ballot for assembly votes, whether in elections or trials, and regulated its functioning; see *lex Gabinia, Cassia, Papiria, Maria, Coelia* (overleaf).

lex

lex Acilia on intercalation, 191 BC: see ACILIUS GLABRIO (1), M'.

lex Acilia repetundarum: a statute known only from passing allusions in *Cicero's Verrines*; it has sometimes been identified with the great epigraphic *lex repetundarum* on the obverse of the *tabula Bembina*; see REPETUNDAE.

lex Aebutia: a statute dealing with private law procedure.

lex Aelia and *lex Fufia*: two separate statutes (Cic. *Har. resp.* 27, 58), mid-2nd cent. BC, about which Cicero and, for a time, modern scholars, got very excited; they regulated *obnuntiatio* in ways which remain obscure; see A. K. Michels, *The Calendar of the Roman Republic* (1967), 94–8.

lex Aelia Sentia, AD 4: see DEDITICII; the significance of declarations of births in Egypt *ex lege Aelia Sentia et Papia Poppaea* remains obscure.

lex Antonia de Termessibus, 68 BC: a statute conferring various privileges on the community of Termessus in *Pisidia; one tablet is preserved, found in Rome in the early 16th cent.; see *Roman Statutes*, no. 19.

leges Antoniae: see ANTONIUS (2), M.

leges Appuleiae: see APPULEIUS SATURNINUS, L.; also *lex latina tabulae Bantinae* (below).

lex Aquilia: the earliest known private law statute, very probably early 3rd cent. BC, amending some of the provisions on *iniuria* of the Twelve Tables; see *Roman Statutes*, no. 41.

fragmentum Atestinum: part of a text found at *Ateste and relating to civil procedure; it has no points of contact with the *lex de Gallia Cisalpina* and its regulations are not limited to Cisalpine Gaul; see *Roman Statutes*, no. 18.

lex Atinia: a statute, of uncertain date, providing for the automatic recruitment of tribunes into the senate.

lex Aurelia, 75 BC, on the tribunate: see AURELIUS COTTA, C.

lex Aurelia iudiciaria, 70 BC: see AURELIUS COTTA, L.; QUAESTIONES.

lex Caecilia Didia, 98 BC: see COMITIA; DIDIUS, T.; see also *lex satura* under LEX (1), § (a).

lex Calpurnia repetundarum, 149 BC: the first statute establishing a regular procedure; see CALPURNIUS PISO FRUGI, L.; REPETUNDAE.

lex Calpurnia on electoral corruption, 67 BC: a statute passed by C. *Calpurnius Piso (1), with the passive support of the other consul, M'. *Acilius Glabrio (3), in opposition to the proposal of the tribune C. *Cornelius.

lex Canuleia: see CANULEIUS, C.

lex Cassia tabellaria: a statute passed by the tribune L. *Cassius Longinus Ravilla, introducing the secret ballot in assembly trials, except for *perduellio*, 137 BC; see ELECTIONS AND VOTING, ROMAN; also *lex Coelia tabellaria* (below).

lex Cassia: a statute passed by the tribune L. Cassius Longinus, excluding from the senate men condemned, or deprived of their *imperium* by the people, 104 BC, aimed at Q. *Servilius Caepio (1).

lex Cincia: a statute probably passed by the tribune M. Cincius Alimentus, 204 BC, forbidding payments to advocates and all gifts beyond a certain limit, except within certain degrees of blood or other relationship; see *Roman Statutes*, no. 47.

lex Claudia, on commercial activity by senators, 218 BC: see CLAUDIUS, Q.

leges Clodiae: see CLODIUS PULCHER, P.

lex Coelia tabellaria: a statute passed by the tribune C. *Coelius Caldus, 107 BC, extending the secret ballot to assembly trials for *perduellio*; see *lex Cassia tabellaria*.

lex Coloniae Genetivae Iuliae: the charter of the Caesarian colony at *Urso, modern Osuna, near Seville; see *Roman Statutes*, no. 25.

leges Corneliae, 87 BC: see CORNELIUS CINNA (1), L.

leges Corneliae, 82–81 BC: see CORNELIUS SULLA FELIX, L. One tablet of the *lex Cornelia de XX quaestoribus* is preserved, found in Rome in the early 16th cent.; see *Roman Statutes*, no. 14.

leges Corneliae, 67 BC: see CORNELIUS, C.

lex Didia, 143 BC: a statute which extended the application of the *lex Fannia* to the whole of Italy and imposed sanctions on guests at, as well as providers of, illegal dinners.

lex Domitia, 104 BC: a statute which provided for the election of the members of the four priestly colleges by 17 out of the 35 tribes; the provision was abrogated by *Sulla and restored by T. *Labienus (1) in 63 BC.

lex duodecim tabularum: see TWELVE TABLES.

lex Fannia, 161 BC: a statute which limited the amount that could be spent on dinners, the kind of food that could be provided and the number of guests.

lex Flaminia agraria: see FLAMINIUS (1), C.

lex Fufia: see *lex Aelia* (above).

lex Fufia Caninia, 2 BC: a statute which limited the number of slaves which an owner could manumit in his will.

lex Gabinia tabellaria, 139 BC: the first statute on the secret ballot, which introduced it for elections (Cic. *leg.* 3. 3. 9, 16. 35–7).

leges Gabiniae (various), certainly or probably 67 BC; see GABINIUS (2), A.: the most famous was that which established a command against the pirates (for *Pompey). In addition there was a statute which fixed February as the month for foreign embassies to appear before the senate, but it is uncertain whether this belongs in 139 or 67 BC. Another *lex Gabinia* forbade the lending of money to provincials in Rome; this probably dates from 67 but might be from Gabinius' consulship of 58 BC.

lex de Gallia Cisalpina, hitherto known as the *lex Rubria*: the statute, of which one tablet is preserved from Veleia, regulating the civil law of Cisalpine Gaul after its incorporation in Italy; see *fragmentum Atestinum* (above); *Roman Statutes*, no. 28.

leges Genuciae: see GENUCIUS, L.

tabula Hebana: see *lex Valeria Aurelia* (below) and separate entry under TABULA HEBANA.

tabula Heracleensis: one of two tablets from *Heraclea (1) containing financial regulations of the Greek city, which contains on the reverse a series of chapters of Roman legislation. We have the end of the text, but not the beginning; there is no *sanctio* and it is clear that we do not have the end of a single statute passed through the assembly. The best view is that we have a locally compiled digest drawing on two statutes, one on maintenance of roads, the other on qualifications for municipal office, local censuses, and *municipia fundana*—the term is obscure; it *may* be that the latter body of material forms part of a *lex Iulia municipalis*, attested by an imperial inscription from *Patavium; see *Roman Statutes*, no. 24.

lex Hortensia: see HORTENSIUS, Q.

lex Icilia: see ICILIUS, L.

lex de imperio Vespasiani: the name given to the text on a bronze tablet found in Rome and already known to Cola di Rienzi in the 14th cent.; it contains the end of a measure conferring certain powers on *Vespasian; see P. A. Brunt, *JRS* 1977, 95–116. One should not too hastily reject the possibility that the tablet was originally a diptych and that the left-hand leaf was seen by Cola; and the conventional view, that although formally a *lex* the text is actually a decree of the senate, is wrong: it is just that the subjunctives of the *rogatio* have not been converted into the imperatives of a *lex*.

lex Iulia, 90 BC: see IULIUS CAESAR (1), L.; also *lex Plautia Papiria* (below).

leges Iuliae: it is often hard to decide whether a measure was passed by *Caesar in 59 or in 49–44 BC, or by *Augustus; for a discussion of a particular case which raises the general issues, see J. D. Cloud, *Athenaeum* 1988, 579–95, 1989, 427–65, 'Lex Iulia de vi'; see also *tabula Heracleensis* (above) and *lex Mamilia Roscia Peducaea Alliena Fabia* (below).

lex Iunia, between 149 and 123 BC: see REPETUNDAE.

lex Iunia, 126 BC: a statute passed by the tribune M. Iunius Pennus, expelling those who were not citizens from Rome, in fear of the impending citizenship bill of M. *Fulvius Flaccus.

lex Iunia: presumably a statute which created the category of Junian Latins. (See LATINI IUNIANI).

lex latina tabulae Bantinae: part of a statute, on the obverse of a tablet from Bantia, but perhaps originally from the nearby Latin colony of *Venusia, of the late 2nd cent. BC; only the enforcement clauses at the end are preserved, but it may be part of the *lex Appuleia maiestatis*; see *Roman Statutes*, no. 7; also *lex Osca tabulae Bantinae* (below). See also TABULA BANTINA.

lex Licinia sumptuaria, just after 143 BC: a statute which replaced the *lex Fannia*; its terms are obscure.

lex Licinia Mucia, 95 BC: a statute which set out to annul the citizenship of those who had usurped it and which according to our sources did more than anything else to provoke the Social War (3); see LICINIUS CRASSUS, L.

leges Liciniae Sextiae: see LICINIUS STOLO, L.

leges Liviae, 122 BC: see LIVIUS DRUSUS (1), M.

leges Liviae, 91 BC: see LIVIUS DRUSUS (2), M.

lex Malacitana: see TABULA (*lex*) IRNITANA.

lex Mamilia, 109 BC: a statute which set up a *quaestio* staffed by *Gracchani iudices* to investigate the conduct of the war against *Jugurtha; see MAMILIUS LIMETANUS, C.

lex Mamilia Roscia Peducaea Alliena Fabia: a fragment of a statute under this name transmitted among the writings of the *agrimensores* (*gromatici) is probably part of the *lex Iulia agraria* of 59 BC; see M. H. Crawford, *Athenaeum* 1989, 179–90.

lex Manilia, 66 BC: see MANILIUS, C.

lex Maria tabellaria, 119 BC: a statute passed by C. *Marius (1) as tribune which narrowed the bridges across which voters passed, in order to reduce the scope for improper influence.

lex Octavia frumentaria: a statute of uncertain date, which perhaps increased the price established for subsidised corn by C. *Sempronius Gracchus, a price which was perhaps restored by L. *Appuleius Saturninus.

lex Ogulnia: see OGULNIUS GALLUS, Q.

lex Oppia: see OPPIUS (1), C.

lex Orchia sumptuaria, 182 BC: the first sumptuary statute, limiting the number of guests at dinners (the *lex Oppia* is an emergency measure of the Second Punic War).

lex Osca tabulae Bantinae: part of the charter of Bantia, on the reverse of a tablet from Bantia, of the 90s BC. (See above, LEX LATINA TABULAE BANTINAE.) It is in *Oscan, but in the Latin script and from left to right. The bulk of the text has been known since the late 18th cent.; but a fragment discovered in 1967 makes it clear that the Oscan text is later than the Latin one: for a nail-hole lies below the Latin text, while the Oscan text is written round it. The surviving chapters of the Oscan text deal with the procedure in the case of a fine, trial before the assembly, the census and penalties for non-registration, procedures *in iure*, and the *cursus honorum. It is virtually certain that the charter is earlier than the *Social War (3); and it is very likely that it represents something very close to the charter of the Latin colony of Venusia. See also TABULA BANTINA.

lex Ovinia, on the composition of the senate: see OVINIUS.

lex Papia, 65 BC: a statute passed by the tribune C. Papius, expelling *peregrini (aliens) from Rome.

lex Papia Poppaea, AD 9: a statute which amended and completed the marriage legislation of Augustus; the jurists treat the two measures as a single piece of legislation. The significance of declarations of births in Egypt *ex lege Aelia Sentia et Papia Poppaea* remains obscure.

lex Papiria tabellaria, 131 BC: a statute passed by the tribune C. Papirius Carbo, introducing the secret ballot for legislation; see PAPIRIUS CARBO (1), C.

lex Pinaria Furia, on intercalation, 472 BC.

lex Plaetoria, about 200 BC: a statute which is remarkable for establishing a public law procedure for a private law affair, the protection of minors in financial matters.

lex Plautia iudiciaria, 89 BC: see PLAUTIUS SILVANUS (1), M.; QUAESTIONES.

lex Plautia Papiria: a statute consequential on the *lex Iulia de civitate*; its only certain provision is that attested by Cicero's *Pro Archia*.

lex Plotia de reditu Lepidanorum: a statute, perhaps of 70 BC, restoring the supporters of M. *Aemilius Lepidus (2), the rebel consul of 78 BC.

lex Poetelia on *nexum: see POETELIUS LIBO VISOLUS, C.

leges Pompeiae: see POMPEIUS MAGNUS (1), CN.

lex Pompeia Licinia, 70 BC: the statute which fully restored the tribunate to the position as it was before *Sulla.

lex Pompeia Licinia, 55 BC: the statute which renewed *Caesar's command in Gaul.

lex Porcia: a statute attested by the *lex de provinciis praetoriis* and the *lex Antonia de Termessibus*; it can now be seen to be earlier than 100 BC and to have begun the process of prescribing precise duties for provincial governors.

leges Porciae: three statutes on *provocatio, explicitly attested by Cicero, *Rep.* 2. 31, 54; no more than circumstantial evidence exists for their precise content or their authors.

lex de provinciis praetoriis: the best name for the statute probably of 100 BC, partially preserved in two Greek translations from *Delphi and *Cnidus, hitherto known as the *lex de piratis* (see PIRACY); it undertook a vast range of organizational tasks in relation to the eastern provinces and interests of Rome; see Roman Statutes, no. 12.

lex Publilia, on plebeian magistrates, 471 BC: see PUBLILIUS VULSO.

leges Publiliae, 339 BC: see PUBLILIUS PHILO, Q.

lex Pupia, on the holding of the senate: see SENATE.

lex Quinctia de aquaeductibus, 9 BC: the only republican statute preserved complete, apart from the *sanctio*, by Sex. *Iulius Frontinus, *De aquis* 129.

lex Remmia: see INIURIA AND DEFAMATION.

lex Roscia theatralis, 67 BC: see ROSCIUS OTHO, L.

lex Roscia: a statute to which the *fragmentum Atestinum* refers; its date and content are quite uncertain.

lex Rubria: the statute by which C. *Sempronius Gracchus founded a colony at *Carthage-Junonia; it was repealed soon after his death.

lex Rufrena: a statute relating to the erection of statues to the deified *Caesar, attested both by inscriptions and by an issue of coins (*RRC* no. 518).

lex Salpensana: see TABULA (*lex*) IRNITANA.

rogationes Scriboniae, 50 BC: see SCRIBONIUS CURIO (2), C.

lex Sempronia, 193 BC: a statute passed by the tribune M. Sempronius Tuditanus, providing that Roman citizens could not enter into agreements relating to loans with Latins (see LATINI) and Italians which were different from those with other Roman citizens.

leges Semproniae, 133 BC: see SEMPRONIUS GRACCHUS (3), TI.

leges Semproniae, 123/2 BC: see SEMPRONIUS GRACCHUS, C.; also *lex Rubria* (above).

lex Servilia iudiciaria: see SERVILIUS CAEPIO (1), Q.

lex Servilia repetundarum: see SERVILIUS GLAUCIA, C.

rogatio Servilia agraria, 63 BC: see SERVILIUS RULLUS, P.

tabula Siarensis: see separate entry under this title; also *lex Valeria Aurelia*.

leges Sulpiciae, 88 BC: see SULPICIUS RUFUS, P.

fragmentum Tarentinum: a statute on a fragment from *Tarentum, of the late 2nd cent. BC; only the reward and enforcement clauses at the end are preserved, but it may be part of the *lex Servilia repetundarum*; see Roman Statutes, no. 8.

lex Tarentina: the charter of Tarentum after the *Social War (3), of which one tablet is preserved; see Roman Statutes, no. 15.

lex Terentia Cassia frumentaria, 73 BC: see TERENTIUS VARRO LUCULLUS, M.

lex Thoria: the second of the agrarian statutes of Appian, *BCiv.* 1. 27, 121–4, to be identified with the great epigraphic *lex agraria* on the reverse of the *tabula Bembina*, winding up the Gracchan agrarian programme and consolidating the situation in Italy and a number of provinces; see Roman Statutes, no. 2; J. A. North, in *Apodosis: Essays Presented to Dr W. W. Cruickshank to Mark his Eightieth Birthday* (1992), 75–83.

lex Titia: the statute which established M. *Aemilius Lepidus (3),

M. *Antonius (2), and Caesar Octavianus (see AUGUSTUS) as *tresviri reipublicae constituendae* on 27 November 43 BC.

lex Trebonia, 55 BC: see TREBONIUS, C.

leges Tulliae, 63 BC: see TULLIUS CICERO (1), M.

lex Ursonensis: see *lex Coloniae Genetivae Iuliae* (above).

leges Valeriae, 509, 449, and 300 BC: a series of statutes dealing, according to tradition, with *provocatio* and other matters; the sources make no coherent distinction between the content of the three statutes and no serious scholar accepts the full historicity of the first two; see for 509 VALERIUS POPLICOLA, P.; for 449 VALERIUS POPLICOLA POTITUS, L.; for 300 VALERIUS (MAXIMUS?) CORVUS, M.

lex Valeria on debt, 86 BC: see VALERIUS FLACCUS (3), L.

lex Valeria Aurelia, AD 20: the centre-piece of a dossier of honours for the dead Germanicus *Iulius Caesar, including also decisions of the senate; the legislation devotes much space to extending an elaborate restructuring of the *comitia centuriata*, originally introduced by the *lex Valeria Cornelia* of AD 5 to honour the dead C. *Iulius Caesar (2) and L. *Iulius Caesar (4) by naming five voting groups after each of them. In AD 20, five were named after Germanicus; and in AD 23, five were named after Drusus *Iulius Caesar. Although the honours for Germanicus and Drusus are attested in the literary sources, neither the legislation nor the system of *destinatio* which it introduced is ever specifically mentioned; the two dossiers are now attested by two inscriptions from Rome, one probably from Rome (the Trivulzio fragment), one from Heba, one from Tuder, one from Siarum in Spain, one from Ilici in Spain; see Roman Statutes, nos. 37–8. See also TABULA HEBANA; TABULA SIARENSIS.

lex Varia maiestatis, 90 BC: see VARIUS SEVERUS (?) 'HYBRIDA', Q.

leges Vatiniae, 59 BC: see VATINIUS, P.

lex Villia annalis: see VILLIUS (ANNALIS), L.; also *leges annales* (above).

lex Visellia, AD 24: a statute which opened an avenue to full citizenship to Junian Latins (see LATINI IUNIANI) and at the same time made access to municipal office more difficult to those who were not free-born.

lex Voconia, 169 BC: one of the very few private law statutes to make any impact on the mainstream historical tradition, restricting the rights of inheritance by women and the proportion of an estate which could go in legacies, as opposed to the heir(s).

*　　　　*　　　　*

lex Hadriana: a set of regulations of *Hadrian for the exploitation of waste land, attested in a document of Severan date (Bruns, *Font.* 115); see *lex Manciana* (below); D. P. Kehoe, *The Economics of Agriculture on Roman Imperial Estates in North Africa* (1988).

lex Hieronica: the set of regulations originally devised for the kingdom of Syracuse and used by the Romans in Sicily for the collection of grain as tax; see HIERON (2) II.

lex libitinaria: contract between a colony or *municipium* and firms of undertakers, for, *inter alia*, executions of slaves; see L. Bove, *Labeo* 1967, 22–48.

lex Manciana: a set of regulations for the exploitation of imperial estates in Africa (see DOMAINS), adopted in a document of Trajanic date (Bruns, *Font.* 114) and attested in use in a document of Hadrianic date (Bruns, *Font.* 115); see *lex Hadriana*, and D. P. Kehoe, cited above.

lex metalli Vipascensis: a set of regulations, 2nd cent. AD, for the running of the mines at Vipasca in Spain and their associated activities, partly in the form of a letter to a procurator; the sources of the rules are largely unknown; see C. Domergue, *La Mine antique d'Aljustrel* (1983).

lex Pompeia: a set of regulations devised by Cn. *Pompeius Strabo as governor of Cisalpine Gaul in 89 BC; their principal importance is that they devised a new function for Latin status after the enfranchisement of all existing Latins by the *lex Iulia de civitate*, by giving Latin status to native communities north of the Po (*Padus) and perhaps in Liguria (see LIGURIANS); they also made use of the technique of government known as *attributio*, of a community without full local autonomy to another community. See TRANSPADANA.

lex Pompeia: the *lex provinciae* of *Pompey for *Bithynia and *Pontus and the only such *lex* to be at all well attested; see M. H. Crawford, in A. Schiavone (ed.), *Storia di Roma* 2. 1 (1990), 91–121.

lex Rhodia: rules governing jettisoning of cargo; see *Digest* 14. 2, and F. di Martino, *Diritto privato e società romana* (1982), 72–147.

lex Rupilia: probably the provincial edict of P. *Rupilius as governor of Sicily in 132 BC, long observed by his successors; all that we know of its content relates to problems of jurisdiction involving *peregrini* (foreigners).   M. H. C.

lex curiata In the late republic a law carried through the curiate assembly (represented by 30 lictors) was deemed necessary to the full legitimacy of those holding the upper, and perhaps also the lower, magistracies (cf. especially M. *Valerius Messalla 'Rufus' (consul 53 BC) in Gell. *NA* 13. 15. 4, although the text is controversial). See COMITIA; MAGISTRACY, ROMAN. The centuriate assembly passed a comparable law for *censors. Again, see COMITIA; MAGISTRACY, ROMAN. This and the use of the archaic *curiae* (see CURIA (1)) suggest that the practice of passing a curiate law is ancient and could even go back to the monarchy, although only *Cicero (*Rep.* 2. 25, etc.) ascribes it to the regal period. See REX; ROME, HISTORY. The most significant modern theories of its (original) function are: (*a*) it conferred *imperium* on those magistrates entitled to it; (*b*) it conferred rights to auspices (see AUSPICIUM); (*c*) it defined, conferred, or confirmed magisterial powers in general; (*d*) it acknowledged or recognized the assumption of office; (*e*) it was an oath of (military) obedience. Uncertainty is created by the elusive quality of the evidence, by the reduction of the *lex curiata* in the late republic to a formality, by possible changes in its perceived function, and different interpretations of its implications. Thus whilst absence of a curiate law was sometimes used to contest the right of a magistrate to hold elections, perhaps exercise jurisdiction, and (particularly) hold military command, other magistrates without a *lex curiata* apparently acted without regard to such restrictions; and obstruction of the curiate law became a political instrument whose effect depended entirely on immediate political argument and circumstances (cf. especially Cic. *Fam.* 1. 9. 25).

K. Latte, *Kl. Schr.* (1968), 341 ff.; E. S. Staveley, *Hist.* 1956, 84 ff.; J. J. Nicholls, *AJPhil.* 1967, 257 ff.; A. Magdelain, *Recherches sur l'imperium* (1968); C. Meier, *Sav. Zeitschr.* 1969, 487 ff.; R. Develin, *Mnemos.* 1977, 49 ff., and *CAH* 7²/2 (1989), 105, 198 f.   A. D.

Lexica Segueriana, so named from a former owner of the MSS (now cod. Paris, Coislin 345 and 347), or ***Bekkeriana***, from the editor (*Anecd. Bekk.* 1), are 1, *Phrynichus (3) the Atticist;

2, *Anonymus Antatticista; 3, Περὶ συντάξεως (On Syntax); 4, Δικῶν ὀνόματα (Names of law-suits); 5, Λέξεις ῥητορικαί (Rhetorical expressions); 6, Συναγωγὴ χρησίμων λέξεων (Vocabulary for an orator). Of the last Bekker prints only A: Bachmann adopts this and edits the rest (*B*, etc.) in his *Anecd.* 1 (1828).

On 2 see K. Alpers, *Das attizistische Lexikon des Oros* (1981), 108; on 4 and 5, H. Erbse in his preface to K. Latte (ed.), *Lexica graeca minora* (1965), p. ix; on 6, G. Wentzel in *Sitz. der preussischen Akademie* (1895), 477–87, reprinted by Latte (1965), as above.
                                   P. B. R. F.; R. B.; N. G. W.

lexicography See ETYMOLOGICA.

Libanius, born at *Antioch (1) (AD 314), died there (*c*.393), was a Greek rhetorician and man of letters who embodied in his work many of the ideals and aspirations of the pagan Greek urban upper classes of late antiquity. He belonged to a wealthy Antiochene curial family (see DECURIONES), and after a careful education at home was sent to study in Athens (336–40). Thereafter he taught *rhetoric successively at *Constantinople (340/1–346) and at *Nicomedia. Recalled to Constantinople by Constantius II, he was offered but declined a chair of rhetoric at Athens; in 354 he accepted an official chair of rhetoric in Antioch, where he passed the rest of his life. His pupils numbered many distinguished men, pagan and Christian alike. John Chrysostom and Theodore of Mopsuestia were almost certainly among them, *Basil and *Gregory (2) of Nazianzus probably, and *Ammianus Marcellinus possibly.

In his later years Libanius became a literary figure of renown throughout the Greek world, and was in correspondence with many of its leading figures, e.g. the emperor *Julian, for whom he had an unbounded admiration, and whose death was a bitter blow to him. In spite of his adherence to *paganism, which for him was uncomplicated by Neoplatonist speculations (see NEOPLATONISM), he enjoyed considerable influence under *Theodosius (2) I, who granted him the honorary title of praetorian prefect (see PRAEFECTUS PRAETORIO). In general, however, he avoided involvement in the politics of the empire.

Works His 64 surviving speeches deal with public or municipal affairs, educational and cultural questions. Many are addressed to emperors or high government officials, with whom he intervenes on behalf of the citizens or the curials of Antioch (e.g. after the riot of 382). Some of these were never actually delivered, but were sent to their addressees and published. Other speeches include his funeral oration on *Julian (*Or.* 17), his encomium of Antioch (*Or.* 11), and the autobiography which he composed in 374 (*Or.* 1). There also survive some 1,600 letters, 51 school declamations, numerous model rhetorical exercises and minor rhetorical works composed in the course of his teaching. The speeches and letters are a mine of information on social, political, and cultural life in the eastern half of the empire in the 4th cent. AD.

Deeply attached to old values, and seeing the rapidly changing world about him through the distorting lens of a pedantic and snobbish literary tradition, Libanius was vain, petty, and wrapped in finicking antiquarianism. Yet his sincerity, his freedom from vindictiveness, his never-failing readiness to use his eloquence to combat injustice, and a certain warmth of character which breaks through the restraints of classicizing purism make him attractive to the patient reader. He writes an Atticizing Greek (see ASIANISM AND ATTICISM) which is always the result of painstaking labour, and often tortuous and difficult. He was much esteemed as a model of style in Byzantine times.

TEXTS *Libanii opera*, ed. R. Foerster, 12 vols. (1903–27); A. F. Norman (ed.), *Libanius' Autobiography (Or. 1)* (1965), and *Selected Works*, 3 vols. (Loeb, 1969–77).

STUDIES P. Petit, *Libanius et la vie municipale à Antioche au IVe siècle* (1956), and *Les Étudiants de Libanius* (1957); J. H. W. G. Liebeschuetz, *Antioch: City and Imperial Administration in the Later Roman Empire* (1972), esp. 1–39.

PLRE 1. 505–7. R. B.

libations, *ritual pouring of *water, *wine, *oil, *milk, or *honey in honour of gods, heroes, or the dead. Libations are an act of surrender, preceding human participation in meals and other acts. They mark commencements and endings, such as mornings and evenings (Hes. *Op.* 724–6); at the banquet (*symposium), the group pours threefold libations to *Zeus and the Olympians (see OLYMPIAN GODS), to the heroes, and to Zeus Teleios, 'He who Finishes'. *Dionysus 'himself' (i.e. wine) is poured to gain divine favour (Eur. *Bacch.* 284–5). Libations express blanket-propitiation when associated with the unknown and new: having arrived in foreign *Colchis, the *Argonauts pour a libation of 'honey and pure wine to Earth (*Gaia) and the gods of the land (*epichōrioi*) and to the souls of dead heroes', asking for aid and a favourable welcome (Ap. Rhod. *Argon.* 2. 1271–5). The common term, *spondē*, usually associated with wine, refers also to the cry of invocation and to the solemn act it accompanies, such as the signing of truces. In iconography sacrificial acts may end with a libation over the fire on the altar (see SACRIFICE). Common is the 'departure of the *hoplite', where a woman is seen to the right, holding a libation vessel; the scene affirms the link between the group, the gods, the house, and the act. *Spondē* is controlled: libation is poured from an *oinochoē* (wine-jug) to a bowl (*phialē*), then onto an altar or the ground. *Choai*, 'total libations', often wineless (*aoinoi*), are characterized by greater quantities, especially for the dead, *chthonian and nature deities, such as *Nymphs, *Muses, and *Erinyes.

J. Rudhardt, *Notions fondamentales de la pensée religieuse et actes constitutifs du culte dans la Grèce classique* (1958), 240–5; Burkert, *GR* 70–3; F. Lissarrague, *The Aesthetics of the Greek Banquet: Images of Wine and Ritual*, trans. A. Szegedy-Maszak (1987); F. Graf in *Perennitas: . . . Studi Brelich* (1980), 209–21; L. Bruit Zaidman and P. Schmitt Pantel, *Religion in the Ancient Greek City*, trans. P. Cartledge (1992), 39–41. I. M.

libel and slander See INIURIA AND DEFAMATION.

libellus See MAGISTER LIBELLORUM.

Liber Pater, Italian god of fertility and especially of *wine, later commonly identified with *Dionysus. There has been much discussion of his origins and possible relation to *Jupiter Liber, but there is no doubt that he was an independent god in Rome by the time (5th cent. BC ?) at which the archaic festival calendar (in capital letters in the *fasti) became fixed, for his festival (the Liberalia, 17 March) appears there. He never had a major temple of his own in Rome, but formed part of the *Aventine Triad, *Ceres, Liber, and Libera, whose joint temple was founded in 493 BC, possibly under south Italian influence, and became a great centre for the plebeians (see PLEBS) in the 5th and 4th cents. BC. Liber and Libera (like other early Roman deities) seem originally to have formed a pair; they were concerned with seeds and therefore with the promotion of fertility both agricultural and human. At Liber's festival, a *phallus was paraded through the fields and into town, accompanied by the singing of crude rustic songs, according to *Augustine, *De Civ. D.* 7. 21. *Virgil

also mentions the crude songs, together with *masks of Dionysus, hung on the trees (*G.* 2. 385–96). At the Liberalia, too, Roman boys commonly put on the *toga of manhood (Ov. *Fast.* 3. 771–90); this is not satisfactorily explained in the sources, but it seems natural to assume that Liber was seen as the patron of the boy's transition (see RITES OF PASSAGE) into fertility.

A. Bruhl, *Liber Pater* (1953); K. Latte, *RR* 161–2; Radke, *Götter*² 175–83; E. Simon, *Die Götter der Römer* (1990), 126–34. J. A. N.

Libertas, 'freedom', personified deity at Rome, linked with *Jupiter in the cult of Jupiter Libertas and the *censors' headquarters, the Atrium Libertatis; worshipped alone on the *Aventine in a temple built by Ti. *Sempronius Gracchus (Livy 24. 16. 9, 238 BC). Her ideological connection with the freedoms of the ordinary citizen is apparent: freedom opposed both to the state of *slavery and to *dominatio* by the powerful. The term was often used in the late republic and early empire to designate the liberty of the politician to develop his career without interference, and so came to focus various types of resistance to the more autocratic aspects of the early Principate. But *Augustus had made a point of restoring the temples of both Libertas and Jupiter Libertas, and the slogan *libertas Augusta* (Mattingly–Sydenham, *RIC*, Claudius 97) was the final response. See FREEDOM IN THE ANCIENT WORLD.

C. Wirszubski, *Libertas as a Political Idea at Rome during the Late Republic and Early Principate* (1968); J. R. Fears, *ANRW* 2. 17. 2 (1981), 869–75. N. P.

Libitina, Roman goddess of burials, which were registered at her grove on the *Esquiline; Dion. Hal. *Ant. Rom.* 4. 15. 5, cf. Plut. *Quaest. Rom.* 23. Both identify her with *Venus, a mere confusion with Lubentina (see also Varro, *Ling.* 6. 47 and cited in Non. 64. 15 f. Mueller).

See Latte, *RR* 138 and 185 n. 2.; Radke, *Götter*, 183 ff., and *Entwicklung*, 184 ff. J. Sch.

libraries By the end of the 5th cent. BC, books were in general circulation, even if some regarded them as a fad of intellectuals like *Euripides (Ar. *Ran.* 943, cf. fr. 506 KA); Athens had booksellers (Eup. fr. 327, Aristomenes (2) fr. 9, KA), and exports reached the Black Sea (Xen. *An.* 7. 5. 14), see EUXINE. Individuals collected the best-known poets and philosophers (Xen. *Mem.* 4. 2. 1); an imagined collection of the later 4th cent. BC includes *Orpheus, *Hesiod, *tragedies, *Choerilus (probably (2)), *Homer, *Epicharmus, and all kinds of prose, including Simus' *Cookery* (Alexis fr. 140 KA). Of famous collectors (Ath. 1. 3a), *Aristotle took first place (Strabo 13. 1. 54); but his library, like that of the other philosophic schools, remained private property (for its chequered history, see Strabo, ibid.; Plut. *Sull.* 26. 1–2).

Institutional libraries begin with the Hellenistic monarchies; the 'public' library of *Pisistratus (Gell. *NA* 7. 17) is no doubt myth. The model was apparently the Peripatos (Strabo, as above; see PERIPATETIC SCHOOL), rather than the temple and palace libraries of the near east. The first Ptolemies (see PTOLEMY (1)) collected ambitiously and systematically; the Alexandrian Library (see ALEXANDRIA (1)) became legend, and *Callimachus (3)'s *Pinakes* made its content accessible. There were rivals at *Pella, *Antioch (1) (where *Euphorion (2) was librarian), and especially *Pergamum. Holdings were substantial: if the figures can be trusted, Pergamum held at least 200,000 rolls (Plut. *Ant.* 58. 9), the main library at Alexandria nearly 500,000 (*Tzetzes, *Prolegomena de comoedia* 11a. 2. 10–11 Koster)—the equivalent, perhaps, of 100,000 modern books. Smaller towns had their own libraries, some at least attached to the *gymnasium: so in the 2nd cent. at *Rhodes, *Cos, and *Tauromenium (SEG 26. 1123).

The Romans inherited some libraries direct (L. *Aemilius Paullus (2) brought home the Macedonian royal library, *Sulla obtained Aristotle's books after the sack of Athens), together with the traditions of private collection and public endowment. *Cicero accumulated several libraries (and visited those of *Varro, Faustus *Cornelius Sulla, and M. Licinius Lucullus, son of L. *Licinius Lucullus (2)); *Persius left 700 rolls of *Chrysippus. The private library became fashionable: Trimalchio boasted both Greek and Latin libraries (Petron. Sat. 48); Seneca the Younger (see ANNAEUS SENECA (2), L.) and *Lucian satirize those whose books serve only for show (Sen. Dial. 9. 9. 4–7; Lucian, Ind.). Successful Greeks and Romans continued to found libraries in their native cities: C. Stertinius Xenophon (*Claudius' doctor) on Cos, *Dio Cocceianus at Prusa, *Pliny (2) the Younger at Como (*Comum). Excavation has uncovered (among others) the libraries of T. Flavius Pantaenus at Athens, Ti. Iulius Aquila at Ephesus ('library of Celsus'), and M. Iulius Quintiana Flavius Rogatianus at Timgad. On the monarchic scale, *Caesar planned a public library in Rome, under Varro's direction; C. *Asinius Pollio actually founded one in the Atrium Libertatis. There followed (among the grandest) *Augustus' library on the *Palatine, *Vespasian's near the *templum Pacis, *Trajan's in his forum (*forum Traiani), M. *Aurelius Severus Alexander's in the *Pantheon; libraries were included in the *baths of Trajan, *Caracalla, and *Diocletian. The Constantinian description of Rome counts 28 libraries; in the 2nd cent. AD at least a procurator bibliothecarum had overseen the whole system. The new capital Constantinople was provided at short order with a library, which eventually reached 120,000 books. *Origen (1)'s library at *Caesarea (2) provided the Christian exemplar.

Hellenistic libraries apparently consisted of simple storage-rooms attached to a *stoa or the like; such is the only ancient library to survive in situ, that of the Villa of the Papyri at *Herculaneum. The great Roman libraries provided reading-rooms, one for Greek and one for Latin (a challenge to parity), with books in niches round the walls. *Vitruvius (De arch. 6. 4. 1) advises that libraries should face east, to provide for good light and against damp; green marble floors might reduce eye-strain, gilded ceilings increase it (Isid. Etym. 6. 11. 2). Books would generally be stored in cupboards (armaria), which might be numbered for reference (SHA Tac. 8. 1). A statue of a divine (or imperial) patron occupied a central niche; busts of authors ('those whose immortal spirits there speak', *Plin. HN 35. 2. 9) adorned the building. Catalogues (indices) listed authors under broad subject-headings; attendants fetched the books (borrowing was for a privileged few). The library of Pantaenus at Athens had its rules inscribed on stone: 'No book shall be taken out, for we have sworn. . . . Open from dawn to midday.' The staff would comprise a librarian; attendants (προσμένοντες in the library of Celsus at *Ephesus, often slaves (as in the Palatine); copyists and restorers (glutinatores, Cic. Att. 4. 4a. 1; antiquarii, Cod. Theod. 14. 9. 2; cf. Suet. Dom. 20). New acquisitions might be provided by gift (each ephebe (see EPHEBOI) at the Ptolemaion of Athens gave 100 rolls on leaving), or by purchase; Pliny's library at Comum had an endowment of 100,000 sesterces (ILS 2927), the library of Celsus 23,000 denarii (Inschriften von Ephesos, 7. 2. 5113).

Libraries came to rank among the grandest civic monuments. In the Bibliotheca Ulpia (forum Traiani), each reading-room covered 460 sq. m. (5,000 sq. ft.). The library of Celsus (see above), founded in honour of Ti. Iulius Celsus Polemaeanus

(consul 92) by his son Aquila (consul 110), has a floor area of 180 sq. m. (2,000 sq. ft.), and Celsus' tomb in the basement; the elaborate façade (re-erected) still impresses. Costs were substantial: 1,000,000 sesterces at Comum, 400,000 sesterces at Timgad. Such libraries celebrated the ruling culture, and its representatives. They also preserved its texts. Ancient books were always vulnerable: material fragile, editions small, circulation desultory. The library offered a safe haven: so Heraclitus of Rhodiapolis, 'the Homer of medical poetry', made sure to donate his works to the libraries of Alexandria, *Rhodes, and Athens (TAM 2. 3. 910). Acceptance into a great library marked a work as authentic (Dictys Cretensis, p. 3. 11 Eisenhut), or politically acceptable (Hor. Epist. 1. 3. 17; Ov. Tr. 3. 1. 59 ff.); emperors promoted favourite authors (Suet. Tib. 70. 2, Calig. 34. 2). But favour could do nothing against fire (the Palatine Library burnt down under *Nero or *Titus, again in AD 191, finally in 363); mould and 'the worst enemy of the Muses' (Anth. Pal. 9. 251), worm, put paid to many immortalities. See also BOOKS, GREEK AND ROMAN.

H. Blanck, Das Buch in der Antike (1992).   P. J. P.

libri coloniarum A catalogue of land allocations in Italy and *Dalmatia from the *Gracchi to the 2nd cent. AD, preserved among the works of the *gromatici; compiled (probably early 4th cent.) from several treatises dating from *Augustus onwards; subsequently some parts were revised (known as Liber coloniarum 2). Despite historical mistakes, there is much potentially useful information on land allocation, partly confirmed by aerial photography and ground survey, for example in the Tavoliere near *Luceria, which have demonstrated Roman field systems.

J. P. Bradford, Antiquity 1949, 58; C. Delano Smith, Transactions of the Institute of British Geographers 1967, 203; F. Grelle, in O. Behrends and L. Capogrossi (eds.), Die römische Feldmesskunst (1992), 67.   J. B. C.

libri pontificales, general name for the records kept by the college of *pontifices at Rome. An idea of part of their contents may be formed from the surviving, inscribed, *commentarii of the *arval brethren and the acta of the *Secular Games; but these are records of rituals performed at particular dates, whereas the pontifical records will have contained in addition rules of procedure and directions for the performing of rituals, including the texts of prayers, vows, and other formulae. So much is clear from the quotations and references preserved in the antiquarian tradition; but hardly any verbatim quotations can be trusted, so that the method of organizing the records and even the question whether there was any organization, remain highly arguable.

G. Rohde, Die Kultsatzungen der römischen Pontifices, RGVV 25 (1936).   H. J. R.; J. A. N.

Liburni, an Illyrian people on the NE coast of the Adriatic, once dominated a large part of the coast of *Illyricum (Strabo 6. 2. 4) but by the Roman period they were confined to the sector between the river Arsia (mod. Raša) on the west side of Istria (2) and the Titius (Krka), where the Delmatae began. The Liburni were famous as seafarers, especially as pirates (Livy 10. 2. 4; see PIRACY), and invented the liburna (or liburnica), a warship adopted by Octavian at Actium. Though part of the province *Dalmatia, some branches of the imperial administration continued to link Liburnia with NE Italy.

J. Wilkes, The Illyrians (1992), 186 ff.   J. J. W.

Libya, Greek name for the country of the Libyans, the indigenous peoples of North *Africa. In *Homer it was a pastoral land of great fecundity near Egypt (Od. 4. 85 f.); later, most commonly the Greek colonial area of Cyrenaica (see CYRENE; COLONIZATION, GREEK), but sometimes other parts, or the whole, of the North African coastal zone, even the whole continent of Africa. Roman informal usage followed Greek; formally it described the Egyptian administrative district west of *Alexandria (1) as the nome (see NOMOS (1)) of Libya and two Diocletianic provinces (see DIOCLETIAN) as Libya Inferior (or *Sicca*), approximately from Alexandria to Darnis (Derna), and Libya Superior (or *Pentapolis*), approximately from Darnis to Arae Philaenorum (mod. Ras el Aali in the Syrtica). On its peoples in the classical period information is currently accruing from anthropological and archaeological surveys. Ancient sources tend to stress their nomadism (see NOMADS), but some always had sizeable settlements; under Greek, Carthaginian, and Roman influence many in the coastal zones seem to have become sedentary farmers. Intermarriage and socio-economic connections with colonists produced racial and cultural mixes here; normally, perhaps, the initiative for raids on the settled areas came from tribes further off.

In Cyrenaica Libya was personified, introduced into the story of the *nymph Cyrene and *Apollo (Pind. *Pyth.* 9. 55. 8), and given a family (variable in detail) which connected her both with Egypt and with Greece, perhaps also with *Babylon. *Pausanias (3) described a (lost) relief at *Delphi (probably of the 5th cent. BC) which showed her crowning Battus, the *founder of Cyrene, who stood in a chariot driven by Cyrene (10. 15. 6). Securely identified representations rarely survive. The clearest is on a Roman-period relief on which she crowns Cyrene who is strangling a lion; she is characterized by corkscrew ringlets, short over the temples and shoulder-length at the sides, a cape, fastened between the breasts and so stiff as to suggest leather, an animal beside her (probably a gazelle), and vine-branches above, with bunches of grapes. Hairstyle and cape seem taken from the real styles of Libyan women, the gazelle evokes the fecundity of pre-desert animals, the vine the fertility of cultivated land. The conceptualization is Greek and embodies the tradition that Libyans helped the founders of Cyrene. Whether it had an origin in Libyan belief is debatable. There is no certain evidence for a native cult of Libya and what there is for a Greek cult is of comparatively late date; the most widespread native cults known are those of *Ammon and of Underworld deities. See CYRENE.

RE 4 A (1932), 1796 f.; *Diz. Epigr.* 4 (1958), 976–8; O. Bates, *The Eastern Libyans* (1914); J. Desanges, *Catalogue des tribus africaines de l'antiquité classique* . . . (1962); S. Stucchi and M. Luni (eds.), *Cirene e i Libyi* (= *QAL* 1987); D. White, *Libyan Studies* 1994, 31–9. Iconography: E. Catani, *QAL* 1987, 385–400; *LIMC* 6/1 (1992), 284 f.   J. M. R.

Licentius, of Thagaste, friend and (probably) relation of St *Augustine to whom (AD 395) he addressed a poem on the difficulty of understanding music and sought Augustine's guidance, asking for a copy of the latter's work *De musica*. The poem is preserved with St Augustine's reply (August. *Ep.* 26f.). It hardly justifies St Augustine's description of Licentius as 'a poet of near-perfection', its language being unoriginal and often obscure.

TEXT *CSEL* 34, 89 ff.

M. Zelzner, *De carmine Licentii* (Diss. Breslau, 1915); *PLRE* 2, 'Licentius' 1.   O. S.

Lichas (d. 411 BC), prominent Spartan, possibly member of the *gerousia*. He gained Panhellenic renown for entertaining visitors to the Gymnopaidia (see SPARTAN CULTS) and, flouting a ban on Spartan participation, emulated his father Arcesilaus by winning the Olympian four-horse chariot race of 420 (see HORSE- AND CHARIOT-RACES). His beating by the umpires later became a

pretext for war with *Elis. *Proxenos of *Argos (2), he concluded the Spartan–Argive treaty of 418/7. In 412/1 he led the commission which negotiated the third Sparto-Persian agreement which conceded Persian claims to Asia.

Thuc. 5. 49–50, 8 *passim*. *RE* 13. 211–12, 'Lichas' 3; PB no. 492; P. Cartledge, *LCM* 1984, 98–102.   S. J. Ho.

Licinianus, Granius See GRANIUS.

Licinius (*RE* 31a), **Valerius Licinianus,** the Roman emperor **Licinius,** born of peasant stock in (new) *Dacia perhaps in the 260s AD, became a close friend and comrade-in-arms of *Galerius, who at Carnuntum (308), when *Diocletian refused to leave retirement, created him a second Augustus (see TETRARCHY). Rather than attack *Maxentius in Italy, Alexander in Africa, or Constantine in Gaul, Licinius undertook the administration of the diocese (*dioecesis*) of *Pannonia; it seems that he did not persecute Christians (see CHRISTIANITY). On the death of Galerius (311) he and *Maximinus raced to acquire Galerius' territories; Licinius obtained those in Europe, and faced Maximinus across the *Bosporus (1), but war was averted by negotiation. Against Maximinus, he formed an alliance with *Constantine I. At Milan (February 313) he married Constantine's half-sister Constantia. His conference with Constantine was interrupted when Maximinus invaded Europe. Licinius defeated him near Adrianople, taking over his Asiatic territories. Licinius and Constantine were now the only claimants to the empire. At *Nicomedia on 15 June he informed his subjects that they had agreed on toleration for all religions, including Christianity, and that confiscated Christian property was to be restored. At the time Christian writers regarded Licinius as a Christian; though he prescribed a monotheistic prayer for use by the army, his later career shows that he was no convert. For obscure reasons he quarrelled with Constantine who defeated him (8 October 316) at Cibalae and then at Campus Adriensis, neither victory being decisive. After Cibalae, Licinius made the *dux limitis* (see LIMITANEI) Valens emperor, but Valens was executed before Licinius negotiated peace with Constantine early in 317. Licinius agreed to surrender all European territory except the diocese of Thracia. On 1 March 317 he made his infant son and namesake Caesar, and Constantine gave this title to his sons Crispus and *Constantine II. Knowing that Constantine would never be happy until he was sole ruler, and suspecting that his own Christian subjects were disloyal, he embarked on a perfunctory persecution. The uneasy peace was broken when Constantine attacked in 324, won a decisive battle at Adrianople (3 July) and besieged Licinius in Byzantium. Licinius put up his *magister officiorum* Martinianus as emperor. Byzantium fell, and at Chrysopolis Licinius was defeated (18 September). He and Martinianus surrendered, and were sent to *Thessalonica, where they were accused of plotting and executed in spring 325. Licinius' son was granted his life but executed in 326. A bastard son who had been legitimized and given high rank was enslaved.

T. D. Barnes, *Constantine and Eusebius* (1981).   R. P. D.

Licinius Archias, Aulus, Greek poet from *Antioch (1) who arrived in Rome c.102 BC, where he celebrated the victories of C. *Marius (1) and L. *Licinius Lucullus (2). His Roman *citizenship under the *lex Plautia Papiria* was contested, and successfully defended by *Cicero's *Pro Archia* (62 BC). Cicero hoped that Archias would write a poem in his honour, but in vain (*Att.* 1. 16. 15). Archias was famous for his ability to improvise on any subject (*Pro Arch.* 18). Some of the 37 epigrams ascribed to various Archiases in the Greek *Anthology are presumably by him, but none were certainly included in *Meleager (2)'s *Garland*.

Gow–Page, *GP* 2. 432–50; A. Cameron, *Greek Anthology* (1993), 55–6.
A. D. E. C.

Licinius (*RE* 113) **Calvus, Gaius** (born 82, dead by 47 BC), politician, orator, and poet, son of the annalist C. *Licinius Macer. In oratory he practised a severe Atticism (see ASIANISM AND ATTICISM) in opposition to *Cicero, but was a lively speaker (Sen. *Controv.* 7. 4. 7; Catull. 53); Cicero himself respected his abilities (*Fam.* 15. 21. 4; *Brut.* 279 ff.), and his oratory was still respected in the times of *Quintilian (*Inst.* 10. 1. 115) and *Tacitus (1) (*Dial.* 18, 21, 25). He left 21 speeches, of which those against P. *Vatinius (one delivered in 54 when Cicero was defending) were most admired (cf. Catull. 53). He was an intimate friend of *Catullus (1) (the two are often paired by subsequent writers), shared his attitudes and tastes, and wrote in the same poetical genres—a miniature epic *Io*, an elegy on the death of his inamorata (perhaps wife) Quintilia (alluded to by Catull. 96), *epithalamia, and satirical *epigrams in varied metres (some of the latter attack *Caesar, with whom, like Catullus, he was eventually reconciled, *Pompey, and Caesar's friend Tigellius Sardus).

FRAGMENTS *ORF*² n. 165; Courtney, *FLP* 201.

E. S. Gruen, *Harv. Stud.* 1966, 217; A. D. Leeman, *Orationis Ratio* (1963), 138.
E. C.

Licinius (*RE* 55) **Crassus, Lucius,** outstanding orator and, even more than M. *Antonius (1), master and model of *Cicero, who idealizes him, particularly in the *De oratore*, where he is the chief speaker. Born 140 BC, he was taught by L. *Coelius Antipater, studied law under P. *Mucius Scaevola and Q. *Mucius Scaevola (1), and married a daughter of Quintus. Aged 21 (*admodum adulescens*: Cic. *Brut.* 158), he successfully prosecuted C. *Papirius Carbo (1), later defended a relative in the Vestal trials (see CASSIUS LONGINUS RAVILLA, L.), and at an uncertain date (conventionally 118), still *adulescens* (*Brut.* 160), supported the popular colony at *Narbo, which, with Cn. *Domitius Ahenobarbus (3), he helped to establish (see *RRC* 282 and, for the date, Sumner, *Orators* 94 ff.). *Quaestor in Asia (see ASIA, ROMAN PROVINCE), he studied philosophy and rhetoric there and in Athens and on his return became a leading orator in the courts. In 106 he supported the jury law of Q. *Servilius Caepio (1) in a great speech attracting popular support for the senate, which P. *Rutilius Rufus condemned on moral grounds. Not politically prominent in the 90s, he became consul 95 with Q. *Mucius Scaevola (2). They passed a law depriving aliens who had been illegally enrolled (probably by the *censors M. Antonius (1) and L. *Valerius Flaccus (2)) of the citizenship and setting up a *quaestio* (see QUAESTIONES) for enforcement. This became one of the main immediate causes of the *Social War (3). In the mid-90s he defended Q. *Servilius Caepio (2) and became an *adfinis* (relation by marriage) of C. *Marius (1). In 92, as censor, he quarrelled with his colleague Ahenobarbus, but they jointly issued an edict prohibiting the teaching of rhetoric in Latin, in part probably in order to restrict access to the powerful weapon of oratory.

Crassus taught a generation of ambitious young aristocrats (see LIVIUS DRUSUS (2), M.; SULPICIUS RUFUS, P.; AURELIUS COTTA, C.), imbuing them with his ideas of aristocratic reform. He supported Drusus, who aimed at putting them into practice, in his tribunate (91), rallying the senate behind him against the consul L. *Marcius Philippus (1) in what Cicero called his 'swan song'. His death soon after led to Drusus' failure. As an orator, he is praised by Cicero for *gravitas*: his style—Asianic, but not to excess (see

ASIANISM AND ATTICISM)—combined rhythm and ornamentation with pure Latinity.

*ORF*⁴ 237 ff.; Cic. *Brut.* and *De or.* Cf. U. W. Scholz, *Der Redner M. Antonius* (1963), 55 f., 94.
E. B.

Licinius (*RE* 68) **Crassus** (1), **Marcus,** son of P. *Licinius Crassus (1), escaped from L. *Cornelius Cinna (1) to Spain, joined *Sulla after Cinna's death, played a prominent part in regaining Italy for him, and made a fortune in Sulla's *proscriptions. After his praetorship he defeated *Spartacus (72–71 BC), but *Pompey, after crucifying many fugitives, claimed credit for the victory, deeply offending Crassus. Formally reconciled, they were made *consuls 70 and presided over the abolition of Sulla's political settlement, though his administrative reforms were retained. During the next few years Crassus further increased his fortune and, relying on his connections, financial power, and astuteness, gained considerable influence. After 67, overshadowed by Pompey's commands (which he had opposed), he is associated by our sources with various schemes to expand his power and perhaps gain a military command. As *censor 65, he tried to enrol the Transpadanes (see TRANSPADANA) as citizens and to have Egypt annexed; he was foiled by his colleague Q. *Lutatius Catulus (2) and their quarrel forced both to abdicate. Always ready to help eminent or promising men in need of aid, he shielded the suspects in the 'first conspiracy' of *Catiline (see CORNELIUS SULLA, P. and AUTRONIUS PAETUS, P.) and supported Catiline until the latter turned to revolution and a programme of cancelling debts. He may have supported the law of P. *Servilius Rullus. A patron of *Caesar (without, however, detaching him from Pompey), he enabled him to leave for his province in 62 by standing surety for part of his debts. On Caesar's return, he was persuaded by him to give up his opposition to Pompey, which during 62–60 had prevented both of them from gaining their political objectives, and to join Pompey in supporting Caesar's candidacy for the consulship. As consul (59), Caesar satisfied him by passing legislation to secure remission of one third of the sum owed by the *publicani* of Asia for their contract (Crassus presumably had an interest in their companies), and he now joined Pompey and Caesar in an open political alliance. After Caesar's departure for Gaul he supported P. *Clodius Pulcher, who soon proved to be too ambitious to make a reliable ally and tried to embroil him with Pompey and Cicero. He welcomed Cicero on his return from exile, but in 56 alerted Caesar to the attempts by Cicero and others to recall him and attach Pompey to the *optimates. Caesar and Crassus met at Ravenna and Pompey was persuaded to meet them at *Luca and renew their alliance. The dynasts' plans were kept secret, but it soon became clear that Pompey and Crassus were to become consuls for a second time by whatever means proved necessary and to have special commands in Spain and Syria respectively assigned to them for five years (see TREBONIUS, C.), while they renewed Caesar's command for five years.

Late in 55, ignoring the solemn curses of the tribune C. *Ateius Capito (1), Crassus left for Syria, determined on a war of conquest against *Parthia. He won some early successes in 54 and completed financial preparations by extorting huge sums in his province. In 53 he crossed the Euphrates, relying on his long-neglected military skills and the recent ones of his son P. *Licinius Crassus (2). Although deserted by *Artavasdes (1) II of Armenia and the king of *Osroëne, he continued his advance into unfamiliar territory. After Publius died in a rash action, he himself was caught in a trap by the *Surenas near *Carrhae and, trying to extricate himself, died fighting.

After playing the game of politics according to the old rules, in which he was a master, he in the end found that unarmed power no longer counted for much in the changed conditions of the late republic, and he died while trying to apply the lesson. His death helped to bring Caesar and Pompey into the confrontation that led to the Civil War.

> Plutarch, *Crassus* is the main source; he appears frequently in Cicero's letters and speeches & in the historians of the late republic, especially Cassius Dio & Appian. For modern discussion (with bibliog.) see B. A. Marshall, *Crassus* (1976) & A. M. Ward, *Marcus Crassus & the Late Roman Republic* (1977), with E. S. Gruen, *AJAH* 1977, 117 ff.   E. B.

Licinius (*RE* 58) **Crassus** (2), **Marcus** (*consul 30 BC), grandson of M. *Licinius Crassus (1), was at first a partisan of Sextus *Pompeius, then an Antonian (see ANTONIUS, M. (2)). The precise date of his desertion to Octavian (see AUGUSTUS) has not been recorded; the consulate was probably his reward. Appointed proconsul (see PRO CONSULE) of *Macedonia, he conducted highly successful campaigns in 29 and 28 (Cass. Dio 51. 23 ff.). Having killed a king of the *Bastarnae with his own hands, he claimed the *spolia opima, to the annoyance of Octavian, himself jealously monopolizing military glory. The claim was rebutted on the grounds that Crassus had not been fighting under his own auspices; Octavian may have used as an argument a linen corslet he claimed to have found in the temple of Jupiter Feretrius, which purported to show that A. *Cornelius Cossus was consul (not merely military tribune; see TRIBUNI MILITUM) when he earned the *spolia opima*. The incident may have accelerated the regulation of Octavian's constitutional position. Crassus was permitted to hold a *triumph (27), after which nothing more was heard of this ambitious (and perhaps dangerous) *nobilis*. His son by adoption is M. Licinius Crassus Frugi (consul 14 BC).

> Syme, *Rom. Rev.*, see index. The constitutional point: E. Groag, *RE* 13. 283 ff., but see E. Badian, in G. Wirth and others (eds.), *Romanitas-Christianitas* (1982), 23 ff.   R. S.; R. J. S.

Licinius (*RE* 61) **Crassus** (1), **Publius**, as tribune passed a sumptuary law (Macrob. *Sat.* 3. 17. 7). In his consulship (97 BC) the senate prohibited human *sacrifice. After commanding in *Iberia (1) for several years, he triumphed (see TRIUMPH) over the Lusitanians (93; see LUSITANIA). He fought in the *Social War (3) under L. *Iulius Caesar (1), was *censor with him 89, but in the uncertainty of the time they could not compile a list of citizens. Earlier probably a friend of C. *Marius (1), he helped to defend Rome against him and L. *Cornelius Cinna (1) and killed himself after their victory (87). His son M. *Licinius Crassus (1) escaped to Spain.   E. B.

Licinius (*RE* 63) **Crassus** (2), **Publius** (*c*.85–53 BC), younger son of M. *Licinius Crassus (1). He accompanied *Caesar to Gaul, first as *praefectus equitum* (cavalry commander) in 58, then as *legatus* (57). In the victory over *Ariovistus his resolute handling of the reserve was decisive. In 57 he subdued the coastal Gallic tribes and perhaps explored the *Cassiterides (Strabo 3. 175–6; see TIN). In 56 he defeated the Aquitanians and returned to Rome where he supported the consular candidature of his father and *Pompey. His elder brother Marcus as quaestor (54) then served under Caesar in Gaul. Publius in 55 married *Cornelia (2), daughter of Q. *Caecilius Metellus Pius Scipio. He commanded a body of Gallic horse under his father in the Parthian War of 53. His vigorous leadership involved them in heavy

losses which he refused to survive. As an augur (see AUGURES), he was succeeded by Cicero.   C. E. S.; R. J. S.

Licinius (*RE* 72) **Crassus Dives Mucianus, Publius**, by birth brother of P. *Mucius Scaevola; brother-in-law of Ap. *Claudius Pulcher (1) and father-in-law of C. *Sempronius Gracchus. Noble, wealthy, and an eminent lawyer and orator (cf. Gell. *NA* 1. 1. 10), he was a central figure in the group opposing P. *Cornelius Scipio Aemilianus that sponsored Ti. *Sempronius Gracchus (3). After Tiberius' death he joined the agrarian commission, acquired popularity as a Gracchan, and became *consul and *pontifex maximus aged about 50 (131 BC). Eager for the Asian command, he used his pontifical power to obtain it, but was defeated and killed by *Aristonicus (1).

> Astin, *Scipio*, see index.   E. B.

Licinius (*RE* 84) **Egnatius Gallienus, Publius**, the Roman emperor **Gallienus**, son of Valerian (P. *Licinius Valerianus), appointed Augustus (see TETRARCHY) with him in AD 253. While his father lived, he commanded in the west and fought a series of successful campaigns on the Danube and Rhine. After the capture of Valerian by the Sasanid Persians (260), he faced serious invasions and internal revolts. He dealt with the most threatening of these (the rebellion of Ingenuus, the Alamannic invasion of Italy, and the advance on Rome of Macrianus senior; see FULVIUS IUNIUS MACRIANUS) with dispatch, making excellent use of the generals he had promoted through the ranks. He then adopted a policy of studied inaction, in effect accepting a tripartite division of the empire. In the east, *Septimius Odenaethus of *Palmyra first disposed of Gallienus' remaining opponents (*Ballista, Quietus) then, as *dux* and *corrector totius Orientis*, was allowed to supervise and defend the region in the emperor's name. In the west, Gallienus left the usurper *Postumus in peace until the abortive campaign of 265, and did not trouble him thereafter. Gallienus thus gave himself the opportunity to consolidate his hold over his 'central' empire (Italy, North Africa, Egypt, the Danubian provinces, and Greece), and pursue significant military, political, cultural, and religious activities. In 268, however, he had to undertake a major campaign in the Balkans, where renewed Gothic invasions over the Black Sea and the Danube had, in 267, resulted in the sacking of Athens and other major Greek cities (see HERULI). He won an important victory on the Nestus, but was unable to exploit it because he had to return to northern Italy to deal with the mutiny of *Aureolus. Though he quickly contained the insurrection, he was murdered by his staff officers as he besieged Aureolus in Milan (*Mediolanum).

The Latin literary tradition is uniformly hostile to Gallienus, probably because he excluded senators from military commands. Modern scholarship tended to rehabilitate his reputation, stressing his recognition of the need for change (e.g. in professionalizing the army, and making greater use of cavalry) and his prudent husbanding of scarce resources. Yet the disenchantment of his senior marshals—who owed their own careers to his patronage—indicates the need for caution; and recent studies have been more qualified in their assessment of him.

> PLRE 1. 383 f.; M. Christol, *ANRW* 2. 2 (1975), 803–27; L. de Blois, *The Policy of the Emperor Gallienus* (1976); W. Kuhoff, *Herrschertum und Weltkrise* (1979).   B. H. W.; J. F. Dr.

Licinius (*RE* 92) **Imbrex**, Latin poet, called by A. *Gellius 'an old writer of comedies', whose *fabula *palliata* entitled *Neaera* he cites (*NA* 13. 23. 16). Perhaps identical with P. Licinius Tegula (*RE* 168), who composed a state hymn in 200 BC.

J. Wright, *Dancing in Chains* (1974).　　　　　P. G. M. B.

Licinius (*RE* 102) **Lucullus** (1), **Lucius,** first *consul of his house (151 BC), tried to enforce the levy for troops for Spain so harshly that he was temporarily imprisoned by the tribunes (see TRIBUNI PLEBIS). When he reached Spain and found that peace had been made with the *Celtiberians, he treacherously attacked the Vaccaei and Cauci. As proconsul, he joined Ser. *Sulpicius Galba (1) in an attack on *Lusitania. He later built a temple to *Felicitas. P. *Cornelius Scipio Aemilianus served under him as military tribune.

H. Simon, *Roms Kriege in Spanien* (1962), see index.　　　　E. B.

Licinius (*RE* 104) **Lucullus** (2), **Lucius,** grandson of L. *Licinius Lucullus (1), nephew of Q. *Caecilius Metellus Numidicus, for whose return from exile he pleaded. He served in the *Social War (3) under *Sulla and, as quaestor (88 BC), was the only officer who supported his march on Rome. As proquaestor in the east, he was Sulla's most reliable officer, charged with diplomatic missions, collecting ships and money, and letting *Mithradates VI escape from C. *Flavius Fimbria in accordance with Sulla's policy. Aedile (79) with his brother M. *Terentius Varro Lucullus, he gave splendid games. Praetor in 78, he became Sulla's literary executor and guardian of Faustus *Cornelius Sulla, and then governed Africa. As consul in 74, he opposed tribunician agitation and, worried by the threats of *Pompey, sent him generous supplies to Spain; after complicated intrigues (see CORNELIUS CETHEGUS, P.), he secured an *imperium* against the pirates for M. *Antonius (Creticus) and the command against Mithradates for himself.

He relieved M. *Aurelius Cotta, raised the siege of *Cyzicus, then occupied much of Pontus, forcing Mithradates to flee to Armenia. In the province of Asia he tried to relieve the cities of financial ruin by drawing up a moderate and ultimately successful plan for payment of their debts and interest at moderate rates. After capturing *Sinope, which he saved from plundering by his army, and *Amaseia, he asked for a senate commission to organize the annexation of Pontus. When *Tigranes (1) II allied himself with Mithradates, Lucullus marched through Cappadocia and invaded Armenia, and in a battle against Tigranes won 'the greatest victory the sun had ever seen' (Plut. *Luc.* 28. 8). He captured the new capital *Tigranocerta, allowed his troops to plunder it and celebrated victory games there. Tigranes had to evacuate his earlier conquests, including *Gordyene and Syria. But the enemy collected fresh forces and the king of *Parthia threatened intervention. An invasion of the Armenian highlands had to be abandoned when the army mutinied, and the capture of *Nisibis did not assuage them. His brother-in-law P. *Clodius Pulcher incited rebellion, and in Rome public opinion was turned against him, chiefly by those who had incurred losses in his organization of Asia. His command was removed by stages (68–67); the army, hearing this, deserted him; and in the end he was superseded by Pompey under the law of C. *Manilius.

Back in Rome, he had to divorce his wife (a sister of *Clodia) for adultery, and a second marriage, to a niece of M. *Porcius Cato (2), turned out no better. After long delays caused by his enemies, he finally triumphed in 63. But he took no leading part in politics, except for an attempt to oppose *Caesar and stop the ratification of Pompey's eastern arrangements (59), which ended in humiliation. He now concentrated on living in refined luxury, but lapsed into insanity before his death (57/6).

He was an able soldier and administrator, an Epicurean, a lover of literature and the arts, and a generous patron. But he lacked the easy demagogy that was needed for success in both war and politics in his day.

Plut. *Luc.* and references in *Cassius Dio and *Cicero are the chief sources. For the war, see also App. *Mith.* A. Keaveney, *Lucullus* (1992).　　　　　E. B.

Licinius Macer, Gaius (*RE* 112), the Roman annalist (see ANNALS, ANNALISTS), was tribune (see TRIBUNI PLEBIS) in 73 BC, when he agitated for popular rights (cf. Sallust, *Hist.* 3. 48); *praetor in 68, he was convicted of extortion in 66 and committed suicide. His history of Rome, in at least sixteen books, began with the origins; *Pyrrhus appeared in book 2; its closing-point is unknown. It reflected democratic and family bias (Livy 7. 9. 5) and was rhetorically composed. At the same time, it rationalized legends and quoted original authorities, particularly the 'linen books', *libri lintei* (Livy 4. 7. 12, 4. 20. 8, 4. 23. 2), in order to reinterpret the old political institutions. *Livy and *Dionysius (7) of Halicarnassus used his work. See HISTORIOGRAPHY, ROMAN.

Peter, *HRRel.* 1². cccl, 298. E. Rawson, *Intellectual Life in the Late Roman Republic* (1985), 219 f.　　　　A. H. McD.; A. J. S. S.

Licinius (*RE* 116a) **Mucianus, Gaius** (*suffect *consul *c.* AD 64, suffect consul for the second time in 70, and for the third time in 72). He served under Cn. *Domitius Corbulo in 58 and was governor of *Lycia-*Pamphylia. *Nero appointed Mucianus governor of *Syria about the time when he sent *Vespasian to *Judaea. Reconciled with Vespasian after earlier disagreements, Mucianus encouraged his designs and secured the allegiance of Syria. Leading the Flavian army through Asia Minor and the Balkans, he was anticipated by *Antonius Primus in the invasion of Italy and defeat of the Vitellians, but was able on the way to repel a Dacian incursion (see DACIA) into *Moesia. He arrived in Rome a few days after its capture, repressed the ambitions of Primus, and controlled the government for Vespasian, whose chief adviser he remained. He is said to have urged that emperor to banish the philosophers from Rome. Mucianus possessed various accomplishments (for a pointed sketch of his character, cf. Tac. *Hist.* 1. 10). He wrote a book of geographical *mirabilia* ('wonders'), much used by *Pliny (1) the Elder. He was dead by 77.

Syme, *Tacitus*, see index.　　　　R. S.; M. T. G.

Licinius (*RE* 123) **Murena, Lucius,** descended from several generations of praetors, served under his father in the 80s BC. He was *quaestor (*c.*75), legate (see LEGATI) of L. *Licinius Lucullus (2), urban *praetor (65), and then governed Transalpine Gaul (see GAUL (TRANSALPINE)). Elected *consul for 62, he was accused of *ambitus by Ser. *Sulpicius Rufus, his defeated rival, and by *Cato (Uticensis); he was defended by *Crassus, Q. *Hortensius, and *Cicero and, though perhaps guilty, he was acquitted. With his colleague D. *Iunius Silanus (1), he passed a *lex Licinia Iunia* on the promulgation of bills. He is not heard of again.

Cic. *Pro Murena.* The speech (§§ 15 ff.) throws light on the concept of *nobilitas.*　　　　E. B.

Licinius (*RE* 161) **Stolo, Gaius,** and **Sextius Sextinus Lateranus** (*RE* 36), **Lucius,** were reputedly plebeian tribunes (see TRIBUNI PLEBIS) from 376 to 367 BC and proposed: (1) the reservation of one consulship each year to a plebeian candidate (see CONSUL; PLEBS); (2) the limitation of individual holdings of public land (**ager publicus*) to 500 *iugera,* roughly 134 ha. or 330 acres

Licinius Sura, Lucius

(App. *BCiv.* 1. 33 gives further alleged provisions); (3) a *debt law providing that *interest should be deducted from the principal and the balance repaid in three annual instalments. Opposition to these proposals prompted Licinius and Sextius to prevent the election of curule magistrates (see MAGISTRACY, ROMAN) for five years of 'anarchy' (375–371 BC). In 367 they secured the sharing of the (enlarged) *decemviri sacris faciundis* (see QUINDECIMVIRI SACRIS FACIUNDIS) between *patricians and plebeians and then the passage of their main proposals. Sextius was consul in 366, Licinius in either 364 or 361.

Our principal narrative of these events (*Livy 6. 34–42) is riddled with political and constitutional absurdities. The anarchy was invented to 'correct' the chronology of the 4th cent. The terms of both the debt law (which Livy alone records) and land law are suspect (although the combination of proposals for structural political change and socio-economic relief is plausible). The apparent reservation of one consulship to plebeians from 366 to 356 is linked to the institution of new, more effective specialized structures for the magistracies and may reflect progressive plebeian advances (a C. Licinius, identified by some sources as Stolo, was reputedly the first plebeian *magister equitum* in 368), perhaps with the support of patricians such as Stolo's reputed father-in-law, M. Fabius Ambustus (consular tribune 381, 369). See AGRARIAN LAWS AND POLICY.

K. von Fritz, *Hist.* 1950, 3 ff.; *CAH* 7²/2 (1989), 323 ff.; K. Bringmann, in J. Bleicken (ed.), *Symposion für A. Heuss* (1986), 51 ff.; B. Forsén, *Lex Licinia Sextia de modo agrorum* (1991). A. D.

Licinius Sura, Lucius (ordinary *consul for the second time AD 102, for the third time 107), from Hispania *Tarraconensis, was a man of great distinction and influence in the reign of *Trajan, whose adoption by *Nerva he allegedly urged. Renowned as an orator, he was interested in literature, a patron of *Martial, and friend of *Pliny (2) the Younger, who in two letters consulted him on questions of physical science and the supernatural (*Ep.* 4. 30, 7. 27). Sura was highly regarded by Trajan, as his third consulship and a statue and public funeral in his honour indicate, and had the complete trust of the emperor, who ignored slanderous stories about him (Cass. Dio 68. 15). He was consul, possibly in 93 or 97, and legionary legate (see LEGATI) or perhaps governor in Lower Germany (see GERMANIA), but his career is obscure, much depending on the attribution to him of an acephalous inscription (*ILS* 1022), which has also been ascribed to Q. *Sosius Senecio. He was present on the first Dacian campaign (see DACIA) where he conducted an unsuccessful diplomatic mission to *Decebalus. Sura may have used his influence with Trajan in support of Hadrian.

*PIR*² L 253; C. P. Jones, *JRS* 1970, 98; R. Syme, *ZPE* 59 (1985), 272 (= *RP* 5. 507). J. B. C.

Licinius (*RE* 173) **Valerianus, Publius,** the emperor **Valerian,** ruled AD 253–60. An elderly (in his 60s) noble senator of great experience, he was sent to *Raetia to gather troops to help *Trebonianus Gallus against Aemilius Aemilianus. On the death of Gallus, he was hailed as emperor by his men, and marched on Italy. Following the murder of Aemilianus, Valerian and his adult son, Gallienus (P. *Licinius Egnatius Gallienus), were universally recognized as Augusti (autumn 253; see TETRARCHY). Both strove to serve the empire in circumstances that, as growing external pressures exacerbated internal economic, political and moral weaknesses, were becoming ever more difficult. However, their joint reign saw the nadir of the 3rd-cent. 'crisis'.

In 254 Valerian moved east to repair the damage done by the

Persians under Gallus and Aemilianus, and to repel new Gothic raids (in 253/4, 254/5, 256) down the eastern and western coasts of the Black Sea into Asia Minor (see HERULI). The strain he was under is reflected in his persecution of *Christianity (rescripts of 257, 258), and his increased reliance on *Septimius Odaenathus of Palmyra. It was perhaps the need for peace which tempted him to negotiate personally with *Sapor I when the latter again invaded the empire in strength, and which led to his capture, with most of his general staff (summer 260). Valerian was subjected to various humiliations, and died a prisoner.

In outlook remarkably similar to *Decius, Valerian may be seen as the last of the senatorial warrior-emperors, who had pursued a combined civilian and military career in the best republican tradition. As Gallienus recognized, new problems demanded new solutions. However, Valerian's courage in captivity in part redeems his incompetence, and may indeed have brought a breathing-space for his empire.

M. Christol, *ANRW* 2. 2 (1975), 803 ff.; J. F. Drinkwater, *RSA* 1989, 123 ff. J. F. Dr.

lictores were attendants (*apparitores*), originally those, *Etruscan in origin, who carried the *fasces for magistrates with *imperium. They accompanied the latter at all times inside and outside Rome, proceeding before them in single file, each carrying his bundle of fasces on his left shoulder. Their function was to announce the approach of the magistrate, clearing everyone except Vestals (see VESTA) and *matronae* (married women) from his path, and to implement his rights of arrest, summons, and, in early times, execution. At Rome the ancient rule was that a consul's lictors only preceded him in the months when he was senior consul. Their number varied according to the nature of a magistrate's *imperium* (a *consul had twelve, a *praetor six). Among the *apparitores* lictors ranked higher than *viatores and lower than *scribae. The lictors who attended magistrates formed a corporation divided into several decuries, each under the presidency of ten men. In the late republic this body also provided lictors for such men as private citizens holding public games and travelling senators, but these are unlikely to have carried fasces. Lictors drawn from a separate decury of *lictores curiati* attended certain religious officials and were responsible for the summoning of the *comitia curiata (see CURIA (1)), while in the imperial age those from a third group—the *lictores populares denuntiatores*—attended at the games of the *magistri vicorum* (magistrates in charge of city wards). Their traditional dress was a toga in Rome, a red cloak (*sagum*) outside Rome and in the triumphal procession, and a black mourning-dress at funerals. Although probably of undistinguished birth, they might derive considerable status from this post.

Mommsen, *Röm. Staatsr.* 1³. 355 f., 373 ff.; N. Purcell, *PBSR* 1983. E. S. S.; A. W. L.

Licymnius (1), brother of *Alcmene and so uncle of *Heracles, killed by Heracles' son *Tlepolemus (*Il.* 2. 653–70). His home was at the gymnasium of *Argos (2) (Paus. 2. 22. 8; Plut. *Pyrrh.* 34), but he was also recognized as eponym of Licymna, the acropolis of *Tiryns (Strabo 8. 373).

C. Harrauer, *Wien. Stud.* 1988, 97–126. E. Ke.

Licymnius (2), of *Chios, dithyrambic poet (see DITHYRAMB) and rhetorician, teacher of *Polus (Pl. *Phdr.* 267c). *Aristotle says that his works were better to read than to hear (*Rh.* 1413ᵇ14). Also wrote on language (ibid. 1414ᵇ15).

Page, *PMG* 768–73.

Ligarius (*RE* 4), **Quintus,** one of three brothers of undistinguished family from Sabinum, was *legatus* in Africa under C. Considius Longus in 50 BC. See LEGATI; AFRICA, ROMAN. Left in charge of the province, he surrendered it in 49 to the Pompeian P. *Attius Varus, helped him to keep out L. *Aelius Tubero who had been appointed governor by the senate, and apparently remained with the Pompeians in Africa till 46, when *Caesar captured him at Hadrumetum. *Cicero and Ligarius' two brothers, who had supported Caesar in 49, pleaded for his recall, but Q. *Aelius Tubero, piqued by his father's humiliation in 49, accused Ligarius before Caesar as a stubborn foe. Cicero defended him and he was restored. In 44, however, he joined the conspiracy against Caesar. His brothers perished in the *proscriptions; his own fate is unknown.

Cic. *Lig.* Schanz–Hosius 1. 439 ff.; G. Walser, *Hist.* 1959, 90 ff.; R. A. Bauman, *The Crimen Maiestatis* (1967), 142 ff.   T. J. C.; R. J. S.

lighthouses Tall monuments which might function as navigational marks were an early feature of ancient harbour-architecture (Archaic examples are known on *Thasos). The idea became celebrated with the building of the 100-m. (328-ft.) tower on the Pharus island at *Alexandria (1), which gave its name to the architectural genre (*c.*300–280 BC, by Sostratus of *Cnidus (Strabo 17. 1. 6)), and the colossus of *Helios at *Rhodes (280 BC, by *Chares (4) of Lindus (Plin. *HN* 34. 41)): both so famous as to be reckoned among the *Seven Wonders of the ancient world. Beacon-fires made such monuments more visible by night as well as by day: but their function as signs of conquest and displays of prestige was as important. Claudius' lighthouse tower at *Portus, intended to rival the Pharus, became a symbol of Rome's port and its activities. The (partly preserved) lighthouse at Dover castle, and its opposite number at Boulogne (*Gesoriacum) suggested the taming of the Channel; another survives at La Coruña (*Brigantium) at the Atlantic extremity of Spain. Such towers became familiar features of the waterfronts of many famous cities.

M.-H. Quet, *MÉFRA* 1984, 789–845; S. Hutter, *Der Leuchtturm von La Coruña* (1973); T. Kozelj and M. Wurch-Kozelj, *BCH* 1989, 161–81.
                                                                                         N. P.

lighting The ancients knew two methods: the burning of oil in a lamp (see LAMPS) and the combustion of a solid substance. In Minoan (see MINOAN CIVILIZATION) and in Classical times lamps were preferred for indoor illumination, and in the Roman empire they were sometimes employed for streets and on exteriors of buildings. The torch (λαμπάς) was more generally used out of doors and also for interiors during the early iron age. The Greek torch was generally of wood (δαΐς), a branch or a bundle of twigs (δετή). The Italians preferred candles of tallow (*candela*) or beeswax (*cereus*), which were mounted on metal *candelabra*. Lanterns were also freely used, candles or lamps enclosed within horn or (in imperial times) glass. *Antioch (1) was one of the few cities in antiquity to provide street lighting (Amm. Marc. 14. 1. 9) along with (late antique) *Ephesus. Torches were also used for signalling in warfare.

Forbes, *Stud. Anc. Technol.* 6. 119 ff.; J. Perlzweig, *Lamps from the Athenian Agora* (1963).   F. N. P.; D. W. J. G.

Ligurians Mentioned from *Hecataeus (1) onwards as the indigenous neighbours of the Greeks at *Massalia. Their territory is first defined clearly (by *Polybius (1) and *Livy) for the 3rd cent. BC. They were then allies of the *Celts and occupied lands adjacent to them: along the coast from the Rhône to the Arno and inland as far as the Durance and the mountains south of the Po (*Padus). Between 238 and 117 BC Rome reduced to submission Ligurian tribes throughout this area. After the Ligurian support of *Mago (2) *c.*205–203, the most important Roman successes were against the Cisalpine Ingauni and Apuani in 181 and 180, against the Alpine Statielli in 173, against the Deciates and Oxybii around Nice (*Nicaea (2)) in 154 (after Massalian appeals for help against Ligurian pirates), and against the 'Celto-ligurian' *Salluvii and their allies near Aix (*Aquae Sextiae) in 123, after further Massalian appeals for help. This marked the major Roman success: only lesser Ligurian tribes remained unconquered and the Roman Province was established. By this time, the western Ligurians at least had become thoroughly Celticized and *Strabo (4. 6. 3) refers to the Salluvii and other tribes near Massalia as Celtoligurian or simply Celtic.

Liguria formed one of the Augustan *regiones* of *Italy. The history of the Ligurians before the 3rd cent. BC is obscure. Contemporary classical writers simply mention them in passing and the traditional account in later works (most notably Justin 43) is semi-mythical. Few ethnographic details are given by early or late authors. The principal account in *Diodorus (3) Siculus (5. 39) insists on the toughness of the Ligurians, both male and female, and of their environment.

Despite claims that some words or place-names (e.g. those ending in -*asco*, like Giubasco) are diagnostically Ligurian, the existence of any Ligurian language is still hypothetical.

Relevant archaeological evidence is scanty and imprecise, and it is not possible to equate any archaeological culture with the historical Ligurians. However, Urn-field traditions, like those of the neighbouring Alpine and *Villanovan groups, are prominent through the Ligurian area at the beginning of the iron age, with influences from Greek colonists and from the La Tène culture north of the *Alps appearing later. There is little evidence to support the tradition of a persisting Mediterranean neolithic tradition in the area.

M. Bats and H. Trézing, *Études Massiliètes* (1986); A. L. F. Rivet, *Gallia Narbonensis* (1988), 9 ff. (for bibliog.).   F. R. H.; J. F. Dr.

Lilybaeum (mod. Marsala), the westernmost point of *Sicily, was the site of a fruitless attempt at colonization *c.*580 BC by Cnidians (see NIBUS) under Pentathlus (Diod. Sic. 5. 9). A small Carthaginian settlement (see CARTHAGE) later grew up there, but *Diodorus (3)'s reference to it in 454 BC (11. 86) is probably mistaken. Its real importance began after 396 (and possibly not before *c.*380), when the Carthaginians developed it as a replacement for *Motya, sacked by *Dionysius (1) I. It became a flourishing port and important Punic stronghold, with powerful defences and an orthogonal street-grid (see URBANISM). *Pyrrhus failed to take it in 276, and it withstood a long siege by the Romans between 251 and 240 (Polyb. 1. 41–59). After 241 it formed part of the Roman province of Sicily as a *civitas decumana* (city liable to pay a tithe, see DECUMA) and was the headquarters, during the republic, of one of the province's two *quaestors. *Cicero resided there and thought it a 'most splendid city' (*civitas splendidissima*: 2 *Verr.* 5. 5. 10). It received the *ius Latii* under *Augustus and became a *colonia* in AD 193. No public buildings have been found (although an amphitheatre, a sanctuary of the Cereres (i.e. *Ceres and *Persephone), and an aqueduct are mentioned in or implied by inscriptions), but several town-houses of Hellenistic and Roman imperial date have been excavated, many with mosaics. Lilybaeum flourished under the empire, when her fortunes were closely linked with those of North Africa. Much damaged in *Vandal raids (440–77), the city was in decline until its capture by the Arabs in 827.

PECS 509–10; C. A. Di Stefano (ed.), *Lilibeo: testimonianze archeologiche dal IV sec. a.c. al V sec. d.c.* (1984), and *Lilibeo punica* (1993); R. J. A. Wilson, *ANRW* 2. 11. 1 (1988), 158–67, and *Sicily under the Roman Empire* (1990), *passim.*   A. G. W.; R. J. A. W.

limes originated as a surveyor's term for the path that simultaneously marked the boundaries of plots of land and gave access between them. It came to be used in a military sense, first of the roads that penetrated into enemy territory (Tac. *Ann.* 1. 50; Frontin. *Str.* 1. 3. 10), and thence, as further conquest ceased, of the land boundaries that divided Roman territory from non-Roman (SHA *Hadr.* 12). At this stage a whole paraphernalia of border control grew up—frontier roads with intermittent watch-towers and forts and fortlets to house the provincial garrisons which moved up to the frontier line. The term *limes* comes to embrace the totality of the border area and its control system (but note the strictures of Isaac, *JRS* 1988 125–47 on this point). In Europe, where the frontiers faced onto habitable lands, and where they did not coincide with a river or other clear natural obstacle, the frontier line came to be marked off (usually no earlier than Hadrian) by an artificial running barrier. In Britain this took the form of a stone wall (*wall of Hadrian) or one of turf (*wall of Antoninus); in Upper Germany (*Germania) and in *Raetia timber palisades were originally built under *Hadrian and *Antoninus Pius; these were strengthened in Upper Germany by a rampart and ditch (*Pfahlgraben*), and replaced in Raetia by a narrow (1.3-m.-/4¼-ft.-wide) stone wall (*Teufelsmauer*) at an uncertain date in the later 2nd or early 3rd cent. In Europe beyond Raetia, the frontier ran along the river Danube (*Danuvius) except where *Dacia projected northwards. Here earthwork barriers were used in discontinuous sectors to the north-west and south-east where there were gaps in the encircling mountain ranges. The Upper German and Raetian frontiers were abandoned under *Gallienus and the whole of Dacia under *Aurelian, leading to an intensification of military control on the rivers Rhine (*Rhenus) and Danube. In the eastern and southern parts of the empire the *limes* took a different form. They lay at the limits of cultivable land capable of supporting a sedentary population and were concerned with the supervision of trade routes and the control of cross-frontier migration by nomadic peoples (see NOMADS) whose traditional *transhumance routes took them into provincial territory. In the east (see ARABIA), military bases were positioned along the major north–south communication line along the edge of the desert (the via nova Traiana), and concentrated on guarding watering-places and points where natural route-ways crossed the frontier line. The threat of raiding Bedouin bands increased in the later Roman period, leading to a considerable build-up of military installations on the desert fringe. The problems were similar in *Africa, where the use of intermittent linear barriers such as the Fossatum Africae was designed to channel and control rather than to halt nomadic movements. In *Tripolitania troops were based at intervals along the Limes Tripolitanus, a route that led right into the major city, *Lepcis Magna, running around the Gebel escarpment which ran through the richest agricultural zone of the province. Three major caravan routes which converged with this road were likewise guarded by the military, with legionaries being outposted in the Severan period to oasis forts at the desert edge. The intermediate area was peppered with fortified settlements, largely of a civilian rather than a military character. The frontiers as a whole were greatly strengthened in the Diocletianic period (see DIOCLETIAN) in response to increasing external pressure. For this later period see LIMITANEI.

G. Forni, *Diz. Epigr.* 4/2, 'limes'; J. Wacher (ed.), *The Roman World* (1987), pt. 4: 'The Frontiers'; C. Whittaker, *The Frontiers of the Roman Empire* (1994). For Britain, D. J. Breeze, *The Northern Frontiers of Roman Britain* (1982); for Germany, D. Baatz, *Der römische Limes*, 2nd edn. (1994); for the east, B. Isaac, *The Limits of Empire: The Roman Empire in the East* (1990); for Syria, A. Poidebard, *La Trace de Rome dans le désert de Syrie* (1934), and D. Kennedy, *Archaeological Explorations on the Roman Frontier in North East Jordan* (1982); for Arabia, S. T. Parker, *Romans and Saracens: A History of the Arabian Frontier* (1986): for Africa, J. Baradez, *Fossatum Africae* (1949), and Y. Le Bohec, *La Troisième Légion Auguste* (1989); for Tripolitania, A. de Vita, *Libya Antiqua* 1964, 65–98; for Tingitana, M. Euzennat, *Le Limes de Tingitane: La frontière méridionale* (1989). For current research see the reports of the International Congresses of Roman Frontier Studies, detailed in J. Wacher (ed.), as cited above, 318, plus H. Vetters and M. Kandler (eds.), *Akten des 14. Internationalen Limeskongresses 1986 in Carnuntum* (1990), and V. A. Maxfield and M. Dobson (eds.), *Roman Frontier Studies 1989: Proc. XVth International Congress of Frontier Studies, Canterbury* (1991).   V. A. M.

limitanei, collective term for units of the late-Roman frontier armies so called because they occupied permanent stations on the frontiers (*limites,* see LIMES), as distinct from units of the mobile army (*comitatenses). This distinction existed earlier, but was completed by *Constantine I. They comprised the surviving *legions and auxiliary units (*alae and cohortes (see COHORS)), now much reduced in size, and new units of cavalry (equites and cunei) and infantry (auxilia and milites). They were grouped into armies commanded by duces (see DUX). They remained fighting troops during the 4th cent. and were sometimes upgraded into the mobile army as *pseudocomitatenses.*

Jones, *Later Rom. Emp.* 97–100, 649–54.   R. S. O. T.

Limyra See PERICLES (2).

Lindum (Lincoln), town in *Britain, lay in the territory of the *Corieltauvi, whose capital was *Ratae (Leicester). It began as a fortress for Legio IX Hispana (see LEGION) c. AD 60 (*RIB* 254–7, 260). Soon after 71 this legion advanced to *Eburacum (York) and Lindum seems to have been held by Legio II Adiutrix perhaps till c.74/5 (*RIB* 253, 258). A *colonia* was founded c.90–6 (*CIL* 13. 6679). The new town, with colonnaded main streets, small *insulae* (blocks of buildings), a piped aqueduct, and notable sewers, occupied the site of the fortress, spreading down the slope to the river Witham, so covering more than 39 ha. (96 acres). The town was an important road-centre and enjoyed good water communications (via the river Witham); in the 4th cent. it was the seat of a bishopric and perhaps the capital of Flavia Caesariensis. Excavations have revealed an early church within the forum.

M. J. Jones, in F. Grew and B. Hobley (eds.), *Roman Urban Topography in Britain and the Western Empire* (1985), and in G. Webster (ed.), *Fortress into City* (1988).   I. A. R.; S. S. F.; M. J. M.

Lindus was the most important of the three independent Dorian cities of *Rhodes until the *synoecism with *Ialysus and *Camirus created the federal Rhodian state in 408/7 BC. The city occupies a prominent headland with good harbours on the central SE side of Rhodes, and controlled most of the southern half of the island. Early cemeteries attest neolithic and Mycenaean occupation (see MYCENAEAN CIVILIZATION), and Lindus appears with the other Rhodian cities in *Homer (*Il.* 2. 656). In the 7th cent. Lindian colonists founded *Gela in Sicily and *Phaselis in Lycia. One of the tyrants governing Lindus in the early 6th cent. was Cleobulus, one of the '*Seven Sages', whose so-called tomb (a round pre-Hellenic structure) lies on a nearby headland. Lindus appears in the Athenian *tribute-lists.

The important cult of *Athena Lindia existed from at least the 10th cent. BC although the existing sanctuary and temple on the acropolis date from the 4th cent. and later. It remained a major Rhodian cult even after the synoecism, as inscribed dedications show. The Lindian *Temple Chronicle* (FGrH 532; see TIMACHIDAS) records mythical and historical dedications to the goddess plus three divine *epiphanies in times of crisis. The priest-list which extends for over 400 years is fundamental in establishing Rhodian chronology. Other remains include a ship relief on the acropolis cliff, a theatre, a temple of Dionysus, and rock-cut tombs.

Famous Lindians include the Stoic philosopher *Panaetius and *Chares (4), sculptor of the Colossus of Rhodes. Tradition maintains that St *Paul landed at Lindus on his way to Rome.

Inscriptions in *IG* 12. 1. C. Blinkenberg, *Lindos 1: Fouilles de l'Acropole 1902–1914: Les Petits Objets* (1931), and *Lindos 2: Fouilles de l'Acropole 1902–1914: Inscriptions* (1941); E. Dyggve, *Lindos 3: Fouilles de l'Acropole 1902–1914 et 1952: Le Sanctuaire d'Athana Lindia et l'architecture lindienne* (1960); S. Dietz, *Lindos 4/1: Excavations and Surveys in Southern Rhodes: The Mycenaean Period* (1984); L. W. Sorensen and P. Pentz, *Lindos 4/2: Excavations and Surveys in Southern Rhodes: The Post-Mycenaean Periods until Roman Times and the Medieval Period* (1992).   E. E. R.

Linear B See MYCENAEAN LANGUAGE; PRE-ALPHABETIC SCRIPTS (GREECE).

linen (λίνον, linum), yarn and cloth, the product of the domesticated flax plant (*Linum usitatissimum* L.), which was developed in the Mediterranean region for oil-seed and fibre from the wild *Linum bienne*. Though hardy, flax grows best in fertile well-watered soils; it was believed by Roman writers to exhaust the land (e.g. Verg. *G.* 1. 77). *Linear B tablets from *Pylos attest significant flax cultivation in the SW Peloponnese around 1200 BC; in later times flax from Elis, further north-west, had a good reputation (Plin. *HN* 19. 20). Outside Greece, Ptolemaic *Egypt was heir to some of the finest linens ever made, but by the Roman period the centre of gravity had shifted to urban centres in *Syria and Palestine, notably *Laodicea-Lycus and *Scythopolis (mod. Beth-Shean; see also TARSUS). In the west there was praise for the linen weavers of the Po Valley (see PADUS) in northern Italy and the coastal tract of SE Spain (Plin. *HN* 19. 1–25). Pliny (ibid.) is also our main source on how linen fibre was extracted from flax stems by retting them in water, breaking them (when dried) into short lengths with a mallet, beating them with a scutching blade, and finally combing on a hackle (aena) set with spikes. Tow (στυππεῖον, stuppa), a by-product of hackling, was used for rope and sacking. The 'Tarsian linens' of Egypt had a special, but so far unexplained, character. Some Greek linen of sound quality survives (e.g. from *Lefkandi on Euboea); in the eastern Roman provinces much linen has been excavated—remains of tunics, cloaks, scarves, and household furnishings, mostly undyed. Netting, sails, and theatre-awnings were all of linen. See TEXTILE PRODUCTION.

F. Olck, *RE* 6/2 (1909), 2435–84 'Flachs'; Forbes, *Stud. Anc. Technol.* 4². 27 ff.; Y. Yadin, *The Finds from the Bar-Kokhba Period in the Cave of Letters* (1963), 252 ff.   J. P. W.

linguistics In its broader sense, linguistics denotes the scientific study of all aspects of language in all forms (including human sign-language and animal communication), whether in isolation or in any of a wide range of interactions. Linguistics is also used more narrowly (often in the phrase *core linguistics*) to mean the

study of the items and their combinations in the grammar at its several levels of analysis, namely: *phonology* (the sound system), *morphology* (word-structure), *syntax* (clause- and sentence-structure, word order), *semantics* (meanings encoded in language), and the *lexicon*.

If modern linguistics in the west owes its birth to a single event, it is to the rediscovery of Sanskrit, by European scholars in the late 18th cent., and the consequent realization that many languages of Europe, Persia, and India must be related and descended from a common ancestor (*Indo-European). Consequently, 19th-cent. linguistics was predominantly historical (*diachronic*) and comparative. Research was devoted above all to writing the histories of languages, to understanding the principles of language-change, to establishing 'family trees' of related languages, and to reconstructing prehistoric ancestral languages by the comparative method of *comparative philology*.

At the beginning of this century, this strong emphasis on diachronic questions gave way to the *synchronic* approach that dominates linguistics today. The focus of interest was no longer, How does a language change over time? but rather, How is a language structured at a given point in time? and, How does it function as 'un système où tout se tient' (Ferdinand de Saussure, 1857–1913)? In America an important factor that reinforced this shift of focus to synchronic descriptive linguistics was the perceived need to record and so preserve the many preliterate languages of the Americas.

Since the late 1950s, the ultimate goal of core linguistics for many researchers, especially under the influence of Noam Chomsky and generative grammar, has been to model formally the knowledge that speakers are hypothesized to have of their language, and the faculty (perhaps innate) that enables children 'on the basis of a finite and accidental experience with language [to] produce or understand an indefinite number of new sentences' (Chomsky).

Language is of central concern to fields other than core linguistics, such as psychology and sociology. Accordingly several more or less discrete interdisciplinary subjects, such as psycholinguistics and sociolinguistics, have come to constitute important branches of modern linguistics in the broader sense. Especially descriptive linguistics and sociolinguistics are of increasing importance in classical studies.

Accessible introductions: J. Lyons, *Language and Linguistics* (1981); R. H. Robins, *General Linguistics*, 4th edn. (1989). Surveys: in 1 vol., J. Lyons and others (eds.), *New Horizons in Linguistics* 2 (1987); in 14 vols.: T. A. Sebeok (ed.), *Current Trends in Linguistics* (1963–76). Reference work, with bibliog.: W. Bright (ed.), *International Encyclopaedia of Linguistics* (1992).   D. R. L.

linguistics, ancient 1. Linguistics, as understood and practised today, arose in western antiquity from two rather different sources: philosophical debate on the origin and nature of language, and the practical requirements of textual criticism and the teaching of Greek. It generally went under the name of grammar (*grammatikē*) which had at first referred simply to the teaching of literacy, and came later to include what would now be called orthographical phonetics, phonology, morphology, and syntax, corresponding to the wider use of 'grammar' among some linguists today. Linguistics developed along with other disciplines concerned with language, in particular *rhetoric and *literary criticism. Several well-known ancient grammarians (see GRAMMATICUS) engaged in one or both of these other subjects as well.

It is clear that, as with so much else in the western intellectual tradition, linguistics began in Greece and was then taken up in the Latin world after the Greek-speaking countries had been absorbed within Roman control. There was some independent thought on language in Roman work, particularly with *Varro (1st cent. BC), but in general the Greeks set the pace and the Romans willingly and explicitly followed them. But it must be kept in mind that Latin linguistics did not chronologically just follow Greek linguistics; from around 150 BC and up to the end of the classical era, around AD 500, when Greek and Latin contacts began to weaken and then fell, Greek and Latin scholars were working contemporaneously and often in direct contact with each other.

2. Linguistic speculations of a sort are known to have occupied philosophers from the *Presocratic period, on such matters as the real-world correspondences of grammatical tenses and genders. *Aristophanes (1) made fun of *Socrates engaging in such studies (in *Clouds*), so presumably this was a familiar topic for the general public in 5th-cent. Athens.

Two rather general questions arose: (*a*), To what extent was language a natural or inborn capacity of human beings, and how far was it the result of a tacit convention or social contract? and (*b*), How far could general statements be made covering large numbers of word-forms and meanings, and how much individual irregularity must be accepted as inherent in language use? This latter went under the name of *analogy and anomaly.

*Plato (1) records a dialogue of Socrates, the *Cratylus*, about the nature of language, and in other dialogues he attributes to him certain linguistic notions such as a nominal-subject element and a verbal predicate as the basic components of sentences. *Aristotle followed Plato's outlines and made reference to linguistic topics in several of his philosophical and literary works.

3. It was the Stoics (3rd cent. BC and after; see STOICISM) who recognized linguistics as a separate and essential part of philosophy or dialectic. They are known to have written a number of specialist books on various aspects of linguistics, and it is unfortunate that these only survive in fragments or in secondary sources, which makes it hard to set out their insightful system of linguistic analysis with any certainty.

Breaking away from the Platonic–Aristotelian school, the Stoics favoured the naturalist origin of language, laying stress on the irregularities necessarily found in it. This was in contrast to the Aristotelian opinions on these matters. Following their devotion to propositional logic as against the predominantly class-membership logic of Aristotle, they gave particular attention to syntax, devising a classification of different predicational constructions. In so far as their system can be reconstructed from the available evidence, it seems to have been logically rather than morphologically based and to have resembled somewhat the format and purpose of the 'logical form' syntax of some modern generative grammarians.

4. Though some details are lacking we are able to follow the successive stages in the recognition of different word-classes (parts of speech) and of the grammatical categories which characterized them. Plato's distinction of nominal subject and verbal predicate was enriched by Aristotle's identification of a complex class of 'form words', without readily ostensive meanings and serving to ensure the unity of whole sentences. He also introduced the word *ptōsis*, 'falling', as a technical term for all grammatically relevant word-form variations. The Stoics later confined the term to its subsequent and current sense of nominal inflexion (Latin *casus* 'case'). This made possible a further subdivision of the Aristotelian class of form words. Their semantic

analysis of Greek verbal tenses into their temporal and aspectual meanings was exploited by *Varro in his analysis of Latin tenses, but was not fully comprehended by the main tradition of antiquity.

Resulting from the conjoint work of Stoic philosophers and *Alexandrian teachers and critics, a system of eight word-classes—noun, verb, participle, (definite) article, pronoun, preposition, adverb, and conjunction—was established and preserved throughout the Greek grammatical tradition.

5. Alexandrian linguistics became the standard model in the Greek and Roman world and very largely formed the basis of both classical and modern grammars of European languages in the Renaissance. Alexandrian grammar, despite its general Aristotelian orientation, was driven less by philosophical considerations than by the needs of teachers of the Greek language and of Greek, especially Homeric, literature. The Macedonian successor states made themselves responsible for promoting Greek studies in their hitherto non-Greek territories. This Hellenizing process (see HELLENISM AND HELLENIZATION) was taken over and continued by the Romans, and during the four centuries of Roman rule the Greek orientation of education and culture was left intact.

*Alexandria (1), a scholarly city founded by *Alexander (3) of Macedon, became a centre of literary and linguistic studies, the latter comprising orthographical phonetics, morphology, syntax, lexical semantics, and dialect studies. *Aristarchus (2) (2nd cent. BC) was both a grammarian and a Homeric scholar, and his pupil *Dionysius (15) Thrax wrote what is probably the first authoritative grammar-book of the Greek language. It soon became known as 'The Manual' (*Ta parangelmata*), and a brief textbook entitled the *Science of grammar* (*Technē grammatikē*) has been attributed to him. There are, however, problems about the genuineness of the text as we have it, except for the first section, and it may be safer to assume that his book, setting out the state of grammatical description and teaching in Alexandria in the 2nd or 1st cent. BC, was subjected to various revisions and that what we have now is a Byzantine version reflecting a standardized edition of the 3rd or 4th cent. AD. In it the sentence and the word were formally defined as the expression of a complete thought and as the minimal unit of syntax, respectively. This was followed by the eight word-classes, their subclassifications, and their categories.

6. A number of Greek grammarians turned their attention to Latin after contacts with the Roman world, and they declared that, subject to just a few exceptions, the framework of Greek grammar would perfectly well fit the Latin language. In their recognition of Greek superiority in intellectual matters this was what the Romans wanted to hear, and as far as possible the Alexandrian classes and categories were handed on to the later Latin grammarians.

However, Varro was the principal link between Greek and Latin linguistics, a man of great and varied learning, knowing both languages well, and acquainted with the grammar-book of Dionysius in its initial state. Following his studies under the Stoic philosopher Stilo Praeconinus (see AELIUS, L.), he understood both the Stoic and the Alexandrian views on language and applied these to Latin in his book *On the Latin Language* (*De lingua Latina*). This is not a grammar of Latin, but a lengthy discussion about the language, its structure, vocabulary, and, so far as he could trace it, its history.

Varro was the most original thinker about language that we know of in the Latin world. In addition to his application of Stoic semantics to the Latin verb he made an extensive study of word formation and inflexion, drawing on the principle of regularity ('analogy'), but recognizing existing irregularities as well. In his books he began the process of grouping Latin case forms together, leading to the later establishment of the traditional five declensions. These five were set out by the late Latin grammarians such as *Priscian (*c.* AD 500) several centuries before a comparable simplified account was applied to Greek, probably under Latin influence, at the end of the Byzantine age, and this must be laid to the credit of Varro's early insights.

Three main differences between Latin and Greek had to be noticed by Varro and others: (*a*) The Latin ablative case, not found in Greek and recognized by Varro as the 'sixth' or 'Latin' case. The term *ablative* was created later by reference to one of its major functions, 'taking away from'. (*b*) The absence of a definite article in Latin. The word-classes were maintained at eight when *Remmius Palaemon (1st cent. AD) made the interjection, which the Greeks treated as a subclass of adverbs, a class in its own right. (*c*) The conflation in Latin of the present completive ('have done') with the plain past ('did'), having differential verb forms in Greek (*pepoiĕka, epoiĕsa*) but a single form in Latin (*feci*). This was duly noted by Priscian.

7. A number of Greek grammarians are known to have been working on syntax in the 1st cent. BC and after, but the first grammarian dealing exclusively with it, whose work is, in part, extant, is *Apollonius (13) Dyscolus, writing in Alexandria and in the Alexandrian tradition around AD 200. He was regarded by Priscian as his principal authority, and later Byzantine grammarians in the main wrote summaries and commentaries on the basis of Apollonius' books. The work of these Byzantine Greek grammarians between 500 and 1500 was the main vehicle for the reintroduction of Greek studies in the western Renaissance.

8. A considerable number of late Latin grammarians are known and their work is extant; the most prominent among them are *Donatus (1) (4th cent.) and Priscian (writing in Constantinople around 500), who became authorities for the later medieval grammarians, both practical and theoretical. Donatus wrote two short grammars of Latin; Priscian wrote at great length, and his principal work, *Institutiones grammaticae* ('The Principles of Grammar') runs to 974 printed pages. The work is divided into eighteen books, the last two being wholly devoted to syntax and drawn largely from Apollonius. Priscian's work recapitulates the entire achievement of the Graeco-Roman grammatical tradition, to which the debt of today's language studies can hardly be exaggerated. See GRAMMAR AND GRAMMARIANS, GREEK AND LATIN.

H. Steinthal, *Geschichte der Sprachwissenschaft bei den Griechen und Römern* (1891; repr. 1961); R. H. Robins, *A Short History of Linguistics* (1990), chs. 2–3; E. Hovdhaugen, *Foundations of Western Linguistics* (1982); P. H. Matthews, in G. C. Lepschy (ed.), *Storia della linguistica* (1990); J. A. Kemp, *The Tekhnē grammatikē of Dionysius Thrax* (Eng. trans.), in D. J. Taylor (ed.), *The History of Linguistics in the Classical Age* (1987); A. A. Long (ed.), *Problems in Stoicism* (1971), chs. 4–5.
R. H. R.

linguistics, historical and comparative (Indo-European)

1. Introduction Historical linguistics studies how language develops in time; comparative linguistics (or comparative philology) uses linguistic comparison to establish that two or more languages are genetically related and descend from an earlier language which may or may not be attested. We know that the Romance languages (French, Italian, Spanish, etc.) are related and descend from a form of Latin, but we can also show that languages like Latin, Greek, Sanskrit, Armenian, Germanic, etc. descend from an unattested parent language. We can reconstruct the main features of this language which we call conventionally Proto-Indo-European (PIE) or simply *Indo-European (IE), and which must have been spoken before writing was developed. Similar techniques allow us to reconstruct Proto-*Semitic, the parent language of Hebrew, Arabic, *Akkadian, etc. or Proto-Algonquian from which a number of Amerindian languages in NE and central North America derive, etc. The question whether all languages descend from one language or many remains open. Within each family we can also establish different degrees of relationship. Greek, Latin, French, English, German are all Indo-European, but Greek and Latin belong to separate branches, English and German to the same branch (Germanic), while French descends from Latin. In general, comparative linguistics may provide evidence for prehistoric events such as the origin or movement of people but it also lengthens the history of the languages studied and throws light onto their features. We should not confuse this comparative linguistics, which aims at identifying genetic relationship, with the homonymous discipline which compares different languages (mostly unrelated) in order to establish language types and general features of language.

General Principles

The comparative and historical study of language requires familiarity with the principles of general linguistics (see LINGUISTICS) which have largely emerged from the study of living languages. In its turn, the general study of language change has much to contribute to the theoretical study of language and has developed as a discipline in its own right (cf. Bynon; Hock; Crowley; McMahon: see bibliog. below). The questions investigated concern the causes and modalities of language change in general and of specific instances of language change. It is now clear that sociolinguistic factors are partly responsible for the occurrence and modalities of language change (prestige forms of language are imitated) and that language variety is much more pervasive than the number of named dialects implies. Ideally all historical studies should take into account the various layers of each language (registers, dialects, etc.) and their correlation with sociohistorical factors, but often the necessary data are not available and we can only speculate.

Good methodology demands that comparison is based on the earliest phases of the languages considered. History must come before comparison; in languages, like Greek and Latin, for which we have a long and uninterrupted documentation, we can use internal evidence to establish what forms are the earliest. Attic forms as, for example, γένη, φιλῶν are shown by Homeric Greek (see HOMER) to be from γένεα, φιλέων, while τιμῶν is from τιμάων, and Attic τιμῶσι is from an earlier τιμάονσι, which derives from †τιμάοντι. This last form is reconstructed through dialect comparison and the dagger indicates that it is not attested.

Modern Linguistic Studies

The ancient Greek and Roman scholars were only interested in describing their own languages (as also were the Indian grammarians); linguistic history and comparison were ignored. Yet one attempt, not entirely free from political overtones, led to the (false) derivation of Latin from Greek in the 1st cent. BC.

Modern historical and comparative linguistics owes its beginnings to a closer study of Sanskrit, the literary and scholarly language of India, and to the encounter with the sophisticated Sanskrit tradition of grammatical analysis. After some earlier tentative statements, and especially after Sir William Jones's paper (1786) asserting the affinity of Sanskrit to the classical languages, it was Franz Bopp who in his work on the *Verbal Inflection of Sanskrit Compared with Greek, Latin, Persian and Germanic* (1816, re-edited in English in 1820) proved by a close comparison of the various verbal forms that the languages mentioned inherited their system from a common ancestor. From then almost to the end of the last century research concentrated on comparison, with Indo-European having the pride of place, and, after a revolutionary upheaval initiated in the late 1870s, found its codification in the monumental grammar of the IE languages by Brugmann and Delbrück (1893–1916). As a result it was established that the IE group embraced Indian and Iranian (the Aryan subgroup) and Armenian in Asia, *Greek, Italic (*Latin with *Oscan and Umbrian, etc. (see also ITALY, LANGUAGES OF)), *Celtic, *Germanic, Balto-Slavic, and Albanian in Europe; poorly known members are *Phrygian, Thracian, *Illyrian, *Messapic, and *Venetic. The 20th cent. brought to light two further groups, previously unknown: *Anatolian, the first attested member of the family (from c.1600 BC), in Asia Minor, and Tokharian in central Asia (cf. Meillet (1); Porzig; Szemerényi (1), (2); Cowgill and Mayrhofer) The detailed study of all these languages has led to spectacular results in all fields; the following survey attempts to outline the variety of problems encountered, with special regard to the classical languages (cf. Buck (1); Meillet–Vendryes; Schwyzer–Debrunner; Leumann–Hoffmann–Szantyr).

2. Phonology The study of the phonological development of ancient languages necessarily starts from written texts, but linguists are mostly concerned with the developments of sounds rather than of letters. Specific techniques allow them to move from spelling to pronunciation (see PRONUNCIATION, GREEK and LATIN). It is now clear that phonological development shows an unexpected form of regularity, which has become the cornerstone of all historical and comparative study and has provided a solid basis for the previously discredited study of etymology. If in a given period a sound changes in one word, then, as a rule, if enough time is allowed, it changes in the same way in all the words in which it appears, provided that the phonological environment (the sounds by which it is surrounded) is the same. Old English (OE) word-initial [kn] (square brackets indicate phonetic transcription) in which the [k] was actually pronounced, becomes [n] in *knight* (now pronounced [nait]) but also in *knot* (i.e. [not]): cf. OE *cniht* and *cnotta*. We state this observation in the form of a 'sound law': OE *kn-* > ME *n-* (> stands for 'becomes'; ME = Middle English), while again noticing that we are interested in the change of sounds and not of letters. 'Sound laws are without exceptions' was the slogan of the 1870s, and, in spite of the great theoretical and practical misgivings voiced ever since, the thesis has been found indispensable, although the conditions must be stated very carefully. Thus Classical Greek [ph] (written ϕ) regularly becomes [f] in modern Greek, while [au] regularly becomes [af] before voiceless stop ([p], [t], etc.) and [av] before voiced stop ([g] etc.). It follows that not only the correspondences between an attested or reconstructed protolanguage and the daughter languages, but also those between cognate languages show regularity; indeed it is the regularity of phonological correspondences that demonstrates that two or more languages are related. If Latin initial *f-* regularly becomes Italian *f-* and Spanish *h-* we expect a regular correspondence between Italian *f-* and Spanish *h-* (> ϕ), which we do indeed find: cf. It. *figlio*, Sp. *hijo* (< Lat. *filius* 'son'), It. *farina*, Sp. *harina* (< Lat. *farina* 'flour'). If so, a word like Sp. *filial* 'filial' must be a learned

borrowing from Latin. It is also this regularity which allows us to reconstruct the sound system of unattested parent languages. The regular correspondences between Gr. *p*, Lat. *p*, Skt. *p*, OE *f* (but *p* after *s*), point to an original IE †*p* and to rules like IE †*p* > Gr. *p* or IE †*p* > OE *f*: 'father' is the direct descendent of IE †*pətēr*, but 'paternal' is a borrowing from Latin.

We may also reconstruct for a protolanguage sounds not attested or scarcely attested in the daughter languages. In addition to liquids, nasals, a sibilant (†*r*, †*l*, †*n*, †*m*, †*s*), and the regular series of voiceless and voiced stops *p*, (*b*), *t*, *d*, *k*, *k*ʷ, *g*, *g*ʷ, IE also had voiced aspirate stops *bh*, *dh*, *gh*, *g*ʷ*h*. An IE *bh* is preserved in Sanskrit but appears in Greek as ϕ (i.e. *p*ʰ, an aspirated *p* in the Classical period), while in Latin in initial position we find *f-* but internally -*b*-. Cf. Skt. *bhrātar-* 'brother' : Gk. $\phi\rho\acute{a}\tau\eta\rho$: Lat. *frāter*, but Skt. *lubh-yati* 'desires' : Lat. *lubet*. Even more complex is the development of IE *dh*: Greek always presents θ (= aspirated *t*ʰ) while Latin has initially *f-* but internally -*d*- and -*b*-, the latter before or after an *r*, after *u*, and before *l*. Cf. Skt. *dhūma-* 'smoke' : Gk. $\theta\upsilon\mu\acute{o}\varsigma$: Lat. *fūmus*; Skt. *madhyas* 'middle' : Lat. *medius*; but Gk. $\dot{\epsilon}\rho\upsilon\theta\rho\acute{o}\varsigma$ 'red' : Lat. *ruber*; Skt. *ūdhar* 'udder' : Lat. *ūber*, etc. We also reconstruct a series of so-called labiovelars (velar sounds of the English *k g* type with lip-rounding; cf. Eng. *qu-*): *k*ʷ, *g*ʷ, *g*ʷ*h*. In historical Greek they merged with labial, dental, and velar sounds, but in the Linear B script they still have distinct signs, so that the development must have taken place after the Mycenaean period. To take a simple case, Latin *quis quid* obviously corresponds to Gk. $\tau\acute{\iota}\varsigma$ $\tau\acute{\iota}$, that is to say while Latin preserves an IE *k*ʷ as *qu*, Greek changed it to τ. But this occurred only before *i* or *e* (cf. Lat. -*que*: Gk. $\tau\epsilon$). Before *a* or *o* Gk. shows π; cf. the interrogative forms $\pi\acute{o}\theta\epsilon\nu$ $\pi\acute{o}\tau\epsilon$ $\pi\acute{o}\tau\epsilon\rho\sigma\varsigma$, etc., from IE †*k*ʷ*o-*. This explains the connection between $\tau\acute{\iota}\nu\omega$ 'I pay' and $\pi\sigma\iota\nu\acute{\eta}$ 'fine, payment', so obvious semantically, and so disconcerting when the sounds are compared; $\tau\iota$-/$\pi\sigma\iota$- represent the regular developments from IE †*k*ʷ*i-* and †*k*ʷ*oi-*.

It used to be believed that vowel changes were too erratic to present any regularity. In fact, vowels develop as regularly as the other sounds. The basic vowels of late IE (*a e i o u*, short and long) are fairly faithfully preserved in the classical languages (though in Latin this is only true for the first syllable of the word). Cf.:

a	IE †*agō*	'I drive'	Gk. $\check{a}\gamma\omega$	Lat. *agō*
ā	†*mātēr*	'mother'	$\mu\acute{a}\tau\eta\rho$	*māter*
e	†*bherō*	'I carry'	$\phi\acute{\epsilon}\rho\omega$	*ferō*
ē	†*plē-*	'full'	$\pi\lambda\acute{\eta}\cdot\rho\eta\varsigma$	*plē-nus*
o	†*oktō*	'eight'	$\dot{o}\kappa\tau\acute{\omega}$	*octō*
ō	†*dō-*	'give'	$\delta\hat{\omega}\rho\sigma\nu$	*dō-num*, etc.

Some apparent exceptions to these rules are explained through the reconstruction for IE of semivowels (approximants) which between consonants function as the nucleus of a syllable (like vowels) but between vowels function as consonants. Thus next to consonantal [j, w] (cf. Eng. *y* and *w*), we have vocalic *i* and *u*; next to consonantal *l, r, m, n*, we have vocalic *ḷ, ṛ, ṃ, ṇ* (the last four symbols indicate vocalic sounds like those indicated by -*le* in *bubble* and -*on* in *button*). The IE vocalic liquids are preserved in one language, Sanskrit, where we often find syllabic *r* (transcribed as *ṛ*); cf. *mṛta-* 'dead', *kṛp-* 'body', etc. In the classical languages the vocalic liquids of IE (*ḷ ṛ*) always develop a vowel, either before the liquid (Lat. *ul ur* or *ol or*; Gk. $\alpha\lambda$ $\alpha\rho$) or after it (Gk. $\lambda\alpha$ $\rho\alpha$). Thus Skt. *ṛksa-* 'bear' corresponds to Gk. $\check{a}\rho\kappa\tau\sigma\varsigma$ but Lat. *ur(c)sus*. The vocalic nasals are preserved in no language. Greek alternations like that of $\tau\epsilon\acute{\iota}\nu\omega$ ($\tau\epsilon\nu$-) 'I stretch' : $\tau\alpha$-$\tau\acute{o}\varsigma$ 'stretched', $\kappa\tau\epsilon\acute{\iota}\nu\omega$ ($\kappa\tau\epsilon\nu$-) 'I kill' : $\check{\epsilon}$-$\kappa\tau\alpha$-$\tau\sigma$ 'he killed', etc., are frequent, but apparently unexplainable; Sanskrit offers similar problems: *tan-* 'stretch' : *ta-tás* 'stretched', *han-* 'kill' : *ha-tás* 'killed', etc. Brugmann pointed out that the relation of εἶμι : (πρόσ)-ι-τος, φευγ- : φυκ-τός, showed that the verbal adjective was formed from the root in its 'weak' form, i.e. without *e* (nil-grade); that τεν- κτεν- were therefore expected to form †*tn-tos*, †*ktn-tos*, with a vocalic nasal (ṇ) which obviously developed into *a* in Greek (and Sanskrit) but *en* in Latin (cf. *tentus* 'stretched'). This at once explained why the aorist of πενθ- 'suffer' was ἐ-παθ-ον (cf. ἔφυγον). Similarly, the aorist of δέρκομαι was ἔδρακον (from †-dṛk-), that of πέρθω, ἔπραθον (from †-pṛth-), etc. In IE, the accusative sing. had the ending *-m*, cf. *rosa-m*. But after a consonantal stem, *-m* had to become syllabic (*-ṃ*) which in Greek gave *-a*, in Latin *-em*; hence, πόδ-α, but *ped-em*, in contrast to νόμο-ν with *-ν* from *-m* and *eru-m*. The same applies to δέκ α : *dec-em*, ἑπτ-ά : *sept-em*, etc.

3. Morphology The study of historical and comparative morphology depends to a certain extent on that of phonology. If we allow for the regular phonetic correspondences we are likely to find that cognate languages often show remarkable morphological and grammatical equivalences, though the degree of conservativism will depend on the type of language studied. Indeed the morphology is often a good indicator of the family to which a language belongs. The classical languages, which are heavily inflected, show considerable agreements between themselves and with their cognates. A simple comparison between nominative sing. Skt. *navas*, Gr. *véos*, Lat. *novus*, accusative Skt. *navam*, Gr. *véov*, Lat. *novum* leads to the reconstruction of the IE nom. and acc. masc. with †*-os*, †*-om* endings. The declension of *familia*, with the old genitive *familiās* (retained in *pater familiās*), closely corresponds to that of οἰκία *-āν -ās -āι*. Equally close parallels can be observed in the other declensions, the pronouns, the verbal inflexions, etc.

Inflexional patterns also reveal another great force at work in the history of languages: the tendency to regularize or at least generalize pre-existing formal patterns even beyond their original locus (analogy). In English, preterites like *sped* tend to be replaced by *speeded*, etc. In Latin the old gen. sing. of *ā*-stems ended in *-ās*. But already in Old Latin, the norm is *-ā-ī* (later *-ai*, *-ae*), obviously on the model of the *o*-stem gen. *domin-ī*. Conversely, the original *o*-stem gen. plural in *-um* or *-om* which survives into classical times in the prosaic *triumuirum*, *liberum*, *talentum* and poetic *deum*, *diuom*, etc., was replaced on the analogy of the *ā*-stems by *-ōrum*: *deōrum*, *sociōrum* after *deārum*, etc. Sound change may disrupt the regularity of a paradigm, but analogy may well restore it, though we are not normally able to predict with certainty whether a specific instance of analogical change will happen or not. 'Speeded' is now in current use but 'readed' for 'read' is not.

4. Syntax The study of historical syntax is at present in a state of flux because of profound changes in the way in which theoretical linguists envisage syntax in general; the same applies to comparative syntax. Our ability to reconstruct syntactical patterns for a non-attested language has been doubted and the most obvious successes of the comparative method concern phonology, morphology, and lexical reconstruction rather than syntax. Yet for a number of languages and especially for the classical languages a great deal of factual work has been done and some results are established; we have a view of the syntactical development in the attested phases and a more sketchy impression of what we can reconstruct for the parent language—more perhaps in the field of morpho-syntax (meaning and use of morphological categories)

than elsewhere. The case-system of the classical languages represents a gradual reduction of an IE system of (at least) eight cases, found as such in Sanskrit (and in a somewhat different form in Old Hittite). Case merger (syncretism) led to a combination of functions; hence the variety of functions performed by, for example, the Latin ablative or the fact that after prepositions like Gr. ἐκ, Lat. *ex* 'from' Greek uses the genitive (which continues an ancient ablative) and Latin the ablative. Syncretism processes continue, of course, after the Classical period, when Greek loses the dative and the languages derived from Latin tend to lose all case distinctions. Similarly in the course of the development of the classical languages we witness a reorganization and simplification of the verbal system which in the late Indo-European phase at least must have been similar to that of Greek and Indo-Iranian (i.e. was based on the three fundamental categories of present, aorist, and perfect, which differed because of their aspect, and on four moods: indicative, subjunctive, optative, and imperative); the contrast of subjunctive and optative was lost in most languages but a future, which did not exist in IE, was independently created. Reconstruction explains some apparent oddities: the Greek rule that after a neuter plural subject the verb is in the singular (τὰ ζῷα τρέχει 'the animals run(s)') is inherited, since it occurs in early Indian and Iranian, and is based on the fact that the neuter plural was originally a collective singular. The so-called Wackernagel's law, a rule of IE word order, is still partly respected in the early phases of the IE languages (and is absolutely regular in Hittite): unaccented words (e.g. particles, pronouns) took second place in the sentence, whatever their meaning: cf. σμίκρα μοι πάϊς ἔμμεν ἐφαίνεο 'you seemed to me a small child' (Wackernagel (1), 1. 1 ff.). Similarly the so-called tmesis of Greek, where preverbs are separated from verbs, reflects an archaic IE pattern where preverbs had much greater autonomy; even in early Latin we find *sub vos placo* 'I beg you', where the pronoun *vos* 'you' (which occurs in second position according to Wackernagel's law) follows the independent preverb *sub*; the later formula is *vos supplico*.

The role of subordination in IE is not clear, but the elaborate sentence construction of the classical languages, in which hypotaxis (subordination) seems the dominant feature, are in many cases based on a shift of earlier paratactic (co-ordinating) constructions. Earlier juxtapositions such as *timeo—ne veniat* 'I am afraid—may he not come', *timeo—ut veniat* 'how could he come', were shifted in meaning 'I am afraid that he might (not) come'; the same explanation applies to φοβοῦμαι μὴ (οὐκ) ἔλθῃ.

Cf. Wackernagel (1) and (2); Debrunner in Schwyzer–Debrunner, vol. 2; Szantyr in Leumann–Hoffmann–Szantyr, vol. 2; Ernout–Thomas; Watkins 1. 242 ff.

*5. Lexicon and *etymology* The meaning of words plays an important role both in historical and in comparative linguistics. When we study the history of a language we want to know not only what new words enter the language or what words are lost, but also what words change meaning, how, and why. We do not believe any longer that to establish the etymology of a word means to know its true meaning, but we are still interested in taking back form and meaning of a word to the earliest possible stage since history of the lexicon (which includes the history of lexical meaning) is an essential part of linguistic history. Semantics (the study of meaning) is also essential for comparative linguistics which depends on establishing correct word equivalences between related languages. While phonological rules give a firm grounding to etymology, what limits can we set to semantic divergence? Should we compare Skt. *yūs* 'broth' with Lat. *iūs* 'law'? The answer is negative since the correct comparison is with the homonymous Latin *iūs* 'broth', but decisions are not always easy. We do not any longer accept the old etymologies of the type *lucus a non lucendo* 'a wood is called *lucus* because there is no light (*lux*)' (see ETYMOLOGY), but we acknowledge that it is difficult to formulate general laws of semantic development. Nevertheless comparative studies have cleared up many problems which would have remained insoluble within Latin or Greek. The word ποινή, mentioned above, would hardly be analysable in Greek. Comparativists can show that it derives from IE †k^w*oi-nā*, represented also by Lithuanian *kaina* 'price', Slavic *cěna* 'id.', Iranian *kainā* 'punishment'; moreover they can also show that this noun derives from a verbal root †k^w*i-* 'to pay' which survives in τίνω (cf. also the verb ἀποτίνω 'pay back' and the noun ἄποινα 'ransom, price' from †ἀποποινα). Lat. *poena* is a borrowing from Greek (just as Eng. *penal, penalty* are borrowed from Latin or Old French). Most of the old etymologies must be discarded but the research of a century has succeeded in amassing a vast corpus of firmly established etymologies, conveniently listed in etymological dictionaries (Walde–Hoffmann and Frisk for the classical languages), some of which also study the way in which words change meaning in the historical period (Ernout–Meillet; Chantraine).

A great deal has also been done to reconstruct the IE lexicon; we have lists of IE roots (Pokorny) and an analysis of the vocabulary of the IE languages divided in semantic fields (Buck (2)); there are also attempts at close semantic reconstruction (Benveniste). Much remains to be done; most of the old reference books do not yet incorporate the results of the recent analyses of the Anatolian languages.

6. Poetics In the middle of the last century A. Kuhn pointed out that Homeric Greek κλέος ἄφθιτον 'fame imperishable' matched exactly in meaning and etymology the Vedic Skt. *śráva(s)* ... *ákṣitam*. This opened the way to a series of comparative studies about formulae, metre, and, in the last resort, cultural features which the individual IE languages inherited from IE and preserved or developed in their literary and poetic traditions. The field is fraught with difficulties since similarity does not guarantee common origin, but is also rich in results. Comparison here operates in terms of sequences longer than the word and in so doing opens the way to a new methodology for the reconstruction of both syntactical and semantic features (cf. Campanile; Watkins, vol. 2).

7. History of the language Languages do not evolve in a vacuum and their development is inextricably linked to the social and political events which affect the life of a community. On the one hand there are contacts with speakers from different linguistic backgrounds, on the other there are individuals who for literary or cultural reasons can impress their mark on the language. Next to the internal history of a language (which is close to its historical grammar) there is an external history which is at least as important. Under the first heading we may mention the change of -τι to -σι in Attic-Ionic or the loss of the dative in late Greek; under the second we shall speak of the expansion of Greek after *Alexander (3) the Great's conquest, of the foreign languages with which it came in contact, of the drastic simplification in its grammar, of the borrowings from Latin, etc., but we shall also discuss the cultural climate which favoured the preservation of some old features (from the case-system to the spelling), the prevailing Atticism, etc. Similar analyses are necessary for all

languages. For the classical languages we have Meillet's masterly (and still unsurpassed) presentations of their history as well as a series of more up-to-date books which discuss equally history and prehistory (see GREEK LANGUAGE; LATIN LANGUAGE).

The works below are those quoted in the text, and are listed in alphabetical order of authors' surnames; different works by the same author are distinguished by numbers in brackets.
É. Benveniste, *Indo-European Language and Society* (1973; Fr. orig. 1969); K. Brugmann–B. Delbrück, *Grundriss der vergleichenden Grammatik der indogermanischen Sprachen* (1893–1916); T. Bynon, *Historical Linguistics* (1977); C. D. Buck, (1) *Comparative Grammar of Greek and Latin*, 8th edn. (1962), (2) *A Dictionary of Selected Synonyms in the Principal Indo-European Languages* (1949); E. Campanile, *Ricerche di culture poetica indoeuropea* (1977); P. Chantraine, *Dictionnaire étymologique de la langue grecque: histoire des mots* (1968–80); W. Cowgill and M. Mayrhofer, *Indogermanische Grammatik* 1. 1/2 (1986); T. Crowley, *An Introduction to Historical Linguistics*, 2nd edn. (1992); A. Ernout–A. Meillet, *Dictionnaire étymologique de la langue latine*, 4th edn. (1959); A. Ernout–F. Thomas, *Syntaxe latine*, 2nd edn. (1953); H. Frisk, *Griechisches etymologisches Wörterbuch* (1954–72); H. H. Hock, *Principles of Historical Linguistics*, 2nd edn. (1991); M. Leumann–J. B. Hofmann–A. Szantyr, *Lateinische Grammatik* 1–3 (1965–79); A. McMahon, *Understanding Language Change* (1994); A. Meillet, (1) *Introduction à l'étude comparative des langues indoeuropéennes*, 8th edn. (1937), (2) *Aperçu d'une histoire de la langue grecque*, 8th edn. (1975), (3) *Esquisse d'une histoire de la langue latine*, 5th edn. (1948); A. Meillet–J. Vendryès, *Traité de grammaire comparée des langues classiques*, 2nd edn. (1953); J. Pokorny, *Indogermanisches etymologisches Wörterbuch* (1951–69); W. Porzig, *Die Gliederung des indogermanischen Sprachgebiets* (1954); E. Schwyzer–A. Debrunner, *Griechische Grammatik* 1–2 (1934–50), 3–4 (indexes, 1953–71); O. J. L. Szemerényi, (1) *Einführung in die vergleichende Sprachwissenschaft*, 3rd edn. (1989), (2) *Scripta minora* 1–4 (1987–91); J. Wackernagel, (1) *Kl. Schr.* 1–2 (1953), 3 (1979), (2) *Vorlesungen über Syntax mit besonderer Berücksichtigung von Griechisch, Lateinisch und Deutsch*, 2nd edn., 1–2 (1926–8); A. Walde–J. B. Hofmann, *Lateinisches etymologisches Wörterbuch* 1–3 (1930–56); C. Watkins, *Selected Writings* 1–2 (1994).

O. J. L. S.; A. M. Da.

Linus (Λίνος), an old song sung either at the vintage as in *Il.* 18. 570, where it is performed by a boy accompanied by the lyre and by a cheerfully dancing and shouting group of young people, or a song of lament using the ritual cry αἴλινον ('alas for Linus'), which was interpreted as a mournful song in honour of Linus. Linus was also a mythical person for whom various *genealogies exist, e.g. son of *Apollo and Psamathe, a local princess of *Argos (2): after she exposed him, he was devoured by dogs and the city was plagued by Apollo till satisfaction was made (Paus. 1. 43. 7–8). He had strong connections with music: (*a*) he invented the *threnos* (Heraclid. Pont. in ps.-Plut. *De mus.* 3); (*b*) he was killed by Apollo in a music contest, because he had boasted that he was as good a singer as the god (Paus. 9. 29. 6 f.); (*c*) he was the music teacher of *Heracles and was killed by his pupil (Apollod. 2. 63); (*d*) he was generally considered a great composer and citharode (Plin. *HN* 7. 204). The Linus song was widely sung under different names in the near east (Hdt. 2. 79), cf. LITYERSES.

H. J. R.; E. Kr.

Liris, river of central Italy, now called Garigliano below *Interamna Lirenas. Rising near the *Fucinus Lacus it flows south-south-east to Sora, turns sharply south-south-west, cascades picturesquely at Isola del Liri, and enters the Tyrrhenian sea through marshy country at *Minturnae. Chief tributaries: Fibrenus (Cicero's natal stream: *Leg.* 2. 6), Trerus, Melpis, mod. Rapido.

E. T. S.; D. W. R. R.

literacy The number of people who could read and write in the ancient world is hard to determine. Without statistical evidence, we must rely mostly on chance information and inference: for example, the institution of *ostracism implies that most Athenian citizens could be expected to write a name. Our evidence (written) indicates the literate, not the illiterate, and especially the highly educated élite. The ancient habit of reading aloud meant that written texts could often be shared the more easily by others; the presence of inscriptions (see EPIGRAPHY, GREEK) does not itself imply that they were read by everyone, since their symbolic value added another dimension to their written contents. There are also many different levels of literacy, which complicate the picture, from the basic ability to figure out a short message, to functional literacy or 'craft literacy', to the skill required for reading a literary papyrus (reading and writing skills may also have been separate). However, certain broad generalizations are possible. The 'mass literacy' of modern industrial countries was never achieved in the ancient world (cf. Harris (see bibliog. below), who believes a maximum of 20–30 per cent literacy was achieved, and that in Hellenistic cities). Women, slaves, and the lower social levels would usually be less literate. Archaic Greece and particularly Archaic Rome have left fewer instances of writing (graffiti, inscriptions), implying sparse literacy, and Archaic Greek cities sometimes attempt to ensure an official's power over the written word was not abused. However, there were pockets and periods where a higher rate of basic literacy among the adult citizen-body is probable: for instance, under the Athenian *democracy, when there was a relatively high level of reading-matter and incentives to read (even the sausage seller can read a little, Ar. Eq. 188–90); Hellenistic cities which made provision for elementary *education, especially *Rhodes; the Roman empire, which probably had widespread craft literacy in the cities (cf. POMPEII) with increasingly elaborate use of writing; Roman Egypt, where the society was permeated by the need for written documentation (the administrative category of 'illiterates' (agrammatoi) denoted illiteracy in Greek). Literacy levels may to some extent be related to the functions of, or needs for, writing: *Sparta used written records very little until the Roman period, hence Classical Spartans were thought illiterate. The contexts in which writing was or could be used are essential in assessing the role or importance of literacy: both Greeks and Romans gave writing a magical, and non-functional role, as well as its more familiar use for preserving literature, public and private records, and inscriptions. It was often supplemented by oral communication and performance (see ARCHIVES; ORALITY; RECORDS AND RECORD-KEEPING). Literacy by itself was not a key to social advancement, and social success was impossible without the accoutrements of high culture. Much reading and writing was done by slaves (see ANAGNŌSTĒS), especially in Rome, ensuring that it was by itself of low status. However, it was not confined at any point in the Graeco-Roman world to scribes: writing is used from very early on in Greece for widely different purposes, informal graffiti and poetry, then inscriptions, suggesting it was not limited to a narrow social group, or to the public sphere. This spread may be partly linked to the comparative ease with which the alphabet can be learned, but the open nature of Archaic Greek society, and the early use of writing for memorials, should also be taken into account.

W. V. Harris, *Ancient Literacy* (1989); R. Thomas, *Literacy and Orality in Ancient Greece* (1992); M. Beard and others, *Literacy in the Roman World* (1991); F. D. Harvey, *Rev. Ét. Grec.* 1966, 585 ff.; H. C. Youtie, *ZPE* 17 (1975), 201 ff., and *GRBS* 1971, 239 ff. (for Egypt); A. K. Bowman and G. Woolf (eds.), *Literacy and Power* (1994). R. T.

literary criticism in antiquity 1. The arts of formal speech played a great part in ancient life, so that it was natural that vocabularies and conceptual frameworks should be developed for the purposes of evaluation, speculation about the nature and role of poetry, and practical advice for successful composition, especially in oratory. In the resulting body of doctrine, this last element—which is the contribution of *rhetoric—is dominant, and it is this which seems the most striking difference between Graeco-Roman 'criticism' and most modern analogues.

2. The first evidences we have of reflection on these subjects are in the early poets. *Homer and *Hesiod speak of their art as a gift of the *Muses, who inspire the poet, know all things, and can tell false tales as well as true (*Il.* 2. 484–92; *Od.* 8. 479 ff.; Hes. *Theog.* 1–104). *Pindar too called himself the 'prophet'— i.e. 'spokesman'—of the Muses (fr. 137 Snell–Maehler), and was proud to think of his 'wisdom' as the product of natural endowment, not of teachable technique, which was for lesser mortals (*Ol.* 2. 83). The poets did not however escape criticism; they were the transmitters of a mythological tradition which had many offensive features—tales of the gods' immorality and the viciousness of heroic figures—and the early philosophers found these an easy target (see XENOPHANES). *Allegory—for example the interpretation of the Battle of the Gods in Homer, *Iliad* 21, as a battle of the elements—began as a mode of defence against such attacks (see THEAGENES (2)), and eventually (especially with the Stoics (see STOICISM) in Hellenistic times and the Neoplatonists (see NEOPLATONISM) later) became the most significant and influential critical approach in all antiquity. The idea of inspiration (of which *Democritus, it seems, made some rational justification) and the demand for a moral and social commitment are not the only achievements of 'pre-Platonic' poetics. More sophisticated reflection is suggested by the paradox of *Gorgias (1), that tragedy 'offers a deception such that the deceiver is more just than the non-deceiver, and the deceived wiser than the undeceived' (Plut. *Mor.* 348c); and delicate connoisseurship is displayed by the comparison of 'high' and 'low' styles, as represented by *Aeschylus and *Euripides, in the great debate in *Aristophanes (1)'s *Frogs*.

3. *Plato (1) pulled the threads together but in a very radical and paradoxical way, in which there may be a good deal of irony. Inspiration, as claimed by the poets, was for him no road to knowledge, indeed a thing of no great worth; and in so far as poets failed to promote the right moral and social values, they were to be banished from the ideal state altogether. In rationalizing this attitude Plato developed for the first time a concept of 'imitation' (*mimēsis*) which, in various guises, was to be a central theme of later theory. He held strongly that the spectacle of degrading emotion nourished the same emotion in the hearer. Parallel to his attack on the poets was his criticism of contemporary *rhetoric; here too he saw fraud, pretence, and contempt for truth. As a critic of style, he was superb, as is shown, not by any refined vocabulary, but by his marvellous parodies (*Symposium*, *Phaedrus*, *Menexenus*), rivalled only by Aristophanes himself.

4. *Aristotle's *Poetics*, the fountain-head of most later criticism, is in part an answer to Plato; this is the context of the improved and very important analysis of *mimēsis* and of the much-debated doctrine that tragedy effects a *katharsis* of pity and fear. This very crabbed and difficult book has many different themes: a general theory of poetry as a 'mimetic' art, and a speculative account of its origins; a detailed analysis of tragedy, stressing the primary importance of plot (*mythos*) over *character and ideas; an account of poetic diction, including a good deal of what we should call

grammatical theory; and finally some discussion of *epic and its inferiority (as Aristotle held) to *tragedy as a poetic *genre. A treatment of comedy is lost, but can to some extent be reconstructed from later writings. The *Poetics* is a truly seminal work, not so much for later antiquity (when it was hardly known, though the dialogue *On Poets*, now lost, was much read) as for the Renaissance and for modern criticism.

5. Whereas Aristotle held poetry and rhetoric to be fundamentally distinct—the one was an 'imitative' art, the other a practical skill of persuasion—his successors tended more and more to blur the difference. *Theophrastus, Aristotle's pupil, is credited with the observation (fr. 84 Wimmer = 78 Fortenbaugh) that, while philosophers are concerned solely with facts and the validity of deductions, poets and orators alike are concerned with their relation with their audience, and this is why they have to use dignified words, put them together harmoniously, and in general produce pleasure (*hēdonē*) and astonishment (*ekplēxis*) in order to cajole or bully their hearers into conviction. For criticism, the consequence of this kind of approach is that form may be judged apart from content. It is thus no surprise that the main achievement of post-Aristotelian criticism is in the analysis of style, rather than in literary theory. The basic distinction between 'high' and 'low' writing, the 'high' being associated with strong emotion and the 'low' with everyday life and character, goes back to Aristophanes; in terms of effect on the audience, it corresponds to the distinction between *hēdonē* and *ekplēxis*, of which Theophrastus speaks. It was of course refined and modified in various ways. *Demetrius (17) for example describes four 'types' of style (*charactēres*), two of which (the 'grand' (*megaloprepēs*) and the 'forceful' (*deinos*)) belong to the higher range, and two (the 'elegant' (*glaphyros*) and the 'plain' (*ischnos*)) to the lower. Particularly influential, however, was a system of three styles, accommodating not only the two extremes but the smooth, flowing style of *Isocrates. This tripartite division was even supposed to be exemplified by Homer's heroes: *Odysseus, whose words come out 'like winter snows', *Menelaus (1), who spoke little but to the point, and *Nestor (1), whose speech was sweet as honey (Quint. *Inst.* 12. 10. 64). All kinds of writing could be pigeonholed in this way: e.g. the representative historians are *Xenophon (1), *Thucydides (2), and *Herodotus (1). A *locus classicus* for the system is *Cicero, *Orator* 75–90. In the Greek critics and rhetors of the empire (*Dionysius (7) of Halicarnassus, *'Longinus', *Hermogenes (2)) there are many refinements of these ideas. 'Longinus' is unique in concentrating not so much on the stylistic means of achieving *ekplēxis*, but on the kinds of subject-matter, thought, and general moral attitude which alone, in his view, could make success in 'the *sublime' possible.

6. Though this rhetorical and stylistic doctrine is the main achievement of critics after Aristotle, there were other developments as well. (*a*) The Stoics (see STOICISM) viewed poetry primarily as an educational instrument, and so in a sense continued Plato's moralizing approach. *Plutarch's essay on *How the Young should Study Poetry* (*Mor.* 14d–37b) is a later example of this tradition: though a Platonist, he tries to overcome Plato's objections to poetry, not (as the Stoics did) by allegory, but by scholarly attention to context and historical circumstances. (*b*) The Epicurean *Philodemus (see EPICURUS) is an important witness to Hellenistic theory: in his *On Poems*, parts of which are preserved in tantalizingly difficult papyrus texts, he discussed and refuted theories of the Stoic *Ariston (1), the scholar *Crates (3) of Mallus, the Peripatetic *Neoptolemus (2), and Aristotle himself. He seems also to have had a positive view of his own, namely

that form and content are inseparable, and cannot be judged separately. If this is a right interpretation, Philodemus makes a sharp contrast with the prevailing 'rhetorical tradition'. (*c*) The *Alexandrian scholars who collected and edited classical poets and orators, and discussed the authenticity of the pieces they found, were also 'critics'. They needed historical, aesthetic, and grammatical insights. Much of Dionysius of Halicarnassus' work on orators is in their tradition; but we know it also from its remains scattered about the many extant commentaries and scholia, all the way down to *Eustathius, which contain critical judgements and insights of interest.

7. The Roman contribution is not a mere appendage to Greek criticism, though the two literary worlds are closely connected, and writers like Dionysius and 'Longinus' actually addressed their works to Roman patrons. In the classical period of Latin literature (as in the days of the Attic Old Comedy) criticism appears in topical writing in quite unacademic contexts; in *Lucilius (1) and *Horace, and later in *Persius and *Petronius Arbiter, it is an ingredient of satire. Horace not only defended his own literary position and expounded literary history in his *Satires* (1. 4, 1. 10, 2. 1) and *Epistles* (1. 19, 2. 1, 2. 2), but wrote a humorous didactic poem (*Ars poetica*) in which he combined traditional precepts on the drama and views on the poet's place in society with witty and urbane reflections on his own literary experience. The *Ars* set a fashion followed in the Renaissance by Vida, Boileau, and Pope.

8. Cicero's achievement as a judge of oratory is unequalled—naturally, for he was himself a great orator. Political oratory died with him, and the age of the declaimers which followed produced critics of a different cast. Seneca the Elder (L. *Annaeus Seneca (1)) makes many shrewd points in commenting on his favourite declaimers. The dominant theme in the early empire seems to have been a consciousness of decline. In itself this was nothing new, since Greek critics of music and art as well as of oratory had long been drawing contrasts between admired works of the past and the degenerate efforts of the present. The younger Seneca (L. *Annaeus Seneca (2)) (esp. in *Epistle* 114) and *Tacitus (1) (*Dialogus*) reflect interestingly on the causes of 'decline'—moral and political, as well as intellectual. With *Quintilian, there is some renewed optimism and a return to Cicero's ideals. The famous chapter (*Inst.* 10. 1) in which he catalogues the authors to be read by the budding orator summarizes traditional teaching on 'imitation' (his account of the Greek authors is based on Dionysius) but shows a capacity for independent judgement.

9. Greek literature, from the time of Dionysius onwards, was increasingly 'classicizing' and archaistic; the critics almost entirely neglected Hellenistic writers and their own contemporaries. In the Latin world, 'archaism', in the form of a preference for the early poets and pre-Ciceronian orators and historians, was in general a development of the 2nd cent. AD (see ARCHAISM IN LATIN). But the Greek model of concentration on the 'classics' was increasingly followed; and the most significant contribution of the later imperial period to literary criticism is to be found in works like *Servius' commentaries on Virgil and *Donatus (1)'s on *Terence.

10. Late antiquity also saw a development in the philosophical criticism of literature. Stoic allegory and Aristotelian theory gave way to Neoplatonist interpretations, which involved allegory of a new, and more metaphysical, kind, and a serious attempt to 'reconcile Homer to Plato' by new means. *Proclus' commentary on the *Republic* of Plato is the main text of this movement. Its importance for the medieval understanding of literature—and

especially of biblical texts—can hardly be exaggerated.

In general see the articles on the authors mentioned and on RHETORIC. Accessible surveys of the whole subject include: G. M. A. Grube, *The Greek and Roman Critics* (1965); D. A. Russell, *Criticism in Antiquity* (1972); M. Fuhrmann, *Einführung in die antike Dichtungstheorie* (1973); G. A. Kennedy (ed.), *Cambridge History of Literary Criticism* 1: *Classical Criticism* (1989). See also W. J. Verdenius, *Mnemos.* 1983, 14–59. D. A. Russell and M. Winterbottom, *Ancient Literary Criticism* (1972) is a selection of the principal texts in English translation.

See also: P. Vicaire, *Platon critique littéraire* (1960); P. Murray, *JHS* 1981, 87–100; S. Halliwell, *Aristotle's Poetics* (1986); G. F. Else, *Plato and Aristotle on Poetry* (1986); R. Janko, *Aristotle on Comedy* (1984); R. Meijering, *Literary and Rhetorical Theories in Greek Scholia* (1987); C. O. Brink, *Horace on Poetry* (1963–82); K. Heldmann, *Antike Theorien über Entwicklung und Verfall der Redekunst* (1982); W. Trimpi, *Muses of One Mind* (1983); W. Bernard, *Spätantike Dichtungstheorien* (1990); R. Lamberton, *Homer the Theologian* (1986); N. O'Sullivan, *Alcidamas, Aristophanes and the Beginning of Greek Stylistic Theory* (1992). D. A. R.

literary theory and classical studies One of the most striking features of 20th-cent. intellectual life has been the attention paid to literary theory, especially from the time of the 1960s. This intellectual ferment has produced a confusing variety of approaches, and especially of terminology, which has in turn given birth to a new minor isagogic genre, that of the 'Introduction to Literary Theory', the modern equivalent of the *Technai rhetorikai* or *Placita philosophorum* of the ancient world. The analogy with the Hellenistic philosophical schools is perhaps particularly close, in that alongside 'school' theorizing there is a mass of more or less eclectic work by practitioners who, like Horace, would claim to be 'bound to swear by no master's words'. Just as no one would regard *Aetius (1)'s account of Platonism as an even half-adequate account of what reading *Plato (1) is like, so summary accounts of literary theory are often embarrassed before their own inadequacy. Many of the most significant 20th-cent. theories of language and literature stress a slippery indeterminacy in discourse that is at odds with the pretence to scientific objectivity which is often (wrongly) taken to be the presupposition of a dictionary like this one: and any attempt to give a history of literary theory instantly encounters the suspicion of plot which is another of the prevalent characteristics of the 'post-modern' age. The field is also one of particularly rapid change and, as another central dogma puts it, there is no point outside history from which it can be surveyed: what seems important in 1996 may seem a quaint byway by the following millennium. The purpose of this article is to offer not so much a path through the minefield as a way in. It is written by two who believe that 20th-cent. theorizing has a great deal to offer classical studies, and that in any case the time when the discipline could even consider trying to pull up the drawbridge and see out the Dark Ages in comfortable isolation has long gone.

In the United States and some European countries (but not in the United Kingdom, where the word is reserved for historical linguistics) 'philology' is the term which is often taken to sum up the traditional methods of classical scholarship. Both defenders of this tradition and critical theorists opposed to it tend to underestimate the degree to which this approach was theorized, the one group in a desire to make it appear as simply natural, the other out of anger at its lack of self-consciousness. In its most developed form it is clearly a product of 19th-cent. German attempts to grant to literary and historical studies the objectivity which was then seen as central to the increasingly powerful physical sciences, and it received its classic formulations from U. von

Wilamowitz-Moellendorff in the course of his quarrel with Nietzsche. The purpose of textual study is to recover the intentions of the authors of the texts, and to this end all conceivable data from the ancient world may be relevant. The fragmentary traces that have come down to us are clues which can enable us to reconstruct the thought processes of the ancients: but the conventions of ancient literature need to be established through painstaking examination of parallels before interpretation can take place. These researches are most typically set forth in editions or especially commentaries, great monuments of learning like Pease's commentaries on *Cicero, Headlam's on *Herodas, or on a higher level Fraenkel's on *Aeschylus and those of Nisbet–Hubbard on *Horace.

There is much in traditional philology of which the discipline can be proud, especially the broad definition of text and the interdisciplinary nature of research implied by the detective metaphor, with the massive learning that that in turn entailed. But there are a number of assumptions made by the method which have come under scrutiny from various different theoretical positions in the 20th cent.: the assumed scientific objectivity of the critic, the focus on the surface psychology of the author, the belief that all the 'clues' will point to a single coherent picture, the aspiration to that overall master interpretation, and especially the belief that the hermeneutic tools used to interpret texts are timeless, based on the common-sense rules used in everyday life. These assumptions are not necessarily to be rejected simply because they are assumptions (though we believe they are all unhelpful), but, paradoxically, if the traditional method is to be sustained, they require a considerably more sophisticated theoretical underpinning than has to date been provided.

The theoretical movements which have brought these assumptions into question may be broadly categorized as *foundational* or *methodological*: the former tackle the basic assumptions of critical practice, that is, they are essentially metacritical, while the latter provide new things to do with texts rather than new reasons to do them. These two categories are naturally not sharply distinct, since assumptions about the point of criticism will affect practice and practice has implications for the foundations of theory, but it is a paradox that the theories which most radically challenge basic assumptions may have less of an effect on practice. It has been argued, for instance, that a 'post-structuralist' view of the self as constructed in language can perversely legitimate an apparently old-fashioned interest in the 'personality' of a figure like Horace (C. Martindale and D. Hopkins, *Horace Made New* (1993), 16–18). In contrast, the narratology of Genette and Bal (see below), with a wealth of new terminology and methods, is often seen as the least 'threatening' approach by traditional scholars, except perhaps in relation to historiography. Nevertheless, the various critical theories cannot be represented simply as a smorgasbord of techniques: more is at stake than methodology (cf. K. Ormand, *Bryn Mawr Classical Review*, 1994).

One popular plot for 20th-cent. literary theory sees the focus of interest moving from the author to the text and then to the reader. In contrast to the traditional focus on the personality of the creator of the text, various movements beginning with the Russian Formalists (to whom we owe such basic concepts as the distinction between 'story'—what happened—and 'narrative'— the way it is told) saw literature as a more or less autonomous system whose workings could be analysed in a manner similar to the formal analysis of language whose foundations were being laid by the linguist F. de Saussure with his *Course in General Linguistics* of 1916, perhaps the single most influential book in

20th-cent. literary theory. Saussure's distinction between a *diachronic* approach to language which looked at how it changed over time and a *synchronic* approach which viewed it as a single coherent system, and his insistence that meaning lay in the relationship between the elements of the system rather than in any external reference, led to a focus on the text rather than on the processes of its creation. This new focus of interest could, however, take radically different forms. In Anglo-American 'New Criticism', whose origins lay in I. A. Richards's experiments with the reading practices of English students reported in his *Practical Criticism* of 1929, the central critical act became the 'reading' of an individual text (usually a lyric poem or novel), exposing the way in which its devices, especially irony and ambiguity, contributed to the unity of its effect. In the continental tradition, on the other hand, interest was concentrated on the *langue* or general system rather than the *parole* or individual utterance within it, to use another distinction made by de Saussure. This eventually led to the movement known as structuralism, whose founding father was the 'Prague school' linguist Roman Jakobson but whose most famous representatives were the anthropologist Claude Lévi-Strauss and the writer Roland Barthes (the movement of people and ideas from eastern Europe to Paris—and later the USA—is another common plot in the history of theory: another distinguished example is the Rumanian poetician Tzvetan Todorov, whose *Encyclopedic Dictionary of the Sciences of Language* (with Oswald Ducrot), originally published in 1972, provides an extremely useful overview of many central concepts). The movement was popularized in England and America by Jonathan Culler's outstandingly approachable *Structuralist Poetics* of 1975.

Structuralist analysis took many forms, but one essential element was this focus not on the individual text but on the underlying system of which it was a part. The analysis of literary and linguistic systems was only one subspecies of a general science of signs or *semiotics* (a concept going back ultimately to the American philosopher C. S. Peirce, who was directly influenced by *Philodemus' On Signs*): a famous early example was Roland Barthes's *System of Fashion* (1985). Myth was particularly a subject of research, as Lévi-Strauss, following in the footsteps of the *Morphology of the Folktale* of the Russian Vladimir Propp (1968; 1st publ. in Russian, 1928), sought, in the bewildering stories told by South American native peoples, the underlying patterns that gave meaning to their lives and enabled them to 'mediate' between the oppositions of nature and culture, men and gods. This phase of structuralism had a particularly profound effect on Greek studies through the 'Paris school' of Jean-Pierre Vernant and Pierre Vidal-Naquet, whose work was based on the earlier pioneering studies of Louis Gernet. Fifth-cent. BC Athenian tragedy and comedy in particular, publicly performed within the context of a religious festival that was also a celebration of social cohesion, proved a fertile ground for analyses which sought common functional patterns in myth, ritual, and literature. It was significant that it was American scholars (particularly Charles Segal and Froma Zeitlin) who did most to welcome the new approaches and put them to use, but their power and suggestiveness were such that they were fairly readily assimilated into the reading practices of Hellenists, as earlier Latin critics had taken to the New Criticism.

One particular offshoot of structuralism, although it took a little longer to establish itself in classical studies, has also been widely employed, that is, the formal study of *narrative* known as *narratology*. The term seems to have been coined by Todorov and many of the methods have their origin in the work of Roland

Barthes, but the father of the approach was the French poetician Gérard Genette, in a discussion of Proust published in a collection with the punning title *Figures III* in 1972 and later translated into English as *Narrative Discourse* (1980). Genette provided a simple but richly suggestive framework for analysing the relationship between story and narrative which proved of great practical utility for the analysis of a wide range of texts, not simply those most clearly 'narrative' in form. His work was carried forward especially by the Dutch theoretician Mieke Bal (*Narratology: Introduction to the Theory of Narrative* (1985; orig. pub. 1977)), and it was the work on point of view (focalization) in *Homer by one of Bal's pupils, Irene de Jong (*Narrators and Focalizers* (1987)) which encouraged use of the methods by classical scholars, though they had already been employed with great success by, for instance, the Italian critic Massimo Fusillo in his book on *Apollonius (1) Rhodius, *Il tempo delle Argonautiche* (1985). Perhaps the most celebrated narratological study of a classical text, however, is John J. Winkler's book on *Apuleius, *Auctor et Actor* (1985), though that largely eschews the more technical terminology of the approach.

Another aspect of the structuralist emphasis on the system of literature rather than individual texts has been a mass of work on what older critics called 'allusion', the recognition in texts of traces of other texts. The detection of these traces has always played an important part in classical philology, partly as 'parallels' and partly in terms of the notions of imitation and literary rivalry that are prominent in ancient literary critical texts. The focus, however, was on allusion as a conscious or unconscious (the question of whether a particular allusion was 'intended' was hotly debated) metaliterary act in which an author chose to pay homage to or otherwise notice a predecessor. Structuralism replaced this with the insight that because all texts participate in literary systems, all texts (and not only literary ones) are always already of necessity shot through with the presence of other texts. A text which did not participate in any system in this way would be literally unreadable, since we would have no possible codes with which to decipher it. Authors cannot decide whether or not to be allusive: whatever they intend, their texts will be read against the 'matrix of possibilities' created by other texts. This phenomenon by which texts are inescapably and multiply allusive was termed by the French critic Julia Kristeva 'intertextuality' and, although in more general usage the term has lost some of its original emphasis and become domesticated as simply a synonym for 'allusion', it gave a powerful impetus to studies of literary relationships which moved beyond comparing and contrasting related passages to an insight into how the presence of earlier texts, if recognized by a critic, can radically affect interpretation. This approach has been of particular fertility in Latin studies, with an important role played by the Italian Latinist Gian Biagio Conte (*The Rhetoric of Imitation* (1986; orig. pub. 1984–5)) and younger Italian figures such as Alessandro Barchiesi (*La traccia del modello* (1984)), whose works have found an enthusiastic echo in English and American Latin studies. It has been central to the revaluation of Silver Latin, and the Flavian epicists in particular, viewed not as servile imitators of Virgil but as machines for producing striking intertextual complexities. See IMITATIO.

After structuralism came post-structuralism, though some figures, notably Roland Barthes, straddle the divide. The year before the famous *événements* of 1968 saw the publication of two major works by the philosopher Jacques Derrida which radically altered the direction of French critical theory. In *On Grammatology* and *Writing and Difference* he expounded a theory whose roots were also in de Saussure but which moved in a very different direction. Like the structuralists, Derrida insisted that there was nothing outside text, that is, everything that constitutes the world for us comes to us as text, already in language. But language is not a stable, self-consistent *langue* that we can hold still under the microscope, but a restless chain of signifiers whose meaning depends on further signifiers, whose meaning . . . In the most celebrated (self-reflexive) pun in 20th-cent. theory, meaning is *différance*, difference / deferral, never wholly present. Drawing on Plato (1)'s *Phaedrus* (particularly in the essay 'Plato's Pharmacy', which is the most concise introduction to his views), Derrida reversed the terms of the hierarchy that made the unmediated 'presence' of everyday speech the original form of which the disembodied and indeterminate voice of writing was an unwelcome perversion. Writing preceded speech, in the sense that all language, however apparently tied down by context and pragmatics, was nevertheless subject to the free-ranging deferral of full meaning that Plato had seen as so threatening. If all writings needed the help of the father, in one important sense the father was never there.

Derrida was not putting forward a literary theory, but a theory of language in general which was also, because of the role played by language in the theory, a general philosophy. Naturally, given the nature of his views, he has always deprecated attempts to turn what he says into a system or a method, but one aspect of what came to be known as 'deconstruction' did have an important effect on the practice of criticism. The structuralists, following the practice of linguistics, where the method had had its origins in phonology, had analysed complex systems into sets of oppositions, like the famous opposition of nature and culture in Lévi-Strauss's analyses. Typically in these oppositions one side was valued over the other: in terms of Derrida's Platonic metaphor, one had paternal authority over the other. Deconstruction was the process by which it was shown that in these oppositions elements apparently possessed by one side could be shown to occur also on the other, and that the relative value of the terms could be 'flipped' (and reflipped, and flipped again). This dismantling of apparently stable hierarchies was not simply a trick, nor was it suggested that there was some way of thinking which avoided the use of oppositions: the point was to stress that any stopping-place in the process of deferral of meaning would be an arbitrary one. But the deconstructive method became an extremely powerful tool for literary critics wishing to challenge dominant views of the '*closure' (a term popularized within a New Critical framework in another work of the late 1960s, Barbara Herrnstein Smith's *Poetic Closure* of 1968) of the texts they were studying. Derrida's views were again enthusiastically received in the United States, particularly by the 'Yale critics' such as J. Hillis Miller and the controversial Belgian Paul de Man, and they were welcome also to a number of classical literary critics precisely because they offered the opportunity to challenge stifling orthodoxies about the harmony and perfection of the classical moment. A conspicuous example was Simon Goldhill's *Language, Sexuality, Narrative: The Oresteia* (1984), which showed how slippery was the teleology even of what many regarded as the most perfectly closed piece of 5th-cent. drama. With his older colleague John Henderson, the father of this movement in the United Kingdom, who published a number of similarly intense and learned deconstructive essays on Latin literature, and the radical ancient historian Mary Beard, Goldhill made Cambridge University a centre for the new approaches.

Deconstruction was an important element in, and also perhaps a product of, the wider cultural phenomenon known as postmodernism, defined succinctly by the French philosopher Jean-Francois Lyotard as 'incredulity towards metanarratives' (*The Postmodern Condition* (1984; orig. pub. 1979), p. xxiv): that is, a belief that there was no fixed plot to human history, no single story that could be told about any human phenomenon, and no 'foundations' outside human discourse that could ground any theory or practice, even those of the supposedly 'hard' sciences. The most important representative of this line in the English-speaking world was the philosopher Richard Rorty. As we mentioned to begin with, however, one paradoxical effect of this radicalism has been to remove the urgency from the question of how to read literary texts. The answer is: however one wants to (in terms of Rorty's pragmatism, 'use' replaces 'meaning' as the central goal of literary study). A central tenet of post-modernism is that there is no single right way to do anything. One aspect of this is that significance is firmly located in the reader, rather than the author or the text, and the reader's own set of beliefs becomes the determining factor in the criticism that he or she produces, rather than any objective features of the text or its historical context: 'meaning is realised at the point of reception.' This leads to a historicism that is the mirror image of the historicism of traditional philology: the emphasis is on the historically determined nature not of the original literary production, but of the modern critic's reading.

In a sense there is no further step beyond post-modernism for criticism to take, no more radical position to adopt than the total denial of foundations. In another sense, however, the question of what an individual reader may wish to do with a text becomes more urgent. There are other 20th-cent. critical traditions that have existed alongside the Saussurean line throughout, and some of these have come into prominence more in the aftermath of post-structuralism. One is the political criticism of literature which has its roots above all in Marxist theory. This has a long history, from the comments on literature of Marx and Engels themselves, through Georg Lukacs to the 'Frankfurt school', and beyond to the influential work of Pierre Macherey (*A Theory of Literary Production* (1978; orig. pub. 1966)) and to Marxists writing in English such as Fredric Jameson and Terry Eagleton. The greatest influence on both recent criticism and in particular the criticism of classical literature has come however not so much from what one might term the main line of Marxist criticism as from the work of critics with a more figured relationship to Marxist theory. The most important of these is the philosopher and 'archaeologist' of human culture Michel Foucault, who enjoyed particularly close relations with classical scholars through association with the ancient historians Paul Veyne and Peter Brown: one of his last major works was a *History of Sexuality* (1990; orig. pub. 1978) which dealt in detail with the ancient world. Like many recent thinkers, Foucault is antifoundationalist and radically historicist: even concepts like 'truth' or 'knowledge' change over time, and there is no possibility of standing outside history. His central contribution was to see that in the light of this, *power* becomes crucial, a power, however, exercised not so much directly from above but more diffusely distributed through every aspect of society. Power in this sense is an inescapable feature of social life, and not simply bad: but it is all encompassing, and any attempt to try to stand outside it is doomed to failure. This insight has been influential in literary studies both directly and through the movement known as 'New Historicism' begun by the American scholar Stephen Greenblatt (e.g. *Renaissance Self-Fashioning* (1980)). Whereas deconstruction tended to figure itself as 'oppositionalist' in the way that it extricated texts from the imprisonment of fixed meanings, the New Historicism saw meaning as necessarily constrained by power. However apparently rebellious a text, it still in the end recapitulates the dominant ideology of the society that produced it: if you shoot the president, you are only confirming that he is setting the agenda for your actions. Methodologically, because power is everywhere in society, New Historicist criticism finds its traces not only in the major official texts of a society but in more marginal texts, and in English studies it has been responsible for a considerable broadening of the range of material which comes under the critic's eye. This has been less important for classical studies, which have always been characterized by the breadth only recently becoming common in 'cultural studies' in other fields, but its influence can be seen in the growing interest in phenomena like drinking, eating, and sex from both a historical and a literary point of view. Again, it is Latin studies where the impact has been greater, particularly in the criticism of Augustan and imperial literature, where the question of the political stance of texts like the *Aeneid* or the *Ars amatoria* is an old one (cf. e.g. T. Habinek and A. Schiesaro (eds.), *The Roman Cultural Revolution* (1995)).

Another Marxist whose views have had especial impact on classical studies is the Russian critic Mikhail Bakhtin, whose work (including some essays published under the names of other scholars but possibly by him, notably V. Voloshinov, *Marxism and the Philosophy of Language* (1973; orig. pub. 1929)) goes back to the 1920s but has had a major impact only more recently (he died in 1975, and his two major studies of Dostoevsky, for instance, were published in 1929 and 1963). Bakhtin's work, which had its origins in Russian Formalism, was wide-ranging, but two related ideas have had the greatest impact. One is the concept of *dialogism*, the manner in which some texts (e.g. *Brothers Karamazov*) are seen as containing many different points of view which are not made subservient to one overall interpretation but coexist as irreducibly multiple: the other is the notion of *carnival*, and the *carnivalesque* text (like that of Rabelais) in which high and low, serious and comic are mixed and all the familiar hierarchies of literature break down. The pre-eminent example of this is the modern novel, which knows no generic boundaries of content or form and can thereby deal with any and every aspect of everyday life. These concepts have been employed in classical literature in relation to genres which are most obviously like Bakhtin's models, such as 5th-cent. Athenian comedy (see COMEDY (GREEK), OLD) and the Latin *novel, but they have also stimulated a more widespread interest in what the philologist Wilhelm Kroll had famously called 'crossing of genres' ('Kreuzung der Gattungen': *Studien zum Verständnis der römischen Literatur* (1924), 202–24), and have been used in relation to the different but still extreme generic complexity of works like *Virgil's Aeneid* and especially Ovid's *Metamorphoses*.

Although Marxist literary theory represents in some ways a separate tradition from the Saussurean line, it has undergone a similar move from a focus on the production of literary texts by individual artists to an analysis of the interpretative practices of readers, conceived however not as their surface reactions but on a deeper level as their underlying ideological configuration, what the sociologist Pierre Bourdieu called their *habitus* (e.g. *The Field of Cultural Production* (1993; orig. pub. 1968–87)). Another tradition that has undergone the shift away from the author to the text and the reader is the psychoanalytic tradition. Like Marx, Freud himself commented at considerable length on literature

and criticism from a variety of points of view, but later psychoanalytic criticism tended to focus solely on the psychology of the author's mental processes, a particularly unrewarding activity in relation to classical antiquity, where our knowledge of the authors is so exiguous. More recent psychoanalytic criticism has turned its attention, again, to the reading process. A particularly sophisticated version of this has been offered by the Italian psychoanalytic critic Francesco Orlando (e.g. *Towards a Freudian Theory of Literature* 1978; orig. pub. 1973), whose *Lettura freudiana della Phèdre* (1971, Eng. trans. in *Towards a Freudian Theory of Literature*) influenced Charles Segal's reading of Seneca's *Phaedra* (*Language and Desire in Seneca's Phaedra* (1986); see ANNAEUS SENECA (2), L.). But the psychoanalyst who has had the most influence on modern theory is the notoriously difficult Jacques Lacan (also an important influence on Segal). For Lacan, there can be no attempt to get beyond language in the psychoanalytic act, and the slippery chains of signifiers seen in Derridan theory *are* the unconscious: he makes extensive use of linguistic concepts such as metaphor and metonymy, but gives them a new, psychological, interpretation. If *power* was the key word for Foucault, for Lacan it is *desire*, but desire working through and in language. The account Lacan gives of this working is complex and his terminology difficult, but one of the important side-effects of his work has been to stimulate interest in a psychological reinterpretation of such typical aspects of the reading process as the desire for and fear of the end and the pleasures of anticipation and recall. This aspect of what has been termed 'reader-response' criticism has been practised with particular suggestiveness by the American critic Peter Brook (*Reading for the Plot: Design and Intention in Narrative* (1984); *Psychoanalysis and Storytelling* (1994)) and has inspired a number of treatments of classical narrative that attempt to go beyond the formalisms of narratology.

Finally, one last tradition of literary theory which will arguably have the greatest impact of all on critical practice but which emphasizes again how difficult it is to confine discussion of theory solely to the contested domain of the 'literary' is feminism, which unites many of the concerns of the other traditions within a new framework. Critical theory both ancient and modern has tended to talk of the author or the reader of a text as a gender-neutral abstraction, in practice often modelled on male responses. But just as the strong historicist line in 20th-cent. criticism has stressed that even the most apparently objective concepts are historically conditioned, so feminist criticism has called into question the universal validity of concepts like reason, coherence, order, and closure: not simply to set against these their opposites as essentially 'feminine' values, but rather to propose the deconstruction of the oppositions. 'Reason' is not a gender-neutral concept, but nor is it simply male and 'emotion' female, though that opposition unconsciously structures unreflective language and thought. The most notable proponent of a new type of 'écriture feminine' is the French critic Hélène Cixous (e.g. *Coming to Writing and Other Essays* (1991); *The Hélène Cixous Reader* (1994)). Early feminist criticism in classics set out either to draw the attention of critics to female writers or subjects previously marginalized, or to expose the more obvious ways in which a literature written by and for men, far from being a model of objective perfection, represented the values of that male world, particularly in relation to *sexuality and violence (e.g. A. Richlin, *The Garden of Priapus*, 2nd edn. (1992; orig. pub. 1983)). But more recent criticism has both attempted a deeper analysis of how gendered writing and reading pervade the texts and their interpretation, and has detected more cracks and fissures in the operation of male power within them (cf. E. Oliensis, *Arethusa* 1991, 107–36). See WOMEN.

This has not been a comprehensive survey either of literary theory in the second half of the 20th cent. or of the classical work inspired by the theories and theorists that we have discussed: nothing, for instance, on the German traditions of hermeneutics and reception theory and scholars like Malcolm Heath and Charles Martindale influenced by them, or on a figure like René Girard (e.g. *Violence and the Sacred* (1977)) whose work has influenced both Greek and Latin studies (e.g. P. Hardie, *The Epic Successors of Vergil* (1993)). Those classical scholars who have been most influenced by modern theory, like Martindale or John Henderson in Britain and Froma Zeitlin and Charles Segal in the United States, cannot and should not be pigeon-holed by those theories, not least because like everyone else's their views have changed over time. But we would like the version of the story we have offered to be seen as stressing both the foundational and the methodological importance of modern literary theory for classics, that is, both as an important and salutary invitation to examine the presuppositions and preconceptions of our individual practices, and as a wealth of techniques and approaches which will enable classical scholars to play their full part in the cultural dialogue that is a central justification for the study of antiquity. See also NARRATIVE; RECEPTION; SPEECH PRESENTATION.

There are a number of introductions to literary theory: see e.g. T. Eagleton, *Literary Theory: An Introduction* (1983), and A. Jefferson and D. Robey, *Modern Literary Theory: A Comparative Introduction*, 2nd edn. (1986). Useful dictionaries of terms include M. H. Abrams, *A Glossary of Literary Terms*, 4th edn. (1981); R. Fowler, *A Dictionary of Modern Literary Terms*, 2nd edn. (1987); G. Prince, *A Dictionary of Narratology* (1987); and J. A. Cuddon, *A Dictionary of Literary Terms and Literary Theory* (1991). Any library-catalogue search for works with 'Literary Theory' in the title will throw up more recent treatments. There is no systematic account of the 'philological tradition', and histories of classical scholarship tend to concentrate on personalities rather than methodological issues. Note however J. E. Sandys, *A History of Classical Scholarship*, 3 vols. (1921³, 1908, 1908); U. von Wila-mowitz-Moellendorff, *History of Classical Scholarship*, ed. H. Lloyd-Jones (1982); R. Pfeiffer, *History of Classical Scholarship*, 2 vols. (1968–76); and, on textual scholarship, E. J. Kenney, *The Classical Text* (1974) and L. D. Reynolds and N. G. Wilson, *Scribes and Scholars*, 3rd edn. (1991). There is an *Introductory Bibliography to the History of Classical Scholarship in the XIXth and XXth Centuries* by W. M. Calder III and D. J. Kramer (1992), which lists some thematic discussions. I. Martin, *The Making of Textual Culture: 'Grammatica' and Literary Theory* (1994), and A. Grafton and L. Jardine, *From Humanism to the Humanities* (1985), offer more sophisticated accounts of the medieval and Renaissance roots respectively of the modern conception of the classical scholar.

For classical literary theory up to the early 1990s, see I. J. F. de Jong and J. P. Sullivan, *Modern Literary Theory and Classical Literature* (1994), which includes bibliographies both of recent literary theories and of classical applications. Note also A. Benjamin (ed.), *Poststructuralist Classics* (1988), and K. Galinsky (ed.), *The Interpretation of Roman Poetry: Empiricism or Hermeneutics?* (1992). The journal *Arethusa* often devotes issues to particular topics: see especially 7. 1 (1974), *Psychoanalysis and the Classics*; 10. 1 (1977), *Classical Literature and Contemporary Critical Perspectives*; 11. 1–2 (1978), *Women and their World*; 16. 1–2 (1983), *Semiotics and Classical Studies*; 19. 2 (1986); *Audience-Oriented Criticism and the Classics*; 26. 2 (1993), *Bakhtin and Ancient Studies*. For the 'Paris school', see the introduction by F. I. Zeitlin to J. P. Vernant, *Mortals and Immortals: Collected Essays* (1991). For the issues raised by feminist approaches, see N. S. Rabinowitz and A. Richlin, *Feminist Theory and the Classics* (1993).   D. P. F., P. G. F.

literature, legal See LEGAL LITERATURE.

Liternum (now Lago di Patria), Roman colony, founded in 194

BC, 8 km. (5 mi.) north of *Cumae. Livy (34. 45), says that it was unsuccessful, but excavation shows a Roman town there until the 4th cent. AD. P. *Cornelius Scipio Africanus retired to a villa there (Livy 38. 52; Sen. *Ep.* 86). It flourished briefly after the *via Domitiana was built in the 1st cent. AD, but later became malarial and declined.   K. L.

litis aestimatio See LAW AND PROCEDURE, ROMAN, §§ 2. 5, 3. 9.

liturgy *Greek* The liturgy (*leitourgia*, 'work for the people') is an institution known particularly from Athens, but attested elsewhere (*Mytilene, Antiphon 5. 77; *Siphnos, Isoc. 19. 36), by which rich men were required to undertake work for the state at their own expense. It channelled the expenditure and competitiveness of rich individuals into public-spirited directions, and was perhaps felt to be less confiscatory than an equivalent level of taxation.

In Athens liturgies were of two kinds: the *trierarchy, which involved responsibility for a ship in the navy for a year; and various liturgies in connection with festivals. The latter included the *chorēgia ('chorus-leading': the production of a chorus at the musical and dramatic festivals), the gymnasiarchy (responsibility for a team competing in an athletic festival), *hestiasis* ('feasting': the provision of a banquet), and *architheōria* (the leadership of a public delegation to a foreign festival). At state level there were at least 97 in a normal year, at least 118 in a year of the Great *Panathenaea, and there were in addition some *deme liturgies.

Liability seems to have begun at a property level of *c.*3–4 talents; in some cases *metics as well as citizens could be called on. Appointment was made sometimes by one of the *archontes, sometimes by the tribes (*phylai). A man who thought that another was richer than himself but had been passed over could challenge the other to perform the liturgy in his place or else accept an exchange of property (*antidosis). The most that could legally be required of a man was to perform one festival liturgy in two years or one trierarchy in three, but in the atmosphere of competition surrounding the liturgies many men performed more liturgies and spent more money on them than the minimum possible.

In the 4th cent. BC it became hard to find sufficient men able to bear the cost of liturgies. Various measures were adopted to spread the cost of the trierarchy more fairly; for festival liturgies a law was proposed in the mid-350s by Leptines to abolish most special exemptions, and the attack on it by *Demosthenes (2) (Dem. 20) was probably unsuccessful. About the 330s the cost of the procession at the Great *Dionysia was transferred from the overseers to the state (*Ath. pol.* 56. 4). Between 317 and 307 *Demetrius (3) of Phalerum abolished all liturgies, and new magistrates styled *agōnothetai* ('contest-setters') were provided with funds for festivals by the state; but in the Hellenistic world there was a tendency to appoint rich men to offices of this kind and to expect them to add from their own pockets to what the state provided. See EUERGETISM.

W. S. Ferguson, *Hellenistic Athens* (1911), 55–8, 99–101; J. K. Davies, *JHS* 1967, 33–40; *DFA*³.   A. H. M. J., P. J. R.

Roman and Graeco-Roman Egyptian In Roman municipal law a sharp distinction was drawn between 'honours' (*honores*) and 'public duties' (*munera*: see MUNUS), the former qualifying their holder for a seat on the council; personal exemption from *munera* was a benefaction conferred by the ruling power through a grant of immunity (*immunitas*). These rules were also applied in the

Greek east, and offices must have been definitely classified into 'magistracies' (*archai*) and 'liturgies' (*leitourgiai*), although by the later 2nd cent. AD the distinction had broken down, as a result of both the logic of *euergetism, which imposed expectations of personal liberality on office-holders indiscriminately, and of compulsion, increasingly applied to both liturgies and magistracies from *Hadrian on (see P. Garnsey, *ANRW* 2/1 (1974), 229–52). By the early 3rd cent., when immunity (*aleitourgesia* in the east) had come to include exemption from magistracies, the most important and onerous liturgies were for the state (notably tax-collection: see DECAPROTI; DECEMPRIMI).

In Graeco-Roman *Egypt a liturgy meant a compulsory state office. Early on under Roman rule a hierarchy of compulsory public services was introduced, 'unparalleled in the ancient world for its comprehensiveness, reaching as it did into the remotest hamlets and compelling service from all levels of the population' (N. Lewis, *Life in Egypt under Roman Rule* (1983), 177–84 at 177). Its origins are detectable in the Julio-Claudian period, and recent scholarship stresses its marked difference in character from the liturgies of the Ptolemaic age (when compulsion in fact was little used). Its chief purpose was to ensure a supply of local officials (*i*) to administer the towns (see METROPOLIS (c)) and villages and (*ii*) to collect the imperial taxes. Liability was based on a property qualification which for the humblest liturgies could be as little as 200 drachmae; unsurprisingly, liturgic evasion was widespread by the later Principate.

J. Oehler, *RE* 12/2 (1925), 1871–9; A. H. M. Jones, *The Greek City from Alexander to Justinian* (1940), 167–8, 175–6; D. Thomas in G. Grimm and others (eds.), *Das römisch-byzantinische Ägypten* (Aegyptiaca Treverensia 2; 1983), 35–9; N. Lewis, *The Compulsory Public Services of Roman Egypt* (Papyrologica Florentina 9; 1982).   A. H. M. J.; A. J. S. S.

lituus, curved staff (without a knot, Livy 1. 18. 7) of the *augures* which they used to delineate their field of vision (*templum*; Cic. *Div.* 1. 30 and Ov. *Fast.* 6. 375, with Pease's and Bömer's notes; Serv. on *Aen.* 7. 187). It also appears in Umbria and Etruria, and earlier in Asia Minor. Frequently represented on republican coins.

RRC; A. J. Pfiffig, *Religio Etrusca* (1975); J. Linderski, *ANRW* 2. 16. 3 (1986), 2252.   J. L.

Lityerses, personification of an Hellenistic reapers' song (schol. Theoc. 10. 41; Poll. 4. 54). Cf. LINUS. Said to be the bastard son of King *Midas (1), he lived in Phrygian Celaenae and forced passing travellers to compete with him at harvesting. When they tired, he whipped them, cut off their heads, and bound the bodies in a stook. He was killed by *Heracles.   H. J. R.; B. C. D.

Livia (*RE* 'Livius' 27) **Drusilla,** b. 58 BC, in 43 or 42 married Ti. *Claudius Nero, whom she accompanied on his flight after the Perusine War. She bore him *Tiberius, the future emperor, and Nero *Claudius Drusus. In 39, in order to marry Octavian (*Augustus), she was divorced though pregnant with her second son. Although she had no further children, she retained Augustus' respect and confidence throughout his life. As consort of the *princeps*, she became an effective model of old-fashioned propriety, her beauty, dignity, intelligence, and tact fitting her for her high position. She played a role in the Augustan system which was unusually formal and conspicuous for a woman, and on Augustus' death became a principal figure in his cult and (by his will) a member of his family, as Iulia Augusta. She was believed to have interceded successfully on behalf of conspirators (see CORNELIUS CINNA MAGNUS, CN.), but some took her influence on Augustus to be malign, and saw her as a ruthless intriguer (her

grandson *Gaius (1) called her 'Ulixes stolatus', 'Odysseus in a matron's gown'), while the tradition grew up that she had manipulated the affairs of Augustus' household on behalf of her sons, especially Tiberius, to the extent of involvement in the deaths of M. *Claudius Marcellus (5), C. *Iulius Caesar (2), L. *Iulius Caesar (4), Agrippa *Iulius Caesar (Agrippa Postumus), and *Germanicus, and even of Augustus himself. But after AD 14 her continuing influence caused discord between her and Tiberius, who was even supposed to have retired from Rome in 26 chiefly to avoid her. She died in 29, but Tiberius' hostility ensured that her will was not executed until Gaius' reign, and that she was not deified until that of *Claudius.

Syme, *Rom. Rev.*, *AA*, and *Tacitus*, see indexes; J. Carcopino, *Passion et politique chez les Césars* (1958), 65 ff.; T. P. Wiseman, *Hist.* 1965, 333 f.; N. Purcell, *PCPS* 1986, 78 ff. Iconography: W. H. Gross, *Iulia Augusta* (1962).   N. P.

Livia (*RE* 'Livius' 38) **Iulia** (or **Claudia),** daughter of Nero *Claudius Drusus and *Antonia (3), often called Livilla. Born *c.*13 BC, she married C. *Iulius Caesar (2) and after his death Drusus *Iulius Caesar (1), to whom she bore Ti. *Iulius Caesar Nero. In AD 25 *Sejanus vainly asked *Tiberius for her hand. After Sejanus' death she was accused of adultery with him and others and of having poisoned her husband. She was put to death and suffered *damnatio memoriae*.   T. J. C.; E. B.

Livius Andronicus, Lucius, a *freedman of the Livii, commonly held to be the first to compose poems of the Greek type in Latin. He produced a comedy and a tragedy at the *Ludi Romani of 240 BC and wrote the text of a hymn to Juno sung by 27 young women at a moment of crisis in 207. Ancient biographers presented him as a half-Greek from *Tarentum who provided grammatical instruction in both Greek and Latin for the children of M. *Livius Salinator (consul 207) and other aristocrats, and who played roles in the stage plays he composed. His prestige persuaded the Roman authorities to permit actors and stage-poets to assemble for religious purposes in the *Aventine temple of *Minerva.

Titles of three comedies (*Gladiolus, Ludius,* †*virgus*†) and ten tragedies (*Achilles, Aegisthus, Aiax, Andromeda, Antiopa, Danae, Equos Troianus, Hermiona, Ino, Tereus*) are transmitted. Varro knew of a tragedy in which Teucer figured. Livius composed for both genres iambic and trochaic verses of the kind that remained current in the Roman theatre until well into the 1st cent. BC. (see COMEDY, LATIN; TRAGEDY, LATIN) Ten words cited by Nonius from an *Equos Troianus* have been plausibly scanned in a mixture of trochaic and cretic short verses and attributed to an actor's monody. The alternating full and 'miuric' (with short penultimate syllable) hexameters cited by Terentianus Maurus from a hymn to *Diana in an *Ino* have often been rejected as spurious.

Twenty-one fragments of a translation of *Homer's *Odyssey* in *Saturnian verses are unambiguously transmitted. Others can be assigned with a fair degree of certainty. Livius ignored the 24-book division introduced at *Alexandria (1). He seems to have kept fairly close to the general wording of the Homeric text but gave both the gods (Μοῦσα = Camena; see MUSES) and the heroes (e.g. Ὀδυσσεύς = Ulixes; see ODYSSEUS) local names and took account of the differences between Roman and Greek notions of story-telling. A peculiarly Roman goddess of prophecy (Morta) replaced a general idea of destiny (μοῖρα; see FATE). Conceptions shocking to Roman ears were toned down (e.g. *Patroclus θεόφιν μήστωρ ἀτάλαντος, 'counsellor equal to the gods' (3. 110), became *vir summus adprimus*, 'first-rate leading man'). Undignified reactions to external events were replaced (e.g. Ὀδυσσῆος λύτο γούνατα, 'Odysseus' knees were loosened', became *Ulixi cor frixit*, 'Ulysses' heart froze'). Livius sought a much grander verbal style in his epic than in his tragic writings, introducing words (e.g. *insece, procitum, ommentans, dusmus*) and forms (e.g. the *-as* genitive singular) quite absent from the ordinary language.

*Cicero thought little of either the *Odyssey* translation or the plays (*Brut.* 71). An eminent schoolmaster of the middle of the 1st cent. BC nevertheless beat the former into the heads of his charges (Hor. *Epist.* 2. 1. 69–71). A revision set in dactylic hexameters of the Ennian type (see ENNIUS) and divided into 24 books was sometimes confused in the grammatical tradition with Livius' original work but seems to have had little general circulation. Those who tried to determine *Virgil's archaic models ignored Livius.

FRAGMENTS E. H. Warmington, *Remains of Old Latin* 2 (Loeb, 1936), 1 ff. (with trans.); dramatic frs.: Ribbeck, *TRF³* 1 ff., *CRF³* 3 ff.; *Odyssia*: Morel, *FPL* 7 ff.

E. Fraenkel, *RE* Suppl. 5 (1931), 598 ff.; S. Mariotti, *Livio Andronico e la traduzione artistica* (1952; rev. 1986); G. Broccia, *Ricerche su Livio Andronico epico* (1974).   H. D. J.

Livius (*RE* 17) **Drusus** (1), **Marcus,** probably a descendant of L. *Aemilius Paullus (1) and M. *Livius Salinator, as tribune (122 BC) combined with the consul C. *Fannius in exploiting the people's reluctance to extend the citizenship as a weapon against C. *Sempronius Gracchus. He proposed the establishment—never carried out—of twelve large citizen colonies and the exemption of Latins (see LATINI) from corporal punishment, and brought about Gracchus' defeat in the tribunician elections. *Consul (112) and proconsul, he fought in *Macedonia, *triumphing in 110. Elected *censor (109) with M. *Aemilius Scaurus (1), he died in office, whereupon Scaurus was forced to abdicate. His daughter married first Q. *Servilius Caepio (2), to whom she bore *Servilia, then M. Porcius Cato, to whom she bore M. *Porcius Cato (2).

For bibliog. see SEMPRONIUS GRACCHUS, C.   E. B.

Livius (*RE* 18) **Drusus** (2), **Marcus,** son of M. *Livius Drusus (1), eldest of a circle of ambitious young nobles around L. *Licinius Crassus (see AURELIUS COTTA, C.; SULPICIUS RUFUS, P.), to whom he owed his oratorical training and some of his ideas. A brilliant, hard-working, and arrogant man, he became tribune 91 BC, having been quaestor and aedile, just after the conviction of his uncle P. *Rutilius Rufus. With the encouragement of M. *Aemilius Scaurus (1), who was himself in danger, and of Crassus he proposed a solution for all of Rome's major problems: 300 *equites were to be raised to the senate (where their influence would be minimal: see NOVUS HOMO) and criminal juries were to be chosen from the enlarged senate. Thus the *equites* would be eliminated as a political force, with the most ambitious creamed off and the rest deprived of power. He also proposed colonies and land distributions to provide for the poor, and the enfranchisement of all Italians. The ruling oligarchy was to reap the political benefit (he is called 'patron of the senate') and hold unchallenged leadership. But those who thought themselves adversely affected combined against him: extreme oligarchs, led by the consul L. *Marcius Philippus (1); *equites* rallied by Q. *Servilius Caepio (2) (once Drusus' friend, but now an enemy); Italians unwilling to give up *ager publicus* as the price of citizenship; probably C. *Marius (1), the enemy of Rutilius. After Crassus' death in September Philippus gained the upper hand and had the laws already passed invalidated by the senate. Shortly

after, Drusus was assassinated. The *Social War (3) and the commission of Q. *Varius were the immediate consequences. Drusus was the grandfather of *Livia Drusilla.

E. Badian, *Hist.* 1962, 225 ff.; P. A. Brunt, *The Fall of the Roman Republic* (1988), see index under 'Drusus'   E. B.

Livius (*RE* 33) **Salinator, Marcus,** was born in 254 BC; *Livius Andronicus was perhaps pedagogue in his father's house. As consul 219 he campaigned against *Demetrius (7) of Pharos with his colleague L. *Aemilius Paullus (1). Both *triumphed, but were accused of peculation. Livius was convicted and fined and withdrew from Rome. (That both served on a commission to *Carthage may be fiction.) His bitterness and the desertion of his father-in-law, Pacuvius of Capua, to the enemy explain his non-participation in the first part of the Hannibalic War (see PUNIC WARS). Recalled by the consuls in 210, he did not speak in the senate until he had to defend a relative against attack in 208. As consul for the second time he was publicly reconciled with his colleague C. *Claudius Nero, who had been a witness against him at his trial. They defeated *Hasdrubal (2) at the *Metaurus, in Livius' province, and Livius was rewarded with a triumph. He was proconsul in Etruria (206/5) and Gaul (204) and became censor, with Nero, in 204, when their quarrel erupted with increasing bitterness. That he imposed a salt-tax may be etymological fiction to explain his (in fact inherited) *cognomen*.

H. H. S.; E. B.

Livy (Titus Livius (*RE* 9)), the Roman historian, lived 59 BC–AD 17 (although Syme has argued for 64 BC–AD 12). He was born and died at *Patavium, the most prosperous city of northern Italy, famed for its stern morality. C. *Asinius Pollio criticized Livy's *Patavinitas* (Paduanism), but the import of this remark is unclear. An epitaph from Padua recording a T. Livius with two sons and a wife Cassia Prima may be his (*ILS* 2919). In a letter he urged his son to imitate *Demosthenes (2) and *Cicero, and this or another son wrote a geographical work. A daughter married L. Magius, a rhetorician. We do not know when Livy came to Rome or how much time he spent there; but he was on good personal terms with *Augustus (see below) and encouraged the young *Claudius, future emperor, to write history. Apart from, perhaps before beginning, his major work he also wrote philosophical dialogues.

Livy entitled his work *Ab urbe condita libri* ('Books from the Foundation of the City'): it covered Roman history from the origins of Rome to 9 BC in 142 books. Of these only 1–10 and 21–45 survive (and 41 and 43–5 have lacunae caused by the loss of leaves in the 5th-cent. manuscript which alone preserves 41–5). We also have two fragments of manuscripts of late antiquity: one, some 80 lines of print, has been known since the 18th cent.; the other, much damaged and containing parts of a few sentences of book 11, was discovered in 1986. We also have passages cited or referred to by later writers, and two kinds of summary of the history. First, there is the so-called Oxyrhynchus Epitome, covering books 37–40 and 48–55, and preserved in a papyrus written in the first half of the 3rd cent. Second, there are the *Periochae* (summaries) of all books except 136 and 137. The *Periochae* were perhaps composed in the 4th cent. and are preserved in a normal manuscript tradition (the summary of the first book survives in two different versions). It is uncertain whether the authors were working directly from the text of Livy or from an earlier summary (or summaries). Conflicts between the summaries and the text of Livy himself can be attributed to errors by the epitomator or to the use of sources other than Livy. Comparison of the summaries with the extant books indicates that we cannot always assume that the summaries of the lost books provide a reliable indication of their contents. The summaries of the final books are very brief, reporting only some foreign wars and events concerning Augustus' family. Livy was also the major source for, among others, *Florus, *Eutropius (1), and *Obsequens (the so-called 'Livian tradition'). The whole work seems to have survived into the 6th cent.

From late antiquity, Livy's history was referred to by 'decades'. This is because ten books were the most that could be fitted into a parchment codex (thus the story of the transmission of the surviving parts varies from decade to decade). But it is disputed whether Livy himself conceived his work as consisting of significant units of five (pentads), ten, or even fifteen books. Book 5 ends with the recovery of Rome after the Gallic sack and book 6 begins with a 'second preface'. The First Punic War began in book 16, while the Second War occupies the whole of the third decade, with the war against *Philip (3) V—the start of Rome's domination of the Hellenistic world—beginning in book 31; the war against *Antiochus (3) III begins in book 36, and books 41–5 contain the whole of the reign of *Perseus (2). But there is no obvious break before books 11 and 26, and it is difficult to discern any pattern in the lost books. Livy was probably attracted by the possibility of beginning and/or concluding a pentad or decade with a significant historical event, but was not prepared to achieve that end by damaging the economy of his work—making books excessively long or short, skimping or padding his material.

Internal indications show that books 1–5 were completed between 27 and 25 BC. It may be, however, that some of the passages which date from that time were additions to an early draft. A note in the best manuscripts of the *Periochae* states that book 121 was said to have been published after the death of Augustus; if that is true (and it may come from Livy's preface) it is likely that this applies to the following books.

Apart from a few references to topography and monuments, indicating autopsy, Livy relied on literary sources; he did not regard it as his duty to consult documents. In books 31–145 it is clear that for events in the east Livy followed *Polybius (1) closely, adapting his narrative for his Roman audience and making additions—sometimes tacitly—and noting variants from the 1st-cent. writers Q. *Claudius Quadrigarius and *Valerius Antias. The common view is that his procedure elsewhere was similar; he followed one main source—Antias, C. *Licinius Macer, and (for books 6–10) Quadrigarius in the first decade, L. *Coelius Antipater, Antias, or Quadrigarius in books 31–45—for longer or shorter sections, supplementing it from other sources. It is also thought that, apart from Antipater in the third decade, he did not use 2nd-cent. Roman writers directly: references to Q. *Fabius Pictor and L. *Calpurnius Piso Frugi were derived from the 1st-cent. writers. Neither conclusion is certain: no Roman writer was so obviously superior on western events as was Polybius on eastern ones, and it could be that Livy sometimes produces an amalgam of the various works he had read (which in many cases had virtually the same story). A passage of the fourth decade (32. 6. 8) is hard to reconcile with the view that Livy read only Polybius, Antias, and Quadrigarius for events in Greece. There is a strong case for holding that he used *Cato (Censorius) directly for the latter's campaign in Spain in 195, and he could well have read other 2nd-cent. writers. Nor can it be excluded that he consulted Polybius directly throughout the third decade

(most scholars agree that he did so for parts of books 24–30). If Livy did read 2nd-cent. historians, he did not necessarily conclude that discrepancies between them and later sources were to be resolved in favour of the former, though he was aware that Antias, and to a lesser extent Quadigarius, were fond of inflating enemy casualty figures.

Livy has been criticized for his failure to inspect the linen corselet which, according to Augustus, proved that A. *Cornelius Cossus was not a military tribune when he dedicated the *spolia opima* (4. 20). But Livy was writing tongue in cheek; it would have been out of the question to refute Augustus, who had political reasons for wanting Cossus not to have been a military tribune. Livy is also criticized for not inspecting the *libri lintei* ('linen books' cited as containing lists of magistrates) when his sources gave differing reports of their evidence (4. 23); it is quite possible that the books were no longer accessible. Nor are Livy's errors—anachronisms, geographical mistakes, misunderstandings of Polybius, and chronological confusions (sometimes caused by fitting Polybius' Olympiad years into a system based on Roman consular years)—all that numerous or striking in relation to the size of his work or in comparison with other writers.

It has often been said that it was Livy who fulfilled Cicero's desire that history should be written by an orator. Cicero wanted a style that 'flowed with a certain even gentleness', and *Quintilian was to write of Livy's *lactea ubertas* ('milky richness'). Livy, reacting against the contorted Thucydideanism of *Sallust (see THUCYDIDES (2)), first introduced fully developed periodic structure into Latin historiography. He had the ability to use language to embellish his material (comparison of Livy with Polybius in individual passages often shows the extent of Livy's originality) to convey an atmosphere and portray emotions. He gives special attention to major episodes, which are particularly numerous in the first decade—e.g. the rape of *Lucretia, the attempted rape of *Verginia, the stories of *Coriolanus, Sp. *Maelius, and M. *Manlius Capitolinus. The mixture of direct and indirect speech is one of the features of his technique. Elsewhere the speed of action in a battle—his battle scenes are often stereotyped—can be conveyed by short vivid sentences, while the dry style normally adopted for lists of prodigies, elections, and assignments of provinces and armies is perhaps a deliberate imitation of early writers, criticized by Cicero for just this, or of the *annales maximi*.

Part of Livy's style is achieved by the use of poetical or archaic words avoided by Cicero and *Caesar. In this respect he is following in a tradition of historiography to which *Sallust also belonged. These usages are most common in books 1–10, least so in 31–45. This phenomenon, however, is not to be explained on the hypothesis that Livy began under the influence of Sallust, but later moved back to a more Ciceronian vocabulary. Rather, Livy makes particular use of vocabulary of this sort in those episodes which specially attracted him, and these became progressively less common as his work proceeded—the diplomatic and military details of the early 2nd cent. did not compare in excitement with the great (and largely fictional) stories of the first decade. But some such episodes do occur in the later books, and it is precisely there that we find the greatest concentration of non-Ciceronian usages, as for example in the story of the *Bacchanalia in book 39 or the account of the death of Cicero preserved by *Seneca the Younger.

Livy was a patriotic writer, though in narrative he never refers to Roman troops as *nostri* or *exercitus noster* ('our men', 'our army'), and often, writing from their opponents' point of view, talks of the Romans as *hostes* ('enemy'). His aim was to chronicle the rise of Rome to mastery first of Italy, then of the rest of the Mediterranean world, and to highlight the virtues which produced this result and enabled Rome to defeat *Hannibal. Livy intended his work to be morally improving (pref. 10), but though there are many passages where he writes with this aim in mind, a moral purpose is not all-pervasive. He believed that a serious moral decline had taken place by his own time, and appears to have lacked confidence that Augustus could reverse it.

Livy doubtless shared Augustus' ideals, but he was by no means a spokesman for the regime. Tacitus (*Ann.* 4. 34) makes A. *Cremutius Cordus, defending himself on a *maiestas* charge, claim that Livy felt free to praise *Brutus and *Cassius; Cordus also claims that Livy was so lavish in his praise of *Pompey that Augustus called him a Pompeian, and adds that this did not harm their friendship. There are signs that Livy regarded the rule of Augustus as necessary, but only as a short-term measure.

CRITICAL EDITIONS (in most cases only the latest is given). Bks. 1–5: Ogilvie (OCT, 1974); 6–10: Walters–Conway (OCT, 1919); 6–7: Bayet (Budé, 1966–8); 8: Bloch–Guillard (Budé, 1987); 21–5: Dorey (Teubner, 1971–6); 26–30: Walsh (Teubner, 1982–9); 31–45: Briscoe (Teubner, 1986–91). *Periochae*: Jal (Budé, 1984), with Briscoe *Gnomon* 1985, 419–24; see also Reeve, *CQ* 1988, 477–91, and 1991, 453–83; an OCT is being prepared by M. H. Crawford. Fragments: Jal (Budé, 1979); an OCT is being prepared by C. B. R. Pelling.

COMMENTARIES The only complete comm. is the revision of Weissenborn by H. J. Müller (further rev. by O. Rossbach for bks. 6–8 and 21) (1880–1924). Bks. 1–5: Ogilvie (1965); 6: C. Kraus (1994); 31–7: Briscoe (1973–81); 36–7: Walsh (1990–2; Walsh is preparing further vols. to cover bks. 38–40); a comm. on bks. 6–10 by S. P. Oakley is in progress.

TRANSMISSION (other than prefaces to editions): G. Billanovich, *JWI* 1951, 137–208, *Traduzione e fortuna di Livio tra medioevo e umanesimo* (1981), and *Studi Petrarcheschi* (1986), 1–115; L. D. Reynolds, in *Texts and Transmission* 205–14; M. D. Reeve, *RFIC* 1986, 129–72; 1987, 129–64, 405–40, and *Studies in Latin Literature and its Influence* (1989), 97–112.

OTHER WORKS A. H. McDonald, *JRS* 1957, 155 ff. (on style); P. G. Walsh, *Livy, his Historical Aims and Methods* (1961); H. Tränkle, *Livius und Polybios* (1977); T. J. Luce, *Livy, the Composition of his history* (1977); Syme, *RP* 1. 400–54; A. J. Woodman, *Rhetoric in Classical Historiography* (1988), 128 ff.; E. Badian, in W. Schuller (ed.), *Livius: Proceedings of Colloquium Held at Konstanz in 1988* (1993), 9–38.   J. Br.

loans See CREDIT; DEBT; HEKTĒMOROI; INTEREST, RATES OF; MARITIME LOANS; NEXUM.

Lobon (*RE* 13), of Argos, perhaps 3rd cent. BC, wrote *On Poets* (Diog. Laert. 1. 112), apparently a tissue of biographical-bibliographical figments: thus he quoted a scolion (see SCOLIA) of *Thales, and his epitaph, and credited him with 200 lines of prose (Diog. Laert. 1. 34).

W. Crönert, Χάριτες F. Leo (1911), 123; O. Vox, *Giornale italiano di filologia* 1981, 83.   P. J. P.

locatio conductio was one of the four consensual *contracts of Roman law. It covered the hiring or leasing of things as well as contracts of employment in the form either of the hire of services or of a contract for work to be done (*locatio conductio rei, operarum*, and *operis*, in modern terminology). The common denominator was that one party 'placed out' (*locare*) a thing, his services, or a job to be done, which the other party 'carried along' or 'took over' (*conducere*), see CONDUCTOR. As in *sale, agreement was required on two essentials: the object of the contract (*res, operae*, or *opus*) and rent or remuneration. Rent/remuneration had to

consist of money and had to be real and certain but not necessarily fair. Neither Roman lease nor labour law was particularly well developed. No effort was made to protect employees or tenants from unfair terms or to grant security of tenure.

Leases for an indefinite period could be terminated at any time. If a third party acquired title over the leased property, he could expel the tenant (*emptio tollit locatum*). The lessee, however, did not have to pay rent and could bring the action on hire (*actio conducti*), if the lessor did not comply with his duty to grant use or use and enjoyment. Where there was a latent defect or a defect in title, the lessor's liability was based, at least occasionally, on an implied guarantee. Risk of destruction due to external force (*vis extraria*) was on the lessor (*periculum locatoris*): the lessee was granted remission of rent. Agricultural *leases were usually concluded for five years but if the lessee remained on the land after that period, the contract was deemed to have been renewed (*relocatio tacita*). Tenant farmers (see COLONUS), as a rule, were required to cultivate the lessor's land. As a contract of employment, *locatio conductio* only covered a small segment of services. Slaves, of course, did not enter into employment relationships. Nor did members of the upper classes; if they rendered (professional) services, they usually did so under a mandate. Both the employee under a contract of services and a contractor who had undertaken to do work were liable if they lacked the required skill (*imperitia culpae adnumeratur*).

F. de Robertis, *I rapporti di lavoro* (1946); T. Mayer-Maly, *Locatio conductio* (1956); H. Kaufmann, *Altrömische Miete* (1964); B. W. Frier, *Landlords and Tenants* (1980); P. W. de Neeve, *Colonus* (1984); S. D. Martin, *Organization of Private Building* (1989); R. Zimmermann, *The Law of Obligations* (1990), 338 ff.   R. Z.

Locri Epizephyrii (mod. Gerace), town in south Italy, a 7th-cent. colony of the Opuntian Locrians (see LOCRIS), 85 km. (53 mi.) north-east of Reggio. Politically, it was notable for the law code of *Zaleucus, one of the earliest written codes, and for the restrictive nature of its hereditary oligarchy. It founded a number of subsidiary colonies in the 6th cent. BC (*Medma, *Hipponium, Metaurus), which may have remained as political dependants. Locri was an ally of *Syracuse, giving assistance to the campaigns against Athens and *Dionysius (1) I's campaigns in Italy. *Dionysius (2) II was given asylum in 356, but, shortly after, the pro-Syracusan élite was overthrown and replaced by a more open constitution. In 280–270, Locri was an ally of *Pyrrhus and made payments to him from the treasury of the sanctuary of *Zeus, but then became an ally of Rome. In 214, it defected to Hannibal after a bout of *stasis but was recaptured after a counter-coup in 208. It remained a *municipium of considerable size under Roman rule, but later declined; it was abandoned in the 5th cent. AD.

A. De Franciscis, *Stato e società in Locri Epizefiri* (1972); F. Costabile, *Municipium Locrensium* (1978); M. Barra Bagnasco, *Locri Epizefiri* (1987).   K. L.

Locrian Maidens, the See AIAS (2) and Walbank, *HCP* 2. 333 ff.

Locris, region in central Greece geographically divided into three parts. In the north-east lay Epicnemidian Locris and southwards Opuntian Locris, both located on the southern shore of the Euboean Gulf. To the west, facing the Corinthian Gulf, lay Ozolian Locris, separated from the others by *Doris and *Phocis. Eastern Locris stretched from *Thermopylae in the north to Cape Stavros in the south, and Western Locris from Phocis near *Delphi in the east to *Naupactus in the west. Eastern Locris was strategically important because its cities commanded the

locus amoenus

narrow corridor between Thermopylae and the open areas of
Phocis and *Boeotia. The Locrians entered the region during the
Dark Ages, and were themselves driven into their three regions
by the later incursion of the Phocians. By the 5th cent. BC the
Eastern Locrians had created an advanced federal government
(see FEDERAL STATES), that included annual officials, the highest
of whom was an *archos*, and a federal assembly of 1,000 members.
There was also a federal judiciary. The government was probably
an oligarchy, with its capital at Opus, the modern Atalanti.
Western Locris had a looser federal government in which the
political authority of tribes and cities were not then definitely
demarcated. (See SEG 12. 480 for Western Locris as a federal
state in the 4th cent. BC.) The Eastern and Western Locrians
retained a strong bond of *kinship, and inscriptions prove that
they retained political contact with each other. They also jointly
contributed two members to the Delphic *amphictiony.

The Locrians sent one colony to Italy, known as Epizephyrian
Locri (see LOCRI EPIZEPHYRII). During the *Persian War the Locrians fought with the Greeks against Xerxes at the battle of Thermopylae, but were forced to serve with the Persians at the battle of
*Plataea. Although the Eastern Locrians took the side of Sparta
during the *Peloponnesian War, notably by supplying troops to
the Boeotians at the battle of *Delion and ships during the Ionian
War (see PELOPONNESIAN WAR), the Western Locrians first joined
Athens, but later supported Sparta. A Locrian dispute with Phocis
figured prominently in the outbreak of the *Corinthian War,
during which Locris supported those opposing Sparta. It allied
itself with Boeotia during the Theban hegemony (i.e. 371–362;
see THEBES (1)). Eastern Locris was the scene of heavy fighting
during the Third *Sacred War, having been repeatedly invaded
by the Phocians. It vacillated between loyalty to Macedonia and
Rome during the Second Macedonian War. After 146 BC Locris
remained loyal to Rome. Although Naupactus in Western Locris
throve until the Venetian period, Eastern Locris declined in prosperity and population during the late Roman empire.

L. Lerat, *Les Locriens de l'ouest* (1952); J. M. Fossey, *The Ancient Topography of Opountian Lokris* (1990). J. Bu.

locus amoenus, 'charming place, pleasance', a phrase (Cic. *Fin.*
2. 107; Isid. *Etym.* 14. 8. 33, etc.) used by modern scholars to refer
to the literary topos of the set description of an idyllic landscape,
typically containing trees and shade, a grassy meadow, running
water, song-birds, and cool breezes. The tradition goes back to
*Homer's descriptions of the grotto of *Calypso and the garden
of *Alcinous (1) (*Od.* 5. 55 ff., 7. 112 ff.); the rural setting for the
dialogue in *Plato (1)'s *Phaedrus* was much imitated. In
*Theocritus and *Virgil's *Eclogues* such landscapes form the backdrop for the songs and loves of shepherds. *Horace criticizes the
fashion for such descriptions (*Ars P.* 16 ff.). This perfect nature is
also the setting for the innocence of the *golden age and the
blessedness of the Elysian Fields (see ELYSIUM); among real places
the vale of *Tempe in Thessaly was idealized as a *locus amoenus*.
There was an analogous fashion for ideal landscapes in Roman
wall-*painting. In later antiquity and the Middle Ages such
descriptions develop into free-standing poems (e.g. Petron. *Sat.*
131; Tiberianus 1). See GARDENS.

E. Curtius, *European Literature and the Latin Middle Ages*, trans. W. Trask
(1953), 195 ff.; G. Schönbeck, *Der locus amoenus von Homer bis Horaz*
(1962). P. R. H.

Locusta (Lucusta), a noted poisoner of Gallic origin, was
employed by Agrippina the Younger (*Iulia Agrippina) to poison
*Claudius and by *Nero for *Britannicus. Nero took with him

on his flight a poison prepared by her. *Galba executed her.

PIR[2] L 414. A. M.

logic, the science of reasoning, developed among the Greeks as
a result of their interest in arguments of all kinds, not only
those occurring in philosophy and mathematics, but also those
occurring in politics and the lawcourts. The comparison of valid
and invalid arguments leads both to the abstraction of logical
form from many arguments of a similar verbal pattern, and to
the analysis of logical constants, i.e. the propositional connectives
such as 'not' and 'if', and the quantifiers, 'every' and 'some'. Both
processes may be observed within the context of philosophical
argument in many of *Plato (1)'s dialogues, e.g. the *Parmenides*
and the *Sophist*. *Aristotle at the end of the *Sophistical Refutations*
claims to have been the first to study the technique of argument
(*dialectic) systematically; in this work and in the *Topics* it can be
seen how the study of argument-forms is gradually disengaged
from the practical study of argument-winning.

Aristotle's main contributions to logic are, first, his theory of
the four forms of general categorical statement (every S is P; no
S is P; some S is P; some S is not P) and of the relations between
them, developed in the *On Interpretation*; and secondly, based on
this theory, the doctrine of the categorical syllogism, presented
in the *Prior Analytics*. Two features distinguish the *Prior Analytics*
as the first great work of formal logic: the use of schematic letters
(A, B, C) to stand in place of terms ('animal', 'white', 'swan'),
which immensely simplifies the presentation of formal argument, and the development of syllogistic as a system, a system
namely of deductive inference. By the theory of reduction, the
syllogistic moods are shown to be interconnected, so that all can
ultimately be reduced to two, later called *Barbara* and *Celarent*.
The syllogistic mood *Barbara* looks like this: 'A belongs to every
B; B belongs to every C; therefore A belongs to every C.' Aristotle
also made a beginning in the study of modal logic, i.e. the logic
of propositions expressed or characterized by the use of the
words 'necessary', 'possible', etc.; but his technical equipment
was insufficient for this task, and his treatment is unsatisfactory.
Aristotle's successor, *Theophrastus, attempted to render the
theory of modal syllogisms consistent by what came to be known
as the *peiorem* rule—without complete success. He also
developed a theory of wholly hypothetical syllogisms, their
prototype being syllogisms composed of three conditional propositions. These, he thought, were in some way reducible to
categorical syllogisms, but his method has not survived.

In the Hellenistic period, largely independently of Aristotle's
term logic, a tradition of logic developed which resembles the
modern logic of propositions, and which was systematized by
the Stoics. Its beginnings may be traced back to the Megarics
(i.e. members of the *Megarian school), who, like Aristotle's
contemporary *Eubulides, seem to have been mainly concerned
initially with the study of logical puzzles. But two Megarics or
Dialecticians, *Diodorus (2) Cronus and *Philon (6) of Megara,
went further, and developed their own theories of the modalities
(both precursors of the Stoic one; see STOICISM) and of conditional
propositions. Philon anticipated some modern logicians by
giving a truth-functional definition of the connective 'if . . . then
. . .'. By far the greatest logician of this second tradition was the
Stoic *Chrysippus. But his numerous works are almost entirely
lost, and Stoic logic in general has to be reconstructed from
fragments. Chrysippus' logic is based on the propositional connectives 'either . . . or . . .' (exclusive disjunction), 'both . . . and
. . .', 'if . . . then . . .', and the prefixed negative 'it is not the case

880

that . . .' The conjunction and the negation were defined as truth-functional. The Stoics used variables, but the values of their variables were propositions ('It is day'), not terms, and the signs they employed were ordinal numbers ('the first', 'the second'), not letters. They, too, elaborated the core of their logic as a system of deductive inference. The resulting hypothetical syllogistic was grounded on five types of indemonstrable arguments (ἀναπόδεικτοι λόγοι) as basic syllogisms and four ground rules (θέματα) by the use of which all other syllogisms were claimed to be reducible to the indemonstrables. The form of the first indemonstrable (later called *modus ponens*) was expressed as follows: 'If the first, then the second; but the first; therefore the second.' Later Stoics introduced further propositional functions, notably the inclusive disjunction (*vel*), and tried to simplify deduction by reducing the number of ground rules.

The two systems of logic, term logic and logic of propositions, were considered as rivals by the Stoics and Peripatetics, each maintaining to cover the whole ground of logic. On either side there were attempts to 'reduce' elements of the competing doctrine to their own—with limited success. It is a moot point whether Aristotle's syllogistic implicitly presupposes a logic of propositions; in any case, because of Aristotle's narrow concept of a proposition, his system covers only part of logic.

In later antiquity, especially among Platonists, some conflation—and some confusion—of the two distinct traditions can be observed. Many Stoic elements found their way into the works of the commentators on Aristotle like *Alexander (14) of Aphrodisias, *Ammonius (2), and *Philoponus, and into the logical writings of *Apuleius and *Boethius. *Galen, in the 2nd cent. AD, made an attempt to synthesize the two systems; but his major work on logic is lost so that we cannot say how successful he was. And he professes to have introduced a third kind of syllogism, named 'relational syllogisms'; one type of simple relational syllogism has the form 'M is equal to N; N is equal to O; therefore M is equal to O'. Such syllogisms are frequent in mathematical reasoning, but again not much is known about Galen's treatment of them.

Inductive logic was comparatively little developed in antiquity. Aristotle discusses ἐπαγωγή in the *Topics* and in the *Posterior Analytics*, but he seems generally to mean by this term what was later called intuitive induction. There is, however, some attempt to formulate principles of scientific research in the Hippocratic writings (see HIPPOCRATES (2)) and in the later medical literature, in particular among the Empiricists. Similarly, some later Epicureans (see EPICURUS) developed a theory of inductive inference.

W. and M. Kneale, *The Development of Logic* (1984); I. M. Bochenski, *Ancient Formal Logic* (1951), and *La Logique de Théophraste* (1947); J. Łukasiewicz, *Aristotle's Syllogistic from the Point of View of Modern Formal Logic* (1957); B. Mates, *Stoic Logic* (1961); G. Patzig, *Aristotle's Theory of the Syllogism* (1968; Ger. orig. 1959); J. Corcoran (ed.), *Ancient Logic and its Modern Interpretations* (1974); M. Frede, *Die stoische Logik* (1974), and 'Stoic vs Aristotelian Syllogistic' and 'The Ancient Empiricists', both in his *Essays in Ancient Philosophy* (1987); P. H. and E. A. De Lacy, *Philodemus on Methods of Inference* (1977); J. Brunschwig (ed.), *Les Stoiciens et leur logique* (1978); M. Burnyeat, 'The Origins of Non-deductive Inference', and D. Sedley, 'On Signs', in J. Barnes and others (eds.), *Science and Speculation* (1982); T.-S. Lee, *Die griechische Tradition der aristotelischen Syllogistik in der Spätantike* (1984); K. Hülser, *Die Fragmente zur Dialektik der Stoiker* (1987–8); P. M. Huby, in W. W. Fortenbaugh (ed.), *Theophrastus of Eresus: Sources for his Life, Writings, Thought and Influence* (1992). S. Bo.

logistai (λογισταί) in Athens in the 5th and 4th cents. BC were public auditors. Three distinct bodies with this title are known:

1. In the 5th cent. 30 *logistai* supervised payments to and from the sacred treasuries.

2. Ten *logistai*, selected by lot from the members of the *boulē, checked magistrates' accounts each prytany (see PRYTANEIS).

3. Ten *logistai* and ten advocates (συνήγοροι), selected by lot from all citizens, examined the accounts of magistrates at the end of their term of office and brought them before a jury, as the first part of the *euthyna. Presumably the *logistai* presided in court and the advocates were the prosecutors. If the jury found a magistrate guilty of theft or of accepting bribes, the penalty was a fine ten times the amount of the offence; if merely of 'malefaction' (ἀδίκιον), which may mean causing loss of public money by neglect or inadvertence, the penalty was a fine simply of the amount lost. See also CURATOR REI PUBLICAE.

M. Piérart, *Ant. Class.* 1971, 526–73. D. M. M.

logistics (Greek, military) In the ancient world, moving and supplying troops was most easily done by sea, and the Greeks believed their 'history' began with an overseas expedition—the Trojan War (see TROY). Certainly, by the 6th cent. BC the *Spartans were capable of attacking *Samos, and in the 5th the Athenians launched seaborne expeditions as far as *Egypt and *Sicily. In the latter case, *Thucydides (2) provides us with details of some of the preparations, including conscripting bakers from mills in Athens (6. 22).

On land, unless they were cavalry, troops went on foot—*Xenophon (1) and his comrades marched anything from 29 (*An.* 1. 2. 10) to 47 km. (1. 2. 6) a day (18–29 mi.) on the way to *Cunaxa until they were near the enemy—and were housed either in skin tents (cf. *An.* 1. 5. 10) or in the open. Foraging was common (cf. e.g. Xen. *Hell.* 2. 4. 25–6, 4. 1. 16), but in friendly or neutral territory food was bought (e.g. Xen. *An.* 1. 5. 6, 2. 5. 30; 1. 5. 10; see MARKETS AND FAIRS). Where there was a likelihood that no provisions would be available, arrangements would be made to carry them (cf. e.g. Xen. *Cyr.* 6. 2. 25 ff.), and there are examples of supply-lines being organized where an army remained in one place for any length of time, for example during the *Plataea campaign (Hdt. 9. 39. 2).

On land ox-carts, pack-animals, and human bearers were used to carry supplies, and Xenophon gives a vivid idea of what these might include (*Cyr.* 6. 2. 30 ff.). Wagons (ἄμαξαι) are often mentioned (see TRANSPORT, WHEELED), and could carry more than pack-animals—Xenophon reckons the average load 'per yoke' as 25 talents (*Cyr* 6. 1. 54—i.e. about 920 kg. or 2,030 lb.). But they could not go everywhere, and Xenophon and his comrades, for example, burned their wagons before their long march home (*An.* 3. 3. 1). The term most frequently used for the animals employed—*hupozugia* (lit. 'beasts under the yoke')—obviously included oxen, but also mules and *horses (Xen. *Oec.* 18. 40), and is sometimes used in addition to 'wagons' clearly to mean 'pack-animals'. Human bearers are usually termed *skeuophoroi* ('baggage-carriers'). *Philip (1) II and *Alexander (3) the Great of Macedonia tended to restrict the size of baggage-trains, and to rely on the soldiers themselves, and their servants, for carrying equipment and supplies; for pack-animals, horses, mules, and *camels were used in preference to oxen or donkeys.

Food consumed obviously varied with circumstances (see FOOD AND DRINK). Xenophon mentions wheat, barley, and chestnut bread, meat, including boiled beef and ass meat (*An.* 2. 1. 6), olives, dates, raisins, vegetables, pickled dolphin, and dolphin fat used instead of olive oil. Most interestingly, the daily rations allowed to the Spartans trapped on Sphacteria, under armistice terms (Thuc. 4. 16. 1), were two *choinikes* (2.16 kg. or 4.75 lb.) of ready-mixed barley meal, two *kotylai* (0.54 lt., 0.95 pints) of *wine, and some 'meat', probably like modern Greek *kima* (mince sauce). This would have provided something like 5,000 calories and 130 g. (4½ oz.) of protein, more than sufficient for a normal, active man, as the Spartan commander showed by hoarding some of it (Thuc. 4. 39. 2). Food brought in by *helots in boats, after the armistice, included wheat flour, wine, and cheese (4. 26. 5), and others swam over with poppy-seed mixed with honey and pounded linseed in skin bags (4. 26. 8).

Xen. *An.*, passim. W. K. Pritchett, *The Greek State at War* 1 (1971); D. W. Engels, *Alexander the Great and the Logistics of the Macedonian Army* (1978).   J. F. La.

logographers The word λογογράφος, as used by the contemporaries of *Demosthenes (2), commonly means a speech-writer for litigants in the courts, or else a writer of prose, as distinct from a poet (cf. Arist. *Rh.* 2. 11. 7 with the note in Cope's edition). Modern practice, however, has followed *Thucydides (2) (1. 21) in applying the term to the predecessors and contemporaries of *Herodotus (1) who were the pioneers of history-writing. Early writers of narrative prose are called λογοποιοί, 'tellers of tales', by Herodotus (2. 134, 143). But like the early philosophers and natural scientists, those who claimed to offer a faithful account of human activities considered their task as an investigation (ἱστορία), as scientific rather than poetic. If we grudge the title of historian to the predecessors of Herodotus, it is largely because they wrote of gods and heroes as well as of men and some of them professed to offer a true and correct version of mythology as well as of history.

No manuscripts of these authors have survived, but there are numerous references to them and occasional direct quotations in later Greek writers. Some later writers (e.g. Strabo 11. 6. 2, 12. 3. 21) have a low opinion of their accuracy and accuse them of fabricating names and incidents; others stress their lack of critical judgement; all agree that they wrote in simple style and language (cf. esp. Dion. Hal. *Thuc.* 23). It would be easier to estimate their talents and their value as historical sources if Herodotus had been more explicit in recording his obligations to them. See HERODOTUS (1).

Many of them came from Ionian cities. Two supposed Milesians, Cadmus and *Dionysius (5), are often given as the earliest logographers; but they are very uncertain figures, and the references to them in later literature are probably not to be trusted (Hellenistic writers were quite capable of fabricating their sources). *Hecataeus (1) of Miletus, on the other hand, is a well-attested historical figure, mentioned several times by Herodotus; he was active politically in Miletus as early as 500 BC (Hdt. 5. 36, 125), and much can be learnt from surviving fragments about the range and character of his literary work. *Acusilaus, *Charon (2), *Damastes, Euagon, *Hellanicus (1), *Pherecydes (2), *Scylax, and *Xanthus (2) can all be considered contemporaries of Herodotus, though there is much uncertainty about precise dates.

The work of the logographers may be classified under various heads:

1. Mythographic treatises, which involved attempts to rationalize and systematize Greek *mythology, and to trace the *genealogies of families who claimed descent from a god or hero. See MYTHOGRAPHERS.

2. Geographical works, often in the form of a *periēgēsis* or *periplous* (see PERIPLOI), describing the peoples and areas met with on a coasting voyage and the neighbouring peoples inland.

3. Accounts of the customs and history of non-Greek peoples. See BARBARIAN.

4. Local histories, especially accounts of the Founding of Cities (κτίσεις), see FOUNDERS, CITY.

5. Chronological works, which might include tables based on lists (real or apocryphal) of kings, magistrates, priests, or priestesses. See TIME-RECKONING.

Herodotus combines the various strains of the logographers' work, and was the first to provide a coherent history, which had for its main theme the contest of Greek and barbarian that culminated in the *Persian Wars.

For fragments and testimonia see *FGrH* (index auctorum, 3. B, 767). L. Pearson, *Early Ionian Historians* (1939), with bibliog.; Thomson, *Hist. Anc. Geog.*, ch. 2; A. Lesky, *A History of Greek Literature* (Eng. trans. 1966), 218 ff.; W. K. Pritchett, *Dionysius of Halicarnassus: On Thucydides* (1975), 54, 78; R. Drews, *The Greek Accounts of Eastern History* (1973); R. Thomas, *Oral Tradition and Written Record in Classical Athens* (1989).   L. P.; S. H.

logos (λόγος) is one of the central terms of classical Greek culture, whose main range is covered by two different sets of terms in English: (*a*) 'speech', i.e. either the activity of speaking (λέγειν) or the thing said (see Hom. *Il.* 15. 393; *Od.* 1. 56), and (*b*) 'reason', either in a wide sense or in the sense of 'argument' (cf. λογίζεσθαι). In role (*a*) the term comes to be used especially of prose speeches (as opposed to poetry), and of non-fictional accounts in general; but at this point it is already merging into role (*b*), for which cf. for example Protagoras' claim to be able 'to make the weaker *logos* the stronger', in those areas of ordinary life—particularly the lawcourts—where argument mattered.

Those ancient Greek philosophers who think of the world as having an ordered structure may express the idea by saying that it runs 'according to *logos*', i.e. is rational or intelligible. But they may also go on to suggest that the world is 'rational' in the sense of *possessing* reason; so, perhaps first, *Plato (1) (whose *Timaeus* makes the world a living, rational creature with a soul which moves itself through the heavens), and after him the Stoics, who see everything as interpenetrated, activated, and ordered by *logos*—also identified with creative *fire, and with god/*Zeus (see STOICISM). According to some (including the Stoics themselves) a view like the last is already to be found in *Heraclitus, and a number of the Heraclitean fragments (DK 22 B1, 2, 50, 72; cf. 45, 115) are more or less consistent with such an interpretation; but Heraclitus is more likely to have had in mind the less extravagant idea of the world as accessible to (speaking to?) human reason.

In later Platonism, and then in early Christian thought (which can be as constructively eclectic as Platonism itself), *logos* often stands for an organizing principle or force separate from, but vitally connected with, cosmic mind (*nous*) or God; in *Neoplatonism, as in Stoicism, the coming-to-be of things in the world may be expressed in terms of the operation of a plurality of such principles or *logoi*. Such thinking seems to combine elements of both the notion of a cosmic *logos* or reason imposing order from the outside (in the philosophers, deriving especially from a literal reading of the figure of the Divine Craftsman in Plato's *Timaeus*) and that of an immanent divine *logos*. The idea in St John's Gospel of the incarnation of *logos* in Christ is no doubt in part a similar reworking and recombination of such older ideas in a new context. See CHRISTIANITY.

C. H. Kahn, *The Art and Thought of Heraclitus* (1979); G. Vlastos, *Plato's Universe* (1975); M. L. Colish, *The Stoic Tradition from Antiquity to the Early Middle Ages* (1985).   C. J. R.

Lollia (*RE* 30) **Paulina** was granddaughter of M. *Lollius and very wealthy: the elder *Pliny (1) had seen her adorned in her fabulous pearls at an ordinary betrothal dinner (*HN* 9. 117). She was forced to abandon her marriage with P. *Memmius Regulus in order that she might marry the emperor *Gaius (1) in AD 38. Divorced by him in the following year, she was an unsuccessful candidate for the hand of *Claudius after the death of *Valeria Messalina in 48. *Iulia Agrippina secured her banishment (on the charge of consulting astrologers) in the following year, and she was driven to suicide.
J. P. B.; M. T. G.

Lollianus, author of Greek *novel *Phoenicica* (Φοινικικά): title and authorship are given by a late 2nd-cent. papyrus fragment (A) of the end of book 1; another (B) straddles two other books. In (A) the narrator loses his virginity with a girl Persis (also mentioned in a third fragment); in (B) he is among Egyptian robbers eating a murdered boy's heart to reinforce an oath of loyalty; after group sex they blacken their faces and dress in white, probably to aid escape rather than to perform religious ritual. Erotic coarseness classes it with *Iolaus* (a novel of probably the 1st cent. AD, preserved on papyrus) and the Lucianic *Ὄνος* ('Ass'; see LUCIAN); tolerance of *hiatus discourages Lollianus' identification with *Philostratus' Ephesian sophist (*VS* 1. 23; see SECOND SOPHISTIC).

> TEXT AND COMMENTARY A. Henrichs, *Die Phoenikika des Lollianus* (1972); S. A. Stephens and J. J. Winkler, *Ancient Greek Novels: The Fragments* (1993).
> TRANSLATION G. N. Sandy, in B. P. Reardon (ed.), *Collected Ancient Greek Novels* (1989).
> INTERPRETATION T. Szepessy, *Acta Antiquae Academiae Scientiarum Hungaricae* 1978; J. J. Winkler, *JHS* 1980; G. Anderson, *Eros sophistes* (1982), 57–8.
E. L. B.

Lollius (*RE* 11), **Marcus** (consul 21 BC), a *novus homo* and prominent partisan of *Augustus, praised or elegantly damned with faint praise by *Horace (*Carm.* 4. 9. 33 ff.) and described by *Velleius Paterculus as crafty, corrupt, and rapacious. He was the first legate (see LEGATI) of *Galatia (25), active in Macedonia, probably as proconsul (*c*.19–18), and then in Gaul, where German raiders inflicted a defeat, the seriousness of which may have been exaggerated. In 1 BC he was chosen to be adviser and overseer of C. *Iulius Caesar (2) in the east. A bitter enemy of *Tiberius, he influenced the young prince against Tiberius. As a result of quarrel or intrigue, however, he fell from favour, was accused of taking bribes from the Parthian king, and died before long, perhaps by suicide (AD 2). Lollius left enormous wealth.

> Syme, *Rom. Rev.*, see index; *RP* 2. 596 f.; S. Mitchell, *Anatolia* (1993), 1. 63 ff.
R. S.; R. J. S.

Lollius Bassus, of Smyrna, author of a dozen epigrams in the Greek *Anthology, from the *Garland* of *Philippus (2). His date is fixed by a pretentious poem on the death of *Germanicus (AD 19; *Anth. Pal.* 7. 391). The satirical epigram 9. 72 is ascribed to Bassus of Smyrna, perhaps a different poet.

> Gow–Page, *GP* 1587–1641.
A. D. E. C.

Lollius (*RE* 21) **Palicanus, Marcus,** 'a Picene of humble origin, loquacious rather than eloquent' (Sall. *Hist.* 4. 43 Maurenbrecher; see PICENUM), father-in-law of A. *Gabinius (2). As tribune 71 BC, he worked on behalf of C. *Verres' victims, the restoration of tribunes' powers, and jury-court reform, all in preparation for *Pompey's consulate (70), during which he was elected praetor 69. His consular candidature (67) was disallowed

by Pompey's enemy C. *Calpurnius Piso (1) (Val. Max. 3. 8. 3).
E. B.

Lollius Urbicus, Quintus, a native of *Numidia, served as military tribune (see TRIBUNI MILITUM) in Germany (*Germania), legionary legate (see LEGATI) in Upper *Pannonia, then as a legate in the Jewish War of AD 132–5, winning military decorations. Consul probably in 135 or 136, he was appointed governor first of Lower Germany and then of Britain, where he is attested from 139 to at least 142. After reoccupying lowland Scotland, he began the construction of the turf-built *wall of Antoninus across the Forth–Clyde isthmus (*RIB* 2191, Balmuildy). Later in the reign of *Antoninus Pius he was prefect of the city (*praefectus urbi*).

> *PIR*[2] L 327.
J. B. C.

Lombards, or **Langobardi,** a Germanic group, described by Tacitus as few but courageous (*Germ.* 40). In the 1st cent. AD they lived along the lower Elbe, but by the 160s they were threatening the upper Danube frontier. After being subsumed into the *Hun federation (*c*.400), victory over the *Heruli (*c*.500) re-established Lombard independence and gave them control over Pannonia; they had by now adopted Arian Christianity (see ARIANISM). They served *Justinian as allies of variable reliability and savage and unruly warriors. In 568, frightened of Avar power (see AVAROSLAV INVASIONS), they migrated to Italy where they maintained an independent kingdom and duchies for two centuries.
L. M. W.

Londinium (mod. London). The Roman settlement had no iron age predecessor and was not established until *c.* AD 50, earlier routes crossing the Thames up river at Westminster. The settlement stood on Cornhill and Ludgate Hill north of the river, with a suburb across the bridge in Southwark. The original settlement was laid out around the northern bridgehead, beside modern London Bridge; it grew to *c*.25 ha. (62 acres) by the time of its destruction in the *Boudiccan revolt of 60/1, when *Tacitus states that it was an important trading centre (*Ann.* 14. 33). There is no evidence for any early military presence and the settlement's early status is uncertain. It was most likely a community of traders from other provinces.

Following AD 61 there was a major public building programme including the construction of two successive fora (Flavian and early 2nd cent.), the latter of enormous size, covering *c*.3.6 ha. (9 acres). There is strong evidence for vibrant economic activity. Substantial timber quays, stretching up to 300 m. (330 yds.) along the river, were constructed from the Flavian period. Epigraphic evidence shows the procurator was based here after 61 (*RIB* 12 and 2443. 2), whilst a substantial Flavian building overlooking the river is interpreted as the provincial governor's palace, implying that London had become the provincial capital. The governor's guard and a staff seconded from other units were based here, probably in the Cripplegate fort, built *c*.90. Adjacent to this was an early 2nd-cent. amphitheatre. The settlement suffered an economic decline during the later 2nd cent., and although there is good evidence for later Roman occupation there was no resurgence of the productive economy. The later Roman city was instead dominated by town houses.

In the late 2nd cent. London was surrounded by a landward wall enclosing 133.5 ha. (330 acres), making it the largest town in Britain. The wall was extended along the riverside in the middle of the 3rd cent., whilst external towers were added in the mid-4th. Excavations show the city to have been more cosmopolitan than the others of the province. A mid-3rd-cent. Mithraeum has been excavated and high-quality sculpture has also been found, including material from a monumental arch reused in the riverside wall.

There is no direct evidence for London's status; it is conjectured to have been successively a *municipium* and *colonia*. It became the capital of Upper *Britain in the early 3rd cent. and Maxima Caesariensis under *Diocletian. The visit of *Constantius I in 306 may have occasioned the grant of its later name, Augusta.

D. Perring, *Roman London* (1991). M. J. M.

Long Walls, the (τὰ μακρὰ τείχη or σκέλη, 'legs'), were built between 461 and 456 BC to connect Athens with her ports, *Phaleron and *Piraeus. (Thuc. 1. 107. 1, 108. 3, remarkably his only references to internal affairs in the *Pentekontaetia, apart from 1. 107. 4: attempt by enemies of the democracy to *stop the* building of the Long Walls, i.e. the walls were identified with *democracy. But see below for—oligarchic—*Corinth.) About 445 the Phaleric wall was replaced by a third, parallel to the north or Piraeus wall. They were destroyed by the Spartans to flute music in 404, rebuilt by *Conon (1) in 393, but allowed to fall into a half-ruined state by 200 (Livy 31. 26. 8). The walls to Piraeus were about 6½ km. (4 mi.) long and c.180 m. (200 yds.) apart; the traces visible a century ago have now almost entirely disappeared. The course of the Phaleric wall is uncertain. The main road from Piraeus to Athens lay outside, the road inside being primarily military. The Long Walls were used in the *Peloponnesian War to make Athens into an isolated fortress, in which most of the population of Attica could live on seaborne provisions. The example of Long Walls was followed elsewhere, notably at *Megara, and even Corinth.

W. Judeich, *Topographie von Athen*, 2nd edn. (1931), 155 ff. (his course for the Phaleric wall is improbable); T. Lenschau, *RE* 19. 88 f.; R. L. Scranton, *AJArch.* 1938, 525 ff.; J. Travlos, Πολεοδομικὴ ἐξέλιξις τῶν Ἀθηνῶν (1960), 48 ff., *Pictorial Dictionary of Ancient Athens* (1971), 158 ff., and *Bildlexikon zur Topographie des antiken Attikas* (1988), 288 ff.; R. E. Wycherley, *The Stones of Athens* (1978), ch. 1; J. F. Hind, *CAH* 9² (1994), 153 (dilapidation by 80s BC); J. R. Ellis, in I. Worthington (ed.), *Ventures into Greek History* (1994), 3 ff. T. J. D.; C. W. J. E.; S. H.

'Longinus' The literary treatise commonly called *On the Sublime* (Περὶ ὕψους), of which about two-thirds survives, is ascribed in the manuscript tradition both to 'Dionysius Longinus' and to 'Dionysius or Longinus'. Until the early 19th cent., it was generally believed to be by *Cassius Longinus. Internal evidence, especially the chapter on the decline of oratory (44), points, however, to a date in the 1st cent. AD. The writer sets out to answer *Caecilius (1) of Caleacte, who had allegedly given an inadequate account of 'sublimity', failing in particular to give due weight to the emotional element (πάθος).

On the Sublime is a very important book. In discussing the quality of thought and style which marks writing as 'sublime' (ὑψηλόν), the author breaks free of the rhetorical tradition within which he works, and makes a connection between 'great writing' and greatness of mind. He is a sophisticated, original, and serious critic. Both his detailed analyses of passages of poetry and prose (e.g. on *Euripides' *Phaethon* (15) and *Demosthenes (2)'s *De corona* 208 (16)), and his general reflections on genius and the limitations of 'correct' writing, are distinguished work, and have deservedly been influential. The period of his greatest influence extends from Boileau's French translation (1674) to the early 19th cent.; but as a stimulus to critical thought and to the understanding of ancient literature he has permanent value. See SUBLIME.

EDITIONS O. Jahn and J. Vahlen, 4th edn. (1910; repr. 1967), with index verborum; W. Rhys Roberts (1907), with notes and trans.; D. A. Russell (1964), with comm.; C. M. Mazzucchi (1992), with comm. and It. trans.

TRANSLATIONS W. Smith (1739); A. O. Prickard (1906); G. M. A. Grube (1957); D. A. Russell (1966); and many others.

Discussion in all general surveys of *literary criticism in antiquity; see also W. Bühler, *Beiträge zur Schrift vom Erhabenen* (1964); J. Bompaire, *Rev. Ét. Grec.* 1973, 323–43; D. A. Russell, *Mnemos.* 1981, 72–86. On the book's influence see S. H. Monk, *The Sublime* (1935); J. Brody, *Boileau and Longinus* (1958); K. Maurer, *Le Classicisme à Rome aux 1ᵉʳˢ siècles avant et après J.-C.* Entretiens Hardt 25 (1979), 213–57. D. A. R.

Longinus, Cassius, rhetorician. See CASSIUS LONGINUS.

Longus, Greek writer of *The pastoral Story of Daphnis and Chloe* (Ποιμενικὰ τὰ κατὰ Δάφνιν καὶ Χλόην), which he presents as a guide's explanation of a painting he saw while *hunting on *Lesbos. His apparently detailed knowledge of Lesbian topography is imprecise and inconsistent, and although Longi appear on Lesbian inscriptions, ours may have been a visitor rather than resident. There are hitherto no papyri, but his mannered sophistic *apheleia* (simplicity), often using short rhyming and rhythmically balanced *cola*, suits the late 2nd or early 3rd cent. AD, as do similarities to passages in *Aelian and *Alciphron (though priority is disputed). Few accept Hermann's identification with the Hadrianic grammarian *Velius Longus.

Longus' four books miniaturize and rusticate the standard novel. Daphnis and Chloe, foundlings brought up by shepherds on the estate of a *Mytilenean aristocrat, gradually fall in love. Obstacles there are—rivals, abductions by pirates and by a taskforce from *Methymna. But everything happens on a few miles of coastline near Mytilene; the chief obstacle to union is their rustic naïvety; and the central theme is their gradual discovery of what love is, by precept, example, and experiment. This is represented as a grand plan of Love (*Eros), and the *Nymphs and *Pan help the couple in trouble; Longus dedicates his work to all three. In book 3 Daphnis is sexually initiated by an older city woman, Lycaenion, but only after eluding further admirers and discovering their aristocratic urban origins do Daphnis and Chloe return from their taste of Mytilene to a country wedding and a life in which their children too will be shepherds. Like the countryside and seasons to which they respond and the incidents which catalyse change, the couple's developing sexual awareness is described in lingering detail. That detail sometimes cloys, the careful motivation of actions sometimes seems contrived, and the teenagers' sexual naïvety may stretch credibility. The style too can be monotonous, albeit well suited to naïve monologues and pretty *ecphrases* (see EKPHRASIS) of rustic scenes and seasons. But the Thucydidean narrative (see THUCYDIDES (2)) of war between Mytilene and Methymna brings variety, and well-educated readers could enjoy recognizing the many allusions to earlier texts, especially to that Hellenistic pastoral poetry which Longus is crossing with the prose tradition of the *novel. Despite the preface's claim, the text is written for entertainment rather than to instruct readers in love or allegorically (as argued by Merkelbach (see bibliog. below)) in the Dionysiac *mysteries; see DIONYSUS.

Among the Greek novelists Longus vies with *Heliodorus (4) for the palm. Readers can admire vivid and convincing detail while aware that they need not be convinced, and, as with *Achilles Tatius (1), Longus' description of physical attractions, bodies, and swelling emotions has attracted more than it has repelled (the latter included Wilamowitz, the former, Goethe, who in his *Gespräche mit Eckermann* recommended reading *Daphnis and Chloe* once a year). Since Amyot's French translation (1559) some 500 translations into modern languages and editions have appeared. In the 18th and early 19th cents. Longus influenced Bernadin de St Pierre (*Paul et Virginie*) and S. Gessner's pastoral idylls in rhythmical prose. Illustrators have been numerous and often distinguished, including Corot, Maillol, Chagall, though many know the story only from Ravel's ballet score (1912).

EDITIO PRINCEPS 1598 (Giunta, Florence).

STANDARD EDITIONS M. D. Reeve (Teubner 1982; 2nd edn. 1985). J.-R. Vieillefond (Budé, 1987). No modern commentary (Bowie and Morgan in preparation) but good notes in O. Schönberger, 4th edn. (1989)

TRANSLATIONS Best by C. Gill, in B. P. Reardon (ed.), *Collected Ancient Greek Novels* (1989). Recent English translations: J. Lindsay (1948); M. Hadas, *Three Greek Romances* (1953); P. Turner (Penguin, 1956; 2nd edn. 1968). J. M. Edmonds' Loeb (1916) prints a revision of Thornley's 1657 trans.

CRITICISM R. L. Hunter, *A Study of Daphnis and Chloe* (1983); B. D. MacQueen, *Myth, Rhetoric and Fiction* (1990); Rohde, *Griech. Roman* 498 ff.; O. Schissel von Fleschenberg, *RE* 13 (1927), 1425–7, 'Longos' 1; Christ–Schmid–Stählin 2/2⁶. 823 ff.; A. Lesky, *A History of Greek Literature* (1966), 867–8; E. L. Bowie, *CHCL* 1. 696–9 (= paperback 1/4 (1989), 136–9); T. Hägg, *The Novel in Antiquity* (1983), 35–41; G. Anderson, *Eros sophistes* (1982), 41–9; H. Reich, *De Alciphronis Longique aetate* (Diss. Königsberg, 1894); A. Valley, *Der Sprachgebrauch des Longus* (Diss. Uppsala, 1926); H. H. O. Chalk, *JHS* 1960; L. Hermann, *Latomus* 1981; E. L. Bowie, *CQ* 1985; R. Merkelbach, *Die Hirten des Dionysos* (1988); J. Winkler, *The Constraints of Desire* (1990); D. Teske, *Der Roman des Longus als Werk der Kunst* (1991).

RECEPTION G. Barber, *Daphnis and Chloe: The Markets and Metamorphoses of an Unknown Bestseller* (1989).   E. L. B.

lot See SORTITION.

Lotus-eaters (Λωτοφάγοι), a mythical people (the ancients liked to locate them in North Africa) living on the lotus plant, which induces forgetfulness and makes its eaters lose all desire to return home (*Od.* 9. 82–104). Those of *Odysseus*' men who ate the lotus had to be dragged back to their ships by force.

J. R. M.

love and friendship Greek philosophers place love and friendship within a structure of eudaimonism: an agent's own happiness or living well (*eudaimonia*) is the final goal of all his deliberate actions. Formal egocentrism frames substantive altruism.

*Plato (1) discusses friendship (*philia*) most fully as an aspect of erotic desire (*erōs*). In the *Symposium*, Plato extends the Socratic psychology by making the ultimate goal of all desire not just being happy, but being happy for ever. Within this world, this may be achieved in a manner through passing on one's physical life to a child, or one's mental life to a beloved; the happiness counts as one's own in that it is a continuation of the life one has led. The ladder of love then advances the lover's attention from persons, through practices, laws, and sciences, to the Form of Beauty, until his goal becomes to beautify his (and arguably also a beloved's) *soul by the light of the Form. In the *Phaedrus*, the lover is reminded by a beloved, congenial as well as beautiful, of the Forms he knew before birth, and of the kind of companionship (imaged in a procession led by a particular god) that determined the manner in which he knew them; he then wishes them to re-create that companionship in a shared life, ideally of philosophy, that will restore to them after death the happiness they lost at birth. In the *Republic*, the pederastic ideal applies between the sexes (viewed as naturally equal, and equally fit for

public life), and yet erotic love is marginalized; the goal of a philosophical polity is a friendship that unites all the citizens, despite their differences of role, so that they identify with one another, applying the term 'mine' ('Mine has fared well' or 'badly') to each other's successes and sufferings.

*Aristotle defines friendship and classifies friendships, applying the term *philos* (in extension even of Greek idiom) far more widely than our 'friend'. Friends wish well to one another according to the manner in which they are friends: friends in utility (such as business partners) wish each other to be useful; in pleasure (such as lovers), to be pleasant; in goodness or virtue, to be good. Since, of these, only being good is intrinsic, and inherently beneficial, to the friend himself, virtue-friendship can alone embody that goodwill (loving another for himself, and wishing him well for his own sake) which is definitive of *philia* in its strict sense. Happiness consists in activity, and is not a state of mind; through beneficence and co-operation, A acts upon and within B's life, making possible actions by B that are owed to A and count as A's also, so that their lives come to overlap. Friends pursue together the activities that they most value; even philosophy can be practised more continuously in company. Each may be improved by the other, taking from him the impression of the characteristics that please them. Aristotle lacks Plato's enthusiasm for pederasty, but concedes that, if the familiarity between a man and a boy produces a similarity of character, it may engender an enduring friendship. Though he views men and *women as naturally unequal, he allows a kind of virtue-friendship to link man and wife, each delighting in the proper virtue of the other. Cities are founded for living, but come to serve living well (see POLIS); through civic co-operation, the motive of self-interest is enriched by goodwill, as each citizen comes to wish every other to be good for his own sake. Women are to contribute to civic friendship not directly (as in Plato's utopias), but indirectly through the influence of the *household on its menfolk.

*Epicurus faces extra difficulties in that his ethic is not only eudaimonist but hedonist. Friendship inspires in him noble sentiments (e.g. the woozy 'Friendship dances round the world announcing to us all that we should wake up and felicitate one another') problematically consistent with the exclusive pursuit of one's own pleasure. The foundation of friendship is utility: it offers us not so much our friends' help, as confidence in their help. Yet it is not only a protector but a creator of pleasures: we rejoice in our friend's joy as in our own, and and are equally pained by his distress; it is more blessed, because more pleasant, to give than to receive. Whether as a pleasure or as an insurance, one may run risks for a friend, take on the greatest pains on his behalf, and even die for him. Later Epicureans tried to explain *how* one can come to take joy in another's joy: perhaps we first form associations for utility, but then affection 'blossoms' out of familiarity, so that we love our friends for their own sake; or else, knowing the advantages of altruism, we contract to love them no less than ourselves. Whether they arise or are adopted, altruistic attitudes make new pleasures possible. Epicurus' hedonism is discriminating, and deprecates the pleasures of love: falling in love is not god-sent, and does not befall the wise; making love never did anyone any good. Characteristic of the Epicureans were calm collegiate friendships.

The Stoic goal was 'living in agreement with nature' by acting virtuously (see STOICISM). A good friend is an external and instrumental good. Having friends is neither valuable in itself, nor necessary for happiness; but it gives virtue new scope. Only good men can be friends, for they do not compete for scarce commodities that are not really good, but co-operate in maintaining wisdom and exercising virtue. Benefiting another benefits oneself, for aiding another's virtue confirms one's own; in this manner, it is social to serve oneself. Ultimately, all good men are friends. This is the culmination of the process of 'appropriation' (*oikeiōsis*): animals have a natural tendency towards self-preservation; as the human animal grows up, it recognizes more and more things as belonging to it, so that its circle of concern extends. Personal familiarity nourishes common values that then create a solidarity uniting all the wise. The early Stoics were more tolerant of erotic relations than the Epicureans. In his Cynic vein, *Zeno (2) took making love to be evaluatively indifferent, whether with boy or girl, whether with boy-beloved or non-beloved. Being in love has real value for the wise: its stimulus is the 'apparent beauty', at once moral and visible, of the immature but potentially virtuous; its goal is a friendship that will foster that virtue. Consistently with that stimulus and goal, the young remain proper objects of love up to the age of 28. Outdoing Plato, Zeno politicizes love: Love is a god who, producing friendship, freedom, and unanimity, furthers the safety of the city.

See also FRIENDSHIP, GREECE; FRIENDSHIP, RITUALIZED; HOMOSEXUALITY.

J.-C. Fraisse, *Philia* (1974); G. Vlastos, *Platonic Studies*, 2nd edn. (1981), 3 ff.; M. C. Nussbaum, *The Fragility of Goodness* (1986); A. W. Price, *Love and Friendship in Plato and Aristotle* (1989); A. A. Long and D. N. Sedley, *The Hellenistic Philosophers* (1987), 1. 137–8; P. Mitsis, *Epicurus' Ethical Theory* (1988), ch. 3; J. Annas, *The Morality of Happiness* (1993), 236–44, 262–76; M. Schofield, *The Stoic Idea of the City* (1991), ch. 2; C. White, *Christian Friendship in the Fourth Century* (1995). A. W. P.

Luca (mod. Lucca), in Liguria (later incorporated in Etruria) on the river Ausar (Strabo 5. 217). Both notices of the town before 100 BC are suspect (Livy 21. 59; Vell. Pat. 1. 15: preferably read *Luna in each case). A border town of the Cisalpine province, Luca became famous when *Caesar and *Pompey met there for their conference in 56 BC (Suet. *Iul.* 24, etc.). Under the late republic Luca was a *municipium* (Cic. *Fam.* 13. 13), under the empire a *colonia* (Plin. *HN* 3. 50). But, although a fairly important station on an extension of the *via Clodia, it is rarely mentioned until late imperial times. E. T. S.

Lucan See ANNAEUS LUCANUS, M.

Lucania (mod. Basilicata), a mountainous region of southern Italy. Together with Bruttium (mod. Calabria, see BRUTTII), it comprised the Augustan Regio III; see ITALY. Sources record Oenotrians, Chones, and Ausonians as its principal inhabitants, but these have not been archaeologically identified. Greek colonization began *c*.700 BC, and *c*.420, the Oscan Lucani (see OSCANS) began to overrun the region. They were related to, although distinct from, the Campanians and Samnites; see CAMPANIA; SAMNIUM. By *c*.390, they held most of the region, with the exception of a number of the Greek cities. They were partially Hellenized (see HELLENISM), adopting Greek coin-types, architectural styles and techniques, alphabet, and political terminology. In the 4th cent. the number of urban and proto-urban sites rose considerably. Like most Oscan towns, they were governed by an elected *meddix*, and they may have been organized into a league, as were the Campanians and Bruttians. They waged intermittent war against the Greeks, and maintained a hostile policy towards Rome. They negotiated a treaty in 326, but fought against Rome in the Pyrrhic (see PYRRHUS) and *Punic Wars and in the *Social War (3). There was extensive *Gracchan and post-Gracchan colonization on confiscated territory. As a result, many cities gained

a new lease of life in the late republic and early empire, although there are signs of depopulation from the 3rd cent. AD.

Le genti non greche della Magna Grecia: Atti di Convegno di Studi sulla Magna Grecia 11 (1972); P. Simelon, *La Propriété en Lucanie depuis les Gracches jusqu'à l'avènement des Sévères* (1993). K. L.

Lucaria, Roman *festival on 19 and 21 July celebrated in a grove (*lucus*) between the *via Salaria and the *Tiber where (Festus 106 Lindsay) the Romans had hidden when fleeing the Gauls. The 18 July, *Alliensis dies*, occasioned this aetiology. *Plutarch (*Quaest. Rom.* 88) indicates that revenue from public groves was called *lucar*; ILLRP 504 confirms that the word originally meant 'grove'. Lucaria must originally have involved clearing groves and propitiating their spirits; cf. Cato, *Agr.* 139–40.

G. Dumézil, *Fêtes romaines d'été et d'automne* (1975), 42 ff.; W. Warde Fowler, *Roman Festivals* (1899) 182–5. C. R. P.

Lucceius (*RE* 6), **Lucius,** as praetor urbanus (67 BC) and friend of *Pompey had his judge's chair broken by the consul M'. *Acilius Glabrio (3) (Cass. Dio 36. 41. 1, with certain emendation). In 64, when *Caesar, in charge of the murder court, encouraged prosecutions of men who had killed the proscribed under *Sulla, Lucceius unsuccessfully prosecuted *Catiline, an ally of Caesar. In 63 he supported Cicero. In 60 he joined Caesar in a joint consular canvass, providing the money on behalf of both; but he was defeated when the *optimates outbid him on behalf of M. *Calpurnius Bibulus (Suet. *Iul.* 19. 1). In the 50s he embarked on a contemporary history starting with the *Social War (3), and Cicero asked him to glorify his exploits in a special monograph (Cic. *Fam.* 5. 12). In 49 he was one of Pompey's trusted advisers, but was pardoned after *Pharsalus. In 45 he wrote to Cicero on *Tullia (2)'s death. We do not hear of him after this. E. B.

Luceria (mod. Lucera), a town on the borders of *Samnium and *Apulia. It is not certainly recorded until 315/4 BC, when it was a Samnite-controlled stronghold, which the Romans captured and made into a Latin colony (see IUS LATII; LATINI). Augustus probably established a colony there, and there is an amphitheatre dating to his reign. Luceria maintained its importance into the Middle Ages, when a great castle was built.

L. J. F. Keppie, *Colonisation and Veteran Settlement in Italy* (1983), 164 ff.; M. Mazzei, *La Daunia antica* (1984). E. T. S.; T. W. P.

Lucian (Λουκιανός), of *Samosata (b. *c*. AD 120), accomplished belletrist and wit in the context of the *Second Sophistic. The details of his life are extremely sketchy, and his own presentations of his biography are literary and therefore suspect. His native language was not Greek but probably *Aramaic; but he practised in the courts, then as an itinerant lecturer on literary-philosophical themes as far afield as Gaul. He presents a '*conversion' to philosophy around the age of 40, and his natural milieu is Athens. He was known to *Galen for a successful literary fraud. We find him late in life in a minor administrative post in Roman *Egypt; he survived the emperor Marcus *Aurelius.

Works Lucian's work is difficult both to categorize and to assign to any sort of literary 'development'. Throughout he is a master of sensibly flexible Atticism (see ASIANISM AND ATTICISM). His *œuvre* runs to some 80 pieces, most of which are genuine. While some can be classified under traditional rhetorical headings such as μελέται ('exercises') and προλαλιαί ('preambles'), the most characteristic products of his repertoire are literary dialogues which fuse Old Comic (see COMEDY (GREEK), OLD) and popular and/or 'literary' philosophy to produce an apparently novel blend of comic prose dialogue. But he is also an accomplished miniaturist, essayist, and raconteur: the Ἐνάλιοι διάλογοι ('*Dialogues of the Sea-Gods') are particularly successful in exploiting the art of prose paraphrase of verse classics from *Homer to *Theocritus; the Πῶς δεῖ· ἱστορίαν συγγράφειν ('How to Write History') gives a wittily commonsensical rather than commonplace treatment of a topical subject; while the Φιλοψευδεῖς ('Lovers of Lies') successfully combines satire of superstition with racy novella. When he chooses he can be a lively and revealing commentator on his cultural and religious environment as when he attacks successful sophists, or figures such as Peregrinus or the oraclemonger *Alexander (13) whom he sees as charlatans. In the Ἀληθῆ διηγήματα ('True Histories') he produced a masterpiece of Munchausenesque parody. His literary personality is engaging but elusive: he is cultivated but cynical, perhaps with a chip on his shoulder, but difficult to excel in his chosen field of versatile prose entertainment. His weakest moments to contemporary taste are perhaps as a repetitive and superficial moralist, his most successful when he plays with the full range of Classical Greek literature in a characteristically amusing way.

ANCIENT SOURCES Suda; Eunap. VS pref. 9; Phot. Bibl. cod. 128. For the new Galen testimony, G. Strohmaier, Philol. 1976.

TEXT M. D. Macleod, 1–4 (OCT, 1972–87).

TRANSLATION A. M. Harmon and others, 8 vols. (Loeb, 1921–67).

SCHOLIA H. Rabe (1906).

STUDIES J. Bompaire, Lucien, écrivain (1958); G. Anderson, Lucian: Theme and Variation in the Second Sophistic (1976); J. Hall, Lucian's Satire (1981); C. P. Jones, Culture and Society in Lucian (1986); R. Bracht Branham, Unruly Eloquence: Lucian and the Comedy of Traditions (1989).
W. M. E.; R. B.; G. A.

Lucilius (1), **Gaius,** Roman satirist, born probably in 180 BC at *Suessa Aurunca on the northern edge of *Campania, died in *Neapolis (Naples) 102 / 1 BC. His family was of senatorial status, a brother probably a senator, but Lucilius remained a knight (eques; see EQUITES), a landowner with large estates who never sought political power himself. It is likely that Lucilius visited Greece. He saw service under P. *Cornelius Scipio Aemilianus at the siege of *Numantia in 134 / 3, continued to enjoy the close friendship of Scipio and his companion C. *Laelius (2) until the end of their lives (see SCIPIONIC CIRCLE), and attacked their enemies. He had other eminent friends in Rome such as *Iunius Congus and *Rutilius Rufus.

Works The extant fragments of Lucilius consist of some 1,400 lines, either isolated verses or small groups. They fall into two main collections, the first chronologically books 26–30 and the second books 1–21. In the first Lucilius used metres found in the saturae of Ennius: the dramatic septenarius (bks. 26–7), a mixture of dramatic metres and hexameters (bks. 28–9). In book 30 he accepted the hexameter alone as the appropriate metre for satire and retained it for the whole of the later collection. References in the poems to historical events seem to confirm that the books in both collections are in chronological order. There are in addition fragments in elegiac couplets in books 22–5, probably epigrams and epitaphs. But in spite of the severe difficulties in the interpretation of poems in a problematical transmission, Lucilius appears as a powerful personality and a major writer.

As a personal poet following *Archilochus, Lucilius attacked enemies by name and described without inhibition his own amatory exploits. In an epistolary poem he reproached a friend for having failed to visit him when he was ill. By recounting such mundane personal experiences he resembles *Catullus (1), but sometimes, when appropriate, he used a persona. His account of a journey to Sicily (bk. 3) suggests a genuine travelogue. Lucilius vilified reprobate consulars such as L. *Opimius and C. *Papirius Carbo (1), also undisciplined tribes and dishonest political lobbying. In denouncing gluttony and extravagance he shows a censorial aptitude for popular moralizing. His definition of virtus ('excellence') proposes a Roman aristocratic ideal with Stoic undertones (see STOICISM). He had philospher friends in Athens but parodied Stoic terminology. Praised by the elder *Pliny (1) for his critical faculty, he wrote on principles of literary criticism and linguistic usage. Particularly noteworthy are Lucilius' own literary intentions, a polemic against *tragedy, and his defence of personal attacks (parts of bks. 26 and 30), the 'Council of the Gods' (bk. 1) on the chequered career of Cornelius Lentulus Lupus, princeps senatus (d. c.125), and the parody of the trial of the Stoic Q. *Mucius Scaevola (1) accused of provincial extortion by the Epicurean T. *Albucius (bk. 2), in which conflicting styles of rhetoric were ridiculed. Lucilius' style is conversational with some unbridled obscenity. He uses many Greek words including technical terms, and sometimes shows calculated elaboration and striking imagery.

At the end of the republic Lucilius was judged to be a writer of cultivated urbanity with characteristic Roman humour but formidable in his vituperation. *Horace discusses him in relation to his own writings: his predecessor's attack on named individuals and his improvisatory manner (Sat. 1. 4), his crude use of Greek words and unrefined style (Sat. 1. 10), and his autobiographical reflections and political invective (Sat. 2. 1). Towards the end of the 1st cent. AD there was a short-lived enthusiasm for Lucilius, in which many preferred him to Horace. Viewed by the satirists *Persius and *Juvenal as the archetypal master of the genre, Lucilius had put a stamp on verse satire which it has retained until the 20th cent. See INVECTIVE; SATIRE.

FRAGMENTS F. Marx, C. Lucilii Carminum Reliquiae (1904–5), text and comm.; E. H. Warmington, Remains of Old Latin 3 (Loeb, 1938), text and trans.; W. Krenkel, Lucilius Satiren (1970), text, Ger. trans., and notes (see F. R. D. Goodyear, CR 1975, 206–9).

STUDIES A. E. Housman, 'Luciliana', Classical Papers 2 (1972); C. Cichorius, Untersuchungen zu Lucilius (1908); I. Mariotti, Studi Luciliani (1960)—useful on Greek words and colloquial language; N. Rudd, Themes in Roman Satire (1986); M. Coffey, Roman Satire, 2nd edn. (1989); E. Gruen, Culture and National Identity in Republican Rome (1992), ch. 7.
M. Co.

Lucilius (2) **(Iunior), Gaius,** friend of L. *Annaeus Seneca (2) (the younger Seneca) and the recipient of the De providentia, Quaestiones naturales, and Epistulae morales; was born in *Campania, perhaps at *Pompeii or Naples (*Neapolis) (Sen. Ep. 49. 1, 53. 1, 70. 1), without wealth or prospects (QNat. 4. pref. 14–15; Ep. 19. 5). He was some years younger than Seneca (Ep. 26. 7). Talent, literary style, and distinguished connections brought him into prominence (Ep. 19. 3). His own energy made him an eques Romanus (Ep. 44. 2; see EQUITES). He was loyal to the memory and to friends or relatives of Cn. *Cornelius Lentulus Gaetulicus after the latter's execution under *Gaius (1), and to victims of *Valeria Messalina or *Narcissus (2) under *Claudius (QNat. 4. pref. 15). Under Claudius and *Nero he held procuratorships (see PROCURATOR) in Alpes Graiae (see ALPS), *Epirus or *Macedonia, Africa (see AFRICA, ROMAN), and *Sicily (Ep. 31. 9, 45. 2, 79. 1; QNat. 4. pref. 1). The date of his death is unknown.

Seneca uses Lucilius as a sounding-board for the philosophical progression of the Epistles. Many of them start from some question Lucilius has supposedly put—generally philosophical, but sometimes literary, linguistic, or social (*Ep.* 9, 29, 39, 43, 71, 72, 106, 108, 109, 111, 113, 114, 117). In spite of business (*Ep.* 17, 19, 22, 24), travel (*Ep.* 69, 84, 104), ill health (*Ep.* 78, 96), and a tendency to grumble (*Ep.* 21, 28, 44, 45, 60, 96, 103), he is depicted as a philosopher, perhaps an ex-Epicurean Stoic (see EPICURUS; STOICISM). On one occasion Seneca says to him 'meum opus es', 'you are my work' (*Ep.* 34. 2), which may also be read as testimony to Seneca's (re-) construction of his friend into the ideal philosophical neophyte and didactic addressee (cf. Griffin (see bibliog. below), 347–53). Seneca also warmly praises Lucilius' own philosophical work (*Ep.* 46).

Lucilius was also a poet (*QNat.* 4. pref. 14 and ch. 2. 2). Four Latin lines (two iambics and two hexameters) are preserved by Seneca (*Ep.* 8. 10, 24. 21; *QNat.* 3. 1. 1). It is unlikely that he is the same as the *Lucillius of the Greek Anthology; but one Greek epigram of twelve lines (*IG* 14. 889 = *Epigr. Gr.* 810) inscribed on stone in Sinuessa with the genitive heading *Iounioros* may well be his. From the passage Sen. *Ep.* 79. 5–7 Wernsdorf and others have attributed the pseudo-Virgilian *Aetna to Lucilius; but the wording suggests a poem including a description of Aetna rather than one devoted to Aetna *per se.*

> Preface to Seneca, *QNat.* 4 and the *Epistulae morales, passim* (esp. 19, 31, 79); J. Delatte, *LEC* 1935, 367 ff., 546 ff.; J. H. Waszink, *Mnemos.* 1949, 224 ff. (supporting the attribution of the *Aetna*); *PIR*² L 388; H. G. Pflaum, *Les Carrières procuratoriennes équestres sous le Haut-Empire romain*, 3 vols. (1960–1), 1, no. 30, p. 70, and 3, pp. 961–2; M. Griffin, *Seneca* (1976), 91, 347–53.   A. M. D.; P. G. F., D. P. F.

Lucilla See ANNIA AURELIA GALERIA LUCILLA.

Lucillius, Greek epigrammatist under *Nero, author of more than 100 satirical epigrams in the Greek *Anthology. Many are jokes about physical types (thin people) or professions (doctors); others are inspired by the world of the Greek *festivals, clever parodies of inscriptions celebrating the victories of athletes (see ATHLETICS); one inspired by a robber burned alive in the amphitheatre (*Anth. Pal.* 11. 184). His work strongly influenced *Martial, not least in its perfection of pointed climax.

> F. J. Brecht, *Motiv- und Typengeschichte des griechischen Spottepigrams* (1930); O. Weinreich, *Epigramm und Pantomimus, Sitz. Heidelberg.* (1948), 82–90; L. Robert, *L'Épigramme grecque*, Entretiens Hardt 14 (1968), 181–295, and *CRAcad. Inscr.* 1968, 280–8 = *OMS* 5. 552 ff. and 6. 317 ff.; W. Burnikel, *Untersuchungen zur Struktur des Witzepigramms bei Lukillios und Martial* (1980).   A. D. E. C.

Lucius Caesar See IULIUS CAESAR (4), L.

Lucretia (*RE* 38), wife of L. *Tarquinius Collatinus, was raped by Sextus, the son of *Tarquinius Superbus; her subsequent suicide because of her dishonour was the catalyst for the expulsion of the Tarquins by L. *Iunius Brutus. The legend, probably originally distinct from that of Brutus but already linked with it in Q. *Fabius Pictor, utilizes Greek notions to explain the overthrow of tyranny; but, particularly in Livy, Lucretia becomes a paradigm of the Roman *matrona* (married woman), heroic in her resolute adhesion to the code of female chastity. In reality, however, she is the victim not only of male violence but also of the ideology of a patriarchal society.

> I. Donaldson, *The Rapes of Lucretia* (1982); S. R. Joshd, in A. Richlin (ed.), *Pornography and Representation in Greece and Rome* (1991), 112 ff.; W. Schubert, *Rh. Mus.* 1991, 80 ff.   A. D.

Lucretius (Titus Lucretius Carus), Epicurean poet (see EPICURUS), author of the *De rerum natura (DRN)*, 'On the Nature of Things' (*c.*94–55 or 51 BC ?). We know less about the life of Lucretius than about almost any other Latin poet. His full name is given only in the manuscripts of his work (pun on *Carus*, 1. 730 ?), and nothing is known of his place of birth or social status, though both have been the subject of much speculation. *Jerome's version of the *Chronicle* of *Eusebius puts his birth in 94 BC, and says that he was 44 when he died, but the *Donatus *Life of Virgil* puts his death in 55, on the same day that Virgil assumed the *toga virilis* (6, though there are textual problems), and a note in a 10th-cent. manuscript (H. Usener *Kl. Schr.* (1913), 156, 196–9) says that he was born 27 years before Virgil, i.e. 97 BC. The only secure date is a reference in a letter of *Cicero to his brother (*QFr.* 2. 10(9). 3) written in February 54, where he praises Lucretius' *poemata* as possessing both flashes of genius (*ingenium*) and great artistry (*ars*), that is, as combining the qualities of an inspired and a craftsmanlike poet. This is certainly a reference to *DRN* (an *Empedoclea* by one Sallustius is mentioned more critically in the same context), and although *poemata* could refer to just selections, the easiest hypothesis is that Lucretius' poem was published by this time. The poem has often been thought to be unfinished (there are problems especially in the prologue to book 4): if so, Lucretius may well have been dead by the time of the letter. But textual corruption rather than incompleteness may be responsible for the problems in the text.

Jerome (whose source was *Suetonius) also reports the story (made famous by Tennyson and others) of Lucretius writing *DRN* in brief intervals of sanity after having been driven mad by a love-potion given him by his wife, and eventually committing suicide. If this story is true, it is surprising that it was not used by *Ovid in his defence of the *Ars Amatoria* in *Tristia* 2 or by the Fathers of the Church attacking paganism and Epicureanism: it may be the result of a biographical reading of parts of books 3 and 4, or of confusion with Lucullus (cf. Plut. *Luc.* 43. 2). Nor is there any reason to believe Jerome's statement that Cicero edited *DRN* after its author's death. More biographical details are provided by the so-called 'Borgia Life' found in a British Museum printed book, but this is a Renaissance compilation (Canfora (see bibliog. below), 35–6).

The addressee of the *De rerum natura* (1. 25–43, 136–48; cf. 1. 411, 1052, 2. 143, 182, 5. 8, 93, 164, 867, 1282) is a Memmius, who must be C. *Memmius (2), a prominent politician associated also with Catullus (28. 9). Memmius was praetor in 58, and a candidate for the consulship of 53: but after a complicated electoral pact that went wrong, he was found guilty of corruption in 52 and went into exile in Athens (E. S. Gruen in *Hommages à Marcel Renard* (1969), 2. 311–21; G. V. Sumner, *Harv. Stud.* 1982, 133–9). In the summer of 51, Cicero wrote to him on behalf of the Epicurean group in Athens, asking him not to demolish what was left of Epicurus' house (*Fam.* 13. 1. 3–4), and suggesting that Memmius was not on good terms with the Epicureans. It is not impossible that he had been annoyed by the dedication of *DRN*: despite its warm praise of him in the prologue, the poem is orthodox in its Epicurean condemnation of political life (3. 59–84, 995–1002, 5. 117–35). But in any case, *DRN* does not imply that Memmius was a convinced Epicurean (cf. 1. 102–3). There can be no clear distinction between Memmius as the didactic addressee and a more generalized second-person, but Memmius' public persona was relevant: *DRN* is not unpolitical (D. Minyard, *Lucretius and the Late Republic* (1985); D. P. Fowler, in M. Griffin and J. Barnes (eds.), *Philosophia Togata* (1989), 120–50).

The poem is in six books of hexameter verse (*c.*7,400 lines, about three-quarters the size of the *Aeneid*) and whether or not it failed to receive the final corrections of its author is substantially complete: it opens with an elaborate prologue, and the prologue to book 6 states explicitly that this is the final book (6. 92–5). The ending is abrupt, and textually corrupt: it is likely that 1247–51 are the actual concluding lines, and should be transposed after 1286, but if this is done, the ending contains a number of closural features, most notably a recall of the end of the funeral of Hector at the end of the *Iliad* (cf. P. G. Fowler, in F. Dunn, D. P. Fowler, and D. Roberts, *Classical Closure* (forthcoming)). The ending on the plague at Athens and the many deaths it caused is in stark contrast to the opening description of the first day of spring and the appeal for help to Venus, but the polarity can be made to have point. The recurrent pattern of the cycle of coming-to-be and passing-away makes a final appearance, while the fixed temporal and spatial location in Athens, which represents the peak of civilization according to the opening of book 6, indicates the inevitable failure of the city-state to provide for the ultimate happiness of human beings.

As well as the great initial prologue to book 1, each of the other books also has a prologue, and the concluding section of each book in some way stands apart from the rest of the book (see especially the attack on love in book 4, and the final plague!). Each book is a unity in terms both of structure and subject-matter. Book 1 deals with the basic metaphysical and physical premises of Epicureanism, beginning with the proposition that nothing comes to be out of nothing, and concluding with a description of the collapse of our world, which is presented as a counterfactual consequence of the belief that all elements tend towards the centre of the earth but which anticipates the Epicurean accounts of the death of our world at the end of book 2 and in book 5. Book 2 deals with the motion and shape of the atoms, and how these are relevant to the relationship between primary and secondary qualities: it concludes with the important Epicurean doctrine of the infinite number of worlds in the universe, and the connected proposition that our world has both a birth and a death (recalling the end of book 1). Book 3 gives an account of the nature of the human soul, and argues both that it is mortal and that, because of this, death is not to be feared. Book 4 discusses a variety of psychological phenomena, especially perception, and argues against scepticism: as remarked above, it concludes with an attack on love, seen as a mental delusion. Book 5 argues for the mortality of our world, and then gives a rationalist and anti-providentialist account of its creation and early history, concluding with the section on the development of human civilization, which is perhaps the most famous part of the poem. Book 6 then proceeds to account for those phenomena of our world which are most likely to lead to false belief in the gods—thunder and lightning, earthquakes, volcanoes, etc.—and ends with the aetiology of disease and the plague at Athens.

This clearly defined book-structure is more typical of prose philosophical treatises than of hexameter poetry, and it is replicated at levels both above and below that of the individual book. The books form three pairs, in which books 1 and 2 deal with atomic phenomena up to the level of the compound (see ATOMISM), books 3 and 4 deal with human beings, and books 5 and 6 deal with the world: there is thus a clear sense of expanding horizons, as we move from the atomic to the macroscopic level. The twin targets of the work as a whole are fear of the gods and of death (1. 62–135; cf. Epicurus, *RS* 1–2, *Ep. Men.* 133): the first and last pairs deal more with the former fear, by explaining phenomena that would otherwise be felt to require divine inter-

vention in the world, while the central books, and especially book 3, tackle the fear of death head on. But the two motives are intermingled throughout the work. The six books may also be organized into two halves, with books 1–3 dealing with basic premises, books 4–6 with what follows from those basic premisses: the problematic prologue to book 4 (repeated almost verbatim from 1. 921–50), with its stress on Lucretius' role as a poet and philosopher and its Callimachean imagery (see CALLIMACHUS (3)), thus functions as a 'proem in the middle' for the second half (cf. G. B. Conte *YClS* 1992, 147–59). The existence of more than one possible structural analysis in this way is typical of *DRN* as a whole (contrast 3. 31–40 with 5. 55–63).

Below the level of the book, the subject-matter is carefully delineated and individual propositions within sections signposted with markers like *Principio*, 'First', *Deinde*, 'Next', and *Postremo*, 'Finally': the verse, in contrast to both the epic verse-paragraph and the neoteric focus on the single line, tends to group itself into blocks of two or more verses, with careful arrangement of words within the block. This division of the text corresponds to the Epicurean stress on the intelligibility of phenomena: everything has a *ratio* or systematic explanation, the world can be analysed and understood. If we are to believe Cicero, however, this is in marked contrast to the formlessness of earlier Epicurean writing in Latin (*Amafinius and Rabirius: cf. Cic. *Acad. post.* 5 with Reid's comm., and esp. *Fin.* 1. 22, 29, 2. 30, 3. 40).

Every major proposition in *DRN* can be paralleled in other Epicurean sources, and it is likely that the majority at least of the arguments for these propositions also existed in the Epicurean tradition. We do not know, however, to what extent the poem had a single main source, and if so, what that source was. The title (cf. 1. 25) recalls that of Epicurus' major treatise, the *Peri physeōs* or 'On Nature', but the structure of that work as we know it from papyrus fragments is not very similar to that of *DRN*, and that presumably also goes for any (lost) epitome. There is a much closer correspondence, however, with the extant *Letter to Herodotus* of Epicurus, passages of which are closely translated (e.g. 1. 159–60 = *Ep. Hdt.* 38), although *DRN* is longer and the order of topics is sometimes changed (e.g. in *Ep. Hdt.* 42–3 Epicurus treats atomic shape before atomic motion (see ATOMISM), while *DRN* reverses the order, 2. 62–729). One plausible hypothesis is that the *Letter to Herodotus* provided the basic core of the poem, but this was expanded from a variety of other sources (cf. also D. Clay, *Lucretius and Epicurus* (1983)). Other prose philosophical and scientific sources are also drawn on (e.g. Plato's *Timaeus*, P. De Lacy in *Syzetesis: Studi Gigante* (1983), 291–307, and the Hippocratic corpus (see HIPPOCRATES (2)), C. Segal, *CPhil.* 1970, 180–2) though we can never be certain that some of this had not already been assimilated into the atomist tradition (cf. F. Solmsen, *AJPhil.* 1953, 34–51). The final part of book 3 in particular (cf. also the prologues to 2 and 3 and the end of 4) contains material from the so-called 'diatribe' tradition of practical philosophical rhetoric (cf. B. P. Wallach, *Lucretius and the Diatribe against the Fear of Death: De Rerum Natura III 830–1094* (1970); T. Stork, *Nil igitur est ad nos* (1970); G. B. Conte, *Genres and Readers* (1994)).

But *DRN* also draws on a wide range of literary texts in both Greek (e.g. *Sappho fr. 31 LP in *DRN* 3. 152–8, *Aeschylus fr. 44 Nauck in *DRN* 1. 250–61, *Euripides fr. 839 Nauck in *DRN* 2. 991–1003, Callimachus fr. 260. 41 Pf. in *DRN* 6. 753, *Antipater (3) of Sidon, *Anth. Pal.* 7. 713 in *DRN* 4. 181–2, and especially *Thucydides (2)'s account of the plague at Athens in 2. 47–53 at the end of *DRN* bk. 6) and Latin (e.g. *Ennius, cf. 1. 117–26, O. Gigon, in

Lucretius Afella, Quintus

Lucrèce, Entretiens Hardt 24 (1978), 167–96, Pacuvius, e.g. *Chryses* fr. 86–92 Ribbeck with 5. 318–23). The main model is the lost philosophical didactic poem of *Empedocles, the *Peri physeōs* or 'On Nature' (cf. W. Kranz, *Philol.* 1943, 68–107; M. Gale, *Myth and Poetry in Lucretius* (1994), 59–75): Empedocles' doctrine is criticized (1. 705–829), but he is praised as a poet especially for his stance as a 'master of truth' offering an important secret to his audience, in contrast to the stress on form in Hellenistic *didactic poetry (*Aratus (1), *Nicander, etc.). Lucretius too writes to save humanity (cf. 6. 24–34 on Epicurus): although the work concentrates on physics and natural philosophy, this ethical purpose is clear throughout (cf. e.g. 2. 1–61, 3. 59–93, 5. 43–54). Epicurus was opposed to poetry as a serious medium of enlightenment, and the Epicurean stress on clarity and simplicity of language and 'sober reasoning' in thought creates problems for an Epicurean didactic poem: by returning to the archaic models of Empedocles and *Parmenides, Lucretius was able to place himself in a tradition which made the alliance of philosophy and poetry more natural (though Empedocles' status as a poet had itself been called into question by *Aristotle, *Poet.* 1447^b 17 ff.). Many of the resources of poetry, particularly the recall to the phenomenal world implicit in the use of metaphor and simile, can easily be made consonant with the needs of Epicureanism: poet and philosopher alike must make the reader *see* (cf. 2. 112–41, A. Schiesaro, *Simulacrum et Imago* (1990)). The effect is a recontextualization of both the traditional devices of poetry and the basic elements of Epicurean epistemology, particularly the 'first image' (*Ep. Hdt.* 38) or prolepsis associated with each word, the basis for live *metaphor (cf. D. Sedley, *Cron. Erc.* 1973, 5–83). The complexity and precision of Lucretius' imagery, always a central part of his claim to poetic excellence (D. West, *The Imagery and Poetry of Lucretius* (1969)), is thus also an aspect of his role as philosopher and scientist.

Nevertheless, the old conception of a conflict between Lucretius the poet and Lucretius the philosopher was not perhaps wholly wrong. The *De rerum natura* became an immensely important text in the Renaissance and modern periods because of its rationalism: when Abraham Cowley celebrated Bacon's victory over 'Authority' and superstition in his ode *To the Royal Society*, it was to Lucretius' image of Epicurus triumphing over *religio* to which he naturally turned (1. 62–79). Similarly, through Pufendorf, Hobbes, and Rousseau (cf. C. Kahn, in G. B. Kerferd (ed.), *The Sophists and their Legacy* (1981), 92–108), the account of the development of civilization in book 5 of *DRN*, and in particular the notion of the 'social contract', enabled historians and philosophers to free themselves from theist models of the foundations of human society. But that very stress on scientific rationalism as providing a single sure and certain (cf. *DRN* 6. 24–34, 4. 507–21) answer to the troubles of life has come under suspicion in the post-modern age. Lucretius the poet offers perhaps more ways of looking at the world than can be accommodated with comfort within the plain and simple truth of Epicureanism. Of necessity, his rationalism has its own sustaining myths, from the clear light of reason which pierces and disperses the clouds of ignorance (2. 55–61, 3. 14–17) to the secure citadel of the wise (2. 7–13), from the nurturing female powers of *Venus, Mother Earth, and Nature (cf. 2. 589–660) to the hellish shadows of 'normal' life (3. 59–86). Nevertheless, those myths in themselves continue to offer a powerful vision of a world by no means providentially ordered for humanity, but in which all humans can find happiness.

LIFE L. Canfora, *Vita di Lucrezio* (1993).

TEXT AND TRANSLATION W. H. D. Rouse, rev. M. F. Smith (Loeb, 1975), with trans. and notes; C. Bailey (1922); K. Müller (1975). There is a bibliography of editions by C. Gordon, 2nd edn. (1985).

COMMENTARIES Complete, in English: H. A. J. Munro, 4th edn. (1886), with text and translation; W. A. Merrill (1907); W. E. Leonard and S. B. S. Smith (1942); C. Bailey (1947), with text and translation; in other languages: C. Giussani (Italian, 1896–8); A. Ernout and L. Robin (French, 1925–8), without a text; and note the Latin commentaries of G. Wakefield (1796–7) and K. Lachmann (1850). Separate editions, in English: Bk. 1, P. M. Brown (1985); Bk. 3, E. J. Kenney (1971); Bk. 4, J. Godwin (1986); see also the comm. on the end by R. Brown (1987); Bk. 5, C. D. N. Costa (1984); Bk. 6, J. Godwin (1992); in German: Bk. 3, R. Heinze (1897).

STUDIES E. J. Kenney, *Lucretius*, *G&R* New Survey 11 (1977), introductory; J. Masson, *Lucretius: Epicurean and Poet*, 2 vols. (1907–9); D. West, *The Imagery and Poetry of Lucretius* (1969); D. Clay, *Lucretius and Epicurus* (1983); E. Asmis, *Epicurus' Scientific Method* (1984); C. Segal, *Lucretius on Death and Anxiety* (1990); M. Gale, *Myth and Poetry in Lucretius* (1994); M. Nussbaum, *The Therapy of Desire* (1994), esp. 140–279; P. Boyancé, *Lucrèce et l'Épicurisme* (1963); P. H. Schrijvers, *Horror ac Divina Voluptas: Études sur la poétique et la poésie de Lucrèce* (1970); A. Schiesaro, *Simulacrum et Imago* (1990).

COLLECTED ARTICLES D. R. Dudley (ed.), *Lucretius* (1965); *Lucrèce*, Entretiens Hardt 24 (1978); C. J. Classen (ed.), *Probleme der Lukrezforschung* (1986).

BIBLIOGRAPHY A. Dalzell *CW* 1972–3, 389–427, and 1973–4), 65–112 (for 1945–72); C. Di Giovine in *Syzetesis: Studi Gigante* (1983), 649–77.

RECEPTION G. D. Hadzits, *Lucretius and his Influence* (1935); W. Schmid, *A & A* 1946, 193–219. P. G. F., D. P. F.

Lucretius (*RE* 25) **Afella, Quintus,** a popular orator and Marian leader, joined *Sulla, captured *Praeneste for him and sent him the head of C. *Marius (2). Persisting, against Sulla's orders, on standing for the consulate (of 81 BC ?), he was cut down at Sulla's command. Appian reports (falsely, it seems) that he had held no previous magistracies.

Sumner, *Orators* 106 f. Greek sources call him 'Ophellas', presumably by contamination with the Hellenistic *condottiere* by that name. E. B.

Lucretius (*RE* 30) **Tricipitinus, Spurius,** the shadowy father of *Lucretia, was credited with a walk-on role in the overthrow of the monarchy. Historians regularized the election of the first *consuls by supposing that Lucretius presided over them as prefect of the city (Livy 1. 59. 12, etc.) or *interrex* (Dion. Hal. *Ant. Rom.* 4. 76. 1, etc.). Lucretius' own brief suffect consulship in 509 BC was not recorded in 'some old authorities' (Livy 2. 8. 5) and must be fictitious, as probably is Lucretius himself. A. D.

Lucrinus Lacus, coastal lagoon between *Puteoli and *Baiae, site of a famous fishery (especially of oysters; see FISHING) and many opulent late republican *villas; it was involved in the harbour-works of Agrippa in nearby Lake *Avernus. The upheaving of Monte Nuovo in 1538 greatly reduced its size.

J. H. D'Arms, *Romans on the Bay of Naples* (1970). N. P.

Lucus Feroniae, a town in the *Tiber valley north of Rome, which grew up around the sanctuary of the Italic rural goddess, *Feronia. Although it became a *colonia* (?after *Actium), it never received a planned street-grid. The forum, a temple, baths, and an amphitheatre are known, as is the nearby villa of the Volusii (L. Volusius Saturninus was consul in 12 BC, and patron of the colony).

Hor. *Sat.* 1. 5. 24–6. M. Moretti and A. M. Sgubini Moretti, *La villa dei Volusii a Lucus Feroniae* (1977), and *I Volusii Saturnini* (1982); L. J. F. Keppie, *Colonisation and Veteran Settlement in Italy* (1983), 168 ff.

E. T. S.; T. W. P.

ludi (including **ludi scaenici**) (games) The chief uses of this word relate to diverse fields of Roman culture.

(1) Religious *festivals came to include formalized competitions and displays as a regular component, counting as religious rites just as much as sacrifices and processions. The numbers of days devoted to *ludi* in Rome increased over time: 57 in the late republic; 77 in the early 1st cent. AD; 177 in the mid-4th cent. AD. There were three types of *ludi*. First, *ludi circenses*, which consisted of chariot-racing, held in the circus in the *Campus Martius and eventually in the Circus Maximus (which could seat 150,000 people), see CIRCUS. Dion. Hal. *Ant. Rom.* 7. 70–3 is the fullest account of the prior procession. Secondly, *ludi scaenici*, originating in 364 BC as *pantomime dances to flute, later including plays, first at the Ludi Romani of 240 BC (see LIVIUS ANDRONICUS, L.); in 200 *Plautus' *Stichus* was produced at the Ludi Plebeii; in 191 the scaenic Ludi Megalenses were instituted; in 169 *Ennius' *Thyestes* was performed at the Ludi Apollinares, instituted in 208 BC; in 160 *Terence's *Adelphoe* was performed at the funeral games of L. Aemilius Paullus (2). Under the empire performances chiefly consisted of *mime and pantomime. The cost was usually shared between state and presiding magistrate. Admission was free, with special seats designated for senators and others; women and slaves were admitted, but sat separately, at least from *Augustus onwards. Plays were staged, initially in temporary settings associated with particular sanctuaries (by the temple of *Apollo in the Prata Flaminia; on the *Palatine next to the temple of Magna Mater; see CYBELE) and from the mid-1st cent BC onwards in permanent theatres (which became increasingly common throughout the empire). Augustus' *Secular Games included both the 'archaic' games 'on a stage without a theatre and without seats', and more 'modern' games (in a purpose-built wooden theatre and in *Pompey's theatre). Thirdly, fights involving *gladiators and *venationes, which under the republic were given under private auspices. These were staged in the republic in the Forum and elsewhere, but from 29 BC in the amphitheatre of T. *Statilius Taurus and from AD 80 in the *Colosseum (which could seat 50,000, with standing-room for another 5,000). Outside Rome, specialist amphitheatres were built and, in the Greek world, existing theatres adapted for the safety of the spectators. See AMPHITHEATRES; COLOSSEUM; THEATRES, STRUCTURE.

(2) Formal and informal games, of which the Romans had at least as many varieties as the moderns, retaining the practice of some of them even in mature years; the Campus Martius contained a 'multitude of those exercising themselves with ball and hoop and wrestling' (Strabo 5. 236). *Ludi*, part sport, part premilitary drill, entered into the routine of the formal associations of young men (see IUVENES), an allegedly ancient institution revived by Augustus; they included the Lusus Troiae (Verg. *Aen.* 5. 545–603; E. Norden, *Aus altrömischen Priesterbüchern* (1939), 188–90). Informal games are attested by numerous archaeological finds of toys, dice, tablets, etc., and also by 'gaming-boards' incised in ancient pavements. Some Christian writers from the late 2nd cent. AD onwards criticized both the *ludi* at festivals, because of their association with the worship of traditional gods, and also games of chance, which could lead to grave abuses (see BALL GAMES; DICING; TOYS).

(3) Schools of instruction, also training-schools for gladiators; there were four training-schools in Rome (including *Ludus Magnus* and *Ludus Matutinus*) which served for the practice of gladiators who were to perform in the Colosseum. Grammatical and literary instruction, originally in the hands of Greeks, was domesticated by the time of the empire; training for public life (law, politics) was acquired through apprenticeship until the schools of rhetoric replaced the old tradition (Quintilian; Tac. *Dial.*). Accommodation for teachers of grammar and rhetoric was generally ad hoc, at street corners, in rooms off porticoes, in private houses and in rented rooms. See EDUCATION, ROMAN.

Wissowa, *RK* 449–67; P. Habel, *RE* Suppl. 5. 608–30; A. Piganiol, *Recherches sur les jeux romains* (1923); A. Ferrua, *Epigraphica* 1946, 53–73; J. P. V. D. Balsdon, *Life and Leisure in Ancient Rome* (1969), 244–339; E. Rawson, *PBSR* 1985; W. Weismann, *Kirche und Schauspiele* (1972), on Christian attitudes. *Ludus Magnus*: Nash, *Pict. Dict. Rome* 2. 24–6; Richardson, *Topog. Dict. Ancient Rome*. 236–8; S. F. Bonner, *Education in Ancient Rome* (1977), 115–25.   A. W. van B., W. B.; S. R. F. P.

Lugdunum (1) *Colonia Copia Claudia Augusta Lugdunum* (mod. Lyon), founded in 43 BC by L. *Munatius Plancus, and to the mid-3rd cent. the metropolis of the north-west of the Roman empire. Its position led to its becoming: the nodal point of M. *Vipsanius Agrippa's Gallic road system; the capital of the province of Lugdunensis (see GAUL (TRANSALPINE)); the religious, administrative, financial, and commercial centre of the Three Gauls and the Germanies; and the residence and birthplace of emperors. It even accommodated a branch of the imperial mint, protected by a *cohors urbana* (see COHORTES URBANAE). The city's large and cosmopolitan population worshipped many deities, including those brought from the east. A Christian community (see CHRISTIANITY) developed early, and in 177 suffered savage and peculiarly well-documented persecution (Euseb. *Hist. Eccl.* 5. 1). Lugdunum declined from c.250, as imperial attention was directed increasingly to the Rhine frontier, and its primacy was usurped by *Augusta Treverorum (Trier). However, in the 4th and early 5th cents. it remained capital of Lugdunensis Prima, the resort of powerful aristocratic families (*Sidonius Apollinaris was probably born here), and the seat of an important bishopric. It became the centre of the *Burgundian kingdom c.461.

Early Roman Lyon occupied the heights of Fourvière, west of the confluence of the Rhône and Saône. At the confluence itself (Gallic *Condate), Drusus (see CLAUDIUS DRUSUS, NERO) established in 12 BC the altar of Rome and Augustus, at which aristocratic representatives of all the Gallic peoples (meeting as the 'Concilium Galliarum') came annually to demonstrate allegiance to Rome. Only a fragment of their amphitheatre survives, though numerous inscriptions have been found. On an island off *Condate developed the city's main shipping and commercial quarter. On Fourvière, the most notable monuments are the theatre and odeum, but the four aqueducts, involving extensive use of syphons, are especially interesting, while the museum contains the bronze tablets of *Claudius' speech on the admission of Gauls to the senate. It was probably neglect of the aqueducts which forced later Roman and medieval Lyon downhill, to a site between Fourvière and the modern Saône.

A. Kleinclausz, *Histoire de Lyon* (1939); P. Wuilleumier, *Lyon, métropole* (1953); A. Audin, *Essai sur la topographie de Lyon* (1956), and *Lyon, miroir . . .*, 2nd edn. (1979); J. F. Drinkwater, *Britannia* 1975, 133 ff.

(2) Lugdunum Convenarum (mod. St Bertrand-de-Comminges), a town in *Aquitania to which *Herod (2) Antipas was banished in AD 40. In 72 BC a hill-fort on the site of the *haute-ville* became the nucleus of *Pompey's resettlement of assorted survivors of the Sertorian Wars (see Q. SERTORIUS), whence the quasi-tribal name of Convenae (Strabo 4. 190). Under the empire a considerable town developed in the plain between the hill and the Garonne. Excavation has uncovered much of its plan,

including forum, temples, baths, theatre, amphitheatre, market, and a 4th-cent. Christian church; extensive use was made of marble from St Béat, 16 km. (10 mi.) to the south. In the later empire the hill was fortified with a wall which largely survives, but the town was sacked by *Vandals in 409 and came under Visigothic control (see GOTHS) in 418. According to *Strabo (4. 191) the Convenae enjoyed *ius Latii; *Ptolemy (4)'s application of colonia to Lugdunum (Geog. 2. 7. 13) may be due to confusion with Lyon.

R. May, St Bertrand-de-Comminges (1985).

(3) A town of the *Batavi, by the mouth of the old Rhine (probably near mod. Katwijk). Its name survives in mod. Leiden.   A. L. F. R.; J. F. Dr.

Luna, Roman moon-goddess. *Varro (Ling. 5. 74) names her among a number of deities introduced by Titus *Tatius and therefore of Sabine origin (see SABINI). The latter statement may be doubted, but the existence of an early cult of Luna remains likely, though Wissowa (RK 315) objects that no trace of it is to be found. This may be mere accident; in historical times she certainly had a cult with a temple on the *Aventine, first mentioned in 182 BC (anniversary on 31 March), but founded between 292 and 219 (Ziolkowski, Temples, 99 f.), and another on the *Palatine, which was illuminated all night long (Varro, Ling. 5. 68; Wissowa, RK 316; cf. C. Koch, Gestirnverehrung im alten Italien (1933), 27; Latte, RR 232; S. Lunais, Recherches sur la lune 1 (1979)).
H. J. R.; J. Sch.

Luna, a Roman colony near the coast of Liguria, on the river Magra, the boundary with Etruria. Founded in 177 BC, it provided a base for expeditions against the *Ligurians; later *Augustus settled further colonists. The city prospered through exploitation of the nearby *Carrara marble quarries (which were imperial property by AD 27), and through export of its great cheeses and celebrated *wine. Laid out largely as a square, the *via Aurelia formed the decumanus (main east–west street). The forum, basilica, theatre, amphitheatre, temples, and town houses have been excavated. The forum was out of use by c. AD 400, but Luna was the seat of a bishopric, and participated in major 7th- and 8th-cent. councils. It was later gradually abandoned.

A. Frova, Scavi di Luna 1–2 (1973–7); L. Lusuardi Siena, Archeologia Medievale 1985, 303 f.   E. T. S.; T. W. P.

Lupercalia, a Roman *festival (15 February), conducted by the association (sodalitas, Cic. Cael. 26; see SODALES) of Luperci (cf. lupus, 'wolf'). It included odd rites (Ov. Fast. 2. 19–36, 267–452; Dion. Hal. Ant. Rom. 1. 32. 3–5 and 80. 1; Plut. Ant. 12, Rom. 21, Iul. 61): goats and a dog were sacrificed at the Lupercal (a cave at the foot of the *Palatine where a she-wolf reared *Romulus and Remus); the blood was smeared with a knife on the foreheads of two youths (who were obliged to laugh), and wiped with wool dipped in milk; then the Luperci, naked except for girdles from the skin of sacrificial goats, ran (probably) round the Palatine (Varro, Ling. 6. 13, 34) striking bystanders, especially women, with goat-skin thongs (a favourite scene in the iconography of Roman months (R. Amedick, MDAI(R) 1990, 197 ff.)). The rite combined purificatory *lustration and fertility magic, but no interpretation is fully satisfactory. It was at the Lupercalia that Antony (M. *Antonius (2)), consul and Lupercus, offered a royal *diadem to Caesar (44 BC). The festival survived until at least AD 494 when Gelasius I, the bishop of Rome, perhaps banned Christian participation and transformed it into the feast of Purification of the Virgin.

A. K. Michels, TAPA 1953, 35 ff.; A. W. J. Hollemann, Pope Gelasius I and the Lupercalia (1974); C. Ulf, Das römische Lupercalienfest (1982); H. Wrede, MDAI(R) 1983, 185 ff.; T. Köves-Zulauf, Römische Geburtsriten (1990).   J. L.

Lupiae (mod. Lecce), the largest city in the Sallentine peninsula. There was a settlement on the site from the 6th cent. BC but urban development did not take place until the Roman period. There are tombs with Greek and Messapian grave goods (see MESSAPII) from the 4th cent., but most of the urban structures are Augustan or later.

G. Susini, Fonti per la storia greca e romana del Salento (1962).   K. L.

Luscius (RE 1a) **Lanuvinus** (= from Lanuvium), author of fabulae palliatae, elder contemporary and rival of *Terence, who offers a spirited reply to criticisms by Luscius in his prologues. Two titles and two lines survive. He seems (if we can trust Terence) to have favoured close fidelity to Greek originals. See PALLIATA.

Ribbeck, CRF; C. Garton, Personal Aspects of the Roman Theatre (1972); J. Wright, Dancing in Chains (1974).   P. G. M. B.

Lusitania, a Celticized region of western *Iberia (1) whose name derives from the people of the Lusitani, but which was also inhabited by other peoples, including the Vettones and Celtici. The Lusitani were mobilized into a coalition against Rome by *Viriatus and defeated in 139 BC. They were overrun by D. *Iunius Brutus Callaicus in 137, defeated by *Pompey during *Sertorius' revolt in 73–72, and again by *Caesar in 61. The region formed part of Further Spain. In 27 it formed the southern part of the Augustan province of Hispania Lusitania. Following the ceding of Gallaecia and Asturia (see ASTURES) to *Tarraconensis at some time after 9 BC, it comprised the whole province, with the rivers Anas (mod. Guadiana) and Durius (Douro) marking its natural boundaries. The capital was at *Emerita Augusta and the province was subdivided into the conventus of Emerita, Scallabis, and Pax Iulia. It was colonized under Caesar and *Augustus, while *municipia were created under Augustus and *Vespasian. Lusitania was an important source of metals and its fish-sauce was exported widely. It had passed from Roman to barbarian control by AD 411.

A. Tovar, Iberische Landeskunde 2: Lusitanien (1976).   S. J. K.

Lusius Quietus was a Moorish chieftain commanding an independent cavalry unit of Moors which operated outside the usual structure of the auxiliaries. He was dishonourably discharged, probably by *Domitian, for misconduct, but volunteered his services during *Trajan's Dacian Wars (see DACIA) since the emperor needed the help of the Moorish cavalry. Quietus and his men distinguished themselves in battle and the Moors are depicted on a scene from *Trajan's Column. He then accompanied Trajan in the invasion of *Parthia, capturing *Singara in NE *Mesopotamia without a fight. In AD 116 he relentlessly suppressed with great slaughter the revolt of the Jews in Mesopotamia; *Nisibis was recaptured and *Edessa destroyed. Probably during the Parthian War, as a reward for his achievements, he was enrolled in the senate with praetorian rank and later became *suffect *consul (possibly in 117, in absence). He also served as governor of *Judaea. His rapid promotion provoked jealousy and hostility and may have contributed to his downfall (Cass. Dio 68. 32). Quietus was removed from Judaea and deprived of his command of the Moors by *Hadrian, and subsequently executed in 118 along with three other senators of consular rank, supposedly for conspiracy against the emperor.

PIR² L 439.   J. B. C.

lustration (*lustratio*), is the performance (*lustrare*) of *lustrum* (*lustrum facere*), a ceremony of *purification and of averting evil. The main ritual ingredient was a circular procession (*circumambulatio, circumagere*, often repeated three times); hence a derived meaning of *lustrare*, 'to move around something'. The instruments of purification, such as torches and sacrificial animals (in particular the *suovetaurilia*), were carried or led (by attendants specially selected on account of their propitious names, *bona nomina*, Cic. *Div.* 1. 102) round the person(s) or the place to be purified, often to the accompaniment of music, chant, and dance. See SACRIFICE, ROMAN. The victims were sacrificed at the end of the ceremony, and their entrails, *exta*, inspected (Tib. 2. 1. 25–6). We hear of *lustratio* of fields (*Cato (Censorius), *Agr.* 141: *fundi, terrae, agri*; Verg. *G.* 1. 338 ff.; Tib. 2. 1), of the village or *pagus* (conducted by the *magistri pagorum*, see F. Blume and others (eds.), *Gromatici veteres* (2 vols., 1848–52), 1. 164–5) of the Roman territory (*ager Romanus* = *Ambarvalia) and the city (*urbs* = *Amburbium*), and of an army (e.g. Livy 23. 35. 5; Cic. *Att.* 5. 20. 2; also represented on *Trajan's Column, scenes 8, 53, 103) and fleet (App. *BCiv.* 5. 401), always before, not after, a campaign or battle; here also belong the old rites of *Armilustrium and *Tubilustrium. But the most important was *lustratio* (by the *suovetaurilia*, Varro, *Rust.* 2. 1. 10) of the Roman people as the concluding part of the *census (*lustrum condere*, Livy 1. 44. 2), performed on the *Campus Martius by one of the *censors (selected by lot). The deity invoked was primarily *Mars (Cato, and for the census, see the so-called altar of Domitius Ahenobarbus; E. S. Gruen, *Culture and National Identity in Republican Rome* (1992), 145 ff. and pls. 2–3), also *Ceres (*Virgil) and *dii patrii* (*Tibullus). The ceremony excluded evil, and kept the pure within the circle, but it also denoted a new beginning, especially for the Roman people at the census or for an army when a new commander arrived or when two armies were joined together. The etymology (and the exact meaning of *lustrum condere*) is disputed: perhaps connected with *lavare* 'to wash', *luere* 'to wash, cleanse', or *lucere*, 'to shine', hence *lustrare* 'to illuminate' (with fire or torches carried at the procession; for the use of *fire at the Iguvine lustrations, cf. *tabulae Iguvinae* I B 11–13 = VI b 49–51; SEE RELIGION, ITALIC).

R. M. Ogilvie, *JRS* 1961, 31 ff.; H. S. Versnel, *MNIR* 1975, 97 ff., and *Visible Religion* (1985–6), 134 ff.; M. Torelli, *Typology and Structure of Roman Historical Reliefs* (1982); H. Petersmann, *WJA* 1983, 209 ff.; F. Lepper and S. Frere, *Trajan's Column* (1988).   J. L.

Lutatius (*RE* 4) **Catulus, Gaius**, the first of his lineage to achieve the consulship (242 BC), concluded the First *Punic War by boldly confronting a relieving Punic naval force off the Aegates islands, west of Sicily, the modern Egadi islands (10 March 241). A wound forced him to cede direction of the battle to Q. Valerius Falto but he was awarded a *triumph and took a leading role in the peace negotiations.   A. D.

Lutatius (*RE* 7) **Catulus** (1), **Quintus**, of noble, but not recently distinguished, family, half-brother of two Iulii Caesares (L. *Iulius Caesar (1) and C. *Iulius Caesar Strabo Vopiscus), and married first to a Domitia, then to a Servilia, sister of Q. *Servilius Caepio (1); was three times defeated for the consulship before succeeding for 102 BC with the help of C. *Marius (1), married to a Iulia and at the summit of his popularity. It was perhaps to improve his chances that he first extended the traditional funeral procession and eulogy of *nobiles* (see Polyb. 6. 53 f.) to a woman, his mother Popillia (Cic. *De or.* 2. 44). Defeated by the *Cimbri

on the upper Adige, he had to give up the Po valley; but in 101, joined by Marius (who treated him with courtesy) and helped by his legate *Sulla, he shared in the victory of the Vercellae (perhaps near Rovigo, on the lower Po). Marius and he triumphed jointly (101) and he built a portico on the Palatine out of the spoils. When Marius received most of the credit for the victory, Catulus became a bitter enemy of his, drawing his friends away from him. He probably fought under L. Caesar in the *Social War (3), opposed Marius and L. *Cornelius Cinna (1) in 88–87, and after their return was prosecuted by M. *Marius Gratidianus and committed suicide.

A cultured man, interested in philosophy, art, and literature, and a patron of literary men (e.g. A. *Licinius Archias and *Antipater (3)), though not the centre of a literary circle, he was a link between the friends of P. *Cornelius Scipio Aemilianus, whom he knew in his youth, and the generation of *Cicero, who greatly admired him and introduced him as a character in the *De oratore*. He wrote light verse (two epigrams survive) and a (lost) monograph on his German campaign, and he was a competent orator.

ORF[4] 218 ff.; H. Bardon, *La Littérature latine inconnue* (1952), 115 ff.; Badian, *Stud. Gr. Rom. Hist.*, see index; *FLP* 75 ff.   E. B.

Lutatius (*RE* 8) **Catulus** (2), **Quintus**, son of (1) above, escaped from Rome at the return of L. *Cornelius Cinna (1) in 87 BC, but seems to have come back and become aedile. On *Sulla's return he joined him and brought about the cruel death of M. *Marius Gratidianus in revenge for his father's. But he opposed lawless murders by the *Sullani*. Consul in 78, he opposed his colleague M. *Aemilius Lepidus (2), carried a law against violence, and secured Sulla a solemn funeral, at which the power of his veterans was displayed. When Lepidus rebelled, Catulus, as proconsul (77), was chiefly responsible for his defeat. Henceforth he was an acknowledged leader of the *optimates*. He was entrusted with the rebuilding of the Capitoline temple and the *Tabularium (public archive) and dedicated the buildings in 69 with lavish games. (Cf. *ILLRP* 367–8.) During the 70s he defended the Sullan settlement, but finally acknowledged the corruption of senatorial juries and accepted its modification (70). He opposed the laws of A. *Gabinius (2) (67) and C. *Manilius (66)—Pompey had offended him in 77—and in 65, as censor, the attempts of his colleague M. *Licinius Crassus (1) to enfranchise the Transpadanes (see TRANSPADANA) and annex Egypt. In 63 he was ignominiously defeated by Caesar in an election for the chief pontificate (see PONTIFEX). He tried to throw suspicion on Caesar as involved in the conspiracy of *Catiline but failed, and his *auctoritas* now declined: in 61 he was asked to speak in the senate after two men much junior to him. He died soon after. He was a mediocre orator (Cic. *Brut.* 222) and never equalled his father's cultural interests.   E. B.

Lutetia (Lutecia) (mod. Paris), *civitas*-capital of the Parisii. The original settlement, on a marshy island in the Seine, was destroyed in 52 BC. Under the empire a new town, built in the Roman fashion, developed on the island and the south bank, where remains of important public buildings still exist. After the invasions of the 3rd cent. AD, settlement was again confined to the island, defended by a wall of reused stones. Now called Parisii, it was a favourite residence of *Julian (proclaimed Augustus here in 360), but its real greatness did not begin until Clovis made it his capital.

P.-M. Duval, *Paris antique* (1961); *TIR* M 31 (1975).   J. F. Dr.

Luxorius or Luxurius

Luxorius or **Luxurius,** of Carthage (5th–6th cent. AD), author of some 90 short poems, in various metres and on various subjects, which afford an insight into the Vandal society of North Africa in which they were written. His identification with an obscure grammarian, Lisorius, is a matter of doubt. In inspiration his poems owe most to the epigrams of *Martial. He apparently held the titles of rank *vir clarissimus* and *spectabilis*.

TEXTS *Anth. Lat.*; M. Rosenblum (1961), with trans. and comm.; H. Happ (1986), with comm.
LITERATURE D. R. Shackleton Bailey, *Towards a Text of the Antholo-gia Latina* (1979), 42–56. PLRE 2. 695.   J. H. D. S.

luxury, laws against See under SUMPTUARY LEGISLATION.

lycanthropy (or werewolves) Those who ate human flesh at the human sacrifice offered on Mt. Lycaeon in *Arcadia were believed to be changed into wolves (see Plato, *Resp.* 8. 565d; ps.-Pl. *Minos* 315c; Theophrastus in Porph. *Abst.* 2. 27. 2). Here *Lycaon (3) would have been the first werewolf. Various stories speak of athletes who lived as wolves for nine years but regained their human form after abstaining from human flesh during this period and subsequently were victorious in contests: thus Demaenetus (Plin. *HN* 8. 82) and Damarchus of Parrhasia (Paus. 6. 8. 2). A comparable episode is given by *Pliny (1) (*HN* 8. 81) and *Augustine (*De civ. D.* 18. 17). But the best-known literary werewolf is probably that of *Petronius Arbiter, *Satyricon* 61–2. Modern scholars suggest that the phenomenon might indicate the existence of a group of 'wolfmen' devoted to the worship of a wolf-god, or a rite of passage like the Spartan *krypteia.

Burkert, *HN* 84–90; M. Jost, *Sanctuaires et cultes d'Arcadie* (1985), 258–67; R. Buxton, in J. Bremmer (ed.), *Interpretations of Greek Mythology* (1987), 60–79; D. D. Hughes, *Human Sacrifices in Ancient Greece* (1991).   M. J.

Lycaon, mythological characters whose name seems to include the Greek word for wolf, λύκος. (1) Son of *Priam and Laothoe, killed by *Achilles (*Iliad* 21. 34–135). (2) Father of *Pandarus (*Il.* 2. 826–7). (3) Son of *Pelasgus and king of *Arcadia. According to *Apollodorus (6) (3. 96–9) he had 50 sons; *Pausanias (3) (8. 3. 1–5) gives the names of 28 of them, all of whom except Nyctimus and Oenotrus founded settlements in Arcadia. Some of his actions depict Lycaon as a *culture-bringer and pious ruler: he founded *Lycosura, and gave *Zeus his epithet Lycaeus, instituting the festival Lycaia in his honour (Paus. 8. 2. 1–7). But his sacrifice to Zeus Lycaeus of a newborn child shows him in a different light. For Pausanias (ibid.) the act appears to be a simple, though horrific, sacrifice; other sources compound Lycaon's impiety by having him entertain Zeus to a feast and offer the god human flesh to test his divinity (cf. already Hesiod, fr. 164 M–W). Sometimes the responsibility for the feast is attributed to Lycaon's sons (Apollod. 3. 8. 1). Zeus punished the transgressors with a thunderbolt, or sent a flood, or changed Lycaon into a wolf (see LYCANTHROPY).

G. Piccaluga, *Lykaon, un tema mitico* (1968); J. Roy, BSA 1968, 287–92; P. Wathelet, in R. Julien and M. Limet (eds.), *Les Rites d'initiation* (1986), 285–97.   M. J.

Lycaonia was the name given to the country round Laranda, the region's metropolis during the Roman empire, covering the northern foothills of the Anatolian *Taurus and the southern part of the central Anatolian plateau. The Lycaonians were first mentioned by *Xenophon (1). The area stretched north as far as Iconium, which was generally reckoned to be the last city of *Phrygia, east to *Cappadocia, and adjoined the genuine highland region of *Isauria on the south-west. Since it lay astride the overland route from western Anatolia to the Cilician Gates and Syria, the successive rulers of Asia Minor—*Persian, *Macedonian, *Seleucid, and Attalid (see PERGAMUM)—attempted to control the region and it was part of the Roman province of Asia by 100 BC, before being assigned to the new province of *Cilicia around 80 BC. After the dissolution of Cilicia the area of Derbe and Laranda was controlled by the dynast Antipater (of Macedonian stock, c.50–36), while Iconium and the region adjoining Cilicia was assigned by Antony (M. *Antonius (2)) first to *Polemon (1) I from 39 to 36 and then to the Galatian *Amyntas (2). All of Lycaonia was included in the province of *Galatia after Amyntas' death in 25 BC, although the mountainous eastern approaches were ruled by client kings (*Archelaus (5) of Cappadocia, his son Archelaus II, *Antiochus (9) IV of Commagene) until the time of *Vespasian. Under *Antoninus Pius it was part of the Triple Province with Isauria and Cilicia, and the southern cities around Karadağ (excluding Iconium and other communities further north) formed a *koinon* (confederacy) and issued bronze coinage, mostly for the first and only time. In the mid-1st cent. AD St *Paul was addressed by the people of Lystra in the Lycaonian language (see ANATOLIAN LANGUAGES), which still apparently survived into late antiquity. The region was famous for its sheep.

L. Robert, *Hellenica* 13 (1965); Jones, *Cities E. Rom. Prov.* 124 ff.; H. von Aulock, *Münzen und Städte Lykaoniens* (1974).   A. H. M. J.; S. M.

Lyceum See ARISTOTLE, § 5; ATHENS, TOPOGRAPHY; PERIPATETIC SCHOOL.

Lycia was a mountainous country in SW Asia Minor between *Caria and *Pamphylia. According to Herodotus (1. 173) the Lycians came there direct from *Crete under *Sarpedon and at that time were called Termilae; they acquired the name Lycians from the Athenian Lycus son of Pandion. In fact the name derives from that of the Lukka tribe of Hittite records. On the other hand the name Termilae, in the form Trmmili, is found on epichoric inscriptions of the 4th cent. BC. The Lycians fought at *Troy as allies of *Priam; by then they already occupied the region of Classical Lycia and their chieftains, Sarpedon and *Glaucus (1), are said to have been rewarded for their martial prowess with land in the *Xanthus valley (*Il.* 2. 876–7).

In 546 BC Lycia was overrun by the *Persians after heroic resistance at Xanthus. Persian influence in the aristocratic culture of the region was very marked, and the Lycians sent ships and men to accompany Xerxes' invasion of Greece in 480. Thereafter they appear fleetingly as subjects of the Athenian empire (see DELIAN LEAGUE), but reverted swiftly to Persian influence and control. In the 4th cent. they were ruled by dynasts, notably *Pericles (2), whose palace and tomb were at Limyra. The region was included for a time in *Mausolus' dominions, submitted readily to *Alexander (3) the Great, and then passed into the hands of the Ptolemies (see PTOLEMY (1)). It was conquered in 197 BC by *Antiochus (3) III, but after his defeat at the battle of *Magnesia in 189 was given by the Romans to *Rhodes. The Lycians bitterly resented and resisted Rhodian control and were rewarded with their freedom in 169 BC. Although they came increasingly under Roman influence (the cult of the goddess Rome was introduced in the early 2nd cent. BC to Xanthus) this freedom was not formally lost until AD 43 when the region was combined with much of *Pisidia and Pamphylia to form a new Roman province.

Lycia's small communities had an unusual capacity for collaboration and federation; see FEDERAL STATES. Even in the 4th cent., when the cities were ruled, under Persian supervision, by dynasts, the uniformity of their coinage, on which the emblem of the triskelion often occurs, hints at some form of confederation. In the Hellenistic period, perhaps before 200 BC a regular Lycian Confederacy (*koinon*) was formed. The east-coast cities of Olympus and *Phaselis were included in Lycia for the first time, to be followed in 83 BC by three cities of the Cibyratis: *Oenoanda, Balbura, and Bubon. In the federal council and assembly the individual cities were represented proportionate to their size and importance (Strabo 14. 664–5). The leading members in the Hellenistic period, entitled to three votes in the league meetings, were *Xanthus, *Patara, Pinara, Tlos, *Myra and Olympus. Until the creation of the Roman province this *koinon* had much of the authority of a sovereign state, including the power to declare war and peace; a federal bronze coinage was struck with uniform types—often featuring a lyre, the symbol of *Apollo, Lycia's patron god—in the name of the various cities, which also issued their own individual types.

The Lycian language and script continued in use down to the end of the 4th cent. BC when it was supplanted by Greek, which had been used alongside Lycian for the previous century. (See LYCIAN LANGUAGE; ANATOLIAN LANGUAGES.) Native culture is also evident in Lycian funerary architecture. Highly distinctive tomb types are often the most prominent material remains to survive on Lycian sites.

Provincial affairs under the Roman empire may have been regulated by a *lex provinciae* introduced in the time of *Vespasian, a period when there is also considerable evidence for new civic building, especially of aqueducts and bathhouses. In the 2nd cent. AD many of the communities benefited from the generosity of *Opramoas of Rhodiapolis and other large-scale local benefactors. A shortage of good land and the relatively limited population, however, prevented any of the Lycian cities from enjoying the level of economic well-being reached in the neighbouring areas of Pamphylia, Pisidia, or Caria.

Jones, *Cities E. Rom. Prov.* 96 ff.; *TAM* 1–2 (inscriptions); Magie, *Rom. Rule Asia Min.* ch. 22; J. A. O. Larsen, *Greek Federal States* (1968), 240 ff.; G. E. Bean, *Lycian Turkey* (1978); T. Bryce, *The Lycians* 1 (1986).   S. M.

Lycian language The Lycian language is documented in somewhat fewer than 200 inscriptions on stone and in several dozen very short imprints on coins, the latter consisting only of personal and place names, often abbreviated. These texts start with the 6th cent. but most of them date from the 5th and 4th cents. BC. They are written in an alphabet derived from or closely related to that of Greek. All but a handful of the stone inscriptions are funerary texts with highly stereotyped contents. One important exception is the 'inscribed pillar' of *Xanthus. Much of this lengthy text remains obscure, owing to problems of vocabulary, but it is clear that it describes the military exploits of a particular dynastic family and the establishment of various cultic centres. Invaluable for understanding the Lycian language is the 'Letoon trilingual', which describes in parallel Lycian, Greek, and *Aramaic versions the establishment of a cult of King Caunius (a cult name evidently connected with *Caunus; see H. Metzger and others, *Fouilles de Xanthos* 6 (1979)).

Two texts thus far discovered in Lycia are composed in a different but closely related language known as 'Milyan' or 'Lycian B'. Its precise dialectal relationship to ordinary 'Lycian A' cannot yet be determined.

Lycian belongs to the Anatolian branch of the *Indo-European family and is thus most closely related to *Hittite, Palaic, Luwian, and *Lydian. Lycian has a particularly close affinity to Luwian, but it also shares several features with Lydian, and the frequent assumption of a pre-historic 'Luvo-Lycian' unity is premature. Lycian shows several highly characteristic features of the Anatolian group of Indo-European: e.g. the demonstrative stem *ebe-* 'this' (= Hittite *apā-* 'that', etc.) and the first-person pronoun *amu* 'I, me' with the same peculiar *u*-vocalism seen in Hittite *ammug*, Lydian *amu/ēmu* etc.

Lycian shares with Luwian and Lydian a tendency to replace the genitive case with an adjectival construction ('paternal house' for 'father's house'). However, it differs strikingly from the other Anatolian languages in its word order. See ANATOLIAN LANGUAGES.

G. Neumann, in B. Spüler (ed.), *Handbuch der Orientalistik* 1/2. 1–2. 2: *Altkleinasiatische Sprachen* (1969), 'Lykisch'; T. Bryce, *The Lycians in Literary and Epigraphic Sources* (1986).   H. C. M.

Lyco (RE 14) (*c.*300/298–*c.*226/4 BC), son of Astyanax of Troas, pupil of *Straton (1) of Lampsacus and his successor as head of the *Peripatetic school, which he directed for 44 years. The sources for his life, mostly derived from a lost biography by *Antigonus (4) of Carystus, show that he was a man of the world, a friend of kings and statesmen, a benefactor of the people, a lover of pleasure and luxury of all kinds—everything but a great philosopher or scientist like his predecessors. He was a fluent and interesting speaker, but had little to teach (Cicero, *Fin.* 5. 13, calls him 'rich in eloquence, but rather lacking in content'), and with him began a long period of decline in the history of the Peripatetic school. Only a few fragments of his writings have survived.

U. von Wilamowitz-Moellendorff, *Antigonos von Karystos* (1881), 78 ff.; F. Wehrli, *Die Schule des Aristoteles* 6, 2nd edn. (1968), 1–26, and in Überweg–Flashar, 576–8.   J. G.; R. W. S.

Lycophron (1), tyrant of *Pherae in *Thessaly *c.*406–390 BC. He may have established his *tyranny by championing a democratic element against the aristocracy, for he was opposed by the nobles of *Larissa and other cities, whom he defeated in 404. He allied with Sparta and in 395 fought against Medius of Larissa, who, with support from *Boeotia and *Argos (2), may have won a temporary advantage over him. In a period of violent struggles between Thessalian cities and factions he played a prominent part, but so little evidence has survived that it is impossible to determine the extent of his success or to assess his ability as a military and political leader. His ambition to dominate Thessaly was achieved by *Jason (2), probably his son.

H. D. Westlake, *Thessaly in the Fourth Century BC* (1935); J. K. Davies, *Democracy and Classical Greece*, 2nd edn. (1993), 236.   H. D. W.; S. H.

Lycophron (2) The name of Lycophron is associated with two writers of the Hellenistic age, the identity of whom is the subject of much debate. They are here distinguished as (*a*) Lycophron and (*b*) ps.-Lycophron.

(*a*) Lycophron, a native of *Chalcis, of the early 3rd cent. BC, active in *Alexandria (1), a member of the tragic *Pleiad, author of a number of tragedies and satyr-plays, and also a grammarian and glossographer of the comic poets, of whom a few glosses survive. The titles of some of the plays are conventional, of others topical (including one on his friend *Menedemus (1) of Eretria and one called the *Cassandreis*, the theme of which is unknown). Only a few fragments survive.

(*b*) Ps.-Lycophron, author of the 'monodrama' *Alexandra*,

written in the immediate aftermath of the victory of T. *Quinctius Flamininus at Cynoscephalae over *Philip (3) V of Macedon in 197/6 BC. The author, whose true name and place of origin are probably concealed beneath the impenetrably enigmatic biographical tradition concerning Lycophron, probably used the name, and some of the literary substance, of Lycophron (a), not in emulation, but as an ironic reminiscence of the earlier writer, who had combined the practice of tragedy and the elucidation of comedy. Only on this assumption of a deliberate pseudepigraphon can the full irony of his work be appreciated. His poem, cast in the form of a prophetic recitation by *Cassandra in iambic trimeters, called in the title of the poem Alexandra, has acquired notoriety on account of its obscure and laboured style and vocabulary, in which individual episodes and persons are alike concealed in memorable metaphorical terms, which defy indisputable rationalization. The poem is nevertheless a powerful, indeed brilliant performance, in which tragic intensity, grim irony, and recondite learning combine to create a memorable *tour de force*.

The framework of the poem (ll. 1–30 and 1461–74) is provided by a report to *Priam by a guard set to watch over Cassandra. The rest is Cassandra's prophecy, which falls into the following main divisions: ll. 31–364, the fall of *Troy and consequent disasters; 365–1089, the sufferings of the Greeks who do not succeed in returning home; 1090–1225, the sufferings of the Greeks who do return home; 1226–80, the wanderings of *Aeneas and the Trojans; 1283–1450, the struggles between Europe and Asia, culminating in the victory of Rome; 1451–60, Cassandra's lamentation on the uselessness of her prophecy.

Three major questions relate to (1) the sources, (2) the purpose, and (3) the occasion of the poem.

1. Sources: (a) stylistic, thematic, and linguistic sources. The use of the iambic trimeter is natural to its tragic theme, and the tragic type of 'monodrama' recitatif (whether iambic or lyric) was current in the Hellenistic age; these features therefore call for no comment here, though they could be illustrated in many ways. (b) For the role of Cassandra as prophetess of post-Homeric catastrophes the author could call on numerous Archaic and Classical sources, and it is inevitable that precise debts, probably incurred by direct loan and not through an intermediary compendium of post-Homeric legends, should be largely unassignable. We may also be certain that, the prophecy apart, many other sources also contributed to the substance of the poem, both in general, and in specific passages. For instance, *Herodotus (1)'s opening passage on the conflict of east and west probably provided the poet with that theme, essential to his version of Cassandra's prophecy, and *Timaeus (2) may have been the channel through which many of the abstruse Western legends, based on *Nostoi* ('Returns' from Troy), which form so significant a part of the poem, reached him. The possibilities extend far beyond the range of our limited knowledge. (c) The poet's language, monstrously obscure and metaphorical, was no doubt his own: a deliberate and successful attempt to wrap the prophetic, Sibylline theme in language that readers might deem appropriate to the occasion, in which echoes of Homeric, lyric, and especially tragic language are evident. The ancients reckoned the poet as 'dark' (σκοτεινός, *ater*), and he would no doubt have agreed.

2. Intent. The poet's purpose in choosing the theme is not explicitly stated, but the emphasis on Italian legends, especially those connected with *Odysseus, and other Greek heroes (irrespective of whether such legends came to him, for example, from a direct reading of an early poet or poets, from a careful study of Timaeus, in some ways a kindred spirit, from an intermediate handbook, or even perhaps by local traditions regarding the heroic past) and the prominence given to the decisive role played by *Macedonia in subduing *Persia, and of Rome in subduing Macedonia, seem to indicate that the ultimate purpose of the prophecy is to commemorate the recent and apparently decisive change in the world order which he associates with the victory of Roman arms.

3. Date. The date of composition has to be determined in the light of this presumed purpose. It has caused much debate and there is no reason, unless more evidence is forthcoming, why the controversy should cease. The problem is well known. Lycophron, as identified under (a), lived in the early 3rd cent. BC, yet the poet clearly refers to a widely recognized Roman supremacy. The two propositions are hardly reconcilable, and the commentator *Tzetzes suggested that the relevant lines had been written by another Lycophron. Since the debate opened in modern times it has been continually discussed whether the lines referring to Rome are acceptable in the context of a date c.275 BC, whether the whole passage relating to Rome should be regarded as an interpolation added after the Roman conquest of Greece had become a reality, or whether the whole poem should be dated to a period when that had happened. The suggestion made here as to authorship is based on the hard-won belief that the reference in the Rome passage to a 'unique Wrestler' refers to Titus Quinctius Flamininus, and was made in the immediate aftermath of his victory at *Cynoscephalae in 197/6 BC, when his praises were being sung, statues being erected to him, and religious festivals in his honour, Titeia, being inaugurated all over Greece. The impact made by the politic and *philhellene Titus, representative of a new ruling power linked by ties of mythological *kinship to the Greek and Trojan past, provides the appropriate background for this speedily produced pro-Roman eulogy from the mouth of the Trojan Cassandra. Independent evidence derived from the use made of 3rd cent. authors, seems to confirm this date.

For Lycophron, (a) above, see the tragic fragments in Snell, *TrGF* 1, no. 100, and for his work as a Comic critic and glossographer see C. Strecker, *De Lycophrone, Euphorione, Eratosthene comicorum interpretibus* (Diss. Gryph. 1884).

Ps.-Lycophron ((b) above): **EDITIONS OF THE *ALEXANDRA*:** (1) Plain texts (without scholia etc.), since 1880: (a) Scheer, vol. 1, Text (1881, repr. 1958), 2, Scholia (1908; repr. 1958); (b) the 'old' Teubner of Kinkel (1880); (c) the new Teubner of Mascialino (1964). (2) Texts with introductory matter, commentaries, notes, translations, etc.: (a) C. von Holzinger, *Lykophron's Alexandra, griechisch u. deutsch mit erklärende Anmerkungen* (1895), the Ger. trans. in iambics—an outstanding edition; (b) G. W. Mooney, *The Alexandra of Lycophron with English Translation and Explanatory notes* (1921), no textual notes, but helpful explanatory notes; (c) A. W. Mair, in the 'old' Loeb *Callimachus and Lycophron; Aratus* (1921), an excellent introduction, more textual information than Mooney, and similar notes; (d) M. Fusillo, A. Hurst, and G. Paduano (eds.), *Licofrone, Alessandra* (1991).

PAPYRI, MSS, SCHOLIA (a) Papyri. The papyri of Lycophron are few and scanty, and do not greatly affect the medieval text. They are listed by U. Criscuolo, *Dioniso* 1970, 722 ff. and S. West, *CQ* 1983, 114 n.; to these lists should now be added *POxy.* 3445 and 3446. All the papyri are of the 1st or 2nd cent. AD. (b) Main MSS. The most important group consists of Marc. 476 of the 11th cent. Coislinianus 345 of the 10th cent., and (a derivative of Marc. 476) Vatic. 1307 of the 11th cent. These form the basis of most modern editions. (c) Paraphrases and scholia: (1) L's text is accompanied in the main MSS by prose paraphrases, either in continuous form or as word for word interpretations. These are printed by Scheer in vol. 1 of his edition, below the text.

(2) *Scholia fall into two classes, (α) the brief *scholia vetera* found in Marc. 476, and, deriving from them, those in Vatic. 1307, which form the earliest surviving interpretations of the text, and (β) the lengthy and independently transmitted commentaries of Johannes Tzetzes, of which there are three different versions. These, along with the scholl. vet. and the paraphrases are all thrown together into one virtually inextricable bundle by Scheer as his vol. 2, described by one authority as 'rivalling in difficulty the *Alexandra* itself'. There is no easy route through these commentaries; the best guide to them are the reviews of Scheer's volume by H. Schulz, *Gött. Anz.* 1910, 19–35, and by Holzinger, *Berliner Philologische Wochenschrift*, 1912, 513–24, and the introduction to Mair's Loeb text, pp. 490–2. (Indexes to Tzetzes, already available in great detail in vol. 3 of C. G. Müller's edition of Tzetzes's scholia (1811), have been published separately by I. Gualandri, *Index Nominum propriorum quae in Scholiis Tzetzianis ad Lycophronem laudantur*, Testi e Documenti per lo studio dell'antichità, 6 (1962), and *Index glossarum quae in scholiis Tzetzianis ad Lycophronem laudantur*, ibid. 12 (1965), with reference to Scheer's edition.)

MODERN STUDIES For work up to *c*.1965 see, in addition to Ziegler's brilliant article in *RE* 13. 888–930, entry under 'Lykophron' 8, the lengthy supplementary entry by St Josifovič, *RE* Suppl. 11 (1968), 114–35, which displays considerable insight, but overstates his case. Since then the main contributions to the study of the text as a whole, date, etc. (omitting discussions of specific sections of the narrative, such as the Locrian Maidens episode; see AIAS (2)) are: A. Hurst, *Mélanges P. Collart* (1976), 231 ff.; S. West, *CQ* 1983 and *JHS* 1984, 127–51; P. Fraser, *Report of Dept. Antiquities, Cyprus* (1979), 328–43.

P. M. F.

Lycortas,

Lycortas, son of Thearidas, of Megalopolis, father of the historian *Polybius (1), friend and political associate of *Philopoemen (d. *c*.167 BC). As hipparch (cavalry commander) of the *Achaean Confederacy under Philopoemen in 192 he fought *Nabis of Sparta, subsequently, both as envoy to Rome (188) and as negotiator with Roman envoys (185 and 184), he supported staunchly Philopoemen's including Sparta and Messene in the confederacy and his refusal to restore all exiles. In 182 he supported Philopoemen's military action against *Messene and *Sparta, which had unilaterally seceded, and after Philopoemen's death succeeded him as *stratēgos* (general and chief magistrate)—which he had already been (185/4)—and restored their membership. *Callicrates (2)'s success in Rome (179) and Roman support for his restoration of exiles to Messene and Sparta (179/8) discredited Lycortas' Philopoemenist policy of asserting Achaean independent interest, even against Rome; the Achaeans rejected his view (170) that the confederacy should remain neutral in the Third Macedonian War. His statues, subsequently removed by Callicrates, were restored in 149.

R. M. Errington, *Philopoemen* (1969); *RE* 13/2. 2202–4, 'Lykortas'.

R. M. E.

Lycosura,

Lycosura, a small town with an important sanctuary in SW *Arcadia, situated in the hills west of the main Megalopolitan basin, belonged to the Parrhasians, but on the foundation of *Megalopolis was allowed, because of its sanctuary, to survive as a separate *polis* surrounded by Megalopolitan territory. Though claiming to be the earth's oldest city, its known history and archaeology run from the 4th cent. BC. The sanctuary and surrounding area have been excavated (but not traces of the walled town). Lycosura was an important religious centre with cults of several deities, but the most significant was *Despoina, who had an imposing Doric temple and colossal cult statuary by *Damophon of Messene. Unfortunately the dates of both the temple and the statuary are disputed, suggestions ranging from the 4th cent. BC to the Hadrianic period; both may belong to

the early 3rd cent. BC (but see DAMOPHON). The cult centre still flourished in the 2nd cent. AD.

E. Meyer, *RE* 13. 2417–32, 'Lykosura'; M. Jost, *Sanctuaires et cultes d'Arcadie* (1985), 172–9.

J. R.

Lycurgus (1)

Lycurgus (1), a mythological personage, according to *Homer, *Il.* 6. 130 ff., a son of Dryas, who attacked *Dionysus, driving him and his nurses before him till the god took refuge in the sea; thereafter Lycurgus was blinded and died soon, having first massacred his family in a divinely induced madness. His death is vaguely placed on Mt. Nysa. Later, as in *Aeschylus (Radt, *TrGF* 3, frags. 57 ff.), he is an Edonian; he and others elaborate the story in various ways. *Apollodorus (6) (1. 35) and *Hyginus (3a) (*Fab.* 132) say Dionysus drove him mad, and further embroider the story of his sufferings and death; their sources are uncertain. For details, see Rapp in Roscher's *Lexikon*, 'Lykurgus'; Marbach, *RE* 13. 2433–40, 'Lykurgus (1)'; Nilsson, *GGR* 1². 580. The myth was popular in art, e.g. (the massacre) on Greek and S. Italian painted pottery (5th–4th cents. BC): A. Farnoux, *LIMC* 6. 1 (1992), 309–19.

H. J. R.; A. J. S. S.

Lycurgus (2)

Lycurgus (2), traditional founder of Classical *Sparta's *eunomia ('good order'). Ancient accounts of his work evolved according to political circumstance. The earliest, in *Herodotus (1) (1. 65–6), reflects official Spartan views: guardian of the early *Agiad king, Leobotes, he was responsible for all Sparta's laws, and military and political institutions which he brought from *Crete. Most later writers attached him to the *Eurypontid king Charillos, perhaps reflecting that royal house's subsequent prominence. A 5th-cent. BC, non-Spartan version that his measures came from Apollo at *Delphi was later incorporated by making Apollo sanction laws he brought from Crete. The view that the ephorate (see EPHORS) was post-Lycurgan, probably originated by King *Pausanias (2) in exile post-395, was invoked by *Cleomenes (2) III when abolishing the office in 227 BC. Later accounts became increasingly wide-ranging and detailed as Lycurgus' achievements were expanded to embrace 4th-cent. and Hellenistic philosophical and political programmes. *Plutarch's 'biography' reflects the culmination of this trend.

Although scholars generally accept that Sparta's *eunomia* was the product of coherent design, few now view it as the work of a single legislator. Many elements emerged through a long-term process of adaptation to Sparta's distinctive political and economic situation. Whether purely legendary or a historical person subsequently invoked as a charter for the regime, Lycurgus' absence from *Tyrtaeus' 7th-cent. account of the 'Great Rhetra' (see SPARTA, § 2) undermines later belief in his significant founding role.

E. N. Tigerstedt, *The Legend of Sparta in Classical Antiquity*, 1 (1965), 70–3.

S. J. Ho.

Lycurgus (3)

Lycurgus (3) (*c*.390–*c*.325/4 BC), Athenian statesman, of great importance after the battle of *Chaeronea (338). The principal evidence about him is the 'Life' in [Plut.] *Lives of the Ten Orators* and the appended honorific decree of 307/6, the original of which is partially preserved (*IG* 2². 457). Clearly he played the major part in the control of the city's finances for a period of twelve years, raising the revenue to perhaps 1,200 talents a year, and financing projects by raising capital from individuals (προδανεισμοί); scattered epigraphic evidence attests the wide range of his activities (note esp. *Syll.*³ 218, *IG* 2². 1627 and 1672, ll. 11 and 303). The powers by which he did it all are obscure.

Lycus

Some have inferred from *Hyperides fr. 118 (OCT Kenyon) and other passages that he was given a general but extraordinary commission to supervise the city's finances, but the manner of the allusions in *Ath. Pol.* to the financial officers tells against such a theory: the passage in Hyperides *In Dem.* (col. 28) frequently taken to describe Lycurgus' position should be referred to *Demosthenes (2)'s powers as theoric commissioner (see THEŌRIKA). Probably he occupied different offices including the position of ταμίας τῶν στρατιωτικῶν (steward of the military fund) and controlled the whole by personal influence (cf. Plut. *Mor.* 841c), which manifests itself to us in the varied decrees which he proposed. Whatever his powers, it is certain that he carried through a diverse building programme including the completion of the Skeuotheke (arsenal) begun by *Eubulus (1), the rebuilding of the theatre of Dionysus, the construction of docks, and the improvement of the harbours. The substantial increase in the navy in this period is ascribed to him. He concerned himself also with the arrangements for processions and festivals, and had statues of the three great tragic poets erected and an official copy made of their works (later borrowed by *Ptolemy (1) II Philadelphus for the library of *Alexandria (1) and never returned). The common belief that Lycurgus instituted, or reformed, the corps of *ephēboi is ill grounded. In politics he was bitterly suspicious of Macedon and was one of those at first demanded by *Alexander (3) the Great in 335. He prosecuted Lysicles who had been a general at Chaeronea and any who after the battle seemed to show signs of defeatism, and, when the revolt of *Agis III in 331/0 put the city in turmoil, Lycurgus used the occasion to attack Leocrates, who had been absent from the city from 338 to 332 but probably not illegally, and very nearly had him condemned for treachery. The fragments of his speeches attest the wide range of his prosecution of corrupt practices. He died shortly before the *Harpalus affair. According to a story contained in a letter ascribed to Demosthenes he was accused by his successor Menesaechmus of having left a deficit; his sons were condemned to repay the money, and were imprisoned when unable to do so. They were released on the appeal of Demosthenes. By 307/6 his great services were generally recognized.

Works Of fifteen speeches regarded as genuine by *Caecilius (1), the only one extant is *Against Leocrates*. The ancient opinion that Lycurgus was mercilessly severe in his prosecutions is supported by the study of this speech. His literary style was influenced by that of *Isocrates, but he is a much less careful writer, being often negligent in the matter of hiatus, and inartistic in the composition of his sentences. Evidently he cared more for matter than style. His disregard of proportion is shown by his inordinately long quotations from the poets.

TEXT N. C. Konomis (Teubner, 1970); with trans.: F. Durrbach (Budé, 1932); J. O. Burtt, *Minor Attic Orators* 2 (Loeb, 1954).

COMMENTARIES A. Petrie (1922); P. Treves (1934); E. Malcovati (1947); N. C. Konomis, 'Notes on the fragments of Lycurgus', *Klio* 1961, 72 ff.

INDEX See ANDOCIDES.

GENERAL LITERATURE See ATTIC ORATORS. Also Rhodes, *CAAP* 515 f.; W. Will, *Athen und Alexander* (1983); S. Humphreys, in J. W. Eadie and J. Ober (eds.), *The Craft of the Ancient Historian: Essays in Honor of C. G. Starr* (1985).   G. L. C.

Lycus (1), 'wolf', a common heroic name. In Attic tradition, Lycus was one of the sons of King *Pandion who at their father's death divided *Attica between them. *Herodotus (1) (1. 173. 3) makes this Lycus the eponym of the Lycians, while *Pausanias (3) (1. 19. 3) connects him with the cult of *Apollo Lycius. It is not clear whether this figure was identified with the Lykus whose shrine was situated near a lawcourt and who appears as a sort of patron of jurors in *Aristophanes (1), *Vesp.* 389–94. A Theban Lycus (see THEBES (1)) was husband of *Dirce, who with her mistreated *Antiope and was killed by her children *Amphion and Zethus.

G. Berger-Doer, *LIMC* 6. 302–7.   E. Ke.

Lycus (2), of *Rhegium, Greek ethnographer and historian, adoptive father of the tragedian *Lycophron (2a) and arch-enemy of *Demetrius (3) of Phaleron (*FGrH* 570 T 1). He lived in *Alexandria (1) *c.*300 BC, where he was held in honour.

Works *On Sicily* and *History of Libya*. Both works contained geographical and much *paradoxographical information. Only fourteen fragments are extant. *Agatharchides of Cnidus (*On the Red Sea* 64) names Lycus as the second most important authority for the west after *Timaeus (2). Used by Timaeus, *Callimachus (3), *Lycophron (2b), and others.

FGrH 570. K. Meister, *Die griechische Geschichtsschreibung* (1990).

K. M.

Lydia was a territory in the west of Asia Minor, centred in the lower Hermus and Cayster valleys, and bordered on the north by Mysia, on the east by *Phrygia, on the south by *Caria; the Phrygian and Carian borders were varied, and the coastal Greek cities (*Cyme, *Smyrna, *Ephesus, etc.) were reckoned sometimes to Lydia, sometimes to *Aeolis or Ionia (see IONIANS). Lydia contained much natural wealth, and lying on two main routes from the coast to the interior of Anatolia it was an entrepôt of trade and lay open to Greek and Anatolian influences, which are reflected in its civilization, art, and cults. Under the Mermnad dynasty (*c.*700–546 BC) Lydia was a powerful kingdom, which by the time of its last king *Croesus had incorporated all the plateau of Anatolia up to the *Halys. After his defeat, Lydia became the chief Persian satrapy in the west, with its headquarters at *Sardis; this satrapy was in close political relations with the Greek city-states throughout the Persian period. The conquest by *Alexander (3) the Great opened Lydia to Graeco-Macedonian colonization; under *Seleucid control (from 280) Lydia was an important satrapy for Seleucid rule in Asia Minor, with Sardis as a royal capital; after the battle of *Magnesia in 189 it became Attalid territory and passed to Rome with the rest of the Attalid kingdom in 133 BC. It remained part of the province of Asia until *Diocletian made it a separate province, with Sardis as *metropolis (sense 'b').

Lydian civilization, architecture, and art were influenced by Anatolian, Iranian, and Greek cultures. Lydia was reputedly the first realm to mint gold–silver coinage (see COINAGE, GREEK) and was the innovator of the 'Lydian mode' (see MUSIC, § 6). The Lydian language is Indo-European. The use of Lydian in inscriptions seems to end in the 2nd cent. BC, but in Strabo's day it was still spoken on the border of Lycia. See also ANATOLIAN LANGUAGES; LYDIAN LANGUAGE.

G. M. A. Hanfmann (assisted by W. E. Mierse), *Sardis from Prehistoric to Roman Times* (1983).   W. M. C.; J. M. C.; S. S.-W.

Lydiadas, son of Eudamus, of *Megalopolis (d. 227 BC). Commanded troops against *Sparta (251), later (*c.*244) became tyrant (see TYRANNY) of Megalopolis. Under threat from the *Achaean Confederacy he abdicated, reintroduced the democratic constitution and united Megalopolis with the confederacy (235), which gave protection against Sparta. He was elected *stratēgos* (general and chief magistrate) of the confederacy, in rivalry to *Aratus (2), in 234/3, 232/1, and 230/29 and began a tradition of Megalopolitan leadership which was later continued by *Philopoemen, *Lycortas, and *Polybius (1); but as hipparch (cavalry commander) in 227, while Aratus was *stratēgos*, according to Aratus' account he disobeyed Aratus' orders in the battle at Ladoceia against *Cleomenes (2) III of Sparta and was killed.

R. Urban, *Wachstum und Krise des achaiischen Bundes* (1979); *RE* 13/2, 'Lydiadas' 1.   R. M. E.

Lydian language Evidence for the Lydian language consists of more than 100 inscriptions, mostly discovered at the site of the ancient capital *Sardis. Only some two dozen of these are long enough and complete enough to be significant in elucidating the language. Aside from a few short imprints on coins, some of which may be as old as the 8th cent. BC, all the texts date from the 5th and 4th cent. BC. Lydian is written in an alphabet related to or derived from that of Greek.

The texts vary in content: many are tomb inscriptions, others appear to be decrees of various kinds. Remarkably, some are in verse, with an accent-based metre and vowel assonance in the last words of each line.

Not all texts found at Sardis are in Lydian. Besides a few graffiti in Carian (see CARIA), there is the 'synagogue inscription', discovered in 1963. It is written in an alphabetic script, but not even the values of the letters, much less the language, have yet been determined.

A short Lydian–Aramaic bilingual text offered a first entry into the Lydian language, but the absence thus far of a substantial Lydian–Greek bilingual limits understanding of Lydian. Grammatical analysis of most sentences is reasonably certain, but many words can be assigned only an approximate meaning, and others are totally obscure.

Lydian is assuredly a member of the Anatolian branch of the *Indo-European family, sharing a number of defining innovations with *Hittite, Luwian, Palaic, and *Lycian. These shared features preclude any suggestion that the appearance of Lydian in Asia Minor is due to a separate development from that of the other languages named above. To cite but one example: Lydian *amu*/*ēmu* 'I, me' shows the same peculiar *u*-vocalism as Hittite *ammug*, Lycian *amu*, etc. Nevertheless, it is undeniable that Lydian differs markedly from the related Anatolian languages in several respects. One development which gives it a very different surface appearance is a massive loss of medial and final vowels, leading in some cases to remarkable consonant clusters: e.g. *ibśimlλ* 'Ephesian' (dative sing.). See ANATOLIAN LANGUAGES.

R. Gusmani, *Lydisches Wörterbuch* (1964), and *Ergänzungsband 1–3* (1980–6).   H. C. M.

Lydus, i.e. **John the Lydian,** civil servant at *Constantinople and Greek author (AD 490–*c*.560). John, son of Laurentius, native of *Philadelphia (2) in Lydia, was well educated in Latin and Greek before travelling to Constantinople in 511. He studied philosophy while awaiting admission to the *memoriales*, an administrative bureau, but when his compatriot Zoticus became praetorian prefect John enrolled as *excerptor* in the prefecture, receiving a privileged position with profitable opportunities (1,000 solidi from fees in 511/2); his patron also arranged a lucrative marriage. John's career progressed less spectacularly after Zoticus' retirement in 512, although his exceptional command of Latin was always an asset. For a time he served as a secretary in the imperial palace, before returning to the prefecture. Under *Justinian, John's literary skills received recognition with imperial requests to deliver a Latin panegyric before foreign dignitaries and describe a Roman victory at Dara (530); perhaps in 543 he was given a professorship at Constantinople, being permitted to combine this with work in the prefecture until retirement in 551/2. The latter half of his bureaucratic career was soured by hatred for Justinian's powerful praetorian prefect, John the Cappadocian, who overhauled central and provincial administration in ways which John disliked, especially since literary learning was devalued. John's three extant works all have antiquarian leanings, though they are not therefore divorced from contemporary concerns. *De mensibus* discusses the Roman calendar, *De ostentis* deals with astrological matters, while *De magistratibus* charts the history of Roman administrative offices, with particular attention to the praetorian prefecture on which John provides valuable inside information.

TEXTS *De mensibus*, ed. R. Wünsch (1898); *De ostentis*, ed. C. Wachsmuth (1897); *De magistratibus*, ed. A. C. Bandy, with Eng. trans (1983). PLRE 2. 612–15, 'Ioannes' 75; M. Maas, *John Lydus and the Roman Past* (1992).   L. M. W.

Lygdamis See NAXOS (1).

Lygdamus, the author of six smooth but tedious elegies addressed to Neaera transmitted at the beginning of book 3 of the Tibullan corpus (see TIBULLUS). Despite much scholarly debate, the identity and date of the poet remain uncertain. At 5. 18, after an allusion to himself as still young, he refers to his birth year (43 BC) in identical language to *Ovid, *Tristia* 4. 10. 6 (published AD 11). Either Lygdamus wrote in the circle of M. *Valerius Messalla Corvinus, and Ovid imitated him because he was his friend, or Lygdamus imitated Ovid here and elsewhere, in which case he must be dated after AD 11 (though not, as some have argued, to the late 1st cent.). Another possibility is that 'Lygdamus' is the young *Ovid.

Text/trans. in editions of Tibullus; comm. in H. Tränkle, *Appendix Tibulliana* (1990). K. Büchner, *Hermes* 1965; W. Erath, *Die Dichtung des Lygdamus* (1971); M. Parca, *Studies in Latin Literature* 4, ed. C. Deroux (1986).   P. W.

lyric poetry

Greek The term 'lyric' (λυρικός) is derived from λύρα, 'lyre'. As a designation of a category of poetry it is not found before the Hellenistic period (earlier writers term such a poem *melos*, 'song', and the poet *melopoios*, 'composer of song'; hence we find 'melic' used as a synonym for 'lyric'). Its use in the ancient world was more precise than the terms 'lyric' and 'lyrical' as now used with reference either to modern or to ancient poetry. Though the term was extended to poetry sung to other stringed instruments or to the flute, it is always used of sung poetry as distinct from stichic, distichic (elegy included), or epodic poems which were recited or spoken.

The 'lyric' age begins in the 7th cent. BC, though the finished metres of the earliest exponents indicate that they are the heirs to a long tradition of popular song. So does the evidence of *Homer, whose narrative mentions sung *paeans (*Il.* 1. 472–3, 22. 391–2; cf. *Hymn. Hom. Ap.* 517–18), *dirges (*Il.* 24. 720 ff.; *Od.* 24. 58 ff.), wedding songs (see EPITHALAMIUM) (*Il.* 18. 491 ff.), the *Linus-song (*Il.* 18. 567 ff.), and more generally choral song and dance (*Il.* 18. 590 ff.). However, the fact that no composer's name survives from this period suggests a context of anonymous folksong. In the 7th cent. a change occurs, as named poets of distinction emerge. The reasons for this change are not clear.

Modern scholars divide lyric into choral and monodic (solo). There is no evidence of any such division in ancient scholarship, and its validity has been disputed, but it does correspond to broad differences in form and content. Choral poetry was performed by a choir which sang and danced. The element of spectacle was enhanced further by the impressive dress of the chorus (Alcm. 1. 64 ff.; Dem. 21. 16). The collective voice was ideally suited to represent the voice of the community, and consequently choral song in general has a pronounced 'public' quality to it. In origin choral performance was sacral, and even in the Classical period 'dance' may be synonymous with 'worship' (Soph. *OT* 896). Accordingly, most of the attested types of choral song are religious or ritual in character: paean, usually addressed to *Apollo but also attested for other gods, *dithyramb, addressed to *Dionysus, processional song (*prosodion*), maiden-song (*partheneion*), dirge (*thrēnos*), wedding song (*hymenaios*). However, the sacral use was not exclusive, for already in Homer we find choral song and dance as festive entertainment. During the late Archaic period there is a further secularization of choral music, as choral songs are composed in praise of rulers and aristocrats, as in the erotic and laudatory songs of *Ibycus and the *encomia* (originally 'party / revel songs', then 'songs of praise') and *epinicia* (victory odes) of *Simonides, *Pindar, and *Bacchylides. Choral lyric is especially associated with 'Dorian' states (*Alcman, *Stesichorus, *Arion (2), Ibycus, Pindar), though not exclusively (since Simonides and Bacchylides were from *Ceos). The dialect is an artificial amalgam of West Greek, Aeolic, and Homeric, though within this framework there are differences between authors. Choral compositions are either strophic (composed of stanzas which correspond metrically, strophe and antistrophe, which later writers associate with the movements of the chorus, 'turn' and 'counterturn') or triadic (each triad being composed of matching strophe and antistrophe, with a third stanza, epode, with a different metrical pattern). The metres are usually elaborate, and the metrical schema of each poem is with rare exceptions unique. The songs are almost invariably tied to a particular occasion. But celebration of the human or divine addressee is usually accompanied by succinct generalizations (*gnōmai*, see GNŌMĒ) which place the present celebration or its occasion in the broader context of human experience, and regularly a myth is narrated, usually occupying the centre of the ode; though not invariable, this persistent pattern is already established for Alcman in 7th-cent. Sparta. The most striking exception is Stesichorus, whose choral lyric narratives are epic in scale and in their lack of explicit attachment to a specific occasion. The choral lyric tradition reached its peak in the late Archaic and early Classical period in the work of Simonides, Bacchylides, and Pindar, the first 'freelance' professional Panhellenic poets. The same period saw the beginning of the decline of choral lyric as a major literary genre. *Aristophanes (1) (*Nub.* 1355 ff.) and *Eupolis (frs. 148, 398 KA) testify to a change in musical tastes at this period. In the age of the *sophists the old practice of learning to sing lyric compositions fell into decline, and so did interest in and knowledge of the choral poets. At the same time, the nature of choral lyric changed, with choral and monody mixed, the abandonment of strophic responsion in the interests of emotional realism, and an increasing dominance of music over words. Choral poems continued to be composed, and major poets emerged who challenged comparison with the old masters (*Xenophon (1) places *Melanippides (2) the dithyrambist in the same category as *Homer and *Sophocles (1), *Mem.* 1. 4. 3). But the number of choral genres still being composed was much reduced.

Monodic lyric is particularly associated with eastern Greece. *Sappho and *Alcaeus (1) were natives of Lesbos and *Anacreon of Teos. The metrical structures of monody are more simple, and unlike choral lyric are repeated from song to song. The dialect tends to be based on the vernacular of the poet. The subject-matter usually derives from the life and circumstances of the poet. The range of solo lyric is very wide. Love, politics, war, wine, abuse of enemies all figure, though to different degrees and with different emphases and approaches from poet to poet. To the modern reader, this personal poetry often seems remarkably impersonal, since there is a marked tendency to generalize personal experience through the medium of myth. As with choral lyric, there is a visible decline in the 5th cent. The latest monodists to be named by Aristophanes are *Timocreon and Anacreon, both active in the late 6th and early 5th cent. There must have been many contemporary and subsequent monodists, but none achieved Panhellenic importance.

The age of scholarly research on the lyric poets begins with the generation after Aristotle. *Dicaearchus wrote a book about Alcaeus (1). *Clearchus (3)'s book *On Love Poetry* included Sappho and Anacreon. *Chamaeleon wrote on Stesichorus, Anacreon, Simonides, and *Lasus; his studies embraced Alcman and probably Ibycus. The major lyric poets were edited by the scholars of the *Library at *Alexandria (1). It is to Alexandrian scholarship that we owe the list of Nine Lyric Poets, Alcman, Alcaeus (1), Anacreon, Bacchylides, Ibycus, Pindar, Sappho, Simonides, Stesichorus (first attested *c*.100 BC, *Anth. Pal.* 9. 184), identical with those who are studied (*hoi prattomenoi* schol. on Dion. Thrax, p. 21. 18 ff.), i.e. subjected to scholarly exegesis; *Corinna is sometimes appended as a tenth, though we do not find a reference to the Ten Lyric Poets as an established grouping before Johannes *Tzetzes. See CANON. The list of nine covers the period 650–450 BC. It includes all those who were studied by the *Peripatetics, with the exception of Lasus and the inclusion of Bacchylides. It is probably a selection, rather than a collection of all surviving lyric, though the surprising exclusion of Lasus suggests that not all Archaic lyric reached Alexandria.

TEXTS E. M. Voigt, *Sappho et Alcaeus* (1971); Page, *PMG*; Davies, *PMGF* 1; with trans., D. A. Campbell, *Greek Lyric 1–5* (Loeb, 1983–93). CRITICISM C. M. Bowra, *Greek Lyric Poetry*, 2nd edn. (1962); A. P. Burnett, *Three Archaic Poets* (1983); D. A. Campbell, *The Golden Lyre* (1983), and *Greek Lyric Poetry* (1967); M. Davies, *CQ* 1988, 180 ff.; D. E. Gerber, *Euterpe* (1970); G. M. Kirkwood, *Early Greek Monody* (1974).
C. C.

Latin The modern definition of lyric (verse neither epic nor dramatic but characterized by brevity, use of stanzas, and the enthusiastic expression of personal experience and emotion) would have meant little in Roman antiquity. Greek lyric could be defined by the social settings of its performance, the accompaniment of the lyre, and the use of certain metrical patterns. Already, however, the classification of the corpus of lyric poetry posed special problems for the scholars of *Alexandria (1), and in the Roman context the only one of these criteria which may be usefully employed is that of metre. The Roman poets knew the Alexandrian *canon of Nine Greek Lyricists, and *Horace, who considers himself to be the first Latin lyric poet, memorably asks to be added to the list (*Carm.* 1. 1. 35). The generic status of *Catullus (1), who combines lyric and iambic metres in his polymetrics (poems 1–60), is disputed by *Martial, *Quintilian, and *Suetonius. For modern scholars the number of lyric poems to be ascribed to him varies between two and sixty-three. Catullan polymetry (and the use of varied metres in a collection can be considered one of the defining features of ancient lyric) may be compared with polymetric experiments involving lyric metres by *Laevius in his *Erotopaegnia*, *Varro in his **Menippean Satires*, and Horace in his *Epodes*. It is Horace who first combines Hellenistic technical refinement with the spirit of the lyric of *Alcaeus (1) and *Pindar, and his *Odes* represent the crowning achievement of Latin lyric poetry. Before them the **cantica* of *Plautus provide genuine examples of lyric verse, as do the unfortunately fragmentary choral odes of early Roman tragedy (see TRAGEDY, LATIN). After Horace, Seneca's tragedies (see ANNAEUS SENECA (2), L.) include choral lyric and *Statius' *Silvae* contain two lyric poems (4. 5 and 7). *Persius (6. 1 f.) and Quintilian (10. 1. 96) mention the lyric verse of Caesius Bassus, while *Pliny (2) (*Ep.* 9. 22. 2) praises *Passennus Paulus as the equal of Horace and provides evidence (e.g. *Ep.* 3. 1. 7, 7. 4. 9) for a considerable amount of amateur lyric versification. The fragments of a number of 2nd-cent. AD poets, conveniently but misleadingly characterized as the *poetae novelli*, also preserve lyric verse of a metrically innovative but alas now very fragmentary nature. Perhaps the greatest, and certainly the most influential, successors of Horace in the tradition of Latin lyric are the Christian poets *Ambrose in his *Hymns* and *Prudentius in his *Cathemerinon* and *Peristephanon*. See further under individual authors.

R. Heinze, *Vom Geist des Römertums* (1960), 172–89; W. R. Johnson, *The Idea of Lyric* (1982); P. A. Miller, *Lyric Texts and Lyric Consciousness: The Birth of a Genre from Archaic Greece to Augustan Rome* (1994).   D. P. N.

Lysander (d. 395 BC), Spartan general. His family, though of Heraclid origin, was poor and when young he was reputedly of *mothax* status, requiring sponsorship through the *agōgē. He subsequently became the *erastēs* ('lover') of *Agesilaus, younger son of King *Archidamus II. Appointed admiral in 408 or 407, he gained the friendship and support of *Cyrus (2) the Younger, commenced the creation of a personal following, and won a victory at Notion which led to the dismissal of *Alcibiades. Resuming command in 405, he transferred his fleet to the *Hellespont and destroyed the Athenian fleet at *Aegospotami. His personal success was celebrated through several monuments and dedications; at *Samos he was worshipped as a god, perhaps the first living Greek ever to receive divine worship. See RULER-CULT, GREEK. Cf. also *Suppl. Hell.* nos. 51, 325, 565.

Lysander established '*decarchies' of his oligarchical partisans in many cities. Obtaining Athens' surrender through blockade (spring 404), he secured the installation of the *Thirty Tyrants, but his policy was overturned by King *Pausanias (2)'s restoration of democracy in 403. At some (disputed) date before 396 the ephors withdrew support from the faltering decarchies. His continuing influence, however, led Sparta to support Cyrus' attempt on the Persian throne (401) and to make his protégé Agesilaus king. Hoping to restore the decarchies, he obtained for Agesilaus the command against Persia in 396. Resentful of Lysander's personal following, Agesilaus frustrated his plans, but gave him an important Hellespontine command where he persuaded the Persian Spithridates to defect. Back in Sparta in 395, he was instrumental in starting war with *Thebes (1). Invading *Boeotia from *Phocis, he was surprised and killed at *Haliartus before the planned rendezvous with King Pausanias' forces.

An abortive scheme to increase his power by making the kingships elective was 'discovered' after his death by Agesilaus. The sources differ as to whether it was planned in 403 or 395; it may be an invention to discredit his posthumous reputation and supporters. Accurate interpretation of Lysander's career generally is impeded by the hostility of most sources to the imperial system he created.

Xen. *Hell.* 1–3; Diod. Sic. 13–14; Plut. *Lys.* RE 13. 2503–6, 'Lysandros' 1; PB no. 504; A. Andrewes, *Phoenix* 1971, 206–26, and in P. Garnsey and C. Whittaker (eds.), *Imperialism in the Ancient World* (1978), 99–102; J.-F. Bommelaer, *Lysandre de Sparte* (1981).   S. J. Ho.

Lysanias (1), of Mallus, local historian who wrote about *Eretria, cited by *Plutarch in his *On the Malice of Herodotus* (861a–d) as providing a corrective to *Herodotus' account of the *Ionian Revolt: he insisted that the Eretrians fought heroically. This may conceivably rest on some genuine (?oral) tradition, but it is more likely to be partisan reworking of the literary tradition including (but not only) Herodotus. Lysanias is difficult to evaluate because his date cannot be fixed.

FGrH 426; Busolt, *Gr. Gesch.* 2². 544 n. 4; O. Murray, *CAH* 4² (1988), 468.   S. H.

Lysanias (2), of Cyrene (fl. 2nd cent. BC), *Alexandrian philologist, taught *Eratosthenes, wrote *Peri iambopoiiōn* and Homeric studies (fragments listed by Gudeman, *RE* 13. 2508 ff.).
      J. S. R.

Lysias, Attic orator. The ancient biographical tradition, that he was born in 459/8 and died *c.*380 BC ([Plut.] *Vit. Lys.* 835c, 836a; Dion. Hal. *Lys.* 1, 12), is clear but problematic. The latter date is plausible; the former less so, and many scholars suggest that a man some fifteen years younger would have been more likely to engage in his range of activities after 403 (the speeches, and cf. also [Dem.] 59. 21–2). He appears as a character in *Plato (1)'s *Phaedrus*; in the *Republic*, his father Cephalus is an elderly *Syracusan, resident as a *metic in Athens, and friend of assorted Athenian aristocrats: the search for dramatic dates, however, is probably vain.

Lysias and his brother Polemarchus left Athens after Cephalus' death to join the panhellenic colony (see PANHELLENISM) of *Thurii in southern Italy, where he is said to have studied *rhetoric. They were expelled as Athenian sympathizers after the Sicilian expedition (see PELOPONNESIAN WAR), and returned to Athens as metics in 412/1. In 403 the *Thirty Tyrants arrested both brothers, alleging disaffection but really (according to Lys. 12. 6) in order to confiscate their substantial property. Polemarchus was executed; Lysias escaped, and gave financial and physical support to the democratic counter-revolutionaries. He was rewarded by *Thrasybulus' decree granting citizenship to all those who assisted in the restoration, but this grant was promptly annulled as unconstitutional.

Works Modern editions contain 34 numbered speeches, although the titles of about 130 others are known, and for several we possess sufficient fragments (either as citations or on papyrus) to determine the nature of the case. Lysias' activity as a speech-writer after 403 was largely confined to that of forensic *logographer (see first sentence), like his fellow metics *Isaeus (1) and *Dinarchus, composing speeches for litigants to deliver in court; but his versatility was very great. Like *Demosthenes (2) and *Hyperides, he wrote for both public and private cases. The two categories, however, are not formally distinguished in the corpus, where few private speeches remain: most striking is 1, in which a cuckolded husband pleads justifiable homicide after killing his wife's lover, and the attack in 32 on an allegedly dishonest guardian. Private cases are better represented among the fragments, including for instance the *Hippotherses*, which deals with Lysias' attempts to recover his confiscated property from those who had purchased it under the Thirty Tyrants. Underlying the public speeches are a variety of legal procedures, most notably

Lysimachus

the *dokimasia or scrutiny of prospective officials, many of them compromised by their record under the *oligarchies of the *Four Hundred or the Thirty Tyrants (16, 25, 26, 31, and the fragmentary *Eryximachus*); other cases concern official malpractice (most notably 12, in which Lysias personally charged Eratosthenes, ex-member of the Thirty, with having killed Polemarchus). The shadow of the Thirty, indeed, hangs over much of Lysias' work, but attempts to discern a consistent political standpoint throughout the corpus have largely foundered.

Lysias' reputation attracted speeches. We are told ([Plut.] *Vit. Lys.* 836a) that no fewer than 425 were circulating in antiquity, but that only 233 of these were agreed to be genuine. Critics since *Dionysius (7) (Dion. Hal. *Lys.* 11–12) have attempted to determine authorship on chronological, stylistic, or, more recently, stylometric grounds, but the search has proved largely inconclusive. Dover (see bibliog. below) has indeed argued that authorship itself may not be a simple concept, and that Lysias and his clients may have collaborated to varying degrees, but this view remains contentious. More important for most purposes (including for instance the use of the speeches as historical sources) is the authenticity not of authorship but of the texts themselves: with the exception of 11, perhaps of 15, and possibly 6, all the forensic works seem to be genuine speeches, written to be delivered on the occasion they purport to be (though we should allow for the probability of unquantifiable revision).

Characteristics Lysias was noted in antiquity as a master of the language of everyday life: this 'purity' of style led to his being regarded by later rhetoricians as the pre-eminent representative of 'Atticism', as opposed to the florid 'Asiatic' school (see ASIANISM AND ATTICISM). Dionysius (*Lys.* 18) criticized him for lacking emotional power in his arguments, but this may be to miss the significance of his admitted mastery in narrative: by the time Lysias has finished telling a story, the audience has been beguiled by his apparent artlessness into accepting as true the most tendentious assertions. Dionysius noted his mastery of *ēthopoiia* (§ 8), by which he evidently meant the ability to portray character attractively, though there are signs in several speeches (notably 1 and 16) of an attempt also to capture the individuality of the speaker in the language given to him.

> TEXTS Hude (OCT, 1912); Thalheim (Teubner, ed. maior, 1913, including citations; ed. minor, 1928); with trans., Gernet and Bizos (Budé, 1924) including longer citations and some papyri; Lamb (Loeb, 1930).
> COMMENTARIES M. J. Edwards and S. J. Usher, *Greek Orators* 1 (1985), *Or.* 1, 10, 12, 16, 22, 24, 25; C. Carey, *Lysias: Selected Speeches* (1989), *Or.* 1, 3, 7, 14, 31, 32.
> GENERAL K. J. Dover, *Lysias and the Corpus Lysiacum* (1968).
>   S. C. T.

Lysimachus (c.355–281 BC), Macedonian from *Pella (late sources wrongly allege Thessalian origins), was prominent in the entourage of *Alexander (3) the Great, achieving the rank of Bodyguard by 328. At *Babylon (323) he received *Thrace as his province, establishing himself with some difficulty against the Thracian dynast, Seuthes (322). He consolidated his power in the eastern coastal districts, suppressing a revolt among the Black Sea cities (313) and founding Lysimacheia in the *Chersonese (1) as a bulwark against the Odrysian monarchy (309). Though he assumed royal titulature (306/5), he made no mark in the wars of the Successors (see DIADOCHI) until in 302 he invaded Asia Minor and fought the delaying campaign against *Antigonus (1) which enabled Seleucus (1) to bring up his army for the decisive

battle of *Ipsus (301). His reward was the lands of Asia Minor north of the *Taurus, the source of immense wealth, which he husbanded with legendary tight-fistedness and a degree of fiscal rapacity. These new reserves (*Pergamum alone held 9,000 talents) supported his impressive coinage and allowed him to consolidate in Europe, where he extended his boundaries north until he was captured by the Getic king, Dromichaetes, and forced to surrender his Transdanubian acquisitions (292). In 287 he joined *Pyrrhus in expelling *Demetrius (4) from Macedon and two years later occupied the entire kingdom. His writ now ran from the Epirote borders to the Taurus, but dynastic intrigue proved his nemesis, when he killed his heir, Agathocles, at the instigation of his second wife, *Arsinoë II, and alienated his nobility (283). *Seleucus (1) was invited to intervene and again invaded Asia Minor. The decisive battle at Corupedium (c. January 281) cost Lysimachus his life. Asia passed to the Seleucids while Macedonia dissolved into anarchy.

> HM 3; S. M. Burstein, in W. Heckel and R. Sullivan (eds.), *Ancient Coins of the Graeco-Roman World* (1984), 57 ff.; H. S. Lund, *Lysimachus* (1992); Heckel, *Marshals* 267 ff.   A. B. B.

Lysippus (1), poet of Old Comedy (see COMEDY (GREEK), OLD). He was victorious in 409 BC (*Inscriptiones graecae urbis Romae*, ed. L. Moretti (1968–90), 216. 7–9 = 6 A 2, 7–9 Mette). His Βάκχαι (*Bacchantes*) contained a jibe on the seer *Lampon (fr. 6).

> FRAGMENTS Kassel–Austin, PCG 5. 618–22, although earlier scholars use the numbering in Kock, CAF 1. 700–3.
> INTERPRETATION Meineke, FCG 1. 215 f.; A. Körte, RE 14/1 (1928), 46, 'Lysippos' 4; G. Norwood, *Greek Comedy* (1931), 35 f.
>   W. G. A.

Lysippus (2) and **Lysistratus**, Sicyonian sculptors (see SICYON), active c.370–315 BC. The two, who were brothers, worked exclusively in bronze. Lysippus was by far the more prolific and famous, producing gods, heroes, agonistic victors, portraits, animals, and even metal vases; Lysistratus is known only for his portrait of Melanippe and for his innovative technique. He took plaster life-masks from his subjects, made adjustments on the wax castings thus obtained, and based his portraits on them (Plin. HN 35. 153). He also took casts from statues, presumably either for workshop consultation or for reproduction (and sale?).

Lysippus was also an innovator. Aggressively independent (Plin. HN 34. 61), he acknowledged the Doryphorus of *Polyclitus (2) as his master only ironically (Cic. *Brut.* 86, 296). This is consistent with *Pliny (1)'s report (HN 34. 65) that he abandoned Polyclitan four-square proportions for a slim physique and small head that made his figures look taller, and cultivated great precision of detail. This approach explains his success as a portraitist (see PORTRAITURE).

His works ranged in scale from an 18.3-m. (60-ft.) *Zeus and a colossal *Heracles for *Tarentum to the 0.3-m. (1-ft.) Heracles Epitrapezius. Roman copies convey their appearance. Many copies of an *Eros with a bow have been connected with his Eros at *Thespiae, and his *Kairos ('Opportunity') appears on reliefs and gems: winged, with a tuft of hair over the forehead but bald behind, and running with a balance supported on a razor, it illustrated the proverb 'Seize time by the forelock', but may also have embodied his artistic credo. His numerous athletes are represented by a contemporary marble version at *Delphi of his Agias (erected 337–332) and by two copies of his Apoxyomenos; the latter both thrusts his arms out into the observer's space and rocks from foot to foot. An original bronze athlete in Malibu

(Getty Museum) is probably a school piece (see LYSIPPUS, SCHOOL OF).

Among his portraits, a late classical *Socrates type ('B') may copy his statue for the Pompeion in Athens. He was *Alexander (3) the Great's favourite sculptor, but few copies remain. If correctly attributed, the so-called Dresden type shows Alexander as crown prince (cf. Plin. *HN* 34. 63), the Schwarzenberg type as the heroic, leonine warrior (Plut. *Mor.* 335b), and the inscribed Azara type as a Zeus on earth (Plut. *Mor.* 335a). Bronze statuettes preserve several different body-types; all once held the spear that proclaimed his kingly authority and martial prowess (Plut. *Mor.* 360d). An equestrian statuette in Naples has been connected with his group at Dium (in *Macedonia) of the king and his 25 Companions who fell at the *Granicus in 334, and a Hellenistic relief from *Messene may reproduce his group at Delphi of *Craterus (1) saving the king from a lion.

Attributions (all copies) include the Farnese Heracles (see GLYCON (2)), the Lateran *Poseidon, a *Dionysus in Venice, a seated *Hermes from *Herculaneum, the Berlin–Santa Barbara Dancer (cf. Plin. *HN* 34. 63), and several athletes. A revolutionary figure, Lysippus transformed the classical tradition in sculpture; his influence lasted into the Hellenistic period through his pupils (see CHARES (4); EUTYCHIDES).

J. J. Pollitt, *Art in the Hellenistic Age* (1986), 20 ff., 47 ff.; P. Moreno, *Lisippo* (1987); B. S. Ridgway, *Hellenistic Sculpture* 1 (1990), 73 ff., 108 ff.; A. F. Stewart, *Greek Sculpture* (1990), 186 ff., 289 ff., figs. 551 ff.

A. F. S.

Lysippus, school of According to *Pliny (1), *HN* 34. 66, Lysippus (2) left three sons and pupils, Laippus (probably Daippus, misreading the initial Δ as Λ), Boedas, and Euthycrates. Elsewhere, he adds *Chares (4) of Lindos and Phanis, and *Pausanias (3) (6. 2. 6) adds *Eutychides of Sicyon. In *HN* 34. 51, Pliny dates Eutychides, Euthycrates, and ⟨D⟩aippus to 296–293 BC, and in 34. 67 and 83 he remarks that Tisicrates of Sicyon and Xenocrates of Athens belonged to the school's second generation. Its last member was Tisicrates' son Thoenias, active *c.*250–230 BC.

Working exclusively in bronze, the school inherited Lysippus' technique, style, and clientele: the Successor-monarchs (*Diadochi), the new eastern cities, those of old Greece, and private individuals. Euthycrates was the most renowned, 'imitating his father's rigour rather than his elegance, preferring to find favour in the austere rather than the graceful style' (*HN* 34. 66). His major works were a *Heracles at *Delphi, an *Alexander (3) the Great Hunting at *Thespiae, a cavalry battle, a *Trophonius at Lebadea, and several chariot groups; he also portrayed famous women like the poetess *Anyte of Tegea. Daippus, on the other hand, specialized in Olympic victors (Paus. 6. 12. 6, 16. 5; Plin. *HN* 34. 87); Boedas and Phanis are each known for only one work, an 'Adorans' and a 'Sacrificing Woman'. The school's two acknowledged masterpieces were the Colossus of Rhodes by Chares and the *Tyche of *Antioch (1) by Eutychides. Xenocrates was its theorist and also wrote on painting (Plin. *HN* 34. 83, 35. 68). *Antigonus (4) of Carystus used him, and he perhaps provided Pliny with his critiques of *Polyclitus (2), *Pythagoras (2), *Myron (1), and Lysippus (cf. Plin. *HN* 1. 34). If so, he is the father of formalist art history.

Attributions (all bronzes) include the 'Getty Bronze' (a youthful Olympic (?) victor of *c.*300), the Ephesus Scraper, a colossal head in Madrid, and a Praying Boy, perhaps a version of Boedas' 'Adorans'. The marble Anzio Girl in Rome is probably not a copy of Phanis' 'Sacrificing Woman', but an original of *c.*200 or later; a herm from the Villa of the Papyri at *Herculaneum perhaps reproduces Tisicrates' portrait of *Demetrius (4) Poliorcetes.

A. F. Stewart, *Greek Sculpture* (1990), 200 f., 297 ff., figs. 617 ff., 721 f.

A. F. S.

Lysis (1), of *Tarentum, a Pythagorean (see PYTHAGORAS (1)) who migrated to *Achaea and then to *Thebes (1) and became the teacher of *Epaminondas. It is uncertain whether he wrote anything.

DK 46; *RE* 14. 64. See also P. Vidal-Naquet, *The Black Hunter* (1986), 68.

Lysis (2) (fl. *c.*300 BC), the originator of λυσιῳδία (a dramatic / musical form named after him, in which female roles were played in male dress). He probably came from *Magnesia (1) on the Maeander in Ionia, like his predecessor Simus, the inventor of the analogously named σιμῳδία. See MAGODIA.

W. G. A.

Lysistratus, sculptor. See LYSIPPUS (2).

Macar, sometimes called *Macareus, in mythology a Lesbian king (*Il.* 24. 544), but usually a son of *Helios and so a Rhodian (schol. Pind. *Ol.* 7. 135); for various accounts of his parentage and adventures, see Schirmer in Roscher's *Lexikon*, under 'Macar'. His name, very strange for a mortal because a stock divine *epithet, has been interpreted as a corruption of Melqart.

H. J. R.

Macareus, when not identical with *Macar, is usually the name of a son of *Aeolus (see (1), for his incestuous love of his sister *Canace). Several minor figures have the same name, e.g. a son of *Lycaon (3) (Apollod. 3. 8. 2); a Lapith (Ov. *Met.* 12. 447; see CENTAURS).

H. J. R.

Maccabees The name Maccabee, probably meaning 'the hammer', was the appellation of Judas son of Mattathias, leader of the Judaean Revolt of 168/7 BC against *Antiochus (4) IV Epiphanes. See JEWS. The name was given also to Judas' fellow rebels, his father and his four brothers. They were the leaders of the traditionalists, reacting against a process of Hellenization in Jerusalem masterminded by a section of the Jewish aristocracy (see HELLENISM AND HELLENIZATION). The high priesthood was usurped by Jason, a member of the Oniad clan, from his brother Menelaus. But the ultimate provocation to the Maccabees was the king's installation of a garrison in the city and a pagan cult in the Temple, and his consequent attempt to suppress Judaism on a wide front. After Mattathias' public killing of an apostate Jew in the act of sacrifice, the Maccabees took to the hills to conduct a guerrilla war, eventually winning concessions from the regent Lysias on behalf of the young Antiochus V. Judas rededicated the Temple on 25 Kislev (December) 164 BC, a date already marked within a few years of the events as the festival of Hanukkah. But he continued to resist the Hellenizers in Jerusalem and successive *Seleucid armies. A memorable victory against Nicanor, the Seleucid general, in 161 was followed by the defeat and death of Judas in 160, in battle against Bacchides, after which his brother Jonathan continued the struggle (see HASMONEANS).

The term Maccabees is also applied to the two Greek books in which the revolt and its sequel are narrated and to two associated books (see JEWISH-GREEK LITERATURE). Finally, the name is sometimes given to the seven children and their mother, whose legendary martyrdom in the persecution of Epiphanes, described in 2 Maccabees 7 and embellished in 4 Maccabees, was remembered in rabbinic literature and gave rise to a cult at *Antioch (1) and to a long-lasting Christian tradition (as well as to the word 'macabre').

E. Bickerman, *From Ezra to the Last of the Maccabees* (1962); Schürer, *History* 1. 164–73; *Cambridge History of Judaism* (1989), 292–351.   T. R.

Macedonia By its geographical position Macedonia forms the connecting link between the Balkans and the Greek peninsula. Four important routes converge on the Macedonian plain: from the Danube (see DANUVIUS) via the Morava and Axius valleys, from the *Adriatic via Lake Ochrid, from *Thrace via Mygdonia, and from the Greek peninsula via *Tempe. In climate Macedonia is intermediate between Europe and the Mediterranean. The original Macedonia was Pieria and Mt. *Olympus (1), and from there the Macedonians acquired the coastal plain of the Thermaic Gulf, which has been formed by the rivers Haliacmon, Lydias, and Axius. These rivers, draining the wide plateaux of Upper Macedonia cut the mountain-ring of the Macedonian plain at Beroea, Edessa, and the defile of Demir Kapu. Of the cantons of Upper Macedonia Elimiotis occupied the middle and Orestis the upper Haliacmon valley, Lyncus and Pelagonia the upper valleys of the Erigon (a tributary of the Axius), Paeonia the upper valley of the Axius, and Eordaea the basin of Lake Arnissa west of Edessa. The Macedonian plain comprised Pieria south of the lower Haliacmon, Bottiaea between the Haliacmon and the Axius, Almopia in the upper Lydias valley, Mygdonia in the Lake Bolbe basin leading towards the Strymon valley, Crestonia and Anthemus north and south respectively of Mygdonia. Upper Macedonia is girt by high mountain-ranges traversed mainly by three important routes mentioned above; when united, it had strong natural defences. The Macedonian plain is vulnerable from the sea and from Mygdonia, but the defiles leading into Upper Macedonia are easily defensible. The natural products were *horses, cattle, sheep, crops, *wine, fruit, *iron, *gold, *silver, and *timber, the last two being exported in antiquity.

Prehistoric Macedonia, occupied continuously from early neolithic times, possessed a uniform culture in the bronze age, little influenced by Mycenae, and was invaded *c.*1150 BC by a northern people, of whom a western offshoot may have provoked the Dorian invasion (see DORIANS; HERACLIDAE). *Hesiod first mentioned 'Makedon', the eponym of the people and the country, as a son of *Zeus, a grandson of *Deucalion, and so a first cousin of *Aeolus (2), Dorus, and *Xuthus; in other words he considered the 'Macedones' to be an outlying branch of the Greek-speaking tribes, with a distinctive dialect of their own, 'Macedonian' (see MACEDONIAN LANGUAGE). He gave their habitat as 'Pieria and Olympus'. In northern Pieria an early iron age cemetery of 300 tumuli, partly excavated, has revealed the rulers there as probably Phrygians (see PHRYGIA) and then *Illyrii until *c.*650 BC, when it went out of use. At that time a new dynasty, the Temenidae (see TEMENUS), ruling the Macedonians, founded their early capital at *Aegae (mod. Vergina), situated above the cemetery, and thereafter gained control of the coastal plain as far as the Axius. The Persian occupation of Macedonia 512–479 BC was beneficial.

*Xerxes gave to *Alexander (1) I the rule over western Upper Macedonia, which was peopled by Epirotic tribes with their own dialect of Greek; and after Xerxes' flight Alexander gained territory west of the Strymon. His claim to be a Temenid, descended from *Heracles and related to the royal house of *Argos (2) in the Peloponnese, was recognized at *Olympia; he issued a fine royal coinage and profited from the export of ship-timber.

The potential of the Macedonian kingdom was realized by *Philip (1) II. By defeating the northern barbarians and incorporating the Greek-speaking Upper Macedonians he created a superb army (see ARMIES, GREEK), which was supported economically by other peoples who were brought by conquest into the enlarged kingdom: *Illyrii, Paeonians, and Thracians—with their own non-Greek languages—and Chalcidians (see CHALCIDICE) and Bottiaeans, both predominantly Greek-speaking. 'He created a united kingdom from many tribes and nations' (Just. *Epit*. 8. 6. 2) by a policy of tolerance and assimilation. His son *Alexander (3) the Great, inheriting the strongest state in eastern Europe, carried his conquests to the borders of Afghanistan and Pakistan. Later the conquered territories split up into kingdoms ruled mainly by Macedonian royal families, which fought against one another and contended for the original Macedonian kingdom (see ANTIGONUS (1–3); DEMETRIUS (4) and (6); PTOLEMY (1); SELEUCIDS). In 167 BC Rome defeated Macedonia and split it into four republics; and in 146 BC it was constituted a Roman province. Thereafter its history merged with that of the Roman empire.

From Philip II onwards the Macedonian court was a leading centre of Greek culture, and the policies of Alexander and his Successors (*Diadochi) spread the Greek-based 'Hellenistic' culture in the east, which continued to flourish for centuries after the collapse of Macedonian power. See COLONIZATION, HELLENISTIC; HELLENISM AND HELLENIZATION.

W. A. Heurtley, *Prehistoric Macedonia* (1939); M. Sakellariou (ed.), *Macedonia: 4,000 years of Greek History and Civilization* (1983); N. G. L. Hammond, *A History of Macedonia* 1–3 (vol. 2 with G. T. Griffith, vol. 3 with F. W. Walbank) (1972–88), *The Macedonian State* (1989), and *The Miracle that was Macedonia* (1991); E. N. Borza, *In the Shadow of Olympus* (1990). R. Errington, *History of Macedonia* (1986; Eng. trans. 1990); R. Billows, *Kings and Colonists: Aspects of Macedonian Imperialism* (1995).
N. G. L. H.

Macedonia, cults Nowadays historians generally agree that the Macedonians form part of the Greek *ethnos* (see ETHNICITY; MACEDONIAN LANGUAGE); hence they also shared in the common religious and cultural features of the Hellenic world. Consequently most of the gods worshipped in Greece can also be found in Macedonia. However, regional characteristics have to be noted. Especially in the areas bordering on *Thrace and among the Paeonians in the north—though these had early contacts with the Macedonians in the centre—local deviants in cult and religion have been attested.

The cult of *Zeus was one of the most important cults in Macedonia. Its places of worship on *Olympus (1), at the foot of the mountain at Dion, and at *Aegae (Vergina) were extremely popular. As father of Makedon he was the Macedonians' eponymous ancestor. The cult of *Artemis was widely practised. Although most of the evidence dates to Roman times one may assume the existence of older religious practices. In the areas in contact with Thrace it is determined by the Thracian cult of Artemis and the worship of *Bendis, probably themselves types of a deity of fertility and vegetation. Herodotus (4. 33) says that women in Thrace and Paeonia always brought wheat-straw in their offerings to Artemis Basileia. In central Macedonia Enodia is attested, on horseback and holding a torch. She has frequently been associated with Artemis. By comparison the cult of *Apollo is not as widespread. Here too local deviants can be found. In Thessalonica, where *Pythian Games were held in honour of Apollo Pythius, the cult of Apollo is even connected with the *Cabiri.

The cult of *Dionysus, whom the Paeonians called Dyalus, was especially popular. However, the sites are unevenly distributed. On the basis of the borders of the later Macedonian provinces there are fewer monuments for Dionysus in the south-west, while one of the cult centres was in the area of the Pangaeus—a region admittedly also settled in by the Thracians.

Zeus, *Apollo, *Heracles, Dionysus, *Athena, and other such gods appear on coins of the 5th and 4th cents. BC. This evidence, however, ought not to be overestimated since these gods were depicted chiefly in order to demonstrate the close links with the Greek world. Especially important was Heracles not only as the ancestor of the Macedonian royal family, but also fulfilling manifold other functions, e.g. as the patron of *hunting. Other cults of not inconsiderable importance were those of *Helios, among the Paeonians worshipped as a disc, *Selene, the *Dioscuri, healing deities—represented by *Asclepius and *Hygieia—*river-gods, *nymphs, the Pierian *Muses, and a strange *snake. Alongside the cult of Dionysus and the Samothracian *mysteries (see SAMOTHRACE), *Orphism too was not unknown (Derveni papyrus *c*.330 BC, see ORPHIC LITERATURE).

The so-called Thracian Rider (see RIDER-GODS) is attested on votive tablets in north and east Macedonia. However, in contrast to Thrace the *Heros Equitans* is frequently depicted on Macedonian tombstones. The numerous deifications of the dead as e.g. *Aphrodite, Artemis, Athena, Dionysus, *Eros, *Hermes, and Heracles belong in this context. These monuments, as well as most of the rider-statues and the votive reliefs depicting various deities, generally date to the second half of the 2nd and the first half of the 3rd cent. AD.

W. Baege, *De Macedonum sacris* (1913); C. Edson, *Harv. Theol. Rev.* 1948, 181 ff.; S. Duell, *Die Götterkulte Nordmakedoniens in römischer Zeit* (1977), and *Ancient Macedonia* 3 (1983), 77–87; D. K. Samsaris, *Ereunes sten historia, ten topographia kai tes latreies ton romaikon eparchion Makedonias kai Thrakes* (1984); M. Hatzopoulos, *Cultes et rites de passage en Macédoine* (1994).
M. O.

Macedonian language The problem of the nature and origin of the Macedonian language is still disputed by modern scholars, but does not seem to have been raised among the ancients. We have a rare adverb μακεδονιστί (important passages in *Plutarch, *Alex*. 51 and *Eum*. 14), but the meaning of this form is ambiguous. The adverb cannot tell us whether Plutarch had in mind a language different from Greek (cf. φοινικιστί, 'in Phoenician'), or a dialect (cf. μεγαριστί, 'in Megarian'), or a way of speaking (cf. ἀττικιστί). We have some 'Macedonian' glosses, particularly in *Hesychius' lexicon, but they are mostly disputed and some were corrupted in the transmission. Thus ἀβροῦτες, 'eyebrows' probably must be read as ἀβροῦϝες (with τ which renders a digamma). If so, it is a Greek dialect form; yet others (e.g. A. Meillet) see the dental as authentic and think that the word belongs to an *Indo-European language different from Greek.

After more than a century we recognize among linguists two schools of thought. Those who reject the Greek affiliation of Macedonian prefer to treat it as an Indo-European language of the Balkans, located geographically and linguistically between *Illyrian in the west and Thracian in the east. Some, like G.

Bonfante (1987, see bibliog. below), look towards Illyrian; others, like I. I. Russu (1938), towards 'Thraco-Phrygian' (at the cost, sometimes, of unwarranted segmentations such as that of Ἀλέξανδρος into †ἀλε- and †ξανδ-). Those who favour a purely Greek nature of Macedonian as a northern Greek dialect are numerous and include early scholars like A. Fick (1874) and O. Hoffmann (1906). The Greek scholars, like G. Hatzidakis (1897, etc.) and above all J. Kalléris (1954 and 1976), have turned this assumption into a real dogma, with at times nationalistic overtones. This should not prevent us, however, from inclining towards this view.

For a long while Macedonian onomastics, which we know relatively well thanks to history, literary authors, and epigraphy, has played a considerable role in the discussion. See NAMES, PERSONAL, GREEK. In our view the Greek character of most names is obvious and it is difficult to think of a Hellenization (see HELLENISM) due to wholesale borrowing. Πτολεμαῖος is attested as early as *Homer, Ἀλέξανδρος occurs next to the Mycenaean feminine *a-re-ka-sa-da-ra* (Alexandra), Λάαγος, then Λᾶγος, matches the Cyprian *Lawagos*, etc. The small minority of names which do not look Greek, like Ἀρριδαῖος or Σαβαττάρας, may be due to substratum or adstratum influence (as elsewhere in Greece). Macedonian may then be seen as a Greek dialect, characterized by its marginal position and by local pronunciations (like Βερενίκα for Φερενίκα, etc.). Yet in contrast with earlier views which made of it an Aeolic dialect (O. Hoffmann compared Thessalian) we must by now think of a link with North-West Greek (Locrian, Aetolian, Phocidian, Epirote). This view is supported by the recent discovery at *Pella of a curse tablet (4th cent. BC) which may well be the first 'Macedonian' text attested (provisional publication by E. Voutyras; cf. the *Bulletin Épigraphique* in *Rev. Ét. Grec.* 1994, no. 413); the text includes an adverb ὅποκα which is not Thessalian. We must wait for new discoveries, but we may tentatively conclude that Macedonian is a dialect related to North-West Greek. See GREEK LANGUAGE; DIALECTS, GREEK (PREHISTORY).

A. Fick, 'Zum makedonischen dialecte', *Zeitschrift für vergleichende Sprachforschung* 1874, 193–235; O. Hoffmann, *Die Makedonen* (1906); repr. 1974); I. I. Russu, *Macedonica* = *Ephemeris Dacoromana* 1938, 105–232; J. Kalléris, *Les anciens Macédoniens* 1 (1954), 2/1 (1976) [no more published; repr. 1988]; G. Bonfante, *Rend. Linc.* 1987, 83–5; C. Brixhe and A. Panayotou, in F. Bader (ed.), *Les langues indo-européennes* (1994), 205–20. O. Ma.

macellum See MARKETS AND FAIRS, *Rome*.

Machaon and **Podalirius**, sons of *Asclepius and physicians already in *Homer, but sons of *Poseidon in the *Iliu Persis* (see EPIC CYCLE). In *Il.* 2. 731–3, they lead the contingent from Tricca in *Thessaly (focus of the later cult of Asclepius), *Ithome, and Oechalia. Their names have an epic ring, Μαχάων being 'Warrior', Ποδα-λείριος apparently 'Lily-foot'. Machaon tends *Menelaus (*Il.* 4. 200–19), but is also active as a fighter and is wounded by *Paris (*Il.* 11. 505–20); Podalirius is too busy in the battle to tend *Eurypylus (*Il.* 11. 836). Their further feats at Troy consist mostly of healing or fighting: they heal *Philoctetes (Soph. *Phil.* 1333 f.; other sources name only one of them), Machaon is killed by Eurypylus (*Little Iliad* fr. 30 Bernabé), Podalirius survives the war and settles in one of several places, especially in *Caria or southern *Italy. They had a cult, both separately (Machaon at Gerenia in *Messenia, Paus. 3. 26. 9; Podalirius an *oracle in Daunia (see DAUNIANS), on Monte Gargano, Lycoph. *Alex.* 1047) and together, generally with their father.

Farnell, *Hero-Cults*; E. J. and L. Edelstein, *Asclepius: A Collection and Interpretation of the Testimonies* (1945). H. J. R.; F. G.

Machon, New Comedy poet and raconteur, born at *Corinth or *Sicyon but resident in *Alexandria (1), where he staged his comedies about the middle of the 3rd cent. BC. From his epitaph by *Dioscorides (1) (Ath. 6. 241 f., *Anth. Pal.* 7. 708 = 24 Gow-Page, *HE*)—'O city of Cecrops, sometimes on the banks of the Nile too the pungent thyme has grown in the garden of the Muses'—it has been inferred ('city of *Cecrops' is Athens) that Machon revived the keen invective of Old Comedy in Alexandria (cf. fr. 21 Gow), but the two surviving comic fragments belong rather to the style of Middle or New Comedy, which was not devoid of pungency. See COMEDY (GREEK), OLD; MIDDLE; NEW.

Machon also composed in iambic trimeters a book of anecdotes (χρεῖαι: see CHREIA) about the remarks and behaviour of notorious Athenian courtesans, *parasites, etc. (462 lines, mainly scurrilous, preserved in Ath. 13).

All the fragments have been edited with introduction and commentary by A. S. F. Gow (1965); comic fragments in Kassel–Austin, *PCG* 5. 623–5. See also Meineke, *FCG* 1. 478 ff.; A. Körte, *RE* 14/1 (1928), 158 f.; I. Gallo, *Teatro ellenistico minore* (1981), 141 ff. W. G. A.

Macrianus See FULVIUS IUNIUS MACRIANUS, T.

Macrinus See OPELLIUS MACRINUS, M.

Macro See SUTORIUS MACRO, Q. NAEVIUS CORDUS.

Macrobius (*RE* 7) **Ambrosius Theodosius,** wrote (1) *De verborum Graeci et Latini differentiis vel societatibus*, (2) *Commentarii in Somnium Scipionis*, (3) *Saturnalia*; in the dedications of (1) and of *Avianus' fables simply 'Theodosius'; in MSS of (2) and (3) styled *vir clarissimus et illustris* (the highest grade of senator); identical with Theodosius, praetorian prefect of Italy in AD 430 (Cameron, see bibliog below), rather than with Macrobius, proconsul of Africa in 410 (Flamant); father of Fl. Macrobius Plotinus Eustathius, city prefect *c.*461, dedicatee of (2) and (3); grandfather of Macrobius Plotinus Eudoxius, who corrected a text of (2).

(1) *De differentiis*. This treatise, addressed to a Symmachus (? the orator *Symmachus (2)'s grandson, consul 446), comparing the Greek verb with the Latin, survives in extracts made at Bobbio and more extensively by Eriugena; it uses *Apollonius (13) Dyscolus and may have been used by *Priscian. Another Bobbio fragment (*De verbo*), addressed to a scholar called Severus, comparing the Latin verb with the Greek, is not Macrobius' work, though possibly based on it.

(2) *Commentarii*. Having discussed how *Cicero's *Republic* differs from *Plato (1)'s, and what *dreams are, Macrobius expounds the *Somnium* philosophically, discoursing on number-mysticism, oracles, moral virtue, astronomy, music, geography, and the *soul (vindicating Plato against *Aristotle); he praises P. *Cornelius Scipio Aemilianus for uniting all the virtues, and the *Somnium* for uniting all the branches of philosophy. The main source is *Porphyry, in particular his commentary on *Timaeus*; but direct knowledge of *Plotinus has been established. Despite frequent inconsistencies and misapprehensions, the work was a principal transmitter of ancient science and Neoplatonic thought to the western Middle Ages. See NEOPLATONISM.

(3) *Saturnalia*. This work is cast in the form of dialogues on the evening before the Saturnalia (16 December, see SATURNUS, SATURNALIA) of AD 383(?) and during the holiday proper. The guests include the greatest pagan luminaries of the time (*Praetextatus, Symmachus, *Nicomachus (4) Flavianus),

Avienus (variously identified with a son of *Avienus the *Aratea poet and with *Avianus the fabulist, if in fact called Avienus), and the grammarian *Servius, still a shy youth but praised in accordance with his later eminence; other names seem taken from Symmachus' letters (Dysarius the doctor, Horus the philosopher, Euangelus the boor). Macrobius himself plays no part. After a few legal and grammatical discussions the night before, the three days are devoted to serious topics in the morning, lighter ones, including food and drink, in the afternoon and evening. Having ranged over the Saturnalia, the calendar, and famous persons' jokes, the speakers devote the second and third mornings to *Virgil, represented as a master of philosophical and religious lore and praised almost without reserve in matters of rhetoric and grammar, including his use of earlier poets, Greek and Roman. The guests then turn to physiology, with special reference to eating and drinking. Sources include *Gellius (constantly used and never named), L. *Annaeus Seneca (2)'s *Epistulae*, *Plutarch's *Quaestiones convivales*, Aelius *Donatus, and [*Alexander (14) of Aphrodisias], *Physical Problems*; they are adapted to Macrobius' own purposes, as when matter from Gellius is used in a preface professing orderly exposition. The work expresses the nostalgia of the Christianized élite in a diminished Rome for the city's great and pagan past; the new religion is ignored. Macrobius' style is elegant, without the extravagance of a *Sidonius Apollinaris or a *Martianus Capella. Though much exploited by John of Salisbury, the *Saturnalia* was less read in the Middle Ages than the *Commentarii*, but returned to favour in the Renaissance.

TEXTS (1) P. De Paolis (1990); (2 and 3) J. Willis (Teubner, 2nd edn. 1970); (2) L. Scarpa (1981), M. Regali (1983–90); (3) N. Marinone (2nd edn. 1977). *De verbo*: M. Passalacqua, *Tre testi grammaticali bobbiesi* (1984).
TRANSLATIONS (2) W. H. Stahl (1952); (3) P. V. Davies (1969).
STUDIES A. Cameron, *JRS* 1966, 25–38; J. Flamant, *Macrobe et le néo-platonisme latin* (1977).
BIBLIOGRAPHY P. De Paolis, *Lustrum*, 1986–7, 107–84.
PLRE 2. 1102 f.   L. A. H.-S.

Madauros (mod. Mdaourouch) in *Numidia was ruled successively by *Syphax and *Masinissa. It was occupied by the Romans to dominate the powerful Musulmani. Probably under *Nerva its native population was supplemented by retired legionaries, and the town received colonial rights as *Colonia Flavia Veteranorum Madaurensium*. *Apuleius was born at Madauros; and since the city was a noted intellectual centre with several schools, *Augustine received part of his education there. Substantial remains of the Byzantine fortifications survive, bisecting the Roman forum and incorporating the adjacent theatre; other visible monuments include temples, two baths, mausolea, and numerous houses. Over twenty oil presses have been identified in the town, indicating the importance of olives in the local agricultural economy. There has been a rich epigraphic haul of nearly a thousand Latin inscriptions.

S. Gsell and C.-A. Joly, *Khamissa, Mdaourouch, Announe* 2 (1922). Inscriptions: *CIL* 8. 4672–763, 16868–907; S. Gsell, *Inscriptions latines de l'Algérie* 1 (1922), nos. 2031–829.   W. N. W.; B. H. W.; R. J. A. W.

Maeander (Μαίανδρος), a river which rises in several sources, including the Marsyas, in and near Celaenae-Apamea in *Phrygia, and flows through the Peltene plain to engage itself first in a narrow valley and then in a canyon 457 m. (1,500 ft.) deep, sunk in the western flank of the Anatolian plateau, whence it emerges to join the Lycus near Colossae, *Laodicea-Lycus, Hierapolis, and Tripolis. Thence to the Sinus Latmius (Latmic gulf) it flows through a flat-bottomed, fertile valley, here dividing *Lydia from *Caria, and passing among other cities *Tralles and *Magnesia (1) ad Maeandrum. In this part of its course it winds much, and the Greeks described it as σκολιός ('crooked') and used its name to describe a winding pattern. Flowing past *Priene in antiquity, the river eventually made a bar across the mouth of the Latmic Gulf, so that the harbours of *Miletus and the island of Lade (scene of a naval battle in 494 BC at the end of the *Ionian Revolt) are now landlocked.

LIMC 6. 1 (1992), 338 ff. (personification in art).   W. M. C.; J. M. C.

Maecenas, Gaius Maecenas is his *nomen*: 'Cilnius' (Tac. *Ann.* 6. 11) may be his mother's name, perhaps descended from an ancient *Etruscan family, the Cilnii of *Arretium (Livy 10. 3. 2). The poets call Maecenas scion of Etruscan kings (Hor. *Carm.* 1. 1. 1). Among Octavian's earliest supporters—he fought at *Philippi—he was his intimate and trusted friend and agent. (See AUGUSTUS.) His great position rested entirely on this: he never held a magistracy or entered the senate, remaining an *eques* (see EQUITES). He arranged Octavian's marriage with *Scribonia, and represented him at the negotiations of the pact of Brundisium (40 BC) and that of Tarentum (37 BC), when he took along his poets (Hor. *Sat.* 1. 5). He went as envoy to M. *Antonius (2) (Mark Antony) in 38, and in 36–33 and 31–29 he was in control of Rome and Italy in Octavian's absence, an unprecedented position: 'no title, only armed power' (Syme, *AA* 272). In 30, claiming to uncover a conspiracy, he executed the son of the triumvir M. *Aemilius Lepidus (3). His enormous wealth must derive partly from the confiscations: by chance we hear that he acquired part of the possessions of the proscribed M. Favonius (schol. Juv. 5. 3). He bequeathed the emperor everything, including his magnificent house and grounds on the *Esquiline, the famous *turris Maecenatiana*. Many inscriptions survive of his slaves and *freedmen. Maecenas was famous, or notorious, for his luxury: wines, gourmet dishes (baby donkey, Plin. *HN* 8. 170), gems, fabrics, and love affairs (that with the dancer Bathyllus became scandalous: Tac. *Ann.* 1. 54). Astute and vigorous at need, he cultivated an image of softness (Sen. *Ep.* 114). His name became proverbial as the greatest patron of poets (Martial 8. 55. 5; see PATRONAGE, LITERARY). Absent from the *Eclogues*, he is the dedicatee of *Virgil's *Georgics*; unnamed in *Propertius 1, he is a rewarding and apparently exigent patron in 2. 1. Virgil introduced *Horace (Hor. *Sat.* 1. 6. 54), who dedicated to Maecenas *Satires* 1, *Epodes*, *Odes* 1–3, and *Epistles* 1. Maecenas gave Horace his Sabine estate. Horace gives the fullest picture of Maecenas and his circle, which included L. *Varius Rufus, *Plotius Tucca, *Domitius Marsus, and his freedman C. *Maecenas Melissus. Maecenas wrote poems which recall the metres and to some extent the manner of Catullus (1): extant fragments of two are addressed to Horace, intimate in tone. He wrote in prose: *Prometheus* (? a *Menippean satire); *Symposium*, Virgil and Horace being speakers; *De cultu suo*. His style was criticized for affectation: 'the preciosity and neuroticism of the author come through strongly in the fragments' (Courtney). They contain no trace of politics, but Maecenas must have been influential in inducing Virgil, Horace, and even Propertius to express support for the regime and the values it fostered. His influence is controversial in detail. He was an important intermediary between *princeps* and poets, who lost contact after his death. His wife Terentia, eventually divorced, was A. *Terentius Varro Murena's sister; apparently Maecenas, departing from his usual discretion, warned her of the detection of her brother's conspiracy (23 BC). Thereafter his relations with Augustus, never openly impaired, seem to have been less close. He died in 8 BC. Two undistinguished *Elegies* on his death survive (see ELEGIAE IN MAECENATEM).

> Syme, *Rom. Rev.* ch. 30, and see index; Schanz–Hosius 2. 17 ff., 116 f.; J.-M. André, *Mécène* (1967); J. Griffin, 'Caesar qui cogere posset', in F. Millar and E. Segal (eds.), *Caesar Augustus* (1984). Prose fragments in André, 149–50; poems, Courtney, *FLP* 276–81; *Elegiae in Maecenatem*, Duff, *Minor Lat. Poets* 115–39.　　　　　J. Gr.

Maecenas Melissus, Gaius, freedman of *Maecenas, invented a short-lived form of light drama, the *fabula trabeata* (named after the *trabea*, a garment worn by *equites*). He compiled a collection of jests in 150 books and was possibly the Melissus quoted several times by *Pliny (1) on natural history. He may also have published works on *Virgil and on grammar.

> Suet. *Gram.* 21; *PIR*² M 38.　　　　　P. G. M. B.

Maecianus, lawyer. See VOLUSIUS MAECIANUS, L.

Maelius (*RE* 2), **Spurius,** was supposedly a wealthy plebeian who aspired to *tyranny at Rome, was denounced by L. *Minucius Esquilinus Augurinus, and killed by C. *Servilius Ahala in 439 BC. The legend, probably already recounted by L. *Cincius Alimentus (fr. 6 Peter) and *Ennius (cf. *Ann.* fr. 150 Skutsch), may have originated as an aetiology of the Aequimaelium, an open space on the southern slopes of the *Capitol which was interpreted as the place where Maelius' house had been 'levelled to the ground' (*aequata*). Sp. Maelius' ambition was traced to his alleviation of a corn shortage and hence implicitly justified aristocratic hostility to such populist benefactions by private individuals.

> A. W. Lintott, *Hist.* 1970, 13 ff.; P. D. Garnsey, *Famine and Food Supply in the Graeco-Roman World* (1988), 167 ff.　　　　　A. D.

maenads, women inspired to ritual frenzy by *Dionysus. Maenadic rituals took place in the rough mountains of Greece in the heart of winter every second year. Having ceremonially left the city, maenads (probably upper-class women) would walk into the mountains shouting the cry 'to the mountains'. Here they removed their shoes, left their hair down, and pulled up their fawn-skins. After a sacrifice of *cakes, they started their nightly dances accompanied by *tympanon* and *aulos* (in sound more similar to the oboe than the flute) (see MUSIC, § 3. 2 and 3). Stimulated by the high-pitched music, the flicker effects of the torches, the whirling nature of the dances, the shouting of *euhoi*, the headshaking, jumping, and running, the maenads eventually fell to the ground—the euphoric climax of their *ecstasy.

Maenadic ritual strongly stimulated the mythical imagination: the *Bacchae* of *Euripides shows us women who tear animals apart, handle *snakes, eat raw meat, and are invulnerable to iron and fire. Most likely, in Euripides' time maenads did not handle snakes or eat raw meat; however, their ecstasy may well have made them insensible to pain. Myth often exaggerates ritual, but the absence of contemporary non-literary sources makes it difficult to separate these two categories in the *Bacchae*, where they are so tightly interwoven.

Maenadism was integrated into the city and should not be seen as a rebellion. It enabled women to leave their houses, to mingle with their 'sisters', and to have a good time. This social aspect, though, could only be expressed through the worship of Dionysus. To separate the social and religious aspect is modern not Greek. See WOMEN IN CULT.

Most likely, maenadism already occurs in *Homer (*Il.* 22. 461 f.). In Athenian art it became popular on pots towards the end of the 6th cent. and again in the 4th cent. BC, with a selective interest expressed in the intervening period by painters of larger pots. Among the tragedians *Aeschylus pictured maenads in various of his lost plays, e.g. the *Bassarids*, as did Euripides, especially in the *Bacchae*. Given these changing periods of interest in maenadism in literature and art, we should be wary of privileging the *Bacchae* by ascribing to it a special influence on later maenadic ritual or by tying it too closely to contemporary new cults. The demise of maenadism started in the Hellenistic period and was complete by the 2nd cent. AD.

> A. Henrichs, *Harv. Stud.* 1978, 121–60; J. N. Bremmer, *ZPE* 55 (1984), 267–86, and *Greek Religion* (1994), 78–80; R. Osborne, in C. Pelling (ed.), *Greek Tragedy and the Historian* (1995).　　　　　J. N. B.

Maenius, Gaius, consul 338 BC, who commemorated his successful war against the Latins (see LATINI) and Volscian *Antium by dedicating the 'beaks' of the captured ships on the exterior of the *Comitium, beneath the speakers' platform, which was hereafter named *Rostra from them. His work in remodelling the *forum Romanum, in an age which is pivotal in the architectural history of the city, is also commemorated in the balconies (*maeniana*) of the Forum porticoes which were used as grandstands for spectacles in the Forum piazza; and in the *columna Maenia* of the Comitium.

> F. Coarelli, *Il Foro Romano* 2 (1985), 39–53.　　　　　N. P.

Maeotis, the sea of Azov, joined to the Black (*Euxine) Sea by the Cimmerian *Bosporus (2) (straits of Kerch). Ancient writers often describe it as a lake or marsh, no doubt because of its shallowness. Its extent was regularly overestimated in antiquity, probably on account of its importance as a waterway and source of slaves and goods. The peoples of its shores are often termed 'Maeotians', especially those to its east and south-east. The Maeotis offered easy access to the Don (*Tanais) and Kuban, stretching deep into the hinterland.　　　　　D. C. B.

Maevius, attacked as a worthless and old-fashioned poet by *Virgil (*Ecl.* 3. 90–1), and the target of *Horace's *Epode* 10. Horace gives no reason for his hostility, except that Maevius 'stinks', but his uncouth versification may be an underlying motive. The internal logic of the *Epode* may support the proposition that Maevius is guilty of sexual misdemeanours.

> E. Fraenkel, *Horace* (1957), 25 ff.; E. A. Schmidt, *Gymnasium* 1977; S. J. Harrison, *CQ* 1989.　　　　　L. C. W.

magi See MAGUS.

magic

1. The concept Antiquity does not provide clear-cut definitions of what was understood by magic and there is a variety of terms referring to its different aspects. The Greek terms that lie at the roots of the modern term 'magic', μάγος, μαγεία, were ambivalent. Originally they referred to the strange but powerful rites of the Persian magi (see MAGUS) and their overtones were not necessarily negative (Pl. *Alc.* 1. 122: 'the magian lore of *Zoroaster'). Soon, however, *magos* was associated with the doubtful practices of the Greek γόης ('sorcerer') and hence attracted the negative connotations of quack, fraud, and mercenary (e.g. Soph. *OT* 386 f.). Through *Aristotle, *Theophrastus, and Hellenistic authors this negative sense also affected the Latin terms *magus*, *magia*, *magicus*. However, in late antiquity, especially in the *Greek Magical Papyri*, the term μάγος regained an authoritative meaning, somewhat like wizard, and was also embraced by philosophers and theurgists (see THEURGY). Since in these late texts prayer, magical formulae, and magical ritual freely intermingle, they challenge modern distinctions between magic and religion (and science). However, definitions being indispensable, we here employ a broad description of the 'family resemblance' of magic: a manipulative strategy to influence the course of nature by supernatural ('occult') means. 'Supernatural means' involves an overlap with religion, 'manipulative (coercive or performative) strategy', as combined with the pursuit of concrete goals, refers rather to a difference from religion.

2. Sources Greek and Roman literature provides abundant examples of magical practice in both narrative and discursive texts. Myth affords many instances. Besides gods connected with magic (*Hermes and *Hecate), we hear of *Telchines, skilful but malignant smiths well versed in magic. The *Idaean Dactyls were masters of medical charms and music. Thracian *Orpheus was a famous magician, and so were *Musaeus (1), *Melampus (1), and others. But, as elsewhere, the female sex predominates. The most notorious witch was *Medea. *Thessaly boasted an old tradition of witchcraft, the Thessalian witches being notorious for their specialism of 'drawing down the moon'.

The earliest literary examples come from *Homer. The witch *Circe (*Od.* 10. 274 ff.) uses potions, salves, and a magic wand to perform magical tricks and teaches *Odysseus how to summon the ghosts from the nether world. Folk magic glimmers through in a scene where an incantation stops the flow of blood from a wound (*Od.* 19. 457). *Hesiod (*Theog.* 411–52) offers an aretalogy (see MIRACLES) of Hecate. Tragedy contributes magical scenes (e.g. the calling up of the ghost of *Darius I: Aesch. *Pers.* 619–842) as well as whole plays (Eur. *Med.*), while comedy ridicules magicians (e.g. Ar. *Plut.* 649–747; *Menander (1)'s (lost) *Deisidaimon* and *Theophoroumenos*). *Theocritus' *Pharmakeutria* ('Drug- or Poisonmonger', hence 'Sorceress') became a model for many later witch scenes (e.g. Verg. *Ecl.* 8, and Hor. *Epod.* 5, describing the gruesome preparation of a love potion). Similarly, magical motifs in Greek epic tradition (e.g. Ap. Rhod. *Argon. passim*) were continued by Roman epic (e.g. Luc. *Civil War* 6. 413–830). Exceptionally informative is *Apuleius' *Metamorphoses*, which contains many a picturesque magical scene.

Another illuminating work by Apuleius belongs to the sphere of critical reflection. His *Apologia* (*De magia*) is a defence against the charge of magic and provides a full discussion of various aspects of ancient magic. Other discussions can be found in the satirical works of e.g. *Theophrastus (for instance the 16th Character (*Deisidaimon*)), and *Lucian, *passim*. Although early philosophers like *Heraclitus, *Pythagoras (1), *Empedocles, and *Democritus were often associated with magical experiments, Greek philosophy generally rejected magic. *Plato (1) wants the abuse of magic (φαρμακεία) to be punished, and *Sceptics, Epicureans (see EPICURUS), and *Cynics never tired of contesting magic. The shift towards a more positive appreciation in late antiquity, in, for example, Hermetic writings (see HERMES TRISMEGISTUS), *Iamblichus (2), and *Proclus (cf. § 1 above), was effected by a new cosmology, also apparent in new demonologies, in *prophecies, and *astrology.

3. Objectives As to the intended effects, a rough distinction can be made between harmful 'black' magic and innocent or beneficial 'white' magic, although the boundaries cannot be sharply drawn. For the category of black magic curse-tablets are the most conspicuous evidence (see CURSES). Numerous other forms of black magic were widely applied and feared: incantations; the use of drugs and poison (significantly φάρμακον may refer to magic, poison, and medicine); the practice of 'sympathetic magic' (*similia similibus*), for instance the use of 'voodoo dolls' melted in fire or pierced with needles (Pl. *Leg.* 933b; Theoc. 2; Verg. *Ecl.* 8; Ov. *Her.* 6. 91); and 'contagious magic', the destruction of the victim's hair, nails, part of his cloak, or other possessions as 'part for all', with the aim of harming the victim himself (Theoc. 2. 53 ff.; Verg. *Aen.* 4. 494 ff.).

Some of these practices can function in 'white' magic as well. Its main objectives are protection against any kind of mishap, the attraction of material or non-material benefits, and the healing of illness. The first two are above all pursued by the use of *amulets or phylacteries, the last by the application of all sorts of materia medica, often activated by charms and ritual (see § 4 below); also by means of *purifications, exorcism, or divine healing.

Mixtures occur: love magic is generally pursued for the benefit of the lover, not for that of the beloved, who is sometimes bewitched in a very aggressive manner and by gruesome means. Other types of magic (e.g. prophecy) are more or less neutral, although uncanny aspects may render them suspect (e.g. nekyomancy or the consultation of spirits of the dead).

4. Techniques Magic is essentially based on secret knowledge of sources of power. The most important are (*a*) utterances, (*b*) material objects, and (*c*) performance.

(*a*) Utterances may consist of inarticulate sounds, cries, various types of noise (e.g. the use of bells), hissing, or whistling. More common are powerful words and formulae. One important category consists of strange, uncanny words not belonging to the Greek or Latin idiom: the 'Ephesian letters' (so called from their alleged origin in *Ephesus), also referred to by terms such as ὀνόματα ἄσημα ('meaningless names'), or *voces magicae* ('magical names/words'), whose (alleged) foreign origin and lack of normal communicable meaning were believed to enhance their magical power. Another category of effective words consists of Greek or Latin expressions in which the illness or the cure is compared with a model taken from myth or legend (esp. Homer, Virgil, the Bible) or nature. Stylistic and prosodic devices, such as metre, anaphora, repetition, and rhyme, add emphasis and efficacy to the formulae, as do other magical devices such as writing normal words from right to left or with foreign letters. A copious stock of magical formulae is provided by the so-called *Greek Magical Papyri*, a corpus of papyrus texts from Egypt that contain extended formulae with magical words and names of great gods and demons, including lists of vowels understood as names of archangels, who are invoked or even forced to assist the practitioner.

(*b*) There is practically no limit to the selection of magical ingredients: any object or material may have a magical force— iron, (precious) stones, pieces of wood, parts of animals, nails, hair, the blood of criminals. Most important are herbs and plants, where magic and folk medicine often coalesce in the wisdom of the root-cutter and herbalist (see PHARMACOLOGY). Drawings of foreign gods and demons may be added and, especially in black magic, 'voodoo dolls', sometimes transfixed with needles, could have a role.

(*c*) In the application of these objects and as independent magical acts, various performative actions play a part. The magical objects must be manipulated in a special way, various gestures are prescribed, etc.

These three technical aspects are often combined, exemplarily so in the famous cure of a fracture in M. *Porcius Cato (1), *Agr.* 160: a knife is brandished and two pieces of reed are brought together over the fracture while a charm is sung: *motas vaeta daries dardares astataries dissunapiter* (untranslatable).

5. Social setting The social and legal standing of magic is basically ambivalent. (Secret) wisdom and expertise in the application of supernatural means was indispensable and widely resorted to, hence highly valued. Many official 'religious' rites, especially in Rome, contained 'magical' elements, which were accepted because and as long as they were publicly executed on behalf of the state. In the private sphere, however, magic's very secretiveness and association with asocial or even antisocial goals fostered suspicion and condemnation. Already in the 5th cent. BC, the author of *The Sacred Disease* (2. 12 f., 4. 36 ff.) made a clear distinction between religious and magical strategies and censured the latter. Plato (see § 2 above) wanted the abuse of magic to be penalized in his ideal state; the Romans, as early as 450 BC, actually did so in the *Twelve Tables. Under the first emperors many laws were issued to repress the growth of magical practices, and the 4th cent. AD saw a renaissance of anti-magical legislation. In this period, however, magic was practically identified with *prava religio* ('bad religion') and *superstitio* ('superstition'), which, together, served as conveniently comprehensive (and vague) classificatory terms to discredit social, political, and/or religious opponents.

R. Heim, *Jahrb. f. cl. Phil.* Suppl. 19 (1892), 463–576; T. Hopfner, *RE* 14 (1928), 301–93; A. M. Tupet, *La Magie dans la poésie latine* 1 (1976); G. E. R. Lloyd, *Magic, Reason and Experience: Studies in the Origins and Development of Greek Science* (1979); G. Luck, *Arcana Mundi: Magic and the Occult in the Greek and Roman Worlds* (1985); C. R. Phillips III, *ANRW* 2. 16. 3 (1986), 2677–773; H. D. Betz, *The Greek Magical Papyri in Translation* 1 (1986); C. A. Faraone and D. Obbink (eds.), *Magika Hiera: Ancient Greek Magic and Religion* (1991); H. S. Versnel, *Numen* 1991, 177–97; F. Graf, *La Magie dans L'antiquité gréco-romaine* (1994).

H. S. V.

magister equitum, 'master of the horse', an emergency magistrate nominated by the *dictator (who was in early times called *magister populi*). Apart from commanding the cavalry, he was the dictator's lieutenant and deputy, whether at Rome or on military service. He held *imperium derived from the dictator and ranked with the praetors. His magistracy ended when his dictator laid down office. A notable but unsuccessful attempt was made in 217 BC to equate the *magister equitum* with the dictator as a colleague. The *magister equitum* for which we have evidence may derive from a regular cavalry commander of the regal period of early republic.

For bibliography see DICTATOR.　　　　A. N. S.-W.; A. W. L.

magister libellorum ('master of petitions'), originally *a libellis* ('secretary for petitions'), an officer on the Roman emperor's staff whose duty was to deal with written petitions from private persons to the emperor and draft replies to them, known as rescripts (*rescripta*: originally written on the petition itself and called subscripts: *subscriptiones*, see SUBSCRIPTIONS). From *Hadrian onwards the office was entrusted to a member of the equestrian order, and, since many petitions concerned points of law, the holder was often a lawyer, such as *Papinianus or *Ulpian. Rescripts composed by these officials for the emperor

formed a large part of the *Codex Gregorianus* and *Hermogenianus* (see CODEX). The office continued in the later empire to be a source of legal expertise but was administratively subject to the *magister officiorum, instituted by *Constantine I. See also MAGISTER MEMORIAE, EPISTULARUM, LIBELLORUM.

A. v. Premerstein, *RE* 13 (1926), 20–5, part of entry '*a libellis*'. *HLL* 4, § 411. 3(g); U. Wilcken, *Hermes* 1920, 1–42; W. Williams, *JRS* 1974, 86–103; Honoré 1981, 24–138; D. Liebs, *ZRG* 1983, 485–509; Millar, *ERW* 240–52, 537–49; J.-P. Coriat, *Studia et documenta historiae et iuris* 1985, 319–48.

T. Hon.

magister memoriae, epistularum, libellorum These three 'masters' replaced the imperial secretaries *a memoria*, *ab epistulis*, and *a libellis*, in control of the bureaux (*scrinia*) in the late Roman secretariat. They are first attested in the 290s AD, and are probably Diocletianic (see DIOCLETIAN). The *magister memoriae* was the senior, and holders included the orator *Eumenius, the jurist *Arcadius Charisius, and the historians *Eutropius (1) and *Festus; the *magister epistularum* also was often a littérateur. Their division of responsibilities is obscure. According to the *Notitia Dignitatum (*Or.* 19), the bureaux all handled petitions to the emperor, but the *memoria* issued memoranda in response, the *epistulae* dealt with embassies from cities, the *libelli* with judicial hearings (*cognitiones*); see further separate entry MAGISTER LIBELLORUM. Literary sources refer to them all as drafting imperial documents, a role which must have overlapped with that of the *quaestor. 'Masters' of bureaux were often promoted to proconsul or *vicarius*, or to the great posts at court including the praetorian prefecture.

Jones, *Later Rom. Emp.* 367–8, 504–5; Millar, *ERW*, ch. 5.　　R. S. O. T.

magister militum, 'master of the soldiers'. *Constantine I deprived the praetorian prefects of their military functions, and to command his enlarged mobile army appointed two new generals, the *magister peditum* (infantry) and the *magister equitum* (cavalry), known collectively as *magistri militum*. Later they were styled *praesentales* ('in attendance') to distinguish them from the other *magistri militum*, generals commanding major regional mobile armies, who were indifferently entitled *magister equitum*, *magister equitum et peditum*, and *magister utriusque militiae* ('master of both arms'). By the time of the *Notitia Dignitatum (*c.* AD 395) there were five eastern *magistri militum* and three western, the latter dominated by the *magister peditum praesentalis* *Stilicho.

Jones, *Later Rom. Emp.* 608–10.　　R. S. O. T.

magister officiorum The 'master of the offices' is first attested in the early 320s AD at the courts of both *Constantine I and *Licinius; so he may be Diocletianic (see DIOCLETIAN). He originally held the rank of tribune, but by an extraordinary accumulation of responsibilities for the working of the central bureaucracy and its communications came to rank second only to the praetorian prefects. He controlled the imperial couriers (*agentes in rebus*) and the inspectors of the *postal service (*curiosi*) drawn from them, and issued postal warrants (*evectiones*). He exercised disciplinary control over the bureaux (*scrinia*) which served the *quaestor, the *magister memoriae, and the other 'masters' responsible for imperial documents. He supervised further groups of court officials whose exact role is often obscure, but who included interpreters, doorkeepers (*decani*), organizers of imperial audiences (*admissionales*), and billeting officers (*mensores*). He was even responsible for the imperial guards (*scholae*), but as a civilian is never known to have commanded them in action. By 390 he also controlled the arms factories (*fabricae*), and in 443 he became inspector-general of the frontier forces (*limitanei*) in the eastern empire.

A. E. R. Boak, *The Master of the Offices in the Later Roman and Byzantine Empires* (1924); Jones, *Later Rom. Emp.* 368–9, 575–84.

A. H. M. J.; R. S. O. T.

magistracy, Greek Magistracies (*archai*) in Greek states were the successors of the *kingships, which rarely survived into the Classical period. By a process which cannot now be followed in detail, and which the sources tend to reconstruct in too systematic a fashion, the powers of a hereditary king came to be divided between a plurality of magistrates, normally appointed for one year and often not eligible for reappointment. In addition to general offices of state, more specialized offices were sometimes created, for example to control a treasury or to supervise public works or the market (see AGORANOMOI). A small state could manage with a small number of magistrates, but in a large one there might be many, and many duties might be given to boards rather than single individuals: Athens in the 5th cent. BC developed a particularly extensive range of offices—700 internal and 700 external, according to the text of *Ath. pol.* 24. 3, though the second 700 is probably corrupt.

Magistrates tended to be more powerful, and to be appointed from a more restricted circle, in *oligarchies than in *democracies. Appointment by lot (see SORTITION) rather than by *election, to civilian posts which were not thought to require special ability, was particularly associated with democracy, but both that and a ban on reappointment to the same office can be found in oligarchies too. Athens and some other democratic states provided small salaries for magistrates (see DEMOCRACY, ATHENIAN, § 2). One office might be regarded as the principal office in a state, but in general there was no hierarchy of offices and no *cursus honorum (see CAREERS, GREEK). The citizens might control their magistrates through such procedures as *dokimasia (vetting their qualifications before they entered office) and *euthynai (examining their conduct after they left office), as well as by making them liable to prosecution for misconduct.

The magistrates of the Hellenistic kings were of a very different kind. They were professionals, paid by their king in money, natural produce, or gifts of land. The higher positions were occupied by Macedonians and Greeks, the lower mostly by natives, who did not rise to higher positions before the 2nd cent. The members of the central administration worked in the chief city, but there were numerous higher and lower officials in every part of the kingdom. The most important provincial officials were usually called *stratēgoi* ('generals'). The administration was strictly centralized in Egypt, but decentralized in the *Seleucid empire. Especially in Egypt, there was a firm hierarchy, bureaucratically organized. Lower officials were often personally dependent on the higher, as the higher were on the king.

For an important further group of offices in the Greek city see LITURGY.

GENERAL G. Busolt, *Griechische Staatskunde*, 3rd edn. (1920–6); V. Ehrenberg, *The Greek State*, 2nd edn. (1969).

ATHENS AND SPARTA G. Gilbert, *Constitutional Antiquities of Sparta and Athens* (1895); H. Michell, *Sparta* (1952); M. H. Hansen, *The Athenian Democracy in the Age of Demosthenes* (1991), ch. 9.

HELLENISTIC H. Bengtson, *Die Strategie in der hellenistischen Zeit* (1937–52); A. H. M. Jones, *The Greek City* (1940).   V. E.; P. J. R.

magistracy, Roman Magistrates at Rome may be divided in various ways according to various criteria. The most general recognizes a distinction between (*a*) the *ordinarii* (regularly elected), namely *consuls, *praetors, *censors, curule *aediles (these four offices were distinguished by privileges as 'curule', so called because they were entitled to use the official curule chair or *sella curulis*), *quaestors, the *vigintisexvirate (vigintivirate under the empire), and (not formally magistrates of the whole *populus Romanus* but only of the *plebs*) the *tribuni plebis and *aediles of the *plebs*, and (*b*) the *extraordinarii* (*extra ordinem creati*, occasionally appointed or elected), namely *interrex, *praefectus urbi (altered by *Augustus), *dictator, *magister equitum, and a number of unique commissions (*decemviri legibus scribundis*—see DECEMVIRATES—*tribuni militum consulari potestate, tresviri rei publicae constituendae* (see TRIUMVIRI), etc.). More important is the distinction between those who possessed *imperium (consuls, praetors, dictators, *magistri equitum*, the *decemviri legibus scribundis*, military tribunes with consular power, and the *tresviri r. p. c.*) and those who did not (the rest). The competences and histories of the individual magistracies varied greatly and are treated separately. Most of them did, however, share certain features. They were elected (apart from the *interrex*, dictator, *magister equitum*, and *praefectus urbi*). They were temporary: all the regular magistracies were annual, apart from the censorship. They were organized in colleges (generally of two, three, or ten members), and thereby subject to the *intercessio (veto) of their colleagues; the dictatorship is the most significant exception, for which reason tenure of it was restricted to six months, until *Sulla and, especially, *Caesar, whose dictatorship for life effectively recreated the *imperium* of the kings. They were unpaid: magistracy was regarded as an honour (*honos* can be a synonym for *magistratus*). The powers of magistrates with *imperium* were restricted over time, by the creation of the tribunate of the *plebs and by the development of *provocatio. But Roman magistrates, unlike Athenian, were never formally accountable to the people who elected them. Around the middle of the 2nd cent. BC it came to be felt that they ought to be, to the point that *Polybius (1) could say, erroneously, that the consuls had, upon laying down their office, to account for their actions to the people (εὐθύνας ὑπέχειν, 6. 15. 10; cf. EUTHYNA). Magistrates and promagistrates (see PRO CONSULE, PRO PRAETORE) could be called to account, but this required special prosecutions which could be (and were) initiated by tribunes. Attempts formally to regulate the conduct, to enforce public scrutiny, and to facilitate public accountability of magistrates and promagistrates were made (chiefly by C. *Sempronius Gracchus and L. *Appuleius Saturninus), but this initiative foundered as the holders of high office dominant in (and, collectively, as) the senate defended their power and privilege, and as political principle gave way to internecine politics in the late republic.

Mommsen, *Röm. Staatsr.* 1, 2; P. Willems, *Le Droit public romain*, 7th edn. (1910); H. F. Jolowicz and B. Nicholas, *Historical Introduction to the Study of Roman Law*, 3rd edn. (1972); W. Kunkel, *An Introduction to Roman Legal and Constitutional History*, 2nd edn. (1973; trans. J. M. Kelly); F. De Martino, *Storia della costituzione romana*, 2nd edn. (1972–5); C. Nicolet, *Rome et la conquête du monde méditerranéen* 1, 2nd edn. (1979), 393 ff.; A. W. Lintott, *Imperium Romanum* (1993), 97 ff.; Broughton, *MRR*.   P. S. D.

magistri (Festus, *Gloss. Lat.* 254). We have to distinguish between (*a*) *magistri*, the presidents of various associations (see CLUBS), religious, funerary, and professional (*collegia*) or territorial (*vici, pagi*), and (*b*) the boards of *magistri* (*collegia magistrorum*) who acted as supervisors of shrines (*curatores fanorum*), such as the *magistri* attested in *Capua, *Delos, and *Minturnae (mod. Minturno) in the last century of the republic. The cult of *Lares* *compitales* was in the late republic and under Augustus supervised by the *magistri* of *vici*. Also the state priesthoods of **quindecimviri*, **fratres arvales*, **Salii*, Luperci (see LUPERCALIA) (and **haruspices*) possessed as administrative officers the (normally) annually elected *magistri*. They also performed sacrifices, often assisted by **flamines*.

Wissowa, *RK*; J. Johnson, *Excavations at Minturnae* 2 (1933); G. Niebling, *Hist.* 1956, 303 ff.; J. Linderski, in M. N. Andreev and others (eds.), *Gesellschaft und Recht im Griechisch-römischen Altertum* (1968), 94 ff.; J.-M. Flambard, *OIRF* 1982, 67 ff.; M. Frederiksen, *Campania* (1984); H. Royden, *The Magistrates of the Roman Professional Collegia in Italy* (1988); J. Scheid, *Romulus et ses frères* (1990).   J. L.

Magna Graecia (Gk. *Megalē Hellas*), the coastal region of **Italy colonized by the Greeks. Definitions varied widely, but most usually it refers to the region between **Cumae and **Tarentum (Serv. on *Aen.* 1. 569). **Strabo (6. 1. 2) includes Sicily, but others exclude both Sicily and Campania (*FGrH* 566 F 13; Plin. *HN* 3. 95; ps.-Scymnus 303). Early sources (Pind. *Pyth.* 1. 146; Eur. *Med.* 439–40) use it to refer to the entire Greek world, not specifically to Italy, while **Justin (20. 1) includes the whole of Italy in the definition. The colonies, founded between *c.*740 (Cumae) and 433 BC (**Heraclea (1)), prospered on the strength of fertile land and trade. In the 4th cent., pressure from the rapidly expanding Oscan peoples of Apennine Italy brought the Greeks into conflict with the Lucani (see LUCANIA) and **Bruttii. By the end of the Pyrrhic war (see PYRRHUS), the entire region was under Roman domination, and by 89 BC all surviving cities were Roman colonies or *municipia*. The wars of the 4th–3rd cent. had undermined the economic prosperity of many cities, and some ceased to exist, but many were still viable. **Neapolis, Cumae, **Paestum, and **Velia flourished, and **Rhegium, **Locri Epizephyrii, **Thurii, **Croton, Heraclea, and Tarentum all maintained municipal status (see MUNICIPIUM).

E. Ciaceri, *Storia della Magna Grecia* (1926–30); M. Napoli, *Civiltà della Magna Grecia* (1970); E. Greco, *Magna Grecia* (1981).   K. L.

Magna Mater See CYBELE.

Magnentius, Flavius Magnus, from a family of barbarian settlers in Gaul, rose to a senior military command under the emperor **Constans. In January AD 350 at Autun (**Augustodunum) he led a coup which overthrew Constans, and rapidly won over the western provinces; although nominally a Christian, he made religious concessions to the pagan senatorial aristocracy. He failed to gain recognition from the eastern Augustus **Constantius II, and his forces were defeated by those of Constantius at the epic battle of Mursa in 351. His resistance finally ended with his suicide in Gaul two years later.   E. D. H.

Magnes is treated by **Aristotle (*Poet.* 1448ᵃ34) as one of the two earliest Athenian comic poets. He won eleven victories at the City **Dionysia, one of them in 472 BC (*IG* 2². 2318. 7, 2325. 44; Anon. *De com.* 9, p. 7). We have eight titles, but the plays ascribed to him in Hellenistic times were of very doubtful authenticity (Anon. ibid.; Ath. 367f and 646e); the titles include *Dionysus*, *Lydians*, *Fig-flies*, *Frogs*, and *Birds*, of which the last three may possibly be mere inferences from Ar. *Eq.* 520 ff., where Magnes is described as πτερυγίζων … καὶ ψηνίζων καὶ βαπτόμενος βατραχείοις ('flapping his wings … buzzing like a gall-fly and dyeing himself frog-green').

Kassel–Austin, *PCG* 5. 626 ff. (*CAF* 1. 7 ff.).   K. J. D.

Magnesia (1) ad Maeandrum, a city of Ionia (see IONIANS) on a tributary of the **Maeander, inland from Ephesus. Colonized by the Magnesians (see MAGNETES), it and **Magnesia (2) ad Sipylum both commanded rich inland valleys. Successively subject to **Lydia and **Persia, it was presented by Artaxerxes I to **Themistocles, whose female relatives were priestesses of the local goddess **Artemis Leucophryene. The temple (a work of **Hermogenes (1)), together with public buildings of the city, which was refounded by the sanctuary in 399 BC, has been excavated; the stoa in the agora yielded an important archive of Hellenistic inscriptions. Like **Magnesia (2) ad Sipylum it sided with Rome against **Mithradates VI, and was made a *civitas libera* (*free city) by **Sulla when he reorganized the province of **Asia.

K. Humann, *Magnesia am Maeander* (1904); O. Kern, *Inschr. Magnesia am Maeander* (1900); S. Mitchell, *Arch. Rep.* 1990, 101.

W. M. C.; J. M. C.; S. S.-W.

Magnesia (2) ad Sipylum, a city of **Lydia lying in the fertile **Hermus valley at the point where the roads from the interior and the Propontis converge on the way to Smyrna; it was the scene of the decisive battle between **Antiochus (3) III and the Scipios in January 189 BC. See also MAGNESIA (1) AD MAEANDRUM; MAGNESIA, BATTLE OF.

Magnesia, battle of The decisive battle of the war between Rome and **Antiochus (3) III of Syria was fought near **Magnesia (2) ad Sipylum in Lydia, probably in January 189 BC. The nominal Roman commander was L. **Cornelius Scipio Asiagenes, consul 190 (see also CORNELIUS SCIPIO AFRICANUS, P.). After the scythechariots on Antiochus' left had been dispersed by **archers and **slingers, Rome's ally, **Eumenes (2) II of Pergamum, led a massed cavalry charge which routed Antiochus' cataphracts (mailed cavalry), also on his left, and drove them into their centre. Meanwhile Antiochus had driven back the Roman left with his Iranian cavalry, but carried the pursuit too far. His **phalanx, drawn up with gaps to accommodate his **elephants, resisted stubbornly until the elephants began to get out of hand, and Eumenes fell on its flank, whereupon it was annihilated.

Livy 37. 39–44. 2; App. *Syr.* 30–5. *RE* 14/1, 'Magnesia' 3; B. Bar-Kochva, *The Seleucid Army* (1976), ch. 14.   J. F. La.

Magnetes, a tribe occupying the mountain-systems of **Ossa and **Pelion on the eastern border of **Thessaly. Their long coastline on the open sea was harbourless, and their chief towns, Meliboea, Homolion, and Rhizus, were very small. They became **perioikoi* to the invading Thessalians and had to surrender the coastal district round **Pagasae, but they retained their two votes on the amphictionic council (see AMPHICTIONY). Pagasae was restored to the Magnetes when **Philip (1) II expelled the tyrants of **Pherae, but they lost the limited *autonomy which they had previously enjoyed and became subjects of Macedonia. In 293 BC **Demetrias (see IOLCUS) was founded through a '*synoecism' of the Magnetes.   H. D. W.

Magnus, of **Carrhae, accompanied **Julian on his Persian expedition in AD 363 and wrote an account of it, of which a summary is quoted by **Malalas. His identification with the tribune Magnus who was decorated for bravery on Julian's Persian campaign is uncertain, as is the extent, if any, to which **Ammianus Marcellinus used him.

FGrH 225. *PLRE* 1, 'Magnus' 3; J. Matthews, *Ammianus Marcellinus* (1989), 163 f., 169 ff.   H. H. S.; A. J. S. S.

Magnus Maximus, Roman emperor (AD 383–8), was a Spaniard who rose to the command of the troops in Britain, where he fought successfully against Picts and Scots. Elevated by the army in Britain, he crossed to Gaul and overthrew *Gratian. He was for a time recognized as emperor by *Theodosius (2) I and controlled Gaul and Spain as well as Britain. He successfully invaded Italy in 387 but in the next year was decisively defeated by Theodosius in battles fought near Siscia and Pola, and was executed on 27 August 388. Maximus was a Catholic and persecuted Priscillian and his followers (see PRISCILLIANISTS). A fictionalized version of his elevation to the throne is presented in the story in the *Mabinogion, The Dream of Macsen Wledig*, and the name of Maximus also occurs in Welsh genealogies.

RE 14, 2546–55; PLRE 1, 'Maximus' 39; J. F. Matthews, *Western Aristocracies and Imperial Court, AD 364–425* (1975), and *Welsh History Review* 1983, 431 ff.   J. F. Ma.

Mago (1) (fl. 550–520 BC), the founder of a family which held quasi-monarchical power at *Carthage from c.550 to 450 BC. He fought in *Sardinia to consolidate the power of Carthage in the island, and changed the basis of the Carthaginian army; previously a citizen levy, it was subsequently a mercenary force, officered and led by Carthaginians.

B. H. Warmington, *Carthage* (1960), 40 ff., 121; L. Maurin, *Semitica* 1962, 5 ff.; G. C. Picard, *CAH* 6² (1994), 365 ff.   B. H. W.; S. H.

Mago (2) (RE 6) was the youngest brother of *Hannibal, under whom he served in Italy (218–216 BC), fighting at *Trebia and *Cannae. He fought in Spain from 215, playing an important part in the events that led to the death in 211 of Cn. *Cornelius Scipio Calvus and P. *Cornelius Scipio (1), until his defeat by P. *Cornelius Scipio Africanus at Ilipa, north of Seville (206; see PUNIC WARS). After failing to seize *Carthago Nova and to re-enter *Gades, he attacked the Balearic isles (*Baleares insulae; Mahon in Minorca perpetuates his name) and in 205 crossed to *Genua. After lengthy recruiting he advanced to the Po valley, where he was defeated by the Romans and severely wounded (203). Soon afterwards he, with Hannibal, was ordered to return to Africa to face Scipio; he died of wounds on the voyage.

J. Briscoe, *CAH* 8² (1989), 56–60.   H. H. S.; J. Br.

magōdia, a type of low-class *mime or lyric, subliterary (like *hilarōdia, simōdia*, and *lysiōdia*), about which ancient sources (Ath. 14. 620d, Strabo 14. 648) are far from clear. *Magōdia* is defined as 'dainty dancing' (ὄρχησις ἀπαλή) by Hesychius (μ 28); an actor, accompanied by kettledrums and cymbals, represented usually in comic style the drunken lover and other low characters. Two papyri provide possible libretti: a lover's complaint before a locked door and a lament for a lost cockerel (texts in Powell, *Coll. Alex.* 177 ff., 182 ff.; I. C. Cunningham, Teubner edn. of Herodas (1987), 36 ff., 40 f.).

P. Maas, *RE* 3 A 1 (1927), 159 f., Σιμῳδοί.   W. G. A.

magus/magi (μάγος, OP *makuš*). Only *Herodotus (1) (1. 101) calls the Magi a Median tribe (see MEDIA). In the pre-Hellenistic Greek tradition they are reciters of theogonies (Hdt. 1. 132), explainers of *dreams, royal educators and advisers (Pl. *Alc.* 122a; Plut, *Artax.* 3; Strabo 15. 1. 68). Magi are experts in the oral tradition rather than a class of priests, although they partake in sacrifices (Strabo 15. 3. 15). In the *Persepolis administrative texts (*PFT*) and in other *cuneiform documents magi often occur without a religious context. The Avesta does not mention magi. In the later Greek tradition the term frequently refers to specialists in exotic wisdom, astrology, and sorcery. See MAGIC; RELIGION, PERSIAN.

R. T. Hallock, *Persepolis Fortification Tablets* (1969); J. Bidez and F.

Cumont, *Les Mages hellénisés* (1938); E. Benveniste, *Les Mages dans l'Ancien Iran* (1938).   H. S.-W.

Maharbal (RE 2), *Hannibal's chief cavalry officer at the beginning of the Second *Punic War, defeated a Roman squadron in Umbria after the battle of Lake *Trasimene in 217 BC. After the battle of *Cannae (216) he is alleged, in a story deriving from M. *Porcius Cato (1), to have urged Hannibal to march on Rome immediately, saying 'Send me with the cavalry; on the fifth day your dinner will be cooked for you on the *Capitol'. In *Livy's version, when Hannibal sensibly declined, Maharbal replied, 'You know how to win a victory, Hannibal, but not how to use it' (Livy 22. 51. 4).

Walbank, *HCP* 1. 420–1.   J. Br.

Maia (1) (Μαῖα, or Μαιάς), daughter of *Atlas, and one of the Pleiades (*Od.* 14. 435; Hes. fr. 217. 2 M–W; Simonides fr. 555 Page, *PMG*; see PLEIAD); her name means simply 'mother' or 'nurse', and she may once have been a goddess of the *kourotrophos type; but apart from conceiving *Hermes with Zeus and bringing him to birth in a cave on Mt. Cyllene in *Arcadia (*Homeric Hymn to Hermes*), she retains little independent identity. (2) Roman goddess associated with *Volcanus (Gell. *NA* 13. 23. 2), to whom the *flamen Volcanalis* sacrificed on 1 May (Macrob. *Sat.* 1. 12. 18); yet the connection with the fire-god is puzzling, since her name appears to come from the root *mag*, and points to growth or increase; cf. the by-form Maiesta (Piso in Macrob. ibid.), and the month-name, appropriate to a season when all plants are growing. By a natural conflation with (1) she was associated with *Mercurius, and worshipped also on 15 May, the *natalis* (anniversary) of his temple; apparently her title in this role was *invicta* (unconquered) ('Maiae invict.', *fasti Antiates* for that date).   A. H. G.

maiestas, used as an abbreviation for the crime *maiestas minuta populi Romani*, 'the diminution of the majesty of the Roman people'. This charge was first introduced by L. *Appuleius Saturninus' *lex Appuleia* (probably of 103 BC). He seems to have been provoked both by the incompetence and corruption of Roman generals in the wars against the *Cimbri and *Teutones and by the frustration of the will of popular assemblies through obstruction (*Rhet. Her.* 1. 21). However, the vagueness of the phrase (Cic. *Fam.* 3. 11. 2; *Inv. Rhet.* 2. 52–3) made this a portmanteau charge, which could be deployed against any form of treason, revolt, or failure in public duty. In the 90s BC it was turned against an allegedly seditious tribune, C. *Norbanus, for his actions in support of Saturninus, and within a short time it virtually replaced charges of *perduellio* ('treason') brought before an assembly. *Sulla's *lex Cornelia maiestatis* of 81 BC was an important part of his reorganization of the criminal law. It incorporated provisions restricting the conduct and movements of provincial governors, now known not to be original but derived from a *lex Porcia* of c.100 BC. However, the law could still be applied to misbehaviour in a popular assembly, for the ex-tribune C. *Cornelius was accused under it in 66 BC for disregarding the veto of a fellow tribune. The *lex Iulia maiestatis* of *Caesar (Cic. *Phil.* 1. 21–3; *Dig.* 48. 4) revised Sulla's law, incorporating banishment (*aqua et igni interdictio*) as the chief penalty. There is no evidence for *Augustus' having passed a new *lex maiestatis*, but the scope of the existing law changed in the light of the existence of an emperor. Conspiracies against the emperor came naturally under the law, but its application was also gradually extended to cover *adultery with his daughter and then libel and slander (*Tiberius was initially reluctant to countenance such charges, but eventually they succeeded). The law was never redrafted to take precise account of these offences and, where conspiracy was concerned, *Domitian was to observe sagely that 'the only time that anybody believed an emperor's statement that he had detected a conspiracy was when the conspiracy had succeeded and he was dead' (Suet. *Dom.* 21). By Tiberius' reign prosecutions for *maiestas* might be brought before not only the *quaestio maiestatis* (see QUAESTIONES) but either the senate, sitting under the presidency of the emperor or consuls, or the emperor himself (Tac. *Ann.* 3. 10–12). Condemned persons were increasingly liable to the death sentence with no opportunity given to retire into exile; their property was confiscated for the imperial *fiscus* and their names were obliterated from public record (*damnatio memoriae*). Since it was even permitted to prosecute those who were dead, one could not be sure of escaping the last two consequences by committing suicide. *Suicide before any formal charge seems in practice to have obtained clemency for the family property and family name until the revival of the law under Marcus *Aurelius (*Cod. Iust.* 9. 8. 6). In the late empire *Arcadius (2) took the view that the sons of those guilty of *maiestas* were lucky to be left alive (ibid. 5).

Information was laid and prosecutions brought by individuals (senators, where the senate was the court used). Certain men came to make a profession of this, being rewarded with at least a quarter of the accused man's property, if they secured condemnation, and were labelled *delatores*. Charges of *maiestas* were increasingly frequent under Tiberius and after AD 23 disfigured his reign. Many were made on apparently trivial grounds or as a complement to other charges, especially *repetundae* and adultery. One reason for this was that a charge of *maiestas* was held to warrant the hearing of a case in the senate, when it would otherwise have been heard in a *quaestio* under more rigid rules and with fewer opportunities for self-display by the accuser. Their political background from AD 23 to 31 was the growing power of *Sejanus at the expense of *Vipsania Agrippina (2), her sons, and friends; from 31 to 37 the determination of Sejanus' enemies to be avenged on his surviving friends. The virulent hatred of one group for another was in the tradition of the late republic and the Civil Wars. A large number of those condemned were guilty of something, but this usually fell short of an attempt to subvert the state.

There were condemnations for *maiestas* under *Gaius (1) and *Claudius and in the latter half of *Nero's reign in contexts where an insecure emperor was being confronted with genuine conspiracies or threats to his position, even if each individual condemned had not necessarily acted treasonably. The condemnations under Domitian fall into the same pattern, but have a special importance for their impact on contemporaries, including the historian *Tacitus (1), in whose work *maiestas* trials are a leitmotiv, and the later emperors *Nerva and *Trajan. These had the courage to follow the example of Titus and guarantee that they would not execute senators, so virtually suspending *maiestas* charges throughout their reigns—though one senator was apparently executed without Trajan's knowledge (Eutr. 8. 4). *Hadrian took a similar oath after executing some consulars for conspiracy but went back on it at the end of his reign. The *maiestas* law then remained dormant until it was revived by Marcus Aurelius after the conspiracy of *Avidius Cassius, and later emperors found it indispensable.

J. L. Ferrary, *CRAcad. Inscr.* 1983; R. A. Bauman, *The Crimen Maiestatis in the Roman Republic and Augustan Principate* (1970), and *Impietas in*

Principem (1974); J. E. Allison and D. Cloud, *Latomus* 1962, 711 ff.; B. Levick, *Tiberius the Politician* (1976). J. P. B.; A. W. L.

Majorian, Iulius Valerius, western Roman emperor (AD 457–61), the last of any ability, was elevated by *Ricimer. His legislative programme to restore the state was combined with systematic reintegration of parts of Gaul and Spain into the empire; his achievement was admired by *Sidonius Apollinaris, whose home city of Lyons (*Lugdunum (1)) he had spared. However, his much-heralded expedition against the *Vandals came to grief at New Carthage (*Carthago Nova) and he was killed by Ricimer soon after.

PLRE 2. 702–3, 'Fl. Iulius Valerius Maiorianus'. J. D. H.

makarismos, or 'calling blessed', is a useful term for expressions of the form 'Blessed is the mortal who has seen these rites' (*Homeric Hymn to Demeter* 480). As in that instance, where the reference is to the Eleusinian *mysteries (see ELEUSIS), such language is particularly commonly used in religious contexts (so also e.g. in *Euripides, *Bacch.* 72 ff., and on the Orphic 'gold plates'; see ORPHISM), and it is plausible that initiates in mystery cults were at a certain stage so acclaimed. But the religious use is only a specialization of a broader formula of congratulation, seen for instance in *Odysseus' complimentary words to the lovely Nausicaa in *Homer, *Odyssey* 6. 154: 'Thrice blessed are your father and lady mother.'

N. J. Richardson, *The Homeric Hymn to Demeter* (1974), 313. R. C. T. P.

Malaca (mod. Málaga), a Phoenician foundation on the southern coast of Spain, was noted by *Artemidorus (2) as an *emporion* for the opposite African shore; it retained a Phoenician character. Its trade and industry, chiefly fish-curing (see FISHING), were not interrupted when it became an ally of Rome. With other Spanish communities, it received the *ius Latii* from *Vespasian. The extant parts of its charter, and those of Salpensa and Irni (see TABULA IRNITANA), are important sources for Latin municipal status (see MUNICIPIUM) in Imperial times.

Dessau, *ILS* 6089; Bruns, *Font.* 147, no. 30.

J. J. van N.; M. I. H.; S. J. K.

Malalas (c. AD 480–c.570), author of an influential universal chronicle in Greek. John Malalas came from *Antioch (1) in Syria where legal expertise probably secured him administrative employment (Malalas is Syriac for 'rhetor', 'lawyer'). His eighteen-book *Chronographia* covers world history from the Creation to AD 563, where the single manuscript of a continuous text breaks off (12th-cent. Oxford MS Bodl. Baroccianus 182): the chronicle probably terminated in 565, less plausibly 574. Apart from lacunae, this MS is also an abridgement of the original, but Malalas was used by later Greek, Syriac, Coptic, Latin, and Slavonic writers and through these adaptations a fuller version of the original has been reconstructed.

The preface proclaims a dual purpose, to narrate the course of sacred history as presented in Christian chronography and present a summary of events from Adam to *Justinian. These motives coalesce in the chronological computations which present an unusual date for Christ's crucifixion, 6,000 years after Creation (normally c.5,500): this permitted Malalas to dismiss contemporary apocalyptic fears that the world would endure for only 6,000 years and hence end in the early 6th cent. Books 1–8 cover the period before Christ, with Greek mythology and history incorporated within a framework of Hebrew affairs. Books 9–10 treat the late Roman republic and early empire, with special attention to the chronology of Christ's incarnation, while 11–17 narrate Roman imperial history from *Trajan to Justin I (uncle of *Justinian); the account becomes increasingly detailed, and from Zeno's reign deserves credit as a major contemporary source, especially for events at Antioch to which Malalas naturally devoted much attention. Book 18 covers Justinian's reign, and at least in part represents a continuation, not necessarily by the same author: the focus of the narrative switches to Constantinople; after a very detailed, document-based account of Justinian's early years (527–32), it abruptly deteriorates into a series of brief notices until the mid-540s when fuller coverage resumes. Malalas' religious views seem orthodox, though theological matters were not a major concern. The *Chronographia* provides important evidence for the interests and attitudes of the educated administrative élite in the eastern empire.

TEXT Standard edn. of the Greek: L. Dindorf (1831).
TRANSLATION The Engl. trans. by E. Jeffreys, M. Jeffreys, and R. Scott (1986) incorporates all scattered testimonies to the lost original.
DISCUSSION AND BIBLIOGRAPHY E. Jeffreys, *Studies in John Malalas* (1990).
L. M. W.

malaria See DISEASE.

Malchus (1), a Carthaginian general (fl. 580–550 BC?). The form of the name is uncertain; possibly it is a misunderstanding of *melek̠*, 'king'. He extended the overseas empire of *Carthage. He strengthened Punic control of western *Sicily, was perhaps checked by *Phalaris of Acragas, and then set off to conquer *Sardinia where he was defeated by the natives. He was 'exiled', that is perhaps ordered to stay with his men (as colonists?) in Sardinia, but the troops insisted on returning home. He seized Carthage, but was soon overthrown and executed. His career represents the first-known threat of a general and army to the civil government of Carthage. He was succeeded in power by *Mago (1).
H. H. S.

Malchus (Μάλιχος) (2) **I**, king of the *Nabataeans, *c.*57–30 BC. He sent cavalry to *Caesar for the Alexandrine war (47). He refused to receive *Herod (I) when he was driven from Palestine by the Parthians (40). See PARTHIA. For his help to the Parthians he had to pay P. *Ventidius a fine, while Antony (M. *Antonius (2)) gave part (but not all) of his territory to *Cleopatra VII who skilfully sowed seeds of discord between Malchus and Herod. Herod was later ordered by Antony to attack Malchus who was defeated (31).

PIR² M 108. G. Bowersock, *Roman Arabia* (1983, corrected reprint 1994), esp. 37 ff.
H. H. S.; A. J. S. S.

Malchus (3), a Byzantine historian (*c.* AD 500) probably from Syrian Philadelphia. His history covered in detail at least the years AD 474–80 in seven books, although the *Suda* reports that it started with the reign of *Constantine I. The majority of the surviving fragments are preserved in Constantine Porphyrogenitus' *De legationibus*; all fall within the period 474–80, and are particularly informative about the *Goths.

FHG 4. 111 ff.; L. Dindorf, *Historici Graeci minores* (1870–1), 383 ff.; C. De Boor, *Excerpta de Legationibus* (1903), 155 ff., 568 ff.; R. Blockley, *The Fragmentary Classicising Historians of the Later Roman Empire*, 2 vols. (text and trans. 1981–3), and LCM 1984, 152 ff.; C. Cresci, *Malco di Filadelfia* (1982) (text, comm., It. trans.).
P. J. H.

Malea, SE promontory of *Laconia, and of the whole Peloponnese (see PELOPONNESUS), a dangerous corner for shipping, chiefly because of the sudden veering of the winds off a harbourless coast. It was denounced on this account from *Homer down to Byzantine writers. But in part this perilousness was a literary tradition, and there was always much traffic through the narrow strait between Malea and *Cythera, even after *Corinth built its *diolkos.

R. Baladié, *Le Péloponnèse de Strabon* (1980), esp. 262–4.
V. E.; A. J. S. S.

Mallius Theodorus (*RE* 70), **Flavius**, held a series of high imperial offices (consul AD 399: PLRE 1. 900–2) and wrote on *On metres* (Keil, *Gramm. Lat.* 6. 585–601); other works, on philosophy and astronomy, are lost.

PLRE. Herzog–Schmidt, § 613.
R. A. K.

Malta See MELITA.

Mamertines (Mamertini—'sons of Mamers', the Oscan form of *Mars), a band of Campanian *mercenaries (see CAMPANIA) who served under *Agathocles (1) in Sicily and after his death (289 BC) seized *Messana, whence they dominated and plundered NE Sicily. Their power was checked temporarily by *Pyrrhus and more seriously by *Hieron (2) II of Syracuse, who defeated them in battle near the Longanus river (? 265). Against the threat of Hieron they appealed in rapid succession to the Carthaginians, who installed a garrison, and to Rome. Roman acceptance of their appeal led to the ejection by the Mamertines of the Carthaginian garrison, to the dispatch to Messana of Appius *Claudius Caudex, and ultimately to the First *Punic War.

Conway, *Ital. Dial.* 1. 1 f.; M. Särström, *A Study in the Coinage of the Mamertines* (1940); A. Vallone, *Kokalos* 1955, 22 ff.; P. R. Franke, *CAH* 7²/2 (1989), 473 f.; H. H. Scullard, ibid., 537 ff.
P. S. D.

Mamilius (*RE* 1), **Lucius,** as chief magistrate (dictator) of *Tusculum intervened decisively against the Sabine adventurer Appius Herdonius, who had seized the *Capitol at Rome (460 BC), and was subsequently rewarded with Roman *citizenship. The legend was perhaps preserved or elaborated by later Mamilii to establish their Roman credentials: M. *Porcius Cato (1), himself from Tusculum, probably recorded it (cf. *Orig.* fr. 25 Peter) and the Mamilii may have had connections with kinsmen of Q. *Fabius Pictor (Münzer, *Röm. Adelsparteien* 66 f.).

Ogilvie, *Comm. Livy 1–5*, 423 ff.; T. J. Cornell, *CAH* 7²/2 (1989), 286.
A. D.

Mamilius (*RE* 4), **Octavius (or Octavus?),** of Tusculum was reputedly son-in-law of *Tarquinius Superbus and died heroically leading the Latins at Lake *Regillus in support of his restoration to the Roman kingship. Inter-communal marriage at the aristocratic or dynastic level is credibly attested for the archaic period and M. *Porcius Cato (1), *Orig.* fr. 58 Peter, may confirm the leading position of *Tusculum among the Latins, but the historicity of Mamilius' own role (particularly his link with the tyrannical Superbus) remains uncertain: the reinforcement of personal power by external alliances (Livy 1. 49. 8) is a stereotype of tyrants, and Latin enthusiasm for Superbus' restoration is probably as fictitious as that of *Porsenna.

T. J. Cornell, *CAH* 7²/2 (1989), 253 n. 8; 257 ff.
A. D.

Mamilius (*RE* 7) **Limetanus, Gaius,** as tribune 109 BC set up three tribunals with equestrian jurors (whom Cicero calls 'Gracchani') to investigate culpable collaboration with *Jugurtha. (M. *Aemilius Scaurus (1) presided over one of them.) Several prominent senators, most with anti-Gracchan backgrounds, including four consulars and an augur, were convicted. He also passed a law regulating boundaries of public land, thus gaining a *cognomen*.

Sall. *Iug.*
E. B.

Mamurra, of *Formiae, *praefectus fabrum* ('officer of engineers') under *Caesar in Spain (61–60 BC) and Gaul, where he accumulated great wealth. His extravagance aroused ill feeling, and *Catullus (1) (poems 29, 41, 43, 57), who had personal reasons for disliking him, claimed that Mamurra had a sexual relationship with Caesar. (On an improbable attempt to identify Mamurra with *Vitruvius see E. Rawson, *Intellectual Life in the Late Roman Republic* (1985), 86 n. 14: the two may, however, have been related.)
C. E. S.; S. H.

manceps has several meanings. Most commonly it denotes the successful bidder in an auction of contracts for the sale or leasing of state lands or for public works. The *manceps* in such contracts usually acted on behalf of associates—in the late republic of a *societas publicanorum* (see PUBLICANI), but the details are obscure. In the late empire, when the functions of the *publicani* have become public duties discharged by guilds (*collegia*), *manceps* is a person charged with an obligatory office (e.g. the conduct of the salt monopoly and the public baths).

Festus also gives a quite different meaning, 'quod manu capiatur', 'because he is taken by the hand', which is presumably related to *mancipatio* and perhaps refers to *res mancipi*.

M. Kaser, *Das altrömische ius* (1949); F. Kniep, *Societas publicanorum* (1896). B. N.

mancipatio This was a solemn transaction with copper and scales, mentioned already in the *Twelve Tables. By historical times it was a symbolic transaction, but it retained the form of a sale, with the scales to weigh the price in copper. It was used to transfer ownership of *res mancipi* (land subject to Roman ownership, and other items including slaves and cattle belonging to land subject to Roman ownership) to create rustic *servitudes and to transfer certain rights over persons. In a set form of words (Gai. *Inst.* 1. 119) before five citizens as witnesses and a weigher (*libripens*) holding the scales, the recipient asserted his ownership of the property, and struck the scales with the copper. The transferor remained silent, though an undertaking given orally and formally (*nuncupatio*) about the property was binding. A recipient who was evicted from the property had an action for twice the price. *Mancipatio* was finally abolished by Justinian.

M. Kaser, *Eigentum und Besitz*, 2nd edn. (1956); A. Prichard, *Law Quarterly Review* 1960, 412; H. F. Jolowicz and B. Nicholas, *Historical Introduction to the Study of Roman Law*, 3rd edn. (1972), 143 ff.; A. Pernice, *Marcus Antistius Labeo* 3. 1, 2nd edn. (1892), 19 ff. B. N.; A. F. R.

mandate (*mandatum*) was one of the four consensual *contracts of Roman law. Based on the Roman notions of good faith, friendship, and moral duty (*officium*) (*Dig.* 17. 1. 1. 4), it dealt with situations where somebody (the mandatary) had agreed to do a service or favour for another (the mandator). The mandator could sue for proper execution of the mandate and for surrender of anything the mandatary had received (*actio mandati*). Condemnation involved disgrace (*infamia). The mandatary, in turn, could bring the counteraction (*actio mandati contraria*) if he had incurred expenses or suffered loss. He could not, however, claim remuneration for his services by this action. In other words, the contract of mandate was necessarily gratuitous. Even though mandate covered (higher) professional services (like those of an advocate), the underlying idea was that the mandatary did not act for personal gain but on account of a moral duty and as a generous and altruistic friend. But the mandator was perfectly free, and increasingly even expected, to show his gratitude by

way of a present (*honorarium*). Late classical law ultimately granted legal protection to the mandatary if a fee (*honorarium, salarium*) had been promised, but only by way of the exceptional procedure (*cognitio extra ordinem*) (Codex 4. 35. 1). Liability of the mandatary, originally only for dishonesty (*dolus*), was handled flexibly in classical law and could include other faults (*culpa*). Whether the mandator's liability covered loss occasioned by mere accident (*casus fortuitus*) is unclear. Mandate, in principle, ended with the death of either of the parties; also, if before the service was due to be performed, the mandator revoked or the mandatary renounced the contract. A 'mandate' purely in the mandatary's interest was not binding; it merely constituted advice.

V. Arangio-Ruiz, *Mandato* (1949); A. Watson, *Contract of Mandate* (1961); R. Zimmermann, *The Law of Obligations* (1990), 413 ff. R. Z.

Mandulis, Hellenized (i.e. Greek) form of the name of the god Merul or Melul, whose cult was centered at Talmis in *Nubia. The name is unknown in pharaonic Egypt, and his shrine at Talmis was built under the Ptolemies (see PTOLEMY (1)) with further work done under *Augustus and *Vespasian. The temple attracted considerable attention in the Roman empire. The range of dated texts at the temple runs from the reign of Vespasian to AD 248/9. According to one of these texts, Mandulis revealed himself to be the 'Sun, the all-seeing master, king of all, all-powerful *Aion'.

A. D. Nock, *Essays* (1972), 357–400. D. S. P.

Manduria (mod. Ionio), an important Messapian city (see MESSAPII) from the 6th to the 3rd cent. BC. *Archidamus III of Sparta fell in battle there in 338, and it must have allied with Rome along with the rest of the Sallentini, *c.*270 (Livy, *Per.* 15). It revolted during the Hannibalic War (see PUNIC WARS) and was sacked in 209, after which it never fully recovered; it did not have municipal status after 89. It is most notable for the well-preserved remains of the Messapian city, including city walls, cemeteries, and houses.

E. Greco, *Magna Grecia* (1981). K. L.

manes, Roman spirits of the dead; probably a euphemism from old Latin *manus* ('good'): P. Kretschmer, *Einleitung in die Geschichte der griechischen Sprache* (1896), 197 n. 4, Latte, *RR* 99 n. 3. The singular did not exist: Pompeius in *Gramm. Lat.* 5. 195. 38 ff. (1) Originally, the dead were undifferentiated, with a collectivity expressed as *di manes*; Cicero (*Leg.* 2. 9. 22) quotes the ancient ordinance *deorum manium iura sacra sunto* ('let there be holy laws of the dead'). Graves had the formulaic dedication DIS MANIBUS SACRUM; they were collectively worshipped at three festivals (*Feralia, *Parentalia, *Lemuria), individually on the dead person's birthday (*RAC* 9. 220, 223). From this come two derivatives: (*a*) the poets used *manes* topographically for 'realm of the dead': Ov. *Fast.* 2. 609; Verg. *G.* 1. 243, *Aen.* 3. 565, 11. 181). (*b*) *Manes* represents all Underworld gods: Verg. *Aen.* 10. 39. (2) Later in a special, still collective sense, *di manes* were identified with the *di parentes* ('family ancestors'): Ov. *Met.* 9. 406 ff. with Bömer's note. (3) *Manes* could represent an individual's *soul. The first evidence: Cic. *Pis.* 16 with Nisbet's note, also *ILLRP* 391; frequently in Augustan writers: Livy 3. 58. 11 (*manes Verginiae*); Hor. *Epod.* 5. 92; Verg. *Aen.* 6. 743 (*quisque suos patimur manes*) with Norden's note; and H. Rose, *Harv. Theol. Rev.* 1944, 45 ff. In the empire it became customary on inscriptions to add to DIS MANIBUS SACRUM the name of the dead person in the genitive or dative

(Pompeius, above); cf. R. Lattimore, *Themes in Greek and Latin Epitaphs* (1942), 90 ff.

F. Cumont, *Lux Perpetua* (1949), 392 ff.; Latte, *RR* 99 ff.; S. Weinstock, *Divus Julius* (1971), 291.　　　　　　　　　　　C. R. P.

Manetho (fl. 280 BC), Egyptian high priest at Heliopolis in the early Ptolemaic period, wrote a history of Egypt in three books (*Aigyptiaka*) from mythical times to 342. The human history was divided into 30 human dynasties (a 31st was added by a later hand) which still form the framework for ancient Egyptian chronology. The original, which contained serious errors and omissions, is lost and the fragments preserved in Christian and Jewish writers are frequently badly corrupted. Nevertheless, his importance in the preservation of Egyptian historical tradition is great, and his influence has been generally benign.

There also exist under the name of Manetho six books of didactic hexameters on *astrology entitled Ἀποτελεσματικά ('Forecasts'). Probably they were composed between the 2nd and 3rd cents. AD. The sole extant MS transmits them in confused order: books 2, 3, and 6 are together a complete poem, and book 4 is another; books 1 and 5 are heterogeneous fragments. The author of the long poem gives his own horoscope (6. 738–50), from which it can be calculated that he was born in AD 80. By claiming knowledge of Egyptian sacred writings and addressing 'Ptolemy', the writer of book 5 seeks extra credibility by implying that he is the famous Manetho; and the whole collection came to be attributed to the same source. The poems are bald catalogues of the likely duties, characteristics, and sexual proclivities of those born under the various combinations and conjunctions of planets and star-signs. The writer of book 4 is notable for his many new compound nouns and adjectives; but in general these poets have little to recommend them.

MANETHO OF HELIOPOLIS *FGrH* 609. Manetho, ed. W. G. Waddell (Loeb, 1940); A. B. Lloyd, in J. Baines and others (eds.), *Pyramid Studies* (1988), 154 ff.; H. J. Thissen, *Lexikon der Ägyptologie* 3. 1180 f.
MANETHO OF 2ND CENT. AD. Text: A. Koechly (ed. maior, Didot, 1851; ed. minor, Teubner, 1858); *POxy*. 2546 (4. 384–415, 417–33, 564–90, 592–604); *ZPE* 21 (1976), 182 (4. 231–5).　　　A. B. L., N. H.

Manichaeism, a developed form of *Gnosticism founded by the Syriac-speaking Babylonian Mani (AD 216–76). At first influenced by a baptismal Gnostic sect such as the Mandaeans (some of whose hymns the Manichees used), he left the sect at the age of 24, after two visions convinced him that he was a manifestation of the Paraclete promised by Jesus. After visiting India he returned to the *Sasanid empire, where he enjoyed friendly relations with the Sasanian royal family and aristocracy including King *Sapor I; but Mazdean opposition under Bahram I led to his execution. A systematic catechism (*Kephalaia*), preserved in Coptic, was edited in his name. His doctrine was a religion of redemption in which dualistic myth provided a rationale for an ascetic ethic. A precosmic invasion of the realm of light by the forces of darkness had resulted in the present intermingling of good and evil, the divine substance being imprisoned in matter. In Jesus the Son of God came to save his own soul, lost in Adam. The Elect, to whom all worldly occupations and possessions were forbidden, participated in redemption, and were destined for deliverance from transmigration. The community also included an inferior order of Hearers who by keeping simple moral rules could hope for rebirth as one of the Elect.

Proscribed in the Roman empire as a subversive foreign cult by *Diocletian (whose edict is preserved) and later emperors, it was attacked by Neoplatonists (Alexander of Lycopolis c.300, *Simplicius c.540; see NEOPLATONISM) and by Christians (Hegemonius, Titus of Bostra, Serapion of Thmuis, *Ephraem Syrus, *Epiphanius, *Augustine). Nevertheless, and despite repeated suppression by imperial legislation, it spread rapidly in the west. Augustine, whose *Confessions* are a prime document of Manichaean influence in the Roman empire, was a Hearer for nine years. Eastwards, the advent of Islam drove it across central Asia to survive in China till the 14th cent. Important texts and paintings were found (1895–1912) at Turfan in Chinese Turkestan, and many Coptic papyri in Egypt in 1933. In the medieval west the legacy of Manichaeism passed to the Paulicians and Bogomils. Significant new material on the early religious experience of Mani, including his break with the baptismal sectarians and his first missionary journeys, is provided by the account of his life in Greek in the so-called Cologne Mani-Codex, published in 1970.

H.-C. Puech, *Le Manichéisme* (1949); G. Widengren, *Mani und der Manichäismus* (1961; Eng. trans. 1965); P. Brown, *JRS* 1969, 92 ff. (= *Religion and Society in the Age of St. Augustine* (1972), 94 ff.); A. Henrichs and L. Koenen, *ZPE* 5 (1970), 97 ff.; S. N. C. Lieu, *Manichaeism in the Later Roman Empire and Medieval China*, 2nd edn. (1992).　　J. F. Ma.

manifestation, divine See EPIPHANY.

Manilius (*RE* 10, cf. 23), **Gaius**, elected tribune (see TRIBUNI PLEBIS) for 66 BC, hence entering office on 10 December 67, on the last day of 67 carried a law distributing freedmen through all the tribes; this the senate annulled next day for non-observance of the *trinundinum*. In 66 Manilius conferred on *Pompey the command against *Mithradates VI and *Tigranes (1) II, with *imperium* over all the provinces of Asia Minor. On laying down his tribunate he was prosecuted for *repetundae by Pompey's enemy C. *Calpurnius Piso (1), but the case was dropped amid the disturbances of January 65, to which date *Cicero, praetor for 66, had postponed it in order to avoid having to deal with the case. But Manilius was soon prosecuted for *maiestas and condemned.

Asc. 60. 64–6 c.; Schol. Bob. *Cic. Mil.* 119 St.; Cass. Dio 36. 42. 4; Plut. *Cic.* 9. R. Seager, *Pompey* (1979), 57 f.　　G. E. F. C.; R. J. S.

Manilius (*RE* 12), **Manius**, unsuccessfully fought against the Lusitani (see LUSITANIA) as proconsul 155 or 154 BC, but became consul 149, perhaps because of his work as a jurist. With his colleague L. Marcius Censorinus he carried out his mission of tricking the Carthaginians into giving hostages and surrendering all their arms before ordering them to abandon their city. Unsuccessful as a commander against their desperate resistance, he returned to Rome in 148. In 133 he persuaded Ti. *Sempronius Gracchus (3) to submit his dispute with M. *Octavius to the senate. A prominent orator (Cic. *Brut.* 108) and distinguished jurist, he appears as a friend of P. *Cornelius Scipio Aemilianus in *Cicero's *De re publica*. His legal writings (we have a few snippets cited by Cicero and *Varro) were still read by Sextus *Pomponius (*Dig.* 1. 2. 2. 39).　　　　　E. B.

Manilius (*RE* 6), **Marcus**, Stoic author (see STOICISM) of the *Astronomica*, a didactic astrological poem whose composition spans *Augustus' final years and *Tiberius' succession (1. 899 mentions P. *Quinctilius Varus' defeat in AD 9; ambivalent references at 1. 7 and 925–6, are disputed, but Augustus is probably alive at 2. 508–9, since Tiberius is not mentioned in 2; by 4. 763–6, 773–7 Tiberius is *princeps*). Manilius may mirror Virgil in choosing didactic at a period of political transition, and he uses his risky topic in support of a continuing Principate.

manipulus (maniple)

The technical content is as follows. Book 1: an introductory theodical account of creation and an astronomy influenced by *Aratus (1); book 2: the characteristics, conjunctions, and twelve-fold divisions (dodecatemoria) of the zodiacal signs, the relationship of cardinals and temples to different areas of human life; book 3: a different circular system of twelve lots (sortes) of human experience, its adjustment, the calculation of the horoscope at birth, length of life, tropic signs; book 4: zodiacal influences at birth, the tripartite division of signs into decans, the 360 zodiacal degrees and their influence, the partition of the world and its nations among the signs, ecliptic signs; book 5: the influence on character of extra-zodiacal constellations at their rising (paranatellonta), a lacuna (709 ff.), stellar magnitudes. The proem to 5 demonstrates that Manilius settled for a five-book structure. Books 2–4 provide a zodiacal central section and the astronomical tour of 5 balances that of 1. Books 1–4 have extensive prologues, 1, 4, and 5 significant finales. Manilius may have abandoned an earlier plan for seven books to include a thorough treatment of planetary influences which can only have received about 200 lines in the lacuna at 5. 709 ff. But since book 5's extensive *Andromeda myth and its closing depiction of stellar magnitudes as a hierarchical star-state analogous with human society echo the bee-state and *Orpheus myth of *Virgil's last Georgic, book 5 should be the final book. Manilius' astrological sources are unclear. Egyptian, Hermetic, and Posidonian influences have been mooted (see HERMES TRISMEGISTUS; POSIDONIUS (2)), and some material only reappears in Arab astrological writings. If not himself the source of *Firmicus Maternus, Manilius shares one with him. His repetitions, contradictions, inaccuracies, and omissions, notably of the promised planetary material, have been justifiably castigated. But his purpose and talents have been obscured by his complex subject and, for English-speakers, by Housman's sarcastic compliments about skilfully versified sums.

The Astronomica is no more a practical treatise than is Virgil's Georgics. Religious philosophy and political ideology are the driving forces. A blistering attack on *Lucretius' republican Epicurean poem underlies the poet's passionate Stoic hymns to the mystical order governing the multiplicity and diversity of creation. *Astrology allows Manilius to link heavenly macrocosm with earthly and human microcosm and he claims the authority of a divinely inspired ascent to justify his vision. His hexameters are fine and his poetic range unusual. Exploiting didactic's formal elements—prologue, 'digression', and epilogue—he reworks Lucretius' and Virgil's greatest excursuses and *Cicero's Somnium Scipionis, but can also frame telling cameos of human foibles in comic and satiric vein, whilst his verbal point marks him as *Ovid's younger contemporary. Today Scaliger's view of Manilius, that he was as sweet as Ovid and more majestic, is returning to favour. See ASTROLOGY; CONSTELLATIONS; DIDACTIC POETRY.

TEXT AND COMMENTARY A. E. Housman, 5 vols. (1903–30); text only (1932). With transl. and comm.: G. P. Goold (1977), introd. on the astrology; H. W. Garrod, Book 2 (1911); D. Liuzzi, Book 1 (1979), Book 2 (1983).
LITERATURE W. Hübner, ANRW 2. 32. 1 (1984), 126–320; F. F. Luhr, Ratio und Fatum: Dichtung und Lehre bei Manilius (1969); R. Helm, Lustrum 1956, 129–58; A. Reeh, Interpretationen zu den Astronomica des Manilius (1973); E. Romano, Struttura degli Astronomica di Manilio (1979).
A. M. W.

manipulus (maniple), a tactical unit of a *legion; its adoption in the 4th century BC, replacing the *phalanx, was associated with the introduction of the throwing spear (pilum) which required a more open and manœuvrable formation. Legionaries were drawn up in three ranks, the first two each containing ten maniples of normally 120 men, the last, ten maniples of 60; light-armed troops (*velites) were assigned in proportion. A maniple consisted of two centuries, each commanded by a centurion (see CENTURIO), the senior having overall responsibility. Intervals between maniples in battle formation were covered by the ranks behind, but were perhaps closed during advance. In the late 2nd cent. BC a larger tactical unit, the cohort (see COHORS), replaced the maniple.

L. Keppie, The Making of the Roman Army (1984).   J. B. C.

Manlius (RE 51) **Capitolinus, Marcus** Manlius' supposed repulse of the Gauls from the *Capitol after being aroused by *Juno's sacred geese (390 BC) was used to explain his cognomen Capitolinus (which in fact probably referred to residence on the hill). The story, possibly already in *Ennius, may also have been an aetiology of an obscure ritual involving geese and dogs and/or the temple of *Juno Moneta (interpreted as 'Juno the Warner'), supposedly built on the site of Manlius' house in 345/4. The earliest version of Manlius' death probably placed it in 385 and represented it simply as punishment for tyrannical ambitions, perhaps issuing in armed revolt. In later (varying) accounts Manlius is tried and executed in 384 (to facilitate a confrontation with M. *Furius Camillus) and his agitation acquires late republican popularis and Catilinarian overtones, focusing especially on the alleviation of debt (here, as with Sp. *Maelius, the general relief offered by a private individual attracts particular aristocratic suspicion). Except by *Diodorus (3) Siculus, he was identified with the *consul of 392, who was credited with an *ovatio over the *Aequi.

T. P. Wiseman, Hist. 1979, 32 f.; O. Skutsch, The Annals of Quintus Ennius (1985), 408; N. M. Horsfall, in J. N. Bremmer and N. M. Horsfall, Roman Myth and Mythography (1987), 63 ff.; A. Ziolkowski, AJPhil. 1993, 206 ff.   A. D.

Manlius (RE 57) **Imperiosus Torquatus, Titus,** consul 347, 344, 340 BC. His dictatorships (see DICTATOR) of 353 (when he reputedly forced *Caere to a 100-year truce), 349, and 320 have all been doubted. In 340 he and his colleague P. *Decius Mus (1) defeated the Latins (see LATINI) and Campani at Veseris in *Campania. Manlius then reputedly defeated the Latins, *Volsci, and *Aurunci near *Suessa and celebrated a *triumph. His career was elaborated with exemplary stories illustrating filial duty, paternal severity, and the role of monomachy (duelling). In one version he saved his father from prosecution for maltreatment of himself (362). His famous duel with a Gaul (variously dated to 367, 361, 358, or 357) explained his cognomen Torquatus by the gold torque taken from his opponent. His execution of his son before Veseris for fighting a duel against orders, already perhaps in *Ennius (Ann. fr. 156 Skutsch, with comm.) and in pointed contrast to Decius' subsequent *devotio (see DECIUS MUS (1), P.), provided an aetiology for the proverbial strictness of 'Manlian orders'.

Beloch, Röm. Gesch. 65, 373; S. P. Oakley, CQ 1985, 392 ff.   A. D.

Manlius (RE 82) **Torquatus, Titus,** was consul 235 BC, when he campaigned in *Sardinia and celebrated a *triumph; he is said to have been the only person between *Numa and *Augustus to have closed the gates of *Janus, signifying that Rome was wholly at peace. He was elected *censor in 231 with Q. *Fulvius Flaccus (1), but they abdicated because of a flaw in their election. He held a second consulship in 224, with Flaccus as colleague; they forced the *Boii to submit. After the battle of *Cannae (216) he opposed the ransoming of Roman prisoners. In 215 he held temporary command in Sardinia; he defeated Sardinian rebels, and later won a victory over combined Carthaginian and Sardinian forces. A *pontifex, he was an unsuccessful candidate for the position of pontifex maximus in 212. He declined to be a candidate for the consulship of 210, was *dictator to hold the elections and celebrate games in 208, and died in 202.

Scullard, *Rom. Pol.* 37–8, 64–5.　　　　　J. Br.

Manlius (*RE* 91) **Vulso, Gnaeus,** was praetor in Sicily 195 BC and consul 189, succeeding L. *Cornelius Scipio Asiagenes in Asia. Without specific authority from senate and people he led his army, by a circuitous route, from *Ephesus to *Ancyra, extracting money from peoples and dynasts as he proceeded, and defeating the *Galatians in two major battles. His justification was that unless the Galatians were subdued, the victory over *Antiochus (3) III would have been in vain; his real motive was a desire for booty and glory. With the assistance of the ten commissioners sent from Rome he concluded the peace with Antiochus at *Apamea in 188, and completed the settlement of Asia Minor. On his return journey he suffered serious losses in *Thrace. He returned to Rome in 187 and, despite the objections of a majority of the ten commissioners, led by L. *Aemilius Paullus (2) and L. Furius Purpureo, was granted a triumph. According to *Livy (39. 6) the return of Manlius' army marked the arrival of foreign luxury in Rome.

Walbank, *HCP* 3. 140–75.　　　　　J. Br.

Manlius (*RE* 101) **Vulso Longus, Lucius,** consul 265 BC, with his colleague M. *Atilius Regulus won a naval victory over the Carthaginians at Ecnomus (near Licata) and landed in Africa; he returned to Rome to celebrate a triumph, leaving Regulus in Africa. Consul again in 250, he and C. Atilius Regulus failed to recapture *Lilybaeum and suffered serious losses.

Walbank, *HCP* 1. 85–9, 103–13.　　　　　J. Br.

Mantias (*c.*165–85 BC), a physician of the 'school' of *Herophilus, was known to the Greeks as the influential first systematic writer on compound drugs (although such drug prescriptions predate Mantias by several millennia, being well attested in Mesopotamian and early Egyptian texts). It is uncertain whether his famous specialized pharmacological books, for example on purgatives, on draughts, on clysters, and 'on remedies according to place' (topical drugs), belonged to his Δυν άμεις ('Powers' or 'Properties' of drugs) and *The Druggist* (or?) *In the Surgery* (or *On the Things in the Surgery*). Many of his compound-drug remedies were found worthy of transmission by the pharmacologists Asclepiades the Younger ('Pharmakion') and Heras, by *Soranus, and in particular by *Galen. Like most Herophileans, Mantias was, however, no narrow specialist: he also wrote on pathology, regimen, and women's disorders (recommending, for example, musical therapy—flute-playing, drums—to ward off imminent *hysteria, but pharmacological agents once hysterical suffocation attacks the patient). See PHARMACOLOGY.

Ed., trans., and comm., H. von Staden, *From Andreas to Demosthenes Philalethes* (1995), ch. 9. Cf. von Staden, *Herophilus* (1989), 515–18.　　　　　H. v. S.

Mantinea, *polis* in the northern part of the upland plain of modern Tripolis in eastern *Arcadia. Mantinea frequently quarrelled with neighbouring *Tegea over the flooding of excess water in the plain, which as a strategic thoroughfare witnessed several important battles (in 418, 362, and 207 BC; see MANTINEA,

BATTLES OF). The main geometric and Archaic settlement and cult centre was the hill of Gourtsouli (ancient Ptolis), a former Mycenaean site (see MYCENAEAN CIVILIZATION). In the mid-6th or early 5th cent. BC the town of Mantinea was founded in the plain in a *synoecism of four or five earlier villages. Although members of the *Peloponnesian League, the Mantineans' relationship with Sparta varied. They supported her during the 470s and 460s, but to protect their newly created hegemony in *Arcadia participated in the unsuccessful anti-Spartan alliance at the battle of 'First Mantinea' in 418. In 385 they were compulsorily dispersed to their original villages (perhaps never entirely abandoned) and their moderate democracy, probably established in the 5th cent., was abolished; but in 370 they restored both town and democracy. Initially prominent in developing the *Arcadian League, they subsequently led the *poleis* who opposed the federal officials and fought against *Thebes (1) at 'Second Mantinea' in 362. Embroiled in the conflicts between *Cleomenes (2) III of Sparta and the *Achaean Confederacy, Mantinea was depopulated by *Antigonus (3) Doson in 223. Given new colonists and renamed Antigonea, the town revived, despite *Strabo's suggestion of ruination (8. 8). Around AD 125 *Hadrian restored its former name and renewed its buildings as the supposed *mētropolis (sense '*a*') of Bithynium, birthplace of his favourite *Antinous (2).

IG 5. 2. 46 ff.; Paus. 8. 6–12. *RE* 14. 1290 ff.; G. Fougères, *Mantinée et l'Arcadie orientale* (1898); S. and H. Hodkinson, *BSA* 1981, 239–96.
　　　　　S. J. Ho.

Mantinea, battles of The three battles of *Mantinea, fought in 418, 362, and 207 BC, exemplify the main stages of Greek warfare. The first (Thuc. 5. 66 ff.), fought between the *Spartans and a coalition mainly of Argives, Athenians (see ARGOS (2); ATHENS), and Mantineans, is the 'classic' *hoplite battle, with both sides edging to the right, as each man sought the protection of his right-hand neighbour's shield, with the result that each side won on its right, and only the discipline of the Spartans in not pursuing led to the rout of the allied right as it returned across the battlefield. The second battle (Xen. *Hell.* 7. 18 ff.; Diod. Sic. 15. 84 ff.), between the *Boeotians and their remaining allies, and a combination of Spartans, Mantineans, Elians (see ELIS), and Athenians, marks the transition between hoplite warfare and the more sophisticated warfare of integration of 'heavy' infantry with other troop types. Here the attack of the Theban *phalanx on the left was preceded by a charge of cavalry mingled with 'light' infantry trained to co-operate with cavalry (*hamippoi*). Finally, with the third battle (Polyb. 11. 11 ff.), between Sparta and the *Achaean Confederacy, we are fully in the Hellenistic age, with both sides using all types of troops and weapons, including catapults (see ARTILLERY).

J. F. Lazenby, *The Spartan Army* (1985); J. Buckler, *The Theban Hegemony* (1980); Walbank, *HCP* 2. 282 ff.　　　　　J. F. La.

Mantua (mod. Mantova), on the river Mincius in Cisalpine Gaul (see GAUL (CISALPINE)). Its *Etruscan origin has been confirmed by archaeological finds. Seldom mentioned in ancient literature, Mantua is famous as the town near which *Virgil was born, and whose territory the Second Triumvirate confiscated (see TRIUMVIRI; PROSCRIPTION).

BTCGI 9 (1991), 'Mantova'; R. De Marinis (ed.), *Gli Etruschi a nord del Po*, 2nd edn. (1988).　　　　　E. T. S.; D. W. R. R.

manubiae (also ***manibiae***), Roman military term, probably derived from *manus* ('hand') and *habere* ('to have'), may mean the funds raised by an official sale of war *booty, or, more likely, that part of the booty legitimately appropriated by an army commander as holder of *imperium*, and of which he was free to dispose as he wished without any legal restrictions. Custom rather than legal rule dictated the amount and type of booty defined as *manubiae*. The commander traditionally expended much of the proceeds of booty in distributions to his troops. Payments were also made to officers—legates, tribunes, quaestors, and even to relatives and friends of the commander, though usually to those who had taken part in the war. Naturally, commanders often used *manubiae* to celebrate their own name through the construction of public buildings and the provision of games and largess for the people. *Augustus suggested that distinguished commanders who had held a triumph could use their *manubiae* to help finance public road-projects. After 19 BC full *triumphs were no longer awarded to senators, and the custom of *manubiae* probably fell into desuetude, all booty coming under the control of the emperor as commander-in-chief.

I. Shatzman, *Hist.* 1972, 177. J. B. C.

manumission of slaves See FREEDMEN, FREEDWOMEN; HIERO-DOULOI; LATINI IUNIANI; SLAVERY.

manus (lit. 'hand') was the power (akin to *patria potestas*) which a husband might have over his wife. In early times it perhaps covered not only (as later) control of property, but the right, after due process, to execute. Entry into *manus* (*conventio in manum*) took place in three ways. *Confarreatio* (so called from a sacramental loaf) was a religious ceremony and requisite for the holders of certain priesthoods; it survived, for the few, probably while polytheism lasted. *Coemptio* ('purchase') was a legal procedure, an imaginary sale. By *usus* ('prescription', obsolete by the 2nd cent. AD), *manus* resulted if a couple lived uninterruptedly as husband and wife for one year: the *Twelve Tables specified that the wife's removal for three successive nights prevented this result. By *conventio in manum* a woman was freed from any previous *paterfamilias* and entered the husband's family, coming under his control or that of his *paterfamilias*, merging her property in his, and gaining succession rights on intestacy equivalent to those of his children (see INHERITANCE, ROMAN). By the end of the republic, *manus* was evidently uncommon; by the 2nd cent. AD at latest a wife *in manu* might initiate divorce and the removal of *manus*. See MARRIAGE LAW, ROMAN. S. M. T., B. N.

manuscripts See BOOKS, GREEK AND ROMAN; PALAEOGRAPHY; SCHOLARSHIP, CLASSICAL, HISTORY OF.

maps Many cultures, including those of *Egypt and *Mesopotamia, use visual representations of aspects of space that cannot be directly perceived. The *Ionian Greeks (perhaps taking the idea from other traditions) produced the first maps in the classical tradition (*Eratosthenes, Strabo 1. 1. 11 (7), attributed the first map to *Anaximander); the famous one shown to *Cleomenes (1) I of Sparta by *Aristagoras (1) of Miletus (Hdt. 5. 49) is an example of such maps: these fit into the context of new world-views that are also found in *Hecataeus (1) and *Herodotus (1). World maps are mentioned at Athens in the late 5th cent. BC, but do not seem to have been widespread.

These early maps were attempts to depict the wider order of the world rather than to survey smaller areas in detail; such local maps, if known, were not related conceptually to the geographers' task. Only the calculation of linear distances on some land routes (such as the *Royal Road) and on *periploi offered a bridge

between the two: but there is no evidence that such linear conceptions of space were represented graphically before the Roman period. The place of maps in the geographical knowledge of *Alexander (3) the Great and his commanders is therefore controversial (see BEMATISTS).

The governmental purposes of the Ptolemies, under whom the ancient agrimensorial techniques of the *Nile valley's agriculture were developed, gave a new status to mapping in Alexandrian geography (see PTOLEMY (1); ALEXANDRIA (1)). Influence from one of the Hellenistic kingdoms may perhaps be postulated for the development in Rome from the 3rd cent. BC of visual representations, in a context of land-divisions (see GROMATICI) on a large scale, long-distance road-building, and widespread city-foundation; and the greatest development of mapping in antiquity was indeed associated with Roman imperial policy. Cadastral plans, especially of land-allotments, were developed to a high degree of sophistication and accuracy: the best-known examples are fragments of the Flavian marble cadasters of the territory of *Arausio (Orange) in the Rhône valley, displayed on the walls of a room near the local forum. The most complex known example of ancient surveying is related in technique and perhaps in purpose, but much larger in scale (about 1 : 300) and more detailed: the *Forma Urbis Romae, a plan of Rome on marble slabs which decorated a hall in the *templum Pacis complex at Rome and dates from the Severan period (the numerous fragments are a source of great value for the nature of the ancient city). A recently discovered fragment of perhaps Flavian date (the 'Via Anicia Fragment') proves that there was an earlier version of neater draftsmanship and greater detail, with records of title to property as well as the names of public buildings.

The scale of Roman land-division (see CENTURIATION) and its connection with world-spanning road-building projects suggested that the wide world of geographic/cosmological description like Eratosthenes' might be represented in this sort of detail, and it is likely that the ambitious plan of world surveying attributed to *Caesar was an attempt, and perhaps the first, to realize this grandiose vision and use it as a sign of knowledge and power. M. *Vipsanius Agrippa's world map, succeeding to Caesar's vision, in the Porticus Vipsania in Rome was a potent symbol of the control of space by the Augustan regime. It is certain that this calibrated distances as well as representing the whole *oikoumenē* ('inhabited world'), but there is dispute over the shape and layout: was it an Eratosthenic world map, a pictorial version of the world-order of the sort that is represented in Roman and late antique art, the progenitor of the *mappae mundi* of the Middle Ages; or an early version of the road-map of the world known as the *Peutinger Table? The practical, as opposed to the symbolic, use of detailed maps in Roman military and governmental planning remains controversial.

O. A. W. Dilke, *Greek and Roman Maps* (1985), 21–38 (Greek and Hellenistic), 39–54 (Agrippa), 87–111 (surveying and planning); C. Nicolet, *Space, Geography and Politics in the Early Roman Empire* (1988, Eng. trans. 1991); R. K. Sherk, *ANRW* 2. 1. (1974), 534–62. N. P.

Marakanda (mod. Samarkand), chief town of *Achaemenid Sogdiana, in the valley of the river Zarafshan, which was the base of *Alexander (3) the Great's tough campaigns in the region. Quintus *Curtius Rufus (7. 6. 10) refers to the existence of a fortified citadel, now identified by excavation, dominating a walled city of 70 stades (roughly 13 km. or 8 miles), while its designation as the 'royal residence of the region' (Arr. *Anab.* 3. 30. 6) implies the existence of an Achaemenid *palace there. Its continued occupation under the *Seleucids is reflected in the archaeological site of Afrasiab (north-east of modern Samarkand), where Hellenistic pottery from levels II–III was initially described as 'Greek–Bactrian'. The exact date of the Hellenistic remains—including typical Greek pottery shapes, building techniques similar to those at *Ai Khanoum, a coin of *Antiochus (2) II, and a short Greek inscription on a vase fragment—now seems likely to be earlier, indicating the probable existence of a Seleucid colony at this nodal point for ancient trade routes and strategic control of the region.

S. Sherwin-White and A. Kuhrt, *From Samarkhand to Sardis* (1993), 106; P. Bernard, F. Grenet, and M. Isamiddinov, *CRAcad. Inscr.* 1992, 275 f.

S. S.-W.

Marathon, a large Attic *deme (see ATTICA) on the NE coast. It is included in *Philochorus' list of twelve townships united by *Theseus (*FGrH* 328 F 94). The earliest archaeological remains from the area are neolithic buildings on the low hill at Plasi and neolithic burials at Agrieleki. Use of both these sites seems subsequently to be almost continuous. Classical remains within the large fertile plain are extensive, and suggest that the Classical deme may have had several centres of habitation. Marathon and the neighbouring demes of Oenoe, Tricorynthus, and Probalinthus formed a religious confederacy known as the Tetrapolis, part of whose calendar is preserved in a 4th-cent. BC inscription (*IG* 2². 1358). An early 5th-cent. inscription (*IG* 1³. 2) found here relates to the celebration of a festival of *Heracles, which by the 4th cent. was one of the major quadrennial festivals administered by central officials. The plain was the scene of *Pisistratus' landing in *c.*545 BC (Hdt. 1. 62) as well as of the Persian landing in 490 BC; see next article. Few well-known Classical figures originated here, and the most famous demesman is Ti. *Claudius Atticus Herodes (2), traces of whose extensive estate can still be identified on the ground.

J. S. Traill, *Demos and Trittys* (1986) 147–8; J. Travlos, *Bildlexikon zur Topographie des antiken Attika* (1988), 216–57. C. W. J. E.; R. G. O.

Marathon, battle of, fought at *Marathon in 490 BC, probably near the surviving mound (*sōros*) covering the cremated remains of the Athenian dead. The Athenians and their allies from *Plataea probably had about 10,000 men, the Persians possibly twice as many. After some delay, probably while the Greeks waited for the Spartans, the battle eventually took place before their arrival, possibly because the Greeks learned that the Persian cavalry was absent, more probably because the Persians began to move on Athens. After lengthening their line by thinning their centre, the Greeks advanced, probably breaking into a run when within bowshot. Their stronger wings won easily and then perhaps turned inwards to envelop the victorious Persian centre as it returned from pursuing the broken Greek centre. The Greeks then pursued the Persian remnants to their ships, capturing seven. In all, 6,400 Persians were allegedly killed for only 192 Athenians. See PERSIAN WARS, various entries.

Hdt. 6. 108–15; Nep. *Milt.* 5; Plut. *Arist.* 5. *RE* 14/2, 'Marathon' 1; J. A. G. van der Veer, *Mnemos.* 1984; J. F. Lazenby, *The Defence of Greece* (1993). J. F. La.

marble Under μάρμαρος, *marmor*, the ancients included granites, porphyries, and all stones capable of taking a high polish. In the third millennium BC the white marbles of the Greek islands were used for Cycladic sculpture. The Minoans employed coloured marbles and breccias for vases and furniture and in architecture for facings and column bases. The Mycenaeans also used coloured marbles, including green porphyry and *rosso antico*, for furniture and architectural decoration. Neither used marble as a building stone or for sculpture.

The fine white marbles of Greece and the Greek islands were widely used for architecture and sculpture from the 7th cent. BC onwards. Grey Naxian and white Parian, the best of the island marbles, were used for both sculpture and architecture. The Pentelic quarries to the north-east of Athens (see PENTELICON) supplied a fine-grained marble for the *Parthenon and other 5th-cent. BC buildings in the city and its territory. In Asia Minor, the white marble quarries at *Ephesus were exploited from the 6th cent. BC; other white marble quarries were opened in the Hellenistic period, for example at *Aphrodisias and *Heraclea (2). It was not until the 2nd cent. BC that quarries of coloured marble were exploited. In Italy the famous quarries at Luna (*Carrara) were not exploited on a large scale by the Romans until the mid-1st cent. BC. *Augustus employed marble extensively, especially *Luna and coloured marbles from the Aegean and North Africa, in his building programmes at Rome. From the time of *Hadrian marble was transported in large quantities to the cities of the empire, spreading architectural and decorative styles. A wide variety of coloured marbles was employed. Columns were often monolithic to exploit the veining in the stones. Apart from architectural decoration marble was also used for veneer and paving. For statuary the Romans used Luna marble, most of the Greek marbles, and some coloured marbles for specific subjects. Many of the major sources of supply were administered directly by the emperor through imperial representatives, or by contractors. The emperor apparently exercised a tight control over the quarrying, use, and distribution of certain stones, for example the granite and porphyry quarries in Egypt (see MONS CLAUDIANUS).

The identification of marbles is problematic. Scientific analysis of white marbles has greatly increased our understanding of their use and distribution. There are various techniques employed, including chemical and petrographic analysis, stable isotope, ESR spectroscopy, and X-ray powder diffractometry. None has been wholly reliable and scholars now believe that a multi-method approach is more appropriate. See QUARRIES.

R. Gnoli, *Marmora Romana* (1988); N. Herz and M. Waelkens (eds.), *Classical Marble: Geochemistry, Technology, Trade* (1988); H. Dodge and B. Ward-Perkins, *Marble in Antiquity* (1992); M. Waelkens and others, *Ancient Stones: Quarrying, Trade and Provenance* (1992).

D. E. S.; H. D.

Marcellinus (1) (probably 2nd cent. AD), author of an extant work Περὶ σφυγμῶν, which incorporates much earlier work on the pulse.

Ed. H. Schöne, *Festschrift zur 49. Versammlung deutscher Philologen und Schulmänner* (1907). V. N.

Marcellinus (2), biographer of *Thucydides (2) (text in Stuart-Jones's OCT of Thucydides, rev. Powell, 1938). His 'Life' contains three sections of which A (chs. 1–45) is probably the 'Life of Thucydides' from [*Proclus'] *Chrestomathia*, worked over by a schoolteacher, and B (chs. 46–53) by a contemporary of *Dionysius (7) of Halicarnassus (perhaps *Caecilius (1)), whose main interest was Thucydides' style. To these Zosimus (5th cent. AD) added C (chs. 54–8) to make the introduction to his edition of *scholia on *Isocrates, *Demosthenes (2), and Thucydides. Marcellinus was probably the scholar who, shortly after *Justinian, isolated the Thucydidean scholia and gave the composition his name. If the biographical parts could be trusted, its value would be great, but there was an ancient tendency to spin biographical facts about an author out of that author's own writings (M. Lefkowitz, *Lives of the Greek Poets* (1981)).

The other Life printed in the Oxford text (*Vit. anon.*) contains some confusion between *Thucydides (1), son of Melesias and (2), the historian.

O. Luschnat, *Philol.* 1954, 42 ff.; A. Momigliano, *Development of Greek Biography* (1971), 87; on the *Vit. anon.*, H. T. Wade-Gery, *Essays in Greek History* (1958), 239, 261 f.; A. Andrewes, *JHS* 1978, 5 ff.

F. W. W.; S. H.

Marcellus, lawyer. See ULPIUS MARCELLUS.

Marcellus, physician and poet from *Side, lived under *Hadrian and *Antoninus Pius. Wrote *On Medical Matters* in 42 books of heroic metre; a work on werewolves (see LYCANTHROPY); a poem *About Fish* (fragments preserved); and two funerary epigrams commissioned by Ti. *Claudius Atticus Herodes (2) to commemorate Regilla, his wife.

M. Wellmann, *Marcellus von Side als Arzt* (1934); W. Ameling, *Herodes Atticus 2* (1983), no. 146; E. Bowie, *BICS* Suppl. 55 (1989), 201 f.

A. J. S. S.

Marcellus, Claudius See CLAUDIUS MARCELLUS (various entries); for other Marcelli see EPRIUS; NONIUS; ULPIUS.

Marcia, concubine of the emperor *Commodus, her full names being Marcia Aurelia Ceionia Demetrias. Daughter of an imperial freedman, she was the mistress of M. *Aurelius' great-nephew Ummidius Quadratus, then of Commodus and of his chamberlain Eclectus, whom she married, although Commodus, over whom she had enormous influence, treated her like a wife. She joined Q. *Aemilius Laetus and Eclectus in the conspiracy which led to Commodus' murder, and was herself killed by *Didius Severus Iulianus in AD 193. She showed favour to the Christians.

Cass. Dio 72; Hdn. 1; SHA *Comm., Pert., Did. Iul.*; Hippol. *Haer.*; *Epit. de Caes. PIR²* M 261.

A. R. Bi.

Marciana See ULPIA MARCIANA AUGUSTA.

Marcianus, lawyer. See AELIUS MARCIANUS.

Marcius (RE 2), the alleged author of prophetic verses (see PROPHECIES) circulating at Rome in the 3rd cent. BC. In 213, verses attributed to him predicting the disaster at *Cannae were circulated at Rome, as were verses to the effect that Rome would only be rid of the foreign enemy if it founded games in honour of Apollo. A subsequent consultation of the Sibylline books (see SIBYL) confirmed this prediction, leading to the foundation of the Ludi Apollinares (Livy 25. 12. 4–12; Macrob. *Sat.* 1. 17. 25; see LUDI).

Subsequent ancient scholarship produced several tales about Marcius (and more than one Marcius). According to *Livy, he (singular) was simply 'a famous prophet' (25. 12. 3). *Cicero mentions the brothers Marcius, 'famous prophets', in two places, and says that 'Marcius' wrote in verse (*Div.* 1. 89, 115, 2. 113); the elder *Pliny (1) says that Marcius was the most famous Roman to write in verse (*HN* 7. 33); while *Ammianus Marcellinus refers to 'Marcius' as a quintessentially Roman prophet, on a par with *Amphiaraus (14. 1. 7). In late antiquity, Symmachus (2) says that Marcius wrote his oracles on the bark of trees, and Servius that he took dictation from the Sibyl (Symmachus, *Ep.* 4. 34; Serv. on *Aen.* 6. 72). The one point that seems certain is that the prophecies of Marcius were in Latin.

Münzer, *RE* 2; Bouché-Leclercq, *Hist. div.*

D. S. P.

Marcius (RE 9), **Ancus,** the fourth king of Rome (traditionally

640–617 BC), reputedly established a settlement at *Ostia (which archaeological investigation has not (yet) confirmed) and exploited the nearby salt-pans. He is also credited with the preceding conquest of Politorium, Tellenae, Ficana, and Medullia, but archaeological evidence refutes his alleged destruction of Ficana and Politorium (if Politorium is modern Castel di Decima). Roman tradition further fleshed out his anonymous reign with the institution of the fetial procedure, annexation of the *Janiculum, and construction of the Marcian aqueduct (certainly anachronistic) and Sublician bridge. *Ennius (*Ann.* 137 Skutsch) characterized him as 'good' (*bonus*), but his supposed settlement of the *Aventine perhaps contributed to his alternative portrayal as a populist, reflected in Verg. *Aen.* 6. 815 f.

Ogilvie, *Comm. Livy 1–5*; O. Skutsch, *The Annals of Quintus Ennius* (1985), 281 ff.; J. Poucet, *Les Origines de Rome* (1985). A. D.

Marcius Barea (*RE* 2) **Soranus, Quintus,** suffect consul AD 52. As consul designate he proposed honours for Claudius' freedman M. *Antonius Pallas. He incurred *Nero's anger for his just proconsulate in Asia (before 63). In 66 he was accused by a knight, Ostorius Sabinus, because of friendship with *Rubellius Plautus and alleged plotting in Asia. He was condemned on false evidence given by his former Stoic teacher Egnatius Celer (Juv. 3. 116; see STOICISM). A niece (or possibly daughter), Marcia Furnilla, was briefly married to *Vespasian's son *Titus, and her sister may have been the mother of *Trajan through whom he presumably inherited the clay-producing estates in Umbria called the *figlinae Marcianae*.

PIR² B 55 and M 218–19; E. Champlin, *Athenaeum* 1983, 257 ff.

M. T. G.

Marcius (*RE* 51, Suppl. 5. 653 ff.) **Coriolanus, Gnaeus** (Gaius in Dion. Hal. and Plutarch), a Roman aristocrat who supposedly received his surname from his part in the Roman capture of Corioli from the *Volsci (493 BC). According to the story he went into exile when charged with tyrannical conduct and opposing the distribution of grain to the starving *plebs. Welcomed by the Volscians of *Antium he became their leader in a war against Rome. In two devastating campaigns he captured a series of Latin towns and led his forces to the gates of Rome, where he was persuaded to turn back by his mother Veturia and his wife Volumnia (in Plutarch they are named as Volumnia and Vergilia respectively). He was then killed by the Volscians (although Q. *Fabius Pictor, fr. 17 Peter, believed that he lived into old age). It is uncertain how much, if any, of this famous story is based on fact. Coriolanus does not appear in the *fasti, and although *Livy makes him a *patrician (as indeed the plot of the story requires), in historical times the Marcii were a plebeian clan (see PLEBS). The setting of the story recalls a time when the Volscians overran southern *Latium and threatened the very existence of Rome; this conforms to what is otherwise known (partly from archaeological evidence) of the situation around 490 BC (see VOLSCI). Finally, the tale of a Roman becoming leader of the Volsci is an example of 'horizontal social mobility', a phenomenon that occurs in other stories of this period (e.g. *Tarquinius Priscus, Appius *Claudius Crassus Inregillensis Sabinus, *Mastarna) and may be a genuine feature of the society of central Italy in the archaic period.

Mommsen, *Röm. Forsch.* 2. 113 ff.; De Sanctis, *Storia dei Romani* (1960), 2². 103 ff.; Ogilvie, *Comm. Livy 1–5*, 314 ff.; C. Ampolo, *Dial. di Arch.* 1976–7, 333–45; T. J. Cornell, *CAH* 7²/2 (1989), 187–8, 261. T. J. Co.

Marcius (*RE* 75) **Philippus** (1), **Lucius,** grandson of Q.

*Marcius Philippus and of Ap. *Claudius Pulcher (1), after a demagogic tribunate (*c*.105 BC) omitted the aedileship, hence (probably) failed to become consul 93. Elected for 91, he disliked M. *Livius Drusus (2)'s plans to enlarge the senate and enfranchise the Italians (see CITIZENSHIP, ROMAN) and led the opposition to him. After the death of L. *Licinius Crassus, he succeeded, as an augur, in having Drusus' laws invalidated. He is not heard of between 90 and 86: a provincial command may be conjectured. Collaborating with the government of L. *Cornelius Cinna (1), he became censor with M. *Perperna (2) in 86, registering the first of the newly enfranchised Italians. They struck his uncle Ap. *Claudius Pulcher (2), then in exile, off the senate list as a supporter of *Sulla. Together with Cn. *Papirius Carbo and Q. *Hortensius Hortalus, he successfully defended Cn. *Pompeius Magnus (1) on a criminal charge. On Sulla's return he joined him, conquered Sardinia for him (82), and as the oldest living consular (except for the inactive Perperna) became a pillar of the Sullan establishment after Sulla's death, leading vigorous action against M. *Aemilius Lepidus (2) and Q. *Sertorius, against whom he persuaded the senate to send Pompey. He frequently, though unsuccessfully, urged the annexation of Egypt under the testament of *Ptolemy (1) X Alexander I. Cicero greatly admired him, characterizes him as a good speaker (though eclipsed by L. Crassus and M. *Antonius (1)), and frequently quotes his witticisms.

J. van Ooteghem, *Lucius Marcius Philippus et sa famille* (1961). E. B.

Marcius (*RE* 76) **Philippus** (2), **Lucius**, son of the above, was governor of *Syria (61–59 BC) and consul (56). He took no part in the Civil Wars. As second husband of *Atia (1) he was stepfather to *Octavian: in March 44 they both tried to dissuade him from accepting the inheritance of *Caesar. In January 43 he went as an emissary of the senate to Antony (M. *Antonius (2)). He was still alive in August 43. L. *Marcius Philippus (3) was no doubt his son by a marriage previous to that with Atia.

Syme, *Rom. Rev.*, see index; J. van Ooteghem, *Lucius Marcius Philippus et sa famille* (1961), 173 ff.; Gruen, *LGRR*, see index.
A. M.; T. J. C.; A. J. S. S.

Marcius (*RE* 77) **Philippus** (3), **Lucius**, son of the last, was tribune in 49 BC, *suffect consul in 38, and governor of Spain (34–33?), whence he triumphed. It was probably he rather than his father who built the Porticus Philippi in Rome. He married *Atia (2), younger sister of his father's second wife.

Syme, *Rom. Rev.*, see index; F. W. Shipley, *Amer. Acad. Rome* 1931.
T. J. C.; A. J. S. S.

Marcius (*RE* 79) **Philippus, Quintus**, was praetor in Sicily 188 BC, and consul 186, when he assisted his colleague Sp. *Postumius Albinus in the suppression of the *Bacchanalia; later that year he suffered a serious defeat in Liguria (see LIGURIANS). In 183 he was an ambassador to Macedon and the Peloponnese; his report on his return was hostile to the *Achaean Confederacy. In 172 he was the leader of an embassy to secure Greek loyalty for the forthcoming conflict with *Perseus (2); among their actions was the break-up of the *Boeotian Confederacy. At a conference with Perseus it was agreed that no hostilities should take place until Perseus had sent envoys to Rome. On his return Philippus boasted that he had thus gained time for Rome to make military preparations. Consul again 169, Philippus penetrated into Macedonia, but lack of supplies forced him to retreat southwards. He declined the offer of troops from the Achaean Confederacy, brought to him by *Polybius (1), and told Polybius privately not

to send any to Ap. Claudius Centho in Illyria. He advised the Rhodians to mediate—it is disputed whether he meant in the war with Perseus or that between Syria and Egypt. He was censor 164 with L. *Aemilius Paullus (2).

Some see Philippus as consistently devious in his dealings with the Hellenistic world; others hold that Polybius was biased against him and that a favourable interpretation of his actions is possible.

J. Briscoe, *JRS* 1964, 6–77; E. S. Gruen, *CQ* 1975, 58–81, and *The Hellenistic World and the Coming of Rome* (1984), see index. J. Br.

Marcius (*RE* 90) **Rex** (1), **Quintus**, as urban praetor 144 BC and propraetor built the great Marcian *aqueduct, the first using arches on a large scale. Its origins were ascribed to his presumed ancestor Ancus *Marcius. See the coins *RRC* 425, showing Ancus and a flight of arches with an equestrian statue, with the legend AQUA MARCIA. E. B.

Marcius (*RE* 92) **Rex** (2), **Quintus**, descended from Q. Marcius Rex (1), married to a daughter of Ap. *Claudius Pulcher (2) and sister of *Clodia, was consul 68 BC (alone for much of the year), then sent as proconsul to Cilicia to fight the pirates, but delayed in Italy by unrest in Transpadane Gaul (see IULIUS CAESAR (1), C.; LICINIUS CRASSUS (1), M.). In his province he refused aid to L. *Licinius Lucullus (2) and received their brother-in-law P. *Clodius Pulcher, trying to stir up trouble against Lucullus. On *Pompey's appointment (66), he was deserted by his army. Hoping (vainly) for a *triumph, he was instructed to use his *imperium* against the Catilinarians (63; see SERGIUS CATILINA, L.), but died almost at once. E. B.

Marcius (*RE* 97) **Rutilus, Gaius**, consul in 357, 352, 344, and 342 BC and founder of a major political lineage was reputedly the first plebeian *dictator (356; ignored by *Diodorus (3) Siculus) and censor (351). See PLEBS. In 357 he supposedly triumphed (see TRIUMPH) over Privernum and in 356 over the *Etruscans and *Faliscans, whose invasion of Roman territory he had repulsed. Clearly one of the earliest dominant plebeian political personalities, he may have won popular support by promoting *debt relief, but the evidence is inconclusive.

K. J. Hölkeskamp, *Die Entstehung der Nobilität* (1987). A. D.

Marcius (*RE* 107) **Turbo, Quintus**, from the Caesarian *colonia* Epidaurum in Dalmatia, is first recorded as centurion in Legio II Adiutrix (see CENTURIO; LEGION) and rose through the primipilate, becoming *praefectus vehiculorum* (see POSTAL SERVICE), tribune in the *vigiles and urban cohorts at Rome, and commander of the imperial horse guard, then procurator of the Ludus Magnus (see LUDI) and prefect of the *classis Misenensis* (fleet based at *Misenum) under *Trajan, the latter post taking him to the east for the Parthian War, at which time he was already one of *Hadrian's friends (SHA *Hadr.* 4. 2). In AD 116 he was given the first of several special missions, to suppress the Jewish revolts in Egypt and Cyrenaica (see JEWS); shortly after Hadrian's accession the next year he was sent to deal with an uprising in *Mauretania. Next he had a special command in *Pannonia (Lower) and *Dacia, with a rank equivalent to prefect of Egypt (SHA *Hadr.* 6. 7, 7. 3). In 119 he became praetorian prefect (see PRAEFECTUS PRAETORIO) and held this post for many years, although ultimately incurring Hadrian's dislike. Turbo, who had the additional names Fronto Publicius Severus, evidently had two adopted sons, one of whom became a senator, the other a procurator; the latter's career-inscription (*AE* 1946, 113) was long mistakenly attributed to Turbo himself until its incompatibility with one of Turbo's own numerous inscriptions (*AE* 1955, 225) was recognized. He is mentioned by M. *Cornelius Fronto, *Cassius Dio, *Eusebius (*Hist. eccl.* 4. 2) and the *Historia Augusta*.

> PIR² M 249; H. G. Pflaum, *Les Carrières procuratoriennes equestres* (1960–1), no. 94; B. Dobson, *Die Primipilares* (1978), no. 107; Syme, *RP* 2. 541 ff., and *Historia Augusta Papers* (1983), 168 ff.   A. R. Bi.

Marcoman(n)i (Stat. *Silv.* 3. 3. 170 scans Marcomăni), a west German (Suebic) tribe, the name meaning the inhabitants of a border country ('march'), are first mentioned by *Caesar. Stirred up by the *Cimbri and *Teutones, the Marcomanni left Saxony and Thuringia (*c*.100 BC) and settled down on the upper and middle Main; they joined *Ariovistus' expedition against Gaul. Attacked by the elder Drusus (*c*.9 BC; see CLAUDIUS DRUSUS, NERO) they emigrated to Bohemia (*c*.8 BC). There *Maroboduus established a powerful kingdom, which *Augustus considered a danger and wanted to destroy, but was hindered by the Pannonian–Illyrian Revolt. Weakened by war against *Arminius, Maroboduus was expelled by Catualda (AD 19), who in turn was overthrown by Vibilius (20), the following kings being more or less dependent upon Rome. After wars under *Domitian and *Nerva peace prevailed till the great Marcomannic Wars (166–73; 177–80) under M. *Aurelius. The Marcomanni must have played their part in the subsequent wars on the middle Danube, though they are not very frequently mentioned. After 500 they left Bohemia and occupied Bavaria. See GERMANS.

> L. Schmidt, *Geschichte der deutschen Stämme . . . Die Westgermanen*, 2nd edn. (1938); E. A. Thompson, *The Early Germans* (1965); A. Garzetti, *From Tiberius to the Antonines* (1974), 484 ff.; M. Todd, *The Northern Barbarians* (1975).   F. A. W. S.; J. F. Dr.

Marcus Aurelius See AURELIUS, MARCUS.

Mardonius, nephew and son-in-law of *Darius I of Persia, took over command in Ionia *c*.492 BC, immediately after the *Ionian Revolt, and removed one major cause of discontent by abolishing government through 'tyrants' (see TYRANNY) and permitting *democracies (Hdt. 6. 43). He *may* have served during the revolt, under *Datis at Lindus (*FGrH* 532 D(1)). He then restored Persian authority in southern Thrace, despite storm damage to his fleet off Mt. *Athos, and being himself wounded by the Brygians. Herodotus makes him the moving spirit of Xerxes' invasion. Left in command in Greece after the battle of *Salamis, he vainly attempted to detach Athens from the Greek alliance by offers of favourable terms. Withdrawing from Attica in 479 in face of the Greek land-forces, he gave battle (perhaps reluctantly) near Plataea and was defeated and killed (see PERSIAN WARS).

> Hdt. 6. 43–5; 7. 5, 9; 8, 9, *passim*. *CAH* 4² (1988), see index; M. M. Austin, *CQ* 1990, 306; J. F. Lazenby, *The Defence of Greece* (1993), chs. 8, 9.   A. R. B.; S. H.

Margites, a humorous narrative poem, apparently composed in Ionia (Colophon?) in the 7th or 6th cent. BC and reputed to be by *Homer ([Pl.] *Alc.* 2. 147b, Arist. *Poet.* 4, etc.; some later sources express doubts). The subject was a moron called Margites and his ludicrous misadventures, especially on his wedding night. The metre was an irregular alternation of hexameters and iambic trimeters. A few fragments survive, including three from papyri.

> FRAGMENTS, TESTIMONIA West, *IE²*.
> TRANSLATION West, *GLP*.
> CRITICISM F. Bossi, *Studi sul Margite* (1986).   M. L. W.

Mari is the name of a kingdom and city north of Abu Kemal in *Syria on the right bank of the *Euphrates, occupied from protodynastic times (*c*.3000 BC) until the *Seleucid period. An early dynasty there is named in the Sumerian king-list as tenth after the Flood. Some third millennium inscriptions and huge archives from the early second millennium have been excavated in two superimposed palaces by French teams led by A. Parrot and then J. Margueron, from 1933 onwards.

> J.-R. Kupper and others, *Reallexikon der Assyriologie* 7 (1987–90), 'Mari'
>   S. M. D.

Mariccus, a Boian of humble stock who declared himself divine 'liberator of the provinces of Gaul', and attracted a large following, before being suppressed on the orders of *Vitellius (AD 69). His activities reflect the uncertainty created by the fall of *Nero, and indicate persisting popular hostility to Rome. However, his failure points up the absence of genuine Gallic *nationalism, soon evident in the collapse of the 'imperium Galliarum' of *Iulius Classicus, Tutor, and Sabinus (70).   J. F. Dr.

Marinus (*c*. AD 130), anatomist, credited by *Galen with reviving anatomical studies (see ANATOMY AND PHYSIOLOGY) at *Alexandria (1).

Works (1) Ἀνατομικαὶ ἐγχειρήσεις ('Practical Anatomy'); (2) an Anatomy in 20 books; (3) a book on the roots of the nerves; (4) an Anatomy of the muscles; (5) a commentary on aphorisms.
         W. D. R.; V. N.

maritime loans were a distinct category of *credit right through antiquity and even into modern times. To pay for a cargo, merchant or shipowner borrowed money for the duration of the voyage. Loan and interest were repaid out of proceeds of sale of the cargo only on condition that the ship arrived safely at its destination; loss was otherwise borne by the lender. High risks justified high interest (*nautikos tokos* or 'maritime interest'): from 4th-cent. BC Athens, anywhere between 12½ and 30 per cent. See INTEREST, RATES OF. As a guarantee against fraud, cargo and even the ship itself (the ship's bottom, as in 'bottomry loan') would be offered as security. Lenders tended to be those with prior experience of sea-trading. The importance of maritime loans in Athens' trade is indicated by their forming the substance of forensic speeches (Dem. 32, [34], [35], [56]). The economic significance of maritime credit in the Greek world is twofold. Apart from the insurance effect (loss of cargo extinguished obligation to repay), traders were generally underfunded, relying on loans to purchase cargoes. Maritime credit appears sporadically in Ptolemaic papyri, and in Roman texts in the guise of *pecunia traiecticia* and *fenus nauticum*. *Cato (Censorius) reputedly lent heavily in maritime loans (Plut. *Cat. Mai.* 21. 6). Sustained treatment comes from legal texts concerned with control of interest. Though maritime credit was regularly excluded from regulation (Paulus, *Sent.* 2. 14. 3), Justinian tried to establish the equivalent of 12 per cent (possibly) per annum) as the maximum interest (*Cod. Iust.* 4. 32. 26. 2).

> G. E. M. de Ste. Croix, in H. Edey and B. S. Yamey (eds.), *Essays in Honour of W. T. Baxter* (1956) 41 ff.; P. Millett, in P. Garnsey, M. K. Hopkins, and C. R. Whittaker (eds.), *Trade in the Ancient Economy* (1983), 36 ff.; R. Bogaert, *Chron. d'É.* 1965, 140 ff.; J. Rougé, in J. H. D'Arms and E. C. Kopff (eds.), *The Sea-borne Commerce of Ancient Rome* (1980), 291 ff.   P. C. M.

Marium-Arsinoë (mod. Polis-tis-Khrysokhou), a city-kingdom of NW *Cyprus, near Khrysokhou Bay, possibly founded in the 11th cent. BC, apparently on a virgin site. It marched with Soli (to the east) and *Paphos (to the south). Though the city is largely unexplored, finds from its extensively excavated cemeteries suggest strong economic links with Greece, especially Athens, in the 6th and late 5th–4th cents.; the copper ore of nearby Limni may have been responsible. Yet the city was ambivalent during the Greek–Persian struggle; though it joined the *Ionian Revolt, *Cimon's siege 50 years later implies a changed loyalty. Its 5th- and 4th-cent. kings are named on their coinage; under the last, Stasioecus II, the city was destroyed in 312 by *Ptolemy (1) I, by whom the survivors were translated to Paphos. It was eventually refounded as Arsinoë by *Ptolemy (1) II c.270 BC.

G. Hill, *A History of Cyprus* 1 (1940); K. Nikolaou, *RDAC* 1964, 131 ff.; O. Masson, *Les Inscriptions chypriotes syllabiques*, rev. edn. (1983), 150 ff.; W. A. P. Childs, *RDAC* 1988, pt. 2, 121 ff.   H. W. C.

Marius (1) (*RE* 14, in Suppl. 6), **Gaius**, born c.157 BC near *Arpinum, of a family probably of recent equestrian standing (see EQUITES), but with good Roman connections, including P. *Cornelius Scipio Aemilianus. He served with distinction under Scipio at *Numantia and, with his commendation, won a military tribunate by election, perhaps serving under M'. *Aquillius (1) in Asia. Quaestor c.123, he was helped to a tribunate by the Metelli (119), but fiercely attacked the consul L. *Caecilius Metellus Delmaticus when he opposed Marius' law ensuring secrecy of individual votes in the *comitia. Because of this breach of *fides* (trust) he failed to gain an aedileship, but became (urban) praetor 115, barely securing acquittal on a charge of *ambitus. Sent to Further Spain as proconsul, he showed aptitude at guerrilla warfare and added to his fortune. On his return he married a patrician *Iulia (1), a distinguished match. In 109 Q. *Caecilius Metellus Numidicus, sent to fight a guerrilla war against *Jugurtha, chose Marius as his senior legate. But when Marius requested leave to seek a consulship, Metellus haughtily rebuffed him. Marius now intrigued against Metellus among his equestrian and Italian friends in Africa and Rome and won election for 107 by playing on suspicions of the aristocracy. He superseded Metellus in Numidia by special legislation. He ended the manpower shortage by the radical step of abolishing the property qualification for service and enrolled a volunteer army. After fighting for two years without decisive success, he captured Jugurtha through the diplomatic skill of his quaestor *Sulla, was elected consul for the second time for 104 by special dispensation, to deal with a threatened German invasion, and triumphed on 1 January.

He found an army reorganized and trained by P. *Rutilius Rufus, his fellow legate under Metellus and his enemy, as consul 105; and, re-elected consul year after year, with friendly colleagues, he improved the army's equipment and organization (see ARMIES, ROMAN) and defeated the *Teutones and Ambrones at Aquae Sextiae (mod. Aix-en-Provence) and, with Q. *Lutatius Catulus (1), the *Cimbri at Vercellae (near Rovigo in northern Italy), in 102 and 101 respectively, consenting to celebrate a joint triumph with Catulus. His immense prestige attracted nobles like Catulus into his following and confirmed the loyalty of *equites* and *plebs. He was elected to a sixth consulship (100), defeating Metellus' quixotic candidacy.

The tribune L. *Appuleius Saturninus had provided land for his African veterans in 103, and in 100 undertook to do so for the veterans of the German war. Marius gladly accepted his co-operation and was pleased when Metellus' intransigence in opposition led to his exile. But when Saturninus, with the help of C. *Servilius Glaucia, threatened to establish independent power, Marius turned against them, rejected Glaucia's consular

candidacy, and, when they tried to force through a law overruling him, 'saved the republic' by forcibly suppressing them. But his stubborn opposition to Metellus' return, delaying it while his friend M. *Antonius (1) was consul, alienated his optimate supporters. When the vote for Metellus' recall passed, he left for the east, 'to fulfil a vow', abandoning hope for a censorship. His firm words to *Mithradates VI earned him election to an augurate in absence and, with his *dignitas* restored, he returned. But he had frittered away his overwhelming stature. Some of his friends and clients were now attacked (M'. *Aquillius (2), C. *Norbanus; the prosecution of T. Matrinius (Cic. *Balb.* 48 f.)), and although he successfully defended them, his noble friends deserted him. In 92, reaffirming his links with the *equites*, he assisted in the prosecution of P. Rutilius Rufus, and in 91 he seems to have opposed M. *Livius Drusus (2) with his equestrian friends, mobilizing his Italian followers against Drusus. When the senate openly expressed support for Sulla by allowing *Bocchus I to dedicate on the Capitol a group showing Jugurtha's surrender, Marius was prevented from violent opposition only by the outbreak of the *Social War (3). In the war he was successful on the northern front, but when not offered supreme command, chose to retire.

With war against Mithradates imminent, Marius hoped to have the command and opposed the attempt of his relative by marriage C. *Iulius Caesar Strabo Vopiscus to win the consulship for 88. He found an ally in Drusus' friend P. *Sulpicius Rufus, tribune 88, in return for supporting his policies. When the *optimates chose Sulla for the consulship and command (he married *Caecilia Metella (1), widow of the *princeps senatus M. *Aemilius Scaurus (1)), Sulpicius had the *plebs transfer the command to Marius. Sulla responded by seizing Rome with his army. Marius, unprepared for this, had to flee (the flight was later embroidered with dramatic detail), finding safety at Cercina, a colony of his veterans off Africa. After the expulsion of L. *Cornelius Cinna (1) from Rome, Marius returned and joined him with an army collected among his veterans. He sacked Ostia and organized Cinna's capture of Rome. Both were proclaimed consuls for 86 and Marius was to supersede Sulla in the east. He now took terrible vengeance on his enemies, especially on faithless former friends; but his health gave out and he died before taking up his command.

A typical *novus homo, like M. *Porcius Cato (1) before him and Cicero after him, Marius wanted to beat the nobles at their own game and win acceptance as a leader of their *res publica*. Unlike some aristocrats, from C. *Sempronius Gracchus to *Caesar, he had no plans for reform. Although favouring rewards for soldiers without distinction between citizens and Italians, he opposed Drusus' attempt to enfranchise the Italians and left it to Saturninus to look after his veterans' interests. His reform of enlistment, due to momentary considerations, accidentally created the client army: it was Sulla who taught him the consequences. However, his early career first demonstrated the power inhering in an alliance of a successful commander with a demagogue and a noble following; and his opponents, in their attitude to him and to Sulla, revealed the lack of cohesion and of political principle besetting the *nobilitas*.

General works on the period necessarily deal with Marius. Broughton, *MRR* 3 has an excellent general bibliography. The only scholarly biographies are T. F. Carney, *A Biography of Gaius Marius* (1961), and J. van Ooteghem, *Gaius Marius* (1964), in French; there is a summary by E. Badian in *Durham University Journal* (1963–4), 141 ff., and more detailed discussion in Badian, *Foreign Clientelae* (1958), ch. 9; on 100 and the 90s, Badian, *Chiron* 1984, 101 ff.   E. B.

Marius, Gaius

Marius (2) (*RE* 15), **Gaius,** son of C. *Marius (1) and of *Iulia (1), born *c*.110 BC, shared his father's flight and return (88–87). Made consul 82, to his mother's distress, with Cn. *Papirius Carbo, to exploit his name, he was defeated by *Sulla at Sacriportus and cut off at *Praeneste. He died during its capture by Q. *Lucretius Afella.   E. B.

Marius (*RE* 42) **Gratidianus, Marcus,** son of a sister of C. *Marius (1) and adopted by his brother; as tribune 87 BC supported L. *Cornelius Cinna (1) and, after Cinna's capture of Rome, prosecuted Q. *Lutatius Catulus (1), a faithless friend of C. Marius (1), who killed himself. Praetor 85, he announced as his own a plan to improve the coinage developed by the praetors and tribunes (its content is unknown) and received heroic honours from the *plebs* (Cic. *Off.* 3. 80 f.). He won another praetorship, but was not allowed to be consul. After *Sulla's victory he was cruelly killed by his brother-in-law *Catiline at the tomb of Catulus (1) at the request of Q. *Lutatius Catulus (2).   E. B.

Marius (*RE* 48) **Maximus,** biographer of twelve emperors from *Nerva to *Elagabalus, continuator and imitator of *Suetonius. He is probably the Marius Maximus who governed Syria, Africa, and Asia, was *praefectus urbi* in AD 217–18, and held his second consulship in 223. His biographies mixed the anecdotal and scurrilous with the diligent quotation of lengthy documents. Like Suetonius, he arranged his material by categories. His work influenced the *Historia Augusta* and provided some of its material (he is quoted there 26 times): he may even have been the main source, at least for some Lives (especially *Elagabalus*), though the issue is fiercely disputed. *Ammianus Marcellinus 28. 4. 14 deplores the taste of those who were still reading him.

> FRAGMENTS Peter, *HRRel.* 2. clxxx–clxxxviii, 121–9.
> LITERATURE R. Syme, *Ammianus and the Historia Augusta* (1968), 89 ff., and *Emperors and Biography* (1971), 113 ff.; T. D. Barnes, *The Sources of the Historia Augusta* (1978).   C. B. R. P.

Marius Victorinus See VICTORINUS, MARIUS.

Mark Antony See ANTONIUS (2), M.

markets and fairs

Greece The arrival of the market as an institution in the 8th cent. BC (see EMPORION; TRADE, GREEK), gradually replacing archaic mechanisms for exchange (see GIFT, GREECE), along with the concomitant beginnings of urbanization, prompted the *polis* to develop marketing arrangements. The installation of permanent retail-markets in urban centres, signalled in the shift in the meaning of ἀγορά (*agora) from 'assembly (place of)' to 'market', is best followed at *Athens, where built shops are attested by *c*.500 and the first public edifice for commercial purposes by 391 BC (Ar. *Eccl.* 686), although temporary 'booths' (*skēnai*) and 'tables' (*trapezai*) still typified the bazaar-area in the 4th cent.; generally, peristylar (colonnaded) markets (*makella*) are a 3rd-cent. development. Elsewhere, as in the 'new town' at *Olynthus, private houses could act as retail outlets. The *polis* controlled the urban market through *agoranomoi and drew revenues from taxing retailers; but it had no larger interest in intervention beyond seeking to assure (for essentially political reasons) an adequate *food supply.

Although urban markets chiefly served an urban populace, additional periodic market-days, attested monthly at Classical Athens (Ar. *Eq.* 43–4; *Vesp.* 169–71), point to their use by peasant farmers; in the 3rd cent. BC one Attic village (*Sunium, perhaps exceptional) had its own built market (J. Travlos, *Bildlexikon zur Topographie des antiken Attika* (1988), 426–9). Although *Demosthenes (2) (23. 39) speaks of the 'border market' (ἀγορὰ ἐφορία) as a thing of the past, periodic rural markets and fairs are attested in remote parts of Roman *Greece (e.g. Paus. 10. 32. 14–16). Periodic markets as a part of religious *festivals (*panēgyreis*), well known from the Hellenistic period, are probably older (as at *Olympia, allegedly existing by *c*.500 BC: Cic. *Tusc.* 5. 3. 9); while all served pilgrims, some were genuine regional fairs too, encouraged by the lifting of import and export duties, as on *Delos (Strabo 10. 5. 4). Negotiation of temporary markets outside city walls for exchanges with campaigning armies was a feature of Greek military *logistics.

Rome The Forum was originally (*i.a.*) a market-site, the word surviving in this sense in the specialized markets of Rome (e.g. *forum Boarium), although by the 1st cent. BC *macellum* was the usual term for an alimentary market. A daily retail market existed in Rome by 210 BC (Livy 26. 27. 1–4) and later was joined by others; wholesaling took place at the riverine Emporium, built in 193 BC (Livy 35. 10. 12). The state supervised Rome's markets through *aediles. State-authorized periodic markets and fairs (*nundinae, mercatus*) have recently been shown to be commoner than usually thought in the Roman world. In cities they included both weekly ('peasant') markets, as for instance in some 25 towns in central Italy of the first cent. AD (attested by inscribed market-calendars), and also regional fairs, as with those following annual games at Rome itself (*Inscr. Ital.* 13. 2. 10) in the same period. In rural areas a distinctly Roman development is the estate market instituted by a landowner, of the type which brought a Roman senator into conflict with an Italian town in 105 (Pliny, *Ep.* 5. 4 and 13) and found too in Roman *Africa and *Asia. Supra-regional fairs (as at Amm. Marc. 14. 3. 3) seem to have been rare, probably because the long-distance seaborne transport of the Mediterranean was ill-adapted for punctuality.

> J. Frayn, *Markets and Fairs in Roman Italy* (1993); L. de Ligt, *Fairs and Markets in the Roman Empire* (1993); P. W. de Neeve, *Athenaeum* 1988, 391 ff.; R. Martin, *Recherches sur l'agora grecque* (1951); R. Wycherley, *The Stones of Athens* (1978), ch. 3.   A. J. S. S.

Marmarica, semi-arid coastal area between the African *Pentapolis and Egypt, approximately from Darnis (mod. Derna) to Catabathmus (Sollum); crossed by routes from the coast to the Ammon-oracle at *Siwa. It included Aziris (?Wadi el Chalig), where Theraeans settled before colonizing *Cyrene, was partly, and then, perhaps, wholly controlled from Cyrene (Plin. *HN* 5. 33), but figures as the Marmaric nome of Egypt (see NOMOS (1)) in *Ptolemy (4) the geographer (4. 5. 2). From *Diocletian it was part of the province of Lower *Libya or Libya Sicca, its capital perhaps at Paraetonium (Marsa Matruh). A cadastral papyrus of AD 191 (*PVat. II*) shows a number of settled farmers with Greek, Libyan, and Latin names, while Greek mariners' guides and Roman *itineraries record small harbours and road stations; but nomadic groups survived. The name Marmaridae, first used of its Libyan inhabitants by Scylax (108; see SCYLAX), was applied over a much wider area; the Marmaridae who raided Cyrenaica in the Roman period seem to have come from further south and west.

> *RE* 14 (1930), 1881 f.; R. G. Goodchild, *TIR* sheet H. 1. 34: *Cyrene* (1954); A. Laronde, *Cyrène et la Libye hellénistique* (1987), ch. 10. On Marmaridae: J. Desanges, *Catalogue des tribus africaines de l'antiquité classique ...* (1962); D. White, *Libyan Studies* 1994, 31 ff. On Aziris: J. Boardman, *BSA* 1966, 150–2.   J. M. R.

Marmor Parium, an inscribed marble stele, originally about 200 cm. high by 69 cm. wide (79 × 27 in.), set up at *Paros (hence its name; also known as the Parian Marble). Two fragments of this important inscription survive, one of which, brought from Smyrna (mod. Izmir) to London in 1627, is now in the Ashmolean Museum, Oxford (save the upper part, which perished during the English Civil War and is known only from a 1628 transcription), while the other, discovered at Paros in 1897, is now in the museum there. The text lists chronological events, not always accurately, and together with other ancient Greek chronicles is important for the understanding of ancient Greek chronology. The events commemorated form a curious medley, drawn chiefly from political, military, religious, and literary history. The compiler of the inscription, whose name is lost, claims to have 'written up the dates from the beginning, derived from all kinds of records and general histories, starting from *Cecrops, the first king of Athens, down to the archonship (see ARCHONTES) of Astyanax (?) at Paros and Diognetus at Athens', i.e. 264/3 BC, presumably the date or near-date of composition. The first fragment covers the period from 1581/0 to 355/4, and the second that from 336/5 to 299/8. The text is written continuously, but comprises a number of items (80 on the first fragment, 27 on the second) each containing one or more events, dated by the number of years separating it from 264/3 and by the name of the Athenian king or archon then in office.

The best editions are *IG* 12, pt. 5 (1903), no. 444 and p. 315, with 12 Suppl. (1939), p. 110; F. Jacoby, *Das Marmor Parium* (1904), and *FGrH* 2 B no. 239 with comm. 2 D no. 239; Tod 205. Cf. F. Jacoby, *Rh. Mus.* 1904, 63 ff.; R. M. Errington, *Hermes* 1977, 478 ff. M. N. T.; E. E. R.

Maroboduus, a prince of the *Marcomanni, persuaded his tribe to migrate from southern Germany to Bohemia (soon after 9 BC), where he built up an organized kingdom, extending his power over Saxony and Silesia. His army was large and well trained. Confronting Roman invasions from the west and south in AD 6, he was saved by the outbreak of the rebellion in *Illyricum. He refused to help *Arminius three years later, and, attacked by the *Cherusci in 17, was saved by the desertion of Arminius' uncle Inguiomerus. In AD 19, however, as the result of troubles fomented by the Romans, Maroboduus was expelled from his kingdom, sought refuge on Roman territory, and was interned at *Ravenna. He survived for eighteen years, his fame diminished by an excessive appetite for life (Tac. *Ann.* 2. 63).

J. Dobiaš, *Klio* 1960, 155 ff. R. S.; B. M. L.

Maron, in *Homer's *Odyssey* son of Euanthes and priest of *Apollo at Ismarus in Thrace (later to be called Maroneia). He gave *Odysseus the wine with which he made Polyphemus drunk (see CYCLOPES), along with other gifts of gold and silver, as thanks for protecting him and his family (*Od.* 9. 197 ff.). According to schol. *Od.* 9. 197 he is grandson of *Dionysus; in *Euripides he is son of Dionysus (*Cycl.* 143–5). See *LIMC* 6. 1 (1992), 362–4.

J. R. M.

Maroneia See MARON; THRACE.

marriage, sacred Ἱερὸς γάμος was a name given to a festival in Athens (Menander fr. 265 Körte), but in modern times the phrase has been given a much wider meaning, and is often used to denote the presentation—conceptual, mythical, or ritual—of a solemn sexual union involving at least one divine partner. The clearest case of a sacred marriage is that of *Zeus and *Hera, marriage indeed being central to Hera's 'meaning'. Rituals which re-enact or allude in some way to this marriage seem to be attested in several parts of Greece: in Athens (the Theogamia or ἱερὸς γάμος), at *Cnossus, and possibly at *Plataea in the curious festival called Daedala, which is explained as the fake marriage, interrupted by Hera, of Zeus with a log dressed as a bride and called Plataea. The great Hera sanctuaries of *Argos (2) and *Samos (see HERAION) may also have celebrated a kind of sacred marriage. Although the description of Zeus and Hera's union in *Iliad* 14. 347–51, where the event is marked by rainfall and the growth of lush vegetation, has led scholars to interpret the scene as a marriage of Sky and Earth resulting in the fruitfulness of nature, it is likely that on the ritual level the divine marriage was concerned not so much with fertility as with the social aspects of human marriage, forming a legitimating model for the institution.

It is possible that the myth of the abduction of *Kore and its related rituals should also be understood as a sacred marriage, one dramatizing the darker side of the bride's experience. Rather different, however, is the annual 'marriage' of *Dionysus with the (human) *basilinna*, the wife of the *basileus* (see ARCHONTES), at the Athenian *Anthesteria. This is clearly a sacral act, perhaps sealing the relationship between the 'stranger' Dionysus and the Athenian people, but it seems not to be called ἱερὸς γάμος.

A. Avagianou, *Sacred Marriage in the Rituals of Greek Religion* (1991); M. Cremer, *ZPE* 48 (1982), 283–90; J. C. Bermejo Barrera, *Quaderni di Storia* 1989, 133–56. E. Ke.

marriage ceremonies

Greek Ceremonies were not identical all over Greece. For example, at Sparta they included a mock abduction (Plut. *Lyc.* 15. 3). But they were shaped by largely similar perceptions about the ceremony and the deities concerned with it. Thus, *Artemis was concerned with the girl's transition to womanhood, *Hera, especially as Hera Teleia, with the institution of marriage, *Aphrodite with its erotic aspect. The evidence is more plentiful for Athens, where it includes images on vases, some of which (e.g. the loutrophoroi) were actually used in the wedding ceremony. What follows is centred on Athens. But the main elements were common to all; thus, the form of the preliminary *sacrifices and offerings may have varied from place to place, but such sacrifices and offerings were made everywhere. After a ritual bath, in water carried in loutrophoroi from a particular spring or river, in Athens *Callirrhoë, the bride and groom were dressed and (especially the bride) adorned. Then the banquet took place at the house of the bride's father, during which (almost certainly) there took place also the rite of the Anakalypteria, the bride's unveiling in front of the groom, followed by gifts to the bride by the groom. Probably also during the banquet, a *pais amphithales* (boy with mother and father still living) carried a winnowing-basket full of bread and said, 'I escaped the bad, I found the better'. After the banquet, in the evening, there was a procession from the bride's house to that of the groom, an important part of the ceremony, and a favourite image on vases with nuptial scenes. The couple went on foot or in a carriage or cart, accompanied by the *parochos* (the groom's best friend). The bride's mother carried torches; the procession included the bride's attendants, musicians, and others who shouted *makarismoi to the couple. The bride was incorporated in her husband's house through the rite of *katachysmata*, the same rite as that by which newly acquired slaves were received into the house: when she first entered the house she was led to the hearth where nuts, figs, and other dried fruit and sweetmeats were showered over her and the bridegroom. They then went to the bridal chamber where the marriage was consummated while their friends sang *epithalamia outside. On the day after they were sent gifts called *epaulia*. See also MARRIAGE LAW, GREEK.

L. Deubner, *JDAI* 1900, 144–54; W. Erdmann, *Die Ehe im alten Griechenland* (1934), 250 ff.; R. Garland, *The Greek Way of Life* (1990), 219–25; J. Redfield, *Arethusa* 1982, 181–201; J. Oakley and R. Sinos, *The Wedding in Ancient Athens* (1993); J. H. Oakley, *Arch. Anz.* 1982, 113–18, R. F. Sutton, in R. F. Sutton (ed.), *Daidalikon* (1989), 331–59; R. Hague, *Archaeology*, May/June 1988, 32–6; I. Jenkins, *Greek and Roman Life* (1986), 38–40.
C. S.-I.

Roman The favourite season was June. Usually on the previous day the bride put away her *toga praetexta*—she had come of age. Her dress and appearance were ritually prescribed: her hair was arranged in six locks (*sex crines*), with woollen fillets (*vittae*), her dress was a straight white woven tunic (*tunica recta*) fastened at the waist with a 'knot of Hercules', her veil was a great flame-coloured headscarf (*flammeum*) and her shoes were of the same colour. Friends and clients of both families gathered in the bride's father's house: the bridegroom arrived, words of consent were spoken, and the matron of honour (*pronuba*) performed the ceremony of linking bride's and bridegroom's right hands (*dextrarum iunctio*). This was followed by a *sacrifice (generally of a pig), and (in imperial times) the marriage contract (involving dowry) was signed. Then the guests raised the cry of *Feliciter!* ('Good Luck!'). There followed the wedding feast, usually at the expense of the bridegroom. The most important part of the ceremony then took place: the bride was escorted in procession to the bridegroom's house (*deductio*), closely accompanied by three young boys, whither the bridegroom had already gone to welcome her. The bridegroom carried her over the threshold to avert an ill-omened stumble; in the house she touched fire and water, was taken to the bedchamber and undressed by *univirae* (women who had known only one husband), and the bridegroom was admitted. Meanwhile an *epithalamium might be sung. This is a generalized account of an upper-class wedding as it appears in literature. There could be many variations of detail and there could be different forms of marriage (see MARRIAGE LAW, ROMAN).

A most important source is Plutarch, *Quaest. Rom.*: see the edition by H. J. Rose (1924), nos. 1, 2, 6, 7, 9, 29, 30, 31, 65, 85, 86, 87, 105, and 107. J. P. V. D. Balsdon, *Roman Women* (1962), 180 ff.; S. Treggiari, *Roman Marriage* (1991), ch. 5.
G. W. W.

marriage law

Greek Marriage in Greece was a process of transfer, by which the *kyrios* ('lord' or 'controller') of a woman (normally her father; if he had died, her nearest adult male relative) gave her away to another man for the procreation of children. Originally this was merely a private arrangement between the two men; but, because the procreation of children affected inheritance of property and membership of the community, cities made laws regulating marriage in order to define legitimacy for those purposes.

In Athens a marriage was legal only if it began with *engye* (see BETROTHAL, GREEK), a formal statement by the *kyrios* granting the woman to a husband. (A woman with no father or brother living could be awarded to a husband by the archon, see ARCHONTES.) The woman's own consent was not legally required. She could not be married to a direct ascendant or descendant, nor to her brother or half-brother by the same mother, but marriage to a half-brother by the same father or to an uncle or cousin was permitted. From 451/0 BC marriage between an Athenian and a foreigner was forbidden (see CITIZENSHIP, GREEK). Bigamy was not allowed; a man could have a concubine as well as a wife,

but the concubine's children were not legitimate. A man could divorce his wife by sending her back to her father, who could then give her in marriage to a second husband.

Marriage was often accompanied by gifts of property or money: in Homeric times usually by gifts from the husband to the father, in Classical Athens by a dowry given by the father to support the wife and her future children. But these were customary, not legal requirements.

See also BETROTHAL; ENDOGAMY; INCEST; INHERITANCE, GREEK.

A. R. W. Harrison, *The Law of Athens* 1 (1968), 1–60; J. Modrzejewski, *Symposion* 1979 (1981), 39–71; C. B. Patterson, in S. B. Pomeroy (ed.), *Women's History and Ancient History* (1991), 48–72.
D. M. M.

Roman Traditional expressions enshrine the view that a man took a wife for the procreation of children. According to the celebrated definition of *Herennius Modestinus adopted in the *Digest*, Roman marriage was 'a joining together of a man and a woman, and a partnership (for life) in all areas of life, a sharing in divine and human law' (*Dig.* 23. 2. 1), an ideal rather than a legal definition. No formalities were legally necessary for the inception of a marriage: the usual ceremonies had social and sometimes religious significance. All that was legally necessary was for a man and woman to live together with the intention of forming a lasting union (*affectio maritalis*, the reciprocal attitude of regarding each other as husband or wife). The initial consent was also given by both partners; if one or both was in paternal power (*patria potestas*) that of the respective fathers was needed. The social consequences of marriage (*honor matrimonii*) followed. Wedding ceremonies, especially the transfer of the bride to the husband's house (for the upper classes a procession) normally attested this intention (see MARRIAGE CEREMONIES, ROMAN). Moreover, the intention was necessary not merely at the beginning of a marriage, but throughout: hence if the intention ceased, the marriage was in principle at an end (see below). Roman marriage was essentially monogamous, for a man could have only one wife at a time for the purpose of breeding legitimate children, and intended to be lasting (provided that *affectio maritalis* persisted). But although the virtue and good fortune of a woman who in her lifetime had only one husband was valued (*univira*), remarriage was acceptable and necessary.

Marriage in the ancient world was a matter of personal law, and therefore a full Roman marriage (*iustae nuptiae, iustum matrimonium*) could exist only if both parties were Roman citizens or had *conubium* (right to contract marriage), either by grant to a group (e.g. Latins) or individually (see COMMERCIUM). Only such a marriage could place the children in the father's power and create rights of succession. Further, parties might have this general *conubium* but still lack *conubium* with each other. Impediments varied: (1) Age. Although consent, not consummation, made a marriage, the partners had to be physically capable. The minimum age became fixed at 12 for women and (apparently) 14, puberty, or both for men. (2) Relationship, by blood, adoption, or marriage, within certain degrees. (3) Disparate rank. A probably innovative prohibition of the *Twelve Tables on intermarriage between *patrician and plebeian (see PLEBS) was abolished in 445 BC; the Augustan marriage laws of 18 BC and AD 9 prohibited marriage between senators and their immediate descendants and freed slaves. (4) Considerations of morals or public policy. *Augustus similarly prohibited marriage between free-born citizens and members of disreputable professions, or with a convicted adulteress. Serving soldiers (below a certain rank) were forbidden to marry (a ban perhaps introduced by Augustus, maintained until *Septimius Severus); later, to avoid undue influence, provincial officials were forbidden to marry women of the province during their term, and guardians to marry their wards. Marriage was usually preceded by a formal *betrothal (*sponsalia*), in early law by solemn exchange of verbal promises (*sponsio*). Later, it became informal (though marked by celebration) and could be broken without legal penalty. But betrothal created relationships and moral obligations similar to those of marriage. In the 4th cent. AD, in imitation of eastern custom, earnest money (*arrha sponsalicia*) guaranteed the promise to marry.

Except when accompanied by *manus (when all the wife's property became the husband's and she was under his control), marriage made no difference to the status or property rights of the wife. She remained either in the paternal power of her father or independent (*sui iuris*), with ownership of her property. Ideally, the separation of property of husband and wife was maintained. Dowry (*dos*), on the other hand, was property transferred to the husband for the duration of the marriage, for the maintenance of the wife. *Dos* was not legally necessary, but it was a moral duty to endow a woman so that she might make an eligible marriage. In early law, whoever gave the dowry could stipulate for its return at the end of the marriage; later, there developed a suit for return of dowry after divorce (*actio rei uxoriae*). The husband could retain fractions of the dowry to cover expenses and compensate him for misconduct or (if there were children) unjustified initiation of divorce by the wife. Later, the husband's ownership diminished; by Justinian's time it amounted to usufruct.

Marriage was ended by the withdrawal of *affectio maritalis* by one or both partners. There was no public authority which had to give permission; even receipt of formal notice was not legally necessary, although in practice a husband or wife would usually inform the partner orally or in writing or by messenger and one would leave the marital home and recover personal property, and arrangements would be made about return of dowry. Augustus introduced documented notification, probably only when the husband needed evidence that he had divorced an adulteress. The husband normally kept any children. If the wife was in *manus*, formalities were necessary to free her. Divorce was by the husband or his *paterfamilias* (see PATRIA POTESTAS) in early times, but by the last century BC could also be decided by the wife (or her *paterfamilias*: the father's powers were gradually curbed). The upper class of the late republic and early Principate exploited the possibility with relative freedom (despite inconvenient economic consequences, possible emotional suffering, e.g. because young children would stay under the father's control, and some public disapproval unless the motives were acceptable, e.g. for *adultery). The Christian emperors penalized unilateral divorce, except on specific grounds; Justinian briefly succeeded in prohibiting consensual divorce (see JUSTINIAN'S CODIFICATION). For *confarreatio* see MANUS.

P. E. Corbett, *The Roman Law of Marriage* (1930); A. Watson, *The Law of Persons in the Later Roman Republic* (1967), chs. 1–7; J. A. Crook, *Law and Life of Rome* (1967); S. Treggiari, *Roman Marriage* (1991).
A. B.; B. N.; S. M. T.

Marrucini, a small tribe on the Adriatic coast of central Italy; chief town: Teate (mod. Chieti). They spoke an *Oscan-type dialect and had very close ties with the *Marsi, *Paeligni, and *Vestini. Allied with Rome before 300 BC, they remained loyal until they joined the *Social-War (3) insurgents under Herius Asinius, grandfather of C. *Asinius Pollio. Their rapid *Romanization ensued.

G. Obletter and others, *Il patrimonio archeologico della città di Chieti* (1985).
E. T. S.; T. W. P.

Mars (Mavors, Mamars, Oscan **Mamers,** Etr. **Maris;** reduplicated **Marmar),** next to *Jupiter the chief Italian god. Months were named after him at Rome (*Martius*, mod. Eng. March), *Alba Longa, Falerii (see FALISCANS), *Aricia, *Tusculum, *Lavinium, and among the *Hernici, Aequiculi, Paelignians (see PAELIGNI), and Sabines (see SABINI) (Ov. *Fast.* 3. 89–95, presumably from *Verrius Flaccus). At Rome his festivals came in March and October, with the exception of the first *Equirria (27 February). They were the *feriae Marti* on 1 March (old New Year's Day), second Equirria (14 March), *agonium Martiale* (17 March), *Quinquatrus (19 March; afterwards extended to five days and supposed to be a festival of *Minerva), and *Tubilustrium (23 March). All these may be reasonably explained, so far as their ritual is known, as preparations for the campaigning season, with performance of rites to benefit the horses (Equirria), trumpets (Tubilustrium), and other necessaries for the conduct of war. On 1, 9, and 23 March also, the *Salii, an ancient priesthood belonging to Jupiter, Mars, and *Quirinus (Servius on *Aen.* 8. 663), danced a sort of war-dance in armour of the fashion of the bronze age and sang their traditional hymn, addressed apparently to all the gods, not to these three only. This is intelligible as further preparation for war. In October the Equus October came on the Ides (15th). A *horse-race took place in the Campus Martius; the off horse of the winning team was sacrificed and his head contended for by the inhabitants of the via Sacra and the Suburra. On the 19th was the *Armilustrium, presumably the purification of the soldiers' arms before putting them away for the winter (see LUSTRATION). In this month again the Salii performed their dances ('arma ancilia movent', the *ancilia* being archaic shields shaped like the figure 8). Before commencing a war the general shook the sacred spears of Mars in the Regia, saying 'Mars vigila'; it is most probable that these were the original embodiments of the god. His priest is the *flamen Martialis* (see FLAMINES) and his sacred animals the wolf and woodpecker (Wissowa, *RK* 141 ff., 555 ff.; see PICUS). It is therefore not remarkable that he is usually considered a war-god and was equated with *Ares. Scholars have hesitated over the function of Mars (Versnel, *Inconsistencies* (see bibliog. below), 2. 290 ff.). Often interpreted as a god of vegetation, Mars is now considered a war- and warrior-god, who exercised his wild function in various contexts, e.g. by his presence on the border of a city, a territory, a field, or a group of citizens. This borderline was materialized, before an action or a period of time, by a *lustration, i.e. a circumambulation of three victims—a boar, a ram, a bull (*suovetaurilia*)—which were then sacrificed.

His mythology is almost entirely borrowed from Ares, the only exception being the comic tale of how he was deceived into marrying *Anna Perenna (Ov. *Fast.* 3. 675 ff.) Under *Augustus he obtained an important new title, Ultor, 'Avenger', in recognition of the victory over *Caesar's assassins (Richardson, *Topog. Dict. Ancient Rome* 244 f. for his other places of worship in Rome).

Latte, *RR* 114 ff.; Dumézil, *ARR* 205 ff.; H. S. Versnel, *Inconsistencies in Greek and Roman Religion* 2 (1992), 289 ff., and *Satricum e Roma* (1990); J. Rüpke, *Domi militiae: Die religiöse Konstruktion des Krieges in Rom* (1990). For the temples: Ziolkowski, *Temples* 101 ff.; G. Alföldy, *Studi sull'epigrafia augustea e tiberiana di Roma* (1992), 17 ff.
H. J. R.; J. Sch.

Marsi inhabited mountains and strategic passes in central Italy near the *Fucinus lacus. Their chief town was Marruvium (Strabo 5. 241). They probably spoke an *Oscan-type dialect, but their early Latinization makes proof of this impossible. They were allied, ethnically and politically, with *Marrucini, *Vestini, and *Paeligni, but from early times were friendly to Rome (cf. App. *BCiv.* 1. 46). In 340 BC they gave Roman troops passage through their territory and remained friendly in the Second Samnite War (see SAMNIUM) (Livy 8. 6, 29; 9. 13; Diod. Sic. 20. 44, 101; records of Marsic hostility are suspect: Beloch, *Röm. Gesch.* 403; Livy 9. 41, 45; 10. 3 probably confuses Marsi with *Aequi). The Marsi were loyal against *Hannibal (Livy 28. 45) but took the initiative in demanding Roman *citizenship in the *Social War (3) (hence often called the Marsic War: Vell. Pat. 2. 21). When this demand was granted, the separate nation of Marsi disappeared. Marsic magicians were famous for miraculous snake-bite cures. A grove, sacred to *Angitia, Italic goddess of healing, stood on Marsic territory (whence mod. Luco ne' Marsi).

C. Letta, *I Marsi e il Fucino nell'antichità* (1972); C. Letta and S. D'Amato, *Epigrafia della regione dei Marsi* (1975).   E. T. S.; T. W. P.

Marsyas (1), a silenus or *satyr. He invented the *aulos* ('double-oboe') or found it, cast aside by *Athena because playing it distorted her face (Apollod. 1. 4. 2), and challenged *Apollo on his *kithara* ('lyre') to a competition. He lost and, suspended from a tree, was flayed alive by Apollo, suffering the proverbial (Solon fr. 33. 7 West, *IE*²) punishment of being 'flayed for a (wine)skin' (*askos*). The moment at which Marsyas catches sight of the abandoned *aulos* was captured in a much-copied bronze statue-group by *Myron (1) *c.*450 BC (Plin. *HN* 34. 57), which perhaps stood on the Acropolis (cf. Paus. 1. 24. 1), and *Zeuxis (1) *c.*400 BC painted a 'Marsyas Bound' (Plin. *HN* 35. 66). Vases from the later 5th cent. on depict the contest and the punishment. *Melanippides (2) wrote a dithyramb *Marsyas* (fr. 2 Page, *PMG* 758), but there were no tragedies on the theme.

The sense of the contest is unclear. It has been thought to demean the Boeotian love of the *aulos* (appropriate around 450 BC), to reflect the *sophistic love of *agōnes* ('competitions'), or to assert the cultural superiority of the *kithara* over the *aulos*.

The story was given a setting at Celaenae in southern *Phrygia, a major road junction, where a local tributary of the *Maeander was named the 'Marsyas' (cf. Hdt 5. 118, 7. 26. 3; Paus. 10. 30. 9) and the *askos* of Marsyas was displayed in the cave from which the river springs (Xen. *An.* 1. 2. 8). This Marsyas later helped repel Gauls with water and flute-music. Beside Celaenae grew the new settlement of Apamea (Kibotos) whose coins in the imperial age alluded to the spring and flutes.

The myth needs a connection with an Apollo cult. The inventive *Ptolemaeus (2) Chennus (Phot. *Bibl.* cod. 190 149a) alleges that Marsyas was born on the day of an Apollo festival and that his flaying is an intriguing coincidence with the flaying of sacrificed animals on that day. Fluting and flaying are certainly part of sacrifice.

Marsyas in art, *LIMC* 6 (1992), 366–78.   K. D.

Marsyas (2), of *Pella, coeval of *Alexander (3) the Great and relative (afterwards admiral) of *Antigonus (1) I, wrote a history of Macedonia in ten books from the origins of the kingship to summer 331 BC. A few uninformative fragments survive.

FGrH 135. W. Heckel, *Hermes* 1980, 444 ff.   A. B. B.

Martial (Marcus Valerius (*RE* 233) **Martialis**), Latin poet, was born at Bilbilis in Spain on 1 March in a year between AD 38 and 41 (in 10. 24, written between 95 and 98, he celebrates his fifty-seventh birthday). He died in Spain, probably at Bilbilis, between 101 and 104 (book 12 is later than 101, but Plin. *Ep.* 3. 21 on Martial's death is not later than 104). Brought up in Spain,

he came to Rome around AD 64 (10. 103 and 104, datable to AD 98, report that he had lived in Rome for 34 years). In Rome he was supported by the younger Seneca (L. *Annaeus Seneca (2)), then the most celebrated Spaniard in the city, and probably by other important patrons (4. 40, 12. 36): C. *Calpurnius Piso (2), Memmius Regulus (consul in 63), and *Vibius Crispus (consul in 61). Already in 65, however, the suppression of the Pisonian conspiracy brought ruin to the families of Seneca and Piso. Martial continued to be on friendly terms with the widow of Lucan (M. *Annaeus Lucanus, Seneca's nephew and another victim) and with Quintus Ovidius, formerly connected with the circle of Seneca (7. 44, 45): it is possible that Martial's property at *Nomentum and the neighbouring estate of Quintus Ovidius were both gifts from Seneca, who had considerable holdings in the area. These links do not, however, mean that Martial was connected with the intellectual opposition to *Domitian, whose favour he assiduously courted. The references to martyrs to republican freedom (*Pompey, *Cicero, *Cato (Uticensis), *Brutus, *Porcia, *Thrasea Paetus) that occur from time to time in Martial are common in literature and by this date innocuous, or indeed had been taken over by Flavian propaganda against Nero. We do not know if Martial attempted a legal career: he expresses strong dislike of the idea, even when endorsed by another important Spaniard, *Quintilian (2. 90), but it was normally considered the most suitable career for an intellectual on the make. In the fifteen years and more that he spent in Rome before his first publications, he was probably already gaining renown and reward through occasional verse and panegyrics of the rich and powerful. He must already have been well known to have been able in 80 to celebrate with a book of epigrams an important public event, the opening games for the new Flavian amphitheatre. It was probably on this occasion that *Titus gave him the *ius trium liberorum*, an honour later confirmed by Domitian (see IUS LIBERORUM). After another two collections with particular purposes (*Xenia* and *Apophoreta*), in 86 he began publishing the series of twelve books of varied epigrams which are his principal claim to fame. They show already in existence a network of patronage and friendship involving a large cross-section of Roman upper-class society. He was also in contact with many of the most significant writers of the period: Quintilian, *Pliny (2), *Silius Italicus, *Frontinus, *Juvenal. There is no mention of *Statius, nor does Statius ever mention Martial, and this silence is usually taken to be a sign of personal enmity between two poets competing for the attentions of the same patrons. Martial's success, already apparently noteworthy before his poems were published in book form (2. 6), grew progressively, and he became extremely popular, being read even in the provinces by a wide public. His relationship with Domitian and the powerful *freedmen of the court also grew, as his popular success gave him a central role in the literary scene and made it more and more natural that his epigrams should be used to celebrate official events connected with imperial propaganda. Martial complains that this success did not bring him financial reward: without any copyright in his works, he was dependent on patrons whose lack of generosity towards their clients and refusal to respect the role and dignity of an intellectual and a poet he constantly laments (see PATRONAGE, LITERARY). He represents himself, doubtless with considerable exaggeration, as just another *cliens* forced to roam the streets of Rome in search of tiny recompense for the humiliating attentions that had to be paid to his patrons. For a long time he rented a house like other persons of moderate means, but he had his property at Nomentum, and from 94 at least he also had a house in Rome: he had a number of slaves, and an honorary tribunate (3. 95. 9) conferred on him the social prestige of equestrian rank. After the death of Domitian he showed no hesitation in repudiating his earlier adulation and turning to Nerva (in book 11; an anthology of books 10 and 11 was also dedicated to Nerva, but this has not survived, though its opening epigrams were placed in book 12) and later Trajan (in a second edition of book 10 from which Domitian's name was expunged, the only version to survive, and in book 12). Both his personal position and his poetry were, however, too closely involved with the court of Domitian, and in the new regime Martial must have felt less at home. Tired of city life and, as ever, nostalgic for the idealized 'natural' life in Spain that he had always set against the falsity and conventionality of Rome, he decided to return there in 98. One of his patrons, Pliny the Younger, helped him with the expenses of the journey, and even in Spain he needed to depend on the generosity of friends, especially a widow, Marcella, who gave him a house and farm which finally enabled him to realize his dream of a free and natural existence. The contradictory and unnatural life of the capital was, however, the source of his poetry, and in book 12, composed in Spain, he expresses with a new bitterness his sense of delusion and emptiness at the loss of the cultural and social stimuli that had made him a poet in the first place.

Works *Epigrammaton liber* (modern title, *Liber de spectaculis*), published AD 80. This described the games for the opening of the Flavian amphitheatre (the '*Colosseum*'): we possess an incomplete selection of about 30 poems from the original volume.

Xenia and *Apophoreta* (now books 13 and 14), published in December of two different years (or less likely a single year) between 83 and 85. They claim to be collections of poetic tickets, each of a single couplet in elegiacs (except for two of the 127 *Xenia* and nine of the 223 *Apophoreta*), and designed to accompany gifts at the Saturnalia (see SATURNUS). They present themselves as collections from which readers can select examples for their own use, and thus form part of the production of works designed to be of practical help to readers during the Saturnalian festivities (cf. Ov. *Tr.* 2. 471 ff.) but they merit literary appreciation for the ingenious brevity with which they characterize everyday objects (in the case of the *Xenia* usually foodstuffs, in the more varied and lively *Apophoreta* every type of gift).

Epigrammaton libri XII (around 1,175 poems in all), published probably as follows. Book 1 at the beginning of 86; 2 in 86–7; 3 in autumn 87, during a long stay at Imola; 4 in December 88; 5 in December 89; 6 in 90–1; 7 in December 92; 8 in January 94; 9 in autumn 94; 10 (lost first edition) in 95; 11 in December 96; 10 (second edition), April–October 98; 12, end of 101/102. Books 1, 2, 8, 9, 12 have prose prefaces.

Martial's production does sometimes include epigrams of the usual Greek type: epitaphs for friends and patrons, dedications celebrating both private and public events, and epideictic poems on contemporary or historical events, unusual happenings, or recoveries from illness. In these cases the traditional conventions are easily recognized, though the treatment may be original. In general, however, Martial's epigrams are very different from those of his Greek predecessors. His main model was *Catullus* (1), not as a love-poet but as a writer who had brought full literary dignity to the minor poetry of autobiography and comic realism. He takes from Catullus many formal elements, above all his metres: as well as the elegiac couplets characteristic of Greek epigram and also predominant in Martial, he includes poems in hendecasyllables and scazons, both common metres in Catullus. Other metres are rare. Catullus had created a genre of minor poetry which joined the influence of the Greek epigram, iambic, and lyric traditions to the Roman tradition (itself influenced by Greek iambic poetry) of satirical verse full of personal and political polemic. Of the other models to whom Martial refers, we know little (*Domitius Marsus) or scarcely anything (*Albinovanus Pedo, Cn. *Cornelius Lentulus Gaetulicus), but they presumably continued the Catullan tradition. Certainly this type of minor poetry on sentimental/autobiographical, satirical, polemical, or complimentary themes was widely practised at Rome both by dilettante amateurs and by 'professional' poets as occasional verse for their patrons. Martial also had important models in late Hellenistic Greek epigram (see EPIGRAM, GREEK), which had already developed the tendency towards a clever final 'point' which marks much of his work: the Neronian poet *Lucillius and his imitator *Nicarchus had cultivated a new type of epigram mocking physical defects and typical characters from social and professional life. Their epigrams are perhaps a little cold and cerebral, but they conclude with striking final effects of surprise.

At first Martial's poems circulated privately, especially through oral delivery (2. 6), or were published in connection with particular events (*Liber de spectaculis*) or for particular 'practical' purposes (*Xenia, Apophoreta*). When he decided to publish them in collections of varied nature divorced from their (real or supposed) occasions, they ceased to be 'practical' verse and became 'literature', although the new form of presentation in its turn fulfilled its roles as entertainment, polemic, or celebration on a higher and more lasting level. Martial's growing success with his readers encouraged the conviction that this type of minor poetry (which he always termed 'epigram', in contrast to the more varied terminology of other writers of the period) corresponded to a real need which the grander and more official genres could not satisfy. It was not a question of formal elegance or emotional intensity—the characteristics that had led *Callimachus (3) and Catullus to affirm the greater dignity of the shorter forms—but of a need for realism, for a closer link between the pages of the text and everyday life (8. 3). The short epigram, able to treat incisively any and every aspect of life, could satisfy this need in a way that the more distant and conventional genres, which continued to produce variations on the same old mythological themes (4. 49, 9. 50, 10. 4), could not. The most typical form of the epigram in Martial, and the reason for his success, is the humorous realistic epigram on contemporary characters and behaviour which moves from witty entertainment to offer a lively and merciless picture of Roman society, revealing its multiple absurdities and contradictions through the mirror of the gestures and behaviour of the various social classes. Martial's attitude, unlike most social description in antiquity, is not moralizing, but he takes pleasure simply in recording with all his verbal art the complexities and contradictions of the spectacle of life. Both as a Spaniard born in a province which still retained a sense of the natural life of the country, and as an intellectual in a world where poets were valued less than he thought their due, Martial observes Rome from the outside. His ambitious view that his chosen poetic form, considered the lowest of all genres (12. 94. 9), might have greater validity than the great works promoted by official culture, and the merciless picture he offers of Roman society together give Martial's work a strongly anti-establishment tone, which, though frequently criticized by opponents, was well received by the general public, and eventually even by the higher classes and the

Martianus Minneus Felix Capella

court, albeit with a certain nervousness. A considerable part of his work in fact represents him as well integrated into the life of the upper classes, who were happy to see themselves described and celebrated in his verse even if at the same time it exposed many sordid aspects of the society of which these same classes were the highest representatives. The epigrams which Martial as a 'professional' poet offered to his patrons as a noble and cultured ornament of their lives give to us a particularly concrete and direct representation of Roman high society, with its houses, parks, possessions, and rituals. The many epigrams devoted to Titus and especially to Domitian are a fundamental document for the history of the imperial cult under the Flavians (see RULER-CULT). The first-person of the comic or satirical poems is mostly simply a device to give vividness to the many social observations so that they appear to have been born from one man's experience, but there is also a more autobiographical 'I', not always easy to separate from the more general figure, the personality of a restless and unsatisfied poet who is proud of his merits but disappointed in society and convinced that he could have achieved much more in different circumstances. We are offered the picture of a simple and candid individual, qualities appropriate to a poet who constantly denounces the falsity and paradoxes of a counterfeit life, a man of delicate affections and a strong sense of friendship, both often depicted in Horatian terms (see HORACE). Love (as opposed to sex) plays little part in the poems, but there are some epigrams of a subtle and sophisticated eroticism, mainly directed towards boys.

Martial's production is extremely varied, and offers both realism and fantasy, subtlety and extravagance. It is rarely that one has a sense of a poem having been written solely for piquant entertainment. His poetic language is influenced not only by Catullus but also by Horace, and above all by *Ovid; it has a cool mastery of expression which knows how to preserve the appearance of nature even when artifice is at its most obvious. His celebratory and adulatory poetry is clearly related to the precious mannerism of Flavian epideictic as we find it in some of Statius' Silvae, albeit with a greater lightness of touch. His realistic epigrams, while maintaining a high literary quality, open themselves to a lower and cruder language, including obscenity: in this area Martial is one of the boldest Latin poets and, in general, many everyday objects and acts, and the words that describe them, enter Latin poetry for the first time with Martial. His most celebrated virtue is the technique with which he realizes his comic effects, either giving his epigrams a novel or surprising conclusion which throws an unexpected light on the situation being described, or else concentrating the entire sense of the poem at the end, in a pointed, antithetical, or paradoxical formulation of extraordinary density and richness of expression. See CLOSURE. This technique derives in part from later Greek epigram (see above), and also shows the same taste for point seen in contemporary rhetoric; Martial's brilliantly inventive use of it made him a model for the modern epigram, and indeed more widely for modern short poetry. The comic mechanisms that he employs, however, are not simply intellectual games, but also the means by which, on each occasion, the reality he is representing can be made the bearer of an intimate contradiction and incongruity, of a violent asymmetry with respect to reason and nature. They are thereby an original and efficacious means to give meaning to the myriad fragments of reality which had attracted his interest and which his large corpus offers in abundance. Within this vast canvas, the generic affinity with real life that epigram derives from its occasional nature is everywhere

employed to the full, but realism is in productive tension with fantasy, play, and the grotesque, as the patterns of behaviour of everyday life are turned about in the brilliant paradoxes of Martial's wit. See also EPIGRAM, LATIN; DEDICATIONS, LATIN.

TEXTS W. M. Lindsay (1929²); W. Heraeus (1925); D. R. Shackleton Bailey (BT, 1990); Loeb ed. (1993).

COMMENTARIES L. Friedlaender (1886); Book 1, M. Citroni (1975), P. Howell (1980); Book 11, N. Kay (1985).

GENERAL STUDIES J. P. Sullivan, Martial: The Unexpected Classic (1991); M. Citroni, Maia (1969, 1988).

DATING L. Friedlaender, see introd. to comm. (1886); M. Citroni, Illinois Classical Studies 1989.

IMPERIAL CULT O. Weinreich, Studien zu Martial (1928); F. Sauter, Der römische Kaiserkult bei Martial und Statius (1934); K. Scott, The Imperial Cult under the Flavians (1936).

POETIC TECHNIQUE K. Prinz, Martial und die zeitgenössische Rhetorik (1959); E. Siedschlag, Zur Form von Martials Epigrammen (1977); W. Burnikel, Untersuchungen zur Struktur des Witzepigramms bei Lukillios und Martial (1980); P. Laurens, L'Abeille dans l'ambre (1989).   M. Ci.

Martianus Minneus Felix Capella composed in Vandalic *Carthage (see VANDALS), probably in the last quarter of the 5th cent. AD, a prosimetric Latin encyclopaedia of the seven Liberal Arts (grammar, dialectic, rhetoric—the medieval 'trivium'—the 'quadrivium', geometry, arithmetic, astronomy, music; see EDUCATION, GREEK, §§ 3 and 4). He subsequently composed a short metrical treatise. Both works were addressed to his son. The encyclopaedia, usually known as the De nuptiis Philologiae et Mercurii, but called the Philologia by its author, comprises a two-book introductory myth describing the ascent to heaven, apotheosis, and marriage of Philology to *Mercury, as well as a seven-book introduction to the Liberal Arts, in which each subject is presented by an elaborately described female personification. The encyclopaedic books are pedestrian compilations, mostly from Latin sources, such as *Aquila Romanus, *Geminus, *Pliny (1) the Elder, *Quintilian, and *Iulius Solinus; whether *Varro's lost Disciplinarum libri were also used is still debated. The myth is fantastic, imaginative, and curiously learned: while strongly influenced by Neoplatonic sources and doctrines on the ascent of the *soul (see NEOPLATONISM), it owes to the parodistic tradition of *Menippean satire such features as councils of the gods, heavenly voyages, and wrangling philosophers. Martianus was pagan (he makes veiled allusions to *Christianity as well as to Chaldaean *theurgy, and elegizes over the silence of the *oracles), and sufficiently well-read in Greek to translate *Aristides Quintilianus' treatise on music. His baroque and intentionally abstruse periodic Latin proved extremely liable to corruption in the extensive and contaminated later manuscript tradition. The Philologia was very influential during the Carolingian period and the 12th-cent. Platonic revival, both as a textbook and as a literary source of mystic cosmology and images of the seven Liberal Arts. Two hundred and forty-one manuscripts of the Philologia have been examined and described by C. Leonardi (Aevum 1959, 443–89, and 1960, 1–99 and 411–524), and much work has been, and is being, done on the medieval commentaries.

EDITIONS Philologia, J. A. Willis (Teubner, 1983), rev. Shanzer, CPhil. 1986, 61–82; M. De Nonno announces an edition of the metrical treatise he has discovered (RFIC 1990, 129–44).

ENGLISH TRANSLATION W. H. Stahl and R. W. Johnson, with E. L. Burge, Martianus Capella and the Seven Liberal Arts, 2 vols. (1971–7).

COMMENTARIES Complete text: U. Kopp (Frankfurt, 1836); Book 1, with trans.: D. R. Shanzer (1986); Book 2, with text and trans.: L.

Lenaz (1977); Book 9, with text and trans.: L. Cristante (1987).
 PLRE 2. 259.   D. R. S.

Martius Verus, Publius, senator from *Tolosa (mod. Toulouse), served with distinction in the Parthian War of L. *Verus (AD 162–6). As legate (see LEGATI) of *Cappadocia (from at latest 172), he remained loyal during the usurpation of *Avidius Cassius in 175, becoming legate of *Syria and consul for the second time (as *ordinarius*) in 180. He died in 190.

Fronto, *Ad Verum*; Cass. Dio 71; SHA *Verus, Avid. Cass. PIR²* M 348.
                                                                                                A. R. Bi.

Marullus (*RE* 4), a rhetor known only from L. *Annaeus Seneca (1), whom he taught along with M. *Porcius Latro.

Schanz–Hosius, § 336. 9. 9.   M. W.

Marxism and classical antiquity Having written his doctoral dissertation on the atomic theories of *Democritus and *Epicurus (1841, published 1928), Karl Marx retained a lifelong interest in classical antiquity, spicing his writings with a wealth of allusions to ancient texts.

The central concern of Marx's intellectual and practical activity was class conflict, but he never provided a definitive account of what he understood by class, and he applied the term to the ancient world in different ways. In the *Communist Manifesto* (with Engels, 1848), Marx spoke of the conflict between 'freeman and slave', but in the *Eighteenth Brumaire of Louis Bonaparte* (1852) he stressed the struggle between wealthy and poor citizens in antiquity, with slaves forming 'the purely passive pedestal for these combatants'. Later, in the first volume of *Capital* (1867), Marx stated that the class struggle in antiquity 'took the form chiefly of a contest between debtors and creditors'; but in the posthumously published third volume (1894) slave and feudal relations of production were amalgamated to form a contrast with capitalism. See CLASS STRUGGLE.

Marx gave primacy in historical explanation to material economic factors, and in his summation of his theory (preface to *Critique of Political Economy* (1859)) he outlined a schema whereby increasing productive capacities led necessarily to strains in the prevailing social relations and the emergence of a new mode of production or social formation. But in the *Grundrisse* notebooks of 1857–8 and elsewhere, he characterized pre-capitalist societies as essentially static in comparison to the revolutionary nature of capitalist production.

In the exploratory *Grundrisse* drafts (published partially in 1939, in full in 1953), Marx identified the classical city as one of four different social formations by which class society emerged from primitive communalism. Whether a relatively stable slave society may be described as the locus of class struggle has been much debated among Marxists. Since Marx defined exploitation as the extraction by one class of a portion of the value (called *Mehrwert* or 'surplus value') created by the labour of another class, class relations are assumed to be antagonistic. But the antagonism between slaves and slave-owners rarely took the form of overt collective conflict. See SLAVERY.

The authority of Stalin's unscholarly *Dialectical and Historical Materialism* (1938), relying largely on Engels's *Origins of Family, Private Property, and the State* (1884) and other writings, imposed a rigid progressivist schema on orthodox Marxist historiography. According to this 'theory of stages', each historical epoch is defined by the prevailing form of labour relation and yields inexorably to the next 'higher' stage as a result of class struggles. Thus, slave society is supposed universally to give way to feudal-

ism, itself in turn replaced by capitalism and then communism. Since the pluralist sixties, various models of ancient society have found supporters among Marxist historians.

In Marxist historiography, classical Greece and Rome are commonly understood to have been slave societies, characterized by a mode of production in which slave labour yields the greatest quantity of surplus value. Slavery need not, on this conception, be the predominant form of labour in respect of numbers of labourers or total quantity of production. While peasant farmers may have been responsible for the larger part of the value produced, slavery will have been the chief form in which the value produced by direct labour was expropriated by the class of large landowners, and thus the basis for the leisure and power of the dominant social class.

Considerable disagreement remains over just when and how slavery took hold in earnest as the primary mode of production in classical antiquity, and when and how it was superseded by feudal labour relations. In regard to the Athenian *democracy, for example, some Marxists have stressed the role of slavery in large-scale agriculture, but others have contended that slave labour was marginal to agricultural production and concentrated rather in household services and, importantly, the *mines. On either conception, overt class struggle consisted basically in a conflict between large landowners, who were in a position to exploit slave and other forms of dependent *labour, and smallholders who ran the risk of being degraded into the ranks of dependent labour.

Slavery did not disappear in late antiquity, but it yielded in importance to the colonate (see COLONUS (*b*)) and other forms of free or semi-free dependent labour. The reasons for this change are again controversial among Marxists, of whom some have attributed the decline of slavery to the higher cost of slaves (and hence the lower profitability of slavery) under the *pax Romana*, whereas others have pointed to the availability of alternative sources of dependent labour as a consequence of the earlier expropriation of the small Roman peasantry (itself a function, in part, of the widespread exploitation of slave labour due to Roman imperial expansion).

Marxist theories of culture have generally emphasized that ideas and institutions depend on a society's underlying relations of production (Marx and Engels, *The German Ideology* (1845–6); Marx's 1859 preface). Marx's own nuanced observations concerning culture were, however, obscured by the mechanical, Stalinist division between base and superstructure, whereby economic relations and interests were held to determine all aspects of culture from morality and the arts to education and law. Neo-Marxist theories, originating especially in Italy and France, have stressed instead the relative autonomy of cultural forms and transcended the purely instrumental view of ideology as a weapon wielded by the ruling class to preserve its hegemony. Marxists have also become increasingly sensitive to analyses of forms of oppression other than the narrowly economic, above all the oppression of *women and other 'outsiders'.

While Marxist historians have been particularly concerned to recover the culture of slaves and other oppressed groups in antiquity directly from the meagre evidence, Marxist critics have also attempted to uncover evidence of class conflict in canonical works of literature, understood to have been shaped by tensions and evasions having their roots in the contradictions of exploitative social relations. Studies of ideology and class relations in the great works of classical antiquity are still rare, but they have contributed substantially to a new interest in the material conditions of the production of classical art. See also LITERARY THEORY AND CLASSICAL STUDIES.

STUDIES G. Thomson, *Aeschylus and Athens* (1941); G. E. M. de Ste. Croix, *The Class Struggle in the Ancient Greek World* (1981); E. M. Wood, *Peasant-Citizen and Slave* (1988); P. Lekas, *Marx on Classical Antiquity* (1988); P. Rose, *Sons of the Gods, Children of Earth* (1992).

BIBLIOGRAPHY Classical antiquity: M. Arthur and D. Konstan, in B. Ollman and E. Vernoff (eds.), *The Left Academy*, 2 (1984); J. P. Sullivan (ed.), *Arethusa* 8 (1975). General: T. Carver (ed.), *The Cambridge Companion to Marx* (1991).   P. A. C., D. K.

Marzabotto, 27 km. (17 mi.) south-west of Bologna (*Felsina), has given its name to the anonymous *Etruscan city (Etr. ? Misa) on the flood-plain of the Reno, which by a subsequent change of course has partially destroyed it. Although Marzabotto has been investigated more extensively than any other Etruscan city, it should not be regarded as typical. It has no direct iron age predecessor, and is accordingly unlikely to be the result of *synoecism: its orthogonal plan and the astronomically precise orientation of its principal axes (identical with that of the temples on the high ground to the north-west) support the hypothesis of a new 'colonial' foundation at the beginning of the 5th cent. BC. The quarters of the city are divided into *insulae* of city-dwellings separated by party-walls; and there is abundant evidence for pottery-making and the working of both bronze and iron. In the 4th cent. the area was invaded by Gauls, who left a cemetery.

BTCGI 9 (1991), 'Marzabotto'; E. Brizio, *Mon. Ant.* 1899, cols. 249 ff.; G. A. Mansuelli in *IBR*, 354 ff.; G. Sassatelli, *La città etrusca di Marzabotto* (1989).   D. W. R. R.

Masada is a small isolated plateau 457 m. (1,500 ft.) high, on the western shore of the Dead Sea, and accessible from there only by the tortuous 'snake path'. *Herod (1), having secured his family in its *Hasmonean fortress during the Parthian invasion of 40 BC, later made it the most spectacular of his own fortress residences, with two ornate palaces, one built onto the northern rock terraces. Archaeology supplements *Josephus' detailed description of the architecture, revealing also a garrison-block, baths, storage rooms for quantities of food and weapons, cisterns, a surrounding casemate wall, and (probably) a synagogue. After the murder of their leader, Menahem, in Jerusalem early in the Jewish Revolt, *sicarii* (Jewish rebels) occupied Masada; and it was the last fortress to hold out after the fall of *Jerusalem, succumbing in AD 73 or 74 to a six-month siege by Flavius Silva. See JEWS. The eight Roman *camps and circumvallation are visible, as well as the earth ramp which supported a platform for artillery. Josephus' graphic account of the mass suicide of the 960 defenders, with their leader, Eleazar ben Yair, after the breaching of the wall, supposedly based on the testimony of two women survivors, has aroused some scepticism. But the remains of the revolutionaries' years of occupation of the site are at any rate extensive. These include domestic and personal objects, as well as Greek papyri and biblical texts of the *Qumran type.

Joseph. *BJ* 7. 252–3, 275–406, etc. Y. Yadin, *Masada* (1966); H. M. Cotton and J. Geiger, *Masada* 2: *The Latin and Greek Documents* (1989); S. J. D. Cohen, *Journal of Jewish Studies* 1982, 385–405; I. A. Richmond, *JRS* 1962, 142–55; E. Stern (ed.), *The New Encyclopaedia of Archaeological Excavations in the Holy Land* (1992).   E. M. S.; T. R.

maschalismos, the practice, mentioned in tragedy (Aesch. *Cho.* 439; Soph. *El.* 445), of cutting off the extremities of a murder victim and placing them under the corpse's armpits (μασχάλαι). The scholiastic tradition (see SCHOLIA) invokes the wish to avoid *pollution, or explains the action as an attempt to incapacitate

the corpse and prevent it from taking vengeance, but parallel practices elsewhere suggest that mutilation for the sake of ridicule may have been an equally prominent motive; certainly the references to its use on the dead *Agamemnon suggest it was a humiliation, the antithesis of proper burial rites. Compare also the mutilation of the living Melanthius, *Od.* 22. 474–7. Whether the practice was common in real life we have no means of knowing.

F. Boehm, *RE* 14. 2060–2; R. C. Jebb, comm. on Soph. *El.*, pp. 211–12; E. Vermeule, *Aspects of Death in Early Greek Art and Poetry* (1979), 236 n. 30; R. Parker, *LCM* 1984, 138.   E. Ke.

Masinissa, king of *Numidia (238–148 BC). In about 213 he helped his father, in alliance with *Carthage, to defeat *Syphax, king of the western or Masaesylian Numidians, and then crossed to Spain, where he first appears in 211, commanding Numidian cavalry against P. *Cornelius Scipio (1) (Livy 25. 34). He continued to serve the Carthaginians in Spain down to Ilipa in 206, but then defected to Rome, pledging his support to P. *Cornelius Scipio Africanus himself should the Romans invade Africa (Livy 28. 34. 12 ff.).

Shortly afterwards, on the death of his father, he returned to Africa, and recovered control of his kingdom from his nephew, only to be driven out again by Syphax. There followed a series of adventures which, according to the more probable version, left him little more than a hunted fugitive. But in 204 he was able to join Scipio Africanus, when the latter landed in Africa (Livy 29. 29. 4), and thereafter his fortunes rapidly improved. His services to Rome culminated in the defeat and capture of Syphax after the battle of the 'Great Plains', and command of the Numidian cavalry on Scipio's right at the decisive battle of *Zama.

His recognition as 'king' by Scipio was confirmed by the senate (Livy 30. 17. 12); and by the terms of the subsequent peace, everything which had belonged to him or his ancestors was to be restored to him. This virtually gave him *carte blanche* in his dealings with Carthage, and by loyally supporting Rome in her wars in Spain, Macedonia, and Greece, he usually, though not invariably, enjoyed her support. His continuous aggression eventually led to Carthage's resorting to war against him, contrary to her treaty with Rome, and though Masinissa was victorious— or perhaps because he was—war with Rome became inevitable, Masinissa living to see its outbreak, though not its end.

Tough, brave, and ruthless, Masinissa was obviously a skilled commander, particularly of cavalry, and a wily statesman. He was one of the very few Mediterranean potentates to grasp the overwhelming power of Rome, and, caught up in a titanic struggle between two great powers, managed to emerge with his own territory significantly enlarged. How far his ambitions extended is doubtful. Inscriptions show that he established diplomatic contacts with eastern Mediterranean kings, but his shrewdness would surely have precluded his thinking in terms of an empire stretching from Morocco to Egypt, as some have claimed. *Polybius (37. 10) and *Strabo (17. 3. 15) also praise his success in turning the Numidians into farmers, though he may have done no more than exploit areas already developed by Carthage. Although there are signs that even the Romans were becoming exasperated by, if not wary of, his ambitions, he managed to die in his bed, at the age of 90, and to bequeath his kingdom to his sons.

RE 14/2, 'Masinissa'; P. G. Walsh, *JRS* 1965; T. A. Dorey and D. R. Dudley, *Rome Against Carthage* (1971).   J. F. La.

masks, as in many other pre-modern cultures, were used in

Greece and Rome in cult and in dramatic representations. We have terracotta representations of grotesque masks worn in adolescent rites of passage in the cult of *Artemis Orthia in Sparta (see SPARTAN CULTS), and depictions of the wearing of animal masks in the cult of *Demeter and Despoina at *Lycosura in Arcadia (see ARCADIAN CULTS AND MYTHS). Masks were often worn in the cult of *Dionysus, and the masks of *satyrs and of Dionysus were sometimes not worn but at the centre of ritual action. Notable among the figures imagined in terms of a frightening mask is the *Gorgon. In Roman religion a notable use was of the *imagines, ancestral masks displayed in the atrium of a noble family and worn by the living at funerals (along with the mask of the deceased). Whereas the Greek word for mask (πρόσωπον) also means face, the Latin persona probably derives from the Etruscan phersu, a masked figure, who is depicted in a 6th-cent. BC tomb.

Greek drama probably inherited the mask from Dionysiac ritual, but there are obvious dramaturgical advantages in the use of masks, especially where the audience is (as often in ancient theatres) at some distance from the action. We have depictions of dramatic masks from the 5th cent. BC onwards, and a classification of dramatic masks by *Iulius Pollux (Onomasticon 4. 133 ff.), written in the 2nd cent. AD but based on earlier Alexandrian scholarship. Numerous terracotta representations of theatrical masks have been discovered on the island of Lipari. Masks were used in all the major dramatic genres (although there is some evidence to the contrary for *Plautus). A common material was linen, and they generally covered the whole head. On the whole the masks of tragedy (naturalistic in the Classical period) and New Comedy represented types rather than individuals (see TRAGEDY, GREEK; COMEDY (GREEK), NEW).

J. P. Vernant and F. Frontisi-Ducroux, Journal de psychologie 1983, 53–69; DFA³ 189–96; D. Wiles, The Masks of Menander (1991).   R. A. S. S.

Massalia (Massilia in Roman writers), mod. Marseille, was founded c.600 BC by settlers from *Phocaea, who obtained the site, on the excellent harbour of Lacydon (Vieux-Port) from the Ligurian Segobriges. Though preceded in the area by Rhodian and other traders, the Massaliotes eventually dominated the coast from *Nicaea (2) to Emporiae (see EMPORION), with outposts further west at Hemeroscopium, Alonae (near Cape Nao), and Maenaca (near Málaga). This last, founded for trade with *Tartessus, was soon lost to the Carthaginians though Massaliote venturing beyond the straits of Gibraltar is reflected in the anonymous 6th-cent. periplous (see PERIPLOI) and in the works of *Pytheas and Euthymenes, who explored the west African coast. In Gaul and eastern Spain the Greek presence had profound effects. Trade up the Rhône (*Rhodanus), especially in the 6th cent., contributed to the evolution of the Hallstatt and La Tène culture of the *Celts, while among the *Ligurian and Iberian tribes of the coast all excavated hill-forts have yielded quantities of imported pottery and many show Greek influence in their fortifications, architecture, and art; occasionally, as at St-Blaise and *Glanum, a native settlement was actually taken over. The introduction of the vine (see WINE) and the *olive completed the picture of 'Gaul transported to Greece' (Just. Epit. 43. 4. 2). Despite Massalia's remoteness and the failure of the Phocaean expedition to Corsica, relations with Greece were maintained with a treasury at *Delphi. Renowned for the stability of its own aristocratic constitution (Strabo 4. 179; Cic. Flac. 26. 63), it was not involved in wars with other Greek cities, but victories over the Carthaginians are recorded in the 6th and 5th cents. Massalia

early enjoyed Rome's *amicitia which later developed into formal alliance; Massaliote ships helped Rome in the Second *Punic War. In 125 BC constant aggression by the *Salluvii prompted an appeal to Rome, which led ultimately to the formation of the 'Province' (later Narbonensis; see GAUL (TRANSALPINE)). Having supported Pompey, the city was taken by *Caesar in 49 BC, and lost most of its territory to *Arelate. Massalia thereafter declined in commercial importance, but retained a high reputation for Greek culture and learning (Cn. *Iulius Agricola was educated there); and in the late empire the city became an important monastic centre, and a haven for refugees fleeing the barbarians in the north (in particular, *Salvianus). It appears also to have begun to recover its economic significance. Excavations since 1945 have revealed many details of both Greek and Roman phases, including a Greek theatre, temples, agora, docks, town walls, and pagan and Christian cemeteries.

F. Benoit, Recherches sur l'hellénisation du Midi de la Gaule (1965); A. L. F. Rivet, Gallia Narbonensis (1988), 9 ff., 219 ff.; S. T. Loseby, JRS 1992, 165 ff.; B. Shefton, in G. Tsetskhladze and F. De Angelis (eds.), The Archaeology of Greek Colonisation (1994), 61 ff.   A. L. F. R.; J. F. Dr.

Massicus mons, mountain spur projecting from the *Apennines towards the Tyrrhenian sea and separating *Latium from *Campania. It is not lofty but very fertile; grapes from its slopes produced some of the choicest *wine in Italy. Sinuessa (mod. Mondragone) controlled the narrow gap between its western extremity and the sea.   E. T. S.

Massilia See MASSALIA.

Mastarna, an *Etruscan adventurer who, according to the emperor *Claudius, became king of Rome after the death of his leader Caeles *Vibenna, whom he had accompanied in all his adventures (ILS 212). One of these adventures is represented in the 4th-cent. BC François tomb-painting from *Vulci, which confirms the friendship between the two heroes and bears out Claudius' claim to have drawn his information from Etruscan sources. More uncertainty surrounds his statement that Mastarna was the Etruscan name of the Roman king Servius *Tullius. It has been suggested that 'Mastarna' is not a name but a title, perhaps an Etruscanized form of the Latin magister ('leader'), which if true leaves open the possibility that his real name was indeed Servius Tullius. Others are more cautious, and prefer to see Mastarna as an otherwise unknown king of Rome.

R. M. Ogilvie, Early Rome and the Etruscans (1976), 87 f.; R. Thomsen, King Servius Tullius (1980), 57 ff.; A. Momigliano, CAH 7²/2 (1989), 94 ff.; and see bibliog. under VIBENNA, CAELIUS.   T. J. Co.

master of the horse See MAGISTER EQUITUM.

Masurius Sabinus (RE 29), probably from *Verona, a leading Roman lawyer of the first half of the 1st cent. AD. He was successful as a law teacher in Rome and counted the powerful C. *Cassius Longinus (2) among his pupils. Not wealthy, he relied on gifts from his pupils and only attained equestrian rank when nearly 50. But his learning was admired, and *Tiberius gave him the privilege of stating legal opinions on the emperor's authority (ius respondendi ex auctoritate principis), the first non-senatorial lawyer to be so honoured. He wrote on sacred and public law but his most celebrated work was three books (libri) on private law (*ius civile). This excluded the law derived from the *praetor's edict, which he and later writers treat separately. Intended for teaching, the Ius civile was widely read and later became the basis of extensive commentaries by Sextus *Pomponius, *Paulus, and

Maternus

*Ulpian. The school (*schola Cassiana*) which Cassius founded with his help and which a century later came to be called the Sabinians seems to have taken a traditional and pragmatic view of the law, to which the Proculians, tracing their intellectual ancestry back to M. *Antistius Labeo, opposed a more principled approach (see LAWYERS (ROMAN)).

Lenel, *Pal.* 2. 187–216; Bremer 2/1. 313–581; *PIR*² M 358; *HLL* 3, § 326. 1; Kunkel 1967, 119–20, 340–5; P. de Francisci, *Bolletino dell'istituto di diritto romano* 1963, 95 ff.; O. Lenel, *Festgabe Ihering* (1892), 1–104; R. Astolfi, *I libri tres iuris civilis di Sabino* (1983); P. Stein, *Cambridge Law Journal* 1972, 8–3 and *Bolletino dell'istituto di diritto romano* 1978, 55–68; D. Liebs, *ANRW* 2. 15 (1976), 197–286.   T. Hon.

Maternus, deserter and leader of a major mutiny on the Rhine *c.* AD 185/6. His activities indicate military unrest and indiscipline after the wars of Marcus *Aurelius, but not widespread social tension in the west. *Herodian (2)'s report (1. 10. 2–7) that the uprising spread throughout Gaul and into Spain, and that Maternus was killed while attempting to assassinate *Commodus in Rome, is unreliable.

G. Alföldy, *Bonner Jahrb.* 1971, 367 ff.; J. F. Drinkwater, *Classical Views* 1984, 349 ff.   J. F. Dr.

mathematics Our knowledge of the origins and early development of mathematics among the Greeks is negligible. In *Mesopotamia an advanced mathematics had existed since at least the time of Hammurabi (*c.*1700 BC). Characteristic of this were problems in arithmetic and algebra, but many facts of elementary geometry were known, e.g. 'Pythagoras' theorem' and the mensuration formulae for a variety of plane and solid figures. It is probable that much of this knowledge reached the Greek world at some time, but the nature of our sources makes it difficult to say what came when, particularly as independent discovery can rarely be excluded. Greek doxographic tradition ascribed the invention of geometry to the Egyptians, whence it was made known to the Greeks in the 6th cent. BC by *Thales in Ionia or *Pythagoras (1) in Magna Graecia. However, there was little to learn from Egypt beyond elementary mensuration formulae, and since neither Thales nor Pythagoras left writings there could be no foundation for the tradition. The most that can be said is that it is probable that 5th-cent. 'Pythagoreans' such as *Philolaus discussed the properties of numbers in the semi-mystical way imitated by *Speusippus in the 4th cent. ('Iamblichus', *Theologoumena tes arithmetikes* 82. 10 ff. de Falco; see bibliog. to IAMBLICHUS (2)).

The first concrete evidence we have concerns the mathematical activity of *Hippocrates (3) of Chios at Athens in the late 5th cent. While investigating the problem of squaring the circle (already considered a typical mathematical problem, cf. Ar. *Av.* 1005), he produced some ingenious theorems on the quadrature of lunes. The *content* of these is reasonably certain, but our knowledge of the *form* is derived via two intermediaries, *Eudemus and *Simplicius (*In Phys.* 60. 22 ff. Diels), and it may have been very different from the Euclidean cast in which we have it. However, these theorems exhibit the concept of proof, the greatest single contribution and the most characteristic feature of Greek mathematics. There must have been a geometrical tradition before Hippocrates; but how old, and of what kind, we cannot say. It is possible that the arguments of *Zeno (1) of Elea in the mid-5th cent., showing that infinite division involved self-contradiction, were in part directed against contemporary mathematical procedures. It is certain that the logical difficulties he raised influenced the later course of Greek mathematics in its

care to avoid infinitesimals. That this was a difficulty in the early stages is shown by *Democritus asking whether the two contiguous faces of a cone cut by a plane parallel to the base are equal or unequal (DK 68 B 155). Another difficulty was the existence of irrationals, specifically the incommensurability of the diagonal of a square with its side. Both arise only when one deals with continuous magnitudes (geometry), not with discrete (arithmetic in the Greek sense). Perhaps this explains the statement of *Archytas in the early 4th cent. that arithmetic can provide proofs where geometry fails (DK 47 B 4). But these logical difficulties did not inhibit the practice of geometry, as is shown by Archytas' own ingenious solution to the problem of finding two mean proportionals (which Hippocrates had already shown to be equivalent to the problem of 'doubling the cube'), and by the work of his contemporary *Theaetetus, who made significant discoveries about irrationals and the five regular solids.

The difficulties were solved, or at least circumvented, by *Eudoxus (1), *c.*360. He formulated a general theory of proportion including both commensurable and incommensurable magnitudes, and also invented the method of approach to the limit which became the standard Greek way of dealing with problems involving infinitesimals. *Euclid's formulation of this is found in book 10, prop. 1: 'If from the greater of (any) two unequal magnitudes more than its half is subtracted, and from the remainder more than its half, and so on, there will (eventually) be left a magnitude less than the smaller of the original two.' *Archimedes (*Quadrature of the Parabola*, pref.) quotes another formulation: 'The amount by which the greater of two unequal areas exceeds the smaller can, by being added continuously to itself, be made to exceed any given finite area.' He says that 'the earlier geometers' used this to prove among other things that pyramid and cone are one-third of prism and cylinder respectively with equal base and height. Since he tells us elsewhere (*Method* pref.) that Eudoxus was the first to prove these theorems (although Democritus had stated them), the second formulation is probably that of Eudoxus. We may guess that Eudoxus, with his interest in logical rigour, was also chiefly responsible for the thorough axiomatization of geometry as we find it in Euclid. The great interest and progress in strict deductive *logic during the 4th cent. is best seen in the logical works of *Aristotle, who also provides valuable evidence for the form of contemporary geometry.

From *Proclus' summary of the early history of mathematics extracted from Eudemus we know many names of mathematicians active in the 4th cent., but few details of what they did. However, Eutocius (*In Arch. circ. dim.* 78–80 Heiberg) preserves an account of a solution by *Menaechmus (2) (mid-4th cent.) to the problem of finding two mean proportionals which is the first attested use of conic sections. Aristaeus wrote a textbook on these not much later, which shows that this branch of higher geometry was rapidly developed.

With the *Elements* of Euclid we come to the first extant mathematical treatise. This, though an introductory textbook, reflects the sophistication of contemporary geometry in both form and content, but the axiomatic method of exposition necessarily obscures the historical development. A particular problem is raised by the propositions concerning the 'application of areas'— 6. 28 gives a general solution of which a particular case can be derived from 2. 5 (see Heath's translation, 383): 'To a given straight line (*b*) to apply a rectangle which shall be equal to a given area (*A*), and fall short of the rectangle formed by the straight line and one of its own sides by a square figure.' In algebraic terms this is $xy = A$, $x + y = b$ (in other words the quadratic equation $bx - x^2 = A$ is to be solved). This is exactly what one would arrive at if one were to transform the 'normal forms' of Babylonian numerical problems involving a quadratic equation into geometrical terms, and it is likely, although not demonstrable, that this 'algebraic geometry' is just such a transformation. If so, some knowledge of advanced Babylonian mathematics had reached Greece by the 4th cent. (the same is true of Babylonian astronomy). As well as plane and solid geometry, the *Elements* comprises number theory, which (like other contemporary branches of mathematics) had not attained the same level of systematization as pure geometry. However, some remarkable results were reached, such as the proof that there is no limit to the number of primes.

In the case of conics this deficiency was supplied by *Apollonius (2), who transformed the approach to the field by extending the 'application of areas' to include it in a *tour de force* of generalization. A generation before him Archimedes created new branches of mathematics by applying the axiomatic approach to *statics and *hydrostatics, but systematization was not his main interest. Most of his surviving work is in higher geometry, where he proves by traditional methods many theorems which are now proved by integral calculus. But his *Method* shows that he arrived at many of these results by using infinitesimals. This is only one of the ways in which his thought was so far ahead of its time that it had no effect in antiquity: thus the profound concept of a numerical system implicit in the *Sand-reckoner* has no echo in surviving literature. However, many of his results, such as the formula for the volume of a sphere and his approximation to π, became mathematical commonplaces.

The 3rd cent. was the great period of pure geometry, represented not only in the work of Apollonius and Archimedes, but also in that of a number of other mathematicians whose achievements can be judged from references by *Pappus and others, although their works are lost. After this, most creative mathematics was done in other fields. Several of these were connected with *astronomy. For instance, the necessity of determining time accurately led to the development of the theory of sundials (see CLOCKS). Although the sundial itself goes back to the 5th cent. or earlier in Greece, mathematical determination of the hour-lines does not predate the 3rd cent., and the particular application to them of the type of descriptive geometry known by the ancients as *analēmma* does not seem to be older than *Diodorus (4) of Alexandria, 1st cent. BC. The most elegant example of this is found in *Ptolemy (4)'s *Analemma*; earlier, cruder methods appear in the works of *Heron and *Vitruvius. The related technique of stereographic projection was probably used by *Hipparchus (3) about 140 BC for mapping circles of the heavenly sphere on to a plane in order to solve certain astronomical problems (exemplified in the plane astrolabe). The same problems led to the development of spherical trigonometry, probably by *Menelaus (3) about AD 100. Plane trigonometry, with the first computed trigonometrical function (a chord table) had already been created by Hipparchus himself, also for astronomical purposes (see TRIGONOMETRY).

It is in later Greek mathematics too that we find the non-axiomatic, numerical and algebraic techniques which are typical of Babylonian mathematics. But it is accidental that the first extant examples occur as late as the work of Heron, *c.* AD 60, for we cannot doubt that they are directly descended from Mesopotamian sources in a continuous tradition, which did not hesitate to borrow from the works of the classical mathematicians,

although apparently ignored by them. It is also found in mathematical papyri, and was evidently 'popular' mathematics (in Heron it is mostly practical). A different branch of the same tradition is found in *Diophantus' *Arithmetica*. This is the Greek work which comes nearest to the modern conception of algebra, although it is not a textbook on the solution of equations, but rather groups of problems, mostly of indeterminate equations. Though the roots of this lie in Mesopotamia, much of the content is probably original, and the form of exposition owes much to the Greek tradition.

In late antiquity, although there were still mathematicians, such as *Pappus, *Theon (4), and Eutocius, competent enough to edit, excerpt, and comment on the classical works, mathematics had become sterile, so that the value of these authors lies in what they preserve from earlier periods. It was only after transmission to the Islamic world (translations into Arabic began in the 9th cent.) that the ancient mathematical tradition was revived and enlarged. This happened again, even more fruitfully, in 16th-cent. Europe, after the recovery of the Greek texts, many of them interpreted in the superb Latin translations of Commandino. Rivault's edition of Archimedes with the commentary of Eutocius (1615) and Bachet's edition of Diophantus (1621) were essential to the work of the great 17th-cent. mathematicians, such as Descartes and Fermat.

For special studies see the articles on the ancient authors referred to. For general accounts see Heath, *Hist. of Greek Maths.* and (sometimes better) G. Loria, *Le scienze esatte nell'antica Grecia*, 2nd edn. (1914). For Babylonian influences see B. L. van der Waerden, *Science Awakening*, 2nd edn. (1961) and O. Neugebauer, *The Exact Sciences in Antiquity*, 2nd edn. (1957). On the history of conics H. G. Zeuthen, *Die Lehre von den Kegelschnitten im Altertum* (1886, repr. 1966) remains fundamental. For Aristotle see T. L. Heath, *Mathematics in Aristotle* (1949). G. J. T.

Matidia Augusta, Salonia, niece of the emperor *Trajan, was daughter of the emperor's sister *Ulpia Marciana and of C. Salonius Matidius Patruinus, a senator from Vicetia. She was much loved by Trajan, whom she accompanied on his travels, and was granted the title Augusta on her mother's death in AD 112. Married twice, Matidia was the mother of two daughters, Matidia and *Sabina, the latter being the wife of Hadrian, who showed great affection for his mother-in-law. She was deified on her death in 119.

PIR^2 M 367. A. R. Bi.

Matius (*RE* 1), **Gaius,** a learned friend of *Cicero and partisan of *Caesar, helped Cicero in his relations with Caesar, especially in 49 and 48 BC. In 44 he shared in the management of the games which *Octavian exhibited in honour of Caesar. Cicero's letter to him about his devotion to Caesar, and his reply, written later in 44, (*Fam.* 11. 27 and 28) are of outstanding interest. Augustus' friend and assistant, C. Matius (*RE* 2), an *eques* and expert on *arboriculture and gastronomy, has been identified with Cicero's friend, but seems to belong to the next generation.

A. M.; T. J. C.; R. J. S.

Matius (*RE* 4), **Gnaeus** (1st cent. BC), translated *Homer's *Iliad* into Latin hexameters and composed *Mimiambi* in imitation of *Herodas; both works are lost. His verse, quoted already by *Varro, is technically proficient; his learning was admired by Aulus *Gellius.

Courtney, *FLP* 99–106. Herzog–Schmidt, § 137. R. A. K.

matriarchy has since J. J. Bachofen (*Das Mutterrecht* (1861)) been used to denote a quite hypothetical and now long discredited

matrilocality

phase in the history of mankind when property was transmitted and descent traced through females, not males. (There has from the outset been a persistent tendency to confuse the specific phenomenon of matrilineal descent on the one hand—a system widely attested among contemporary peoples worldwide—with female supremacy in a more general and altogether less clearly defined sense on the other). The system of descent is stated by Herodotus (1. 173) to have been operative as a going concern among the non-Greek people of *Lycia in his own time, but this assertion is flatly contradicted by the conventional family structure reflected in their funeral inscriptions, including well over 150 in the *Lycian language itself, many of which go back to the 4th cent. BC.

The statement of *Aristotle (fr. 547 Rose; cited by Polyb. 12. 5–6) that the people of *Locri Epizephyrii in southern Italy derived all their ancestral honours from women, not from men, has long been viewed as indicating a similar descent system, but in fact refers to the first generation only. It reflects the ancient tradition that the city was founded by runaway slaves who (unlike the accompanying womenfolk) necessarily and by definition lacked full civic status, from which alone honours of any kind could be derived. Crucial to the correct interpretation of Aristotle's statement (even as summarized: the verb is lacking) is the distinction between the first and second preposition, which on a casual reading it is only too easy, but mistaken, to assimilate: 'among them all ancestral distinction (is derived) from the women, not from the men . . .' (πάντα τὰ διὰ προγόνων ἔνδοξα παρ' αὐτοῖς ἀπὸ τῶν γυναικῶν, οὐκ ἀπὸ τῶν ἀνδρῶν . . .).

The Greek term 'gynaecocracy' ('women in control'), used much more widely, denotes not a specific set of institutions, or descent system, but a disturbing threat to, and reversal of, the state of masculine supremacy on all fronts, the normality (and desirability) of which is effectively taken for granted by ancient sources, which are throughout antiquity hardly notable for even an incipient feminism. Mythical all-female societies such as the *Amazons or the women of *Lemnos appear to reflect projected male anxiety on this score rather than any sort of recollection (itself a highly questionable notion) of prehistoric data. Equally, ancient speculations as to what preceded the institution of marriage (the invention of *Cecrops: Varro in August. De civ. D. 18. 9, cf. Just. Epit. 2. 6. 7 and the Suda entry for *Prometheus) are simply imaginative reconstructions for which no real historical foundation was necessary. They were, however, enthusiastically taken up and even generalized in the second half of the 19th cent., which saw a plethora of universal evolutionary schemas along 'matriarchal' lines and speculative reconstruction on a breathtaking scale. (A conspicuous feature of these theories is the constant resort to such dubious (because uncontrollable) hypothetical props as the doctrine of 'survivals'.) There were, or should have been, definitively scotched by anthropological fieldwork at the beginning of the present century (e.g. B. Malinowski, The Family among the Australian Aborigines (1913); and see ANTHROPOLOGY AND THE CLASSICS); regrettably, the theories themselves, though not impossible to disprove, have continued to exercise such an attraction in some quarters as to guarantee them a kind of extended though strictly unhistorical half-life.

S. Pembroke, JWI 1967, 1–35; P. Vidal-Naquet, in R. L. Gordon (ed.), Myth, Religion and Society (1981), 187–200, with references; B. Wagner-Hasel (ed.), Matriarchatstheorien der Altertumswissenschaft (1992); see also B. Wagner-Hasel, in R. R. Bolgar (ed.), Classical Influences on Western Thought, AD 1650–1870 (1979), 275–91, Journal of the Economic

and Social History of the Orient 1965, 217–47 (for Lycia: not significantly affected by subsequent finds), and Annales ESC 1970, 1240 ff.

S. G. P.

matrilocality denotes a pattern of *marriage in which the groom resides with the bride's parents, as opposed to the more common patrilocal marriage, where the bride goes to live with the groom's kin. Both patterns occur in Greek myth and saga and may have coexisted in bronze age society. An essential concomitant of Homeric patrilocal marriage is the suitor's presentation of hedna, 'gifts', to the prospective bride-giver. In exceptional cases the girl is bestowed anaednon, 'without gifts', in restitution or as recompense for service (e.g. *Agamemnon's promise to *Achilles at Il. 9. 146). Although hedna were once reckoned as 'bride-price' to compensate for the loss of a daughter, they are more plausibly explained as a pledge for the daughter's security. Instances of marriage by capture and marriage by contest are variants of the patrilocal pattern. Conversely, for families without surviving sons, matrilocal marriage permits a daughter's husband to perform a resident son's duties and claim the estate. This custom must be distinguished from matriliny, or regular succession through the female line, as the son-in-law only inherits by default. In *Homer such unions with heiresses involve close male kin: *Diomedes (2) (Il. 5. 410–15) and Iphidamas (Il. 11. 221–6) marry their mother's sisters, and *Alcinous (1) (Od. 7. 63–6) weds his brother's daughter. That Iphidamas is reported to have given gifts in exchange for his bride (Il. 11. 243) indicates conflation of patterns. By the offer of daughters as wives, rulers with living sons attract foreign warriors into their service: so the king of *Lycia acknowledges the prowess of *Bellerophon (Il. 6. 191–3) and Alcinous attempts to obtain *Odysseus as a husband for *Nausicaa (Od. 7. 311–14). *Priam's extended family, consisting of fifty sons and twelve sons-in-law, is the most striking Homeric example of matrilocal residence. The kinship terminology used in descriptions of Priam's household (e.g. the distinction of galoōs, 'husband's sister', and einatēr, 'husband's brother's wife', at Il. 6. 378) implies that families in which married sons and daughters and their spouses lived with parents were a historical reality. After Homer, these terms disappear and patrilocal marriage becomes the rule. Nevertheless, it is possible that in Classical Athens the kinsman who married an epiklēros, 'fatherless heiress', was still expected to reside with the bride's legal guardian. See INHERITANCE, GREEK.

M. I. Finley, RIDA 1955, 167 ff.; W. K. Lacey, The Family in Classical Greece (1968), 39 ff.; G. Wickert-Micknat, Die Frau, Archaeologia Homerica 3, pt. R (1982), 89 ff.

M. B. S.

Matris, of *Thebes (1) (3rd cent. BC ?), rhetor, wrote an Encomium of Heracles with Asianist characteristics (see ASIANISM AND ATTICISM).

FGrH 39. H. Hobein, RE 14 (1930), 2287.

M. B. T.

Matron, of Pitane in *Aeolis (late 4th cent. BC), parodist (see PARODY, GREEK), wrote a poem called Δεῖπνον Ἀττικόν, 'Attic Dinner', quoted by *Athenaeus (1) (4. 134–7), beginning Δειπνά μοι ἔννεπε, Μοῦσα, πολύτροφα καὶ μάλα πολλά ('Tell me, Muse, of the many nourishing dinners'), a parody of the opening of *Homer's Odyssey.

Suppl. Hell. frs. 534–40.

J. S. R.

Matuta Mater, goddess of the dawn (Lucr. 5. 656; Prisc. Inst. 2. 53, ed. M. Hertz (Keil, Gramm. Lat. 3. 76, ll. 18 ff.)) sometimes assimilated to *Leucothea, had an ancient temple in the *forum Boarium, beside that of *Fortuna. During her festival, the Matralia of 11 June (Ov. *Fast.* 6. 475), matrons made a *cake, expelled a slave from the temple, and recommended to the goddess the children of their sisters over their own. The meaning of the rituals and of the goddess's name has prompted a difference of views between G. Dumézil and H. J. Rose. Dumézil sees Matuta as a goddess of the dawn and has proposed an interpretation of the known elements of the Matralia based on comparison with Vedic mythology. Rose wanted to recognize a goddess of growth. Other interpretations base themselves on the assimilation to Leucothea (see INO-LEUCOTHEA). Matuta Mater also had a temple at *Satricum (1).

G. Dumézil, *ARR* 50 ff., and *Mythe et épopée* 3 (1973); H. J. Rose, *CQ* 1934, 156 ff.; Radke, *Götter* 206 ff.; R. Bloch, *CRAcad. Inscr.* 1968, 366 ff.; F. Coarelli, *Il Foro Boario* (1988).   J. Sch.

Mauretania, the land of the Moors, stretching from the Ampsaga to the Atlantic and embracing the western half of the *Atlas range. Most of the country is high and rocky, supporting sheep and producing a little wine; corn and olives grew on the coast, in the Mulucha valley, and on the plains of *Volubilis and Sala. The chief exports were wine, ebony, precious woods, and purple dyes.

There seems to have been communication with Spain from early days, binding Europe and Africa by piracy and colonization. The bulk of the population belonged to the Moorish branch of the Berber race, while a string of Phoenician trading-stations was established on the Mediterranean and Atlantic coasts during the 8th and 7th cents. BC.

By the late 3rd cent. BC the small Moorish tribes had formed kingdoms: the earliest ruler known by name, Baga, who had 4,000 soldiers at his disposal (Livy 19. 30. 1), was a contemporary and ally of *Masinissa. *Bocchus I played an important part in the Jugurthine War, as a result of which western Numidia was incorporated into the Mauretanian kingdom. Mauretania was divided on the death of Bocchus' successor Mastanesosus in 49 BC: *Bocchus II received eastern Mauretania, and *Bogud the western part; but the latter lost his kingdom when he sided with Antony, probably in 38, and Bocchus then ruled over a united Mauretania until his death in 33, when it was left to Octavian. Octavian handed it over, in 25 BC, to *Juba (2) II, whose capitals were at Iol (Caesarea) and probably Volubilis. The murder in Rome of *Ptolemy (2), Juba II's son and successor (AD 23–40), led to disturbances. Mauretania was pacified by *Suetonius Paulinus (41–2) and Cn. *Hosidius Geta. In or about 44 *Claudius constituted two Mauretanian provinces, ruled by *procurators, with capitals at *Tingis and *Caesarea (3). Moorish cavalry served in the Roman armies, and the Moor *Lusius Quietus won distinction under Trajan. A number of *coloniae* were founded. Defence was provided by auxiliary units posted in forts. Large tracts, however, remained under Moorish chieftains; there were serious rebellions in the late 3rd and the 4th cents. Mauretania Tingitana was attached by *Diocletian to the diocese (see DIOECESIS) of Spain, while at the same time Mauretania Caesariensis, in the diocese of Africa, was divided into two new provinces, Mauretania Caesariensis (with its capital still at Caesarea) and Mauretania Sitifiensis (its capital at Sitifis).

J. Carcopino, *Le Maroc antique*, 2nd edn. (1947); L. Chatelain, *Le Maroc des Romains*, 2nd edn. (1968); *De l'Empire aux villes imperiales: 6000 ans d'art au Maroc* (1990), 21–44, 96–180, 333–89. Inscriptions: M. Euzennat and J. Marion, *Inscriptions antiques de Maroc 2: Inscriptions latines* (1982). Early Roman settlement: N. K. Mackie, *Hist.* 1983, 332–58.
                                                        W. N. W.; R. J. A. W.

Mauryas, the first major dynasty ruling virtually the entire Indo-Pakistan subcontinent from *c*.324/21–185/80 BC. Established by Chandragupta (see SANDRACOTTUS) with the assistance of Chanakya/Kautilya, the establishment of empire involved overthrowing the existing Nanda dynasty. Chandragupta consolidated the kingdom north of the Narmada. *Seleucus (1) I Nicator ceded territory to him and sent *Megasthenes to his court. Chandragupta was succeeded *c*.300/297 by Bindusara, who is believed to have extended the boundaries southwards into the peninsula. Both rulers received envoys and gifts from the *Seleucids and the Ptolemies (see PTOLEMY (1)). Links with Hellenistic kings were furthered in the reign of the next king, *Ashoka, the date of whose succession—either 272 or 268—is debated, since the Buddhist chronicles of Sri Lanka mention a four-year interregnum on the death of Bindusara occasioned by rivalries over the succession. The short-lived but extensive empire was governed from the capital at Pataliputra (see PALIBOTHRA).

The edicts of Ashoka provide evidence on the areas included within the empire as well as its administration. The degree of centralization suggested by earlier studies has been recently reconsidered. The empire served to link various regions of the subcontinent through administration and through encouraging trade, the latter being suggested by the widespread distribution of punch-marked coins and the growth of urban centres. The agricultural economy was extended through the state bringing land under cultivation by settling families of cultivators. Both royal patronage and trade assisted in the spread of Buddhism and in the generally sympathetic reception of heterodox ideas.

The succession after Ashoka remains confused. By *c*.180 BC the empire had declined for a variety of reasons including weak successors, fiscal crises, and a top-heavy administration. See INDIA.

R. Thapar, *Asoka and the Decline of the Mauryas*, 2nd edn. (1973), and *The Mauryas Revisited* (1988); G. Fussman, *Annales* 1982, 621–47; T. R. Trautmann, *Kautilya and the Arthasastra* (1971); J. W. McCrindle, *Ancient India as Described by Megasthenes and Arrian* (1877).   R. Th.

Mausoleum at Halicarnassus, the One of the *Seven Wonders of the world, it was the tomb of the satrap *Mausolus of Caria (reigned 377–353 BC). Begun shortly after 367, when Mausolus refounded *Halicarnassus, it was finished after his wife *Artemisia (2) died in 351, and is perhaps best interpreted as his hero-shrine (see HERO-CULT) as city-*founder. Its architect was *Pythius of Priene; *Vitruvius (*De arch.* 7 pref. 12) records that he and Mausolus' court sculptor Satyrus wrote a book on the building, and he and Pliny (*HN* 36. 31) note that four other sculptors joined them: *Scopas, Bryaxis, *Leochares, and either *Praxiteles or *Timotheus (3). Pliny also outlines the building's form, reports that Scopas and his colleagues each took one side of it, and adds that Pythius made the chariot-group that crowned it. It stood until the 15th cent., when the Knights of Rhodes quarried it for their castle.

Excavation has supplemented and corrected the ancient accounts. The building consisted of a high podium measuring 30 × 36 m. (100 × 120 ft.), a colonnade of 36 Ionic columns, and a pyramid of 24 steps. With the crowning chariot-group, it reached a total height of 42.7 m. (140 ft.). The tomb-chamber was encased in the podium, and sacrificial remains suggest the existence of a hero-cult. The podium's steps carried quantities of freestanding sculpture (hunts, battles, audience scenes, sacrifices, and portraits), and was crowned by an *Amazon frieze; portraits stood between the columns; coffer-reliefs embellished the peristyle's ceiling; lions ringed the cornice; and the base for the chariot carried a *Centaur frieze. The chariot frieze may have ringed the interior of the tomb-chamber.

C. T. Newton, *A History of Discoveries at Cnidus, Halicarnassus, and Branchidae* (1862); G. B. Waywell, *The Free-Standing Sculpture of the Mausoleum at Halicarnassus* (1978); K. Jeppesen and others, *The Maussolleion at Halikarnassos* (1981–); S. Hornblower, *Mausolus* (1982), ch. 9; A. F. Stewart, *Greek Sculpture* (1990), 180 ff., figs. 524 ff.   A. F. S.

Mausolus (Maussollos in inscriptions), son of *Hecatomnus. Ruler of *Caria 377–353 BC, in conjunction with his sister and wife *Artemisia (2), and an important figure in the diffusion of *Hellenism in 4th-cent. Asia Minor, who nevertheless promoted or retained the local Carian element. (He made dedications in Greek, but only at local, culturally mixed sanctuaries like *Labraunda; he is not directly attested at the other important Carian sanctuaries *Amyzon or *Sinuri, though this may be chance because his brother *Idrieus features at both places and *Ada and Hecatomnus at Sinuri.) Greek artists worked on his *Mausoleum, though again this has some definitely non-Greek features.

He ruled under Persian auspices (see PERSIA), and used the title *satrap in inscriptions (Tod 138 = Syll.³ 167; Syll.³ 170). That he was a proper satrap has been denied on grounds such as that 'real' satraps did not rule jointly or were always Iranians, but these are not ancient definitions; it has further been urged that literary sources do not call him satrap, but the combination of *FGrH* 115 F 297 and A. Gell. 10. 18 imply that *Theopompus (3) did. The same applies to other members of the Hecatomnid family (see ADA; ARTEMISIA (2); HECATOMNUS; IDRIEUS; PIXODARUS). It is nevertheless true that Mausolus seems to act as a free agent in foreign and internal affairs, but that may merely indicate that the kings of Persia wisely left a lot to the men (and women) on the spot.

Mausolus moved his capital from *Mylasa to *Halicarnassus (which he enlarged by *synoecism, *Callisthenes *FGrH* 124 F 25) in the 370s, perhaps announcing thereby an interest in Aegean politics. He joined the *Satraps' Revolt of the 360s, but seems to have smoothly returned to his Persian allegiance when things got rough. Thereafter his activities promoted or at least coincided with Persian interests, most notably when he fomented the *Social War (1) of 357–355 between Athens and its allies in the *Second Athenian Confederacy. *Demosthenes (2) in his Rhodian Speech (15) is our main source for this and he has every motive for exaggerating Mausolus' role, thus sparing Athens (see RHODES) and the Rhodian democrats whom Mausolus had seduced away from their democratic solidarity with Athens and into the arms of Caria. But the fact of Mausolus' interference is certain (Diod. Sic. 16. 7, from *Ephorus, is independent corroboration). On Rhodes and elsewhere Mausolus' regime resulted in oligarchies, whether at his insistence or not. But Syll.³ 169 (Mausolan *Iasus) has a fairly democratic formula, cf. Michel 466 (assembly pay at the same city).

Mausolus' area of direct control was large and his sphere of influence larger, taking in, as we now know, *Cnossus on Crete (*ILabraunda* no. 40, Greek text which starts 'it seemed good to Mausolus and Artemisia'). But he also had relations with communities in *Pisidia (the Solymoi), *Pamphylia (*Phaselis), and Ionia (*Erythrae, see Tod 155 and cf. IDRIEUS). Mausolus definitely annexed Rhodes, *Chios, and *Cos in the 350s (Dem. 15, cf. 5. 25). By the time of his brother *Pixodarus (337), *Lycia was included in satrapal Caria, but it is not certain that this was so under Mausolus, who was, however, on good terms with *Caunus on the Lycia–Caria border (*SEG* 12. 471).

Strabo 14. 2. 16–17. L. Robert, *Études anatoliennes* (1937), 570–3; J. Crampa (ed.), *Labraunda … 3: The Greek Inscriptions* 2 (1972); S. Hornblower, *Mausolus* (1982), esp. 364 ff. for the inscriptions, and *CAH* 6² (1994), ch. 8a; T. Petit, *BCH* 1988, 307 ff.; S. Ruzicka, *Politics of a Persian Dynasty: The Hecatomnids in the Fourth Century BC* (1992).

S. H.

Mavortius, possibly the consul of AD 527 (*PLRE* 2. 736–7) wrote a Virgilian *cento entitled *Iudicium Paridis*. The Christian Virgilian cento *De ecclesia* is sometimes ascribed to him, through a dubious emendation.

Ed. Baehr. *PLM* 4. 198 ff. G. Salanitro, *Enc. Virg.* 'Mavorzio'.   S. J. Ha.

Maxentius (*RE* 1), **Marcus Aurelius Valerius** (b. *c.* AD 283), son of *Maximian, married *Galerius' daughter but was, like Constantius I's son *Constantine I, passed over when Diocletian and Maximian abdicated and Galerius and *Constantius I succeeded as Augusti (305). On Constantius's death Flavius Valerius *Severus became Augustus, but Constantine's proclamation and the attempt by Severus to register the *plebs* at Rome provoked the praetorian guard to proclaim Maxentius as *princeps* (306). In 307 he took the title Augustus and reconferred this on his father, calling him from retirement to assist him. Severus failed to suppress Maxentius, who had him executed; Galerius invaded Italy but failed against Maxentius, who now controlled all Italy and Africa, but not Spain. Maximian secured an alliance with Constantine in Gaul by giving him the title Augustus and his daughter Fausta in marriage. In 308 Maximian quarrelled with his son, failed to depose him, and fled to Constantine; at *Carnuntum Galerius declared Maxentius a public enemy. A revolt in Africa by the **vicarius* Domitius Alexander (*c.*308–9) was defeated by Maxentius's praetorian prefect (see PRAEFECTUS PRAETORIO); famine at Rome was averted. Maximian's renewed attempt to become Augustus (310) caused Constantine to sever his alliance with the family and (312) invade Italy. He killed Maxentius's prefect near *Verona, marched on Rome and defeated Maxentius's forces (said to have been four times as numerous) at Saxa Rubra; Maxentius was drowned near the Mulvian bridge (*pons Mulvius). He may have been no soldier, and his need for cash caused resentment among senators, but Constantinian propaganda gives a wholly misleading impression of him. Twice in the interests of public order he intervened in squabbles in the Roman Church, but he tolerated *Christianity and restored property to the Church.

T. D. Barnes, *Constantine and Eusebius* (1981).   R. P. D.

Maximian (Marcus Aurelius Valerius Maximianus (*RE* 1)) Born *c.* AD 250, the son of shopkeepers near Sirmium, he rose through the ranks of the army. An excellent general, he was called by his old comrade-in-arms *Diocletian to assist him as his Caesar (21 July 285), with responsibility for Italy, Africa, Spain, Gaul, and Britain. Sent against the insurgent *Bacaudae in Gaul, he soon dispersed their irregular bands under Amandus and Aelianus; he repelled a German invasion of Gaul, and was promoted Augustus (1 April 286; see AUGUSTUS, AUGUSTA AS TITLES). Against *Carausius he was less successful: an expedition by sea failed, and the usurper was able to hold Britain and part of Gaul for some years, while Maximian was heavily engaged on the Rhine. He acted in close accord with Diocletian, with whom he conferred in 289 and 290/1 and to whom he remained utterly loyal.

In 293, under Diocletian's tetrarchic system (see TETRARCHY), he received *Constantius (1), probably his praetorian prefect (see praefectus praetorio) since 288 and already married to his (?step-) daughter Theodora, as his Caesar. In 296 he came to guard the Rhine while Constantius recovered Britain from *Allectus, who had killed Carausius. After fighting in Spain in autumn 296, Maximian crossed to Africa to deal with a revolt by the Quinquegentanei and other Mauretanian tribes; *c.*299 he entered Rome in triumph, and there he began the building of the baths of Diocletian. Late in 303 Diocletian joined him in Rome to celebrate a joint triumph and the *vicennalia* (twentieth anniversary of his reign). Maximian enforced the persecution of Christians (303–5) in Italy and Spain, and with some severity in North Africa where they were numerous.

When Diocletian abdicated on 1 May 305, Maximian, at Milan, reluctantly did the same, but his son *Maxentius, proclaimed emperor at Rome (28 October 306), named his father Augustus for the second time and called him from retirement. In spring 307, assisting his son, Maximian forced Flavius Valerius *Severus to abdicate at Ravenna; then, to secure for Maxentius an alliance with *Constantine against *Galerius, he went to Gaul (*c.* Sept.) and gave Constantine the title Augustus and his daughter, Fausta, in marriage (see constantine i). In April 308 Maximian failed to depose his son, with whom he had quarrelled, and fled to Constantine who sheltered him. Forced to abdicate again at the conference of *Carnuntum (November 308), Maximian could not settle down to honourable inactivity. In revolt against Constantine he assumed the purple for the third time, but was quickly captured at Massilia (see massalia) and died by his own hand (*c.* July 310). Proclaimed *Divus* by Maxentius and the senate, his memory was damned (see damnatio memoriae) by Constantine; after the Mulvian bridge (*pons Mulvius) his widow Eutropia swore that Maxentius had not been his son, and he was rehabilitated.

See bibliog. under diocletian.   R. P. D.

Maximianus, Latin poet, wrote six elegies of varied length (686 verses in total), from which we can deduce a few biographical data: his name (4. 26), Italian origin (5. 5, 40), youth spent in Rome (1. 37, 63), successful political career (1. 9–10, 13–14), participation in an embassy to the east (5. 1–4), and relations with the philosopher *Boethius. In consequence, most people place Maximianus in the period of Gothic rule in Italy (middle of the 6th cent. AD; see goths). He represents himself as an old man lamenting his lost youth and his love affairs with various women (Lycoris in 2; Aquilina, his youthful passion, in 3; the dancer Candida in 4; a young Greek girl in 5). The language and style are inspired by Augustan love-elegy, with metrical 'errors' attributable to the late date: the rhetorical and sententious tone was appreciated in the Middle Ages. The text presents serious difficulties, not resolved in the existing editions.

TEXT Baehr. *PLM* (1883).
COMMENTARIES R. Webster (1900); F. Spaltenstein (1983).
STUDIES R. Ellis, *AJPhil.* 1884, 1 ff., 145 ff.; H. E. Wedeck, *Latomus* 1952, 487 ff.; W. Schetter, *Studien zur Überlieferung und Kritik des Elegikers Maximian* (1970). PLRE 2. 739 f.   P. P.

Maximinus Thrax, Roman emperor. See iulius verus maximinus, c.

Maximinus (*RE* 'Daia'), **Gaius Galerius Valerius,** originally named Daia, born in Illyricum *c.* AD 270, son of a sister of *Galerius, was rapidly promoted in the army, and made Caesar when Galerius became Augustus (305). Charged with governing Syria and Egypt, he was resentful that Galerius made *Licinius Au-

gustus (308). Spurning the title *filius Augustorum* ('son of the Augusti'), he had his troops proclaim him Augustus; Galerius recognized this (309/10). On Galerius's death (311), as senior Augustus he seized Asia Minor while Licinius occupied Galerius' European territories; war with Licinius was averted, but to balance the latter's alliance with Constantine (see constantine i) he drew closer to *Maxentius. Learning of the latter's defeat, and that the senate had made Constantine senior Augustus, he crossed the Hellespont. Defeated by Licinius near Adrianople (30 April 313), he fled and committed suicide at Tarsus. Like Galerius, he was an ardent *pagan. In 306 and 308 he ordained that all in his dominions should sacrifice: city magistrates and census officials drew up lists and individuals were called on by name. From 307 he used the death penalty only rarely, but mutilated recusants and sent them to the mines; outside Egypt there were relatively few executions. When Galerius ended the persecution Maximinus acquiesced but in autumn 311 recommenced. With little genuine support, he incited cities and provinces to petition against the Christians. 'Acts of Pilate' and confessions of ex-Christians to *incest were published as propaganda. To revive paganism he organized the pagan priesthood hierarchically. The persecution was relaxed and then called off just before his defeat.
                                                            R. P. D.

Maximus (1), of Tyre (2nd cent. AD), the author of 41 extant *Dialexeis* ('Lectures'), apparently delivered in Rome in the reign of *Commodus. They present undemanding expositions of a range of (broadly) philosophical themes, always with an eye to their ethical implications, in a calculatedly lively and ostentatiously literary style; frequent Homeric quotation and regular evocation of *Plato (1) and the Platonic *Socrates give the collection much of its distinctive flavour. The doctrinal content is in effect (Middle) Platonic (see platonism, middle), though Maximus officially poses as a spokesman for a unified and non-sectarian philosophical truth. As a philosophizing declaimer he may be compared with *Dio Cocceianus, *Favorinus, and *Apuleius.

Ed. H. Hobein (1910); new edns. forthcoming. M. Trapp, *ANRW* 2. 34. 3 (forthcoming).   M. B. T.

Maximus (2) (probably 2nd cent. AD), author of the extant astrological poem *Peri katarchōn* (on forecasts), part of which later passed under the name of *Orpheus. The *Suda* calls the author an Epirote or Byzantine, but identifies him with *Julian's teacher *Maximus (3), who came from Ephesus; this, however, seems improbable, as the poem is quite unphilosophical.

Ed. A. Ludwich (1877).   W. D. R.; J. S. R.

Maximus (3) (*RE* 40), of Ephesus (d. AD 370), Neoplatonist philosopher; see neoplatonism. A pupil of *Aedesius, who was himself a pupil of *Iamblichus (2), Maximus followed his master's tendency to emphasize *theurgy and *magic. However, like many Neoplatonists, he combined this interest in the supernatural with rigorous philosophy, producing work on Aristotelian logic and in particular a (lost) commentary on *Aristotle's *Categories*. Maximus' own most distinguished pupil was the future emperor *Julian. He is said to have foretold Julian's subsequent elevation to the throne and no doubt encouraged the young prince in his rejection of Christianity. In 361 Maximus was invited by Julian, now emperor, to join his court at Constantinople and remained with him until his death during his Persian campaign. For some time he enjoyed the confidence of *Valens but fell into disfavour and was imprisoned in 364. His release was due to the intervention of *Themistius. In 370 he was put to death for complicity in a plot to assassinate Valens. He is not the author of an astrological poem in hexameters sometimes attributed to him.

Eunap. *VS* 7. 473–81 (Loeb trans. by W. C. Wright); Julian, *Ep.* 26, 190, 191 (Loeb trans. by W. C. Wright); Simplicius, *Categories* 1. 15 f.

A. D. S.

Maximus (Roman emperor) See MAGNUS MAXIMUS.

'Maximus Victorinus' (also 'Maximinus' or 'Maximianus'), name under which is transmitted a brief treatise on Latin prosody (*De ratione metrorum*: Keil, *Gramm. Lat.* 6. 216–28); the name is probably a corruption of 'Marius Victorinus' (cf. Herzog–Schmidt, 5. 354 f.). Early editors attributed various other treatises to the same 'Maximus Victorinus' (*Gramm. Lat.* 6. 187–205, 206–15, 229–39, and Keil, ibid. pp. xviii ff.), without good manuscript authority.

R. A. K.

Mazaeus (*c.*385–328 BC), Persian noble, governed *Cilicia and *Syria under *Artaxerxes (3) III and *Darius III. After *Issus (333) he vacated his satrapy and held high command at *Gaugamela (331), where he came close to breaking *Alexander (3) the Great's left. Taking refuge in *Babylon (his wife's home), he formally surrendered the city to his conqueror and in return was appointed to Babylonia as Alexander's first Iranian *satrap, a position which he held until his death.

Berve, *Alexanderreich* 2, no. 485.

A. B. B.

meals Among the Greeks the times and names of meals varied at different periods. In early times breakfast (ἄριστον) was taken shortly after sunrise, followed by a main meal (δεῖπνον) at midday and supper (δόρπον) in the evening. In Classical Athens two meals—a light lunch (ἄριστον) and dinner (δεῖπνον) in the evening—appear to have been usual. From the 4th cent. BC onwards an earlier breakfast (ἀκράτισμα) was again added, or substituted for lunch.

Among the Romans dinner (*cena*) was eaten in the middle of the day in early times, with a light supper (*vesperna*) in the evening. Eventually an evening *cena*, often commencing in the late afternoon, became usual. Lunch (*prandium*), consisting of fish or eggs and vegetables together with wine, was eaten towards midday and replaced supper. In the morning there was a very light breakfast (*ientaculum*), which might consist of only bread and salt. Cheese and fruit were sometimes added.

The *cena*, the biggest meal of the day, was eaten after the day's work was finished. It consisted of three parts. The hors d'œuvre (*gustatio*), of eggs, shellfish, dormice, and *olives, with honeyed wine (*mulsum*), was followed by the *cena* proper, comprising up to seven courses (*fercula*), with one chief item (*caput cenae*). This might be a whole roasted pig, accompanied by smaller, but substantial courses (e.g. lampreys, turbot, roast veal). The meal ended with dessert (*mensae secundae*), consisting of snails, nuts, shellfish, and fruit. *Apicius, On the Art of Cookery (Eng. trans. J. Edwards, 1984) describes the meals of the rich, to whom most of our information relates. The appearance of ostriches, peacocks, cranes, etc. on the tables of the rich was largely due to the search for novelty. The pseudo-*Virgilian poem *Moretum* (Eng. trans. E. J. Kenney, 1984) describes a peasant's lunch (see APPENDIX VERGILIANA).

See COOKERY; FOOD AND DRINK.

RE 3. 1895–7), 'cena', 11. 944–82, 'Kochkunst', and 14. 524–7, 'Mahlzeiten'; J. Carcopino, *Daily Life in Ancient Rome* (1956); D. and P. Brothwell, *Food in Antiquity* (1969); K. D. White, *Progress in Food and Nutrition Science* 2 (1976), 143–91.

J. R. S.

meals, sacred, either as part of a religious festival or functioning as religious festivals. The notion that a divinity is a participant in the meal with mortals distinguishes these meals from those in which acts of devotion are part of the standard ritual of dining because the act of devotion is the occasion for the meal.

The notion that a divinity could share in a meal with mortals was common to many cultures in the ancient Mediterranean and near east (we are insufficiently informed about the cult practices of Celtic, Germanic, and indigenous African peoples to say anything about their beliefs in this regard). In some cases (banquets with the god *Sarapis, for instance), invitations would be issued in the name of the divinity, e.g. 'Sarapis invites you to dine at his temple'; in other cases the invitation would be issued by a priest (Youtie 1948; Montserrat 1992 (see bibliog. below)). *Homer may illustrate the ideology of these events when he specifically says that the gods could be seen eating with the Phaeacians (*Od.* 7. 201–3). In all such cases, it is generally understood that a god would participate with humans at a sacrificial banquet. The underlying principle was that the divinity shared the sacrificial food with those who had offered the sacrifice. Under such circumstances a specific portion of the sacrificial meal that was thought to be appropriate to the divinity in question was set aside, burned, or otherwise disposed of (it might be buried in the case of *chthonian gods, or thrown into the sea in the case of maritime immortals). It was not uncommon for a place to be set at the table for the divinity, and for the divinity to be the titular master of the banquet: thus numerous references in the sources to such items as 'the table of *Zeus', the 'couch of Sarapis', or 'the meal of the gods'. In some ceremonies certain priests might themselves eat the god's food (e.g. the festival of the Iobacchi at Athens) where individuals ate the portion of the divinity whom they represented in the procession), and thus be thought to partake directly of the divinity. This belief is most familiar in the Christian Eucharist.

The concept of the 'sacred meal' is of great importance in classical polytheism since it represented the direct involvement of the divinities in the life of a community and generated numerous associations of worshippers (see THIASOS) who celebrated their own meals with divinities for their own benefit, in addition to those meals held in conjunction with state cults. It is also symbolic of the essential connection between group dining and the concept of community in the ancient world. See DINING-ROOMS; SACRIFICE, GREEK and ROMAN; SANCTUARIES.

A. D. Nock, *Harv. Theol. Rev.* 1944, 141–74; H. C. Youtie, *Harv. Theol. Rev.* 1948, 9–29; D. Montserrat, *JEg. Arch.* 1992, 301–7; J. Rudhart and O. Reverdin (eds.), *Le Sacrifice dans l'antiquité* (1981); Burkert, *HN* and *GR*.

D. S. P.

measures of length, capacity, and weight were linked to water weight in ancient systems of mensuration. The basic units are recorded in near eastern sources from the early third millennium BC.

1. Measures of length Greek

Measures of length were based on parts of the human body, with the foot as unit both for fractions like finger and palm and for multiples like pace and arm-span. *Pylos tablets designate tables as six-footers (*we-pe-za*) or nine footers (*e-ne-wo-pe-za*); whether this is a measure or description of supports is uncertain. Homer is acquainted with the foot-standard, but the length of his foot is unknown. In historic Greece many standard feet are found, the absolute values for which are derived from surviving stadia (preserved with starting and finishing lines; see STADIUM)), and literary evidence providing correspondences with the Roman foot. The Olympic foot, said to have been taken from that of *Heracles, was of 320 mm. (12.6 in.); it is surpassed by other standards, e.g. the Pergamene of 330 mm. (13 in.), and the so-called Aeginetan of 333 mm. (13.1 in.). The latter correspond with the *pes Drusianus* of Gaul and Germany in the 1st BC (330 mm.). They were presumably based on a shod foot; contrast the Attic foot of only 295.7 mm. (11.64 in.) Subdivisions of the foot are taken from the fingers: thus

2	finger-breadths, δάκτυλοι	= 1	κόνδυλος, middle joint of finger
4	,, ,,	= 1	παλαιστή (or δῶρον), palm
8	,, ,,	= 1	διχάς or ἡμιπόδιον half-foot
10	,, ,,	= 1	λιχάς, span of thumb and first finger
12	,, ,,	= 1	σπιθαμή, span of all fingers
16	,, ,,	= 1	πούς, foot.

Higher dimensions are taken from the arms; thus

18 δάκτυλοι	= 1	πυγμή, short cubit, elbow to start of fingers
20 ,,	= 1	πυγών, short cubit of Homer and Herodotus, elbow to end of knuckles of closed fist
24 ,,	= 1	πῆχυς, normal cubit, elbow to tips of fingers
27 ,,	= 1	πῆχυς βασιλήιος, royal cubit.

For longer distances:

2½ feet	= 1	βῆμα, pace
6 feet	= 1	ὄργυια, fathom, stretch of both arms
100 feet	= 1	πλέθρον, breadth of the γύης, acre.

Beyond this Homer uses phrases such as the cast of a stone or quoit or spear. The later Greek unit, the στάδιον (*stadion*, stade, see STADIUM), originally the distance covered by a single draught by the plough, contained 600 feet, no matter what the length of the foot might be, and its exact length is therefore often doubtful (see R. Bauslaugh, *JHS* 1979, 1–6). The παρασάγγης (parasang) of 30 stadia was adopted from Persia.

Roman

The Roman foot (*pes*) of 296 mm. (11.65 in.) was generally divided into 12 inches, corresponding to the division of the *libra* into 12 *unciae*; the names of the subdivisions are the same (see WEIGHTS). There was also a division into 16 *digiti*, similar to the Greek system and possibly derived from it.

For longer distances:

5 pedes	= 1	passus, pace
125 paces	= 1	stadium
1,000 paces	= 1	Roman mile (1,480 m.: 1,618½ yds.).

2. Measures of area

Measures of area in both Greece and Rome were based on the amount ploughed in a day by a yoke of oxen. The Greek unit is the πλέθρον (*plethron*), measuring 100 × 100 = 10,000 square 'Greek' feet. Another unit, the μέδιμνος, found in Sicily and in Cyrenaica, represented the amount of land that could be sown by a *medimnus* of wheat. (Similarly, Mycenaean land measures seem to have been expressed by volumes of grain.)

The Romans employed the *actus quadratus*, a square of 120 feet, two of which formed the *iugerum* of 28,800 square Roman feet. Two *iugera* formed a *heredium*, 100 *heredia* a *centuria*.

3. Measures of capacity Greek

Measures of capacity fall into two divisions, dry and wet (μέτρα ξηρά, μέτρα ὑγρά), corresponding to the primary products, corn and wine, of ancient agriculture. In the Mycenaean system the two divisions share the same symbols and ratios for the smaller measures; absolute values are not certain. In historic Greece the *kotylē*, which is basic to both wet and dry, is made up of six *kyathoi* or four *oxybapha*; its absolute value in various local systems ranges from 210 ml. to more than 330 ml. (7.4–11.6 fl. oz.), the most usual being 240 and 270 ml. (8.5 and 9.5 fl. oz.). The dry measures are:

4	kotylai	= 1	χοῖνιξ, at Athens a day's corn ration for a man
8	choinikes	= 1	ἑκτεύς
6	hekteis	= 1	μέδιμνος.

For liquid measure the table continues:

6	kotylai	= 1	ἡμίχους
12	kotylai	= 1	χοῦς
12	choes	= 1	μετρητής, or wine-amphora.

Roman

The basic unit in the Roman system is the *sextarius* (546 ml.: 19.2 fl. oz.), which is equivalent to the Greek *dikotylon*; its components are:

48	cochlearia
12	cyathi
8	acetabula
4	quartaria
2	heminae.

For dry measures the higher denominations are:

8	sextarii	= 1	semodius
16	sextarii	= 1	modius.

For liquid measures:

12	heminae	= 1	congius
8	congii	= 1	amphora
20	amphorae	= 1	culleus.

The *amphora* was the unit by which the burden of ships was determined (e.g. Livy 21. 63). See H. T. Wallinga, *Mnemosyne* 1964, 1 ff.

See also WEIGHTS.

Ventris–Chadwick, *Docs.*; O. Viedebantt, *Forschungen zur Metrologie des Altertums* (1917); F. Hultsch, *Reliquiae Scriptorum Metrologicorum* (1882); P. Tannery, Dar.–Sag. 'Mensura'; M. A. Powell, *Reallexikon der Assyriologie* 9 (1987–90), 457–517, 'Masse und Gewichte'.

F. N. P.; M. L.; M. V.

mechanics, specifically the description and explanation of the operations of machines (*mēchanai*); the ancient discipline embraces physical, geometric, and practical aspects. The earliest systematic effort to account for mechanical phenomena, the *Peripatetic Mechanica* (sometimes ascribed to *Aristotle himself), adopts as its paradigm the lever, turning on the principle that weights are moved more easily as the distance of the moving force from the fulcrum increases. In his mechanical writings *Archimedes takes an alternative approach based on the principle of static equilibrium, as exemplified by the balance: that equilibrium holds when the weights are inversely proportional to their distances from the point of suspension. Accordingly, in his efforts in *statics and *hydrostatics Archimedes introduces the conception of the centre of gravity (*kentron bareōs*), the point at which one can locate a body's entire contribution to a configuration of weights. Discussions extant with *Heron of Alexandria (mid-1st cent. AD, *Mechanics* 1. 24, 2. 35–41) and *Pappus of Alexandria (early 4th cent. AD, *Collection* 8. 5–18) extend only slightly our knowledge of the ancient barycentric theory, but include some valuable testimonia to certain lost mechanical writings by Archimedes and *Ptolemy (4). In a more practical genre, treatises on machines were compiled by *Ctesibius of Alexandria (early 3rd cent. BC), *Philon (2) of Byzantium (late 3rd cent. BC), *Vitruvius (late 1st cent. BC, *De architectura*, primarily book 10), Heron, and others. Such of these works as survive include accounts of a wide range of machines, including water- and steam-powered devices, automata, ballistic engines and their deployment in sieges, and so on. The art of the ancient *mēchanikos* apparently combined enquiries into the theory and design of devices with meticulous concern over details of their manufacture and operation.

W. Schmidt and L. Nix (eds.), *Heronis Opera* 1–2 (1899–1900); E. W. Marsden, *Greek and Roman Artillery*, 2 vols. (1969–71); A. G. Drachmann, *Mechanical Technology of Greek and Roman Antiquity* (1963); J. G. Landels, *Engineering in the Ancient World* (1978); D. Hill, *History of Engineering in Classical and Medieval Times* (1984). W. R. K.

meddix *tuticus* or *summus*, assisted by a *meddix minor*, was the senior magistrate among the *Oscan-speaking peoples. His authority differed from that of the Romano-Latin *praetura*, to which some communities, notably *Bantia, tended to assimilate the office, in being non-collegiate and yet lacking the absolute character of *imperium*, though supreme in jurisdiction and administration. The relation of *meddix minor* to *meddix tuticus* recalls that of *magister equitum* to *dictator*.

E. Salmon, *Samnium and the Samnites* (1967), esp. 87 ff.

A. N. S.-W.; A. J. S. S.

Medea, in mythology, granddaughter of *Helios, and daughter of Aeëtes, king of Colchian Aia (see COLCHIS), and his wife Eidyia; ancient writers frequently associate her name (perhaps rightly) with μήδεσθαι, 'to devise', and she became the archetypal example of the scheming, *barbarian woman. Already in our earliest testimony, *Hesiod's *Theogony*, she is associated with the completion of *Jason (1)'s challenges in Aia in his quest for the golden fleece, and leaves Aia with him to live in *Iolcus (vv. 992–1002), but her mastery of drugs and potions, a skill she shares with her aunt *Circe, is not mentioned. This passage appears in a catalogue of goddesses who slept with mortal men, and Medea was clearly always conceived as a divine being (cf. Pind. *Pyth*. 4. 11; West on Hes. *Theog*. 992). In one Archaic legend she married *Achilles in the Elysian Fields (see ELYSIUM) after the hero's death (Ap. Rhod. *Argon*. 4. 814–15 with schol.). In the best known account, that of *Pindar, *Pythian* 4 and *Apollonius (1), *Argonautica*, Jason succeeds in gaining the golden fleece because Medea is made to fall in love with him and supplies him with a potion to protect him in the tasks Aeëtes sets him; she then charms the dragon which guarded the fleece so that Jason could steal it. In a story first attested for *Pherecydes (2) (*FGrH* 3 F 32) and *Sophocles (1) (fr. 343 Radt), Medea protected the *Argonauts from the pursuit of the Colchians by killing her baby brother, Apsyrtus, and scattering his limbs either in the palace itself or at the later *Tomis ('the cutting') on the Black Sea coast. Apollonius, however, makes Apsyrtus a young man, and Medea plots his murder by Jason on an Adriatic island (4. 395–481). On their return to Iolcus, Medea rejuvenated Jason's aged father, Aeson, (first in the cyclic *Nostoi*, fr. 6 Davies, *EGF*) and in some

versions also Jason himself (Page, *PMG* 548; Pherec. *FGrH* 3 F 113); as the instrument of Hera's revenge, she then punished *Pelias by persuading his daughters to cut him up and boil him so that he too could be rejuvenated (cf. Braswell on Pind. *Pyth*. 4. 250 (c)). After this, Jason and Medea fled to *Corinth, the setting of *Euripides' famous *Medea*, which, more than any other text, influenced later traditions about and iconographic representations of Medea. If Euripides did not actually invent Medea's deliberate killing of Jason's new bride and her own children to punish Jason for abandoning her, he certainly gave it fixed form; in earlier tradition Medea had sought to make her children immortal, and in the historical period they were the object of cult in Corinth (cf. Eur. *Med*. 1378–83). Her association with that city, attested in a complex variety of stories, goes back at least to the early Archaic period; in his epic *Corinthiaca*, *Eumelus (*c.* 700) made Aeëtes king first of Corinth and then of Colchis, and the Corinthians subsequently summoned Jason and Medea from Iolcus (frs. 2–3 Davies, *EGF*).

Medea fled from Corinth to Athens in a chariot of the Sun drawn, according to a tradition at least as old as the 4th cent. BC, by dragons; there she took shelter with King *Aegeus (cf. Eur. *Med*. 663–758). When Aegeus' son, *Theseus, came to Athens from *Troezen, Medea recognized him and sought to remove a threat to her position by attempting to poison him or having him sent to fight the bull of *Marathon, or both; fragments of *Callimachus (3)'s *Hecale* refer to these stories.

L. Séchan, *Rev. Ét. Grec.* 1927, 234–310; A. Lesky, *RE* 15. 29–64; D. L. Page, *Euripides, Medea* (1938); K. von Fritz, *A&A* 1959, 33–106; A. Brelich, *Stud. mat. hist. rel.* 1959, 213 ff. R. L. Hu.

Medea in art Medea first appears on an *Etruscan olpe of *c.*630 BC showing the cauldron of rejuvenation, with which she tricks the Peliads (i.e. daughters of *Pelias) on Attic vases from a century later, and on a Roman copy of a Classical relief, probably from the Altar of the Twelve Gods in the Athenian Agora. The slaughter of the children appears mainly on south Italian vases, also a painting by Timomachus, mid-1st cent. BC (Plin. *HN* 35. 136). From the later 5th cent., Medea usually wears eastern garb and carries potions. She appears in the capture of *Talos (1). Her snake-chariot is shown. She appears with Theseus. In Roman art, she appears particularly on *sarcophagi, contemplating the murder of her children.

LIMC 6/1. 386–98; H. Meyer, *Medeia und die Peliaden* (1980).

K. W. A.

Media, the country of the Medes, was situated in mountainous country south-west of the *Caspian Sea. The Medes spoke a language akin to Old *Persian. Fragments of the language (as either loanwords or part of a Medo-Persian *koinē*) have been identified in OP inscriptions. No Median writing has been found. Medes are attested in the annals of *Assyria from the 9th cent. BC. Sargon II (722–705) and Esarhaddon (680–669) report on Medes and their kings causing trouble. At present, 7th-cent. archaeological evidence for the Medes consists of isolated manors (Godin Tepe, Nush-i Jan, deserted in the 6th cent.); a Median style in art has so far not been identified. *Ecbatana, the main city of the Medes, still awaits excavation. Around 612 BC attacks on the major Assyrian cities by the Medes, under their king Umakištar (= Cyaxares), and Babylonians resulted in the fall of Assyria (Fall of Nineveh chronicle, Grayson (see bibliog. below)). The Babylonian Nabonidus chronicle reports that Ištumegu (Astyages) attacked *Cyrus (1) of Persia and was defeated.

Current views on the Median empire depend more on *Herodotus (1)'s *Mēdikos logos* than on near eastern (contemporary) evidence. According to Herodotus, Deioces founded the empire and instituted a court ceremonial (1. 96–101). His grandson Cyaxares organized the army and was successful against Assyria (1. 103–5). Most modern scholars regard Cyaxares as the real founder of the Median empire. Cyaxares' son Astyages is said to have ruled as a despot and was attacked and defeated by his grandson Cyrus the Persian (1. 123–30). It is debated whether Herodotus' report on Median state-formation is essentially correct and based on a reliable oral tradition, or a Greek reconstruction based on scraps of Babylonian information (Cyaxares, Astyages). It is therefore uncertain to what extent the Persians inherited political institutions from the Medes.

I. Starr, *Queries to the Sungod: Divination and Politics in Sargonid Assyria* (1990); A. K. Grayson, *Assyrian and Babylonian Chronicles* (1975); I. M. Diakonov, *Cambridge History of Iran* 2. 36–148, 'Media'; L. D. Levine, *Iran* 1974, 99–124; B. Genito, *EW* 1986, 11–81; O. W. Muscarella, *JNES* 1987, 109–26; S. Brown, *JCS* 1986, 107–19; H. Sancisi-Weerdenburg, in A. Kuhrt and H. S.-Weerdenburg (eds.), *Achaemenid History* 3: *Method and Theory* (1988), 197–212, and *Achaemenid History* 8 (1994).

H. S.-W.

Media Atropatene (mod. Azerbaijan), the NW corner and least accessible part of *Media, in the isolated mountainous zone of the Urmia basin, named after the Achaemenid satrap, Atropates (328/7–323 BC). It was left independent by the *Seleucids under local Iranian dynasts (this probably dating from 323 BC). *Antiochus (3) III made a successful show of force against the then ruler, the aged Artabarzanes, to prevent possible collaboration with potential rebels in the context of Molon's revolt (Polyb. 5. 55. 1). Seleucid garrisons at the Karafto caves and Arvoman, on the borders of Media Atropatene, are likely to have been founded to keep an eye on the region. The area was regarded as an independent kingdom (Strabo 11. 13. 1) under first the Seleucids, then *Armenia and Rome.

P. Bernard, *StIr* 1980, 301 f.; M. Schottky, *Media Atropatene und Gross-Armenien in hellenistischer Zeit* (1989); S. Sherwin-White and A. Kuhrt, *From Samarkhand to Sardis* (1993).

S. S.-W.

Medicina Plinii, an extant compilation made (probably AD 300–50) from *Pliny (1)'s account, in books 20–32 of the *Naturalis historia*, of the plants and animals used for medicinal purposes. Marcellus Empiricus describes it as being the work of a second Pliny. This work has to be distinguished from a work commonly but falsely ascribed to Plinius Valerianus, of which the first three books are a garbled version (6th or 7th cent.) of the earlier work, while the last two books come from a different source.

A. Önnerfors, *CML* 3.

W. D. R.; V. N.

medicine

1. Introductory survey 1. Western literature begins with a *disease; in the first book of *Homer's *Iliad* the god *Apollo (associated with the medical arts directly or through his Asclepiad progeny; see ASCLEPIUS) sends a plague on the Greeks camped before Troy to avenge Chryses' treatment at the hands of *Agamemnon. No attempt is made to treat the plague; the activity of doctors in the Homeric epics is generally limited to the treatment of wounds and injuries sustained in combat. Many later authorities (e.g. A. *Cornelius Celsus) argued that this was a sign of the high moral standards which then prevailed. If disease had its own moral force in literature—note, for example, *Hesiod's account of diseases escaping from *Pandora's jar (*Op.* 69–105), the role of illness and *deformity in the *Oedipus legends, in *Sophocles'

Philoctetes, in Attic comedy, and down to the Roman Stoic (see STOICISM) disapproval of over-reliance on medical help—the status and social function of those who treated diseases was similarly a matter for moral ambivalence. Mad doctors in Greek Middle and New *Comedy speak with strange, Doric accents—see *Crates (1), fr. 41 Kock; *Epicrates, fr. 11 Kock; *Menander (1), *Aspis* 439 f. (Sicily was the home of an influential group of medical theorists who claimed an ultimate connection with *Empedocles of Acragas, and Doric was also spoken on *Cos and *Cnidus.) The first Greek doctor traditionally to arrive in Rome, Archagathus, was nicknamed '*carnifex*' or 'butcher'. On the other hand, Homer had allowed that 'a doctor is worth many other men' (*Il.* 11. 514), and even in post-heroic times the number of inscriptions commemorating doctors suggests to some scholars a possible problem of undersupply. Medicine was never a profession in any strict modern sense; the vast amount of medical literature which survives from the pens of educated, philosophically literate men does not necessarily present a balanced view of the range and diversity of medical traditions, which seem to have competed on more or less equal terms. The pluralism of ancient medicine is very striking. An increasing amount of archaeological evidence which has come to light this century especially from Roman sites—medical instruments, votive objects from temples, prescription stamps, wall-paintings, and so on—goes some way towards providing a fuller picture, but the gulf between the archaeological and literary study of ancient medicine remains wide.

2. Most of the literary evidence for early medical practice and theory is preserved either in the Hippocratic writings (see HIPPOCRATES (2)) or by *Galen, but there is much besides in early literary texts, especially the Homeric epics. From earliest times, therapies might involve incantation (for example, to staunch the flow of blood from a wound sustained fighting a wild boar, at *Od.* 19. 452–8), or the use of analgesic drugs (e.g. by *Patroclus at *Il.* 11. 837–48), or the magical herb *moly* to defend *Odysseus against *Circe's witchcraft (*Od.* 10. 203–347), down to the use of *amulets and charms by the so-called 'purifiers' (καθαρταί; see PURIFICATION) and 'mages' (μάγοι; see MAGUS). Medical treatment and advice was also supplied by drug-sellers (φαρμακοπῶλαι), 'root-cutters' (ῥιζοτόμοι), *midwives (μαῖαι), gymnastic trainers, and surgeons (see SURGERY). In the absence of formal qualifications, anyone could offer medical services, and the early literary evidence for medical practice shows doctors working hard to distinguish their own ideas and treatments from those of their competitors. Some Hippocratic treatises, like *On the Sacred Disease,* indicate by their hostility the importance of medical services offered by these root-cutters, drug-sellers, and purveyors of amulets, incantations, and charms. If the traditional picture of rational Hippocratic medicine dominating ancient medical practice still attracts many modern scholars, the reality seems to have been a good deal more complicated. See MAGIC.

3. Various authorities, both ancient and modern (starting with *Herodotus (1)) have sought links with Egypt to explain the origins of certain medical practices, especially surgery, in the Greek world. Others have found links with the near east, and with Babylonian medicine in particular, although these have proved very difficult to prove. Some argue that the Hellenistic doctors working in *Alexandria (1) continued to be influenced by Egyptian traditional medicine in the 4th and 3rd cents. BC. In the 5th cent. BC, when Herodotus told (3. 129–37) the story of Darius' Greek physician, *Democedes of Croton, the really surprising feature of his career—apart from its conspicuous

success—was Democedes' technical superiority over the Egyptian doctors.

4. Medical practitioners often took their skills from town to town, visiting communities in the same way, ironically enough, as the diseases they sought to treat. (The word 'epidemic' (from ἐπιδημέω) means 'visitation'.) Little is known of the careers of such doctors. *Thucydides (2)'s account of the great *plague at Athens (2. 47) provides one of our few non-medical accounts of reaction to a great public crisis; he has little to say, however, about the doctors who treated the plague beyond the important observation that they were often the first to succumb. Herodotus is aware of the practice followed by various Greek states of hiring public physicians—he notes that Democedes held such a position at *Aegina—but very little is known of the exact role of these doctors. The question of just how public these public physicians were is a difficult one; there is little evidence, for instance, to indicate that they were hired to provide free care for the citizenry, and some scholars simply see some kind of semi-official recognition of medical status lying behind these positions.

5. Nor is it clear how common were contracts and agreements like those contained in the Hippocratic Oath. The Oath is probably aimed at a specific, and perhaps rather small, group of doctors—in it, the doctor swears by Apollo, by Health (*Hygieia), and *Panacea amongst other things to revere his teacher and his teacher's family, and never to administer poison, use the knife, abuse his patients, or breach their confidences. The Oath could be as much a symptom of general medical anarchy, as of a coherent acceptance of general standards. Anyone could choose to practise; some were ex-slaves but many were free-born. In Rome, where traditional Italian medicine competed with foreign imports to an unknown extent, many doctors were Greek. Sometimes training might take the form of an apprenticeship to another doctor, attendance at medical lectures, or even at public anatomical demonstrations.

6. In the 1st cent. AD, A. *Cornelius Celsus reiterated the traditional division of medical therapy into *dietetics, *pharmacology, and surgery. The use of exercise and the regulation of one's way of life was traditionally associated with the training of athletes and gymnasts. Some dietetic lore is preserved outside medical writings in cookery books like that of the Roman *Apicius and the Greek epicure *Athenaeus (1) of Naucratis. Surgery too, was employed from earliest times although dangers in its use meant that the more invasive procedures were generally used as a last resort. The drug lore contained in book 9 of *Theophrastus' *Historia plantarum* (written probably in the 4th cent. BC) gives a good idea of the persistence of certain beliefs about the magical powers of drugs and herbs, but Theophrastus also preserves a good deal of information new and old about the very real powers of medicinal plants. This is equally the case with the much later *Materia medica* of *Dioscorides (2) (fl. *c.* AD 60). See BOTANY; PHARMACOLOGY.

2. Temple medicine Shrines and temples to the god *Asclepius formed one important focus for religious medicine. Most of the detailed evidence we have for temple medicine comes from later writers and inscriptions; and it is not altogether clear when Asclepius, rather than his father Apollo, began to become the object of veneration. That the practice of temple medicine was widespread in the 5th and 4th cents. BC, however, seems clear from the extended parody in *Aristophanes (1)'s *Plutus* (653–744). The most important temple was at *Epidaurus. Many inscriptions from here detail the practical help and advice that the faithful

received from the god as they slept in the temple precincts (it was called ἐγκοίμησις, Lat. *incubatio*, '*incubation': see Diod. Sic. 1. 53). All manner of problems were solved here, not all of them strictly medical—monuments erected by grateful patients record cures for lameness, baldness, infestations with worms, blindness, aphasia, and snakebite. One case involves the god repairing a broken wine-cup brought to the temple by a worried slave. It is widely believed that the development of the cult of Asclepius at Epidaurus received a new impetus after the great plague at Athens.

Relations between temple medicine and the medicine of the Hippocratic corpus are difficult to determine. One later tradition has it that disciples of Hippocrates established a rival temple to Asclepius on Cos but there is considerable disagreement over the antiquity of the cult here; there was another at Tricca in *Thessaly, and throughout antiquity the medical, magical, and religious seem to have coexisted in this context. In Greek and Roman temple sites, many stone and terracotta votive objects survive—models of affected parts of the body which the god was able to cure. Important later accounts of experiences of temple medicine are preserved in the *Sacred Orations* of P. Aelius *Aristides (2nd cent. AD), and the importance of *dreams is shown by the *Onirocritica* of *Artemidorus (3) of Daldis (2nd cent. AD). In many cases, it seems, diagnoses of physicians could be rejected in favour of those acquired through dreams.

3. Early medical theory Little is known about the activities of early—pre-Hippocratic—theorists who offered physiological and pathological accounts of the human body. Certain Presocratic philosophers had well-attested interests in medical theory; most important perhaps was *Empedocles of Acragas, a version of whose four-element theory was applied to the basic fluid constituents in the body. It is mirrored in a dominant strain of Hippocratic humoral pathology, as well as in the physiological theories of *Plato (1) (in the *Timaeus*) and, in all probability, those of *Philistion of Locri (see HUMOURS). Speculative theories about the origins of man, human reproduction, the internal structure of the body, and the nature of various biological processes are a feature of the cosmologies of *Anaxagoras and *Diogenes (1) of Apollonia amongst others. An early statement of the idea that health can be ascribed to some kind of balanced state of affairs in the body (the political undertone is significant) is attributed to *Alcmaeon (2) of Croton, who is also credited (controversially) with some of the the first anatomical work based on dissection. Nearly all ancient doctors ascribed disease to an imbalance of some kind or other, and Plato's pathological theory in the *Timaeus* (e.g. at 82a) similarly ascribes certain conditions to 'surfeit' or 'lack'.

4. Hippocratic medicine 1. The large and heterogeneous corpus of writings which bears the name of *Hippocrates (2) forms the core of our literary evidence for early Greek medicine. It was always agreed, even in antiquity, that the writings were not all by one person, even though some favoured Hippocratic authorship of, or inspiration behind, certain treatises. Galen, for instance, argued that the treatise *On the Nature of Man*, which is partly the work of *Polybus (3), largely represented the views of Hippocrates himself and that other works similar in character could be attributed to Hippocrates' own medical school on Cos. Galen in fact, may well have encouraged the idea that there are two distinct intellectual strains in the corpus, one 'Hippocratic', 'Coan', philosophically refined, the other more primitive, less theoretically sophisticated, and originating from a rival medical school at Cnidus. This model of medical thought has come under attack in recent years, partly due to more detailed work on the ways in which Galen reacted to his predecessors, and partly through closer analysis of these supposedly 'Cnidian' works. Moreover, although certain places seem to have been a focus for medical activity—various places in *Magna Graecia and around *Cyrene especially, as well as Cos and Cnidus—it is not at all clear that they were sites of schools in any formal sense. Intellectually and culturally, the Hippocratic corpus shows signs of influence from all areas of Greek life, not just medical life.

2. The contents of the Hippocratic corpus had apparently stabilized by the time of the Roman emperor *Hadrian, when Artemidorus Capito put together a canon of Hippocratic works. Galen still felt the need to write a treatise (now lost) entitled *The Genuine Hippocratic Treatises*. It seems that the corpus in its present form dates from this time. In common with several other ancient (and modern) authorities, the Hippocratic lexicographer *Erotian divided the writings into five categories. These form a useful framework for a brief survey.

(a) 'Semiotic' works
(b) Aetiological and physiological works
(c) Therapeutic works: Surgery; Regimen; Pharmacology
(d) 'Mixed' works (treatises which are summaries of others, or compilations)
(e) Works on the art of medicine (dealing with medical method, knowledge, deontology)

(a) Semiotic works

'Expertise at making prognoses seems to me one of the best things for a doctor' (*Prognostic* 1). The ability to interpret the signs presented by the patient and the patient's circumstances is regarded as a skill of the first importance throughout the corpus. The patient, understandably enough, was interested solely in the outcome of the disease, or the preservation of his health. Hippocratic *diagnosis had to be based on careful study of a wide range of different phenomena, from the general—age, climate, sex, way of life—to the very specific. The author of *Prognostic* (ch. 2) offers the following advice about observing an acute, potentially fatal, case, which came later to be known as the *Hippocratic facies*: 'In acute diseases, the doctor needs to pursue his investigation thus: first, examine the face of the patient to see if it resembles the face of healthy people, and in particular if it is as it is normally. Such a resemblance is a very good sign; the opposite a very grave one. The opposite signs might appear as a sharp nose, hollow eyes, sunken temples, cold ears drawn in with their lobes turned outwards, and skin hard around the face, tight, and desiccated. The colour of the whole face is pale or dark. If the face is like this at the beginning of the disease, and if one cannot yet build up a complete picture on the basis of the other signs, the doctor needs to ask if the man is having trouble sleeping, if his bowels are disturbed, or if he is hungry. If he answers 'yes' to any of these, then the danger can be considered less serious. The crisis occurs after a day and a night, if it is through these causes that the face appears thus. But if the patient does not answer 'yes', and if recovery does not take place within the above-mentioned period, one should realize that it is a sign of death.' Apart from *Prognostic*, *Prorrhetic* is an important work in this class, and there is much relevant material, especially on charting the likely course of incurable diseases, in the case histories of the *Epidemics*. Health faddists are catered for in works like *Regimen in Health*, which stand at the head of a long tradition of similar handbooks outlining precepts for healthy living.

(b) Physiology

Hippocratic doctors, by and large, were committed to the idea that the phenomena of health and disease are explicable in the same way as other natural phenomena. Many treatises, notably *On the Nature of Man*, *Regimen*, *On Fleshes*, *On the Sacred Disease*, and *On Breaths* offer answers to the basic questions that most divided ancient doctors—how is the body constructed? how is it generated? what makes it prey to disease? what is disease? and so on. Whilst concepts of balance and morbid imbalance underly many pathological theories, the nature of the balance and the elements implicated in it could be explained in many ways. For the author of *On the Nature of Man*, the balance was one of fluids or 'juices' in the body (see HUMOURS). In this treatise, the humours are blood, yellow bile, black bile, and phlegm, and they are linked to the four *elements earth, air, fire, and water, the four qualities associated with the elements, and the four seasons. Predominance of yellow bile and phlegm is particularly associated with disease. This is not the only humoral pathological system in the Hippocratic corpus—but its adoption and adaptation by Galen much later ensured its subsequent association with 'true' Hippocratic doctrine. *On the Nature of Man* opens with a blistering attack on those who explain disease by reference to one causal agent. The treatise *On Breaths*, for example, attributes all disease to 'breaths'. This debate about the extent to which the search for causes can be narrowed down continued throughout antiquity. Theoretical disagreements apart, the names and symptoms of the major diseases were broadly accepted by Hippocratic doctors. Diseases tended to be named after the affected part, or the seat of the most significant symptoms; so pneumonia (πνεύμων 'lung'), pleurisy (πλευρά 'sides'), hepatitis (ἧπαρ 'liver'), arthritis (ἄρθρον 'joint'), and so on; this was even the case for those doctors (like the later Methodists (see § 5. 3 below)), who either took a whole-body view of all disease, or denied altogether that diseases exist as specific entities. Difficulties could arise over fundamental terminological disagreements: phrenitis, for example, was named after the φρήν, which stood at various times for the diaphragm, the cerebral membranes, and even the lungs.

(c) Therapeutic works

Hippocratic therapy took many forms: treatises like *On Ancient Medicine* and *Airs, Waters, Places* stress the historical and practical debt of medicine to dietetics, which focused attention on the whole of the patient's way of life, diet, and environment. The applications of dietetics were not confined to the sick; 'precepts of health' showed the way to the prevention of disease. Yet the drug-based treatment of disease is also an important strand in Hippocratic therapy. Pharmaceutical therapies and tests (for example, for pregnancy or fertility) are especially characteristic of the gynaecological treatises (see *Diseases of Women 1–2*, *On the Nature of Woman*). Much ingenuity was expended in devising drugs to promote and test for conception—*On Barren Women* provides many examples. Explanations of why these treatments work tell us much about ancient speculative views on the internal structure of the female body (see GYNAECOLOGY). Surgery and invasive physical manipulation were also widely used, although the status of surgery was problematic because of the dangers involved. Several treatises deal with methods of reducing dislocations (*Joints*, *Instruments of Reduction*, *Fractures*), bandaging (*In the Surgery*), excision of haemorrhoids (*Haemorrhoids*), treatment of cranial trauma (*Wounds in the Head*), surgical removal of the dead foetus (*Excision of the Foetus*), and so on.

(d) 'Mixed' works

Erotian's category of 'mixed' works includes practical compendia of material dealt with under the other headings. The seven books of *Epidemics* fell into this category, as did the highly influential and pithy summaries of Hippocratic practice contained in the *Aphorisms*.

(e) The art of medicine

Authors of many of the theoretical works in the corpus take care to describe their own epistemological as well as practical methods. They often distinguish their enterprises from those of philosophers on one side, and alternative healers on the other. The author of the treatise *On Ancient Medicine* insists that medicine cannot be approached in the same way as those subjects which 'stand in need of an empty postulate' (see HYPOTHESIS, SCIENTIFIC), an attack which seems to be directed at cosmologists and meteorologists, but may also be directed at doctors tempted to import fledgling deductive methods from geometry and mathematics into medicine. The constant concern with establishing the status of medicine as a *technē*, an art, gives us some idea how tenuous this status could be. The difficulty of the task faced by the author of *On Ancient Medicine* can be seen in the use of postulates that he himself seems to make later in the treatise, when he privileges the physiological position of certain qualities such as bitter and sweet in the body. In addition to these studies, a number of works deal with the problem of how the doctor should behave with his patients and in his dealings with society generally (e.g. *In the Surgery*).

5. From the Hippocratics to Galen 1. The dominating figure of *Galen eclipsed many of his predecessors, and very little Hellenistic medical writing survives intact. None the less, recent work on Hellenistic and Graeco-Roman medicine has brought to light a great deal of new material and goes some way towards rediscovering the 500 odd years of lost medical research. After the conquests of *Alexander (3) the Great, medicine like so much else spread east to the great new centres of learning and research in the Aegean, Egypt, and Asia Minor whilst remaining in its traditional homes in the west. Medical theorists and doctors like *Diocles (3) of Carystus, Plistonicus, Phylotimus, *Praxagoras of Cos, Mnesitheus, and Dieuches of Athens were still important enough in the 2nd cent. AD to be cited by Galen. Diocles' anatomy and Praxagoras' study of the diagnostic value of the pulse and the nature of its origins in the blood-vascular system were of great importance. Aristotle's pioneering work on scientific method, psychology, and zoology proved central to much post-Hippocratic medical research, even if figures like Galen insisted that Aristotle was heavily dependent on Hippocrates for his medical and on Plato for the philosophical details. (The physiology of Plato's *Timaeus* proved a rich source of theory throughout the rest of antiquity.) Aristotle's famous exhortations to anatomical research found particular resonances in Ptolemaic Alexandria (1), where *Herophilus and *Erasistratus made extraordinary progress in anatomy and physiology. It seems likely that they even employed highly controversial techniques such as human *vivisection, using condemned criminals as subjects. *Herophilus found the Greek language insufficient to the task of describing his discoveries, and he is credited with a series of anatomical coinages, several of which remain in use today. He undertook pioneering work on the anatomy of the eyes, on neural anatomy, and the male and female reproductive systems, and his work on the diagnostic use of the pulse, following on from Praxagoras, is highly elaborate.

2. If most of the doctors mentioned immediately above subscribed to various types of humoral system (though there is some doubt about Herophilus), Erasistratus developed or adopted a strikingly different theory which shows an awareness of post-Aristotelian physical theory. Erasistratus argued that the body is composed of a 'threefold web' of elemental nerve, vein, and artery 'perceptible to the intellect'. The activities of macroscopic nerves, veins, and arteries also figure prominently in his pathological system, which accounted for disease in terms of the morbid seepage of blood into the arteries through anastomoses (a term especially associated with his theory) in their walls. Veins, for him, distributed blood through the body, and arteries the vital *pneuma* which had its origins in inspired air. Erasistratus' anatomical work, in harness with his physical theory, supported him in his conviction that the arteries did not naturally carry blood— a view quite conceivably supported by inspection of corpses. The blood we see in the arteries on dissection rushes in to prevent the formation of an unnatural vacuum, as *pneuma* leaves through the point at which the incision is made. This view was fiercely attacked by Galen in his treatise *On Whether Blood is Naturally Contained in the Arteries*.

3. The literary evidence for later Hellenistic medicine also documents the rise of sectarian groups (αἱρέσεις) of doctors who espoused different methodological approaches to medicine. If in practice the pool of treatments on which they drew remained more or less constant, the debate over how medicine should be studied, which can be discerned in much Hippocratic writing, became far more vigorous. Much of what is known about their activities is known through Galen; he insisted that he was himself a slave to no sect, often affecting what appears a rather disingenuous respect for 'common sense'. The so-called 'Empiricists' (see PHILINUS (1); SEXTUS EMPIRICUS), who espoused a medicine in which theory and speculation about diseases had no place, determined treatments on the basis of earlier experience of similar conditions, research into other doctors' experience, and, in special cases, a kind of analogical inference which justified thinking that what works for a complaint afflicting one part of the body may well work on a similar affection in another part. The complex details of their medical method are preserved mainly by Galen in a series of treatises on Empiricism, *On Medical Experience*, *Outline of Empiricism*, and *On Sects for Beginners*. These doctors, including figures like *Serapion (1) and *Heraclides (4) of Tarentum, saw themselves as quite apart from so-called rationalist or dogmatic physicians who were committed to the value of theory in various ways. This latter group was never strictly a sect— adherents of medical theories hardly make up a coherent group— and frequently the term 'dogmatic' is used in a critical sense.

One sect which went so far as to name itself after its method became particularly successful in Rome. 'Methodism' was grounded on the idea that the whole of the diseased body (and not just the affected part) presents one of two morbid, phenomenally evident states or 'communities', one called 'stricture', the other 'flux'. (Some Methodists allowed a third state, a mixture of the other two.) Theoretical reflection on the origins of these states was unnecessary for many Methodists, and the appropriate treatment followed directly on the correct identification of the general state of the whole body. The most famous Methodist physician was *Soranus of Ephesus; his work on gynaecology survives in the original Greek, and there is a paraphrastic version of his treatises *On Acute and Chronic Diseases* by Caelius Aurelianus, a 6th-cent. Methodist.

4. However much the medical sects may appear to us as a series of monolithic entities, it should be stressed that sectarian orthodoxy was rare, and a great deal of theoretical and practical

variation can be found in all the groupings, including the less well known like the *Pneumatists and other more eclectic groups. (It might reasonably be thought that Soranus' Methodism, for instance, would explicitly discourage the anatomical investigation of the human body on the ground that this is an unnecessary luxury in view of the fact that indications for treatment simply follow on from correct visual recognition of the prevailing morbid state. Yet Soranus' highly detailed gynaecological research shows that his methodological faith did not stifle his curiosity.) It should equally be stressed that not all doctors were sectarian; evidence from inscriptions points to the existence of large numbers of independent medical practitioners who were very likely to have been largely innocent of the theoretical debates going on in other quarters. Mention should also be made at this point of the important anatomical work of *Rufus of Ephesus.

6. *Galen* of Pergamum (probably AD 129–99) dominates later Greek medicine, and indeed the whole subsequent western medical tradition. He is our most important source for post-Hippocratic medicine, and the modern appreciation of Hippocratic medicine owes much to his own version of Hippocratic doctrine. A daunting amount of his work survives—nearly three million words in Greek alone—and much remains to be edited and translated to modern standards. He wrote several guides to his own works, one of which, *On the Order of his Own Books*, provides a convenient starting-point for this briefest of surveys. Here, surprisingly perhaps, he stresses before anything else the importance of what he calls 'demonstrative knowledge' (ἐπιστήμη ἀποδεικτική) in all medical work. He advises those embarking on medical studies to examine the methodological weakness of the medical sectarians, who lack, he claims, the logical equipment necessary to tell truth from fiction. (Galen's bluff and bluster and his claim to possess the means to real knowledge need to be treated with caution, but his logical skill is indeed considerable.) He then recommends an introductory study of anatomy and basic physiology. Of his own works which survive, he recommends that anatomy should begin with *On Pulses for Beginners*, and *On Bones for Beginners*, culminating in the great teleological analysis of the human body, *On the Usefulness of the Parts*. Important evidence for the nature of Galen's debt to the Hippocratics, Plato, Aristotle, and the Stoics is presented in *On the Doctrines of Hippocrates and Plato*, in which Galen investigates in very general terms the 'physical and psychical faculties of the body'. *On the Natural Faculties* presents Galen's reaction to the physiology of his Hellenistic medical predecessors.

Galen's physiological theory is based on a four-humour system which closely resembles the theory of the Hippocratic treatise *On the Nature of Man*, although many details of Galen's version draw on Stoic mixture theory—see *On the Elements according to Hippocrates* and *On Mixtures*. The application of the theory to the behaviour of drugs is dealt with in a series of extensive pharmacological treatises which draw together drug lore and theory from a variety of earlier sources. Galen is able to draw on all kinds of pharmacological writers, from the Greek Empiricist Heraclides of Tarentum to Dioscorides, Asclepiades the Pharmacist, and the Roman *Scribonius Largus. See also separate entry GALEN.

7. *After Galen* important medical compendiums were compiled by *Oribasius, *Aetius (2) of Amida, *Paul of Aegina, Marcellus of Bordeaux and *Alexander (16) of Tralles, to name only a few.

Modern scholarship is only now beginning to re-examine these figures in any detail.

See also: ANATOMY AND PHYSIOLOGY; DIAGNOSIS; DIETETICS; DISEASE; GYNAECOLOGY; HUMOURS; PHARMACOLOGY; PNEUMA; SURGERY; VIVISECTION.

TEXTS For ancient texts, see entries for individual doctors.
LITERATURE There is a great deal of modern work on ancient medicine.
Early medicine
F. Kudlien, *Der Beginn des medizinischen Denkens bei den Griechen* (1967), and *Clio Medica* 1968, 305–36; G. E. R. Lloyd, *Magic, Reason and Experience* (1979), *Science, Folklore and Ideology* (1982), and his collected papers in *Methods and Problems in Greek Science* (1991).
Temple medicine
The ancient testimony relating to the cult of Asclepius is collected in E. and L. Edelstein, *Asclepius*, 2 vols. (1945). For historical and archaeological background to the cult of Asclepius on Cos, see S. Sherwin-White, *Ancient Cos* (1978). See also G. Luck, *Arcana Mundi* (1985), and C. A. Behr, *Aelius Aristides and the Sacred Tales* (1968) (for Pergamum).
Hippocratic medicine
A selection of treatises is translated with introduction in G. E. R. Lloyd (ed), *Hippocratic Writings* (1978); see also W. D. Smith, *The Hippocratic Tradition* (1979); P. Potter, *A Short Handbook of Hippocratic Medicine* (1988) provides a general bibliographical guide. L. Edelstein's collected papers, ed. O. and C. L. Temkin, *Ancient Medicine* (1967), remain important. In general, see also the papers in V. Nutton, *From Democedes to Harvey* (1988).
Hellenistic and Graeco-Roman medicine
T. C. Allbutt, *Greek Medicine in Rome* (1921). Herophilus: B. F. Meyer and E. P. Saunders (eds.), *Jewish and Christian Self-Definition* 3 (1982), 76–100, 199–206; H. von Staden, *Herophilus: The Art of Medicine in Early Alexandria* (1989), which surveys the whole period with great authority. J. T. Vallance, *The Lost Theory of Asclepiades of Bithynia* (1990).
Greek medicine in the Roman world
J. Scarborough, *Roman Medicine*, (1969); R. Jackson, *Doctors and Diseases in the Roman Empire* (1988).
Galen
M. Frede, *Galen: Three Treatises on the Nature of Science*, (1985); M. T. May, *Galen on the Usefulness of the Parts of the Body*, 2 vols. (1968), trans. with good introd.; D. J. Furley and J. S. Wilkie, *Galen on Respiration and the Arteries* (1984); R. J. Hankinson, *Galen 'On the Therapeutic Method', Books I and II* (1991). See also bibliog. under GALEN.
Later medicine
O. Temkin, *Hippocrates in a World of Pagans and Christians* (1991).
J. T. V.

medieval Latin See LATIN, MEDIEVAL (LITERARY).

Mediolanum (mod. Milan), founded *c*.396 BC, near *Etruscan Melpum (Plin. *HN* 3. 125), by the *Insubres. Under permanent Roman control from 194 BC, it grew steadily as a *municipium* and, later, as a *colonia*. As the principal north Italian road-centre, Mediolanum became the western Roman capital at the end of the 3rd cent. AD, when *Maximian enlarged its walls: from AD 300 it was also seat of the governor of Liguria (see LIGURIANS), the praetorian prefect (see PRAEFECTUS PRAETORIO), and the vicar (see VICARIUS) of Italy. It had a circus, mint, and warehouses, and became an important centre for the applied arts. It also prospered from its position in the heart of the fertile plain of *Cisalpine Gaul. Bishop *Ambrose (374–97) built many churches, all outside the walls, making it a major Christian centre. In 403, *Arcadius (2) abandoned Mediolanum as a capital in favour of *Ravenna, and *Attila (452), *Odoacer (476), *Theoderic (1) (493), Uraia (539), and Alboin (569) successively captured it. The *Lombard city was small, with unpaved streets and wooden houses.

R. Krautheimer, *Three Christian Capitals* (1983); M. Mirabella Roberti,

Milano romana (1984); A. Salvioni, *Milano, capitale dell'impero romano 286–402 d.c.* (1990); D. Caporusso, *Scavi MM3*, 5 vols. (1991).

E. T. S.; T. W. P.

Medism (rarely Persism, though see Strabo 14. 657: the 'med-' root is a linguistic fossil from the era of *Cyrus (1)'s conquest of *Lydia) is a term whose application is normally confined to states or individuals (Gongylus (Xen. *Hell.* 3. 1. 6 with Thuc. 1. 128. 6), *Pausanias (1), *Themistocles) that voluntarily collaborated with Persia in connection with invasions of mainland Greece; see PERSIAN WARS. Exceptions (Hdt. 4. 144; Paus. 9. 6. 3; Thuc. 3. 34; Satyr. in Diog. Laert. 2. 12; Plut. *Ages.* 23; Philostr. *VS* 580; Procop. *Bell.* 8. 9, 16) cover similar situations at different periods. The context is always concrete; the word describes neither e.g. puppet-tyrants in Greek Anatolia nor generalized 'pro-Persian' feelings. Sources rarely state motives for Medism: one modern explanation, lure of the Persian lifestyle, is debatable, if more is meant than simple envy of Persian wealth (cf. *Critias DK 88 B 31 on Thessalians in 480 BC). Enforced émigrés might adopt Persian mores, though sources hardly stress it, but such assimilation is difficult to demonstrate in a Greek context. Fear of attack or hatred of Greek rivals outweighing distaste for *barbarians (itself perhaps less prescriptively solid before 480/79) seem more relevant considerations.

See also HELLENISM; ORIENTALISM.

D. Graf, *JHS* 1984, 15 ff.; M. M. Austin, *CQ* 1990, 289 ff.; C. J. Tuplin, *Achaemenid History* 7 (1991), 37 ff.

C. J. T.

Mediterranean The Mediterranean Sea, very deep and, over substantial areas, out of sight of land, little affected by tides, and less rich in marine life than many of the world's enclosed seas (but see FISHING), provided the coherence which united the classical world. It was regarded as a unity (and distinct from the encircling Ocean) from the Archaic period; both Greeks and Romans named it as being distinctively theirs (the name Mediterranean is not found before *Iulius Solinus).

This sea represents (and has done, in the shape of its predecessor the *Tethys, for some 200 million years) the complex and shifting abutment of the tectonic plates, fragmented at their edges, which make up the adjoining continents. This structural instability produces the characteristic tangled chains of high mountains interspersed with deep down-faulted basins, valleys, and plains, and an intricate coastal topography with numerous indentations, and very many *islands of every size (as well as volcanoes and frequent *earthquakes).

With its inner branch the Black (*Euxine) Sea, the Mediterranean is a major climatic feature (see CLIMATE): the distinctive pattern of summer drought and very variable winter rainfall promotes some uniformity in agricultural production. The sea is very prone to bad weather and notoriously changeable, but its numerous beaches and anchorages make it readily adaptable to the needs of communication and exchange. Contacts by sea have therefore shaped the orientation of most of the cultures of its seaboards at all periods, whether they have identified it with home like Xenophon (1)'s Greeks with their famous cry of 'thalatta, thalatta!' ('the sea, the sea!': *An.* 4. 8); built their power on what was known in systematic historiography as a thalassocracy (see SEA POWER); or rejected it like some Romans and some of the Islamic states as an inimical and alien element.

V. Burr, *Nostrum Mare: Ursprung und Geschichte der Namen des Mittelmeeres und seiner Teilmeere in Altertum* (1952); F. Braudel, *The Mediterranean in the Age of Philip II* (Eng. trans. 1972); E. C. Semple, *The Geography of the Mediterranean Region and its Relation to Ancient History* (1932); S. Arenson, *The Encircled Sea* (1990).

N. P.

Meditrinalia, Roman festival on 11 October, from *mederi* ('be healed'), that is to say, by tasting old and new *wine (Varro, *Ling.* 6. 21; Festus 110 Lindsay). The *Vinalia Priora (23 April) appropriately involved new wine; Meditrinalia probably 'healed' by mixing new wine with old.

F. Bömer, *Rh. Mus.* 1941, 51 ff.; G. Dumézil, *Fêtes romaines d'été et d'automne* (1975), 98 ff.; Latte, *RR* 74 ff.

C. R. P.

Medma (mod. Rosarno in S. Italy), a 7th-cent. Locrian colony (see LOCRI EPIZEPHYRII), which may have remained a Locrian dependency. The earliest coinage appears *c*.350 BC, and an anti-Locrian alliance of *Hipponium, Medma, and *Croton in 422 may represent an unsuccessful bid for independence. It probably suffered damage during the *Bruttian and *Syracusan raids of the 4th cent. and perhaps was abandoned by the end of the 3rd cent. BC.

M. Paoletti and S. Settis, *Medma e il suo Territorio* (1981); Hornblower, *Comm. on Thuc.* 2 (1996), n. on 5. 5. 3.

K. L.

Medon (Μέδων), name of several mythological persons, the only one of importance being the herald in *Homer's *Odyssey*, who warns *Penelope of the suitors' plot against *Telemachus (4. 677 ff.) and is spared by *Odysseus (22. 357 ff.).

Medusa See GORGO.

Mefitis, Italic goddess, protectress of fields and flocks and provider of water, associated with sulphurous vapours (Verg. *Aen.* 7. 84). Her sanctuaries were widespread in Italy, from *Cremona in the north (Tac. *Hist.* 3. 33) to the *Esquiline in Rome (Varro, *Ling.* 5. 49), and to Rossano di Vaglio (in Lucanian territory; see LUCANIA) and Amsanctus (in the region of the Hirpini Samnites; see SAMNIUM) in the south.

E. T. Salmon, *The Making of Roman Italy* (1982), *passim.*

T. W. P.

Megacles, son of Alcmaeon, of the family of the *Alcmaeonidae at Athens. He was the successful suitor of Agariste, daughter of *Cleisthenes (1), tyrant of Sicyon (perhaps in 575 BC). Later he appears as factional leader of the *Paralioi*, in opposition to the *Pedieis* ('of the Plain') led by Lycurgus, and the *Hyperakrioi* (or *Diakrioi*) led by *Pisistratus (Hdt. 1. 59–62). The precise significance of these groups, probably representing regional support, and their relation to later Cleisthenic *deme divisions (see CLEISTHENES (2)), are unclear, but *Paralioi* ('of the Coast') perhaps refers to the SE promontory of *Attica where Alcmaeonid estates may have been. When Pisistratus seized power (*c*.560), Megacles joined with Lycurgus to expel him, but then helped him to a second period of tyranny on condition that Pisistratus married his daughter. This led to a further quarrel and Pisistratus again retired before a combination of the other two factions (*c*.556). Nothing further is recorded of Megacles. He may have shared a family banishment in Pisistratus' third tyranny after 546. He was father of *Cleisthenes (2) and of Hippocrates, the father-in-law of *Xanthippus (1), and grandfather of *Pericles (1).

Hdt. 1. 59–62, 6. 126–31. Davies, *APF* 9688, pp. 371–2; R. J. Hopper, *BSA* 1961, 189 ff.; D. M. Lewis, *Hist.* 1963, 189 ff.; A. Andrewes, *CAH* 3²/3 (1982), 393–7.

R. T.

Megalopolis (*Megalē Polis*, 'Great City'), a new foundation in SW *Arcadia in the period following *Leuctra (sources differ on the date, in the range 370–367 BC). Existing communities were combined to produce a new state with a new urban centre; five

Arcadian *poleis* (see POLIS) provided *founders, but the Theban *Epaminondas is credited with strong influence. The main accounts (Diod. Sic. 15. 72. 4; Paus. 8. 27) differ on the number of communities incorporated into Megalopolis, but its territory clearly covered SW and central Arcadia, which had had no major state. The main part of the territory was a large upland basin crossed by the river *Alpheus, an area crucial for access to northern Messenia, and for travel across the Eurotas/Alpheus watershed between upper *Laconia and southern Arcadia. The new city, built in the era of liberation from Sparta, was fortified (cf. MANTINEA; MESSENE) by walls enclosing a large area; its buildings included a notable theatre and a meeting-place (the Thersilion). Some communities incorporated in Megalopolis sought to regain independence, both in the 360s and under *Philopoemen. None the less Megalopolis became the largest Arcadian *polis*, influential in the Peloponnese (see PELOPONNESUS) from the 4th to the 2nd cent. BC, often supporting Macedon. In 235 the tyrant *Lydiadas took Megalopolis into the *Achaean Confederacy, where it played a major part, despite being sacked by the Spartan *Cleomenes (2) III in 223. Megalopolis was the birthplace of the writers *Cercidas and *Polybius (1). It declined under Roman domination, but continued to exist until late antiquity.

RE 15. 127–40; A. Petronotis, *Megalopolis in Arcadia* (1973, in Greek); M. Moggi, *I sinecismi interstatali greci* (1976); M. Jost, *Sanctuaires et cultes d'Arcadie* (1985); G. A. Pikoulas, *Southern Megalopolitan Territory* (1988, in Greek).　　　J. R.

Megara, city between *Athens and *Corinth. It had only difficult access through mountains to the Corinthian Gulf, at *Aegosthena and Pagae (Pegae); its best territory, the plain near the city, was close to Nisaea, the Saronic Gulf port. Two important routes led through Megarian territory from the *Peloponnese to central Greece: the Saronic Gulf coast road to *Eleusis, and the western route to *Boeotia known (N. G. L. Hammond, *BSA* 1954) as the Road of the Towers. Megara suffered throughout her history from her more powerful neighbours. There was a doubtful tradition of early subjection to the *Bacchiadae of Corinth; but an independent Megara founded colonies after the mid-8th cent. BC, in *Sicily at *Megara Hyblaea but especially in the east, on the *Bosporus (1) (*Chalcedon, *Byzantium) and the Black Sea (see EUXINE). The tyrant *Theagenes (1) (rather after 650?) assisted his son-in-law *Cylon in an unsuccessful attempt on the tyranny at Athens; we know little more except that he 'slaughtered the flocks of the wealthy'. *Salamis (1) was disputed with Athens until *Pisistratus established Athenian control. Megara joined the Spartan alliance (see PELOPONNESIAN LEAGUE) towards 500 and fought in the *Persian Wars, but Corinthian aggression *c*.460 caused her to join the Athenians, who helped to erect the first known *Long Walls, between the city and Nisaea; the First *Peloponnesian War soon followed. Another change in Megarian allegiance enabled Sparta to invade Attica in 446, and the *Thirty Years' Peace was agreed, under which Athens agreed to give up Pagae and Nisaea. Athens' Megarian Decree (432?) restricted Megarian access to the Athenian Agora and harbours in the Athenian empire; it was a response to Megarian cultivation of sacred land on the border. Spartan diplomacy (and popular opinion) made it a significant factor in the outbreak of the *Peloponnesian War; but *Thucydides (2) was right to judge that other issues were more important. Megara suffered two destructive invasions each year until 424. In that year democrats, having recently exiled oligarchic opponents, attempted to betray the city; Nisaea was taken, but *Brasidas saved Megara itself, and an extreme oligarchy was established. Megara rejected the terms of the Peace of *Nicias (1), since they did not include the return of Nisaea; it was not recovered until 410/9. The city is rarely mentioned in the 4th cent. It is unclear whether that reflects insignificance or a skilful ability to avoid involvement in contemporary struggles, even something approaching neutrality; but *Isocrates (8.117) represents her as enjoying the fruits of peace *c*.355 BC, though another border dispute with Athens followed shortly afterwards. Although the Megarians were 'the only Greeks whom not even the emperor *Hadrian could make prosper' (Paus. 1. 36. 3), the refortified city acquired strategic significance once more from the 4th cent. AD on.

RE 2 (1931) and Suppl. 12 (1970), 'Megara' 2; T. J. Figueira and G. Nagy, *Theognis of Megara* (1985); R. Legon, *Megara* (1981).　　J. B. S.

Megara Hyblaea, on the east coast of *Sicily 22 km. (14 mi.) north of *Syracuse, was founded by Megarian colonists (see MEGARA) who had previously failed to establish themselves at Trotilon and Thapsus nearby. The traditional foundation date, 728 BC, now seems confirmed by the earliest finds, which are approximately contemporary with those of Syracuse founded only five years earlier (Thuc. 6. 3–4). A dozen one-roomed square houses of the 8th cent. have been identified. Also of great importance is the location of the trapezoidal agora, which was laid out with two stoas and two temples in the second half of the 7th cent., at the same time as a regular street-grid (on two different alignments). This is one of the earliest examples of orthogonal town-planning known in the Greek world (see LAND DIVISION; URBANISM).

The city's proximity to Syracuse conditioned its history. After flourishing for some 250 years, during which time it colonized *Selinus, it was destroyed by *Gelon in 483 BC (Thuc. 6. 4. 1–2). The firm date is a valuable *terminus ante quem* for the archaeology of Greek Sicily. Restored under *Timoleon, Megara prospered in the 3rd cent., to which period a small Doric temple (? of Aphrodite), a bathhouse, and many of the houses belong, but despite new defences the city was again destroyed, in 213 BC by M. *Claudius Marcellus (1) (Livy 24. 35). Limited occupation, however, continued to the end of the republican period, and in late Roman times farms were installed in the ruins.

PECS 565–6; *BTCGI* 9 (1991), 511–34; Gabba–Vallet, *Sicilia antica* 1. 601–14; G. Vallet, F. Villard, and P. Auberson, *Megara Hyblaea* 1 (1976), 2 (1964), 3 (1983), 4 (1966). Date of temple: W. von Sydow, *MDAI(R)* 1984, 282–7.　　A. G. W.; R. J. A. W.

Megarian school, the Socratic school of philosophy founded by *Euclides (1) of *Megara in the early 4th cent. BC. Its last known head, *Stilpon, died about a century later.

Its preoccupations were ethical and metaphysical. The combined influence of *Socrates and *Parmenides is captured in its slogan 'The good is one thing, called by many names'. It taught the unity and invulnerability of virtue, reduced potentiality to actuality, and espoused some provocative metaphysical theses. 'Megarian questionings' became a byword for sophistry.

An independent branch, the Dialectical school, was founded by Dionysius of Chalcedon and included *Diodorus (2) Cronus and *Philon (6) among its members. Its work became a formative influence on Stoic logic (see STOICISM).

E. Zeller, *Socrates and the Socratic Schools* (Eng. trans. 1868); G. Giannantoni, *Socratis et Socraticorum Reliquiae* (1990); K. von Fritz, *RE* Suppl. 5. 707 ff.　　D. N. S.

Megasthenes

Megasthenes (c.350–290 BC), diplomat and historian, who lived with Sibyrtius, whom *Alexander (3) the Great appointed *satrap of Arachosia and Gedrosia (which he governed until at least 316). Megasthenes served on several embassies, 302–291, and his mission (perhaps more than one) to Chandragupta (*Sandracottus), founding king of the *Maurya empire in north India, was especially significant to his work. He embodied his firsthand experience in an Indian history (Ἰνδικά) which covered geography, including peoples and cities, system of government, classification of the citizens and religious customs, and archaeology, history, and legends. Like *Herodotus (1), Megasthenes received much of his information first hand, through interpreters. But also like Herodotus and *Hecataeus (2) of Abdera on Egypt, he idealized Indian civilization by imposing Greek philosophical notions, and he accepted uncritically native fables. But appearing at a time when western interest in India had been stimulated by the campaigns of Alexander and his Successors (*Diadochi), the *Indika* provided the Greeks with the fullest account yet of India. Together with the lesser works of the historians of Alexander's expedition, it was the source for many centuries of the western world's knowledge of the country. It was used by *Diodorus (3), *Strabo, and *Pliny (1) the Elder, and was the chief source of *Arrian's Ἰνδική.

FGrH 715. T. S. Brown, *The Greek Historians* (1973), 141–51; A. Zambrini, *ASNP* 1982, 71–149; S. Sherwin-White and A. Kuhrt, *From Samarkhand to Sardis* (1993), 95 ff. G. L. B.; K. S. S.

Meidias See DEMOSTHENES (2); LAW AND PROCEDURE, ATHENIAN, 3(h).

Meilichios, a cult epithet meaning roughly 'who can, but needs to, be propitiated'. The primary Meilichios was *Zeus. He was a god of individuals and of semi-familial groups (K. Forbes, *Philol.* 1956) more often than of cities, a frequent recipient of private dedications, and a giver of wealth (Xen. *An.* 7. 8. 1–6). *Sacrifices to him were often of non-standard type (wineless *libations, victims burnt whole), and his festival at Athens, the *Diasia, was marked by 'a certain grimness'. He was sometimes associated in cult with the Eumenides (*Erinyes), and could be portrayed as a giant *snake. Moderns therefore categorize him as a '*chthonian' god, one threatening but powerful to confer benefits.

Nilsson, *GGR* 1. 411–14; Burkert, *GR* 428 n. 24; M. H. Jameson, *BCH* 1965, 159–65; *SEG* 38. 997. R. C. T. P.

Mela See ANNAEUS MELA; POMPONIUS MELA.

Melampus (1), mythical seer and ancestor of the Melampodids, Greece's most renowned family of seers. The young, unmarried seer Melampus won a bride for his brother Bias, and for himself a part of a kingdom with its kingship. The kernel of this myth belongs to the older strata of Greek mythology, as Melampus' knowledge of the language of snakes and woodworms demonstrates (*Od.* 11. 281–97, 15. 231–6). But his kingship is almost certainly the invention of the Melampodids, who probably tried to strengthen their position by this myth. Melampus is also connected with girls' *initiation. He is the king's son who with a band of youths catches the daughters of *Proetus and cures them of madness. Melampus was worshipped in *Arcadia, witness his Melampodeon and the personal name Melampodorus.

K. Dowden, *Death and the Maiden* (1989), 96–115; E. Suárez de la Torre, *LEC* 1992, 3–21; M. Jost, *BCH* Suppl. 22 (1992), 173–84 (Arcadia); E. Simon, *LIMC* 'Melampous'. J. N. B.

Melampus (2) (3rd cent. BC), author of two extant works on *divination, Περὶ παλμῶν μαντικῆς ('On Divination by Palpitation': ed. H. Diels, *Abh. Berl. Akad.* 1907) and Περὶ ἐλαιῶν τοῦ

σώματος ('On Birthmarks': ed. J. G. F. Franz, *Scriptores Physiognomoniae Veteres*, 1780).

Melanippides (1) (late 6th/early 5th cent. BC), *dithyrambic poet, of Melos, grandfather of Melanippides (2). The *Marmor Parium testifies to a victory at the Athenian *Dionysia in 494/3. So the notice in the *Suda* which distinguishes two dithyrambographers named Melanippides seems to be reliable.

D. F. Sutton, *Dithyrambographi Graeci* (1989), 18 f.; M. L. West, *Greek Music* (1992), 357. B. Z.

Melanippides (2) (2nd half of the 5th cent. BC), *dithyrambic poet, of *Melos, grandson of Melanippides (1). *Pherecrates (fr. 155. 3 ff. KA) introduces him as musical innovator and corrupter of the traditional dithyrambic music. He altered the structure of the dithyramb by writing astrophic compositions (*anabolai*) (Arist. *Rh.* 3. 9). His scanty remains are of a *Danaides*, a *Marsyas* (in which *Athena flings away a flute in disgust), and a *Persephone*. His fame is attested by *Xenophon (1) (*Mem.* 1. 4. 3).

TEXT Page, *PMG* 392 ff.; D. F. Sutton, *Dithyrambographi Graeci* (1989), 43 ff.
LITERATURE P. Maas, *RE* 15/1. 422 f.; M. L. West, *Greek Music* (1992), 357 f.; B. Zimmermann, *Dithyrambos* (1992), 125 f. B. Z.

Melanippus, one of the Theban champions who opposed the *Seven Against Thebes. Aesch. *Sept.* 407–16 tells us only that he was a descendant of the Spartoi and defended the Gate of *Proetus against Tydeus. But a fuller story, attested at e.g. Statius *Theb.* 8. 716–66 and ps.-Apollod. 3. 6. 8 and illustrated on 5th-cent. BC vases, must already have existed in epic. Here Melanippus wounds *Tydeus but is killed by him or by *Amphiaraus. Amphiaraus or *Capaneus brings the head of Melanippus to Tydeus, who sucks out the brains. *Athena, who had intended to give immortality to Tydeus, withholds the gift in disgust, and he dies.

Herodotus 5. 67 records that *Cleisthenes (1) of Sicyon, being at war with *Argos (2), brought an image of Melanippus from Thebes and transferred to him certain rites that the Sicyonians had previously paid to his enemy, the Argive *Adrastus (1).

The same name is borne by several other figures in myth and epic.

J. D. Beazley, *JHS* 1947, 1–7. A. L. B.

Melanthius (1), a 5th-cent. BC tragic poet, possibly son of *Philocles and brother of *Morsimus, was often mocked by comic poets for expensive gastronomic tastes and other faults: Ar. *Peace* 803–18, 1009–15 (where a *Medea*, probably by him, is parodied), *Birds* 150–1; Ath. 8. 843c. He can hardly be the same as the Melanthius whose elegiac verses addressed to *Cimon are cited by *Plutarch, *Cim.* 4. Yet another Melanthius (of Rhodes) was a tragic poet and philosopher of the 2nd cent. BC.

TrGF 1². 136–8, 303, 348; West, *IE*² 2. 82–3. A. L. B.

Melanthius (2) (4th cent. BC), painter. Pupil of *Pamphilus (1), whom he probably succeeded as head of the Sicyonian 'school'. The picture of Aristratus in his victorious chariot was painted by 'all those about Melanthius' including *Apelles; no other work by him is mentioned. Apelles admitted his superiority in composition. He wrote on painting, and said that works of art, like characters, should show a certain stubbornness and harshness (in contrast to Apelles' boasted 'charm'). See PAINTING, GREEK.

T. B. L. W.

Melanthius (3). Probably an Athenian, maybe an *exēgētēs, he wrote an *Atthis in at least two books. Only one fragment (describing an earthquake) has survived. He also wrote on the Eleusinian *mysteries (see ELEUSIS). Three fragments remain. The most interesting concerns *Diagoras of Melos. He flourished sometime between 350 and 270 BC.

FGrH 326.   P. E. H.

Meleager (1), in mythology son of *Ares or of *Oeneus, king of the Aetolians of Calydon (see AETOLIA), and Althaea. He was the great hero of the Calydonian boar-hunt, the story of which is first found in Homer, told by *Phoenix (2) during the Embassy to *Achilles. Oeneus forgot to sacrifice to Artemis, and she, in anger, sent a great wild boar to ravage the country. Meleager gathered huntsmen and hounds from many cities and killed the boar. The goddess then stirred up strife between Aetolians and *Curetes over the head and hide of the boar, and a violent battle ensued (*Il.* 9. 529 ff.). From this point on, Homer seems to develop the traditional story in order to create a *paradeigma* (example) paralleling Achilles' situation, the better for Phoenix to persuade him back to battle. While Meleager fought, all went well for the Aetolians, but when he withdrew from battle (out of anger with his mother, who had cursed him for the 'slaying of a brother') the Curetes attacked their city more and more violently. Meleager was offered gifts and was entreated to return to battle by priests, his father, mother, and sisters; but he refused. Only when his wife Cleopatra entreated him did he go and fight, but then too late to receive the offered gifts. Elsewhere (2. 642) the fact of his death is mentioned, but not the manner of it. In other epic versions, the *Ehoiai* (fr. 25 M–W) and the *Minyas* (see Paus. 10. 31. 3), he is killed by Apollo.

In later legend the manner of his death changes. Shortly after his birth the Moirai (see FATE) had said that he would live until a brand then on the fire burned away. His mother extinguished the brand and kept it safe for many years until, after the boar-hunt, Meleager killed her two brothers, either accidentally (Bacchyl. 5. 93 ff.), or in anger when, after he had given the hide of the boar to *Atalanta with whom he was in love, they took it away from her (Apollod. 1. 8. 2–3; ultimately from *Euripides' *Meleager*? Cf. Ov. *Met.* 8. 268 ff.). At this Althaea threw the brand into the fire and Meleager died, whereupon she killed herself.

The hunt of the Calydonian boar was a popular subject in art from the 6th cent. BC. For this and other scenes relating to Meleager, see S. Woodford and I. Krauskopf, *LIMC* 6/1. 414–35; see also, in general, J. R. March, *The Creative Poet, BICS* Suppl. 49 (1987), 29–46.   J. R. M.

Meleager (2) (fl. 100 BC), poet and philosopher from Gadara in *Syria; lived in *Tyre and retired to *Cos in old age. His autobiographical poems claim that he was trilingual, speaking Greek, Syrian, and Phoenician (*Anth. Pal.* 7. 417–19; M. Luz, *SIFC* 1988, 222–31). He wrote *Menippean satires, Cynic discourses in a medley of prose and verse, now lost. But his chief claim to fame is his *Garland*, a substantial collection of epigrams by poets of the preceding two centuries, artistically arranged by alternation of authors and thematic links between poems. His preface (*Anth. Pal.* 4.1) names all his contributors, assigning each the name of a flower. His own poems are almost entirely erotic, addressed indifferently to boys and girls. His themes are taken from predecessors like *Callimachus (3) and *Asclepiades (2), but developed with extraordinary versatility and felicity of expression. His language is sometimes simple but often flamboyant, with all the traditional imagery of Cupids, bows, torches, thunderbolts, and honey, but his metre follows precise rules.

See too ANTHOLOGY; CYNICS; EPIGRAM, GREEK.

Gow–Page, *HE*; D. L. Page, *Miscellanea ... Rostagni* 1963, 544–7; D. H. Garrison, *Mild Frenzy* (1978); S. Tarán, *The Art of Variation in the Hellenistic Epigram* (1979).   A. D. E. C.

Meletus (1), an Athenian tragic poet attacked by *Aristophanes (1) (frs. 117, 156 KA). The name is very common and causes much confusion. This Meletus is thought to have been the father of *Meletus (2), the accuser of *Socrates, but it may have been the son, not the father, who wrote an *Oedipodeia* (Ar. fr. 453 *KA*). The writer of erotic *scolia mentioned at Ar. *Frogs* 1302, Epicrates fr. 4, may be another man, as may the accuser of *Andocides (*On the Mysteries* 94).

TrGF 1². 186–8. D. MacDowell, *Andokides: On the Mysteries* (1962), 208–10.   A. L. B.

Meletus (2), perhaps son of Meletus (1); the titular accuser of *Socrates in 399 BC, though *Anytus was Socrates' real opponent. He may be the Meletus who in 399 accused *Andocides of impiety (Andoc. 1. 94) and the author of the speech against Andocides preserved as Lysias 6.

H. J. Blumenthal, *Philol.* 1973.   M. Ga.

Melicertes was flung by his mother Ino (see INO-LEUCOTHEA), when pursued by *Athamas, into the sea. A dolphin carried his body ashore; he received a new name, Palaemon, and the *Isthmian Games were instituted in his honour (Paus. 1. 44. 7 f.). His cult took place in *Poseidon's sanctuary and received new impetus in Roman times, when a temple and precinct were built under Hadrian; the temple is illustrated on coins of the period.

Burkert, *HN* 197 f.; E. Vikela, *LIMC* 'Melikertes'; E. R. Gebhard, in T. Gregory (ed), *The Roman Corinthia* (1993).   J. N. B.

Melinno, author of poem in five sapphic stanzas on the world-power of Rome, quoted in error by *Stobaeus (3. 7. 12), who calls her a native of *Lesbos, though the dialect is more akin to that of choral lyric. Her date is much disputed; suggestions range from the 3rd cent. BC to the early Principate (the latter dating is based on metrical features shared with *Statius), though the absence of a reference to the *princeps points to the republican period. The first half of the 2nd cent. BC seems the most likely date. Despite some similarities in images and ideas, there is no reason to suppose that she was influenced by Latin poetry.

TEXT *Suppl. Hell.* 268 f.
TRANSLATION D. J. Rayor, *Sappho's Lyre* (1991), 141 f.
CRITICISM C. M. Bowra, *JRS* 1957, 21 ff. (= *On Greek Margins* (1970), 199 ff.); R. Mellor, *Thea Roma* (1975), 122 ff.   C. C.

Melissa (Μέλισσα, 'Bee'). Like its Hebrew equivalent Deborah, this is occasionally found as a proper name, also as a title, especially of priestesses of *Demeter (according to schol. Pind. *Pyth.* 4. 104); of *Artemis (Aesch. *TrGF* 3 fr 87); of *Rhea (Didymus (1) quoted below), besides the Asianic cult of the Ephesian *Artemis, whose regular symbol is a bee; that, however, her priestesses were called *melissai* is not quite certain, see C. Picard, *Éphèse et Claros* (1923), 183 f. One or two minor heroines of mythology are so named, the best known being the sister of *Amaltheia; both were daughters of Melisseus king of Crete, who was the first to sacrifice to the gods. While her sister fed the infant *Zeus with milk, she provided honey for him, and was afterwards made the first priestess of the Great Mother, meaning presumably Rhea (Didymus in Lactant. *Div. inst.* 1. 22, from his commentary on *Pindar, the probable source of the above scholion). *Columella (*Rust. 9. 2. 3) mentions a 'very beautiful woman Melissa whom

Melissus

Jupiter turned into a bee', generally taken to refer to the same story. See HONEY.

LIMC 6. 1 (1992), 444–6.   H. J. R.

Melissus, of *Samos, the admiral who defeated the Athenians in 441 BC, was the last important member of the *Eleatic school of philosophy. Like *Parmenides, he saw reality as changeless and single, but he went further, describing it as boundless, with past and future, maintaining (apparently) that it is incorporeal, and denying the existence of void and thus of motion. These innovations seem intended to defend Eleaticism against theories of change proposed by *Anaximenes (1) and *Diogenes (1) of Apollonia (rarefaction and condensation), *Empedocles (rearrangement in a plenum), and probably the atomists (motion in a vacuum; see ATOMISM).

DK 30; Kirk–Raven–Schofield, *Presocratic Philosophers* 390–401; R. Vitalis, *Melisso di Samo* (1973).   M. Ga.

Melissus, Aelius See AELIUS MELISSUS.

Melissus, Gaius See MAECENAS MELISSUS.

Melita (mod. Malta), an island with highly important megalithic monuments and, later, a *Phoenician trading post. It was taken over by the Carthaginians in the 6th cent. BC and, always of strategic importance, it was acquired by Rome in 218 BC and made part of the province of Sicily. By the early 2nd cent. AD, Malta and the neighbouring island of Gozo had been granted municipal status (see MUNICIPIUM), and were administered by an imperial procurator. Punic traditions remained strong throughout the Roman period, and the island prospered from olive-oil and textile production. There are extensive 4th- and 5th-cent. AD *catacombs.

Plin. *HN* 3. 92; Diod. Sic. 5. 12; Livy 21. 51; Cic. *Verr. passim*. D. H. Trump, *Malta: An Archaeological Guide* (1972); A. Bonanno, *Journal of the Faculty of Arts, Univ. of Malta* 1977, 73 ff.; M. Buhagiar, *Late Roman and Byzantine Catacombs in the Maltese Islands* (1986).

E. T. S.; J. B.; T. W. P.

Melitene (mod. Eski Malatya), a city in eastern *Cappadocia close to the *Euphrates. The ancient *Hittite metropolis, Milid, gave its name to the district of Melitene and this in turn became the name of the city when it emerged as an important garrison town and road junction, part of the eastern frontier defences of the Roman empire. In *Strabo's time (12. 2. 6, 537) there was no *polis*, but in AD 70 the Legio XII Fulminata was stationed there (see LEGION) and the town was given municipal status (see MUNICIPIUM) by Trajan. The position controlled the approach to the important crossing of the Euphrates at Tomisa, which led to Sophene, a district east of the river assigned by *Pompey to the king of Cappadocia and still ruled by a client of Rome in AD 54 (Tac. *Ann*. 13. 7). By the late 4th cent. Melitene was part of the new province of Armenia Secunda. Remains of a legionary fortress of the imperial period have been identified as well as well-preserved fortifications which can be attributed to the time of *Justinian (Procop. *Aed*. 3. 4).

T. B. Mitford, *ANRW* 2. 7. 2 (1980), 1186.   E. W. G.; S. M.

Melito (d. *c*. AD 190), bishop of *Sardis, addressed a defence of Christianity to Marcus *Aurelius (only fragments extant), in which he sees Christ's birth as providentially coinciding with Augustus' establishment of the *pax Romana*. A sermon on the Eucharist (preserved in three Greek papyri, a Coptic papyrus, some Syriac fragments, a Georgian version, and a Latin epitome),

is both an early essay in typology and a rhetorical exercise. It is written in a florid style, with many parallels to that of *Maximus (1) of Tyre, making much use of isocolon with anaphora and homoeoteleuton.

B. Altaner, *Patrology* (1960), 133 ff.; M. Testuz, *Papyrus Bodmer XIII* (1960); S. Hall, *On Pascha and Fragments* (1979).   H. C.; M. J. E.

Melos, a volcanic island (151 sq. km.: 58 sq. mi.) in the SW *Cyclades, exceptionally fertile and rich in minerals, including sulphur, alum, pumice, and fuller's earth. It is the main source of obsidian in the Aegean, used extensively in the neolithic and early bronze age for tools and projectiles.

Widely settled in the early bronze age, from *c*.2200 BC population concentrated at Phylakopi on the north coast. Phylakopi became an important fortified administrative centre with Minoan and, later, Mycenaean connections, eventually deserted in the 11th cent. Its sanctuary has produced important evidence for bronze age cult. Melos was resettled *c*.900 BC from Laconia during the *Dorian colonization of the southern Aegean. The ancient city (mod. Trypiti/Plaka) occupied an acropolis overlooking the Great Bay, its early wealth apparent in its cemeteries. From the 8th to the 6th cent. BC farmsteads and villages were widespread, contracting in the unsettled conditions of the later 6th cent. Melos contributed two pentekontors (50-oared warships) to the Greek fleet in 480 BC (see SALAMIS, BATTLE OF) and remained independent until the *Peloponnesian War, when Athens could no longer tolerate its neutrality. Following a failed expedition in 426, a more determined campaign in 416–15 ended in execution of the men, enslavement of the women and children, and establishment of an Athenian *cleruchy. This was expelled by *Lysander in 405, and Melos was resettled with its former inhabitants. Prosperity returned and increased under the Roman empire. Large villas attest local affluence, fed by demand for its mineral products, processed and exported from extensive coastal installations. *Catacombs at the ancient city imply a large early Christian community. Commercial activity continued into the Dark Ages, outliving the ancient city, deserted by *c*. AD 650.

Thuc. 3. 84. *RE* 15/1 (1931), 567 ff.; *PECS* 570–1; *IG* 12. 3; T. D. Atkinson and others, *Excavations at Phylakopi in Melos* (1904); C. Renfrew and M. Wagstaff (eds.), *An Island Polity* (1982); C. Renfrew and others, *The Archaeology of Cult* (1985); I. Malkin, *Myth and Territory in the Spartan Mediterranean* (1994), 73 ff.   R. W. V. C.

Memmius (1) (*RE* 5), **Gaius,** tribune 111 BC, attacked the nobles for corruption in dealing with *Jugurtha. He summoned Jugurtha to Rome, but a colleague prevented his interrogation. He was a vigorous prosecutor before the tribunals of C. *Mamilius Limetanus. Praetor after 107, he was prosecuted for extortion (probably) in Macedonia, but acquitted despite M. *Aemilius Scaurus (1)'s testimony. Standing for the consulship of 99, he was killed by his competitor C. *Servilius Glaucia. He was probably military tribune at *Numantia and censured by P. *Cornelius Scipio Aemilianus, though this has been doubted (Sumner, *Orators* 85 f.).   E. B.

Memmius (2) (*RE* 8), **Gaius,** married *Sulla's daughter Fausta. In 66 BC, apparently as tribune, he attacked the Luculli and succeeded in delaying the *triumph of L. *Licinius Lucullus (2). As praetor 58 he was hostile to *Caesar. In 57 he went as governor to Bithynia. In 55 he divorced Fausta, who now married T. *Annius Milo, in 54 stood for consul with Caesar's support; but his chances were ruined by an electoral scandal which he himself revealed (see CLAUDIUS PULCHER (3), AP.); eventually condemned for *ambitus, he went into exile in Athens (52). In 50 he had hopes of restoration; we do not know if they were realized. He died before 46. Gaius, his son, was suffect consul in 34. Memmius was something of an orator and poet, and a literary patron; *Catullus (1) and C. *Helvius Cinna accompanied him to Bithynia, and *Lucretius dedicated his De rerum natura to him.

Schanz–Hosius 1. 276, 310 f.; A. Biedl, *Wien. Stud.* 1930, 98 ff.; 1931, 107 ff.; G. della Valle, *Rend. Linc.* 1939, 737 ff.; *ORF*⁴ 401 ff.; B. Farrington, *Anales de filología clásica* 1959, 13 ff.; D. R. Dudley (ed.), *Lucretius* (1965), 19 ff.   T. J. C.; R. J. S.

Memmius (*RE* 29) **Regulus, Publius,** a *novus homo, probably from Narbonensis (Syme, *Tacitus* 787; see GAUL (TRANSALPINE)), served as quaestor to *Tiberius and was promoted by him. He was *suffect consul in AD 31 and handled the overthrow of *Sejanus for Tiberius in the senate. He governed Moesia, Macedonia, and Achaia 35–44, but was forced to come to Rome in 38, to give his wife *Lollia Paulina in marriage to *Gaius (1), pretending to be her father. At least since that year, he belonged to the *fratres arvales. He was proconsul of Asia (probably) 48–49 and remained influential under Claudius and Nero until his death (61). Tacitus gives him a warm eulogy (*Ann.* 14. 47. 1).

Syme, *AA*, see index, and *Some Arval Brethren* (1980), 67.   E. B.

Memnon (1), a mythical king of *Ethiopia, was the son of *Eos and Tithonus (Hes. *Theog.* 984 f.). He went with a large force to Troy to assist *Priam, his uncle; and there, wearing armour made by *Hephaestus, he killed many Greeks including *Antilochus, the son of *Nestor (1) (*Od.* 4. 187 f.), who died saving his father's life (Pind. *Pyth.* 6. 28–42). Finally he fought with *Achilles while the two mothers, Eos and *Thetis, pleaded with *Zeus for their sons' lives. Memnon was killed, and Eos asked Zeus to show him some special honour. Either he was made immortal (*Aethiopis*, Proclus), or Zeus turned the smoke from his funeral pyre into birds, which circled the pyre and then, separating into two groups, fought and killed each other, falling into the flames as offerings to the hero. After this, fresh flocks of birds, named Memnonides, gathered annually at Memnon's tomb, and fought again and died again (Ov. *Met.* 13. 576–622). The dew was said to be the tears shed by Eos in grief for her son.

Many ancient writers connect Memnon with *Susa (e.g. Paus. 10. 31. 7; Strabo 15. 3. 2). On his march to Troy, he was said to have left several great steles along his route, and *Herodotus (1) notes that this has caused him to be confused with Sesostris (2. 106). He also has unmistakable connections with Egypt: there was a Memnoneion at both *Thebes (2) and Egyptian Abydos, a little to the north of Thebes; and the 'Colossi of Memnon' (see MEMNON, COLOSSI OF) were huge statues inscribed with the name of Amenophis III, one of which, when the first rays of the dawn struck it, was said to emit a musical note, as though it were Memnon greeting his mother's light (Paus. 1. 42. 3).

Memnon's final combat with Achilles and his body carried away by Eos were favourite themes in Archaic and Classical vase-painting. He is given regular heroic features, but often has black African attendants. See A. Kossatz-Deissmann, *LIMC* 6/1. 448–61.   H. J. R.; J. R. M.

Memnon (2), of Rhodes, military commander. First attested (*c*.360 BC) with his brother *Mentor (2) in the service of the Persian satrap *Artabazus, whose daughter (Barsine) they successively married, Memnon supported Artabazus' revolt against *Artaxerxes (3) III and shared his subsequent exile in Macedonia (*c*.352–342). He was reinstated in Persian favour and his estates

in the Troad after his brother's successes in Egypt, and in 336/5 he fought effectively against the Macedonian expeditionary force in Asia Minor. He was present at the *Granicus, where his fellow generals rejected his scorched-earth strategy, and his opposition to the fateful decision to engage *Alexander (3) the Great probably won him the overall command in the Aegean. He successfully organized the defence of *Halicarnassus (334), and after the demobilization of the Macedonian fleet he used his overwhelming naval superiority to capture *Chios and *Lesbos and threatened to attack Macedonia. His death at the siege of *Mytilene (summer 333) is represented as a serious blow to the Persian resistance, but it can be argued that he failed to exploit his military advantage to the full.

Berve, *Alexanderreich* 2, no. 497; A. J. Heisserer, *Alexander the Great and the Greeks* (1980).   A. B. B.

Memnon (3), of *Heraclea (3) Pontica, probably 2nd cent. AD, wrote the history of his city in at least sixteen books, perhaps following *Nymphis; books 9–16 are substantially preserved by *Photius. The work supplies a broad historical context, and from book 13 there survives a long digression on the rise of Rome.

FGrH 434. W. R. Nethercut, *Vergilius* (1976), 30–3; P. Desideri, *Studi classici e orientali* 1970/1, 487–537.   A. H. McD.; K. S. S.

Memnon, colossi of, two seated statues of Amenophis III on the west bank of the Nile at *Thebes (2) below the mortuary temples and necropolis of the Memnoneia. The latter is mentioned in *UPZ* 174 of 150 BC. *Strabo (17. 1. 46) visited the colossi with *Aelius Gallus in 26/5 BC. One of them, damaged by earthquake, regularly emitted a sound at dawn until repaired by Septimius Severus, and attracted numerous 'touristic' graffiti (see IULIA BALBILLA).

A. Bataille, *Les Memnoneia* (1952). A. and É. Bernand, *Les Inscriptions du Colosse de Memnon* (1960).   W. E. H. C.

Memor, Scaevus, tragedian, brother of the satirist *Turnus (2) (Mart. 11. 10). He was victorious at the Capitoline Games in AD 94 and was honoured with a statue (Mart. 11. 9). We have a fragment probably from a lament by Trojan prisoners (Ribbeck, *TRF* p. 269). Fulgentius, *Expositio sermonum antiquorum* 25 quotes a fragment from a tragedy *Hercules* which he ascribes to one Memos (or Memmius?): this might be by Scaevus Memor.

E. Diehl, *RE* 2 A 344.   M. Ci.

Memphis (now Mit Rahina and Saqqara), though replaced as capital under *Ptolemy (1) I, remained an important city of both Ptolemaic and Roman Egypt. At least from the reign of Ptolemy V Epiphanes (and possibly earlier) the Ptolemies were crowned according to the Egyptian rites in the city's temple of *Ptah. Important priestly edicts, including that of the Rosetta Stone (196 BC), derive from the city. Connected to the Ptah temple was the cult of *Apis—in its Osiriac form precursor to *Sarapis—which, together with other necropolis animal-cults, made the city a centre for tourists and pilgrims. Caches of Greek and demotic papyri from the necropolis illuminate the Hellenistic city. Less is known of Roman Memphis, which served as a legionary camp less important than neighbouring Babylon.

D. J. Thompson, *Memphis under the Ptolemies* (1988).   D. J. T.

Men (Μήν, also Μείς), one of the most important gods of west Anatolia (see ANATOLIAN DEITIES). Etymology uncertain, but the name must derive from a native language. From its home territory of Mysia Abbaitis and west *Phrygia, the cult spread south and east to *Pisidia and *Lycaonia, and down the *Hermus valley.

Menaechmus

The earliest iconography was formed in *Attica, where a few dedications by *metics (4th–3rd cent. BC) survive. Almost all the other evidence is Anatolian, from the Principate (no significant literary evidence). The c.370 surviving inscriptions suggest a high god (Τύραννος, Οὐράνιος, Μέγας) invoked to obtain healing, safety, and prosperity, confirmed by the iconography of Men riding a horse, or carrying spear or sceptre. His most characteristic sign is the crescent moon, either alone or behind his shoulders; as moon-god, Men was linked with the Underworld, agricultural fertility, and the protection of tombs. The cult was highly local: Men almost always bears a native local epithet, and sometimes the name of the local cult-founder too. Different aspects of the god seem to be stressed in each area. There were several large temple-estates with tied villages (Strabo 12. 3. 31; 8. 14, 20).

A quarter of the epigraphic evidence comes from the temple of Men Askaenus near *Antioch (2) in Pisidia, revealing the gradual assimilation of the Roman military colonists into local religious life. Many of these votives 'testify' to the god's intervention. Men is also the god whose power is most commonly 'written up on a *stele' in the 'confession texts' of Maeonia (border of Lydia/Mysia). Typically they recount how the dedicant was punished with misfortune after committing an offence against the god (e.g. impurity) or a neighbour (especially theft). These steles are important evidence for the symbolic role of inscriptions (see EPIGRAPHY, GREEK, text attached to n. 28).

E. N. Lane, *Corpus monumentorum religionis dei Menis*, 4 vols. (1971–8), and *ANRW* 2. 18. 3 (1990), 2161–74; A. van Haepern-Pourbaix, *Mélanges P. Naster* (1983), 221–57; R. Vollkommer, *LIMC* 6 (1992), 462–73.

R. L. G.

Menaechmus (1), of *Sicyon, Greek historian who wrote about *Alexander (3) the Great, about his native Sicyon, and about music. *Aristotle's list of Pythian victors (see PYTHIAN GAMES) is supposed to have superseded a work by Menaechmus.

FGrH 131. Pearson, *Lost Histories of Alexander* 250 ff. S. H.

Menaechmus (2) (fl. mid-4th cent. BC), geometer, disciple of *Eudoxus (1) of Cnidus, offered a solution of the problem of two mean proportionals. A text of the solution is reported in the Archimedes commentary by Eutocius of Ascalon. As the solution employs conic sections (a hyperbola and two parabolas), Menaechmus must have anticipated in some manner the theory of conic sections, first compiled about a half-century later by *Euclid and by the mathematician Aristaeus of Croton. *Proclus cites Menaechmus for views on the nature of geometric propositions. See MATHEMATICS.

W. R. Knorr, *Ancient Tradition of Geometric Problems* (1986), 61–6, 351–2, and *Textual Studies in Ancient and Medieval Geometry* (1989), 94–100; H. R. Mendell, 'Aristotle and the Mathematicians' (Ph.D. diss., Stanford University, 1986) 320–6. W. R. K.

Menander (1) (Μένανδρος, ? 344/3–292/1 BC), the leading writer of New Comedy (see COMEDY (GREEK), NEW), although in his own time less successful (with only eight victories) than *Philemon (2). An Athenian of good family, he is said to have studied under the philosopher *Theophrastus and the playwright *Alexis, and to have been a friend of *Demetrius (3) of Phaleron, the pro-Macedonian regent of Athens from 317 to 307. Making his début probably in 324 or 323, he wrote over 100 plays, many of which must have been intended for performance outside Athens. Nearly 100 titles are known, but some may be alternatives attached to plays restaged (as happened frequently) after Menander's death.

Menander's plays were lost in the 7th and 8th cents. AD as a result of Arab incursions and Byzantine neglect, but in modern times many papyri have been discovered, attesting great popularity in Ptolemaic and Roman Egypt. These include one virtually complete play, *Dyskolos* ('Old Cantankerous': victorious at the *Lenaea in 316), and large enough portions of six others to permit some literary judgement: *Epitrepontes* ('Arbitration', a mature work half-preserved intact and named after a brilliant scene), *Perikeiromene* ('Rape of the Locks', nearly half of its clear plot surviving), *Samia* ('Girl from Samos', four-fifths preserved), *Aspis* ('Shield', first half), *Sikyonios* ('Sicyonian', some 180 lines more or less complete, fragments of 250 or so others), and *Misoumenos* ('Man She Hated', tantalizing remains of a popular and exciting comedy, about 175 lines complete or comprehensible). There are smaller but important fragments of *Dis Exapaton* ('Double Deceiver'), *Georgos* ('Farmer'), *Heros* ('Hero'), *Theophoroumene* ('Girl Possessed'), *Karchedonios* ('Carthaginian'), *Kitharistes* ('Harpist'), *Kolax* ('Flatterer'), *Koneiazomenai* ('Drugged Women'), *Perinthia* ('Girl from Perinthus'), *Phasma* (Phantom), and of several still unidentified plays.

In addition ancient authors have preserved over 900 quotations, ranging from a single word to sixteen lines. Some are witty, some impressively moving, some sententious, but the lack of dramatic context normally prevents evaluation of serious or ironic intent. There also exist several collections of one-line maxims (μονόστιχοι) attributed to Menander, but only a few of these actually originated with him.

It has always been difficult to assess how far his Latin adaptors *Plautus and *Terence modified Menander's works for the Roman stage, although the tattered fragments of *Dis Exapaton* now reveal that Plautus' adaptation at *Bacchides* 494–562 was freer than most scholars had previously imagined. Plautus' *Cistellaria* was based on Menander's *Synaristosai* ('Women Lunching Together'), *Stichus* on *Adelphoi* ('Brothers') 1, Terence's *Adelphoe* on *Adelphoi* 2, *Andria* on *Andria* ('Woman of Andros') and *Perinthia*, *Eunuchus* on *Eunouchos* ('Eunuch') and *Kolax*; Plautus' *Aulularia* has often been thought to derive from Menander.

Menander's plays are always set in contemporary Greece, often *Athens or *Attica, but although the characters are aware of events in the wider world, the plots focus on private domestic problems. These often include situations less common probably in real life than on the stage (foundling babies, raped or kidnapped daughters, for instance). There is always a love-interest, but the range of situations is wide—a young man in love with a country girl or an experienced courtesan, an older man believing his mistress has been unfaithful, a husband doubting the paternity of his wife's new baby. Yet love is often only one ingredient in the drama; thus in *Dyskolos*, Sostratos' infatuation shares the limelight with his developing friendship with Gorgias and Knemon's misanthropy.

Menander was a skilful constructor of plots, an imaginative deviser of situations, and a master of variety and suspense. He wrote for the theatre, highlighting the memorably emotive detail both in scenes of psychologically convincing dialogue and in long, vivid narrative speeches which sometimes recall the messengers of 5th-cent. tragedy. Tragedy may also have influenced the use of divine prologues, either beginning the play or following an appetite-whetting initial scene; these provided the audience with facts still unknown to the characters and enabled them to appreciate the irony of characters' ignorance.

Menander's plays were written in non-realistic verse (mainly iambic trimeters), yet his lines give an illusion of colloquial speech, while variations of rhythm subtly modulate tone, emotion and presentation of character. In his earlier comedies at least he introduced variety by sometimes using, for both lively and serious scenes, the trochaic tetrameter; and the last scene of *Dyskolos* employs iambic tetrameters accompanied by pipes.

The characters are firmly rooted in a comic tradition of two-generation families, with important roles for slaves, courtesans, soldiers, parasites, and cooks. Although they retain hints of the traits that were developed in Middle Comedy (see COMEDY (GREEK), MIDDLE), they are presented as credible individuals, and here two aspects of technique are significant. Menander often takes a type figure and either adds to it some unexpected touches (thus the courtesan Habrotonon in *Epitrepontes* is turned into a planning slave), or develops the expected traits in a new direction (thus the soldier Polemon in *Perikeiromene* characteristically boasts, but about his mistress's wardrobe, not military exploits). Secondly, although virtually every character speaks the same late Attic dialect, many of them are given individual turns of phrase that set them apart (e.g. in *Dyskolos* the cook Sikon's flamboyant metaphors and Knemon's simplistic exaggerations).

Menander attempts no profound psychological insights and leaves to his audiences the pleasure of deducing emotions and motives. Dialogue often moves so quickly that an alert brain is needed to grasp all the implications. A single sentence may simultaneously forward the action, describe another person, and illuminate the speaker. Characters are portrayed typically with mingled irony and sympathy, and although the dramatist is primarily an entertainer, he quietly inculcates a lesson that understanding, tolerance, and generosity are the keys to happiness in human relationships.

TEXTS F. H. Sandbach (1972[1], 1990[2]): papyri, selection of quoted fragments; A. Körte and A. Thierfelder (1959): quoted fragments; S. Jäkel (1964): μονόστιχοι. *Aspis, Samia*: C. Austin (1969–70), with notes. *Dis Exapaton*: E. W. Handley (1965). *Dyskolos, Samia*: J.-M. Jacques (1976[2] and 1971), with Fr. trans. and notes. *Sikyonios*: R. Kassel (1965).

COMMENTARIES On all the then published papyri and selected quoted fragments: A. W. Gomme and F. H. Sandbach (1973): authoritative. *Dyskolos*: E. W. Handley (1965). *Epitrepontes*: U. von Wilamowitz-Moellendorff (1925). *Misoumenos*: F. Sisti (1985). *Samia*: D. M. Bain (1983).

TRANSLATIONS N. Miller (Penguin, 1987). New Loeb edition by W. G. Arnott, in progress: *Aspis–Epitrepontes* (1979), 2 vols. to follow.

CRITICISM W. G. Arnott, *Menander, Plautus, Terence* (1975); A. Blanchard, *Essai sur la composition des comédies de Ménandre* (1983); H.-D. Blume, *Menanders Samia* (1974); J. Blundell, *Menander and the Monologue* (1980); K. B. Frost, *Exits and Entrances in Menander* (1988); S. Goldberg, *The Making of Menander's Comedy* (1980); E. W. Handley and A. Hurst (eds.), *Relire Ménandre* (1990); N. Holzberg, *Menander: Untersuchungen zur dramatischen Technik* (1974); R. L. Hunter, *The New Comedy of Greece and Rome* (1985); A. G. Katsouris, *Tragic Patterns in Menander*, and *Linguistic and Stylistic Characterization* (both 1975); F. H. Sandbach, *The Comic Theatre of Greece and Rome* (1977); A. Schäfer, *Menanders Dyskolos* (1965); E. G. Turner (ed.), *Ménandre, Entretiens Hardt* 16 (1970); T. B. L. Webster, *Studies in Menander*, 2nd edn. (1960), and *Introduction to Menander* (1974); D. Wiles, *The Masks of Menander* (1991); G. Vogt-Spira, *Dramaturgie des Zufalls: Tyche und Handeln in der Komödie Menanders* (1992).   W. G. A.

Menander (2) **'Soter'** (*c*.150–130 BC) carried Greek rule ('Yavana-raja') in *India to its greatest extent. He later embraced Buddhism and remains the only Indo-Greek king remembered in Indian literary sources. Born in the village of Kalasi (probably near *Alexandria (6), i.e. Alexandria-in-Caucaso, mod. Begram), Menander ('Milinda' in Buddhist tradition) was the son and successor of an unnamed king. He conquered the Punjab and made Sagala (Sialkot?) his capital. Then, according to both Indian and

Greek sources, he advanced deep into the heart of India and probably reached *Palibothra (Patna) in the Ganges valley. This campaign may have been aborted due to the civil wars in *Bactria and NW India associated with the rise of *Eucratides I, whose assassination in *c*.145 left Menander free to regain at least some of his lost territories. He may have been married to Agathocleia, a daughter of King Agathocles (one of the Euthydemid foes of Eucratides). She and their son, Strato I, ruled together after Menander's death in *c*.130. Plutarch records that his ashes were divided among numerous cities competing to build funerary monuments in his honour. The greatest of Indo-Greek kings, Menander successfully bridged the cultural divide between Greece and India. His reign may have influenced the development of the Buddha's image in art and the building of stupas (see GANDHARA). Likewise, his coinage beautifully blends Greek and Indian iconography.

A. K. Narain, *CAH* 8[2] (1989), 406 ff.   F. L. H.

Menander (3), of Ephesus, compiled, from native records, a Greek chronicle of the Phoenician kings 'among both Greeks and barbarians', from which *Josephus derives information on Hiram, king of *Tyre. Menander is perhaps to be identified with the Menander of Pergamum to whom a Phoenician chronicle is ascribed by Tatian and by Clement of Alexandria. See DIOS.

Joseph. *AJ* 8. 144–6; *Ap.* 1. 116–20; *FGrH* 3. 783.   T. R.

Menander (4) (*RE* 16) **'Rhetor'**, of *Laodicea-Lycus (? late 3rd cent. AD) wrote commentaries on *Hermogenes (2) and *Minucianus the Elder. Two treatises on 'epideictic speeches' pass under his name. The first (3. 329 ff. Spengel) deals with hymns, prayers, encomia of countries and cities, etc.; the second (ibid. 368 ff.), probably the work of a different writer, less polished but more lively, gives rules for ceremonial addresses to the emperor and other officials, and for birthdays, weddings, invitations, leave-takings, funerals, and special festivals. Both books (like the sections on epideictic speeches in the *Art of Rhetoric* attributed to *Dionysius (7) of Halicarnassus) deal with a branch of rhetoric remote from lawcourts and deliberative assemblies, and in some ways a substitute for the poetry of cult or special occasion. They thus contain much material useful for the interpretation of the poets. See EPITAPHIOS; EPITHALAMIUM; PROPEMPTIKON.

TEXT Spengel, *Rhet.* 3; C. Bursian (1882); D. A. Russell and N. G. Wilson (1981), with trans. and comm., including trans. of the relevant parts of the Dionysian *Art of Rhetoric*.

See also W. Nitsche, *Der Rhetor Menandros und die Scholien zu Demosthenes* (1883); J. Soffel, *Die Regeln Menandros für die Leichenrede* (1974); F. Cairns, *Generic Composition in Greek and Roman Poetry* (1972).

D. A. R.

Menander Protector (Menander Phylax or Menander the Guardsman) See AGATHIAS.

menarche See MENOPAUSE; MENSTRUATION.

Mende, city in north Greece, roughly half-way down the western side of the western (Pallene) prong of *Chalcidice. A colony of *Eretria in *Euboia (Thuc. 4. 123. 1), it was famous for its wine which features on its coins. A prosperous member of Athens' *Delian League, its normal tribute was 8 talents. It was won over by the Spartan *Brasidas in 423 BC but went back to its Athenian allegiance soon after, an episode brilliantly recounted by *Thucydides (2). It declined after the foundation of Cassandreia (see POTIDAEA) in 316. Part of the ancient city (near modern

Mendes

Kalandra) has been excavated, as has a temple of *Poseidon by the beach on the nearby promontory of Possidi. The sculptor *Paeonius was from Mende. Finds from excavations on the site can be seen in the museums at Polygiros and Thessalonike.

Thuc. 4. 123 ff.; B. D. Meritt, *AJA* 1923, 447 ff.; M. Zahrnt, *Olynth und die Chalkidier* (1971), 200–3 and in *Lexikon der historischen Stätten* 421; S. G. Miller, *PECS* 572; Hornblower, *Comm. on Thuc.* 2 (1996).   S. H.

Mendes, a he-goat often represented on Egyptian monuments as a ram and identified by Herodotus as the Greek god *Pan, was the god of Mendes (mod. Djedet) in the NE Delta where a cemetery of sacred rams has been uncovered. The cult was widespread in Hellenistic Egypt. An important hieroglyphic inscription, the Mendes Stele, from 270 BC records the divinization and entry into the Mendes temple of *Arsinoë II as a full Egyptian goddess; local taxes financed the cult. By decree her worship was thus joined to that of the chief god of each temple throughout Egypt.   D. J. T.

Menecrates (1), of *Xanthus, a 4th-cent. BC writer of the history of *Lycia (Λυκιακά) in Ionic Greek (see GREEK LANGUAGE, §§ 3, 4).

FGrH 769.

Menecrates (2), of *Ephesus, probably born c.340 BC, wrote a didactic poem called *Erga* in imitation of *Hesiod, and probably another poem on apiculture i.e. *bee-keeping (*Melissurgica*).

Ed. Diels, *PPF* 171–2.   J. S. R.

Menedemus (1) (*RE* 9), of *Eretria (c.339–c.265 BC) was sent by his city to *Megara on military service. He was there won over to philosophy (perhaps after a visit to the *Academy in Athens), and studied under *Stilpon. He moved to Elis and joined the school founded by *Phaedon; he became leader of it and transferred it to Eretria (see ERETRIA, SCHOOL OF). He involved himself in politics and attained high office, but was forced into exile by political opponents. He took refuge at the court of *Antigonus (2) Gonatas in Macedonia and died there. As a philosopher he was called an eristic, and his positive contributions, if any, are unknown.

Diog. Laert. 2. 125–44. K. von Fritz, *RE* 15. 788–94; D. Knoepfler, *La Vie de Ménédème d'Érétrie de Diogène Laërce* (1991).   D. J. F.

Menedemus (2), *Cynic philosopher of the 3rd cent. BC, from western Asia Minor, first a pupil of *Colotes the Epicurean, later of Echecles the Cynic, both of Lampsacus. He is best known from Colotes' polemic against him.

Menelaion, the *Laconian shrine of *Menelaus (1) and *Helen at ancient Therapne (Hdt. 6. 61; Isoc. 10. 63; Polyb. 5. 18. 21; Paus. 3. 19. 9); from c.700 BC occupied a commanding position on a spur high above the Eurotas, 2.5 km. (1½ mi.) south-east of *Sparta. A high rectangular terrace reached by a ramp, and retained by massive rectangular conglomerate ashlars, surrounded a *naiskos* ('small temple') built on a conspicuous knoll. Excavations (1900, 1909–10, 1973–7) recovered dedications for Helen and for Menelaus. The site survived until the 1st cent. BC. There was an extensive bronze age settlement on the spur. Though occupied in early and middle Helladic times, its ascendancy was in the 15th cent., when an embryonic Mycenaean palace (see MYCENAEAN CIVILIZATION) was built, the earliest of its kind on the Greek mainland. The 'palace' was demolished and rebuilt on a new axis soon after its completion. 'Palace' and size of settlement combine to suggest that here, and not at the Palaeopyrghi site by the Vaphio tholos 5.5 km. (3½ mi.) south-south-

east, was the Mycenaean centre of the upper Eurotas valley. Parts of the site were burnt c.1200 BC; it was abandoned shortly afterwards. Doubtless its significance was understood by the later builders of the Menelaion.

ΠΑΕ 1900, 74 ff; *BSA* 1908–9, 108 ff; 1909–10, 4 ff; *Arch. Rep.* 1976–7, 24 ff.; R. Barber, in J. Sanders (ed.), *Philolakon* (1992), 11 ff.

H. W. C.

Menelaus (1), younger brother of *Agamemnon and husband of *Helen; king of *Sparta (though *Aeschylus, *Ag.* 400, makes him share his brother's palace at *Argos (2)). The abduction of his wife by *Paris caused the Trojan War. In *Homer's *Iliad* he is sometimes effective in battle (notably in book 17, where most of the other Greek leaders are absent), and he defeats Paris in a duel at 3. 340–82. He is consistently portrayed, however, as a (relatively) 'gentle warrior' (17. 588), inferior to the best fighters but honourable and courageous (at 6. 37–65 he wishes to spare the Trojan Adrestus until overruled by Agamemnon, and at 7. 94–122 he volunteers for a hopeless duel with the far stronger *Hector). In Homer, *Odyssey* 4, he is seen at Sparta as a wealthy and hospitable king and recounts his adventures on his way home from Troy. These include his visit to Egypt and his encounter with *Proteus, who prophesied that instead of dying he would finally be translated to *Elysium (4. 561–9).

In tragedy his character deteriorates, like that of Helen. In *Euripides' *Trojan Women* he is a weak man, who clearly lacks the resolve to kill his guilty wife, while in *Sophocles (1)'s *Aias* and Euripides' *Andromache* and *Orestes* he shows varying degrees of unpleasantness. He is a sympathetic character, however, in Euripides' more light-hearted *Helen*. *Herodotus (1), 2. 119, surprisingly makes him sacrifice two Egyptian children.

He shared a tomb and cult with Helen at Therapne near Sparta (see MENELAION).   A. L. B.

Menelaus (2), Greek sculptor, pupil of Stephanus and member of the school of *Pasiteles, working at Rome in the 1st cent. AD. Known from a signature on a group of Orestes and Electra in the Terme, for which he has adapted motives of the 4th cent. BC, but Orestes wears his cloak Roman fashion. Identified with M. Cossutius Menelaus who signed a lost statue, one of the *Cossutii.

J. Pollitt, *Art in the Hellenistic Age* (1986), 175; A. F. Stewart, *Greek Sculpture* (1990), fig. 861.   T. B. L. W.; A. J. S. S.

Menelaus (3) (*RE* 16), of *Alexandria (1) (fl. AD 95–8), mathematician and astronomer, made astronomical observations at Rome in 98 (Ptol. *Alm.* 7. 3), and was known to *Plutarch (*De fac.* 17). The following works by him are extant (only in Arabic translation). (1) *Sphaerica*, in three books, is a textbook of spherical geometry, which contains the earliest theorems on spherical trigonometry. Book 1 gives the definition of a spherical triangle (τρίπλευρον), and develops theorems modelled on *Euclid's for the plane triangle. Book 2 is concerned with the solution of problems important for spherical astronomy, in a more elegant way than such predecessors as *Theodosius (4). Book 3 treats the basis of spherical trigonometry. Proposition 1 is 'Menelaus' Theorem', which was used by subsequent astronomers (e.g. *Ptolemy (4)) to solve spherical triangles. It is probable that much of this treatise was original: it superseded earlier methods of solving spherical problems (see TRIGONOMETRY). (2) *On Specific Gravities*, dedicated to the emperor *Domitian.

Other works by Menelaus included a chord-table (Theon (4), *Comm. on Almagest* 1, ed. A. Rome, 451) and a treatise on the elements of geometry in three books (cited by al-Bīrūnī, see Suter, *Bibl. Math.* 3 F. 11, 31 ff.).

TEXTS AND TRANSLATIONS *Sphaerica*: ed. M. Krause (1936), with Ger. trans.; Lat. trans. by Halley (1758). *On Specific Gravities*: Arabic unedited, in MS Escurial 960; Ger. trans. by Wurschmidt, *Philol.* 1925, 377–409.

COMMENT A. A. Björnbo, *Studien über Menelaos' Sphärik*, *Abh. zu Gesch. d. Math.* 14 (1902); Heath, *Hist. of Greek Maths.* 2. 260 ff. HAMA 1. 26 ff. On the Arabic tradition see F. Sezgin, *Geschichte des arabischen Schrifttums* 5 (1974), 158 ff. G. J. T.

Menenius (*RE* 12) **Lanatus, Agrippa,** consul 503 BC, reputedly used a (Greek) political parable of the self-destructive refusal of the limbs to feed the stomach to convince the *plebs* of the futility of *secession in 494/3. In *Livy (2. 32. 8 ff.), the fable apparently justifies aristocratic economic power and leisure; in *Dionysius (7) of Halicarnassus (*Ant. Rom.* 6. 86. 1 ff.) it less effectively legitimizes the political dominance of the senate. The entire story, with its élitist assumptions about effective popular oratory, was probably concocted by one of the Graecizing early Roman historians (cf. Dion. Hal. *Ant. Rom.* 6. 83. 2); Menenius' role as mediator was perhaps invented on the assumption that he was of plebeian birth (Livy 2. 32. 8).

Ogilvie, *Comm. Livy 1–5*, 275, 312 f.; L. Bertelli, *Index* 1972, 224 ff.; D. Peil, *Der Streit der Glieder mit dem Magen* (1985). A. D.

Menestheus, leader or joint leader of the Athenian forces at Troy in the account in *Homer's *Iliad*. He is remarkable for his lack of prominence in the story, and in later Athenian accounts is at least partially eclipsed by the sons of *Theseus (see ACAMAS; DEMOPHON (1)).

F. Cantarelli, *Rend. Ist. Lomb.* 108 (1974), 459–505; *LIMC* 6. 1 (1992), 473–5. E. Ke.

Menestor, a south-Italian Greek botanist, traditionally a Pythagorean (see PYTHAGORAS (1)) from *Sybaris (Iamb. *VP* 267). *Theophrastus occasionally quotes from Menestor's lost books on botany, which considered particular plants and their growth according to warmth or frigidity. Mulberries sprout late, but ripen quickly, growing in cold weather (Theophr. *Caus. pl.* 1. 17. 3), an application of the Pythagorean theory of opposition of the warmth and cold to plants: mulberry requires cold for growth, from its warm nature. Plants needing warmth due to their cold nature included rush, reed, galingale, silver fir, pine, prickly cedar, Phoenician cedar, and ivy (ibid. 1. 21. 6). *Empedocles had posited a theory of why the warm evergreens withstood cold weather by means of their pores, so Menestor is dated sometime between Empedocles and Theophrastus (*c*.400 BC), and is the author of the first known Greek works on inductive botany. Theophrastus (*Caus. pl.* 1. 22. 1–7) refutes Menestor's arguments in a succinct manner. See BOTANY.

TESTIMONIA AND FRAGMENTS DK 32.

GENERAL LITERATURE E. Steier, *RE* 15/1. 853–5, 'Menestor' (refs. to E. Meyer, *Geschichte der Botanik* 1 (1854), 21–2, are superseded by more modern works); A. G. Morton, *History of Botanical Science* (1981), 24. J. Sca.

Menexenus, of Athens, pupil of *Socrates, was one of those present at the conversation in prison related in *Plato (1)'s *Phaedo*. He plays a considerable part in the *Lysis* and a less prominent one in Plato's dialogue named after him.

L. Dean-Jones, *CQ* 1995, 51 ff. M. Ga.

Menippe, name of a Nereid (see NEREUS) in Hesiod, *Theog.* 260, and of two or three insignificant heroines, as the mother of

*Eurystheus (schol. *Il.* 19. 116, which also gives her several other names); the mother of *Orpheus, generally a *Muse (Tzetzes, *Chiliades* 1. 12. 306).

Menippean satire in the sense of a mixture of prose and many verse forms was, according to *Quintilian (*Inst.* 10. 1. 95), introduced by *Varro, who in early compositions (Cic. *Acad.* 1. 8) freely adapted works of *Menippus (1), combining jocularity with social comment and popular, especially *Cynic philosophy. Some of the titles suggest inventive fantasy; many have a second explanatory title in Greek. Some 600 fragments have been preserved but their exiguous or mangled state makes exegesis and reconstruction particularly daunting.

In late AD 54 L. *Annaeus Seneca (2) wrote *Apocolocyntosis* ('Pumpkinification'), a compact and savage satire on the recent apotheosis of the emperor *Claudius, which is the only near-complete classical Menippean to have survived. The prose narrative is studded with quotations placed in incongruous situations; the verses include parody of a tragic speech and a mock funeral lament in anapaests.

The *Satyrica* of *Petronius Arbiter is a unique fusion of two genres, Menippean satire and the comic novel. Menippean elements are found in the mockery of a tasteless dinner party, the *Cena Trimalchionis*. Literary criticism and the long verse excerpts, tragic senarii and epic hexameters, are spoken by a disreputable vagabond. Vulgar Sotadean verses (see SOTADES (2)) occur in the *Satyrica* and in the tale of Iolaus, a Greek comic romance in prose and verse (1st cent. AD) found in a papyrus fragment (*POxy.* 3010). Petronius will have drawn on this tradition.

A mixture of prose and verse as a miscellany (*per saturam*) is used in late antiquity by *Martianus Minneus Felix Capella and by *Boethius in his *Consolatio*. A closer connection with satire in Martianus is problematical. See SATIRE.

C. A. van Rooy, *Studies in Classical Satire* (1965); M. Coffey, *Roman Satire*, 2nd edn. (1989); R. Astbury (ed.), *Varronis saturae Menippeae* (1985); J.-P. Cèbe, *Varron: Satires Ménippées* (1972–); P. T. Eden (ed.), *Seneca: Apocolocyntosis* (1984); P. J. Parsons, *Oxyrhynchus Papyri* 42 (1974); D. Shanzer, *Martianus Capella, Book I* (1986); G. O'Daly, *The Poetry of Boethius* (1991); J. C. Relihan, *Ancient Menippean Satire* (1993); P. Dronke, *Verse with Prose from Petronius to Dante* (1994). M. Co.

Menippus (1), of Gadara (Syria), influential *Cynic writer, probably of first half of 3rd cent. BC. An untrustworthy Life (Diog. Laert. 6. 99–101) makes him a pupil of Metrocles and associates him with *Thebes (1). Twice referred to as σπουδογέλοιος or satirist (Strabo 16. 2. 29; Steph. Byz., entry under Γάδαρα), a term he might have applied to himself, he seems to have specialized in humorous moralizing; it is tempting, but perhaps dangerous, to assume that his works closely resembled those of Lucian in which he is a character. Very little is known of his work except titles, among which are: *Diathekai* or 'Wills' (parodying the wills of philosophers ?); *Letters Artificially Composed as if by the Gods* (? cf. Lucian, *Saturnalia*); *Nekyia* or 'Necromancy' (presumably in the parodistic tradition of *Crates (2) and *Timon (2), and possibly influential on *Horace, *Sat.* 2. 5, the younger *Seneca, *Apocol.*, and various works of *Lucian; a trace of this work may survive at Diog. Laert. 6. 102; *Symposium* (cf. Ath. 14. 629 f.); *Arcesilaus* (presumably *Arcesilaus (1) the head of the Academy); Διογένους πρᾶσις ('Sale of Diogenes') (Diog. Laert. 6. 29–30; cf. Lucian, *Sale of the Philosophers*). Menippus is said to have used *omnigenum carmen* in his works ('Probus' on Verg. *Ecl.* 6. 31, discussing *Varro's *Menippean Satires*), and there is no reason to doubt that, in keeping with the general Cynic tradition, both quotation and parody had a prominent role; the influence of Semitic and Arabic 'prosimetrum' has been suggested (cf. LUCIAN; MELEAGER (2)). It must be stressed that ancient theory did not use '*Menippean satire' to denote all prosimetric forms in the loose fashion still too common in modern scholarship.

R. Helm, *Lucian und Menipp* (1906); J. Hall, *Lucian's Satire* (1981).
R. L. Hu.

Menippus (2), of *Pergamum, wrote a *periplous* (see PERIPLOI) of the Black (*Euxine) Sea (partly preserved) and *Mediterranean in three books, dated to the early Augustan period by an epigram of *Crinagoras (*Anth. Pal.* 9. 559).

GGM 1. cxxxv f., 563 f.; A. Diller, *The Tradition of the Minor Greek Geographers* (1952), 147–64, 188.
N. P.

Meno (*RE* 17), pupil of *Aristotle. His summary of medical doctrines was known to *Plutarch (*Quaest. conv.* 8. 9. 3) and *Galen (15. 25 Kühn). Parts are thought to be preserved in the 'Anonymus Londinensis' papyrus, which is one of the most important sources for the early history of Greek *medicine.

Ed. H. Diels, *Anonymi Londinensis ex Aristotelis iatricis Menoniis et aliis medicis eclogae* (1893); trans. W. H. S. Jones (1947).
J. T. V.

Menodorus or **Menas** was a *freedman of *Pompey and perhaps previously a pirate. In 40 BC he captured *Sardinia from *Octavian for Sextus *Pompeius. In 39 he advised Sextus not to make the Pact of Misenum with M. *Antonius (2) (Mark Antony) and Octavian, and was said to have suggested making away with them at the subsequent celebration. In 38, after Sextus had become suspicious of his loyalty, Menodorus restored Sardinia to Octavian, was rewarded with equestrian rank, and fought in the naval war against Sextus under C. *Calvisius Sabinus. In 36 he returned to Sextus, but failed to recover his trust and again deserted to Octavian. He was killed in Octavian's Illyrian campaign of 35, at the siege of *Siscia.
G. W. R.; T. J. C.; E. B.

Menodotus (1), of *Perinthus, author of a fifteen-volume Greek history (Ἑλληνικαὶ πραγματεῖαι) beginning c.217 BC and perhaps to be identified with *Menodotus (2) of Samos, the author of List of Remarkable Things on Samos (τῶν κατὰ τὴν Σάμον ἐνδόξων ἀναγραφή).

FGrH 82 and 541.
K. S. S.

Menodotus (2), Samian Greek (? identical with Menodotus (1), Diod. Sic. 26. 4), wrote a *List of Remarkable Things on Samos* (including the temple of Hera).

FGrH 541.

Menodotus (3), of *Nicomedia (fl. probably c. AD 120), follower of *Pyrrhon, pupil of *Antiochus (11) of Ascalon, and leader of the empirical school of medicine (see MEDICINE, § 5. 3). He was a voluminous author, and is often referred to by *Galen.

Menoeceus, in mythology, (1), descendant of *Echion (1), one of the Sparti, and father of *Creon (1) and Iocasta (e.g. Soph. *OT* 69–70; full genealogy in schol. Eur. *Phoen.* 942—from Aeschylus?). His charioteer Perieres killed the *Minyan king *Clymenus (2b) thus starting the war between *Orchomenus (1) and *Thebes (1), which ended with the defeat of the former by *Heracles and the Thebans ([Apollod.] 2. 4. 11). (2) Son of *Creon (1), who sacrificed himself that Thebes might survive the assault of the Seven (Eur. *Phoen.* 905–1018, 1090–2) see SEVEN AGAINST THEBES. See *LIMC* 6. 1 (1992), 475 f.
A. Sch.

Menoetius, son of Actor and Aegina, and one of the *Argonauts.

He was father of *Patroclus, and lived at Opoeis in *Locris; but, when Patroclus accidentally killed a comrade in a dice game, Menoetius brought him to *Peleus' house in Phthia to grow up with *Achilles (*Il.* 23. 84–90).
J. R. M.

menopause, in contrast to menarche, was not regarded by medical writers as being a critical time in a woman's life. This may have been because the onset of fertility was culturally far more significant than its decline, or because it is experienced not as a single event, but as a gradual process. No discussion of menopause by a woman survives, so it is not clear whether the lack of interest in this stage of life merely reflects a primary male interest in women as childbearers. In ancient medical theory, menopause occurs because women, despite being naturally 'wetter' than men to the extent that they need to lose the excess fluid in *menstruation, eventually dry out as a result of ageing (e.g. Hippoc. *Mul.* 2. 111). According to *Aristotle (*Hist. an.* 582^a 21–4, 583^b 23–8), women age more quickly than men. He placed menopause at around the age of 40, although it could be later (ibid. 585^{b}3–5). Although the theory of ageing in periods of seven years meant that 42 was a theoretically appropriate age for menopause, later medical writers accepted an even wider age range; for example, *Soranus (*Gyn.* 1. 4. 20) believed it could occur as late as 60. *Oribasius (*Medical Collections* 142) gave the range from 50 to 60, but he believed that it could occur in a woman as young as 35 if she were overweight. See AGE.

D. W. Amundsen and C. J. Diers, *Human Biology* 1970, 79–86; G. Clark, *Women in Late Antiquity* (1993); L. Dean-Jones, *Women's Bodies in Classical Greek Science* (1994).
H. K.

Mens, personified Roman deity of good counsel (*gnōmē* or *euboulia* in Greek), whose temple on the Capitoline (see CAPITOL) was vowed after the disaster at *Trasimene (217 BC) and dedicated in 215. It was restored by M. *Aemilius Scaurus (1) at a time (after 115 BC) when senatorial *euboulia* was in need of some advertisement (Plut. *De fort. Rom.* 5, cf. 10). More generally, the cult of Mens Bona was popular in the imperial period among slaves and freedmen.

H. Scullard, *Festivals and Ceremonies of the Roman Republic* (1981), 148–9; F. Cenerini, *Epigraphica* 1986, 99–113; *LIMC* 6. 1 (1992), 477–9.
N. P.

menstruation was, in Hippocratic medicine (see HIPPOCRATES (2)), regarded as essential to female health. The age of menarche was believed to be the fourteenth year, as the network of internal channels in the girl's body developed sufficiently to allow the collection and evacuation of blood. In antiquity, the first sign of puberty was generally taken to be not menarche, but breast development (Arist. *Hist. an.* 581^{a}31–^{b}24; Sor. *Gyn.* 1. 20 and 24; cf. Pl. *Leg.* 925a). Mature women's bodies, being wetter and softer than those of men, absorbed a greater amount of fluid from their diet and, due to women's supposedly less active lifestyle, this would accumulate in the body (e.g. Hippoc. *Mul.* 1. 1). The excess needed to be evacuated both regularly—the most common terms for the menses translate as 'monthlies'—and heavily, the expected blood loss being about half a litre (nearly one pint) over two to three days (*Mul.* 1. 6). If it remained in the body, the blood would exert pressure on vital organs and cause disease, possibly threatening life. A missed period was an impossibility in this construction of the female body; the blood is described as 'hidden', and must be purged by irritant pessaries and other remedies.

In *Aristotle's model of the female body, menstruation is a

sign of inadequacy; only the male body is hot enough to concoct blood into semen (e.g. Arist. *Gen. an.* 775ᵃ14–20). *Parmenides and others apparently believed, in contrast, that women were the hotter sex, since they clearly have more blood and blood is humorally hot and wet (Arist. *Part. an.* 648ᵃ28–30; *Gen. an.* 765ᵇ19; see HUMOURS). Aristotle, *Diocles (3), and *Empedocles thought that all women menstruated at the same time of the lunar month, with the waning moon (Arist. *Gen. an.* 767ᵃ2–6; Sor. *Gyn.* 1. 21).

In Roman medicine menstruation was separated from women's health, *Soranus arguing that exercise or singing could stop menstruation entirely, but the woman would remain healthy (*Gyn.* 1. 5, 1. 22–3).

In addition to being a purging of a substance dangerous to a woman's health if retained, menstruation was valued as a sign of potential conception, indicating that the womb was open to receive the male seed. In contrast to the Christian tradition, intercourse while menstruating was not generally seen as polluting, the best time for fruitful intercourse being thought to occur towards the end of a menstrual period while the womb was still open (Hippoc. *Nat. mul.* 8; *Nat. puer.* 15; Arist. *Gen. an.* 727ᵇ12–25). Menstrual blood was also thought to provide the raw material out of which the foetus was formed, hence the cessation of menstruation during pregnancy (e.g. Arist. *Gen. an.* 727ᵇ11–14).

In terms of quality, Greek writers thought that menstrual blood was no different from any other blood, although some argued that it was a cold, corrupt form (e.g. Plut. *Mor.* 651c–e). In a passage which may be a later interpolation, Aristotle describes the clouding effect on a mirror of the gaze of a menstruating woman (*Div. somn.* 459ᵇ26–460ᵃ23). Some Roman writers attributed further magical powers to menstrual blood; *Pliny (1) passes on the belief that it increases agricultural fertility and can cure a number of diseases (*HN* 28. 23). Ritual laws including prohibitions on contact with menstruation, death, *childbirth, and intercourse are known from the Hellenistic era.

We know little of menstrual protection in antiquity, but folded rags were used (e.g. Hippoc. *Mul.* 1. 11; Plut. *Mor.* 700e). The *Suda*'s account of the life of the philosopher *Hypatia includes the story that she once threw one at an unwanted suitor. Mommsen's suggestion that the use of *rhakos* in the inventories of Artemis Brauronia should be interpreted as a dedication of menstrual rags after menarche is erroneous (see BRAURON); this probably indicates only that the condition of dedicated garments had deteriorated. See GYNAECOLOGY; POLLUTION.

G. Clark, *Women in Late Antiquity* (1993); L. Dean-Jones, *Women's Bodies in Classical Greek Science* (1994); H. King, in A. Cameron and A. Kuhrt, *Images of Women in Antiquity* (1983), 109–27, and in *Helios* 1987, 117–26; A. Mommsen, *Philol.* 1899, 343–7.   H. K.

Menthe (μένθη) or **Minthe** (μίνθη), i.e. spearmint or green mint (*Mentha viridis*). Strabo, 8. 3. 14 (cf. Ov. *Met.* 10. 729–30), states that she was *Hades' mistress (a Naiad (see NYMPHS), daughter of *Peitho, Phot. *Bibl.*, entry under μίνθα). *Persephone trampled her underfoot, and she was transformed into the plant named after her, which smells sweeter when trodden upon.

Roscher, *Lex.* 2. 2, 2801.   J. R. S.

Mentor (1), in mythology, an old Ithacan (see ITHACA), friend of *Odysseus, who left his household in his charge (*Od.* 2. 225 ff.). *Athena takes his shape to help *Telemachus (*Od.* 2. 401 and elsewhere; cf. 24. 548).

Mentor (2), Rhodian mercenary leader, brother-in-law of the satrap *Artabazus, whose service he and his brother *Memnon

(2) entered. He married his niece Barsine, Artabazus' daughter. Both brothers took part in the *Satraps' Revolt (362–360 BC) and received some territory in *Troas. In 353 they fled with Artabazus. Mentor went to Egypt, entered again the king's service, and was general at the conquest of Egypt (343). He rose high in Persian service and was ordered to quell the dynasts of Asia Minor. Among them was *Hermias (1), whom he put to death (341). He had previously obtained the recall of Artabazus and Memnon. He probably died soon after.

Dem. 23. 150 ff.; Diod. Sic. 16. 42 ff.; Tod 199. H. W. Parke, *Greek Mercenary Soldiers from the Earliest Times to the Battle of Ipsus* (1933); P. A. Brunt, *Riv. Fil.* 1975, 26 ff.; Bosworth, *HCA* 1. 112 f., and *Conquest and Empire* (1988), 252.   V. E.; S. H.

mercenaries

Greek and Hellenistic For there to be mercenaries, three conditions are necessary—*warfare, people willing to pay, and others to serve. Warfare existed almost throughout Greek history, and there were probably also always those whom love of adventure, trouble at home, or poverty made willing to serve. Alcaeus (1)'s brother, Antimenidas, and *Xenophon (1) himself are, perhaps, examples of the first; the latter's comrades, the Spartans *Clearchus (1) and Dracontius, of the second. But in the heyday of the city-state, when military service was the duty of all citizens, mercenaries usually only found employment with tyrants or with near eastern potentates. *Psammetichus I of Egypt, for example, used *Carians and *Ionians to seize power around 660 BC, and Pabis of Colophon and Elesibius of *Teos were among those who carved their names on the statue of Ramesses II at Abu Simbel, while serving Psammetichus II.

There was probably always also a market for specialist troops like Cretan *archers and Rhodian *slingers, particularly when warfare became more complex. Cleon, for example, took *Thracian *peltasts to *Pylos (Thuc. 4. 28. 4), and Cretan archers and Rhodian slingers joined the Sicilian Expedition in 415 (Thuc. 6. 43. 2). By the end of the *Peloponnesian War there were enough Greeks eager for mercenary service for the Persian prince, *Cyrus (2), to raise more than 10,000 for his attempt on his brother's throne, including Athenians, Spartans, Arcadians, Achaeans, Boeotians, and Thessalians, as well as the usual Cretan and Rhodian specialists.

Poverty had probably always been the main factor in driving Greeks to become mercenaries—it is significant how many were Arcadians—and the increasing number in the 4th cent. BC was probably partly due to the worsening economic situation (cf. Isoc. 4. 167 ff.). Greek mercenaries were now in great demand in Persia, and it is said that the Persian king promoted the *Common Peace of 375 in order to be able to hire Greeks for the reconquest of Egypt. But Greek states also increasingly employed mercenaries. *Jason (2) of Pherae is said to have had up to 6,000 (Xen. *Hell.* 6. 1. 5), and the 4th cent. saw many other 'tyrants' who relied on mercenaries to keep them in power, the most conspicuous being *Dionysius (1) I of Syracuse. In the '*Sacred War' of 356–346, the Phocians showed how even a small state could rival larger ones provided it had the financial resources—in this case the treasures of *Delphi—to hire troops.

*Philip (1) II and *Alexander (3) the Great of Macedonia certainly employed mercenaries, particularly as specialists and for detached duties such as garrisons, and the *Diadochi increasingly employed mercenaries in their *phalanxes as the supply of real Macedonians declined. However, as the Hellenistic world settled down after *Ipsus, the great powers developed supplies of phalanx-troops from their own national resources—often the descendants of Greek mercenary settlers—and most mercenaries of the 3rd and 2nd cent. BC appear to have been, once again, light-armed and specialist troops.

> H. W. Parke, *Greek Mercenary Soldiers from the Earliest Times to the Battle of Ipsus* (1933); G. T. Griffith, *Mercenaries of the Hellenistic World* (1935).
> J. F. La.

Roman Contact with foreign powers such as *Carthage and Macedon exposed Rome's weakness in cavalry and light-armed troops. This deficiency she remedied principally by obtaining contingents outside Italy. Some came from independent allies like *Masinissa, others were raised by forced levies or paid as mercenaries. Gauls served in the First *Punic War, 600 Cretan archers fought at Lake *Trasimene, Numidian cavalry (see NUMIDIA) turned the scale at the battle of *Zama. During the next two centuries the number and variety of contingents increased. Spain was a favourite recruiting-ground for cavalry and light infantry, while Caesar obtained his cavalry from Numidia, Gaul, and Germany, and his archers and slingers from Numidia, Crete, and the Balearic Islands.

Under the Principate such troops became formalized within the *auxilia, but supplementary irregular troops were always employed on campaign (Germans, Cantabrians, Dacians, Palmyrenes, Sarmatians, Arabs, Armenians, Moors, etc.).

> J. Kromayer and G. Veith, *Heerwesen und Kriegführung der Griechen und der Römer* (1928), 311–13; L. Keppie, *The Making of the Roman Army* (1981); P. Southern, *Britannia* 1989, 84–104; J. C. N. Coulston, in M. C. Bishop (ed.), *The Production and Distribution of Roman Military Equipment* (1985), 282–6, 292–8.
> J. C. N. C.

Mercurius (Mercury), patron god of circulation, known as well in Campania (at *Capua and in the *Falernus ager, Vetter nos. 136, 264) and Etruria (the *Etruscan deity Turms). According to ancient tradition, in 495 BC Mercury received an official temple on the SW slope of the *Aventine, its anniversary falling on 15 May (Festus 135. 4 Lindsay). He was foreign in origin in the view of some scholars (Latte, *RR* 162), but others see him as an Italic and Roman deity (Dumézil, *ARR* 439 f.; Radke, *Götter*, 214 ff.). On any view his cult was old, and it had close links with shop-keepers and transporters of goods, notably grain; also, at the *lectisternium of 399 BC he was associated with *Neptunus, and, at that of 217 BC, with *Ceres. But his function was not simply the protection of businessmen (see NEGOTIATORES) or 'the divine power inherent in *merx* [merchandise]' (Combet-Farnoux). If all the evidence for his cult, notably Ovid, *Fast.* 5. 681–90, and *ILS* 3200, is taken together, he emerges, like the Greek *Hermes, as the patron god of circulation, the movement of goods, people, and words and their roles. Mediator between gods and mortals, between the dead and the living, and always in motion, Mercury is also a deceiver, since he moves on the boundaries and in the intervening space; he is patron of the shopkeeper as much as the trader, the traveller as well as the brigand (see BRIGANDAGE). Hence it is not astonishing that *Horace, with a certain malice, assigns to *Augustus the traits of this ambiguous mediator (*Carm.* 1. 2. 41 ff.).

> B. Combet-Farnoux, *Mercure romain* (1980); E. Vetter, *Handbuch der italischen Dialekte* 1 (1953); *LIMC* 6. 1 (1992), 500–54.
> J. Sch.

Merobaudes, Flavius, probably of Frankish origin, but resident in Spain. By AD 435 he was count of the consistory (*Consistorium): in 443 he became *magister utriusque militiae* (see MAGISTER MILITUM), and subsequently *patricius* (see PATRICIANS,

end). He probably died *c*.460. In the 430s and 440s he composed a number of panegyrics for Flavius *Aetius and for the imperial family, and he is also the author of some devout Christian poetry.

> Ed. F. M. Clover, *TAPhS* 61/1 (1971).
> I. N. W.

Meroe, a capital of Kush (*Nubia), on the east bank of the Nile, between the Fifth and Sixth Cataracts. It was occupied from the 7th cent. BC until the 4th cent. AD when the Meroitic state fragmented, in part owing to the military—and perhaps commercial—activities of the neighbouring state of Aksum (see AXUMIS). First referred to by Herodotus (2. 29), it figures more prominently in Hellenistic and Roman literature, especially after the conflict with Rome in 25 BC. In late literature, most notably *Heliodorus (4)'s *Aethiopica*, it was a romanticized, exotic place. Classical tradition claimed that Meroe was ruled by a line of queens called Candace.

> L. Török, *ANRW* 2. 10. 1 (1988), 107–341.
> R. G. M.

Merope (Μερόπη), in mythology, (1) a Pleiad (see CONSTELLATIONS no. 23), wife of *Sisyphus; she is the nearly invisible star of the group, for she hides her face for shame at having married a mortal, while all her sisters mated with gods (see Apollod. 1. 85; Hyg. *Fab.* 192. 5). (2) Wife of Cresphontes king of Messenia; see AEPYTUS. (3) Wife of *Polybus (1) of Corinth, Oedipus' foster-father (Soph. *OT* 775); see OEDIPUS. (4) Daughter of Oenopion (see ORION; Apollod. 1. 25). For more Meropae see Stoll in Roscher's *Lexikon*, entry under the name.
> H. J. R.

Mesatus, a tragic poet, came third in the year (perhaps 463 BC) in which *Aeschylus was victorious with his Danaid tetralogy. Restoration of his name in an inscribed victor list implies that he won two, three, or four victories, the first shortly after 468.

> *TrGF* 1². 87–8.
> A. L. B.

Mesene, from Aramaic *Maišān*, the southernmost part of Iraq, around modern Basra, basically coterminous with the Seleucid satrapy of the Erythraean Sea, the capital of which was Alexandria-on-the-Tigris (later refounded as Antioch). Following the death of *Antiochus (7) VII, Spaosines (Hyspaosines), his former *satrap there, restored Antioch, renaming it after himself as Spasinou Charax, 'City of Spaosines' (Plin. *HN* 6. 31. 138; Charax from Aramaic *karekā*, 'city'), and establishing the independent kingdom of Characene. The kingdom survived, enjoying varying degrees of independence from *Parthia, until it was incorporated into the *Sasanid empire by Ardashir around AD 222. From the mid-1st to the late 2nd cent. AD Palmyrene caravans regularly travelled between Charax and *Palmyra, transporting goods arriving via the *Persian Gulf from the east. In 131 Meredat, king of Charax, employed a Palmyrene named Yarhai as *satrapēs Thilouanōn*, 'satrap of the Thilouanoi', i.e. inhabitants of *Tylos (mod. Bahrain).

> E. Drouin, *Le Muséon* 1890, 129–50; S. A. Nodelman, *Berytus* 1960, 83–121; D. T. Potts, in D. T. Potts (ed.), *Araby the Blest* (1988), 137–67; H. H. Schaeder, *Der Islam* 1945, 11–42; D. Sellwood, *Cambridge History of Iran* 3/1 (1983); F. H. Weissbach, *RE* 15/1 (1931), 1082–95.
> D. T. P.

Mesomedes (fl. AD 144), a Cretan and a *freedman of *Hadrian, wrote short and highly original poetry for accompaniment by the lyre. His fourteen surviving lyrics include hymns, beast-fables, descriptions of a sundial and of a sponge, and a piece on glass-making; for four of them the MSS preserve musical notation. In his striving for ingenious effects and in his originality of expression can be seen the influence of the epideictic epigram and of the *progymnasmata*. His poems have a flavour of Doric dialect, and use a variety of metres.

TEXT Heitsch, *Griech. Dichterfr.* 1². 24–32; U. von Wilamowitz-Moellendorff, *Griechische Verskunst* (1921), 595–607; E. Pöhlmann, *Denkmäler altgr. Musik* (1970), 13–31.

GENERAL E. L. Bowie, in D. A. Russell (ed.), *Antonine Literature* (1990), 85–90; M. L. West, *Greek Music* (1992), 303–8, etc. and GM 165–74.
N. H.

Mesopotamia, the country between the *Tigris and the *Euphrates. The name is generally used to include the whole alluvial country south of the mountains, and the deserts on either side, i.e. the ancient kingdoms of *Assyria and *Babylonia, modern Iraq. Classical writers usually regarded Mesopotamia as excluding Babylonia.

As an important political and commercial link between *Syria, *Cappadocia, and Babylonia, Mesopotamia was colonized extensively by the *Seleucids. It was a frequent battle-ground of Roman and Parthian armies. Mesopotamia was overrun by *Trajan (AD 114–17) (his *Provincia Mesopotamia* was promptly abandoned by *Hadrian) and again overrun by L. *Verus (162–5) and *Septimius Severus (197–9) but was not permanently occupied. Part of Upper Mesopotamia, however, became Roman after the campaigns of Verus and was formed into a separate province, 'Mesopotamia', by Severus. See also HATRA; OSROËNE.

Jones, *Cities E. Rom. Prov.* ch. 9; L. Dilleman, *Haute Mesopotamie et pays adjacents* (1962); M. Colledge, *Parthian Art* (1977).
M. S. D.; E. W. G.; S. S.-W.

Messallina See STATILIA MESSAL(L)INA (third wife of Nero); VALERIA MESSAL(L)INA (wife of emperor Claudius).

Messana (mod. Messina), an 8th-cent. colony, originally called Zancle, founded by Cumaean and Euboean settlers on the straits of Messina (see CUMAE; EUBOEA). It prospered, founding colonies at Mylae and *Himera, but was overshadowed by *Rhegium, whose tyrant, *Anaxilas (1), seized it in 490/89. Samian and Messenian settlers arrived in 486, with Rhegine assistance, and changed the name of the city to Messana. It remained under Rhegine domination for most of the 5th cent., but by 427 was independent again. It was destroyed by Carthaginians in 396 and rebuilt by *Dionysius (1) I, falling under Syracusan domination. In 288 it was seized by the *Mamertines, who ruled it until 264, when *Hieron (2) II attempted to oust them. Their appeal to Rome for help, and Roman agreement, was the occasion of the First *Punic War. After 241 BC it became a *civitas foederata* (allied city) and prospered throughout the empire, thanks to its harbour and domination of the straits. It was occupied by the Saracens in AD 843. Much of the archaeological evidence was destroyed in the earthquake of 1908, but cemeteries of the Hellenistic period and the 1st–3rd cents. AD have been found, and the acropolis located. The area around the harbour was the heart of the archaic city. Traces of archaic and Roman houses, Hellenistic and Roman tombs, and an archaic sanctuary have been located, and of an orthogonal street-plan dating to the Greek period of the city's history.

G. Vallet, *Rhegion et Zancle* (1959); F. Coarelli and M. Torelli, *Sicilia* (1980).
K. L.

Messapic language The term Messapic refers to the pre-Roman language attested in some 600 inscriptions, mostly funerary, found in the second Augustan district (*regio*) of Italy, *Apulia et Calabria*. See ITALY; MESSAPII. The Messapic inscriptions are written in two similar alphabets, both of Greek origin. Given the present state of knowledge, it is wise to speak of Messapic only for the inscriptions of the modern Sallentine peninsula (*Calabria), including also some epigraphic evidence from Monopoli, Caglie, and Brindisi. The name *Messapii* is also used as quasi-synonymous of *Iapyges*, *Sal(l)entini*, and *Calabri* (cf. e.g. Strabo 6. 277), but in origin *Iapygia* indicated the Sallentine peninsula; thus we have no evidence that the Greeks called Messapic the local language of Daunia (see DAUNIANS) and Peucetia. There may have been a local unitary language spoken in an area which went from Gargano to the Capo di Leuca, but so far this can only be a hypothesis. It would also be possible to think of some form of linguistic unity subsuming a number of dialects and one could compare e.g. the position of *Oscan in Campania as contrasted with that of Umbrian in the *tabulae Iguvinae*. A recent inscription of *Arpi (Daunia) from the 3rd cent. BC has *Artos pinave* 'Artos painted', the signature of the artist who decorated the tomb; the form of the name (*Artos* and not †*Artas*) shows Greek influence; yet the verb *pinave* is Messapic. The oldest known Messapic texts belong to the 6th cent. and the beginning of the 5th cent. BC. During the 1st cent. Messapic was replaced by Latin, which is the origin of modern Sallentine dialects.

For many years the study of Messapic was based on the assumption that the language was genetically related to *Illyrian. The main supporter of this theory was the German scholar H. Krahe, though he eventually modified his views considerably. At present we prefer to see Messapic as an autonomous linguistic unit, with its own history, to be studied within the context of the other languages and the history of ancient Italy. Yet it may still be possible to establish links between Messapic, which is certainly an *Indo-European language, and other languages genetically close to it. In fact we cannot exclude that Messapic was introduced into Italy (in several waves?) by 'Illyrian' speakers who came from the Balkans, though at present this cannot be verified.

The majority of Messapic texts consist of onomastic formulae, which cause no difficulties of comprehension. However there are also votive inscriptions (for Aphrodite and Demeter); an important term is the word *tabaras*, 'priest'. New possibilities of interpretation seem to be opened by the discovery of an important set of epigraphic data in the 'Grotta della Poesia' near Lecce.

E. Polomé, in H. Birnbaum and J. Puhvel (eds.), *Ancient Indo-European Dialects* (1966), 59–76.
C. de S.

Messapii were the inhabitants of the 'heel' of Italy, the Sallentine peninsula (see CALABRIA). Together with the Daunians and Peucetii they made up the people known collectively as 'Iapygians' (Polyb. 3. 88. 3, contrast 2. 24. 11, with Walbank, *HCP* on both passages). For their language see MESSAPIC LANGUAGE. There was constant tension and warfare between the Messapians and Sparta's nearby colony *Tarentum: see *Syll.*³ 21 and 40 a (Jeffery, *LSAG* pp. 281 and 284 nos. 6 and 7); and Hdt. 7. 170 for a massacre of Tarentines and allied Rhegines (see RHEGIUM) by Messapians. King Artas of Messapia, a *proxenos of Athens (M. Walbank, *Athenian Proxenies of the Fifth Century BC* (1978), no. 70), was allied to Athens against Sparta by 413 BC: Thuc. 7. 33; this is consistent with usual Messapian policy against Tarentum (see above). But despite this hostility, there was some cultural and religious borrowing from Tarentum, and the traffic may have been two-way on the evidence of the appearance of the words 'Zeus Messapeus' on an inscribed 6th-cent. Laconian bowl. In 338 the Messapians helped to defeat Tarentum's mercenary King *Archidamus III of Sparta. But in the Roman war against *Pyrrhus the Messapians changed policy and supported Tarentum and were consequently subjugated by Rome (see Broughton, *MRR* under 266 BC). Although only casually mentioned thereafter, they were never completely assimilated. Their chief towns were Uria, *Rudiae, Caelia, *Brundisium, Uzentum. See also IAPYGIA; MESSAPIC LANGUAGE; MESSAPUS.

T. Potter, *Roman Italy* (1987), 37–8; R. W. V. Catling and D. G. J. Shipley, *BSA* 1989, 187–200 (the bowl); K. Lomas, *Rome and the Western Greeks 350 BC–AD 200* (1993), see index; N. Purcell, *CAH* 6² (1994), ch. 9b.

E. T. S.; S. H.

Messapus, (1) eponym of Messapia in southern Italy (Strab. 9. 2. 13, see MESSAPII). (2) In Virgil, Etruscan ally of *Turnus (1), son of *Neptunus (*Aen.* 7. 691–705, etc.). *Virgil innovates in his parentage, and probably takes his name from (1). *Ennius claimed descent (Sil. *Pun.* 12. 393, Skutsch on Enn. *Ann.* 524).

N. M. Horsfall, *Enc. Virg.* 'Messapo'.

S. J. Ha.

Messene (Μεσσήνη, mod. Mavromati), *polis founded in 369 BC by *Epaminondas as part of a Theban strategy (see THEBES (1)) to contain Sparta; named after the eponymous heroine (*LIMC* 'Messene'), recipient of a temple (newly identified) and lively cult. Situated on the western slopes of Mt. *Ithome in the lower plain of *Messenia, its natural strength was reinforced by exceptionally fine city walls, largely preserved. The excavated remains include a stadium associated with a gymnasium, a theatre, and an elaborate cult-complex centred on a temple of *Asclepius, all aligned on a 'Hippodamian' plan (see HIPPODAMUS). Surviving attacks by Hellenistic dynasts and capture by the *Achaean Confederacy (182 BC), after a shaky start under Augustus (a plea for imperial rescue from 'evils' in AD 15 is attested), the city became a prosperous regional centre of *Achaia, producing a Roman consular family in the 2nd cent. It administered the important mystery-sanctuary of Andania.

Paus. 4. 31. 4 ff. *IG* 5. 1. 1425 ff.; *SEG* 23. 201 ff. (inscriptions). Current Greek excavations: ΠΑΕ from 1987; Ἔργον from 1988. C. Habicht, *Pausanias' Guide to Ancient Greece* (1985), 36 ff.; L. Migeotte, *BCH* 1985, 597 ff. (Augustan Messene); N. Deshours, *Rev. Ét. Grec.* 1993, 39 ff. (cult).

A. M. W.; R. J. H.; A. J. S. S.

Messenia, the SW region of the Peloponnese (see PELOPONNESUS), bounded on the north by *Elis—along the lower course of the river Neda—and *Arcadia, and on the east by *Laconia, where the frontier follows at first the main ridge of Taygetus, but further south runs to the west of it (here lay the *ager Dentheliatis*, long disputed between *Messene and *Sparta), and terminates at the river Choerius a few miles south of the head of the Messenian Gulf. Western Messenia, dominated by Mt. Aegaleos, is hilly but well watered, with settlements concentrated on the coast. In Classical times the central and eastern region watered by the (partly navigable) river Pamisus was more populous; this area was well known for stockraising (Strabo 8. 5. 6, 366), and the lower plain, Macaria, was famous for its fertility.

Prehistory Survey work (see ARCHAEOLOGY, CLASSICAL) has provided a wealth of information on prehistoric Messenia, demonstrating that for much of the bronze age eastern Messenia was less significant than the western region, where the majority of important sites have been found. Neolithic finds remain scanty, but major early Helladic II buildings have been identified at Akovitika (near mod. Kalamata) and Voïdhokoilia (near Osmanaga lagoon). The later prehistoric sequence is best known from Nichoria, close to Rizomylo at the NW edge of the Messenian Gulf, which was occupied for the middle and most of the late Helladic periods, and again for much of the Dark Age. Middle

Helladic Messenia has a markedly local character, without much evidence for contacts with the Aegean civilizations, but several of its more substantial settlements seem to have become the centres of small early Mycenaean principalities, to judge from the distribution of tholos-tombs, a type probably first developed in this province (early examples at *Pylos, Nichoria, and elsewhere). These principalities seem to have been combined from the mid-14th cent. BC onwards, to form one of the more important Mycenaean states, whose centre was at Pylos. As indicated by the Linear B texts found in the Pylos palace, the state was divided into two provinces incorporating sixteen regions, which were taxed on a proportional system. While the importance allotted to Pylos and *Nestor (1) its king in the Homeric poems may reflect dim memories of this state, the almost total mismatch between its regional centres and the sites named in the Homeric Catalogue of the Ships (in *Iliad* 2) and other Greek legends elsewhere demonstrates the lack of reliable information about the prehistoric period in the Greek traditions (cf. *MME* 113; J. Chadwick, *Minos* 1975, 55 ff.). The collapse of this state *c.*1200 BC is reflected in a massive decline in the number of identifiable settlements. A reasonable number of Dark Age sites can be identified (W. Coulson, *The Dark Age Pottery of Messenia* (1986)), but information derives principally from Nichoria, where substantial structures and habitation-strata have produced pottery of markedly local character, but a relative abundance of metalwork whose types suggest wider contacts. Dark Age Messenia may have become important enough to be involved in the foundation of *Olympia (C. Morgan, *Athletes and Oracles* (1990), ch. 3), but the conflict with Sparta cut its development short.

O. T. P. K. D.

Myth-history This conflict dominates the patriotic historical tradition of the Messenians preserved in *Pausanias (3) (4. 1–24). According to this the descendants of Neleus were expelled on the arrival of the *Dorians in Messenia, led by the returning *Heraclidae, one of whom, Cresphontes, had won the region by lot, founding the royal line of the Aepytids; when this failed, *Aristodemus (1) was elected king and he, followed by *Aristomenes (1), were the heroes of the Messenian resistance to Spartan expansionism during the so-called Messenian Wars. This tradition was worked up, perhaps largely fabricated, following the foundation of Messene in 369 BC; note too the 4th-cent. BC 'historical' murals at Messene seen by Pausanias (4. 31. 11); for other reminiscences of this tradition in local cult and onomastics see *IG* 5. 1. 1469 and *SEG* 23. 14 (Augustan bull-sacrifice to Aristomenes).

History The Spartans had conquered central Messenia by (?) 700 BC, reducing the old population to the status of *helots (cf. *Tyrtaeus fr. 6 West, *IE*²) or *perioikoi; the Messenian diaspora dates from now. The Third Messenian War, after the great earthquake of 464 BC, terminated, like the first war, in the surrender of the stronghold of *Ithome after a long siege. Granted a safe conduct, many of the survivors (of the *perioikoi* only?) were settled by the Athenians at *Naupactus (455). During the Peloponnesian War the Messenian helots were encouraged to sporadic revolts by the Athenian garrison established at Pylos after the victory at Sphacteria (425), in which Messenians from Naupactus played a decisive part. In 369 Messenia was liberated with the help of the Theban *Epaminondas. Its subsequent history is bound up with that of Messene. Of the lesser Messenian communities now emerging as autonomous *poleis*, the most important were Asine, Corone, and *Methone (2) on the western peninsula; all three prospered in imperial times, partly as stages for east–

west shipping. Sparta's influence in eastern Messenia lingered until well into the 2nd cent. AD.

PREHISTORY *MME*; *GAC* map D; *Excavations at Nichoria in Messenia*: vol. 1, G. Rapp and S. Aschenbrenner (1978), vol. 2, W. McDonald and N. Wilkie (1992), vol. 3, W. McDonald, W. Coulson, and J. Rosser (1983).

HISTORY M. Valmin, *Études topographiques sur la Messénie ancienne* (1930); C. Roebuck, *A History of Messenia from 369 to 146 BC* (1941); F. Kiechle, *Messenische Studien* (1959); P. Cartledge, *Sparta and Lakonia*, 2nd edn. (2002), ch. 8; R. Baladié, *Le Péloponnèse de Strabon* (1980), *passim*; P. Cartledge and A. Spawforth, *Hellenistic and Roman Sparta*, 2nd edn. (2002), esp. 138 ff., 174 f.   A. M. W.; R. J. H.; A. J. S. S.

Messenian cults and myths Since the Messenians were subject to Sparta from the Third Messenian War (see MESSENIA, *myth-history*; SPARTA, § 2) to the refoundation of *Messenia as a state in 370/69 BC, little is known of their traditions in the early period. There are few excavated sanctuaries (e.g. Pharae, Corone), and most of the evidence is from Hellenistic times or even, in the case of *Pausanias (3) and of imperial coins, from the age of the Antonines or the Severi.

Among the older cults, we can pick out that of *Zeus Ithomatas (i.e. of *Ithome) at *Messene (Paus. 4. 33. 1–2), which was already important during the Messenian Wars. On the *Laconian border and common to both territories was the sanctuary of Artemis Limnatis at Kombothekra, whose origins date back to legendary times. Archaeology has made known to us the temples of Apollo Corythus near Corone, and of the *river-god Pamisus, near Thuria. And the cult of Hagna and *Demeter at Andania, best known for a *lex sacra* of 92/1 BC (*IG* 5. 1. 1390) may also go back to an early period.

Other cult figures seem to belong to the period of Spartan domination, like the *Dioscuri at Messene, or *Apollo Carneius (see CARNEA). But most of the gods are represented: at Messene, Pausanias (4. 31. 6–32. 6) mentions *Zeus *Soter (linked with the 4th-cent. foundation of the city), *Poseidon and *Aphrodite, *Artemis Laphria (whose epithet comes from *Naupactus), *Eileithyia, the *Curetes, Demeter, *Asclepius, *Sarapis, and *Isis, while inscriptions give in addition Artemis Oupesia, the imperial cult, etc. In addition, excavations at the Asclepieum (formerly thought to be the civic agora) have revealed a temple and cult-room of Artemis Orthia overseen by a sacred council of 'elders of Oupesia', (an alternative name for the goddess) and the Sebasteum or chamber for the Roman imperial cult. Elsewhere in Messenia, we can point to Athena as city-goddess at Corone and Thuria, and Aphrodite as 'Syrian Goddess' (see ATARGATIS) at Thuria. *Hero-cult is also found (*Aristomenes (1), the heroine Messene). The chief characteristic of Messenian myths is an evident wish to confer antiquity on cults; hence local legends which place the births of Zeus and Asclepius in Messenia. Other myths, such as that of Caucon at Andania, are concerned with the establishment of cults, or with the central figure of Aristomenes, who in the tradition of the Second Messenian War symbolizes the Messenian wish for freedom. His saga, mixing epic elements from *Rhianus with themes of tragedy, was put together in order to create a glorious past as a foundation for Messenian identity.

P. Themelis in R. Hägg (ed.), *Ancient Greek Cult Practice from the Epigraphic Evidence* (1994), 101–22 (Artemis Orthia).   M. J.

Messiah, messianism See CHRISTIANITY; RELIGION, JEWISH; VIRGIL (section on Eclogues).

Messius (*RE* 9) **Quintus Decius, Gaius,** the emperor **Decius** (AD 249–51), born in *Pannonia, but of an old senatorial family, had already achieved high office before being appointed by Philip (M. *Iulius Philippus) to restore order on the Danube. His success, and Philip's unpopularity, caused his troops to declare him emperor and compel him to overthrow his patron. In 250 the Carpi invaded Dacia, the *Goths, under Kniva, Moesia. Decius was defeated near Beroea. The following year, in an attempt to intercept the Goths on their way home, he and his son Herennius were defeated and killed at Abrittus.

Decius was a staunch upholder of the old Roman traditions. His assumption of the additional surname of Trajan promised an aggressive frontier policy; and his persecution of Christians resulted from his belief that the restoration of state cults was essential to the preservation of the empire. See CHRISTIANITY. However, his approach was outdated and his reign initiated the worst period of the 3rd-cent. 'crisis'.

R. Syme, *Emperors and Biography* (1971); H. A. Pohlsander, *ANRW* 2. 16 (1986), 1826 ff.; H. Wolfram, *History of the Goths* (1988).   B. H. W.; J. F. Dr.

Metagenes, Athenian comic poet, won two victories at the *Lenaea in the last decade of the 5th cent. BC (*IG* 2². 2325. 128). We have fragments of four plays; in *Thurio-Persians* Thurii is eulogized fantastically as a land of abundance (see CRATES (1) and PHERECRATES); Ὅμηρος ἢ Ἀσκηταί ('Homer or the Athletes') mentions (fr. 10) the betrayal of *Naupactus to the Spartans in 400 (Diod. Sic. 14. 34. 2).

Kassel–Austin, *PCG* 6. 4 ff. (*CAF* 1. 704 ff.).   K. J. D.

metallurgy

Greek Metallurgy covers all processes involving native metal or metallic ores after mining (concentration, smelting, refining) up to the production of artefacts. Understanding these depends less on literary references (mainly Roman: *Strabo, *Pliny (1)) than on archaeological and scientific research, analytical, comparative, and experimental. Only the richest ores could be smelted directly; generally, enrichment was needed to avoid wasting fuel. So, mined rock was sorted underground and above, poorer material rejected, and the richer crushed with stone mauls or iron hammers on anvil-stones; deeply worn boulders are recognizable as such in *Laurium. Washing aided concentration of ores, especially those (gold, argentiferous lead) heavier than gangue; it could be done in pans or cradles, with rough cloth or fleeces (as in *Colchis, giving rise to the golden fleece legend). Milling to a fine grain, in rotary mills or hopper-querns, and sieving preceded washing. Laurium best exemplifies the elaborate arrangements for ore treatment which local conditions necessitated. Stone-built cement-surfaced rectangular washing tables had stand-tanks with funnelled jet-holes (perhaps serving wooden sluices), level floors, sunken channels, and sedimentation basins, which separated the milled ore from gangue and recycled water. There are also four known round washeries with helicoidal stone sluices. Repeated washing ensured the desired enrichment. Smelting was done with wood or carbon fuel in ovens of various forms, with heat intensified by means of bellows. Laurium offers three excavated furnace sites with a row of banked oven-rooms, filling-platforms, and traces of stone and clay chimney-ovens. Furnace techniques depended on the melting-point of metals, the ores used, the need to use fluxes or cope with slag, whether reduction or oxidization took place, and whether the process produced a liquid metal (copper, bronze, gold, a silver–lead mix) to be tapped into moulds to form ingots, or a livid mass (iron bloom) requiring hot hammering. Remelting and refining generally followed; so, 'work-lead', remelted under blown air produced metallic silver (for minting coins) and lead-oxide, which again remelted produced lead (for sealing cramps in masonry etc.). The Greeks used crucible and cupellation methods, developed an early knowledge of alloys (e.g. copper, then arsenical coppers, true copper–tin bronzes, and lead-bronzes for casting), and mastered various hot and cold treatments for metals, smithing, and soldering. Some vase-paintings usefully illustrate workshop activities, like smithing and casting of bronze statues. See MINES AND MINING, GREEK.

R. F. Tylecote, *A History of Metallurgy*, 2nd edn. (1992), and *Historical Metallurgy* 1984, 65–81; 1992, 1–18.　　　　　　　　　J. E. J.

Roman In the Roman period most metals were obtained not in a natural state directly from mining, but as a result of metallurgical processing of compound mineral deposits (ores). Ores, once mined, were crushed with stone mortars and as much sterile rock as possible was removed by hand-sorting. Manual millstones, or occasionally handle-powered, 'hourglass' mills (similar to the grain-mills from *Pompeii) were used to grind the ore to a powder, which was often further concentrated by washing. This was carried out using portable sievelike instruments or in a permanent installation (washery), where water was channelled over the ore, forcing the heavier metal-bearing grains to settle in basins while carrying off the lighter dross.

Few complete Roman smelting-furnaces have survived, and so knowledge of metallurgical techniques depends on scattered finds of parts of furnaces and on ancient authors such as *Diodorus (3) Siculus, *Strabo, and the elder *Pliny (1), who describe the main techniques, sometimes conflating different processes. Scientific analyses of metal objects and slag-heaps, as well as experiments conducted in reconstructed furnaces, have revealed much about the nature and efficiency of Roman metallurgy. No major innovations in metallurgical techniques were introduced under the Romans, but slag-heaps show that the scale of smelting at many sites was significantly increased to match the increased scale of mining. The main types of furnace were the bowl-furnace and the shaft-furnace. The latter allowed continuous production, since fresh fuel and ore could be added at the top of the shaft while slag and molten metal were tapped at the base. These became more widespread throughout the empire under Roman rule. In both types charcoal was the main fuel used and the high temperatures required were achieved by channelling air from hand-worked bellows directly over the ore through a clay pipe (tuyère) fitted into the base of the furnace. Certain metals were more in demand than before, especially lead, which had previously been of interest mainly for its silver content. *Orichalcum* (brass), an alloy of copper and zinc, was probably only discovered in the Roman period. It played an important role in *coinage from Augustus onwards, being used for sestertii and dupondii.

The Romans used various techniques to separate out individual metals from ores. *Gold was refined by cementation (Diod. Sic. 3. 14; Strabo 3. 2. 8; Plin. *HN* 33. 84) or by amalgamation with mercury (Plin. *HN* 33. 99). In the former process ore was heated with salt or sulphureous substances in a clay crucible. Other metals and impurities were converted into chlorides or sulphides and burnt off or absorbed into the crucible, leaving behind the gold. Amalgamation was possible because all other substances float on mercury, while gold combines with it. The resultant amalgam was pressed on a leather hide. The mercury passed through it, leaving behind pure gold. Cupellation was used to refine silver from galena (lead sulphide). The galena was

heated in a crucible (cupel) and oxidized by the air forced into the furnace. Some of the resultant lead-oxide (litharge) was absorbed into the crucible, while the rest was removed with cold iron rods. The silver and any gold present were left in globular form at the bottom of the crucible. Pyrites and copper-rich ores, especially chalcopyrite, often contained some silver and gold. Such ores were first smelted to produce an impure ingot, which was alloyed with lead and reheated. Since lead melts at a much lower temperature than copper, by the process of liquation the molten lead carried the silver and gold with it, leaving the copper in the ore. The precious metals were then separated from the lead by cupellation, and then from each other by cementation.

Iron has an extremely high melting-point (1,540 °C: 2,804 °F). Since furnaces could not achieve such temperatures until the 19th cent., wrought, rather than cast, iron was produced in Roman times. Iron ore was reduced in a furnace until it formed a lump (bloom) of iron, slag, and charcoal, which settled at the bottom of the furnace. A smith later hammered these blooms to remove pieces of relatively pure iron, which were then welded into the tools or implements required. The Romans understood the process of carburization, whereby iron, when heated with charcoal, absorbed carbon and gained strength, which could be enhanced if the hot iron was rapidly cooled by being plunged into cold water (i.e. quench-hardening). See MINES AND MINING, ROMAN. See also under individual metals.

O. Davies, *Roman Mines in Europe* (1935); R. J. Forbes, *Metallurgy in Antiquity* (1950), revised as *Stud. Anc. Technol.* 8, 9; J. Ramin, *La Technique minière et métallurgique des anciens* (1977); J. F. Healy, *Mining and Metallurgy in the Greek and Roman World* (1978; rev. It. trans. 1992); W. A. Oddy (ed.), *Aspects of Early Metallurgy* (1980); R. F. Tylecote, *A History of Metallurgy*, 2nd edn. (1992), and *The Early History of Metallurgy in Europe* (1987).　　　　　　　　　J. C. E.

metamorphosis, a type of tale focusing on a miraculous transformation into a new shape. Tales of transformations of a divine or human being into an animal, plant, or inanimate object were very popular throughout antiquity. Already attested in Homer, they were given a literary form later. Collections of these tales are known to have existed from the Hellenistic period onwards. *Nicander of Colophon (2nd cent. BC) wrote Ἑτεροιούμενα, *Parthenius of Nicaea (1st cent. BC) Μεταμορφώσεις. These and similar collections are now lost except for a book of excerpts by *Antoninus Liberalis. They provided the model and material for *Ovid's *Metamorphoses*, recording some 250 transformations from the creation of the world to the reign of Augustus. After Ovid the most famous literary metamorphosis is that in *Apuleius' *Metamorphoses* (2nd cent. AD), relating the transformation of Lucius into an ass and his final, miraculous, restoration to human shape by the goddess Isis. Outside the realm of fiction, magicians (and gods) were generally believed to be able to change their own shapes and those of others.

S. Jannaccone, *La letteratura greco-latina delle metamorfosi* (1953); P. M. C. Forbes Irving, *Metamorphosis in Greek Myths* (1990); F. Celoria, *The Metamorphoses of Antoninus Liberalis* (1992), trans. and comm.

　　　　　　　　　H. S. V.

Metanira (Μετάνειρα), in mythology, wife of *Celeus, king of *Eleusis; she received *Demeter hospitably, but spoiled her plan to make Metanira's child immortal by screaming when she saw him laid on the fire; see DEMETER. She had a cult in Eleusis (Paus. 1. 39. 2) near the well where Demeter sat; cf. Athenagoras, *Leg. pro Christ.* 14.

metaphor and simile are features of literary language that have been extensively discussed by theorists and critics since antiquity. The first purposeful investigations are *Aristotle's (*Poet.* 21–2; *Rh.* 3. 2. 6–4. 4, 3. 10. 7–11. 15). By the time of *Quintilian (*Inst.* 8. 5. 35–9. 3. 102) metaphor and simile have a place in an elaborate apparatus of 'tropes' (τρόποι, *tropi/modi*) and 'figures' (σχήματα, *figurae*), with metaphor (μεταφορά, *translatio*) classed among the tropes, and simile (εἰκών, *similitudo*) generally associated with the figures (e.g. Cic. *De or.* 3. 205, cf. Quint. *Inst.* 9. 2. 1–2). Figures comprise a variety of supposedly special 'conformations' (Quint. *Inst.* 9. 1. 4), from homoeoteleuton to rhetorical question. Tropes comprise all deviations (except for errors) from established word usage, including in particular (*a*) deviations based on contiguity or association, in modern analysis generally grouped together as 'metonymy' ('arma virumque cano', 'arms and the man I sing', Verg. *Aen.* 1. 1, where *arms* implies *war*) and (*b*) metaphor, a deviation based on similarity or analogy (a swarm of bees '*nare* per aestatem liquidam', *swim* through the summer air, Verg. *G.* 4. 59).

Ancient discussion of metaphor is frequently vitiated by confusion of metaphor proper with literary cliché and 'dead metaphor': i.e. deviation from established usage is equated with colourful usage perhaps once deviant but now established. For languages no longer spoken, distinguishing deviant from established instances is difficult, but remains essential. It is not helpful to discuss as metaphor Homeric 'shepherd of the people' (ποιμένα λαῶν *Il.* 1. 263 etc.), which may 'sound metaphorical' in translation, but in Homeric Greek is an established usage. Likewise we should distinguish metaphor from usages like 'sitire agros' ('the fields are *parched*'), which Cicero says was current among rural speakers in his own time, yet himself grotesquely calls 'bold metaphor' (*Orat.* 81–2).

Modern theorists generally associate metaphor with simile and with comparison in general, including informal analogy, under the general heading, 'imagery', but (less plausibly and unlike the ancients) dissociate metaphor from the other tropes. In ancient theory, notwithstanding the figure/trope distinction, metaphor and simile are commonly linked (as Arist. *Rh.* 3. 4. 1; Quint. *Inst.* 8. 6. 8), and metaphor is the most important of the tropes (as Quint. *Inst.* 8. 6. 4), but not detached from them. More constructively, modern analysts of metaphor distinguish the vehicle (deviant element) from the tenor (non-deviant element) and both from the image as a whole, and likewise with the corresponding elements of similes and other forms of comparison.

In much Greek and Latin literature metaphor and allied figures occur sporadically without any intensive or intense use. Representative are the short explanatory comparisons that crop up in technical prose ('in tetanus the jaws set hard like wood', αἱ γένυες πεπήγασιν ὡς ξύλιναι Hippoc. *Morb.* 3. 12) and the orator's isolated and often half-familiar metaphors, commended by generations of rhetoricians ('Italiam tumultus expergefecit', 'the insurrection *awoke* Italy', Anon. in *Auct. ad. Her.* 4. 34. 45). The significant usage of imagery is in poetry and poetic prose. With the antiphonal epic simile, usage is more drastically restricted: 'And *as when* a man *packs* the wall of a high house tight with stones . . . , *even so packed* were their helmets and bossed shields' (ὡς δ᾽ ὅτε τοῖχον ἀνὴρ ἀράρῃ . . . Ι ὣς ἄραρον . . . *Il.* 16. 212–4). This is much the most important mode of imagery in Homer, from whom it is transmitted as part of the epic repertoire to Apollonius (1), Virgil, and beyond; outside epic poetry, instances are few.

The main poetic functions of metaphor and simile in ancient usage are:

1. To make clearer, as through a diagram, usually by appeal to familiar experience. The function is chiefly associated with epic simile (as in the *Iliad* example just cited) or simile or analogy in scientific or philosophical contexts: *Plato (1)'s long comparison (*Ion* 533d–e) between the inspirational power of poetry and the magnet and *Lucretius' analogy (5. 1056–90) between human speech and animal communication are representative. With poetic metaphor the function is rarely dominant, except where the goal is imagery that expresses the inexpressible, as when Plato (*Resp.* 509e) uses the very word εἰκόνες ('images') to express the relation between sense-objects and ideal reality. Many of the best examples come from earlier Greek literature: Aesch. *Ag.* 218 ἀνάγκας ἔδυ λέπαδνον ('he put on the yoke-strap of necessity'); *Heraclitus 52 αἰὼν παῖς ἐστι παίζων, πεσσεύων ('time is a boy playing draughts').

2. To make immediate, as if to the senses (not necessarily to the sight, *pace* Arist. *Rh.* 3. 11. 1–4 etc.). This is less a matter of making clear than of making alien ('defamiliarizing', in modern theoretical terminology) and thereby making listener or reader experience anew: Archil. 120. 2 οἴνῳ συγκεραυνωθεὶς φρένας ('my wits are *thunderstruck* with wine'), Ar. *Ach.* 274 f. καταβαλόντα καταγιγαρτίσαι ('laying her down and *crushing* her *grape*'), Verg. *G.* 4. 59 'nare per aestatem liquidam' (the 'swimming' bees, cited above), Petron. *Sat.* 1 'mellitos verborum globulos' ('phraseological *honey-balls*'). The mechanism is usually short metaphor.

3. To exploit the associations, including the contrary associations, of the vehicle, beyond any limited point or ground of comparison. *Il.* 8. 306 ff.: Gorgythion is killed and 'his head dropped down like a poppy, weighed down with its fruit and the spring rain' (μήκων . . . Ι καρπῷ βριθομένη νοτίησί τε εἰαρινῆσιν): poignant contrast of death with life and growth. Aesch. *Ag.* 40 f.: Menelaus (1) is Πριάμου μέγας ἀντίδικος, 'Priam's great adversary *at law*': the implication that the Trojan War is somehow a legal event prefigures the way the whole cycle of conflict is eventually resolved in *Eumenides*. Verg. *Aen.* 12. 948–9 (*Aeneas killing *Turnus (1)): 'Pallas te hoc vulnere, Pallas immolat' ('this wound is for you from Pallas; you are Pallas' *sacrificial offering*'): the vehicle evokes the nexus of religious duty and destiny to which Aeneas is committed, even as he avenges himself on Turnus for the murder of young *Pallas (2d).

Different functions readily coexist in a complex whole, as in many of the instances quoted. Complexity is often intensified by clusters of imagery. The richest examples are in Aeschylus: *Ag.* 1178 ff. (Cassandra): ὁ χρησμὸς οὐκέτ᾽ ἐκ καλυμμάτων Ι ἔσται δεδορκὼς νεογάμου νύμφης δίκην, Ι λαμπρὸς δ᾽ ἔοικεν ἡλίου πρὸς ἀντολὰς Ι πνέων ἐφήξειν, ὥστε κύματος δίκην . . . ('no longer shall my prophecy look out from a veil like a young bride, but *lampros* it will come, blowing against the rising sun, and like a wave . . .'). Here interaction between tenor and vehicle is a further poetic resource: the untranslatable *lampros* is both 'lucid' (of the plain speech to come), 'fresh' (of the bride's face), 'keen' (of the dawn wind), and 'bright' (of the rising sun). Complex poetic relationships of a different kind are created by the use of imagery to develop or create themes within a larger work. A wide range of thematic images exists, from 'law' in Aeschylus' *Oresteia* (glanced at above) to 'food and drink' in Persius' first satire.

In some of the best ancient literature, however, metaphor and simile are not predominant. In particular, the most characteristic tropical movements in much Latin poetry and literary prose involve not metaphor but metonymy: Hor. *Ars P.* 80 'hunc socci cepere pedem grandesque coturni ('both the slipper [= comedy] and the big boot [= tragedy] have accepted the iambic foot'); Tac. *Ann.* 4. 67 'aestas in favonium obversa' ('[the island in] summer faces the west wind'); Juv. 1. 51 'Venusina digna lucerna' ('crimes worthy of the Venusian lamp', i.e. crimes that the satirist Horace, born at Venusia, might have got up early, or stayed up late, to write about). And in Virgil's *Aeneid*, which begins with a simple metonym ('arma'), the representative trope of the closing lines is not the metaphor in 'immolat' discussed above, but the agonized metonymic cluster that precedes it, 'Pallas te hoc vulnere, Pallas . . .'. Here 'wound' (i.e. weapon that deals the wound) and the repeated 'Pallas' (i.e. 'I, Aeneas, on behalf of Pallas') combine to create a harsh and powerful image: the absent Pallas is 'there' in the weapon's stroke to avenge his own 'wound' and Aeneas' too.

V. Pöschl, H. Gärtner, and W. Heyke, *Bibliographie zur antiken Bildersprache* (1964); W. B. Stanford, *Greek Metaphor* (1936); M. H. McCall Jr., *Ancient Rhetorical Theories of Simile and Comparison* (1969); M. S. Silk, *Interaction in Poetic Imagery* (1974) (on 'dead metaphor', 27 ff., 228 ff.); G. Williams, *Figures of Thought in Roman Poetry* (1980); D. H. Porter, *Symb. Osl.* 1986, 19 ff. (bibliog. on thematic imagery, esp. in Greek tragedy). Among work on imagery in particular authors that sheds light on imagery in general, D. A. West, *The Imagery and Poetry of Lucretius* (1969), C. Moulton, *Similes in the Homeric Poems* (1977), and D. Steiner, *The Crown of Song: Metaphor in Pindar* (1986), are noteworthy.

M. S. Si.

Metapontum (mod. Metaponto), an Achaean colony (see ACHAEA), at the mouth of the river Basento. It was a prosperous city, controlling extensive territory. Its early history is dominated by rivalry with *Siris, which it destroyed, and *Tarentum. In 413 BC it supported the Athenian expedition against *Sicily and S. Italy (Thuc. 7. 33. 4–5, mentioning an earlier alliance, and 7. 57. 11. See however 6. 44. 2 for 415). By the 4th cent., it was declining. *Dionysius (1) I captured it in the 390s, as did the Lucanians (see LUCANIA). As a member of the Italiote League of Greek cities, it was under the domination of *Tarentum from *c.*370 onwards. It contracted an alliance with the Molossian king *Alexander (6) I, but fell foul of another *condottiere*, *Cleonymus of Sparta, who captured it in 302/1. It supported *Pyrrhus but fell to Rome in 272, and was a Roman ally (see SOCII) until 212, when it revolted, supporting Hannibal until his retreat from Italy. After the war, it disappears from the historical record, although a Roman *municipium continued to exist on the site. The territory has been extensively surveyed, revealing one of the earliest and largest Greek systems of centuriation (see LAND-DIVISION, GREEK) and numerous rural settlements, the number of which declines sharply after the 4th cent. BC.

D. Adamesteanu, *Rev. Arch.* 1967; J. C. Carter, in G. Barker and T. Hodges (eds.), *Archaeology and Italian Society* (1981); Various authors, *Metaponto: Atti di Convegno di Studi sulla Magna Grecia*, 13 (1974).

K. L.

Metaurus (mod. Metauro), river in Umbria, midway between Rimini (*Ariminum) and *Ancona. The consuls C. *Claudius Nero and M. *Livius Salinator, and the praetor L. Porcius Licinus confronted *Hasdrubal (2), bringing reinforcements to *Hannibal from Spain and Gaul, north of Sena Gallica (Senigallia). He fell back to the high ground south of the river, where he was defeated (with heavy losses on both sides) and killed, on 23 June 207 BC, so ending Hannibal's last faint hope of victory in Italy.

Livy 27. 43–9. Walbank, *HCP* 2. 267 ff.; Caven, *Punic Wars* 208–16.

B. M. C.

Metelli See CAECILIUS.

meteorology (μετεωρολογία) strictly means 'the study of things aloft', but the term was widely used in antiquity to cover the study both of what might now be called meteorological phenomena and the investigation of (supposedly) related phenomena on and within the earth itself, such as tides, earthquakes, volcanoes, and the formation of minerals and metals. Presocratic interest in meteorology is well attested, but the difficulty of providing explanations of such intractable phenomena sometimes made students of the subject figures of fun. *Aristophanes (1) in the *Clouds* parodies 'meteorosophists' for their arcane and silly speculations about atmospheric and subterranean marvels. The author of the Hippocratic treatise *On Ancient Medicine* (see HIPPOCRATES (2)) attacks those who are forced by the very nature of the subject to base their speculations on indemonstrable premisses (see HYPOTHESIS, SCIENTIFIC). Even *Socrates (in Plato's *Phaedrus* 270a) offers *Anaxagoras a backhanded compliment, claiming that he filled people with 'lofty' (i.e. meteorological) thoughts.

The earliest surviving work on the subject is *Aristotle's *Meteorology*. Aristotle describes his own work as an account of the *physics of the sublunary sphere—that is, the sphere closest to the earth; he includes accounts of comets and shooting stars (which were thought to originate in the upper atmosphere), and moves on to discuss weather, earthquakes, the origins of rivers, and the seas. Book 3 ends with an account of the formation of minerals. Book 4 (still of disputed authenticity) deals with the physical properties of materials found in and around the earth and their behaviour. The later commentators on this work, especially *Alexander (14) of Aphrodisias, and John *Philoponus, preserve a great deal more information on the subject, and Aristotle himself preserves important evidence about the views of his predecessors.

Aristotle's successor *Theophrastus also wrote a *Meteorology*, of which parts survive in a Syriac version. After Theophrastus, a wide variety of explanations of meteorological phenomena continued to circulate; accounts of unusual or terrifying phenomena like *earthquakes and storms were especially common. Epicurean meteorological theory (outlined most conveniently in the *Letter to Pythocles*, and in book 6 of *Lucretius' *On the Nature of Things*) is directed at banishing fear through the discovery of natural explanations of frightening phenomena. See EPICURUS. The anonymous Latin poem *Aetna* is also of considerable interest in this respect.

The Stoic natural philosopher *Posidonius (2) of Apamea was perhaps the most important ancient meteorologist after Aristotle; his own work does not survive, but much of it is thought to be reproduced in the younger Seneca's *Natural Questions* (see ANNAEUS SENECA (2), L.) and *Strabo's *Geography*. (The relation to Posidonian theory of the Ps.-Aristotelian treatise *On the Universe* remains unclear.) Posidonius' work on terrestrial phenomena forms part of a grand scheme in which the structure and nature of operations in the upper atmosphere are united with those of the entire organic whole of the cosmos.

TEXTS Aristotle, *Meteorology*, trans. H. D. P. Lee (Loeb, 1952); Ps.-Aristotle, *On the Universe*, trans. D. Furley (Loeb, 1955); *Theophrastus of Eresus*, ed. W. W. Fortenbaugh, 2 vols. (1992); Epicurus, *Letter to Pythocles*, in Diogenes Laertius, *Lives of the Philosophers* 10. 3–117, trans. R. D. Hicks (Loeb, 1925; vol. 1 repr. with new intro. 1972); Lucretius, *On the Nature of Things* 6, trans. M. F. Smith (Loeb, 1975); *Posidonius*, L. Edelstein and I. G. Kidd, 2nd edn. with comm., 3 vols (1988–9);

Seneca, *Natural Questions*, trans. T. H. Corcoran (Loeb, 2 vols. 1971–2); Alexander's and Philoponus' commentaries on Aristotle's *Meteorology* are edited by M. Hayduck (1899 and 1901).

LITERATURE The classic work is O. Gilbert, *Die meteorologischen Theorien des griechischen Altertums* (1907; repr. 1967), and see the bibliographies in the texts cited above. J. T. V.

Methana, a volcanic peninsula in the Saronic Gulf, 10 km. (6 mi.) north of *Troezen. In 425 BC Methana was captured by the Athenians, who fortified the isthmus, but was restored to Sparta in 421. Coins issued in the 4th cent. suggest a period of independence and this may have prompted the fortification of the ancient city at Palaiokastro. In the 3rd cent. there was a spectacular volcanic eruption, described by *Strabo (1. 3. 18). Subsequently, in 226 BC, Methana was taken by the Ptolemaic admiral Patroclus and used as a military base by the Ptolemies, the city being renamed Arsinoë in honour of Arsinoe III, the wife of *Ptolemy (1) IV. C. B. M.

Methodism, Methodists, medical. See MEDICINE, § 5. 3.

Methodius, according to (an unreliable) tradition, bishop of Olympus in *Lycia and martyr (3rd cent.), author of the Greek treatises *The Banquet, or On Virginity* (*Symposium*; in praise of chastity, modelled on *Plato (1)), *Aglaophon, or On the Resurrection* (against *Origen (1); fragments), *On the Freedom of the Will* (against *Gnosticism; fragments), *On the Life and the Reasonable Action* (in Old Slavonic translation), and of several other writings.

TEXTS Complete edition: N. Bonwetsch, *Methodius, GCS* 27 (1917); *The Banquet:* H. Musurillo and V.-H. Debidour, *Méthode d'Olympe—Le Banquet*, SC 95 (1963), with Fr. trans.

TRANSLATIONS A. Roberts, J. Donaldson, and A. C. Coxe, *The Ante-Nicene Fathers: Translations of the Writings of the Fathers down to AD 325* 6 (1886; repr. 1979), 309–402; H. Musurillo, *Symposium* (1958).

R. Williams, *Theologische Realenzyklopädie* 22 (1992), 680 ff. W. K.

Methone (1), Greek town (a colony of *Eretria) in Pieria (see MACEDONIA), granted privileges by Athens early in the *Peloponnesian War (ML 65 and N. G. L. Hammond and G. T. Griffith, *History of Macedonia* 2 (1979), 124 ff.); taken by *Philip (1) II in 354 (Diod. 16. 31. 6). S. H.

Methone (2), or Mothone, strong place on the western peninsula of *Messenia, south of *Pylos. See BRASIDAS.

Methymna (now Mithymna), the second most powerful *polis of *Lesbos, on the NW coast; birthplace of the poet *Arion (2). The earliest finds are geometric; later remains include an Archaic street, a theatre-like building, an aqueduct tower, cemeteries, and a harbour mole. Its limited arable was increased by the incorporation of *Arisbe (2) and the Kalloni plain in the Archaic period; cult sites at Klopedi and Mesa may have lain within its territory. It had important sanctuaries of Apollo and Dionysus, and its wine was esteemed.

Methymna's independent history is dominated by rivalry with *Mytilene. It did not back the Mytilenean Revolt in 428, but broke with Athens after the Sicilian expedition. The Spartans resisted *Thrasybulus' attempt to recapture Methymna; later it joined the *Second Athenian Confederacy. After the *Social War (1) it endured tyrannies and was briefly held by Persia before *Alexander (3) the Great freed Lesbos. There followed a long period of Ptolemaic rule (see PTOLEMY (1)). Methymna concluded an alliance with Rome in 129 BC. Archaeology testifies to the existence of the Roman town but not, as yet, to prosperity.

H.-G. Buchholz, *Methymna* (1975); N. Spencer, *BSA* 1995; *RE* 15/2 (1932), 1391–5. D. G. J. S.

metics As the Greek *polis evolved it sought to differentiate, amongst its inhabitants, between insiders and outsiders. Insiders *par excellence* were its own members, the citizens; palpable outsiders were its slaves, indigenous or imported (see SLAVERY); but this simple dichotomy would have sufficed only for communities like *Sparta which discouraged immigration. Elsewhere it was necessary to recognize free persons who lived, temporarily or permanently, in the *polis* without becoming its citizens. Several -*oikos* words are attested of such persons, with *metoikos* ('metic') most common. The precise nature and complexity of metic-status doubtless varied from place to place; evidence approaches adequacy only for Athens, atypical in its allure and, consequently, the numbers of those who succumbed thereto (half the size of the (reduced) citizen body of c.313 BC (Ath. 272c); perhaps proportionately larger in the 5th cent. BC (R. Duncan-Jones, *Chiron* 1980, 101 ff.)). With *Solon having created only indirect incentives to immigration, Athenian metic-status probably owes its formal origins to *Cleisthenes (2), after whom the presence of metics was recognized in law and could develop in its details at both city and local (*deme) level. The dividing line between visitors and residents seems to have been drawn on a common-sense basis in the 5th cent. BC but became more mechanical in the 4th (thus Gauthier and Whitehead, below; *contra*, E. Lévy in R. Lonis (ed.), *L'Étranger dans le monde grec* (1987), 47 ff.). Definition as a metic brought some privileges but many burdens, largely fiscal (including the *metoikion*, 'poll-tax') and military; various exemptions came with higher-status niches such as *isoteles*. Socio-economically, Athens' metics were highly diverse, and contemporary attitudes to their presence deeply ambivalent.

Athens: M. Clerc, *Les Métèques athéniens* (1893), sentimentalized but still worth consulting; P. Gauthier, *Symbola* (1972), ch. 3; D. Whitehead, *The Ideology of the Athenian Metic* (1977). General: D. Whitehead, *Ant. Class.* 1984, 47 ff. D. W.

Metiochus and Parthenope, hero and heroine of a lost Greek *novel reconstructed chiefly from the 11th-cent. Persian *Vamicq and Adhra*. In a fragment preserved on a papyrus of the 2nd cent. AD, the scene is a *symposium of the court of *Polycrates (1) of Samos; Anaximenes proposes discussion of love, and Polycrates' daughter Parthenope responds angrily to the speech of a metic, Metiochus son of Miltiades, questioning conventional images of Eros and himself abjuring love. Style and presumably date are close to *Chariton's.

TEXTS H. Maehler, *ZPE* 23 (1976); S. A. Stephens and J. J. Winkler, *Ancient Greek Novels: The Fragments* (1993).

TRANSLATION G. N. Sandy, in B. P. Reardon (ed.), *Collected Ancient Greek Novels* (1989).

INTERPRETATION A. Dihle, *Würzburger Jahrbücher* 1978; T. Hägg, *The Novel in Antiquity* (1983), 18, *Eranos* 1985, *Cl. Ant.* 1987, and *Symb. Osl.* 1989. E. L. B.

Metis, intelligence personified. According to *Hesiod (*Theog.* 886–900), she was the wife of *Zeus, who swallowed her when she was pregnant, since he knew she would first bear *Athena and then another child, who would become ruler of the universe. She was also connected with the birth of *Hephaestus (?Hes. fr. 343 M–W). The myth explains the close connection of Zeus and Athena with *mētis*.

M. Detienne and J.-P. Vernant, *Cunning Intelligence in Greek Culture and Society* (1978), *passim*. J. N. B.

Meton (*RE* 2), Athenian astronomer, is dated by his observation of the summer solstice, together with *Euctemon, in 432 BC (Ptol. *Alm.* 3. 1). He is famous for his introduction of the luni-solar calendaric cycle named after him, with 19 solar years and 235 months, of which 110 were 'hollow' (containing 29 days) and 125 full (containing 30 days), making a total of 6,940 days. The basis of the cycle (though not the year-length of 365⁵/₁₉ days) was undoubtedly derived from Babylonian practice. We may presume that Meton intercalated a thirteenth month in the same years as the Babylonians, and prescribed a fixed sequence of full and hollow months, but this is conjectural. He used the month-names of the Athenian calendar, but his cycle was intended not as a reform of that, but to provide a fixed basis for dating astronomical observations (in which it was later superseded by the cycle of *Callippus), and for Meton's own astronomical calendar (*parapēgma*). Meton erected an instrument for observing solstices (see ASTRONOMICAL INSTRUMENTS) on the Pnyx (Philochorus, *FGrH* 328 F 122), and appears as a character in *Aristophanes (1),s, *Birds* (992 ff.), produced in 414. See ASTRONOMY.

> G. J. Toomer, *Dict. Sci. Biogr.* 9. 337–40, 'Meton' (with ancient references to Meton and further literature). G. J. T.

Mētragyrtēs (Μητραγύρτης), lit. 'beggar of the Mother', a mendicant servitor of *Cybele. *Mētragyrtai* travelled in bands, begging, dancing, and prophesying. They are attested in 5th-cent. BC Athens (Arist. *Rh.* 1405ᵃ20), and Cicero (*Leg.* 2. 22, 40; cf. Dion. Hal. *Ant. Rom.* 2. 19) implies that these *famuli* were tolerated at Rome. They were generally *eunuchs, the Galli. Similar *agyrtai* ('beggars') existed in other cults (Pl. *Resp.* 364b), chiefly oriental, and *Apuleius (*Met.* 8–9) gives a lively picture of those of the Dea Syria (see ATARGATIS). An inscription from Syria (*BCH* 1897, 59, no. 68) records the collections made on his travels by one such slave (δοῦλος) of Atargatis (cf. *SEG* 7. 358, 801).

> H. Graillot, *Le Culte de Cybèle* (1912), ch. 8; A. D. Nock, *Essays* (1972), 1. 7–15; F. Poland, *RE* 15/2 (1932), 1471–3. F. R. W.; D. S. P.

metre, Greek (The different types of metre are described in § 4, and cross-references to individual metres within this section are indicated by the letters (a)–(i).)

Greek verse is quantitative: syllabic length is its patterning agent.

1. Prosody A syllable is long either φύσει ('by nature'), when its vowel-sound is long (long vowel or diphthong), or θέσει (traditionally rendered 'by position'), when its vowel-sound is short, but followed by two or more consonants, whether or not they belong to the same word. In this case, the consonants are said to 'make position'. ζ ξ ψ are double consonants. However, plosive ('mute') followed by nasal (μ ν) or liquid (λ ρ) does not always make position, depending on whether the plosive closes the syllable or not: πᾰτ-ρός, but πᾰ-τρός. The plosives are: π β φ (labials), τ δ θ (dentals), κ γ χ (velars). The voiced plosives, β δ γ, are the strongest. Thus, βλ and γλ usually make position until the 5th cent. BC, and γμ γν δμ δν always make it. The treatment of plosive + nasal/liquid varies between periods and types of poetry. In *Homer, the early iambographers and lyric poets, the combination makes position usually or more often than not. It is least likely to make position in Attic poetry, especially comedy. Hence the term *Attic correption*.

The meeting of vowels at the junction between words gives rise to various modifications, some of which are shown typographically. *Elision* means the suppression (for metrical purposes) of short final vowel before initial vowel. Certain short vowels (e.g. -ŭ, -ῐ as noun or adjective ending) are unelidable, and are not placed before words beginning with a vowel. The diphthongs -αι and -οι are occasionally elided (e.g. in Homer, βούλομ' ἐγώ).

Occasionally, an initial vowel is suppressed following a final vowel (*prodelision, aphaeresis*). A final long vowel or diphthong may be shortened before an initial vowel. This is common in *Homer (whence the term *epic correption*), and continues to be found in post-Homeric poetry in dactylic and other single-long-double-short metres. Correption may occur within a word (note, especially, πŏιεῖν, τŏιοῦτος, etc. in Attic). *Crasis, synizesis, synecphonesis* are processes by which final and initial vowel are conflated into one sound. Sometimes this is shown typographically (e.g. κᾱπό = καὶ ἀπό), sometimes not (e.g. μὴ οὐ). Where final and initial vowel meet without modification there is said to be *hiatus*. Hiatus in the absence of metrical discontinuity is exceptional. In Homer, the now unwritten consonant *digamma* (ϝ) produces certain apparent metrical anomalies: *hiatus (αἴθοπα οἶνον = αἴθοπα ϝοῖνον) and lengthening of seemingly short syllables (τῖς εἴπεσκε = τις ϝείπεσκε). Also in Homer, in the first half of the dactylic metron (see § 4 (b) below), naturally short syllables are sometimes made to count as long (*metrical lengthening*) for less obvious reasons (see W. F. Wyatt, *Metrical Lengthening in Homer* (1969)).

2. Basic Concepts While actual verse is composed of syllables (components of words), verses in the abstract can be thought of as patterns of three types of *position* (West's term): *long* (-), *short* (∪) and *anceps* (×). This last admits either a long or a short syllable. Thus, ×-∪- can be realized as either ∪-∪- or --∪-. While in Greek music a long might have the value of two, three, or four shorts (χρόνοι πρῶτοι, *morae*), in metre, long is treated as equivalent to two shorts. In some metres (dactylic (b), anapaestic (c)), double short and long are freely interchangeable, at least in certain positions. Such positions are sometimes called *biceps* (Maas's term). In other types of metre (iambic and trochaic (a) etc.), double short can take the place of long with restrictions. This is called *resolution*. Word-end is avoided between double shorts produced by resolution. In yet other metres (aeolo-choriambic (h), dactylo-epitrite (g)), long cannot normally be resolved or replaced by double short. In Attic drama, especially comic spoken verse, ∪∪ is sometimes found in place of short or anceps (a). This is properly called *substitution*. The use of - as an alternative to ∪∪ (as in dactyls) is sometimes called *contraction*.

Much Greek verse is composed in sequences of uniform *metra*: short rhythmic phrases with their own rules for internal variation (e.g. ×-∪- *iamb*, -∪∪ *dactyl*, etc.) Thus, ×-∪- ×-∪- is an *iambic dimeter*, -∪∪ -∪∪ -∪∪ -∪∪ a *dactylic tetrameter*. Three types of Greek metre (dactylo-epitrite (g), aeolo-choriambic (h) and iambo-choriambic (i)) are composed in non-uniform phrases.

The larger rhythmic sections of Greek verse (*verses, minor periods*) are marked off by verse-end (*metrical pause*). At verse-end, full word-end, without elision, is obligatory. Certain short 'words' (the definite article, prepositions, interrogative τίς, relative ὅς, conjunctions) are *prepositive*, meaning that they are treated as part of the following word, and may not be divided from it by verse-end. Certain others (τις indefinite, particles) are *postpositive*: they belong to the preceding word, and, again, may not be divided from it. Verse-end may (but need not) also be marked by hiatus and/or *brevis in longo* (short syllable occupying long position). Verse-end never follows a short position and relatively rarely an anceps, so a short syllable at verse-end may be defined as *brevis in fine versus* (symbol ⌣). Verse-end is also sometimes marked by *catalexis*. This involves the suppression of the final or penultimate position of the verse, with the result that a naturally blunt rhythm (e.g. . . . ∪-∪-ׅ) becomes *pendent* (. . .∪--ׅ), and, conversely, a pendent rhythm (e.g. . . . . –∪–×ı) becomes blunt (. . . –∪–ı). We do not know how catalexis was realized in performance in the Classical period, but the Seikilos musical inscription of the 1st cent. AD (E. Pöhlmann, *Denkmäler altgr. Musik* (1970), 55–7 no. 18) shows catalectic . . . ∪–– rhythmized as . . . ∪–⌐ (⌐ = ∪∪∪). Catalexis is rarely found in the absence of word-end. Suppression of a position other than the final or penultimate is admitted in some metres (iambic and trochaic (*a*), ionic (*e*)). This phenomenon is called *syncopation*. It is particularly common in Attic lyric. As with catalexis, we do not know how it was realized in performance.

Within a verse, anceps is found neither beside anceps nor beside short. This is a universal rule of Greek metre, to which the only exceptions are the base in aeolo-choriambic (*h*) and a few passages in *Sophocles (1) and *Euripides where iamb follows dactyl without intervening verse-end (see T. C. W. Stinton, *CR* 1965, 142–5; *Collected Papers* (1990), 11–15).

Cola are relatively short rhythmic phrases (although a single colon can constitute a verse). Colon-end need not generally coincide with word-end, but in rhythms composed in repeating metra (iambic, dactylic, etc.) word-end is required to define cola. In others (especially aeolo-choriambic), cola are defined by their own metrical shape. Colon-division can be a matter of editorial judgement, but there is enough certainty to enable us to recognize the more common patterns. Metrical continuity, as shown by the absence of any of the indications of verse-end, is called *synapheia*. Where a word overlaps from one colon to the next, there is said to be *synartesis*.

3. Verse and stanza Stichic verse is composed in sequences of verses, or 'lines' (στίχοι), of from three to six metra, uniform in metrical type and length. This method of composition is associated with spoken delivery or with recitative (παρακαταλογή). Stichic verses have obligatory word-end at or near mid-verse. Such word-end is called *caesura* if it falls within a metron, *diaeresis* if it falls between metra. Elision may occur at caesura and diaeresis. Various types of catalectic tetrameter (in particular, iambic, trochaic (*a*), anapaestic (*c*)) are used in sequence. These are, in fact, *dicola*: they are made up of a dimeter and a catalectic dimeter, with diaeresis between. Such compounds are first found in *Archilochus, and are much used in comedy. There are also dicola in non-uniform rhythm, such as the *archilochean* (×–∪∪–∪∪– ×–∪–∪––), which apparently combines dactylic and iambic rhythms (West, *IE²* 168; Ar. *Vesp.* 1529–37). The *system*, a sequence in uniform rhythm (iambic, trochaic, anapaestic) ending in catalexis and traditionally laid out in dimeter-lengths, is also a typically recitative structure. *Distichs* are couplets of unequal verses. The most common is the *elegiac* distich (dactylic hexameter + –∪∪– ∪∪–ı–∪∪–∪∪– *b*), which, again, occurs first in Archilochus, and was extensively used in the archaic period (*Theognis (1), *Mimnermus, *Solon), and, as the typical metre of epigrams, survived into Byzantine times. Archilochus also composed short, three-verse stanzas (see, especially, West, *Delectus ex iambis et elegis graecis* (1980), 196a), although these have been laid out as couplets since antiquity. The *sapphic* and *alcaic* stanzas (*h*), although traditionally laid out as four lines, also consist of three verses, the last of which is a dicolon, with occasional synartesis between the cola. Anacreon sometimes composed in short stanzas of three or four uniform cola, rounded off by the same colon in its catalectic version (*PMG* 347, 348). All these poets of the Aegean islands use short stanzas which reappear in different poems.

The stanzas of Dorian lyric are usually much longer, and are

individual in design, not repeated from one poem to another. Characteristically, poems are composed in *triads*, groups of three stanzas of which the first two (*strophe* and *antistrophe*) correspond (are in *responsion*; meaning that they are metrically identical), while the third, the *epode*, is different. The whole triad may be repeated a number of times: AAB, AAB, AAB. . . . *Alcman (*PMG* 1) shows a rudimentary triadic structure, but triadic composition first appears full-blown in *Stesichorus, and is general in *Pindar and *Bacchylides. The lyric stanzas of Attic drama follow the Dorian method of composition, but often combine different types of metre (compare Alcman, *PMG* 1). Songs are not triadic, although a single strophic pair is occasionally followed by an epode. Most commonly they are made up of one or more strophic pairs, each pair having its own distinctive metrical pattern. Astrophic lyric is also used, especially in monodies (solos). Certain, strictly limited, variation occurs in corresponding stanzas. Thus, in iambic and trochaic (*a*) short anceps may correspond with long and resolved long with unresolved, and in dactyls (*b*) –– occasionally corresponds with – ∪∪.

4. Types of metre Types of poetic rhythm are associated in origin with different regions and poetic genres. In the 5th cent. BC, the Attic dramatists made a synthesis of metrical styles.

(a) **Iambic and trochaic**

These two metres can be seen as different segments of the sequence . . . ×–∪–× . . ., which also features in some other types of metre (*g*, *h*). The iambic metron is ×–∪ –, the trochaic –∪–×. Transition from one rhythm to the other is almost always accompanied by verse-end. Longs may be resolved (. . . ×∪∪–∪∪∪× . . .), but word-end between shorts so produced is avoided. In serious poetry, word-end (except following a monosyllable) is avoided after long anceps, except at caesura or diaeresis (*extended Porson's Law*; see L. P. E. Parker, *CQ* 1966, 1–26). In sung verse, short and/or anceps can be suppressed by syncopation, to produce, in iambic, (×)–∪– (*cretic*), ∪–(∪)– (*bacchiac*), ––(∪)– (*molossus*); and, in trochaic, –∪–(×) (*cretic*), –(∪)–∪ (*palimbacchiac*), –(∪)–– (*molossus*), and, in both metres, (×)–(∪)– (*spondee*).

The term ἴαμβος first occurs in Archilochus (West, *IE²* 215). In origin, it seems to have designated a type of occasion, and the verse associated with it, whether or not in iambic metre (see IAMBIC POETRY, GREEK). There is a traditional connection between iambus and ritual invective (*Hymn. Hom. Cer.* 202 ff. and Richardson on 213–17). Archilochus used the iambic trimeter and the catalectic trochaic tetrameter, and also verses combining iambic with dactylic (see § 3 and (*b*) below). *Hipponax is regarded as the originator of the *choliamb*, a trimeter in which the last metron takes the form ×–––. This verse was revived in the Hellenistic period (*Callimachus (3), *Herodas). The iambic trimeter of the early iambographers is subject to two sets of restrictions on word-end (*Knox's Laws*, see A. D. Knox, *Philol.* 1932, 18–39): first, the early iambographers and some of their later imitators, including Callimachus, avoid trimeters (including choliambs) ending with exactly three words of the form ı–∪–ı–∪–ı; secondly, the iambographers, but not Callimachus, avoid following word-end after the second short with two words of the form ı–∪ı–∪–ı. In the early trimeter, caesura falls in the second metron, after anceps or after short: ×–∪– ×ı–∪ı– ×–∪–.

In the 5th cent., the iambic trimeter became the standard spoken verse of drama. Caesura is found not only after second anceps and second short, but also after the third long (most often with elision). Porson's Law is observed in tragedy, but not in comedy. Euripides used resolution with increasing frequency as his career advanced (E. B. Ceadel, *CQ* 1941, 66–89), but no such tendency is observable in the other dramatists. Substitution of double short for the first anceps of the verse is permitted in tragedy. In comedy, any anceps or short, except the short of the last metron, may be replaced by double short. Tragic-type trimeters were used by the Hellenistic poet *Lycophron (2) (*Alexandra*). Comic-type trimeters survived in satiric and humorous writing (e.g. *Machon). The catalectic trochaic tetrameter is used occasionally in tragedy by *Aeschylus (e.g. *Pers.* 215–48) and Euripides, very rarely in Sophocles, and extensively in comedy, the catalectic iambic tetrameter only in comedy. Iambic and trochaic systems are also used in comedy.

In lyric iambic, the Attic dramatists (Aeschylus in particular) exploit syncopation (e.g. *Ag.* 192–257). Resolution came to be used with increasing frequency in later tragedy, especially in Euripides and in lamentation (e.g. *HF* 114 ff. = 126 ff.). *Aristophanes (1) uses both tragic-style iambic in parody (e.g. *Ach.* 1190–1225, *Ran.* 1353–5) and, extensively, very simple iambic in songs of comic type, including invective (e.g. *Ran.* 420–43). Lyric trochaic is much more common in comedy than in tragedy, but in later Euripides highly-resolved trochees are used in lamentation in much the same way as iambic (e.g. *Hel.* 173 ff. = 184 ff.). Two short cola, the iambic *ithyphallic* (–∪–∪––) and the ambiguous *lecythion* (–∪–×–∪–) are frequently used as *clausulae*, to round off stanzas or sections of stanzas in various metres.

Hellenistic poets used iambic in short stanzas, in combination with dactylic, trochaic, and even aeolo-choriambic (e.g. Theoc. *Epigr.* 17, 18, 21; Callim. *Epigr.* 38, 39). The catalectic trochaic tetrameter is little used after the Classical period, but see *Theocritus, *Epigr.* 18.

(b) Dactylic

Metron: –∪∪ or ––. To the best of our understanding, verse-end must be preceded by a metron of the form –– (which may be called 'spondee', but should be distinguished from the syncopated iambo-trochaic metron (*a*)). Catalexis (. . . ∪∪–I) is very rare and confined to sung dactylic. The dactylic hexameter is the metre of Homeric epic. *Aristotle (*Poet.* 1459[b]) describes it as στασιμώτατον καὶ ὀγκωδέστατον τῶν μέτρων ('most solid and massive of metres'), although that may reflect literary associations rather than the inherent character of the rhythm. The hexameter usually has caesura in the third metron, either after the long or between the two shorts: –∪∪ –∪∪ –I∪I∪ –∪∪ –∪∪ ––. The fifth metron tends to be a dactyl rather than a spondee. Various tendencies observable in the incidence of word-end in Homer's hexameters harden into rules for Hellenistic poets (particularly Callimachus) and, still later, for *Nonnus. Thus, word-end between the shorts of the fourth metron is comparatively rare in Homer and strictly avoided by Callimachus and Nonnus (*Hermann's Law*). Word-end following a spondaic metron was clearly felt to be disruptive within the verse, and is avoided after spondaic second, third, and fourth metra. Word-end after dactylic fourth metron (*bucolic diaeresis*) is, however, common. A word of the form ∪–∪ may stand in only two places in the Callimachean hexameter: at the end (where it has the value ∪–– by *brevis in fine versus*), or immediately before caesura (–∪∪ –∪I∪ –∪∪ –∪∪ –). Exceptions are *Hymn* 2. 41 and 6. 91.

In the elegiac distich (see § 3), hexameters alternate with a verse made up of –∪∪–∪∪– twice over, with intervening diaeresis and long for double short permitted only in the first half. The phrase –∪∪–∪∪– (*hemiepes*), although clearly dactylic in affiliation, is not analysable into metra, and we do not know how it was understood by the Archaic poets who first used it (see also (*g*)). Archilochus combined it with iambic (West, *IE²* 168, 182–6) in his dicola and short stanzas, as he also combined dactylic in repeating metra (*IE²* 188–95). Alcman combined dactylic with trochaic in a lyric stanza (*PMG* 1). He is said by *Hephaestion (2) (see § 5) to have made extensive use of tetrameters of the form –∪∪–∪∪–∪∪–∪∪ (*PMG* 27). He also used tetrameters ending –– (*PMG* 17, 56). Both types of tetrameter, as well as hexameters, are common in Attic dramatic lyric, but dactyls occur in sequences of any length from 2 to 28 (Ar. *Eccl.* 1170–6) The longest sequence in tragedy uninterrupted by coincidence of word-end with spondaic metron is 26 metra (Soph. *OC* 229–35). In such sequences, cola cannot be identified. The pentameter is a favourite length with Aeschylus. In his plays there are several predominantly dactylic stanzas (e.g. *Pers.* 852–906, *Eum.* 347 ff. = 360 ff.). The combination of dactylic with a little iambic (*Ag.* 104 ff. = 123 ff., 140 ff.) must have been used in a number of lost plays, to judge from the cento at Ar. *Ran.* 1264 ff. The only predominantly dactylic stanza in Sophocles' surviving plays, *OT* 151 ff. = 159 ff., has clear affinities with this type of Aeschylean stanza. Typically, Sophocles introduces substantial dactylic passages in *kommoi* (e.g. *El.* 121–250, *Phil.* 1170–1217), usually in tetrameters. The dactylic stanza returns with Euripides (e.g. *Supp.* 271 ff., *Andr.* 1173 ff. = 1186 ff., *Phoen.* 784 ff. = 801 ff.). Aristophanes is sparing in his use of dactylic, more or less confining it to parody (*Pax* 114 ff., *Ran.* 1264 ff.) and to passages aiming at a solemn, pseudo-solemn or consciously poetic effect (e.g. *Nub.* 275 ff. = 298 ff., *Ran.* 814 ff.) There are occasional dactylic cola in *Timotheus (1)'s *Persae* (*PMG* 791. 132–3, 139, 190, 196), but after the 5th cent. dactylic tends to disappear from literary lyric. It occurs in three sub-literary *paeans of the 4th cent. or later (*Coll. Alex.* pp. 136–40).

(c) Anapaestic

In the earliest surviving anapaestic verse, Spartan marching songs (*PMG* 856–7), the metron seems to be ∪∪–∪∪–, and ∪∪– . . . remains the dominant movement. In Attic poetry, however, all positions are biceps: ∪∪–‾∪∪–‾∪∪, so that a metron may even take the form –∪∪–∪∪. Consecutive double short (∪∪∪∪) is only admitted in sung anapaests. Syncopation is only used to produce catalexis, and a catalectic metron may only take the forms ∪∪–– or –––. Word-end between metra is usual. Anapaestic is predominantly a recitative metre. In Attic tragedy, recitative anapaests appear in systems which vary in length from two or three dimeters to over fifty (e.g. Aesch. *Ag.* 40–103; Soph. *Ant.* 110–17, 127–33; Eur. *Alc.* 1159–63). The catalectic tetrameter is much used in comedy, especially in the parabasis, which is sometimes referred to as 'the anapaests' (e.g. Ar. *Ach.* 627, *Eq.* 504). Sung anapaests are used in Attic drama. As well as consecutive double short, they admit sequences of catalectic dimeters, and the rhythm is often heavily spondaic. They have a strong association with lamentation (e.g. Aesch. *Pers.* 907–1001; Soph. *El.* 86–250; Eur. *Med.* 96–183, *Tro.* 98–229). Euripides makes notable use of them in monody (*Ion* 82–183 and 859–922). Hellenistic anapaests are scarce (*Coll. Alex.* pp. 113, 126, 187–9; *PMG* 1033).

(d) Cretic

Metron: –∪–. Apparent cretics are produced in iambic and trochaic by syncopation, but it seems clear that there was also a distinct cretic rhythm in which –∪– equalled five *morae*. The subject is dealt with in *POxy.* 2687, a fragment of a treatise on rhythm, which, however, remains enigmatic. Ancient metricians used the term *paeon* (παιών) for resolved cretics (∪∪∪–, –∪∪, ∪∪∪∪), but this is a needless complication. According to

*Ephorus (*FGrH* 70 F 149 = Strabo 10. 480), the metre was 'invented' by *Thaletas of Gortyn, said by ps.-Plutarch (*De mus.* 1134b) to have carried out the second organization of music at Sparta. Ancient authorities associate the rhythm with the hyporcheme. Our earliest cretics are among the fragments of Alcman (*PMG* 58): hexameters, with final – –. The term 'cretic' first occurs in *Cratinus (*PCG* 237). Pindar, *Ol.* 2 is predominantly cretic. Here, some verses open with *acephalous* ('headless') metra: ‚∪– or ‚∪∪∪. The second long is more often resolved than the first. There are also two cretic fragments of Bacchylides (15, 16 Snell–Maehler). In tragedy, there is one pure cretic stanza: Aesch. *Supp.* 418 ff. = 423 ff. A fragment of satyric drama, Soph. *Ichneutae* 329 ff. = 371 ff. (*TrGF* 4. 314) is predominantly cretic, and cretic sequences are found in iambo-trochaic contexts (e.g. Aesch. *Cho.* 783 = 794; Eur. *Tro.* 1092 = 1110). Aristophanes uses pure cretic extensively in his earlier plays (especially *Ach.* and *Eq.*). –∪∪ is very common; ∪∪– is not found (except, possibly, in *PGC* 113, from Γεωργοί). Resolution of both longs is very rare in the Classical period (Aesch. *Ag.* 1142 = 1153; Eur. *IT* 897, *Or.* 185 = 206), but the Hellenistic poet, *Simmias (2), experimented with it (*Coll. Alex.* p. 114). The first *Delphic Paean*, inscribed with musical notation in the second half of the 2nd cent. BC (see MUSIC § 10(2)), is in cretics, and uses all four possible forms (*Coll. Alex.* pp. 141–8).

(e) Ionic

Metron: ∪∪– –. This is a rhythm of the eastern Aegean which does not combine readily with other metres. Tetrameters are quoted from Alcman (*PMG* 46) and *Alcaeus (1) (LP 10). *Anacreon seems to have introduced a variation on the dimeter: ∪∪–∪–∪– (occasionally ∪∪– – –∪– –), supposedly produced by switching the fourth and fifth positions (*anaclasis*, an ill-authenticated phenomenon). Poems in the *anacreontic* metre continued to be composed even into the Byzantine period. In spite of comastic associations (Anacreon in general and Eur. *Cyc.* 495 ff.), anacreontics are found in contexts of lamentation in tragedy (e.g. Aesch. *Cho.* 327 ff. = 357 ff.; cf. schol. on Aesch. *PV* 128, cited by Page, *PMG* 412). More generally, ionic metre had oriental connotations: it is used extensively in *Persae* and *Bacchae*, two plays with oriental choruses. Cult associations with Dionysus are possible, but the evidence is thin (see Dodds on Eur. *Bacch* 72). Catalexis (∪∪–I) seems to occur in Anacreon (*PMG* 411 (b)). Attic poets use ∪∪– to begin verses, as well as to end them. They also introduce occasional resolution (e.g. *Bacch.* 373, 398). The *galliambic* dicolon (dimeter + catalectic dimeter, with resolution) is cited by Hephaestion (see § 5) and said by Choeroboscus (§ 5) to have been used by Callimachus. Hephaestion includes the ionic *a maiore* (– –∪∪) among his 'feet' (§ 5), but its existence has not been proved from actual texts. Passages in ionic which open with cola beginning –∪∪ . . . pose unresolved problems of analysis (Anacreon, *PMG* 346 and, with iambic prefix, Aesch. *Sept.* 720 ff. = 727 ff., *Ag.* 448 ff. = 466 ff., etc.).

(f) Dochmiac

Metron: ×– –×–. All longs may be resolved. Theoretically, 32 forms are possible, but by no means all have actually been found, and, out of some 2,000 dochmiacs, more than two-thirds belong to three forms: ∪∪∪–∪– (c.650), ∪– – –∪– (c.500), –∪∪–∪– (c.250). Also quite common are: ∪∪∪∪∪∪– (c.90) and ∪∪∪∪∪∪∪∪ (c.60). The *hypodochmiac*, –∪–∪–, is a well-authenticated equivalent to the dochmiac. Dochmiac differs interestingly from iambo-trochaic in that word-end between two shorts produced by resolution is freely admitted. Substitution is extremely rare. Word-end tends to coincide with metron-end, and there is no catalectic

form. Different forms of dochmiac may correspond, within limits of compatibility. Thus, a dochmiac with two short ancipitia may not correspond with one with two long ancipitia (exceptions: Soph. *Ant.* 1320 = 1344, *OC* 1561 =1573). The ratio of resolved long in corresponding dochmiacs may either be the same, e.g. 1:1, as ∪∪∪–∪– = ∪–∪∪∪–, or may differ by one, as 0:1, 1:2, etc. (exception: Eur. *Or.* 330 =346, ∪∪∪∪∪∪∪ = ∪∪∪–∪–). Dochmiac metre is virtually confined to Attic drama, where it is distinctively the rhythm of violent emotion (Aesch. *Sept.* 78–180; Soph. *OT* 1313–68; Eur. *Bacch.* 977–1016, 1024–42; Ar. *Ach.* 353 ff. = 385 ff.). Dochmiac-shaped phrases can be found in Pindar, but other characteristics of dochmiac composition are absent, and other interpretations are possible. From the Hellenistic period, one composition in (rather free) dochmiacs survives: *Coll. Alex.* pp. 177–9.

Two major types of metre are not constructed in repeating metra.

(g) Dactylo-epitrite

This metre combines dactylic with iambo-trochaic phrases, and belongs originally to Dorian lyric. The discovery of major fragments of *Stesichorus has made it possible to trace the development of the rhythm (see M. W. Haslam, *Quaderni urbinati di cultura classica* 1974, 7–57 and *GRBS* 1978, 29–57). Even in Stesichorus' purely dactylic stanzas (*POxy.* 2617, *Geryoneis*), a distinction is observable between some double shorts which are contractible to long and others which are not. Contractible ∪∪ (biceps) is used to mark off recurring patterns, especially to 'link' phrases of the form –∪∪–∪∪– (hemiepes). *POxy.* 2619 (*Iliu Persis*) includes short iambo-trochaic phrases (. . . ×–∪×. . .), and in the last verse of the strophe, the place of the biceps in linking hemiepe is taken by anceps: –∪∪–∪∪–∪̱–∪∪–∪∪–×̄–∪–×̄. *PLille* 76 a b c (*Thebaid*) shows ∪,–, and ∪∪ in the same 'link' positions, but ∪ never corresponds with ∪∪ within the same strophic pair. *POxy.* 2360 consists exclusively of –∪∪–∪∪– and –∪– linked by ancipitia. This can be identified with the fully-developed dactylo-epitrite which is used extensively by Pindar and Bacchylides. Here, the most common constituents, –∪∪–∪∪– and –∪–, are linked together by ancipitia, usually long, into seemingly rambling verses, such as *Ol.* 3. 1–2: –∪∪–∪∪– – –∪– – – –∪∪–I–∪∪–∪∪– – –∪–. Less common phrases are the *choriamb* (–∪∪–) and the lengthened hemiepes (–∪∪–∪∪–∪∪–). Headless phrases are sometimes found at the beginnings of verses (‚∪–, ‚∪∪–, ‚∪∪ ∪∪–), and – – is occasionally found at verse-beginning or verse-end. Occasionally, too, link anceps is omitted, e.g. *Pyth.* 1. 2: –∪– – –∪∪– –∪– – –∪∪–∪∪– – –. Resolution of long and contraction of double short are both generally excluded, except for occasional resolution of one or other long in cretic phrases (∪∪∪– or –∪∪∪).

In Attic poetry, unambiguous dactylo-epitrite is not found in Aeschylus, apart from *PV*. There are some largely or predominantly dactylo-epitrite stanzas in Sophocles and Euripides (e.g. Soph. *Aj.* 172 ff. = 182 ff., *Trach.* 94 ff. = 103 ff.; Eur. *Med.* 410 ff. = 421 ff., 627 ff. = 635 ff.). Among surviving plays, *Medea* has the largest concentration of dactylo-epitrite. Aristophanes uses dactylo-epitrite allusively in *Eq.* 1264 ff. = 1290 ff., where he quotes Pindar, and in *Pax* 775 ff. = 796 ff., where he incorporates quotations from Stesichorus. The metre has no catalectic form, but the Attic poets import the (strictly alien) bacchiac as clausula, preceded by (×)–∪–. Aristotle's *Hymn to Virtue* (*PMG* 842) is a notable example of late dactylo-epitrite.

We are unable to distinguish cola in dactylo-epitrite, because within the verse we cannot determine whether link anceps belongs with what follows or with what precedes. Maas (see § 5) devised a code, based on D = –∪∪–∪∪– and e = –∪–, which obviates verbal description and the need to identify cola.

Among Pindar's dactylo-epitrites there are a few examples of (–)∪∪–∪∪–∪–. Otherwise, the cadence . . .–∪∪–∪– is peculiar to aeolo-choriambic (h), and, unless the Pindaric phrases come by 'infection' from that type of metre, they may perhaps be explained as rare survivals of the Stesichorean link biceps: –∪∪–∪∪–∪–. In tragedy, cola of varying lengths based on the pattern (×–)∪∪–∪∪–∪–(–) are found in dactylo-epitrite (as well as aeolo-choriambic) contexts. Dale (§ 5) classified these as 'prosodiac-enoplian', but their true genesis and affinities remain uncertain.

(h) Aeolo-choriambic

The signature-phrase of this metre is –∪∪–∪– (*dodrans*), and cola typically begin with *base*, which seems originally to have been two ancipitia (××), realizable as –∪, ∪–, ––, or ∪∪. However, ∪∪ is only found in Lesbian poetry (*Sappho, LP 47. 2, 94. 22, 98. 8). In Anacreon and in Attic and later poetry the base may take the forms –∪, ∪–, ––, and, in later Attic drama, ∪∪∪. The base may be said to be treated as –× or ×–, but, even so, forms with resolved long and long anceps (∪∪–, –∪∪) seem to be excluded (on forms of base and correspondence, see K. Itsumi, *CQ* 1984, 66–82). The colon is the unit of analysis, and the most common colon, the *glyconic*, consists of base + dodrans (××–∪∪–∪–). Its catalectic (pendent) form, the *pherecratean*, lacks the penultimate short (××–∪∪––). Anacreon composed poems in stanzas consisting of two, three, or four glyconics, with pherecratean as clausula (*PMG* 348, 358, 359), and such groups of cola are quite often incorporated into the more elaborate stanzas of Attic drama (e.g. Soph. *Phil.* 169–71 = 180–2). A colon found in Sappho (*LP* 95. 9, 96. 7), Anacreon (*PMG* 357. 5), *Corinna (*PMG* 654, col. 3. 10–50) and in later Attic drama, the *polyschematist* or *wilamowitzianum*, combines base with a reversed form of the dodrans: ××–×–∪∪–. Polyschematist can correspond with glyconic.

Aeolo-choriambic cola seem capable of endless variation. A bacchiac added to the end of the glyconic produces the *phalaecian*. The initial –∪∪. . . of the dodrans can proliferate, as in the so-called *aeolic dactyls* of Sappho: ××–∪∪–∪∪–∪∪– (*LP* 44). Choriambs can be inserted between base and dodrans to produce *asclepiads* (lesser: ××–∪∪––∪∪–∪–, *LP* 350; greater: ××–∪∪––∪∪––∪∪–∪–, *LP* 347). The base can be reduced to a single anceps, as in the *telesillean* (×–∪∪–∪–, *PMG* 717) and its catalectic form, the *reizianum* (×–∪∪––), in Sappho's pendent asclepiad (×–∪∪––∪∪–∪––, *LP* 148) and in the earliest known colon of the type, ×–∪∪–∪––, in Alcman, *PMG* 1. Base can also be completely eliminated (e.g. Soph. *Ant.* 134–5 = 147–8: –∪∪∪–∪∪–∪∪–∪∪–). The sapphic and alcaic stanzas combine variations on the dodrans with the iambo-trochaic sequence. Both consist of three verses, of which the last is a dicolon: sapphic: –∪–×–∪∪–∪–– (twice), ∪–×–∪∪–∪– + –∪∪––; alcaic: ×–∪–×–∪∪–∪– (twice), ×–∪–×–∪–× + –∪∪–∪∪––. Pindar uses a highly individual version of aeolo-choriambic (*Ol.* 1, 4, 9, 14, etc.).

Aeolo-choriambic is much used in the lyric of Attic drama. There, the cadence . . .–∪– occasionally becomes . . .––– (*drag*), and Sophocles and Euripides very occasionally admit resolved long (e.g. Soph. *Ant.* 788; Eur. *El.* 445). Stanza-forms range from simple sequences of identical cola rounded off by their own catalectic forms, in the manner of Anacreon (Ar. *Eq.* 973 ff. = 985 ff., *Av.* 1731 ff. = 1738 ff. and, with a little variation, Soph. *OT* 1186 ff. = 1196 ff.), to patterns of some complexity, involving other types of metre. Sophocles, in particular, makes frequent

and sophisticated use of the metre, and he alone among the dramatists favours asclepiad-type cola (e.g. *Ant.* 944–51 = 955–61, *Phil.* 707–15 = 718–27). In Attic popular poetry, aeolo-choriambic appears in scolia: *PMG* 902–5 (greater asclepiads) and 893–6, the 'Harmodius songs' (in which the third verse opens with what seems to be a headless dodrans: ⌣∪∪–∪–). A section of Timotheus' *Persae* (*PMG* 791. 203–34) consists almost exclusively of glyconics and pherecrateans.

Hellenistic poets used various aeolo-choriambic cola in sequence, thereby sometimes bequeathing their names to pre-existing cola: phalaecian (Phalaecus, Gow–Page, *HE* 3; Theoc. *Epigr.* 22), asclepiads (Asclepiades, *Suppl. Hell.* 15; Theoc. 30), aeolic dactyls (Theoc. 29). The eponymous poet of the glyconic is unknown.

Glyconic + pherecratean make up the *priapean* dicolon. The *eupolidean* dicolon is a compound of polyschematist + lecythion, in which the first two positions of the lecythion came to be treated like aeolic base (Ar. *Nub.* 518–62).

(i) Iambo-choriambic

This metre is unique in combining two types of metron: –∪∪– and ×–∪– (with catalectic ∪–). Poems in the rhythm first appear in Anacreon (*PMG* 384–89). Dimeters of the form ×–∪––∪∪– and –∪∪–×–∪– are used by the Attic dramatists, often in aeolo-choriambic contexts. ×–∪––∪∪– must, however, be distinguished from the polyschematist, with which it does not correspond. The *aristophanean* (–∪∪–∪–), analysable either as the catalectic form of –∪∪–×–∪– or as a pendent extension of the dodrans, is a common, all-purpose clausular colon in drama.

5. History of metrical studies Stichic verse was, as far as we know, written out in lines even in the earliest texts, but *Dionysius (7) of Halicarnassus (*Comp.* 22. 17, cf. 26. 14) associates the division of lyric into cola with *Aristophanes (2) of Byzantium or 'some other metrician'. The very few papyri that can be reliably dated earlier than Aristophanes' scholarly activity support this (*PBerol.* 9864 and 13270). The level of understanding with which these *Alexandrian scholars did their work remains doubtful. The metrical *scholia vetera* on Aristophanes cite the metrician *Heliodorus (2), who may be dated to the late 1st cent. BC/early 1st cent. AD, but the most important Greek metrical work to come down to us from antiquity is an abridgement of a treatise by Hephaestion (2nd cent. AD). His system is based on a list of 'feet' of from two to eight *morae* (from ∪∪, the 'pyrrhic', to ––––, the 'dispondee') which looks like the result of an exercise in permutations and combinations. He does not explain the principles on which feet may be combined, nor why a given passage should be analysed into long feet which are merely compounds of shorter ones. Hephaestion provided the base for Byzantine metrical studies. In the early period, George Choeroboscus (second half of the 8th cent.) produced a commentary on him; Isaac Tzetzes (d. 1138) used him to compose a treatise in verse on the metres of Pindar. Demetrius Triclinius (early 14th cent.) grasped the principle of strophic correspondence, and used it, with his metrical knowledge derived from Hephaestion, to emend poetic texts. Many of his emendations are inadequate or otiose; some have never been bettered.

Careful observation and increasing metrical knowledge produced much improvement to texts in the 17th and 18th cents., but modern understanding of the structures of Greek metre begins with the work of G. Hermann (*De metris poetarum Graecorum et Romanorum libri iii* (1796), *Elementa doctrinae metricae* (1816)). A. Boeckh, in his edition of Pindar (1811), demonstrated the significance of verse-end in lyric. Theories evolved in the 19th cent. by German scholars (Westphal, J. H. H. Schmidt) designed to assimilate Greek rhythms to those of European classical music have now been generally abandoned (see L. E. Rossi, *Metrica e critica stilistica* (1963)). Likewise, argument about the existence and, if it existed, the nature of beat (*ictus*) in Greek verse is now generally in abeyance. In the 20th cent., Wilamowitz's work, though unsystematic and uncertain in matters of principle, is still worth consulting on individual passages. Paul Maas played a decisive part in the creation of modern metrics both by clarifying principles and by distinguishing genuine contributions to knowledge from theorizing in the work of his predecessors. His rigour and sobriety remain unequalled. A. M. Dale's work, especially on the lyric of drama, remains of central importance. M. L. West's general treatise adopts a historical approach and provides, in particular, a wealth of information on prosody and on the poetry of the pre- and post-classical periods.

A. M. Dale, *The Lyric Metres of Greek Drama*, 2nd edn. (1968), *Collected Papers* (1969), and *Metrical Analyses of Tragic Choruses* (1971–83); P. Maas, *Griechische Metrik*, 3rd edn. (1929), and *Greek Metre*, trans. H. Lloyd-Jones (1962); M. L. West, *Greek Metre* (1982), and *Introduction to Greek Metre* (1987); U. von Wilamowitz-Moellendorff, *Griechische Verskunst* (1921; repr. 1962).

SURVEYS E. Kalinka, Bursian, *Jahresb.* Suppl. 250 (1935), 290–507; A. M. Dale, *Lustrum* 1958, 1–51; L. P. E. Parker, *Lustrum* 1972, 37–98.

L. P. E. P.

metre, Latin

1. Introduction A tradition of writing Latin verses on the quantitative model of those of Classical Greek literature maintained itself from 240 BC down to the end of the western empire, although drastic changes began to affect the phonological system of the spoken language well before AD 476 even among the urban upper classes. The relation of the so-called *Saturnian verse to the classical tradition is disputed, as are the precise dates and places of the first conscious efforts to construct verses on accentual rather than quantitative principles.

The practice of writing quantitative poetry continued through the Middle Ages and was given great emphasis in the Humanist schools of the 16th and 17th cents. Dactylic and trochaic verses were recited with a metrical stress ('ictus') on the first element (the 'rise') of the foot; anapaestic and iambic verses with one on the second. *Horace's 'aeolic' verses were analysed as combinations of trochees, iambuses, dactyls, and anapaests and stressed accordingly. Richard Bentley (1662–1742) taught his Cambridge pupils how the apparently prosaic *Terence could usually be read in the same rhythmical way with even less clash between the metrical stress and the word-accent and at the same time warned against the imposition of an excessively regular pattern of stresses on a piece of classical epic poetry.

In the course of the 19th cent. German and French students of classical poetry questioned whether the scholastic practice of reading quantitative verses with a metrical stress corresponded with anything in the reality of ancient recitation. Italian scholars have recently argued with particular vigour against the notion of an ictus. The continuing influence of the humanistic verse-writing tradition has made the British loath to regard classical Latin verse as entirely quantitative.

A number of conscious changes in prosodic and metrical practice were made by the Latin poets of the 1st cent. BC. Those

have to be distinguished from the changes which growing insensitivity to syllabic quantity brought about in late antiquity. The 3rd- and 2nd-cent. poets had exploited uncertainties of the language itself. The conventional certainties imposed in the 1st were accepted for a remarkably long time. Pressure to conform to the metrical rules apparent in the texts of the Greek classics was frequently applied by the more sophisticated kind of *grammaticus, but there always remained features of Latin practice either stricter or looser than the Greek. Our own uncertainty about various aspects of Latin phonology will always prevent a full appreciation of the metres of archaic and classical Latin poetry.

2. Survey of verse types (*a*) **Narrative and didactic poetry**
In the 3rd cent. BC some poets offered advice or information, others told stories in the Saturnian verse. Early in the 2nd cent. *Ennius proclaimed himself a Latin *Homer and composed an account of Roman history in a verse (the 'dactylic hexameter') modelled on that of the *Iliad*, which he sometimes called the *versus longus*, perhaps to distinguish it from the notably short Saturnian. Overall he did not permit himself nearly as much prosodic liberty as Homer seemed to have done. He even barred the shortening of the iambic sequence allowed in Latin stage-poetry and set limits to the synizesis of adjacent vowels. On the other hand he introduced the Homeric practice of distributing adjacent mute and liquid consonants between different syllables. He avoided as far as possible phrases which conjoined a word ending in a vowel with one so beginning. He permitted /i/ and /u/ to be treated as glides in some contexts. Where metre as distinct from prosody was concerned he contracted the first four biceps elements much more often than Homer did but normally left the fifth biceps be. He tended to place a caesura after the third longum rather than in the middle of the third biceps. At all events the *versus longus* differentiated itself radically from the Saturnian in having its second colon longer than its first. Ennius felt under no obligation to avoid a break of words in the middle of the fourth biceps (Hermann's 'bridge') or after a contracted fourth biceps (the bucolic 'bridge'). He restricted the number of word arrangements permitted at the end of the verse and showed a marked preference for a break of words either in the middle or at the end of the fifth biceps.

First-century composers of hexameters dispensed with the licence of giving no phonetic value to final -*s* preceded by a short vowel. They reduced sharply the amount of other prosodic variation permissible in final syllables. Ennius' preferences with regard to break of words both in the middle and towards the end of the verse began to develop into hard and fast rules. Some 1st-cent. composers affected a peculiar kind of verse associated with *Aratus (1) and *Apollonius (1) of Rhodes, in which a dactylic sequence was brought to an end with a contracted fifth biceps (e.g. Catull. 64. 71 *a misera assiduis quam fluctibus externavit*). *Virgil's versification set itself consciously apart from the Homeric, the Ennian, and the 1st-century 'neoteric'. The hiatus of *Aen.* 3. 211 (*insulae Ionio...*), the final monosyllable of 3. 375 (... *deum rex*) and the στήριγμα (lengthening) of 3. 517 (... *circumspicit Oriona*) were untypical of the general style of the *Aeneid*; in each case the poet sought surprise. He was followed by all later composers of hexameters in not permitting, as Ennius and *Catullus (1) had done, a word of spondaic or molossic shape immediately to precede the fifth element. On the other hand, the freedom with which he admitted elision to the verse found no imitators among the 1st-cent. AD poets.

(b) Dramatic poetry

For dialogue carrying vital information and unaccompanied by any music the early stage-poets used a verse (the 'iambic senarius') clearly related to the iambic trimeter of the Athenian theatre but which was by no means a straight literary adaptation. It did not keep short its third and seventh elements. On the other hand it did not admit every kind of long syllable or pair of short syllables to those elements. Nor did it allow an iambus-shaped word or word-end to precede a final iambus-shaped word. It tried to avoid filling the seventh and eighth elements with a spondee-shaped word or word-end. Much the same sort of rules governed the construction of resolved elements as did in the Attic trimeter. The tragic verse did not differ from the comic except in so far as it admitted fewer resolutions and availed itself less of the licence to shorten iambic sequences. It preferred to have the ninth element long but did not bar absolutely a short final syllable in this position. The impure third and seventh elements were a particular offence to Hellenizing taste, and the Augustan tragedians got rid of the licence. The younger Seneca (L. *Annaeus Seneca (2)), and probably the Augustans before him, insisted that the final syllable of a word preceding the final cretic should be long.

Monologues and dialogues of some degree of excitement intended to be accompanied by the pipes were often set in a verse (the 'trochaic septenarius') related to the Athenian trochaic tetrameter. This had the same general characteristics as the iambic dialogue verse. Its occurrence in triumphal songs and the like suggests that it had a long history preceding its use in the theatre.

Other iambic and trochaic lengths and various anapaestic, cretic, bacchiac, ionic, and what may be roughly termed 'aeolic' patterns were also used with an accompaniment on the pipes in both genres. Terence's sparing use, or avoidance, of many of these may be part of an eccentric ambition to get closer to the down-to-earth rhythmical character of the Athenian New Comedy (see COMEDY (GREEK), NEW). They reappear in the stage poets of the second half of the 2nd cent. Nothing like the elaborate strophic responses constructed by the 5th-cent. Athenian poets is known from the Roman theatre. Theme and tone always dictated the change of metre.

The younger Seneca followed Classical Greek rather than archaic Latin practice in writing anapaests for his choruses. Horace's monostrophic poems on the other hand were preferred as models to the elaborate lyric structures of Sophocles and Euripides.

(c) Satura

The iambic and trochaic verses of drama and the dactylic hexameter dominate the remains of the *saturae* of Ennius and *Lucilius (1). The Lucilian hexameter was rather less rule-bound than that of Ennius' *Annales*. It admitted more readily, for example, a shortened iambic sequence. In his *Menippean satires *Varro used as well as prose all Lucilius' verse forms and a number not evidenced in Latin before. *Horace used only the hexameter and dispensed with Lucilius' more outrageous liberties in his *Sermones* and *Epistulae*. Nevertheless his hexameter stood a recognizably long way from the verse of Virgil's *Eclogues*, *Georgics*, and *Aeneid*. *Persius and even more so *Juvenal tried to reduce the number of metrical distinctions between *satura* and its more dignified sister genre.

(d) Iambus

(See IAMBIC POETRY, LATIN.) Even the Saturnian verse could be used for vulgar lampoons and the like in the 2nd cent. BC. The verses of dramatic dialogue were, however, the principal vehicles of *invective. In the middle of the 1st cent. Catullus produced a number of close imitations of the iambic trimeters and tetrameters and the choliambics of the Ionian iambists, Archilochus and Hipponax. He got as far as he could from the iambic verse of the local stage, sometimes dividing a mute + liquid pair between syllables in the Ionian way and ignoring the Latin ban on the iambic word or iambic word-ending in front of a final iambus. Horace imitated the more elaborate Archilochian patterns (see ARCHILOCHUS) in his *Epodes* in a similar spirit.

In the same general category may be placed the Phalaecian verse used by Varro in his *saturae* and much used by Catullus for invective pieces. This had some relation to the forms of ionic verse used by Sotades (2) and imitated by Ennius and *Accius. Noteworthy is the liberty Varro and Catullus permitted themselves in forming the first two elements.

(e) Lyric poetry

The *Erotopaegnia* of the late 2nd- or early 1st-century BC *Laevius contained experiments with iambic, ionic, and 'aeolic' verse-forms. Catullus, and doubtless other contemporaries, adapted some of the monostrophic patterns of the Lesbian and Ionian lyric poets, again avoiding anything that smacked of stage *cantica of the same general metrical type. Horace produced imitations of a much greater variety of Greek lyric patterns. Whereas, however, Catullus had followed the apparent freedom of the Greek poets over the length of certain elements and the internal divisions of the strophe and its constituent cola, Horace turned into rules a number of observable tendencies of the Greek models.

(f) Elegy

A number of Romans of the 1st cent. BC took an interest in the elegies of *Philitas and *Callimachus (3). Old Ionian elegy never meant much to them. (See ELEGIAC POETRY, GREEK.) Catullus' translation of the passage of Callimachus' *Aetia* relating to the stellification of Berenice's lock of hair adapted closely the metrical pattern of the original. Old Latin liberties like the shortening rather than complete elimination of a long vowel before an initial short vowel continued to be accepted by *Cornelius Gallus. By the time of *Ovid, however, the elegiac couplet was bound by a set of rules much tighter than the set applied by the Alexandrian Greeks. Most striking was the demand that the couplet should end in a dissyllable.

(g) Epigram

In the 3rd and 2nd cents. BC the Saturnian verse was used for epitaphs, commemorative inscriptions, and perhaps also for inscribed insults. Some poets preferred the iambic senarius. Ennius composed an epitaph for P. *Cornelius Scipio Africanus in elegiac couplets. This form competed more and more successfully as time passed. The term *epigram was extended in Latin, as in Greek, to cover the impromptu poem written on wax tablets at a social occasion or surreptitiously scribbled on a wall. Here the Phalaecian verse joined the elegiac couplet and the iambic senarius. The pattern of the couplet of Catullus' epigrams was much looser than that of his more ambitious elegies. He used a Greek-style iambic trimeter rather than the stage senarius. Whether Catullus believed his Phalaecian poems and his short elegiac poems to belong to the one genre may be doubted, but *Martial certainly thought both metrical forms appropriate to the 'epigrams' he published at the end of the first cent. AD. The latter did not, however, admit a short syllable to either of the first two elements of the Phalaecian, and his elegiac couplet resembled more that of Ovid's elegies than that of Catullus' epigrams. See EPIGRAM, LATIN.

P. W. Harsh, *Lustrum* 1958, 215 ff.; R. J. Getty, *Lustrum* 1964, 103 ff.; J. Leonhardt, *Dimensio syllabarum* (1985); W. S. Allen, *Accent and Rhythm* (1973); H. Drexler, *Einführung in die römische Metrik* (1967); S. Boldrini, *La prosodia e la metrica latina* (1992); C. Questa, *Introduzione alla metrica di Plauto* (1967); J. Soubiran, *Essai sur la versification dramatique des romains* (1988); L. Müller, *De re metrica poetarum Latinorum praeter Plautum et Terentium* (1894); R. Heinze, *Die lyrischen Verse des Horaz* (1918); M. Plautnauer, *Latin Elegiac Verse* (1951). H. D. J.

Metrodorus (1), of *Chios, pupil of *Democritus, lived in the 4th cent. BC. His *On Nature* seems to have combined *atomism with the attempt to apply the Eleatic denial of change (see ELEATIC SCHOOL) to the universe as a whole. He occupied himself mainly with the explanation of meteorological and astronomical phenomena (see ASTRONOMY; METEOROLOGY). He also wrote historical works—*Trojan Chronicles* and perhaps also *Ionian Chronicles*.

DK 70. W. D. R.

Metrodorus (2) (*RE* 15), of *Lampsacus (*c.*331–278 BC), was one of the four καθηγεμόνες ('founders') of Epicureanism, and the most important after Epicurus; *Epicurus dedicated to him his *Eurylochus* and his *Metrodorus*, besides writing letters to him and mentioning him often in his works. He reckoned him not among original thinkers, but as first among those who could reach the truth with the help of others, and ordered that Metrodorus' memory as well as his own should be celebrated on the 20th of every month. Metrodorus' brother Timocrates notoriously left the Epicurean Garden over doctrinal disputes. The list of Metrodorus' writings, preserved by *Diogenes (6) Laertius (book 10) is a long one, and considerable fragments remain.

Fragments collected by A. Körte, *Jahrb. f. cl. Phil.* Suppl. 17 (1890), 531–97; *PHerc.* 831, ed. A. Körte, ibid. 571 ff. R. Westmann, *Plutarch gegen Kolotes* (1957). W. D. R.; D. O.

Metrodorus (3), of *Stratonicea, an adherent first of the Epicurean school (see EPICURUS), then of that of *Carneades (Diog. Laert. 10. 9; Cic. *De Or.* 1. 45).

Metrodorus (4), of *Scepsis in Mysia, was a friend of *Mithradates VI, but later joined *Tigranes (1) II, with the result that Mithradates had him killed. A man by this name is several times mentioned by *Cicero, as celebrated especially for his memory (he wrote a treatise expounding his system: Plin. *HN* 7. 88). He may be identical with the other Metrodorus, known for his hatred of Rome. Among works by this man (or one of these men) we hear of a book on Tigranes, a book on gymnastic training, one on custom (the meaning of the title is uncertain), and a geographical treatise.

FGrH 184, with Jacoby's comm. H. H. S; E. B.

metronomoi, overseers of *weights and *measures in Athens; five for the city and five for the *Piraeus, appointed by lot for one year (*Ath. pol.* 51. 2). In other states their duties were carried out by the *agoranomoi. P. J. R.

mētropolis ('mother-city') has several senses.
(*a*) The 'mother-city' of a Greek colony (*apoikia) usually nominated the *founder (*oikistēs*), conducted rituals of *divination and departure, organized a body of settlers, and formulated the charter of their individual status. Major mother-cities, such as *Chalcis or *Miletus, sometimes led mixed groups of settlers

but would insist on their own founder and customs. The latter, *nomima*, would identify a colony either ethnically ('Dorian') or more specifically, as originating from a particular *polis. *Nomima* could include cults, *calendar, script, *dialect, names and number of tribes (see PHYLAI) and other social divisions, titles of office-holders, and so on, and can aid modern research to determine colonial connections. Our sources in general are meagre, especially for early mother-cities (8th–7th cents. BC) but three salient facts of the civic identity of colonies seem to emerge, stressing the importance attached to the *mētropolis*: the identity of the mother-city, the date of foundation, and the name of the founder. The annual founder's cult in the colony probably commemorated, simultaneously, both the independence of the colony and its metropolitan, dependent origins. Taking sacred fire from the common hearth at the *prytaneion of the mother-city to light a new fire in the colony, a rite analogous both to marriage and military sacrifices, similarly stressed both continuity and new sovereignty. Mostly colonies were independent *poleis* (unlike modern colonialism, e.g. of France in Algeria; see POLIS); the Locrian foundation decree of *Naupactus, for example, repeats the formula 'when he becomes a Naupactian' (ML 20. 1, 22). On the other hand the articulation 'as parents to children', is also found in such decrees. The kinship-links were both real and metaphorical: descendants could point out graves of ancestors in the mother-city (Thuc. 1. 26. 3), and citizens from colonies could participate in cults and sacrifices in the *mētropolis*, a right usually denied to strangers. Religion was often the only, albeit meaningful, expression of continuing relations. Whether or not a mother-city controlled its colonies depended on distance (e.g. *Thasos and its opposite mainland, *Syracuse and *Acrae and Casmenae) or on ambition combined with maritime capabilities. *Corinth is known for its 'imperial' colonization in the Adriatic; its colony *Corcyra fought wars against it from the 7th cent. on, sometimes fell under its domination, and argued before the *Peloponnesian War that it was founded not to be a slave but an equal to its *mētropolis*. Corinthian art, however, continued to dominate in Corcyra regardless of politics. Primacy was naturally accorded to mother-cities (e.g. in the Argive *arbitration (see ARGOS (2)) between *Cnossus and Tylissus), expressing a common and consistent opinion in Greece. War between a mother-city and colony was considered shameful and alliance or military aid would rather be expected. Spartan generals kept appearing in Taras (see TARENTUM) centuries after its foundation in 706, and Sparta twice set out with exceptionally large contingents to help its motherland *Doris in 457 and 426. *Isopoliteia, the right to exercise *citizenship in both mother-city and colony, seems to have been exceptional in spite of some indications to the contrary (e.g. a man called Aceratus was archon in both Paros and its colony Thasos in the later 6th cent.). In spite of their (modern) 'peripheral image', colonies often eclipsed the mother-cities (e.g. *Cyrene and *Thera), reached more advanced forms of urban and country planning (*Megara Hyblaea) and political development (Achaean colonies were *poleis* when the *polis*-form had not yet reached *Achaea), articulated law codes (see LAW IN GREECE) and significantly contributed to the abstraction and formation of the Greek *polis* in general.

See also APOIKIA; ARCHĒGETĒS; COLONIZATION, GREEK; FOUNDERS, CITY; KINSHIP.

J. Bérard, *Expansion et colonisation grecques* (1960); A. J. Graham, *Colony and Mother City in Ancient Greece*, 2nd edn. (1983); I. Malkin, *Religion and Colonization in Ancient Greece* (1987). I. M.

(*b*) In Roman times an honorary title granted usually to the capitals of κοινά (provincial organizations), sometimes to other important cities.

J. Deininger, *Die Provinziallandtage der römischen Kaiserzeit* (1965), 143 n. 5; C. P. Jones, *The Roman World of Dio Chrysostom* (1978), see index under 'metropolis'.

(c) In Egypt the administrative capital of a *nomos (1). Under the Ptolemies (see PTOLEMY (1)) the *mētropoleis*, though they usually had many Greek residents, possessed no official communal organization. *Augustus placed on a special register the Hellenized residents of the *mētropoleis* (οἱ ἀπὸ μητροπόλεως), and these henceforth formed a hereditary class, paying poll-tax at a lower rate. He also established in each *mētropolis* a body of magistrates (ἄρχοντες), who managed the *gymnasium and the ephebic training (see EPHĒBOI), the market and corn supply, and the Greek temples. These were chosen—in theory probably by popular election—from a hereditary class styled ἡ ἀπὸ γυμ νασίου, 'from the gymnasium'. *Septimius Severus established in each *mētropolis* a council (βουλή), which co-opted its members and nominated the magistrates and the principal officials of the *nomos* except the στρατηγός ('governor') and βασιλικὸς γραμ ματεύς ('royal scribe'); these were appointed by the prefect. The *mētropoleis* officially became cities probably in AD 297, perhaps ten years later.

P. Jouguet, *La Vie municipale dans l'Égypte romaine* (1911); Jones, *Cities E. Rom. Prov.* ch. 11; Rostovtzeff, *Roman Empire*[2], 296–8 and n. 51; A. K. Bowman and D. Rathbone, *JRS* 1992, 120–7.   A. H. M. J.; S. H.

Mettius Pompusianus (*RE* entry under L. Pompusius Mettius; the identification is very doubtful) became *suffect consul AD 70–5 in spite of being alleged to possess an imperial horoscope. *Domitian in the early 90s first relegated him (see RELEGATIO) to *Corsica, then executed him, because of the horoscope, his map of the world, his volume of extracts of royal speeches from *Livy, and his slaves named after Carthaginian generals.

Suet. *Vesp.* 14; *Dom.* 10. 3; Cass. Dio 67. 12. B. Jones, *The Emperor Domitian* (1992), 186; cf. M. Corbier, *L'Aerarium Saturni* (1974), 88 ff.   G. E. F. C.; B. M. L.

Mezentius, king of *Caere in Etruria, whose aid was invoked by *Turnus (1) against *Aeneas. According to the story, told in the *Origines* of *Cato (Censorius), Mezentius helped the Rutulians in exchange for the first-fruits of the vintage; the Latins (see LATINI) then promised their first-fruits to *Jupiter, who gave them victory, Mezentius himself being killed by *Ascanius in single combat. In the *Aeneid* of *Virgil, Mezentius appears as a bloodthirsty and impious tyrant, and is killed by Aeneas. Attempts to interpret the story as a reflection of historical events, such as the war between *Veii and Rome (Ogilvie, comm. 628), or a supposed *Etruscan conquest of Latium in the 6th cent. BC (A. Alföldi, *Early Rome and the Latins* (1965), 209–12), are misguided. The story remains a legend, although an inscription on a 7th-cent. Etruscan vase from Caere attests to the presence there of a family of Mezentii in the Archaic age (D. Briquel, *CRAcad. Inscr.* 1989, 105–13).

Cato, *Orig.* 1. 9–12 Chassignet; Verg. *Aen.* 7–10; Ov. *Fast.* 4. 877–900.   T. J. Co.

miasma See POLLUTION.

Micon, painter and sculptor, of Athens. His painting was closely connected with that of his contemporary *Polygnotus, but Polygnotan ethos is never attributed to him. He painted in the Theseum (soon after 475 BC) *Theseus and *Minos; probably also an Amazonomachy and Centauromachy (see AMAZONS;

CENTAURS). In the *Stoa Poecile he is variously credited with Marathon and the Amazonomachy. The Amazonomachy and Centauromachy are reflected on vases: one Amazon is named Peisianassa, perhaps after Peisianax, who built the stoa. In the Anakeion were his *Argonauts (Paus. 1. 18. 1). He painted the Peliads (see PELIAS; MEDEA), naming them Asteropea and Antinoe; he also painted Butes so that only head and eye appeared above a hill; analogies can be found on contemporary vases. *Aelian (*NA* 4. 50) says he excelled at painting horses (similarly, *Pausanias (3) says he took most care in painting Acastus' horses in the Anakeion). He made a statue in *Olympia of Callias, victor in 472; the Mariémont warrior may reproduce an original by him. Micon's daughter Timarete was a painter (Plin. *HN* 35. 147). See PAINTING, GREEK.   K. W. A.

Midas (1), legendary king of *Phrygia, a comical figure famous in Greek tradition for his interview with Silenus (see SATYRS AND SILENS), his golden touch, and his ass's ears (best single source: Ovid, *Met.* 11. 90–193). Eager to learn the secret of life, the universe, and everything, he captured the wild nature-spirit Silenus by spiking the pool at which he drank—on the borders of *Macedonia, according to Hdt. 8. 138—with wine; the *daimon was brought before him bound (a scene attested in Greek art from *c.*560 BC, see Miller in bibliog. below) and revealed either (Theopompus, *FGrH* 115 F 75, in Ael. *VH* 3. 18) the existence of a world beyond our own divided between the two races of the Blest and the Warriors, or (Arist. fr. 65 Gigon, in Ps.-Plut. *Cons. ad Apoll.* 27) the melancholy insight, which became proverbial, that the best thing for mankind was never to be born, otherwise to leave this world as soon as possible. Verg. *Ecl.* 6 is a variant on this theme.

*Dionysus, grateful for Silenus' safe return to the wild, offered to grant the king any wish; Midas asked that everything he touched should turn to gold, but regretted his request when it became apparent that this made it impossible for him to eat or drink. The unwanted gift was washed off into the source of the Lydian river Pactolus, which thereafter carried gold dust down in its streams. A second divine encounter confirmed Midas' lack of judgement: invited to judge a musical contest between *Apollo and *Pan (or, according to Hyginus (3), *Marsyas), he preferred Pan, and was rewarded by the god with the ironical gift of donkey's ears. A turban hid his shame from all except his barber who, unable to contain the secret, told it to a hole in the ground; but reeds grew over the spot, and their wind-blown whispering propagates the unhappy truth for all time: 'Midas has ass's ears.'

Behind the character of legend there probably lies the historical king (of 'Mushki') whom the Assyrians knew as Mita (Hawkins, in bibliog. below; see also MIDAS (2)); the eastern evidence is compatible with the traditional dates given for Midas by *Eusebius, 738–696/5 BC. The recent excavation of the largest of the tomb-mounds outside the Phrygian capital *Gordium recovered a skeleton which may be his; it shows no sign of auricular abnormality (Prag, in bibliog. below).

L. E. Roller, *Cl. Ant.* 1983, 299–313, and 1984, 256–71; M. C. Miller *AK* 1988, 78–89; D. Hawkins, *Reallexikon der Assyriologie* 8. (1994), 271–3; A. J. N. W. Prag, *Anat. St.* 1989, 159–65.   A. H. G.

Midas (2), historical king of *Phrygia, 738–696/5 BC (dates from *Eusebius). He was the first *barbarian king to make presents to *Delphi (Hdt. 1. 14), and is said to have married the daughter of Agamemnon king of *Cyme (Arist. fr. 611. 37 Rose; Poll. 9. 83, mentioning Agamemnon, who is not the famous one), and to have committed suicide by drinking bull's blood when the *Cimmerians overthrew his kingdom (Strabo 1. 3. 21). In Assyrian records he appears as Mita: he joined a confederacy against King Sargon (717), but became his vassal (707). His story anticipates that of the Lydian *Gyges.

J. D. Hawkins, *CAH* 3² 1 (1982), 417 ff.; M. Mellink, *CAH* 3²/2 (1991), 622 ff. (spectacular 'tomb of Midas' at Gordium: fig. 42). On the marriage, H. T. Wade-Gery, *Poet of the Iliad* (1952), 7, 65 n. 21.

P. N. U.; S. H.

Midias See MEIDIAS.

midrash, a type of exegesis of scriptural texts practised by *Jews. The genre of midrash is characterized by the use of an explicit citation of, or clear allusions to, a passage in an authoritative text in order to provide a foundation for religious teachings often far removed from the plain meaning of the passage employed. In halakhic midrash such teachings comprise legal rulings. In aggadic midrash scriptural passages are exegeted for their own sake or for homiletic sermons. Midrashic techniques are found embedded in much post-biblical Jewish literature but they also engendered a large body of works devoted to this technique alone.

Midrashic exegesis is found already within the Hebrew Bible, where the books of Chronicles act as a midrash on the books of Samuel and Kings. Various types of midrash are attested in Jewish writings from the Hellenistic period, notably the *pesher*, found only among the *Dead Sea Scrolls, in which biblical texts are treated as complex codes from which the secret meaning has to be explicated, and the *Liber Antiquitatum Biblicarum*, attributed in the Renaissance to *Philon (4) of Alexandria but actually composed in Hebrew by an unknown Jew, probably in the 1st cent. AD. But most extant midrashim were produced and preserved by *rabbis from the 2nd cent. AD to the medieval period.

In rabbinic midrash, the rules of interpretation were eventually subjected to codification, but in earlier texts the authors were often creative, particularly in the use of exegesis to support legal views already reached for reasons independent of biblical support. Rabbinic midrashim reflect varied interests. On the whole, the halakhic midrashim are earlier (2nd and 3rd cents.), the aggadic midrashim are later (3rd to 6th cents., and on into the Middle Ages), but the distinction between these genres is not precise. All the midrashim contain teachings passed down from earlier generations (sometimes in oral form), and it is extremely difficult to give a date and place for the final redaction of many of the texts found in the medieval manuscripts.

The main extant halakhic (legal) midrashim from the Roman period are the *Mekhilta de Rabbi Ishmael* and the *Mekhilta de Rabbi Shimon bar Yohai* (both on Exodus), *Sifra* (on Leviticus), and *Sifre* (on Numbers and Deuteronomy), all probably compiled in Palestine by the early 3rd cent. AD. Of the exegetical and homiletic midrashim, *Lamentations Rabbah* may have been redacted in the 4th cent., *Genesis Rabbah*, *Leviticus Rabbah*, and *Pesikta de Rab Kahana* in the 5th cent., all probably in Palestine. However, all these texts certainly include material from earlier generations and may contain insertions from later periods. See RABBIS; RELIGION, JEWISH.

H. L. Strack and G. Stemberger, *Introduction to the Talmud and Midrash* (Eng. trans. 1991), 254–393, with bibliog. (Ger. 8th edn. in Stemberger, *Einleitung* (1992), 231–349). M. D. G.

midwives and normal labour are rarely mentioned in the Hippocratic treatises (see HIPPOCRATES (2)), perhaps because Hippocratic doctors concerned themselves with abnormal labour only. Occasional references to female 'helpers' and 'cord-cutters' survive (e.g. Hippoc. *Mul.* 1. 46 and 1. 68). However, it is also possible that midwives are not discussed because any woman was thought able to take on the role if necessary. In *Soranus, in contrast, the midwife appears as a literate and highly knowledgeable professional, the ideal midwife being trained in all areas of therapy—diet, surgery, and drugs—and able to decide how each case should best be treated (*Gyn.* 1. 2–3). Soranus' midwife does not have to have given birth herself, and can be old or young so long as she is sufficiently strong for the job. She must be free from superstition; labour, as a dangerous time for both mother and baby, was hedged around with taboos, and Soranus ridicules midwives who refuse to use iron when cutting the cord because they believe it is unlucky (*Gyn.* 2. 6).

It has been argued that the shift from the Hippocratic invisible midwife to Soranus' highly trained midwife reflects real development in women's health care. The names of 25 midwives are given in *CIL*, and the imperial women of the early empire were served by slave- and freedwomen in this role. There is some evidence that midwifery training was received from family members who were either doctors or midwives. *Galen dedicated *On the Anatomy of the Uterus* to a midwife, and his description of the midwives consulted by the wife of Boethus rates them as 'the best in Rome' (*On Prognosis* 8). However, we know neither how good were 'the best', nor how poor 'the rest'. From the later Roman empire there is also evidence that midwifery was not necessarily a full-time role; *Eunapius (*VS* 463) mentions a midwife who was called out to a woman in labour while working in a wine-bar. This gives particular significance to another of the features of Soranus' ideal midwife; his insistence that she should be sober. In Justinian's Code for the year 531 (see JUSTINIAN'S CODIFICATION), the price of a slave midwife is the highest for any female slave (6. 43. 3).

Whatever the relationship between Soranus' ideal and the reality, the ideal continued to have enormous influence through the abridged versions of the text which circulated in the world of late antiquity. Late antique Latin treatises such as those of Muscio, Caelius Aurelianus, Theodorus Priscianus, and the anonymous *Liber ad Soteris* are all based on Soranus and address themselves specifically to an audience of female midwives who read Latin, but not Greek.

The scope of the midwife's role in antiquity appears to have extended far beyond labour and the care of the newborn. She could give judgement on whether or not a woman was pregnant, and was called in when any woman—even a virgin—was ill. Male midwives cannot be ruled out, although the evidence is difficult to interpret; it is however clear from inscriptions that male doctors sometimes delivered babies. See CHILDBIRTH; MOTHERHOOD.

G. Clark, *Women in Late Antiquity* (1993); V. French, *Helios* 1987, 69–84; A. Hanson, in S. Pomeroy (ed.) *Women's History and Ancient History* (1991), 73–110; N. Kampen, *Image and Status* (1981); S. Treggiari, *AJAH* 1976, 76–104; L. C. Youtie, *ZPE* 65 (1985), 123–49. H. K.

migration See COLONIZATION (various entries); EXILE; LIMES; METICS; NEGOTIATORES; NOMADS; POPULATION, GREEK and ROMAN; SYNOECISM; TRANSHUMANCE.

milestones (*mil(l)iarium*), a typical feature of Roman (not Classical Greek) road-building. The earliest surviving Roman milestone (*ILS* 5801) dates from *c*.250 BC; in the Roman east they are found as late as *Justinian's reign. Under the republic they are inscribed with the names of consuls or other magistrates concerned with the building or repair of roads. In the Principate the full names and titles of the emperor usually appear; in the Roman east the inscriptions are often bilingual. They may attest the date of new roads (e.g. *ILS* 208, 5834), or methods of funding construction (e.g. *ILS* 5875). On trunk roads in Italy the distance given is often that from Rome, in the provinces from the administrative capital; but in most cases the distance is from the city on whose territory the milestone stood—often useful for the delimitation of those territories. In the Three Gauls and Germany from the time of Trajan distances were measured in *leugae* (1,500 paces—*c*.823 m. or 900 yds.). Milestones were usually cylindrical, about 1.8 m. (6 ft.) high. See ROADS; also entries under VIA.

K. Schneider, *RE* Suppl. 6 (1935), 395–431. Latin milestones are being republished in *CIL* 17 (1985–). Greek milestones are scattered in the epigraphic publications. Among regional studies, note D. French, *ANRW* 2. 2 (1980), 698–729 (Asia Minor); L. Gounaropoulou and M. Hatzopoulos, *Les Milliaires de la Voie Égnatienne*, Meletemata 1 (1985). See also bibliogs. under EPIGRAPHY, GREEK and LATIN.

G. H. S.; J. C. M.; A. J. S. S.

Milesian tales See ARISTIDES (2); NOVEL, GREEK and LATIN.

Miletus, southernmost of the great *Ionian cities of *Asia Minor, claimed partly Cretan origin (see CRETE); the successive strata of Minoan and Mycenaean settlement uncovered on the site (see MINOAN and MYCENAEAN CIVILIZATION) lend colour to this claim, as also the equation with Milawanda (acknowledged in the *Hittite records to have belonged to *Ahhiyawa). In *Homer the people of Miletus were Carians (see CARIA) who fought against the Achaeans (i.e. Greeks) at *Troy; and in later Greek prose tradition the Ionian settlers, under their Codrid founder *Neleus, seized Miletus from Carians (whose women they married). During the 7th and 6th cents. BC Miletus founded many colonies on the Black (*Euxine) Sea and its approaches (including *Abydos, *Cyzicus, *Sinope, *Panticapaeum, *Olbia, *Istria (1)), led the way in Greek penetration of Egypt (Milesians' Fort and *Naucratis; Necho's offering to the nearby temple at *Didyma after Megiddo, 608 BC), and had close contacts with *Sybaris till its destruction in 510. Miletus' sea power and colonies were partly cause, partly result of her long struggle with the Lydians (see LYDIA). *Alyattes made terms with Miletus (then under a tyrant Thrasybulus, the friend of *Periander), which apparently kept a privileged position when *Croesus subdued Ionia and when *Persia conquered Croesus' dominions *c*.546. See NEUTRALITY. In 499 Miletus, instigated by its ex-tyrant *Histiaeus and *Aristagoras (1), started the *Ionian Revolt. After the naval disaster at Lade the city was captured, the temple at *Didyma was burnt, and Miletus was destroyed (494).

Lade ended a long period of prosperity, interrupted by intervals of internal political struggles; to this period belong the Presocratic Milesian philosophers *Thales, *Anaximander, and *Anaximenes (1) and the chronicler and map-maker *Hecataeus (1). Finds from recent excavations of local pottery of the 7th–6th cents. BC, richly decorated with animal friezes, seem to indicate that Miletus was the main production centre of these types, rather than, as had previously been thought, *Rhodes.

After the Persian defeat at Mycale (479) Miletus joined the *Delian League, but in the mid-5th cent. (probably after a revolt) the Athenians imposed a garrison and imperial controls on the city. In 412, during the *Peloponnesian War, Miletus revolted from Athens, and became the main Spartan naval base in the region. It became a Persian possession after the *King's Peace,

until captured and liberated by *Alexander (3) the Great.

Delivered from the rule of Asander in 312, Miletus maintained friendly relations with the Hellenistic kings, especially the Ptolemies (see PTOLEMY (1)) and *Seleucids, who strove to incorporate it within their empires and who funded some of the buildings uncovered in the great German excavations of the site. It made treaties of *isopoliteia with its neighbours and colonies, and there was a large Milesian element resident in Athens. Miletus became part of the province of *Asia (129 BC). St *Paul visited it (AD 51). Its prosperity in the Roman period, from which many of the monuments date, was diminished by the silting up of its harbour (now 14.5 km. (9 mi.) from the sea). See EPHESUS.

Miletus suffered from the Gothic attacks of the 3rd cent. (see GOTHS); but the city continued to be maintained in late antiquity, with regular work to prevent the silting of the harbour. There was a period of lively building activity in the 6th and 7th cents., including several impressive churches. In the 7th cent. the theatre was fortified and the city contracted into a walled town.

Milet 1–5 / 1 (1903–90), publications of the German excavations; G. E. Bean, *Aegean Turkey*[2] (1980), ch. 10; *PECS* 578–82; N. Ehrhardt, *Milet und seine Kolonien: Vergleichende Untersuchung der kultischen und politischen Einrichtungen* (1983); P. J. Rhodes, *CAH* 5[2] (1992), 58–9 on the tangled evidence for Miletus in the Delian League; S. Mitchell, *Arch. Rep.* 1985, 70–105, see 85, and 1990, 102–6; C. Foss, *AJArch* 1977, 469–86, see 477–8 (repr. in C. Foss, *History and Archaeology of Byzantine Asia Minor* 2 (1990)). P. N. U.; J. M. C.; S. S.-W., C. R.

military training (Greek) Perhaps the most surprising thing about Greek warfare is that there is little or no evidence that any troops, other than Spartans, were trained before the 4th cent. BC, and the implication of what the sources say is that the Spartans were unique. Thus *Thucydides (2) has *Pericles (1) contrast the courage instilled in the Spartans by 'laborious training' (2. 39. 2) with the natural courage of the Athenians, and implies that the only trained troops opposed to the Spartans at the battle of *Mantinea in 418 were the thousand picked Argives trained at the state's expense (5. 67. 2). *Xenophon (1) implies that it was only *after* Leuctra that the Boeotians began to train (*Hell.* 6. 5. 23), and the author of the treatise on the Spartan constitution attributed to him (see XENOPHON (1), *Constitution of the Spartans*) claims (11.8) that manœuvres practised by the Spartans were beyond other Greeks. One must remember that in the normal Greek state the main element in the armed forces, the *hoplites, consisted of men of a comparatively high social standing, and that any kind of training might have been resented: it was much easier to train rowers for the fleet, since they came from a relatively humble background, whether free or slave.

Even the level of training among the Spartans should not be exaggerated. It is true that the Xenophontic treatise on the constitution implies that Spartan soldiers were trained to carry out manœuvres such as deploying from column-of-march into line-of-battle in various ways, depending on the direction of the enemy's approach, and that without training they could not have carried out such drills as the one whereby files from the left or right wings of the *phalanx were withdrawn behind the centre to double its depth (*anastrophē*), or the counter-march (*exeligmos*) for about-facing a phalanx. Nevertheless, much of this would have been at the level of 'square-bashing', and there is no evidence for any tactical training whether of officers or men.

In the 4th cent. there is increasing evidence for training. Xenophon's *Cyropaedia* is fictional, but presumably he would not have had *Cyrus (1) train his troops, if such training was still unthinkable outside Sparta, and it seems unlikely that he would have written his pamphlet on the cavalry commander unless there had also been works on infantry tactics, such as, perhaps, some of the lost parts of the 'Stratagems' of *Aeneas Tacticus. After Leuctra, the Thebans began to train, the new *Arcadian League had a standing army of 5,000 eparitoi, and there is some reason to believe that the two years' 'national service' of Athenian *ephēboi, mentioned by the Aristotelian Athenian Constitution, began in the first half of the 4th cent. There was also an increasing use of specialized troops such as *peltasts, some of whom—e.g. those of Iphicrates—were highly trained, and of *mercenaries, who were at least experienced. Xenophon has an interesting passage on the methods *Iphicrates used to train his fleet as it sailed round the Peloponnese in the 370s (Hell. 6. 2. 27 ff.), and he and other commanders probably trained land forces in similar ways.

It seems likely that *Philip (1) II instituted regular training in all branches at least of his Macedonian army, and when *Alexander (3) the Great succeeded, he was able to put on an impressive display for the Illyrians (Arr. Anab. 1. 6. 1–3). There can be no doubt that the army with which he conquered the Persian empire was highly trained, and with this and Hellenistic armies we enter the period of 'professional' soldiering at all levels.

J. K. Anderson, Military Theory and Practice in the Age of Xenophon (1970); G. L. Cawkwell, CQ 1972, 262 n. 4; W. K. Pritchett, The Greek State at War 2 (1974); J. F. Lazenby, The Spartan Army (1985); A. B. Bosworth, Conquest and Empire (1988).　　　　　　　　　　　　　　J. F. La.

milk (γάλα, lac). Fresh milk was not very important in the Greek and Roman diet, for climatic reasons, and many people in southern Italy and Greece cannot digest lactose in milk. However, northern *barbarians, especially nomads like the *Scythians, were known to drink milk. The milk that was consumed, normally in the form of cheese or curds (ὀξύγαλα), was usually that of goats or sheep. Cows' milk found little favour. Butter (βούτυρον) was used only by barbarians, since the Greeks and Romans preferred *olive oil. Horses' milk was also known. Receptacles identified as feeding-bottles for infants have been found on archaeological sites, but breast-milk was much more important (see BREAST-FEEDING). Milk was highly valued in medicine. The physicians recommended the internal or external use of milk (both human and animal) or whey for numerous ailments. It was also used for *cosmetic purposes, and in religious ceremonies as a first-fruit offering (see APARCHĒ), although its early use in this domain was often superseded by that of *wine.

RE 15. 1569–80, 'Milch'.　　　　　　　　　　　　　　J. R. S.

mills 'Saddle-querns', in which grain (see CEREALS) was rubbed between a fixed flat lower stone and a smaller hand-held upper stone, had been in general use for thousands of years before the 'hopper-rubber' mill appeared in Greece by the 5th cent. BC. Mechanized versions consisted of a rectangular upper stone, with a cavity that acted as a hopper for grain, pivoted at one end to allow a side-to-side action; grooves cut into the grinding surfaces improved the flow of grain and the removal of flour from the lower stone. Perhaps as early as the 3rd cent. BC, the introduction of a pair of round stones made a dramatic improvement, for a central (adjustable) pivot took the weight of the upper stone, which could be moved in a continuous rotary motion, assisted by its own momentum, and propelled by a crank-like vertical handle set into the upper surface. This development did not take place in Greece, for rotary mills did not appear there before the Roman period. Rotary mills were also scaled up into the hourglass-shaped 'Pompeian' form, powered by animals or slaves, in contexts such as commercial bakeries.

The invention of the water-mill (first described by *Vitruvius (De arch. 10. 5. 2) in the late 1st cent. BC) involved the combination of several existing devices. A type of a vertical, undershot water-lifting wheel was connected to a rotary mill, using power transmitted through 90 degrees by the engaged cog-wheels of a saqiya gear, an *Alexandrian invention used in Egypt for animal-powered water-lifting equipment. It is now known from archaeological evidence that 'Vitruvian' mills were used extensively in the Roman empire; they survived in widespread use into the 20th cent., supplemented by windmills from the 12th cent.. The date of 'Norse' water-mills, driven by a horizontal wheel that does not require gears, is uncertain, but their modern distribution and suitability for small irregular Mediterranean watercourses suggest Graeco-Roman origins. Hand-powered rotary mills always remained common in domestic settings, in contrast to the medieval period, when they were frequently banned in order to ensure custom for manorial water-mills or windmills.

L. A. Moritz, Grain-mills and Flour in Classical Antiquity (1958); O. Wikander, Exploitation of Water-power or Technological Stagnation? A Reappraisal of the Productive Forces in the Roman Empire (1984). K. T. G.

Milo See ANNIUS.

Milon, an athlete from *Croton of the later 6th cent. BC; six times victor in wrestling at the *Olympian Games, six times at the *Pythian. He is said to have carried a heifer down the course, killed it with one blow, and eaten it all in one day. Trying to rend a tree asunder he was caught in the cleft and eaten alive by wolves. See also DEMOCEDES.　　　　　　　　　　　　　F. A. W.

Miltiades, Athenian aristocrat and general, a member of the wealthy and powerful family of the Philaïdai. Archon (see ARCHONTES) in 524/3 BC, he was sent to recover control of *Chersonesus (1) by the tyrant *Hippias (1) in succession to his brother, Stesagoras, and his namesake and uncle, the elder Miltiades. There he married the daughter of the Thracian king, Olorus (see THUCYDIDES (2), Life). Subsequently he submitted to *Persia, and served *Darius I in the latter's Scythian campaign, allegedly supporting the Scythian suggestion that he and his fellow Greek tyrants should destroy the bridge over the Danube that Darius had left them to guard, though *Histiaeus of Miletus persuaded the majority not to agree. Shortly afterwards he was driven out of Chersonesus by a Scythian invasion, but returned when the nomads withdrew. He then appears to have joined in the so-called *Ionian Revolt early in the 5th cent., and it was possibly then that he won control of *Lemnos. But he was forced to flee to Athens when the revolt was crushed, and was prosecuted for having held tyrannical power in Chersonesus. Acquitted, he was shortly afterwards elected one of the ten generals (see STRATEGOI) for the year 490/89, and, according to tradition, it was he who was responsible for the Athenian decision to confront the Persians at *Marathon (see MARATHON, BATTLE OF), for persuading the *polemarchos *Callimachus (1) to give his casting-vote for fighting, and for choosing the moment, possibly when the Persian cavalry was absent; modern scholars have also credited him with deploying the phalanx with strong wings and a weak centre with the deliberate intention of bringing about the 'double envelopment' which won the battle. However, some of the details of the story are possibly anachronistic—for example, the polemarchos was probably still the real commander-in-chief—and Miltiades' alleged military experience should not be exaggerated. He had never commanded a hoplite army of any size—and even *Herodotus (1) does not make him responsible for the Athenian deploy-

mime

ment, which, in any case, was probably defensive. Since Callimachus was killed, and Miltiades' son *Cimon subsequently became the most influential man in Athens in the 470s and 460s, one suspects that Miltiades' image as the victor of Marathon owes much to family tradition.

After the victory, he commanded an Athenian fleet in an attack upon *Paros, but having failed to take the town, and been severely wounded, he was brought to trial and condemned to pay a fine of 50 talents. He died of gangrene before he could pay, but his son dutifully discharged the debt.

RE 15/2, 'Miltiades' 2; A. R. Burn, *Persia and the Greeks*, 2nd edn. (1985); M. M. Austin, *CQ* 1990, 303 f.; J. F. Lazenby, *The Defence of Greece* (1993).
J. F. La.

mime The *mimus* (μῖμος) was an imitative performance or performer.

Greek In Greece, as elsewhere, the instinct for imitation found its expression in the mimetic dance. From early times solo performers, by play of gesture, voice, and feature, gave imitations of neighing horses, etc. (Pl. *Resp.* 396b), and small companies, called in Sparta δεικηλίκται (? 'masked men'), elsewhere αὐτοκάββαλοι ('improvisers') or in Italiot towns φλύακες (*phlyakes*), presented short scenes from daily life (e.g. 'The Quack Doctor') or mythology, probably on a hastily erected stage in the market-place or in a private house; such performers belonged to the social class of acrobats, etc. *Xenophon (1) (*Symp.*) tells of a mime 'of *Dionysus and *Ariadne', danced at a private banquet by a boy and girl; we note the connection with *Syracuse, the musical accompaniment, the use of dialogue, and the fact that the girl is also a sword-dancer and the concubine of the Syracusan dancing-master. In the 5th cent. BC *Sophron of Syracuse wrote 'men's' and 'women's' mimes in Dorian rhythmic prose; the language was popular and included frequent proverbs; the surviving titles (e.g. 'The Old Fishermen', 'The Women Quacks', 'The Women Visitors to the Isthmia') indicate stock mime themes. Of the mimes of Sophron's son, *Xenarchus (1), virtually nothing is known. In the 3rd cent. the taste for realism brought the mime to the fore; *Theocritus dressed traditional themes in his courtly hexameters (Idyll 2: the deserted heroine resorts to magic; 15: two Syracusan women visit the festival of *Adonis in *Alexandria (1); 21 (probably by an imitator of Theocritus): two old fishermen converse; 14 is also dramatic in form); these pieces, like those of the more realistic *Herodas, were probably intended for semi-dramatic recitation. Meanwhile the popular mime invaded the theatre; it now took the form either of παίγνια (? slight, often vulgar, performances) or of ὑποθέσεις, 'plots' (Plut. *Quaest. conv.* 712e), taken over from drama proper and presented in mimic fashion by the μαγῳδοί (Ath. 621c; see MAGODIA) or μιμολόγοι (the meaning of the various terms for performers, whether they suggest spoken or musical delivery, is uncertain); cf. the 3rd-cent. Athenian lamp with its representation of three maskless performers and the inscription 'Mimologi', hypothesis: Mother-in-law'. The 'Alexandrian erotic fragment' is perhaps a sung mime: theme, the deserted heroine. In *POxy.* 413 we have (a) a farce mostly in prose, based on the plot of *Iphigenia among the Taurians* (?): a Greek girl, named Charition, aided by her brother, escapes from an Indian king and his followers by making them drunk; the barbarians speak pseudo-Indian; there is a low clowning part; (b) a prose mime: theme, the jealous mistress (cf. Herodas 5), who tries to poison her husband and make love to her slaves; there are six or seven short scenes and seven roles, all unimportant except that of the archimima; here, as always, the interest of the mime is in character and situation rather than in action. In the Marissa wall-inscription we have a song-dialogue between a hetaira and the *exclusus amator* ('shut-out lover').

TEXTS I. C. Cunningham (Teubner, 1987).
On *phlyakes*, O. Taplin, *Comic Angels* (1993).
W. B.

Roman Barefoot clowns (*planipedes*, Festus 342 Lindsay) playing without masks improvised sketches in the streets of Rome and Italy before the popularity of mime won it regular official presentation at the Floralia (first instituted 241 BC, made annual in 173 BC, cf. Ov. *Fast.* 5. 287–352). Early performers bear Greek names like Protogenes, slave of Cloulius (epitaph, Warmington, *Remains of Old Latin* (1940), 4. 14; *CIL* 1. 2. 1861); no doubt many were Greek. Leading mimes (*archimimi*) trained their own companies, devising or modifying scenarios for their use. After Sulla associated with mime artists, mime became smart, displacing the *Atellana as an *exodium* ('after-piece'). Both men and women took part, exploiting sexual innuendo and display. Mime actresses like Arbuscula and Dionysia won wealth and notoriety, and Cytheris, an ex-slave, was mistress of both Antony (M. *Antonius (2)) and the elegist *Cornelius Gallus.

The scripts of literary mime composed by gentlemen like Cn. *Matius and Decimus *Laberius probably used the same plots based on change of fortune ('from rags to riches', Cic. *Phil.* 2. 65), the pursuit and escape of tricksters (Cic. *Cael.* 65), and disguise or concealment of adulterous lovers (Ov. *Tr.* 2. 513–14), but would be more carefully constructed, like traditional comedy. Surviving excerpts are unrepresentative, quoted only for Laberius' eccentric word-forms or the literary aphorisms of *Publilius Syrus. Non-dramatic literary texts could be performed as mime: *Ovid reports that his elegies were staged (*Tr.* 2. 519–20), as were *Virgil's *Eclogues* in his lifetime, and versions of the tales of *Dido and *Turnus (1) in later centuries (Macrob. *Sat.* 5. 17. 4). *Augustus and his successors delighted in mime and presented it to win favour from the city crowd; audiences were entertained with 'real' fires, and the *crucifixion or rape on stage of condemned criminals and slaves (see K. M. Coleman, *JRS* 1990, 44–73). Star performers exploited their popularity to insert innuendos against emperors into their performance, or, like Latinus (Juv. 1. 36; Mart. 9. 29), became imperial lovers or informers. The glamour of mime defeated the denunciations of *Tertullian and later of the official Christian Church: *Justinian made a mime actress his empress, and, free from constricting laws of form or performance, the mongrel genre survived to be reborn as *commedia dell'arte*.

No Latin scenarios survive and few fragmentary texts, but the subjects of mime clearly influenced Rome's formal literature: in particular they provided themes for the invented genres of *satire and *elegiac poetry (Latin): the adulterer's escape (Hor. *Sat.* 1. 2; Prop. 2. 23; Ov. *Am.* 3. 4), the scene of witchcraft (Hor. *Sat.* 1. 8; *Epod.* 5 and 17), the interrupted or ruined party (Prop. 4. 8; Hor. *Sat.* 2. 8; Petron. *Sat.* 53, 78). The 'Menippean' combination of prose and verse (see MENIPPEAN SATIRE) in the narrative satire of *Varro and *Petronius Arbiter reflects the popularity of the same combination in mime. Petronius borrows its narrative devices (quarrels, theft, and arrest, or escape in disguise), drawing attention to the mimic or play-acting element: his heroes even devise and enact the scenario of a real-life mime to trick the legacy hunters of *Croton (*Sat.* 117). In the empire the Greek and Roman traditions blended, and the many echoes and features of mime in *Apuleius' *Metamorphoses* are as likely to be Greek in origin as Roman.

TEXTS M. Bonaria (ed.), *Mimorum Romanorum Fragmenta* 1: *Fragmenta*; 2: *Fasti mimici et pantomimici* (1955).

E. Wüst, *RE* 15 (1932), 1727 ff.   E. F.

mimesis See IMITATIO; LITERARY CRITICISM IN ANTIQUITY; MUSIC, § 5 (*b*); PLAGIARISM.

Mimnermus, Greek elegiac poet from *Smyrna (fr. 9 West), later claimed by Colophon whose foundation he described (frs. 9. 3, 10). His name may commemorate the Smyrnaeans' famous resistance to *Gyges at the river *Hermus sometime before 660 BC, which would imply his birth at that time. He commented on a total solar *eclipse (fr. 20), more likely that of 6 April 648 than that of 28 May 585. He was apparently still alive when *Solon (fr. 20 West) criticized a verse of his, but there is no sign that he survived *Alyattes' destruction of Smyrna *c.*600. Ancient reckoning set his floruit in 632–629 (*Suda*). His poetry was divided into two books, probably corresponding to the titles *Smyrneis* and *Nanno* (cf. Callim. fr. 1. 11–12 pf.). The *Smyrneis* was a quasi-epic on the battle against Gyges, with elaborate proemium and ample narrative with speeches (frs. 13–13a). The shorter elegies stood under the collective title *Nanno*, said to be the name of a girl aulete whom Mimnermus loved; though she is not mentioned in fragments, and he also celebrated the charms of boys (cf. frs. 1. 9, 5, Hermesianax 7. 38 Powell, Alexander Aetolus 5. 4 f. Powell). He was especially famous for poems on the pleasures of love, youth, and sunlight. But fr. 14 seems to come from a call to arms, contrasting the citizens' present spirit with that of a hero of the Hermus battle. Mimnermus was also remembered as an aulete or oboist (Hipponax 153 West; Hermesianax 7. 37 f.; Strabo 14. 1. 28). See ELEGIAC POETRY, GREEK.

TEXT B. Gentili and C. Prato, *Poetae Elegiaci* 1 (Teubner, 1979); West, *IE*[2] 2.

TRANSLATION M. L. West, *Greek Lyric Poetry* (1993).

COMMENTARY T. Hudson-Williams, *Early Greek Elegy* (1926); D. A. Campbell, *Greek Lyric Poetry* (1967); A. Allen, *The Fragments of Mimnermus: Text and Commentary* (1993).

DISCUSSION *RE* Suppl. 11. 935–51; M. L. West, *Studies in Greek Elegy and Iambus* (1974), 72–6; C. W. Müller, *Rh. Mus.* 1988, 197–211.
                                                          M. L. W.

Mindarus, Spartan admiral, 411/10 BC. When the Phoenician ships promised by *Tissaphernes failed to arrive, he transferred the main Peloponnesian fleet to the *Hellespont where *Pharnabazus was offering assistance and the Athenian grain route could be threatened. His fleet was defeated off Cynossema and again off *Abydos (autumn 411). Early in 410 he recaptured *Cyzicus; but there his ships, either by surprise (*Xenophon (1)) or strategy (*Diodorus (3) Siculus), were caught out of harbour by a superior Athenian fleet. Forced to flee to land, he died defending his ships which were all captured or burned. The battle's outcome prompted Sparta's peace offer of 410 and temporarily re-established Athens' naval supremacy.

Thuc. 8. 99–107; Xen. *Hell.* 1. 1. 2–18; Diod. Sic. 13. 38–51. *RE* 15. 1767–9; PB no. 536; D. Kagan, *The Fall of the Athenian Empire* (1987), ch. 9.   S. J. Ho.

mineralogy The modern term for the systematic study of the character and diversity of chemical elements and compounds which occur naturally within the earth. How far the Greeks could be said to have engaged in this kind of study is highly questionable, yet there is evidence that the diversity of mineral substances was recognized, and names given to a few minerals. There is no doubt that the ancients had experience of the use of ores, precious and semi-precious stones, and *building materials.

Archaeological evidence for ancient mining and *metallurgy, however, suggests degrees of technical sophistication and understanding which are not equally evident in the surviving literary sources.

Epistemologically-based hierarchies of nature like those of *Plato (1) and, to a lesser extent, *Aristotle seem effectively to have discouraged the systematic investigation of anything but the most unusual, valuable, or beautiful of mineral substances. Yet speculation about the origins of earth-materials in general is a feature of certain Presocratic cosmologies (notably those of *Anaximenes (1), *Heraclitus, *Anaxagoras, and *Empedocles). There is little sign of any generally accepted distinction between rocks and minerals, but Plato (*Ti.* 59b–60c) distinguishes between the modes of formation of rocks ($\pi\epsilon\tau\rho\alpha\iota$) and metals. He argues that metals (of which the most perfect is *gold) are formed when a fusible type of water melts and then congeals in the earth. Varying degrees of admixture with earth explain the variety of the products of the process. Stones are formed when earth is compressed by the air above it. At the end of book 3 of the *Meteorology*, Aristotle divides substances found in the earth into metals ($\mu\epsilon\tau\alpha\lambda\lambda\epsilon\upsilon\tau\acute\alpha$), characterized by their fusibility and ductility and which result from the action of his 'vaporous exhalation', and 'things dug up' ($\acute{o}\rho\upsilon\kappa\tau\acute\alpha$), including what he calls the 'infusible stones'—ochre, sulphur, etc.—which result from the burning action of the so-called dry and fiery exhalation on the earth.

Aristotle's successor *Theophrastus preserves the distinction between substances which originate in water and in earth. His short treatise *On Stones*, companion to a lost treatise on metals to which he refers in passing, covers stones and earth-materials with a particular interest in the rare and unusual. He discusses the properties of mineral substances and stones—particularly those endowed with special qualities—without attempting any systematic classification. By modern standards, the number of 'stones' he mentions is remarkably small.

Much of Theophrastus' research was used later by the elder *Pliny (1), in books 33–7 of the *Natural History*. Book 33 deals with precious metals, their origins, modes of extraction and uses. Book 34 covers less valuable metals and alloys, like copper, *lead, *iron, and *bronze, and Book 35 begins the coverage of earths, focusing first on their utility as artists' pigments. Book 36 treats stone, especially architecturally useful varieties like *marble, limestone, granite, before moving on to more unusual, in some cases marvellous, substances like the lodestone, and the 'eagle stone'. The introduction of Hellenistic material on the magical and extraordinary properties of certain stones, especially *gems, is a striking feature of book 37, which also contains (37. 42) the first surviving account of the true origin of *amber. This tradition is preserved and developed in the later, often mystical, Lapidaries. *Dioscorides (2) treats minerals with medicinal importance in the fifth book of his *Materia medica*, as does *Galen in his great pharmacological treatises.

TEXTS AND TRANSLATIONS Aristotle, *Meteorology*, trans. H. D. P. Lee (Loeb, 1952); Theophrastus, *On Stones*, ed. and trans. E. R. Caley and J. F. C. Richards (1956); another edn. and trans. by D. E. Eichholz (1965); Pliny, *Natural History*, books 33–7, trans. H. Rackham and D. E. Eichholz (Loeb, 1952, 1962); Dioscorides, *Materia medica*, ed. M. Wellmann, 3 vols (1906–14); F. de Mély, *Les Lapidaires de l'Antiquité et du Moyen Âge* 1 (1898); R. Halleux and J. Schamp, *Les Lapidaires grecs* (1985).

LITERATURE C. E. N. Bromehead, *Proceedings of the Geologists' Association* 1945, 89–134; D. E. Eichholz, *CQ* 1949, 141 f.; J. F. Healy, *Mining and Metallurgy in the Greek and Roman World* (1978), and in R. French and F. Greenaway (eds.), *Science in the Early Roman Empire*

Minerva

Minerva

Minerva

(1986); R. Halleux, *Le Problème des métaux dans la science antique* (1974); J. T. Vallance, *Rutgers Studies in Classical Humanities* 1988, 25–40.

J. T. V.

Minerva (archaic **Menerva**), an Italian goddess of handicrafts, widely worshipped and regularly identified with *Athena. Altheim (*RE* 'Minerva'; cf. *Hist. Rom. Rel.* 235 and n. 34; *Griechische Götter* (1930), 142 n. 4) believes her actually to be Athena, borrowed early through Etruria (see ETRUSCANS); but most scholars think her indigenous, and connect her name with the root of *meminisse* ('to remember') etc. At all events there is no trace of her cult in Rome before the introduction of the Capitoline Triad, where she appears with *Jupiter and *Juno in an Etruscan grouping. Apart from this she was worshipped in a (possibly) very ancient shrine on mons Caelius (see CAELIUS MONS), which was called Minerva Capta by *Ovid, from the taking of Falerii in 241 BC (Ov. *Fast.* 3. 835 ff.). But it seems that this name was derived from a statue captured in Falerii (see FALISCANS) and offered to the Caelian Minerva (see Ziolkowski, *Temples* 112 ff.). A much more important cult lay *extra pomerium* ('outside the *pomerium*') on the *Aventine; it was supposedly vowed in 263 or 262 BC (see Ziolkowski, *Temples* 109 ff.). The Aventine Minerva was of Greek origin and was the headquarters of a guild of writers and actors during the Second Punic War (Festus 446. 26 ff. Lindsay) and seems to have been generally the centre of organizations of skilled craftsmen. Minerva's worship spread at the expense of *Mars himself, the *Quinquatrus coming to be considered her festival, apparently because it was the *natalis* ('anniversary') of her temple (Ov. *Fast.* 3. 812); it was also extended to five days, from a misunderstanding of the meaning ('fifth day after' a given date; see Frazer on Ov. *Fast.* 3. 812). 13 June was called the *Quinquatrus minusculae* ('Lesser Quinquatrus') and was the special feast-day of the professional flute-players (*tibicines*; cf. Ov. *Fast.* 6. 651 ff., and G. Dumézil, *Mythe et épopée 3* (1973))

Latte, *RR* 163 ff.; Radke, *Götter* 217 ff.; F. Castagnoli, *Il culto di Minerva a Lavinium* (1979) Dumézil, *ARR* 303 ff.; J.-L. Girard, *ANRW* 2. 17. 1 (1981), 203 ff.; W. Schürmann, *Typologie und Bedeutung der stadtrömischen Minervakultbilder* (1985); *LIMC* 2/1 (1984), 1051 ff.

H. J. R.; J. Sch.

mines and mining

Greek Greeks obtained *gold and *silver and 'utility' metals, copper, *tin (for bronze), *iron and *lead by mining and by trade; *colonization extended their scope for both. Literary evidence for mining is mainly historical not technical; later references to Egyptian and Roman methods are only partly applicable. Epigraphical, archaeological, and scientific evidence has extended knowledge of industrial organization and techniques, and proved the early exploitation of certain ore-fields. Climate, geography, and geology dictated methods: panning for gold (as in Asia Minor and Black Sea regions) and hushing of placer deposits were rarely practicable in Greece and its islands, while low rainfall reduced mine-drainage problems and accounted for the elaborate catchment channels, cisterns and ore-washeries designed to recycle water in the *Laurium area. There the Athenian lead-silver mines were extremely extensive (copper and iron ores were also exploited). *Thoricus has revealed sherd evidence for mining in the early bronze age (third millennium BC), late Mycenaean (see MYCENAEAN CIVILIZATION), and late Roman times, with marks of prehistoric hammer-stones and later metal chisels and picks. Sporadic mining continued in Laurium till the boom period of the 5th and 4th cents. BC, with small-scale working and re-exploitation of minehead and furnace spoil-heaps thereafter.

Opencast pits, oblique and vertical shafts (with cuttings for ladders, stagings, and windlasses), and underground galleries (some only 1 m. (39 in.) high) and chambers mark hillsides and valleys, along with extensive surface-works (cisterns, washeries), some in seemingly haphazard juxtaposition, others segregated in compounds. Cycladic *Siphnos, prosperous and famed for its gold- and silver-mines in Archaic times, has also produced evidence for silver-lead mining in the early bronze age, with opencast pits, trenches, shafts, ovoid galleries, and chambers, repacked ritually on abandonment. In northern Greece also, in Macedonia and Thrace (Mt. *Pangaeus) and on *Thasos, gold and silver were mined. Control of the mainland mines yielded *Philip (1) II of Macedon an income of 1,000 talents annually. See METALLURGY, GREEK; SLAVERY.

J. F. Healy, *Mining and Metallurgy in the Greek and Roman World* (1978); C. E. Conophagos, *Le Laurium antique* (1980); *Thorikos* 8 (1984), 151–74, and 9 (1990) 114–43; *Der Anschnitt*, Beiheft 3: *Silber, Blei und Gold auf Sifnos* (1985).

J. E. J.

Roman Imperial expansion gave Rome control over a wide variety of mineral resources. The Iberian peninsula (see SPAIN), *Gaul (Transalpine), *Britain, the Danubian provinces (*Dalmatia, *Noricum, and *Dacia), and Asia Minor came to be the major mining regions of the Roman empire, and gold, silver, copper, lead, and tin the main metals extracted. *Iron was found in many parts of the empire and despite the presence of large-scale iron-mining districts in Noricum and the Kentish Weald was usually exploited in smaller local units of production. It is difficult to trace precisely the history of Roman mining, since mining areas and individual mines came into and went out of production, and because archaeological research has been more thorough in some areas than others; but the main lines can be drawn. Italy contained few precious metals, and so Rome initially had to rely on imports from mines controlled by Hellenistic kings in the east and the Carthaginians in the west. After the defeat of *Hannibal in 201 BC, Romans and Italians were soon exploiting the *silver-mines in SE Spain around New Carthage (*Carthago Nova). After the conquest of the Macedonian kingdom in 167 BC, Rome regulated the operation of the Macedonian *gold-mines to suit its needs. The apogee of production at the major mines of Iberia, Gaul, Britain, and the Danubian provinces took place in the first two centuries AD. After the disruption of the 3rd cent., some mines were operating again in the 4th cent., but, as far as we can tell, on a reduced scale and under a different organizational regime.

The Romans rarely opened up new areas of mining, but often expanded the scale of production and the variety of metals mined in regions already known for their mineral potential. Techniques of prospection relied heavily on observation of visible veins of mineralization in rock deposits and changes in soil colour. Of the precious metals only gold (and to a lesser degree copper) existed in a natural state. Silver, copper, *lead, and *tin occurred in compound metal deposits (ores) and required metallurgical processing to convert them into usable metals. Three main types of mining were practised: the exploitation of alluvial deposits; opencast mining of rock-deposits found near the surface; and underground mining of deeper-lying rock-deposits. The Romans exploited alluvial deposits (placers) of gold and tin by panning or, if they were larger in scale, by flushing the alluvium with large quantities of water released at high speed in sluices to separate the metal-bearing sands from the dross. In NW Spain especially deep alluvial deposits were undermined before being flushed with water to separate out the gold-nuggets (Plin. *HN*

33. 70–8). In underground mines vertical shafts were sunk often in pairs occasionally to an impressive depth: 340 m. (1,115 ft.) at one mine near New Carthage. Horizontal galleries, often strengthened with wooden props, connected the shafts, increased ventilation, and allowed ore once mined to be removed from the ore-face. Terracotta oil-lamps were placed in niches to provide lighting. Drainage was a problem in deeper mines. Manual bailing was practised (Pliny, *HN* 33. 97), but if possible, drainage adits were cut through sterile rock. In some mines chain-pumps, Archimedean screw-pumps, or a series of water-lifting wheels were used. Mining tools, including picks, hammers, and gads, were mainly of iron, while ore was collected in buckets made of esparto grass before being hauled, in some cases by pulleys, to the surface.

Many mines (especially gold- and silver-mines) over time became the property of the Roman state, but cities and private individuals continued to own and operate mines. In state-owned mines the state either organized production directly, as probably occurred in the gold-mining region of NW Spain, or it leased out contracts to work the mines to individuals, small associations or the larger *societates publicanorum* (see PUBLICANI). Mineworkers were often slaves, but prisoners of war, convicts, and free-born wage labourers also formed part of the workforce. Tombstones from mining settlements show that people often migrated long distances to work at mines. Soldiers were stationed at the larger mines, not just to supervise the labour force, but also to provide technological expertise. Any mining site needed a large number of ancillary workers to keep the labour force fed, clothed, and equipped, and to assist in processing ore into usable metals. See METALLURGY, ROMAN.

The most important ancient sources are Pliny (*HN* 33–6), Strabo, and Diod. Sic.; see *RE* Suppl. 4 (1924), 111–24, 'Bergbau'. For the leasing of state-owned mines see the *lex Metalli Vipascensis* (*ILS* 6891 = *FIRA* 1. 105) and the *lex Metallis Dicta* (*FIRA* 1. 104) with D. Flach, *Chiron* 1979, 399–448; C. Domergue, *La Mine antique d'Aljustrel (Portugal) et les tables de bronze de Vipasca* (1983). In general see O. Davies, *Roman Mines in Europe* (1935); U. Täckholm, *Studien über den Bergbau der römischen Kaiserzeit* (1937); J. F. Healy, *Mining and Metallurgy in the Greek and Roman World* (1978; rev. It. trans. 1992); P. Rosumek, *Technischer Fortschritt und Rationalisierung im antiken Bergbau* (1982); *Minería y metalurgía en las antiguas civilizaciones mediterraneas y europeas* (1989); J. C. Edmondson, *JRS* 1989, 94–102 (later empire); J. Andreau, *RN* 1989, 86–112, and 1990, 85–108; C. Domergue, *Les Mines de la péninsule ibérique dans l'antiquité romaine* (1990).   J. C. E.

Minicius Fundanus, Gaius, *suffect consul AD 107, had a wide circle of friends who included the younger *Pliny (2) and *Plutarch. As proconsul of Asia (in 122–3) he received *Hadrian's rescript (see CONSTITUTIONES; MAGISTER LIBELLORUM) about procedure concerning Christians. A copy of this was later attached to the end of *Justin Martyr's *First Apology* (c.150).

PIR² M 612.   H. H. S.

Minoan civilization, the bronze age civilization of *Crete (c.3500–1100 BC). See also RELIGION, MINOAN AND MYCENAEAN. The term 'Minoan' (after the legendary *Minos) was coined by Sir Arthur Evans to distinguish the prehistoric culture of Crete revealed in his excavations beginning in 1900 at the site of *Cnossus (Κνωσσός) from the *Mycenaean civilization revealed by Schliemann on the Greek mainland. Evans, using the pottery styles found at Cnossus divided the civilization into three phases, early, middle, and late Minoan (EM, MM, LM), a scheme subsequently refined to produce complex subdivisions (e.g. EM IIA,

LM IIIA1), although a simpler tripartite division into pre-Palatial, Palatial (subdivided into proto- and neo-Palatial), and post-Palatial better reflects cultural developments. The absolute chronology of prehistoric Crete, established through connections with the 'historical' chronology of Egypt, has been refined using radiocarbon dating techniques together with tree-ring calibration. Chief among the refinements are the dates for the earliest permanent settlers on the island (c.7000 BC), for the beginning of the bronze age (EM I) (c.3500 BC), and for the beginning of the late bronze age (LM I) (c.1700 BC, based on a likely date for the destruction of the Akrotiri site on *Thera of 1628 BC). The beginning of the iron age is conventionally placed at the end of the sub-Minoan phase (c.1000 BC), although functional iron objects are known from LM IIIC onwards.

Pre-Palatial (neolithic to MM IA: c.7000–2000 BC). Although humans may have visited Crete earlier, it was first colonized before c.7000 BC possibly from SW Anatolia. The only attested site of that date is Cnossus, some 5 km. (3 mi.) from the sea on the west side of the Kairatos valley—in its earliest phase perhaps only 0.25 ha. (0.6 acre) in size with a population of about 70 (cf. *Antiquity* 1991, 233 ff.). The first colonists there brought with them a fully developed farming lifestyle and the ancestor of one of the island's later languages. For the next 2,500 years very few sites are known until numbers increase dramatically in the late and final neolithic periods (c.4500–3500 BC), by which time Cnossus has reached a size of 5 ha. (12.4 acres), its population perhaps as high as 1,500. The rise in site numbers seems too large to be explained solely by indigenous population increase, suggesting some new settlers in a period when many of the smaller Aegean islands were being colonized for the first time. The appearance of new ceramic traditions in the earliest bronze age ('Agios Onouphrios' and 'Pyrgos' wares) and material culture links with the *Cyclades have been cited as further evidence for immigration.

Although the EM I phase conventionally marks the beginning of the bronze age, this term is misleading: copper metallurgy was already known in the final neolithic at Cnossus, but true bronze metallurgy does not become widespread until EM II (c.2,500 BC). See METALLURGY. Our understanding of society in EM I–MM IA Crete (c.3500–2000 BC) depends to a large extent on burials (particularly those in circular tombs in the Mesara region) and on a handful of small excavated sites, such as Debla, Myrtos Phournou Koriphi (0.09 ha.: 0.25 acre), and Vasiliki (which lends its name to a characteristic ceramic of the EM II period). The evidence of these sites (with populations perhaps in the order of 30–50 individuals) suggests a relatively egalitarian society, in contrast to the larger settlements that certainly existed in this phase (Cnossus, Phaestus, Malia, Mochlus) with populations perhaps ranging from 450 (Phaestus) to 1,500 (Cnossus) (cf. T. Whitelaw, *Minoan Society*, ed. O. Kryszkowska and L. Nixon (1983), 337 ff.). Their sizes, together with poorly understood monumental structures at Cnossus and élite burials at Mochlus, imply the emergence of a social hierarchy already by EM II. In the latest pre-Palatial phase (MM IA in central Crete, EM III in the east), élite burials become more widespread (Archanes, Malia, Gournia, Mochlus), as do indicators of connections with the eastern Mediterranean, suggesting the importance of social stratification and external contacts as factors associated with the emergence of the palaces (cf. *PCPS* 1984, 18 ff.).

Palatial (MM IB to LM IB: c.2000–1470 BC). The first structures referred to as 'palaces' are built at the central Cretan sites of

Minoan civilization

Cnossus, Malia, and Phaestus in the MM IB phase. Architecturally they are distinguished by monumentality (floor areas range from 1.3 ha. (3.2 acres) at Cnossus to 0.75 ha. (1.85 acres) at Malia), by their arrangement around a paved central court, with a paved western court, and by sophisticated masonry techniques such as ashlar orthostate blocks. The uniformity of plans of the first palaces is somewhat illusory and Malia in particular seems to have had a more dispersed layout, while it is possible that architecturally distinct palaces did not appear all over the island in MM IB, notably in east Crete, where an extensive network of roads, way-stations, and watch-towers established in MM II, linked the sites of Palaikastro and Kato Zakros with the SE section of the island.

Innovations in economic and social organization of the late pre-Palatial period are more clearly articulated in the architectural environment of the early palaces. The palaces mobilized agricultural surplus within their territories, necessitating the construction of large-scale storage facilities for food to support the élite and their workforce, to provide relief in times of stress, and, probably, to support ritual feasting. To record such storage two scripts were used—so-called Cretan Hieroglyphic (chiefly at Cnossus and Malia) and Linear A (at Phaestus; see PRE-ALPHABETIC SCRIPTS (GREECE))—while clay sealings were used at Phaestus as a direct means of controlling storage rooms and containers. Élite craft production was centred on the palaces and it seems likely that the palaces also monopolized the acquisition of raw materials, such as copper (from *Attica and other sources: see LAURIUM), tin, and ivory (through Syria). Finds of the polychrome 'Kamares' ware characteristic of the proto-Palatial period are widespread if not numerous at various sites in the eastern Mediterranean and Egypt, suggesting exchange links with the major circum-Mediterranean powers. Overseas contacts with the Greek mainland and the Aegean islands (especially the Cyclades) are intense during the proto-Palatial period and become more so in the neo-Palatial period.

Iconographic and artefactual evidence suggest that the palaces also functioned as centres for ritual, while cult sites, including cave (e.g. the Idaean, Dictaean, and Arkalochori caves), spring (e.g. Kato Symi), and peak-top sanctuaries—particularly characteristic of Minoan culture (e.g. Iouchtas, Petsophas: *Cambridge Archaeological Journal* 1992, 59 ff.)—were widely distributed in the rural landscape. The alignments of Cnossus on Mount Iouchtas and Phaestus on the Kamares cave suggest a close connection between the palace centres and these rural cult places, which may have functioned to unify territories around a prominent visual marker.

The palaces became focal points for settlement, as the growth of the settlement at Cnossus by the neo-Palatial period to an estimated 75 ha. (185 acres), its population to perhaps 12,000, demonstrates. (By comparison, late Helladic *Mycenae was 30 ha. (74 acres) in area, including the walled citadel.) The territories controlled from Cnossus, Phaestus, and Malia may each have been over 1,000 sq. km. (386 sq. mi.) in extent.

The transition from the old or first palaces (the proto-Palatial) to the new or second palaces (the neo-Palatial period) is defined by reconstruction of the palaces, after destructions—perhaps by earthquake—at all three major sites in MM II and IIIA. It is the new palaces that are best understood and which show the greatest architectural similarities. They retain many of the functions of their predecessors: storage, ritual, élite craft production (including the dark-on-light 'Plant'- and 'Marine'-style fine-ware ceramics), also the acquisition of raw materials through contacts

with the Greek mainland and the Aegean islands and with the eastern Mediterranean and Egypt. Striking among these links are examples of frescoes in Minoan style at Tel Kabri in Israel and Tell el-Daba'a (ancient Avaris) in the Egyptian Delta.

However, there are changes in the neo-Palatial period. The palaces are extensively decorated with frescos containing figured scenes drawn from the natural world and from ritual, public display and possibly narrative; the best preserved examples are not from Crete, but the Minoanized settlement of Akrotiri on Thera. It seems that the extent of storage space and access to the central structures was more restricted in this phase, suggesting a devolution of agricultural storage and some administrative control to subordinate settlements, including a new class that appears in the neo-Palatial period, conventionally called 'villas': small, rural settlements with storage and processing facilities for agricultural produce (e.g. Vathypetro) and links to the palaces in architectural details and the use of Linear A script and clay sealings (e.g. Myrtos Pyrgos, Tylissos, Sklavokampos). These 'villas' may have been subordinate to towns, each perhaps controlling specific sectors of the palatial territories and in some cases producing Linear A finds (Archanes, Agia Triada, Gournia, Palaikastro). Ports are also important, notably at Kommos on the western coast of the Mesara plain, 6 km. (3.7 mi.) from Phaestus and Agia Triada, and the small (only 0.31 ha. (0.8 acre) in area) palace constructed at Kato Zakros on the east coast of the island, perhaps over a proto-Palatial predecessor, which may have functioned to control exchange.

The Linear A script is now in almost exclusive use for administrative recording and is also found on items of jewellery (gold and silver pins) and stone offerings-tables found at rural sanctuaries (Iouchtas, Kato Symi), implying close links between the palaces and rural cult sites. The architectural uniformity of the new palaces, together with the widespread use of Linear A and the discovery of near identical seal impressions at a number of sites has suggested to some a unification of the island under a single authority, probably the palace at Cnossus (e.g. *Kadmos* 1967, 15 ff.), but this need not necessarily have been the case (J. F. Cherry, *Peer Polity Interaction* (1986), 35 ff.).

Post-Palatial (LM II to SM: *c*.1470–1000 BC). The end of the Neo-Palatial period is marked by a series of burnt destructions in the pottery phase known as LM IB; sites affected include the palaces of Kato Zakros, Malia, and Phaestus and many smaller sites as far west as Chania. The following period is conventionally referred to as the post-Palatial, although some scholars prefer to extend the term neo-Palatial to include the final destruction of the palace at Cnossus, which continued in use. The date of the final destruction at Cnossus hinges on the material Evans published as belonging to the final palace and has been controversial since the 1960s, when rival dates were proposed of *c*.1375 and *c*.1200 BC. The discovery at the western site of Chania (Linear B *ku-do-ni-ja*) in a LM IIIB context of Linear B tablets, one of them at least probably written by a Cnossian scribe (*Kadmos* 1992, 61 ff.; *BCH* 1993, 19 ff.), not only supports a late date for the Cnossus destruction, but also confirms the existence of close administrative ties between the two sites.

The Linear B documents record the final year of the economic administration centred on Cnossus in an early form of the Greek language, a fact that implies—along with archaeological evidence for features of mainland material culture—that Mycenaean Greeks had taken over control there and had perhaps been responsible for the destructions at the end of the LM IB phase (see MYCENAEAN LANGUAGE). From the documents it is possible to demonstrate that Cnossus managed the economy of much of central and western Crete, a territory of perhaps 3,000–4,000 sq. km. (1,200–1,500 sq. mi.), incorporating the territories of former palatial centres, which continued to be occupied but were now subordinate to Cnossus.

As in other parts of the Aegean, many sites on Crete are abandoned or destroyed in the latter half of the LM IIIB pottery phase (c.1250–1200 BC). The final destruction of Cnossus may be part of this pattern. A number of settlements are founded in inaccessible or easily defensible locations in the LM IIIC–SM periods, notably at Karphi (altitude 1,100 m.: 3,600 ft.), at Vrokastro, and Kavousi, and at Kastri near Palaikastro. Some Minoan settlements continue in use or are reoccupied after the bronze age (Cnossus, Phaestus, Kydonia), while some attract later cult (Kommos, Palaikastro). Relatively few cult sites (notably the Idaean and Dictaean caves) are reused in the iron age, but the spring sanctuary at Kato Symi, dedicated to *Hermes and *Aphrodite in the historical period, is in continuous use.

GENERAL A. J. Evans, *The Palace of Minos at Knossos* 1–4 (1921–36, repr. 1964); *Proceedings* of the six International Cretological Congresses (1961–91); R. Hägg and N. Marinatos (eds.), *The Minoan Thalassocracy* (1984), and *The Function of the Minoan Palaces* (1987); O. Krzyszkowska and L. Nixon (eds.), *Minoan Society* (1983); C. G. Doumas (ed.), *Thera and the Aegean World II* 1–2 (1978–80); D. A. Hardy (ed.), *Thera and the Aegean World III* 1–3 (1990); W. V. Davies and L. Schofield, *Egypt, the Aegean and the Levant* (1995).
SITES Bibliography on sites (including those mentioned above): J. W. Myers, E. E. Myers, and G. Cadogan (eds.), *The Aerial Atlas of Ancient Crete* (1992); J. F. Cherry, J. Bennet, and A. L. Wilson, *A Gazetteer of Aegean Civilisation in the Neolithic and Bronze Age 2: Crete* (1995), updates in *Nestor*. Brief annual reports on archaeological work in *Archaeological Reports* (JHS) or *Chronique des fouilles* (BCH).
TOPICS
Cult: N. Marinatos, *Minoan Religion: Ritual, Image and Symbol* (1993).
Burial: K. Branigan, *Dancing with Death* (1993); O. Pelon, *Tholoi, Tumuli, et cercles funéraires* (1976); I. Pini, *Beiträge zur minoischen Gräberkunde* (1968); J. S. Soles, *The Prepalatial Cemeteries at Mochlos and Gournia* (1992).
Pottery: P. P. Betancourt, *The History of Minoan Pottery* (1985).
Chronology: S. W. Manning, *The Absolute Chronology of the Aegean Early Bronze Age* (1994); P. M. Warren and V. Hankey, *Aegean Bronze Age Chronology* (1989). Knossos destruction: M. Popham, *Studies in Mediterranean Archaeology* 12 (1970); E. Hallager, *The Mycenaean Palace at Knossos* (1977); J. Driessen, *An Early Destruction in the Mycenaean Palace at Knossos* (1990).
Architecture: J. W. Graham, *The Palaces of Crete*, rev. edn. (1987); J. W. Shaw, *Minoan Architecture: Materials and Techniques* (1971).
Art and Iconography: P. Darcque and J.-C. Poursat (eds.), *L'Iconographie minoenne* (1985); S. Hood, *The Arts in Prehistoric Greece* (1978); S. A. Immerwahr, *Aegean Painting in the Bronze Age* (1990); F. Matz, H. Biesantz, and I. Pini (eds.), *Corpus der Minoischen und Mykenischen Siegel* 1– (1964–); L. Morgan, *The Miniature Wall Paintings of Thera* (1987).
J. Be.

Minoan scripts See PRE-ALPHABETIC SCRIPTS (GREECE).

Minos (Μίνως), legendary king of *Crete who lived three generations before the Trojan War. The island's bronze age civilization has been named Minoan after him (see preceding entry). He was a son of *Zeus (Il. 13. 449; Od. 11. 568) and *Europa (daughter of Agenor, Diod. Sic. 5. 78. 1, or of *Phoenix (1), Il. 14. 321) whom Zeus had carried to Crete from *Tyre or *Sidon in the shape of a bull. According to another tradition, which implies a prehistoric *Dorian presence on Crete, he was the son of Asterius (Asterion) and descendant of Dorus (Diod. Sic. 4. 60. 2–3). In a contest for

the kingship Minos prayed to *Poseidon to send him a bull from the sea for sacrifice. The god complied, but the bull was so handsome that Minos kept it for himself. Poseidon therefore caused Minos' wife Pasiphaë to fall in love with the bull, and from their unnatural union the Minotaur, half-man, half-bull, was born and kept in the *labyrinth built by *Daedalus (Diod. Sic. 4. 77. 4). Labyrinth occurs in Linear B (*dapurito*, KN Gg 702, X 140; see MYCENAEAN LANGUAGE) and has been connected with the double axe (λάβρυς), a Minoan religious symbol, and with the palace of Cnossus. The myth probably conceals bronze age cult involving Zeus, the bull, and Minos, although the king was not divine.

Minos may have been a dynastic title rather than an individual: *Diodorus (3) distinguishes between two with that name over three generations (Diod. Sic. 4. 60. 2–5). Minos was the most royal of mortal kings (Hes. fr. 144 M–W.), the favourite of Zeus who granted him kingship and renewed it every nine years in his cave on Mt. Ida (Od. 19. 179; Pl. Leg. 624d; Strabo 16. 2. 38). With his brother *Rhadamanthys he gave the first laws to mankind ([Pl.] Minos 318d), and acted as judge of the living and the dead (Od. 11. 568). Minos' reputation as first thalassocrat (Hdt. 1. 171, 3. 122; Thuc. 1. 4. 1, 8. 7; Diod. Sic. 4. 79. 1, 5. 78. 3; see SEA POWER) recalls Minoan influence in the bronze age. Attic legend called him cruel. He made war on *Megara (see NISUS (1)) and Athens to avenge his son *Androgeos, and he forced the Athenians to send an annual tribute of seven young men and women to be sacrificed to the Minotaur until *Theseus slew the monster (Plut. Thes. 15–19). Minos died violently in Sicily (Hdt. 7. 170). He had followed the fugitive Daedalus to the court of Cocalus, king of Camicus, whose daughters scalded him to death in his bath (Apollod. Epit. 1. 15; cf. Diod. Sic. 4. 79. 2). His companions built him a large tomb, but the bones were later returned to Crete in the reign of *Theron of Acragas (d. 472 BC) (Diod. Sic. 4. 79. 4).

The Minotaur appears on Minoan neo-palatial seals (once on the mainland at Midea (Arch. Rep. 1991/2, 14 (LH IIIB)) but without mythological context. The legend of the killing of the Minotaur by Theseus remained a popular subject in Greek painting from the Archaic period (e.g. red-figure cup by Epictetus, Beazley, ARV² 72, no. 17); but King Minos was rarely represented on his own in art, generally in his function as judge of the dead. See RELIGION, MINOAN AND MYCENAEAN.

F. Poland, RE 15 (1932), 1890–1927; R. F. Willetts, *Cretan Cults and Festivals* (1962); N. Schlager, in *Fragen und Probleme der bronzezeitlichen ägäischen Gyptik: Corpus der minoischen und mykenischen Siegel*, Beiheift 3 (1989), 225–39; M. Robertson, *History of Greek Art* (1975), 804, 815.
H. J. R.; H. W. P.; C. M. R.; B. C. D.

Minotaur See DAEDALUS; LABYRINTH; MINOS; THESEUS; THESEUS IN ART.

mint (for coins) see COINAGE, GREEK and ROMAN; (plant) see MENTHE.

Minturnae, important town on the *via Appia, where it crossed the river *Liris near its mouth. Rome reduced the *Aurunci, originally inhabitants of the region, in the Latin and Second Samnite Wars (see SAMNIUM) and established a citizen colony there in 295 BC, with a small rectangular *castrum* or fortress (c.3 ha.: 7½ acres) with polygonal walls. The settlement soon expanded, with a republican forum and *capitolium* (shrine of the Capitoline triad: see CAPITOL; JUPITER) outside the old defences. Augustus recolonized Minturnae, and added an 11-km. (7-mi.)

aqueduct and a theatre (for c.4,500 spectators). A new forum was eventually built, and the old *capitolium* was eclipsed by three new temples, one incorporating manumission records of the Sullan period; see CORNELIUS SULLA, L. Minturnae was an important shipbuilding centre including vessels with huge storage jars (*dolia*), and there were some 200 m. (220 yds.) of docks along the Liris. One kilometre (just over half a mile) downstream was the sanctuary of the sea-goddess, Marica, mother of *Latinus, venerated from the 6th cent. BC. Minturnae remained of significance throughout imperial times, and was destroyed by the *Lombards in AD 590. The visible remains (which include an amphitheatre, baths, shops, etc.) are extensive.

F. Coarelli (ed.), *Minturnae* (1989); M. P. Guidobaldi, *Dial. di Arch.* 1988, 125 ff.; P. Arthur, *Romans in Northern Campania* (1991), 37 ff.

E. T. S.; T. W. P.

Minucianus the Elder (2nd cent. AD), Athenian orator and rhetorician. Besides speeches (Himer. *Or.* 7. 4), he wrote a *Progymnasmata*, a *Rhetoric* (Τέχνη) dealing with *stasis*-theory (see RHETORIC, GREEK), and a commentary on *Demosthenes (2). The *On Rhetorical Arguments* (Spengel–Hammer, *Rhet.* 1. 340) is probably by a 3rd-cent. namesake. His work was much criticized by his younger contemporary *Hermogenes (2), but continued to be read into the 5th cent.

W. Stegemann, *RE* 15/2 (1932), 1975.

M. B. T.

Minucius (*RE* 30) **Augurinus, Gaius,** according to *Cornelius Nepos, as tribune (probably 187 BC) prosecuted L. *Cornelius Scipio (2), who was saved by the intervention of Ti. *Sempronius Gracchus (2) (Gell. *NA* 6. 19). The facts are inextricably confused by the fictional elaboration of the 'trials of the Scipios' (see PETILLIUS Q.).

E. B.

Minucius (*RE* 40) **Esquilinus Augurinus, Lucius,** was consul or suffect consul in 458 BC. The story that he was trapped on the Algidus by the Aequi, rescued by *Cincinnatus, but deposed from office is modelled on the experiences of M. *Minucius Rufus (1) in 217 BC. Minucius appears among the Second *Decemvirate but although supposedly exiled, he was apparently identified with the corn commissioner who denounced Sp. *Maelius in 439. The earliest accounts probably simply credited him with alleviating a corn shortage, to explain a column-statue supposedly erected to him by the grateful populace near the Tiber harbour, though a 5th-cent. date for such an honorific column-statue is implausible. His (subsequent) introduction into the Maelius narrative was prompted or facilitated by a (Greek) etymologizing interpretation of his name as 'informer'. He was recorded as holding office (even perhaps as 'prefect of the corn supply') in 440–439 in the Linen Books unearthed by C. *Licinius Macer (Livy 4. 13. 7) and some asserted that he became a plebeian and supernumerary tribune, clearly to justify the claims of later plebeian Minucii to descent from their presumed patrician 5th-cent. namesakes.

Momigliano, *Quarto contributo*, 331 ff.; Ogilvie, *Comm. Livy 1–5*; *RRC* nn. 242–3.

A. D.

Minucius Felix, Marcus, fl. AD 200–40, author of a dialogue in elegant, ironic Latin between a Christian, Octavius, and a *pagan, Caecilius Natalis of *Cirta (perhaps identical with a Caecilius Natalis mentioned in Cirta inscriptions of c.210–17). The pagan case uses M. *Cornelius Fronto's discourse against

*Christianity. The Christian rejoinder uses Stoic matter (see STOICISM) from *Cicero and L. Annaeus Seneca (2), and has a long-disputed relation to *Tertullian's *Apologeticum* which must be one of dependence. The target is philosophical scepticism without the *sinceritas* to abandon polytheism. See APOLOGISTS, CHRISTIAN.

Ed. J. Beaujeu (1964); B. Kytzler (Teubner, 1982); Eng. trans.: G. Clarke (1974). C. Becker, *Der Octavius des M. F.* (1967). *RE* Suppl. 11. 952 ff., 1365 ff. *PIR²* M 611.

H. C.

Minucius Fundanus See MINICIUS FUNDANUS.

Minucius (*RE* 5 and 52) **Rufus (1), Marcus,** as consul 221 BC helped in reducing the Istri. Dictator (probably for holding elections) shortly before 218, he attempted to make C. *Flaminius (1) his *magister equitum*, but was foiled by an omen (Plut. *Marc.* 5. 5; cf., not contradicting this, Val. Max. 1. 1. 5). After the battle of Lake *Trasimene (217) he was elected *magister equitum* to Q. *Fabius Maximus Verrucosus in an unprecedented procedure. Disobeying Fabius' orders to refrain from battle, he won a minor victory, whereupon his power was raised to equal Fabius'. He seems to have interpreted this (as *Polybius (1) and some other sources later did) as making him joint dictator (a constitutional absurdity) and vowed an altar to Hercules as dictator (*ILLRP* 118). After a serious error he was trapped by *Hannibal, but was rescued by Fabius. Aristocratic tradition has him salute Fabius as his 'father' (Livy 22. 29 f.). He died fighting bravely at *Cannae.

Polyb. 3 and Livy 22 are the main sources. For the first dictatorship see Broughton, *MRR* 3. 143 f., with bibliog.

H. H. S.; E. B.

Minucius (*RE* 54) **Rufus (2), Marcus,** consul 110 BC and proconsul in Macedonia, won major victories over native tribes and triumphed 106. From the spoils he built the Porticus Minucia, used under the empire for grain distributions. As hereditary patrons of Liguria, he and his brother Quintus settled a boundary dispute between *Genua and a tribe (*ILS* 5946).

E. B.

Minyans (Μινύαι), the descendants of *Minyas, an *Ur*-Greek population-group believed in Classical times to have inhabited Aegean lands in the heroic age (see DRYOPS; PELASGIANS), with centres at *Orchomenus and *Iolcus. Western Peloponnesian communities of so-called Minyans existed in the lifetime of Herodotus (4. 148). In myth they appear outside the mainland mainly linked to the itinerary of the Minyan *Argonauts (Teos, Lemnos, Cyrene, etc.).

Archaeologists since Schliemann call 'Minyan' a grey, wheel-made pottery ubiquitous on the pre-Mycenaean mainland of Greece from c.1900 BC and once, but now no longer, thought to mark that phantom, 'the coming of the Greeks'.

A. R. B.; A. J. S. S.

Minyas, known almost entirely from legendary genealogies (see Nilsson, Fiehn, and West (below): the epic, *Minyad*, survives only in fragments, which tell us nothing about him). He was the eponym of the *Minyans, who were based in Boeotian *Orchomenus (1) (the tholos-tomb there being called the Treasury of Minyas: Paus 9. 38. 2), with strong connections to parts of Thessaly, and others to the SW Peloponnese: it was the Minyans of *Iolcus who dispatched the *Argo* (e.g. Pindar, *Pyth.* 4, and see Bacon); the Minyan *Athamas reigned—according to varying traditions—at Orchomenus and at Halus; *Neleus of Pylos wed

Chloris daughter of Amphion son of *Iasus, a former king of Orchomenus (*Od*. 11. 281–6, and see Kiechle).

J. R. Bacon, *The Voyage of the Argonauts* (1925); Bernabé, *PEG* 1. xxi, 137–42; Davies, *EGF* 144–5; K. Fiehn, *RE* 15 (1932), 2014–18; F. Kiechle, *Lakonien und Sparta* (1963), 31–7; M. P. Nilsson, *The Mycenaean Origin of Greek Mythology* (1932), 127–37; M. L. West, *The Hesiodic Catalogue of Women* (1985), 64–6.

A. Sch.

mirabilia See PARADOXOGRAPHERS.

miracles Stories of the power of the gods were common throughout antiquity, many of them rooted in personal devotion, as appears, for instance, from votive inscriptions expressing gratitude for a miraculous recovery. A large group is linked with particular cults and cult places allegedly founded following miraculous deeds by the deity involved, who thus showed his/her divine power. Early instances can be found in the Homeric *Hymns*, for example those to *Dionysus, *Demeter, and *Apollo. From the 4th cent. BC onwards there is a rapid increase in miracle-stories, and the connection with *epiphany receives ever more emphasis. Under the title *Epiphaneiai* collections of miracles abounded, the term ἐπιφάνεια signifying both the appearance and the miraculous deeds of the god; see EPIPHANY. Among the epigraphic evidence the miracles performed by *Asclepius in Epidaurus (4th cent. BC) are particularly significant. Slightly earlier, literature reveals a new impetus in the *Bacchae* of *Euripides. Miracles (healing, punitive, and other) are now explicitly pictured as divine instruments to exact worship, obedience, and submission. In the same period the term ἀρετή—literally the 'virtue' of a god—develops the meaning 'miracle', which entails the rise of so-called ἀρεταλογίαι, aretalogies: quasi-liturgical enumerations of the qualities, achievements, and power (all could be referred to by the term δύναμις) of a specific god. All these features abound in and after the Hellenistic period in the cults of great foreign gods, for instance *Sarapis and *Isis, and no less in Christian texts. The fierce competition between, and radical demand of devout submission to, these new gods fostered a propagandistic tendency to publicize the gods' miraculous deeds. 'Miracle proved deity' (Nock) and as such it was often welcomed with the exclamation εἷς ὁ θεός ('one/unique is the god'), thus contributing to the shaping of 'henotheistic' religiosity.

O. Weinreich, *Antike Heilungswunder* (1909); R. Herzog, *Die Wunderheilungen von Epidauros*, *Philol.* Suppl. 22 (1931); A. D. Nock, *Conversion* (1933); H. C. Kee, *Miracle in the Early Christian World* (1983); H. S. Versnel, *TER UNUS. Isis, Dionysos, Hermes: Three Studies in Henotheism* (1990).

H. S. V.

mirrors (κάτοπτρον, *speculum*) (see also CATOPTRICS) Mirrors in the Graeco-Roman world were made of various materials—mostly copper alloy, but *silver and *iron examples have been found. Earliest surviving pieces date to the Mycenaean period *c*.1200–1100 BC, with bone and ivory handles carved with animal motifs. Egyptian mirrors have been found in some burials and as temple offerings in the classical world. Greek hand-mirrors were made in one piece from the 7th cent. BC, becoming more elaborate with time. Mirrors of the 5th cent. BC include those with a heavy disc and a separate ornamental tang slotting into a handle or stand. The most elaborate examples are the so-called *Caryatid mirrors where the disc is supported by a female figure, rarely a youth, on a stool or plinth. The date-span covers the period *c*.620–*c*.400 BC. The other important group are the 4th–3rd-cent. BC mirrors with a hinged cover to protect the reflecting surface. The lid may be decorated with a plaque showing a female head or a mythological event. The inside cover was sometimes engraved

with a related scene, or silvered to give a second mirror surface. This form was copied by the *Etruscans, and is found in light-weight versions in southern France during the 1st cent. AD.

The most characteristic Etruscan mirror was the hand-mirror, originally with a tang cast in one piece with the disc and inserted into an organic handle, and dated from the late 6th to the 5th cent. BC. In later versions the handle was cast in one piece with the disc. The series ended in *c*.200 BC. Engraved scenes on the reverse side of the mirror may show named figures from mythology.

Roman mirrors from the Augustan period onwards have been found in most provinces of the empire, with applied engravings, a decorative plaque on the reverse, or figurative ornament. Silver mirrors, including examples with handles across the back, are well known. *Glass mirrors have been found but are more common in the north-eastern provinces and the eastern mediterranean than in the west. They were set into lead frames with simple ornament or inscriptions; plaster, wood, amber, and ivory were also used. The glass was backed with a variety of materials including plaster, wax, and metal foil.

L. O. Keene Congdon, *Caryatid Mirrors of Ancient Greece* (1981); W. Züchner, *Griechische Klappspiegel* (1942); E. Gerhard, *Etruskische Spiegel*, 5 vols. (1840–97); N. T. de Grummond, *A Guide to Etruscan Mirrors* (1982); *Corpus Speculorum Etruscorum* (1981–); R. Adam, *Recherches sur les miroirs prénestins* (1980); I. Mayer-Prokop, *Die Gravierten Etruskischen Griffspiegel* (1967); U. Fischer-Graf, *Spiegel Werkstätten in Vulci* (1980); G. Lloyd-Morgan, *Description of the Collections in the Rijksmuseum G. M. Kam at Nijmegen 9: The Mirrors* (1981); G. Zahlhaas, *Römische Relief Spiegel* (1975); B. Zouhdi, *Miroirs de verre de l'époque romaine conservés au Musée de Damas* (1970).

G. Ll.-M.

Mise (Μίση), an obscure goddess, first mentioned in Hero(n)das 1. 56, where the name of the festival, κάθοδος ('descent'), suggests chthonian ritual. The forty-second Orphic hymn (see ORPHIC LITERATURE) says she is bisexual and seems to identify her with both *Dionysus and *Demeter; she may well be Asianic.

H. J. R.

Misenum, the northern headland of the bay of Naples (*Neapolis) (reputedly the tomb of *Aeneas' trumpeter Misenus, Verg. *Aen*. 6. 162 f.) and the adjoining harbour and town. A villa resort in the late republic (the most famous estate belonged to C. *Marius (1), L. *Licinius Lucullus (2), and later to the emperors), it became one of the principal imperial naval bases (with *Ravenna) under Augustus (see NAVIES). The fleet (commanded in AD 79 by the elder *Pliny (1), Plin. *Ep*. 6. 16. 20) has left many inscriptions and a huge cistern, the 'Piscina Mirabilis'. Its civic status, eventually *colonia*, is reflected in the recently excavated shrine of the *Augustales. The harbour was abandoned in the 5th cent. AD.

M. Borriello and A. D'Ambrosio, *Baiae-Misenum* (1979).

E. T. S.; N. P.

Mishnah, a collection of legal opinions which became the foundation document of rabbinic Judaism. Compiled in *c.* AD 200 in Palestine by the patriarch Judah haNasi and his school, the Mishnah comprises the legal statements of the *tannaim*, i.e. *rabbis, and the sages they considered to be their forebears, from Hellenistic times to the early 3rd cent. AD. This material, expressed in a spare post-biblical Hebrew, is arranged in 63 tractates divided into six orders: *Zeraim* ('seeds'), dealing with agricultural matters; *Moed* ('set times'), on the observance of festivals; *Nashim* ('women'), primarily on relations between women and men; *Nezikin* ('damages'), on civil and criminal law; *Kodashim*

Mithradates

('holy things'), on sacrifices in the Jerusalem Temple; *Tohorot* ('purities'), on the transfer, avoidance, and removal of ritual pollution. The division into tractates was already more or less established by the 3rd cent., but their arrangement within each order varies in different manuscript traditions. Tractate *Abot* ('Fathers'), a collection of wisdom sayings by a range of rabbis included within the order *Nezikin*, belongs to a different literary genre from the rest of the Mishnah. It includes a few quotations by rabbis of the generation after Judah haNasi, and may have been added to the Mishnah after its initial redaction.

Since the legal opinions expressed by the rabbis cited in the Mishnah frequently contradict each other explicitly, it is unlikely that the compilation was intended simply as a law code. On the other hand, the redactor imposed a clear literary structure on the material and did not simply collect earlier traditions. It may be best to view the work as a teaching manual.

The imprint of the editor is clear in all tractates despite the persistence of minor textual variants for several centuries after Judah haNasi. Such variants are best explained by the oral transmission of the text within rabbinic academies by professional reciters who painstakingly committed it to memory (hence the name 'Mishnah', from the Hebrew root *shnh* ('repeat')). The date when the Mishnah was written down is uncertain. It may have been only after the compilation of the *Talmuds (i.e. *c*. AD 500), or even later.

According to later rabbinic tradition there existed already at the time of the redaction of the Mishnah compilations of rabbinic legal materials of which Judah haNasi made use. Of such non-Mishnaic collections from this period, only the Tosefta survives; it was compiled probably in *c*. AD 250 and has a literary form similar to the Mishnah. Other tannaitic material was preserved in early works of *midrash and as independent traditions (*beraitot*) in the Talmuds.

Since the Mishnah was not composed as a work of historiography, its use as a source for Jewish social, political, and religious history in the period before AD 70 is hazardous, but the text contains much information about the social history of Palestine in the 2nd cent. AD. The attribution of legal opinions in the Mishnah to particular rabbis is in general reliable, so that it is possible to reconstruct from the text the development of rabbinic law between AD 70 and 200. See RABBIS; RELIGION, JEWISH.

TEXT *Shisha Sidrei Mishnah*, ed. H. Albeck (1952–8).
TRANSLATIONS H. Danby, *The Mishnah* (1933); J. Neusner, *The Mishnah: A New Translation* (1987).
Introduction and bibliography: H. L. Strack and G. Stemberger, *Introduction to the Talmud and Midrash* (Eng. trans. 1991), 119–66 (Ger. 8th edn. in Stemberger, *Einleitung* (1992), 113–52)..   M. D. G.

Mithradates Persian name borne most famously by six of the eight Hellenistic kings of *Pontus in Asia Minor. Later propaganda invented a noble ancestry for the royal line—*Cyrus (1), *Darius (1), and *Alexander (3) the Great were among those claimed as ancestors—but its origins lie almost certainly in a Persian family of local dynasts who held sway in the city of Cius on the Propontis during the 4th cent. BC.

Mithradates I The family history is obscure, but it was probably Mithradates III of Cius, who, having been forced to flee to *Paphlagonia, took advantage of the major powers' lack of interest in northern Asia Minor to carve out a principality in the area, and proclaim himself the first king of Pontus, Mithradates I Ctistes or '*Founder' (302–266 BC). His consolidation of Pontic independence included in *c*.280 the acquisition through his son

and successor Ariobarzanes (266–*c*.250) of the coastal city of Amastris, the kingdom's first foothold on the Black Sea.

Mithradates II (*c*.250–*c*.220 BC) initiated an important policy of dynastic alliance with the Seleucids. He himself married the sister (see *HCP* 3. 772) of *Seleucus (2) II, while one of his daughters, *Laodice (3), married *Antiochus (3) III, and another Antiochus' minister *Achaeus (3). In the dispute between Seleucus II and *Antiochus (8) Hierax, Mithradates supported the latter. When *Rhodes was devastated by an *earthquake in 227/6, he joined other benefactors in sending aid. In 220 either he or his successor planned, but failed, to capture the strategically important city of *Sinope.

Mithradates III The sources speak of six Pontic kings named Mithradates, and as we have certain knowledge of only five, the sixth is usually assumed and inserted in the line at this point as Mithradates III (*c*.220–*c*.189/8 BC). He was succeeded by his forceful son *Pharnaces I (*c*.189/8–*c*.155/4).

Mithradates IV Philopator Philadelphus (155/4–152/1 BC) abandoned the aggression of his brother Pharnaces I, and established cordial relations with *Cappadocia, and with Rome, whose ally *Pergamum he helped in a war against *Bithynia.

Mithradates V Euergetes (152/1–120 BC) skilfully increased the power and influence of Pontus. He helped Rome against *Carthage (149–146) and against *Aristonicus (1) (132–129), and was rewarded with *Phrygia. He invaded Cappadocia, but apparently was content to exert indirect control through the marriage of his daughter to the young king of Cappadocia, *Ariarathes VI. He probably married a Seleucid princess, and in other ways presented a Greek face to the world: many of his courtiers were Greeks; he was honoured as a benefactor at Athens and *Delos; and his coins display a special devotion to *Apollo. He was assassinated in 120.

Mithradates VI Eupator Dionysus (120–63 BC), elder son of Euergetes, was the greatest, most famous king of Pontus, and Rome's most dangerous enemy in the 1st cent. BC. After murdering his mother and brother, his first major enterprise was the conquest of the Crimea (see CHERSONESUS (2)) and northern *Euxine. Ultimate control of most of the circuit of the Black Sea gave him almost inexhaustible supplies of men and materials for his military campaigns. In Cappadocia he continued to try to exert indirect control through agents: his creature Gordius, a Cappadocian noble; his sister Laodice; her son *Ariarathes VII; and eventually his own son, whom he installed as king *Ariarathes IX. For the more aggressive annexation of Paphlagonia he took as ally his most powerful neighbour, *Nicomedes (3) III of Bithynia, but subsequently fell out with him. A famous meeting with C. *Marius (1) in 99/8, and the armed intervention of *Sulla in Cappadocia a little later, made it clear that war with Rome was inevitable, and he prepared carefully. While Italy was preoccupied by the *Social War (3), he annexed Bithynia and Cappadocia. Skilful diplomacy, masterful propaganda and Roman overreaction enabled him to cast Rome in the role of aggressor and cause of the First Mithradatic War which followed (89–85). His armies swept all before them in Asia, where he ordered a massacre of resident Romans and Italians (the 'Asian Vespers'). He failed to capture Rhodes, but was welcomed in Athens (see ARISTION) and won over most of Greece. The Roman response came in 87, when Sulla arrived in Greece with five legions. He defeated the Pontic armies, besieged and captured Athens, and took the war to Asia. Mithradates surrendered at the Peace of Dardanus, and was allowed to retire to Pontus. The Second Mithradatic War (c.83–81) was no more than a series of skirmishes with Sulla's lieutenant L. *Licinius Murena, but when *Nicomedes (4) IV of Bithynia died in 76 or 75 and bequeathed his kingdom to Rome, Mithradates again prepared for war. Having allied himself with Quintus *Sertorius, the Roman rebel in Spain, he invaded Bithynia in the spring of 73 (possibly 74), thus precipitating the Third Mithradatic War. The advance faltered immediately with a disastrous failure to capture *Cyzicus, and the Roman forces, ably commanded by L. *Licinius Lucullus (2), pushed Eupator out of Pontus into *Armenia, where he took refuge with King *Tigranes (1) II, his son-in-law. He failed to win *Parthian support, but was able to return to Pontus in 68. The great *Pompey, newly appointed to the Mithradatic command, easily defeated him, and forced him to retreat to his Crimean kingdom. He was said to be planning an ambitious invasion of Italy by land, when his son Pharnaces led a revolt against him (see PHARNACES II). Inured to poison by years of practice, he had to ask an obliging Gallic bodyguard to run him through with a sword. Mithradates presented himself both as a civilized philhellene—he consciously copied the portraiture and actions of Alexander the Great—and as an oriental monarch, and although in many ways he achieved a remarkably successful fusion of east and west, he failed either to understand or to match the power of Rome.

App. *Mith.* E. Meyer, *Geschichte des Königreichs Pontos* (1890); T. Reinach, *Mithridates Eupator, König von Pontos* (1895); E. Olshausen, *RE* Suppl. 15 (1978), 'Pontos'; B. McGing, *The Foreign Policy of Mithridates VI Eupator* (1986); J. Hind, *CAH* 9² (1994), ch. 5.   B. C. McG.

Mithras, an ancient Indo-Iranian god adopted in the Roman empire as the principal deity of a mystery cult which flourished in the 2nd and 3rd cents. AD. Iranian Mithra was a god of compact (the literal meaning of his name), cattle-herding, and the dawn light, aspects of which survive (or were re-created) in his western manifestation, since Roman Mithras was a sun-god ('deus sol invictus Mithras', 'invincible sun god Mithras'), a 'bull-killer', and 'cattle-thief', and the saviour of the sworn brothers of his cult.

The cult is known primarily from its archaeological remains. Over 400 find-spots are recorded, many of them excavated meeting-places. These and the c.1,000 dedicatory inscriptions give a good idea of cult life and membership. Some 1,150 pieces of sculpture (and a few frescos) carry an extraordinarily rich sacred art, although the iconography remains frustratingly elusive in default of the explicatory sacred texts. Literary references to Mithras and Mithraism are as scarce as the material remains are abundant.

Mithraism was an organization of cells. Small autonomous groups of initiates, exclusively male, met for fellowship and worship in chambers of modest size and distinctive design which they called 'caves' ('Mithraea', like 'Mithraism' and 'Mithraist', are neologisms). A cave is an 'image of the universe', and according to *Porphyry (*De antr. nymph.* 6) the archetypal Mithraeum was designed and furnished as a kind of microcosmic model. Mithraea were sometimes sited in real *caves or set against rock-faces (e.g. at Jajce in Bosnia) or were made to imitate caves by vaulting or decoration or by sequestering them in dim interior or underground rooms (see the Barberini, San Clemente, and Santa Prisca Mithraea in Rome, those at Capua and Marino, and the many Mithraea of *Ostia, among which the 'Seven Spheres' Mithraeum with its mosaic composition of zodiac and planets arguably exemplifies Porphyry's cosmic model). The Mithraeum is the antithesis of the classic temple, totally lacking in exterior decoration and space for solemn public ritual. The Mithraeum's most distinctive (and unvarying) feature is the pair of platforms flanking a central aisle. It was on these that the initiates reclined for a communal meal. Visual representations (see esp. the Santa Prisca frescoes and the relief from Konjic in Bosnia) show that this meal was the human counterpart of a divine banquet shared by Mithras and the sun-god (the latter appearing on the monuments as a separate being) on the hide of the bull killed by the former in his greatest exploit.

As is now known from the Santa Prisca frescos and the pavement of the Felicissimus Mithraeum in Ostia, initiates were ranked in a hierarchy of seven grades, each under the protection of one of the planets: Raven (Mercury), 'Nymphus' (Venus), Soldier (Mars), Lion (Jupiter), Persian (Moon), 'Heliodromus' (Sun), Father (Saturn). It is generally accepted that this was a lay hierarchy, not a professional priesthood. Mithraists, as their monuments attest, remained in and of the secular world. It is unlikely that the full hierarchy was represented in each Mithraeum, although probable that most were presided over by one or more Fathers. The disparate connotations of the various ranks, the two idiosyncratic coinages ('Heliodromus' and 'Nymphus'—the latter would mean, if anything, 'male bride'), and the unique planetary order all bespeak an unusually inventive and evocative construct.

Actual Mithraea or traces of the cult have been found in virtually every quarter of the Roman empire, though with two notable areas of concentration. The first was Rome itself and its port of Ostia. In Ostia, some 15 Mithraea have been discovered in the excavated area that comprises about half of the town's total. Extrapolation to Rome, where some 35 locations are known, would yield a total of perhaps as many as 700 Mithraea. The number is impressive (if speculative), but individual Mithraea were small, and even if all were in service contemporaneously they would accommodate no more than 2 per cent of the population—scarcely the great rival to Christianity that inflated views of the cult have sometimes made it. The other area of concentration was the empire's European frontier from Britain to the mouth of the Danube. As inscriptions confirm, Mithraism's typical recruits were soldiers and minor functionaries, e.g. employees of the Danubian customs service headquartered at *Poetovio (mod. Ptuj in Slovenia). Many were *freedmen or slaves. Mithraism did not generally attract the upper classes (except as occasional patrons) until its final days as the rather artificial creature of the pagan aristocracy of 4th-cent. Rome. It was always better represented in the Latin west than the Greek east.

By the middle of the 2nd cent. AD the cult was well established. The routes of its diffusion and its earlier development are much debated, problems complicated by the question of transmission from Iran. Did the cult develop from and perpetuate a stream of Zoroastrianism, or was it essentially a western creation with 'Persian' trimmings? (See RELIGION, PERSIAN; ZOROASTER.) There is no agreement, because there is so little evidence. Almost the only firm datum is *Plutarch's remark that the Cilician pirates suppressed by *Pompey (*Pomp.* 24) had secret initiatory rites (*teletai*) of Mithras which had endured to his own day. These may have been a prototype of the developed *mysteries.

The cult's theology and its sacred myth must be recovered, if at all, from the monuments. Principal among these is the icon of Mithras killing a bull, which was invariably set as a focal point at one end of the Mithraeum. Mithras is shown astride the bull, plunging a dagger into its flank. The victim's tail is metamorphosed into an ear of wheat. Mithras is accompanied by dog, snake, scorpion, and raven; also by two minor deities, dressed like him in 'Persian' attire and each carrying a torch (one raised, the other inverted), whose names, Cautes and Cautopates, are known from dedications. Above the scene, which is enacted in front of a cave, are images of *Sol and *Luna. This strange assemblage challenges interpretation. Clearly, the killing is an act of sacrifice, but to what end? It has been seen variously as an action which creates or ends the world (support for both can be adduced from Zoroastrian sources) or which in some sense 'saves' the world or at least the initiates within it. The line from Santa Prisca 'et nos servasti [. . .] sanguine fuso' ('and you saved us with the shed blood') probably refers to the bull-killing Mithras qua saviour, though one must beware of reading into this 'salvation' inappropriate Christian connotations.

The bull-killing has also been interpreted as an astrological allegory, the initial warrant for this being the remarkable correspondence, certainly not an an unintended coincidence, between elements in the composition and a group of constellations. But there is no consensus on the extent to which learned astrological doctrines should be imputed to the cult, let alone on their theological or soteriological function. This contributor holds that *astrology was central and that its function was to provide the specifics of a doctrine of the soul's celestial journey (descent to earth and ascent to heaven), initiation into which, Porphyry says (De antr. nymph. 6), was the ritual enacted in Mithraea.

The bull-killing is but one episode, albeit the most important, in a cycle of Mithraic myth represented (frustratingly, in no set order) on the monuments. Other episodes are Mithras' birth from a rock, the hunt and capture of the bull, and the feast celebrated with Sol. The banquet scene is sometimes shown on the reverse of bull-killing reliefs, as salvific effect from salvific cause. There are fine examples in the Louvre (from Fiano Romano), Wiesbaden (from Heddernheim), and—still, one hopes—Sarajevo (from Konjic). See MYSTERIES.

F. Cumont, *Textes et monuments figurés relatifs aux mystères de Mithra* 1 (1899); M. J. Vermaseren, *Corpus Inscriptionum et Monumentorum Religionis Mithriacae*, 2 vols. (1956–60), and *Mithras, the Secret God* (1963); R. Turcan, *Mithra et le mithriacisme*, 2nd edn. (1993); R. Merkelbach, *Mithras* (1984); M. Clauss, *Mithras: Kult und Mysterien* (1990); J. R. Hinnells (ed.), *Mithraic Studies*, 2 vols. (1975), J. Duchesne-Guillemin (ed.), *Études mithriaques* (1978); U. Bianchi (ed.), *Mysteria Mithrae* (1979); *Journal of Mithraic Studies*, vols. 1–3 (1976–80); R. Beck *ANRW* 2. 17. 4 (1984) 2002–2105, and *Planetary Gods . . . in the Mysteries of Mithras* (1988).   R. L. B.

Mithridates See MITHRADATES.

Mitylene See MYTILENE.

Mnasalces, of *Sicyon, author of eighteen epigrams in the Greek *Anthology, mainly funerary or dedicatory. He was honoured with *proxeny at *Oropus (IG 7. 395; A. Wilhelm, *Sitz. Wien* 1915, 3–6). Six epigrams, two new, are partially preserved on a 2nd-cent. BC papyrus headed $M[\nu]\alpha\sigma\dot{\alpha}\lambda\kappa\sigma\nu$ (PKöln 204). HE 2671–4 is an elaborate reworking of an epigram by *Asclepiades (2) (HE 946–9). A mock epitaph by *Theodoridas (Anth. Pal. 13. 21) describes him as $\dot{\epsilon}\lambda\epsilon\gamma\sigma\pi\sigma\iota\dot{\sigma}$ (elegiac poet) and attacks him for bombast and slavish imitation of *Simonides.

Gow–Page, *HE*; W. Seelbach, *Die Epigramme des Mnasalkes und Theodoridas* (1964); A. Cameron, *The Greek Anthology* (1993), 3, 32, 392.
                                                          A. D. E. C.

Mnaseas, 3rd-cent. BC Greek traveller of *Lycia; he was probably a student of *Eratosthenes who wrote on the myths and geo-

graphy, and separate works on the antiquarian details, of Europe, Asia, and Africa.

FHG 3. 149 ff., 4. 659 ff.; and see esp. *RE* 15. 2250 ff.   K. S. S.

Mnesimachus, a Middle Comedy writer (see COMEDY (GREEK), MIDDLE) (Ath. 7. 329d, 9. 387a), one place after *Antiphanes in the *Lenaean list with one victory (IG 2². 2325. 147 = 5 C 1 col. 3. 8 Mette). His seven known titles include mythological burlesque, comedies of everyday life, and probably political attack (his *Philip*, see PHILIP (1) II).

FRAGMENTS Kassel–Austin, *PCG* 7. 16–26.
INTERPRETATION Meineke, *FCG* 1. 423; A. Körte, *RE* 15/2 (1932), 2378 f., 'Mnesimachos' 2; K. Maidment, *CQ* 1935, 22.
                                                          W. G. A.

Moderatus, of *Gades (c. AD 50–100) wrote 'Lectures on Pythagoreanism' (*Pythagorikai scholai*) in eleven books; see PYTHAGORAS (1). A polemical *Neopythagorean, he tried to derive the main principles of *Plato (1)'s metaphysics from Pythagorean teaching, and treated the Pythagorean theory of number as a symbolic representation of metaphysical doctrine, the monad being the principle of change and multiplicity. Ancient references suggest that his interpretation of the hypotheses of Plato's *Parmenides* may have played a significant part in the formation of *Neoplatonic doctrine, since he appears to foreshadow the Plotinian system of hypostases.

E. R. Dodds, *CQ* 1928, 135 ff.; J. M. Rist, *TAPA* 1962, 389 ff.; J. Dillon, *Middle Platonists* (1977), ch. 7.   J. M. D.

Modestinus, lawyer. See HERENNIUS MODESTINUS.

Moeris, the classical name for the lake (mod. Birket Qārūn) lying in the northern section of the *Fayūm depression, southwest of Cairo. The Fayūm, and so ultimately Lake Moeris, which forms a sump for water entering the area, was fed by the Bahr Yusuf, a branch of the Nile; it was rich in fish. Drained first in the Twelfth Dynasty, this area was again intensively developed under the early Ptolemies (with both drainage and new canals) and renamed the Arsinoite nome (see PTOLEMY (1); ARSINOË (1); NOMOS (1)). *Herodotus (1)'s description of the whole Fayūm lying beneath this lake (2. 149) appears to record a misunderstanding of basin *irrigation rather than contemporary reality.

A. B. Lloyd, *Herodotus Book II: Comm.* (1988), with bibliog.   D. J. T.

Moeris, an Atticist lexicographer (see ASIANISM AND ATTICISM), to be dated (probably) not long after *Phrynichus (3), and author of the extant $\Lambda\dot{\epsilon}\xi\epsilon\iota\varsigma$ $A\tau\tau\iota\kappa\dot{\omega}\nu$ $\kappa\alpha\dot{\iota}$ $E\lambda\lambda\dot{\eta}\nu\omega\nu$ $\kappa\alpha\tau\dot{\alpha}$ $\sigma\tau\sigma\iota\chi\epsilon\iota\dot{\sigma}\nu$ (alphabetically arranged Attic and Greek glossary, sometimes called $A\tau\tau\iota\kappa\iota\sigma\tau\dot{\eta}\varsigma$, 'Atticist'). The work deals with sundry points of grammar (accidence and syntax) and, mainly, with diction—the choice of words and their correct, 'Attic', forms and proper meanings. It was based on Aelius *Dionysius (3), Phrynichus (3), *Philemon (7), and the *Synonyms* of Herennius *Philon (5) of Byblos. Moeris recognizes the distinction between Old and New Attic; as models he accepts *Plato (1), *Aristophanes (1), *Thucydides (2), *Xenophon (1), the orators (see ATTIC ORATORS), *Herodotus (1), and *Homer, but, unlike Phrynichus, none of the tragedians; both reject Middle and New Comedy (see COMEDY (GREEK), MIDDLE and NEW). In the nature, merits, and limitations of his work he resembles Phrynichus.

EDITIONS Pierson (1759); Bekker (1833).
CRITICISM A. Maidhoff in M. Schanz, *Beitr. z. hist. Syntax d. Griech.* 19 (1912).   P. B. R. F.; R. B.

Moero, of Byzantium, female poet of late 4th–early 3rd cent. BC.

Only scanty remains survive: ten verses from the hexameter *Mnemosyne*, two epigrams, a summary of a story of cruelty and mad passion from her Ἀραί ('Curses'), and the mention of a *Hymn to Poseidon*. Her son, Homeros, was one of the tragic *Pleiad in *Alexandria (1).

FRAGMENTS Powell, *Coll. Alex.* 21–3; Gow–Page, *HE* 2. 413–15.
R. L. Hu.

Moesia was in the first instance the country of the Moesi, a Thracian tribe (see THRACE) situated on the lower Danube in present-day Serbia. Little is heard of the Moesi before 29 BC, when they were defeated and subdued by M. *Licinius Crassus (2) (Cass. Dio 51. 25. 1). Along with those of the Triballi, their neighbours to the east, the *civitates* of Moesia were administered by a *praefectus* (*CIL* 5. 1838 = *ILS* 1349, *CIL* 5. 1839) and attached to the province of Macedonia. The date at which Moesia was constituted a separate province is still uncertain. The first imperial legate (see LEGATI) recorded in the territory is A. *Caecina Severus (Cass. Dio 15. 29. 3), who left his province in AD 6 to defend *Sirmium against the Pannonians (see PANNONIA). It is possible that an earlier legate was P. *Vinicius (consul AD 2), attested on a dedication at Callatis (*IGRom.* 1. 654). In AD 33/4 the legions IV Scythica and V Macedonica (see LEGION) were engaged in cutting the vital tow-path through the Danube gorge below Belgrade (*CIL* 3. 1698 and 13813b; see DANUVIUS). A separate province of Moesia first emerges in 45/6 after the breakup of the great Balkan command which had united responsibility for the lower Danube, *Macedonia, and the Thracian kingdom. Henceforth Moesia extended along the lower Danube from near the river Drinus to the Black Sea (*Euxine); its southern frontier ran roughly along the main Balkan range. The governor of Moesia also had under his supervision the Black Sea coast to the straits of Kerch' (see BOSPORUS (2)), and from the time of *Vespasian, if not before, a *classis Moesica* (Moesian fleet) patrolled its northern waters. With a widely dispersed army along the lower Danube the legates in Moesia had to deal with turmoil among the semi-nomadic peoples of the plains beyond the river and the Pontic steppes (*CIL* 14. 3608) or the commercial privileges claimed by the ancient Greek colonies on the Black Sea coast such as *Istria (1) (*Inscriptiones Scythiae Minores Graecae et Latinae* (ed. D. M. Pippidi), vol. 1, nos. 67–8). Under *Domitian (AD 85–6) Moesia was split into two consular provinces, *Upper* and *Lower*, with the river Ciabrus as the boundary. For a brief period (until 117) after the Dacian Wars of *Trajan (see DACIA) units of the army of Upper Moesia were stationed in the plain between the Danube, the lower Theiss, and the Marisus (Mureş); that of Lower Moesia was similarly deployed across the north of the Wallachian plain east of the Alutus (mod. Olt).

Moesia always remained a military borderland. Apart from the old-established Greek cities on the Black Sea coast and from *Naissus on the upper Morava, all its chief towns grew out of Roman camps on the Danube—Singidunum (Belgrade), *Viminacium, Ratiaria, Oescus, Novae, Durostorum (Silistra), and Troesmis. Under *Hadrian or soon after, these places were constituted colonies or *municipia* of Italian pattern. Under the Roman peace the wheat and orchard lands of the lower Danube valley were well developed, and the *Latin language obtained a firm hold among the indigenous population, which had received repeated increments by transplantations of Dacians and kindred peoples across the Danube. During the invasions of the 3rd cent. (see GOTHS; HERULI) Moesia became a principal storm-centre, but its cities at any rate survived until the 6th or 7th cent.

A. Mócsy, *Pannonia and Upper Moesia* (1974); R. F. Hoddinott, *Bulgaria in Antiquity* (1975); B. Gerov, *Landownership in Roman Thracia and Moesia* (1st–3rd cent.) (1988); *Inscriptions de la Mésie Supérieure* 1– (1976–).
M. C.; J. J. W.

Mogontiacum (mod. Mainz) commanded important routes into the heart of Germany (see GERMANIA), and was a bulwark of Roman power on the Rhine (*Rhenus). Between 18 and 13 BC a fortress was built here to hold two legions. The timber fortress was replaced in stone in the second half of the 1st cent. AD and the garrison reduced to one legion after the rebellion of L. *Antonius Saturninus (89). A large and thriving town grew up between the fortress and the Rhine, and the seat of the governor of Upper Germany was here. From the 1st cent. there was a fort on the right bank of the river guarding an important bridgehead (mod. Kastel).

The legionary fortress was still garrisoned around 300 and possibly later. By the later 4th cent. it had been abandoned and part of its area was included within the new town walls, though a military presence was still maintained. Mogontiacum was the seat of a bishopric. It fell to the barbarians in 406: *Alans and *Burgundians proclaimed Jovinus here in 411.

K. H. Esser, *Bonner Jahrb.* 1972, 212 ff.; K.-V. Decker and W. Selzer, *ANRW* 2. 5. 1 (1976), 457 ff.; L. Schumacher, *Römische Kaiser in Mainz* (1982); W. Selzer, *Römische Steindenkmäler* (1988). P. S.; J. F. Dr.

Moliones (Aktorione), the twin sons of Molione and Actor, her mortal husband. In *Homer (*Il.* 11. 750–3) they are sons of *Poseidon (or born from a silver egg, Ibyc. fr. 4 Page, *PMG*). They were 'Siamese twins' in *Hesiod (fr. 17 M–W); at *Il.* 2. 621 they are named Cteatus and Eurytus, are married, and have sons. In Homer they fight *Nestor (1), elsewhere (Pherec. *FGrH* F 79a; Apollod. 2. 7. 2) they fight *Heracles and are killed by him at Cleonae, where *Pausanias (3) (2. 15. 1) saw their tomb.

'Siamese twins' appear on vases and *fibulae of the second half of the 8th and early 7th cents. BC, and the 6th-cent. throne of *Amyclae (Paus. 3. 18. 15). Their identification as the Molione is disputed: they may rather be inseparable twins or sworn brothers.

LIMC 1/1. 472–6, 'Aktorione'. K. W. A.

Molon See ANTIOCHUS (3); MEDIA ATROPATENE.

Molossi, common name of tribes forming a tribal state (*koinon*) in *Epirus, which originated in northern Pindus (including the Orestae, *FGrH* 1 F 107) and expanded southwards, reaching the Ambraciote Gulf (see AMBRACIA) c.370 BC. The king exchanged oaths with his people in an annual ceremony and commanded the tribal army, and the royal house, 'The Aeacidae', claimed descent from *Neoptolemus (1), son of *Achilles. The earliest inscriptions, of the reign of Neoptolemus in 370–368 BC, mention ten *damiorgoi* (a kind of magistrate: see DĒMIOURGOI), a *prostatēs* (president), and a *grammateus* (scribe), all named by one of the ten constituent tribes. 'The Molossians and their Allies' formed a military coalition, analogous to 'The Lacedaemonians and their Allies' (see PELOPONNESIAN LEAGUE), in which the Molossian king held the command as *hēgemōn*; *Alexander (6) I the Molossian demonstrated its potentiality in south Italy in 334–330 BC. When the state was absorbed into the Epirote Alliance, the Molossian king commanded the army of the alliance, and in this capacity *Pyrrhus won his victories in Italy and Sicily. After the fall of the monarchy c.232 BC the Molossian state was a constituent part of the Epirote Confederacy, until it alone sided with *Perseus (2) of Macedon in 170 and was annihilated by Rome in 167 BC.

Arkhaiologike Ephemeris 1956, 3 (inscriptions); Hammond, *Epirus*, and *CAH* 6² (1994), ch. 9d.   N. G. L. H.

Momos (Μῶμος), fault-finding personified, a literary figure, hardly mythological (though he occurs in *Hesiod, *Theog.* 214, among the children of Night, see NYX) and quite divorced from cult. He advises *Zeus to foment the Trojan War (*Cypria* fr. 1, Davies, *EGF*; see EPIC CYCLE; TROY). *Callimachus (3) makes use of him (*Hymn* 2. 113 and fr. 393 Pf.) as the mouthpiece of views which he opposes, while in *Lucian (as *Iupp. trag.* 19 ff.) he amusingly voices the author's satires on the conventional, popular Stoic theology (see STOICISM), or otherwise makes fun of his fellow gods. He is a figure in a fable, also cited by Lucian (*Nigr.* 32; cf. *Hermot.* 20, *Ver. Hist.* 2. 3).   H. J. R.; J. S. R.

Mona (mod. Anglesey). As a centre of Druidism (see RELIGION, CELTIC) it was attacked by *Suetonius Paulinus (AD 60/1), who withdrew to tackle the Boudiccan revolt (see BOUDICCA). It was reduced by Cn. *Iulius Agricola in 78/9. A collection of iron age metalwork from Llyn Cerrig Bach is probably associated with the cult. The island shows scant traces of Romanization, but there was copper-mining and Roman material is found on native sites. A late 3rd- or 4th-cent. Roman fort exists at Holyhead (Caer Gybi). Welsh tradition speaks of an Irish invasion (5th cent.) repelled by Cunedda, whose descendants ruled here.

RCHM (Wales), *Anglesey*; C. Fox, *Finds of the Iron Age at Llyn Cerrig Bach* (1946).   C. E. S.; M. J. M.

monarchy See KINGSHIP.

money may be regarded as a conventional means of representing a claim or a right to goods or services. Its existence may result from everything on a scale between a tacit understanding within a society and state legislation. And a wide variety of objects may function as money in the different uses which this possesses— for payments, for storing wealth, for measuring value, and as a means of exchange. It is likely that at an early stage valuable and imperishable objects, such as metal, served to convert surplus produce into a means for the acquisition of other produce in the future; at the same time, any commodity, such as cattle, may have served for measuring value. A decisive step was taken when an organized community designated an official monetary unit, normally of precious metal, for collective purposes, whether for measuring value or for payments, for fines, or for taxes. This step had been taken in most near eastern kingdoms by the beginning of the iron age, in many Greek communities by 800 BC, in Rome by 500 BC. The production of money in the form of coinage began in western Asia Minor about 600 BC and spread rapidly in the Greek world, more slowly in the Phoenician world, in the Roman world from the late 4th cent. BC. In the Greek world, the use of spits, *oboloi*, as objects of value is reflected in the use of *oboloi* as monetary units and denominations of most Greek coinage systems. See COINAGE, GREEK and ROMAN.

Despite the spread of coinage, not only in the Greek, Phoenician, and Roman worlds, but also to communities on their fringes—from Parthia to Spain—even in the high Roman empire, there were large areas of the Mediterranean world in which coinage played a minimal role; and many areas are likely at all times to have operated without any significant use of monetary institutions.

The ratio between the principal metals—*gold, *silver, *bronze—varied over time, with such factors as the increasing transfer to the Greek world of gold from Persia or the exploitation of silver-mines in Spain; these shifts naturally affected the rela-

tionships between different monetary units and different coin denominations.

The Hellenistic period saw the development of systems of paper transfers of money, mostly in connection with the levy of taxes; and the Roman state was able to a limited extent to function on anticipated revenues. But the ancient world never developed any form of paper money, let alone the use of credit mechanisms to increase the money supply.

See also BANKS; CREDIT.

M. H. Crawford, *La moneta in Grecia e a Roma* (1982); M. F. Hendy, *Studies in the Byzantine Monetary Economy* (1985).   M. H. C.

monopolies, in the sense of exclusive control of the supply of a product or service, were known in antiquity, but restricted in scope. In no case was the declared aim an increase in productivity through efficient planning or economies of scale. Instead, monopolistic control aimed above all at increasing revenues and was the prerogative of the state: 'cornering the market' by individuals was an almost mythical occurrence (Arist. *Pol.* 1259ᵃ5 ff.). State control and leasing of silver deposits in Attica (see LAURIUM) marks a long-term revenue-raising monopoly. Other Greek states invented and sold monopolies in time of fiscal emergency ([Arist.] *Oec.* 2). In Ptolemaic *Egypt, monopoly control of goods and services, usually by sale and lease of rights, was a way of life (from oil and textiles to beer and goose-breeding). In the Roman empire, sale of monopolies by cities was a regular revenue-raising device. See ECONOMY, GREEK, HELLENISTIC, and ROMAN.

F. M. Heichelheim, *RE* 16, 'Monopole'; M. I. Finley, *The Ancient Economy* (1973; 2nd edn. 1985); K. Riezler, *Über Finanzen und Monopole im alten Griechenland* (1907); C. Préaux, *L'Économie royale des Lagides* (1939).   P. C. M.

monotheism Apart from the influence of developed Judaism (see RELIGION, JEWISH) and *Christianity, no such thing as monotheism in the strict sense, i.e. the refusal to use the predicate 'god' of any but one being, existed in classical antiquity; even theistic philosophers, such as *Plato (1), *Aristotle, or the Stoics (see STOICISM), acknowledged the existence of subordinate deities (even if no more than planetary gods) beside the supreme one. Locally, it was usual enough to refer to one particular deity as 'the god' or 'the goddess', e.g. *Athena at Athens, *Apollo at *Delphi. But a further tendency towards monotheism may be detected, at any rate in Greek popular religion as interpreted by non-philosophical authors. This takes the form of the increasing supremacy of *Zeus. Even in *Homer (*Il.* 8. 18–27) he is much stronger than all the other gods put together; later authors tend to use 'Zeus', 'the gods', 'God' indiscriminately, e.g. Hesiod, *Op.* 42 and 47, where the same act is ascribed, first to 'the gods', then to Zeus. To *Aeschylus (*Ag.* 160 f.) Zeus is the supreme moral governor of the universe, though even there the existence of other gods is clearly recognized (169 ff.). Hellenistic writers favour vague phrases like τὸ θεῖον, τὸ δαιμόνιον. In the philosophical tradition, especially that of Platonism, an attitude of virtual monotheism is taken up, though there the single organizing principle of the universe is very much an impersonal force. See ANGELS.

Nilsson, *GGR* 1. 220, 421, 2. 546; L. P. Gerson, *God and Greek Philosophy* (1990).   H. J. R.; H. W. P.; J. D.

Mons Claudianus in the eastern desert mountains of Egypt was a Roman fortified village and imperial quarry 120 km. (75 mi.) east-north-east of Qena (ancient Cainē) on a route to the Red Sea. Occupied intermittently from the 1st to the 3rd cent.

AD it supplied granite columns for the *forum Traiani in Rome. Its buildings and 130 quarries are well preserved. Excavation between 1987 and 1993 has provided over 8,000 Greek and Latin ostraca detailing its occupation by a Roman garrison and civilian workmen. The extensive organic finds include 30,000 cloth fragments from dated contexts. See QUARRIES.

J. Bingen and others, *Mons Claudianus—Ostraca Graeca et Latina* (1992–). W. E. H. C.

mons Sacer, a hill near Rome just beyond the *Anio on the road to *Nomentum. In 494 and 449 BC the plebeians left Rome, returning only when the patricians granted concessions guaranteed by a *lex sacrata*. The mons Sacer, for obvious aetiological reasons, was represented as the destination of the seceding plebeians (Livy 2. 32, 3. 52; Festus 422, 423 Lindsay); see SECESSIO.
E. T. S.

monsoon, a system of perennial winds which regulate navigation between southern *Arabia and India. The SW monsoon (August–September) allows ships to sail through the gulf of Aden and the Arabian sea straight to the east coast of *India, departure from the *Red Sea taking place in July (Plin. *HN* 6. 104; *Peripl. M. Rubr.*). The return from India uses the NE monsoon, in November–December. It has been argued (S. Mazzarino, *Helikon* 1982/87) that the Greek word ὕφαλος refers to a 'submarine' wind, not to the navigator *Hippalus (on this view a misreading of *Pliny (1) *HN* 6. 100), as usually held. This does not make the adventures of *Eudoxus (3) in the 2nd cent. BC less credible; his voyages probably marked the first exploitation of the monsoon by classical mariners—notwithstanding earlier use by Arabs or Indians.

L. Casson, *The Periplus Maris Erythraei* (1989), 283 ff.; J. Rougé, *AMB* 1. 59 ff.; L. Casson, in V. Begley and R. De Puma (eds.), *Rome and India* (1991), 8 ff. J.-F. S.

Montanism was a prophetic movement among Christians in Asia Minor. It emerged in *Phrygia, probably *c*. AD 172 (Euseb. *Chron.*, under twelfth year of M. *Aurelius), since the conflicting evidence of Epiphanius (*Adv. haeres.* 48. 1) is otherwise unreliable. Montanus is a shadowy figure, and his sect owed its growth to the prophetesses Prisca and Maximilla, who proclaimed the approaching descent of the New Jerusalem near the Phrygian village of Pepuza. Their message seems to have been purely eschatological, with a strong emphasis on the glory of martyrdom, the attainment of ritual purity by rigorous fasts and penances, and freedom from the encumbrances of daily life. The movement was forcefully opposed throughout Asia Minor by bishops who denied the validity of prophecy through women or in *ecstasy. Yet, despite the failure of the original prophecies, it gained a firm hold in the country areas of Asia Minor, where an important series of Montanist inscriptions openly proclaiming the Christian beliefs of those commemorated have been found in the Tembris valley of northern Phrygia. Dating to 249–79 they are the earliest undisguisedly Christian inscriptions outside the Roman *catacombs. Montanism became an organized Church whose hierarchy included the ranks of patriarch and *koinōnos* ('companion' of Christ) as well as bishops, presbyters, and deacons. It persisted in Asia Minor until the 8th cent., but had a brilliant flowering in North Africa, where it won the allegiance of *Tertullian about 207. The martyrology of Perpetua and Felicitas is perhaps of Montanist origin. The sect had a great appeal for anyone who maintained a strong opposition between Chris-

tianity and the institutions of the world; hence, no doubt, its greater frequency in rural areas.

Eusebius, *Hist. eccl.* 5. 16 f., and Epiphanius, *Adv. haeres.* 48, preserve fragments of Montanist prophecies and anti-Montanist works. N. Bonwetsch, *Texte zur Geschichte des Montanismus*, Lietzmann's *Kleine Texte* 129, 1941.

See also P. de Labriolle, *La Crise montaniste* (1913); W. Schepelern, *Der Montanismus und die phrygische Kulte* (1929); W. M. Calder, *Bull. Rylands Libr.* 1923, 309 ff., and *Anat. St.* 1955, 27 ff.; W. H. C. Frend, *Martyrdom and Persecution in the Early Church* (1965), 290 ff.; T. D. Barnes, *JTS* 1969 and 1970. W. H. C. F.; M. J. E.

Monte Testaccio, an artificial hill, 36 m. (118 ft.) high and covering roughly 22,000 sq. m. (26,300 sq. yds.), in the Emporium district of Rome south of the *Aventine near the *Tiber. It is composed entirely of broken *amphorae dating from the 1st to the mid-3rd cent. AD, mostly oil amphorae from *Baetica in Spain with a smaller amount from North Africa, analysis of which has contributed to debate on the Roman economy.

E. Rodríguez Almeida, *Il Monte Testaccio* (1984); Nash, *Pict. Dict. Rome* 2. 411 ff. J. D.

months See CALENDAR, GREEK and ROMAN; TIME-RECKONING.

Monumentum Ancyranum See RES GESTAE.

moon See ASTROLOGY; ASTRONOMY; CALENDAR, GREEK and ROMAN; LUNA; MENSTRUATION; PHOEBE; SELENE; TIME-RECKONING.

Mopsus, famous mythological seer(s?), who is already the *Argonauts' seer in Archaic epic (*POxy.* 53. 3698). He is the son of Ampyx or Ampycus, comes from Titaresos (i.e. *Dodona), and dies on the journey, bitten by a serpent in Libya (Ap. Rhod. *Argon.* 4. 1502 ff.). Another tradition makes him the son of Manto, daughter of *Tiresias (Paus. 7. 3. 2). This Mopsus founds the oracle of *Claros and then emigrates to *Cilicia, where the city of Mopsuestia carries his name. Here he defeats *Calchas in a contest of *divination (Hes. fr. 278 M–W). As a *Hittite inscription mentions a 'Muksus' and the 7th-cent. BC Luwian–Phoenician inscription at Karatepe the 'house of Mopsus', this Mopsus probably derives from Anatolia. But how does this fit with the name *mo-qo-so* in Linear B (see MYCENAEAN LANGUAGE)? Was there a family of seers called Mopsus?

E. Simon, *LIMC* 'Mopsos' 1, 2; T. Scheer, *Mythische Vorväter* (1993), 153–271. J. N. B.

Morgantina (Lat. Murgentia?), a city of east-central *Sicily almost certainly to be identified with Serra Orlando, a steep-sided ridge 4 km. (2½ mi.) east of Aidone. Its acropolis, still called 'Citadella', commands a wide expanse of the western part of the plain of Catania, and is the site of the earliest settlement, in the 10th cent. BC. The Italic affinities of the latter community appear to reflect Strabo's (6. 1. 6) story of Morgetes. Greek pottery, masonry styles, and architectural *terracottas suggest that Greek settlers, probably from *Catana or *Leontini, established themselves *c*.560, on good terms with the indigenous settlers. In the 5th cent. and later the city was within the Syracusan orbit, apart from the short period (459–450) when it was under the control of *Ducetius (Diod. Sic. 11. 78. 5), and after 424 when it was ceded to *Camarina (Thuc. 4. 65). Refortified under *Timoleon with a walled circuit 7 km. (4.3 mi.) long, it was replanned and resettled under *Agathocles (1) and *Hieron (2) II. The agora on two levels, linked by a monumental stairway, was flanked by three stoas, a theatre, and other public structures, including a fountain, a granary, and the *prytaneion*. Many of the excavated houses, some with *mosaics, also belong to the 3rd cent. On Hieron's death in 215, Morgantina threw in its lot with *Carthage rather than support Rome, but three years later it fell to M. *Claudius Marcellus (1) after a siege, and was handed over for settlement to Rome's Spanish *mercenaries. A market building in the lower agora is the only new public building of this phase. By the end of the republic, Morgantina had lapsed into decay: Strabo (6. 2. 4) refers to it as no longer existing, although both pottery and *Pliny (1)'s reference (HN 3. 91) to the Murgentini (if they were indeed here) show that occupation did not finally peter out until the 1st cent. AD.

PECS 594–5; Gabba–Vallet, Sicilia antica 1. 731–7; S. Raffiotta, Morgantina (1985); E. Sjøqvist, R. Stillwell, H. L. Allen, and M. Bell, twelve excavation reports in AJArch. between 1957 and 1988; Morgantina Studies 1–4 (1981–93). A. G. W.; R. J. A. W.

Mormo, a vicious female spirit (like *Empusa, *Gello, and *Lamia (1)) used to frighten children, whose name is perhaps connected with Latin formido ('fear'). She was a queen of the *Laestrygones who lost her own children and so murders other children (schol. Theoc. 15. 40), or a Corinthian who ate her own children (schol. Aristid. p. 42 Dindorf).

J. Tambornino, RE 16/1 (1933), 309–11; Gow on Theoc. 15. 40; Rohde, Psyche, app. 6. K. D.

Morpheus, in Ovid Met. 11. 633–8 a son of Sleep, who sends dream visions of human forms ($\mu o \rho \phi a \iota$). Medieval and later authors use the name more generally for the god of *dreams or simply of sleep. E. Ke.

Morsimus, son of *Philocles and great-nephew of *Aeschylus, was an eye-doctor (see OPHTHALMOLOGY) and also a tragic poet, but regarded by *Aristophanes (1) as a particularly bad one (Eq. 401; Pax 802; Ran. 151).

TrGF 1². 147–8. A. L. B.

Morychus ($M \acute{o} \rho \upsilon \chi o \varsigma$). Lexicographers and *paroemiographers explain a saying 'sillier ($\mu \omega \rho \acute{o} \tau \epsilon \rho o \varsigma$) than Morychus, who neglects inside affairs and sits outside' as alluding to a statue of *Dionysus in Sicily, surnamed Morychus, which was outside his temple; their authority is *Polemon (3). H. J. R.

mosaic Floors paved with natural pebbles arranged in simple geometric designs were used in the near east in the 8th cent. BC. In the Greek world, unpatterned pebble floors were known in the Minoan and Mycenaean periods (see MINOAN and MYCENAEAN CIVILIZATION); decorated pebble mosaics are first attested at the end of the 5th cent., at *Corinth and *Olynthus. The earliest examples had simple two-dimensional designs, both geometric and figured, usually light on a dark ground. Their use, mainly in private houses, spread throughout Greece during the 4th cent.; by its end a wider range of colours and shades was used, and attempts were made to achieve more three-dimensional effects. Outstanding examples of this phase come from the palatial houses at *Pella in Macedonia, dated to the late 4th cent.; some artificial materials such as strips of lead or terracotta for outlines were used here to reinforce the natural pebbles. See HOUSES, GREEK.

The technique of tessellated mosaic (opus tessellatum), in which pieces of stone or marble were cut to approximately cubic shape and fitted closely together in a bed of mortar, was invented in the course of the 3rd cent. BC; the exact date is controversial. There were probably experiments in various places; mosaics at *Morgantina in Sicily are often cited as early

examples. Tesserae were cut irregularly at first, then with greater precision; by the 2nd cent. the technique sometimes known as opus vermiculatum had appeared, in which tiny pieces, sometimes less than 1 mm. square, in a wide range of colours, were fitted so closely together as to imitate the effects of painting. Mosaics in this last technique often took the form of emblemata: panels produced in the artists' studio, and then inserted into the floor at the centre of a coarser surround of tessellated mosaic. Outstanding examples have been found near *Alexandria (1) (at mod. Thmuis), and in *Pergamum; *Pliny (1) (HN 36. 184) records the mosaicist Sosus of Pergamum, famous for his representation of an 'unswept floor' (asarōtos oikos) littered with the debris of a meal, and for a scene of Drinking Doves, reflected in several Roman copies. The largest number of mosaics of the Hellenistic period is found in *Delos, dating from the late 2nd and beginning of the 1st cent. BC; they range from pavements of unshaped chips to very fine emblemata.

In Italy mosaics of Hellenistic style are found in Rome, *Pompeii, and elsewhere from the late 2nd cent. BC onwards; outstanding examples are the Alexander mosaic (see ALEXANDER (3) III, THE GREAT) from the House of the Faun in *Pompeii and the Nile mosaic from *Praeneste (mod. Palestrina). Tessellated mosaics with geometric patterns, coloured or black-and-white, became increasingly common in the 1st cent. BC. Alongside them appeared more utilitarian types of floor, especially those of signinum, coloured (usually red) mortar-and-aggregate, their surface often decorated with tesserae or other pieces of stone strewn at random or arranged in simple patterns. The antecedents for these may have come from Carthage, where pavements of related type are dated at least as early as the 3rd cent., perhaps to the 4th. Another technique developed in Italy in the late republic is that of opus sectile ('cut work'), where larger pieces of stone or marble were cut to the shape of specific parts of a design; this was later used on walls as well as floors, for both ornamental and figured designs.

Under the empire mosaics became mass-produced; they were widespread in private houses and better-quality apartments, and in large public buildings such as *baths. Geometric designs were much more common than figured work, and fine emblemata, always objects of luxury, became rare. In Italy throughout the first three centuries AD, the great majority of mosaics were black-and-white, with all-over geometric or floral designs, or with figures in black silhouette. The figures might be set in panels, or as abstract all-over designs covering the greater part of the floor; examples are found above all in *Ostia.

Much of the western empire adopted the use of mosaic under Italian influence during the 1st and 2nd cents. AD; a taste for polychromy generally prevailed over the black-and-white style. Each province tended to develop its own regional character, with a repertory of favourite designs and methods of composition. Among the most distinctive are those of North Africa; elaborate polychrome geometric and floral designs were favoured, and figure scenes often formed all-over compositions covering large areas of floor with minimal indication of depth or recession. Subject-matter here was often directly related to the interests and activities of the patrons, with scenes from the amphitheatre, the hunting-field, or the country estate. Closely related are the pavements of the great 4th-cent. villa at *Piazza Armerina in Sicily, very probably laid by a workshop from Carthage. In Spain the most striking mosaics come from villas of the late empire: they have much in common with the African floors, but include a higher proportion of mythological or literary subjects. In Britain a number of individual workshops have been distinguished, especially from the 4th cent.

The development in the eastern empire is less well known, but a fine series has been excavated at *Antioch (1), dating from *c.* AD 100 to the 6th cent. The Hellenistic tradition of the pictorial figure scene persisted much longer here, and black-and-white mosaics were rare. Very fine pictorial mosaics of the 4th cent. AD have been found at several sites in *Syria (e.g. Shahba-Philippopolis, *Apamea). At the end of the 4th cent. these gave way to all-over two-dimensional designs, both geometric and figured, best exemplified by the 5th-cent. 'hunting-carpets' of Antioch. Some eastern (*Sasanid) influence is perceptible in these late mosaics, but the dominant influence seems to come from fashions developed slightly earlier in the west.

The use of mosaic on walls and vaults (*opus musivum*) was a Roman invention. In the late republic grottoes and fountains were decorated with shells, pumice-stone, and pieces of glass, from which the use of regular glass tesserae developed. Numerous small fountains in Pompeii were decorated in this way, and more extensive mosaic decoration on walls is found there and in Rome in the 1st cent. AD; patterns and designs were more closely related to wall-painting than to floor mosaic. The technique was used on a large scale for vaults and walls in buildings such as baths and tombs in the 2nd and 3rd cents. The use of mosaic in Christian *churches from the 4th cent. onwards is an extension of this development.

D. Salzmann, *Untersuchungen zu den antiken Kieselmosaiken* (1982); P. Bruneau, *Exploration Archéologique de Délos 29: Les Mosaïques* (1972); E. Pernice, *Die hellenistische Kunst in Pompeii 6: Pavimente und figürliche Mosaiken* (1938); J. Clarke, *Roman Black-and-White Figural Mosaics* (1979); K. Dunbabin, *Mosaics of Roman North Africa* (1978); A. Carandini, A. Ricci, and M. de Vos, *Filosofiana: The Villa of Piazza Armerina* (1982); D. Levi, *Antioch Mosaic Pavements* (1947); J. Balty, *Mosaïques de Syrie* (1977); F. Sear, *Roman Wall and Vault Mosaics* (1977).

K. M. D. D.

Moschion, an Athenian tragic poet, probably of the 3rd cent. BC, is known almost exclusively from fragments quoted by *Stobaeus. He wrote a *Telephus* and two historical plays, *Themistocles* (see THEMISTOCLES) and *Men of Pherae*, the theme of which was perhaps the death of *Alexander (5) of Pherae. A long fragment on the origin of civilization (fr. 7) recalls in some points [Aesch.] *PV* 436 ff. His style is elegantly conventional, with some boldness of vocabulary.

TrGF 1². 263–8; *Musa Tragica* 200–7, 295–6. A. L. B.

Moschus, of *Syracuse, elegant hexameter poet of the mid-2nd cent. BC; counted as second in the *Suda*'s canonical list of Three Bucolic Poets, between *Theocritus and *Bion (2). Like most Hellenistic poets, he combined creative writing with scholarship; the *Suda* calls him a γραμματικός (grammarian) and pupil of *Aristarchus (2), and he may be the Moschus whom Athenaeus (11. 485e) mentions as author of a work on Rhodian lexicography.

His masterpiece is the *Europa*, a 166-line pocket epic narrating the abduction of the Phoenician princess by Zeus in bull-form. It exhibits all the stigmata of the classic '*epyllion': neat exposition of the situation in time and space, brief but rhetorical speeches, dreams and prophecies of the future, a summary conclusion, and in particular the elaborate, 25-line *ekphrasis* of the golden basket which *Europa takes to the seaside meadow, inlaid by *Hephaestus with scenes which (unbeknown to her) prefigure her own imminent fate. Echoes of *Homer dominate

the poem, both at the linguistic level and in the way the heroine recalls *Nausicaa; the influence of *Apollonius (1) and Theocritus can also be traced, besides that of earlier works like the *Homeric Hymn to Demeter* (flower-gathering) and Aeschylus (dream of the two continents; cf. Aesch. *Pers.* 176 ff.). The language is highly polished; indeed, polished can become precious, and (like *Catullus (1), in poem 64) Moschus is rather over-fond of certain stylistic mannerisms, e.g. iterative forms in -εσκε.

Five other shorter pieces have an erotico-pastoral flavour; poem 1 ('*Eros on the Run') is a cleverly-motivated description of the god's characteristics cast in the form of a 'Wanted' proclamation delivered by his mother *Aphrodite. Also of considerable interest is the *Megara*, a 125-line hexameter dialogue between the wife of *Heracles and his mother *Alcmene, concerning their anxieties about the absent hero; but there is no justification for its traditional place in editions as 'Moschus IV'.

TEXT A. S. F. Gow, *Bucolici Graeci* (1952).
TRANSLATION A. S. F. Gow, *The Greek Bucolic Poets* (1953).
COMMENTARY On the *Europa*: W. Bühler (1960; in German); M. Campbell (1991); N. Hopkinson, in N. Hopkinson (ed.), *A Hellenistic Anthology* (1988).
INTERPRETATION K. Gutzwiller, *Studies in the Hellenistic Epyllion* (1981), 63–73.
On the *Megara*: T. Breitenstein, *Recherches sur le poème Mégara* (1966).

A. H. G.

mother-city See MĒTROPOLIS.

motherhood

Greek Women were deemed to have a natural right to *marriage and *children. Physicians maintained that intercourse and *childbirth were necessary to female health and prescribed pregnancy to cure pathological conditions; records of miraculous cures at the sanctuary of *Asclepius in *Epidaurus reflect a high level of sterility anxiety. Views of the maternal contribution to genetic inheritance differ: *Apollo's denial of female parentage at Aesch. *Eum.* 658–61 and *Aristotle's restriction of procreative agency to male spermatic fluid (*Gen. an.* 721ᵇ7–724ᵃ12) are countered by the Hippocratic belief (see HIPPOCRATES (2)) that the embryo results from the union of male and female seed, its sex determined by the stronger of the two (see EMBRYOLOGY). From a judicial standpoint, *Pericles (1)'s law of 451/0 BC restricting citizenship to children of two Athenian parents had the practical effect of making the mother's civic status fundamental to *inheritance questions.

Contrary to the Spartan practice of delaying marriage, Athenian girls married and bore children soon after puberty. Early pregnancy and inadequate hygiene made labour hazardous, as the cultural homology between war and childbirth attests (Eur. *Med.* 248–51). The male foetus was considered to be more active, healthier for the mother to bear, and easier to deliver. *Artemis was the chief divinity presiding over childbirth, although numerous lesser powers were also invoked (see EILEITHYIA). Women gave birth at home, attended by *midwives and friends; all participants incurred ritual *pollution, the mother's possibly lasting until post-partum bleeding terminated. Brides were not fully assimilated into conjugal families until after the birth of the first child.

Maternal love was idealized as unconditional, selfless, and stronger than that of a father (Xen. *Mem.* 2. 2. 5; Arist. *Eth. Nic.* 1159ᵃ28–33, 1161ᵇ26–7). Though often assisted by wet-nurses (see BREAST-FEEDING) or dry-nurses, the mother was accordingly viewed as the infant's primary care-giver. Boys were raised in the women's quarters until they began formal education at about age 6; girls remained with their mothers until marriage. Physical separation of mother and child was a regular consequence of divorce, as fathers retained custody. *Widows, however, might go on caring for their offspring, residing either in the dead husband's house or with other kin. Mothers continued to play an active part in the lives of adult children. Although the bond between mother and son was felt to be especially close, hints of strain occur. Slater's psychoanalytic use of myth and tragedy as evidence for maternal hostility is problematic (see bibliog. below), but *Aristophanes (1)'s comic representation of a spoiled only son in the *Clouds*, *Plato (1)'s family history of the timocratic man (*Resp.* 549c–550b), and *Herodas' vignette of a mother exasperated by a truant boy (*Mime* 3) all depend upon the recognizable cultural stereotype of a domineering female parent. The legendary 'Spartan mother' may be a fictive projection of similar tensions. Real sons and mothers were nevertheless expected to assume mutual responsibilities to one another throughout their lives, the grown son becoming his mother's protector in her widowhood and old age. See LOVE AND FRIENDSHIP; WIDOWS.

P. E. Slater, *The Glory of Hera* (1968); R. Garland, *The Greek Way of Life* (1990).
M. B. S.

Roman The Roman word for mother (*mater*) is reflected in such words as *materfamilias* and *matrona*, a respectable wife (Cic. *Top.* 14; Gell. *NA* 18. 6. 8–9). The legendary 'first' Roman divorce was of a virtuous wife unable to bear children and thus fulfil the formal purpose of *marriage (Gell. *NA* 17. 21. 44; 4. 3. 2). The promotion of citizen marriage and procreation (see CHILDBIRTH) by the legislation of the emperor *Augustus included some honorific awards for mothers (Prop. 4. 11. 61; *Inst. Iust.* 4. 18. 4; Gai. *Inst.* 3. 44–53; see IUS LIBERORUM).

Roman ideal mothers tended to be praised for instilling the foundations of traditional morality and rhetorical skills, with the emphasis on the mother's influence on the education of her adolescent or young adult son. Where modern ideologies stress the intensive relationship of the (biological) mother with her infant and very young child and idealize maternal nurture and patience, Roman authors praised the moral severity and hard-headedness of the ideal mother's guidance (Tac. *Dial.* 28), as in the case of *Cornelia (1), mother of the *Gracchi, or Caesar's mother *Aurelia (Cic. *Brut.* 211; Quint. *Inst.* 1. 1. 6). Being widows by the time their sons reached adolescence, these mothers might have taken on socializing roles otherwise performed by fathers, but Roman marriage and mortality patterns meant that a father-less adolescence was not abnormal. The bias of Roman literary historical sources leads to an emphasis on the role played by such mothers in forming the character of famous sons of the political élite or imperial family (Tac. *Agr.* 4; Suet. *Ner.* 52). References to mothers and young children or mothers and daughters are rare and incidental. Mother–daughter combinations tend to figure in the context of *betrothal, where mothers played a greater role than might be expected from the legal concentration on the powers of the *paterfamilias*. The symbolic story (Plut. *Ti. Gracch.* 4 and Livy 38. 57. 7) of a mother's exclusion from the process contrasts with more circumstantial accounts (Cic. *Att.* 5. 4. 1, 6. 1. 10, 6. 6. 1 on *Tullia (2); 13. 42. 1 on young Quintus). Icono-graphic, inscriptional, and legal sources flesh out our knowledge, but, like the literary sources, concentrate on ideal (or, in the case of law, problematic) aspects of family relations (e.g. the pathos of the baby 'snatched from his mother's breast' by death in *CIL* 6. 23790). Imaginative literature, such as satire, provides larger-

than-life model mothers, monster mothers, and wicked step-mothers. Speculation continues about Roman attitudes to child-hood, but we do know that Roman *children from an early age were likely to enjoy relations with a variety of care-givers rather than exclusively with the biological mother. Maternal *breast-feeding, advocated by male moralists, would have depended in practice on social and economic considerations (Gell. *NA* 12. 1; Tac. *Dial.* 28; Plut. *De amore prolis* 3; *De liberis educandis* 5). Maternal mortality and morbidity imposed flexibility at all social levels. The élite child was likely to have a number of servile care-givers and frequent contact with a range of relatives; slave children might be reared communally within the *familia* and the young children of free(d) lower class parents might intermittently be cared for by friends, neighbours, and relatives to release the mother (like the slave mother) for labour of various kinds. Epi-taphs chosen at random from the vicinity of Rome give some indication of the variety of relationships: *CIL* 6. 21334, 11005, 25808, 34421, 11592.

S. Dixon, *The Roman Mother* (1988).
S. Di.

Mothone See METHONE (2).

Motya (mod. Mozia), an islet of *c*.45 ha. (111 acres) which an artificial causeway, now submerged, joined to western Sicily. Colonized by the *Phoenicians at the end of the 8th cent. BC, it became one of the great military and commercial strongholds of Carthaginian Sicily (*Panormus and Soloeis being the others). Nevertheless it underwent a good deal of Hellenic cultural influ-ence, well exemplified by the life-size marble statue found in 1979, of a charioteer, carved *c*.460 BC undoubtedly by a Greek hand. *Dionysius (1) I sacked Motya in 397 BC after a memorable siege, and it was not resurrected thereafter (*Lilybaeum replacing it as the Carthaginian stronghold in western Sicily), although there was some Hellenistic occupation of the site, at least until 241. The defences, two sanctuaries, one of which contains burnt human and animal sacrifices (*tophet*), an artificial harbour (*kōthōn*), and several houses, are the chief excavated monuments.

J. I. S. Whitaker, *Motya* (1921); Dunbabin, *Western Greeks*, esp. 22, 326–35; B. S. J. Isserlin and J. du Plat Taylor, *Motya* 1 (1974); V. Tusa and others, *Mozia* 1–9 (1964–78); A. Ciasca and others, *Mozia* (1989).
A. G. W.; R. J. A. W.

mountain cults Mountains as such were not worshipped in classical Greece or in Italy, but they were places of special cult, to the point that Mt. Maenalus in *Arcadia was considered sacred to *Pan in its entirety (Paus. 8. 36. 8). The location of a sanctuary was rarely the exact summit of the mountain (*Zeus Lycaeus on Mt. Lycaeon is an exception), but more often in the passes or on the slopes. The sanctuary could include a temple, as at *Bassae, or might be more rustic and simple (the cave at Phigalia, the Corycian cave above *Delphi; see CAVES). Worshippers were mainly shepherds, depicted on their votives. The deities most frequently worshipped were *Zeus, the weather-god, *Artemis, goddess of the animal world and of boundaries, *Hermes, a country god and patron of shepherds, *Apollo, another pastoral god, and Pan, the divine herdsman and hunter of small game. Overall there are no special cult acts proper to mountain sites. However, two rituals at Mt. Lycaeon, unparalleled elsewhere, can be linked to the wildness of the place: the magic ritual attached to the spring Hagno, performed with an oak branch by the priest of Zeus after a long period of drought to cause rain (Paus. 8. 38. 4), and the human sacrifice practised at the Lycaea on the top of the mountain, the origin of which was traced to *Lycaon (3). Certain types of myths have a more particular connection with mountains, such as those of the births of gods (Zeus on Lycaeon, or in *Crete on Mt. Ida, Hermes on Cyllene). The mountain solitude and the presence of divinities of nature in the form of *kourotrophos-type nymphs would give the young gods a secluded and suitable upbringing before their integration into divine society.

La Montagne dans l'antiquité. Actes du Colloque de la SOPHAU, Pau (mai 1990) (1992).   M. J.

mountains, like *islands, were a familiar feature of real Greek life, but they also had a fantastic literary life of their own, often standing for wildness, origins, and reversal.

R. Buxton, JHS 1992, 1 ff., and Imaginary Greece (1994), 81 ff.; G. Fowden, JHS 1988, 48 ff.; M. Jameson in J. F. Bergier (ed.), Montagnes, fleuves, forêts dans l'histoire (1987), 7–17. See also GREECE (GEOGRAPHY), and under particular mountains, e.g. ATLAS, HYMETTUS, OLYMPUS (1), etc.   S. H.

Mucia (RE 'Mucius' 28) **Tertia,** daughter of Q. *Mucius Scaevola (2) and cousin of Q. *Caecilius Metellus Celer and Q. *Caecilius Metellus Nepos, married Pompey c.80 BC and bore him Cn. *Pompeius Magnus (2) and Sex. *Pompeius Magnus and a daughter. Unfaithful to him during his long absence in the 60s, she was divorced by him on his return, which antagonized the two Metelli. She later married M. *Aemilius Scaurus (2) and bore him a son, whose pardon she secured after *Actium. In 39 she tried to mediate between Sextus and Octavian.

Bauman, WPAR 78 ff.   E. B.

Mucius (RE 10) **Scaevola, Gaius,** features in the cycle of legends surrounding the figure of Lars *Porsenna. According to the story, Mucius stole into Porsenna's camp in an attempt to assassinate him, but failed to recognize the king and mistakenly killed his secretary who was sitting beside him. On being arrested he showed his indifference to the prospect of torture by thrusting his right hand into a fire—whence his surname Scaevola ('left-handed'). The story appeared in *Cassius Hemina (fr. 16 Peter), and was probably an old legend; the burning of the right hand may have a ritual significance (cf. Val. Max. 3. 3. 2), and the presence of the secretary sitting beside the king is a genuine *Etruscan detail.

Ogilvie, Comm. Livy 1–5, 262–3; G. Colonna, Mélanges J. Heurgon (1976), 187–95.   T. J. Co.

Mucius (RE 17) **Scaevola, Publius,** brother of P. *Licinius Crassus Dives Mucianus whom he succeeded as pontifex maximus. As tribune in 141 BC he instituted a tribunal to try the corrupt ex-praetor L. Hostilius Tubulus, who went into exile. As consul (133), being an eminent lawyer and enemy of P. *Cornelius Scipio Aemilianus, he was one of the senior advisers of Ti. *Sempronius Gracchus (3). Despite the request of some senators, he refused to use violence against the tribune, but later defended the action of P. *Cornelius Scipio Nasica Serapio in killing them. He followed in the footsteps of his father (consul 175) as a jurist, firmly establishing his family's pre-eminence in this field, and he seems to have published the series of *annales maximi.

E. S. Gruen, Athenaeum 1965, 321 ff., and see under SEMPRONIUS GRACCHUS (3), TI. For his legal views, R. A. Bauman, RIDA 1978, 223 ff.E. B.

Mucius (RE 21) **Scaevola (1), Quintus,** called 'Augur' (cf. next article), Stoic (see STOICISM), eminent lawyer, son-in-law of C. *Laelius (2), but probably, like P. *Mucius Scaevola, moderately Gracchan in sympathy (his daughter married M'. *Acilius Glabrio (2)). Praetor c.120 BC, he was accused repetundarum after gov-

erning Asia, but acquitted. (The trial was satirized by *Lucilius (1).) He was consul in 117, and in 100 opposed L. *Appuleius Saturninus. He taught (among others) his son-in-law L. *Licinius Crassus and, in his old age, *Cicero, who venerated his memory and introduced him into several dialogues. Alone among the principes present in the city, he opposed *Sulla after his march on Rome (88) and aided C. *Marius (1) who had married his granddaughter. He died soon after.   E. B.

Mucius (RE 22) **Scaevola (2), Quintus,** called 'Pontifex' (cf. preceding article), son of P. *Mucius Scaevola, whom he surpassed both as an orator and a lawyer. In his most famous case, the causa Curiana (Cic. De or. 1. 180 f.), he defended the strict wording of a will, against the defence of aequitas (equity) and intention by L. *Licinius Crassus. As consuls (95 BC), he and Crassus passed the lex Licinia Mucia instituting a quaestio (see QUAESTIONES) against aliens who had been illegally enrolled as citizens. Perhaps on the motion of M. *Aemilius Scaurus (1), he was sent as proconsul to govern Asia, either after his praetorship, or more probably after his consulship (see RUTILIUS RUFUS, P.). He reorganized the troubled province with the aid of his legate Rutilius and, departing after nine months, left Rutilius in charge. When Rutilius was prosecuted in 92, he escaped prosecution, probably through his remote connection with C. *Marius (1) and because of his high prestige, and in 89 he became *pontifex maximus, the last civil lawyer known to have held this office. After Marius' death he was threatened by C. *Flavius Fimbria, but escaped harm and remained in Rome under the government of L. *Cornelius Cinna (1) and Cn. *Papirius Carbo, loyal to the government and advising compromise with *Sulla. He was killed by L. *Iunius Brutus Damasippus in 82, probably when on the point of joining Sulla.

Scaevola, known in legal circles as 'Quintus Mucius', was perhaps the leading lawyer of the later Roman republic. His eighteen books (libri) on the civil law (De iure civili) was the most famous legal treatise of the period and was still the subject of commentary by Sextus *Pomponius and others in the 2nd cent. AD. He also compiled a book of definitions (Horoi: the title comes from *Chrysippus). He was the first lawyer to give serious attention to classification; thus, he distinguished five types of *guardianship. But, despite his grounding in Greek, especially middle Stoic, culture he did not succeed in reducing the civil law to a system, though he helped to make it morally more acceptable. Thus he fixed on the conscientious head of a family (diligens paterfamilias) as the pattern of correct behaviour in avoiding harm to others. His large legal practice was attended by many pupils including C. *Aquil(l)ius Gallus and, after his father P. Mucius Scaevola's death, *Cicero.

Badian, Stud. Gr. Rom. Hist., see index, and see further under RUTILIUS RUFUS, P.; Lenel, Pal. 1. 757–64; Bremer 1. 48–104; Wieacker, RRG 1. 549–51, 596–600; F. Schulz, Roman Legal Science (1946); Watson (1974), ch. 11.   E. B.; T. Hon.

Mulciber See VOLCANUS.

mulomedicina See VETERINARY MEDICINE.

Mulvian Bridge See PONS MULVIUS.

Mummius (RE 7a, vol. 16. 1192 ff.), **Lucius,** as praetor and proconsul (153–2 BC) defeated the Iberian Lusitani (see LUSITANIA), triumphing 152. As consul 146 he succeeded Q. *Caecilius Metellus Macedonicus in Macedonia and in the command against the revolt of the *Achaean Confederacy, which he defeated. He destroyed Corinth, making the land *ager publicus, then, with a senatorial commission, organized the province of Macedonia and dealt with the Greek cities, calling on *Polybius (1) for advice. He punished those involved in the revolt, dissolved the confederacy as a political unit, and arranged for Greece to be supervised by future commanders in Macedonia. The works of art taken, on an unprecedented scale, from Corinth and other cities (see BOOTY) were largely given to his friends or to Italian and provincial communities in his *clientela* (see CLIENS), or set up for display in Rome. (See *ILLRP* 327 ff.) He celebrated a triumph and became *censor (142) with P. *Cornelius Scipio Aemilianus, moderating his severity. He died soon after. His descendants, perhaps as early as c.100 BC, adopted the victory name 'Achaicus', never given to him.

App. *Hisp.* 56. 236 ff.; Polyb. 39. 2 ff.   E. B.

Munatia Plancina was in Syria with her husband, Cn. *Calpurnius Piso (3), governor of the province, when *Germanicus and *Vipsania Agrippina (2) were in the east (AD 18–19). By temperament no less domineering than Agrippina, she was, moreover, a friend of *Livia Drusilla. It was inevitable, therefore, that she should quarrel with Agrippina, and when Germanicus died in AD 19 Agrippina accused her of murder. Livia's intercession saved her life when Piso was condemned in 20. Accused again in 33, she committed suicide. For the recently discovered *senatus consultum* about Piso see CALPURNIUS PISO (3), CN.   J. P. B.; R. J. S.

Munatius (*RE* 30) **Plancus, Lucius,** of senatorial family, served under *Caesar in the Gallic and Civil Wars, was probably praetor late 47 BC, and in 45 was one of Caesar's six prefects of the city (see *RRC* 475). Proconsul of Gallia Comata (see GAUL (TRANSALPINE)) after Caesar's death, he invaded *Raetia, winning a minor victory, and founded the colonies of *Lugdunum (1) and Raurica (later *Augusta Raurica). In letters to Cicero (*Fam.* 10) he asserted his loyalty to the republic, while advising peace with M. *Antonius (2). He left D. *Iunius Brutus Albinus, probably after Octavian's march on Rome, joining Antonius and M. *Aemilius Lepidus (3). In the triumviral *proscriptions he was said to have put his brother's name on the list. In December 43 he triumphed (over Gaul or Raetia), became consul 42 with Lepidus, and then or later restored the temple of Saturn (see SATURNUS) out of his triumphal spoils (*ILLRP* 43; cf. Suet. *Aug.* 29. 5). In the Perusine War he failed to assist L. *Antonius (Pietas), then escaped with *Fulvia to M. Antonius in Greece. After governing Asia (40) and, during Antonius' Parthian campaign, Syria as Antonius' deputy (35: he is said to have ordered the execution of Sextus *Pompeius Magnus), he joined Antonius in *Alexandria (1) and outdid himself in flattery of *Cleopatra VII. Before *Actium he joined Octavian with his nephew M. *Titius, later claiming that he had refused to fight for Cleopatra. In 27 he moved that Octavian be called Augustus. In 22 he was censor, with Paullus *Aemilius Lepidus. He was buried at Caieta (mod. Gaeta), where his tomb inscription was found (*ILS* 886). His son Lucius was consul AD 13, his daughter *Munatia Plancina married Cn. *Calpurnius Piso (3).

Broughton, *MRR* 3. 146; G. Walser, *Der Briefwechsel des L. Munatius Plancus mit Cicero* (1957).   G. W. R.; T. J. C.; E. B.

Munatius (*RE* 32) **Plancus Bursa, Titus,** brother (or perhaps cousin) of L. *Munatius Plancus, as tribune 52 BC was prominent in trying to avenge the death of P. *Clodius Pulcher and punish T. *Annius Milo. With Q. Pompeius Rufus, he was responsible for the burning of the *Curia (2), and in *Pompey's interest he delayed the holding of elections. Convicted by Cicero of *vis (51)

despite Pompey's support, he was supported in exile and, in 49, restored by Caesar, but held no higher office. In the war of *Mutina he unsuccessfully fought for M. *Antonius (2) against *Pontius Aquila and is not heard of after.

Cic. *Pro Milone*, with Asc. *Mil.* and Marshall, Asconius *Comm.*
                T. J. C.; E. B.

mundus (etymology uncertain), the world, the ornament (cf. Gk. *kosmos*), also a round pit at Rome, *mundus Cereris* (Festus, *Gloss. Lat.* 261; *CIL* 10. 3926 from Capua, *sacerdos Cerialis mundalis*), with its upper part vaulted, and the lower (*inferior*) giving access to the Underworld. It was open (*mundus patet*) on 24 August, 5 October, and 8 November. On these days (*dies religiosi*) no public business (unless necessary) or marriages could be transacted (Ateius Capito and Cato Licinianus in Festus, *Gloss. Lat.* 273; Varro in Macrob. *Sat.* 1. 16. 18). It is unlikely that this *mundus* was identical with the foundation pit *Romulus excavated in the *Comitium (or the *Palatine) to deposit clods of earth and first-fruits (Plut. *Rom.* 11; Ov. *Fast.* 4. 821 ff.). See also PITS, CULT.

H. Le Bonniec, *Le Culte de Cérès* (1958); J. Puhvel, *AJPhil.* 1976, 54 ff.; A. Magdelain, *Rev. Ét. Lat.* 1976, 99 ff.; F. Coarelli, *Dial. di Arch.* 1976–7, 346 ff., and *Il Foro Romano* 1 (1983); H. Solin, *Zu lukanischen Inschriften* (1981), 47 ff. (*mundus Attinis*); F. Castagnoli in *Festschrift G. Radke* (1986), 32 ff.   J. L.

Munichia (1) (or **Munychia**), mod. Kastella, is a steep hill to the north-east of *Piraeus which rises to a height of 86 m. (282 ft.). Directly below is Munichia Port and to the south-east Zea Port. In 510 BC *Hippias (1) began fortifying the hill, intending to make it his seat of government (*Ath. pol.* 19. 2). The SW slope saw fighting in 403 when *Thrasybulus defeated the *Thirty Tyrants (Xen. *Hell.* 2. 4. 10–19). The theatre of Dionysus on its NW flank was used for dramatic festivals, *deme assemblies, and in 411 and 404 for political rallies. Munichia played an important strategic role throughout Athenian history, notably during the Macedonian occupation (322–229) when by garrisoning it the enemy were able to control both Athens and Piraeus. Its most prominent shrines were those of Artemis Munichia (see MUNICHIA (2)) and *Bendis. Remains of ancient houses are visible on the summit.

R. Garland, *The Piraeus* (1988); J. Travlos, *Bildlexicon zur Topographie des antiken Attika* (1988), 340.   R. S. J. G.

Munichia (2), an Attic festival held on the 16th of the month Munichion (roughly, early May) in honour of the *Artemis of *Munichia (1). There was sacrifice and a procession, in which *cakes ringed with 'little torches', like birthday cakes, were brought to the goddess (who was herself a φωσφόρος, 'light-bringer' or saviour). The festival came also to serve as a commemoration of the Greek victory at the battle of *Salamis. In addition, archaeological evidence now supports the ancient reports that young girls served as *arktoi*, 'bears', at Munichia as well as *Brauron.

E. Simon, *Festivals of Attica* (1983), 81–2, 86; L. Palaiokrassa, Τὸ ἱερὸ τῆς Ἀρτέμιδος Μουνιχίας (1991), esp. 34–6.   R. C. T. P.

Munichus (later **Munychus**), eponym of *Munichia (1), the acropolis of *Piraeus, where he received refugees from Boeotian *Orchomenus (1) (Diodorus, *FGrH* 372 F 39) and founded the temple of *Artemis Munichia (*Suda*, entry under Ἔμβαρος εἰμι). Though he is connected with *Theseus, appearing in the fight against the *Amazons on Beazley, *ARV²* 1174. 6, he is distinct from Munitos, son of *Acamas or *Demophon (1).

L. Palaiokrassa, Τὸ ἱερὸ τῆς Ἀρτέμιδος Μουνιχίας (1991), 23–9 (sources), 36–7, and *LIMC* 6. 635–7.   E. Ke.

municipium, one of the most significant institutions of Roman administrative law, the organism through which the Roman polity became incorporative, and thus developed from the institutional framework of a city-state to accommodate much greater numbers of enfranchised citizens than had any *polis.

The term means 'the undertaking of duty'. Originally the duty in question was no doubt various and resembled the diverse mutual obligations which were found in diplomatic relations between states in the Mediterranean of the 5th cent. BC. As the institution evolved in Roman practice, the duty to provide military assistance, and the reward of incorporation in the Roman body politic on settling in Rome, became paramount, and were always there in the theory of the *municipium*. In actuality, an asymmetry between Rome and any of its municipal partners grew steadily. Municipal status originally in many cases went with *civitas sine suffragio*, citizenship without the vote at Rome, though the *ius suffragii* might be added (as to *Arpinum, *Fundi, and *Formiae in 188 BC), or acquired through movement to Rome. Roman supervision, through *praefecti*, became more systematic. The line between second-class citizenship and subjugation was fine, and in the 3rd cent., for instance in the case of *Capua, it can be hard to tell who in a municipal relationship with Rome thought the deal a privilege and who a disgrace. After the Hannibalic War (see PUNIC WARS) choices became more limited.

Municipia that had been given the *suffragium* retained the title *municipium*, and it was on this model that after the enfranchisement of Italy in 89 BC, all communities that were not *coloniae* became *municipia*. In a somewhat piecemeal way, some regularity in the charters and institutions of these communities was achieved, and a process of formation of civic nuclei in areas where there had been only villages was encouraged: this continued under *Augustus. Most of the cities of Italy from this point on were thus *municipia*, usually governed by magistrates called *quattuorviri*. But the institution was still mutating.

On the analogy of practice in Italy before the *Social War (3), some loyal communities in the provinces were made *municipia*: rewarded for military service, that is, by a sort of citizen right, usually the *ius Latii. C. Marius (1) seems to have done this in Africa; *Caesar did it in Cisalpine Gaul (see GAUL (CISALPINE)), and then on a very grand scale in *Baetica. Augustus regularized the process in a law (the *lex Iulia municipalis*) which also established a model charter. This is known through the versions of it which were used in the Flavian continuation of the process of municipalization in southern Spain, especially the charters of *Malaca, Salpensa, and the very full version of the insignificant community of Irni, which proves the existence of an Augustan prototype (see TABULA IRNITANA). Under this charter the *quattuorviri* are replaced by two pairs of magistrates, and every five years there are to be censor-like special magistrates. Various other officers, such as a quaestor, are envisaged. Even the non-Roman inhabitants of the *municipium* are assimilated to Roman citizens in various ways under the law.

In its imperial form, as we see it in the Augustan use at Autun (*Augustodunum), or the Claudian at *Volubilis, the old theory of military service and reward is still present. As a way of spreading the citizenship and rewarding loyalty of a political kind, while encouraging responsible and governmentally helpful behaviour on the part of local élites, it became a standard benefaction from the centre to the provinces of the west; though the higher status of *colonia* replaced this function in the 2nd cent. AD. There remained in Gaul and Britain, and in the Rhine and Danube provinces, many *civitates*, communities with a legal status which had not been incorporated in this way. The dissemination of the citizenship, complete by 212, rendered the partial citizen rights of the *ius Latii* obsolete. See CITIZENSHIP, ROMAN; CIVITAS; COLONIZATION, ROMAN.

A. N. Sherwin-White, *The Roman Citizenship*, 2nd edn. (1973); M. Humbert, *Municipium et civitas sine suffragio* (1978); P. A. Brunt, *Italian Manpower* (1971).   N. P.

munus, a gift or service, given or rendered freely (a lover's gift, or the gifts of gods to men) or, more commonly, out of a sense of duty (burial of the dead, sacrifices, or funeral games). The latter sense leads to its use in Roman public life, for what a person owes to the state or community of which he is a citizen or in which he lives. There are personal *munera*, especially military service or service as a magistrate—for the latter, the word becomes common as such service, under the empire, turns into an onerous obligation—and financial *munera*: taxes and contributions corresponding to Greek *liturgies. Thus, a *municeps* is originally a man who accepts *munera* towards Rome, whether personally or within a *municipium. At least by the middle republic, men could be exempted by law from *munera* for various kinds of services, and such *immunitas spread under the empire to whole classes of citizens deemed essential to the state, with increasing pressure on those not exempt. (See *Dig.* 50. 4 and 5, for details under the middle empire.) *Immunitas* could similarly be conferred on communities that would normally have owed taxes to Rome (see TRIBUTUM).   E. B.

murder See LAW AND PROCEDURE, ATHENIAN and ROMAN (§ 3); PARRICIDIUM.

murrina vasa, luxury tableware imported into Rome from the middle east and, being extremely costly, a status symbol. According to *Pliny (1), the chief source (*HN* 37. 18. 22), it was made from a soft mineral found in *Persia, and especially in Carmania. The mineral showed a variety of pleasing colours, purple and red predominating; his description suits fluorspar. Roman *Thebes (2) produced imitations in *millefiori* *glass, of which examples survive (*Peripl. M. Rubr.* 6. 26. 6: μορρίνη).

C. E. N. Bromehead, *Antiquity* 1952, 65 ff.; L. Casson, *The Periplus Maris Erythraei* (1989), 112.   D. E. E.; A. J. S. S.

Musaeus (1) (Μουσαῖος), a mythical singer with a descriptive name ('He of the Muses'). He belongs particularly to *Eleusis, where he is either autochthonous (see AUTOCHTHONS) or an immigrant from *Thrace, the country of mythical singers. He is father or son of *Eumolpus, the eponymous hero of the sacred sacerdotal family of Eleusis, and his wife Deiope has her grave beneath the Eleusinian Telesterion; the couple and their son Eumolpus are shown on a red-figure vase of the Meidias Painter (Beazley, *ARV*² 1313. 7).

He is closely connected with *Orpheus, whom he follows together with *Hesiod and *Homer in a canonical list (see CANON) of the quintessential Greek poets (deriving from *Hippias (2) of Elis, DK 86 B 6). *Plato (1) called Orpheus and Musaeus descendants of the Moon (*Resp.* 364e); to others, Musaeus is Orpheus' son (Diod. Sic. 4. 25. 1), disciple (Tat. *Adv. Graec.* 39), or, after his identification with Moses, teacher (in Hellenistic Jewish writers). Like Orpheus, Musaeus is said to have invented the hexameter or even the *alphabet.

Like Orpheus, Musaeus became, in the late 6th cent. BC, the exponent of apocryphal poetry; their works share some titles.

Musaeus

Among Musaeus' works are *oracles (Ar. *Ran.* 1033), collected around 500 BC by Onomacritus whom *Hipparchus (1), the son of Pisistratus, exiled for having added a forgery (Hdt. 7. 6. 3). See also DIVINATION. More important are poems which make him the chief exponent of an Attic and Eleusinian '*Orphism'. *Plato alludes to a poem (or poems) on eschatology used by 'Orphic' vagrant priests (*Resp.* 364e), later sources know a *Theogony* and a *Hymn to Demeter* used in the Attic family cult of the Lycomidae (Paus. 4. 1. 5). A vase in the Louvre depicts a young Musaeus learning epic (theological) poetry from his teacher *Linus (Beazley, *ARV*² 1254. 60), a cup in Cambridge perhaps shows Musaeus writing down the utterances of Orpheus' singing head.

See ORPHEUS; ORPHIC LITERATURE.

Testimonia in O. Kern, *Orphicorum Fragmenta* (1922). See also I. M. Linforth, *The Arts of Orpheus* (1941); F. Graf, *Eleusis und die orphische Dichtung Athens in vorhellenistischer Zeit* (1974); A. Kaufmann-Samaros, *LIMC* 6 (1992), 685–7, 'Mousaios'.   F. G.

Musaeus (2), of *Ephesus (3rd cent. BC), author of an epic *Perseis* in ten books and poems in honour of *Eumenes (1) I and *Attalus I of Pergamum. Known only from the *Suda*.   R. L. Hu.

Musaeus (3). See HERO AND LEANDER.

Muses, goddesses upon whom poets—and later other artists, philosophers, and intellectuals generally—depended for the ability to create their works. They were goddesses, not lesser immortals, not only because of their pedigree(s) and their home on *Olympus (1). They are called goddesses from the earliest sources on, and their attitude to mankind is identical to that of gods: they do not hesitate to destroy a mortal who dares to usurp their place (so *Thamyris, whom they maimed and deprived of his skill: Hom. *Il.* 2. 594–600), and they are divinely contemptuous of humankind (it does not matter to them whether the poetry they inspire is true or false: Hes. *Theog.* 26–8). Muses appear both singly and in groups of varying sizes (West, on *Theog.* 60). Homer, for example, addresses a single goddess or Muse but knows there are more (the Thamyris story). The canonical nine and their names probably originated with *Hesiod (West on *Theogony* 76). They were: Calliope (epic poetry), Clio (history), Euterpe (flute-playing), Terpsichore (lyric poetry and dancing, esp. choral), Erato (lyric poetry), Melpomene (tragedy), Thalia (comedy), Polyhymnia (hymns and pantomime), Urania (astronomy). But their names, functions, and number fluctuated.

The earliest sources locate the Muses at Pieria, just north of Olympus, and on Olympus itself; they are associated with so-called 'Thracian' bards, *Orpheus, Thamyris, and *Musaeus (1). That region appears to have been their first home. A southern group, the Muses of *Helicon, is identified by Hesiod with the Muses of Olympia and Pieria, perhaps because of an underlying connection between the two regions (compare Mt. Leibethrion and its nymphs in the Helicon massif with Leibethra in Pieria in *Macedonia), but possibly because the young poet himself saw fit to make the association as a means to enhance his own reputation (on the introduction to the *Theogony*, see Thalmann (below), 134–52).

Hesiod's influence led eventually—but possibly not before the 4th cent. BC—to the establishment of a formal cult and sanctuary below Mt. Helicon in the Vale of the Muses. This may have been the first 'Mouseion' (*Museum: it housed, in the open air, statues of both legendary and historical notables, and possibly contained an archive of poetic works), and it is not surprising that a Ptolemy (probably *Ptolemy (1) IV Philopator, whose queen *Arsinoë III

was worshipped as the Tenth Muse) was among the benefactors when part of the musical *agōn, the Mouseia, was reorganized towards the end of the 3rd cent. BC (for the Heliconian cult, see Schachter, 147–79).

Philosophers, traditionally beginning with *Pythagoras (1), adopted the Muses as their special goddesses, in some cases organizing their schools as *thiasoi under their patronage (Boyancé, esp. 229–351). From Hellenistic times they were a popular subject, individually or as a group, in sculpture (especially *sarcophagi) and *mosaics.

There is no satisfactory etymology (see Frisk and Chantraine).

P. Boyancé, *Le Culte des Muses chez les philosophes grecs* (1937); P. Chantraine, *Dictionnaire étymologique de la langue grecque* 3 (1974); H. Frisk, *Griechisches etymologisches Wörterbuch* (1963); A. Schachter, *Cults of Boiotia* 2 (1986); W. G. Thalmann, *Conventions of Form and Thought in Early Greek Epic Poetry* (1984); *LIMC* 7. 1 (1994), 991–1059.   A. Sch.

Museum (Μουσεῖον), originally a place connected with the *Muses or the arts inspired by them. *Euripides speaks of the μουσεῖα of birds, the places where they sing. When a religious meaning was attached an altar or a temple was built to mark the spot. But the predominant significance of the word was literary and educational. Thus Mt. *Helicon had a Museum containing the manuscripts of *Hesiod and statues of those who had upheld the arts (Ath. 14. 629a). Almost any school could be called 'the place of the Muses' (*Libanius). There was a Museum in *Plato (1)'s *Academy and in *Aristotle's Lyceum.

By far the most famous Museum was that of *Alexandria (1), founded by *Ptolemy (1) I Soter probably on the advice of Aristotle's famous pupil, *Demetrius (3) of Phaleron. It was distinct from the *Library. Both were near the palace, but the exact site of neither is clearly identifiable. The Museum housed a band of scholars, who were supported by a generous salary granted by the Ptolemies and later by the Caesars, who appointed a president (ἐπιστάτης) or priest (ἱερεύς) as head of the institution. If lectures were given at all, they were secondary to research, but there were many discussions in which the kings joined. Dinners or symposia (see SYMPOSIUM), illuminated by witticisms, epigrams, and the solution of problems, were frequent and characteristic. According to one source a record war kept of the solutions offered. The papyri suggest that the influence of the Museum stabilized the texts of authors, especially *Homer, and ensured that a supply of *books could reach the smaller towns. The buildings, splendidly furnished by the Ptolemies, included a communal dining-hall, an *exedra* (arcade with seats) for discussions and lectures, a *peripatos* (covered walk) planted with trees.

Circa 146 BC political upheavals caused learned men, including the great *Aristarchus (2), to flee from Alexandria, which was henceforth rivalled by *Pergamum as well as by Athens, *Rhodes, *Antioch (1), *Berytus, and Rome. The Museum suffered in reputation, but *Cleopatra VII, the last of the Ptolemies, still took part in its discussions. According to a doubtful tradition Mark Antony (M. *Antonius (2)) gave the Pergamene library to Alexandria to make up for loss by fire during Caesar's siege, 47 BC. Renewed prosperity came under the *pax Augusta*. The early emperors visited the Museum and extended its buildings, and *Hadrian bestowed special care on it. The Museum was visited by famous litterati like *Plutarch, *Dio Cocceianus, *Lucian, and *Galen. In AD 216 it suffered under the tyranny of *Caracalla. It was destroyed, after the occupation of Alexandria by *Zenobia, in 272, but seems to have resumed its activities. It is unlikely to have survived long after *Theodosius (2) I's edict of 391 requiring the destruction of pagan temples. The *Suda* gives the last member of the Museum as *Theon (4), the father of *Hypatia (c. AD 380). In the Ptolemaic period the Museum was famous for science and literary scholarship; in the 2nd cent. AD for the New Rhetoric; in the 3rd cent. for *Neoplatonism. In the 4th cent. *Ammianus Marcellinus (22. 16) reports scientific activity, but admits a decline.

E. Müller-Graupa, *RE* 16, 797–281, 'Museion'; Wilamowitz, *Hell. Dicht.* 1. 160 ff.; G. Faider-Feytmans, *Hommages à Joseph Bidez et à Franz Cumont* (1949), 97 ff.; M. El-Abbadi, *Life and Fate of the Ancient Library of Alexandria*, 2nd edn. (1992).   T. J. H.; N. G. W.

music

1. In Greek and Roman Life 'Let me not live without music', sings a chorus of greybeards in *Euripides (*HF* 676). Expressions such as 'without music', 'chorusless', 'lyreless' evoked the dreary bitterness of war, the *Erinyes' curse, or death, 'without wedding song, lyreless, chorusless, death at the end' (Soph. *OC* 1221–3). Poetic pictures of unblemished happiness are correspondingly resonant with music; and in every sort of revel and celebration, Greeks of all social classes sang, danced (see DANCING), and played instruments, besides listening to professional performances. Music was credited with divine origins and mysterious powers, and was the pivot of relations between mortals and gods. It was central to public religious observance, and to such semi-religious occasions as weddings, funerals, and harvests. At the great panhellenic *festivals (see PANHELLENISM) and their many local counterparts, choruses and vocal and instrumental soloists competed no less than athletes for prizes and glory (cf. Pind. *Pyth.* 12): these showcase occasions provided a matrix for the development of sophisticated forms of art-music, and fostered rapid stylistic elaborations and technical advances (see AGŌNES).

The best Greek soloists and composers were usually in some sense professionals, and professionals are already familiar in *Homer, though apart from *Thamyris (*Il.* 2. 594–600) they are neither competitors nor independent agents, but retainers in a noble house. In historical times poet-composers such as *Terpander, *Thaletas, and *Alcman may have been 'retained' by the public purse in Sparta, and there were eminent musicians in the retinues of 6th-cent. tyrants. Others, *Sappho for example, and many in 5th-cent. Athens, made their living as teachers. But not all public performers were professionals. Choruses of singers and dancers remained citizen-amateurs until Hellenistic times, whether in Homer's Phaeacia (see SCHERIA), in Alcman's Sparta, in Archaic *Delos, or in the dithyrambic and dramatic contests of Classical Athens (see DITHYRAMB; COMEDY (GREEK), OLD; TRAGEDY (GREEK)), and often later, even on occasion in Augustan Rome. Well-bred Greek citizens normally had a competence on an instrument (usually the lyre, sometimes the pipes) as well as in singing and choral dance. When *Achilles, the toughest of the Greek warriors, is found playing the lyre and singing in his tent (*Il.* 9. 186–9), no one is surprised. Humbler folk sang at their work, piped to their flocks, or kept time to music at their oars. Guests at the *symposium listened to girl-pipers and other hired entertainers, but also sang and played instruments. Women made music in their domestic quarters. Music, all in all, was essential to the pattern and texture of Greek life at all social levels, providing a widely available means for the expression of communal identity and values, and a focus for controversy, judgement, and partisanship in which all citizens could enthusiastically engage.

It has generally been held, perhaps rightly, that music was much less important in Roman life than in Archaic or Classical Greece. It was nevertheless indispensable at Rome to all religious rituals and civic celebrations, prominent in public theatrical performance and private merrymaking, a fully institutionalized ingredient of military activities, and a common element in the education of well-bred citizens (see EDUCATION, GREEK, § 3). Professional performers won great acclaim. There are perhaps three main reasons for its apparently less significant status. First, we are ill-informed about relations between music and poetry in early Roman times. Unlike their Greek counterparts, most surviving Latin poets belong to a period in which sophisticated poetry had emancipated itself from occasions of musical performance and was primarily designed to be spoken or read. Secondly, Roman writers on music are typically educated men with a deep respect for Hellenic culture, inclined to compare the deliberate theatricality and the cosmopolitan variousness of contemporary performance unfavourably with the supposedly pure, simple, and ethically edifying music of the Greek past (but Greeks themselves regularly made similar complaints from the 5th cent. onwards). Finally, Greek lore about music's effects on character and its distinctive role in moral education had been elaborately articulated by philosophers and theorists, and such theorizing continued through imperial times: but in whichever language they wrote, Roman intellectuals invariably related these ideas to the older Greek music, seldom reflecting on matters within their own experience. Romans seem to have thought of the musical elements in education either as a source of peripheral gentlemanly adornments, or as part of a thoroughly ungentlemanly professional training. Even where one would most expect it, in the ethical writings of the Roman Stoics (see STOICISM), there are few traces of the doctrine that musical education moulds the moral core of a citizen's dispositions and sensibilities. To most reflective Roman minds, music in their own milieu was no more than trivial entertainment, and the polemics of the Epicurean *Philodemus against Greek Stoics' and Platonists' conceptions of music's ethical significance found a ready audience (see PLATO (1)). Technical analyses of musical structures continued similarly to focus wholly on Greek models: we have only the most impressionistic accounts of the music the Romans heard. Given the state of our literary evidence, the bulk of the article is inevitably devoted to Greek music, and says rather little about Rome.

2. The Evidence Our knowledge of Greek and Roman music comes from seven main sources. (*a*) A number of Greek musical scores survive: most are fragmentary, and almost all date from the Hellenistic period or later. (*b*) We have remnants of various instruments: the majority are reed-blown pipes, some quite well preserved (for a list see West, *Anc. Gr. Mus.* 1992 (in bibliog. below), 97–8). Conclusions can be drawn about their tuning, but the loss of the reeds leaves inevitable uncertainties. There are also some percussion instruments, relatively uninformative fragments of several lyres and a *hydraulis* ('water organ'), and parts of the frames and some tuning-pins from stringed instruments of uncertain type, excavated in a Greek context in Anatolia. Most of our information about instruments comes from sources of other kinds. (*c*) There are abundant non-technical references to music in ancient literature, shedding light on the practice of music, its social roles and perceived aesthetic qualities. The works of poets and philosophers are especially rich in musical allusions, though their remarks can be hard to interpret. Poetry carries with it other traces of its own musical performance, particularly in pitch-accent and rhythm. Essays more centrally concerned with the nature and history of musical practice are few but crucial: the most important are some passages of *Athenaeus (1), and the pseudo-*Plutarchan dialogue *De musica*. (*d*) Inscriptions and certain other non-literary documents give occasional evidence about the economics and institutional organization of music, recording such things as prizes awarded, fees paid, or details of the affairs of a musicians' guild (see DIONYSUS, ARTISTS OF). (*e*) Greek technical treatises in musical theory offer analyses of melodic and rhythmic structures. These give the clearest insights we have into the formal characteristics of ancient music, though their scope is admittedly limited, and we cannot assume that theory was always a faithful reflection of practice. Technical issues are also addressed on occasion by philosophers, scientists, and mathematicians. (*f*) Musical subjects are often depicted in painting and sculpture, giving valuable information about instruments and the manner and contexts of their performance: more tentative conclusions can be drawn about the artists' conceptions of the atmosphere and significance of various musical occasions. (*g*) Finally, and with great caution, we may draw upon the resources of ethnomusicology for comparisons with other cultures relatively untouched by later western music.

3. *Instruments* Through contact with their neighbours, especially in the east, the Greeks knew of many kinds of instrument; yet they made substantial use of only two main sorts, lyres and αὐλοί (pipes). The reasons are obscure. Rome was more accommodating, but even so the same families of instrument remained predominant.

1. Strings

All ancient stringed instruments were plucked with the fingers or struck with a plectrum: the bow is a much later invention.

(*a*) Instruments of the lyre family have two arms, joined by a crossbar, fixed to a soundbox in roughly the plane of its face. (In Greece the arms were always of equal length: evidence of the asymmetrical lyres common in the middle east is occasionally found in Rome.) Strings are stretched from the crossbar over a bridge on the face of the box, and secured near its base. There are two main subgroups, bowl-lyres and box-lyres.

Bowl-lyres are principally represented in Greece by the *lyra* proper (λύρα or χέλυς). Its soundbox was a tortoiseshell, or perhaps sometimes wood, shaped and painted to resemble one. A thin sheet of hide fixed across the opening formed the face and supported the bridge. The arms were sticks curved like horns (horns may sometimes have been used): its manufacture is described in the *Homeric *Hymn to Hermes*. Like all Greek lyres it was usually played with a large plectrum, made of horn, bone, or wood. It was the prime instrument of education in Classical times, and was used everywhere for amateur music-making: its tone was too light for serious public performance. A variant, the *barbitos*, appeared during the 6th cent. BC and was common in the 5th, differing only in its longer, differently shaped arms. The pitch must have been lower, but its soundbox was no bigger and it cannot have supported much tension or been capable of much volume. Vase-paintings link it with Sappho and *Alcaeus (1), but most commonly with male revellers and satyrs.

Box-lyres, whose soundbox is wooden and has sides distinct from the back and face, appear much earlier than the tortoiseshell instrument in art and literature. Quite elaborate versions are shown in Minoan and Mycenaean painting (see MINOAN and MYCENAEAN CIVILIZATION), simpler ones in geometric art. The *phorminx* of Homeric epic was of this simple type. To judge from the statuettes and paintings, it was heavily built: its box was convex at the bottom, straight or concave at the top, and its back was probably rounded. The arms were strong and usually straight.

Late in the 7th cent. BC, apparently after a period of experimentation, the great *kithara* that became the major instrument of professional and public performance first appears in art. The base of the much enlarged box is flat, the straight sides angled outwards: the back bulges along its vertical axis. On the box, at least, no sound-holes are shown. At the upper corners the box tapers into curved, horn-shaped extensions, connecting with the arms at narrow, delicate, elaborately supported junctions. The arms are broad and rectangular: the crossbar extends outwards beyond them, usually ending in circular or elliptical bosses. The bridge is wide, and raised on four feet. At the base, the strings are fixed to a solid rectangular tailpiece, or to a bar. This striking design was evidently successful: it remained largely unchanged for 200 years. Debates continue about the significance of the devices at the junction of box and arms. One hypothesis posits a complex arrangement of movable parts and springs, designed to tighten or relax the whole structure (e.g. Paquette 1984). Alternatively, the narrow junction serves to isolate vibrations in the upper and lower parts of the instrument (e.g. Wegner 1949). Possibly the arms were subsidiary soundboxes, the spirals at their bases concealing sound-holes. Something similar appears on a third type of box-lyre, now called the 'cradle *kithara*', which appears between the late 6th cent. and the late 5th. It is much smaller, and unlike the concert *kithara* is often played by women. It is evidently a development of the old *phorminx*. The box has a convex base and concave top: the back seems to be flat. The arms are certainly hollow, with sound-holes near the bottom; and though the junction between them and the box lacks the elaboration of the larger instrument, they are always set in from the line of the box's sides, touching the box only at one corner of their bases. The separation of resonating chambers is obvious and seems deliberate. A few other forms of box-lyre were used in Classical times (e.g. the 'Thamyris *kithara*'); but the big *kithara* described above remained unchallenged for serious purposes until around 400 BC, when a new type with rectangular box and straight arms appeared, becoming predominant in the 4th cent. and remaining so, with modifications, into the imperial period. On *kitharai* in Roman sculptures, and in some earlier depictions of lyres, the arms curve forwards. Quite probably this was so also on the classical *kithara*, but Greek artists never successfully portrayed that instrument in profile.

(*b*) No other kinds of stringed instrument found a major niche in Greek music-making. Several types of harps were known: literary evidence associates them with composers of Archaic lyric, but we know them principally from paintings of the late 5th and 4th cent., BC where they are always played by women. The names *trigōnos*, *psaltērion*, *pēktis* and perhaps *magadis* belong to harps. A three-stringed, lutelike instrument, the *pandoura*, is occasionally mentioned and represented in art. All other stringed instruments were variants on these types.

Strings were made of gut or sinew, sometimes flax. Early lyres probably had only four strings: from the 7th cent. BC through Classical times the standard number was seven or eight, though 5th-cent. innovators made a few additions (harps had many more). Devices for adjusting the strings' tension (κόλλοπες) were originally strips of hide wound with the string round the crossbar to form a roll: levers were sometimes bound into the roll to facilitate tuning. Tuning-pins with triangular heads, probably turned with a separate key, are sometimes shown on Roman sculptures: the Anatolian remains suggest a Greek origin, perhaps in the 4th cent. Classical paintings seem to depict several kinds of device, but there is little agreement on their interpretation. Strings on lyres and harps were normally not stopped, but sounded open. Harps were plucked with the fingers, lyres usually struck with a plectrum: several strings could be struck in a single sweep, while the left hand's fingers damped those not intended to sound.

2. Wind

(a) The pipe called αὐλός in Greece, *tibia* in Rome, was common throughout the Mediterranean. Despite the usual mistranslation it was not a flute, but was sounded with a reed. Both double reeds (akin to those of oboes and shawms) and single or 'beating' reeds (as on the clarinet) were apparently known: the issue has been much disputed, but double reeds probably predominated at all periods. The body of the instrument was a cylindrical tube, equipped with finger-holes. The reed was inserted into a separate, short, bulbous section (ὅλμος), fitted in turn into the top of the tube, sometimes with a second ὅλμος in between. A cloth band (φορβειά) around the player's head and face was sometimes used to support the cheeks. These pipes were normally played in pairs, one fingered by each hand. The musical function of this practice is uncertain, and probably varied. Where each pipe had few finger-holes they might supplement each other's scale. Some evidence suggests the use of a drone. There are hints also of both antiphony and rudimentary harmony (especially [Plut.] *De mus.* 1137b–d). The pipes were most often equal in length, but in 'Phrygian' *auloi* (*tibiae impares*) the left-hand pipe was longer and ended in a bell. They varied in size and pitch: *Aristoxenus classifies them by pitch into five types. Early *auloi* had between three and five finger-holes. We have remains of several with six, where one is presumably a vent. Later instruments might have many more (up to 24 on surviving examples). Such an instrument could modulate between several different scales, holes not currently in use being closed with rotating metal collars: the development is credited to the Theban aulete Pronomus around 400 BC. The conclusions of Schlesinger (1939) about scales played on *auloi* have been modified in the light of more recent work, especially on the archaeological remains; but the problems are complicated by the fact that the placing of finger-holes is by no means the only determinant of pitch. Pipe music was emotionally stirring, capable of a wide range of expressive and dramatic effects. It was used in many religious contexts, in drama and other forms of choral performance, at weddings, symposia and revels generally, and in a multitude of other contexts: it was the principal instrument of Dionysiac cult and the mystery religions (see DIONYSUS; MYSTERIES). Conservative social theorists and educationalists disapproved of its mimetic and emotional versatility. It is banned from Plato's ideal city (*Resp.* 399d), and on *Aristotle's view citizens may listen to it but not learn to play it, for it is not a 'moral' instrument (*Pol.* 1341ᵃ).

(b) Several other wind instruments were known. The σῦριγξ πολυκάλαμος is the familiar pan-pipe, sounded by blowing across the ends of the tubes. The Greek variety had pipes of equal length, plugged to different depths with wax to create different notes: the stepped form is Etruscan and Roman. It was best known in rustic settings, but appears often elsewhere in informal music-making. The σῦριγξ μονοκάλαμος, a single, end-blown flute with finger-holes, is found occasionally from the 4th cent. BC onwards, as are side-blown flutes (probably indicated by the words πλαγίαυλος and φῶτιγξ). Bagpipes were known in both Greece and Italy from the 2nd cent. BC, perhaps earlier. The ὕδραυλις, an organ whose pumped air-supply was converted into a steady flow hydraulically, was invented by the engineer *Ctesibius of Alexandria in the 3rd cent. BC, and became very popular in Rome. Its pipes were generally flues. The hydraulic mechanism was replaced, perhaps in the 2nd cent. AD, by a bag inflated by bellows and subjected to pressure. Some organs of the late Roman empire were impressively large and loud. Instruments of the brass family were used primarily for signalling, in the army and at the games: the Roman army had an extensive repertoire of such signals, and the instruments were used also for ceremonial fanfares. A straight type (σάλπιγξ) with a narrow cylindrical bore and a small bell was the commonest in Greece, though a curved form (κέρας) was known: Romans used both straight (*tuba*) and curved (*cornu*) varieties, both with conical bores, and the *lituus*, of *Etruscan origin, which was straight and cylindrical but sharply curved upwards at its bell.

3. Percussion

Greeks used percussion instruments in light entertainment and revelry, and especially in the more exotic kinds of cult. Wooden clappers (κρόταλα), analogous to castanets but larger and differently shaped, small cymbals, and hand-held drums (τύμπανα) like tambourines (but without jingles) are much the commonest. The sistrum, originally Egyptian, appears in some post-Classical Greek paintings and was well known at Rome.

4. History Elegant marble statuettes from the *Cyclades and paintings from Minoan Crete and Mycenaean Greece hint at cultivated musical skills in very early times. Folk music and dance, and informal singing, were no doubt common too, as in the background of Homer's world. In Homer the one specialized, professional musician is the minstrel who sings epic lays to his *phorminx*, accompanied, in one episode (*Od.* 8. 246–65) by a dancing chorus. Later Greeks thought of sophisticated art-music as originating in the east. The development of *kitharōidia* (the art of singing to one's own stringed accompaniment) in the context of the competitive festivals was associated with *Terpander, who came from *Lesbos to Sparta (then a major cultural and artistic centre) perhaps as early as 680 BC: Terpander won victories at the *Carnea, and four times at the *Pythian Games. Many innovations were later attributed to him, most notably the establishment of a canon of set pieces known as citharodic *nomoi*; and the citharodes of Lesbos were the recognized masters for several generations. (*Nomoi*, at least in 5th-cent. and later Greek usage, were solo pieces whose formal and stylistic outlines were regulated and distinguished by fixed rules, not unnaturally in a competitive setting. See NOMOS (2).) The art of the *aulos* was said to have been brought to Greece by the Phrygian Olympus: he may be legendary, but pieces attributed to him survived in Aristotle's time. Aulodic *nomoi*, sung to a piper's accompaniment, were reputedly 'established' by a certain Clonas, roughly contemporary with Terpander. Auletic *nomoi*, for pipes without the voice, were performed at *Delphi from the early 6th cent.: they included the famous *Pythikos nomos*, a piece of programme music representing the battle between *Apollo and the Python, whose most distinguished performer was Sacadas of *Argos (2). Instrumental solos for *kithara*, citharistic *nomoi*, were also sometimes performed. Later writers assert that all this virtuosic music, indeed all significant music up to the early 5th cent., was composed and performed (often by its composer) in a simple, unornamented melodic style, using relatively few notes and no modulations; and each type of piece had its own clearly distinct form and character. It is clear nevertheless that 6th-cent. musicians pioneered major stylistic and technical developments. Innovations in the structure and use of instruments and the relation between soloists and choruses, and experiments with the forms of compositions, were credited especially to musicians in the northern Peloponnese (see PELOPONNESUS). Novel melodic styles were attributed also to Sappho and other Archaic composers of lyrical monody. The jewel-like art-songs of these composers and the massive pieces of *Stesichorus, for example, however significant their backgrounds in folk-song and epic respectively, self-evidently embody sophisticated and original conceptions of musical form.

Choral lyric, an indissoluble blend of poetry, melody, accompaniment and, dance, was already an admired art in the 7th cent., notably in Sparta and at the Delian festivals; competition was endemic and essential in this genre too (see particularly Alcman fr. 1 *PMG*, and the *Homeric Hymn to Apollo*). We hear of many types: the story of the two that later achieved highest status, *dithyramb and *tragedy, cannot be retold here. Both originated in the singing and dancing of choruses to the *auloi*, which always remained the accompanying instrument: the dialogue of drama perhaps grew out of interchanges between the chorus and its leader. Other choral genres, such as paeans, maiden-songs, and victory-songs, were often accompanied by a *kithara*, sometimes by *aulos* and *kithara* together (but the question whether *Pindar's victory-songs were indeed choral, or were solo pieces prefacing choral singing, is now the subject of lively dispute). Poet-composers of the late 6th and early 5th cents.—*Lasus, *Pratinas, Pindar, *Simonides, and others—were often self-consciously reflective about their art: traces of various musical controversies survive, and Lasus is said to have written the first treatise on music. Pindar repeatedly proclaims himself a musical innovator (e.g. *Ol.* 3. 4–6, fr. 61 Snell–Maehler). But to moralists from Aristophanes (1) onwards, their period marks the pinnacle of the ancient, simple, educative, and edifying style: afterwards there is nothing but decline into theatricality and populism. As the 5th cent. progressed, melodies came to be embroidered with ornaments and turns, both in the vocal line and independently in its accompaniment. Modulations between scale-systems, facilitated by developments in instruments (more finger-holes on *auloi*, added strings on the *kithara*) became common, undermining old links between genre and musical structure. Traditionally distinct genres, such as *kitharōidia* and choral dithyramb, began to merge into new and indeterminate forms. Technical expertise and startling dramatic effect were untiringly pursued: star instrumentalists and singers were idolized by the public, and like their modern counterparts enhanced their musical acts with striking costumes and histrionic bodily movements. Whereas previously the sense, rhythm, and cadence of the words had dictated their musical interpretation, now they were progressively subordinated to musical ideas worked out in their own terms and for their own sake. These developments spelled the downfall of an integrated art closely allied to religion and civic tradition; but it also meant the emancipation of pure music from ritual and, crucially, from poetry, which came gradually to be seen as a separate art. This musical revolution went hand in hand with the radical political and social changes of the later 5th cent., and with the individualistic, questioning modes of thought exemplified in the sophists and Socrates. The main names associated with it are Phrynis, *Melanippides (2), *Cinesias, *Philoxenus (1), and especially *Timotheus (1): Cinesias and other purveyors of the 'new music', including *Agathon and Euripides, are regularly pilloried by *Aristophanes (1). The Theban school of auletes (see THEBES (1)), notably Pronomus and Antigenidas, achieved astonishing new levels of technical virtuosity and emotional expression.

The new music met with resistance not only from Aristophanes and Plato. A 4th-cent. source paraphrased at [Plut.] *De mus.*

1137–8 lists a string of musicians who deliberately rejected the elaborate styles and theatrical tricks of Timotheus in favour of older and severer forms. But as always in musical history, the new music gradually became old hat. The subtle nuances of intonation and the complex modulations characteristic of Timothean music came to seem heavy and 'classical' in their turn, and were supplanted by straightforward diatonic progressions lightly flavoured with chromaticism. The vogue in the late 4th cent. was for saccharine melodies and medleys of popular tunes without rhythmic or structural interest—or so the critics asserted. But in Hellenistic times, what passed for the music of Euripides, Timotheus, and others was still performed, though commonly as excerpts, 'concert arias', shorn of their context; and the religious music of the Delphic *paeans (2nd cent. BC) shows persisting allegiance to the older styles. Greek writings of the imperial period show that theorists still perceived the structures of contemporary music as continuous with those of the past, and the surviving scores broadly confirm this. We hear of few innovative composers after the 4th cent.: thereafter the emphasis is always on great performers, playing variations on a standard repertoire.

Professional musicians existed from early times, not all of them eminent composers or performers. There was a steady demand for instrumental accompanists, chorus-trainers, elementary teachers, and other hacks. Pipe-girls and other entertainers hired to perform at symposia were professionals too, in their way, relying on music for a living: a number of them might form a 'troupe' run by an enterprising impresario (see Xen. *Symp.* 2. 1). Fourth-century Greece teemed with professionals of one sort and another, many of them second-rate (see e.g. the anecdotes about *Stratonicus at Ath. 347f–352d). During the subsequent 500 years the profession flourished, with rich opportunities provided by the proliferating festivals, by royal, proconsular, and imperial patronage, and by the public's insatiable appetite for theatrical entertainment in *Alexandria (1), Rome, and other major centres. Early in the 3rd cent. BC musicians and other performing artists began to band together in guilds—the so-called artists of Dionysus. In Rome there were guilds for particular categories of musician. The *collegium tibicinum* ('guild of pipe-players'), for instance, was allegedly founded in the reign of Numa *Pompilius: Livy (9. 30) records a strike by its members in 311 BC.

Of the historical development of Roman music we know little in detail, but its cultural importance is indisputable. Despite much pious condemnation of music and musicians, high-class Romans generally arranged musical instruction for their children: their teachers were normally slaves. Women were expected to be competent domestic performers. Well-born girls and boys, trained by *Horace, sang at the Ludi saeculares (*Secular Games) of 17 BC. At the professional level, brass-players were essential to the military machine, their signals used for innumerable purposes (e.g. Cass. Dio 47. 43. 1 ff.). Pipe-players (*tibicines*), supposedly of Etruscan origin, always attended the rituals of sacrifice and libation, occasionally joined by performers on brass or lyre. Ancient indigenous rites included the strange songs of the *fratres arvales* and the ferocious war-dances of the *Salii, who swarmed twice a year through the streets singing and leaping to the sound of pipes, lyres, and percussion. Pipes and brass instruments were regularly played in funeral processions. The many foreign cults adopted in Rome brought their music with them. *Isis, for instance, was worshipped in daily hymns with pipes and sistra, and at an annual festival where the *Osiris story was recounted in song and represented in dance. Pipes, cymbals, hand-drums, and ecstatic dancing were characteristic of Bacchic ritual, as in Greece; see BACCHANALIA; DIONYSUS; MAENADS. Musicians were most fully at the centre of attention, however, in the various manifestations of public entertainment. In Plautine comedy (see PLAUTUS), an overture was played on the pipes, and there were interval performances of piping and dancing. Both comedies and tragedies included set-piece songs, often excerpted for the concert platform. *Pantomime, whose executants won great fame in the early empire, was essentially dramatic solo dance, with a chorus and piper, and sometimes other instruments too. In the romantic and comic *mime, the actors sang and danced accompanied by pipes, brass, and percussion. Non-dramatic entertainments included large-scale 'orchestral' concerts (Sen. *Ep.* 84. 9) and performances in the amphitheatres by exotic musicians and dancers. Trumpets and later the *hydraulis* sounded an accompaniment to gladiatorial combat (see GLADIATORS). Solo recitals by pipe-players and citharodes were common: *Nero and *Domitian organized competitive festivals. Small groups of musicians entertained guests in wealthy households: streets and taverns were alive with buskers. Most musicians were of modest social class, but the best, whatever their origins, attained extraordinary wealth and prestige: the spectacular case of the piper and singer Tigellius is particularly well documented from *Cicero's letters and Horace *Sat.* 1. 2, 3.

5. Theory, philosophy, and science

People described as μουσικοί, *musici*, are often not musicians but students of musical theory and philosophy. The usage owes much to Plato, but its roots are earlier. Music became the object of abstract thought in the context of three related enterprises: (*a*) investigations into the mathematical aspects of musical phenomena; (*b*) philosophical studies of the effects of music on character and its role in education; and (*c*) the empirically based project of analysing and systematizing the structures underlying musical compositions themselves.

(*a*) Early Pythagoreans (see PYTHAGORAS (1)) were struck by correspondences between relations in two apparently distinct domains, musical and mathematical. They observed that when a stretched string was divided by a bridge so that its two segments yielded notes in the fundamental musical relations of octave, fifth, and fourth, the ratios of lengths formed the simple, orderly series 2:1, 3:2, 4:3. They inferred that all genuinely musical relations correspond to elegant mathematical formulae and are governed by intelligible mathematical principles; and since music is a paradigm of harmonious order, they sought to describe the ordering of the whole cosmos and of the soul in terms of similar numerical relations and principles. *Philolaus (late 5th cent.) gave a complete mathematical analysis of the diatonic octave, allied to speculations about cosmic *harmonia* (DK 44 B 6). Plato, besides providing (in *Resp.* 10) the first extant account of the 'harmony of the spheres', insisted that the proper business of harmonic science is with the mathematical principles governing harmonious systems of numbers, not with the imperfections of human musical practice (*Resp.* 531c). Musical beauty is just the reflection, in one perceptible domain, of an ordering that is essentially formal and mathematical. Harmonics became the fifth and highest of the mathematical disciplines in the philosopher's intellectual curriculum. Plato apparently believed he had found the key principle. In an influential passage of the *Timaeus* (34b–36d) he uses the ratios of a musical attunement to describe the structure of the soul of the universe. The attunement is essentially identical with that of Philolaus, but Plato finds a basis for it

in a sophisticated theory of means and proportions. This theory was the brainchild of his Pythagorean contemporary *Archytas, who used it to underpin his own analysis of three distinct scale systems (see Ptol. *Harm.* 1. 13, 14, 2. 14), all quite different from Plato's ideal attunement. Unlike Plato, Archytas evidently intended his analyses and mathematical explanations to apply to the attunements of real musical practice; but he also made important advances in strictly mathematical aspects of the subject. The purely rationalistic approach reappears in the Euclidean *Sectio canonis* (see EUCLID), and later in the works of *Nicomachus (3), *Theon (2) and many others, often associated with wider metaphysical speculations: it was transmitted to the Middle Ages through *Boethius. An impressive development of the Archytan project is found in *Ptolemy (4)'s *Harmonics*, which seeks both to derive the structures of musical attunements from mathematical principles, and to confirm by experiment on specially contrived instruments that these theoretical results matched those accepted in practice by the ear. Such researches were regularly associated with investigations in the science of *acoustics, also pioneered by Archytas (DK 47 B 1), designed primarily to explain the phenomenon of pitch in physical terms amenable to quantification within a theory of ratio.

(*b*) It was widely believed in 5th-cent. Greece that music affects moral *character; that music of different styles and structures affects it differently; that appropriate musical training is essential to a citizen's education; and that music of the 'wrong' sort is morally and socially pernicious. Such ideas are regularly taken for granted in Aristophanes. They were first deliberately articulated by the Athenian sophist and musicologist *Damon (2). Plato draws explicitly on his work when he bans from his ideal city ethically unsuitable rhythmic and melodic forms, on the grounds that they represent inappropriate or excessive emotions, and that the tendency of all music is to mould the structure of the listener's *soul in its own image. Only those melodic forms that represent and engender courage (Dorian) and moderation (Phrygian) are permitted. Also outlawed are instruments, including *auloi* and many-stringed harps, designed to modulate readily between 'ethically' distinct musical structures (*Resp.* 397a–400e). Plato applauds Damon's view that changes in musical styles invariably lead to change in fundamental political laws and social customs (*Resp.* 424c). Detailed plans for the ethical and social training of citizens through music, and critiques of contemporary musical practice, are elaborated in the *Laws* (653c–673a, 700a–701b, 795a–812e). Perhaps the most thoughtful discussion of the subject is Aristotle's (*Pol.* 1339^a–1342^b). He considers carefully the grounds for claims about music's powers and functions, the reasons why citizens should not only listen to music but learn to perform it (though not to professional levels), the emotional and ethical characteristics of instruments, melodic and rhythmic structures, and much else. While more pragmatic in approach than Plato, and more ready to value music for non-moral reasons too, he nevertheless agrees that different rhythms and melodies are representations (μιμήματα) of different ethical characters, and have corresponding effects on the listener's soul. Plato offers only veiled hints about the way in which relations between musical and psychic character might be analysed mathematically, and Aristotle is silent on the issue; but later writers often argue and speculate about it in some detail. *Aristides Quintilianus, for example, after a fascinating discussion of musical ethics and education in *De musica* 2, devotes the bulk of book 3 to mathematical and numerological analyses of musical, psychic, and cosmic structures, and of the relations between them: analogous computations appear in the third book of Ptolemy's *Harmonics*, and in many other sources. Certain writers, however, notably the Epicurean *Philodemus (see EPICURUS) in his *De musica*, argued that the conception of music as possessing moral attributes and influencing character is baseless and wholly mistaken.

(*c*) Not all studies of musical structures were mathematical in the Pythagorean style. The musical ear does not hear an interval or measure it as a ratio between quantities, but as something more like a distance on a linear continuum. Given an identifiable auditory 'measure' of such distance, one may seek to analyse patterns of attunement and their interrelations in language that reflects more directly the listener's experience. Attempts at such analyses, based on painstaking empirical attention to the audible phenomena, began towards the end of the 5th cent.: their pioneering authors perhaps deserved better than Plato's ridicule (*Resp.* 531a–b) and the waspish criticisms of Aristoxenus. But Aristoxenus, in his writings on rhythmics and especially on harmonics, is indisputably the giant of this musicological tradition. His account of the elements of melody, their organization into systems, and the relations between systems of different sorts is a colossal achievement, and the principal source of our knowledge of Greek musical structures. Though it lacks the mathematical precision of the Pythagorean approach, it is incomparably richer in musical content; and though it demands system and order where practice was probably more erratic, its claims to reflect the framework within which Greek composers worked should be taken seriously. Analysis of the surviving scores does much to confirm its credentials.

6. *Melodic Structure* Greek music was primarily melodic, and the science of harmonics was concerned with the structures underlying melodies, not with 'harmony' in our sense. A lyre, for instance, cannot play an acceptable melody with its strings tuned at random. Harmonics seeks to analyse patterns of attunement and the features distinguishing them from uncoordinated jumbles of pitches, and to identify relations between patterns of different kinds. The following account sets out from Aristoxenus: earlier systems and later variants will be discussed briefly at the end.

Tetrachords and genera

The relations fundamental to any scale or attunement were the concords (συμφωνίαι), octave, fifth, and fourth (no smaller or intermediate intervals were conceived as concordant). According to Aristoxenus, every extended system is essentially a sequence of tetrachords, groups of four notes spanning the interval of a fourth. The notes bounding any tetrachord are fixed (ἑστῶτες) in relation to one another. The two notes between them, however, can vary in position: they are 'moving' notes (κινούμενοι). The different 'genera' of attunement are defined by the way these notes, particularly the higher, are related to the tetrachord's boundaries. Three genera were recognized. In diatonic, the highest interval in the tetrachord is no greater than the other two together. When it is greater, the two lower intervals jointly constitute a πυκνόν (a 'compressed' group of intervals: the distinction between πυκνά and larger structures falls approximately where modern sensibilities distinguish a 'wide' tone from a 'narrow' minor third). Tetrachords containing πυκνά are of either chromatic or enharmonic genus. An enharmonic tetrachord may be conceived either as one whose two lowest intervals constitute the smallest possible scalar steps, or as one whose highest interval is the largest that can be grasped as a single step. Between this extreme and the diatonic all tetrachordal divisions are chromatic. Aristoxenus held that

though the range within which each moving note can fall has determinate limits, it can fall on any of indefinitely many points between them: hence each genus has indefinitely many variants or 'shades' (χροαί). But he identifies six as especially familiar. The intervals of their tetrachords, measured in tones and reading from the lowest upwards, are these.

Tense (σύντονον) diatonic	½	1	1
Soft (μαλακόν) diatonic	½	¾	1¼
Tonic (τονιαῖον) chromatic	½	½	1½
Hemiolic (ἡμιόλιον) chromatic	⅜	⅜	1¾
Soft (μαλακόν) chromatic	⅓	⅓	1⅚
Enharmonic	¼	¼	2

Greek melodies plainly embraced many intervals that later western music has lost. Followers of Aristoxenus never disputed these quantifications: they usually treated the first, third, and sixth as fundamental. The tetrachordal divisions proposed by 'Pythagorean' theorists, however, commonly differ significantly both from Aristoxenus and from one another (see especially Ptol. *Harm.* 2. 14). As Aristoxenus himself explicitly recognized, practice was in these respects quite variable.

Extended systems and species of the octave

Tetrachords linked to form larger structures may be conjoined (συνημμένα), sharing a note as their common boundary, or disjoined (διεζευγμένα), separated by the interval of a tone. Aristoxenus' contention that every note in a system must stand either in the concord of a fourth to the fourth note (inclusive) from it or in that of a fifth to the fifth note reflects these two possibilities, and entails also that every tetrachord in a system is divided identically. An octave can be made up of two tetrachords and a tone, taken in any order, or by two complementary part-tetrachords with a tetrachord and a tone between them: thus notes covering an octave, in any one genus, can be variously arranged. Fifth-century analyses of attunements span no more than (roughly) an octave: neither the range of any one instrument nor the compass of any one melody is likely to have exceeded these limits. Aristoxenus and all later writers relate their attunements to a system spanning two octaves. This does not reflect a sudden widening of melodic compass: rather, the system was designed as a framework within which every octave-attunement could be located simultaneously. This structure, the Greater Perfect System (GPS), is set out below, with the names of 'fixed' notes capitalized.

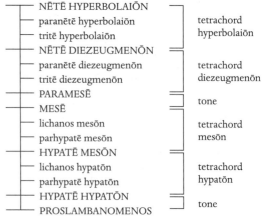

Within the GPS, taken in any genus, every possible form or 'species' of an octave made up as described above is represented.

There are seven: they can be found by taking the intervals upwards through an octave from each of seven successive notes in turn. Thus in Aristoxenus' tense diatonic, the sequence of intervals from *hypatē hypatōn* upwards is ½, 1, 1, ½, 1, 1, 1; from *parhypatē hypatōn* it is 1, 1, ½, 1, 1, 1, ½, and so on: the last member of the set begins on *mesē* (the sequence from *proslambanomenos* is identical). Each species constitutes a different way in which an attunement can be formed using the intervals of a single genus. These seven attunements took the old title *harmoniai*. Their representation in this form is due to 5th-cent. theorists: the original *harmoniai* of musical practice were less systematically related (see 'Before and after Aristoxenus', below). Along with the general title they inherited the ethnic names of the earlier attunements: that beginning on *hypatē hypatōn* is Mixolydian, the next is Lydian, then Phrygian, Dorian, Hypolydian, Hypophrygian, Hypodorian (the names are assigned differently in medieval modal theory).

From harmoniai to tonoi

Each octave attunement can be conceived as projected onto a central range between the 5th and 12th of 15 positions in the double octave. When the *harmonia* in this range is Dorian (regularly treated as basic), the sequence of its notes and intervals is the same as that in the corresponding part of the GPS: note 5, for instance, is still *hypatē mesōn*. But when it is e.g. Phrygian, note 5 becomes *lichanos hypatōn*, and the series of notes in the GPS has moved upwards by one position. This situation may be thought of in two ways. On one conception, the number of notes above and below the central octave remains constant. The sequence of notes and intervals that would overshoot one end of that range in non-Dorian *harmoniai* is relocated at the other end, *proslambanomenos* and *nētē hyperbolaiōn* being treated as equivalent. All the two-octave systems to which the *harmoniai* belong thus occupy the same range, but their interval-sequences differ: they are in effect different species of the double octave. Alternatively, each *harmonia* is part of a two-octave system following the normal course of the GPS from *proslambanomenos* to *nētē hyperbolaiōn*. Then each system contains the same sequence of intervals but starts at a different pitch, and the complete set covers a range of nearly three octaves. It begins to look like an organization of keys. However musically important distinctions between octave-species still were in Aristoxenus' time, distinctions of key were rapidly overtaking them. The two-octave systems containing the *harmoniai* are called *tonoi*; and to project every *harmonia* onto the same range only seven are needed. But Aristoxenus devised a set of thirteen *tonoi*, identical in structure and arranged a semitone apart, so that the distance between the lowest *proslambanomenos* and the highest was an octave. Their Aristoxenian names, from lowest to highest, are these: Hypodorian, low Hypophrygian, high Hypophrygian, low Hypolydian, high Hypolydian, Dorian, low Phrygian, high Phrygian, low Lydian, high Lydian, low Mixolydian, high Mixolydian, Hypermixolydian. The names evidently reflect the scheme's original connection with the seven *harmoniai*. Where we find high and low variants, one of them has been inserted in the process of filling out the semitonal series: Hypermixolydian merely completes the octave. Later a different set of names appears: Hypodorian, Hypoionian, Hypophrygian, Hypoaeolian, Hypolydian, Dorian, Ionian, Phrygian, Aeolian, Lydian, Hyperdorian, Hyperionian, Hyperphrygian, above which are added two more, Hyperaeolian and Hyperlydian. This scheme presents five basic *tonoi* in the centre, each with its 'hypo' and 'hyper' versions at the interval of a fourth below and above. No connection with

the octave-species remains, and the scheme appears quite artificial. As Ptolemy argues (*Harm.* 2. 7–11), even the thirteenth *tonos*, at an octave from the first, has little musical significance: the fourteenth and fifteenth have none at all. Ptolemy holds also that key-relations as such are musically trivial, significant only when bringing different octave-species into play. This entails a return to a system of just seven *tonoi*. Nevertheless the scheme of fifteen *tonoi* persisted: each is separately represented, for instance, in Alypius' notational tables. The main purpose of any system of *tonoi* was to clarify the relations involved in modulation, whether between octave-species or between keys. Modulations were reckoned smoother where more notes and intervals in the two attunements coincided; and by this criterion the best modulations are between *tonoi* separated by a concordant interval (Cleonides *Eisagoge* 13). Others are possible, but progressively more startling. The comprehensive system of *tonoi* thus provides a map of the most natural routes between species or keys, and also a means of judging just how aesthetically unsettling any given modulation would be. Aristoxenus' reconstruction of these relations was perhaps in its time an unrealistically systematic *tour de force*: previous practice had been chaotic and little understood (*Harm.* 37. 8–38. 5). Many theorists, Aristoxenus included, recognized another structure, the Lesser Perfect System (LPS), alongside the GPS. The two are identical over the first octave; but at *mesē*, instead of proceeding through a disjunctive tone to the tetrachord *diezeugmenōn*, the LPS adds a further tetrachord in conjunction, the tetrachord *synēmmenōn*, at the top of which it ends.

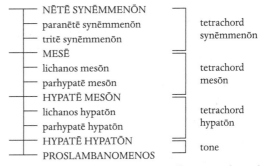

The system may reflect the structure of an ancient heptachord attunement (from *hypatē mesōn* to *nētē synēmmenōn*) of which we occasionally hear. From the 4th cent., however, GPS and LPS were conceived as variants within a single structure, whose series of notes and intervals branched into alternative routes at *mesē*. They were often combined in a composite representation, known as the Unmodulating System. As both theorists and scores make clear, modulations between a disjoined and a conjoined tetrachord above *mesē* were so common and natural that they were felt as possibilities equally inherent in the same scalar framework. In fact, as Ptolemy argues (*Harm.* 2. 6), the LPS is otiose: the shift from the disjunct to the conjunct tetrachord can be straightforwardly understood as a modulation of *tonos* through a fourth, where the pitch of *mesē* in the first *tonos* is occupied by *hypatē mesōn* in the second.

Before and after Aristoxenus

The evidence of later writers and surviving scores shows that Aristoxenian analyses remained intellectually and musically relevant for nearly a millennium. Certainly there were changes. Already in Aristoxenus' time the enharmonic genus, central to much 5th-cent. practice, was shifting towards the chromatic, and it eventually disappeared, except from textbooks. By the 2nd cent. AD, according to Ptolemy, even the chromatic had lost ground; only a form very close to the diatonic survived in common practice. It had also become normal for differently divided tetrachords to appear in the same attunement (*Harm.* 1. 16, 2. 16). Some scores interpolate extra notes into Aristoxenian structures, or use anomalously formed tetrachords: a few late specimens suggest that the tetrachordal framework itself was beginning to break down. But beneath these variations the old structures survived: there was no revolution.

The relation between Aristoxenus' analyses and earlier music is more obscure. In the 7th cent. the space between notes a fourth apart was probably occupied by only one note, and melodies and attunements were of very limited compass. Their expansion to about an octave belongs to the 6th and 5th cent., as does the insertion of a further note within each fourth, and regular distinctions between what Aristoxenus (and no earlier writer) calls 'genera'. Ethnic names like those associated with the seven *harmoniai* appear occasionally in the 7th and 6th cent., commonly in the 5th. Though early distinctions between Dorian and Phrygian music, for instance, were certainly not exhausted by structural differences of attunement, the notion that such differences were importantly involved is not just a 4th-cent. intellectual's fantasy. It is clearly attested in the later 5th century (Ar. *Eq.* 987–91), makes good sense of difficult passages in Pindar and earlier lyric, and is probably genuinely old. The series of seven octave species, however, is evidently a product of theorists' systematizing. Our only detailed evidence about the structures of earlier attunements comes from a late source (Aristid. Quint. 18. 5–19. 10), where six *harmoniai*, allegedly those mentioned in Plato's *Republic*, are tabulated. Some of their ranges and structures are irregular, by later standards, but there are enough correspondences for them to be construed as those on which the systematic theorists went to work. Their credentials have been much debated, but they are our most promising clue, and are worth recording here. Aristides represents them in a form proper to the enharmonic genus, and we do not know whether diatonic and chromatic variants existed.

Lydian: ¼, 2, 1, ¼, ¼, 2, ¼
Dorian: 1, ¼, ¼, 2, 1, ¼, ¼, 2
Phrygian: 1, ¼, ¼, 2, 1, ¼, ¼, 1
Iastian: ¼, ¼, 2, 1½, 1
Mixolydian: ¼, ¼, 1, 1, ¼, ¼, 3
Tense Lydian: ¼, ¼, 2, 1½

7. *Melody and Accompaniment* In performance, clarity, smoothness, and precision were admired: slides between notes were reckoned unmusical. Various compositional strategies and melodic figures are classified by theorists (especially Aristid. Quint. 1. 12), but the scores themselves are more illuminating. Phrases, for instance, tend to rise before falling. Single scalar steps are the commonest, but large leaps are used for special effect. There are identifiable melodic clichés, and some obvious specimens of word-painting. Phrases are seldom repeated or recognizably echoed within a composition. In some pieces the melodic focus ('tonic') lies high in the range, in others low: this feature, along with others, suggests that distinctions between octave species retained some importance (but the issue of where 'tonics' lay is often controversial). The pitch-relations embedded in the words of spoken Greek and indicated by written accents are generally respected in musical settings, though less consist-

ently in later pieces. The exception is in the setting of pieces with strophe and antistrophe: the same melody generally served for both, but their pitch accents are never likely to match.

Singing was usually accompanied, typically by one instrument, occasionally more: melodies played on an instrument were sometimes accompanied on the same instrument or another (on instrumental figures in general see Ptol. *Harm.* 2. 12). Often, melody and accompaniment were in unison or octaves, as choral singing was invariably; but though there were no developed concepts of harmony or polyphony, nonunison accompaniments were also common (see especially Pl. *Leg.* 812d–e), and were said to be as old as *Archilochus* ([Plut.] *De mus.* 1141b). Their function was not always merely ornamental: their discordant fragmentations and concordant reunifications of the musical sound (cf. [Arist.] *Pr.* 19. 39; [Plut.] *De mus.* 1137b–e) were conceived as having structural implications, left tantalizingly unclear in our sources but perhaps related primarily to the emphatic articulation of rhythm (but in this area nothing is certain). The harmonic theorists' unhelpful silence on the matter is due to their concentration on melody in the abstract: accompaniment was regularly considered part of a composition's realization in performance, not part of the composition itself.

8. *Rhythm and Rhythmic Notation* Rhythm, as Greek theorists acknowledged, is what gives music life; and the rhythmic intricacy of music before the mid-5th cent. was reckoned among its great merits. In vocal music it was closely allied to the patterns of long and short syllables codified as metre, and much can be learned from poetic texts designed for singing and dancing, since these patterns were usually preserved in performance. But rhythm is not just metre. For Aristoxenus it is essentially a relation between two elements in a temporal structure, up-beat (ἄνω χρόνος) and down-beat (κάτω χρόνος), or arsis and thesis: these concepts, derived from dance, apparently represent relaxation and stress, though the matter is disputed. These relations can be expressed as ratios: Aristoxenus recognizes as musically rhythmic the ratios 1:1, 2:1, 3:2; some theorists add 4:3. The ratio of arsis to thesis is not, on Aristoxenus' view, inherent in words or metrical relations as such, but is brought to them by the distinct act of rhythmic composition: hence a given stretch of poetic text might be 'rhythmized' without violence in different ways by different dispositions of arsis and thesis. It follows that our knowledge of metre leaves important issues of rhythmical interpretation uncertain. In written music these ambiguities could be resolved by marking a dot (στιγμή) over the arsis, as is sometimes done in surviving scores. Other rhythmic symbols also appear, and are explained in the treatise known as Bellermann's Anonymous.

The signs ‿, ⌐ (or ⌐), ⊔, ⊔⊔, placed over a note indicate lengths of two, three, four, or five time-units respectively (but the last two do not occur in our scores). The sign ∧ or ⌒ indicated a rest, or sometimes a lengthening of the preceding note. By itself it is one time-unit's length: longer rests were marked by combining the 'rest' sign with a sign of quantity (e.g. ∧̄). A ligature under a pair of note-symbols, or sometimes a colon before them, indicates that they are sung to the same syllable. Three notes are sometimes written with the sign meaning 'two time-units' over them, a colon in front of them, and the ligature joining two of the notes: here the group occupies two time-units, and the ligatured notes are each half the length of the third. Certain other signs are used to show divisions of notes in instrumental music, to mark phrase boundaries, or to separate stretches of singing from instrumental interludes.

9. Melodic Notation The melodic notations achieved the form found in surviving scores by the 3rd cent. BC, and remained in use until about the 5th cent. AD. They were not used to publish music to a general readership, only to serve the needs of performers: this may account for the scarcity of the scores. Our knowledge of their meaning derives mainly from tabulations in the *Eisagoge* of *Alypius (perhaps 3rd cent. AD): other sources of the period give briefer discussions and occasional examples of notated melody. There are two systems, equivalent in significance: our sources explain that one was used for vocal music, one for instrumental (but usage in the scores, where 'vocal' notation predominates, is rather erratic). The signs, based on letters of the alphabet, are arranged in groups of three, of which the lowest indicates a note in a simple diatonic series, while the second and third represent sharpenings of the note by one or two degrees. The amount of this sharpening is in theory a quarter-tone but in practice variable, depending on genus and on various other considerations. (According to Alypius and Boethius, movable notes in chromatic can be distinguished from those in enharmonic by a diacritical mark, not found in our scores.) Other principles involved in these notations' use are too complex to be explored here. The sequence of symbols covered just over three octaves. Alypius' tables show the series which is extracted from the whole to notate a two-octave scale in each of the fifteen *tonoi*, taken in any genus. A melody could then be written in any key that projected the appropriate pattern of intervals onto a suitable range (though certain keys are much more commonly used than others). Despite the complexities, our scores use these notations consistently and efficiently. Most commentators hold, probably rightly, that in its essentials the instrumental notation is the older (but contrast Bataille 1961). Its arcane symbols seem to be derived from an early regional script, perhaps Argive. They display the triadic structure clearly, the members of each group being rotations of one another. The vocal notation, by contrast, uses the letters of the Ionic alphabet, widely adopted from about 400 BC, in simple sequence: it seems likely to reflect performers' need for a more straightforward symbolism. Though in their existing form both notations must postdate the 4th-cent. system of *tonoi*, the instrumental may well have its origins in the early 5th. There is evidence of the existence of other notations in the 4th cent., possibly earlier, but they were soon extinct, and may never have been used except by theorists. Late sources also record a system of solmization, of which possible traces have been found in a painting of about 500 BC.

10. The Surviving Scores Our collection of Greek scores, mostly fragmentary, continues slowly to grow, and now stands at 46, perhaps 47 (see no. 47 below). They are as follows.

Inscriptions

(1–2) Extensive fragments of a paean by Athenaeus and a paean and processional by Limenius, inscribed on the Athenian treasury at *Delphi and now in Delphi museum. Both were composed for the Athenian mission to Delphi in 127 BC. They are much the longest surviving compositions. (See also METRE, GREEK, § 4*d*.) Athenaeus' paean is in vocal notation, that of Limenius, a citharist, in instrumental: both are in paeonic rhythm (5/8). They strikingly exemplify Aristoxenian structures without appearing scholastic: they are fluent, sophisticated and expressive, and demand highly trained performers. (3) Small fragments of a piece inscribed (perhaps 1st cent. BC) in a sanctuary in *Caria. (4) The

four-line Song of Sicilus survives complete, carved on a Carian tombstone, now in Copenhagen: it carries both melodic (vocal) and rhythmic notation. The simple words, on the theme 'enjoy life while you've got it' are set to an equally simple but appealing diatonic melody. Probably 1st cent. AD. (5) Inscription from *Epidaurus (*SEG* 30. 390), about AD 300, a brief fragment of a hexameter *hymn to *Asclepius, in the chromatic genus, followed by an instrumental phrase (in vocal notation).

Papyri

(6) *PVienna* G2315, Rainer inv. 8029 (*c*.200 BC), a fragment of Euripides, *Orestes* 338–44. The enharmonic melody could be Euripides' own. There are accompanying instrumental notes, different from those of the melody. (7–8) *PLeid.* 510 (3rd cent. BC), fragments of Eur. *IA* 784–92 and 1499–1509, perhaps from a collection of excerpts. Notes are clearly identifiable only in the former, and with many gaps. The melody is enharmonic, and contains wide leaps in pitch. (9) *PHib.* 231 (3rd cent. BC), two tiny fragments of notation, possibly examples in a treatise. (10) *PZenon* 59533 (3rd cent. BC), two notated phrases, basically diatonic but with 'accidentals', perhaps from a tragedy. (11) *PVienna* G13763 and 1494 (about 200 BC), small vocal fragments with instrumental interludes. (12) *PVienna* G29825a–f (about 200 BC), brief fragments of uncertain type. (13) *POxy.* inv. 89B. 29–33 (3rd–2nd cent. BC), fragments of text with notation, not yet published. (14) *POxy.* 2436 (1st–2nd cent. AD), perhaps from a satyr-play, showing features of florid post-classical styles. (15) *POsl.* inv. 1413 fr. a, 1–15, b–e (1st–2nd cent. AD), setting of an anapaestic passage, probably from a tragedy, in an ornate post-classical style: possibly the composer's own copy. (16) *POsl.* inv. 1413 fr. a, 15–19, a speech in iambics, set in the style of 15, not necessarily from the same play. (17) *PMich.* inv. 2958, lines 1–18 (2nd cent. AD), a substantial passage of tragic dialogue, the setting flamboyantly decorated. A line of seventeen notes, still in vocal notation but without text, is presumably an instrumental interlude. (18) *PMich.* inv. 2958, lines 20–27, a fragment of uncertain type. (19) *POxy.* 3704 (2nd cent. AD), five fragments of uncertain type, probably tragic. (20–1) *POxy.* inv. 102/58(c), 105/31(c) (2nd cent. AD), fragments of uncertain type, not yet published. (22–4) *POxy.* inv. 63 6B 63/K(1–3) (b)–, 72. 13(g)–, 100/122(c) (2nd–3rd cent. AD), not yet published. (25–9) *PBerol.* 6870 (2nd–3rd cent. AD), apparently an anthology: lines 1–12 from a paean, in Hellenistic style, diatonic; lines 13–15, from an instrumental piece, similar to the paean in metre and key; lines 16–19, from a lament, in a late melismatic style, uniquely set in a female register; lines 20–2, from an instrumental piece in a complex rhythm; line 23, a brief and macabre phrase of lyric. (30) *POxy.* 3161 recto (3rd cent. AD), four fragments from a dramatic lament in a late style. (31) *POxy.* 3161 verso, three fragments of lament in a similar style, on a different theme. (32) *POxy.* 3162 (3rd cent. AD), a dramatic fragment, content obscure. (33) *POxy.* 3705 (3rd cent. AD), four alternative settings of a fragmentary verse, presumably from a textbook. (34–5) *POxy.* inv. 100/81(b), 100/125(a) (3rd cent. AD), fragments of obscure type, not yet published. (36) *POxy.* 1786 (late 3rd cent. AD), substantial fragments of a Christian hymn, the earliest surviving. Its melodic shape and ornamentation have suggested a non-Greek, oriental origin, but it can be interpreted as a development of late Greek models.

Manuscripts

(37) A four-line invocation of the Muse, transmitted with 38–40 but probably rather earlier: diatonic, with decorative chromaticisms. (38) A three-line invocation of Calliope (see MUSES) by *Mesomedes, a Cretan composer at the court of Hadrian:

diatonic, using something like a major scale; the one apparent 'accidental' may be a scribal error. (39) A nineteen-line hymn to the Sun by Mesomedes, diatonic without accidentals, with a well established tonal focus and a preference for small melodic steps; a polished if unexciting composition. (40) A twenty-line hymn to *Nemesis by Mesomedes (the last line incomplete). Rather wider in compass than 39, otherwise similar; the last five lines have the air of a coda. (41–6) Six brief instrumental passages recorded at Anonymus Bellermanni 97–101, 104, either to illustrate rhythms or as students' exercises, or both.

Painted pottery

(47) Eleusis Museum 907, a black-figure painting (about 500 BC) depicting an Amazon with *salpinx* and written syllables that may represent notes of a solmization system. If it counts as a score, it is much the earliest we possess.

BIBLIOGRAPHICAL SURVEYS R. P. Winnington-Ingram, *Lustrum* 1958; T. J. Mathiesen, *A Bibliography of Sources for the Study of Ancient Greek Music* (1974); H. Oki, *Répertoire de littérature musicale de la Grèce antique* (1981); A.-J. Neubecker, *Lustrum* 1990; earlier surveys in Bursian, *Jahresb.* 1877–1935.

ANCIENT SOURCES Musical writings

(1) Collections. C. von Jan, *Musici scriptores Graeci* (1895): Aristotle excerpts, Euclid, Cleonides, Nicomachus, Bacchius, Gaudentius, Alypius; L. Zanoncelli, *La manualistica musicale greca* (1990): Jan's text, omitting Aristotle, with It. trans.; A. Barker, *Greek Musical Writings* 1–2 (1984–9): annotated Eng. trans. of various works (cited below as *GMW*). (2) Individual authors. Anonymus Bellermanni: ed. D. Najock (1975). Aristides Quintilianus: ed. R. P. Winnington-Ingram (1963), Ger. trans. R. Schäfke (1937), Eng. trans. in *GMW* 2. Ps.-Arist.: *Problems*, Books 11 and 19, ed. G. Marenghi (1957), Eng. trans. of most in *GMW* 1–2. Aristoxenus: *Elementa Harmonica*, ed. H. S. Macran, with Eng. trans. (1902), R. da Rios, with It. trans. (1954), Eng. trans. in *GMW* 2; *Elementa Rhythmica*, ed. G. B. Pighi (1969), L. Pearson, with Eng. trans. (1990), Eng. trans. in *GMW* 2; other fragments, ed. F. Wehrli, 2nd edn. (1967). Athenaeus: ed. G. Kaibel (1887–90), C. B. Gulick, with Eng. trans. (1950), Eng. trans. of excerpts in *GMW* 1. Baccheius: Eng. trans. O. Steinmayer, *Journal of Music Theory* 1985. Boethius: ed. G. Friedlein (1867), Eng. trans. C. Bower (1989). Bryennius: ed. G. H. Jonker (1970). Cleonides: ed. J. Solomon, with Eng. trans. (1980). Euclid: Eng. trans. in *GMW* 2. Nicomachus: Eng. trans. in *GMW* 2. Philodemus: ed. J. Kemke (1894), D. A. van Krevelen (1939); Book 1, ed. G. M. Rispoli (1969); Book 4, ed. A.-J. Neubecker, with Ger. trans. (1986). Ps.-Plutarch, ed. H. Weil and T. Reinach (1900), F. Lasserre, with Fr. trans. (1954), B. Einarson and P. H. De Lacy, with Eng. trans. (1967), Eng. trans. in *GMW* 1. On Tragedy, ed. R. Browning (1963). Ptolemy: ed. I. Düring (1930), and Ger. trans. (1934), Eng. trans. in *GMW* 2. Porphyry's commentary on Ptolemy: ed. I. Düring (1932), Eng. trans. of excerpts in *GMW* 2. Sextus Empiricus: *Adversus musicos*, ed. J. Mau (1954), R. G. Bury, with Eng. trans. (1961). Theon of Smyrna, ed. E. Hiller (1878), Eng. trans. of excerpts in *GMW* 2.

Musical fragments

Incomplete collection in C. von Jan, *Musici scriptores Graeci*, Suppl. (1899); nearly complete collection, with commentaries, E. Pöhlmann, *Denkmäler Altgriechischer Musik* (1970); complete listing with bibliographies, and transcriptions and discussions of major fragments, in M. L. West, *Ancient Greek Music* (1992).

MODERN LITERATURE F. A. Gevaert, *Histoire et théorie de la musique de l'antiquité* (1875–81; repr. 1966); R. Westphal, *Griechische Harmonik und Melopoeie*, 3rd edn. (1886); T. Reinach, *La Musique grecque* (1926); W. Vetter, *RE* 16/1 (1933), 823–76, 'Musik'; R. P. Winnington-Ingram, *Mode in Ancient Greek Music* (1936); O. Gombosi, *Die Tonarten und Stimmungen der antiken Musik* (1939); K. Schlesinger, *The Greek Aulos* (1939); C. Sachs, *The Rise of Music in the Ancient World* (1943); M. Shirlaw, 'The Music and Tone-systems of Ancient Greece', *Music Review* 1943, see also *Music and Letters* 1951; I. Düring, 'Studies in Musical Terminology', *Eranos* 1945; T. Georgiades, *Der griechischer Rhythmus* (1949); M. Wegner, *Das Musikleben der Griechen* (1949); F.

Behn, *Musikleben im Altertum und frühen Mittelalter* (1954); W. Vetter, 'Griechenland: antike', *Die Musik in Geschichte und Gegenwart* 5 (1956); I. Henderson, *New Oxford History of Music* (1957), 'Ancient Greek Music'; E. Moutsopoulos, *La Musique dans l'œuvre de Platon* (1959); A. Bataille, 'Remarques sur les deux notations mélodiques', *Recherches de Papyrologie* (1961); Pickard-Cambridge–Webster, *Dithyramb*[2]; B. Aign, *Die Musikinstrumente des ägäischen Raum* (1963); M. Vogel, *Die Enharmonik der Griechen* (1963); M. Wegner, *Musikgeschichte in Bildern* 2/4 (1963), 'Griechenland'; G. Fleischauer, ibid. 2/5 (1964), 'Etrurien und Rom'; E. A. Lippman, *Musical Thought in Ancient Greece* (1964); W. D. Anderson, *Ethos and Education in Greek Music* (1966); A. Baines, *Woodwind Instruments and their History*, 3rd edn. (1967); G. Wille, *Musica Romana* (1967); L. Richter, *Die Musik der griechischen Antike* (1968); M. Wegner, *Musik und Tanz* (1968); T. B. L. Webster, *The Greek Chorus* (1970); W. Burkert, *Lore and Science in Ancient Pythagoreanism* (1972; Ger. orig. 1962); A. Baudot, *Musiciens romains de l'Antiquité* (1973); F. A. G. Beck, *Album of Greek Education* (1975); A.-J. Neubecker, *Altgriechische Musik* (1977); A. Barker, 'The Predecessors of Aristoxenus', *PCPS* 1978; S. Michaelides, *The Music of Ancient Greece: An Encyclopedia* (1978); M. Pintacuda, *La Musica nella tragedia greca* (1978); J. Chailley, *La Musique grecque antique* (1979); R. P. Winnington-Ingram, *New Grove* (1980), 'Greece, ancient'; M. L. West, 'The Singing of Homer and the Modes of Early Greek Music', *JHS* 1981; A. Barker, 'Aristides Quintilianus and Constructions in Early Music Theory', *CQ* 1982; D. Restani, 'Il *Chirone* di Ferecrate e la "nuova" musica greca', *Rivista italiana di Musicologia* 1983; D. Paquette, *L'Instrument de musique dans la céramique de la Grèce antique* (1984); B. Gentili and R. Pretagostini (eds.), *La Musica in Grecia* (1988); G. Comotti, *Music in Greek and Roman Culture* (1989; expanded from It. orig. 1979); M. Maas and J. M. Snyder, *Stringed Instruments of Ancient Greece* (1989); A. Riethmüller and F. Zaminer (eds.), *Musik im Altertum* (1989); C. Burnett, M. Fend, and P. Gouk (eds.), *The Second Sense* (1991); C. Carey, 'The Victory Ode in Performance: The Case for the Chorus', *CPhil.* 1991; M. Heath and M. Lefkowitz, 'Epinician Performance', *CPhil.* 1991; R. W. Wallace and B. MacLachlan (eds.), *Harmonia Mundi* (1991); M. L. West, 'Analecta Musica', *ZPE* 92 (1992), 1–34; M. L. West, *Ancient Greek Music* (1992).

A. D. B.

music in worship Both in Greece and Italy *music, vocal and instrumental, formed an important part of worship at all periods. To begin with *Homer, the embassy sent to Chryse in *Iliad* 1. 472–4 spend the whole day after their arrival singing a hymn (παιήων) to *Apollo, who is pleased with it. This *paean remained typical of his worship, and the quintuple rhythm characteristic of it was named after it. In like manner the *dithyramb was appropriated to *Dionysus. Neither of these, however, was exclusively the property of Apollo or Dionysus; e.g. paeans were composed to *Asclepius (see Powell, *Coll. Alex.* 133 ff.). The singing of some kind of *hymn appears regularly to have accompanied any formal act of worship, and instrumental music (strings and wind) also is commonly mentioned: see SACRIFICE, GREEK.

Much the same is true for Italy. Hymns are continually met with, some traditional, as those of the *Salii (see MARS) and arval brothers (W. Henzen, *Acta Fratrum Arvalium* 1874, cciv; see FRATRES ARVALES). Instrumental music was so regular and necessary an accompaniment of ritual (e.g. Cic. *Har. resp.* 23, the proceedings are vitiated 'si . . . tibicen repente conticuit'—'if the pipe-player suddenly falls silent') that the *collegium tibicinum et fidicinum qui sacris publicis praesto sunt* formed an ancient and important guild with a holiday of its own, cf. MINERVA. One reason for this was doubtless to drown any slight noises which might be of ill omen.

Very little is known of the style of this music, but it is fairly certain that there was no prohibition of the introduction of new forms.

H. J. R.

Musonius (*RE* 1) **Rufus, Gaius,** of *Volsinii, Roman *eques* (see EQUITES) and Stoic philosopher (see STOICISM), seems to have been born before AD 30 and to have died before 101/2. About AD 60 *Rubellius Plautus was banished by *Nero to Asia Minor, and Musonius followed him. After Rubellius' death he returned to Rome, but in 65, on the discovery of the Pisonian conspiracy (see CALPURNIUS PISO (2), C.), he was banished to Gyaros in the *Aegean. He returned to Rome, probably under Galba and tried to preach peace to the Flavian army approaching Rome. He was again banished by *Vespasian, but returned again in the reign of *Titus. We do not know of his having written books, but many of his apophthegms (pithy sayings) and discourses have been preserved. Among his pupils were many philosophers (notably *Epictetus) and many leading Roman citizens.

Ed. O. Hense (1905); one letter in R. Hercher, *Epistolographi Graeci* (1873), 401–4. M. Pohlenz, *Die Stoa*, 2nd edn. (1955–9); M. P. Charlesworth, *Five Men* (1936), 33 ff.; C. E. Lutz, *YClS* 1947, 3 ff.; A. C. van Geytenbeck, *Musonius Rufus and Greek Diatribe* (1963); R. Laurenti, *ANRW* 2. 36. 3 (1989), 2113–20; A. Jagu, *Musonius Rufus, Eutretiens et fragments* (1979). W. D. R.; M. T. G.

Mutina (mod. Modena), a prosperous wool-trading town in Cisalpine Gaul (see GAUL (CISALPINE)), on the *via Aemilia and controlling other important roads and passes (Strabo 5. 218). First settled in the neolithic period, it was an *Etruscan and Boian centre (see BOII), and by 218 BC a walled Roman stronghold (Livy 21. 25; Polyb. 3. 40 (inexact)). It became a citizen colony in 183 BC, and was famous for its successful resistance to *Pompey in 78 and Antony (M. *Antonius (2)) in 43 BC. Subsequently it is rarely mentioned, although it retained its importance well into the 5th cent. AD. The surrounding landscape was extensively centuriated (see CENTURIATION).

Misurare la terra: Centuriazione e coloni nel mondo romano, il caso modenese (1984); A. Cardarelli and others, *Modena dalle origini all'anno mille* (1989). E. T. S.; T. W. P.

Mycenae is a rocky hill, flanked by ravines to north and south, situated on the NE edge of the Argive plain between larger hills. There are few remains from the earliest phases of occupation, apart from the 'Prehistoric Cemetery', containing mainly children's graves, on the SW slope, and there is no indication that Mycenae was a significant settlement before the period to which it gives its name. The increasingly rich and elaborate burials in the shaft-graves of Circle B, on a knoll to the west, and Circle A, in the middle of the SW slope, reflect its rise to power and wealth during the 16th cent. BC, and the number (probably seven) and quality of tholos-tombs constructed during the 15th cent. similarly reflect the maintenance of this position, but only scanty traces of contemporary buildings have been found.

The finest tholos-tombs (the 'Treasury of Atreus' and 'Tomb of Clytaemnestra') were most probably constructed during the 14th cent. BC, to which the oldest parts of the surviving palace and fortifications belong; in the 13th cent. these were expanded and many other buildings were constructed, notably the concentration of likely shrines known as the 'Cult Centre' on the SW slope, and the West House group south of Circle B, most probably a combination of administrator's residence, offices, and storerooms. By this time there was an extensive settlement around the citadel and a wide spread of chamber-tomb cemeteries, probably used by satellite settlements, over the surrounding slopes to north, west, and south-west. Mycenae was now at the height of its wealth and power, probably controlling a consider-

able territory and able to exert influence widely in the Aegean, though there is no evidence that it dominated the whole Mycenaean world in an organized political system, like the contemporary Hittite 'empire', and only a few Linear B tablets survive to illuminate aspects of its organization (see MYCENAEAN LANGUAGE).

In the mid-13th cent. BC there was widespread damage by fire, followed by repairs and further building, mostly within the citadel. It is unclear whether this represents hostile attack, but the cutting of a stepped passage through the rock to a water supply below the north wall, fed by an aqueduct from the nearby spring, could well be a precaution against siege. Around 1200 there was considerable further destruction, especially within the citadel. This was reoccupied on some scale, but there is little evidence for continued occupation elsewhere, and few chamber-tombs remained in use: Mycenae was evidently in decline, and by about 1100 was no more than a village. It remained inhabited throughout the Dark Age, and had become reasonably prosperous by about 600 BC, when some structure decorated with fine relief sculptures was built, but politically it was surely subordinate to *Argos (2). In a brief period of independence (probably as a result of Argos' disastrous defeat in 494) it sent forces to the *Persian War in 480–479, but was destroyed by Argos c.468. It was re-established as a fortified town by Argos in the 3rd cent. BC, but decayed again, although some local population presumably survived to point out the tombs of the heroes to Pausanias (3). But little genuine tradition of its importance survived: the prominence of Mycenae in Homer is not matched in the other legends, which consistently allot greater antiquity and importance to Argos.

GAC A 1; *LH Citadels*, 23 ff.; G. Karo, *Die Schachtgräber von Mykenai* (1930–3); A. J. B. Wace, *Chamber Tombs at Mycenae* (1932), *Mycenae* (1949), and (with others) in E. B. French (ed.), *Excavations at Mycenae 1939–1955* (1980); G. E. Mylonas, *Grave Circle B of Mycenae* (1973, in Greek), *Proc. Brit. Acad.* 1981, 307 ff.; S. Iakovidis, *BICS* 1977, 99 ff.; E. B. French, in R. Hägg and N. Marinatos (eds.), *Sanctuaries and Cults in the Aegean Bronze Age* (1981), 41 ff.; W. D. Taylour, *Well-Built Mycenae 1: The Excavations* (1981); A. Xenaki-Sakellariou, *The Chamber Tombs of Mycenae; Tsountas' Excavations (1887–1898)* (1985, in Greek); D. M. Lewis, *CAH* 5² (1992), ch. 5. O. T. P. K. D.

Mycenaean civilization (see also RELIGION, MINOAN AND MYCENAEAN) takes its name from the spectacular finds made by Heinrich Schliemann at *Mycenae, and was first systematically defined by Christos Tsountas. He applied the term Mycenaean to all Aegean late bronze age material, but it is now confined to the culture which developed on the mainland in the late bronze age. The stylistic divisions of the Mycenaean pottery style (LH (late Helladic) I, IIA, etc.) provide a well-defined relative chronology, but historically the Mycenaean age is better divided into a formative period, covering LH I and IIA (c.1575/50–1450 BC), a Palace period, covering LH IIB, IIIA1, IIIA2, IIIB1, and IIIB2 (c.1450–1200 BC), and a post-Palatial period, covering LH IIIC (frequently subdivided into early, middle, and late) and sub-Mycenaean (c.1200–1050/1000 BC).

The most striking feature of the formative period is the emergence of wealthy ruling groups in the southern mainland, who were surely native to the territories that they controlled; theories that they represent alien invaders have not identified the new and consistently occurring cultural assemblage that should appear, or explained the variability of the earliest Mycenaean developments in different regions and the strong links with the preceding middle Helladic culture. Their emergence and acquisition of considerable wealth, displayed mostly in lavish burials (see below), remains hard to explain, but the expanding influence of *Minoan civilization in the *Aegean and the increasing involvement of the Aegean with the east Mediterranean trading systems may have been major stimuli. Minoan influence is most marked in the crafts (see below) that they patronized, and was hardly felt at the level of the ordinary settlements.

During the formative period features that were at first localized, like the Messenian tholos-tombs (see MESSENIA (prehistory)), were combined into something more like a homogeneous culture; by its end not only the Mycenaean pottery style but the characteristic burial practices had spread through the Peloponnese (see PELOPONNESUS) and central Greece. The new principalities were organized rather simply—there is no trace of the administrative use of the seal or writing—and the popularity of weapons as high-status grave-goods suggests that society was more turbulent than that of Crete and the south Aegean islands. The discovery of early Mycenaean pottery in the north Aegean and central Mediterranean suggests that the mainlanders could have played a significant role in the expansion of trade connections, but their contacts with the near east will still have been largely indirect while Minoan civilization dominated the Aegean.

Theories of Mycenaean responsibility for the collapse of Minoan civilization c.1450 BC remain questionable, but the following period certainly saw a great expansion of Mycenaean culture and the establishment of a state in *Crete, centred on Cnossus, whose ruling class had strong Mycenaean connections in its burial customs and use of Greek, written in the Linear B script (see MYCENAEAN LANGUAGE; PRE-ALPHABETIC SCRIPTS (GREECE)), as the administrative language. The administrative skills of Crete were probably transmitted to the mainland at this time, when the first well-preserved antecedents of the later Mycenaean palaces were built (*Tiryns, *Menelaion); but tombs continued to be richly provided with grave-goods at both mainland and Cretan sites. The final destruction of Cnossus during the 14th cent. BC removed the last major competitor to the mainland centres, and Mycenaean civilization now reached its zenith, dominating the south Aegean and extending along the Asia Minor coast from *Miletus to Cnidus.

The organizing centres of this civilization were the great palaces best preserved at Mycenae, Tiryns, *Pylos, and *Thebes (1). While considerably smaller than the Minoan palaces and differently laid out, they evidently functioned similarly, as centres of administration, ceremonial, storage, and craftwork. They presided over societies that were small in scale: most settlements ranged in size from a few households to some hundreds, and even the greatest, with populations probably in the thousands, do not have a very townlike appearance. But there were more settlements on the mainland than ever before; exploitation of the land was being expanded, probably to provide commodities for trade as well as to support an increasing population. The most recent study (P. Halstead, *PCPS* 1992, 57 ff.) distinguishes between the highly specialized economies of the palaces, which concentrated on large-scale cultivation of a few crops and the production of perfumed olive oil, fine textiles, and other craftwork, and the mixed economies of the ordinary settlements, which were not controlled from the palaces but interacted with them, providing some agricultural products in taxes and others, like pulses, on an irregular basis. To judge from the Pylos texts, which provide most of the documentary information, the palace directly maintained a workforce of many hundreds, and controlled most of the distribution and working of bronze. Resources

were now expended mainly on building and engineering projects rather than tombs, though the finest tholoi belong to the period.

The Linear B texts do not make the palaces' administrative system wholly clear, but at the top in Pylos was the *wanax*, a monarch-like figure; below him were various administrators, who may well have been drawn from a class of major landowners. Texts concerning land-holdings indicate that people of very varied status could hold land, generally by some form of lease, including priests, craftsmen, herdsmen, and, at *Pa-ki-ja-ne*, an important religious site relatively near Pylos itself, many 'slaves of the god', both male and female (see HIERODOULOI). Land could be leased from different owners and in various ways, but its tenure may always have entailed payment to the palace in taxes or service.

Mycenaean pottery of this period is found in considerable quantities in much of the Mediterranean, reaching rarely as far as northern Italy and eastern Spain. It was clearly popular, for it was widely imitated, but the most significant element may have been containers for perfumed *olive oil and other substances. Its conspicuousness should not lead to overestimation of the Mycenaean position either in Mediterranean trade, whose most important organizing centres were probably in *Syria and *Cyprus, or politically: there remain difficulties in identifying the state *Ahhiyawa, mentioned in *Hittite sources, with Mycenaean Greece, and likely references to Mycenaeans are hard to identify in other near eastern sources. The masses of exported Mycenaean pottery may rather symbolize the strenuous effort necessary to maintain the inward flow of raw materials and luxuries necessary to the Mycenaean style of life.

Indications of trouble during the later 13th cent. BC may reflect strains within Mycenaean society rather than any external threat. Some major sites had already suffered severe damage (Thebes) and begun to decline, or been abandoned (*Gla), before the main series of destructions around 1200 BC; these have been attributed to earthquakes in the Argolid, but this explanation can hardly apply all over the mainland (e.g. Menelaion, Pylos, Teikhos Dymaion, *Crisa). Subsequently some regions recovered and prospered at a simpler level, centring on large nucleated settlements (Tiryns, *Lefkandi, Perati) that were still essentially Mycenaean in culture and retained contacts with the Aegean and near east. But exchange systems had been badly dislocated, and there seems to have been growing instability; ultimately the surviving centres were abandoned or dwindled to villages. Culture reverted to an essentially pre-Mycenaean level, parochial and impoverished, with limited external contacts, and surviving Mycenaean features disappeared (e.g. figurines, chamber-tomb cemeteries).

Burial customs Most characteristically, an open passage (*dromos*) would be cut to a chamber hollowed in soft rock (chamber-tomb) or built of stone; best known of the latter are the tholos-tombs, which have a circular ground-plan, domed vault, and covering mound, and were probably always high-status tombs. A series of burials, averaging 6–8 but often more or fewer, were inhumed in these chambers, often with complex two-stage rites. Although showing similarities to earlier Aegean forms, these tomb types seem specifically Mycenaean developments. They were used by a variable but increasingly large proportion of the population; the rest may have used cists and pits, but these nowhere occur in large numbers.

Architecture Ordinary houses mostly consisted of a few rooms grouped on various plans, built largely of mud-brick on stone foundations, with timber fittings and some kind of thatched roof. The palaces and some smaller buildings were built in the Minoan style, with fine stone façades, wooden columns, plastered walls around a timber frame, and fresco decoration in major areas. Although clay roof-tiles have been identified at several major sites, they seem a late development hardly used in the palaces, which were probably flat-roofed like the Minoan. Where fully preserved, palace plans centre on the 'megaron' suite of rooms, essentially a hall containing an elaborate hearth and 'throne' emplacement, approached through an ante-room and porch, which surely had a ceremonial purpose. Other rooms open off flanking corridors, and there are traces of an upper storey and further associated structures, including storage buildings and workshops. Also notable architecturally are the 'Cyclopean' fortifications, of two faces of massive blocks containing a rubble fill, generally 5–8 m. (16–26 ft.) thick and averaging 8 m. (26 ft.) high; the same style was used for terraces, dikes, dams, bridges, etc., mainly in the Argolid and Boeotia.

Crafts Many luxury crafts were established on the mainland in the formative period, as demonstrated by the rich grave-goods from many tombs. Their first practitioners may have been largely immigrants: Minoan influence is marked from the beginning in the weapons, precious vessels, seals, and decorated pottery, although native elements can be identified, and this steadily increases in jewellery. As a result, no separate Mycenaean artistic tradition developed; individuality is shown mainly in preferences for particular motifs, themes, or materials (e.g. metal rather than stone for vessels). The crafts of the Palace period maintained high standards technically, but generally repeated the established themes of earlier art; some, like the production of seals, progressively declined. More use was made of *ivory than before, especially for inlays on luxury furniture, but also for occasional works in the round. Decorative stone reliefs are occasionally found in palaces and the finest tholoi, but the Lion Gate relief at Mycenae remains unique. Worth mentioning as particularly characteristic are the clay figurines, especially standing female figures and bovids, which evidently served several ritual purposes. In the post-Palatial period, elaborate classes of pictorial pottery are conspicuous for a while, but all but the most basic crafts eventually disappeared.

GENERAL G. E. Mylonas, *Mycenae and the Mycenaean Age* (1966); J. T. Hooker, *Mycenaean Greece* (1976); J. Chadwick, *The Mycenaean World* (1976); O. Dickinson, *The Origins of Mycenaean Civilisation* (1977), and *The Aegean Bronze Age* (1994); W. Taylour, *The Mycenaeans*, 2nd edn. (1983); K. Demakopoulou, *The Mycenaean World* (1988); K. Kilian, in E. B. French and K. Wardle (eds.), *Problems in Greek Prehistory* (1988), 115 ff.

SITES *GAC*; R. Hope Simpson, *Mycenaean Greece* (1981); *LH Citadels*.

TRADE A. F. Harding, *The Mycenaeans and Europe* (1984); M. Marazzi, S. Tusa, and L. Vagnetti, *Traffici micenei nel Mediterraneo* (1986); papers in N. H. Gale (ed.), *Bronze Age Trade in the Mediterranean* (1991).

LINEAR B See MYCENAEAN LANGUAGE; PRE-ALPHABETIC SCRIPTS (GREECE).

RELIGION C. Renfrew, *The Archaeology of Cult* (1985); B. Rutkowski, *The Cult Places of the Aegean* (1986), chs. 9–11.

CRAFTS Relevant portions of M. S. F. Hood, *The Arts in Prehistoric Greece* (1978), and R. Higgins, *Minoan and Mycenaean Art*, 2nd edn. (1981). O. T. P. K. D.

Mycenaean language is the name given to the form of the Greek language written in the Linear B script and found in the Mycenaean palaces (see PRE-ALPHABETIC SCRIPTS (GREECE)). The incompleteness of the script makes it impossible to give a full account of the dialect. In contrast to the Classical situation there appears to be considerable uniformity between all the sites so far known. It is clear that the dialect forms part of the Greek language because of the presence of characteristic sound-changes, inflexions, and vocabulary. The genitive singular of *o*-stems in -οιο, of masculine a-stems in -āο, the formation of substantives (including names) in -εύς, the feminine of the perfect participle of the verb in -υιᾶ, and the medio-passive participles in -μενος are all typically Greek features. The vocabulary contains specifically Greek words (both Indo-European and non-Indo-European), such as Fάναξ (Homeric ἄναξ) 'king', ἔχει 'he has', ἀμφιφορῆϜες 'amphoras', ξέυϜια 'for guests'.

A dialect 500 years earlier than Homer can be expected to show archaic forms later abandoned. For instance, ā is maintained, where Attic-Ionic substitues η. The labio-velar stops of Proto-Indo-European appear to have survived: so 'and' is not τε but kʷe, 'attendants' not ἀμφίπολοι but amphikʷoloi, 'halter' not φορβειά but phorgʷewia. The vowel contractions of later Greek are absent, partly because Ϝ and the aspirate still blocked the hiatus (e.g. φάρϜεha 'cloths', χαλκῆϜες 'bronzesmiths'). A case ending in -φι is used far more consistently than in Homer for the instrumental plural in some declensions (e.g. andrian(t)phi, 'with statues'). The vocabulary contains a number of words later either unknown or in very restricted use (e.g. the word κτοίνā apparently meaning 'estate', later known only as a technical term in Rhodian inscriptions, or its epithet κτιμένā, which recurs in the Homeric ἐυκτίμενος). The dialect does not fit the pattern of the first millennium dialects, but appears to be most closely related to Classical Arcadian and Cypriot. It shares with them and with Attic-Ionic the shift of final -τι to -σι, and this distinguishes it from the whole of the West Greek group. Since these dialects are in some respects more archaic than Mycenaean, it follows that their ancestor must already have been in existence.

M. Ventris and J. Chadwick, *Documents in Mycenaean Greek*, 2nd edn. (1973); E. Vilborg, *A Tentative Grammar of Mycenaean Greek* (1960).
J. C.

Myconos See CYCLADES and *Syll*³ 1024.

Mygdon (Μυγδών). In *Homer, *Iliad* 3. 184 ff. *Priam relates that he went as an ally to a Phrygian army gathered under Mygdon and Otreus to fight the *Amazons on the Sangarius. The Coroebus of Verg. *Aen.* 2. 407 was Mygdon's son, [Eur.] *Rhes.* 539. Mygdon is apparently the eponym of the Thracian or Phrygian Mygdones. H. J. R.

Myia, daughter of *Pythagoras (1), is called a Pythagorean philosopher (Clem. *Strom.* 4. 19. 121, 224).

RE 16/1, 'Myia' 2. V. L. H.

Mylasa (mod. Milâs), the principal non-Greek city of *Caria and capital of the area under the Hecatomnid rulers (see HECATOMNUS). It is probable (*BSA* 1961, 98 f.) that the early seat of government was at Peçin Kale, some 8 km. (5 mi.) south of Milâs, and that the city at Milâs was founded by *Mausolus. Mausolus later transferred the capital to *Halicarnassus. The Hellenistic and Roman city at Milâs continued to be of importance, but its site at the foot of a mountain was considered ill-chosen (Strabo 659). Mylasa had three notable temples of *Zeus: Zeus Osogos, Zeus Karios, and Zeus Stratios or Labraundos, the last situated in hills to the east at *Labraunda and approached by a paved sacred way. Swedish excavations have revealed much about this site. After the battle of *Magnesia (190 BC) Mylasa was exempted from the grant of Caria to the Rhodians (see RHODES), and in 167 joined in an uprising of the subjects of Rhodes on the mainland; this was suppressed, but immediately afterwards the senate revoked its gift of territory to Rhodes (Polyb. 21. 46, 30. 5). In 40 BC, when Q. *Labienus, at the head of a Parthian army, overran Caria, the Mylasans were persuaded by Hybreas, a distinguished citizen and rhetorician, to resist him; for this Labienus punished the city savagely, but it soon recovered, probably with help from Augustus (Dittenberg. *Syll.*³ 768). Strabo's assertion (659) that Physcus was the port of Mylasa is an error: the name of the port (mod. Kül]ük) was Passala (Steph. Byz., entry under the name; cf. *Stadiasmus Maris Magni*, ed. C. Müller, 291). Mylasa is listed as a bishopric in Caria; the site has produced important inscribed legal documents of the 5th cent. (W. Blümel, *Die Inschriften von Mylasa* (1987), 611–13).

Among the ruins at Milâs the most notable are a handsome mausoleum of Roman date (modelled on the *Mausoleum?) and an arched gateway bearing a relief of a double axe, a symbol which also occurs on coins of the Hecatomnids and of Mylasa. Recent archaeological discoveries include a fragment of an altar (c. mid-5th cent. BC) and an acroterion (c.400 BC), valuable as the earliest evidence for monumental architecture, when Mylasa was under control of Mausolus' father, Hecatomnus.

G. E. Bean, *Turkey Beyond the Maeander* (1980), 31 f.; S. Hornblower, *Mausolus* (1982), see index; S. Mitchell, *Arch. Rep.* 1990, 88.

G. E. B.; S. S.-W., C. R.

Mylitta is the Greek transcription for the Assyrian goddess Mullissu (Sumerian *Ninlil*). She was the spouse of Aššur (the Assyrian Enlil) in *Assyria. Herodotus (1. 199), who associated prostitution with her cult (see PROSTITUTION, SACRED), identified her with *Aphrodite.

S. Dalley, *Revue d'Assyriologie* 1979, 177–8. S. M. D.

Myllus Probably a stock figure of Greek farce ('The Squinter', cf. Cratinus fr. 96 KA = 89 Kock), but named by the *Suda* (ε 2766) and others as an early writer of Old Comedy (see COMEDY (GREEK), OLD).

Meineke, *FCG* 1. 26 f.; U. von Wilamowitz-Moellendorff, *Hermes* 1875, 338 f.; A. Körte *RE* 16/1 (1933), 1074; Pickard-Cambridge–Webster, *Dithyramb*², 188 f.; Kassel–Austin, *PCG* 7. 28. W. G. A.

Myos Hormos, port on the Egyptian *Red Sea linked by caravan with *Coptus on the Nile (Strabo 2. 5. 12, 16. 4. 5, 17. 1. 45), important for the *India trade. It is securely identified with Quseir al-Qadim.

A. Fuks, *JJP* 1951, 207–16; A. Bülow-Jacobsen and others, *BIFAO* 1994, 27–42; D. P. S. Peacock, *JRA* 1993, 226–32; S. E. Sidebotham, *Roman Economic Policy in the Erythra Thalassa* (1986). W. E. H. C.

Myra (mod. Demre) was one of the six most important cities of Hellenistic *Lycia, with three votes in the federal assembly, and was called *mētropolis* (see MĒTROPOLIS (*b*)) in inscriptions of Roman imperial date. Its most important asset was the harbour at nearby Andriace, where St *Paul changed ships *en route* to Rome in AD 60. A civic ferry service linked the city with Limyra to the east (*OGI* 572). The principal pagan cult of the city was of (*Artemis) Eleuthera; in late antiquity it was famous as the see of St Nicholas. The ruins of the city have mostly been covered by aggredation, leaving only the impressive Roman theatre—reconstructed after an earthquake in the 140s AD with funds provided by *Opramoas of Rhodiapolis—and the acropolis hill behind it, which offers an impressive backdrop of Lycian rock-

tombs, some dating back to the 4th cent. BC. At the harbour of Andriace there is a well-preserved *granary built by the emperor *Hadrian.

G. E. Bean, *Lycian Turkey* (1978), 120–33; J. Borchhardt and others, *Myra: Eine lykische Metropole* (1974). S. M.

Myrina, one of the cities of the Aeolian League, situated on the coast north of Cyme at the mouth of the river Pythicus or Titnaeus. Its reputed founder was Myrrhine, queen of the *Amazons. In the Athenian empire (see DELIAN LEAGUE) it was assessed at one talent, the highest figure in *Aeolis after *Cyme. The city was rebuilt with *Tiberius' help after the earthquake of AD 17 and for a while named Sebastopolis (Plin. *HN* 5. 121). In imperial times the ancient white marble temple of *Apollo at Gryneum was situated in a beautiful grove on Myrina's territory (Strab. 13. 3. 5, 622; Paus. 1. 21. 7). Late Hellenistic tombs excavated between 1880 and 1882 have produced hundreds of *terracotta figurines, for which Myrina is famous. Other remains are very scanty.

E. Pottier and A. J. Reinach, *La Nécropole de Myrina* (1887); G. E. Bean, *Aegean Turkey* (1966), 106–10; D. Kassab, *Statuettes en terre-cuite de Myrina: Corpus des signatures, monogrammes, lettres et signes* (1988). G. E. B.; S. M.

Myron (1), sculptor from Eleutherae (on the Boeotian-Attic border), active *c*.470–440 BC. Reputed pupil of Hageladas and rival of *Pythagoras (2) (Plin., *HN* 34. 57). He was the greatest representative of the post-Archaic period of experimentation in Greek bronze sculpture, and was much interested in proportion (Plin. *HN* 34. 58); his œuvre encompassed gods, heroes, athletes, and animals. A detailed description by *Lucian (*Philops*. 18) has enabled the identification of copies of his Discobolus. Poised between the back- and fore-swings, it is a brilliant study in arrested movement. His group of *Athena and *Marsyas has also been recognized in copy. Composed like a temple metope, it represented a moment of high drama: Athena has just thrown down the flutes, and Marsyas tentatively advances to pick them up. His *Heracles and *Perseus have also been recognized in copy, several athlete types have been attributed to him, and his famous cow may be reproduced in Roman bronze statuettes and marbles. It was a frequent subject of *epigrams (*AP* 9. 713–42, etc.; see Gow–Page, *HE* 2. 63–4.

J. Boardman, *Greek Sculpture: The Classical Period* (1985), 80, figs. 60 ff., 71 f.; A. F. Stewart, *Greek Sculpture* (1990), 147, 148 f., 255 ff., figs. 290 f., 300. A. F. S.

Myron (2), of *Priene (3rd cent. BC?), historian and possibly rhetorician (if so, then a friend of *Chremonides); author of a *Messenian History (Μεσσηνιακά) probably used by *Diodorus (3) Siculus in book 8. *Pausanias (3) criticizes his account of the First Messenian War (see SPARTA) as inaccurate. He also wrote *In Praise of Rhodes* ('Ρόδου 'Εγκώμιον) and possibly some untitled rhetorical works.

FGrH 106 and 265 with comm. to FF 38–46. E. Schwartz, *Hermes* 1899, 453 ff.; L. Pearson, *Hist.* 1962, 410 ff. K. S. S.

Myronides, son of Callias, Athenian general, commanding the 'oldest and youngest' in the Megarid (the territory of *Megara), and the armies which were defeated at *Tanagra and victorious at Oenophyta and then continued campaigning in northern Greece (*c*.458–456 BC). Comedians praised Myronides as a representative of the good old days: if he had only recently died when he was featured in *Eupolis' *Demoi* (412), it can hardly be the same

Myronides who was ambassador to *Sparta and general at the battle of *Plataea in 479.

PA 10509 (one man); D. L. Page, *Select Papyri* 3 (Loeb, 1941), 202–17; K. R. Walters, *AJAH* 1978, 188–91.   V. E.; P. J. R.

myrrh, a thorny bush (*Commiphora myrrha*), native to Somalia and Yemen, which yields a reddish resin. Unlike frankincense (see INCENSE), which was principally used in ritual contexts, myrrh was valued for its use in perfumes, cosmetics, and medicines (Theophr. *Hist. pl.* 9. 4. 2–9; Plin. *HN* 12. 35). The *Peripl. M. Rubr.* § 24 names Muza as a south Arabian port which exported Arabian myrrh.

F. N. Hepper, *Bulletin on Sumerian Agriculture* 1987, 107–14; A. Steier, *RE* 16, 1134 ff.   D. T. P.

Myrrha, or **Smyrna,** or **Zmyrna,** legendary Levantine beauty who conceived an incestuous passion for her father (Theias of Assyria or *Cinyras of Cyprus) and, consequently, *Adonis; she was transformed into a tree whose bark weeps the eponymous *myrrh. See Ov. *Met.* 10. 298 ff. (no doubt influenced by the lost poem of the neoteric C. *Helvius Cinna (see HELLENISTIC POETRY AT ROME), praised in *Catullus (1) 95) and Ant. Lib. *Met.* 34.

A. H. G.

Myrsilus, of *Methymna (fl. *c*.250 BC), wrote a history of *Lesbos and *Historical Paradoxes*. *Dionysius (7) of Halicarnassus (*Ant. Rom.* 1. 23) quotes him extensively on the *Pelasgians or Tyrrhenians. See PARADOXOGRAPHERS.

FGrH 477. S. Jackson, *Myrsilus of Methymna: Hellenistic Paradoxographer* (1995).   K. S. S.

Myrtilus, Athenian comic poet and brother of *Hermippus (1), won a victory at the *Lenaea *c*.427 BC (*IG* 2². 2325. 125). We have two titles, *Titanophanes* and *Erotes* (Loves).

Kassel–Austin, PCG 7. 29 ff. (CAF 1. 253 ff.).   K. J. D.

Myrtis, poet, of *Anthedon in Boeotia; according to later tradition (*Suda*, entries under Κόριννα, Πίνδαρος) teacher both of *Pindar and *Corinna. Her date depends on that of Corinna, who (fr. 15) criticizes her for competing with Pindar. No fragment of her work survives, but a paraphrase in *Plutarch (*Quaest. Graec.* 40 = *Mor.* 300d–f) on the Boeotian hero Eunostus indicates an interest in local myth and in aetiology.

Page, PMG 371; J. M. Snyder, *The Woman and the Lyre* (1989), 40 f.   C. C.

mysteries For much of the 20th cent. the term 'mystery religions' has been current, denoting a special form of personal religion linking the fate of a god of Frazer's 'dying-rising' type with the individual believer. The two scholars whose authority made soteriology the central issue were Fr. Cumont (1904) and R. Reitzenstein (1910). The concealed agendum was the question of the uniqueness, and by implication, validity, of Christianity; at the same time, it was the model of that religion which provided the agreed terms of discussion. In this perspective, the earliest and most influential Greek mystery cult, of *Demeter and Kore (see PERSEPHONE) at *Eleusis, appeared a crude forerunner of more developed mystery religions from the near east, which in the Hellenistic period filled a spiritual vacuum left by the etiolation of Archaic and Classical civic cult. 'Mystery' was taken to be the essence of oriental religiosity.

This entire scenario, and with it the coherence of the notion 'mystery', has now been seriously eroded. U. von Wilamowitz and C. Schneider showed in the 1930s that mysteries in the Greek (Eleusinian) sense were unknown in the homelands of the oriental cults, and were only attached to them on their entry into the Graeco-Roman world. M. P. Nilsson later made a similar point about Dionysiac mysteries (see DIONYSUS); and it is now agreed that all the 'oriental' divinities were thoroughly Hellenized in the process of being assimilated. The validity of Frazer's typology of the dying-rising god (*Osiris, *Attis, *Adonis) was undermined in the 1950s by H. Frankfort and others. The nature of the soteriology of mystery cults has been critically reviewed by the 'School of Rome' since the 1960s, especially by U. Bianchi (see bibliog. below) and his pupils, and redefined as 'the mass of benefits and guarantees which the worshipper expected from the celebration of the cult' (Sfameni Gasparro). In the light of this revisionism, the uniqueness of the claims of Pauline *Christianity (see PAUL, ST.) against the background of Judaic Messianism (see RELIGION, JEWISH) has been re-emphasized, and the issue of the Christianization of the Roman empire opened to fresh debate. The category 'mysteries' is looking decidedly limp. For it is clear that they cannot be considered independent movements, let alone religions, but as merely an ingrained modality of (Greek, later Graeco-Roman) polytheism—they have been compared with a pilgrimage to Santiago di Compostela in the Christian context. And they are only a specialized, often highly local, form of the cult of ill-assorted divinities. Their prominence in modern scholarship is quite disproportionate to their ancient profile.

The most useful recent typology of Graeco-Roman mysteries as forms of personal religious choice is that of Bianchi and others. Three modes are distinguished: 'mystery' proper, an entire initiatory structure of some duration and complexity, of which the type (and in many cases the actual model, e.g. Celeia near Phlius (Paus. 2. 14. 1–4) or the mysteries of *Alexander (13) of Abonuteichos (Lucian, *Alex.* 38 f.)) is Eleusis; 'mystic' cult, involving not initiation but rather a relation of intense communion, typically ecstatic or enthusiastic, with the divinity (e.g. Bacchic frenzy (see DIONYSUS), or the κύβηβοι of *Cybele); and 'mysteriosophic' cult, offering an anthropology, an eschatology, and a practical means of individual reunion with divinity—the primitive or original form is *Orphism, consistently represented as a 'mystery' (e.g. Paus. 9. 30. 4 f., 10. 7. 2), the most typical, Hermeticism and Gnosis (see GNOSTICISM), though these are late Egyptian and Judaeo-Christian forms of religiosity. Bianchi himself has sought to provide an element of thematic unity by adapting Frazer's 'dying-rising god' typology: these cults are all focused upon a 'god subject to some vicissitude'. This tack has rightly been criticized, but the scheme has heuristic value without it.

Of their very nature, ideal types simplify to offer insight. The real world is always much more confused. The word τελετή (see TELETĒ), which often denotes initiatory rituals of the Eleusinian type, could also be applied to any kind of unusual rite in some way analogous. One of the costs of conceptual clarity is the exclusion from consideration of numerous minor cults of Greece and Asia Minor, such as the *teletē* of *Hera at Nauplia, where she bathed annually to 'become a virgin' (Paus. 2. 38. 2). 'Mystery' shifts uneasily between indigenous term and analytical concept. Further complications are the intermingling of the three types in practice and the clear evidence of changes over time: early Orphic lore cannot be neatly distinguished from Bacchic 'mystic' experience; Orphic texts are intimately connected with the formation of Eleusinian myth; the cult of Cybele and Attis is marked by 'mystic' *ecstasy but also, in the Hellenistic period and after, by mysteries of uncertain content analogous to those of Eleusis, and, from the 2nd cent. AD, by a fusion of sacrifice, substitute-castration, and personal baptism—the *taurobolium* ('bull-sacrifice'); the cult of *Mithras may have taken on a 'mysteriosophic' tone.

The variety of mystery cults makes them exceptionally difficult to summarize both briefly and accurately. The aim of the 'mystic' form is best contrasted with that of the collective, integrative, political value of sacrificial civic religion: the individual seeks through possession/'madness' to transcend the constraints of the everyday and become a member of a privileged but temporary community of bliss (Eur. *Bacch.* 64–169; Strabo 10. 3. 7). Religious imagery and style offer a complex counterpoint to those of civic cult. A brusquer world-rejection inspired the 'mysteriosophic' form, based upon a myth accounting for the separation between god and man, flesh and spirit (Kern, *Orph. frag.* 232), evident in the gold plaques from Pelinna in *Thessaly (late 4th cent. BC; see ORPHISM). The 'mystery' type is much more integrated into dominant social values. The modal form, the Eleusinian mysteries, was a full and regular part of Athenian civic cult from the late 6th cent. BC, institutionalizing many aspects of religious aspiration otherwise excluded from public ceremonial: collective purification, the dramatic representation of mythical narrative, the opportunity for awe, fear, wonder, scurrility, and humour (the γεφυρισμοί (ritual abuse) at the bridge over the Cephissus), explicit exegesis by the *mystagōgoi*, the privilege bestowed by an open secret 'that may not be divulged', and public reaffirmation of a theodicy of moral desert linked to good fortune. In this perspective, the offer of a blessed existence in the Elysian fields after death (e.g. *Hymn. Hom. Cer.* 480–9, comm. N. J. Richardson (1974); see ELYSIUM) received no special emphasis, being a projection of complacency into the world beyond, not a compensation for the sorrows of this one. The point probably holds good for all mystery cults, indigenous or 'oriental' (cf. Diod. Sic. 5. 49. 5 f.), until the 3rd cent. AD. See CABIRI.

W. Burkert, *Ancient Mystery Cults* (1987); G. Wagner, *Pauline Baptism and the Pagan Mysteries* (1967; Swiss orig. 1962); K. Prümm, *Dictionnaire de la Bible*, Suppl. 6 (1960), 10–173, 'Mystères'; P. Lévêque, *SMSR* 1982, 185–208. Eleusis: G. E. Mylonas, *Eleusis and the Eleusinian Mysteries* (1962); F. Graf, *Eleusis und die orphische Dichtung Athens in vorhellenistischer Zeit* (1974); Clinton, *Sacred Officials*. Samothrace: S. G. Cole, *Theoi Megaloi* (1984). Dionysus: G. Casadio, *SMSR* 1982, 209–34, and 1983, 123–49; F. Matz, *Dionysiake Telete* (1963). Cybele and Attis: G. Sfameni Gasparro, *Soteriology and Mystic Aspects in the Cult of Cybele and Attis*, 2nd edn. (1985). Isis: F. Le Corsu, *Isis: Mythe et mystères* (1977). Mithras: R. Turcan, *Mithra et le mithriacisme*, 2nd edn. (1993). Soteriology: U. Bianchi and M. J. Vermaseren (eds.), *La soteriologia dei culti orientali nell'impero romano* (1982). Iconography: U. Bianchi, *The Greek Mysteries* (1976). Philosophic appropriation of initiatory language: C. Riedweg, *Mysterienterminologie bei Platon, Philon und Klemens von Alexandrien* (1987); J. Smith, *Drudgery Divine* (1990): debate about Christian 'mysteries'. R. L. G.

mythographers The first comprehensive collection of heroic myths was the *Catalogue of Women* ascribed to *Hesiod, and myths formed a substantial element in the writings of the genealogists (*Hecataeus (1), *Acusilaus, *Pherecydes (2) of Athens, *Hellanicus (1)) in the 5th cent. BC, and the Atthidographers (see ATTHIS) in the 4th. *Asclepiades (1) of Tragilus, a pupil of *Isocrates, treated the myths of tragedy in particular, and compared them with earlier versions.

But the main mythographic collections date from Hellenistic or early imperial times, and fall into two broad categories. The first type attempts to collect relevant myths to elucidate major authors such as *Homer, *Pindar, the tragedians (see TRAGEDY, GREEK), and the Hellenistic poets. Scattered in the ancient scholia

to Pindar, *Euripides, *Theocritus, *Apollonius (1) of Rhodes, and *Lycophron (2) are rich collections of mythography. The most remarkable such collection consists of hundreds of stories (*historiai*) in the scholia to the *Iliad* and *Odyssey*, which papyrus discoveries now show to have been an independent book (dubbed the 'mythographus Homericus') in antiquity; only later was it incorporated with the scholia. See SCHOLIA.

The second category comprises independent collections of myths organized around a particular theme and attributed (usually falsely) to a famous name, such as the star-myths of *Eratosthenes (see CONSTELLATIONS, § 3), the love stories of *Parthenius, the 'Tales from Euripides' of *Dicaearchus, the narratives of *Conon (3) and the *Metamorphoses* of *Antoninus Liberalis. The greatest of these is the *Library* ascribed to *Apollodorus (6) of Athens (the genuine Apollodorus had a scholarly interest in myths, but cannot be the author of this handbook). It contains a continuous account of Greek myths from the Creation to the Dorian invasion, arranged by family genealogies; the Hesiodic *Catalogue of Women* is a likely structural model, although the sources are seldom named, and (for individual details) may be countless.

In Latin, *Ovid's *Metamorphoses* offered in poetry a comprehensive mythography (although of a very different sort) to match the *Catalogue of Women*, and several works in Latin either translate or imitate Greek predecessors: mythographic narratives are found in *Servius and other scholia, and traces of earlier sources can be glimpsed in the *Fabulae* and *Astronomia* of *Hyginus (3) (another suspicious attribution) and the miscellanies of *Fulgentius and the so-called *Mythographi Vaticani* (ed. G. H. Bode (1834)).

TEXTS The Teubner *Mythographi Graeci* (1894–) was never completed; still useful is A. Westermann, *Mythographoi: Scriptores poeticae historiae graeci* (1843).
A. Henrichs, in J. Bremmer (ed.), *Interpretations of Greek Mythology* (1987). J. S. R.

mythology is the field of scholarship dealing with myth but also a particular body of myths. Myth goes back to the Greek word *mythos*, which originally meant 'word, speech, message' but in the 5th cent. BC started to acquire the meaning 'entertaining, if not necessarily trustworthy, tale'. The Romans used the word *fabula*, which was also used in modern discussions until c.1760, when the Göttingen classicist C. G. Heyne (1729–1812) coined the word *mythus* in order to stress the inner veracity of myth. No universally accepted definition of myth exists, but Walter Burkert's statement that 'myth is a traditional tale with secondary, partial reference to something of collective importance' gives a good idea of the main characteristics of myth.

Let us start with the problem of tradition. *Homer already mentions the *Argonauts, the Theban Cycle, and the deeds of *Heracles. The presence in Linear B texts (see MYCENAEAN LANGUAGE) of the formulae 'Mother of the Gods' and 'Drimius, son of *Zeus' suggests a divine genealogy, and the myths of *Achilles, *Helen, and the cattle-raiding Heracles all seem to go back to *Indo-European times (and Heracles maybe further back than that). The connection with central institutions or pressing problems of society—*initiation, marriage, food—makes their continuity persuasive: Achilles' myth can hardly be separated from rites of initiation, whereas wedding poetry probably stands in the background of Helen's mythology. See INITIATION; RITES OF PASSAGE.

Other myths were certainly also of considerable age, such as the birth of Athenian *Erechtheus from the seed of *Hephaestus or the birth of the famous horse *Arion (1) from the union of *Poseidon with the goddess Erinys (see ERINYES). It is typical of Greek myth that Homer and other Archaic poets tended to suppress such strange and scandalous details, which survived only in locally fixed traditions. The trend of Greek mythology was firmly anthropomorphic and away from the fantastic.

Another ancient complex was constituted by initiatory myths. Strikingly, all early *Panhellenic expeditions—the Trojan War (see TROY), *Jason and the Argonauts, and the Calydonian Hunt (see ATALANTA; MELEAGER (1))—contain many male initiatory elements, just as the myths of *Iphigenia, *Io, *Europa, and the daughters of *Proetus reflect the final transition into womanhood. Although many other Indo-European peoples had initiatory myths, its prominence is one of the distinctive features of Greek mythology.

A more recent complex of myths came from the east. The Indo-Europeans had at the most only rudimentary theogonical and cosmogonical myths. It is not surprising, therefore, that in this area Greece became very much indebted to the rich mythologies of Anatolia and Mesopotamia. *Cronus' castration of his father *Uranus ultimately derives from the Hurrians, having passed through *Hittite and *Phoenician intermediaries; the division of the world between Zeus, Poseidon, and *Hades through the casting of lots, as described in the *Iliad* (15. 187–93), derives from the Akkadian epic *Atrahasis*; and when *Hera, in a speech to deceive Zeus, says that she will go to *Oceanus, 'origin of the gods', and *Tethys, the 'mother' (*Il.* 14. 201), she mentions a couple derived from the parental pair Apsu and Tiamat in the Babylonian creation epic *Enuma Elish.* New clay tablets will surely present further surprises in this direction.

The fertile contacts with the east probably took place in the early iron age. Somewhat later, the foundations of colonies (see COLONIZATION, GREEK) in the Mediterranean and the Black Sea (*c.*750–600 BC) led to the last great wave of mythological inventions. In particular, the myths about the return of the heroes after the Trojan War, but also the expedition of the Argonauts, enabled many colonies to connect their new foundations to the Panhellenic past as created through these great myths. It is surprising how quickly traditional story-patterns here transformed historical events.

It is clear that poets were always prepared to assimilate or borrow new material. Another way of 'staying in business' was to vary the traditional myths by introducing new details—e.g. new names and motivations—or by restructuring the myth into a different direction. Whereas archaic myth concentrated more, for example, on dynasties and heroic feats, in a later, more regulated society, myth tended to concentrate on relations within the family and, especially in Athenian tragedy (see TRAGEDY, GREEK), on the relation between individual and *polis* or the value of democratic institutions (see DEMOCRACY, ATHENIAN).

Rome, on the other hand, was situated at the margin of the 'civilized' world and was late to assimilate Greek myth (see further below). When the Roman élite started to write down its history at the end of the 3rd cent. BC, it had one fixed mythological complex at its disposal: the foundation of Rome by *Romulus and Remus. A few names, such as *Janus and *Picus, hint at the sometime existence of other myths, but nothing suggests an originally rich mythology, and the absence of a *Götterapparat* has even led some scholars to the suggestion that the Romans lacked a mythology altogether. Moreover, the 'brain drain' of neighbouring élites into Rome did not favour the survival of Italic myths: the founding of *Praeneste by Caeculus is the only full

myth from *Latium that we still have. The foundation myths show that the temporal horizon was not the creation of gods or men but the birth of the native city; the foundation of the city was also the most important mythological theme in public declamations in imperial times (see FOUNDERS, CITY).

Unlike Rome, which lacked a native expression for poets and poetry, Greece knew many poets who were the main producers of mythology; the tradition of formal narrative prose, which existed as well, is only discoverable in bare outlines. Poets performed at courts or local festivals in various genres, which successively became popular: epic in the 8th cent., choral lyric in the 6th and, finally, tragedy, the last public performance of myth, in the 5th. Yet myths were also related in other contexts. Temple friezes, sculptures, and vases (see IMAGERY; PAINTING; SCULPTURE) made myth as a subject visible virtually everywhere. Women told myths during weaving-sessions (Eur. *Ion* 196 f.); old men will have related them in the *leschai* (club-like meeting-places), and mothers and nurses told them to children (Eur. fr. 484 Nauck; Pl. *Leg.* 887d). 'Indoctrination' by mothers and nurses will have been a significant, if usually neglected, factor in the continuing popularity of myth all through antiquity.

The uses of myth varied over time, but the entertainment value was always important. Indeed, Homer himself points to the delight of songs (*Od.* 17. 385). Choral lyric, with its combination of music, dance, and song, must have been quite a spectacle, and for the thousands of spectators Athenian tragedy was a welcome break in the winter months. Other uses included the foundation of the social and political order. Myth explained how in Athens males had arrived at their dominant position through the chaos caused by women; how cities originated, such as *Thebes (1) through a struggle against a dragon, or how tribal groupings arose, such as the *Ionians from *Ion (1) and the Aeolians (see AEOLIS) from *Aeolus (2). It explained why, for example, the Spartans ruled their extended territory, or why Athens could claim *Aegina.

Myth also helped the Greeks to define the world around them and their own place in relation to the gods. By situating murderous women on mountains, by letting girls in their prime play on flowery meadows, or by ascribing the ancestry of the leading family to a river-god, these features of the landscape were assigned negative or positive values. Moreover, by relating the unhappy endings of love affairs between gods and humans, for example *Semele being burnt to ashes through the appearance of Zeus in full glory, myth stressed the unbridgeable gap between mortals and immortals.

Finally, the aetiological function of myth was substantial. Many myths explained the birth or function of rituals; even the tragedian *Euripides often recounted the origins of vital Attic cults. Other myths highlighted or 'explained' unusual features of ritual: the myth of the Lemnian women concentrated on the separation of the sexes but totally left out the new fire, which was actually very prominent in the corresponding ritual. (See Burkert, *HN* 190 ff.) The exaggeration by myth of the ritual separation of the sexes into the mythical murder shows up an important difference between myth and *ritual: myth can depict as real what in ritual has to remain symbolic. Over time, myth could free itself from one specific ritual and be connected with other ones, or the ritual could disappear while the myth continued to be narrated: in the 2nd cent. AD the traveller *Pausanias (3) recorded many myths of which the rituals had already long disappeared.

Myth was originally the product of an oral society (see

ORALITY), but the arrival of writing brought important changes. Poets had now to share their leading intellectual roles with philosophers and historians—authors who wrote in prose and did not have to subject their opinions to the scrutiny of a public. The new intellectuals soon started to systematize and criticize mythological traditions. On the other hand, the force of tradition weighed heavily and that explains why the two most popular strategies in dealing with mythology were rationalization, which in our sources starts with *Hecataeus (1) of Miletus (c.550–480 BC), and allegorization, which probably started with the late 6th-cent. rhapsodist *Theagenes (2) of Rhegium; the adoption of this approach by the Stoics (see STOICISM) caused its survival until late antiquity. In this way, intellectuals could have their mythological cake and eat it.

These developments strongly diminished the public influence of poets as prime producers of mythology. In Hellenistic times, the myths recorded and adapted by *Callimachus (3) and his contemporaries were directed at a small circle of connoisseurs not the general public. However, it was these poets who exercised an enormous influence in Rome, where in the last two centuries of the republic and during the early Principate a proliferation of mythical themes can be noted—to the extent that in *Ovid one ritual can receive several aetiological myths. However, it is hard to say what degree of authority, if any, these myths had in Rome.

In the Hellenistic and early imperial period scholars started to collect myths in order to elucidate allusions in the Classical authors; most important in this respect was the collection of mythological *scholia on Homer which circulated as a separate book at least from the 1st to the 5th cent. AD. Other collections concentrated on one theme, such as *Eratosthenes' book of star-myths (see CONSTELLATIONS, § 3) or the famous *Library* ascribed to *Apollodorus (6), which organized the mythological material by families (see MYTHOGRAPHERS). It is especially these collections which have ensured modern knowledge of the less familiar myths of Greece.

The modern study of Greek mythology started in France in the 18th cent., but the centre of interest soon shifted to Germany, where there was more philological expertise. It was the insights of Heyne in particular—myth as history, myth as explanation of natural phenomena, myth as the product of a specific people—which dominated the field in the 19th cent. However, the excesses of the naturalist interpretation were an important factor in the shift of scholarly interest away from mythology towards ritual at the end of the 19th cent. Since the middle 1960s interest in Greek myth has revived, notably through the work of Walter Burkert (1931–   ). The focal points of the new approaches are the relationship between myth and ritual and the explanatory and normative functions of myth. Roman myth has also profited from this revival, but the scarcity of material and the élite's view of myths as *fabulae*, 'fictional stories', make it difficult to see what exactly the place of myth was in Roman society. The differences between Greek and Roman mythology still await further analysis.

GREECE W. Burkert, *Structure and History in Greek Mythology and Ritual* (1979); E. Risch, *ZPE* 60 (1985), 1–9 (Indo-European tradition of narrative prose); J. Bremmer (ed.), *Interpretations of Greek Mythology* (1987); T. Carpenter, *Art and Myth in Ancient Greece* (1991); K. Dowden, *The Uses of Greek Mythology* (1992); W. Burkert, *The Orientalizing Revolution* (1992), ch. 3 (influence from the east); F. Graf, *Greek Mythology: An Introduction* (1993) contains an excellent historiographical survey; I. Malkin, *Myth and Territory in the Spartan Mediterranean* (1994); R. Buxton, *Imaginary Greece* (1994).

ROME J. N. Bremmer and N. M. Horsfall, *Roman Myth and Mythography* (1987); F. Graf (ed.), *Mythos in mythenloser Gesellschaft: Das Paradigma Rom* (1993).

ICONOGRAPHY *LIMC*.   J. N. B.

Mytilene (the official form; also Mitylene; now Mytilini), the most important *polis* in *Lesbos, situated on an islet (now a promontory) adjoining the east coast. Its walls, extending on to the mainland, enclosed an area similar to that of Athens; it possessed land in Asia Minor. Archaeology has revealed harbour moles, cemeteries, aqueducts, a theatre (possibly Pompey's prototype for Rome's first theatre), and a major sanctuary of *Demeter and Kore (see PERSEPHONE). As *Vitruvius observed, the streets were open to the north wind.

Greek finds begin in the protogeometric period. As the city grew powerful, its élite helped found the Hellenion at *Naucratis, and fought Athens over *Sigeum. 'Lesbian' transport *amphorae, widely exported now and later, may in fact be Mytilenean. The poet *Alcaeus (1) led one side in a civil war; his arch-enemy *Pittacus became sole ruler (see AISYMNĒTĒS), but was reputedly a just man. Following a lengthy Persian domination, interrupted by the *Ionian Revolt, Mytilene became a steadfast ally of Athens; after its revolt in 428 a *cleruchy was installed. Mytilene remained mostly pro-Athenian until the Persians returned in 357. Liberated by *Alexander (3) the Great, it was successively ruled by *Antigonus (1), *Lysimachus, and the Ptolemies (see PTOLEMY (1)).

The Hellenistic town produced metals, textiles, terracottas, and *garum* (see FISHING). The Romans sacked it in 79 BC for supporting *Mithradates VI. *Pompey freed it (see THEOPHANES); the citizens celebrated their links with Rome through monuments, and Romans often visited Mytilene for recreation. Its public buildings and houses indicate prosperity in Roman and late Roman times.

Mytilene became a bishopric and several Christian basilicas have been identified; a unique series of *mosaics (3rd/4th cent. AD) depicts scenes from theatrical works, with scenes and actors named.

N. Spencer, *BSA* 1995; H. and C. Williams, *Échos du monde classique/Classical Views* 1991 ff.; *Arch. Rep.* 1987–8 ff.; *RE* 16/2 (1935), 1411–27; D. L. Page, *Sappho and Alcaeus* (1955); S. Charitonidis, L. Kahil, and R. Ginouvès, *Les Mosaïques de la maison de Ménandre à Mytilène* (1970); basilicas: *AΔ* 1968, 10–69.   D. G. J. S., C. R.

Naassenes, Christian splinter group that took its name from the Hebrew word for serpent (*nahash*), Hellenized (i.e. turned into Greek) as *naas* (Hippol. *Haer.* 5. 1); the word in Hebrew, perhaps not coincidentally, had the same numerical value as the word for Messiah. In Greek, the serpent was connected by false etymology with the word for temple (*naos*), and the Naassenes believed that nothing mortal or immortal, animate or inanimate could exist without Naas. They taught that the universe derived from an hermaphroditic monad (Adam), who produced three elements as offspring, Nous (Mind), *Chaos, and *Psyche (Hippol. *Haer.* 5. 5). The three elements of Adam descended into one man, Jesus, who revealed knowledge, *gnōsis*, to humans. Just as Adam and Naas created without sex, they also preached strict sexual abstinence. It appears that they claimed that their doctrine originated with James, the brother of Jesus, who had revealed it to Mariamme. Numerous quotations from their works, including a Naassene hymn, are preserved in Hippolytus' *Refutatio omnium haeresium*. *PFayum* 2, which had been identified as a second Naassene hymn, is now generally thought to be simply a poem about the Underworld (C. H. Roberts, *Manuscript, Society and Belief in Early Christian Egypt* (1977), 81–2).

K. Rudolph, *Gnosis* (1983); T. Wolbergs, *Griechische Gedichte der ersten nachchristlichen Jahrhunderte* (1971), on Naassene hymn (with bibliog.); J. Frickel, *Hellenistische Erlösung in christlicher Deutung* (1984).   D. S. P.

Nabataeans The Nabataean Arabs, whose kingdom was centred on *Petra, achieved great wealth by conveying luxury goods from southern Arabia to the Mediterranean. In 312 BC *Antigonus (1) I tried unsuccessfully to conquer them and, though they had been forced into a treaty with Rome as early as 62 BC, their kings retained independent status until Trajan transformed their kingdom into the Roman province of Arabia (AD 106). More important kings included Obodas I (*c.*96–87 BC), Aretas III Philhellenos (87–62), Aretas IV Philopatris (9 BC–AD 40), Malichus II (40–70), and Rabel II (70–106). Their religious traditions are 'Arabian' and their main deity, Dushara/Dusares, was probably astral in character. Although they normally spoke some form of Arabic, they used *Aramaic for inscriptions. See ARABS; ARETAS; MALCHUS (2) I.

A. Negev, *ANRW* 2. 8 (1977), 520–686; J. Starcky, *Dictionnaire de la Bible*, Suppl. 7 (1966), 886–1017; R. E. Brünnow and A. von Domaszewski, *Die Provincia Arabia* (1904–9); J. Hornblower, *Hieronymus of Cardia* (1981), 144 ff., 178; G. W. Bowersock, *Roman Arabia* (1983, corr. repr. 1994), esp. chs. 2–5; F. Millar, *The Roman Near East 31 BC–AD 337* (1993), see index.   J. F. H.

Nabis, son of Demaratus, probably descended from the deposed Spartan king *Demaratus (2), seized the crown—now a single crown—in 207 BC on the death of his royal ward Pelops. Forming a mercenary guard in the manner of the Archaic tyrants (see TYRANNY), and with the aid of Cretan pirates, he is said to have drastically restored the revolutionary programme of *Cleomenes (2) III abrogated by Macedon in 222. Opponents were exiled or, following torture, executed, and their wives were forcibly married to enfranchised ex-helots—or so the mainly hostile sources allege. A less excited view would be that Nabis got under way the necessary modernization of Sparta and began finally to bring the city out of its 'Lycurgan' shadow (see LYCURGUS (2)). In foreign affairs, his fortunes were mixed. In 204–3 he raided *Megalopolis, but was in 201 repelled from *Messene and in 200 defeated by the *Achaean Confederacy general *Philopoemen. In the Second Macedonian War he gained *Argos (2), betrayed to him by *Philip (3) V of Macedon, and instituted revolutionary measures there. But T. *Quinctius Flamininus rejected his overtures, and in 195 he found himself charged with tyranny and forced to surrender Argos and the Laconian ports. This was the effective end of Sparta's *perioikoi. In 193, attempting to regain the ports, he was subdued by Philopoemen and Flamininus. In 192 he was assassinated in Sparta in an Aetolian coup. A revolutionary type, his career and policy have suffered unduly in the pro-Achaean tradition of *Polybius (1).

J.-G. Texier, *Nabis* (1975); P. Cartledge and A. J. S. Spawforth, *Hellenistic and Roman Sparta* (1989), ch. 5.   P. A. C.

Naevius, Gnaeus, stage poet of Campanian birth (see CAMPANIA) and obscure social attachments, possibly a client of the Claudii Marcelli (see CLAUDIUS MARCELLUS entries). He saw military service in the last years of the First *Punic War. His theatrical career began as early as 235 and was over by 204. Many stories were told of the insulting remarks he made about men of the nobility from the stage or in other contexts. Plautus, *Mil.* 210–12 was interpreted to refer to a spell by him in prison. He died in the Punic city of *Utica.

Titles of 32 plays on themes of the Attic 'New' Comedy (see COMEDY (GREEK), NEW) are transmitted (*Acontizomenos, Agitatoria, Agrypnuntes, †assitogiola†, Carbonaria, Chlamydaria, Colax, †cemetria†, Corollaria, Dementes, Demetrius, Dolus, Figulus, Glaucoma, Gymnasticus, Hariolus, Lampadio, Leo, Nagido, Neruolaria, †pellicus†, Personata, Proiectus, Quadrigemini, Stalagmus, Stigmatias, Tarentilla, Technicus, Testicularia, †tribacelus†, Triphallus, Tunicularia*). According to *Terence (*An.* 9–21), Naevius was one of those who set a precedent for treating an Attic model with some liberty. He put both dialogues and monologues into musically accompanied metres of the type used by his contemporary

Naiads

*Plautus (see METRE, LATIN). On occasion he made his Greek personages allude to features of Italian life. There is thus no need to deduce from an allusion to the tastes of the men of *Praeneste and *Lanuvium (Macrob. *Sat.* 3. 18. 6) that the *Hariolus* was a play of the kind composed by *Titinius and L. *Afranius (1), i.e. a *fabula* *togata*. The *Satyra* cited by *Verrius Flaccus (Festus, p. 306. 29, Lindsay) is a mystery.

Six titles (*Danae, Equos Troianus, Hector proficiscens, Hesiona, Iphigenia, Lycurgus*) suggest tragedies of the Attic type. An account of *Danae's disgrace (Non. p. 456. 25, Lindsay) seems to have been set in bacchiac verse rather than in spoken senarii. Naevius also composed original tragedies, one on the story of *Romulus the first Roman king, another (the *Clastidium*) on the defeat of a Gallic army in 222 by M. *Claudius Marcellus (1). The latter may have been performed at funeral games for Marcellus in 208 or at the dedication in 205 of the temple of Virtus (see HONOS) vowed by the consul before the battle of *Clastidium.

Only one of the plays survived into the 1st-cent. BC stage repertoire. A narrative poem in *Saturnian verses concerning the 264–241 war with *Carthage, the *Carmen belli Poenici*, lasted longer. The grammarian C. *Octavius Lampadio divided it into seven units towards the end of the 2nd cent. Naevius could hardly have been unaware of the pro-Carthaginian account of the war by *Philinus (2) of Acragas. Whether he knew of *Fabius Pictor's has been the subject of much speculation. A digression filling a large part of the first of Lampadio's units, all the second, and a large part of the third related the early history of Rome and Carthage and provided a divine, perhaps even a cosmic, setting for the 3rd-cent. clash of arms. Naevius claimed inspiration by the *Camenae and used a metrical and verbal style hard now to distinguish from that of *Livius Andronicus' translation of *Homer's *Odyssey*.

Despite strong criticism by *Ennius (Cic. *Brut.* 72) Naevius' poem continued to find readers in the 1st cent. BC. Two grammarians, a Cornelius and a Vergilius, composed commentaries on it (Varro, *Ling.* 7. 39). *Horace used its survival to make fun of the claims of Ennius' *Annals* (*Epist.* 2. 1. 53–4). The collectors of 'thefts' in *Virgil's *Aeneid* detected a number from Naevius. The matter was still of interest in the 5th cent. AD (cf. Macrob. *Sat.* 6. 2), but there is no evidence that the older poem itself could be found in any library of this time.

TEXTS E. H. Warmington, *Remains of Old Latin* 2 (Loeb, 1936), 46 ff. (with trans.). Dramatic frs.: O. Ribbeck, *TRF*³ 7 ff., *CRF*³ 6 ff. *Carmen belli Poenici*: W. Morel, *FPL* 17 ff.

DISCUSSIONS E. Fraenkel, *RE* Suppl. 6 (1935), 622 ff.; L. Strzelecki, *De Naeviano Belli Punici carmina quaestiones selectae* (1935); S. Mariotti, *Il 'Bellum Poenicum' e l'arte di Nevio* (1955); K. Büchner, *Humanitas Romana* (1957), 13 ff.; H. D. Jocelyn, *Antichthon* 1969, 32 ff.; M. Barchiesi, *Nevio epico* (1962); *La Tarentilla revisitata: Studi su Nevio comico* (1978). H. D. J.

Naiads See NYMPHS.

Naïssus (modern *Niš*) in *Moesia (after *Diocletian in Dardania), first visited by Roman troops in 75/72 BC, was probably the earliest permanent military camp in Moesia. Though of great strategic importance, little is known of its history: it became a *municipium* under M. *Aurelius or later. Here *Claudius II decisively defeated the *Goths in AD 269. Frequently visited by Roman emperors, especially by *Constantine I the Great, who was born there, it was destroyed by *Huns in 441, but was partially restored. Under *Justinian, Naïssus flourished anew, but

was seriously threatened by the Slavs. It was destroyed or at least sacked by the Avars in 596 (see AVARO-SLAV INVASIONS), but continued to exist as a Slav town.

Inscriptions de la Mésie Supérieure 4, ed. P. Petrović (1979).

F. A. W. S.; J. J. W.

names, personal, Greek Greek nomenclature conformed in many important respects to the *Indo-European pattern; its main features can be seen already in Mycenaean texts (see MYCENAEAN LANGUAGE) and in *Homer. One name only was the norm for men and women. Secondary names given in the Classical and Hellenistic periods to public figures such as politicians, courtesans, and kings, usually linked by ὁ/ἡ, ὁ/ἡ ἐπικαλούμενος/η, etc., did not break this rule, since they were nicknames and were not handed down in the family.

While the single name was sufficient in private life, in public contexts, such as decrees, dedications, and tombstones, it was normally followed by the name of the father, the patronymic (very rarely that of the mother, the metronymic), or by the name of the husband (for women). It became standard practice to express the patronymic in the form of the father's name in the genitive: thus, Ἀλέξανδρος Φιλίππου, 'Alexander [son] of Philip'. An early type of patronymic, detectable in Mycenaean texts and evident in Homer, an adjectival form with the suffix -ιος (Αἴας Τελαμώνιος, 'Ajax son of Telamon'), survived in the historical period only in regions of *Aeolic dialect, *Boeotia, *Thessaly, and *Lesbos, where the parent's name took the suffix -ιος, or -ειος, and variants, according to the stem and the dialect (e.g. Ἀγάθων Θρασώνιος, 'Agathon son of Thrason'; Νικίαιος, 'son of Nikias'; Φιλίννα Ἀριστάρχεια, 'Philinna daughter of Aristarchos'). A second patronymic form common in Homer, with the suffix -ίδης and variants (Ἕκτωρ Πριαμίδης, 'Hektor son of Priam') formed independent names with no active patronymic force (Ἀγαθωνίδης, Θράσων Θρασωνίδου). The name and patronymic could in certain circumstances be further qualified by an indication of location (*deme, tribe (see PHYLAI), or *phratry). In cities with a deme structure, for example, the demotic was regularly given after the patronymic when at home, but seldom used abroad; city or regional ethnics (indicators of origin or of political affiliation) would not be used except when abroad.

The name-giving is associated in our sources with the ceremony of the Amphidromia, and is assigned variously to the fifth, seventh, or tenth day after birth. It was common practice to name the first son after his paternal grandfather, the second after his maternal grandfather, paternal uncle, etc. Naming a son after his father was much less common. Daughters were also often named after family members, but the evidence is less plentiful than for men.

Greek names could be simple or compound. In the first case a name could be identical to any noun or adjective (except for the compulsory retraction of the accent in some instances), but it could also be a derivative of any word, formed by means of various suffixes (masc. -ων, -ιων, etc., fem. -ω, -ις, etc.) including diminutive suffixes (-υλος, -ισκος, -ιλλα, -υλλα, etc.). Thus from the adjective θρασύς 'bold', Θράσυς, Θρασίων, Θράσυλλα, etc.

Compound names such as Ξάνθιππος, which were probably felt to have higher status (cf. Ar. *Nub.*, 60 ff.), were often replaced by shortened forms (hypocoristics) according to rules of formation which are not entirely predictable. Normally a large part of the second element of the compound is replaced by a suffix with or without gemination of the previous consonant: Πάτροκλος from Πατροκλῆς (originally Πατροκλέης), Ἐπικτᾶς from Ἐπίκτητος, Κλεομμᾶς from Κλεομένης, etc. Names of men were masculine and declined according to the normal rules for words belonging to their declension; names of women normally were feminine but could also be neuter (e.g. Ἡδίστιον) and again declined in a predictable manner. It is notable, however, that names allow types of formation which common adjectives or nouns avoid; an epitheton like ἀγέστρατος is both masculine and feminine but the name Τιμόστρατος can only be used for a man, and a new form Τιμοστράτη is created for a woman. Similarly ἀκρατής is both masculine and feminine but Ξενοκράτης can only be a man and the woman's name is Ξενοκράτεια, etc.

It is not possible to do more than hint at the enormous range of concepts drawn on to form names. Among the substantives forming simple names (and combining in compound names) were the names of animals (λέων 'lion' → Λέων, Λέαινα, Λεοντίσκος), weapons (θώραξ 'breastplate' → Θώραξ, Θωρακίδης), parts of the body (κέφαλος 'head' → Κέφαλος, Κεφαλίων), plants (ἄμπελος 'vine' → Ἄμπελος, Ἀμπελίων, Ἀμπελίς, Ἀμπελίδης), rivers (Ἀσώπιος, Ἀσωπίων, Ἀσώπιχος, Ἀσωπόκριτος, etc. common in *Boeotia, from the river Asopus). Abstract nouns, including neuter nouns, were used particularly for women's names (Ἀρέτη, Εὐταξία, Δώρημα). Compound names could, with certain exceptions, take their elements in either order. They commonly carried notions of leadership and military prowess (Ἀγέ-στρατος/Στράτ-ηγος, Ἀρχέ-δημος/Δήμαρχος, Στρατο-νίκη/Νικο-στράτη, Πολεμο-κράτης/Εὐ-πόλεμος), civic organization (Ἀστυ-νόμος, Ἀρχέ-πολις/Πολί-αρχος, Δημο-δίκη, Πεισί-δημος), saving or defending (Σωσί-πολις, Ἀλεξί-δημος), strength (Κράτ-ιππος, Δημο-κράτεια), beauty or nobility (Ἀγαθό-βουλος, Καλλί-ξενος, Καλλιστ-αρέτη, Εὐ-κρίτη), liking, honouring (Φιλο-τίμη, Ἀστύ-φιλος, Ἐράσ-ιππος, Τιμο-λέων, Θρασύ-τιμος), reputation (Κλεο-μήδης, Θρασυ-κλῆς, Φιλό-κλεια). These and many other words combined to create thousands of different name-forms, some occurring in more than 50 different forms. While there was a natural tendency for desirable attributes to be chosen, it was not always the case, and it remains a matter of psychological curiosity why some forms were chosen, and even handed down within families: thus, αἰσχρός 'ugly' forming Αἴσχρος, Αἴσχρα, Αἰσχρίων, Αἰσχρώ; κόπρος 'dung' forming Κοπρίων, Κοπρία, Κόπρις; σιμός 'snub-nosed' forming Σῖμος, Σιμύλος, Σιμίσκος.

Many studies have focused on particular categories of names. Theophoric names were a recognized category in antiquity (ὀνόματα θεοφόρα and ἄθεα, Ath. 10. 448e). They were based not only on gods' names, but also on their cult titles, and on months named after them. Adjectival derivatives of a deity's name, Ἀπολλώνιος/α, Διονύσιος/α, Δημήτριος/α, were among the most common of Greek names. Compound forms were likely to carry notions of giving/given (-δωρος, -δοτος), birth (-γένης/-γένεια), repute or favour (-κλῆς/-κλεια; -φάνης/-φάνεια; -χάρης/-χαρις, etc.). Thus, based on the name of *Zeus, with the root Dio-: Διόδωρος, Διόδοτος, Διογένης, Διοκλῆς, Διοφάνης, Διοχάρης, Διόγνητος, etc. Some theophoric names reflect a local cult, for example Καρνεάδης, Κάρνις, etc. common at *Cyrene, a centre of the cult of *Apollo Carneius (see CARNEA). Non-Greek deities were also absorbed into nomenclature, as is shown by the spread, from the late 3rd cent. BC, of the names Σεραπίων, Σεραπιάς, Σεραπίς, etc., derived from the Egyptian god *Sarapis. With time, however, these and other names became neutralized, as

the survival into the Christian period of names deriving from pagan deities shows.

The justification for believing in a category of distinctively 'slave' names has been undermined by the epigraphical evidence of manumission documents. It is true that certain types of name were common among slaves, notably those derived from ethnics, especially of those countries which were a regular source of slaves (e.g. Σύρος/α, Αἰγύπτιος/α, Θρᾶιξ/Θράισσα, but also Ῥόδιος/α, Θεττάλη, Λάκων, etc.; less commonly, the name of a country, Ἀσία, Ἰταλία); names associated with certain regions (Τίβειος from *Paphlagonia); names of heroic and historical figures (Πάρις, Κροῖσος); names derived from suitable qualities conveyed in abstract nouns or adjectives (Εὐκαρπία, Ἁρμονία, Γλυκέρα, Εὔνους); transactions (Κτῆμα, Δόσις). Many of these names, however, were also borne by free people, and many slaves had 'good' names indistinguishable from those of free people. The naming and renaming of slaves (see SLAVERY), on enslavement or at birth into slavery in the household, or at manumission, and the passing of manumitted slaves into the local population, are all factors tending to loosen the concept of a 'slave-name'. Servile status can never be deduced from the name alone, without supporting circumstantial evidence.

In the Roman, and especially the imperial, period significant changes in nomenclature took place. The practice developed, particularly in *Asia Minor, of having two or more names, often linked by a formula such as ὁ/ἡ καί, ἐπικλήν, ὁ χρηματίζων (Ἱεροκλῆς Λέων ὁ καὶ Θράσων). This can be seen as a development of earlier practice; with the spread of Roman *citizenship, however, the fundamental pattern of Greek nomenclature was broken. A Greek with Roman citizenship would usually record the praenomen and nomen (abbreviated and spelt in various ways, Τ., Τί., Τίτος, Φλ., Φλάβιος, Φλαούιος), and retain the Greek name in the cognomen (Τ. Φλ. Ἀλκιβιάδης, Αὐρηλία Φιλοκράτεια). Under the impact of the *tria nomina* (see NAMES, PERSONAL, ROMAN, § 1) the patronymic was adapted in various ways, sometimes recorded in the Roman fashion before the cognomen, with or without υἱός, sometimes retained after the cognomen (Αὐρ. Νικόστρατος Νίκωνος, Αὐρ. Ἀγησᾶς ὁ πρὶν Ἀγαθία), approximating to Greek practice, and sometimes conveyed in a patronymic adjective formed in -ιανός/-ιανή (Ἡρωδιανός, Εὐτυχιανή). Practice was very varied. In absorbing Roman citizenship into their nomenclature Greeks showed as much ingenuity and licence as they had in forming their own names. In the Christian period, the single name became once more the norm, usually without the patronymic. By that time names had undergone a fundamental change under the influence of the new religion, though it was still possible to come across monks called Alcibiades and bishops called Serapion.

Reflecting as they do the full range of language, landscape, cults, and institutions, names offer an important means of understanding ancient Greek society. Since J.-A. Letronne pointed out their potential in a pioneering article (*Annali dell'Istituto* 1845, 251 ff.), there have been enormous advances in both the evidence for names and the study of them. The following bibliography can do no more than indicate the major studies.

W. Pape and G. E. Benseler, *Wörterbuch der griechischen Eigennamen* (1863–70); F. Bechtel, *Die historischen Personennamen des Griechischen* (1917); O. Landau, *Mykenisch-Griechische Personennamen* (1958); L. Robert, *Noms indigènes dans l'Asie Mineure gréco-romaine* (1963), and many other studies throughout his *Opera Minora Selecta*, 7 vols. (1969–90); G. Daux, in *L'Onomastique latine* (1977), 405 f.; H. von Kamptz, *Homerische Personennamen* (1982); L. Zgusta, *Kleinasiatische Personen-*

namen (1984); P. M. Fraser and E. Matthews, *A Lexicon of Greek Personal Names*, 1987–   (vol. 1, 1987, vol. 2, 1994, vol. 3A, 1997, vol. 3B, 2000); O. Masson, *Onomastica Graeca Selecta*, 2 vols. (1990); C. G. Fragiadakis, *Die attischen Sklavennamen* (1988).   E. M.

names, personal, Roman 1. In the classical period, the Romans shared with other peoples of Italy, including the Etruscans, a system of personal nomenclature in which the central element was a hereditary family-name. The official designation of a freeborn male Roman citizen embraced five components. Thus *M. Tullius M. f. Cor. Cicero* consists of the praenomen, *M(arcus)*; the nomen or *gentilicium*, the family-name, *Tullius*; the indication of the father's name, *M(arci) f(ilius)*; the indication of the Roman voting tribe (see TRIBUS) to which the citizen belonged, *Cor(nelia tribu)*; and the cognomen, *Cicero* (optional in the republican age). The *tria nomina* or 'three names' were thus: praenomen, nomen, and cognomen.

2. It is probable, however, that the Italic peoples originally used a single name only, as suggested in the case of the Romans by grammarians' statements and the oldest Latin inscriptions. This would have been the inherited *Indo-European pattern that survives in some other language groups (as for instance *Celtic, where single names, often compounds, are the rule, or *Venetic), but which was swept away by a revolution in Italic nomenclature: the creation of the hereditary family-name (*gentilicium*) from what had originally been patronymics, normally derived with a suffix *-ius* from the name of the father (so *Quintius* = 'son of *Quintus*'). The prehistoric existence of such adjectival patronymics in Latin can be inferred from their occurrence in other Indo-European languages (cf. Greek *Telamốnios Aías* 'Ajax son of Telamon', see NAMES, PERSONAL, GREEK) and from their appearance in the literary sources for the regal period (e.g. *Hostus Hostilius, Numa Marcius Marci filius*); they are also attested as such in some other Italic languages, *Faliscan and *Umbrian, albeit within the context of a gentilicial name system. At some unspecified time, these patronymics, having formerly changed from generation to generation, became invariable, a development reflecting the need to indicate membership of a large *gens*. The switch from patronymics to gentile names could have occurred from around 700 BC somewhere between the lower *Tiber and the Tyrrhenian sea—that is, in the area of interaction between the *Etruscans, the central Italic peoples, and the Latins (see LATINI). The social and linguistic prerequisites would have been offered by the Italic peoples; on the other hand, the Etruscans may have carried out the actual change-over by reinterpreting the complicated Italic patronymic system. The gentile name system seems to have become established in Rome around the end of the 7th cent.

3. Most gentile names of the early republic are in origin patronymics (another patronymic suffix beside *-ius* was *-ilius*, whence e.g. *Lucilius* to *Lucius*). Many of them are derived from names attested only as cognomina (*Claudius* from *Claudus*, *Plautius* from *Plautus*), which may represent old individual names that did not survive as praenomina. For many gentile names resembling patronymics, the base is no longer attested, at least not as a name (*Cornelius, Sulpicius, Terentius*). Some such names may be of non-Latin origin, but the majority of Roman gentile names are probably derived from Latin individual names that vanished as a result of the praenomen reduction (see § 4). Names in *-i(e)dius* are of Oscan origin; those in *-na*, and many in *-nius*, are of Etruscan origin (e.g. *Ovi(e)dius, Peperna, Volumnius* from Etr. *Velimna*); note too the Latinized gentile names of Etruscans

and Osco-Umbrians given Roman citizenship: thus Etr. *Cafate* became *Cafatius*; Umbr. *Kluviier* (gen.) gave *Cluvius*. Ethnics were another source for the formation of gentile names: the oldest Roman example is *Tarquinius*, derived from the name of the home town of two kings of Rome (see TARQUINIUS PRISCUS and SUPERBUS); *Gabinius* from *Gabii, Gabinus*, and *Sabinius* from *Sabinus* are later examples. In the imperial period, especially in the provinces, new forms were coined from common cognomina (e.g. *Frontonius* from *Fronto*) and from native names (e.g. *Adnamatius, Solimarius* in *Gaul).

4. After the establishment of the gentile name system, the numerous old single names became the praenomina, identifying the individual within the family. For this purpose a limited selection was sufficient, and the number of praenomina was gradually reduced. In the late republic some eighteen praenomina only were in general use: *Aulus, Decimus, Gaius, Gnaeus, Lucius, Manius, Marcus, Numerius, Publius, Quintus, Servius, Sextus, Spurius, Tiberius*, and *Titus*, and the Oscan *Salvius, Statius, Vibius*. The popularity of these praenomina varied considerably, the most frequent at all times being *Gaius, Lucius, Marcus, Publius, Quintus*. In inscriptions from the imperial period, *Tiberius* and *Titus* are also very frequent, but the popularity of *Tiberius* is entirely due to the Claudian emperors and to the numerous descendants of their freedmen, regularly called *Ti. Claudii* (see § 9); *Titus* primarily owes its wide diffusion to the Flavian emperors (see VESPASIAN; TITUS; DOMITIAN). Some praenomina were popular in particular provinces, like *Sextus* in Gaul. As the number of praenomina was limited, in extra-familial use they were almost always abbreviated: *A. = Aulus, P. = Publius, Q. = Quintus, S(p). = Spurius, Ser. = Servius, Sex. = Sextus, T. = Titus, Ti. = Tiberius*, etc. These abbreviations perhaps go back to the 6th cent., as is shown by the use of *K.* for *Kaeso* and *Ɱ = M'.* (the archaic form of *M* with five strokes), for *Manius*; their introduction coincides with the emergence of the gentile name and the drastic reduction in the number of praenomina.

Indo-European compound names, of the type seen in e.g. Greek *Aristo-krátēs*, were abandoned very early in the proto-Italic period, giving way to simple names, the origin of which often remains obscure. Many are certainly Latin, for example the numerical praenomina such as *Quintus, Sextus*, and *Decimus*, which perhaps originally indicated the month of birth; *Marcus* and *Manius* might also refer to the month of birth (thus a Marcus would have been born in March, the month consecrated to Mars, a Manius in February, the month of the *manes). *Tiberius* is derived from the name of the river-god *Tiberis, Servius* apparently from *servus*. Others are definitely of Etruscan origin, as *Aulus* from *Avle* < *Avile* (derived from *avil* 'year').

5. The last component in the name of a Roman citizen was the cognomen. Originally unofficial surnames for individuals, thus complementing the function of the praenomina, the early cognomina of the Roman nobility became for the most part hereditary, designating a branch of a larger *gens*. Thus the Cornelii were split into several branches, the most famous being the *Cornelii Scipiones*; other branches were distinguished as the *Cossi, Dolabellae, Lentuli*, etc. Such a family could split still further, with an additional cognomen, e.g. the *Cornelii Scipiones Nasicae*. Cognomina were long a characteristic of *patrician families; in the republican period noble plebeian families (see PLEBS) also normally bore a cognomen (e.g. the *Sempronii Gracchi*). See CORNELIUS and SEMPRONIUS entries. It is not certain when the cognomina came into use, but those attested for the aristocracy of the early republic are surely authentic in part. Ordinary people began

to bear individual cognomina regularly only as late as the transition from the republic to the empire, but the usage established itself very quickly, and from the beginning of the empire the *cognomen* gradually superseded the praenomen as the individual name of a Roman.

There was a great variety of cognomina. They could be Latin, Greek, or '*barbarian*'. They denote physical peculiarities (*Longus, Callistus*), mental qualities (*Clemens, Agatho*), circumstances, especially the so-called wish-names (*Felix, Eutyches*), circumstances of birth or sex (*Natalis, Masculus*), occupations (*Agricola*), fauna and flora (*Leo, Arbuscula, Anthus*), other substantives used metonymically (*Oriens, Silva, Sagitta, Spinther*), and abstracts (*Victoria, Helpis*). Cognomina derived from other names, directly or with suffixes, are very popular: from praenomina (*Marcus, Marcellus*), gentile names (*Iulianus*), other cognomina (*Frontinus*), names of historical figures (*Sulla, Alexander*), divine and mythological names (*Saturninus, Romulus, Diodorus, Hermes*), and place-names (*Romanus, Macedo*; metonymically *Italia, Corinthus*; such names did not necessarily denote origin); derivatives from appellatives are also common (*Cato* from *catus*). A person could bear more than one cognomen, especially in old aristocratic families, where the first (and eventually the second) cognomen had become hereditary: *P. Cornelius Scipio Nasica Corculum*. Another type of cognomen should be mentioned, the so-called *cognomina ex virtute*, given to victorious generals and derived from the name of the town or people conquered; some of these names became hereditary, as with *Messalla*, obtained by M'. *Valerius Maximus Messalla in 263 BC after the relief of *Messana and retained by the family into the imperial period. See VALERIUS MESSALLA entries. Comparable are the emperors' honorific titles, such as *Germanicus, Dacicus*, or *Arabicus*.

6. The indication of the father's name and the *tribus* was optional, because these two parts of the name do not designate a person directly. However, their use is required in legal texts like the Acilian law on extortion (122 BC) or the *tabula Heracleensis* (45 BC), although the *tribus* indication is often lacking even in official documents. In Latin (other Italic languages had different practices), the indication of the father, in the form of his praenomen in the genitive and the word *filius* (normally abbreviated to *f.*) was placed after the gentile name. The praenomen of the grandfather was sometimes added too (in the genitive, followed by *n(epos)*), even outside the upper classes, e.g. *L. Samiarius C. f. N. n.*

7. *Women's names. The nomenclature of free-born women was similar to that of free-born men except that, normally, women did not have a praenomen in the Classical period. A woman inherited her gentile name from her father and did not usually change it at marriage. Thus the normal form of a woman's name in the republican period was—to take *Cicero's daughter as an example—*Tullia M. f.* (a woman was not inscribed in a *tribus*). In earlier times, women could bear praenomina, and these are often attested in inscriptions outside Rome, e.g. at Pisaurum or *Praeneste. They were either feminine forms of men's praenomina or descriptive designations, which probably indicated order of birth: *Maior, Minor, Maxuma, Paulla, Secunda, Tertia*.

8. An adopted son took his adoptive father's full name, but could add an extra cognomen formed with the suffix *-ianus* from his original gentile name (*Scipio Aemilianus*, natural son of *L. Aemilius Paullus*). See CORNELIUS SCIPIO AEMILIANUS, L. He could also retain his original cognomen unaltered (*Varro Lucullus*; see TERENTIUS VARRO LUCULLUS, M.). In the imperial period there are

yet other ways to indicate a variety of family connections.

9. Names of foreigners, slaves (see SLAVERY), and *freedmen. Slaves and provincials without Roman (or Latin) *citizenship were known by an individual name, and thus lacked a praenomen and nomen; *peregrini* used their individual name followed by the father's name in the genitive and (optionally) by *f(ilius -ia)*, e.g. *Tritano Acali* and *Tritano Lani f.*, from Dalmatia. When enfranchised, new citizens normally retained their individual name as their cognomen. They were free to choose their praenomen and nomen; during the empire, it became common for new citizens to adopt those of the reigning emperor, less often of the intermediary (e.g. the provincial governor) who brokered their enfranchisement. Inscriptions show that soldiers of auxiliary units (see AUXILIA), who normally became Roman citizens only on discharge, could bear their prospective praenomen and nomen even before enfranchisement.

We do not know much about the older forms of the nomenclature of slaves. The earliest attested form is a compound consisting of the owner's praenomen and *-por = puer* (e.g. *Marcipor*), but in inscriptions slaves bear single Latin and above all Greek names (indeed at Rome, Greek names were for a long time limited to the servile onomasticon). These were followed by the owner's name: the usual form in the 1st cent. BC was *Pamphilus Servili M. s(ervus)*; from the Augustan age, the order of elements in the indication of the owner's name usually follows the pattern *Dama L. Titi ser(vus)*, but it can also be represented by the cognomen only: *Amethystus Orfiti ser(vus)*. When manumitted, slaves took the nomen of their master and, from the end of the republic, usually his praenomen too, retaining their slave name as a cognomen (this, however, was regularly omitted in inscriptions until the end of the 2nd cent. BC). The gentile name was followed by the indication of freed status, achieved by adding the master's praenomen in the genitive and the abbreviation *l.* or *lib.* for *libertus -a* (the official name of Cicero's freedman Tiro would thus have been *M. Tullius M. l. Tiro*); if the former owner was a woman, an inverted C (Ɔ) was used instead of the praenomen. An imperial freedman was usually designated as *Aug. l.* or *lib. = Augusti libertus -a*.

10. The *supernomen*, a sort of cognomen, falls roughly into three categories: (a) the so-called *agnomina*, added to the rest of the name with *qui/quae et* or with *sive* (a custom which spread during the second century AD from the Greek east and characterized the lower classes); (b) the so-called *signa* proper, connected to the main name with the word *signo*; these are attested from the end of the 2nd cent. AD and also characterized the lower classes (e.g. *Trebius Iustus signo Asellus*); (c) the so-called detached *signa*, derived from Greek acclamations (from the end of the 2nd cent. AD), mostly new coinages in *-ius*; these *signa* were detached from the main text of an inscription and placed above or below it, more rarely in other positions; e.g. in *CIL* 6. 1507, *L. Ranius Optatus c(larissimus) v(ir)*, with *Aconti* chiselled above the text. Detached *signa* appear mostly in aristocratic inscriptions from late antiquity. Most of the *signa* were probably nicknames, but, in the course of time, they could become the main name of the person or family. A example is *Gregorius*, derived from the Greek acclamation *grēgorei*, but attested as a cognomen as early as the end of the 2nd cent. AD.

11. From the early imperial age, the nomenclature of the Roman citizen began to undergo radical changes, as a result of the adoption of an individual cognomen by ordinary citizens, and of the sharing of the same praenomen by the sons of new citizens and freedmen. As the first step praenomina began to

disappear, having lost their identifying function (their total number was small, and in old Roman families only a few were in use); instead the cognomen took on the role of principal individual name. Later, gentile names also began to lose their identifying function as a result of the wide diffusion of the imperial nomina, especially after 212, when all provincial *peregrini* (i.e. non-Romans) became citizens and *Aurelii* (see CONSTITUTION, ANTONINE). In the Christian period, the tendency to revert to a single name was gradually strengthened, and, by the end of antiquity, Roman nomenclature once more adopted, except amongst the aristocracy, the system of a single name. Hereditary family names were revived at the end of the first millennium in the populous towns of northern Italy, spreading from there all over Europe. The influence of *Christianity on name-giving was slight before the last centuries of antiquity. Explicitly Christian names came into use slowly, starting from the 4th cent.; but the majority of names used by the Christian communities in the west were still firmly anchored in the old pagan world (names such as *Aphrodite*, *Eros*, *Hermes* remained common). Biblical names, such as *Iohannes* or *Petrus*, as well as names of martyrs (*Laurentius*), became popular only from the 5th cent.

General: J. Marquardt and A. Mau, *Das Privatleben der Römer* 1, 2nd edn. (1886), 7 ff.; E. Fraenkel, *RE* 16. 1611 ff., 'Namenwesen'; H. Rix, *Römische Personennamen: Namenforschung: Ein internationales Handbuch zur Onomastik* 1 (1995), 724–32. For § 2: H. Rix, *ANRW* 1. 2 (1972), 700 ff. For § 3: W. Schulze, *Zur Geschichte lateinischer Eigennamen* (1904; repr. with addenda by O. Salomies 1991). For § 4: O. Salomies, *Die römischen Vornamen* (1987). For § 5: I. Kajanto, *The Latin Cognomina* (1965); H. Solin, *Beiträge zur Kenntnis der griechischen Personennamen in Rom* 1 (1971), and *Die griechischen Personennamen in Rom* 1–3 (1982); P. Kneissl, *Die Siegestitulatur der römischen Kaiser* (1969). For § 7: M. Kajava, *Roman Female Praenomina: Studies in the Nomenclature of Roman Women* (1995). For § 8: D. R. Shackleton Bailey, *Two Studies in Roman Nomenclature*, 2nd edn. (1991), 53 ff.; O. Salomies, *Adoptive and Polyonymous Nomenclature in the Roman Empire* (1992). For § 9: G. Vitucci, *Diz. Epigr.* 4. 909 ff. 'libertus'; H. Chantraine, *Freigelassene und Sklaven im Dienst der römischen Kaiser* (1967); H. Solin, *Die stadtrömischen* (1996). For § 10: I. Kajanto, *Supernomina* (1966). For § 11: I. Kajanto, *Onomastic Studies in the Early Christian Inscriptions of Rome and Carthage* (1963). For the nomenclature of the Roman aristocracy: T. Mommsen, *Die römischen Eigennamen der republikanischen und augusteischen Zeit: Römische Forschungen* 1, 2nd edn. (1864), 3 ff.; R. Syme, *Hist.* (1958), 172 ff.; for onomastic customs in Roman society: H. Solin, *Namenpaare* (1990). H. So.

Naples See NEAPOLIS.

Naqš-i Rustam, 7 km. (4½ mi.) north of *Persepolis, impressive rock-cut tombs of *Darius I, *Xerxes I, *Artaxerxes (1) I, and *Darius II. Kings standing on thrones supported by subject peoples are carved in relief above palatial porticoes. Trilingual inscriptions proclaim the royal virtues of Darius I. See also SAPOR.

R. G. Kent, *Old Persian*, 2nd edn. (1953); E. F. Schmidt, *Persepolis* 3 (1971). M. V.

Narbo (mod. Narbonne), the first Roman colony in *Gaul, founded in 118 BC to protect the road to *Spain. It succeeded a Celto-Iberian hill-fort (at Montlaurès). *Caesar's tenth *legion was settled here, and under *Augustus Narbo became the capital of Narbonensis, the seat of the imperial cult and an important trading centre. Enlarged by *Claudius, its full title was *Colonia Iulia paterna Claudia Narbo Martius decumanorum*. Always rivalled by *Nemausus (Nîmes), in the 2nd cent. it declined in prosperity, and in the later empire was eclipsed by *Arelate (Arles). However, it produced the emperor *Carus (282–3), and remained an important local administrative and episcopal centre: an expensive

new cathedral was completed in 445. In 462, it fell to the *Visigoths. Narbonne has few visible remains, but a fine series of inscriptions illustrating public and private life.

M. Gayraud, *Narbonne antique* (1981); A. L. F. Rivet, *Gallia Narbonensis* (1988), 43 f., 130 ff. J. F. Dr.

Narce, a *Faliscan town 5 km. (3 mi.) south of Falerii. The river Treia (a tributary of the *Tiber) has exposed an uninterrupted stratigraphical sequence from middle bronze to iron age below the acropolis, on which the remains of later walls and fortifications are visible. Further evidence comes from the cemeteries, where the latest material belongs to chamber-tombs of the mid-3rd cent. BC, just before the Roman conquest of the area.

Mon. Ant. 1894, *passim*; E. H. Dohan, *Italic Tomb-groups in the University Museum* (Philadelphia, 1942); T. W. Potter, *A Faliscan Town in South Etruria* (1976). D. W. R. R.

Narcissus (1), in mythology, a beautiful youth, son of *Cephissus (the *Boeotian river) and Liriope, a *nymph. He loved no one till he saw his own reflection in water and fell in love with that; finally he pined away, died, and was turned into the flower of like name. *Ovid, who preserves the fullest version, claims that Narcissus was punished for his cruelty to *Echo: he repulsed her and she so wasted away with grief that there was nothing left of her but her voice (Ov. *Met.* 3. 342 ff.). Other ancient explanations, Paus. 9. 31. 7–8; *Conon (3), 24. The story appealed to Roman taste: it is depicted in nearly 50 murals from *Pompeii alone.

LIMC 'Narkissos'. H. J. R.; A. J. S. S.

Narcissus (2), *freedman secretary (*ab epistulis*) to *Claudius, acquiring 400 million sesterces and great political influence. He went to Gaul in AD 43 to embark the invasion force for Britain and received *quaestoria *ornamenta* in 48 for exposing *Valeria Messallina, with whom he had collaborated in removing threats to Claudius. The limits of his power appeared when he was given command of the praetorians for one day only. It was weakened by the Messallina affair, involving the deaths of leading men, and eclipsed by that of M. *Antonius Pallas, whose ally *Iulia Agrippina married Claudius (Narcissus favoured another bride), and who obtained *praetoria ornamenta*. Narcissus mismanaged the draining of the Fucine Lake (*Fucinus lacus) (52) and he failed to promote *Britannicus. On Claudius' death in 54 he was immediately forced to suicide.

F. Millar, *JRS* 1967, 9 ff.; P. Weaver, *Familia Caesaris* (1972); B. Levick, *Claudius* (1990), see indexes. J. P. B.; B. M. L.

Narnia (mod. Narni), formerly the *Umbrian hill town of Nequinum. Made into a Latin colony (see IUS LATII; LATINI) in 299 BC, it became a flourishing *municipium* on the via Flaminia, with a famous Augustan *bridge, part of which survives. The emperor Nerva was born here.

M. H. Ballance, *PBSR* 1951, 91 ff.; M. Bigotti, G. A. Mansuelli, and A. Prandi, *Narni* (1973). E. T. S.; T. W. P.

narratio From the first, *rhetoric saw the need for a legal speech normally to contain a 'statement of the facts' (*diēgēsis*, *narratio*) following the proem, and it was soon agreed that it should have the interconnected qualities of brevity, clarity, and plausibility. A narrative might be omitted, or be introduced elsewhere in a case, for some special reason. The aim was always to put one's case in the best possible light. Training was provided in the schools, for narration was one of the *progymnasmata; and in this connection an important division was established into legendary (*fabula*), historical (*historia*), and realistic (*argumentum*), corresponding to three degrees of 'truth-content' (e.g. Quint. *Inst.* 2. 4. 2).

See e.g. *Rhetorica ad Herennium* 1. 12–16 with H. Caplan's helpful notes; R. Volkmann, *Die Rhetorik der Griechen und Römer*, 2nd edn. (1885; repr. 1963), 148–64.   M. W.

narrative, narration In the last 30 years, interest in narrative has developed at an incredible pace. Two branches of this 'narratology' may be distinguished. The one is oriented towards the 'story' as signified ('what happened': cf. especially the work of Greimas and Bremond, looking back to Propp's famous *Morphology of the Folktale*); the other is oriented rather towards the narrative as signifier ('the way it is told': Stanzel, Genette, in the line of the Russian formalists, Henry James, and E. M. Forster). Both approaches have been widely applied in classical studies, but the first has perhaps been more successful in the anthropological study of myth (see MYTHOLOGY), the second in literary studies, in that it focuses on the rhetorical construction of the work rather than its underlying functional structure. The sophisticated armoury of methods that is modern narratology is one of the products of structuralism and semiotics, and like those more general movements it has in recent times been subject to qualifications and criticisms from post-structuralists and from reception theorists and students of literary pragmatics with their greater focus on the audience or readership of a work.

An interest in the theory of narrative is already apparent in *Aristotle, whose *Poetics* may be considered the first treatise of narratology. Obviously there are differences between the prescriptive and evaluative character of ancient *aesthetics and the descriptive and interpretative character of the semiotic approach: but it is significant that Aristotle assigns a central place to *mythos* or 'plot', which is the criterion (rather than metre) that he uses to distinguish poetry from other forms of discourse. *Mythos*, analyzed both in terms of content and of its representation, is required to have an organic unity which calls to mind the concept of *closure as defined in Anglo-American criticism. The Aristotelian theory of narrative includes drama, and many modern theorists such as Ricoeur include drama (and historiography) within the boundaries of narrative theory. More recently however, the idiosyncratic nature of the dramatic text, which is realized fully only in performance, has been stressed. One may certainly study narrative elements in non-narrative genres (e.g. *Pindar or the messenger speeches of tragedy; see TRAGEDY, GREEK), but it is important to remember that these genres have different contexts of *reception and different purposes. For this reason, a narrower conception of *fictional* narrative, above all *epic and the *novel, may be preferable. The question of the applicability of narratological approaches to *historiography has been particularly controversial, especially in relation to the work of the American historian Hayden White (see now S. Hornblower in Hornblower (ed.), *Greek Historiography* (1994), ch. 5).

The basic forms of western narrative occur already in Homer. Genette distinguishes four categories: the *order* in which events are narrated, their *duration* at the level of narrative in comparison to that of the underlying story, the mode or *mood* in which the information is conveyed ('focalization', point of view), and the *voice* which delivers it. A fifth category, that of the *frequency* with which an event is related, plays a less central role. Homeric narrative knows various possible ways of manipulating the linearity of story-time, such as the 'analeptic' flashbacks of *Nestor in the *Iliad* and the beginning *in medias res* of the *Odyssey*. At the level of duration, 'scenes' with dialogue predominate over more

rapid 'summaries': the opposition is a version of the Platonic one (see PLATO (1)) between *mimēsis* 'representation' and *diēgēsis* 'narration', or Henry James' distinction between 'showing' and 'telling'. At the level of mood and voice, we are presented with a narrator who is (on the surface at least) impersonal, objective, and with a point of view superior to that of his characters. In comparison with this model, *Apollonius (1) Rhodius and *Virgil, under the influence of Hellenistic *epyllion, show a desire for a denser and more 'subjective' mode more oriented towards the present moment of narration: hence the greater use of 'proleptic' anticipation of later events, of summary narration, and of focalization from the point of view of the characters (e.g. *Medea, *Dido).

The equivalence between poetry and fiction established by Aristotle had a long history in antiquity, and prose fiction developed late. The love novel or romance at first used a linear narrative technique (*Chariton, *Xenophon (2) of Ephesus) but later turned to more complex forms in the phase influenced by the *Second Sophistic (*Achilles Tatius (1), *Longus, *Heliodorus (4)). In these, we find frequent use of a restricted point of view and 'metadiegesis' (the device of 'stories within stories' used e.g. also by *Ovid). This last technique is particularly prevalent in Heliodorus: the ultimate model is the *Odyssey*. In contrast, the Latin novel, associated more closely with that cultural tradition which the theorist Bakhtin called 'Menippean', tended towards more free and open forms, as in Greek did the *Life of Aesop*. See also LITERARY THEORY AND CLASSICAL STUDIES; SPEECH PRESENTATION.

M. Bakhtin, *The Dialogic Imagination* (1981); G. Genette, *Narrative Discourse* (1980); P. Ricoeur, *Time and Narrative* (1984); M. Bal, *Narratology* (1985); H. White, *The Content of the Form* (1987); S. Cohan and L. M. Shires, *Telling Stories* (1988); M. J. Toolan, *Narrative: A Critical Linguistic Introduction* (1988); G. Prince, *A Dictionary of Narratology* (1987). There is a bibliography of classical work in I. J. F. de Jong and J. P. Sullivan (eds.), *Modern Critical Theory and Classical Literature* (1994), 282 f.: note especially de Jong's own *Narrators and Focalizers: The Presentation of the Story in the Iliad* (1987).   M. F.

narratology See LITERARY THEORY AND CLASSICAL STUDIES; NARRATIVE, NARRATION.

Narses (AD 478–573), a Persarmenian *eunuch prominent throughout *Justinian's reign as member of the imperial bedchamber, envoy, and general. In 530/1 he exploited local contacts to welcome Persarmenian deserters, while in 532 his role in suppressing the Nika riot was crucial. In 535 Theodora used him in *Alexandria (1) to reinstate a Monophysite bishop (Narses' doctrinal attachment), and in 541 to spy on her enemy, John the Cappadocian. Quarrels with *Belisarius blighted his first military command in Italy (538–9), but he returned as commander-in-chief in 551 after careful preparations in *Thrace and recruitment of *Heruli and *Lombards. He defeated the Ostrogoths (see GOTHS) in pitched battles at Tadinum and mons Lactarius, and thereafter gradually recaptured all Italy south of the Alps, which he now governed from Rome as patrician. Though recalled to *Constantinople in 568 he remained in Italy until his death to oppose the Lombards.

PLRE 3. 912–28.   L. M. W.

nationalism

Greece, Archaic and Classical

Lewis has observed that 'to say that the Athenians built the Parthenon to worship themselves would be an exaggeration, but not a great one'. Such self-worship would make 5th cent. BC

Athenians into 'nationalists' by one modern criterion (cf. Gellner, drawing on E. Durkheim: 'in a nationalistic age, societies worship themselves brazenly and openly'). But in the strong sense familiar from the history of the 19th-cent. rise of certain European nation-states, nationalism was hardly a feature of, or problem experienced by, the Classical Greek world. City-state particularism (see POLIS), and the consciousness of the religious and linguistic differences between *Dorians and *Ionians, are not the same as nationalism. Such feelings are best considered under the heading of *ethnicity. The idea that Greece was a 'nation', in a way that transcended local differences, does occur in our sources, but only at special moments like the *Persian Wars (see e.g. Hdt. 8. 144). In the following period the Persian Wars affected Greek thinking (see PERSIAN-WARS TRADITION); but the effect was negative rather than positive: in the 5th cent. BC '*barbarians' were viewed more disparagingly as a result of the Persian Wars, just as the opposition between Dorians and Ionians became sharper as tensions between Athens and Sparta increased in the same period. But no correspondingly increased sense of Greek national identity is traceable. However, it has been well said (Finley) that it is point-less to castigate the Greeks for their 'failure to achieve unity' when there is so little evidence that this was an aim they had or even understood. Nationalism, like ethnicity, is a matter of attitude. The rhetorical nature of much of our literary evidence makes the truth about real attitudes hard to reach: before the invading Athenians arrive in *Sicily in 415 BC, the Syracusan *Hermocrates in *Thucydides (2) is made to say, in effect 'let us unite! Sicily for the Sicilians' (4. 61. 2; 6. 34. 4); but once the Athenians have arrived he plays the Dorian card, to create bad feeling against the invading Ionians (6. 77. 1).

D. M. Lewis, *CAH* 5² (1992), 139; E. Gellner, *Nations and Nationalism* (1983), 56; M. I. Finley, *The Use and Abuse of History*, 2nd edn. (1986), 120 ff.; F. W. Walbank, *Selected Papers* (1985), 1 ff.; E. Hall, *Inventing the Barbarian* (1989). S. H.

Hellenistic and Roman

The Graeco-Macedonian kingdoms were essentially dynastic states under personal rule. This was true even of the 4th-cent. BC ethnic state of Macedonia, sometimes seen today as a 'national' monarchy: but it is notable that *Alexander (3) the Great's invasion of Asia not only promoted no vital Macedonian interest but led to the undoing of the traditional Macedonian state.

Early Rome did not evolve into a nation because initial expansion was based, not on incorporation, but treaty-relationships (see SOCII); even when she extended her citizenship to all Italy, a Roman citizen belonged to a city, not a country.

Subject-resistance to the Hellenistic and Roman empires is sometimes scanned for 'national feeling'. But there was rarely a tradition of political unity even among ethnic groups sharing a common culture (e.g. the Gauls), so that nationalism in the modern sense could not exist. Important exceptions are the indigenous Egyptians under the Ptolemies, and the Jews of *Judaea, who rebelled under both the *Seleucids and Rome; both groups could look back to a tradition of political independence. Otherwise, revolts against imperial Rome, when not occurring shortly after incorporation and constituting a continuation of the initial armed struggle, were chiefly occasioned by Roman misgovernment (e.g. the revolt of *Boudicca), the political ambitions of individuals (e.g. AVIDIUS CASSIUS, C.), or other factors. Generally, Rome's political integration of subject élites (much more successful, and indeed purposeful, than in the Ptolemaic and Seleucid empires) kept local nationalisms underdeveloped. The assertion of local cultures in (e.g.) the African and Greek-speaking prov-

inces has been thought to be fuelled by anti-Roman sentiment, but this interpretation is controversial (2nd-cent. AD nostalgia among Greek-speakers for the Classical past, for instance, was actually encouraged by Rome); it is no easier here than in the regional schisms of early Christianity (see DONATISTS) to detect provincial quests for political independence.

R. Errington, *History of Macedonia* (1990), ch. 4; F. W. Walbank, cf. bibliog. to preceding section; Brunt, *RIT*. A. J. S. S.

natural law See LAW OF NATURE

nature See ANATOMY AND PHYSIOLOGY; ANIMALS (various entries); ANTHROPOLOGY; ASTRONOMY; BODY; BOTANY; CLIMATE; CONSTELLA-TIONS; EARTHQUAKES; ECOLOGY; EMBRYOLOGY; FAMINE; GEOGRAPHY; GYNAECOLOGY; LANDSCAPES; LAW OF NATURE; METEOROLOGY; MINERALOGY; PETS; PHARMACOLOGY; PHYSICS; PHYSIOGNOMY; POLIT-ICAL THEORY (for *nomos* (3), 'law, convention', as opp. *physis* ('nature')); TIMBER.

nauarchos, 'admiral', a general term for the commander of a navy, of a squadron however small, and even of a single ship. As an official title it appears comparatively late, since full-time *navies were hugely expensive and the geographical conditions of Greek warfare, which demanded amphibious operations, discouraged the separation of naval from military commands. Thus at Athens, for example, Athenian and allied fleets were always commanded by *stratēgoi. But with the greater specialization of warfare, especially in states lacking an established naval tradition, the title began to appear, most importantly in *Sparta (c.430–360 BC), Syracuse under *Dionysius (1) I and (2) II, Ptolemaic *Egypt, the *Achaean Confederacy, and *Rhodes. The *nauarchos* was everywhere admiral of the fleet, with no colleague; in the Greek republics such as Sparta his tenure was normally a single year (a rule that had to be circumvented to accommodate *Lysander, but admirals who served monarchs (e.g. in Syracuse and Egypt) might enjoy long commands.

M. Strack, *RE* 16. 1889–96, 'Nauarchos'; R. Sealey, *Klio* 1976, 335–58. P. A. C.

Naucratis (Kōm Ga'if), a Greek city in the Saite nome (see NOMOS (1)) on the east bank of the Canopic branch of the *Nile 83 km. (52 mi.) south-east of *Alexandria (1). It was founded as a trading station in the reign of *Psammetichus I (664–610 BC). Under *Amasis the Hellenion was erected by the Ionians from *Chios, *Teos, *Phocaea, *Clazomenae, the *Dorians of *Rhodes, *Cnidus, *Halicarnassus, *Phaselis, and Aeolian *Mytilene. *Aegina, *Samos, and *Miletus had their own temples in honour of *Zeus, *Hera, and *Apollo. Officials named *timou-choi* were in charge of the Hellenion. The excavations of Petrie and Gardner (1884–6) and Hogarth (1899, 1903) found great quantities of datable Greek pottery with dedications to the Greek gods. American excavations began in 1977. According to *Strabo, Naucratis was founded by Milesians, who had established the 'Milesians' Fort' near the Bolbitine mouth of the Nile. Charaxas, *Sappho's brother, went there on business. Bresson argues that it only became a *polis* after *Alexander (3) the Great's conquest, when it struck the only civic *coinage of gold and silver known in Egypt. Papyri rarely survive in the wet conditions of the Delta, but the Zenon archive (see APOLLONIUS (3)) gives evidence of trade in the mid-3rd cent. BC. Ptolemaic inscriptions survive from newly erected buildings. *OGI* 120 refers to a *syngraphophylax* ('registrar of contracts') under *Ptolemy (1) VI Philometor. In the Roman period it retained its Greek constitution, the model for *Antinoöpolis. Under *Hadrian, Naucratites had no right of intermarriage with Egyptians. Between AD 261 and 289 annual public games were held. Victors from *Oxyrhynchus were granted Naucratite citizenship. It had a *boulē in the 4th cent. AD.

Hdt. 2 (comm. A. B. Lloyd); Strabo 17, *passim*; Sappho fr. 82 LP. Extensive testimonia in A. Bernand, *Le Delta égyptien d'après les textes grecs*, (1971), 575–863.

W. M. Flinders Petrie, E. A. Gardner, *Naukratis* 1–2 (1886–8); D. G. Hogarth, *BSA* (1899), and *JHS* (1905); W. Coulson and others, *Ancient Naucratis* 3 (1989); E. R. Price, *JHS* 1924; R. M. Cook, *JHS* 1937; J. Boardman, *The Greeks Overseas*, 3rd edn. (1980); M. M. Austin, *Greece and Egypt in the Archaic Age* (1970); F. von Bissing, *Bulletin de la Société royale d'archéologie d'Alexandrie* 1951, 33 ff.; C. Roebuck, *CPhil.* 1951; A. Bresson, *DHA* 1980; R. Coles, *ZPE* 18 (1975), 199–204; Wilcken, *Chr.* 27. *PGen.* 10. Papyri: A. Calderini, *Dizionario dei nomi geografici dell'Egitto* 3 (1983), 320–1.   W. E. H. C.

naukrariai, early divisions of the population of *Attica. The name used regularly to be derived from *naukraros* as 'ship-chief', implying a connection with the Athenian *navy, and although alternatives have been suggested that remains the likeliest explanation. There are said to have been twelve *naukrariai* in each of the four old tribes, *phylai (*Ath. pol.* 8. 3), and naucraric funds were mentioned in laws of *Solon. According to *Cleidemus (*FGrH* 323 F 8) *Cleisthenes (2) raised their number to 50, to fit his new tribes, but according to *Ath. pol.* 21. 5 they were replaced by Cleisthenes' *demes. There is no evidence of their existence after 500 BC, and if they did survive Cleisthenes' reforms, and were concerned with ships, they presumably disappeared in the wake of the enlargement of the fleet by *Themistocles. Herodotus (5. 71. 2) in his account of *Cylon says that at that time the *prytanies* ('presidents', see PRYTANEIS) of the *naukraroi* were the most important officials of Athens: this seems to be an attempt to divert the responsibility for killing Cylon's supporters from the archons, and particularly from Megacles the *Alcmaeonid.

V. Gabrielsen, *C&M* 1985, 21–51.   A. W. G.; T. J. Ca.; P. J. R.

naumachia The word was used for a naval battle, shown as a great spectacle, or for an artificial lake constructed for the purpose, the best known being that excavated by *Augustus in 2 BC on the right bank of the Tiber (near S. Cosimato), 550 m. long and 365 wide (1,800 × 1,200 ft.) with an island in the middle, fed with water from a new aqueduct, the aqua Alsietina. *Caesar had been the first to give such an exhibition in 46 BC, on the left bank of the *Tiber. Prisoners of war and condemned criminals did the fighting; and some famous sea fight of history (e.g. *Salamis, the Athenians at *Syracuse (413 BC), *Actium) was re-enacted. *Claudius exhibited a great *naumachia*, with 19,000 combatants, on the Fucine Lake (*Fucinus lacus) in AD 52 (Tac. *Ann.* 12. 56 f.). Similar displays were sometimes given on private estates and by flooding amphitheatres (the *Colosseum at Rome in AD 80 and elsewhere, as archaeology shows, e.g. at Capua and at Nîmes (*Nemausus)).

K. Coleman, *JRS* 1993, 48 ff.   J. P. B.; A. J. S. S.

Naumachius (perhaps as early as the 2nd cent. AD), author of a poem on the 'duties' of wives, of which *Stobaeus (68. 5, 74. 7, 93. 23) cites portions.

Naupactus, a town in western (Ozolian) *Locris commanding the entrance to the Corinthian Gulf. It has a small protected harbour and small coastal plain cut off from the interior by mountains. A legend, probably derived from the city's name

('ship-construction'), records that the *Dorians built their ships here before crossing to invade the Peloponnese (see PELOPONNESUS). The site's value as a naval base was appreciated by the Athenians, who seized it and peopled it with exiled *Messenians in 456 BC. During the *Peloponnesian War, Naupactus was the main Athenian base in the west. After Sparta had expelled the Messenians (399), *Achaea colonized and held the city until *Philip (1) II captured it and gave it to Aetolia in 338. With the collapse of the *Aetolian Confederacy, Naupactus lost its importance. *Augustus reassigned it to the Roman colony of *Patrae. Excavations have revealed a bath complex and building remains on the town's east side while blocks from the ancient city wall are incorporated into the medieval and Turkish fortifications. See MESSENIA.

L. Lerat, *Les Locriens de l'Ouest* (1952), 1. 38–41, 86–93; P–K, *GL* 2. 320–1; *Lexikon der historischen Stätten* 456–7; A. B. Bosworth, *AJAH* 1976, 164 ff.; E. Badian, *From Plataea to Potidaea* (1993), ch. 5.   W. M. M.

Nauplius, (1) eponym of Nauplia near *Argos (2); son of *Poseidon and *Amymone. (2) His descendant, often confused with (1) (Nauplius (1)–*Proetus–Lernus–Naubolus–Clytoneus–Nauplius (2), Ap. Rhod. 1. 134–8), an *Argonaut, navigator, and slave-trader. He was given *Catreus' two daughters, Clymene and *Aërope, to sell overseas, but married Clymene and fathered *Palamedes and Oeax (Apollod. 3. 2). He was also given Aleus' daughter Auge, after she gave birth to *Telephus (1), to sell overseas, but instead gave her to Teuthras, king of Teuthrania, who married her (Apollod. 2. 7. 4). To avenge the death of Palamedes, he caused some of the Greek leaders' wives to be unfaithful; then later he was instrumental in wrecking the Greek fleet on its return from *Troy, when he lit false beacons at Cape Caphereus in *Euboea (Eur. *Hel.* 767, 1126 ff.; Apollod. *Epit.* 6. 7–8). See also HESIONE.   H. J. R.; J. R. M.

Nausicaa, in *Homer's *Odyssey* the young daughter of *Alcinous (1), king of the Phaeacians (see SCHERIA), and Arete. In book 6, moved by *Athena in a dream, she goes to the river-mouth to do the family washing, and is playing ball with her maids when the shipwrecked *Odysseus comes out of hiding and begs her help. He is almost naked, and the maids run away in fear; but Nausicaa, given courage by Athena, stands her ground and promises him her help. She gives him food, drink, and clothing, shows him the way to the city, and advises him on how to behave to her parents. She admits to herself that she would like to marry him, and Alcinous is ready to agree to this (7. 311 ff.), but Odysseus is eager to return home to *Penelope. He bids farewell to Nausicaa, assuring her that he owes her his life and will remember her always (8. 457–68). According to a later story, she married *Telemachus (Hellanicus, *FGrH* 4 F 156).   H. J. R.; J. R. M.

Nausiphanes, of Teos (fl. *c.*340–320 BC), Democritean philosopher (see DEMOCRITUS), and teacher of *Epicurus, who however claimed to have learnt nothing from him. A pupil of *Pyrrhon of Elis (the putative founder of Scepticism (see SCEPTICS)), he exhibited some of the sceptical tendencies typical of 4th-cent. Democriteanism. His work the *Tripod* was an epistemological one, said to have influenced Epicurus' treatise on criteria, the *Canon*. He taught a broad educational curriculum, and advocated the study of *physics as a foundation for success in rhetoric and politics—a stance pilloried by the Epicureans.

DK 75; F. Longo Auricchio, in *Ricerche sui papiri ercolanesi* 1 (1969); K. von Fritz, *RE* 16, 2021–7.   D. N. S.

nautodikai (ναυτοδίκαι) were Athenian magistrates who presided over trials involving men who travelled by sea, either as merchants or as overseas residents (cleruchs; see CLERUCHY). They are first heard of around 445 BC, when Athenian commercial and imperial success probably increased the number of such trials. They were abolished around 350, when new arrangements for mercantile cases (δίκαι ἐμπορικαί) were established.

D. M. MacDowell, *The Law in Classical Athens* (1978), 229–31.

D. M. M.

navicularii were private shipowners. In the Principate *navicularii* who contracted to provide a certain minimum tonnage for the service of the *annona*, the public *food supply of Rome, were given special rewards by emperors: *Claudius offered benefits of status, and by the time of *Hadrian the great boon of exemption from the public liturgies imposed locally by cities had been added (see LITURGY, ROMAN). Most of the known *navicularii* were members of municipal élites, often freedman or their descendants. The *navicularii* were encouraged to form associations (*collegia* or *corpora*: see CLUBS, ROMAN) which made it easier for the state to supervise their activities and check entitlement to the privileges. In the late empire shipment for the *annona* (now to *Constantinople too) became a public obligation imposed corporately on these associations, whose membership was made hereditary.

A. B. J. Sirks, *Food for Rome: The Legal Structure of the Transportation and Processing of Supplies for Imperial Distributions in Rome and Constantinople* (1991); L. De Salvo, *Economia privata e pubblici servizi nell'impero romano: I corpora naviculariorum* (1992). D. W. R.

navies The oldest navy in the ancient world was probably that of the Egyptian pharaohs; see EGYPT. Very little is known about Egyptian naval development, however, until the *Saites (672–525 BC), one of whom, Necho II (610–595), reorganized the navy to protect Egyptian interests against the Babylonians. The introduction of *triremes, probably under *Amasis (570–526), further strengthened Egypt's navy prior to the Persian conquest.

The Persian navy was created under *Cambyses (530–522). It utilized triremes and was crewed by the king's maritime subjects, arranged in territorial or ethnic squadrons (e.g. Egyptians, *Phoenicians, *Ionians). During much of the 5th cent. BC this navy fought in the eastern Mediterranean against the Greek city-states, led by Athens, whose ships were crewed by her citizens and subject allies. From the battle of *Salamis (480) to the battle of Aegospotami (405) the Athenians were the dominant naval power in the region. They developed considerable expertise in trireme warfare, which was put to good use in the *Peloponnesian War. During the 4th cent. the Athenian navy remained a powerful force, although lack of money and manpower prevented a return to its former position of dominance. Defeat by the Macedonians at the battle of *Amorgos in 322 BC effectively marked the end of the Athenian navy.

The Hellenistic period saw the development of larger warships as the Hellenistic monarchs apparently tried to outbuild each other in an attempt to achieve supremacy and assert prestige. The Ptolemaic kings (see PTOLEMY (1)) used their navies extensively in the effort to secure their overseas possessions, but no single state gained lasting naval dominance until the Romans were forced to create a series of large fleets from the resources of Italy, initially in order to defeat the Carthaginians, and then to fight a series of wars in the Greek East.

Roman naval forces in the 2nd and 1st cents. BC were mainly drawn from allies in Italy and the Greek east. The value of a strong navy had been demonstrated to Octavian in his struggle

with Sextus *Pompeius. He established permanent naval forces soon after the battle of *Actium. These consisted of a fleet to guard the NW coast of Italy and the Gallic coast, based at *Forum Iulii (mod. Fréjus), two praetorian fleets to secure the Italian coasts, based at *Ravenna and *Misenum, a small fleet based at *Alexandria (1) and, probably, another at *Seleuceia (2) in Pieria. Later emperors added units in the Black (*Euxine) Sea, *Africa, *Britain, and on the Rhine and Danube rivers (see RHENUS; DANUVIUS). The Forum Iulii fleet disappeared before the end of the 1st cent. AD, but most of the others seem to have continued to exist well into the third cent. Considerable reorganization took place under *Constantine I who divided the fleets into smaller squadrons and created extra commands.

The duties of the Roman navy included transporting Roman troops, supporting land campaigns, protecting coastal settlements, suppressing *piracy, and dealing with hostile incursions by barbarians into Roman waters. The fleets of the Roman imperial navy contained mainly triremes and smaller vessels, with only a few *quinqueremes or larger ships in the two praetorian fleets. After the defeat of *Licinius in AD 324 triremes ceased to be the main ships of the imperial fleets, and the navy of the Byzantine empire consisted largely of two-banked galleys, called *dromones*.

Naval craft were expensive to build and maintain. Most warships could not be used for *trade and their crews were normally free men who required payment as well as provisioning. The creation of a navy was, therefore, a momentous step for any ancient state. *Samos acquired its navy during the prosperous period of *Polycrates (1)'s tyranny, possibly with Egyptian backing. The Athenian navy of the 5th cent. BC was founded on the proceeds of a rich silver strike in the *Laurium mines in 483, and maintained through tribute payments and the wealth of private citizens (see TRIERARCHY). During the Peloponnesian War the Spartans were only able to sustain their naval presence in the Aegean with the support of the Persian king, who provided money for the wages of the crews. The achievement of the Rhodians (see RHODES), who maintained a substantial navy from the 4th to the 1st cent. BC, was exceptional and surpassed only by the Roman empire. See SEA POWER; SHIPS.

J. Rougé, *Ships and Fleets of the Ancient Mediterranean* (1981; Fr. orig., *La Marine dans l'antiquité* (1975)); H. T. Wallinga, 'The Ancient Persian Navy and its Predecessors', in H. Sancisci-Weerdenburg (ed.), *Achaemenid History 1: Sources, Structures and Synthesis* (1987) and *Ships and Sea-Power before the Great Persian War* (1993); B. Jordan, *The Athenian Navy in the Classical Period* (1975); E. E. Rice, 'The Rhodian Navy in the Hellenistic Age', in W. Roberts and J. Sweetman (eds.), *New Interpretations in Naval History* (1991); J. H. Thiel, *Studies on the History of Roman Sea-power in Republican Times* (1946), and *A History of Roman Sea-power before the Second Punic War* (1954); C. G. Starr, *The Roman Imperial Navy*, 2nd edn. (1960); M. Reddé, *Mare Nostrum: Les Infrastructures, le dispositif et l'histoire de la marine militaire sous l'empire romain* (1986). P. de S.

navigation can be defined as the art of taking a ship successfully from one chosen point to another. From a very early stage the relatively calm, tideless waters of the Mediterranean encouraged travel by sea. Seagoing *ships were not normally used in the winter months, because storms and poor visibility made navigation hazardous, but *Hesiod's suggestion that sailing be limited to July and August is overcautious (Hes. *Op.* 663–5), the period between the vernal and autumnal equinoxes being the best season, with some leeway at either end. Ancient vessels were either paddled, rowed, or sailed. Their speed depended upon size, type of propulsion, and the weather. Sailing speeds of between four and six knots seem to have been the norm with favourable winds. Light or unfavourable winds might reduce speed to less than one knot, making it preferable to lie up and wait for a change in the weather.

Ancient seafarers guided their vessels without the benefit of instruments or charts. Wherever possible they followed the coastline or sailed between fixed points on land. On clear nights the stars could be used to plot a course, as could the moon. Experienced ancient mariners would have had a good, practical understanding of the phases of the moon and the movement of the stars, which they would have passed on by oral transmission. They would also have needed detailed knowledge of local conditions such as prevailing winds and currents, the presence of reefs, rocks, and shallows, and how to follow a course according to local landmarks.

Basic navigational equipment included oars and sails, steering oars, anchors, usually made of stone or wood, or both, and a variety of lines and cables. Leaded lines for checking the depth of the water were common, often featuring a hollow weight that could be used to sample the nature of the seabed. Flags and pennants were used to identify warships, or sometimes deliberately to misidentify them (Polyaenus, *Strat.* 8. 53. 3), and lanterns were employed at night or in fog to enable flotillas to follow a flagship (App. *BCiv.* 2. 89). Although the theoretical skills and the basic knowledge needed to produce quite detailed *maps were available from the early Hellenistic period onwards, there is no evidence that charts intended for use at sea were ever produced. A few descriptions of sea routes and coastlines (*periploi) have survived from antiquity, but it is unlikely that they circulated among the mariners themselves.

Navigable rivers were also heavily used, especially the *Nile, the Rhine (*Rhenus), and the Rhône (*Rhodanus). In late republican and imperial times the Tiber would have been crowded with vessels carrying people and goods up to Rome from *Ostia. River-craft were mostly rowed, paddled, or sailed, but towing, either by teams of men or animals, or by use of a line fixed on shore and a capstan was also common. See LIGHTHOUSES; NAVIES.

L. Casson, *Ships and Seamanship in the Ancient World*, 2nd edn. (1986), and *CAH* 6² (1994), 512 ff.; S. McGrail, *Ancient Boats in NW Europe: The Archaeology of Water Transport to AD 1500* (1987). P. de S.

Naxos (1), the largest (430 sq. km.: 166 sq. mi.) of the *Cyclades, noted for its *marble and emery. Its fertile west contrasts with its rugged east side. In mythology it was birthplace of *Dionysus, burial-place of the *Aloadae and scene of *Ariadne's abandonment by *Theseus. Naxos, first occupied in the middle neolithic, flourished in the early bronze age. During the second millennium Grotta on the west coast (mod. Chora) emerged as the prime settlement. No clear break is detectable before the arrival of Ionian settlers from Athens c.1025 BC. The ancient city grew over the ruined Mycenaean town (see MYCENAEAN CIVILIZATION). A geometric tumulus cemetery at Tsikalario exhibits links with Macedonia. Naxos colonized *Amorgos c.900 BC and joined in founding Sicilian *Naxos (2) in 735. Its Archaic prominence is revealed in dedications and monuments at *Delos (a colossal statue of *Apollo, the House of the Naxians, a Naxian stoa and, perhaps, the Lion Terrace) and the Sphinx column at *Delphi, as well as in the marble temples and sculpture found on Naxos itself. Its craftsmen were pioneers in the development of monumental marble sculpture and architecture. At the peak of its power, following the overthrow of the tyrant Lygdamis (see TYRANNY) c.525 BC, Naxos dominated the Cyclades, including its inveterate

enemy *Paros, allegedly with 8,000 soldiers and a fleet at its command. In 500 it withstood a Persian siege but in 490 city and temples were burnt and those captured enslaved. In 480 Naxian *triremes defected to the Greek fleet at the battle of *Salamis. Naxos was the first to revolt from the *Delian League c.467, subsequently being reduced to tributary status. Later, c.450 BC, an Athenian *cleruchy was imposed, reflected in Naxos' low tribute of six and two-thirds talents. A well-preserved Hellenistic tower (Pyrgos Cheimarrou) survives in the south-east.

R. E. Herbst *RE* 16, 2079 ff.; *PECS* 611–12; *IG* 12. 5; *ΠΑΕ* 1949–51, 1959, and most subsequent years; *AΔ* 1965 B, 515 ff., 1966 B, 391 ff.; *Arch. Anz.* 1968, 693 ff., 1970, 135 ff., 1972, 319 ff., 386 ff., 431 ff., 1982, 159 ff., 1987, 569 ff.; *Les Cyclades* (1983), 15 ff.; *ASAA* 1983, 109–36; R. Barber and O. Hadjianastasiou, *BSA* 1989, 63 ff.; A. Hoffman (ed.), *Bautechnik der Antike* (1991), 63 ff. R. W. V. C.

Naxos (2), on what is now Capo Schisò, near Giardini on the east coast of *Sicily, was the first Greek colony (see COLONIZATION, GREEK) in the island (734 BC). Founded by the Chalcidians (see CHALCIS) under Thucles, its sanctuary of Apollo Archegetes (still unlocated) was particularly venerated by the Siceliot Greeks (Thuc. 6. 3. 1, cf. ARCHĒGETĒS). Chiefly important as colonizer of *Leontini and *Catana, it was not itself a powerful city. Captured by *Hippocrates (1) c.495 BC, when its citizens were expelled, it was resettled in 461 when a new street-grid was laid out. Now in opposition to *Syracuse, it concluded alliances with Leontini (427) and Athens (415). In 403 *Dionysius (1) I captured and destroyed it. There was a smaller settlement on the site in the 4th cent. BC, and a Roman and Byzantine roadside settlement along the coast immediately to the north-east of the Greek city, but Naxos was effectively replaced after 403 by *Tauromenium, on the hill above Capo Schisò. Our knowledge of the ancient topography has been dramatically increased by excavation over the past three decades, when a sanctuary in the SW quarter (probably to *Hera rather than *Aphrodite), the 5th-cent. walls on the west, a potters' quarter, areas of housing, and the necropoleis have all been investigated. Naxian wine, celebrated on the city's Archaic and Classical coinage, was widely exported in the Hellenistic and Roman periods.

PECS 612–13; Gabba–Vallet, *Sicilia antica* 1. 619–35; Dunbabin, *Western Greeks, passim*. Excavation reports by P. Pelagatti, G. M. Bacci, and M. C. Lentini at intervals in *Boll. d'Arte* between 1964 and 1990; cf. also *Not. Scav.* 1984–5 [1988], 253–497. Foundation period: *ASAA* 1981, 291–311. Sanctuary: N. Valenza Mele, *MÉFRA* 1977, 508–24. Houses: M. C. Lentini, *Xenia* 1990, 5–22. Coinage: H. A. Cahn, *Die Münzen der sizilischen Stadt Naxos* (1944). Wine: R. J. A. Wilson, *Sicily under the Roman Empire* (1990), 23, 264. A. G. W.; R. J. A. W.

Neanthes, of *Cyzicus (3rd cent. BC), historian, pupil of *Philiscus (1) of Miletus. The precise identity of his extensive writings is unclear. They include a *Hellenica* ('Ελληνικά) in at least six books, two works on *Cyzicus, divided into the legendary (Τὰ κατὰ πόλιν μυθικά) and the historical periods ('Ώροι Κυζικηνῶν), and a series of biographies (Περὶ ἐνδόξων ἀνδρῶν) notable for the first recorded literary treatment of the life of *Timon (1) the misanthrope. His accuracy is unreliable. A history of *Attalus I of Pergamum is by a younger Neanthes (*FGrH* 171).

FGrH 84. G. L. B.; K. S. S.

Neapolis (mod. Naples), Cumaean colony founded c.600 BC (see CUMAE; COLONIZATION, GREEK). It remained under Cumaean and *Syracusan influence until c.450, when a second foundation was made by the Athenian Diotimus (*FGrH* 566 F98). After the fall of *Cumae (421), it was the principal Greek city of *Campania.

Unlike Cumae, it made an accommodation with the *Oscans, admitting a number of them into the Neapolitan élite. In 327, it was drawn into the conflict between Rome and the Samnites, initially supporting the Samnites (see SAMNIUM). After a siege, during which the Tarentines (see TARENTUM) failed to produce promised support, a pro-Roman faction staged a coup and made peace, obtaining favourable terms. Naples remained a Roman ally (see SOCII) throughout the Pyrrhic (see PYRRHUS) and *Punic wars, and became a *municipium in 89. In 82, it was sacked by *Sulla and its war fleet destroyed, but it recovered and became a fashionable resort for Romans attracted by its Greek culture. Greek *agōnes were established in honour of *Augustus in 2 BC and its *Hellenism ensured the patronage of many *philhellene emperors. The Greek language and Greek *magistracies survived until the 3rd cent.

> M. W. Frederiksen, *Campania* (1984); M. Napoli, *Napoli Greco-Romana* (1959); various authors, 'Napoli Antica', *PP* 1952; J. D'Arms, *Romans on the Bay of Naples* (1970); various authors, *Neapolis, Atti di Convegno di Studi di Magna Graecia* (1985); various authors, *Napoli Antica* (1987).
> K. L.

Nearchus, of *Crete, boyhood friend of *Alexander (3) the Great and *satrap of *Lycia/*Pamphylia (334–329 BC); he commanded the fleet on the *Hydaspes and circumnavigated the coast from south *India to the *Tigris. Prominent at Babylon in 323 (see GREECE (HISTORY), *Hellenistic period*), he served on the staff of *Antigonus (1) between 317 and 312. His memoirs of Alexander's campaign were popular, used *in extenso* by *Strabo and *Arrian, but their title, economy, and dimensions are hard to fathom. The extant citations refer to events in India and to Nearchus' own voyage in the southern Ocean. Valuable detail is preserved, and there are traces of a critical attitude to Alexander (his account of the transit of Gedrosia is a catalogue of horrors); but there is much fantasy and his own importance is systematically exaggerated.

> FGrH 133; Pearson, *Lost Histories of Alexander*, ch. 5; E. Badian, *YClS* 1975, 147 ff.; Heckel, *Marshals*, 228 ff.
> A. B. B.

Nechepso, pseudonymous author, with Petosiris, of an astrological treatise in at least fourteen books, written, perhaps in Egypt, by a late Hellenistic Greek who used the Egyptian names to convey a spurious antiquity. Its great influence is shown by the frequent citations in later astrological works. See ASTROLOGY.

> E. Riess, *Philol.* Suppl. 6 (1891–3), 325 ff., collected the fragments, but many can be added from *CCAG* and *Vettius Valens. See further W. and H. G. Gundel, *Astrologumena* (1966), 27 ff. (whose views on Egyptian influence are untenable).
> G. J. T.

nectar See AMBROSIA.

negotiatores, the businessmen of the Roman world. In literary sources of the republican period, most notably *Cicero, *negotiatores*, or people who *negotia gerunt* ('conduct business deals'), are found as members of resident communities of Italian and Roman citizens in all the provinces of the empire, most frequently in the major urban centres and ports. The term is used very broadly and is rarely defined in any particular way. It is clear that many who are described by Cicero as *negotiatores* were of high equestrian status (see EQUITES). There were close links and involvement with the work of the *publicani (tax companies), bankers, landowners, and shipping. Indeed, one rhetorical remark of Cicero's (*Font.* 46) about 'all the publicans, farmers, cattle-breeders, and the rest of the *negotiatores*' suggests that the term *negotia* could cover all those activities. The considerable

expansion of trade in the Mediterranean in the Roman period depended upon organization of markets, investment in shipping, and, in a world where the money-supply was uncertain, *credit to facilitate deals (see also BANKS; MARITIME LOANS). This is what *negotiatores* provided. Such money-men invariably also had investments in land, which provided security. The scale and importance of the activities of the *negotiatores* was emphasized by Cicero in his speech on the command of *Pompey (*Leg. Man.* 17 ff.; 66 BC) at the time of *Mithradates VI's disruption of Asia. The term *negotiator* was rarely defined precisely, because most such money-men had investments in a whole range of property and activities. The term had an air of respectability, which *mercator* ('trader') did not (people prided themselves in inscriptions on being *negotiatores*, much more rarely on being *mercatores*). The distinction may be that, while the *negotiator* might invest in or own ships, he did not actually sail them. Given the social nuance of the term and its close connection with the financing of trade, it is no surprise to find it changing over time. So in the imperial period it came to be appropriated as the normal term for trader or merchant (see *ILS* 7273: '*mercatores* who *negotiantur*'). So for the first time specialist adjectives were regularly ascribed to the term (e.g. *negotiatores vinarii*, 'wine-traders').

Negotiatores, their families and their freed slaves, as Roman residents in the provinces, were significant vectors of *Romanization, although, at least in the Greek east, the process of acculturation was importantly two-way (Errington). Their overall impact on the provinces is debated: that many—if well-connected enough—exploited Roman status to enrich themselves (especially in the late republic) at provincials' expense is clear (e.g. Chr. Le Roy, *Ktèma* 1978); but some at least also used their wealth to support the cities in which they resided (e.g. *Atticus, a 'super-*negotiator*', at Athens) and—in the east—local (Greek) culture. The scale of the eventual fortunes of a few settler-families is shown by the return of descendants to Italy as provincial senators from the 1st cent. AD on (see SENATORS, PATTERNS OF RECRUITMENT). See also TRADE, ROMAN.

> J. Hatzfeld, *Les Trafiquants italiens dans l'orient hellénique* (1919; pioneering and not yet superseded); J. Rougé, *Recherches sur l'organisation du commerce maritime en Méditerranée sous l'empire romain* (1966); A. J. N. Wilson, *Emigration from Italy in the Republican Age of Rome* (1966); J. H. D'Arms, *Commerce and Social Standing in Ancient Rome* (1981); P. Brunt, in *The Fall of the Roman Republic and Related Essays* (1988), 144 ff.; R. M. Errington, in *Festschrift für K. Christ* (1988), 140 ff.
> J. J. P.; A. J. S. S.

Nekyomanteion See THESPROTI.

Nelei carmen ('The Song of Neleus'), a work as old as Livius Andronicus' *Odissia*, according to Charisius. Five fragments (19 words) survive. The title suggests a narrative poem, but the metre of three fragments is probably iambic, suggesting a drama.

> E. H. Warmington, *Remains of Old Latin*, 2 (Loeb, 1936), 626–9; Ribbeck, *TRF.* Schanz–Hosius 1. 49.
> P. G. M. B.

Neleus (Νηλεύς), son of *Tyro and *Poseidon (Ποσειδῶν Πετραῖος Pind. *Pyth.* 4. 136, who has an important cult in *Thessaly), twin of *Pelias, with whom he is exposed but saved by a herdsman or an animal. After a quarrel, he leaves Pelias as king of *Iolcus and either conquers or founds *Messenian *Pylos. Here he fathers twelve sons, with *Nestor (1) the youngest (Hom. *Od.* 11. 235–259 and Hes. *Cat.* fr. 33 M–W, both without the exposure). He reigns without playing a major role in the wars of Nestor's youth (Hom. *Il.* 7. 132–56, 11. 670–762). But when he refuses to cleanse *Heracles from the murder of Iphitus (see

POLLUTION; PURIFICATION), Heracles conquers Pylos and kills all the sons, except Nestor (Hes. fr. 35). Exposure and miraculous survival are typical for founders of dynasties and empires (*Romulus, *Darius (1), Moses), while the geographical dislocation hides the combination of different local traditions. The later events, as they appear already in the *Iliad*, are determined by Pylian story telling about the youth of Nestor.

Neleus (also written Νειλεύς) had cult in *Attica, together with *Basile, was believed the ancestor of the noble families of the Medontidae, Paeonidae, and *Alcmaeonidae, and founder of *Erythrae, *Miletus, or the entire *Ionian dodecapolis ('twelve cities'), and he had a grave in *Didyma (Paus. 7. 2. 6). Athenian tradition made him a younger son of *Codrus who emigrated to Ionia after a quarrel with his brother; at least some Ionian traditions preferred to derive him from Pylos.

F. Bader, in R. Bloch (ed.), *Recherches sur les religions de l'antiquité classique* (1980), 9–83; Kearns, *Heroes of Attica*, 188; E. Simon, *LIMC* 6 (1992), 727–31. F. G.

Nemausus, a town in Gallia Narbonensis (modern Nîmes), originally a *Celtic settlement, perhaps capital of the Volcae Arecomici. It was probably a *colonia Latina* (see IUS LATII; LATINI) by 28 BC and the seat of an important mint. In 16 BC it was laid out with walls enclosing c.220 ha. (543 acres). Very important remains exist: amphitheatre, precinct of *Deus Nemausus*, and a temple erected c. AD 2, and eventually dedicated to C. *Iulius Caesar (2) and L. *Iulius Caesar (4) (the 'Maison Carrée'). The Pont-du-Gard forms part of its *aqueduct. Nemausus rivalled *Narbo as a social and economic centre, and was among the most successful cities of Roman Gaul, producing a number of leading figures, including ancestors of the emperor *Antoninus Pius.

R. Amy and P. Gros, *La Maison Carrée* (1979); M. Christol and C. Goudineau, *Gallia* 1988, 87 ff.; A. L. F. Rivet, *Gallia Narbonensis* (1988), 85, 162 ff. J. F. Dr.

Nemea (Νεμέα). (1) Fertile upland valley in the NW Argolid sandwiched between the territories of ancient Phlius and Cleonae; legendary scene of *Heracles' encounter with the lion; site of the Panhellenic sanctuary of *Zeus, its accompanying festival (see NEMEAN GAMES) wandering between here and *Argos (2), where it remained for good from c.50 BC. American excavations have revealed remains of an Archaic heroon (see HERO-CULT), perhaps for Opheltes, and a 6th-cent. temple; this last was replaced in the late 4th cent. by the temple still partly standing, evidently built to mark the festival's (temporary) return c.330 BC under Macedonian patronage, along with the stadium, baths, and guest-house; a row of nine treasury-like buildings, evidently 'club-houses' or *leschai* for foreign states, dates from the early 5th cent. By the mid-2nd cent. AD the temple was roofless (Paus. 2. 15. 3). A small Christian *basilica of the 5th–6th cents. and the settlement which it served have been found.

(2) Name of the river flowing north and forming the boundary between *Corinth and *Sicyon, the scene of the battle of the Nemea (see NEMEA, BATTLE OF THE).

S. G. Miller (ed.), *Nemea: A Guide to the Site and Museum* (1990). Excavations: D. Birge and others, *Nemea* 1 (1992). T. J. D.; A. J. S. S.

Nemea, battle of the (394 BC). Perhaps the greatest of *hoplite battles, the battle was fought east of the river Nemea in the NE Peloponnese (see NEMEA), between 6,000 *Spartan hoplites, with perhaps 12,500 from their allies, and 24,000 *Athenians, Argives (see ARGOS (2)), *Boeotians, *Corinthians, and *Euboeans. The Spartans on the right, facing east, appear to have marched to the right in column until somewhat over half were beyond the Athenians facing them, while a similar manœuvre took the Boeotians on the allied left beyond the left of Sparta's allies. The result was that both sides won on their right, but whereas the Boeotians and those next to them simply went off in pursuit, the Spartan right wheeled left and was thus in a position to catch the enemy on their shieldless side as they attempted to return across the battlefield, killing perhaps 2,800, for the loss of only 1,100.

Xen. *Hell.* 4. 2. 15–23; Diod. Sic. 14. 83. 1–2. J. F. Lazenby, *The Spartan Army* (1985). J. F. La.

Nemean Games These were held in the sanctuary of *Zeus at *Nemea (1). They were said to have been founded by *Adrastus (1) of *Argos (2), in memory of the child Opheltes, killed there by a snake during the expedition of the *Seven against Thebes, or by *Heracles after he had killed the Nemean lion. They were reorganized as a Panhellenic festival in 573 BC, held in July every second and fourth year in each Olympiad, and were at first managed by Cleonae, later by Argos. The prize was a crown of fresh celery.

K. Hanell, *RE* 16. 2322–7; S. G. Miller, *Hesp.* 1975–88, and (ed.), *Nemea: A Guide to the Site and Museum* (1990); Stella G. Miller, in W. J. Raschke (ed.), *The Archaeology of the Olympics* (1988), 141–51; *CAH* 5² (1992), 106 f. (Lewis), 232 (Richardson). N. J. R.

Nemesianus, Marcus Aurelius Olympius, from *Carthage, late in the 3rd cent. AD composed four pastorals, long ascribed to *Calpurnius Siculus, and an incomplete didactic poem on hunting (*Cynegetica*). He is recorded as having distinguished himself in poetic contests, and himself states an intention (apparently never fulfilled) to write an epic on the deeds of the imperial brothers *Numerianus and *Carinus (*Cyn.* 63–78). His *Cynegetica* is datable to the period between the death of the emperor *Carus (283) and that of *Numerianus (284). If *Cyn.* 58–62 means—as it surely does—that he has turned from pastoral to didactic poetry, his *Eclogues* will have been written first.

The *Eclogues*, four short poems, 319 lines in all, are strongly influenced by *Virgil and Calpurnius. In the first the shepherd Thymoetas' threnody on Meliboeus recalls the praises of Daphnis in Verg. *Ecl.* 5. The second, in which two young shepherds express their longing for the girl Donace, shut up at home by her parents, is indebted especially to Calp. *Ecl.* 2 and 3. Verg. *Ecl.* 6 is the model for the third, in which Pan sings in praise of Bacchus. The fourth, like the second an *amoebean song, owes to Verg. *Ecl.* 8 the use of a refrain, which was part of the Theocritean tradition (see THEOCRITUS). Both Virgilian and Calpurnian elements appear in all four poems.

Of the *Cynegetica*, 325 lines survive. After a long introduction, Nemesianus turns to the necessities for *hunting–*dogs (he discusses rearing, training, diseases, breeds), *horses, nets, and traps. The poem breaks off on the verge of the chase. It is a vexed question whether the poet used the work of *Grattius 'Faliscus'; if so he is at least independent of the order of the material in Grattius' poem.

Two fragments of a poem on bird-catching (*De aucupio*, 28 hexameters) are also ascribed to Nemesianus, though the attribution is doubtful.

Nemesianus is essentially an imitator—sometimes whole lines are borrowed from a predecessor—but he is at least competent, and his poems are not unattractive. With a few exceptions, his diction and metre are classical.

TEXTS P. Volpilhac (1976); with comm. (*Eclogues* and *Cynegetica* only), H. Williams (1986); with trans., Duff, *Minor Lat. Poets*.

Nemesis

STUDIES B. Luiselli, *Stud. Ital.* 1958, 73–95; W. Schetter, in C. Gnilka and W. Schetter (eds.), *Studien zur Literatur der Spätantike* (1975), 1–43; J. Küppers, *Hermes* 1987, 473–98. PLRE 1. 622.　　　J. H. D. S.

Nemesis, both goddess and abstract concept from νέμειν (to deal or distribute); often a personified moral agent ('Retribution') like Lachesis and Praxis. She was daughter of Night (*Nyx), according to Hesiod, and born after the Moirai (see FATE) and *Keres as 'an affliction to mortal men' (*Theog.* 223). An Attic tradition names *Oceanus as father (Paus. 1. 33. 3, 7. 5. 3; cf. schol. on Lycoph. 88), perhaps to indicate that she belonged to an older generation of gods (Herter, *RE* 16/2. 2362). Homer did not know the goddess (schol. on Hes. *Theog* 223), although he was familiar with *Themis. He probably introduced the negative sense of anger, disgrace, and censure which is absent from the verb but reflected in Hesiod's genealogy. The moral element becomes more distinct in Hesiod's juxtaposition of Nemesis beside Aidos (*Op.* 200), echoing *Il.* 13. 122 (cf. 6. 351), in which she expresses public indignation and Aidos the offender's sense of shame.

Nemesis' oldest cults were Ionic: at the Attic *deme of *Rhamnus (6th cent. BC; Paus. 1. 33. 2–8), and in *Smyrna where she was worshipped in dual form (Paus. 7. 5. 3). Her first Rhamnusian temple (Doric distyle) was destroyed by the Persians and replaced in the late 5th cent. (V. Petrakos, *Rhamnous* (1983)). A smaller temple belonged to *Themis whose 4th-cent. marble statue was dedicated by Megacles. *Agoracritus' (or *Phidias', Paus. 1. 33. 3) image of Nemesis—its fragmentary remains partly excavated by Petrakos—held an apple branch in her left hand and a bowl, decorated with Ethiopians, in her right. A crown on her head showed figures of *Nike and deer. In myth Zeus pursued her in the shape of a fish and various animals (*Cypria* fr. F7 Davies, *EGF*); he finally changed into a swan and she into a goose. She laid an egg which a shepherd found and took to *Leda who nurtured *Helen after she was hatched (Apollod. 3. 10. 7; Paus. 1. 33. 7). The account in the *Cypria* shows Homeric influence (Nemesis feels *aidōs* and *nemesis*, fr. F7 Davies, *EGF*); but her affinity with animals and connection with *Artemis point to Nemesis' original chthonian divine nature (Farnell, *Cults* 2. 487 ff.), as do the Nemeseia (schol. Dem. 41. 11). See CHTHONIAN GODS. Like Themis, Nemesis' cultic past is obscured by her nature as indignant avenger. Both as an impersonal and personified power, she is merciless (Pind. *Pyth.* 10. 44), envies good fortune (*Ol.* 8. 86; cf. Hdt. 1. 34), and punishes *hubris (Eur. *Phoen.* 183). There is a Nemesis of gods, men, and even of the dead (Aesch. fr. 266 *TrGF*; Soph. *El.* 792). As relentless Fate, she is identified with Adrasteia (Aesch. fr. 158 *TrGF*) and guards against excess, hence her attribute of an ell or measuring-rod. Later she shared cult with *Tyche (Hsch.).

Rossbach, *RML* 3. 117–66; H. Herter, *RE* 16/2 (1935), 2338–80; *LIMC* 6. 1 (1992), 733 ff.　　　H. J. R.; B. C. D.

Nemesius (fl. *c.* AD 400), bishop of *Emesa in Syria, perhaps identical with the former advocate to whom, as governor of *Cappadocia Secunda (*c.*386/7), *Gregory (2) of Nazianzus addressed four letters and a protreptic poem inviting him to become a Christian. His essay in Christian Platonism, *On the Nature of Man*, is remarkable not only for its wide reading in medical and philosophical sources, e.g. *Galen and *Porphyry, but also for its Christian standpoint and its thesis that the spiritual life of man is conditioned by the body's natural limitations.

WORKS Ed. Migne, *PG* 40. 508 f.; trans. and comm. W. Telfer (1955); J. Quasten, *Patrology* 1960, 351 ff. PLRE 1. 622, 'Nemesius' 2.　　　J. F. Ma.

Nemi See ARICIA; REX NEMORENSIS.

Nemrut Dag (Mt. Nemrut), the highest mountain in *Commagene, its peak—commanding spectacular views over SE Turkey—the site of a monumental *hierothesion* (mausoleum-cum-cult-centre) built *c.*40 BC by the Commagenian king *Antiochus (9) I; of interest for its grandiose divinizing (see RULER-CULT, GREEK) of this Roman *client king and for its mix of Greek and Persian imagery and religious ideas (see SYNCRETISM). The complex comprised a vast tumulus (probably the royal burial-mound) flanked by two terraces for sculpture, each repeating the same row of colossal enthroned divinities (8–9 m. (26–9 ft.) high), among them Antiochus himself, and the same two series of inscribed relief-slabs portraying respectively his Persian and Macedonian ancestors. In two long (Greek) inscriptions (duplicates), Antiochus expounded his lifelong piety and prescribed details of the cult (*OGI* 383; partial Eng. trans.: S. Burstein, *The Hellenistic Age from the Battle of Ipsos to the Death of Kleopatra VII* (1985), no. 48). See ARSAMEIA (2).

PECS 618–19; K. Akurgal, *Ancient Civilizations and Ruins of Turkey*, 4th edn. (1978), 346–51. Texts: *OGI* 383–402; H. Waldmann, *Die kommagenischen Kultreformen unter König Mithridates I* (1973); H. Waldmann, *Der kommagenische Mazdaismus*, MDAI(1) Beiheft 37 (1991).　　　A. J. S. S.

nenia A dirge containing lamentation and praise of a deceased person (Diomedes, Keil, *Gramm. Lat.* 1. 485; Festus, 158 Lindsay). It was sung to a flute accompaniment by a hired mourner (*praefica*), whose assistants made responses (Serv. on *Aen.* 6. 216) before the house of mourning, during the funeral procession, and beside the pyre. It never became a literary genre. No example has reached us: we have only an anapaestic parody (Sen. *Apocol.* 12). The derivation from νηνίατον [Φρύγιον] (a Phrygian tune for the flute) is given by Pollux 4. 79 [80] but it may be an independent Latin onomatopoeia. Nenia or Naenia was also the goddess of funerary lamentation according to Arn. *Adv. nat.* 4. 7; August. *De civ. D.* 6. 9. She had a temple in front of the porta Viminalis (Wissowa, *RK* 245; Latte, *RR* 52; Radke, *Götter*, 227).

From the idea of empty repetition (cf. Plaut. *Asin.* 808 and Cato in Gell. 18. 7. 3), it came to mean children's rhymes (Hor. *Epist.* 1. 1. 63), a magical litany, a senseless rigmarole (*nugae*), it could also signify 'end' (Plaut. *Pseud.* 1278) or coda (Hor. *Carm.* 3. 28. 16). In *Ausonius it signifies *epicedion; in *Sidonius Apollinaris, a metrical epitaph.　　　C. F.; G. W. W.; J. Sch.

neōkoros ('temple warden'), originally a temple official; from the late 1st cent. AD formalized as a title for a city which held a provincial temple to the Roman emperor. Ambitious cities could claim by the 3rd cent. AD to be 'thrice *neōkoros*', e.g. Ephesus. See TEMPLE OFFICIALS.

S. R. F. Price, *Rituals and Power* (1984).　　　S. R. F. P.

Neophron, of *Sicyon, a tragic poet, wrote 120 plays according to the *Suda*, which also says that he 'was the first to introduce *paedagogi* and the torture of slaves'. A hypothesis to *Euripides' *Medea* cites *Dicaearchus and (pseudo-)*Aristotle as saying that that play is adapted from a *Medea* by Neophron; and the surviving fragments of Neophron's *Medea* reveal close links between these two plays. Some scholars, however, have argued that Euripides' play must really be the model, and Neophron's the adaptation.

TrGF 1². 92–4; *Musa Tragica*, 200–7, 295–6. D. L. Page, *Euripides: Medea* (1938), pp. xxx–xxxvi; B. Manuwald, *Wien. Stud.* 1983, 50–6.　　　A. L. B.

Neoplatonism, a modern term for *Plotinus' renewal of Platonic philosophy (see PLATO (1)) in the 3rd cent. AD. It became the dominant philosophy of the ancient world down to the 6th cent. The following phases may be distinguished in its history. (*a*) After the Sceptical period of Plato's *Academy, philosophers in the 1st cent. BC, notably *Antiochus (11) and *Posidonius (2), initiated a revival of dogmatic Platonism. This revival (called today 'Middle *Platonism') became widespread in the 2nd cent. AD when such writers as *Albinus (1) (Alcinous) and *Numenius, having recourse sometimes to Aristotelian and Stoic ideas, drew from Plato's dialogues a systematic philosophy. (*b*) Working in this intellectual context, *Plotinus developed an unorthodox, compelling interpretation of Plato, a philosophy containing profound metaphysical and psychological ideas which provided his successors with a fruitful basis of reflection. Plotinus' *Enneads* (published posthumously, *c.*300–5) are Neoplatonism's most important philosophical product. (*c*) Plotinus' school at Rome did not survive his death in 270. However his closest pupils (*Porphyry, *Amelius Gentilianus) did much to promote his philosophy. Porphyry published Plotinus' biography and works, on which he commented. He also innovated, in particular in metaphysics and in integrating Aristotle's logic into Neoplatonism, contributing also to the influence of Neoplatonism among Latin writers, pagan and Christian, such as Marius *Victorinus, Calcidius, *Augustine, and *Macrobius. Plotinus and Porphyry were also read in the east and used by *Eusebius of Caesarea and *Gregory (3) of Nyssa. (*d*) *Iamblichus (2), who founded an influential school in Syria, introduced a new phase. In particular his systematic harmonization of Neoplatonic metaphysics with supposedly ancient pagan theologies made Neoplatonism suitable to the needs of the pagan reaction led by *Julian the emperor. *Sallustius' *On the Gods and the World* (ed. and trans. A. D. Nock (1926)) summarized the Neoplatonic interpretation of pagan religion, whereas *Eunapius made out of the lives of his Neoplatonic teachers a pagan hagiology (*Lives of the Sophists*, ed. and trans. W. C. Wright (Loeb, 1922)). (*e*) Iamblichean philosophers contributed to the emergence of a Neoplatonic school at Athens (*Syrianus, *Proclus, Damascius, *Simplicius, etc.) which produced works of learning and philosophical sophistication and had close relations with a Neoplatonist school in *Alexandria (1) (*Hypatia, *Synesius, Hierocles, *Ammonius (2) Saccas, John *Philoponus, etc.) from which came important commentaries on *Aristotle. *Justinian closed the Athenian school in 529. Its members took temporary refuge in Persia, whereas the Alexandrian school, perhaps through an understanding with the Church, continued on for another century. Neoplatonism strongly influenced Byzantine thought (through *Dionysius (4) the Areopagite, *Psellus), Islamic philosophy, Medieval Latin thinkers (through Augustine, John the Scot) and the Renaissance (through Ficino, Pico).

GENERAL R. Wallis, *Neoplatonism* (1972); A. H. Armstrong (ed.), *The Cambridge History of Later Greek and Early Medieval Philosophy* (1967); C. Zintzen (ed.), *Die Philosophie des Neuplatonismus* (1977); *Le Néoplatonisme. Colloque du CNRS* (1971). See also bibliog. under IAMBLICHUS (2); PLOTINUS; PORPHYRY.

ORIGINS J. Dillon, *The Middle Platonists* (1977); H. Dörrie, *Platonica minora* (1976), and in *Les Sources de Plotin*, Entretiens Hardt 5 (1960); P. Merlan, *From Platonism to Neoplatonism*, 2nd edn. (1960).

DIFFUSION P. Courcelle, *Late Latin Writers and their Greek Sources* (1969; Fr. orig., 2nd edn. 1948); S. Gersh, *From Iamblichus to Eriugena* (1978), and *Middle Platonism and Neoplatonism: The Latin Tradition* (1986); *Plotino e il Neoplatonismo in oriente e in occidente* (1974).

D. O'M.

Neoptolemus (1), son of *Achilles and Deidamia; also known (but not to *Homer) as Pyrrhus.

The *Odyssey* of Homer relates how, after the death of Achilles, *Odysseus fetched Neoptolemus from *Scyros to Troy, where he distinguished himself in counsel and battle and was one of the warriors in the Wooden Horse (11. 505–37). After his return to Greece he married *Hermione, daughter of *Menelaus (1) and *Helen (4. 5–9). Cyclic epics (see EPIC CYCLE) told how, in the sack of Troy, he killed *Priam and (according to the *Little Iliad*) the infant *Astyanax (but the *Capture of Troy* attributed this to Odysseus), and chose *Andromache as his prize. *Ibycus made him responsible for the sacrifice of *Polyxena (fr. 26 Page, *PMG*), as he is in *Euripides, *Hecuba* 523–68, and in the younger Seneca's *Trojan Women* (see ANNAEUS SENECA (2), L.).

He had a tomb at *Delphi. *Pausanias (3) is probably wrong in claiming (1. 4. 4) that this did not receive cult honours until after the hero had been seen helping to repulse an attack by Gauls in 279/8 (see CELTS). Of his death at Delphi various accounts are given. *Pindar says at *Paean* 6. 98–120 that *Apollo was angry with him for killing Priam at the altar of *Zeus Herkeios and swore that he would not return home; so, after a visit to Molossia (where the royal house in historical times claimed descent from him, see MOLOSSI), he came to Delphi and was killed by the god during an argument with the temple servants. At *Nemean* 7. 34–47, however, apparently wishing to correct the Paean with a version more favourable to Neoptolemus, Pindar does not mention Apollo's anger and says that Neoptolemus was killed, to the Delphians' distress, in a quarrel over sacrificial meat.

Yet another account is given by *Euripides' *Andromache*: his death at the hands of the Delphians is brought about by the treachery of *Orestes, his rival for the hand of Hermione. *Virgil, who depicts him as a monster of savagery in the sack of Troy (*Aen.* 2. 526–58), has him killed by Orestes in person (3. 330–2), a version dubiously referred to the *Little Iliad* (see EPIC CYCLE).

*Sophocles (1) in *Philoctetes* makes Neoptolemus a companion of Odysseus on the expedition to fetch *Philoctetes from *Lemnos. Here he is an essentially honourable youth, persuaded at first to assist in the plots of Odysseus but then finding his true nature through pity for Philoctetes.

Various episodes from his career are depicted on vase-paintings, especially the killing of Priam or Astyanax in scenes of the sack of Troy.

LIMC 6 'Neoptolemos'; J. Fontenrose, *The Cult and Myth of Pyrros at Delphi* (1960).
A. L. B.

Neoptolemus (2), of *Parium (3rd cent. BC; earlier than *Aristophanes (2) of Byzantium, probably later than *Eratosthenes), Greek writer. His works included poems, literary criticism, and philological treatises. His views on poetry, known to us through a summary by *Philodemus, are said by *Porphyrio to have been adopted in essentials by *Horace in the *Ars Poetica*. See also GLOSSA, GLOSSARY, GREEK; LITERARY CRITICISM IN ANTIQUITY, § 6.

A. Rostagni, *Arte poetica di Orazio* (1930); C. O. Brink, *Horace on Poetry* (1963).
J. D. D.; K. J. D.

Neopythagoreanism, a renewed interest in Pythagorean ideas and practices (see PYTHAGORAS (1)) that took widely different forms, appears first in the Hellenistic period with the emergence of apocryphal texts, often inspired by Platonic, Aristotelian, or Stoic sources (see PLATO (1); ARISTOTLE; STOICISM), usually decked out in Doric dialect, and claiming to be the work of *Pythagoras (1) or of Pythagoreans such as *Archytas, *Timaeus (1) of Locri,

*Ocellus. Individuals described as 'Pythagoreans' appear in the 1st cent. BC in *Alexandria (1) (*Eudorus (2)) and Rome (*Nigidius Figulus, his circle, and others) and are found in the 1st cent. AD (*Moderatus of Gades, *Apollonius (12) of Tyana) and in the 2nd (*Nicomachus (3) of Gerasa, *Numenius, *Alexander (13) of Abonuteichos). Some were philosophers who, in the context of a revival of dogmatic Platonism and inspired by Pythagorizing in Plato's *Academy, took an interest in Pythagorean metaphysics, mathematics, and number symbolism. Thus Eudorus and Moderatus spoke of an ultimate Pythagorean cause, the 'One', source of numbers and of all else. The Pythagorean way of life, which had a strong religious bent and involved ascetic and vegetarian practices, was followed by Moderatus and by Apollonius, whose activities as magician show another Neopythagorean tendency also found in Alexander of Abonuteichos. Much of Neopythagoreanism and the legend of Pythagoras as a source of religious revelation were incorporated in *Neoplatonism by Porphyry and by Iamblichus (2). Neopythagoreanism also exercised influence on Jewish thought through *Philon (4) and Christian thought through *Clement of Alexandria.

TEXTS H. Thesleff, *The Pythagorean Texts of the Hellenistic Period* (1965); B. Centrone, *Pseudopythagorica ethica* (1990); D. Fideler (ed.), *The Pythagorean Sourcebook* (1987); 'Timaeus Locrus', ed. and trans., W. Marg (1972); 'Ocellus Lucanus', ed. R. Harder (1926); pseudo-Archytas, ed. T. Szlezák (1972). See bibliog. under NICOMACHUS (3); NIGIDIUS FIGULUS; NUMENIUS.

DISCUSSION W. Burkert, *Philol.* 1961, 16 ff., 226 ff.; W. Burkert and H. Thesleff in *Pseudepigrapha* 1, Entretiens Hardt 18 (1972); H. Thesleff, *An Introduction to the Pythagorean Writings of the Hellenistic Period* (1961); H. Dörrie, *RE* 24. 268 ff.; J. Dillon, *The Middle Platonists* (1977).

D. O'M.

neoterics See HELLENISTIC POETRY AT ROME.

Nepet (e) (mod. Nepi, a small but strategically important town, 40 km. (25 mi.) north-west of Rome, situated on the edge of the territory of the *Faliscans and together with *Sutrium controlling the road through the Ciminian forest into central Etruria, as well as the direct route to southern Umbria, later the via Amerina. After the conquest of *Veii in 396 BC it fell into Roman hands, receiving a Latin colony either in 383 (Livy 6. 21. 4) or in 373 (Vell. Pat. 1. 14. 2). Created a *municipium* after the *Social War (3), it was modestly prosperous under the empire. In late antiquity (Procop. *Goth.* 4. 35) it became once more of strategic importance, a role which it retained throughout the Middle Ages.

Not. Scav. 1910 and 1918; M. W. Frederiksen and J. B. Ward-Perkins, *PBSR* 1957, 89 ff. J. B. W.-P.; D. W. R. R.

Nepos, biographer. See CORNELIUS NEPOS.

Neptunus, Italic god of *water. He extended his protection to watercourses and to expanses of water threatened by evaporation in the heat of summer as well as to human activities linked with water; hence, under the influence of *Poseidon, he could become patron of journeys on water. During *sacrifice (Roman), the cooked *exta* ('entrails') were thrown into water (Livy 29. 27. 5); it is in virtue of this capacity that the absurd identification of *Consus with 'Neptunus Equester', i.e. Poseidon Hippios, takes place, Livy 1. 9. 6. The etymology of his name is quite uncertain; in Etruscan it is Neθun(u)s. His festival is of the oldest series (Neptunalia, 23 July); we know concerning its ritual only that arbours, *umbrae*, of boughs were commonly erected (Festus 519, 1 Lindsay), but it may be conjectured that its object was to obtain

sufficient water at this hot and dry time of year. Neptune is attested at Rome before the first *lectisternium* (399 BC); his association there with *Mercurius seems to refer to the circulation of merchandise (Livy 5. 13. 6). His cult-partner is Salacia (Gell. 13. 23. 2); she may be the goddess of 'leaping', i.e. springing water (*salire*), but was identified with Amphitrite as he was with Poseidon.

For his temples see Ziolkowski, *Temples*, 117 ff. Cf. Wissowa, *RK* 225 ff.; G. Dumézil, *Mythe et épopée* 3 (1973), 21 ff.; and *Fêtes romaines d'été et d'automne* (1975), 25 ff. H. J. R.; J. Sch.

Neratius (*RE* 15) **Priscus, Lucius,** an influential Roman lawyer from *Saepinum in *Samnium, was descended from the family of *Antistius Labeo's wife. He was *suffect consul in AD 97 and later governor of *Germania Inferior, i.e. Lower Germany (?) and *Pannonia, but the story that *Trajan considered him a possible successor is a fiction. He headed the Proculian school along with his junior colleague *Celsus, belonged to Hadrian's council, and was still alive in 133. Probably as a teaching aid he wrote *Regulae* ('Guidelines'), a genre of literature which soon became popular. He also published seven books (*libri*) of *Membrana* ('Notes') and, drawing on his practice, three of *Responsa* ('Opinions'). Basically conservative, he was nevertheless open to the subjective and moralizing influence of Stoic thought. *Paulus and *Ulpian used him as a source and Justinian's compilers (see JUSTINIAN'S CODIFICATION) took some 70 passages from his works, some of which have, without good ground, been assigned by scholars to later centuries.

Lenel, *Pal.* 1. 763–88; Bremer 2/2. 286–359; *PIR²* N 60; *HLL* 3. § 396. 3; Kunkel 1967, 144–5; Syme, *RP* 1. 339–52; R. Greiner, *Opera Neratii: Drei Textgeschichten* (1973); T. Honoré, *Revue historique de droit français et étranger* 1974, 504–14; Honoré 1962, 168–9; V. Scarano Ussani, *Empiria e dogmi: La scuola proculiana fra Nerva e Adriano* (1989), 19–81. T. Hon.

Nereus, an old sea god, son of *Pontus and father by the Oceanid Doris of the Nereids; see NYMPHS. He lives with the Nereids in the depths of the sea (*Il.* 1. 358; Hes. *Theog.* 233–6), particularly in the *Aegean Sea (Ap. Rhod. *Argon.* 4. 771–2). *Hesiod and *Pindar extol his righteousness. Like other 'Old Men of the Sea' he has great wisdom and even the gift of prophecy (Hor. *Carm.* 1. 15. 3–5). These abilities bring him into strenuous contest with *Heracles. *Bacchylides (*dithyramb 17) and *Pherecydes (*FGrH* 3 F16) relate that Heracles had to catch Nereus unawares in order to learn the whereabouts of the golden apples (see HESPERIDES). Panyassis (Ath. 11. 469d) makes Nereus give the bowl of the Sun to Heracles. In his contest with Heracles Nereus transforms himself into fire, water, and many other shapes (*Stesichorus; Pherecydes; Apollod. 2. 5. 11). In addition to his 50 or 100 daughters, he is said by *Lucian (*Trag.* 87) to have educated *Aphrodite.

The earliest representations of him are of the early 6th cent. BC, as a fishtailed old man fighting Heracles and mutating. Vases from the mid-6th cent. to the early Classical show him fully human and holding a fish rather than mutating, distinguished from *Triton, whom he watches fighting Heracles. Nereus attends the wedding of *Peleus and *Thetis (François vase), and c.510–425 watches them wrestle. Some late Archaic vases show Nereus riding a hippocamp (i.e. a monster with a horse's body and a fish's tail), others Heracles destroying Nereus' house, sometimes in his presence. His only post-Classical appearance is on the *Pergamum altar, where he is named, helping Doris and *Oceanus.

LIMC 6/1. 824–37; G. Ahlberg-Cornell, *Herakles and the Sea-monster in Attic Black-figure Vase-painting* (1984). On the Nereids, see J. M. Barringer, *Divine Escorts* (1995)   G. M. A. H.; J. R. T. P.; K. W. A.

Nero (Nero Claudius Caesar, *RE* Suppl. 3, 'Domitius' 29), Roman emperor AD 54–68, was born 15 December 37 of Cn. Domitius Ahenobarbus (consul AD 32) and *Iulia Agrippina.

To strengthen his doubtful claim to the throne, stories had been spread of his miraculous childhood (Suet. *Ner.* 6; Tac. *Ann.* 11. 11) and stress laid on his descent from the divine *Augustus. In 49 his mother, as *Claudius' new wife, was able to have the younger Seneca (L. *Annaeus Seneca (2)) recalled from exile in order to teach her son rhetoric and to secure his betrothal to Claudius' daughter *Octavia (3); in 50 Lucius Domitius Ahenobarbus was adopted by Claudius, thus becoming Tiberius Claudius Nero Caesar or, as he is sometimes called, Nero Claudius Caesar Drusus Germanicus. In the next year he assumed the *toga virilis* at the early age of 13 and was clearly marked out for the accession by being given the same privileges as Augustus' grandsons Gaius and Lucius had received (see IULIUS CAESAR (2), C. and IULIUS CAESAR (4), L.). When Claudius died on 13 October 54, Nero was escorted into the praetorian camp by the prefect Sex. *Afranius Burrus. The senate then conferred the necessary powers on Nero and declared his adoptive father a god and Agrippina his priestess.

The ancient tradition is unanimous in regarding Nero's initial years of rule as excellent, a period hailed as a golden age by contemporary poets. Two 4th-cent. writers ascribe to the later emperor *Trajan the view that Nero surpassed all other *principes* for a *quinquennium*, apparently referring to the first five years. Of our three major ancient authorities, *Suetonius and *Cassius Dio suggest that the young emperor at first left government to his mother and Dio adds that Seneca and Burrus soon took over control, leaving the emperor to his pleasures. *Tacitus (1), however, regards the influence of Agrippina (visible on coins of December 54 showing her head facing Nero's on the obverse) as more apparent than real and the role of his advisers as one of guiding his activities, as in Seneca's *De clementia*, and managing court intrigue and public relations. Nero's first speech to the senate, written by Seneca, is described by Suetonius (*Ner.* 10) as a promise to rule according to Augustan precedent; Tacitus (*Ann.* 13. 4) adds a renunciation of the abuses of the Claudian regime—excessive influence of palace minions and monopolization of jurisdiction by the *princeps*, in particular, the trying of (political) cases behind closed doors—and a pledge to share the responsibilities of government with the senate. The historian vouches for the fulfilment of these promises, clearly interpreting the last, not in the sense of a surrender of power by the *princeps* but of an attitude of respect towards that body. Symbolic of the new attitude was the legend '*ex s c*' ('in accordance with a senatorial decree') appearing regularly on the gold and silver coinage for the first ten years, though whether it is an authorization mark or relates to the types and legends is uncertain.

Nero at first heeded his advisers because they protected him from his domineering mother and indulged him within limits. She had always used the menace of rivals to threaten him, and the presence of a considerable number of dynastic claimants was inevitable under the Augustan Principate, which, not being an avowed monarchy, could have no law of succession to regulate the actual practice of hereditary succession. When Agrippina decided to show sympathy for Claudius' natural son *Britannicus in 55, she sealed his doom, though the poisoning was not overt and could be dissembled, as by Seneca, who wrote praising

Nero's clemency in the next year. In 59 Agrippina's resistance to his affair with *Poppaea Sabina led Nero to enlist the prefect of the fleet of *Misenum to drown her in a collapsible boat. When that failed, she was stabbed at her villa. This spectacular crime marked the end of the good part of Nero's reign, according to a contemporary view (Tac. *Ann.* 15. 67), echoed in the later tradition of the 'Quinquennium Neronis'. But for Tacitus, the political deterioration did not set in until 62 when a treason charge of the unrepublican sort, based on irreverence towards the emperor, was admitted for the first time in the reign (see MAIESTAS), and Burrus died, thereby ending Seneca's influence as well. One of the new prefects, *Ofonius Tigellinus was seen by Tacitus as Nero's evil genius, rather like *Sejanus to *Tiberius. Nero now divorced his barren wife Octavia and married Poppaea who was pregnant: the child was a girl, Claudia Augusta, who was born in January of 41 and died four months later.

The death of his mother already made him feel freer to indulge his artistic passions. His enthusiasm for art, chariot-racing, and Greek *athletics seems to have been genuine; he wanted to lead Rome from gladiatorial shows (see GLADIATORS) to nobler entertainments. At the Iuvenalia, private games held in 59 to celebrate the first shaving of his beard, he sang and performed on the cithara (lyre) but also encouraged members of the upper classes to take lessons in singing and dancing. A year later he introduced for the first time at Rome public games in the Greek fashion (see AGŌNES) to be celebrated every five years. In 61 he opened a *gymnasium and distributed free *oil to competitors. His interest in re-educating Rome was genuine: it was not until the second celebration of these games in 65 that the *princeps* himself performed, though he had already made his début in the Greek city of Naples (*Neapolis) a year earlier. His voice, described as 'slight and husky', may have been passable; his poetry was probably his own, for *Suetonius had seen his notebooks with their erasures (*Ner.* 52).

The emperor's popularity with the propertied classes had been further undermined by a fire which devastated the city and strained the economy. It broke out in the early hours of 19 June 64 in shops around the Circus Maximus, and spread north through the valley between the *Palatine and the *Esquiline. It lasted for nine days in all and reduced three of the fourteen regions (*regiones) of the city to rubble, leaving only four regions untouched. The emperor provided emergency shelter and helped with reconstruction, but he soon revealed that he would take the opportunity, not only to introduce a new code of safety for buildings, but to use land previously in private occupation for a grand palace and spacious parks (the Golden House or *Domus Aurea) in the centre of Rome. The precious metal coinage shows the financial strain, to which the expense of the disastrous revolt of *Boudicca in *Britain in 60 and the protracted wars with *Parthia over *Armenia contributed: both the gold and silver were reduced in weight and the silver content of the denarius lowered by more than 10 per cent. With rumours circulating that Nero had instigated the fire and recited his own poems over the burning city, Nero made the Christians scapegoats, burning them alive to make the punishment fit the alleged crime (see CHRISTIANITY).

Nero never lost his popularity with the ordinary people of Rome, who loved his generosity and his games. The threat came from the upper classes and especially from senators governing provinces where the propertied élite had become discontent as a result of confiscations after the Rome fire: they are attested in Gaul, Spain, Africa, Britain, Judaea, and Egypt. But meanwhile his paranoiac prosecutions in Rome led to a conspiracy in 65 to

Nerva, Marcus Cocceius

assassinate him and make C. *Calpurnius Piso (2) emperor. The scheme was betrayed. Piso and his accomplices, senators including *Lucan, knights, officers of the praetorian guard, and one of the prefects, Faenius Rufus, were executed. Nero now suspected all, and more deaths followed, including Seneca, *Petronius, and the Stoics *Thrasea Paetus and *Barea Soranus (see STOICISM). In the year after Poppaea's death, Nero married *Statilia Messallina, and, also in 66, *Tiridates (4), a member of the ruling Parthian dynasty, came to Rome to receive the diadem of Armenia from Nero's hand. This represented an adjustment of Roman foreign policy in the east, where independent client kings had always been imposed on this buffer state with Parthia. In September of 66, despite another conspiracy at *Beneventum, Nero himself left for Greece, to perform in all the Greek games. The highpoint of his tour was his liberation of Greece from Roman administration and taxation, announced at a special celebration of the *Isthmian Games at Corinth on 28 November 67. The text of Nero's speech in Greek is preserved on an inscription (ILS 8794; Syll.³ 814; Sherk, Hadrian 71 for translation).

While in Greece *Vespasian was selected from the emperor's entourage to deal with a revolt in Judaea (see JEWS). But Nero deposed and executed three senatorial commanders, Cn. *Domitius Corbulo who had served him well in the east, and the Scribonii brothers who governed the two Germanies (see GERMANIA). Disaffection was rumbling in the west. At last Nero, in response to the warnings of his freedman Helius, returned to Italy. Soon after, in March of 68, C. *Iulius Vindex, governor of Gallia Lugdunensis (see GAUL, TRANSALPINE), rose in arms. Although he was defeated two months later by the governor of Upper Germany, Nero's failure to respond decisively had encouraged others to defect. In Spain *Galba declared himself 'Legate of the Senate and Roman People', and in Africa L. *Clodius Macer revolted. The praetorians were told that Nero had already fled abroad and were bribed by C. *Nymphidius Sabinus, one of their prefects, to declare for Galba. The senate followed suit, decreeing Nero a public enemy. Nero took refuge in the villa of his freedman Phaon and there he committed suicide, reputedly lamenting, 'What an artist dies with me!' (Suet. Ner. 48–9).

Nero's *philhellenism earned him the devotion of many in the Greek-speaking provinces, and within the next twenty years, three false Neros appeared there, all playing the lyre and all attracting followers. But the Christians naturally hated him for their persecution of 64 and the Jews for the mistreatment that led to the revolt which ultimately lost them the Temple in Jerusalem.

Smallwood, Docs. . . . Gaius; J. Tresch, Die Nerobücher in den Annalen des Tacitus (1965); K. R. Bradley, Suetonius' Life of Nero: An Historical Commentary (1978); B. H. Warmington, Suetonius' Nero (1977), and Nero, Reality and Legend (1969); M. T. Griffin, Nero: the End of a Dynasty (1984); U. Hiesinger, AJArch. 1975; A. Boethius, The Golden House of Nero (1960); L. Fabbrini, Città e architettura nella Roma imperiale, Analecta Romana Instituti Danici, Suppl. 10 (1983), 169 ff.; F. A. Lepper, JRS 1957, 95 ff.; D. MacDowall, The Western Coinages of Nero (1979).
M. P. C.; G. E. F. C.; M. T. G.

Nerva, Marcus Cocceius (RE 16), Roman emperor AD 96–8, grandson of M. *Cocceius Nerva (2), was born possibly in AD 35. His family, which came from the old Latin colony of *Narnia and acquired distinction during the Civil Wars, had a remote connection with the Julio-Claudian dynasty. Nerva it seems did not serve as a provincial governor or hold any senior administrative post, but was influential as a confidant of *Nero, who admired his poetry and presented him with triumphal ornaments and other honours after the suppression of the conspiracy of C.

*Calpurnius Piso (2) in 65. Despite this he was high in the Flavians' favour, being ordinary *consul with *Vespasian in 71 and again in 90 with *Domitian.

Nerva was seemingly not party to the plot to murder Domitian and was approached by the conspirators only after several others had rebuffed them. But he had qualities of good birth, a pleasant disposition, and long experience in imperial politics, and immediately set out to be a contrast to Domitian, who had been detested by the upper classes and whose memory was damned by the senate (see DAMNATIO MEMORIAE). The slogans on Nerva's coinage ('Public Freedom', 'Salvation', 'Equity', 'Justice') reflect his wish to create a new atmosphere. He released those on trial for treason, banned future treason charges, restored exiles, returned property confiscated by Domitian, displayed moderation in the public honours he accepted, and took advice from leading men. He built *granaries in Rome, dedicated the forum Transitorium (see FORUM NERVAE) begun by Domitian, distributed a largess to the people and the soldiers, removed the burden of the imperial post (vehiculatio, see POSTAL SERVICE) from communities in Italy, and initiated moves to buy up land for distribution to the poorest citizens; he may also have begun the alimentary scheme, which aimed to provide funds for the maintenance of poor children in rural Italy, although major responsibility for its execution probably lay with Trajan (see ALIMENTA). According to Tacitus, Nerva combined two incompatible elements—liberty and imperial rule (Ag. 3).

However, Nerva was elderly and infirm and had no children. Naturally there was speculation about the succession, and further problems appeared. The desire for vengeance against supposed agents of Domitian came close to anarchy. The appointment of a senatorial committee in 97 to effect economies suggests that there were some financial difficulties, which arguably were the result of extravagance in Nerva's regime. The most serious signs of disquiet occurred among the soldiers, with whom Domitian had been popular. One army was close to mutiny on the news of his death, and subsequently there were rumours about the intentions of a governor of one of the eastern provinces in command of a substantial army (Philostr. VS 488; Plin. Ep. 9. 13). Coins celebrating 'Concord of the armies' probably express hope rather than confidence. There was also a plot against the emperor in Rome. Most ominously, rebellion broke out among the praetorians who had been stirred up by their prefect Casperius Aelianus into demanding the execution of the murderers of Domitian. Nerva had to accede, and was forced to give public thanks for the executions, thereby losing much of his authority and prestige. In October 97 amid gathering political crisis, he adopted *Trajan, whom he had previously appointed governor of Upper Germany, as his son, co-emperor, and successor. His own title Germanicus, granted for a minor victory over the Germans in Bohemia, was conferred on Trajan. It is impossible to discover the exact circumstances of Trajan's adoption. Pliny suggests that the empire was tottering above the head of an emperor who now regretted his elevation to imperial power (Pan. 6. 3, 7. 3), but this may have been exaggerated in order to please Trajan. However if Nerva's regime faced increasing discontent, his advisers would doubtless take into consideration Trajan's distinguished background and career, popularity with the troops, and proximity to Rome. Nerva's death on 28 January 98 marks an important point in the development of the empire, since he was the last strictly Italian emperor.

ANCIENT SOURCES Cass. Dio 67. 15–18, 68. 1–4; Plin. Pan., Ep.; Eutr. 8; Aur. Vict. Caes. 12; [Aur. Vict.] Epit. 12.

DOCUMENTS AND COINS *BM Coins, Rom. Emp.* 3; Smallwood, *Docs. . . . Nerva.*

LITERATURE A. Garzetti, *Nerva* (1950), and *From Tiberius to the Antonines* (1974; It. orig. 1960); Syme, *Tacitus*; M. Hammond, *The Antonine Monarchy* (1959). Imperial finances: R. Syme, *JRS* 1930, 55 (= *RP* 1. 1); G. Biraghi, *PP* 1951, 257. Forum Transitorium: J. C. Anderson, *Collection Latomus* 182 (1984), 55.   J. B. C.

Nervii, a Belgic people (see BELGAE) occupying parts of Hainault and Flanders, who were defeated by *Caesar after a fierce struggle in 57 BC. Under the empire they contributed six cohorts to the *auxilia* and ranked as a *civitas libera* ('free community'; Plin. *HN* 4. 106). Numerous villas and potteries indicate general prosperity and their capital Bagacum (mod. Bavay) became an important commercial centre. After the barbarian invasions of the 3rd cent., however, its forum was converted into a *castellum* (fort); much of the wall of this survives, with an important cryptoporticus.

Caes. *BGall.* 2. 15–28; C. Jullian, *Histoire de la Gaule* 2 (1909), 462 ff.; Grenier, *Manuel* 3. 315 ff.; *TIR* 31 (1975), 42 f.; E. M. Wightman, *Gallia Belgica* (1985).   A. L. F. R.; J. F. Dr.

Nestor , in mythology the youngest son of *Neleus and Chloris, and the only one to survive the massacre by *Heracles. He was king of Pylos (*Il.* 2. 77), and went with *Menelaus (1) around Greece to assemble the heroes ready for the expedition against *Troy (*Cypria*, Proclus; see EPIC CYCLE), then himself accompanied them with 90 ships (*Il.* 2. 591 ff.) and his sons *Antilochus and *Thrasymedes, even though he was at that time a very old man (1. 250 ff.). Homer portrays him as a highly respected elder statesman, the archetypal wise old man, but one still strong (11. 635 f.) and valiant in battle. He is always ready with advice: he tries to make peace between *Achilles and *Agamemnon (1. 254 ff.), and later suggests the Embassy to Achilles (9. 111 ff.), giving the ambassadors many instructions (179); he also suggests the spying raid on *Hector's camp in which Dolon is killed (10. 204 ff.); he even offers to his son *Antilochus advice on chariot-racing which he himself admits is superfluous (23. 306 ff.). He is much given also to long, rambling stories of the distant past, rich in reminiscences of his own achievements: how he excelled in war against the *Centaurs (1. 260 ff.) and the Epeians (11. 670 ff.), killed the Arcadian hero Ereuthalion (4. 319) and almost killed the *Moliones (11. 749 ff.), and performed outstandingly at the funeral-games of Amarynceus (23. 626 ff.). But he is always listened to by his comrades with patience, and indeed with respect (see Agamemnon's comments, 2. 370 ff.).

The *Aethiopis* (see Proclus) told how *Memnon killed Antilochus, who died to save his father's life (Pind. *Pyth.* 6. 28–42). The *Odyssey* records that, at Achilles' funeral, Nestor stopped the panic of the Greeks at the wailing of *Thetis and her attendants (24. 47 ff.). After the fall of Troy he realized that disaster impended (3. 165 ff.) and sailed safely home to Pylos, where he entertained *Telemachus who was seeking news of *Odysseus (3. 4 ff.). No tradition about the manner of his death has survived.

LIMC 7. 1 (1994), 1060 ff.   J. R. M.

Nestor (2). See SEPTIMIUS NESTOR, L.

neutrality, a word with no single Greek or Latin equivalent. In Greek the idea is expressed by terms meaning e.g. 'keeping quiet', 'helping neither side'. Individuals may be neutral between parties, and states between states. The first, domestic, sort of neutrality was allegedly prohibited by *Solon (*Ath. pol.* 8), and though possibly fiction this is not actually absurd because *Pericles (1), according to *Thucydides (2) (2. 40. 2), later expresses high Athenian expectations about civic involvement. In his ana-

lysis of faction (see STASIS) at *Corcyra (3. 82. 8) Thucydides says that 'middle people' fell victim to both parties; this carries the idea 'moderate' as well as 'neutral'. Neutrality in wars between Greek states, and even in wars between Greeks and '*barbarians', was possible: Archaic *Miletus formalized its neutral status with Lydia then Persia; Argive neutrality in the *Persian Wars (see ARGOS (2)) amounted in Herodotus' view (8. 73) to *Medism, but Argos' reputation did not stink for this later, contrast the outright Medizer *Thebes (1). Neutrality became harder in the *Peloponnesian War (though the Argives, again, maintained in the *Archidamian War the neutrality guaranteed to them since 446 BC). The topic interested Thucydides, who reports both the initial neutrality of *Melos (2. 9) and later Athenian efforts to violate it, first unsuccessful (3. 91) then successful (5. 85 ff., the occasion of the famous Melian Dialogue of 416 BC). He also tells us (4. 78, *Thessaly) about rules for crossing neutral territory. Small states, like the Ionian states in the final phase of the *Peloponnesian War, often tried to avoid commitment to either side. In the 4th cent., some (but not all) *Common Peace treaties allowed neutrality; Tod 145 of ?362 BC, a Greek reply to the satraps planning revolt from Persia, announces a neutrality policy (interestingly, in view of Argive neutrality at other times, the stone was found at Argos). Women in *Aristophanes (1)'s *Lysistrata* are pacifists, that is, neutrals of a kind, and this may have been true of many women at all times.

Republican Rome, by the *foedus Cassianum* of *c*.493 BC which first regulated Roman relations with the other Latin peoples, and which developed into the *foedus aequum* or 'equal treaty', permitted a sort of limited neutrality by imposing terms which did not require military help in Rome's aggressive wars but only if Rome were attacked (see FOEDUS). Though the Romans' early alliances with e.g. the Achaeans were of this type, Rome came to avoid the 'treaty' method of dealing with the Greeks. In practice, as Rome's power grew, it became harder for its Italian allies (see SOCII) to avoid contributing militarily, even when not strictly obliged to do so (e.g. the Camertes in the Second *Punic War), and harder for third parties to try to mediate between Rome and its enemies. Thus the Rhodians felt Rome's displeasure when they tried to mediate between Rome and *Perseus (2) in 168 BC (Polyb. 28–30). The Cretans were lucky to get away with no more than diplomatic protests from Rome about their ambiguous neutrality at the same period (Livy 43. 7). Evidence for neutrality in domestic politics is hard to find before the time of *Cicero, who after much hesitation rejected requests by *Caesar and the Caesarians that he should remain neutral in the Civil War with *Pompey. Others of Cicero's class did stay neutral.

In the ancient world neutrality was theoretically possible at many periods, and sometimes explicitly provided for, but difficult to maintain in face of overwhelming power like that of Classical Athens or Rome.

R. A. Bauslaugh, *The Concept of Neutrality in Classical Greece* (1990); H. D. Westlake, *Studies in Thucydides and Greek History* (1989), ch. 10; A. J. Toynbee, *Hannibal's Legacy* 1 (1965), 263 ff.; P. A. Brunt, *JRS* 1986, 12 ff. (Cicero).   S. H.

news, dissemination of. See EPIGRAPHY, GREEK and LATIN; POSTAL SERVICE; S. Lewis, *News and Society in the Greek Polis* (1996).

nexum appears to have been a solemn transaction of the oldest Roman law, with copper and scales (*per aes et libram*), by which a man subjected himself to somebody else's power of seizure. Because of the ambiguity of our literary sources (Varro, Festus, Livy), all details concerning this transaction are rather obscure.

Nicaea

Its very existence has even been disputed (most recently by O. Behrends). If it did exist, its original economic purpose may have been to ensure repayment of a loan: if the borrower did not redeem himself by paying back promptly what he had received, the lender could proceed with personal execution on the debtor, possibly even without prior lawsuit and judgement. But *nexum* may then also have been used (*nummo uno*, i.e. involving merely a symbolical payment) as a kind of self-pledge by which the debtor enslaved himself to the creditor until he had worked off a debt. *Nexum* was prohibited sometime during the 4th cent. BC as a result of the class struggles; as a loan transaction it was replaced by the informal *mutuum*. See also DEBT.

M. Kaser, *Altrömisches ius* (1949), 119 ff., 138 ff., 233 ff., and *Römisches Privatrecht* 1, 2nd edn. (1971), 166 f.; H. F. Jolowicz and B. Nicholas, *Historical Introduction to the Study of Roman Law*, 3rd edn. (1972), 164 ff.; O. Behrends, *RIDA* 1974, 137 ff., and *Iura* 1982, 78 ff.; M. Talamanca, *Enciclopedia del diritto* 29 (1979), 4 ff. R. Z.

Nicaea (1), modern Iznik, a city in *Bithynia founded by *Antigonus (1) as Antigoneia and renamed by *Lysimachus. According to *Strabo (12. 4. 7, 565–6), it formed an exact square with four gates, the central position being occupied by a *gymnasium. The gates, located at the four cardinal points, can be seen from the principal crossroads. The Roman and late Roman walls still stand and the theatre, identified by the younger *Pliny (2) as an example of bad engineering (*Ep.* 10. 39), has been excavated. *Pompey assigned it a vast territory, which was mainly divided between large landowners, who are identifiable from inscriptions of imperial date. It was a bitter rival of its neighbour *Nicomedia, but lost ground definitively by opting for *Pescennius Niger in the Civil War with *Septimius Severus. Constantine I chose Nicaea for the first great ecumenical Church council in AD 325, when the Nicene Creed was formulated.

A. M. Schneider, *Istanbuler Forschungen* 1938 and 1943; L. Robert, *Harv. Stud.* 1977, 1–37 (rivalry with Nicomedia); S. Şahin, *Die Inschriften von Iznik*, 4 vols. (1979–87), with testimonia; *Arch. Rep.* 1989/90, 89 (theatre excavations); C. Foss and D. Winfield, *Byzantine Fortifications* (1986); N. L. Boncasa, *PECS* 622–3. O. A. W. D.; S. M.

Nicaea (2) (mod. Nice), a Greek colony, was founded on Ligurian territory by *Massalia, to whose jurisdiction it continued to belong. In 154 BC, Q. Opimius relieved it and the neighbouring port Antipolis (mod. Antibes) from attacks by *Ligurians. Under the empire it was overshadowed by its neighbour Cemenelum (now Cimiez), *c*.3 km. (2 mi.) inland, which—in contrast to Nicaea, of which little survives—has substantial remains: an amphitheatre, shops, baths, and a Christian baptistery: in the late empire, indeed, both centres were, anomalously, the seats of bishoprics.

L. Duchesne, *Fastes épiscopaux de l'ancienne Gaule* 1 (1894); N. Gauthier and G. C. Picard (eds.), *Topographie chrétienne des cités de la Gaule* 2 (1986); A. L. F. Rivet, *Gallia Narbonensis* (1988). O. A. W. D.; J. F. Dr.

Nicaenetus, of *Samos or *Abdera, late 3rd-cent. BC epic poet, author of a (lost) *epyllion *Lyrkos* quoted by *Parthenius (*Amat. Narr.* 1); a (lost) *Catalogue of Women* mentioned by *Athenaeus (1) (590b); and a handful of epigrams in the *Garland* of *Meleager (2). *Epigram* 1 (Gow and Page) draws on *Callimachus (3) and *Apollonius (1) Rhodius; 4 describes a picnic at the temple of Hera on Samos (see HERAION).

Powell, *Coll. Alex.* 1–4; Gow–Page, *HE*. A. D. E. C.

Nicander, of Colophon. Nicander says he was 'nurtured by the snow-white city of Claros' (*Theriaca* 958), and that he lives among 'the tripods of Apollo in Claros' (*Alexipharmaca* 11), indicating that he was probably a priest of *Apollo at *Claros. Nicander of Colophon is not the Nicander, son of Anaxagoras, cited as an epic poet in a Delphian inscription (*Syll.*³ 452), dated 258 BC; internal evidence suggests a floruit for Nicander of Colophon of *c*.130 BC.

Works

Surviving intact are two didactic poems in hexameters, the *Theriaca* and *Alexipharmaca*. Forming the subject-matter of the *Theriaca* are snakes, spiders, scorpions, presumably poisonous insects, and related creatures (centipedes, millipedes, solifuges), accompanied by remedies for their bites and stings; the *Alexipharmaca* retails botanical, animal, and mineral poisons and antidotes. Nicander is a gifted Homeric glossator, but he is neither zoologist nor toxicologist: the lost tracts *Poisonous Animals* and *Poisonous Drugs* by *Apollodorus (4) of Alexandria (early 3rd cent. BC) were plagiarized for specifics. Noteworthy are descriptions of several cobras, the black widow spider, a number of scorpions, the blister beetle (from which came the infamous aphrodisiac, *kantharis*), the velvet ant (a wingless wasp), the wind scorpion or solifuge, and others. Important are the accounts of opium, aconite, hemlock, and the thorn apple (*Datura stramonium* L.), showing careful study of widely known poisons. Extant as fragments or known only by title or subject are the metaphrastic epics *Oetaica*, *Thebaica*, *Sicelia*, *Cimmerians*, and *Europia*; *Ophiaca* was in elegiacs, retelling snake-legends; *Heteroeumena* ('Metamorphoses') was employed by *Antoninus Liberalis and *Ovid; *Cicero (*De or.* 1. 69) admires Nicander's *Georgica*, used by *Virgil for his poem of the same name; and probably Nicander's *Melissurgica* ('Bee-keeping') underlies bk. 4 of Virgil's *Georgics*; Nicander's *Cynegetica* was a hunting-poem in elegiacs; the scholia on the *Theriaca* incorporate a *Hymn to Attalus* (fr. 104 Schneider), often cited as a Vita Nicandri; the scholiasts know a *Colophoniaca*, *Poets from Colophon*, *Glosses*, and *Temple Tools* (the last two in prose), and *Aetolica* has perished almost without a trace; two epigrams in the Greek Anthology (7. 526; 11. 7) carry Nicander's name, the former about the Spartan Othryadas, the latter addressed to Charidemus about the boredom attending sex with one's own wife.

The *Suda* entry on Nicander (ν 374) makes him a grammarian, poet, and physician, the last falsely adduced from his ersatz medical poems, or from Nicander's versifying of the pseudo-Hippocratic *Prognostics*. Nicander has little poetic talent; his efforts generally lack digressions, and in spite of some lofty subjects, there are woefully few similes and metaphors. His borrowing from Apollodorus indicates near-slavish dependence, and Nicander has little comprehension of the toxicology or zoology he carefully purloined. Yet as a grammarian and glossator, Nicander is among the most diligent of the Alexandrians in searching for puns, double meanings, and allusions in the Homeric epics, and like *Euphorion (2), Nicander frequently alters word-meanings, fitting fresh spellings into his lines, often violating the norms of Greek grammar. *Callimachus (3) was Nicander's guide in handling metre.

Nicander's two poems became standard for later students of toxicology, and these obscure hexameters owe their survival to their ease on the memory: one recalled Nicander's scanned lines far more easily than (e.g.) the lengthy treatises of Apollodorus or the poisonous animals in *Philumenus. Nicander's poems were authoritative until the Renaissance, even with the large scholiastic literature alongside, attempting to explain many of Nicander's patently murky terms. The scholia contain numerous quotations of lost authors, or unknown from other sources, and the delicious replication of superstitions about snakes, spiders, toads, frogs, salamanders, wasps, spiders, and so on are lodes for the folklorist and the historian of medicine, who note the meld of *magic and *Galen. See PHARMACOLOGY.

TEXTS A. S. F. Gow and A. F. Scholfield, *Nicander: The Poems and Poetical Fragments* (1953), with trans., clipped notes, and general bibliog.; O. Schneider, *Nicandrea* (1856), with comm. A. Crugnola, *Scholia in Nicandri Theriaka* (1971); M. Geymonat, *Scholia in Nicandri Alexipharmaca* (1974).

GENERAL LITERATURE W. Kroll, *RE* 17 / 1. 250–65; H. Schneider, *Vergleichende Untersuchungen zur sprachlichen Struktur der beiden erhal-tenen Lehrgedichte des Nikander von Kolophon*, Klass. Phil. Stud. 24 (1962), J. Scarborough, *Pharmacy in History* 1977, 3–23, and 1979, 3–34, 73–92, *Coleopterists' Bulletin* 1977, 293–6, and *Melsheimer Entomological Series* 1979, 17–27; H. White, *Studies in the Poetry of Nicander* (1987); I. C. Beavis, *Insects and Other Invertebrates in Classical Antiquity* (1988).

J. Sca.

Nicanor (1), of Stagira, named in *Aristotle's will as the future husband of his daughter. Intimate with the philosopher, he served with *Alexander (3) the Great in Asia and was commissioned to proclaim the Exiles' Decree at the Olympian Games of 324 BC (see EXILE, Greek). He also acted as diplomat, negotiating person-ally with *Demosthenes (2), and received honorary citizenship at Ephesus. Nothing more is attested of his activities, but it is a common speculation to identify him with *Cassander's garrison commander in the *Piraeus, condemned and executed after his victory near the *Bosporus (1) in 318.

H. Berve, *RE* 17. 267, 'Nicanor' 4. A. B. B.

Nicanor (2), of *Alexandria (1) (2nd cent. AD), wrote on the punctuation of the *Iliad*, of the *Odyssey* (see HOMER), and of *Callimachus (3); also a general work Περὶ στιγμῆς (on punctuation). He recognized three kinds of full stop, three of the comma, and two of the colon. In punctuation he dominates the Homeric *scholia as *Herodian (1) does in accentuation, *Aristonicus (2) in Aristarchan textual criticism (see ARISTARCHUS (2)), and *Didymus (1) in erudition.

FRAGMENTS Περὶ Ἰλ. στιγμῆς, Friedlaender (1851); Περὶ Ὀδ. στιγμῆς, Carnuth (1875). P. B. R. F.

Nicarchus, author of some 40 Greek satirical epigrams in the Greek Anthology much influenced by *Lucillius, some of them vulgar but some also very funny.

F. J. Brecht, *Motiv- und Typengeschichte des griechischen Spottepigrams* (1930); W. Burnikel, *Untersuchungen zur Struktur des Witzepigramms bei Lukillios und Martial* (1980). A. D. E. C.

Niceta, bishop of Remesiana (mod. Bela Palanka, former Yugoslavia) c. AD 400. Missionary to barbarians and a friend of *Paulinus of Nola, he wrote amongst other works an *Explanatio symboli*: an exposition of the Apostle's Creed. Reputedly he com-posed the great Church hymn, *Te Deum laudamus*.

Ed. A. E. Burn, *Niceta of Remesiana* (1905); trans. *Fathers of the Church* 7 (1949). A. H.-W.; P. J. H.

Nicias (1) (c.470–413 BC), Athenian politician and general. During the period after the death of *Pericles (1) he became the principal rival of *Cleon in the struggle for political leadership. He was a moderate and opposed the aggressive *imperialism of the extreme democrats, his aim being the conclusion of peace with Sparta as soon as it could be attained on terms favourable

to Athens. Elected frequently to serve as *stratēgos*, he led several expeditions in which, thanks to his cautious competence, he suffered no serious defeat and won no important victory. He was largely responsible for the armistice concluded in 423, and the Peace of 421 appropriately bears his name.

He now favoured a policy of retrenchment and objected to the ambitious schemes of *Alcibiades, who advocated Athenian intervention in the Peloponnese and later an expedition to Sicily. Despite his disapproval Nicias was appointed with Alcibiades and *Lamachus to conduct this enterprise. Alcibiades was soon recalled, and little was accomplished in 415, but in 414 Syracuse was besieged and almost reduced to capitulation. The death of Lamachus, the arrival of the Spartan *Gylippus, and the inactivity of Nicias, now seriously ill, transformed the situation, and in spite of the efforts of *Demosthenes (1), who brought reinforce-ments in 413, the Athenians were themselves blockaded. Nicias, who refused to withdraw by sea until too late, led the vanguard in a desperate attempt to escape by land. His troops were over-whelmed at the river Assinarus, and he was subsequently exe-cuted. The narrative of *Thucydides (2), though giving due credit to Nicias for his selfless devotion, shows very clearly that the Athenian disaster was largely due to the inadequacy of his mili-tary leadership.

He was very wealthy (Xen. *Vect.* 4. 14 says he had 1,000 slaves working in the silver *mines; see SLAVERY) and spent lavishly; see esp. Plut. *Nic.* 3, mentioning the splendid festival procession he led to *Delos, where Athens has recently re-established the festi-val of the Delia (Thuc. 3. 104). Thucydides may have this in mind when he speaks of Nicias' *aretē* (civic virtue, a notion which could include open-handed outlay on *liturgies.). See Thuc. 7. 86. 5.

Thuc. bks. 3–7; Plut. *Nicias*. H. D. Westlake, *Individuals in Thucydides* (1968), chs. 6 and 11; W. R. Connor, *The New Politicians of Fifth-Century Athens* (1971), see index; A. W. H. Adkins, *GRBS* 1975, 379 ff.; D. Kagan, *The Peace of Nicias and the Sicilian Expedition* (1981); D. M. Lewis, *CAH* 5² (1992), ch. 9, and A. Andrewes, ibid., ch. 10. H. D. W.; S. H.

Nicias (2), painter, especially of women (Plin. *NH* 35. 130), pupil of Antidotus (pupil of *Euphranor), Athenian. *Pliny (1) dates him 332 BC. He painted statues for *Praxiteles (about 340) and refused to sell a picture to *Ptolemy (1) I (after 306). His works included Nemea—signed as encaustic (see PAINTING (TECHNIQUES))—Necyomantea (after *Homer, *Od.* 11), Alexan-der (3) the Great, Io, Andromeda. The Io and Andromeda are reflected in versions in *Pompeii and Rome which have a similar colour scheme to the 4th-cent. Alexander *sarcophagus. He advised the choice of large subjects such as cavalry and sea battles (contrast *Pausias). See PAINTING, GREEK.

M. Robertson, *History of Greek Art* 1 (1975), 436–9. T. B. L. W.

Nicias (3) (*RE* 26a, Suppl. 7), of *Nicaea (1), of uncertain date (100 BC–AD 200), author of philosophical *Successions* (Διαδοχαί), used as a source by *Diogenes (6) Laertius. D. N. S.

Nicochares, Athenian comic poet and son of *Philonides (1), produced *Lakones* in 388 BC (hyp. 4 Ar. *Plut.*) and in *Galatea* (fr. 4) ridicules the same person as *Aristophanes (1) in *Plut.* 303 f. We have ten titles, several implying mythological burlesque; *Galatea* could possibly be one ancestor of Theoc. 11.

Kassel–Austin, *PCG* 7. 39 ff. (*CAF* 1. 700 f.). K. J. D.

Nicocles See EVAGORAS.

Nicolaus of Damascus, versatile author; friend and historian

Nicomachus

of *Herod (1) the Great; born c.64 BC of distinguished family, outstandingly well-educated. He became a *Peripatetic and came into contact with leading figures of his day: he was tutor to the children of M. *Antonius (2) and *Cleopatra VII (FGrH 90 T 2) and from 14 BC close adviser of Herod I, who employed him on diplomatic missions (F 136). Herod also studied philosophy, rhetoric, and history with Nicolaus and encouraged him to write (F 135). When Herod incurred *Augustus' displeasure on account of the campaign in Arabia in 8/7, Nicolaus succeeded in placating the *princeps* in Rome; in 4 he supported Herod Archelaus who had come to Rome to have his succession to the throne confirmed (F 136).

Works

(1) *Historiai*, universal history in 144 books from the earliest times to the death of Herod the Great, the most comprehensive work of universal history since *Ephorus. Books 1–7, known through the Constantinian excerpts, dealt with the ancient east (Assyrians, Medes, Lydians, Persians) and early Greece (F 1–102). Sources: chiefly *Ctesias and *Xanthus (2) for the east, Ephorus and *Hellanicus (1) for Greece. Only meagre fragments of books 8–144 are extant. Books 123–4, preserved in *Josephus *AJ* 14–17, contained the history of Herod the Great, for which Nicolaus, despite his tendentious and extenuating presentation (cf. T 12, F 96. 101 f.), was an excellent primary source: he drew on his own experiences and on the king's *hypomnēmata* or memoirs (FGrH 236). (2) *Ēthōn synagōgē* ('collection of (Strange Peoples') Customs'), dedicated to Herod and of Peripatetic character (F 103–24, all in *Stobaeus). (3) *Bios* ('Life') *of Augustus*, apologetic and panegyric account based on Augustus' autobiography, which reached down to c.25 BC. The fragments (F 125–30, in the Constantinian excerpts) treat of Octavian's youth and education, *Caesar's assassination, and the conflict between Octavian and Antonius until Octavian's levy of an army in *Campania in 44; the terminal point and date of composition have been much discussed, but he probably wrote sometime between 25–20 BC (Jacoby) and AD 14 (Steidle). (4) *On My Own Life and Education*, autobiography (F 131–9). Education is seen from the viewpoint of Aristotelian ethics (see ARISTOTLE) and compared to 'a journey to one's own hearth' (F 132); an important source for the contemporary system of education. (5) (Lost) tragedies and comedies. (6) Philosophical writings, known through Greek fragments and, chiefly, texts in Arabic and Syriac: *On Aristotle's Philosophy*, a handbook of paraphrases and commentaries, e.g. on natural philosophy, metaphysics, and the after-life. Nicolaus therefore plays an important part in the *reception of Aristotle.

FGrH 90. A. Lesky, *History of Greek Literature* (1966); M. Toher, *The Bios Kaisaros of Nicolaus of Damascus: An Historiographical Analysis* (Diss. Brown Univ. Providence, 1985) (microfilm); O. Lendle, *Einführung in die griechische Geschichtsschreibung* (1992).   K. M.

Nicomachus (1), son of *Aristotle; to him, according to an ancient account, Aristotle dedicated the *Nicomachean Ethics*; but possibly the name is due to his having edited the work, as *Eudemus may have edited the *Eudemian Ethics*.

Nicomachus (2), New Comedy poet (see COMEDY (GREEK), NEW) of the mid-3rd cent. BC, when he was praised by both *Delos and *Samos in honorary decrees (IG 11. 4. 638; C. Habicht, *MDAI(A)* 1957, 224 ff.). Fr. 1, a cook glories in his art.

FRAGMENTS Kassel–Austin, PCG 7. 56–61.
INTERPRETATION Meineke, FCG 1. 496 ff.; A. Körte, RE 17/1 (1936), 461 f. 'Nikomachos' 15; A. Giannini, Acme 1960, 165 f.; H.

Dohm, *Mageiros* (1964), 192 ff.; G. M. Sifakis, *Studies in the History of Hellenistic Drama* (1967), 27.   W. G. A.

Nicomachus (3) (RE 21), of *Gerasa, *Neopythagorean mathematician and musicologist (fl. c. AD 100); wrote (1) *Introduction to Arithmetic* (Ἀριθμητικὴ εἰσαγωγή), in two books, on the Pythagorean theory of numbers (see PYTHAGORAS (1)). Among much trivia it includes some valuable historical information, e.g. on the 'sieve' of *Eratosthenes (1. 13). It was extremely influential, especially in the Middle Ages, having been translated into Latin (by *Apuleius, see Cassiodorus in Migne, PL 70. 1208 B) and Arabic, and adapted for his *De institutione arithmetica* by *Boethius. Among extant commentaries are those by *Iamblichus (2), Asclepius of Tralles, and *Philoponus. (2) *Manual of Harmonics* (Ἐγχειρίδιον ἁρμονικῆς), see MUSIC, § 5. Lost works include Θεολογούμενα ἀριθμητικῆς (extracts preserved in the work of the same name attributed to *Iamblichus) and an *Introduction to Geometry* (see Introd. arith. 2. 6. 1).

EDITIONS AND TRANSLATIONS Arithmetic: ed. R. Hoche (Teubner, 1866); Eng. trans., D'Ooge, Robbins, and Karpinski (1926); Arabic trans., *Ṭābit b. Qurra's Arabische Übersetzung der Ἀριθμητικὴ Εἰσαγωγή des Nikomachos von Gerasa*, ed. W. Kutsch (1958). Harmony: ed. C. von Jan, *Musici Scriptores Græci* (1895), with other fragments; trans. with comm., F. R. Levin, 'Nicomachus of Gerasa, Manual of Harmonics' (Ph.D. Diss. Columbia University, 1967).
ANCIENT COMMENTARIES Iamblichus, ed. H. Pistelli (Teubner, 1894; repr. 1975); Asclepius, ed. L. Taran, TAPhS NS 59/4 (1969); Philoponus, ed. R. Hoche (1864: bk. 1; 1867: bk. 2).
COMMENT Heath, *Hist. of Greek Maths.* 1. 97 ff.   G. J. T.

Nicomachus (4) **Flavianus, Virius** (c. AD 340–94), Roman senator, who with Vettius Agorius *Praetextatus and his close friend and associate Q. Aurelius *Symmachus (2) was a champion of the old *paganism. After a distinguished public career—he was *vicarius* of Africa in 376, and under *Theodosius (2) I *quaestor sacri palatii* (388–90; see QUAESTOR, end), and praetorian prefect of Italy and Illyricum (390–2)—he wholeheartedly supported the usurper *Eugenius, under whom he was also praetorian prefect and conducted a full-scale pagan revival. On Eugenius' defeat by Theodosius he committed suicide. His reputation was restored in 431 through the influence of his son and grandson (ILS 2948). He was the author of *Annales* dedicated to Theodosius, which have often been seen as a source for *Ammianus Marcellinus and other late 4th-cent. writers, but the scope of this work is entirely unknown. It is also debated whether he or Praetextatus was the 'prefect' attacked by the author of the anonymous *Carmen contra paganos* (Cod. Par. 8084; Riese, *Anth. Lat.* 1. 1. 4, 20 ff.). His son Nicomachus Flavianus *iunior* held the prefecture of Rome under Eugenius but was forgiven by Theodosius. He participated in the revision of the text of Livy carried out by the Nicomachi and others in the early 5th cent.; he married the daughter of Symmachus.

ILS 2946–8; PLRE 1. 347–9, 'Flavianus' 15. H. Bloch, in A. Momigliano (ed.), *The Conflict between Paganism and Christianity in the Fourth Century* (1963), ch. 8; J. F. Matthews, *JRS* 1973, 179 ff.; A. M. Honoré and J. F. Matthews, *Xenia* 1989, 9 ff.   J. F. Ma.

Nicomedes, the name of several kings of Bithynia:

(1) Nicomedes I

(c.279–c.255 BC), son of Zipoetes (before 315–c.279), who had taken the royal title in 298, inherited his father's struggle against *Antiochus (1) I. He joined the Northern League, purchasing the aid of *Heraclea (3) by returning Cierus, invited the Gauls (see CELTS) across the *Bosporus (1), and assisted them to settle in

*Phrygia (see GALATIA). He founded *Nicomedia *c.*265, and received honours at *Cos and *Olympia. At his death his son Ziaëlas (*c.*255–*c.*230) seized the throne in defiance of the guardians of his father's will in favour of his minor children, but continued his Hellenizing policy.

(2) Nicomedes II Epiphanes

(149–*c.*127 BC), son of *Prusias (2) II, cultivated the favour of the Greek cities, and, a faithful ally, aided Rome in the war against *Aristonicus (1) (133–129), but his request for territory in *Phrygia was refused in favour of *Mithradates V of Pontus.

(3) Nicomedes III Euergetes

(*c.*127–*c.*94 BC), son of Nicomedes II. His gifts to Greek cities won him the title Euergetes ('Benefactor'). Yet because of the condition of Bithynia, when C. *Marius (1) requested aid from him against the *Cimbri (104) he declared that most of his men had been seized and enslaved by Roman *publicani, and the senate decreed that no free man from an allied state should be held in slavery. His attempts to divide *Paphlagonia with *Mithradates VI of Pontus and to win *Cappadocia by marrying Queen Laodice were foiled by Roman intervention (see ARIARATHES VII–IX).

(4) Nicomedes IV Philopator

(*c.*94–75/4 BC), son of Nicomedes III. *Mithradates VI of Pontus promptly drove him out in favour of his brother Socrates (*c.*92), but a Roman commission under M'. *Aquillius (2) restored him (90–89). Under pressure from Aquillius and his Roman creditors he raided Pontic territory, and precipitated the First Mithradatic War (88). Restored by *Sulla in 85/4, he ruled thereafter in such peace as Roman officials and businessmen allowed him. *Caesar was sent as envoy to him to get ships for the siege of Mytilene (81/0). At his death (late 75 or early 74) he bequeathed his impoverished kingdom to Rome.

App. *Mith.*; references in Polybius, Diodorus Siculus, and Memnon; *OGI* 340–6. T. Reinach, *Trois royaumes de l'Asie mineure* (1888); *Mithridate Eupator* (1896); *L'Histoire par les monnaies* (1902), 167 ff.; Rostovtzeff, *Hellenistic World*, see index; Magie, *Rom. Rule Asia Min.* 311 ff. and index; G. Vitucci, *Il regno di Bitinia* (1953); R. Sullivan, *Near Eastern Royalty and Rome* (1990), 30 ff.　　　　T. R. S. B.; S. M.

Nicomedes (5) (*RE* 16), mathematician (? *c.*200 BC), was the discoverer of the cochloidal or conchoidal curves, by means of which he solved the problem of trisecting the angle and that of doubling the cube. See especially Eutocius, *Comm. in Arch. de Sph. et Cyl.* (Heiberg²), 98 ff.

Heath, *Hist. of Greek Maths.* 1. 238 ff., 260 ff.; G. Toomer, *Dictionary of Scientific Biography* 10, entry under the name.　　T. L. H.; G. J. T.

Nicomedia (mod. Izmit) was founded *c.*265 BC by *Nicomedes I, supplanting the ancient Greek colony of Astacus. It became the chief city of Hellenistic *Bithynia and later of the Roman province. In 29 BC *Augustus authorized a provincial temple dedicated to Rome and to himself at Nicomedia, which presumably became the meeting-place of the provincial assembly (see CONCILIUM). It accumulated titles in competition with *Nicaea (1) and in the 3rd cent. AD was styled 'greatest metropolis, leading city of Bithynia and Pontus, Hadrianic Severianic Nicomedia, twice *neocorus* (see NEŌKOROS), sacred asylum, friend and ally of the Roman people'. Although it suffered from frequent earthquakes and was sacked by the *Goths in the mid-250s, it was chosen by *Diocletian as his eastern capital, and scanty traces of the imperial palace have been identified. Its prosperity derived from a large and fertile territory, good harbours both on the

Black (*Euxine) Sea and on the *Propontis, and a favourable location on the trunk road from the Danube region to the eastern frontier of the Roman empire. Nicomedian traders appear in almost every province of the empire, particularly in the neighbouring Balkans, and its seamen in most ports of the eastern Mediterranean. Numerous buildings of the Roman city are mentioned by the sources, but apart from the fortifications of late antiquity only modest remains have been detected beneath the modern city.

W. L. MacDonald, *PECS* 623–4; W. Ruge, *RE* 17. 468–92, 'Nikomedeia'; Rostovtzeff, *Hellenistic World*, see index; Magie, *Rom. Rule Asia Min.*, see index; *TAM* 4/1 (inscriptions); L. Robert, *Harv. Stud.* 1977, and *Documents d'Asie Mineure* (1987), 91 ff.; *BCH* 101 and 102 (1977–8).
　　　　T. R. S. B.; S. M.

Nicophon, Athenian comic poet, won one or more victories at the City *Dionysia and the *Lenaea in the last decade of the 5th cent. BC (*IG* 2². 2325. 67, 131) and produced *Adonis* in 388 (hyp. 4 Ar. *Plut.*). We have six titles, mostly implying mythological burlesque (including *Birth of Aphrodite*; see POLYZELUS).

Kassel–Austin, *PCG* 7. 63 ff. (*CAF* 1. 775 ff.).　　K. J. D.

Nicopolis, 'victory city', *Alexander (3) the Great's foundation to commemorate the battle of *Issus (333 BC), and, more importantly, its imitations in the east Mediterranean (with a Greek-speaking population), built to commemorate the victories of Roman commanders and emperors, starting with *Pompey.

(1) Nicopolis of Pontus, the site of *Pompey's victory in 66 BC over *Mithradates VI, where he settled a mixed colony of veterans, wounded, and natives; the scene of *Pharnaces II's victory over Caesar's lieutenant Cn. *Domitius Calvinus in 47 BC. Being a strategic point in the system of frontier roads it grew in importance under the empire, received *ius Italicum, and became the *metropolis (sense b) of Lesser *Armenia.

(2) Nicopolis ad Istrum, founded in northern *Thrace by *Trajan after the Dacian Wars (see DACIA) and survived until the mid-5th cent. AD when it was destroyed by the *Huns. The city lies on a tributary of the Iatrus (mod. Yantra), which flows into the Danube. The plan was based on a regular grid of paved streets, within stone defences, probably constructed in the 170s, enclosing an area of 25 ha. (62 acres) at the centre of which was the nearly square agora (42 × 41 m.: 138 × 135 ft.) and a double-aisled stoa completed under *Hadrian (*IGBulg.* 2. 601). The city flourished in the 2nd cent. and was rebuilt after damage by the Costoboci in 170 (*IGBulg.* 2. 615).

(3) Nicopolis in Epirus, the most successful of these cities, on the isthmus of the Preveza peninsula opposite *Actium at the entrance to the Ambracian Gulf. Founded by Octavian (see AUGUSTUS) on the site of his army encampment (specially revered, as at Nicopolis (1), which provided the model), Nicopolis was not only a 'victory city' honouring his defeat of Antony (M. *Antonius (2)) and *Cleopatra VII in this region, but was also a *synoecism of older cities (Strab. 10. 2. 2; Paus. 5. 23. 3). It was settled soon after 31 BC, and dedicated, perhaps, in 29. A *free city minting its own coinage, Nicopolis served as a regional administrative, economic, and religious centre, especially following the creation of a separate province of *Epirus. Augustus chose the city as the new site for the Actian Games (*Actia*), an ancient festival once held on Cape Actium, but now celebrated every four years under Spartan stewardship and ranked equal to the major Panhellenic *agōnes; he also enrolled it in the Delphic *amphictiony. Surviving structures include impressive city walls,

a theatre, stadium, bath structure, odeum, Actian victory monument, aqueduct, and four early Christian basilicas. It was home to *Epictetus.

(4) Nicopolis in Egypt, by *Alexandria (1), founded by Octavian to commemorate his Egyptian campaign (30 BC), once more on the site of his camp.

(1) F. Cumont, *Studia Pontica* 2 (1906), 302 ff.

(2) A. Poulter, *Ancient Bulgaria* 2 (1983), 74–118; H. J. Schalles, H. von Hesberg, and P. Zanker (eds.), *Die römische Stadt im 2. Jahrhundert n. Chr.* (1992), 69–86.

(3) Hammond, *Epirus*, 62; E. Chrysos (ed.), *Nicopolis I. Proceedings of the First International Symposium at Nicopolis, 23–29 September 1984* (1987, actually 1988); W. M. Murray and P. M. Petsas, *Octavian's Campsite Memorial for the Actian War* (1989).   S. M., J. J. W., N. P., W. M. M.

Nicostratus (1), Middle Comedy poet (see COMEDY (GREEK), MIDDLE), regarded by *Apollodorus (6) as a son of *Aristophanes (1). Some of the 21 titles known may be of comedies by Nicostratus (2); they are intriguing, e.g. *Hesiod*, *Parakolumbosa*, *Pseudostigmatias* or 'Pretended Mortgagee', but the 40-odd citations give very little away.

Kassel–Austin, PCG 7. 74 ff. (*CAF* 2. 219 ff.).   K. J. D.

Nicostratus (2), New *Comedy poet, mentioned in the *Lenaean victors' list after *Menander (1), *Philemon (2), *Apollodorus (3), *Diphilus, and *Philippides (*IG* 2². 2325. 165 = 5 C 1 col. 4. 14 Mette), probably winner of the second prize at the *Dionysia of 311 BC (*IG* 2². 2323. 43 = 3 B 2 col. 1. 18 Mette). On a Delian inscription (see DELOS) of 280 BC (*IG* 11. 107 = 2 D 1c, 24 f. Mette) he is named with two other comic poets, Philemon and Ameinias.

FRAGMENTS Kassel–Austin, *PCG* 7. 74–92, although earlier scholars use the numbering in Kock, *CAF* 2. 219–30.

INTERPRETATION Meineke, *FCG* 1. 346 ff.; A. Körte, *RE* 17/1 (1936), 545, 'Nikostratos' 20.   W. G. A.

night See NYX.

Nigidius Figulus, Publius (praetor 58 BC), scholar and mystic, 'after Varro the most learned of men' (Gellius), friend of *Cicero, active supporter of *Pompey, died in exile in 45. He displayed an enthusiasm for Pythagoreanism (see PYTHAGORAS (1)) and along with it *astrology, and was said to engage in *magic. He wrote comprehensive works on grammar (*Commentarii grammatici*: see GRAMMAR, GRAMMARIANS, LATIN), theology (in particular *De dis*, 'On the Gods'), and various branches of natural science. His scholarship was too abstruse to win public esteem and he was eclipsed by his contemporary, M. Terentius *Varro. Fragments of his works survive in Gellius and other writers. See also SCHOLARSHIP, ANCIENT, ROMAN.

TEXT A. Swoboda, *P. Nigidii Figuli operum reliquiae* (1889); A. della Casa, *Nigidio Figulo* (1963).

E. Rawson, *Intellectual Life in the Late Roman Republic* (1985), *passim* (see index).   A. H.-W.; A. J. S. S.

Nike, the goddess of Victory, is first mentioned by *Hesiod (*Theog.* 383–4) as daughter of the Titan (see TITANS) Pallas and *Styx, and sister of Zelos, Kratos, and Bia ('Rivalry', 'Strength', and 'Force'). With these she was honoured by *Zeus because she fought with the gods against the *Titans. *Bacchylides (11. 1) depicts her standing next to *Zeus on *Olympus (1) and judging the award for '*areta*' (virtue) to gods and men. The victorious athlete sinks into the arms of Nike (Pind. *Nem.* 5. 42). Here Nike is already victory of an athletic, not only a military, contest.

Nike has no mythology of her own, and in cult may be assimilated with other gods, like Zeus at *Olympia (Paus. 5. 14. 8) or *Athena at Athens, where from *c.566* BC, she had an altar on the Acropolis, and subsequently a Classical temple. *Pausanias (3) (1. 22. 4) calls this Nike wingless, adding (3. 15. 7) that the Athenians and Spartans had a wingless Nike so that she would always stay with them. In art, her winged appearance is readily confused with orientalizing figures, and subsequently with Iris, especially when she holds a *kērykeion* (caduceus). She appears from the early 6th cent., on vases, freestanding or as acroteria, always in the 'Knielauf' pose. She may have two or four wings. The Nike of *Archermus (supposedly the first to give Nike wings) *c.550* BC and that of Callimachus *c.480*, are representative.

In the Classical period, her iconography is fully developed, attributes including garland, jug, phiale, and *thymiatērion* (censer). She is particularly popular on vases after the battle of *Marathon, often alone, or pouring a libation over an altar, for both gods and men; also in athletic and military contexts, sometimes holding weapons, or decorating a *trophy. She strides, runs, or flies. Sculptural representations attempt to evoke flight, such as the Nike of Paros (*c.470*) where she hovers or alights; so too the Nike of *Paeonius at Olympia of *c.420*. She was shown alighting on the hand of the Athena Parthenos and the Zeus at Olympia (where she was also an acroterion). The sculpted parapet of her temple on the Acropolis (*c.410*) shows her as messenger of Victory, setting a trophy, administrating libations, leading bulls to sacrifice, and, characteristically, binding her sandal. She appears as charioteer on Classical vases, especially south Italian.

In the Hellenistic period, Nike is used for political ends by *Alexander (3) the Great and the *Diadochi on coins and *gems. The striding type is represented by the Nike of *Samothrace (*c.306–250*), and continues in attachments to Canosan vases and terracotta statuettes to the 1st cent.

RE 17, 'Nike' 2; *LIMC* 6/1. 850–904; R. Carpenter, *The Sculpture of the Nike Temple Parapet* (1929).   K. W. A.

Nile, Egypt's river (explored by ancient Egyptians to the Upper Blue Nile) and the confluence of the Bahr-el-Gazal with the White Nile, was known to *Homer as 'Aegyptos river', to *Hesiod as 'Neilos'. *Cambyses (*c.525* BC) reached the desert south of Korosko, but *Herodotus (1) knew little beyond *Meroe. *Anaxagoras made a good guess that the Nile flood was caused by melting snows, but the true cause was unknown. *Alexander (3) the Great's explorations disproved that the Nile joined the Indus. Under the Ptolemies (see PTOLEMY (1)) the White Nile (Astapous), the Blue Nile, and sources of the Astaboras (Atbara) became known. It was confirmed that the annual flood came from rains in *Ethiopia, as *Aristotle had guessed. According to *Juba (2) II, the Nile rose in the *Atlas mountains and emerged in the east Sudan after two journeys underground. Nero's explorers passed the confluence of the Sobat with the White Nile, but were blocked by papyrus marshes (sudd). *Circa* AD 100 a traveller, Diogenes, reported from near Zanzibar (Rhapta) that snowcapped 'Mountains of the Moon' supplied two lakes feeding an affluent of the Nile, an indication of Lakes Victoria and Albert, and Mts. Kenya and Kilimanjaro. Neilus (Egyptian Ḥapi), the god of the inundation, is widely represented in Roman art. The use of nilometers to measure the annual flood made it possible in Egypt, alone in the ancient world, to calculate tax revenue in advance. The building of the Aswan High Dam in 1963 has raised the water-table throughout Egypt affecting ancient sites and leaching salts from below.

ANCIENT SOURCES Hdt. 2 (comm. A. B. Lloyd); Strabo *passim*; Seneca, *QNat.* 6. 8. 3–4; Plin. *HN* 5. 9. 48–59, 6. 184–6; Ptol. *Geog.* 1. 9. 4, 4. 8. 3; [Arist.], *De inundatione Nili: Ét. de Pap.* 1971, 1–33.

LITERATURE D. Bonneau, *Le Crue du Nil* (1963), and *Le Fisc et le Nil* (1971); Cary–Warmington, *Explorers* (Pelican), 202–15.

W. E. H. C.

nimbus, a circular cloud of light which surrounds the heads of gods or emperors (Serv. on *Aen.* 2. 616, 3. 587) and heroes. The belief that light radiates from a sacred or divine person is a common one and the nimbus only a special form which was developed in classical religion and art. Assyrian art, for instance, represents some gods with rays around their shoulders, and Greek art shows deities of light, such as *Helios, with a radiate crown. Greek vases and Etruscan mirrors of the 5th cent. BC afford the earliest examples of nimbus, often combined with the crown of rays. This hybrid form is also found at *Palmyra in the 1st cent. AD. Under the Roman empire the plain, smooth form tends to prevail. In Pompeian wall-paintings (see POMPEII) it is still associated primarily with the deities of light, such as *Apollo-Helios and *Diana, but almost all pagan gods of any importance are occasionally represented with a nimbus; in the 2nd and 3rd cents., for example in the mosaics of *Antioch (1) and Africa, its use becomes more indiscriminate. In late ancient art emperors, consuls, and other dignitaries, and sometimes even portraits of dead commoners have the nimbus. In Christian art only Christ was represented with the nimbus at first, but it was soon extended to the Virgin, the major saints, and angels.

M. Collinet-Guérin, *Histoire du nimbe des origines aux temps moderns* (1961).

G. M. A. H.; R. J. L.

Nimrud (ancient Kalhu, biblical Calah), Assyrian city *c.*35 km. (22 mi.) south of *Nineveh (1) on the east bank of the *Tigris near the confluence of the Greater Zab; the patron deity was Ninurta (corruption Nimrod). Palaces, temples, and a ziggurat on the citadel, and the arsenal of Shalmeneser III (858–824) in the lower city have been excavated intermittently since 1845. A temple library, various archives, metal objects, Phoenician and Syrian ivories, and stone relief sculptures were found. The site was occupied from prehistoric times and mainly abandoned after its sack by the Medes and Babylonians in 612 BC. It was the capital city of *Assyria from the reign of Assurnasirpal II (883–859), who built the monumental NW palace and nine temples, until the late 8th cent. when it was superseded by Khorsabad and then Nineveh. A Hellenistic settlement has been uncovered.

J. N. Postgate and J. E. Reade, *Reallexikon der Assyriologie 5* (1976–80), 'Kalhu'.

S. M. D.

Nineveh (1) Assyrian city of Ninua (mod. Kuyunjik and Nebi Yunus) on the east bank of the *Tigris beside modern Mosul, also called 'Old Babylon' in astronomical tradition. Continuously inhabited from prehistoric times into late antiquity, it was the capital city of *Assyria in the 7th cent. BC. The patron deity was *Ishtar, with a cult strongly Hurrian in the second millennium. Intermittent excavations from 1842 onwards have uncovered monumental palaces with sculptures and libraries of Sennacherib (704–681) and of Ashurbanipal (668–627) as well as religious buildings and city gates. Texts and sculptures attest fine gardens designed by Sennacherib. Although sacked in 612 BC, its revival was encouraged by *Cyrus (2) II. In classical tradition its eponymous founder was Ninus.

H. W. F. Saggs, *The Might That Was Assyria* (1984).

(2) *Aphrodisias in Caria was known as Ninoe and claimed foundation by Ninus. (3) Hierapolis in Syria was called 'Old Nineveh' by Philostr. *VA* 1. 3 and 19; Amm. Marc. 14. 7.

S. M. D.

Ninnius Crassus (early 1st cent. BC?), author of a translation of *Homer's *Iliad*.

Courtney, *FLP* 107.

Niobe, in mythology, daughter of *Tantalus and wife of *Amphion of *Thebes (1). They had a large family, though the number varies in different accounts: six children of either sex according to *Homer (*Il.* 24. 604, the oldest mention of Niobe, which seems to imply that the story was well known and that she was already a stock type of bereavement), seven of either sex according to *Ovid (*Met.* 6. 182–3), five or ten in other versions (see, for instance, Hes. fr. 183 M–W, and cf. Apollod. 3. 5. 6). Niobe boasted that she was superior to *Leto, who had only one son and one daughter, *Apollo and *Artemis. So Leto called on her children to avenge the insult, whereupon Apollo shot down all Niobe's sons and Artemis her daughters (*Il.* 24. 604 ff., cf. Apollod. 3. 5. 6.). Sometimes it was said that there were either one or two survivors (Apollod. ibid.). Homer seems to have adapted the story of Niobe in *Iliad* 24 to suit *Priam's situation (see Richardson's notes): after the children were killed they lay unburied for nine days because *Zeus had turned the people to stone, then on the tenth day the gods themselves buried them (cf. HECTOR). Niobe, 'worn out with weeping', ate, just as Priam is being urged to eat, and then became a rock on Mt. Sipylus (see MAGNESIA (2)), an image of everlasting sorrow with water flowing down her face like tears. The rock, according to *Pausanias (3) (1. 21. 3), was a natural formation looking something like a woman. Niobe remains to this day a symbol of grief.

In art the deaths of the children and the grief of their mother are a favourite subject: see M. Schmidt and W. Geominy, *LIMC* 6/1. 908–29.

J. R. M.

Nireus, after *Achilles the best-looking man in the Achaean expedition against *Troy (*Il.* 2. 671–5), became a byword for male beauty: Horace, *Carm.* 3. 20. 15, *Epod.* 15. 22; Prop. 3. 18. 27, etc. No certain representation in art is identified.

E. Ke.

Nisa (mod. Baghir), among the hills east of the Caspian near Ashkhabad, Turkmenistan; was a capital of *Parthia, 3rd cent. BC on, called by *Isidorus (1) (1st cent. AD) 'Parthaunisa . . . Greeks call it Nisaea', with (undiscovered) 'royal tombs' (*Parthian Stations*, 12—see ISIDORUS (1)). It occupied two mounds. New Nisa (unexcavated) was a mud-brick city till *c.* AD 1700. Old Nisa (partly excavated 1950s–1960s, 1990s) was a pentagonal, 14-ha. (35-acre), frequently refurbished royal fortress-palace of mud- and fired brick, with terracotta and stone ornaments; it had walls 8–9 m. (26–9 ft.) thick, 43 towers, gardens, northern clay-vessel wine-stores, and 2,000 graffiti in *Aramaic script of the Parthian era giving the name Mihrdatkert, 'made by Mithradates'—I, II, 2nd cent. BC?—; there were also a Treasury 60 m. (197 ft.) square containing Hellenistic marble statuettes and ivory rhyta with Greek-style relief figures, a central Tower, a Round (17-m.: 58-ft.) Hall, and a Square ('Quadrate') Hall, later with quadrilobate columns and wood-framed, painted, Greek-style male and female ancestor (?) wall reliefs of clay, all illustrating Hellenized 'Parthian' culture, deliberately destroyed (3rd cent. AD ?).

M. A. R. Colledge, *Parthian Art* (1977), see index; V. M. Masson, *Old*

Nisaea

Nisa—A Parthian Royal Residence (1985), (good, popularizing); M. Durdiev, Nisai—Parfia dovletinin paitagti (1992) (popularizing).
M. A. R. C.

Nisaea See MEGARA.

Nisibis (mod. Nusaybin), a city in NE *Mesopotamia. After the end of the Assyrian empire it disappeared from history until the Hellenistic age when it was temporarily known as Antioch Mygdonia. It reverted quickly to its old name and became part of the Parthian (129) and then the Armenian empire (after 80 BC) (see ARMENIA; PARTHIA). It was stormed by L. *Licinius Lucullus (2)'s troops in 68, but—after a short Armenian interval—was eventually recovered by the Arsacid king Artabanus III, who assigned it to his 'vassal', Izates of Adiabene. Nisibis thereafter was part of *Adiabene with a mixed population of Arabs, Aramaeans, Greeks, and Iranians. Apart from *Trajan's ephemeral occupation, it first became a Roman city as a result of *Verus' campaign. *Septimius Severus rewarded it for its loyalty to him by making it a *colonia* (Cass. Dio 75. 3. 2) and it received the honorary title *mētropolis* from *Severus Alexander onwards. As a frontier fortress city it suffered many vicissitudes during the wars of the Romans against the *Sasanids. In his peace treaty with Sapor II (AD 363) *Jovian ceded it to Persia, its population, loyal and Christian, preferring to abandon the city rather than to live under Persian rule (Amm. Marc. 25. 7. 9). Partly resettled with Persians, the Sasanians were able to retain it in their struggle against Byzantium until the Arab invasion of 640.

Nisibis was always an important centre of trade. In the treaty of AD 297 between *Diocletian and *Narses it was specified that Nisibis should be the only Roman market for trade exchanges between the two empires, and 4th- and 5th-cent. regulations continued to enforce this monopoly (Cod. Iust. 4. 63. 4). Nisibis was the birthplace and place of work until 363 of *Ephraem Syrus and later the intellectual centre of the Nestorian Church, and continued to flourish long after the Arab conquest.

L. Dillemann, Haute Mésopotamie orientale et pays adjacents (1962); M. H. Dodgeon and S. N. C. Lieu (eds.), The Roman Eastern Frontier and the Persian Wars AD 226–363 (1991), passim; J.-M. Fiey, Nisibe, métropole syriaque orientale (1977).
J. Wi.

Nisus (1), legendary king of *Megara and evidently an important hero there (e.g. Thuc. 4. 118. 4, and compare the name of the harbour, Nisaea). His life and the fate of his city depended on his red or purple lock of hair; this was cut off by his daughter Scylla in order to betray the city to the besieging general *Minos, either for a bribe (Aesch. Cho. 612–22) or for love (Ov. Met. 8. 1–151). Nisus was turned into a sea-eagle, Scylla into the bird ciris pursued by him. The story is told at length in the pseudo-Virgilian poem Ciris (see APPENDIX VERGILIANA). Nisus was also worshipped in Athens, where he was made into a son of *Pandion, who received the Megarid (the territory of Megara) when his father divided *Attica among his four sons.

Roscher, in Roscher, Lex. 3. 425–33; R. O. A. M. Lyne, Ciris (1978).
E. Ke.

Nisus (2), Trojan hero in *Virgil's Aeneid, son of Hyrtacus, sympathetically presented as the devoted older lover of the young and headstrong Euryalus. He helps Euryalus to victory in the foot-race at Aen. 5. 286–361, and dies avenging him in the night-episode at Aen. 9. 176–502.

M. Bellincioni, Enc. Virg. 'Eurialo'.
S. J. Ha.

Nisus (3), Roman grammarian. His younger contemporary *Suetonius heard him retail an anecdote on the original 'editing' of *Virgil's Aeneid (Donat. Vit. Verg. 42 Hardie). His writings (now lost) are cited by *Velius Longus, *Charisius, *Macrobius, and *Priscian.

PIR² N 105. Mazzarino, Gramm. Rom. Frag. 332–41; Herzog–Schmidt, § 392.
R. A. K.

Nisyros is a small, circular, volcanic island of the Dodecanese lying south of *Cos. Mentioned in *Homer (Il. 2. 676), and occupied perhaps in prehistoric but certainly by early Archaic times, in the Classical period it appears in the Athenian *tribute lists. Nisyros remained independent in the 4th–3rd cents. but was controlled by *Philip (3) V of Macedon for a short period after c.205. Its freedom was soon restored. By about 200 Nisyros was incorporated into the Rhodian state (see RHODES), probably as a *deme of the city of *Camirus. A fine fort (4th cent.?) stands on the ancient acropolis south-west of Mandraki town. Nisyros remained prosperous into the Christian period. See GIANTS.

INSCRIPTIONS IG 12. 3, and pt. 3 Suppl. (1904); W. Peek, Inschriften von den dorischen Inseln (1969), and Wissenschaftliche Zeitschrift, Universität Halle 1967, 369 ff.
LITERATURE Clara Rhodos 1932–3, 471 ff.; P. M. Fraser and G. E. Bean, The Rhodian Peraea and Islands (1954); G. E. Bean and J. M. Cook, BSA 1957, 118 ff.; R. Hope Simpson and J. F. Lazenby, BSA 1962, 169.
E. E. R.

nobilitas When the *plebs attained legal equality with the *patricians, the magistracies were in theory open to all citizens (cf. Cic. Sest. 137). In fact, the ruling class gradually co-opted powerful plebeian families into association, until (by the 3rd cent. BC) a new, increasingly plebeian, oligarchy emerges. In lists of consuls and priests, the same names again tend to recur, with a slow trickle of newcomers. These new rulers are the nobiles, 'known' men—known (presumably) because they had the right to *imagines, and actors representing their ancestors in full ceremonial dress were a common sight in the streets of Rome. These 'known' men naturally had an advantage in elections, and it was increased by a network of family and client relationships (see CLIENS) built up over generations. Since we have no earlier relevant sources, we do not know how and when the word 'nobilis' acquired a more exclusive meaning: 'descended from a consul' (or comparable magistrate). This, as Matthias Gelzer first brilliantly realized, is its quasi-technical meaning in the 1st cent. BC (although the general meaning 'known' always coexists with it outside the political sphere). Perhaps praetorships (six by 197/6, eight by 81) had become too common, and aedileships too humble.

As *Sallust says (Iug. 63. 7), with pardonable exaggeration, the nobiles tended to regard the accession of an outsider to the consulship as 'polluting' it. By the late republic, the defeat of a nobilis by an outsider sufficed to raise a presumption of *corruption (see Cic. Mur. and Planc.). Nobilitas was never a necessary or a sufficient qualification for the consulship. There was fierce competition among nobiles for only two posts, and some outsiders of senatorial background gained admission. (We usually do not know their maternal descent.) But very few men not born to senatorial families became consuls, and those few normally through the support of eminent families. They tended to be perfectly absorbed into the ethos of the oligarchy and became its defenders. (See NOVUS HOMO.) The proportion of nobiles in the consulate is never, over any lengthy period, less than 70 per cent (and this is a minimum, since we do not know the background of many, especially 2nd-cent., holders); by the age of *Cicero, when many old families long unrepresented revive, it is close to

90 per cent. These proportions are remarkably untouched by the most violent political crises.

Under the empire the word was a social label, still chiefly applied to descendants (on either side) of republican, or at most triumviral, consuls. *Nobiles* were raised to (usually harmless) dignity by 'good' emperors (the success of a patrician *Galba showed how dangerous they could be) and persecuted by 'bad' emperors. Most noble families were extinguished by the Antonine period; though the *Acilii Glabriones survived to the 4th cent. AD.

M. Gelzer, *Die Nobilität der römischen Republik* (1912) is basic—reprinted as the first item in his *Kleine Schriften* 1 (1962) and translated, with numerous corrections and the addition of a later essay on the *nobilitas* under the Principate, by Robin Seager: *The Roman Nobility* (1969). P. A. Brunt, *JRS* 1982, 1 ff., tried to rebut Gelzer's case (which admittedly shows flaws in presentation), but was refuted by D. R. Shackleton Bailey, *AJPhil.* 1986, 255 ff.; see also L. A. Burckhardt, *Hist.* 1990, 77 ff. For the statistics see E. Badian, *Chiron* 1990, 371 ff. On origins and early history: K.-J. Hölkeskamp, *Die Entstehung der Nobilität* (1987).

E. B.

Nola (mod. Nola), 28 km. east of Naples (*Neapolis). Founded in the 7th cent. BC it enjoyed great prominence in the 6th and 5th cents. It was later captured by the Campani (see CAMPANIA), and came under Roman domination *c.*313. It revolted during the *Social War (3) and became a Sullan colony (see CORNELIUS SULLA, L.). Further colonization took place under Augustus.

S. De Caro and A. Greco, *Campania* (1981). K. L.

nomads Greek (followed by Roman) writers lumped together as nomads (νομάδες, formed on νομός, 'pasture') all pastoral groups for whom wandering was a way of life, without distinguishing (as does the modern concept of nomadism) between semi-nomads—including those practising *transhumance—and fully nomadic societies of no fixed abode, such as the ancients met on the desert fringes of *Libya and *Arabia and in *Scythia. *Homer's portrayal of the pastoral *Cyclopes as uncivilized and savage (*Od.* 9) inaugurates a persistent hostility in Greek literature to nomads, whose lifestyle as 'cultivators of living fields' (γεωργίαν ζῶσαν γεωργοῦντες, Arist. *Pol.* 1256ᵃ 34–5), in particular their different diet (see MILK) and desert habitat, set them apart from the sedentary communities of Greek farmers and encouraged a stereotyping taken to extremes in *Herodotus (1)'s account of the nomadic Scythian 'man eaters' (4. 106). Thus to turn nomads into settled agriculturalists ranked among the self-evident achievements of the Macedonian kings *Philip (1) II and *Alexander (3) the Great (Arr. *Anab.* 7. 9. 2, 8. 40. 8). Modern ethnographic work denies this rigid conceptual separation of cultivators from nomads in real life, stressing rather their economic symbiosis, for which there is some ancient evidence from Roman *Africa, where the old view, that the Roman state tried to blockade out the Libyan nomads by means of a *limes, is now questioned. See BARBARIAN; PASTORALISM.

B. Shaw, *Anc. Soc.* 1982–3, 5–31; C. Whittaker, *Land, City and Trade in the Roman Empire* (1993), ch. 1; R. Rebuffat in *L'Afrique dans l'occident romain*, CEFR 134 (1990), 231–47. A. J. S. S.

nomen See NAMES, PERSONAL, ROMAN.

Nomentum (mod. Mentana), old Latin town on the edge of Sabine territory (see LATINI; SABINI), 23 km. (14 mi.) north-east of Rome. Rome annexed it in 338 BC. Famed in imperial times for its wine and country *villas, it was linked with Rome by the via Nomentana, which crossed the *Anio by a still-standing bridge.

C. Pala, *Nomentum*, Forma Italiae 1/12 (1976). E. T. S.; T. W. P.

nomophylakes (νομοφύλακες) were 'guardians of the laws'. In Athens, according to one authority (*Philochorus), officials with this title were instituted when *Ephialtes (4) deprived the *Areopagus of most of its powers in 462/1 BC; but this statement is disbelieved by some modern scholars, and even if it is true the office cannot have become permanent, since it is not heard of again until the late 4th cent. It was probably instituted or reinstituted in the 320s. At this period there were seven *nomophylakes*. Their chief duty was to attend meetings of the *boulē and the *ekklēsia and veto actions or proposals which were illegal or contrary to the interests of Athens. They had some kind of power to check magistrates (see MAGISTRACY, GREEK) who acted illegally, and they also had some religious functions.

F. Jacoby, comm. on *FGrH* 328 F 64; G. L. Cawkwell, *JHS* 1988, 12.

D. M. M.

nomos (1), 'nome', the Greek term for the administrative districts of ancient *Egypt. Under the *Seleucids the term is also found in Palestine, probably introduced there by the Ptolemies (see PTOLEMY (1)). Though differing in number over time, traditionally there were 42 nomes—22 in Upper and 20 in Lower Egypt; by the 3rd cent. AD the number was almost 60. Nomes were further divided into toparchies, and these into villages. Each was governed by a *stratēgos* who by the late Ptolemaic period was purely an administrative official. He was assisted by many lower officials, particularly royal scribes (*basilikoi grammateis*), who continued into the Roman period. Under *Septimius Severus nome capitals (*mētropoleis*; see MĒTROPOLIS (c)) acquired town councils with administrative responsibilities. In the 4th cent. they gave way to *pagi* (see PAGUS). D. J. T.

nomos (2). The word νόμος means 'a style of song with a prescribed *harmonia* (tuning) and a definite rhythm' (Suda). There were seven canonical types used either with *kithara* (lyre) (the citharodic nomes originated by *Terpander in the 7th cent. BC, Procl. in Phot. *Bibl.* 320a, 32 ff; Poll. 4. 66) or with *aulos* (pipe) (the aulodic nomes, of which Clonas was the originator, [Plut.] *De mus.*). Among the nomes for solo instrument the most famous was the (auletic) Pythian nome originated by Sacadas of Argos (early 6th cent.) with five parts representing *Apollo's fight against the Python snake (Poll. 4. 84). The 'new style' of music in the 5th cent. BC (e.g. Phrynis; *Timotheus (1)'s *Persae*) broke with the strict rules of the old nomes and created new and experimental forms of artistic solo performances. See MUSIC, § 4.

M. L. West, *Ancient Greek Music* (1992); A. Barker, *Greek Musical Writings* 1 (1984); H. Grieser, *Nomos* (1937); U. von Wilamowitz-Moellendorff, *Timotheos: Die Perser* (1903), 89 ff.; H. Färber, *Die Lyrik in der Kunsttheorie der Antike* (1936). C. M. B.; E. Kr.

nomos (3), Greek for 'law'. See LAW IN GREECE, and cf. ISONOMIA. For *nomos* as opp. *physis* (nature) see CALLICLES; POLITICAL THEORY.

nomothetai (νομοθέται), 'law-makers', were usually individuals like *Draco and *Solon, but in Athens in the late 5th and the 4th cent. BC large groups with this title were appointed. The earliest known was appointed in 411 in connection with the Five Thousand (Thuc. 8. 97. 2) and must have lapsed when that regime fell. In 403, when democracy was restored, one group of *nomothetai* was appointed by the *boulē to draft and display proposed additions to the laws, and another body of 500 *nomothetai* was elected by the demes to consider these proposals in conjunction with the *boulē (Andoc. 1. 82–4).

Thereafter *nomothetai* were appointed regularly to consider proposed changes in the laws, on which they, not the *ekklēsia*, now took the final decisions. In some cases (or in all, according to one view) they were drawn by lot from the list of 6,000 jurors; thus they were ordinary citizens, without special expertise, but their function was to examine proposals more closely than the *ekklēsia* would do. The intention seems to have been to make legislating more difficult and less casual, and to prevent inconsistencies and contradictions arising within the legal code. Details of the procedure, which was probably changed at least once, are hard to ascertain; the information in *Demosthenes (2)'s speeches *Against Leptines* and *Against Timocrates* is incomplete and tendentious. For three different interpretations see bibliog.

D. M. MacDowell, *JHS* 1975, 62–74; P. J. Rhodes, *CQ* 1984, 55–60; M. H. Hansen, *GRBS* 1985, 345–71.   D. M. M.

non-verbal communication See GESTURES.

Nonius Asprenas, Publius, declaimer (see DECLAMATION), occasionally cited by L. *Annaeus Seneca (1) (who also mentions a Lucius Asprenas); perhaps the consul of AD 38 of that name.

PIR² N 122. Schanz–Hosius, § 336. 9. 12.   M. W.

Nonius (*RE* 38) **Marcellus** (early 4th cent. AD?), author of an encyclopaedic dictionary in twenty books (*De compendiosa doctrina*, ed. W. M. Lindsay, 3 vols. (1903); book 16 is lost). The first twelve books deal with grammatical and semantic matters (e.g. *de numeris et casibus* (on numbers and cases), *de differentia similium significantionum* (on the differences between similar meanings), the rest with terms for clothing, weapons, and the like (but not religion); the words discussed (arranged alphabetically only in books 2–4) are all illustrated by quotations, save in the last book (*de propinquitate*, on kinship-terms). The work was based on Nonius' own excerpts from a broad range of republican authors, whose texts he used in a fixed order. He also consulted earlier learned compilations (e.g. Aulus *Gellius, *glossaries) from which he took other citations. For the fragments of several early authors, and especially of *Varro's poetry, Nonius is our chief source.

PLRE 1. 552. Method of composition: W. M. Lindsay, *Nonius Marcellus' Dictionary of Republican Latin* (1901); D. C. White, *Studi Noniani* 1980, 111–211. Herzog–Schmidt, § 615.   R. A. K.

Nonnus, of Panopolis in Egypt (fl. AD 450–70), the main surviving exponent of an elaborate, metrically very strict style of Greek *epic that evolved in the Imperial period. His huge *Dionysiaca* is in 48 books, the sum of the books of the *Iliad* and *Odyssey*; Nonnus' stated intention is to rival *Homer, and to surpass him in the dignity of his divine, not human, subject (25. 253–63). The poem describes at length the antecedents of *Dionysus' birth, the birth itself, and the new god's fight for recognition as a member of the pantheon in the face of hostility from Hera; the central section (books 13–40), which describes the war of Dionysus and his Bacchic forces against the Indians and their king Deriades, is Nonnus' equivalent of the *Iliad*. Nonnus' highly rhetorical and extraordinarily luxuriant style is an attempt to create a new type of formulaic composition, recognizably similar to that of Homer but with greater variety and with far more lexical permutations. In his mythological learning and countless allusions to earlier poetry he is a true successor to Hellenistic writers of the Callimachean school (see CALLIMACHUS (3)); the episodes that describe Dionysus' love affairs with youths and nymphs are influenced also by the *novel.

Nonnus' other extant work is a hexameter version of St John's Gospel. Stylistic analysis suggests that it may be earlier than the *Dionysiaca*; but the *Dionysiaca* clearly lacks final revision. These two facts have led scholars to make ingenious conjectures about Nonnus' life, religion, and possible conversions. But there is evidence that amongst intellectuals in the 5th cent. it was not felt contradictory for a Christian to write heavily classicizing verse.

Dionysiaca:
    TEXT R. Keydell, 2 vols. (1959); W. H. D. Rouse, 3 vols. (Loeb, 1940); F. Vian and others, in progress (Budé, 1976–   ).
    CRITICISM W. Fauth, *Eidos poikilon* (1981); J. Lindsay, *Leisure and Pleasure in Roman Egypt* (1965), 359–95; P. Chuvin, *Mythologie et géographie dionysiaques* (1991); N. Hopkinson (ed.), *Studies in the Dionysiaca of Nonnus*, PCPS Suppl. 17 (1994).
Paraphrase of St John's Gospel:
    TEXT A. Scheindler (Teubner, 1881); bk 18, ed. E. Livrea (1989).
    CRITICISM E. Livrea, *Prometheus* 1987, 97–124.   N. H.

Norba (mod. Norma), an important *Volscian town from at least the early 5th cent. BC, situated on a bluff overlooking the *Pomptine Marshes, south-east of Rome. It received a Latin colony (491–492 BC) to contain the Volsci. Although always loyal to Rome, it was destroyed by *Sulla (82 BC) and never recovered. There are fine polygonal walls (4th cent. BC) and several temples.

L. Quilici and S. Quilici Gigli, *Arch. Laz.* 1988, 233–56.   T. W. P.

Norbanus (*RE* 5), **Gaius,** *novus homo* with a non-Roman nomen, began his career with the tribunate (103 BC), in which he successfully prosecuted Q. *Servilius Caepio (1), using force against the intercession of T. *Didius and a L. Aurelius Cotta. He was quaestor under M. *Antonius (1) (101) and, when prosecuted for *maiestas*, probably in 95, by P. *Sulpicius Rufus for his actions in 103, was successfully defended by Antonius (Cic. *De or.* 2. 97 f.), like him an early associate of C. *Marius (1). Praetor *c*.91, he kept Sicily safe during the *Social War (3) and defeated an Italian attack on *Rhegium. Consul 83 with L. Cornelius Scipio Asiagenus, to symbolize the unity of patrician *nobiles* and new men behind the government, he was several times defeated, as consul and as proconsul 82, by *Sulla and Q. *Caecilius Metellus Pius. He fled to Rhodes and there committed suicide to escape extradition.

F. Münzer, *Hermes* 1932, 260 ff.; E. Badian, *Stud. Gr. Rom. Hist.*, see index, and *AJPhil.* 1983, 106 ff.   E. B.

Noricum, a Roman province in the eastern Alps, south of the Danube, between *Raetia and *Pannonia with a predominantly *Celtic population. Though the Taurisci were the chief tribe, Noricum (apparently derived from the *Norici* dwelling round *Noreia*, the ancient capital) became in the first part of the 2nd cent. BC the name of the Celtic *federal state, which had its own coinage. It was of considerable importance in *Caesar's time, as shown by the fact that Caesar accepted aid from Noricum. The Romans were soon attracted by the quality of *iron from Noricum and in the 1st cent. BC a flourishing emporium existed on the Magdalensberg in southern Carinthia (see VIRUNUM), probably the site of Noreia. To secure the NE frontier of Italy, the Taurisci north of the Ocra were made tributary (35 BC), and then the kingdom of Noricum was incorporated into the Roman empire following operations by P. Silius Nerva in *Transpadana and *Illyricum (16 BC). Perhaps for some time under a *praefectus civitatium* (CIL 5. 1838–9), Noricum was put under an equestrian governor who resided at *Virunum and commanded the *auxilia* and the body of picked local youths called the *iuventus Noricorum* (Tac. *Hist.* 3. 5, 3. 70). During the *Marcomannic wars the newly raised Legio II Italica (see LEGION) was quartered in Noricum (first at Ločica near Celeia, then Albing and by 191 at *Lauriacum). Its commander became the governor of Noricum as an imperial legate (see LEGATI) or *legatus Augusti pro praetore*, residing at Ovilava; the financial procurator remained at Virunum. Under Diocletian Noricum was divided into two parts under *praesides* (see DIOCLETIAN): Noricum Ripense on the Danube and Noricum Mediterraneum in the south, the former also having a *dux* as military commander. In the 5th cent. Noricum was overrun by German tribes and was occupied after 493 by *Goths, by *Franks (c.536), by *Lombards (568), and shortly before 600 by Slavs and Avars (see AVARO-SLAV INVASIONS).

G. Alföldy, *Noricum* (1974).   F. A. W. S.; J. J. W.

Nortia, an *Etruscan goddess (the Etruscan name-form is uncertain). In her temple at *Volsinii each year a nail was affixed; Livy 7. 3. 7 compares the old Roman custom of the *praetor maximus* affixing on the Ides of September a nail in Jupiter's temple, and interprets these yearly nails (*clavi annales*) as markers of years (cf. Festus, *Gloss. Lat.* 161). They could serve that purpose, but the goal of the rite (with Mesopotamian and Hittite parallels) was rather to fix the fates for the coming year. Nortia was identified with *Fortuna (schol. Juv. 10. 74) and *Nemesis (Martianus Capella, 1. 88). *Necessitas* (Hor. *Carm.* 1. 35. 17–20, 3. 24. 5–8) and the Etruscan *Athrpa* appear with nails of destiny. Akin to this rite was the practice of driving nails to ward off disaster or pestilence.

H. S. Versnel, *Triumphus* (1970); L. Aigner Foresti, *AJAH* 1979, 144 ff.; J.-P. Thuilier, *MÉFRA* 1987, 605 ff.   J. L.

Nossis (fl. *c.*300 BC), Greek poetess from Epizephyrian Locri (see LOCRI EPIZEPHYRII), author of a dozen epigrams from *Meleager (2)'s *Garland* in the Greek *Anthology, mostly inscriptions for votive offerings and works of art. She compares herself to Sappho (*Anth. Pal.* 7. 718), and 5. 170 implies that she also wrote love poetry.

Gow-Page, *HE*. M. Gigante, *PP* 1974, 22–39; M. Skinner, *Arethusa* 1989, 5–18.   A. D. E. C.

Notitia Dignitatum The 'List of Offices' is a late Roman illustrated manuscript which survived in a Carolingian copy. This is lost, but at least four copies were made, which are now in Oxford, Cambridge, Paris, and Munich. The Notitia is divided into two parts, each entitled 'a list of all offices, civil and military' in the eastern and western halves of the empire respectively, as divided in AD 395. Each part was kept by a senior member of the court secretariat, the *primicerius notariorum*, and contains an index followed by more than 40 chapters, one for each of the high officers of state, from the praetorian prefects, masters of the soldiers (see MAGISTER MILITUM), and other court dignitaries to the lesser generals (*comites* and *duces*) and the provincial governors, in order of precedence or geographical sequence. For the provincial governors, however, only one specimen of each grade (*consularis, corrector, praeses*) is given. Each chapter gives the title and rank of the dignitary, a brief description of his functions, including a list of his subordinate officers, if any, and the members of his staff (*officium*); for generals, a list of units under his command, with their stations in the case of *duces*. Each chapter is accompanied by an illustration of *insignia*, a schematic picture of the dignitary's responsibilities; for *magistri militum* these are the shields of their regiments, for *duces* their forts. The Notitia outlines the late Roman order of battle and administrative structure in great detail, but its date and purpose are obscure. It may have listed dignitaries who received letters of appointment (for a fee), our

copy being derived from the western working copy, since some eastern chapters are in abbreviated form and contain nothing which is demonstrably later than 395, whereas the western chapters have been altered thereafter. Both parts contain internal inconsistencies due to piecemeal revision, and material which reached its present form in earlier reigns. Revision later than 395 is most apparent in the western military chapters, which must reflect the supremacy (395–408) and strategy of the *magister militum* *Stilicho.

Ed. O. Seeck, *Notitia Dignitatum* (1876). Jones, *Later Rom. Emp.* 3. 347 ff.; D. Hoffmann, *Das Spätrömische Bewegungsheer* (1969–70); R. Goodburn and P. Bartholomew (eds.), *Aspects of the Notitia Dignitatum* (1976).
                    R. S. O. T.

Notus (south wind) See WIND-GODS; ZEPHYRUS.

Novaesium (mod. Neuss on the Rhine), the site of a series of military stations. An auxiliary-sized fort, built *c.*20/10 BC, was followed by several for forces larger than one legion, before the construction of a single-legionary fortress in stone under *Claudius. Rebuilt after the troubles of AD 69–70, this was evacuated under *Trajan and superseded by an auxiliary fort, destroyed during the 3rd-cent. invasions. In the 4th cent., *Julian repaired the fortifications of Neuss, perhaps those of the old legionary fortress. All stations had their attached civil settlements (see CANABAE) and there was also a separate civil settlement.

H. von Petrikovits, *Bonner Jahrb.* 1961, 475 ff.; C. M. Wells, *The German Policy of Augustus* (1972), 127 ff.; H. Chantraine and others, *Das römische Neuss* (1984).   J. F. Dr.

Novatianus, Roman presbyter and 'anti-pope'. On failing to be elected to the see of Rome in AD 251, he had himself consecrated counter-bishop to Cornelius, perhaps from a mixture of personal and theological motives, and certainly under pressure. His schismatic Church of καθαροί ('pure ones'), which lasted for centuries, was strongly rigorist, refusing all reconciliation to those who lapsed or committed serious sins. Surviving works, written in stylish Latin, include at least two letters in the Cyprianic corpus (30, 36; perhaps 31), an impressive treatise on the Trinity, and another on Jewish dietary laws; the *De spectaculis* ('On Spectacles') and *De bono pudicitiae* ('On the Excellence of Chastity') attributed to *Cyprian are now also widely accepted as his. His debt to *Stoicism has been exaggerated. He was apparently martyred under Valerian (P. *Licinius Valerianus).

TEXT G. Diercks, CCSL 4 (1972).
TRANSLATION R. J. DeSimone (1974).
STUDIES H. J. Vogt, *Coetus sanctorum: Der Kirchenbegriff des Novatian und die Geschichte seiner Sonderkirche* (1968).   J. H. D. S.

novel, Greek Extended prose narrative fiction is a latecomer to Greek literature. It is first recognizable in a lively account of the Assyrian king Ninus' courtship of a 14-year old *Semiramis, preserved on a papyrus dated by a document on its verso to earlier than AD 100–1 and by its script to between 50 BC and AD 50. Its composition need not be earlier, though some conjecture *c.*100 BC. Of the five novels to survive complete, *Chariton (like *Metiochus and Parthenope*, known from papyri and oriental descendants) probably belongs to the later 1st cent. AD, though a date as late as *Hadrian is possible; *Xenophon (2) to the first half of the 2nd cent., and *Achilles Tatius (1) to the 2nd; *Longus is perhaps late 2nd or early 3rd cent. AD, while both early 3rd and late 4th cent. AD are claimed for *Heliodorus (4). Only *Iamblichus (1)'s *Babylonian History*, known from fragments and

*Photius' epitome, is firmly dated by its author's claimed career, to c. AD 165–80.

These narratives (two in eight books, the others in four, five, and ten) vary a shared pattern. Boy and girl fall in love: Xenophon (2)'s heroine is also 14, his hero 16, Longus' 13 and 15. Either before marriage (Achilles Tatius, Heliodorus, ? Ninus) or soon after (Chariton, Xenophon (2)) they are separated and survive storms, shipwreck, imprisonment, attempted seduction or rape, torture, and even what readers and characters believe to be death, before reunion at the book's end. Their ordeals usually traverse Egypt or other near eastern lands; but Heliodorus' couple have Ethiopian *Meroe as their goal, Xenophon (2)'s reach south Italy, and Longus compresses his pastoral couple's adventures into a corner of *Lesbos, substituting sexual naïvety for external forces as obstacles to their union. The heroine typically preserves her virginity/fidelity to her husband, although Chariton's accepts a cultivated Greek as her second husband (to protect the hero's child she is carrying). Achilles' hero, however, succumbs to a married Ephesian, and Longus' receives sexual instruction, crucial to the plot's advancement, from a married city woman.

Love stories are found in earlier Greek literature, both verse (especially of the Hellenistic period) and prose (above all *Xenophon (1)'s Cyropaedia); *historiography is evoked by the setting of the Ninus, of Chariton (5th/4th-cent. *Syracuse), and of a scene from Metiochus and Parthenope; the centrality of a young couple's love, their city origins and some speeches recall New Comedy (see COMEDY (GREEK), NEW); analogous story-patterns can be found in Mesopotamian or Egyptian literature. But the novel evolves from none of these. Rather it is a late Hellenistic or early imperial creation, whose literary effects include evocation of all these Greek predecessors and of *Homer's Odyssey and Attic tragedy too (see TRAGEDY, GREEK). Elaborate 'documentation' of the story's 'origin' and apparently exact geographical detail entice readers to accept the 'events' as having once happened, albeit in the distant (Ninus) and particularly Classical past: only Xenophon (2)'s world seems to be that of the empire, though Achilles' might be taken as such, and the élites from which the novels' characters are drawn (even the foundlings Daphnis and Chloe) resemble those of Greek cities of the Roman empire. But all authors exclude Rome and Romans. *Piracy is commoner than in the pax Romana, coincidences are far-fetched, but the impossible is avoided and only such miraculous events admitted (e.g. prophetic *dreams) as contemporary belief credited.

Characters are less convincing. Anglophone critics often adduce shallow characterization as a reason for denying that these works are 'novels': in continental Europe they are Roman (Ger.), roman (Fr.), romanzo (It.), romance (Portug.) rather than novela (Sp.). The main characters, albeit morally admirable, are indeed rarely interesting, though the often stronger heroines engage readers more effectively, and some minor characters (e.g. Heliodorus' Calasiris and even Cnemon) are more fascinating because less predictable. Descriptions of actions and thoughts (usually conveyed by dialogue or monologue) are deployed rather to delineate emotion and raise suspense or excitement. The speeches attest rhetorical training, as do *ekphraseis of scenes or works of art, especially in Achilles Tatius, Longus, and Heliodorus, authors whose mannered and Atticizing style has caused their novels to be classed as 'sophistic' (see SECOND SOPHISTIC). Yet Chariton too, though not Atticizing, both claims to be a rhetor's secretary and deploys rhetorical speeches, while all four avoid hiatus and allude extensively to Classical literature. These features mark literary aspirations as high and the intended reader-

ship as educated. Philostratus (see PHILOSTRATI) and *Julian betray knowledge of the genre, but the silence of other writers has puzzled scholars, and been used (along with the lack of an ancient generic name) to argue that it was despised and of low status. Few, however, dispute the dexterity with which all but Xenophon (2) unfold their plot and manipulate their readers. Achilles, Longus, and Heliodorus can be seen as variously parodying the genre's basic tropes, and the complexity, irony, and suspense created by Heliodorus' opening in mediis rebus, and gradual unfolding of the couple's story through Calasiris' long and sometimes misleading narrative, mark him as a master of plot-construction, with Calasiris and Fate or Fortune sometimes taking his part.

Such 'ideal' romances were not the only novels. *Antonius Diogenes retained romantic love but gave more emphasis to travel in a chinese-box plot occupying 24 books. In the lost Metamorphoses ascribed by Photius (cod. 129) to Lucius of Patrae and in its surviving epitome, the Lucianic (see LUCIAN) Ὄνος ('Ass'), the first-person narrator who is turned into an ass strings together in a travel-framework incidents involving witchcraft and obscene or titillating sexual escapades in the tradition of Milesian Tales (see ARISTIDES (2)). Similar coarse and melodramatic treatment of sex is found in the papyrus of *Lollianus' Phoenician Tales and in a prosimetric scrap in which one Iolaus may intend disguise as a eunuch priest to achieve a boy's seduction (POxy. 42. 3010, early 2nd cent. AD). Remoter still, and with only a minor role for love or sex, are *Dictys Cretensis' rewriting of the Trojan War and the Alexander Romance (see PSEUDO-CALLISTHENES).

Of the five 'ideal' romances all but Longus were still read in the 6th cent.; in the 9th Photius summarized Antonius, Lucius' Metamorphoses, Heliodorus, Iamblichus, and Achilles, commending their Attic style but condemning erotic content. Only the last two, and Xenophon (2), get Suda entries, but in the 11th cent. *Psellus wrote a comparison of Achilles and Heliodorus, while both they and Longus inspire writers of four 12th-cent. Byzantine novels, three verse and one prose.

In the Renaissance Heliodorus, the first to be printed (1534) and translated (into French, 1547), was most influential; but later the others, especially Longus, were much read too, vernacular translations preceding editiones principes.

TEXTS Besides those listed under individual authors, note B. Lavagnini, Eroticorum Graecorum Fragmenta Papyracea (Teubner, 1922); F. Zimmermann, Griechische Roman-Papyri und verwandte Texte (1936), with comm. and index; S. A. Stephens and J. J. Winkler, Ancient Greek Novels: The Fragments (1993).

TRANSLATIONS B. P. Reardon (ed.), Collected Ancient Greek Novels (1989).

CRITICISM E. Rohde, Der griechische Roman (1876; 4th edn. 1960); Christ–Schmid–Stählin 2/2⁶. 819 ff.; K. Kerenyi, Die griechisch-orientalische Romanliteratur (1927; repr. 1962); R. Merkelbach, Roman und Mysterium (1962); A. Lesky, A History of Greek Literature (1966), 857–70; B. E. Perry, The Ancient Romances (1967); B. P. Reardon, Phoenix 1969, and The Form of Greek Romance (1991); M. D. Reeve, CQ 1971; G. Anderson, Eros Sophistes (1982), and Ancient Fiction (1984); T. Hägg, The Novel in Antiquity (1983); E. L. Bowie, in CHCL 1. 683–99 (= paperback 1/4 (1989), 123–39), and with S. J. Harrison, JRS 1993, 159–78; N. Holzberg, Der antike Roman (1986); M. Fusillo, Il romanzo greco (1989) = La Naissance du roman grec (1991); A. Billault, La Création romanesque (1991); G. Bowersock, Fiction as History (1994). E. L. B.

novel, Latin The Latin novel is mainly represented for us by two extant texts, the Satyrica of *Petronius Arbiter (1st cent. AD) and the Metamorphoses or Golden Ass of *Apuleius (2nd cent. AD); no previous long fictions are known in Latin. An important influence on both were the lubricious *Milesian Tales* of L. *Cornelius Sisenna in the 1st cent. BC (Ov. *Tr.* 2. 443–4), short stories translated from the Greek Μιλησιακά of *Aristides (2) (2nd cent. BC; cf. Plut. *Crass.* 32, [Lucian], *Amores* 1). The adaptations by *Varro of the prosimetric Greek satires of *Menippus (1) of Gadara (see MENIPPEAN SATIRE) also contributed something to the prosimetric form and satirical content of Petronius, and were followed by L. *Annaeus Seneca (2) in his *Apocolocyntosis*; there is also recent evidence in the Iolaus-papyrus (*POxy.* 42. 3010) that there existed at least one work of low-life prosimetric fiction in Greek.

Petronius' *Satyrica* survives only in parts, but was clearly lengthy, in at least sixteen books. Its plot concerns the comic adventures of a homosexual couple as narrated by one of them, Encolpius; as its title implies, it has connections with Roman *satire, in terms both of its prosimetric form (see above) and of its content, for example the comic meal (the *Cena Trimalchionis*). Two of its inserted tales clearly reflect the tradition of *Milesian Tales* (above)—the Widow of Ephesus (111–12) and the Pergamene Boy (85–7); it also contains literary and social criticism and some complex narrative technique. Apuleius' *Metamorphoses* in eleven books, concerning the metamorphosis of a young man into an ass and his comic adventures before retransformation by the goddess Isis, contains like the *Satyrica* a number of inserted tales, the most famous being that of Cupid and Psyche in two books (4. 28–6. 24). Some of these are clearly *Milesian Tales*, which Apuleius explicitly claims to use (1. 1. 1, 4. 32. 6); the inserted tales make up a large proportion of the plot but also lend it unity and coherence by their close thematic relation to the main narrative. The *Metamorphoses* has marked Isiac and Platonic elements; in the final book, the conversion of Lucius to Isiac cult and the resulting reassessment of his adventures (11. 15. 1–5), coupled with the apparent revelation that the narrator is no longer Lucius but Apuleius himself (11. 27. 9), provide a problematic conclusion in both ideological and narratological terms (see NARRATIVE).

Both Petronius and Apuleius use the existing genre of the Greek ideal novel, but both alter its flavour in a characteristically Roman way, parodying its stress on virtuous young love, adding low-life realism, bawdy humour, and elements from other established literary genres, and using narrators, narrative levels, and inserted tales in a complex way. All these features appear to some extent in Greek novelistic texts, but are fundamentally characteristic of the two main Latin novels. There are two further Latin novels extant from late antiquity, translations from the Greek, belonging essentially to the Greek rather than Latin tradition—the *Story of Apollonius, King of Tyre* (see APOLLONIUS (14)) (5th-6th cent. AD) and the Alexander Romance of *Iulius Valerius (4th cent. AD; see PSEUDO-CALLISTHENES). Christian texts in Latin make use of the ancient novel for fictionalized hagiography: the pseudo-Clementine *Recognitiones* (4th cent. AD), translated from an earlier Greek original, shows many novelistic elements in its melodramatic story of the young Clement, Peter's successor as bishop of Rome, as does *Jerome's similar *Life of St Paul the First Hermit* (text in Migne, *PL* 23. 17–30) from the same period. There are also fictionalized histories in Latin with some novelistic colouring from late antiquity, particularly the Troy-narratives of *Dictys Cretensis (4th cent. AD) and *Dares of Phrygia (5th/6th cent. AD).

B. E. Perry, *The Ancient Romances* (1967); J. P. Sullivan, *The Satyricon of Petronius* (1968); P. G. Walsh, *The Roman Novel* (1970); T. Hägg, *The Novel in Antiquity* (1983); J. J. Winkler, *Actor and Auctor: A Narrato-*

logical Reading of Apuleius' Golden Ass (1984); N. W. Slater, *Reading Petronius* (1989); C. C. Schlam, *The Metamorphoses of Apuleius* (1992); G. Bowersock, *Fiction as History* (1994).   S. J. Ha.

novensides, a group of Roman deities of totally unknown function. In Wissowa's system this group was supposed to embrace, in contrast to the di *indigetes, divinities newly installed at Rome (*nov-en-sides*, 'newly settled-in'. H. Wagenvoort (*Roman Dynamism* (1947), 83), in view of the spelling *novensiles*, attested in the literary sources, derived their name from *nuere*: hence 'mobile, active' deities. More recently these two interpretations have been dropped in favour of a connection with *novem*, 'nine', already made in antiquity (Arn. *Adv. nat.* 3. 381; Marius Victorinus, *Gloss. Lat.* 6. 25. 5 ff. Keil). The epigraphic testimony from the land of the *Marsi (*esos novesede*, R. S. Conway, *The Italic Dialects* (1897), 261), along with the literary references to their Sabine origin (Varr. *Ling.* 5. 74; Calpurnius Piso fr. 45 Peter), suggests that these 'nine gods' were originally from central Italy and were introduced fairly early to Rome, a colony of which, Pisaurum, mentions (*deiv. no[v]esede*, *ILLRP* 20). But others give them an Etruscan origin.

S. Weinstock, *RE* 17. 1185; G. Capdeville, *Secondo Congresso Internazionale Etrusco* (1985), 1171 ff.; Radke, *Entwicklung*, 113 ff.   J. Sch.

Noviomagus, a *Batavian settlement near Nijmegen (perhaps the *oppidum Batavorum* of Tac. *Hist.* 5. 19). It was destroyed in AD 70, and the Romans established a legionary fortress (garrisoned until *c.*100) nearby. The civil population settled on lower ground to the west, where an important commercial town developed, which traded extensively with Britain and the north and was raised to colonial status (as *Ulpia Noviomagus*) by *Trajan. It suffered badly in the invasions of the 3rd cent. Pottery finds persist beyond the 4th cent., but by then a new settlement was growing up further east.

J. Bogaers and others, *Noviomagus* (1980).   O. B.; J. F. Dr.

Novius (*RE* 5), early 1st cent. BC, author of *fabulae Atellanae*, which he and his contemporary L. *Pomponius made literary. We have 44 titles and over 100 lines. Three of his jokes are praised in Cicero, *De or.* 2 (dramatic date 91 BC). See ATELLANA.

P. G. M. B.

novus homo (= 'new man'), term used in the late republic (and probably earlier) in various related senses: for the first man of a family to reach the senate, where he normally remained a 'small senator' (*BAfr.* 57); in a special sense, for such a man actually to rise to the consulship; and (although in our sources less frequently) for the first man of a senatorial family to reach the consulship (e.g. Cic. *Off.* 1. 138). The first of these achievements was not very difficult, provided a man had at least equestrian standing (see EQUITES), some military or oratorical ability, and good connections. The last was also far from rare: it was in this way that the *nobilitas was constantly reinvigorated. But few men rose from outside the senate to a consulship, and the most frequent use of the term in fact characterizes this unusual achievement. It took unusual merit and effort and either noble patronage (e.g. that of the Flacci for M. *Porcius Cato (1)) or a public emergency, as in the cases of C. *Marius (1) and *Cicero. (For *novi homines* in this sense see also COELIUS CALDUS, C.; NORBANUS, C.; POMPEIUS, Q.; and for statistics on all these classes between the *lex Villia* (see LEX (2), at *lex Villia*) and Caesar, see *Chiron* 1990, 406 ff.)

The *novus homo* become consul contrasts with the *nobiles* (the 'known' men) as *per se cognitus* ('known (only) through himself').

He has to win his own connections and *clientelae* to balance those inherited by the *nobiles*. Hence a typical pattern of career and outlook develops, best seen in Marius and Cicero, about whom we have the fullest information. During his rise the *novus homo* prides himself on his *virtus* and achievements and tends to compare them with those of the founders of noble families, as contrasted with their degenerate descendants. (See e.g. Sall. *Iug.* 85; Cic. 2 *Verr.* 5. 180 ff.) Cicero readily returns to this motif when it suits him in his later speeches.) But he is not a reformer of the system. After rising to the top, he aims at defending the order in which he has risen and gaining recognition as an equal from his social superiors. Some (e.g. Cato, in part through longevity) more or less fully succeed in this; others (e.g. Marius and Cicero) are never quite accepted. But they never favour the advancement of other new men.

Under the empire, men of this sort, of equestrian background, at first from Italy and gradually from the provinces, can rise high on their own merits, promoted by the emperor, to whom they give less cause for jealousy and suspicion.

J. Vogt, *Homo novus* (1926); D. R. Shackleton Bailey, *AJPhil.* 1986, 255 ff.; T. P. Wiseman, *New Men in the Roman Senate, 139 BC–AD 14* (1971).

E. B.

Nubia, part of the classical *Ethiopia, is the region of the middle Nile valley from Aswan to the Fourth Cataract. Modern literature also includes the central Sudan (the Butana, or island of *Meroe) as far as Khartoum within the definition. After Egyptian domination during the New Kingdom (*c.*1550–1080 BC), indigenous kingdoms flourished into medieval times. The region from the Second Cataract to the central Sudan (Upper Nubia) was the kingdom of Kush, with its major centres at Napata and Meroe. There was conflict between the Ptolemies and the kings of Meroe for control of Lower Nubia (First–Second Cataracts), and a number of temples were built there. Roman annexation of Egypt saw further conflict; an expedition by P. *Petronius in 25–24 BC (Strabo 17. 1. 53–4) fixed the frontier at Hiera-Sycaminus, where it remained until the reign of Diocletian. Lower Nubia was fairly prosperous in the Roman period and large quantities of imported goods are found in the Nubian cemeteries. During the later Roman empire the region was occupied by the Blemmyes who moved into the Nile valley from the Eastern Desert and by the Nobades, who came from the south-west. Philae, just south of Aswan, became a pilgrimage centre in the Roman period, and Nubians are often depicted as priests of the goddess Isis. Because of Nubian devotion to the cult of *Isis, Philae was left open when *Theodosius (2) I closed the remainder of the temples in the empire. By the reign of Justinian, much of Nubia had been converted to Christianity. In Greek and Roman literature Nubia appears most frequently as the borderland between Egypt and Meroe. It is usually characterized as an uninhabited region where 'silent trade' is performed (Philostr. *VA* 6. 2).

W. Y. Adams, *Nubia: Corridor to Africa* (1984). R. G. M.

Nuceria (1), large town at foot of peninsula of *Surrentum: (mod. Nocera Inferiore). Originally peopled by *Oscan-speaking Alfaterni, it regularly changed hands whenever war visited *Campania. In AD 59 it and neighbouring *Pompeii staged a bloody riot.

M. and A. Fresa, *Nuceria Alfaterna* (1974).

(2) Large town on the *via Flaminia in *Umbria: mod. Nocera Umbra. The campaign of *Sentinum, 295 BC, probably brought it under Roman control.

G. Sigismondo, *Nucera in Umbria* (1979). E. T. S.; T. W. P.

Numa See POMPILIUS, NUMA.

Numantia (now Garray, near Soria), a strategic site on the upper Douro (Durius) in Spain; initially occupied in the bronze age, walled by the 4th cent. BC, and culturally *Celtiberian by this date. Numantia played a pivotal role in the Celtiberian resistance to Rome, repelling attacks by *Cato (Censorius) (195), Q. Fulvius Nobilior (153), M. *Claudius Marcellus (3) (152), Q. *Pompeius (140), and *Popillius Laenas (139–8); the capitulation of *Hostilius Mancinus (137) crowned a series of failures and defeats. Finally, after an eight-month blockade, Numantia's 4,000 inhabitants capitulated to the overwhelming forces of *Scipio Aemilianus in 133 BC, a date which marks the end of concerted resistance to Rome in Iberia. C. *Marius (1), *Jugurtha, and *Rutilius Rufus witnessed Numantia's destruction. Thorough excavations have uncovered the town, Scipio's works of circumvallation, and thirteen Roman camps at Numantia or in the neighbourhood (one each of Marcellus and Pompeius, two of Cato and Nobilior, and seven of Scipio). The town had reappeared by *Augustus and was on the *Caesaraugusta-to-Asturica road. This now modest centre began to decline in the 3rd, and was probably finally abandoned in the 4th, cent. AD.

A. Schulten, *Numantia*, 4 vols. and atlas (1914–31); M. Salinas, *Conquista y romanización de Celtiberia* (1986), 91 ff. J. J. van N.; S. J. K.

numbers, Greek

Greek Numeral Notations

There were two main systems:

(1) The 'alphabetic' or 'Milesian', probably originating in Ionia and the older of the two. It consisted of the ordinary letters of the Ionian alphabet plus ϛ = 6, ϙ = 90, and ↑ or ↗ = 900. Thus α to θ represent 1 to 9, ι to ϙ 10 to 90, and ρ to ↗ 100 to 900. Thousands from one to nine are represented by ,α to ,θ, and 10,000 by *M*. Multiples of 10,000 are written by putting the multiplier above; thus 126,763 is written $\overset{\iota\beta}{M}\,\varsigma\psi\xi\gamma$.

(2) The 'acrophonic'. Apart from I, the unit, the signs were the initial letters of the numeral words: Γ = πέντε, Δ = δέκα, Η = ἑκατόν, Χ = χίλιοι, Μ = μύριοι. Quintuples of the latter four were represented by a combination with Γ; thus ⊡, Ⓕ, or ⊡ = 50, ⊡ = 500, ⊡ = 5,000, ⊡ = 50,000. Other multiples were expressed by repetition of the sign; thus 126,763 is written ΓΓΜΜΜΡΧΓΗΗΗΡⅢ. These signs were frequently used in Attic inscriptions to express sums of money; in that case they represented drachmas, except that ⊢ = 1 drachma and I = 1 obol. Ϲ was used for a ½-obol, ⊃ or Τ for ¼-obol, and Τ for a talent. The latter sign was combined with the numerals to express numbers of talents, e.g. ⊡ΔΗⅢΧ.

On present evidence we may tentatively say that (2) was the system used in all public inscriptions in *Attica (with the possible exception of *IG* 1³. 1387) down to *c.*100 BC, and sporadically later. It is also the main system used (with local variations) in other Greek states from the 5th to the 3rd cent. (1) is found in the earliest Attic vase-inscriptions, but from *c.*480 wide (but not universal) use of (2) is found in Attic private inscriptions. (1) ousted (2) in other Greek states during the 3rd cent. BC. It is almost universal in surviving papyri.

A zero sign ō is found in astronomical papyri and MSS. *Fractions*: Like the Egyptians, the Greeks preferred to express fractions as the sum of unit fractions (fractions with 1 as numerator); they expressed the unit fraction by the sign for the number with an accent; thus γ´δ´ = ⅓ + ¼ = ⁷⁄₁₂. There were special signs ∠ for ½ and β´ for ⅔. However, proper fractions could also be expressed by the word (or the sign) for the numerator and the accented letters for the denominator, e.g. $\delta\acute{v}o~\mu\epsilon' = {}^{2}/_{45}$ (*Aristarchus (1)), $\theta~\iota\alpha' = {}^{9}/_{11}$ (*Archimedes), or by expressions like $\delta^{\omega\nu}s = {}^{6}/_{4}$, $\nu~\kappa\gamma^{\omega\nu} = {}^{50}/_{23}$ (*Diophantus). Most convenient was the practice, regular in Diophantus and occasional in *Heron, of placing the denominator *above* the numerator, e.g. ${}^{\phi\iota\beta}_{\beta\nu s} = {}^{2456}/_{512}$ (Diophantus). Sexagesimal fractions are standard in the later astronomical works (e.g. *Ptolemy (4)). In this system e.g. $\iota\beta~\lambda\delta'\nu s'' = 12 + {}^{34}/_{60} + {}^{56}/_{60.60}$.

Artificial Systems

Archimedes, in his lost Ἀρχαί and in the *Sand-reckoner* (*Psammites*), sketched a system for expressing very large numbers going by powers of a myriad myriads (100,000,000 or 10^{8}). The first *order* consists of numbers from 1 to 10^{8}, the second *order* those from 10^{8} to 10^{16}, and so on, up to the 10^{8} *order* concluding the first *period*. Other *periods* follow ad lib. This system amounts to taking 100,000,000 in place of 10 as the base of a scale of notation. *Apollonius (2) of Perge formulated a 'position-value' system going by powers of 10,000, i.e. with 10,000 substituted for 10 as the base (see Pappus 1. 8 f.).

Articles by M. N. Tod, *BSA* 1911–12, 1926–7, 1936–7, and *JHS* 1933, give full evidence for the acrophonic system, and in *BSA* 1950 for the alphabetic. On the early vase-inscriptions: R. Hackl in *Münchener archäologische Studien dem Andenken A. Furtwängler gewidmet* (1909), esp. 79 ff. Best general account: G. E. M. de Ste. Croix, *Studies in the History of Accounting* (ed. Littleton and Yamey, 1956), 50 ff. See also K. Menninger, *Zahlwort und Ziffer*, 2nd edn., 2 (1958), 73 ff. Fractions: Heath, *Hist. of Greek Maths.* 1. 41 ff. In the papyri, E. Mayser, *Grammatik d. gr. Papyri* (1926–38), 52 f. On computation with alphabetic numerals: J. G. Smyly in *Mélanges Nicole* (1905), 513 ff. For the use of *a*–*ω* for 1– 24 see F. Dornseiff, *Das Alphabet in Mystik und Magie* (1922), 11.

T. H.; G. J. T.

numbers, Roman The numbers are based on seven signs: I = 1, V = 5, X = 10, L = 50 (formerly, before the 1st cent. BC, ↓), C = 100, Ð = 500, ∞ (or a recognizable variant) = 1,000 (M was not used as a figure, only as an abbreviation of the words *mille, milia*). The system's origins are debated. Modern scholarship rejects the late and complex theory of *Priscian (mixing alphabetic and acrophonic principles); Mommsen's influential dual explanation argues for both pre-alphabetic (i.e. pictographic) origins (I, V, and X) and a putative Roman adaptation of 'unused' Greek (Chalcidic; see CHALCIS) letters (↓, C, ∞); most recently an origin in the *Etruscan system of tally-marks has been proposed (Keyser).

A notation could be constructed on this basis both by the additive method (IIII = 4; XXXX = 40) and by the subtractive (IV = 4; XL = 40) and both methods were employed, sometimes even in the same document. Inscriptions seem to show a preference for the additive method, especially in official contexts, and this preference is occasionally carried to the extent of ignoring the signs V and L (so IIIIIIviri often for VIviri and such forms as XXXXXX for LX). The rule is that when two figures stand side by side, the smaller, if to the right, is to be added to its neighbour, if to the left, to be subtracted from it (VI = 6; IV = 4); exceptions occur, but are very rare. For numbers above 1,000, for which the additive method might be clumsy, modifications of the basic signs were evolved (so Ð = 5,000; ⊕ = 10,000) and, later, as an alternative, the use of superscript bars to denote that a figure is to be multiplied by 1,000 (so $\overline{X}$ = 10,000), and of superscript bars with dependent verticals at either side to denote that it is to be multiplied by 100,000 (⊠ = 1,000,000).

From the 2nd cent. BC the figure-signs began to be used also as *sigla* for words or components of words with a numerical reference (so X = *denarius*, IIviri = *duoviri*) and eventually for ordinal adjectives and adverbs and for distributives as well as for cardinal numbers. It was probably to distinguish such usages, in circumstances where confusion with letters or with cardinal numbers might occur, that the practice of using a medial bar was introduced (so ✕ = *denarius*) and subsequently a superscript bar (so *IIviri* = *duoviri*; $\bar{V}$ = *quinquies*). From the Augustan period onwards this use of a superscript bar was extended, although it never became invariable. In a comparatively small number of cases it appears also above an ordinal number, presumably in error, and creates confusion with the use of the bar to denote multiplication by 1,000.

Cursive forms of the figures are usually recognizable without undue difficulty (cf. ⧣ = 30), though ɕ = 6, common especially in Christian texts, is at first sight obscure.

For fractions, a duodecimal system was used. A horizontal stroke was the sign for the unit of $\frac{1}{12}$ (*uncia*) and S, from *semis*, for $\frac{1}{2}$. The appropriate number of horizontal strokes provided the notation for $\frac{1}{12}$ to $\frac{5}{12}$ (= = = — is $\frac{5}{12}$) and, when preceded by S, for $\frac{7}{12}$ to $\frac{11}{12}$ (S = = — is $\frac{11}{12}$). For smaller fractions a number of *sigla* were developed; lists may be found in the epigraphic handbooks, see EPIGRAPHY, LATIN, bibliography.

E. Hübner, *Exempla Scripturae Epigraphicae* (1885), pp. lxx f.; T. Mommsen, *Hermes* 1887, 596 f., 1888, 152 f.; J. S. and A. E. Gordon, *Contributions to the Palaeography of Latin Inscriptions* (1957), 166 ff.; B. E. Thomasson, *Opuscula Romana* 3 (1961), 179 ff.; P. Keyser, *AJArch.* 1988, 529 ff.

J. M. R.; A. J. S. S.

numbers, sacred, certain numbers taken to represent or control divine actions. The derivation of such numbers can be extremely complex, deriving at times from natural phenomena, at times from linguistic coincidence, this last being the result of the use of letters for counting in a majority of ancient societies, in turn resulting in the practice of numerology, or the representation of a person or concept by the sum of the letters in a word. Thus in *Aramaic, the name of Nero Caesar, written as *nrwn ksr*, is 666 (100 + 60 + 200 + 50 + 200 + 6 + 50), and in the *Sibylline Oracles* emperors are often represented by the sum of the letters in their names.

Interest in the number seven seems to derive from the belief that there were seven planets, in five from the number of fingers on a hand (and, possibly, ten for similar reasons), in three, possibly from the tripartite division of the cosmos into air, land, and sea, and twelve from the numbers of signs in the zodiac. Multiples of these numbers may also be regarded as significant (e.g. nine), as could numbers that exceeded a significant number by one (e.g. 13). After the adoption of the Julian calendar (see CALENDAR, ROMAN), the number 365 seems also to have attracted considerable attention.

In addition to calculations based upon numbers derived from nature, there were calculations based upon broader eras of human history. Here the number ten seems to have been of particular interest in the Roman world as the number of *saecula* (ages) before an eschatological catastrophe (the succession of nine, or, more often, ten *saecula* derived from Etruscan speculation), even though there was considerable dispute as to how *saecula* should be counted. The Egyptian scheme of the Great Year (1,461 ordinary years) was derived from the fact that the Egyptian year was a quarter-day too short, and thus the calendar corresponded exactly with the natural year only once every 1,461 years. In Judaeo-Christian thought, a belief in a 'sabbatical millennium' developed out of the view that a day of the Lord lasted for a thousand years, and that he had created the world in six days resting upon the seventh (R. Landes, in W. Verbeke, D. Verhelst, and A. Welkenhuysen (eds.), *The Use and Abuse of Eschatology in the Early Middle Ages* (1988), 141–9). This scheme generated much heated debate so long as schemes based upon the age of the world were used.

G. Ifrah, *From One to Zero: A Universal History of Numbers* (1985); D. S. Potter, *Prophets and Emperors* (1994). D. S. P.

numen, the 'expressed will of a divinity', a term generating much modern debate. Basing themselves on the pre-deist theories of the beginning of this century, W. W. Fowler and J. Frazer, followed by H. J. Rose, H. Wagenvoort, and K. Latte, supposed that by *numen* the Romans meant an impersonal divine force. This conception has been challenged by W. Pötscher and G. Dumézil (see bibliog. below), in particular on grammatical grounds. In fact, until the beginning of our era (and later), *numen* is always construed with the genitive of the name of a divinity (a term like *deus*, or with the adjective *divinus*), and can only mean 'the expressed will of a divinity'. This assent was indicated notably by the *nutus*, an inclination of the head. Such at any rate was the interpretation of the ancient grammarians (Festus 178 Lindsay; Varro, *Ling.* 7. 85). The concept of *numen*, which without doubt was very old, serves to represent the action of both mortals and immortals. The *numen* of a divinity shows the actual and particular will of this deity, and it is different both from his or her person and *genius (which describes the capacity for action of a being or a thing at the moment of its constitution). In general the *numen* concerns the gods and, under the empire, the ruling emperor, but exceptionally it applies to the senate and the Roman people, endowed like the ruler with a quasi-divine power of action. The *numen Augusti* received a cult from the beginning of our era, its function being to represent the exceptional power of the ruler, and enabling the attribution of divine honours to him in his lifetime. Later on, writers considered the *numen* as an 'integral part of the particular will of the deity' (Dumézil)— i.e. as a synonym of divinity, taking the manifestation of power for the divinity who exercises it. This usage was never general, however, and only applied in earlier times. See RULER-CULT.

Dumézil, *ARR* ch. 3; W. Pötscher, *ANRW* 2. 16. 1 (1978), 355 ff.; D. Fishwick, *Harv. Theol. Rev.* 1969, 356 ff. (= his *The Imperial Cult in the Roman West*, 2 vols. in 4 (1987–92)), 2. 1 (1991), 325 ff. J. Sch.

Numenius, of Apamea (2nd cent. AD), leading Platonist (also referred to as a Pythagorean). Substantial fragments of two of his works survive: a metaphysical dialogue *On the Good* and a history of the *Academy designed to show how much it had corrupted *Plato (1)'s teaching. This teaching was Pythagorean, he claimed, relating it to the ancient wisdom of the Brahmans, Magi (see MAGUS), Egyptians, and Jews whose scriptures he interpreted allegorically. He shared ideas with *Gnosticism and with the *Chaldaean Oracles. His metaphysics includes a first god (the Good, which is absolutely transcendent) and a second god who imitates the first and organizes the world. Matter is evil, as is life in the body for our soul. He had considerable influence on *Plotinus, who was accused of plagiarizing from him, on *Origen (2), *Porphyry, and later *Neoplatonists. See NEOPYTHAGOR-EANISM.

FRAGMENTS Ed. and trans. E. des Places (1973).
DISCUSSION J. Dillon, *The Middle Platonists* (1977), 361 ff.; G. Martano, *Numenio d'Apamea* (1960); E. R. Dodds in *Les Sources de Plotin*,

Entretiens Hardt 5 (1960), 1 ff.; M. Frede, *ANRW* 2. 36. 2 (1987), 1034 ff. D. O'M.

numeri in a military context was simply a term for bodies of soldiers; consequently *numerus* was often applied to a formation lacking a formal title, like *frumentarii* (grain-collecting agents) or *equites singulares Augusti*, and to units recruited from unromanized peoples, which, preserving their military customs and techniques, in some cases remained distinct from the usual army structure. However, since *numerus* was also used to designate a *cohors, ala* (see ALAE), or *legion, it was not a technical term applied only to special types of unit. Therefore, the use of *numerus* to describe a national or ethnic unit, for instance *numerus Syrorum sagittariorum* ('unit of Syrian archers'), does not imply that such units had uniform conditions of service, organization, and function; the formation of national units was probably a gradual process beginning in the 1st cent. AD.

In military bureaucracy the phrase *in numeros referre* relates to registration of new recruits on the rolls of their unit.

H. Callies, *Die fremden Truppen im römischen Heer des Principats und die sogenannten nationalen Numeri* (1964); M. P. Speidel, *ANRW* 2. 3 (1975), 202. J. B. C.

Numerianus, Marcus Aurelius (*RE* 174), younger son of *Carus, was appointed Caesar in AD 282 and participated in the Persian campaign. After the death of Carus he became Augustus (see AUGUSTUS, AUGUSTA AS TITLES), though real power lay with his praetorian prefect and father-in-law, Aper. Having withdrawn from Persia he died in Bithynia in mysterious circumstances (late 284). The army chose Diocles (later *Diocletian) to succeed him. Diocles' immediate condemnation and slaying of Aper as Numerian's murderer have aroused suspicion that he too may have been involved in conspiracy against both Carus and Numerian.

PLRE 1. 634. See bibliog. under CARUS, M. AURELIUS.
H. M.; B. H. W.; J. F. Dr.

Numicus (or **Numicius**) (mod. Fosso di Pratica), the creek near *Lavinium in *Latium where *Aeneas allegedly perished. He was subsequently venerated in the sanctuary of *Sol Indiges at the mouth of the river, where he is supposed to have landed. Finds show that the sanctuary was in existence by the 5th cent. BC.

Enea nel Lazio, archeologia e mito (Rome, 1981), 167. T. W. P.

Numidia, originally the country of the Numidae or African *nomads, lying west and south of Carthaginian territory (see CARTHAGE). Later the title was given to a Roman province, covering a much smaller area of land, a triangle broadening out from its apex on the Mediterranean coast north of *Cirta, across the High Plateaux (*Atlas mountains), down to the Saharan *limes. This Numidia was bounded by *Mauretania Caesariensis on the west and the province of Africa (see AFRICA, ROMAN) on the east. Although not as fertile as the latter, Numidia produced corn, wine, and olives in the plains, and bred horses, cattle, and sheep on the uplands. Its bears, lions, and leopards were much in demand in the amphitheatres of Italy and elsewhere; *elephants were also numerous, one place near Cirta being called Elephant Castle (*castellum Elephantum*). The label 'Numidian' however, was applied to products from the whole area of (pre-Roman) Numidia rather than just from the narrow confines of the Roman province; one example is *marmor Numidicum*, the yellow marble of *Simitthus in Proconsularis.

The original Berber inhabitants of Numidia were *nomad herdsmen, who sometimes practised a simple agriculture. Those on the coast came under the influence of *Utica, Carthage, and other Phoenician settlements. By the time of the Second Punic War their small clans had coalesced into tribal confederacies of the Masaesyli under *Syphax (the more westerly of the two, occupying western Algeria north of the Sahara), and the Massyli under *Masinissa. Their cavalry was formidable, but disunion made them difficult allies politically. Under Masinissa nomadism was abandoned for agriculture, and town life developed; Punic was adopted as the language of the élite, and worship of Baal-Hammon became popular alongside native cults. Masinissa was followed by Micipsa (148–118 BC), Adherbal (118–112), *Jugurtha (118–106), Hiempsal (106–60), and *Juba (1) (69–46). Royal capitals included Siga (in western Algeria near the Moroccan border), *Hippo Regius, *Cirta, Iol (later *Caesarea (3)), *Zama Regia, and *Bulla Regia. Little archaeologically remains of this period except for the monumental stone-built mausolea, at Siga, *Thugga, 'The Tomb of the Christian Woman' near *Tipasa, El Khroub near Cirta, and the Medracen near Batna; all date probably between c.200 and c.50 BC. As Numidia supported *Pompey (47–46), the indigenous dynasty was overthrown. Eastern Numidia was established as the province of Africa Nova (46 BC), and in 25 BC the area west of Cirta was made the client kingdom of Mauretania under *Juba (2) II. Also under *Augustus Africa Nova was united with the old province of Africa again (and the whole called Africa Proconsularis) until divided by Septimius Severus, when a separate province of Numidia was created for the first time (AD 197/8). *Christianity spread rapidly in the 3rd cent., and in the 4th Numidia became the stronghold of the *Donatists.

When the frontiers of Africa Proconsularis were placed on the river Ampsagus (mod. Rhummel), the Legio III Augusta (see LEGION) moved into Numidia under its legate (see LEGATI), and was stationed successively at *Theveste and *Lambaesis. Military colonies were founded at *Thamugadi, *Madauros, and elsewhere. On its southern frontier Numidia was protected by the forts of the limes, which ran from the Tunisian shotts (salt lakes) westwards and north-west to Aumale. Between the military roads were districts ruled by indigenous chieftains, who occasionally rebelled. The frontier held until the 5th cent. when Saharan raiders and Berber tribesmen sacked a number of towns during the *Vandal occupation of Africa.

C. Saumagne, La Numidie et Rome (1966); H. G. Horn and C. B. Rüger (eds.), Die Numider (1979); E. W. B. Fentress, Numidia and the Roman Army (1979); A. Berthier, La Numidie: Rome et le Maghreb (1981); H. W. Ritter, Rom und Numidien: Untersuchungen zur rechtlichen Stellung abhängiger Könige (1987).   W. N. W.; R. J. A. W.

nummularius, a banker, whether one who exchanged coins of different monetary systems or one who tested coins to see whether they were forgeries; and in the 3rd cent. AD a mint official, though it is not clear whether he tested incoming or outgoing coin. The principal surviving evidence for the activities of a nummularius has been seen since the work of R. Herzog in the small bone or ivory labels now known as tesserae nummulariae (see TESSERA). They typically bear the name of a slave, his owner, the statement spectauit, 'he inspected', and a date by day, month, and year; and they are supposed to have been attached to sealed bags of coin which had been inspected. The interpretation is attractive, but not without problems, since it is quite unclear why it should matter on which precise day a bag of coin had been inspected. See BANKS.

R. Herzog, RE 18/2. 1415–55; J. Andreau, La Vie financière dans le monde romain (1987), 177–219, 485–525.   M. H. C.

nymphaeum In the Classical Greek world a nymphaeum was a shrine to the *Nymphs, often a rural cave or grove with no architectural adornment. Several sculptured reliefs dedicated to *Pan and the Nymphs are known from Classical *Attica (see CAVES, SACRED).

The Nymphs were with river-gods the guardian spirits of sources of pure *water. When the tyrant *Theagenes (1) of *Megara diverted fresh water for his city, he sacrificed to the *river-god at the point where the waters had been captured. By the Roman imperial period such sentiment was more publicly expressed at the urban terminus of *aqueducts, where the waters were filtered into a fountain, often richly decorated with statues and inscriptions recording the generosity, piety, and social status of the donor, and in many instances referring to the river or spring from which the waters originated. The most intelligible surviving example was built by Ti. *Claudius Atticus Herodes (2) in the sanctuary at *Olympia about AD 150. The modern term nymphaeum applied to such buildings derives from late antique usage; in the early empire urban fountains were called munera, onerous burdens to those who held public office (see MUNUS). Ornate fountains were built in many wealthy cities of the Roman empire, notably *Miletus, *Lepcis Magna, and *Carthage. Grotto-nymphaea were built as rustic conceits in some late republican and early imperial *villas of the Roman Campagna and the bay of Naples. Some sacred nymphaea survived in remote areas: several Greek sites were noted by *Pausanias (3), who commended their oracular or healing powers; many were associated with *baths.

R. Ginouvès, Balaneutiké (1962), and in J. des Gagniers (ed.), Laodicée du Lykos: Le Nymphée (1969); N. Neuerburg, Fontane e ninfei nell'Italia antica (1965); S. Settis, ANRW 1. 4 (1973), 661–745; S. Walker in S. Macready and F. H. Thompson (eds.), Roman Architecture in the Greek World (1987), 60–72.   S. E. C. W.

Nymphidius (RE 5) **Sabinus, Gaius,** son of a court freedwoman, claimed to be the son of the emperor *Gaius (1). He probably commanded an auxiliary regiment in Pannonia (ILS 1322) and then became a tribune in the guard. In 65 he was given the consularia *ornamenta by *Nero for his part in suppressing the Pisonian conspiracy (see CALPURNIUS PISO (2), C.) and made *praefectus praetorio with *Tigellinus. In 68, by promise of an enormous donative, he induced the praetorians to desert Nero for *Galba, but he had designs upon the Principate himself. He forced Tigellinus to resign, and intended to demand from Galba the prefecture for life without colleague. But he met with unexpected opposition from the praetorians when Galba refused to honour his promises of money, and was killed by them.

R. L. J.; G. E. F. C.; M. T. G.

Nymphis, of *Heraclea (3) in Bithynia, 3rd-cent. BC statesman and historian. Enough remains of his thirteen-volume history of Heraclea (in *Memnon (3)'s epitome) to show how good it was; his 24-volume history of *Alexander (3) the Great and his successors (perhaps to 246 BC) is almost completely lost.

FGrH 432; cf. FGrH 434 (Memnon).   W. W. T.; G. T. G.; K. S. S.

Nymphodorus, *Syracusan author of the Hellenistic period.

Works

(1) Peri tōn en Sikelia thaumazomenōn ('On Strange Things in Sicily', FGrH 572 F 1–3). (2) Periploi (F 4–8); F 4 on the slave revolt in *Chios is especially noteworthy. His interests were not so much geographical as *paradoxographical.

nymphs

FGrH 572. A. Giannini, *Paradoxographorum graecorum reliquiae* (1966), 112 ff. K. M.

nymphs A varied category of female divinities anthropomorphically perceived as young women (the word *nymphē*, means also 'bride'). They inhabit and animately express differentiated nature: *water (rivers, springs, the sea), *mountains, trees, and 'places' (regions, towns, states). Their ubiquitous presence in popular imagination, folklore, art, myth, and cult, provides a vivid illustration of ancient pantheism.

Cult of Nymphs, particularly associated with caves, is mentioned already in *Homer and corroborated by archaeology. In the Polis cave at *Ithaca, there was a cult both to *Odysseus and the Nymphs; in western *Crete, at Lera was a cave sacred to *Pan and the Nymphs. The grotto on Mt. *Hymettus above Vari (*Attica) was sacred to Pan, *Apollo, and the Nymphs; at the Corycian cave in Phocis were found hundreds of small vessels (aryballoi), thousands of figurines, and 16,000 knucklebones. See CAVES, SACRED. Nymphs were closely associated (mythically perceived as daughters or lovers) in worship with *river-gods, such as the archetypical *Acheloüs. They received both animal and cereal *sacrifices; *wine was usually forbidden in their worship. Nymphs are intimately, albeit vaguely, linked with productive and life-enhancing powers. Although mostly belonging to the countryside or to particular spots (streams, groves, hills), nymphs appear also in official state cult. *Dionysus' nurse, Nysa (a place-name), had a state cult at Athens led by official 'hymn-singers', *hymnētriai*. Pandemos was the 'All the People' nymph in Athens. There was a fountain-house sacred to the Nymphs in the Athenian Agora. At *Cos magistrates were responsible for 'ancestral sacrifices' to the Nymphs. At *Thera each *Dorian tribe (Hylleis and Dymanes; see PHYLAI) had its own nymph. In Illyrian Apollonia the crackling of *incense (burning on the altar of the Nymphs) served for divination (Strabo 316).

The association with other gods, such as Pan (especially), *Hermes, and *Artemis appears both in cult and myth. Apollo and Dionysus are addressed as 'Nymph-leaders', *nymphagetai*. Often regarded as daughters of Zeus, nymphs were also perceived as belonging to an earlier stratum: the Meliads, nymphs of ash trees, emerged from the drops of blood of *Uranus' castrated genitals. Nymphs are either lovers or mothers of gods, heroes, or satyrs; as virgins they roam the woods and mountains with Artemis. Eponymous nymphs (or mothers of eponymous heroes), such as Aegina (cf. AEGINA) and Aeacus, or Satyra (Satyrion) the mother of Taras (both the name of a river and the city, see TARENTUM), filled up the landscape.

Nymphs may have other nymphs attending them (*Calypso). They are either immortal or endowed with super-human longevity. They are often named after their respective elements: Hamadryads die with the particular trees with which they are identified; Oreads are mountain-nymphs; Naiads and Hydriads, water-nymphs, often daughters of the river-god, e.g. Asopus; the Nereids are nymphs of the calm sea (daughters of the Old Man of the Sea, *Nereus); Alseids reside in groves (*alsos*); Oceanids are daughters of *Oceanus and *Tethys; other nymphs were named after geographical features, such as the Leimoniads, nymphs of meadows, or the Acheloids, nymphs of the river Acheloüs.

Most nymphs are benevolent, although they may abduct handsome boys (*Hylas). They bring flowers, watch with Apollo and Hermes over the flocks, and, as patronesses of healing springs (e.g. in the Asclepieum at Athens, *IG* 2². 4960), aid the sick. See SPRINGS, SACRED. As divinities of woods and mountains they may help hunters. Folk-tales, similar to those about fairies and mermaids, are told about nymphs. A man who sees them becomes 'possessed by nymphs'. They punish unresponsive lovers, as did the nymphs who blinded *Daphnis. See also NYMPHAEUM.

Nilsson, *GGR* 1³. 244–55; J. Ferguson, *Among the Gods: An Archaeological Exploration of Ancient Greek Religion* (1989); A. D. Nock, *Essays 2* (1972), 919–27; A. W. Gomme and F. H. Sandbach, *Commentary on Menander* (1973), 134–5; W. R. Connor, *Cl. Ant.* 1988, 154 ff. I. M.

Nyx (*Νύξ*), personification of night. In Greek mythology she was a great cosmogonical figure, feared and respected even by *Zeus (Hom. *Il.* 14. 259). In *Hesiod she is born of *Chaos and mother of Aether, Hemera, and lesser powers. Frequent touches in the description recall her nocturnal aspect, but this is scarcely seen in the Orphic theogonies, where her influence over creation is immense (cf. ORPHIC LITERATURE; ORPHISM). In the Rhapsodies she is daughter of *Phanes and succeeds to his power. When in turn she hands the sceptre to her son *Uranus she continues to advise the younger generations, Uranus, *Cronus, and especially *Zeus, in the task of world-making. Her influence is due to her oracular powers, exercised from a cave. There are signs that in an earlier Orphic version Phanes was absent and Nyx the primal power. The theogony of the *Birds* (Ar. *Av.* 693 ff.) makes her prior to Eros (= Phanes), and this supposition suits the awful dignity of Nyx which Homer and '*Orpheus' alike emphasize, and the vague reference of *Aristotle (*Metaph.* 1071ᵇ27) to *theologoi* who derive everything from Night. Nyx was primarily a *mythographer's goddess, with little cult, but one may mention her connection with *oracles (not confined to Orphic literature, see Plut. *De sera* 22; schol. Pind. *Pyth. argumentum*). In Greek and Roman art her identification is problematic as she has no canonical form (fig. N on the Parthenon's east pediment, for example, may either be Nyx or *Selene).

LIMC, 'Astra' (A); 'Nyx' 6. 1 (1992), 939–41 (Nyx); 2. 1 (1984), 905–9 (Astra (A)). W. K. C. G.; A. J. S. S.

oasis, derived from Egyptian, was the Greek term for watered, habitable land in deserts, particularly in N. Africa. Though really depressions, oases were regarded as islands in a dried-up sea (Olympiodorus, *FHG* 4. 64–5). Those of Egypt were important as trading stations and as sources of wheat, dates, and alum. They were garrisoned by the Ptolemies (see PTOLEMY (1)) and Romans, and were linked to the Nile valley and each other by caravan. The Oasites were considered a separate race from the Egyptians. The oases of the Sahara were described by Herodotus (4. 181–5) as a chain extending from east to west at ten-day intervals. The most renowned oases of Egypt were (1) *Siwa—the Oasis of *Ammon on the border of Libya twelve days from *Memphis, famous for its oracle; (2–3) Kharga and Dakhla—Oasis Magna exterior and interior, both west of *Thebes (2); (4) Bahariya—Oasis Minor, 200 km. (125 miles) west of *Oxyrhynchus. Kellis in the Kharga oasis was capital of the Mōthite nome (see NOMOS (1)). All these have artesian water. (2–3) have produced numerous Greek inscriptions and *ostraca; (1) is rich in ancient sites (sanctuaries, tombs). See WATER.

G. Wagner, *Les Oasis d'Égypte* (1987). L. L. Giddy, *Egyptian Oases* (1987).
W. E. H. C.

oath (in Roman law) An oath (*iusiurandum*) was used in several ways in the stage before the magistrate (*in iure*) in Classical Roman civil proceedings. (1) In almost every action either party might exact from the other, on pain of losing the case, an oath that he was proceeding in good faith (*iusiurandum calumniae*). Justinian made this oath compulsory for both parties and for their representatives (see JUSTINIAN'S CODIFICATION). (2) In a few actions only the plaintiff might invite the defendant to swear to the validity of his claim (*deferre iusiurandum*); the defendant might then either swear and win the case, or refuse and lose, or invite the plaintiff to swear instead, with the same alternatives before him (*referre iusiurandum*), or, finally, might invite the plaintiff to swear a *iusiurandum calumniae*. (3) Either party in any action (or at any stage of any dispute) might invite the other to swear an oath of this kind; the other might either swear and win or refuse with impunity. These last two oaths are distinguished by the modern names of *iusiurandum necessarium* and *voluntarium* respectively.

In the proceedings *apud iudicem* an oath served only as evidence or (*iusiurandum in litem*) for the assessment by the plaintiff of the value of the thing in issue in certain actions.   B. N.

oaths An oath (ὅρκος, *iusiurandum*, see preceding article) was a statement (assertory) or promise (promissory) strengthened by the invocation of a god as a witness and often with the addition of a *curse in case of perjury. A defendant in a lawsuit, for example, might swear by a god that his testimony was truthful and might specify the punishment for perjury. If the oath was false, the god, by effecting the provisions of the curse, would punish the individual, not for lying in court but for committing perjury. (See EVIDENCE, ANCIENT ATTITUDES TO.) Throughout antiquity oaths were required of signatories to treaties, of parties to legal disputes, commercial and private contracts, conspiracies, and marriages, of governmental officials, judges, and jurors, and, particularly by the Romans, of soldiers (*sacramentum*), and, under the empire, of citizens to affirm their allegiance to the emperor.

Virtually any deity could be invoked as a witness, but in formal oaths the Greeks often called upon a triad of gods representing the sky, earth, and sea (*Helios or *Zeus, Ge (see GAIA) or *Demeter, and *Poseidon); the Romans upon *Jupiter (Dius Fidius) and 'all the gods'. Everyday language was apparently sprinkled with casual oaths, and Greek women often invoked *Artemis, the men Zeus or *Heracles; Roman women named Castor and the men Hercules or Pollux (see DIOSCURI). The gods themselves swore by the *Styx. The punishment for perjury, when specified, might suit the particular circumstances of the oath-taker, but often called for 'the complete destruction of the perjuror and his family' (Andoc. 1. 98; Plin. *Pan.* 64). An oath itself could be strengthened by being taken in a *sanctuary (Pl. *Prt.* 328 BC) or by an act of sympathetic *magic. As an example of the latter, in *Homer's *Iliad* (3. 295 ff.) the combatants, as they prayed to Zeus and poured a *libation to accompany their oath, said, 'Whoever first cause suffering contrary to this oath, may their brains flow to the ground like this wine.' Animal *sacrifice was performed for the same purpose (Dem. 23. 67 ff.; Livy 1. 24. 5 ff.).

The maintenance of oaths was an essential element of public and personal piety. The Spartans imagined that their defeats at *Pylos and elsewhere were caused by their disregard of an oath (Thuc. 7. 18. 2), and *Plato (1) saw in the growing disregard of oaths signs of a breakdown of belief in the gods (Pl. *Leg.* 12. 948b–e; cf. E. *Med.* 492–5; see ATHEISM). See also MEDICINE, § 1.5 (Hippocratic Oath).

R. Hirzel, *Der Eid* (1902); J. Plescia, *The Oath and Perjury in Ancient Greece* (1970).   J. D. M.

obligation (*obligatio*) was defined by Justinian (see JUSTINIAN'S CODIFICATION) as 'a legal tie which binds us to the necessity of making some performance in accordance with the laws of our state' (*Inst.* 3. 13 pr.). It implied both 'duty' and 'liability': a relation existed in terms of which the debtor ought to make performance; only if he failed to comply with this duty did he become liable in the sense that his body and/or property were exposed to execution. Ancient Roman law, in contrast, had merely been concerned with liability: payment of a composition (if a wrongful act had been committed) or performance of whatever a person had undertaken to do (like repayment of a loan in the case of *nexum) was merely a means of warding off the impending execution to which the victim of the wrong or the lender were entitled by virtue of a pledge-like power of seizure over the body of wrongdoer or borrower. The carving out of this very advanced concept of an *obligatio* and the development of a law of obligations was one of the great contributions of Classical Roman jurisprudence to the science of law. Obligations could arise, according to Justinian's famous scheme (*Inst.* 3. 13. 2) from a contract, as though from a contract (*quasi ex contractu*), from a wrong, or as though from a wrong (*quasi ex maleficio*). Justinian, who appears to have delighted in the number four, proceeded to give a fourfold subdivision of contractual obligations and mentioned four delicts—*furtum* (*theft); *rapina* (robbery); *damnum* (wrongful damage); *iniuria* (insult)—as well as four quasi-delicts: *iudex qui litem suam fecit* (the judge who makes a case his own); *deiectum vel effusum* (pouring or throwing things out of buildings); *positum vel suspensum* (things placed or hanging which might endanger the traffic if they fell); *furtum vel damnum in navi aut caupone aut stabulo* (stealing or damaging property entrusted to a sea carrier, innkeeper, or stablekeeper). Payment of money not due (*indebitum solutum*) and unsolicited services (*negotiorum gestio*) were two of the most important sources of quasi-contractual obligations.

E. Betti, *La struttura dell' obbligazione romana* (1955); M. Kaser, *Römisches Privatrecht*, 1, (2nd edn. 1971), 146 ff., 474 ff.; R. Hochstein, *Obligationes quasi ex delicto* (1971); O. Behrends, *Der Zwölftafelprozess* (1974); M. Talamanca, *Enciclopedia del diritto*, 29 (1979), 1 ff.; R. Zimmermann, *The Law of Obligations* (1990), 1 ff.   R. Z.

Obsequens (*RE* 2), **Iulius,** tabulator of Roman prodigies (see PORTENTS), most plausibly dated to the 4th or early 5th cent. AD. His collection covered prodigies from 249 to 12 BC, and is extant for 190–12. It is based on *Livy, though comparison with books 37–45 shows that he exercised selectivity; he also notes the events which he thought the omens presaged or reflected. There is little basis for the common view that he knew Livy only or largely in *epitome.

Ed. O. Rossbach (1910), with Livian *Periochae.* P. L. Schmidt, *Iulius Obsequens und das Problem der Livius-Epitome* (1968).   C. B. R. P.

Oceanus (geographical) A circumambient ocean-river, the final destination of all streams, predates Greek and Roman culture, appears in *Homer and *Hesiod, and was confirmed by geographical theory: the accessible land-mass could only cover a small portion of the earth's surface. Some Homeric commentators thought that Homer had deliberately practised *exokeanismos*—removing the experience of *Odysseus into a world beyond the domain of factuality. *Phoenician contacts with the metalliferous and fertile Guadalquivir valley (*Tartessus) took them into Atlantic waters early, and that Greeks followed quite soon is reflected in *Herodotus (1)'s story of the voyage of Colaeus (4. 152). Such pioneer navigators were a feature of the literary tradition about the Ocean from at least the 6th cent., and exchanges certainly reached the Atlantic coasts of Gaul and S. Britain from the Classical period. Southward exploration to verify the circumnavigability of Africa (see AFRICA (LIBYA), EXPLORATION; EUDOXUS (3)), and northward to explore the seas around Europe were inconclusive, and the idea that the *Caspian Sea was an inlet like the *Red Sea, the *Persian Gulf, and the *Mediterranean

itself, persisted. The Indian Ocean, despite its size and the tides that in the Atlantic were regarded as a distinctive and worrying feature of Ocean, was regarded as analogous to these other inlets rather than being a part of Ocean proper; but the crossing to Britain, conversely, was, for political purposes, represented as going beyond Ocean in its most awesome sense.

J. Romm, *The Edges of the Earth in Ancient Thought* (1992).   N. P.

Oceanus (mythological), son of *Uranus (Sky) and Ge (*Gaia, Earth), husband of *Tethys (a combination probably derived from the Babylonian creation-epic *Enuma Elis*), and father of the Oceanids and river-gods (Hes. *Th.* 133, 364); the name has no *Indo-European etymology and is probably a loan-word. The Homeric Oceanus is the river encircling the whole world, from which through subterranean connections issue all other rivers; its sources are in the west where the sun sets. Monsters such as Gorgons (see GORGO / MEDUSA), *Hecatoncheires, *Hesperides, Geryoneus, and outlandish tribes such as *Cimmerians, Aethiopians (see ETHIOPIA), and *pygmies, live by the waters of Oceanus (*Il.* 3. 3; *Od.* 1. 22; 2. 13).

In Greek theories of the world Oceanus is conceived as the great cosmic power (*Il.* 14. 201, 246, 302), water, through which all life grows, and in Greek mythology as a benign old god. Sometimes the elemental, sometimes the personal, aspect is more emphasized. The belief that sun and stars rise and set in the ocean is expressed mythologically in the statement that stars bathe in Oceanus (*Il.* 18. 489), and the Sun traverses it in a golden bowl by night to get back to the east (Mimnermus fr. 12 West). See HELIOS. The rise of rational geographical investigation in *Herodotus (1) and others narrowed the significance of Oceanus down to the geographical term of 'Ocean'.

In art Oceanus appears early (François vase), is represented on the famous Gigantomachy (see GIANTS) of *Pergamum, and becomes really common in Roman times, especially on *sarcophagi, with Earth as a counterpart. See TITAN.

H. A. Cahn, *LIMC* 'Okeanos'.   G. M. A. H.; J. N. B.

Ocellus (or Occelus) of *Lucania occurs in *Iamblichus (2)'s list of Pythagoreans (*VP* 36; see PYTHAGORAS (1)), along with a brother, Occilus, but the surviving work *On the Nature of the Universe* bearing his name and known as early as the 1st cent. BC is certainly spurious. It shows considerable traces of Aristotelian influence (e.g. arguments for the eternity of the world), as well as many Platonist formulations (see ARISTOTLE; PLATO (1)), and may probably be dated around 150 BC.

Ed. R. Harder (Berlin, 1926).   J. M. D.

Ocnus ("Οκνος, 'Hesitancy' personified), a proverbial figure made famous by *Polygnotus' Underworld mural in the Cnidian *leschē* (club-house for the citizens of *Cnidos) at *Delphi (Paus. 10. 29. 1). The painter showed him seated in *Hades, plaiting a straw rope which an ass, behind him, ate up as fast as he could weave it; presumably, since for the Greeks the future lies 'behind', the allegorical point was that chronic indecision can lead only to futile consequences (though Pausanias was told by the locals that Ocnus, in life, had been a hard-working man whose wife spent all his money). It may also be relevant that 'donkey' (ὄνος) is the Greek for windlass; as if winches 'ate' rope. His eternal labour recalls that of the Danaides (see DANAUS); he looks like a popular moralist's humorous, scaled-down version of the great criminals in hell.

LIMC 7. 1 (1994), 33–5.   A. H. G.

Ocriculum, near modern Otricoli, an *Umbrian settlement on the *Tiber, and later on the *via Flaminia. It became allied to Rome early (in 308 or 297/95 BC), and was sacked in the *Social War (3). A theatre, amphitheatre, baths, and other structures survive from the Roman town, which remained important in the late empire, and was probably sacked by the *Lombards. T. *Annius Milo had a villa there.

T. Ashby and R. Fell, *JRS* 1921, 163 ff; C. Pietrangeli, *Otricoli* (1978).
E. T. S.; T. W. P.

Octavia (1) (*PIR*² O 65), daughter of C. *Octavius and Ancharia and so half-sister of *Augustus, married Sextus Appuleius; their sons Sextus and Marcus were consuls in 29 and 20 BC respectively.

Syme, *Rom. Rev.*, see index; M. W. Singer, *TAPA* 1948, 268 ff.   T. J. C.

Octavia (2) (*PIR*² O 66), daughter of C. *Octavius and *Atia (1), and sister of *Augustus, married (by 54 BC) C. *Claudius Marcellus (1). In 40 Marcellus died and, to seal the Pact of Brundisium, she was immediately married to Antony (M. *Antonius (2)). She spent the winters of 39/8 and 38/7 with him in Athens, and in 37 helped with the negotiations which led to the Pact of Tarentum. When he returned to the east, Antony left her behind. In 35 Octavian (the future Augustus) sent her to Antony with token reinforcements for his army; Antony forbade her to proceed beyond Athens. She rejected Octavian's advice to leave Antony's house, and though divorced by him in 32 brought up all his surviving children by *Fulvia and *Cleopatra VII along with their two daughters and her three children by Marcellus. Her nobility, humanity, and loyalty won her wide esteem and sympathy. She died in 11 BC. The Porticus Octaviae in Rome (see Nash, *Pict. Dict. Rome*) was named after her.

Syme, *Rom. Rev*, see index; M. W. Singer, *CJ* 1947, 173 ff.
PORTRAITURE *CAH*, pl. 4. 166 f.; H. Bartels, *Studien zum Frauenporträt der aug. Zeit* (1963), 14 ff.; V. H. Poulsen, *Les Portraits romains*, 1 (1962), 76 f.   G. W. R.; T. J. C.

Octavia See CLAUDIA OCTAVIA.

Octavia, the one extant *fabula praetexta*, dramatizes in 983 lines the fate of *Nero's neglected empress (see CLAUDIA OCTAVIA). It is generally doubted that L. *Annaeus Seneca (2), who is brought in as a character trying to restrain Nero's cruelty with Stoic advice, can be its author. Style and metrics, though different in several respects from Senecan practice, do not yield conclusive evidence about the author. Moreover, *Iulia Agrippina's ghost foretells Nero's doom in words so true that they were probably written after Nero's death in 65. Specifically Senecan features, however, are clearly visible in the structural organization of the play, and especially in the portrayal of Nero as a cruel tyrant who embodies the opposite of the ideal Stoic ruler set forth in Seneca's own *De clementia*; see KINGSHIP.

RE 17. 2. Texts: with Senecan *corpus*, most recently by O. Zwierlein (1986); with comm.: G. Ballaira (1974); L. Y. Whitman (1978). F. Giancotti, *L'Ottavia attribuita a Seneca* (1954); C. J. Herington, *CQ* 1961; D. F. Sutton, *The Dramaturgy of the O.* (1973); G. Williams, in J. Elsner-J. Masters (eds.), *Reflections of Nero* (1994).   A. Schi.

Octavian See AUGUSTUS.

Octavius (*RE* 15), **Gaius,** from a wealthy equestrian family (see EQUITES) of *Velitrae, rose to the praetorship (61 BC) (see PRAETOR) and governed *Macedonia with conspicuous ability. (Being the father of *Augustus, he receives unreserved praise in our sources, for instance Velleius, 2. 59. 2). By his first wife Anchaia he was

father of *Octavia (1) and by *Atia (1) of *Octavia (2) and Gaius, the later Augustus.

Syme, *Rom. Rev*, index.   T. J. C.; R. J. S.

Octavius (1) (*RE* 17), **Gnaeus,** was one of two envoys sent to various Greek states by C. *Hostilius Mancinus in 170 BC, assuring them of their rights and strengthening their loyalty to Rome. In 168 he was praetor in charge of the fleet; *Perseus (2) surrendered to him at *Samothrace after the battle of *Pydna. He triumphed in 167 and built a portico (Porticus Octavia) near the Circus Flaminius. He was consul 165, and in 163 led the embassy sent to the East after the death of *Antiochus (4) IV Epiphanes with orders to burn the *Seleucids' warships and hamstring their *elephants; in 162 he was murdered in the *gymnasium at Laodicea. He had been a member of the *decemviri sacris faciundis since 169.

Briscoe, *Hist.* 1969, 63–4.   J. Br.

Octavius (2) (*RE* 20), **Gnaeus** failed to be elected aedile, but became consul 87 BC with L. *Cornelius Cinna (1), whose attempt to reverse *Sulla's legislation he opposed, finally driving Cinna and his supporters out of Rome after a massacre in the Forum and thus starting what Cicero calls the *bellum Octavianum*. He had Cinna deposed and the *flamen Dialis* (see FLAMINES) L. *Cornelius Merula elected in his place, thus assuring himself of sole power. Cinna collected an army, was joined by C. *Marius (1), Cn. *Papirius Carbo and Q. *Sertorius. Besieged in Rome, Octavius summoned Cn. *Pompeius Strabo and Q. *Caecilius Metellus Pius to aid him, but after Pompeius' death Metellus withdrew and his army disintegrated. The senate finally surrendered Rome to Cinna, and Octavius, refusing to flee, was killed wearing his consular robes and his head was displayed in the Forum.

E. B.

Octavius (*RE* 31), **Marcus,** as tribune 133 BC (see TRIBUNI PLEBIS) vetoed the agrarian bill of Ti. *Sempronius Gracchus (3) and, refusing (contrary to constitutional tradition) to withdraw his veto (see INTERCESSIO), was deposed by the *concilium plebis* on Gracchus' motion. This action, equally contrary to tradition, had dangerous implications, which, when pointed out by a senior ex-consul, turned many men of all classes against Gracchus; but it was never judged illegal. A bill directed at Octavius by C. *Sempronius Gracchus in 123 was withdrawn, allegedly at *Cornelia (1)'s request.

For bibliog. see SEMPRONIUS GRACCHUS (3), TI.   E. B.

Octavius (*RE* 67) **Lampadio, Gaius,** a Roman scholar and (probably) *freedman, who arranged *Naevius' Bellum Punicum in seven books. He was allegedly influenced by the critic *Crates (3) of Mallus, in the second half of the 2nd cent. BC (Suet. *Gramm.* 2).

Herzog–Schmidt, § 193.   R. A. K.

Octavius (*RE* 59; suppl. 12,500) **Tidius Tossianus Iavolenus Priscus, Gaius (**or **Lucius),** the jurist **Iavolenus Priscus,** came from either Nedinum (Nadin) in former Yugoslavia or *Iguvium (Gubbio) in Umbria (see UMBRIANS). He had an active career in imperial administration and the law. He may have been promoted from equestrian to senatorial standing with praetorian rank. His earliest recorded posts involved two legionary commands, and the role of legal assessor (*iuridicus*) in Britain. After his consulship (AD 86), he was governor of Upper Germany (90; see GERMANIA), then of *Syria, possibly at the end of *Domitian's reign, and soon after proconsul of *Africa. He also served on *Trajan's *consilium, and was an eminent jurist: *Pliny (2) describes him as deeply involved in public affairs and a recognized expert on civil law, but rather eccentric (*Ep.* 6. 15). He was the last sole head of the Sabinian law school (see MASURIUS SABINUS) and, probably as a teaching aid, epitomized and commented on *Antistius Labeo, *Cassius Longinus (2), and *Plautius, thus initiating an important genre of legal literature, besides publishing fifteen books (*libri*) of letters (*epistulae*) dealing with difficult legal problems.

Lenel, *Pal.* 1. 277–316; Bremer (1901) 111. 394–494; *HLL* 3 (forthcoming) § 395.7: Kunkel (1967), 138–40; B. Eckhardt, *Iavoleni Epistulae* (Berlin 1978); U. Manthe, *Die libri ex Cassio des Iavolenus Priscus* (1982); Honoré (1962), 153–4. J. B. C.; T. H.

Octavius Titinius Capito, Gnaeus (*PIR²* O 62), a Roman knight (see EQUITES) who after a successful army career held the post of *ab epistulis* (imperial secretary) continuously under *Domitian, *Nerva, and *Trajan, and later became *praefectus vigilum* (*ILS* 1448; see VIGILES). He was a friend of the Younger *Pliny (2), whom he advised to write history and received a notable reply (*Ep.* 5. 8). A painstaking patron of literature (ibid. 8. 12), he himself wrote of the deaths of famous men: he also commemorated the traditional republican 'martyrs' by keeping statues of *Brutus, *Cassius, and M. *Porcius Cato (2) in his house. G. E. F. C.

October horse See MARS.

Odaenathus See SEPTIMIUS ODAENATHUS.

odeum (ᾠδεῖον), a small theatre or roofed hall for musical competitions and other assemblages.

The Odeum of *Pericles (1) at Athens, an exceptional structure, placed in the area of the then undeveloped theatre, was a square hall having a pyramidal roof supported on rows of internal columns supposedly utilising the masts taken from the Persian fleet after the battle of *Salamis (Vitr. *De Arch.* 5. 9. 1). It was used for the choral elements in the competitions of the *Dionysia festival (see PROAGON). There are no traces of the provision for the audience, but *Plutarch (*Per.* 13) says it contained seats.

Developed odea are generally smaller and, when roofed, avoid the need for supports intruding into the auditorium. They usually take the form of miniature theatres, with seats arranged in a semicircle, contained within a rectangular outer structure which often truncates the uppermost rows of seats. Since this form may also be used for *theatres (e.g. *Priene, *Thera) the distinction depends on size, the larger theatres not being roofed. There is an odeum at *Argos (2), where the seating was originally straight-sided; in origin it was a political meeting place or law court, rather than a concert hall. The developed type occurs at *Pompeii, where inscriptions refer to it as a covered theatre (*theatrum tectum*). A large example, the Odeum of Agrippa (see VIPSANIUS AGRIPPA, M.), filled the centre of the Athenian agora. This had a free span of 25 m (82 ft.), roofed only as a result of Roman technological advance (and even this collapsed, so that the span had to be reduced).

Such odea with curvilinear seats are Roman rather than Hellenistic in date, though in architectural terms they cannot be distinguished from similar political buildings such as the Bouleuterion of *Antiochus (4) IV at *Miletus. *Pausanias (3) also calls the large theatre built by Ti. *Claudius Atticus Herodes (2) on the south side of the acropolis of Athens an odeum; architecturally it

is indistinguishable from a normal Roman theatre, unless, as has been suggested, it was roofed. See ATHENS, TOPOGRAPHY.

J. Travlos, *Pictorial Dictionary of Ancient Athens* (1971), under the entries, Odeion of Agrippa; Odeion of Herodes; Odeion of Perikles. R. A. T.

Odoacer, ruler of Italy (AD 476–93), was the son of Edeco, an important follower of *Attila, and perhaps a Germanic Scirian. He served under Roman commanders before rebelling in 476, deposing the last emperor, *Romulus Augustulus. He recognized the sovereignty of the eastern emperor and cultivated the Roman senate. An Arian (see ARIUS), he had good relations with the Catholic Church and little trouble in governing Italy. He was overthrown after 489 by *Theoderic (1), and murdered at a banquet in *Ravenna.

A. H. M. Jones, *JRS* 1962; A. Chastagnol, *Le Sénat romain sous le règne d'Odoacre* (1966). P. J. H.

Odysseus ('Οδυσσεύς, Latin Ulixes from one of several Greek variants; hence English Ulysses), king of *Ithaca; son of *Laertes and *Anticlea; husband of *Penelope; hero of *Homer's *Odyssey*.

In Homer's *Iliad*, despite his out-of-the-way kingdom, Odysseus is already one of the most prominent of the Greek heroes. He displays martial prowess (e.g. at 11. 310–488, where he delays the rout of the Greeks), courage and resourcefulness (e.g. in the *Doloneia* of book 10, a late addition), and above all wisdom and diplomacy (e.g. at 2. 169–335, where he prevents the Greek army from disbanding, and in the embassy to *Achilles, especially 9. 223–306). He shows little of the skill in deceit which is characteristic of him in the *Odyssey*, but such epithets as 'much enduring' and 'cunning', which occur in both epics, must refer to his exploits after the Trojan War (see TROY), and show that these were always his principal claim to fame.

In the *Odyssey* he is in some ways the typical 'trickster' of folktales, who uses guile and deception to defeat stronger opponents. His maternal grandfather is the knavish *Autolycus (1) (19. 392–466). Besides spear and sword he uses the bow, which was often considered a less manly weapon, and he even procures arrow-poison (1. 261–2). He not only resorts to trickery by necessity but sometimes revels in it, as when he boasts of his triumph over the Cyclops (9. 473–525; see CYCLOPES); and his lying tales on Ithaca are elaborated with relish, as Athena observes (13. 291–5). But Homer was concerned to make him a worthy hero, not just for a folktale, but for an epic. Books 1–4, where his son *Telemachus takes centre-stage, are largely devoted to building up our sense of his greatness: he is the ideal king, whose return is necessary to establish order on Ithaca, and a friend deeply honoured by *Nestor and *Menelaus. When we first see him in book 5—longing for home after his long detention by *Calypso, then no sooner released than shipwrecked—the emphasis is on his noble patience and endurance. At his lowest point, naked and destitute on the shore of *Scheria in Book 6, he is still resourceful, and can be seen by the princess *Nausicaa as an ideal husband (6. 239–45). Even in the fantastic and magical episodes which he relates as bard-like storyteller to the Phaeacians in books 9–12 (the Lotus-Eaters, the Cyclops, the Bag of the Winds, the *Laestrygonians, the witch *Circe, the visit to the Underworld, the *Sirens, *Scylla and *Charybdis, the Cattle of the Sun), there is pathos as well as adventure. When he finally reaches Ithaca he spends much of the rest of the poem (books 17–21) in the most humiliating condition, disguised as a beggar in his own house; but in his final revenge over Penelope's suitors, although he takes the crafty and necessary precaution of removing their weapons

(19. 1–52), the main emphasis is on his strength in stringing the great bow and the skill with which he wields it (books 21–2).

(For the works mentioned in the following paragraph see EPIC CYCLE.) A later epic, the *Telegonia* of *Eugammon of Cyrene, continued the story with further travels and martial adventures for Odysseus, who was finally killed unwittingly by Telegonus, his son by Circe. Other early poetry seems to have presented him less favourably. In the *Cypria* he feigned madness to evade his obligation to join the Trojan expedition, but the trick was exposed by *Palamedes. In revenge he and *Diomedes (2) later brought about Palamedes' death. In the *Little Iliad* Odysseus and Diomedes stole the *Palladium, a Trojan talisman; and by some accounts Odysseus tried to kill Diomedes on the way back. The dispute with *Aias over the arms of Achilles, first mentioned at *Odyssey* 11. 543–51, was related in the *Aethiopis* and *Little Iliad*, and *Pindar (*Nemean* 8. 23–34) claims that Odysseus won the arms by dishonest trickery. The killing of the infant Astyanax was attributed to *Neoptolemus (1) by the *Little Iliad* but to Odysseus by the *Sack of Troy.*

The tragedians tended to be similarly unfavourable. *Sophocles, while presenting a noble and magnanimous Odysseus in *Aias*, makes him an unprincipled cynic in *Philoctetes*. *Euripides depicts the Homeric Odysseus straightforwardly in *Cyclops*, but evidently made him a villain in his lost *Palamedes* (as does the *sophist *Gorgias (1) in his *Defence of Palamedes*), and his character in other plays (on stage in *Hecuba*, reported elsewhere) is in keeping with this. His detractors now often call him the son, not of Laertes, but of the criminal *Sisyphus, who had allegedly seduced Anticlea before her marriage.

*Virgil's references to Ulixes in *Aeneid* 2 follow the Euripidean conception (ignoring a tradition which made him a founder of Rome and father of *Latinus), as does Seneca (L. *Annaeus Seneca (2)) in *Troades*. The dispute over the arms of Achilles, treated as a rhetorical debate by *Antisthenes (1), is again so treated by *Ovid, *Met.* 13.

At a few sites Odysseus was honoured as a cult hero, evidently because of his prestige in epic. His name has been found on a dedication on Ithaca.

In art he is always a popular figure. The more spectacular adventures are illustrated especially often in the Archaic period (the blinding of Polyphemus (see CYCLOPES) and the escape under the ram are found as early as the seventh century). Later these are joined by quieter subjects, such as the embassy to Achilles and the dispute over the arms. From the 5th cent. Odysseus is often depicted in a conical hat, the *pilos*.

> LIMC 'Odysseus'; W. B. Stanford, *The Ulysses Theme*[2] (1963), and with J. V. Luce, *The Quest for Odysseus* (1974). Cult: L. Farnell, *Greek Hero-Cults* (1921), 411.   A. L. B.

Odyssey See HOMER; ODYSSEUS.

Oea (neo-Punic Wy't; mod. Tripoli), a harbour town, one of three cities which gave its name to *Tripolitania or 'three-*polis*-land' (*Sabratha and *Lepcis Magna are the others). Oea was the only city of the three to survive into medieval times (thus the modern name). It is assumed to have been a *Phoenician foundation, but it is not explicitly so stated by *Sallust (*Iug.* 19. 1), and the earliest archaeological evidence is so far of the 5th cent. BC. Under Rome a city of *Africa Proconsularis, it became a *colonia* in the 2nd cent. AD. In 69 Oea summoned the Garamantes to her aid against Lepcis, and Valerius Festus had to drive them out of the province (Tac. *Hist.* 4. 50). It was visited by *Apuleius (*Apol.* 73), who married a rich widow from Oea; he indicates that Punic

was the principal language spoken in his day (*Apol.* 98). It was a bishopric by AD 256. Little remains of ancient Oea except a well-preserved four-way arch of AD 163–4. A temple to the *genius coloniae* is known nearby, and some painted tombs survive from its necropolis.

> PECS 639; D. E. L. Haynes, *Antiquities of Tripolitania* (1956), 101–6; S. Aurigemma, *L'arco quadrifronte di Marco Aurelio e di Lucio Vero in Tripoli*, Suppl. to Libya Antiqua 3 (1969).   O. B.; R. J. A. W.

Oebalus, an early Spartan king, who had a hero-shrine (see HERO-CULT) at Sparta (Paus. 3. 15. 10). He has no legend, merely a place in several mutually contradictory genealogies, for which see Wörner in Roscher's *Lexikon*, under the name. Hence *Oebalius*, *Oebalides*, etc., in Latin poetry often mean Spartan, and the name itself is now and then used for some minor character of Spartan or Peloponnesian origin (as Verg. *Aen.* 7. 734).

> H. J. R.

Oecists See ARCHĒGETĒS; FOUNDERS, CITY; MĒTROPOLIS (sense (*a*)).

Oecles (Οἰκλῆς) or **Oicleus** (Οἰκλέους), in mythology, father of *Amphiaraus (Aesch. *Sept.* 609 and often).   S. H.

Oedipus, son of Laius, the king of *Thebes (1) who killed his father and married his mother. The name appears to mean 'with swollen foot', but the reason for this is obscure, as the explanation given by ancient authors—that his feet were swollen because his ankles were pierced when he was exposed as a baby—looks like rationalizing invention.

*Homer's *Iliad* mentions him only (23. 679) in the context of the funeral games held after his death, implying that he died at Thebes and probably in battle. Homer's *Odyssey*, however (11. 271–80), tells how he unwittingly killed his father and married his mother Epicaste (the later Iocasta), but the gods soon made this known (this version allows no time for the couple to have children) and Epicaste hanged herself. Oedipus continued to reign at Thebes, suffering all the woes that a mother's *Erinyes can inflict.

Of the epic *Oedipodia* (see EPIC CYCLE) we know little except that it mentioned the *Sphinx (also in *Hesiod, *Theog.* 326), who killed *Haemon (3) son of *Creon (1) and must have been killed (perhaps in fight) by Oedipus, and that Oedipus had children, not by his mother, but by a second wife, Euryganeia. The children must have included *Eteocles and Polynices, and probably also *Antigone (1) and Ismene.

Another epic, the *Thebais*, told how Oedipus, now probably blind, twice cursed his sons, first when Polynices disobeyed him by serving him wine in a gold cup on a silver table (fr. 2, cf. *TrGF* 2 fr. adesp. 458), and again when his sons served him the wrong joint of meat (fr. 3). He prayed that they would quarrel over their patrimony and die at each other's hands, and the epic went on to describe the Theban War that ensued. See SEVEN AGAINST THEBES.

It is uncertain when Oedipus was first said to have had children by his mother (see INCEST), and when the motif of his *exile arose. In a fragment of *Stesichorus (*PMGF* 222b) the mother of Eteocles and Polynices attempts to mediate between them, presumably after the death of Oedipus, but she could be either Iocasta (Epicaste) or Euryganeia. Pindar, *Pyth.* 4. 263–9, may allude to Oedipus in exile.

In 467 *Aeschylus produced a tetralogy consisting of *Laius*, *Oedipus*, the surviving *Seven against Thebes*, and the satyr-play *Sphinx*. Though much is debatable, the outlines of the Oedipus story can be gathered from fragments and from allusions in the

Oeneus

Septem (esp. 742–91). Laius learned from the *Delphic oracle that to save the city he must die childless. Overcome by lust, however, he begot Oedipus, and sought to have the baby exposed. Oedipus somehow survived to kill his father at a fork in the road near Potniae. He came to Thebes and rid the city of the man-eating Sphinx, probably by answering its riddle. He married Iocasta, became an honoured king, and begot Eteocles and Polynices. The patricide and incest came to light (we do not know how, but the prophet *Tiresias may have played a role), and Oedipus in his anguish blinded himself and cursed the sons born of the incest: they were to divide their patrimony with the sword. In the *Septem* Oedipus is dead, having probably died at Thebes.

*Sophocles' *Antigone* (49–54) mentions how Oedipus blinded himself and died and Iocasta hanged herself. But Sophocles' *Oedipus Tyrannus* (*King Oedipus*) became the definitive account. Here Laius received an *oracle from *Apollo that his son would kill him, so he ordered a shepherd to expose the infant Oedipus on Mt. Cithaeron. The shepherd, however, took pity on the baby, and Oedipus survived to be brought up as the son of *Polybus (1), king of *Corinth, and his wife *Merope (3). An oracle warned him that he would kill his father and marry his mother, so he fled from Corinth. At a junction of three roads near Daulis he killed Laius in a quarrel, not knowing who he was. Coming to Thebes he answered the riddle of the Sphinx, married Iocasta, and became king. When the play opens, the city is being ravaged by a *plague, caused, so the oracle reveals, by the polluting presence of the killer of Laius (see POLLUTION). Oedipus, an intelligent and benevolent king, pronounces a *curse on the unknown killer and begins an investigation, which ends in the discovery of the whole truth. Iocasta hangs herself and Oedipus blinds himself with pins from her dress. The ending is problematic, as Oedipus does not go into the immediate exile foreshadowed earlier but remains, for the moment, in the palace.

*Euripides too wrote an *Oedipus*, in which the king was blinded by the servants of Laius, not by his own hand. In Euripides' *Phoenissae* he is self-blinded and is still living in the palace at the time of his sons' death.

At the end of his life Sophocles returned to Oedipus with his *Oedipus at Colonus*. Here the blind man, led by Antigone, comes to the grove of the Eumenides (see ERINYES) at *Colonos near Athens, where he knows that he must die. Protected by *Theseus, he resists the attempts of Polynices and Iocasta's brother Creon, who banished him from Thebes, to bring him back there for their selfish purposes. He curses his sons for their neglect, and finally, called by the gods, he dies mysteriously at a spot known only to Theseus, where his angry corpse will protect Athens against Theban attack. Tombs and *hero-cults of Oedipus are reported from Colonos and from Athens itself (among other places), but the antiquity of these, and their relation to Sophocles' play (where he has *no* tomb), are uncertain.

Roman authors of an *Oedipus* tragedy included *Caesar. The *Oedipus* of Seneca (L. *Annaeus Seneca (2)) is based on Sophocles' *Oedipus Tyrannus*. The role of Oedipus in *Statius' *Thebaid* is derived from Euripides' *Phoenissae*.

In art the confrontation with the Sphinx is often portrayed, other episodes more rarely. See *LIMC* 7. 1 (1994), 1–15.

C. Robert, *Oidipus* (1915); L. Edmunds, *Harv. Stud.* 1981, 221 ff. and *Oedipus* (1985); J. R. March, *The Creative Poet* (*BICS* Suppl. 49, 1987), 119–54; D. J. Mastronarde, *Euripides: Phoenissae* (1994), 17–30.

A. L. B.

Oeneus, mythical king of Calydon in *Aetolia and father by Althaea of *Meleager (1) and *Deianira. His name (from οἶνος, *wine) and the story in Hyginus (*Fab.* 129) that Deianira's real father was *Dionysus suggest that he was a hero associated with that god. His second wife Periboea was the mother of *Diomedes (2)'s father *Tydeus, whose paternity is variously given; either Tydeus or Diomedes took the aged Oeneus' side in a quarrel over the throne with his brother Agrius (Pherecydes *FGrH* 3 F 122, Apollod. 1. 8. 4–6, Paus. 2. 25. 2).

An *Attic hero Oeneus was among the tribal *eponymoi; he was said to be son of Dionysus (Dem. 60. 30) or of Pandion (Paus. 1. 5. 2), but we know nothing else about him.

E. Ke.

Oeniadae, a city of southern *Acarnania located at modern Trikardokastro near the mouth of the *Achelous river. Hostile to Athens in the 450s (*Pericles (1) unsuccessfully besieged the place), Oeniadae eventually joined the Athenians and served as a base for her warships in the 4th cent. In the 3rd cent., it fell to *Aetolia, was restored to Acarnania by *Philip (3) V in 219, returned to Aetolia in 212 by M. *Valerius Laevinus, and finally returned to Acarnania by Rome in 189. Thereafter, progressive silting of its harbours by the nearby river diminished the city's usefulness. Impressive remains, including city walls, a theatre and shipsheds, still mark the site of the ancient city.

PECS 640; W. M. Murray, *The Coastal Sites of Western Akarnania*, diss. (1982).

W. M. M.

Oenoanda, a city in N. *Lycia, whose Hellenistic walls enclose ruins largely of the Roman period. The city was also known as Termessus Minor, having been colonised from the homonymous Pisidian city (see PISIDIA) probably around 200 BC. It has produced four remarkable inscriptions, whose importance is out of all proportion to their unremarkable provenance: the enormous genealogical inscription carved on the funerary monument of Licinia Flavilla, which traces the family's descent back to the Spartan Cleander, allegedly founder of Oenoanda's northern neighbour Cibyra (*IGRom* 3. 500; see GENEALOGY); the most complete epigraphic dossier from the Roman world concerning the creation of an *agon*, an artistic festival, by a local citizen C. Iulius Demosthenes in AD 125 (see AGŌNES); the literary works of the local Epicurean philosopher *Diogenes (5), which were engraved for public display in the centre of the Roman city; and a theological *oracle of the 3rd cent. AD, which was to be quoted by *Lactantius and is a key text for the understanding of pagan religious mentality in the later Roman empire (see ANGELS).

M. Wörrle, *Stadt und Fest im kaiserzeitlichen Kleinasien* (1988); J. Coulton, *Anat. Stud.* 1982, 115–31 (Termessus Minor); J. Coulton, *PCPS* 1983, 1–20.

S. M.

Oenomaus See HIPPODAMIA (1); PELOPS.

Oenomaus of Gadara (fl. *c.* AD 120), *Cynic; seemingly the *pagan philosopher 'Abnimos' of the *Talmud, so perhaps a Hellenized *Jew (see HELLENISM). He wrote: 'Exposure of the Charlatans' (or 'Against the Oracles'), a witty and inventive polemic extensively preserved by Eusebius; various works effectively known by title only; and tragedies (lost). An ambitious and important literary voice of later Cynicism, he imitated *Diogenes (2) (*Politeia* and tragedies), *Crates (2) (verse parodies) and *Menippus (1) of Gadara ('Exposure of the Charlatans'). He himself became a literary influence on *Lucian, a philosophical influence on fourth-century Cynics, a target of *Julian's vilification and a source for Christians of arguments against paganism. See also CYNICS.

J. Hammerstaedt, *Die Orakelkritik des Kynikers Oenomaus* (1988), *ANRW*
2. 36. 4 (1990), 2834–65, and in M. O. Goulet-Cazé and R. Goulet
(eds.), *Le cynisme ancien et ses prolongements* (1993), 399–418.   J. L. Mo.

Oenone (Οἰνώνη), a *nymph of Mt. Ida, loved by *Paris. When
he deserted her for *Helen she was bitterly jealous, and on
learning that he had been wounded by *Philoctetes with one of
*Heracles' arrows, she refused to cure him. Relenting too late,
she came to *Troy and found him already dead, whereat she
hanged herself or leapt upon his funeral pyre.

Apollod. 3. 154–5; Parth. 4; Quint. Smyrn. 10. 259 ff., all with small
variations; *LIMC* 7. 1 (1994), 23–6.   H. J. R.

Oenophyta See ORCHOMENUS (1); THEBES (1), *Historic*.

Oenopides of Chios (fl. late 5th cent. BC) was said by *Eudemus
to have 'discovered' the obliquity of the ecliptic and some constructions in elementary geometry. A luni-solar period ('Great
Year') of 59 years and 730 months is credibly attributed to him.

DK 41. See I. Bulmer-Thomas, *Dict. Sci. Biogr.* 10. 179 ff.   G. J. T.

Ofonius Tigellinus, (see *RE*), a low-born Sicilian, was brought
up in the households of the emperor *Gaius (1)'s sisters, and in
AD 39 was exiled for adultery with them. Under *Claudius he
lived in obscurity, but *Nero made him first *praefectus vigilum* (see
VIGILES) and then in 62 *praefectus praetorio*. He recommended
the numerous executions of the following years; and for his part
in unmasking the Pisonian conspiracy of 65 (see C. CALPURNIUS
PISO (2), C.) he was given triumphal ornaments and other distinctions. After accompanying Nero on his Greek tour, he deserted
him at the last, but after Nero's death he was removed from his
prefecture by his colleague *Nymphidius Sabinus. Through the
influence of *Vinius he lived unharmed through *Galba's reign,
but under *Otho he was forced to suicide (Tac. *Hist.* 1. 72).

G. E. F. C.; M. T. G.

Ogulnius (*RE* 5) **Gallus, Quintus** (consul 269 BC), as tribune
of the plebs (see TRIBUNI PLEBIS) together with his brother Gnaeus,
in 300 carried a law (*lex Ogulnia*), despite the opposition of Appius
*Claudius Caecus, by which the two major priestly colleges (see
PRIESTS) were to be shared between *patricians and plebeians (see
PLEBS). From then on five of the nine augurs (see AUGURES), and
four of the eight pontiffs (see PONTIFEX), were always plebeians
(Livy 10. 6–9). As curule aediles in 296 the Ogulnii used fines
from usurers for dedications and to set up near the *Ficus Ruminalis*
a statue-group of the infants *Romulus and Remus beneath the
teats of the she-wolf (Livy 10. 23. 11–12); in 269, when Q. Ogulnius was consul, this group appeared on the reverse of Rome's
earliest silver *coinage (Crawford, *RRC* no. 20). In 292, after a
*plague, Q. Ogulnius led a delegation to bring the serpent of
*Asclepius from *Epidaurus to Rome, and in 273 he was one of
three Roman ambassadors to the court of *Ptolemy (1) II.

P. T.; T. J. Co.

Ogygus (Ὤγυγος, etymology and meaning uncertain), a primeval king, generally of *Boeotia (as Paus. 9. 5. 1), but of *Lycia,
Steph. Byz. s.v. Ὠγυγία; of Egyptian *Thebes (2), schol. Lycophr.
1206; of the Titans (see TITAN), Theoph. *ad Autol.* 3. 29. The first
Deluge was in his time, Euseb. *Praep. Evang.* 10. 10. 7.

H. J. R.

oikists See ARCHĒGETĒS; FOUNDERS, CITY; MĒTROPOLIS (sense '*a*').

oil See OLIVE.

ointment (μύρον, *unguentum*) was used for medical and cosmetic
purposes, and in religious ceremonies and funeral rites (see DEAD,
DISPOSAL OF), in which the restorative, the aromatic, the sacrifi-

cial, and the sumptuary combined in varying degrees. Vegetable
oils and animal fats served as the vehicles for herbal remedies
and fragrant salves, lotions, and unguents. Exotic ingredients,
such as cassia (κασία, *casia*), cinnamon (κιννάμωμον,
cinnanmum), frankincense (λιβανωτός, *thur*), *myrrh (σμύρνα,
myrrha) were inevitably more costly and carried greater status.
Many of these were imported into the Mediterranean from
Arabia and beyond, either via Egypt or through the agency of
coastal cities that served as outlets for luxury goods brought
across the desert from the *Red Sea. The trade is well attested
for Hellenistic and Roman times, when it was largely in the hands
of *Nabataean merchants (see INCENSE; SPICES). At the point of
consumption, expensive ointments were kept in costly containers, of *gold (cf. Theoc. 15. 116), *silver, agate, rock-crystal
or *ivory; cheaper ones in vessels of alabaster, *bronze, *glass or
ceramic; the archaeological record is heavily biased in favour of
the latter.

RE 1 A 'Salben'; A. Schmidt, *Drogen und Drogenhandel im Altertum*
(1924); L. Casson, *The Periplus Maris Erythraei* (1989); G. Donato and
M. Seefried, *The Fragrant Past* (1989); H.-P. Bühler, *Antike Gefässe aus
Edelstein* (1973); G. M. A. Richter and M. J. Milne, *Shapes and Names of
Athenian vases* (1935).   L. E.; M. V.

Olbia, a city by the village of Parutino, near the mouth of the
Hypanis (Bug) and within easy reach of the estuary of the
*Borysthenes (Dnieper). The date of its foundation is derived
from archaeology and is placed *c*.550 BC, rather later than once
thought (cf. Ps.-Scymn. 804–12). Excavation has revealed buildings from the 6th cent. BC to the 4th cent. AD. Its history is divided
into two large periods, pre-Getic and post-Getic, divided by the
sack of the city by *Burebistas in the mid-1st. cent. BC.

From *c*.550 an *agora and *temenos are known, while monumental stone architecture was erected. From *c*.500 BC housing-
styles changed markedly: dug-out dwellings were replaced by
commonplace surface housing. A series of wine-presses have
been found: defensive structures are known from *c*.450 BC.
Archaeology also indicates the close relations between Olbia and
the peoples of the hinterland, which were sometimes tense (e.g.
Dittenberg. *Syll.* 495). Numerous small settlements fringed the
lagoons and waterways around Olbia. The island of Berezan was
of particular importance, situated at the mouth of the Dnieper
lagoon: settlement there now seems to have begun at much the
same time as at Olbia, contrary to the old view that it was the
first stage in the settlement of Olbia.

*Herodotus (1) visited Olbia, as did *Dio Cocceianus *c*. AD 100.
Dio presents an Olbia in decline, but hanging on to a Greek
identity. See also DIONYSUS; ORPHISM.

Y. Vinogradov, *Olbia* (1981), and *Politicheskaya istoria Ol'viyskovo polisa,
VII-I vv. do n.e.* (1989); A. J. Graham, *CAH* 3². 3 (1982), 124–9; D.
Kacharava and G. Kvirkvelia, *Goroda i poseleniya Prichernomor'ya
antichnoy epokhi* (1991), 188–201.   D. C. B.

Old Oligarch is the modern name given to a short pamphlet
about 5th-cent. BC Athens, preserved among the works of *Xenophon (1) and sometimes referred to as ps.-Xenophon, *Constitution of the Athenians*. There are three chapters.

The work aims to show that the *demos* (people) or lower
classes at Athens run affairs in their own interests, and it takes
the curious form of a salute from an anti-democratic viewpoint.
See OLIGARCHY. The author stresses the importance of the link
between *sea power and *democracy: 'it is right that the the the
poor and the *demos* have more power there than the noble and
rich because it is the *demos* which mans the fleet' (1. 2).

Old Persian

The ostensible date is disputed (440s or—the more usual dating—mid-420s?). See however below.

It is hard to know what to make of the treatise: nothing else quite like it survives from the 5th cent. and it had little influence on later anti-democratic thought in antiquity (no contemporary author quotes it). It may belong in the category of *symposium literature, note the second person singular at 1.8—perhaps a sign that what we have is the dazzling second half of a kind of *dialogue written to entertain. If so, we cannot be sure how seriously to take it or whether it constitutes good first-hand evidence for what it mentions. There are passages which would be valuable evidence for Classical Athens if they were straightforwardly usable (and they are often so used), e.g. 1. 10 on the licence allowed to slaves (see SLAVERY), 1. 16 on the use of the law-courts for the maintenance of the democracy (see LAW AND PROCEDURE, ATHENIAN), ch. 2 on sea power generally, 2. 18 on the refusal of the people to let dramatists mock the *demos* (something less than outright censorship may be meant; but see INTOLERANCE, INTELLECTUAL AND RELIGIOUS), the figure of 400 trierarchs (3. 4; see TRIERARCHY), and occasional Athenian imperial toleration of non-democratic regimes (3. 11). But some of this could have been concocted out of *Thucydides (2), cf. e.g. 1. 8 with Thuc. 3. 45. 6 for the link between *freedom and ruling others; and the end of 3. 11 (*Messenians) could be elaborated from Thuc. 1. 102 ff. If the above doubts are justified, the 'date' question reduces to one of intended *dramatic* date and there may be no such single date, i.e. we cannot even press the argument from the assumed existence of the Athenian Empire (see DELIAN LEAGUE). But the above is heretical and the usual view sees the pamphlet as good evidence for facts and attitudes about Athenian democracy.

EDITIONS AND COMMENTARIES E. Kalinka (1913); H. Frisch (1942); G. W. Bowersock (in Loeb Xenophon vol. 7) with Lewis *CR* 1969, 45 ff.; J. Moore *Aristotle and Xenophon on Democracy and Oligarchy* (1975), 19–61; LACTOR (xli).

MODERN STUDIES A. Momigliano, *Secondo contributo* (1962), 57–67 (sea power); A. W. Gomme, *More Essays* (1962) 38 ff.; G. W. Bowersock, *HSCP* 1966, 33 ff.; W. G. Forrest, *Klio*, 1970, and *YClS* 1975; W. R. Connor, *New Politicians of Fifth-Century Athens* (1971), 207 ff.; S. Cataldi, *La Democrazia ateniese e gli alleati* (1984) (on 1. 14–18); J. T. Roberts, *Athens on Trial* (1994), 52 ff.; G. de Ste. Croix, *The Origins of the Peloponnesian War* (1972), app. 6; M. Treu, *RE* 9A, 1928–82. S. H.

Old Persian See PERSIAN, OLD.

Olen, mythical poet, before *Musaeus (1); a *Hyperborean or *Lycian; said to have brought the worship of *Apollo and *Artemis from Lycia to *Delos, where he celebrated their birth among the Hyperboreans in hymns which continued to be recited there (Hdt. 4. 35; Callim. *Hy.* 4 304–5); individual Delian hymns of Olen are mentioned by *Pausanias (3) in several places.

M. L. West, *The Orphic Poems* (1983), 53. R. C. T. P.

oligarchy ('the rule of the few'), with monarchy (see KINGSHIP) and democracy one of the three basic categories of constitution commonly used by the Greeks from the 5th cent. BC onwards. Whereas a democratic regime gave basic political rights to all adult males in the free non-immigrant population, and had slight or non-existent limitations on eligibility for office, an oligarchic regime excluded some of the free population even from basic political rights, and might exclude even more of them from office-holding and reduce the amount of business which came the way of the full citizen body. In practice those who were admitted to political activity by democracies but not by oligarchies were the poor, and *Aristotle, after listing the three categories of constitu-

tion and distinguishing correct and deviant versions of each, went on to say that really oligarchy is the rule of the rich and democracy is the rule of the poor (*Pol.* 3. 1279^a 22–1280^a 6).

Before the 5th cent. the constitutions of most states were in fact oligarchic, though the term did not yet exist. In the 5th cent. Athens developed a self-conscious democracy (see DEMOCRACY, ATHENIAN) and posed as a champion of democracy elsewhere in Greece, while those who disliked that labelled themselves oligarchic, and Sparta, though not itself a typical oligarchy, posed as the champion of oligarchies. At the end of the 5th cent. there were oligarchic revolutions in Athens, resulting in the regimes of the *Four Hundred and of the (moderate but still not fully democratic) Five Thousand in 411–410, and of the *Thirty Tyrants in 404–403. In the Hellenistic period the distinction between oligarchy and democracy was still sometimes taken seriously, but it mattered less than in the classical period as even states which were democratic in form tended in practice to be run by the rich; and government by the rich was preferred by the Romans. See also DEMOCRACY, NON-ATHENIAN AND POST-CLASSICAL; PATRIOS POLITEIA; POLITICS.

L. Whibley, *Greek Oligarchies* (1896); V. Ehrenberg, *The Greek State*^{2} (1969); M. Ostwald, *Popular Sovereignty*, see index; P. J. Rhodes, *CAH* 6^2 (1994), 580. V. E.; P. J. R.

olive The olive is probably native to the Mediterranean region. It is long-lived and highly drought-resistant, though sensitive to frost, and thrives best at relatively low altitudes. Olives generally only crop every other year, and usually trees are regionally synchronized. Despite the attempts of farmers from antiquity to the present to break this habit, it has never successfully been circumvented.

Olives are easily propagated by cuttings, ovules (trunk growths, Gk. *premna*), or by grafting, a well-known technique in the classical world. Domesticated scions were frequently grafted onto wild stocks. Trees grown from cuttings planted in a nursery beds seem to have been more characteristic of Roman than Greek regimes. Greek farmers apparently preferred planting ovules, which have a greater success-rate under conditions of water-stress than cuttings. Olives do not grow true to type from seed. Many varieties were known and cultivated for both oil and table use in classical antiquity.

Rarely grown under a monocultural system, olives were usually part of mixed farming regimes, including arable and other tree crops since cropping and yields can be erratic. Sometimes olive cultivation was combined with *pastoralism, as in M. *Porcius Cato (1)'s (*Agr.* 10) model olive grove which included a shepherd, 100 sheep, and a swineherd. Sheep ate grass and weed growth under trees, while pigs utilized the presscake.

Olives are harvested in autumn and winter. Greeks and Romans felt that the best-quality oil came from 'white' ('green') olives, picked early, a belief not in accord with modern practice. Ripe, 'black' olives contain more oil than green ones—the scarcity of oil in the latter may partially explain why it was more highly valued. Today the crucial factor is felt to be acidity, which increases in oil which is old, or which has been made from olives (black or green) stored for some time between picking and pressing.

Olives can be processed for either table-olives or oil: they are not edible raw. The most basic table-olives are packed in salt, but the Roman agronomists provide other recipes. Olive oil was used for food, medicine, *lighting, perfume (see OINTMENT), and bathing, as well as *athletics.

Producing oil entails crushing, pressing, and separating. Many different devices were known in antiquity for crushing and pressing olives. The simplest crusher is a flat bed with a stone roller. However the Romans (and probably the Greeks) believed that crushing the olive stones (almost inevitable with most machines) lowered oil quality. For luxury-quality oil they tried to keep crushed stones to a minimum, although this reduced the yield. Machines were invented to achieve this end, although it is questionable how effectively they worked. The most common olive crusher found in archaeological contexts is the rotary mill generally known as the *trapetum*, invented around the 4th cent. BC (it is debated whether the earliest examples from *Chios and *Olynthus used one millstone or two). They remained common throughout the Roman world until late antiquity. See MILLS. The most usual presses were beam presses. Earlier examples were weighted with large stones, but later many used capstans. Screw presses came into use during Roman times, though the date of their invention is uncertain, perhaps around the 2nd cent. BC. Crushed olives were placed in bags or frails on the pressbed (many stone examples survive), and the press was fastened. The first pressing produced best quality 'green' oil, sometimes kept separate and sold at high prices. Hot water was poured on the frails before further, lower quality, pressings.

The mixed oil, water, and olive juice (*amurca*) was left to settle in vats until the oil floated. Then oil was skimmed off the top or the waste let out via a tap from the bottom. Oil was stored in large jars (*dolia*, *pithoi*) or sold in *amphorae*. Though most ordinary oil was probably consumed locally, high-quality oil was a luxury product traded over long distances, like vintage wine. Certain regions, e.g. *Attica, *Samos, *Venafrum, *Baetica, and Cyrenaica (see CYRENE; LIBYA), became famous for oil. In the case of Attica, the olive was an important symbol of Athena and Athens and oil from the sacred trees (*moriai*) was given as prizes at the Panathenaic Games (see PANATHENAEA). However, it was probably never the most important Attic crop and oil may not have been the primary export. See AGRICULTURE; AMPHORAE.

A. Pease, *RE* 17 (1937), 2454 ff., 'Oleum'; J. Hörle, *RE* 6 A 2 (1937), 1727 ff., 'Torcular' and 2187 ff. 'Trapetum'; M.-C. Amouretti and J.-P. Brun (eds.), *La Production du vin et de l'huile en Méditerranée* (1993); A. G. Drachmann, *Ancient Oil Mills and Presses* (1932); L. Foxhall, *Olive Cultivation In Greek Farming: The Ancient Economy Revisited* (1995).

L. F.

Olympia, *panhellenic sanctuary of *Zeus located in hill country beside the river *Alpheus in *Elis.

1. Before 500   There is evidence of extensive prehistoric settlement in the vicinity including a large EH tumulus in the Altis which remained visible into the early iron age, MH houses, and Mycenaean tombs (see MYCENAEAN CIVILIZATION) in the vicinity of the archaeological museum.

Votives (tripods and figurines) in an ash layer in the Altis indicate cult activity at least from the late 10th cent. (perhaps with an early ash altar). The first Olympiad was traditionally dated 776 BC (see TIME-RECKONING). According to *Pindar, *Heracles founded the *Olympian games; an alternative tradition attributed the foundation to *Pelops after his victory over Oenomaus (see next article). A sequence of wells on the eastern side of the sanctuary beginning in the late 8th cent. served visitors.

The first temple (ascribed to *Hera) was built *c.*590. A row of eleven treasuries (primarily of W. Greek i.e. Italian and Sicilian states) lay under Cronus Hill. The first phase of the *stadium (*c.* mid-6th cent.) consisted of a simple track west of the later

stadium, extending into the Altis. The first bouleuterion (building for the *boulē) was built in *c.*520. From at least the 6th cent., sanctuary and festival were managed by Elis. (See also PHEIDON; PISA.)

C. A. M.

2. Classical   The Greeks of the west (see (1) above) always had close connections with Olympia, cp. ML 10 of *c.*525 (treaty between *Sybaris and the Serdaioi); ML 29, bronze helmet commemorating *Hieron (1) I's victory over the *Etruscans at *Cumae in 474 (cf. *BCH* 1960, 721 and *SEG* 33 no. 328); ML 57 (victory dedication of *Tarentum over *Thurii) and *I. Olympia* 266 (statues dedicated by Praxiteles of *Syracuse and *Camarina). But Olympia, the paramount athletic sanctuary (P. *Ol.* 1), was properly panhellenic. Thus the *Persian Wars were commemorated at Olympia, though less spectacularly than at *Delphi; for instance (Mallwitz 32 ff.) the Athenians dedicated at Olympia a helmet 'taken from the Medes'; another splendid helmet-dedication by *Miltiades might be from Marathon (see MARATHON, BATTLE OF) but is probably earlier. The battle of *Plataea prompted a colossal bronze Zeus (Paus. 5. 23), inscribed with a roll of honour of the participating states, including Ionian Athens in second place after Sparta. But the *Dorian character of Olympia is marked, even if we deny political symbolism to the labours of *Heracles depicted on the temple metopes of the mid-5th-cent. Zeus temple, the second to be built within the Altis. Thus the Olympian Games of 428 were turned by Sparta into an overtly anti-Athenian meeting, Thuc. 3. 8 ff. But Athens was never, even in the *Peloponnesian War, formally denied access to Olympia, any more than to Delphi; and to balance ML 22 (Spartan victory dedication over *Messenians, 490s?) we have, from the 420s, ML 74, the lovely *Nike of *Paeonius—a dedication by Athens' friends the Messenians at *Naupactus (cf. Thuc. 1. 103). We do hear of a classical exclusion from the Olympic games, but of Sparta not Athens: Thuc. 5. 49–50, a rare Thucydidean glimpse of the continuing political importance of *athletics.   S. H.

3. Hellenistic and Roman   Hellenistic kings affirmed by their dedications Olympia's panhellenic standing. New buildings included a *palaestra, *gymnasium, and (*c.*100 BC) the earliest Roman-style *baths found in Greece. Roman domination, signalled by the dedications of L. *Mummius (146 BC), at first saw Olympia decline in prestige: by 30 BC the games had dwindled into an essentially local festival. Imperial patronage prompted a marked revival: M. *Vipsanius Agrippa repaired the temple of Zeus and both *Tiberius and *Germanicus won chariot-races, to be outdone by *Nero, who performed in person at irregularly convened games (67) including (uniquely) musical contests (full refs.: N. Kennell, *AJPhil.* 1988, 241). In the 2nd cent., with the popularity of the games never greater, Olympia once more attracted orators (see SECOND SOPHISTIC), as well as cultural *tourism (*Phidias' statue of Zeus was among the *Seven Wonders of the ancient world); facilities saw a final expansion, including a *nymphaeum, attracting conservative attack (Lucian, *Peregr.* 19). From fear of the *Heruli, the sanctuary was fortified (*c.*268) at the cost of many classical monuments. Cult survived well into the 4th cent. A Christian *basilica was built *c.*400–450; the temple was only toppled by earthquake in the 6th cent.

A. Mallwitz, *Olympia und seine Bauten* (1972), and in W. Raschke, *The Archaeology of the Olympics* (1988); B. J. Peiser, *Das dunkle Zeitalter Olympias* (1993), *Olympia Bericht*, 5, 10, 11 and *Olympische Forschungen* vols. 3, 5, 7, 8, 10, 12, 13; A. Hönle, *Olympia in der Politik der griechischen Staatenwelt* (1968); C. Morgan, *Athletes and Oracles: The Transformation of Olympia and Delphi in the Eighth Century BC* (1990); N. J. Richardson, *CAH* 5² (1992), 223 ff.   A. J. S. S.

Olympiad

Olympiad, four-year period between occurrences of the *Olympian Games; see HIPPIAS (2); TIMAEUS (2); TIME-RECKONING. See also D. M. Lewis, *Notes and Queries* 1960, 403.

Olympian Games These were held in the precinct of *Zeus (the Altis) at *Olympia, once every four years in August or September. They were in honour of Zeus, and were said to commemorate the victory of *Pelops in his chariot-race with king Oenomaus of Pisa (cf. Pindar, *Ol.* 1. 67–88), but also to have been founded by *Heracles (Pind. *Ol.* 10. 24–77). Lists of victors begin in 776 BC (see HIPPIAS (2); TIME-RECKONING), and a catalogue of the winners down to AD 217 is preserved by *Eusebius. They were abolished in AD 393 by the emperor *Theodosius (2) I.

The original contest was the *stadion*, a sprint of about 200 m. (see STADIUM). Other contests were added between the late 8th and 5th cents. BC, including races for chariots and single horses. Early victors were often from Sparta, but by the 6th cent. competitors were coming from all over the Greek world. In the 5th cent. the festival lasted five days. The main religious ceremony was the *sacrifice of a hecatomb on the great altar of Zeus (Paus. 5. 13. 8). The contests were preceded by a procession from *Elis (the host-city) to Olympia, and a ceremony at which athletes and officials swore an oath to observe the rules of the games, and they were followed by victory celebrations, with processions and banquets. From 472 BC the main sacrifice was preceded by the *pentathlon and horse-races, and on subsequent days there were the boys' contests, men's foot-races, *wrestling, *boxing, *pankration, and finally the race in armour. The prizes were crowns of wild *olive.

RE 17. 2520–36, 18. 1–45 (Ziehen); E. N. Gardner, *Olympia: Its History and Remains* (1925); H. Bengtson, *Die Olympischen Spiele in der Antike* (2nd edn. 1972); H.-V. Herrmann, *Olympia, Heiligtum und Wettkampfstätte* (1972); M. I. Finley and H. W. Pleket, *The Olympic Games* (1976); see also bibliog. for OLYMPIA. N. J. R.

Olympian gods, Olympians See APHRODITE; APOLLO; ARES; ARTEMIS; ATHENA; DEMETER; DIONYSUS; HEPHAESTUS; HERA; HERMES; POSEIDON; ZEUS (these are the twelve on the *Parthenon frieze; but see RELIGION, GREEK, *Gods and other cult figures*).

Olympias, daughter of Neoptolemus of Molossia (see MOLOSSI), married *Philip (1) II of Macedon (c.357 BC) and bore him two children, *Alexander (3) 'the Great' and Cleopatra. Her husband's last marriage (to Cleopatra, niece of Attalus) led to a serious quarrel in which she retired to her native *Epirus. Returning after Philip's assassination, she savagely murdered her erstwhile rival along with her infant daughter. After Alexander's departure (334) her relations with his viceroy, *Antipater (1), were turbulent, and by late 331 she had resumed residence in Epirus, which she treated as her fief. There she remained until 317, when *Polyperchon enlisted her aid against *Eurydice (2), who had disowned him and sided with *Cassander. She invoked the memory of her husband and son, and the royal couple fell into her hands without a blow. That good will disappeared after she forced Eurydice and her wretched consort to their deaths and conducted a bloody purge in Macedon. Her armies in turn melted away before Cassander and she was forced to surrender at *Pydna (spring 316). She was condemned by the Macedonian assembly (see ASSEMBLY, MACEDONIAN) and killed by relatives of her victims. Implacably passionate in her political hatreds, she was passionately devoted to ecstatic Dionysiac cults (see DIONYSUS; ECSTASY; MAENADS; WOMEN IN CULT), and her influence

may have helped engender his son's belief in his divinity. See RULER-CULT.

Berve, *Alexanderreich* ii. no. 381; *HM* 3 (1988). A. B. B.

Olympichus See LABRAUNDA.

Olympieum, the temple of *Zeus Olympius at Athens; begun by Antistates, Callaeschrus, and Antimachides, architects employed by *Pisistratus, but abandoned after the latter's death, and the expulsion of his son, *Hippias (1), and not resumed until *Antiochus (4) IV Epiphanes employed the Roman architect Cossutius (see COSSUTII) to continue the work. It was completed for *Hadrian. The Pisistratean building was planned as a Doric temple. Cossutius changed the order to Corinthian, but in general seems to have adhered to the original plan, dipteral at the sides, tripteral at the ends (Vitr. *De Arch.* 3. 2). The stylobate measured 41. 11 × 107. 89 m. (135 × 355. 75 ft.), and the Corinthian columns were 4. 88 m. (16. 89 ft.) in height. The capitals are carved from two blocks of marble. *Vitruvius says the temple was open-roofed (hypaethral), which may have been true in its unfinished state at that time. It would have been roofed when completed by Hadrian to contain a gold and ivory cult-statue. Hadrian certainly is responsible for the impressive buttressed peribolos wall, decorated with Corinthian columns on its interior, and with a gateway of Hymettan *marble (see HYMETTUS) on its north side.

W. B. Dinsmoor, *Architecture of Ancient Greece*³ (1950), 91, 280 f.; D. Willers, *Hadrians panhellenisches Programm* (1990); J. Travlos, *Pictorial Dictionary of Ancient Athens* (1971), under 'Olympieion'; R. Tölle-Kastenbein, *Das Olympieion in Athen* (1994). R. A. T.

Olympiodorus (1) (fl. 307–280 BC), democratic Athenian commander, secured *Aetolian help against *Cassander (c.306), whom he subsequently repulsed from *Elatea. At some time before 295 he rescued the *Piraeus from an attempted Macedonian capture (on the most probable interpretation of Paus. 1. 26. 3, the most important source for Olympiodorus' career, based on *Pausanias (3)'s knowledge of inscriptions); after the recapture of Athens by *Demetrius (4) Poliorcetes he became virtually tyrant, holding the archonship for two successive years (294–292). In 287 he led an insurrection against Macedon, seizing the Museum (see ATHENS, TOPOGRAPHY, *Pnyx*); later he helped *Demochares to take *Eleusis.

W. S. Ferguson, *Hellenistic Athens* (1911); W. B. Dinsmoor, *Archons of Athens* (1931); B. D. Meritt, *Hesp.* 1938; T. Sarikakis, *The Hoplite General in Athens* (1951), 23, 77; C. Habicht, *Untersuchungen zur politischen Geschichte Athens in 3. Jahrhundert v. Chr.* (1979), esp. 10 n. 42, 58 ff, 95–112, and *Pausanias' Guide to Ancient Greece* (1985), 90–92 and 100 f.; T. L. Shear, *Kallias of Sphettos and the Revolt of Athens in 286 BC*, Hesp. Supp. 17 (1978) see index.; G. M. A. Richter, *Portraits of the Greeks*, rev. R. R. R. Smith (1984), 170. F. W. W.; S. H.

Olympiodorus (2) of Gaza, pupil of the Academic sceptic *Carneades (who lived 214–129 BC).

Philodemus, *Index Acad.* col. 24. 6. G. S.

Olympiodorus (3) of *Thebes (2) (Egypt), Greek historian. Born before AD 380, he died after 425. We do not know where he lived, but we are informed that in 412 he was sent as an ambassador to the *Huns and in 415 he visited Athens. A typical Egyptian 'intellectual' of the later 4th cent., he remained a *pagan. He gave poetry as his profession, but is known to us as the writer of twenty-two books of history from AD 407 to 425 which, despite his paganism, he dedicated to the Christian emperor *Theodosius (3) II. The work is lost, but is known from over forty fragments as summarized by *Photius (*Bibl.* 80), and from the use made of it by *Philostorgius, *Sozomen, and *Zosimus. It contained many references to personal experiences, learned excurses, details on intellectual life at Athens, and on the life of the contemporary Roman governing class (his fragments on the city of Rome are particularly revealing) and of the *barbarians, and on superstitious beliefs which he probably shared. His work is notable for its rare favour to *Stilicho, and in general for its insight into early 5th-cent. western history, on which he was clearly well informed. He claimed *Homer as a countryman from Egyptian Thebes, and for twenty years owned a parrot which could 'dance, sing, call out names, and do other things'. A fragment of an epic poem, *Blemyomachia* or 'Battle against the Blemmyes', has been assigned to him.

Fragments in *FHG* 4. 58 and in R. C. Blockley, *The Fragmentary Classicising Historians of the Later Roman Empire* (1981–3). See also E. A. Thompson, *CQ* 1944, 43 ff.; A. Cameron, *Hist.* 1965, 470 ff.; J. F. Matthews, *JRS* 1970, 79 ff.. On the *Blemyomachia*, E. Livrea, *Beitr. zur Klass. Philol.* 1978.
J. F. Ma.

Olympus (1), the highest mountain in the Greek peninsula, dominating the *Aegean to the east and, to the north and south, the Macedonian and Thessalian plains. Rising at one point to 2,918 m. (9,573 ft.), with several other heights exceeding 2,900 m. (9,500 ft.), it forms a ponderous limestone cupola relieved by an aureole of lesser mountains and foothills pierced by valleys. Considered to be the throne of *Zeus and home of the gods, it held an important place in religion, mythology, and literature. Olympus proper was Macedonian; for the ancients the rest of the massif, shared between *Macedonia and *Thessaly, marked the northernmost limit of Greece. It was not, however, an obstacle to communication, which was achieved by way of *Tempe or the basin of Karya to the east, and the col of Petra and the valley of Titarese to the west.
B. H.

Olympus (2), in *Cyprus (mod. Troodos), rises to 1,952 m. (6,403 ft.) and constitutes the main mountain mass of the southwest part of the island. It is heavily wooded; on its lower slopes are modern mines of asbestos, and in antiquity there are said to have been gold-mines.
T. B. M.

Olynthus, a city north of *Potidaea on the mainland of the Chalcidic peninsula (see CHALCIDICE). Originally Bottiaean, it became a Greek city after its capture by *Persia (479 BC) and repopulation from Chalcidice; its position and mixed population made it the natural centre of Greek Chalcidice against attacks from Athens, Macedonia, and Sparta. In 433 the city was strengthened by further migration and received territory from Macedon (Thuc. 1. 58), and it soon became the capital of a Chalcidian Confederacy issuing federal coinage (see FEDERAL STATES); by 382 the growth of the Confederacy aroused the enmity of Sparta, which reduced Olynthus after a two-year siege and disbanded the Confederacy (Xen. *Hell.* 5. 2. 11 f.). When Sparta collapsed, Olynthus re-formed the Confederacy and resisted Athenian attacks on Amphipolis; when that city fell to *Philip (1) II of Macedon Olynthus allied with him against Athens (Diod. 16. 8), expelled the Athenian *cleruchy from Potidaea, and received Anthemus from Philip (357–356). Alarmed by the growing power of Philip, Olynthus intrigued with Athens, harboured rivals to the Macedonian throne, and with Athenian assistance defied Philip; the city fell to Philip by treachery (Dem. 19. 266 f.) and was destroyed (348). Excavations have revealed the layout of the city (see URBANISM).

A. B. West, *The History of the Chalcidic League* (1919); D. M. Robinson, *Excavations at Olynthus* (1929–52); M. Gude, *A History of Olynthus*

(1933); F. Hampl, *Hermes* 1935, 177 ff.; J. A. O. Larsen, *Greek Federal States* (1968), 55 ff; M. Zahrnt, *Olynth und die Chalkidier* (1971) and in *Lexicon der historischen Stätten* 488 f.
N. G. L. H.

Omphale, daughter of Iardanus and queen of *Lydia. According to Lichas at Soph. *Trach.* 248–80, *Heracles killed Iphitus, son of Eurytus of Oechalia, by treachery, and *Zeus decreed that he should expiate this crime by being sold in slavery to Omphale. Having endured this humiliation for a year, Heracles sacked Oechalia in revenge. Other details are given elsewhere, e.g. ps.-Apollod. 2. 6. 2–3: after the killing of Iphitus *Apollo refused to give Heracles an oracle, so Heracles carried off the *Delphic tripod. The quarrel was halted by Zeus, and Apollo then decreed that Heracles should be sold to Omphale for three years (not one year in this version) and the price should be paid to Eurytus. *Hermes took him to her, and during his servitude he performed various exploits. Others again, e.g. Ovid *Her.* 9. 53–118, say that as Omphale's slave Heracles had to dress as a woman and perform women's work (a paradox popular with Hellenistic and Roman authors), and that he was her lover and had one or more children (Lamus according to *Ovid, other names elsewhere) by her.

LIMC 7. 1 (1994), 45–53.
A. L. B.

omphalos, the navel. Metaphorically, the centre of a geographical area, e.g. the sea (*Odyssey* 1. 50), a city (= the agora: Pindar, fr. 75. 3 S–M), the world. Title to the last was claimed by *Delphi, at least by early in the classical period (e.g. *Pindar, *Pythian* 4. 74; *Bacchylides 4.4; *Aeschylus, *Eumenides* 40 and 166), and reinforced by identification with a concrete object, namely an egg- (or navel-) shaped stone. *Strabo 9. 3. 6 (419–20) gives the fullest description of the Delphic omphalos: it was covered by wreaths and had two images on it representing the two birds sent by *Zeus, one from the west, one from the east, meeting at Delphi. This stone was in the temple. The marble stone seen by *Pausanias (3) 10. 16. 3—and preserved to this day (Roux 130–1, cf. Morgan 225)—is a man-made object, the wreaths depicted in relief. It stood on the esplanade outside the temple.

Burkert (127) takes the omphalos to represent a sacrificial stone (see SACRIFICE, GREEK) over which a fleece or goatskin was spread. Hermann associates it with a pre-Greek chthonic goddess (see CHTHONIAN GODS). On Delphi's claim to be the centre of the world, see Defradas 108–110. The earliest known depiction of an omphaloid object is on a Tyrrhenian amphora of the second quarter of the 6th cent. (*CVA* Munich Inv. 1426), showing *Hector and *Achilles fighting over the body of *Troilus. Here it is draped with a cross-hatched covering and labelled 'altar'. The event took place in the sanctuary of *Apollo Thymbraios: the use of the omphalos to identify the site not only reflects the influence of Delphi, but also confirms the sacrificial function of the omphalos.

Burkert, *HN*; J. Defradas, *Les Thèmes de la propagande delphique* (1972); H. V. Herrmann, *Omphalos* (1959); C. Morgan, *Athletes and Oracles* (1990); G. Roux, *Delphes* (1976).
A. Sch.

Onasander, traditionally a Platonic philosopher, wrote a treatise on generalship, addressed to Quintus Veranius (consul AD 49, governor of *Britain 57–8). He emphasized the importance of strong character and moral uprightness in a commander, while offering sound advice on military psychology, troop deployment, and the use of stratagems. Onasander claimed a practical purpose: 'I may say confidently that my work will be a training school for good generals' (Prologue, 4).

TEXT AND DISCUSSION *Aeneas Tacticus, Asclepiodotus, Onasander* (Loeb, 1923). See also B. Campbell, *JRS* 1987, 13 ff.
J. B. C.

Onesicritus

Onesicritus, of Astypalaea, pupil of *Diogenes (2) and head steersman of *Alexander (3) the Great. On the ocean voyage of 325/4 he acted as lieutenant to *Nearchus, who gave a sharp account of their disagreement. Onesicritus later wrote an encomiastic account of Alexander (which had a reputation for fiction), purportedly modelled on *Xenophon (1)'s *Cyropaedia*. The extant citations focus upon *India, particularly the philosophy of the Brahmans and the kingdom of Musicanus which he depicted as an egalitarian utopia. But he was the first author to give details of Ceylon (see TAPROBANE), and his description of the southern ocean overlapped and perhaps inspired that of Nearchus.

FGrH 134; T. S. Brown, *Onesicritus* (1949); Pearson, *Lost Histories of Alexander*, ch. 4.   A. B. B.

Onomacritus See MUSAEUS (1).

Onomarchus, Phocian *stratēgos* (see PHOCIS). Second-in-command to *Philomelus, he rescued survivors of Neon (355). *Boeotian inaction allowed him to outface minority Phocian opposition and—after further pillaging of *Delphian treasuries—assemble a new army. With western *Locris pressured into alliance, Thronium enslaved and *Doris cowed (354), he invaded Boeotia (354, 353), re-establishing *Orchomenus (1) and seeking victory in the Third *Sacred War by targeting the principal antagonist. Both invasions were interrupted by developments in *Thessaly where his destabilizing Pheraean (see PHERAE) alliance provoked Macedonian intervention. In 354, after *Phayllus (2)'s failure, he defeated *Philip (1) II twice (a unique feat), driving him from Thessaly. Further northern conquests are controversial, but this was Phocis' apogee—symbolized by resumption of *naopoioi* meetings at Delphi (spring 353). Later that year, diverted from *Coronea and in loose conjunction with Athenian *triremes, Onomarchus faced Philip at Crocus Field (near *Pagasae) and died with c.6,000 soldiers in a bloodbath. His corpse was crucified and 3,000 prisoners were drowned as temple-robbers.

RE 18, 'Onomarchos' (1); J. Buckler, *Third Sacred War* (1989); *CAH* 6² (1994), see index.   C. J. T.

onomastics See NAMES, PERSONAL, GREEK and ROMAN.

Opellius (*RE* 2) **Macrinus, Marcus,** from *Mauretania, became praetorian prefect under *Caracalla and from motives of personal safety rather than ambition contrived his assassination (AD 217). Saluted Augustus by his troops (see AUGUSTUS, AUGUSTA, AS TITLES), he was the first Roman emperor who was not a senator. He ended Caracalla's *Parthian war, but his subsequent retrenchments in pay and the retention of the European legions in Syria made the army regret the death of Caracalla. Through the agency of *Iulia Maesa the story was put about that her grandson Bassianus was Caracalla's natural son. The soldiers of Legio III Gallica (see LEGION) saluted him emperor (218), and Macrinus was routed in a battle near *Antioch (1) and subsequently captured and put to death.

Herodian 4. 14–5. 4; Dio Cassius bk. 78; *B. M. Coins Rom. Emp.* 5, pp. ccxiii f., 494 ff.; H. Halfmann, *Itinera Principum* (1986); P. Cavuoto, *Macrino* (1983).   H. M. D. P.; J. F. Dr.

Ophellas, Macedonian officer under *Alexander (3) the Great and one of the *hetairoi*; sent by the satrap Ptolemy (see PTOLEMY (1) I) to subdue *Cyrene (322 BC). He became governor there; but we know nothing certain of his attitude in the Cyrenean revolt of 313/12, nor whether he was concerned with the constitutional reforms of that period (see CYRENE). At any rate, he became almost independent. There is little information about his relations with *Carthage. But he took part in *Agathocles (1)'s campaign to Africa, when, overestimating his forces, he hoped to subdue Carthage, and to found an African realm. Married to the Athenian Euthydice (Plut. *Dem.* 14 wrongly calls her Eurydice) of the Philaid family (see MILTIADES), he was able to induce many Athenians to join him. Having assembled a large body of Greek soldiers and colonists, he lost many of his men during the march through the desert. Eventually the two Greek generals joined forces. But soon after (probably 309), Ophellas was murdered by Agathocles, who took over his troops. Almost all the colonists perished. See also THIBRON (2).

Diod. 18. 21; 20. 40 ff.; Justin 22. 7. 4 ff.; Tod 203. V. Ehrenberg, *Polis und Imperium* (1965), 539 ff.; S. Applebaum, *Jews and Greeks in Ancient Cyrene* (1979) 48 ff.; K. Meister, *CAH* 7². 1 (1984), 396 ff.; E. Will, *HP* 1² (1979) 39, 69, 115 f.   V. E.; S. H.

Opheltes See NEMEA; NEMEAN GAMES.

Ophion ('Ὀφίων), Orphic god (see ORPHISM), husband of Eurynome and ruler of the universe before *Cronus; Ap. Rhod. 1. 503 ff.; Kern, *Orph. frag.* 98, no. 29.

ophthalmology was greatly advanced by the Greeks. Twenty operations were devised; until the beginning of the 18th cent. only four were added. The treatment of more than thirty *diseases was not essentially changed until the beginning of the 17th cent. This great achievement, mostly due to the Hellenistic physicians, was closely connected with the development of human *anatomy and probably with that of mathematical *optics. Other factors may have contributed to a special interest in the subject and thereby to the amazing success: the frequency of eye diseases in the Mediterranean world, the importance of sight for every human being, the valuation of sight peculiar to the Greeks.

As regards anatomy, the fabric of the eye was almost entirely unravelled. Seven membranes were distinguished, the optic nerve was accurately described. The theories of vision were less satisfactory, depending too much on the various philosophical conceptions; *Galen assumed that a sight-spirit proceeds from the brain along the nerves, envelops the object seen, and then returns to the crystalline humour, thus completing the act of vision. The explanation of diseases, in spite of all anatomical knowledge, was based mainly on humoral conceptions (see HUMOURS). The therapy consisted in certain dietetic measures and also in the local application of collyria, the great variety of which is attested by the innumerable seals of Roman oculists. As for *surgery, it suffices to refer to the astounding operations for cataract, as described by A. *Cornelius Celsus and as practised by *Antyllus (2nd c. AD).

TEXTS Celsus, bks. 6 and 7; Aetius, bk. 7; the only Greek treatise preserved: Th. Puschmann, 'Nachträge z. Alexander Trallianus', *Berl. Stud. f. class. Philol. u. Archaeol.* v. 2 (1886). Medieval compilations, probably based on ancient material now lost: P. Pansier, *Collectio ophthalmologica Veterum Auctorum* (1903), (fasc. vi ps.-Galen, *De oculis*). Fragments of the canon of ophthalmology, written by the Herophilean Demosthenes (1st cent. AD) and dependent on Herophilus' book on eye diseases, collected J. Hirschberg, *Arch. f. Gesch. d. Med.* (1918–19); concerning a medieval translation of this work, M. Wellmann, *Hermes*, 1903. Translation of Antyllus, M. Meyerhof, *Die Antike* 1933.

LITERATURE. General survey. J. Hirschberg, *Gesch. d. Augenheilkunde im Altertum* (1890); E. Savage-Smith, *DOP* 1984, 169–85. Theories of vision, G. M. Stratton, *Theophrastus and Greek Physiological Psychology* (1917); R. E. Siegel, *Galen on Sense Perception* (1970); D. Lindberg, *Theories of Vision* (1976); B. S. Eastwood, *The Elements of Vision* (1982). Operations, J. Ilberg, *Arch. pap.* (1908). Instruments, J. S. Milne, *Surgical

Instruments in Greek and Roman Times (1907); M. Feugère, *JRGZM* 1985, 436–508; R. Boyer, *Gallia*, 1990, 215–49. Stamps, *CIL* 13. 3. 100021 (Espérandieu); H. Nielsen, *Ancient Ophthalmological Agents* (1974). Oculists, V. Nutton, *Epigraphica* 1972, 16–29; H. Lieb, *ZPE* 43 (1981), 207–15; G. C. Boon, *Britannia* 14 (1983), 1–12. For attitudes to blindness, A. Esser, 'Das Antlitz der Blindheit in der Antike', *Janus* Suppl. 4 (1961).
L. E.; V. N.

Opillus (Opillius) See AURELIUS OPILLUS.

Opimius (*RE* 4), **Lucius**, as praetor 125 BC crushed the revolt of *Fregellae, but was not allowed to *triumph (Val. Max. 2. 8. 4). C. *Fannius, supported by C. *Sempronius Gracchus, defeated his bid for the consulship of 122, but he became consul 121 and, with his colleague Q. *Fabius Maximus Allobrogicus fighting in Gaul, was in charge of Rome. When Gracchus and M. *Fulvius Flaccus took to violence, he obtained the first '*senatus consultum ultimum' from the senate, interpreted it to give him unlimited powers, and crushed the rebellion with considerable loss of life. He then (we are told) condemned a large number to death in a special *quaestio. To commemorate this, he restored and dedicated the temple of *Concordia and built a *basilica in the Forum. Prosecuted by P. *Decius Subulo, he was defended by C. *Papirius Carbo (1) and acquitted (120). This secured constitutional recognition of the '*senatus consultum ultimum'. He headed a commission that divided Numidia between *Jugurtha and his brother Adherbal, was later convicted by the 'Gracchan jurors' (Cic. *Brut.* 128) of the court set up by C. *Mamilius Limetanus and went into exile. He was buried at *Dyrrhachium. The *wine produced in his consulship became proverbial for excellence.
E. B.

Oplontis (a name listed in Roman road-itineraries), between *Pompeii and *Herculaneum at Torre Annunziata, is famous for an extremely opulent and well-preserved *villa (which may have belonged to the family of *Poppaea Sabina) destroyed in the eruption of AD 79. Approached through a formal garden (see GARDENS) with avenues of oleanders, it comprised a series of atria and peristyles on the hill-slopes overlooking the sea: to the east was a huge piscina flanked by colonnades, statues and mature plane trees. The frescoed decoration is of great beauty and importance.

A. De Franciscis, *Die Pompejanischen Wandmalereien in der Villa von Oplontis* (1975); W. Jashemski, *The Gardens of Pompeii II* (1993).   N. P.

Oppian of *Cilicia (late 2nd cent. AD) wrote the *Halieutica*, a five-book hexameter work on sea-creatures and how to catch them (see FISHING). Amongst didactic poems the *Halieutica* is particularly noteworthy for its varied and imaginative use of myth and simile and for the way in which it assimilates man and fishes, hunter and hunted. At the end of the final book we learn of the horrid fate of the sponge-diver, as the sea at last gains its revenge.

The *Cynegetica*, a four-book hexameter poem on the animals and techniques of the chase, is ascribed to Oppian in the MSS but is clearly not by him: its metre is less polished, its use of epic language and syntax is less correct, and its style is more overtly rhetorical. The poet tells us that he is a Syrian from *Apamea, and the work is dedicated to the emperor *Caracalla; probably it was published between 212 and 217 AD. It contains several imitations and echoes of the *Halieutica*.

TEXT A. W. Mair (Loeb, 1928); *Cyn.* only, P. Boudreaux (1908).
CRITICISM B. Effe, *Dichtung u. Lehre* (1977) 137–53, 173–84.
N. H.

oppidum, 'town', principally a descriptive word for an urban nucleus, in descriptions the antithesis of a village (see PAGUS), the Roman equivalent for *polis as opposed to *kōmē*. Thus in the lex

Rubria (49 BC) the *oppida* are listed before their three subdivisions, *municipium, *colonia, *praefectura. Also a term of Roman administrative law for places from which a territory was practically administered, though that territory was not in formal terms allotted to the community juridically. Cities of the Latins (*Latini) which were incorporated into Roman territory before 89 became *oppida* in this sense, and the term was also used for communities of Roman citizens in the provinces. Both types eventually became ordinary *municipia*. In modern archaeological usage, *oppidum* has become a conventional label for the pre-Roman defensive enceintes of the iron age peoples of north-west Europe, especially the La Tène cultures (see CELTS).

For *oppida* in Italy, A. N. Sherwin-White, *Roman Citizenship*[2] (1973); in the north-west, B. Cunliffe, *Iron Age Communities in Britain*[3] (1991).
N. P.

Oppius (1) (*RE* 8), **Gaius**, as tribune of the plebs (see TRIBUNI PLEBIS) 215 BC, carried a law, occasioned by the exigencies of the Hannibalic War (see PUNIC WARS), imposing restrictions on women in respect of clothing, ownership of gold, and the use of horse-drawn vehicles. See LEX (2), *leges sumptuariae*. It was repealed in 195, despite strong opposition from M. *Porcius Cato (1). *Livy (34. 1–8) devotes considerable space to the debate, inventing a speech for Cato.

Briscoe, *Comm.* 34–7, 39–63.   J. Br.

Oppius (2) (*RE* 9), **Gaius**, *Caesar's friend of equestrian rank (see EQUITES) and, with L. *Cornelius Balbus (1), manager of his affairs. He corresponded with *Cicero on Caesar's behalf and after Caesar's death helped *Octavian. He wrote a number of biographies, certainly of P. *Cornelius Scipio Africanus, probably of Caesar and *Cassius; and he also wrote for *Octavian (perhaps *c.*32 BC) a pamphlet to prove that *Caesarion was not Caesar's son. Some ancient critics wrongly attributed to him the *Bellum Alexandrinum, *Bellum Africum, and *Bellum Hispaniense*.

Peter, *HRR* 2, pp. lxiii f., 46 ff.; Syme, *RR*, see index.
A. M.; T. J. C.; E. B.

Opramoas of Rhodiapolis in *Lycia is known from a huge inscription engraved on his temple tomb (*TAM* 2. 905), which records the honours decreed to him by the Lycian confederacy (see FEDERAL STATES) between AD 124 and 152 and the letters of the procurators and legates (see PROCURATOR; LEGATI) of Lycia-*Pamphylia and of the emperor *Antoninus Pius relative to these decrees, and from other inscriptions of Lycia. These imply that he gave more than 1,000,000 denarii to the confederacy and its cities for games, buildings, distributions, etc.; if an inscription from *Xanthus (*Xanthos* VII no. 67) is rightly attributed to him, further donations of some 900,000 denarii are also on record, and his benefactions offer the fullest documented example of civic *euergetism by an individual in the eastern provinces of the Roman Empire. His descendants became Roman senators but he played the role of *domi nobilis*.

P. Veyne, *Le Pain et le cirque* (1976), 295 ff.; R. Heberdey, *Opramoas Inschriften vom Heroon zu Rhodiapolis* (1897); A. Balland, *Fouilles de Xanthos* 7 (1981), 173–224; J. J. Coulton, *JHS* 1987, 171 ff. (contesting the attribution of the Xanthus inscription to him).   A. H. M. J.; S. M.

Ops, personified Abundance, seen by the Romans as very ancient (Varro, *Ling.* 5. 74), was honoured above all during the Opiconsiva of 25 August and the Opalia of 19 December, in conjunction with the god *Consus. Ops consiva was patron of the reserved (*condere, Consus) portion of the harvest (*ops*). This important function earned her a shrine in the *Regia (Varr. *Ling.* 5. 74; Festus 202,

19 ff. Lindsay), a temple on the *Capitol (Liv. 39. 22. 4, where she bears the epithet *opifera*, bearer of abundance), and, after her late association with a reinterpreted *Saturnus, an altar in company with Ceres, 'at the forum', on the Vicus iugarius (10 August AD 7, *Inscr. Ital.* 13. 2. 493), no doubt coinciding with a time of *famine (Dio Cass. 55. 31. 3).

> G. Dumézil, *Idées romaines* (1969), 289 ff.; Ziolkowski, *Temples* 122 ff.; P. Pouthier, *Ops et la conception romaine de l'abondance dans la religion romaine jusqu'à la mort d'Auguste* (1981, to be used with caution).
>
> J. Sch.

Optatianus Porfyrius, Publilius (*PLRE*. 649) (3rd–4th cent. AD), Latin poet. Exiled by *Constantine I, he owed his recall to a set of poems presented to the emperor. He was twice *praefectus urbi*. His poems are full of *acrostics and other ingenuities; some are arranged to have the shape of an object such as an altar or organ.

> TEXTS. E. Kluge (1926); with comm., G. Polara (1973).
> STUDIES. T. D. Barnes, *AJPhil.* 1975, 173–86; W. Levitan, *TAPA* 1985, 245 ff. J. H. D. S.

optics, in the modern sense (since Johannes Kepler in the 17th cent.) conceived as the science of light, among the ancients it is viewed primarily as the theory of vision. The ancient atomists (e.g. *Democritus, *Epicurus, *Lucretius; see ATOMISM) advocated an intromissionist theory: that vision entails the reception into the eye of corpuscular emanations from the surfaces of the objects seen. Alternative conceptions were proposed by *Aristotle (*De anima* 2. 7) and by the Stoics. But the most widely held view was extramissionist, as perhaps already formulated by Pythagoreans (see PYTHAGORAS (1)) in the 4th cent. BC: that vision is mediated by a type of fire emanating from the eye outward to the objects seen (cf. Pl. *Ti.* 45b–46c). This is the view adopted by *Euclid and those in the tradition of geometric optics. The visual ray (specifically *opsis*, or more generally *aktis*) proceeds along a straight line from eye to object (cf. Euc. *Catoptrica*, posts. 1–2, *Optica*, post. 1), so that the angle between the rays to the extremities of the object becomes the measure of its apparent size (*Optics*, post. 4). One thus can account geometrically for visual phenomena, such as why objects appear larger as they are nearer, why less of a sphere or cylinder is seen as the eye approaches it, why more distant points on an elevated plane appear lower, and so on. The earliest extant compilation of optical theorems is the *Optica* of Euclid (early 3rd cent. BC), which receives an interesting commentary and extensions by *Pappus of Alexandria (early 4th cent. AD; *Collection* 6. 80–103). The field is developed in its geometric, experimental, physical, and even psychological aspects in the *Optica* attributed to *Ptolemy (4) (mid-2nd cent. AD), of which there is extant only a partial text in Latin via a lost Arabic translation. Separate treatises are extant also in the subfield of *catoptrics, or vision mediated by mirrors. See also OPHTHALMOLOGY.

> J. L. Heiberg (ed.), *Euclidis Opera*, 5 (1895); A. Lejeune (ed.), *Optique de Claude Ptolémée*², (1989), and *Euclide et Ptolémée* (1948); D. C. Lindberg, *Theories of Vision from al-Kindi to Kepler* (1976) ch. 1; W. R. Knorr, *Archives internationales d'histoire des sciences* 35 (1985), 28–105; G. Simon, *Le Regard, l'être et l'apparence dans l'optique de l'antiquité* (1988). W. R. K.

optimates, populares Perhaps following the model of Greek, Romans seem from an early time to have used words for 'good' (*bonus*, sup. *optimus*) to denote high birth and social standing, as well as moral excellence, qualities the upper class regarded as inherently combined. The social meaning is already found in *Plautus and *Ennius, though 'optimates' in a political sense

does not appear in our sources until the 1st cent. BC. These 'best' men naturally assumed the right to rule the state. A 4th-cent. *lex Ovinia* ordered the censors to enrol in the senate *optimum quemque* ('all the best men'), *patricians and plebeians (see PLEBS). In due course this was understood to mean all men elected to high office (*de facto* limited to a small upper class). The senate was in charge of making policy, guided by the new *nobilitas*. Its successful leadership in the Second *Punic War and the great wars in the east that followed led to unquestioning acceptance of its authority, though the assemblies' rights were respected, poverty was alleviated by colonization and distribution (at times reluctant) of conquered land, and candidates for election conspicuously courted the favour of individual voters. The second half of the 2nd cent. BC saw a marked decline both in the success of senate leadership and in its care for the less fortunate. In foreign affairs the unpopular levies for the protracted wars in Spain led to resentment and actual resistance, organized by tribunes (see TRIBUNI PLEBIS). By the end of the century, the inglorious war against *Jugurtha and the disasters against the Gauls and Germans demolished the prestige of those born to command, and they came under increasing attack from men (usually tribunes) later described as 'populares' ('supporters of the people'). Successive tribunician laws provided for ballot in assemblies (a tribunician law of C. *Marius (1) made it secret ballot), and such laws were supported by aristocrats (e.g. P. *Cornelius Scipio Aemilianus) who believed in a 'mixed constitution'. At home the decline and proletarianization of the peasantry caused serious military, as well as social, problems, yet the senate majority resisted any attempt at distributing *ager publicus*. Finally a group of eminent senators supported Ti. *Sempronius Gracchus (3) in putting a moderate law for the distribution of some *ager publicus* directly to the plebs (133 BC). Stubborn resistance to this caused increasing tensions, which led to Tiberius' violent death. His younger brother Gaius *Sempronius Gracchus (tribune 123–122) then embarked on an ambitious programme of reform. In particular, while recognizing the senate's right to supervise administration, he sought to balance its power by subjecting senators serving in provinces to a new class, the later *equites, in *repetundae* trials. When Gaius also was killed in a riot, the Gracchi became martyrs to later populares. Ambitious tribunes continued to provide leadership, and the tribunal set up by C. *Mamilius in the Jugurthine War made it clear that the *equites*, although of the same class as senators, resented the death of the Gracchi and despised senatorial incompetence. The election of the *novus homo* C. Marius to the consulship and continued command seemed to threaten the birthright of the *nobilitas*, and his admission of the *proletarii to the legions created a potential armed pressure group of the poor, which L. *Appuleius Saturninus and C. *Servilius Glaucia tried to combine with the *equites*, largely for their own political advantage.

The optimates never recovered the qualities of leadership and readiness to compromise that had made them successful and dominant. Attempts at reform met with resistance, which led to violence on both sides. M. *Livius Drusus (2), an aristocratic tribune in the mould of C. Gracchus, tried, again with the support of some aristocrats, to rally some of those who had usually supported populares (especially poor citizens and the Italians seeking the Roman citizenship) behind the senate, but again the senate majority defeated the reforms on which the plan was based, resisting Italian enfranchisement (and thus causing the *Social War (3)), land distribution (see AGRARIAN LAWS AND POLICY), and colonization. While refusing to assume the duty of providing for the veterans of proletarian armies, leaving them to become clients of their commanders, the senate merely opposed the commanders' attempts to secure benefits for their veterans. In the end, after prolonged civil war, *Sulla established personal power with the support of his client army, which he amply rewarded with land expropriated from his enemies. His legislation tried to eliminate the populares, establishing the Senate securely in power against threats from *equites*, tribunes and ambitious commanders.

But the inefficiency and corruption of his senate led to the disintegration of his system within a decade. The consulship of *Pompey and M. *Licinius Crassus (1) in 70 saw the abolition of all restrictions on tribunes, compromise with the *equites* (see AURELIUS COTTA, L.) and the integration of the Italians into the citizen body, which, by greatly enlarging that body, made it less amenable to senate control. Since the senate persisted in doing nothing for veterans and opposing their commanders' attempts to secure benefits for them, commanders were driven into opposition to the senate, alliance with tribunes, and the use of *populatis* methods, especially the passing of legislation by the people and plebs despite senate opposition. Pompey and *Caesar thus secured the distribution of corn to the city plebs and of land to veterans—and powerful commands for themselves. The Gracchi and Marius were so successfully cited as precedents, as heroes and martyrs, that even Cicero, at heart a convinced optimate, had to act as a *populatis* and claim the heritage of those men when addressing people or plebs.

The populares of Cicero's age were generally devoid of serious principle. Whether new men like P. *Vatinius or patrician nobles like *Catiline, P. *Clodius Pulcher, and Caesar, they traded on the old traditions for personal advancement. Violence came to be used of set policy, with the poor and veterans hoping for benefits providing ready armies of the Forum. Men like Caesar and Catiline incurred huge debts to engage in unprecedented corruption. Characteristically, no *populatis* attempted to introduce elements of democracy into the system of Roman *comitia*, for real democracy might have counteracted optimate resistance and superseded the tactics on which they themselves relied for their own advancement (see DEMOCRACY, NON-ATHENIAN AND POST-CLASSICAL). The senate, on the other hand, while powerless against those tactics, continued in its failure to formulate any policy to set against them, but shielded continuing refusal to admit reforms by appeal to its traditional prestige. Many optimates now regarded their right to rule as divorced from any obligation for service, and most as limited to service in traditional offices, for their own political benefit. The decline that had begun after *c.*150 thus led to polarization and disintegration, without any organized movement for reform, which appeared to be in nobody's interest but that of the governed, who had no initiative.

Cicero saw a senate reawakened to its traditions as the only source for leadership. He tried to rally the *equites* behind it in a *concordia ordinum* (concord of the highest two orders in society) and all right-thinking citizens, concerned for the welfare of their country, in a consensus of all *boni* (lit. 'good men'), a term that he used in this wide extension. In a programmatic passage in a speech before a jury of senators and *equites* (*Sest.* 96 ff.) he claimed the term 'optimates' for all (even *freedmen) who, under the leadership of the senate, resisted the attacks of unscrupulous and dangerous self-professed populares. However, he never went so far as to give positive programmatic content to his appeal.

Augustus, after disintegration had led to nearly two decades of bloody civil wars, found the heirs to the optimates willing to give up the struggle for real power in return for peace and recognition of their social eminence and economic security. With the old populares, he saw that the people did not want real power either (for they had no experience of it), but would be satisfied with moderate, but secure, economic benefits. He also used the one point in which the optimates, populares, and the actual people had agreed, glory and the expansion of the empire, to cement unity behind a policy aiming at, and for a long time actually delivering, those objectives. As in a way the heir to both optimates and populares, he secured power for himself without permitting the revival of political conflict.

RE entries for 'Optimates' (H. Strasburger), 'Populares' (C. Meier: Suppl. 10. 550 ff.); P. A. Brunt, *The Fall of the Roman Republic* (1988), esp. ch. 1 (and see index).   E. B.

oracles Among the many forms of *divination known to the Greeks, the responses given by a god or hero when consulted at a fixed oracular site were the most prestigious (see e.g. Soph. *OT* 498–501). Such oracles were numerous. *Herodotus (1) lists five in mainland Greece and one in Asia Minor which king *Croesus supposedly consulted in the 6th cent. BC (1. 46), and at least another five (including one 'oracle of the dead') appear in his pages; *Pausanias (3) mentions four lesser local oracles, and at least five more can be added from epigraphical evidence (cf. C. Michel, *Recueil d'inscriptions grecques* (1900–27), 840–56; *Syll.*³ 1157–66).

Healing oracles, those of *Asclepius above all, are a specialized group, though even these never confined themselves exclusively to medical questions. The business of a general purpose oracle is best revealed by the lead question-tablets found at *Zeus' oracle at *Dodona. The majority of enquiries are from individuals; of the minority addressed by states, most ask whether a particular alteration to cult practice is acceptable, or more generally by what sacrifices divine favour is to be maintained; one or two concern political issues. Individuals enquire, for instance, whether their wife will conceive (or conceive a son), whether a proposed marriage or journey or change of career is wise, whether a child is legitimate; they also ask about health problems, and more generally about ways of winning and keeping divine favour. The kind of answer envisaged is either 'yes' or 'no' or 'by sacrificing to X'.

According to *Plutarch (*De Pyth. or.* 408c), similar everyday questions about 'whether to marry or to sail or to lend', or, from cities, about 'crops and herds and health' ('and cults', he might have added) formed the staple of Delphi's business in his day (see DELPHIC ORACLE). Before about 400 BC, states had certainly also consulted Delphi about political issues, but even then a decision, to go to war for instance or dispatch a colony (see COLONIZATION, GREEK), had normally been made by the state before approaching the oracle. What was sought was a divine sanction. And since no mortals were endowed with religious authority in the Greek system, all oracles at all dates had an especially important role in sanctioning adjustments to cult practice.

Techniques by which responses were given were very various. The most prestigious was 'inspired' prophecy, the sayings of a priest or more commonly a priestess who spoke, probably in a state of trance, in the person of the god. This was the method of several oracles of *Apollo in Asia Minor and almost certainly of that of Delphi too, though a process of drawing bean-lots seems also to have played some part there. The prophetic dream was characteristic of healing oracles such as those of Asclepius and *Amphiaraus, though not confined to them: the consultant slept a night or nights in the temple (*incubation), during which the god in theory appeared in a dream and issued instructions (or even, in pious legend, performed a cure direct). The oracle of Zeus at *Olympia worked by 'empyromancy', signs drawn from the flames on Zeus' *altar. To consult the hero *Trophonius at Lebadea, the client made a simulated descent to the Underworld: how the revelation then occurred is not recorded. Nor do we know anything certain about the practice at Zeus' oracle at Dodona.

Apart from the Egyptian–Libyan oracle of *Ammon at the *oasis of *Siwa in the Sahara, which many Greeks consulted as an oracle of Zeus from the 5th cent. BC onwards, the great oracular shrines were Greek. In Italy, the oracle of the *Sibyl at *Cumae is well-known from *Virgil, *Aeneid* 6. 9–101, who describes an ecstatic form of prophecy (see ECSTASY). Also prominent was the lot-oracle of *Fortuna Primigenia at *Praeneste. On extraordinary occasions the Roman government or ruler consulted the Sibylline books (see SIBYL), which were kept by the *duoviri* (later *quindecimviri) *sacris faciundis*.

H. W. Parke, *Greek Oracles* (1967), and *The Oracles of Zeus* (1967); R. Parker, in *Crux: Essays Presented to G. E. M. de Ste. Croix* (1985), 298–326; I. Malkin, *Metis* 4. 1 (1989); and see the bibliog. to the articles on individual oracles. R. C. T. P.

Late antiquity The first two centuries AD witnessed a great flourishing of oracular shrines throughout the Greek-speaking portion of the Roman empire. These oracles took many different forms. *Delphi, *Didyma, and *Claros delivered responses from a god through a prophet, whose words were interpreted for consultants by priests at the shrine. At Mallus in Cilicia and the sanctuary of *Amphiaraus at *Oropus (for example), the consultant slept (after a period of some preparation) in the shrine, hoping to have a dream of the god (also interpreted by priests). Other oracles, such as that of Bel at *Apamea appear to have worked by indicating passages in Classical literature (see also *POxy.* 3831). Lot-oracles of various sorts are known from southern Asia Minor and Egypt. The oracle of Glycon (see ALEXANDER (13)) offered a wide variety of methods of consultation.

Many responses are concerned with cult activity and personal crises; others, however, appear to have been more philosophic and provided important material for some pagan opponents of Christianity—they were taken as proof that the gods existed and as a proper guide to religious belief. Two oracles, of Didyma and Zeus Philios, the last opening at *Antioch (1) under Maximin Daia (305–13; see MAXIMINUS, GAIUS GALERIUS VALERIUS), also played significant roles in the great persecutions of the early 4th cent. Christians argued in turn that these responses were the work of demons, and those oracular shrines that survived the problems of the 3rd cent. appear to have been closed very soon after *Constantine I's defeat of Valerius *Licinius in 324.

L. Robert, *Opera Minora Selecta 5* (1989), 584–686, 747–69; R. Lane Fox, *Pagans and Christians* (1986); D. S. Potter, *Prophets and Emperors* (1994). D. S. P.

orality Coined as the opposite of *literacy, to denote the phenomenon of extensive reliance on oral communication rather than the written word, it is a useful concept for the ancient world, where writing was often used less than modern readers would assume. Various forms of orality are not incompatible with some use of writing, and it can be helpfully sub-divided into (1) oral composition, (2) oral communication, (3) oral transmission.

Oral composition, entirely without the help of writing, is best

known in relation to the Homeric poems (see HOMER) and the long tradition of oral poetry through the Greek Dark Ages. The influential work of Parry and Lord sought to show how an oral poet could compose in performance. Spontaneous oral composition can also be found, however, in later symposiastic poetry, and oratory. The importance of oral communication can be seen e.g. in the political activity of democratic Athens (see DEMOCRACY, ATHENIAN); in the use of contracts or wills relying on witnesses, not writing, in Athens and Rome (see EVIDENCE, ANCIENT ATTITUDES TO); in the habit of hearing literature (see ANAGNŌSTĒS). Oral transmission is the transmission without writing of any information, literature, traditions about the past etc. This usually involves some distortion, especially over generations of oral tradition, unless there is a deliberate effort to maintain the accuracy of the tradition (e.g. through poetry). Until the development of 5th-cent. Greek *historiography, most Greeks knew about their past from oral tradition; and it was crucial in preserving traditions about early Rome. Its character and reliability depends heavily on who is transmitting the traditions and why (e.g. notions of honour, patriotism). Thus Archaic Greece was almost entirely an oral society: even poetry that was written down (e.g. *Sappho) was primarily meant to be heard and performed.

As written documents and the centrality of written literature increase in the 5th. and 4th. cents., elements of orality still remain fundamental, notably the performance of poetry and prose (e.g. *Herodotus (1)), and oratory and extempore performance; the value of the written word was not uniformly accepted (cf. *Plato (1)'s criticisms in *Phaedrus*). Roman society was more book- and library-oriented, but even at the level of high culture one finds literary readings, the accomplishments of oratory, memory, and improvisation (see Quint. *Inst. Or.* 10. 7. 30–2; 11; the skill and advantages of shorthand were despised, Sen. *Ep. Mor.* 90. 25). The balance between oral communication and writing varied immensely over the period and in different areas. Some see a fundamental mentality engendered by orality (e.g. lack of individualism and/or analytical skills), but both Greece and Rome have their own particular manifestations of oral culture, and the theory may be exaggerated.

R. Thomas, *Literacy and Orality in the Ancient World* (1992), and *Oral Tradition and Written Record in Classical Athens* (1989); B. Gentili, *Poetry and its Public in Ancient Greece* (1988); A. Lord, *The Singer of Tales* (1960); C. J. Herington, *Poetry into Drama* (1985); E. Havelock, *Preface to Plato* (1963). R. T.

orators See ATTIC ORATORS and entries under names there listed; also RHETORIC, GREEK and LATIN; SECOND SOPHISTIC.

Orbilius Pupillus, Lucius, grammarian (Suet. *Gramm.* 9) who migrated from his native *Beneventum to Rome aged 50 (63 BC). A cross-grained character and severe critic of the capital's scholastic milieu, in which he did not prosper, he is recalled by his pupil *Horace for the beatings administered during lessons on *Livius Andronicus' *Odyssey* (*Epist.* 2. 1. 69 ff.); yet he was honoured at Beneventum with a statue on the town's Capitolium.

Herzog–Schmidt, § 280. R. A. K.

Orcades, the Orkney and Shetland Islands, were probably discovered by *Pytheas, and were visited by the fleet of Cn. *Iulius Agricola, who temporarily subdued them. *Pomponius Mela gave their number as 30–40; *Ptolemy (4) mentioned the islands, but placed them incorrectly. Orcas Headland of Britain was the northern end of Scotland—Dunnet Head or else Duncansby

Head. There is only a small amount of Roman material from the islands, which were hardly touched by the Roman world.

Mela 3. 54; Tac. *Agr.* 10; Ptol. *Geog.* 2. 3. 31. E. H. W.; M. J. M.

Orchomenus (mythological) (*a*) *Eponym of the Boeotian *Orchomenus (1), a vague genealogical figure. He is son of *Zeus and the Danaid Isonoe (schol. Ap. Rhod. 1. 230; obviously late, cf. DANAUS AND THE DANAIDS) and father of *Minyas; son of Minyas (Paus. 8. 36. 6 and elsewhere); his brother, and so son of Eteocles (not the Theban) (schol. Pind. *Isthm.* 1. 79). (*b*) Eponym of the Arcadian *Orchomenus (2) (Paus. 8. 36. 1). H. J. R.

Orchomenus (1), city in NW *Boeotia located between the foot of Mt. Akontion and the NW bay of Lake *Copais, whose W. basin it dominated. See the preceding article for the name. In prehistory Orchomenus was probably always one of the most important prehistoric settlements in Boeotia, although none of its phases is very well known; significant neolithic, Early Helladic, and Middle Helladic strata were found in early excavations, and there is a good range of Mycenaean pottery (see MYCENAEAN CIVILIZATION), including LH IIIC. The importance of the site in later Mycenaean times can be gauged from the 'Treasury of Minyas', a tholos tomb virtually identical in size and quality to the 'Treasury of Atreus' at *Mycenae, and finds of fresco-fragments comparable in themes and quality with those from Mycenaean palaces (S. A. Immerwahr, *Aegean Painting in the Bronze Age* (1990), 195). Some of these are associated with a building which may have been the palace; but if so, it was off the acropolis, uncharacteristically, and no trace of a fortification has been reported. It is the best placed centre to have undertaken the partial drainage of Lake Copais, and *Gla may have been an outpost of its power. The legends of Orchomenus's wealth (especially *Il.* 9. 381) and importance may dimly reflect this period. Its history after *c*.1200 BC is extremely obscure for a long period.

A rich city in the Classical period, Orchomenus was famed as the city of the Graces (see ORPHISM), to whom a venerable sanctuary was dedicated. Notable also were the graves of Minyas and Hesiod. Its principal existing monuments include the 'Treasury of Minyas' (above) and its well preserved circuit-walls. A small, still unpublished, theatre dates from the 4th cent. BC, and remains of various sanctuaries survive.

Rivalry between Orchomenus and *Thebes (1) for the hegemony of Boeotia became a constant factor throughout the Classical period. That tension notwithstanding, Orchomenus joined the *Boeotian Confederacy by the time of *Xerxes' invasion (see PERSIAN WARS), when it medized (see MEDISM). Upon the re-establishment of the Boeotian Confederacy, Orchomenus possessed two units within it. During the *Pentekontaetia Athens overran Boeotia after the battle of Oenophyta in 457 BC, after which Orchomenus formed the principal base for the liberation of the region. Joining with other Boeotians, Orchomenus defeated Tolmides at the battle of *Coronea in 447. In the new confederacy that was created in the wake of victory, Orchomenus maintained its position of importance. At the battle of *Delion in 424 BC Orchomenians held a position on the left wing, but about this time the city lost its control of *Chaeronea, which weakened its position within the confederacy. It seceded from the confederacy during the Corinthian War by taking the side of Sparta. Left independent after the *King's Peace of 386, it fell to Thebes after *Leuctra, and was destroyed in 364. *Phocis held it during much of the Third *Sacred War, but *Philip (1) II restored it to Boeotia after his victory at *Chaeronea in 338 BC. Its prosperity declined

in the Hellenistic period, and under Rome it became an unimportant place.

GAC G 1; P. A. Mountjoy, *Orchomenos, 5* (1983), ch. 1; S. Lauffer, *Kopais* 1 (1986); J. Knauss, *Kopais* 2 (1987). J. Fossey, *ANRW* 2. 1 (1979), 229 ff. (Roman). O. T. P. K. D.; J. Bu.

Orchomenus (2), polis in E. *Arcadia whose main territory lay in an upland basin (also the site of Mycenean settlement; see MYCENAEAN CIVILIZATION). The extensive site was fortified by the later 5th cent. BC, with public buildings on the higher ground; in the Roman period, and perhaps earlier, housing lay below the walls on the south. Tradition (partly conflicting with tradition about Arcadian Trapezus) accorded Orchomenus great prominence under Archaic kings, fighting with *Messenia against *Sparta (evidently in the Second Messenian War). Whatever the truth of these reports, such prominence faded in the Archaic period. In the 5th and earlier 4th cent. Orchomenus was a loyal ally of Sparta, resisting anti-Spartan Arcadians in the Peloponnesian War and after *Leuctra, but occasionally extending control over smaller neighbours. Later it changed allegiance frequently, and by the Roman period was in decline.

RE 18. 887–905; D. M. Leahy, *Phoenix*, 1958, 141–65; M. Jost, *Sanctuaires et cultes d'Arcadie* (1985), 113–22; R. Osborne, *Classical Landscape with Figures* (1987), 118–21; F. E. Winter, *EMC* 1987, 235–46. J. R.

orders (of architecture) The main Greek orders of architecture are Doric, Ionic, and Corinthian. The definitive form of Doric is established by the beginning of the 6th cent. BC, representing the translation into stone of forms which originated in wooden structures of the 7th cent. Ionic evolved at the same time, but took longer to reach definitive form; there are important local variations at least until the early-Hellenistic period.

The origin of these systems is uncertain. Wooden columns similar to Doric (but with no evidence for the entablature) had been used in Aegean late bronze age architecture, but these cannot have survived to the early evolution of Doric in the 7th cent. BC. The structural origin of elements in the entablature (e.g. the guttae which represent the wooden pegs fixing different elements together) is certain, but cannot be extended to all parts. The triglyph and metope frieze may be an adaptation of decorative patterns found in carpentry and the decorative arts, though a structural origin has been argued.

The Ionic order is inspired by Near Eastern architecture, copied even more closely in the variant Aeolic form of the NW Aegean. Both have volute capitals. Aeolic has two separate spirals springing from a central triangle, Ionic links the volutes across an abacus. In the entablature the architrave is normally surmounted by a row of dentils. Attic Ionic replaces this with a continuous carved frieze (which may echo parapet-like gutters of major East Greek buildings). In the Hellenistic period the Attic base is standard, while the entablature includes both continuous and dentil friezes.

Corinthian evolves in the 4th cent. BC, using more ornate capitals decorated with acanthus leaves under volutes springing from the centre to all four corners (see CALLIMACHUS (4)). Another variant, Composite, combines the acanthus leaves with an Ionic four volute system. The earliest example of Corinthian (now lost) was in the Temple of Apollo at *Bassae. Corinthian columns were used internally in temples and other buildings at Epidaurus and Delphi in the 4th cent. BC. It gained favour as an external system in the Hellenistic period, culminating in the *Olympieum donated to Athens by *Antiochus (4) IV. Though surviving examples are rare, its more ornate form probably found favour in the Hellenized east and Egypt.

All three orders are taken over by Roman architects: Doric in a primitive, variant form dating back to Archaic times, Ionic and Corinthian in the standardized Hellenistic models.

P. P. Betancourt, *The Aeolic Style in Architecture*, (1977); W. Kirchhoff, *Die Entwicklung des Ionischen Voluten Kapitells in 6. und 5. Jhd.* (1988); B. Wesenberg, *Kapitelle und Basen* (1971); J. J. Coulton, *BSA* 1974 and 1979. R. A. T.

ordinary consuls (*consules ordinarii*) See CONSUL; SUFFECT, SUFFECTIO.

Ordovices See OSTORIUS SCAPULA, PUBLIUS.

Oreads See NYMPHS.

Oreithyia See BOREAS.

Oreos See HISTIAEA (cf. Andrewes, *HCT* 5 (1981), 320 on Thuc. 8. 95. 7).

Orestes, in mythology son of *Agamemnon and *Clytemnestra, and avenger of his father's murder by his mother and her lover *Aegisthus. Homer (*Od.* 1. 29 ff.; 298 ff.; 3. 303 ff.) says that Orestes killed Aegisthus, having returned home from Athens in the eighth year after Agamemnon's death, and implies that he also killed Clytemnestra. The vengeance was an entirely praiseworthy deed, for which he won great reputation; no regrets are expressed by anyone at his having to kill his mother, and there is no hint of any pursuit by the *Erinyes, who later play so important a part in the legend. Clytemnestra was simply 'hateful' (*Od.* 3. 310), and Orestes, as head of the family, would necessarily have been her judge and executioner.

*Stesichorus wrote an *Oresteia* running to at least two books, but few fragments are left (see frs. 210–19 Davies *PMGF*). We know, however, that he included a recognition scene between Orestes and *Electra, and also the pursuit by the Erinyes, against whom *Apollo provided Orestes with a bow (fr. 217). But it is 5th-cent. tragedy which provides the fullest details of Orestes' legend. At the time of Agamemnon's murder Orestes was taken to Strophius, king of *Phocis and brother-in-law of Agamemnon, and brought up by him together with his own son Pylades, who later accompanies Orestes when he returns secretly home, on the instruction of Apollo, to avenge his father's death. Here he encounters his sister Electra, and they recognize each other with mutual joy. In *Aeschylus' *Choephori*, brother and sister join together in an invocation to Agamemnon's ghost, but the focus of this play is still mainly on Orestes, and Electra is not actively involved in the killings. Orestes gets access to the palace as a stranger, bringing news of his own death, and can scarcely bring himself to kill Clytemnestra. After her murder he is at once pursued by her Erinyes, who form the Chorus of the following play (*Eumenides*) where Orestes is put on trial and finally absolved by the homicide court on the *Areopagus, once Athena has given the casting vote in his favour. She also calms the Erinyes, who are to be settled in a shrine with the beneficent title of the Eumenides, 'the Kindly Ones'.

Electra's role in helping her brother is developed by *Sophocles (1) and Euripides: in Sophocles' *Electra* she urges Orestes on from outside the door while he is inside killing their mother, and in Euripides' *Electra* she is by far the more dominant figure, driving the weak and indecisive Orestes to kill Clytemnestra and even grasping the sword with him when his own hand fails (1217, 1225). Here in Euripides, quite unlike Sophocles' play, brother

and sister are entirely overcome with guilt and remorse once the deed is done; here too, again unlike Sophocles' version, the Erinyes will pursue Orestes (1252 ff.). Elsewhere in Euripides we are aware of these Furies as the imagined phantoms of Orestes' guilty conscience (*Orestes*); and his release from their pursuit is a long process involving a journey to the land of the Tauri (*Iphigenia in Tauris*). In his *Andromache*, Orestes murders *Neoptolemus (1) and carries off *Hermione, whom he later marries, having by her a son, Tisamenus (Paus. 2. 18. 6).

Various local traditions are recorded: for instance *Pausanias (3) was shown (1. 28. 5) an altar which Orestes set up in commemoration of his being freed from the Erinyes by the verdict of the Areopagus (as in Aeschylus), a stone at *Troezen (2. 31. 4) on which he had been purified, and another at Gythium in *Laconia where he was cured of madness (3. 22. 1); also a place near Megalopolis where he had bitten off a finger in his madness and so been cured (8. 34. 1–3).

Orestes, killing Aegisthus, was a popular scene in art, occurring possibly in the 7th cent., and with certainty from the 6th. Also popular was Orestes' meeting with Electra at Agamemnon's tomb. See also RELICS.

R. M. Gais, *LIMC* 1. 1. 372 ff. I. McPhee, *LIMC* 3. 1. 709 ff.
H. J. R.; J. R. M.

Orestheus, in mythology, a king of *Aetolia, grandfather of *Oeneus and son of *Deucalion. He had a bitch which brought forth a stick; this he buried and from it sprang a vine. From its branches, ὄζοι, the Ozolian Locrians were named, and Orestheus called his son Phytios, 'Plant-man'. (Athenaeus, 35a–b and Pausanias, 10. 38. 1 = Hecataeus of Miletus). For the connection of the family with *wine cf. OENEUS. H. J. R.

orgeōnes (ὀργεῶνες) are members of a society devoted to the rites (ὄργια) of a particular hero or god; they are in effect confined to *Attica. A group of *orgeōnes* was an organized corporation with a precinct (sometimes leased out when not in use), funds, a constitution and officers; it met periodically (in several attested cases once a year) to *sacrifice and feast, to pass decrees, and to enrol new members. See CLUBS, GREEK.

A complication arises with a law, probably of the 5th cent. (Philochorus *FGrH* 328 F 35), which required *phratries to grant membership to (among others) *orgeōnes*. This seems to show that groups of *orgeōnes* were not wholly private bodies but had some relation to sub-structures of the city. On the most plausible view (A. Andrewes, *JHS* 1961), the law did not force phratries to admit persons of lower status, but rather confirmed that those already admitted after scrutiny to more exclusive groups should be given phratry membership without more ado. If *orgeōnes* enjoyed such privilege, it is natural to wonder whether their cults (like those of their grander relatives the *genē*: see GENOS) were in some sense public. Not all *orgeōnes* can have benefited from this law, however; for of the attested groups at least one consisted of non-citizens, the Thracians who, exceptionally, organised a procession in the Athenian public cult of *Bendis (see RELIGION, THRACIAN). Several groups of prosperous citizens who are *orgeōnes* of heroes (such as the healer Amynos) may represent the old type envisaged by the law; other groups that honoured gods—Mother, *Asclepius, *Dionysus, the Syrian goddess (see ATARGATIS)—were perhaps *orgeōnes* only in a looser sense.

W. S. Ferguson, *HTR* 1944; Andrewes (see above); E. Kearns, *The Heroes of Attica* (1989), 73–7. R. C. T. P.

Oribasius (*c.* AD 320–*c.*400), Greek medical writer. Born in Pergamum, he studied medicine at *Alexandria (1) under *Zeno (2) of Cyprus, and practised in Asia Minor. He became the personal physician of *Julian, who took him to Gaul (355). Closely involved in the proclamation of Julian as Emperor (361), Oribasius accompanied him until his death in *Mesopotamia (363). Banished for a time to foreign courts, Oribasius was soon recalled by the Emperor *Valens and continued to practise his profession until an advanced age. His principal works are a collection of excerpts from *Galen—now lost—and the *Collectiones medicae* ('Ἰατρικαὶ συναγωγαί), a vast compilation of excerpts from earlier medical writers, from *Alcmaeon (2) of Croton (c.500 BC) to Oribasius' contemporaries Philagrius and Adamantius. Both of these works were written at the behest of Julian. Of the 70 (or 72) books of the *Collectiones* only 25 survive entire; but the rest can be in part reconstructed from the *Synopsis ad Eustathium*, and the treatise *Ad Eunapium*, epitomes of the *Collectiones* in 9 books and 4 books respectively made by Oribasius himself, and from various excerpts and summaries, some of which are still unpublished. Oribasius was a convinced *pagan, and his medical encyclopedia is a product of the vain effort of Julian and his circle to recall the classical past. For the medical historian its importance lies in the large number of excerpts from lost writers—particularly those of the Roman period—which it preserves, usually with a precise reference to the source; Oribasius adds nothing of his own. His work was constantly quoted and excerpted by early Byzantine medical writers, the *Synopsis* and the *Ad Eunapium* were twice translated into Latin in Ostrogothic Italy (see GOTHS), and Syriac and Arabic translations of portions of Oribasius' work form one of the principal channels by which knowledge of Greek medicine reached the Islamic world. See MEDICINE, § 7.

CMG 6; I. Bloch in M. Neuburger and J. Pagel, *Handbuch der Geschichte der Medizin* 1 (1902), 513 ff.; H. O. Schröder, *RE* Suppl. 7. 797 ff.; B. Baldwin, *Acta Classica* 18 (1975), 85 ff.   R. B.; V. N.

oriental cults and religion Although eastern influences, real or imagined, were by no means absent from Greek mythology and cult prior to *Alexander (3) the Great, the term 'oriental religions' typically designates the cults of a variety of divinities originating in Anatolia and the Fertile Crescent, which, spreading beyond their homeland, arrived in Italy and the W. Mediterranean between the late 3rd cent. BC and the 3rd cent. AD. Though the outlandish character of individual cults was noted in antiquity, the term corresponds to no ancient distinction.

The history of the term may be roughly divided into three phases. From the Renaissance to c.1900, it was used casually to account for 'decadence', whether of Italo-Roman religion or paganism in general. For one strand of post-Renaissance Humanism, exemplified by Gibbon, it embraced Christianity. F. Cumont's *Les Religions orientales dans le paganisme romain* (1906), however, was the first attempt to give the notion explanatory power: he assimilated religious movements from Asia Minor, Egypt, Syria, and Persia to one another as mystery religions concerned with a promise of after-life. As such, they prepared the way for Christianity. Cumont himself, by including *astrology and *magic, and by introducing Bacchic cult (see DIONYSUS) into the 4th edition (1929), muddied the claim. A. D. Nock's *Conversion* (1933) began a process of reaction. Do the similarities between these cults outweigh their differences? What was the role of post-mortem salvation? Is the contrast civic cult/personal religion satisfactory? Why exclude *Christianity? An index of current confusion is the list of titles in *Études préliminaires aux religions orientales dans l'Empire romain* (1961–92). There

have been uneven attempts to rework Cumont's term. See MYSTERIES.

R. MacMullen, *Paganism in the Roman Empire* (1981); M. J. Vermaseren (ed.), *Die orientalischen Religionen im Römerreich* (1981); R. Turcan, *Les Cultes orientaux dans le monde romain*[2] (1992).   R. L. G.

Orientalism *Orientalism* is the title of a study by the distinguished Palestinian literary critic, Edward Said; published in 1978, its impact has been enormous. The central thesis is that the concepts 'Europe' and 'Orient', as polar opposites, have been created by Europeans, particularly in the context of European imperialism, to provide a positive, strong image of Europe, with which eastern civilizations (especially the Muslim world) can be negatively contrasted. The 'Orient' is thus presented as lacking all desirable, active characteristics: it is effeminate, decadent, corrupt, voluptuous, despotic, and incapable of independent creative development. This pervasive perception of 'the east' underlies most studies of Middle Eastern history and culture and has profoundly shaped scholarly analysis. Although most of Said's study is devoted to the 18th to 20th cents. he argues that Oriental stereotypes derive much of their imagery from early Greek literary works (e.g. *Herodotus (1); *Aeschylus' *Persae*). This has led several classicists and ancient historians to refocus their work and explore consciously the assumptions made in some traditional areas of study. As a result, standard approaches to several subjects are now being scrutinized and radically reassessed. Most prominent among these are: the development of Greek art, in particular the '*orientalizing' phase, Greek tragedy, and Achaemenid and Hellenistic history. An interesting, though in several respects maverick, study of Greek civilization, which adopts part of Said's political agenda, is M. Bernal's *Black Athena* (London 1987–   ); he takes an extreme position to argue that Greece was colonized by black Africans and *Phoenicians and owed its culture to them.

See also HELLENISM, HELLENIZATION.

E. Said, *Orientalism* (1978); H. Sancisi-Weerdenburg, in A. Cameron and A. Kuhrt (eds.), *Images of Women in Antiquity* (1983, 2nd edn. 1993), 20–33; *Achaemenid History* 1 (ed., 1987), 33–45, and *Achaemenid History* 2 (ed. with A. Kuhrt, 1987), 117–131; E. Hall, *Inventing the Barbarian* (1989), and in J. Rich and G. Shipley (eds.), *War and Society in the Greek World* (1993), 108–33; A. C. Gunter, in H. Sancisi-Weerdenburg and J. W. Drijvers, (eds.), *Achaemenid History* 5 (1990), 131–47; P. Briant, in P. Bilde and others (eds.), *Religion and Religious Practices in the Seleucid Kingdom* (1990), 40–65; M. C. Root, in H. Sancisi-Weerdenburg and A. Kuhrt (eds.), *Achaemenid History* 6 (1991): 1–29; S. P. Morris *Daidalos and the origins of Greek art* (1992).   A. T. L. K.

orientalizing, an expression applied to certain phases of *Etruscan, Greek, Hellenistic, Roman, and Byzantine art when they appear to adopt stylistic traits characteristic of the Near East. Examples include the influence of (see CYPRUS; SILVER) Phoenician and Cypriot silverware on Etruscan metalwork and pottery, or that of eastern textiles on the decoration of Greek Geometric and Archaic vessels; the 'Achaemenidizing' character of some of the architectural details of Hadrian's Villa at Tivoli, which are probably dependent on Persian *booty won by *Alexander (3) the Great; and the *Sasanian motifs employed in the design of *Anicia Iuliana's church of St Polyeuctus in *Constantinople in the early 6th cent. AD.

H. Payne, *Necrocorinthia* (1931); T. J. Dunbabin, *The Greeks and their Eastern Neighbours* (1957); R. M. Harrison, *A Temple for Byzantium* (1989).   M. V.

orientation The patterning of the human environment according to generally accepted calibrations of ambient space took a number of forms in ancient Mediterranean cultures, and particularly in religious contexts, such as the laying out of *sanctuaries according to the cardinal points (that is to solar phenomena: there is little evidence of lunar or stellar orientations), or to face parts of ritually or mythically important landscapes (note the orientation of sanctuaries in Latium towards the *Albanus mons). A connection between the sunrise quarter and the right hand was found in Greek practice (cf. *Il.* 12. 237 f.), and an eastward orientation is common but not mandatory for *temples (e.g. the *Parthenon). Conversely the west was inauspicious and used in cursing (e.g. Lysias 6. 51), though many Anatolian goddess-temples faced west (see ANATOLIAN DEITIES). Roman augury (see AUGURES) was one of the most developed of such systems, with a complex division of the sky and the land beneath it from the observer's viewpoint, which was closely related to the cardinal points and to the practices of land division (augural sanctuary of *Bantia; orientation of the *centuriation of the *ager Campanus*; see CAMPANIA).

Geographers developed a system based on the principal winds, which was related to theories of *meteorology and adapted to town-planning (see URBANISM). Fixed orientation was hampered by the absence of the compass.

A. V. Podossinov, *Cartographica Helvetica*, 1993, 33–43; B. L. Gordon, *History of Religions* 10 (1971), 211–18; M. Eliade and L. E. Sullivan, *Encyclopaedia of Religion* 11 (1987), 105–8.   N. P.

Orientius, a Gaul of the 5th cent. AD, who composed an elegiac exhortation to a Christian life.

TEXT Ed. C. A. Rapisarda, *Commonitorium et Carmina Orientio Tributa* (1958).   J. D. H.

Origen (1) (**Origenes Adamantius**), (probably AD 184 or 185–254 or 255: Euseb. *Hist. Eccl.* 7. 1, Jerome, *De Vir. Ill.* 54) was born at *Alexandria (1) of Christian parents. Our chief source of information on his life is the sixth book of *Eusebius' *Ecclesiastical History*, together with the *Panegyric* by *Gregory (4) Thaumaturgus and the surviving book (translated by *Rufinus (2)) of the *Apology for Origen* which Eusebius wrote with Pamphilus (Migne, PG 17. 521–616). Educated by his father Leonides (who perished in the persecution of 202 under Septimius Severus) and later in the Catechetical School of Alexandria under Pantaenus and *Clement (of Alexandria), he became a teacher himself, with such success that he was recognized, first informally, then in 203 officially, as head of the school. He learned pagan philosophy from one Ammonius, perhaps not *Ammonius Saccas but another Ammonius who was a *Peripatetic (Porphyry, in Eus. *HE* 6. 19, *Vita Plotini* 20). The story of his self-castration in accordance with Matthew 19: 12 is supported by Eusebius (*HE* 6. 8), but doubted by *Epiphanius (*Panarion* 64. 3). His career as a teacher was interrupted in 215 by *Caracalla's massacre of Alexandrian Christians. He withdrew to Palestine, but after a time was recalled by his bishop, Demetrius. Through his extensive literary work he now acquired such influence in the eastern Church as to become its unofficial arbiter, and, on a journey to Greece in this capacity, allowed himself to be ordained priest by the bishops of *Caesarea (2) and Jerusalem. Demetrius, who had not given his consent, took offence at this and perhaps also at parts of Origen's teaching. On obscure grounds, Origen was banished from Alexandria and deposed from the presbyterate, but the decision was ignored in Palestine, and Origen settled at Caesarea in 231. He continued his labours until, after repeated torture in the Decian persecution (250–1; see MESSIUS), his health gave way and he died at Tyre at the age of 69.

Origen's works were voluminous and of wide scope, but only a fraction has survived. He was a pioneer in textual criticism of the Bible, exegesis and systematic theology.

Critical. His chief work in this sphere was the *Hexapla*, begun before 233 and not completed till 244–5. In it were set out in six columns: (*a*) the Hebrew text of the OT, (*b*) the same transliterated into Greek characters, (*c*) and (*d*) the two Greek versions by Aquila and Symmachus, (*e*) the *Septuagint, (*f*) the revision of this by Theodotion. Only fragments survive. A conservative redactor, Origen defended the Greek portions of Daniel against Sextus *Iulius Africanus.

Exegetical. He wrote commentaries on the greater part of Scripture. Some took the form of scholia on obscure passages, others of homilies on numerous books of the OT and NT, many of which are preserved in the original or in Latin translation by *Jerome or Rufinus. There were also elaborate commentaries on diverse books of the OT and on the Gospels of Matthew and John (parts survive). Origen sought, though not consistently, a moral sense pertaining to the soul and a typological sense to instruct the spirit, occasionally discarding the historical sense where data were in conflict.

Doctrinal. The *De Principiis* is an original exposition of Christianity written before Origen left Alexandria. Setting out from points of doctrine in the Church tradition, he proceeds by (often tentative) speculation to support these by rational inference or by Scriptural quotation, and thus produce a system at once philosophical and pious. Large fragments of the Greek survive, but the only complete version is the Latin of Rufinus.

Apologetic. The *Contra Celsum*, written *c*.249, replies in detail to the learned attack of the Middle Platonist *Celsus, which probably appeared in 176. This is the only extant work in which Origen avows his philosophic education. Part of the *Dialogue with Heraclides* was discovered on papyrus at Tura near Cairo in 1941.

Devotional. Two of Origen's works in this category, the *De oratione* and *Exhortatio ad martyrium* have come down to us complete. The former was probably written *c*.231, the latter was addressed *c*.235 to his friends Ambrosius and Protoctetus, who suffered persecution under Maximin. His spiritualizing treatise *On the Pasch* was also discovered at Tura.

The *Philocalia* is a collection of excerpts from Origen's writings by *Gregory (2) of Nazianzus and *Basil of Caesarea. It preserves the original Greek of many passages otherwise known only in Latin, and shows what the Cappadocians found valuable in his teaching. But Origen had already come under attack by Methodius for his denial of a carnal resurrection, and at the end of the 4th cent. he was condemned by Epiphanius and (eventually) Jerome. The translations by his champion Rufinus are often freer and more periphrastic than those of Jerome, in the interests of orthodoxy and of clarity. Despite this advocacy, Origen was finally condemned under Justinian at the Council of Constantinople (553).

TEXTS *Origenes Werke*, ed. P. Koetschau (1899 ff); *Vier Bücher von Prinzipien*, ed. H. Karpp (1976); *Traité des Principes*, ed. H. Crouzel and M. Simonetti (1978–84); *Contre Celse*, ed. M. Borret (1967–9); *The Philocalia of Origen*, ed. J. A. Robinson (1893). *Philocalie 1–20*, ed. M. Harl (1983). Tura Papyri ed. J. Scherer (1947–); *Entretien avec Heraclide*, ed. J. Scherer (1960).

TRANSLATIONS *Philocalia*, G. Lewis (1911); *De Principiis*, G. W. Butterworth (1936); *Contra Celsum*, H. Chadwick (1953); *On Prayer* etc., R. A. Greer (1979).

GENERAL LITERATURE E. de Faye, *Origène*, 3 vols. (1923–8); R. Cadiou, *La Jeunesse d'Origène* (1936); J. Daniélou, *Origène* (1948, Eng. trans. 1955); H. Chadwick, *Early Christian Thought and the Classical*

Tradition (1966); R. P. C. Hanson, *Allegory and Event* (1959); M. Fédou, *Religion paienne et chrétienne chez le Contre Celse d'Origène* (1989); H. Crouzel, *Origène* (1985, Eng. trans. 1989), and *Les Fins dernières selon Origène* (1990); N. Pace, *Richerche sulla traduzione di Rufino del 'De principiis' di Origene* (1990); E. A. Clark, *The Origenist Controversy* (1992); M. J. Edwards, *Journal of Ecclesiastical History* 1993.　　H. C.; M. J. E.

Origen (2) (*RE* 4), Platonist philosopher (see NEOPLATONISM), 3rd cent. AD. Like his Christian namesake and contemporary, he is said to have studied under *Ammonius (2) Saccas, but it is generally agreed that the two Origens were different people. The pagan wrote only two works, both now lost, *On the Demons* and *That the King is the Only Creator* (Porph. *Plot.* 3); the latter title refers to his refusal to distinguish the Creator from the Supreme God as *Numenius and *Plotinus did (Procl. *Theol. Plat.* 2. 4).

R. T. Wallis, *Neoplatonism* (1972), 38; K.-O. Weber, *Origenes der Neuplatoniker* (1962: includes collection of fragments).　　A. D. S.

Orion, of whom various tales are told, was a mighty hunter and prodigious lover (father of fifty sons by as many *nymphs: Corinna, fr. 655 *PMG*, cf. 654. 3. 27–30, 37–43; he also pursued the Pleiades, and assaulted *Merope (1) and *Artemis), who was favoured and/or punished by the gods (in particular Artemis), and eventually transformed into the *constellation (no. 35). One version of the myth (that he was beloved of *Eos, for which reason Artemis killed him in Ortygia) was known to *Homer (*Od.* 5. 121–4): see also *Od.* 11. 572–5 (Orion in the underworld, gathering the beasts he had slain in his lifetime), and *Il.* 18. 487–9 (= *Od.* 5. 273–5), where, on the shield of *Achilles, the Bear keeps a watchful eye on Orion. *Hesiod also knew the constellation (*Op.* 598, 609–10, 614–16, 619–20). See Apollodorus 1. 4. 3–5.

Orion's tomb was shown to *Pausanias (3) at *Tanagra, where there was also a place called the Pole, at which *Atlas (father of the Pleiades) sat and meditated (9. 20. 3). Both *Euphorion (2), *CA* 101 and Corinna associate Orion with Tanagra, and one of the stories of his parentage makes him son of Hyrieus. According to another he was a son of *Poseidon and Euryale.

Apollodorus, *The Library* (trans. J. G. Frazer) (1921); J. Fontenrose, *Orion* (1981); A. Griffiths, *JHS* 1986, 58–70; M. P. Speidel, *Mithras-Orion* (1980), esp. 31–7; *LIMC* 7. 1 (1994), 78–80.　　A. Sch.

Ormenus, name used by *Homer for miscellaneous Trojan warriors (see TROY), slain at *Il.* 8. 274 and at 12. 187, and for miscellaneous grandfathers, of *Phoenix (2) at *Il.* 9. 448, and of *Eumaeus at *Od.* 15. 414. Also, the eponym of a city Ormenion (*Il.* 2. 734), the later Orminion on the Gulf of *Pagasae, with which *Demetrius (12) of Scepsis speciously associated Phoenix in the light of his grandfather (Strabo 9. 5. 18).　　K. D.

ornamenta were the decorations, costume, and status of a specific senatorial rank, quaestorian, praetorian, or consular, and in the republic were granted only in exceptional cases. In the imperial period these honours were granted more frequently, both to senators, who received precedence in voting associated with a higher rank without actual promotion (contrast *adlectio*; see ADLECTION), and to non-senators, for whom conferment of *ornamenta* was a mark of imperial favour, bestowing the appropriate senatorial status on public occasions, but not involving admission to the senate. Grants to non-senators were made most commonly to praetorian prefects, who, from the Flavians onwards, probably received consular ornaments, but also under *Claudius to freedmen officials (*Narcissus (2) receiving quaestorian, M. *Antonius Pallas praetorian ornaments). These develop-

opments indicate increasing imperial control of senatorial magistracies. The *ornamenta* of local magistrates were also voted to individuals by communities in Italy and the provinces.

After 19 BC no senator outside the imperial family was permitted to celebrate a *triumph. Instead deserving commanders were on imperial initiative awarded *triumphalia ornamenta*—the insignia normally carried by a general in his triumphal procession.

J. B. C.

Orodes (*RE* 1), king of *Parthia from *c.*58/7 to 37 BC. He disputed the throne for some years with his brother Mithradates III, whom he finally captured and executed in 55/4. When Parthia was threatened by a Roman invasion in 54/3, Orodes marched against Rome's ally *Artavasdes (1) of Armenia, while his general *Suren opposed *Crassus in Mesopotamia and won the decisive victory at Carrhae. Suren, too powerful for Orodes' comfort, was soon executed. Orodes' son Pacorus then invaded Syria unsuccessfully in 51. During the civil wars the Parthians sided against Caesar and the Caesarians, and Parthian contingents fought in the Philippi campaign; then in 40 Parthian armies under Orodes' son Pacorus and the Roman Q. *Labienus overran Syria, Palestine, Cilicia, and much of southern Asia Minor. In 39/8 Mark Antony's general P. *Ventidius (see ANTONIUS (2), MARCUS) won several victories and ejected them; Pacorus died in the fighting, and the inconsolable Orodes abdicated in favour of another son, *Phraates IV, who promptly killed him.

A. N. Sherwin-White, *Roman Foreign Policy in the East* (1984); R. D. Sullivan, *Near Eastern Royalty and Rome, 100–30 BC* (1990).　　C. B. R. P.

Orontes (mod. *Nahr el 'Āsī*), chief river of *Syria. It rises near *Heliopolis (*Baalbek*), flows north-east past *Emesa (*Homs*) and Arethusa, bends west past Epiphania (*Hama*) and then, below *Apamea, flows due north, and finally south-west through *Antioch (1), into the Mediterranean below *Seleuceia (2) in Pieria, after a journey of 272 km. (170 miles). Strabo's statement (16. 2. 5 ff.) that it flows partly underground and his aetiological story of Orontes, who is said to have bridged it and given it its name, are without foundation. Its valley was renowned for its fertility (Strabo, loc. cit.) and has always been the main route followed by traffic and armies from the north making for Egypt. The Macedonian colonists of Syria (see COLONIZATION, HELLENISTIC) renamed it after the R. Axius (see MACEDONIA).

E. W. G.

Oropus, a major city in SE *Boeotia. Much of the Oropia is hilly, but Oropus itself dominates both a small plain in the Asopus valley and a harbour (see Austin no. 83: greedy customs-collectors). Remains of the city are scanty, consisting of traces of a circuit-wall, agora, and scattered tombs. Prominent, however, is the healing sanctuary of *Amphiaraus, who legend said was swallowed up there on his exile from Thebes. Oropus was a notorious bone of contention between *Thebes (1) and *Athens, despite the fact that it was geographically an extension of the plain of *Tanagra. It enters history as a subject of Athens (Thuc. 2. 23). In 411 BC *Eretria and Oropians handed the city to Boeotia, only to have Athens regain control of it until 402 BC, when Thebes again annexed it. It came again under Athenian control probably after the *King's Peace, but Thebes recovered it in 366 BC. *Philip (1) II returned it to Athens after the defeat of Thebes, but it became independent after the *Lamian War. In 313 BC *Cassander gave it back to Boeotia, and it remained a member of the *Boeotian Confederacy from 311 to 171 BC.

D. Knoepfler, *Chiron*, 1986, 71 ff; J. M. Fossey, *Topography and Population*

Orosius

of Ancient Boiotia (1988), 29 ff.; Hornblower, Comm. on Thuc. 1 (1991) on 2. 23.　　　　　　　　　　　　　　　　　　　　　　　　　J. Bu.

Orosius, a young presbyter who arrived in Africa from NW Spain (Braga) in AD 414; his memorandum (*Commonitorium*) against the *Priscillianist and Origenist heresies (see ORIGEN (1)) led *Augustine to address a reply to him on the subject. On Augustine's commendation he moved on to *Jerome in Bethlehem. While in the Holy Land he argued against the Pelagians (see PELAGIUS), and received a portion of the recently discovered remains of St Stephen to take back to the congregation in Braga; unable to make the crossing to Spain, he left these relics with the Christians of the island of Minorca (Migne, PL 41. 805 ff.). Returning to Africa, with Augustine's encouragement he compiled the seven books of his *Histories against the Pagans*, stretching from the Creation to the history of Rome down to AD 417—an apologetic response (see APOLOGISTS) to the *pagan argument that the coming of Christianity had brought disaster to the world.

Ed. M.-P. Arnaud-Lindet (Budé, 1990–1); CSEL 18 for *Commonitorium*.　　　　　　　　　　　　　　　　　　　　　　　　　E. D. H.

Orpheus, the quintessential mythical singer, son of *Apollo and a Muse (see MUSES), whose song has more than human power. In archaic Greece, Orpheus appears among the *Argonauts whom he saves from the *Sirens by overcoming their song with his own; other attestations exalt the power of his song (*Ibycus, *Simonides). In the 5th cent. Orpheus enlarges his field of competence: his powerful song encompasses epic poetry, healing songs, oracles, and initiatory rites.

His main myth is his tragic love for *Eurydice (1), narrated by *Virgil (*Georg.* 4. 453–525) and *Ovid (*Met.* 10. 1–11. 84) but known already in some form in the 5th cent. BC. In Virgil's version Eurydice, newly wed to Orpheus, died of a snakebite, and the singer descended to Hades to bring her back. His song enchanted *Hades; Eurydice was allowed to return provided Orpheus did not look back when leading her up; he failed, losing Eurydice for ever. He retired into wild nature where his lamenting song moved animals, trees, and rocks; finally a band of Thracian women or Bacchic *maenads (see DIONYSUS) killed him. The first representation of Eurydice, Orpheus and *Hermes is the relief from the Athenian Altar of the Twelve Gods: earlier is the allusion in Eur. *Alc.* 357–62 (438 BC). Orpheus' death at the hands of maenads is presented in *Aeschylus' drama *Bassarae* as the result of Dionysus' wrath (470/460 BC). Vases depicting Thracian women murdering him are somewhat earlier, without giving a reason for the killing; later, it is the aloofness of the widowed (and turned homosexual) singer which provokes the women. But even after his death, Orpheus' voice was not silenced: his head was carried by the sea to the island of *Lesbos where for a while it gave prophecies.

Generally, Orpheus is called a Thracian. A grave and a cult belong not to *Thrace but to Pieria in *Macedonia, north-east of Mt. *Olympus (1), a region which formerly had been inhabited by Thracians and with which the Muses had some relations. It may have been a recent invention, or point to the original home of Orpheus who has no certain place in the web of Greek mythological *genealogy.

An important consequence of his miraculous song was his authorship of the so-called Orphic poetry: as early as the late 6th cent. the powerful singer who went down into Hades was thought especially competent to sing about eschatology and theogony. Pythagoreans (see PYTHAGORAS (1)) and adherents of Bacchic mystery cults adopted him as their figurehead, and the

Neoplatonist philosophers (see NEOPLATONISM) especially discerned deep theosophical knowledge in these poems and promoted Orpheus to the role of prime theological thinker.

In art the myth of Orpheus is treated from c.550 BC to late antiquity (main themes: as Argonaut; murder; in Hades; with the animals).

See MUSAEUS (1); ORPHIC LITERATURE; ORPHISM; PYTHAGORAS (1), PYTHAGOREANISM.

Testimonia in O. Kern, *Orphicorum Fragmenta* (1922). See also W. K. C. Guthrie, *Orpheus and Greek Religion* (1934, 2nd edn. 1952, repr. 1993); I. M. Linforth, *The Arts of Orpheus* (1941); F. Graf, in J. Bremmer (ed.), *Interpretations of Greek Mythology* (1987), 80–106; C. Segal, *Orpheus: The Myth of the Poet* (1989); LIMC 7. 1 (1994), 81–105.　　　　　　　　F. G.

Orphic literature, the pseudepigraphical literature ascribed to *Orpheus. Neoplatonist authors especially cite hexameters from different poems attributed to Orpheus 'the theologian', and an entire corpus of hymns is preserved. The fragments of his poetry have often been collected (Gesner 1764. Hermann 1805. Lobeck 1829. Kern 1922); the remains of a 4th-cent. papyrus commentary on a theogony of Orpheus, found in 1962 in the remains of a funeral pyre in Derveni (Macedonia), considerably enlarged the corpus of texts.

The main texts attributed to Orpheus are theogonies. The Neoplatonists (see NEOPLATONISM) relied chiefly on the 'Rhapsodic Theogony', a late Hellenistic work incorporating earlier theogonies; at least four earlier works are known, the earliest of which one goes back to the first half of the 5th cent. BC. They follow the Oriental succession scheme established by *Hesiod, but extend it in both directions: *Uranus and *Gaia, Hesiod's first ruling couple, are preceded by Night (see NYX) and Protogonos or Phanes, and *Zeus' reign was succeeded by that of *Dionysus. The decisive invention is a double birth myth of Dionysus. Dionysus is the incestuous offspring of Zeus and his daughter *Persephone; *Hera, in anger, ordered the Titans (see TITAN) to kill the young god, which they did; they cooked and ate the boy. Zeus in turn killed the Titans with his thunderbolt. From the ashes of the burning Titans sprang mankind; from the heart of Dionysus which had been saved, Zeus reproduced with *Semele the second Dionysus. This myth is told only in Neoplatonist sources, and the consequence that man has a double nature, from the Titans and from the divine child that has eaten, is the one drawn by Olympiodorus, not by the Orphic poet. Still the story explains why man's nature is wicked (he is an offspring of the wicked Titans), and why Dionysus could intercede on man's behalf with Persephone after death (Dionysus alone, if anyone, can assuage his mother's wrath against the offspring of the Titans). These elements are present already in Classical times— in a much-discussed fragment of a Pindaric threnos or dirge (see PINDAR), the overcoming of Persephone's 'ancient grief' is vital for the human *soul to attain the supreme stage in metempsychosis (fr. 133). *Plato (1) knows man's Titanic nature, and in a recently discovered gold tablet from *Thessaly (Pelinna, c.320 BC), the dead person has to appeal to Dionysus' help before the tribunal in the underworld.

Incidentally, these references show the role Orphic poetry played in Bacchic mystery cults, and their syncretistic nature. Other Orphic texts (as those of *Musaeus (1)) contained ritual prescriptions (τελεταί, 'rites': see TELETĒ). Others again were concerned with eschatology and especially with Eleusinian mythology (κατάβασις, 'descent to Hades'; see ELEUSIS), as were the related ones, by Musaeus and *Eumolpus. In Classical times,

Pythagorean Orphica were important; Pythagoras himself was said to have published poems under the name of Orpheus, according to *Ion (2) of Chios (d. 422 BC), and Epigenes (4th cent. BC) gave a list of Pythagoreans responsible for Orphica; some titles seem to indicate poems about cosmogony and natural history.

The corpus of 87 *hymns stands somewhat apart. They centre again round Dionysus and presuppose the Orphic theogony, and they seem to have been used in actual rituals: they must have belonged to a local Dionysiac community. Details of cult and language point to western Asia Minor (*Pergamum?) as place and the late Hellenistic or early imperial epoch as date of origin; such groups are well attested in this region and epoch. Even more loosely connected to Orpheus are two poems from late antiquity, under Orpheus' name, the *Orphic Argonautica* and the *Lithica*. In the *Argonautica*, Orpheus narrates the myth of the *Argonauts, with some superficial knowledge of Orphic cosmogony. The *Lithica* reveal the secret qualities of stones; it was only the Byzantine *Tzetzes who attributed them to Orpheus as a specialist in arcane lore.

See DIONYSUS; ORPHEUS; ORPHISM; PYTHAGORAS (1), PYTHAGOREANISM.

The *Orphica* of G. Hermann (1805) are a still useful collection of all poetry attributed to Orpheus, but recent edns. exist for most parts: fragments, O. Kern, *Orphicorum Fragmenta* (1922), the hymns, W. Quandt, *Orphei Hymni* (1955, 1963); *Argonautica*, G. Dotin (1930); *Lithica*, E. Abel (1881, repr. 1971); for the Derveni papyrus see the provisional publication in *ZPE* 47 (1982), after p. 300; for the best overall account M. L. West, *The Orphic Poems* (1983). See also bibliog. to ORPHISM.   F. G.

Orphism, a set of beliefs and religious practices thought to derive from Orphic literature. The concept is modern; it develops ancient and Florentine Neoplatonist ideas (see NEOPLATONISM) about the crucial role *Orpheus had as a theologian of all mystery cult (see MYSTERIES) in Greece. Reacting to F. Creuzer (1771–1858) who, though he denied that Orpheus was a historical figure, still thought that Orphic literature contained the essential knowledge of Eleusinian and Dionysiac mysteries (see ELEUSIS; DIONYSUS), C. A. Lobeck (*Aglaophamus*, 1829) had distinguished Eleusis, Bacchic (i.e. Dionysiac), and Samothracian mysteries (see CABIRI; SAMOTHRACE) from the Orphica; this opened the way to assimilate Orphic literature to Pythagoreanism and to see Orphism as a religious movement on its own, beginning in the late archaic age and combining ideas from Dionysian mysteries and Pythagorean philosophy. Formulated by E. Rohde (*Psyche*, 1894) and refined, among others, by M. P. Nilsson, A.-J. Festugière, and W. K. C. Guthrie, the concept of Orphism as a religious movement and part of a wider mystic and ascetic movement of late archaic Greece, or even as 'Orphic religion', gained general acceptance in 20th-cent. scholarship. However, Wilamowitz had pointed out that to the Greeks, there existed only Orphic literature and lowly religious quacks called Ὀρφεοτελεσταί, 'initiators according to Orpheus'; I. M. Linforth, later G. Zuntz and esp. W. Burkert went on to deny the existence of Orphism as a religious movement in the strict sense of the word, and recent archaeological finds have helped to change previously accepted opinion about Orphism.

Orphism is basically Orphic literature; it comprised, besides the dominant theogonical and eschatological poems, ritualistic texts, *hymns sung in ritual and prescriptions about specific *initiation and other rites. They were used by two sets of people, followers of Bacchic mystery groups, and individual ritual spe-

cialists, the itinerant Orpheotelests. The specialists used rituals to heal demonic possession, to harm by *magic, and to bring about eschatological hopes (Plat. *Rep.* 364be; *Derveni Papyrus* col. 16; see preceding article); they belong to the wide group of initiators, cathartic priests, and soothsayers attested from archaic Greece to imperial Rome, who often had oriental origins (see ORIENTAL CULTS AND RELIGION) and who performed outside the bounds of *polis religion. Bacchic rituals begin to have distinctive eschatological beliefs and rituals at least in the early 5th cent.; an inscription from *Cumae attests an exclusive burying ground, bone tablets from *Olbia in S. Russia show Bacchic belief in an afterlife (or even metempsychosis) and connect this with Orpheus, *Herodotus (1) connects Bacchic burial customs with Orpheus and derives them via Pythagoras from Egypt (Hdt. 2. 81). By the end of the century, the first gold leaf appears in a woman's grave in S. Italian *Hipponium (Vibo Valentia); it prescribes what the deceased must to do in the nether world in order to join the other 'initiated bacchoi'. More such leaves are known from N. Greece, S. Italy, and *Crete, ranging from the 4th cent. BC to a late Roman one. Some follow the Hipponium pattern, others describe an underworld tribunal under *Persephone where the deceased has to give the correct answer; a series from *Thurii attests belief in metempsychosis (see SOUL) and is influenced by S. Italian Pythagoreanism; a text from Pelinna in *Thessaly shows Dionysus as decisive helper with Persephone, which recalls the Orphic anthropogony. Vase paintings from S. Italy confirm the connection of Orpheus with eschatology (amphora by the Ganymede painter in Basle, c.325 BC) and Dionysus (crater by the Darius painter, c.375 BC), as does a terracotta group of Orpheus overcoming the Sirens from a Tarentine grave (J. Paul Getty Museum, later 4th cent.). The general impression is that many Bacchic mystery groups in the ancient world, ranging in time from the 5th cent. BC to the 2nd cent. AD and later, derived part of their beliefs and rituals from Orphic literature, without however striving for a unified doctrine or abstaining from other influences, like Pythagoreanism.

See DIONYSUS; MYSTERIES; ORPHEUS; ORPHIC LITERATURE; PYTHAGORAS (1), PYTHAGOREANISM.

M. P. Nilsson, *Harv. Theol. Rev.* 1935, 181–230, repr. in *Opuscula Selecta* 2 (1952), 628–83; W. K. C. Guthrie, *Orpheus and Greek Religion* (1934, 2nd edn. 1952, repr. 1993); I. M. Linforth, *The Arts of Orpheus* (1941); G. Zuntz, *Persephone. Three Essays in Religion and Thought in Magna Graecia* (1971); W. Burkert, *Colloquy*, 1977, 1–10; F. Graf, in T. Carpenter and C. Faraone (eds.), *Masks of Dionysus* (1993), 239–58; R. Parker in A. Powell (ed.), *The Greek World* (1995), 483–510; L. Brisson, *Orphée et l'Orphisme dans l'antiquité gréco-romaine* (1995).   F. G.

Orsippus, Megarian victor (see MEGARA) in the foot race at *Olympia in 720 BC. What passed as his epitaph, though it was written well after his death, claimed two feats for him. In a border dispute he established a larger territory for Megara than ever before; and he was the first athlete to compete naked at Olympia (*IG* 7. 52). Orsippus was not the only candidate for the latter distinction; Greeks considered their lack of shame at nakedness an important difference between themselves and *barbarians. The border dispute, which was presumably later than his Olympic victory, may have been with *Corinth; but Athens is another candidate. See ATHLETICS.

RE 18. 2, 'Orsippos'; J. B. Salmon, *BSA* 1972, 198 f. and *Wealthy Corinth* (1984), 71.   J. B. S.

Ortygia, old name of *Delos ('Quail Island'); its *nymph was identified with *Asteria. But as some half-dozen other places

Oscan and Umbrian

were also called Ortygia, it is by no means certain that all references (e.g. *Od.* 5. 123) are to Delos. See SYRACUSE.

Höfer in Roscher's *Lexikon*, under the name.　　　　J. A. W.

Oscan and **Umbrian** are the principal representatives of a group of closely related languages belonging to the Italic branch of *Indo-European. The usual name for this group is 'Osco-Umbrian' but a less cumbersome label 'Sabellic' has recently been introduced, based on what seems to have been the native term for the peoples of this linguistic community: an element *sab-/saf-* may be recognized in such names as *Samnium* (Oscan *safinim*) and *Sabini*. (It is clear from recorded glosses and from personal names that the *Sabini spoke a form of Osco-Umbrian, but there are virtually no inscriptions that can be assigned to them apart from an unintelligible text on a vase from Poggio Sommavilla.)

Oscan was spoken over a large part of S. Italy down to the 1st cent. BC. The best evidence comes from *Campania, where it was the language of the Samnites who took over the region in the 5th cent. There are a few early Oscan vase inscriptions written in the *Etruscan alphabet, but from the 4th cent. onwards, after the creation of the Oscan alphabet, there are found inscriptions of many kinds—coin legends, building inscriptions, texts painted on walls at *Pompeii, dedications, *curses, funerary inscriptions, religious texts (the *iúvilas* from *Capua). Oscan inscriptions in the same alphabet are also found inland, right across to *Apulia: some dialectal variation might be expected within such a large area, but there are only limited traces of this. There are more striking differences in the Oscan of *Lucania, written with the Greek alphabet and eventually—a sign of advancing *Romanization—the Latin alphabet, as in the *tabula Bantina, the longest Oscan text, a compilation of laws from the early 1st cent. BC. Sample text: *avt púst feíhúis pús fisnam amfret, eíseí tereí nep abellanús nep núvlanús pídum tríbarakattíns* 'but behind the walls that surround the temple, on that land neither the Abellani nor the Nolani are to build anything' (from *Nola, Ve. 1, B18–21); amongst features shared with Umbrian (see UMBRIANS) one may note the nom. pl. in *-ús*, inherited in nouns and extended to pronouns (*pús*), while characteristically Oscan is the perfect stem in *-tt-*.

Umbrian is known principally from the *tabulae Iguvinae* a collection of bronze tablets with texts relating to religious rituals, partly in the Umbrian alphabet, partly in the Latin alphabet, dating from *c*.200 to the early 1st cent. BC. There are in addition some two dozen miscellaneous short inscriptions from various places in Umbria, again in both alphabets; the earliest is dated to *c*.400 BC. Sample text: *este persklum aves anzeriates enetu pernaies pusnaes preveres treplanes iuve krapuvi tre buf fetu …* 'Begin this ceremony by observing the birds, those in front and those behind. Before the Trebulan gate sacrifice three oxen to Jupiter Grabovius …' (*TI* 1a. 1–3); a characteristic difference from Oscan is the elimination of diphthongs, cf. *preveres* beside Oscan *prai* and *veruís*.

Between Umbria and the Oscan-speaking south there is relatively meagre evidence (some inscriptions in the Latin alphabet from the last three centuries BC) for a number of related languages: Paelignian, Marrucinian, Vestinian, Volscian, Marsian, Aequian. Precise identification and classification of these is difficult and the conventional labels rest essentially on geographical correlation with peoples of ancient Italy, but in the case of Marrucinian there is internal confirmation from a bronze tablet from Rapino (Ve. 218) that proclaims a *toutai maroucai lixs* 'a law

for the Marrucinian people' (see MARRUCINI). These languages show features in common with both Oscan and Umbrian, and cannot be regarded simply as variants of one or other of them. In the mountainous central region there had no doubt always been several varieties of Osco-Umbrian spoken, and regular contact between dialectal groups combined with frequent population shifts resulted in a complex pattern of linguistic relationships.

The earliest substantial remains of any Osco-Umbrian language are the so-called South Picene inscriptions from east central Italy (and inland as far as Cures, in Sabine territory). These are mainly epitaphs on stone, written in a distinctive alphabet and dated to the 6th and 5th cents. BC. They are imperfectly understood, but there is no doubt that the language belongs within the Osco-Umbrian group: characteristic features are seen, for instance, in the phrase *safinas tútas* (gen. sg.) 'of the Sabine people', where a form of the *sab-/saf-* word occurs, and with Osco-Umbrian internal *-f-* (see below), and also the word for 'people' *t(o)úta* that is found in Oscan *touto*, Umbrian *tota* (and cf. Marrucinian *toutai* above).

Characteristic phonological features that distinguish the Osco-Umbrian languages from Latin include the treatment of inherited labiovelars as labials (cf. Oscan *pís*, Umbrian *pisi*: Lat. *quis*) and of internal voiced aspirates as fricatives (cf. Oscan *tfei*, Umbrian *tefe*: Lat. *tibi*). These features allow the recognition of loan-words: Osco-Umbrian forms in Lat. *popina* beside native *coquina*, *rufus* beside *ruber*, or conversely Lat. *quaestor* borrowed as Oscan *kvaísstur*, Umbrian *kvestur*. Distinctive morphological features include the o- stem gen. sg. in Oscan *-eis*, Umbrian *-es* (later *-er*) and the future perfect in *-us-*. See ITALY, LANGUAGES OF.

TEXTS E. Vetter, *Handbuch der italischen Dialekte* (1953); P. Poccetti, *Nuovi documenti italici* (1979); A. Marinetti, *Le iscrizioni sudpicene* (1985).
GRAMMAR R. von Planta, *Grammatik der oskisch-umbrischen Dialekte* (1892–7); C. D. Buck, *A Grammar of Oscan and Umbrian*[2] (1928); G. Meiser, *Lautgeschichte der umbrischen Sprache* (1986).　　J. H. W. P.

Oscans ('Οπικοί, Opici, Obsci, Osci), prehistoric inhabitants of S. Italy. Their original habitat, *Campania and much else, gradually shrank. They may be identical with the historical *Aurunci (Ausones, with rhotacism and *-co* suffix). When *Sabelli replaced them in Campania and elsewhere, their name survived for the newcomers' language, which the ancients called 'Oscan'. Samnites (see SAMNIUM), *Frentani, Campani, Lucani, *Bruttii, Mamertini (see MAMERTINES), and Apuli all spoke Oscan, the three first-named writing in a modified Etruscan alphabet, the others in Greek or Latin characters. The dialects of the central Italian *Paeligni, *Marrucini, *Vestini, *Marsi, *Sabini, and *Aequi (?) resembled Oscan. Many Oscan inscriptions survive, mostly dating from 300 to 90 BC. Oscan with Volscian (see VOLSCI) and Umbrian forms one group of Italic languages, *Latin and *Faliscan forming the other. It differs greatly from Latin in sound changes, word forms, and vocabulary, less in syntax (see ITALY, LANGUAGES OF; OSCAN AND UMBRIAN). Official and educated classes in Italy long continued to use Oscan; but the *Social War (3) ensured its ultimate displacement by Latin. *Strabo (5. 233) makes the astonishing statement that Atellan farces (see ATELLANA), the only Oscan literary form known to us, were performed in Oscan *at Rome* in his day. Certainly the language was still spoken at *Pompeii in AD 79 and in country districts survived even longer.

J. Whatmough, *Foundations of Roman Italy* (1937), 110, 301 (with bibliog.); E. Vetter, *Handbuch der italischen Dialekte* (1953), 1 ff.; E. Pulgram, *The Tongues of Italy* (1958); M. Pallottino, *Storia della prima Italia* (1984).　　E. T. S.; T. W. P.

Oschophoria (Ὠσχοφόρια), an *Attic festival celebrated early in the autumn month Pyanopsion, and organised by the *genos of Salaminioi (see SALAMIS (1); SUNIUM). The main rites were (1) a procession from a temple of *Dionysus to the shrine of *Athena Skiras at *Phaleron, led by two young men 'outstanding in wealth and nobility' (Salaminioi?), dressed as women and carrying ὠσχοί, i.e. bunches of grapes on the branch; (2) (probably) a race along the same course between ephebes of each tribe (see EPHĒBOI; PHYLAI), also holding ὠσχοί, the winner of which received first taste of a special five-ingredient brew (πενταπλόα); (3) a banquet, with which female 'dinner-bearers' (δειπνοφόροι) were involved. The libations were accompanied by a mixed cry, of joy, ἐλελεῦ, and of grief, ἰού, ἰού. The elements of abnormality in the rite (*transvestism, and the ambiguous cry) were explained aitiologically by reference to incidents accompanying the homecoming of *Theseus.

I. Rutherford and J. Irvine, ZPE 72 (1988); C. Calame, Thésée et l'imaginaire athénien (1991), 143–8.   R. C. T. P.

Osiris (Egypt. wsỉr), the Egyptian god whose death and resurrection provided the model for the fate of each Pharaoh, and, from the Middle Kingdom, also of non-royal persons. The association with Pharaoh is most marked at Abydus in Upper Egypt. In the Pyramid Texts, he is killed by his brother *Set, but his body is prevented by *Isis and Nephthys from rotting, and restored to life. The myth gradually grew in complexity, esp. in the Late Period: Plut., De Is. et Os. 12–19 (indispensable comm. and trans., by J. G. Griffiths, 1970). In iconography, Osiris, as 'lord of the west', appears as a mummy holding crook and 'flail', most commonly in the New Kingdom as judge with *Anubis at the 'weighing of the heart'. The basis of the Hellenistic/Roman Osirian *mysteries however was probably the 'festival of Choiak', the celebration of Osiris' death and resurrection (cf. Apul. Met. 11. 27–30). In the Roman period (from the 1st cent. BC), the Osiris Canopus, a jar with the head of Osiris carried in processions (ibid., 11. 11), becomes the preferred public form, alluding to the water of life given by Osiris. See EGYPTIAN DEITIES.

J. G. Griffiths, The Origins of Osiris² (1980); W. Helck, in RE Suppl. 9 (1962), 469–513; LIMC 7. 1 (1994), 107 ff.   R. L. G.

Osroëne, in NW *Mesopotamia, bounded on three sides by the Khabur and *Euphrates, and on the north by Mt. Masius. In the later 2nd cent. BC it broke away from *Seleucid control and formed a separate kingdom with *Edessa as capital. Its kings bore Semitic names, and the population was mainly Aramean, with a Greek and *Parthian admixture. As a Parthian vassal state and a buffer between two empires, Osroëne played a prominent and ambiguous role in the struggle between Rome and *Parthia. After the campaigns of L. Verus it became a Roman dependency, later a province. Long coveted and more than once overrun by the *Sasanids, it was conquered by the Arabs (AD 638).

A king-list survives in a Syriac chronicle ascribed to Dionysius of Tell-Mahre (probably c. AD 800). Of its kings, named Abgar, the following may be noted: Abgar I (92–68 BC); II (68–53 BC), the betrayer of Crassus; V (4 BC–AD 7 and 13–50), famous for his spurious correspondence with Christ; VII (109–116), who entertained Trajan in Edessa; L. Aelius Septimius Abgar VIII (177–212; 212–14 jointly with his son), who became a Christian.

A. von Gutschmid, Untersuchungen über die Geschichte des Königsreichs Osroene, Mem. acad. St Petersbourg, 7th ser. 35, 1 f.; A. Bertinelli, ANRW 2. 9. 1 (1976), 3–45; M. Colledge, Parthian Art (1977).   M. S. D.; E. W. G.; S. S.-W.

Ossa, a mountain of 1,978 m. (nearly 6,500 ft.) in Thessalian Magnesia (see THESSALY). On the north it is separated from the massif of *Olympus (1) by the defile of *Tempe, but on the south it forms with *Pelion an almost unbroken wall which shuts off the interior of Thessaly from the sea.

Ostia, city at the mouth of the *Tiber, colonia at least by the late 4th cent. BC, heavily involved with Rome's naval history, commerce, and communications, and one of the best-known Roman cities archaeologically. Abandoned in the 5th cent. AD, Ostia was covered with drifting sand from coastal dunes, and the area was sparsely populated until this century because of malaria. With the coast southwards, and the remains of *Portus, this therefore makes an archaeological site of the highest importance.

Tradition ascribed the foundation to King Ancus *Marcius, and claimed that the trade in salt from the adjacent lagoons (which was certainly significant in historical times) dated back to that epoch (cf. the *via Salaria). The Latin civilization is well represented in the immediate hinterland by the important discoveries at Castel di Decima on the via Laurentina and Ficana, overlooking the confluence of the Tiber and the Fossa Galeria, an important route leading inland towards *Veii, and dominating the coastal plain just inland from Ostia. No remains have been found at Ostia earlier than those of the small (c.2 ha.) fortified settlement, typical of the coloniae maritimae of the time, constructed at the Tiber mouth, from which it took its name at the end of the 4th cent. (the so-called 'Castrum').

The Tiber was the route to the arsenal of Rome, the Navalia, and needed strategic protection throughout the *Punic wars, and on into the age of the depredations of *piracy, which destroyed a Roman fleet at Ostia in 67 BC. Since the 6th cent. BC it had also provided access for travellers and traders to the wharves of Rome (greatly improved and embellished during the 2nd cent.). The imperial power won by Rome at that time gave its sea access new importance, and, as the grain-supply (see FOOD SUPPLY, Roman) of the city came under increased governmental supervision from the time of C. *Sempronius Gracchus, a resource of huge political sensitivity began to pass through the difficult and insecure waters of Ostia regularly. A circuit of walls (probably of the end of the 2nd cent. BC) enclosed 69 ha.; C. *Marius (1) captured Ostia by treachery in 87 and sacked it. In the Civil War the loyalty to Octavian's cause of members of the local élite, Cartilius Poplicola and Lucilius Gamala, benefited the city under the victorious regime. But Strabo describes Ostia in the Augustan period as 'a city without a harbour' (5. 3. 5 (232)), and says that the huge merchant-ships of southern Spain 'make for *Puteoli and Ostia, the shipyard of Rome' (3. 2. 6 (145)); the city was still only a way-station on the route up the river, and the ports of *Campania (which long received much of the grain trade and retained their prosperity until the third century) were unrivalled until the construction of the basins of *Claudius and *Trajan at Portus.

The good communications of the coastal area attracted the villas of the Roman élite even before the discomfiture of the pirates in the 60s, and there were spacious houses of the Pompeian type within Ostia's new walls as well as large estates in the territory. These increased in number greatly at the end of the republic, and Ostia became the centre of a resort coast which stretched south to *Antium, the litus Laurentinum where *Pliny (2) the Younger had a maritime *villa. It was to service this community that Ostia became the 'very comfortable and convenient city' (amoenissima civitas) of the proem to *Minucius Felix' dialogue Octavius.

These comforts are very apparent. Most of the houses are good quality *insulae* which, when they were first studied, gave an exaggeratedly optimistic idea of what Roman urban conditions were like (some of the apartments have as many as seven rooms), the streets were often colonnaded or arcaded, and there are areas of very spacious houses, like the area outside the seaward gate, (where the synagogue was excavated in 1962). An aqueduct supplied at least 17 bath-houses (some very grand, like the forum baths). Ostia was well-equipped with taverns and similar places of resort, and provides important information about them (see INNS, RESTAURANTS). A lavish theatre was originally probably a benefaction from M. *Vipsanius Agrippa, perhaps because of the town's contributions to the war against Sex. Pompeius. The buildings of the *forum (first given monumental form under Augustus and his successors; the large Capitoline temple is Hadrianic) occupied most of the area of the former *colonia*, and are on a magnificent scale.

The principal testimony to Ostia's economic life are the great *horrea* or storehouses (see GRANARIES, Roman), including many used by the *annona* (in the 3rd cent. increasingly transformed into other uses). There are a number of headquarters of *collegia*, associations among other things connected with commerce, the river, the harbour, or warehousing (see CLUBS, ROMAN); the elaborately decorated premises were intended to provide a place of visible, semi-public social interaction for the bosses rather than the rank and file. The 'Square of the Corporations' is the most remarkable building of this kind, taking the form of a piazza surrounded by colonnades and *tabernae* for the representatives of ports involved in the grain-trade, and for others connected with the harbour: its precise function remains unclear. Our understanding of the relationship of the city to the river is hampered by changes in the Tiber's course and erosion of the site: there are some indications that important dependencies of the city extended to the north on both banks of the river. But the main extent of the town was a long development beside the via Ostiensis, stretching towards Rome, and dense occupation to the west around two roads which forked beyond the seaward gate and gave access to different parts of the littoral.

Most of what is visible at Ostia is a development of the Flavian, Antonine, and Severan periods. The uniformity of the kiln-fired brick construction and the regularity of the plan suggest wholesale redevelopment, and large-scale investment in urban property. Much of what we know of Ostia refers to the 2nd and 3rd cents. when the city appears to have been home to a social milieu who had made their money in harbour-activities; their descendants and successors saw a further move away from economic activity in the direction of *amoenitas* and in late antiquity the *domus*, small and elegant, with elaborate water-decorations, returned to the city-centre (e.g. the famous House of Cupid and Psyche).

Ostia is relatively small (there is no sign that the built-up area was ever larger than about 50 ha., and much of this was not primarily dwelling-places). It was overwhelmingly a service-town, for the countryside around, for the spread-out activities of the Tiber-bank, and the harbours of Portus, and for the numerous passers-by on their way to and from Rome (wide horizons are apparent in the diversity of its religious cults). Such service functions supported an economically relatively privileged population and a considerable number of their slaves who are archaeologically largely invisible. Otherwise labour is likely to have been available on a seasonal basis from Rome and other parts of the densely populated region around it. Ostia was thus rather a focal point in a port-region rather than a harbour-town in the strict sense, and its importance is much more as an example of the social and economic, architectural and urban conditions prevailing in Rome itself than as either a typical example of a Mediterranean port or a normal Italian regional centre.

The serious study of the site was made possible by the eradication of malaria, and very large areas were uncovered during 1938–42, so that about three-quarters of the inner part of the city is visible today. Work has concentrated more recently on the detailed publication of the building-history of sections of the excavated site, on stratigraphic excavation of small areas (the Baths of the Swimmer (Terme del Nuotatore) are a particularly celebrated case) and on the exploration of the urban periphery and territory. See HOUSES, ITALIAN.

Excavations published in the occasional but continuing series *Scavi di Ostia*; inscriptions, *CIL* 14. The landmark of Ostian studies remains the great synthesis by R. Meiggs, *Roman Ostia* (1960, 2nd edn. 1973). Archaeological guide: C. Pavolini, *Ostia* (1983). Other studies: G. Hermansen, *Ostia: Aspects of Roman City Life* (1981); Boersma, *Amoenissima civitas: Block V ii at Ostia, Description and Analysis of the Visible Remains* (1985); J. E. Packer, *MAAR* 31 (1971); J. T. Barker, *Living and Working with the Gods* (1994). N. P.

Ostorius Scapula, Publius (suffect consul before AD 46), of equestrian background, succeeded Aulus *Plautius as governor of *Britain in 47. He consolidated Roman control by disarming some of the previously conquered peoples, and invaded north Wales, but was forced to turn back by a revolt of the *Brigantes. Legion XX (see LEGION) was moved *c*.49 from *Camulodunum (Colchester), which was then secured by a colony, for campaigns against the *Silures and Ordovices in south and central Wales, which ended in the defeat of *Caratacus, although the war dragged on. Ostorius received *ornamenta triumphalia* but died in 52, worn out by his responsibilities.

Tac. *Ann.* 12. 31–9. D. R. Dudley and G. Webster, *The Roman Conquest of Britain, AD 43–57* (1965), 131; A. R. Birley, *The Fasti of Roman Britain* (1981), 41. J. B. C.

ostraca are potsherds used for writing. Almost all found in Greece are incised; in Athens they were used particularly in voting in *ostracism. In Egypt the great majority are written with pen and ink. There the preferred fabric is the neck or shoulders of an *amphora. The discrepancy is probably due to humid conditions of survival in Europe. In Egypt the Ptolemaic ostraca from the Nile valley are mainly tax receipts written in abbreviated form; later, orders and lists are common. Letters, school exercises, and religious texts, pagan and Christian, increase. The military ostraca from *mons Claudianus and the Wadi Fawakhir in the Eastern Desert are of a different character: documents and letters are more extensive, there is more Latin, and ostraca are used where papyrus would have been the norm in the Nile valley. The Greek-Demotic *Archive of Hor* from Saqqara provides important evidence for the chronology of Antiochus IV Epiphanes' invasion of Egypt. The Thebaid is the most prolific source in all periods. Outside Egypt Latin ostraca have been found in *Tripolitania, *Carthage and *Masada. The commonest sources are rubbish mounds or house ruins. See POTTERY (GREEK), INSCRIPTIONS ON.

M. L. Lang, *The Athenian Agora 25—Ostraca* (1990). Ink ostraca in Rhodes: *AR* 34 (1988), 81–3. U. Wilcken, *Griechische Ostraka aus Ägypten und Nubien* (1899)—the standard introduction. Earlier publications listed in J. F. Oates and others, *Checklist of editions of Greek Papyri and Ostraca*[3], *BASP* suppl. 4 (1985). J. C. Shelton, *Greek Ostraca in the Ashmolean Museum from Oxyrhynchus* (1988); C. Gallazzi and others,

Ostraka greci del Museo egizio del Cairo (1988); H. Cuvigny and G. Wagner, Ostraca grecs de Douch (= Kysis) (1986–); J. Bingen and W. Clarysse, Elkab III (= Eileithuias Polis) (1989); J. D. Ray, Archive of Hor (1976); R. S. Bagnall, 'Papyri and Ostraka from Quseir al-Qadim (Leukos Limen)', BASP 23 (1986), 1–60. C. Tsiparis, Ostraca Lundensia (1979); C. Gallazzi, Ostraka da Tebtynis dell' Univ. di Padova (1979–); O. Guéraud, 'Ostraca de la Wadi Eawâkhir', BIFAO 41 (1942), 141–96; R. Marichal, 'Ostraca de Bu Njem', CRAcad. Inscr. 1979, 436–52; R. Cagnat and A. Merlin, 'Ostraka latins de Carthage', JS 1911, 514; H. M. Cotton and J. Geiger, Masada II (1989).　　　　W. E. H. C.

ostracism in Athens in the 5th cent. BC was a method of banishing a citizen for ten years (cf. EXILE, Greek). Each year in the sixth *prytany the question whether an ostracism should be held that year was put to the *ekklēsia. If the people voted in favour of holding an ostracism, it was held on a day in the eighth prytany in the *Agora under the supervision of the *archontes and the *boulē. Each citizen who wished to vote wrote on a fragment of pottery (ostrakon) the name of the citizen whom he wished to be banished. The voters were marshalled by *phylai in an enclosure erected for the occasion, to ensure that no one put in more than one ostrakon. When all had voted, the ostraka were counted and, provided that there was a total of at least 6,000, the man whose name appeared on the largest number was ostracized. (An alternative view, attributed to *Philochorus, FGrH 328 F 30, is that the ostracism was valid only if at least 6,000 votes were cast against one man.) He had to leave the country within ten days and remain in exile for ten years, but he did not forfeit his citizenship or property, and at the end of the ten years he could return to live in Athens without any disgrace or disability.

The date of the institution of ostracism has been a matter of dispute. According to the standard account (Arist. Ath. Pol. 22) the law about it was introduced by *Cleisthenes (2) in 508/7, but the first ostracism was not held until 487. Some modern scholars accept this account and offer various conjectural explanations of the twenty years' interval. Others maintain that the law cannot have been passed until shortly before the first ostracism in 487, and that Cleisthenes therefore was not its author; a statement attributed to *Androtion (FGrH 324 F 6) has been adduced in support of this view, but its interpretation and value are doubtful. A third view, based on later sources, is that Cleisthenes introduced a different method of ostracism by the boulē and was himself ostracized by this method, which was subsequently replaced by the method first used in 487.

The man ostracized in 487 was Hipparchus son of Charmus, a relative of the ex-tyrant *Hippias (1). He was followed in 486 by Megacles, one of the Alcmaeonids (see ALCMAEONIDAE), and in 485 by some other adherent of Hippias' family, probably Callias son of Cratius. No doubt these three had all become unpopular because it was thought that they favoured the Persian invaders and the restoration of the tyranny. Xanthippus was ostracized in 484 and *Aristides (1) in 482, but both of these returned from exile in 480 when an amnesty was declared in an attempt to muster the full strength of Athens to resist the invasion of Xerxes. Other prominent men known to have been ostracized are *Themistocles about 470, *Cimon in 461, and *Thucydides (1) son of Melesias in 443. *Hyperbolus was the last victim of the system; his ostracism is usually dated in 417, though some scholars have placed it in 416 or 415. Ostracism then fell out of use, although the law authorizing it remained in force in the 4th cent. The *graphē paranomōn was found to be a more convenient method of attacking politicians.

It is often hard to tell why a particular man was ostracized.

Sometimes, as in the cases of Cimon and Thucydides (1), the Athenians seem to have ostracized a man to express their rejection of a policy for which he stood and their support for an opposing leader; thus an ostracism might serve a purpose similar to that of a modern general election. But no doubt individual citizens were often actuated by personal malice or other non-political motives, as is illustrated by the story of the yokel who wished to vote against Aristides because he was tired of hearing him called 'the Just' (Plut. Arist. 7. 7).

Over 10,000 ostraka, dumped in the Agora or *Ceramicus after use, have now been found. The names include not only men whom we know to have been actually ostracized but also a considerable number of others. Some are men quite unknown to us, and it may well be that they were not prominent politicians but merely had an odd vote cast against them by some malicious personal acquaintance. Particularly interesting is a find of 190 ostraka in a well on the north slope of the Acropolis (see ATHENS, TOPOGRAPHY), all inscribed with the name of Themistocles by only a few different hands. Presumably they were prepared for distribution by his opponents. This suggests that he was the victim of an organized campaign, and it illustrates the importance of ostracism as a political weapon in 5th-cent. Athens. See also LITERACY.

R. Thomsen, The Origin of Ostracism (1972); E. Vanderpool, Lectures in Memory of L. T. Semple 2 (1973), 217–70; M. L. Lang, The Athenian Agora 25: Ostraka (1990); P. Harding, Androtion and the Atthis (1994), 94–8; P. J. Rhodes, in R. Osborne and S. Hornblower (eds.), Ritual, Finance, Politics (1994), ch. 5. S. Brenne in W. Coulson and others (eds.) The Archaeology of Athens and Attica under the Democracy (1994) 13–24: illustrations.　　　　D. M. M.

Ostrogoths See GOTHS.

Otacilius (RE 12) **Crassus, Titus,** was praetor 217 BC, and from then until his death in 211 was in continuous charge of a fleet off *Lilybaeum; he raided Africa in 215 and 212. In 215 he and M. Aemilius Regillus appeared to be about to be elected consuls for 214, but Q. *Fabius Maximus Verrucosus, whose niece was married to Otacilius, intervened and secured the election of himself and M. *Claudius Marcellus (1), the half-brother of Otacilius. Otacilius received a second praetorship. He appears again in a similar story concerning the elections for 210, but his part is probably a doublet of the episode in 215. He was a *pontifex and is also described as an augur (see AUGURES), but this is based on a mistake by Livy or a corruption in his text (see MRR 1. 284 n. 6 and 7, cf. 406 n. 4).

Scullard, RP 59, 64–5; Briscoe, CAH 8². 66–7, 70.　　　　J. Br.

Otho (Marcus Salvius (RE 21) **Otho)** (AD 32–69), whose father received *patrician rank from *Claudius, was husband of *Poppaea Sabina and friend of *Nero. As Nero fell in love with his wife (afterwards divorced), he was sent to *Lusitania as governor in 58 and remained there until Nero's death (68). He supported *Galba and hoped to be his heir. Disappointed, he organized a conspiracy among the *Praetorians and was hailed emperor (15 Jan. 69). He tried to appear as the legitimate successor of Nero. Egypt, Africa, and the legions of the Danube and the Euphrates declared for him. But the legions of the Rhine had already chosen *Vitellius, and their military preparations were far advanced. By early March their advanced guard had crossed the Alps, and an Othonian expedition to southern Gaul achieved little. His generals *Vestricius Spurinna and *Annius Gallus held the line of the Po, but his armies from the Danube arrived only gradually. Though defeated in a minor engagement the Vitellians were soon heavily reinforced: yet Otho insisted on a decisive battle before he could oppose equal strength. His troops advanced from *Bedriacum, *c.*35 km. (22 miles) east of *Cremona, and were irretrievably defeated. He committed suicide on 16 Apr. 69. Otho's profligacy seems not to have impaired his energy or his interest in government. But he was a slave to the Praetorians who had elevated him.

Plutarch, *Otho* (comm. E. G. Hardy, 1890); Suetonius, *Otho* (comm. G. W. Mooney, 1930). A. Passerini, 'Le due battaglie presso Bedriacum', *Studi di antichità offerti a E. Ciaceri* (1940); F. Klingner, 'Die Geschichte Kaiser Othos bei Tacitus', *Sächsische Sb. Phil.-hist. Kl.* 1940. See also on GALBA.   A. M.; G. E. F. C.; M. T. G.

otium See LABOUR.

Ouranos See URANUS.

ovatio was a form of victory celebration less lavish and impressive than a *triumph, probably of native Roman or Latin origin. It could be granted to a general who was unable to claim a full triumph, e.g. because his victory had not involved the destruction of a large number of the enemy or because he had handed over his army to a successor. He entered Rome on foot or horseback instead of in a chariot, dressed in a *toga praetexta* (not *picta*) and without a sceptre, wearing a wreath of myrtle instead of laurel, and the procession was much less spectacular. For a list of Roman *ovationes* see *RE*. The last recorded one is in AD 47, that of A. *Plautius.

H. S. Versnel, *Triumphus* (1970), ch. 5.   H. H. S.; A. W. L.

Ovid (Publius Ovidius Naso, 43 BC–AD 17), poet, was born at *Sulmo in the Abruzzi on 20 March. Our chief source for his life is one of his own poems, *Tr.* 4. 10. As the son of an old equestrian family, Ovid was sent to Rome for his education. His rhetorical studies under *Arellius Fuscus and *Porcius Latro, in which he evidently acquitted himself with distinction, are described by the elder Seneca (L. *Annaeus Seneca (1)) (*Controv.* 2. 2. 8–12; cf. 9. 5. 17). His education was rounded off by the usual Grand Tour through Greek lands (*Tr.* 1. 2. 77–8, *Pont.* 2. 10. 21 ff.). After holding some minor judicial posts, he apparently abandoned public life for poetry—thus enacting one of the commonplaces of Roman elegiac autobiography. With early backing from M. *Valerius Messalla Corvinus (*Pont.* 1. 7. 27–8) Ovid quickly gained prominence as a writer, and by AD 8 he was the leading poet of Rome. In that year he was suddenly banished by *Augustus to *Tomis on the Black (*Euxine) Sea. Ovid refers to two causes of offence in his exile poetry: *carmen*, a poem, the *Ars Amatoria*; and *error*, an indiscretion. He has much to say concerning the first of these counts, especially in *Tr.* 2; concerning the second he repeatedly refuses to elaborate—though, since the *Ars* had already been out for some years in AD 8, the *error* must have been the more immediate cause. Amid the continuing speculation (cf. J. C. Thibault, *The Mystery of Ovid's Exile* (1964); Syme, 215–22), all that can be reconstructed from Ovid's own hints is a vague picture of involuntary complicity (cf. *Tr.* 2. 103–8) in some scandal affecting the imperial house. Tomis, a superficially Hellenized town with a wretched climate on the extreme edge of the empire, was a singularly cruel place in which to abandon Rome's most urbane poet. Public and private pleading failed to appease Augustus or (later) *Tiberius: Ovid languished in Tomis until his death, probably (so *Jerome) in AD 17. Several of the elegies from exile are addressed to his third wife (connected somehow with the *gens Fabia: *Pont.* 1. 2. 136), who remained behind

him in Rome; Ovid also mentions a daughter and two grandchildren.

Works (all extant poems written in elegiac couplets except the *Metamorphoses*).

Amores, 'Loves'. Three books of elegies (15, 20, and 15 poems) presenting the ostensibly autobiographical misadventures of a poet in love. What we have in this three-book collection is a second edition, published not before 16 BC and perhaps somewhat later (1. 14. 45–9); work on the original five books mentioned in Ovid's playful editorial preface may have begun *c.*25 BC. (For the vexed chronology of all Ovid's amatory works see McKeown 1. 74–89.) The *Amores* continue the distinctive approach to elegy taken by Ovid's older contemporaries *Propertius and *Tibullus and by the shadowy *Cornelius Gallus before them (cf. *Tr.* 4. 10. 53–4); the frequent use of mythological illustration recalls especially Propertius. Corinna, the named mistress of Ovid's collection, owes much to Propertius' Cynthia and Tibullus' Delia; her name itself (along with the pet bird mourned in *Am.* 2. 6) acknowledges a debt to an important forerunner of the Augustan elegiac woman, *Catullus (1)'s Lesbia ('Lesbia' looks to *Sappho; 'Corinna' names another Greek female poet; see CORINNA). Erotic elegy before Ovid had featured a disjunction in the first-person voice between a very knowing poet and a very unknowing lover. Ovid closes this gap, and achieves a closer fit between literary and erotic conventions, by featuring a protagonist who loves as knowingly as he writes. Ovid's lover is familiar with the rules of the genre, understands the necessity for them, and manipulates them to his advantage. The result is not so much a parody of previous erotic elegy as a newly rigorous and zestful exploration of its possibilities.

Heroides, 'Heroines' (so called by *Priscian, *Gramm. Lat.* 2. 544 Keil; but cf. *Ars Am.* 3. 345 *Epistula*. The correct form may have been *Epistulae Heroidum*, 'Heroines' Epistles'). Of the 'single *Heroides*' 1–14 are letters from mythological female figures to absent husbands or lovers; *Her.* 15, whose Ovidian authorship is in doubt, is from the historical but heavily mythologized Sappho. In their argumentative ingenuity these poems show us the Ovid who was a star declaimer in the schools; in that they speak of female subjectivity under pressure they also testify to an admiration for Euripidean tragedy (see EURIPIDES), and give us a glimpse of what we have lost in Ovid's own *Medea*. The heroines tend to be well known rather than obscure: some of the interest of the letters lies in locating the point at which they are to be 'inserted' into prior canonical works, usually epic or tragic, and in considering the operations of revision and recall. The epistolary format is sometimes archly appropriate ('what harm will a letter do?', Phaedra asks *Hippolytus (1)), sometimes blithely inappropriate (where on her deserted shore, one wonders, will *Ariadne find a postman?); above all, perhaps, it effects a characteristically Alexandrian modernization by Ovid (see HELLENISTIC POETRY AT ROME) of the dramatic monologue by presenting the heroine as a writer, her impassioned speech as a written text, and the process of poetic composition as itself part of the action. Ovid claims the *Heroides* to be a new kind of literary work (*Ars Am.* 3. 346); they owe something to an experiment in Propertius (4. 3). The idea for the 'double *Heroides*' (16–21) may have come from the replies which Ovid's friend *Sabinus is said to have composed for the 'single *Heroides*' (*Am.* 2. 18, a poem which probably places the 'single *Heroides*' between the two editions of the *Amores*). Formerly doubted, 16–21 are now generally accepted as Ovid's own, stylistic discrepancies with 1–14 being explained by a later com-

Ovid

positional date (perhaps contemporary with the *Fasti*). Arguably it is in these paired letters that the potential of the epistolary format is most fully realized.

Medicamina Faciei Femineae, 'Cosmetics for the Female Face'. A didactic poem which predates the third book of the *Ars* (*Ars Am.* 3. 205–6). Only the first 100 lines survive, the latter 50 of which, a catalogue of recipes, show Ovid matching *Nicander (in the *Theriaca* and *Alexipharmaca*) in virtuoso ability to make poetry out of abstruse drug-lore. See COSMETICS.

Ars Amatoria, 'Art of Love' (for the title cf. Sen. *Controv.* 3. 7. 2). A didactic poem (see DIDACTIC POETRY) in three books on the arts of courtship and erotic intrigue; the mechanics of sexual technique receive but limited attention (2. 703–32, 3. 769–808), perhaps reversing the proportions of works such as the manual of Philaenis (*POxy.* 2891). Books 1–2, datable in their present form to about 1 BC (1. 171 ff.), advise men about women; book 3, presented as a sequel (3. 811 may or may not imply a substantial gap in real time), advises women about men—arguably with one eye still firmly upon the interests of the latter. The situations addressed owe much to previous elegy; at times the preceptor seems to explore the rules of love poetry as much as of love (*ars amatoria* functioning as *ars poetica*). Mythological illustration is more fully developed than in the *Amores*, anticipating the full-scale narratives of *Metamorphoses* and *Fasti*. The actors themselves are firmly located in contemporary Rome: the vivid specificity of the social milieux is sometimes more reminiscent of satire than of earlier elegy. As didactic, the *Ars* takes many traits from Virgil's *Georgics* and Lucretius. It has an irreverent and parodic feel, however, deriving not from the theme alone (other didactic poems, as Ovid was to point out (*Tr.* 2. 471 ff.), could be frivolous too) but from the combination of theme and metre. Conventionally, didactic was a subset of epic written in hexameters; Ovid's choice of elegiac couplets, as it signals a continuity with his own *Amores*, signals a felt discontinuity with mainstream didactic. As successor to the *Amores*, the *Ars* achieves much of its novelty through a reversal of the implied roles of poet and reader: in the *Amores* the reader oversees the poet's love affair; in the *Ars* the poet oversees the reader's love affair. It may be (for we cannot but read with hindsight derived from later events) that this newly direct implication of the Roman reader in the erotic text made the *Ars* the poem most likely to be picked on when the climate turned unfavourable to Ovid's work. The poet's attempts to forestall moral criticism in this area (1. 31–4; cf. *Tr.* 2. 245–52) seem disingenuous.

Remedia Amoris, 'Remedies for Love'. A kind of recantation of the *Ars Amatoria*; the poet now instructs his readers how to extricate themselves from a love affair. The *Remedia* (date between 1 BC and AD 2 indicated by 155–8) appropriately concludes Ovid's early career in erotic elegiac experimentation.

Metamorphoses, 'Transformations'. An unorthodox *epic in fifteen books, Ovid's only surviving work in hexameters, composed in the years immediately preceding his exile in AD 8. The poem is a collection of tales from classical and Near Eastern myth and legend, each of which describes or somehow alludes to a supernatural change of shape (see METAMORPHOSIS). Metamorphic myths enjoyed an especial vogue in Hellenistic times and had previously been collected in poems (all now lost) by Nicander, by the obscure Boios or *Boio (whose *Ornithogonia*, 'Generation of Birds', was apparently adapted by Macer, *Tr.* 4. 10. 43), and by *Parthenius. In Ovid's hands metamorphosis involves more than just a taste for the bizarre. Throughout the poem (and with programmatic emphasis in the opening cosmogony) the theme calls attention to the boundaries between divine and human, animal and inanimate, raising fundamental questions about definition and hierarchy in the universe. Structurally the *Metamorphoses* is a paradox. The preface promises an unbroken narrative, epic in its scope, from the creation to the poet's own day; but throughout much of the poem chronological linearity takes second place to patterns of thematic association and contrast, book divisions promote asymmetry over symmetry (see BOOKS, POETIC), and the ingenious transitions (criticized by the classicizing Quintilian: *Inst.* 4. 1. 77) do as much to emphasize the autonomy of individual episodes as to weld them into a continuum. In some ways the poem's closest analogue (structurally; but also for its interest in the mythic explanation of origins) is *Callimachus (3)'s *Aetia*, whose avowed aesthetic, influential on all Augustan poetry, the *Metamorphoses* seems both to reject and to embrace (1. 4; E. J. Kenney, *PCPS* 1976, 46 ff.). There is a real flirtation with the Augustan model of epic teleology established in the *Aeneid*; but it can be argued that the metamorphic world of Ovid's poem is structurally and ideologically incompatible with such a vision. Wherever his sources are wholly or partly extant, Ovid's dialogues with the literary past repay the closest attention. He engages with an unprecedented range of Greek and Roman writing; every genre, not just epic, leaves its mark in the poem's idiom. But in the final analysis the *Metamorphoses* renders its sources superfluous: with its many internal narrators and internal audiences, with its repeated stress on the processes of report and retelling whereby stories enter the common currency, the primary intertextual reading which the poem insists on is one internal to itself. As narrative it brilliantly captures the infinite variety and patterning of the mythological tradition on which it draws (and which, for many later communities of readers, it effectively supersedes). Ovid's poetic imagination, intensely verbal and intensely visual, finds here its finest expression. The *Metamorphoses* tells utterly memorable stories about the aspirations and sufferings which define and threaten the human condition; from the poem's characteristic aestheticization of those sufferings comes both its surface brightness and its profound power to disturb.

Fasti, 'Calendar'. A poetical calendar of the Roman year with one book devoted to each month (see CALENDAR, ROMAN). At the time of Ovid's exile it was incomplete, and only the first six books (January–June) survive. These show evidence of partial revision at Tomis (e.g. 1. 3, 4. 81–4); the silence which is books 7–12 abides as a reminder of a life interrupted. The poem's astronomy (1. 2) is influenced by *Aratus (1)'s *Phaenomena*, its aetiological treatment of history and religion (1. 1) by Callimachus. These debts show Ovid at his most overtly Alexandrian; but, like Propertius in his fourth book (4. 2, 4, 9, 10), he is applying Callimachean aetiology to distinctively Roman material. The *Fasti* belongs equally in the tradition of *Varro's lost *Antiquitates*; and the figure without whom the poem is ultimately inconceivable is the emperor Augustus, whose recuperation and appropriation of Roman religious discourse constitutes the basis of Ovid's own poetic appropriation (1. 13–14). The restrictiveness of the day-to-day format as a determinant of both subject-matter and structure is repeatedly stressed by the poet (4. 417, 5. 147–8). However, comparison with other calendrical sources (cf. A. Degrassi, *Inscr. Ital.* 13, *Fasti et Elogia* (1963), esp. the *Fasti Praenestini* compiled by *Verrius Flaccus) reveals the extent to which Ovid has been free to select and order his emphases; and the very fragmentation of the narrative material (e.g. the life of Romulus is split and chronologically shuffled between five or six different dates) offers an interesting contrast with the contemporaneous (and more fluid) *Metamorphoses*. The poet is a prominent character in his own poem: he appears in expository passages as an eager antiquarian weighing aetiological and etymological variants with himself or with interlocutors who range from the *Muses (as in books 1–2 of Callimachus' *Aetia*) to random bystanders. Long mined for its detailed information about the perceived roots of Roman religion and ritual, the *Fasti* has begun to attract new attention both as a complex work of art and as an exploration of religious thinking at a time of ideological realignment.

Tristia, 'Sorrows'. A series of books dispatched from exile between AD 9 and 12, containing (so *Tr.* 1, 3, 4, 5) poems addressed by Ovid to his wife and to various unnamed persons in Rome. The 'sorrows' of the title are the past, present, and anticipated sufferings associated with the relegation to the Black Sea: the *Tristia*, like the later *Epistulae ex Ponto*, function as open letters in which the poet campaigns from afar for a reconsideration of his sentence. *Tr.* 2, addressed to Augustus, differs in format from the other four books. A single poem of over 500 lines, it uses an ostensibly submissive appeal for imperial clemency as the point of departure for a sustained defence of the poet's career and artistic integrity. The mood of the *Tristia* is deeply introspective, with all the rich opportunities for geography and ethnography subsumed within the narrative of an inner journey: the ships on which Ovid voyages into exile merge with his metaphorical 'ship of fortune' (1. 5. 17–18); the icy torpor and infertility of the Pontic landscape become indices of the poet's own (allegedly) frozen creativity. The books read at times as *post mortem* autobiography, with exile figured as death and the elegiac metre reclaiming its supposed origins in funereal lament. On one level the insistently self-deprecatory poetics (e.g. 1. 1. 3 ff.) offer an artful fiction of incompetence, extending a *topos* of mock modesty familiar from earlier literary programmes in the sub-epic genres. But only on one level. The pervasive imagery of sickness and barrenness, decay and death, though belied by the continued technical perfection of Ovid's writing, captures an erosion of the spirit which feels real enough, in and between the lines, in the later books from Tomis.

Epistulae ex Ponto, 'Epistles from Pontus'. Four books of poems from exile, differing from the *Tristia* only in that the addressees are named (1. 1. 17–18), and characterized with greater individuality. The letters in books 1–3 were gathered into a single collection ('without order': so claims 3. 9. 51–4) in AD 13; book 4 probably appeared posthumously (4. 9 written in AD 16).

Ibis. An elaborate curse-poem in elegiacs (perhaps AD 10 or 11) directed at an enemy whose identity is hidden under the name of a bird of unclean habits; both title and treatment derive from a lost work of Callimachus (55–62). As at the beginning of the *Tristia*, Ovid dramatizes a forced break with his former self: a previously benign poet now seeks to wound; his elegy has become a prelude to Archilochean iambic (see ARCHILOCHUS; IAMBIC POETRY, GREEK and LATIN). In fact, the *Ibis* displays much continuity with Ovid's earlier work. The poem's ferociously dense catalogue of sufferings achieves a mythological comprehensiveness (despite its small compass) comparable to that of the *Metamorphoses* or *Fasti*; even its 'unOvidian' obscurity (57–60) comes across as a thoroughly Ovidian experiment (cf. G. Williams, *PCPS* 1992, 174 ff.).

Lost and spurious works. Our principal loss is Ovid's tragedy *Medea* (*Tr.* 2. 553). Two verses survive, one cited by Quintilian (*Inst.* 8. 5. 6), the other by the Elder Seneca (*Suas.* 3. 7). The poet of the *Fasti* was among those who translated Aratus' *Phaenomena*

into Latin hexameters; two brief fragments remain. It is most unlikely that either the *Halieutica* or the *Nux* is by Ovid (cf. J. A. Richmond in *ANRW* 2. 31. 4, 2744 ff., with bibliography).

Ovid is not only one of the finest writers of antiquity; he is also one of the finest readers. Not since Callimachus, perhaps, had a poet shown such understanding in depth and in detail of the literary traditions of which he was the inheritor; never was such understanding carried so lightly. In a national literature dominated by anxious gestures towards the past, Ovid's relationship with his predecessors is exuberantly unanxious. Moreover, the same revisionary energy which he brings to alien texts is applied no less to his own. Ovid constantly reworks himself, at the level of the poem (the *Ars* reframes the *Amores*, the *Remedia* the *Ars*), of the episode (cross-referential Persephones in *Metamorphoses* and *Fasti*), and even of the individual line and phrase (cf. A. Lueneburg, *De Ovidio sui imitatore* (1888)). This paradigm of self-imitation, together with the deceptively easy smoothness and symmetry which he bequeaths to the dactylic metres, make his manner (once achieved) endlessly imitable to later generations as a kind of Ovidian *koinē*. What remains inimitable, however, is the sheer wealth of the poet's invention. Ovid devoted most of his career to a single genre, elegy, so that by the time of the *Remedia* he was already able to claim (*Rem. Am.* 395–6) that 'elegy owes as much to me as epic does to Virgil'. (The *Metamorphoses* still lay ahead, an epic which—although it is much else besides—can justly be said to be the epic of an elegist.) But within elegy he achieved an unparalleled variety of output by exploiting and extending the range of the genre as no poet had before— not by ignoring its traditional norms, but by carrying to new extremes the *Alexandrian and Augustan tendency to explore a *genre's potentiality by testing its boundaries.

No Roman poet can equal Ovid's impact upon western art and culture; only the critics, stuffy as *Quintilian (*Inst.* 10. 1. 88, 98), have sometimes stood aloof. Especially remarkable in its appropriations has been the *Metamorphoses*—from the Christianizing ingenuities codified in the 14th-cent. *Ovide moralisé* to the bold painterly narratives of Titian's *poesie* in the Renaissance. In the Anglophone world the terms of Ovid's *reception in the modern era have largely been defined by Dryden and Pope; behind these influential Ovids can still be sensed the Naso of Shakespeare's Holofernes, 'smelling out the odoriferous flowers of fancy', and the figure of 'Venus clerk, Ovyde' in Chaucer's *Hous of Fame*. Though not immune to the challenges which the 20th cent. has posed to the continuity of the classical tradition, Ovid's poetry, now entering upon its third millennium, still reaches artists as well as scholars: a 1979 preface to the *Metamorphoses* by Italo Calvino is at once an academic essay and an assimilation of Ovid's narrative aesthetic to Calvino's own 'postmodern' fiction ('Ovid and Universal Contiguity' translated in *The Literature Machine* (1987), 146 ff.). See ELEGIAC POETRY (LATIN).

BIBLIOGRAPHICAL SURVEYS *ANRW* 2. 31. 4 (1981); J. A. Barsby, *G&R* New Surveys 1978 (addenda J. Booth 1991).

TEXTS *Am., Medic., Ars Am., Rem. Am.* E. J. Kenney (OCT, 1961). *Her.* H. Dörrie (1971). *Met.* W. S. Anderson (Teubner, 1977); R. J. Tarrant (OCT, in prep.). *Fast.* E. H. Alton, D. E. W. Wormell, and E. Courtney (Teubner, 1978). *Tr., Pont., Ib.,* frag. S. G. Owen (OCT, 1915; ed. maior of *Tr.* 1889). *Tr.* G. Luck (see (c)). *Pont.* J. A. Richmond (Teubner, 1990). *Ib.* A. La Penna (see (c)). Complete: G. P. Goold (Loeb, rev. 1977–89). Cf. R. J. Tarrant in *Texts and Transmission* (1983).

EDITIONS WITH COMMENTARY (T= with Eng. trans.). *Am.* J. C. McKeown (1987–   ); P. Brandt (1911); (1, T) J. A. Barsby (1973); (2, T) J. Booth (1991). *Her.* A. Palmer (1898); (1–3) A. Barchiesi (1992).

Medic. G. Rosati (1985). *Ars. Am.* E. Pianezzola, G. Baldo, and L. Cristante (1991); P. Brandt (1902); (1) A. S. Hollis (1977). *Rem. Am.* P. Pinotti (1988); A. A. R. Henderson (1979). *Met.* (comm. only) F. Bömer (1969–86); M. Haupt, O. Korn, R. Ehwald, and M. von Albrecht (1853–1966); (1) A. G. Lee (1953); (8) A. S. Hollis (1970); (6–10) W. S. Anderson (1972). *Fast.* F. Bömer (1957–8); (T) J. G. Frazer (1929). *Tr.* G. Luck (1967–77). *Pont.* (1) A. Scholte (1933); (4. 1–7, 16; comm. only) M. Helzle (1989). *Ib.* A. La Penna (1957).

ANNOTATED TRANSLATIONS Complete: Loeb (see (*b*)). *Am.*, *Medic.*, *Ars Am.*, *Rem. Am.*, *Met.*, *Tr.* A. D. Melville, with E. J. Kenney (1986–92). *Am.* (with text) A. G. Lee (1968). *Her.* H. Isbell (1990). *Met.* A. Golding (1567) ('Shakespeare's Ovid') in edn. of J. F. Nims (1965); (1–8, with text) D. E. Hill (1985–92).

LIFE AND TIMES R. Syme, *History in Ovid* (1978); J. Fairweather, *CQ* 1987, 181 ff. Cf. A. Barchiesi, *Il poeta e il principe: Ovidio e il discorso augusteo* (1994).

LITERARY STUDIES General: E. J. Kenney in *Cambridge History of Classical Literature*, 2 (1982); S. Mack, *Ovid* (1988); L. P. Wilkinson, *Ovid Recalled* (1955); H. Fränkel, *Ovid: A Poet Between Two Worlds* (1945); on the *Met.*, J. Solodow, *The World of Ovid's Metamorphoses* (1988); G. Galinsky, *Ovid's Metamorphoses* (1975). Cf. A. Barchiesi, *MD* 16, 1986, 77 ff.; S. Hinds, *Ramus* 1987, 4 ff. Literary and artistic reception: C. Martindale (ed.), *Ovid Renewed* (1988); L. Barkan, *The Gods Made Flesh* (1986).　　　　　　　　　　　　　　　　　　　　　　　　　　S. E. H.

Ovinius (*RE* 1) *Pompeius Festus 290 Lindsay records the bill of a tribune (see TRIBUNI PLEBIS) Ovinius which provided that the *censors should enrol in the *senate *optimum quemque* ('the best fitted individuals'?) from every rank either by *curia* (reading *curiatim*) or under oath (reading *iurati*). Festus apparently interprets this as ending the system whereby the chief annual magistrates (see MAGISTRACY, ROMAN) enrolled their own nominees. The Ovinian plebiscite is therefore assumed (not necessarily correctly) to have been a general norm transferring control of the senatorial list from consuls to censors between 339 (when one censorship was reserved to plebeians) and 318 or 312 BC (the first recorded censorial revision). If so, it may have increased the independence of the senate vis-à-vis the consuls. The terms of the plebiscite (which Festus may not reproduce *verbatim*) are problematic: if it required the censors to give precedence to all worthy ex-magistrates (P. Willems, *Le Sénat de la république romaine* (1885) 1. 153 ff.), it formalized the criteria for senatorial membership, perhaps particularly benefiting potential plebeian recruits.

CAH 7². 2. 393 f.; K.-J. Hölkeskamp, *Die Entstehung der Nobilität* (1987), 142 ff.　　　　　　　　　　　　　　　　　　　　　　　　　　　　A. D.

ownership, Greek ideas about There was no Greek term for 'ownership'. For *Aristotle (*Rhet.* 1361ᵃ21) the mark of a thing being one's own is that one is free to give or sell it, but under Classical Athenian law a man could sell property which he could only give in bequest if he had no surviving legitimate son. While a distinction between 'ownership' and 'possession' was recognized, the distinction was not elaborated in the body of law at Athens, or, as far as we know, elsewhere.

The sense in which an individual could be said to 'own' property depended on what that property was. There are traditions which attest inalienable, heritable but not marketable, grants of land to individuals; in Classical Athens, there was no bar on the sale of land, but the regulation of bequests and the aspersions cast in court on those who sell ancestral land suggest that in some sense land was held to belong to the family and not simply to the individual. Regulations about dowries (see BETROTHAL; MARRIAGE LAW), which passed through the husband to the wife's children and could be used but not alienated by the husband,

similarly suggest a sense of 'family' property. Mineral resources seem to have been regarded as belonging to the community: their exploitation required an agreement with the state as well as with the owner of the land surface. See MINES AND MINING.

*Women's legal rights to buy, sell, and inherit property varied from state to state, being minimal at Athens but much more extensive elsewhere, although women were often forbidden to buy and sell property except through a male *kyrios*. But even at Athens it is clear that women's stake in family property was recognized socially if not by law. See INHERITANCE, *Greek*; LAW IN GREECE.

A. R. W. Harrison, *The Law of Athens*, 1 (1968); L. Foxhall, *CQ* 1989, 22–44; M. I. Finley, *Studies in Land and Credit in Classical Athens 500–200 BC* (1951); S. Todd, *The Shape of Athenian Law* (1994), index under 'Owner, Ownership'.　　　　　　　　　　　　　　　　　　　R. G. O.

ownership, Roman Ownership (*dominium*), though apparently not defined by the Roman jurists, is the right to a thing, irrespective of whether the owner has any control or enjoyment of it. The owner's right to use his property was at all times subject to restrictions, whether to secure advantages for a neighbouring owner or for the public interest. These restrictions might derive from servitudes, from legislation or from the general law, especially the remedies granted by the praetor in terms of his *edict.

Ownership of a thing could be acquired in various ways. Someone who took possession of an ownerless object would become owner. In particular someone who caught a fish or wild animal would own it so long as it remained in his possession. More commonly people would become owners by acquiring an object from its previous owner, e.g. under a contract of sale. The transferor would often make actual delivery of a movable, but delivery of the keys of a store could transfer its contents. Even when the transferor was not owner, a person who acquired the thing in good faith (*bona fides*) by a recognized transaction (*iustus titulus*) e.g. sale, which would normally transfer ownership, became the full civil-law owner if he possessed it, if movable, for a year, or if immovable, for two years, provided always the thing had at no time been stolen. This form of acquisition by prescription, called *usucapio*, also applied to *res mancipi* (see MANCIPATIO), i.e. to things like Italic land which under the civil law could be transferred only by formal conveyance (*mancipatio*) or a collusive lawsuit (*in iure cessio*). If instead *res mancipi* were simply delivered e.g. by pointing out to the acquirer the boundaries of the land, pursuant to a suitable transaction such as sale, the recipient would become full civil-law owner of the movable or immovable after one or two years respectively. Until the period of prescription was over, the old civil law would not have protected either the transferee from a non-owner or the person who acquired a *res mancipi* without a formal conveyance. But in the late republic the praetor intervened in both cases by granting an action to protect the acquirer (*actio Publiciana*). This put the transferee of a *res mancipi* for almost all purposes in the position of the full civil-law owner, while the acquirer from a non-owner was protected against everyone except the true owner of the object. Indeed by the time of *Gaius (2) (*Inst.* 2. 40) for practical purposes the concept of ownership extended beyond the full civil-law owner at least to the informal transferee of a *res mancipi* (so-called 'bonitary owner'). Justinian (see JUSTINIAN'S CODIFICATION) abolished the distinction between *res mancipi* and other property, and with it the idea of two sorts of ownership.

An owner of a thing could assert his title against anyone

possessing it by an action known as a *rei vindicatio* (claim for a thing). The term signified in the early Roman process the formal assertions of the right of ownership made by both parties. The *actio Publiciana*, which protected people who were acquiring a thing by prescription, was a variant form of *rei vindicatio* with the fiction that the time necessary for prescription had elapsed (Gai. *Inst.* 4. 36). In the formulary procedure the successful plaintiff in a *rei vindicatio* could not compel the defendant to return the thing, but the plaintiff was allowed to swear its value and thus by judicious over-valuation to encourage its return. If indeed the defendant lost the *vindicatio* and paid the plaintiff's valuation of the thing, he became its full civil law owner.

Two or more persons could have common ownership (*communio*) of a thing, including land, or of an undivided group of things, such as an inheritance, originating in a contract of partnership (*societas*), or, independently of their intention, in a common inheritance or legacy. In early law (*consortium, societas ercto non cito*: Gai. *Inst.* 3. 154a, b) a legal transaction in relation to the thing by one owner affected the rights of all (e.g. alienation transferred ownership of the whole), but in Classical law such a transaction affected only the particular co-owner's notional share, or, if it did not admit of such divided effect, was void. Thus a purported creation of a usufruct over the whole affected only the creator's share, and a creation of a right of way was void. There were special rules as to manumission of a common slave. In the material enjoyment of the property each co-owner could exercise the full rights of an owner, subject to the veto of any other co-owner (*ius prohibendi*). Disputes were adjusted by an action for division of the property (*actio communi dividundo*) or inheritance (*actio familiae erciscundae*). The judge divided the property among the co-owners in proportion to their shares, with equalizing payments where necessary. Profits, expenses, and damages, incurred by individual joint owners, were also apportioned by the judge.

Provincial land belonged to the State (Gai. *Inst.* 2. 7), and could not be owned by individuals, unless by special grant of Italic right (**ius Italicum*) it had been assimilated to land in Italy. The distinction was, however, technical rather than practical since the interest of individuals in such land was effectively protected. Since the civil law system of *usucapio* could not apply to provincial land, a system of acquisition by long prescription (*longi temporis praescriptio*) developed, giving a title after ten years when the persons with competing interests were both present, and after twenty years when one was absent. Justinian in effect merged *usucapio* and *longi temporis praescriptio*.

P. Bonfante, *Corso di diritto romano*, 2. 1 (1926); M. Kaser, *Eigentum und Besitz*² (1956); A. Watson, *The Law of Property in the Later Roman Republic* (1968); G. Diósdi, *Ownership in Ancient and Preclassical Law* (1970); A. Rodger, *Owners and Neighbours in Roman Law* (1972); P. Birks, *Acta Juridica* 1985, 1; J. M. Rainer, *Bau- und nachbarrechtliche Bestimmungen im klassischen römischen Recht* (1987); P. Birks (ed.), *New Perspectives in the Roman Law of Property* (1989).   A. B.; B. N.; A. F. R.

Oxus (Ὦξος, mod. Amu Darya), central Asian river bounding *Bactria to the south before flowing north-west into the Aral Sea. Known by name to *Herodotus (1) and *Aristotle, it was apparently confused by them with the *Araxes. It was discovered by *Alexander (3) the Great, and some Indian trade was known to come by it, and thence by the *Caspian and the rivers Cyrus and Phasis (see COLCHIS) to the Black (*Euxine) Sea. The Graeco-Bactrian settlement of *Ai Khanoum was founded on its left bank. A Greek dedication to the river-god (2nd-cent. BC) was found at Takht-i Sangin (Tadzhikistan).

Strabo 11. 514–18; Ptol. *Geog.* 6. 9–18. S. Sherwin-White and A. Kuhrt, *From Samarkhand to Sardis* (1993), 185 and pl. 16 (dedication).
E. H. W.; A. J. S. S.

Oxus treasure A rich hoard of gold and silver objects of 5th- and 4th-cent. BC date, found on or near the river *Oxus in 1877 and mostly now in the British Museum. It is uncertain, however, whether the objects belong to a single hoard, since the purported assemblage included coins as late as the 2nd cent. BC. Many of the pieces are, however, distinctively Achaemenian in character and must be earlier. These include a pair of gold penannular armlets with finials in the form of winged, horned griffins, of a kind seen carried by tribute bearers on reliefs at *Persepolis. In common with other armlets and rings from the hoard, they were once inlaid with semi-precious stones. There are gold and silver statuettes; especially notable is a model four-horse chariot, in which sits a Persian nobleman. The plate consists of a gold jug, and some gold and silver bowls; a single handle in the form of a wild goat had gilded ears, eyes and hoofs. There are many gold appliqués of a kind known to have been sewn on the garments of Persian kings and high officials.

O. M. Dalton, *The Treasure of the Oxus* (1964).   M. V.

Oxylus See HERACLIDAE.

Oxyrhynchus (Behnesa), a nome capital (see NOMOS (1)) beyond the Bahr Yusuf west of the Nile, was the richest source of papyri ever found in Egypt. Grenfell and Hunt excavated for papyri (1897–1906) and were succeeded by Pistelli and Breccia (1910–34). The finds came from rubbish mounds north-west and south-east of the town; they are now worked out. Most are Roman or Byzantine; the Ptolemaic levels lay beneath the water table. Over 70 per cent of surviving literary papyri come from Oxyrhynchus.

Sculptured funeral stelae of the 1st–3rd cents. AD from a cemetery west of the town came on the market in the 1970s.

POxy. 1–59 (1898–   ). *Pubblicazioni della Società Italiana*, 1–15 (1912–   ). J. Krüger, *Oxyrhynchos in der Kaiserzeit* (1990). E. G. Turner, *JEg. Arch.* 1952. H. D. Scheider, *Beelden van Behnasa* (1982).
W. E. H. C.

Oxyrhynchus, the historian from *Hellenica of Oxyrhynchus*: two sets of papyrus fragments found at *Oxyrhynchus in Egypt, both 2nd cent. BC: POxy 842 (London Papyrus, found in 1906, edited by Grenfell and Hunt, who named the unknown author P. = Papyrus) and PSI 1304 (Florentine Papyrus, found in 1942). Both belong to the same historical work dating from the first half of the 4th cent. BC and contain a total of about 20 pages of Greek history, with some gaps. The London Papyrus deals with the political atmosphere in Greece in 397/6, the naval war between Athens under *Conon (1) and Sparta, the conflict between *Thebes (1) and *Phocis (including a valuable excursus on the constitution of the Boeotian Confederacy (see BOEOTIA; FEDERAL STATES)), and *Agesilaus' campaigns in Asia Minor. The Florentine Papyrus deals with events of the Ionian–Decelean War (final phase of the *Peloponnesian War), esp. the sea-battle at Notium 407/6.

The Oxyrhynchus historian (henceforth 'P.') represents a valuable independent tradition parallel to *Xenophon (1), *Hell.* 1 and 2, and is, via *Ephorus, the basis of *Diodorus (3)'s books 13–14. P. wrote shortly after the events related in his narrative; he is a primary author whose work is based on autopsy and personal research. The presentation is objective and factual, the style moderate, no speeches, frequent excursuses; the chronological arrangement is by summers and winters, like *Thucydides (2) (quoted in ch. 2. of the Florentine Papyrus). Hence it is a continuation of Thucydides from 411 to 395. P. wrote after the *King's Peace in 387/6 (cf. 11. 2) and before the end of the Third *Sacred War in 346 (13. 3).

Numerous attempts have been made to determine the author's identity. Among the names put forward are Ephorus (Walker, Gelzer), *Theopompus (3) (E. Meyer, Laqueur, Ruschenbusch und Lehmann), *Androtion (Momigliano, Canfora), *Daimachus (Jacoby), *Cratippus (Breitenbach, Accame, Harding). Ephorus and Theopompus are not primary sources; Ephorus writes κατὰ γένος, that is he arranged his material by topic; furthermore P. is hardly a writer of universal history. Style, ethos, and presentation exclude Theopompus. P. is no atthidographer either (see ATTHIS): Androtion arranged his material by *archontes. Daimachus, the local historian of Boeotia, can be ruled out: P. does indeed show valuable knowledge of *Boeotia and the Boeotian Confederacy, but betrays no sympathy for

Theban policy (cf. 12. 4–5). Detailed knowledge of the situation at Athens, sympathy for Conon, and the close continuation of Thucydides suggest an Athenian author (see above): The most likely candidate is a Cratippus (*FGrH* 64) whom Jacoby called a 'später Schwindelautor', a late fraud—unjustly, since he seems to have been a historian of great importance. This identification is based on the correspondences between, on the one hand, what we know of Cratippus' work from T2 = Plut. *Mor.* 345c–e and, (on the other) Ephorus in Diod. 13 and 14 (cf. Accame).

EDITIONS V. Bartoletti and M. Chambers (Teubner, 2nd edn. 1993); P. R. McKechnie and S. J. Kern (1988).

COMMENTARIES I. A. F. Bruce, *A Historical Commentary on the Hell. Ox.* (1967) McKechnie and Kern (1988), see above.

OTHER WORKS H. R. Breitenbach, *RE* Suppl. 12, 1970, 383 ff. (fundamental); G. Bonamente, *Studi sulle Elleniche di Ossirinco* (1973); G. A. Lehmann, *ZPE* 26, 1977, 181 ff.; S. Accame, *MGR* 6, 1978, 125 ff.; P. Harding, *AHB* 1, 1987, 101 ff.; K. Meister, *Die griechische Geschichtsschreibung* (1990). See also CRATIPPUS.   K. M.

Pacuvius, Marcus (*c*.130–220), stage poet and painter of South Italian birth, nephew and pupil of Quintus *Ennius. His family belonged to *Brundisium, and he spent his last years in *Tarentum. He seems to have had relations with L. *Aemilius Paullus (2) (consul for the first time 182), or with Paullus' sons, and C. *Laelius (2) (consul 140).

Titles of 13 tragedies of the Attic (see TRAGEDY, GREEK) type (*Antiopa*, *Armorum iudicium*, *Atalanta*, *Chryses*, *Dulorestes*, *Hermiona*, *Iliona*, *Medus*, *Niptra*, *Pentheus*, *Periboea*, *Teucer*, *Thyestes* [?]) are transmitted. The themes of 8 relate to the Trojan War. *Cicero approved of the way in which, when translating *Sophocles (1)'s *Niptra*, Pacuvius made Ulysses' reaction to pain more appropriate to a great hero (*Tusc*. 2. 48). Several plots seem to have come from post-Euripidean pieces (see EURIPIDES). The *Paulus* must have dealt with some episode in the life of L. Aemilius Paullus or in that of his father. *Fulgentius cites (*Serm. ant.* 12) a comedy *Pseudo*, while *Pomponius Porphyrio (Hor. *Sat*. 1. 10. 46) and *Diomedes (3) (*GL* 1. 485. 32–4) refer to *saturae*. In the time of *Pliny (1) the Elder the temple of *Hercules in the *forum Boarium boasted the possession of a painting by him (*HN* 35. 19).

Pacuvius' borrowings of Greek poetic vocabulary, neologisms (cf. e.g. the description of some dolphins as *Nerei repandirostrum incuruiceruicum pecus*, '*Nereus*' snub-nosed, curved-necked flock') and unusual items of syntax brought him criticism from the grammatical purists of his own time. In the 1st cent. he was regarded as the greatest of the Latin tragic poets, surpassing *Accius in the artistry of his deployment of the high tragic style. Cicero cites a number of extended passages in his rhetorical and philosophical dialogues. The *Armorum iudicium*, *Chryses*, *Iliona*, and *Teucer* remained in the 1st-cent. BC repertoire. *Nonius Marcellus had access to copies of the *Atalanta*, *Periboea*, *Dulorestes*, and *Hermiona* and possibly others. The several references to borrowings from Pacuvius in the late commentaries on *Virgil's *Aeneid* doubtless go back to the scholarship of the 1st cent. AD.

E. H. Warmington, *Remains of Old Latin* 2 (1936), 158 ff. (with trans.); Ribbeck, *TRF*³ 87 ff. G. d'Anna, *M. Pacuvii fragmenta* (1967); I. Mariotti, *Introduzione a Pacuvio* (1960).   H. D. J.

Padus (Ligurian *Bodincus*, Greek Ἠριδανός, mod. Po): Italy's longest river, with numerous tributaries. It rises in the Cottian *Alps, flows about 400 miles eastward through Cisalpine Gaul (see GAUL (CISALPINE)), and enters the *Adriatic near *Ravenna. Its valley was inhabited in prehistoric times by *terramaricoli* (see TERRAMARA), and from *Etruscan days dikes have protected its reclaimed riparian lands. In antiquity navigation as far as Turin (*Augusta Taurinorum) was possible but hazardous owing to the swift current. Since ancient times floods and the silt carried down have considerably altered its lower course and delta. See also ERIDANUS; TRANSPADANA.

Polyb. 2. 16; Strabo 4. 203 f.; 5. 212, 217; Plin. *HN* 3. 117–22. C. Jacini, *Il viaggio del Po* (1937) with full bibliography.   E. T. S.

Paean (Παιάν). Originally a healing god later equated with *Apollo and *Asclepius, also a ritual exclamation (ἰὲ Παιάν) and a name for the song addressed to these gods. In Archaic and Classical times it is used in various religious, political and personal situations, the common function being to create a dialogue between man and god, the latter being petitioned or thanked for well-being and salvation. Typical situations for paean-singing were: (1) a religious festival (esp. for Apollo), (2) illness or *plague, where Apollo is addressed in his role as Healer (*Il*. 1. 473), (3) a military action (*Il*. 22. 391, Aesch. *Sept*. 635), (4) a sympotic context (see SYMPOSIUM, SYMPOSIUM LITERATURE), where all sang it in unison after the *libations and before the symposium (Alcm. fr. 98. 2; Aesch. *Ag*. 247; Pl. *Symp*. 176a; Athen. 149c), (5) on public occasions such as the ratification of peace (Xen. *Hell*. 7. 4. 36; Arr. 7. 11). Paeans were not confined to Apollo, but were also sung to *Zeus (Xen. *An*. 3. 2. 9), *Poseidon (*Hell*. 4. 7. 4), *Dionysus, Asclepius, and *Hygieia. From the 4th cent. BC the songs become more formalized and are also addressed to individuals such as *Lysander (Plut. *Lys*. 18) and T. Quinctius Flamininus (Plut. *Flam*. 16). See also HYMNS.

L. Käppel, *Paian* (1992).   C. M. B.; E. Kr.

Paeligni, a central Italian tribe always closely associated with the *Marrucini, *Marsi, and *Vestini. Their language greatly resembled *Oscan. Allies of Rome before 300 BC, the Paeligni remained loyal until the *Social War (3), when their principal town, *Corfinium, became the Italic capital. After 90 BC, they were rapidly Romanized. *Ovid, born at *Sulmo, is their most celebrated native son.

F. van Wonterghem, *Ant. Class.* 1973, 36 ff., *Superaequum, Corfinium, Sulmo* (Forma Italiae 4: 1, 1984).   E. T. S.; T. W. P.

Paeonius, Greek sculptor from *Mende in *Thrace, active *c*.420. Known from an original work found at *Olympia in 1875—a marble statue of a flying *Nike (Victory), mounted on a high triangular base, and displayed just to the east of the temple of *Zeus. The inscription on the base states that the monument was erected by the Messenians and Naupactians (see MESSENIA, *History*; NAUPACTUS), and that Paeonius both made it and won the competition for the acroteria for the temple (of Zeus). This latter statement clarifies *Pausanias (3)'s report (5. 10. 8) that he and *Alcamenes made the temple's east and west pediments, which is impossible on stylistic grounds.

Pausanias (5. 26. 1) guessed that the Nike commemorated the battle of *Oeniadae in 452, but reported a Messenian tradition that it celebrated Sparta's defeat at Sphacteria in 425 (see PYLOS), and that they omitted to say so out of fear of the Spartans. The statue's style, which is certainly post-Parthenonian (i.e. later than the *Parthenon at Athens), proves the latter correct. A virtuoso essay in marble-carving, the Nike represents the 'birthday' of the flamboyant or 'Rich' style in Greek sculpture, just as the Tyrannicides had announced the birth of the Severe style (see CRITIUS). Her wet and windswept drapery clearly alludes to a battle at sea; she is also the first partially nude divinity in Classical Greek art.

A. F. Stewart, *Greek Sculpture* (1990), 89 ff., 165, 271, figs. 408–11.
A. F. S.

Paestum (mod. Pesto), a Sybarite colony (see SYBARIS), founded as Posidonia *c*.600 BC 60 km. south-east of Naples (see NEAPOLIS). It grew rapidly, exploiting its agricultural resources and control of communications, and there was a period of intense urban expansion in the 6th cent., during which a series of temples was constructed. In 410, it fell to the Lucanians and gradually became Oscanized (see LUCANIA; OSCANS). In 273 a Latin colony was founded there (see COLONIZATION, ROMAN); it continued to flourish under Roman control. It retained the right to issue coins until the 1st cent. AD. A second colony was founded in AD 71, and inscriptions reveal a thriving civic body until late antiquity, when malaria (see DISEASE) and marshy conditions became a problem. Both the Greek and Roman cities were orthogonally planned, and there are extensive remains of all phases of the city's history, and of extramural sanctuaries at Santa Venere and Foce del Sele.

U. Zanotti Bianco, *Heraion al Foce del Sele* (1951–4); J. G. Pedley, *Paestum* (1990); M. Mello, *Paestum Romana* (1974); M. Mello and G. Voza, *Le iscrizioni latine di Paestum* (1968); M. Napoli, *Paestum* (1970). K. L.

Pagae See MEGARA.

pagan, paganism The Latin word *paganus* means literally one who inhabits a *pagus*: see Festus, 247 Lindsay, and *Servius'* comment on *Virgil's phrase *pagos et compita circum* (G. 2. 382). By imperial times (e.g. Tac. *Hist.* 3. 24. 3, Plin. *Ep.* 10. 86 B), the term was applied to one who stayed at home or lived a civilian life. Christian reference implied one who was not a *miles Christi* (hence *fides pagana* and *paganus fidelis* in Tert. *De corona* 11. 4 f. and numerous examples thereafter). *Paganismus* was first used in the 4th cent. by Marius Victorinus (*Ep. ad Galatios* 2. 4. 9) and *Augustine (*De diversis quaestionibus* 83. 83). Traditional usage nevertheless persisted (Prudent. *Cath.* 11. 87, Macrob. *Sat.* 1. 16. 6).

Both expressions, in the Christian era, may have been colloquial (see *Cod. Theod.* 16. 5. 46 of AD 409 and Augustine *Ep.* 184. 5). *Paganus* occurs more in sermons than in treatises, where it appears to demand explanation (as by Augustine *Retract.* 2. 43)— the implication being that the more sophisticated were aware of a misleading facility. Literary usage had long preferred *gentes* and associated forms. Such also was the custom in the *Vetus Latina*, with Greek analogues in the *Septuagint, which suggests that a readiness to group all other believers under one heading owed something to the exclusiveness of the *Jews. *Orosius (*Hist. adv. paganos* 1, prologue 9) and *Prudentius (*c. Symm.* 1. 449) were

wrong in supposing an allusion to mere rusticity and in any case referred to *gentiles/gentilia* as well (see also Filastrius 111. 2).

Use of the terms in English has encouraged the risky assumption that religious belief and practice, outside the Christian and Jewish spheres, formed a unity. Christian convenience and a late Roman inclination to *syncretism contributed to the habit. The English word 'paganism' was transferred from Latin at least as early as the 14th cent. In more modern times it has been applied to non-European peoples, with a suggestion of 'natural religion'.

Such language ignores only with prejudice the sheer variety of ancient cult. A modern and objective writer might justify its use by the undoubted desire of men and women, especially among the more philosophical from the 3rd cent. AD, to stress the exalted nature of an ultimate and single god and to associate as divinities the different objects of local devotion. The prayer of Lucius in *Apuleius is a useful example of the latter (*Met.* 11. 2). *Plotinus' 'flight of the alone to the alone' is notorious (*Enn.* 6. 9) and *Julian (particularly in his *Hymn to King Helios*) carried that quasi-monotheistic process to a cultic peak. Even apparently less reflective men were increasingly eclectic in their practical observance: note the priesthoods of *Symmachus (2) and his peers (J. F. Matthews, *JRS* 1973, 175–95). We may have our suspicions about the historicity of the erudite catholicity of the emperor Severus Alexander (see AURELIUS SEVERUS ALEXANDER, M.), who supposedly revered in private a statue of Christ along with those of Abraham, *Orpheus, and *Apollonius (12) of Tyana (SHA. *Sev. Alex.* 29. 2); but the capacity for shared perception in *Apoph. Patr.* Olympios 1 and the charming tolerance of bishop Pegasius of Ilium (Julian, *Ep.* 78 Hertlein) are less open to doubt. Deliberate competition with Christianity is difficult to document, except in Julian's case (*Ep.* 49 Hertlein; *Frag. Ep.* ed. Hertlein, pp. 371 f., esp. 305 B).

For those who continue to baulk at the taint of judgement in the word, alternatives (like 'polytheism', which is not always accurate) have been hard to identify and harder to enforce.

R. MacMullen, *Paganism in the Roman Empire* (1981); R. Lane Fox, *Pagans and Christians* (1986). P. R.

Paganalia, Roman public festival (*publica sacra*: Festus, 284. 20 Lindsay) of the *pagi*, (village communities; see PAGUS). Listed as one of the movable feasts (*feriae conceptiuae*) by Macrob. *Sat.* 1. 16. 6; anachronistically attributed to Servius *Tullius by Dion. Hal. *Ant. Rom.* 4. 15. 1–4. Sometimes linked with the January 24– 6 Sementiuae (Ov. *Fast.* 1. 655–704 with Bömer's notes) but Varro (*Ling.* 6. 24, 26), while noting both festivals' agricultural basis, clearly differentiates the Paganalia as one 'that the entire *pagus* might celebrate in the fields' (*ut haberent in agris omnis pagus*). Wissowa connects it with the Compitalia of January 3–5 (*Ges. Abhl.* 236–40; cf. *RE* 4. 793–4). Certainty on its date of celebration thus becomes impossible.

RE 18. 1. 2293–5; J. Bayet, *Rev. Hist. Rel.* 1950, 172–206; L. Delatte, *Ant. Class.* 1937, 103–10, and cf. 1936, 381–91; Wissowa, *RK* 439–40.
C. R. P.

Pagasae, city in *Thessaly, on the gulf of Volos; archaeologists place its site variously at Soros near Alykes Volou and Pefkakia, the later *Demetrias. After the decline of *Iolcus, it formed part of the domain of the Magnetes, but rapidly developed into the principal maritime outlet for the Thessalian trade in grain, livestock and slaves, along with Pyrasus and Phalara near *Lamia. Incorporated into *Pelasgotis and dependent on *Pherae, it remained prosperous until the tyrannies of *Jason (2) and *Alexander (5). *Philip (1) II of Macedon acquired it in 353 BC, ended Pherae's control of the port and appropriated the revenues. After the foundation of Demetrias (293 BC), Pagasae became one of its satellites.

F. Stählin and others, *Pagasai und Demetrias* (1934).   B. H.

pagus, term of Roman administrative law for subdivisions of territories, referring to a space rather than a point, and thus convenient for subdividing areas where there was no focal settlement, and the extended territories of those which did. It had three important applications: (1) subdivisions of the territories of 'tribal' peoples, as in Transalpine Gaul (see GAUL (TRANSALPINE)), before or after they were given the Roman status of *civitas*; (2) (attested in epigraphy, though not in late republican municipal law) communities of dispersed settlement in Italy which had no urban nucleus, but still a separate status: these survived in Italy at least to the Augustan period, and had assembly, communal funds, and a board of magistrates to administer them and relate to the authorities of Rome, whose *euergetism beautified and equipped a focal sanctuary where their meetings took place, in place of the *forum of a town; and (3) the constituent subdivisions of the territory of a full city, as we see for instance in the Veleia table (see ALIMENTA) and also some of the urban subdivisions of the city of Rome (cf. *vicus). The *pagi* were the base units out of which Roman administrators, largely for fiscal reasons, constructed the municipal system.

E. Sereni, *Comunità rurali dell'Italia antica* (1955); M. W. Frederiksen in P. Zanker (ed.), *Hellenismus in Mittelitalien* (1976), 341–55; *Epigrafia del Villaggio* (1993).   N. P.

paignion, the Greek equivalent of *jeu d'esprit*: an equivocal literary-critical label applied to various writings by their critics (dismissively) or their authors (apologetically or tongue-in-cheek). Negatively, *Plato (1) applies it to *comedy (*Leg.* 816e), *Aelian to *Theocritus' *Idylls* (*NA* 15. 19). On the positive side, *Gorgias (1) uses it of his *Encomium of Helen* (21, end), *Philitas as the title of a collection of poems (Powell, *Coll. Alex.* 92–3). There is no sign that the word ever becomes a technical term.

M. S. Si.

painting (techniques) For the technique of panel-pictures, most of which were executed on wood, we have little direct evidence, but *Pliny (1) divides his account of Greek painters (*HN* 35) into those who worked with the brush (*penicillo*) and those who painted in encaustic. The distinction was probably between a tempera technique (in which pigments are mixed with an organic medium such as size to help them to adhere to the surface) and a method of applying colours with heated wax, using either a brush or a spatula. Encaustic was also suitable for painting on stone, and was evidently employed for colouring statues, which explains Pliny's statement that the technique was perfected by *Praxiteles. In wall-painting the famous murals of the 5th cent. BC by *Polygnotus and *Micon seem to have been on wooden panels attached to the walls, but the normal method was to paint on coats of plaster, using fresco. In this technique the pigments are applied while the plaster is still soft and are fixed by a chemical reaction between lime in the plaster and carbon dioxide in the air. That fresco was used in antiquity has often been doubted, but the account of *Vitruvius (*De arch.* 7)

and tell-tale traces in surviving decorations (notably the seams between the 'giornate di lavoro', the areas of fresh plaster laid for each day's work) put the issue beyond doubt.   R. J. L.

painting, Greek (see also POTTERY, GREEK). When the Mycenaean palaces fell, c.1200 BC (see MYCENAEAN CIVILIZATION), the art of painting was lost. It is next practised in the early Archaic period. Sources for Archaic to Hellenistic are: literary references; artefacts echoing painting (primarily vases); surviving examples, mostly recent discoveries.

Writers of the Roman period are most informative (J. J. Pollitt, *The Art of Greece* (rev. 1990), 124–80). *Pliny (1) (*HN* 35) gives a history of painting, detailing many works and careers, dividing artists into regional schools, notably (as in sculpture) a 4th-cent. Sicyonian school; see SICYON. Pliny acknowledges debts to Xenocrates of Sicyon, hence the conspicuousness of the Corinthia (i.e. the territory of *Corinth) in the sources (although much has been found there). *Pausanias (3)'s autopsy and interest in art *per se* distinguish him from other writers. Philosophers like *Plato (1) and *Aristotle made moral and aesthetic judgements on art (see ART, ANCIENT ATTITUDES TO); the *ekphrasis* employed by rhetoricians like Philostratus (see PHILOSTRATI), *Lucian, and Aelius *Aristides involved describing art for effect, not accuracy.

Classical painters enjoyed high social standing (hence perhaps their prominence in the sources): most notably, *Polygnotus' association with *Cimon, and *Apelles' with *Alexander (3) the Great. Slaves (see SLAVERY) were excluded from painting (*HN* 35. 77); Pliny lists female painters (*HN* 35. 147). Painting was introduced into the school curriculum by *Pamphilus (1) (below).

Pliny denies Egyptian influence on early painting, placing its beginnings at Corinth or Sicyon. The invention of linear painting is attributed to Philocles of Egypt or Cleanthes of Corinth, dating early Archaic. The temples at Corinth and neighbouring *Isthmia, c.690–650, have painted walls: the former has blocks of colour, the latter figures c.30 cm. (12 in.) high and border patterns on stucco, using several colours. Contemporary is the rare use of a brown wash for flesh on vases from several regions, notably Corinth (Chigi (MacMillan) Painter). However, these are explicable ceramically, as are the clay 'metopes' from *Thermum, c.630, and Corinthian red-ground vases, c.575–550. Also from the Corinthia, the wooden Pitsa plaques, c.540–500 (largest, c.15 × 30 cm. (6 × 12 in.)) use a white ground and a range of colours, including (like Isthmia) blue.

Tomb paintings preserved in Etruria appear to have been undertaken for Greek patrons (see ETRUSCANS); at *Paestum in Southern Italy, the Tomb of the Diver, c.480, bears close resemblance in pose and (in the *symposium) subject-matter to contemporary Athenian vases. In *Lycia, tomb paintings discovered at Elmalı in 1969–70 (M. Mellink, *CRAcad.Inscr.* 1979, 476–96), c.525 and c.475, include a funeral feast and a hunt, mixing Greek, Persian, and local elements. A painting on a stone plaque from *Persepolis c.500 (*JHS* 1980, 204–6) further attests to a mix of Greek and local elements.

Cimon of Cleonae (between *Argos (2) and Corinth) is credited with inventing *katagrapha* (three-quarter views) and a new disposition of figures, matching renderings on late 6th-cent. Pioneer vases, a date supported by *Simonides against Pliny's early Archaic. Substantial advances occur c.475–450, the age of Polygnotus and *Micon. Their work, often on historical and heroic themes in prominent public buildings, was characterized by variable groundlines, grouping, and disposition of figures, reflected in some contemporary vases. *Panaenus (brother of *Phidias) is said to have painted portraits (among the earliest) in the Marathon painting of the *Stoa Poecile. The use of perspective was greatly developed by *Agatharchus, and *Sophocles (1) is said to have introduced *skene*-painting (Arist. *Poet.* 1449ᵃ) (A. L. Brown, *PCPS* 1984).

Apollodorus of Athens (fl. 407–404 BC) opened 'the door of the art of painting' (Pliny, *HN* 35. 61), developing *skiagraphia*, balancing light and shade. Through the 'door', says Pliny, walked *Zeuxis (1). He is often contrasted with *Parrhasius of Ephesus (fl. 397 BC), who worked mainly in Athens. Zeuxis was the painter of shade and mass, Parrhasius of contour lines (Plin. *HN* 35. 65–72), reflected e.g. in the lekythoi of Group R. Euphranor (fl. 364 BC) contrasted himself with Parrhasius, saying that the latter's Theseus was fed on roses, his own on meat (Plin. *HN* 35. 129). A debate on painting styles is reflected in *Xenophon (1) (*Mem.* 3. 10. 1–5) where Parrhasius talks with *Socrates. The most highly regarded of all painters was Apelles (fl. 332 BC), pupil of Ephorus of Ephesus and Pamphilus (1) of Sicyon, and court painter to Alexander. His contemporary, *Protogenes of Rhodes, could not quite match Apelles in drawing straight lines freehand.

Classical paintings were (at least mainly) painted on whitened wooden panels (probably hung on a frame by pegs, as in the Stoa of Attalus at *Delphi). The removal of the Stoa Poecile paintings by *c.* AD 400 supports this. Pliny and *Cicero give (differing) lists of four-colour painters, implying that the Classical range was limited to red, yellow, black, and white. Pliny divides colours into 'austeri' (earth) and 'floridi' (artificial). The absence of blue (used at Archaic Isthmia and Pitsa) may be explained if black acts as a darkening agent. The absence of green is incompatible with Vergina (see AEGAE) and Aineia (below), although the Alexander mosaic (if it accurately reflects a late classical painting) argues for the four-colour scheme.

Most paintings were done with brushes, but encaustic, applying pigments mixed with heated wax, is regularly used from the 4th cent. (a statue is being painted in encaustic on an Apulian vase of *c.*370–360, G. Richter, *Handbook of Greek Art*, 288 fig. 403), although Polygnotus used it (Plin. *HN* 35. 122). *Pausias of Sicyon first became well-known for encaustic, learning it from Pamphilus, teacher of Apelles. Pausias is said (anachronistically) to have begun the practice of painting on panelled ceilings, and to have painted small panels, but is best known for introducing many kinds of flowers, and for his *stephanoplokos*, or girl making garlands (Plin. *HN* 35. 123–5). 'Pausian' florals occur regularly on contemporary South Italian vases, and on mosaics and paintings from *Macedonia (below), Illyria (see ILLYRII), and elsewhere. Pausias painted *Eros and Drunkenness at *Epidaurus (Paus. 2. 27. 3). Encaustic was used by *Nicias (2) (fl. 332) on paintings, and perhaps on the statue he painted for *Praxiteles; he was famed for painting women (Plin. *HN* 35. 131), and animals, or living figures in general (Paus. 1. 29. 15).

Recent finds include tomb paintings from Macedonia, notably Vergina (M. Andronikos, *Vergina* (1984)), from 1976. See AEGAE. The smaller tomb (*c.*340?) contains a *Hades and *Persephone which eschews outline, painted impressionistically, with subtle shades of colour, hatching giving shading and depth. The 'tomb of *Philip (1) II' (if so, soon after *c.*336) features a hunt where human figures dominate, as in later Hellenistic and early Roman wall-painting. The treatment of landscape is paralleled in the Alexander mosaic from *Pompeii. Hades and Persephone are also painted on the back of a throne found at Vergina in 1987 (*Arch. Rep.* 1988–9, cover, 78–9).

The tombs at Aineia (found 1979–82), *c.*350–325, use at least six colours, and include 'Pausian' florals (I. Vokotopoulou, *Οι ταφικοί τυμβοί της Αινείας* (1990)). The late-4th-cent. paintings at Lefkadia feature 'Pausian' florals, and imitation relief sculpture, including suggested shadow. The figures are reminiscent of the Roman paintings at *Boscoreale. The contemporary tomb at Kazanlak in Bulgarian Thrace (L. Zhivkova, *The Tomb at Kazanlak* (1974)) depicts battle, chariot race, and feast (and 'Pausian' florals). Outline is emphasized, with shading and little subtlety of colour, a different approach from the Macedonian, indicating that several trends were current, as must have been true of all periods of Greek painting. These tomb paintings were apparently executed on wet plaster, with a binding medium. See IMAGERY; PAINTING (ROMAN); PAINTING (TECHNIQUES); POTTERY (GREEK).

V. J. Bruno, *Form and Colour in Greek Painting* (1977); C. M. Robertson, *A History of Greek Art* (1975).   K. W. A.

painting, Roman In late republican times Roman collectors avidly acquired Greek 'old master' pictures (see ART, ANCIENT ATTITUDES TO), and contemporary painters provided new works for the market; Greek artists such as Metrodorus of Athens in the 2nd cent. BC and Iaia of Cyzicus in the 1st cent. BC were brought to, or migrated to, Rome to meet the demand. Pictures commemorating military campaigns were carried in triumphs (see TRIUMPH). But the advent of the empire saw a gradual shift of interest from portable panels to wall-paintings, a trend lamented by *Pliny (1) (*HN* 35. 118).

Wall-painting on plaster is attested in tombs at Rome from an early date (a well-known fragment from the *Esquiline shows historical episodes from the Samnite wars; see SAMNIUM) and became increasingly normal in private houses. At *Pompeii and *Herculaneum virtually every residence eventually contained extensive paintings, ranging from simple schemes in minor rooms to rich, polychrome schemes in important rooms. The evidence from the Vesuvius region, together with contemporary material from Rome (including remains in *Augustus' properties on the *Palatine and Nero's *Domus Aurea), enable us to follow changing fashions up to the late 1st cent. AD. The so-called First Style, the Italian version of a fashion current throughout the Hellenistic world, modelled plaster in relief to imitate drafted masonry and marble veneer. Pictures were admitted in narrow friezes at eye-level, and the veins of imitation marble were occasionally shaped into figures and other motifs. The Second Style began early in the 1st cent. BC and reproduced architectural forms by illusionistic means upon a flat surface; the illusion became increasingly elaborate, with receding planes, baroque forms and rich colouring, but the architecture remained essentially solid and constructible. The painted architecture of the Third Style (*c.*15 BC–AD 50) was delicate and unreal, and all illusion of depth was removed from the wall, which was now divided into broad areas of colour (red and black especially favoured, but blue and green also becoming more popular) supplemented by fine miniaturist detail; interest was now focused on a central picture, often very large and showing academic groups set against a landscape backcloth. The Fourth Style (extending to the end of the Flavian period) retained both the central pictures, now smaller and squarer, and the unreal architecture, but reintroduced effects of depth, if only as a foil to large 'tapestry' fields framed by stencil-like borders; yellow appeared as a dominant colour alongside red and black.

The evidence from the 2nd, 3rd, and 4th cents. AD is more fragmentary and difficult to date, but includes important decorations from the provinces. Architectural schemes remained popular but often without the organic structure and internal logic of the Pompeian period; sometimes, as in the Inn of the Peacock at *Ostia, they were reduced almost to abstract patterns. Surviving ceiling-decorations show inventive schemes in which emphasis was laid upon the centre and diagonals, reflecting the influence of structural forms such as cross-vaults. In the 3rd cent. AD there was a fashion for a cheap kind of decoration in which walls and ceilings were divided into compartments by a tracery of red and green stripes or lines on a white ground, a style much favoured in the early Christian *catacombs. The early 4th cent. saw something of a classical revival. A richly coloured ceiling from the Constantinian palace at *Augusta Treverorum (Trier), painstakingly reconstructed from thousands of fragments, was divided into rectangular compartments containing busts of poets or philosophers and nimbed females (see NIMBUS) alternating with pairs of winged Cupids, all on blue backgrounds.

Portable panel-pictures certainly continued to be produced throughout the Roman period, but most are lost; an exception is a wooden roundel found in Egypt which depicts *Septimius Severus with his empress and sons. Also from Egypt comes a series of mummy portraits, usually executed on wooden panels which were inserted in the mummy-case; the painting was done either directly on the wood or on a thin coat of gypsum-plaster. The first known paintings in manuscripts belong to late antiquity; they include the well-known series of illustrations in two 5th-cent. codices of Virgil now in the Vatican Library. See IMAGERY; PORTRAITURE (ROMAN); SCULPTURE (ROMAN).

M. Borda, La pittura romana (1958); R. Ling, Roman Painting (1991).
R. J. L.

palaces In bronze-age Crete and Greece palaces serve as complex administrative centres, as well as the residence of presumed monarchs (see MINOAN and MYCENAEAN CIVILIZATION). With the rise of Macedon, monarchy is once more a significant political institution. The palace now in course of excavation at *Pella (late-4th cent.?), and the palace (late-4th or 3rd cent.) of *Aegae (Vergina), consist of rooms around substantial colonnaded courtyards. The ground floor rooms at Aegeae are arranged almost entirely for formal feasting, one, with an antechamber, and marble and mosaic embellishment, being presumably that of the king and his closest 'friends' (see DINING-ROOMS).

Only written descriptions survive of the palace of the Ptolemies (see PTOLEMY (1)) in *Alexandria (1). Here there was a mixture of separate administrative and related structures, together with special feasting buildings, one, built for Ptolemy II in the form of a Macedonian dining tent, having sufficient space for 130 feasting couches.

In Rome the favoured area was the Palatine Hill (which gives its name to palaces as a type). The definitive construction is that of *Domitian (incorporating some earlier work by *Claudius and part of *Nero's Domus Transitoria). This comprises two large brick and concrete structures arranged around courtyards, one with large rooms designed for public receptions and functions, the other with smaller rooms and dining-rooms, presumably the residential area. Before this Nero had built his *Domus Aurea (Golden House), sprawling over a large part of the city in imitation of the palace at Alexandria. Left unfinished at his suicide it was then demolished, or subsequently incorporated into the

baths of *Trajan. The rambling rural 'Villa' of *Hadrian at *Tibur (Tivoli) probably reflects the type. See also AI KHANOUM; EUROPUS.

A. G. McKay, Houses, Villas and Palaces in the Roman World (1975); F. Sear, Roman Architecture (1982); I. Nielsen, Hellenistic Palaces (1994).
R. A. T.

Palaemon See ISTHMIA; MELICERTES; REMMIUS.

palaeography

Introduction Palaeography is the study of the history of writing upon papyrus (see PAPYROLOGY), wax, parchment, and paper, while *epigraphy deals with inscriptions carved in hard materials; from it we learn how to read old scripts and to observe their development, which may provide us with criteria for establishing the date and place of origin of a piece of writing. It is also concerned with the layout of the written page and the form of the book. The separate study of the book as an archaeological object, much developed recently, is usually called codicology. We here confine ourselves to Greek and Latin writing. In both languages the written letters change under the influence of three forces: the first, the desire to form the letters with less effort, and the second, the need to be legible, oppose each other; the third, a concern for beauty, in the individual letter, the line as a whole or the page, makes the scribe careful, but sometimes, in his search for regularity and uniformity, he makes the letters hard to distinguish from each other.

Scripts may be classified as *Book-hands* and *Cursives* or everyday hands: both have always existed side by side; the book-hand is conservative, but the cursive can change very quickly and its forms tend to invade the book-hand. Hands are also divided into *majuscules* and *minuscules*: in majuscules, which comprise *capitals*, *uncials*, and early *cursives*, the letters mainly lie between two parallel lines (bilinearity), e.g. φ in Greek or F in Latin Capitals and several letters in Latin Uncials (e.g. h and q) project above and below them. *Uncials* is the name given to the earliest book-hand deviating from Capitals, which is marked by certain rounded forms. The term means 'inch-high', and was taken by Mabillon from *Jerome's attack upon the de-luxe Christian manuscripts of his day, written in elaborate gold and silver letters on purple parchment; in reality the letters were never more than 16 mm. (⅝ in.) high. In Later Cursive, both Greek and Latin, many letters with long 'ascenders' and 'descenders' developed, and these were taken over by the subsequent book-hands. Such hands are called *minuscules*, scripts in which the bodies of the letters lie between two inner lines but the ascenders and descenders reach out towards two outer lines above and below (quadrilinearity); in most cases only one is actually ruled: the one on which the letters stand, or from which in Greek after AD 1000 they hang.

The *materials* used for writing deeply influence its development; parchment, as opposed to papyrus and paper, encourages a more careful, heavier style; because it was difficult to make curves in wax, it produced special deformations in letters that left their mark on all subsequent Latin writing, e.g. in d, g, f. Papyrus (see BOOKS, GREEK AND ROMAN; PAPYROLOGY, GREEK) was the main material used from classical times until the 4th cent. AD, after which it was a mere survival, except in Egypt. In the 4th cent. parchment, hitherto rarely found though of very ancient use, gained the upper hand. Paper, adopted from China by Islam and introduced by the Arabs to Spain and Sicily, gradually spread through the rest of western Europe in the 13th to 15th cents.

Papyrus, which did not stand folding well, was mostly used in the form of a roll, the text being in narrow columns, normally written on one side only; the criss-cross structure of papyrus guided the scribe in keeping the columns vertical and his lines regular. The bound book, or codex, formed of folded quires of parchment, written on both sides, existed already in the 1st cent. AD, when it was mentioned by *Martial, but this first appearance may represent an abortive experiment. The papyrus codex, perhaps a parallel development, first emerges in the 2nd cent., from which time a number of fragments survive. Until the 4th cent. papyrus codices predominated, but the form, which was probably inspired by the codex of joined wax tablets, was better suited to parchment. The codex probably owed its eventual dominance over the roll to its adoption by the early Christians, especially for their copies of the Gospels. It should be noted, however, that non-Christian texts also were being copied in codex form as early as the 2nd cent. (SEE BOOKS, GREEK AND ROMAN). Writing on parchment involves elaborate folding and cutting of whole skins to make up the double leaves or bifolia which form the quires, and pricking and ruling of the leaves to guide the scribe. The methods used for this can sometimes be used to date and localize individual manuscripts.

The ink used on papyrus is a mixture of carbon and gum ('Indian ink'), chemically very stable but sensitive to damp. That used on parchment is a solution of oak-galls and iron, not always satisfactory chemically. Pens were of reed at first and in medieval times of quill. Writing on parchment was often erased and a new text written over it: this is called a *palimpsest. The under writing may sometimes be read with the help of an ultra-violet lamp. Difficulties in reading manuscripts are caused, apart from bad preservation, by the unfamiliar forms of the letters, the lack of divisions between words, and the use of abbreviations. The first trouble is much increased by the presence, under cursive influence, of *ligatures*, i.e. combinations in which two or more letters are tied together and lose their original shapes, e.g. &, a combination of ε and ϛ.

Abbreviations are divided into *suspensions*, in which the first letter or the beginning of the word is given but not the ending (sign, a dot or transverse stroke); *contractions*, giving the first letter, generally some of the middle of a word and always the last letter (sign a tittle or horizontal stroke above); and *specific signs* denoting particular words, syllables or letters. These largely go back to ancient shorthand, e.g. in Latin to the *Notae Tironianae* (see TACHYGRAPHY). Numerals are marked by tittles, also sometimes foreign words, or by flanking signs, also used for 'quotes'. A letter wrongly written may be dotted above, or more usually, below (expunctuation).

These difficulties tend to increase as time goes on, save that later manuscripts begin to divide the words. Division into paragraphs is at first rare and inconspicuously marked; later it is indicated by the methods still in use. Punctuation, too, is at first scarce and irregular.

A scribe sometimes, especially in later times, adds at the end of a manuscript a note, called a *colophon*, giving his name with the place and date of writing: note that the Greek era runs from 5508 BC. We also find *subscriptiones*, notes by scribes or correctors, and these are sometimes dated.

The study of decoration and miniatures can often be helpful for dating and localizing medieval manuscripts. Since the field of study is vast, the inexperienced non-specialist is however advised to solicit the help of expert librarians or art historians whenever possible.

Greek palaeography Most of the earliest specimens of Greek

writing are inscriptions on stone, the study of which is usually regarded as constituting the separate auxiliary science of *epigraphy. A large number of short inscriptions on Greek vases also survive from the 8th cent. BC onwards; in this category the Athenian vases are the most important, and they have recently been studied by H. R. Immerwahr, *Attic Script: A Survey* (1990). The palaeography of literary texts can now take as its starting-point two specimens which survive from the second half of the 4th cent. BC, PBerol. 9875 of *Timotheus (1)'s *Persae* and the Derveni papyrus of a commentary on an Orphic text (see ORPHIC LITERATURE; ORPHISM). The script shows a close affinity to contemporary inscriptions on stone. Papyri of Hellenistic and subsequent centuries are very numerous. In Hellenistic times a more cursive style was developed for use in documents, while literary texts were usually copied in a formal style (though there are famous exceptions such as *Aristotle's *Athenaion politeia*); and whereas many documents are dated so that the development of the script can be charted, the same is not true of literary texts (colophons including a date seem to be a medieval invention), and the exact dating of some literary papyri remains difficult. On these questions one should consult C. H. Roberts, *Greek Literary Hands 350 B.C.–A.D. 400* (1956) and E. G. Turner, *Greek Manuscripts of the Ancient World* (2nd edn. rev. and enlarged by P. J. Parsons, 1987).

Important changes in book production occurred in the first two centuries of the Roman empire: parchment became available as an alternative and more durable, though probably much more expensive, writing material, while the codex was gradually adopted in place of the roll, in a process lasting from the 2nd to the end of the 4th cent. The part played by the Christians in this latter development is examined by C. H. Roberts and T. C. Skeat, *The Birth of the Codex* (1983). By the middle of the 4th cent. a new calligraphic script, of which anticipations can be seen in a few earlier specimens, had emerged. Commonly called uncial by analogy with a Latin script, it is often associated with biblical texts, as its most striking representatives are seen in the famous Codex Sinaiticus and Codex Vaticanus of the Bible; it is quite wrong, however, to label this script biblical, as it was also used in the transcription of classical texts. Uncial script had a long history, and several varieties of it developed; but it never dominated the production of literary texts to the exclusion of other less calligraphic styles. The variety of scripts in use in the late Roman and early Byzantine periods is well illustrated in G. Cavallo and H. Maehler, *Greek Bookhands of the Early Byzantine Period A.D. 300–800* (1987).

But radical change was inevitable, as capital-letter scripts are extravagant in their use of writing material, and it looks as if the supply of papyrus may have become less abundant. Probably in the 8th cent. copyists began to look for acceptable alternatives to uncial, and they experimented with modifications of types of script currently used in documents. All these new scripts are known as minuscule. The result of one of the experiments is seen in MS Vaticanus gr. 2200; it requires considerable skill on the part of the reader to decipher it. Traces of other experiments can also be seen, especially in some fragments found at St Catherine's monastery on Sinai in 1975 (some plates are given in the provisional publication by L. Politis, *Scriptorium* 1980, 5–17). But the solution which found general favour is a script capable of great elegance while posing relatively few problems for the reader; although it was probably devised towards the end of the 8th cent. and some extant specimens may be as early as that, the first securely dated example is from AD 835 (MS St Petersburg 217, a copy of the Gospels). Uncial continued in use for a while, particularly for certain liturgical books; but minuscule was adopted for almost all purposes in the course of the 9th cent. It could probably be written more quickly by a skilled copyist, and it brought with it the possibility of further economy of space through the use of abbreviations (otherwise known as compendia). In antiquity abbreviations had been used frequently in documentary texts, but not very often in literary texts. Key terms of Christian theology were abbreviated by the special system known as *nomina sacra* (see L. Traube, *Nomina sacra* (1907)). From the 9th cent. onwards the scribes used a system of abbreviations which catered for grammatical inflections and some technical terms of specialist topics. Such abbreviations were used very extensively in marginal notes; but many scribes avoided them in the main body of the text or used them only at the end of the line, presumably in order to achieve the effect of justification.

It is not certain where the successful form of minuscule was invented; T. W. Allen associated it with the monastery of St John the Baptist founded by Stoudios in Constantinople (*JHS* 1920, 1–12). Nor is it easy to distinguish by their script books produced in the Byzantine capital from those originating in the far-flung regions of the empire; but in recent years close study of the hands has made it possible to identify a fair number of MSS written in the Greek monasteries and communities of Sicily and southern Italy, which remained bilingual even after the Byzantine government had lost control of those areas. However, individual cases continue to arouse controversy, and in this respect Greek palaeography has progressed much less than Latin.

Another change that took place about the same time as the adoption of minuscule was the introduction of paper, an invention borrowed by the Arabs from the Chinese. Scraps of it are found among the latest papyri, and MS Vaticanus gr. 2200 is the oldest complete Greek manuscript on paper. Exactly how quickly the use of paper spread is uncertain; but it is clear that by the 11th cent. Byzantine scribes, including those in the imperial chancery, were using it quite frequently, and by the middle of the 14th cent. parchment had been largely replaced by paper, much of it now produced in western Europe and datable within fairly narrow limits thanks to the evidence of watermarks.

Minuscule held the field for the rest of the Byzantine period. Many scribes displayed a remarkable conservatism, copying earlier models with a skill that has often deceived scholars into assigning an incorrect date. Such conservatism was applied more often to biblical and theological than to secular texts; the latter were usually written purely for personal use and the result was a cursive or even careless script. In dating these copies scholars until recently were often misled. At various dates, particularly in the 11th and 14th cents. one can point to styles of script that represented a calligraphic canon; but in the late 15th cent. when printing types had to be cut no such canon held the field, and some of the type-faces bear a suspicious resemblance to the script of identifiable copyists (see N. Barker, *Aldus Manutius and the Development of Greek Script and Type in the Fifteenth Century* (1992²)). As a consequence Greek printing types did not achieve the high standard of elegance found in much Latin printing, and for centuries certain Byzantine features remained which purists could reasonably criticize.

Latin palaeography The earliest Latin book-hand, in use for copying whole books, almost entirely non-Christian, from the

1st cent. BC to the 6th cent. AD, is the *capital*, closely related in structure to inscriptional capitals, but differing in appearance because it is written not carved; the writing implement used (a reed pen) and the soft material used (papyrus or parchment), give the script a fluidity and accented chiaroscuro, or contrast of thick and thin strokes; right angles become curves and spatular serifs are added to vertical strokes. This capital script has traditionally been called *rustic* to distinguish it from the rigid *monumental* or *square* capitals, which until recently were thought to be the earliest manifestation of capital book-script but which in fact appear to have been an artificial creation of the 5th to 6th cent., directly modelled on inscriptions. The best-known example of the use of monumental capitals is the *Virgilius Augusteus* (MS Vat. lat. 3256). The capital scripts continued to be used later for headings, *explicits* and *incipits* and verse initials. The everyday Roman script used for documents and letters, a currently written version of capitals known as *capital* or *Older Roman cursive*, was also used for some literary works and was in use until the 3rd cent. AD. This was replaced by a *minuscule* cursive known as *Later* or *New Roman cursive*, which had already emerged by the 3rd cent. By the 5th cent. this script was also being used in manuscripts. It is largely erect, with marked ascenders and descenders and many new letter forms, especially aubdefℑhlmnpqrⲅⲅτu, and uses many ligatures, which substantially change the appearance of the joined letters and often make the script very hard to decipher. As Bischoff says, 'With this script the structure of Latin letters in principle reached a final and definite form, and the dual system which still holds good today—majuscule and minuscule—was created' (*Latin Palaeography*, p. 65).

Soon elements of the Roman cursives were blended with capitals to form new book-scripts: the so-called *uncial* and *half-uncial*. An early experiment is seen in the fragment *De bellis Macedonicis* (*CLA* 5. 676), perhaps of *c.* AD 100. *Uncial* script is found in about 500 manuscripts of the 4th cent. or later; it may however have originated as early as the 2nd cent. Its elements derive from capital cursive. It is a broad majuscule script with a marked tendency to roundness. and the characteristic letters are: aꝺꞓhlmqu. It continued to be widely used as a book-script until the 8th cent. The so-called *half-uncial* is a minuscule script and has a different origin, being a calligraphization of Later Roman cursive, which apparently originated in Africa. Early versions are found in the East between the 3rd and 5th cents. In the fully developed Western form, found from the 5th cent. onwards, the letters are mostly separate but a few ligatures are retained, especially with ℮. Characteristic letters are abdeℑmnprⲅⲅτu. The script was less widely used than uncial, although it was popular in parts of Italy and continued to be used in post-classical times also in Spain and France. At Tours and elsewhere in the 9th cent. it was used as part of the hierarchy of scripts. A cursive version of the script, *cursive half-uncial* or *literary cursive* (Lowe's 'quarter-uncial'), which may be older in origin than half-uncial itself—a small, current script using rather more ligatures—is found in some late antique schoolbooks and in scholia and marginalia of the 4th and 5th cents. It appears to have been brought to Ireland by Christian missionaries in the 5th cent. and to be the parent of the Insular hands.

The earliest surviving examples of Irish script probably date from the turn of the 6th cent. Two types of script develop: a heavy round half-uncial type script with wedge-shaped serifs, and a cursive minuscule. These scripts were taken to Scotland and England and also to the Continent in the late 6th cent. by Irish missionaries and underwent further elaboration in England after the introduction of manuscripts from Rome as a result of St Augustine's mission to Canterbury in the late 6th cent. and subsequent contacts of English churchmen with Rome. Thus uncials came to be used at Canterbury and Wearmouth/Jarrow as well as the *Insular half-uncial* (used for example in the Lindisfarne Gospels), and an elaborate system of minuscules and hybrid hands. The *Anglo-Saxon minuscule* script of the late 9th cent. develops out of the Insular pointed minuscule. This minuscule in turn underwent several phases and was used for texts in both Latin and Anglo-Saxon until the mid-10th cent., when Caroline minuscule was introduced into England.

On the Continent numerous 'national', 'sub-Roman', or 'pre-Caroline' minuscule book-hands developed in the period following the gradual decline and dissolution of the Roman empire, although uncial and half-uncial continued to be used in some centres. These scripts were generally calligraphic developments of Later Roman cursive with some half-uncial admixture and were often highly stylized, with elaborate ligatures. Two of the best-known types of script that emerged are the *Visigothic* script of Christian Northern Spain (from the 8th cent.) and the *Beneventan* of South Italy and Dalmatia (also found from the 8th cent.); both of these survived the spread of Carolingian script to the rest of the Continent, Visigothic until the late 11th cent. Beneventan, although largely displaced by the 13th cent., was still practiced occasionally as late as the 16th cent. In monastic centres such as Bobbio (from the 7th cent.) and Nonantola (8th to 9th cent.) in Italy and Corbie (8th cent.) and Luxeuil (7th to 8th cent.) in France, other distinctive minuscules emerged. In north Italy some minuscules remained very close to their Roman cursive origins, while in south Germany and Switzerland minuscule scripts were developed which looked forward to the Carolingian developments.

Caroline or *Carolingian minuscule* emerges in the second half of the 8th cent., perhaps first at Corbie under Abbot Maudramnus (*c.*772–81). It seems to have been not a deliberate creation but a natural development of a calligraphizing tendency and an imposition of discipline and simplification on existing scripts, eliminating most ligatures, symptoms of which are also found elsewhere. The main basis of the script seems to have been half-uncial, with some alternative letter forms persisting for a time but g, n, and r taking their modern forms. The success of the script was ensured by the active promotion by Charlemagne (768–814, emperor from 800) of scholarship and education, typified by his *Admonitio generalis* of 789. This led to the promotion and adoption of the new script (with local variations in detail) in writing centres throughout his realm in the late 8th and the 9th cent., through exemplars sent to them from the library of the Palace School (where the script was already in use in the 780s). Alcuin, an Anglo-Saxon from Northumbria and former librarian of York, who was summoned to Charlemagne's court in 782 and became abbot of Tours in 796, was influential in the diffusion of the script. It was at Tours that a 'hierarchy of scripts' was first developed, influenced by Anglo-Saxon models, with monumental and 'rustic' capitals being used for headings, uncial and half-uncial for 'incipits' and 'explicits', and the new Caroline minuscule for the main text.

Forms of Caroline minuscule continued in use until the 12th cent., or later in some places. The letter forms changed little after the mid-9th cent., but the script tended to become larger in module, and often stiffer and less even, and there was an increasing use of abbreviations. Caroline minuscule is the main vehicle

of classical literature; only twenty-odd manuscripts in capitals survive from the late antique period, predominantly copies of Virgil; only a few manuscripts in uncials are classical and of the other early scripts only Insular and Beneventan are of importance for the classics. For most authors a 9th- or 10th-cent. Caroline manuscript is the best authority. In the first instance scholars of this period were copying still-surviving ancient manuscripts, many of them, it seems, collected at the Palace Libraries of Charlemagne and his son Louis the Pious, and most of these ancient exemplars subsequently perished.

In the late 11th and early 12th cents. in northern France and England a tendency to angularity in script steadily developed which led first to the type of script known as *protogothic* or *late Caroline* and then, by the end of the 12th cent. to the so-called *Gothic* system of scripts (the name is later and the script has nothing to do with the *Goths), which carried the tendency to angularity and compression even further in the highest grades of book-script, known as *textualis*, except in Italy, where textualis always retains a certain roundness. In the less formal hands, especially, there was often a high degree of currency (writing rapidly which causes deformation) and abbreviation could be very heavy. Cursive (*cursiva*) scripts were developed at the same time, originally for documentary use, and by the late 13th cent. these were being taken over as book-hands, to begin with for cheaper books, for example for the students of the new universities or for texts in the vernacular. By the mid-14th cent., however, calligraphic versions had been developed of the cursive book-hands. In north Italy, in the second half of the 14th cent., such 'chancery' hands were often used for copying classical texts. In the 15th cent., especially in Germany and the Low Countries, small, neat, simplified *hybrid* gothic book-hands were developed which combined elements of both *textualis* and *cursiva* and were more legible than either. Gothic scripts continued to be used in most of Europe until the 16th cent. or later. The huge variety of scripts developed in the Gothic period still awaits systematic study.

In the mid- and later 14th cent. some scholars in Italy felt a need for scripts that were easier to read than the gothic hands: simpler, clearer and less abbreviated. Petrarch developed a simplified *semi-gothic* hand for copying and annotating his own manuscripts. This script was much imitated in north Italy in the late 14th and early 15th cent. Led by Coluccio Salutati, an admirer of Petrarch who was Chancellor of Florence from 1375 to 1406, younger scholars in Florence, especially Poggio Bracciolini and Niccolò Niccoli, took things further, and imitating the hands of the Carolingian and protogothic manuscripts that they owned in large numbers, they developed by 1400 a new script which they called *littera antiqua* (probably using the term to imply 'old' rather than 'antique'), which is now usually called *humanistic* because of its origins. This hand, in varying manifestations, was rapidly taken up over most of Italy for the copying of literary texts in Latin and in the 1460s it was used as the model for the *Roman* type used for such texts by the first printers in Rome. Niccoli developed a cursive hand to complement the formal *antiqua* and used it to make copies on paper of classical and other texts newly discovered by Poggio and other friends, which served as exemplars for their further diffusion. The humanistic *cursiva* was to begin with mainly used by humanists copying or annotating texts for themselves, but by the later fifteenth century it had become acceptable as a hand to be used in even the most de-luxe copies of literary texts, especially in the form known as *italic* developed in the Veneto and diffused also in Rome, which served as the model for the italic type of Aldus Manutius. See also VINDOLANDA TABLETS.

INTRODUCTION General: E. Maunde-Thompson, *Introduction to Greek and Latin Palaeography* (1912, repr. 1975); A. Dain, *Les Manuscrits* (1949; 3rd edn. 1975).

Scribes and bookmaking: W. Wattenbach, *Das Schriftwesen im Mittelalter* (1866; 4th edn., 1958); T. Birt, *Das antike Buchwesen* (1882); C. H. Roberts and T. C. Skeat, *The birth of the codex* (1983); H. J. Martin and J. Vezin (ed.), *Mise en page et mise en texte du livre manuscrit* (1990); F. G. Kenyon, *Books and Readers in Ancient Greece and Rome* (1932; 2nd edn. 1951); *Libri, editori e pubblico nel mondo antico: guida storica e critica*, ed. G. Cavallo (1975); B. L. Ullman, *Ancient Writing and its Influence* (1934; 2nd edn. 1980); F. W. Hall, *Companion to Classical Texts* (1913); L. D. Reynolds and N. G. Wilson, *Scribes and Scholars: A Guide to the Transmission of Greek and Latin Literature* (1968; 3rd edn. 1991).

General series of facsimiles: Palaeographical Society, *Facsimiles of Ancient MSS and Inscriptions*, ser. 1 and 2 (1873–94); New Palaeographical Society, ser. 1 and 2 (1903–30); *Archivio paleografico italiano*, ed. E. Monaci and others (1882–); G. Vitelli and C. Paoli, *Collezione fiorentina di facsimili paleografici*, 2 vols. (1884–97); A. Chroust, *Monumenta palaeographica*, 3 ser., rarely found complete (1899–1907; 1907–17; 1931–40); *Codices e vaticanis selecti phototypice expressi* (1899–); *Codices graeci et latini phototypice depicti*, ed. W. N. du Rieu, S. G. De Vries, and G. I. Lieftinck (1897–).

GREEK PALAEOGRAPHY For the period from AD 800 onwards there is no standard modern treatment of the subject. A good deal can be learned from V. Gardthausen, *Griechische Paläographie* (1911–13²). For abbreviations one still has to consult T. W. Allen, *Notes on Abbreviations in Greek Manuscripts* (1889) and the much fuller epoch in G. F. Cereteli, *Sokraščenija v' grečeskich' rukopisjach'* (1904², repr. 1969). An album of specimens accompanied by brief notes is provided by N. G. Wilson, *Medieval Greek Bookhands* (1972–3). Otherwise up-to-date information on specific topics should be sought in the proceedings of the conferences on Greek palaeography held from 1974 onwards: (1) *La Paléographie grecque et byzantine* (Colloques internationaux du CNRS 559) (1977); (2) D. Harlfinger and G. Prato (eds.), *Paleografia e codicologia greca* (1991); (3) G. Cavallo, G. De Gregorio, and M. Maniaci (eds.), *Scritture, libri e testi nelle aree provinciali di Bisanzio* (1991). See also R. Barbour, *Greek Literary Hands A.D. 400–1600* (1981); K. and S. Lake, *Dated Greek Minuscule Manuscripts to the year 1200*, 10 vols. (1934–9); A. Turyn, *Codices Graeci Vaticani Saeculis xiii et xiv scripti annorumque notis instructi* (1964), and *Dated Greek Manuscripts of the Thirteenth and Fourteenth Centuries in the Libraries of Italy*, 2 vols. (1972); D. Harlfinger, *Specimina griechischer Kopisten und Schriftstilen des 15. und 16. Jahrhunderts* (1974); H. Hunger, *Repertorium der griechischen Kopisten 800–1600* (1981–).

LATIN PALAEOGRAPHY General: L. E. Boyle, *Medieval Latin Palaeography: A Bibliographical Introduction* (1984); L. N. Braswell, *Western Manuscripts from Classical Antiquity to the Renaissance: A Handbook* (1981); B. Bischoff, G. I. Lieftinck, and G. Battelli, *Nomenclature des écritures livresques du ixᵉ au xviᵉ siècles* (Premier colloque internationale de paléographie latine, Paris, 1953, 1954); E. A. Lowe, *Handwriting, Our Medieval Legacy*, ed. W. B. Ross (1969); T. J. Brown, 'Latin Palaeography since Traube', *Trans. Cambridge Bibliog. Soc.* (1963), repr. in *A Palaeographer's View* (see Collected Essays below); J. J. John, 'Palaeography, Western European', in *Dictionary of the Middle Ages*, ed. J. R. Strayer, 9 (1987); *Lo spazio letterario del Medioevo. I. Il Medioevo latino*, ed. G. Cavallo, C. Leonardi, and E. Menesto, vol. 1: *La produzione del testo* (2 parts, 1992); A. Cappelli, *Dizionario di abbreviature latine ed italiane* (3rd edn. 1929; 6th rev. edn. 1987); W. M. Lindsay, *Notae latinae* (1915: abbreviations, *c.*700–850); D. Bains, *A Supplement to Notae latinae* (1936: continues to 1100); M. B. Parkes, *Pause and Effect: An Introduction to the History of Punctuation in the West* (1992).

Manuals: G. Battelli, *Lezioni di paleografia* (1949); H. Foerster, *Abriss der lateinischen Paläographie* (1949; 2nd edn. 1963); G. Cencetti, *Lineamenti di storia della scrittura latina* (1954); J. Stiennon, *Paléographie du moyen âge* (1973); B. Bischoff, *Paläographie des römischen Altertums und des abendländischen Mittelalters* (1979); 2nd rev. edn. 1986; Fr. trans.

1985; Eng. trans.: *Latin Palaeography: Antiquity and the Middle Ages* (1990); A. Petrucci, *Breve storia della scrittura latina* (1989).

Collected essays: L. Traube, *Vorlesungen und Abhandlungen* (1909–20); P. Lehmann, *Erforschung des Mittelalters* (1941–62); B. Bischoff, *Mittelalterliche Studien* (1966–7; 1981), *Manuscripts and Libraries in the Age of Charlemagne* (trans. M. Gorman, 1994, of selected essays mostly from the earlier collection); E. A. Lowe, *Palaeographical Papers, 1907–65*, ed. L. Bieler (1972); T. J. Brown, *A Palaeographer's View: The Selected Writings . . .*, ed. J. Bately and others (1993); M. B. Parkes, *Scribes, Scripts and Readers. Studies . . .* (1991).

Catalogues: *Latin Manuscript Books before 1600: A List of the Printed Catalogues and Unpublished Inventories of Extant Collections*, by P. O. Kristeller, 4th rev. enlarged edn. by S. Kramer (Mon. Germ. Hist. Hilfsmittel 13) (1993); *Classical MSS*: B. Munk Olsen, *L'Étude des auteurs classiques latins aux xiᵉ et xiiᵉ siècles*, 1– (1982–) (vols. 1–2 are a catalogue of Latin classical MSS copied between the 9th and 12th cents.); C. Jeudy and Y.-F. Riou, *Les Manuscrits classiques latins des bibliothèques publiques de France*, 1– (1989–); L. Rubio Fernandez, *Catálogo de los manuscritos clásicos latinos existentes en España* (1984); E. Pellegrin and others, *Manuscrits classiques latins de la Bibliothèque Vaticane*, 1– (1975–).

Facsimiles: W. Wattenbach and C. Zangemeister, *Exempla codd. lat. litteris maiusculis scriptorum* (1876–9); E. Chatelain, *Paléographie des classiques latins* (1884–1900), *Uncialis scriptura codd. lat. novis exemplis illustrata* (1901); W. Arndt and M. Tangl, *Schrifttafeln zur Erlernung der lat. Paläographie* (1904–7); F. Steffens, *Lateinische Paläographie* (1903; 2nd edn. 1909; repr. 1929; Fr. trans. 1910); F. Ehrle and P. Liebaert, *Specimina codd. lat. vaticanorum* (1912); A. Millares Carlo, *Tratado de paleografia española²* (1932); E. A. Lowe, *Codices latini antiquiores*, 12 vols. (1934–71) = *CLA*; B. Bischoff and others, 'Addenda to CLA', *Mediaeval Studies*, 1985, 1992; J. Mallon, A. Marichal, and C. Perrat, *L'Écriture latine de la capitale romaine à la minuscule* (1939); I. Kirchner, *Scriptura latina libraria* (1955; 2nd edn. 1970); G. Turrini, *Millennium scriptorii veronensis*, 1967; M. Brown, *A Guide to Western Historical Scripts from Antiquity to 1600* (1990); collections of dated or datable MSS in Latin script published under the auspices of the Comité internationale de paléographie latine: Austria, F. Unterkircher and others, 1–7 (1969–86); Belgium, F. Masai and others, 1–6 (1968–91); France, C. Samaran and R. Marichal, 1–7 (1959–84); Germany, J. Autenrieth, 1– (1984–); Great Britain, in progress: A. G. Watson, London, British Library (1979), and Oxford (1984), and P. Robinson, Cambridge (1988); Italy 1– (1974–) (pub. by Univ. degli studi di Roma. Scuola speciale per archivisti e bibliotecari); Netherlands, G. I. Lieftinck and J. P. Gumbert, 2 vols. (1964–88); Sweden, M. Hedlund, 2 vols. (1977–80); Switzerland, B. M. Scarpatetti and others, 3 vols. (1977–91).

INDIVIDUAL SCRIPTS Late antique scripts: J. Mallon, *Paléographie romaine* (1952); A. Pratesi, 'Considerazioni su alcuni codici in capitale della Biblioteca Apostolica Vaticana', *Mél. E. Tisserant* 7 (Studi e testi 237, 1964); A. K. Bowman and J. D. Thomas, *Vindolanda: The Writing Tablets* (1983).

Uncial: E. A. Lowe and E. K. Rand, *A 6th-Century Fragment of the Letters of Pliny the Younger* (1922); E. A. Lowe, *English Uncial* (1960); A. Petrucci, 'L'onciale romana', *Studi medievali*, 3rd ser., 1971.

Half-uncial: E. A. Lowe, *Codd. lugdunenses antiquissimi* (1924), see also his *Pal. Papers*.

Insular: W. M. Lindsay, *Early Irish Minuscule Script* (1910), *Early Welsh Script* (1912), (ed.), *Palaeographica latina* (1922–9); *Evangelia quattuor Codex lindisfarnensis*, facsimile, introd. T. D. Kendrick and others (1956–60); T. O'Neill, *The Irish Hand* (1984); see also collected papers of Brown and Parkes.

Beneventan: E. A. Lowe, *The Beneventan Script* (1914; 2nd edn., enlarged by V. Brown, 1980), *Scriptura Beneventana* (1929, plates); V. Brown, 'A Second New List of Beneventan MSS', *Mediaeval Studies*, 1988.

Visigothic: P. Ewald and G. Loewe, *Exempla scripturae visigoticae* (1883); J. M. Burnham, *Palaeographia iberica* (1912–25); Z. García Villada, *Paleografía española* (1923); R. P. Robinson, 'MSS. 27 and 107 of the Municipal Library at Autun', *Amer. Acad. Rome*, 1939; *Bobbio*: C. H. Beeson, 'The Palimpsests of Bobbio', *Misc. G. Mercati* 6 (Studi e testi, 126), 1946; P.

Collura, *Studi paleografici: La precarolina e la carolina a Bobbio* (1965).

Early Caroline: E. K. Rand, 'The Vatican Livy and the Script of Tours', *Amer. Acad. Rome*, 1917, *Studies in the Script of Tours*, 1–2 (Amer. Acad. Rome, 3, 20: 1929, 1934); L. W. Jones, *The Script of Cologne from Hildebald to Herman* (ibid. 10, 1932), 'The Script of Tours in the 10th Cent.', *Speculum*, 1939; B. Bischoff, *Die Abtei Lorsch im Spiegel ihrer Handschriften* (2nd rev. edn., 1989), *Kalligraphie in Bayern. Achtes bis zwölftes Jh.* (1981), *Die südostdeutschen Schreibschulen und Bibliotheken in der Karolingerzeit* (1974, 1980); see also Bischoff's collected papers; B. Bischoff and J. Hofmann, *Libri sancti Kyliani. Die Würzburger Schreibschule und die Dombibliothek im viii und ix Jh.* (1952); D. Ganz, *Corbie in the Carolingian Renaissance* (1990); R. McKitterick, 'Script and Book Production', in *Carolingian Culture: Emulation and Innovation* (1994: with useful bibliog.).

Late Caroline: L. W. Jones, 'The Art of Writing at Tours 1000–1200', *Speculum*, 1940; T. A. M. Bishop, *English Caroline Minuscule* (1971); P. Supino Martini, *Roma e l'area grafica romanesca (secoli x–xii)* (1987); J. Vezin, *Les scriptoria d'Angers au xiᵉ siècle* (1974).

Protogothic and Gothic: N. R. Ker, *English Manuscripts in the Century after the Norman Conquest* (1960); I. Kirchner, *Scriptura gothica libraria* (1966); A. Petrucci, *La scrittura di Francesco Petrarca* (Studi e testi, 248, 1967); S. H. Thomson, *Latin Bookhands of the Later Middle Ages 1100–1500* (1969).

Humanistic: B. L. Ullman, *The Origin and Development of Humanistic Script* (1960); A. J. Fairbank and R. W. Hunt, *Humanistic Script of the Fifteenth and Sixteenth Centuries* (Bodleian picture book; 1960, repr. 1993); J. Wardrop, *The Script of Humanism* (1963); J. J. G. Alexander and A. C. de la Mare, *The Italian Manuscripts in the Library of Major J. R. Abbey* (1969); E. Casamassima, 'Literulae latinae. Nota paleografica', introd. to S. Caroti and S. Zamponi, *Lo scrittoio di Bartolomeo Fonzio umanista fiorentino* (1974); A. C. de la Mare, *The Handwriting of the Italian Humanists*, 1– (1974–); C. F. Bühler, *The Fifteenth-Century Book* (1960); A. Petrucci (ed.), *Libri, scrittura e pubblico nel Rinascimento* (1979).

ILLUMINATION C. de Hamel, *A History of Illuminated Manuscripts* (2nd edn. 1994: useful introd. with basic bibliog.); J. J. G. Alexander, *The Decorated Letter* (1978); for the early period: K. Weitzmann, *Late Antique and Early Christian Book Illumination* (1977); C. Nordenfalk, *Die spätantiken Zierbuchstaben* (1970), *Early Medieval Book Illumination* (2nd edn. 1988); E. H. Zimmermann, *Die vorkarolingischen Miniaturen* (1916); see also the useful catalogues of illuminated MSS in individual libraries: H. J. Hermann on Vienna (1905–1933); O. Pächt, J. J. G. Alexander, and E. Temple on Oxford (1966–85); F. Avril and others on Paris, Bibl. Nationale, in progress (1980–); and for the British Isles, J. J. G. Alexander (ed.), the *Survey of MSS. Illuminated in the British Isles*, 9 vols. (1975–94). A similar series is in preparation for France.

A. C. de la M. (*Introduction*; *Latin*), N. G. W. (*Greek*)

Palaephatus, *mythographer, wrote (? in the late 4th cent. BC) a *Peri apiston*, 'on incredible things', extant only in an excerpt, in which myths are rationalized. It had considerable influence in the Byzantine period. The name Palaephatus is perhaps a pseudonym.

N. Festa, *Mythographi Graeci* 3. 2 (1902); *FGrH* 44; W. Nestle, *Vom Mythos zum Logos* (1941), 148–52.   J. D. D.; J. S. R.

palaestra (παλαίστρα) was a wrestling ground, a place for athletic exercise, whether public or private, which eventually took the conventional form of an enclosed courtyard surrounded by rooms for changing, washing, etc. The application of the term to actual buildings is often uncertain; conventionally it is used for structures significantly smaller in size than the developed gymnasia (see GYMNASIUM) which are similar in arrangement. However the palaestra at *Olympia, distinguished as such from the gymnasium by *Pausanias (3) (6. 21. 1), measures altogether 66.35 × 66.75 m. (217½ × 219 ft.), larger than gymnasia elsewhere (e.g. *Priene). It is, however, adjacent to a normal, larger colon-

naded court, only partly preserved, which here constitutes the gymnasium. The distinction is one of usage, rather than form. See ATHLETICS; WRESTLING.

A. Mallwitz, *Olympia und seine Bauten* (1972), 278; S. Glass in W. J. Raschke (ed.), *The Archaeology of the Olympics* (1988).   R. A. T.

Palamedes (Παλαμήδης, 'the handy or contriving one'), a proverbially (cf. Ar. *Ran.* 1451) clever hero, son of *Nauplius (2) and Clymene. Tradition from the *Cypria* on (Proclus; see EPIC CYCLE) makes *Odysseus his enemy because he was forced by Palamedes to serve in the Trojan War (see TROY): *Odysseus pretended to be mad to avoid going to Troy, but Palamedes exposed him, either by putting the infant *Telemachus in front of his ploughshare (Hyg. *Fab.* 95. 2) or by threatening the baby with a sword (Apollod. *Epit.* 3. 7). Odysseus saved his son, and thus gave himself away. In revenge he later forged a letter from *Priam to Palamedes, promising him a sum of gold if he would betray the Greeks, then buried this same amount of gold in Palamedes' quarters. *Agamemnon read the letter, found the gold, and handed over Palamedes to the army to be stoned (Apollod. *Epit.* 3. 8; Hyg. *Fab.* 105). His father Nauplius avenged his death by causing some of the Greek leaders' wives to be unfaithful, and later by lighting false beacons at Cape Caphereus in *Euboea, with the result that the Greek fleet was wrecked (Apollod. *Epit.* 6. 7–8).

Palamedes was credited, alongside *Cadmus, with having invented certain letters of the *alphabet (see Hyg. *Fab.* 277. 1) and the games of draughts (πεσσοί) and dice (see DICING) to help while away the Trojan War (Paus. 2. 20. 3).   H. J. R.; J. R. M.

Palatine, the chief of the *seven hills of Rome, traditionally (Tac. *Ann.* 12. 24; Dion. Hal. 1. 87; Livy 1. 7, etc.) the site of the oldest settlement there; in legend, the home of *Evander and *Romulus. Tradition assigns fortifications to the hill, and this seems to be confirmed by recent archaeological work. Early settlement is represented by two archaic cisterns and rock-cut post-holes for Iron age huts; one example, above the Lupercal (see LUPERCALIA) and *forum Boarium, is identified as the 'hut of Romulus' which was preserved in historic times. Temples on the hill included those dedicated to *Victoria (294 BC) near the Clivus Victoriae, Victoria Virgo (193), and the Magna Mater (191; see CYBELE). Many aristocratic houses occupied the hill and the slopes which led down to the Forum, from the late 6th cent. BC onwards; famous owners including M. *Fulvius Flaccus, Q. *Lutatius Catulus (2), *Cicero, *Crassus, T. *Annius Milo, M. *Antonius (2) (Mark Antony), M. *Livius Drusus (2), M. *Aemilius Scaurus (2) (whose house has recently been excavated), and Q. *Hortensius Hortalus. The house of Hortensius was acquired by *Augustus (Suet. *Aug.* 72) and became the nucleus of a group of palace-buildings which included a portico and libraries as well as the new temple of *Apollo (Vell. Pat. 2. 81). In the early Julio-Claudian period, the palace continued to be composed of individual houses (Joseph. *AJ* 19, 117), but Caligula (*Gaius (1)) extended it to the Forum and 'made the temple of Castor and Pollux his vestibule' (Suet. *Calig.* 22; see CASTOR AND POLLUX), as recent excavations confirm. *Nero made important additions to the palace-buildings both before and after the great fire of AD 64. *Domitian was responsible for the Flavian palace-buildings, designed by the architect Rabirius and conventionally known as Domus Flavia and Domus Augustana, which included a monumental garden (*hippodromus*). Further construction was undertaken by *Hadrian, *Commodus, and *Septimius Severus, who built out towards the south-east, where the *Septizodium provided a monumental façade. The palace remained in use even after *Constantinople became the new imperial capital (see PALACES).

Nash, *Pict. Dict. Rome* 2. 163 ff.; P. Zanker, *The Power of Images in the Age of Augustus* (1988; Ger. orig. 1987); Coarelli, *Roma⁶*, 124–48; M. Cristofani (ed.), *La grande Roma dei Tarquini* (1990), 79–107; Richardson, *Topog. Dict. Ancient Rome*, 279–82.   I. A. R.; D. E. S.; J. R. P.

palatini is a collective term used in the late empire for the members of the central bureaucracy, the privileged *comitatus*, so called because they belonged to the imperial 'palace'. The adjective 'palatine' was also added to the classification of some units of the mobile army: the guards cavalry (*scholae*) and new-style infantry *auxilia*, and the most senior of the cavalry detachments (*vexillationes*) and legions. This usage is first attested in 365, and seems to have been largely honorific.

Jones, *Later Rom. Emp.* 572–86; D. Hoffmann, *Das spätrömische Bewegungsheer* (1969–70), 396–404.   R. S. O. T.

Palestine See JEWS; JUDAEA; SYRIA.

Palfurius (*RE* 2) **Sura**, in Suet. *Dom.* 13 took the prize for Latin oratory at *Domitian's Capitoline Games (Greek-style games (*agōnes*) in honour of *Jupiter Capitolinus, first celebrated 86) after being expelled from the Senate; the crowd begged Domitian to restore him, but were silenced. In Juv. 4. 53 a Palfurius is a *delator*, informer (cf. Dio Cass. 68. 1. 2: 'Seras' condemned by *Nerva), and the Scholiast claims that he had performed in the Neronian arena (see NERO) but turned Stoic pleader (see STOICISM) and poet after expulsion by *Vespasian; he was son of a consul (suff. 56, of Spanish origin).

R. Syme, *Ktèma*, 1981, 281 (= *RP* 4. 88).   B. M. L.

Palibothra (Pataliputra, mod. Patna), situated near the confluence of the Ganges and the Son and on the Mauryan Royal Road linking northern and eastern *India, was the capital of the Mauryan empire (*c*.324/1–181/0 BC). The *Seleucid kings kept Greek residents, *Megasthenes and *Daimachus, at the court of the first two Mauryan kings, Chandragupta and Bindusara (the classical Amitrochates). In his account of India, Megasthenes describes the city's fortifications, stockade, and moat, some of which have been excavated. It remained an important city though little noticed by later Greek and Roman visitors to India. See MAURYAS.

Strabo 2. 70. 15 (702); Plin. *HN* 6. 63; Ptol. *Geog.* 1. 12. 9 etc. L. A. Waddell, *Discovery of the Exact Site of Asoka's Classic Capital at Pataliputra* (1892).   E. H. W.; R. Th.

Palici (Παλικοί), *Sicel twin-gods of the small lake (Lago dei Palici) near Menaeum in the Sicilian interior, which sends up a considerable amount of natural gas. Allegedly a suspected person might go to the lake and swear he was innocent; if he lied, he lost his life by the power of the gods (the gases are in fact somewhat poisonous); if not, he returned safe and might claim damages from his accuser. Their legend was that a local *nymph, Thalia, being pregnant by *Zeus, begged to be swallowed up in the earth to escape Hera; this was granted to her, and when she bore twins they made their way up through the pools known as Delloi. Traces of the sanctuary described by Diod. Sic. 11. 89. 8 are extant.

Macrob. *Sat.* 5. 19. 15 ff.; Servius on *Aen.* 9. 581. Bloch in Roscher's *Lexikon* 3. 1281; E. Manni, *Sicilia Pagana* (1965), 173 ff.   H. J. R.; A. J. S. S.

palimpsest (παλίμψηστος), a term applied to manuscripts in which the original text has been scraped or washed away, in order that another text may be inscribed in its place. As the term properly implies scraping, it must have originally been applied to such materials as leather, wax, or parchment, and only by analogy to papyrus, which could be washed, but not scraped. The term seems to occur first in *Catullus (22. 5); cf. Plut. *Mor.* 504 d, 779 c, where it is treated as synonymous with ἔκπλυτος. When parchment was scarce (especially, it seems, about the 9th cent. in western Europe) early manuscripts were not infrequently treated thus; and since the removal of the original writing was seldom complete, valuable texts of the Bible, *Cicero's *De re publica*, *Plautus, *Gaius (2), Licinianus, etc., have been recovered from such palimpsests. In the Byzantine world the shortage of writing material was often severe, especially in the Italo-Greek areas. An important palimpsest of early date has yielded some fragments of Euripides' *Phaethon*; still more significant is the codex from which J. L. Heiberg recovered an unknown treatise of *Archimedes. See also PALAEOGRAPHY, *Introduction*.

L. D. Reynolds and N. G. Wilson, *Scribes and Scholars* (3rd edn. 1991), 192–5, 286.   F. G. K.; N. G. W.

Palinurus, in mythology, helmsman of *Aeneas (Dion. Hal. 1. 53. 2). In *Virgil's *Aeneid* he is overcome by the god Sleep (Somnus), falls overboard, is washed up on the shore of Italy, and there killed by local inhabitants; his loss is negotiated by *Venus as the price to *Neptunus of the Trojans' safe arrival in Italy (5. 779 ff.). Aeneas sees his ghost in the Underworld, and promises to bury him at the site of his death, named after him as Cape Palinurus (6. 337 ff.), modern Capo Palinuro in *Lucania, where a settlement of the 6th cent. BC has been excavated.

M. Lossau and E. Greco, *Enc. Virg.* 'Palinuro'.   S. J. Ha.

Palladas, a Greek epigrammatist, was a schoolmaster at *Alexandria (1) in the 4th cent. AD. It is hardly possible to infer from his poems whether he was a Christian, a pagan, or an agnostic. About 150 of his epigrams are to be found in the Greek *Anthology. Some are written in hexameters or iambics, but most are in metrically unrefined elegiac couplets. Though most of his themes are by no means original, his poetic voice is highly distinctive: black, bitter, and cynically humorous, his brief poems satirize and reflect with disillusion on human ambitions and beliefs, and on life in general.

A. Franke, *De P. epigrammatographo* (1899); A. Cameron, *JRS* 1965, 17–30 and *The Greek Anthology* (1993), see index; H. Beckby, *Anthologia graeca* (2nd edn., undated, *c*.1965), 1. 57–62.   N. H.

Palladium Miraculous guardian statues were common in ancient cities, but none was more famous than the Trojan Palladium, a small wooden image of armed *Athena. It fell from the sky, and the safety of *Troy depended on its possession. *Odysseus and *Diomedes (2) carried it away, thus enabling the sack of Troy (variants of the story in Ov. *Fasti* 6. 419–60; Dion. Hal. 1. 68–9; Verg. and Serv. *Aen.* 2. 162–79; Sil. *Pun.* 13. 36–70). But in the canonical Roman tradition (dating perhaps to the late 4th cent.) it was *Aeneas who rescued the Palladium and brought it to *Lavinium, whence it ultimately reached Rome (Dion. Hal.). Ovid adduces both legends, but others tried to reconcile them: the image robbed by the Greeks was only a copy (Arctinus in Dion. Hal.), or: Diomedes came to Italy and returned the Palladium to Aeneas (Cassius Hemina, fr. 7 Peter; Varro in Serv.; Sil. Ital.). Also other cities claimed the Trojan Palladium: Athens, *Argos (2), Sparta, and in Italy *Heraclea (1), *Luceria, *Siris, and Lavinium (Strabo 6. 264). In Rome it was kept as a pledge of Rome's fate (*fatale pignus*) in the innermost part of *Vesta's temple (*penus Vestae*), where only the chief Vestal could enter; when in 241 BC the temple burnt, the pontifex maximus L. *Caecilius Metellus saved the Palladium, but (so some authorities) lost his sight (Cic. *Scaur.* 48; *Phil.* 11. 24; Livy 26. 27. 14; Ovid; Dion. Hal. 2. 66; Val. Max. 1. 4. 4; Sen. *Controv.* 4. 2; Plin. *HN* 7. 141; Luc. 1. 598; illustrated on the coins of *Galba, *RIC* 1. 206). It was still there in AD 191 (Herodian 1. 14. 4), but *Augustus may have placed it (or its copy) temporarily in Vesta's chapel in his *Palatine house.

R. G. Austin, Verg. *Aen.* 2 (1964), 83 ff.; A. Dubourdieu, *Les Origines et le développement du culte des Pénates* (1989); R. Cappelli, *BdA* (1990), 29 ff.; C. A. Faraone, *Talismans and Trojan Horses* (1992). J. L.

Palladius (1), **Rutilius Taurus Aemilianus,** author of the only surviving agricultural treatise from late antiquity (*c.* mid-5th cent. AD: the date is disputed) in 15 books: book 1 contains 32 wide-ranging short topics; books 2–13 outline the year's work by month; book 14 treats veterinary matters, book 15 (in elegiacs) grafting. Palladius owned properties in Italy near Rome, 3. 25. 20) and Sardinia (4. 10. 16) and possibly Gaul (cf. the detailed description of a Gallic reaping machine, 7. 2. 2–4). His practical experience (cf. 2. 2. 1; 4. 10. 24) ensured a critical approach to his main sources *Columella and *Gargilius Martialis (cf. 1. 28. 5, 4. 10. 16). The purposefully plain prose style (cf. 1. 1. 1) and absence of discussion of slaves (except for 1. 6. 18) suggest that he was writing instructions for a workforce of free tenants—against a background of agricultural recession (cf. 3. 18. 6; 7. 1).

TEXT R. H. Rodgers (complete work), Teubner (1975); R. Martin (bks. 1, 2), Budé (1976); J. Svennung (bk. 14), (1926).
STUDIES J. Svennung, *Untersuchungen zu Palladius und zur lateinischen Fach- und Volkssprache* (1935); K. D. White, *Roman Farming* (1970); R. H. Rodgers, *BICS* 1971, 46–52, *An Introduction to Palladius* (1975); A. Cossarini, *Atti dell'Istituto Veneto di Scienze, Lettere ed Arti*, 1977–8, 175–85; E. Frézouls, *Ktèma* 1980, 193–210. M. S. Sp.

Palladius (2) Born in *Galatia in AD 364, Palladius, like his brother and sister, adopted an ascetic life. He settled first on the Mount of Olives, where he associated with Melania the Elder and *Rufinus (2) and came under the influence of *Origen (1)'s works. He moved to Egypt *c.* AD 388—first to *Alexandria (1), then to the monastic centre Nitria during the heyday of Arsenius, and finally to the Kellia, where he remained for nine years in the company of Macarius of Alexandria and Evagrius of Pontus. Always restless and with a wide-ranging curiosity, he kept in touch with Palestinian associates and explored the ascetic communities established further south under the influence of Pachomius; see ASCETICISM. Poor health forced him eventually to leave Egypt. He returned north to Bithynia, came under the influence of John *Chrysostom after *c.* AD 400, and was appointed bishop of Helenopolis. Heavily involved in the controversies surrounding Chrysostom in Constantinople, he helped plead his cause with Innocent, bishop of Rome, AD 404–5, and suffered consequently a short period of exile thereafter. It was at that time, *c.* AD 408, that he wrote his *Dialogue* in Chrysostom's memory, a vital source for the events surrounding the patriarch's disgrace. He was appointed to the see of Aspona in Galatia in AD 412. He wrote his *Historia Lausiaca c.* AD 420, dedicated to Lausus, imperial chamberlain (*PLRE* 2. 660 f.). The association reflects the audience for ascetic literature among the pious laity of the capital. Although based on memories by that time old and in some respects unreliable, this collection of short biographical sketches (including women as well as men and urban ascetics as well as recluses) is lively, detailed, and witnesses to the breadth of

Palladius' own experience as well as to the tastes of his patrons and admirers. It enjoyed great popularity, and was woven into many later collections. Ascribing to Palladius the *De gentibus Indiae et Bragmanibus* raises a number of difficulties; but the work is undoubtedly of his period broadly speaking. In addition to its interest for the development of the Alexander legend (see PSEUDO-CALLISTHENES), it hints at geographical information and religious attitudes peculiar to that time. See ASCETICISM.

WORKS *The Lausiac History of Palladius*, ed. Dom. C. Butler (1898, 1904); *Palladios. Dialogue sur la vie de Jean Chrysostome*, ed. A.–M. Malingrey with P. Leclercq, 2 vols. (Sources chrétiennes, nos. 341–2, 1988); see also *Palladii Dialogus de vita s. Joannis Chrysostomi*, ed. P. R. Coleman-Norton (1928); *Palladius. De gentibus Indiae et Bragmanibus*, ed. W. Berghoff (1967); J. D. M. Derrett, *C&M* (1960) 64–99 (with edn.); and 100–35.
ADDITIONAL SURVEYS D. J. Chitty, *The Desert a City* (1966); E. D. Hunt, *JTS* 1973, 456–80; E. A. Clark, *The Origenist Controversy* (1992). P. R.

Pallas (1) (Pallas, -ados), a name of *Athena, apparently said to be derived either from a playmate of the same name accidentally killed by the goddess (Apollod. 3. 12. 3) or from a giant Pallas (-antos) whom Athena overcame (ibid. 1. 6. 2). E. Ke.

Pallas (2), an Attic hero, one of the four sons of *Pandion among whom *Attica was divided (Soph. *TGrF* F 24). His division was usually said to be the Paralia (south coast), but he was evidently also, rather awkwardly, the eponym of the inland *deme of Pallene. Together with his sons, who were *Giants, he opposed *Theseus, but their ambush near Gargettus was unsuccessful and they were killed. The story has an oblique relation to the regional factions of the late 6th cent. BC.

The name was borne also by other characters in myth, notably the son of *Evander and protégé of *Aeneas, killed by *Turnus (1) (Verg. *Aen.* 8. 104 ff., etc.). E. Ke.

Pallas, Marcus Antonius See ANTONIUS PALLAS, M.

palliata (sc. *fabula*, 'drama in a Greek cloak (*pallium*)'), the type of comedy written at Rome by *Plautus and *Terence, either known or assumed in nearly all cases to be adaptations of (Greek) New Comedy (see COMEDY (GREEK), NEW); since the plays of Plautus and Terence are the only complete Latin comedies to have survived from antiquity, this term has come to be synonymous with Latin *comedy. Almost certainly a masked drama from the start (though the ancient evidence is contradictory), it shows Greek characters in a Greek setting, and in general the authors are believed to have preserved many of the essential elements of plot from their Greek originals. But Roman details sometimes intrude, particularly in Plautus, who adapted the Greek plays with considerable freedom and whose portrayal of stereotyped stock characters may as well have been influenced by the *Atellana. Plautus was the first Latin playwright to devote himself exclusively to comedy; *Livius Andronicus, *Naevius, and *Ennius all wrote tragedies as well.

The Latin authors abandoned the five-act structure and choral interludes of Greek New Comedy, writing almost throughout for continuous performance; the act- and scene-divisions found in modern editions of Plautus and Terence do not go back to the authors. Like the Greek authors, they wrote in verse, but they increased the proportion of text with musical accompaniment (see CANTICA). They were not restricted to the use of three speaking actors and wrote many scenes requiring more.

It was through Plautus and Terence that Greek New Comedy

became the dominant type of comedy in the European dramatic tradition, with plots portraying love affairs, confusion of identity, and misunderstandings, and with casts including boastful soldiers, rediscovered foundlings, and scheming servants. The influence of the *palliata* is clear in Udall's *Ralph Roister Doister*, Shakespeare's *The Comedy of Errors*, Molière's *L'Avare* and *Les Fourberies de Scapin*, and many other plays.

See ARGUMENTUM; COMEDY, LATIN; CONTAMINATIO; and, as well as the authors mentioned above, AQUILLIUS or AQUILIUS; ATILIUS; CAECILIUS STATIUS; C. FUNDANIUS; LICINIUS IMBREX; LUSCIUS LANUVINUS; TRABEA; TURPILIUS; VERGILIUS ROMANUS. Other named authors include Juventius, Quintipor Clodius, and Vatronius.

W. G. Arnott, *Menander, Plautus, Terence* (1975); CHCL 2. 93–127; G. E. Duckworth, *The Nature of Roman Comedy* (1952); D. R. Dudley and T. A. Dorey (eds.), *Roman Drama* (1965); K. Gaiser, in H. Temporini (ed.), *ANRW* 1. 2 (1972), 1027–113; H. Haffter, *Untersuchungen zur altlateinischen Dichtersprache* (1934); R. L. Hunter, *The New Comedy of Greece and Rome* (1985); E. Lefèvre (ed.), *Die römische Komödie: Plautus und Terenz* (1973); F. H. Sandbach, *The Comic Theatre of Greece and Rome* (1977); J. Wright, *Dancing in Chains: The Stylistic Unity of the Comoedia Palliata* (1974). P. G. M. B.

Palmyra (Tadmor) gained wealth, power, and splendour particularly in Roman times. From it, a central Syrian desert oasis with hills, wadi, and spring (*Efqa*), routes ran in all directions. Efqa yielded stone tools, some *c.*7,500 BC, others neolithic, *c.*7000 BC. A community, Tadmor (of uncertain etymology), enters the records *c.*2000 BC. Puzur-Ishtar the 'Tadmorean' made a contract at Kanesh (Kultepe), Asia Minor (19th cent. BC); Syrian archives mention Tadmoreans, Suteans (nomads) pillaging, and the Amurru king's demand for taxes. The *Assyrians (1115–1077) defeated, near Tadmor, Aramaeans (Semites whose language, *Aramaic, spread throughout western Asia) and (645–644) *Arabs (Semites), who penetrated western Asia and comprised half Roman Tadmor's population. Hellenistic Old Testament *Chronicles* (and Josephus) reported that Solomon 'rebuilt Tadmor'; *c.*150 BC. *Parthia reached the Euphrates, and a Tadmor family built a hypogeum in Hellenized, hybrid 'Parthian' style. Tadmor rose rapidly after Seleucid extinction (64/3 BC), becoming semi-independent, and exploiting caravans between Roman (coastal) Syria and Parthia. Crafts-people developed Tadmor's 'Parthian' art style. From 44 BC there are Aramaic inscriptions, often with Seleucid-era dating, documented (profile-figured) art and architectural commissions. In 41 M. *Antonius (2) raided Palmyra unsuccessfully; shrines were refurbished and from now on, striking stone tomb towers lined routes. Roman control, from *Tiberius (*Germanicus' eastern mission, AD 17–19), brought soldiery, use of Greek and occasionally Latin alongside Aramaic, the name 'Palmyra', taxation (Tariff Law, 137), administration (tribes, Senate, City, People), urbanization, and religious *syncretism. *Hadrian visited Palmyra *c.*129. Caravans, often organized and policed by Palmyrenes, brought luxuries. The Palmyrenes created a handsome, largely limestone city, combining Semitic, Greek, Roman, and Parthian features. Walls, gates, the great Temple of Bel (32), Romanized temples (Baalshamin, 130/1), a piazza, market (agora), houses, streets (including the Grand Colonnade, with bracket statuary), the Tetrapylon, arch, tower tombs, hypogea, and 'house'-tombs arose. The local, stylized, frontal-figured 'Parthian' art comprised statues depicting deities and notables, reliefs of deities, lions and ceremonial, funerary busts (for closing burial slots) and sarcophagi showing the deceased, wall-paintings, including funerary Roman allegories

(Achilles, Ganymede), plaster heads and friezes, and (from *c.*200) coins. Imports included Chinese silks, imperial and Athenian marble statues, and mosaicists (Cassiopeia). The Palmyrene king *Septimius Odaenathus' (murdered 267–8) and queen *Zenobia's brief, Roman-style empire was ended by *Aurelian (272–3). *Diocletian (284–305) built a camp, walls and baths; Justinian (527–65) refurbished the walls and churches. Arabs took Tadmor (634); a late medieval fortress arose. Palmyra's 18th-cent. rediscovery influenced European neo-classicism.

T. Wiegand, *Palmyra* (1932); M. A. R. Colledge, *The Art of Palmyra* (1976), with bibliog. 'Parthian' style: M. A. R. Colledge, *Parthian Art* (1977), with bibliog.; *Iconography of Religions*, 14, 3: *The Parthian Period* (1986); K. Parlasca, *Syrische Grabreliefs* (1982); J. Starcky and M. Gawlikowski, *Palmyre* (1985); E. M. Ruprechtsberger (ed.), *Palmyra* (1987). Context: D. Strong, *Roman Art*, 2nd edn. rev. R. Ling and M. A. R. Colledge (1988), index; W. A. Daszewski and M. Gawlikowski (eds.), *Polish Archaeology in the Mediterranean*, 2: *Reports 1989–90* (1991), 85–93 (house, fortress); ibid. 3 (1992); ibid. 4 (1993), 115–18 (Zenobia's camp); E. Will, *Les Palmyréniens* (1992), with bibliog. Neo-classicism: e.g. I. Browning, *Palmyra* (1979), 89–96 (popularizing). M. A. R. C.

Pamphila (*RE* 1) of *Epidaurus, a scholar and anecdotal historian under *Nero. Her chief work, ἱστορικὰ ὑπομνήματα, 'Historical Notes', of which *Diogenes (6) Laertius and Aulus *Gellius preserve ten fragments from the original thirty-three books, was a *varia historia*, according to *Photius. It may have been summarized by *Favorinus.

FHG 3. 520. M. T. G.

Pamphilus (1) (4th cent. BC), painter, of *Amphipolis. Pupil of Eupompus of Sicyon (contemporary of *Parrhasius); teacher of *Apelles, *Pausias, *Melanthius (2). He painted a 'Battle at Phlius' (probably 367 BC) and the *Heraclidae, referred to by *Aristophanes (1) (*Plut.* 385: before 388 BC). His pupils paid him a talent for a course lasting 12 years. He insisted on a knowledge of arithmetic and geometry, and had panel-painting introduced in Sicyon as a school subject. See PAINTING, GREEK.

Overbeck, 1746–53; M. Robertson, *History of Greek Art* 1 (1975), 484–5. T. B. L. W.; A. J. S. S.

Pamphilus (2) of *Alexandria (1) (fl. AD 50), lexicographer. He wrote a Τέχνη κριτική, Φυσικά, Περὶ βοτανῶν 'Critical art', 'Physics', 'Botany', and, in ninety-five books, a great lexicon—Περὶ γλωσσῶν ἤτοι λέξεων 'on words and expressions'—which absorbed many previous specialist collections (see GLOSSA, GLOSSARY). It was used by *Athenaeus (1), and abridged by a succession of epitomators; the surviving lexicon of *Hesychius of Alexandria represents the last stage in this process. See also DIOGENIANUS (2). P. B. R. F.; R. B.

Pamphus, cited by *Pausanias (3) as a pre-Homeric writer of *hymns, but judged from the extant fragments to have been a Hellenistic poet.

P. Maas in *RE* 'Pamphos'. R. P.

Pamphylia, 'land of all tribes', the southern coastal plain of modern Turkey between Antalya (*Attaleia) and *Side, was traditionally settled by a mixed multitude of Greeks led by *Amphilochus, *Calchas, and *Mopsus. The local dialect (see ANATOLIAN LANGUAGES), which has affinities with Cypriot and Arcadian as well as additional Anatolian forms and vocabulary, confirms the tradition of an early Greek settlement, but there is no certainty that this extends back as far as the late bronze age. There are no archaeological traces of settlements of any kind during this period, and Greek immigration is perhaps better assigned to the period after 800 BC. The ancient sources are at odds with one another about the geographical limits of Pamphylia, but the term is best applied to the southern coastal plain enclosed by the mountains of eastern *Lycia, *Pisidia, and Rugged *Cilicia. The main cities were Attaleia, Magydus (unidentified), *Perge, Sillyum, *Aspendus, and Side. During the 5th and 4th cents. BC *Persian influence and control may be surmised, but Pamphylia must have been won over to the Athenian empire (see DELIAN LEAGUE) by *Cimon's victory at the *Eurymedon in the 460s, and Aspendus, Perge, and Sillyum appear in the Athenian tribute assessment of 425 BC. In the Hellenistic period the cities emerged as thriving independent civic communities, although overall control of the region was a bone of contention between the Ptolemies (see PTOLEMY (1)) and *Seleucids in the 3rd cent. and between the Attalids (see PERGAMUM) and the Pisidians in the 2nd cent. BC. A milestone found near Side belonging to the road built by M'. *Aquillius (1) between 129 and 126 BC from Pergamum shows that Pamphylia was part of the Roman province of *Asia from its creation in 133. Around 80 BC it was attached to Cilicia; it reverted to Asia during the 40s, and was assigned to *Galatia from 25 BC. Probably from AD 43 until the 4th cent. it formed a joint province with Lycia, also including the Pisidian highlands to the north. The cities of Pamphylia had fertile territories and good *harbours, which laid the basis for great prosperity. Settlers of Italian origin played a leading role in civic life during the 1st and 2nd cents. AD at Attaleia, Perge, and Aspendus, and several of the earliest Roman senators from the eastern provinces came from this background (see NEGOTIATORES). The well-preserved remains of the region show the spectacular flowering of civic life, which lasted deep into the 3rd cent., when Pamphylia, protected by its geographical position from Gothic and Persian raids (see GOTHS; SASANIDS), played a key role in the defence and recovery of the eastern part of the empire.

Jones, *Cities E. Rom. Prov.* 124 ff.; G. E. Bean, *Turkey's Southern Shore*[2] (1979); H. Brandt, *Gesellschaft und Wirtschaft Pamphyliens und Pisidiens im Altertum* (1992) (with full bibliog.); E. Blumenthal, *Die altgriechische Siedlungskolonisation im Mittelmeerraum unter besonderer Berücksichtigung der Südküste Kleinasiens* (1963). S. M.

Pan, a god whose original home was *Arcadia. His name, attested on Mount Lykaion in the form Πάονι, is certainly derived from the root †pa(s), and means 'guardian of flocks' (cf. Latin *pascere*). His appearance is mixed, half man and half goat, not surprising in a region where divine theriomorphism is well attested (see ARCADIAN CULTS AND MYTHS). His usual attributes of syrinx and *lagobolon* (a device for catching hares) mark him out as a shepherd. Pan became a kind of national god of Arcadia, being shown in the fourth century on the reverse of coins of Zeus Lycaeus type of the *Arcadian League. Starting at the beginning of the 5th cent., Pan spreads into Boeotia and *Attica, continuing in the 4th cent. to reach the rest of the Greek world.

The principal myths concern his birth, and there are no fewer than fourteen different versions of his parentage. Most often his father is *Hermes, another Arcadian god, but the name of his mother varies, though most often she is a *nymph, in harmony with the god's rustic nature. In some versions Pan's mother is *Penelope. Otherwise, there are few stories about Pan before Hellenistic times: he loves the nymphs *Echo, Pitys, and *Syrinx, of whom the last two escape him, and *Selene, the moon.

Pan's activities and functions are basically concerned with the pastoral world (see PASTORALISM, GREEK). He is a shepherd god and protector of shepherds, who sacrifice in his honour kids (*Anth. Pal.* 6. 154), goats or sheep, and who dedicate to him statuettes showing herdsmen, with or without offerings. He is also a hunting god, concerned with small animals such as hares, partridges, and small birds, while it is *Artemis who presides over larger game. This function is illustrated by an Arcadian ritual, whereby after an unsuccessful hunt, young men would beat Pan's statue with squills (Theoc. 7. 106–8, with scholia). In this way they would stimulate Pan's powers of fertility and direct it towards the animal domain. Pan is also linked to the world of those soldiers patrolling the rocky, lonely places where he lives. During the *Persian Wars, he intervened among the Athenian ranks at Marathon (see MARATHON, BATTLE OF.) *Herodotus (1) (6. 105. 2–3) has the story of his appearance to the runner *Phidippides, who was near Mount Parthenion in Arcadia on his way to *Laconia to get help from the Spartans; he offered to help the Athenians, in return for which the cult of Pan was established in Athens. From the Hellenistic period onwards, Pan is the god responsible for sowing panic (πανεῖον) in the enemy, a sudden, unforeseeable fear. Soldiers therefore pay cult to him. In the case of the individual, too, Pan can exercise a type of savage and violent possession (*panolepsia*). In Attica (cf. *Menander (1), *Dyskolos* 571–2; see PHYLE), Arcadia, and at the Corycian cave at *Delphi, Pan is credited with oracular and prophetic powers. See CAVES, SACRED; ORACLES.

The Greeks liked to worship Pan, together with Hermes and the nymphs, in sacred *caves, recalling the figure of the Arcadian goatherd. But in his homeland of Arcadia, though he is fond of mountains, well away from human habitation, Pan does not live in caves, and he is not absent from cities. Little is known of his public cult. In Athens, it involved the sacrifice of a castrated goat and a torch-race. Individual offerings are typified by votives such as vases, golden grasshoppers, oil-lamps (in the cave at Vari in *Attica), and reliefs, which show the God in his cave in front of his worshippers, playing the syrinx and accompanied by Hermes, three nymphs, and sometimes the river *Achelous (see RIVER-GODS). In the *Dyskolos* of Menander, the mother of Sostratos organizes a religious celebration in honour of Pan at *Phyle, in Attica, after the god appears to her in a dream. The sacrifice of a sheep is followed by a meal, and the happy and rowdy celebration continues all night at the cave, with drinking and dancing in the presence of the god.

The ancients quite early associated Pan with the word πᾶν, 'all' (Homeric *Hymn to Pan* 47). From this, word-play leads to the association which made Pan in the Roman period into a universal god, the All. It is in this context that we should see the well-known story in *Plutarch (*Mor.* 419 c), which has sometimes been linked with the rise of Christianity, of a mysterious voice announcing the death of 'great Pan'. Despite these developments, as *Pausanias (3) bears witness, in cult the god remained the god of shepherds.

M. Jost, *Sanctuaires et cultes d'Arcadie* (1985), 456–76; P. Borgeaud, *The Cult of Pan in Ancient Greece* (1988); Parker, *ARH* 163–8. M. J.

Panacea (Πανάκεια), 'All-Healer', daughter of *Asclepius (Plin. *HN* 25. 30 and often).

Panactum (border fort between *Attica and *Boeotia) See Hornblower, *Comm. on Thuc.* 5. 3. 5 (1996).

Panaenus (fl. 448 BC, acc. to *Pliny (1)), painter, brother (or nephew) of *Phidias, Athenian. He helped Phidias with the colouring of the Olympian Zeus (see OLYMPIA) and painted mythical scenes on screens between the legs of the throne. In the temple of *Athena in *Elis he put on a plaster mixed with saffron (for fresco?), and painted the inside of the shield of Colotes' Athena.

Panaetius

The best sources ascribe to him, rather than to *Micon or *Polygnotus, the 'Battle of *Marathon' in the *Stoa Poecile.

Overbeck, 696, 698, 1054, 1083, 1094–108; M. Robertson, *History of Greek Art*, 1 (1975), 322 ff. T. B. L. W.

Panaetius (*c*.185–109 BC), son of Nicagoras; a Stoic philosopher (see STOICISM) from *Rhodes. At some point he was made a priest of *Poseidon Hippios at *Lindus. From a noble family, he studied with *Crates (3) of Mallus at *Pergamum and with the leaders of the Stoic school at Athens, *Diogenes (3) of Babylon and his successor *Antipater (2) of Tarsus. He moved to Rome in the 140s and became, like *Polybius (1), part of the entourage of P. *Cornelius Scipio Aemilianus. He accompanied Scipio on a major journey in the eastern Mediterranean (140/139). It is said that he lived alternately in Rome and Athens. In 129 he succeeded Antipater as head of the school. He died in Athens in 109.

Panaetius seems to have been more open to the views of *Plato (1) and *Aristotle than were many Stoics, and to have questioned the earlier belief in a periodic world-conflagration. Unlike earlier Stoics, he doubted the efficacy of *astrology and *divination, though he retained a belief in divine providence. It is possible that he made some changes in moral psychology, in the direction of Platonic or Aristotelian dualism. But the evidence on this point is not as clear as for *Posidonius (2). In ethics, he is associated with a more practical emphasis on the moral situation of ordinary men and a reduced emphasis on the morally perfect sage. His account of the virtues also shows signs of revision, but not radical change. Books 1–2 of *Cicero's *De Officiis* were heavily influenced by Panaetius' Περὶ καθήκοντος ('on duty'). His student *Hecaton was influential in ethics.

M. van Straaten, *Panaetii Rhodii Fragmenta*[3] (1962) is the basic collection of evidence. His *Panétius, sa vie, ses écrits et sa doctrine . . .* (1946) replaces earlier work. Pohlenz's discussion in *Die Stoa* (1948–55) is badly out of date. B. I.

Panathenaea, the great civic festival of Athens in honour of its patron goddess *Athena, celebrated in Hekatombaion (roughly August). Its core was the great procession, evoked on the *Parthenon frieze, in which representatives of different sections of Athenian society and even *metics marched or rode from the *Ceramicus through the agora to the acropolis (see ATHENS, TOPOGRAPHY). There followed large sacrifices, the meat from which was publicly distributed. The night before, choirs of boys and maidens had celebrated a 'night festival' (*pannychis). Every four years, the Panathenaea was extended to become the 'greater Panathenaea'. Only then, probably, did the procession bring to Athena the famous Panathenaic robe, embroidered with scenes from the battle of Gods and Giants. The greater Panathenaea also included major athletic and musical competitions (see AGŌNES), open to all Greece and lasting several days, winners in which received money prizes or *olive oil contained in the distinctive Panathenaic prize *amphoras. The games were added to the Panathenaea in the 6th cent. (in or near 566), doubtless to set it on a par with other recently founded panhellenic athletic festivals (Pythia, Isthmia, Nemeia; see PANHELLENISM; PYTHIAN, ISTHMIAN, and NEMEAN GAMES). In the 5th cent. Athens' allies were required to participate in the procession, which thus became a symbol of imperial power; see DELIAN LEAGUE.

J. Neils, *Goddess and Polis* (1992). R. C. T. P.

Pandareos (Πανδάρεως), name of either one or two obscure mythological persons, the father of *Aëdon, and, if this is not the same Pandareos, the father of two daughters whose story is told

in *Od.* 20. 66 ff., on which see the ancient commentators. Their names were Cleothera and Merope, and they were left orphans (the scholiast says *Zeus killed their father and mother because Pandareos had stolen his dog from Crete). *Hera, *Athena, *Artemis, and *Aphrodite befriended them, brought them up, and gave them all manner of good qualities; but while Aphrodite was visiting Zeus to arrange their wedding, the *Harpyiae carried them off and gave them to be servants to the *Erinyes. Cf. Roscher, *Lexikon*, 'Pandareos'.

LIMC 7. 1. 159–60. H. J. R.

Pandarus, a Trojan, son of *Lycaon (2) (*Il.* 2. 826–7), and an *archer favoured by *Apollo. Urged on by *Athena, he breaks the truce between the Greeks and Trojans by shooting at and wounding *Menelaus (1) (4. 86 ff.); wounds *Diomedes (2) (5. 95 ff.), and is killed by him while fighting alongside *Aeneas (5. 166–296).

LIMC 7. 1. 160–1. J. R. M.

Pandion, a Megarian hero (see MEGARA) and a mythical king of Athens, later identified as the name of two Athenian kings. For Athenians, his Megarian connections would have bolstered aggressive territorial claims, linked with the tradition of the division of Attica (including the Megarid, i.e. the territory of Megara) between his four sons. He was also one of the tribal *eponymoi. See also NISUS (1).

Kron, *Phylenheroen*, 104–19, 262–4; *LIMC* 7. 1. 162–3. E. Ke.

Pandora, whose name combines 'all' and 'gifts', was a goddess connected with the earth, but she is better known as the first human female, the cause of all man's woes. If the name has any relevance here, it sounds ironic; but the two Pandoras may in fact be connected through the idea of the earth as first ancestor. In the account of the Hesiodic poems (see HESIOD; *Op.* 53–105 is the fuller version) *Zeus caused Pandora to be created in order to punish *Prometheus and the human race. She was fashioned out of clay by *Hephaestus, given 'gifts' by 'all' the *Olympian gods, and sent as a gift herself to Prometheus' brother Epimetheus. Here she opened a large jar and released all manner of evils into the world; only Hope was left to counterbalance these.

O. Lendle, *Die Pandorasage bei Hesiod* (1957); G. Fink, *Pandora und Epimetheus* (1958); H. Neitzel, *Hermes*, 1976, 387–419; M. L. West, *Hesiod: Works and Days* (1978), 164–6; N. Loraux, *The Children of Athena* (1993, Fr. orig. 1981), 72–84; D. and E. Panofsky, *Pandora's Box*[2] (1962); P. Lévêque, *Kernos*, 1988, 49–62. E. Ke.

Pandosia, unidentified site in the Crathis valley in S. Italy, and Oenotrian capital, which was later captured by the *Bruttii. The 5th-cent. coinage is closely related to that of *Croton. In 331, *Alexander (6) I, the Molossian king, was defeated by the Lucanians (see LUCANIA) at Pandosia. It became a Roman ally but defected during the Hannibalic war (see PUNIC WARS).

V. Panebianco in *Magna Grecia* (1974). K. L.

Pandrosus, daughter of the Athenian king *Cecrops, to whom with her sisters *Aglaurus and Herse the infant *Erichthonius was entrusted. In some versions she was the only sister not to disobey *Athena's command not to open the chest in which the baby was concealed, which probably reflects her close association with Athena and her role in the *Arrephoria rite and her role as a nurse of children. Pandrosus had a sanctuary on the Athenian acropolis separately from her sisters, but may have been worshipped together with them elsewhere in *Attica.

Kron, *LIMC* 1. 283–98; Kearns, *Heroes of Attica*, 23–7, 192–3; P. Brulé, *La Fille d'Athènes* (1987), 34–41. E. Ke.

panegyric (Latin) The origins of Latin panegyric are to be sought in the ancient institution of the *laudatio funebris or 'funeral eulogy', and in the custom by which consuls entering upon office thanked the people for their election. Later came fertilization from Greek *rhetoric, whose precepts for praise are best seen in the treatises of *Menander (4) Rhetor. The continuous Latin tradition was much influenced by *Cicero's praise of *Pompey in the *Pro lege Manilia* and of *Caesar in the *Pro Marcello*, and later by the younger *Pliny (2)'s *Panegyricus*, in which he gave thanks to *Trajan when Pliny took up his consulship in AD 100. By that time praise was ordinarily reserved for the emperor, and the *XII Panegyrici Latini* show us the tradition flourishing in the 3rd and 4th cents.

This collection was found by Giovanni Aurispa in 1433, in a now lost Mainz manuscript. Its contents are (using the numbering according to Mynors's edition): 1 Pliny's *Panegyricus*; 2 Latinius Pacatus Drepanius' panegyric of 389 congratulating *Theodosius (2) I in the senate on his victory over *Magnus Maximus; 3 *Claudius Mamertinus' speech of thanks for his consulship to *Julian at *Constantinople (362); 4 Nazarius' panegyric, given in Rome, of (the absent) *Constantine I (321); 5–8 are by anonymous Gallic orators and were given probably or certainly at *Augusta Treverorum (Trier), 5 to Constantine in 311 or 312 for benefits conferred on *Augustodunum (Autun), 6 again to Constantine (310), 7 to Constantine on the occasion of his marriage to Fausta (307), and 8 to *Constantius I after the recovery of Britain (297); 9 is the *Pro restaurandis scholis* ('On restoring the schools') of *Eumenius (297 or 298); 10 and 11 were given by one and the same unknown Gallic orator at Trier, 10 to *Maximian on Rome's birthday (289) and 11 to Maximian on his (291); finally, 12 is an anonymous speech given at Trier in praise of Constantine after the defeat of *Maxentius (313).

The 3rd- and 4th-cent. *Panegyrics* are written in flowery but correct Latin, Plinian rather than Ciceronian. They throw considerable light on the history of their times, especially in Gaul, and on the themes and procedures of imperial propaganda. It was the speaker's task to place the deeds of the emperor being praised in the best possible light; exaggeration and economy with the truth are naturally prevalent, just as they are in historical works influenced by panegyric (Cicero's letter to L. *Lucceius (*Fam.* 5. 12) and the correspondence between L. *Verus and M. *Cornelius Fronto on the Parthian War (Fronto 2. 194–218 Haines) are significant here).

Prose panegyrics not included in this collection but wholly or partly extant are by *Symmachus (2) (between 369 and c.388), *Ausonius (379), *Merobaudes (437), *Ennodius (c.507) and *Cassiodorus (6th cent.).

Verse panegyric is represented for us by the *Panegyricus Messallae preserved in the Tibullan corpus, the equally anonymous *Laus Pisonis, *Statius' *Silvae 4. 1 and 5. 2, and various poems of *Claudian, *Sidonius Apollinaris, *Corippus, and *Venantius Fortunatus.

TEXTS R. A. B. Mynors (1964); V. Paladini and P. Fedeli (1976). E. Galletier's Budé (1949–55) contains Fr. trans.
CONCORDANCE T. Janson (1979).
GENERAL K. Ziegler, *RE* 'Panegyrikos'; Schanz–Hosius §§ 445a, 578–91, 814–5 (for the *XII Panegyrici*); S. MacCormack in T. A. Dorey (ed.), *Empire and Aftermath* (1975), ch. 7; and (for the Greek background) *Menander Rhetor*, ed. D. A. Russell and N. G. Wilson (1981). W. S. M.; M. W.

Panegyricus Messallae, a eulogy of M. *Valerius Messalla Corvinus, in 212 hexameters, by an unidentified poet, preserved

in the Tibullan corpus as 3. 7 (= 4. 1; see TIBULLUS). Following the long-established tradition of panegyric by clients celebrating the military exploits of a wealthy patron, the poet compares Messalla to *Odysseus, and, it has been argued, to *Alexander (3) the Great. The piece is generally agreed to be on a lower artistic level than the other poems in the corpus, and it suffers in comparison with Tibullus' elegy (1. 7) on Messalla's *triumph (27 BC); some have nevertheless argued for Tibullan authorship. The poem is usually dated to 31 BC, on the grounds that Messalla's consulship (31) is the latest event explicitly mentioned; reminiscences of Tibullus, however, suggest a date after 27 and this view gains support if lines 118–34 are interpreted as an oblique reference to Messalla's triumph.

Text and trans. in edns. of Tibullus; text/commentary in Tränkle, *Appendix Tibulliana* (1990); Schoonhoven, *ANRW* 2. 30. 3 (1983), 1681–707; Bright, *Quaderni Urbinati* (1984); Papke in *Concentus Hexachordus*, ed. Krafft and Tschiedel (1986). P. W.

Pangaeus, a mountain in *Thrace, east of *Amphipolis and not far from the coast; it extends for some 25 km. from south-west to north-east, and at its highest point reaches 1,956 m. The name appears first in *Pindar, *Pyth.* 4. 180, and in *Aeschylus, *Persae* 494; *Herodotus (1) (6. 46; 7. 112) mentions *gold and *silver *mines worked by Thracian tribes and by the islanders of *Thasos, who controlled part of the mainland ('*peraea') and in particular a mine at Scapte Hyle. Geologically the higher part of the mountain is not of a metalliferous nature, consisting, as it does, of crystalline white marble. Since 1981 the Greek Geological Institute (IGME) and the Archaeological Ephorate have discovered numerous shafts, smelting furnaces, and metallurgical complexes of ancient times. Their final reports will revolutionize our knowledge of mining in the Pangaeus area. In the mid-6th cent. BC the wealth of the area attracted *Pisistratus of Athens (*Ath. Pol.* 15. 2), and in 463 BC Athens defeated Thasos and acquired the Thasian settlements on the mainland. With the collapse of the Athenian empire (see DELIAN LEAGUE) Thasos regained control but only to lose it again to Athens c.375 BC. A stronger enemy, *Philip (1) II, incorporated the Pangaean area into the Macedonian kingdom; he destroyed two Thasian settlements (Galepsus and Phagres) and converted a third, Oesyme, into a Macedonian city, 'Emathia'. The output of the mines was increased by improved mining techniques, and helped to make *Amphipolis the chief mint of *Alexander (3) the Great's domains. Thereafter, and especially in Roman times, Pangaeus declined progressively in importance. See MINES AND MINING.

D. Lazaridis, *Thasos and its Peraea* (1971); D. K. Samsares, *Historical Geography of Eastern Macedonia in Antiquity* (1976); IGME report in *AΔ* 37. 326 and 38. 322. N. G. L. H.

Panhellenion, Attic, Athens-based loyalist organization of eastern cities, founded by *Hadrian in 131/2, but probably not fully operational before 137; known almost entirely from inscriptions. Drawn from five Roman provinces (*Achaia, *Thrace, *Asia, and *Crete-and-*Cyrene), member-cities sent representatives ('Panhellenes') to a council presided over by an archon; personnel were provincial notables. Admission-criteria were a 'noble' Greek foundation (notably from Athens and Sparta) and loyalty to Rome. On present evidence the Panhellenion was chiefly a cultic organization (an inscription from Aezani (Wörrle) shows that Panhellenes, like provincial priests of the emperors, wore crowns with imperial busts), centred on the worship of its deified founder ('Hadrian Panhellenius') and on the cult of *Demeter at *Eleusis; there are slight indications of administrative functions. It indirectly promoted the economic and cultural revival of Achaia and inter-city ties across the *Aegean, surviving at least as late as the 250s, when its festival, the Panhellenia, is last attested.

J. H. Oliver, *Hesperia* suppl. 13 (1970); A. Spawforth and S. Walker, *JRS* 1985, 78 ff., 1986, 88 ff.; M. Wörrle, *Chiron*, 1992, 337 ff.; C. P. Jones, *Chiron* 1996; A. Spawforth, *Chiron* 1999.   A. J. S. S.

panhellenism, the idea that what the Greeks have in common as Greeks, and what distinguishes them from *barbarians, is more important than what divides them. The word is not an ancient one, though *Panhellenes* is used of the Greeks in the *Iliad* (2. 530) and elsewhere in early poetry (see HELLENES). The beginnings of the idea should be sought in the Greeks' resistance to the Persian invasions of 490 and 480–479 BC (see PERSIAN WARS), and in the *Delian League as a Greek alliance formed to continue the war against Persia. In the 4th cent., after the *Peloponnesian War, the argument that the great days of the Greeks were when they were united against Persia rather than fighting among themselves, and that to recover their greatness they should again unite against Persia, was advanced by *Gorgias (1) and *Lysias and became a recurrent theme in the works of *Isocrates. The invasion of the Persian empire planned by *Philip (1) II of Macedon and accomplished by *Alexander (3) the Great was partly inspired by this idea. Panhellenic Games were games open to all Greeks; see AGŌNES, § (2). The four great panhellenic *sanctuaries were *Delphi, *Olympia, *Isthmia, and *Nemea, though there were panhellenic aspects to e.g. the *Panathenaea at Athens.

N. H. Baynes, *Byzantine Studies and Other Essays* (1955), ch. 8; C. Morgan in N. Marinatos and R. Hägg (eds.), *Greek Sanctuaries* (1993), 18 ff.   P. J. R.

Panionium, meeting place of the Ionian League (see IONIANS) from very early (early 7th cent. BC?), where the common festival (Panionia) of the twelve member-cities took place and their *probouloi* met to discuss common policy in time of need. *Herodotus (1) (1. 148) places it on Mt. Mycale; for security it was later moved near *Ephesus (by 426/5 BC: see Hornblower on Thuc. 3. 104. 3, where the festival is called Ephesia), before returning (373 BC?) to Mt. Mycale, where it was still celebrated under the Principate (*Strabo 14. 20. 1). Sacrifice was made to Heliconian *Poseidon; the priesthood was reserved for men from *Priene. The site has been excavated: there was no temple, it seems, but an altar, 18-m. long (*c*.500 BC); also a bouleuterion.

PECS 670; Hornblower, *Comm. on Thuc.* 1 (1991), 527 ff.
J. M. C.; A. J. S. S.

pankration (παγκράτιον). In this event *boxing and *wrestling were combined with kicking, strangling, and twisting. It was a dangerous sport, but strict rules were enforced by the umpires. Biting and gouging were forbidden (except at Sparta, Philostr. *Imag.* 348), but nearly every manœuvre of hands, feet, and body was permissible. You might kick your opponent in the stomach, twist his foot out of its socket, or break his fingers (cf. Pausanias 6. 4, 8. 40. 1–2). All neck holds were allowed, a favourite method being the 'ladder-grip', in which you mounted your opponent's back, and wound your legs round his stomach, your arms round his neck. See ATHLETICS.

M. Poliakoff, *Combat Sports in the Ancient World* (1987), 54–63.
F. A. W.; S. J. I.

Pannonia, a Roman province established in AD 9 and named after the Pannonii, a group of Illyrian peoples (see ILLYRII) who had absorbed Celtic influences to varying degrees (see CELTS),

lay south and west of the Danube (*Danuvius) in the valleys of the Drava and Sava and the latter's Bosnian tributaries. In 119 BC the Romans campaigned against them, not for the first time, seizing *Siscia. In 35 BC Octavian (see AUGUSTUS) advanced against them and recaptured Siscia, where he established a garrison. Fighting broke out in 16 BC with a Pannonian invasion of Istria and continued in 14. In 13 M. *Vipsanius Agrippa and M. *Vinicius advanced eastward down the Sava and Drava valleys. After Agrippa's death (12 BC) the conquest of the Pannonians, notably the Breuci in the Sava valley, was completed ruthlessly by *Tiberius and Roman control was extended to the Danube (*Res Gestae Divi Augusti* 100. 30). Pannonia north of the Drava appears to have accepted Roman rule without a struggle, probably owing to fear of the Dacians to the east. Some fighting is attested in 8 BC by Sex. Appuleius but Pannonia remained more or less at peace until AD 6 when the Breuci joined the Daesitiates in revolt, under two chiefs called *Bato (1–2). After AD 9 Pannonia was governed by *legati Augusti pro praetore* of consular rank; see LEGATI. When *Dacia was annexed in 106, Pannonia was subdivided into two provinces, the larger *Superior* in the west under a consular legate and facing the *Germans, and *Inferior* in the east facing the Sarmatians under a praetorian. The latter was upgraded to consular under *Caracalla by a boundary alteration which equalled the strength of the two provincial armies. Following the reforms of *Gallienus the senatorial legates were superseded by equestrian *praesides*. Under *Diocletian both provinces were subdivided, Pannonia Superior into Pannonia Prima in the north (capital Savaria), under a *praes* and a *dux*, Pannonia Ripariensis or Savia in the south (capital Siscia) under a *dux*; Pannonia Inferior into Valeria in the north (chief places: *Aquincum and Sopianae) under a *praes* and a *dux*, and Pannonia Secunda in the south (capital *Sirmium) under a *consularis* and a *dux*. During the 4th cent. Pannonia suffered greatly from barbarian invasions. The end appears to have come with the incursion of Radagaisus and the Ostrogoths (see GOTHS) in AD 405, causing large numbers of Romans to flee to Italy.

A. Mócsy, *Pannonia and Upper Moesia* (1974); A. Lengyel and G. T. B. Radan (eds.), *The Archaeology of Roman Pannonia* (1980); Z. Visy, *Der Pannonische Limes in Ungarn* (1985).   J. J. W.

pannychis, an 'all-night' festival, with rites appropriate for the deity but often including banquets, hymns, and dances, as in Athens for *Athena Polias at the *Panathenaea (Eur. *Heracl.* 777–83) and for *Artemis at the Tauropolia (Men. *Epit.*). In comedy such night festivals could be made the occasion of illicit sexual encounters (ibid.). Pannychis was also a common name for a *hetaira* (see HETAIRAI), as in *Lucian, *Dial. Meret.* 9.   J. D. M.

Panormus (modern Palermo), town in *Sicily founded by the *Phoenicians early in the 7th cent. BC, became the main Carthaginian *point d'appui* in north-western Sicily. Despite its name it was never Greek, and save for a brief capture by *Pyrrhus in 276 was continuously in Punic i.e. Carthaginian hands until taken by the Romans in 254 (Polyb. 1. 38). It is mentioned sporadically in the sources, usually as a Carthaginian base of operations (e.g. in 480). A *civitas libera et immunis* (see FREE CITIES) under Roman rule, it became a *colonia* under *Augustus, with recolonization under *Vespasian and *Hadrian (*Lib. Colon.* 211). Its superb position, with a notable harbour backed by the fertile Conca d'Oro, ensured its importance and prosperity; it became the capital of Arab, Norman, and modern Sicily. The Punic city-wall and cemetery have been found, also Punic inscriptions.

There is no good ancient description, but cf. Diod. Sic. 22. 10; Callias fr. 2 (*FGrH* no. 564); Silius Ital. 14. 261–3. Geography and antiquities: *PECS* 'Panormus'; B. Rocco, *Annali dell' Ist. Orientale di Napoli* 34 (1974), 469 ff. (inscriptions); *Di terra in terra: Nuove scoperte archeologiche nella provincia di Palermo* (1991), 255 ff. See also HAMILCAR (2), HEIRCTE.

A. G. W.; A. J. S. S.

Pantheon, a temple in the *Campus Martius dedicated to all the gods. The first Pantheon, built by M. *Vipsanius Agrippa in 27–25 BC, was completely rebuilt early in the reign of *Hadrian but retained Agrippa's name in the dedicatory inscription (*CIL* 6. 896); it was later repaired by *Septimius Severus and *Caracalla. The building was entered from a long rectangular forecourt through a traditional octastyle Corinthian portico (33.1 × 13.6 m. (109 × 45 ft.)) of red and grey granite columns, 48 Roman feet (11.8 m.) high, although the original design may have been for 60 (Roman) ft. columns. A rectangular block links this to the circular cella, 43.3 m. (142 ft.) in both diameter and height, lit from a single central oculus, 9 m. (30 ft.) in diameter. The cylindrical wall of the brick-faced concrete rotunda (6.2 m. (20 ft.) thick) supporting the dome is divided into eight piers by the doorway and alternating semi-circular and rectangular recesses at the lower level with internal key-shaped chambers above, all linked by a complex series of relieving arches extending to the haunches of the dome. The six lateral recesses were divided off by marble columnar screens crowned by a continuous entablature while small aedicules framing statue niches decorated the piers between them. Richly coloured marble veneer, substantially preserved in the lower zone, decorated the interior; a small section of the attic decoration has been restored to its original form. The great bronze doors are ancient. The play of light from the oculus across the vast surface of the richly coffered dome is largely responsible for the building's enduring fascination.

K. de Fine Licht, *The Rotunda in Rome* (1968); W. L. MacDonald, *The Architecture of the Roman Empire I* (1982²), 94 ff.; Nash, *Pict. Dict. Rome* 2. 171 ff.; P. Davies, *Art History* (1987), 131 ff.
J. D.

Panthous (Πάνθους, Πάνθοος), Trojan elder in *Homer's *Iliad* (3. 146); his son *Polydamas is protected by *Apollo (*Il.* 15. 522), who may have rescued Panthous himself from Troy (Pindar, *Paean* 6.73 ff.). *Virgil makes Panthous priest of Apollo, killed at Troy's fall (*Aen.* 2. 318 ff.).

L. Lehnus, *Enc. Virg.* 'Panto'.
S. J. Ha.

Panticapaeum, a city at modern Kerch on the west side of the Cimmerian *Bosporus (2): a Milesian foundation *c.*600 BC (see COLONIZATION, GREEK; MILETUS), which some consider to have replaced an earlier local settlement there. Its site incorporates a low coastal terrace and so-called Mt. Mithradates. Archaeology has shown substantial structures with tiled roofs by *c.*500 BC.

Around 300 BC a substantial defensive wall had been constructed, reinforced with bastions. At the same time, its gold coinage and fine tombs attest its prosperity. The 1st cent. AD saw the erection of fine buildings on the acropolis, decorated with marble. Among economic activities at Panticapaeum was the salting of fish in cisterns, and also wine production.

Panticapaeum was the principal city of the Crimean portion of the Bosporan kingdom (see SPARTOCIDS). Damaged by Gothic onslaughts of the mid-3rd cent. AD (see GOTHS) and sacked by *Huns at the end of the 4th cent., the city survived into the Middle Ages.

V. F. Gajdukevich, *Das bosporanische Reich*² (1971); G. A. Koshelenko, I. T. Kruglikova, and V. S. Dolgorukov (eds.), *Antichnye gosudarstva Severnovo Prichernomor'ya* (1984), 59–63; D. Kacharava and G. Kvirk-velia (eds.), *Goroda i poseleniya Prichernomor'ya antichnoy epokhi* (1991), 208–16.
D. C. B.

pantomime, popular art-form under the Roman empire in which a solo dancer (*pantomimus,* παντόμιμος) represented mythological themes without voice, supported by instrumental music and a chorus. The apparent meaning is 'one who imitates everything', but the distinctive quality of pantomime is that the artist did everything by imitation, as in modern mime. The art (called the 'Italian dance' in the Greek east) was introduced at Rome in 22 BC by the Cilician Pylades and Bathyllus of *Alexandria (1) (see MAECENAS, C.); Hellenistic antecedents are suggested too by e.g. the *pantomimos* of an inscription from *Priene of *c.*80 BC (*IPriene* 113). Pylades' innovation, according to himself (Macrob. *Sat.* 2. 7), was to add the orchestra and the chorus. Bathyllus seems to have specialized in light themes related to comedy or satyric drama, such as Pan playing with a satyr; Pylades' style is said to have been 'high flown, passionate' (Ath. 1. 20e) and related to tragedy. Tragic subjects were in fact a favourite, and Greek inscriptions grandly describe pantomime-performers as 'actors of tragic rhythmic dance' (ὑποκριταὶ τραγικῆς ἐνρύθμου κεινήσεως). A highly sophisticated art, demanding much from both performers and spectators, pantomime was essentially serious, and so enjoyed a higher status than the *mime.

Performance took place in the theatre or privately. The artist, usually a handsome, athletic figure, wore a graceful silk costume (Suet. *Calig.* 54) permitting free movement and a beautiful mask with closed lips (Lucian, *Salt.* 29). Behind him stood the chorus, the musicians and the *scabillarii,* who beat time by pressing with the foot on the *scabillum,* a wooden or metal instrument fastened underneath the sandal. Beside the artist there sometimes stood an assistant—perhaps an actor with a speaking part (Lucian, *Salt.* 68). The dancer might in one piece have to appear in five different roles, each with its own mask (Lucian, *Salt.* 66; cf. 63). The dancer's power to convey his meaning by steps, postures, and above all gestures (Quint. *Inst.* 11. 3. 88) was aided by certain conventions, e.g. there was a traditional dance for 'Thyestes devouring his children' (cf. ATREUS). The songs of the chorus were of secondary importance (Libanius, *Pro Saltatione* 381); surviving fragments are in Greek. Men of letters such as Lucan (M. *Annaeus Lucanus) and *Statius wrote libretti for the pantomime. Pantomime-artists were popular in both halves of the empire. In the east they performed not just in special shows but also in *agōnes, including, eventually, such old sacred festivals as the *Pythian Games. In late antiquity the pagan content of the pantomime drew the fire of church fathers, especially John *Chrysostom; but it still flourished in the 6th century.

Lucian, *Salt.*; Libanius, *Pro saltatione.* L. Robert, *Hermes,* 1930, 106 ff.; C. Roueché, *Partisans and Performers* (1993), ch. 3.
W. B.; A. J. S. S.

Panyassis of *Halicarnassus (5th cent. BC), uncle or cousin of *Herodotus (1), wrote an epic about *Heracles in fourteen books, which was quite well regarded by literary critics (Dion. Hal. *De Imit.* fr. 6. 2. 4, Quint. *Inst.* 10. 1. 54). Some thirty fragments survive.

TEXT M. Davies, *Epicorum Graecorum Fragmenta* (1988), 113 ff.; A. Bernabé, *Poetae Epici Graeci,* 1 (1987), 171 ff.
COMMENTARY V. J. Matthews (1974).
M. L. W.

paper See PALAEOGRAPHY, *Introduction.*

Paphlagonia, a territory of northern Asia Minor, which included the mountainous coastal region between *Bithynia and *Pontus and extended inland as far as *Galatia on the Anatolian plateau. It was traversed by the overland route which led east from *Byzantium to the northern section of the eastern Roman frontier. It was noted for its timber production. Its social structure was similar to that of Pontus: villages predominated, organized in administrative districts, while the cities of the interior (Pompeiopolis, Neapolis or Neoclaudiopolis, Gangra or Germanicopolis; Hadrianopolis) only developed between the organization of *Pompey's province of Pontus and Bithynia in 63 BC and the time of *Hadrian. In 3/2 BC, when the inhabitants of Paphlagonia took the *oath of allegiance to *Augustus, they were still mostly organized by rural *eparchiae* (*OGI* 532). Greek colonial settlements dotted the coast from *Heraclea (3) to *Sinope, but *Hellenism did not affect the population of the interior. In the time of *Mithradates VI the region was controlled by castles and other fortified strong-points. From the 3rd cent. BC, the area south of Mt. Olgassys around Gangra at first kept its independence under native kings, was then divided between Pontus and Bithynia, was again entrusted to various dependent kings by the Romans, and was finally attached to the province of Galatia by Augustus in 6 BC. The rulers of this region include: Morzius (before 189 to after 179 BC); Pylaemenes *c.*132; Pylaemenes, son of *Nicomedes (3) III of Bithynia *c.*107; Attalus Epiphanes and Pylaemenes *c.*62; Castor, son of Castor Tarcondarius, *c.*40–37/6; Deiotarus Philadelphus (his son), 37/6—6–5 BC. Coastal Paphlagonia meanwhile remained part of the province of Pontus and Bithynia. The two regions were reunited as a single province by the time of *Diocletian. Paphlagonia has a role to play in the religious history of antiquity. A Christian author observed that its pagan inhabitants were noted for their strict morality (*Socrates Scholasticus 4. 37), and Olgassys, one of the highest mountain chains in northern Anatolia, was reputed to be the home of the Olympian gods (see RELIGION, GREEK). According to *Lucian the credulity of the local Paphlagonians led *Alexander (13) to dupe them with his new oracular cult of Glycon, the new *Asclepius, at the coastal town of Abonuteichus.

L. Robert, *Noms indigènes dans l'Asia Mineure gréco-romaine* (1963), *À travers l'Asie Mineure* (1980); Strabo 12. 3. 4–9, 542–4; R. Leonhardt, *Paphlagonia* (1915); Jones, *Cities E. Rom. Prov.* 148 ff.   T. R. S. B.; S. M.

Paphos, city-kingdom of SW *Cyprus. (1) Palaepaphos (mod. Kouklia) built on a bluff near the coast, site of a famous sanctuary of *Aphrodite, by tradition born nearby of sea-foam. Alternative cult-*founders are the pre-Greek *Cinyras, ambivalent friend of Agamemnon, (the Paphos royal house was Cinyrad throughout its history) and *Agapenor of *Tegea, post-Trojan War settler. Archaeology supports both traditions. The first temple (pillar-hall and temenos) is of 12th-cent. BC date; contemporary tombs nearby contain imported and local Mycenaean pottery (see MYCENAEAN CIVILIZATION). 11th-cent. chamber tombs suggest actual Aegean colonization; so does a grave-gift inscribed in the Cypriot syllabary (see PRE-GREEK LANGUAGES) with the Greek name Opheltes. Little remains of the early-iron-age and Archaic city, only its cemeteries. At the (excavated) NE gate in the Archaic defences are Persian siege works of 498 BC, rich in debris (sculpture etc.) from a destroyed extra-mural sanctuary. The Archaic-Hellenistic Aphrodite temples are lost; a sanctuary complex of *c.* AD 100 replaced one destroyed in the AD 76–7 earthquake. Its plan hardly matches depictions of the sanctuary and its aniconic cult figure on 1st–2nd-cent. AD coins. Though its sanctuary was still renowned in Hellenistic and Roman times (many dedications by foreign grandees, including the future emperor *Titus) from the 4th cent. BC, the city was replaced by

(2) Nea Paphos, a harbour city 16 km. north-west, apparently founded *c.*320 BC by the last king, Nicocles. The port and ship-building resources were strategically important to the *Diadochi; under the Ptolemies (see PTOLEMY (1)) it became, and remained, the island's capital, at the expense of *Salamis (2) (traces of its mint, and a *nomophylakeion*, are known). Though the Hellenistic city is concealed by the Roman, *Alexandrian influence is clear in its cemetery of rock-cut peristyle atrium tombs. Three huge Roman mansions with excellent 3rd-cent. floor-mosaics are partly excavated.

M. R. James, *JHS* 1888, 175 ff.; T. B. Mitford, *BSA* 1961, 1 ff.; K. Nikolaou, *Mélanges Michaelowski* (1966), 561 ff.; W. A. Daszewski, *Report of the Department of Antiquities, Cyprus*, 1987, 171 ff.; V. Karageorghis, *Palaepaphos-Skales* (1983): F. G. Maier and V. Karageorghis, *Paphos: History and Archaeology* (1984); F. G. Maier, *CAH* 6² (1994), 300 ff.
H. W. C.

Papinianus, lawyer: see AEMILIUS PAPINIANUS.

Papirianus (*PLRE* 1. 666 f.) (date unknown, perhaps 5th cent. AD), writer on orthography cited by *Priscian and excerpted by *Cassiodorus (Keil, *Gramm. Lat.* 7. 158–65; cf. ibid. 216, a fragment of 'Q. Papirius,' probably the same man).

R. Herzog and P. L. Schmidt (eds.), *Handbuch der lateinischen Literatur der Antike* 8/5 (1989), § 702.   R. A. K.

Papirius (*RE* 33) **Carbo (1), Gaius,** supported Ti. *Sempronius Gracchus (3), on whose agrarian commission he later served (from 130 BC). As tribune 130 (?), he passed a law extending vote by ballot (see GABINIUS (1), A.; CASSIUS LONGINUS RAVILLA, L.) to legislative assemblies and unsuccessfully proposed one to allow iteration of the tribunate (see TRIBUNI PLEBIS). After turning against C. *Sempronius Gracchus, he won the consulship for 120, when he successfully defended L. *Opimius against P. *Decius Subulo. Much disliked, he was prosecuted by young L. *Licinius Crassus and committed suicide (119). He is widely named among the alleged murderers of P. *Cornelius Scipio Aemilianus. He was an orator of some distinction.

*ORF*⁴ 152 ff.; Astin, *Scipio* (see index).   E. B.

Papirius (*RE* 34) **Carbo (2), Gaius,** cousin of *Cn. Papirius Carbo and *C. Papirius Carbo Arvina, as tribune 89 or 88 BC was joint author of the *Lex Plautia Papiria* (see PLAUTIUS SILVANUS (1), M.). Like his cousin C. Arvina, he was praetor under Cinna or Carbo, then commanded troops under Sulla and was killed in a mutiny.   E. B.

Papirius (*RE* 38) **Carbo, Gnaeus,** a seditious tribune (see TRIBUNI PLEBIS) in 92 BC; he passed a law reorganizing the coinage. He fought in the *Social War (3) and supported L. *Cornelius Cinna (1) in 87. He became Cinna's colleague as consul 85 and 84 and, as sole consul after Cinna's death, abandoned Cinna's Liburnian campaign and continued his moderate policy, giving citizenship to the last of the Italians and supporting a senate vote for disarmament. At the end of 84 he gave up the consulship, but with Sulla advancing in Italy, became consul 82 with C. *Marius (2) and, with newly-raised levies, fought unsuccessfully in Picenum, Etruria, and Cisalpine Gaul against *Sulla, Q. *Caecilius Metellus Pius, and *Pompey. After failing to relieve Marius at *Praeneste he fled to Africa, was proscribed, captured by Pompey (whom he had once defended on a criminal charge) and ignominiously executed at Lilybaeum.

On the coinage reform, see M. H. Crawford, *Coinage and Money under the Roman Republic* (1985), 183 ff.   E. B.

Papirius (*RE* 40) **Carbo Arvina, Gaius,** son of Gaius (1) and cousin of Gaius (2) and Gnaeus (above), was an active tribune (see TRIBUNI PLEBIS) in 90 BC. He co-operated with the government of L. *Cornelius Cinna (1) and Cn. Carbo and advanced to a praetorship. Like three other senior senators, he seems to have been preparing to join *Sulla when he was killed on the orders of L. *Iunius Brutus Damasippus. It was no doubt his death that made him the only Carbo praised by *Cicero.

> On the four Carbones above, see Cic. *Fam.* 9. 21. 3, with Shackleton Bailey's commentary (2. 379 ff., with stemma).   E. B.

Papirius (*RE* 52) **Cursor** (1), **Lucius,** Roman general and hero of the Second Samnite War (see ROME (HISTORY); SAMNIUM), was five times consul (326, 320, 319, 315, 313 BC) and at least twice dictator (325, 310). According to *Livy (8. 28. 8), he was joint author, with his colleague C. *Poetelius Libo Visolus, of a law abolishing debt-bondage (326). As dictator in 325 he quarrelled famously with his Master of the Horse (see MAGISTER EQUITUM), Q. *Fabius Maximus Rullianus, whom he attempted to execute for fighting without orders. But he was most clearly remembered in later tradition as the man who took command after the disaster of the *Caudine Forks, defeating the Samnites at *Luceria (320) and *Satricum (319). Livy praises his speed as a runner (whence his surname), his capacity for food and drink, his physical strength and his strict discipline, and notably compares him to his contemporary, *Alexander (3) the Great (9. 16. 11–19).

> E. T. S.; T. J. Co.

Papirius (*RE* 53) **Cursor** (2), **Lucius,** son of (1), Roman general. As consul in 293 BC he defeated the Samnite 'Linen Legion' (troops clad in *linen) at Aquilonia (Livy 10. 38–42), and in his second consulship (272) he ended the Pyrrhic War (see PYRRHUS) by subduing the Lucani (see LUCANIA), *Bruttii, and Tarentines (see TARENTUM) (Zonaras 8. 6). He erected the first sundial at Rome (Plin. *HN* 7. 213; see CLOCKS).

> E. T. S.; T. J. Co.

Papirius Fabianus, a declaimer and philosopher, pupil of Q. *Sextius and of Blandus, teacher of and model for L. *Annaeus Seneca (2). His declamations are copiously illustrated in Sen. *Controv.* bk. 2: cf. *praef.* 4–5.

> M. Griffin, *Seneca* (1976), esp. 39 ff.   A. J. S. S.

Papius (*RE* 12) **Mutilus, Gaius,** Samnite noble (see SAMNIUM), commanded the southern group of rebels in the *Social War (3). After considerable successes in *Campania, he was defeated by the consul L. *Iulius Caesar (1) (90 BC) and by *Sulla (89). Unmolested during Sulla's absence in the east, he perhaps accepted Roman citizenship, but fought against Sulla after his return, was proscribed and killed himself. A descendant was consul AD 9 (see LEX (2), lex Papia Poppaea).

> His coins: E. A. Sydenham, *The Coinage of the Roman Republic* (1952), nos. 635–41, most with Oscan legends, two with title *embratur* (= *imperator*).   E. B.

Pappus (*RE* 2), of *Alexandria (1), (fl. AD 320) mathematical commentator. The most important of his surviving works is Συναγωγή (*Collection*), a compilation (probably made after his death) in eight books of eight originally separate treatises and commentaries on different parts of the mathematical sciences. Book 8, an introduction to mechanics, is referred to as a distinct work by Eutocius, and exists as such in Arabic translation (in a fuller version than the Greek). Book 1 is missing, but was perhaps Pappus' commentary on *Euclid, *Elements* 10 (see below). Book 2, of which the first part is also missing, contains number games

based on a lost work of *Apollonius (2) with a notation for expressing large numbers. Book 3 is a miscellany of geometrical problems for the use of students, book 4 on higher geometry and special curves, book 5 on isoperimetric problems and the regular and semi-regular polyhedra, book 6 a commentary on the collection of astronomical treatises known as the 'Little [Domain] of Astronomy' (Μικρὸς ἀστρονομούμενος). Book 7, the longest and most interesting, entitled *Domain of Analysis* (Ἀναλυόμενος τόπος), is a commentary on Hellenistic works of higher geometry, mostly lost. The *Collection* is invaluable (and of considerable influence in European mathematics) as a source for lost works from the great period of Greek mathematics. Pappus' own contributions, in the form of 'lemmas' and proofs, are mostly trivial, and it is probable that all significant theorems are taken from earlier works, even when unattributed.

Pappus wrote a commentary to *Ptolemy (4)'s *Almagest*, of which the part on books 5 and 6 survives. This is superficial, but provides valuable information on lost works of *Hipparchus (3). His commentary to Euclid *Elements* 10, which survives in Arabic translation, is of interest because of its discussion of 'unordered irrationals', with references to a work of Apollonius on the same topic and to *Theaetetus. Among other lost works are Χωρογραφία οἰκουμενική, a universal geography used in an early Armenian text, and commentaries on the *Planispherium* of Ptolemy (4) and the *Analemma* of *Diodorus (4). See MATHEMATICS.

> EDITIONS AND TRANSLATIONS *Collection*, ed. F. Hultsch, 3 vols. (1876–8, with Lat. trans.); Fr. trans. by P. Ver Eecke, 2 vols. (1933); book 7 ed. with trans. and commentary by A. Jones, 2 vols., 1986 (see 1–3 for Pappus' biography; 15 ff. for the nature of the *Collection*; 9–15 for Pappus' other works); *Comm. on Almagest*, ed. A. Rome (1931). *Comm. on Euclid Bk. 10*, ed. with trans. by Junge and Thomson (1930).
> COMMENT *Collection*: Heath, *Hist. of Greek Maths.* 2. 355 ff.; A. Jones, *Scriptorium*, 1986, 16–31. On the Arabic version of bk. 8 see D. E. P. Jackson, *CQ* NS 1980, 523–33. The geography: R. H. Hewsen, *Isis*, 1971, 187–207.   G. J. T.

papyrology, Greek Papyrus, manufactured in Egypt since *c*.3000 BC from a marsh plant, *Cyperus papyrus* (see BOOKS, GREEK AND ROMAN), was the most widely used writing material in the Graeco-Roman world. The object of papyrology is to study texts written on papyrus (and on ostraca, wooden tablets, etc. in so far as they come from the same find-spots) in Egyptian (hieroglyphs, demotic, Coptic), Hebrew, *Aramaic, Greek, Latin, Pahlavi, and Arabic. Greek papyrology also deals with Greek texts written on parchment (see PALAEOGRAPHY, *Introduction*). The vast majority of Greek papyri have been found in Egypt, preserved in the dry sand; with the exception of some carbonized papyri from *Bubastis and Thmouis, no papyri have survived in the damp soils of the Delta or *Alexandria (1). Outside Egypt, Greek papyri have been found at *Herculaneum, at Dura-*Europus, in Palestine, and one text has come from Greece: the carbonized Orphic commentary found in a burial at Derveni near Salonica; see ORPHIC LITERATURE; ORPHISM.

After the excavations of the Villa dei Pisoni at Herculaneum in 1752–4, the first Greek papyrus from Egypt to become known in Europe was the *Charta Borgiana*, now in Naples, bought in Egypt in 1778 and donated to Cardinal Stefano Borgia (= *Sammelbuch* 1. 5124). Several substantial papyrus rolls with literary texts were acquired by travellers in Egypt in the 19th cent. and brought to Europe. Excavations of Graeco-Roman sites in Egypt for the sake of papyri began in 1895 in the *Fayûm and in 1896/7 at Behuesa (*Oxyrhynchus), following the discovery of large quantities of documentary papyri at Ashmunein (*Hermopolis) and the Fayûm (the Arsinoite nome; see NOMOS (1)) in 1877 and 1887. Today the sites which produced most of this material have been more or less exhausted; the most promising source of papyrus texts is now mummy cases made of papyrus cartonnage, i.e. layers of discarded papyri, sometimes reinforced with linen cloth, covered with plaster and painted; they often contain Egyptian (demotic) and/or Greek texts of the Ptolemaic or Augustan periods.

To date, an estimated 30,000 papyrus texts have been edited, while substantial quantities of unpublished texts, mostly documents, remain in collections in Europe, Egypt, and North America. They cover the period from the mid-4th cent. BC to the early 8th cent. AD, during most of which (332 BC to AD 641) Greek was the official language in Egypt. The latest surviving dated papyri are a papal document in Latin of AD 1057 and an Arabic document of AD 1087; a papyrus codex leaf from the *Life of St Niphon*, written in Southern Italy, now in Yale, is dated to the 11th or 12th cent.

The papyrologist's first tasks are decipherment and transliteration. The main difficulties here may be (*a*) the great variety of handwritings, ranging from clear and easily legible literary hands to rapidly written cursive hands with many abbreviated words; (*b*) the fragmentary, often very tattered state of the papyri, and therefore the need to restore missing letters, syllables, whole words or phrases; (*c*) misspellings, omissions, and other mistakes in the texts. Literary papyri are usually (but by no means exclusively) written in book-hands which are often 'bilinear', i.e. unconnected and regularly formed letters tend to fit between two ideal parallel lines. Documents and official and private letters show a wide range of hands, from the clumsy and semi-illiterate to highly skilled professional cursives and stylized 'chancery' hands. See PALAEOGRAPHY. The language of the Greek documents is the *Koinē* (*sc. dialektos*), the 'common' or standard Greek of the Hellenistic and Roman periods; see GREEK LANGUAGE. Spelling and other mistakes often reveal changes in pronunciation and syntax which herald the development of the colloquial Greek *koinē* into Byzantine and Modern Greek.

The second task is the interpretation and evaluation of the texts. Papyrus texts of known literary works can help to clarify the history of the textual transmission, as well as contributing new readings or confirming, as ancient variants, readings which had previously been dismissed as Byzantine conjectures. Many papyri, especially those of commentaries (*scholia, ὑπομνήματα*), have also provided new information on the activities of Alexandrian scholars. Being nearly always older, in some cases by up to 1,000 years, than the medieval manuscripts, papyrus texts have been of great importance for textual criticism, as they have produced many new correct readings and have confirmed earlier scholars' conjectures. On the whole, they bear witness to the general soundness of our textual tradition, by showing that the texts as established by Alexandrian scholars and known to the Graeco-Roman world differed little from that we now have. The impact which papyri of lost literary works have had on classical scholarship cannot be overestimated; much of what we can read today of the works of the lyric poets (especially *Stesichorus, *Sappho, *Alcaeus (1), *Bacchylides, and *Pindar), of Attic tragedy (see TRAGEDY, GREEK) and satyr play (see SATYRIC DRAMA), of New Comedy (*Menander (1)), of Hellenistic poetry (*Callimachus (3)), and of many other areas of Greek literature has survived only on papyrus. Among the hitherto unknown prose texts, medical and scientific writings, philosophy and his-

toriography are well represented; the *Constitution of Athens* (see ATHENAION POLITEIA), the *Hellenica Oxyrhynchia* (see OXYRHYNCHUS, THE HISTORIAN FROM), and the medical Anonymus Londiniensis are among the most noteworthy. Substantial parts of unknown Greek novels have come to light, as well as religious, astrological, and magical texts. From the 2nd cent. AD onwards, Christian texts appear; of these, more than half are biblical, the OT being more often represented than the NT; of particular interest are the *Apocrypha*, some of which also survive in Coptic versions (*Acta Pauli*, Gospels of St Peter and Thomas, etc.). The Chester Beatty papyri, which contain large portions of eleven papyrus codices, and several codices in Greek and in Coptic in the Bodmer Library, take our knowledge of the text of the Bible back to the 2nd cent. AD. While confirming that the textual tradition of the *Septuagint and the New Testament is generally sound, they have nevertheless modified and clarified our knowledge of the history of biblical texts.

By far the greatest number of Greek papyri are documents—official correspondence, edicts, petitions and complaints, legal contracts, lists and receipts, letters, and private papers of every description. They have contributed a wealth of information on the administration, the economy, the social and cultural life of Greeks and Hellenized Egyptians, so that Graeco-Roman Egypt has become by far the best-documented area and period in the ancient world. The edicts of the Ptolemies (see PTOLEMY (1)), together with the petitions addressed to them (*enteuxeis*), show how the kings tried to satisfy both Egyptians and Greeks, playing the traditional role of Pharaohs while at the same time promoting the gradual Hellenization of Egypt and its integration into the Hellenistic world. Under Roman rule, the documents reveal significant changes to the administrative and financial system: the 'planned economy' which the Ptolemies had inherited from the Pharaohs gives way to private enterprise, the state monopolies disappear, tax-farmers are replaced by government-appointed officials. From the later 2nd cent. onwards the continuous drain on the country's resources makes itself felt, as is shown by the cumulative evidence of documents and, above all, *archives, such as the family archives of the farmers Philosarapis at Tebtunis and Sarapion at Hermoupolis, of Heroninus at Theadelpheia in the 3rd cent., of Flavius Abinnaeus, the last garrison commander of Dionysias in the Fayûm, in the 4th, while the administrative duties as well as business affairs of a wealthy government official are illustrated by the archive of the *stratēgos* *Apollonius (3) of the early 2nd cent. The effects of the introduction of town councils under Severus, of the *Constitutio Antoniniana* in AD 212 (see CONSTITUTION, ANTONINE), and of Diocletian's and Constantine's reforms are reflected in the papyri, as are the growth of the large estates and the growing power of their owners, e.g. in the archives of Dioscorus of Aphrodito, and of the Taurinus family at Hermoupolis.

Lawsuits are amply documented in Greek papyri, which have made it possible to reconstruct the legal systems and judicial procedures of Ptolemaic and Roman Egypt, and to verify the gradual intrusion of Roman law in the later Roman and Byzantine periods. Many private contracts show how civil law was applied in practice. Legal historians can thus study the interaction of different legal systems (Egyptian, Hellenistic, and Roman).

Papyrologists not only decipher and edit documents but also point out the specific interest each text may have for administrative, economic, social, legal, or religious history, making new information available to specialists. To do this effectively, it is often necessary to assemble all available documents of the same kind, or dealing with the same subject, e.g. Ptolemaic petitions to the king (*enteuxeis*), royal decrees, census returns, notifications of death, wet-nurse contracts, etc. Documents and letters which had once formed a public or a family archive are often dispersed in many collections and need to be reassembled and studied in context. Some of the most interesting archives are bilingual, either Demotic/Greek (e.g. the Zenon archive (see APOLLONIUS (3)), the Adler papyri, the Amenothes archive in Turin, or that of Dionysius son of Kephalas), or Greek/Latin (the family papers of Claudius Terentianus and Claudius Tiberianus), or Greek/Coptic (Dioscorus of Aphrodito, or Pachymius of Panopolis). Graeco-Roman Egypt always had a multicultural and multilingual society; therefore Greek papyrologists need to be aware of the partial nature of the Greek evidence, which often has to be complemented with the relevant texts in other languages.

E. G. Turner, *Greek Papyri*² (1980) (excellent, mainly on literary papyri), *The Papyrologist at Work* (1973); O. Montevecchi, *La papirologia*² (1988) (excellent on documentary papyrology, with useful bibliogs.); P. W. Pestman, *New Papyrological Primer* (1990); I. Gallo, *Greek and Latin Papyrology* (1986); L. Mitteis and U. Wilcken, *Grundzüge und Chrestomathie der Papyruskunde*, 4 vols. (1912) (still very useful; selection of 882 documentary papyri with introductions and notes); M. Capasso, *Manuale 9: papirologia ercolanese* (1991); R. Taubenschlag, *The Law of Graeco-Roman Egypt in the Light of the Papyri*² (1955); H. J. Wolff, *Das Recht der griechischen Papyri Ägyptens* (1978).

Publications of papyri and ostraca, including *SB* or *Sammelbuch* etc., are quoted according to the lists in Turner, *Greek Papyri*, 154–79, and in J. F. Oates and others, *Checklist of Editions of Greek and Latin Papyri, Ostraca and Tablets*⁴ (1992). The inventory of R. A. Pack, *The Greek and Latin Literary texts from Greco-Roman Egypt*² (1965), has still not been replaced; Christian and Jewish literary texts are listed in J. van Haelst, *Catalogue des papyrus littéraires juifs et chrétiens* (1976). For publication of new texts and bibliography on all branches of the subject see the annual surveys in *Aegyptus*, *Gnomon*, and *L'Année philologique*.

Documentary texts published in journals, Festschriften, etc. are republished in *Sammelbuch griechischer Urkunden aus Aegypten*, vols. 1–18; corrections to documentary texts, re-editions, etc. are listed in *Berichtigungsliste der griechischen Papyrusurkunden aus Aegypten*, vols. 1–8.   H. Ma.

papyrology, Latin In comparison with Greek papyri Latin papyri are uncommon, even when 'papyri' is understood in a wide sense so as to include *ostraca and parchment scraps. This is because the vast majority of papyri come from the eastern Mediterranean where the language of administration was Greek even under the Roman empire. Latin was in regular use in this area until *c.* AD 300 only in the military sphere; and although *Diocletian made an effort to encourage the use of Latin in the eastern provinces, this did not have any great effect.

In the last 100 years some 600 Latin papyri have been published, less than a quarter of which are literary. Most come from Egypt, but finds have also been made at Dura-*Europus, Nessana, and *Masada, as well as in the west. Two literary papyri dating from the reign of *Augustus are known: the much discussed elegiac verses from Qasr Ibrim attributed to *Cornelius Gallus (*JRS* 1979, 125–55) and a fragment of *Cicero, *In Verrem* (*CPL* 20). Otherwise literary texts before AD 300 are rare. They include a few lines of *Virgil and a handful of historical texts, notably an *Epitome* of Livy (*CPL* 33), a piece of *Sallust, *Histories* (*CPL* 28), and a text relating to Servius *Tullius (*CPL* 41). Most *Herculaneum papyri are in Greek; exceptions are the *Carmen de Bello Aegyptiaco* (re-edited G. Zecchini, 1987), and a few scraps of *Ennius and *Lucretius. After AD 300 literary texts are less unusual. Commonest are Virgil and Cicero, often for school use and accompanied by Greek glosses. Also for school use are a number of grammat-

ical texts and glossaries (see GLOSSA, GLOSSARY). New verse is represented by 124 lines of a hexameter poem concerning *Alcestis (see below); known verse by, among others, *Terence, *Andria* (Pack² 2933a, 2934) and *Juvenal with Greek *scholia (*CPL* 37).

One or two legal texts may date from as early as *c.* AD 100, but most texts in this category belong to the 4th–6th cents. and indicate the importance at this time of Roman legal studies. Especially noteworthy are a fragment of *Gaius (2), *Institutiones* (*CPL* 78), near-contemporary texts of the *Codex Justinianus* (*CPL* 99–101), and *Pauli Sententiarum Fragmentum Leidense* (re-edited G. Archi and others, 1956); see JUSTINIAN'S CODIFICATION; IULIUS PAULUS. Among Christian texts we have some from the Old Latin version of the Bible, a fragment of Luke with a Gothic translation (*CPL* 53), a Latin–Greek lexicon of St Paul (A. Wouters, *The Chester Beatty Codex AC 1499*), and an extensive Hymn to the Virgin. This last forms part of a remarkable codex, now in Barcelona, which also includes Cicero, *Cat.* 1–2, the poem of Alcestis referred to above (published by R. Roca-Puig, in 1965, 1977, and 1982 respectively), and Christian liturgical texts in Greek.

In the first three centuries of the empire most Latin papyri are military documents, including large rosters, strength reports, a military calendar (the *Feriale Duranum*), and numerous accounts and pay records. A small but interesting find from the 1st cent. has been made at *Masada and there are two important 3rd-cent. archives, from Dura-Europos (Syria) and Bu Njem (Libya). Over 130 military documents from Egypt and Dura are to be found in Fink's collection and a score or more have since been published. For Masada see H. M. Cotton and J. Geiger, *Masada II* (1989), and for Bu Njem, R. Marichal, *Les Ostraca de Bu Njem* (1992). Many other Latin documents such as wills and private letters are no doubt also from military sources. The former are of legal interest, while the latter offer us a glimpse of Latin 'as she was spoke'; see LATIN LANGUAGE. There are also some imperial edicts and rescripts. In the 4th cent. it was normal for proceedings before high Egyptian officials to use Latin to record the preamble and decisions of cases written down in Greek. Apart from these bilingual texts and a few official letters, non-literary papyri in Latin are uncommon after AD 300. From the West we have an extensive collection of papyri from the papal chancery at *Ravenna. Although these fall outside the classical period (5th–8th cents.), they are of value for their information on palaeography, Roman law, and the development of the language (J.-O. Tjäder, *Die nichtliterarischen lateinischen Papyri Italiens* (1954–82)).

The contribution of Latin papyri to classical studies is far from negligible. They provide our earliest information about the shape and format of the Roman book and the diplomatic of Roman documents, and they have revolutionized our understanding of early Latin *palaeography. A few new texts have been recovered, and we have learnt a good deal about the textual transmission of some works (e.g. Cicero, *In Catilinam*) and the spread of Latin culture. Most important of the non-literary texts are those of a military nature. Our knowledge of the Roman army has been increased considerably by documentary evidence of the way things worked in practice, which provides a useful counterbalance to the evidence from literary sources and archaeology. See ARMIES, ROMAN.

Latin papyri known up to 1958 are collected in R. Cavenaile, *Corpus Papyrorum Latinarum* (*CPL*); Cavenaile has updated the information in *Serta Leodiensia Secunda* (1992), 47–62. Literary texts are listed in R. A. Pack, *Greek and Latin literary texts from Egypt* (2nd edn., 1965 = Pack²), nos. 2917–3026 (updated by P. Mertens, *Miscellània Roca-Puig* (1987), 189–204). Military documents are collected in R. O. Fink, *Roman Mili-*

tary Records (1971), and letters in P. Cugusi, Corpus Epistularum Latinarum (1992). For facsimiles of literary papyri see E. A. Lowe, Codices
Latini Antiquiores, and for documents A. Bruckner and R. Marichal,
Chartae Latinae Antiquiores; see also R. Seider, Paläographie der lateinischen Papyri (1972–81).   J. D. T.

papyrus See BOOKS, GREEK AND ROMAN; PALAEOGRAPHY, Introduction; PAPYROLOGY, GREEK and LATIN.

paradoxographers Interest in the unexpected or unbelievable
(paradoxa, thaumasia, apista) is prominent in the Odyssey and
*Herodotus. Collections of marvels attributed to 4th-cent.
authors (*Aristotle, *Theopompus (3), *Ephorus) are not
genuine, but paradoxography as a distinct literary genre came
into existence in the 3rd cent. with paradoxa by *Callimachus (3)
(fr. 407–411) and his pupil *Philostephanus, *Antigonus (4) of
Carystus, Archelaus of Egypt, *Myrsilus of Methymna, and
others. In the Roman period there are substantial collections
of marvels by *Isigonus and *Phlegon, and several anonymous
collections survive in medieval manuscripts. The material is
taken from geography, botany, zoology, and human culture.
Several ancient writers dabbled in the subject (*Cicero, Michael
*Psellus) and others (*Varro, *Pliny (1) the Elder, *Aelian) used
paradoxographers as sources.

A. Westermann, Paradoxographi (1839); O. Keller, Rerum naturalium
scriptores graeci minores, 1 (1877); A. Giannini, Paradoxographorum Graecorum reliquiae (1966).   J. S. R.

paragraphē (παραγραφή) in Athenian law was a procedure for
objecting that a prosecution was inadmissible because it was in
some way contrary to law. Before the main trial (εὐθυδικία) could
proceed, the objection had to be heard at a separate trial, in
which the objector (the defendant in the original case) spoke first
and his opponent replied. If the objector won, the original case
was dropped; if he lost, it went to trial. Whoever lost at the
hearing of the paragraphē had to pay his opponent one-sixth of
the sum at stake in the case (ἐπωβελία); this discouraged the use
of paragraphē as a device for delaying a trial without justification.
The procedure was instituted under a law proposed by Archinus
in 403/2 BC, permitting paragraphē against prosecutions which
contravened the *amnesty of that year. The first paragraphē heard
under this law was the one for which *Isocrates wrote his speech
Against Callimachus. Soon the procedure was being used also for
objections on other grounds to the admissibility of private cases,
but it seems not to have been used for public cases.

H. J. Wolff, Die attische Paragraphe (1966); D. M. MacDowell, The Law
in Classical Athens (1978), 212–19.   D. M. M.

paraklausithyron, a lover's song at his beloved's door, in which
he begs for admission and laments his exclusion. It occurs in a
variety of poetic genres (e.g. lyric, idyll, epigram, comedy, mime,
elegy). Originating in the real-life situation of the komos ('revel')
through the streets following a drinking party, it later it became
a vehicle for the expression of romantic love, especially in *elegiac
poetry (Latin), where the door itself receives greater prominence
and is often addressed as a god (e.g. Ovid, Am. 1. 6).

F. O. Copley, Exclusus Amator (1956); F. Cairns, Generic Composition in
Greek and Roman Poetry, 'komos'; Yardley, Eranos, 1978.   P. W.

parasang See MEASURES.

parasite, a stock character of Greek and Roman comedy. At
first called kolax ('toady', 'flatterer', as in Eupolis' Kolakes of 421
BC, named after its chorus), the type acquired as a joke in the 4th
cent. the alternative label parasitos or 'sponger' (in origin a 'fellow

diner', particularly denoting certain religious functionaries).
Thereafter the two terms were largely interchangeable, though
sometimes distinguished, and they overlap with other character-
labels such as the sykophantēs ('swindler'; see SYCOPHANTS).

Parasites attach themselves to their social superiors for their
own advantage, above all for free meals; in return they flatter or
entertain their patron, run errands, and suffer much ill-treatment. Sometimes the patron is a vainglorious soldier, and soldier
and parasite made a stock pair.

*Athenaeus (1) 6. 234 ff. preserves many anecdotes and quota-
tions from Greek comedy (from *Epicharmus onwards), several
mocking notorious parasites from real life. The studies of parasites in *Lucian's Parasitos, *Alciphron's Epistles, and *Libanius'
Declamations 28, 29 are partly indebted to comedy.

O. Ribbeck, Kolax (1883); E. W. Handley on Menander, Dyskolos 57 ff;
W. G. Arnott, GRBS 1968; H.-G. Nesselrath, Lukians Parasitendialog
(1985), Die attische mittlere Komödie (1990), 309 ff.; P. G. McC. Brown,
ZPE 92 (1992).   P. G. M. B.

Parcae See FATE.

parchment See BOOKS, GREEK AND ROMAN; PALAEOGRAPHY, Introduction.

Parentalia, Roman festival of ancestors on the dies parentales
(13–21 Feb.), the last of which was a public ceremony (*Feralia),
while the rest were days for private devotions to the family dead
(di parentum, parentes). These were dies religiosi (see FASTI) during
which the magistrates did not wear the praetexta, temples were
closed and no weddings celebrated, but not all were nefasti
(*Lupercalia, 15th, Quirinalia, 17th, 18th–20th all comitiales).
Often distinguished from the *Lemuria by benevolence, but
*Ovid (Fasti 2. 547 ff.) implies otherwise.

Ov. Fast. 2. 533 ff. F. Cumont, Lux Perpetua (1949), 396 ff., 435.   C. R. P.

Parian Marble See MARMOR PARIUM.

Parilia, Roman festival of the god, or goddess (both genders are
attested), Pales, held on 21 April. In early times it seems to have
been a ritual concerned with the flocks and herds of the Roman
community; *Ovid (Fasti 4. 721 ff.) describes the lighting of bonfires (through which the celebrants are supposed to jump)
and the purification of the animals (with material made by the
*Vestals from the ashes of the calf of the *Fordicidia and blood
of the October Horse; see MARS). By the late republic (Cicero,
Div. 2. 98; Varro, Rust. 2. 1. 9) it was also identified as the 'birthday'
of the city of Rome; and in the 2nd cent. AD it gained the
alternative title 'Romaia' (Ath. 8. 361 e–f).

M. Beard, PCPS 1987, 1–15; M. Beard, J. North, and S. Price,
Religions of Rome (1998).   M. B.

Paris, also called Alexandros (his usual name in *Homer), son
of *Priam and *Hecuba. Homer refers several times to his abduction of *Helen, which was the cause of the Trojan War (see TROY).
At an earlier stage in the development of the legend he was
perhaps the principal warrior on the Trojan side. Even in the
Iliad he is sometimes effective in battle (e.g. 13. 660–720), and he
will be responsible, with *Apollo's help, for the death of *Achilles
(22. 359–60). In general, however, he is seen as greatly inferior to
*Hector, who taunts him as handsome but unwarlike at 3. 38–
57, 6. 325–31, 13. 768–73. He uses the bow, which tends (see
ARCHERS, GREEK AND HELLENISTIC) to be regarded as an unmanly
weapon. He is defeated in a duel by *Menelaus (1), has to be

rescued by *Aphrodite (3. 313–82), and then consoles himself by making love to Helen (3. 383–447).

The *Cypria* (see EPIC CYCLE) told the story of the Judgement of Paris, often mentioned in subsequent literature. Incited to rivalry by *Eris, the goddesses *Hera, *Athena, and Aphrodite appointed Paris to decide between them. They were brought to him by *Hermes, and, bribed by the promise of Helen, he chose Aphrodite as the most beautiful. The story is mentioned at *Iliad* 24. 27–30, in a passage which some scholars (following *Aristarchus (2)) reject on the grounds that Homer shows no knowledge of the Judgement elsewhere; but others argue that he did know of it but in general suppressed it as unsuitable for his epic.

According to the *Little Iliad* Paris was killed by *Philoctetes.

*Sophocles and *Euripides each wrote an *Alexandros*, and *Ennius an *Alexander*. We are now well-informed about Euripides' influential play: Hecuba, before the birth of Paris, dreamt that she had given birth to a fire-brand (this motif goes back to *Pindar's eighth *Paean*, fr. 521). So the child was exposed, and Hecuba initiated athletic games (*agōnes*) in his memory. But he survived and was brought up among herdsmen. Grown to manhood, he was brought to Troy, where he competed in the games himself, winning several events. His brother *Deiphobus, furious at being defeated by a mere herdsman, urged Hecuba to kill him, and *Cassandra, recognizing him, prophesied disaster for Troy; but his identity was revealed and his life was spared.

The motif of the nymph *Oenone, who loved Paris when he lived as a herdsman on Mount Ida, was abandoned by him for Helen, and later refused to cure him of the wound that killed him, was known as early as *Hellanicus (1) (*FGrH* 4 F 29), and is exploited by *Ovid in *Heroides* 5.

In art various episodes from his career are represented. The Judgement is especially popular, and is identifiable as early as the 7th cent.

LIMC, 'Alexandros'; T. C. W. Stinton, *Euripides and the Judgement of Paris*, JHS Suppl. 11 (1965 = *Collected Papers on Greek Tragedy* (1990), 17–75); R. A. Coles, *A New Oxyrhynchus Papyrus: The Hypothesis of Euripides' Alexandros*, BICS Suppl. 32 (1974). A. L. B.

Paris (mod. city). See LUTETIA.

Parisi, a British tribe (see BRITAIN, ROMAN) on the north bank of the Humber, well known for its La Tène cemeteries (see CELTS), which became a self-governing *civitas* under Roman rule (*RIB*. 707). Their only centre to be mentioned by *Ptolemy (4) (*Geog.* 2. 3. 17) is Petuaria (Brough on Humber), where a small town (5.6 ha. within its defences), most likely the *civitas*-capital, developed in the 2nd cent. on the site of a fort. An aedile of the *vicus* erected a stage-building in the reign of *Antoninus Pius (*RIB*. 707). There are a series of other lesser towns in the territory but none as Romanized as Brough. Rural settlement was extensive but villas are few and developed late; the mosaic from Rudston is famous for the rustic execution of its classical theme.

J. S. Wacher, *Excavations at Brough-on-Humber 1958–61* (1969); H. Ramm, *The Parisi* (1978). S. S. F.; M. J. M.

Parisii See LABIENUS (1), T.; LUTETIA.

Parium, now Kemer, a city on the Asian coast of the Sea of Marmora (*Propontis) near the entrance to the *Hellespont. Its importance is due in part to its excellent position in a protected harbour. Parium was founded in the late 8th cent. BC by colonists from *Miletus, *Erythrae, and *Paros, from the last of which it took its name. In the 5th cent. BC it was tributary to Athens (see DELIAN LEAGUE), but little is known of its 4th-cent. history. During

the Hellenistic era it was a free city under the protection of the Attalids of *Pergamum, who permitted it to annex a considerable portion of the territory of its neighbour, Priapus. Under *Augustus it flourished as a colony, Colonia Pariana Iulia Augusta, to which *Hadrian added Hadriana at its refounding during his reign. In Roman times it was connected to the other towns of the southern shore of the Propontis by a good road that continued along the Asian coast of the Hellespont. It retained its importance as the seat of a bishopric in the 4th cent. In early times it was the site of an oracular temple (see ORACLES) to *Apollo Actaeus, which ceased to exist. There stood in Parium two works of art that are depicted on the coins of the city: an altar to Apollo which is said to have measured one stade in length, and a famous statue of Eros by *Praxiteles. Little is now to be seen on the site, which lies largely unexcavated.

E. Olshausen, *RE* Suppl. 12 (1970); W. Ramsay, *Historical Geography of Asia Minor* (1890). E. N. B.

Parma, on the *via Aemilia, south of the Po (*Padus), in Cisalpine Gaul (see GAUL (CISALPINE)). First settled in the late bronze age, it was developed by the *Etruscans and Gauls. From 183 BC a Roman colony, it was sacked by Mark Antony (M. *Antonius (2); 43 BC). Restored under *Augustus, it remained important, and its walls were repaired by *Theoderic (1). It flourished as Chrysopolis in Byzantine times.

L. Grazzi, *Parma romana* (1972). E. T. S.; T. W. P.

Parmenides of *Elea is said to have legislated for his native city and (*c.*450 BC) to have visited Athens in his sixty-fifth year (Pl. *Parm.* 127b). His philosophical poem, in hexameters, survives in large fragments. It opens with the narration of a journey taken by the initiate poet-speaker, apparently from the world of daily life and light to a mysterious place where night and day cross paths and opposites are undivided. Here he is greeted by a goddess whose instruction forms the remainder of the work. She urges him to cease relying on ordinary beliefs and to 'judge by reason the very contentious refutation' of those beliefs that she offers. Her address attends closely to logical rigour and connection. The proem is suffused with religious language, and one might conjecture that an initiation in reason is being substituted for the perception-suffused initiations of religious cult.

Every aspect of this difficult argument is disputed; one can only offer one plausible account. Central to the goddess's teaching is the idea that thought and speech must have an object that is there to be talked or thought about. This being the case, if something is sayable or thinkable, it must *be*: 'You cannot say or think that it is not.' On this basis, she concludes not only that nothingness or the non-existent cannot figure in our speech, but also that temporal change, internal qualitative variation, and even plurality are all unsayable and unthinkable—on the grounds that talk about all these will commit the speaker to making contrasts and entail the use of negative language. Thus, whatever can be talked or thought about must be 'without birth or death, whole, single-natured, unaltering, and complete'.

A subsidiary argument invokes an idea of sufficient reason to rule out cosmogony: if what is had a beginning in time, there must have been some reason for that beginning. But what reason could there be, if (by hypothesis) there was nothing there previously?

Having described the 'Way of Truth', the goddess then acquaints her pupil with the deceptive contents of mortal beliefs. The cosmogony that follows is not intended to have any degree of truth or reliability. It is presumably selected because it shows the fundamental error of mortals in its simplest form. The decision to 'name' two forms, light and night, commits mortals to contrastive negative characterizations.

Parmenides was a great philosophical pioneer, who turned away from the tradition of Ionian cosmogony to attempt something fundamentally different: a deduction of the character of what is from the requirements of thought and language. His views were developed further by his followers *Melissus and the distinguished *Zeno (1). *Empedocles, *Anaxagoras, and *Democritus all felt the need to respond to his arguments in defending plurality and change, though they did so without addressing his fundamental concern about language and thought. The core of his argument thus remained untouched until *Plato (1)'s *Sophist*, in which the Eleatic Stranger proposes a new understanding of the relation between language and the world in order to break the strong grip of the argument of 'father Parmenides'. See also ELEA; ELEATIC SCHOOL (medical society which looked back to Parmenides).

DK 28; W. Burkert, *Phronesis*, 1969; D. Furley, *Exegesis and Argument*, *Phronesis* Supp. 1 (1973); M. Furth, in A. Mourelatos (ed.), *The Pre-Socratics* (1974); D. Gallop, *Parmenides of Elea* (1984); Kirk–Raven–Schofield, *The Presocratic Philosophers*, 239–62; A. Mourelatos, *The Route of Parmenides* (1970); G. E. L. Owen, in Owen (ed.), *Language, Science, and Dialectic* (1986).
M. C. N.

Parmenion (*c*.400–330 BC), Macedonian noble, the most respected general of *Philip (1) II. Active in senior command as early as 356, he headed the expeditionary force in Asia Minor (336) and eased *Alexander (3) the Great's accession by helping remove his colleague Attalus, the new king's bitterest enemy. Consequently he was the automatic choice as Alexander's second-in-command in Asia, and two of his sons had command of the Companion cavalry and the hypaspists. At the major battles (the *Granicus, *Issus, and *Gaugamela) he controlled the Macedonian left and had an indispensable defensive role. There is a tradition of disagreement between Parmenion and his king which is in part fabrication, but there appears to have been a genuine divergence of views on the terminus for conquest in Asia. As a result Parmenion was detached with increasing frequency on independent missions, and in the summer of 330 he was deputed to escort the treasures of *Persepolis to the Median capital, where he remained, gradually isolated as his Macedonian troops rejoined Alexander in the east. When his son *Philotas was executed for alleged treason, he was murdered at the king's command (autumn 330). He had been a long-standing curb on the king's ambitions and was too dangerous to be left alive.

Berve, *Alexanderreich*, 2. 606; Heckel, *Marshals*, 13 ff.
A. B. B.

Parmeniscus, pupil of *Aristarchus (2) and defender of his texts against *Crates (3) of Mallos, wrote Πρὸς Κράτητα, Περὶ ἀναλογίας, 'against Crates'; 'on *Analogy' (recognizing eight noun declensions), and commented on *Euripides.

M. Breithaupt, *De Parmenisco grammatico* (1915).
N. G. W.

Parmeno of *Byzantium, choliambic poet (see METRE, GREEK, § 4 (*a*)) of (?) first half of 3rd cent. BC. His scanty fragments suggest that he wrote at least partly in Egypt.

Powell, *Collectanea Alexandrina*, 237–8; *Suppl. Hell.* 604 A; Maas, *RE* 18. 1572.
R. L. Hu.

Parnassus, outlying spur of the Pindus range, running southeast and rising to 2,457 m. It separates the (Boeotian) *Cephissus valley from that of *Amphissa and runs into the Corinthian Gulf at Cape Opus. Its limestone mass is mostly barren, but its lower

slopes are well watered; they carry the Phocian towns (see PHOCIS) on its eastern flank and the plain of *Crisa with the high valley of *Delphi on the south. The best ascent is from Daulis; the passes which cross its spurs run from *Cytinium to Amphissa and from Daulis to Delphi via 'the cross-roads' of *Sophocles, *OT* 733, where it is joined by the route from Lebadea (see TROPHONIUS) to Delphi. A sacred mountain especially to the *Dorians.
N. G. L. H.

Parnes, the mountain range separating *Attica from *Boeotia, rising to 1,413 m. (4,636 ft.). *Pausanias (3) 1. 32. 2 refers to a statue and altars of *Zeus near the summit, and a cave on the lower summit has yielded geometric, Archaic, and Roman dedications. In the 4th cent. a series of watch-towers was built as part of the systematic defence of this frontier.

J. Travlos, *Bildlexikon zur Topographie des antiken Attika* (1988), 319–28.
R. G. O.

Parnon See LACONIA.

parody, Greek (παρῳδία). Parody entails imitation, but an imitation which is intended to be recognized as such and to amuse. By exaggerating distinctive features, it may simply invite ridicule and criticism of the original; or it may exploit the humour of incongruity, coupled with exaggeration for ease of recognition, by combining the language and style of the original with completely alien subject-matter. In both cases, but particularly where incongruity is intended to achieve its effect, the targeted original may be a whole genre of literature rather than an individual author. The parodies of Aeschylean and Euripidean lyrics (see AESCHYLUS; EURIPIDES; TRAGEDY, GREEK) in *Aristophanes (1)'s *Frogs* are outstanding examples of the parody of individuals, while there are very many passages of Aristophanes in which high tragic style, identifiable by vocabulary and metre, is combined with matter which is down-to-earth (*Lys.* 706–17 is a good example of this).

*Aristotle (*Poet.* 1448²12) mentions *Hegemon as ὁ τὰς παρῳδίας ποιήσας πρῶτος ('the first parodist'), but *Athenaeus (1) (15. 699 a) says, more precisely, that he was the first to enter τοὺς θυμελικοὺς ἀγῶνας ('theatrical competitions') and win contests at Athens for parody. (For similar contests cf. an Eretrian inscription of *c*.400 BC, Ἐφημερὶς Ἀρχαιολογική 1902, 98 ff.). Athenaeus (15. 698 B), following *Polemon (3), regards *Hipponax as the real inventor of the genre, and quotes from him four burlesque hexameters on a parasite. The *Margites*, generally attributed to *Homer in antiquity, was known to *Archilochus in the early 7th cent. BC (Fr. 303). It described the adventures of a Simple Simon, and had iambics mixed up with its hexameters. Virtually nothing of it or of the *Cercopes* remains. The extant *Batrachomyomachia* (Battle of the Frogs and Mice), written perhaps during the *Persian Wars, narrates the fate of small creatures with epic grandiloquence and pathos. The tradition of Homeric parody runs through comedy to the gastronomists (*Matron, *Archestratus, etc.) and the Sillographers or lampoonists (see TIMON (2)).

Parody of tragedy in Aristophanes is not confined to language; characteristic constituents of tragedy, such as the messenger-speech, are also parodied (e.g. *Ach.* 1174–89), and so are whole scenes from particular tragedies (e.g. *Thesm.* 849–923, utilizing Eur. *Hel.*). Nor is tragedy the only target: *Pindar is parodied in *Av.* 904–53, religious ritual in 863–88, experts on oracles in 959–91, scientists in 992–1020, and would-be connoisseurs of oratory in *Eq.* 1375–80. It should not be imagined that elevated language in the lyrics of Aristophanes is necessarily an indicator of parody;

he often composes serious choral (e.g. *Nub.* 275–90) or solo (e.g. *Av.* 209–37) lyrics for dramatic functions to which such language is entirely appropriate, and although there is undoubtedly a strand of incongruity in the frogs' chorus (*Ran.* 209–67) the effect is attractive and it is hard to discern any target of ridicule.

Parody is by no means unknown in later comedy—*Eubulus (2) fr. 9 is a very obvious parody of Euripidean prologues—but it diminishes. *Sam.* 325 f. is one instance in *Menander (1); *Diphilus fr. 29 labours the point by adding ὡς οἱ τραγῳδοί φασιν ('as the tragedians say').

*Plato (1)'s parodies are often on a much larger scale than those of the comic poets, and he shows great subtlety and judgement in sustaining the character of the originals without lapsing into absurdity. *Agathon's speech in the *Symposium* (194e–7e) is a notable example; it is described as being in the style of *Gorgias (1) (198c), and we can compare it with what survives of Gorgias' work. The epideictic speech of *Protagoras in *Prt.* 320 c–8 d is obviously parody, but our limited acquaintance with Protagoras' own work makes assessment of its success difficult. Eryximachus' speech (*Symp.* 185e–8e) parodies the grandiloquent generalizations of a type of quasi-scientific literature current in the age of the *sophists. The first part of the funeral speech in the *Menexenus* is certainly parody, but the point (and purpose) of transition from the humorous to the serious in that speech remains an enigma. See ASPASIA; EPITAPHIOS; MENEXENUS. Whether *Phaedrus* 230e–4e, purporting to be an epideictic speech by *Lysias, is parody or quotation is disputed. Shorter passages of parody in Plato are sometimes identifiable, e.g. *Prt.* 337 a–c, which we can see to be a skit on *Prodicus; some may possibly be quotation, e.g. *Grg.* 448c (Polus).

There is much amusing parody of *Herodotus (1) and *Ctesias in *Lucian's *True Histories*, but the equally amusing incongruities of his *Dialogues of the Gods* belong rather to mythological burlesque, a genre which Lucian inherited from Old and Middle Comedy (see COMEDY (GREEK), OLD and MIDDLE).

W. H. S. Bakhuyzen, *De parodia in comoediis Aristophanis* (1877); P. Rau, *Paratragodia* (1967); S. Goldhill, *The Poet's Voice* (1991), ch. 3.   K. J. D.

parody, Latin No Latin *genre gives as central a place to literary parody as does (Greek) Old Comedy (see COMEDY (GREEK), OLD), and traditionally parody has been seen as playing a more restricted role in Latin, the concept being reserved for instances such as the broader para-tragedy of *Plautus and *Terence (cf. G. E. Duckworth, *The Nature of Roman Comedy* (1952), 335 n. 16), and self-standing poems such as the parody of *Catullus (1) 4 (to a ship), in *Catalepton* 10 (to a magistrate), and the parodies of *Virgil, *Ecl.* 1 and 3 by Numitorius (Courtney, *FLP, Obtrectatores Vergili* 1–2). Increased attention given to intertextuality in general, however (see LITERARY THEORY AND CLASSICAL STUDIES), with perhaps some influence from those modern theories which offer broad definitions of parody (cf. esp. L. Hutcheon, *Poétique*, 1981, 140–55, *A Theory of Parody* (1985)), has led to the concept being employed more widely. In general, any intertextuality with a 'higher' genre in a lower may be read as parody, and hence parody has been seen especially in genres like *satire (e.g. the parody of the council of the gods in *Ennius' *Annales* book 1 in *Lucilius (1), book 1, or the burlesque of Homer *Od.* 11 in *Horace, *Serm.* 2. 5; for *Menippean satire, see E. Courtney, *Philologus*, 1962, 86–100). In love-elegy *Propertius and *Tibullus parody *epic (e.g. Prop. 4. 8 with the killing of the suitors in *Od.* 22), and *Ovid both continues that tradition in the *Amores* and produces a travesty of it (contrast K. Morgan, *Ovid's Art of Imita-*

tion (1977) and J. T. Davis in *ANRW* 31. 4 (1981), 2460–506). In general, much of Ovid's work approaches parody (e.g. the travesty of Virgil's *Aeneid* in *Met.* 13–14 and the parody of it in the story of *Anna Perenna in *Fasti* 3. 545–656). But the work in which parody plays the most central role is perhaps *Petronius Arbiter's *Satyricon*, which 'parodies an astonishingly wide range of other literature' (N. W. Slater, *Reading Petronius* (1990), 18; cf. Courtney above). The poem on civil war recited by Eumolpus at *Satyricon* 119–24, which is very close in many respects to Lucan's *Bellum Civile* (see ANNAEUS LUCANUS, M.), has been variously seen as completely serious and either entirely or partially parodic, which underlines the difficulty of determining the boundaries of parody (cf. F. T. Baldwin, *The Bellum Civile of Petronius* (1911), 13–22, 71–88, and F. Zeitlin, *Latomus*, 1971, 56–82). The rise of Christianity offered a particularly elevated subject-matter for the sort of burlesque familiar from the Middle Ages: one text, the *Cena Cypriani*, occasioned a celebrated discussion by M. Bakhtin (cf. C. Modesto, *Studien zur Cena Cypriani* (1992)). See also IMITATIO.

J. P. Cèbe, *La Caricature et la parodie dans le monde romain antique des origines à Juvenal* (1966: also on non-literary and visual parody); P. J. C. Lehmann, *Die Parodie im Mittelalter* (2nd edn. 1983, with selection of texts); W. Karrer, *Parodie, Travestie, Pastiche* (1977); M. Bakhtin, *The Dialogic Imagination* (1981); G. Genette, *Palimpsestes* (1982); L. Hutcheon (see text); M. A. Rose, *Parody: Ancient, Modern, and Post-Modern* (1993).   P. G. F., D. P. F.

paroemiographers The proverb (παροιμία), or concise saying in common and recognized use, often summarizing experience or embodying practical wisdom, is a constant feature in Greek literature, both prose and verse, from *Homer onwards. It not only provided an ingredient calculated to please the ordinary hearer, but contributed to the formulation of moral philosophy. It might be in prose or metrical form, and gave its name to the Paroemiac. Many quotations from literature, and especially from poetry, enjoyed an independent life as proverbs or *sententiae* (γνῶμαι; see SENTENTIA; GNŌMĒ).

Paroemiography, or the making of collections of proverbs for specific purposes, may be said to have begun with *Aristotle in a work entitled Παροιμίαι, *Proverbs* (Diog. Laert. 5. 26); he was followed in this by his pupil, the *Peripatetic *Clearchus (3) of Soli, and later by the Stoic Chrysippus (see STOICISM); *Theophrastus also wrote Περὶ παροιμιῶν, *On Proverbs*. So far such collections were made for the purposes of philosophy. In the *Alexandrian age collections for literary purposes began to be made by such writers as the antiquarian *Demon (*On Proverbs*, of which a fragment has been recovered); *Aristophanes (2) of Byzantium, who made prose and metrical collections; *Didymus (1) (thirteen books); and Lucillus of Tarrha (in Crete). The later sophistic movement (see SECOND SOPHISTIC) led to a great demand for the proverb as an ornament of style, as may be seen, for example, in the works of Lucian (W. Schmid, *Atticismus* i. 411) and Libanius.

The origins of the existing *Corpus Paroemiographorum* go back to Zenobius, a sophist of the time of Hadrian; he made an epitome in three books of the collections of Didymus and Lucillus Tarrhaeus (*Suda*, Ζηνόβιος), obliterating the book-divisions in the process; the collections appear to have been already arranged according to literary genres. The Corpus in its original form, as constituted in the early Middle Ages, consisted of (1) the work of Zenobius, arranged alphabetically for scholastic purposes; (2) a collection of *Proverbs of Plutarch used by the Alexandrians*, probably deriving from *Seleucus (6) of Alexandria (*Suda*, Σέλευκος); and

Paros

(3) an alphabetical list of *Popular Proverbs*, derived from the same sources as Zenobius, ascribed to the lexicographer Diogenianus (time of Hadrian), but probably the work of an anonymous writer. From these were formed later the collections of Gregory of Cyprus (13th cent.), Macarius (14th cent.), and Apostolius (15th cent.). There exist a number of smaller medieval collections of proverbs, published and unpublished, mostly prepared by and for teachers of rhetoric. Some contain proverbs not in the *Corpus*.

EDITIONS T. Gaisford (1836); E. v. Leutsch and F. G. Schneidewin (1839); W. Bühler, in progress (1982–   ).
CRITICISM O. Crusius and L. Cohn, *Philol.* Suppl. 6 (1891–3) (sources and MS tradition); O. Crusius, *Analecta critica ad Paroem. gr.* (1883); *Paroemiographica, Sitz. Münch. Ak.* 1910; K. Rupprecht, *RE* 18 (1949), 1735 ff.

W. M. E.; R. B.; N. G. W.

Paros, a large island (196 km.²) in the central *Cyclades, its fine white marble prized by sculptors and masons from Archaic times. A middle-neolithic settlement at Saliagos, an islet between Paros and Antiparos (ancient Oliaros), is among the earliest in the Cyclades. A late-bronze-age fortified acropolis at Koukounaries was destroyed in the 11th cent. BC. Resettled by *Ionians in the 10th cent. BC, the ancient city (mod. Paroikia) occupied the site of a mid- to late-bronze-age town. After resettlement Koukounaries was deserted *c.*700 BC; its temple of *Athena survived until Classical times. Parian prosperity and power are exemplified in the 7th cent. by the poetry of *Archilochus and the colonization of *Thasos, and in the 6th by marble temples, massive fortifications and its sculpture workshops. The 'Melian' style of Orientalizing pottery (cf. MELOS) is now attributed to Paros. A noteworthy 6th-cent. monument is the heroon of Archilochus, where later the Parian Chronicle (see MARMOR PARIUM) and Life of Archilochus were inscribed. Frequently at odds with *Naxos (1), its Ionian connections are revealed by its art and friendship with *Miletus, perhaps influencing Paros to Medize (see MEDISM) in the *Persian wars. Successfully resisting *Miltiades' attempt to punish collaboration but subject to an indemnity after the battle of *Salamis, its high tribute of 16–18 talents under the Athenian empire (see DELIAN LEAGUE) demonstrates continuing prosperity. In 385 BC, with Syracusan support, Paros colonized the island of Pharos (modern Hvar) on the Dalmatian coast. In late antiquity the great church of Katapoliani was built at Paroikia.

O. Rubensohn, *RE* 18, 1781 ff.; *PECS* 677–9; *IG* 12 (5); *MDAI(A)* 1917, 1 ff.; O. Rubensohn, *Das Delion von Paros* (1962); J. D. Evans and C. Renfrew, *Excavations at Saliagos* (1968); *AA* 1970, 144 ff., 1972, 366 ff., 431 ff., 1982, 171–290, 621 ff.; *JdI* 1985, 321 ff.; *ΠAE* 1974–91; M. Schuller, *Der Artemistempel im Delion auf Paros* (1991); D. Berranger, *Recherches sur l'histoire et la prosopographie de Paros à l'époque archaïque* (1992).
R. W. V. C.

Parrhasius, famous painter, son, and pupil of Euenor of Ephesus, later Athenian. *Pliny (1) dates Euenor 420 BC and Parrhasius 397 (with *Zeuxis (1), his great rival); but he made designs for Mys' reliefs on the shield of *Phidias' Athena Promachus (before 450). He was arrogant and wore a purple cloak and a gold wreath. He painted a 'rose-fed' *Theseus, *Demos, 'Healing of *Telephus (1)', *Philoctetes, 'Feigned madness of *Odysseus'. Such pictures displayed the details of expression which he discusses with *Socrates in the *Memorabilia* of *Xenophon (1). He wrote on painting. He was famed for subtlety of outline; therefore perhaps made less use of shading. His gods and heroes became types for later artists; his drawings on parchment and wood were used by craftsmen (probably metal workers) in Pliny's time.

Overbeck, 637, 1130, 1649, 1680, 1692–730; M. Robertson, *History of Greek Art* 1 (1975), 411 ff., 421 ff.
T. B. L. W.

parricidium meant the killing of a *par*, i.e. originally perhaps a member of a sib or clan, later a close relative. In a law attributed to king *Pompilius Numa (Festus, entry under Parricidium) any deliberate (*dolo sciens*) killer of a free man is declared equivalent to a *paricidas*: in other words a killer outside the clan group is declared as heinous as a killer within it. That *parricidium* was in early Rome the word used for any murder of which the state took cognizance is also suggested by the early office of *quaestores parricidii* (see QUAESTOR). By the late Republic *parricidium* had come to mean the murder of *parentes* (near relations), as in *Cicero's speech for Sex. *Roscius and the *lex Pompeia de parricidiis* of 70 or 55 BC; it retained this meaning in classical texts and *Justinian's codification, which defines precisely for this purpose the circle of persons considered as near relations (*Dig.* 48. 9). A wider general sense came to be given to the term *homicidium* (rarely used in earlier texts, but more frequent in the legislation of the later Empire). Under the republic the convicted murderer of close relatives was drowned in the sea, tied up in a sack (*culleus*) with a dog, cock, ape, and viper. In later legislation the penalty was differentiated according to the gravity of the act, but the death-penalty remained the normal sanction.

D. Cloud, *ZSS* 1971.
A. B.; B. N.; A. W. L.

Parthenius of Nicaea or Myrleia (1st cent. BC), Greek poet and scholar taken to Rome as prisoner during the Third Mithradatic War (see MITHRADATES VI) and subsequently freed. He seems to have had some influence (the extent of which is disputed) on younger Latin poets such as C. *Helvius Cinna, C. *Cornelius Gallus, and *Virgil (according to *Macrobius, *Sat.* 5. 17. 18 he was Virgil's tutor in Greek), encouraging the study and imitation of *Callimachus (3) and *Euphorion (2), whose influence is evident in the remains of his own poetry. Only fragments survive of his numerous works in elegiacs, notably an *Encomium* in three books on his wife Arete, and in hexameters. Extant is the *Erotika Pathemata*, a collection of summaries in prose of esoteric love stories selected from a wide range of Greek poets and prose writers; this is dedicated to Cornelius Gallus, and ostensibly presented as material for the Latin poet to work into hexameter poems or elegies.

TEXT (fragments) A. Meineke, *Analecta Alexandrina* (1843), 255 ff.; *Suppl. Hell.* 605–66 (with *testimonia*); (*Er. Path.*) E. Martini, *Mythographi Graeci* 2: 1 (1902), (with trans.) S. Gaselee (Loeb, 1916).
GENERAL W. V. Clausen, *GRBS* 1964, 181–96; T. P. Wiseman, *Cinna the Poet* (1974); N. B. Crowther, *Mnemos.* 1976, 65–71; R. O. A. M. Lyne, *CQ* 1978, 167–87.
F. W.

Parthenon The Parthenon was the temple of *Athena built on the highest part of the Acropolis at Athens south of the Archaic temple. The name is properly that of the west room, but is generally extended to the entire building. The title Parthenos (virgin) is descriptive; her status is Polias, protector of the city. It was begun in 447 BC in the time of *Pericles (1); the temple and cult statue were dedicated in 438, but work continued, notably on the pedimental sculptures, until 432. A temple had been begun on the site after *Marathon (490) (see MARATHON, BATTLE OF), but work was abandoned on the approach of the second *Persian war (480–79). What had been built was destroyed by the Persians when they captured the city.

The Periclean building adapts the foundations and platform of this earlier structure, and, possibly, some of the marble elements prepared for it. It was built to house the gold and ivory statue by *Phidias, who must have been responsible for at least the design of its sculptural decoration; it is unlikely that he also directed the architectural design, which was determined more by the existing foundations than the statue it was to house.

The architect was *Ictinus together with *Callicrates (1). In the Parthenon the Doric *order is seen at its most perfect in proportions and in refined details, though there are some unusual features. The material is fine marble readily available from the quarries of *Pentelicon a few miles north-east of Athens and generally used in the important Athenian buildings of the Periclean period. The temple measures about 69.5 × 30.8 m. (228 × 101 ft.) on the top step. It has eight columns at the ends, and seventeen on the sides. The inner structure has a porch of six columns at each end. The larger eastern room had a two-tiered inner colonnade running not only along the sides but round the western end, behind the great cult statue; recent study has shown that there were windows high to the sides of the east door. The smaller western room opened off the back porch, and had its roof supported by four Ionic columns; it served as a 'treasury'.

The sculpture was more elaborate, more unified in theme, and more relevant to the cult than in most temples. It was also more extensive: every metope is carved, while the porch colonnades have instead a continuous frieze, extended abnormally the entire length of the cella outer walls. The metopes must have been made first, and then the frieze. The pediments were the latest addition. They showed, in the east, Athena newly sprung from the head of *Zeus, and in the west, the contest of *Poseidon and Athena for the land of Attica. The metopes, in high relief, showed mythical combats, on the south side, best preserved, Lapiths and *Centaurs, on the east, Gods and *Giants, on the west, Greeks and *Amazons, on the north—less certainly, since this side is very badly preserved—Trojan scenes (see HOMER; TROY). Some of these themes were echoed in the minor decoration of the cult statue. The frieze, in low relief, comprises a Panathenaic procession (see PANATHENAEA). It has been suggested this depicts or honours the young Athenian citizens who died at the battle of Marathon. A general allusion on these lines is certain. The whole temple, like its predecessor, is best interpreted as a thank-offering (after a false start) for the final, successful outcome of the wars with Persia, and it is clear that the reliefs allude to this, to the glorification of the Greek, and specifically Athenian, contribution to the victory.

The temple was subsequently converted into a church, dedicated to the Virgin, and then a mosque. It remained almost intact, though reroofed, until 1687, when a Turkish powder-magazine in it was exploded by the besieging Venetians. Earlier reconstruction work has been dismantled, and a thorough programme of conservation is being carried out, which has led to the identification of many of the fallen fragments. See also NATIONALISM.

G. P. Stevens, *The Setting of the Periclean Parthenon, Hesperia* Suppl. 3, (1940); W. B. Dinsmoor, *Architecture of Ancient Greece*[3] (1950), 149 f., 159 ff., 358 bibliog.; C. J. Herrington, *Athena Parthenos and Athena Polias* (for the cults) (1955); F. Brommer, *Die Skulpturen der Parthenon-Giebel* (1963), *Die Metopen des Parthenon* (1967), *Der Parthenon Fries* (1977); A. K. Orlandos *He Architektonike tou Parthenonos* (1977); J. Boardman in *Festschrift für Frank Brommer* (1977); R. Osborne, *JHS* 1987, 98 ff.; M. Korres, *Die Explosion des Parthenon* (1990); E. Berger (ed.), *Parthenon-Kongress* (1984); M. Beard, *The Parthenon* (2002). R. A. T.

Parthenopaeus (Παρθενοπαῖος), one of the *Seven against Thebes. Sometimes he is Argive (see ARGOS (2)), brother of *Adrastus (1), sometimes *Arcadian, the son of *Atalanta. With *Telephus (1), he was exposed on Mount Parthenion, and he accompanied Telephus to Mysia. He was victorious in the archery contest at the games founded at *Nemea in honour of Archemorus-Opheltes; see NEMEAN GAMES. He took part in the expedition of the Seven against his mother's wishes, and was killed in front of Thebes by *Periclymenus (or Asphodicus or *Amphilochus).

Schol. Soph. *OC.* 1320; [Apollod.] 1. 9. 13, 3. 6. 3 ff., 9. 2 ff.   M. J.

Parthia, Parthian empire The people whom Greeks and Romans called Parthians were originally Parni, members of the semi-nomad Dahae confederacy north of Hyrcania. Their Greek name is derived from the Achaemenian (see ACHAEMENIDS) and then *Seleucid satrapy (see SATRAP) called Parthia (*Parthava*), which they occupied, traditionally in 247 BC, the year with which the Parthian ('Arsacid') era begins; later they ruled from the *Euphrates to the Indus, with *Ctesiphon as their main residence. The territorial gains under Mithradates I and II not only changed their former eastern Iranian empire into an ethnically, politically, socially, and culturally diverse one needing new forms of administration and organization, but also deeply influenced the relationship between the Parthian aristocracy and the rulers. It was the conflict between kings and nobles which shaped later history and often allowed foreign powers like Rome to intervene in Parthian affairs. Although we hear of large estates of Parthian aristocrats in the conquered parts of the empire we do not know very much about the way in which their rights of possession and use were transferred to, and retained by them. It is therefore dangerous to call the Parthian state a 'feudal' one. Ambitious members of the great Parthian families (Suren, Karin, Gev and others), governors, petty and 'vassal' kings temporarily gained total or limited independence (like the rulers of *Mesene and Seistan). We do not know very much about Parthian rule in Persis, apart from the fact that in their time south-western Iranian historical and mythical tradition was replaced by eastern Iranian stories and legends, and that Parthian rule was finally brought to an end by local dynasts from Istakhr (see SASANIDS).

The structure of Parthian society and the titulature of their élite are best known from the administrative documents from Nisa, the Sasanian inscriptions of the 3rd cent. AD and the classical reports of Parthian warfare. They distinguish between a higher and a lower nobility and their dependants (cf. the *ordo probulorum, liberi*, and *servi* in *Justin), the last group not being slaves but people with the belt of 'vassalage' (Iran. *bandag*). Apart from these groups we find a kind of middle stratum of artists, traders, doctors, bards, and other specialists and the non-Iranian native population of the conquered territories. Scholarship for a long time classified the Parthians as culturally dependent, without great political aspirations and inferior to Rome in almost all respects. New findings (texts from Mesopotamia, archaeological remains) provide a more differentiated view which, e.g., allows us to see the 'Philhellenism' of the kings (on their coins and in cultural affairs; cf. HELLENISM) and the Iranian traits of their rule as ways of ensuring the co-operation of two important groups of subjects. In warfare they were famous for their mailed cavalry (*cataphractarii* / *clibanarii*) and their horse archers, and they bred the Nisaean horses which were known even in China. The Parthians spoke Parthian, a western Middle Iranian language; they seem to have adopted the Zoroastrian cult of fire and its calendar (see ZOROASTER), but tolerated every other religion.

A stronger emphasis on the Iranian heritage is characteristic of the second half of their empire (cf. the legends on the coins and the role of *Vologeses I (?) in the Zoroastrian tradition), but it is very dangerous to see this as a consequence of the revolt of *Seleuceia (1), the reasons for which are not known to us. The Parthians played an important role as middlemen in the trade between China (see SERES), India and Syria. Their art—a revived Iranian art, which absorbed both Mesopotamian and Greek elements—spread far and is historically interesting.

N. C. Debevoise, *Political History of Parthia* (1938); K. Schippmann, *Grundzüge der parthischen Geschichte* (1980); M. A. R. Colledge, *The Parthian Period* (1986); *The Cambridge History of Iran* 3. 1–2 (1983).

J. Wi.

Pasargadae (Πασαργάδαι), an *Achaemenid centre north-east of *Persepolis, where *Cyrus (1) the Great 'conquered Astyages the Mede in his last battle ... founded a city, and constructed a palace as a memorial of his victory' (Strabo 15. 3. 8; cf. MEDIA). The tomb of Cyrus the Great, visited by *Alexander (3) the Great (Arr. *Anab.* 6. 29; Strab. 15. 3. 7; Plut. *Alex.* 69. 4), lies to the south-west of an area which in Achaemenian times was a well watered 'paradise' of palaces and gardens, overlooked by a citadel on the Tall-i Takht, or 'Throne Hill'. Excavation has revealed over 1 km. of stone-lined conduits.

C. Nylander, *Ionians in Pasargadae* (1970); D. Stronach, *Pasargadae* (1978).

M. V.

Pasion (d. 370/69 BC) was the wealthiest banker and manufacturer of his time in Athens (see BANKS). He began his career as a slave with a banking firm in the *Piraeus, was made a freedman and subsequently acquired ownership of the bank. By his wife Archippe he had two sons, *Apollodorus (2) and Pasicles. He later became an Athenian citizen, having spent lavishly on donations to the city. Although associated with *Callistratus (2) and *Timotheus (2), he appears to have taken no part in politics. Information about his business activities derives from a speech written in the 390s for a disgruntled client (see Isoc. 17), and from the later speeches of Apollodorus (see esp. Dem. 36, 45, 46). He left real estate of 20 and outstanding loans of almost 40 talents.

RE 18/2, 'Pasion 2'; Davies, *APF* no. 11672; J. Trevett *Apollodoros the Son of Pasion* (1992) with earlier bibliog.

J. C. T.

Pasiphae See MINOS.

Pasiteles, a Greek sculptor from S. Italy given Roman citizenship and a contemporary of *Pompey the Great (106–48 BC). A scholar-artist in the tradition of *Antigonus (4) of Carystus, he wrote five volumes entitled 'Noble [or Marvellous] Works of Art Throughout the World' (Plin. *HN* 1. 34, 36. 39). His reputation was based on these and on his metalwork. Several anecdotes describe his working methods, which included sketching from life and always making a preparatory model in clay. Though his ivory *Jupiter in the temple of Q. *Caecilius Metellus Macedonicus was his only work of sculpture to be individually recorded (Plin. *HN* 36. 39), he represents a decisive shift in Greek sculpture towards production for purely Roman tastes. Only a single signed statue-support in marble has survived, though two generations of his workshop are represented in costively neo-classical creations of marked sentimentality: an athlete (or hero) signed by his pupil Stephanus and the *Orestes and *Electra signed by Stephanus' pupil *Menelaus (2), both in Rome.

A. F. Stewart, *Greek Sculpture* (1990), 230 f., 306 f., figs. 860 f.; D. E. E. Kleiner, *Roman Sculpture* (1992), 29 f., figs. 6 ff.

A. F. S.

Passennus Paullus Propertius, an *eques* (see EQUITES) from Assisi (*Asisium), whose contemporary *Pliny (2) (*Ep.* 6. 15, 9. 22) praises him for his elegies as being, like his actual descent, Propertian (see PROPERTIUS). He also wrote Horatian lyric (see HORACE).

See Courtney, *FLP* 371.

E. C.

Passienus (*RE* 1), Augustan orator and declaimer (d. 9 BC), father of the consul of BC 4. He is mainly known from the Elder Seneca (L. *Annaeus Seneca (1)).

Schanz–Hosius § 336.9.13.

M. W.

pastoral poetry, Greek For as long as peasants have tended their flocks and herds on grazing lands away from the village, song and music (especially that of the pipe, which is easily cut, fashioned and carried) have served as an anodyne against rustic tedium and brutality; the Taviani brothers' film *Padre Padrone* (1977) provides a powerful illustration from modern Sardinia. This is especially true of the goatherd, who ranges furthest into the wild territory of *Pan in search of shrubs on which only his chalcenteric and omnivorous charges will browse; and in these lonely wastes it is natural that two herdsmen whose paths cross should not only perform in each other's company but that their songs should be competitive. This real-world situation provided the foundation upon which a literary genre was established by the Sicilian poet *Theocritus in the 3rd cent. BC and developed by his followers in Hellenistic Greece (*Moschus, *Bion (2), and a school of epigrammatists), Rome (*Virgil, *Calpurnius Siculus), and the post-Renaissance world.

Bucolic poetry was not created *ex nihilo*. Two piping herdsmen are among the figures depicted on the Shield of Achilles (*Homer, *Il.* 18. 525 f.), and *Eumaeus in Homer's *Odyssey* shows early literary interest in peasant characterization; even the *Cyclops Polyphemus, communing with his ram, arouses a moment of sympathy which will later stimulate his re-creation as a youthful lover in *Philoxenus (1) (frr. 2–4 P) and Theocritus (6, 11). The Sicilian lyric poet *Stesichorus is credited by *Aelian (*VH* 10. 18) with having been the first to sing of the local bucolic hero *Daphnis, back in the 6th cent. (fr. 102 P). But the conditions needed for pastoral themes to gain critical mass as a viable genre were not met until literary life became concentrated in the great Hellenistic cities, alienated from the villages in which so many Greek cultural traditions (tales, folksong, dance, ritual competition) had developed. One thread in the cultural amalgam of the 3rd cent. is an understandable nostalgia for the simpler world once dominated by Daphnis, Pan, *Priapus, and the *Nymphs; a world now largely vanished but whose continued existence could at least be fantasized in the mountains of *Magna Graecia and *Arcadia.

As already mentioned, the basic form elaborated by Theocritus seems to have been essentially agonistic. Theocritus 5 provides the clearest example. Two peasants meet; one proposes a contest; stakes are wagered, and a judge is sought; jockeying for the most favourable ground takes place; and after some preliminary boasting and badinage, each attempting to unsettle the other, the competition begins. This takes the form of an alternating ('*amoebean') sequence of couplets or quatrains in which the first singer, as proposer of each subject, has an inbuilt advantage, while the respondent must follow suit and if possible cap each theme. This goes some way to offset the fact that the initiator of the challenge—in this case, Lacon—has chosen the time and place (contrast 6. 5). In poem 5, victory is suddenly and confidently claimed by Comatas at v. 136, and immediately confirmed by the judge. Why? The explanation of G. Serrao (*Problemi di poesia alessandrina* 1 (1971)) is attractive: not only must the respondent follow suit but (to continue the card-game analogy) each singer must remember every trick that has been played; the first one to contradict a previous statement is the loser. There is thus a natural limiting factor to the bucolic agon, for the longer it goes on the harder it gets.

The genius of Theocritus' creativity was to realize the possibilities offered by this half-crude, half-sophisticated model to the modern style of self-conscious urban literature. His chosen form is artificial from the start; the Doric *dialect may impart a rustic flavour, but the metre is the classical Homeric hexameter. Each poem works its own elegant variation on the fundamental pattern. The brief exchanges of the original contest are substituted with single songs (6, 7); rivalry is replaced by a friendly and voluntary exchange of gifts (6); the scenes of peasant life acquire a distancing layer of sophistication by being framed as notional letters (6. 2, Ἄρατε) or poetic autobiography (7); the dialogue may become an end in itself without ever reaching the stage of competition (4), or may be dropped in favour of a lover's monologue (3). Full circle is reached in poem 1, where the obscene teasing is inverted to become exquisite politeness and in which, though the diptych structure is retained, the first 'performance' is not a competition effort at all but an ekphrastic description (deliberately recalling the Iliadic *Shield of Achilles*, only recast on a miniature scale) of the decorative carving on a wooden cup (see EKPHRASIS) which is freely offered as reward for a song by the other character. The coarse duels of the grubby, garlic-chewing rustics have been alchemically transmuted into allusive mandarin elegance, without ever quite pulling free of their roots in the vigorous Sicilian soil. The literary conventions which lead on to *Virgil, Milton, and Marie-Antoinette are all in place.

B. Snell, *The Discovery of the Mind* (1953), ch. 13; R. Merkelbach, *RhM* 1956, 97–133; T. G. Rosenmeyer, *The Green Cabinet: Theocritus and the European Pastoral Lyric* (1969); C. Segal, *Poetry and Myth in Ancient Pastoral* (1981); D. M. Halperin, *Before Pastoral: Theocritus and the Ancient Tradition of Bucolic Poetry* (1983); E. A. Schmidt, *Bukolische Leidenschaft oder über die antike Hirtenpoesie* (1985); K. J. Gutzwiller, *Theocritus' Pastoral Analogies: The Formation of a Genre* (1991). A. H. G.

pastoral poetry, Latin Latin pastoral poetry is, in strict terms, represented by *Virgil's ten eclogues, *Calpurnius Siculus' seven, the two *Einsiedeln eclogues and *Nemesianus' four. But pastoral (or 'bucolic') is often defined by theorists as a 'mode' rather than a *genre, and, in this sense, one may speak of pastoral colouring or attitudes in *Tibullus, *Lucretius, the *Culex, Dirae,* and *Lydia* of the *Appendix Vergiliana, Aeneid* 8, and numerous other texts besides. It is unlikely that Virgil's contemporary *Cornelius Gallus wrote pastoral elegies, although the tenth *Eclogue* has frequently been interpreted to that effect.

Among Latin pastoralists Virgil stands supreme. He significantly extended the boundaries of the genre which he had inherited from *Theocritus, whose inspiration he explicitly acknowledges, and upon whom he draws extensively in all the *Eclogues*, with the exception of 4 and 6, in which the poet strives to lift pastoral to a higher plane (cf. 4. 1 *Sicelides Musae, paulo maiora canamus,* 'Sicilian Muses, let us sing a somewhat grander strain'). Virgil's innovativeness is proclaimed at the outset of the *Eclogue*-book. Whereas Theocritus had kept pastoral and court poems rigidly distinct, contemporary politics and pastoral are strikingly blended in the first *Eclogue*, which describes, in the persons of Meliboeus and Tityrus, the effects upon the Italian

countryside of the triumviral dispossessions of the late 40s BC (see TRIUMVIRI; PROSCRIPTION). In consequence of this, the pastoral world may be said to exist no longer in a hermetic space, but to suffer encroachments from without, which have the effect of disrupting the shepherds' traditional *otium* ('ease, tranquil existence').

Also to Virgil's credit is the creation of the Arcadian setting—Snell's famous 'spiritual landscape'—which was to prove so influential in European pastoral. But it is important to note that references to *Arcadia in the *Eclogues* are actually rather few, and are moreover combined with features of Italian topography (cf. *Eclogue* 7). The precise import of Arcadia is much disputed. It seems best to regard it as a remote, solitary setting for lovers' plaints and for song (at which the Arcadians were especially skilled). Both topics are central to pastoral. It is probably to the former of these that *Horace's famous verdict on the *Eclogues*, *molle atque facetum* ('gentle' and 'elegant') (*Sat.* 1. 10. 44) refers, though both adjectives have a stylistic connotation as well.

The *Eclogues* are self-reflexive, experimental, and challenging, but none of the authors who follow Virgil can rival him in complexity and suggestiveness. With Calpurnius, and to a lesser extent the Einsiedeln eclogues, one has a sense that pastoral is being pushed to its furthest limits. Indeed, Calpurnius' fifth *Eclogue* is concerned with purely georgic matters, while his seventh provides no more than a pastoral framework for extensive praise of *Nero's Roman amphitheatre. Similarly, both Neronian pastoralists show a readiness to talk explicitly of political matters which are properly extraneous to the pastoral world (though they naturally impinge upon it).

Certain aspects of Virgilian pastoral are taken up and developed by Calpurnius—not necessarily in a felicitous way. Whereas Virgil (in *Ecl.* 1 and 9) had hinted at an opposition between city and country, in Calpurnius' final poem, this opposition is made explicit, and resolved in favour of the former, so that the pastoral ethic is in a sense betrayed by its own representative Corydon. Virgil's youthful 'god' (Octavian) had exercised his (questionable) influence on the land at long range; Calpurnius pictures the city-dwelling Nero as a veritable *deus praesens,* 'god made manifest' in the countryside, at the mere sound of whose name the fields are instinct with joy and fertility (4. 97 ff.). So too the praise which Virgil had proffered to several patrons becomes concentrated, in Neronian pastoral, in the figure of the emperor. The richly textured, prophetic millenarianism of Virgil's fourth *Eclogue* is transmuted into the prosy assertion that the *golden age—a favourite theme both of pastoral and imperial *propaganda—has returned under the presidency of Nero. Virgil's experimentation with the possibilities of the genre and his musings on which direction his future work should take are commuted by Calpurnius (*Ecl.* 4) into pastoral encomium, culminating in a baldly-phrased request for imperial patronage. One can only commend Nero for shutting his ears.

The *Eclogues* of Nemesianus, written it seems in the early 280s AD, are far more conventional than those of Calpurnius, whom Nemesianus nevertheless assiduously echoes, and, it is arguable, outshines. Verbally and thematically, the influence of Virgil is paramount. The fourth *Eclogue* restores to pastoral the Theocritean refrain, which Calpurnius had dropped. Also noteworthy is *Eclogue* 2, in which two young shepherds rape the girl of whom both are enamoured while, like Proserpina, she is picking flowers. The motif of sexual violence is new to pastoral poetry, although the idea of erotic conquest—in this case by force—

recalls [Theocritus] 27 and, to some extent, anticipates the medieval *pastourelle*.

GENERAL AND ANCIENT T. Rosenmeyer, *The Green Cabinet* (1969); D. Halperin, *Before Pastoral* (1983); J. Hubaux, *Les Thèmes bucoliques dans la poésie latine* (1930); *Ramus*, 1975; *Arethusa*, 1990.
VIRGILIAN PASTORAL G. Binder, *Gymnasium* 1987; H. J. Rose, *The Eclogues of Vergil* (1942); E. A. Schmidt, *Poetische Reflexion. Vergils Bukolik* (1972); E. W. Leach, *Vergil's Eclogues: Landscapes of Experience* (1974: good on theory of pastoral); W. Berg, *Early Vergil* (1974); N. Rudd, *Lines of Enquiry* (1976), 119 ff.; E. Coleiro, *An Introduction to Vergil's Bucolics* (1979); W. Briggs, *ANRW* 31. 2 (1981), 575; M. Lee, *Death and Rebirth in Vergil's Arcadia* (1989; useful introduction to the *Eclogues*).
ARCADIA B. Snell, *The Discovery of the Mind* (1953), 281 ff.; D. Kennedy, *Hermathena*, 1982; R. Jenkyns, *JRS* 1989.   L. C. W.

pastoralism, Greek Although animals were ubiquitous throughout the Greek countryside, animal husbandry has until recently received little systematic attention; hence current interpretations are frequently embryonic. Zooarchaeological studies of animal bone assemblages from the historical period are particularly needed.

Evidence of domesticated animals goes back to the 7th millennium BC. In the early neolithic modest flocks of ovicaprines (sheep and goats), kept primarily for meat, were integrated into small-scale gardening, grazing on fallow and stubble and supplying manure. More specialized stock-keeping arose in the late neolithic and bronze age, with increased exploitation of 'secondary products', especially ox traction and ovicaprine textile fibres, culminating in the large-scale wool production of the Minoan and Mycenaean palaces (see MINOAN and MYCENAEAN CIVILIZATION). Older views of the Dark Age as one of nomadic pastoralism (often associated with the 'Dorian invasions'; see DORIANS; HERACLIDAE) are now under challenge. 'Homeric society' rested upon arable production, with large herds as a store for surplus wealth. The period of independent *poleis* (discussed further below) witnessed smaller herd sizes; Hellenistic and Roman Greece a subsequent increase. Within the Roman, especially later Roman, empire demand for pastoral products made ovicaprine stock-raising (often conducted from isolated, tenant-run farmsteads) important on larger Greek estates.

The animals reared in different regions were partly influenced by environmental conditions, with more larger livestock in the moister north and west. Older studies assumed that environmental conditions also dictated a pattern of long-distance seasonal *transhumance, as practised frequently in modern times. Transhumance, however, is now regarded as the product of specific economic and political circumstances (especially weak lowland agriculture and unified political authority) which did not apply under the independent *poleis* (see POLIS). Despite occasional cross-border agreements, seasonal movements were generally limited to upland areas within *polis* boundaries. Many citizens possessed a few 'house' animals; but larger herds (typically not more than 50–100 strong) were owned by wealthy landowners employing individual hired or slave herders, rather than—as recently—by independent, low-status mobile pastoralist groups. Recent research has emphasized the income-generating capacity of such modest-sized ovicaprine flocks reared for their marketable high-quality wool and cheese. The extent of animal husbandry's integration with arable farming is controversial. One opinion stresses the role of agro-pastoral farms whose animals fed at least partly on fodder crops, fallow, and agricultural waste-products, providing manure in return; another asserts greater reliance upon pastures distant from arable cultivation.

Animal husbandry also performed important religious and social functions. The requirements of official sacrificial calendars mirrored the seasonal availability of surplus animals from local flocks and conditioned the age at which animals were sold. war-horses, chariot-horses (see HORSES), and hunting *dogs were powerful status symbols, playing important roles in élite lifestyles. (See also BRIGANDAGE; PAN.)

J. F. Cherry, S. Hodkinson, J. E. Skydsgaard, and M. H. Jameson, in C. R. Whittaker (ed.), *Pastoral Economies in Classical Antiquity* (PCPS, Suppl. 14, 1988), 6–119; P. Halstead, in I. Hodder, G. Isaac, and N. Hammond (eds.), *Pattern of the Past* (1981), 307–30; J. Killen, *BSA* 1964, 1–15; S. Hodkinson, *Rivista di studi liguri* 1990, 139–64; S. Isager and J. E. Skydsgaard, *Ancient Greek Agriculture* (1992), chs. 5, 14; C. Mee and others, in G. Barker and J. Lloyd (eds.), *Roman Landscapes* (BSR Archaeological Monographs 2, 1991), 223–32; S. Payne, in N. C. Wilkie and W. D. E. Coulson (eds.), *Contributions to Aegean Archaeology* (1985), 211–44; D. Kehoe, *JRA* 1990, 386–98.   S. J. Ho.

pastoralism, Roman Pastoralism, whether good, bad or indifferent, provided the most lucrative returns, according to *Cato (Censorius) (Cicero, *Off*. 2. 89; Columella, *Rust*. 6 praef. 4–5; Plin. *HN* 8. 29–30). Thus scholars have traditionally focused on such profitable forms of stockbreeding (sometimes described as 'ranching') as *Varro's long-distance, large-scale *transhumance of sheep between *Apulia and the Abruzzi (*Rust*. 2. 2. 9)—entreprenerial pastoralism largely divorced from, or even in competition with, settled *agriculture, which exploited Rome's post-Hannibalic control of Italy (see PUNIC WARS; ROME (HISTORY), § 1.4). More recently, evidence from archaeology (patterns of rural settlement, *villa excavation and analysis of animal bones and plant remains) and ethnography (the study of still-extant traditional forms of pastoralism), together with a close reading of the Roman *agricultural writers, has begun to round out the picture by emphasizing the more widespread, if less prominent, closer integration of pastoralism with agriculture. Subsistence *peasants, who owned a few sheep for clothing, milk, cheese, and manure (Columella, *Rust*. 7. 2. 1) and an ass for transport and the plough (*id*. 7. 1. 1), sowed their limited cultivable land with crops for their own consumption but found pasture for their animals most of the year round in local scrub and woodland (cf. Varro, *Rust*. 2. 5. 11; Columella, *Rust*. 1. 2. 5). A *c*.60 ha. (240 *iugera*) estate with 6 plough-oxen, 4 asses, 100 sheep, and an unspecified number of pigs (Cato, *Agr*. 10) could produce additional fodder resources of its own: surplus grain, forage crops rotated with cereals, dry and/or irrigated meadows (which might also be profitably leased, Cato, *Agr*. 9; 149; Varro, *Rust*. 1. 21), grass grown on fallow land, grazing of the cereal crop while still in the leaf, foliage, and grape pressings. Besides sheep, which were always in the majority—with parts of Apulia and the Po plain (see PADUS) gaining reputations for particular breeds (Columella, *Rust*. 7. 2. 3)—Roman pastoralism included cattle, horses, mules, asses, goats, pigs, dogs, and slave herdsmen (Varro, *Rust*. 2. 10. 6; 2 passim) and, from the late republic onwards, the specialized breeding, known as *pastio villatica*, of peacocks, dormice, boars, snails, fish, etc. (Varro, *Rust*. 2, esp. 10. 6). See BRIGANDAGE.

J. E. Skydsgaard, *Analecta Instituti Danici*, 1974, 7–36; E. Gabba and M. Pasquinucci, *Strutture agrarie e allevamento transumante nell'Italia romana* (1979); J. M. Frayn, *Sheep Rearing and the Wool Trade in Italy during the Roman Period* (1984); M. S. Spurr, *Arable Cultivation in Roman Italy* (1986); C. R. Whittaker (ed.), *Pastoral Economies in Classical Antiquity*, PCPS 14 (1988); G. Barker and A. Grant (eds.), *PBSR* 1991, 15–88.   M. S. Sp.

pasturage See PASTORALISM, GREEK; PASTORALISM, ROMAN.

Patara, Lycian Pttara, modern Kelemiş, was one of the most important cities of *Lycia, situated near the mouth of the Xanthus river, south of *Xanthus. *Herodotus (1) (1. 182) mentions the *oracle of *Apollo at Patara and the discovery of red-figure pottery confirms that the site was occupied in Classical times. *Alexander (3) the Great offered its revenues to *Phocion, who turned them down. The harbour was (now blocked by sand-dunes) occupied by *Antigonus (1) in 315 and *Demetrius (4) Poliorcetes in 304 during the wars of the *Diadochi; the city was temporarily renamed Arsinoe under *Ptolemy (1) II and was taken in 197 BC by *Antiochus (3) III, when Livy refers to it as the capital of the Lycian nation. It may have been one of the main residences of the Roman governors of Lycia and *Pamphylia under the empire. The surviving buildings include a bath-house (see BATHS) partly funded with money released for the purpose by the emperor *Vespasian, the arch built by the governor Mettius Modestus on the occasion of *Hadrian's visit in AD 129, a granary built by the emperor himself (as at Andriake, see MYRA), and the theatre whose stage building was constructed in AD 147 by a local benefactress, Vilia Procula.

> G. E. Bean, *Lycian Turkey* (1978) 82–91; *TAM* 2.   S. M.

Patavinitas, the provincial smack of *Livy's native *Patavium (Padua), declared by C. *Asinius Pollio (Quint. 1. 5. 56; 8. 1. 3) to typify Livy's writing. *Quintilian himself seems puzzled as to Pollio's point, but took it as referring to expression and vocabulary; pronunciation too was perhaps relevant. Some speculate that Pollio was thinking of a wider provincialism of mentality, but this is unlikely. His charge enraged Morhof (1639–91), who retorted on Pollio's 'Asinity' in *De Patavinitate Liviana* (1685).

> J. Whatmough, *Harv. Stud.* 1933, 95–130; P. G. Walsh, *Livy* (1961), 267–71; E. S. Ramage, *Urbanitas* (1973), 109–10.   C. B. R. P.

Patavium, a city situated near celebrated springs in a fertile part of Cisalpine *Gaul (Strabo 5. 212 f.; Plin. *HN* 2. 103); modern Padua. The *Veneti probably founded Patavium and it became their capital, successfully resisting a Spartan attack in 301 BC (Livy 10. 2). By 174 it was subject to Rome, but retained local autonomy (Livy 41. 27). C. *Asinius Pollio temporarily oppressed Patavium, probably because it opposed Antony (M. *Antonius (2)), 43 BC (Macrob. 1. 11. 2; Cic. *Phil.* 12. 10). But in general it prospered. It was a road-centre, and canals connected it with the sea. Its flourishing woollen industries made Patavium the wealthiest north-Italian city in *Augustus' time. Later *Mediolanum and *Aquileia outstripped it, but Patavium always remained important, even after *Huns (452) and *Lombards (601) sacked it. Its most famous sons were *Livy (see preceding article), *Asconius, and *Thrasea Paetus.

> G. Fogolari and A. M. Chieco Bianchi, *Padova preromana* (1976), *Padova antica* (1981).   E. T. S.; T. W. P.

Pater Patriae ('Father of the Fatherland'), the title conferred on *Cicero for his action against the Catilinarian conspirators (see SERGIUS CATILINA, L.), on *Caesar after the battle of Munda, and on *Augustus in 2 BC (when he had reached the age of 60), in a gesture of unanimity by the Roman community, coinciding with the dedication of the *forum Augustum. *Tiberius never accepted the title, but after a show of refusal all the later emperors (before Pertinax, who accepted it at accession) took it if they lived long enough. The title was eloquently suggestive of the protecting but coercive authority of the *paterfamilias*.   N. P.

paterfamilias See PATRIA POTESTAS.

pathology As defined in medical handbooks from at least AD 150 onwards, pathology was that part of medicine specifically concerned with the causes of disease. As such it went beyond the observation and classification implicit in diagnosis to an identification of what might be invisible to the senses. From seeing, smelling, hearing, and touching the patient, and occasionally even tasting sweat or urine, the true physician could identify the cause of the illness, and work to eliminate or alleviate it. While this skill was used primarily in treatment, doctors might be called upon to testify in a lawcourt, and in Graeco-Roman Egypt medical certification in cases of wounding or suspicious death (*POxy.* 3926) was apparently a common procedure.

The investigation of the causes of illness was difficult in a pre-technological age. Although *Herophilus is said to have invented a clock to time the pulse (recognized as a diagnostic guide by his master, *Praxagoras), and *Galen mentions urine being heated for examination, these are rare exceptions to what were otherwise impressionistic and qualitative judgements. In such circumstances establishing a cause of illness might be the mark of the truly distinguished medical expert or, as the Empiricist physicians argued, a waste of time. There was little agreement as to what these causes might be, as well as overlapping schemes of explanation.

For some conditions, especially pestilence, stroke, epilepsy, and some skin disfigurements like leprosy, divine punishment was suspected. An insult to a god or goddess, even by a member of one's family, or, according to some Jewish and Christian authors, an individual's generally sinful behaviour, had called down physical retribution. A religious cause thus demanded, at least in part, a religious remedy, whether the direct intervention of the divinity or secular healing following on an appropriate apology.

Below the gods lay the heavens. For some, illness was determined by one's stars—hence the frequent mention of medical horoscopes and iatromathematicians (doctor-astrologers). More sceptical writers like *Rufus of Ephesus and Galen preferred to think of climate and seasons, each with their own particular air and mirroring in their ordered progression the cycle of remissions and relapses of febrile diseases like malaria, with their mathematically predictable 'critical days'. The importance of good air had been argued even before the Hippocratic text *Airs, Waters, and Places* (see HIPPOCRATES (2)), which asserted a paramount role for environment in disease and assigned physical and moral peculiarities of the Scythians or Libyans to the effects of *climate and geography. Many writers thought that the air itself became polluted, or miasmatic, and hence brought about large-scale epidemic *diseases or *plagues, but there was little agreement over what this *pollution was. Some considered the air itself a poison, avoidable only by flight or by taking smaller breaths; others believed in an alteration in the general quality of the air (particularly becoming hot and moist) which produced adverse reactions in individuals of a certain bodily constitution; others, the 'Democriteans' (cf. DEMOCRITUS), suggested that there were airborne 'seeds of disease', a neat explanation for the apparently random spread of an epidemic.

The notion of miasms was favoured by the Hippocratics, who ascribed them either to wider atmospheric causes, mephitic vapours coming from the ground, stagnant pools, rotting corpses, or even the breaths and excretions given off by the sick. All had power to change the atmosphere and infect (a metaphor taken from the dyeing of cloth) those who came close to the miasma. That those who had most to do with the sick were most likely to fall ill themselves was recognized by *Thucydides (2) in his account of the plague of Athens—he also, on equally empirical grounds, noticed that those, like himself, who had recovered from one attack were less likely to fall ill of it again—and by *Isocrates. The author of the Aristotelian *Problems* 1. 7 and 7. 8 acknowledged the existence of what modern physicians would term contagious diseases, but was uncertain how and why they spread. This uncertainty is also reflected in the fact that no Greek word has yet been securely identified as the equivalent of the Latin *contagium* (contagion). Interest in contagion appears among Methodists (see MEDICINE, § 5.3), whose mechanistic philosophy of the body lent itself more readily to such an explanation, and among writers on *veterinary medicine (whose advice to separate or kill infected animals was not easily applied to humans.) The Latin word was also frequently used by non-medical authors to describe the spread of unpopular or heretical beliefs.

Most surviving Greek medical texts are largely in the Hippocratic tradition, and emphasize internal causes of disease within the individual patient. *Plato (1) in his *Timaeus* talked about diseases caused by the decomposition of substances into their original components, the later Hippocratics and Galen discussed lesions of continuity, *Erasistratus thought in terms of blood seeping into areas of the body where it ought not, and *Asclepiades (3) explained disease as resulting from the blockage or fluidity of pores of the body, but these were exceptions to the general tendency to account for disease as either imbalance or a consequence of the production within the body of harmful substances. In the so-called Anonymus Londinensis papyrus one writer, perhaps *Meno, the pupil of *Aristotle, listed the explanations given for disease by at least eighteen authors. Some, like Euryphon of Cnidus and the mysterious Ninyas the Egyptian, attributed disease to unassimilated, rotting residues within the body. A similar explanation, that the residues produce harmful airs, breaths or gases, appears in *On breaths*, and is ascribed by Meno to the historical Hippocrates. Others demurred. An ancient (pre-AD 170) editor of Meno's list declared instead that Hippocrates had considered disease the result of an imbalance of *humours, as in *On the Nature of Man*, the tract later regarded by Galen as quintessentially Hippocratic.

The idea of imbalance was widely shared by many physicians, even though there was little agreement on precisely what was out of balance. For some, it was the body's elements; for others its humours; the Methodists thought in terms of three common conditions, stricture, laxity, and a combination of the two; and the Hippocratic author of *Ancient medicine* posited a whole variety of competing opposite powers within a veritable corporeal battleground. Some placed particular emphasis on the production of bile or phlegm, others of blood, water, or the near-deadly black bile.

This imbalance might show itself in one's general health, or in one place or series of symptoms. Some imagined noxious substances (*materia peccans*) or fluxes being carried around the body until they fixed on one particular place; the author of *Sacred Disease* described how in epilepsy excess phlegm blocked air from circulating freely around the body, while in frenzy excess bile burnt up the brain's moisture. Others explained how an imbalance led to the inability of a bodily part to function properly— such damage, like heat, swelling, or redness, was a cardinal sign of something wrong.

Once identified, the cause of disease was to be removed allopathically, by applying opposing therapies. Galen attempted to describe drugs in terms of their intensity of action (ranging from imperceptible to deadly), but although some authors also suggested that diseases varied in their intensity, neither he nor they succeeded in calibrating the two together. Ancient pathology always remained an inexact science. See DISEASE; PLAGUE.

V. Nutton, *Medical History*, 1983, 1–34; M. D. Grmek, *Mém. Centre Jean Palerne*, 1984, 53–70.   V. N.

Patrae (Patras), port on the mod. Gulf of Patras in western *Achaea. The city (centred on an acropolis and controlling an extensive plain), was occupied from Mycenaean times, and formed part of the historical Achaean ethnos; see ETHNICITY.

Patrae's early history is obscure. It supported Athens in the *Peloponnesian War (Thuc. 5. 52), possibly via an independent alliance. In 419 *Alcibiades failed to persuade the assembly to extend the city walls to the sea following intervention by pro-Corinthian and Sicyonian elements.

In *c.*280 Patrae joined *Dyme in expelling the Macedonians and reforming the *Achaean confederacy. Losses sustained in repelling the Gallic invasions of 279 encouraged the people of Patrae to disperse into villages throughout their territory (Paus. 7. 18. 6).

In *c.*14 BC *Augustus planted a veteran colony, to which he attached the neighbouring Achaean towns. Excavated remains of the Hellenistic-Roman city include the agora, *odeum, amphitheatre, cemeteries, Augustan shrines and an extensive road system.

A. Rizakis in S. Walker and A. Cameron (eds.), *The Greek Renaissance in the Roman Empire* (1989), 180 ff. and *Achaïe* 1 (Meletemata 20, 1995).
                                                                                C. A. M.

patria potestas was the power of a Roman male ascendant, normally father or grandfather (*paterfamilias*), over descendants through males (*liberi*), provided that his marriage was valid in Roman law (see MARRIAGE LAW, *Roman*), and over adopted children. This power was seen by lawyers as practically unique to Roman citizens. Any male who became independent (*sui iuris*) by being freed from *patria potestas* became a *paterfamilias*, even if he were a child too young to be a father. There was no comparable power held by women. It was not terminated on a child's arrival at any age of majority, but most commonly by the death or voluntary decision of the *paterfamilias*. Thus a woman might leave *patria potestas* if her *paterfamilias* transferred her into the control of a husband, *manus*, or a child of either sex if the *paterfamilias* emancipated him or her (by fictitious sale to a third party, followed by manumission, thrice repeated). *Adoption or becoming the *priest of *Jupiter (*flamen Dialis* (see FLAMINES)) or Vestal Virgin (see VESTA) or exile (see EXILE, *Roman*) of either party ended *patria potestas*; becoming a war captive or the father's insanity suspended it. If a son in power (*filiusfamilias*) married and his wife entered his marital power (*manus*), the daughter-in-law was in his father's power, as were their subsequent children. Sons and daughters in power (*filii/filiaefamilias*) owned no property, though they might be allowed to administer property held by permission of the *paterfamilias*: this was called *peculium*. Anything they acquired (as earnings, by gift or bequest, etc.) belonged in law to the father. Action for delict by a child in power had to be brought against the father. Father's consent was necessary for the marriage of *filii/filiaefamilias* and he might bring about a divorce. The *paterfamilias* also had power of life and death over children. This was exercised soon after birth, when a father chose to acknowledge and rear a child or not to do so. Legends and some accounts from the historic period show *patresfamilias* executing, banishing, or disowning adult children. Private judicial action, normally on the advice of a council, shows the exercise of *patria potestas*; execution of traitorous or insubordinate sons by public officials, such as the famous execution of the Bruti (509 BC) or Torquatus (340) by consular fathers (see IUNIUS BRUTUS, L.; MANLIUS IMPERIOSUS TORQUATUS, T.), exemplify paternal severity in a public role. Sons are portrayed as liable to punishment chiefly for offences against the state, daughters for unchastity. The Augustan adultery law (see AUGUSTUS) gave *patresfamilias* specific rights (with strict provisos) to kill on the spot adulterous daughters taken in the act. In historic times, paternal monopoly of control of property (mitigated by the emperors for serving soldiers: *Digest* 49. 17) will have been more relevant to most *filiifamilias* than the father's theoretical capital jurisdiction. But the *peculium* might in practice be left in a child's control, and moral obligations were reciprocal. Relatively low expectation of life will have meant that many fathers died before their children reached full adulthood. *Sui heredes*, those who gained independence by emerging from *patria potestas* or *manus* on the death of the *paterfamilias*, on his intestacy divided his property equally. If he made a will, he could make his own decisions, but children had a strong moral claim and anyone who would become independent of *patria potestas* on the father's death had to be formally disinherited if not named *heres* (heir and executor): this would not preclude a legacy. *Patria potestas* remained a living institution throughout the classical period and was still important under Justinian (e.g. *Inst.* 2. 9; see JUSTINIAN'S CODIFICATION), while the comparable *manus* atrophied. Its continued relevance in changing times, though probably more prominent in the minds of legal theorists than in those of ordinary fathers and children (M. *Tullius Cicero (1) and his brother Q. *Tullius Cicero (1) fail to invoke it when their teenage sons pose problems) illustrates the Romans' conservatism and ability to adapt and exploit old structures. It was ideologically acceptable and presumably useful or neutral in specific circumstances.

Gai. *Inst.* 1. 55–107, 124–37, 3. 1–44; *Dig.* 1. 6–7. J. A. Crook, *CQ* 1967, 113–22; W. V. Harris in *Studies A. Arthur Schiller* (1986), 81–95; R. P. Saller, in *Continuity and Change* 1 (1986), 7–22, and in *Festschrift Karl Christ* (1988), 393–410.   B. N.; S. M. T.

patriarchy See MATRIARCHY.

patrilocality See MATRILOCALITY.

patricians formed a privileged class of Roman citizens. The word is probably connected with *patres* ('Fathers'), a formal collective term for patrician senators (see SENATE). In the republican period patrician status could be obtained only by birth; and it may be surmised that in early times both parents had to be patricians, if the law of the *Twelve Tables which stated that patricians could not legally marry plebeians (see PLEBS) was a codification of long-established practice rather than an innovation by the Decemviri (see DECEMVIRATES, FIRST AND SECOND); this law was repealed by C. *Canuleius in 445 BC. It is also possible, but not certain, that patrician marriages had to be by *confarreatio*. (See MANUS.)

The origin of the patriciate is disputed. Tradition made it the creation of *Romulus, but also suggested that it was augmented by the admission of aristocratic clans (see GENS) from outside Rome, such as the 'Trojan families' (including the Iulii) who were brought to Rome after the sack of *Alba Longa, and the Claudii, a Sabine clan (see SABINI) that migrated to Rome at the beginning of the republic. The mysterious distinction among the patricians

between the 'greater and lesser clans' (*gentes maiores, gentes minores*) was explained as a consequence of the elevation of new men to the patriciate by the kings. These stories suggest not only that the patriciate originated under the monarchy, but also that patrician status was characteristic of whole clans (though the modern view that only patricians had clans is untenable). Even so, many clans developed plebeian branches, for instance the plebeian Claudii Marcelli.

In contrast with the tradition, some modern scholars believe that the patricians emerged only under the republic. Their strongest argument is that the kings themselves do not appear to have been patricians. But the nature of patrician privilege suggests a different interpretation. One of the most notable patrician prerogatives was their control of affairs during an interregnum (when, it was said, the 'auspices returned to the Fathers'—*auspicia ad patres redierunt*; see AUSPICIUM). Only a patrician could hold the office of *interrex ('between-king'), evidently a relic of the regal period (see REX). It may be correct to say that it was the patricians who chose the king, but that the king could not himself be a patrician. This would explain both the origin of patrician power and the fact that most of the kings were in some sense outsiders (many of them, indeed, foreigners).

There is some evidence that patricians served in the cavalry, and that six centuries were reserved for them; but it is doubtful if this was the definitive criterion of patrician status. The theory that the republican patricians were the descendants of the royal cavalry is probably mistaken.

We know that the patricians monopolized all the important priesthoods, and it is most probable that they were essentially a group defined by religious prerogatives. The nature of their political power is, by contrast, much less certain. Membership of the senate was not confined to patricians, since the senators were formally known as 'Fathers and Conscripts' (*patres et conscripti*) of whom only the former were patricians (the *patrum auctoritas* was confined to them). The most controversial question is whether it was necessary to be a patrician in order to hold a magistracy. Our sources assume that it was, but the Fasti suggest that in the earliest decades of the republic not all consuls were patricians. The patrician monopoly of political office developed gradually in the course of the 5th cent., and was successfully challenged in the 4th by the increasingly powerful *plebs*.

Although by 300 BC the patricians had lost their monopoly of office and of the major priestly colleges, they continued to exercise power out of all proportion to their numbers. Until 172 BC one of the two annual consuls was always a patrician, and they continued to hold half the places in the major priestly colleges as of right. Other priesthoods, such as the *flamines maiores, the *rex sacrorum, and the *Salii, remained exclusively patrician.

As an aristocracy of birth, the patriciate was unable to reproduce itself, and patrician numbers gradually declined. Of around 50 patrician clans that are known in the 5th cent., only 14 still survived at the end of the republic. *Caesar (by a *Lex Cassia*, 45 or 44 BC) and *Octavian (by a *Lex Saenia*, 30) were given the right to create new patricians. Later emperors used their censorial powers to confer patrician status on favoured individuals, who then passed it on to their descendants. The hereditary patriciate seems finally to have disappeared in the third century, but *Constantine revived the title *patricius* as a personal honour, in recognition of faithful service to the empire.

Mommsen, *Röm. Forsch.* 1 (1864), 69 ff., *Röm. Staatsr.* 3 (1887), 3 ff.; A. Magdelain, in *Hommages J. Bayet* (1964), 427 ff.; A. Momigliano, *JRS* 1966, 16 ff., and *Entretiens Hardt*, 13 (1967), 199 ff.; P. C. Ranouil,

patrimonium

Recherches sur le patriciat (1975); F. De Martino, *PP* 1980, 143–60; E. S. Staveley, *Historia*, 1983, 24–57; K. Raaflaub (ed), *Social Struggles in Archaic Rome* (1986); A. Drummond, *CAH* 7²/2 (1989), 178 ff.; R. E. Mitchell, *Patricians and Plebeians* (1991); M. A. Levi, *Patrizi e plebei* (1993). A. M.; T. J. Co.

patrimonium and **res privata** were divisions of the property of the Roman emperors, whose precise nature and interrelation remain obscure. Through a complex process of gifts, legacies, and confiscations the emperors, from *Augustus onwards, accumulated extensive properties in Italy and the provinces. These properties (the *patrimonium*) came to be regarded as crown property which passed on the death of an emperor not to his private heirs but to his successors in office. Overall responsibility for their supervision lay with the *procurator patrimonii* (of ducenarian rank; see DUCENARII) at Rome. In turn the provincial procurators possessed responsibility for the supervision of patrimonial properties in their province. See PROCURATOR. In the late 2nd and early 3rd cents. increasingly frequent epigraphic references throw light on the lower-ranking equestrian and freedmen procurators responsible for individual domains or sets of domains within a province.

The unreliable *Historia Augusta* (*Sept. Sev.* 12. 4) states that *Septimius Severus established the *privatarum rerum procuratio*, although a procurator of the *ratio privata* is attested under Marcus Aurelius (*AE* 1961, 280). The statement in the *Historia Augusta* finds some support from the fact that between 193 and 235 considerable numbers of regional procurators of the *res privata* appear, especially in areas of Italy and in Africa and Asia Minor. In this period both terms are used in the legal sources (*Dig.* 30. 39. 10.; *Cod. Iust.* 2. 1. 7.) in referring to imperial properties. Given the widespread confiscations which occurred under Severus it is a plausible hypothesis that the *res privata* was created at this time to administer the newly confiscated properties which were, thus, treated as distinct from pre-existing crown lands. In the course of the 3rd cent. the post of *procurator patrimonii* at Rome ceases to be attested; the *procurator rationis privatae*, of trecenarius rank, develops into the *magister rationis summae privatae*; and in the 4th cent. into the *comes rei privatae*, head of one of the major financial departments of the late empire. In the 4th cent. *res privata* seems to be the standard term for all imperial property, though *patrimonium* and its cognates are still used (e.g. *Cod. Theod.* 4. 12. 2)

F. Millar, *The Emperor in the Roman World* (1977), ch. 4; Jones, *Later Rom. Emp.* 411 ff. G. P. B.

patrios politeia, 'ancestral constitution (or way of life)', slogan apparently (but see below) used in the late 5th cent. BC at Athens by proponents of *oligarchy, as a reassuring but fraudulent way of justifying constitutional change. See e.g. *Ath. Pol.* 29. 3 (411); also 34. 3 (404), stressing explicitly the role of *Theramenes, which can be conjectured for 411 also. The fraud lay in the implied claim that earlier reformers like *Solon and *Cleisthenes (2) had denied full citizen rights (see CITIZENSHIP, GREEK) to *thetes, the lowest Athenian property class, confining them to *hoplites (*zeugitai) and above. Such general nostalgia for the imagined world of Solon and Cleisthenes is found in the 4th cent. (see e.g. Isoc. 7. 20, although *Isocrates actually avoids the expression *patrios politeia*, and some of the tradition about the 5th cent. may reflect 4th-cent. arguments. See however Thuc. 8. 76. 6 for what may be a near-contemporary echo of the debate about the ancestral constitution at the time of the *Four Hundred; the reference is to oligarchic subversion of the 'ancestral laws'. More explicitly and fully, Xen. *Hell.* 2. 4. 20–1 (speech of Cleocritus)

illustrates and exploits the normal as opposed to fraudulent sense of 'ancestral' political arrangements. *Thrasymachus (DK 85 B1, at end) says that the ancestral constitution was common to all, perhaps a way of saying that the idea was used or abused by all sides. The phrase 'ancestral constitution' had a long life ahead of it; for early Hellenistic Athens contrast Plut. *Phoc.* 27. 5 and Diod. 20. 46. 3.

A. Fuks, *The Ancestral Constitution* (1953); M. I. Finley, *Use and Abuse of History*² (1986), 34 ff.; M. Ostwald, *From Popular Sovereignty to the Sovereignty of Law* (1986), see index; J. T. Roberts, *Athens on Trial* (1994), 60 f., 64 ff. S. H.

Patrocles, Greek commander at *Babylon after 312 BC under *Seleucus (1) I, whom he assisted against *Demetrius (4). Under Seleucus and *Antiochus (1) I, he governed lands from the *Caspian towards India, gathering geographical material including north-west India. About 285 he was sent to explore the Caspian, voyaged up its western and then its eastern sides, learned about Indian trade down the *Oxus, but mistakenly asserted that the Oxus and Jaxartes flowed into the Caspian. His reports confirmed the belief that this sea opened into the supposed near-by Northern Ocean, and, according to *Pliny (1) the Elder, Patrocles claims to have sailed by this imaginary route from the Caspian to India. He was part of a group of Hellenistic explorers and generals who were intent on recording geographical and anthropological discoveries of lands coming under their purview. His work survives only in a few fragments, mostly in *Strabo, and its title and scope are unknown.

FGrH 712; W. W. Tarn, *Greeks in Bactria and India* (1951); J. O. Thomson, *History of Ancient Geography* (1948); S. Sherwin-White and A. Kuhrt, *From Samarkhand to Sardis* (1993), 19. E. H. W.; K. S. S.

Patroclus, in mythology, son of *Menoetius. Having accidentally killed a playfellow, the young Patroclus took refuge with *Peleus (*Homer, *Iliad* 23. 85 ff.). He and his father were kindly received, and Patroclus, who was somewhat older than *Achilles (11. 787), was assigned to him as a personal attendant. For the rest see HOMER; ACHILLES. H. J. R.

patronage, literary

Greek Literary patronage in Greece is associated chiefly with autocratic rulers (though at classical Athens the *chorēgia was a kind of democratization of the patronage principle; see DEMOCRACY, ATHENIAN). The tyrants of Corinth, Pisistratid Athens, Samos, and the Greek cities of Sicily were notable examples, patronizing such writers as *Arion (2), *Alcman, *Anacreon, *Pindar, *Simonides, and *Bacchylides. See TYRANNY and the tyrants there listed. Later *Archelaus (2) of Macedonia collected at his court a literary coterie which included *Agathon, *Timotheus, and *Euripides. Later still the Hellenistic monarchs were often literary patrons, especially the Ptolemies (see PTOLEMY (1)), who established and maintained at *Alexandria (1) the famous *Museum and Library (see LIBRARIES). Similar patronage was exercised by the Attalids in *Pergamum.

D. M. Lewis, *CAH* 4² (1988), 292 ff. and 6² (1994), 154 f.; *DFA*³ 86–91 (democratic Athens); C. M. Bowra, *Pindar* (1964), ch. 3; Fraser, *Ptol. Alex.* ch. 6; C. Préaux, *Le Monde hellénistique* (1978), 214 ff.; S. Hornblower, *Mausolus* (1982), 332 ff.; B. Meissner, *Historiker zwischen Polis und Königshof* (Hypomnemata 99, 1992); P. J. Parsons in A. W. Bulloch, E. S. Gruen, and others (eds.), *Images and Ideologies: Self-Definition in the Hellenistic World* (1993), 152 ff. A. E. A.; S. H.

Roman In Rome, it was not until the 1st cent. BC that literary texts began to circulate through the book-trade, and this was never the only means of publication. Normally, an author received no money from booksellers, and publication of a work was thus costly. A large part of the circulation of contemporary texts at any time took place through the private dispatch of copies or the organization of recitations, through the network of social relations which connected the élite of Rome, of Italy, and eventually of the provinces: an élite which was almost exclusively the public for literary production. Even when, from Augustan times on, the book-trade became more important and the social composition of the reading public broadened, the fame of an author continued to depend considerably on the appreciation of those élite circles who determined fashion and taste in every sector of life. For this reason, writers needed the support of leading members of this élite, both materially if they were not themselves rich and more generally to enable them to become well known and appreciated. Such support was given within the codified framework of patronage and *amicitia* ('friendship') that was a feature of Roman society, in forms which varied according to the respective social and economic level of the author and patron and the degree of prestige enjoyed by intellectual activity in a particular period or with a particular patron. Writers might in one sense be in a similar position to other *clientes* (see CLIENS) and *amici* of lower social standing, and be required to accompany the patron in leisure pursuits, on voyages, etc. But it was clear that they were in a special category because they could offer their patron in exchange something greater than other clients: the appreciation of their patrons' merits by the entire reading public, and even, perhaps, immortality. Similarly, while writers received the same benefits as other clients—presents, hospitality, and social status—they also needed a particular favour, access to the channels of literary reception, and thus that fame amongst the contemporary public which was the necessary precursor of future glory. Writers could limit themselves to inserting the name of their patron in a work as a dedicatee, or they could celebrate the achievements of the patron or his family in epic poems or tragedies (*praetextae*; see FABULA) or compose occasional poems on various aspects of the patron's public or private life. The degree to which the author's inspiration was thus constrained depended on the breadth of vision of the patron and the degree of autonomy that the writer was able to preserve. To an extent patronage did lead to courtly literature, especially in the imperial period, but as a system which brought writers into relation with the social and political élite it may also be seen as forcing writers to confront important political and civic themes, without necessarily cramping their inspiration. The numerous *recusationes* (refusals to compose a work requested by the patron) in Augustan poetry show the broad boundaries allowed by a patron like *Maecenas, albeit in the interests of *Augustus' power. For generosity and foresight, and for the high level of poetry produced, Maecenas' circle came to be viewed as the ideal already in the Neronian period.

In the Archaic period literary activity, with the exception of historiography and oratory, was considered the activity of artisans, and thus the province of people of lower social class. Theatrical pieces were commissioned by the city, and their authors received payment for them from the *aediles in charge of the performances: writers for the theatre continued in later periods also to be the only authors to get paid for their work. But writers also frequently entered into private relationships with one or more leading families interested in their work, sometimes as teachers (a lower class activity, attested for *Livius Andronicus and *Ennius). Through the support of these families they might

obtain their freedom (Livius Andronicus, *Terence; see FREEDMEN) or Roman *citizenship (Ennius) and also probably help with getting their plays performed. *Naevius, Ennius, *Pacuvius, and *Accius wrote *praetextae* celebrating the families of their patrons, and Ennius did the same with his patrons in the *Annales*. Ennius also presents for the first time, as *Cicero noted with distaste (*Tusc.* 1. 3), the figure of the poet who accompanies his patron (M. *Fulvius Nobilior, 189 BC) on a military expedition in order to create a cultured environment and to be better able to celebrate his exploits: a practice known first in the courts of Hellenistic rulers but later common at Rome. Literary patronage was already becoming an ostentatious tool that leading Roman politicians could use for their own ends, rather than a means of support for public benefactors, as Cicero pretended that it still was in his day (*Pro Archia*). The great Roman families from the 2nd cent. BC on welcomed Greek intellectuals more and more warmly as clients to help them with their studies (now a sign of prestige), look after their rich *libraries, and commemorate them in learned works or celebrate them in verse. But as time went on, Latin literary production became separated from its craftsman associations: most of what we have from the 2nd cent. BC on is the work of senators (see SENATE), or more often of *equites and members of well-off provincial families who through talent or family connections came to participate in the life of the Roman élite but were not involved in the normal military and political careers of that élite. Patronage by the great Roman families, which by the 1st cent. BC had made Rome a centre of attraction for Greek as well as Roman intellectuals, reached a peak in the triumviral period and the first years of Augustus' principate, when figures like C. *Asinius Pollio (patron of *Horace and *Virgil, founder of the first public library in Rome; see LIBRARIES), M. *Valerius Messalla Corvinus (patron of *Tibullus, *Ovid, *Valgius Rufus, and others), and Maecenas gathered round them the greatest intellectual figures of the period and gave them both economic support and cultural stimulus. Maecenas in particular, in his role as both close ally of Augustus and amateur of new poetry, gave to Virgil, Horace, *Propertius, and others personal friendship and extremely generous financial support. The concentration of power in a single person made the patronage of the *princeps* himself a sort of state patronage: this was a novelty in Rome, but Augustus used it more and more directly as time went on, particularly after Maecenas faded from power around 20 BC and the regime became more rigid. *Caesar had already begun the process in the brief years of his dictatorship, inducing poets to write of his military exploits and planning a large public library, which Augustus was to realize. In the imperial period, the ostentatious patronage of those figures who had competed for power at the end of the republic no longer had any point. The social prestige of literary pursuits remained high, but private individuals showed their greatness of spirit through a diffuse patronage which on occasions might be notably generous but which was always *ad hoc* and on a restricted scale. The ultimate source of all patronage was the emperor, and this was true also of literary patronage. Some emperors were not interested in letters, but others employed patronage widely to make poetry an instrument of propaganda and courtly celebration, as in the case of *Nero and *Domitian, both of whom gave a powerful impetus to literature in their reigns. Nero introduced into Rome the Greek custom of literary contests (see AGŌNES), taken up again later by Domitian, and this gave Rome for the first time an official occasion for the publication of literary works and a means of public support for writers. *Pliny (2) the Younger offers in his letters an optimistic portrait of imperial literary patronage, but this is contradicted by *Juvenal (*Sat.* 1 and 7), who depicts the Rome of his day as inhabited by a host of starving writers in search of support from greedy and sadistic patrons. *Martial also in part offers a more pessimistic picture, but while he laments that Rome no longer contains a Maecenas willing to give a poor poet the leisure to pursue his art, he also shows throughout his verse how the emperor and private patrons alike provided gifts and favours, sometimes considerable, even to a poet like himself writing within the minor genre of epigram. In fact, it would have been impossible to obtain regular financial support solely from the free exercise of literature—in this sense Juvenal's picture is correct. But literary talent could provide an entrée into the social élite, and thus to the many and various benefits such access to the friendship of the great could provide, from minor gifts to lucrative positions in private or public service. This sort of direct or indirect support could still enable a man like Martial to devote himself full time to literature.

B. K. Gold (ed.), *Literary and Artistic Patronage in Ancient Rome* (1982); P. White, *Promised Verse: Poets in the Society of Augustan Rome* (1993), *Harv. Stud.* 1975, and *JRS* 1978; R. P. Saller, *CQ* 1983; A. Hardie, *Statius and the Silvae* (1983); A. Dalzell, *Phoenix*, 1956. M. Ci.

patronage, non-literary Greek and Roman society were both heavily stratified, and many forms of dependence tied people to their superiors in *wealth, power and *status. The study of these relations is a central part of ancient social history. (Classical Athens was perhaps untypical, though see PATRONAGE, LITERARY (Greek) for the *chorēgia.)

Sources such as the letters of *Cicero and the younger *Pliny (2) combine with the legal evidence and epigraphy to give a more complete picture of patronage in the Roman world. In addition, the special relationship between *patronus* and *cliens among Roman citizens was recognized as being distinctive (e.g. Dion. Hal. *Ant. Rom.* 2. 9), and has received a great deal of scholarly attention.

By the Augustan period it could be believed that *Romulus had assigned all the plebeians at Rome to individual aristocratic patrons. In practice, the title of *cliens* was odious (Cicero, *Off.* 2. 69) and the patterns of formal patronage of this type are hard to discern. Much is made of the institution in early imperial literature, but that may be largely a literary reflection in traditional guise on current problems of status. Certainly the role of *clientes* in late republican politics has been much exaggerated. This is partly because of the tendency to confuse it with other Roman social institutions such as *amicitia (friendship), or *hospitium* (hospitality) and to adduce practices such as the morning *salutatio*, a deferential and potentially humiliating paying of respects, but a practice which entailed only a more general dependence.

Two further forms of patronage, for which the word *patronus* was indeed used, have also complicated the picture. The first is the relationship of the master to a slave or former slave, which had precise definition in Roman law, and which entailed *operae* or duties for *freedmen. This was of course a common form of dependence everywhere in the ancient world, and in Roman cities there must have been many blurred and difficult borderline cases in mixed freedman and free households as to who owed what kind of duty to which former owners or their relatives. The second is the relationship of Roman leaders to whole communities either in Italy or the provinces, and their protection of influential foreigners, for whom they might even obtain the Roman *citizenship. This relationship essentially derived from

the circumstances of Rome's growth as an imperial power, and in many ways drew on the behaviour of Hellenistic kings and their families. Augustus and his successors combined enormous households and very numerous dependents with an unsurpassed range of opportunities for bestowing favours of this second sort on communities and individuals all over the inhabited world. But that did not mean that they ruled through a vast extension of the institution of *clientela*.

Cicero's patronage is our most systematic guide to the late republican practice. He acquired relations with communities in southern Italy on his way to his province of Sicily as quaestor; in the troubles of 63, retainers from *Atella, *Volaterrae, and particularly *Reate gave him their physical support; he had a close tie with the important city of *Cales; around his villa at *Pompeii most of the towns were in his *clientela*; his governorship in Cilicia gave him a special relationship with the whole of *Cyprus; and (in an area where his friend T. *Pomponius Atticus had important financial interests) he had the city of *Buthrotum as clients, and so on. All these places could count on Cicero for *commendatio: a way into the personal politics of Rome, and in particular legal guidance and support. *Civitates* were a natural object of this kind of patronage, but other collectivities, such as *collegia*, acquired patrons in this way too (see CLUBS, ROMAN).

The example of Cicero provides us with an insight into the importance of the general phenomenon of patronage. Chains of this sort of relationship offered a way of dealing with the scale of ancient society: with the mechanics of representing, and making decisions concerning the rival interests of, either very numerous individuals in a large community, or thousands of communities in a world-empire. It thus offered a sort of brokerage, and promoted both active communication and reciprocal exchanges of information and esteem, and served to retain a real political role for patrons under a system in which their constitutional political position had been greatly weakened by the advent of the imperial system. *Commendatio*, moreover, could only work if there were in place agreed principles of comparison and standards of assessment, the maintenance of which fostered cultural cohesion. Finally, the system reflected and maintained change in hierarchic order, and worked against sclerotic immobility, since the effectiveness of chains of influence varied, and the fortunes of the client with them. All of these effects ultimately worked in favour of the social stability which is such an interesting feature of the Roman world. See PATRONUS.

ABSENCE OF PATRONAGE AT ATHENS: P. Millett, in A. F. Wallace-Hadrill (ed.), *Patronage in Ancient Society* (1989), 15 ff.

ROME: P. A. Brunt, *Roman Republican Themes* (1988), 382–442; R. Saller, *Personal Patronage under the Early Empire* (1982); E. Deniaux, *Clientèles et pouvoir à l'époque de Cicéron* (1993); J.-M. David, *Le Patronat judiciaire* (1992). N. P.

patronomos (πατρονόμος), official instituted c.227 BC by *Cleomenes (2) III (Paus. 2. 9. 1) in his reform of Sparta's polity, attested from the 1st cent. BC as Sparta's eponymous magistrate. Roman inscriptions link his duties with the 'Lycurgan customs' (cf. LYCURGUS (2)), so favouring the title's translation as 'guardian of the ancestral traditions'. Probably the first *patronomoi* oversaw Cleomenes' revived *agōgē.

P. Cartledge and A. Spawforth, *Hellenistic and Roman Sparta* (2nd edn. 2002), 201–2; N. Kennell, *ZPE* 85, 1991, 131–7. A. J. S. S.

patronus, at Rome, was a man who gave assistance and protection to another person, Roman or non-Roman, who thereby became his client. In return clients gave their patrons respect, deference and services, which included personal attendance and political support. The social prestige and political influence of a Roman noble was made evident by the size and standing of his clientele, and competition for political office among the republican élite was partly (exactly how much is disputed) a matter of obtaining the support of other powerful individuals and their personal followings. Under the empire patronage was the means by which imperial appointments were dispensed, and was fundamental to the working of the administration (see further CLIENS).

A special type of patronage (which was clearly defined by law) was exercised by a slave-owner over his *freedmen. He retained a certain amount of domestic jurisdiction over them and inherited their property if they died childless or intestate. Patrons and freedmen were often buried together, and inscriptions (especially from the 2nd cent. AD onwards) suggest that genuine feelings of friendship often subsisted between them.

Under the later republic the function of legal assistance by patrons was extended to include cases where practised speakers supported litigants in return for a fee. In 204 BC a *Lex Cincia* (see LEX (2)) forbade the payment of fees to patrons, but this law was frequently circumvented. The forensic *patronus* is to be held distinct from the technical legal adviser or *advocatus* (see ADVOCACY).

Roman generals assumed a general patronage over peoples conquered by them, and this patronage was transmitted to their descendants. As early as 278 BC C. *Fabricius Luscinus took the Samnites as his clients, while the Claudii Marcelli undertook to look after the interests of the province of Sicily (conquered in 210 BC by M. *Claudius Marcellus (1)). The patronage of *Pompey extended widely over the empire; in 83 BC he raised three legions of clients in his home region of Picenum, and his son Sextus *Pompeius could get help in Spain and Asia from his family's clients. It is probable that the emperors too exercised a patronage of this type over the provinces.

A similar form of patronage, which became common under the empire, originated in the action of Roman municipalities, which appointed one or more influential Romans to defend their interests in Rome and to provide them with personal access to the emperor (cf. the list of patrons of *Canusium, *ILS* 6121). During the same period many *collegia* or clubs (see CLUBS, ROMAN) appointed leading men as their patrons in the same way as the municipalities.

In the late empire powerful men offered protection to individual *peasants against the tax collector and other public obligations in return for money, services or even the surrender of the ownership of land. The emperor's legislation against this type of patronage was hardly successful. See PATRONAGE, NON-LITERARY.

M. Gelzer, *The Roman Nobility* (1969; German orig. 1912); R. Saller, *Personal Patronage under the Early Empire* (1982); A. von Premerstein, *Vom Werden und Wesen des Prinzipats* (1937); L. Harmand, *Le Patronat sur les collectivités publiques* (1957); Jones, *Later Rom. Emp.* (1964), 2. 775; R. Van Dam, *Leadership and Community in Late Antique Gaul* (1985), and see bibliog. under 'Cliens'. For patronage over freedmen, M. Kaser, *ZSS* 1938, 88 ff.; S. Treggiari, *Roman Freedmen during the Late Republic* (1969). Municipia: J. Nichols, *ANRW* 2. 13 (1980), 535 ff., and *Hermes*, 1980, 365 ff. Collegia: J. P. Waltzing, *Étude historique sur les corporations professionelles*, (1895), 425 ff., 2 (1896), 367 ff. See also CLIENS.

A. M.; T. J. Co.

patronymics See NAMES, PERSONAL, GREEK and ROMAN.

patrōoi theoi (πατρῷοι θεοί), literally 'gods associated with a father', hence commonly 'ancestral' or 'inherited gods'. There is

a clear similarity between the use of the epithet here and in phrases such as ἱερὰ πατρῷα, ancestral shrines, and οὐσία πατρῷα, a man's patrimony: gods, like their altars, are in sense inherited property (whence the names of *patrōoi theoi* are often followed by a possessive genitive or other similar construction). Two usages can be distinguished: (1) in patriotic appeals (e.g. Aesch. *Pers.* 404) and similar contexts, the *patrōoi theoi* seem to be the whole established pantheon of the state; (2) particular gods are *patrooi* to particular groups or individuals; put in other terms, particular individuals or groups traditionally worship at particular shrines (which they own). Thus in the Thesmophorion of *Thasos a series of altars have been found bearing inscriptions such as '[altar] of *Zeus Patroos of the Neophantideis' (a kinship group), 'of Zeus Alastoros Patroos of the Phastadeis'. At Athens, candidates for the archonship were asked 'if they possessed an *Apollo Patroos and a Zeus of the Courtyard, and where these shrines were' (*Ath. Pol.* 55. 4). Here the cult of a particular *patroos* is in principle universal or at least widespread, though diffused through the separate altars of a series of individual groups; and it was primarily in this sense that Apollo could be said to be *patroos* to the *Ionians (Pl. *Euthyd.* 302b–d), or Zeus to Dorian states; see DORIANS.

Patrōoi theoi normally belonged, it seems, to hereditary extended groups based on fictitious kinship such as the *patra* on Thasos and the *phratry and *genos at Athens; but individual families could probably also have *patrōoi* of their own (cf. Pl. *Leg.* 717b). One Leocrates was accused by *Lycurgus (3) (Lycurg. *Leoc.* 25) of having exported his ἱερὰ πατρῷα, 'family *sacra*', in a crisis.

Zeus *patroos* is sometimes (e.g. Ar. *Nub.* 1468) spoken of as if he were 'Zeus who protects the rights of fathers'; this is an exceptional interpretation of the epithet, not its basic meaning. More common and influential (in modern accounts too) is the idea that an ancestral god is also an ancestor god: we are told for instance that it is as father of the Ionian ancestor *Ion (1) that Apollo is *patroos* to the Ionians (Pl. *Euthyd.* 302b–d; so too with the Zeus *patrōos* of the Dorians, via *Heracles: see Apollod. 2. 8. 4). But the virgin Athena is a *patroa* on Thasos, and there are other like cases; the idea of paternity is not, therefore, fundamental. The emotional appeal of the *patrooi* (the strength of which is visible above all in Lycurgus's speech against Leocrates) derives primarily not from the idea of parenthood but from that of tradition, continuity, the transmission to one's children of that which was one's parents'.

J. Ilberg, 'Patrooi theoi' in Roscher, *Lex.*; C. Rolley, *BCH* 1965.

R. C. T. P.

patrum auctoritas was the assent given by the 'fathers' (*patres*) to decisions of the Roman popular assemblies. The nature of this assent is unclear, but it may have been a matter of confirming that the people's decision contained no technical or religious flaws. The 'fathers' in question were probably only the *patrician senators, not the whole *senate (Livy 6. 42. 10; Sall. *Hist.* 3. 48. 15; Cic. *Dom.* 14. 38; Gaius 1. 3). During the middle republic the *patrum auctoritas* became a formality. A *Lex Publilia* of 339 BC (Livy 8. 12, see PUBLILIUS PHILO, Q.) established that it must be given to new laws before the voting of the *comitia, thus ensuring that the patricians could no longer overturn measures on technical grounds. The rule was extended to elections in the 3rd cent. by a *Lex Maenia* (Cic. *Brut.* 4. 55). The relevance of the *Lex Hortensia* (see HORTENSIUS, Q.) of *c*.287 BC to the *patrum auctoritas* is disputed (cf. App. *BCiv.* 1. 59. 266 with E. Gabba's commentary). The *patrum auctoritas* affected the *comitia curiata* and *centuriata* and (probably) the *comitia tributa*. There is no clear evidence that it also affected the *concilium plebis*. On all these see COMITIA.

Mommsen, *Röm. Forsch.* 1 (1984), 233 ff. and *Staatsr.* 3. 155 ff., 1036 ff.; P. Willems, *Le Sénat de la République romaine*, 2 (1885), 33; De Sanctis, *Stor. Rom.* 2 (1907), 220 ff.; E. S. Staveley, *Athenaeum*, 1955, 3 ff.; V. Mannino, *L'auctoritas patrum* (1979); A. Drummond, *CAH* 7². 2 (1989), 185; T. J. Cornell, ibid. 343.

A. M.; T. J. Co.

Paul, St St Paul, a Roman citizen from *Tarsus, was a convert (see CONVERSION) from Pharisaic to Messianic Judaism as a result of a mystical experience (Gal. 1: 12 and 16) when he believed himself called to be the divine agent by whom the biblical promises about the eschatological ingathering of the pagans would be fulfilled. That transference of allegiance led him to renounce his previous religious affiliations (Phil. 3: 6 f.), even though the form of his religion remains in continuity with apocalyptic Judaism; see RELIGION, JEWISH. We know him as the result of letters which he wrote over a period of about ten years to maintain communities of Jews and gentiles in Rome and several other urban centres in a pattern of religion which enjoined faithfulness to Jesus Christ as the determining factor in the understanding of the Mosaic Law. This subordination of the Law inevitably led to conflict with Jewish and Christian opponents who suspected him of antinomianism and apostasy. He commended Christianity as a religion which was both the fulfilment of the Jewish tradition and also the negation of central precepts like food laws and circumcision, though he was emphatic in his rejection of idolatry. In his letters we have clear evidence of the emergence of identifiable Christian communities separate from Judaism with a loose adherence to the Jewish tradition as interpreted by Paul. At the end of his life he organized a financial offering for the poor in Jerusalem from the gentile churches he had founded. According to *Acts his journey to Jerusalem with this collection preceded his journey to Rome where later Christian tradition suggests that he died in the Neronian persecution. The letters in the New Testament which are widely assumed to be authentic are Romans, 1 and 2 Corinthians, Galatians, Philippians, 1 Thessalonians, and Philemon, and possibly Colossians and 2 Thessalonians. Ephesians, and 1 and 2 Timothy and Titus are probably pseudonymous. This last group of documents indicates the direction of the Pauline tradition after the apostle's death when accredited teachers began to be ordained to ensure the preservation of the apostolic traditions and institutions in the face of emerging *gnosticism and antinomianism. See also CHRISTIANITY; PHARISEES.

H. D. Betz, *Galatians* (1979); W. Meeks, *The First Urban Christians* (1983); C. Rowland, *Christian Origins* (1985); E. P. Sanders, *Paul and Palestinian Judaism* (1977); A. F. Segal, *Paul the Convert* (1990); G. Theissen, *The Social Setting of Pauline Christianity* (1982). C. C. R.

Paul of Aegina, physician, died after AD 642 in *Alexandria (1). Arabic texts ascribe to Paul works on *gynaecology, toxicology, and medical practice and procedures, but extant only is his tract in seven books called the *Epitome of Medicine*, which borrows liberally from *Galen and *Oribasius. Paul outlines the important aspects of medicine, with his *pharmacology (bk. 7) resting on *Dioscorides (2): there are precise accounts of 90 minerals and metals, nearly 600 botanicals, and almost 200 animal products (milks to insects) used as drugs. Paul's summary of *surgery (bk. 6) had wide influence in later Arabic and Latin traditions.

TEXTS I. L. Heiberg, *Paulus Aegineta* 2 vols. (1921, 1924); Eng. trans. F. Adams, *The Seven Books of Paulus Aegineta*, 3 vols. (1844, 1846, 1847).

GENERAL LITERATURE M. Tabanelli, *Studie sulla chirurgica bizantina* (1964); I. Brotses, *Ho byzantinos iatros Paulos ho Aiginetes* (1977); J. Scarborough in *DOP* 1984, 228–32; O. Temkin, *Hippocrates in a World of Pagans and Christians* (1991), 230–1. J. Sca.

Paulinus (1) of Nola (AD 353/4–431), born at Bordeaux, was a favourite pupil of *Ausonius. After governing *Campania (381) and *Magnus Maximus' usurpation in Gaul (383–8), he turned to a Christian ascetic life with his wife Therasia first in Spain then, from 395, as a priest and bishop at *Nola. His poems, mostly in hexameters, celebrated the cult of St Felix of Nola and made him one of the leading Christian Latin poets. Over fifty of his letters also survive, revealing an extensive network of correspondents, including *Augustine. Emotional, devout, often prolix, and occasionally humorous, Paulinus is an important witness to the religious character of his age.

Text ed. W. Hartel, *CSEL* 29, 30; Eng. trans. and notes, P. Walsh (letters 1966, poems 1975). J. T. Lienhard, *Paulinus of Nola and Early Western Monasticism* (1977), with bibliog. J. D. H.

Paulinus (2) of Pella, a Gallo-Roman aristocrat, wrote the *Eucharisticon*, a Christian poem of thanks for his misfortunes, *c.* AD 460, when in his eighties. The grandson of *Ausonius, he was born at Pella but reared at Bordeaux. He experienced the Germanic invasions of 407 and served with the usurper Priscus Attalus (414–15) in Aquitaine. His two sons died young and he was reduced to poverty by barbarian inroads and the dishonesty of his relations but later made a partial recovery when he unexpectedly received payment from a *Goth who had settled on his land.

Text ed. H. G. Evelyn White with trans., *Ausonius*, 2 (1921), 304–51. J. D. H.

Paullus See AEMILIUS PAULLUS.

Paulus, the most learned and technically accomplished Greek poet of *Justinian's reign. Of wealthy family and distinguished education, he served as silentiary (usher), ultimately chief silentiary, under Justinian and Justin II. His major work is an *epic celebrating the rededication of the Church of St Sophia in 562/3, restored after damage in the 557 earthquake; this combines panegyric of emperor and patriarch with architectural description in an intellectual *tour de force* that demonstrates the ability of traditional Homeric epic (see HOMER) to accommodate contemporary Christian themes. A subsidiary section describes the pulpit (*ambo*). The Palatine *Anthology includes about 80 of his epigrams (half on erotic topics, a quarter about works of art), originally from the *Cycle* of his friend, the poet *Agathias.

P. Friedländer, *Johannes v. Gaza und P. Silent.* (1912, repr. 1969); C. Mango, *Art of the Byzantine Empire* (1972), 80–96; *PLRE* 3. 979–80 (Paulus 21); M. Whitby, *CQ* 1985; A. Cameron, *The Greek Anthology* (1993). L. M. W.

Paulus, lawyer. See IULIUS PAULUS.

Pausanias (1), son of the *Agiad regent Cleombrotus (d. 480 BC), and nephew of *Leonidas. As regent for Pleistarchus, he commanded the combined Greek land forces at *Plataea in 479, while his Eurypontid co-king *Leotychides assumed the overall command at sea. Not prone to modesty, he ascribed the Greek victory to his leadership, thereby earning a reminder of his mortality from *Simonides and a rebuke from the Spartan authorities. Nevertheless in 478 he was placed in command of an allied 'Hellenic League' fleet and captured *Byzantium, but his arrogant behaviour and possibly treasonable negotiations with the Persian enemy provoked a mutiny that redounded to the benefit of Athens. Recalled to Sparta for trial on this charge, he escaped conviction and returned to Byzantium, apparently still on official business, since he was entrusted with the *skytalē* (message-stick). Expelled in c.475 by *Cimon, leader of the new Athenian sea-league (see DELIAN LEAGUE), he removed to the Troad (see TROAS) where he was believed to be continuing to negotiate with Persia on his own behalf. He was again recalled to Sparta and tried c.470, but yet again acquitted. His enemies had more success with accusations of complicity with a *helot uprising and an alleged promise of citizenship to helot rebels. To escape arrest by the *ephors, he took refuge in the sanctuary of Athena on the Spartan acropolis, where he was left to starve; but shortly before he died, he was removed from consecrated ground to avoid *pollution. Later, the Spartans made reparations with the erection of two statues and the founding of a hero-shrine in his (and Leonidas') honour; see HERO-CULT.

Hdt. bk. 9; Thuc. 1. 95, 131–4. M. E. White, *JHS* 1964, 140–52; ML p. 60; T. Kelly in J. W. Eadie and J. Ober (eds.), *The Craft of the Ancient Historian: Essays in Honor of Chester G. Starr* (1985), 141–69.   P. A. C.

Pausanias (2), grandson of *Pausanias (1), *Agiad king of Sparta 445–426 and 408–395 BC: his first reign was as a minor during the temporary deposition of his father Pleistoanax. In 403 he undermined *Lysander's dominance in Athens by obtaining command of a *Peloponnesian League expedition against the democratic resistance at *Piraeus, promoting reconciliation between them and the Three Thousand in Athens, and securing a treaty which restored democracy and brought Athens into Sparta's alliance. Back in Sparta he was prosecuted but acquitted. In 395 his army arrived at *Haliartus after Lysander's defeat and retired without battle, partly due to Athenian military opposition. Sentenced to death, he fled to *Tegea. In exile he continued to oppose his enemies in Sparta. He interceded with his son Agesipolis I to save the democratic leaders at *Mantinea in 385, and wrote a pamphlet which seemingly accused his enemies of violating traditional Lycurgan laws (see LYCURGUS (2)) and advocated abolition of the ephorate. The pamphlet probably disseminated much basic documentation about Sparta, such as the 'Great Rhetra', but also contributed significantly to the distorted idealization of her society, the 'Spartan mirage'.

RE 18. 2578–84 (Pausanias 26); PB no. 596; C. D. Hamilton, *Sparta's Bitter Victories* (1979), index; E. David, *PdP* 1979, 94–116.   S. J. Ho.

Pausanias (3), from *Magnesia (2) ad Sipylum (?) (fl. c. AD 150), periegetic writer (see TOURISM), wrote an extant *Description of Greece* (Περιήγησις τῆς Ἑλλάδος) claiming to describe 'all things Greek' (πάντα τὰ Ἑλληνικά); in fact limited essentially to the province of *Achaia with the omission of Aetolia and the islands. Contents: 1. Attica, Megara; 2. Argolis etc.; 3. Laconia; 4. Messenia; 5–6. Elis, Olympia; 7. Achaea; 8. Arcadia; 9. Boeotia; 10. Phocis, Delphi.

His chief concern in his selective account was with the monuments (especially sculpture and painting) of the Archaic and Classical periods, along with their historical contexts, and the sacred (cults, rituals, beliefs), of which he had a profound sense. His work is organized as a tour of the *poleis* and extra-urban sanctuaries of Achaia, with some interest in topography, but little in the intervening countryside. His concern for objects after 150 BC is slight, although contemporary monuments attracted his attention, especially the benefactions of *Hadrian. He wrote from autopsy, and his accuracy (in spite of demonstrable muddles) has been confirmed by excavation. Although his approach was personal, his admiration for old Greece (Athens,

Sparta, Delphi, and Olympia figure prominently) and its great patriots (see 8. 52) belongs to the archaizing enthusiasm for the Greek motherland fanned by the *Second Sophistic and Hadrian's *Panhellenion, which attracted many overseas (especially Asian) Greeks to Antonine Achaia; presumably Pausanias wrote partly with these in mind.

TEXTS W. Jones, with trans. (Loeb, 1918–35); M. Rocha-Pereira, (Teubner, 1973–81); D. Musti, trans. and comm. (1982–).
COMMENTARIES J. Frazer (1898); H. Hitzig and H. Bluemner (1896–1910); N. Papahatzis (1974–81).
STUDIES O. Strid, *Über Sprache und Stil des Periegeten Pausanias* (1976); C. Habicht, *Pausanias' Guide to Ancient Greece*, rev. edn. (1998); C. Bearzot, *Storia e storiografia ellenistica in Pausania il periegeta* (1992); K. Arafat, *Pausanias' Greece* (1996); S. Alcock and others, *Pausanias* (2001).   A. J. S. S.

Pausanias (4) and **Aelius *Dionysius** (3) were important Atticists at Rome in the 2nd cent. AD (see ASIANISM AND ATTICISM). From *Aristophanes (2) of Byzantium, *Didymus (1), *Pamphilus, and others they compiled Attic Lexica, used by *Photius and *Eustathius.

FRAGMENTS H. Erbse, *Untersuchungen zu den attizistischen Lexika* (1950).   P. B. R. F.; J. S. R.

Pausias (4th cent. BC), painter, son and at first pupil of Bryes, then of *Pamphilus, a Sicyonian. According to *Pliny (1) he was the first to paint ceiling-coffers, a claim not supported by archaeology. He liked small pictures of boys and flowers (thereby advancing the art of still life); he also painted a Sacrifice with a frontal view of an ox and Methe i.e. drunkenness personified (in the Tholos at *Epidaurus, about 350 BC) drinking from a glass cup through which her face could be seen. Such subjects displayed the encaustic technique (see PAINTING (TECHNIQUES)) of which he was the first great master. Echoes have been detected in the *Pella mosaics and early *Gnathia vases. See PAINTING, GREEK.

Overbeck, 1062, 1726, 1760–5; M. Robertson, *History of Greek Art* 1 (1975), 485 ff.   T. B. L. W.

Pausilypon, name of an extensive, highly-landscaped villa (παύσων λύπην, sans souci) belonging to *Augustus' luxurious equestrian friend (see EQUITES) P. *Vedius Pollio, and developed by the emperors, on the ridge between *Puteoli and Naples (*Neapolis): now Posilippo. The area is notable for the 700 m. tunnel for the Naples–Puteoli road, probably the work of M. *Vipsanius Agrippa's architect Cocceius; another long gallery forms part of the villa.

R. T. Günther, *Pausilypon* (1913).   N. P.

Pax, the personification of (political) peace, cf. EIRENE. Scarcely heard of before Augustus, she comes (as Pax Augusta) to represent one of the principal factors which made the imperial government both strong and popular, the maintenance of quiet at home and abroad (cf. Tac. *Ann.* 1. 2. 1: Augustus 'seduced everyone with the sweetness of peace'). The most famous, but not the only, monuments of the cult were the *Ara Pacis Augustae and the Flavian Templum Pacis, dedicated AD 75 (see Richardson, *Topog. Dict. Ancient Rome*, 286 f.).

Wissowa, *RK* 334 f.   H. J. R.

pay, political See DEMOCRACY, ATHENIAN, § (2); EKKLĒSIA; LAW AND PROCEDURE, ATHENIAN, § (2).

peace See EIRENE; JANUS; LIBATIONS; PAEAN; PAX; WARFARE, ATTITUDES TO (GREEK AND HELLENISTIC).

peasants are like postholes: it is much easier to see where they ought to have been in the classical world than where they actually were. By 'peasants' most scholars have meant, small-scale, low-status cultivators, whether free, tenant, or otherwise dependent, farming at subsistence level. Such people left little impact on the historical or archaeological record except perhaps in Egypt. Finds of modest farmsteads in archaeological survey or excavation (see ARCHAEOLOGY, CLASSICAL) can rarely be placed on the socio-economic scale with any certainty. Our suppositions are based largely on indirect evidence.

Much of the literary evidence is anecdotal, depicting the peasant as a 'type', e.g. Dicaeopolis (Ar. *Ach.*). Characters sometimes identified as 'peasants' (e.g. *Hesiod) are difficult to place in socio-economic terms, but are highly unlikely to be peasants. The peasant eventually becomes an 'ideal type' in classical literature, redolent of wholesome, simple, 'old-time' ideals (e.g. Verg. *G.* 4). The peasant ethos of self-sufficiency appealed to élite classical writers as a moral ideal, surfacing frequently in treatises on farming (e.g. Xen. *Oec.* 5. 1–17, Cato, *Agr. praef.* 2. 7; Varro, *Rust.* 2. 1–3). Peasants and similar types were romanticized, notably in the *pastoral poetry of the Hellenistic period, though this tradition continued into Roman times, e.g. *Dio Cocceianus' Euboean idyll (Dio Chrys. *Or.* 7; see EUBOEA).

In Athens it is generally assumed that peasants composed the bulk of the citizen population, and were thus the majority in the *ekklēsia* (assembly). It is not certain to what extent this applied to other states. Even in Athens, though many owned small amounts of land, the bulk of the acreage was held by the rich. To what extent the peasantry co-operated or could be mobilized as a political force is much debated. Their geographical distribution is also problematic.

Our view of the peasantry of republican and imperial Rome is equally blurred. Though ancient writers bemoaned the demise of small-scale cultivators in the countryside, recent studies have treated these complaints more as a rhetorical position than reality. The status of Roman 'peasants' is unclear and probably varied regionally. Many may have been tenants of or similarly dependent on the wealthy élite. The place of veterans' allotments and small-town market-centres in the social demography of the Italian countryside has also been much debated. Only in Egypt where there are surviving tax-collection documents from the Ptolemaic and Roman periods are very small-scale cultivators, often tenants, recorded. Though 'peasant values' were an important ideal in Roman thought, we can only guess at the political impact of 'real' peasants.

L. Foxhall, *JRS* 1990, 97–114; P. Garnsey, *Famine and Food Supply in the Graeco-Roman World: Responses to Risk and Crisis* (1988) ch. 4, and *PCPS* 1979, 1–25; M. H. Jameson, *CJ* 1977, 122–45; J. M. Frayn, *Subsistence Farming in Roman Italy* (1979); E. M. Wood, *Peasant Citizen and Slave: The Foundations of Athenian Democracy*, (1988). L. F.

peculium Persons in (someone else's) power could not own property, but, while technically having ownership, a father could allow his son, and a master his slave, to administer certain assets. These assets were known as *peculium* and could be extensive, including money, goods, land and slaves. In practice the assets were regarded as belonging to the son or slave, and a slave given his liberty on condition that he paid a sum of money (*statuliber*) could use his *peculium* to fulfil the condition. Much commercial and financial activity was conducted by slaves with their *peculium*. Where a son or slave entered into a transaction, the father or master was liable to the extent of the *peculium*, subject to deductions, at the time of the judgement and/or to the extent to which the estate of the father or master had profited from the transaction (*actio de peculio et in rem verso*: Gai. *Inst.* 4. 72a). Where the son or slave traded with his *peculium* with his knowledge, the father or master was liable to the extent of the *peculium* without deductions (*actio tributoria*). From *Augustus anything acquired by a son as a result of military service formed his 'service assets' (*peculium castrense*), which he could dispose of as if he were of full capacity. *Constantine I extended this to cover a son's earnings from a range of public offices (*peculium quasi castrense*). The son enjoyed the same right as with the *peculium castrense*, except that until the time of Justinian he could not generally dispose of the assets by will. See SLAVERY.

H. Fitting, *Das castrense peculium* (1871); W. W. Buckland, *The Roman Law of Slavery* (1908); G. Micolier, *Pécule et capacité patrimoniale* (1932). A. F. R.

Pedanius Fuscus Salinator, Gnaeus, senator (see SENATE) from *Barcino (Barcelona), whose character and eloquence were highly rated by *Pliny (2). He was married to *Hadrian's niece Julia, the daughter of L. *Iulius Ursus Servianus. Fuscus was Hadrian's first colleague in the consulship, in AD 118, but is not heard of again. His son of the same names, Hadrian's grandnephew, aspired to the throne, and was forced to suicide at the end of the reign.

Pliny, *Epp.* R. Syme, *RP* 4–5 (1988), 5–7 (1991). A. R. Bi.

pederasty See HOMOSEXUALITY.

Pedius (*RE* 1), **Quintus,** perhaps of Campanian origin, son of an *eques* (see EQUITES) and of Iulia, *Caesar's elder sister (hardly her grandson as Suet. *Iul.* 83 says), served as Caesar's *legatus* (see LEGATI) in Gaul (58–56 BC?) and supported him in 49. Praetor 48, he suppressed the rising of T. *Annius Milo. In 46 he and Q. Fabius Maximus commanded Caesar's forces in Spain; in 45 they took part in the campaign of Munda and and were allowed to triumph. In 44 Pedius inherited one eighth of Caesar's estate but was induced by *Octavian to place it at his disposal. In 43 he became consul with him (19 August), carried a law providing for the trial of Caesar's murderers, and was left in charge of the city during Octavian's negotiations with M. *Antonius (2) (Mark Antony) and M. *Aemilius Lepidus (3) at Bononia. Ordered to initiate the *proscriptions, he obeyed but died of anxiety over his task and the future.

Syme, *RR*, see index; T. P. Wiseman, *CQ* 1964, 129. G. W. R.; T. J. C.; E. B.

Pedius (*RE* 3), **Sextus,** a Roman lawyer probably of the mid-2nd cent. AD, known only from citations by *Iulius Paulus and *Domitius Ulpianus which point to a powerful mind. He may be identical with the *suffect consul Sex. Pedius Hirrutus of 158 or a member of the same family. He wrote on stipulations and on the *praetor's *edict; Ulpian repeatedly cites his views on the edict of the curule aediles.

Lenel, *Pal.* 2. 1–10; Bremer (1901), 111, 79–99; *PIR*[1] P 149; *HLL* 4 (forthcoming) § 421. 1; Kunkel (1967), 168–9; A. Cenderelli, *Studia et documenta historiae et iuris*, 1978, 371–428. T. Hon.

Pegae See MEGARA.

Pegasus (1), in mythology the immortal winged horse who carries the thunder and lightning of *Zeus; he was born from Medusa's severed neck (see GORGO) when she was pregnant by *Poseidon (Hes. *Theog.* 278–86). Pegasus was caught and tamed at the fountain of Pirene at *Corinth by the hero *Bellerophon, with the help of *Athena Chalinitis or of Poseidon (Paus. 2. 4. 1; cf. Pind. *Ol.* 13. 63–86). He helped Bellerophon to kill the *Chimaera, the *Amazons, and the Solymi (Pind. ibid. 87–90; Apollod. 2. 3. 1–2). Bellerophon took vengeance on Stheneboea by flinging her off Pegasus from a great height into the sea (Eur. *Stheneboea*); and in turn was himself flung off when he tried to fly on him to *Olympus (1) (Eur. *Bellerophon*). Pegasus was said to have created various springs from the earth by a stamp of his hoof, including Hippocrene on Mt. *Helicon near the *Muses' sacred grove, and another spring of that name at *Troezen (Paus. 9. 31. 3, 2. 31. 9). Pegasus' birth is represented in the early archaic pediment of *Corcyra, and he appears on early coins of Corinth, the city with which he is most closely connected by legends. With Bellerophon he is a popular subject in art from before the mid-seventh century, where their attack on the Chimaera first appears in Corinthian vase-painting (see Brommer, *Vasenlisten*³, 292–8; *LIMC* 7). In Roman times Pegasus became a symbol of immortality.

H. J. R.; J. R. M.

Pegasus (2) (*RE* 4), **(Plo?)tius**, an erudite Roman lawyer ('a book, not a man'), son of a naval captain, who despite his father's low status as a freedman became suffect consul about AD 71, when he was responsible for two important decrees of the senate. He governed *Dalmatia and was urban prefect (**praefectus urbi*) under *Domitian (Juv. *Sat.* 4. 71–81). He succeeded *Proculus as head of the school named after the latter and is cited by later writers but no texts from his work, loosely called *Ius Pegasianum* ('Law according to Pegasus'), have survived.

Lenel, *Pal.* 1. 9–12; Bremer (1901) 111 199–210; *PIR*¹ P 164; *HLL 3* (forthcoming) § 396.1; Kunkel (1967) 133–4; E. Champlin, *ZPE 32* (1978), 269–78; Syme, *RP 5.* 611 ff. T. Hon.

Peiraeus See PIRAEUS.

Peitho, the personification of 'Winning Over' (Buxton 49 f.), more loosely, 'Persuasion', that makes woman available to man in the context of love and marriage. Her divine status is not fixed, allowing *Euripides' wilful lines (fr. 170): 'There is no shrine of Peitho except words, ɪ And her altar is in human nature.' Thus she appears as a minor figure in the entourage of *Aphrodite (like Pothos and Himeros—'longing' and 'desire'), e.g. on vases from the early 5th cent. onwards, or as an epithet of Aphrodite or *Artemis. More substantially, she has a shrine at *Sicyon connected with Apollo and Artemis (Paus. 2. 7. 7), whilst at *Argos (2) there is a shrine of Artemis Peitho founded by Hypermestra (Paus. 2. 21. 1). At Athens *Theseus established the worship of Aphrodite Pandemos and (of?) Peitho (Paus. 1. 22. 3), where she has a priestess and receives annual sacrifices (Isoc. 15. 249). Her name is used at Argos (2) for the aunt or wife of the culture-hero *Phoroneus (see CULTURE-BRINGERS), and in *Hesiod for an Oceanid (*Theog.* 349; see NYMPHS) and a Lady Peitho (*Op.* 73). The existence of Peitho from early times perhaps shows something about men's awareness of the independent minds of *women.

LIMC 3. 1 (1984), 121 ff. and 7.1 (1994), 242 ff.; R. G. A. Buxton, *Persuasion in Greek Tragedy: A Study of Peitho* (1982), ch. 2.; F. Voigt, *RE 19* (1937), 194–217. K. D.

Pelagius Now agreed to have been British by birth, educated in rhetoric and possibly in law, Pelagius settled in Rome after AD 380. Noted for his *asceticism, though formally neither monk nor priest, he enjoyed (like *Jerome, Priscillian (see PRISCILLIANISTS), and *Rufinus (2)) the patronage of Christian aristocrats, especially women, and responded similarly to their interest in scripture. His *Letter to Demetrias* is a vivid monument. His commentaries on Epistles of *Paul are straightforward and polished, following in a Roman tradition dating to Marius *Victorinus and including *Ambrosiaster, reminiscent of the 'Antiochene' school, but informed also by Latin translations of *Origen (1). He was inevitably engaged with protagonists of the controversy over Origen's theology. His asceticism was moderate, his attachment to freedom intense. He aroused the scorn of Jerome for the one and criticized *Augustine on account of the other. Anxious to maintain a balance between *Manichaeism and a disparagement of virginity, he rejected current views of original sin, defending the justice of God and the individual's ability to rise by deliberate choice above moral weakness. Protected in Rome by his patrons, he left the city at the time of the Gothic sack (see GOTHS) in AD 410, taking brief refuge in Africa and seeing his supporter Cælestius condemned at the Council of Carthage in 411. Pelagius moved east and was supported at synods by John of Jerusalem in 415. Western enemies in both Africa and Rome were relentless, however, and were reinforced by imperial condemnation in 418 (*Coll. Quesnelliana* 14, 19, *PL* 56. 490–3, 499–500. See also *C.Th.* Sirm. 6 of AD 425). The remaining course of his life and the circumstances of his death are unknown. The soundness of his judgement has been hard to suppress, in spite of Augustine's reputation, and was proliferated in numerous pamphlets and defended by Julian of Eclanum.

WORKS Souter, *Pelagius's Expositions of Thirteen Epistles of St Paul*, 3 vols. (1922); see now also T. de Bruyn, *Pelagius's Commentary on St Paul's Epistle to the Romans* (1992) (includes full introd. and bibliog.); B. R. Rees, *The Letters of Pelagius and his Followers* (1991) (ET with full refs. to edns.).

STUDIES Best modern study: B. R. Rees, *Pelagius: A Reluctant Heretic* (1988). Still important: G. de Plinval, *Pélage* (1943); R. F. Evans, *Four Letters of Pelagius* (1968), and *Pelagius: Inquiries and Reappraisals* (1968); O. Wermelinger, *Rom und Pelagius*, (1975). See also F. G. Nuvalone and A. Solignac, *Dict. Spir.* 12. 2 (1986), 2889–942. P. R.

Pelasgians (*Πέλασγοι*), a mythic population-group mentioned by *Homer (*Il.* 2. 840, 17. 301) as Trojan allies 'from Larisa' (apparently in *Thrace). In Homer's Greece, *Achilles' domain includes 'Pelasgian Argos' (*Il.* 2. 684) and Achilles worships 'Pelasgian *Zeus' of *Dodona (16. 233); in *Od.* 19. 177 Pelasgi are among the mixed population of *Crete. Thus installed in the heroic age as a group with an Aegean home, 'Pelasgians' became a descriptive category for the *Ur*-peoples of the Aegean more generally, as with *Herodotus (1), who ascribes the minority-language of the Crestonians in *Chalcidice a Pelasgic origin (1. 57); since the Athenians claimed to be autochthonous (see AUTOCHTHONS), they too were 'Pelasgians'. Myths of Pelasgian colonization in (especially central) Italy, including Rome, essentially reflect the desire to Hellenize, first *Etruscan, then Roman, origins; cf. HELLENISM. See also PELASGUS.

D. Briquel, *Les Pélasges en Italie* (1984). A. R. B.; A. J. S. S.

Pelasgiotis, the most important and densely populated of the four Thessalian *tetrades* (districts). Organized by Aleuas the Red *c.*550–500 BC, it was based on land seized by the Thessalians from the so-called *Pelasgians, earlier occupants of what today is the eastern plain of Thessaly. As the term 'tetrad' indicates, this district like the three others originally comprised only four cities: *Larissa, *Crannon, Scotussa, and *Pherae. From *c.*500 BC the Thessalians extended the limits of the Pelasgiotis up to *Tempe and the edges of Mts. *Ossa and *Pelion. The Perrhaebian, Magnesian, and Aenianian cities on the plain were integrated into the

Pelasgus

Pelasgiotis (Atrax, Argussa, Condaea, Mopsium, Elatea, Gyrtum, Sycurium, Armenium). The Thessalians of Pherae even managed to gain access to the sea: *Pagasae and Pyrasus formed part of the tetrad until *c*.350 BC, when *Philip (1) II of Macedon decided to take control of these two ports himself along with their revenues. The agricultural wealth of the eastern plain around Larissa and Pherae formed the basis for the economic and political strength of these two cities, and their rivalry was a determinant of Thessalian history in the 5th and 4th cents. BC. By contrast, Crannon and Scotussa, sited in the central Revenia hills, remained relatively unimportant.

F. Gschnitzer, *Hermes*, 1954, 451 ff.; E. Kirsten in A. Philippson, *Griechische Landschaften*² 1 (1953), 259 ff.; B. Helly, *L'état Thessalien: Aleuas le Roux, les tétrades et les tagoi* (1995). B. H.

Pelasgus, eponym of the *Pelasgians, the mythical pre-Hellenic inhabitants of Greece. A hero of that name is found in *Arcadia, *Argos (2), and *Thessaly, i.e. the regions said to have been occupied by the Pelasgians. The Arcadians claimed Pelasgus as their first-born man, king, and godlike inventor of culture (he was the son of Earth, Asius in Paus. 8. 1. 4–6; Apoll. 3. 8. 1). According to one genealogy, he was the son of *Niobe and *Zeus, father of *Lycaon (3) (Paus. 8. 2. 1; Apoll. 3. 8. 1; Strabo 5. 2. 4) who in turn had fifty sons, the eponymous founders of the Arcadian cities. The Argive Pelasgus was king at the time of the arrival of *Danaus and the Danaids (Aesch. *Suppl.* 250); he welcomed *Demeter during her search for *Persephone and built a temple for her as Pelasgis (Paus. 2. 22. 1). His daughter Larissa (Hygin. *Fab.* 145. 2) gave her name to the Argive citadel (Paus. 2. 24. 1). Son of Larissa and *Poseidon in Thessalian legend, Pelasgus left his native Peloponnese with his brothers *Achaeus (1) and Phthius and settled in *Thessaly, from then on called Haemonia. They divided the land into three parts which were named after them Achaea (i.e. Achaea Phthiotis, see PHTHIOTIS), *Phthiotis, and *Pelasgiotis: Dion. Hal. *Ant. Rom.* 1. 17. H. J. R.; B. C. D.

Peleus, in mythology son of *Aeacus, king of *Aegina, and Endeis. He and *Telamon (1) killed their half-brother *Phocus (Apollod. 3. 12. 6), at which their father banished them both (see EXILE, Greek), and Peleus went to Phthia (see PHTHIOTIS) where he was purified (see PURIFICATION, GREEK) by Eurytion, son of Actor, and married his daughter *Antigone (2). But at the Calydonian boar-hunt (see ATALANTA; MELEAGER (1)) he accidentally killed Eurytion and was again exiled. This time he reached *Iolcus, where *Acastus son of Pelias purified him, and he took part in Pelias' funeral games in which he wrestled with Atalanta. But Astydamia, Acastus' wife, fell in love with him; and when he refused her advances she sent a lying message to Antigone that Peleus was about to marry Acastus' daughter Sterope. Antigone hanged herself. Astydamia then lied to Acastus that Peleus had tried to rape her. Acastus, unwilling to kill the man whom he had purified, instead took him hunting on Mt *Pelion and hid his sword while he slept, thus leaving him defenceless against the *Centaurs. Either the gods sent Peleus a sword (Ar. *Nub.* 1063 with schol.) or Chiron gave him back his own sword (Apollod. 3. 13. 3). So he escaped, and took vengeance on Astydamia by capturing Iolcus and cutting her to pieces. He was given the extraordinary privilege of marriage to the goddess *Thetis, though he had to win her by wrestling with her while she changed into many different shapes—fire, water, wind, tree, bird, tiger, lion, snake, and cuttle-fish. The gods came to their wedding-feast and brought gifts. But Thetis left Peleus because he interfered when she tried to make their son *Achilles immortal by burning

away his mortality (Apollod. 3. 13. 6). In old age Peleus was alone and afflicted (*Il.* 24. 486–9), but finally in death was reunited with Thetis and made immortal (Eur. *Andr.* 1253 ff.).

His wrestling at the funeral games for Pelias, his wrestling with Thetis, their wedding, and his bringing the infant Achilles to be brought up by Chiron, are favourite subjects in 6th- and 5th-cent. art (the last already in the mid-7th cent.); he also appears in pictures of the Calydonian boar-hunt.

Brommer, *Vasenlisten*³, 316–31; J. R. March, *The Creative Poet* (BICS Suppl. 49, 1987), 3–26; LIMC 7. H. J. R.; J. R. M.

Pelias, in mythology, son of *Tyro and *Poseidon and father of *Alcestis; his name was etymologized from the dark (πελιός) mark on his face left by the kick of a horse when he was exposed as a child (Apollod. 1. 9. 8). Already in *Hesiod he is portrayed as an evil man (*Theog.* 995–6); when king of *Iolcus he devised the expedition for the Golden Fleece to rid himself of *Jason (1)'s rightful claims to his throne. After the expedition Jason and *Medea persuaded his daughters to cut him up so that Medea could rejuvenate him by boiling; thus did *Hera punish him for neglecting to honour her. The funeral games in his honour were a famous subject for Archaic epic and vase-painting.

Scherling, RE 19. 317–26; P. Dräger, *Argo Pasimelousa* (1993); LIMC 7. 1 (1994), 273 ff. R. L. Hu.

Peligni See PAELIGNI.

Pelion (τὸ Πήλιον ὄρος), a mountain of over 1,615 m. (5,300 ft.) in Thessalian Magnesia (see THESSALY). It was the reputed home of the centaur Chiron (see CENTAURS). The mountain system of Pelion with that of *Ossa cut off the plain of *Pelasgiotis from the Aegean. On the east the steeply rising coast was harbourless, but beneath its south-western slopes, which were fertile and enjoyed a mild climate, it sheltered good harbours on the Bay of Volo. H. D. W.

Pella, city of *Macedonia, situated beside the river Lydias, navigable from Pella to the sea (Livy 44. 46; Strabo 7. fr. 20), at the crossroads where the route down the Axius valley meets the *Via Egnatia. Known to *Herodotus (1) (7. 123) and *Thucydides (2) (2. 1. 4), it was developed by *Archelaus (2) and became the largest Macedonian city (Xen. *Hell.* 5. 2. 13). Recent excavations have revealed besides cemeteries dating from the time of Archelaus the layout of its grid street-plan, of wide streets with a regular covered system of drains. Excavated houses are single storey, built on a most generous scale. The agora, approached by a broad street, covers 70,000 m² (84,000 sq. yds.), surrounded by continuous colonnades. In the northern part of the city, the remains of a royal palace (see PALACES) have been found.

Excavation reports in *Arch. Rep.* esp. 1981 and following; recent work in *AEMΘ* 1 (1987), 119 f., 137 f.; M. Lilibaki-Akamati in S. Drougou (ed.), *Hellenistic Pottery from Macedonia* (1991). R. A. T.

Pelopidas, Theban general. First attested at the Spartan siege of *Mantinea (386), he was exiled by the pro-Spartan junta (382). His contribution to the liberation of *Thebes (1) (379/8) earned the first of thirteen boeotarchies (see FEDERAL STATES). Returning from an attack on *Orchomenus (1), he inflicted a psychologically important defeat on two Sparta *morai* at *Tegyra (375). At *Leuctra (about which he had a prophetic dream) he and the *Sacred Band helped to execute *Epaminondas' battle-plan. After the historic Theban invasion of *Laconia (370/69), he was (like Epaminondas) acquitted on a politically inspired charge of acting *ultra vires*. In 367 he visited *Artaxerxes (2) II, extracting a rescript which suited Theban interests but proved hard to enforce. Latterly his special interest was *Thessaly. In 369 he threatened *Alexander (5) of Pherae and freed *Larissa from *Alexander (2) of Macedon, receiving *Philip (1) as a hostage. In 368 he bargained with Ptolemaeus (Alexander's murderer), but was arrested by Alexander of Pherae (Boeotian military intervention eventually 'negotiated' his release). In 364 Thessalians under his command worsted Alexander of Pherae at *Cynoscephalae, but he was killed. (The Thessalians erected his statue at Delphi, SEG 22. 460.) With Epaminondas (their friendship is much stressed in the tradition esp. Plut. Pelop., for which see Westlake, CQ 1939, 11 ff.) he embodies the post-Leuctra 'Theban Hegemony', though neither consistently exercised political control in Thebes.

RE 19, 'Pelopidas'; J. Buckler, Theban Hegemony (1980); J. Roy, CAH 6² (1994), ch. 7.   C. J. T.

Peloponnese See PELOPONNESUS.

Peloponnesian League, the earliest known and the most long-lived Greek summachia or offensive and defensive *alliance. The name is modern and strictly inaccurate, since the alliance was neither all- and only Peloponnesian nor a league (the members were not all allied to each other, and when no League war was in progress, members were free to carry on separate wars even with other members); the usual ancient name was 'the Lacedaemonians (Spartans) and their allies'. In the 6th cent. Sparta used personal ties of xenia (see FRIENDSHIP, RITUALIZED) to negotiate treaties of alliance with Peloponnesian cities, the first being with either *Tegea or *Elis. Some hold that a period of separate treaties with individual cities was followed shortly before 500 by the organization of the League as a permanent alliance (see CLEOMENES (1) I); others date the organization earlier (see CHILON), others later. Allies swore to have the same friends and enemies as Sparta whithersoever they might lead; Sparta did not reciprocate these oaths, but did bind itself to go to the aid of an ally attacked by a third party with all strength and to the utmost of its ability. Sparta thus summoned and presided over the assembly of its allies, each of whom had one vote. Sparta could not be committed by the allies to a policy which it did not approve, but did require the approval of a majority vote of an allied congress to implement any joint policy it advocated. In war Sparta always held the command, appointed Spartan officers to levy and command allied contingents, and decided how many troops each ally must commit and the terms of engagement. In peace the League's main function from Sparta's standpoint was to act as a shield around its vulnerable domestic economic base (see HELOTS); for the allies the benefits were less clear-cut, except for aristocrats and oligarchs whom Sparta tended to champion, not always successfully, against incipient democratic movements. After victory over Athens in 404 a tendency to transform the League into an empire became more apparent, although tribute was never directly levied on League members, and the violations of allied political autonomy more flagrant. The sharp decline in Spartiate manpower was one of the major reasons behind a reform of the organization in the early 370s, but this did not halt the disaffection which culminated in allied satisfaction at Sparta's humiliation on the battlefield of *Leuctra in 371. Five years later, on the initiative of *Corinth, always the most important single ally, the League quietly dissolved.

Thuc. 1. 19, 67–86, 144. G. E. M. de Ste. Croix, The Origins of the Peloponnesian War (1972), ch. 4, app. 5, xvii–xxi; F. Gschnitzer, Ein neuer spartanischer Staatsvertrag (1978); J. B. Salmon, Wealthy Corinth: A

History of the City to 338 BC (1984), esp. ch. 17; P. Cartledge, Agesilaos and the Crisis of Sparta (1987), esp. ch. 13; W. T. Loomis, The Spartan War Fund: IG V. 1, 1 and a New Fragment (1992); G. L. Cawkwell, CQ 1993, 364 ff.   P. A. C.

Peloponnesian War, of 431–404, fought between *Athens and its allies (see DELIAN LEAGUE) on the one hand and *Sparta and its allies (see PELOPONNESIAN LEAGUE) on the other; most of it (down to 411) was recorded by the great historian *Thucydides (2) and that is the most interesting thing about it. The first ten years were the *Archidamian War, a title first used by *Lysias, as far as we know, for what Thucydides called the 'ten-years war', 5. 25. 1. This phase was ended by the inconclusive Peace of *Nicias (1). (Strabo 13. 600 subdivides yet further, referring to the 'Pachetian' part of the Peloponnesian War, i.e. the first half of the present book 3 of Thucydides, which deals with the revolt of *Mytilene; the name is from the Athenian commander Paches). The second main phase of the whole war, which Thucydides insisted on regarding as a unit, began with Athens' disastrous expedition to *Sicily (415–413) and continued with the 'Ionian' (cp. Thuc. 8. 11. 3) or 'Decelean' (Strabo 9. 396) War until the Athenian surrender in 404. That is the Second or Main Peloponnesian War. The First Peloponnesian War is the modern name for the struggle between Athens and Corinth (with Sparta occasionally exerting itself) in c.461–446; it was ended by the *Thirty Years Peace. See further ARCHIDAMIAN WAR; ATHENS; CORINTH; GREECE (PREHISTORY AND HISTORY); SPARTA.

On the First Peloponnesian War see D. M. Lewis, CAH 5² (1992), ch. 5. On the main war D. Kagan, The Outbreak of the Peloponnesian War (1969), The Archidamian War (1974), The Peace of Nicias and the Sicilian Expedition (1981), and The Fall of the Athenian Empire (1987); D. M. Lewis and A. Andrewes CAH 5² (1992), chs. 9–11; on the expressions used for the war and its sub-divisions see S. Hornblower, JHS 1995, 60 n. 65.   S. H.

Peloponnesus the large peninsula of southern mainland Greece, joined to *Attica and *Boeotia by the Isthmus of *Corinth, a mountainous area of complex topography. All the north is highland, from the lower chains of the Argolic peninsula (see ARGOS (2)) westwards successively through Cyllene (Ziria), Chelmos, Panachaicum, and to the south Erymanthus and Maenale towards the centre of the Peloponnese: all with extensive areas above 1,500 m. Three chains run southwards from this mass, the lowest to the west beginning with Lykaion and running through *Ithome to form the Messenian peninsula (see MESSENIA); Taygetus (see LACONIA) in the centre, with the highest summit of the Peloponnese (2,409 m.), forming the peninsula now called the Mani, running to Cape *Taenarum (Matapan); and Parnon to the east, running to cape *Malea. The (mainly limestone) mountains are agriculturally unproductive, being densely wooded, and used for forest-grazing and other *pastoralism.

Within this armature are located a number of sizeable alluvial lowlands (especially the plain of Argos; the Eurotas valley; the Pamisus valley and plain of Messenia; the *Alpheus valley and plain of *Elis; and the central basin of *Megalopolis), and many other small basins, including a series of characteristic polje in the limestone mountains. Along the north and west coasts are well-watered and well-drained terraces, the uplifted remnants of earlier coastal plains. Except where drainage was very poor, the agriculture of all these lowlands supported nucleated settlements at some period. The deep gulfs between the mountain chains provided some good harbours; the capes were all dangerous, Malea notoriously so. Smaller landfalls were numerous, and are not far apart even on the most mountainous coasts (like eastern Laconia).

Pelops

The landscape helped the regions retain some identity throughout antiquity. Elis to the north-west with the panhellenic sanctuary of *Olympia was the region of the Alpheus plain and adjacent coasts. The steep northern valleys, their outfalls, and the coastal strip made up *Achaea. The central mountains and basins, including the plain of Megalopolis, constituted *Arcadia; the south-western peninsula and Pamisus plain Messenia; the Eurotas valley and south-eastern peninsula Laconia. The Isthmus and its adjacencies were controlled by Corinth; Argos was the principal focus of its plain (and some neighbouring districts: but the Saronic Gulf and the ambiguous allegiances of *Aegina confused the political geography of this area).

The siting of major centres has varied, though a perennial factor has been the combination of control of fertile bottomland and routes within and away from the Peloponnese. Thus the sea/land crossroads of the Isthmus gave Corinth rather stable geographical circumstances, but similar natural advantages in the Roman period, when routes to north-western Greece and beyond were of ever greater importance, were enjoyed by *Patrae (which became a *colonia*), at the western mouth of the Corinthian gulf and close to the easy crossing from Rhium to Antirrhium. The plain of Argos supported important communities in the bronze age, throughout antiquity, and again in the medieval and early modern periods. To the south Lacedaemon/*Sparta was a central place for the Laconian plain throughout antiquity; its inhabitants fled to the coastal refuge of Monemvasia in the troubles thereafter, but in late Byzantine times Mistra used the resource base of the central Eurotas plain once again. Bronze-age settlements in Messenia were of considerable importance, and after the end of Spartan control, *Messene as a city had some prosperity; the Hellenistic and Roman periods saw a growing role for the southern coastal cities of Gythium and *Methone (2) which were useful stations on long-haul east–west routes (an importance which Methone in particular retained until the 19th cent.). The inland districts supported a considerable population, particularly the cities of eastern Arcadia, *Tegea, *Mantinea, and *Orchomenus (2), the three ingredients of Byzantine and early modern Tripolis; internal routes played a part here.

'Peloponnesos' is first attested in the *Cypria* (see EPIC CYCLE) and the Homeric Hymn to Apollo, and the inhabitants seem to have thought of themselves as really resembling islanders (in Mediterranean comparison slightly smaller than Sicily, twice the size of Cyprus). The fragmentation of the topography encouraged various forms of federalism (see FEDERAL STATES) and *sympoliteia; the hegemony of Sparta promoted a regional solidarity, though it was never complete. In later times geographers saw the Peloponnese on a smaller scale, likening it to a plane-tree leaf (the medieval name Morea derives from a similar analogy to the mulberry) or to the acropolis of Greece (Strabo 8. 334).

W. Leake, *Travels in the Morea* (1830); E. Curtius, *Peloponnesos* (1851–2); A. Philippson, *Der Peloponnes* (1892); R. Baladié, *Le Péloponnèse de Strabon* (1980).   N. P.

Pelops, father of *Atreus, a hero worshipped at *Olympia and believed to be the eponym of the Peloponnese (see PELOPONNESUS). As a child, he was killed and served up by his father *Tantalus, in order to test his guests the gods. Only *Demeter, mourning the loss of her daughter, failed to notice, and ate part of his shoulder; the other gods restored him to life and replaced his shoulder with ivory. Later, he wooed *Hippodamia, daughter of Oenomaus of *Pisa, the area round Olympia.

Oenomaus had promised his daughter to any man who could carry her off in a chariot and escape his pursuit; unsuccessful contenders would be killed. Though skilled in horsemanship through the favour of his former lover *Poseidon, Pelops won (in the usual version) by bribing Oenomaus' charioteer Myrtilus to loosen the linchpins on his master's chariot. Oenomaus was thus killed, but in dying cursed Pelops; or he was cursed by Myrtilus, whom he killed on the homeward journey, either because he was ashamed by the manner of his victory or because Myrtilus loved Hippodamia. The curse took effect only in the next generation; Pelops himself prospered greatly, and had six sons by Hippodamia.

*Pindar speaks of Pelops' burial near the great altar at Olympia 'amidst blood-offerings' (*Ol.* 1. 90–3), but no burial was found in the tumulus there, and *Pausanias (3) (6. 22. 1) records that the hero's bones were kept in a chest near the temple of *Artemis Kordax at Pisa. However, just as Pelops' myth suggests a connection with the *Olympian games, so his cult was most prominent at Olympia, where he had a large sanctuary inside the Altis grove; numerous archaic dedications were found here. There was a ritual opposition between this cult and that of Olympian *Zeus, whereby those who had eaten meat sacrificed to Pelops were refused entry to the precinct of Zeus (presumably for a specified time, or until purified; see PURIFICATION, GREEK).

In art, Pelops appears at Olympia itself, where the preparations for the chariot-race are the subject of the east pediment of the temple of Zeus, and the preparation and race are found occasionally in 5th- and 4th-cent. vase-painting (Brommer, *Vasenlisten*[3], 539–40.)

Pindar, *Olympian* 1 with scholia; Paus. 5. 13. 1–7; Apollod. *Epit.* 2. 6–9. H. V. Herrmann, in *Stele: Festschrift Kondoleon* (1980) 59–74; A. Brelich, *Gli eroi greci* (1958) 94–106; Burkert, *HN* 93–103; *LIMC* 7. 1 (1994), 282 ff.   E. Ke.

peltasts Term originally used of Thracians (see THRACE) equipped with a small, light shield (*peltē*), but later probably of any light infantry similarly armed, their main offensive weapon being the javelin. Judging by contemporary vase-paintings, *Pisistratus may have recruited some, but their first certain appearance was at *Pylos (Thuc. 4. 28. 4), where they are said to have come from *Aenus, in Thrace. They were subsequently used by *Brasidas in *Chalcidice (e.g. Thuc. 4. 111. 1) and in 409 *Thrasyllus (1) had 5000 sailors equipped as peltasts (Xen. *Hell.* 1. 2. 1). They were particularly useful in a skirmishing role, or as an advanced guard, for example for seizing passes and other strategic points. They could not hope to defeat *hoplites in pitched battle, but if they managed to keep their distance, they could wear them down by missile fire, as at *Amphipolis in 422 (Thuc. 5. 10. 9). Their greatest exploit was the defeat of a Spartan *mora* (brigade) near *Corinth in 390 (Xen. *Hell.* 4. 5. 11–8), when they they were commanded by *Iphicrates. With the introduction of more integrated tactics by the Macedonians, peltasts become more difficult to identify, since the term was sometimes used (e.g. Polyb. 5. 23. 3) of troops described as being among the more heavily armed.

RE 19. 1, 'Peltastai'; J. G. P. Best, *Thracian Peltasts and their Influence on Greek Warfare* (1969); A. M. Snodgrass, *Arms and Armour of the Greeks* (1967).   J. F. La.

Pelusium, the city at the easternmost mouth of the *Nile (modern Tell el-Farama) which formed the natural entry to Egypt from the north-east, on the route upriver to *Memphis. It was near this stategic entry-point that *Cambyses defeated the

Egyptians in 525 BC. *Pharnabazus and *Iphicrates were stopped here by floods in 374, but many successful invaders of Egypt came this way, among them *Artaxerxes (3) III (342), *Alexander (3) the Great (332), *Antiochus (4) IV (169/8), A. *Gabinius (2) and M. *Antonius (2) (55), and Octavian (see AUGUSTUS) in 30 BC. Under the Roman empire, Pelusium was a station on the route to the *Red Sea. Salt-pans lay in the area, which was also famed for its flax.   D. J. T.

Penates, di, Roman spirits connected with the inner part (*penus, penitus,* etc.) of the house (Cic. *Nat.* 2. 67, Servius on *Aen.* 1. 378); the name only exists in the plural and as an adjective with *Di* (gods). They were worshipped in *Vesta's temple (Tac. *Ann.* 15. 41. 1) and also on the *Velia (Platner–Ashby p. 388). Roman legal scholars theorized about and expanded on the content of the *penus* (S. Treggiari, *Roman Marriage* (1991) 389 ff.) and it is tempting to parallel this with the expanding province of the Penates: officials sacrificed to them (Ogilvie on Livy 1. 14. 2, Servius on *Aen.* 2. 296) and they received offerings as *Publici* and of the imperial house (Latte, *RR* 89 ff., *RE* 19. 440 ff.). Moderns assert they were regularly conjoined with the *Lares, but the ancient evidence does not support this.

Although *Virgil's *Aeneid* crystallized the tradition of a Trojan/Greek origin, the precise Greek origins and route to Rome remain disputed. At *Lavinium they were equated with the *Dioscuri (Servius on *Aen.* 3. 12) and represented by statues. But they had aniconic representations at another shrine there according to *Timaeus (2) (Dion. Hal. *Art. Rom.* 1. 67 = *FGrH* 566 F 59 with Jacoby's notes); cf. S. Weinstock, *JRS* 1960, 112 ff. The former group probably influenced the Velia shrine, the latter the *penus Vestae.*

RE 19. 417 ff.; A. Alföldi, *Early Rome and the Latins* (1965), 258 ff.; A. Dubourdieu, *Les Origines et le développement du culte des Pénates* (1989).
                                                    C. R. P.

Peneleos (Πηνέλεως; also Πηνέλαος, *Etym. Magn.* 670. 50 Sylburg, but reading uncertain; Peneleus, Hyg. *Fab.* 81, cf. Πηνέλεον, read by *Aristophanes (2) in *Homer, *Iliad* 13. 92), son of Hippalcimus or Hippalcus (Diod. Sic. 4. 67. 7; Hyg. *Fab.* 97. 8); one of the Boeotian leaders (*Iliad* 2. 494); killed by *Eurypylus (Quint. Smyrn. 7. 104); wooed *Helen (Apollod. 3. 130); an *Argonaut (ibid. 1. 113).   H. J. R.

Penelope, daughter of *Icarius (1) (*Tyndareos' brother), wife of *Odysseus, and mother of *Telemachus. In *Homer's *Odyssey* she faithfully awaits Odysseus' return, although pressed to marry one of the many local nobles. She pretends that she must first finish weaving a shroud for Laertes, Odysseus' father, which she unravels every night for three years, until detected by a maid and forced to complete it (*Od.* 2. 93 ff., 19. 137 ff., 24. 128 ff.). Finally, twenty years after Odysseus' departure, in despair she resolves to marry the suitor who can string Odysseus' bow and perform a special feat of archery. Odysseus, who has returned disguised as a beggar, achieves this and kills the suitors with the bow. She tests his identity by another trick concerning their marriage-bed (23. 174–206) and they are reunited. Homer portrays her as a model of fidelity, prudence, and ingenuity, and most later writers echo this view.

In the *Telegony* (see EPIC CYCLE) Odysseus, Penelope, and Telemachus are immortalized by *Circe after Odysseus' death. Telemachus marries Circe, Telegonus Penelope (*Epicorum Graecorum Fragmenta,* ed. M. Davies, p. 73). Italus is their son in Hyginus (*Fab.* 127). In the epic *Thesprotis* Penelope bears Odys-

seus a second son, Ptoliporthes, on his return from Troy (called Arcesilaus in *Telegony* fr. 2 ed. Davies). But in Arcadian legend Odysseus expels her because of infidelity and she dies at *Mantinea, where *Pausanias (3) saw her tomb (8. 12. 5–6). In another version she is seduced by the suitor Amphinomus and killed by Odysseus (Apollod. *Epit.* 7. 38). Arcadian legend seems also to be behind the odd tradition which made her the mother of *Pan, by *Apollo or *Hermes (Pindar fr. 100 Snell, Hdt. 2. 145, Apollod. *Epit.* 7. 38, *FGrH* 244 F 134–6, etc.), or even by all the suitors (Duris of Samos, *FGrH* 76 F 21)!

In art she is shown mourning Odysseus' absence (seated at her loom with head on hand, elbow on knee), at the departure of Telemachus, receiving gifts from the suitors, conversing with Odysseus, at the foot-washing scene, and at the suitors' death. Zeuxis is said to have portrayed her character (*mores*) in a painting (Plin. *HN* 35. 63).

RE 19. 460–93 (E. Wüst); Roscher, *Lex.* 3. 1901–20 (J. Schmidt); W. B. Stanford, *The Ulysses Theme* (1968); M.-M. Mactoux, *Pénélope: Légende et mythe* (1975); R. B. Rutherford, *Homer, Odyssey Books 19 and 20* (1992), 27–38; N. Felson-Rubin, *Regarding Penelope* (1994); *LIMC* 7. 1 (1994), 291 ff.   N. J. R.

Penia, poverty personified, differentiated from πτωχεία or destitution (Ar. *Plut.* 548–54); an allegorical and not a cult figure, though described humorously as a local divinity at Hdt. 8. 111. 3.   E. Ke.

Pennus See LEX (2), Lex Iunia, 126 BC.

Pentadius (*PLRE* 1,687) (3rd or 4th cent. AD), author of elegiac poems in 'echoic' or 'serpentine' verse (where the opening words of each hexameter are repeated as the second half of the following pentameter) on fortune, spring, and *Narcissus (1), and (less certainly) of a number of short epigrams.

TEXTS *Anth. Lat.*; with trans., Duff, *Minor Lat. Poets.*   J. H. D. S.

pentakosiomedimnoi, 'five-hundred-bushel men', at *Athens, members of the highest of the four property classes devised by *Solon, comprising men whose land yielded at least 500 *medimnoi* of corn or the equivalent in other produce (the other classes were the *hippeis, *zeugitai, and *thētes). Under Solon's constitution the treasurers of Athena and perhaps also the archons (see ARCHONTES) were appointed exclusively from this class, and for the treasurers the requirement survived to the 4th cent., though by then either it was not enforced or a poor man might technically be rated as a *pentakosiomedimnos* (*Ath. Pol.* 7. 3–8. 1).
                                        A. W. G.; T. J. C.; P. J. R.

Pentapolis (African), the five Greek cities of central Roman Cyrenaica (the northern Gebel Akhdar and its coastal fringe), *Cyrene (Shahat), with (from east to west) Apollonia or Sozusa in late antiquity (Marsa Susa), Ptolemais/Barca (Tolmeita), Taucheira (Tocra), for a time called Arsinoe, *Berenice (a) (Benghazi), originally Euesperides. The name, first attested c. AD 79 (Plin. *HN* 5. 31), must post-date the creation of the fifth city by promotion of the dependent 'Port of Cyrene' to be the city of Apollonia, perhaps early in the 1st cent. BC (probably already before *SEG* 20. 709, of c.67 BC, but the earliest certain reference is in Strabo 17. 837. 20–1). It may have been associated with the Roman provincial *koinon* (see CONCILIUM); certainly Cyrene, where the *koinon* met, became 'Metropolis of the Hexapolis' (*SEG* 20. 727) after *Hadrian founded Cyrenaican Hadrianopolis; and when Hadrianopolis failed, Pentapolis reappeared as an informal name for the Diocletianic province (see DIOCLETIAN) of Libya Superior. But there was some political coherence in the area long before there were five cities. Cyrene had claimed to be leader of all Greek settlements there at first, apparently, through the authority of her kings, later as mother-city, until it and they were subjected to the Ptolemaic monarchy in c.322 (see EGYPT, *Ptolemaic*); and when, perhaps, Ptolemaic control was interrupted in the mid-3rd cent., it is possible that a free federation was briefly substituted, the work of Ecdelus and Demophanes. It is not clear whether any such organization existed, after the death of the last king in 96 BC, when Rome, his heir, gave all the cities freedom; whether so or not, maintenance of order broke down until Roman provincial government was introduced following a decision of the Roman *senate in 75/4.

For the history of these Greek settlements written records are limited, and do not always distinguish the city of Cyrene from the cities of Cyrenaica. Archaeological exploration is providing supplementary information for all city sites (least satisfactorily so far for Barca (el Merj), where thick silt covers the earlier levels), but often controversially. *Cyrene is treated separately. Early settlements are attested elsewhere, quite soon after the foundation of Cyrene, many of them dependent villages, e.g. on the sites later known as Apollonia and Ptolemais, but also at Taucheira, which is so far westwards that one might expect it to have had a civic organisation from the first (but its territory was of limited extent, so that she was always liable to be overshadowed by a richer neighbour; thus for *Herodotus (1) it was a city, but within the orbit of Barca, 4. 171). There was a second wave of settlements in the 6th cent., again probably, including many dependencies, along with two more cities. Barca was founded c.570 by dissident members of Cyrene's royal family, in the extensive and fertile inland plain south of the later Ptolemais and of Taucheira, so rich that it was a potential rival of Cyrene (and was able, apparently without great difficulty, to recover after the *Persians sacked her at the instigation of Queen Pheretime of Cyrene, Hdt. 4. 165 f.). The westernmost city, Euesperides (Sidi Ubeid, near Benghazi), a site revealed by aerial photography, has produced pottery of the mid-6th cent., which was presumably her approximate foundation date. Although in one of the areas where tradition placed the Gardens of the *Hesperides, she controlled land less rich than its reputation and was disadvantaged both by the tendency of her harbour to silt, and by exposure to Libyan raids from the Syrtica (see SYRTES). Where evidence exists, it shows clear links between the institutions of these three cities and those of Cyrene.

In the mid-3rd cent. they acquired Ptolemaic dynastic names (precise dates and circumstances disputed). The Euesperideans became 'Bereniceans from Euesperides' (the adjunct apparently soon dropped) when, or soon after, they moved *en bloc* to a site under modern Benghazi with better harbour facilities; Queen *Berenice (3) II is said to have given them a city wall and her name. The Barcaeans became 'Ptolemaitans from Barca' (the exact form of the adjunct varies, but a reference to Barca might still be included in the 2nd cent. AD) when city government was moved from the inland site (whose status became that of a village) to that of its dependent port, now renamed Ptolemais (probably by *Ptolemy (1) III) and provided (presumably by royal gift) with grand civic buildings. Both moves could have been voluntary, if under royal patronage; but it has been suggested that they were made under punitive compulsion. The Taucheirans probably became 'Arsinoeans' at approximately the same time, but we know nothing more about this change; the new name was dropped in the Roman period. The Ptolemies needed to

strengthen the ports on which they depended for quick connections with Egypt, and perhaps desired to dim the prestige of Cyrene; it is surprising that nothing analogous is attested for the Port of Cyrene before the Roman period.

As free cities from 96 to c.74 BC they suffered from internal *staseis* (see STASIS), piratical and Libyan raids, famine, and, following provincialization, stresses due to Rome's civil wars; after Actium, from some misgovernment, and from difficult relations with the Jewish communities (see JEWS) established in them by the Ptolemies, which culminated in a serious revolt in AD 115–17 (the Jews vanish from the record after that; the heavy casualties inflicted were made up by new settlers who were Roman legionary veterans); there were also damaging Libyan raids under *Augustus, held in check from the end of his reign until the mid-3rd cent. (there were small Roman forces in the Syrtica at any rate for part of this time), but recurring thereafter and vividly described in the early 5th cent. in the letters of *Synesius. Under the early Roman empire they seem to have enjoyed a modest prosperity, show standard loyalist reactions to Rome and something of the intercity rivalry common in the eastern provinces. In Diocletian's reorganization Ptolemais (probably an assize-town earlier) became the capital instead of Cyrene; in the late 5th or early 6th cents. the emperors Anastasius and *Justinian sponsored a revival in which new church buildings and rebuilding or redecoration of others are notable features. In the 7th century, in the context of the Arab invasions, the capital was moved westwards to Taucheira. After the Arab conquest, some life continued in all the cities until the 10th cent.

RE 19 (1938), 509, no. 3; E. S. G. Robinson, *British Museum Catalogue of Coins: Cyrenaica* (1927), 'Koinon', 'Barce', 'Euhesperides', 'Minor Mints', 'Cyrenaica under the Romans'; Jones, *Cities E. Rom. Prov.*[2] ch. 12; F. Chamoux, *Cyrène sous la monarchie des Battiades* (1953); A. Laronde, *Cyrène et la Libye hellénistique* (1987), partly contested by T. V. Buttrey in *Libyan Studies*, 1994; P. Romanelli, *La Cirenaica romana* (1943); B. Jones in G. Barker, J. Lloyd, and J. Reynolds, *Cyrenaica in Antiquity* (1985) 27–41; S. Applebaum, *Jews and Greeks in Ancient Cyrene* (1979); G. Lüderitz, *Die Juden der Cyrenaika* (1993); R. G. Goodchild, *Cyrene and Apollonia: An Historical Guide* (1963), *Kyrene und Apollonia* (1971), and in *Libyan Studies* (Select papers of R. G. Goodchild, ed. J. Reynolds, 1976) 216–28, 256–67; J. Reynolds, in *JRS* 1978, 111–21, with Oliver, 274–8, 281–4.

SITES J. H. Humphrey (ed.), *Apollonia, The Port of Cyrene: Excavations by the University of Michigan 1965–7* (1976); A. Laronde in A. Bresson and P. Rouillard (eds.), *L'Emporion* (1993), 89 f.; J. N. Dore, *Libyan Studies*, 1990, 19–22, see also 1991, 91–105, 1992, 101–5, 1993, 117–19, 1994; C. H. Kraeling, *Ptolemais, City of the Libyan Pentapolis* (1962); J. Little, in G. Barker, J. Lloyd, and J. Reynolds (see above), 43–7; J. Reynolds in S. Stucchi (ed.), *Giornata Lincea sulla Archeologia Cirenaica* (1990); J. Boardman, *BSA* 1966, 149–56; J. Boardman and J. Hayes, *Excavations at Tocra 1963–5*, (1966), 2 (1973); M. Vickers, *Libyan Studies* 1994, with earlier bibliog. for Euesperides; R. G. Goodchild, *Benghazi, Story of a City* (1963); J. A. Lloyd and others, *Excavations at Sidi Khrebeish, Benghazi* 1 (1977), 2 (1979), 3 (1985).
J. M. R.

pentathlon, a contest held at the *Olympian Games and elsewhere consisting of five events (long-jump, running, *discus, *javelin, *wrestling; cf. Simonides *Epig.* 41P ἅλμα, ποδωκείην, δίσκον, ἄκοντα, πάλην), precursor of the modern decathlon. Victory in three events was sufficient, but not necessary, for overall victory; if one competitor did not win three events, it is not known on what basis it was decided who was the overall winner. Pentathletes would train and compete, especially when long-jumping, to the sound of aulos music. See ATHLETICS.

SCORING SYSTEM How and Wells on Hdt. 9. 33. 2; T. F. Scanlon,

Greek and Roman Athletics: a Bibliography (1984), 80–2; W. E. Sweet, *Sport and Recreation in Ancient Greece* (1987), 56–9.

USE OF MUSIC M. L. West, *Ancient Greek Music* (1992), 30 n. 86.

R. L. Ho.; S. J. I.

pentecontor See SHIPS.

Pentekontaetia. the 'period of (almost) fifty years' (Thuc. 1. 118. 2) between the end of the *Persian Wars in Greece in 479 and the beginning of the *Peloponnesian War in 431. The term is often applied to the selective account given by *Thucydides (2) at 1. 89–118 of the period from 478 to the early 430s, offered to justify his claim that the truest cause of the Peloponnesian War was Athens' power and Sparta's fear of it. The account is brief, selective, and lacking in precise dates.

Modern works: HCT; Hornblower, *Comm. on Thuc.*; CAH 5² (1992); E. Badian, *From Plataea to Potidaea* (1993); W. K. Pritchett, *Thucydides' Pentekontaetia and Other Essays* (1995).

V. E.; P. J. R.

Pentelicon, mountain east of Athens, known in antiquity as Brilessus. From the 6th cent. BC onwards the high-quality *marble was exploited by quarrying on both western and northern slopes. All the major building projects in Athens in the late 5th cent. employ Pentelic marble, and the ancient *quarries and quarry roads remain visible today. Traces of both a fort and a sanctuary have been found at the summit.

Paus. 1. 32. 1. J. Travlos, *Bildlexikon zur Topographie des antiken Attika* (1988), 329–34.

R. G. O.

Penthesilea, in mythology daughter of *Ares and the *Amazon queen Otrere. She accidentally killed her comrade Hippolyte in the battle which followed *Theseus' marriage to Phaedra, then went to *Troy to be purified (see PURIFICATION, GREEK) of her blood-guilt by *Priam. As a consequence, she led an army of Amazons to Troy to help Priam after *Hector's death (Apollod. *Epit.* 5. 1–2). Here, according to the *Aethiopis* (see Proclus, and cf. Quint. Smyrn. 1. 18 ff.), she performed valiantly in battle until finally overcome and killed by *Achilles. She was buried by the Trojans, and Achilles grieved over her; whereupon *Thersites jeered at him for being in love with her and Achilles killed him. Since in this version Thersites was of good family—son of Agrius brother of *Oeneus, and thus a kinsman of *Diomedes (2) (schol. *Il.* 2. 212, Quint. Smyrn. 1. 767 ff.)—a dispute arose and Achilles had to sail to *Lesbos to be purified.

Penthesilea's death at Achilles' hands is often shown in art from the mid-6th cent., and was the subject of one of the panels painted by *Panaenus round *Phidias' Zeus.

A. Kossatz-Deissmann, LIMC 1. 1. 161–71; A. Kauffmann-Samaras, LIMC 1. 1. 597–601; D. von Bothmer, *Amazons in Greek Art* (1957), 4 f., 72, 145 ff.

J. R. M.

Pentheus, in mythology son of Agave, daughter of *Cadmus, and her husband *Echion (1). Euripides' *Bacchae* gives the most familiar version of his legend. The disguised *Dionysus returns from his conquests in the east to *Thebes (1), where the young king Pentheus is refusing to recognize his deity or to allow his worship. Pentheus imprisons Dionysus, in ignorance of his true identity and seeing him simply as a corrupting influence on the women of Thebes; but Dionysus escapes, and, by making Pentheus mad, inveigles him up on to Mt. Cithaeron to spy on the *maenads there. Pentheus, deranged and himself dressed as a maenad, is torn to pieces by the women led by his mother Agave. She carries his head home in triumph, believing it to be that of a lion killed in the hunt, where she is gently brought to sanity and grief by Cadmus.

Pentheus with the maenads is found occasionally in vase-paintings from the late 6th cent. on (Brommer, *Vasenlisten*³, 485–6; LIMC 7); but these seem to reflect a different tradition in which an armed Pentheus went into battle against the maenads.

J. R. March, BICS 1989, 33–65; LIMC 7. 1 (1994), 306 ff. J. R. M.

Peparēthos (*Πεπάρηθος*; now Skópelos), a fertile *Aegean island (95 sq. km., 37 sq. miles) in the Sporades. The main town (founded from *Chalcis) has fortification walls, Mycenaean tombs (see MYCENAEAN CIVILIZATION), and a cemetery; *Thucydides (2) mentions public buildings damaged by a tidal wave in 427 BC (3. 89. 4). The other towns were Selinus and Panormus; rural sites include watchtowers. Peparethos' harbour and position made it strategically valuable: it was often an Athenian possession. Its *Delian League tribute of 3 talents suggests it was wealthier than neighbouring *Sciathos and Icos; it exported wine. Under Rome it was free until Antony (M. *Antonius (2)) gave it to Athens. The late Roman remains suggest a certain prosperity.

A. A. Sampson, *Ἡ νῆσος Σκόπελος* (1968); C. Fredrich and A. J. B. Wace, MDAI (A) 1906; P. Bruneau, BCH 1987; RE 19. 1 (1937), 551–8; [British Admiralty] Naval Intelligence Division, *Greece* 3 (1945), 397–9.

D. G. J. S.

Perachora ancient *Peiraion*, the promontory opposite *Corinth, in Corinthian territory. At the western extremity, sited on a narrow shelf of land by a small harbour is the sanctuary of *Hera Akraia (oracular according to Strabo; see HERAION; ORACLES), of considerable importance in the Archaic period, attracting offerings from a wide area. A small apsidal temple of *c*.750 BC must have resembled the terracotta models found among the offerings. The final temple of *c*.525 BC is abnormally long and narrow because of the restricted site. Other buildings include a formal dining building *c*.500 BC and a two-storey stoa of *c*.300 BC. There are complex waterworks, by the sanctuary and in the area above its 'sacred valley'.

H. G. G. Payne and others, *Perachora* 1 (1940), 2 (1962); R. A. Tomlinson, in O. Reverdin and B. Grange (eds.), *Le Sanctuaire grec*, (1992); U. Sinn, MDAI(A) 1990, 53 ff.

R. A. T.

peraea territory opposite, and controlled and often economically exploited by, an *island. See PANGAEUS; RHODES; THASOS.

Perdiccas (1) **I,** the first king of *Macedonia (Hdt. 8. 139), who probably conquered the Macedonian coast *c*.640 BC.

HM 2, 1979, see index. N. G. L. H.

Perdiccas (2) **II,** king of *Macedonia *c*.450–413 BC. By astute diplomacy Perdiccas survived rebellions in Upper Macedonia, invasion by *Sitalces, and intervention by Athens and Sparta, and succeeded in uniting Macedonia and diminishing the Athenian control of his coast. In alliance with Athens until the Athenians founded *Amphipolis in 436, he subsequently promoted the revolt of *Potidaea and the Chalcidians, whom he advised to concentrate at *Olynthus. The Athenians aided by Derdas, prince of Elimiotis, and by Philip, exiled brother of Perdiccas, captured Therme before they came to terms with Perdiccas in order to besiege Potidaea. Perdiccas assisted Potidaea until Sitalces negotiated a treaty for him with Athens, who ceded Therme (431); probably Derdas also submitted to Perdiccas. In 429 the invasion of Sitalces was checked by the Macedonian cavalry, and a marriage-alliance was contracted; in 425 Perdiccas allied with *Brasidas to oust Athens and to reduce the Lyncestian prince Arrabaeus, but when the campaign in Lyncus failed, allied with

Athens (422). Allying in 417 with Sparta and Argos, he allied again with Athens when attacked in 415, and died c.413.

HM 2 (1979) see index; E. Badian, *From Plataea to Potidaea* (1993), ch. 6. N. G. L. H.

Perdiccas (3) (d. 321 BC), son of Orontes, *Macedonian noble of the princely house of Orestis, commanded his native battalion in the phalanx of *Alexander (3) the Great. His military distinction, somewhat obscured by the hostile account of *Ptolemy (1) I, won him elevation to the rank of Bodyguard by 330. Subsequently he ranked second only to *Craterus in his effectiveness as marshal and succeeded *Hephaestion in his cavalry command and his position as chiliarch (Grand Vizier). The settlement at Babylon (323) confirmed him in the chiliarchy with command of the central army and gave him custody both of the new king, *Philip (2) Arrhidaeus, and the unborn child of Alexander. In 322 his position strengthened after his successful invasion of *Cappadocia, but his dynastic intrigues alarmed the commanders in Europe, *Antipater (1) and *Craterus (1), who declared war in winter 322/1 (the chronology is disputed). Perdiccas himself quarrelled with Ptolemy, whom he suspected of separatist ambitions, and invaded Egypt (summer 321). After protracted and costly operations around *Pelusium and *Memphis his troops were incited to mutiny, and he was killed.

Berve, *Alexanderreich*, 2. no. 627; R. A. Billows, *Antigonus the One-Eyed* (1990); Heckel, *Marshals*, 134 ff. A. B. B.

perduellio (from *perduellis* = *hostis*) was the crime of activity hostile to the state. It covered a much wider field of offences than consorting with the enemy against the state (*proditio*), but it was probably not clearly defined. In the early republic it came under the jurisdiction of *duumviri perduellionis*, who seem to have had the discretion to condemn without further reference but became subject to *provocatio. By the 3rd cent. BC prosecutions were mounted by tribunes in an assembly (see IUDICIUM POPULI). In the late republic such prosecutions became obsolete when crimes of this kind were actionable in the *quaestio de maiestate* (see MAIESTAS; QUAESTIONES). *Perduellio* is still used in *Digest* 48. 4. 11 (Ulpian) to designate a specially heinous type of *maiestas*.

C. H. Brecht, *Perduellio* (1938); R. A. Bauman, *The Crimen Maiestatis in the Late Republic and Augustus' Principate* (1970). B. N.; A. W. L.

peregrini, foreigners—the term used by Romans for the free citizens of any other community than the Roman people. This was the status of the peoples of non-Roman Italy, except the Latins (see LATINI), until 90 BC and of allied and subject communities outside Italy until *Caracalla's reign (see CONSTITUTION, ANTONINE). The Latins were considered separate from the *peregrini* under the republic, though this distinction disappeared under the Principate. The principle that no Roman could be a citizen of two communities remained true until the end of the republic (Cic. *Balb.* 28–30), but it seems to have been modified before the death of *Caesar. From the triumviral period onwards *peregrini* could receive Roman citizenship but remain effective members of their own communities. Indeed *Augustus' third *Cyrene edict confirms the liability of such Roman citizens to perform public services (*munera*; see MUNUS) in their own communities.

A. N. S.-W.; A. W. L.

Peregrinus (later called Proteus), from a wealthy family in the Roman colony of *Parium. A *Cynic philosopher, he is the subject of a satirical essay by *Lucian 'On the death of Peregrinus', unfortunately preserving most of what is known about him, including dubious allegations of parricide and pederasty. Visiting Palestine, he became a Christian convert (see CONVERSION). Returning to Parium, he gave away his property to his fellow-citizens; apostasy led to a period of study in Egypt under the Cynic Agathobulus. According to Lucian a visit to Rome ended with banishment for verbal abuse of the emperor (*Antoninus Pius). Based in *Achaia, he made speeches at *Olympia exhorting a Greek revolt and attacking the ex-consul Ti. *Claudius Atticus Herodes (2), a local benefactor. He achieved posthumous fame by self-immolation at the *Olympian Games of AD 165. Although Lucian paints him as a mad charlatan, Aulus *Gellius thought him a man of 'dignity and fortitude' (*NA* 12. 11. 1).

C. P. Jones, *Culture and Society in Lucian* (1986), ch. 11; L. Holford-Strevens, *Aulus Gellius* (1988), 104 f.; G. Anderson, *Sage, Saint and Sophist* (1994), index. A. J. S. S.

Pergamum, in Mysia c.24 km. (15 miles) from the *Aegean, a natural fortress of great strategic importance commanding the rich plain of the river Caïcus; important historically as the capital of the Attalid kings and, later, as one of the three leading cities of provincial *Asia, and archaeologically as the only excavated Hellenistic royal capital outside *Macedonia. First attested in Greek sources in 401 BC, Pergamum enters history's mainstream as a treasury of *Lysimachus, who entrusted it (c.302) to *Philetaerus (2), founder of Attalid fortunes (for the political history of the dynasty see also EUMENES (1–2) and ATTALUS I–III). An indigenous community (in spite of the Attalid claim to foundation by the Heraclid *Telephus (1)), Pergamum had adopted Greek civic organization (see POLIS) by c.300 (*OGI* 265) at the latest, and this was upheld by the Attalids, who maintained control in practice through their assumption (from Eumenes I) of the right to appoint the chief magistrates (*stratēgoi*). As a royal capital as well as a *polis*, the city was the chief showcase of Attalid patronage. From Attalus I on the kings promoted *Athena, the city's presiding deity, as dynastic protectress, especially of military success; she acquired the title Nikephoros, 'victory-bearer', and her sanctuary in the upper city was adorned with the famous statues of defeated Galatians (see EPIGONUS). *Strabo (13. 4. 2) credits above all Eumenes II, his power and wealth vastly augmented by the Peace of Apamea, with the enlargement and beautification of the city. To his reign dates the 'Great Altar', masterpiece of the Pergamene 'school' of Greek *sculpture, as well as the royal *libraries and the terraced, fan-shaped plan of the upper city, its focus the royal palace—a remarkable statement of royal absolutism (see URBANISM); an inscription (*SEG* 13. 521; Eng. trans. in Austin no. 216) preserves a royal law on municipal administration showing the efforts made to keep the city clean and in good repair (see ASTYNOMOI). This royal programme aimed at transforming Pergamum into a Hellenistic cultural capital, for which the model was *Athens, recipient of generous Attalid patronage in the 2nd cent. BC. Declared free in his will by Attalus III, Pergamum lost its Roman status of allied city for its support of *Mithradates VI (88–85 BC); ensuing hardship at the hands of Roman troops and businessmen was mitigated by the diplomacy of Diodorus Pasparos, a leading citizen, deified by the grateful city (C. Jones, *Chiron*, 1974, 183 ff. for the redating). Although politically and economically subordinate to *Ephesus, Pergamum under the Principate was head of a *conventus and a centre of the (Roman) *ruler-cult. Its prosperity and prestige can be gauged from such new monuments as the temple of *Trajan and *Zeus Philios and, in the lower city, the Asclepieum (see ASCLEPIUS), transformed under *Hadrian, and from its tally of six senatorial families by AD 200 (H. Halfmann, *Die Senatoren aus dem östlichen Teil des Imperium Romanum* (1979), 68). Attacked by the *Goths in the mid-3rd cent., the city contracted. Despite unimpressive physical remains from late antiquity, it remained an important intellectual centre, where the future emperor *Julian studied philosophy and the medical writer *Oribasius worked.

EXCAVATIONS *Altertümer von Pergamon*, 1– (1912–); *Pergamenische Forschungen*, 1– (1972–).

MODERN STUDIES E. Hansen, *The Attalids of Pergamon* (1971), 485 ff.; *PECS* 688 ff.; R. Allen, *The Attalid Kingdom* (1983), ch. 7; S. Price, *The Roman Imperial Cult in Asia Minor* (1984), esp. 252 ff.; W. Radt, *Pergamon. Geschichte und Bauten* etc. (1988).   A. J. S. S., C. R.

Perge, near modern Aksu, a city of *Pamphylia on the river Cestrus, which was supposedly founded by the 'mixed multitude' of Greeks who wandered across Asia Minor after the Trojan War (see TROY), led by *Calchas, *Mopsus, and *Amphilochus. A Hittite document shows that it had previously been one of the towns of the southern kingdom of Tarhuntassa. Statues of Calchas and Mopsus stood with those of other, more recent, 'city-*founders' inside the remodelled Hellenistic south city gate. The Pergaeans welcomed *Alexander (3) the Great and served him as guides. By the late-Hellenistic period the lower town was fortified with walls which still stand; the original settlement was on the hill to the north. The city was famous for the native cult of Pergaean *Artemis, called Vanassa Preiia in the local dialect; she was depicted on coins as a baetyl, doubtless orginally a meteoritic stone, but the site of the temple has not been located. Perge was a leading city of the early empire and was visited by St *Paul, *en route* to the interior of Asia Minor. In the early 2nd cent. AD much fine building was completed, in large measure due to the generosity of Plancia Magna, wife of the Roman senator C. *Iulius Cornutus Tertullus, and herself member of an important local *émigré* Italian family, which had wide interests in Asia Minor. Distinguished Pergaeans were the mathematician *Apollonius (2) and the 2nd-cent. philosopher Varus, called 'the Stork', from the same family as Plancia Magna. Perge vied with its neighbour *Side for the rank of first city in Pamphylia and became particularly important in the third century, when the whole region served as a bulwark of Roman military resistance against Gothic and Persian invasions (see GOTHS; SASANIDS). Most of the city's public buildings, as well as the fortifications, are well preserved.

Lanckoroński, *Städte Pamphyliens*, 1 (1890), 33–63; G. E. Bean, *Turkey's Southern Shore*[2] (1979), 25–38; *Epigraphica Anatolica*, 1988, 97–169 (inscriptions); P. Weiss, *Chiron*, 1991, 353–92 (rivalry with Side and the 3rd cent.).   G. E. B.; S. M.

Periander, tyrant of *Corinth c.627–587 BC, after his father *Cypselus; he was for many the typical oppressive tyrant; see TYRANNY. Advice that he should eliminate rivals is said by *Herodotus (1) to have been given to Periander by Thrasybulus of *Miletus, who walked silently through a field of corn lopping off ears that were taller than the rest; *Aristotle made the advice pass in the opposite direction. Unlike his father, Periander recruited a bodyguard; he sent 300 Corcyraean boys to *Lydia for castration as punishment when Corcyraeans killed his son (see CORCYRA); he himself killed his wife Melissa, made love to her corpse and took the fine clothes off Corinthian women to burn for her spirit. There was also, however, a more favourable tradition: he was in many lists of the *seven sages, and 'he was neither unjust nor insolent, but hated wickedness' (Arist. fr. 611. 20 Rose). The burning of clothes probably reflects a more general attack on

luxury, and restrictions on slave ownership may have been similar; his measures against idleness are a misinterpreted memory of the labour which his extensive building programme required: among other things, he constructed the *diolkos and an artificial harbour at *Lechaeum, and levied dues upon the use of them. If Cypselus had not brought Corcyra under control after the *Bacchiadae fled there, Periander did, and installed his son as tyrant; this is the context of the joint Corinthian/Corcyraean foundations of *Apollonia and *Epidamnus. He founded *Potidaea, the only Corinthian colony in the *Aegean. He had a warlike reputation; probably his activity in particular lay behind *Thucydides (2)'s account of early naval affairs, which attributes more or less the naval practices of his own day, including suppression of *piracy, to Corinth. He attacked *Epidaurus and captured its tyrant, his father-in-law Procles. He arbitrated between Athens and *Mytilene in their dispute over *Sigeum (see ARBITRATION). He gave Thrasybulus of Miletus advice, and probably naval assistance, during his successful resistance to the Lydian siege. On his death, the tyranny passed to his nephew Cypselus, also called Psammetichus, who was soon killed; opposition will have begun much earlier, under Periander himself.

RE 19, 'Periandros 1'; J. B. Salmon, *Wealthy Corinth* (1984).   J. B. S.

Pericles (1) (c.495–429 BC), Athenian politician, was the son of *Xanthippus (1) and the *Alcmaeonid Agariste, niece of *Cleisthenes (2) and granddaughter of Agariste of *Sicyon (see CLEISTHENES (1)) and *Megacles. See ALCMAEONIDAE. He was *chorēgos (paying for the production) for *Aeschylus' Persae in 472, but first came to prominence as one of the elected prosecutors of *Cimon in 463/2. In 462/1 he joined with *Ephialtes (4) in the attack on the *Areopagus.

According to *Plutarch he became popular leader and one of the most influential men in Athens after Ephialtes' death and the *ostracism of Cimon. Little is recorded of him for some years, but it is reasonable to assume that he was in favour of the more ambitious foreign policy pursued by Athens in the 450s and of the further reforms of that decade. He is credited with a campaign in the Gulf of Corinth c.454 and with the sending out of *cleruchies to places in the *Delian League, and with the introduction of pay for jurors and the law limiting citizenship to those with an Athenian mother as well as an Athenian father. His proposal for a congress of all the Greeks, which came to nothing because of opposition from *Sparta (Plut. *Per*. 17: its authenticity has been challenged) perhaps belongs to the early 440s and was an attempt to convert the Delian League into a league of all the Greeks under Athens' leadership now that the Delian League's war against Persia had ended. In 446 he commanded the expedition to put down the revolt of *Euboea; he returned to Athens when the Peloponnesians invaded, and was alleged to have bought off the Spartan king Pleistoanax; and he then went back to deal with Euboea.

Pericles was greatly involved in Athens' public building programme of the 440s and 430s. This was the issue on which opposition to him was focused by *Thucydides (1) son of Melesias, a relative of Cimon, but Thucydides was ostracized (see OSTRACISM) c.443 and the building continued. According to Plutarch, Pericles was elected general (see STRATĒGOI) every year after that and was Athens' unchallenged leader; but it seems likely that attacks on Pericles and his friends, probably from the democratic end of the political spectrum, are to be dated to the early 430s. His mistress *Aspasia and the *sophist *Anaxagoras were perhaps prosecuted, the sculptor *Phidias was prosecuted and left Athens, and Pericles himself was charged with embezzlement but presumably acquitted.

In the 430s he led an expedition to the Black Sea (see EUXINE SEA). The policies pursued by Athens in the late 430s, which led to the outbreak of the *Peloponnesian War, are presumably his: *Aristophanes (1) represents him as being particularly obstinate over the decree imposing sanctions on *Megara, and *Thucydides (2) gives him a speech claiming that a policy of appeasement will not work. According to Thucydides his strategy for the Peloponnesian War was to stay inside the walls when the Peloponnesians invaded, and to rely on Athens' sea power and superior financial resources to outlast the Peloponnesians; but there are indications in the scale of Athens' expenditure and naval activity in the opening years of the war that Thucydides' picture may be distorted. In 430, when the hardship of the war was beginning to be felt, the Athenians deposed him from the generalship and attempted unsuccessfully to negotiate with Sparta; he was afterwards re-elected, but he was one of the many Athenians to suffer from the *plague, and he died in 429.

Pericles was an aristocrat who became a democratic leader. He won the admiration of Cimon's relative, the historian *Thucydides (2), as a man who was incorruptible and far-sighted, and who led the people rather than currying favour with them (2. 65). Plutarch reconciled this with the less favourable picture given by *Plato (1) by supposing that Pericles was a *demagogue in the earlier part of his career and a great statesman in the later. He was an impressive orator. His manner was aloof, and he is said to have been uninterested in his family's concerns. His marriage (possibly to his cousin and *Alcibiades' mother, Deinomache) was unhappy, but he formed a liaison with the Milesian Aspasia, and when his two sons by his Athenian wife had died from the plague his son by Aspasia, Pericles, was made an Athenian citizen.

Prosop. Att. 11811; APF 455–60. F. J. Frost, JHS 1964, 69–72, Hist. 1964, 385–99; R. Seager, Hist. 1969, 129–41; K. J. Dover, Τάλαντα 1976, 24–54 = The Greeks and their Legacy (1988), 135–58; A. Andrewes, JHS 1978, 1–8; R. D. Cromey, GRBS 1982, 203–12, Hist. 1984, 385–401.

A. W. G.; P. J. R.

Pericles (2), early 4th-cent. BC dynast of Limyra (east *Lycia). His name suggests imitation of Athenian culture. He defeated Artembares, ruler of Pinara and Tlos (TAM 1. 67, 104) and (?) successor of Arbinas son of Gergis in West Lycia (ML 93 + SEG 28. 1245; see XANTHUS). Pericles led the united Lycians against Telmessus (Fethiye), west of Lycia: FGrH 115 Theopompus F 103. 17. All this looks like a bid for pan-Lycian supremacy, and new inscriptions found at Limyra (M. Wörrle, Chiron, 1991, 203–39) do indeed show Pericles calling himself ruler of the Lycians, Λυκίων βασιλεύς; they also attest dealings between Pericles and a Lycian community called the Pernitai. A fine tomb, with Greek-style *caryatids, may be his. By 337 Lycia was absorbed into the Hecatomnid Carian satrapy (see PIXODARUS).

T. Bryce, Historia, 1980, 377 ff.; M. Wörrle (as above). Tomb: J. Borchhardt, Die Bauskulptur des Heroons von Limyra (1976). S. H.

Periclymenus, in mythology, (1) son of *Poseidon and a daughter of *Tiresias (schol. Pind. Nem. 9. 26). One of the Theban defenders against the *Seven against Thebes; according to the epic Thebais (fr. 4 Davies; see EPIC CYCLE) and *Euripides (Phoen. 1157), he killed *Parthenopaeus, and *Pindar tells how he would have killed the seer *Amphiaraus, had not Zeus intervened. (2) Son of Pylian *Neleus. His grandfather, Poseidon, gave him the power of *metamorphosis which made him a great warrior; he

was finally killed by *Heracles with the assistance of *Athena (Hes. frr. 33, 35 M–W; schol. Ap. Rhod. Arg. 1. 156–60a).

Lewy, Roscher, Lex. 3, 1967–8; LIMC 7. 1 (1994), 322–3. R. L. Hu.

Perinthus, a city on the European coast of the Sea of Marmora (*Propontis) halfway between *Byzantium and the *Hellespont. Founded by the Samians (see SAMOS; COLONIZATION, GREEK) sometime in the 6th cent. BC, Perinthus was an important Greek settlement on the frontier of the Thracian world, with which it maintained a precarious relationship. The site was a steep, banked headland protected by walls that ran across the neck of the peninsula. Its early history was marked by attacks of Thracians and the hostility of the Megarians (see MEGARA), the latter of whom had established their own colonies nearby at the entrance to the Bosporus. Perinthus' founding Samians turned back a Megarian expedition directed against the city. After *Darius I's Scythian expedition (c.513–512 BC), the city was taken over by the Persians. Perinthus was later attached to the empire of Athens (see DELIAN LEAGUE) to which it paid an annual tribute of ten talents, after Byzantium the highest amount of any city in the Propontic region. The city gave refuge to *Alcibiades in 410 BC, and *Xenophon (1) and the Ten Thousand stopped there on their return to Greece, Perinthus then being ruled by the Spartan governor of Byzantium. Throughout the 4th cent. Perinthus was the chief *emporion of the region. In 377 it joined the *Second Athenian Confederacy, which protected it against the Thracian king, Cotys I, in 365. By 355 it had regained its *autonomy and joined Byzantium as allies of *Philip (1) II of Macedon. When Perinthus refused to assist Philip against the Athenians in the *Chersonesus (1) (340) the king besieged it. After a vain three-month attempt to overcome the city's defences Philip was forced to withdraw. Perinthus enjoyed a third-century federation with Byzantium, but became subject to *Philip (3) V of Macedon in 202. Rome restored its freedom in 196. In 189 it became part of the Attalid kingdom (see PERGAMUM), and by the end of the 2nd cent. BC it was again ruled by Rome. In the 3rd cent. AD Perinthus' name was changed to Heraclea, preserved today as Eregli. The city's importance declined with the foundation of *Constantinople, although it continued to be the second city of the Propontis.

ATL 1; B. Isaac, The Greek Settlements in Thrace Until the Macedonian Conquest (1986). E. N. B.

Periochae see LIVY.

perioikoi, 'dwellers round about', was the name employed usually to describe neighbouring people frequently constituting groups of subjects or half-citizens, normally with local self-government; but it could also be applied to outright slaves. Perioikoi of the usual, personally free type were found in Argolis (see ARGOS (2)), *Crete, *Elis, *Thessaly, and elsewhere, but the best-known group are those of the Spartan state. Here, the origins of their status and ethnic affiliation are unclear, though their *dialect was the Laconian Doric (see LACONIA) common to all the state's inhabitants.

Like the full citizen Spartiates, perioikoi were counted as Lacedaemonians in military contexts, not only serving in the Spartan army but (after c.450) in the same regiments. But they had no say in the making of Spartan policy and seem to have been subject to special taxation, so can be considered at best half- or second-class citizens of Sparta. One unreliable ancient source states that they were controlled by a system of *harmosts, as if they were Sparta's imperial subjects, but the only certainly attested harmost in a perioikic area was based on the strategically sensitive island of *Cythera (called *Kutherodikes* in Thuc. 4. 53. 2, but 'harmost' in the 4th-cent. inscription *IG* 5. 1. 937). *Isocrates (*Panath.* 177) was also almost certainly wrong to claim that the Spartans could put *perioikoi* to death without trial. Rather, the status of the *perioikoi* vis-à-vis Sparta was more akin to that of an ally of the *Peloponnesian League. The perioikic *poleis* (regularly so called, e.g. at Thuc. 5. 54. 1; see POLIS) possessed local political *autonomy and their own religious sanctuaries but were entirely subject to Sparta in their foreign policy. Social stratification within the Perioikic communities is on record; we hear in *Xenophon (1) both of 'gentlemen' *perioikoi* (*kaloikagathoi*: *Hell.* 5. 3. 9) and of a named Perioikic cavalryman (*Hell.* 5. 4. 39); these were presumably substantial landowners. But humbler *perioikoi* profited from the Spartans' abstention from all economic activity, by providing them with raw materials (especially iron) and objects of manufacture and trade; Gytheum, the most important community, served Sparta both as chief port and as naval dockyard and muster-station. In 370 Sparta was deprived of the (less numerous) Perioikic communities in Messenia, and in 368 some northern Laconian communities were incorporated in *Megalopolis, but those of the rest of Laconia remained intact until 195 (see NABIS).

F. Gschnitzer, *Abhängige Orte im griechischen Altertum* (1958); A. J. Toynbee, *Some Problems of Greek History* (1969); G. E. M. de Ste. Croix, *The Origins of the Peloponnesian War* (1972), app. 22; R. T. Ridley, *Mnemosyne*, 1974, 281–92; P. Cartledge, *Sparta and Lakonia* (1979), esp. ch. 10; J. F. Lazenby *The Spartan Army* (1985); A. Andrewes in *Owls to Athens* 1990 (Argos); G. Shipley in J. M. Sanders (ed.), *ΦΙΛΟΛΑΚΩΝ, Lakonian Studies in honour of Hector Catling* (1992), 211 ff. P. A. C.

Peripatetic school The name belongs to a series of philosophers of whom *Aristotle was the first and by far the most significant. Geographically the school was located in a sanctuary dedicated to *Apollo, called the Lyceum, a public space outside the city wall of Athens but within easy walking distance (the *Academy was another such place). A *gymnasium was built there; by the end of the 5th cent. BC it was a favourite gathering place for young Athenian men. Visiting *sophists lectured there, *Socrates met his young conversational partners there. As in other similar places, there were 'walks' (*peripatoi*). The name 'Peripatos' stuck to the school begun there by Aristotle, formerly a member of the Academy, when he returned to Athens in 336.

The school was originally, perhaps always, a collection of people rather than a building: Aristotle, a non-Athenian with the status of *metic, could not own property. His successor *Theophrastus could and did, and he bequeathed real estate and a library to a group of his students, including *Straton (1) who was then elected Head. Straton was succeeded by *Lyco, Lyco by *Ariston (2) of Ceos, who was Head until *c*.190. After that the succession is obscure, but there is evidence of continuous philosophical activity until the 1st cent. BC, when Athens was captured by *Sulla and the Peripatetic library removed to Rome. (For detailed discussion of this period, and the complexities of the succession, see Lynch, *Aristotle's School.*)

In the time of Aristotle and Theophrastus, the foundations were laid for systematic, co-operative research into nearly all the branches of contemporary learning. After Theophrastus' death in 287, however, Aristotle's 'school-treatises'—the works that have survived to this day—seem to have been mishandled: Theophrastus left the library to Neleus of Scepsis in Asia Minor, and if the story in Strabo 13. 1. 54 is to be believed it was removed from Athens. It is clear at least that Aristotle's fame then began to depend on his 'exoteric', more popular works. Straton con-

tinued the great tradition, especially in physics, but later members of the school devoted themselves to literary criticism, gossipy biography, and unimportant moralizing.

There was a revival in the 1st cent. BC, under the leadership of *Andronicus of Rhodes. The school-treatises of Aristotle had been in some sense rediscovered (they had been sold to Apellicon of Teos and brought by him to Athens, thence taken to Rome by *Sulla, passed on to *Tyrannio (1) the grammarian and friend of Cicero, and from him to Andronicus; see Strabo 13. 1. 54 and Plutarch, *Sulla* 26), and Andronicus published an edition of them (date uncertain; probably after Cicero). In this period Peripatetic philosophy was not specifically located in Athens, and was not sharply distinguished doctrinally from the Academy and the Stoa; the Epicureans were opposed to them all.

In the 2nd cent. AD Marcus *Aurelius established teachers in the four main schools, including the Peripatos, in Athens. But the inheritance of Aristotle passed to the great commentators on his work, many of whom were themselves Neoplatonists; see NEOPLATONISM.

Fragments of *Dicaearchus, *Aristoxenus, Clearchus, *Demetrius (3), Straton, Lyco, Ariston, *Heraclides (1) Ponticus, *Eudemus, *Phaenias, *Chamaeleon, *Praxiphanes, *Hieronymus (2), and *Critolaus in F. Wehrli, *Die Schule des Aristoteles* (1944–59; 2nd edn. 1967–78; texts with Ger. comm.). K. O. Brink, *RE* Suppl. 7 (1940); J. P. Lynch, *Aristotle's School: A Study of a Greek Educational Institution* (1972); H. B. Gottschalk, *ANRW* 2. 36. 2 (1987); R. Sorabji (ed.), *Aristotle Transformed: The Ancient Commentators and their Influence* (1990); M. G. Sollenberger, *ANRW* 2. 36. 6 (1992); M. Ostwald and J. P. Lynch, *CAH* 6² (1994), 614 ff. D. J. F.

Periphetes (*Περιφήτης*, 'famous', 'notorious'), name of several minor mythological figures, see Höfer in Roscher under the name, and especially of a brigand, also called Corynetes (*Κορυνήτης*, 'club-wielder'), killed by *Theseus on his way to Athens. He was son of *Hephaestus and Anticlea, Apollod. 3. 217, who adds that he lived in *Epidaurus, was weak in the legs (or feet, *πόδας*) and killed all passers-by with an iron club. This Theseus took from him and afterwards carried (another resemblance between Theseus and *Heracles). *Hyginus (3a) (*Fab.* 38. 1) says he was son of *Poseidon; no other author mentions his mother. See further Höfer, above, and bibliography under THESEUS. For representations in art see *LIMC* 7. 1 (1994), 929. H. J. R.

periploi, 'voyages around' (i.e. around a sea, following the coastline) were the standard basis of ancient descriptive *geography. Sequences of *harbours, landings, watering-places, shelters from bad weather, landmarks, or hazards could be remembered in an oral tradition as a sometimes very long list, and in written culture provided a summation of space that could be easier to intuit, and which offered much more room for detail, than cartography (see MAPS). As a technique the *periplous* is the ancestor of the terrestrial equivalent, the *Itineraries, and offered a peg on which to hang more information than the purely navigational. The first literary version was believed to have been prepared for *Darius I by *Scylax of Caryanda, and the earliest Mediterranean *periplous* (actually late 4th cent.) goes by his name. The best preserved and in some ways most characteristic is the late-antique *Stadiasmus Maris Magni*. The genre was used for routes beyond the Mediterranean; from the Atlantic we know of a late 6th-cent. Massalian account of the Spanish seas northward to Britain (*Avienus, 95–115), the remarkable journey along the Moroccan coast attributed to the Carthaginian *Hanno (1), and the voyage of *Pytheas of Massalia to Britain and beyond; all these have many points of contact with wonder-literature (see PARADOXOGRAPHERS). More sober are the well-attested descriptions of the important routes into and round the Indian Ocean. Following the real Scylax, *Alexander (3) the Great's captain *Nearchus (2) left a description of the coast between the *Persian Gulf and the Indus; *Agatharchides of Cnidus in the 2nd cent. gave a detailed survey of the Red Sea, partly in the interests of Ptolemaic revenues; and the surviving Periplous Maris Erythraei of the 1st cent. AD is a source of the highest importance for the really extensive knowledge of the routes to southern India and south along the East African coast that had been opened up (see MONSOON). Other examples of the genre include *Arrian's own *Periplous of the Black Sea*, a personal record of a Roman commander's experience as well as a description; and Marcian's late compilation, the Periplous of the Outer Sea.

P. Janni, *La mappa e il periplo* (1984); A. Peretti, *Il periplo di Scilace* (1979); G. W. B. Huntingford, *The Periplus of the Erythraean Sea* (1980); L. Casson, *The Periplus Maris Erythraei* (1989); Arrian, A. Diller, *The Tradition of the Minor Greek Geographers* (1952), 102–46; O. A. W. Dilke, *Greek and Roman Maps* (1985), 130–44.   N. P.

perjury See CURSES; OATHS.

Perperna (1) (*RE* 4), **Marcus,** first bearer of a non-Latin type of *nomen* (see NAMES, PERSONAL, ROMAN) to become consul (130 BC), was of *Etruscan, but long Romanized and municipal family: his father had served as an officer in 168–7. In or after his praetorship he decisively defeated the Sicilian slaves near Henna, thus preparing the victory of P. *Rupilius, and was awarded an ovation (Flor. 2. 7. 7–8). Sent to Asia as consul, he defeated and captured *Aristonicus (1), but died at Pergamum (129), so that his successor Manius *Aquillius (1) ended the war.   E. B.

Perperna (2) (*RE* 5), **Marcus,** son of the preceding, born *c.*148 BC, was consul 92 and censor 86 with L. *Marcius Philippus (1). They registered the first of the newly enfranchised Italians. He died in 49, surviving all but seven of the men he had put on the senate list as censor (Plin. *HN* 7. 156), but is hardly ever heard of and had no political influence.   E. B.

Perperna (*RE* 6) **Veiento, Marcus,** probably son of the preceding, sent to Sicily as praetor *c.*82 BC, he refused to join *Sulla, but abandoned Sicily to Cn. *Pompeius Magnus (1). He returned (perhaps via Liguria) to join M. *Aemilius Lepidus (2) in his rebellion and after its failure fled with him to Sardinia, from where he took an army to join *Sertorius (late 77). Frequently defeated by Pompey, he resented Sertorius' ascendancy and assassinated him at a banquet. 'As unable to exercise as to submit to command' (Plut. *Sert.* 27. 2), he was decisively defeated by Pompey, who thus ended the war. He offered Pompey Sertorius' correspondence, but Pompey burnt it unread and executed him.

MRR 3. 155 f.   E. B.

Perrhaebi, a tribe occupying a district on the northern border of *Thessaly and commanding passes from *Macedonia. Although most of their country was mountainous and sparsely inhabited, their principal towns, Oloosson, the tribal capital, and Phalanna were situated in fertile plains. Neither, however, played any significant role in history. The Perrhaebi, who had been thrust northwards by the invading Thessalians, were reduced to the status of *perioikoi. Though liable to a war-tax, they enjoyed some degree of autonomy whenever the Thessalian *koinon* (league) was weak, and they held two votes on the Amphictionic

Council (see AMPHICTIONY). With the growth of Thessalian cities in the 5th cent. they found themselves increasingly dominated by *Larissa. *Philip (1) II of Macedon severed Perrhaebia from Thessaly, and it remained under Macedonian control until liberated by T. *Quinctius Flamininus in 196.

F. Stählin, *Das hellenische Thessalien* (1924), 5 ff.; M. Sordi, *La lega tessala* 1958; *HM* 2 (1979), see index.   H. D. W.; S. H.

Persaeus of Citium (*c.*306–*c.*243 BC), Stoic (see STOICISM), brought up by *Zeno (2), whose pupil he became. In 277, when Zeno declined the invitation of *Antigonus (2) Gonatas to come to his court at *Pella, Persaeus was sent instead. He educated Antigonus' son Halcyoneus and acquired great political influence. He wrote works on *kingship, the Spartan constitution, on applied topics such as marriage, criticisms of *Plato (1)'s *Laws*, and dialogues on symposia (see SYMPOSIUM). In 244 he was made commander of Acrocorinth (see CORINTH), but lost the town and citadel to *Aratus (2) in 243, and committed suicide.

Testimonia: H. von Arnim, *SVF* 1. 96–102.   J. A.

persecution, religious See CHRISTIANITY; INTOLERANCE, INTELLECTUAL AND RELIGIOUS; SEMITISM (PAGAN), ANTI-.

Persephone/Kore, goddess, *Demeter's daughter by *Zeus, *Hades' wife and queen of the Underworld. Her most important myth is that of her abduction by Hades, her father's brother, who carried her off when she was picking flowers in a meadow and took her to the underworld, Demeter's unsuccessful search for her daughter (which took her to *Eleusis) and consequent withdrawal from her normal functions caused the complete failure of crops, and men would have starved if Zeus had not intervened. When Demeter did not respond to the persuasion of the divine messengers he sent to mediate, Zeus sent Hermes to persuade Hades to release Persephone, which he did; but Hades tricked Persephone and made her eat some pomegranate seeds, with the consequence that she could not leave Hades for ever, but had to spend part of the year with her husband in the underworld and part of the year with her mother in the upper world. The story is told in the Homeric *Hymn to Demeter*, a text which has a complex relationship with what may well have been the most important cult involving Persephone and Demeter, that of the Eleusinian *mysteries, the celebration of which included a ritual search for Kore with torches.

In the images Kore/Persephone is represented as a young woman, often with the addition of attributes, among which torches, stalks of grain, and sceptres are common, while some, like the cock at *Locri Epizephyrii, are found especially in the iconography of particular cults.

The name Kore stresses her persona as Demeter's daughter, Persephone that as Hades' wife. (Her name also occurs in other forms, for example, Phersephone, or, in *Attic, Pherrephatta). The myth of her rape was perceived as, among many other things, a polarized articulation of some perceptions pertaining to marriage from the viewpoint of the girl. Her cult in some places, notably Locri Epizephyrii, stresses this aspect. Her wedding had an important place in Locrian cult and myth and she was worshipped also as the protector of marriage and the women's sphere, including the protection of children. Demeter does not seem to have had a prominent place in the Locrian cult. Persephone's wedding and the flower-picking that preceded the abduction were also celebrated in other places, as, for example, in Sicily, where her flower-picking and marriage were celebrated, and in the Locrian colony of *Hipponium. The Sicilians also celebrated *Korēs katagōgē*, the bringing down of Kore.

Of course she also had an awesome and dread aspect as the queen of the underworld. Everyone will eventually come under her authority. But she was not implacable, and she and Hades listened to reasonable requests, such as that to return to the upper world to request the performance of proper burial or other rites—a trait abused and exploited by the dishonest *Sisyphus who refused to return to Hades.

She was often worshipped in association with Demeter; a most important festival in honour of the two goddesses was the *Thesmophoria, which was celebrated by women all over the Greek world (Demeter also bore the cult-title Thesmophoros, 'law-giving'). At *Cyzicus Persephone was worshipped with the epithet Soteira (Saviour) and her festival was called Pherephattia or Koreia or Soteria. (Cf. also Paus. 8. 31. 1 for Arcadia). Not surprisingly, Persephone had an important place in the texts inscribed on the gold leaves that were buried with people who had been initiated into *Orphism. In one strand of belief Persephone was the mother of Dionysus-Zagreus.

M. P. Nilsson, *Griechische Feste* (1906), 354–62, and *Geschichte der griechischen Religion*, 1³ (1967), 462–6, 469–81; L. R. Farnell, *The Cults of the Greek States*, 3 (1907); J. S. Clay, *The Politics of Olympus* (1989), 202–66; G. E. Mylonas, *Eleusis and the Eleusinian Mysteries* (1961); W. Burkert, *Greek Religion: Archaic and Classical*² (1985), 159–61, and *Homo Necans* (1983), 248–97; E. Simon, *Die Götter der Griechen* (1985) 91–117; C. Sourvinou-Inwood, 'Reading' Greek Culture (1991) 147–88. C. S.-I.

Persepolis, in Persis, a residence of the *Achaemenid kings. *Alexander (3) the Great in 331 BC took and looted Persepolis and set fire to the palaces (Diod. 17. 71–2); this served to bake a number of clay sealings. The royal quarters, built on a hill-terrace, contained a treasury and symmetrically planned palaces with immense square columnar halls.

Excavations on the site have revealed that *Darius I levelled the rock-terrace and began the great *Apadana (audience hall), the main palace-buildings, and the 'harem'. These were completed by *Xerxes I; *Artaxerxes (1) I finished the Hall of a Hundred Pillars and built his own palace. Around the whole complex was a fortification wall, and a great gate and stairway led up to the terrace. The bas-reliefs of these palaces are among the finest extant examples of Achaemenid art. These include the Audience reliefs originally flanked by lions attacking bulls, and 23 delegations of tribute bearers. The tombs of the Achaemenid kings are near by. In the palace and walls two collections of thousands of administrative texts written in *Elamite have been found.

E. F. Schmidt, *Persepolis* 1–3 (1953–70); R. G. Kent, *Old Persian*² (1953); R. T. Hallock, *Persepolis Fortification Tablets* (1969); A. B. Tilia, *Studies and Restorations at Persepolis and other Sites of Fars*, 1–2 (1972–8); G. G. Cameron, *Persepolis Treasury Tablets* (1984); E. Porada, *Cambridge History of Iran* 2 (1985), 793–827. M. S. D.; M. V.

Perses of *Thebes (1), a poet of the later 4th cent. BC, has a few sepulchral and dedicatory epigrams in the Greek Anthology, apparently written as real inscriptions (e.g. *Anth. Pal.* 7. 445) but more emotional than similar poems in the Classical era (e.g. 7. 730).

Gow–Page, *HE* 2859 ff.; Page OCT *Epigrammata Graeca*, 834 ff. G. H.; S. H.

Perseus (1), a mythological hero. The following, founded on Apollod. 2. 4. 1–5, is the usual legend. *Acrisius, brother of *Proetus, being warned by an oracle that his daughter *Danaë's son would kill him, shut her away in a bronze chamber. *Zeus visited her there in a shower of gold. Acrisius, learning that she had borne a son, whom she called Perseus, set mother and child adrift at sea in a chest. They drifted to the island of Seriphus, where a fisherman called Dictys rescued them and gave them shelter. When Perseus became a young man, Polydectes, the king of Seriphus and Dictys' brother, having fallen in love with Danae contrived to send him away to fetch the head of the Gorgon Medusa (see GORGO). This Perseus achieved, with the help of *Athena and *Hermes through whom he acquired the necessary implements of sickle, bag, cap of darkness for invisibility, and winged shoes. While returning home he came upon *Andromeda about to be devoured by a sea-monster, fell in love with her, rescued and married her. When they returned to Seriphus he used the Gorgon's head to turn Polydectes and his followers into stone for persecuting Danaë. He now gave the head to Athena, who put it in the centre of her *aegis, and returned the bag, cap and shoes to Hermes. Leaving Dictys as king of Seriphus, he came with his wife and mother to *Argos (2) to see his grandfather. But Acrisius, learning of this and still fearing the oracle, hurried away to *Pelasgiotis. Perseus followed, and, while competing in the funeral games of Teutamides, king of *Larissa, he threw the discus and accidentally struck and killed Acrisius, thus fulfilling the oracle. Leaving Argos to the son of Proetus, Megapenthes, he became king of *Tiryns and founder of the Perseidae dynasty. The adventures of Perseus, and particularly those relating to the beheading of Medusa, are favourite themes in art from the 7th cent.

Brommer, *Vasenlisten*³, 271–91, and *LIMC* 7. H. J. R.; J. R. M.

Perseus (2), king of *Macedonia (179–168 BC), elder son and legitimate successor of *Philip (3) V, was born about 213/2. He took part in his father's campaigns against the Romans and then, as ally of Rome, against the *Aetolians. Perseus stood against the pro-Roman policies and royal aspirations of his brother Demetrius (executed for treason by Philip in 180) and succeeded to the throne on Philip's death in 179. After renewing his father's treaty with Rome, he secured his popularity at home with a royal amnesty and set about extending his influence and connections in the Greek world at large. In the early 170s he married Laodice, daughter of *Seleucus (4) IV, gave his sister in marriage to *Prusias (II) of Bithynia, won the goodwill of *Rhodes, and restored Macedon's position in the Delphic *Amphictiony. The mid-170s saw his popular involvement in social conflicts in Aetolia and *Thessaly, his reduction of Dolopia, and a remarkable *tour de force* through central Greece. Perseus' success evoked at Rome hostile suspicion, evident from the early 170s and increasing thereafter as Perseus came to be for many an alternative focus to Rome in the states of Greece. Much of the expansion of Perseus' influence was at the expense of *Eumenes (II) of Pergamum, widely and correctly perceived theretofore as supporter of Rome. Eumenes denounced Perseus at length to the Romans (172) and provided them with a series of pretexts for war with Macedon, declared in 171. That Perseus had warlike designs against Rome must be doubted, as his susceptibility to the deceptive diplomacy of Q. *Marcius Philippus in the winter of 172/1 suggests. His aim was to restore the prestige of Macedon in Greece, and a situation wherein 'the Romans would be chary . . . of giving harsh and unjust orders to the Macedonians' (Pol. 27. 9. 3). Perseus' decision to accept war with Rome has, with reference to the military manpower available to Rome, been viewed as foolish; it has also, with different sort of reason, been compared to the decision of the Greeks in October 1940. His strategy of defence on the

Macedonian frontiers was at first successful, and a cavalry victory in 171 revealed a groundswell of support in Greece. But his diplomacy won over only the Illyrian king Genthius, whose support proved of little moment. The Romans entered Macedonia, and the Macedonian phalanx fought its last battle on unfavourable ground at *Pydna, on the morrow of the lunar eclipse in June 168. Perseus himself, after firing the royal records, was taken on *Samothrace later in the year. He graced the triumphal procession (see TRIUMPH) of L. *Aemilius Paullus (2) in 167 and died in captivity a few years later at *Alba Fucens.

P. Meloni, *Perseo e la fine della monarchia macedone* (1953); F. W. Walbank, *HCP*; V. M. Warrior, *AJAH* 1981, 1 ff.; E. S. Gruen, *The Hellenistic World and the Coming of Rome* (1984), 505 ff.; *HM* 3. 488 ff.; P. S. Derow, *CAH* 8² (1989), 303 ff.
P. S. D.

Perseus (3) (2nd cent. BC), mathematician. *Proclus describes him as the discoverer of the sections of the σπεῖρα (tore or anchor-ring).

W. Knorr, *The Ancient Tradition of Geometric Problems* (1986), 263 ff.
A. S.

Persia In the narrow sense (Persis, Pārsa), Persia defines the country lying in the folds of the southern Zagros mountains. From the start of the first millennium BC, an Iranian population lived in close contact with the Elamite inhabitants here (see ELAM). This led to the emergence of the Persian *ethnos* and the kingdom of Anshan, which appears fully on the historical scene beginning with the conquests of *Cyrus (1) the Great. Even with the extension and consolidation of the *Achaemenid empire under *Darius I, Persia proper retained a prominent place in the way in which the Great Kings visualized their territorial power. At the same time, members of the Persian aristocracy received the highest governorships and offices in the central and provincial government. In this respect, the empire created by Cyrus and his successors may be described as Persian.

The history of this large empire has been neglected for a long time: between the fall of *Babylon (539) and *Alexander (3) the Great's arrival, the Near East has resembled a gigantic historiographical 'no-man's land'. This neglect cannot be blamed on a lack of documents, and finds of material continue to be made. Besides the archaeological and iconographical evidence, the historian has at his disposal royal inscriptions, thousands of *Elamite and Babylonian tablets and *Aramaic documents, not to mention Greek accounts and other regional bodies of material. But Achaemenid history has been viewed for a long time through the distorting lenses of Greek authors, not least because the Persians themselves left virtually no narrative accounts of their own history. The find of central government documents (especially the Elamite tablets from *Persepolis, combined with a different vision of Near Eastern history, has given a new and powerful impetus to intensive study of a fascinating period of ancient history.

On the historical scale, the Achaemenid period represents a turning point in Middle Eastern history: for the first time, countries from the Indus to the Balkans, from Central Asia to Elephantine in Upper Egypt were embraced by one, unifying, political structure. This political unification did not result in the disappearance of local ethno-cultural identities. In 334, despite the marked process of acculturation, Asia Minor, *Egypt, *Babylonia, and *Bactria were still countries clearly distinguishable in terms of language, culture, and religion. This was also true of Persia proper. In spite of partial and/or temporary setbacks (notably the secession of Egypt between 399 and 343), the overall assessment must be that the empire held together for more than two centuries. Alexander himself frequently did little more than take over to his own advantage the Achaemenid ideological heritage and administrative techniques. *Mutatis mutandis*, the splintered geo-political pattern of the Near East *c.*280 recalls the one which had prevailed before Cyrus the Great's conquests.

J. M. Cook, *The Persian Empire* (1983); P. Briant *HEA*, *passim*; J. Wiesehöfer, *Die 'dunklen Jahrhunderte' der Persis* (1994); A. Kuhrt, *The Ancient Near East* (1995), 647 ff.
P. B.

Persian, Old (abbr. OP), an *Indo-European language of western Iran (first millennium BC). Its writing is limited to royal inscriptions. The syllabic script has only 44 signs. The oldest extant and largest inscription is that of *Bisitun. It is debated whether the script was invented by *Darius I or had predecessors in western Iran. The majority of texts dates from the reigns of Darius and *Xerxes I. Thereafter texts are scarcer and contain more errors. OP was the first *cuneiform script to be deciphered (Grotefend, Rawlinson).

R. G. Kent, *Old Persian, Grammar, Texts, Lexicon* (1953); P. Lecoq, *ActIr.* 2 (1974), 55–62, and *ActIr.* 3 (1974), 25–107; I. M. Diakonov, in *W. B. Henning Memorial Volume* (1970), 98–124; W. Hinz, *Neue Wege im Altpersischen* (1973), 15–38.
H. S.-W.

Persian Gulf, a shallow, epicontinental sea located between lat. 24°–30° 30' N. and long. 48°–56° 30' W., *c.*1,000 km. long (625 mi.), 200–350 km. wide (125–200 mi.), narrowing to *c.*60 km. (40 mi.) where it debouches through the Straits of Hormuz into the Indian Ocean. Human settlement on the coast of the Persian Gulf can be traced from *c.*5,000 BC onward. Fragments from a lost periplus of *Scylax of Caryanda have suggested to some scholars that Scylax explored the Persian Gulf sometime between *c.*519 and 480 BC, but this view is considered untenable by others. The Persian Gulf is possibly mentioned in Greek literature for the first time as Περσικὸς κόλπος in a no longer extant work by *Hecataeus (1) (*c.*500 BC), cited by Steph. Byz. (*Ethn.*), by which name it was known to *Eratosthenes (Strab. 15. 2. 14; 16. 3. 2) and *Arrian (*Anab.* 5. 26. 2). *Pliny (1) calls it *sinus Persicus* (*HN* 6. 108–9, 138, 144) or *mare Persicum* (*HN* 6. 114, 130, 149). The voyage of *Nearchus in 325 BC afforded the first real opportunity for the Greeks to observe the Persian Gulf, resulting in the collection of detailed botanical information on the region (Theophr. *Hist. Pl.* 4. 7. 7–8; 5. 4. 7–8; *Caus.* 2. 5. 5). *Alexander (3) the Great's interest in exploring the east coast of *Arabia and offshore islands led him to send out three expeditions in 324 BC, under Archias, *Androsthenes, and Hieron, which resulted in the collection of more data on the region. Although Alexander's plans to conquer and colonize eastern Arabia remained unfulfilled, the native peoples of the Persian Gulf did come under a certain degree of Hellenistic influence, though less by direct colonization than by trade. Many cemeteries and the large mound of Ras al-Qalat bear witness to strong Hellenistic influence on Bahrain (see TYLOS); sites in eastern Saudi Arabia, such as the walled-city of Thaj (see GERRHA), have yielded Attic black-glazed pottery and other Greek imports; and excavations at the site of Mleiha, in the emirate of Sharjah (UAE), have uncovered stamped Rhodian *amphora handles. Mleiha is also known to have been a mint, where coinage was mould-made. The *Seleucids never established many colonies along the Persian Gulf, and most of these were at the head of the Gulf only (e.g. Seleuceia-on-the-Erythraean Sea (in Elymais/southern *Mesene?); *Antioch (4)-

Persis; Alexandria-on-the-Tigris (i.e. Spasinou Charax); and Are-thusa, Larisa, and Chalcis (lower Tigris or north-easternmost Arabia?)). A Hellenistic fortification and sanctuary was estab-lished on Failaka, an island off the coast of Kuwait (see ICAROS (2)). During the Roman era, a major axis of trade linked *Palmyra, Spasinou Charax, and *India in a network which must have existed parallel to that described in the *Peripl. M. Rubr.*, *Juba (2) II of Mauretania's *De Expeditione Arabica*, prepared for the young Gaius Caesar (C. *Iulius Caesar (2)), contained detailed information on the peoples and places of the Arabian side of the Gulf, as the citations from it in Pliny attest, and the *Geography* of *Ptolemy (4) preserves many toponyms and ethnic names attesting to a large population, both settled and tribal, in the area. The archaeology of this period is less well-known, but the large site of ed-Dur, in the emirate of Umm al-Qaiwain (UAE), has yielded e.g. much imported Roman glass and ceramics, largely datable to the 1st cent. AD, as well as half-a-dozen coins minted by the kings of Characene, at the head of the Gulf, and an aureus of *Tiberius.

H. Bretzl, *Botanische Forschungen des Alexanderzuges* (1903); A. Hermann, *RE* 37 (1937), 1030–3; J.-F. Salles in A. Kuhrt and S. Sherwin-White (eds.), *Hellenism in the East* (1987), 75–109; J.-F. Salles in H. Sancisi-Weerdenburg and A. Kuhrt (eds), *Achaemenid History*, 4 (1990), 111–30; D. T. Potts, *The Arabian Gulf in Antiquity*, 2 (1990), 1–21 and *The Pre-Islamic Coinage of Eastern Arabia* (1991). D. T. P.

Persian Wars, term usually applied to the two Persian attempts to conquer Greece in 490 and 480/79 BC. The origins of the conflict go back to mainland Greek involvement in the rebellion of the Asiatic Greeks against Persian rule, earlier in the 5th cent. (see IONIAN REVOLT), but although *Herodotus (1) dramatizes their desire for revenge, the Persians already ruled many European Greeks in *Thrace and *Macedonia, and their primary reason for seeking to conquer the rest may well have been that their rule over existing Greek subjects would never be secure while others remained independent.

The first attack was by sea. After ravaging *Naxos (1) and subdu-ing other islands, forcing Carystus (see EUBOEA) to terms, and taking *Eretria by treachery, an invasion-force eventually reached *Marathon, where it was confronted by an army of Athenians and Plataeans (see PLATAEA). After several days' delay during which the Persians possibly hoped for support to materialize for the ex-tyrant of Athens, *Hippias (1), who had accompanied them, they perhaps provoked a battle by beginning to move on Athens, but were decisively defeated. See MARATHON, BATTLE OF.

The death of *Darius (1) and a revolt in Egypt delayed renewal of the attack, but when it came, it was on a more massive scale and led by Darius' successor, *Xerxes I, in person. How large his forces actually were is an intractable problem: the fleet may have con-tained the 1,207 triremes of tradition, but the army is unlikely to have had more than 100,000 men at most. Persian strategy clearly involved co-operation between the two, but the view that the army depended on sea-borne supplies is probably mistaken, since it continued to operate in 479 after the fleet had been defeated. More likely, naval forces were intended to prevent Greek ships from interfering with communications or in Asia Minor, and also, possibly, to turn Greek defensive positions on land.

Once aware of the Persian preparations, the Greeks consulted the *Delphic oracle and received a series of gloomy prognostica-tions. The Athenians, in particular, were advised to flee to the ends of the earth, and even a second approach only elicited the enigmatic response to rely on the 'wooden wall'. But interpreting this to refer to their newly-built navy, they determined to resist,

and probably late in 481, conferred with others of like mind. It was decided to patch up quarrels, to send spies to *Asia Minor, and to appeal for help from uncommitted states. The appeals failed, and the spies were caught, to be released on Xerxes' orders to spread alarming reports of his power. But, crucially, under Spartan leadership, an alliance was created.

At a second meeting, probably in spring, 480, a Thessalian appeal to defend the *Tempe pass led to the dispatch of 10,000 *hoplites by sea via the Gulf of *Pagasae. These withdrew before Xerxes even crossed the *Hellespont, allegedly because of a warning from the Macedonian king about Persian numbers, and the realization that the pass could be turned. But the episode clearly shows that there was as yet no Peloponnesian reluctance to defend northern and central Greece, and that preparations by both land and sea were well in hand.

It was then decided to defend the *Thermopylae pass and to send the fleet to *Artemisium on the north-east coast of *Euboea. But Thermopylae was turned through treachery, and what was probably a rear-guard under the king of Sparta, overwhelmed (see LEONIDAS (1); THERMOPYLAE, BATTLE OF), while at sea, though the Persians suffered severely in storms, and the Greeks held the initiative for two days, they were so battered in the third day's fighting that they had virtually decided to withdraw before the news from Thermopylae arrived. See ARTEMISIUM, BATTLE OF.

Falling back to *Salamis (1), the Greek fleet helped the Atheni-ans to complete the evacuation of *Attica, which had probably been decided upon and largely carried out some months previ-ously, but there then followed a pause. Eventually, either because of a message from *Themistocles or because it was decided to try a surprise attack before the onset of winter, the Persian fleet entered the channel between Salamis and the mainland where its numbers and manoeuvrability were nullified. Decisively defeated (24 September?), it withdrew to Asia. See SALAMIS, BATTLE OF.

Xerxes himself now also returned to Asia, but probably left most of his army in Greece under *Mardonius, who wintered in Thessaly and offered Athens generous terms to weaken her resolve. When this failed, he reoccupied the city (June 479), sending another envoy over to Salamis with a renewed offer. Despite stirring expressions of an undying will to resist, and the lynching of an unfortunate councillor who suggested the offer be considered, Athenian resolution was severely tested by Sparta's reluctance to take the offensive. But in the end, a combination of scarcely veiled Athenian threats and allied warnings broke the deadlock.

Mardonius withdrew from Attica, allegedly because it was not suitable for cavalry and a potential trap, but possibly, in reality, to avoid confrontation and thus continue to let diplomacy do his work, The Greeks followed him to *Boeotia, but clung to the foothills of Cithaeron (the mountain range which separates this part of Boeotia from Attica) until a success against the Persian cavalry in which its commander was killed, led them to move nearer to the Asopus, where Mardonius' main camp lay. There followed a delay during which they suffered increasingly from the harassment of Persian cavalry, and eventually, with their supply-lines severed and their water-supply at risk, they had to retreat.

Despite modern suggestions that the withdrawal was skilfully planned to lure Mardonius into attacking the apparently isolated right wing, whereupon the centre and left would converge to crush him, it is more likely that everything went wrong, as Herodotus suggests, with the centre's precipitate retirement to Plataea leaving the wings dangerously divided. However, in the ensuing battle, the Lacedaemonians (i.e. Spartans) and Tegeates (see TEGEA) on the right routed the Persians, while the Athenians on the left defeated their Greek allies. Mardonius himself was killed and most of his Asiatic troops with him, either on the field or in their palisaded camp. Only the Persian centre which had never become involved, managed to retreat in good order. See PLATAEA, BATTLE OF. According to Greek legend, on the very same day, across the Aegean, a Greek fleet under *Leotychidas, king of Sparta, landed its men on the Mycale peninsula, defeated a Persian army and stormed the palisaded base where their ships had been beached. Thus the Greek triumph was complete.

Some modern explanations for their victory can be discounted. There is no reason to believe, for example, that Persian soldiers, even those conscripted from subject peoples, fought any less conscientiously for their king than the Greeks for their freedom. Fighting for freedom is no guarantee of success, and the Indian army under the Raj shows that subjects of an imperial power can make superb soldiers. Nor is there any reason to believe that the Greeks, with the possible exception of the Spartans, were more highly trained or more disciplined than their opponents (see MILITARY TRAINING, GREEK). Indeed, at sea, the reverse was probably the case. However, it is true that even if most hoplites were untrained and inexperienced, they were at least accustomed to the *idea* of hand-to-hand combat, whereas this was not true of the Persians.

Again, Greek commanders were certainly no more highly trained or experienced than their Persian counterparts. If anything, the latter had probably had more experience, but the officers of both sides largely owed their positions to social standing. Thus it is unlikely that tactics or strategy played a decisive part. Only at Marathon is there any good evidence for Greek tactics, and even there the thinning of the Greek centre was probably defensive, and the converging of the wings accidental.

As for strategy, it has been alleged that the positioning of the Greek fleet at Salamis virtually compelled the Persians to fight it under unfavourable circumstances, even that the Greeks had decided, from the start, to fall back on Salamis and the Isthmus, and to win the war at sea, while, in effect, refusing their land forces. But these views largely depend on the erroneous notion that the Persian army depended on their fleet for supplies. Nevertheless, it is true that the Greeks both achieved a sufficient measure of unity to put up a defence in some strength, and that they acted together in a simple but effective plan, occupying defensive positions to nullify the enemy's strength in numbers and mobility, and as far north as possible. In the end there is no simple explanation for what happened. Perhaps the simplest is that in the two decisive battles the Greeks were better equipped. At Salamis, in confined waters, their possibly more stoutly constructed ships—Herodotus has Themistocles describe them as 'heavier' (βαρυτέρας: 8. 60a)—stood up better to ramming head-on; at Plataea, as he emphasizes (9. 62. 3, 63. 2), their hoplites were certainly better equipped for hand-to-hand fighting. The Persians could have avoided both battles, and thus, as *Thucydides (2) has some speakers from *Corinth imply (1. 69. 5), it might be truer to say that they lost through their own mistakes.

C. Hignett, *Xerxes' Invasion of Greece* (1963); A. R. Burn, *Persia and the Greeks* (2nd edn. 1985); J. F. Lazenby, *The Defence of Greece* (1993); P. Green, *The Greco-Persian Wars* (1996).   J. F. La.

Persian Wars: the Persian viewpoint One of the great problems for the historian is the absence of any direct reflection of the Persian angle on this celebrated conflict. In fact, besides the *Bisitun inscription and relief, which recounts *Darius I's accession, the Persians have not left us any narrative accounts of their history. The changes in the lists of provinces which appear regularly in the royal inscriptions cannot be used as a reliable criterion for tracing the growth or shrinkage of Persian territorial power. We find the only Persian version of the wars (at least, it is presented as such) in a late account by *Dio Cocceianus (Dio. Chrys. *Or.* 11. 148–9). Dio cites the oral testimony of a fictional Mede, and asserts that the mission entrusted by Darius to *Datis and *Artaphernes in 490 was to sail against *Naxos (1) and *Eretria; according to this version, the Marathon episode (see MARATHON, BATTLE OF) was an unimportant failure; similarly, *Xerxes' victory at *Thermopylae, his punishment of Athens and the tribute imposed on the Greeks allowed him to present himself in a flattering light as a returning victor. Dio adds that this was clearly the official version, intended to prevent any restlessness on the part of the 'peoples of the upper land (τὰ ἄνω ἔθνη)'. Otherwise, in view of the Persian silence on the wars, *Herodotus (1) is practically our only source. For him, the expeditions of 490 and 480 were the culmination of a long series of conflicts and misunderstandings. In his perspective, the *Ionian Revolt and decisions taken as a result played a key-role. This is true of the burning of *Sardis (*c.*499) which, he says (5. 102), gave the Persians the opportunity to declare a war of reprisals against the Greeks; similarly, the participation of an Athenian contingent alongside the Ionians 'was the beginning of disaster for Greeks and barbarians' (5. 97). According to Herodotus' logic, Persian actions on the western frontier were part of a planned series of steps leading inevitably towards an expedition against the cities of Europe: the conquest of *Samos by Syloson (3. 139–47), the mission supposedly entrusted to *Democedes (3. 135–8), the Scytho-Thracian expedition of Darius in 513 and *Mardonius' campaign in *Thrace following the Ionian Revolt were all part of this plan. Herodotus' presentation is very debatable, as it is a questionable assumption that Darius had determined on a plan for the conquest of Balkan Greece from the moment of his accession. He certainly did pursue a consistent Aegean policy, following that of *Cambyses, who is known to have been the real founder of Achaemenid naval power. Thucydides understood this, when he set Darius' conquest of the islands into the *longue durée* of thalassocracies (see SEA POWER). Thus, what we traditionally call the first Persian war was nothing more than the last stage of the Persian seizure of the eastern Aegean. This also means that the expedition of Datis and Artaphernes was rather different in aim from the campaign led by Xerxes in 480. The punishment meted out to Eretria and Athens in 490 was little more than a secondary by-product of successful maritime conquest; in 480, the aim was to compel the European Greeks to acknowledge Xerxes' sovereignty, although nothing definite is known of Xerxes' precise territorial ambitions and plans for organizing his European conquests. Although the Persian Wars as such ended in 479, the Greek struggle against the Persians continued, with the Ionian cities asking Sparta, then Athens, to protect them in order to forestall a renewed Persian offensive. This request led to the birth in 478, under Athenian hegemony, of the *Delian League, 'whose guiding principle was to ravage the lands of the King in revenge for the wrongs suffered' (Thuc. 1. 96. 1). The hostilities between Athens and Persia spanned the length and breadth of the Aegean front from Thrace to Egypt. In the first stage they were marked by a series of victorious Athenian offensives under the command of *Cimon (victor at *Eurymedon in 466), until the Athenians suffered a serious defeat in Egypt. We have the first mention of direct intervention by the Persian court in Greek affairs on this occasion, i.e. when *Artaxerxes (1) I sent Megabazus to Sparta 'to bring about the retreat of the Athenian troops from Egypt' (Thuc. 1. 109. 2). Around 449/8, according to Diodorus (13. 4. 4–6) and other ancient writers, a peace was concluded between the Great King and Athens, by whose terms Artaxerxes undertook not to intervene with military force on the Asia Minor coast. But, given Thucydides' silence on the matter, the historical veracity of this 'Peace of Callias' is a subject of continuing debate. See CALLIAS, PEACE OF. In the following years Persian *satraps intervened repeatedly in the cities of Asia Minor, e.g. Pissouthnes who, c.440, sent auxiliary troops to help the Samian exiles wishing to overthrow the island's democracy and Athenian hegemony. The Athenian disaster in Sicily spurred the satraps *Pharnabazus (Dascylium) and *Tissaphernes (Sardis) into making an alliance with Sparta (412). This led to the Ionian War (see PELOPONNESIAN WAR), when Spartans and Athenians fought each other under the watchful eye of the representatives of the Great King, who had ordered his satraps to collect the tribute due from the Greek cities of Asia. The Athenian defeat (404) did not put an end to hostilities, which resumed in Asia Minor and the islands in the early years of the 4th cent.; they continued down to 387/6, when *Artaxerxes (2) II imposed the *King's Peace, which gave control of the Greek cities of Asia Minor to Persia. This treaty was still determining relations between *Darius III and the Asiatic cities when *Alexander (3) the Great began his campaign in Asia Minor (cf. Arrian *Anab.* 2. 1. 4; 2. 2).

In his *Panegyricus* *Isocrates denounced the Persian-imposed treaty, which he contrasted with the Peace of Callias: 'Then it was we who fixed the frontiers of the barbarian empire . . . Now it is he who regulates Greek affairs' (118–20). The passage shows that, beginning in antiquity, the great periods of Graeco-Persian hostilities were set into an ideological vision of Greek–*barbarian relations. In Athens, in particular, the memory of the Persian wars became a tenet of Athenian self-glorification and was deliberately transformed in the process. This 'vulgate' appears from *Aeschylus' *Persians* (472) onwards; thereafter all the orators of the 4th cent. appealed to the memory of the great moments of Marathon and Salamis (see SALAMIS, BATTLE OF) in order to justify Athenian pretensions to hegemony. This is especially true of the theoreticians of *panhellenism, from *Gorgias (1) and *Lysias to Isocrates and *Ephorus. Among all the great deeds of the past, Marathon was particularly favoured by the orator obliged to declaim the annual *epitaphios. When *Diodorus (3) (drawing on Ephorus) wishes to stress the courage of the Greek soldiers fighting with the Pharaoh Inarus against the Persians in 460, he maintains that they knew how to be worthy of their elders at Thermopylae (11. 77. 3–4). A century later, *Chares (1) again invoked the precedent of the Persian Wars after his victory over Persian detachments in Hellespontine Phrygia, not scrupling to present it to the Athenians as 'the sister of the Battle of Marathon' (Schol. ad Dem. 4. 14; Plut. *Arat.* 16. 3). *Alexander (3) the Great, too, took up the theme of the war of revenge: conceptually his destruction of *Persepolis corresponded to the destructions wrought by Xerxes on the Athenian acropolis, and so put an official end to the confrontation between Greeks and barbarians. The mythologized memory of the Persian Wars continued to be transmitted in Hellenistic Athens (*BCH* 99 (1975): 63–75). See PERSIAN-WARS TRADITION.

G. Nenci *Introduzione alle guerre persiane* (1958); N. Loraux *L'Invention d'Athènes* (1981; Eng. trans. 1986); M. Nouhaud *L'Utilisation de l'histoire par les orateurs attiques* (1982); *CAH* 5² (1992); P. Briant, *HEA* chs. 4, 13.
P. B.

Persian-Wars tradition The glory-days of the Persian wars loomed large in defining mainland Greek identities until well into the Roman age. In *Thucydides (1) 5th-cent. Athens justified its empire by them (1. 74. 4), in the tradition of the *epitaphios they are a cause for Athenian boasting (accompanied by distortion of the facts), and in *Aristophanes (1) for nostalgia. In the 4th cent. *Macedonia's rise prompted rhetorical appeals by Athenian politicians to ancestral resolve and self-sacrifice in the Persian wars, notably after the fall of *Olynthus in 348 BC (Dem. 19. 303), the context in which a group of documents allegedly from the Persian wars first appear (see PLATAEA, OATH OF), stigmatized by *Theopompus (3) (*FGrH* 115 F 153), and most modern historians, as Athenian inventions. *Philip (1) II and *Alexander (3) the Great countered this (mainly) Athenian rhetoric by presenting Macedon's Persian adventure as a Greek war of revenge for Persian sacrilege in 480 BC (Arr. *Anab.* 2. 14. 4; 3. 18. 11–12). The prestige-seeking Attalid kings of Hellenistic *Pergamum explicitly paralleled their victories over the Gauls (see GALATIA) with earlier Greek ones over Persia (esp. Paus. 1. 24. 2). Roman emperors from *Augustus on equated Persia with *Parthia in presenting eastern policy and warfare, along the way fuelling subject-Greek memories of the Persian wars, a favourite theme of the *Second Sophistic.

C. Habicht, *Hermes* 1961, 1–35; R. Thomas, *Oral Tradition and Written Record* (1989), esp. 225, 84–93; A. Spawforth, in S. Hornblower (ed.), *Greek Historiography* (1994), ch. 9.
A. J. S. S.

Persius Flaccus, Aulus (AD 34–62), Neronian satirist; see NERO. His ancient biography records that he was a rich equestrian of *Etruscan stock who died young and who was connected with the Stoic opposition to Nero (see STOICISM) through his links with P. *Clodius Thrasea Paetus and the philosopher L. *Annaeus Cornutus. However, Persius' satires are isolated and introverted works, more concerned with inner, philosophical freedom than with political liberty. The 'biting truth' he reveals (1. 107) is confined to moral crassness, literary bad taste, and his own failings.

Persius claims to take his lead from *Lucilius (1), but his language and ideas are similar to those of *Horace. He reduces Horace's 18 satires to 6 and a mere 650 hexameters, offering 'something more concentrated' (1. 120), with 'the taste of bitten nails' (1. 106). This format provoked violent reactions in antiquity: Lucan (M. *Annaeus Lucanus) admired the satires as 'real poetry'; *Martial considered them a precious elixir worth more than bulky epics; but Jerome is said to have burned them because of their obscurity. Persius certainly stretches satire to un-Horatian extremes: his characters are either aged or immature, tutors or students; his ideal is uncompromising Stoicism, not easy Epicureanism (see EPICURUS); Horace's mocking conversations become diatribes filled with bitter spleen.

Persius opens with a prologue in limping iambics (scazons), the metre of cynical sneering, exposing satire as a hybrid, semi-poetic genre, and the patronage system as mutual back-scratching. (1) lifts the curtain on a disgusting orgy of modern poetry, in which specimens of literary decadence, possibly parodies of Nero's own works, corrupt Persius' avowedly straightforward style. His disgust with 'confused Rome' eventually explodes, and he mutters a cherished secret into a hole in the ground: all Romans have asses' ears. This echo of the Midas story (see MIDAS (1)) prompted an ancient legend that Cornutus, who edited Persius after his death, had been forced to change a specific attack on Nero to this vaguer generalization. (2) strips bare the hypocrisy of Roman citizens who sacrifice to the gods in the hope of material gain, not moral virtue. (3) is most often read as a dialogue between a lazy student in bed with a hangover and a Stoic tutor who urges him to pursue philosophy before it is too late (though both may be voices inside Persius' own head). (4) is a dialogue between a young politician (*Alcibiades) and a philosopher (*Socrates) where, again, self-knowledge is encouraged. In (5) Persius pays homage to his own tutor Cornutus, who has taught him to use unadorned language. The two are united by their devotion to Stoicism in a topsy-turvy world where others are enslaved to material desires. In (6), a Horatian-style epistle to *Caesius Bassus from the coastal resort of *Luna, Persius meditates on the contrast between his own tiny and worthless-seeming legacy to his profligate heirs and the infinite heaps of wealth coveted by others.

Persius is often regarded as a paragon of Stoic virtue, but in fact he makes no secret of his own imperfections; in the confusion of different voices, he speaks as an erring student as well as a stern tutor. It is a mistake to try to extract clear messages from his disjointed outbursts. Although he claims to aspire to bluntness, his language is a tortuous mixture, full of jarring juxtapositions and strained links (*iunctura . . . acri*, 5. 15); he uses a dense tissue of images, often graphically anatomical, to revitalize dead metaphors and fuse disparate ideas. It was this black wit which struck a chord with the church fathers, and with later satirists, especially John Donne. See SATIRE, ROMAN.

TEXT W. V. Clausen, OCT (1992²).

COMMENTARIES O. Jahn (1843, repr. 1967); J. Conington and H. Nettleship (1893, repr. 1967); D. Bo (1969); R. A. Harvey (1981); W. Kissel (1990).

STUDIES K. J. Reckford, *Hermes* 1962, 476–504; C. S. Dessen, *'Iunctura Callidus Acri': A Study of Persius' Satires* (1968); R. G. M. Nisbet in *Critical Essays on Roman Literature: Satire*, ed. J. P. Sullivan (1963); J. C. Bramble, *Persius and the Programmatic Satire* (1974).

TRANSLATIONS J. Dryden (1692); W. Gifford (1821, repr. 1991); W. S. Merwin (1961); N. Rudd (1973); G. Lee (1987). E. J. G.

persuasion See PEITHO; RHETORIC, GREEK and LATIN.

Pertinax (emperor). See HELVIUS PERTINAX, P.

Perusia, mod. Perugia, an ancient Italian hill city with interesting walls and Etruscan tombs. Originally perhaps *Umbrian, Perusia first appears in history as an *Etruscan city. In 295 BC, despite a treaty, it fought against Rome, then submitted and signed a lengthy truce (Serv. on *Aen.* 10. 201; Diod. 20. 35; Livy 10. 30, 31, 37). Thereafter it remained loyal, e.g. against Hannibal (Livy 23. 17; 28. 45). When Perusia sheltered L. *Antonius in 41 Octavian (see AUGUSTUS) besieged, captured, and plundered it (Perusine War: App. *BCiv.* 5. 32–49). Subsequently called *Augusta Perusia*, Perusia always flourished but is rarely mentioned before the 6th cent.

C. Shaw, *Etruscan Perugia* (1939); G. Pianu, *Perugia* (1985); *Antichità dell'Umbria* (exhibition catalogues: see UMBRIANS).

E. T. S.; D. W. R. R.

Pervigilium Veneris, a Latin poem of 93 trochaic tetrameters catalectic, has caught the romantic imagination perhaps more than any other poem in ancient literature. But while its beauty is unquestioned, interpretation is problematic; date and authorship are uncertain, and many editors have contributed to the difficulties by the wholesale and unnecessary transposition of lines. The setting is *Sicily, on the eve of the spring festival of *Venus, and the poem celebrates the procreative power of the goddess in nature. For the most part the mood is one of exhilaration, which is reflected in the metre and in numerous cases of verbal repetition, most notably the famous refrain (*Cras amet qui numquam amavit, quique amavit cras amet* 'Let who has never loved love tomorrow, and tomorrow let who has loved love'); but a serious, philosophical side is also evident, and the poem ends on a disquieting note as the poet asks anguishedly when *his* spring will come. However it is to be interpreted, the poem is not to be thought of (as has been done) as a genuine liturgical hymn. As to the date, the reign of *Hadrian has been a popular conjecture, but the 4th cent. is on various grounds more likely (perhaps post-368; see Shanzer); it is certainly earlier than *Fulgentius, who quotes from it. The ascription to *Tiberianus (Baehrens, Cameron) is at best precarious.

TEXTS *Anth. Lat.* 200 Riese, 191 Shackleton Bailey; R. Schilling (1944); with trans. and comm., L. Catlow (1980); with trans., G. Goold, *Catullus, Tibullus, Pervigilium Veneris* (Loeb, 2nd edn. 1988).

STUDIES A. Cameron, in *La poesia tardoantica* (1984), 209–34 (incl. text); D. Shanzer, *RFIC* 1990, 306–18; H. M. Currie, *ANRW* 2. 34. 1 (1993), 207–24. J. H. D. S.

Pescennius (*RE* 2) **Niger Iustus, Gaius,** won distinction in a minor campaign in *Dacia in the 180s AD and became governor of *Syria *c.*191; he was proclaimed emperor there in April 193, on the news of P. *Helvius Pertinax's murder. He was an Italian and had support from the *plebs* at Rome, but was recognized only in the eastern provinces. L. *Septimius Severus moved rapidly against him, expelling his forces from *Thrace (except *Byzantium) in summer 193. Niger's army was defeated again at *Cyzicus and Nicaea before the end of the year, leading Egypt to renounce allegiance, with Arabia and some Syrian cities following suit. In spring 194 Niger was decisively defeated near Issus and was captured and killed near *Antioch (1), fleeing to the Parthians.

Dio Cass. 73–4; Herod. 2–3; SHA *Did. Iul.*; *Sev.*; *Pesc. Nig.* (largely fiction). B. M. *Coins, Rom. Emp.* 5; A. R. Birley, *The African Emperor Septimius Severus* (2nd edn. 1988). A. R. Bi.

Pessinus, mod. Balıhisar, was one of the most important cult centres of the goddess *Cybele in *Phrygia; the temple, built and adorned with marble porticos by the Attalids (see PERGAMUM), was controlled by priests (*galli, archigalli*). In 204 BC the sacred stone of the goddess was taken to Rome (Livy 29. 10. 4); see PHILHELLENISM. The Galatians assumed control over the priesthood, and in imperial times Pessinus became the centre of the Tolistobogian tribe (see GALATIA). The cult of Cybele was maintained until AD 362, when the emperor *Julian visited the sanctuary and attempted to revive it. Excavations to date have yielded no trace of the main sanctuary, but have uncovered a temple of the imperial cult from the time of *Tiberius and the central street of the city, which ran along the valley of the river Gallus and served as a canal during periods of high rainfall, when flood water swept through the city from the slopes of nearby Mount Dindymus.

B. Virgilio, *Il tempio-stato di Pessinunte* (1981); J. Devreker and M. Waelkens, *Les Fouilles de Pessinonte* (1982); M. Waelkens, *EA* 1984, 37–73 (imperial temple). S. M.

Petelia (*Strongoli*), Bruttian city (see BRUTTII) in S. Italy, 30 km. (19 mi.) north of *Croton. Originally a Chonian foundation, with Greek influences reflected in material culture and in the myth of foundation by *Philoctetes (Verg. *Aen.* 3.402), it fell to the Bruttii *c.*350, came under Roman control *c.*270, and was the only Bruttian city to remain loyal in the Hannibalic war (see PUNIC WARS).

E. Arslan in *Magna Grecia* (1974). K. L.

Petillius (*RE* 4, 11), **Quintus** Two tribunes (see TRIBUNI PLEBIS) of this same name are said by *Livy, following *Valerius Antias, to have prosecuted *Scipio Africanus in 187 BC, and later to have proposed the bill to set up a court to try L. *Cornelius Scipio Asiagenes and others on charges of corruption. These statements form part of the highly disputed evidence for the 'Trials of the Scipios'; the Petillii may indeed have been involved, if not in the way reported by Livy. One of the two will be the Q. Petillius (*RE* 11) Spurinus, who, as praetor 181, burnt the 'Pythagorean' books claimed to have belonged to King *Numa Pompilius, and as consul 176 died fighting in Liguria (see Ligurians).

Scullard, *RP* 290–303; J.-M. Pailler, *Bacchanalia* (1988), 623–67; E. S. Gruen, *Studies in Greek Culture and Roman Policy* (1990), ch. 5. J. Br.

Petillius (*RE* 8), **Cerialis Caesius Rufus, Quintus** (*suffect consul for the second time in AD 74), possibly son-in-law of *Vespasian, suffered a humiliating defeat while commanding *legion IX Hispana in Britain during *Boudicca's revolt (60). Entrusted with a cavalry force during the Flavian march on Rome, he was sent by Vespasian in 70 as governor of Lower Germany to put down the revolt of C. *Iulius Civilis in the Rhineland. Despite some setbacks which Tacitus attributes to rashness and carelessness, he won a victory at Rigodulum, occupying Trier (*Augusta Treverorum) the following day, and suppressed the rebellion by the end of 70. Cerialis probably held his first consulship in absence, then as governor of Britain (71–73/4), he crushed the *Brigantes, Britain's largest people, penetrating to the northern Pennines. The Q. Petillius Rufus, ordinary consul in 83, may be Cerialis himself, or possibly a son or brother.

A. R. Birley, *The Fasti of Roman Britain* (1981), 66. J. B. C.

Petra (*Aramaic *reqem* or *raqmū*) was the capital of the *Nabataeans from before 312 BC until the establishing of the Roman province of *Arabia in AD 106, from which date *Bostra was the base for Roman administration. Even in this late period Petra retained considerable significance and eventually became an important Christian centre. The town lies in a hollow surrounded by steep mountains. Most of its visible and excavated remains, including temples, a theatre, and a colonnaded street, date to the 1st cent. AD. The surrounding rock-faces have tombs cut in them. Some are small and have simple stepped patterns, others are extremely elaborate, have *triclinia* associated with them, and show artistic and architectural influence from Ptolemaic/Roman Egypt. Some fine tombs have been identified as royal and the general prominence of funeral architecture has even led to the suggestion that Petra might have been a necropolis rather than a normal settlement site. The possibility exists, however, that Nabataean dwellings were rather insubstantial, perhaps even tents as reported by *Diodorus (3) Siculus/*Hieronymus (1) of Cardia (Diod. 19. 94. 2–6). Such dwellings would have left little trace. There are other important monuments in the hills around Petra, approached by monumental stairways, including a sacrificial 'High Place' overlooking the centre. Nabataean inscriptions at Petra itself are not numerous, but one important inscription indicates that king Obodas I was deified. Another is a well-preserved tomb-inscription giving details of the installations associated with the tomb.

G. Dalman, *Petra und seine Felsheiligtümer* (1908); J. Starcky, *Dictionnaire de la Bible. Supplément* 7 (1966), cols. 886–1017; J. McKenzie, *The Archi-tecture of Petra* (1990); G. W. Bowersock, *Roman Arabia* (1983, corr. repr. 1994), see index. J. F. H.

Petreius (*RE* 3), **Marcus,** probably son of a Marian *primipilaris* (senior centurion), had already had thirty years' military experience in 63 BC (Sall. *Cat.* 59. 6) when, as legate of C. *Antonius 'Hybrida', he defeated *Catiline at Pistoria. In 59 he vehemently opposed *Caesar. From 55 he governed Hispania Ulterior as *Pompey's legate and in 49 brought his two legions to the Ebro to join *Afranius (2) against Caesar. He unsuccessfully tried to prevent the surrender of their armies after *Ilerda, but was dismissed unharmed. He is not mentioned at *Pharsalus, but in 48, with Faustus *Cornelius Sulla, joined M. *Porcius Cato (2) at *Patrae and sailed with him to join the Pompeians in Africa. After an initial success against Caesar, he submitted to Q. *Caecilius Metellus Pius Scipio's command and after Thapsus, by arrangement with *Juba (1) I, killed the king and then himself.

G. E. F. C.; E. B.

Petronius (*RE* 29), senator of consular rank and courtier of *Nero. His praenomen is uncertain (at Tac. *Ann.* 16. 17 'Gaius' is supplied from 16. 18, but it is more likely that a cognomen has fallen out); Pliny, *HN* 37. 20, and Plut. *Mor.* 60 D seem to give the praenomen (see NAMES, PERSONAL, ROMAN) Titus to the same man, and a T. Petronius Niger is attested as consul on *Herculaneum tablets. However, a document from *Ephesus attests a Publius Petronius Niger as suffect consul with the same colleague in July of AD 62. According to *Tacitus (1) he had been outstanding for his indolence, though this did not prevent him from being energetic as proconsul in Bithynia and as consul (*Ann.* 16. 18). For a time he was influential enough to guide Nero in his choice of pleasures, and even when forced by *Tigellinus' intrigues to commit suicide in 66, he showed himself not merely fearless but contemptuous of Stoic posturings. Instead of a will full of flattery of Nero or his current favourites, Petronius left a document denouncing him in embarrassing detail. Scholars have long ago discarded the notion that this denunciation has anything to do with the *Satyricon* (see PETRONIUS ARBITER), which, however, reflects the *philhellenic atmosphere of the Neronian court, having affinities with the *Odyssey* (see HOMER) and the Hellenistic novel and being set in places around the Bay of Naples (*Neapolis).

W. Eck, *ZPE* 42, 1981, 227; J. P. Sullivan, *The Satyricon of Petronius* (1968); M. Smith, *Cena Trimalchionis* (1975); G. Luck, *AJP* 1972, 133 ff. M. S. S.; M. T. G.

Petronius (*RE* 24), **Publius,** probably grandson of a prefect of Egypt; an augur from AD 7 and suffect consul in 19 with M. Iunius Silanus: they passed the *lex Iunia Petronia*. Petronius was proconsul of Asia (29–35?) and *legatus* of Syria (39–42). Commanded to erect a statue of the emperor *Gaius (1) in the Temple at Jerusalem, he demurred, pleading Jewish opposition. Gaius replied with an order to commit suicide, but the news of the emperor's death arrived first. T. J. C.; R. J. S., E. B.

Petronius Arbiter, author of the extant *Satyrica* (Σατυρικά), possibly identical with *Petronius, the politician and *arbiter elegantiae* at the court of Nero, forced to suicide in AD 66. Given that scholars now agree that the *Satyrica* belongs stylistically and in terms of factual detail to the Neronian period, and that *Tacitus (1)'s account of the courtier Petronius describes a hedonistic, witty, and amoral character which would well suit the author of the *Satyrica* (*Ann.* 16. 17–20), many find it economical to identify the two, but the matter is beyond conclusive proof; the occurrence of the name T. Petronius Arbiter in the MSS of the *Satyrica* gives no aid, since this may simply be the supplement of a later copyist who had read Tacitus.

Of the *Satyrica* itself we seem to have fragments of books 14, 15, and 16, with book 15 practically complete, containing the *Cena Trimalchionis* (26. 6–78.8). The commonly used but misleading title *Satyricon* (sc. *libri*) conceals not Σατυρικόν (neuter singular) but Σατυρικῶν (neuter genitive plural) and alludes both to influence from Roman *satire and (ironically) to Encolpius' far from satyric sexual capacity (see below for both). The whole work was evidently lengthy; one conjectural reconstruction has suggested twenty books and a length of 400,000 words. It is prosimetric in form, an inheritance from the similar satires of *Varro, though there is now extant a Greek low-life prosimetric fictional text in the Iolaus-papyrus, *POxy.* 42 (1974). The outline of the plot is naturally difficult to reconstruct; the main characters are the homosexual pair Encolpius (the narrator) and the younger Giton, who undergo various adventures in a southern Italian setting. They encounter a number of characters, some of whom, such as the unscrupulous adventurer Ascyltus and the lecherous poet Eumolpus, try to divide the lovers; Giton is not particularly faithful, and this, like the sexual orientation of the lovers and many other elements in the novel, constitutes an evident *parody of the chaste fidelity of the boy–girl pairings of the ideal Greek *novel. Encolpius seems to be afflicted with impotence as the result of the wrath of the phallic god Priapus, and there are several episodes describing his sexual failures; the wrath of Priapus is evidently a parody of the wrath of *Poseidon in the *Odyssey* of *Homer, and other parallels between Encolpius and *Odysseus are present, particularly when he encounters a woman named Circe (126 ff.).

Many themes familiar from Roman satire appear, such as legacy-hunting (the episode set in Croton (Crotone), 116–41) and the comic meal (the *Cena Trimalchionis*); in the latter Encolpius, Giton and Ascyltus attend a dinner given by the rich *freedman Trimalchio, probably in *Puteoli, in the narrative of which both Trimalchio's vulgar and ignorant display of wealth and the snobbishness of the narrator emerge very forcibly, and which contains in a parody of *Plato (1)'s *Symposium* a collection of tales told by Trimalchio's freedman friends which gives some evidence for vulgar Latin, though Petronius has naturally not reproduced colloquial speech exactly. Several other inserted tales are told in the novel, especially those of the Pergamene Boy (85–7) and the Widow of Ephesus (111–12), suitably lubricious stories for their narrator Eumolpus, but also clearly drawing on the Hellenistic tradition of Milesian tales (see NOVEL, LATIN). The inserted poems in various metres sometimes appear to comment on the novel's action; the two longest, presented as the work of the bad poet Eumolpus, seem to relate to other Neronian writers, the 65-line *Troiae Halosis* (89) written in the iambic trimeters of Senecan tragedy, and the *Bellum Civile* in 295 hexameters (119–24), closely recalling *Lucan's homonymous epic on the same subject (and restoring the divine machinery which Lucan had excluded). Literary and cultural criticism is certainly a concern of the novel; there are prominent attacks on contemporary oratory, painting, and poetry (1–5, 88–9, 118).

Petronius' novel seems not to have been widely known in antiquity, though a more extensive text than ours was available; it was rediscovered between the 15th and 17th cents., with great impact. The fragmentary text which has come down to us is likely to have some degree of interpolation, though scholars disagree as to how much. A number of poems in various metres

transmitted separately from the *Satyrica* are also attributed to Petronius. See NOVEL, LATIN.

TEXT AND COMMENTARIES Text ed. K. Müller (3rd edn. 1978); cf. also M. D. Reeve in *Texts and Transmission*, 295–300. There is no complete commentary on Petronius; M. S. Smith, *Cena Trimalchionis* (1975); G. Guido, *Bellum Civile* (1975); O. Pecere, *Widow of Ephesus* (1975); on the poems (other than the *Bellum Civile* and *Troiae Halosis*) E. Courtney's edn. (1991). Eng. trans. of *Sat.* by J. P. Sullivan (1965).
CRITICISM Bibliog. for 1945–82 by M. S. Smith, *ANRW* 2. 32. 3 (1985); J. P. Sullivan, *The Satyricon of Petronius* (1968); P. G. Walsh, *The Roman Novel* (1970); K. F. C. Rose, *The Date and Author of the Satyricon* (1971); H. Petersmann, *Petrons Urbane Prosa* (1977); N. W. Slater, *Reading Petronius* (1989). S. J. Ha.

Petronius (*RE* 75) **Turpilianus, Publius** (consul AD 61), succeeded *Suetonius Paulinus as governor of Britain. His policy was one of peace. In 63 he was *curator aquarum* in Rome. He contributed to the repression of the Pisonian conspiracy (see C. *Calpurnius Piso (2)). In 68 Nero entrusted to him the command against the rebels. His conduct was ambiguous (Dio 63. 27. 1; Plut. *Galba* 15, 17) and he was killed by *Galba. A. M.; M. T. G.

pets (companion animals). Animals were kept, inside and outside the house, as pets and for show, from early times. *Dogs that fed from their master's table are mentioned by *Homer (*Od.* 17. 309) and *Penelope found pleasure in watching her flock of geese though there is complicated symbolism here, geese = suitors (*Od.* 19. 536–7). For *Odysseus' *Argos (1d) see *Od.* 17. 290 ff.

The commonest pet was the small white long-coated Maltese dog, represented on 5th-cent. BC Attic vases and gravestones. In *Aristotle (*HA* 9. 6. 612^b 10–11), it is used as a comparative standard of size for the marten. *Athenaeus (1) says that this dog was especially popular among the Sybarites (see SYBARIS), accompanying its owner even to the gymnasia (12. 518 f; 519 b). Publius' dog, Issa, was probably a Maltese (Mart. 1. 109). Epitaphs show the affection felt for pet dogs by their owners (*Anth. Lat.* 1176; 1512).

Tamed birds, especially starlings, magpies, ravens, and crows, which could be taught to talk, were popular (Stat. *Silv.* 2. 4. 18–19; Plin. *HN* 10. 42. 120). Lesbia's 'sparrow' (Catull. 2; 3) was possibly a bullfinch. The more exotic parrot, introduced from India, was rarer (Varro, *Rust.* 3. 9. 17; Plin. *HN* 10. 42. 117; Ov. *Am.* 2. 6; Mart. 14. 73). Nightingales and blackbirds were kept for their song (Plin. *HN* 10. 29. 81 ff.; Plin. *Ep.* 4. 2. 3). Monkeys amused the household with tricks they had been taught (Plaut. *Mil. Glor.* 102; Plin. *HN* 8. 80. 215). Harmless snakes and the *lagalopex* (long-eared fox) and ichneumon mentioned by Martial (7. 87) were less usual pets. The cat was a late introduction into the Roman house, probably because, being a sacred animal in Egypt, its export from that country was forbidden. But L. *Annaeus Seneca (2) (*Ep.* 121. 19) and *Pliny (2) (*HN* 10. 73. 202) assume their readers' acquaintance with it as a household animal. In earlier times, its function in controlling vermin was performed by the ferret. Other animals were kept outside the house, more as a hobby and for showing off to visitors. The fishponds of the wealthy contained murenas and bearded mullet which might be trained to eat from their masters' hands (Cic. *Att.* 2. 1. 7; Plin. *HN* 9. 81. 171). Aviaries and vivaria were fairly common from the late republic onwards. Here were kept singing birds, doves, pigeons, peacocks, flamingos, boars, hares, deer, and antelopes (Varro, *Rust.* 3. 3; 12–13; Columella 8. 9. 1; 9. 1. 1). See ANIMALS, ATTITUDES TO; DOGS.

W. R. Halliday 'Animal Pets in Ancient Greece', *Discovery* (1922), 151 ff.; J. M. C. Toynbee, *PBSR* 1948, 24 ff., and *Animals in Roman Life and Art* (1973); R. Lane Fox, *PCPS* 1996, 168 n. 245.　　　　　S. W.; S. H.

Peucestas, son of Alexander, Macedonian, came to prominence in 326/5 BC when he saved the life of *Alexander (3) the Great at the Malli town (in southern Punjab) and was promoted to the élite bodyguard. Appointed satrap of Persis (325/4) he won Alexander's commendation (and the army's reprobation) by adopting Persian *mores* and language. Subsequently confirmed in office at Babylon (323) and Triparadeisus (321), he led the coalition of satraps which resisted the ambitions of Peithon in Central Asia (319/18). Relinquishing authority grudgingly to *Eumenes (3), he played an important part (somewhat invidiously reported by Eumenes' encomiast, *Hieronymus (1)) in the great campaign in Iran. Finally he surrendered to *Antigonus (1) (early 316), who removed him from Persis but apparently retained him in his service. He was active in *Caria (c.312?) and survived into the reign of *Demetrius (4).

Berve, *Alexanderreich*, 2 no. 634; R. A. Billows, *Antigonus the One-Eyed* (1990), 417 f., no. 90.; Heckel, *Marshals*, 263 ff.　　　　　A. B. B.

Peucetii See MESSAPII.

Peutinger Table conventional name for a MS made at Colmar c.1200 of a late Roman world-map, itself a 4th-cent. modification of a 2nd-cent. and perhaps even earlier design. The most important document of ancient cartography (see MAPS), it is also a very important source for ancient topography. It represents the inhabited world from Spain and Britain (all but a fragment of which are missing) to India, though the *Mediterranean world occupies ⅙ of the whole (and Italy a third) of the scroll. The elongated form (6.82 m. long by 34 cm. high (approx. 22 × 1 ft.)) precludes constant scale or recognizable visual form for most land-masses and seas; but the dense and topologically correct network of roads (with posting-stations and distances) has a practical value like the *Itineraries. Major cities have pictorial images, middle-ranking ones conventional signs. Important rivers, mountains, and some other features of historical or thaumatological significance are included.

K. Miller, *Die Peutingersche Tafel* (1916, repr. 1962); L. Bosio, *La Tabula Peutingeriana* (1983).　　　　　N. P.

Phaea, the ferocious Sow of Crommyon, killed by *Theseus, first called Phaea in Apollod. *Epit.* 1. 1 (1st cent. AD). It is named by (or maybe 'after') the old woman who reared it. Crommyon was a village belonging to *Corinth (previously to *Megara). The deed invites association with *Heracles' slaughter of the Erymanthian boar and is depicted on 17, mainly red-figure, vases (often including the old woman egging the sow on), as well as on a metope of the Hephaisteion (see ATHENS, TOPOGRAPHY, *Agora*), as once it had on the Athenian treasury at *Delphi. It presumably entered literature with the lost late 6th-cent. BC epic *Theseid* (see EPIC CYCLE).

Bacchylides 17 (18). 23–5 (the earliest, c.470 BC); Eur. *Suppl.* 316–17; Apollod. *Epit.* 1. 1; Plut. *Thes.* 9; Diod. 4. 59; Hyg. *Fab.* 38 (a boar, by confusion with Erymanthian/Calydonian boars); Ov. *Met.* 7. 435. F. Brommer, *Theseus: Die Taten des griechischen Helden in der antiken Kunst und Literatur* (1982), 9–13.　　　　　K. D.

Phaeacians See SCHERIA.

Phaeax, Athenian politician. First mentioned in Ar. *Eq.* 1377–80; in 422 BC he was sent to *Sicily in an attempt to reopen the

opportunities for Athenian involvement which had been closed at the congress of *Gela (424), but had little success (Thuc. 5. 4–5). He is best known for the assertion by *Theophrastus that it was not *Nicias (1) but he who combined with Alcibiades to secure the *ostracism of *Hyperbolus (cf. Plut. *Nic.* 11, *Alc.* 13). The speech preserved as *Andocides 4, *Against Alcibiades*, was written in the character of Phaeax with reference to that ostracism: its authenticity continues to be disputed.

PA 13921; APF 521–4; LGPN 2 (1994), Phaiax no. 1. W. D. Furley, *Hermes*, 1989, 138–56; P. J. Rhodes in R. Osborne and S. Hornblower, *Ritual Finance Politics* (1994), ch. 5.　　　　　H. H. S.; P. J. R.

Phaedon of *Elis (5th–4th cent. BC), narrator of *Plato (1)'s *Phaedo*, was evidently a young member of *Socrates' circle, who originally came to Athens as a prisoner of war (see *Méthexis* 2, 1989, 1–18). His reported foundation of a 'school of Elis' suggests a notable philosophical career based there. He probably wrote two Socratic dialogues (*Zopyrus*, cf. Cic. *De fato* 10 and *Tusc.* 4. 80–1; *Simon*), possibly others; none survives.　　　　　C. J. R.

Phaedra See HIPPOLYTUS (1).

Phaedrus (1) (*RE* 7) of Athens (b. c.450), member of the Socratic circle (see SOCRATES), a character in *Plato (1)'s *Prt.* and *Symp.* as well as in the *Phdr.* (in which, though Socrates pretends otherwise, he must be middle-aged). He is marked by a naïve enthusiasm for rhetoric.　　　　　A. W. P.

Phaedrus (2), son of Thymochares, Athenian from the *deme of Sphettos (d. after c.258 BC). Member of a rich *mine-working family with a tradition of active political participation, Phaedrus' career is known only from an honorary decree, passed in his lifetime in the 250s (IG 2². 682). He was twice general for equipment under *Lachares (296/5 and 295/4) several times home-defence general (see STRATĒGOI) and twice mercenary general (dates unknown). During the revolution of 287 he was hoplite general and cooperated with his brother *Callias (6), who was in Ptolemaic service (see PTOLEMY (1)), and the Ptolemaic admiral Sostratus to supply the city, expel *Demetrius (4)'s garrison and negotiate the subsequent peace agreement, which he then recommended in the assembly. The next year he was the first hoplite general freely elected by the restored democracy. Subsequently he negotiated a subsidy of 50 talents from *Ptolemy (1) I, was agonothete (festival organizer) and fulfilled all liturgies (see LITURGY (GREEK)).

Davies, *APF* no. 13964; C. Habicht, *Untersuchungen zur politischen Geschichte Athens im 3. Jh. v. Chr.* (1979); T. L. Shear, *Kallias of Sphettos and the Revolt of Athens in 286 BC* (1978).　　　　　R. M. E.

Phaedrus (3) (c.140–70 BC), Epicurean philosopher (see EPICURUS), perhaps an Athenian by birth, was in Rome, where *Cicero heard him lecture, before 88. He was head of the Epicurean school in Rome for a short time. He appears in Cicero as one of the most respected Epicureans of the time: Cicero thought him of decent character and an excellent stylist (*Nat. D.* 1. 93 *Phaedro nihil elegantius nihil humanius*). Cicero when he was writing *On the Nature of the Gods* 1 asked his friend T. *Pomponius Atticus (*Att.* 13. 39. 2) to send him Phaedrus' work Περὶ θεῶν, 'about the gods' (according to a convincing emendation). He is also attested in dedications at *Eleusis. While still living, he was succeeded by Patro as head of the school.

R. Philippson, *RE* 19 (1938), 'Phaidros (8)'; A. E. Raubitschek, in *The School of Hellas* (1991), 337–44. On Phaedrus' dates see T. Dorandi,

Phaedrus, Gaius Iulius

Ricerche sulla cronologia dei filosofi ellenistici, Beiträge zur Altertumskunde 19 (1991).   W. D. R.; D. O.

Phaedrus (4) or **Phaeder, Gaius Iulius** (*c*.15 BC–*c*. AD 50), a slave of Thracian birth (possibly from *Pydna: see 3, prol. 17 ff.), received a good schooling perhaps in Italy, became a freedman of Augustus, and composed five books of verse fables. Under *Tiberius, he offended L. *Aelius Seianus through suspected allusions in his fables and suffered some unknown punishment. Scarcely noticed by Roman writers (he is not mentioned by either L. *Annaeus Seneca (2) (the younger Seneca) or *Quintilian in their references to fable), he is first named (though identification is uncertain) by *Martial (3. 20. 5 *improbi iocos Phaedri*, 'the jokes of mischievous Ph.') and next by *Avianus (*praefat.*). Prose paraphrases of his and of other fables were made in later centuries, in particular the collection entitled 'Romulus', and in the Middle Ages enjoyed a great vogue. The five books are clearly incomplete and thirty further fables (*Appendix Perottina*), included in N. Perotti's epitome of fables (*c*.1465) drawn from a MS now lost, have been shown to belong to them; additional fables deriving from Phaedrus are contained in the prose paraphrases.

Phaedrus' achievement, on which he greatly prides himself, lies in his elevation of the fable, hitherto utilized in literature only as an adjunct, e.g. in satire (cf. Hor. *Sat.* 2. 6. 79 ff., the town and country mouse; *Epist.* 1. 7. 29 ff., the fox and the corn-bin), into an independent *genre. His fables, written in iambic senarii, consist of beast-tales based largely on '*Aesop', as well as jokes and instructive stories taken not only from Hellenistic collections but also from his own personal experience. His main source is likely to have been a collection of Aesopic fables compiled in prose by *Demetrius (3) of Phaleron. Philosophic weight is sought by borrowings from the *chreiai* ('maxims') and *diatribe; moral instruction is generally self-contained at the beginning (*promythia*) or ending (*epimythia*) of the tale. Besides his professed purpose of providing amusement and counsel, Phaedrus sometimes satirizes contemporary conditions both social and political. His work evidently evoked considerable criticism and retorts to his detractors are frequent. The presentation is animated and marked by a humorous and charming brevity of which Phaedrus is rightly proud (2 *prol.* 12, 3 *epil.* 8, 4 *epil.* 7), but which sometimes leads to obscurity. In language he stands in the tradition of *Terence; skilfully adapting the *sermo urbanus*, he shows a classical purity and clearness (apart from a frequent use of abstract nouns and occasional vulgarisms or other unorthodoxies). His iambic senarius goes back to the early metre of Latin *comedy and is very regular. See FABLE.

RE 19. 2.
    TEXTS L. Havet (with notes, 1895); J. P. Postgate, (OCT 1919); A. Brenot (with trans., Budé, 1961²); B. E. Perry (with trans., Loeb 1965); A. Guaglianone (1969).
    CONCORDANCE C. Cremona (1980).
    BIBLIOG. H. MacL. Currie, ANRW 2. 32. 1 (1984); N. Holzberg, *Anregung* 37 (1991), 226 ff.   A. Schi.

Phaenias of Eresus (fl. 320 BC), a pupil of *Aristotle who inherited the *Peripatetic interest in literary and historical research. Amongst various writings may be noted Τυράννων ἀναίρεσις ἐκ τιμωρίας ('On the slaying of tyrants for motives of revenge'), an expansion of Aristotle, *Pol.* 1311ᵃ25, marked by moral judgements characteristic of the period, and Περὶ τῶν ἐν Σικελίᾳ τυράννων ('On the tyrants in Sicily'). References in *Plutarch's 'Lives' of Solon and Themistocles suggest that Phaenias was a valuable addition to Plutarch's sources.

FGrH 3 B pp. 443 and 658; Wehrli, *Schule des Aristoteles* 9² (1969); F. J. Frost, *Plutarch's Themistocles: A Historical Commentary* (1980).   G. L. B.; S. H.

Phaethon (Φαέθων), in mythology, son of *Helios (the Sun-god) and the heroine Clymene. Learning who his father was, he set out for the East to find him, and arriving at his palace, asked him a boon. The Sun granting him in advance anything he liked, he asked to guide the solar chariot for a day. But he was too weak to manage the immortal horses, which bolted with him and were likely to set the world on fire till *Zeus killed Phaethon with a thunderbolt. He fell into the *Eridanus, and his sisters, mourning for him, turned into amber-dropping trees. See Euripides, fragments of *Phaethon*, with J. Diggle's comm. (1970).

Eur. *Hipp.* 735 ff.; Ovid, *Met.* 1. 750 ff.; LIMC 7. 1 (1994), 350–4.   H. J. R.; S. H.

Phalaecus, Phocian *stratēgos* (see PHOCIS). Son or nephew of *Onomarchus, he succeeded *Phayllus (2) alongside another relative, Mnaseas (351), who was soon killed, leaving Phalaecus in control. Military success sometimes eluded him, Phocis became vulnerable to Boeotian invasion (see THEBES (1))—but by 347 he had captured *Orchomenus (1), *Coronea, and Corsiae and helped Clitarchus in *Euboea. As with Onomarchus, success provoked self-seeking Macedonian intervention. Phocian opponents reacted by deposing him, but he quickly regained power and (distrusting his external allies) ended the Third *Sacred War by negotiating safe-passage out of Nicaea (346). Strategic control of eastern *Locris thus only protected leader and army, while Phocis endured Amphictionic and Macedonian revenge (see AMPHICTIONY; MACEDONIA). The mercenaries found employment in Crete and Phalaecus accidentally burned to death in a siege-machine at Cydonia.

J. Buckler, *Third Sacred War* (1989).   C. J. T.

phalanx In Homer the word is usually in the plural and means 'ranks', but in the singular it came to mean the close-packed formation characteristic of Archaic and Classical hoplites. It usually formed eight deep, but as early as *Delion (424 BC) the Thebans (see THEBES (1)) were twenty-five deep (Thuc. 4. 93(?)), and at *Leuctra (371 BC) fifty deep (Xen. *Hell.* 6. 4. 12). Though inflexible and unwieldy and thus vulnerable if caught on rough ground or attacked in flank or rear, the phalanx was extremely formidable when driving forward, as the Persians found to their cost, and in the hands of the Spartans not even as cumbersome as it might seem. By articulating it down to units of 30–40 men, and by training, the Spartans were able to wheel wings forward at right angles to the main line of advance, or back behind the rest of the phalanx so as to double its depth, and even to countermarch it to face an attack from the rear; they also developed a technique for dealing with the threat of missile-armed troops—ordering the younger men in the front ranks to charge out and drive off the enemy (cf. e.g. Xen. *Hell.* 4. 2. 20; 6. 5. 18–9; 4. 3. 18; 4. 5. 14, 16).

The same term was applied to the infantry-of-the-line in Macedonian armies, though their task was primarily to pin the enemy while the cavalry exploited any opportunity so created. See ARMIES, GREEK AND HELLENISTIC. The Macedonian version was probably the creation of *Philip (1) II (cf. Diod. 16. 3. 1 f.), and it too achieved considerable flexibility through training and proper articulation into sub-units; its main offensive weapon was a formidable long pike (the *sarisa*). Philip and *Alexander (3) the Great's 'phalangites' were probably recruited from the rural peasantry of Macedonia, rather than the rather better-off class from whom the hoplites had been drawn.

This created problems after Alexander's conquest of the Persian empire, and for those of Alexander's successors who could not recruit in Macedonia. Alexander was already experimenting with a mixed force of Macedonians and Asiatics before his death, and the *Seleucids and Ptolemies (see PTOLEMY (1)) used military settlers who received land in return for military service (see CLERUCHY for the Ptolemies). Though formidable enough to perturb even L. *Aemilius Paullus (2), the victor of *Pydna (Polyb. 29. 17. 1), Alexander's successors forgot that the secret of his and his father's success had been the integration of the phalanx with other arms: by itself it was no match for the legion. See MILITARY TRAINING (GREEK).

F. E. Adcock, *The Greek and Macedonian Art of War* (1957); J. K. Anderson, *Military Theory and Practice in the Age of Xenophon* (1970); V. D. Hanson, *The Western Way of War* (1989). J. F. La.

Phalaris (RE 1), of *Acragas (Agrigento), the first important Sicilian tyrant (c.570–c.549). Of Rhodian descent (see RHODES), he exploited a building contract on the acropolis to acquire a body of adherents, seized the acropolis and disarmed the ruling aristocracy. Probably enlisting mercenaries, he attacked the native Sicans and created an empire that stretched to the north coast with the acquisition of *Himera (near Termini Imerese), threatened perhaps by its *Phoenician neighbours. He fortified Acragas and enlarged its territory, taking in and fortifying the Ecnomus (Licata) promontory. He ruled for 16 years, and was then overthrown (by the great-grandfather of *Theron). A byword in antiquity for cruelty (he was said to have roasted his enemies alive in a brazen bull), he established the pattern of Sicilian *tyranny—militarist and imperialistic—for the future.

H. Berve, *Die Tyrannis bei den Griechen* (1967), 129–32. B. M. C.

Phalaris, letters of See LETTERS, GREEK; PSEUDEPIGRAPHIC LITERATURE.

Phaleron, the harbour (*epineion*) of Athens as late as 490 BC (Hdt. 6. 116); offering little shelter, it was thereafter soon displaced by *Piraeus. The site is uncertain—probably at the low hill of Agios Georgios in mod. Old Phaleron. In late Archaic times the settlement was large, to judge from its quota of nine seats on the Cleisthenic *boulē; to it probably belonged an 8th–6th-cent. BC cemetery at the bottom of Syngrou Ave.

C. J. Eliot, *PECS* 698; R. Garland, *The Piraeus* (1987), esp. 176–7. A. J. S. S.

phallus, an image of the penis, often as erect, to be found in various contexts, in particular (*a*) in certain rituals associated with fertility, notably Dionysiac *processions (see DIONYSUS): see e.g. Ar. *Ach.* 243 on the Attic rural Dionysia (see ATTIC CULTS AND MYTHS), *Semos in Athen. 622b-c on groups of 'ithyphallics' and 'phallus-bearers', *Varro in Aug. *Civ.* 7. 21 'for the success of seeds' at the Liberalia (see LIBER PATER); (*b*) as a sacred object revealed in the Dionysiac *mysteries, as in the Villa of the Mysteries fresco at *Pompeii; *Iamblichus (2) (*Myst.* 1. 11) mentions it as a symbol of secret doctrine; (*c*) in the costume of comedy (see COMEDY (GREEK), OLD), *satyric drama and various low theatrical genres; *Aristotle (*Poet.* 1449ᵃ11) says that comedy originated in phallic songs; (*d*) on permanent display, often as part of a statue such as those of *Priapus or the *herms identified with *Hermes; (*e*) as apotropaic: e.g. *Pliny (1) (*HN* 28. 39) says that it guards not only babies but also triumphal chariots (against envy). In general its appeal is as an expression of fertility and regeneration,

but also of masculine strength (e.g. in the case of the herms marking boundaries).

Nilsson, *GGR* 1³. 118 ff., 590 ff.; W. Burkert, *HN* 69 ff. R. A. S. S.

Phanes (Φάνης), a god in several Orphic theogonies, 'the one who makes (or is) manifest', born from an egg fashioned by Chronos in the *Aither, also called Πρωτόγονος, the Firstborn. He is the first ruler and the creator of all, bisexual, invisible but radiant with light, gold-winged, and has the heads of various animals. His daughter with whom he mates is Night (see NYX), who bears *Gaia and *Uranus. He is also called *Eros, Bromios, *Zeus, *Metis, and Erikepaios. See ORPHIC LITERATURE, ORPHISM.

M. L. West, *The Orphic Poems* (1983); *LIMC* 7. 1 (1994), 363–4. M. P. N.; F. G.

Phanocles, Greek poet of uncertain date and provenance, but probably of the 3rd cent. BC. Six fragments or testimonia of his poetry survive; all seem to belong to the same elegiac poem entitled Ἔρωτες ἢ Καλοί ('Love Affairs, or Beautiful Boys'). This seems to have contained a series of accounts of the passions of heroes (e.g. *Orpheus, *Tantalus, *Agamemnon) or gods (e.g. *Dionysus) for boys; possibly each episode was introduced by the formula ἢ ὡς ('or as . . .') in the manner of *Hesiod's *Ehoiai*, as in frs. 1 and 3. The longest fragment (1) describes the death and mutilation of Orpheus by Thracian women, jealous of his love for *Calais: their descendants were ever afterwards tattooed as a punishment; the pre-eminence of *Lesbos in poetry is explained by the fact that Orpheus' head and lyre were washed ashore and buried there. The importance of aetiologies in frs. 1, 5, and 6 might suggest a connection with *Callimachus (3), but Phanocles' language is simpler, being more straightforwardly imitative of *Homer, and his narrative more direct. He has more in common with *Hermesianax (who is more likely than Phanocles to be the author of the tattoo-poem *PBrux.* 8934); *POxy.* 3723 (?imperial date) may be an imitation of Phanocles.

TEXTS Powell, *CA* 106–9; Diehl, *Anth. Lyr. Graec.* 6². 71–3. F. W.

Phanodemus, son of Diyllus, Athenian atthidographer (see ATTHIS) and father of the historian *Diyllus, was born before 374/3 BC, since he was a *bouleutēs* (see BOULĒ) in 344/3 (*IG* 2². 223). He was crowned in 343/2 for his service to the *dēmos (people). His next post may have been governor of the island of Icos, of which he wrote a history (*Ikiaka*). Probably, therefore, he agreed with the confrontational policy of *Demosthenes (2) towards Macedon. His later association with *Lycurgus (3) (Jacoby calls him his 'minister of public works and education') and other leading politicians of Athens after the battle of *Chaeronea (*IG* 7. 4252–4) confirms this impression. But his interest was more in cult than politics. He was especially involved with the cult of *Amphiaraus at *Oropus, but was also *hieropoios* for the Pythais to *Delphi in 330 (that is, he had responsibility for the Athenian delegation to the festival at Delphi, see PYTHIAN GAMES).

He wrote an *Atthis* for which nine books are attested. Only 27 fragments remain. The last datable fragment (F23) treats the death of *Cimon. We do not know how close to his own time he carried his account. Of the extant fragments all except three concern the mythical period and the cults. His Atheno-centricity is extreme (e.g. F13—the Trojans emigrated from Athens; F14—the Greeks sailed to *Troy from *Brauron not *Aulis).

FGrH 325. P. E. H.

Phaon, a mythical ferryman, made young and beautiful by *Aphrodite, who also hid him among lettuces like her beloved

Pharisees

*Adonis. *Sappho among others is said to have loved him, finally leaping from the cliff at *Leucas (Lefkas) for his sake: the story, which echoes other legends, appears first in Attic comedy.

G. Nagy, *Greek Mythology and Poetics*, 1990; *RE* 19. 2; *LIMC* 7. 1 (1994), 364–7.   M. Wil.

Pharisees, an influential religious group among *Jews in the late Hellenistic and early Roman periods. Explicit references to Pharisees are found in *Josephus and the New Testament and in Christian writings dependent upon them. The evidence found there can be supplemented from rabbinic references to Jewish religious figures before AD 70, since some of those to whom they referred may have been Pharisees. There may also be allusions to Pharisees in the *Dead Sea Scrolls. Pharisees are mentioned in Josephus' histories as a political party in the time of the *Hasmonean ruler John Hyrcanus (135–104 BC). After a period of opposition to Alexander Janneus (103–80 BC), their influence over the Hasmonean dynasty reached a peak during the rule of his widow Alexandra Jannaea (80–67 BC). Under *Herod (1) the Great (37–4 BC) the Pharisees won the support of some members of the royal court, but in general they seem to have stopped interfering in Judaean politics as a group, although individual Pharisees sometimes had prominent political roles. The last attestation of any individual who described himself as having been a Pharisee at least at some stage in his life was Josephus in the 90s AD (*Vita* 12).

The sources on the Pharisees are largely second-hand accounts and hence are too contradictory to permit a clear and convincing analysis of their beliefs and influence. No one source is satisfactory, and discrepancies abound. Josephus described the Pharisees as a philosophy within Judaism, equivalent to the Stoics (see STOICISM) among the Greeks. According to his account (*BJ* 2. 162–6), Pharisees taught that there is a life after death and that man controls his own destiny, although fate also plays a role in human fortunes. In contrast to the *Sadducees, they accept ancestral traditions in interpreting the law. Josephus' account may have been coloured by his own Pharisaic leanings and by a desire to appeal to his gentile Greek readers. In one passage, he described the Pharisees as particularly influential among Jews with regard to prayers and sacrifices (*Ant.* 18. 12–15). In the Gospels, Pharisees appear as opponents of Jesus, attacked for hypocrisy, in particular in the scrupulous observance of biblical laws about the sabbath, the tithing of agricultural produce and the avoidance of pollution. In the *Acts of the Apostles the Pharisee Gamaliel is portrayed as a powerful opponent of the Sadducees in a meeting of the sanhedrin in Jerusalem, and as the teacher of St *Paul. Paul's own writings are those of a former Pharisee, but how much his theology reflects Pharisaic rather than common Jewish or novel Christian ideas is debated. Rabbinic texts may refer to Pharisees when they report the teachings of those Jewish sages before AD 70 whom they see as their forebears. In particular, the sayings of Hillel (fl. *c*. AD 10–30) and his descendants are probably to be accounted those of Pharisees, since Hillel's family included both Rabban Gamaliel (mentioned as a Pharisee in the New Testament) and Simon son of Gamaliel (described as a Pharisee by Josephus). Many of those rabbinic traditions about the sages before AD 70 which are specifically attributed to named individuals concern purity, tithing and the sabbath; some deal with the rules governing dining clubs (*haburoth*) in which purity and tithing regulations were carefully observed by all members. However, it cannot be securely deduced from this that sages before AD 70 were believed by later rabbis to have had no other religious interests, since many traditions on moral and ethical issues, on civil and criminal law, and on the conduct of worship in the Jerusalem Temple, were preserved anonymously. Many such teachings may have been promulgated before AD 70 by Pharisees, but there is no evidence to confirm or disprove the possibility.

There is no agreement among scholars about the best way to reconcile this confused evidence. It may be that the self-description 'Pharisee', which probably derives from the semitic root *prs* ('separate'), was adopted by a large group in which some (in rabbinic terminology, *haberim* ('fellows')) were particularly zealous over purity and tithing while others were less so. The only figure given in ancient sources for the number of Pharisees is the 6,000 who refused to take an oath of loyalty to Herod in 12 BC (Joseph. *Ant.* 17. 42). See RELIGION, JEWISH.

TEXTS J. Neusner, *Rabbinic Traditions about the Pharisees before 70* (1971); J. Bowker, *Jesus and the Pharisees* (1973); A. Schürer, *The History of the Jewish People in the Age of Jesus Christ*, ed. G. Vermes and others, 2 (1979), 382–7.

MODERN DISCUSSIONS A. I. Baumgarten, *JBL* 1983, 411–28, and *Harv. Theol. Rev.* 1987, 63–77; E. P. Sanders, *Jewish Law from Jesus to the Mishnah* (1990), 97–254, and *Judaism: Practice and Belief* (1992), 380–451.   M. D. G.

pharmacology From earliest times, drugs formed an important part of *medicine, and *Homer has the first record of good drugs and bad drugs (poisons). Folklore incorporated many data on toxic substances, and in the legends Homer's *Circe and *Euripides' *Medea link *magic with poisons. Yet simultaneously there is another understanding of drugs and their actions: Pindar (*Pyth.* 3. 51–3) reflects *Asclepius' medicine as curative with drugs, surgery, and magical incantations. Drugs were contrasted to foods, but ancient thought overlapped the two, much as moderns fuse medical and culinary uses of *spices. Mycenaean Linear B tablets (see PRE-ALPHABETIC SCRIPTS (GREECE)) record prized spices (e.g. saffron, cumin, etc.), and they were basic in drug lore throughout antiquity. Pharmaceuticals included animal products (*honey, beeswax, blister beetle solutions, fats, marrows, bloods, etc.), as well as oil seeds (e.g. sesame, linseed (flax)); odours identified specific cheeses, taste determined high-quality drugstuffs, and the study of aromatics led to the widespread production of perfumes, exotic and otherwise (Theophrastus, *On Odours*). Until the *Enquiry into Plants* by *Theophrastus (esp. *Hist. Pl.* book 9 (lii)), Greek pharmacal *botany had not received clear organization, and folklore encompassed many famous drugs, e.g. the pennyroyal (*Mentha pulegium* L.), used in a tea for female *contraception; the poisonous hemlock (*Conium maculatum* L.), infamous as the drug that killed *Socrates in 399 BC; the now-extinct silphium from *Cyrene (prob. among the *Ferula* spp.), used as a cure-all distinguished by its fetid pungency; rose-oils of many varieties (*Rosa* spp.) employed as essential in the manufacture of perfume. For female ailments, there are several hundred botanical substances recorded in the Hippocratic *Diseases of Women* and similar tracts (see GYNAECOLOGY).

Book 9 of Theophrastus' *Hist. Pl.* is mostly a collection of material derived from *rhizotomoi* ('rootcutters'), and incorporates their oral traditions and experiences with drugs, both beneficial and toxic; about 300 species appear, ranging from the detailed preparation of the hemlock to the use of licorice (*Glycyrrhiza glabra* L.). The *rhizotomoi* knew their pharmaceuticals as plant-parts, and Theophrastus reflects this ancient expertise as he classes his 'herbs' as seeds, roots, leaves, stems, and so on. Of interest is the inclusion of *myrrh (*Commiphora myrrha* (Nees.)

Engl.) and frankincense (*Boswellia carteri* Birdw.), showing long-term activity of trade routes from southern *Arabia. *Nicander of Colophon (fl. *c*.130 BC) summarized in hexameters the toxicology of many plants, minerals, and animals; his *Theriaca* and *Alexipharmaca* became references for many later physicians and pharmacologists, but it is the *Materia Medica* by *Dioscorides (2) of Anazarbus (fl. *c*. AD 65) which gave the fullest and most accurate disquisition of drugs and drug lore of Greek, Hellenistic, and early Roman imperial times. About 600 pharmaceuticals are described according to a drug affinity system (Riddle, *Dioscorides*), and this magnificent work became *the* textbook on the subject; Dioscorides' tract entered Arabic traditions, with Latin renditions from Arabic and Greek descending into the European Renaissance to provide blueprints for the beginnings of modern pharmacy. *Galen of Pergamum (AD 129–after 210) assiduously copied many works on drugs, especially those of early Roman imperial physicians: lengthy quotations give us extracts from the lost writings of Andromachus the Elder, his son also named Andromachus (both fl. in the reign of Nero (AD 54–68)), T. *Statilius Crito (physician to Trajan (AD 98–117)), and a number of others. Among Latin authors on pharmacology, A. *Cornelius Celsus (fl. AD 14–37), *Scribonius Largus (fl. in reign of Claudius (AD 41–54): Scribonius was Sicilian, writing in both Latin and Greek), and *Pliny (1) the Elder (his famous *Natural History* appeared in AD 77) delineate western traditions of herbal lore combined with Greek and Hellenistic data on drugs; Pliny shows how commonplace were drugs of all varieties in every social stratum.

Exemplified by Galen, Graeco-Roman pharmacology explained drug action through the venerated theoretical constructs of *elements, qualities, and *humours; frequently drug therapy treated by opposites (a cold disease received pharmaceuticals which were hot: pepper (*Piper* spp.) treated an excess of the cold, wet phlegm; hot rashes were best alleviated with cooling rose oils, etc.). Of course, moderns explain drug actions by means of saponins, glycosides, alkaloids, and the like; significantly, Graeco-Roman pharmacology had grouped many pharmacally active plants among the Umbelliferae, Liliaceae, Ranunculaceae, Gentianaceae, Compositae, Iridaceae, Solanaceae, Piperaceae, and Papaveraceae, each family yielding goodly amounts of active principles. Of long-standing use, even down to our own day, are e.g. the opium poppy (Fam. Papaveraceae: *Papaver somniferum* L., with its major alkaloids morphine, codeine, thebaine, noscapine, narceine, papaverine, and several dozen more) and the autumn crocus (Fam. Liliaceae: *Colchicum autumnale* L., used in the treatment of gout and bronchitis (and occasionally for leukaemia), due to the presence of the amorphous, yellow-white alkaloid, named appropriately colchicine).

TEXTS J. Chadwick and M. Ventris, *Documents in Mycenaean Greek* (2nd edn. 1973), nos. 92–3, 98–107. See also under individual authors.
GENERAL LITERATURE R. Sigismund, *Die Aromata* (1884; repr. 1974); R. von Grot, *Über die in den hippokratischen Schriftensammlung enthaltenen pharmakologischen Kenntnisse* (1889; repr. 1968); J. Berendes, *Die Pharmazie bei den alten Kulturvölkern* (1891; repr. 1989); H. Schelenz, *Geschichte der Pharmazie* (1904; repr. 1965) (esp. chs. 1–10); E. Strantz, *Zur Silphionfrage* (1909); A. Schmidt, *Drogen und Drogenhandel im Altertum* (1924; repr. 1979); J. Stannard, 'The Plant Called Moly,' *Osiris*, 1962, 254–307; J. Innes Miller, *The Spice Trade of the Roman Empire* (1969); U. Räth, *Zur Geschichte der pharmazeutischen Mineralogie* (1971); C. Fabricius, *Galens Exzerpte aus älteren Pharmakologen* (1972); D. Goltz, *Studien zur Geschichte der Mineralnamen in Pharmazie. Chemie und Medizin von den Anfängen bis Paracelsus* (1972); S. Lilja, *The Treatment of Odours in the Poetry of Antiquity* (1972); J. Stannard, 'Squill in Ancient and Medieval Materia Medica', *Bulletin of the New York Academy of Medicine*, 1974, 684–713. J. Scarborough, 'The Drug Lore of Asclepiades of Bithynia', *Pharmacy in History* 1975, 43–57, 'Nicander's Toxicology, I: Snakes' and 'Nicander's Toxicology, II: Spiders, Scorpions, Insects and Myriapods', *Pharmacy in History* 1977, 3–23, and 1979, 3–34, 73–92, id. 'Theophrastus on Herbals and Herbal Remedies', *Journal of the History of Biology*, 1978, 353–85, and 'Some Beetles in Pliny's *Natural History*', *Coleopterists Bulletin*, 1977, 293–6; M.-H. Marganne, *Inventaire analytique des papyrus grecs de médecine* (1981); J. Stannard, 'Medicinal Plants and Folk Remedies in Pliny, Historia naturalis', *History and Philosophy of the Life Sciences*, 1982, 3–23; J. Scarborough, 'Roman Pharmacy and the Eastern Drug Trade', *Pharmacy in History* 1982, 135–43; G. E. R. Lloyd, 'Theophrastus, the Hippocratics and the Root-Cutters', in *Science, Folklore and Ideology* (1983), 119–35; J. Scarborough, 'On Medications for Burns in Classical Antiquity', *Clinics in Plastic Surgery*, 1983, 603–10, id. 'Theoretical Assumptions in Hippocratic Pharmacology' in F. Lasserre and P. Mudry (eds.), *Formes de pensée dans la collection hippocratique: Actes du IVᵉ Colloque international hippocratique Lausanne . . . 1981* (1983), 307–25; J. M. Riddle, *Dioscorides on Pharmacy and Medicine* (1985); C. Wright Shelmerdine, *The Perfume Industry of Mycenaean Pylos* (1985); J. Scarborough, 'Criton, Physician to Trajan: Historian and Pharmacist', in J. W. Eadie and J. Ober (eds.), *The Craft of the Ancient Historian: Essays in Honor of Chester G. Starr* (1985), 387–405; K. Nielsen, *Incense in Ancient Israel* (1986); J. Scarborough, 'Pharmacy in Pliny's *Natural History*: Some Observations on Substances and Sources', in R. French and F. Greenaway (eds.), *Science in the Early Roman Empire: Pliny the Elder, his Sources and Influence* (1986), 59–85. P. Faure, *Parfums et aromates de l'Antiquité* (1987). J. Scarborough, 'Texts and Sources in Ancient Pharmacy, 1: Ancient Near Eastern and Greek Texts', and '2: Hellenistic Pharmacy, Toxicology, and Medical Entomology', *Pharmacy in History*, 1987, 81–4, 133–9. J. M. Riddle, 'Folk Tradition and Folk Medicine: Recognition of Drugs in Classical Antiquity', in J. Scarborough (ed.), *Folklore and Folk Medicines* (1987), 33–61. J. Scarborough, 'Contraception in Antiquity: The Case of Pennyroyal', *Wisconsin Academy Review*, 1989, 19–25, and 'Pharmaceutical Theory in Galen's Commentaries on the Hippocratic Epidemics', in G. Baader and R. Winau (eds.), *Die hippokratischen Epidemien* (1990), 270–82; D. Brent Sandy, *The Production and Use of Vegetable Oils in Ptolemaic Egypt* (1989); J. Scarborough, 'The Pharmacology of Sacred Plants, Herbs, and Roots', in C. A. Faraone and D. Obbink (eds.), *Magika Hiera: Ancient Greek Magic and Religion* (1991), 138–74; R. I. Curtis, *Garum and Salsamenta: Production and Commerce in Materia Medica* (1991); J. Scarborough, 'The Pharmacy of Methodist Medicine: The Evidence of Soranus' Gynecology', in P. Mudry and J. Pigeaud (eds.), *Les Écoles médicales à Rome* (1991), 203–16; R. J. Durling, *A Dictionary of Medical Terms in Galen* (1993). J. Sca.

pharmakos, a human scapegoat. During the *Thargelia, but also during adverse periods such as *plague and *famine, Athenians and Ionians expelled scapegoat(s), who were called 'offscourings', in order 'to purify' the cities. These *pharmakoi* were chosen from the poor and the ugly, received a very special treatment in the *prytaneion ('townhall': *Massalia), were led in a procession to the sound of unharmonious music around the city, beaten with wild or infertile plants like the squill, and finally pelted with stones and chased over the border. Corresponding myths speak about aristocrats, princesses, or kings sacrificing themselves for the city. Clearly, myth exaggerates, but saviours have to be important: with a less valuable sacrifice the city cannot be saved. The occurrence of comparable rites among *Hittites and Israelites suggests a Near-Eastern origin. See POLLUTION.

J. Bremmer, *Harv. Stud.* 87 (1983), 299–320; Parker, *Miasma* (1983), 257–71; D. Hughes, *Human Sacrifice in Ancient Greece* (1991). J. N. B.

Pharnabazus, son of Pharnaces, hereditary *satrap of *Dascylium or *Hellespontine Phrygia, distant cousin and son-in-law of *Artaxerxes (2) II. Instructed like *Tissaphernes to recover control of Asiatic Greek cities, he co-operated undeviously with Sparta, appearing personally at *Abydos, *Cyzicus (410), and *Chalcedon (408) and providing relief after Cyzicus. Cyrus (2)'s arrival (407) aborted Athenian negotiations with *Darius II via Pharnabazus, and he temporarily disappears (though his appointment of a female governor in the *Troas perhaps falls hereabouts). He had *Alcibiades murdered at *Lysander's request (404/3) but after Sparta's intervention in Anatolia his territory was invaded. *Agesilaus invited him to rebel but conceded his right to remain loyal to Artaxerxes (395). His advice had already prompted *Conon (1)'s naval counter-offensive, and after Cnidus he took the fleet to mainland Greece (393)—unparalleled for a Persian after 479—attacked Spartan territory and supplied money to Athens and her allies. By 388/7 he had left to marry the king's daughter (Ariobarzanes took the satrapy) and he subsequently commanded unsuccessful attacks on Egypt in c.386–384 and 373, on the latter occasion rejecting the good advice of *Iphicrates.

Thuc. 8; Xen. *Hell.* 1–5; *RE* 19, 'Pharnabazos 2'; J. M. Cook, *Persian Empire* (1983); D. M. Lewis, *Sparta and Persia* (1977); *CAH* 5² (1992), ch. 11 (Andrewes); 6² (1994), chs. 3 (Hornblower) and 4 (Seager); A. Kuhrt, *The Ancient Near East* (1995), 691, 697 f.　　　　　　　　　　　C. J. T.

Pharnaces I, king of *Pontus c.189/8–c.155/4 BC. Realistic coin portraits reflect the ambition and aggression of his actions. His most important successes were the capture of *Sinope, and the establishment of diplomatic ties with the cities of the north and west coasts of the Black (*Euxine) Sea. His resources proved insufficient, however, to bring victory in the war of expansion he launched against almost all his neighbours in Asia Minor (c.183–179); see PRUSIAS (2) II CYNEGUS. Although dismissive of Roman diplomatic intervention during the war, defeat forced him to become the first king of Pontus to enter a relationship of 'friendship' with Rome. He probably married a *Seleucid princess, and was honoured as a benefactor at Athens and *Delos. If not entirely successful, Pharnaces' reign provided valuable lessons for his grandson *Mithradates VI Eupator.

For bibliog. see MITHRADATES.　　　　　　　　　　B. C. McG.

Pharnaces II, son of *Mithradates VI Eupator and king of *Bosporus (2) (63–47 BC). After supplanting his father, he was given the throne of Bosporus by *Pompey. Little is heard of him until Rome was distracted by the civil war of *Caesar and Pompey, when he overran *Lesser Colchis, *Armenia, *Cappadocia, and eastern *Pontus. With Caesar absent in Egypt, he defeated the Roman forces under Cn. *Domitius Calvinus. The following year, 47, Caesar arrived and defeated him with spectacular speed at the battle of Zela, the occasion of Caesar's famous claim 'veni, vidi, vici' ('I came, I saw, I conquered'). On his return to Bosporus Pharnaces was killed by his opponent Asander.

R. Sullivan, *Near Eastern Royalty & Rome 100–30 BC* (1990).　B. C. McG.

Pharos See PHARUS.

Pharsalus, city in *Thessaly, on the southern border of the central valley of the river *Enipeus, near a crossroads linking the *Adriatic to the *Aegean and central Greece and Thessaly to *Macedonia. Occupation of the site has been continuous from the neolithic until today. A few Mycenaean remains are insufficient to ensure identification with Phthia, home of *Achilles (see PHTHIOTIS); the name, unknown to *Homer, is relatively late. From the 6th cent. BC Pharsalus dominated the tetrad of Phthiotis and played an active role in Thessaly. Two aristocratic families,

the Echecratids and the Daochids, shared power over the city, which was allied to Athens in the *Persian Wars, and several times received the supreme command of the Thessalians. Around 500 BC Pharsalus minted coins and constructed its walls. From the end of the 5th cent. it was involved in the struggles between *Larissa and *Pherae; its citizens expelled the Echecratids and *Jason (2) of Pherae took over the city. Its prosperity revived under Macedonian domination. In 197, occupied by T. *Quinctius Flamininus after *Cynoscephalae, it fell under Roman control. *Caesar defeated *Pompey at *Pharsalus in 48. The city is last attested under Justinian, who repaired its walls. Apart from vestiges of these, little survives of ancient Pharsalus.

F. Stählin, *Das hellenische Thessalien* (1924), 133 ff.; Y. Béquignon, *RE* suppl. 12, cols. 1071 ff.; B. Helly, *L'état Thessalien* (1995).　　B. H.

Pharus See ALEXANDRIA (1); LIGHTHOUSES; SEVEN WONDERS.

Phaselis (mod. Tekirova), was a Greek settlement founded from *Rhodes on the mountainous east coast of *Lycia c.690 BC. Its triple harbour laid the foundation for commercial success. It was one of the communities which shared in the foundation of *Naucratis and was part of the Athenian empire, presumably after the battle of *Eurymedon. The so-called Phaselis decree regulates judicial relationship between it and Athens (ML 31).

In the 4th cent. the city struck a pact with *Mausolus (*TAM* 2. 3. 1183). It gave *Alexander (3) the Great a friendly reception, came under Ptolemaic control (see PTOLEMY (1)), and was for a short time after 197 BC subject to *Antiochus (3) III. It was included in the Lycian Confederacy (see FEDERAL STATES), although with lower status than its neighbour Olympus. In the 1st cent. BC it became a base for the pirate chieftain Zenicetes and was subsequently sacked by P. *Servilius Vatia Isauricus. Under the empire it rejoined the Lycian League and was visited by *Hadrian in 129, when a monumental gateway whose remains survive was built to link the south harbour with the main street.

G. E. Bean, *Turkey's Southern Shore²* (1979), 121–33, and *Lycian Turkey* (1978), 150–2; H. T. Wade-Gery, *Essays in Greek History* (1958), 180 ff., and G. E. M. de Ste. Croix, *CQ* 1961, 100 ff. (treaty with Athens); J. Schäfer and others, *Phaselis*, *MDAI (I)* Beiheft (1985).　G. E. B.; S. M.

Phasis The ancient river Phasis is the modern Rioni, with its tributary the Quirila, which traverses the lowland of *Colchis and joins the Black (*Euxine) Sea at the town of Phasis, near modern Poti. The lowland itself might be called Phasis. The river was sometimes seen as the division between Europe and Asia. It was also regarded as the home of the pheasant (or 'Phasian bird'). The town of Phasis claimed Milesian origin (see MILETUS; COLONIZATION, GREEK), with one Themistagoras as its oecist (see FOUNDERS, CITY), probably c.550 BC. Its site has been located, partly submerged under modern Lake Palaeostomi. By the reign of Hadrian there was a Roman fort there, with an associated civilian settlement close by.

D. C. Braund, *Georgia in Antiquity* (1994); *LIMC* 7. 1 (1994), 368–70 (personification).　　　　　　　　　　　　　　D. C. B.

phasis See LAW AND PROCEDURE, ATHENIAN.

Phayllus (1), an athlete (see ATHLETICS) from *Croton in south Italy who gained three victories in the Pythian Games and also fought at Salamis (480 BC; see SALAMIS, BATTLE OF) in a ship which he fitted out at his own expense. He is presumed to be the athlete of this name who is said in an epigram (*Anth. Pal.*, appendix 297) to have jumped 16.8 m. (55 ft.).

Hdt. 8. 47; Paus. 10. 9. 2; Plut. *Alex.* 34 with J. R. Hamilton's Comm. (1969); Tod 21 (not in ML); M. Guarducci, *Epigrafia Greca* 1.

113–15 no. 6; C. Habicht, *Pausanias' Guide to Ancient Greece* (1985), 115 f.   F. A. W.; S. H.

Phayllus (2), Phocian *stratēgos* (see PHOCIS). First attested as his brother *Onomarchus' lieutenant in 354. Defeated in *Thessaly by *Philip (1) II, he inherited the Phocian command after the battle of the Crocus Field (353). Philip's immediate interest was in Thessaly, not central Greece, which gave Phayllus time to organize his allies to defend *Thermopylae against the Macedonians' eventual advance (353/2) and—like Onomarchus after Neon—restore Phocian fortunes in the Third *Sacred War by assembling a new mercenary army (at double pay). Despite three serious defeats in *Boeotia (352) and an unsuccessful night-battle at Abae (351), he retained authority and established complete control of Epicnemidian *Locris (351), only to succumb to an unidentified illness.

RE 19, 'Phayllos 1'; J. Buckler, *Third Sacred War* (1989).   C. J. T.

Phegeus (Φηγεύς), in mythology, father of Arsinoë, wife of *Alcmaeon (1); his sons murdered Alcmaeon when he remarried (see CALLIRHOË; Apollod. 3. 87 ff.). An undatable but probably late story (*Certam. Hom. et Hes.* 249 Rzach) says *Hesiod stayed for some time at his court and was put to death by his sons, who suspected him of seducing their sister.   H. J. R.

Pheidon, king of *Argos (2), who ended up as a tyrant (Arist. *Pol.* 1310ᵇ). According to *Herodotus (1) (6. 127) he acted 'with the most *hubris of all the Greeks', and drove out the *Elian organizers of the *Olympian Games, presiding himself; he also established, perhaps standardized, Peloponnesian *weights and *measures. Beyond this, the tradition, mostly late, is diffuse and unhelpful. His reign is most probably dated to the early 7th cent. BC (? 680–660), to coincide plausibly with the height of Argive power, a defeat of Sparta at Hysiae (669/8). *Pausanias (3) dates his interference at *Olympia to 748 (6. 22. 2) but a plausible emendation would give 668. Herodotus' placing of a 'son of Pheidon' amongst Agariste's wooers, c.575 (see CLEISTHENES (1)), may merely represent the distortions of folk-tale (6. 127). It is now clear that the attribution to Pheidon of the first Greek *coinage in the later sources is anachronistic and need have no bearing on his dating (see Kraay, *CAH* 4². 432–3). The dedication of spits found at the Argive *Heraion, if his at all, could well be a standard set preserved there after his reform of weights and measures. He is said to have restored 'the lot of *Temenus', expanded Argive power over the NE Peloponnese, perhaps *Corinth, where he supposedly died interfering in stasis, even *Aegina. *Strabo says he took the leadership of the Peloponnese from Sparta. It has been suggested that he was a pioneer in the development of the *hoplite *phalanx (an early Argive grave, c.710–700, has the main elements of the hoplite panoply) and that this was what enabled Argos to defeat Sparta. Argive expansion would thus precede the rise of strong tyrannies in Corinth and *Sicyon.

Strabo 8. 358, 376 (cf. 355); FGrH 90 (Nic. Dam.) F 35; A. Andrewes, *The Greek Tyrants* (1956); E. Will, *Korinthiaka* (1955), 344 ff.; R. A. Tomlinson, *Argos and the Argolid* (1972), ch. 7.   R. T.

phēmē (φήμη), a rumour of unknown origin which springs up among the people at large; unprompted and unguided popular opinion. It is a god (Hes. *Op.* 763–4 with West's comm. (1978), also Parker, *ARH* 234 f.) and is never quite in vain (οὐ ... πάμπαν ἀπόλλυται).   S. H.

Pherae, a city of *Thessaly situated on a hill commanding a fertile district near the southern verge of the plain of *Pelasgiotis. It lay close to important land-routes and, alone among Thessalian cities, enjoyed easy access to the sea. When in possession of *Pagasae, it controlled the export of Thessalian corn. Though prominent in mythology as the home of Admetus, it remained politically insignificant except during the half-century (c.406–352 BC) when it was ruled by the family of Jason (see LYCOPHRON (1); JASON (2); ALEXANDER (5)). *Philip (1) II of Macedon expelled the tyrant-house and established a Macedonian garrison. He also effectively ended the prosperity of Pherae by depriving it of Pagasae.

The walls of the city date probably from the period of the tyrants. A temple, built in the 6th cent. but reconstructed in the 4th, may be that of *Artemis Ennodia, whose head appears on the local coinage.

E. Kirsten, *RE* Suppl. 7. 984 ff.; M. Sordi, *La lega tessala* (1958); HM 2 (1979), see index; fuller treatment than the above in T. S. Mackay, *PECS*; B. Helly, *L'état Thessalien* (1995).   H. D. W.; S. H.

Pherecrates, Athenian comic poet (see COMEDY (GREEK), OLD), won his first victories at the City *Dionysia and the *Lenaea between 440 and 430 BC (IG 2². 2325. 56, 122) and produced *Agrioi* at the Lenaea in 420 BC (Pl. *Prt.* 327d, Ath. 218d), depicting the fortunes of men who have left civilization (cf. Ar. *Av.*) to live among savages. We have nineteen titles and only 300 citations, which bear out the judgement of Anon. *De Com.* 29 p. 8 that Pherecrates was εὑρετικὸς μύθων ('inventor of stories'). In *Deserters* the parabasis appears to have been uttered by a chorus of deities (fr. 28; cf. Ar. *Nub.* 607 ff.). In *Miners* the underworld is depicted (fr. 113) as a land of fantastic abundance, and a similar theme appears (fr. 137) in *Persians* (see also CRATES 1 and METAGENES). Μυρμηκάνθρωποι ('Ant-Men') contained the story of *Deucalion's flood and *Zeus' repopulation of the earth by turning ants into men—a conflation of the Flood myth with a story of the origin of the Myrmidons (Hes. fr. 205). *Tyrannis* may possibly have had a plot similar to that of Ar. *Eccl.* The long and interesting fr. 155 (from *Chiron*) is a speech by Music, complaining of her treatment by contemporary musicians.

PCG 7. 102 ff. (CAF 1. 145 ff.).   K. J. D.

Pherecydes (1) of Syros, fl. 544 BC, reputed to be the first writer of Greek prose. His subject was the birth of the gods and the creation of the cosmos. Fragments and testimonia attest the following features: (1) Zas (*Zeus) was the first god, and with him Chronos (*Cronus) and Chthonie (Ge, 'Earth', see GAIA); (2) subsequent gods were born from five (or seven) 'recesses' (μυχοί: their cosmogonic significance is variously interpreted); (3) Zas married Chthonie in a formal ceremony, and presented her with a robe he had decorated with Earth and Ogenos (Ocean (see OCEANUS (mythological))), providing the model for a human marriage-ritual; (4) Cronus battles Ophioneus ('the snake'). Points of comparison exist with Hesiod's *Theogony*, the 'Orphic' cosmogony in the papyrus from Derveni (see ORPHIC LITERATURE), and Near-Eastern cosmogonies. Biographical fragments attribute to Pherecydes world travels, miracles, and an uncanny death. His belief in the immortality of the soul led doxographers to make him the teacher of *Pythagoras (1).

DK 7; H. Schibli, *Pherekydes of Syros* (1990).   J. S. R.

Pherecydes (2) of Athens, 'the genealogist' (later confused with (1)), wrote copious *Histories* mythical and genealogical, commended by Dion. Hal. *Ant. Rom.* 1. 13. 1. *Eusebius' date for him is 456 BC (Olympiad 81. 1).

Phidias

FGrH 3; cf. 333; R. Thomas, *Oral Tradition and Written Record in Classical Athens* (1989), 161–73, 181 ff. See also GENEALOGY.   S. H.

Phidias, Athenian sculptor, son of Charmides, active *c*.465–425 BC; reputed pupil of Hegias and Hageladas. His early works included the colossal bronze *Athena Promachos on the Acropolis; her spear-point and helmet-crest were supposedly visible from *Sunium (Paus. 1. 28. 2). His Athena Lemnia, perhaps preserved in Roman copy, and his Marathon group at *Delphi (see MARATHON, BATTLE OF) may also be early; some attribute the Riace bronzes (see 'RIACE WARRIORS') to the latter.

Phidias' reputation rested chiefly on his chryselephantine Athena Parthenos and his *Zeus at *Olympia (Quint. 12. 10. 9). Both were of gold and ivory over a wooden core, with embellishments in jewels, silver, copper, enamel, glass, and paint; each incorporated numerous subsidiary themes to demonstrate the divinity's power. *Plutarch (*Per*. 13) puts Phidias in charge not merely of the Athena but of *Pericles (1)'s entire building programme. He certainly belonged to Pericles' inner circle, and at the least probably directed the *Parthenon's exterior sculpture. The Athena recapitulated several of its themes. Almost 12 m. (40 ft.) high and draped in over a ton of gold, she was begun in 447 and installed in 438; descriptions by *Pliny (1) (*HN* 36. 18) and *Pausanias (3) (1. 24) have enabled the identification of many copies (see RETROSPECTIVE STYLES). Her right hand held a *Nike, and her left a spear and a shield embellished outside with the Amazonomachy and inside with the Gigantomachy (see AMAZONS; GIANTS). Lapiths and *Centaurs adorned her sandals, and her base carried the Birth of *Pandora in relief. A Gorgoneion (see GORGO) occupied the centre of her *aegis, and a sphinx and two Pegasi (see PEGASUS (1)) supported the three crests of her helmet; griffins decorated its cheek-pieces.

Plutarch (*Per*. 31 f.) reports that Pericles' enemies prosecuted Phidias for embezzling the Parthenos' ivory and for impiety, and that he died in prison; *Philochorus dated his trial to 438, but says that he fled to Olympia, where the Eleans killed him after he made the Zeus (*FGrH* 328 F121). This seems more likely, for his workshop there belongs to the 430s and has yielded tools, terracotta moulds (for a colossal female statue), and even a cup bearing his name. As *Strabo (8. 353 f.) and Pausanias (5. 10. 2 ff.) describe it, the Zeus was even larger than the Parthenos. Enthroned, he held a Nike in his right hand and a sceptre in his left; coins and vase-paintings reproduce the composition. The throne was richly embellished with Graces (see CHARITES), Seasons (see HORAE), Nikai (see NIKE), *sphinxes and Theban children, the slaughter of the children of *Niobe (of which marble copies survive), and an Amazonomachy; paintings by *Panaenus (Phidias' brother) on the screens between its legs included Hellas (Greece) and Salamis (see SALAMIS, BATTLE OF), some of the Labours of *Heracles, *Hippodamia and *Sterope (1), and *Achilles and *Penthesilea. Another Amazonomachy adorned Zeus' footstool, and the statue's base carried the Birth of *Aphrodite.

Ancient critics regarded Phidias as the greatest and most versatile of Greek sculptors (Quint. 12. 10. 9, etc.). His pupils dominated Athenian sculpture for a generation (see AGORACRITUS; ALCAMENES; CALLIMACHUS (2); PAEONIUS), and Hellenistic and Roman neo-classicism looked chiefly to him. Attributions (all copies) include the Medici Athena, the 'Sappho-Ourania', the Kassel Apollo, and the Mattei-Sciarra Amazon (after Pliny's account of the contest at Ephesus, *HN* 34. 53).

N. Leipen, *Athena Parthenos: A Reconstruction* (1971); J. Boardman, *Greek Sculpture: The Classical Period* (1985), 96 ff., 203 ff., figs. 79 ff., 180 ff.; A. F. Stewart, *Greek Sculpture* (1990), 60 f., 150 ff., 257 ff., figs. 312 ff.   A. F. S.

Phidippides, a long-distance courier (*hēmerodromos*) who *Herodotus (1) (6. 105 f.) says ran from Athens to Sparta in 490 BC to enlist help for the battle of Marathon (see MARATHON, BATTLE OF), reaching his destination 'next day'; a possible feat, since the winner of a race over the same ground in 1983 managed to cover the distance (*c*.240 km.; 149 miles) in under 22 hours. On the way Phidippides encountered the god *Pan, who asked him why the Athenians did not yet honour him with a state cult; this was subsequently put right. Later sources confuse his run with that of a messenger who brought the news of the Marathon victory back to Athens; they also call him Philippides (as do some manuscripts of Herodotus).

F. J. Frost and E. Badian, *AJAH* 1979, 159–66.   A. H. G.

Philadelphia (1) (Darb El-Gerza), a village in the Arsinoite nome (*meris* of Heracleides; see NOMOS (1)) in the NE *Fayūm, founded by *Ptolemy (1) II Philadelphus during drainage round lake *Moeris. Berlin Museum excavations (1908–9) uncovered Ptolemaic rectangular *insulae*. In 1914–15 illicit digging revealed the archive of Zenon, bailiff of *Apollonius (3), Philadelphus' finance minister, who held a royal estate of 10,000 aruras. Roman papyri include Claudius' Letter to the Alexandrians (*PLondon* 1912) and the Edict of Ti. *Iulius Alexander (*BGU* 1563). *Maecenas, Germanicus *Iulius Caesar, *Livia Drusilla, C. Petronius (governor of Egypt from 24 BC), M.*Antonius Pallas, *Narcissus (2), and D. *Valerius Asiaticus had imperial estates there. The site was abandoned by the 5th cent.

Papyri: A. Calderini, *Dizionario dei nomi geografici dell'Egitto* 5. 74–7 with bibliog.; *PDiog.* (1990); É. Bernand, *Recueil des inscriptions grecques du Fayoum* 1 (1975), 196–208. P. Viereck, *Philadelpheia* (1928). M. Rostovtzeff, *A Large Estate in Egypt in the Third Century BC* (1922); G. M. Parassoglou, *Imperial Estates in Roman Egypt* (1978).   W. E. H. C.

Philadelphia (2) of *Lydia, founded in the Cogamis valley by *Attalus II Philadelphus (159–138 BC). The site is fertile but lies on the edge of the Catacecaumene, and was so constantly troubled by earthquakes that according to *Strabo (13. 628) few of the citizens lived actually in the city. Philadelphia struck coins almost from its foundation, and celebrated games in honour of *Zeus-*Helios and Anaitis (see ANAHITA). Wrecked by the disastrous earthquake of AD 17, it quickly recovered; under *Gaius (1) it added to its name the title of Neocaesarea, and under *Vespasian that of Flavia. In the 3rd cent. it became *neōkoros and merited the title of metropolis. It was one of the Seven Churches of Asia in Revelation. A theatre, a 2nd-cent. AD city-gate and a late-antique city-wall are among the ruins at mod. Alaşehir (*AR* 1989–90, 97).

T. S. Mackay, *PECS* 703.   G. E. B.; A. J. S. S.

Philammon (Φιλάμμων), legendary musician and poet, son of *Apollo (Hes. fr. 64 M–W), and famous citharode in the time of *Orpheus and the *Argonauts. He won the citharodic contest at the Pythian festival (see PYTHIAN GAMES) (Paus. 10. 7. 2), instituted choruses singing about the birth of *Leto, *Artemis, and Apollo (Heracl. Pont. in ps. Plut. *De mus.* 3) and was first to use choruses of maidens (*Pherecydes (2) *FGrH* 3 F120). He also founded the mysteries at Lerna (Paus. 2. 37. 2).   H. J. R.; E. Kr.

Philargyrius, Iunius (*PLRE* 2. 874), commentator on *Virgil, author of an extant *Explanatio in Bucolica*, transmitted in two versions, a longer and a shorter, both containing Celtic glosses, of some interest and quality; it is generally dated to the 5th cent. AD. Two later Virgilian commentaries, the *Scholia Bernensia* on the *Eclogues* and *Georgics* and the *Brevis Expositio Georgicorum*, seem to owe much to him, though their spellings of his name leave room for uncertainty (one calls him 'Iunilius Flagrius', the other 'Filagrius').

Text in H. Hagen, *Appendix Serviana* (1902). M. Geymonat, *Enc. Virg.* 'Filargirio'.

S. J. Ha.

Philemon (1), **Baucis and** See BAUCIS AND PHILEMON.

Philemon (2), 368/60–267/63 BC, New Comedy poet (see COMEDY (GREEK), NEW) from *Syracuse (*Suda* φ 327) or Soli in *Cilicia (Strabo 14. 671), but granted Athenian *citizenship before 307/6 (*IG* 2². 3073 = *Syll.*³ 1089 = 2 B 1a Mette). In a long life (97 or 99 or 101 years: sources differ) he wrote 97 comedies, of which over 60 titles are known; he won 3 times at the *Lenaea, coming immediately after *Menander (1) in the victors' list (*IG* 2². 2325. 161 = 5 C 1 col. 4. 10 Mette), while his first victory at the *Dionysia is dated to 327 (*Marm. Par.*, *FGrH* 239 B 7). *Alciphron (4. 18) implies that Philemon received an invitation to the court of *Ptolemy (1) I; it is not certain that this was taken up, although another anecdote (Plut. *Mor.* 449e, 458a) brings him before King Magas of *Cyrene. Accounts of his death differ, but all agree that he was physically and mentally active to the end.

Most of the titles seem typical of New Comedy; only two (*Myrmidons, Palamedes*) sound like myth burlesques. Contemporary judgement awarded Philemon frequent victories over Menander, though this verdict was reversed by posterity (Quint. *Inst.* 10. 1. 72; Apul. *Flor.* 16.; Gell. *NA* 17. 4. 1). Just under 200 fragments survive, emphasizing the moralizing aspect of Philemon's thought: e.g. fr. 22 KA and K, a slave is a human being; 74 KA = 71 K, peace the only true good; 97 KA = 94 K, real justice. There are many gnomic lines and couplets (see GNŌMĒ), often lacking Menander's terse precision, and Jachmann's attack (*Plautinisches und Attisches* (1931), 226 f.) on Philemon's flat-footed, repetitive, and platitudinous verbosity is not unjustified. Of greater interest perhaps are the pompous cook who parodies *Euripides' *Medea* (82 KA = 79 K: see H. Dohm, *Mageiros* (1964), 122 ff.; cf. PARODY, GREEK) and part of a long-winded prologue spoken by Air (95 KA = 91 K).

Of Philemon's capacities in complete plays Plautine adaptations (see PLAUTUS) furnish some evidence—*Mercator* (from ῎Εμπορος, Merchant), *Trinummus* (from Θησαυρός, Treasure), and possibly *Mostellaria* (? from Φάσμα, Phantom). Here the fondness for surprises is probably the most interesting common factor; there is little, however, to make anyone quarrel with *Apuleius' judgement (*Flor.* 16) that Philemon's plays contained wit, plots neatly turned, recognitions (or solutions) lucidly arranged, realistic characters, maxims agreeing with life, and few seductions.

In Athens Philemon's comedies were revived after his death (B. H. Meritt, *Hesperia*, 1938, 116 ff. = 4a 25 Mette); in the 2nd cent. AD a statue was erected in his honour (*IG* 2². 4266). But it is an index of diminished popularity in comparison with Menander that there are far fewer quotations from Philemon in later writers, and no papyrus or other text identified with certainty as Philemon has been recovered, although several attributions have been suggested (cf. C. Austin, *CGFP* 244, 255, 296, 297); of these perhaps the second is the most plausible, in view of the long-windedness of part of that fragment.

FRAGMENTS Kassel and Austin, *PCG* 7 (1989), 221–317, although earlier scholars use the numbering in Kock, *CAF* 2. 478–539.

INTERPRETATION C. A. Dietze, *De Philemone comico* (Diss. Göttingen 1901); Wilamowitz, *Menander, Das Schiedsgericht* (1925), 165; A. Körte in *RE* 19. 2 (1938), 2137 ff, 'Philemon 7'; E. Rapisarda, *Filemone comico* (1939); B. Krysiniel-Józefowicz, *De quibusdam Plauti exemplaribus graecis* (1949); T. B. L. Webster, *Studies in Later Greek Comedy*² (1970), 125 ff.; F. Conca, *Acme*, 1973, 129 ff.; H. Hommel, *Grazer Beiträge*, 1984, 89 ff.; D. Averna, *Dioniso*, 1988, 39 ff.

W. G. A.

Philemon (3) **the Younger,** son of the celebrated *Philemon (2), and himself a New Comedy poet; wrote fifty-four plays (none known to us by name) and won six victories.

PCG 7 (1989), 318 ff.

S. H.

Philemon (4) A fourth Philemon, whether of the same family as (2) and (3) or not, is known from didascalic inscriptions (see DIDASKALIA) as author of Μιλησία, 'The Milesian Woman', 183 BC.

PCG 7 (1989), 321.

S. H.

Philemon (5) In the middle of the 4th cent. BC lived a fifth Philemon, an actor, mentioned by *Aeschines (1) (1. 115) and *Aristotle (*Rhet.* 1413ᵇ 31).

S. H.

Philemon (6) of Aixone (an Attic *deme) (probably early 2nd cent. BC), grammarian, edited Homer and compiled *Attikai glossai*, 'Attic glosses', see GLOSSA.

J. S. R.

Philemon (7) of Athens (c. AD 200), an Atticist grammarian, wrote Σύμμικτα ('miscellanea') and Περὶ Ἀττικῆς ἀντιλογίας (? ἀναλογίας) τῆς ἐν ταῖς λέξεσιν, a linguistic work on contradiction or perhaps analogy, see ANALOGY AND ANOMALY.

L. Cohn, *Philol.* 1898, 353 ff.

J. S. R.

Philetaerus (1), Middle Comedy poet (see COMEDY (GREEK), MIDDLE), said by *Dicaearchus to be the son of *Aristophanes (1), but this was disputed; however, allusions assign him to the earlier period of Middle Comedy. He won first prize twice at the *Lenaea (*IG* 2². 2325. 143). Of twenty-one comedies (*Suda*) thirteen titles are preserved; four or five are mythological burlesques, but there are many topical references.

PCG 7 322 ff. (*CAF* 2 230 ff.).

W. G. W.; K. J. D.

Philetaerus (2) (c.343–263 BC), son of Attalus (a Macedonian?) and a Paphlagonian mother, founder of the Attalid dynasty (see PERGAMUM). First an officer of *Antigonus (1) (before 302), and next commander of Pergamum for *Lysimachus, who kept a large treasure there, he deserted opportunely to *Seleucus (1) (282), and henceforth was ruler of Pergamum under *Seleucid suzerainty. He enlarged his territories to include much of the Caïcus valley, was a benefactor of Greek cities (e.g. Cyzicus: *OGI* 748 = Austin 194), and defended Pergamum from the Galatian invaders of Asia Minor (278–276). He adopted his nephews, one of whom (*Eumenes (1)) succeeded him. He was himself said to be a *eunuch.

R. B. McShane, *The Foreign Policy of the Attalids* (1964), 30 ff.; S. N. Davis and C. M. Kraay, *The Hellenistic Kingdoms* (1973), 250 ff.; R. E. Allen, *The Attalid Kingdom* (1983), 49 ff., 183 ff.; H. Heinen *CAH* 7². 1. 426–8. R. Smith, *Hellenistic Royal Portraits* (1988), 74–5, 159.

G. T. G.; A. J. S. S.

Philetas See PHILITAS.

philhellenism (in Roman republican history) refers to the nexus of two developments in the late 3rd and 2nd cent. BC. One of these is cultural, characterized by the actively favourable reception of Greek language, literature, and philosophy within the Roman ruling class. The other, political, is signalled by the adoption of policy and behaviour actively represented as beneficial to, and respectful of, Greece and Greeks. The phenomenon is associated especially with T. *Quinctius Flamininus, L. *Aemilius Paullus (2), and P. *Cornelius Scipio Aemilianus and his *Scipionic Circle. Instances of approbation of aspects of Greek culture go back a very long way. Advice was taken from *Apollo at *Delphi and thanks rendered to him (398, 394) long before Delphi was 'freed' from Aetolian control (see AETOLIA) in 189. On instruction from Apollo during the Samnite wars (see SAMNIUM) statues of *Alcibiades and *Pythagoras (1) were erected in the *Comitium (Plin. *HN* 34. 26), long before C. *Laelius (2) welcomed Athenian philosophers. The serpent of *Asclepius was brought to Rome from *Epidaurus (292) long before the black stone of the Magna Mater (see CYBELE) was imported from *Pessinus (204). Greek plays (in translation) were first performed in Rome in 240. In the sphere of diplomacy, L. *Postumius Megellus, when envoy to *Tarentum in 282, spoke Greek long before Flamininus dealt with Greeks in their own language, and as early as 228 Rome's victorious treaty with the Illyrian queen *Teuta was presented to Greeks as in their interest (Polybius 2. 12). The name 'Atticus' was first borne by the censor of 247 (and consul 244, 241) A. Manlius Torquatus Atticus.

Early instances of 'philhellenic' behaviour, collective and individual, abound, as do indications of 'hellenization' (though it is difficult to say how far this ever happened and what exactly it means to say that it did). But these instances are disparate, and the disparate sources for them are not such as to suggest ideological coherence or consistency. From the end of the 3rd cent. the pace quickens and the picture changes. This is partly a matter of evidence—the availability of a comparatively continuous contemporary account (*Polybius (1)) and the tendency of writers of the 1st cent. (esp. *Posidonius (2) and *Cicero) to find philhellenism in their favoured Romans of the second, but not only that. Q. *Fabius Pictor wrote his *annals in Greek early in the 2nd cent., and by the 160s Greek purveyors of hellenism were flocking to Rome (Polyb. 31. 24. 7); things Greek were much sought and genuinely admired, if occasionally to excess. A. *Postumius Albinus had his self-imposed literary hellenism castigated by M. *Porcius Cato (1); Polybius (39. 1) concurred and more. (Cato's hostility to particular representatives and manifestations of Roman philhellenism should not be taken to indicate general hostility to hellenism.) T. *Albucius was lampooned by *Lucilius (1) for preferring to be called Greek rather than Roman (Cic. *Fin.* 1. 9).

Alongside all this, the Romans in 200 announced to Greeks that they would go to war against *Philip (3) V of Macedon to prevent him from attacking any Greeks and protected Athens from Macedonian attack. From 198 Flamininus adopted the language of Greek diplomacy and used the rhetoric of Greek freedom to great advantage, most strikingly at the Isthmian games of 196. This was the efflorescence of political philhellenism. It was effective. Philip was defeated, and Greek cities honoured Flamininus; *Lampsacus with an embassy (196) and *Smyrna with a *templum urbis Romae* (temple of the city of Rome) (195) sought Roman favour and protection against *Antiochus (3) III. But the philhellenic posture was less in evidence during the war with Antiochus and thereafter, as a policy of partisan intervention took hold. L. *Aemilius Paullus (2) celebrated his victory over *Perseus (2) in Greece in explicitly hellenistic fashion, but he also oversaw the deportation or slaughter of Rome's opponents in the Greek cities and mass enslavement in Epirus. At the same time, the Romans were often referred to in

Greek inscriptions of the period as 'common benefactors' (κοινοὶ εὐεργέται; see EUERGETISM), and the goddess Roma was worshipped: Greeks participated in the construct that was Rome's political philhellenism and so continued to make it as real as Rome's dominion. See also HELLENISM, HELLENIZATION.

G. Colin, *Rome et la Grèce* (1905), 97 ff.; W. G. Forrest, *JRS* 1956, 170 f.; A. E. Astin, *Scipio Aemilianus* (1967), 294 ff. and *Cato the Censor* (1978), 157 ff.; E. Badian, *Lectures in Memory of Louise Taft Semple* (1970); C. Gallini, *Dialoghi di Archeologia* 1973, 175 ff.; R. Mellor, *ΘΕΑ ΡΩΜΗ* (1975); J.-L. Ferrary, *Philhellénisme et impérialisme* (1988; with Gruen, *Class. Phil.* 1990, 324 ff. and Derow, *JRS* 1990, 197 ff.); E. Rawson, *CAH* 8² (1989), 422 ff. (with 585 ff.); T. P. Wiseman, *JRS* 1989, 129 ff.; E. S. Gruen, *Studies in Greek Culture and Roman Policy* (1990); A. W. Erskine, *Historia* 1994, 70 ff.   P. S. D.

Philicus of *Corcyra, poet, tragedian (member of 'The *Pleiad'), and priest of *Dionysus in *Alexandria (1) under *Ptolemy (1) II Philadelphus (*Suda* φ 358; Hephaestion p. 30. 21 Consbruch; ? *Callixeinus in Ath. 5. 198c). No fragments or certain titles of the forty-two tragedies ascribed to him are known, but a substantial, though fragmentary, section remains from his *Hymn to Demeter* in stichic choriambic hexameters (five metra of -◡◡- followed by ◡-◡) and Attic dialect, *Suppl. Hell.* 676–80. In what survives of this fascinating poem, which Philicus explicitly presents to the *grammatikoi* i.e. grammarians, scholars (*Suppl. Hell.* 677), we see *Demeter consoled for the loss of her daughter by the promise of cult honours at *Eleusis, and cheered by the jokes of *Iambe, here presented as an old woman from the Attic countryside; in a move typical of Hellenistic poetry, Philicus reports Iambe's speech, whereas the *Homeric Hymn to Demeter* merely recorded its effect. *Suppl. Hell.* 980 is a partly preserved epitaph, probably for this Philicus.

F. Schramm, *Tragicorum graecorum hellenisticae quae dicitur aetatis fragmenta* (1929); K. Latte, *MH* 1954, 1–19 (= *Kleine Schriften* 539–61); Fraser, *Ptol. Alex.* 1. 651–2; C. G. Brown, *Aegyptus* (1990), 173 ff.
R. L. Hu.

Philinus (1) of Cos (fl. *c.*240 BC), an apostate pupil of *Herophilus. According to most ancient sources—A. *Cornelius Celsus (*Med.* prooem. 10) being the only significant exception—he was the founder of the Empiricist 'school' of medicine. The origins of the Empiricist school in a polemical rivalry with Herophileans become visible in his works. He rejected a conspicuous feature of the Herophilean tradition, namely the diagnostic and prognostic interpretation of pulse 'signs', and wrote a treatise in six books in response to *Bacchius' Hippocratic lexicon. Like many subsequent Empiricists, he also made major contributions to *pharmacology, as *Pliny (1) the Elder and *Galen confirm. Here, too, Philinus was attentive to language, introducing etymologizing explanations of the names of botanical ingredients. Some of his compound drug prescriptions were transmitted by Andromachus the Younger and are preserved by Galen.

To what extent Galen's detailed characterizations of the epistemological and methodological foundations of medical Empiricism (e.g. their famous 'tripod') apply to Philinus, remains uncertain in the absence of more specific evidence. Also uncertain is whether the Empiricist is identical with a Philinus who wrote in the theriac tradition. See MEDICINE § 5. 3.

Ed., comm.: K. Deichgräber, *Die griechische Empirikerschule* (1930; 1965²). H. Diller, *RE* 19. 2. 2193–4.   H. v. S.

Philinus (2) (*RE* 8), of Acragas, pro-Carthaginian historian of the First *Punic War (see Polybius 1. 14); used by *Polybius (1) and perhaps by *Diodorus (3). He is the authority for the so-called Treaty of Philinus of 306, between Rome and *Carthage, rejected by Polybius (3. 26. 3) and by some modern historians, but accepted as authentic by others.

Walbank, *HCP* 1. 27–355. B. M. C.

Philip (1) **II** (382–336 BC), king of Macedon and architect of Macedonian greatness. In his youth he witnessed the near dissolution of the kingdom through civil war and foreign intervention, and spent some time (probably 369–367) as hostage in *Epaminondas' *Thebes (1). The nadir came when his brother, Perdiccas III, died in battle against Illyrian invaders (360/59; see ILLYRII), who occupied the north-western borderlands. On his accession (perhaps initially as regent for his nephew, Amyntas) his priority was to save Macedon from dismemberment by hostile powers, poised for the kill; and from the outset he displayed a genius for compromise and intrigue. The Athenians, who backed a pretender (Argaeus), were defeated in a skirmish near *Aegae but wooed by the return of their prisoners (and by hints that he would recognize their claims to *Amphipolis). Other belligerents (Paeonians and Thracians; see THRACE) were bought off, and Philip used the time he acquired to train a new citizen army in mass infantry tactics, introducing the twelve-cubit pike (*sarisa*) as its basic weaponry (see PHALANX). His efforts bore fruit in 358, when he decisively defeated the Illyrians near Lake Lychnitis and used his victory to integrate the previously independent principalities of upper Macedonia into his kingdom. Their nobility joined the companions of his court and the commons were recruited into the army. Philip's increased power was immediately deployed against Athens. While the city was enmeshed in the *Social War (1) (357–355) he annexed Amphipolis and *Pydna in 357, captured *Potidaea in 356, ceding it to the Olynthian federation (see CHALCIDICE; OLYNTHUS) in return for alliance, and acquired *Methone (1) (354)—at the cost of his right eye and permanent disfigurement. From the conquests came land which he distributed in part to a new aristocracy, recruited from all parts of the Greek world (e.g. *Nearchus of Crete, Laomedon of Mytilene and *Androsthenes of Thasos, all settled at Amphipolis). Most important was Crenides, the Thracian settlement by Mt. *Pangaeus, which Philip occupied and reinforced in 356, naming it *Philippi after himself. The exploitation of the neighbouring gold mines allegedly engrossed 1,000 talents *per annum*, which enabled him to maintain a large mercenary army and win the services of politicians in southern Greece.

*Thessaly rapidly became an annex of Macedon. An early marriage alliance with the *Aleuadae family of *Larissa brought an invitation to intervene in the murderous internecine war between the Thessalian League and the tyrants of *Pherae. Initial defeats in 353 were redeemed in 352 by the great victory of the Crocus Field and the expulsion of Lycophron and Peitholaus from *Pherae. In return Philip was appointed archon of Thessaly with its revenues and superb cavalry at his disposal. In 349 he attacked another traditional enemy, *Olynthus, and by September 348 had captured the city through internal treachery. The population was enslaved and Olynthus' land absorbed, but despite the shock of this exemplary treatment there was no response to the Athenian appeal for an international alliance against him, and in despondency the Athenians entered peace negotiations early in 346. Peace and alliance were concluded in April 346 (Peace of *Philocrates) at the same time that Philip accepted an appeal to lead an Amphictionic campaign against the Phocians (allies of Athens; see AMPHICTIONY; PHOCIS). With

masterly prevarication he delayed ratifying the peace until he was in the vicinity of *Thermopylae, preventing the Athenians reinforcing their allies, and forced the Phocians to terms (July 346). The settlement which resulted left him master of Thermopylae with voting rights in the Amphictiony.

The years after 346 saw further expansion. Campaigns against the Illyrians (notably in 345) brought the Dardanians and Taulantians to subject status, and between 342 and 340 Philip crowned a long series of campaigns against the Thracians with a prolonged war in the Hebrus valley. The old Odrysian kingdom became a dependency under a Macedonian *stratēgos*; military colonies (notably *Philippopolis/Plovdiv) were implanted, and the Thracians supplied his largest pool of auxiliary troops. Meanwhile Philip's influence had expanded in southern Greece. He championed *Megalopolis and *Messenia against Sparta, supported a coup at Elis (343) and sent mercenaries to Euboea (343/2: date disputed). By 342 Athenian interpretations of his motives had more conviction. In 341 the Euboean regimes at *Eretria and Oreos (*Histiaea) were overthrown by an Athenian-led invasion and Athenian overtures were sympathetically received in the Peloponnese. The situation became graver in 340, when Philip laid siege to *Perinthus and *Byzantium, and open war erupted in the late summer, when he commandeered the Athenian grain fleet. He left the sieges incomplete to launch a successful attack on the Scythian king Ateas, and returned to Macedon in mid-339.

The final act came when he assumed command of an Amphictionic expedition against the Locrians of *Amphissa and used the campaign as a fulcrum to attack Thebes and Athens, now united in alliance against him. Its denouement was the battle of *Chaeronea (August 338), fought with a fraction of the forces at his disposal, which destroyed Thebes as a military power and made him undisputed master of the Greek world. Garrisons at *Corinth, *Thebes (1), *Ambracia, and (probably) *Chalcis policed the settlement he imposed, and a conference at Corinth (summer 337) approved a common peace which guaranteed the stability of all governments party to it, prohibited constitutional change and entrenched Philip as executive head (*hegemon*) of the council (*synedrion*) which directed its enforcement (see CORINTH, LEAGUE OF). It was intended to perpetuate Macedonian domination and did so effectively. The meeting also witnessed Philip's proclamation of his war of revenge against Persia, a project doubtless long in gestation but only now publicized, and in 336 an expeditionary force crossed the Hellespont to begin operations in Asia Minor.

Philip's last year was overshadowed by domestic conflict. His love match with Cleopatra provoked a rift in the royal house which saw his wife *Olympias in angry retirement and the heir-apparent, Alexander (see ALEXANDER (3) III, THE GREAT), in temporary exile in Illyria. There was a formal reconciliation; but tensions persisted, and Philip fell by an assassin's hand in autumn 336. The sources give personal motives, but there are also hints of a multiplicity of conspirators and the background to the murder is beyond speculation. He was interred at *Aegae (many believe, in the splendid barrel-vaulted Tomb II in the Great Tumulus of Vergina), leaving his kingdom a military and economic giant but internally almost as distracted as it had been at his accession.

ANCIENT SOURCES *Theopompus (3)'s *Philippica*, originally in 58 books, survives only in fragments (*FGrH* 115). Brief historical outlines are provided by Diod. bk. 16 and Justin bks. 7–9, and there is a wealth of (often contentious) detail in the orations of *Demosthenes

(2), *Aeschines, and *Isocrates. For inscriptional evidence and more abstruse literary material see P. Harding, *From the End of the Peloponnesian War to the Battle of Ipsus* (1985).

MODERN LITERATURE J. R. Ellis, *Philip II and Macedonian Imperialism* (1976) and *CAH* 6² (1994), chs. 14, 15; G. L. Cawkwell, *Philip of Macedon* (1978); *HM* 2 (1979)—fundamental; J. Buckler, *Philip II and the Sacred War* (1989).   A. B. B.

Philip (2) **Arrhidaeus** (c.357–317 BC), son of *Philip (1) II and Philinna of Larissa. Mentally impaired, he left no trace in the tradition of *Philip (1) II's and Alexander (3) the Great's reigns and came unexpectedly to prominence in June 323 when the Macedonian phalanx troops found him at Babylon and proclaimed him Alexander's successor. Joint ruler with the infant *Alexander (4) IV, he assumed the regnal name Philip (III) and became a cipher in the hands successively of *Perdiccas (3), who had him marry his cousin Adea (*Eurydice, 2), *Antipater (1) and *Polyperchon. He came to grief in 317, when his wife usurped his authority against the regent Polyperchon and was defeated and captured. *Olympias had him murdered (October 317); but his memory was honoured by *Cassander, who reinterred his and his wife's remains. Some have identified their burial place as the controversial Tomb II at Vergina (see AEGAE).

Berve, *Alexanderreich* 2, no. 781; Bosworth, in *Chiron* 1992.1.   A. B. B.

Philip (3) **V** (238–179 BC), king of Macedon, son of *Demetrius (6) II and Phthia (Chryseis) and adopted by *Antigonus (3) Doson, whom he succeeded in summer 221. He quickly showed that his youth did not betoken weakness in Macedon, initially against the *Dardani and others in the north. The *Social War (2) (220–217), in which he led the Hellenic League against *Aetolia, *Sparta, and *Elis, saw him establish his own authority in the face of intrigues amongst his ministers and brought him considerable renown at home and abroad. After the Peace of Naupactus (217), he sought to take advantage of Rome's discomfiture in Italy and to replace Roman with Macedonian influence along the eastern shore of the *Adriatic: first by sea with limited success (after an aborted expedition in 216 he lost his fleet in 214) and later by land with considerably more (he captured Lissus on the Adriatic in 213). His treaty with *Hannibal (215) defined spheres of operation and interest but led to no useful action. Rome's alliance with the *Aetolian League (211) did much to neutralize Philip's advantage on land, and the intervention of *Attalus I of Pergamum on the Roman-Aetolian side further distracted him. Remarkable energy and tactical skill were devoted to assisting and protecting his allies, the Achaeans against Sparta and those on the mainland against Roman–Aetolian rapacity. With the withdrawal of Attalus, a biennium of Roman inactivity (207–206), and the development by *Philopoemen of a competent military force in Achaea (see ACHAEAN CONFEDERACY), the balance shifted. After sacking *Thermum, Philip forced terms on the Aetolians (206), and concluded the temporizing (on the Roman side at least) Peace of Phoenice in 205. Philip then turned eastward: he employed the piratical Dicaearchus to gain resources and from 203/2 sought to gain control of territory in the Aegean and Asia Minor subject to the infant *Ptolemy (1) V; the nature and extent of his co-operation with *Antiochus (3) III in this venture is disputed. This expansion, along with that achieved by his lieutenants on the mainland, alarmed many, especially Attalus and the Rhodians (see RHODES). Their naval engagements with Philip off *Chios and Lade (near *Miletus) in 201 were of mixed outcome, but their *démarche* at Rome late that year came at an opportune juncture: the Romans were victorious over Carthage

and already inclined against Philip and towards the east. In 200 they declared war and lost no time in announcing that they had come as protectors of the Greeks (see FREEDOM IN THE ANCIENT WORLD; PHILHELLENISM); many believed them. After campaigns in Macedonia (199) and Thessaly (198), Philip was defeated at *Cynoscephalae in Thessaly in 197. By the subsequent peace settlement the Romans confined him to Macedonia, exacted 1,000 talents indemnity, most of his fleet, and hostages, amongst them his younger son, Demetrius. After securing an alliance with the Romans, Philip co-operated with them, sending help against *Nabis (195) and Antiochus and the Aetolians (192–189), and made acquisitions in Thessaly. For facilitating the advance of the Scipios (P. *Cornelius Scipio Africanus and L. *Cornelius Scipio Asiagenes) through Macedon and Thrace (190) he had the rest of his indemnity remitted and his son restored. He then set about consolidating Macedon: finance was reorganized, populations were transplanted, mines reopened, central and local currencies issued. Accusations by his neighbours (especially *Eumenes (2) II of Pergamum) led to constant interference by an already suspicious Rome. Adverse decisions by the senate in 185 convinced him that his destruction was intended and quickened his efforts to extend his influence in the Balkans by force and diplomacy. Meanwhile, the pro-Roman policy of Demetrius (fostered by T. *Quinctius Flamininus and others who encouraged him to entertain hopes of succession) led to a quarrel with the crown prince *Perseus (2) and ultimately to Philip's reluctant decision to execute Demetrius for treason (180). From this Philip never recovered, and in 179, amidst an ambitious scheme for directing the *Bastarnae against the Dardani, he died at *Amphipolis.

M. Holleaux, *Rome, la Grèce et les monarchies hellénistiques au IIIème siècle avant J.-C.* (1921); F. W. Walbank, *Philip V of Macedon* (1940), *HCP*, and *CAH* 7². 1 (1984), 473 ff. (with bibliog.); E. S. Gruen, *The Hellenistic World and the Coming of Rome* (1984), 359 ff.; *HM* 3 (1988), 367 ff.; R. M. Errington, *CAH* 8² (1989), 94 ff., 244 ff. (with bibliog.); P. S. Derow, *CAH* 8² (1989), 290 ff. (with bibliog.).   P. S. D.

Philip (4), following the will left by his father *Herod (1), was confirmed by *Augustus tetrarch (see TETRARCHY) of the northern part of his kingdom—designated as Batanea, Trachonitis, Auranitis, Gaulanitis (the Golan), and including Panias, where Philip founded the city of Caesarea Philippi. His rule, over a largely non-Jewish, Syrian population, is highly praised by *Josephus. When he died in AD 34, his territory was briefly part of the province of *Syria until it was put under *Iulius Agrippa (1) I in 37.   T. R.

Philippi, a city in eastern *Macedonia on the *via Egnatia, overlooking an inland plain to the east of Mt. *Pangaeus. Its territory was remarkable for its rich gold mines (Strabo 7 fr. 34, distinct from those of Mt. Pangaeus), which were worked by Thracians (see THRACE) until in 360 BC *Thasos annexed it and founded a city 'Crenides', probably known also as 'Datum' (Strab. 7 fr. 36). The citizens of Crenides invoked the help of *Philip (1) II against the Thracians. He enlarged the city, renamed it Philippi, and derived 1,000 talents a year from its mines (Diod. 16. 8. 6). He treated it as a 'free' Greek city within his kingdom, drained its swamps and increased its territory. It became well known in 42 BC, when the forces of M. *Antonius (2) (Mark Antony) and Octavian (see AUGUSTUS) defeated those of M. *Iunius Brutus (2) and C. *Cassius Longinus (1); and the victors developed and enlarged Philippi as a Roman colony. The Apostle *Paul founded the first Christian church at Philippi in AD 49. The site is remarkable for a fine theatre and four magnificent basilicas.

P. Collart, *Philippes* (1937); P. Lemerle, *Philippes et la Macédoine orientale à l'époque chrétienne et byzantine* (1945); D. Lazaridis, *Philippi* (in Greek, 1956). N. G. L. H.

Philippides of Athens, New Comedy poet (see COMEDY (GREEK), NEW), who won a victory at the *Dionysia in 311 BC (*IG* 2². 2323a. 41 = 3 B 2 col. 1. 16 Mette) and two, three, or four victories at the *Lenaea (*IG* 2². 2325. 164 = 5 C 1 col. 4. 13 Mette). Of forty-five comedies (*Suda* φ 345) we know fifteen titles. As a friend of *Lysimachus, king of Thrace, Philippides possessed great influence; an honorific decree of 283/2, which records his services to Athens, is still extant (*IG* 2². 657 = *SIG*³ 374 = 3 A 4a 6 Mette). Fr. 6: The Good in *Plato (1); 9: the ways of *nouveaux riches*; 18: *Euripides quoted for consolation in trouble; 25: denunciation of the sacrilegious behaviour of *Demetrius (4) I Poliorcetes.

FRAGMENTS Kassel and Austin, *PCG* 7 (1989), 333–52, although earlier scholars use the numbering in Kock, *CAF* 3. 301–12.

INTERPRETATION Meineke, *FCG* 1. 470 ff.; Körte in *RE* 19. 2 (1938), 2204 ff., 'Philippides 7'; J. K. Davies, *Athenian Propertied Families 600–300 BC* (1971), 541; G. B. Philipp, *Gymnasium* 1973, 493 ff.; I. Gallo, *Sileno*, 1980, 225 ff. W. G. A.

Philippopolis (Plovdiv) was at the centre of the road-system of inland *Thrace. *Philip (1) II founded it in 342 BC as a mixed settlement of Thracians and 2,000 Macedonian and Greek settlers, whom *Theopompus (3) said were rascals; hence its nickname 'Poneropolis', meaning 'Crookham' (*FGrH* 115 F 110). Sometimes Macedonian, sometimes Odrysian (see THRACE), it was reoccupied by *Philip (3) V in 183 BC, and *Perseus (2) was supported by the Odrysians in the final conflict with Rome in 168 BC. Renamed Trimontium under Roman rule, it was the centre of the provincial government of Thrace. Later it was a stronghold against Gothic invaders (see GOTHS), in AD 250–70.

RE 19 (1937), 2244 (Danov); G. Mihailov, *Inscriptiones Graecae in Bulgaria repertae* 3. 1 (1961). N. G. L. H.

Philippus (emperor). See IULIUS PHILIPPUS, M.

Philippus (1) (*RE* 42) of Opus (fl. *c*.350 BC), astronomer, was thought by some (Diog. Laert. 3. 37) to have transcribed the *Laws* of his teacher *Plato (1) and to have written the *Epinomis*. He is probably the Philippus who composed an astronomical calendar (see ASTRONOMY) and primitive shadow-tables.

HAMA 2. 574, 739 ff. A. E. Taylor, *Proc. Brit. Acad.* 15 (1929). G. J. T.

Philippus (2) of Thessalonica, epigrammatist and editor of a *Garland* of epigrams written since *Meleager (2). The *Garland*, probably published under *Nero, was arranged alphabetically by the first word of each poem (substantial blocks survive in the Greek Anthology). Within each letter group poems are arranged by community or contrast of theme. Some eighty of Philip's own epigrams are included, mainly ecphrastic (see EKPHRASIS) and rhetorical, often variations on poems by his authors—sometimes juxtaposed with their models by a deliberately engineered alphabetical link.

Gow–Page, *GP* 2628 f.; Alan Cameron, *Greek Anthology* (1993), 33–43, 56–65. A. D. E. C.

Philiscus (1) (4th cent. BC), a pupil of *Isocrates, wrote a *Rhetoric* (τέχνη), a life of the orator *Lycurgus (3), and political pamphlets. See TIMAEUS (2).

FGrH 337bis (addenda p. 757); 496 F 9. L. Radermacher, *Artium Scriptores* (1951), 194. M. B. T.

Philiscus (2), Middle Comedy poet (see COMEDY (GREEK), MIDDLE). Eight titles are known, the majority mythological burlesques; 14 lines in a papyrus (*PSI* 1175: C. Austin, *CGFP* fr. 215) have been attributed to his Διὸς γοναί (Birth of *Zeus).

FRAGMENTS Kassel and Austin, *PCG* 7 (1989), 356–9.

INTERPRETATION Meineke, *FCG* 1. 423 f.; C. Gallavotti, *RFIC* 1930, 214 n. 2; A. Körte, *Hermes*, 1930, 475 and in *RE* 19. 2 (1938), 2381 f., 'Philiskos 5'. W. G. A.

Philiscus (3) of Aegina (4th cent. BC) came under the teaching of *Diogenes (2) of Sinope at Athens and joined the *Cynic school. He is said to have taught *Alexander (3) the Great, but this is doubtful. Seven tragedies were ascribed to him in antiquity.

TrGF 1². 258–9. W. D. R.; J. S. R.

Philiscus (4) of Thessaly (*c*. AD 153–220), sophist and rhetorician, held the chair of rhetoric at Athens.

Philostr. *VS* 2. 30 (621–3); comm. S. Rothe (1988), 252. M. B. T.

Philistion (*RE* 4) of *Locri Epizephyrii, physician and perhaps a contemporary of *Plato (1) (*c*.427–347 BC), provides important evidence for early medical theory outside the Hippocratic corpus (see HIPPOCRATES (2)). According to *Callimachus (3) (in Diog. Laert. 8. 86) he was a teacher of *Eudoxus (1) of Cnidus. None of his work survives intact but he is connected doctrinally by *Galen with an influential group of Sicilian doctors, and especially with *Empedocles. Galen notes that he was regarded by some as the author of the Hippocratic treatises *Regimen*, and *Regimen in Health*. Like Empedocles, he posited four *elements, fire, earth, air, and water, and the related qualities hot, dry, cold, and moist. The author of the Anonymus Londinensis papyrus preserves (20. 25) Philistion's view that disease could be the result either of an imbalance of these elements within the body, or of respiratory dysfunction leading to morbid internal air blockages, or be caused by external factors such as physical trauma. He apparently wrote extensively on *dietetics, and his treatments for a variety of disorders are quoted by a number of later authorities including *Athenaeus (3), Galen, and *Oribasius (frs. 9–16 Wellmann). It is widely suspected that he influenced the pathological theory presented by Plato at *Timaeus* 81e–86a.

TEXTS M. Wellmann, *Die Fragmente der Sikelischen Aerzte*, (1901), 109–16.

LITERATURE On Philistion's influence, M. Wellmann, *Hermes*, 1900. His influence on Plato, see A. E. Taylor, *A Commentary on Plato's Timaeus* (1928), 599. On the physiological theory in its wider medical context, H. von Staden, *Herophilus: The Art of Medicine in Early Alexandria*, (1989), 388. J. T. V.

Philistus of *Syracuse, *c*.430–356 BC, friend, adviser, officer, and historian of *Dionysius (1) I and (2) II. He successfully supported Dionysius I in his bid for power in 406/5 (T3) and served for a long time as commander of the tyrants' stronghold in Ortygia (T 5c). He was exiled for personal reasons in *c*.386 and on his return put in charge of the organization of colonies along the Adriatic coast (T 5a). He served as Dionysius II's political adviser and *nauarchos* ('admiral', T 9b). A staunch opponent of *Plato (1)'s and *Dion's reforms (T 5c and 7), he died in 356 in the fight against the insurgent Syracusans, maybe through suicide (T 9c).

Work The History of Sicily (*Sicelica*) contained two *syntaxeis* (parts), covering the time from the mythical beginnings until 363/2. The seven books of the first part brought the narrative down to the capture of *Acragas by the Carthaginians (see CARTHAGE) in 406/5, the second part dealt in four books with the reign of the elder Dionysius from his accession to power in 406/5 until his death in 368/7 (T 11a). In addition there were two books on Dionysius the Younger reaching down to 363/2. The work was continued by Athanis or rather Athanas of Syracuse until *Timoleon's resignation in 337/6 (Dion. 15. 94. 4). Philistus showed very favourable tendencies towards the tyrants. Plutarch (Dion. 36. 3 = T 23a) calls him 'the greatest lover of the tyrants (*philotyrannotatos*) and more than any one else an admirer of luxury, power, wealth, and marriage alliances of tyrants'. Similar opinions are found in *Cornelius Nepos (Dion. 3. 1 = T 5d), *Diodorus (3) (16. 16. 3 = T 9c), *Dionysius (7) of Halicarnassus (T 16a) and *Pausanias (3) (1. 13. 8 = T 13a). The scant fragments that deal with Dionysius I (esp. F 57 and 58) also show Philistus' favourable attitude. He was nevertheless a very competent and important historian: the ancients regarded him unanimously as an imitator of *Thucydides (2), e.g. Dionysius of Halicarnassus (T 16), *Cicero (T17) and *Quintilian (T 15c). Many parts of Diodorus' narrative which are based on *Timaeus (2), e.g. the siege of *Gela 13. 108–13, the building of the wall in Syracuse 14. 18, the preparations for the war against Carthage 14. 41–6, ultimately derive from the vivid and knowledgeable account of Philistus. Several details in Diodorus' account of the Sicilian expedition by Athens (12. 82–13. 10) which are not mentioned in Thucydides, but do appear in Diodorus' source *Ephorus, argue for Philistus as their source of origin. Only 76 direct fragments are extant, 42 of which in the geographical lexicon of *Stephanus of Byzantium: these contain scarcely more than place names. E. Meyer regarded this as 'one of the most serious losses for ancient historiography'.

FGrH 556. R. Zoepffel, *Untersuchungen zum Geschichtswerk des Philistos*, Diss. Freiburg/Brg. (1965). F. W. Walbank, *Kokalos* 1968/9, 476 ff. L. Pearson, *The Greek Historians of the West: Timaeus and his Predecessors* (1987); M. Sordi, *Studia Hellenistica*, 1990, 159 ff.; K. Meister, *Die griechische Geschichtsschreibung* (1990), 68 f.; Ch. Sabattini, *Filisto storiografo e politico. Tradizione, forma, immagine*, Diss. San Marino (1992). O. Lendle, *Einführung in die griechische Geschichtsschreibung* (1992), 206 ff.; D. M. Lewis, *CAH* 6² (1994) ch. 5. K. M.

Philitas (also spelt **Philetas**) of *Cos, poet and scholar, born *c*.340 BC, became tutor of *Ptolemy (1) II Philadelphus (b. Cos 308); reputedly also taught *Zenodotus, *Theocritus, and *Hermesianax. He presumably spent some time in *Alexandria (1), but probably died in Cos, where a bronze statue or relief was erected in his honour.

Works (1) *Poetry*. Five titles are attested: *Hermes, Demeter, Telephus* (?), *Epigrammata, Paegnia*; only small fragments are extant. *Hermes* (the reason for the title is unclear), in hexameters, narrated *Odysseus' visit to *Aeolus (1)'s island and his love-affair with his daughter Polymele (fr. 5 Pow. (= Parthenius, *Er. Path.* 2) is not necessarily a full or accurate summary). *Demeter*, a narrative elegy, recounted the goddess's mourning and search for Kore (*Persephone), including perhaps her visit to Cos. *Telephus* (if the title is right: Telephus was also the name of P.'s father) included a reference to the marriage of *Jason (1) and *Medea. *Paegnia* and *Epigrammata* may have been alternative titles for the same collection of epigrams. It is not clear in which of his works Philitas may have written love-poetry to Bittis (cf. Hermesianax fr. 7. 77–8; Ovid, *Tr.* 1. 6. 2), or treated the subject of *bougonia* (fr. 22 Pow.), possibly alluded to by Theocritus (*Id.* 7. 78–89) and Virgil (*G.* 4. 281 ff., see ARISTAEUS, end).

(2) *Prose*. Thirty-odd fragments survive of a work variously entitled Ἄτακτοι γλῶσσαι, Γλῶσσαι, or Ἄτακτα (i.e. *Miscellaneous Glosses*: an alleged work Ἑρμηνεία may be identical) which explained Homeric glosses, dialect forms, and technical terms (see GLOSSA, GLOSSARY); this is already referred to as a standard work of reference in a 3rd-cent. comedy, the *Phoenicides* of *Straton (2).

Although so little of his work has survived, it is clear that Philitas' influence on Hellenistic and Latin poetry was very great. He rather than *Antimachus came to represent the combination of literary scholarship and poetic creativity emulated by *Callimachus (3) and other *poetae docti* or 'learned poets' (e.g. Propertius 3. 1. 1, 3. 3. 52). His poetry was admired for its learning, small scale, and high polish; *Demeter* in particular was highly esteemed (cf. Callimachus, fr. 1. 9–10) and is thought to be the object of many allusions by later poets. It has been conjectured that the character of Philetas in *Longus' novel *Daphnis and Chloe* may be the vehicle for reminiscences of P.'s poems, in which some scholars have detected pastoral elements.

TEXTS Powell, *CA* 90–6 (poetic frs. only); G. Kuchenmüller, *Philetae Coi Reliquiae* (1928); *Suppl. Hell.* 673–5.

GENERAL A. von Blumenthal, *RE* 19 (1938), 2165–70; R. Pfeiffer, *Hist. Class. Schol.* (1968), 88–92; (on Philetas in Longus) F. Cairns, *Tibullus* (1979), 25–7, E. Bowie, *CQ* 1985, 67–91; (on P. and Latin poetry) P. E. Knox, *Papers of the Leeds International Latin Seminar* 7 (1993), 61–83. F. W.

Philo See PHILON (4).

Philochorus (*c*.340–260 BC), son of Cycnus, was a truly Hellenistic man. The mini-biography of him in the *Suda* reveals a man of religion (he was official prophet and diviner in 306), a patriot, who was arrested and put to death by *Antigonus (2) Gonatas for supporting *Ptolemy (1) II Philadelphus at the time of the Chremonidean War (see CHREMONIDES), and a scholar-historian, who wrote at least twenty-seven works, of which the most famous was his *Atthis. His scholarly interests ranged from local history (of *Attica, *Delos and *Salamis (1)) to chronography (Olympiads), cult (monographs on *Prophecy, Sacrifices, Festivals*, and the *Mysteries at Athens*) and literature (studies on *Euripides and *Alcman). He was the last atthidographer (see ATTHIS) and the most respected, to judge from the number of times his work was cited. Jacoby considered him 'the first scholar' to write an *Atthis*, though this may be unfair to his predecessors.

The *Atthis* was seventeen books long. We have over 170 fragments. From these we can form a good impression of the structure and character of his work. It was arranged in the standard chronological format of the genre, by kings and archons (see ARCHONTES), and presented its information in succinct factual notices in unadorned prose, a good example of which can be found in Dion. Hal. *To Ammaeus* 1. 9. Despite his professional interest in religion, Philochorus only devoted two books to the early period down to *Solon, and two more to the end of the 5th cent. The fourth century, which had been treated in detail by *Androtion, was also reduced to two books. The remaining eleven books covered the 60 years from 320–260. So, Philochorus' main interest was the period of his mature years. Unfortunately nothing of significance has survived from these books, because this period did not interest the later scholars who cited him.

In his research Philochorus used documents and his own experience for his own time. For the earlier period he used the *Atthis* of Androtion, as is shown by the frequency with which the two are cited together. By contrast he did not approve of the *Atthis* of his immediate predecessor, *Demon, which he criticised in a monograph entitled *Atthis against Demon*. The fragments show that Philochorus was familiar with the works of *Herodotus (1), *Thucydides (2), *Ephorus, and *Theopompus (3). His *Atthis* was a source for the Hellenistic chronographers.

FGrH 328; F. Jacoby, *Atthis* (1949); P. E. Harding, *Androtion and the Atthis* (1994). P. E. H.

Philocles, nephew of *Aeschylus, is said by the *Suda* to have written 100 plays, and was victorious on the occasion when *Sophocles (1) produced *Oedipus Tyrannus*. However, he was nicknamed Gall and Son of Brine because of his harsh style, and was mocked by comic poets (e.g. Ar. *Vesp.* 461–2, *Av.* 1295, *Thesm.* 168). Ar. *Av.* 281–3 probably alludes to his *Tereus*, from a *Pandionis* tetralogy.

TrGF 1². 139–42; *Musa Tragica* 94–7, 281–2. A. L. B.

Philocrates, Athenian politician, already active in the 350s BC, but principally connected with the Atheno-Macedonian peace of 346. An attempt at negotiations in 348 was thwarted by a *graphē paranomōn*, though *Demosthenes (2) secured Philocrates' acquittal. In 346 he proposed crucial decrees authorizing despatch of the first embassy, acceptance of peace and alliance by Athens and her allies, and extension of the treaty to *Philip (1) II's descendants and political abandonment of Phocis, and served on associated embassies. Athenian dissatisfaction with the outcome exposed him to prosecution by *Hyperides for *bribery—alleged evidence included commercial ventures involving wheat and *timber (a major Macedonian commodity), house-building, income from land provided by Philip, and ostentatious sexual and gastronomic self-indulgence—and he fled into exile (343).

RE 19, 'Philokrates 5'; J. R. Ellis, *Philip II* (1976), and *CAH* 6² (1994), chs. 14, 15; G. L. Cawkwell, *Philip of Macedon* (1978). C. J. T.

Philoctetes, in mythology son of Poeas and leader of seven ships to *Troy (*Homer, *Il.* 2. 718), but left behind in *Lemnos suffering from a snakebite (ibid. 722–3). The *Epic Cycle* adds that while the Greeks were sailing to Troy they sacrificed in Tenedos, and there Philoctetes was bitten and left behind because of the stench of his festering wound (*Cypria*, Proclus). Ten years later *Odysseus captured *Helenus, the Trojan seer, and learned from him that Troy could only be taken if Philoctetes was present, so *Diomedes (2) fetched him from Lemnos. He was healed by *Machaon, then fought a duel with *Paris and killed him (*Little Iliad*, Proclus). *Aeschylus, *Sophocles (1), and *Euripides each wrote a *Philoctetes* (Dio Chrys. *Or.* 52, cf. 59), but only Sophocles' play survives. Sophocles adds that Philoctetes had the bow and inescapable arrows of *Heracles given to him (801 ff.; or given to his father, Apollod. 2. 7. 7) for lighting the pyre on Mt. Oeta. Without the bow Troy would not fall (68–9), so *Neoptolemus (1) is ordered by Odysseus to obtain it by trickery. But Neoptolemus' basic honesty causes complications in the plot, and the play ends with Heracles *ex machina* ordering Philoctetes to Troy. Homer's *Odyssey* says that Philoctetes returned safely home after the war (3. 190); but some later accounts say that he wandered to *Magna Graecia and founded cities there: cf. *Apollodorus (6) in Strabo 6. 254. He certainly had *hero-cult in more than one place (near *Sybaris and at Macalla in the territory of *Croton, *Lycophron (2(b)), 919 ff., cf. [Aristotle] *Mir. Ausc.* 107).

LIMC 7. 1 (1994), 376–85. H. J. R.; J. R. M.

Philodamus of Scarphea, author of a '*paean to *Dionysus' apparently performed, by demand of the Pythia (see DELPHIC ORACLE), at the Delphic festival of *Theoxenia and inscribed in the sanctuary in 340/39. A paean to Dionysus, rather than *Apollo, is a novel hybrid; but at Delphi the two gods were traditionally closely associated, and the paean itself interweaves themes of Dionysiac legend with such local concerns as the rebuilding of Apollo's temple.

Powell, *Coll. Alex.* 165–71 (accessible but outdated text); A. Stewart in B. Barr-Sharrar and E. N. Borza, *Macedonia and Greece in Late Classical and Early Hellenistic Times* (1982); L. Käppel, *Paian* (1992). R. C. T. P.

Philodemus (*RE* 5) (*c*.110–*c*.40/35 BC), born at Gadara in *Syria, died probably at *Herculaneum; he came to Rome *c*.75 BC and eventually enjoyed the favour and powerful friendship of the Pisones. One of them, L. *Calpurnius Piso Caesoninus (consul 58), was especially attached to him and was perhaps the owner of the magnificent *villa at Herculaneum. *Cicero's somewhat ironical praise of Philodemus (*Pis.* 28. 68 ff.) shows that he was already well known to a Roman audience for his poetry in 55 BC. His connections with Piso brought Philodemus the opportunity of influencing the brilliant young students of Greek literature and philosophy who gathered around him and Siron at Herculaneum and Naples (*Neapolis), as is shown by Philodemus' addresses to and the responses of *Varius Rufus (who wrote a *De morte*), *Virgil (cf. his *Appendix* and *Georgics* 3), *Plotius Tucca, and *Horace (who names Philodemus in his *Satires*). Although his prose work, discovered in about a thousand papyrus rolls in the philosophical library recovered at Herculaneum (see PAPYROLOGY, GREEK), is detailed in the strung-out, non-periodic style typical of Hellenistic Greek prose before the revival of the Attic style after Cicero (see ASIANISM AND ATTICISM), Philodemus like *Lucretius greatly surpassed the average literary standard to which most Epicureans aspired (see EPICURUS). In his elegant and often indecently frank erotic epigrams, some thirty-five which are preserved in the *Anthologia Palatina* (see ANTHOLOGY), together with a hundred or so incipits of these and additional epigrams in a papyrus from *Oxyrhynchus, he displays taste and ingenuity worthy of his fellow-citizen *Meleager (2). The success of these poems is proved by the allusions to, and imitations of, them in several passages of Horace, *Propertius, Virgil, and *Ovid. Although Cicero seems to imply that Philodemus' main activity was poetry, he makes clear that he also devoted himself, for Piso's benefit, to popularizing Greek philosophy, which he dealt with both systematically (Rhetoric, Poetics, Music, Ethics, Physics or, rather, Theology) and historically (in his comprehensive History of Philosophers, Σύνταξις τῶν φιλοσόφων, comprising an outline of the chronology of the Greek philosophical schools in ten books). His works covered a wide field, including in addition psychology, logic, aesthetics, and literary criticism. Particularly remarkable was his theory of art, which he conceived as an autonomous, non-philosophical activity, independent of moral and logical content, according to which artistic worth is determined not by its content or meaning, but by its form or aesthetic value. His particular originality is obscured by the fact that his works were not selected for preservation in the manner of other canonical authors. Philodemus succeeded in influencing the most learned and distinguished Romans of his age. No prose work of Philodemus was known until rolls of papyri, charred but largely legible, containing his writings, were discovered among the ruins of the villa at Herculaneum (now at Naples). See also PHILOSOPHERS ON POETRY.

TEXTS No complete edn. of Philodemus has hitherto been pub. Epigrams ed. G. Kaibel (1885); Gow–Page, *GP*; with and trans. and comm., D. Sider (forthcoming). Prose works, after the published facsimiles of the Herculaneum papyri (*Herculanensium Voluminum*), continue to appear in drastically improved new editions due to progress in reading and reconstructing the charred papyri: first in the Teubner series (Sudhaus: *On Rhetoric*, Olivieri: *On Speaking Frankly*, Jensen: *On Household Economy* and *On Vices*, Kemke: *On Music*), omitting those that have been replaced by more recent editions in the series of editions

Philogelos

(with Italian translation and commentary) directed by F. Sbordone, *Ricerche sui Papiri Ercolanesi*, 1–4 (1969–83: *On Poems*, ed. Sbordone; *On Rhetoric* 1–2, ed. L. Auricchio), and M. Gigante, *La scuola di Epicuro* (1978–), as follows: *On the Good King According to Homer* (ed. Dorandi, 1982); *On Anger* (ed. Indelli, 1988); *On Music* (end of bk. 4, ed. Neubecker, 1986); *On Poems*, bk. 5 (ed. Mangoni, 1993); *Against the* [?] (*P. Herc.* 1005, Angeli, 1988); *On Signs* (De Lacy and De Lacy, 1978). From P.'s *History of Philosophers: Index Academicorum* (ed. Dorandi, 1991) and *Index Stoicorum* (ed. Dorandi, 1994), while Diog. Laert. bk. 10 draws on the section on Epicureans. Many texts originally edited elsewhere by Gomperz (*On Piety: Herk. Stud.* 2, 1866), Crönert (*Kolotes u. Menedemos*, 1906), Diels (*On Gods: Abh. Berl. Akad.* 1915–16), and Jensen (*On Poems* bk. 5, 1923, Weidmann series), Kuiper (*On Death*, 1925) have been re-edited piecemeal in *Cronache Ercolanesi* (Naples, 1, 1971–). For *On Piety* see A. Henrichs, *Cronache Ercolanesi* 4 (1974) and 5 (1975) and the edn. by D. Obbink (forthcoming). *Lexicon Philodemeum* publ. C. J. Vooys (2 vols., 1934); H. Usener's, *Glossarium Epicureum*, ed. M. Gigante (1977) indexes many of Philodemus' texts.

GENERAL LITERATURE Susemihl, *Gesch. Griech. Litt. Alex.* 2. 267 ff.; R. Philippson, *RE* 19 (1938), 2444–82; M. Gigante, *Ricerche Filodemee²*, (1983). On the philosophical background: Long and Sedley, *The Hellenistic Philosophers*, 2 vols. (1987); J. Annas, *Hellenistic Philosophy of Mind* (1993); and essays and bibliog. in Griffin and Barnes, *Philosophia Togata* (1989). On the papyri in general see M. Capasso, *Manuale di papirologia ercolanese* (1991); for a listing by inventory number with bibliog. in M. Gigante (ed.), *Catalogo dei Papiri Ercolanesi* (1979), suppl. by M. Capasso, *Cronache Ercolanesi* 19 (1989), 193–265. On the morphology of the Greek of the papyri see W. Crönert, *Memoria Graeca Herculanensis* (1903). For Ph.'s life and villa, M. Gigante, *Philodemus in Italy* (Eng. trans. 1994; Ital. orig. 1990), and the essays collected in *La Villa dei Papiri*, Suppl. 2, *Cronache Ercolanesi*, 13 (1983). For Ph.'s theory of poetry and aesthetics see the essays collected in D. Obbink, *Philodemus and Poetry* (1994); R. Janko, *Philodemus: On Poems, Book One* (2000).
P. T.; D. O.

Philogelos A collection of 265 funny stories, compiled in late antiquity and ascribed to the otherwise unidentifiable Hierocles and Philagrius. We may perhaps compare the joke-books used by *Plautus' *parasites (*Pers.* 392–5, *Stich.* 400, 454 f.), but the work's purpose and intended audience are obscure. The jokes are not about named persons, but about typical representatives of various characters or professions, or of physical or (alleged) regional peculiarities—misers, cowards, wits, doctors, astrologers, eunuchs, Abderites, and so on. Well over half feature the *scholastikos*, a fool whose wits have been so addled by study that he overlooks some factor obvious to ordinary common sense. Thus (255) a *scholastikos* bought a raven with a view to testing the belief that the bird frequently lived over 200 years. (A very similar story is related of a modern politician who took up tortoise-keeping in retirement.) Some anecdotes are associated elsewhere with historical figures, e.g. 148: cf. Plut. *Mor.* 177a (*Archelaus (2) of Macedon); 193: cf. Cic. *De Or.* 2. 276 (*Ennius and P. *Cornelius Scipio Nasica); 264: cf. Plut. *Mor.* 178 f (*Philip (1) II).

TEXT *Philogelos: der Lachfreund* (ed., Ger. trans., comm.), A. Thierfelder (Munich, 1968).

TRANSLATION B. Baldwin, *The Philogelos or Laughter-Lover* (1983). See also *RE* Suppl. 11. 1062–8 (Thierfelder).
S. R. W.

Philolaus of *Croton or perhaps *Tarentum (*c.*470–390 BC) wrote one book which was probably the first by a Pythagorean (see PYTHAGORAS (1)). He was a contemporary of *Socrates and is mentioned in *Plato (1)'s *Phaedo* (61 d6) as arguing that *suicide is not permissible. A consensus has emerged that, although many of the fragments are from spurious works, some fragments from the genuine book survive (1–7, 13, 17). These show that Philolaus'

book was the primary source for *Aristotle's account of Pythagoreanism and influenced Plato's *Philebus*. The book contained a cosmogony and presented astronomical, psychological, and medical theories. Philolaus argued that the cosmos and everything in it was made up not just of the unlimiteds (continua that are in themselves without limit, e.g. earth or void) used as elements by other Presocratics, but also of limiters (things that set limits in a continuum, e.g. shapes). These elements are held together in a harmonia ('fitting together') which comes to be in accord with pleasing mathematical relationships. Secure knowledge is possible in so far as we grasp the number in accordance with which things are put together. Philolaus was the first to make the earth a planet. Along with the fixed stars, five planets, sun, moon, and a counter-earth (thus making the perfect number ten), the earth orbits the central fire.

Fragments, testimonia, and translation in C. Huffman, *Philolaus of Croton* (1993). See also W. Burkert, *Lore and Science in Ancient Pythagoreanism* (1972; Ger. orig. 1962).
C. A. H.

philology, comparative. See LINGUISTICS, HISTORICAL AND COMPARATIVE (INDO-EUROPEAN).

Philomela, daughter of *Pandion and sister of Procne, transformed into a bird. The earliest version of the story (*Od.* 19. 518–23) makes the nightingale daughter of *Pandareos, who killed her own son in a fit of madness. In the more familiar version, crystallized by *Sophocles (1)'s lost play *Tereus*, the story began when Procne's husband Tereus raped Philomela and then attempted to guarantee her silence by cutting out her tongue. Philomela depicted her story in a piece of weaving which she sent to Procne, whereupon the latter took revenge by killing Itys, her son by Tereus, and serving him up to his father. Tereus pursued the two women to punish them, but was turned into a hoopoe, while Philomela became a swallow and Procne a nightingale (or vice versa).

Apollod. 3. 14. 8; Ov. *Met.* 6. 424–674. Burkert, *HN* 179–85.
E. Ke.

Philomelus, son of Theotimus, of Ledon persuaded *Phocis to challenge Amphictionic control of *Delphi (see AMPHICTIONY). Elected *stratēgos autokrator* (commander with full powers) and with Athenian and Spartan support, he hired mercenaries, recruited Phocian *peltasts and seized Delphi in a bloody *coup* (summer 356). Military responses from western *Locris and *Boeotia were averted (details are controversial) and he publicized Phocis' claim to Delphi while denying any designs on the sanctuary's wealth. Such propriety crumbled when the Amphictiony declared a (Third) *Sacred War. He invaded eastern Locris, aiming to meet Thessalian and Boeotian components of the Amphictionic army separately, but despite superiority at Argolas (? Mendhenitsa) had to retreat into Phocis and committed suicide after the ensuing defeat at Neon.

RE 19, 'Philomelus 3'. J. Buckler, *Third Sacred War* (1989).
C. J. T.

Philon (1) of *Eleusis (4th cent. BC), architect. He designed the arsenal at *Piraeus, and added a porch to the Telesterion at Eleusis. The former building, one of the most admired in antiquity (Plin. *HN* 7. 37. 135), was destroyed by *Sulla, and no vestiges of it have been identified; but we possess a detailed specification (*IG* 2². 1668), allowing a detailed reconstruction. His books on the arsenal, and on the proportions of sacred buildings (Vitr. 7 praef.), have not survived.

R. Garland, *The Piraeus* (1987), 156 ff.; J. Travlos, *Bildlexikon zur Topographie des antiken Attika* (1988), 342.
H. W. R.; A. J. S. S.

Philon (2) (*RE* 48) of Byzantium, writer on technology (fl. *c.*200 BC) was an imitator of *Ctesibius and was himself used by

*Heron. He wrote a compendium of technology (μηχανικὴ σύνταξις) in nine (?) books. Of this there are preserved: book 4, βελοποιικά, on the construction of war-catapults (see ARTILLERY); book 5, πνευματικά (in Arabic translation, itself partially translated into Latin), on the construction of siphons and other devices worked by the action of heated air and fluids (see PHYSICS); parts of book 7, παρασκευαστικά, and of book 8, πολιορκητικά, on the construction of offensive and defensive works and other siege operations. The lost book 6, on automata-making, is referred to by Heron (ed. Schmidt 1. 404 ff.). Though not uninterested in theory (see *Pneumatica*, introd.), his primary concern is the construction of devices for utility or amusement.

Eutocius (*Comm. in Arch.* 60–2 Heiberg[2]) informs us of a solution by Philon to the problem of finding two mean proportionals ('doubling the cube'). It is essentially the same as those by *Apollonius (2) and Heron. Philon refers to this (*Belopoeica* 7) as coming from book 1.

EDITIONS AND TRANSLATIONS *Belopoeica*: ed. with trans. E. W. Marsden, *Greek and Roman Artillery: Technical Treatises* (1971), 105 ff.; *Pneumatica*: ed. Carra de Vaux (with Fr. trans.) in *Notices et extraits des manuscrits* 38.1 (1903), 27 ff. Eng. trans. with facsimile of the medieval Latin by F. D. Prager, *Philo of Byzantium, Pneumatica* (1974); preferable for the Latin text is V. Rose, *Anecdota Græca et Græcolatina* (1870), 297 ff.; *Parasceuastica* and *Poliorcetica*: ed. Y. Garlan, *Recherches de poliorcétique grecque* (1974), 279 ff. (with Fr. trans.).

COMMENT *Belopoeica*, E. W. Marsden, *Greek and Roman Artillery: Historical Development* (1969). *Pneumatica*: A. G. Drachmann, *Ktesibios, Philon and Heron* (1948), 41 ff. Siege works: Garlan, above. Doubling the cube: Heath, *Hist. of Greek Maths.* 1. 262 ff.   G. J. T.

Philon (3) of *Larissa (159/8–84/3 BC), the last undisputed head of the *Academy. Philon studied for eight or nine years in his native town under Callicles, a pupil of *Carneades, before he went to Athens at the age of 24, to study under Clitomachus, whom he succeeded as head of the Academy in 110/9. In 88, during the Mithradatic wars (see MITHRADATES VI), he left for Rome, where he numbered among his pupils Catulus, father and son (see LUTATIUS CATULUS (1–2), Q.), and *Cicero, who became his most devoted pupil and follower. Philon probably remained in Rome until his death.

Although Philon may have published many books, none of them, not even their titles, have survived, and we know nothing about their form. Some of his teachings are represented in a long passage in *Stobaeus and in Cicero's *Academicus primus* and *Lucullus*.

Under the scholarchate of Philon, the sceptical Academy modified its attitude of strict suspension of judgement and adopted Carneades' account of the 'plausible impression' (πιθανόν, Lat. *probabile*) as an epistemological theory that would allow philosophers to accept the views they found most convincing, with the proviso that certain knowledge could not be achieved. This may have led to the revival of a more radical version of scepticism (see SCEPTICS) by *Aenesidemus, who accused the Academics of his time of being 'Stoics fighting other Stoics' (Phot. *Bibl.* cod. 212; see STOICISM). It was probably in the two books he wrote at Rome towards the end of his life that Philon went a step further and claimed that knowledge (κατάληψις) was indeed possible, though not by the stringent standards of the Stoic definition. He proceeded to ascribe this view to the Academics from *Plato (1) on, which provoked an angry reaction from his pupil *Antiochus (11) of Ascalon in the *Sosus*.

In accordance with the new fallibilism of his school, Philon also taught other philosophical subjects. Like the Stoics, he compared the philosopher to a doctor, and divided the teaching of ethics into five parts corresponding to the stages of a medical therapy (Ar. Did. in Stob. 2. 7. 2), from persuading the pupil of the benefits of philosophy through the elimination of erroneous beliefs and the implanting of healthy views about goods and evils to teaching about the goal of life (τέλος) and advice for everyday living. Cicero tells us that Philon also taught rhetoric alongside philosophy; a combination that Cicero obviously found congenial.

While Philon's mitigated scepticism may be discerned in later self-styled Academics like *Plutarch, his influence on the development of Middle Platonism remains doubtful. See PLATONISM, MIDDLE.

SOURCES H. J. Mette, *Philon von Larisa und Antiochos von Askalon*, Lustrum 28/9, 1986/7.

MODERN DISCUSSIONS H. Tarrant, *Scepticism or Platonism?*, 1985, and see bibliog. under Antiochus, Sceptics.   G. S.

Philon (4), **'Philo'**, often known as **Philo Judaeus**, philosopher, writer and political leader, was the leading exponent of Alexandrian-Jewish culture (see ALEXANDRIA (1)), and, together with *Josephus, the most significant figure in *Jewish-Greek literature. Philo's voluminous works were a formative influence on *Neoplatonism and on Christian theology, from the New Testament on. His family was prominent in the Jewish diaspora and in the service of Rome in the east. The two sons of his brother, Alexander the Alabarch, were Marcus Iulius Alexander, husband of *Iulius Agrippa (1) I's daughter Berenice (4), and Tiberius *Iulius Alexander. The only fixed date in Philo's own life is AD 39/40, when, as an old man, he led the Jewish embassy to *Gaius (1); see section on *Gaius and the Jews*. Apart from those events, he himself seems to have confined his activities to the Alexandrian Jewish community. He made a pilgrimage to Jerusalem, but need not otherwise have had much contact with Palestine. Virtually all his surviving works were apparently preserved in the library of *Caesarea (2) built up by *Origen (1) and then by *Eusebius, who catalogues most of them at *HE* 2. 18. Some three-quarters of the corpus consists of exposition of the Pentateuch, in three series, whose order of writing is obscure: *Quaestiones*, which are brief catechetical commentaries in the form of questions and answers, *Legum allegoria*, a more extended and systematic exegesis, and *Exposition*, which sets out the Mosaic laws. The *Life of Moses* was perhaps a separate enterprise, as also the *De vita contemplativa*, which describes the way of life of a group of Egyptian Jewish ascetics called the Therapeutai. Two tracts, *In Flaccum* and the *De legatione ad Gaium*, probably originally one composite work, give a graphic account of the persecutions of the Jews under Gaius and of their political consequences. The *In Flaccum* gives much space to the divine punishment inflicted on the persecutors of the Jews (see AVILLIUS FLACCUS, A.).

Philo operated within the Greek philosophical tradition and deployed an elaborate Greek literary language. At the same time, he was at home with the Greek Bible on which his commentaries were based. The sole authority of the Mosaic law was fundamental to him. The spuriousness of his Hebrew etymologies suggests, but does not prove, that he did not know Hebrew. His ontology was markedly Platonic: to provide a medium for the operation of a perfect God upon an imperfect world, he introduced a range of mediating powers, notably *dunameis* and the *logos*. Philo's ethics are close to *Stoicism, but for him true morality is imitation of the Deity.

Philon

L. Cohn, P. Wendland, and S. Reiter, *Philonis Opera Quae Supersunt*, 1–6 (*ed. maior*, 1896–1930, repr. 1962; *ed. minor* 1896–1915); F. H. Colson and G. H. Whitaker, Loeb, Philo 1–10. Schürer, *History* 3.2 (1987), 809–89; *ANRW* 2. 21. 1 (1984); H. A. Wolfson, *Philo* (1947); E. R. Goodenough, *An Introduction to Philo Judaeus*[2] (1962).   T. R.

Philon (5) of Byblos (*RE*, 'Herennius 2'), scholar, born *c.* AD 70 and died *c.* AD 160, composed in Greek a learned work on *Phoenician history, providing a markedly euhemeristic account (see EUHEMERUS) of Phoenician religion. Extensive fragments of this history were preserved by *Eusebius in his *Praeparatio evangelica* 1. 9. 22 ff. Philon's claim to have translated much of his material directly from the ancient writer Sanchuniathon, who had devoted a treatise in the Phoenician language to theology, cosmogony, and the origins of civilization, should be regarded with considerable scepticism, since Philon's versions of the ancient myths have clearly been moulded to conform to Hellenistic expectations. On the other hand, similarities between the stories ascribed by Philon to Sanchuniathon and the evidence for Phoenician myths discovered in *Ugaritic texts demonstrate that some of the material used by Philon may derive from genuine Phoenician traditions, which have, however, been modified over the intervening centuries.

Herennius Philon's other writings included a work *Concerning the Acquisition and Selection of Books*, a work *Concerning Cities and the Illustrious Men each of them Produced*, and another *Concerning the Reign of Hadrian*. See also PHOENICIANS; SANCHUNIATHON.

FGrH 790. L. Troiani, *L'Opera storiografica di Filone da Byblos* (1974); A. I. Baumgarten, *The Phoenician History of Philo of Byblos: A Commentary* (1981) (the most useful study); R. A. Oden and H. W. Attridge, *Philo of Bylos: The Phoenician History: Introduction* (1981).   M. D. G.

Philon (6) (*RE* 39) the Dialectician, an innovative logician, active in the late 4th and early 3rd cents. BC. Often erroneously called Philo of Megara by scholars (his birthplace is unknown), he belonged to the Dialectical school—an independent offshoot of the *Megarian School, not geographically linked with Megara—where he studied under *Diodorus (2) Cronus. He defended a truth-functional account of a valid conditional, and formulated a definition of possibility in terms of the subject's bare 'fitness' for receiving the predicate in question, regardless of circumstances.

G. Giannantoni, *Socratis et Socraticorum Reliquiae* (1990); W. and M. Kneale, *The Development of Logic* (1962).   D. N. S.

Philonides (1) Athenian comic poet, produced *Aristophanes (1)'s *Wasps*, *Amphiaraus*, and *Frogs*; we have three titles of his own plays, and he may be the Φιλ[who won first prize at the City *Dionysia *c.*410 BC (*IG* 2². 2325. 64). It is stated by the first *hypothesis to Ar. *Wasps* that he won first prize with *Proagon* at the *Lenaea in 422 BC, but *Proagon* is everywhere else attributed to Aristophanes.

PCG 7. 363 ff. (*CAF* 1. 254 ff.).   K. J. D.

Philonides (2) (*RE* 5 and 7), Epicurean philosopher (see EPICURUS), mathematician and statesman (fl. 200–160 BC). A fragmentary biography of him is preserved in a Herculaneum papyrus, which is important for dating *Apollonius (2), *Zenodorus, and other Hellenistic mathematicians whom Philonides knew. Inscriptions reveal him as an honorary citizen of Athens and a leading citizen of his birthplace, Laodicea in Syria.

Biography ed. I. Gallo, *Frammenti Biografici dei Papiri*, 2 (1980), 23–166. W. Crönert, *Sitz. Kgl. pr. Ak. Wiss.* 1900, 2. 942–59. For the inscriptions see U. Köhler ibid. 999–1001.   G. J. T.

Philopator, Stoic (see STOICISM), probably of the time of *Hadrian (AD 117–38). See Zeller, *Phil. d. Griechen* 3. 1⁴. 169, 714.   J. A.

Philopoemen (*c.*253–182 BC), son of Craugis of *Megalopolis, statesman and general of the *Achaean Confederacy, called 'the last of the Greeks' by an anonymous Roman. Philopoemen's first known activity dates from the 220s, when he helped defend Megalopolis against *Cleomenes (2) III (223) and impressed *Antigonus (3) III Doson at the battle of Sellasia. He subsequently spent ten years in Crete as mercenary captain, perhaps serving Macedonian interests. During the First Macedonian War as hipparch (cavalry commander) of the Confederacy (209) and twice *strategos* (chief magistrate and general: 208/7 and 206/5) he defeated and killed the Spartan ruler Machanidas at Mantinea (207); see MANTINEA, BATTLES OF. Under *Nabis Sparta continued to trouble the Peloponnese. Philopoemen campaigned against him both as volunteer (202/1) and as *strategos* (201/299) and, after six more years in Crete, again as *strategos* (193/2) when, after Nabis' murder by the *Aetolians, he united Sparta with the Confederacy, against *Flamininus' wishes.

Sparta's entry to the Confederacy raised the problem of dealing with the masses of Spartans exiled by the social-revolutionary regimes of the last generation. Philopoemen wished to restore only Achaean supporters, but by adopting an uncompromising hostility to traditional Spartan concerns (in 188, after massacring a group of exiles at Compasion, he destroyed Sparta's city-walls and dismantled the characteristic education (*agōgē*) and legal systems, replacing them with Achaean institutions) he provoked opposition even among Achaean friends in Sparta. Spartan opponents appealed against Achaean policies to the Roman senate, which repeatedly suggested solutions, all of which Philopoemen and his supporters (especially *Lycortas) rejected—indeed, they refused on principle to recognize any Roman competence in Achaean internal affairs, since Rome had formally recognized Achaean independence by granting a treaty. This rigorous and offensive attitude split Achaean politics also on this issue (Aristaenus, *Callicrates (2)), but Philopoemen died before a solution was reached. He was said to have been poisoned after being captured by renegade Messenians (182). At his public funeral Lycortas' son *Polybius (1) carried the urn and later wrote a biography (not extant), and defended his memory in his *Histories*.

Plutarch, *Life of Philopoemen*; R. M. Errington, *Philopoemen* (1969).   R. M. E.

Philoponus, John, *c.* AD 490 to 570s, a Christian Neoplatonist (see NEOPLATONISM) in *Alexandria (1), influenced subsequent science down to Galileo by replacing many of *Aristotle's theories with an account centred on the Christian idea that the universe had an absolute beginning. But because his own Christian theology was unorthodox, he was anathematized in 680, and his scientific influence came to the West belatedly through the Arabs. Seven early commentaries on Aristotle survive, four described as taken from the seminars of his Alexandrian teacher Ammonius son of Hermeias, although he added his own ideas. The commentary on Aristotle's *Physics* (datable to 517) among others may have been revised after 529 to accommodate more anti-Aristotelian theories. In that year, the Christian emperor *Justinian closed the other great Neoplatonist school at Athens, and Philoponus published an attack on the Athenian Neoplatonist *Proclus, who had been Ammonius' own teacher. This attack (*Against Proclus On the Eternity of the World*) was followed by

Against Aristotle on the Eternity of the World. The most influential of Philoponus' anti-Aristotelian ideas concerned dynamics. Motion in a vacuum is theoretically possible. Again, projectiles are moved by an internal impetus impressed from outside, not by Aristotle's external forces. Later (*De opificio mundi*), Philoponus expanded impetus theory into a unifying system by having God impress different kinds of impetus into bodies at the time of the Creation. From 553, Philoponus concentrated on Christian theology in a series of heretical works which have survived mostly in Syriac. Some, including the *Arbiter* (= *Diaetētēs*) of that year, upheld the Monophysite view that Christ had only one nature, not two, one human and one divine. Later works, including *On the Trinity* (= *On Theology*) published in 567, are apparently committed to Tritheism, the view that the three members of the Trinity are three gods. Still later ones including *On the Resurrection*, written around 574, argued that we will have new resurrection bodies and, as immortal, will cease to be human. Philoponus never held the Alexandrian philosophy chair. He was known as Grammaticus, and two of his works on grammar survive, as do works on many other subjects.

Commentaria in Aristotelem Graeca 13–17 (1887–1909), partly Englished, with other works, in R. Sorabji (ed.), *The Ancient Commentators on Aristotle* (1987–); *De aeternitate mundi*, ed. H. Rabe (1890); Syriac in *Opuscula Monophysitica*, ed. A. Sanda (1930), A. van Roey, *Orientalia Lovanensia Periodica* (1979; 1980) and *Antidoron, hommage à Maurits Geerard* (1984). R. Sorabji (ed.), *Philoponus and the Rejection of Aristotelian Science* (1987); K. Verrycken in R. Sorabji (ed.), *Aristotle Transformed* (1990); *RE* 9. 2 (1916), 'Ioannes 21'.   R. R. K. S.

philosophers and politics *Plato (1) (*Rep*. 473d) regarded good government as unattainable 'unless either philosophers become kings in our cities or those whom we now call kings and rulers take to the pursuit of philosophy'. He already recognized, however, that philosophers would either be reluctant to leave the contemplation of truth for the task of governing any but an ideal city, or would be ridiculed and rejected if they tried (*Rep*. 516d–517a; 519e–521b).

Philosopher-leaders were rare in the ancient world: *Cicero (*Leg*. 3. 14) named only *Demetrius (3) of Phaleron, the *Peripatetic philosopher who ruled Athens from 317 to 307 BC, ignoring less respectable examples, like the Peripatetic Athenion and the Epicurean *Aristion (see EPICURUS) who ruled Athens for brief periods in his youth; see also DION. The Romans themselves sent philosophers to rule *Tarsus (Strabo 14. 675), but it was in the 2nd cent. AD that admirers of Marcus *Aurelius, the emperor, could claim that Plato's ideal was finally fulfilled (SHA *Marc*. 27. 6–7, cf. *Med*. 9. 29). Philosophers more commonly served their cities by educating and advising rulers or serving as ambassadors. In the 3rd cent. BC *Hermippus (2) wrote a treatise entitled 'On Those who Have Converted from Philosophy to Tyrannies and Positions of Power', in which he described such cases as the Stoic *Persaeus who served *Antigonus (2) Gonatas (unsuccessfully) as a general. Another Stoic, *Sphaerus, advised King *Cleomenes (2) of Sparta (Plut. *Cleom*. 11). In 155 BC when the Athenians wanted the senate to reduce a fine imposed on the city, they sent as envoys the Stoic *Diogenes (3), the Peripatetic *Critolaus and the Academic *Carneades. They succeeded in their missions, but also gave such attractive lectures that *Cato (Censorius) objected that they were seducing Roman youth away from traditional values (Plut. *Cato* 22).

The charge of corrupting the youth, already employed against *Socrates, was used at Rome as a reason for expelling philosophers from the city as early as 161 BC. As a preparation for public life, philosophy was suspect on several counts: (1) Philosophers, as Plato surmised, might reject practical politics. The Epicureans in fact advocated such abstention except in exceptional circumstances, though many of them in fact participated (e.g. Athen. 5. 215b; Cic. *Fin*. 2. 76; *Tusc*. 5. 108; Joseph. *BJ* 19. 32; Epict. 3. 7, cf. Plin. *Ep*. 8. 24). Stoics (see STOICISM) took the opposite line, so that their failure to participate was, or could be construed as, criticism of the existing regime. (2) Philosophers might insist on unrealistic moral standards in public life (e.g. Cic. *Mur*. 60 f.; Sen. *Clem*. 2. 5. 2). The Romans were particularly prone to this view (Tac. *Agric*. 4. 4), so that whereas philosophers, except Epicureans, were regularly honoured at Athens and elsewhere in the Greek world for their contribution to educating the young (e.g. Diog. Laert. 7. 10–12), at Rome they were at first excluded from the privileges offered to doctors and teachers of rhetoric and literature for their services to the community.

It is often said that philosophers made a theoretical contribution to politics only in the age of the independent Greek city-state or *polis, and that before, and after, Academic and Peripatetic political theory was applied to Rome in the age of the republic, philosophers living under the Hellenistic and Roman monarchical systems limited their concerns to the individual. That is an oversimplification of the fact that the Hellenistic schools were not interested in discussing ideal constitutions, but rather in prescribing moral conduct for rulers of any kind and in teaching their subjects how to preserve their integrity and exercise free speech. See KINGSHIP.

C. Habicht, *Hellenistic Athens and her Philosophers* (1988); M. L. Clarke, *Higher Education in the Ancient World* (1971); F. L. Vatai, *Intellectuals in Politics in the Greek World* (1984); A. Erskine, *The Hellenistic Stoa: Political Thought and Action* (1990); M. Griffin and J. Barnes (eds.), *Philosophia Togata* (1989); E. Rawson, *Intellectual Life in the Late Roman Republic* (1985); H. D. Jocelyn, *Bull. Rylands Libr.* 1976/7; C. Wirszubski, *Libertas as a Political Idea at Rome during the Late Republic and Early Principate* (1950); P. A. Brunt, *PBSR* 1975.   M. T. G.

philosophers on poetry The engagement of philosophers with poetry was a recurrent and vital feature of the intellectual culture of Graeco-Roman antiquity. By around 380 BC, *Plato (1) could already refer to 'a long-standing quarrel between philosophy and poetry' (*Rep*. 10. 607b). Early Greek philosophy, while closely related to poetry (*Xenophanes, *Parmenides, and *Empedocles wrote in verse, with various debts to poetic tradition), set itself to contest and rival the claims of 'wisdom', *sophia*, made by and on behalf of poets. Xenophanes, repudiating anthropomorphic religion, cast ethical and theological aspersions on the myths of *Homer and *Hesiod (DK 21 B 1.21–4, 11–12); Heraclitus expressed caustic doubts about the idea of poets as possessors and teachers of insight (DK 22 B 40, 42, 56–7). Philosophy and poetry could be considered competing sources of knowledge and understanding. The stage was set for lasting debates about their relationship.

Plato, while emulating poetry in his myths and in features of his dramatic writing, produced a far-reaching critique of poetry's credentials as an educational force within Greek culture (*Rep*. bks. 2–3, 10). Though sometimes scantily concerned with complexities of context, he responds to an existing tendency to regard poetic works as carrying normative significance: the putative 'truth' of poetry, which he so frequently (though not invariably) impugns, was in part a matter of paradigmatically interpreted images of human behaviour and morality. Plato's anxieties over poetry are based, besides, on an awareness of its immense psychological power, especially in the theatre. Yet despite the *Republic*'s proposals for severe political censorship, Plato's dealings with poetry remain ambivalent and deeply felt: he quotes, echoes, and competes with it throughout his dialogues. But his critique rests, from first to last, on the premiss of philosophy's superior wisdom and judgement.

*Aristotle too is committed to the superior range of philosophical thought, but much readier than Plato to allow the independent cultural value of poetry. *Poetics* 25. 1460^{b}13–15 asserts that poetic standards are not identical to those of *politikē* (ethics/politics), and the treatise as a whole, respecting generic traditions and recognizing the status of poetry as a distinct art (*technē*), elaborates categories that focus upon the internal organization of poetic works. Yet Aristotle's stance is still markedly philosophical, not only in its method and many of its concepts, but also in discerning an affinity between poetry and philosophy. Poetry 'is more philosophical than history', because it 'speaks more of universals' (9. 1451^{b}5–7). Aristotle's discussion of tragedy and epic ascribes to them the capacity to reveal deep features of human 'actions and life'; the pleasure of poetry arises from an experience that is simultaneously cognitive and strongly emotional.

By the later 4th cent., philosophical schools had established an institutional status which made their relationship to a traditional education in *mousikē* (poetry and music) an urgent question. Both *Epicurus (Diog. Laert. 10. 6) and *Zeno (2), founder of *Stoicism (id. 7. 32), are said to have rejected such conventional *paideia*. Yet the attitudes of their schools towards poetry were more complex and divergent than this suggests. Epicurus followed Xenophanes and Plato in attacking poetic myths as purveyors of false religious beliefs, to which the proffered antidote was his own natural philosophy. He asserted the need for philosophical judgement of poetry: 'only the wise man can discourse correctly about music and poetry' (Diog. Laert. 10. 121). Epicureans acquired a reputation for rejecting poetry; *Metrodorus (2), Epicurus' follower, provocatively declared it unnecessary to know even the openings of Homer's epics (Plut. *Mor.* 1094e). But the possibility of a more positive evaluation remained available, given the school's commitment to pleasure as the criterion of value: Epicurus himself allowed that philosophers could enjoy artistic performances (Diog. Laert. 10. 120). An Epicurean rapprochement with poetry was eventually effected both by *Lucretius' great work, and by the critical writings of *Philodemus, who regarded poetry as principally pleasurable, morally neutral in itself, yet capable of conveying ideas compatible with Epicurean philosophy. Lucretius and Philodemus demonstrate that Epicureanism had, by the 1st cent. BC, space for a subtle range of stances towards these issues.

Stoicism, by contrast, was solidly tied to a moralistic view of poetry—a view influenced by Plato, yet largely unplatonic in its inclination to 'save' poetry, wherever possible, either by allegorical interpretation or by exploiting the principle, propounded by Zeno himself (Dio Chrys. 53. 4), that not everything in poetry need be judged in terms of truth. Stoics as different as *Chrysippus and *Strabo, while acknowledging the scope (and sometimes the pleasures) of fiction, unequivocally sought ethical and didactic value in poetry; the habits of reading to which this led—habits immensely influential on later ages—can be seen in such figures as L. *Annaeus Seneca (2), *Epictetus, and Marcus *Aurelius. At an extreme, Stoic subordination of poetry to philosophy amounted to redefinition: 'only the wise man can be a poet' (Strabo 1. 2. 3).

Interpretative control, even to the point of appropriation, was

perhaps the dominant tendency in ancient philosophy's dealings with poetry; Aristotle and Philodemus stand out as exceptionally liberal. Appropriation, but also reconciliation, reached a climax in the Neoplatonic reinterpretation of Homer as a fount of esoteric wisdom, symbolically expressed (see NEOPLATONISM). Thus, on the threshold of a new Christian synthesis of learning and culture, the 'ancient quarrel' was temporarily silenced.

G. Kennedy (ed.), *The Cambridge History of Literary Criticism*, 1 (1989).
F. S. H.

philosophy, history of The *sophists of the later 5th cent. BC were probably the first to trace affiliations between the ideas of philosophers and their poetic predecessors (*Hippias (2)), and to classify views on the number and nature of the basic realities (*Gorgias (1)). Both procedures are echoed in *Plato (1) (e.g. *Cra.* 402a–c, *Soph.* 242c ff.), but it is *Aristotle whose respect for the beliefs of the wise makes their employment a principled ingredient in philosophical enquiry, e.g. in the introductions to the *Physics* (1. 2), *De Anima* (1. 2), and especially the *Metaphysics* (A. 3–6), where he identifies and criticizes the first anticipations by previous thinkers of each of his four causes. Aristotle also composed monographs on the philosophies of individual thinkers or schools (e.g. *Democritus, the Pythagoreans; see PYTHAGORAS (1)). It was left to his pupils to write systematic accounts of the growth of e.g. natural philosophy (*Theophrastus) and mathematics (*Eudemus), again focused on initial discoveries of key ideas. To the same period belong the first biographies of philosophers, as evidenced e.g. in surviving information about *Aristoxenus' account of Pythagoras. This genre of writing was particularly favoured by early Hellenistic authors, among whom *Antigonus (4) of Carystus was especially notable.

The Hellenistic period also saw the development of three further genres. (1) Successions (*diadochai*). Following the model of formal institutions like the *Academy, where the headship of the school passed from one philosopher to his successor, scholars such as *Sotion (1) drew up lineages of teachers and pupils which included all the major and many of the minor figures known to us. *Philodemus' accounts of the Academy and the Stoa (see STOICISM) are early surviving examples. (2) Doxographies. For the dialectical purposes of dogmatists and *sceptics alike it was convenient to have to hand systematic accounts of the views of philosophers on given topics, so arranged as to exhibit contradictions or at least differences between them. *Aëtius (1)'s *Placita* is our fullest example; for Hellenistic evidence we may cite e.g. the famous *Carneadea divisio* (of theories of the goal of life). Sometimes (as reflected e.g. in Sext. Emp. *Math.* 7) chronological sequence might be used as a supplementary ordering principle. (3) περὶ αἱρέσεων ('On schools of thought'). Useful also are summary or introductory accounts of the main doctrines of different schools, such as those supplied in many of *Cicero's philosophical writings or *Arius Didymus' treatment of Stoic and *Peripatetic ethics. These might include mention of variations or innovations introduced by later members of the schools. *Galen's little introduction on the medical 'sects' is a formal example of the genre. Much of the philosophical content of *Diogenes (6) Laertius' *Lives of the Philosophers* will originally have belonged to it, although his work is principally biography organized according to the principles of succession literature.

Philosophers of our day recognize that the title of history of philosophy may be claimed by various intellectual enterprises. If it is taken to involve sympathetic reconstruction of an alien world of thought, no ancient writer practised history of philosophy. Mostly the past was simply appropriated for present use: whether to show the ingrained nature of another's error, or to invoke ancient authority, where the construction of an intellectual pedigree might be particularly useful, or to illustrate the inevitability of contradiction between philosophers—or simply to provide materials for one or other of these purposes.

GENERAL H. Diels, *Doxographi Graeci* (1879); J. Glucker, *Antiochus and the Late Academy* (1978); J. Mansfeld, *Studies in the Historiography of Greek Philosophy* (1990). Biography: U. von Wilamowitz-Moellendorff, *Antigonos von Karystos* (1881). Diog. Laert.: J. Meyer, *Diogenes Laertius and his Hellenistic Background* (1978); articles in *Elenchos* 7 (1986). The concept of history of philosophy: R. Rorty and others (eds.), *Philosophy in History* (1984). M. Sch.

Philostephanus of Cyrene (3rd cent. BC), pupil or friend of *Callimachus (3), wrote: (1) geographical works, full of marvels and fables (Ath. 7. 297f, 8. 331d; Aul. Gell. 9. 4. 2; Harpocr. under Βούχετα, Στρύμη; schol. Pind. *Ol.* 6. 77); (2) a mythological and antiquarian treatise *Note-books* (Ὑπομνήματα) (schol. Ap. Rhod. 2. 124); (3) *On Discoveries* (Clem. Al. *Strom.* 1. 308a).

R. Pfeiffer, *History of Classical Scholarship*, 1 (1968), 151.
J. F. L.; J. S. R.

Philostorgius (c. AD 368–c.440 (?)), ecclesiastical historian; born in Boryssus (*Cappadocia), into a clerical family who had been won over to neo-*Arianism (Eunomianism). By the age of 20, he was in *Constantinople where he spent much of his life. An adherent of Eunomius, he wrote in continuation of *Eusebius of Caesarea an ecclesiastical history to AD 425 in twelve books, each beginning with a letter of his name. It is now fragmentary, surviving in an extended epitome by *Photius, and in other fragments, especially the *Passio of Artemius*. It is noted in a separate *Biblioteca* entry and two epigrams in the Greek *Anthology. The work is valuable in presenting an alternative view of church history from the time of *Constantine I, with praise for Constantius II and condemnation in apocalyptic tones of the policies of *Theodosius (2) I and (3) II, together with secular material and geographical digressions partly based on his own travels. Other (lost) works of Philostorgius include a refutation of *Porphyry, an encomium on Eunomius and a life of Lucian of Antioch.

Ed. Bidez–Winkelmann, *GCS* (1981). *RE* 20 (1941), 119–22; *ODB* 3 (1991) under the name. A. M. N.

Philostrati Up to four members of this originally Lemnian family (see LEMNOS) can be separated, but not securely. (1) Philostratus son of Verus, a writer of sophistic works of which probably none now survives. (2) His son L. Flavius Philostratus ('the Athenian'), who enjoyed both a distinguished local career and a place in the circle of *Iulia Domna, wife of *Septimius Severus. She commissioned his 'Life' of *Apollonius (12) of Tyana (τὰ ἐς τὸν Τυανέα Ἀπολλώνιον), a philosophic holy man of the 1st cent. AD; later he produced Βίοι σοφιστῶν ('Lives of the Sophists'), and he is probably the author of most of a number of minor pieces, including the Ἡρωϊκός, a dialogue on the heroes of the Trojan War and their cults, a Γυμναστικός, (On Athletic Training) and 'Erotic Epistles'; he died under Philip the Arab (AD 244–9) (*Suda*). He mentions (3) Philostratus the Lemnian, probably great-nephew and son-in-law. Two sets of Εἰκόνες, descriptions of pictures, survive, attributed to two Philostrati who were grandfather and grandson, either (2) and the exceptionally well connected (3), or (3) and an otherwise unknown (4). Two Διαλέξεις and a brief dramatic dialogue Νέρων also survive.

The *Life of Apollonius* offers pagan hagiography under a sophistic veneer, and remains suspect both in sources and details; the *Lives of the Sophists* offer the foundation for our knowledge of the *Second Sophistic: they are sketches, sometimes affected and tendentious, of prestigious public speakers in action. The *Heroikos* offers an entertaining *aperçu* into how a sophistic writer might extend and 'correct' still vibrant Homeric materials. The first *Eikones* are often charming mythological sketches, purporting to instruct a child on the content of perhaps imaginary pictures; the later set are more perfunctory (see EKPHRASIS).

The *œuvre* of the Athenian Philostratus so far as we can judge it offers an illuminating glimpse into sophistic interests and the capacity to infiltrate them into a wide variety of literary fields. But fluency and charm are often at odds with idiosyncrasy and rhetorical bravura, as well as a constantly equivocal attitude to facts and 'the real world'. Philostratus ranks as something of an arbiter of sophistic tastes and values; he is also an index of sophistic shortcomings.

NOTICE *Suda* (confused).
EDITIONS C. L. Kayser, (Teubner 1870–1); Ἡρω., L. de Lannoy, (Teubner 1977).
TRANSLATIONS Loeb now covers Βίοι σοφιστῶν, W. Cave Wright (1921); Τὰ ἐς Ἀ, F. C. Conybeare (1912); Εἰκόνες A, B, A. Fairbanks (1931); Ἐπιστολαὶ ἐρωτικαί A. R. Benner and F. H. Fobes (1949); Νέρων, M. D. Macleod (Loeb Lucian, vol. 8, 1967). Commentaries on Select Lives by S. Rothe (1989); Γυμν. by J. Juethner (1909); Εἰκόνες A. (E. Kalinka and O. Schoenberger, 1968).
CRITICISM F. Solmsen, *RE* 20. 124 ff.; E. L. Bowie, *ANRW* 2. 16. 2 (1978); G. Anderson: *Philostratus: Biography and Belles-Lettres in the Third Century AD* (1986), and *The Second Sophistic* (1993); S. J.-J. Flintermann, *Politiek, Paideia & Pythagorisme* (1993). W. M. E.; R. B.; G. A.

Philotas (d. 330 BC), Macedonian noble, son of *Parmenion and commander of the Companion cavalry during the early campaigns of *Alexander (3) the Great. After a career of distinction, in which he fought in all the major actions, he came to grief sensationally late in 330, when he was accused of complicity in a court conspiracy, condemned by the Macedonian army, and executed after interrogation under torture. The details are mysterious, but nothing was proved against him other than failure to pass on information about the conspiracy. He was already under suspicion, victim of a covert investigation, and the conspiracy gave Alexander's younger marshals the opportunity to eradicate the influence of Parmenion.

Berve, *Alexanderreich* 2. 802; Badian, *TAPA* 1960, 324 ff.; Bosworth, *Conquest & Empire*, 101 ff.; Heckel, *Marshals*, 23 ff. A. B. B.

philotimia, literally the love of honour (timē). The pursuit of honour(s), tangible or intangible, was a constant of élite behaviour throughout Graeco-Roman antiquity; all that changed was its context and the extent to which it was given unbridled expression or else harnessed to the needs of the community at large. Of the latter phenomenon classical Athens (see DEMOCRACY, ATHENIAN) provides rich literary and epigraphic documentation, at city level and elsewhere; *philotimia* was good if its fruits brought communal benefit, and *timē* duly bestowed on the naturally competitive served as an object-lesson for all. See AGŌNES, EUERGETISM.

GENERAL A. R. Hands, *Charities and Social Aid in Greece and Rome* (1968), ch. 3 and *passim*; K. J. Dover, *Greek Popular Morality* (1974), 226 ff.; P. Veyne, *Le Pain et le cirque* (1976; abr. Eng. version *Bread and Circuses*, 1990), esp. chs. 1–2.
CLASSICAL ATHENS D. Whitehead, *C&M.* 1983, 55 ff, and *The Demes of Attica* (1986), 234 ff. D. W.

Philoxenus

Philoxenus (1) (*c*.435–380 BC), of *Cythera, *dithyrambic poet. He lived at the court of *Dionysius (1) of Syracuse, who sent him to the quarries. *Pherecrates (fr. 155. 26 Kassel-Austin) introduces him as a musical innovator and corrupter of the traditional music. In the *Mysians* he seems to have composed a dithyramb in a mixture of the Dorian and Phrygian modality. In his most famous work, the *Cyclops*, parodied in Aristoph. *Plut.* 290 ff., the Cyclops (see CYCLOPES) sang a solo to the lyre, which suggests that Philoxenus introduced solos into the choral genre. See MUSIC, § (4).

> TEXT Page, *PMG* 423 ff.; Sutton, *Dithyrambographi Graeci* (1989), 68 ff.
> CRITICISM *RE* 20. 1. 192 ff. (Maas); M. L. West, *Greek Music* (1992), 364 ff.; B. Zimmermann, *Dithyrambos* (1992), 122 ff.   B. Z.

Philoxenus (2), of Leucas, contemporary of *Philoxenus (1), author of the poem *The Banquet*, the description of a splendid dinner written in dactylo-epitrites and in dithyrambic language. The *Cookery-book* quoted by *Plato (2) Comicus (fr. 189 Kassel-Austin) and written in dactylic hexameters is probably another poem of the same author.

> TEXT Page, *PMG* 433 ff.; Montanari, *Archestrato* 1 (1983), 121 ff.
> CRITICISM Wilamowitz, *Textgeschichte der griechischen Lyriker* (1900), 85 ff.; B. Zimmermann, *Dithyrambos* (1992), 143 f.   B. Z.

Philoxenus (3), Eretrian painter, dated by *Pliny (1) to 330 BC. He painted for *Cassander (after 306?) a Battle of *Alexander (3) the Great and *Darius III (Plin. *HN* 35. 110). A *mosaic in *Pompeii of the 2nd cent. BC depicting the two kings in battle is proved by the likeness of Alexander's breastplate to that from Tomb II at Vergina (see AEGAE) to represent faithfully a 4th-cent. original. Philoxenus has been suggested as the artist. See PAINTING, GREEK.

> H. Fuhrmann, *Philoxenos von Eretria* (1931); J. Pollitt, *Art in the Hellenistic Age* (1986), 45–6.   T. B. L. W.

Philoxenus (4) of *Alexandria (1) (1st cent. BC) wrote on the text of *Homer, accents, metre, verbs, and Atticism, and compiled important (lost) lexica of Homeric and other *dialects. See ETYMOLOGICA.

> R. Pfeiffer, *History of Classical Scholarship*, 1 (1968), 273–4, C. Theodoridis, *Die Fragmente des Grammatikers Philoxenos* (1976).   J. S. R.

Philumenus of *Alexandria (1), member of the eclectic school of medicine, *c.* AD 180. An excerpt from his work *De Venenatis Animalibus* (on poisonous animals), the basis of the thirteenth book of *Aelian, has been edited by M. Wellmann in *CMG* (1908). He also wrote a book on diseases of the bowels (only part extant, in a Latin tr., ed. Michaeleanu, 1910), and one Περὶ γυναικείων (on gynaecology, not extant).   W. D. R.

Philyllius, Athenian comic poet, won the first prize once at the *Lenaea at the beginning of the 4th cent. BC (*IG* 2². 2325. 137). We have ten titles, mostly implying mythological burlesque, and thirty-three citations.

> PCG 7. 374 ff. (*CAF* 1. 781 ff.).   K. J. D.

Philyra, 'Linden-tree', an Oceanid (see NYMPHS) loved by *Cronus, who, being surprised by Rhea while making love to her, turned himself and Philyra into horses. Their child was the *centaur Chiron, whose monstrous shape horrified the mother so that she prayed to change her own form, and thus became the tree called after her. The myth is consistently located in northern Greece.

> A. Kossatz–Deissmann, *LIMC* under the name.   J. N. B.

Phineus, a Thracian seer-king (see THRACE), whose myth derives from the *Peloponnesus. According to *Hesiod (fr. 254) Phineus had been blinded because he had shown Phrixus the way or because he had preferred a long life over eye-sight. *Apollonius (1) of Rhodes (2. 177 ff.) adds that he revealed the plans of the gods against their will. They penalized him through the Harpies (see HARPYIAE), who stole or defiled all his food. When the *Argonauts came, he made a compact with them: he would prophesy the further course of their adventures, if they would deliver him from the Harpies. This was achieved by the sons of Boreas, whose action already appears on 6th-cent. vases.

In his *Phineidaei* and *Phineus* (twice) *Sophocles (1) probably preferred a different version. After a first marriage with Cleopatra, daughter of *Boreas, Phineus remarried. His new wife so slandered her stepsons that Phineus either blinded them himself or let her do so. When the Argonauts arrived in Thrace, the sons of Boreas liberated their cousins against the will of Phineus, who now directed his army against the Argonauts and was killed by *Heracles. The stepmother was handed over to her father and executed.

> L. Kahil, *LIMC* under the name.   J. N. B.

Phlegon of *Tralles, a freedman of *Hadrian, author of a work covering all the *Olympiads, from the first to that of AD 140. He also wrote works on Sicily, Roman festivals, Roman topography, and wondrous events.

> *FGrH* 257, A. Giannini, *Paradoxographorum Graecorum Reliquiae* (1966); J. D. Gauger, *Chiron*, 1980, 223–61.   K. S. S.

Phlegyas, eponym of the Phlegyae, a Thessalian people, son of *Ares (Apollod. 3. 41 and elsewhere; his mother's name varies). He is also represented as living near Lake Boebeis (Pind. *Pyth.* 3. 34), or in *Orchomenus (1) (Paus. 9. 36. 1), while the Epidaurian legend (Paus. 2. 26. 4; see EPIDAURUS) brings him to the *Peloponnesus. He was father of Coronis, the mother of *Asclepius (Pind. ibid. and elsewhere); of *Ixion (Eur. fr. 424 Nauck). Verg. *Aen.* 6. 618, on which see *Servius, puts him in *Tartarus.

> J. Fontenrose, *Python* (1959), 25 ff., 477 ff.   H. J. R.

phlyakes, farces (also called ἱλαροτραγῳδίαι, cheerful tragedies) which were performed in S. Italy and also perhaps at *Alexandria (1) in the 4th and 3rd cent. BC. The chief authors of these ludicrous scenes from daily life or from mythology were *Rhinthon, *Sciras, and *Sopater (1) of Paphos; vase-pictures illustrate an earlier (? pre-literary) stage in their development.

> The fragments are collected in G. Kaibel, *CGF* (1899), 183–97, and A. Olivieri, *Frammenti della commedia greca e del mimo nella Sicilia e nella Magna Grecia*, 2² (1947), 7–42. See also E. Wüst in *RE* 20. 1 (1941), 292 ff., 'φλύακες'; M. Bieber, *The History of the Greek and Roman Theater*² (1961), 129 ff.; O. Taplin, *PCPhS* 1987, 92 ff., and *Comic Angels* (1993). On the vase-paintings see esp. A. D. Trendall, *Phlyax Vases*² (*BICS* Suppl. 19, 1967), and in *EAA* 3 (1960), 706 ff., 'Fliacici, Vasi'; cf. also *The Red-figured Vases of Lucania Campania and Sicily* (1967), and (with A. Cambitoglou) *The Red-figured Vases of Apulia* (1978, 1982); V. Mayo, *The Art of South Italy* (1982).   W. G. A.

Phocaea, the most northerly of the *Ionian cities in Asia Minor, occupying a site with twin harbours midway between the Elaitic and Hermaean gulfs. Poorly endowed with land, the archaic Phocaeans were renowned seafarers and traders, and *Herodotus (1) (1. 163 ff.) stresses their close contacts with *Tartessus in S. Spain; Greek *colonization of the French and Spanish coasts was essentially their doing, above all *Massilia and *Emporion, with lesser trading-ports *en route*, as at Alalia in *Corsica (Hdt. 1.

165. 1). Besieged by a Persian army in 540, most citizens preferred emigration to submission, finally settling at *Elea in Italy. Phocaea never recovered from their loss: Dionysius, the general-issimo of the Greek fleet in the *Ionian Revolt, was a Phocaean; but his city only contributed three ships. Even so the city survived into late antiquity. The scanty remains (at mod. Foça) include an archaic temple.

PECS 708 f.; CAH 3². 3 (1982), 139 ff.   D. E. W. W.; A. J. S. S.

Phocas (5th cent. AD), grammarian, author of an *Ars de nomine et verbo* (ed. Keil, *Gramm. Lat.* 5. 410–39) and a *Vita Vergilii* in hexameters (often published, e.g. in Baehrens, *PLM* 5. 85). A *De aspiratione* attributed to him (ed. Keil, *Gramm. Lat.* 5. 439–41) is apocryphal.

Schanz–Hosius, § 1106.   J. F. Mo.; R. H. R.

Phocion (402/1–318 BC), son of Phocus, Athenian statesman and general, pupil of *Plato (1) and friend of *Xenocrates (1), called 'the Good'. No Athenian was *strategos more often than Phocion's 45 times between 371 and 318. An incorruptible inde-pendent political thinker with basically conservative views, he served with *Chabrias and was probably attached to *Callistratus (2) and *Eubulus (2). He opposed *Demosthenes (2)'s agitation against Macedonia throughout, probably on grounds of practic-ability. This attitude did not prevent his pursuing Athenian inter-ests as *strategos*: he led military action in *Euboea in 348 and 341, at *Megara (perhaps 342) and at *Byzantium (340/39, here against *Philip (1) II). After *Chaeronea and again in 335 he negotiated milder treatment for Athens from the Macedonian kings. The same attitude characterised his stance in the *Lamian War (322): he opposed the war, but did his duty as *strategos* in defending Attica and was chief negotiator with the victorious *Antipater (1). The constitutional changes limiting political rights introduced by Antipater were probably his idea, but his co-oper-ation with the Macedonians, for whom he was the most influen-tial Athenian, and his toleration of the Macedonian garrison in *Munichia ruined his reputation with the Athenian democrats; the brief democratic revolution under *Polyperchon (318) saw his condemnation and death.

Plutarch, *Life of Phocion*; H.-J. Gehrke, *Phokion* (1976); L. Trittle, *Phocion the Good* (1988).   R. M. E.

Phocis, a country of central Greece comprising the middle Cephissus valley (see CEPHISSUS, Boeotian) and the valley of *Crisa, which are linked loosely by passes over the southern spurs of Mt. *Parnassus. Both areas were fertile, the former possessing pasture and agricultural land, and the latter olives, vines, and corn. In the 6th cent. BC Phocis was organized in a strong feder-ation (see FEDERAL STATES), issuing federal coinage and levying a federal army. Phocis' internal unity enabled it to resist the aggression of its neighbours, who coveted the control of *Delphi and of the route to northern Greece via the Cephissus valley and the pass of Elatea to *Thermopylae, and the Phocians showed skill in their diplomacy. Deprived of Delphi and the Crisaean plain in the First *Sacred War (c.596) and overrun by *Thessaly, their ambition was to regain her outlet to the sea; checked from expanding at the expense of *Doris by Sparta, the Phocians allied with Athens (457), seized Delphi, and were confirmed in their control by an expedition under *Pericles (1) (448), to whom a Phocian alliance was valuable for encircling Boeotia. After the battle of *Coronea (447) Phocis joined Sparta, was loyal to Sparta during the *Peloponnesian War and in the early fourth century, until *Boeotia impressed Phocis into its Central Greek Confeder-

acy. The Phocian bid for independence in the Third *Sacred War broke Theban power but exhausted Phocis. See PHILOMELUS, ONOMARCHUS.

P–K, *GL* 1. 2. 422 ff.; E. Kase and others (eds.), *The Great Isthmus Corridor Route* 1 (1991).   N. G. L. H.

Phocus (Φῶκος), in mythology, son of *Aeacus by the *nymph Psamathe, who took the shape of a seal, φώκη; hence the name of her son (Apollod. 3. 158). He proved a distinguished athlete, thus arousing the jealousy of the legitimate sons, *Peleus and *Telamon (1); they drew lots to see which should kill him, and Telamon, to whom the task fell, murdered him while they were exercising; Aeacus found out and banished them both (ibid. 160).

LIMC 7. 1 (1994), 396.   H. J. R.

Phocylides (1) A gnomic hexameter poem (see GNŌMĒ) com-posed in Miletus in the first half of the 6th cent. BC had successive maxims introduced by the formula 'This too from Phocylides'; he may have been the poet, as later assumed, or a fictitious sage. Evidence for elegiacs by Phocylides is unreliable. (2) A late moralizing poem in 230 hexameters, probably composed by an *Alexandrian Jew around the turn of our era, also claims Phocyl-ides as its author. It is generally cited as 'Pseudo-Phocylides'. See JEWISH-GREEK LITERATURE.

M. L. West, *JHS* 1978, 164–7, and *Theognidis et Phocylidis Fragmenta* (1978); P. W. van der Horst, *The Sentences of Pseudo-Phocylides* (1978); J. Thomas, *Der jüdische Phokylides* (Novum Testamentum et orbis anti-quus, 23), 1992 (pp. xv, 534).   M. L. W.

Phoebe, in Hesiod (*Theog.* 136) one of the race of *Titans, daugh-ter of Ge (*Gaia) and *Uranus and mother by Coeus of *Leto. Both name (*Aeschylus derives Phoebus from Phoebe, *Eum.* 7) and kinship suggest an Apolline connection (see APOLLO), although the use of the name for Artemis/Diana, or for the moon, appears to be confined to late authors. The name belongs also to a heroine, sister of Hilaeira (see LEUCIPPIDES).   E. Ke.

Phoebus i.e. radiant; name or description of *Apollo. See also PHOEBE.

Phoenicians (Φοίνικες, *Poeni*), a people (rather than a nation) occupying the coast of the Levant; they are thus described only in the classical sources and etymologically their name is Greek; their own name for themselves is unknown, although the Bible classes them as Canaanites (for the Greek tradition on Chna see *Hecataeus (1) in Steph. Byz.; also *Philon (5) of Byblos). The royal Assyrian inscriptions (9th–7th cent. BC) refer to the cities of *Tyre, *Sidon, *Byblos, etc., as (in the form of ethnics) do the Phoenician inscriptions; but they are silent about 'Phoenicia' and 'Phoenicians', which were classical constructs.

A common view derives *Phoinikes* from the Greek φοίνιος, φοῖνος, meaning 'red'. The Phoenicians were so designated (runs this view) from their copper skin, and/or their expertise in the *purple industry; other theories relate their name to the copper trade, the palm-tree and dates, textiles (based on a tablet of ambiguous sense from Minoan Cnossus; see MINOAN CIVILIZATION), or to an Egyptian word for 'woodcutters'.

The land of the Phoenicians (Phoenicia) extended along the E. Mediterranean coast from modern Syria to S. Lebanon and Galilee. Its limits are debated: either from *Tarsus to *Gaza, or, more conventionally, from Tell Sukas (Syria) south of *Ugarit, to Akko (Galilee). For the classical Greeks, Phoenicia was no more or less than the Phoenician homeland, without the precise boundaries later assigned by Rome. The Phoenicians were divided into several city-kingdoms, the most famous being Sidon (for 'Sidonian' as a synonym for 'Phoenician' see Hom. *Od.* 4. 84), Tyre, and Byblos, although *Aradus, Amrith, *Berytus, and *Sarepta were important too.

The Phoenicians were said by *Herodotus (1) (1. 1; 2. 44; 7. 89) to have migrated from the *Persian Gulf 2,300 years before his time. Whatever the basis of this tradition, it takes the existence of the Phoenicians back to the 3rd millennium, when their presence in Lebanon is well-attested archaeologically. The port of Byblos was known in Early Dynastic Egypt. The history of the Phoenicians is intimately related to the sea, as shown e.g. by their island-harbours at Tyre and Aradus and their harbour-settlements in the western Mediterranean; also by their expertise in ship-building (using wood from the Lebanon forests) and seafaring. This relationship inspired two dominant trends in their history: their role in international trade—notably metals (both ore and processed), textiles, purple, foodstuffs, exotic materials, and craft-goods (see the trade of Tyre in Ezekiel 27)—and what is misleadingly called Phoenician 'colonization': i.e., the spread of Phoenician settlements (trading posts and farming communities) from Spain (see GADES) via Africa (see UTICA) to Egypt; of these *Carthage was the most famous. This movement began early in the 11th cent., reaching its climax in the 9th-8th cents., when Phoenician culture (arts, religion, and inscriptions) left traces almost all over the Mediterranean.

The Phoenicians were also a vital element of the Near East: the maritime strength of the region caused Assyrian and Babylonian kings to conquer it several times, and the Phoenicians formed the backbone of the Persian navy in Achaemenid times. They maintained close links with Palestine, Egypt (along with the Red Sea), Assyria and Arabia, and their arts were strongly influenced by the east.

From the beginning of their expansion, the Phoenicians came into contact with the Greeks, but it was only after the *Persian Wars that the Hellenization of Phoenicia commenced; see HELLENISM, HELLENIZATION. After their conquest (Tyre included) by Alexander, the Phoenician cities were gradually integrated into the Hellenistic *koinē* or shared culture, first under the Ptolemies (see PTOLEMY (1)), then the *Seleucids and finally Rome; but their political identity (based on their cities) and cultural character (notably their language) were partly preserved, and the Phoenicians maintained their own specific place in the Graeco-Roman world. See PHILON (5).

SOURCES G. Bunnens, *L'Expansion phénicienne* (1979).

MODERN STUDIES The collection *Studia Phoenicia*; The journal *Rivista di Studi Fenici* (1988); S. Moscati, *I Fenici* (1988); M. Gras, P. Rouillard, and J. Texidor, *L'Univers phénicien* (1989); C. Baurain and C. Bonnet, *Les Phéniciens* (1992); F. Millar, *PCPS* 1983, 55 ff. and *The Roman Near East* (1993). J.-F. S.

Phoenicides, New Comedy poet (see COMEDY (GREEK), NEW) with two victories at the *Dionysia (*IG* 2². 2325. 76 = V B 1 col. 5. 17 Mette). Fr. 1 refers to a peace made in the 280s BC; in fr. 4 a courtesan on retirement describes her experiences of past lovers.

FRAGMENTS Kassel and Austin, *PCG* 7 (1989), 388–92.

INTERPRETATION Meineke, *FCG* 1. 481 f.; A. Körte in *RE* 20. 1 (1941), 380. W. G. A.

Phoenix (1) Eponym and founder of the *Phoenicians, son of Agenor, Eur. fr. 819, Apollod. 3.1.1. In *Homer, *Iliad* 14. 321, however, he is the father of *Europa; and in *Hesiod (*Cat.* fr. 138) his wife Cassiepea bears him Cilix, Phineus, and Dorcylus. (2) In *Iliad* 9 (otherwise only 16. 96), an ambassador sent by

*Agamemnon together with *Odysseus and *Aias to persuade *Achilles to give up his wrath. Phoenix has been appointed by *Peleus to accompany Achilles to *Troy and teach him heroic values. In an extensive and powerful oration, he illuminates Achilles' situation through a story of his own conflict with his father Amyntor over a concubine, leading to his reception by Peleus, and by a story of *Meleager (1)'s withdrawal from fighting in anger at his mother. *Sophocles (1) wrote a *Phoenix*, as did *Euripides whose influential version accounts for *Apollodorus (6)'s story (3. 13. 8) that Amyntor blinded Phoenix and Peleus had him healed by the *centaur Chiron. In Soph. *Phil.* (and probably earlier in Lesches' *Little Iliad*, see EPIC CYCLE) he is again an ambassador with Odysseus, to persuade *Neoptolemus (1) to enter the war, and the latter buries him *en route* for the Molossians (see MOLOSSI) in Hagias' *Nostoi* (returns of the Heroes). K. D.

Phoenix (3) of Colophon, iambic poet of early 3rd cent. BC (see IAMBIC POETRY, GREEK); six choliambic fragments, on ethical subjects, moralizing rather than specifically *Cynic, survive; best known is fr. 6, a literary elaboration of a begging-song from *Rhodes.

TEXT Diehl, *Anth. Lyr. Graec.* 1. 3. 104–10; Powell, *Coll. Alex.* 231–6; (with trans.) A. D. Knox, *The Greek Choliambic Poets* (Loeb, 1929).

GENERAL J. A. Martín García, *Fénice de Colofón* (diss. Madrid 1981); G. Wills, *CQ* 1970, 112–18. F. W.

Phoenix (*De Ave Phoenice*), poem in 170 elegiac lines on the fabulous bird whose life, eternally renewed through death, was a potent symbol for both pagans and Christians. The ascription to *Lactantius has been questioned, but there are strong hints of Christian authorship.

TEXTS *Anth. Lat.* 475a Riese; with trans., Duff, *Minor Lat. Poets*. See also C. F. Heffernan, *The Phoenix at the Fountain* (1988). J. H. D. S.

Phorbas, a common heroic name; many of its bearers seem particularly associated with violence. One was a Lapith (*Hymn. Hom. Ap.* 211; Ov. *Met.* 12. 322; see CENTAURS). Another was a brigand who forced travellers to *Delphi to box with him and so killed them; eventually he was killed by *Apollo (schol. *Il.* 23. 660; Fontenrose, *Python* (1959), 24–7). At least one Phorbas was also worshipped in Athens (e.g. Andoc. *Myst.* 62), though in myth there are two figures: one was a foreign ally of *Eumolpus, killed by *Erechtheus in the Eleusinian war (e.g. Andron *FGrH* 10 F 1), the other an associate of *Theseus, his charioteer (Pherecydes *FGrH* 3 F 152) or tutor and inventor of wrestling (Polemon fr. 55 Preller, cf. *ARV*² 1268. 1).

Höfer, in Roscher, *Lex.* 3. 2424 f. E. Ke.

Phorcys, in mythology, son of *Nereus and Earth i.e. *Gaia (Hes. *Theog.* 237). Marrying his sister Ceto, he became father of the *Graeae and *Gorgo (ibid. 270 ff.). Other children are ascribed to him in various sources, as Thoosa, mother of the Cyclops, Polyphemus (*Od.* 1. 71; see CYCLOPES); the *Sirens (Sophocles in Plut. *Quaest. conv.* 745 f.). In general he is the father or leader of sea-monsters, such as the *Tritons (Verg. *Aen.* 5. 824).

LIMC 7. 1 (1994), 398. H. J. R.

Phormion (1), Athenian admiral, *stratēgos* of the *phylē Pandionis (this is not certain), first mentioned in 440 BC before *Samos. In the next years he proved an excellent military leader in *Acarnania, at *Potidaea, and in *Chalcidice. In 430 he blockaded *Corinth from *Naupactus; and next summer, by brilliant tactics, he defeated two superior Peloponnesian fleets, thus restoring Athenian influence in Acarnania. After his return (428), he is said to have been sentenced for peculation (*FGrH* 324 F 8). Probably he died at this time. (See the commentaries of Rhodes and Hornblower on Thuc. 2. 103, 3. 7.)

Thuc. bks. 1 and 2; *PA* 14958. V. Ehrenberg, *AJPhil.* 1945, 119; D. M. Lewis, *JHS* 1961, 118 f. *CAH* 5² (1994) ch. 9; Fornara, *Generals*, 49 f., 77 f.; Develin, *AO* 91 f., 117 ff.; J. S. Morrison and J. F. Coates, *The Athenian Trireme* (1986), esp. 72 ff. V. E.; S. H.

Phormion (2) (4th cent. BC) was the slave and subsequently *freedman of the Athenian banker *Pasion (see BANKS), and himself worked in the bank. Shortly before Pasion's death he leased the bank from him, and later married his widow Archippe in accordance with his will. Persistent bad relations between him and his stepson *Apollodorus (2) led in *c.*349 to the latter unsuccessfully prosecuting him on a charge of embezzling money from the bank (see Dem. 36, 45, 46). Like Pasion, he was awarded Athenian *citizenship. He owned a number of ships, but it is unclear whether he continued as an independent banker after the lease of Pasion's bank expired.

J. Trevett, *Apollodoros the Son of Pasion* (1992). J. C. T.

Phormis (or Phormus), Syracusan writer of comedy. *Aristotle (*Poet.* 5. 1449ᵇ6) seems to treat him as a contemporary of *Epicharmus. The *Suda* adds that he was tutor to the sons of *Gelon (d. 478 BC), and attributes to Phormis the invention of long cloaks for his actors and (?) a new form of *skēnē*. Paus. 5. 27. 1 mentions a notable Arcadian soldier Phormis who fought for *Hieron (1) and Gelon; whether or not the same man, is not known.

CGF 148; Pickard-Cambridge–Webster, *Dithyramb*², 289. K. J. D.

Phoroneus, a very ancient figure of Argive tradition (see ARGOS (2)). He was son of *Inachus and Melia; father of Apis and the Argive Niobe, the first earthly love of *Zeus; and king of the whole *Peloponnesus (Apollod. 2. 1, which also gives his descendants). He was reputedly the first to gather together scattered families into cities (Paus. 2. 15. 5). The Argives credited him with the discovery of fire, and kept a flame burning in his memory (Paus. 2. 19. 5). J. R. M.

Phosphorus (Φωσφόρος = Ἑωσφόρος; Lucifer), son of *Eos, the Dawn, and Astraeus, a Titan (Hes. *Theog.* 381); personification of the morning star which announces the approach of dawn, and thus 'light-bearer', bringer of the light of day (*Il.* 23. 226, cf. *Od.* 13. 93–4), i.e. the planet Venus, and the only planet mentioned in Greek literature before the 4th cent. (see West on Hes. *Theog.* 381). Phosphorus was father of *Ceyx, king of Trachis (Apollod. 1. 7. 4). J. R. M.

Photius, (*c.*810–*c.*893) the best of the Byzantine scholars and patriarch of *Constantinople in AD 858–67 and 878–86. 'At the pressing intreaty of the Caesar (Bardas), the celebrated Photius renounced the freedom of a secular and studious life, ascended the patriarchal throne, and was alternately excommunicated and absolved by the synods of the East and West. By the confession even of priestly hatred, no art or science, except poetry, was foreign to this universal scholar, who was deep in thought, indefatigable in reading, and eloquent in diction' (Gibbon, ch. 53). His most important work is the *Bibliotheca*, 'Library' (not his title; the alternative *Myriobiblion*, 'Ten Thousand Books', has even less justification), 'a living monument of erudition and criticism' (Gibbon, as above). It is a hastily compiled, ill-arranged critical account in 280 chapters of books read by Photius in the absence of his brother, Tarasius, for whose information, and at whose request, the work was composed. There is conflicting evidence

about the date of composition. Theology and history predominate; oratory, romance, philosophy, science, medicine, and lexicography also come within its scope. Besides its intrinsic value (the criticisms are often felicitous and acute, both from the literary and the bibliographical point of view), it has a considerable adventitious importance as the best or sole source of our information about many notable lost works; it mentions some sixty non-theological works not now surviving. Poetry is almost entirely neglected; but there is other evidence that Photius had read at least the usual school authors, *pace* the implication of Gibbon's remark cited above. The *Lexicon*, which is an earlier work, is a glossary based ostensibly and in fact indirectly upon Aelius *Dionysius (3), *Pausanias (4), and *Diogenianus (2), but immediately drawn from such later compilations as *Timaeus (3)'s Platonic lexicon, and chiefly from the Συναγωγή (see LEXICA SEGUERIANA). The *Lexicon* was long known only from the *Codex Galeanus* at Cambridge, defective at the beginning. Part of the missing portion was then supplied by MSS in Athens and Berlin, and finally in 1959 a MS containing the complete *Lexicon* was found at Zavorda in Macedonia. Some aspects of Photius' scholarship can be illustrated from his *Letters* and *Amphilochia*.

EDITIONS *Bibl.*: Bekker, 1824–5; R. Henry, 1959–77, with index by J. Schamp, 1991. *Lexicon*: Naber, 1864–5; C. Theodoridis, in progress (1982–). *Letters and Amphilochia*: B. L. Laowdar–L. G. Westerink (1983–8).
CRITICISM K. Ziegler, *RE*; N. G. Wilson, *Scholars of Byzantium* (1983), 89–119, and *Photius' Bibliotheca: A Selection Translated with Notes* (1994). P. B. R. F.; R. B.; N. G. W.

Phraates (1) **IV** (*c.*38–3/2 BC), king of *Parthia. He secured his succession by murdering his father *Orodes II and many Parthian princes and nobles. In 36 he had to face a Roman invasion, when Antony (M. *Antonius (2)) penetrated into Media, but the Parthians made an attack on the rear of the Roman army, annihilated the two legions and forced Antony to raise the siege of Praaspa and to withdraw through the mountains of Armenia with heavy losses. From 31 to 25 BC Phraates had to contest his throne with the rebel *Tiridates (2), both of them asking for Roman military support. *Augustus' request for the lost Roman standards and the prisoners of war were fulfilled by Phraates, but not until 20 BC and only when the Romans made a grand show of force near the Parthian border. A few years later he sent his four sons to Rome; his reasons for doing so are debated. He was assassinated by his wife Musa, a former Roman slave presented to Phraates by Augustus. For the other kings named Phraates, see ARSACIDS.

M. Karras-Klapproth, *Prosopographische Studien zur Geschichte des Partherreiches* (1988), under the name; E. Nedergaard, *Acta Hyperborea*, 1988, 102 ff. J. Wi.

Phraates (2) **V (Phraataces)** (3/2 BC–AD 2), king of *Parthia; the son of *Phraates IV by Musa. Wife and son secured the murder of Phraates IV, and Phraataces succeeded. He drove a certain Artavasdes, who was the nominee of *Augustus, out of Armenia and tried to take a strong line with Augustus. Because of heavy Roman protest and the expedition of C. *Iulius Caesar (2) against him Phraates gave in, met the Emperor's grandson on an island in the Euphrates (AD 1) and promised not to interfere in Armenia again. In AD 4 Phraates, who had married his mother Musa in AD 2, was deposed by the Parthian nobles who chose Orodes III. Neither he nor his successor Vonones, one of the four sons of *Phraates (1) IV at Rome, were able to secure this noble support and pursue an active foreign policy. This changed when *Artabanus II prevailed.

M. Karras-Klapproth, *Prosopographische Studien zur Geschichte des Partherreiches* (1988), under the name. J. Wi.

phratries (φρατρίαι, with dialectal variations), in Greek states, groups with hereditary membership and probably normally associated with specific locality(ies). The members were 'phrateres', related to words which in other *Indo-European languages mean 'brother'. Phratry names often, but not always, had the patronymic ending -*idai*. The relationship between a phratry's eponym and its members, however, is largely obscure. Though the institution probably originated in the Mycenaean period or earlier, two references in *Homer's *Iliad* (2. 362–3 and 9. 63–4) are the earliest secure evidence.

Phratries are attested in a wide range of Greek states, including *Sparta and *Argos (2) in *Dorian Greece and several *Ionian states, including *Athens. We are especially well informed about the Labyadai at *Delphi (*Insc. Jur. Gr.* 2 no. 28). At Argos and *Syracuse phratries were subgroups of *phylai, and may also have been elsewhere, though this is nowhere securely attested in Ionian states. Phratries could contain subgroups such as the *genos. They could be reorganized, e.g. by democratic reformers (Arist. *Pol.* 1319[b]. 19–27; see also, on Chios, W. G. Forrest, *BSA* 1960, 172–89).

Ionian Greeks, including Athenians, conceived of the institution as part of their Ionian heritage (see IONIANS). Like the Ionian *phylai*, their origin was attributed to *Ion (1), and celebration of the phratry festival *Apaturia was regarded as a criterion of Ionian identity (Hdt. 1. 147).

We know much more about phratries at Athens than anywhere else. In addition to numerous references in literary sources, especially the orators, inscriptions attest them from the 7th to the 2nd cents. BC. At least about nine phratries are now known by name. In total there were probably at least about thirty. Before the reforms of *Cleisthenes (2) (508 BC) every Athenian male belonged to a phratry and phratries functioned as social groups concerned with matters of family and descent. Under *Draco's law on homicide, dating from the 620s, and re-enacted at the end of the 5th cent., members of the phratry of a victim of unintentional homicide are required to support the victim's family, and, if the victim has no family, to take on its role. This function as natural unit of community beyond the family was characteristic. The 4th-cent. author of the *Athenaion Politeia believed that the phratries had been subdivisions of the four old Ionian *phylai* (*Ath. Pol.* fr. 3), which, for most practical purposes, were abolished by Cleisthenes. This may, however, have no firmer basis than his belief, probably false, that the phratries were identical with the old *trittyes, which were *phylē* subdivisions. It has been thought that, before Cleisthenes, phratries played a wider political role and were the main structures through which aristocratic power was exercised. Some, however, now think this unlikely, at least for the 7th and 6th cents., when it seems that the financial, military, political and judicial administration was organized through the old *phylai* and their subdivisions, the *trittyes* and *naukrariai. It seems that it was rather at these institutions that Cleisthenes' reforms were directed.

After Cleisthenes phratry membership continued to be necessary for a native-born Athenian citizen, along with membership of Cleisthenes' new institutional structure of *phylai*, *trittyes* and *demes. The phratry apparently continued to play a major role in controlling matters relating to legitimacy of descent, including access to citizenship and inheritance of property. Phratry members appear as witnesses in 4th-cent. legal cases where matters of descent are in dispute. Down to the 2nd cent., natural-ized citizens were normally enrolled in a phratry and a deme. The most substantial evidence for an individual Athenian phratry is three decrees, inscribed on stone in the early 4th cent., which regulate in detail admissions procedures (IG 2[2]. 1237).

The nature and relationship of the two groups mentioned in the decrees, the Demotionidai and the House of the Dekeleieis, are uncertain. Unlike the demes, however, phratries could split and fuse in response to social and demographic pressures, and it has been suggested that the House of the Dekeleieis were in the process of splitting away from their parent phratry, the Demotionidai, at the time these decrees were passed. Male children probably underwent a dual process of phratry introduction, in infancy at the *meion* and in adolescence at the *koureion*. In addition there might be a separate process of scrutiny (*diadikasia*), including a vote by the phratry on a candidate's eligibility. Under *Pericles (1)'s citizenship law, citizen descent was necessary in the female line as well as the male. The phratries seem to have taken greater account than the demes of women, who, while not normally regarded as phratry members, might sometimes be introduced to their fathers' phratries and were presented to their husbands' phratries at the *gamelia*.

While phratries might pursue common activities throughout the year, phratry admissions normally took place at the annual phratry festival, *Apaturia, at which there was also religious observance, especially cult of *Zeus Phratrios and *Athena Phratria, feasting and e.g. competitions. Phratries could own property, which provided a source of income to support cultic and other activities and e.g. for loans to members; see CREDIT.

A variety of subgroups (possibly sometimes known as *thiasoi*) is found in Athenian phratries: *genē*, groups whose members were *orgeōnes and others. Philochorus (*FGrH* 328 F 35) records that it was obligatory for phratries to accept (i.e. as members) both *orgeones* and *homogalaktes* (said to be an old word for *gennetai*) and this is reflected in the evidence of late 5th- and 4th-cent. orators. It has been supposed that this was representative of archaic aristocratic dominance of phratries, but this is unlikely. The internal constitution of phratries seems to have reflected contemporary norms. In the 4th cent., decrees were voted on by all members, ballots were secret and officials accountable to the group. The chief officer of a phratry, elected annually, was the phratriarch, responsible for phratry administration and for representing it externally. Phratry subgroups might contain priests, but it is unclear whether there were also separate phratry priests.

S. D. Lambert, *The Phratries of Attica* (1993); C. W. Hedrick, *The Decrees of the Demotionidai* (1990); N. F. Jones, *Public Organisation in Greece* (1987); D. Roussel, *Tribu et Cité* (1976); M. Guarducci, *L'Istituzione della fratria*, MAL (1937–8); Parker, ARH 104 ff. S. D. L.

Phrygia (see ASIA MINOR, *Classical*) was the large and ill-defined geographical region which stretched across much of west central Anatolia. During the Roman period the region extended north to *Bithynia, west to the upper valley of the *Hermus and to *Lydia, south to *Pisidia and to *Lycaonia, and east as far as the Salt Lake. Phrygian, one of the *Anatolian languages, is attested within these boundaries by neo-Phrygian inscriptions, mostly of the 3rd cent. AD; see PHRYGIAN LANGUAGE. Another useful criterion by which the presence of Phrygian culture may be determined is the distribution of grave monuments depicting a door, a typical Phrygian motif. At earlier periods, however, artefacts of Phrygian type were distributed over a much wider area; so-called Old Phrygian inscriptions (of the 8th and 7th cents. BC) have been found as far apart as *Dascylium in the Hellespont and Tyana in western *Cappadocia.

Virtually nothing is known about Phrygian society between the 5th and the 2nd cents. BC. Macedonian settlers, following in the wake of *Alexander (3) the Great's campaigns, established themselves around the Anatolian plateau, for instance at *Docimium, Philomelium, and Lysias, and introduced a partly Hellenized culture which was imitated by the native aristocracy. Cities and city institutions emerged during the 3rd cent. BC in S. Phrygia under *Seleucid influence. Phrygian culture, however, is best attested in the Roman period. The region was then divided between the provinces of *Asia and *Galatia. It has produced thousands of inscriptions from its cities (mostly agricultural townships which acquired city status under the empire) and above all from the village-communities, which were the most characteristic form of settlement. Apart from funerary texts the commonest type of inscriptions are religious dedications to Greek and *Anatolian deities. Phrygian religious life, which doubtless perpetuated traditions which stretched far back into Anatolian prehistory, can be described and analysed in considerable detail. Alongside those of *Zeus and various mother goddesses, the most widespread cults were for the Anatolian god *Mēn, and for deities associated with righteousness, vengeance, and justice, including the abstract couple 'Holy and Just' (see ANGELS). They enjoined a strict moral code of behaviour, and it is no coincidence that Jewish and early Christian communities flourished on Phrygian soil in the 2nd and 3rd cents. AD.

W. M. Ramsay, *The Cities and Bishoprics of Phrygia* (1895–7); MAMA 1, 4–7, 9–10; C. H. E. Haspels, *The Highlands of Phrygia* (1971); C. Naour and T. Drew Bear, ANRW 2. 18. 3 (1990), 1907–2044; M. Waelkens, *Die kleinasiatischen Türsteine* (1984). S. M.

Phrygia, Hellespontine the district of *Asia Minor closest to the *Hellespont. See DASCYLIUM; PHARNABAZUS.

Phrygian language Phrygian is known mainly from inscriptions, both at an early (Old Phrygian) and at a later (New Phrygian) stage. At some time in the 8th cent. BC, the Phrygians devised an alphabet adapted from Greek and Semitic models. In this are written some 250 Old Phrygian texts (mostly short, but with a few of reasonable length) ranging from the second half of the 8th cent. to the second half of the 3rd cent. BC, the majority belonging to the pre-*Achaemenid period (8th–6th cents. BC). They include monumental rock inscriptions, e.g. *ates . . . midai lavagtaei vanaktei edaes*, lit. 'Ates . . . to Midas chief [and] king has dedicated'. During the Hellenistic and early Roman periods, Phrygian must have been reduced to use as a spoken vernacular, but from the 1st to the 3rd cents. AD it turns up again in written form, in the Greek alphabet. We have over 100 short New Phrygian inscriptions, most of them consisting of curse formulae, often added to epitaphs that are otherwise in Greek; e.g. *iosni semoun knoumanei kakon abberet etitetikmenos eitou*, lit. 'whoever to this grave harm should bring, cursed may he go'. Phrygian is an Indo-European language, but in spite of its geographical location it does not belong to the Anatolian sub-group (Hittite, Lycian, etc.); its closest connections are rather with Greek. But our knowledge of Phrygian remains altogether rather poor.

J. Friedrich, RE 20. 1 (1941), 882 ff.; C. Brixhe and M. Lejeune, *Corpus des inscriptions paléo-phrygiennes* (1984). M. Lej.

Phrynichus (1), an early Athenian tragic poet; see TRAGEDY, GREEK. The *Suda says that he won his first victory between 511 and 508 BC, was the first to introduce female characters in tragedy, and invented the trochaic tetrameter (the last claim, at least, being certainly false). *Themistocles was his *choregus for a

victorious production in 476 (Plut. *Them.* 5), probably near the end of his career.

At least two of his tragedies were on historical subjects. Soon after 494, when the city of *Miletus, which had been aided by Athens, was sacked by the Persians (see IONIAN REVOLT), Phrynichus produced a *Capture of Miletus*, which, according to *Herodotus (1) 6. 21, so distressed the Athenians that they fined him a thousand drachmas 'for reminding them of their own troubles'. The hypothesis to the *Persians* of *Aeschylus quotes *Glaucus (5) of Rhegium as saying that Aeschylus modelled the play on the *Phoenician Women* of Phrynichus, but that Phrynichus began his play with a eunuch who related the defeat of *Xerxes while setting out chairs for the royal councillors (but there may be a confusion here between Phrynichus' *Phoenician Women* and his *Persians*).

Plays on mythical subjects included *Egyptians* and *Danaids* (titles which recall Aeschylus's Danaid tetralogy); *Alcestis*, which influenced *Euripides' *Alcestis* (at least at lines 74–6); *Women of Pleuron*, concerning *Meleager (1); *Actaeon*, *Antaeus*, and *Tantalus*.

He was remembered for the beauty of his lyrics (Ar. *Wasps* 220, 269, *Birds* 748–51) and for inventive choreography (Ar. *Wasps* 1490, Plut. *Quaest. Conv.* 8. 9. 3). In general he seemed to *Aristophanes (1) to exemplify the 'good old days' of tragedy (also *Thesm.* 164–6, *Frogs* 910, 1299 f.).

TrGF 1². 69–79; *Musa Tragica* 40–9, 270–1; H. Lloyd-Jones, *Greek Epic, Lyric, and Tragedy* (1990), 230–7. A. L. B.

Phrynichus (2), Athenian comic poet, produced his first play in 434 (*Suda*) or 429 BC (Anon. *De Com.* 9 p. 7); the latter statement probably refers to his first victory—at the *Lenaea, where he won two victories (IG 2². 2325. 124), his first victory at the City *Dionysia being some time after 420 (ibid. 61). He produced *Monotropos* in 414 (hyp. 1 Ar. *Av.*) and *Muses* in 405 (hyp. 1 Ar. *Ran.*). We have eleven titles and over 90 citations; two of the titles, *Connus* and *Revellers*, are also attributed to *Ameipsias, and this attribution is to be preferred, since it is given by the fifth *hypothesis (1) to *Aristophanes (1)'s *Clouds* and the first hypothesis to his *Birds*, the composers of which will have derived their information ultimately from the *didaskaliai*. Fr. 61 (play unnamed) refers humorously to the mutilation of the *herms in 415.

PCG 7. 393 ff. (CAF 1. 369 ff.). K. J. D.

Phrynichus (3) **Arabius**, of Bithynia, Atticist (see ASIANISM AND ATTICISM), rhetorician, and lexicographer under M. *Aurelius and *Commodus. He compiled Σοφιστικὴ προπαρασκευή, a lexicon of 'Attic' words in thirty-seven books, preserved only in a summary by Photius and in fragments; also Ἀττικιστής (περὶ κρίσεως καλῶν καὶ δοκίμων ὀνομάτων 'Attikistes (on the choice of correct and excellent words)'), extant in an abridgement, our *Eclogē* ('Ἐκλογή, 'selection'). They were based on *Eirenaeus and Aelius *Dionysius (3); see also PAUSANIAS (4). Phrynichus criticizes Pollux, his successful rival for the chair of rhetoric at Athens, for his laxity in the choice of words, and, with Moeris, ranks among the strictest of the 'Atticists'. He recognizes different levels of style within 'Atticism'. His models are *Plato (1), the Ten Orators (see ATTIC ORATORS), *Thucydides (2), *Aeschines (2) Socraticus, *Critias, Antisthenes, Aristophanes, Aeschylus, Sophocles, and Euripides. Nor would he accept the usage of even the best of these without cavil. In the letter to the Imperial Secretary, Attidius Cornelianus, which introduces the *Eclogē*, he reprobates those who try to justify their diction by citing the impeached words from classical authors: ἡμεῖς δὲ οὐ πρὸς τὰ διημαρτημένα ἀφορῶμεν ἀλλὰ πρὸς τὰ δοκιμώτατα τῶν ἀρχαίων, 'we look at the excellent usage of the ancients not at their mistakes'. Such critical scrutiny, however, if at all possible, would demand a clearer perception than the Atticists ever had of the nature and relations of spoken and literary Attic, and of the diverse sources from which the language of the poets was drawn. Nevertheless, Phrynichus' work contains many acute and accurate observations.

EDITIONS Soph. Pr.: J. von Borries (1911) (with the fragments); Ecl.: E. Fischer (1974). P. B. R. F.; R. B., N. G. W.

Phthiotis, one of the *tetrades* (districts) of *Thessaly. Phthiotis was used in Greek, from the Classical period, to designate three distinct geographical and political entities: (1) the territory of Homeric Phthia, kingdom of *Achilles; (2) the SE tetrad of Thessaly; and (3) the peripheral part of Thessaly called Achaea Phthiotis, which disappeared as a political unit in the Roman period after its incorporation into the Thessalian League.

Centred on the middle and lower valley of the river Enipeus, the tetrad of Phthiotis was bounded to the north by the Revenia hills separating the two plains of Thessaly, to the south by the Othrys foothills, and to the east by the hills which, from the Revenia to the Othrys range, dominate the plain of Halmyrus, the E. part of Achaea. To the west the border with *Hestiaeotis passed through the plain of Karditsa.

In the 6th cent. BC, when Aleuas the Red (see ALEUADAE) introduced the division into tetrads, Phthiotis comprised four cities: *Pharsalus, Euhydrium, Phyllus, and Pirasia. They incorporated villages (*komai*): for Pharsalus the sources mention Palaeopharsalus, as well as a sanctuary, Thetideum, near the site of the two battles of *Cynoscephalae (364 and 198 BC). From the end of the 4th cent. BC, Phthiotis included a fifth city, Eretria, sited on the borders with Achaea Phthiotis.

F. Gschnitzer, *Hermes* 1954, 451 ff.; J.-C. Decourt, *La Vallée de l'Enipeus* (*BCH* suppl. 21 1991), 147 ff. B. H.

Phylacus, protector-hero of *Delphi, whose sanctuary was near that of *Athena Pronaia. Together with Autonous, he appeared in heroic form and attacked the Persian invaders in 480 BC (Hdt. 8. 38–9; see PERSIAN WARS), and in some accounts he joined three other heroes for the same purpose at the attack of *Brennus (2) and the *Celts in 279 BC (Paus. 10. 23. 2).

G. Nachtergael, *Les Galates en Grèce* (1975), 161–4. E. Ke.

phylai The Greek word *phyle*, usually but misleadingly translated 'tribe', was widely but not universally used in the Greek world to denote the principal components or divisions of the citizen body. Their origins are unclear. Entities so called are unknown to epic, except for the anomalous line *Homer, *Iliad* 2. 363, but their use in Aegean and colonial contexts suggests that they existed well before the 8th cent. BC. Two sets are well attested in the Archaic period: the *Dorian tribes Hylleis, Dymanes, and Pamphyloi, known as such in 7th-cent. Sparta (Tyrtaeus F 19 West) and elsewhere, and the *Ionian–Attic tribes Geleontes, Hopletes Argadeis, Aigikoreis, Oinopes, and Boreis, known in Archaic Athens (the first four), some Aegean islands and Ionia. North-western Greece, Boeotia, Thessaly, and the areas of Aeolic dialect (Lesbos etc.) used no such divisions till the Hellenistic period, using instead *phratries (Thessaly) or the formalized *merē* ('parts', 'sections') of federal *Boeotia (*Hell. Oxy.* 19 Chambers; see FEDERAL STATES). Hence the systematization of the Dorian and the Ionian-Attic tribe-systems is likely to reflect on the one hand the processes which yielded the main *dialects of Greek, and on the other the process of city-state formation in the Dark Age, which was slow to affect central and northern Greece.

Archaic tribes appear to have functioned as military units (as *Tyrtaeus explicitly says) and as constituencies for the selection of magistrates (hence boards of eight treasurers of Athena in 6th-cent. Athens) or councillors (ML 8—*Chios). They developed or incorporated various subdivisions, such as *trittyes and *naukrariai at Athens, or groups called Thousands or Hundreds, or occasionally phratries and *genē*. However, few states continued such tribal systems unchanged into or beyond the classical period. The renaming of existing units is occasionally visible, as perhaps at *Megara (Hdt. 5. 68), as is the addition of new tribes to accommodate newcomers or the hitherto disfranchised. In *Crete, for example, some seventeen tribe names are known besides the Dorian triad. Moreover, many states evidently used the occasion of a *synoecism, a refoundation, or a liberation to start afresh on different principles, which might reflect territorial divisions or ethnic origins but would normally aim at equality of size and status. *Corinth's creation of an eight-tribe structure may be among the earliest, followed by those of Demonax at *Cyrene (Hdt. 4. 161), of *Cleisthenes (2) in Attica, and the new starts at *Elis (Paus. 5. 9. 4–6) and *Thurii (Diod. 12. 11. 3). In such new dispensations, tribes might be named after geographical features, constituent or immigrant ethnic groups (hence the later *Rhomaioi* or *Rhomeis*), gods or heroes, local dynasts or benefactors, kings or Roman emperors, and even at the extreme (*Heraclea (1) in Lucania) common objects such as 'box', 'tripod', 'shield', etc.

The best-attested such new system was that created by Cleisthenes for Attica in or just after 508/7 BC. The landscape was regarded as comprising three zones, City, Shore, and Inland. Each zone was split into ten sections called *trittyes* ('thirdings'), to each of which were assigned between one and ten of the 139 existing settlements, villages, or town-quarters, which were henceforth termed *demoi* (*demes*). Three sections, one each from City, Shore, and Inland, were then put together to form a tribe. The thirty sections therefore yielded ten tribes, each named after a local hero and each with a geographically scattered membership roughly equal in size and hereditary in the male line thenceforward. They rapidly took on various functions. They became the brigading units for the army and in some way for the navy; constituencies for the election of magistrates, especially the ten generals (see STRATĒGOI), for the selection of members of the Council of 500 (see BOULĒ) and of the 6,000 jurors, and for the selection of boards of administrative officers of every kind; cult groups; and bases for the selection of competing teams of runners, singers, or dancers at various festivals. They had their own corporate life, with officials and sanctuaries (*IG* 2². 1138–71), and came to have an official order: Erechtheis, Aigeis, Pandionis, Leontis, Akamantis, Oineis, Kekropis, Hippothontis, Aiantis, and Antiochis. Later, by the reallocation of demes, new tribes were occasionally created in honour of certain kings and rulers (Antigonis and Demetrias from 307/6 till 201/0; Ptolemais from 224/3; Attalis from 200; and Hadrianis from AD 124/5). Though the vitality of the tribes diminished with time, the system gave the Athenian citizen body a stable and effective internal articulation throughout antiquity. Other equally complex systems in other cities seem to have had comparable purposes and effects.

IN GENERAL D. Roussel, *Tribu et cité* (1976); N. F. Jones, *Public Organization in Ancient Greece* (1987).

FOR SPECIFIC AREAS AND TOPICS Forrest, *BSA* 55 (1960), 172–89 (Chios); A. Andrewes, *Hermes*, 1961, 132–3 (epic); C. Roebuck, *TAPA* 1961, 495–507 (Ionia); D. M. Lewis, *BSA* 1962, 1–4 (Ceos); J. S. Traill, *The Political Organisation of Attica* (1975) (Athens); N. F. Jones, *CPhil.* 1980, 197–215 (Dorian tribes); J. B. Salmon, *Wealthy Corinth* (1984), 413–19 (Corinth); J. S. Traill, *Demos and Trittys* (1986) and Parker, *ARH*, see index (Athens).   J. K. D.

Phylarchus from Athens or *Naucratis (T 1), Greek historian who lived in the 3rd cent. BC. He wrote *Historiai* covering the period from *Pyrrhus' death, 272, to the death of the Spartan king *Cleomenes (2) III in 220/19, thereby continuing *Hieronymus (1) of Cardia and *Duris (2) of Samos; he adopted Duris' tragic and sensational mode of presentation: cf. Polyb. 2. 56–63 = F 53–6. Phylarchus' partisanship of Cleomenes and his anti-Achaean bias were harshly criticized by *Polybius (1) (see above), himself not an admirer of the king, who denounces Phylarchus' arbitrary and erroneous reporting. His work included numerous digressions of all kinds: miraculous events (F 10, 17, 35), strange animal tales (F 4. 26–28. 38. 61), multifarious anecdotes (F 12, 31, 40, 41, 75), love affairs (F 21, 24, 30, 32, 70, 71, 81). Phylarchus' reliability cannot be rated very highly: despite Strasburger, Polybius' reproach of *terateia* ('sensationalism') is justified. *Plutarch used Phylarchus as his chief authority for the *Agis and Cleomenes* and as one of his sources for the *Pyrrhus* and *Aratus*. Pompeius *Trogus also drew on him. The Atticists' low opinion of his style (cf. Dion. Hal, comp. 4; see ASIANISM AND ATTICISM) may account for the loss of his work. Only 60 fragments are extant.

Shorter works (see testimonium 1): *The History of Antiochus and Eumenes of Pergamum* (probably a supplement to the *Historiai* dealing with *Antiochus III, 223–187, and *Eumenes II, 198–160/59); *Mythical Epitomes*, apparently a brief mythical story; *Agrapha* ('Unwritten'), maybe a compilation of mythical traditions which had received no previous literary treatment, cf. fr. 47; *On Inventions*.

FGrH 81; J. Kroymann, *RE* Suppl. 8, 1956. 471 ff.; E. Gabba, *Studi su Filarco* (1957); T. W. Africa, *Phylarchos and the Spartan Revolution* (1961); K. Meister, *Historische Kritik bei Polybios* (1975); H. Strasburger, *Die Wesensbestimmung der Geschichte durch die griechische Geschichtsschreibung* (1975); H.-D. Richter, *Untersuchungen zur hellenistischen Historiographie* (1987); P. Pedech, *Trois historiens méconnus: Théopompe, Duris, Phylarque* (1989). K. Meister, *Die griechische Geschichtsschreibung* (1990), 100 f.; O. Lendle, *Einführung in die griechische Geschichtsschreibung* (1992), 195 ff..   K. M.

Phylas, name of four minor mythological persons, the least unknown being a king of the Dryopes (see DRYOPS). He sinned against the shrine at *Delphi, and consequently *Heracles overthrew him and gave his people to *Apollo as serfs. Many of them, either escaping or being sent by Apollo's command, went to the *Peloponnesus, where they settled at *Asine and other places. Heracles had by Phylas' daughter a son Antiochus, after whom the Attic tribe (see PHYLAI) Antiochis was named (Diod. Sic. 4. 37; Paus. 1. 5. 2; 4. 34. 9–10). See EPONYMOI.   H. J. R.

Phyle, a small Attic *deme with a fort controlling one of the major routes through Mt. *Parnes to *Boeotia. The deme figures as liable to raiding by Boeotians in *Aristophanes (1) (*Ach.* 1023), and from a fort there *Thrasybulus led the force which overthrew the *Thirty Tyrants (Xen. *Hell.* 2. 4. 2–22). The fort now visible is a splendid example of 4th-cent. construction. In the depth of a gorge to the east is a Cave of *Pan (see CAVES, SACRED), from which remains from Middle Helladic on have been recovered,

and close to which lay the fictional plot of land of *Menander (1)'s *Dyscolus*.

W. Wrede, 'Phyle', *MDAI(A)* 49 (1924), 153–224; Ἀρχ. Ἐφ. 1905, 99–158; 1906, 89–116.   C. W. J. E.; R. G. O.

Phyromachus, Athenian sculptor and painter, active *c.*200 BC, included in an Alexandrian list (*Laterculi Alexandrini* 7. 3 ff) among the four principal Greek 'sculptors of men' (ἀνδριαντοποιοί); he often collaborated with the Athenian Niceratus, who was perhaps his father. With *Antigonus (4), *[Ep]igonus, and Stratonicus, he 'did the battles of Attalus and Eumenes against the Gauls' (Plin. *HN* 34. 84). His Antisthenes and his Asclepius for *Pergamum are apparently preserved in copy; if the attributions hold, he was an early exponent of the Pergamene baroque, and perhaps invented or perfected the style. His date is controversial: *Pliny (1)'s floruit of 296 (*HN* 34. 51) is too early, for his pupil, the painter Heraclides, left *Macedonia for Athens in 168 (ibid. 34. 146; 35. 135). He was evidently active during the period when Pliny's source believed that 'the art (i.e. of bronze-casting) stopped' (ibid. 52: 293–156 BC) and so was redated accordingly.

A. F. Stewart, *Greek Sculpture* (1990), 207 f., 302 f., figs. 678 f; B. Andreae (ed.), *Phyromachosprobleme* (1991).   A. F. S.

physics today involves the investigation of the nature and behaviour of matter and energy, and it is often thus distinguished from chemistry and biology. The same term, derived from the Greek word for 'nature', '*physis*', is used to describe a number of ancient inquiries, including *peri physeos historia* (the inquiry into nature), '*ta physika*' (natural things) and *physikē* [sc. *epistēmē*], where no such distinction is implied. These ancient expressions are to some extent context-relative and they covered a range of interests far wider than that encompassed by modern physics. 'Theory of Nature' might be a reasonable general characterization of ancient physics. Notably, for some ancient authorities 'physics' explicitly excluded mathematics and even mathematical attempts at modelling nature. For early doctors physical inquiry was equivalent to what we might now call physiology; the cognate terms in English, 'physic' and 'physician', tend to relate, on the other hand, to the practice of what is now called pathology.

Before Aristotle, physical investigation ranged from the cosmological through to the observation and explanation of discrete natural phenomena. Early studies of the material origins of the world (see ELEMENTS), the position of the earth in space, along with speculation about what we now call magnetism, and the nature of sound and light, could all be thought of as parts of physical inquiry. In the first book of the *Metaphysics*, *Aristotle reports in summary fashion that many of the earliest philosophers based their speculations about nature on the idea that the physical world is reducible to one or more basic starting points or principles. *Thales is supposed to have given water a special status, *Anaximenes air, and so on. The atomists *Leucippus (2) and *Democritus (see ATOMISM) invented a theory of matter which, they hoped, would satisfy *both* strict logical demands for certain, immutable, knowledge about reality (laid down by people like *Parmenides of Elea) *and* account for the changing and unpredictable phenomena of the visible world. They posited an ontologically real world of first principles—atoms and void—and a secondary world of appearances, the result of the movement of the atoms in the void. (Aristotle praised Democritus for arguing 'physically' and not just 'logically', but criticized nearly all his predecessors for leaving important questions unanswered, notably about the origins of physical motion.)

2. *Plato (1)'s physical system is similarly based on a distinction between what is real and intelligible (the Forms) and the particulars we can see in the world around us, which share in different ways (though never completely) in the perfection of the idealized Forms. Doubts about the extent to which the mathematical perfection of ultimate reality can ever be fully present in physical objects lie behind the reservations expressed by Plato about the reliability of the physical theory in the *Timaeus* (5. 27–30). Matter, for Plato, is inherently chaotic, and the creator of Plato's universe had to struggle hard with the recalcitrant material substrate of physical being as he sought to model it in the image of the Forms.

Yet the desire to describe mathematically the behaviour of natural—physical—objects and phenomena did not always clash, even for Plato, and relations between mathematics and the physical world were studied throughout antiquity. Early evidence comes from the Pythagorean investigations into harmonics, but the idea that a mathematically describable order has left its imprint on at least some levels of creation was encouraged by Plato. In *Republic* 9, Plato prescribed a curriculum of physical subjects including astronomy, stereometry, and harmonics for the education of the Guardians of his ideal state, because their study shows that the perfect order of the Forms is reflected to some extent at least in the world around us.

3. Aristotle is the author of the earliest surviving detailed work bearing the title *Physics*. For him, *Physikē* is distinguished (e.g. at *Metaphysics* E 1, 1026[a]) from the abstract study of number and shape in *mathematika* (see MATHEMATICS) and from the science of divinity in *theologikē*. Physics involved going back to the first principles which underlie the phenomenal world of natural objects, and investigating their origins, number, behaviour, and interactions. The 'inquiry into nature' in Aristotle's view is the study of those things which do not exist independently of matter. It can thus be thought to include both the theoretical material contained in the *Physics* itself, the biological and zoological material in, for example, the *History of Animals*, what we might call the geophysical material in the *Meteorology*, along with the inherently more mathematical material of astronomy in *On the Heavens*.

In Aristotle's *Physics*, the first principles governing the behaviour of matter are investigated in great detail. The nature of physical existence, of weight, qualitative variety, different types of motion and their origins, the nature of purpose-directed activity and its sources are all examined. It is here that the four types of causal question necessary for a full account of something's existence are formulated—the formal, final, material, and efficient. Aristotelian ideas about motion—notably his statements implying that the velocity of falling objects is inversely proportional to the resistance they meet and directly proportional to their weight (see *Physics* 4. 8), which made velocity in a void undefinable—were famously criticized and developed by much later commentators, including *Simplicius and *Philoponus. Aristotle's successors as head of the Lyceum, *Theophrastus of Eresus and *Straton (1) of Lampsacus, continued to stress the importance of the types of physical inquiry initiated by their master.

4. It is widely believed that Aristotle's criticisms of early atomic physics (especially in *On Generation and Corruption*) led *Epicurus and his followers to modify Democritean atomism in a number of respects. The exact extent of Epicurean innovation is hard to gauge, partly because of our lack of evidence for Democritus' own theory, and partly because Epicurus himself acknowledges few positive debts to any predecessors. Driven by the need to find arguments to dissolve away fear, and especially fear of death, Epicurean physics centres on proving the existence of ungenerated and permanent forms of matter—atoms—whose unpredictable and unpremeditated motion in the void can explain all natural phenomena. The Epicureans developed new arguments to prove the possibility of indivisible atoms, explain their motion and combination, and found new language to describe void. The phenomena of sensation and action at a distance (magnetic attraction, for instance) are all explained in terms of influxes or effluxes of atoms moving across the void. Purpose-directed activity in the domain of natural phenomena, and the active intervention of divine power in human life for good or ill, are denied. The study of the physical world is of value only insofar as it aids in the search for peace of mind.

5. With ethics and logic, physics was one of the cornerstones of Stoic philosophy. Although there is doctrinal variation within *Stoicism on the level of detail, *Diogenes (6) Laertius (7. 132) reports that the Stoics divided physics into the study of the world, of the elements, and the inquiry into causes. Stoic physics is an essential part of the broad Stoic inquiry into our place in the universe, and into the divine and guiding active principle which permeates everything, designing and steering it. Unlike the Epicureans, but following Plato and Aristotle, the Stoics denied the possibility of void within the cosmos, and many of the more sophisticated explanations of action at a distance in a continuum can be laid at their door (see PNEUMA).

6. Mathematical—geometrical—models of the behaviour of physical bodies developed rapidly in *mechanics, and also in what Aristotle calls the more 'physical' branches of *mathematics or the more 'mathematical' branches of physics, such as *optics, *acoustics and *astronomy. (Mathematical geography, *statics and *hydrostatics might be added to Aristotle's list.) Quite apart from the mathematical sophistication of these ancient inquiries, the level of methodological controversy, particularly between empiricist and rationalist positions, is striking. In the Aristotelian corpus there is a treatise on mechanics, almost certainly not by Aristotle himself, which deals with the theory and practical uses of balances, pulleys, and levers. *Archimedes' theoretical work on the behaviour of basic mechanical elements is characteristic of the subsequent application of strict geometry to the practical explanation of physical contrivances. Archimedes' *On the Equilibrium of Planes* deals amongst other things with the problem of how to determine the centre of gravity in different types of figures. Other important ancient mechanical theoreticians include *Heron of Alexandria (*Mechanics*) and *Pappus of Alexandria (esp. the *Collectio*, bk. 8.)

7. A group of ancient writers dealt with applied as well as theoretical mechanics. Figures like *Ctesibius are little more than names to us, but Heron of Alexandria and *Philon (2) of Byzantium wrote elaborate works on the subject, Philo dealing with the theory and practice of machines of war, Hero with mechanical automata. (See PNEUMATICS.)

8. The physics of sight, light, and colour occupied both physiologists and mathematicians. Natural philosophers and physiologists offered theories to explain the mechanisms of visual perception (e.g. Plato, *Timaeus*, Aristotle *On the Soul* 2, and Theophrastus, *On the Senses*, which includes a review of earlier theories of sight). Theoretical debate focused on the nature of light—was it a type of wave, or a tension in the continuum (a Stoic view), or the transport of something through the atomists'

void? Geometrical optics was based on the assumption that light—or the visual ray—travels from the eye in straight lines. Systematic research into the behaviour of these lines begins (for us) with *Euclid's *Optics*, which also survives in a late version by *Theon (4) of Alexandria, but important treatises on optics were also composed by *Ptolemy (4), by Heron of Alexandria and an optician of the 4th cent. AD, Damianus (of Larissa?). *Geminus, quoted by *Proclus (*Commentary on Euclid's Elements* 1), divides optics into (a) the study of problems related to the perception of objects at a distance (including perspective), (b) *catoptrics, or the study of reflection and refraction, and (c) scenography, which dealt originally with the problem of representing in drawing and painting objects of different sizes and at different distances from the observer. In addition, dioptrics (the subject of a work by Heron of Alexandria) was concerned with the construction of optical instruments used to investigate all these phenomena.

9. 'Pythagoras had no faith in the human ear', reports *Boethius (*On Music* 1. 10). He sought instead fixed, mathematical ways of measuring consonances; the Pythagoreans were credited even in antiquity with the discovery of the connection between the length of a vibrating body and its pitch. Further work on the subject was done by the Pythagorean *Philolaus of Croton, and on the properties of vibrating bodies generally by *Archytas, Euclid, Ptolemy, and *Nicomachus (3). Aristotle deals with the physiology of sound, speech and hearing in *On the Soul*, and there is a spurious tract in the Aristotelian corpus entitled *On Things Heard*. Ancient harmonics was profoundly influenced by more general epistemological debates over how far the senses—the ear in this case—should be trusted over reason. There was also a long-running dispute over the fundamental nature of sound itself which mirrors in certain respects disagreements about the nature of light—is sound continuous, or discrete, to be analysed geometrically or arithmetically? The greatest ancient authority on harmonics is the Aristotelian physicist and musicologist *Aristoxenus, whose *Elements of Harmonics* provided the basis for most subsequent treatments of both mathematical and practical harmonics. See MUSIC.

TEXTS See entries for individual authors. A selection of the most important Epicurean and Stoic texts may be found in A. A. Long and D. N. Sedley, *The Hellenistic Philosophers*, 2 vols. (1987); the ancient evidence for Greek musical theory is now best consulted in A. D. Barker, *Greek Musical Writings*, 2 vols. (1984–9).

LITERATURE S. Sambursky, *The Physical World of the Greeks* (1956), *Physics of the Stoics* (1959), and *The Physical World of Late Antiquity* (1962); G. E. R. Lloyd, *The Revolutions of Wisdom* (1987), with full ref. to earlier work.   J. T. V.

physiognomy, the art of observing and making inferences from physical features of the body, was practised from *c.*1,500 BC (when it is mentioned in Mesopotamian handbooks on divination). A focus on personal character (and a reflection on the relation between physical and psychical facts) seems to be a Greek innovation. *Aristotle attempted to give an inductive basis to assertions of the interdependence of body and *soul (*An. Pr.* 70^{b}7); and the *Historia animalium* provided empirical evidence that corroborated early ideas about moral types among animals. In the first extant treatise on the subject, the *Physiognomonica* (a Peripatetic work of the 3rd cent. BC long attributed to Aristotle), the comparison with animal, racial and gender types presupposes that moral perfection is embodied in the (free) male Greek citizen. This treatise is the forerunner of a tradition embracing M. Antonius *Polemon (4) in the 2nd cent. AD and Adamantius in the 4th, as well as medieval and modern writers. As a sign-based form of

knowledge, physiognomy has been used in (and has drawn on) medicine, ethnography and astrology: *Posidonius (2) may have been the author of a description of mankind from a physiognomical viewpoint, and *Galen proposed a systematic conflation with the humoral theory (see HUMOURS). Physiognomical judgements were prized by orators because of their persuasive force; artists too were well versed in physiognomy. The key to the popularity of the discipline, and its semblance of scientific objectivity, lies in its claim to being a comprehensive interpretation of the human world. This was based on a rationalization of everyday intuitions, social prejudices, and folklore.

R. Förster, *Scriptores physiognomonici graeci et latini*, 2 vols. (1893): the principal (though incomplete) collection of texts and ancient references, with still valuable *Prolegomena*; J. Schmidt, *RE* 20 (1941), 'Physiognomik'; E. C. Evans, *Physiognomics in the Ancient World* (1969); J. André, *Traité de physiognomonie par un anonyme latin* (1981), has a useful introduction; G. Dagron in *Poikilia. Études offertes à Jean-Pierre Vernant* (1987); M. M. Sassi, *La scienza dell'uomo nella Grecia antica* (1988).   M. M. S.

Physiologus ('the Natural Scientist'), an exposition of the marvellous properties of some 50 animals, plants, and stones, with a Christian interpretation of each (e.g. the pelican, which kills its offspring then revives them after three days with its own blood, figures the salvation of mankind through the Crucifixion). Both place and date of composition are disputed: perhaps Syria, perhaps Egypt; perhaps as late as the 4th cent. AD, perhaps (more likely?) as early as the 2nd. In any event, the work draws heavily on earlier traditions of Greek natural historical writing, particularly that of the *paradoxographers, with their concentration on the marvellous in nature and on occult natural sympathies and antipathies. The *physiologus* of the title is not the (entirely anonymous) author, but the (equally anonymous) authority from whom he claims to derive his information; it is however unclear whether he drew on a single proximate source or on several. No neat separation of the entries into borrowed (pagan) 'information' and superimposed Christian interpretation is possible, as in many cases the 'information' has already been reshaped to fit its new context (e.g. in the highlighting of the number three, to allow reference to the Trinity and the three days of the Passion).

The work enjoyed extraordinary popularity in late antiquity and the Middle Ages. After the first version there were two subsequent (shorter) re-editions in Greek, between the 5th and the 11th cents. At least two, possibly three separate Latin translations were made, beginning perhaps as early as the 8th cent., and there were translations into Armenian, Georgian, Slavic, Syriac, Coptic, and Ethiopic. Illustrated versions were also produced. Via the Latin translation, it had a profound influence on medieval Bestiaries.

TEXT F. Sbordone (1936); D. Offermanns (1966); D. Kaimakis (1974). Eng. trans. M. Curley (1979).

STUDIES B. Perry, *RE* 20 (1941), 1074; M. Wellmann, *Philol.* Suppl. 22. 1 (1930); O. Seel, *Der Physiologus* (1960).   M. B. T.

physiology See ANATOMY AND PHYSIOLOGY.

physis (nature) as opp. **nomos* (3) (law, convention) See POLITICAL THEORY.

Phytalus, a hero associated with the sacred fig-tree at Laciadae in *Attica, he was said to have been taught the culture of *figs by *Demeter. His descendants purified *Theseus (see PURIFICATION, GREEK) after his shedding of blood on the road from *Troezen to

Athens, clearly a story legitimating certain sacral duties performed by the *genos Phytalidai.

Plut. *Thes.* 23; Paus. 1. 37. 2–4. Kearns, *Heroes of Attica*, 121.　　E. Ke.

Piazza Armerina, a hill-town of central southern *Sicily known to students of antiquity for the remains of the most sumptuously appointed Roman *villa so far discovered in the Roman empire; it lies in the Casale district, 5 km. (3 mi.) south-west of the modern town. The complex, covering 1.5 ha., consists of four parts: a triple-arched entrance with court beyond; the main heart of the residential villa grouped around a peristyled garden, with a large reception hall and the private living quarters opening off a 70-m.-long corridor; a banqueting suite to the south, set around another court; and an elaborate bath-suite. There are some 45 rooms in all; service quarters still await identification. The reception hall was paved in marble, the remaining rooms and corridors with *mosaic floors of varying quality, some geometric but the majority figured. All are likely to have been laid by mosaicists from North Africa, probably based in *Carthage. The columns were of polychrome marble, the walls for the most part frescoed. The date of construction falls within the first three decades of the 4th cent. AD. The owner must have been a wealthy member of the senatorial order who held magistracies at Rome—the assembling of animals for the games, and a chariot race in the Circus Maximus, are among the subjects depicted in the mosaics—but his identity has proved elusive. Various candidates have been proposed, including Q. Aradius Valerius Proculus and the Ceionii Rufii, but none convincingly. The earlier hypothesis, that the villa was an imperial residence for either *Maximian or his son *Maxentius, is now discredited. Other large and well-appointed 4th-cent. villas were discovered in the 1970s in Sicily, at Patti Marina on the north coast, and at Caddeddi on the Tellaro near Noto, but neither match the villa at Piazza Armerina for size or luxury.

B. Pace, *I mosaici di Piazza Armerina* (1955); G. V. Gentili, *La villa erculia di Piazza Armerina. I mosaici figurati* (1959); H. Kähler, *Die Villa des Maxentius bei Piazza Armerina* (1973); A. Carandini, A. Ricci, and M. De Vos, *Filosofiana. The Villa of Piazza Armerina* (1982); R. J. A. Wilson, *Piazza Armerina* (1983); *Opus* 2 (1983), 535–602; G. Rizza (ed.), *La villa romana del Casale di Piazza Armerina* (= *CronASA* 33) (1988).

R. J. A. W.

Picenum is situated east of the *Apennines in the mid-Adriatic region, the warlike iron-age inhabitants of which practised inhumation. The inscriptions in the area fall into two groups: northern, from Novilara, Fano, and Pesaro, and southern (the so-called 'Old Sabellic'), which, like the material culture of the region, has strong affinities with the opposite shores of the Adriatic. The extensive use of *amber from the *Orientalizing period onwards points in addition to commercial contact with the head of the Adriatic. The area was conquered by Rome in the early 3rd cent. BC. See PICUS; POMPEIUS MAGNUS (1), GNAEUS.

D. Lollini in *PCIA* 5 (1976), 107 ff.; E. T. Salmon, *The Making of Roman Italy* (1982).　　D. W. R. R.

Picus, king of pre-Roman *Latium, son of *Saturnus, and father of *Faunus (Verg. *Aen.* 7. 47–9, 171; cf. Festus 228, 288 Lindsay), later transformed into a woodpecker (*picus*) by a jealous *Circe (*Aen.* 7. 189–91, Ov. *Met.* 14. 308–415 with Bömer's notes) which afterwards appeared in a dream to Rhea Silvia (Ov. *Fast.* 3. 37; see ROMULUS and REMUS) and brought food to the Twins (Plut. *Quaest. Rom.* 21). *Ovid's account utilized *Aemilius Macer's *Ornithogonia* (fr. 1 Morel with Courtney, *FLP* 293) which relied

on Boeus' (Boeo?) account (Hollis' introduction on Ov. *Met.* 8. 236–59; Courtney 294); thus Italic traditions are conflated with *Alexandrian.

Q. *Fabius Pictor (fr. 3 Peter) knew the woodpecker as *Mars' bird (*picus Martius*) while *Valerius Antias (fr. 6 Peter) knows Picus as a king, thus indicating early variability of the human/bird traditions. Further, some felt the Picentes (inhabitants of *Picenum) were descended from Picus, although this probably relies on folk etymologies: *RE* 20. 1189, Latte, *RR* 51 n. 4, J. Bremmer, *BICS Suppl.* 52 (1987), 31. The *Picus Martius* (Roscher, *Lex.* 2. 2430–1) was clearly associated with prophecy (Festus 214 Lindsay) and according to Ovid (*Fast.* 3. 291–4) had to be bound, a prophetic commonplace: Hom. *Od.* 4. 410–60, Verg. *Ecl.* 6. 19, *G.* 4. 405. The *Tabulae Iguvinae (Vb8–18; cf. VIaI) name spelt to be drawn from fields sacred to it, and augural Picus may be reflected in the names of St Picentia (R. Palmer, *The Archaic Community of the Romans* (1970), 103) and Tiora Matiene or Martiana (Palmer, *Roman Religion and Roman Empire* (1974), 93–4). These many conflations make certainty impossible; cf. Wissowa, *Ges. Abh.* 137–9.

RE 20. 1214–18; *Kleine Pauly* 4. 847; Roscher, *Lex.* 3. 2494–6; Wissowa, *RK* 66, 212, 244 n. 3. L. Preller, *Römische Mythologie*² (1865), 331–4; U. Scholz, *Studien zum altitalischen und altrömischen Marskult und Marsmythos* (1970), 50 n. 4, 113–14.　　C. R. P.

pietas is the typical Roman attitude of dutiful respect towards gods, fatherland, and parents and other kinsmen (Cic. *Nat. D.* 1. 116: '*pietas* is justice towards the gods'; Cic. *Inv. Rhet.* 2. 66: 'religion is the term applied to the fear (*metus*) and worship (*caerimonia*) of the gods. *Pietas* warns us to keep our obligations to our country or parents or other kin'). Pietas, personified, received a temple in Rome (vowed 191 BC, dedicated 181; Livy 40. 34. 4; cf. Festus 228, 28 Lindsay); it was destroyed in 44 BC. See Richardson, *Topogr. Dict. Anc. Rome*, 290). She is often represented in human form, sometimes attended by a stork, symbol of filial piety; during the empire, Pietas Augusta appears on coins and in inscriptions. Some Romans adopted as cognomen the term Pius; *Virgil's 'Pius *Aeneas' significantly expresses the Roman ideal in his religious attitude, in his patriotic mission, and in his relations with father, son, and comrades. The decision to construct an Ara Pietatis Augustae was taken in AD 43 (M. Torelli, *Typology and Structure of Roman Historical Reliefs* (1982), 63 ff.). See RELIGION, ROMAN, TERMS RELATING TO.

Latte, *RR* 238.　　W. C. G.; J. Sch.

Pietrabbondante, a cult centre of the Pentri Samnites (see SAMNIUM), in the Abruzzi mountains of Molise. It has been quite erroneously identified as *Bovianum Vetus, and lies close to the citadel site of Monte Saraceno, with defences of the 4th cent. BC. The sanctuary, which has commanding views, was established in the 3rd cent. BC, and was apparently destroyed by *Hannibal. A small Ionic temple was then built. An inscription in *Oscan mentions *Samnium, suggesting that it was a national shrine; another records a *meddix tuticus (chief magistrate of the Samnites), Cn. Staiis Stafidins. Between c.120 and 90 BC, a second much larger temple, of Latian form, and a Hellenistic-type theatre, were added to the sanctuary. It went out of use, however, at the end of the *Social War (3), although the site was frequented down into the 4th cent. AD.

M. J. Strazzulla and B. di Marco, *Il santuario sannitico di Pietrabbondante* (1971). A. La Regina in *Hellenismus in Mittelitalien* (1976), 219 ff., and *Sannio. Pentri e Frentari dal VI al I sec. A.C.* (1980), 131 ff.; S. Capini and A. Di Niro, *Samnium* (1991), 113 ff.　　T. W. P.

piety See INTOLERANCE, INTELLECTUAL AND RELIGIOUS (for action against impiety); PIETAS; PRAYER; RELIGION (various entries); RITUAL; SACRIFICE.

Pigres, Carian poet; brother of *Artemisia (1); said to have interpolated pentameters into *Homer's *Iliad*, and to have written the *Margites*.

EGF 65.   S. H.

pilgrimage (Christian) Despite the New Testament's disavowal of the localized cults of Judaism and the surrounding pagan world—the need was for holy lives rather than holy places—early Christians still clung to their sacred sites. Jesus' followers preserved some memory of the location of his tomb in *Jerusalem and (at least by the mid-2nd cent.) of his birthplace in Bethlehem; while further afield the burial places of martyrs on the outskirts of their cities attracted local gatherings. In maintaining these recollections of their sacred past, the first Christian pilgrims tried to assert some communal identity in a world indifferent or hostile to their faith.

As the first emperor to favour Christianity, *Constantine I actively promoted holy places through imperial church-building in the Holy Land, as well as at the shrines of Peter and *Paul and other Roman martyrs; and his mother Helena Augusta personified the official interest in sacred sites by visiting Palestine as part of a tour of the eastern provinces (c. AD 327). Pilgrimages to the Holy Land were no longer just a local preserve, but might bring travellers from the opposite end of the empire. The earliest such journey on record is that of an unknown pilgrim from Bordeaux, who reached Jerusalem in 333: the surviving document is both a 'secular' itinerary of the route and the account of a pilgrimage round the biblical sites of the Holy Land. The religious significance attached not to the journey itself, but to its objective of locating and—with the aid of the 'eyes of faith' and a very literal reading of the text—entering into the scriptural past of both Old and New Testaments.

In 381–4 the western pilgrim Egeria journeyed round the Holy Land and Egypt (see ITINERARIUM EGERIAE). Besides visiting martyr-shrines *en route*, she endeavoured to search out 'on the ground' the places of the Bible, attempting e.g. to retrace the movements of the children of Israel out of Egypt. Holy men were as much an object of pilgrimage for her as holy places: the monks who now populated the region formed part of Egeria's scriptural landscape, perceived as successors of the Holy Land's biblical occupants. These 4th-cent. Christian travellers engaged in a species of devotional *tourism which had eyes only for the biblical past re-created in the contemporary Holy Land. The many other associations of pilgrimage—ascetic (see ASCETICISM), therapeutic, penitential—would emerge only later.

J. Wilkinson, *Egeria's Travels* (rev. edn. 1981); E. D. Hunt, *Holy Land Pilgrimage in the Later Roman Empire AD 312–460* (1982); P. Maraval, *Lieux saints et pèlerinages d'Orient* (1985); R. Ousterhout (ed.), *The Blessings of Pilgrimage* (1990).   E. D. H.

Pindar, lyric poet, native of Cynoscephalae in *Boeotia. He was born probably in 518 BC (*Suda*, fr. 193, if the latter refers to Pindar). The tradition (one of several competing accounts) that he lived to the age of eighty is at least roughly correct, since his last datable composition (*Pyth.* 8) belongs in or shortly after 446. On the basis of *Pyth.* 5. 72 it is widely believed that he belonged to the aristocratic family of the Aegeidae. He achieved panhellenic recognition early; at the age of 20 he was commissioned by the ruling family of *Thessaly to celebrate the athletic victory of a favourite youth, Hippocleas (*Pyth.* 10). His commissions covered most of the Greek world, from *Macedonia and *Abdera in Thrace in the north (fr. 120–1, *Pae.* 2) to *Cyrene in Africa in the south (*Pyth.* 4, 5, 9), from *Italy and *Sicily in the west (*Ol.* 1–5, 10, 11, *Pyth.* 1, 2, 3, 6, *Nem.* 9, *Isthm.* 2) to the seaboard of *Asia Minor in the east (*Ol.* 7, *Nem.* 11, fr. 123). He probably travelled a great deal, but we have little information on his movements. He is already a classic for *Herodotus (1) (3. 38), and was regarded by many in antiquity as the greatest of the nine poets of the lyric canon (Quint. 10. 1. 61, Dion. Hal. *On imitation* 2).

The *Alexandrian editors divided Pindar's works into 17 books: *hymns, *paeans, *dithyrambs (2 books), *prosodia* (processional songs, 2 books), *partheneia* (maiden-songs, 3 books), *hyporchemata* (dance songs, 2 books), encomia, *threnoi* (dirges) and *epinicia* (victory songs, 4 books). Of these, the only books to survive intact are the choral victory songs composed for the formal celebration of victories in the four panhellenic athletic festivals (see AGONES). His patrons were the great aristocratic houses of the day, and the ruling families of Cyrene, *Syracuse and *Acragas. The scale of this section of the corpus indicates the value which Pindar, in common with other Greeks, placed on *athletics as a testing ground for the highest human qualities. The victory ode was normally performed either at the athletic festival shortly after the victory or after the victor's return to his native city. Since time for composition and choir training was limited, the former type tends to be brief. Odes composed for performance after the victor's return are usually, though not invariably, lengthier and more elaborate. The longer odes usually have three sections, with the opening and closing sections devoted to the victor and his success and the central section usually containing a mythic narrative. The opening is always striking, often elaborate, consisting either of an abrupt announcement of victory or a focusing process which sets the victory against a general background, usually through a hymnal invocation or a preparatory list of objects, experiences, or achievements (*priamel). In the sections devoted to the victor conventional elements recur. The god of the games is honoured. Place of victory and event are announced, with details frequently surrendered slowly in order to maintain a forward tension (description of victory is rare, however). Earlier victories by the patron or other members of his family are listed; such lists are carefully crafted to avoid monotony. The city is praised, and in the case of boy victors the father and usually the trainer. Self-praise by the poet is also common. More sombre notes, surprising to the modern reader, are struck. The poet often reminds the victor of his mortality or offers prayers to avert misfortune; these elements reflect the archaic fear of divine envy and awareness of the psychological dangers of success; they function both to warn and to emphasize the extent of the achievement. *Gnomai* (succinct generalizations, see GNŌMĒ) are frequent. Recurrent themes are the impossibility of achievement without toil, the need for divine aid for success, the duty to praise victory, the vulnerability of achievement without praise in song, the importance of inborn excellence and the inadequacy of mere learning. The effect of this moralizing is to give the ode a pronounced didactic as well as celebratory quality.

Pindar usually chooses myths dealing with the heroes of the victor's city. As with most Greek *lyric, the myth is not narrated in full. Usually a single incident is selected for narration, with other details dealt with briskly. Even the lengthy quasi-epic myth of *Pyth.* 4 proceeds by a series of scenes, not an even narrative. Audience familiarity with the myth is assumed. Unlike his contemporary *Bacchylides, Pindar regularly adopts an explicit

1183

moral stance with reference to the events narrated. The role of myth in the odes varies. Sometimes the myth has only a broad relevance to the victor, in that the deeds of the city's heroes highlight the tradition which has produced the victor's qualities. On occasion myth presents a negative contrast to the victor (such as the *Tantalus myth in *Ol.* 1, the *Orestes myth of *Pyth.* 11). Often it appears to reflect an aspect of the victory or the victor's situation as developed in the direct praise.

The fragmentary nature of the rest of the corpus makes it difficult to generalize about other genres. The same moralizing quality is present. The structure where ascertainable corresponds to the tripartite structure of the victory odes. The myth is in most cases uncontroversial, since it arises from the location and occasion of the performance.

His poems are written in regular stanzas, either strophic or triadic. With the exception of *Isthm.* 3 and 4, no two poems are identical metrically. Most are composed in the dactylo-epitrite or aeolic metres. His manner of writing is both dense and elaborate. Words are used sparingly. Compound adjectives abound. The style is rich in *metaphor, and rapid shifts of metaphor are common. Transition between themes is rapid, and is often effected by formalized claims to be constrained by time or rules of composition or to have lost the way. As his earliest and last datable compositions (*Pyth.* 10 and 8) show, he adhered throughout his life to a conservative set of standards. His thought impresses not for its originality but the consistency and conviction with which he presents the world view of the aristocrat of the late Archaic period. His religion is the traditional Olympian religion (see RELIGION, GREEK), combined in *Ol.* 2 and the dirges with elements of mystery cult and Orphico-Pythagorean belief (see ORPHISM; PYTHAGORAS (1), PYTHAGOREANISM).

TEXT H. Maehler, *Pindari Carmina cum Fragmentis* (1987, 1989).
TRANSLATION F. Nisetich, *Pindar's Victory Odes* (1980).
COMMENTARIES AND CRITICISM G. Bona, *I Peani* (1988); E. L. Bundy, *Studia Pindarica* (1962); R. W. B. Burton, *Pindar's Pythian Odes* (1962); J. B. Bury, *Nemean Odes* (1890), and *Isthmian Odes* (1892); M. Cannatà Fera, *Threnorum Fragmenta* (1990); F. Dornseiff, *Pindars Stil* (1921); C. Carey, *A Commentary on Five Odes of Pindar* (1981); L. R. Farnell (1932); B. L. Gildersleeve, *Olympian and Pythian Odes*² (1890); E. Krummen, *Pyrsos Hymnon* (1990); S. Lavecchia, *Dithyramborum Fragmenta* (2000); L. Lehnus, *Olimpiche*² (1989), C. A. Privitera, *Le Istmiche* (1982); I. Rutherford, *Pindar's Paeans* (2001); E. Thummer, *Die isthmischen Gedichte* (1968–9); W. H. Race, *Pindar* (1986); M. J. H. van der Weiden, *The Dithyrambs* (1991); D. C. Young, *Three Odes of Pindar* (1968); *RE* 20. 1606 ff.; L. Kurke, *The Traffic in Praise* (1991).   C. C.

Pindarus, named in some manuscripts as the author of the *Ilias Latina*, perhaps arising from confusion in transmission with *Dares of Phrygia.

M. Scaffai, *Latomus*, 1979, 932–9.   S. J. Ha.

piracy can be defined as armed robbery involving the use of ships. The greater mobility which the sea provides is a major factor in differentiating between piracy and *brigandage, although the Greek and Latin vocabulary for the two was largely the same. It is often very difficult to distinguish piracy from warfare in the ancient sources, especially when the labelling of certain activities as piracy seems to be a way of illegitimizing the perpetrators, similar in some ways to the modern practice of describing political violence as terrorism.

The earliest references to pirates are in the Homeric poems (see HOMER), particularly the *Odyssey*, where piracy is an activity which brings no shame upon its practitioners, although it may be disapproved of for the misery it brings to the victims (e.g. Hom. *Od.* 3. 71–4; 14. 222–34). None of the Homeric heroes is ever called a pirate, but they carry out seaborne raids which are very similar to the actions of those referred to as pirates (e.g. *Od.* 9. 39–52).

Piracy begins to be differentiated from war in the Classical period of Greek history, when the political aims of the Greek city-states began to take precedence over the economic goals of raiding and plundering. Nevertheless, pirates are mentioned frequently by *Thucydides (2) and *Xenophon (1) in their accounts of the wars of the 5th and 4th cents. BC, and the works of the Attic orators show that accusations of piracy were made by both sides in the rivalries between Athens and *Macedonia in the second half of the 4th cent. BC.

In the Hellenistic period the main difference between piracy and warfare was the scale of activity. Many pirates operated on the fringes of wars in this period, taking advantage of the political confusion, but they do not seem to have played a major part in the conflicts of the Hellenistic monarchs. Although attacks on ships at sea are mentioned occasionally in the ancient sources, the main threat from piracy seems to have been to coastal settlements. Numerous inscriptions from this period record sudden attacks by unidentified pirates on the islands and coastal cities of the Aegean, in search of both plunder and prisoners to be ransomed or sold. The abduction of a well-born young man or woman by pirates who sell their captive as a slave (see SLAVERY) became a common theme in Greek and Latin literature.

The custom of plundering enemies, or even third parties, in reprisal for injuries or insults suffered could be used by some groups to justify acts which others might have called piracy. A great deal of the piracy found in sources from the 5th to the 2nd cents. BC involves reprisals (see SYLE). The rules governing reprisals were rather vague, allowing considerable latitude for interpretation. *Polybius (1) criticized the *Aetolians in particular for their abuse of this custom (Polyb. 4. 3–6; see AETOLIA). Cities and communities attempted to deter attacks by concluding treaties which guaranteed them immunity from reprisals, but it is unclear how effective this system was in practice. See ASYLIA.

Thucydides credited *Minos with clearing the seas of pirates (Thuc. 1. 4), but, until the 1st cent. BC, no ancient state possessed the resources to suppress piracy on anything more than a local scale, although even small successes might win fulsome praise and help to legitimize political power. A significant problem was the fact that successful suppression of piracy meant depriving pirates of bases on land, which entailed the conquest and control of territory. Without co-operation between states, or the imposition of a policy by a single imperial power, piracy could easily flourish in many parts of the Mediterranean. The Athenians took some action to limit piracy in their own interests in the 5th and 4th cents. BC, as did the Rhodians (see RHODES) in the Hellenistic period. Both were strongly applauded by later writers. The rise of Roman power in the Mediterranean was accompanied by a gradual realization that the Romans should take a stand against those perceived as pirates, but little action had been taken by the 2nd cent. BC, when pirates based in *Cilicia began to cause serious problems in the E. Mediterranean.

The attitude of the Romans towards piracy in the Mediterranean seems to have changed towards the end of the 2nd cent. BC. The campaign of Marcus *Antonius (1) in Cilicia in 102 was specifically directed against pirates, and a law of 100 BC concerning praetorian provinces enjoins all Rome's allies and friends to assist in the suppression of piracy. See LEX (2), Lex de provinciis praetoriis. Further campaigns by Roman magistrates in the 70s and 60s BC, most famously that of *Pompey in 67, reduced the areas from which pirates were able to operate, but piracy remained a problem at the start of Augustus' reign. It was only after the Roman emperors had secured control of the entire coastline of the Mediterranean that they were able to reduce piracy to a minimum, through the use of their powerful army and navy.

Piracy was thus largely confined to the margins of the Roman empire with some strong incursions by *barbarian tribes in the second half of the 3rd cent. AD. When the empire began to break up in the 5th cent. AD, however, piracy again became a serious problem, especially when the *Vandals seized *Carthage and used it as a base for their own plundering raids. The Muslim conquests of the 7th cent. were followed by a widespread resurgence of piracy in the Mediterranean. See BRIGANDAGE; NAVIES; SEA POWER; SLAVERY; SYLĒ.

P. de Souza in A. Powell (ed.), *The Greek World* (1995), 179–98; D. C. Braund in J. Rich and G. Shipley (eds.), *War and Society in the Roman World* (1993); P. Brulé, *La Piraterie crétoise hellénistique* (1978); A. H. Jackson, in M. R. D. Foot (ed.), *War and Society* (1973); H. A. Ormerod, *Piracy in the Ancient World* (1924). P. de S.

Piraeus (Πειραιεύς), the great harbour complex of Athens, is a rocky limestone peninsula some 7 km. (4–5 mi.) south-west of Athens which *Themistocles began to fortify in 493/2 (Thuc. 1. 93. 3–7) as a strong base for Athens' rapidly expanding fleet in preference to the open roadstead of *Phaleron. It has three harbours, Zea (modern Pasalimani) and *Munichia (1) (Mikrolimani) on the east, used exclusively by naval shipping. Zea possessed 196 shipsheds and *Philon (1)'s Arsenal. The biggest harbour, Kantharos (Goblet) or Megas Limen (Great Harbour), lies to the west and accommodated, in addition to warships, a thriving emporium on its northern and eastern shoreline comprising 'five stoas round about the harbour' (schol. to Ar. *Pax* 145), of which some traces remain. Its urban development dates to c.450 BC when *Hippodamus of Miletus 'cut up' (κατένεμε) Piraeus' by laying it out according to an orthogonal plan (Arist. *Pol.* 2. 1267ᵇ23). The presence of a very large number of *metics led to the establishment of many foreign cults here, including *Bendis, *Isis, *Men, Mother of the Gods (see CYBELE), and Nergal. In 458/7 Piraeus was joined to Athens by *Long Walls and in c.446 the building of the Middle Wall eliminated Phaleron from the fortified area. In 429 moles were constructed on either side of each harbour's mouth which could be closed by chains in time of war. The fortifications were destroyed by the Spartans in 404 but rebuilt by *Conon (1) in 393. Though the port revived in the mid-4th cent. BC, it never became more than the ghost of its former Periclean self (see PERICLES (1)). During the Macedonian occupation (322–229 (see ATHENS, *History*)) it rapidly lost its pre-eminence as the trading capital of the eastern Mediterranean and its population dwindled accordingly. To this period, however, dates the well-preserved theatre in Zea. *Sulla's destruction of the town in 86 was so ruthless that little was visible to *Pausanias (3) (1.1.2–5) when he visited it in the 2nd cent. AD. Several important bronze statues, including those of *Apollo, *Artemis, and *Athena, which were deliberately buried at the time to escape destruction, came to light in 1959. As headquarters of the fleet, Piraeus constituted the heartland of Athenian *democracy and was the focus of the resistance to the *Thirty Tyrants, thereby justifying *Aristotle's claim that its population was 'more democratic' (μᾶλλον δημοτικοί) than that of Athens' (*Pol.* 5. 1303ᵇ10–12). There are few traces of the city visible today, apart from extensive portions of the circuit walls, Zea theatre, and a few shipsheds.

R. Garland, *The Piraeus* (1987); J. Travlos, *Bildlexikon zur Topographie des antiken Attika* (1988), 340 ff. R. S. J. G.

Pirithous (Π(ε)ιρίθοος or -θους), in mythology, a Lapith (see CENTAURS), son by *Zeus of *Ixion's wife Dia (*Il.* 14. 317–18; Pherecydes in schol. Ap. Rhod. 3. 62). *Homer knows of him as fighting the *Centaurs (*Il.* 1. 263 ff.), presumably in the quarrel mentioned in *Od.* 21. 295 ff., and a doubtfully genuine verse (*Od.* 11. 631) mentions him in Hades. In the first and last of these passages he is associated with *Theseus, whose close friend he is in later authors. Hence, as our mythological tradition is largely Attic (see ATTIC CULTS AND MYTHS), he tends to appear as little more than the pendant of his friend. He is actually an Athenian in schol. *Il.* 1. 263.

One of the few adventures which are his rather than Theseus' is his wedding-feast. Marrying *Hippodamia, daughter of *Boutes (*Il.* 2. 742 and schol. on 1. 263), he forgot, according to one account, to include *Ares among his guests (Servius on *Aen.* 7. 304). For that or some other reason (the simplest is that they were very drunk, cf. *Od.* 21. 295, where one Centaur is responsible for the disturbance) the Centaurs abused his hospitality by offering violence to Hippodamia, and a great fight began (Ov. *Met.* 12. 210 ff.; the earlier accounts of a story which the *Olympia pediments and *Parthenon metopes show to have been well known in the 5th cent., if not before, have not survived), ending in the victory of the Lapiths.

For the rest, Pirithous took his share in the carrying off of *Helen, the war against the *Amazons, and finally Theseus' descent to *Hades, which, indeed, in one account (Hyg. *Fab.* 79. 2) was undertaken to get *Persephone as wife for Pirithous, in return for his services in the matter of Helen. Theseus in most accounts escapes; Pirithous generally does not (but cf. Hyg. ibid. 3).

The fight of Lapiths and Centaurs appears in early archaic art (François vase and elsewhere) as a pitched battle in armour. The brawl at the feast first appears in the early classical period, in Attic vase-painting, and the West pediment of the Temple of *Zeus at Olympia; no doubt also in the picture in the Theseum at Athens probably by *Micon. Pirithous is also shown aiding Theseus to abduct Helen, pictured from the mid-6th cent. Theseus and Pirithous were shown in the Underworld by *Polygnotus, and in a few surviving works from the mid-5th cent. on.

LIMC 7. 1 (1994), 232–42. H. J. R.; C. M. R.; A. H. G.

Pisa was the district round *Olympia. Opinions are divided whether there was ever a town of this name; some have suggested that it is represented by a site at Frangonisi (*BSA, Arch. Rep.* 1959–60, 11). The Pisatans were in early times a power independent of the Eleans. After *Pheidon's usurpation of the *Olympian Games (668 BC) they held the presidency until c.580, under the tyranny of the house of Pantaleon. Their claim was revived by the Arcadians in 364 (Xen. *Hell.* 7. 4. 28; see ARCADIA). See ELIS; OLYMPIA.

A. Andrewes, *The Greek Tyrants* (1956), 62 f.; H. Berve, *Die Tyrannis bei den Griechen* (1967), 1. 35; J. Roy, *CAH* 6² (1994), 204 f. (giving refs. to inscriptions). T. J. D.; R. J. H.

Pisae (mod. Pisa), on the Arno. Quite possibly a *Ligurian settlement, it was by the 5th cent. BC an important *Etruscan town and port. It is first mentioned in 225 BC, when the Romans used the harbour (Polyb. 2. 16 f.; Livy 21. 39) against the Ligurians. They were defeated by c.177, when nearby *Luna was made a colony (see COLONIZATION, ROMAN), although one did not materialize at Pisa (Livy 33. 43; 40. 43). It did however become a colony in Augustan times, and was a prosperous town, if seldom mentioned. Traces of a theatre, amphitheatre, baths, and a temple of *Vesta survive, and there are important museum collections.

N. Toscanelli, *Pisa nell'antichità* (1933–4); A. C. Gabba, *Camposanto monumentale di Pisa. Le antichità* (1977); M. Pasquinucci and S. Storti, *Pisa antica* (1989).　　　　　　　　　　　　E. T. S.; T. W. P.

Pisander (Πείσανδρος) (1) of *Camirus in Rhodes (7th or 6th cent. BC), author of the oldest *epic about *Heracles known to the *Alexandrians, in two books. The ascription of other poems to him was disputed.

M. Davies, *Epicorum Graecorum Fragmenta* (1988), 129 ff.; Bernabé, *PEG*, 1. 164 ff.; G. L. Huxley, *Greek Epic Poetry* (1969), 100–5.　　M. L. W.

Pisander (2), Athenian politician, often attacked in comedy for corruption and cowardice, and ridiculed for his fatness (see COMEDY (GREEK), OLD). As an apparent democrat he took a principal part in the investigation into the mutilation of the *herms (415 BC), but in 412 he showed still more energy in organizing the oligarchic revolution (see OLIGARCHY): he travelled between *Samos and Athens, and seems to have been the author of the motion which brought the régime of the *Four Hundred into being. On the fall of that régime he fled to the Spartans and was condemned in his absence for treason.

PA 11170. A. G. Woodhead, *AJPhil.* 1954, 131–46; Andrewes, *HCT* 5 (1981), 116–17.　　　　　　　　　　A. W. G.; A. A.; P. J. R.

Pisander (3) of Laranda (early 3rd cent. AD) wrote a comprehensive epic on world history in 60 books, the Ἡρωικαὶ θεογαμίαι, *Heroic Marriages of the Gods*. See SEPTIMIUS NESTOR.

Keydell, *RE* 19. 145–6, and *Hermes*, 1935, 301–11; Heitsch, *Die griechischen Dichterfragmente der römischen Kaiserzeit* (1964), 2. 44–7.　　R. L. H.

Pisidia, a mountainous region of southern Asia Minor which extended from the Pamphylian plain (see PAMPHYLIA) to lakes Burdur, Eğridir, and Beyşehir. Protected by difficult terrain the inhabitants of its strongly fortified cities were able to maintain their independence from the Persians and were never effectively controlled by any of the Hellenistic kings. In the late republic Rome preferred to strike deals with individual cities rather than to exercise direct control; *Amyntas (2) the Galatian was made king of Pisidia in 36 BC but the area was not thoroughly controlled until it had been included in the province of *Galatia. To maintain security Augustus founded a group of 'Pisidian' colonies in and around the region, including *Antioch (2), Cremna, Olbasa, and Comama, and built a new military road through the region, the *via Sebaste. The most important cities of the Hellenistic period were Termessus, Selge, and Sagalassus; they and smaller centres such as Pednelissus, Adada, Ariassus, Etenna, and Cremna were throughly Hellenized (see HELLENISM, HELLENIZATION), although native cults and the Pisidian language (which was carried west to the Cibyratis by Pisidian settlers in the Hellenistic period, Strabo 13. 4. 17, 631) persisted in the country districts until the late empire. The cities, above all Sagalassus, the metropolis, and the colony at Cremna prospered and grew under Roman rule. See LEX (2), Lex Antonia de Termessibus.

H. von Aulock, *Städte und Münzen Pisidiens*, 1 and 2 (1978, 1980); G. E. Bean, *Anat. Stud.* 1959 and 1960; B. Levick, *Roman Colonies in Southern Asia Minor* (1967); S. Mitchell, *Mediterranean Archaeology*, 1991, 119–45; E. Schwertheim (ed.), *Forschungen in Pisidien, Asia-Minor-Studien* 6 (1992); H. Brandt, *Gesellschaft und Wirtschaft Pamphyliens und Pisidiens*

in Altertum, Asia-Minor-Studien 7 (1992); S. Mitchell, *Anatolia*, 2 vols. (1993); S. Mitchell and J. Nollé, *Pisidien. Antike Welt Sonderheft* (forthcoming).　　　　　　　　　　　　　　　S. M.

Pisistratus (Πεισίστρατος), tyrant of Athens (see TYRANNY), claimed descent from the Neleids (see NELEUS) of *Pylos and Pisistratus, archon (see ARCHONTES) at Athens 669/8 BC. He first came to prominence through his success in the war against *Megara (c.565). In a period of aristocratic faction between Lycurgus and the *Pedieis* (party 'of the Plain') and *Megacles and *Paralioi* (coast party), he created a third faction, the *Hyperakrioi* or *Diakrioi* (referring to 'hill country', probably NE *Attica: the factions probably reflect regional bases of support, Hdt. 1. 59). He first seized power with the bodyguard granted him by the Athenians (c.560). Ousted by the other two factions, he returned again with Megacles' allegiance and, if we can extract anything from the ruse in *Herodotus (1) (1. 60), a claim to the protection of *Athena. However the *Alcmaeonid alliance disintegrated and he went into a 10-year exile, settling Rhaecelus in *Macedonia, mustering support from *Eretria, other cities (e.g. *Thebes (1)) and from the mines of Mt. *Pangaeus (*Ath. Pol.* 15; Hdt. 1. 64). Armed with money and Argive *mercenaries (see ARGOS (2)), he landed near *Marathon, c.546, defeated opposition at the battle of Pallene, and established the tyranny for 36 years. He died in 527.

Sources agree that Pisistratus' rule, financed by a 5 per cent tax and perhaps family resources from the Strymon area (see THRACE), was benevolent and law-abiding: (esp. Thuc. 6. 54; a 'golden age', *Ath. Pol.* 16. 7). Despite the mention of exiles (Hdt. 1. 64), he seems to have achieved a *modus vivendi* with other aristocratic families (who are later found holding archonships: see HIPPIAS (1)). Strained relations with the Philaids may have been eased by *Miltiades' colonization of the *Chersonesus (1) (Hdt. 6. 34–41), whose strategic importance suggests it had Pisistratus' blessing. Athenian interests were strengthened by Pisistratus' control of *Naxos (1) (Hdt. 1. 64), and recapture of *Sigeum, foreshadowing Athens' later maritime expansion. He lent money to poor farmers and instituted travelling judges (*Ath. Pol.* 16).

From the 560s, Athens begins to acquire a monumental appearance and become a *panhellenic artistic centre (Herington). The archaeological record indicates rapidly increasing prosperity, as Attic black figure becomes (from the 560s) the dominant exported pottery. How much can be linked to Pisistratus' personal efforts, rather than to the indirect effects of internal peace and external expansion, is uncertain and controversial, and purely archaeological evidence is inconclusive. The *Panathenaea, reorganized in 566/5, and City *Dionysia prospered, but Pisistratus cannot securely be credited with establishing the former, nor erecting the (so-called 'old') temple of Athena on the Acropolis built about the same time. The beginning of Athenian *coinage, attested archaeologically by 550, might imply the ruler's support. It is likely, however, that, like other archaic aristocrats, he used religious cult to consolidate his position (Davies *APF* pp. 454–5; Lewis) or enhance *polis cohesion; and that he was a great builder, like his sons. He purified the *Ionian religious centre of *Delos and instituted a festival there (Thuc. 3. 104). Other cults to Apollo were probably fostered by him in Athens, that of Pythian *Apollo and (perhaps) Apollo Patroos (first temple built, in the Agora, c.550); and perhaps other cults (see Shapiro). It has been suggested, purely on pottery evidence, that he claimed special association with *Heracles (Boardman) as well as Athena's protection. Of secular buildings, as well as the

Placentia

Enneakrounos fountain-house (Paus. 1. 14. 1), he can probably be associated with other building in the Agora in the third quarter of the 6th cent., including the Stoa Basileios and the mysterious 'Building F': in short with the further clearing of the Agora and its development as civic centre. (See ATHENS, TOPOGRAPHY; HIPPIAS (1); HIPPARCHUS (1); IMAGERY; PROPAGANDA).

Hdt. 1. 59–64; Thuc. 6. 54–5; *Ath. Pol.* 13–17. A. Andrewes, *CAH* 3².3 (1982), ch. 44; H. Shapiro, *Art and Cult under the Tyrants in Athens* (1989); P. J. Rhodes, *Phoenix* 1976, 219 ff., for chronology; J. S. Boersma, *Athenian Building Policy from 561/0 to 405/4 BC* (1970); J. Boardman, *Rev. Arch.* 1972, 57 ff.; D. Lewis, *Hist.* 1963, 22 ff.; T. L. Shear, in *Athens Comes of Age: From Solon to Salamis* (Sympos., Princeton, 1978), 1 ff.; J. Herington, *Poetry into Drama* (1985), ch. 4; Parker, *ARH* ch. 6.   R. T.

Pithecusae (Pithekoussai), modern Ischia (Aenaria; Inarime at Verg. *Aen.* 9. 715 f. and in other poets), the largest island in the Bay of Naples (see NEAPOLIS) and the site of the first and most northerly Greek establishment in the west. See COLONIZATION, GREEK. The acropolis, Monte di Vico (Lacco Ameno), was in continuous use between the mid-8th and the 1st cents. BC; traces of earlier indigenous Apennine bronze age settlement have been found there and elsewhere on the island, and more particularly on the neighbouring islet of Vivara, where there had also been a substantial Mycenaean presence (see MYCENAEAN CIVILIZATION). An *emporion* rather than an *apoikia*, Pithecusae was settled by Chalcidians and Eretrians (Strabo 5. 4. 9). Throughout the second half of the 8th cent. it served as a large and vital 'pre-colonial' staging post—with a stable population numbered in thousands—at the western end of the route from the Aegean and the Levant. The suburban industrial complex (Mezzavia) has yielded abundant evidence for early metallurgical production; competent local versions of Euboean Late Geometric pottery were produced en masse, and expatriate Protocorinthian potters were also active. The graves excavated (1952 onwards) by Giorgio Buchner in the Valle di San Montano were arranged from the outset in family plots, and in addition to local products contain vases and other artefacts imported before *c.*700 from *Euboea, *Corinth, Athens, North *Syria (or *Cilicia: seals of the 'Lyre Player Group'), Phoenicia (see PHOENICIANS), *Egypt (scarabs, including one with the cartouche of Bocchoris: 718–712), and Etruria (see ETRUSCANS). A Rhodian Late Geometric kotyle (grave 168; see RHODES) is inscribed in the alphabet of *Chalcis with verses that offer a playful challenge to the cup of Homeric *Nestor (1); a local krater depicts a shipwreck scene, and is the oldest example of figurative painting in Italy.

On the Italian mainland, the 8th-cent. operations at Euboean Pithecusae did much to create the *orientalizing atmosphere in which, prior to his emigration to Tarquinia (*Tarquinii) in 657, *Demaratus (1) of Corinth could acquire great wealth by trading with the Etruscan cities (Dion. Hal. 3. 46. 3–5). In this as in other respects, Pithecusae declined in importance at the end of the eighth century, following the foundation of Euboean *Cumae on the nearby mainland of *Campania (Livy 8. 22. 5–6).

BTCGI 8 (1990), 'Ischia'; D. Ridgway, *The First Western Greeks* (1992; Ital. orig. 1984); G. Buchner and D. Ridgway, *Pithekoussai I* (Mon. Ant. 1993); G. Tsetskhladze and F. De Augelis (eds.), *The Archaeology of Greek Colonisation* (1994).   D. W. R. R.

pits, cult The Greeks placed in pits (βόθροι) offerings and libations to the dead and to those deities (*chthonian) thought to reside in the earth or in the underworld. Offerings in pits could form part of funerary or tomb cult (Cleidemus, *FGrH* 323 F 14) or of a fertility ritual (e.g. the *Thesmophoria in Athens) and

could be used to honour or invoke the dead or deity for a variety of purposes, including prophecy (*Od.* 11. 24 ff.). Water and blood used in rites of *purification could also be buried (*Morb. Sacr.* 148. 44 ff. (Jones)). In the cults of Olympian deities (see RELIGION, GREEK) worn-out or broken dedications and other consecrated objects as well as the bones and ashes of sacrificed animals were buried in pits. Because such things, however useless, had been consecrated to the deity, they were still sacred and hence were buried within the *sanctuary. See also the Roman MUNDUS.

J. D. M.

Pittacus of *Mytilene (*c.*650–570 BC), statesman, lawgiver, and sage. He commanded in the war against Athens for *Sigeum, on which *Periander of Corinth later arbitrated (see ARBITRATION); helped to overthrow the tyrant Melanchros, then after further complex factional struggles in Mytilene, was elected *aisymnētēs for ten years. *Alcaeus (1) accused him of being tyrant, but he laid down office and died ten years later. One of his sayings was that 'painted wood', i.e. law, was the best protector of the city. His best-remembered law doubled the penalty for all offences if committed while drunk. A moderate reformer, like his contemporary *Solon, he was violently attacked by his fellow citizen and former ally Alcaeus, whose family had helped overthrow tyranny but wished to perpetuate the old aristocratic rule.

Alcaeus; Strabo 13. 617; Ar. *Pol.* 1274ᵇ, 1285ᵃ⁻ᵇ; Diog. Laert. 1. 4; Pl. *Prt.* 26 ff; Plut. *Conv. sept. sap.* D. Page, *Sappho and Alcaeus* (1955); C. M. Bowra, *Greek Lyric Poetry*² (1961), ch. 4; A. Andrewes, *The Greek Tyrants* (1956).   R. T.

Pittheus, legendary king of *Troezen in the N. *Peloponnesus; quick to grasp the meaning of the Pythia's oracle to the Athenian king *Aegeus, he got him drunk and put him to bed with his daughter Aethra, thus becoming the grandfather of *Theseus and creating a family tie between his own small state and the powerful city over the water.   A. H. G.

Pixodarus, son of *Hecatomnus and youngest brother of *Mausolus, was *satrap (see MAUSOLUS) of *Caria 341–336 BC, after ousting his sister *Ada; he tried to attach himself by marriage to the Macedonian royal house, a curious episode (Plut. *Alex.* 10). After 336 he shared the satrapal rule with a Persian by blood, Orontobates, until *Alexander (3) III the Great's arrival (see ADA). An important trilingual inscription from 337, in Greek, *Lycian, and *Aramaic, was published in 1974, and the Aramaic text calls Pixodarus 'satrap in Caria and *Lycia', not just Caria (*SEG* 27. 942 for the Greek text; for the position earlier in the 4th cent. see PERICLES (2) of Limyra). This inscription, and *ILabraunda* no. 42 (cf. *Syll.*³ 311: Mausolus), are interesting as showing that Pixodarus gave local Carian and Lycian communities a say in running their own affairs, though his own satrapal authority is not left in doubt.

Strabo 14. 2. 17. J. Crampa, *Labraunda, the Greek Inscriptions* 2 (1972); E. Badian, *Schachermeyr Studies* (1977), 40 ff.; H. Metzger and others, *Fouilles de Xanthos*, 6 (1979); S. Hornblower, *Mausolus* (1982; inscriptions at 364 ff.), and *CAH* 6² (1994), ch. 8a; S. Ruzicka, *Politics of a Persian Dynasty: The Hecatomnids in the Fourth Century BC* (1992).   S. H.

Placentia (mod. Piacenza), near the confluence of the Po (*Padus) and the Trebbia. Established as a Latin colony (see COLONIZATION, ROMAN) of 6,000 settlers in 218 BC, despite Boian opposition, it was frequently attacked by Gauls, Carthaginians (see CARTHAGE), and *Ligurians. In 187 BC the *via Aemilia became its *decumanus maximus* and, although often contested for, it became prosperous, first as a *municipium* and later as a *colonia*. Little is known of its later history, but the square plan of the

1187

original *castrum*, with sides of *c*.480 m. (525 yds.), is still visible in the modern street layout. Notable finds include the bronze liver of *c*.200 BC, used by *Etruscan augurs (see AUGURES) for *divination (see RELIGION, ETRUSCAN).

M. L. Pagliani, *Piacenza* (1991). E. T. S., T. W. P.

Placidia, Galla, daughter of *Theodosius (2) I (b. *c*. AD 390). She was captured by the Goths at Rome in 410 and married to their leader, Athaulf, at Narbonne (*Narbo; 414). After his murder, she was restored to the Romans (416) and married Constantius, later *Constantius III. Her son by this marriage became *Valentinian III. She beautified *Ravenna and died at Rome in 450.

S. I. Oost, *Galla Placidia Augusta* (1968). E. A. T.; J. D. H.

Placidus (*PLRE* 2. 890) (5th cent. AD?), author of a glossary (ed. Goetz, *CGL* 5. 3–158; and Pirie and Lindsay, *Gloss. Lat.* 4. 12–70) which contains entries of two distinct kinds: brief glosses on archaic words, extending to the end of the letter P (treated as pseudo-Placidus in *Gloss. Lat.* 4); and more discursive notes on matters of grammatical and antiquarian interest. See GLOSSA, GLOSSARY.

Herzog–Schmidt, § 706. R. A. K.

plagiarism The more sophisticated ancient critics distinguished 'imitation' of earlier writers (Gk. *mimēsis*, Lat. *imitatio*) from 'theft' (Gk. *klopē*, Lat. *furtum*). 'Theft' involves derivative copying and is condemned: this, and only this, is plagiarism. 'Imitation' is an acceptable, even normal, re-use (in part, relatable to the modern structuralist's notion of 'intertextuality'; see LITERARY THEORY AND CLASSICAL STUDIES), such that the 'borrowed' material is recreated as the borrower's 'own property' ('privati iuris', Hor. *Ars P.* 131) and (perhaps because the original is well known and informs the new context) the relationship between new and old is acknowledged rather than concealed. When L. *Annaeus Seneca (1) suggests that *Ovid imitates *Virgil 'not as pilferer but as open appropriator' ('non subripiendi causa sed palam mutuandi', *Suas.* 3. 7), the distinction is clear; so too when 'Longinus' (*Subl.* 13) praises a whole tradition of writers, from *Archilochus to *Plato (1), for their re-use of *Homer.

More often, however, the damaging label, 'plagiarism', was applied fairly mechanically to imitation in general. In this spirit the Greek world produced numerous dissertations 'On Plagiarism' (περὶ κλοπῆς: a list is given by *Porphyry in Euseb. *Praep. Evang.* 10. 3. 12); the earliest known is *Aristophanes (2) of Byzantium's study of *Menander (1) (but cf. Pfeiffer, *Hist. Class. Schol.* I, 191). In earlier times, in particular, charges of, or fears of, plagiarism are common and are rarely complicated by any thought of more subtle relationships. *Theognis (1) (19 ff.) put a 'seal' (*sphragis) on his verses to forestall their misappropriation. The playwright *Aristophanes (1) (*Nub.* 553–4) claimed that *Eupolis' *Maricas* was his own *Knights* 'worn inside out', and that other comic writers were 'imitating' (μιμούμενοι) his comparisons (ibid. 559, where the vocabulary of 'imitation' is clearly negative). *Isocrates (5. 94) said other orators made use of his work. In Rome, *Terence was accused of 'theft' for reworking Greek material already translated or adapted by his predecessors (*Eun.* 23 ff., *Ad.* 6 ff.). Philosophers as eminent as *Anaxagoras, Plato, and *Epicurus were all accused of stealing other thinkers' ideas (Diog. Laert. 9. 34; 3. 37; 10. 7, 10. 14).

The preoccupation with plagiarism over many centuries serves as a reminder that, contrary to some modern misstatements, ancient literature, especially poetry, was expected to be 'new'. Certainly, many writers, Greek and Roman, are anxious to assert the necessity of originality or their own claim to it: among them, *Pindar (*Ol.* 9. 48–9), Aristophanes (1) (e.g. *Nub.* 547), *Choerilus (2) (fr. 2 Bernabé), *Timotheus (1) (fr. 20 Page), *Xenarchus (2) Com. (7. 1 ff. Kock), *Callimachus (3) (*Aet.* fr. 1. 25–8), *Lucretius (1. 926–7), *Virgil (*G.* 3. 291–3), *Horace (*Epist.* 1. 19. 21–34), *Propertius (3. 1. 3 ff.), *Diodorus (3) (40.8).

RE 20 (1950), 1956–97 ('Plagiat': Ziegler); E. Stemplinger, *Das Plagiat in der griech. Lit.* (1912); W. Kroll, *Stud. zum Verständnis der röm. Lit.* (1924), 139–84; G. B. Conte, *The Rhetoric of Imitation* (1986: Ital. orig. 1974, 1984); D. A. Russell in D. A. West and A. J. Woodman (eds.), *Creative Imitation and Latin Literature* (1979), 1–16. M. S. Si.

plague (λοιμός, Lat. *pestis*), a term confusingly employed by ancient historians to designate epidemics of infectious *diseases. Epidemics in antiquity were not necessarily caused by the disease now called plague (*Yersinia pestis*), although *Rufus of Ephesus cites some evidence for true plague in Hellenistic Egypt and Syria. The major epidemic diseases are density-dependent. The 'plague of Athens' (see below) was an isolated event in Greek history, but there is more evidence for great epidemics during the Roman Empire. This increase in frequency was a consequence of *population growth in antiquity. Most of the epidemics described by Roman historians, e.g. *Livy who relied on the annalistic tradition, are described so briefly that there is no hope of identifying the diseases in question. Epidemics are neglected in the major theoretical works of ancient medicine (the Hippocratic corpus (see HIPPOCRATES (2)) and *Galen) because doctors had no knowledge of the existence of micro-organisms and had difficulty applying the types of explanation they favoured (in terms of the diet and lifestyle of individuals; also, later, the theory of the four *humours) to mass outbreaks of disease.

*Thucydides (2) (2. 47–58, 3. 87) described the so-called 'plague of Athens' (430–426 BC), the most famous epidemic in antiquity. Unfortunately there is no agreement regarding the identification of the disease. Around 30 different diseases have been suggested as the cause. Most of these are highly implausible, either because they do not correspond to Thucydides' description, or because they cannot be transmitted in such a way as to cause large epidemics. Epidemic typhus and smallpox are the strongest candidates, but true plague has also attracted a considerable number of advocates, along with the hypothesis that the disease organism is now extinct. Thucydides recognized the role of contagion in transmitting the infection.

The second famous plague in antiquity was the 'Antonine plague', which attacked the Roman empire in the 2nd cent. AD. Galen, the main source, does not provide a comprehensive description, but gives details which permit a more definite resolution of the problem than in the case of the 'plague of Athens': this evidence indicates smallpox. Subsequently there were other great epidemics, e.g. the 'plague of Cyprian' in the 3rd cent. AD. However, the descriptions are so inadequate that it is impossible to identify them. Typhus and smallpox were probably the most important causes of epidemics in antiquity.

J. R. Sallares *The Ecology of the Ancient Greek World* (1991); M. D. Grmek *Diseases in the ancient Greek world* (1989; Fr. orig. 1983). J. R. S.

Plancina See MUNATIA PLANCINA.

Plancius (*RE* 4), **Gnaeus,** son of a prominent *eques* (see EQUITES) and *publicanus of *Atina and protégé of his compatriots, the Saturnini (see SENTIUS SATURNINUS, C.), served in Africa, Crete, and (as military tribune) in Macedonia. As quaestor 58 BC in Macedonia, he visited and aided the exiled *Cicero. He was tribune 56 and curule aedile 55 or 54. (For his coins see *RRC* 432.) After election to that office he was accused of *ambitus* by a defeated competitor, M. *Iuventius Laterensis, and successfully defended by Q. *Hortensius Hortalus and Cicero, whose surviving speech (with the commentary by the Bobbio scholiast, *Cic. Or. Schol.* pp. 153–69) is the chief evidence on his life. He fought for *Pompey in the Civil War and unsuccessfully begged Cicero to procure him a pardon from *Caesar.

> *MRR* 3. 158. E. B.

planets See ASTROLOGY; ASTRONOMY; PTOLEMY (4), § (2).

plants, knowledge of See BOTANY.

plants, sacred Plants are associated with particular gods by virtue of their special properties of *purification and healing (see PHARMACOLOGY), or because of their symbolic value usually connected with fertility and growth. Thus corn is sacred to *Demeter who taught its cultivation to man. Similarly the vine belongs to *Dionysus as the god of *wine. Mugwort (*parthenis* or *artemisia*, Plin. *HN* 25. 73) is a healing plant connected with *Artemis in her function as goddess of *childbirth. The sexual symbolism of the pomegranate as the attribute of *Persephone and *Hera, goddess of women and marriage (Paus. 2. 17. 4), is well known. In ritual plants symbolized the annual death and rebirth of vegetation, as in the pre-Greek cult of *Hyacinthus. The papyrus flower, lily, and crocus have the same significance in the Minoan frescoes of *Thera (S. Immerwahr, *Aegean Painting in the Bronze Age* (1989), 60, 62; N. Marinatos, *Art and Religion in Thera* (1984), 118).

Corn also symbolized the recurring cycle of vegetation in the Eleusinian *mysteries (see ELEUSIS) but acquired moral and political overtones after 600 BC under Orphic influence (see ORPHISM) and after the annexation of Eleusis by Athens. Plants had *magic and medicinal properties: the withy (λύγος, *agnus castus*) bound the image of Spartan Artemis Orthia (Lygodesma, Paus. 3. 16. 11) in *Sparta and of Samian Hera during the Tonaea festival on the island of *Samos (Athen. 15. 672c). The use of the *lygos* in Demeter's *Thesmophoria was intended to reduce the sexual drive of the women worshippers. The *moly* plant cured *Circe's spell (*Od.* 10. 305. Other references to Homer in *RE* 19. 2. 1446–56). But it is doubtful if such plants were intrinsically sacred, any more than the wild olive awarded to the Olympic victor (see OLYMPIAN GAMES), the bay leaves of the *Pythian Games or the wild celery of the *Nemean Games.

Lively Roman interest in herbal medicine produced some specialist, also much superstitious and unscientific (Galen 12. 498 f. Kühn), literature in the early empire. *Pliny (1) the Elder wrote extensively on healing and magic plants in *HN* 20–32. Some of this learning was excerpted in the popular 4th-cent. collection known as the *Medicina Plinii*.

> F. Pfister, *RE* 19. 2 (1938), 1446–56; Steier, *RE* 16. 1 (1931), 81–5.
> H. J. R.; B. C. D.

Plataea, a city in southern *Boeotia situated between Mt. Cithaeron and the Asopus river, commanding a small plain. Mentioned as 'green' in *Homer's *Iliad* (2. 504), it was inhabited from the neolithic to the Byzantine periods. In the last quarter of the 6th cent. BC *Thebes (1) tried to force it into the Boeotian Confederacy (see FEDERAL STATES). An appeal to *Sparta for support having failed, Plataea entered into an alliance with *Athens. The border between Plataea and Thebes became the Asopus river. The Plataeans turned out in force to support Athens at the battle of *Marathon, despite the often specious denials of

the Athenian orators. A site on the battlefield has been claimed as the mass grave of the Plataeans. The greatest fame of Plataea comes from the final battle there between the Greeks and the Persians in 479 BC, when some 600 Plataeans fought alongside the other Greeks (Hdt. 9. 28); in celebration of the victory the Greeks erected the altar of *Zeus Eleutherius. See PLATAEA, BATTLE OF.

Plataea faded into temporary obscurity in the early 5th cent. BC. After the defeat of the Athenian Tolmides in 447 BC, however (see CORONEA), it joined the new Boeotian Confederacy, commanding two votes. The Theban attack on it in 431 BC was the real start of the *Peloponnesian War. Most inhabitants having fled to Athens, the survivors, after a spirited defence, surrendered in 427. Rebuilt after the war, Plataea was independent under the terms of the *King's Peace until 373 BC, when Thebes again seized it. Again survivors found refuge in Athens, their plight bemoaned by *Isocrates (14 *Plataikos*). After the battle of *Chaeronea in 338, *Philip (1) II restored it. *Alexander (3) the Great gave Plataea its opportunity for revenge when he destroyed Thebes in 335 BC. Plataea and other Boeotians wreaked havoc during the fighting, and strengthened their power within the Boeotian Confederacy. The wars of the Hellenistic period and those resulting from the Roman entry into Greek affairs wasted Plataea along with other Boeotian cities. It remained loyal to Rome during the Third Macedonian War, but shared the sufferings of other Boeotian cities during *Sulla's campaign of 86 BC. Although its everyday insignificance made it a comic butt, Hellenistic and Roman Plataea retained symbolic importance for a larger Greek world through its two cults commemorating the famous battle, of which that of Hellenic *Homonoia had been added around the time of the Chremonidean war (see CHREMONIDES). Panhellenic games, the Eleutheria, at least as old as the 3rd cent. BC, were still celebrated in the mid-3rd cent. AD; their centrepiece was a hoplite-race, of which the victor was proclaimed 'Best of the Greeks'. See PERSIAN-WARS TRADITION.

> M. Amit, *Great and Small Poleis* (1973), pt. 2; L. Prandi, *Platea* (1988); E. Badian, *From Plataea to Potidaea* (1993), ch. 3. J. Bu.; A. J. S. S.

Plataea, battle of (479 BC). The battle, which finally put paid to *Xerxes' attempt to conquer Greece (see PERSIAN WARS), falls into three stages. In the first, the Greeks, commanded by the Spartan, *Pausanias (1), clung to the lower slopes of Cithaeron (the mountain range which separates this part of *Boeotia from *Attica), and fought off the Persian cavalry, killing its commander. This encouraged them to move down towards the river Asopus, where water-supplies were better, but exposed them to continuous harassment by Persian cavalry, eventually leading to their being denied access to the Asopus, and the choking up of the Gargaphia spring (now Retsi?). A planned night withdrawal then went disastrously wrong, leaving the Athenians isolated on the left, the Lacedaemonians (*Spartans) and Tegeates (see TEGEA) on the right, and the centre just outside Plataea itself. This perhaps tempted the Persian commander, *Mardonius, to order a general attack, but his Asiatic troops were decisively beaten by the Spartans and their comrades, and his Boeotian allies by the Athenians.

> *RE* 20. 2, 'Plataiai', § 10; Hdt. 9. 20 ff. C. Hignett, *Xerxes' Invasion of Greece* (1963); J. F. Lazenby, *The Defence of Greece* (1993). J. F. La.

Plataea, oath of Fourth-cent. BC Athens knew an anti-Persian oath sworn by the Greek allies before the battle of Plataea (see preceding article), preserved in three nearly identical versions (Lycurg. *Leocr.* 81; Diod. 11. 29. 3; Tod 2. 204). *Theopompus (3) (*FGrH* 115 F 153) denounced it as an Athenian invention, although there is a linguistic case for authenticity (Siewert), saving the undertaking not to rebuild sanctuaries destroyed by the Persians. This clause is sometimes invoked (none the less) to explain an apparent Athenian tardiness in repairing ruined temples after 479 BC (even though on this point the archaeological evidence remains controversial). See PERSIAN-WARS TRADITION.

P. Siewert, *Der Eid von Plataia* (1972); *CAH* 4². 604, 5². 34, 314–15.

A. J. S. S.

plate, precious (Greek and Roman) Vessels of *gold and *silver are frequently mentioned in literary texts. *Pindar (*Ol.* 7. 1–4) described a gold *phiale* as 'the peak of all possessions'. Greek temple inventories list large quantities of plate and they frequently provide information about the weights of items. Herodotus (1. 14, 25, 50–2, 92) also records the gold and silver dedications made by various Lydian kings such as *Gyges, *Alyattes, and *Croesus. As silver and gold can be reworked, few items of ancient plate have survived in their original form. Likewise sanctuaries as depositories of such wealth were frequently looted; the inscribed dedication on a silver *phiale* found in a grave at Kozani was to *Athena at *Megara. Outstanding pieces of Greek plate include the silver vessels decorated in gold-figure from Duvanli in Bulgaria (see also ROGOZEN) and Semibratny in southern Russia. Although much plate has been lost it is possible (but this is controversial) that metallic shapes, and perhaps even colours, influenced the production of fine Greek pottery.

The study of Roman plate is assisted by the discovery of plate lost in the eruption of *Vesuvius in AD 79. Two major hoards have been recovered: one at *Boscoreale and the other in the House of Menander at *Pompeii. Several major hoards also come from late antiquity although the precise circumstances surrounding their burial are not always clear; these include the Mildenhall Treasure from Suffolk, and the Kaiseraugst Treasure. See HILDESHEIM TREASURE; OXUS TREASURE.

D. E. Strong, *Greek and Roman Gold and Silver Plate* (1966); A. Oliver, Jr., *Silver for the Gods* (1977); D. von Bothmer, *A Greek and Roman Treasury* (1984); J. P. C. Kent and K. S. Painter, *Wealth of the Roman World AD 300–700* (1977); M. Vickers and D. Gill, *Artful Crafts: Ancient Greek Silverware and Pottery* (1994).

D. W. J. G.

Plato (1) of Athens, *c*.429–347 BC, descended from wealthy and influential Athenian families on both sides. His own family, like many, was divided by the disastrous political consequences of the *Peloponnesian War. His stepfather Pyrilampes was a democrat and friend of *Pericles (1), but two of his uncles, *Critias and *Charmides, assisted the oligarchic revolution of 404. At some point Plato renounced ambition for a public career, devoting his life to philosophy. The major philosophical influence on his life was Socrates, but in three important respects Plato turned away from the example of *Socrates. He rejected marriage and the family duty of producing citizen sons; he founded a philosophical school, the *Academy; and he produced large quantities of written philosophical works (as well as the shadowy 'unwritten doctrines' produced at some point in the Academy, for which we have only secondary evidence).

Plato's works are all in the form of *dialogues in which he does not himself appear. The philosophical point of this is to detach him from the arguments which are presented. Plato is unique among philosophers in this constant refusal to present ideas as his own, forcing the reader to make up his or her own mind about adopting them—a strategy which works best in the shorter dialogues where arguments are presented in a more lively

way. For Plato this detachment and use of dialogue is not a point of style, but an issue of epistemology: despite various changes of position on the issue of knowledge, he remains convinced throughout that anything taken on trust, second-hand, either from others or from books, can never amount to a worthwhile cognitive state; knowledge must be achieved by effort from the person concerned. Plato tries to stimulate thought rather than to hand over doctrines.

This detachment also makes Plato himself elusive, in two ways. First, we know very little about him personally. Later biographies are patently constructed to 'explain' aspects of the dialogues. The seventh of a series of 'letters by Plato' has been accepted as genuine by some scholars, and has been used to create a historical background to the dialogues. But such 'letters' are a recognized fictional genre (see FORGERIES, LITERARY); it is very unwise to use such material to create a basis for the arguments in the dialogues, which are deliberately presented in a detached way. To try to explain the dialogues by appeal to a 'life and letters', though tempting since antiquity, is to miss the point of Plato's procedure, which is to force us to respond to the ideas in the dialogues themselves, not to judge them by our view of the author.

Second, the dialogues themselves are extremely varied and interpretatively often quite open. Since antiquity there has been a debate as to whether Plato's philosophical legacy should be taken to be one of a set of doctrines, or of continuing debate and argument. The middle, sceptical Academy (see PLATONISM, MIDDLE) read Plato for the arguments, and Plato's heritage was taken to be a continuation of the practice of argument against contemporary targets. The dialogue most favourable to this kind of interpretation is the *Theaetetus*, in which Socrates presents himself as a barren midwife, drawing ideas out of others but putting forward none himself. However, in antiquity we find the competing dogmatic reading of Plato, in which the dialogues are read as presenting pieces of doctrine which the reader is encouraged to put together to produce 'Platonism', a distinctive system of beliefs. The dogmatic reading has to cope with the diverse nature of the dialogues and the unsystematic treatment of many topics, with apparent conflicts between dialogues and with the changing and finally disappearing role of Socrates as the chief figure. These problems are often solved by appeal to some development of Plato's thought, although there have been 'unitarians' about Plato's ideas since *Arius Didymus declared, 'Plato has many voices, not, as some think, many doctrines' (Stobaeus, *Eclogae* 2. 55. 5–6).

Since the 19th cent. much energy has been expended on the chronology of the dialogues, but, in spite of computer-based work, no stylistic tests establish a precise order. In any case a chronology of the dialogues is only interesting if it tracks some independently established development of Plato's thought, and attempts to establish this easily fall into circularity where they do not rest on the dubious 'life and letters'. Stylistically, however, the dialogues fall into three comparatively uncontroversial groups: (1) the 'Socratic' dialogues, in which Socrates is the main figure, questioning others about their own positions but arguing for none himself, though characteristic views of his own emerge. This group includes *Ion, Laches, Lysis, Apology, Euthyphro, Charmides, Menexenus, Hippias Major, Hippias Minor, Protagoras, Crito, Cleitophon, Alcibiades, Lovers, Hipparchus* (the last two are often doubted as Plato's work, and since the 19th cent. this has been true of the *Alcibiades*, never doubted in antiquity). Two dialogues generally regarded as transitional between the Socratic and middle dialogues are *Gorgias* and *Meno*. Two dialogues which use the Socratic format but have much in common with the later works are *Euthydemus* and *Theaetetus*. (2) the 'middle' dialogues, in which Socrates remains the chief figure, but, no longer undermining others' views, sets out, at length, many positive ideas: this group includes *Phaedo, Republic, Symposium,* and *Phaedrus.* (3) the 'later' dialogues, in which Socrates retreats as the main interlocutor, and Plato deals at length, sometimes critically, with his own ideas and those of other philosophers, in a newly detailed and increasingly technical and 'professional' way: this group includes *Cratylus, Parmenides, Sophist, Statesman, Philebus,* and *Laws. Timaeus* and *Critias* are most often put in this group, but there are arguments for placing them with the middle dialogues.

There is no uncontroversial way of presenting Plato's thought. Many aspects of his work invite the reader to open-ended pursuit of the philosophical issues; others present her with more developed positions, substantial enough to be characterized as 'Platonic' even for those who reject the more rigid forms of the dogmatic reading. While no brief survey of Plato's varied and fertile thought can be adequate, some major themes recur and can be traced through several works.

Ethical and Political Thought Plato is throughout insistent on the objectivity of values, and on the importance of morality in the individual's life. The 'protreptic' passage in the *Euthydemus* anticipates the Stoics in its claim that what are called 'goods' (health, wealth, and so on) are not really so; the only good thing is the virtuous person's knowledge of how to make use of these things in a way consonant with morality. The assumption is explicitly brought out that everyone pursues happiness, though we have, prior to philosophical reflection, little idea of what it is, and most confuse it with worldly success; the choice of virtue is embodied in the worldly failure Socrates. Many of the Socratic dialogues show Socrates trying to get people to rethink their priorities, and to live more morally; he is sure that there is such a thing as virtue, though he never claims to have it. He further identifies virtue with the wisdom or understanding that is at its basis, the unified grasp of principles which enables the virtuous to act rightly in a variety of situations, and to explain and justify their decisions and actions.

In the *Protagoras*, we find the claim that this wisdom will be instrumental in achieving pleasure; this view is examined respectfully, and although we find attacks on the idea that pleasure could be our end in the *Phaedo* and *Gorgias*, Plato reverts to some very hedonistic-seeming thoughts in the *Philebus* and *Laws.* Arius Didymus compares Plato with *Democritus as a kind of hedonist, and clearly he is tempted at times by the idea that some form of pleasure is inescapably our aim, although after the *Protagoras* he never thinks that our reason might be merely instrumental to achieving it. Apart from cryptic and difficult hints in the *Philebus*, he never achieves a substantive characterization of the virtuous person's understanding.

In some of the early and middle dialogues Plato conflates the wisdom of the virtuous individual with that of the virtuous *ruler*; the skill of running one's own life is run together with that of achieving the happiness of others. The culmination of this is the *Republic*, where individual and state are similar in structure, and the virtuous individual is produced only in the virtuous state. Later Plato divides these concerns again, so that the *Philebus* is concerned with individual, and the *Laws* with social morality.

Plato's treatment of social and political matters is marked by a shift of emphasis between two strands in his thought. One is his conviction that the best solution to political problems is the exercise of expert judgement: in an individual life what is needed is overall grasp based on correct understanding of priorities, and similarly in a state what is needed is expert overall understanding of the common good. This conviction is triumphant in the *Republic*, where the rulers, the Guardians, have power to run the lives of all citizens in the state in a very broadly defined way: laws serve the purpose of applying the Guardians' expert knowledge, but do not stand in its way. Expert knowledge gives its possessor the right to enforce on others what the expert sees to be in their true interests, just as the patient must defer to the doctor and the crew to the ship's captain.

Plato is also, however, aware of the importance of law in ensuring stability and other advantages. In the *Crito* the Laws of Athens claim obedience from Socrates (though on a variety of unharmonized grounds). In the *Statesman* Plato admits that, although laws are in the real world a clog on expertise, they embody the past results of expertise and are therefore to be respected, indeed obeyed absolutely in the absence of an expert. In the *Laws*, where Plato has given up the hope that an actual expert could exist and rule uncorrupted by power, he insists that problems of political division and strife are to be met by complete obedience to laws, which are regarded as the product of rational reflection and expertise, rather than the haphazard product of party strife.

Plato's best-known contribution to political thought is his idea, developed in the *Republic*, that individual (more strictly the individual's *soul) and state are analogous in structure. Justice in the state is the condition in which its three functionally defined parts—the rulers, the rulers' auxiliaries, and the rest of the citizens (the producers)—work in harmony, guided by the expert understanding of the rulers, who, unlike the others, grasp what is in the common interest. Analogously, justice in the individual is the condition where the three parts of the individual's soul work in harmony. What this condition will be will differ for members of the three classes. All the citizens have souls whose parts are: reason, which discerns the interest of the whole or at least can be guided by grasp of someone else's reason which does; 'spirit', the emotional side of the person; and desire, the collection of desires aimed at their own satisfaction regardless of the interests of the whole. For all, justice consists in the rule of reason, and the subordination of spirit and the desires; but what this demands is different for the rulers, who understand and can articulate the requirements of reason, and for the producers, who do not. It is notable that Plato identifies this condition of soul, which he calls psychic harmony, with justice, quite contrary to Greek intuitions about political justice. In the *Republic*, the citizen's justice consists in identifying his or her overall interest, to the extent that that is possible, with the common interest, and this idea is taken to notorious lengths in the central books, where the rulers are to live a life in which individuality is given the least possible scope. Opinions have always differed as to whether the *Republic* is a contribution to political theory, or a rejection of the very basis of political theory, one which refuses to solve political conflicts, but unrealistically eliminates their sources. The *Republic* has always been most inspiring as a 'pattern laid up in heaven' for individuals to use in the pursuit of individual justice.

Knowledge and its Objects In the early dialogues, Socrates is constantly in search for knowledge; this is provoked, not by sceptical worries about knowledge of matters of fact, but by the desire to acquire, on a larger and deeper scale, the kind of expert knowledge displayed by craftspeople. Socrates does not doubt that such globally expert knowledge, which he calls wisdom, exists, nor that it would be most useful in the understanding and running of one's life, but he never claims to have it, and in the Socratic dialogues differences show up between it and everyday kinds of expert knowledge. Sophists, particularly *Hippias (2), are ridiculed as people who uncontroversially have everyday skills, but are shown up as totally lacking in the kind of global understanding which Socrates is seeking.

Socrates' conception of wisdom is an ambitious one; the person with this expert knowledge has a unified overall grasp of the principles which define his field and (as is stressed in the *Gorgias*) he can give a *logos* or account of what it is that he knows, enabling him to explain and justify the judgements that he makes. In several dialogues this demand for giving a *logos* becomes more stringent, and prior conditions are set on an adequate answer. The person who putatively has knowledge of X is required to give an answer as to what X is which is in some way explanatory of the way particular things and kinds of thing are X. The answer is said to provide a 'form' which is itself in some way X, indeed X in a way which (unlike the Xness of other things) precludes ever being the opposite of X in any way. A number of complex issues arise over these 'forms', hotly disputed by scholars and with respect to which the text gives suggestive but incomplete solutions.

In the Socratic dialogues there is a noteworthy mismatch between the goal of wisdom and the method that Socrates employs; for the latter is the procedure of *elenchus*, the testing of the opponent's views by Socrates' tenacious arguments. But the *elenchus* is a method that shows only inconsistency between beliefs; it has no resources for proving truth. Its result is negative; we have demonstrations as to what friendship, courage, piety, and the like are not, but none as to what they are. In the *Meno* a different approach emerges; the theory of 'recollection' stresses that a person can get knowledge by thinking in a way not dependent on experience, and therefore entirely through his own intellectual resources. Although the *Meno* is careful not to restrict knowledge entirely to such *a priori* knowledge, Plato goes on to develop an account of knowledge in which the model of skill is replaced by that of non-empirical, particularly mathematical reasoning. In the *Phaedo* and *Republic* Plato stresses both the non-empirical nature of the objects of knowledge, the forms, and the structured and hierarchical nature of knowledge. Understanding now requires grasp of an entire connected system of thought, and insight into the difference between the basic and the derived elements, and the ways in which the latter are dependent on the former. As the conditions for having knowledge become higher, knowledge becomes an ever more ideal state; in the *Republic* it is only to be achieved by an intellectually gifted élite, who have spent many years in unremittingly abstract intellectual activities, and have lived a life strenuously devoted to the common good. In the *Republic* Plato's account of knowledge, theoretically demanding yet practically applicable, is his most extensive and ambitious.

In later dialogues this synthesis, though never repudiated, lapses. In the *Statesman* we find that theoretical and practical knowledge are now carefully separated; in the *Laws* a continued stress on the importance of mathematics does little work, and contrasts with the work's extensive and explicit reliance on experience. The *Theaetetus* examines knowledge with a fresh and lively concern, attacking various forms of relativism and subjectivism, but without reference to the *Republic* account.

Plato continues to talk about forms, but in elusive and often puzzling ways. The one sustained passage which appears to discuss forms as they appear in the *Phaedo* and *Republic* is wholly negative—the first part of the *Parmenides*, where various powerful arguments are brought against this conception of forms, and no answers are supplied. Whatever Plato's own opinion of these arguments (some of them resembling arguments in early *Aristotle), forms in later dialogues revert to a role more like their earlier one. They are the objective natures of things, the objects of knowledge, and are to be grasped only by the exercise of thought and enquiry, not by reliance on experience. *Statesman* 262b–263d discusses the way that language can be misleading: there is no form of foreigner, since 'foreigner' simply means 'not Greek', and things are not put into a unified kind by not being Greek. There is no single method, other than the continued use of enquiry, to determine which of our words do in fact pick out kinds that are natural, rather than merely contrived. However, Plato, though never renouncing forms as a demand of objectivity in intellectual enquiry, ceases to attach to them the mystical and exalted attitudes of the middle dialogues.

Soul and the Cosmos Throughout the dialogues Plato expresses many versions of the idea that a person's soul is an entity distinct from the living embodied person, attached to it by a relation which is inevitable but unfortunate. In the *Phaedo* several arguments for the soul's immortality show that Plato is dealing indiscriminately with a number of different positions as to what the soul is: the principle of life, the intellect, the personality. The latter two are the ideas most developed. Soul as the intellect is the basis of Plato's tendency to treat knowledge as what transcends our embodied state; in the *Meno* learning a geometrical proof is identified with the person's soul recollecting what it knew before birth. Soul as the personality is the basis of Plato's use of myths of *transmigration of souls and afterlife rewards and punishments. In the middle dialogues these two ideas are united: the *Phaedrus* gives a vivid picture of souls caught on a wheel of ongoing rebirth, a cycle from which only philosophical understanding promises release.

Plato's use of the idea that souls are immortal and are endlessly reborn into different bodies is a metaphorical expression of a deep body–soul dualism which also takes other forms. He tends to draw sharp oppositions between active thinking and passive reliance on sense-experience, and to think of the senses as giving us merely unreflected and unreliable reports; the middle dialogues contain highly coloured disparagements of the world as revealed to us through the senses. However, there is also a strain in Plato which sets against this a more unified view of the person. In the *Symposium* he develops the idea that erotic love can be sublimated and refined in a way that draws the person to aspire to philosophical truth; in the *Phaedrus* he holds that this need not lead to repudiation of the starting-point. In the *Republic* the soul has three parts, two of which are closely connected with the body; but in the final book only the thinking part achieves immortality.

The *Timaeus*, an account of the natural world cast in the form of a description of how it was made by a creator god, treats the world itself as a living thing, with body and soul, and a fanciful cosmic account is developed. Other later dialogues, particularly the *Philebus*, also introduce the idea that our souls are fragments of a cosmic soul in the world as a whole. Many aspects of the *Timaeus*' cosmology depend on the assumption that the world itself is a living thing.

Later Problems and Methods The later dialogues do not display the same literary concerns as the Socratic and middle ones, nor do they contain the same themes. Rather, Plato moves to engaging with the ideas of other philosophers, and his own earlier ones, in a way strikingly unlike his earlier way of doing philosophy by the use of dialogue. In the later works the dialogue form is often strained by the need for exposition, and they are sometimes heavy and pedagogical. However, dialogue is often used brilliantly for long stretches of argument, as in the *Parmenides* and *Sophist*.

The *Sophist* presents, in a passage of challenging argument, Plato's solution to *Parmenides' challenge about the coherence of talking about not-being. The *Timaeus* takes up the challenge of cosmology, replying to earlier thinkers with different cosmological assumptions. More fanciful treatment of cosmology is found in the *Statesman*. The *Cratylus* discusses questions of language and etymology in a semi-playful but systematic way. The unfinished *Critias* and the *Statesman* take up questions of political theory, discussing them by means previously rejected, like fiction and accounts which take folk memory and myth seriously. The *Philebus*, discussing the place of pleasure in the good life, does so in a context of Pythagorean metaphysics. The *Laws* sketches an ideal state with considerable help from the lessons of history and of actual politics. These works show a larger variety of interests than hitherto, and an increased flexibility of methodology. Plato in these works shows both a greater respect for the views of others and an enlarged willingness to learn from experience, tradition and history. *Laws* 3 is a precursor of Aristotle's detailed research into political history. It is not surprising that we find many ideas which remind us of his pupil Aristotle, and the latter's methods and concerns, from the 'receptacle' of the *Timaeus*, suggestive of matter, to the treatment of the 'mean' in the *Statesman*.

Plato is original, radical, and daring, but also elusive. His ideas are locally clear and uncompromising, and globally fragmented, perennially challenging the reader to join in the dialogue and take up the challenge, following the argument where it leads. See DIALECTIC.

LIFE A. Riginos, *Platonica: the anecdotes concerning the Life and Writings of Plato* (1976).
TEXT OCT, Burnet, rev. New edn. in progress (1995–).
SCHOLIA C. F. Hermann, *Platonis Dialogi*, 6.
WORD INDEX TO PLATO L. Brandwood (1976).
TRANSLATIONS There are large numbers of modern translations of nearly all the dialogues. Most can be found in Penguin and Hackett; there are numerous translations of the *Republic* in particular. No authoritative translation of all the dialogues by a single person has replaced that of Jowett, itself currently being revised.
STUDIES In the 20th cent. there has been voluminous work on all aspects of Plato, but it has been fragmented and divided between different dialogues; there have been few studies of Plato as a whole apart from brief introductions. R. Kraut (ed.), *The Cambridge Companion to Plato* (1993), is, however, a useful introduction, and has an extensive bibliog. An older comprehensive discussion can be found in I. M. Crombie, *An Examination of Plato's Doctrines*, 2 vols. (1962, 1963). The important work of G. Vlastos can be found in *Socrates, Ironist and Moral Philosopher* (1992), *Socratic Studies* (1994), and *Platonic Studies* (2nd edn., 1981). G. E. L. Owen's influential articles on Plato can be found in his collected papers, *Logic, Science and Dialectic* (1986). A collection of articles on *Socrates* ed. G. Vlastos (1971) has now been followed by H. Benson (ed.), *Essays on the Philosophy of Socrates* (1992). For Plato see *Plato I* and *II*, ed. G. Vlastos (1971); also R. E. Allen (ed.), *Studies in Plato's Metaphysics* (1965). See also M. Ostwald and J. Lynch, *CAH* 6² (1994), 602 ff.; R. B. Rutherford, *The Art of Plato* (1995; on literary aspects). J. A.

Plato (2), Athenian comic poet (see COMEDY (GREEK), OLD), won

his first victory at the City *Dionysia *c.*410 BC (*IG* 2. 2325. 63). He produced *Hyperbolus* at some date during 420–416 BC, *Victories* after 421 (it referred to Ar. *Pax*), *Cleophon* in 405 and *Phaon* (probably) in 391. We have thirty titles and 300 citations. Many of the citations refer to people known to us from Aristophanes (esp. *Av.*) and from historians. The titles (see CLEOPHON (1); HYPERBOLUS) show that many of his plays were strongly political, and at least one of them, *Envoys*, belongs to the 4th cent., since it mentions an embassy of Epicrates and Phormisius to Persia (fr. 127). Other titles, e.g. *Zeus kakoumenos*, point to mythological burlesque; *Sophists* ridiculed contemporary artistic (and possibly, though not certainly, philosophical) innovations (see SOPHISTS).

PCG 7. 431 ff. (*CAF* 1. 601 ff.). K. J. D.

Platonism, Middle The Platonism of the period between *Antiochus (11) of Ascalon (d. *c.*68 BC) and *Plotinus (b. AD 205), characterized by a revulsion against the sceptical tendency of the New *Academy and by a gradual advance, with many individual variations, towards a comprehensive metaphysic, including many elements drawn from other schools. In *logic and ethics, especially, these philosophers oscillated between the poles of Aristotelianism (see ARISTOTLE) and *Stoicism, but in their metaphysics, after Antiochus, at least, they remained firmly transcendentalist, drawing varying degrees of inspiration from the Pythagorean tradition; see PYTHAGORAS (1). Chief figures (apart from Antiochus) are: *Albinus (1), *Alcinous (2), *Apuleius, *Atticus, *Eudorus, *Numenius, *Plutarch. The only surviving corpus of work is that of Plutarch, but there are useful summaries of Platonist doctrine by Alcinous and Apuleius. The Jewish philosopher *Philon (4), and the Christians *Clement of Alexandria and *Origen (1), are deeply influenced by contemporary Platonism, and are often good evidence for its doctrines.

J. Dillon, *The Middle Platonists* (1977). J. M. D.

Platonius, of unknown date (Kaibel speculated 9th or 10th cent. AD), whose writings 'On the distinction among comedies' and 'On the distinction of styles' are preserved in extracts. He argues that Old Comedy gave way to Middle because of political repression, but shows no knowledge of any author of Middle Comedy. See COMEDY (GREEK), OLD, and MIDDLE.

W. J. W. Koster, *Scholia in Aristophanem* 1. 1A: *Prolegomena de comoedia* (1975), pp. 3–7; H.-G. Nesselrath, *Die attische mittlere Komödie* (1990), 30–4. J. S. R.

Platorius (*RE* 2) **Nepos, Aulus,** possibly of Spanish origin, consul AD 119, was appointed governor of *Thrace, probably by his friend *Hadrian in 117. Nepos was sent to Lower Germany (see GERMANIA) in 119 or 120, then moved straight from there to Britain (122 until after September 124); he may have accompanied the emperor himself and apparently brought with him Legio VI Victrix (see LEGION), which was now to be permanently stationed in Britain. Inscriptions from several milecastles and two forts (Benwell and Halton Chesters, *RIB* 1340; 1427) show that he began work on Hadrian's wall (see WALL OF HADRIAN). Subsequently Nepos fell out of favour with the emperor. J. B. C.

Plautius (*RE* 60), a Roman lawyer of the later 1st cent. AD, known only through excerpts in Justinian's Digest (see JUSTINIAN'S CODIFICATION) from commentaries on his work by L. *Neratius Priscus, *Javolenus Priscus, Sextus *Pomponius, and *Iulius Paulus (*Ex Plautio, Ad Plautium*), who clearly admired him and arrange what seems to have been the same basic text in a very varying order.

Plautius, Aulus

Lenel, *Pal.* 2. 13–14; Bremer (1901), 111. 218–39; *PIR*[1] P 342; *HLL* 3 (forthcoming) § 395.4; Ferrini, *Opere* 2 216–228; S. Riccobono, *Scritti di diritto romano* 1 (1957), 1–44; Kunkel (1967), 34.   T. Hon.

Plautius (*RE* 39), **Aulus** (*suffect consul AD 29), of a family from Trebula Suffenas that became consular under *Augustus. He was governor of *Pannonia in AD 42 and his loyalty to *Claudius, whose first wife Urgulanilla had been been a member of the family, probably helped to make the revolt of L. *Arruntius Camillus Scribonianus futile. In 43, commanding the British expedition, he defeated *Cunobelinus' sons in battle, probably at the Medway and at the Thames, and staged Claudius' entry into the *Belgic capital *Camulodunum. Most of lowland Britain had been overrun before his departure (47) for the last ovation (see OVATIO) awarded to a subject, a measure of Claudius' favour and of the family's ascendancy. In 57 (during a senatorial revival) Plautius tried his wife 'according to ancient custom' on charges of foreign religious practices—and acquitted her. He was probably dead by 65.

E. M. Clifford, *Bagendon* (1961), 57 ff.; G. Webster and D. R. Dudley, *The Roman Conquest of Britain, A.D. 43–57*[2] (1973), ch. 4; M. Todd, *Roman Britain 55 BC–AD 400* (1981), chs. 3 f.; A. Birley, *The Fasti of Roman Britain* (1981), 37 ff.; S. Frere, *Britannia*[3] (1987), 48 ff.; J. Hind, *Britannia* 1989, 1 ff.; B. Levick, *Claudius* (1990), index.   C. E. S.; B. M. L.

Plautius (*RE* 23) **Hypsaeus, Publius**, of consular family, was quaestor and proquaestor of *Pompey in the east and became curule aedile with M. *Aemilius Scaurus (2) in 58 BC, when they issued the striking coins *RRC* 422. (The moneyer of *RRC* 420 is a different person.) In 56 he supported Pompey's desire for an Egyptian command. In 53 he was a candidate for the consulship with Q. *Caecilius Metellus Pius Scipio and T. *Annius Milo. The campaign, in which he and Scipio were supported by Pompey and P. *Clodius Pulcher, was corrupt and violent, and the elections were repeatedly postponed. After Clodius' death (January 52) the partisans of Plautius and Scipio attacked the *interrex* M. *Aemilius Lepidus (3) in his house in order to force him to fix the election-day. When Pompey had been made sole consul he abandoned Plautius, who was convicted of *ambitus*. He was perhaps restored by *Caesar, if it is he who witnessed a *senatus consultum* in April 44 (Jos. *AJ* 14. 220). The identification is persuasive, but speculative.   T. J. C.; E. B.

Plautius (*RE* 42) **Lateranus**, nephew of Aulus *Plautius, deprived of his senatorial rank in AD 48 as a lover of *Valeria Messallina, was restored by Nero (55). Consul designate (65) he took part in the Pisonian conspiracy (see C. CALPURNIUS PISO (1)) and was executed. For his palace on the Caelian hill (see CAELIUS MONS) *Juvenal 10. 15–18. The Lateranus of 8. 146 ff. is not modelled on this man, who did not see his consulship and to whom is ascribed genuine patriotism by *Tacitus (1), *Ann.* 15. 49; nor probably on a son, cf. Tac. *Ann.* 15. 60. 1.   G. E. F. C.; B. M. L.

Plautius (*RE* 41) **Silvanus** (1), **Marcus**, tribune 89 or 88 BC. With his colleague C. *Papirius Carbo (2) he passed a law supplementing that of L. *Iulius Caesar (1) by offering the Roman citizenship to men *adscripti* (added to the rolls as having received local citizenship) in Italian cities who appeared before a praetor within 60 days to claim it. This particularly concerned Greek cities in Italy, which, like other Hellenistic cities, had freely made outstanding men citizens. One who thus became a Roman citizen was A. *Licinius Archias. Plautius may also be the tribune who changed the composition of the criminal juries, perhaps only for a year, by substituting a panel of fifteen men from each tribe for the *equites* who had previously had a monopoly. This led to juries dominated by senators, which even convicted Q. *Varius under his own law.

Cic. *Arch.* 7; Asc. p. 79c, with Marshall, *Commentary*; Schol. Bob. 125 St. (confused: see E. Badian, *JRS* 1973, 128 ff.); E. Badian, *Stud. Gr. Rom. Hist.* 75 ff.   E. B.

Plautius (*RE* 43) **Silvanus** (2), **Marcus**, grandson of a praetor, was consul 2 BC, proconsul of Asia (AD 4–5), and *legatus* of Augustus in Galatia, in which capacity he may have fought the mountaineers of *Isauria in AD 6. He brought two legions from Galatia to Europe, served with distinction in the Pannonian War under *Tiberius and received *ornamenta triumphalia* in 9 (*ILS* 921). He is surely not the subject of the *elogium ILS* 918 (see SULPICIUS QUIRINIUS, P.). His mother *Urgulania was a friend of *Livia Drusilla, his daughter Urgulanilla married the future emperor *Claudius.

Syme, *AA* 338 ff.; *RP* 3 (1984), 876 ff.   R. J. S.

Plautius (*RE* 47) **Silvanus Aelianus, Tiberius** (*suffect consul AD 45, consul for the second time in 74), is known mainly from the inscription extant at the Mausoleum of the Plautii near Tibur. Son of the patrician L. Aelius Lamia (consul AD 3), he entered the family of M. *Plautius Silvanus (2) (consul 2 BC). After serving as quaestor to *Tiberius and tribune of Legio V in Germany (see LEGION; GERMANIA), Plautius attended *Claudius as legate in the conquest of Britain (for Claudius' favour see PLAUTIUS SILVANUS (2), M. and PLAUTIUS, AULUS). After his proconsulship of Asia (? AD 53/4), he was legate of *Moesia (60–66 or 67). He transplanted more than 100,000 natives south of the Danube; weakened by the dispatch of troops to the East for Cn. *Domitius Corbulo's campaigns, he prevented a Sarmatian disturbance; secured the province by dealing with the chieftains; relieved the siege of *Chersonesus (3); and sent corn to Rome. These services were not honoured by Nero; it was left to *Vespasian to grant him the *ornamenta triumphalia*. In 70 he was sent to govern Hispania *Tarraconensis, but was probably recalled at once to be Prefect of the City (see PRAEFECTUS URBI).

ILS 986 (= *MW* 261) trans. D. Braund, *Augustus to Nero* no. 401; L. Halkin, *Ant. Class.* 1934, 121; U. Vogel-Weidemann, *Die Statthalter von Africa u. Asia in den Jahren 14–68* (1982), 405 ff.; P. Conole and R. Milns, *Hist.* 1983, 183 ff.   R. S.; B. M. L.

Plautus (Titus Maccius (*RE* Maccius) **Plautus)**, comic playwright, author of *fabulae palliatae* (see FABULA) between *c*.205 and 184 BC; plays by Plautus are the earliest Latin works to have survived complete. The precise form of his name is uncertain, and in any case each element of it may have been a nickname (see A. S. Gratwick, *CQ* 1973, 78 ff.). He is said to have come from Sarsina in Umbria, inland from *Ariminum (Jerome, Festus; an inference from the joke at *Mostellaria* 769 f.?), made money in some kind of theatrical employment, lost it in a business venture, and been reduced to working in a mill (Gell. *NA* 3. 3. 14 f., probably all fictitious). Gell. *NA* 3. 3 records that 130 plays were attributed to him but that the authenticity of most was disputed; *Varro had drawn up a list of 21 plays which were generally agreed to be by Plautus, and there can be little doubt that these are the 21 transmitted in our manuscripts and listed at the end below (though Varro himself believed some others to be genuine as well). Nearly 200 further lines survive in later quotations (many of one line or less), attributed to over 30 named plays.

The *didascaliae* give dates of 200 BC for *Stichus* (at the Plebeian Games) and 191 for *Pseudolus* (Megalesian Games, on the dedication of the temple of *Cybele). See LUDI. There is general agreement that *Cistellaria* and *Miles Gloriosus* are relatively early plays, *Bacchides*, *Casina*, *Persa*, *Trinummus*, and *Truculentus* late, but the dating of most plays is quite uncertain; the criteria usually invoked are (alleged) contemporary references and relative frequency of *cantica*, but neither yields indisputable results.

The plays are nearly all either known or assumed to be adaptations of (Greek) New Comedy, with plots portraying love affairs, confusion of identity and misunderstandings; the strongest candidates for (Greek) Middle Comedy are *Amphitruo* (Plautus' only mythological comedy) and *Persa* (because of the reference to a Persian expedition into Arabia at line 506). See COMEDY (GREEK), MIDDLE and NEW. For eight plays the prologue names the author or title, or both, of the Greek original: *Diphilus is named as the author for *Casina* and *Rudens*, *Philemon (1) for *Mercator* and *Trinummus*, the otherwise unknown Demophilus for *Asinaria*; titles alone are given for *Miles Gloriosus* and *Poenulus*; the prologue of *Vidularia* is very fragmentary but seems to have given at least the title of the original. In addition, *Bacchides*, *Cistellaria*, and *Stichus* are known to be based on plays by *Menander (1), and *Aulularia* is widely believed to be. We cannot always be sure what titles Plautus himself gave his plays, but in about half these cases he seems to have changed it from the Greek original, and the titles of nearly all his plays have at least been Latinized. Scholars influenced by *Terence's invocation of Plautine precedent at *Andria* prologue 18 used to think they could show that Plautus had in some cases incorporated material from another Greek play into his adaptation (see CONTAMINATIO); it is now commoner to believe in free invention of some material by Plautus. Attempts have even been made to show that he sometimes took no specific Greek original as his model, so far without success. But he adapted his models with considerable freedom and wrote plays that are in several respects quite different from anything we know of New Comedy. There is a large increase in the musical element. The roles of stock characters such as the *parasite appear to have been considerably expanded. Consistency of characterization and plot development are cheerfully sacrificed for the sake of an immediate effect. The humour resides less in the irony of the situation than in jokes and puns. There are 'metatheatrical' references to the audience and to the progress of the play (e.g. *Pseudolus* 388, 562 ff., 720–1), or explicit reminders (as at *Stichus* 446–8) that the play is set in Greece. Above all, there is a constant display of verbal fireworks, with alliteration, wordplays, unexpected personifications (e.g. *Rudens* 626, 'Twist the neck of wrongdoing'), and riddling expressions (e.g. *Mercator* 361, 'My father's a fly: you can't keep anything secret from him, he's always buzzing around'). Both the style of humour and the presentation of stock characters may well have been influenced by the *Atellana*, but the verbal brilliance is Plautus' own.

The Greek originals have not survived, but a tattered papyrus published by Handley in 1968 contains the lines on which *Bacchides* 494–561 are based (from Menander's *Dis Exapaton*, 'The Double Deceiver'), for the first time enabling us to study Plautus' techniques of adaptation at first hand, and confirming the freedom of his approach. Plautus has preserved the basic plot and sequence of scenes, but he has cut two scenes altogether and has contrived to avoid a pause in the action where there was an act-break in the original. The tormented monologue of a young man in love has had some jokes added to it. Passages spoken without musical accompaniment in the original Greek are turned into accompanied passages in longer lines. The play is still set in Athens, and the characters have Greek-sounding names; but Plautus has changed most of them, in particular that of the scheming slave who dominates the action, called Syrus (The Syrian) in Menander's play; Plautus calls him Chrysalus (Goldfinger) and adds some colour elsewhere in the play by punning on this name. Chrysalus even boasts of his superiority to slaves called Syrus (649)!

The plots show considerable variety, ranging from the character study of *Aulularia* (the source of Molière's *L'Avare*) to the transvestite romp of *Casina*, from the comedy of mistaken identity in *Amphitruo* and *Menaechmi* (both used by Shakespeare in *The Comedy of Errors*) to the more movingly ironic recognition comedy of *Captivi* (unusual in having no love interest). *Trinummus* is full of high-minded moralizing; *Truculentus* shows the triumph of an utterly amoral and manipulative prostitute. In several plays it is the authority-figure, the male head of the household, who comes off worst: *Casina* and *Mercator* show father and son competing for the love of the same girl, while at the end of *Asinaria* the father is caught by his wife as he tries to share his son's beloved; other plays (above all *Bacchides*, *Epidicus*, *Mostellaria*, and *Pseudolus*) glorify the roguish slave, generally for outwitting the father. These plays have been seen as providing a holiday release from the tensions of daily life, and their Greek setting must have helped: a world in which young men compete with mercenary soldiers for a long-term relationship with a prostitute was probably quite alien to Plautus' first audiences, a fantasy world in which such aberrations as the domination of citizens by slaves could safely be contemplated as part of the entertainment.

Plautus is at his most exuberant in the *cantica*, operatic arias and duets written in a variety of metres, with considerable technical virtuosity, and displaying many features of high-flown style. They often do little or nothing to advance the action, and we know of nothing like them in Greek New Comedy. *Cantica* come in many contexts, e.g. in the mouth of young men in love (as at *Cistellaria* 203–28, *Mostellaria* 84–156, *Trinummus* 223–75), or of 'running slaves', who rush on to the stage in great excitement to deliver an important piece of news but take the time to deliver a lengthy monologue about its importance (as at *Mercator* 111–30, *Stichus* 274–307, *Trinummus* 1008–58). Chrysalus has two strikingly boastful *cantica* at *Bacchides* 640–66 and 925–77. Some of his boasting is embroidered with triumph-imagery and other peculiarly Roman references; it is part of the fantasy of Plautus' Greek world that it can include Italian elements. Thus at *Pseudolus* 143 and 172 the pimp Ballio in addressing the members of his establishment speaks as a Roman magistrate issuing an official edict, and at *Menaechmi* 571 ff. the complaints about the duties of a patron are concerned entirely with social problems at Rome in Plautus' day. But such explicit comment on Roman matters is rare.

Plautus' plays continued to be performed with success at Rome at least until the time of Horace, and they were read by later generations. The earliest surviving manuscript is the 6th-cent. 'Ambrosian palimpsest'. Plautus was well known in Renaissance Italy, particularly after the rediscovery of twelve plays in a manuscript found in Germany in 1429, and his plays were performed and imitated all over Europe until the seventeenth century, and more sporadically thereafter. Terence was more widely read in schools, but both contributed to the development of the European comic tradition (see COMEDY, LATIN; PALLIATA).

TEXT F. Leo (1895–6); W. M. Lindsay (OCT); P. Nixon (Loeb, with Eng. trans.); A. Ernout (Budé, with Fr. trans.). On the MSS, R. J. Tarrant, in *Texts and Transmission*. (O. Zwierlein, *Zur Kritik und Exegese des Plautus* 1–4 (1990–2; more vols. to follow) argues that the transmitted texts have been heavily interpolated and that Plautus himself preserved faithfully the elegance of his Greek originals. The case for widespread interpolation is strong; but few are likely to be convinced that so much of what has been seen as characteristically Plautine is in fact post-Plautine.)

LIST OF SURVIVING PLAYS (WITH SELECTION OF EDITIONS AND COMMENTARIES) *Amphitruo*: W. B. Sedgwick (1960). *Asinaria* ('The Comedy of Asses'): F. Bertini (Lat. 1968). *Aulularia* ('The Pot of Gold'): W. Stockert (Ger. 1983). *Bacchides* ('The Bacchis Sisters'): C. Questa (1975²; no comm.), J. Barsby (1986). *Captivi* ('The Prisoners'): W. M. Lindsay (1900, school edn. 1921²), J. Brix, M. Niemeyer, and O. Köhler (Ger. 1930⁷). *Casina*: W. T. MacCary and M. M. Willcock (1976). *Cistellaria* ('The Casket Comedy'). *Curculio* ('The Weevil'): J. Collart (Fr. 1962), G. Monaco (Ital. 1969). *Epidicus*: G. E. Duckworth (1940). *Menaechmi* ('The Menaechmus Brothers'): A. S. Gratwick (1993); companion to the Penguin trans., F. Muecke (1987). *Mercator* ('The Businessman'): P. J. Enk (Lat. 1932). *Miles Gloriosus* ('The Boastful Soldier'): J. Brix, M. Niemeyer, and O. Köhler (Ger. 1916⁴), M. Hammond, A. M. Mack, and W. Moskalew (1970²). *Mostellaria* ('The Haunted House'): E. A. Sonnenschein (1907²), J. Collart (Fr. 1970), F. R. Merrill (1972). *Persa* ('The Persian'): E. Woytek (Ger. 1982). *Poenulus* ('The Punic Chappie'): G. Maurach (Ger. 1988²). *Pseudolus*: A. O. F. Lorenz (Ger. 1876), M. M. Willcock (1987). *Rudens* ('The Rope'): E. A. Sonnenschein (1901²), F. Marx (Ger. 1928), H. C. Fay (1969). *Stichus*: H. Petersmann (Ger. 1973). *Trinummus* ('Threepence'): J. Brix, M. Niemeyer, and F. Conrad (Ger. 1931⁶). *Truculentus* ('The Ferocious Fellow'): P. J. Enk (Lat. 1953). *Vidularia* ('The Suitcase'—only *c.*100 lines survive): R. Calderan (Ital. 1982). Lat. comm. on all the plays: J. L. Ussing (1875–92).

TRANSLATIONS E. F. Watling (Penguin, 9 plays); E. Segal (*Miles Gloriosus, Menaechmi, Mostellaria*: 1969); C. Stace (*Rudens, Curculio, Casina*: 1981); J. Tatum (*Bacchides, Casina, Truculentus*: 1983); P. L. Smith (*Miles Gloriosus, Pseudolus, Rudens*: 1991).

BIBLIOGRAPHIC SURVEYS J. D. Hughes, *A Bibliography of Scholarship on Plautus* (1975); D. Fogazza, *Lustrum* 1976; E. Segal, *Classical World*, 1981; F. Bubel, *Bibliographie zu Plautus 1976–1989* (1992).

LANGUAGE AND LEXICON W. M. Lindsay, *Syntax of Plautus* (1907); G. Lodge, *Lexicon Plautinum* (1924 and 1933).

METRE W. M. Lindsay, *Early Latin Verse* (1922); C. Questa, *Introduzione alla metrica di Plauto* (1967), and *Numeri innumeri* (1984); L. Braun, *Die Cantica des Plautus* (1970); A. S. Gratwick (ed.), *Menaechmi* (1993).

STUDIES W. S. Anderson, *Barbarian Play: Plautus' Roman Comedy* (1993); M. Bettini, *Verso un' antropologia dell'intreccio* (1991); F. Della Corte, *Da Sarsina a Roma* (1967²); E. Fraenkel, *Plautinisches im Plautus* (1922) = *Elementi Plautini in Plauto* (1960, with additional notes); E. W. Handley, *Menander and Plautus: A Study in Comparison* (1968); G. Jachmann, *Plautinisches und Attisches* (1931); E. Lefèvre, E. Stärk, and G. Vogt-Spira, *Plautus barbarus* (1991); F. Leo, *Plautinische Forschungen* (1912²), *Geschichte der römischen Literatur* (1913), 93 ff; E. Segal, *Roman Laughter* (1987²); N. Slater, *Plautus in Performance* (1985); N. Zagagi, *Tradition and Originality in Plautus* (1980).   P. G. M. B.

plebiscitum, as opposed to *lex (1), was in theory a resolution carried by any Roman assembly in which no patrician cast his vote. In practice, except perhaps on a few occasions in the late republic, it was a resolution of a plebeian tribal assembly (*concilium plebis*: see COMITIA) presided over by a plebeian magistrate. At first the plebiscite was no more than a recommendation, and it attained the force of law only if re-enacted at the instance of a consul in the full assembly of the *populus*; but from an early date—possibly 449 BC—all plebiscites were recognized as universally binding which received the prior sanction of the patrician senators (**patrum auctoritas*). By the *lex Hortensia* of 287 BC (see HORTENSIUS, QUINTUS) they were afforded unconditional validity, and, with plebeian tribunes being drawn increasingly from within the governing class in the years which followed, they embodied much of the official routine legislation of the middle republic. In the post-Gracchan period they again became instruments of challenge to senatorial authority. Sulla therefore required in 88, and again in 81 BC, that all tribunician proposals should be approved by the senate before being put to the vote. This restriction was removed in 70 BC.

Mommsen, *Röm. Forsch.* 1. 177 ff., *Röm. Staatsr.* 3³. 150 ff.; H. Siber, *Die plebejischen Magistraturen* (1936), 39 ff.; A. Roos, *Comitia Tributa–Concilium plebis, Leges–Plebiscita* (1940); E. S. Staveley, *Athenaeum* 1955, 3 ff.; A. Drummond, *CAH* 7²/2 (1989), 222 ff.   E. S. S.; A. J. S. S.

plebs, the name given to the mass of Roman citizens, as distinct from the privileged patricians, perhaps related to the Greek term for the masses, *plethos*. A modern hypothesis that the *plebs* was racially distinct from the *patricians is not supported by ancient evidence; and the view of some ancient writers (Cic. *Rep.* 2. 16; Dion. Hal. 2. 9; Plut. *Rom.* 13) that the plebeians were all clients (see CLIENS) of the patricians in origin may simply be an overstatement of the truism that clients were plebeians. Although we can confidently believe in the differentiation of an aristocracy of wealthier and more powerful families in the regal period, a clear-cut distinction of birth does not seem to have become important before the foundation of the republic, except perhaps in the field of religion, where the view that the plebeians did not originally have *gentes* (Livy 10. 8. 9; see GENS) may be of some value. Our sources maintain that in the early republic the plebeians were excluded from religious colleges, magistracies, and the senate; a law of the *Twelve Tables confirmed an existing ban on their intermarriage with patricians, only to be repealed within a few years by the *lex Cannuleia*. However, they were enrolled in *curiae (see CURIA (1)) and *tribus, they served at all times in the army and could hold the office of *tribunus militum. The 'Conflict of the Orders', by which the *plebs* (or, more precisely, its wealthier members) achieved political equality with the patricians, is an essential part of the story of the development of Rome. The *plebs* owed its victory to the fact that it organized itself into an association, which held its own assemblies (*concilia plebis*; see COMITIA), appointed its own officers, the *tribuni plebis and *aediles (usually selected from the wealthier members of the order) and deposited its own records in the temples of *Ceres and *Diana on the *Aventine. Its major tactic in crises was *secessio, secession *en masse* from Rome (note that the term *seditio* also means a going apart). During the first secession it secured inviolability for the persons of its officers by a collective undertaking to protect them. In fact the tribunes and aediles became in due course magistrates of the *populus Romanus*. The final secession in 287 BC led to the *lex Hortensia, which made *plebiscita binding on the whole community. This is normally regarded as the end of the Conflict of the Orders, since the plebeians were no longer significantly disadvantaged *qua* plebeians. However, there continued to be clashes between the interests of the aristocrats and the wealthy and those of the humbler citizens over issues such as public land, which had first emerged in the early republic. Under the later republic the name 'plebeian' acquired in ordinary parlance its modern sense of a member of the lower social orders. Hence from at least *Augustus' reign onwards those who did not belong to the senatorial or equestrian orders or to the order of the local senate (*decuriones*) in colonies or *municipia* were often called the *plebs*.

A. Momigliano, *JRS* 1963; J.-C. Richard, *Les Origines de la plèbe romaine* (1978); A. Guarino, *La rivoluzione de la plebe* (1975); K. Raaflaub, *Social Struggles in Archaic Rome* (1986); Z. Yavetz, *Plebs and Princeps* (1969); M. Griffin in L. Alexander (ed.), *Images of Empire* (1991), 19 ff.

A. M., A. W. L.

Pleiad The name given to eight or more tragic poets in *Alexandria (1): *Alexander (8) of Aetolia; Homerus of Byzantion, son of *Moero; *Sosiphanes of Syracuse; *Sositheus of *Alexandria (7) Troas; *Lycophron (2); *Philicus; Dionysiades of Tarsus; Aeantides. These are the eight names usually included in the group though there are fluctuations in the ancient lists (cf. SEVEN SAGES; SEVEN WONDERS OF THE ANCIENT WORLD; CANON). Strictly there ought to have been only seven members of the Pleiad, to correspond to the stars in the astronomical *constellation (no. 23) of that name. (See ATLAS; MAIA; MEROPE (1); ORION; STEROPE; for the Pleiades in myth, who gave their names to the stars.) See also TRAGEDY, GREEK, § II. 1.

F. Stoessl, *Kleine Pauly* 4 (1979), 923; Fraser, *Ptol. Alex.* 1. 619; both on the literary Pleiad. Full evidence (complicated) for the mythical and astronomical Pleiades: E. Boer, *Kleine Pauly* 4 (1979), 922 f.   S. H.

Pleminius (*RE* 2), **Quintus**, was put in charge of *Locri Epizephyrii by P. *Cornelius Scipio Africanus after its recapture in 205 BC. He committed atrocities against the citizens and plundered the temple of *Persephone. A dispute with two military tribunes led to his being almost murdered by Roman soldiers. Scipio left him in charge after an enquiry, whereupon he tortured and executed both the tribunes and those Locrians who had complained to Scipio. In 204 the Locrians complained to the senate, and a commission was sent to investigate. The Locrians exonerated Scipio, but Pleminius and his accomplices were sent to Rome for trial. In one version he died before the trial could take place, in another he was executed in 194 after plotting to commit arson in Rome and thus escape from prison.

Briscoe, *Comm. 31–33*, 87.   J. Br.

Pleuron, an *Aetolian city originally settled between the *Acheloüs and Evenus rivers near ancient Mt. Kourion (at Gyfotokastro and Petrovouni). Originally ascribed to the Curetes as well as to the sons of *Aetolus (Pleuron and Calydon), the settlement is quite ancient and is listed in the catalogue of ships (Hom. *Il.* 2. 638). When *Demetrius (6) II of Macedonia destroyed the city *c.*230 BC (Strabo 10. 2. 4), the inhabitants moved 1.5 km. (*c.*1 mi.) northward to a large, fortified site (Kastro Kyra Eirinis) on Mt. Aracynthus (near Kato Retsina). Remains include an impressive, well-preserved circuit wall, a theatre, stoa, gymnasium, large cistern, and numerous building foundations.

Woodhouse, *Aetolia* (1897) 115–32; *PECS* 717–18; S. Bommelje and P. Doorn, *Aetolia and the Aetolians* (1987), 104.   W. M. M.

Pliny (1) **the Elder** (AD 23/4–79), Gaius Plinius Secundus, prominent Roman equestrian, from Novum *Comum in Gallia Cisalpina (see GAUL (CISALPINE)), commander of the fleet at *Misenum, and uncle of *Pliny (2) the Younger, best known as the author of the 37-book *Naturalis Historia*, an encyclopaedia of all contemporary knowledge—animal, vegetable, and mineral—but with much that is human included too: *natura, hoc est vita, narratur* ('Nature, which is to say Life, is my subject', *pref.* 13).

Characteristic of his age and background in his range of interests and diverse career, Pliny obtained an equestrian command through the patronage of Q. Pomponius Secundus (consul 41), and served in Germany, alongside the future emperor *Titus. Active in legal practice in the reign of *Nero, he was then promoted by the favour of the Flavians (and probably the patronage of *Licinius Mucianus, whose works he also often quotes) through a series of high procuratorships (including that of Hispania *Tarraconensis), in which he won a reputation for integrity. He became a member of the council of *Vespasian and Titus, and

was given the command of the Misenum fleet. When *Vesuvius erupted on 24 August 79, duty and curiosity combined, fatally; he led a detachment to the disaster-area, landed at *Stabiae, and died from inhaling fumes. For his career and death two letters of his nephew (Pliny, *Ep. 3. 5* and *6. 16*) are the primary source (also Suet. *Illustr.* fr. 80 Reifferscheid).

Throughout this career Pliny was phenomenally productive of literary work. His cavalry command produced a monograph on the use of the throwing-spear by cavalrymen, piety towards his patron demanded a biography in two books. The *Bella Germaniae* in 20 books recounted Roman campaigns against the Germans, and was used by *Tacitus (1) in the *Annales* and *Germania*. *Studiosi* in 3 long books (two rolls each) was a collection of *sententiae* from *controversiae* for use by orators, and *Dubius sermo*, reconciling the claims of *analogy and anomaly in Latin diction, reflect his period of legal employment—and the dangers of composing anything less anodyne in the latter years of Nero. The years of his procuratorships produced a 31-book history continuing *Aufidius Bassus and covering the later Julio-Claudian period; and, dedicated to Titus, the *Naturalis Historia*.

Pliny was clearly impressed by scale, number, comprehensiveness, and detail. It is characteristic that he claims that there are 20,000 important facts derived from 2,000 books in his work (*pref.* 17), but this is a severe underestimate. The value of what he preserves of the information available to him (the more so since he usually attributes his material to its source) far outweighs the fact that when he can be checked against the original (as with *Theophrastus, for instance), he not infrequently garbles his information through haste or insufficient thought. To give only four examples: our study of ancient *agriculture, *medicine, the techniques of *metallurgy, and the canon of great artists in antiquity, would all be impoverished if the work had perished (see ART, ANCIENT ATTITUDES TO). So dependent are we on him for many technical fields, that it becomes essential to remember that, mania for inclusiveness notwithstanding, his was a selection of what was available to him (and is indeed—creditably—slanted where possible towards his own experience). The argument from literary silence about many matters of economic and social importance is thus often essentially an argument from the silence of Pliny, and therefore methodologically very limited. It still has to be said that he can scarcely be blamed for not applying the standards of empirical enquiry to ancient medical lore, or for sharing widespread misconceptions about the world. Indeed, one of the interesting aspects of the work is the eloquent witness that he provides for precisely these pre-scientific ways of thinking.

Pliny was no philosopher. It may indeed be thought refreshing to have a view of the ancient world from an author who did not have some claim to the philosophical viewpoint; certainly the sections where Pliny's thought is least accessible are often those where subject matter such as the Cosmos or the Divine take him away from the relatively concrete. Even here, though, there is an engaging personality at work, and there are enough asides and reflections on the world to give an impression of the author which, though it resembles, to an extent, the persona adopted by other Latin technical writers such as *Vitruvius or Sex. *Iulius Frontinus (and is deeply conscious of what literary work it is proper to expect from an important equestrian, but not a senator) is still highly individual: as is the style and the imagery, which was often misunderstood in later antiquity, and can still baffle today. The standard ethical *diatribe against luxury and aristocratic excess of the man from the municipality is given vivid historical and geographical colour, and if the Roman past is idealized it is partly through the evocation of an image of the *populus Romanus* which is among the least hostile treatments of the many in any ancient author. The themes of the sufficient excellence of the natural endowment of Italy, and the terrible moral threat posed by the differential value of the exotic, form a laconic and memorable conclusion to book 37 (described in book 1, end as *Comparatio naturae per terras; comparatio rerum per pretia,* 'nature compared in different lands; products compared as to value').

Vita vigilia est (*pref.* 18): Life is being awake. The *Naturalis Historia* is a monument to keeping alert, and to the useful employment of time. Pliny's energy and diligence astonished his nephew, were intended to impress his contemporaries, and still amaze today; they were, moreover, not just a contingent habit of mind, but intended as an ethical statement. For all his defects of accuracy, selection, and arrangement, Pliny achieved a real summation of universal knowledge, deeply imbued with the mood of the time, and the greatness of his work was speedily recognized. It was a model for later writers such as *Iulius Solinus and *Isidorus (2), and attained a position of enormous cultural and intellectual influence in the medieval west.

Syme, *RP* 2 (1979), 742–73; M. Beagon, *Roman Nature* (1992), with other bibliog.

EDITIONS R. König and G. Winckler (Munich 1973– , with frags. of other works in vol. 1); various editors in Budé edn., now nearly complete, variable in quality; trans. (but unreliable text) H. Rackham and W. H. S. Jones (Loeb, 1938–63); C. Mayhoff (Teubner, 1899–1906).
N. P.

Pliny (2) **the Younger** (*c.* AD 61–*c.*112), Gaius Plinius Caecilius Secundus, is known from his writings and from inscriptions (e.g. *ILS* 2927). Son of a landowner of *Comum, he was brought up by his uncle, *Pliny (1) the Elder, of equestrian rank (see EQUITES), who adopted him, perhaps in his will; see ADOPTION. He studied rhetoric at the feet of *Quintilian and Nicetes at Rome. After the usual year's service on the staff of a Syrian legion (*c.*81), he entered the senate in the later 80s through the patronage of such distinguished family friends as *Verginius Rufus and Sex. *Iulius Frontinus. He practised with distinction in the civil courts all his life, specializing in cases relating to inheritance, and conducted several prosecutions in the senate of provincial governors charged with extortion. He rose up the senatorial ladder, becoming praetor in 93 (or less probably 95) and consul in 100, and he also held a series of imperial administrative appointments, as *praefectus aerari militaris* (*c.*94–6), *praefectus aerari Saturni* (*c.*98–100) (see AERARIUM for both posts), and *curator alvei Tiberis,* i.e. in charge of the banks of the river *Tiber (*c.*104–6). He was thrice a member of the judicial council of *Trajan (*c.*104–7), who sent him as *legatus Augusti* to govern *Bithynia-*Pontus (*c.*110; see LEGATI), where he apparently died in office (*c.*112). His career, very similar to that of his friend *Tacitus (1), is the best-documented example from the Principate of municipal origins and continuing ties, of the role of patronage, of the nature of senatorial employment under emperors tyrannical and liberal, and of the landed wealth that underpinned the system.

Pliny published nine books of literary letters between 99 (or 104) and 109 at irregular intervals, singly or in groups of three. Some letters comment elegantly on social, domestic, judicial, and political events, others offer friends advice, others again are references for jobs or requests for support for his own candidates in senatorial elections, while the tone is varied by the inclusion of short courtesy notes and set-piece topographical descriptions. Each letter is carefully composed (*Ep.* 1. 1), with great attention

to formal style; Pliny uses the devices of contemporary rhetoric, with intricate arrangement and balance of words and clauses in sentences and paragraphs. Letters are limited either to a single subject treated at appropriate length, or to a single theme illustrated by three examples (cf. *Epp.* 2. 20; 3. 16; 6. 31; 7. 27). Great care was also taken with the sequence of letters within each book. Pliny and his friends regularly exchanged such letters (*Ep.* 9. 28), which Pliny distinguished from boring business letters (*Ep.* 1. 10), from mere trivialites (*Ep.* 3. 20), and from the philosophical abstractions of Seneca's letters (*Ep.* 9. 2; see ANNAEUS SENECA (2), L.). The letters do have their origins in day-to-day events, but Pliny aimed to create a new type of literature. He set out to write not an annalistic history, but a picture of his times with a strong moral element. He censures the cruelty of slave masters, the dodges of legacy hunters, and the meanness of the wealthy, but the targets of his criticisms are normally anonymous. He dwells for preference on positive aspects of the present, the benign role of Trajan, the merits of friends and acquaintances, the importance of education, and the literary life of Rome. Other letters describe the public life of senatorial debates, elections and trials, without concealing the weaknesses of senators, and recount, in a manner anticipating Tacitus, heroic episodes of the political opposition to *Domitian, with which Pliny liked to claim some connection. See LETTERS, LATIN.

Pliny was also active in other fields of literature. He wrote verses enthusiastically, publishing two volumes in the manner of his protégé *Martial, of which he quotes a few indifferent specimens. His surviving speech, the *Panegyricus,* the only extant Latin speech between *Cicero and the late imperial panegyrics, is an expanded version of the original he delivered in the senate in thanks for his election to the consulship. Rhetorically a success (its popularity in the late-Roman rhetorical schools is responsible for its survival), it contrasts Trajan with the tyrannical Domitian. It is a major statement of the Roman political ideal of the good emperor condescending to play the role of an ordinary senator. See PANEGYRIC, LATIN.

The tenth book of letters contains all of Pliny's correspondence with Trajan: the first fourteen letters date between 98 and *c.*110, the remainder to Pliny's governorship of Bithynia-Pontus. The letters are much simpler in style than those in books 1–9 and were not worked up for publication, which probably occurred after Pliny's death. The provincial letters are the only such dossier surviving entire, and are a major source for understanding Roman provincial government. Each letter concerns a particular problem, such as the status of foundlings or the condition of civic finances, on which Pliny sought a ruling from Trajan. In *Ep.* 10. 96 Pliny gives the earliest external account of Christian worship, and the fullest statement of the reasons for the execution of Christians; see CHRISTIANITY.

TEXT *Ep.* R. A. B. Mynors (1963); *Pan.* M. Durry (1938); R. A. B. Mynors, in *XII Panegyrici Latini* (1964).

STUDIES R. Syme, *Tacitus* (1958), chs 7–8, app. 17, 19–21; A. N. Sherwin-White, *The Letters of Pliny: A Historical and Social Commentary* (1966), with review by F. Millar, *JRS* 1968, 218–24; R. P. Duncan-Jones, *The Economy of the Roman Empire*[2] (1982), ch. 1. A. N. S.-W.; S. R. F. P.

Plotina See POMPEIA PLOTINA.

Plotinus (*Πλωτῖνος*) (AD 205–269/70), Neoplatonist philosopher. The main facts of his life are known from *Porphyry's memoir (prefixed to editions of the *Enneads*). His birthplace, on which Porphyry is silent, is said by *Eunapius and the *Suda* to have been Lyco or Lycopolis in Egypt, but his name is Roman, while his native language was almost certainly Greek. He turned to philosophy in his 28th year and worked for the next eleven years under *Ammonius Saccas at *Alexandria (1). In 242–3 he joined *Gordian III's unsuccessful expedition against Persia, hoping for an opportunity to learn something of eastern thought. The attempt was abortive, and at the age of 40 he settled in Rome as a teacher of philosophy, and remained there until his last illness, when he retired to *Campania to die. At Rome he became the centre of an influential circle of intellectuals, which included men of the world and men of letters, besides professional philosophers like *Amelius and Porphyry. He interested himself also in social problems, and tried to enlist the support of the emperor Gallienus (see LICINIUS EGNATIUS GALLIENUS, P.) for a scheme to found a Platonic community on the site of a ruined Pythagorean settlement in Campania (see PYTHAGORAS (1)).

Writings Plotinus wrote nothing until he was 50. He then began to produce a series of philosophical essays arising directly out of discussions in his seminars (συνουσίαι), and intended primarily for circulation among his pupils. These were collected by Porphyry, who classified them roughly according to subject, arranged them rather artificially in six *Enneads* or groups of nine, and eventually published them c.300–5. From this edition our manuscripts are descended. An edition by another pupil, the physician *Eustochius, is known to have existed (schol. *Enn.* 4. 4. 30); and it has been argued by some scholars (Henry, *Recherches*, etc., see bibliog.) that the extracts from Plotinus in *Eusebius, *Praep. Evang.* are derived from this Eustochian recension. Save for the omission of politics, Plotinus' essays range over the whole field of ancient philosophy: ethics and aesthetics are dealt with mainly in *Enn.* 1, physics and cosmology in *Enns.* 2 and 3; psychology in *Enn.* 4; metaphysics, logic, and epistemology in *Enns.* 5 and 6. Though not systematic in intention, the *Enneads* form in fact a more complete body of philosophical teaching than any other which has come down to us from antiquity outside the Aristotelian corpus. Plotinus' favourite method is to raise and solve a series of ἀπορίαι ('difficulties'): many of the essays give the impression of a man thinking aloud or discussing difficulties with a pupil. Owing to bad eyesight, Plotinus never revised what he wrote (Porph. *Vita Plot.* 8), and his highly individual style often reflects the irregular structure of oral statement. Its allusiveness, rapid transitions, and extreme condensation render him one of the most difficult of Greek authors; but when deeply moved he can write magnificently.

Philosophical Doctrine In the 19th cent. Plotinus' philosophy was often dismissed as an arbitrary and illogical syncretism of Greek and oriental ideas. Recent writers, on the other hand, see in him the most powerful philosophical mind between *Aristotle and Aquinas or Descartes; and in his work a logical development from earlier Greek thought, whose elements he organized in a new synthesis designed to meet the needs of a new age. These needs influenced the direction rather than the methods of his thinking: its direction is determined by the same forces which resulted in the triumph of the eastern religions of salvation, but its methods are those of traditional Greek rationalism. Plotinus attached small value to ritual, and the religious ideas of the Near East seem to have had little direct influence on the *Enneads*, though Bréhier would explain certain parallels with Indian thought by postulating contact with Indian travellers in Alexandria. To *Christianity Plotinus makes no explicit reference; but *Enn.* 2. 9 is an eloquent defence of Hellenism against Gnostic superstition (see GNOSTICISM).

Plotinus holds that all modes of being, whether material or mental, temporal or eternal, are constituted by the expansion or 'overflow' of a single immaterial and impersonal force, which he identifies with the 'One' of the *Parmenides* and the 'Good' of the *Republic* (see PLATO (1)), though it is strictly insusceptible of any predicate or description. As 'the One', it is the ground of all existence; as 'the Good', it is the source of all values. There is exact correspondence between degrees of reality and degrees of value, both being determined by the degree of unity, or approximation to the One, which any existence achieves. Reality, though at its higher levels it is non-spatial and non-temporal, may thus be pictured figuratively as a series of concentric circles resulting from the expansion of the One. Each of these circles stands in a relation of timeless dependence to that immediately within it, which is in this sense its 'cause'; the term describes a logical relationship, not an historical event. Bare Matter (ὕλη) is represented by the circumference of the outermost circle: it is the limiting case of reality, the last consequence of the expansion of the One, and so possesses only the ideal existence of a boundary.

Between the One and Matter lie three descending grades of reality—the World-mind (νοῦς), the World-soul (ψυχή), and Nature (φύσις). The descent is marked by increasing individuation and diminishing unity. The World-mind resembles Aristotle's Unmoved Mover: it is thought-thinking-itself, an eternal lucidity in which the knower and the known are distinguishable only logically; within it lie the Platonic Forms, which are conceived not as inert types or models but as a system of interrelated forces, differentiations of the one Mind which holds them together in a single timeless apprehension (νόησις). The dualism of subject and object, implicit in the self-intuition of Mind, is carried a stage further in the discursive thinking characteristic of *Soul: because of its weaker unity, Soul must apprehend its objects successively and severally. In doing so it creates time and space; but the World-soul is itself eternal and transcends the spatio-temporal world which arises from its activity. The lowest creative principle is Nature, which corresponds to the immanent World-soul of the Stoics (see STOICISM): its consciousness is faint and dreamlike, and the physical world is its projected dream.

Man is a microcosm, containing all these principles actually or potentially within himself. His consciousness is normally occupied with the discursive thinking proper to Soul: but he has at all times a subconscious activity on the dreamlike level of Nature and a superconscious activity on the intuitive level of Mind; and his conscious life may lapse by habituation to the former level or be lifted by an intellectual discipline to the latter. Beyond the life of Mind lies the possibility of unification (ἕνωσις), an experience in which the Self by achieving complete inward unity is momentarily identified with the supreme unity of the One. This is the Plotinian doctrine of ecstasy. The essays in which he expounds it, on the basis of personal experience, show extraordinary introspective power and are among the classics of mysticism. It should be observed that for Plotinus unification is independent of divine grace; is attainable very rarely, as the result of a prolonged effort of the will and understanding; and is not properly a mode of cognition, so that no inference can be based on it.

Plotinus also made important contributions to psychology, particularly in his discussion of problems of perception, consciousness, and memory; and to aesthetic, where for Plato's doctrine that Art 'imitates' natural objects he substitutes the view that Art and Nature alike impose a structure on Matter in

Plotius Tucca

accordance with an inward vision of archetypal Forms (see ART, ANCIENT ATTITUDES TO). His most original work in ethics is concerned with the question of the nature and origin of evil, which in some passages he attempts to solve by treating evil as the limiting case of good, and correlating it with Matter, the limiting case of reality.

TEXTS P. Henry and H.-R. Schwyzer, *editio maior*, 3 vols. (1951–73), *editio minor* (OCT 1964–82); E. Bréhier (Budé, 1924–38), with Fr. trans.; A. H. Armstrong, (Loeb, 1966–88), with Eng. trans. and nn.

TRANSLATIONS Eng. S. MacKenna and B. S. Page (4th. edn. 1969; Penguin edn., with some tractates omitted, ed. J. M. Dillon, 1991); Ger.: R. Harder (1930–7), rev. edn., with Gk. text, and comm. by R. Beutler and W. Theiler (1956–67); Ital. V. Cilento (1947–9). A new Fr. series of trans. and comms. by P. Hadot (1988–   ).

PHILOSOPHY E. Bréhier, *La Philosophie de Plotin* (1928, Eng. trans., 1958); W. R. Inge, *The Philosophy of Plotinus* (1929); A. H. Armstrong, *The Architecture of the Intelligible Universe in the Philosophy of Plotinus* (1940, repr. 1967); P. Hadot, *Platin, ou la simplicité du regard* (1963, 2nd edn. 1973); J. M. Rist, *Plotinus, The Road to Reality* (1967); H. Blumenthal, *Plotinus's Psychology* (1971); R. T. Wallis, *Neoplatonism* (1972); G. P. O'Daly, *Plotinus's Philosophy of the Self* (1973); E. Emilsson, *Plotinus on Sense-Perception* (1988); D. O'Meara, *Plotinus* (1993). H.-R. Schwyzer, in *RE*, is still most useful.

See also NEOPLATONISM.   E. R. D.; J. M. D.

Plotius Tucca, friend of *Virgil and *Horace and member of *Maecenas' circle (Hor. *Sat.* 1. 5. 30, 1. 10. 81), also associated with *Philodemus (*Pap. Herc. Paris* 2). He is claimed to have assisted *Varius Rufus in the posthumous editing for publication of Virgil's *Aeneid* on the orders of *Augustus (Donatus, *Vit. Verg.* 38–41, Servius, *Praef. ad Aen.*), but the evidence concerning the extent and nature of this edition is unreliable and problematic.

R. Scarcia, *Enc. Virg.* s.v. 'Tucca'; G. P. Goold, *Harv. Stud.* 74 (1970), 122–30.   S. J. Ha.

ploughing (Roman) 'What is good cultivation? Good ploughing.' (Cato, *Agr.* 61. 1; see PORCIUS CATO (1), M., *Appendix*). While ploughing was of paramount importance for the intensive *villa agriculture described by the Roman agricultural writers, *Pliny (1) the Elder's observation that mountain peoples 'ploughed' with hoes (*HN* 18. 176) indicates that ploughs were common enough elsewhere. Roman ploughs were ards (which worked the soil without turning the sod, cf. *Columella, *Rust.* 2. 2. 25), sole-ards being common to Mediterranean regions, beam-ards to northern provinces. *Peasants might possess an inexpensive plough drawn by the versatile ass (cf. Plin. *HN* 8. 167; Columella, *Rust.* 7. 1. 2). Villas bred oxen of different sizes and used a variety of ploughs and detachable ploughshares for diverse soils, crops (e.g. the smallest ploughs for fenugreek, Columella *Rust.* 2. 10. 33) and ploughing operations (e.g. working the soil in the vineyard, Columella *Rust.* 2. 2. 24; 3. 13. 3). The introduction of the coulter (Plin. *HN* 18. 171) and the wheeled plough (*HN* 18. 172–3: 'a recent invention', the diffusion of which is disputed) illustrates the continuing exploitation of heavier soils noted first in Cato (*Agr.* 135. 2). Biennial fallowing predominated, except where fertile soil allowed rotation or when the pressures of subsistence demanded continual cropping. The fallow was ploughed first in spring, after providing pasture over the winter (Varro, *Rust.* 1. 27. 2). Further ploughings with lighter ploughs provided a well-aereated seed-bed, to absorb rainfall but minimize evaporation, for the autumn sowing. To cover the seed and to create drainage channels (which also facilitated later weeding), a ridging plough was developed (Varro, *Rust.* 1. 29. 2–3; Palladius 1. 42. 1). See AGRICULTURE, ROMAN.

(In addition to the works cited for AGRICULTURAL IMPLEMENTS) A. G. Haudricourt and M. J.-B. Delamarre, *L'homme et la charrue à travers les ages* (1955); W. H. Manning, *JRS* 1964, 54–64 and *British Museum Quarterly* 35 (1971), 125–136; G. Forni, *Tecnologia, economia e società nel mondo romano. Atti del convegno di Como 27–29 settembre 1979* (1980), 89–120.   M. S. Sp.

Plouton See HADES.

Ploutos See PLUTUS.

Plutarch (L.(?) Mestrius Plutarchus) of *Chaeronea; b. before AD 50, d. after AD 120; philosopher and biographer. The family had long been established in Chaeronea, and most of Plutarch's life was spent in that historic town, to which he was devoted. He knew Athens well, and visited both Egypt and Italy, lecturing and teaching at Rome. His father, Autobulus, his grandfather, Lamprias, and other members of his family figure often in his dialogues; his wide circle of influential friends include the consulars L. Mestrius Florus (whose gentile name he bore), Q. *Sosius Senecio (to whom the *Parallel Lives* and other works are dedicated), and C. *Minicius Fundanus, as well as magnates like the exiled Syrian prince *Iulius Antiochus Philopappus (see COMMAGENE). For the last thirty years of his life, Plutarch was a priest at *Delphi. A devout believer in the ancient pieties and a profound student of its antiquities, he played a notable part in the revival of the shrine in the time of Trajan and Hadrian; and the people of Delphi joined with Chaeronea in dedicating a portrait bust of him 'in obedience to the decision of the Amphictions' (*Syll.*³ 843 A); see AMPHICTIONY. Late authorities (*Suda*, Eusebius) report that he received *ornamenta consularia* from Trajan, and was imperial procurator in Achaea under Hadrian; whatever lies behind this, he was a man of some influence in governing circles, as he was in his writing an active exponent of the concept of a partnership between Greece, the educator, and Rome, the great power, and of the compatibility of the two loyalties.

The 'Catalogue of Lamprias', a list of his works probably dating from the 4th cent., contains 227 items. Extant are 78 miscellaneous works (some not listed in the Catalogue) and 50 Lives. We have lost the Lives of the Caesars (except *Galba* and *Otho*) and some others (notably *Epaminondas, Pindar, Daiphantus*), and probably two-thirds of the miscellaneous works. Nevertheless, what remains is a formidable mass; Plutarch was a very prolific writer, especially (it seems) in the last twenty years of his life. The relative chronology of his works however is very difficult to establish (C. P. Jones, *JRS* 1966, 61–74). For a complete list of titles, see e.g. any volume of the Loeb *Moralia*, or D. A. Russell, *Select Essays and Dialogues* (World's Classics, 1993), pp. xxiii–xxix. In what follows, we can only mention a few. (The numbers attached to the titles refer to the order of treatises in all editions.)

1. The group of *rhetorical* works—epideictic performances—includes 'The Glory of Athens' (22), 'The Fortune of Rome' (20), 'Against Borrowing Money' (54). Plutarch's richly allusive and metaphorical style does not seem very well adapted to rhetorical performance, and these—with the exception of 'Against Borrowing' which is a powerful, satirical piece—are not very successful; it is often thought, though without clear evidence, that Plutarch's epideictic rhetoric was something that he gave up in later life.

2. The numerous treatises on themes of popular moral philosophy are derivative in content, but homogeneous and characteristic in style. Among the best are 'Friends and Flatterers' (4), 'Progress in Virtue' (5), 'Superstition' (14), 'The Control of

Anger' (29), 'Talkativeness' (35), 'Curiosity' (36), and 'Bashfulness' (38). In 'Rules for Politicians' (52), Plutarch draws both on his historical reading and on his own experience, to give advice to a young man entering politics. The warm and sympathetic personality never far beneath the surface appears particularly in 'Consolation to my Wife' (45) and 'Advice on Marriage' (12). Plutarch's teaching is less individualistic than that of many ancient moralists: family affections and friendly loyalties play a large part in it.

3. Many of Plutarch's works are *dialogues, written not so much in the Platonic tradition as in that of *Aristotle (and indeed *Cicero), with long speeches, a good deal of characterization, and the frequent appearance of the author himself as a participant. The nine books of 'Table Talk' (46) are full of erudite urbanity and curious speculation. 'Socrates' Daimonion' (43) combines exciting narrative (liberation of *Thebes (1) from Spartan occupation in 379/8; see PELOPIDAS) with philosophical conversation about prophecy (a favourite theme) and an elaborate Platonic myth (see PLATO (1)) of the fate of the soul after death (Plutarch attempted such myths elsewhere also, especially in 'God's Slowness to Punish' (41)). 'Eroticus' (47) also combines narrative with argument, this time in a near contemporary setting: the 'kidnapping' of a young man by a widow who wishes to marry him forms the background to a discussion of heterosexual and homosexual love in general. Delphi is the scene of four dialogues, all concerned with prophecy, *daimones*, and divine providence; and it is in these (together with *Isis and Osiris* (23)) that the greater part of Plutarch's philosophical and religious speculation is to be sought.

4. He was a Platonist, and a teacher of philosophy; and the more technical side of this activity is to be seen in his interpretation of the *Timaeus* (68) and a series of polemical treatises against the Stoics (70–2) and Epicureans (73–5).

5. We possess also important antiquarian works—'Roman Questions' and 'Greek Questions' (18), mainly concerned with religious antiquities—and some on literary themes ('On Reading the Poets' (2) is the most significant).

Plutarch's fame led to the inclusion in the corpus of a number of *spuria*, some of which have been very important: 'The Education of Children' (1) was influential in the Renaissance; 'Doctrines of the Philosophers' (58) is a version of a doxographic compilation to which we owe a lot of our knowledge of Greek philosophy, while 'Lives of the Ten Orators' (55) and 'Music' (76) are also important sources of information.

The 'Parallel Lives' remain his greatest achievement. We have 23 pairs, 19 of them with 'comparisons' attached. Plutarch's aims are set out e.g. in *Alexander* 1: his object was not to write continuous political history, but to exemplify individual virtue (or vice) in the careers of great men. Hence he gives attention especially to his heroes' education, to significant anecdotes, and to what he sees as the development or revelation of character. Much depends of course on the sources available to him (*Alcibiades* is full of attested personal detail, *Publicola* is thin and padded out, *Antony* full of glorious narrative, especially about *Cleopatra VII, *Phocion* and *Cato Maior* full of sententious anecdotes), but the general pattern is maintained wherever possible: family, education, début in public life, climaxes, changes of fortune or attitude, latter years and death. The *Lives*, despite the pitfalls for the historian which have sometimes led to despair about their value as source-material, have been the main source of understanding of the ancient world for many readers from the Renaissance to the present day.

Indeed, Plutarch has almost always been popular. He was a 'classic' by the 4th cent., and a popular educational text in Byzantine times. The preservation of so much of his work is due mainly to Byzantine scholars (especially Maximus Planudes). His wider influence dates from Renaissance translations, especially Amyot's French version (*Lives* 1559, *Moralia* 1572) and Sir T. North's English *Lives* (1579; largely based on Amyot) and Philemon Holland's *Moralia* (1603). Montaigne, Shakespeare, Dryden, Rousseau, and Emerson are among Plutarch's principal debtors. In the 19th cent., however, his influence, at least among scholars, diminished: he was seen as a derivative source both in history and in philosophy, and his lack of historical perspective and his rather simple moral attitudes earned him much disrespect. Recent scholarship has done much to reverse this negative view; as understanding of his learning and the aims and methods of his writing has deepened, so he has come again to be seen, not as a marginal figure, but as a thinker whose view of the classical world deserves respect and study. See also BIOGRAPHY, GREEK.

TEXTS Complete edns. of Plut. in Teubner (*Moralia*, H. Wegehaupt and others; *Vitae*, K. Ziegler and others) Collection Budé (R. Flacelière and others); Loeb (*Moralia*, F. C. Babbitt and others; *Lives*, B. Perrin). These naturally vary in quality: the Loeb *Lives* and the first 6 vols. of the Loeb *Moralia* are in need of revision. Of older edns., D. Wyttenbach (1795–1830) has a commentary on part of the *Moralia* and a *Lexicon Plutarcheum* not yet replaced. The *Index Rerum* in F. Duebner's edn. (1846) is still a useful tool, as is W. C. Helmbold and E. N. O'Neil, *Plutarch's Quotations* (1959).

Edns. of individual works have multiplied in recent years: e.g. B. P. Hillyard, *De audiendo* (1981); S. Schröder, *De Pythiae oraculis* (1990); J. Gwyn Griffiths, *De Iside et Osiride* (1970); S.-T. Theodorsson, *Quaestiones Convivales* (1989–); J. R. Hamilton, *Alexander* (1969); C. B. R. Pelling, *Antony* (1988); P. A. Stadter, *Pericles* (1989); J. L. Moles, *Cicero* (1988). Recent Ital. edns. include the series of *Lives* by M. Manfredini, L. Piccirilli and others, and the *Corpus Plutarchi Moralium* begun by I. Gallo and others.

GENERAL WORKS K. Ziegler, 'Plutarchos', *RE* 22. 1. 636–962 (rev. separate repr. 1964) is indispensable. See also C. P. Jones, *Plutarch and Rome* (1971); D. A. Russell, *Plutarch* (1972); and the long introd. by R. Flacelière and J. Irigoin in the Budé Œuvres Morales 1 (1987). R. Hirzel, *Plutarch* (1912), gives the best available account of Plutarch's influence.

OTHER BOOKS R. Hirzel, *Der Dialog* 2 (1895); R. M. Jones, *The Platonism of Plutarch* (1916); D. Babut, *Plutarque et le Stoïcisme* (1969); F. E. Brenk, *In Mist Apparelled* (1977); H. D. Betz (ed.), *Plutarch's Ethical Writings and Early Christian Literature* (1978), and *Plutarch's Theological Writings and Early Christian Literature* (1975). *ANRW* 33.6 (1992) is devoted to Plutarch. For recent bibliog. on *Lives*, See also P. A. Stadter (ed.), *Plutarch and the Historical Tradition* (1992).

TRANSLATIONS The classic 16th-cent. translations of the *Lives* have been often reprinted (e.g. Amyot in Bibliothèque de la Pléiade (1951), North in Tudor Translations (1895), and Temple Classics (1898) and often in selections (e.g. T. J. B. Spencer, *Shakespeare's Plutarch*, 1964)); 'Dryden's Plutarch' is in Dent's Everyman's Library, as is a selection from Philemon Holland's *Moralia*. For a complete Eng. *Moralia* (apart from the Loeb), see W. W. Goodwin's revision of the 18th-cent. version 'by various hands', 5 vols. (Boston, Mass., 1874–8). Modern versions of many *Lives* and some *Moralia* are in Penguin Classics; there are other selections from the *Moralia* by T. G. Tucker (1913), A. O. Prickard (1918), and D. A. Russell (1993).

Ploutarchos, the journal of the International Plutarch Society, reports on current scholarship on Plutarch and related subjects..   D. A. R.

Pluto, Pluton See HADES.

Plutus, Wealth, originally and properly abundance of crops, hence associated with *Demeter at *Eleusis. He is son of Demeter and *Iasion according to Hesiod (*Theog.* 969–74), but at

Plynteria

Athens, where he had an important role in the *Mysteries, he is attested simply as son of Demeter. Demeter and Kore (see PERSEPHONE/KORE) send him to those whom they favour (*Hymn. Hom. Cer.* 488–9), especially of course Eleusinian initiates. Unlike the fertility god Plouton (see HADES), he is only a personification, never the object of formal worship. In Eleusinian art he is represented in the company of Demeter and Kore usually as a boy a few years old, naked, holding a cornucopia or bunch of grain stalks, and wearing (in the Classical period) a loosely draped himation, as in the Great Eleusinian Relief. At a climactic moment in the Mysteries he evidently made a dramatic appearance.

Outside the Mysteries he is found in a variety of popular traditions and is associated with several gods and goddesses, including *Eirene and *Dionysus. In one tradition, represented by *Aristophanes (1)'s *Plutus*, he personifies wealth in general, appearing in the form of a blind old man.

Clinton, *Iconography*, chs. 2–3, and *LIMC*, 'Ploutos'; J. Zwicker, *RE* 21, 'Ploutos'. K. C.

Plynteria, an Attic festival (see ATTIC CULTS AND MYTHS) celebrated (in Athens) near the end of the early summer month Thargelion, at which the ancient image of *Athena Polias was undressed and washed ($\pi\lambda\acute{v}\nu\omega$) by women of the *genos* Praxiergidai; it was probably taken in procession to the sea. The day of the cleansing counted as impure, and temples were closed. The festival is probably old *Ionian in origin, as several Ionian communities have a month-name Plynterion. See IONIAN FESTIVALS.

R. Parker, *Miasma* (1983), 26 ff. R. C. T. P.

pneuma ($\pi\nu\epsilon\hat{v}\mu\alpha$, Lat. *spiritus*) is connected etymologically with $\pi\nu\acute{e}\omega$, breathe or blow, and has a basic meaning of 'air in motion', or 'breath' as something necessary to life. In Greek tragedy it is used of the 'breath of life' and it is the 'Spirit' of the New Testament. In early Greek thought *pneuma* is often connected with the *soul; in *Aristotle it frequently denotes 'warm air', sometimes 'heat', and the term is also used of seismic winds which are trapped within the earth. Its precise meaning, then, must always be determined in its context. The word may have been used first by *Anaximenes (1) of Miletus to describe both elemental air in motion in the world, and 'psychic air' in man. 'Psychic pneuma' also constitutes the soul and underlies sensory and motor activities in a number of ancient medical theories. In Hippocratic and post-Hippocratic writings (see HIPPOCRATES (2)) it is widely used of inspired air or breath inside the body, with no apparent reference to any particular theory. In the medical theory of *Erasistratus, 'vital pneuma' travels from the lungs via the heart into the arteries. One ancient medical sect, the 'Pneumatic' (see PNEUMATISTS), was called after its central use of such concepts. Pneuma-theory forms a cornerstone of Stoic *physics (see STOICISM), and the Stoics are particularly associated with the doctrine that pneuma provides the universe both with cohesion and its dynamic properties.

W. Jaeger, *Hermes*, 1913, 29–74; G. Verbeke, *L'Évolution de la doctrine du pneuma du stoicisme à S. Augustin* (1945); F. Solmsen, *MH* 1961, 150–97. J. T. V.

pneumatics in ancient contexts, suggests the fusion of the theoretical study of the properties of air (*pneuma) with its practical applications. (It might be more accurate to say 'fluids' generally rather than air if we are to characterize an ancient science which corresponds to what we now call hydraulics.) The investigation of the behaviour of fluids in motion attracted many disciples

from doctors to cosmologists to the inventors and builders of mechanical marvels.

It is unclear exactly when pneumatics came to be thought of as a subject in its own right. Its traditional founder was *Ctesibius of Alexandria, who worked in the early 3rd cent. BC and invented a number of mechanical toys operated by air, water, and steam under pressure. None of his work survives intact, but the fifth book of *Philon (2) of Byzantium's *Mechanical Syntaxis* (probably composed in the mid-3rd cent. BC, and existing now only in Arabic and Latin translations) is thought to draw heavily on Ctesibius' theoretical and practical work, as does book 10 of *Vitruvius' *On Architecture*. The earliest surviving work in Greek is *Heron of Alexandria's *Pneumatica*, which was probably composed in the 1st cent. AD. In the preface to this work the author is keen to acknowledge his debt to early 'philosophers' as well as mechanics. A number of early experiments in this area had been aimed at establishing the corporeality of air—Anaxagoras, for instance, is credited with a test involving the lowering of a tube closed at its upper end into water, in order to show that the water's entrance into the tube is somehow blocked by the air contained in the tube (DK 59 A 69). Many other such early investigations by natural philosophers were concerned with the explanation of biological phenomena such as respiration and the propulsion of fluids through the body, often by analogy with other more readily visible processes such as the operation of the water clock or *klepsydra* (see CLOCKS) which features in the Empedoclean account of the mechanics of respiration (DK 31 B 100; see EMPEDOCLES). In some later physiological theories, 'pneumatic motion' is invoked to explain the phenomena of pulsation and fluid dynamics generally, (eg. by *Erasistratus), as well as the activities of the motor nerves (perhaps by *Herophilus, although the evidence is not secure.) The central theoretical problem, however, concerned the nature of the vacuum and its role in the dynamics of fluid motion. Pneumatic motion was explained in a number of different ways depending on how the status of void was viewed. Some of those, including Heron and perhaps *Straton (1) of Lampsacus, who believed that large-scale void does not exist naturally within the cosmos, nevertheless allowed that it could be created on a small scale by force. Any vacuum so created will then draw in contiguous matter until the natural state is reached again. Others (ultimately following *Plato (1)) denied even the possibility of this kind of small scale, interstitial void, and insisted that void cannot exist in any form within the cosmos; for these people (who include the Stoics) pneumatic motion is explicable in terms of special dynamic properties inherent in *pneuma* itself in the cosmic continuum.

TEXTS For Philon see Carra de Vaux, *Notices et extraits des manuscrits de la Bibliothèque Nationale*, 38 (1903), 27–235. For Heron, W. Schmidt, *Heronis Alexandrini Opera*, 1 (1899) (Lat. version of Philo's *Pneumatics* is printed at the end of Schmidt's vol., pp. 458–89). The Eng. trans. of Hero by J. G. Greenwood in the 1851 edn. of Bennet Woodcroft repr. with additional material, in M. B. Hall (ed.), *The Pneumatics of Hero of Alexandria* (1971).

LITERATURE M. Boas, *Isis*, 1949, 38–48; A. G. Drachmann, *Acta Historica Scientiarum Naturalium et Medicinalium*, 1948, and *The Mechanical Technology of Greek and Roman Antiquity*, (1963). On the different conceptions of void, J. T. Vallance, *The Lost Theory of Asclepiades of Bithynia* (1990), ch. 2. J. T. V.

Pneumatists, term used in antiquity to describe a group of doctors influenced by Stoic *physics (see STOICISM), but also continuing an important Hippocratic tradition (see HIPPOCRATES (2)) which underlined the importance of *pneuma in explanations of psychological, physiological and pathological phenomena. (The spurious Hippocratic treatise *on Nutriment* which may date to the 1st cent. BC is often thought to show their influence.) Their founder was probably *Athenaeus (3) of Attaleia, and other influential doctors from this far from monolithic sect included *Archigenes of Apamea, *Agathinus of Sparta, *Aretaeus of Cappadocia, and *Herodotus (2) the Doctor. None of their works survive. They are associated with the division of the art of medicine into parts corresponding to the Stoic division of the parts of dialectic, along with much highly elaborate work on the nature and classification of the pulse, and with a lively interest in doxography. They had a reputation as eclectics and *Galen shows them a certain amount of sympathy. They may have claimed an affiliation with *Posidonius of Apamea (on the basis of a disputed reference in Aetius of Amida (Posidonius T 114 Kidd)), and also with the much earlier physician *Herophilus of Chalcedon, although both of these connections is uncertain.

M. Wellmann, *Philologische Untersuchungen* 14, 1895; H. Diller, *Sudhoffs Archiv* 1936, 178–95; F. Kudlien, *Hermes*, 1962, 419–29 and *RE* Suppl. 11. 1097–108.   J. T. V.

Pnyx, hill at Athens, 400 m. (*c.*440 yds.) south-west of the *Agora, where the Classical assembly or *ekklēsia* usually met. The auditorium was reconstructed, and its orientation altered, at the end of the 5th cent. BC, perhaps in connection with the introduction of pay for assembly attendance. See ATHENS, TOPOGRAPHY.

K. Kourouniotes and H. A. Thompson, *Hesp.* 1932, 96 ff.; M. H. Hansen, *The Athenian Assembly,* 2 (1989), 129–53.   S. H.

Po See PADUS.

Podalirius See MACHAON.

Poetelius (*RE* 7) **Libo Visolus, Gaius,** one of the lordly plebeians (see PLEBS) raised to public power by the *Leges Liciniae Sextiae* (see LICINIUS STOLO, C.), was consul 360 (when he triumphed over Gauls and Tiburtines), 346 and 320 BC. He is probably the tribune of 358 who passed a law against *ambitus*, necessitated by the consequences of those laws. In 326 (according to the Livian tradition), with his colleague L. *Papirius Cursor, he passed a law considerably alleviating debt bondage (*nexum*): the details are uncertain and debated. *Varro ascribes the law to his son as dictator 313.

Livy 7. 15. 12 f., 8. 28; Varro, *LL* 7. 105. G. MacCormack, *Labeo* 1973, 306 ff.   E. B.

Poetovio (mod. Ptuj in Slovenia), was a Roman legionary base and city in *Pannonia where the prehistoric Amber Route crossed the river Drava. During the 1st cent. AD it was occupied successively by Legions VIII Augusta (before *c.* AD 43–5) and XIII Gemina (see LEGION) until a veteran colony was established there under *Trajan (*colonia Ulpia Traiana*). Later the city was a headquarters of the customs organization for *Illyricum (*portorium publicum Illyrici*) and in the crisis of the 3rd cent. was again a military base. The city began on the site of the fortress and *canabae on the south bank of the river (Igornja and Hajdina) but later its centre moved to higher ground across the river (Ptuj) following construction of a stone bridge. Under *Diocletian the city passed from Pannonia into *Noricum and survived as a fortified Christian centre into the 5th cent.   J. J. W.

Poggio Civitate (Murlo), 24 km. (15 mi.) south of Siena, is the site of an anonymous early *Etruscan complex in the territory of *Clusium. Excavation (1966 onwards) has revealed an *orient-

alizing building, constructed between 675 and 650 BC, accidentally destroyed by fire *c.*610 and soon replaced by a similar Archaic complex which was dismantled and ritually obliterated *c.*530. Both phases are exceptionally rich in architectural terracottas; those of the earlier building combine with their counterparts at *Acquarossa to add a new (and fundamentally indigenous) dimension to previous knowledge of 7th-cent. Etruscan architecture. The excavators identify the orientalizing and Archaic complexes as 'meeting halls' of a religious and political (federal) nature. Others prefer to see the Archaic building as the private 'palace' of a local aristocrat; specific features of its plan have suggested direct derivation from Near Eastern models, and the decorative programme of its frieze-plaques includes the earliest representation in Italy of the characteristically Near Eastern reclining banquet.

Case e palazzi d'Etruria (exhibition catalogue, Siena 1985); K. M. Phillips, Jr., *In the Hills of Tuscany* (1993), with full previous bibliog.; R. D. De Puma and J. P. Small (eds.), *Etruscan Art and Society: Studies on Murlo and Ancient Etruria* (1994).   D. W. W. R.

Pola, at the southern end of the Istrian peninsula in the northern Adriatic, has always owed its importance to its fine land-locked harbour. This ancient town was probably founded by *Illyrii, certainly not by Colchians in pursuit of *Argonauts (reject Strabo 1. 46; 5. 215). Presumably it came under the Romans' control when they conquered the head of the Adriatic (178 BC: Livy 41. 13). Destroyed in the Civil Wars, Pola was rebuilt by *Augustus as the colony *Pietas Iulia* and became a flourishing town whose magnificent Antonine amphitheatre still survives (Plin. *HN* 3. 129).

PECS 'Pola'.   E. T. S.; D. W. R.

polemarchos (πολέμαρχος), one of the nine *archontes appointed annually in Athens. The name indicates that the polemarchos' original function was to command the army; presumably the office was created to take over this function from the king. Eventually military command was transferred to the *stratēgoi, but the date and stages of the transfer are not clear. At *Marathon in 490 BC the strategoi debated and voted on strategy but Callimachus (1) the polemarch had a casting vote (Hdt. 6. 109), and he was the 'leader' (ἡγεμών, Arist. *Ath. Pol.* 22. 2); it is disputed whether that means he was the real or merely the titular commander-in-chief. Certainly the polemarchos no longer had military authority after 487/6, when *archontes were appointed by lot (see SORTITION) and it could not be expected that every polemarch would make a competent commander.

Thereafter the polemarch's main functions were legal. In the 4th cent. he had charge of trials of *metics' family, inheritance, and status cases, and of the allocation to tribe-judges (members of the Forty) of other private actions involving metics; and it is likely that at an earlier period his responsibilities for cases involving aliens were more extensive. He also conducted certain *sacrifices and arranged the funeral ceremony for men killed in war.

E. Badian, *Antichthon*, 1971, 1–34; N. G. L. Hammond, *Studies in Greek History* (1973), 346–64; D. M. MacDowell, *The Law in Classical Athens* (1978), 221–4.   D. M. M.

Polemon (1) (*RE* 3) **I,** king of *Pontus and accomplished survivor. He probably aided his father, the wealthy rhetorician Zeno, to defend his city *Laodicea-Lycus against the *Parthians in 40–39 BC. Antony (M. *Antonius (2)) first made him ruler of parts of *Lycaonia and Cilicia (39), then promoted him to rule the recently enlarged kingdom of Pontus (37) and subsequently

Polemon

Lesser *Armenia (?33). He was captured during Antony's Parthian expedition and ransomed (36); the next year he mediated between Antony and *Artavasdes (2) of Media. After *Actium *Augustus confirmed his title but took away Lesser Armenia. In 15/14 he was awarded the turbulent Bosporan kingdom (see BOSPORUS (2)); *Agrippa helped him to occupy it, but local opposition was bitter, and he was eventually captured and killed in 8/7. His widow Pythodoris succeeded him in Pontus.

H. Buchheim, *Die Orientpolitik des Triumvirn M. Antonius* (1960); R. D. Sullivan, *ANRW* 2. 7. 2 (1980), 915–20; G. W. Bowersock, *Augustus and the Greek World* (1965), see index.　　　　　C. B. R. P.

Polemon (2) (*RE* 8a, vol. 21. 2. 2524–30) of Athens, head of the *Academy 314/313–270/269 BC. Primarily a moralist, he dismissed the purely theoretical side of philosophy as sterile. He formulated the ideal of 'living according to nature'—later the official goal of *Stoicism, founded by his pupil *Zeno (2)—and maintained that virtue is both necessary and sufficient for happiness while accepting (unlike the Stoics) that there are bodily and external goods. He wrote prolifically.

TESTIMONIA M. Gigante, *Rendic. Archeol./Lettere e Belle Arti Nap.* 51 (1976), 91–144. H. Dörrie, *Der Platonismus in der Antike* 1 (1987).
　　　　　D. N. S.

Polemon (3), a Greek of *Ilium (fl. *c.*190 BC), Stoic geographer (see STOICISM) who collected geographical, epigraphic, and artistic material in Greece, including especially dedications and monuments at *Delphi, Sparta, Athens. In another work Polemon attacked *Eratosthenes (Ath. 6. 234d; 10. 436d; 442e, etc.). See EPIGRAPHY, GREEK.

FHG 3. 108–48; L. Preller *Polemonis Periegetae Fragmenta* (1838).
　　　　　E. H. W.

Polemon (4) (*RE* 10), **Marcus Antonius** (*c.* AD 88–144), of *Laodicea-Lycus, was a member of an old and influential family who became a prominent sophist (see SECOND SOPHISTIC) and enjoyed the friendship of *Trajan, *Hadrian and *Antoninus Pius. He was a citizen and benefactor also of *Smyrna, and was chosen to deliver the inaugural oration for Hadrian's *Olympieum at Athens in AD 130. His oratory was in the grand manner, his delivery passionate and excited. Extant are two short declamations, in which the fathers of two heroes of Marathon (see MARATHON, BATTLE OF), *Callimachus (1) and *Cynegirus, present their sons' claims for the prize of valour (ἀριστεία). The subjects of other declamations are known from Philostratus (see PHILOSTRATI), all very conventional. More important was his work on *physiognomy, known from Latin and Arabic translations and a later Greek paraphrase. He gave examples of tell-tale physical features from contemporaries, mostly unnamed; but he also, for example, describes Hadrian's eyes as 'full of light and bright', a characteristic (we are told) of the 'pure Greek'. Polemon is a fascinating example of the tastes and talents of his age and class.

Philostratus, *VS* 1. 25; extant declamations ed. H. Hinck (1873). See H. Jüttner, *De Polemonis rhetoris vita operibus arte* (1898); B. P. Reardon, *Les Courants littéraires grecs* (1971), 107 ff., 243 ff.　　　　　D. A. R.

pōlētai (πωληταί), 'sellers', were Athenian officials. The date of their institution is not known, but they already existed in the time of *Solon. In *Aristotle's time there were ten, appointed annually by lot from the ten *phylai. They conducted the selling or leasing of property belonging to the state, especially property confiscated from convicted offenders. They sold as slaves *metics who failed to pay the metics' tax, and they let rights to work

*mines, to collect taxes, and to carry out public works. The method generally used was an auction held in the presence of the *Boulē. The *pōlētai* then made out lists of the payments due from purchasers and tenants; sales of confiscated property and mining leases were inscribed on stone, and numerous fragments of these inscriptions have been found.

M. K. Langdon, *The Athenian Agora*, 1991, 53–143, and in R. Osborne and S. Hornblower (eds.), *Ritual, Finance, Politics* (1994), ch. 15.
　　　　　D. M. M.

police In any discussion of police it is necessary to distinguish between the function of policing, that is, maintaining public order and enforcing the law, and the existence of a specialized agency of repression, i.e. a police force, to carry out these tasks on behalf of the state. Police forces as such, though taken for granted as a necessity, or at least a necessary evil, in modern societies, did not exist in the ancient world. They are a creation of the 18th and 19th cents., and reflect the growth of state power in the increasingly complex and bureaucratic societies of the modern industrialized world, and the extent to which mechanisms of social control have been centralized and monopolized by the state.

On the other hand, ancient city-states recognized the need for publicly appointed officials to carry out functions of social regulation. For example, in Classical Athens annual boards of magistrates (*astynomoi, *agoranomoi, *sitophylakes, etc.) were charged with keeping the streets clean, supervising market transactions, and controlling grain prices (*Ath. Pol.* 50–1, with Rhodes's commentary). Officials of this kind are attested in Greek cities throughout the Hellenistic and Roman periods, and the same functions were performed in Rome and cities of the Latin west by the aediles and their equivalents.

There were also magistrates appointed to deal with certain aspects of criminal activity. At Athens a board of citizen officials called the *Eleven, appointed by lot, had the task of guarding prisoners in the city gaol, carrying out executions and occasionally arresting criminals. In Rome these functions were carried out by minor magistrates called *tresviri capitales*, who may also have exercised summary jurisdiction over slaves and humble citizens. But these magistrates, who were assisted by only a small number of public slaves, had neither the authority nor the resources to act as a police force. At Athens after the *Persian Wars a special force of 300 Scythian slaves, armed with bows, was used to keep order in the assembly and the law courts, but the Scythian archers acted as policemen only in the most rudimentary sense; they were of low status, enjoyed little public respect and had no authority to investigate, arrest or prosecute. At Rome the *lictors who attended the senior magistrates were only symbols of the state's authority to discipline and punish; they had no effective power to coerce. The authority of magistrates depended absolutely on the acceptance by the citizens of their political institutions and the men who operated them.

A remarkable feature of ancient societies is how little the authorities were involved in the suppression, investigation, and prosecution of criminal activity. These matters were left to the private initiative of citizens who relied on networks of kin, friends, and dependants in a system of self-help. Small-scale disturbances were resolved locally by neighbours and passers-by, who were expected to take sides and usually did so. The state became involved only when violence had a political dimension or when it became a threat to the community as a whole. In such circumstances the authorities mobilized ordinary citizens who took up arms on behalf of the state. This happened in Athens in the crisis of 415 BC (Andocides 1. 45), and in Rome in 186 BC at the time of the Bacchanalian affair (Livy 39. 16. 13; see BACCHANALIA). In the political crises of 121 and 100 BC the senators and knights armed themselves and their dependants in order to crush C. *Sempronius Gracchus and L. *Appuleius Saturninus. The need to call upon the armed support of the citizens in a crisis was widely recognized, and is for example laid down in Roman colonial charters (e.g. *lex Coloniae Genetivae* 103).

After the breakdown of public order in the late republic the Roman emperors instituted more permanent forces to police the city of Rome. These were the urban cohorts, commanded by the prefect of the city (see PRAEFECTUS URBI), and the *vigiles*, a corps of 7,000 freed slaves under an equestrian prefect, whose principal task was to act as a fire brigade, but could be used to enforce order if necessary. The praetorian guard (see PRAETORIANS) was also on hand to suppress major public disturbances. Urban cohorts similar to those at Rome existed at certain large cities, including *Lugdunum (1) and *Carthage, and several cities apparently had fire brigades; but these were treated with suspicion by the central government which saw them as potentially subversive. *Trajan advised *Pliny (2) to provide fire-fighting equipment for the citizens of *Nicomedia to use when needed, rather than to set up a permanent fire brigade (Plin. *Ep.* 10. 34, a most revealing document). But these paramilitary forces of the Roman empire, although closer to a police force than anything else in antiquity, were not involved in day-to-day law enforcement, which remained the responsibility of private citizens acting on their own behalf.

O. Hirschfeld, *Kl. Schr.* (1913), 576 ff.; R. Macmullen, *Enemies of the Roman Order* (1967), 163 ff.; P. A. Brunt, in M. I. Finley (ed.), *Studies in Ancient Society* (1974), 74 ff.; A. W. Lintott, *Violence, Civil Strife and Revolution in the Classical City* (1982); M. I. Finley, *Politics in the Ancient World* (1983), 20 ff.; W. Nippel, *JRS* 1984, 20–9, *Aufruhr und 'Polizei' in der römischen Republik* (1988), and *Public Order in Ancient Rome* (1995); V. Hunter, *Policing Athens* (1994). See also VIGILES; COHORTES URBANAE, etc.   T. J. Co.

polis (pl. *poleis*), the Greek city-state. The *polis* is the characteristic form of Greek urban life; its main features are small size, political *autonomy, social homogeneity, sense of community and respect for law. It can be contrasted with the earlier Mycenaean palace economy (see MYCENAEAN CIVILIZATION), and with the continuing existence of tribal (*ethnos*) types of organization in many areas of northern Greece. (See ETHNICITY. For a different sense of 'tribe' see below.) The *polis* arose in the late Dark Ages. It is present in *Homer; the archaeological signs of city development (public space, temples, walls, public works, town planning) appear in an increasing number of sites in the 8th–7th cents. (Old *Smyrna, *Eretria); the peaceful abandonment of smaller sites and the general decline of archaeological evidence from the countryside in the 7th cent. suggest early *synoecism or concentration of population in specific *polis* sites. The foundation of organized settlements in new areas (see COLONIZATION, GREEK) is not distinct, but part of the same process.

Each *polis* controlled a territory (*chora*) delimited geographically by mountains or sea, or by proximity to another *polis*; border wars were common, as were inter-city agreements and attempts to establish religious rights over disputed areas; *Athens and *Sparta were exceptional in possessing large territories. Autonomy was jealously guarded, but the necessities of collaboration made for a proliferation of foreign alliances, leagues, and hegemonies; and a constant struggle for domination or independence

developed (see IMPERIALISM, *Greek and Hellenistic*). There was also constant interchange and competition between cities, so that despite their separate identities a common culture was always maintained. Economically the *polis* served an agrarian economy as a centre for local exchange, processing and manufacture; many cities were located on the sea, and had also important overseas trading interests (see ECONOMY, GREEK and HELLENISTIC). Socially the citizens comprised an ethnically homogeneous or limited group, organized according to 'tribes' (*phylai*) and smaller *kinship groups, such as *phratries, *demes and families (see HOUSEHOLD); new cities would replicate these, and they were often reorganized more or less artificially to serve new civic functions. Each city had a specific patron deity and a religious calendar (see CALENDAR, GREEK) with other lesser cults and festivals; the older priesthoods belonged to specific aristocratic families, later ones were often appointed by the people (see PRIESTS). Animal sacrifice (see SACRIFICE, GREEK) was accompanied by equal distribution of the meat at civic festivals, which from the 6th cent. became the focus for city-organized competitions in sport, dancing, and theatre (see AGŌNES). New cities required religious authorization, traditionally from the oracle of Apollo at Delphi (see COLONIZATION, GREEK; DELPHIC ORACLE); sacred fire was brought from the mother city, and established at the *prytaneion*, which in all cities acted as the common hearth, where magistrates and others took meals provided at public expense; the *founder of a new city was given heroic honours after death, with a tomb within the walls and public rites. See HERO-CULT.

Economy, kinship groups, and religion were subordinate to the main focus of the *polis*, which was broadly political; and its development may be seen largely in terms of the adaptation of these forces to a political end. Originating as an aristocratic system, the *polis* became a 'guild of warriors', in which the military power of the community (*hoplites, and later at Athens the 'naval mob'; see THĒTES) controlled the political and institutional life. Women were therefore never admitted to political rights and were effectively excluded from public life. In origin all cities seem to have possessed similar institutions: magistrates (see MAGISTRACY, GREEK) elected annually, a council of elders (see GEROUSIA), and a warrior assembly; the common later contrast between *oligarchy and *democracy simply relates to relatively minor differences in the distribution of powers and eligibility for office. The first stage in the development of the *polis* (7th–6th cents.) was usually the establishment of a written or customary lawcode (often attributed to a named *nomothetēs* (*Lycurgus (2), *Solon)), which limited the arbitrary powers of the aristocratic magistrates and regulated social conflict; the ideal was often referred to as *eunomia* (see SPARTA, § (2); TYRTAEUS). The second stage (late 6th cent.) was the evolution of the concept of the citizen with defined privileges and duties; this often involved the establishment of equality in political rights (*isonomia, or democracy), but also the establishment of clear membership rules excluding non-citizens, and creating subordinate statuses (see CLEISTHENES (2); METICS). The *polis* was indeed always defined in terms of its members, rather than geographically: the city of Athens is always called 'the Athenians', and citizenship generally implied equality and participation in all political, judicial, and governmental activities. In the 5th and 4th cents. a fully political society developed, centred on the making of complex decisions in the citizen assembly (see POLITICS).

This elaboration of a political culture affected all aspects of the *polis*. Religious and social institutions were not autonomous, but were continually being adapted to conform to the needs of *polis* organization. Sparta is a striking example: an initially normal Greek city substituted universal military commensality (the **syssitia*) in place of family structures, and adapted all religious *rituals to the needs of a hoplite *polis*. Other cities underwent less extreme forms of adaptation, but the constant subordination of family and religious structures and large parts of the legal system (such as inheritance) to the needs of the *polis* is striking, and creates an impression of rationality in the development of social forms. Equally the dominance of the political led to an early recognition of the difference between the various spheres of social activity (Max Weber's 'formal rationality'), and of the possibility of conflict between them, which is especially exemplified in the public art of tragedy (see TRAGEDY, GREEK).

In the late 4th cent. the gradual loss of political autonomy eroded the power of the armed citizens, and increased that of wealthy notables. The Hellenistic *polis* was marked by a conflict between rich and poor citizens (see CLASS STRUGGLE), mediated by the willingness of the rich to spend their *wealth on the duties of office and to engage in *euergetism, or subsidizing the expenses of office and of public festivals and culture, and providing buildings and other public works; this is expressed in the ideal of *homonoia*. The extension of the *polis* as a civic form across the areas conquered by *Alexander (3) 'the Great' under his successors created a colonial-style system, in which a Greek urbanized élite lived off the labour of a non-Greek countryside (see COLONIZATION, HELLENISTIC). The criterion of citizenship became education at the *gymnasium* in Greek letters and sport, and the concept of the *polis* became as much cultural as political.

The *polis* of the Roman age inherited a tradition of independence and competition within an imperial system, of civic pride expressed in public building programmes, and of cultural superiority over Romans and native peasantry; this was exemplified in the Greek renaissance of the '*Second Sophistic'. The Greek cities of the eastern empire were thus able to develop and continue a rich economic, cultural and social life into the early Byzantine period.

The origins of the rationalization and idealization of the *polis* lie deep in the reforming tendencies of the Archaic age. Greek political philosophy emerged in the fifth century with various attempts to imagine utopian cities whose institutions were directed towards specific ends; *Plato (1)'s *Republic* and *Laws* stand in this tradition. *Aristotle's *Politics* begins from the claim that 'man is by nature an animal of the *polis*', and seeks to draw conclusions from the whole experience of the *polis*, but fails to create an ideal philosophical state. Later thinkers (the *Cynics, *Zeno (2), *Epicurus) rebelled against the conception of man as subordinate to the *polis*, either by claiming his freedom from it, or by redefining the institution as a *cosmopolis*, in which all wise men were free. It is this mystical universalization of the *polis* which enabled first the Roman imperial panegyrists (see PANEGYRIC) and then the Christian writer *Augustine to conceive of the *polis* as a transcendental city embracing all the members of a community, whether empire or church.

See also CITIZENSHIP, GREEK; ETHNICITY; FEDERAL STATES; FREEDOM IN THE ANCIENT WORLD; GREECE (PRE-HISTORY AND HISTORY); ISOPOLITEIA; LAW IN GREECE; POLITICAL THEORY; POLITICS; STASIS; SYMPOLITEIA; URBANISM.

Max Weber, *Economy and Society* (1968), part 2 ch. 16; C. Renfrew and J. Cherry (eds), *Peer Polity Interaction and Socio-political Change* (1986); V. Ehrenberg, *The Greek State* (1960); O. Murray and S. Price (eds.), *The Greek City from Homer to Alexander* (1990); D. Roussel, *Tribu et cité* (1976); F. de Coulanges, *The Ancient City* (1874); P. Schmitt Pantel, *La Cité au banquet* (1992); I. Malkin, *Religion and Colonization in Ancient Greece* (1987); A. H. M. Jones, *The Greek City, from Alexander to Justinian* (1940); P. Veyne, *Bread and Circuses* (1990); M. Schofield, *The Stoic Idea of the City* (1991); P. Flensted-Jensen and others (eds.), *Polios and Politics* (2000). O. Mu.

Polites, in mythology, son of *Priam by *Hecuba, a swift runner and consequently employed as a scout (*Iliad* 2. 791 ff., cf. 24. 250). He takes a minor part in the fighting (13. 533; 15. 339). In Verg. *Aen.* 2. 526 ff. he is killed by *Neoptolemus (1); cf. Quint. Smyrn. 13. 214; source unknown.

LIMC 7. 1 (1994), 424. H. J. R.

political theory Greek and Roman authors reflected constantly about justice, good government, the nature of law. Epic, tragedy, comedy, history, and oratory are rich in political thought, frequently intensely interacting with the thought of the philosophers. To single out the philosophers, as must be done here, is potentially distorting.

Greek and Roman political theory is distinctive in its focus on the *soul. All the major thinkers hold that one cannot reflect well about political institutions without reflecting, first, about human flourishing, and about the psychological structures that facilitate or impede it. Their thought about virtue, education, and the passions is integral to their political theory, since they hold, for the most part, that a just city (*polis*) can only be achieved by the formation of balanced and virtuous individuals—although they also hold that institutions shape the passions of individuals and their possibilities for flourishing.

The 5th cent. BC in Athens saw a flowering of political theory and a turning of philosophy from cosmology to human concerns. The *sophists and those influenced by them exchanged arguments about the status of ethical and political norms—whether these norms exist by nature (*physis*) or by convention or law (*nomos (3)), and whether they are absolute, or relative to the species and/or the individual. *Protagoras' famous saying that 'The human being is the measure of all things' was probably not intended as the claim that each individual is the subjective judge of value for himself; the human species is the standard. But even such anthropocentrism constituted a challenge to the primacy of religious sources of value. Other thinkers championed more thoroughgoing forms of relativism. While Protagoras strongly defended conventions of justice as essential to well-being, others offered an immoralist teaching, urging individuals to pursue their own pleasure or power in so far as they could escape the tyranny of constraining law and custom.

*Socrates portrayed his relation to the Athenian democracy (see DEMOCRACY, ATHENIAN) as that of a gadfly on the back of a 'noble but sluggish horse': democracy was on the whole admirable but in need of critical self-examination. Although charged with oligarchic sympathies, he remained on good terms with *Lysias and other prominent democrats after the restoration; it is likely that he preferred democracy to other regimes, while advocating a larger role for expert judgement. In *Plato (1)'s *Crito*, he justifies his refusal to escape his penalty by insisting on the obligation of obedience to law imposed by a citizen's acceptance of the benefit and education of those same laws.

Plato's search for a just city, in the *Republic*, begins with the attempt to defend the life of the just person against *Thrasymachus' immoralist challenge, showing that this life is more *eudaimōn* (see DAIMŌN) than the unjust life. In order to understand justice in the individual, the interlocutors imagine an ideal city, in whose class relations justice may be seen. The relation between city and *soul turns out to be more complex than analogy, however, since the institutions of the ideal city prove necessary for the production of full justice in individuals; and the rule of just individuals is necessary for the maintenance of ideal institutions. The just individual is characterized by psychic harmony in which each part of the soul does its proper work, reason ruling and appetite and spirit being ruled; so too, in the just city, the reasoners are to rule and people dominated by appetite are to be ruled. On this basis Plato's Socrates develops his institutional proposals, which include: an education for the ruling class in which all traditional poetry is banished as bad for the soul; the abolition of the nuclear family and a communal scheme of marriage and child-rearing; the equal consideration of women for all functions, including that of ruler; a selective cultivation of the best souls to produce a ruling class of philosophers with knowledge of the good. Plato seems unconcerned about the limits he imposes on free choice, since he views most citizens as psychically immature and in need of permanent supervision.

Plato's later political works, *Statesman* and *Laws*, re-examine these psychic and institutional questions. *Stateman* develops the idea of practical wisdom as a flexible ability to grapple with the changing circumstances of human life, thus anticipating a prominent theme in the thought of *Aristotle. In *Laws* the emphasis on the guiding political role of wisdom is maintained, but, apparently, with a new emphasis on the importance of consent by and rational persuasion of the ruled, who now seem to be judged capable of some sort of fully-fledged virtue. The dialogue reflects at length about the justification and nature of punishment (see PUNISHMENT, GREEK THEORIES ABOUT).

Aristotle's political thought includes an account of the nature of human flourishing or *eudaimonia*, since, as he argues, the good things that politics distributes (property, possessions, offices, honours) are good not in themselves but as means to flourishing; an account of flourishing thus gives a 'limit' to the legislator, whose task will be to make an arrangement such that, barring catastrophic accidents, 'anyone whatsoever may do well and live a flourishing life'. Aristotle justifies the *polis* as essential to the complete realization of human ends, and details its development from the household and the village. While critical of 'artificial slavery', he defends a 'natural slavery' whose subjects are beings who 'altogether lack the deliberative faculty'. A more co-operative type of subordination is justified for women, apparently on the grounds that they deliberate ineffectually. Because he holds that virtue requires leisure, he denies citizenship to farmers, craftsmen, and resident aliens. These exclusions aside, Aristotle's preferred regime is that of free and equal citizens, ruling and being ruled by turns. His ideal city subsidizes the participation of poor citizens in common meals and other institutions out of the revenue from publicly held land; on the other hand, Platonic communism of property is thoroughly repudiated, as is Plato's attack on the family. Education is central, and Aristotle seems almost as insensitive as Plato to the issue of state control. In the central books of the *Pol.*, Aristotle describes various types of actual regime and their alternations.

For *Epicurus, justice is a necessary condition for *eudaimonia*, not an end in itself. Political involvement is to be avoided as a source of disturbance. The moderation of bad desires, such as the fear of death and aggressive wishes, will ameliorate many social ills. *Lucretius either preserves or innovates a fuller account of politics, which includes the idea that justice arose out of an implicit contract for the sake of protecting the weak.

The Stoics (see STOICISM) also focus on the therapy of the soul, holding that anger, fear, and the other 'passions' should be extirpated by removing excessive attachments to external goods such as money and reputation. This will change politics by removing various bad forms of contention and self-assertion. *Zeno (2) and *Chrysippus propose an ideal city in which virtuous citizens will live in concord, inspired by bonds of love. Women are given full equality; the institution of marriage is replaced by free consensual sexual relations. To all Stoics, local and national affiliations are less morally salient than our membership in the worldwide community of reason; this theme of the *kosmou politēs* ('world citizen') is developed vividly in Roman Stoicism, especially in Marcus *Aurelius. Roman Stoics debated the question of the best regime: some preferred monarchy and conceived of the emperor as (ideally) a Stoic sage; others, such as *Thrasea Paetus, understanding the Stoic ideal of self-command to entail republican government, invoked Stoicism in their anti-imperial politics.

Other major contributors to Hellenistic political theory include *Cicero, with his account of the mixed regime, and *Plutarch, with his wide-ranging reflections on virtue and rulership. See DEMOCRACY; FREEDOM IN THE ANCIENT WORLD; KINGSHIP; OLIGARCHY; POLIS; POLITICS.

COMMENTARIES C. C. W. Taylor, *Plato: Protagoras* (1976); E. R. Dodds, *Plato: Gorgias* (1959); J. Adam, *The Republic of Plato* (1926–9); S. H. Halliwell, *Plato: Republic V* (1993); E. B. England, *The Laws of Plato* (1921); W. L. Newman, *The Politics of Aristotle* (1887–1902).

STUDIES G. Grote, *A History of Greece* (1888), ch. 67; F. Heinimann, *Nomos und Phusis* (1945, repr. 1965); W. K. C. Guthrie, *A History of Greek Philosophy*, 3 (1971); E. Havelock, *The Liberal Temper in Greek Politics* (1957); C. J. Classen (ed.), *Sophistik* (1976); G. Kerferd, *The Sophistic Movement* (1981); E. Barker, *Greek Political Theory* (1918), and *Political Thought of Plato and Aristotle* (1959); K. Popper, *The Open Society and Its Enemies*, 5. 1 (5th edn. 1966); G. Vlastos, *Socrates* (1991), *Socratic Studies* (1994), and *Platonic Studies* (1981); T. Saunders, *Plato's Penal Code* (1991); G. Morrow, *Plato's Cretan City* (1960); D. Keyt and F. Miller (eds.), *A Companion to Aristotle's Politics* (1991); A. A. Long and D. Sedley, *The Hellenistic Philosophers* (1987); M. Schofield, *The Stoic Idea of the City* (1991).
M. C. N.

politics

In Greece 1. Politics as power struggle. This is the dominant interpretation of politics in the modern world since Macchiavelli; it requires organized groups, either operating out of group self-interest or with differing conceptions of the common interest. In the archaic age of Greece there is some evidence for the existence of aristocratic groups supported by retainers, notably in the poetry of *Alcaeus (1) and at Athens before *Cleisthenes (2); in the Classical period organized aristocratic *hetaireiai* occasionally emerged as politically important, but usually as a consequence of lack of success in normal political life. Organized political parties never existed, and political programmes were confined to groups trying to change the constitution.

2. Politics as ritualized decision-making. Specific political institutions and methods for decision-making are first found in the archaic age, and were highly developed by the Classical period; the best-known examples are *Sparta and *Athens (see LYCURGUS (2); SPARTA; DEMOCRACY, ATHENIAN). They involved a specific location for taking decisions, religious rituals for demarcating space and time, and a fixed procedure. In principle all citizens with full rights could participate in the assembly. The aim was to achieve consensus through structured discussion; arguments usually took the form of opposed speeches, and speakers were expected to maintain certain conventions of dignified behaviour: scandal

was caused when these were infringed by the Athenian dem-agogues in the late 5th cent. At Athens political leaders were initially of aristocratic birth, but after the death of *Pericles (1) they were simply those who spoke most often (*prostatai tou dēmou, dēmagōgoi* (see DEMAGOGUES), *rhētores*); they were regarded as responsible for decisions, and prided themselves on consist-ency of advice. There were four main issues on which they were expected to possess knowledge: city revenues, war and peace, defence, corn supply (Aristotle *Rhet.* 1. 4; Xen. *Mem.* 3. 6). Seven-teen assembly speeches survive from the period 403–322 BC, by *Lysias, *Andocides and (especially) *Demosthenes (2); they are brief and well organized; their arguments are based on rational calculation of advantage and consequence, rather than appeals to sentiment, religion, or historical rights. The controls on assembly procedure in the 5th cent. were customary; but in the 4th cent. the formal distinction between laws and decrees, and the limita-tion of the assembly to the making of decrees, led to the constitu-tional check of the *graphē paranomōn*, whereby decrees could be challenged in the courts as being contrary to the laws. A decision once taken was accepted as the will of the community expressed in such phrases as 'the Athenians decided', and was binding on all: there was no mechanism for continued dissent.

This absence of a means for structuring permanent political oppositions such as class conflict (see CLASS STRUGGLE) was a basic weakness of Greek political life: *stasis*, armed revolution, had as its aim the overthrow of the existing consensus, in order to return to a different political unity through the extermination of the opposition; it was common in many cities, and focused on the conflict between democracy and oligarchy, or the question of equal or unequal distribution of political privileges in relation to social class; it caused much instability of political life. *Stasis* was regarded as a disease of the body politic, capable of destroying the community (Thuc. 3. 82–3). Philosophers were unable to offer any solution to the problem.

At Rome Roman society had a strong gentilicial framework, and throughout the republic politics was largely based on the *clientela* (see CLIENS) or kinship group; the late republic saw also the growth of military clientship among the dynasts. Much of Roman political life was concerned with the struggle for election to those offices which gave access to legal power, military command, and the possibility of conquest (see IMPERIUM; MAGISTRACY, ROMAN; PRO CONSULE; PRO PRAETORE; PROVINCIA); it therefore involved a measure of participation by the people. Individuals might espouse conservative or radical attitudes and be designated by the political labels, *optimates* and *populares*; but there was much inconsistency, and these claims seldom involved clear differences in policy. Decision-making was divided between the aristocratic *senate and a number of different assemblies, and was therefore complex and open to challenge. Roman political life seems closer to modern practices than does Greek, for it distanced the people from the process of *decision-making and possessed a complex constitutional law based on precedent; but it still lacked the concept of institutionalized party politics. The political leader-ship was always aristocratic, and much concerned with its own dignity, privileges and 'equality'. The emperors continued to respect the claims of the senate to play a major role in the political system at least in principle during the 1st cent. AD, but the power of the people was not preserved under the principate; *libertas* (see FREEDOM) became an aristocratic ideal.

See DEMOCRACY, ATHENIAN; DEMOCRACY, NON-ATHENIAN AND POST-CLASSICAL; FREEDOM IN THE ANCIENT WORLD; OLIGARCHY; POLIS; STASIS; TYRANNY.

Thuc. 3. 82–3; Arist. *Rhetoric* 1, *Politics* 4–6. M. I. Finley, *Politics in the Ancient World* (1983); G. E. M. de Ste. Croix, *The Class Struggle in the Ancient Greek World* (1981); W. Rösler, *Dichter und Gruppe* (1980); G. M. Calhoun, *Athenian Clubs in Politics and Litigation* (1913); J. Ober, *Mass and Elite in Democratic Athens* (1989); H. Ryffel, *Metabole Politeion* (1949); M. Gelzer, *The Roman Nobility* (1969); P. A. Brunt, *Social Conflicts in the Roman Republic* (1971); C. Meier, *Res publica amissa* (2nd edn. 1980); J. Hellegouarc'h, *Le Vocabulaire latin des relations et des partis politiques sous la République* (1963); Ch. Wirszubski, *Libertas* (1950).   O. Mu.

pollution, the Greek concept of Societies create order by stigmatizing certain disorderly conditions and events and persons as 'polluting', that is, by treating them metaphorically as unclean and dangerous. Very roughly, the pollutions generally recognized by the Greeks were birth, death, to a limited degree sexual activity, homicide except in war, and sacrilege; certain diseases, madness above all, were also sometimes viewed in this way, while mythology abounds in instances of extreme pollutions such as incest, parricide, and cannibalism.

Different pollutions worked in different ways (local rules also varied). We get some indication of the attendant casuistry from, above all, a long code from Cyrene (*SEG* 9. 72) and the rules of purity attached to certain Coan priesthoods (F. Sokolowski, *Lois sacrées des cités grecques* (1969), nos. 154, 156). To give some illus-trations: contact with a dead person of one's own family pollutes for longer than with an unrelated person; a person entering a house of birth becomes polluted, but does not transmit the pollution further; sexual contact only requires purification if it occurs by day . . .

Pollution has a complicated relation to the sacred. In one sense they are polar opposites: the main practical consequence of (for instance) the pollutions of birth and death was that the persons affected were excluded from temples for a period of days, and *priests and priestesses had to observe special rules of purity. But offenders against the gods became 'consecrated' to them in the sense of being made over to them for punishment; and such negative consecration (which could also be imposed by a human curse) was comparable to a pollution. This is why ἄγος and ἐναγής, words that appear to be related to a root †ἀγ conveying the idea of sacredness, to some extent overlap in usage with μίασμα and μιαρός, the standard terms for pollution and pollut-ing. In consequence, the boundaries are blurred between the concepts of 'pollution' and of 'divine anger'.

Since some pollutions are natural and inescapable, rules of purity are obviously not simply rules of morality in disguise. But the very dangerous pollutions were those caused by avoidable (if sometimes unintentional) actions such as bloodshed and sacri-lege. In theory, one man's crime could through such pollution bring disaster to a whole state. There is a common mythological schema (best seen at the start of *Sophocles (1), *OT*), whereby pollution causes plague, crop-failure, infertility of women and of animals. Such pollution is fertility reversed, which is why such powers as the Eumenides (*Erinyes) are double-sided, agents of pollution and also givers of fertility (see above all Aeschylus, *Eum.*). Orators often attempted to brand political opponents as polluting demons, the source of the city's misfortunes; and a question actually put to the *oracle of *Zeus at *Dodona shows that this conception of the polluting individual was not a mere anachronism in the historical period: 'is it because of a mortal's pollution that we are suffering the storm?' (*SEG* 19. 427).

But pollution is also often envisaged as working more select-ively. According to *Antiphon (1)'s *Tetralogies*, for instance, murder pollution threatens the victim's kin until they seek vengeance or prosecute, the jurors until they convict. Thus the threat of pollution encourages action to put right the disorder.

Fear of pollution is often said by modern scholars to be absent from the world of Homer; the emergence of such anxieties becomes therefore a defining mark of the succeeding centuries. But it is wrong to interpret pollution beliefs, an ordering device, as primarily a product of fear; and the natural context for, for instance, a doctrine of blood pollution of the type discussed above is a society such as Homer's where legal sanctions are weak. As we have seen, pollution belief is a complex phenomenon, a vehicle for many different concerns: it has no unified origin or history. See also PURIFICATION, GREEK.

L. Moulinier, *Le Pur et l'impur dans la pensée des Grecs* (1952); J.-P. Vernant, *Myth and Society in Ancient Greece* (1980; Fr. orig. 1974), ch. 6; R. Parker, *Miasma* (1983). R. C. T. P.

Pollux (mythical character) See CASTOR AND POLLUX; DIOSCURI.

Pollux, Iulius, of *Naucratis (2nd cent. AD), scholar and rhetorician. His *Onomasticon* was composed in the lifetime of *Commodus, to whom are addressed epistles prefixed to each of its ten books: that introducing book 8 indicates that the author's appointment to a chair of rhetoric at Athens (not before AD 178) preceded the completion of the work. In books 8–10 he replies to *Phrynichus (3)'s criticism of points in 1–7. As an example of Atticism (see ASIANISM AND ATTICISM) and other profitable vices of the age he comes under Lucian's lash in ῥητόρων Διδάσκαλος (*Rhetorum Praeceptor, a Teacher of Rhetoric*): cf. ch. 24—οὐκέτι Ποθεινὸς ὀνομάζομαι ἀλλ' ἤδη τοῖς Διὸς καὶ Λήδας παισὶν ὁμώνυμος γεγένημαι ('I am no longer called Potheinos—the Desired One—but have become the namesake of the children of Zeus and Leda'; i.e. the *Dioscuri, Castor and Pollux). Like his other works, the *Onomasticon* in its original form has perished: the extant manuscripts are derived from four incomplete, and interpolated copies, all descending from an early *epitome possessed (and interpolated) by Arethas, archbishop of Caesarea, *c.* AD 900. The arrangement is by topic, not alphabetical. The work partly resembles a rhetorical handbook, e.g. in its collections of synonyms and of subject-vocabularies, in collections of compounds (ὁμο- and some others), in the fifty-two terms for use in praising a king, or the thirty-three terms of abuse to apply to a tax-collector. The story of *Heracles' discovery of *purple is added expressly as a light relief for the student. Wider philological and encyclopaedic interests appear in the citations from literature and in the treatment of music and the theatre. Besides these, his subjects include religion, private and public law, human anatomy and ethics, war, the sciences, arts, crafts and trades, houses, ships, husbandry, cookery, children's games, and a host of other matters. The sections on stage antiquities (book 4) and on the Athenian constitution (book 8) are of especial interest to scholars. But the work is predominantly a thesaurus of terms, not of information. It is also mainly derivative, but useful to us because the sources no longer survive.

EDITION
Bethe, in Teubner's *Lexicog. Gr.* 9. 1–3, 1900–37.

P. B. R. F.; R. B.; N. G. W.

Polus of *Acragas (Agrigentum), pupil of *Gorgias (1) and teacher of rhetoric. He is a principal character in *Plato (1)'s *Gorgias*, which mentions his *Rhetoric* (τέχνη: 462b) and may parody its opening words (448c). Plato also makes fun of his readiness to coin new technical terms (*Phaedr.* 267b–c).

L. Radermacher, *Artium Scriptores* (1951), 112. M. B. T.

Polyaenus (1), (*RE* 6) of Lampsacus (d. before 271 BC), the παιδαγωγός, 'chaperon' of the celebrated Epicurean Pythocles, and one of the chief original disciples of *Epicurus, who turned Polyaenus' attention from mathematics to philosophy. Epicurus addressed him in well-known letters (Sen. *Ep.* 18. 9: Epicurus told Polyaenus that less than an obol a day was necessary to live, though *Metrodorus (2), who had not progressed so far in philosophy might require a whole obol) and his life was memorialized in the literature of the school, including Epicurus' own works.

WORKS *Against Aristo* (Πρὸς τὸν Ἀρίστωνα, probably the Stoic); *On Definitions* (Περὶ ὅρων).
FRAGMENTS A. Tepedino Guerra, *Polieno. Frammenti*, La scuola di Epicuro 11 (1991).
FURTHER DISCUSSION A. Angeli, *Cronache Ercolanesi*, 1981, 41–101, *Filodemo. Agli amici di scuola (PHerc. 1005)*, La scuola di Epicuro 7 (1988), and *Cronache Ercolanesi* 1988, 27–51. W. D. R.; D. O.

Polyaenus (2), a Macedonian rhetorician, dedicated his collection of *Strategemata* (stratagems) in eight books to Marcus *Aurelius and Lucius *Verus. It is wide-ranging, including exploits by gods, heroes, and famous women, and uses excerpts from earlier collections; some entries are historically valuable, others fictitious. However, the underlying theme is didactic, to expound the methods of protecting an army and overcoming the enemy, and along with traditional clichés of military life, he recounts stratagems employed by historical Greek commanders, with some examples from Roman history, notably *Hannibal, *Caesar, and *Augustus. Polyaenus even claims a practical purpose, to assist the emperors in the Parthian war (AD 162–6): 'You consider it part of the art of winning victories to study the ways by which commanders in the past triumphed.'

TEXT J. Melber, Teubner (1887, repr. 1970).
TRANSLATION P. Krentz and E. L. Wheeler, 2 vols. (1994).
J. B. C.

Polybius (1) (*c.*200–*c.*118 BC), Greek historian of Rome's rise to Mediterranean dominion and of the world in which that happened. His father, *Lycortas of Megalopolis, was a leading figure of the *Achaean Confederacy in the 180s and, along with *Philopoemen, one of the architects of the doomed Achaean attempt to treat with Rome on a basis of equality during those years. Polybius bore Philopoemen's ashes to burial in 182, was appointed in 180 as envoy to Alexandria, and in 170/69 served as Hipparch of the Confederation. After Rome's victory over *Perseus (2) of Macedon at *Pydna, he was denounced as insufficiently friendly to the Romans by *Callicrates (2) and became one of the thousand prominent Achaeans deported to Rome and subsequently detained without trial in various towns of Italy. Polybius became friend and mentor to P. *Cornelius Scipio Aemilianus, was allowed to remain in Rome during his captivity, and formed part of the *'Scipionic Circle'. He probably accompanied Scipio to Spain (151) and to Africa (where he met *Masinissa), returning to Italy over the Alps in *Hannibal's footsteps. After the release of the surviving detainees in 150 Polybius witnessed the destruction of *Carthage (146) in Scipio's company and undertook an exploratory voyage in the Atlantic. He helped to usher in the Roman settlement of Greece after the sack of Corinth (146), visited *Alexandria (1) and *Sardis, and may have

Polybius

been at *Numantia in 133. He is reported to have died at the age of 82 after falling from a horse.

His minor works—an early encomiastic biography of Philopoemen, a work on tactics, a history of the Numantine war (see NUMANTIA), and a treatise on the habitability of the equatorial region—are all lost. Of his *Histories* a substantial amount survives; he is the only Hellenistic historian of whom a significant amount does remain. Only books 1–5 of the original forty survive intact. After that we are dependent upon excerpts and occasional quotations by other writers. The 'Excerpta Antiqua' are a continuous abridgement of books 1–18 and provide the majority of what remains of books 6–18. For the remainder the main source is the slightly later collection of excerpts, by a number of hands under various headings and from many Greek historians along with Polybius, made for the emperor Constantine VII Porphyrogenitus (AD 912–50). From five books there are no excerpts at all (17, 19, 26, 37, 40); they were presumably lost already. A few quotations from 19, 26, and 37 are found in other authors. Book 34 (devoted to geographical matters) was much referred to, especially by *Strabo; it survives only in quotations. Books 17 and 40 have perished without trace. For the arrangement of what does survive of books 7–39, a matter beset with difficulty, see Walbank, *HCP* 3. 1–62.

Polybius' original purpose was to tell the story of (that is, to describe and explain) Rome's rise to world dominion, to answer the question 'how and by a state with what sort of constitution' (πῶς καὶ τίνι γένει πολιτείας) almost the whole of the known world was conquered and fell under the single rule of the Romans in a space of not quite 53 years' (1. 1. 5; from the beginning of the 140th Olympiad in 220 to the end of the Macedonian monarchy in 167: books 3–30). He was profoundly impressed by this process, both by the simple fact of the end of the monarchy that had dominated the affairs of Greece for almost two centuries and by the way in which the course of events seemed almost calculated to produce the final result. A metaphor of supernatural guidance is often invoked in the form of τύχη (fortune), which, though sometimes very close to seeming an active, even a vengeful, agent, is never invoked as an explanation of anything. He later extended his purpose to show how the Romans exercised their dominion, how the world under them reacted to it, and how both were affected (books 30–39; book 40 contained a recapitulation and chronological survey). For his task Polybius developed both a structure and a kind of history. Given his theme and his belief that the process at issue was fundamentally unitary, the structure must allow at once for universality and focus. This was made possible by combining chronological and geographical organization in an original way. Vertically, the arrangement is by Olympiads, each Olympiad containing four numbered years; these years were not rigidly fixed but were adapted to the flow of events. Horizontally, the framework is geographical. Within each year there is a fixed progression from west to east: first, events in Italy (with Sicily, Spain, and Africa), then Greece and Macedonia, then Asia, then Egypt. Books 1 and 2 are something apart. They focused primarily on Rome from the first Punic war to 220, providing a background for those little acquainted with the Romans and an explanation of how the Romans could with reason come to develop the aim for universal dominion (ἡ τῶν ὅλων ἐπιβολή, 1. 3. 6, etc.) that informed their actions after the Hannibalic war.

For the kind of history he wrote Polybius invented the term *pragmatikē historia*, 'pragmatic history'. This kind of inquiry involves study of documents and written memoirs, geographical

study (especially autopsy), first-hand knowledge of some events, and the most careful examination of eye-witnesses about the rest. The focus is upon political actions (αἱ πράξεις αἱ πολιτικαί, 12. 25e), but the scope of 'political' was for Polybius very wide indeed, as may be inferred from the breadth of his account of the Roman *politeia* in book 6: this embraced military, economic, religious, social, and political institutions and practice. (It also included the formulation of the theory of a tripartite constitution, incorporating elements of monarchy, aristocracy, and democracy, that influenced political thinking for the next two thousand years.) Apprehension of all these was needed in order to describe things properly and, above all, to explain them. For Polybius the historian's primary task was explanation. 'The mere statement of a fact may interest us, but it is when the reason is added that the study of history becomes fruitful: it is the mental transference of similar circumstances to our own that gives us the means of forming presentiments about what is going to happen . . .' (12. 25b). This resembles *Thucydides (2) (1. 22), as does Polybius' insistence upon true and accurate narration of historical action (both deed and speech), but Polybius goes beyond his predecessor in his insistence upon the element of explanation and beyond everybody in his explicit formulation (3. 6–7) about beginnings (ἀρχαί) and reasons (αἰτίαι). (*Prophasis* is reserved for 'pretext'.) Beginnings are actions; actions are preceded by decisions to act; decisions to act are processes involving various elements: a proper explanation, for Polybius, must delineate these processes and identify these various elements. In dealing with the wars that led to Rome's dominion Polybius adheres rigorously to his principles: he aims to explain in a properly multifaceted way rather than to assign responsibility.

Having brought the writing of history to a methodological acme (and having access to Rome and Romans in a way that his Greek predecessors and contemporaries did not), Polybius was regularly critical of past and contemporary historians, often polemically and sometimes excessively, whether for their method or their bias (book 12 is the most concentrated statement about method and what survives of it contains much hostile criticism of *Timaeus (2)). From bias he was himself manifestly not free, whether positive (as for Philopoemen, Scipio Aemilianus, or the Achaean Confederacy as a whole) or negative (as for T. Quinctius Flamininus, the *Aetolian Confederacy, many of Rome's opponents and supporters alike, and the lower classes generally). But he was, though of course not neutral, honest, and he was, above all, concerned about the effect of undisputed dominion upon the society that wielded it and upon those who inhabited the world in which it was wielded.

TEXTUAL Editio princeps: V. Opsopaeus (1530, Gk. text of bks. 1–5; a Lat. trans. by N. Perotti had appeared in 1473). Major mod. texts: I. Casaubon (1609); J. Schweighäuser (1789–95, 8 vols. in 9, with excellent Lat. trans., extensive textual notes, geographical and historical index, and a lexicon of Polybian usage); Fr. Hultsch (1867–72, 1888–92, upon which is based the Eng. trans. by E. S. Shuckburgh, 1889); Th. Büttner-Wobst (Teubner, 1889–1904, 1905); W. R. Paton (Loeb, 1922–7, with Eng. trans. of text based upon Büttner-Wobst); P. Pédech and others (Budé, 1969– , with Fr. trans. and nn.). Also: F. W. Walbank, *A Historical Commentary on Polybius*, 3 vols. (1957–79); J. M. Moore, *The Manuscript Tradition of Polybius* (1965); A. Mauersberger, *Polybios-Lexikon* (1956–).

FURTHER STUDIES *RE* 21. 2, 'Polybios' (1); E. Mioni, *Polibio* (1949; here and *RE* for earlier literature); M. Gelzer, *Kleine Schriften*, 3 (1964), 111 ff.; P. Pédech, *La Méthode historique de Polybe* (1964); G. A. Lehmann, *Untersuchungen zur historischen Glaubwürdigkeit des Polybios* (1967); K.-E. Petzold, *Studien zur Methode des Polybios und zu ihrer histor-*

ischen Auswertung (1969); J.-A. de Foucault, *Recherches sur la langue et le style de Polybe* (1972); F. W. Walbank, *Polybius* (1972), *Selected Papers* (1985), *passim*, and in I. Worthington (ed.), *Ventures into Greek History* (1994), 28 ff.; E. Gabba (ed.), *Polybe* (1974, Entretiens Hardt 20); K. Meister, *Historische Kritik bei Polybios* (1975); K. Sacks, *JHS* 1975, 92 ff. and *Polybius on the Writing of History* (1981); P. S. Derow, *JRS* 1979, 1 ff., in T. J. Luce (ed.), *Ancient Writers: Greece and Rome* (1982), 525 ff., and in S. Hornblower (ed.), *Greek Historiography* (1994), 73 ff.; M. Dubuisson, *Le Latin de Polybe* (1985); J. Davidson, *JRS* 1991, 10 ff.; A. M. Eckstein, *AJPhil.* 1992, 387 ff.   P. S. D.

Polybius (2) (*RE* 5), a *freedman, one of *Claudius' secretaries, particularly concerned with patronage (*a studiis*); whether he was *a libellis* (concerned with petitions) also is doubtful. His power was manifest (he went about between the two consuls) and his literary gifts helped his rise (he translated *Homer into Latin and *Virgil into Greek). In AD 42 or 43 L. *Annaeus Seneca (2) addressed to him from exile a *Consolatio* for the death of a brother, hoping that it would be construed as a petition for recall. His death in 46 or 47 by the contrivance of *Valeria Messallina provoked the other freedmen to counter-measures in 48.

Sen. *Consolatio ad Polybium* (ed. J. D. Duff, 1915). A. Momigliano, *Claudius*[2] (1961), 43 n., 75 f.; F. Giancotti, *Rend. Linc.* 1953, 59 ff.; F. Millar, *JRS* 1967, 16 f.; P. Weaver, *Familia Caesaris* (1972); B. Levick, *Claudius* (1990), indexes.   A. M.; T. J. C.; B. M. L.

Polyboea, (1) name of several mythological heroines; (2) a goddess, sister of *Hyacinthus, identified with *Artemis and Kore (*Persephone) (Paus. 3. 19. 4; Hesych.).   S. H.

Polybus (1), in mythology, a king of *Corinth married to Merope. Being without sons, they adopted the infant *Oedipus and reared him as their own (Soph. *OT* 1016 ff.). (2) A king of *Sicyon who died without sons and left his kingdom to *Adrastus (1), the son of his daughter who had married Talaus, king of *Argos (2) (Hdt. 5. 67. 4).   J. R. M.

Polybus (3) Hippocratic physician, and according to one tradition the son-in-law of *Hippocrates (2) himself. Attempts have been made to assign authorship of various Hippocratic treatises to him (eg. parts of *On the Nature of Man*, *On Birth in the Eighth Month*). His view that all blood vessels originate in the head is quoted by *Aristotle (*HA* 511[b]24–513[a]7), and some of this material is repeated in more detail in the Hippocratic treatises *On the Nature of Bones* (9. 174–8 Littré) and *On the Nature of Man* (6. 58–60 Littré). There is a somewhat garbled account of his pathological system—in which diseases are caused by imbalances of blood, phlegm, and bile—in the Anonymus Londinensis papyrus, 19. 1 ff.

H. Grensemann, *Abhandlungen der Geistes- und sozialwissenschaftliche Klasse der Akademie der Wissenschaften und der Literatur in Mainz*, 1968.2; J. Jouanna, *Rev. Ét. Grec.* 1969, 552–62; H. von Staden, *Hermes*, 1976, 494–6.   J. T. V.

Polycarp (c. AD 69–c.155), bishop of *Smyrna and correspondent of Ignatius of Antioch. His martyrdom at the age of 86 is described in a letter from the Smyrnaean church to that at Philomelium, Phrygia. That the MSS preserve an interpolated text is probable from *Eusebius of Caesarea's quotations (*Hist. Eccl.* 4. 15). Eusebius' *Chronicle* mentions his death next to the year AD 167, but a (post-Eusebian?) addition to the Smyrnaean letter (ch.

21) dates it to 23 Feb. 'in the high-priesthood of Philip of Tralles in the proconsulate of Statius Quadratus'. The chronology based by 19th-cent. authors on Aelius *Aristides may be dubious, but, since Quadratus was consul in 142, his proconsulate of Asia cannot fall later than 161. Lightfoot's date of 155 fits well with Quadratus' career and with the Asiarchate of Philip, which commenced in 148. Time must be allowed for his return to Smyrna after his visit to Rome (c.154/5) to defend the old Asiatic custom of keeping Easter with the Jewish Passover. His extant letter to the Philippians (a warning against apostasy) speaks of Ignatius as dead in ch. 9, but implies that he is not yet known to be dead in ch. 13; the view that it conflates two letters has commended itself to many scholars.

Ed. J. B. Lightfoot, *Apostolic Fathers* 2. 3 (1889). P. N. Harrison, *Polycarp's Two Epistles* (1936).   H. C.; M. J. E.

Polycles, name of three Athenian sculptors. According to *Pliny (1), *HN* 34. 50, a Polycles (1) 'flourished' in 372 BC. At least two descendants were active in the 3rd and 2nd cents.: Polycles (2) was Aetolian *proxenos (see AETOLIA) in 210/9 (*IG* 9[2]. 1. 29[17]), and Pliny (*HN* 34. 52) lists a Polycles of Athens (3) among those who 'revived the art' (sc. of bronze-casting) in 156. The family's genealogy and sculptural activities are problematic, for the names Polycles, Timarchides, and Dionysius often recur. The sources give many works to 'Polycles', including an *Alcibiades, a 'noble hermaphrodite', several athletes, hunters, and warriors, and a *Hercules, *Apollo, and *Jupiter in Rome (with Dionysius). Most of them were perhaps by Polycles (3), who was apparently among the first Greek sculptors to work in Rome. The head of the Hercules survives, and the hermaphrodite has been recognized in the Capitoline type; both are neo-classic (pseudo-Praxitelean) works of c.150 BC.

A. F. Stewart, *Greek Sculpture* (1990), 220, 225, 230, 304 f., figs. 819 f., 858.   A. F. S.

Polyclitus (1) of *Larissa, author of *Historiae* relating to *Alexander (3) 'the Great' (*FGrH* 128), is known primarily as a geographical source for *Strabo.   A. B. B.

Polyclitus (2), Argive sculptor, active c.460–410 BC. Supposedly a pupil of Hageladas, Polyclitus worked exclusively in metal; all his works were in bronze except the *Hera of *Argos (2) (after 423), which was in chryselephantine. He made gods, heroes, and athletes, and his statues of mortals were unsurpassed (Quint. 12. 10. 9). His reputation rested largely on a single work, the *Doryphorus* or Spearbearer; he also wrote a book called the *Canon, or Rule, that explained the principles of his art, apparently basing it on this statue. In it, he stated that 'perfection comes about little by little through many numbers' (*Philon (2) Mechanicus 4. 1, 49. 20), and described a system of proportion whereby, starting with the fingers and toes, every part of the body was related mathematically to every other and to the whole (Galen, *De plac. Hipp. et Plat.* 5, p. 3. 16 Kühn).

The Doryphorus (perhaps an *Achilles) is nowhere described in detail; we only know that it was a nude, 'virile boy', 'suitable for both war and athletics', and 'aimed at the mean' (Plin. *HN* 34. 55; Quint. 5. 12. 21; Galen, *De temperamentis*, p. 566. 14 Kühn). Since 1863, however, it has been unanimously identified with a youth known in over 50 copies, the best in Naples (from *Pompeii), Berlin, and Minneapolis. A bronze herm by *Apollonius (6) is the best copy of the head. He stands on his right leg with his left relaxed; his right arm hangs limp and his left is flexed to hold the spear; his head turns and inclines somewhat to his right. This compositional scheme, which unifies the body by setting up cross-relationships between weight-bearing and relaxed limbs, is called chiastic after the Greek letter *chi* (χ), and thereafter becomes standard practice in Greek and Roman sculpture. His proportional scheme was equally influential (though no single reconstruction of it has yet gained universal acceptance), as was his system of modelling, which divided the musculature into grand (static) and minor (mobile) forms, alternating in ordered sequence throughout the body. Though sculptors such as *Euphranor and *Lysippus (2) introduced their own variations upon this ideal, the Polyclitan ideal remained widely influential, and was particularly popular in Roman imperial sculpture. This and the longevity of Polyclitus' own school accounts for *Pliny (1)'s observation that later artists followed his work 'like a law' (*HN* 34. 55).

*Varro criticized Polyclitus's work as being 'virtually stereotyped' (Plin. *HN* 34. 56—an inevitable consequence of a rigorously applied ideal), and a series of copies that apparently reproduce his other statues bear this out. These include his Diadoumenus (a victor binding a fillet around his head), Discophorus, Heracles, and Hermes; the 'Westmacott Boy' in the British Museum may copy his statue of the boy-boxer Cyniscus at *Olympia. His *Amazon, placed first in the contest at Ephesus, is plausibly identified in the Sosicles (Capitoline) type, who rests on a spear held in her right hand. The Hera is described by Pausanias (2. 17), but no secure copies of her survive, presumably because antiquity rated her inferior to the great chryselephantine statues of *Phidias (cf. Strabo 8. 372).

Boardman, *Greek Sculpture: The Classical Period* (1985), 205 f., 203 ff., figs. 160 ff., 191, 195; A. F. Stewart, *Greek Sculpture* (1990), 75 f., 150 ff., 263 ff., figs. 378 ff.; H. Beck and others, *Polyklet. Der Bildhauer der griechischen Klassik* (1990).   A. F. S.

Polycrates (1), tyrant (see TYRANNY) of *Samos, son of Aeaces, seized power *c.*535 BC, with his brothers Pantagnotus and Syloson, but soon made himself tyrant. Almost unrivalled in magnificence (Hdt. 3. 125, 122), he made Samos a great naval power (see NAVIES; SEA POWER), subjected neighbouring islands (Hdt. 3. 39, 122; Thuc. 1. 13), including Rheneia near *Delos which he dedicated to *Apollo (Thuc. 1. 13; 3. 104). He formed a defensive alliance with Amasis, king of Egypt, but seems to have broken it off deliberately (contrast the moralizing tale of Polycrates' ring in Hdt. 3. 39 ff.) when *Cambyses tried to acquire Egypt, and supplied Samian ships. The Samians mutinied and went over to Sparta; *Sparta and *Corinth, apparently to prevent Polycrates medizing, tried to overthrow him, unsuccessfully (525 BC). He was lured to the mainland, *c.*522, by the *satrap Oroetes, who pretended to be plotting against *Darius I, and was crucified. He pursued a piratical and opportunist thalassocracy (see Hdt. 3. 39 for *piracy), upset by the gradual extension of Persian power, which he tried to court. He attracted artists, craftsmen, and poets (*Anacreon, *Ibycus, *Theodorus (1)). The three famous building achievements praised by *Herodotus (1) (3. 60), the great temple of *Hera (see HERAION), the harbour mole, and the tunnelled *aqueduct bringing water to the city, may all in fact be attributable to Polycrates (as Arist. *Pol.* 1313^b), though the chronology on which this hinges is disputed.

Hdt. 3. 39–60, 120–5; Thuc. 1. 13, 3. 104; Arist. *Pol.* 1313^b; Ath. 540d.

G. Shipley, *History of Samos* (1987); B. Mitchell, *JHS* 1975, 75 ff.; M. M. Austin, *CQ* 1990, 289 ff.; J. Barron, *CQ* 1964.   R. T.

Polycrates (2) (*c.*440–370 BC) was an Athenian *sophist who spent his latter years in Cyprus, and is best known for his (lost) fictitious 'Accusation of *Socrates' ($\kappa\alpha\tau\eta\gamma\rho\rho\iota\alpha$ $\Sigma\omega\kappa\rho\acute{\alpha}\tau\sigma\nu\varsigma$), written after 393/2 BC, and put in the mouth of *Anytus. The defences of Socrates by *Plato (1) and *Xenophon (1) seem to be responses to Polycrates. His speech was known to *Libanius, who composed an elaborate 'defence' partly at least in reply to it. Polycrates also practised the genre of 'paradoxical encomia'; his encomium on Busiris roused *Isocrates to criticize it in his own *Busiris*; and we hear also of encomia of *Clytemnestra and *Paris, and of mice and salt.

L. Radermacher, *Artium Scriptores* (1951), 128–32; J. Humbert, *Polycratès* (1930); E. R. Dodds, ed. of Plato's *Gorgias* (1959), 28–29; H. Markowski, *De Libanio Socratis defensore* (1912); H. Erbse, *Hermes*, 1961, 257–87.   D. A. R.

Polydamas ($\Pi o(\upsilon)\lambda\upsilon\delta\acute{\alpha}\mu\alpha\varsigma$), in mythology, son of Panthoos (Homer, see below). In the *Iliad* he takes some part in the fighting, but is chiefly noteworthy for his sage advice, which Hector rejects to his cost (18. 249 ff.). His death is nowhere recorded and he seems to be thought of as surviving the war.   H. J. R.

Polydeuces (i.e. Pollux) See CASTOR AND POLLUX; DIOSCURI.

Polydorus, in mythology youngest son of *Priam, by Laothoë (Hom. *Il.* 21. 84–91) or Hecuba. In the *Iliad* he is killed by *Achilles (20. 407–18). But according to *Euripides' *Hecuba*, Priam had sent him with much gold to be kept safe by Polymestor, a Thracian king, who murdered him for the gold after the fall of Troy; and Hecuba avenges his death by blinding Polymestor and killing his two sons. Cf. Verg. *Aen.* 3. 22 ff.   J. R. M.

Polyeidus (1), a seer, one of the Melampodidae, a Corinthian (see MELAMPUS (1); CORINTH). When Glaucus, son of *Minos, was drowned in a honey-jar, Polyeidus, after passing a test imposed by Minos, found the body and afterwards restored it to life by using a herb revealed by a snake.

See Hyg. *Fab.* 136; Roscher's *Lexikon*, under the name.   H. J. R.

Polyeidus (2) 'the Sophist' is known only from *Aristotle (*Poet.* 16, 17), who refers to the recognition scene in his *Iphigeneia* (if that was the title).

Polygnotus, painter, son and pupil of Aglaophon, of Thasos. *Pliny (1) dates him before 420 BC, calling him also a sculptor. He may also be dated by his friendship with *Cimon, for whom he painted in the *Stoa Poecile (depicting Cimon's sister Elpinice as Laodice), refusing a fee. This or his Anakeion painting gained him Athenian citizenship. He painted the 'Iliu Persis' and 'Nekyia' in the Cnidian *Lesche* (club-house for the citizens of *Cnidus) at *Delphi probably between 458 and 447, and probably the Theseum (Athens) soon after 475. The 'Rape of the Leukippides' (see DIOSCURI; LEUCIPPUS (1)) in the Anakeion, '*Odysseus having slain the suitors' in Plataea, '*Achilles in Scyros' and '*Nausicaa' (both later in the Pinacothece) are undated.

*Pausanias (3)'s description of the Cnidian *Lesche* (10. 25–31) reveals Polygnotus' innovative variable groundline and distribution of figures, reflected in such contemporary vases as the Niobid Painter krater. He was praised by *Aristotle and *Lucian for livelier and more expressive faces than before. Pliny credits him with originating transparent drapery, and representing open mouths. Many of the elements of his art had appeared sporadically before, but he combined them to represent men of high moral purpose (ethos) and 'better than ourselves', often either taking a decision or in the reaction after the event. For Theophrastus and others he was a primitive (he did not use shading), but still the first great painter. See PAINTING, GREEK.

R. Kebric, *The Paintings in the Knidian Lesche at Delphi* (1983); M. Stansbury-O'Donnell, *AJArch.* 1989, 203–15, and 1990, 213–35.

K. W. A.

Polynices See ANTIGONE (1); ETEOCLES; OEDIPUS; SEVEN AGAINST THEBES.

Polyperchon, son of Simmias, Macedonian from Tymphaea (close to *Epirus, and on the east side of N. Pindus), campaigned with *Alexander (3) 'the Great'. After *Issus (333 BC) he was given command of the Tymphaean battalion of the phalanx, which he retained until 324. Already of advanced years, he returned with the veterans demobilized at Opis (324). As *Craterus (1)'s second-in-command he acted as governor in Macedonia during the first coalition war (321–19), and was rewarded for his loyalty and military success with the regency, to which the dying *Antipater (1) appointed him over the head of *Cassander. In the war which ensued he encouraged democratic revolution at Athens (318), but was frustrated at Megalopolis and withdrew to Macedon. There he invoked the aid of *Olympias against the challenge from *Eurydice (2) but shared her unpopularity and lost his army—and Macedon—to Cassander (spring 316). Returning to the Peloponnese, he surrendered the regency to *Antigonus (1) (315); and in 309 he invaded Macedon, hoping to replace Cassander with Heracles (an illegitimate son of Alexander), but murdered his charge in return for recognition by Cassander and ended his life (at an uncertain date) in comparative obscurity in the Peloponnese.

HM 3 (1988); Heckel, *Marshals*, 188 ff.

A. B. B.

Polyphemus See CYCLOPES; GALATEA.

Polyphrasmon, son of *Phrynichus (1), was also a tragic poet, winning his first victory between 482 and 471. His *Lykourgeia* tetralogy was defeated in 467 by the Theban tetralogy of *Aeschylus and by *Aristias.

TrGF 1²/84–5.

A. L. B.

Polystratus (*RE* 7) (first half of the 3rd cent. BC), one of the original adherents of *Epicurus and founders of Epicureanism, followed *Hermarchus (successor of Epicurus) as head of the school. Like *Aristotle, he wrote a protreptic treatise *On Philosophy* (though not apparently directed against Aristotle). One of his books (on the methodology of inference from commonly held beliefs) is remarkably preserved as part of the philosophical library from *Herculaneum. Polystratus follows *Colotes in his attack on Sceptical philosophers (see SCEPTICS) who denied the certainty of knowledge derived from sensation (Polystr. *De contemptu* col. 24. 2–7 Indelli μάχεσθαι τοῖς φανεροῖς; cf. Colotes' characterization of *Arcesilaus (1) at Plut. *Adv. Col.* 1123a: μάχεται τοῖς ἐναργεσιν, 'he is in conflict with plain facts').

WORKS *Against those who Irrationally Despise Popular Beliefs* (Περὶ ἀλόγου καταφρονήσεως): ed. G. Indelli, *Polistrato. Sul disprezzo irrazionale delle opinioni popolari*, La scuola di Epicuro 2 (1978); selection

with Eng. trans. and comm. in Long and Sedley, *The Hellenistic Philosophers* 1–2 (1987), no. 7D pp. 35–7; D. Fowler, *Oxford Studies in Ancient Philosophy* 2 (1984), 244–6. Περὶ φιλοσοφίας: frs. ed. Crönert, *Kolotes und Menedemos* (1906), 36, with discussion by M. Capasso, *Cronache Ercolanesi*, 1976, 81–4.

W. D. R.; D. O.

Polyxena, in mythology a daughter of *Priam and *Hecuba, though she is not mentioned by *Homer. In the *Cypria* (see EPIC CYCLE) she is mortally wounded at the fall of Troy by *Diomedes (2) and *Odysseus and buried by *Neoptolemus (1) (fr. 27 Davies). In the *Iliu Persis* (Proclus; again, see EPIC CYCLE) and later she is sacrificed on the tomb of *Achilles by Neoptolemus (Eur. *Hec.* 220 ff.) to appease the ghost of Achilles and thus to raise winds to take the Greek ships home (ibid. 35 ff., 534 ff.). In later times the story arose that Achilles, during his life, had been in love with her (e.g. Hyg. *Fab.* 110).

In art she is often shown present in scenes of *Troilus ambushed at the fountain and pursued by Achilles.

A. Kossatz-Deissmann, *LIMC* 1. 1. 72–95.

J. R. M.

Polyzelus, Athenian comic poet, won four victories at the *Lenaea, the first in the last decade of the 5th cent. BC (*IG* 2². 2325. 130). We have six titles and a dozen citations; four of the titles indicate theogonic burlesque; a fifth, *Demotyndareos*, is certainly political, but its occasion and point are disputed.

PCG 7. 553 ff. (*CAF* 1. 789 ff.).

K. J. D.

pomerium—explained in antiquity as meaning what comes after, or before, the wall—was the line demarcating an augurally constituted city. It was a religious boundary, the point beyond which the *auspicia urbana* (see AUSPICIUM) could not be taken (Varro, *Ling.* 5. 143), and was distinct both from the city-wall and the limit of actual habitation, although it might coincide with the former and was often understood as the strip inside or outside the wall (cf. Livy 1. 44; Plut. *Rom.* 11). Almost every aspect of the history of the *pomerium* of Rome is debatable. Our sources refer to an original Palatine *pomerium*, later extended by Servius *Tullius and then unchanged until *Sulla's day (sources in Lugli, *Fontes* 2. 125 ff.); Tacitus (*Ann.* 12. 24), perhaps following the emperor *Claudius, describes a circuit round the *Palatine. Although this circuit has been thought to result from confusion with the circuit of the *Lupercalia, recent excavations on the north-east slope of the Palatine have revealed a series of ditches and walls from the regal period, which seem from their size to be more of symbolic value than a real system of defence and thus perhaps confirm the literary tradition. *Varro's account (*Ling.* 5. 46–54) of the city of the four regions may correspond to the *pomerium* at some early date. *Gellius (*NA* 13. 14. 4–7, quoting the augur M. *Valerius Messalla 'Rufus', consul 53 BC), mentions extensions by Sulla—perhaps to be connected with the boundary-stones to the Campus Esquilinus (*ILLRP* 485)—and also by *Caesar (cf. Cic. *Att.* 13. 20; Dio 43. 50. 1). On the other hand, *Augustus' silence in *Res gestae* suggests that he made none, despite the statement of Tacitus (*Ann.* 12. 23). Later extensions were made by Claudius, who was the first to include the *Aventine (Tac. loc. cit.; Gell. loc. cit.; *CIL* 6. 31537a–d, 37023–4; *Not. Scav.* 1912, 197; 1913, 68), and by Vespasian (*CIL* 6. 31538a–c; *Not. Scav.* 1933, 241; cf. *CIL* 6. 930. 14–16). The *cippi* (boundary stones) dating from *Hadrian (*CIL* 6. 31539a–c; *Not. Scav.* 1933, 241) seem only to be restorations, while the account of *Aurelian's later extension is doubtful (SHA *Aurelian* 21). The imperial *pomerium*, as loosely defined by the *cippi*, is thought to have coincided on the east with the republican wall, breaking away to include the

Aventine and the Emporium, the southern half of the *Campus Martius and all the Pincian hill, at the last point extending beyond *Aurelian's later wall.

Labrousse, *Mél. d'Arch.* 1937; Grimal, ibid. 1959; Rodríguez-Almeida, *Rend. Pont.* 1978–9; *BCAR* 1986, 411 ff.   I. A. R.; J. N.; A. W. L.

Pometia (near mod. Cisterna?), also known as Suessa, gave its name to the *Pomptine Marshes. *Volsci and Romans often disputed its possession in primitive *Latium. About 495 BC Rome obliterated it. It was never rebuilt. Spoils from Pometia enabled *Tarquinius Superbus to found the Capitoline temple at Rome (Livy 1. 53). See CAPITOL; TARQUINIUS PRISCUS.   E. T. S.; T. W. P.

Pomona, Italo-Roman goddess of *poma*, i.e. fruits, especially such as grow on trees (apples etc.). Her *flamen was lowest in rank of all (*minimus*, Festus 144, 14 Lindsay), corresponding apparently to the small importance of her province. She had a sacred place, *pomonal*, 20 km. (12 mi.) out of Rome on the via Ostiensis (Festus 296, 15 ff. Lindsay), but no known festival. *Ovid (*Met.* 14. 623 ff.) has a story (unconnected with facts of cult and clearly his own or another comparatively late author's invention) that *Vertumnus loved her, pleaded his own cause in disguised shape, and finally won her. In another version she is the spouse of *Picus (Serv. on *Aen.* 7. 190).   H. J. R.; J. Sch.

Pompeia (*RE* 'Pompeius' 52), granddaughter of Q. *Pompeius Rufus and of *Sulla, married *Caesar in 67 BC. After the Bona Dea scandal (see CLODIUS PULCHER, P.) he proclaimed her innocence, but divorced her since his household had to be above suspicion.   E. B.

Pompeia Plotina, (*RE* 'Pompeius' 131), wife of *Trajan, evidently from Nîmes (*Nemausus). She did not accept the title *Augusta* (offered in AD 100) until 105 (see AUGUSTUS, AUGUSTA AS TITLES) and did not feature on the coinage until 112. She had no children and strongly supported *Hadrian, stage-managing his adoption by the dying Trajan at Selinus in Cilicia in August 117 (leading to rumours that it had been faked). She took a personal interest in the Epicurean philosophical school (see EPICURUS) at Athens. On her death, probably early in 123, she was deified and Hadrian built a basilica in her memory at Nîmes (*Nemausus).

H. Temporini, *Die Frauen am Hofe Trajans* (1978); M.-T. Raepsaet-Charlier, *Prosopographie des femmes de l'ordre sénatorial* (1987), no. 631.   A. R. Bi.

Pompeii Archaeologically the best-known Roman city, this port and regional centre in the Sarnus plain of south *Campania, destroyed by the eruption of AD 79, is central to the study of Roman art and domestic life, but surprisingly hard to fit in to general accounts of local politics, or economic and social history.

The oldest architecture (fragments from the Doric Temple and the Temple of *Apollo) belongs in the Greek milieu around the Campanian *apoikiai* of the 6th cent. BC (see APOIKIA): scattered finds suggest links with the *Etruscan cultures of the Archaic and Classical periods, and the wider Mediterranean world. Pompeii appears as a dependent port-settlement of *Nuceria in 310 BC (Livy 9. 38. 2–3), and at no earlier point—either in the Greek, Etruscan, or early Samnite (*Oscan-speaking; see SAMNIUM) milieux of 6th, 5th, and 4th cents.—does there seem to have been a substantial urban nucleus or an autonomous political community. Even now there has been little stratigraphic excavation, but the early Pompeii appears at present as a village on the lava hill above the sheltered mouth of the river Sarno, with a

couple of prominent sanctuaries and a likely role as an anchorage for coasting vessels and a local market.

There have been suggestions of a 6th-cent. enceinte on the line of the later substantial fortifications (enclosing some 63 ha. on the summit of the lava spur, and perhaps, if so early, a refuge-enclosure). Debate continues, but the walls are most probably to be linked with the introduction of new methods and aspirations in such architecture now widely attested among the indigenous populations of south Italy at the end of the 4th cent., and linked with a widespread urbanising process. The layout of the greater part of the street-plan is probably also of 4th/3rd-cent. date (perhaps in two phases with rather different orientations), though the 9 ha. nucleus of somewhat irregular lanes and small blocks around the Forum may reflect earlier circumstances.

The impetus for the impressive transformation involved in the creation of streets and walls escapes us: otherwise, the basics of Pompeii as we know it are 2nd cent. Campanians were prominent participants in late Hellenistic economic prosperity, and the Oscan culture (see OSCANS) of this period is of particular interest for its participation—alongside, and blending with, the similar contemporary experience of Rome—in the currents of fashion and display that were found in the eastern Mediterranean. The formation, out of earlier local prototypes, of the distinctive 'Pompeian house', belongs in this setting. Benefactors who could afford dwellings like the palatial House of the Faun equipped the city with the larger theatre, the earlier palaestra, and the temple of Isis, the first baths, the gymnasium around the Doric temple, the first systematization of the forum, and the paving of the main streets. This phase undoubtedly saw activity in the harbour district, of which little is still known.

On this flourishing community, *Sulla imposed a *colonia* of Roman veterans, led by his nephew, as a penalty for siding with the enemy in the *Social War (3) (during which he had himself laid siege to Pompeii). See COLONIZATION, ROMAN. Latin subsequently replaced Oscan (completing a process that had been at work for some time) in the town's inscriptions, and the *meddix tuticus* was replaced by *aediles. The new community continued the tradition of architectural benefaction with important monuments: the amphitheatre, the covered theatre, the temple of Jupiter which formed the main feature of the forum. Further important houses date from this period (like that of the Silver Wedding), as do the first monumental tombs of the inner suburbs and the first villas of the territory (Cicero was one proprietor).

Yet another phase of public building marked the city's response to the initiatives and ideologies of the new Augustan regime. Important monumental complexes like the Macellum or the Porticus of Eumachia (which echoes themes in contemporary architecture in the capital) were added to the forum; the Great Palaestra was built alongside the amphitheatre, and the larger theatre remodelled.

The sudden destruction crystallized a problematic moment: the damage of the earthquake of 62 was still being patchily repaired and the opulence and modishness of some private and public projects of the last phase (the temple of the town's patron Venus and the 'central' baths were both ambitious in scale) contrast with chaos and squalor. The centre of gravity of Campania was shifting towards *Puteoli, and servicing the luxury villas had perhaps become the town's principal activity. But the inscriptions painted on the walls attest vigorous political life, and the removal of decorative and documentary material from the easily identified public zones in the immediate aftermath of the eruption may have skewed the evidence towards the private sphere. Most important, earlier phases might have looked like this too, if they had been interrupted: the constant disruptions of rebuilding and social discontinuity, and the enormous complexity of the social history of a community like this, are among Pompeii's most important lessons.

Neither the composition by place of origin nor the total size of the population is easily established, though the inscriptions attest frequent links by family-name (implying blood-ties or manumission-relationships) with other cities of the area. Local contacts also included rivalry over spectacles (vividly illuminated by the slogans and notices painted on the walls), like that with Nuceria which caused a major riot in AD 59, untypically attracting attention from Rome (Tac. *Ann.* 14, 17), and the economic relations which stemmed from the city's important function as a port (for *Nola, Nuceria, and Acerrae, Strabo 5. 4. 8). The city was the centre of a vigorous and varied cash-crop agriculture (an export *wine of middling reputation was of some importance); excavation has revealed the intensiveness of cultivation on small garden-lots even within the walls. See GARDENS. The territory had been centuriated at an uncertain date. The processing of agricultural produce is visible in many small commercial premises, but the extent and economic standing of activities such as textile-manufacture remain controversial. Any assessment of Roman Pompeii must take into account the wealth of Campania, its dense network of overseas contacts (which are reflected in many aspects of the life of the city, especially its religion), and the investment in the area that derived from its popularity as a resort.

The site (only haphazardly reoccupied in antiquity) was first rediscovered in 1748, rapidly acquiring a sensational fame. Systematic recording began in 1861; the new excavations of the 1950s set a new standard; contemporary work today concentrates more on recording, conservation, and analysis, since the discoveries of the first excavators have often decayed irreparably. Some four-fifths of the walled area have been disinterred.

W. Jongman, *The Economy and Society of Pompeii* (1988); L. Richardson, *The Architecture of Pompeii* (1988); A. and M. De Vos, *Pompei, Ercolano, Stabia* (1982: Guide archeologiche Laterza), 7–240; W. Jashemski, *The Gardens of Pompeii*, 1 (1979), 2 (1993); P. Arthur, *Ant. Journ.* 1986, 29–44. N. P.

Pompeius (*RE* 143) (late 5th–early 6th cent. AD), African grammarian, commented on *Donatus (1)'s *ars* (*GL* 5. 95–312), perhaps also on *Virgil and *Terence (very uncertain).

Kaster, *Guardians of Language*, 139–68, 343–6. Herzog–Schmidt, § 702. R. A. K.

Pompeius (*RE* 12), **Quintus**, a *novus homo* attached to P. *Cornelius Scipio Aemilianus, became consul in 141 BC by trickery and against Scipio's will (it was said). *Cicero (*Brut.* 96) ascribes his success to his oratorical ability. He succeeded Q. *Caecilius Metellus Macedonicus in the Numantine command, blaming his lack of success on his predecessor. In 140 he was forced to negotiate a treaty, but repudiated it on his successor's arrival and gained the senate's approval for this action. Prosecuted *repetundarum* (see REPETUNDAE), in a *cause célèbre*, by Metellus and other distinguished men, he was acquitted, and in 136 he and Metellus served together as legates in Spain under L. *Furius Philus. A prominent opponent of Ti. *Sempronius Gracchus (3), he became *censor (131) with Metellus (the first pair of plebeian censors; see PLEBS).

Astin, *Scipio*, see index. E. B.

Pompeius Falco, Quintus, senator from Sicily, friend and correspondent of *Pliny (2) the Younger, was married to a daughter of Q. *Sosius Senecio. Falco commanded a legion in the First Dacian War (see DACIA), then governed *Lycia-*Pamphylia and *Judaea, becoming consul in AD 108. Governor of Lower *Moesia during the crisis there at the end of *Trajan's reign, Falco was appointed by *Hadrian governor of *Britain, also a troubled province, serving until 122, and may have begun the building of the *wall of Hadrian. He was proconsul of Asia (see ASIA, ROMAN PROVINCE), from 123–4. He was still alive *c*.140, when the young Marcus *Aurelius inspected his tree-grafting.

Plin. *Epp.*; Fronto, *Ad M. Caes.* A. R. Birley, *The Fasti of Roman Britain* (1981), 95 ff.; W. Eck, *Catania antica. Atti della S. I. A. C. Catania 1992*. A. R. Bi.

Pompeius Festus, Sextus (late 2nd cent. AD), scholar, abridger of the *On the meaning of words* of *Verrius Flaccus. Of his work (alphabetically arranged in twenty books) the first half is lost. Festus himself was epitomized in the 8th cent. by Paulus Diaconus. The standard edition (including Paulus) is that of W. M. Lindsay (1913) whose later edition in *Glossaria Latina* 4 (93–467) incorporates Festus material gleaned from glossaries. See SCHOLARSHIP, ANCIENT.

Schanz–Hosius, § 341. J. F. M.

Pompeius Lenaeus, a learned *freedman of *Pompey, taught in Rome and, loyal to his patron's memory, attacked the character and style of *Sallust who had described Pompey as 'honest on the surface, but in fact without shame' (Suet. *Gram.* 15). At Pompey's request he made a Latin translation of the writings of *Mithradates VI on *pharmacology, according to *Pliny (1) (*HN* 25. 5 and 7) the first work of its kind in Latin.

J. Christes, *Sklaven und Freigelassene als Grammatiker und Philologen im antiken Rom* (1979), 57 ff. J. W. D.

Pompeius (*RE* 31) **Magnus** (1), **Gnaeus (Pompey),** b. 106 BC (the official *cognomen* meaning 'the Great', in imitation of *Alexander (3), was assumed after 81 BC). He served with his father Cn. *Pompeius Strabo at *Asculum (89) and brought a private army of three legions from his father's veterans and clients in *Picenum to win victories for *Sulla in 83. He was then sent *pro praetore* to Sicily, where he defeated and killed Cn. *Papirius Carbo, and from there to Africa, where he destroyed Cn. Domitius Ahenobarbus and King Iarbas. Though Pompey was still an *eques*, Sulla grudgingly allowed him to triumph (12 March 81); and in 80, after the death of his wife Aemilia, Sulla's stepdaughter, he married *Mucia Tertia, a close connection of the Metelli. He supported M. *Aemilius Lepidus (2) for the consulship of 78, for which Sulla cut him out of his will, but assisted Q. *Lutatius Catulus (2) to overcome Lepidus next year. Later in 77 he was sent *pro consule* to reinforce Q. *Caecilius Metellus Pius against Q. *Sertorius in Spain. Thence he returned in 71 and attempted to steal from *Crassus the credit for finishing off the Slave War (see SPARTACUS). He was rewarded with a second triumph and as his first magistracy, despite his youth, the consulship of 70, with Crassus as his colleague. They restored the legislative powers which Sulla had removed from the tribunes; and L. *Aurelius Cotta reversed another of Sulla's arrangements by ending the senate's monopoly of representation on the courts: judges were now to be drawn equally from senators, *equites*, and *tribuni aerarii* (a group similar to the *equites*).

Pompey took no consular province. But in 67 the *lex Gabinia* (see A. GABINIUS (2); LEX (2)) empowered him to deal with *piracy. The command, for three years, covered the whole Mediterranean, and gave him unprecedented powers; but Pompey's campaign required only three months. In 66 a law of the tribune C. *Manilius gave him the Asiatic provinces of Cilicia, Bithynia, and Pontus, earlier held by L. *Licinius Lucullus (2), and the conduct of the war against *Mithradates VI. Pompey's eastern campaigns were his greatest achievement. Mithradates was defeated immediately, and though attempts to pursue him over the Caucasus failed, he committed suicide in the Crimea in 63. Pompey founded colonies, annexed *Syria, settled *Judaea, and laid the foundation of subsequent Roman organization of the East (though he reached no agreement with *Parthia).

In 62 he returned, disbanded his army, and triumphed, no longer a *populy* as hitherto (for the new role, Cic. *Att.* 2. 1. 6 and for *populares* see OPTIMATES). He made two requests: land for his veterans, and ratification of his eastern arrangements. But he had divorced Mucia for adultery, allegedly with *Caesar; and the Metelli, aided by Lucullus and M. *Porcius Cato (2), frustrated him until in 60 Caesar succeeded in reconciling him with Crassus. In 59 the three men formed a coalition and Pompey married Caesar's daughter *Iulia (2). His demands were satisfied by Caesar as consul; but his popularity waned, and in 58/7 P. *Clodius Pulcher flouted and attacked him. In 57, after securing *Cicero's return from exile, he received control of the corn-supply for five years with proconsular *imperium* and fifteen legates. But no army was attached, nor could he secure the commission to restore *Ptolemy (1) XII Auletes in Egypt. In April 56 the coalition with Caesar and Crassus was renewed at *Luca. Pompey became consul with Crassus for 55, and received both Spanish provinces for five years; he governed them through legates, staying in the suburbs of Rome. After Iulia's death in 54 he declined a further marriage alliance with Caesar, and the death of Crassus in 53 increased the tension between Caesar and Pompey. In 52 after Clodius' murder Pompey was appointed sole consul, with backing even from Cato. Pompey's immediate actions—the trial of T. *Annius Milo and his legislation on violence, on bribery, and on the tenure of *magistracies—were not necessarily intended specifically to injure Caesar, but the prolongation of his *imperium* for five years from this date destroyed the balance of power, and he took as his colleague Q. *Caecilius Metellus Pius Scipio, whose daughter *Cornelia (2) he married about the time that he became consul. At first he resisted attempts to recall Caesar, but his desire to pose as the arbiter of Caesar's fate was challenged in 50 by C. *Scribonius Curio (2), who insisted that both or neither should lay down their commands. Unable to accept the implications of parity, Pompey conditionally accepted from the consul C. *Claudius Marcellus (1) the command of the republic's forces in Italy. In 49 he transported his army from *Brundisium to Greece and spent the year mobilizing in *Macedonia. He met Caesar on the latter's arrival in 48 with a force powerful in every arm, and inflicted a serious reverse when Caesar attempted to blockade him in *Dyrrhachium. But later (9 August), perhaps under pressure from his senatorial friends, he joined in a pitched battle at *Pharsalus, and was heavily defeated. He fled to Egypt, but was stabbed to death as he landed (28 September 48).

The violence and unconstitutional character of Pompey's early career invite comparison with *Augustus whose constitutional position his powers often prefigured: in 67 he had 15 (or even 24) legates; from 55 he governed Spain through legates (see LEGATI), and while doing so was made consul in 52. But still more significant was his wealth and his unofficial power: by 62 in Spain, Gaul, Africa and the east, and parts of Italy, there were colonists

and clients (see CLIENS) bound to him by the relationship of *fides* (loyalty) and surrounding him with a magnificence unsurpassed by a Roman senator hitherto; the climax was reached with the dedication of his theatre in the *Campus Martius in 55. His military talents are hard to evaluate. Other commanders—Metellus, Crassus, Lucullus—often paved the way to his successes, and at Pharsalus he clearly panicked. Logistics seem to have been his strong point, as in the campaign against the pirates. But in politics he showed a mastery which it was easy for clever men to underrate (e.g., for all its brilliance, the epigram of M. *Caelius Rufus in Cic. *Fam.* 8. 1. 3: 'he is apt to say one thing and think another, but is not clever enough to keep his real aims from showing'). 'Moderate in everything but in seeking domination' (Sallust, *Histories* 2. 14), by superb skill and timing he rose from his lawless beginnings to a constitutional pre-eminence in which he could discard the use of naked force. His aim was predominance, but not at the expense of at least the appearance of popularity. He did not wish to overthrow the republican constitution, but was content if its rules were bent almost but not quite to breaking-point to accommodate his extraordinary eminence. His private life was virtually blameless, and two women, Iulia and Cornelia, married to him for dynastic ends, became deeply attached to him, and his love for Iulia was noted by contemporaries. Cicero, though he never understood Pompey's subtleties, remained a devoted admirer; and despite the disappointments of the war years Pompey's death brought from him a muted but moving tribute: 'I knew him to be a man of good character, clean life, and serious principle' (*Att.* 11. 6. 5).

For the sources see CAESAR; M. Gelzer, *Pompeius²* (1959); R. Seager, *Pompey* (1979). G. E. F. C.; R. J. S.

Pompeius (*RE* 17) **Magnus** (2), **Gnaeus,** elder son of Pompey (Cn. *Pompeius Magnus (1); see preceding article) and *Mucia Tertia, was born 79 BC. About 54 he married a daughter of Ap. *Claudius Pulcher (3). In 49 he secured an Egyptian fleet, with which before the battle of *Dyrrhachium he destroyed *Caesar's transports. Early in the African War he occupied the Balearic Islands and crossed to Spain, where he was joined after Thapsus by his brother Sextus *Pompeius Magnus and T. *Labienus (1), raised thirteen legions, and won most of the southern part of the province. But after manoeuvres which drove him south from Corduba he was defeated by Caesar in 45 in the hard-fought battle of Munda, and later captured and executed. (For the battles here mentioned see further IULIUS CAESAR (1), C.)

G. E. F. C.; E. B.

Pompeius (*RE* 33) **Magnus (Pius), Sextus,** younger son of Pompey (Cn. *Pompeius Magnus (1)) and *Mucia Tertia, was born probably *c.*67 BC. Left in Lesbos with *Cornelia (2) during the campaign of Pharsalus (48), he accompanied his father to Egypt and after his murder went to Africa; after Thapsus (46) he joined his brother Cn. *Pompeius Magnus (2) in Spain, and during the campaign of Munda (45) commanded the garrison of *Corduba. Subsequently he contrived to raise an army, partly of fugitive Pompeians, and won successes against *Caesar's governors in Further Spain, C. Carrinas, who was *consul suffectus* (see CONSUL) in 43, and after him C. *Asinius Pollio. In summer 44 M. *Aemilius Lepidus (3) arranged a settlement between him and the senate, under the terms of which he left Spain; but instead of returning to Rome, he waited on events in *Massalia with his army and fleet. In April 43 the senate made him its naval commander, with the title *praefectus classis et orae maritimae* (see RRC

511); but in August he was outlawed under the *lex Pedia* (see PEDIUS, Q.) and then used his fleet to rescue fugitives from the *proscriptions and to occupy Sicily, at first sharing authority with the governor Pompeius Bithynicus, but later putting him to death; and using the island as a base for raiding and blockading Italy. He repelled an attack by *Octavian's general Q. *Salvidienus Rufus in 42, supported Antony against Octavian in 40 (when his lieutenant *Menodorus occupied Sardinia) and in 39 concluded the Pact of *Misenum with the triumvirs (see TRIUMVIRI), who conceded to him the governorship of *Sicily, *Sardinia and *Corsica, and *Achaia, an augurate (see AUGURES) and a future consulship (see *ILLRP* 426) in return for the suspension of his blockade. In 38 Octavian accused him of breaking the pact and again attacked him, but was defeated in sea fights off *Cumae and *Messana. In 36 the attack was renewed, and after M. *Vipsanius Agrippa's victory off Mylae, Octavian's defeat off *Tauromenium, and Lepidus' occupation of southern and western Sicily, the war was decided by the battle of Naulochus (3 September). Sextus escaped with a few ships to Asia, where he attempted to establish himself, but was forced to surrender to M. *Titius, who put him to death.

Sextus was, like his father, an able and energetic commander. His brief career was spent entirely in the continuation—symbolized by his adoption of the surname Pius (he gives his name as Magnus Pompeius Magni f. Pius)—of an inherited struggle. Despite his long absence from and blockade of Italy, he seems to have been popular in Rome. His wife was *Scribonia, daughter of L. *Scribonius Libo.

M. Hadas, *Sextus Pompey* (1930); Syme, *RR* index, *AA* 255 ff.
T. J. C.; R. J. S.

Pompeius (*RE* 103) **Planta, Gaius,** in AD 69 fought in the war between *Otho and *Vitellius. He was *procurator of *Lycia (*c*.75 or 76), an *amicus* of *Trajan, and prefect (see PRAEFECTUS) of *Egypt (98–100). He wrote an account of battle of *Bedriacum, which *Tacitus (1) may have used for his *Histories*.

Peter, *HHRel.* 2. 116. H.-G. Pflaum, *Les Carrières procurat.* (1960), 140 f.
H. H. S.; B. M. L.

Pompeius (*RE* 39) **Rufus, Quintus,** son or grandson of Q. *Pompeius, as tribune (100 BC) unsuccessfully worked for the recall of Q. *Caecilius Metellus Numidicus and remained closely attached to his family. He was *praetor urbanus* 91, and consul 88 with *Sulla, whose daughter married his son. He opposed P. *Sulpicius Rufus, his former friend, and was driven from Rome, but then occupied it with Sulla. Sent (by a *senatus consultum* whose validity could be impugned) to supersede his distant relative Cn. *Pompeius Strabo, he was killed by the latter's soldiers with the commander's acquiescence.

For a coin-portrait see *RRC* 434/1 (p. 456).
E. B.

Pompeius Saturninus, dilettante friend of *Pliny (2) the younger, who admired his oratory, history, and poetry (*Ep.* 1. 16).

Schanz–Hosius § 450. 7.
M. W.

Pompeius Silo, rhetor of the Augustan era.

Sen. *Contr.* 3, pr. 11; etc.
M. B. T.

Pompeius (*RE* 45) **Strabo, Gnaeus,** father of Pompey (Cn. *Pompeius Magnus (1)), after his quaestorship *c*.106 BC tried to prosecute his commander. As tribune (104) he successfully prosecuted Q. Fabius Maximus Eburnus (censor 108) in an epoch-making case limiting *patria potestas*. In the *Social War (3) he fought in the northern sector, as legate (90) and—after a victory

over T. Lafrenius—as consul (89). Pompey, *Cicero, and *Catiline, among others, served under him (Cichorius, *Röm. Stud.* 144). Capturing *Asculum Picenum, he ended the northern war and triumphed late in 89 before resuming his command. His distant relative Q. *Pompeius Rufus was sent to supersede him and was killed, with Strabo's acquiescence. In 87, asked to defend Rome against *Cinna, he behaved ambiguously; he negotiated with Cinna (he probably had connections with Cn. *Papirius Carbo) over a joint consulship, excluding both *Marius (1) and the *optimates. His death (perhaps in an epidemic) was thought fit punishment and his body was dragged through the streets. He was one of the first, in the light of Sulla's march on Rome, to see the possibilities offered to unscrupulous leaders by the new army (see MARIUS (1) and SULLA) and the spread of citizenship. As consul he had given Latin rights to *Transpadana and enfranchised some Spaniards on the battlefield (*ILLRP* 515). In those regions and in *Picenum he built up the following later inherited and exploited by his son.

M. Gelzer, *Kl. Schr.* (1962–3), 2. 106; E. Badian, *Historia*, 1969, 465 ff., and *Klio*, 1984, 306 ff.
E. B.; R. J. S.

Pompeius (*RE* 142) **Trogus,** a Romanized Vocontian from Gallia Narbonensis (see GAUL (TRANSALPINE)), author of zoological, and perhaps botanical works, now lost, and the 'Philippic Histories' (*Historiae Philippicae*), usually dated to the reign of *Augustus and known only through the *epitome of *Justin and the tables of contents (*prologi*). Beginning with the ancient Near East and Greece (bks. 1–6), he covered Macedon (bks. 7–12) and the Hellenistic kingdoms to their fall before Rome (bks. 13–40); books 41–2 contained Parthian history to 20 BC, books 43–4 the regal period of Rome, and Gallic and Spanish history to Augustus' Spanish wars. His sources continue to be debated. Although heavy or even exclusive reliance on *Timagenes of Alexandria is now thought unlikely, he may well have used extensively the *Histories* of *Posidonius (2), perhaps through an intermediary source.

TEXT O. Seel (Teubner, 1956).

STUDIES Seel, *Eine römische Weltgeschichte* etc. (1972); G. Forni and M. Angeli Bertinelli, *ANRW* 30. 2 (1982), 1298–361 (review article); J. Alonso-Nuñez, *G&R* 1987, 56; Syme, *RP* 6. 358 ff.
A. H. McD.; A. J. S. S.

Pompey See POMPEIUS MAGNUS (1), CN.

Pompilius, a tragedian (Varro *LL* 7. 93) whose elegiac epitaph (?) for himself also survives.

See Courtney *FLP* 51.
E. C.

Pompilius (*RE* Numa 1), **Numa,** legendary second king of Rome (traditionally 715–673 BC), from whom the Aemilii, Calpurnii, Marcii, Pinarii, and Pomponii later claimed descent. Reputedly a Sabine (see SABINI) from Cures, he supposedly created much of the basic framework of Roman public religion through his institution of cults, rituals, priesthoods, and calendar reforms (so Ennius, *Ann.* 113–19 Skutsch). Already in Ennius he claimed to have received instruction from *Egeria and (an originally distinct?) Greek or Graecizing tradition, going back at least to 181 BC (when alleged 'books of Numa' were discovered and destroyed), made him a pupil of *Pythagoras (1). Rationalistic historians reinterpreted Egeria as a political fiction and the discarding of the Pythagoras story on chronological grounds enables *Cicero (*Rep.* 2. 28 f.) and *Livy (1. 18. 2 ff.) to stress Numa's native credentials. Accounts of Numa's reforms (including e.g. the encouragement of settled agriculture) are hardly historical and are elaborated according to individual taste: Livy (1. 18 ff.), for example, discards stories of divine instruction and miraculous encounters with deities (Valerius Antias fr. 6 P.) to focus on religion as a matter of human ordinance and an ethico-political instrument. Alleged 'laws of Numa' (Cic. *Rep.* 2. 26; etc.) will be (at best) supposedly ancient ordinances preserved by the *pontifices*.

Ogilvie, *Comm. Livy 1–5*, 88 ff.; P. Panitschek, *Grazer Beiträge* 1990, 49 ff.; V. Buchheit, *Symb. Osl.* 1991, 71 ff.   A. D.

Pomponius (*RE* 101, fl. 89 BC, according to Jerome), **Lucius,** of *Bononia; author of *fabulae Atellanae*, which he and his contemporary *Novius made literary. We have seventy titles and nearly 200 lines. Ps.-Acro on Hor. *Ars P.* 288 lists him as an author of *praetextae* and *togatae*, perhaps wrongly. *Pomponius Porphyrio on *Ars P.* 221 lists *Atalante*, *Sisyphos*, and *Ariadne* as satyr-plays by Pomponius; they are generally taken to have been *Atellanae*, but T. P. Wiseman, *JRS* 1988 argues that Porphyrio was right. See ATELLANA.   P. G. M. B.

Pomponius (*RE* 107), **Sextus,** a Roman lawyer of the 2nd cent. AD who wrote under *Hadrian, *Antoninus Pius, and Marcus *Aurelius. A teacher and prolific writer, the author of over 300 books (*libri*), he seems not to have given *responsa* (consultative opinions) nor to have held public office. His relation to the Sabinian and Proculian schools (see MASURIUS SABINUS; PROCULUS, SEMPRONIUS) is problematic; but there is (disputed) evidence that he was at one time an associate of *Gaius (2) (*Dig.* 45. 3. 39). His *Enchiridium* (Introduction to Law), from which Justinian's compilers excerpted a long passage (*Dig.* 1. 2. 2; see JUSTINIAN'S CODIFICATION), is of great interest for its account of the history of the Roman constitution and the legal profession. It was the first and for long the only work on legal history. But the text, perhaps taken from a student's notes of lectures shortly before 131 AD, is garbled and contains many errors. Pomponius' large-scale commentaries included thirty-nine books of readings on Quintus Mucius (see Q. MUCIUS SCAEVOLA (4)), thirty-five on Masurius Sabinus' *ius civile* (Civil Law), and perhaps 150 on the praetor's *edict: we know of a citation from book 83 which deals with a topic that comes little more than halfway through the edict. *Domitius Ulpianus, an admirer, made great use of this work, which was not available to Justinian's compilers. There were also extensive casuistic works, *Epistulae* (Letters) and *Variae lectiones* (Varied Readings). In all Justinian's compilers included over five hundred passages from Pomponius in their *Digesta*. Dealing meticulously with unlikely as well as likely hypotheses, Pomponius' work not only founded the study of legal history but made a solid contribution to the analysis and structure of Roman private law.

Lenel, *Pal.* 2. 15–160; *PIR*[1] P 521; *HLL* 4 (forthcoming) § 422; Kunkel (1967), 170–1; Mommsen, *Ges. Sch.* 2 (1905), 21–5; T. Honoré (1962), 1–11, 18–26, 171–4; D. Liebs, in A. Guarino and L. Bove (eds.), *Gaio nel suo tempo* (1966), 61–75; H. Ankum, in A. Watson (ed.), *Daube Noster* (1974), 1–13; D. Nörr, *ANRW* 2. 15 (1976), 497–604.   T. Hon.

Pomponius (*RE* 102, Suppl. 8) **Atticus, Titus,** b. 110 BC as the son of a cultured *eques* of a family claiming descent from *Pompilius Numa, was later adopted by a rich uncle (Q. Caecilius), whose wealth he inherited. He was a friend of *Cicero from boyhood (Cicero's brother Quintus married Atticus' sister), and Cicero's *Letters to Atticus*, probably published in the reign of *Nero (though parts were known to some before), are the best source for his character, supplemented by an encomiastic bio-

graphical sketch by his friend Nepos (see CORNELIUS NEPOS). In 85 Atticus left Italy after selling his assets there, in order to escape the civil disturbances he foresaw. He lived in Athens until the mid-60s (hence his *cognomen*), among other things studying Epicurean philosophy (see EPICURUS), to which however he never wholly committed himself. Henceforth he combined a life of cultured ease (*otium*) with immense success in various business activities and an infallible instinct for survival. He privately urged Cicero to determined action on behalf of the *optimates, with whom he sympathized, but himself refused to take sides in politics and personally assisted many prominent politicians from C. *Marius (1) to Octavian (see AUGUSTUS), without regard for their differences and conflicts. He was Cicero's literary adviser and had his works copied and distributed. He himself wrote a *Liber Annalis* (a chronological table of world, and especially Roman, history), which became a standard work, eulogistic histories of some noble families, and minor works. (All are lost.) He lived to become a friend of M. *Vipsanius Agrippa, who married his daughter. In 32 he committed suicide when incurably ill.

D. R. Shackleton Bailey, *Cicero's Letters to Atticus*, esp. 1 (1965), introd. (3 ff.); Nepos, *Atticus*. E. Rawson, *Intellectual Life in the Roman Republic* (1985), esp. 100 ff. On Nepos see F. Millar, *G&R* 1988, 40 ff.   E. B.

Pomponius Bassulus, Marcus (probably time of *Trajan or *Hadrian). His epitaph from Aeclanum (*CIL* 9. 1164) says he translated *Menander (1) and wrote original comedies (probably not staged).   P. G. M. B.

Pomponius (*RE* 104) **Mela** of Tingentera (near Gibraltar) in *Baetica, and proud of his home province (2. 86), author of a pioneering Latin *geography (*De chorographia*) in three books, composed at the moment of *Claudius' invasion of Britain (AD 43–4), which it may be designed to celebrate (3. 49–52). The work was already used by the elder *Pliny (1). Mela systematically delineates the order of the lands and seas on the globe, and lists names of peoples and places with a few ethnographic details in an order which follows the sea coasts and is therefore vague on the interior of Europe and more surprisingly, Asia, but which does give a (distorted) account of the Baltic and Scandinavia. His base material resembles that of *Strabo, and more obviously suggests, though it does not establish, the use of a map (see MAPS). Mela is interested in wonders and the mythological and historical past, but little in geographical mathematics.

RECENT EDITIONS G. Ranstrand (1971); P. Parroni (1984); A. Silberman (1988); K. Brodersen, *Pomponius Mela: Kreuzfahrt durch die antike Welt* (1994).   N. P.

Pomponius (*RE* 105) **Porcellus** (not 'Marcellus'), **Marcus** (early 1st cent. AD), grammarian whose extreme pedantry is reported by *Suetonius (*Gramm.* 22, cf. Cass. Dio 57. 17. 1–3) and the elder Seneca, L. *Annaeus Seneca (1) (*Suas.* 2. 12 f.).

Kaster, *Studies on the Text of Suetonius* (1992), 99–102.   R. A. K.

Pomponius (*RE* 106) **Porphyrio** (early 3rd cent. AD), scholar whose commentary on *Horace is extant (ed. Holder, 1894), though only in a redaction dating to the 5th(?) cent. The commentary, which touches lightly on *Realien* and concentrates on grammar and rhetoric, seems intended for school-use; it incorporates the work of earlier commentators, including *Helenius Acro.

Herzog–Schmidt, § 446.   R. A. K.

Pomponius Proculus Vitrasius Pollio, Titus (*RE* 'Pomponius' 67 and 'Vitrasius' 8), a member of the Vitrasii family from *Cales in *Campania which provided two prefects of Egypt (see PRAEFECTUS) in the Julio-Claudian period and gained senatorial rank under Trajan. Pollio's father was suffect consul *c.* AD 137, he himself gained patrician rank and married Annia Fundania Faustina, cousin of M. *Aurelius. *Suffect consul *c.*151, he governed two imperial provinces (*Moesia Inferior and Hispania Citerior; see SPAIN) and was proconsul of Asia, was *comes* of Marcus in the northern wars and consul for the second time (*ordinarius*; see CONSUL) 176.

G. Alföldy, *Konsulat und Senatorenstand unter den Antoninen* (1977).
A. R. Bi.

Pomponius Rufus, of unknown date, in whose *Collecta* *Cornelia (1) declared 'My jewels are my children' (Val. Max. 4. 4. pr.), is sometimes identified with C. *Sempronius Gracchus' friend and diehard supporter M. Pomponius (Cic. *Div.* 2. 62; Vell. Pat. 2. 6. 6, Val. Max. 4. 7. 2).
L. A. H.-S.

Pomponius (*RE* 103, Supp. 14) **Secundus, Publius [?Calv]isius Sabinus** (Quint. *Inst.* 8. 3. 31; 10. 1. 98), was *suffect consul AD 44 after governing *Crete and *Cyrene. Endangered by prosecution in 31, he survived (Tac. *Ann.* 5. 8). He was uterine brother of Caesonia, *Gaius (1)'s wife. His brother Quintus (suffect consul AD 41), who favoured the restoration of the republic after Gaius' death, perished as an accomplice of L. *Arruntius Camillus Scribonianus in 42. *Pliny (1) the Elder, who saw the handwriting of the *Gracchi in his possession (*NH* 13. 83), wrote his biography (Pliny, *Ep.* 3. 5), calling him 'consular poet' and 'bard and most distinguished citizen' (*HN* 7. 80; 13. 83). He wrote *Aeneas*, a *praetexta* (see FABULA). In 47 his verses on the stage drew insults from the crowd (Tac. *Ann.* 11. 13). Legate (see LEGATI) of Upper Germany (see GERMANIA), he checked the *Chatti in 50, winning triumphal ornaments (see ORNAMENTA)—to be rated less highly than his literary achievement (ibid. 12. 28; cf. 5. 8 for his refinement). He is not attested after 51.

Cichorius, *Röm. Stud.* 423 ff.; W. Otto, *Philol.* 1935, 483 ff.; Schanz–Hosius 2⁴. 475; W. Eck, *Die Statthalter d. germ. Prov.* (1985), 19 ff.
J. W. D.; B. M. L.

Pomptine Marshes, a malaria-stricken region (see DISEASE), formed by the stagnation of the Ufens and other streams, lying south-east of Rome between Volscian mountains and Tyrrhenian Sea. *Pliny (1)'s statement that twenty-four cities once flourished here (*HN* 3. 59) is an exaggeration: Suessa Pometia, like the lands later assigned to citizens of the Pomptina and Oufentina tribes (see TRIBUS), lay outside the marshes proper (Livy 6. 21; 7. 15; 9. 20). The *via Appia crossed the marshes, but travellers apparently preferred to use the parallel, 30 km. (19-mile-long) ship-canal, since the marshes included highwaymen among other perils (Strabo 5. 233; Hor. *Sat.* 1. 5. 10 f.; Juv. 3. 307). From 160 BC or earlier numerous attempts were made by M. Cornelius Cethegus, *Trajan, and others to drain them—a task successfully accomplished in the 20th cent. Traces of *centuriation are known.

M. Cancellieri, in *La Via Appia* (1990), 61 ff. (= *Arch. Laz.* 10); A. Voorips, S. H. Loving, and H. Kamermans, *The Agro Pontino Project* (1991).
E. T. S.; T. W. P.

pons Mulvius carried the *via Flaminia across the *Tiber north of Rome; it is first mentioned in 207 BC. The existing bridge, the modern *Ponte Milvio*, was first built by M. *Aemilius Scaurus (1) in 109 BC and there has been much later rebuilding. Of the four main 18-m. (60 ft.) arches, only the southern pair are ancient. Above the pointed cutwaters, both up- and downstream, there

are arched flood-passages. The road makes a sloping approach on either side. The Allobroges were trapped here during the Catilinarian conspiracy in 63 BC (see SERGIUS CATILINA, L.) and here *Maxentius was defeated by *Constantine I in AD 312. See BRIDGES.

M. H. Ballance, *PBSR* 1951, 79 ff.; Nash, *Pict. Dict. Rome* 2. 191–2.
I. A. R.; D. E. S.; J. R. P.

Pontecagnano important archaic settlement (perhaps the ancient Picentia) in south *Campania overlooking the Gulf of Salerno. Its extensive cemeteries show close connections with the cultures of the *Etruscans of north Campania and central Italy, and with the Latin communities (see LATIUM), and important contacts with the wider Mediterranean world of the 8th cent. BC. The *colonia* of *Salernum (197 BC) was its eventual successor.

B. D'Agostino and P. Gastaldi, *Pontecagnano* (1988), 38–42, 112–15.
N. P.

pontifex/pontifices, one of the four major colleges of the Roman priesthood. The college of *pontifices* was a more complicated structure than the other three, containing as full members the **rex sacrorum* (the republican priest who took over the king's religious functions) and the three major **flamines* as well as the *pontifices* proper; the Vestals (see VESTA) and the minor *flamines* together with the pontifical scribe were also part of and under the authority of the college. The *pontifices* themselves were originally three in number, all *patricians; new members were co-opted by the old ones. In an archaic priestly order preserved by Festus (299 L), the *rex* and the *flamines* take precedence over the *pontifex*, but this may reflect the situation of the regal period, not that of the early republic.

The college's duties were wide-ranging: they had general oversight of the state cult—sacrifices (see SACRIFICE, ROMAN), games (see LUDI), festivals and other rituals; they advised magistrates and private individuals on the sacred law and kept books which recorded their rules and decisions; they had special areas of concern in relation to families and clans (*gentes*; see GENS)—the control of adoptions, burial law, the inheritance of religious duties (*sacra familiaria*); some argue that their legal role originally extended far more widely into the civil law. They had no authority over priests outside the college; and their relationship with the state remained an advisory one—their rulings (*decreta*, *responsa*) had to be put into effect by magistrates or by the assemblies.

The *pontifices'* position evolved gradually during the republic: the *lex Ogulnia* of 300 BC abolished the monopoly of the patricians and added extra places for the plebeians. From then till the end of the republic the college, together with the augurs (see AUGURES), had as its members the dominant figures in the ruling élite, including C. *Iulius Caesar (1), M. *Aemilius Lepidus (3) the triumvir, and *Augustus himself.

The leading member of the college—the *pontifex maximus*—who had originally been selected by the college, was from the mid-3rd cent. BC onwards elected by a special procedure (only seventeen of the thirty-five tribes voted), which was later extended to the rest of the college—and the other colleges—by the *lex Domitia* of 104 BC. He acted as spokesman for the college, particularly in the senate; but could be overruled by his colleagues. Perhaps as a result of the selection by popular vote, the *pontifex maximus* came to be seen as the most prominent and influential of the priests; but it was not until Augustus united the position with other priesthoods and with the power of the *princeps*, that the *pontifex maximus* came to resemble a 'High

Priest'. From then on the position was always held by the reigning emperor until *Gratian refused to accept it.

Wissowa, *RK*² (1912), 501–23; J. A. North in *CAH* 7²/2 (1989), 585–7; M. Beard in Beard and North (eds.), *Pagan Priests* (1990), 34–48; A. Watson, *The State, Law and Religion* (1992). J. A. N.

Pontius (*RE* 4), **Gavius** was the Samnite general (see SAMNIUM) who engineered the entrapment of the Roman army at the *Caudine Forks in 321 BC (so already Q. *Claudius Quadrigarius fr. 19; 21P.). *Pontius Telesinus (hence from Telesia, probably in the territory of the Caudini) reputedly claimed descent from him; if so, he perhaps preserved (or invented) his ancestor's role. In Roman sources Pontius is credited with a father of great wisdom (cf. especially Cic. *Sen.* 39 ff. with Powell *ad loc.*), Roman honour was avenged when he himself was sent under the yoke in 320, and his capture and execution by Q. Fabius Maximus Gurges in 292 marked the effective end of Samnite resistance. None of this is historical.

E. T. Salmon, *Samnium and the Samnites* (1967). A. D.

Pontius (*RE* 17) **Aquila,** of undistinguished family, probably from *Sutrium, tribune 45 BC, annoyed *Caesar by not standing up as he passed in triumph after Munda. He was one of Caesar's murderers, and in 43 served under D. *Iunius Brutus Albinus in the war of Mutina. After defeating T. *Munatius Plancus Bursa he was killed in the battle of 21 April, and shared the honour of a public funeral with A. *Hirtius and C. *Vibius Pansa Caetronianus. T. J. C.; E. B.

Pontius Pilatus, prefect of *Judaea AD 26–36 (see PRAEFECTUS). A famous inscription (EJ 369) from *Caesarea (2) attests to the name of his post. Offences against religious sentiment, perhaps not deliberate, created several serious disturbances which Pilatus handled badly. He yielded to determined protests against image-bearing standards being brought into *Jerusalem by troops. Shields set up in the palace, treated also as iconic, were removed at *Tiberius' behest. Control of a crowd objecting to the use of Temple funds for the building of an aqueduct was achieved with heavy violence. A military attack on Samaritans gathering at Mt. Gerizim finally led to accusations before L. *Vitellius, legate (see LEGATI) of *Syria, and then to Pilatus' recall. A reliable account of his conduct of the trial of Jesus, mentioned also in *Josephus' *testimonium*, cannot be extracted from the conflicting Gospel accounts. John's portrayal of him giving judgement from a tribunal in front of his *praetorium* is plausible. Later Christian tradition and an apocryphal literature proliferated around him and his wife.

Josephus, *AJ* 18. 55–89; *BJ* 2. 169–77; Philo, *Legatio*, 299–306; Matthew 27; Mark 15; Luke 23; John 18: 28, 19. J.-P. Lémonon, *Pilate et le gouvernement de la Judée: Textes et monuments* (1981); Schürer, *History* 1. 383–7. T. R.

Pontius (*RE* 21) **Telesinus,** descendant of Gavius *Pontius, Samnite 'praetor' (see SAMNIUM) in the *Social War (3), though not mentioned in any action in it. In 82 BC, after failing to relieve C. *Marius (2) at *Praeneste, he marched on Rome and, after a fierce and fluctuating battle, was defeated by *Sulla outside the Colline gate. He and many of his soldiers died in the battle, the survivors were massacred after surrendering.

A. Keaveney, *Sulla* (1982), 142 ff., 146 n. 28. E. B.

Pontus (Πόντος), the sea mythologically personified; he is son of Earth, *Gaia (Hes. *Theog.* 131–2); father of *Nereus, Ceto, and

Eurybia (233 ff.); husband of Mare, i.e. Thalassa, the sea under yet other names (Hyg. *Fab., praef. 5*). S. H.

Pontus was the region of northern *Asia Minor including the south coast of the Black (*Euxine) Sea between *Paphlagonia and *Colchis and extending southward to *Cappadocia. It is dominated by a series of mountain ranges, separated by deep valleys, which run parallel to the coast and dictate the lines of overland communication. The valleys of the rivers *Halys, Iris, and Lycus, lead to fertile coastal deltas, and the basins of the last two belonged to the territories of the cities of the Pontic heartland—*Amaseia, *Zela, and Comana. The best traverse route from coast to interior ran from *Amisus to Sebasteia. Pontus is well watered and fertile, with a mild, damp climate on the coast and in the valleys. Olives and other fruits, nuts, pasture, and grain were in abundant supply near the coast; the coastal ranges supplied timber, especially for ship-building, and the mountains were rich in iron (see CHALYBES), copper, silver, salt, and alum.

The social and political structure resembled that of Cappadocia, with villages organized into territorial units, large temple territories (notably at Comana and Zela) with numerous sacred slaves ruled by priests, and a quasi-feudal nobility which had strong Iranian connections. The mountainous regions of the east above *Trapezus remained the home of uncivilized barbarian tribes—the Sanni refused to pay their taxes to Rome (due in the form of bees' wax!) as late as the time of *Hadrian. The Greek colonies on the coast were essentially trading stations, with no hinterland territory before the Roman period.

The centre and strength of the Pontic kingdom was based on the valleys of the Lycus and Iris, especially the royal centre of Amaseia, but the kings continually added to their territory until it reached its greatest extent under Mithradates VI Eupator (see MITHRADATES I–VI; PHARNACES I), who used it as the basis of his challenge to Roman power in Asia Minor. The kings apparently brought the priests and nobility under control and established an overall administration, but did little to develop the cities. In 63 BC *Pompey gave parts of Pontus to dynasts (Trapezus and Pharnaceia in the east to *Deiotarus, Comana to its priest-rulers), but organized the rest into a province consisting of eleven cities with large co-terminous territories: Amastris, *Sinope, Amisus, Neapolis, Pompeiopolis, Magnopolis, Amaseia, Cabeira-Diospolis, Zela, Megalopolis, and *Nicopolis (1). Most of these reverted to native rulers under Antony (M. *Antonius (2)) but they were gradually brought back, sometimes with new names, into the Roman provincial regime in the early empire to form the north-eastern districts of *Galatia known as Pontus Galaticus (mostly 3/2 BC, *metropolis (sense (b)) Amaseia) and Pontus Polemoniacus (AD 64, metropolis Neocaesareia). Both districts were hived off to become part of Cappadocia by *Trajan. A separate Pontic province emerged in the third century. To the end Pontus kept much of its native character; the cities remained regional and artificial, the feudal aristocracy important, and the native people were only lightly touched by Hellenic civilization.

T. Reinach, *Mithridates Eupator* (1895); J. G. C. Anderson, F. Cumont, and H. Grégoire, *Studia Pontica*, 1–3 (1903–10): Jones, *Cities E. Rom. Prov.* 148 ff. T. R. S. B.; S. M.

Popillius Laenas, Gaius, praetor 175 BC, consul 172 and 158. In his first consulship he was instrumental in sabotaging the attempts of the senate to deal with his brother Marcus (consul 173) after exception was taken to the latter's enslavement of *Ligurians. After serving in Greece under A. Hostilius Mancinus (consul 170) in both military and diplomatic capacities (170–169), he led an embassy which compelled *Antiochus (4) IV to withdraw his army from Egypt (168): Popillius drew a circle in the sand around the king and demanded that he signal obedience or disobedience to Rome's behest before stepping outside it.

RE 22. 1, 'Popillius (18)'; Broughton, MRR (with Suppl. p. 168); L. Moretti, *Iscrizioni Storiche Ellenistiche*, 42. P. S. D.

Popillius (RE 28) **Laenas, Publius,** son of the preceding, as consul 132 BC severely punished supporters of Ti. *Sempronius Gracchus (3) and was forced into exile by a law of C. *Sempronius Gracchus (123). After the vindication of L. *Opimius, a law of the tribune L. *Calpurnius Bestia allowed him to return. As consul he built the *via Popillia in north-east Italy. If the inscription ILLRP 454 was set up by him (the name is lost), he was praetor in Sicily, built a road from *Rhegium to *Capua with a Forum Popillii (see VIA POPILLIA), and as consul furthered agrarian reform as an *optimate response to Ti. Gracchus. But there are good reasons for ascribing that text to T. Annius Rufus (consul 128) (see VIA ANNIA (2)).

T. P. Wiseman, *Roman Studies* (1987), 108 ff., 122 ff. E. B.

Poplifugia An obscure Roman festival on 5 July. Its name resembles that of the equally puzzling *Regifugium. The ancients explained it as the flight of the people at the death of *Romulus (Dion. Hal. *Ant. Rom.* 2. 56. 5, Plut. *Vit. Rom.* 29) or the ritual routs of Latin armies celebrated by offerings to Vitula on July 8 (Macrob. *Sat.* 3. 2. 11 ff.). Wissowa (RK 116) implausibly linked it to Jupiter, while Latte (RR 128) conjectured that it and the Regifugium involved some ritual to evoke terrible powers whose presence must be avoided.

R. E. A. Palmer, *Roman Religion and Roman Empire* (1974), 10 ff. C. R. P.

Poppaea (RE 4) **Sabina,** daughter of T. Ollius (d. AD 31), and named after her maternal grandfather C. Poppaeus Sabinus (consul AD 9, governor of Moesia 12–35), was married first to Rufrius Crispinus, prefect of the praetorians under Claudius, by whom she had a son later killed by *Nero. By 58, during her second marriage, to the future emperor *Otho, she became mistress of Nero (so Tac. *Ann.* 13. 45 f.; another version in *Hist.* 1. 13). It was allegedly at her instigation that Nero murdered *Iulia Agrippina in 59 and in 62 divorced, banished, and executed *Claudia Octavia. Nero now married Poppaea, who bore a daughter Claudia in 63; both mother and child received the surname Augusta but the child died at four months. Through Poppaea's influence, her native *Pompeii became a colony (see also OPLONTIS). *Josephus, who secured a favour from her in Rome, apparently attests to her Jewish sympathies (though the word θεοσεβής is problematic), but she actually did the Jews a disservice in securing her friend's husband, *Gessius Florus, the procuratorship (see PROCURATOR) of *Judaea in 64 (*Vita* 16; *Ant. Jud.* 2. 195). In 65, pregnant again, she is supposed to have died from a kick which Nero gave her in a fit of temper, and was accorded a public funeral and divine honours.

T. J. C.; M. T. G.

Poppaedius (RE 'Poppaedius') **Silo, Quintus,** noble Marsian (see MARSI), friend of M. *Livius Drusus (2), in the *Social War (3) commander of the northern group of rebels. After vainly trying to negotiate with C. *Marius (1) (Diod. 37. 15), he defeated and killed Q. *Servilius Caepio (2) (90 BC) and the consul L. Porcius Cato (89). Defeated by the army of Cn. *Pompeius Strabo

and forced to abandon the Italian capital *Corfinium, he withdrew southwards and recovered *Bovianum Vetus, where he built up a large army (89). In 88 he was defeated and killed by Q. *Caecilius Metellus Pius or one of his legates.

A. Keaveney, *Rome and the Unification of Italy* (1987), see index. His coins: Sydenham, CRR 634, cf. 619. E. B.

populares See OPTIMATES.

population, Greek The demography of Greece is a very difficult subject to investigate because of the shortage of statistical data. The Greeks did not have the modern concept of 'population' as a breeding group. Ancient authors did not write any books about demography and give hardly any figures for population sizes. Owing to the stress on war in historiography most estimates relate to the size of military forces or to the manpower available for military purposes, i.e. adult males only. Extrapolations must be attempted from such information to total population sizes because women, children, and slaves were usually not enumerated at all. The Greeks had a very poor grasp of numbers and were prone to exaggeration, for example in relation to the size of Persian armies. *Thucydides (2) was a notable exception to this rule. Even in Classical Athens it seems unlikely that there was a central register of *hoplites, in addition to the deme registers. Greek states did not have taxes payable by all inhabitants that would have required the maintenance of records for financial purposes. Censuses of citizens were rare in the ancient Greek world.

Estimates of ancient population sizes inevitably involve a lot of guesswork. It is often necessary to use estimates of carrying capacity based on land areas, soil fertility, etc. The assumptions underlying such estimates are usually controversial. Intensive archaeological field surveys are yielding information about changes in settlement patterns in ancient Greece, which are probably connected with population fluctuations. The general pattern is of a thinly populated landscape in the 11th–10th cents. BC, followed by substantial population growth in most areas from the 9th cent. BC, suggesting that *colonization from the eighth century BC onwards was at least partly a product of population growth. A peak was reached in the fifth to the third centuries BC. The period of colonization after *Alexander (3) 'the Great' (see COLONIZATION, HELLENISTIC) was at least partly a consequence of population increase. There was a substantial decline in the last two centuries BC, which continued into the early Roman empire. There were many local variations on this broad pattern in all periods. However it is very striking that the inference drawn from the field surveys, namely that Greece was more densely populated in the classical period than at any time before or since until the late 19th cent. AD, correlates with the fact that even the lowest estimates of the size of the population of Classical Greece made by modern scholars, on the basis of the fragmentary literary sources, are substantially higher than figures derived from census data for parts of late medieval and early modern Greece. The total population in the 4th cent. BC may have been about two million people.

Demography is not just a matter of population size. It is also concerned with the age-structure of populations, which is determined principally by fertility rates and also by mortality rates. Fertility and mortality rates are determined by many factors, especially average age of marriage for fertility, and disease patterns for mortality. There is as little information for vital rates in ancient Greece as for population size.

1221

population, Greek

Excavations of *cemeteries suggest a high level of infant and early child mortality in Classical Greece (c.30 per cent at *Olynthus). Physical anthropologists attempt to determine the age of death of ancient skeletons. However their methods suffer from various sources of uncertainty, especially in relation to the age of death of adults. Individuals who survived infancy and early childhood (i.e. survived weaning) may have had a reasonable chance of reaching old age. Moreover conclusions drawn from cemeteries about populations, rather than individuals, are often controversial because it is not certain whether the individuals buried there were a representative sample of the whole population. Scholars are suspicious of ages given in literary sources because there were no birth or death certificates. The Greeks in the Classical period seldom recorded ages or causes of death on tombstones.

There is even less evidence for fertility rates than for mortality rates. However, fertility levels were almost certainly much higher than in modern advanced countries. In the context of high infant mortality (see CHILDBIRTH) parents needed several children to ensure that some reached adulthood, to provide an heir to the estate, support for the parents in old age, and additional farm labour. These considerations are also important motives for high fertility in developing countries today. Each adult woman would have had to give birth four or five times to reproduce the population. There is very little evidence for average age of marriage, particularly for women, which is the most important factor influencing fertility levels. There were no marriage certificates. A few passages in literary sources suggest a pattern of late marriage for men (around the age of 30) and early marriage for women (mid- to late-teens). Early marriage for women made very high fertility rates possible. Consequently family limitation measures such as *infanticide or *abortion may have been practised in some social classes, regions, or periods. Marriage patterns are themselves influenced by the nature of the economic system, social structure, and even conceivably by political organization.

Apart from calculations based on land areas, and scattered references to army strengths, the main body of information comes from *Athens, especially for the 4th cent. BC. Such promising contemporary epigraphic sources as lists of *ephēboi (two age-classes of young men undergoing military training), bouleutai (councillors, see BOULĒ) and diaitētai (an age-class of elderly men serving as arbitrators, see ARBITRATION, GREEK) are usually fragmentary. It is unclear whether these groups were recruited from the entire adult male citizen body or only from the hoplite and upper classes (see PENTAKOSIOMEDIMNOI; HIPPEIS; ZEUGITAI). At Athens every boy at 18 was registered in his father's deme. The total of deme registers formed the list of those entitled to attend the assembly, and the basis of lists of zeugitai liable to hoplite service and *thētes liable to service in the Athenian navy. Unfortunately *deme registers were not inscribed on stone. Other methods for calculating population size are hardly any more promising: *cereal production (the one extant figure may well refer to a year of drought); cereal imports (one estimate made in a year of drought, which may in any case total the imports for several years). Boys and girls were enrolled in their *phratries; but there were no other records of citizen women. *Metics were required to pay a tax and were registered in their deme of residence. The biggest source of uncertainty is the number of slaves (see SLAVERY).

For Classical Athens only one census is recorded, namely that carried out by *Demetrius (3) of Phaleron in the late 4th cent. BC. According to information preserved by *Athenaeus (1) (6.

272c) this census enumerated 21,000 citizens, 10,000 metics and 400,000 slaves. The number of citizens seems plausible, but it is uncertain whether it includes all citizens or merely those liable and fit for hoplite service. The number of metics is the only preserved figure for this status-group, whose numbers probably varied in accordance with the prosperity of Athens. The number of slaves is incredible, as are similar figures for slaves in *Corinth and *Aegina. Attempts have been made to emend the text, but it is more likely that these figures for slaves were simply invented. Nevertheless there were probably considerably more slaves in the 5th cent. BC, at the time of the Athenian empire (see DELIAN LEAGUE), than there had been earlier. *Herodotus (1) (5. 97. 2) suggests that there were about 30,000 Athenian citizens in the early 5th cent. BC. This stock figure for the number of citizens was frequently repeated: the citizen body probably did not significantly exceed it during the 4th cent. BC. Multiplication by four to account for women and children indicates a total (citizen) population of around 120,000 then. There is no evidence that the sex-ratio diverged significantly from parity. Evidence for the size of Athenian military forces during the 5th-cent. empire suggests that by c.450 BC there were at least 50,000, or possibly even 60,000, citizens, revealing a substantial increase since the early 5th cent. BC. This level was maintained until the beginning of the *Peloponnesian War. According to Thucydides (2. 14) most Athenians still lived in the countryside then, rather than in Athens. During the war the citizen population gradually declined, first because of the great '*plague', and second because of heavy casualties in battle, especially during the Syracusan expedition (415–413).

*Sparta suffered from a serious problem of manpower shortage, which *Aristotle (Politics 1270ᵃ29–34) identified as the reason for her downfall. Herodotus (7. 234. 2; 9. 10. 1) states that Sparta had 8,000 potential soldiers in 480 BC, and 5,000 actually took part in the battle of Plataea (see PLATAEA, BATTLE OF) in 479 BC. By *Aristotle's time Sparta probably had fewer than 1,000 citizens. There is much debate about the causes of this decline. Such diverse factors as the structure of Spartan society, casualties in war, inheritance patterns, and the *earthquake of c.464 BC have been invoked to explain it. In any case, it is clear that the Spartan citizen body was only a small fraction of the total population of *Laconia and, before 371 BC, *Messenia. Field-survey data suggest that these parts of the *Peloponnesus were as densely populated in the 4th cent. BC as the rest of Greece.

There is even less evidence for other parts of Greece. Judging by evidence for military strengths, *Argos (2) and *Boeotia had citizen bodies not dissimilar in size to that of Athens in the 4th cent. BC, but probably had fewer resident aliens and slaves. Corinth's population was at most half the size of the Athenian population. The mountainous country of *Arcadia produced many emigrants. However, migration occurred on a substantial scale from most regions of Greece from the Dark Age until well into the Hellenistic period, resulting in the foundation of many colonies abroad. The Greek colonies in *Sicily and Italy were particularly prosperous. The population of *Syracuse may have exceeded in size all the states of mainland Greece, including Athens. Several other colonies in these areas, such as *Acragas and *Tarentum, probably also surpassed virtually all states in mainland Greece in respect of population size, although there is little detailed information available.

J. R. Sallares, The Ecology of the Ancient Greek World (1991); K. J. Beloch, Die Bevölkerung der griechisch-römischen Welt (1886); T. J. Figueira, TAPA 1986, 165–213; L. Gallo, Alimentazione e demografia della Grecia antica (1984); A. W. Gomme, The Population of Athens in the Fifth and Fourth

Centuries (1933); M. H. Hansen, Demography and Democracy (1985), and Three Studies in Athenian Demography (1988).   J. R. S.

population, Roman There are two different kinds of questions which historians might wish to ask about the population of the Roman world: how large was it or any of its constituent parts? and what were the patterns and tendencies of such things as birth rates and death rates? Four kinds of information are available to offer imperfect answers to the first question: *census figures, mostly but not exclusively, for the Roman republic and early empire, where they served for the levy and, originally, taxation; figures relating to the feeding of (part of) the population of the city of Rome; occasional references to the population of particular cities or areas, usually without any possibility of knowing on what they were based; and figures for the carrying capacity of different areas of the Roman world in the earliest periods for which reasonably reliable figures exist. The first to collect such material systematically was K. J. Beloch and it is with him that serious study of the population of the Roman world begins. Almost no information is available for the second question; and one has to try to find the best fit of such scraps as there are with the model life tables compiled in the modern period for a variety of populations at different stages of economic development.

As far as the Roman census figures are concerned, they purport to give the adult male population from the early republic to the early empire. Leaving aside the problem of the reliability of the early figures, some scholars have argued that they give for the republic only the adult male population above the property qualification for military service, excluding *proletarii. If the figures really were only of those eligible, however, it would be hard to see why the Romans ever had problems of recruitment to the legions. On the other hand, it has also been argued that the rise in the total under Augustus is so large that it can only be explained on the assumption that the figures now included women and children, probably over the age of one:

70/69 BC	910,000
28 BC	4,063,000

This view is principally associated with the name of P. A. Brunt. It is by no means universally accepted; and the alternative view argues that the difference is to be explained by the enfranchisement of Transpadane Gaul (see TRANSPADANA) in 49 BC and by the greater efficiency of registration. In any case, the figure of 4,063,000 will have included large numbers of Romans living overseas and comparisons with guesses as to the total (male) population of Italy in any earlier period are hazardous. Similarly, we cannot know how far rises in numbers after *Augustus are due to manumissions of slaves (see SLAVERY) and enfranchisements of provincials (see CITIZENSHIP, ROMAN).

There will always have been some under-registration in the census, probably substantial after *tributum ceased to be collected after 167 BC. The rise in numbers between 131 and 125 BC is probably to be related to the Lex agraria of Ti. *Sempronius Gracchus (3); but it is not clear whether it is due to recipients of plots of land bothering to register for the first time or to men registering in order to prove their eligibility. The relatively low rise in 86 BC, after the enfranchisement of peninsular Italy in 90 is probably to be explained by the difficulty of conditions in the aftermath of the *Social War (3).

All arguments about trends are made difficult by uncertainty over the scale of losses due to war casualties and the removal of Roman citizens to Latin colonies (see COLONIZATION, ROMAN),

and of additions to citizen numbers through the manumission of slaves and the incorporation of new citizens from other communities.

The conventional view of Rome is that in the imperial period it had a total population of about 1 million; but it seems not to have been widely noticed that a fragment of *Livy, quoted in a scholium on Lucan 1. 319 (see SCHOLIA; ANNAEUS LUCANUS, M.), implies that this figure had already been reached when *Pompey was curator annonae in 57 BC.

Figures exist for a number of other cities, plausibly attesting that *Alexandria (1), *Carthage, *Antioch (1), *Pergamum, *Ephesus, *Apamea in Syria, and Lyon (*Lugdunum (1)) had free populations in the range 300,000 to 100,000, probably including the free inhabitants of their chora or territory. The numbers of slaves to be added to these figures are obviously uncertain, though *Galen implies that there were as many slaves in Pergamum as free male inhabitants. (Attempts to estimate size of cities from carrying capacity of *aqueducts are hopelessly flawed: many cities never had aqueducts at all and relied on cisterns; aqueducts therefore form an unknowable part of the total water supply.)

For the total population of the Roman empire, Beloch estimated about 54 million at the death of Augustus; it is a plausible guess and compatible with the figure of 7.5 million reported for Egypt, excluding Alexandria (1). The total may have risen slightly thereafter, declining with the series of *plagues which begin in the 160s AD and culminate in that under *Justinian.

When we turn to patterns and tendencies in the population as a whole, the best guess is that the population of the Roman world was relatively stable, both in size and in structure, with a high birth-rate and a high death-rate, particularly in infancy. Some confirmation for the use of model life tables as parallels comes from the small number of declarations of death which survive from Egypt, and a few other documents. It should by now be clear that ages of death recorded on tombstones are wholly worthless as demographic evidence; the surviving evidence is hopelessly skewed by underlying differences in who was commemorated and who was not.

The existence of the *ius (trium) liberorum obviously indicates that three surviving children was regarded as an attainable goal. There is very limited evidence for the sex-ratio at birth or for the scale of infanticide, let alone specifically female infanticide.

K. J. Beloch, Die Bevölkerung der griechisch-römischen Welt (1886); R. T. Duncan-Jones, Hist. 1964, 199–208; P. A. Brunt, Italian Manpower (2nd edn. 1987); C. Nicolet, in Epigrafia (1991), 119–31 'Les recensements augustéens'; T. G. Parkin, Demography and Roman Society (1992); R. S. Bagnall and B. W. Frier, The Demography of Roman Egypt (1994).   M. H. C.

Populonia (Etr. Pupluna), in Italy, on the promontory overlooking Porto Baratti, was the port of the metal-rich zone of northwest Tuscany (see ETRUSCANS), and the smelting centre for the iron of Elba. There is evidence of early contact with nuraghic *Sardinia; and Populonia was the only Etruscan city established directly on the sea. Limited remains of sacred and habitation areas (c.600 BC onwards) below the acropolis are supplemented by the impressive walls, the metal-working facilities in the 'industrial quarter', and extensive cemeteries ranging in date from the *Villanovan to the Hellenistic period.

Atti XII Convegno Studi Etruschi 1979 (1981); F. Fedeli, Populonia: storia e territorio (1983); L'Etruria mineraria (exhibition catalogue, 1985); A. Romualdi (ed.), Populonia in età ellenistica: Atti del Seminario 1986 (1992).   D. W. R. R.

populus, a collective term for the Roman citizen body. The Roman People (*populus Romanus*) comprised the entire community of adult male citizens, but excluded women and children, as well as slaves and foreigners. At first it may have signified the people in arms, since the original title of the *dictator* was *magister populi* (and cf. the word *populari*, 'to lay waste'). This merely confirms that military service was one of the earliest functions of citizenship. It is probably not legitimate to infer from the formula *populus plebsque* (e.g. Cic. *Pro Mur.* 1. 1) that plebeians were excluded from the citizen body (or from the army; see PLEBS). In the later republic and during the early centuries of the empire *populus Romanus* was the technical designation of the Roman state, which indicates that the Romans had no abstract concept of 'the State' as an impersonal entity independent of the individuals who composed it. By means of its formal procedures in the *comitia*, the *populus Romanus* elected magistrates, passed laws, declared war and ratified treaties; and it was the *populus Romanus* that had dealings with the gods in public religious ceremonies. The *res publica* was the affair (or property) of the people, as *Cicero observed (*Rep.* 1. 39), noting the formal equivalence 'res publica res populi'.

Mommsen, *Röm. Forsch.* 1. 168 ff.; *Röm. Staatsr.* 3. 3 ff.; Brunt, *Fall of the Roman Republic* (1988), 2, 299, 326. T. J. Co.

Porcia (*RE* 28) was daughter of M. *Porcius Cato (2) and wife first of M. *Calpurnius Bibulus and from 45 BC of *Brutus. She shared the political ideals of her father and her husbands, insisted on being let into the secret of the plot to murder *Caesar, and took part with her mother-in-law *Servilia in the conference of republicans at Antium on 8 June 44. When Brutus sailed for the east she returned to Rome, where she became ill and in the early summer of 43 took her life, perhaps by inhaling fumes from a brazier (Plut. *Brut.* 53, Cic. *Ad Brut.* 1. 9. 2, 17. 7). The less good tradition makes her do this on the news of Brutus' death in 42.

T. J. C.

Porcius (*RE* 5) **Cato** (1), **Gaius**, grandson of M. *Porcius Cato (1) and of L. *Aemilius Paullus (2), was a friend of Ti. *Sempronius Gracchus (3), but seems to have turned against him (see the context in Cic. *Lael.* 39). Probably praetor in Sicily (Cic. *2 Verr.* 4. 22), he was consul 114 BC, was disastrously defeated by the *Scordisci and convicted *repetundarum* (see REPETUNDAE), but made to pay only 8,000 sesterces (ibid.). He was condemned by *Gracchani iudices* under the law of C. *Mamilius Limetanus and went into exile, becoming a citizen of *Tarraco. E. B.

Porcius (*RE* 6) **Cato** (2), **Gaius**, towards the end of 59 BC called *Pompey 'privatus *dictator' ('unofficial dictator') when prevented from prosecuting A. *Gabinius (2) (Cic. *Off.* 1. 2. 15). As tribune 56 he attacked Pompey again over his desire for an Egyptian command and proposed a bill to abrogate the command of P. *Cornelius Lentulus Spinther; he procured a 'Sibylline oracle' (see SIBYL) that *Ptolemy (1) XII Auletes must not be restored by force. After the conference of *Luca he postponed the elections for 55 in the interests of Pompey and *Crassus. He was probably praetor 55 (see *MRR* 3. 169 f.). In 54 he was prosecuted, and though apparently acquitted is not heard of again. G. E. F. C.; R. J. S.; E. B.

Porcius (*RE* 9) **Cato** (1), **Marcus**, 'Cato the Censor' (234–149 BC) ('Censorius') was a dominant figure in both the political and the cultural life of Rome in the first half of the 2nd cent. BC. A *novus homo*, he was born at *Tusculum, but spent much of his childhood in the Sabine country (see SABINI), where his family owned land. He served in the Hannibalic War (see PUNIC WARS), winning particular praise for his contribution at the battle of the *Metaurus in 207. He embarked on a political career under the patronage of the patrician L. *Valerius Flaccus (1), who was his colleague in both consulship and censorship. As quaestor 204 he served under P. *Cornelius Scipio Africanus in Sicily and Africa; a constant champion of traditional Roman virtues, he looked with disfavour on Scipio's adoption of Greek customs and relaxed military discipline in Sicily, but the story that he came back to Rome to express his criticisms should be rejected. He is said to have returned from Africa via Sardinia, bringing thence the poet *Ennius to Rome. He was plebeian aedile 199 and praetor 198, when he may have carried the *lex Porcia* (see LEX (2)) which extended the right of *provocatio* to cases of scourging. He governed Sardinia, expelling usurers and restricting the demands made on the Sardinians for the upkeep of himself and his staff. He reached the consulship in 195: after unsuccessfully opposing the repeal of the *lex Oppia* (see OPPIUS (1)), he went to Spain, where, in a campaign which may have extended into 194, he suppressed a major rebellion, extended the area under Roman control, and arranged for the exploitation of the gold and silver mines; he returned to Rome to celebrate a triumph. In 191, as military tribune, he played an important part in the defeat of *Antiochus (3) III at Thermopylae, and was sent to Rome by M.' *Acilius Glabrio (1) to report the victory.

Cato was constantly engaged in court cases, both as prosecutor or prosecution witness and as defendant. He was an instigator of the attacks on the Scipios (Africanus and his brother L. *Cornelius Scipio Asiagenes), and two of his other targets, Q. Minucius Thermus and Glabrio, can be seen as allies of the Scipios. The attack on Glabrio was connected with the censorial elections of 189, when Cato and Flaccus stood unsuccessfully. See CENSOR. Five years later they were elected, having stood on a joint programme of reversing the decline of traditional morality. They were severe in their review of the rolls of the senate and the *equites*, removing L. *Quinctius Flamininus from the senate and depriving L. *Cornelius Scipio Asiagenes of his public horse. High levels of taxation were imposed on what the censors regarded as luxuries, and the public contracts were let on terms most advantageous for the state and least so for the contractors. They undertook extensive public works, including major repairs and extensions to the sewage system. The controversies caused by his censorship affected Cato for the rest of his life. But he courted conflict and spoke his mind to the point of rudeness. He rigidly applied to himself the standards he demanded of others and made a parade of his own parsimony: when in Spain he had made a point of sharing the rigours of his soldiers.

Though he held no further public offices Cato continued to play an active role in politics. He was probably an augur (*MRR* 3. 170). He opposed the modification of the *lex Baebia* of 181 (see BAEBIUS TAMPHILUS, M.) which had provided for the election of only four praetors in alternate years, and of the *lex Orchia* (see LEX (2)), a sumptuary law. Soon after 179 he attacked M. *Fulvius Nobilior, and in 171 was one of the patrons chosen by the peoples of Spain to present their complaints against Roman governors. A critical remark about *Eumenes II of Pergamum in 172 and speeches in 167 against declaring war on Rhodes and in favour of leaving Macedonia free are probably part of a general reluctance to see Rome too directly involved in eastern affairs. It was also in 167 that he opposed the attempt by Ser. *Sulpicius Galba (1) to block the *triumph of L. *Aemilius Paullus (2); Cato's son later married a daughter of Paullus, and it thus seems that the old enmity between Cato and the family of the Scipios was at an end. In the last years of his life, after serving on an embassy to *Carthage in 153, Cato convinced himself that the existence of Carthage constituted a serious danger to Rome; he ended each speech in the senate by saying that Carthage must be destroyed. Despite the opposition of P. *Cornelius Scipio Nasica Corculum war was eventually declared in 149. Shortly afterwards came the last speech of Cato's life, against Ser. Sulpicius Galba (1).

Cato has rightly been called the 'virtual founder of Latin prose literature'. Among works that were known to later generations—though not necessarily intended for publication by Cato himself—but of which we know little, are the *Ad filium* ('to his son'), perhaps no more than a brief collection of exhortations, a letter to his son, the *De re militari* ('on military matters'), a work dealing with civil law, the *Carmen de moribus*, probably a prose work on behaviour, and a collection of sayings.

Cato was the foremost orator of his age, and made many speeches. Over 150 were known to *Cicero, and we possess fragments of eighty. There can be little doubt that he intended his speeches to survive, though it is an open question whether he revised them for publication and conceived of himself as creating Latin oratory as a literary genre.

Previous Roman historians, starting with Q. *Fabius Pictor, had written in Greek; Cato's *Origines*, begun in 168 and still in progress at the time of his death, was the first historical work in Latin. It consisted of seven books. The first dealt with the foundation of Rome and the regal period; Cato had little or nothing to say about the early republic. The second and third covered the origins and customs of the towns of Italy (the title of the work is appropriate only for these three books). His approach was probably influenced by Greek κτίσις (foundation) literature and/or *Timaeus (2). The remaining books described Rome's wars from the First Punic war onwards. Cato is said to have written in a summary fashion, though some episodes were given detailed treatment, and he devoted more space to the events of the period during which he was writing; the last two books cover less than twenty years. He chose to omit the names of generals and included at least two of his own speeches (those on behalf of the Rhodians and against Ser. Sulpicius Galba).

The only work of Cato which survives intact is the *De agri cultura* ('on agriculture'). It is concerned not with agriculture as a whole, but principally with giving advice to the owner of a middle-sized estate, based on slave labour, in Latium or Campania, whose primary aim was the production of wine and olive oil for sale. It also includes recipes, religious formulae, prescriptions, and sample contracts. The work is disordered and some have wondered whether Cato himself is responsible for the shape of the text as we have it. See further separate article, below.

Cato sometimes expressed great hostility to all things Greek: in the *Ad filium* he called the Greeks a vile and unteachable race; in 155, worried by the effect their lectures were having on Roman youth, he was anxious that an embassy of Athenian philosophers should leave Rome rapidly. But he knew Greek well and had a good knowledge of Greek literature. His objections were to an excessive *philhellenism and he probably thought that contemporary Greeks were very different from the great figures of the past.

Cato was married twice, to Licinia and to Salonia (daughter of one of his clients), and had a son by each wife; the first died as praetor-designate in 152; the second, born when his father was 80, was the grandfather of Cato (Uticensis); see next article.

EDITIONS Jordan, *M. Catonis praeter librum de re rustica quae exstant* (180); speeches: *ORF*[4] 18–97; *Origines*: *HRR* 1[2]. 55–97 and ed. Chassignet (Budé, 1986); see below for the *Agr.*

OTHER WORKS A. Astin, *Cato the Censor* (1978); Briscoe, *Comm.* 34–37, see index.   J. Br.

Appendix: Cato (Censorius), De agricultura 'Cato first taught agriculture to speak Latin' (Columella *Rust.* 1. 1. 12). The work (c.160 BC) was both innovative and part of an established Greek genre. Indications of acquaintance with Greek technical literature are clear, while the largely shapeless structure of the treatise reflects the infancy of Roman prose writing. Later authors (Varro *Rust.* 1. 2. 12–28) defined and systematized *agriculture, discarding Cato's recipes and encomium of cabbage. Cato wrote for the young man who expected to make money and to enhance his public reputation by successful agriculture (3. 2). Thus the *villa should be sited near good access routes (1. 1. 3), and wine and oil stored until prices are high (3. 2). The treatise's essential subject is the slave-staffed villa in Latium or Campania practising mixed farming with an emphasis on vines and olives. The archaeological record documents a gradual spread of villa sites in these regions from the beginning of the 2nd cent. BC and a remarkable diffusion of Italian *wine-*amphorae in the western Mediterranean from the mid-2nd cent. BC.

TEXT W. Hooper and H. Ash (Loeb) (1967); R. Goujard (Budé) (1975); A. Mazzarino (Teubner) 2nd edn. (1982), G. Purnelle, *Cato de agricultura fragmenta omnia servata* (1988).

STUDIES E. Brehaut, *Cato the Censor on Farming* (1933); P. Thielscher, *Des Marcus Cato Belehrung über die Landschaft* (1963); S. Boscherini, *Lingua e scienza greca nel de agricultura di Catone* (1970); E. Rawson, *Intellectual Life in the Late Roman Republic* (1985); J.-P. Morel, *CAH* 8[2] (1989), 495 ff.   M. S. Sp.

Porcius (*RE* 20) **Cato** (2), **Marcus**, 'of Utica' ('Uticensis') (95–46 BC), great-grandson of Cato (Censorius) (see preceding entry), nephew of M. *Livius Drusus (2), and brought up in the Livian household with the children of his mother's marriage to Cn. Servilius Caepio. Quaestor probably in 64, in 63 he became tribune-designate in order to check Q. *Caecilius Metellus Nepos, supported L. *Licinius Murena's prosecution, and intervened powerfully in the senate to secure the execution of the Catilinarians (see SERGIUS CATILINA, L.). As tribune he conciliated the mob by increasing the numbers eligible to receive cheap corn, but in all else remained uncompromising; *Cicero (*Att.* 1. 18. 7; 2. 1. 8) deplores his lack of realism which prevented revision of the Asian tax-contracts (61)—thus alienating the *equites—and which frustrated every overture of *Pompey until the coalition between Pompey, *Caesar, and *Crassus was formed. In 59 he opposed Caesar obstinately and was temporarily imprisoned, but next year P. *Clodius Pulcher removed him by appointing him to undertake the annexation of *Cyprus. Though King Ptolemy of Cyprus (an illegitimate son of *Ptolemy (1) IX and brother of *Ptolemy (1) XII Auletes) killed himself and Cato's accounts were lost on the voyage home, his reputation for fairness remained unimpaired. After *Luca he persuaded his brother-in-law L. *Domitius Ahenobarbus (1) not to give up hope of being elected consul for 55, but Domitius' candidature collapsed because of physical intimidation by the supporters of Pompey and Crassus. P. *Vatinius defeated Cato for the praetorship by bribery, but Cato was eventually praetor in 54. In 52, abandoning his constitutional principles, he supported Pompey's election as sole consul; he himself stood for 51 but failed. In the war he tried to avoid citizen bloodshed but resolutely followed Pompey: he served in Sicily, but was expelled from there by C. *Scribonius Curio (2). Then he served in Asia, and held *Dyrrachium during the campaign of *Pharsalus. After Pompey's defeat, Cato joined the quarrelling Pompeians in Africa and reconciled them; he had Q. *Caecilius Metellus Pius Scipio made general. During the war he governed *Utica with great moderation, and was honoured by the city's inhabitants when after Thapsus in April 46 he committed suicide rather than accept pardon from Caesar, an act which earned him the undying glory of a martyr.

Cato's constitutionalism, a mixture of *Stoicism and old Roman principles, was genuine. After death he was more dangerous than ever to Caesar, who in his *Anticato, a reply to Cicero's pamphlet Cato, pitched the hostile case too high, and allowed the fame of Cato's life and death to give respectability to the losing side, and to inspire later political martyrs: 'the victors had their cause approved by the gods, the vanquished by Cato' (Lucan 1. 128).

SOURCES Plutarch's Cato Minor is laudatory but rich in anecdotes. See also the sources cited under C. *Iulius Caesar.

STUDIES On Cato's portrait see Acta Archaeologica 1947, 117 ff.; on Cyprus, E. Badian, JRS 1965, 110 ff.; R. Fehrle, Cato Uticensis (1983).
G. E. F. C.; M. T. G.

Porcius Festus, *procurator of *Judaea, AD ?60–62, was, like his predecessor Felix, harassed by sicarii terrorists and by a pseudo-prophet. He supported *Iulius Agrippa (2) II against the priests in a dispute over a palace extension. He carried on the trial of St *Paul, before sending him to Rome (Acts 25–6). He died in office.
T. R.

Porcius (RE 49) **Latro, Marcus,** Augustan rhetor, from Spain. His contemporary and close friend L. *Annaeus Seneca (1) vividly describes (Controv. 1 pr. 13–24) his obsessive nature and extraordinary memory. Though not at home in court (Quintilian 10. 5. 18), he was ranked among the four best declaimers of the period (Controv. 10 pr. 13). Among much quoted by Seneca is the extended extract forming Controv. 2. 7. Latro was admired and exploited by Ovid (Controv. 2. 2. 8) and criticized by M. *Valerius Messalla Corvinus (ibid. 2. 4. 8). He committed suicide, perhaps in AD 4.

Schanz–Hosius § 336. 3.
M. W.

Porcius (RE 48) **Licinus** (fl. probably at the end of the 2nd cent. BC) wrote a literary history of Rome in trochaic septenarii; notable are two lines which date the coming of the Muse to Latium in the Second *Punic War (probably a reference to *Naevius), and twelve on *Terence and his relations with the so-called *Scipionic Circle (the hostile tone suggests that Licinus was a Gracchan). An elegiac epigram clearly based on Hellenistic literary themes is a representative of the beginnings of the influence of *Hellenistic poetry at Rome.

See Courtney FLP 82.
C. J. F.; E. C.

pornography has been defined as material which presents people—particularly women—as mute, available, and subordinate sexual objects, often shown in a context of violence. In its most extreme form, pornography theory argues that all representation produced by men in patriarchal societies is, by very definition, pornographic. In antiquity the rare term pornographos is used in a far more limited sense, to mean a writer about, or a painter of, whores (see PROSTITUTION, SECULAR). It first appears in *Athenaeus (1) 13. 567b 3–8. The lost Hellenistic erotic handbooks, probably written by men despite being assigned to female authors (e.g. Philaenis) suggest that part of their purpose was to teach women to be whores, presenting themselves as objects for male pleasure. It has been argued that at least some forms of representation from the ancient world should be seen as pornographic in a modern sense. In particular, types of production sometimes read in this way include vase paintings, wall paintings, and oil lamps.

Attic red-figure ware includes scenes of abuse and degradation of women, including some sado-masochism, in which women are typically threatened with a sandal. Kilmer argues that scenes on pottery are deliberately left open-ended, so that the viewer can decide whether to see a figure as male or female, and can use his or her own preferences in deciding what form of sexual activity will happen next. It is possible to read homosexual images on Athenian vases as more 'romantic' in tone than the heterosexual images.

Erotic wall paintings from cities such as Pompeii were once used to define buildings as brothels, but it is now clear that erotic wall paintings as exemplars were found on the walls of private houses as well. Roman literary references to such images refer to small painted pictures (Ov. Tr. 2; Suet. Tib. 43) on the bedroom walls of the Julio-Claudian emperors. Mirror covers and oil lamps also show heterosexual couples in a range of poses.

A further category of ancient material used in a rather different way is *Suetonius' Lives of the Twelve Caesars. The erotic scenes here were illustrated in the 18th cent. and these images were then passed off as recently discovered ancient *cameos. Some scenes were subsequently used to illustrate privately printed sex manuals—an example of using the classical past as pornography. See HETEROSEXUALITY; HOMOSEXUALITY; PAINTING; SEXUALITY.

J. Boardman and E. La Rocca, Eros in Greece (1978); F. K. Forberg, Apophoreta (1824); P. F. Hugues d'Hancarville, Monumens de la vie privée des douze Césars (1786); C. Johns, Sex or Symbol (1982); M. F. Kilmer, Greek Erotica (1993); H. King in R. Porter and M. Teich (eds.), Sexual Knowledge, Sexual Science (1995); A. Richlin (ed.), Pornography and Representation in Greece and Rome (1992).
H. K.

Porphyrio See POMPONIUS PORPHYRIO.

Porphyry (AD 234–c.305), scholar, philosopher, and student of religions. He was born probably at Tyre; originally bore the Syrian name Malchus; studied under *Cassius Longinus at Athens; became a devoted disciple of *Plotinus with whom he studied in Rome (263–268 AD). His varied writings (sixty-nine titles can be listed with reasonable certainty) may be put into the following categories.

1. Commentaries and introductions to *Aristotle: only the influential Isagogē and the shorter commentary on the Categories survive. There are fragments of a larger commentary on the Categories and of commentaries on De interpretatione, Ethics, Physics, and Metaphysics.

2. Commentaries on *Plato (1): extensive fragments of a Timaeus commentary, evidence for commentaries (or at least treatment of select topics) on Cratylus, Parmenides, Phaedo, Philebus, Republic, and Sophist.

3. Our edition of Plotinus' Enneads arranged into sets of nine treatises; also a lost commentary on the Enneads.

4. Historical work includes scholarly research on chronology which may have formed a separate work (Chronica) or part of his Against the Christians and a history of philosophy down to Plato, from which the extant Life of Pythagoras (see PYTHAGORAS (1)) is an excerpt.

5. His metaphysical works are almost entirely lost but included treatises on the principles, matter, the incorporeal, the soul and

the surviving *Sententiae*, a succinct, but probably incomplete, introduction to Plotinian metaphysics which displays some divergences from Plotinus. An anonymous commentary on the *Parmenides*, even if not by Porphyry himself, suggests strongly that Porphyry is the ultimate source for some important developments in the concepts of being, existence, and transcendence with particular reference to the One and Nous. It can no longer be held that Porphyry made no original contribution to philosophy.

6. Although his publications on religion have been commonly interpreted as pointing to an intellectual development from credulous superstition to critical rejection, a fairer assessment of the evidence demonstrates a consistent interest in and respect for most traditions allied to a searching but constructive critique of the workings and significance of many pagan rituals. *On Abstinence* (a treatise on vegetarianism; see ANIMALS, ATTITUDES TO) and the *Letter to Marcella* show a traditional piety, *On Statues* a conventional interest in ritual symbolism, *Philosophy from Oracles* acceptance of ritual with some questioning, the *Letter to Anebo* a searching critique of ritual religion, and *De regressu animae* a limitation of the scope of *theurgy. Porphyry raised but did not solve the problem of the relationship of philosophy to religion. In *Against the Christians* he used historical criticism e.g. to establish the lateness of the Book of Daniel. Elsewhere he similarly proved the 'Book of Zoroaster' to be a forgery.

7. Philological works include *Homeric Enquiries*, a landmark in the history of Homeric scholarship (see HOMER); an allegorizing interpretation of the Cave of the Nymphs in the *Odyssey*; writings on grammar, rhetoric, and the history of scholarship.

8. Extant works on technical subjects are a commentary (incomplete) on *Ptolemy (4)'s *Harmonica*; an introduction to Ptolemy's *Tetrabiblos* and a treatise on the entry of the soul into the embryo (formerly attributed to *Galen but probably by Porphyry).

LIFE AND WORKS J. Bidez, *Vie de Porphyre* (1913); *RE* 22.1 (1953) 'Porphyrios'; H. Dörrie and others, *Porphyre* (1966); A. Smith, *ANRW* 2. 36. 2 (1987).

TEXTS Works on Arist. in *Comm. in Arist. graeca* 4. 1; frs. of comm. on Plato's *Timaeus*, A. R. Sodano (1964); *anon. comm. in Parm.* in *Porphyre et Victorinus*, P. Hadot (1968); frs. of *Κ. Χριστιανῶν*, A. Harnack, *Abh. Berl. Ak.* 1916 and *Sitzb. Berl. Ak.* 1921; *Porphyrii Opuscula²* (1886) Nauck; *De l'Abstinence*, J. Bouffartigue and M. Patillon (2 vols. 1977, 1979); *Vie de Pythagore, Lettre à Marcella*, E. Des Places (1982); *Πρὸς Ἀνεβῶ*, Sodano (1958); *Sententiae*, Lamberz (1975); *Life of Plotinus* in edns. of Plot.; *Ὁμηρικὰ ζητ.*, H. Schrader (1880–90), Liber I, Sodano (1966); *Εἰς τὰ Ἁρμονικὰ Πτολ.*, I. Düring (Goteborg, 1932); *Πρὸς Γαῦρον*, K. Kalbfleisch, *Abh. Berl. Ak.* (1895 Anhang); frs. of *Σύμμικτα ζητ.* with comm., H. Dörrie (1959); *Porphyrii Fragmenta*, ed. Smith (1993).   A. Sm.

Porphyry's music theory Like *Augustine and other Christian fathers, *Porphyry was suspicious of real *music but held musical theory in high esteem. In arguing that *Ptolemy (4)'s *Harmonics* relies heavily on unacknowledged sources, his incomplete *Commentary* preserves much important earlier material (selections translated in A. Barker, *Greek Musical Writings*, 2 (1989)). It became well known in the Renaissance for championing a non-Ptolemaic, partly qualitative theory of pitch.

TEXT I. Düring (1932); notes in his *Ptolemaios und Porphyrios über die Musik* (1934).   A. D. B.

Porsen(n)a, Lars, king of *Clusium, who besieged Rome at the beginning of the republic in a vain attempt to reinstate the exiled *Tarquinius Superbus. The standard version of the story is that Porsenna was so impressed by the heroism of Romans such as *Horatius Cocles and C. *Mucius Scaevola that he gave up the siege and made peace with the Romans. He withdrew from Rome, and instead sent his forces, under the command of his son Ar(r)uns, against the Latin town of *Aricia. This expedition ended in failure, however, when Arruns was defeated and killed by the Latins and their allies from *Cumae. The survivors of his army made their way back to Rome, where they were hospitably received. There are many contradictory elements in this romantic tale, which is further complicated by an alternative tradition which maintained that the Romans had surrendered to Porsenna (Tac. *Hist.* 3. 72), and that he imposed a humiliating treaty on them (Plin. *HN* 34. 139). This unflattering version, which is unlikely to have been invented by the Romans, has given rise to a modern theory that Porsenna used Rome as a base from which to launch his attack against the Latins, and that it was his defeat at Aricia that finally caused him to withdraw. The battle of Aricia is probably an authentic event, since it appears to have been independently recorded in Greek sources (see ARISTODEMUS (2)), but it is unlikely that Porsenna's original aim was to restore the Tarquins. Since Tarquinius Superbus was closely associated with Porsenna's enemies, the Latins and Aristodemus, it is more probable that, so far from attempting to restore the Roman monarchy, Porsenna actually abolished it, and that the republic emerged after his withdrawal.

Alföldi, *Early Rome and the Latins* (1965), 47 ff.; Ogilvie, *Comm.* (1965), 255; E. Gjerstad, *Op. Rom.* 7 (1969), 149–61; M. L. Scevola, *RIL* 109 (1975), 3–27; CAH 7². 2. 93–4, 257–9; J. R. Jannot, *MÉFRA* 100 (1988), 602–11.   T. J. Co.

portents may be defined as phenomena seen as in some way indicating the future, which are generally believed to be of divine origin. Such signs frequently occur spontaneously, although they may be sought. Roman theory thus distinguished the two types respectively as *oblativa* and *impetrativa* (see AUGURES). Some sort of belief in portents was general (though not universal) in antiquity, but scepticism on particulars was widespread; there was much room for disagreement on what constituted a portent and on what it portended, as well as on its importance in relation to other factors.

Already in *Homer we can observe much that is characteristic of portents in the Greek world. Signs from the behaviour of birds are frequent, and are sometimes explicitly said to come from *Zeus; they may simply confirm something that has been said (e.g. *Il.* 13. 821–3) or they may use symbolism to convey a more complex message. Typical of the latter kind is the portent at *Il.* 12. 200 ff., where an eagle is bitten by a snake it is carrying and forced to drop it. This is interpreted by *Polydamas to mean that the Trojans will eventually fail in their attack on the Achaean ships. Scepticism is shown by *Hector, who regards such signs as trivial ('one omen is best, to fight for your country', 243)—but events will prove him wrong. Other portentous events in Homer include thunder (e.g. *Il.* 8. 170–1) and sneezing (*Od.* 17. 541–7). Most of the portents recorded from later periods, Greek and Roman, conform to basically similar types. They are drawn from meteorological or astronomical phenomena (strange types of rainfall, *eclipses—also *earthquakes), from the behaviour of animals (birds, swarms of bees), and from the involuntary actions or unknowing words of humans. Other sources include the entrails of sacrificial victims, the unusual appearance of statues, and (especially in Rome) deformed births, human or animal. Wishing to interpret such an event, Greeks might consult a professional *mantis* (seer) or even send to an oracle, or they might, like Polydamas, draw their own conclusions. As with other forms of prophecy, much latitude was possible here. *Xenophon (1) relates, for instance, that when a Spartan expedition was demoralized by an earth tremor their leader and king Agesipolis interpreted it to indicate *Poseidon's approval, since the expedition was already under way. Once he had achieved part of his aim, however, he was prepared to accept a thunderbolt and a lobeless sacrificial liver as signs that the expedition should be disbanded (*Hell.* 4. 7. 4–7).

Similar phenomena were regarded as portentous in the Roman world, but were conceived in a different way. Whereas certain signs, as among the Greeks, were simple indicators of the future, in particular of the success or otherwise of an undertaking, the more unusual or sinister-seeming—rains of blood, monstrous births—were classified as *prodigia* and seen as signs of divine anger. Rather than exact interpretation, what was needed therefore was expiation, and the matter was likely to be the concern of the state. Prodigies were reported to the consuls, who prepared a list for the senate; the senate then decided which were authentic and of public concern. It might then take immediate action or more usually refer the matter to the *pontifices* (see PONTIFEX) or *haruspices, or arrange a consultation of the Sibylline Books (see SIBYL). With this elaborate state mechanism in place, it is not surprising that perhaps even more than in Greece portents were closely connected with politics and could be the subject of manipulation, conscious or unconscious. *Publica prodigia* decline in frequency during the 1st cent. BC, but omens and portents of other types continue to be reported throughout antiquity and beyond.

See also DEFORMITY; DIVINATION; PROPHECIES.

A. Bouché-Leclercq, *Histoire de la divination dans l'antiquité* (1879–82, repr. 1975), vols. 1, 4; R. Bloch, *Les Prodiges dans l'antiquité classique* (1963); B. MacBain, *Prodigy and Expiation* (1982).   E. Ke.

portico, in a general sense, an extended colonnade and thus a possible translation of the Greek *stoa. The Latin term *porticus* can refer similarly to extended free-standing colonnades which are simply stoas erected in a Roman context. On the other hand, the Porticus Aemilia in the *forum Romanum, dating originally to 193 BC, was an extended, enclosed, market-hall 487 × 60 m. (1,595 × 495 ft.) with at least six rows of internal columns. Often in Latin the term is used to designate enclosed courtyards with colonnades surrounding all four sides, such as the Porticus Octaviae at Rome, shown on the Severan *Forma Urbis; some fragments still stand. This was a temple precinct, enclosing the temples of Juno Regina and Jupiter Stator (and comparable with the precinct of Artemis Leucophryene at *Magnesia (1) ad Maeandrum). The distinction between stoa and portico is thus unreal.

E. Nash *Pict. Dict. Rome*, entries under 'Porticus'.   R. A. T.

portoria were in origin duties on goods entering or leaving harbours, the upkeep of which was a charge on public funds. Such levies were made in Italian harbours under the republic, though they were temporarily abolished between 60 BC and *Caesar's dictatorship. In the late republic and Principate internal customs-duties (raised for revenue, not protective, purposes) were extended to the provinces and levied on the major traffic-routes; for this purpose several provinces might form a single unit (e.g. the Gallic or the Danubian provinces) in the sense that duty was raised at a uniform rate (often, as in Gaul, 2½ per cent) within the area. On the eastern frontiers, at least, customs duties,

apparently fixed at 25 per cent, were levied on goods crossing the empire's borders. The collection of *portoria* had been let out to *publicani during the republic. In the main this procedure remained in force during the Principate, although there is some evidence in the 2nd cent. (from Illyricum at least) for a change to direct collection by state officials. In the Principate the process of collection was supervised either by the provincial procurator or by specially designated procurators responsible for the tax in a province (or group of provinces). For the inscription from *Ephesus detailing the schedule of the Asian *portoria* see *AE* 1989, 681. See FINANCE, ROMAN; PUBLICANI (bibliog.).

S. J. de Last, *Portorium* (1949); P. A. Brunt, *Roman Imperial Themes* (1990), ch. 17.   G. P. B.

portraiture, Greek Although archaic gravestones and other sculpture already represented specific individuals (see ANTENOR (2); THEODORUS (1)), Greek portraiture proper begins after the Persian invasions of 480. The Tyrannicides (see CRITIUS) were generic representations of men long dead, but the *Themistocles from Ostia (a copy) modifies a pre-existing *Heracles type to make him into a heroic figure (cf. Plut. *Them.* 22. 2). Such 'role' portraiture, whereby standard types were personalized to a greater or lesser degree, was normative during the classical period and into the Hellenistic. Examples (all copies) include *Pericles (1) (c.425: see CRESILAS), *Herodotus (1), *Thucydides (2), and *Socrates 'A' (c.380), *Xenophon (1) (c.350), *Plato (1) (c.345: see SILANION), 'Acropolis' *Alexander (3) the Great (c.338), *Sophocles (1) (c.336), *Aristotle and Socrates 'B' (c.320: see LYSIPPUS (2)), *Demosthenes (2) (280), *Epicurus (c.270), *Metrodorus (2) and *Hermarchus (c.260), and *Carneades (c.150). Most if not all are Attic. Coiffure, attributes, posture, and gesture helped to locate the subject as belonging to a particular citizen and/or character type within the *polis.

Though *Demetrius (2) of Alopece apparently excelled at specific likenesses, they chiefly appear outside Athens or in other media: good surviving examples are the Porticello 'philosopher' (c.400) and an engraved gem by Dexamenus (c.430). Portraits of barbarians, outside the *polis* and its social and characterological norms, also tend to be quite specific: compare the '*Mausolus' from the *Mausoleum and the coins of the early 4th-cent. Lycian and other dynasts.

Alexander's conquests both revolutionized the genre of ruler-portraiture and stimulated a massive demand for portraits at all levels. *Lysippus (2) idealized his features and blended them with a version of the nude spear-bearing Doryphoros (see POLYCLITUS (2)) in order to show him as a latter-day *Achilles, while *Apelles represented him as a *Zeus on earth, complete with thunderbolt (Plut. *Mor.* 335a f. 360d; *Alex.* 4). They and others also first portrayed the ruler in narrative situations (hunts, battles, processions), and with gods and personifications. Alexander's successors eagerly followed suit, choosing the *diadem (which he had assumed in 330) as their royal symbol. Whether equestrian, armoured, cloaked, or nude; striding, standing, or seated; spear-bearing or with trident, sceptre, or cornucopia; or wearing solar crown, winged *petasos, panther-scalp, elephant-scalp, or horns, their statues, pictures, coins, and gems represented them as charismatic and often semi-divine rulers in their own right. While most are idealized, this seldom obscures their individuality, for easy recognition is one of their prime aims; indeed, some Bactrian (see BACTRIA) and Asian rulers opted for a no-nonsense realism as an alternative, attention-getting, device.

After Alexander, portraiture became the central Hellenistic art form. While the old categories continue, and bourgeois portraits are mostly conventional, others are markedly original. Most striking are the sharp-featured *Menander (1) (c.290), the aged *Chrysippus (c.200), the bronze 'Worried Man' from *Delos (c.100: see AGASIAS (2)), and some inspired 'baroque' portraits: the Antisthenes (c.200: see PHYROMACHUS), the 'pseudo-Seneca' (c.150; perhaps *Hesiod), and the Homer IV (c.150). Portraits of Romans conformed both to traditional Greek attitudes about barbarians and the sitters' own tastes: examples range from the aquiline, impetuous T. *Quinctius Flamininus (after 197; cf. Plut. Flam. 1. 1) to the hard-boiled Italian merchants who settled on Delos between 166 and 88 (see NEGOTIATORES). Athletes represent the opposite pole: surviving examples suggest hardly any individualization in the majority of cases. See PORTRAITURE, ROMAN.

G. M. A. Richter, *The Portraits of the Greeks*, 3 vols. (1965); rev. edn. in 1 vol. by R. R. R. Smith (1984); J. J. Pollitt, *Art in the Hellenistic Age* (1986); R. R. R. Smith, *Hellenistic Royal Portraits* (1988); A. F. Stewart, *Greek Sculpture* (1990), and *Faces of Power: Alexander's Image and Hellenistic Politics* (1993).   A. F. S.

portraiture, Roman Roman portraiture is especially noted for its verism, the meticulous recording of facial characteristics including such unflattering features as wrinkles, warts, and moles. The origins of the veristic style remain obscure, but republican customs suggest that portraits were used by the Romans to exemplify noble behaviour. *Polybius (1) (6. 53) records the practice at the funeral processions of great men of dressing young men of the family in the clothes and death masks of those distinguished ancestors whom they most resembled; he and the elder *Pliny (1) describe the ancestral portraits kept in genealogical order in noble houses together with a written record of the achievements of the dead. The right to keep and display such portraits (see IMAGINES) was restricted to the nobility and to the families of serving magistrates.

Most surviving republican Roman portraits date to the 1st cent. BC, when the ancestral portrait was used in the competitive environment of the intense struggle for political leadership in the late republic. Some aspiring political and military leaders adopted the fashions of Hellenistic court portraiture, but *Caesar favoured the veristic style, discrediting its republican origins by becoming the first Roman to have his own portrait on coins minted during his lifetime, and permitting his images to be carried on litters and set up on sacred platforms. *Augustus developed an idealised image drawn from the repertoire of Classical Greece, but recognizably Roman in its often modest presentation. From the beginning of Empire, men and women copied court portraiture from images of the emperor and his family on coins and statues intended for wide use and public view at Rome and in the provinces. The veristic style continued to be used by some nobles, but was also adopted by *freedmen who wished to celebrate the right of their families to Roman citizenship following legislation passed under Augustus; in the conventionalized portraits of freedmen and their families it is difficult to trace the documentation of individual features that was so marked a feature of republican portraiture of the aristocracy. Verism is also marked in the portraiture of emperors of modest origin such as *Vespasian and some of the 3rd-cent. emperors.

The Julio-Claudian emperors and their successors were mostly clean-shaven, though *Nero and *Domitian were occasionally portrayed bearded. It is likely that his beard, comparable to that of *Pericles (1), expressed *Hadrian's commitment to Greek culture. During his reign women adopted the simple bun worn high on the crown, a revival of Hellenistic Greek fashion and a striking contrast to the elaborate tiered coiffures fashionable from the time of Nero to that of Trajan. Hadrian's adoption of the beard and the contemporary innovation of engraving the pupil and iris of the eye influenced subsequent imperial and private portraiture. Among beards there were idiosyncratic variations: Marcus *Aurelius wore the long beard of the philosopher, and *Septimius Severus the forked beard marking his interest in the cult of the Graeco-Egyptian god *Sarapis. The soldier-emperors and tetrarchs (see TETRARCHY) of the later 3rd cent. were ill-shaven rather than bearded, with close-cropped hair; *Gallienus, in contrast, presented an image of Hadrianic refinement. The clean-shaven portrait was revived by *Constantine I and his successors. Commemorative and funerary portraits were introduced to many regions under the empire, and proved an influential form of individual commemoration. Portraits, whether of imperial or private subjects, were made in a wide variety of media including silver, bronze, stone, terracotta, glass, mosaic, ivory, bone, and painted wood. Of the last the most striking examples are the mummy portraits made in the *Fayûm (Egypt), the only naturalistically coloured portraits to survive from antiquity (see PAINTING, ROMAN). Many of these seem to represent individuals as they appeared in life; some present a type still current in north-east Africa. These and the limestone funerary reliefs of *Palmyra (Syria) offer the best surviving evidence for the wearing of *dress and jewellery.

Roman portrait busts may be dated not only by their relationship to the fashions of the imperial court, but by changes in the shape and size of the bust, which by Flavian times had enlarged from head and neck to incorporate the shoulders, and in the early third century grew to a half-length figure, after which it shrank again. See ART, FUNERARY, ROMAN.

J. L. Breckenridge, *ANRW* 1. 4 (1973), 826–54; 2. 12. 2 (1981), 477–512; P. Zanker, *The Power of Images in the Age of Augustus* (1988); K. Fittschen and P. Zanker, *Römische Porträts in den kapitolinischen Museen, Rom: 1. Prinzenbildnisse* (1983); *3. Prinzessenbildnisse* (1985).
                                                F. N. P.; J. M. C. T.; S. E. C. W.

Portunus god worshipped in the *Tiber harbour at Rome (festival, the Portunalia, 17 August; a *flamen* is attested). Originally linked with 'ways in' in the wider sense, his cult came to concern *harbours in general, and at Rome was associated, probably from the 6th cent. BC, with the Corinthian sea-faring cults of Palaemon (see ISTHMIA; MELICERTES) and Leucothea (see INO-LEUCOTHEA). His temple at the head of the Pons Aemilius, long wrongly known as that of Fortuna Virilis, one of the best-preserved in Rome, is part of the monumental remodelling of the waterfront of the Tiber harbour by members of the *gens Aemilia* in the mid 2nd cent. BC.

F. Coarelli, *Il Foro Boario* (1988). H. Scullard, *Festivals and Ceremonies of the Roman Republic* (1981), 56–8.   N. P.

Portus *Claudius undertook the construction, which *Caesar had planned, of an enclosed harbour two miles north of *Ostia, linked to the Tiber by a *canal: to remedy the very difficult conditions of transshipment at Ostia; to provide Rome with a worthy gateway for seaborne visitors; and to help mitigate floods at Rome by improving the flow of the *Tiber. A deep basin was excavated and protected from the sea by two moles (the arrangement is still not fully understood), with a *lighthouse rivalling that of *Alexandria (1) (excavation has proved that its foundation was indeed a scuttled merchant-ship filled with concrete, cf. Suet. *Cl.* 20. 3).

Portus Itius

The new harbour was not safe, as its wide open expanse was prone to squalls; disaster struck in 62, and *Nero's plan for ship-canals between *Cumae and Ostia perhaps represents a falling back on the natural superiority of the ports of *Campania. *Trajan however undertook the construction of an inner basin at Portus, hexagonal in plan, covering 32 ha., which rendered the harbour usable (despite some problem with silting) throughout antiquity. Indeed although the commercial life of 2nd-cent. Ostia certainly embraced both the Tiber-bank wharves of that town and the facilities (especially large warehouses) at Portus, in the 3rd cent. Portus (where the Alexandrian grain-fleet docked from the reign of *Commodus) began to function more independently, a process which was reflected in a Christian bishopric by 314 and a grant of independent status by Constantine I.

Much of the layout of the Claudian harbour has been revealed by the construction and continuing development of the Leonardo da Vinci airport at Fiumicino since the late 1950s. Important finds of large and small ships from the harbour silts are preserved in a museum in the airport complex. Also of Claudian date is the fine basilica-like vestibule on the main quayside, with files of heavily rusticated columns, originally perhaps the principal exit towards Rome. There was some sort of imperial residence in the complex, like that of Trajan overlooking the harbour of Centumcellae. There are also very imposing remains of several phases of enormous warehouses, and a late antique wall, but archaeological work in the Trajanic harbour has been long delayed by the intransigence of the landowners. The exploration of the cemetery and the environs of the important early Christian complex of S. Ippolito on the island between Portus and Ostia, the Isola Sacra, is more advanced. See HARBOURS.

O. Testaguzza, *Portus* (1970); R. Meiggs, *Roman Ostia* (2nd edn. 1970), 148–71. N. P.

Portus Itius, a harbour of the Morini, used by *Caesar (*BGall.* 5. 2 and 5) in the second British expedition (54 BC). The words seem to mean 'Channel Harbour', so that Boulogne, the port normally used, is the obvious identification, though there are arguments for Wissant.

R. Dion, *Latomus*, 1963, 203 ff. E. Wightman, *Gallia Belgica* (1985), 37. C. E. S.

Porus (d. 318 BC), eponymous ruler of the Pauravas, an Indian people (see INDIA) between the rivers Jhelum and Chenab, refused to acknowledge the superiority of *Alexander (3) 'the Great' and organized a brave but futile defence. Defeated crushingly at the battle of the *Hydaspes (spring 326 BC), he displayed a heroism which commended him to his conqueror. Alexander expanded his kingdom and in 326/5 declared him paramount ruler of all territories east of the Jhelum (Hydaspes). By 324 his sway may have included Sind, now cleared of European occupation, but he could give no cohesion to his disparate realm, and his assassination at the hands of Eudamus (Macedonian commander at Taxila) left western *India an easy prey for Chandragupta (*Sandracottus).

Berve, *Alexanderreich*. 2, no. 683; Bosworth, *Conquest and Empire* (1988). A. B. B.

Poseidon 'All men call Poseidon god of the sea, of *earthquakes, and of horses', wrote *Pausanias (3) (7. 21. 7) in the 2nd cent. AD, describing the three principal aspects of one of the most widely, and anciently, worshipped of the Greek gods. Pausanias' term for god of the sea, *pelagaios*, is descriptive, not cultic, but his epithets for the earthquake god, Asphaleios, 'He who keeps things

steady', and god of horses, Hippios, were common cult titles. In the form Posedaon (= Ποσειδάων, as in epic poetry) he is attested on Mycenaean tablets from the palace archives at *Cnossus on Crete and at Pylos in Messenia, where there are more references to him than to any other divinity (see MYCENAEAN LANGUAGE; PRE-ALPHABETIC SCRIPTS (GREECE)); he has a sanctuary (Posidaion) and Posidawes (cult personnel?), while a female figure, Posideia, owes her name to him. His local importance at Pylos is reflected in *Homer's *Odyssey* (3. 4–8, *Nestor (1) and nine groups of 500 Pylians sacrifice nine black bulls to the god on the seashore) and in later traditions of the Neleids in Athens and Ionia, who claimed descent from Pylian kings (see NELEUS). According to Homer, in a division of realms, *Zeus received the sky, Poseidon the sea, and *Hades the underworld, while all three shared *Olympus (1) and earth. He is a powerful figure, resistant to pressure from his brother Zeus while acknowledging the latter's seniority (15. 184–99); this is in contrast to the story of Zeus being the last child of *Cronus and Rhea (Hes. *Theog.* 454–506, and often later). In Homer he is largely the god of the sea, aside from the implications of earthquake in the epithets *enosichthon*, *ennosigaios* ('earth-shaker'). He causes storms and calms the waters; his wife is Amphitrite, a sea-creature. Poseidon supports the Greeks in the Trojan War (see TROY), but is hostile to *Odysseus, the supreme seafarer. Eventually Odysseus will establish the god's cult far from the sea where an oar is mistaken for a winnowing fan (*Od.* 11. 119–34).

Poseidon begets various monstrous figures such as Odysseus' enemies the *Cyclopes. He is not associated, in myth or cult, with civic institutions. The violence of natural phenomena, sea and earthquake, are central to the Greek conception of him. In art he is always a grave, mature male, indistinguishable from Zeus when not accompanied by attributes.

Numerous sanctuaries of the god on coastal sites, such as the 5th-cent. BC marble temple on the promontory of *Sunium in Attica, where quadrennial boat races were held in his honour, and the oracular shrine at *Taenarum in Laconia which boasted a passage to the underworld, show that his ties to the sea were also prominent in cult, as do the dedications of sailors and fishermen. Many coastal settlements were named after him.

But there were also important cult places inland where clefts in rocks, pools, streams and springs (cf. Aesch. *Sept.* 308–11) were signs of his activity. Heliconius, his title as common god of the *Ionians at the *Panionium near Mycale, and similar epithets on the Greek mainland (cf. also Mt. *Helicon in Boeotia with its spring Hippocrene), may refer to the blackness of deep waters. A concern with fertility is seen in the worship of Poseidon Phytalmios ('of plants') which was said to be almost universal among the Greeks (Plut. *Mor.* 675f). This aspect of the god may have stemmed from his association with fresh waters and lightning, for which the trident was an instrument. There is, however, in general an emphasis on masculinity and potency in his myths and cults (so stallions, bulls, and uncastrated sheep are sacrificial victims, cf. *Syll.*[3] 1024 from Myconos).

Mating with grim figures (a single Erinys (see ERINYES) in Boeotia, Schol. *Il.* 23. 347, with *Demeter Erinys at Arcadian Telphusa (see ARCADIA), she in the form of a mare, he as a stallion, Paus. 8. 25. 4–5), he begets the marvellous horse *Arion (1) and, at Telphusa also a daughter with a secret name. Again in Arcadia, at Phigaleia (Paus. 8. 42. 1–2), Black Demeter is represented with a horse's head and her child by Poseidon is *Despoina which is also the public name of the daughter of Demeter and Poseidon Hippios at Lycosura (Paus. 8. 37. 9–10). With the Gorgon Medusa (see GORGO) he begets Chrysaor and the winged horse *Pegasus (1) whose name was connected with the springs (*pēgai*) of Ocean (Hes. *Theog.* 278–83). He had herds of horses in Arcadian Pheneus (Paus. 8. 14. 5–6), and horses were sometimes sacrificed to him (Paus. 8. 7. 2). In his sanctuary at Onchestus in Boeotia a horse with chariot but no driver was allowed to run loose and if the chariot crashed it was dedicated to the god (*Hymn Hom. Ap.* 229–38). This close association with the horse has led to the theory that he was introduced to Greece along with the horse by the speakers of an ancestral form of Greek early in the second millennium BC. Whatever the reasons for the original connection, the aristocratic and non-utilitarian associations of the horse were appropriate for a god often named as the ancestor of aristocratic families.

He was worshipped widely in inland Arcadia and Boeotia ('All Boeotia is sacred to Poseidon', *Aristarchus (2), in *Et. Mag.* 547. 17) and he had important cults around the Saronic Gulf. In the Archaic period, on the island of *Calauria off Troezen, his sanctuary was the centre of an *amphictiony of originally five small *poleis* on the Argolic and Saronic gulfs, together with Athens and Boeotian *Orchomenus (1) (Strabo 8. 6. 14; Poseidon's son *Theseus moves in myth, as his cult may have moved historically, from Troezen to Athens). The organization seems to have lapsed in the Classical period but revived briefly in the Hellenistic. The Athenian orator and statesman *Demosthenes (2) killed himself in the sanctuary while fleeing from the Macedonians in 322 BC. *Corinth, not a member of the amphictiony, developed the open-air shrine of the god on the Isthmus, dating from the Dark Age, into a major regional and then panhellenic sanctuary (see ISTHMIA) with one of the earliest ashlar-built temples (mid-7th cent. BC) and, in the early 6th cent., a biennial festival with games (see ISTHMIAN GAMES). It was the seat of the Hellenic League first formed at the time of *Xerxes' invasions (see PERSIAN WARS) and revived more than once by the Macedonian kings. The sanctuary was destroyed by the Romans in 146 BC. and rebuilt by them more than a century later. On the southern tip of *Euboea was the sanctuary of Poseidon Geraistius.

In Athens Poseidon was shown contending with *Athena for the patronage of the city in the west pediment of the *Parthenon. He bore the epithet *Erechtheus while Erechtheus himself (originally a local form of the god?) was regarded as a heroized early king of the city. The same Attic *genos* ('clan') provided the priest of Poseidon Erechtheus and the priestess of Athena Polias (the goddess of the Acropolis). Even so, no major Athenian festival was celebrated in his honour. The annual Posideia, held in the winter month of Posideon, is more likely to have been concerned with his agricultural than his maritime role. His priest, along with the priestess of Athena, also marched to Sciron, west of Athens, the site of a sacred ploughing (Plut. *Mor.* 144b).

The etymology of the name is not certain. The first two syllables seem to contain the Greek word for 'Lord', 'Husband', cf. Sanskrit (*páti-*). *da*, in the second part of his name, may be an alternative form of Ga = Ge, Earth (cf. GAIA), for which the Pindaric epithet (see PINDAR) Ennosidas and the first syllable of Damater (Demeter) may provide support. He would then be 'Husband of Earth' (cf. the epic epithet *gaieochos*, 'holder of the earth').

Burkert, *GR*; M. Gérard-Rousseau, *Les Mentions religieuses dans les tablettes mycéniennes* (1968, 181–5); M. P. Nilsson, *Griechische Feste* (1906); W. Pötscher, 'Poseidon', *Kl. Pauly* 4 (1972); F. Schachermeyr, *Poseidon und die Entstehung des griechischen Götterglaubens* (1950); E. Wüst, *RE* 22 (1953), 'Poseidon'; N. Robertson, *CQ* (1984) 1 ff.; *LIMC* 7. 1 (1994), 446–83.
M. H. J.

Poseidonia See PAESTUM.

Posidippus (1), New Comedy poet (see COMEDY (GREEK), NEW), born in *Macedonia; he won four victories at the *Dionysia (*IG* 2². 2325. 71 = 5 B 1 col. 5. 12 Mette), competing from 289/8 BC onwards (*Suda* π 2111). Fr. 13 KA = 12 K, a version of the story of Phryne's acquittal; 28 KA = 26 K, a cook instructs his pupils; 30 KA = 28 K, a Thessalian claims that his dialect is not inferior to Attic; see GREEK LANGUAGE, § (3).

Posidippus' importance is clear; he is alleged to have introduced slave cooks onto the stage (Ath. 14. 658f); his Ἀποκλειομένη, 'Girl Locked Out' (? or 'In'), which ended with the formula now known to be typical in New Comedy (fr. 6 KA), was re-enacted twice in the late 180s (*IG* 2². 2323. 163 = 3 B 3 col. 3b 17 Mette, and a new fragment edited by A. P. Matthaiou, *Horos*, 1988, 13); his work was adapted on the Roman stage (Gell. 2. 23. 1); and his statue is extant (G. M. A. Richter, *The Portraits of the Greeks*, 2 (1965), 238 f.).

FRAGMENTS Kassel–Austin, *PCG* 7 (1989), 561–81, although earlier scholars use the numbering in Kock, *CAF* 3. 335–48.
INTERPRETATION Meineke, *FCG* 1. 482 ff.; A. Körte in *RE* 22. 1 (1953), 426 ff, 'Poseidippos' (1); A. Giannini, *Acme*, 1960, 170 f.; G. Sifakis, *Studies in the History of Hellenistic Drama* (1967), 28.   W. G. A.

Posidippus (2) of Pella, author of 20 mainly erotic and sympotic *epigrams in the Greek *Anthology, much influenced by *Callimachus (3) and *Asclepiades (2), though said to have been one of Callimachus' literary enemies (1 p.3 Pfeiffer). He is named as ἐπιγραμματοποιός (composer of epigrams) in a proxeny inscription (see PROXENOS) from *Thermum dated to 264/3 (*IG* 9². 1. 17. 24). An elegy on old age survives on wooden tablets (*Suppl. Hell.* 705). Another 100 epigrams, mainly ecphrastic and dedicatory (see EKPHRASIS; DEDICATIONS), divided into broad categories (e.g. twenty on victors in chariot races), are preserved on a 3rd-cent. BC papyrus roll in Milan (due to be published by G. Bastianini and C. Gallazzi).

Gow-Page, *HE*; H. Lloyd-Jones, *JHS* 1963, 75 f. = *Academic Papers* 2, 158; R. Keydell, *KP* no. 2; *Suppl. Hell.* 698–708; A. Cameron, *Greek Anthology* (1993), 369–76, and *Callimachus and his Critics* (1995).
A. D. E. C.

Posidonius (Ποσειδώνιος) (1) of Olbiopolis, sophist and historian, author of works on the Dniester region, *Attica and *Libya, has been identified, though this is very uncertain, with the Posidonius (*FGrH* 169) who, according to *Plutarch (*Aem.* 19), was contemporary with *Perseus (2) of Macedon (179–168 BC) and described his reign, including the battle of *Pydna.

FGrH 279.   A. H. McD.

Posidonius (2) (*c*.135–*c*.51 BC), Stoic philosopher (see STOICISM), scientist, and historian. A Syrian Greek from *Apamea on the Orontes, he was educated at Athens under *Panaetius, but settled in *Rhodes, a prosperous free city with already a reputation for philosophy and science. Granted citizenship, he took a significant part in public life as *prytanis, and as a member of at least one embassy to Rome in 87/6. Probably in the 90s he embarked on long tours of research to the west, visiting certainly Spain, southern Gaul, and of course Rome and Italy. Thereafter his School in Rhodes became the leading centre of Stoicism, and a general mecca not only for intellectuals, but for the great and powerful of the Roman world such as *Pompey and *Cicero.

The range of his writing is astonishing. In addition to the

Posidonius

conventional departments of philosophy (natural philosophy or *physics, ethics, *logic), he wrote penetratingly on *astronomy, *meteorology, *mathematics, *geography, hydrology, seismology (see EARTHQUAKES), zoology (see ANIMALS, KNOWLEDGE ABOUT), *botany, *anthropology, and history (see HISTORIOGRAPHY, HELLENISTIC). Some thirty titles survive over this field, but no complete work. This has led to a crux of methodology in Posidonian scholarship. Earlier this century research inspired by K. Reinhardt concentrated on a wide range of supposed echoes of Posidonian influence conjectured from horizontally parallel passages in later authors as the main tool for reconstructing his philosophy; but the uncertainty and dangerously subjective nature of this process, although at times illuminating, produced contradictory results. A fresh start has been made by the collection and study of the attested fragments which form a more secure base for what can be accepted as evidence, and offer a new picture.

Posidonius has been dubbed unorthodox in his Stoicism, but this is a misconception. He was not so regarded by his contemporaries, and he did not diverge from the fundamental tenets. He believed rather in the development of philosophy by continued interpretation in the light of subsequent criticism of the basic ideas of the founders and 'the old authorities'. At that level there had always been divergence of interpretation in the Stoa, as between *Ariston (1) and *Chrysippus. So Posidonius had strikingly original things to say within the context of Stoic natural philosophy in defence of the ultimate principles as material without quality or form; on problems of destruction, generation, continuity and change related to the individual; on the problem of 'now' in time viewed as a continuum; on a finite cosmos surrounded by infinite void; and in logic, on the criterion of truth, *dialectic, and on the relational syllogism.

On the other hand he was convinced that in ethics Chrysippus had seriously distorted Stoicism with his monolithic rational psychology which defined emotion as mistaken judgement, and so failed to explain the cause and operation of emotions and hence the major questions in moral behaviour. Posidonius argued for a return to irrational faculties of mind with affinities towards pleasure and power. These were natural, but not good. Only our rational affinity for moral virtue he recognized as good and absolute. Hence the uncompromising Stoic end of virtue alone is preserved, despite some ancient and modern misunderstandings. Posidonius claimed that he could now explain the mechanics of moral choice, moral responsibility (since the root of evil lies within us), and moral education which required behavioural therapeutics as well as rational argument. His attack on Chrysippus in his book *On Emotions* as culled from *Galen's *De Placitis* rests on three grounds: respect for the facts, consistency derived from deductive proof, and understanding sprung from explanation of the causes of phenomena. Posidonius was himself famed for all three in antiquity. They are the key for the coherence of his own work.

In the first place, he promoted logic from being the organon or tool of philosophy to that organic part of it which as bones and sinews supplied the articulation and dynamic of its structure. From the model of Euclidean mathematics, in whose foundations he was much interested, he regarded axiomatic deductive proof as the top-down causal explanation of the cosmic nexus. The tools of philosophy, and this is explicitly stated, now become the special sciences, a completely original concept peculiarly apposite for the material continuum of the Stoic universe. The sciences were thus necessary for natural philosophy, and the two

complementary, but not equal. For while science supplied the descriptive factual pattern of phenomena as the cosmic map on which their rational organization may be traced, and so included the plotting of their immediate relationship of antecedent causation, and even offered possible alternative explanatory hypotheses at that level, only philosophy could provide final and complete explanation of causes or aetiology by its incontrovertible method of deductive proof from assured axiomatic premisses established by the natural philosophers. These procedures demanded precise distinction between different kinds of cause, but the details of the synthesis and interaction of natural philosophy and science are largely missing because of the lack of interest of reporters like *Strabo. Some of Posidonius' own research in the sciences is remarkable, such as a lunar theory of the periodicity of tides which held sway until Newton; or his ingenious method of measuring the circumference of the earth leading to the establishment of latitudinal bands. *On Ocean* was an extraordinary work ranging from the astronomical establishment of geographical zones and so physical and climatic conditions, to human geography and anthropology. It is one of the lost books of antiquity one would most like to recover.

The same relationship holds for history and ethics, for history with its descriptive framework of actual social behaviour was his necessary tool for moral philosophy. The *History* was a major work in its own right of 52 books covering the period from 146 BC probably to the mid-80s and possibly unfinished. Its scope was all-embracing of the Mediterranean-centred world, from the histories of *Asia Minor to *Spain, *Egypt and *Africa to Gaul and the northern peoples, Rome and Greece. It was packed with formidable detail of facts and events, both major and minor, global and local, and of social and environmental phenomena. But the unifying factor of the huge canvas, factually drawn and sharply critical of credulous legend was, as *Athenaeus (1) implied and the tone and presentation of the brief Athenian tyranny of Athenion (see ARISTION) in 88 BC demonstrates, a moralist's view of historical explanation, where events are caused by mind and character in the relationship between ruler and ruled, and by tribal or racial character in social movement and motives. Hence his detailed interest in ethnology (Italian, Roman, Gallic, Germanic), i.e. ethology operating as cause. Again, such studies offer immediate historical explanation; final aetiology and principal causes come from the philosophical study of psychology and ethics.

His style, vivid, forceful and highly-coloured still gleams fitfully through the fragments. It so impressed such an authority as Cicero that he importuned Posidonius to write up his cherished consulate. The manner of declining showed a diplomat of enviable tact.

Posidonius' position in intellectual history is remarkable not for the scattered riches of a polymath and savant, but for an audacious aetiological attempt to survey and explain the complete field of the human intellect and the universe in which it finds itself as an organic part, through analysis of detail and the synthesis of the whole, in the conviction that all knowledge is interrelated.

A dominant figure in his lifetime, his subsequent reputation and influence have been overstressed to pandemic proportions and require re-examination; but the impact was considerable and continued at least to the 6th cent. AD. In mainstream Stoicism he did not supplant Chrysippus, and it was often outside the School, and not least in the sciences and history that he was consulted. The riches of the details tended to obliterate the grand design.

TEXTS The standard collection of the attested fragments is L. Edelstein and I. G. Kidd, *Posidonius I, The Fragments* (1972, 1989), with full comm. and bibliog. by I. G. Kidd, *Posidonius II, The Commentary* (2 vols. 1988). W. Theiler, *Poseidonios: Die Fragmente* (1982) is the culmination of the older Reinhardt tradition and methodology, and should be treated with caution. For the historical fragments only: F Jacoby, *FGrH* 87; J. Malitz, *Die Historien des Poseidonios* (1983).

STUDIES In general: M. Laffranque, *Poseidonios d'Apamée* (1964). Studies for the 'new' Posidonius: I. G. Kidd, in: A. A. Long (ed.), *Problems in Stoicism* (1971); *A&A* 1978, 7 ff.; J. Brunschwig (ed.) *Les Stoïciens et leur logique* (1978); Fondation Hardt, *Entretiens* 32 (1986), 1 ff; P. Huby and G. Neal (eds.), *The Criterion of Truth* (1988); J. Barnes and M. T. Griffin (eds.), *Philosophia Togata* (1989). K. Bringmann, in Fondation Hardt, *Entretiens* 32 (1989), 29 ff.; D. E. Halm, *ANRW* 36. 3 (1989), 1325 ff. Key volumes for the older tradition were K. Reinhardt, *Poseidonios* (1921), and *Kosmos und Sympathie* (1926).   I. G. K.

possession, legal Classical Roman law distinguished ownership and possession. While *ownership is the right to a thing, irrespective of whether the owner has any control or enjoyment of it, possession is, essentially, the control of a thing irrespective of whether the possessor has any right to it. A thief may therefore have possession.

According to the jurist Paul (see IULIUS PAULUS), a person acquired possession by an act of the mind and an act of the body (*animo et corpore*): the object had to be placed in the person's effective control and the person had to intend to exercise control. What was effective control varied with the type of object involved. Possession is a 'fact' in the sense that, in principle, it lasts only so long as the control continues. But the principle came to be stretched and it was held that once acquired possession could in certain circumstances continue by intention alone (*animo solo*) where, as in the case of summer pastures which were not used in winter, actual control was lost for a time. While possession is essentially the control of a thing, it must (usually) be an exclusive control in the manner of an owner. A tenant (*conductor, colonus*), a borrower, a depositee did not have possession; nor did a usufructuary.

The praetor protected possession by interdicts, orders forbidding its disturbance or restoring it once disturbed. The praetor may have begun by protecting holders of public land (*ager publicus*) or those who held by grant at will (*precarium*) from a great landowner. Here it was impossible or inappropriate for the holder to be owner, and yet it would be inconvenient to deny the holder direct protection against an interloper. Once established in these cases, protection by interdict was extended to others, including owners and those in the course of acquiring by prescription. The possessor can (broadly) recover or retain his possession against any person interfering with it, provided that he has not himself obtained possession from that person by force, secretly, or by grant at will (*vi, clam, precario*). If therefore a thing is taken from a thief, the thief can recover possession, provided the taker is not the person, whether owner or not, from whom the thief himself took it. If the thing passes from the dispossessor into the hands of a third party, the thief cannot recover possession. For possession is protected only against the immediate dispossessor: against any subsequent holder the claim must be by *vindicatio* (see ownership). In classical law this is subject to a limited exception in the case of movables.

The terminology of possession in the Roman law sources is by no means clear. The possession protected by interdicts is often simply termed '*possessio*', though many texts avoid the term and speak of 'holding' (*tenere*) or 'being on the land' (*morari in fundo*). Control not protected by interdicts, e.g. by a tenant, is sometimes

called natural possession (*naturalis possessio*). Civil possession (*civilis possessio*) is possession that can lead to the acquisition of ownership by prescription. The civil possessor is usually protected by interdicts, but, if property was pledged for a debt, the debtor might have civil possession and the creditor interdict possession.

P. Bonfante, *Corso di diritto romano* 2. 2 (1928), 3 (1933); M. Kaser, *Eigentum und Besitz²* (1956); M. Lauria, *Possessiones²*(1957); E. Levy, *West Roman Vulgar Law, The Law of Property* (1951); A. Watson, *The Roman Law of Property in the Later Roman Republic* (1968).   B. N.; A. F. R.

possession, religious That a human being might become possessed by a supernatural power was a fairly common ancient belief. The effect might be a prophetic trance as in the case of the Pythia (see DELPHIC ORACLE). Plato (*Phdr.* 244a ff., esp. 265) further distinguishes between telestic (inspired by *Dionysus), poetic (inspired by the *Muses), and erotic (inspired by *Aphrodite and *Eros) possession. Words expressing the notion 'possessed by (a) god', such as θεόληπτος or θεοφόρητος, carried an ambivalent meaning. On the one hand they referred to terrifying pathological experiences, as for instance epileptic strokes or various types of insanity. On the other, possession involved direct contact with a god and thus could effect a kind of sacralization. Around 400 BC inscriptions (*IG* 1². 784, 785, 788) mention Archedemus from *Thera, ὁ νυμφόληπτος ('seized by the nymphs'), who withdrew to a cave to devote himself to a monk-like worship of the *Nymphs; see CAVES, SACRED. Closely related are the various κάτοχοι or κατεχούμενοι of later pagan and Christian creeds, especially in Asia Minor and Egypt: people who retired from the world to become the possession of their gods, whom they served in slavish submission. Belief in the pathological connotations of possession, especially possession by demons, grew stronger in the post-Classical period (cf. the many stories about demoniacs in the NT) and reports of magical cures and exorcisms, pagan and Christian, abound. See ASCETICISM.

J. H. Waszink, *RAC* 2 (1954), 183–5; Fr. Pfister, *RAC* 4 (1959), 944–87; N. Himmelmann-Wildschütz, *Theoleptos* (1957); W. R. Connor, *Cl. Ant.* 1988, 155–89.   H. S. V.

postal service The Greek *poleis* communicated by professional messengers (*hemerodromoi*, like *Phidippides, on land; there were also messenger-ships), but developed no other general infrastructure for communications. The Assyrian state (see ASSYRIA), however, with its developed and centralized requisitioning system, used relays of mounted couriers. These were the model for the efficient Persian arrangements (see ROYAL ROAD) which were maintained at the expense of local communities. From the first, the carrying of messages, the movement of goods due to the state, and the journeys of the ruler and his representatives were closely linked, and this is the system bequeathed by the *Achaemenid kingdom to the (*Diadochi) Successors of *Alexander (3) the Great, in *Syria and in Egypt, where the Ptolemies (see PTOLEMY (1)) developed it to a high level of complexity and dependability (here the duty to maintain the post was liturgical (see LITURGY), like military service, though it could be commuted into a tax).

Rome in the republic knew only the essentially private, though quite large scale, networks of messengers (*tabellarii*) maintained by important men, governors, or *publicani* (entitled to requisition in certain circumstances). No doubt most movements of information and materials continued to be organized in this essentially private way: *Augustus' bold introduction (Suet. *Aug.* 49. 3) of a public postal system for the whole empire was modelled rather on the Hellenistic kingdoms, and designed specifically for governmental purposes. The original system (Augustus' experiment made use of long-distance, rather than relay-, messengers called *iuvenes*) and its 1st cent. development are still relatively little known (our best information derives from legal regulations for the system in the 4th cent.), but its developed form (the so-called *cursus publicus*) was clearly one of the largest-scale administrative initiatives of antiquity. It could only work through a system of local requisitioning of animals, vehicles, and provisions, and the system for arranging this (*vehiculatio*, in Greek *angareia*) rapidly became one of the most burdensome and unpopular forms of state imposition. Nerva freed Italy from it: a series of measures preserved on inscriptions from different provinces (most recently *Galatia under Tiberius, see Mitchell in bibliog. below) attests the scale of the problem, the level of unrest, the state's concern, and the inefficacy of attempts to reform. The principal check, the limiting of use of the service to those with warrants (*diplomata*) was very prone to abuse, and even *Pliny (2) the Younger defends his use of the system for his wife in a letter to *Trajan (*Ep.* 10, 120). Valid *diplomata* were very valuable documents. The appointment of supervisory officials (*a vehiculis*, later *praefectus vehiculorum*) does not seem to have helped, though the appointment of imperial contractors (*mancipes*, SHA, *Hadrian* 7. 5) relieved local magistrates of burdensome involvement in the running of the system, and various attempts to shift parts of the cost of the system, at least in some places, to the state, are attested.

The system was centred on the posting stations (*mansiones*, originally the larger and most important stations, and *mutationes*) and, naturally on the road network (some visual signalling was used, but with relatively simple content only, cf. Polyb. 10. 45. 6); many of the imperial *maps and *itineraries were also probably adjuncts of the *cursus*. Any specialized personnel was military, first *tabellarii* like those used in the republic, then *speculatores*, eventually the more secret-agent-like *frumentarii* (2nd cent.) and *agentes in rebus* (Diocletianic). The existence of this administrative infrastructure invited its use for other state purposes: it rapidly became linked with the wholesale movement of state goods, especially the food-supplies exacted by the development of the *annona* into a tax in kind (see FOOD SUPPLY), for which Septimius Severus created the *cursus clabularis*, with provision of ox-carts, as opposed to the *cursus velox*; and with troop movements in general.

The government communication network (a better description than 'postal service') was thus potentially very effective (50 miles per day was a not uncommon speed for messages, but the news of the revolt of the Rhine army in 69 travelled to *Galba at the rate of *c.*150 miles per day), and its existence is certainly one of the distinguishing features of the Roman empire. What is more problematic is the question of the density of written communications and their role in day-to-day government: the relationship between potential and actuality remains in need of clarification. See TRAVEL.

E. J. Holmberg, *Zur Geschichte des Cursus Publicus* (1933); H. G. Pflaum, *Essai sur le Cursus Publicus sous le haut Empire* 1940); L. Casson, *Travel in the ancient world* (1974), 182–90; R. Chevallier, *Roman Roads* (1976), 181–4. S. Mitchell, *JRS* 1976, 106–31; B. M. Levick, *The Government of the Roman Empire: A Sourcebook* (1985), 99–115. N. P.

postliminium A Roman citizen captured by the enemy was regarded by Roman law as a slave (see BOOTY; SLAVERY), except that his rights were not extinguished but in suspense. By virtue of the right of *postliminium* (literally return behind the threshold)

a captive who returned recovered all his rights retrospectively, just as if he had never been captured. The principle applied only to rights, not to 'facts', i.e. to legal relationships which require for their existence some physical manifestation. Such relationships did not revive automatically, but had to be physically resumed. Thus *ownership revived automatically, but *possession did not; nor did marriage (but this rule was altered by Justinian; see JUSTINIAN'S CODIFICATION). If the captive died in captivity, he died a slave; but a *lex Cornelia* (of the dictator *Sulla) preserved the validity of his will by the fiction that he died a citizen. This fiction was applied to successions on intestacy and was further extended in the post-classical law. *Postliminium* was applied also to land and to certain things important in war (slaves, ships, horses used in military service) which fell into enemy hands and were later recovered by their owner.

J. Imbert, *Postliminium* (1944); L. Amirante, *Captivitas e postliminium* (1950); E. Levy, 'Captivus redemptus', *Ges. Schr.* 2 (= *CPhil.* 1943; = *Bull. Ist. dir. rom.* 1951). B. N.

poststructuralism See LITERARY THEORY AND CLASSICAL STUDIES.

Postumius (*RE* 31) **Albinus, Aulus,** served under L. *Aemilius Paullus (2) against *Perseus (2) and was praetor 155 BC, when, presiding in the senate, he used a procedural trick to prevent the release of the Achaean hostages. In 154 he was a member of an embassy which ended the war between *Attalus II and *Prusias II. Consul 151, he and his colleague L. *Licinius Lucullus (1) were imprisoned by the tribunes for the severity of their conduct of the levy. He was in Greece, perhaps as an ambassador, in 146, and was later one of the ten commissioners for the settlement after the Achaean War. An enthusiast for Greek culture, he wrote a history of Rome, from its origins, in Greek (there may have been a Latin translation) and also a poem. According to *Polybius (1) he was mocked by *Cato (Censorius) for apologizing, in the preface to his history, for his inadequate knowledge of Greek. In the same passage (39. 1), Polybius presents a hostile picture of him, influenced, no doubt, by his conduct in 155, but *Cicero (*Brutus* 81) praises his literary work and culture.

FRAGMENTS HRR 1². 53–4, FGrH no. 812. Walbank, HCP 3. 542–3, 726–8. J. Br.

Postumius (*RE* 45) **Albinus, Spurius,** as consul in 110 BC renewed the war with *Jugurtha after L. *Calpurnius Bestia's treaty and left his brother Aulus in charge when he went to Rome to hold elections. Aulus was defeated and his army was sent under the yoke (early 109). Spurius, returning as proconsul, failed to repair the disaster, was superseded by Q. *Caecilius Metellus Numidicus and convicted by the tribunal set up by C. *Mamilius Limetanus. E. B.

Postumius (*RE* 55) **Megellus, Lucius,** a colourful and controversial political figure of the age of the Samnite Wars (see ROME (HISTORY); SAMNIUM). He was three times consul (305, 294, 291 BC), and is said to have triumphed over the Samnites on all three occasions, and on the last two over the Etruscans as well. But *Livy mentions confusion in his sources over these campaigns; the 305 triumph is not listed in the *Fasti Capitolini* and that of 294 was unauthorized (Liv. 10. 37. 6–12). In 291 he was fined for using soldiers under his command as agricultural labourers on his own estates, an episode dealt with in a newly discovered fragment of Livy book 11. When sent as envoy to demand restitution from *Tarentum in 282, he was publicly humiliated, an event that led to war and ultimately to the expedition of *Pyrrhus to Italy.

Broughton, *MRR* 1; fragment of Livy 11; B. Bravo and M. T. Griffin, *Athenaeum*, 1988, 447–521; R. E. A. Palmer, *Athenaeum* 1990, 5–18.

H. H. S.; T. J. Co.

Postumius (*RE* 63) **Tubertus, Aulus,** reputedly defeated the *Aequi (and *Volsci according to Livy) as *dictator at the *Algidus pass on 17 June (Ov. *Fast.* 6. 721 ff.) in 432 (Diodorus) or 431 BC (Livy). Livy's 'Homeric' narrative of the battle (4. 27 ff.) resembles accounts of Lake Regillus (see REGILLUS, LAKE), won by the dictator A. Postumius Albus; both may derive from popular or family tradition. If Postumius' supposed execution of his son for indiscipline is not modelled on T. *Manlius Imperiosus Torquatus, it perhaps exemplified the restrictions on individual inititative necessitated by heavy infantry warfare.

Ogilvie, *Comm. Livy 1–5*, 576 ff.; *CAH* 7². 2. 289. A. D.

Postumus (*PLRE* 1. 720), **Marcus Cassianius Latinius,** *Gallienus' military commander on the Rhine from AD 259, quarrelled with the young prince, Saloninus, and his civilian advisers during the barbarian attacks following the capture of *Valerian (260). He seized power and established himself as Roman emperor in Gaul, Britain and Spain. He defended his 'Gallic empire' against both Germanic invaders and Gallienus (265), but was killed by his own troops after defeating the rebel Laelianus (269).

Postumus' strength and weakness was his determination not to march on Rome. This enabled him to defend the west, but strained the loyalty of his army and allowed no 'legitimate' emperor to trust him entirely.

I. König, *Die gallischen Usurpatoren* (1981); J. F. Drinkwater, *The Gallic Empire* (1987). J. F. Dr.

Potamon (1) of Mytilene (*c.*75 BC–AD 15), orator and rhetorician, undertook embassies on behalf of his city to *Caesar at Rome (47, 45) and *Augustus (26). He wrote encomia of *Brutus and Caesar, a history of *Alexander (3) the Great and *On the Perfect Orator.*

FGrH 147; *PIR* 3 (1898), P675; Sen. *Suas.* 2. 15. M. B. T.

Potamon (2) of *Alexandria (1), of the time of *Augustus; the only ancient philosopher to describe himself as an 'eclectic' (see ECLECTICISM). *Diogenes (6) Laertius (*Proem.* 21) describes him as founding a school, but whether he had followers is doubtful. He seems to have attempted to combine Platonic (see PLATO (1)), *Peripatetic, and Stoic doctrines (see STOICISM).

J. Dillon, *Middle Platonists*, 138, 147. J. M. D.

Potentia (*Potenza*), in S. Italy, 6th-cent. BC Lucanian city (see LUCANIA) in the Basento valley. The earliest settlement was at Serra di Vaglio, notable for its urban expansion and hellenization (see HELLENISM, HELLENIZATION) in the 4th cent. Around 200 BC, this was abandoned in favour of Potentia, 8 km. (5 mi.) northeast. Inscriptions indicate a flourishing *municipium, but there is little archaeological evidence. K. L.

Potidaea, a Corinthian colony (see CORINTH; COLONIZATION, GREEK), founded *c.*600 BC for trade with *Macedonia and along the line of the later *via Egnatia. It struck coins from *c.*550 BC. A strongly fortified port, it withstood a siege by Artabazus (480–479). It joined the *Delian League; but its connection with Corinth, which supplied its annual chief magistrate, rendered it suspect to Athens. After an increase of its tribute to fifteen talents (434 BC) it revolted (432), but although it received help from *Peloponnesus it was reduced in 430. Athenian cleruchs (see CLERUCHY) occupied the site until 404, when it passed to the

Chalcidians (see OLYNTHUS). It was recovered by Athens in 363 and received another cleruchy in 361; but in 356 it fell into the hands of *Philip (1) II of Macedon. It was perhaps destroyed in the Olynthian War (348); but it was refounded by *Cassander under the name of Cassandreia (*c.*316).

J. A. Alexander, *Potidaea* (1963); G. E. M. de Ste. Croix, *OPW* 79 ff.; E. Badian, *From Plataea to Potidaea* (1993), ch. 4. N. G. L. H.

potsherds See OSTRACA; OSTRACISM.

pottery, Greek

1. General Pottery is a primary source of evidence throughout the Greek period. Pervasive and almost indestructible, its generally predictable development means that it provides a framework to which other arts can be related. The presence of clay in every region fostered local styles, whence trade patterns can be detected. Factors determining origin are clay, shape, and decoration, the latter varying from none (most cookpots, coarsewares, storage amphoras) to the elaborate mythological scenes exemplified by Archaic and Classical Athenian vases (see IMAGERY). Recent advances in clay analysis have further refined provenance studies (see POTTERY, SCIENTIFIC ANALYSIS OF). Regular inscriptions give names of potters and painters and clues to workshop organization (see POTTERY (GREEK), INSCRIPTIONS ON) as do excavations like those in the Athenian Agora, the area of *Plato (1)'s *Academy, the Potters' Quarter at Corinth, or Figaretto on *Corcyra. Sir John Beazley (1885–1970) adopted Renaissance attribution methods to reconstruct the careers of many Archaic and Classical Athenian vase-painters, and to gauge master–pupil relations and workshop patterns. The method has been criticized as unduly subjective, but has been extensively applied to Etruscan, S. Italian, Laconian, and Corinthian pottery (D. A. Amyx, *Corinthian Vase-Painting of the Archaic Period* (1988)). Recent trends have moved from attributions towards the social significance of pottery, with renewed interest in factors influencing shapes, imagery and composition, especially wall-painting (see PAINTING, GREEK). Thus metalwork has been seen as a complete model for Classical vase shapes and decoration, although surviving examples do not permit this conclusion and literary sources are late. The *Corpus Vasorum Antiquorum* (CVA) continues publishing vase collections worldwide. Recent advances in computing have facilitated access to extensive archives of Athenian (Oxford) and Corinthian (Amsterdam) vases; computers are now being used for profile and even figure-drawing.

2. Prehistoric During the neolithic period, handmade burnished wares were characteristic over a wide area (e.g. *Cnossus, Saliagos, *Thessaly). The surface is sometimes blackened or reddened and may have relief, incised or impressed decoration (sometimes with white or red paste fill); ripple (MN) and pattern (LN) burnish are especially popular on *Crete. On the mainland, painted (abstract linear) designs occur from an early stage; notable are the MN Sesklo (dark-on-light) and LN Dimini (light on dark and bichrome) wares.

In the early bronze age, dark-on-light painted wares with simple geometric designs dominate. On Crete, Ag. Onouphrios and Pyrgos wares (the latter with pattern burnish) were followed by the mottled Vasiliki ware. In the *Cyclades, the Pelos phase (incised ornament) was followed by Syros (stamped and incised) with its characteristic sauceboats and frying pans. Mainland styles were dominated by burnished wares (initially similar to Cycladic). During the middle bronze age (when the fast wheel came into use), matt-painted wares were popular on the Cyclades and the mainland, and dark-on-light was fashionable on Crete. Influences of metalwork are widespread (eg. in mainland grey Minyan ware). During the late bronze age, dark-on-light returned, initially with a naturalistic, Minoan-influenced style (mainly floral and marine subjects), followed by more standard linear decoration uniform over a wide area. Hand-made burnished ware appeared during late LHIIIB, and there was a brief vogue during middle LHIIIC for the elaborate Close, Granary, and Pictorial styles. Thereafter Submycenaean wares were more austerely Geometric (P. A. Mountjoy, *Mycenaean Pottery* (1993)).

3. *Historic* After the austere geometry of Submycenaean, the Protogeometric and Geometric periods (1050–700 BC) saw the addition of new shapes and motifs (notably the meander). From restricted beginnings, decoration came to cover the whole vase in horizontal bands. This period is characterized by local schools, notably Argive and Attic; here the 8th cent. saw the development of figure scenes, including funerary subjects (prothesis and ekphora), chariot processions and battles. From the 8th cent. onwards, it is possible to identify 'hands' such as the Dipylon Master (J. N. Coldstream, *Greek Geometric Pottery* (1968)).

From the late-8th cent. the Geometric style developed into *Orientalizing, with the addition of motifs including florals and animals (real and fantastic) which replaced Geometric patterns. Although silhouette continued, the black-figure technique (invented in Corinth c.720) was most innovative; here lines are incised into a silhouette, with the addition of red and white. The human figure was drawn with increasing naturalism, and mythological representations become complex. The chief 7th-cent. fabrics are Proto-Corinthian and Proto-Attic; contemporary is the peak of the island and East Greek schools (A. Lemos, *Archaic Pottery of Chios* (1991)). A mid-7th-cent. series of vases of various schools may reflect contemporary free-painting, using such elements as a brown paint for flesh and mass battle scenes (e.g. works of the Corinthian Chigi (MacMillan) Painter).

By 600, black-figure was fully established in Attica (J. D. Beazley, *The Development of Attic Black Figure* (1951/1986); J. Boardman, *Athenian Black-Figure Vases* (1974)), and by soon after 550 Corinth, Athens' main rival, had effectively ceased producing figured wares, continuing with the patterned 'conventionalizing' style. Athenian potters produced a wider range of vases, introducing such shapes as the volute- and kalyx-krater, and a range of cups, such as the Siana, lip, band, and types A and B, which are among the finest of Attic potting. Notable among painters are Sophilus, the first whose name we know (c.580–570), Nearchus (c.570–555) and his son Tleson, and the rivals Execias and the Amasis Painter (c.560–525). The regular practice of inscribing vases is of inestimable value: the words *epoiesen* and *egrapsen* probably name the potter and painter, although it is possible that the former indicates the workshop owner, often the head of an extended family.

Around 525, the red-figure technique was invented at Athens, possibly by Psiax or the Andocides Painter (perhaps the same man as the black-figure Lysippides Painter) (M. Robertson, *The Art of Vase-Painting in Classical Athens* (1992); J. Boardman, *Athenian Red-Figured Vases: the Archaic Period* (1978), *Athenian Red-Figured Vases: the Classical Period* (1989)). Other innovations of this period include Six's technique, coral or intentional red, and white ground. In red-figure the decoration is left in the clay colour, and the background painted black; inner details are painted with lines of varying thickness. The use of the brush rather than the engraver allowed greater fluidity of drawing. Accessory colours are used sparingly in the 6th cent., white becoming common towards its end. The first generation trained in red-figure (c.520–500) Beazley called the Pioneers (e.g. Euphronius, Phintias, Euthymides); they are characterized by adventurous anatomical depictions. Late Archaic vase-painting saw further advances by, for example, the Berlin and Cleophrades Painters (who preferred large vases), and the cup specialists Duris and the Brygus Painter. Black-figure continued in quantity until the end of the Archaic period and, for Panathenaic prize amphorae, until the 2nd cent. BC.

In the early Classical period, some vases of the Niobid Painter and others reflect the free painting recorded in literary sources as current in Athens and elsewhere in the works of such artists as *Polygnotus and *Micon (c.475–450). The later 5th cent. saw the ornate miniaturism of the Meidias Painter (L. Burn, *The Meidias Painter* (1987)) and others, often featuring boudoir scenes. There is a parallel, broader tradition exemplified by the Dinos Painter. White ground, at first mainly on cups, is used in the later 5th cent. for funerary lekythoi, often painted with delicate colours (D. C. Kurtz, *Athenian White Lekythoi* (1975); L. Wehgartner, *Attische Weissgrundige Keramik* (1983)).

4th-cent. vases are characterized by greater use of accessory colours and gilding; red-figure ceased by c.320 but although much late work is poor, artists such as the Marsyas and Eleusinian Painters (c.350–330) gave unprecedented depth to their figures. In the late-4th cent., fineware production was restricted to cheap clay substitutes for the costly metal vessels which suited Hellenistic taste. Painted decoration was limited to floral scrolls and patterns: both light-on-dark and dark-on-light styles are found, but painted wares are secondary to the new metallic styles in which relief ornament predominates. Moulded reliefs may be added to wheelmade vases or vases may be thrown in a mould (e.g. the particularly widespread Megarian bowls). During the 3rd cent., the black ground colour inherited from Athens was modified in E. Greece into red or bronze, and thence developed *terra sigillata, the standardized fine pottery of Roman times.

In Italy, painted wares imitating the contemporary Greek styles appeared from the 8th cent. BC, and by 525 native pottery was largely displaced by Greek (mainly Attic) imports and local copies. Independent schools of pottery in Apulia borrowed painted techniques from Greece, but remained local in style. Red figure production began in S. Italy about 440, perhaps introduced by immigrant Athenian potters. There are five main schools: Apulian, Lucanian, Paestan, Campanian, and Sicilian (A. D. Trendall, *Red Figure Vases of South Italy and Sicily* (1989)). A considerable output of vases, often large and elaborately decorated, continued into the early 3rd cent. Their inspiration was initially Athenian, but they increasingly diverged; their iconography owes much to the theatre, especially the 'phlyax' vases (A. D. Trendall and T. B. L. Webster, *Illustrations of Greek Drama* (1971); O. P. Taplin, *Comic Angels* (1993); see PHLYAKES). In Gnathian (mid-4th to early 3rd cent.), the pot is painted black and decoration added.

In Hellenistic times, Apulia and Campania were the chief areas of production. Light-on-dark painted ware and vases with applied reliefs were most popular. *Alexandria (1) was the principal source of inspiration, and Italy was long uninfluenced by E. Greek experiments in red glazes and moulded wares; after 30 BC, however, it took the lead with the appearance of Arretine ware. See AMPHORAE.

R. M. Cook, *Greek Painted Pottery* (1972); B. A. Sparkes, *Greek Pottery*

(1991); J. Y. Noble, *The Techniques of Painted Attic Pottery* (1965/1988).

K. W. A., C. A. M.

pottery (Greek), inscriptions on Inscriptions can be painted on pots (*dipinti*), before or after firing, or incised (*graffiti*), normally after firing. Post-firing dipinti consist mainly of notations of a broadly commercial character on plain *amphorae. The bulk of written material from many parts of the Greek world earlier than *c*.400 BC, and especially in the first generations of writing, before *c*.650, consists of texts on pots. Most are informally inscribed, though pre-firing dipinti can be used to aesthetic effect on decorated ware, and some graffito dedications (notably on Panathenaic amphorae; see PANATHENAEA) are in full 'lapidary' style. Vase inscriptions are a prime source of evidence for e.g. the identification of painted figures, names of potters and painters, distributors of pottery and its cost, aspects of local scripts, variations of *dialect and spelling, identity of cults (see OSTRACA). Painted inscriptions are most commonly labels for figures, commencing as near the head as possible; sometimes words uttered by the figures appear. Signatures of potters and painters are first attested soon after 700 BC, become common on Attic vases of *c*.525–475, but thin out over the following century. We also find the names of favoured youths (rarely girls) with the epithet *kalos*, 'beautiful'; these are of chronological, historical and social interest. Graffiti cover an enormous range; owner's marks and dedications, often abbreviated, are frequent; alphabets, shopping-lists and messages can be exciting, but are much rarer. See also EPIGRAPHY, GREEK; OSTRACA; POTTERY, GREEK.

M. L. Lang, *The Athenian Agora*, 11, *Graffiti and Dipinti* (1976); H. R. Immerwahr, *Attic Script: A Survey* (1990); Jeffery, *LSAG*; A. W. Johnston, *Trademarks on Greek Vases* (1980); F. Lorber, *Inschriften korinthischer Vasen* (1979); D. M. Robinson and E. J. Fluck, *Greek Love Names* (1937).

A. W. J.

pottery, Roman Roman pottery was used for a wider range of purposes than in most periods of prehistory or the Middle Ages, providing a comprehensive range of vessels for table and kitchen functions, and for use in storage and transportation. At the top of the quality scale were vessels with a smooth glossy surface designed for the table, notably the bright red *terra sigillata*, or Samian ware, mass-produced in Italy (Arretine ware) and elsewhere from the 1st cent. BC. Elaborately decorated cups and beakers with coloured surface coatings were used alongside this dinner service, while ornate pottery oil *lamps provided light. The majority of Roman pots were plain earthenware vessels designed for everyday household cooking and storage functions. The only really specialized forms were *amphorae, used for transporting wine and oil, globular *dolia*, employed on farms for storage and fermentation, and *mortaria*, large bowls suitable for grinding and mixing. Many Roman buildings were constructed (wholly or partly) from bricks and roofed with ceramic tiles, while specialized clay elements aided the construction of bath-buildings and vaulted ceilings (see BUILDING MATERIALS).

The study of pottery is an essential part of the investigation of sites by excavation, and an important part of Roman 'industrial archaeology'. It reveals details of technology and methods of manufacture, and the analysis of patterns of production and distribution illuminates aspects of society and the economy. Pottery production ranged from a part-time activity that supplemented farming to full-time employment for specialized craft workers. Most vessels were formed on a potter's wheel and fired in carefully constructed kilns, although some widely distributed kitchen wares were handmade and fired in bonfires. Some industries made ranges of forms, others concentrated on particular categories. Most Roman pottery seems to have been traded, rather than manufactured, for the exclusive consumption of individual households or estates. Distribution patterns of wares varied enormously; Italian *terra sigillata* could be found throughout the empire, whereas unspecialized kitchen wares might only supply a single town and its surrounding region.

Rome conquered areas of Italy that already possessed well-established ceramic traditions—Celtic in the north, Etruscan in central Italy and Greek in the south. In areas north of the Alps, the term 'Roman' may indicate new forms and wares introduced by trade or conquest, in contrast to 'native' pottery of local origin, but the term is best used in its broadest sense, simply to mean pottery of Roman date. The kitchen and storage vessels made in most conquered areas were not markedly different from those of Italy, and they were normally adopted by the invaders once permanent garrison forts had been established. Studies of kiln sites show that some specialized vessel forms, such as flagons, were rapidly added to the repertoire of local potters. However, name-stamps on *terra sigillata*, lamps and *mortaria* all confirm that some manufacturers either migrated to new provinces or set up branch workshops, presumably to avoid high transport costs involved in supplying distant markets. We are particularly well informed about the diffusion of *terra sigillata* production from Italy to the provinces, for styles of decoration and name-stamps, combined with typological studies of the evolution of plain vessels, allow us to identify production centres that may then be corroborated by scientific analysis of clays; see next entry.

Roman military units included skilled artisans who frequently established facilities for the manufacture of bricks and rooftiles, commonly stamped the name of their unit or legion. If local pottery supplies were inadequate (e.g. in northern parts of the Rhineland or in northern Britain and Wales) they also turned their hands to potting. Since many soldiers had been recruited in Italy or heavily Romanized provinces, the majority of vessel forms made by military potters are closely comparable to those found in Italy itself, with the addition of some forms that reveal Celtic or other regional influence. Military production tended to be short-lived, for when frontier areas were stabilized, supplies could be brought safely from non-military sources in the hinterland. Alternatively, civilian potters might set up production in a military region in order to take advantage of new markets created by forts and the civilian settlements (*canabae*) which grew up around them.

From the end of the 1st cent. AD, sites around the Mediterranean were increasingly supplied with Red Slip Ware from North Africa and Asia Minor rather than *terra sigillata* made in Europe. Although sharing common origins, these wares diverged after the 1st cent. AD. In general, recognizably 'Roman' forms and wares still dominated ceramics used around the Mediterranean as late as the 7th cent. AD.

D. P. S. Peacock, *Pottery in the Roman World: An Ethnoarchaeological Approach* (1982); K. Greene, *Interpreting the Past: Roman Pottery* (1992).

K. T. G.

pottery, scientific analysis of Petrographical and chemical analysis are the two main ways to characterize pottery. The former treats the pottery as a geological sediment which has been used for a particular purpose. Thus by scanning thin sections of pottery under a polarizing microscope, mineral inclusions can be visually identified; this allows a parallel to be drawn with other

poverty

ceramic material, which may lead in turn to an identification of the clay source. This technique is particularly useful for coarse wares such as transport *amphorae. However in the case of fine pottery where inclusions have been removed, the clay can be treated as a bulk material. The sample can be studied by three main means: neutron activation analysis, optical emission spectroscopy, and atomic absorption spectrophotometry. In addition to the three main elements within clay (silicon, aluminium, and oxygen), an analysis will seek to determine the percentage of other elements in the composition: iron, calcium, magnesium, potassium, sodium, and titanium. These proportions can then be plotted and the results compared with other tests from pottery or indeed from clay sources.

One of the main uses for these analyses has been in provenance studies. This is particularly important for the bronze age in determining which items are imported or made locally, and this in turn allows an archaeological site to be placed within a regional setting. For example some late Minoan IB marine-style pottery found outside Crete was shown not to be consistent with Cretan compositions; however the clay beds, and therefore the place of production, have yet to be identified. Some plastically moulded Archaic terracottas from the E. Greek world seem to have clay which is consistent with pottery known to have been made at Miletus.

R. E. Jones, *Greek and Cypriot Pottery: A Review of Scientific Studies* (1986).
D. W. J. G.

poverty See CYNICS; DIOGENES (2); PENIA; WEALTH, ATTITUDES TO.

praefectura was the term for an assize-centre in Roman territory. When, for example, *Capua became a *municipium, praefecti (see praefectus) delegated by the *praetor urbanus were sent there from time to time, to perform jurisdiction and perhaps to promote the assimilation of Roman law by the Capuans, who were now citizens without the vote (cives sine suffragio). The praefecti are found later on a regular basis in other municipia and towns and in agrarian centres (fora and conciliabula) in the areas of full-citizens (e.g. CIL 1². 583. 31). They did not replace but assisted the local authorities of municipia; in small centres of Roman citizens they were sometimes the only judicial authority, while in *Campania, after the abolition of autonomy following the revolt of 215–211 BC, a special set of praefecti, elected at Rome, was instituted to take sole charge of local jurisdiction. After the *Social War (3) the old praefecturae in Italy were assimilated to municipia, but this seems to have been a gradual process, since we find the term praefectura in the texts of the Table of *Heraclea (1) (see LEX (2) for the Tabula Heracleensis) and the lex Iulia agraria (lex Mamilia Roscia). Praefecturae also continued to be areas of jurisdiction in Cisalpine Gaul at least until the triumviral period to judge from the Ateste fragment (see under LEX (2))) and the lex Rubria.
A. N. S.-W.; A. W. L.

praefectus means 'placed in charge' and describes a great variety of men set in authority—officers in the army and navy, major imperial officials, judicial officers delegated by the praetor (see PRAEFECTURA) and deputies for local magistrates.

Before the *Social War (3) each wing (ala) of allied cavalry had six praefecti, three of whom were Roman officers. In *Caesar's time cavalry continued to be commanded by praefecti, while the praefectus fabrum (chief of engineers), e.g. Caesar's officer *Mamurra, became an aide-de-camp to the commander. Under the Principate units of allied troops (*auxilia), both wings of cavalry and cohorts of infantry, were commanded by praefecti,

who were of equestrian rank (see EQUITES). The administrative post of legionary camp commandant, praefectus castrorum, was from *Claudius' reign onwards regularly held by an ex-centurion who had reached the rank of primus pilus (see PRIMIPILUS) but was unlikely to have further promotion. Praefecti also held extraordinary appointments, e.g. praefectus orae maritimae, praefectus levis armaturae (prefects with coastal duties, command of light-armed troops).

Some of the major appointments were also military: praefecti commanded the praetorian guard (see PRAEFECTUS PRAETORIO), the *vigiles and the imperial fleets of *Ravenna and *Misenum (see NAVIES), while the urban cohorts were under the *praefectus urbi, a senator of consular rank. In the early Principate some governors of (mainly minor) imperial provinces were called praefecti (this was the correct title of Pontius Pilate (*Pontius Pilatus) in Judaea) and this remained the title of the equestrian governor of Egypt. The legions in Egypt were commanded by equestrian praefecti instead of the normal senatorial legati; *Septimius Severus followed this precedent when he raised Legiones Parthicae I–III (see LEGION) and it was extended by *Gallienus. In the late empire praefecti were commanders in the *limitanei of legions and detachments of legions, alae, numeri, and fleets.

J. Suolahti, *The Junior Officers of the Roman Army in the Republican Period* (1955); L. Keppie, *The Making of the Roman Army* (1984); J. B. Campbell, *The Emperor and the Roman Army 31 BC–AD 235* (1984); D. Saddington, *The Development of the Roman Auxiliary Forces from Caesar to Vespasian 49 BC to AD 79* (1982); A. N. Sherwin-White, *PBSR* 1939.
H. M. D. P.; G. R. W.; A. W. L.

praefectus praetorio *Augustus first appointed praetorian prefects (see praefectus) to command the *praetorians in 2 BC; there were usually two, of equestrian rank (see EQUITES, Imperial period). He recognized the potential importance of the prefecture, since it controlled the only significant military force in Rome. Prefects were selected personally by the emperor more for reliability than any specialist expertise, and their status and power increased because they had the ear of the emperor, who tended to confide in them and delegate some of his increasing administrative burden. The prefect was the only official permitted to bear a sword in the emperor's presence. The personal influence gained by several prefects enhanced the role of the prefecture itself, e.g. L. *Aelius Seianus, who also persuaded *Tiberius to concentrate the guard in one camp in Rome and became sole prefect (there were several further instances of this), Sextus *Afranius Burrus, *Ofonius Tigellinus, C. *Fulvius Plautianus. By AD 70, prefects were usually granted consular ornaments (see ORNAMENTA), and the prefecture had become the most important equestrian post, the climax of a career which had often begun with the equestrian military offices or even a chief centurionate (e.g. *Bassaeus Rufus—ILS 1326). Prefects were frequently to become involved in political intrigues, and many met violent deaths, though *Macrinus was the first to make himself emperor (217).

As regular members of the emperor's advisory council (*consilium principis), they helped to formulate imperial policy; they also had significant military responsibilities, since one prefect usually travelled with the emperor on campaign, sometimes even commanding an army in the field. Gradually they also acquired judicial functions (perhaps arising from their police powers in Rome), and by the late second century exercised independent jurisdiction in Italy (CIL 9. 2438); *Septimius Severus confirmed their jurisdiction in Italy beyond the hundredth milestone from Rome (within was the responsibility of the prefect of the city; see next entry).

With the growth of the system of requisition in kind during the 3rd cent. AD and the extensive administrative reforms of *Diocletian and his successors, the duties of the praetorian prefects underwent further progressive change. Though under Diocletian and *Constantine I praetorian prefects are still occasionally found in military functions, their regular responsibilities were increasingly concentrated upon civil, and especially financial, administration, and the prefects themselves were normally promoted from the civil branches of the imperial service. They were still formally attached to the persons of Augusti and Caesars (under Constantine there were at one point no fewer than five prefects), but as the responsibilities of the members of the imperial college became more regionalized, so too the praetorian prefects were increasingly associated with specific areas, which eventually emerged as the territorial prefectures of the Gauls (including Britain and Spain), Italy (with Africa and usually Illyricum), and the east. In the 4th cent. the office was one of the few imperial administrations in which members of the senatorial aristocracy showed consistent interest, and in the 5th cent. the praetorian prefectures of Gaul and of Italy were the vehicle by which the upper classes of these areas maintained their influence over the residual imperial administration.

M. Durry, *Les Cohortes prétoriennes* (1938; reissued 1968); A. Passerini, *Le coorti pretorie* (1939); L. L. Howe, *The Praetorian Prefect from Commodus to Diocletian* (1942); F. Millar, *The Emperor in the Roman World* (1977), 122; Jones, *Later Rom. Emp.* 13. 448–62. J. B. C., J. F. Ma.

praefectus urbi 'Prefect of the City' (of Rome), an office which antedated the Roman republic and outlasted the western empire. (1) The temporary deputy of the absent king or consuls, not often needed after the institution of praetors, except once a year when all regular magistrates attended the Latin festival on the Alban Mount, and so after the institution of (2) known as *praefectus urbi feriarum Latinarum*. The prefect had *imperium at Rome, and in early times when he had real responsibility he was usually an ex-consul; later, men at the beginning of their public career were chosen.

(2) A magistrate instituted by *Augustus to be the emperor's deputy at Rome. After a false start with M. *Valerius Messalla Corvinus *c.*25 BC, the regular series seems to have begun with L. *Calpurnius Piso (2) in AD 13 (Tac. *Ann.* 6. 11). The prefect was always a senator (see SENATE), usually a senior ex-consul, and served for a number of years. He was nominally an independent magistrate, with the duty of keeping order in the city, and for this purpose had *imperium* and the command of the urban cohorts (see COHORTES URBANAE). He also presided in his own court of justice, which by the 3rd cent. had practically superseded those of the regular magistrates; it heard cases both from Rome and outside, within a radius (from *c.*200) of 100 miles. By the 4th cent. the prefect also presided over the senate and supervised, but did not appoint, the officials responsible for the city's food supply and public works. He was still responsible for public order, even though the urban cohorts had been disbanded by *Constantine I. The prefecture was now regarded as the crown of a senatorial career, and was held on average for about a year; most prefects were senators by birth, and did not necessarily achieve the consulship. The *Theodosian Code and the correspondence of *Symmachus (2) as prefect (in 384) give a detailed picture of the prefect's duties, which are much the same as those summarized by *Cassiodorus (*Var.* 6. 4). In 359 a separate prefect was instituted for *Constantinople.

E. Sachers, *RE* 22 (1954), 2502–34; T. J. Cadoux, *JRS* 1959, 152–60; A. Chastagnol, *La Préfecture urbaine à Rome sous le bas Empire* (1960), and *Les Fastes de la préfecture de Rome au bas Empire* (1962); R. H. Barrow, *Prefect and Emperor* (1973). T. J. C.; R. S. O. T.

Praeneste (mod. Palestrina), with interesting polygonal walls, occupied a cool, lofty spur of the *Apennines 37 km. (23 mi.) east-south-east of Rome. Traditionally founded in the mythical period (Verg. *Aen.* 7. 678), the oldest finds belong to the recent bronze age. Immensely rich burials of *Etruscan type and 7th-cent. date show it to be the pre-eminent city in this region at that time. It first appears in history in the 5th cent. BC as a powerful Latin city (see LATINI) whose strategic site facing the Alban Hills was inevitably attacked by *Aequi. In the 4th cent. it frequently fought Rome and, after participating in the Latin War, was deprived of territory and became a *civitas foederata* which still possessed *ius exilii* 200 years later (Polyb. 6. 14) and apparently preferred its own to Roman citizenship (Livy 23. 19 f.; see CITIZENSHIP, ROMAN). After 90 BC Praeneste became a Roman *municipium* devoted to C. *Marius (1)'s cause, which *Sulla sacked (82), transferred to lower ground, and colonized with veterans. It remained a *colonia* in imperial times, famed chiefly as a fashionable *villa resort and seat of the ancient and oracular *sortes Praenestinae* which Roman emperors, foreign potentates, and others consulted in the huge temple of *Fortuna Primigenia, perhaps Italy's largest sanctuary (Polyb. 6. 11). Its impressive remains probably belong to the second half of the 2nd cent. BC, and it was still venerated in the 4th cent. AD: sweeping ramps carry the edifice up the hillside in a series of terraces.

Praeneste has yielded a very early specimen of Latin, the Manios brooch (second half of 7th cent. BC), whose peculiarities (if it is genuine) confirm *Pompeius Festus' statement (157, 488 Lindsay) that Praenestine Latin was abnormal (but see EPIGRAPHY, LATIN, § (4), and A. E. Gordon, *Introduction to Latin Epigraphy* (1983), 76); it is also known for a spectacular marine mosaic (cf. Plin. *HN* 36. 25), and *Verrius Flaccus' calendar. Flaccus probably, and the Greek writer *Aelian certainly, were natives of Praeneste. The Anicii (see ANICIA IULIANA; ANICIUS FAUSTUS, Q.; BOETHIUS), originally African, were also prominent Praenestines.

Strabo 5. 238; Livy 2. 19; 3. 8; 6. 21, 26 f.; 8. 12 f.; 23. 10 f.; Diod. 16. 45; App. *BCiv.* 1. 65. 94; Cic. *Div.* 2. 41. F. Fasolo and G. Gullini, *Il Santuario della Fortuna Primigenia a Palestrina* (1953); P. Romanelli, *Palestrina* (1967); L. Quilici, *Mondo archeologico* 1980, 21 ff; F. Coarelli, *I santuari del Lazio in età repubblicana* (1987); *Urbanistica ed architettura dell'antico Praeneste* (Atti del Convegno 1988). E. T. S.; T. W. P.

praenomen See NAMES, PERSONAL, ROMAN.

praerogativa was the *centuria in the *comitia centuriata* of the Roman people which had the right of voting first. In early times the eighteen *centuriae* of the knights voted first *en bloc*; but not later than 215 BC the right was conferred upon one of the seventy *centuriae* of the first class chosen on each occasion by lot. Even after the introduction of the ballot (see ELECTIONS AND VOTING) the decision of the *centuria praerogativa* was made known before the rest of the assembly recorded its vote. According to Cicero its influence upon the final outcome of the voting was very considerable. The ten centuries created by the *lex Valeria Cornelia* of AD 5 are best interpreted as *praerogativae* (see TABULA HEBANA).

Mommsen, *Röm. Staatsr.* 3³. 290 ff., 398; Taylor, *RVA* 91–6. E. S. S.; B. M. L.

praetexta See FABULA.

Praetextatus, Vettius Agorius (*c.* AD 320–84), pagan senator,

1239

praetor

a resolute opponent of Christianity and friend of *Symmachus (2), who held many high state offices and various priesthoods, both in the traditional public cults and in the so-called 'oriental' cults such as *Isis, Magna Mater (see CYBELE), and *Mithras. His joint epitaph with his wife Aconia Fabia Paulina, in which husband and wife address one another (CIL 6. 1779 = Dessau 1259; Carm. epigr. 111), shows how a synthesis of pagan cults was attempted in face of the common enemy *Christianity; Praetextatus is said to have saved his wife from the fate of death by her initiations into the mysteries. Like other anti-Christians, Praetextatus was attached both to philosophy (cf. Macrob. Sat. 1. 24. 21) and to the ancient writers, 'by whom the gates of heaven are opened'. He produced a Latin version of *Themistius' adaptation of *Aristotle's Analytics, and his work in translating Greek prose and poetic works into Latin and in revising their texts is also mentioned on his epitaph. He also used his public offices to promote the interests of his religion. Having held both the prefecture of Rome (367–8) and the praetorian prefecture of Italy (384), Praetextatus died as consul designate for 385. It is debated whether he rather than Nicomachus Flavianus is the subject of the anonymous Carmen contra Paganos (Cod. Par. 8084; Riese, Anth. Lat. 1. 1. 4. 20 ff.).

PLRE 1. 722–4, 'Praetextatus 1'; T. W. J. Nicolaas, Praetextatus (Dutch diss., 1940); P. Lambrechts, Op de Grens van Heidentum en Christendom. Het Grafschrift van Vettius A. P. en Fabia Aconia Paulina (1955); H. Bloch, in A. Momigliano (ed.), The Conflict between Paganism and Christianity in the 4th Century (1963), ch. 8; A. Chastagnol, Les Fastes de la Préfecture de Rome au Bas-Empire (1962), 171–8; J. F. Matthews, JRS 1973, 175 ff.
J. F. Ma.

praetor

Republic 'Praetor' (from prae-ire, 'to precede', i.e. in battle) was originally the title borne by the two republican magistrates who were chosen annually to serve as eponymous heads of state. In 367 BC the Romans, as part of the Licinian-Sextian compromise (see LICINIUS STOLO, C.) decided to add a patrician 'praetor' as third colleague to these two chief magistrates, who were now (or were soon to be) called '*consuls'. The new praetor held *imperium, which was defined as being of the same nature as the consuls' but minus, 'lesser', in relation to theirs. As a magistrate with this type of imperium, the praetor could perform almost all the activities of the consul, both in Rome and in the field, unless a consul stopped him; however, a praetor could not interfere with the consuls. Livy's statement (6. 42. 11) that the praetor was created specifically to hear cases of law at Rome may simply reflect an annalist's guess, based on the most familiar aspect of the urban praetor in later times. The administration of law was merely one of the praetor's areas of competence, which came with the grant of imperium. The praetor was, in the (quite common) absence of the consuls from the city, the chief magistrate in Rome and, as such, in charge of the legal system, as well as acting president of the senate and legislative *comitia; but he also had the right to lead an army, and indeed that is the capacity in which we mostly find him in Livy books 7–10. Plebeians (see PLEBS) were first admitted to the office in 337.

The acceptance (first in 327) of extension of imperium beyond the year of the magistracy ('prorogation'), allowed the Romans, despite ever-increasing military commitments, to retain the system of two consuls and a sole praetor down to almost the end of the First *Punic War. Around 244 there was an increase from one to two praetors, now designated as urbanus and inter peregrinos ('over foreigners')—the latter perhaps originally a military

commander, rather than a legal magistrate who heard cases involving non-citizens as some late sources (anachronistically) have it. The Romans doubled the number of praetors to four c.228 to provide regular commanders for *Sicily and *Sardinia, and in 198 created another two (with enhanced, i.e. consular, imperium) to serve in the Spanish provinces (see SPAIN). These additions made possible the transformation of the peregrine praetorship into a (mainly) city jurisdiction; they also led to an eventual insistence on the praetorship as a prerequisite for the consulship (c.197).

In 146, when *Macedonia and Africa (see AFRICA, ROMAN) were organized as praetorian provinces, the senate decided to keep the number of praetors at six, probably to control competition for the consulship. This decision made it impossible for all the provinces to be governed by regular magistrates in their year of office; routine prorogation of overseas commanders had to become actual policy. The Romans soon exploited what was, in effect, a new system of provincial government. In 126 came the annexation of Asia as a praetorian province, and in 123, C. *Sempronius Gracchus introduced a praetor's court at Rome to try cases of provincial extortion. Additional standing courts on the Gracchan model were established between 123 and 91 (see QUAESTIONES), while more territorial provinces were instituted— with no increase in praetors. By the 90s, even the city praetors (i.e. urban, peregrine and those in charge of a permanent court) had to be regularly prorogued, so that they could proceed to overseas provinces.

In 81 as dictator *Sulla raised the number of praetors to eight. He also institutionalized some earlier developments in a scheme aimed at ensuring regular annual succession, in which all praetors were restricted to Rome to tend to the city jurisdictions and the various courts, and were sent (with consular imperium) to govern an overseas province only after their year of office. However, the introduction of new standing courts (in 65 and then again in 55) coupled with increased bribery and violence at the consular elections (a praetor now had only a one-in-four chance of reaching the consulship) contributed to the collapse of this system by the late 50s BC.

Mommsen, Röm. Staatsr. 2³. 1. 193–238; E. Badian, Gnomon, 1979, 792–4; J.-C. Richard, Rev. Phil. 1982, 19–31.
T. C. B.

Caesar and imperial period The number of praetors was increased by *Caesar to sixteen, as much to provide offices for partisans as to fulfil functions, although there were more posts in civil and criminal jurisdiction than could be filled by the praetors available in the late republic. Some praetors are found in military commands during their year of office in the period of the civil wars, but there is no clear evidence that this continued under *Augustus, who restricted the number of praetors at first to ten and then to twelve. Under the Principate the praetors retained their traditional republican functions at Rome—performing civil jurisdiction (for the consolidation of the edict of the urban praetor under Hadrian see EDICT), presiding over criminal courts, overseeing the games and occasionally presiding over the senate (e.g. Sex. Iulius *Frontinus in AD 70). Some of their juridical functions were partially taken over by the consuls, e.g. the provision of guardians from *Claudius' reign to that of Marcus *Aurelius'. Certain among them acquired specific new functions, such as the praetors of the treasury between 23 BC and AD 44 and the praetors in charge of fidei commissa. In general they retained a high profile through presiding over and financing major games and also because the office was still an important step in the *cursus honorum*, the first occasion when a man received *imperium* as a magistrate. This enabled a holder to go on to be governor of a public province or to be a legate of a legion in an imperial province.

Mommsen, *Röm. Staatsr.* 2³. 1. 193 ff.   A. W. L.

praetorians The *cohors praetoria* was a small escort which accompanied an army commander in the republic, taking its name from his tent (**praetorium*). During the civil wars the military dynasts had kept large personal bodyguards, and in 27 BC *Augustus established a permanent force consisting of nine cohorts, each containing 500 (or possibly 1000) men, recruited mainly from Italy and Romanized provinces. The praetorians had superior service conditions, receiving more than three times legionary pay and serving for 16 years, which marked them out as élite troops. Three cohorts, armed but in undress uniform, were stationed in Rome; the rest were dispersed among neighbouring towns, perhaps to ameliorate the politically sensitive idea of troops in the capital. In 2 BC Augustus appointed two prefects (see PRAEFECTUS PRAETORIO) to take overall charge, although he retained personal command, and the name of the reigning emperor, not the praetorian prefect, always appeared on *diplomas granting privileges to the praetorians.

In AD 23 L. *Aelius Seianus, now sole prefect, persuaded *Tiberius to base the praetorians in one permanent camp in the eastern suburbs of Rome. This made the guard a more coherent corps which could be directly and speedily deployed in a crisis. Also in Tiberius' reign, the guard was probably increased to twelve cohorts (*AE* 1978. 286). Its role was to protect the emperor and members of the imperial family, suppress disturbances, and discourage plots. A detachment of the guard accompanied the emperor on campaign, although it had no special tactical role.

*Vitellius increased the guard to sixteen cohorts of 1,000 men by adding legionaries from his army of the Rhine. In *Domitian's reign the number of cohorts was set at ten, each comprising 1,000 men and commanded by a tribune, who had usually served as a legionary chief centurion and as tribune in the other city troops, the *vigiles* and urban cohorts (see COHORTES URBANAE). The praetorians were still largely Italian and were supported by a cavalry arm—the *equites singulares Augusti*.

Inevitably the praetorians were drawn into political intrigue as it became obvious that their support could be crucial for a new emperor. In 41 after the murder of *Gaius (1), *Claudius won them over with a huge donative, and thereafter every emperor at his accession granted a donative and, if in Rome, addressed the guard. *Commodus' indulgence subverted the praetorians' discipline and in 193 his successor, *Pertinax, was murdered by the guardsmen who then proceeded to offer their support to the highest bidder for the purple. When later in 193 *Septimius Severus seized power he disbanded the disgraced praetorians and replaced them with legionaries from the Danubian armies which had first supported him. But the guard retained its role until 312 when *Constantine I disbanded it after his defeat of *Maxentius.

Despite their special relationship with the emperor, the praetorians had no formal position of power, and lacked the political awareness to sustain the influence that circumstances sometimes gave them.

M. Durry, *Les Cohortes prétoriennes* (1938; reissued 1968); A. Passerini, *Le coorti pretorie* (1939); D. L. Kennedy, *Anc. Soc.* 1978, 275.   J. B. C.

praetorium denoted the tent of a Roman commander (Polyb. 6. 27; Caes. *BC* 1. 76), and also his council of senior officers (Livy

26. 15. 6). Probably the *via praetoria* and the *porta praetoria* of a military camp were originally the road and gate adjacent to the commander's tent (see CAMPS). From this, *praetorium* came to mean the headquarters of a provincial governor (Cic. *Verr.* 4. 65), and in permanent forts of the imperial period indicates the private dwelling of the commanding officer, located close to the headquarters building or *principia* (e.g. *RIB* 1685–6; 1912—'praetorium . . . and principia'). But the meaning of *praetorium* was diverse: a hostel for officials travelling along main roads (*CIL* 3. 6123); a large house or imperial palace (Suet. *Tib.* 39; Juv. 10. 161; D 50. 16. 198); the emperor's bodyguard—*diplomas refer to soldiers serving 'in praetorio meo' (*ILS* 1993).   J. B. C.

pragmatic history See POLYBIUS (1).

Prasutagus, client king of the *Iceni of East Anglia in *Britain, was renowned for his wealth (Tac. *Ann.* 14. 31). His death in AD 60 precipitated the rebellion of his wife *Boudicca, for the king's will dividing his property between his daughters and *Nero in the hope of preserving the kingdom was disregarded.   S. S. F.

Pratinas of Phlius, according to the *Suda* competed with *Aeschylus and *Choerilus (1) in the 70th *Olympiad (i. e. 499–496 BC), was the first to write satyr-plays, and exhibited fifty plays of which thirty-two were satyric. His son Aristias won second prize with a production of his father's plays in 467 BC. The main surviving fragment (Ath. 14. 617b) attacks the tendency of the pipe to dominate the song. Probably it is from a satyr-play, and parodies the dithyrambic style (see DITHYRAMB). But it is also possible that it is in fact an Attic dithyramb by another, otherwise unknown Pratinas of the late 5th cent. BC.

TrGF 4; Pickard-Cambridge–Webster, *Dithyramb*² 17–20, 65–8; P. H. J. Lloyd-Jones, *Cuadernos de la Fundación Pastor* 13 (1966), 11–33; R. Seaford, *Maia*, 1977–8, 81–94.   R. A. S. S.

Praxagoras of Cos (*RE* 1), a physician of the second half of the 4th cent. BC. He is known only through the testimony of others, but it seems likely that he was a teacher of the great anatomist *Herophilus of Chalcedon, and what little is known of him suggests that he was himself an anatomist of importance. *Galen rather grudgingly acknowledges this, at the same time attacking his view that the nerves originate in the heart. He made important observations about the connection of the brain and spinal cord, and drew a distinction (perhaps being the first to do so) between veins and arteries, and their functions. He argued that the venous vascular system carried blood around the body, the arterial, *pneuma*. Details are lacking, but blood was apparently a product of healthy digestion, and *pneuma* was derived from inspired air, supplemented possibly by certain gaseous by-products of digestion. *Pneuma* assumed a special status in Praxagoras' physiology, and was associated with the generation and communication of movement both in the arteries and the heart, and throughout the body. Praxagoras' complex physiological and pathological system ascribed the origins of most diseases to alterations in the state of *humours, brought about by imperfect digestion. The four humours were themselves divided into as many as eleven sub-categories on grounds of taste, colour, and other properties. Little is known of his therapeutic practice, but it seems to have reflected closely his theoretical concerns with redressing highly complex humoral imbalances by means of dietary regulation and purging.

TEXTS The ancient testimony is collected and discussed in F. Steckerl, *The Fragments of Praxagoras of Cos and his School* (*Philosophia Antiqua* 8, 1958).

Praxidikai

LITERATURE On Praxagoras' date, see H. von Staden, *Herophilus: The Art of Medicine in Early Alexandria* (1989), 41–4 with refs. to earlier lit.
J. T. V.

Praxidikai, 'the exactors of justice'; goddesses worshipped at *Haliartus (Paus. 9. 33. 3). Their temple was roofless (it is common for *oaths to be taken in the open air) and they were sworn by, but not lightly. They were daughters of *Ogygus, i.e. ancient Boeotian (Dionysius of Chalcis quoted by *Photius). In the singular an epithet of *Persephone (*Hymn. Orph.* 29. 5).
H. J. R.

Praxilla, lyric poet (fl. 451 BC, according to *Eusebius), native of *Sicyon, composer of *hymns (747), *dithyrambs (748), and drinking-songs or *scolia (749), possibly wedding-songs (754). Her mythic narratives contained distinctive innovations (751–3). A line in her hymn to *Adonis was proverbial for its silliness (Zenob. 4. 21).

Page, *PMG* 388–90; D. A. Campbell, *Greek Lyric Poetry* (1967), 446.
C. C.

Praxiphanes, *Peripatetic philosopher (end of 4th–mid-3rd cent. BC). Probably he was born in *Mytilene and worked in *Rhodes. At some time he was publicly honoured in *Delos (*IG*. 11. 613). The few traces of his work remaining suggest that he concentrated on *grammatikē* (grammar) and literary criticism. He was involved in controversy with the Epicurean *Carneiscus on the subject of friendship, and also with *Callimachus (3), who wrote a book *Against Praxiphanes*.

F. Wehrli, *Die Schule des Aristoteles* 9 (1957; frs. and comm.); C. O. Brink, *CQ* 1946, 11 ff.; W. Aly, *RE* 22 1769; J. P. Lynch, *Aristotle's School* (1972); A. Momigliano, *The Development of Greek Biography* (1971), 66–7 and C. J. Tuplin, *Archaiognosia* 1993–4, 181 ff. (both on Praxiphanes' handling of *Thucydides (2)).
D. J. F.

Praxiteles, Athenian sculptor, probably son of Cephisodotus (1), active *c*.375–330 BC. *Pliny (1) (*HN* 34. 50) dates him to 364–361, perhaps after his *Aphrodite of *Cnidus ('Cnidia'). He worked in both bronze and marble, though was more successful at the latter (Plin. *HN* 36. 20); he paid great attention to surface finish, by preference employing the painter *Nicias (2) for the final touches (*HN* 35. 133). A prolific artist, he specialized in statues of the younger gods, particularly Aphrodite, *Dionysus, and their respective circles, and in portraits, though some architectural sculpture is also attributed to him.

His masterpiece was the Cnidia (Pliny, *HN* 36. 20 f.; ps.-Lucian, *Amores* 13; etc), supposedly modelled after his mistress Phryne; reproductions on local coins have led to the identification of numerous copies. Chief among them is the so-called Venus Colonna in the Vatican, though recent research suggests that it and others like it may copy a Hellenistic version rather than the Cnidia herself. Displayed amid gardens in a colonnaded, circular shrine, remains of which have been discovered on the site (see CNIDUS), the goddess was completely nude. Sculptors of the previous generation had occasionally represented her in transparent drapery or baring a breast, and Praxiteles himself may already have shown her topless if the Arles Aphrodite is correctly attributed to him and is earlier than the Cnidia. In the Cnidia, he simply took the final, logical step: the essence of the love-goddess was her body, so it must be revealed. His pretext was apparently her cult-title 'Euploia', referring to her 'fair voyage' from *Cyprus (see PAPHOS); accordingly, he showed her at the bath, with a hydria beside her, holding her cloak in her left hand.

No certain originals by Praxiteles exist: the base of his *Apollo group from *Mantinea and the bronze Marathon boy are probably workshop pieces, and the Aberdeen and Leconfield heads could be by his sons (see CEPHISODOTUS (2)). The *Hermes and Dionysus at *Olympia, long attributed to him on the basis of *Pausanias (3) 5. 17. 3, is almost certainly post-Praxitelean; among other anomalies, Hermes' shoes are unparalleled in the 4th cent. but have clear descendants in the second. A bust from Eleusis, however, may be his 'Eubuleus', cut down from a free-standing statue after the Costobocian sack of AD 170. His Apollo Sauroctonos survives in copy, and other plausible attributions (all copies) include two satyrs, the Arles Aphrodite, the Dresden and Gabii *Artemis types, and the Palatine *Eros; the Apollo Lycius, recognized from *Lucian, *Anach.* 7 is often added to them on stylistic grounds even though no text specifies its author.

Praxiteles' vision of a dreamy *Elysium inhabited by divine beings remote from the cares of mortals anticipates the philosophy of *Epicurus, and was widely influential. His fastidious manner was often imitated, particularly in *Alexandria (1), where it tended to degenerate into a facile slurring of surfaces enlivened by a luminous polish. His canon for the female nude (wide hips, small breasts, oval face, centrally-parted hair, etc.) remained authoritative for the rest of antiquity (see BODY).

A. F. Stewart, *Greek Sculpture* (1990), 64, 66, 176 ff., 277 ff., figs. 492 ff.; B. S. Ridgway, *Hellenistic Sculpture*, 1 (1990), 90 ff.
A. F. S.

prayer Prayer was the most common form of expression in ancient religion. It could be formal or informal and was often accompanied by other acts of worship, e.g. *sacrifice or vow (the Greek word *euchē* meant both prayer and vow). The earliest instance of an independent formal prayer, namely the prayer of the priest Chryses to *Apollo in *Il.* 1. 37 ff., presents a complete set of the fixed constitutive elements of ancient prayer. These are: (1) *invocation*. The god is addressed with his (cult) name(s), patronymic, habitual residence, functions, and qualities. This part serves both to identify and to glorify the god. (2) The *argument* (in older literature called *pars epica*), consisting of considerations that might persuade a god to help, e.g. a reminder of the praying person's acts of piety, or a reference to the god's earlier benefactions or his natural inclination to help people. This part often expanded into a eulogy with narrative aspects, especially in *hymns. (3) The *prayer* proper, the petition. For the great majority of both private and public prayers contain a wish. There is a large variation in 'egoistic' motifs ('Gebetsegoismus'). Drought, epidemics, or hail, for instance, can be prayed away (ἀποπομπή), but also passed on to enemies or neighbours (ἐπιπομπή). This comes very close to the *curse, which, too, may contain elements of prayer: the term ἀρά (*ara*) denoted both prayer and curse. Although feelings of gratitude were not lacking, the prayer of gratitude was extremely rare. It did exist but instead of terms for gratitude (χάρις, *gratia*) expressions of honour (τιμή, ἔπαινος, *laus*) were generally employed, glorification being the most common expression of gratitude, as in human communication. Private prayer often lacked these formal aspects, but in public cultic prayer too very simple invocations occurred, as e.g. in the famous Eleusinian prayer (see ELEUSIS): ὗε κύε ('rain, conceive' Hippol. *Haer.* 5. 7. 34. 87 Wendland). There were also linguistically meaningless sounds which accompanied certain dances and processions and which could be interpreted as invocations of the god, such as *ololuge, thriambe, euhoi, paian*. They could even develop into the name of a god: the cry *iakche* became the divine name *Iacchus.

Although Greek influence is noticeable, especially with respect to the formal aspects, Roman, and generally Italic, prayers (*preces*) distinguished themselves by their elaborate accuracy. Prayers for individual use were often equally formulaic (cf. Cato, *Agr.* 132. 2), but both officially and privately less elaborate prayers occurred as well, e.g. *Mars vigila* ('Mars, wake up', Serv. at *Aen.* 8. 3).

Ancient prayer used to be spoken aloud. Silent or whispered prayer was reserved for offensive, indecent, erotic, or magical uses, but was later adopted as the normal rule in Christian practice. Kneeling down, though not unknown, was unusual, the gesture of entreaty being outstretched arms, with the hands directed to the god invoked (or his cult-statue).

G. Appel, *De Romanorum Precationibus* (1909); A. Corlu, *Recherches sur les mots relatifs à l'idée de prière d'Homère aux tragiques* (1966); E. von Severus, *RAC* 8 (1972), 1135–52; O. Michel, *RAC* 9 (1976), 11–13; H. S. Versnel, in *Faith, Hope and Worship* (1981), 1–64; D. Aubriot-Sévin, *Prière et conceptions religieuses en Grèce ancienne jusqu'à la fin du Ve siècle av. J.-C.* (1992).   H. S. V.

pre-alphabetic scripts (Greece) Writing in the Aegean area appears to be a native growth, although no doubt inspired by earlier scripts used in Anatolia and Egypt. The pre-alphabetic scripts may be grouped into four classes, plus an isolated case.

The so-called *hieroglyphic* script was used on seal-stones dating from about 1900–1625 BC, rarely on other materials. Its signs are pictorial in character.

These were later simplified into outlines, hence named Linear A and B. *Linear A* was widely used in Crete during the period approximately 1800–1450 BC and has been found in Minoan settlements in the *Cyclades, in *Thera, *Melos, and *Ceos. It was clearly similar in type to Linear B, many of the signs being closely similar, if not identical. The inscriptions in Linear A are of three kinds: (1) clay tablets, which from their use of numerals and ideographic signs can be identified as accounts; (2) short inscriptions on movable objects, many of which appear to dedicatory in character; (3) a small number of ill-preserved graffiti. The script is plainly of the same type as Linear B, but so far it has proved impossible to identify the language.

Linear B is a later form of the script which was employed to write the Greek language (see MYCENAEAN LANGUAGE). It was used to keep records of personnel and produce on tablets of unbaked clay at the main centres with palatial buildings: *Mycenae, *Tiryns, *Thebes (1), and *Pylos on the mainland, *Cnossus and Khaniá (ancient Cydonia) in *Crete (see MYCENAEAN CIVILIZATION). Most of the documents date to the 13th cent. BC, though some of the Cnossus tablets may be a little earlier. Storage jars with Linear B inscriptions have been found at a number of sites both in Crete and the mainland; analysis of the clay, as well as some of the inscriptions, suggests that they were made in western Crete.

The script, which runs uniformly from left to right, is composed of signs of three types. (1) Commodities, including people and animals, are noted by special signs called ideograms or logograms, in origin pictorial, but often developing into unrecognizable patterns. These stand before numbers to show what is being counted. There are signs of this class to denote the smaller fractions of major units of volume and weight. (2) The numeral signs are decimal-based, signs for 1, 10, 100, 1,000, and 10,000 being repeated up to nine times. (3) Syllabic signs, usually noting a consonant followed by a vowel, are used to spell out names and vocabulary words. There are signs for the five vowels, but length is not indicated. There are also a small number of signs with the value: consonant + semivowel + vowel (e.g. *nwa, dwo, rja*, perhaps to be read as *rra*). One series of signs has to do duty for

plain, aspirated and voiced stops (e.g. *ka* can be read as κα, χα, or γα), though in the dental series special signs are used for the voiced sounds. The two liquids are not distinguished (*ra* can be read as ρα or λα). Clusters of consonants can be spelled out by adding extra vowels or, in certain cases, omitting the first; final consonants are not written. Thus *a-re-ku-tu-ru-wo* is the man's name Ἀλεκτρύω(ν), *ko-no-so* = Κνωσ(ο)ς, *pe-ma* = (σ)πέ(ρ)μα, *ko-wa* = κό(ρ)ϝα (Att. κόρη). Words are divided, but monosyllables are treated as part of the following or preceding word (e.g. *da-mo-de-mi* = δᾶμο(ς) δέ μι(ν)). The system would rarely cause a speaker of the Mycenaean language any trouble, but offers major difficulties for the modern investigator. There is an internationally agreed system of transcription; the commodity signs are represented by the meaning, where known, expressed in Latin (e.g. *vir, equus, hordeum, ficus*).

Cypro-Minoan is the name given to a related script from bronze age *Cyprus. It occurs in at least three forms at dates ranging from the fifteenth to the twelfth centuries BC; a variant is also known from *Ugarit on the coast of *Syria. It appears to be the origin of the *Classical Cypriot* script, which was in use for writing the local dialect of Greek from the 7th to the 3rd cents. BC. An isolated example giving a single Greek name is dated to the 11th cent. BC. Some of the simpler signs are identical, or almost so, with Linear B signs with the same value. The syllabic signs are of the same basic type, but there are none incorporating semivowels. Final consonants are always written by using the sign for the consonant + e (e.g. *pa-si-le-u-se* = βασιλεύς). The liquids are distinguished by separate signs. A few inscriptions cannot be interpreted as Greek, so it is proable that the script was also used for a native language, now known as Eteo-Cyprian.

The *Phaestus Disk* is an isolated document found in a Middle Minoan context at Phaestus in Crete. It is almost certainly written in a syllabic script from right to left, but its place of origin is uncertain, and its relationship to the Minoan scripts doubtful. Any attempt at decipherment of such a small sample is bound to fail. See GREEK LANGUAGE, and the next entry.

J. Chadwick, *Linear B and Related Scripts* (1989) and *The Decipherment of Linear B* (1958); J.-P. Olivier, in R. Treuil, *Les Civilisations Égéennes* (1989).
                                             J. C.

pre-Greek languages The Greek language is known to have been well established in mainland Greece and *Crete by the 13th cent. BC. But the presence of an earlier language in this area can be inferred from the classical place names, the majority of which are without meaning in Greek. In a few cases the resemblance to a Greek word may be fortuitous or the result of deliberate adaptation (e.g. Σπάρτη, Ῥόδος, Ναυπλία); most inhabited sites with Greek names are foundations of historical date (e.g. Ναύπακτος, Μεγαλόπολις). The elements used in the pre-Greek names can only be reliably identified if of sufficient length. The best examples are: (1) -ινθος, -υνθος as in Κόρινθος, Ζάκυνθος); since this suffix is absent from Asia Minor, but -ανδα is common there, it has been suggested that these have a common origin, but this cannot be proved. (2) -σσος (Attic and Boeotian -ττος) as Παρνασσός, Ἁλικαρνασσός (Λυκαβηττός, Γαργηττός); this should be distinguished from -σος (which is also Attic) as in Κηφισός, Πάμισος, often river names, but in Crete settlements such as Κνωσός, Ἀμνισός, Τυλισός. (3) -ᾱνᾱ, -ᾱναι (-ηνη, -ηναι) as in Παλλήνη, Μεσσήνη, Ἀθῆναι, Μυκῆναι; these may be connected with the ethnic names in -ᾱνες, -ηνες, as in Ἀκαρνᾶνες and surprisingly Ἕλληνες. This conclusion is supported by the presence of a large number of words in the Greek vocabulary without known etymology, which may well be loan-words from an earlier language of the region. Many of them are the names of plants and animals native to the Mediterranean area, but they include artefacts. Some of these show the same suffixes as the place names. (1) appears in e.g. τερέβινθος / τέρμινθος 'turpentine-tree', ἐρέβινθος 'chick-pea', ἄψινθος 'wormwood', ἀσάμινθος 'bath', λαβύρινθος 'labyrinth'; (2) in κυπάρισσος (Attic κυπάριττος) 'cypress', νάρκισσος 'narcissus', κολοσσός 'statue', πεσσός 'piece used in games', ὑσσός 'javelin'; (3) in τενθρήνη 'kind of wasp', ἀπήνη 'cart', σαγήνη 'drag-net'.

Greek tradition knew of a pre-Greek people called *Pelasgians (Πελασγοί), but *Herodotus (1) (1. 57) declared himself unable to say what language they spoke. The name has in modern times been used for a hypothetical *Indo-European language reconstructed from these place names and loan-words, but this theory has not been generally accepted.

We have direct evidence of a pre-Greek language in Crete. The Linear A inscriptions (see PRE-ALPHABETIC SCRIPTS (GREECE)) of the Minoan period are evidently not in Greek, but their language cannot yet be reliably identified. At a later date a few alphabetic inscriptions are known from eastern Crete which are not in the Greek language.

A famous stele from *Lemnos contains an early alphabetic inscription in a language which appears to have affinities with Etruscan (e.g. AFIZ = Etr. avils 'years'). This has been taken as confirmation of the story in Herodotus (1. 94) that the Etruscans (Τυρσηνοί) were an offshoot of the Lydians (See ETRUSCAN LANGUAGE). In *Cyprus there are undeciphered inscriptions in the Cypro-Minoan script, but which do not seem to be in Greek, but in classical times there are syllabic inscriptions from *Amathus which are certainly not Greek. Their unknown language is conventionally referred to as Eteo-Cyprian.

J. Chadwick, 'Greek and Pre-Greek', Trans. Philol. Soc. 1969, 80–98; F. Schachermeyr, RE 22. 2. 1350–548.   J. C.

Precatio terrae, Precatio omnium herbarum, two short anonymous prayers of uncertain date to Mother Earth and to all herbs; the second may show Christian influence. Attempts to read these texts as iambic senarii have resulted in much misguided conjecture.

TEXTS Anth. Lat. 4–5 Shackleton Bailey; with trans., Duff, Minor Lat. Poets.   J. H. D. S.

prejudice See HOMOSEXUALITY; INTOLERANCE, INTELLECTUAL AND RELIGIOUS; RACE; SEMITISM (PAGAN), ANTI-; WOMEN.

Presocratic philosophers, thinkers who lived not later than *Socrates. See e.g. ANAXAGORAS; ANAXIMANDER; ANAXIMENES (1); ATOMISM; DEMOCRITUS; EMPEDOCLES; HERACLITUS; HIPPIAS (1); LEUCIPPUS (3); PROTAGORAS; PYTHAGORAS (1); SOPHISTS; THALES; XENOPHANES; ZENO (1).

Priam (Πρίαμος), in mythology son of *Laomedon and originally called Podarces; king of *Troy at the time of its destruction by *Agamemnon. When Laomedon refused to pay *Heracles the promised reward for saving *Hesione from the sea-monster, Heracles killed Laomedon and all of his sons except Priam, whom he spared and made king of Troy. Priam's principal wife was *Hecuba, though he had other wives and concubines. He was father of fifty sons (Il. 24. 495) including *Hector, *Paris, *Deiphobus, *Helenus, *Troilus, *Polydorus, and *Lycaon (1), and daughters including *Cassandra and *Polyxena (though the latter is not mentioned by *Homer). When the Greeks came to

Troy with Agamemnon, Priam was already an old man. Homer depicts him as an amiable character, tender to *Helen although he disapproves of the war and its cause (Il. 3. 162 ff.), respected even by his enemies for his integrity (ibid. 105 ff., 20. 183) and esteemed by most of the gods (though *Hera and *Athena are hostile) for his piety. He takes part in the treaty (3. 259 ff.) and has returned to the city before it is broken (305 ff.). He tries to persuade Hector to come to safety within the walls after the rout of the Trojans (22. 38 ff.) and after his death goes to the Greek camp to ransom his body, moving *Achilles to pity (Il. 24 passim). The lost Iliu Persis (see EPIC CYCLE) told of his death at the fall of Troy, killed by *Neoptolemus (1) while taking refuge at the altar of *Zeus Herkeios in his own palace. The most powerful description in surviving literature is *Virgil's (Aen. 2. 506 ff.). Priam's name became almost proverbial for a man who had known the extremes of contrasting fortunes.

Neoptolemus killing Priam at the altar is a popular scene in art from the early 6th cent. on, as a separate scene or as the centre of a Sack of Troy, and is often associated with the death of *Astyanax (see O. Touchefeu, LIMC 2. 1. 931–3). Priam is also shown coming to ransom Hector's body from Achilles (see A. Kossatz-Deissmann, LIMC 1. 1. 147–61).

LIMC 7. 1 (1994), 507–22.   H. J. R.; J. R. M.

priamel Literary term for a kind of paratactic comparison (i.e. comparison by listing or enumeration). Examples are *Sappho fr. 16, 'some people like x, others y, but I say the best thing is to get your heart's desire', cf. *Pindar, Ol. 1, first lines, or *Homer, Il. 13. 636 ff. with Janko's n. (see also Thuc. 1. 86. 3 with Schmid 62). It is a focusing device: to understand D you need to compare it with A, B, and C. It is nothing to do with Greek melos, a song. The derivation is supposed to be from Latin praeambulum, 'a preamble'.

Pl. Symp. 221c. W. H. Race, The Classical Priamel from Homer to Boethius (1982) and Classical Genres and English Poetry (1988), ch. 2; U. Schmid, Die Priamel der Werte im griechischen von Homer bis Paulus (1964); Nisbet & Hubbard on Hor. Carm. 1.1 (pp. 2 f.).   S. H.

Priape(i)a are poems about the phallic god *Priapus, addressed to him, spoken by him, or invoking him. The genre is well represented in Hellenistic and later *epigram, but the range of topics is limited. It was enriched and developed by the Romans, whose Priape(i)a are distinguished from Greek exemplars by their focus on the god's aggressive, anally-fixated, sexuality, by the absence of any discernible religious sentiment, and by the almost invariable treatment of Priapus as a figure of fun. There are notable specimens by *Horace (Sat. 1. 8), *Tibullus (1. 4), and *Martial, and in the *Appendix Vergiliana. The main Latin material is assembled in the corpus of eighty poems known as the Carmina Priapea or Corpus Priapeorum, believed by most recent authorities to be the work of one poet, who has been dated to the Augustan period, to AD 100, and various points in between. The collection is distinguished by its extreme obscenity, genuine wit, fierce mockery of the ridiculous or grotesque, clever use of verbal borrowings and *parody, amusing tension between the sophistication of the literary form and the crudity of the subject-matter, and elegant variations on a number of recurrent themes.

TEXTS Buecheler ed. minor of Petronius (1904); Cazzaniga, Carmina Ludicra Romana (1959); Kytzler and Fischer (1978).
STUDIES V. Buchheit, Studien zum Corpus Priapeorum (1962); A. Richlin, The Garden of Priapus (1983), 116 ff.; W. Parker, Priapea (1988; incl. text and trans. into rhyming doggerel), E. O'Connor, Symbolum Salacitatis (1989).   L. C. W.

Priapus (Πρίαπος, Πρίηπος), an ithyphallic god most familiar from the sportively obscene short poems (Greek and Latin) called Priape(i)a: in these he typically threatens to punish by penetration any male or female intruder into the garden of which he is guardian. He was said to be a son of *Dionysus (the god he is most closely linked to in cult) by a *nymph or *Aphrodite (Strabo 13. 1. 12; Paus. 9. 31. 2). He is first mentioned in the 4th cent. BC (in the title of *Xenarchus (2)'s comedy *Priapus*) and allusions become common in the 3rd, when his cult seems to have spread rapidly out from the *Lampsacus region, probably absorbing some pre-existent ithyphallic deities on the way; he was later to be well known almost throughout the Roman empire. He is associated with sexuality, human fertility, gardens, herds, in Greek texts with fishermen and occasionally in Roman texts with tombs; a text of the 3rd cent. BC presents him simply as a bringer of wealth and a general helper (*IG* 12. 3. 421 = 1335 Thera). His image was typically sited in a garden or house, though temples are sometimes also attested. His preferred victim in Lampsacus was the lustful ass, but elsewhere he received animal sacrifice of more normal type or, very commonly, offerings of fruit, flowers, vegetables (and fish).

In the Priape(i)a he presents himself as a minor and disreputable god, and in texts of all kinds he is humorously handled. It has often been suggested that this embodiment of generative power had once been treated with more reverence. But the prurience, embarrassment, depreciation, and humour associated with him are appropriate responses to that image of sexuality which, as much as of fertility, he presents. The association between ithyphallic display and protection of territory is also found among primates; how to fit this analogy into a broader account of the god is uncertain. See PHALLUS.

H. Herter, *De Priapo* (1932), and in *RE* and *Kl. Pauly* under 'Priapos'; D. Fehling, *Ethologische Überlegungen auf dem Gebiet der Altertumskunde* (1974), 7–38; see also BAUBO. R. C. T. P.

Priene, an Ionian city situated on the ancient mouth of the *Maeander. Apart from controlling the *Panionium, it was unimportant, suffering disastrously in the 7th–6th cents. at the hands of the *Cimmerians, Lydians, and Persians. At an uncertain date in the 4th cent., but by the reign of *Alexander (3) the Great and perhaps at his instigation (S. Hornblower, *Mausolus* (1982), 323 ff.), the city was refounded at the foot of Mt. Mycale facing *Miletus, on a site dominated by a precipitous spur (the Teloneia) forming its acropolis. Priene's chief importance is archaeological. The German excavations (1895–8) revealed one of the best surviving examples of a Greek planned city with almost all its essential public buildings; historically valuable too is the Hellenistic 'archive' of public documents carved on the temple of *Athena Polias. Only the harbours remain to be discovered under the accumulation of river silt, which had already left the city high and dry by the Augustan age (Strabo 12. 8. 17). Inside the wall-circuit, a grid-pattern was laid out to the points of the compass, with level main streets running east-west and the *agora and other public buildings mostly concentrated in the central panel of the grid, with residential blocks to either flank. Although later modified, in their original form the house-plans seem to show a deliberate uniformity of design, a feature reflecting, it has been claimed, the egalitarian ethos of 4th-cent. BC Greek *democracy. See also PYTHIUS; URBANISM.

T. Wiegand and H. Schrader, *Priene, Ergebnisse* (1904); F. Hiller, *Inschriften von Priene* (1906); R. E. Wycherley, *How the Greeks built Cities* (1962) *passim*; G. Bean, *PECS* 737 ff.; S. Sherwin-White, *JHS* 1985, 69 ff.

('archive'); W. Hoepfner and E.-L. Schwandner, *Haus und Stadt* (1986), 141 ff. (house-plans). J. M. C.; A. J. S. S.

priests (Greek and Roman) Cities in the Graeco-Roman world always had men and women, often of high rank, specially chosen for the service of the gods and goddesses. They might be serving for life or for a fixed term; they might be holding a hereditary position, or be publicly elected or selected by some other method, or the office might (at least in the Greek world) be put up for sale. The offices always carried honour, but often too, especially in later periods, the expectation of high expenditure by the holders. (See EUERGETISM.) The duties varied a great deal, from quite humble service to high authority and power.

Greek and Latin have several terms referring to these positions—*hiereis* and *sacerdotes* are only the most common; in English, 'priest' is used as a generic term for all of them, but implies a potentially misleading unity of conception and an analogy with the roles of priesthood in later religions. Pagan priests did not form a separate group or caste and seldom devoted their whole lives to religious activity; characteristically, they performed their religious duties on special occasions or when required and otherwise continued with the same range of social or political activities as other members of their social groups. Above all, there was no religious community, separate from the civic community, with its own personnel or power-structure. Nor did priests monopolize religious action or communication with the gods and goddesses: fathers of families, leaders of social groups, officials of the city, all had the power of religious action, with priests as advisers or helpers. So far as the city itself was concerned, it might well be the city authorities who took the religious decisions and the magistrates (elected officials), not the priests, who took religious actions on the city's behalf.

To this extent, there was not much difference between the pagan practice of Greece and of Rome; but differences appear on a more detailed examination. Greek cities have female as well as male priests, female for goddesses, male for gods. They do not form priestly groups or colleges, but are attached to particular cults and even to particular temples, sanctuaries, or festivals; there is an alternative pattern where priesthood is carried in families. Priests seldom act as advisers to individuals, who consult ritual experts (*exēgētai*; see EXĒGĒTĒS) or diviners (see DIVINATION). They seem not to have been consulted on religious issues by the state, except the priests of an oracle speaking on behalf of a god or when special *purifications or remedies were needed and a religious expert might be brought in.

In Rome on the other hand priests are (with the exception of the Vestal Virgins) males, formed into colleges or brotherhoods (see SODALES). They are not attached to particular deities or temples, but rather to special festivals (as the Luperci to the *Lupercalia) or areas of religion (the *augures to the taking of auspices). The *flamines are a spectacular exception, perhaps preserving a more archaic and far closer relationship between priest and deity; they therefore provide the model for the priesthood of the emperors after death (the Divi; see RULER-CULT). The most senior colleges were above all expert advisers, consulted by the senate when religious problems were to be dealt with. The *pontifices* (see PONTIFEX/PONTIFICES) are also available to private individuals, in need of advice on the religious law (see HIEROMNĒMONES).

In both Greece and Rome, the powers associated with priesthood were narrowly defined. They superintended particular cultic activities, but the financing of these activities was often carefully controlled by state officials and the priests controlled no great temple incomes or resources, as equivalent officers did in other parts of the ancient world. The city would often vote funds for religious expenditure and might regard the treasures stored in temples as state reserves to be used in case of emergency (see, famously, Thuc. 2. 13. 3–4) and repaid later. There might also at all periods be city officials taking overall responsibility for state religious expenditure.

In the imperial period, both in the east and west, priesthood became closer than ever to the expression of public power. The flaminate in its new guise of an imperial priesthood became widespread in the provinces and cities, held by the leading members of the local élites as a mark of their authority and an opportunity for public generosity. Meanwhile, the emperor's image in priestly garb became one of the empire-wide expressions of his rule.

Apart from these official civic priesthoods, there was a great range of religious expertise available for private consultation—diviners of all sorts, magicians, and astrologers; these had no official recognition and often attracted criticism. The mystery-cults also had their priests, who might attain to great authority within a less controlled cultic environment than that of the civic priests; religious groups devoted to a particular cult might appoint priests of their own; the Bacchist movement of 186 BC (see BACCHANALIA) had priests and priestesses, differentiated from lay magistrates in the senate's decree; but the clearest example of this development is the figure of the *Isis priest in *Apuleius' novel (*The Golden Ass* 11), who acts as mentor and spiritual adviser to the hero after his rescue from the spell that turned him into the ass. It seems clear that there were new currents within pagan religious life that corresponded to, if they were not imitating, the new religious types evolving at the same time amongst Jews and Christians. Nothing, however, in pagan religious life corresponded to the Christian hierarchic structure of deacons, priests and bishops. See ORACLES; QUINDECIMVIRI SACRIS FACIUNDIS.

J. Scheid, in C. Nicolet (ed.), *Des ordres à Rome* (1984), 243–80; M. Beard and J. North (eds.), *Pagan Priests: Religion and Power in the Ancient World* (1990). J. A. N.

primipilus In the army of the imperial period the *primipilus* or *primus pilus* was chief centurion (see CENTURIO) of a legion, commanding the leading century of the five in the first cohort, the centurions of which comprised the *primi ordines: primus pilus, princeps, hastatus, princeps posterior, hastatus posterior*. The *primus pilus* probably held office for one year and usually gained equestrian rank immediately afterwards, with the opportunity of promotion to the camp prefecture and possibly the tribunates of the urban troops—*vigiles, urban cohorts (see COHORTES URBANAE), and *praetorian guard (e.g. ILS 2701); favoured men could then be appointed to more senior equestrian posts, possibly first holding the position of chief centurion for a second time (*primus pilus bis*—e.g. ILS 1385), who ranked below the senior military tribune.

B. Dobson, *Die Primipilares* (1978). J. B. C.

princeps When *Augustus selected 'Princeps' as the word which indicated most satisfactorily his own constitutional position, he chose, typically, a word which had good republican associations.

It was not an abbreviation of *princeps senatus, though that, also, was a republican title and one which Augustus held. The *princeps senatus*, or First Senator, was before the time of *Sulla the man who had been placed by censors at the head of the list

of members of the senate, and ranked as the senior member of that body. Augustus in the census of 28 BC enrolled himself as *princeps senatus* (Dio Cass. 53. 1; *Res Gest.* c. 7), and succeeding emperors held the same position.

Principes in the plural, meaning the 'chief men of the state', was a phrase commonly employed by late republican writers, as *Cicero, and it continued to be used in the empire (Suet. *Aug.* 66; *Res Gest.* c. 12).

It was the singular *princeps*, however, applied to *one* prominent statesman, especially *Pompey, in republican times, which supplied *Augustus with something of a precedent (e.g. Sall. *H.* 3. 48. 23 M.; Cic. *Har. Resp.* 46, *Pis.* 25, *Dom.* 66, *Sest.* 84, *Red. Sen.* 5 and 29, *Red. Pop.* 16). Early in 49 BC Cornelius Balbus wrote to Cicero (*Att.* 8. 9. 4): 'Caesar wants nothing more than to live without fear while Pompey is Princeps.' Cicero used this designation of other statesmen besides Pompey. In 46 BC he used it of *Caesar (*Fam.* 9. 17. 3). He used it also of himself in connexion with the renown that he won by his action against the Catilinarian conspirators (*Phil.* 14. 17; see SERGIUS CATILINA, L.) and by his rallying of the Senate against Mark Antony (M. *Antonius (2)) at the end of 44 BC (*Fam.* 12. 24. 2). The phrase *princeps ciuitatis* is also used of the *moderator reipublicae* in Cicero's *De Republica* (5. 7. 9, where the reading is probably sound in spite of the doubts of Dessau, *Gesch. der röm. Kaiserzeit* 1. 61 n. 2), though here, almost certainly, he was not thinking of Pompey. In this work Cicero stressed the need for statesmen (in the plural) of wisdom and moral standing to ensure that a revived republic functioned properly. Augustus' choice of the word *princeps* to designate his position was typical of his respect for tradition; it contrasted strongly with the Dictatorship and the suspected monarchical intentions of Caesar and, in indicating an unquestioned but not a narrowly defined or clearly determined primacy, the word suited perfectly Augustus' definition of his own authority in the *Res. Gest.* c. 34: 'I excelled all in influence, although I possessed no more official power than others who were my colleagues in the various magistracies.' *Principatus* was in sharp opposition to *dominatio, princeps* to *dominus*, and both Augustus and *Tiberius took pains to suppress the use of the title *dominus*, though it remained a conventional form of polite address within Roman society (Ov. *Fasti* 2. 142; Suet. *Aug.* 53; Plin. *Ep.* 10; Dio Cass. 57. 8). The importance of this choice of title was appreciated by Roman historians; cf. Tac. *Ann.* 1. 1: 'He assumed control over a state exhausted by civil discord under the title of *princeps*'; 1. 9: 'He had put the commonwealth in order not to make himself king or dictator, but under the title of *princeps*' (cf. 3. 28).

Princeps was not an *official* title (as e.g. *pater patriae). It was assumed by Roman emperors at their accession and not conferred upon them by definite grant of the senate; nor does it appear in the list of official titles in documents and inscriptions. On the other hand, by itself it might be used in inscriptions (e.g. on the funerary urn of *Vipsania Agrippina: 'Ossa Agrippinae . . . matris C. Caesaris Aug. Germanici principis', ILS 180). *Claudius, in his edict *de Anaunorum civitate*, wrote: 'Gai principatu', 'in the principate of Gaius' (Dessau, ILS 206). The Greek form of the word, ἡγεμών, appears in the fifth Cyrene edict of Augustus (line 86, JRS 1927, 36): Αὐτοκράτωρ Καῖσαρ Σεβαστός, ἡγεμὼν ἡμέτερος (see CYRENE, EDICTS OF).

The nuance of the word, chosen by Augustus for its inoffensive character, was soon lost (though the use of the word itself persisted) as the government of the Roman emperors became more autocratic. It may be doubted whether the Greeks ever appreciated its subtlety; *Cassius Dio, for instance, in recording

Tiberius' very typical remark (57. 8. 2), 'I am *dominus* (lord, master) of my slaves, *imperator of my troops, and *princeps* of the rest', loses the point by using, for *princeps*, not ἡγεμών, but πρόκριτος, which means *princeps senatus*. The title *princeps* in Latin survived the reorganization of *Diocletian, though such phrases as *gloriosissimus princeps* show that its original significance had been lost.

Further light is thrown on the significance of the word *princeps* by the title *princeps iuventutis*, meaning Leader of the Equestrian Order, or, more probably, of the *iuventus* of that Order (see EQUITES, *Imperial period*; PRINCEPS IUVENTUTIS), which was given in certain cases in the early empire to princes of the imperial house who might be considered as 'heirs apparent', the relation of the *princeps iuventutis* to the *princeps* being well illustrated by *Ovid's words (*Ars. Am.* 1. 194): 'now *princeps* of the young, in future of Rome's seniors'.

M. Hammond, *The Augustan Principate* (1933); Mommsen, *Röm. Staatsr.* 2. 2. 3; A. Gwosdz, *Der Begriff des römischen Princeps* (1933); A. von Premerstein, *Vom Werden und Wesen des Prinzipats* (1937); Syme, *Rom. Rev.*² Full bibliog. up to 1954 in *RE* 22, 1998 ff. by L. Wickert who supplements his *RE* article and bibliog. in *ANRW* 2. 1 (1974), 3–76; this deals with work up to 1970. P. A. Brunt, *Fall of the Roman Republic* (1988).   J. P. B.; M. T. G.

princeps iuventutis or ***princeps iuvenum*** The phrase occurs in the republic (Cic. *Vat.* 24, the younger Curio, see SCRIBONIUS CURIO (2), C.), but first appears with constitutional significance after the reorganization of the *iuventus* by *Augustus (*see* IUVENES). Probably in 5 and 2 BC respectively the equestrian order gave silver shields and spears to Augustus' grandsons Gaius *Iulius Caesar (2) and Lucius *Iulius Caesar (4), and hailed them as *principes iuventutis*. The same honour was paid informally to Germanicus *Iulius Caesar and Drusus *Iulius Caesar (1), sons of Tiberius (Ovid, *Ex Pont.* 2. 5. 41); certainly to Drusus' son Tiberius *Iulius Caesar Nero 'Gemellus', adopted son of *Gaius (1), in AD 37; to *Nero in 51, to *Vespasian's sons *Titus and *Domitian, and to *Commodus. The title was sometimes retained when the holder was no longer a *iuvenis*, and had something of the significance of 'crown prince' (Ovid, *Ars Am.* 1. 194. Titus, taking tribunician power in AD 71, gave it up; with Gemellus and Domitian, who kept it in 80 as consul for the seventh time, it relegated a claimant to the Principate by putting him in a later generation than current incumbents. Occasionally after Domitian, however, and regularly in the 3rd cent., reigning emperors used the title; its connection with the equestrian order also disappeared then.   J. P. B.; B. M. L.

princeps senatus The senator whose name was entered first on the *senate list compiled by the censors (see CENSOR). Once selected, he maintained his position for life and longevity conferred increased influence. The *princeps senatus* had to be a *patrician, but apparently one of a limited number of *gentes* (perhaps the *maiores gentes*, not known to us in detail: Mommsen, *Str.* 3. 31; see GENS). Thus Cn. Servilius Caepio, as censor 125 BC, was not eligible. By the 3rd cent. BC it was customary to appoint the senior living ex-censor who was qualified, but the censors had no legal obligation to do so. In 209, Q. *Fabius Maximus Verrucosus was chosen, though junior in standing to another ex-censor, and in 136 Ap. *Claudius Pulcher (1) appointed himself and not P. *Cornelius Scipio Aemilianus who was his enemy. A censor in office was first appointed in 179 and a non-censorian ex-consul in 125. Apart from great dignity, the rank conferred the privilege of speaking first on any motion in the senate. Since

there was usually not much debate, the *princeps senatus* moved all routine *senatus consulta* (see SENATUS CONSULTUM), and he influenced many debated ones. M. *Aemilius Lepidus (1), appointed six times, was the most powerful man of his generation. M. *Aemilius Scaurus (1), appointed five or perhaps six times, 'almost ruled the world by his nod' (Cic. *Font.* 24): it was he who moved the **senatus consultum ultimum* against L. *Appuleius Saturninus and ceremonially handed C. *Marius (1) a sword, and he pressed the legislation of M. *Livius Drusus (2). *Sulla abolished the office, since he did not want any one senator to have such dominant power. Augustus revived it, appointing himself when he revised the senate list in 28 BC (Dio 53. 1. 3), even though Iulii were probably not eligible under the republic, and he held the office until his death (cf. *RG* 8. 2). His successors took it as a matter of course.

J. Suolahti, *Arctos* NS 7 (1972) 207 ff.; Mommsen, *Str.* 3. 31 and 970 is still useful. There is no reliable published list of *principes senatus*, but they can be found in *MRR* under each censorship.   E. B.

Principate, the regime established by *Augustus (see PRINCEPS); also, the period of Roman history between Augustus and the late 3rd cent. AD (the 'Dominate' – a near-obsolete word – conventionally began AD 284). See ROME, HISTORY, §§ 2, 3.

Priscian (Priscianus Caesariensis) (5th–6th cent. AD) was the most prolific and important member of the late Latin grammarians. His grammatical works have been edited by Heinrich Keil (*Grammatici Latini* 2, 3), and they amount to over 1,000 printed pages in all.

Born in Mauretania, Priscian spent most of his life as a teacher of Latin in *Constantinople (Byzantium), then the capital of the eastern Roman empire. His surviving works include the *Institutio de nomine et pronomine et verbo*, the *Praeexercitamina*, a set of grammatical exercises based on each first line of the twelve books of the *Aeneid*, and the *Institutiones grammaticae*. The *Institutio* was an important authority for the teaching of Latin in the early Middle Ages before the much longer and more comprehensive *Institutiones* (974 printed pages) became widely known in and after the Carolingian age.

This work comprises eighteen books, the first sixteen setting out, after a brief introduction to orthography, the eight Latin word classes (parts of speech) in great detail. Books 17 and 18 provide an account of the syntax of Latin, the first systematic treatment of Latin syntax of which we have knowledge.

The *Institutiones* represents a summation in Latin of the whole of grammatical theory and practice as it had developed in the Graeco-Latin world hitherto. The two books on syntax were, as Priscian acknowledges, very largely based on the work of the *Alexandrian Greek grammarian *Apollonius (13) Dyscolus. The original purpose of the *Institutiones* was the teaching of Latin to Greek speakers, as is shown by repeated references to classical Greek texts. Latin was still the official language of the eastern empire, but by the 8th cent. it had become largely unused and unremembered except by some scholars.

In western Europe it became, along with the shorter grammars of *Donatus (1), the authority for the teaching of grammar and of Latin, the *lingua franca* of educated medieval Europe. Several hundred individual manuscripts are known to have existed, and the work was subjected to many epitomies and commentaries. In the later Middle Ages it became the linguistic basis of the scholastic speculative grammars, particularly in the University of Paris. This arose gradually through the attempted philosophical explanation by commentators on Priscian's descriptive account of Latin, after the study of the Aristotelian texts became more widespread and profound.

The established and intended purpose of Priscian's teaching and writing had become void after a few centuries in the east, but his principal work remains of the greatest importance in the western Middle Ages for the teaching of Latin and for philosophical grammar, some of whose concerns, e.g. universal grammar, are still with us today. See GRAMMAR, GRAMMARIANS, LATIN.

R. H. R.

Priscillianists The Priscillianists were members of a Christian ascetic movement which flourished in Spain and Aquitaine during the last quarter of the 4th cent. AD. Its founder, Priscillian, was a well-educated Spanish layman, possibly of senatorial standing. From c.375 his teachings spread rapidly, attracting a considerable following and the opposition of bishops Ithacius of Ossonoba and Hydatius of Mérida. Affinities with *Gnosticism and *Manichaeism laid them open to charges of heresy, but a council convened at Saragossa (October 380) failed to condemn the Priscillianists by name. Shortly thereafter Priscillian was consecrated bishop of Avila by Instantius and Salvianus, his episcopal supporters. Their opponents obtained from *Gratian an imperial rescript expelling the Priscillianists from their churches (381). Although the exiled bishops were unable to win an audience with either Pope *Damasus or *Ambrose, they did secure from Macedonius, Gratian's master of the offices, a rescript authorizing them to resume possession of their sees.

Gratian's murder by *Magnus Maximus (383) had disastrous consequences for the Priscillianists. To bolster his tenuous political position, the usurping emperor convened a new council at Bordeaux at which Priscillian and Instantius were condemned (384). After these appealed directly to Maximus at Trier, Ithacius and Hydatius accused them of sorcery and the case was tried as a criminal rather than ecclesiastical matter. Using confessions acquired by torture, Evodius, Maximus' praetorian prefect (see PRAEFECTUS PRAETORIO), found the accused guilty. Despite the protests of Martin of Tours, Priscillian was executed and Instantius banished to the isles of Scilly (385). The condemnation of clerics by a lay tribunal and episcopal complicity in prosecuting a capital case shocked contemporaries. Ithacius and Hydatius were forced to resign their sees while Priscillian's followers hailed him as a martyr. The Council of Toledo (400) reconciled moderate Priscillianists, but the movement remained strong in Galicia until c.600.

Priscillian's teachings included advocacy of celibacy, vegetarianism (see ANIMALS, ATTITUDES TO), lay spirituality, and the spiritual equality of men and women. Priscillianist theology exhibits a fondness for apocryphal scriptures, numerology, and esotericism, as well as tendencies toward Sabellian Monarchianism. Priscillian's followers included wealthy aristocrats and common people alike. The movement represents both the theological variety and social turmoil which characterized the ascendancy of *asceticism in the west.

Priscillianist texts edited by G. Schepps, *CSEL* 18 (1889). E.-C. Babut, *Priscillien et le priscillianisme* (1909); A. d'Alès, *Priscillien et l'Espagne chrétienne* (1936); B. Vollmann, *RE* Suppl. 14 (1974), 485–559, 'Priscillianus'; H. Chadwick, *Priscillian of Avila* (1976).   T. R. B.

Priscus, east Roman bureaucrat and historian of the 5th cent. AD. Born in Panium in *Thrace and a professional rhetorician, he accompanied Maximinus on an embassy of *Theodosius (3) II to *Attila in 449. His history included an extant detailed account of this episode. In 452 he followed the same Maximinus to Arabia and Egypt, and later became *assessor* to the *Magister Equitum* Euphemius under the emperor Marcian. He visited Rome at least once, perhaps in 450. The *Suda reports that he published now lost declamations and letters, as well as his eight-book history which included events from at least 433/4 to 472, although some kind of digression seems to have covered the arrival of the *Huns on the fringes of Europe (c. AD 375). It is unclear whether he consciously picked up where *Olympiodorus (3) left off. The history is lost, but long excerpts from it are preserved in Constantine Porphyrogenitus' *De legationibus* and other Byzantine sources. It also underlies substantial sections dealing with the Huns in the *Getica* of *Jordanes. Three quarters of the surviving material deals in great detail with the Huns in the time of Attila; whether this reflects the balance of the original is impossible to know. What survives suggests that he wrote as a critic of appeasement. His style is deliberately classicising, owing much to *Herodotus (2) and somewhat less to *Thucydides (2).

Müller, *FHG* 4 (1851), 69; Dindorf, *Hist. Gr. Min.* 1 (1870), 275; (partially, though a better edn.) De Boor, *Excerpta de Legationibus* (1903), 121 and 575; R. Blockley, *The Fragmentary Classicising Historians of the Later Roman Empire*, 2 vols. (1981–3), ch. 3 and 221 ff. respectively (discussion, text, and trans.).   P. J. H.

prison Roman criminal law, like that of Athens, did not in general use public imprisonment of free persons as a form of punishment, although under the republic some criminals suffered private imprisonment at the hands of those they had wronged and, occasionally, a special kind of criminal might be detained either inside or outside Rome. The public prison (*carcer*, *publica vincula*) served normally only for a short incarceration, whether used as a coercive measure by magistrates against disobedience to their orders (see COERCITIO) or for convicted criminals awaiting execution (though such detention lasted several years for Q. *Pleminius, c.200 BC). During inquiry in a criminal trial the accused person could be detained so as to be at the disposal of the authorities, but this was not necessarily in a public prison. Larger households had arrangements for imprisoning slaves, especially in workhouses (*ergastula*) in the countryside. These were also used for convicted debtors and (under the republic) thieves, as well as other free men improperly seized.   A. B.; A. W. L.

pro consule, pro praetore, a magistrate (see MAGISTRACY, ROMAN) in place of a *consul or *praetor respectively, operating outside Rome and outside the regular annual magistracy.

The first instance is Q. *Publilius Philo, who was about to take Naples (*Neapolis) in 326 BC, when his consulate ran out. The people voted that he should retain his *imperium in place of a consul (*pro consule*). He later triumphed as such. In the following centuries Rome's imperial expansion produced an endemic shortage of magistrates with *imperium*. Extensions were henceforth voted (*prorogatio imperii*) for both consuls and praetors whenever necessary for military purposes or to enable the holder of *imperium* to *triumph. This became a routine measure requiring only a decree of the senate, not a popular vote. Similarly the magistracies of quaestors could be prorogued *pro quaestore*.

In 295 BC four private citizens were given commands *pro praetore*; at least two of them had been delegated by a consul on his own authority. Such delegation of a promagistracy occurred later, when a magistrate or promagistrate was leaving his post abroad without receiving a successor sent from Rome (whatever his former status, the recipient would be given *imperium pro praetore*). However, the multiplication of Roman commanders or officials in a particular *provincia was normally achieved by the appointment of *legati, usually with more limited powers. Their nomination had to be approved by the senate, though it usually acceded to the wishes of the magistrate whose legati they were to be.

A promagistracy was exercised within a provincia, normally defined by the senate, in order to avoid collisions of rival authorities, and the holder was not permitted to go beyond it except in an emergency or for essential travel. This last tradition was enshrined in legislation—lex Porcia and lex de provinciis consularibus of 101–100 BC, lex Cornelia de maiestate, lex Iulia de repetundis (see LEX (2); CORNELIUS SULLA, L.; IULIUS CAESAR (1), C.). During the Hannibalic War (see HANNIBAL; PUNIC WARS) prorogation for long periods became common and several private citizens were given imperium pro magistratu by the people (but not, in this period, allowed to triumph). After the war long promagistracies became rare and the grant of imperium to private citizens was abandoned, but these practices revived (and a private citizen like *Pompey even triumphed) amid the troubles and shortage of commanders in the last century of the republic. Quaestors and legati could be given imperium pro praetore if necessary. Meanwhile, the multiplication of provinces and the development of *quaestiones perpetuae entailed the integration of prorogation into the administrative system. By the late second century BC praetors normally went to their provinces abroad after their year of office and the allocation of such provinces did not occur until then. Before Sulla consuls still undertook major wars in their year of magistracy. This practice became rare in the late republic and in any case they tended to continue as proconsuls after their consular year. The increase of the number of provinces in the 60s and the poor health or unwillingness of some magistrates to serve abroad led to a great increase in long tenures and this trend was accelerated by the series of emergencies characterizing that period.

Consuls were always prorogued pro consule, praetors at first usually pro praetore; but both during and after their office their imperium might be raised to pro consule (with twelve *lictors), when the size of their armies or the importance of their tasks required it. After Sulla all governors seem to have ranked pro consule. Legates of proconsuls assigned extraordinary major commands by the people (e.g. Pompey and Caesar) were now granted imperium pro praetore on appointment. The number of their lictors is not certain. Pompey in 52 BC fixed a compulsory interval between magistracy and provincial government and seems to have tried to limit tenure of a promagistracy in principle to a year, in order to break the nexus of electoral bribery and corruption abroad and to prevent the dangerous accumulation of power. This meant that in the short term promagistracies had to be conferred on private citizens chosen by the senate (such as Cicero, who had declined a promagistracy after his consulship). This move Caesar denounced as unconstitutional and he rescinded Pompey's law. However, *Augustus seems to have returned to Pompey's ideas in his organization of the 'public provinces', though not with regard to his own. The emperor himself was consul from 27 to 23 BC and thereafter had proconsular imperium. So the governors on the spot of the provinces assigned to him ranked as legati pro praetore (with five lictors)—these would be either ex-praetors or ex-consuls, depending on the importance of their command. From 23 BC the emperor's proconsular imperium was also defined as greater (maius) with respect to that of proconsuls in the public provinces.

Mommsen, Röm. Staatsr.; W. F. Jashemski, Origin and History of Procon-sular and Propraetorian Imperium to 27 BC (1950); A. Giovannini, Consulare Imperium (1983). E. B.; A. W. L.

Pro(h)aeresius, (AD 276–367/8). Greek rhetorician. Born in *Cappadocia, he studied in *Antioch (1) and Athens, where he succeeded his teacher Julianus as professor of rhetoric. He gained an immense reputation through his ability to improvise and his phenomenal memory. Invited by the emperor *Constans to his court in Gaul, he had honours showered upon him both there and in Rome; the senate set up a statue of him, and offered him a chair of rhetoric in the city, which he declined. Among his students in Athens were *Basil and *Gregory (2) and the future emperor *Julian. When Julian in 362 issued his edict forbidding Christians to teach, special exception was made for Proaeresius, who was a Christian; he preferred, however, to resign his chair, but took it up again after Julian's death. None of his speeches survives.

Eunap. VS Giangrande 63–79; Jerome, Chron. a. 2378. G. A. Kennedy, Greek Rhetoric under Christian Emperors (1983), 138–41; PLRE 1. 731. R. B.

proagōn The proagōn at Classical Athens was an official theatrical presentation which took place a few days before the Great *Dionysia began. It was held in the *Odeum, a building east of the theatre reconstructed by *Pericles (1) c.445 BC, where the poets appeared before the public with their choruses, actors, and presumably chorēgoi (see CHORĒGIA), to give an exposition of some kind of the dramas with which they were to compete, perhaps little more than an indication of their general plot or subject-matter. Those involved in the forthcoming competitions were thereby identified before their civic peers: for, though garlanded, actors and choruses appeared without costumes or masks. We hear only of tragedy being presented in this way, but the procedure may have included comedy.

The evidence for the proagon is meagre, its interpretation controversial. One source implies that it involved a competition (agon); perhaps, it has been suggested, to determine the order of performance. *Aristophanes (1) wrote a comedy called Proagon (prob. 422 BC) in which *Euripides was ridiculed; and an anecdote tells how at the proagon following Euripides' death, *Sophocles (1) appeared in mourning, his troupe ungarlanded (Vit. Eurip.). (Aeschin. In Ctes. 66–7 with schol.; schol. Ar. Vesp. 1109; Pl. Symp. 194a).

A. Pickard-Cambridge, The Dramatic Festivals of Athens, 2nd edn. with addenda, rev. J. Gould and D. M. Lewis, 1988 (1968). P. J. W.

Proba, Faltonia Betitia, Christian poetess and wife of Clodius Celsinus Adelphius, prefect of Rome in AD 351. She composed a lost epic on the civil war between Constantius II and Magnentius (under whom her husband held his prefecture), and later an extant Virgilian *cento on the creation of the world and the life of Christ (CSEL 16. 568 ff.).

PLRE 1. 732, 'Proba 2'. J. F. Ma.

probolē See LAW AND PROCEDURE, ATHENIAN.

probouloi (πρόβουλοι) was a name used for officials in various Greek states. In *Athens probouloi were appointed in 413 BC. They were ten men over 40 years of age, including *Sophocles (1) the tragedian and Hagnon the father of *Theramenes. They were appointed immediately after the failure of the Sicilian expedition (413 BC, see ATHENS, HISTORY), evidently because it was felt that the *ekklēsia and the *boulē could not conduct the war efficiently. They had some executive powers, but the precise extent is not known; they may have taken over some functions from the *prytaneis. In 411 they were included in a commission appointed to draft a new constitution; this led to the revolution of the *Four Hundred, after which they are not heard of again.

F. Ruzé, in J. Tréheux (ed.), Mélanges d'histoire ancienne offerts à W. Seston (1974), 443–62; S. Alessandri, Symposion 1988 (1990), 129–47.

D. M. M.

Probus (1), **Marcus Aurelius** (RE 194; PLRE 1, 736), b. *Sirmium AD 232, commanded the eastern army in 276. He challenged *Florianus after the death of *Tacitus (2) and, as the better general, emerged as sole emperor (autumn).

He was an active warrior-emperor. In Gaul from 277 to 278, he expelled Alamannic and Frankish invaders (see ALAMANNI; FRANKS) and restored the Rhine frontier. Between 278 and 280 he defeated the *Burgundians and *Vandals in *Raetia and campaigned on the middle Danube. In 280 he moved to *Antioch (1), whence he directed the suppression of Isaurian banditry (see ISAURIA) and nomadic incursions into Upper Egypt. His main intention was probably to deal with the Persian question (see SASANIDS), but he soon had to leave Syria to subdue mutinies on the Rhine and in Britain. Another rebellion, by Saturninus, in his rear, also failed. In 281 he celebrated a triumph in Rome. In 282 he was at Sirmium when *Carus claimed the purple in Raetia. Probus was killed by his own troops (autumn).

His problems with the army suggest growing military discontent. This is traditionally ascribed to Probus' disciplinarian tendencies and his use of soldiers as labourers on agricultural and civil-engineering schemes. However, possibly he also seemed to his troops and officers to be increasingly careless of the empire's real needs. Indeed, though in his military, civil, and religious policies he projected himself as the authentic successor of *Aurelian, his end is reminiscent of that of *Gallienus. His main historical significance is his acceleration of the settlement of barbarians on Roman territory.

K. Pink, NZ 1949, 13 ff.; S. Vitucci, L'imperatore Probo (1952); R. Syme, Emperors and Biography (1971); L. Polverini, ANRW 2. 2 (1975), 1013 ff.; G. E. M. de Ste. Croix, Class Struggle (1981); H. Halfmann, Itinera principum (1986).

J. F. Dr.

Probus (2), **Sextus Claudius Petronius** (c. AD 328–390), Roman senator, four times praetorian prefect (see PRAEFECTUS PRAETORIO) between 364 and 383, and loyal supporter of the dynasties of Valentinian (see VALENTINIAN (1) and (2)) and Theodosius (see THEODOSIUS (2) and (3)). Unusual among senators in his commitment to a political career in the service and entourage of emperors, Probus' character and ambitions drew from *Ammianus Marcellinus one of his most vivid character studies (27. 11), in which he was described as 'gasping like a fish out of water' when not holding the prefectures into which he was forced by the pressure of his clan, the Christian Anicii, in order to defend their interests. Probus' financial administration of Illyricum in his third and longest prefecture is criticized by *Jerome, and he is regarded with great reserve in the letters of *Symmachus (2). Probus was buried at St Peter's, and the now lost epitaph erected in his mausoleum was transcribed by the antiquarian Mafeo Vegio, c.1450.

CIL 6. 1756b (= Diehls, ILCV 63); PLRE 1. 736–40, 'Probus 5'; J. F. Matthews, Western Aristocracies and Imperial Court, AD 364–425 (repr. of 1990), 195 ff., 400 f.; A. Cameron, JRS 1985, 164 ff. J. F. Ma.

processions are an extremely common feature of Greek and Roman religious practice. It is above all in the procession that a

group may ritually display its cohesion and power to itself and others. And the route taken may express the control of space. The group may embody the whole community, as in the splendid festivals of the Greek *polis—the Panathenaic procession (see PANATHENAEA) represented on the *Parthenon frieze, for example, with its various subgroups of virgins, youths, old men, musicians, chariots, and so on. Smaller groups form processions at funerals, weddings, and the like. Or a great procession may be centred around a single individual, as in the Roman *triumph. The procession almost always leads up to some action at its destination, frequently animal *sacrifice in a precinct (with the victims led in the procession); but also mystic *initiation (see MYSTERIES), as in the mass of initiands proceeding on the sacred way from Athens to *Eleusis; theatrical performances, as at the Athenian City *Dionysia; the offering of a robe to the deity, as at the Panathenaea; fire ritual on a mountain top, as at the Boeotian Daedala; games, as in the Roman pompa circensis; and so on. Special types of procession include those which escorted a deity (generally *Dionysus) into the city, as at the Anthesteria, and those conducted by children collecting contributions. Among the objects carried in processions were phalloi (see PHALLUS), baskets, the sacred objects of the mysteries, and branches hung with wool and fruit (eiresionai). Detailed accounts survive of magnificent processions at *Alexandria (1) (Ath. 196a–203b, the procession of *Ptolemy (1) II Philadelphus, see CALLIXEINUS) and at Rome (Dion. Hal. 7. 72, preceding the *Ludi Magni). Christian antipathy to pagan festivals is expressed in the idea of the pompa diaboli (devil's procession).

RE 21. 1878–994, 'Pompa'; H. S. Versnel Triumphus (1970); Burkert, GR 99–102; G. Rogers, Sacred Identity of Ephesus (1989). R. A. S. S.

Proclus, Neoplatonist philosopher (AD 410 or 412–485; see NEOPLATONISM). Born in *Lycia of wealthy parents, he was destined for the law, but after some study in *Alexandria (1), came to Athens in search of philosophical enlightenment, where he spent the rest of his life. He studied with Plutarch of Athens and *Syrianus, whom he succeeded as head of the Platonic school (diadochos) in 437. His importance as a creative thinker has sometimes been exaggerated: most of the new features which distinguish his Neoplatonism from that of *Plotinus, such as the postulation of triadic 'moments' within each hypostasis, or of 'henads' within the realm of the One, are traceable, at least in germ, to *Iamblichus (2) or Syrianus. But he is the last great systematizer of the Greek philosophical inheritance, and as such exerted a powerful influence on medieval and Renaissance thought, and even, through Hegel, on German idealism. His learning was encyclopaedic and his output vast. Extant works include the following:

1. Philosophical treatises: Elements of Theology, a concise summary of Neoplatonic metaphysics; Platonic Theology, a more elaborate account of the same; Elements of Physics, based on *Aristotle's theory of motion; Opuscula: On Providence, On Fate, and On Evil, long known only in William of Moerbeke's Latin trans., but now rediscovered in Greek, plagiarized by Isaac Sebastocrator.

2. Commentaries on *Plato (1): On the Timaeus; On the Republic, really a series of independent essays; On the Parmenides; On the Alcibiades; On the Cratylus (excerpts).

3. Scientific works: Outline of Astronomical Theories; Commentary on the First Book of *Euclid's Elements. There are also a commentary on *Ptolemy (4)'s Tetrabiblos and a work on eclipses, which have received no modern edition.

4. Literary works: *Hymns*; *Chrestomathia*, a handbook of literature extant in epitome only, authorship disputed (see EPIC CYCLE); *scholia on *Hesiod, *Works and Days*.

LIFE Marinus, *Vita Procli*, ed. J. F. Boissonade (1814).

WORKS *Elem. Theol.* ed. E. R. Dodds (2nd edn. 1963); *Elem. Phys.* ed. A. Ritzenfeld (1912); *Theol. Plat.* ed. H.-D. Saffrey and L. G. Westerink (Budé, 1968–94); *In Tim.* ed. E. Diehl (Teubner, 1903–6); *In Rep.* ed. W. Kroll (Teubner, 1899–1901); *In Alc.* ed. Westerink (1954); A. Ségonds (Budé, 1985–6); *In Crat.* ed. G. Pasquali (1908); F. Romano (1989); *Hymns*, ed. E. Vogt (1957); *Chrest.* ed. A. Severyns (1938–63).

PHILOSOPHY L. J. Rosán, *The Philosophy of Proclus* (1949); R. Beutler, *RE* 'Proklos'; W. Beierwaltes, *Proklos: Grundzüge seiner Metaphysik* (1965); R. T. Wallis, *Neoplatonism* (1972), ch. 5; S. Gersh, *Kinesis Akinetos: A Study of Spiritual Motion in the Philosophy of Proclus* (1973); J. Trouillard, *La Mystagogie de Proclus* (1982); J. Pépin and H.-D. Saffrey (eds.), *Proclus, lecteur et interprète des anciens* (1987).   J. M. D.

Procne See PHILOMELA.

Proconnesus See PROPONTIS.

Procopius Greek historian, born in *Caesarea (2) in Palestine *c.* AD 500. After a thorough rhetorical and legal education—where he studied we do not know—he obtained by 527 a post on the staff of *Justinian's great general *Belisarius, and soon became his *assessor* (πάρεδρος) and counsellor (σύμβουλος), and carried many difficult and sometimes dangerous missions for his commander. After accompanying Belisarius on his Persian (527–31), African (533–6), and Italian (536–40) campaigns, he returned to *Constantinople by 542, where he may have continued to pursue an official career. His fortunes no doubt fluctuated with those of his great patron, who incurred the enmity of Theodora. He is not to be identified with the Procopius who was prefect of the city (see PRAEFECTUS URBI) in 562. The date of his death is unknown.

His principal work is his *History of the Wars of Justinian* in eight books. Books 1–2 deal with the first Persian war, 3–4 with the war against the *Vandals in Africa, 5–7 with that against the *Goths in Italy; these were probably published in 551. Book 8 contains supplementary material and a short history of the years 551–3. The *History* deals primarily with *Justinian's campaigns, but there are many digressions on the political scene in Constantinople and on events elsewhere in the empire. Procopius, as Belisarius' confidant, had direct and comprehensive acquaintance with military affairs and was favourably placed to interrogate eyewitnesses of what he had not himself seen. These are the main sources upon which his *History* relies. But he also made use of documents and other written sources in Greek and Latin, and probably also in Syriac. His strength lies in clear narrative rather than in analysis. Procopius was a careful and intelligent man, generally of balanced judgement, though he had a slight prejudice in favour of his hero Belisarius. His attitude is somewhat old-fashioned and backward-looking. His claim to a sincere desire to establish the truth is somewhat vitiated by the very different picture which he paints of Justinian's regime in his *Secret History*, written at the same time as books 1–7 of his *History of the Wars*. It is a virulent, uncritical, and often scurrilous attack on the whole policy of Justinian and on the characters of the emperor and his consort, which can only have been circulated clandestinely so long as Justinian was alive. It provides a kind of sub-text to the *History of the Wars*, and reveals Procopius as a diehard, if occasionally almost paranoiac, adherent of the aristocratic opposition, which had briefly shown its hand at the time of the Nika riot of 532. Whether this was his attitude since his youth or had been occasioned by his later experience we do not know.

The general reliability of his account of military events is unlikely to have been seriously affected by his reservations concerning Justinian's regime. His work *On Justinian's Buildings*, was composed (*c.*553–5) at the emperor's behest, and is panegyrical in tone. Whether this betokens a change in the author's views or merely proves his ability to ride two different horses at once, we cannot tell. The work is a first-class source for the geography, topography, and art of the period, and Procopius displays an unexpected talent for lucid architectural description.

All the works are written in a classicizing but generally clear Greek, with many echoes and reminiscences of earlier historians, particularly *Thucydides (2). Procopius, however, is no imitative epigone, but a historian of the first rank, helped rather than hindered by the literary tradition within which he wrote.

Ed. J. Haury, 3 vols. (1914–40, repr. 1963–4); H. B. Dewing, 7 vols. (Loeb, 1914–40). B. Rubin, *Prokopios von Kaisareia* (1954); J. A. S. Evans, *Procopius* (1972); A. M. Cameron, *Procopius and the Sixth Century* (1985); *PLRE* 3. 1060–6.   R. B.

Procris, an Attic heroine (see ATTIC CULTS AND MYTHS; HERO-CULT), best known for her stormy marital relationship with *Cephalus. When the disguised Cephalus discovered her willingness to be unfaithful, she fled in shame to *Crete, where she cured *Minos of his childlessness and, being a great huntress, was presented by him with a hound which never missed its mark, which in turn she gave to Cephalus. Having then tricked her husband with his own method, she remained suspicious of him, and was accidentally killed by him while spying on him as he was hunting. Her father *Erechtheus then buried her and prosecuted Cephalus.

For bibliog. see CEPHALUS; also *LIMC* 7. 1 (1994), 529–30.   E. Ke.

Procrustes, familiar epithet of one of *Theseus' adversaries on his journey from *Troezen to Athens, also known as Damastes, Polypemon, and perhaps Procoptas. He was a brigand who lived between *Eleusis and Athens. Having overcome his victims he would force them to lie down on a bed, or on one of two beds; if they were too short, he would hammer them out or rack them with weights to fit the longer bed, if too tall he would cut them to fit the shorter. Theseus disposed of him in like manner.

Diod. 4. 59. 5; Apollod. *Epit* 1. 3. 4; Hyginus, *Fab.* 38.   E. Ke.

Proculus (*RE* 9a), **Sempronius** (?), a Roman lawyer of the mid-1st cent. AD, perhaps from Spain, who gave his name to the Proculian school, which emphasized principle and consistency, in contrast with that founded by *Masurius Sabinus and C. *Cassius Longinus (2). Sextus *Pomponius calls him 'powerful' (*plurimum potuit*), an indication of senatorial rank. He is known for eleven books (*libri*) of *Epistulae* (Letters), derived from practice and teaching, the first time this title was used by a lawyer. His views are often cited by later lawyers and Justinian's compilers took 34 passages from him for their *Digesta* (see JUSTINIAN'S CODIFICATION).

Lenel, *Pal.* 2. 159–84; Bremer (1901), 111. 99–170; *PIR*[1] P 741; *HLL* 3. (forthcoming) § 327.2; Kunkel (1967) 113–19; T. Honoré, *RHD* 1962, 472–509; C. Krampe, *Proculi Epistulae* (1970).   T. Hon.

procurator signified an agent or, in legal proceedings, representative, and under the Principate came to be the distinctive term for the employees of the emperor in civil administration. They might be freedmen from the imperial *familia* (slave household), but the majority, especially of the holders of the more important posts, were normally *equites*. The principal types of procuratorial post were:

Prodicus

1. Praesidial procurators governed minor provinces such as *Corsica, *Judaea, *Noricum, *Thrace, and the Mauretanias (see MAURETANIA). These governors had originally been called *praefecti*; thus Pontius Pilate (*Pontius Pilatus) was officially entitled *Praefectus Iudaeae*, AE 1963, 104. However this term came to be reserved for the equestrian governors of Egypt and, from 198, *Mesopotamia where legionary troops were stationed. Praesidial procurators commanded the auxiliary units in their provinces, exercised full civil and criminal jurisdiction, and supervised all fiscal matters. If at any time legionary forces were permanently stationed in such a province, the role of governor was transferred to a senatorial *legatus pro praetore* (e.g. Judaea from the time of the revolt of AD 66; see LEGATI).

2. Procurators of imperial provinces, governed by *legati*, supervised the collection of direct taxes, indirect taxes (when special officials were not appointed, see below (4)), and of the revenues accruing from imperial properties. They were also responsible for the commissariat and pay of the troops. They had small detachments of troops at their disposal and official entitlement to requisitioned transport.

3. Procurators of the public provinces, governed by annual proconsuls, were originally only in charge of the properties of the emperor. They came, by a process whose details remain obscure, to acquire responsibilities analogous to those of the procurators of the imperial provinces and, thus, to exercise joint supervision, with the proconsuls, of public taxation.

Both of these types of procurators (2 and 3) also acquired legitimate jurisdiction in fiscal litigation. Occasionally they are found exercising powers, in the realms of civil and criminal jurisdiction or of non-fiscal administration (e.g. supervision of construction of roads), which were routinely the preserve of senatorial governors. These occasional extensions of their role are probably best understood as matters of administrative expediency. Also both types of procurator might act in place of the senatorial governor of the province. The first known occasion was in Asia about 88 (after the execution of the incumbent proconsul), and this function became increasingly common from the first half of the 3rd cent.

4. Procurators of imperial estates (see DOMAINS) were responsible for their general supervision. They issued regulations about the mutual obligations of *coloni* and *conductores* and possessed wide policing powers.

5. Procurators responsible for the supervision of specific indirect taxes appear in the 1st cent. and more widely in the 2nd (see PORTORIA and VECTIGAL). Their responsibility normally encompassed a set of geographically contiguous provinces.

6. Throughout the first two centuries there was a steady accretion of procuratorial posts connected with the organization of matters such as the aqueducts, the *annona* (see FOOD SUPPLY), the mint, and imperial *ludi* or *familiae gladiatoriae*.

Entry to procuratorial posts followed normally on military service, either (for men who were already *equites*) the 'tres militiae' (*praefectus cohortis*, *tribunus legionis*, *praefectus alae*), or from the rank of *primipilus bis* for men who had risen from the ranks. The 1st cent. saw the formation of the 'praetorian cursus' by which a *primipilus went as tribune of a cohort successively in the three urban units (*vigiles*, urban, and praetorian cohorts), went to another legion as *primipilus bis*, and then moved to important procuratorships. Under *Hadrian we meet for the first time the junior equestrian post of *advocatus fisci* which served as a non-military point of entry to the equestrian cursus. A minority of the most successful procurators could hope to gain promotion to the major prefectures, Egypt, the *annona*, and the praetorian cohorts and from the late 1st cent. to the secretarial posts with the emperor, previously the preserve of imperial freedmen. Procurators were the direct appointees of the emperor and received a codicil of appointment (see AE 1962, 183 for a fine example).

By the reign of *Septimius Severus 163 procuratorial posts are attested; many of those only attested in the 2nd cent. may have existed earlier (our surviving evidence is seriously deficient). A regular hierarchy of promotion evolved (see CAREERS; CURSUS HONORUM) which by the mid second century ran (after military service or the post of *advocatus fisci*) from minor procuratorial posts, to provincial procuratorships, praesidial procuratorships, 'secretarial posts', and major prefectures. In this evolution procuratorial posts came to be graded by level of pay—*sexagenarii* (those receiving 60,000 sesterces per annum), *centenarii* (100,000), *ducenarii* (200,000), and, rarely, *trecenarii* (300,000). The number and the duties of the freedmen procurators are ill known; but most, probably, acted as assistants to equestrian procurators.

In the second half of the 3rd cent. equestrians steadily replaced senators as provincial governors, a process completed by *Diocletian (except for the surviving proconsulates of Africa and Asia); the word *praeses*, increasingly common for both types of governor in the third century, was now universal for equestrian governors. *Procuratores* survived as the officials in charge of imperial mints, mines, factories, and landed properties.

O. Hirschfeld, *Die kaiserlichen Verwaltungsbeamten* (1905); H. G. Pflaum, *Les Procurateurs équestres* (1950), and *Les Carrières procuratoriennes* (1960–1); F. Millar, *Hist.* 1964, 180 ff; *Hist.* 1965, 362 ff; R. P. Saller, *JRS* 1980, 44 ff; P. A. Brunt, *JRS* 1983, 42 ff, and *Roman Imperial Themes* (1990), ch. 8.   G. P. B.

Prodicus of Ceos, a *sophist and contemporary of *Socrates (1). Little is known about his life. We learn from *Plato (1) that he served on diplomatic missions and that he took advantage of the opportunities these afforded to build up his clientele and to demand high fees. He was chiefly a teacher of *rhetoric, with a special interest in the correct use of words and the distinction of near-synonyms. Plato represents Socrates as being on friendly terms with him and paying tribute to the value of his teaching, though usually with a touch of irony. Of his writings all that survives is *Xenophon (1)'s paraphrase of his myth of the Choice of *Heracles between Virtue and Vice. He gave naturalistic accounts of the origin of religion, in some respects anticipating *Euhemerus, and is counted as an atheist by some sources. See also CULTURE-BRINGERS.

DK 84, Eng. tr. in R. K. Sprague (ed.), *The Older Sophists* (1972); W. K. C. Guthrie, *A Hist. of Greek Philosophy*, 3 (1969); A. Henrichs, *Harv. Stud.* 1975, 93 ff., and *Cronache Erculanese* 6 (1976), 15 ff.; C. W. Willink, *CQ* 1983, 25 ff.; M. Ostwald, *CAH* 5² (1992), 345 f., 368 f.   C. C. W. T.

prodigies See PORTENTS.

proedroi (πρόεδροι) were chairmen. In the 5th cent. BC in Athens the chairman at meetings of the *boulē and *ekklēsia was the foreman of the *prytaneis; but later, probably from 403/2 onwards, this duty was taken over by *proedroi*, presumably because the foreman of the *prytaneis* was thought to be overburdened. At each meeting of the *boulē* or *ekklēsia* the foreman of the *prytaneis* picked nine *proedroi* by lot from the other members of the *boulē*, one from each of the ten *phylai except that to which the *prytaneis* themselves belonged, and then he picked by lot one of these nine *proedroi* to be their foreman (ἐπιστάτης). One man could not be a *proedros* more than once in a prytany, nor foreman of the *proedroi* more than once in a year. The *proedroi* kept order at the meeting, brought forward the various items of business in accordance with the agenda, counted or estimated the votes given by show of hands, and finally dismissed the meeting.

P. J. Rhodes, *The Athenian Boule* (1972), 25–8; M. H. Hansen, *The Athenian Assembly* (1987), 37–9.   D. M. M.

Proetus, the first king of Tiryns, who quarrelled with his brother *Acrisius in their mother's womb. See also BELLEROPHON; LETTERS, GREEK. The only other important myth, which is fragmented into various local traditions, concerns his daughters, the Proetides. These insulted the statue of *Hera (*Acusilaus, *FGrH* 2 F 28), or refused the rites of *Dionysus (Hes. fr. 131). They were driven mad by the offended deity and wandered about the country 'with all sorts of indecent behaviour'. In particular, they took themselves for cows and roamed the *Peloponnesus mooing. *Melampus (1), being asked to heal them, demanded a share of the kingdom; this was refused, and they went madder still, now being joined by all the other women who had killed their own children. Finally, Proetus agreed to Melampus, although his terms had been raised. The women were then caught by Melampus and a band of youths at Sicyon and cured, except one, Iphinoe, who had died. Melampus married one of the daughters and became king. The myth with its 'mooing' girls, a stay outside the city, a chase by youths and a concluding marriage strongly suggests a background in initiation. As daughters of the primeval king, the Proetides were the exemplary initiates; see INITIATION.

Homer, *Il.* 6. 157 ff. with Kirk's comm. G. Casadio, *Storia del culto di Dioniso in Argolide* (1994), 51–116; L. Kahil, *LIMC* under the name; K. Dowden, *Death and the Maiden* (1989), 70–95.   H. J. R.; J. N. B.

progress See ANTHROPOLOGY.

progymnasmata (Lat. *prae-exercitamina*) were the 'preliminary exercises' which made up the elementary stage of instruction in schools of rhetoric. It is not clear that there was a recognized 'cycle' of such exercises before Roman times, but a number of extant collections from the time of the empire survive. The treatise by Aelius *Theon (3) (1st cent. AD) is the earliest; that of Aphthonius (*c*. AD 400) the most influential. A set of exercises attributed to *Hermogenes was translated into Latin by *Priscian. *Libanius and Nicolaus of Myra are also important, and the genre continued to be developed in Byzantine times. The principal exercises were μῦθος (*fable), διήγημα (*narrative), χρεία (anecdotal apophthegm), γνώμη (maxim, see GNŌMĒ), ἀνασκευή and κατασκευή (refutation and confirmation), κοινὸς τόπος (commonplace, see TOPOS), ἠθοποιΐα (speech written in character), ἔκφρασις (description, see EKPHRASIS), θέσις (general question), νόμου εἰσφορά (introduction of a law). While some of these exercises might prove useful for forensic or deliberative oratory, others (especially 'narrative' and 'description') were closer to the needs of epideictic oratory or history. The influence of these exercises on literature was very great and very long-lasting. See RHETORIC, GREEK.

Texts in L. Spengel, *Rhetores Graeci*; Theon, ed. J. R. Butts (1987); Aphthonius, ed. H. Rabe (1926), trans. by R. Nadeau in *Speech Monographs* 19 (1952), 264–85; Nicolaus ed. J. Felten (1913); Libanius' *Progymnasmata* are in vol. 8 of R. Foerster's edn. (1913). See in general: R. F. Hock and E. N. O'Neil, *The Chreia in Ancient Rhetoric* (1986); G. A. Kennedy, *Greek Rhetoric under Christian Emperors* (1983), 52–73; W. Kroll in *RE* Suppl. 7. 1117–19; C. S. Baldwin, *Ancient Rhetoric and Poetics* (1924), and *Mediaeval Rhetoric and Poetics* (1928); A. Grafton and L. Jardine, *From Humanism to the Humanities* (1986), 130–5.   D. A. R.

Prohaeresius See PRO(H)AERESIUS.

proletarii, as opposed to *assidui*, were the citizens of Rome too poor to contribute anything to the state except their children (*proles*). They seem to have been equated with the *capite censi* as persons who paid no tribute and were exempt from military service except in an emergency (*tumultus), when they were issued with armour and weapons. The alternative explanation produced in *Gellius (*NA* 16. 10), that the *proletarii* had property between 1,500 and 375 asses, while the *capite censi* had 375 or less, is not confirmed elsewhere nor can it be easily reconciled with the single century of *capite censi/proletarii* in the *comitia centuriata*.

In the mid-2nd cent. BC direct taxation for Romans was suspended (see TRIBUTUM) and the property qualification for military service was lowered. Nevertheless, the distinction between those who were sufficiently wealthy to be regarded as both sound citizens and reliable defenders of their country, and those who were not, remained important in Roman political ideology. C. *Marius (1) in 107 BC set a precedent by enrolling *capite censi* volunteers, when there was no emergency, but conscription from those financially qualified remained the main source of the legions throughout the republic. Although in Ciceronian times the *proletarii* must have constituted a major part of the total population, they had virtually no strength in the *comitia centuriata*, being collected in a single century, which only voted if the decision was still open after the decision of the five propertied classes had been declared.

Mommsen, *Röm. Staatsr.* 3. 237 f.; E. Gabba, *Republican Rome: The Army and the Allies* (1976), ch. 1; P. Brunt, *Fall of the Roman Republic* (1988), ch. 5.   A. W. L.

promagistrates See PRO CONSULE, PRO PRAETORE.

Prometheus, divine figure associated with the origin of *fire and with *Hephaestus, developed by *Hesiod into a figure of greater weight. The name, of unknown significance, was given the sense 'Forethought' by Hesiod, who added a contrasting figure Epimetheus ('Thinking after the event'). His father is *Iapetus.

Local Myth and Cult: (1) At Athens Prometheus and Hephaestus are worshipped by potters (because of the firing of clay?) and in the *Academy. A torch-race in honour of Prometheus probably formed part of a ritual renewal of fire (Deubner, *Attische Feste*, 211–12, cf. Nilsson, *Feste*, 173–4). (2) In *Thebes (1) (Paus. 9. 25. 6) one of the *Cabiri is named Prometheus and his son is Aetnaeus ('of Mt. Etna', where Hephaestus and the *Cyclopes worked as smiths). (3) *Deucalion is the son of Prometheus (Hes. fr. 2, Acusilaus *FGrH* 2 F 34, Pind. *Ol.* 9. 55) and after the flood first lived at Opus (just north of *Boeotia in *Locris). Prometheus has a memorial at Opus, as also at *Sicyon (Paus. 2. 19. 8). (4) At Panopeus (just west of Boeotia in *Phocis) a building housed a statue of Asclepius or possibly Prometheus (Paus. 10. 4. 4). The mythic inhabitants of Panopeus were the Phlegyes ('Blazing men'), etymologically identical with the Indian Bhṛgus, a priestly clan responsible for sacrificial fire received from a divine being Mātariśvan.

In the *Theogony* of the Boeotian Hesiod (506–616) Prometheus is bound to a pillar, his liver eaten daily by an eagle and nightly renewed until finally he is freed by *Heracles. This is traced back to a meal shared by men and gods where Prometheus tricks the gods into feasting on bones and fat, explaining the division of victims after *sacrifice and also the distance which now separates men and gods. *Zeus in anger removes fire from men, but Prometheus steals it and gives it to man, who is then further punished by Hephaestus' creation of woman, foolishly accepted by Epimetheus (see PANDORA). The portrait of Prometheus was developed by later authors: (Pseudo-?) *Aeschylus' *Prometheus Bound* makes him yet more of a *culture-bringer, responsible for man's skills and sciences (442–525). There is also a persistent tradition that Prometheus created man from clay (cf. Ar. *Av.* 686; Paus. 10. 4. 4; Hor. *Carm.* 1. 16. 13–16), as commonly in mythologies (Stith Thompson A1241), and this might lie behind Hephaestus' creation of woman in Hesiod.

Prometheus' defiance of the gods captured the romantic imagination and has profoundly influenced most modern artistic and literary genres (see H. Hunger), notably because of the monumental nobility in the *Prometheus Bound* of Prometheus chained to the rock, hurling defiance at Zeus, and despising mere thunderbolts. The trickery with which Hesiod characterizes this culture-hero has attracted interest in the light of trickster heroes in other mythologies, notably North American. In any case, myths of the origin of fire and of man bring Greek myth closer than usual to world mythologies and folk-tale (Stith Thompson A1415).

His release by Heracles is depicted in art since Archaic times; his theft of fire and creation of man are generally later and less frequent.

K. Bapp, in Roscher, *Lex.* 3. 2 (1909), 3032–110; L. Eckhart, *RE* 23. 1 (1957) 653–730; J. G. Frazer, 'The Origin of Fire' in Apollodorus (Loeb), vol. 2, Appendix 3; H. Hunger, *Lexikon der griechischen und römischen Mythologie* (1959), 353–6; L. Séchan, *Le Mythe de Prométhée* (1951); M. L. West, *Hesiod: Theogony* (1966); J.-P. Vernant, *Myth and Society in Ancient Greece* (1980), 168–85; *LIMC* 7. 1 (1994), 531–53.   K. D.

pronoia (foresight) See PROVIDENTIA.

pronunciation, Greek The main features of the pronunciation of ancient Greek may be established through the study of contemporary documents, literary texts, spelling mistakes, puns, grammarians' statements, etc. (see PRONUNCIATION, LATIN). In many points we may claim only approximate accuracy, but it is certain that the pronunciation of ancient Greek was different from that of Modern Greek and also differed from most modern scholarly pronunciations which inevitably show the influence of national traditions and the scholar's first language. What follows mostly refers to Classical (5th cent. BC) Attic written in the Ionic alphabet (see ALPHABET, GREEK) and offers a traditional view of Attic pronunciation different from that of those scholars like Theodorsson who believe that by the 4th cent. this had already advanced a great deal further in the Modern Greek direction.

A. Vowels and Diphthongs Attic had five short and seven long vowels: [a, i, y, e, o, a:, i:, y:, ɛ:, e:, ɔ:, o:]. Square brackets and symbolism refer to phonetic transcriptions. Note that there are different conventions in transcription and e.g. short [a] may be indicated by [a] or [ă]; long [a] by [a:] or [ā]. Also, in what follows, [e:] = [ē], [ɛ:] = [ẹ̄], [o:] = [ō], [ɔ:] = [ǭ], [y] = [ü].

1. Three letters indicated both short and long vowels: α, ι, υ. Of these [a] and [a:], written α, were central or, more likely, slightly fronted vowels (for the quality cf. *a* in Italian or in Northern English *cat*); [i] and [i:], written ι, were high front vowels similar in quality to French *i* and to the vowel of Engl. *see*. In Attic, in part of Ionic, etc. υ represented [y] and [y:], i.e. front vowels with lip-rounding similar to French *u* or German *ü*. Other dialects used the same sign to indicate [u] and [u:], back vowels similar to German *u* and the vowel of Engl. *too*.

2. In Ionic and Attic there was a long open *e*-vowel [ɛ:] written

η (cf. *aî* in French *maître*) as well as a closer counterpart [e:] (cf. French *été*). This was originally written ɛ, but by the end of the 5th cent. BC a digraph ɛι was used (see below). The letter ω indicated [ɔ:], a long open back vowel (cf. French *fort*), whose close counterpart [o:] (cf. French *beau*) was written first with ο and then with the digraph ου. Later on (c.350 BC ??) the pronunciation changed to [u:] still written ου. The equivalent short mid vowels were written ɛ and ο; the exact quality is uncertain—presumably higher than that of [ɛ:] [ɔ:] and lower than that of [e:] [o:].

3. In the history of Greek diphthongs tend to disappear. By the end of the 5th cent. BC Attic had changed the original diphthongs [ei] [ou], written ɛι ου, into long vowels [e:] [o:]; this explains the use of the digraphs for long vowels (see above). The diphthongs [ai] [oi] (as in Eng. *my* and *boy*), which were written αι and οι, survived longer but at a much later stage [ai] changed into [ɛ:] and still later [oi] into [y:]. Similar changes had occurred in Boeotian many centuries earlier. The [au] and [eu] diphthongs, written αυ and ɛυ, were preserved all through the Classical period; the second element was [u] and not [y]. The status of υι is not clear but in Attic it occurs before vowel only; before consonant it had been replaced by [y:], written υ.

4. The long diphthongs αι, ωι, ηι, αυ, ωυ, ηυ were probably pronounced with a later onset of the glide and were unstable. The *i*-element was lost in pronunciation, if not in spelling, by the second or first century BC. Spellings like ᾳ, ῳ, ῃ with *iota subscript* are a Byzantine innovation.

Later developments. In Modern Greek the significant distinctions of quantity have disappeared though stressed vowels tend to be long. ι, η, υ, ɛι, οι, υι are all pronounced [i]. The second element of the *u*-diphthongs turned into a fricative [f] or [v] according to the sound that followed. Most of these changes were probably complete by the early Byzantine period.

B. Consonants 1. The letters π, τ, κ and β, δ, γ indicated voiceless and voiced stops of the bilabial, dental, and velar series: [p t k b d g] as in French *p*, *t*, 'hard' *c*, *b*, *d*, 'hard' *g*. It is likely that [t, d] (and [n s]) were dental and not alveolar as English [t d n s]. A set of voiceless aspirates [pʰ], [tʰ], [kʰ] were written with φ, θ, χ: cf. the southern English pronunciation of *p* in *pin* and such words as *top-hat*.

2. The labial and dental nasals [m, n] were indicated by μ and ν (cf. French *m* and *n*). A velar variant of the latter sound (cf. [ŋ] in Eng. *ink*) was found before velar sounds and was frequently, though not exclusively, indicated with γ (as in συγγράφω), which in this use was called ἄγμα by the grammarians. Greek [r], written ρ, was probably a voiced rolled tip-tongue sound, similar to Italian *r* or Scottish *r*. The initial variant (ῥ) was probably voiceless. λ indicated a dental lateral sound [l] as in English *leave* and σ a voiceless dental sibilant [s]; cf. French *son* and Eng. *see* where, however, [s] is alveolar. A voiced variant [z] was found before voiced consonants.

3. The rough breathing (ʽ) indicated a breathed glottal fricative (like English *h*) found at the beginning of some words before vowel; the smooth breathing (ʼ), first used by the Alexandrian grammarians, indicated its absence.

4. Three letters indicated consonantal clusters. The value of ζ is disputed and probably varied from dialect to dialect; in Classical Attic it indicated a [zd] cluster but at various stages it may have corresponded to an affricate [dz]. However as early as the 4th cent. BC Attic shows signs of a pronunciation [zz] or [z]. ξ and ψ represented the clusters [ks] and [ps] respectively.

5. Some dialects still knew the voiced semivowel [w], similar to English *w*, which was expressed by the letter Ϝ (digamma) and which had disappeared in Attic. A voiceless variant of it may underlie the spelling Ϝh found in some inscriptions.

6. The spellings ππ, λλ, νν, etc. indicated long or geminate stops and continuants [pp], [ll] etc., similar to those of modern Italian. In the case of Attic ττ corresponding to Ionic σσ the real pronunciation, at least for the early period, is disputed.

Later developments. We have evidence from an early period for the tendency of the voiced and aspirated stops to change into continuants; the full change, however, took place only in the imperial and early Byzantine period. ϕ, θ, χ came to indicate [f] (like English *f*), [θ] (like Eng. *th* in *thing*), [χ] (like *ch* in Scottish *loch*); β and δ indicated [v] and [ð] (like *th* in Eng. *other*); [g] (γ) was changed into [γ] (the voiced equivalent of [χ]) or [j] (cf. *y* in Eng. *yes*). The long geminate consonants were lost and replaced by the corresponding non-geminate consonants.

C. Syllables The ancients divided words into syllables and established rules for this division. From the point of view of metre what counts is the alternation of long (or heavy) and short (or light) syllables, but syllabic quantity should not be confused with vocalic quantity. All syllables which contain a long vowel or diphthong are long (μή, αἰ), but syllables are also long if they contain a short vowel and a final consonant, i.e. if the vowel is followed by more than one consonant (the first syllable of ἀι νήρ is light, that of ἀν ι δρός heavy, but in both forms [a] is short). In contrast with Latin, the distribution of the Greek accent is determined by the length of vowels, not of syllables.

D. Accent 1. Much of our information on the nature of the Greek accent comes, directly or indirectly, from the ancient grammarians. The early Greek accent was one of pitch, i.e. the prominence given within the word to the accented syllable was obtained through a rise of the pitch, followed by falling pitch; differences of stress, if present, were not a relevant factor and it has also been argued that stress had a distribution independent from that of high pitch (Allen). The date at which the 'musical' or pitch accent was replaced by an accent like that of Modern Greek where stress is a primary component is not easy to establish. The change may have developed for a long time, but probably was completed by the end of the 4th cent. AD. Most modern pronunciations follow Modern Greek in replacing high pitch with stress; the 'Henninian' pronunciation (still in use in England), which uses for Greek the same rules of accentuation as for Latin, ought to be rejected.

2. The Greek inscriptions did not normally indicate the word accent or even the division of words (see EPIGRAPHY, GREEK). For this and for the distinctions among the various kinds of accent we depend on the information provided by ancient authors, by some papyri, and by the late manuscripts in which the accents are marked. Most words had one main accent but some so-called enclitic and proclitic elements (mostly pronouns or particles like τις, μοι, ὁ) formed an accentual unit with the word which preceded or followed (the rules cannot be discussed here). The rise in pitch was followed by falling pitch mostly on the next syllable, though sometimes on the second *mora* (unit/element) of a long vowel. The usual signs were first introduced by the *Alexandrian grammarians (probably by *Aristophanes (2)), but the distinction between acute and grave is already mentioned in *Plato (1) (*Cra.* 399). Of the three types of accent the acute (ὀξεῖα) indicated a high pitch which according to one interpretation of a disputed passage by *Dionysius (7) of Halicarnassus (*De comp. verb.* 11), differed by a musical fifth from the grave. It could rest on both

short or long vowels or diphthongs; in the second case it is likely, though not generally accepted, that the higher pitch concerned only the second *mora* of the vowel (⌐ = ◡◌́). In the ancient tradition all unaccented syllables were seen as bearing a grave accent (βαρεῖα), which therefore indicated a lack of accentuation. The fact that an acute resting on the last syllable of a word was changed into a grave within a phrase (θεοί but θεοὶ ἄλλοι) is variously interpreted: loss of accent, partial lowering of pitch, purely graphic convention, etc. Note, however, that this use of the grave is relatively late; the papyri prefer spellings like κἀλὸς ἀνήρ (for καλὸς ἀνήρ), περίκλυτος (for περικλυτός), etc. The circumflex (περισπωμένη) is found only on long vowels or diphthongs and, as the original sign indicates, represents a high pitch on the first mora followed by a falling pitch on the second (◌͡ = ◌́◌̀); in other words it is a combination of an acute and a grave (ἡ ὀξυβαρεῖα, according to another terminology).

3. The Greek accent was different from Latin in that it was free, i.e. its position was not determined merely by phonological rules, but also by a number of different factors: grammatical, lexical, etc. Yet, as in Latin, the accent was limited to one of the last three syllable of a polysyllabic word. In Greek further limitations depended on the quantity of the vocalic element of the last syllable. If this was short, an acute could be found on any of the last three syllables; if the penultimate syllable was long and carried the accent in Attic this had to be a circumflex. If the last vocalic element was long, the accent had to rest on one of the last two syllables and if it was on the penultimate could only be an acute.

E. H. Sturtevant, *The Pronunciation of Greek and Latin*[2] (1940); M. Lejeune, *Phonétique historique du mycénien et du grec ancien* (1972); S.-T. Teodorsson, *The Phonemic System of the Attic Dialect 400–340 BC* (1974), *The Phonology of Ptolemaic Koine* (1977), and *The Phonology of Attic in the Hellenistic Period* (1978); J. P. Postgate, *Short Guide to the Accentuation of Ancient Greek* (1924); J. Vendryes, *Traité d'accentuation grecque* (1904, repr. 1945); Ch. Bally, *Manuel d'accentuation grecque* (1945); W. S. Allen, *Accent and Rhythm* (1973), and *Vox Graeca*[3] (1978); A. M. Devine and L. D. Stephens, *The Prosody of Greek Speech* (1994).
A. M. Da.

pronunciation, Latin Our knowledge of the pronunciation of classical Latin is derived from a variety of sources. Most direct are the specific statements of Latin grammarians and other authors (though allowance must be made for the fact that the former tend to be of later date). Other sources are: puns, word-play, contemporary etymologies, and onomatopoeia; the representation of Latin words in other ancient languages; later developments in the Romance languages; the spelling conventions of Latin, and especially any deviations from these; the internal structure of Latin itself and of its metrical patterns (see GRAMMAR, LATIN; ETYMOLOGY).

In England the pronunciation of Latin has been particularly subject to change over the centuries, owing to influence first from Old English, then from Norman French, and lastly above all by the 'Great Vowel Shift' of Early Modern English. The result was that from the 16th cent. the English pronunciation of Latin was so far removed from the classical original and from other 'national' pronunciations (though these also had their own peculiarities) that it was virtually unintelligible elsewhere. A valuable source for this period is provided by the phonetic transcription of a Latin passage by the phonetician Robert Robinson in his *Art of Pronunciation* of 1617. Despite the reforming efforts of Erasmus (*De recta Latini Graecique sermonis pronuntiatione*, 1528) and early support for these particularly in Cambridge and in

France, vested interests prevented their successful adoption; and in England it was not until the early 20th cent. that official approval, from Oxford and Cambridge and the Classical Association, was secured for a new and generally acceptable reconstruction. In France reaction to change has been even stronger. The old 'English' pronunciation survives mainly in legal Latin and in loan-words (e.g. *genius*). Ecclesiastical pronunciation tends to an 'Italianate' style derived from the Roman Catholic Church.

It is impossible to reconstruct the vocal totality of a dead language; but at least for the individual sounds it is feasible to reach an approximation which is probably as close as the average classical scholar makes to the sounds of a living foreign language.

A. Vowels and Diphthongs The simple vowels of Latin are divisible into two mutually symmetrical systems, long and short, each of five members—*a, i, u, e, o*. These may be described phonetically in terms of the degree of raising of the tongue and the part of the tongue involved. Thus *a* is low (or 'open') central, *i* is high (or 'close') front, *u* is high back, *e* is mid front, and *o* is mid back. The back vowels are also accompanied by lip-rounding. Whilst the short *ă* and the long *ā* were of similar quality, the other long vowels were distinctly higher than their short counterparts: in fact in the Romance languages the mid long *ē* and *ō* developed in the same way as the high short *ĭ* and *ŭ*. The approximate values of these vowels in terms of modern languages are as follows:- *ă/ā* as first/second vowels of Italian *amare* (less correctly as in Southern English *cup/path*); *ĭ/ī* as in Eng. *bit/beat*; *ŭ/ū* as in Eng. *put/fool*; *ĕ* as in Eng. *pet*; *ē* as in Fr. *gai* or Ger. *Beet*; *ŏ* as in Eng. *pot*; *ō* as in Fr. *beau* or Ger. *Boot*.

In addition to the main short-vowel system there is also evidence for an unstressed vowel of 'intermediate' quality between *ĭ* and *ŭ*. In certain words, in middle syllables followed by a single labial consonant (*u, p, b, f*), early Latin writes a vowel *u* which later generally changes to i; e.g. *optumus → optimus*. The earliest, inscriptional example of this change dates from 117 BC, and its official recognition is said to have been due to *Caesar. It is likely that at some time both the *u* and the *i* written in such words were different from the normal vowels so written, most probably being more centralized, the latter like the ы in Russian горы or the *y* in Welsh *felly*. There is no good evidence that these spellings indicated, as sometimes stated, a fully front lip-rounded vowel like the German *ü* or ancient Greek *υ*. In any case, perhaps already in the classical period, it soon merged with the *ĭ* of the main system. The sound of the Greek *υ* was, however, adopted in loan-words from Greek and written with *y*, as *nympha* etc.

The diphthongs *ae* (earlier written *ai*) and *au* had much the same values as those in Eng. *high* and *how*. Each of these consists of a glide from a low to a high vowel-quality, and in rural districts the two elements merged into (long) simple mid vowels; in late Latin this change became more general. Though represented in spelling as *e* and *o*, it is likely that they were of a lower (more open) quality then the normal *ē/ō*, as in Fr. *tête* and Eng. *saw*, since they developed in the Romance languages in the same way as *short ĕ* and *ŏ*. The rarer diphthong *oe* was similar to that in Eng. *boy*; and the infrequent *ui, eu* and *ei* were glides of the type suggested by their spelling (note that the *u* of *ui*, as in *cui, huic*, is *not* a consonant, i.e. this digraph is not pronounced as Eng. *we*).

B. Consonants The pronunciation of the Latin consonants calls for no general systemic comment. They were mostly pronounced with the common values of the letters used, with a few special exceptions. In particular *c* and *g* were in classical times pronounced as voiceless/voiced velar plosives, i.e. as in Eng.

cap/gap or *kit/get*, even before the front vowels *i* and *e*, where later, by the process of palatalization, they developed first to 'affricates', as in Italian *cento*, or by a further process to fricatives, as in Fr. *cent* or Spanish *ciento* (the original value survives in Sardinian dialect *kentu*). In the group *gn*, as in *dignus*, it is likely that the *g* was nasalized, so that the group will have sounded like the *ngn* in Eng. *hangnail*.

In its consonantal value the letter *u* (V) stood for a semivowel, like the English *w*, and not a fricative *v*; the change to the latter value took place around the end of the 1st century AD. The other semivowel, written as *i* (I), had the value of the English *y*.

h in colloquial Latin, even in classical times, tended to be dropped, and has completely disappeared in the Romance languages. In initial position it may be considered simply as a voiceless onset of the following vowel, and as such does not prevent elision of a preceding final vowel. Similar considerations apply to the labial nasal *m* in final position before a following initial vowel; the explanation here is presumably that the consonant developed simply into a nasalization of the preceding vowel (as in Fr. *rien* from L. *rem*).

Consonants written double were pronounced long: thus *nn* in *annus* as in Eng. *unnamed* (not as in *manner*).

C. Quantity For accentual and metrical purposes (see METRE, LATIN) it is important to distinguish between *length of vowels* (long/short) and *quantity of syllables* (heavy/light, using terms adopted from Sanskrit grammar). A heavy syllable is one containing either a long vowel (or diphthong) *or* a short vowel followed by more than one consonant; all other syllables are light. An exception to this rule is provided by groups of consonants comprising a plosive (*p, t, c, b, d, g*) followed by a liquid (*r, l*); in *Plautus and *Terence, and in spoken Latin, these groups were treated as single consonants for quantitative (and hence accentual) purposes. But in dactylic verse they may also be treated as a normal group, in imitation of Greek models: thus in *Aen.* 2. 663 *patris* has a light first syllable but *patrem* a heavy.

Note that in the pronouns *hic* (nom. masc.) and *hoc* (nom./acc. neut.) the *vowel* is short; but in the latter, and after Plautus and Terence the former, *c* stands for *cc*, giving heavy quantity, before a following vowel (except by occasional archaism in the case of *hic*). But in ablative *hoc* and adverb *hic* the vowel itself is long.

D. Accent The placing of the classical accent was governed by quantity. By the so-called 'Penultimate Law', in words of more than two syllables the accent falls on the penultimate syllable if this is heavy, but on the antepenultimate, regardless of quantity, if the penultimate is light: thus e.g. *conféctus* but *confícere, cónficit*. In disyllables the accent falls on the first.

As regards the nature of the accent, there are clear indications that in prehistoric and in late Latin it was manifested by stress, and it is unlikely that the intervening classical accent would have been of a different nature. Grammarians, following Greek models, tend to describe it in terms of musical pitch as in ancient Greek, but the detailed plagiarism of their descriptions and the very different placement rules in the two languages, as well as other internal and typological evidence in Latin, make this highly improbable. Admittedly stress is often accompanied by variation in pitch, but this does not make pitch the primary feature.

One result of the different nature of the accent in Greek and Latin was that in the last two feet of the Latin hexameter, unlike Greek, poets increasingly aimed at agreement between the verse rhythm and the linguistic accent. But in the rest of the line discord rather than concord prevails, and there is evidence that the

Romans themselves recited poetry with stress on the linguistic accents rather than on the verse rhythm where these conflicted. There seems also, however, to have been a pedagogical practice, used for the teaching of metre, whereby each foot was accented as if it were a word, resulting in a 'scanning' delivery such as is practised by some readers to-day. See PROSE RHYTHM, LATIN.

E. H. Sturtevant, *The Pronunciation of Greek and Latin*[2] (1940); F. Brittain, *Latin in Church*[2] (1955); J. Marouzeau, *La Prononciation du latin* (1955); E. Liénard, *Prononciation du latin classique* (1963); A. Traina, *L'alfabeto e la pronunzia del latino*[2] (1963); W. S. Allen, *Accent and Rhythm: Prosodic Features of Latin and Greek* (1973), and *Vox Latina*[2] (1978).   W. S. A.

prooemium

1. Verse See HYMNS (GREEK); LYRIC POETRY, GREEK.

2. Prose Applied originally to poetry (Pind. *Pyth.* 1. 4, *Nem.* 2. 3), the term προοίμιον was taken over by rhetorical theory to designate the first of the four (sometimes more) sections into which classical rhetoricians divided the prose speech. It is, with the peroration (ἐπίλογος), the part of the speech which contains the greatest accumulation of recognizable commonplaces, and the typical themes are already discernible in the 5th cent. Toward the end of the 5th cent. the custom arose of compiling collections of stock openings (and also perorations) to forensic and political speeches. Such collections are attested for *Antiphon (1), *Critias, *Thrasymachus and perhaps Cephalus (see *Suda*, below Κέφαλος; for deployment of stock prooemia cf. Lys. 19. 2–5, 11 with Andoc. 1. 1, 6–7, 9, Isae. 8. 5 with Dem. 27. 2–3). The extant set attributed to *Demosthenes (2) numbers fifty-six, five of which are identical with the openings of Dem. 1, 4, 14, 15, 16. Blass argues cogently for the authenticity of the set, often impugned, pointing out that the historical background, in the few places where it is defined, is everywhere that of the *first war against *Philip (1) II, a restriction only explicable on the supposition that Demosthenes himself wrote the prooemia between 349 and 346 for his own use when required (cf. Cicero's practice, *Att.* 16. 6. 4). *Ephorus wrote a prooemium to each book of his history, a practice followed by *Diodorus (3) (Diod. Sic. 16. 76. 5). The theory of the prooemium is discussed by *Aristotle (*Rh.* 3. 14), *Hermogenes (2) (*Inv.* 1. 1–5), and *Apsines (*Rhet.* ad init.).

R. Swoboda, *De Dem. quae feruntur prooemiis* (1887); F. Blass, *Die attische Beredsamkeit*, 3[3] (1962), 322 ff.   C. C.

propaganda

propaganda is not easy to define. It means active manipulation of opinion and some distortion of the truth; it also perhaps aims at exclusive indoctrination of one set of opinions, contrast ideology (a value-system which may admit the possibility of other value-systems) or mentality (values unconsciously subscribed to rather than actively promoted). Propaganda has been divided (Ellul) into agitation propaganda and integration propaganda; the first seeks to change attitudes, the second to reinforce them. This division is helpful (see below) for the understanding of the ancient world.

Lacking modern techniques for the dissemination of information, the ancient world was spared some modern manifestations of propaganda; nor were conditions suitable for the emergence of professional governmental 'propaganda machines' of a modern sort (*decision-making was amateur and theoretically in the hands of the citizens). There were however ways of making general proclamations. Thus Rome exploited *Delphi to make pronouncements adverse to *Perseus (2) of Macedon, see *Syll.*[3] 643; this builds on a long Greek tradition of making pro-

clamations at panhellenic *sanctuaries (see PANHELLENISM) like Delphi and *Olympia. There were other less direct ways of moulding opinion; it has been suggested (Boardman) that vase-painting and architecture directly reflect *Pisistratus' foreign, domestic, and religious policies, and if so this would be integration propaganda; but the interpretation of the evidence is controversial (see IMAGERY). Pisistratan 'control' of vase-painters was hardly close enough to justify talk of propaganda.

The Spartan educational system or *agōgē can also be seen as a kind of integration propaganda; equally, Sparta's policy of 'freeing the Greeks' was originally agitation propaganda, a way of undermining Athens' *Delian League. (The 'freedom of the Greeks' motif was later taken up by Hellenistic rulers and eventually by Romans down to *Nero. See FREEDOM IN THE ANCIENT WORLD. The 'agitation' element became less prominent over time). Classical Athens for its part used religion, myth (esp. *Ionian themes), and manipulation of the past, exploiting different types of literary and artistic discourse, to promote its empire (see ATHENS; AUTOCHTHONS; BARBARIAN; DELIAN LEAGUE; DORIANS; IONIANS; PANATHENAEA). In particular, imperial Athens exploited and exaggerated the idea of *kinship (*syngeneia*) between states, and treated its subject allies as if they were all its Ionian colonists owing quasi-familial obligations: cf. MĒTROPOLIS (a). But 'Athens' and 'Sparta' are abstractions and it is a question how far Athenian or Spartan individuals set out consciously to manipulate opinion. In any case Thuc. 6. 82. 3–4 is strikingly out of line (Euphemus at *Camarina justifies Athenians' coercion of their Ionian 'kin' by reference to Ionian participation in *Xerxes' invasion).

Autocrats are more promising propagandists. Hellenistic rulers promoted their regimes through sculpture and spectacle, but not all self-advertisement of this sort is strictly propaganda. We get closer with the Rome of *Augustus, who had the power, the wealth, and the motive to promote a specific set of values and beliefs, using art, architecture, coinage, sculpture, and literature, including and especially Augustus' own *Res Gestae (see AUGUSTUS). At the outset there was an 'agitation' element to his propaganda, which was aimed at Mark Antony (M. *Antonius (2)), but Augustan propaganda turned into the integrative type as opposition became less of a threat. But even the most loyal Augustan poets were not crude propagandists. Subsequent imperial propaganda tends to be of the integrative type, and takes sophisticated forms (thus the *Persian-Wars tradition, strictly a story of *Greek* achievement, is taken over by Rome as a way of reconciling Greeks to Roman power). With the aggressive paganism of *Julian we perhaps encounter agitation propaganda again.

GENERAL J. Ellul, *Propaganda: The Formation of Men's Attitudes* (1973).

SPARTA Hdt. 1. 65 ff.; J. Hooker, in A. Powell (ed.), *Classical Sparta: The Secrets of her Success* (1989), ch. 5.

PISISTRATID ATHENS J. Boardman, *Rev. Arch.* 1972, 57 ff., *JHS* 1975, 1 ff., in D. Kurtz and B. Sparkes (eds.), *The Eye of Greece* (1982), *CAH* 4[2] (1988), ch. 7c, and *JHS* 1989, 158–9; R. M. Cook, *JHS* 1987, 169 ff.; R. Osborne, *Hephaistos*, 1983–4, 61–70; J. Blok, *Bulletin Antieke Beschaving* (1990), 17 ff.

CLASSICAL (IMPERIAL) ATHENS R. Meiggs, *The Athenian Empire* (1972), ch. 16; N. Loraux trans. A. Shapiro, *The Invention of Athens* (1986); S. Goldhill, *JHS* 1987, 58 ff. = J. Winkler and F. Zeitlin (eds.) *Nothing to Do With Dionysos* (1990), 97 ff.; R. Parker, in J. Bremmer (ed.), *Interpretations of Greek Mythology* (1987), 187 ff.; E. Hall, *Inventing the Barbarian* (1989); S. Hornblower, *Harv. Stud.* 1992, 169 ff.

HELLENISTIC On the 'freedom of the Greeks' see Seager and Tuplin, *JHS* 1980, 141 ff.; Seager, *CQ* 1981, 106 ff.; cf. already Thuc. 2.

8 (Sparta); E. Rice, *The Grand Procession of Ptolemy Philadelphus* (1983); R. R. R. Smith, *Hellenistic Sculpture* (1993), 103.

ROME K. Scott, *Mem. Amer. Acad. Rome* 1933, 1 ff.; P. Hardie, *Virgil's Aeneid: Cosmos and Imperium* (1986), P. Zanker trans. A. Shapiro, *The Power of Images in the Age of Augustus* (1988); J. Griffin, in F. Millar and E. Segal (eds.) *Caesar Augustus* (1984), 189 ff.; A. Spawforth in S. Hornblower (ed.), *Greek Historiography* (1994), ch. 9.   S. H.

propemptikon (προπεμπτικόν), a composition expressing wishes for a prosperous journey to a departing friend. This was a common poetical theme, attempted also in prose in late antiquity (*Menander (4) Rhetor 395–9 Spengel; *Himerius, *Oration* 10. 1 Colonna). Poetical examples are found in Greek lyric (e.g. Sappho fr. 5 L–P), in Hellenistic poetry (*Callimachus (3) fr. 400 Pfeiffer, *Theocritus 7. 52–89) and in the Roman poets (*Helvius Cinna's *Propemptikon to Pollio* (56 BC) was famous but is lost; extant examples include *Horace, *Odes* 1. 3, 3. 27; *Propertius 1. 8; Statius, *Silvae* 3. 2). These poems were often very learned and allusive, as is natural for the occasional poetry of literary cliques, but there was a fairly standard set of expected topics: complaints of 'desertion' by the departing friend, encomium of the place he is going to, dangers of the voyage, prayer for safe return. The late rhetoricians (see Menander above) codified and enumerated these topics, and their prescriptions parallel and illuminate the practice of the poets.

D. Wachsmuth, *Kl. Pauly* 4. 1179; F. Cairns, *Generic Composition in Greek and Roman Poetry* (1972), with full lists of relevant texts; D. A. Russell and N. G. Wilson, commentary on Menander Rhetor (1981), 303–8.   D. A. R.

Propertius, Sextus, born between 54 and 47 BC, at *Asisium, where his family were local notables (4. 1. 121 ff.). His father died early, and the family property was diminished by Octavian's confiscations of 41–40 BC (4. 1. 127 ff.; see AUGUSTUS; PROSCRIPTION)—not so diminished however that Propertius needed to earn a living. In the two last poems of book 1 the poet notably identifies with the side vanquished by Octavian at *Perusia in 41 BC. It is the first sign of a political independence that continues throughout his life, despite involvement in *Maecenas' circle. As the Augustan regime toughened, Propertius' modes of irreverence become more oblique, but irreverence towards the government is maintained none the less: see e.g. 2. 7, 2. 15. 41 ff., 3. 11, 4. 9.

Propertius' first book was probably published before Oct. 28 BC; the latest events mentioned in books 2, 3, and 4 belong to the years 26, 23, and 16 respectively. Propertius was certainly dead by 2 BC (Ov. *Rem. Am.* 764).

It is as a love poet that Propertius is best known. He celebrated his devotion to a mistress whom he called Cynthia (a name with Apolline and Callimachean associations; see APOLLO; CALLIMACHUS (3)). Apuleius says her real name was Hostia (*Apol.* 10). Many of the incidents suggested in the poems seem conventional, but there is no reason to doubt Cynthia's basic reality. Her social status is uncertain.

Characteristic of Propertian love poetry is the claim to be the slave of his mistress (1. 1 etc.), and the claim that love is his life's occupation; it replaces the normal career move of a young equestrian (service in the cohort of a provincial governor, *militia*). Propertius distils this last point by referring to love as his *militia* (esp. 1. 6. 29 f.). Typical too of his love poetry is his use of mythology: he cites figures and events from myth as 'romantic standards', as examples of how things in a romantic world might be.

Book 1, consisting almost entirely of love poems, is addressed to a variety of friends, most prominently a Tullus (1. 1, 1. 6, 1. 14, 1. 22; 3. 22) who seems to have been nephew to L. Volcacius Tullus, consul in 33 BC with Octavian. Book 2 (which some think an amalgamation (by a later hand) of two books), still largely devoted to love poems, evidences his entry to the circle of Maecenas (2. 1), but there is no suggestion that he was ever economically dependent on the great patron in the way that *Virgil and *Horace were (see PATRONAGE, LITERARY). Book 3 also contains a prominent poem to Maecenas (3. 9), but book 4 omits all mention of his name. Maecenas fades from Propertius' poetry as he fades from Horace's: this is probably due to the great patron's loss of favour with Augustus in the wake of the conspiracy of 23 BC.

Book 3 shows a greater diversity of subject-matter than the first two books, and it is here that Propertius first makes an ostentatious claim to be a Roman Callimachus (3. 1 and 3. 3). Some scholars think the claim is not very justified: Horace had claimed to be the Roman *Alcaeus (1) (*Ode* 3. 30); with some humour Propertius responds by making his claim to be the first Roman to adopt the mantle of another Greek poet. Among the many non-Cynthia poems in book 3 one might note 3. 18 on the death of Augustus' nephew M. *Claudius Marcellus (5). It is hard to imagine Propertius writing this a few years earlier. The toughening of the Augustan regime and the fading influence of the mediating Maecenas was having its effect. But Propertius can still be irreverent (see above). The concluding poems of the book recall book 1 in various ways, and mark the end both of the affair with Cynthia and of his career as a love-poet (or so it seems).

Book 4 is more successful than book 3, and in it Propertius has a more valid claim to be called a Roman Callimachus. It consists partly of poems descended from Callimachus' *Aetia*; but these are Roman *Aetia* (1, 2, 4, 6, 9, and 10), one (6) indeed explaining the *aition* of the Temple of Apollo as a thank-offering for the victory at *Actium. 4. 6 is an example of Propertius' later subtle irreverence. It is largely devoted to an account of the battle of Actium, but tells it all in the manner of Callimachus, a style wholly unsuited to the subject-matter. The total result is amusing to those with literary taste. To these aetiological poems are added poems on various subjects. The two in which he returns to the theme of Cynthia (7 and 8) are among Propertius' most original, and the speech from beyond the grave by Cornelia (11) is moving, though marred by textual corruption.

Some Romans, though not *Quintilian, thought Propertius the most 'refined and elegant' of the Roman elegists (Quint. 10. 1. 93; cf. also Plin. *Ep.* 9. 22). Such epithets apply to many of his poems, but others seem to the modern reader obscure and jagged. Part of this is the reader's fault. The poet's wit is a demanding one. Other and real obscurities are due to a very corrupt manuscript tradition. The fact remains that Propertius is difficult in a way that *Tibullus is not, and—perhaps owing to his Callimachean aspirations—often seems to cultivate complexity and convolution.

His vivid recreation of his affair with Cynthia, his literary range, and his political independence make Propertius one of the most captivating of the Latin poets.

TEXTS E. A. Barber, 2nd edn. (1960); R. Hanslik (1979); P. Fedeli (1984); G. P. Goold (1990).

COMMENTARIES M. Rothstein, 1² (1920), 2² (1924); H. E. Butler and E. A. Barber (1933); P. J. Enk (bk. 1, 1946; bk. 2, 1962); D. R. Shackleton Bailey, *Propertiana* (1956); W. A. Camps (bk. 1, 1961; bk. 4, 1965; bk. 3, 1966; bk. 2, 1967); P. Fedeli (bk. 1, 1980; bk. 3, 1985). *Selections*, J. P. Postgate (1905).

TRANSLATIONS G. P. Goold (1990); Guy Lee (1994).

BIBLIOGRAPHY P. Fedeli and P. Pinotti *Bibliografia Properziana* (1985). H. Harrauer *A Bibliography to Propertius* (1973).

CRITICISM J.-P. Boucher, *Études sur Properce* (1965); M. Hubbard, *Propertius* (1974); R. O. A. M. Lyne, *The Latin Love Poets From Catullus to Horace* (1980), 65–148; H.-P. Stahl *Propertius: "Love" and "War"* (1985), T. D. Papanghelis *Propertius: A Hellenistic Poet on Love and Death* (1987).   R. O. A. M. L.

property classes, Athenian See HIPPEIS; PENTAKOSIOMEDIM-NOI; THĒTES; ZEUGITAI.

prophecies, texts purporting to be the work of inspired sages, had an important role in Graeco-Roman thought. Collections of prophecies, which are attested as early as the 6th cent. BC (Hdt. 7. 6), might be attributed to a divine or semi-divine character such as *Orpheus, *Bacis, or a *Sibyl; they could be presented as accounts of moments where an individual was seized by a prophetic fit, or collections of significant oracles that either emanated, or were claimed to have emanated, from major oracular shrines. The priests of *Delphi are said to have assembled such a collection for *Croesus in the 6th cent. (Hdt. 1. 91), *Porphyry assembled a collection of such texts in the 3rd cent. AD to offer explanations of cult practices, and Christians took over portions of these collections to illustrate intimations of Christian truth in pagan texts.

The purveyors of such texts, usually called *chresmologoi* in Greek and by a number of different titles in Latin (including *vates*, *prophetes*, and *hariolus*), ordinarily did not claim inspiration for themselves, and it is impossible to know what role they played in the actual composition of such works. Evidence from Egyptian sources (most importantly the *Oracle of the Potter*) and from the manuscript traditions of the Sibylline Oracles does, however, suggest that there was considerable fluidity in their texts.

Recitation of these prophecies is often noted at times of public unrest. *Thucydides (2), *Aristophanes (1), and *Plutarch provide a sample of such prophecies (and parodies of the same) during the *Peloponnesian war; *Phlegon of Tralles preserves a number of anti-Roman texts that circulated in the east during the 2nd and 1st cents. BC; and *Cassius Dio provides several examples of their use in the imperial period (e.g. Thuc. 2. 8. 2; 54. 2; 5. 26. 4; 8. 1. 1; Ar. *Eq.* 61; *Pax* 1065; Plut. *Nicias* 13; FGrH 257 fr. 36 III; Dio 56. 25). Other authors (e.g. *Plutarch and *Pausanias (3)) show that the appearance of such writings was not an epiphenomenon of crisis, but rather that they were in general circulation at all times.

The most significant extant collections of prophecies are the corpus of *Sibylline Oracles*, the *Chaldaean Oracles*, the *Tübingen Theosophy*, a Syriac collection of the 6th cent. AD, and in Phlegon of Tralles. There are obvious connections in theory and use, if not necessarily in form or content, between the prophecies of the classical world and the ancient Near East, especially the so-called 'Akkadian Apocalypses', the books of the Hebrew Prophets, and some Egyptian Wisdom Literature. See also DIVIN-ATION.

TEXTS FGrH 257; J. Geffcken, *Die Oracula Sibyllina* (1902); E. des Places, *Oracles Chaldaïques* (1971); H. Erbse, *Fragmente griechischer Theo-sophien* (1941); S. Brock, *Orientalia Lovaniensia Periodica* 13 (1983).

DISCUSSIONS A. Bouché-Leclercq, *Histoire de la divination dans l'antiquité* (1872–82); D. S. Potter, *Prophets and Emperors* (1994).   D. S. P.

prophētēs (προφήτης), the title of the mortal who speaks in the name of a god or interprets his will. It is properly used only of seers and functionaries attached to an established oracular shrine; the unattached seer is called *mantis* or *chresmologos*. And it is more often used of the officials who presided over oracular shrines than of the actual receivers of mantic inspiration: *Pindar can distinguish the two functions, inviting the Muse (see MUSES) to 'prophecy, and I will be your mouthpiece' (*prophētēs*) (μαντεύεο Μοῖσα, προφατεύσω δ ἐγώ, fr. 150 Sn.). At Delphi (see DELPHIC ORACLE) and *Didyma the immediate reception of the divine revelation was a woman, while the 'prophets' were males who oversaw the oracular session: at Didyma, an annually elected magistrate, at Delphi (where the title was not official) two priests who served for life. The distinction is not absolute, however, as the term προφῆτις was also sometimes applied to the inspired woman. It used to be supposed that at Claros a male *prophētēs* spoke the oracles, but according to a recent suggestion the θεσ-πιωδός, 'oracular singer', did so instead.

E. Fascher, ΠΡΟΦΗΤΗΣ (1927); J. Fontenrose, *The Delphic Oracle* (1978), 218–19, and *Didyma* (1988); H. W. Parke, *The Oracles of Apollo in Asia Minor* (1985).   R. C. T. P.

Propontis (ἡ Προποντίς), now the sea of Marmara, an intermediate sea between the *Aegean and the *Euxine, whence its ancient name. Its length, just over 225 km. (140 mi.), and its greatest breadth, hardly 64 km. (40 mi.), are overstated by *Herodotus (1) (4. 85) at 1,400 stades, i.e. 248 km. (155 mi.), and 500 stades, i.e. 88 km. (55 mi), whereas *Strabo (2. 5. 22) gauges the length accurately but exaggerates the breadth absurdly. The Propontis is connected with the Euxine by the deep, narrow, and winding channel of the Thracian *Bosporus (1), and with the Aegean by that of the *Hellespont; these waterways were commanded by *Byzantium and *Troy respectively. The principal cities on its shores are: Byzantium and *Chalcedon at the mouth of the Bosporus; *Nicomedia at its eastern extremity; Selymbria, *Perinthus-Heraclea, and Bisanthe-Rhaedestus on its Thracian coast; Cius and *Cyzicus on its south side. The largest island in the Propontis is Proconnesus, now Marmara, meaning '*marble', which has given its modern name to the whole sea. There are other islands, including Ophiusa and Halone, in the same neighbourhood, and at the other end, in full view from Byzantium, are the four small islands now known as the Princes' Islands (Demonnesi); their ancient names seem to have been Prote (now Kinali), Elaea (Burgaz), Chalcitis (Heybeli), and Pityodes (Büyük Ada). A list of islands is given by *Pliny (1) (*HN* 5. 151). The rivers *Granicus, Aesepus, Macestus, and Rhyndacus enter the Propontis on its south side; on the north side there are no rivers of any consequence.   G. E. B.

Propylaea A propylon is a monumental roofed gateway: the derivative term, propylaea, is applied to more complex structures, specifically the Periclean gateway (see PERICLES (1)) to the acropolis of *Athens designed by Mnesicles and built between 436 and 432 BC. It is approached by an inclined ramp continuing the natural slope of the rock. It was preceded by an earlier gateway, apparently less complex, on a different alignment, anticipating in part the arrangements of Mnesicles' building. Started before the Persian Wars, it was burnt by *Xerxes' forces, but afterwards repaired; part still survives behind the south-west wing of Mnesicles' building. Mnesicles' plan was elaborated by lower flanking wings to north and south. On the west front are structures with porches each with 3 columns *in antis*. That to the north was once decorated inside with paintings. Since it is approached by an off-centre door, it was in all probability a formal feasting room, holding 17 couches (see DINING ROOMS). A similar façade on the south cleverly embellishes an approach passage to the Nike bastion. These were the last sections to be built, work being hastened (when all other building activity was stopped) at the approach of the *Peloponnesian War. The eastern rooms of the wings, clearly intended, were abandoned unbuilt. The central gateway building comprises two rooms with Doric hexastyle porticos facing outwards and inwards, the inner hall at a higher level. The dividing cross wall is pierced by five doors; the largest, centre, door is for a continuous inclined passage, used only for the ceremonial *processions and animals. The others are at the top of a flight of five steps from the lower hall.

The Propylaea is constructed of Pentelic *marble, with the innovatory use of dark grey ('black') Eleusinian limestone for contrasting orthostats and string-courses (see PENTELICON; ELEUSIS). The front-gate hall has its roof supported on two rows of Ionic columns, the central passage having a span of nearly 4.26 m. (14 ft.). The architraves of the Ionic colonnades were reinforced with iron beams because of the weight superimposed on them by the ceilings which were formed of marble beams and of slabs with deeply hollowed square coffers, richly decorated in blue and gold. Much admired in antiquity, the building was part-replicated in the (2nd cent. AD) 'Greater Propylaea' at Eleusis.

W. B. Dinsmoor, *Architecture of Ancient Greece*[3] (1950), 198 ff.; J. Bundgaard, *Mnesicles; A Greek Architect at Work* (1957); W. B. Dinsmoor, Jnr., *The Propylaia to the Athenian Acropolis. 1. The Predecessors* (1980); T. Kalpaxis, *Hemiteles* (1986); R. A. Tomlinson, *BSA* 1990, 405 ff.; H. Eiteljorg, *The Entrance to the Athenian Acropolis before Mnesides* (1995).

R. A. T.

prorogation See PRO CONSULE, PRO PRAETORE; SENATE, *Regal and Republican Age: Procedure*.

proscription, the publication of a notice, especially (1) a notice of a sale; (2) a list of Roman citizens who were declared outlaws and whose goods were confiscated. This procedure was used by *Sulla in 82–81 BC, and by M. *Antonius (2) (Mark Antony), M. *Aemilius Lepidus (3), and *Octavian in 43–42 as a means of getting rid of personal and political opponents and obtaining funds in virtue, or anticipation, of special powers of inappellable jurisdiction conferred on them as *dictator and *triumviri respectively. The proscribed were hunted down and executed in Rome and throughout Italy by squads of soldiers, and the co-operation of the victims' families and slaves and of the general public was sought by means of rewards and punishments.

Despite some wild exaggeration in ancient sources and modern calculations, Sulla's proscription, in part an act of revenge for massacres in 87 and 82 by *Marius (1) and (2), targeted no more than perhaps 520 persons. The lists were closed on 1 June 81. The sons and grandsons of the proscribed were debarred from public life until restored by *Caesar in 49. The impression left was profound, and similar conduct was feared from Caesar or *Pompey, whichever should win the Civil War: as it was, Caesar's clemency was made an excuse for the proscriptions of the triumvirs (see above). Their lists included about 300 senators and *equites*; but many escaped, and some of these, including a fair proportion of senators, were afterwards restored.

Syme, *RR* 187 ff.; M. Fuhrmann, *RE* 23. 2440 ff. (Nachträge); F. Hinard, *Les Proscriptions de la Rome républicaine* (1985). T. J. C.; R. J. S.

prose-rhythm, Greek The earliest surviving discussion of prose-rhythm is to be found in *Aristotle *Rhet.* 1408[b]21–9[a]21, where he distinguishes between 'rhythm' (ῥυθμός) and 'metre' (μέτρον) and emphasizes that if prose makes too much use of μέτρα, i.e. the patterns of long and short syllables whose regular

repetition is familiar in poetry, 'it will be a poem'. In his view, dactylic rhythm (- ∪∪ - ∪∪ etc.), characteristic of epic, is too solemn, too remote from normal communication; iambic rhythm (× - ∪ - × - ∪ - etc.) has the opposite fault, because it is the 'natural' rhythm of conversation and therefore fails to strike (ἐκστῆσαι) the hearer, while trochaic rhythm (- ∪ - × - ∪ - × etc.) is undignified to the point of vulgarity. He therefore recommends paeonic rhythm (- ∪ ∪ ∪ and ∪ ∪ ∪ -), which, except for a few passages of Old Comedy (see COMEDY (GREEK), OLD), was not used for continuous passages of poetry and thus had no strong poetic associations.

Aristotle (*Rhet.* 1409[a]2) regards *Thrasymachus of Chalcedon as the pioneer of paeonic rhythm in oratory, though it is by no means conspicuous in the only substantial citation of Thrasymachus' work which has survived. *Isocrates certainly prided himself on εὐρυθμία (5. 27, 13. 16), but we do not know what theoretical principles he taught his pupils, except the strict avoidance of *hiatus, apparent in all his own work. It is possible that *Gorgias (1) experimented with rhythms which an audience would associate with lyric poetry, for the peroration of *Agathon's speech in Pl. *Smp.* 197c–e, a speech which we are explicitly invited (198c) to regard as a *parody of Gorgias, contains many such, e.g. θεατὸς σοφοῖς, ἀγαστὸς θεοῖς (a pair of dochmiacs), but the experiment seems to have had no influence. The verse-forms used in Greek poetry were so numerous that 'accidental' verses in prose texts are quite common, and the justification for calling them accidental is the absence of anything in the context to suggest why the writer should have wished to write poetically.

It is difficult, for several reasons, for us to scan Greek prose. Not only are there many syllables which can be treated as long or as short (e.g. the first syllable of τοιοῦτος or of πατρός), but also there is much room for disagreement over the points at which the speaker may have made a slight pause and therefore may not have elided a short final vowel which in the dialogue of drama would always have to be elided. The manuscript texts are inconsistent in respect of elision. For example, in Lys. 12. 3, where the transmitted text is οὔτ' ἐμαυτοῦ πώποτε οὔτε ἀλλότρια πράγματα πράξας, did the speaker say just that, or . . . πώποτ' οὔτ' ἀλλότρια . . .? And (ibid.) is πειράσομαι ὑμᾶς . . . διδάξαι to be scanned as - - ∪ - - - etc., with hiatus after -μαι, or - - ∪ ∪ - etc. (as commonly in poetry), or even (not impossible) - - ∪ - - etc.? Similar problems are presented by καὶ οὐ (κοὐ), τὰ ἐμά (τἀμά ?) and the like.

We can, however, observe that *Demosthenes (2) has a strong tendency to avoid a succession of more than two short syllables; so strong, in fact, that uncertainties over elision hardly affect the issue (it is, of course, incompatible with Aristotle's recommendation of the paeon). This observation was first made by Blass; no ancient critic or rhetorician mentions it, but in the 2nd cent. AD Aelius *Aristides shows precisely the same tendency.

We can also see that in the 'clausula', i.e. the last four or five syllables immediately preceding a major pause, some authors show distinctive preferences. There is an early manifestation of preoccupation with clausulae in the two short surviving works of *Plato (1)'s contemporary, *Antisthenes (1), where - ∪ - × appears with monotonous regularity at 49 out of a total of 59 major pauses (and ∪ ∪ ∪ - × at eight of the rest). Demosthenes is noticeably fond of the clausula - - - × (the final syllable should probably always be counted as long, as at verse-end in poetry). Plato in *Laws* uses the clausulae ∪ - - ∪ × and - - - ∪ × nearly twice as often as in *Republic*, and ∪ - ∪ ∪ × only a quarter as often; a gradual shift in his preferences is discernible in the works which have been dated on other grounds between *Republic* and *Laws*.

The sensitivity of Greek writers, audiences, and critics to prose-rhythm attests an aesthetic dimension which is generally lacking in modern criticism. It is only rarely that we are 'struck' by a particular sequence of longs and shorts. The famous double cretic ἑσπέρα μὲν γὰρ ἦν at the start of a narrative passage in Dem. 18. 169 may be an exception, but would hardly impress us in a less dramatic context. The critic *Dionysius (7) of Halicarnassus is obsessed by rhythm to the neglect of other aspects of language (including, at times, meaning), e.g. in his discussion (*Comp. Verb.* 113–15) of the opening sentence of the Periclean Funeral Speech (see EPITAPHIOS) in Thuc. 2. 35. 1. His enthusiastic analyses, however, remind us that prose-rhythm is a creative art; the writer is no more bound by 'rules' than a composer of music is bound to construct a melody out of pre-fabricated phrases. Ten syllable-places can accommodate more than one thousand different sequences of longs and shorts.

In late antiquity, when long and short vowels were no longer differentiated and the ancient tonic accent turned into a stress-accent, many authors (e.g. *Procopius and *Himerius) developed individual preferences in patterns of stress for clausulae.

F. Blass, *Die Rhythmen der attischen Kunstprosa* (1901); A. W. de Groot, *Der antike Prosarhythmus* (1921), and *La Prose métrique des anciens* (1926); W. H. Shewring, *CQ* 1930, 164–73, and 1931, 12–22; S. Skimina, *État actuel des études sur le rhythme de la prose grecque* (1937); D. R. Cox and L. Brandwood, *Journal of the Royal Statistical Society,* Series B, 1959, 195–200; D. F. McCabe, *The Prose-Rhythm of Demosthenes* (1981).

K. J. D.

prose-rhythm, Latin

Quantitative In the classical period, the Roman ear was clearly sensitive to patterns of quantity in formal spoken prose. An effective rhythm could provoke spontaneous applause (Cic. *Or.* 214). Doubtless Roman orators built up preferences for some rhythmical patterns over others by instinct and by trial and error, but some influence from Greek theory and practice is certain. *Cicero's rhythmical practice, evident not only in his formal speeches but also in his treatises and even in his private letters, seems to have become a standard which many authors followed more or less consciously, though some rejected it.

Theoretical discussions of prose rhythm in Roman writers are generally much influenced by the Greek rhetoricians, and do not show a perfect analytical grasp of the principles of Latin prose rhythm as shown in the actual practice of authors. Indeed, these principles were not fully worked out in explicit terms until the fundamental work of Zieliński on Cicero's speeches. Scholarship since then has added considerably to the available data and has refined our understanding of prose rhythm in various ways, but no radically new analysis has gained acceptance.

Generalizations about a particular author's rhythmical practices can be made in terms of (*a*) a marked avoidance of rhythms that one would expect to occur in a random sample, and (*b*) marked preferences for particular patterns in a given position, usually the end of a sentence. The term *clausula* is used to refer both to the end of a sentence and, by extension, to the rhythmical patterns used there. The usefulness of statistical analysis of clausulae is, however, subject to certain limitations: it is difficult to define the norm of unrhythmical prose against which the practice of particular authors can be measured, and the question what is to count as a clausula admits of some degree of latitude owing to variations in editorial punctuation.

It is clear from what remains of pre-Ciceronian oratory that 'Ciceronian' rhythmical preferences were already in evidence before Cicero's time, and it is not clear that he himself added anything except, perhaps, a greater regularity. Certain clausulae, particularly the ditrochee (– ∪ – ×) and its expanded form (– ∪ – ∪ – ×), are associated with the florid and exuberant style known as 'Asian', and do indeed appear to have been cultivated on the model of the Asian school of Greek rhetoric, exemplified particularly well in the inscription of *Antiochus (9) I of Commagene from *Nemrut Dag (E. Norden, *Die antike Kunstprosa* (2nd edn. 1909) 1. 141–5; see ASIANISM AND ATTICISM).

The basic clausula patterns preferred to a marked extent by Cicero are the ditrochee (– ∪ – ×) and its expansion with a preceding cretic (– ∪ – – ∪ – ×), the double cretic (– ∪ – – ∪ ×), and the cretic + trochee or spondee (– ∪ – – ×) (the quantity of the final syllable is in all cases immaterial). The ditrochee becomes less common in Cicero's later work, indicating a gradual abandonment of the more obvious features of 'Asian' style.

Cicero also cultivates 'resolved' forms of these three rhythms, in which one of the long syllables is replaced by two short syllables; successions of three short syllables (but not of two or four) are thus favoured. The *esse videatur* rhythm, a resolved version of (– ∪ – – ×), became so much a trademark of Cicero's style that later writers almost always avoided it except when consciously imitating him. Variations are also found in which a molossus (– – –) is substituted for a cretic, giving rise to the patterns (– – – – ∪ ×) (largely avoided by later writers, even those whose practice is otherwise 'Ciceronian') and (– – – – ∪ – ×); the spondaic clausula (– – – ×) is not favoured by Cicero but does occur, and is used more often by his successors.

Anything reminiscent of verse tends to be avoided by Cicero, both in the clausula and elsewhere; this applies to sequences of iambo-trochaic rhythm, to dactyls and to choriambs. The hexameter ending (– ∪ ∪ – ×) or 'heroic clausula' is not altogether avoided, as long as the coincidence of accent and ictus characteristic of the epic hexameter is not present.

Neither word-accent nor the pattern of word-division appears to play a major part in Cicero's rhythmical preferences. He does, however, show a marginal preference for coincidence of accent and ictus in his favoured rhythms; and in the ditrochaic clausula, a sonorous quadrisyllable (such as *comprobavit*) would be preferred to a pair of dissyllables (such as *ipse dixit*).

The preference for the above-mentioned rhythms is most marked at sentence-end, but has also been detected at the boundaries between cola (i.e. at natural sense-breaks within sentences). Rhythmical considerations can thus be useful for determining how to articulate a long sentence into smaller units. They can also be relevant to textual criticism. Emendations which noticeably 'improve' the rhythm (i.e. bring it into line with Cicero's normal practice) are, prima facie, more plausible than those which create a rhythmical anomaly.

Reactions against Ciceronianism in style brought varying practices with regard to rhythm. We do not know enough of the work of the anti-Ciceronian (or 'Atticist') orators of Cicero's time to make significant generalisations as to their practice. However, the historians Sallust and Livy show a marked avoidance of the Ciceronian favourites (– ∪ – ×), (– ∪ – – ×) and *esse videatur*. The double cretic, however, is not avoided by them, and (– ∪ – – ×) comes back into favour with *Tacitus (1). *Livy in particular is more tolerant of poetic or near-poetic rhythms, both in the clausula and otherwise; this is consistent with the frequently poetic colouring of his narrative.

Accentual (In what follows, ´ = accented syllable; x = unaccented syllable; . = break between words.) Like verse, prose rhythm in classical Latin was firmly based on quantity, and stress patterns played at most a secondary role. However, the rhythmical structure of the spoken language changed radically in the course of time (see PRONUNCIATION, LATIN), until the stress accent became paramount and distinctions of quantity as such were lost. There was, clearly, an intermediate stage, in which stress was becoming more important at the expense of quantity but quantitative distinctions had not yet been erased; the distinctions of quantity were artificially preserved as an elegance when they were ceasing to be observed in normal speech. Since the position of the Latin accent is dependent on syllabic quantity, it will be seen that there is a tendency for certain accentual patterns to predominate even in a fully quantitative system of clausulae. The preference for coincidence of accent and ictus in the clausula is seen to have increased by the 3rd and 4th cents. AD. Later still, a fully accentual system of clausulae evolved. In medieval *Latin, the preferred rhythms are the so-called *cursus planus* (´×.×´×), the *cursus tardus* (´×.×´××), and the *cursus velox* (´××.××´×). Each of these represents a coalescence of two or more of the favoured Ciceronian patterns: thus the *planus* incorporates (– ∪ . – ı – ×) and (– ∪ –ı– . ∪ – ×), while the *tardus* incorporates (– ∪ . – ı – ∪ ×) and the resolved pattern (– ∪ . – ı ∪ ∪ ×). The *velox* presumably derives from (× ∪ – . ∪ – ı – ×) or (– ∪ – . ∪ . – ı – ∪ ×). But each *cursus*-form also permits quantitative patterns that would be rejected by Cicero. All accentual clausulae in this system are subject to two general rules: (*a*) the last word must never be accented on the first syllable, and (*b*) there must always be an even number of unaccented syllables between accents. This latter rule applies also to Greek accentual prose of the Byzantine period. According to Nicolau, these rules grew up as a result of the development of a theory of prose-rhythm in which word-division played a large part, exemplified by the treatise of Marius Plotius *Sacerdos (writing under *Diocletian) which is a refinement of that of *Caesius Bassus in the 1st cent. AD.

QUANTITATIVE T. Zieliński, *Philologus* Suppl. 1904, 591–844, and ibid. Suppl. 1914; H. D. Broadhead, *Latin Prose Rhythm* (1922); H. Bornecque, *Les Clausules métriques latines* (1907); L. Laurand, *Étude sur le style des discours de Cicéron*, 4th edn. (1938), 2; W. Schmid, *Über die klassische Theorie und Praxis des antiken Prosarhythmus*, Hermes Einzelschriften 12 (1959); J. Wolff, [*Neue*] *Jahrb.* Suppl. 1901; E. Fraenkel, in *Kl. Beiträge* 1. 73–92, and *Leseproben aus Reden Ciceros und Catos* (1968); R. G. M. Nisbet in E. Craik (ed.), *Owls to Athens* (1990); A. Primmer, *Cicero Numerosus* (1968). There have been a considerable number of special studies of the rhythmical practices of particular Latin authors.

ACCENTUAL M. G. Nicolau, *L'Origine du 'cursus' rythmique et les débuts de l'accent d'intensité en latin* (1930); T. Janson, *Prose Rhythm in Medieval Latin* (1975).   J. G. F. P.

Proserpina, Proserpine See PERSEPHONE.

proskynēsis See ALEXANDER (3) THE GREAT, § 10; CALLISTHENES; RULER-CULT, *Greek*.

prosopography is a modern term for the study of individuals, and is derived from the Greek *prosōpon*, one meaning of which is 'person'. There is no agreed or official definition of prosopography, which goes under different names in different disciplines (to the social scientist, prosopography in one of its manifestations is 'multiple career-line analysis': see L. Stone in bibliog. below). Prosopography, as used in ancient history, is a historical method which uses onomastic evidence (see NAMES, PERSONAL, GREEK and ROMAN) to establish (i) regional origins of individuals and (ii)

family connections, esp. via marriage-ties but also via *adoption (which leaves traces on nomenclature), between individual and individual and between group and group. (See GENOS and GENS for the basic large *kinship units; but 'group' theories of Roman politics, see below, presuppose units made up of more than one *gens*. Thus Scullard posited a 'Fulvian-Claudian group' in late 3rd cent. Rome, see various entries under FULVIUS and CLAUDIUS.) Conclusions about the origins and family connections of individuals then classically lead to inferences about their likely political sympathies and allegiances.

The prosopographic method is specially associated with Roman history, and in particular with the work of R. Syme (1903–89; see esp. *Rom. Rev.*, *AA*, and *RP*), who once wrote of 'the science (or rather the art) of prosopography' (*RP* 2. 711). Syme however had his German predecessors at one level (E. Groag, F. Münzer, and the editors of the first ed. of *Prosopographia Imperii Romani*, 1897–). Prosopography of the Syme–Scullard sort has always had its critics; for an early reply to such critics see H. H. Scullard's preface to the 2nd edn. of his *Roman Politics 220–150 BC* (1973, but reprinted from *BICS* 1955. Scullard's book, first published in 1951 and much indebted to Münzer's *Römische Adelsparteien und Adelsfamilien* (1920), had argued for the existence and importance of family 'groups' at Rome in the late 3rd and early 2nd cents. BC. For a more cautious approach to this issue, but still retaining the central idea, see J. Briscoe, *Hist.* 1969, 67 ff., dealing with the mid 2nd cent. BC). But fundamental scepticism persisted, see for instance P. A. Brunt, *Gnomon* 1965, 189 ff. and K. Hopkins, *Death and Renewal* (1983), ch. 2. One obvious line of criticism is that the prosopographic approach is too narrow, thus it is alleged to neglect ideas in favour of 'matrimonial bulletins' (A. N. Sherwin-White, *JRS* 1969, 287, apparently approved by Brunt, *PBA* 1994, 463, cf. *JRS* 1968, 231; see also Stone 63) or in favour of strictly economic evidence about ownership and transmission of property (Stone 59). These are however hardly objections to the prosopographic method itself, but rather to its mechanical and unimaginative implementation. Again, W. V. Harris, *War and Imperialism in Republican Rome 327–70 BC* (1979), 32 explicitly rejects the prosopographic approach of Scullard, by putting the emphasis on the fighting and military success which were the justification for election to political office which in turn made possible further military success, and so on. Another objection (Brunt 1965, see above) is that for the age of *Cicero, where political evidence of a direct sort is for once relatively plentiful, members of the same family go different ways, ties seem generally loose and loyalties changeable. As for individuals, 'we seldom have access to their minds'. Again, this is an argument for sophisticated and flexible use, not for abandonment, of the technique. More generally and recently, some of the assumptions about Roman political life made by Syme (and before him by M. Gelzer, *The Roman Nobility* (1969, Ger. orig. 1912)) are now disputed. Extensive use of prosopographic technique tended to go with a belief in the pervasiveness of *clientela* relationships and political friendships: the powerful individual or group (it was held) was capable of mobilizing vast *clientelae*. But see Brunt, *Fall of the Roman Republic* (1988), chs. 7, 8 for scepticism about the importance of domestic *clientela* (cf. CLIENS; AMICITIA); see also (for the idea that Roman republican politics was more democratic, and less securely in the control of a small élite, than has usually been thought in the present century) the Roman works cited in the bibliog. to DEMOCRACY, NON-ATHENIAN AND POST-CLASSICAL. Finally (Stone; Hopkins) traditional prosopography can be criticized for undue attention to the doings of élites and exceptional individuals (Hopkins 41 speaks of the 'Everest fallacy', i.e. the 'tendency to illustrate a category by an example which is exceptional'); but the paucity of evidence for low-status groups and individuals is not a problem peculiar to prosopography but one which faces most attempts to investigate the ancient world. Notwithstanding the above-noted objections, it is one premise of the present dictionary that Roman republican history in its human and political complexity cannot be understood without proper and expertly guided attention to prosopographical detail. The complexity can be grasped by a glance at the multiple entries under the name of any one of the great *gentes* (Aemilii, Cornelii, Fulvii, Iulii, Sempronii, and so on). As for imperial Rome, prosopography, allied with *epigraphy, has transformed understanding of the Roman governing class under the Principate, not only by documenting the gradual absorption of subject-élites into the *senate and order of *equites* (see SENATORS, PATTERNS OF RECRUITMENT; EQUITES, *Imperial period*), but also by providing the basis for estimates of the biological maintenance-rates of senatorial families (cf. the statistical approach of Hopkins himself in the book cited above), and discussion of the relative claims of merit versus patronage in advancing individual *careers. At a lower social level, present knowledge of the diffusion and activities of the *negotiatores* owes much to prosopography.

Prosopography has made less impact on Greek history, though the example of *PIR* was followed by J. Kirchner, *PA* for Athens (1901), P. Poralla, *Prosopographie der Lakedaimonier* (1913) for Sparta, and by Berve, *Alexanderreich* (1926), a massive study of the extended entourage of *Alexander (3) the Great; see also now Heckel, *Marshals*. But it was not till E. Badian's acute study of Harpalus, *JHS* 1961, that approaches more familiar from Roman history were applied to Alexander's court. In 1958 C. Habicht made remarkable use of prosopography in aspect (i) above—i.e. the study of the ethnic and regional origins of individuals, rather than aspect (ii), their marriage connections—for the illumination of *Seleucid policy towards indigenous personnel: see HELLENISM, HELLENIZATION. In Athenian history, J. K. Davies, the author of *Athenian Propertied Families* (1971, a family-based study of the Athenian 'liturgical class' i.e. those liable to perform liturgies, see LITURGY, GREEK), has shown that there is a basic mutual incompatibility between Athenian history and the method of Münzer': *Rivista Storica Italiana* 1968, 209 ff. (in Italian). But simple prosopographic methods can, naturally, be used for Classical Athens, see for instance Dover, *HCT* 4. 276 ff. on the 'politics and prosopography' of the affairs of the Herms and Mysteries (see ANDOCIDES), with good general cautionary remarks at 288 on the dangers of believing 'that kinsmen and acquaintances consistently support each other's policies'. Another example is the association of *Cleon with the tribute re-assessment of 425 BC (ML 69), the proposer of which was called Thudippus (a rare name). Now the 4th.-cent. orator *Isaeus (1) reveals (9.17) a second Cleon, who is a son of a Thudippus, and it is a plausible inference that Thudippus married the daughter of the famous Cleon. Again, prosopography has shown that there is surprisingly little overlap between politics at *deme level and at city level (D. Whitehead, *The Demes of Attica* (1986), 325, cf. 237). Large differences nevertheless remain between Athenian and Roman politics, despite recent shifts (see above) in the study of Roman republican history and despite attempts actually to categorize Rome of the middle and late republic as a democracy with some affinities to the classical Athenian model. But politics is not the only kind of history, and, as we have seen, there is more than one way of doing prosopography. Syme, for instance, was as much

interested in names as indicators of origin and of social as well as geographical mobility, as in the evidence they provided for family connections. He drew in particular on W. Schulze, *Zur Geschichte lateinischer Eigennamen* (1904). When P. M. Fraser and E. Matthews, *Lexicon of Greek Personal Names* (*LGPN*; so far 2 vols., 1987 and 1994), is complete, the possibilities for the Greek social historian, interested in origins and migration, will be enormous.

GENERAL DISCUSSIONS L. Stone, 'Prosopography', *Daedalus*, 1971, 46 ff.; T. F. Carney, *Phoenix*, 1973, 16 ff.; E. Badian, *JRS* 1967, 218; T. R. S. Broughton, *ANRW* 1.1 (1972), 250 ff. (Roman republic); A. J. Graham, *ANRW* 2.1 (1974), 136 ff. (Roman empire). S. H., A. J. S. S.

Prosper Tiro (*c.* AD 390–*c.*455), of Aquitaine, became a monk and may have taken deacon's orders. At Marseille (*Massalia) he supported *Augustine's doctrine of Grace against more moderate interpretations put forward in John *Cassian's *Collationes* (426). In 431 he journeyed to Rome to seek Pope Celestine's support for Augustinianism, and on the accession of *Leo I (1) (440) he returned to Rome where he acted as the Pope's secretary. According to Gennadius he drafted Leo's letters against Eutyches.

He was important, first as a champion of Augustine in the 'Semi-Pelagian' controversy (427–32), and second as the compiler of the Chronicle. Though he did not know Augustine he wrote (427/8) telling him that Pelagianism (see PELAGIUS) was rife in Marseille, and after Augustine's death (430) Prosper wrote three books in his defence. He attacked the anti-predestinarian views of John Cassian in a sarcastic work, *Contra Collatorem*, a reference to Cassian's *Collationes*. After the latter's death in 435 his *Expositio super Psalmos* contained more friendly estimates of his views, but also expressed Prosper's distaste for the current misbeliefs of Nestorius, the *Donatists, and Pelagians. While at Rome he popularized Augustine's memory in two works of extracts from Augustine's writings, *Liber Sententiarum ex operibus Sancti Augustini delibatarum* and *Epigrammata ex sententiis Sancti Augustini*, the latter in verse.

At Rome he compiled his Chronicle; down to 378 it was based on *Jerome's translation of *Eusebius' Chronicle, and thereafter to 417 borrowed from Sulpicius Severus (see SEVERUS, SULPICIUS) and *Orosius. He continued it first to 443 and finally to 455. From 417 to 455, Prosper's jejune entries are valuable for contemporary events, e.g. the intrigues which led to the invasion of Africa by *Gaiseric (429) and also for the early years of Leo's pontificate. The tendency of the work is heavily anti-heretical. This coupled with vindication of St Augustine rather than historical accuracy was his main interest.

His lasting memorial lay in the canons of the Council of Orange (529), which were based partly on the *Epigrammata*. His style, often modelled on Cicero, was good and the author's liveliness of spirit survives the rather rigid framework of his subjects.

Critical text of Chronicle ed. T. Mommsen, *MGH* 9. 341–499. Other works, Migne, *PL* 51 (Vienna Corpus edn. in preparation); P. Callens, *Exp. Psalm.* and *Lib. Sent.* (CCL 18 A, 1972). See articles in *DCB* and *DTC*. Also, E. M. Pickman, *The Mind of Latin Christendom* (1937), 418 ff. W. H. C. F.

prostitution, sacred is a strictly modern, not ancient, term and misleading in that it transfers to the institution, or rather a variety of institutions, an adjective which in ancient sources denotes only the status of the personnel involved (sometimes also their earnings, which likewise became sacred on dedication). In the cult of *Aphrodite at *Corinth, Strabo (8. 6. 20, C378; cf. 12. 3. 36, C559), admittedly writing long after the city's destruction in

prostitution, secular

146 BC, gives a total of over 1,000 *hetairai* dedicated by both men and women. Much earlier *Pindar (fr. 122; Chamaeleon fr. 31 Wehrli), in a *scolion* (see SCOLIA) which explicitly anticipates a degree of moral opprobrium and seeks to forestall this with a coy invocation to 'necessity' (ἀνάγκη), celebrates the dedication of up to 100 by the contemporary Xenophon of Corinth (the figure given is strictly a total of limbs rather than of persons). The modern view that their professional activities were ritually significant is not borne out by the down-to-earth, matter-of-fact ancient term 'earning from the body' (ἐργάζεσθαι ἀπὸ τοῦ σώματος), elsewhere and no less casually also used of wet-nursing (see CHILDBIRTH). Dedication is also emphasized in the cult of Aphrodite at *Eryx in Sicily (Strabo 6. 2. 6, C272; once again a thing of the past by his time), some women being sent from outside the island; *Diodorus (3) (4. 83. 6) emphasizes relaxation and entertainment rather than religious solemnity. In the cult of Ma (*Bellona) at Comana Pontica, *Strabo (559) says most but not all such women were sacred. In all these cases, the adjective denotes no more than manumission by fictive dedication of a kind already attested in the cult of Poseidon at *Taenarum in the 5th cent. BC (Schwyzer 52. 3–4).

A quite distinct institution, reported only from the margins of the Greek world, is the practice of pre-marital sex with strangers, sometimes sustained over a period of time, sometimes strictly delimited, but invariably presented as followed by a lifetime of strict conjugal fidelity, the *locus classicus* being *Herodotus (1)'s often hilarious description of *Babylon (1. 199, not confirmed but not contradicted by *cuneiform sources; some distinctive features repeated in LXX Epist. Jerem. 42–43, c.300 BC). This is a one-off rite, compulsory for all, in the service of the goddess *Mylitta, to whom earnings are dedicated, the act itself (by contrast with Corinthian practices) involving a strictly religious obligation (ἀποσιωσαμένη 199.4, cf. Justin (Trogus) *epit.* 18. 5. 4 (*Cyprus), Val. Max. 2. 6. 15 (*Sicca Veneria, Numidia)). By contrast, Herodotus' picture of Lydian girls (see LYDIA) earning their dowries by prostitution (and giving themselves away in marriage, 1. 93) could be a strictly secular (economic) phenomenon; not only did the Lydians invent coined money, they were the world's first 'hucksters', κάπηλοι (ibid. 94).

Distinct again but poorly attested (that is to say indirectly and in the rather suspect context of tyrannical misdeeds) is the vow supposedly taken by the citizens of *Locri Epizephyrii (S. Italy) to prostitute all their unmarried girls (*virgines*, Justin (Trogus) *epit.* 21. 3. 2) in the event of victory over *Rhegium in 477/6 BC, a one-off and clearly desperate measure which must if authentic be explained in quite different terms, perhaps connected with the highly unusual circumstances of the city's foundation. But oriental origins (or influence), so often invoked to exorcise the Hellenist's embarrassment at the Corinthian data (see ORIENTALISM), the real problem remaining the fact of their reception (and naturalization), however comforting on the Greek mainland, are certainly not applicable to Locri.

The ἱαρὰν μίστωμα, or 'contract-price of the [pl.] sacred (—)', mentioned in a number of inscriptions from the 4th-cent. archive of the temple of *Zeus at Locri (A. de Franciscis, *Stato e società a Locri Epizefiri* (1972), nos. 22, 30, 31) must certainly denote sacred lands, not sacred women: for the ellipse cf. the μίσθωσις τῆς νέας ('rental of the new (land)') in F. Sokolowski, *Lois sacrées* (1969), no. 33, ll. 11–18 (Athens, 335/4–330/29 BC).

GENERAL SURVEY E. M. Yamauchi in H. A. Hoffner (ed.), *Orient and Occident (Essays . . . Cyrus H. Gordon*, 1973), 213–22.

CORINTH C. K. Williams, II, in *Corinthiaca (Studies . . . Darrell A. Amyx*, 1986), 12–24.

LOCRI (the *votum*): C. Sourvinou-Inwood, *CQ* 1974, 186–98.

S. G. P.

prostitution, secular The prostitution of women (broadly defined here as the exchange of a female's sexual service, with or without her consent, for some other resource) may have arisen in Greece out of contact with earlier Near Eastern manifestations of so-called sacred prostitution (see preceding entry); this may have been 'temple prostitution', 'prostitution' in order to gain a dowry, or both. The exchange of sexual service for the economic benefits conferred by marriage is remarked upon by *Hesiod (*Works and Days* 373–5). In both Greece and Rome, prostitution was considered to be as necessary an institution as the institutions of *marriage, concubinage (see CONTUBERNIUM), or *slavery. Social attitudes and legislation generally stigmatized the prostitute, who—whether female or male—generally was of low status. In the Greek world there is a constant emphasis on the economic perils of the transaction for men (Archilochus 302 W) and its concomitant provision of sexual release (Philemon, *Adelphoi* fr. 3K–A). The very terms *porneion* (brothel) and *pornē* (whore) are related to *pernēmi* (to sell); cf. Latin *meretrix, merx, mereo*. The major written sources—fictional literature, historiography, the orators, and law codes—frequently set into collision medical, moralizing, regulatory, tolerant, and oppressive ideologies, and must be analysed with great care. Much work remains to be done on this important aspect of social history. See HETAIRAI; HOMOSEXUALITY (for male prostitutes); PROSTITUTION, SACRED.

H. Herter, *Jahrbuch für Antike und Christentum* 1960, 70 ff.; K. J. Dover, in J. Peradotto and J. P. Sullivan (eds.), *Women in the Ancient World: The Arethusa Papers*, 143–57; W. A. Krenkel, in M. Grant and R. Kitzinger (eds.), *Civilization of the Ancient Mediterranean: Greece and Rome* (1988), 1291–7; C. J. Pateman, *The Sexual Contract* (1988); T. A. J. McGinn, *Helios*, 1989, 79–110; D. M. Halperin, ibid. 88–112, and *One Hundred Years of Homosexuality and Other Essays on Greek Love* (1990).

M. M. H.

Protagoras of *Abdera (c.490–420 BC), the most celebrated of the *sophists. He travelled widely throughout the Greek world, including several visits to Athens, where he was associated with *Pericles (1), who invited him to write the constitution for the Athenian colony of *Thurii. The ancient tradition of his condemnation for impiety and flight from Athens is refuted by *Plato (1)'s evidence (*Meno* 91e) that he enjoyed a universally high reputation till his death and afterwards. See INTOLERANCE, INTELLECTUAL AND RELIGIOUS. He was famous in antiquity for agnosticism concerning the existence and nature of the gods, and for the doctrine that 'Man is the measure of all things', i.e. the thesis that all sensory appearances and all beliefs are true for the person whose appearance or belief they are; on the most plausible construal that doctrine attempts to eliminate objectivity and truth altogether. It was attacked by *Democritus and Plato (in the *Theaetetus*) on the ground that it is self-refuting; if all beliefs are true, then the belief that it is not the case that all beliefs are true is itself true. In the *Protagoras* Plato represents him as maintaining a fairly conservative form of social morality, based on a version of social contract theory; humans need to develop social institutions to survive in a hostile world, and the basic social virtues, justice and self-control, must be generally observed if those institutions are to flourish.

DK 80, English trans. in R. K. Sprague (ed.), *The Older Sophists* (1972); A. Capizzi, *Protagora* (1955); W. K. C. Guthrie, *A History of Greek*

Philosophy 3 (1969); G. B. Kerferd, *The Sophistic Movement* (1981); C. Farrar, *The Origins of Democratic Thinking* (1988). **C. C. W. T.**

Protesilaus, leader of a Thessalian contingent at *Troy (see THESSALY). According to *Iliad* 2. 698–702 he was the first of the Greeks to disembark and was immediately killed, 'and his wife was left tearing her cheeks and his house half-built'. This is later elaborated, mainly (to our knowledge) in Latin authors (Catullus 68. 73–130; Ovid, *Her.* 13, Laodamia to Protesilaus; Hyginus 103–4). Here Protesilaus had offended the gods by failing to sacrifice before he began his house. An oracle prophesied that the first man ashore at Troy would die and he deliberately sacrificed himself. His wife Laodamia grieved so for his loss that the gods allowed her to see him for three hours, after which she killed herself; or she spent so much time with an image of him that her father burnt it and she flung herself on the fire.

LIMC 7.1 (1994), 554–60. **A. L. B.**

Proteus, a minor sea-god or 'Old Man of the Sea', herdsman of seals. At *Homer, *Odyssey* 4. 349–570 *Menelaus (1) encounters him on the island of Pharos off the coast of Egypt. The god takes on various shapes in an effort to escape (his shape-changing became proverbial), but Menelaus holds him fast and forces him to answer questions. This episode must have been the subject of *Aeschylus' *Proteus*, the satyr-play of the *Oresteia*. Later writers, including *Virgil, who imitates the Homeric account at *Georgics* 4. 387–529, associate the god with *Chalcidice.

At *Herodotus (1) 2. 112–20, however (cf. Eur. *Hel.* 4), Proteus is not a god but a virtuous Egyptian king, who keeps *Helen with him for the duration of the Trojan War.

K. O'Nolan, *Hermes*, 1960, 1 ff.; P. Plass, *CJ* 1969, 104 ff.; S. West on *Od.* 4. 384 ff., in A. Heubeck, S. West, and J. B. Hainsworth, *Comm. on Homer's Odyssey* 1 (1988), 217 f.; LIMC 7.1 (1994), 560–1. **A. L. B.**

Protogenes (late 4th cent. BC), famous painter and sculptor of *Caunus or *Xanthus; friendly rival of *Apelles, working mainly in Rhodes. His masterpieces were an Ialysus and Resting Satyr. He wrote two books on painting. See PAINTING, GREEK.

Overbeck, 1907–36; M. Robertson, *History of Greek Art*, 1 (1975), 495 f. **T. B. L. W.; A. J. S. S.**

protrepticus, an exhortation (to philosophy), first developed as a genre by the 5th-cent. *sophists, who thus persuaded students to take their courses in philosophy and other arts, especially those required for politics. No early examples are extant, but *Plato (1)'s *Euthydemus* includes an example (278e–282d), and something similar is found in *Isocrates' *Against the Sophists*, *Helen*, *Busiris*, and *To Nicocles*. The most famous example in antiquity was *Aristotle's *Protrepticus* (now lost), addressed to Themison, king of *Cyprus. This is known to have influenced *Cicero's *Hortensius* (also lost), and was excerpted, to an extent that remains controversial, by the neo-Pythagorean *Iamblichus (2) (see NEOPYTHAGOREANISM) in his *Protrepticus*, which is extant. A later extant example is *Galen's protreptic to medicine (Kühn, *Med. Graec. Opera*, vol. 1).

P. Hartlich, *De exhortationum a Graecis Romanisque scriptarum historia* (1889); K. Gaiser, *Protreptik und Paränese bei Platon* (1959); I. Düring, *Aristotle's Protrepticus* (1961); P. Moraux (ed.), *Frühschriften des Aristoteles* (1975); G. W. Most, in *Studi su codici e papiri filosofici: Platone, Aristotele, Ierocle* (1992). **D. J. F.**

proverbs See PAROEMIOGRAPHERS; and cf. GNŌMĒ; SENTENTIA.

Providentia, learned term for *prudentia*, 'foresight', the capacity to distinguish good from bad, which became, under the influence of the *pronoia* ('forethought') of *Stoicism, a virtue of statesmen. *Providentia Augusti* became the object of cult at the beginning of the Principate. It expressed the wise forethought of *Augustus in regulating the succession in AD 4, before being extended to other fields of imperial forethought. The altar of Augustan *Providentia* was sited in the *Campus Martius near the *Ara Pacis Augustae. Its anniversary fell on June 26, date of the *adoption by Augustus of the future emperor *Tiberius. The date of the altar's construction is unknown. It was already in existence by AD 20, since it is mentioned in the *senatus consultum* about Cn. *Calpurnius Piso (2). The *Providentia Augusti* was invoked on the discovery of conspiracies and was a frequent theme in imperial coinage. From the time of *Hadrian, *Providentia deorum*, protectress of the imperial family and the empire, was invoked alongside *Providentia Augusti*.

M. Charlesworth, *Harv. Theol. Rev.* 1936, 107 ff.; J. Béranger, *Principatus. Études de notions et d'histoires politiques dans l'Antiquité gréco-romaine* (1975), 331 ff.; H. Broise, *MÉFRA* 1980, 232 ff.; J. Martin, *Providentia deorum: Aspects religieux du pouvoir romain* (1982–5). **J. Sch.**

***provincia*/province** 1. The etymology of the word *provincia* is obscure: it was mistakenly derived from *pro* + *vincere* by Roman antiquarians. Its basic meaning is the sphere in which a magistrate (perhaps originally a magistrate with *imperium*) is to function. See MAGISTRACY, ROMAN. By the 3rd cent. BC, the two consuls normally had their *provinciae* assigned by the *senate or by mutual agreement (*comparatio*); later allotment was normal. A law of C. *Sempronius Gracchus (123) provided that the senate was to decide, before the consular elections, in a vote protected against tribunician *intercessio, which *provinciae* were to be consular: this was to prevent personal or political influences on that decision. At the beginning of the year the senate would decide which *provinciae* were to be praetorian (and, before 123, consular): for these, the magistrates would then draw lots. Any others would be filled by designated promagistrates (see PRO CONSULE, PRO PRAETORE). By the late 3rd cent., a magistrate or promagistrate was expected to confine his activities to his *provincia*, except in emergencies or by special permission. By 171 this had become a formal rule, enforced by the senate (see Livy 43. 1): perhaps in the process of administrative reform that produced the law of L. *Villius. It was at various times reaffirmed in legislation on provincial administration.

Originally the two consuls normally divided all duties between them. Since they had to campaign nearly every year, a *praetor with *imperium* was appointed (traditionally in 367) and given the *provincia urbana* (affairs in the city, especially legal business and the presidency of the senate and legislative assemblies when necessary). Until c.100, when consuls began most often to stay in Rome, this remained his task, but he came to specialize in civil law and in the end to confine himself to this. A second praetor was created at the end of the First *Punic War, probably to supervise the newly-won territory of Punic *Sicily and perhaps later *Sardinia. In 227 two new praetors were created for these overseas *provinciae* and the second praetor, though freely used in fighting in the Second Punic War, was normally assigned to judicial duties in the city, in due course those affecting aliens (hence the popular title *praetor peregrinus*). Two more praetors were created in 198/7, to command in the two newly won territories in *Spain, hitherto in the charge of private citizens with special *imperium*. Henceforth the word *provincia*, although it never lost its original meaning, was mainly used for overseas territories under permanent Roman administration, i.e. it came mainly to mean 'province'; but the two city *provinciae* were the highest in prestige. By the second century (and probably from the start) provincial commanders were attended by *quaestors. The praetor of Sicily, where the territory of *Syracuse, annexed in the Second Punic War, remained under its traditional administration, separate from that of the originally Punic province, was given two quaestors. Characteristically for Roman conservatism, he retained the two quaestors to the end of the republic, even after the administration of Sicily was unified, in the settlement of P. *Rupilius after a slave war, on the more profitable model of the old kingdom of Syracuse.

After 197 the senate was unwilling to create more praetors (see PRAETOR) and, as a necessary consequence, on the whole to annex more territory. *Macedonia was 'freed' after the battle of *Pydna; *Numidia was not annexed after *Jugurtha's defeat; Transalpine Gaul (see GAUL (TRANSALPINE)), which provided the land connection with Spain, was not organized as a province until after the wars with the *Cimbri and their allies had shown the danger this presented; *Cyrene, bequeathed by its king (96), was not properly organized until the 60s; and the bequest of Egypt by *Ptolemy (1) X Alexander I (87) was refused by *Sulla. But some annexation became necessary, or was regarded as such: Macedonia and Africa (the territory of *Carthage; see AFRICA, ROMAN) in 146, Asia after the war with *Aristonicus (129), Transalpine Gaul after 100. Unwillingness to create more praetors meant that the traditional city-state system of (in principle) annual magistracies was abandoned and promagistrates became an integral part of imperial administration. New quaestors were probably created, since quaestors, at that time not even guaranteed membership of the senate, did not endanger the political system. In 123–2, C. Gracchus, reforming the *repetundae court, put a praetor in charge of it. Over the next generation, other *quaestiones were established on this model, so that by c.90 most, perhaps all, praetors were occupied in Rome during their year of office. Since consuls were not involved in routine provincial government, provinces were almost entirely left to promagistrates. As early as 114, the *praetor urbanus* C. *Marius (1) was sent as proconsul to Spain after his year of office—a major innovation as far as our records go. By the nineties praetors serving in the city might expect to be sent overseas the following year. Major foreign wars, the *Social War (3) and civil wars added to the strain on the system, and tenures of promagistrates increased until they could reach six years. This, combined with the growth of the client army (see MARIUS (1)), posed a serious danger to the republic, as Sulla soon showed.

Sulla, after his victory, aimed at stabilizing the state under senate control. He added at least two *quaestiones*, but also added two praetorships (and raised the number of quaestors to 20). Consuls (it seems) were encouraged to go to prestigious provinces (like Cisalpina) at the end of their year. It was apparently Sulla's idea that ten magistrates with *imperium*, normally governing provinces after their year of office, would suffice to keep provincial tenures down to a year or at most two. But after 70 various factors—especially the rise of *populares* (see OPTIMATES) with their programmes and ambitions and increasing, hence increasingly expensive, competition for the consulship—led to accelerated annexation. *Crete was annexed by Q. *Caecilius Metellus (Creticus) to end Cretan *piracy—and to prevent its annexation by *Pompey. *Cyprus was annexed to pay for P. *Clodius Pulcher's corn distributions; Pompey annexed Syria and added Pontus to Bithynia, as well as first organizing several territories (e.g. Judaea) as dependencies of provinces. He claimed

to have added 85 million denarii to Rome's previous revenue of 50 million (Plut. *Pomp.* 45. 4). *Caesar, for reasons of personal ambition, extended Transalpine Gaul to the Rhine and the English Channel. Yet men not seeking glory or fortunes were often unwilling to serve in provinces, and Sulla had omitted to make acceptance of a promagistracy compulsory, as a magistrate's *provincia* always had been. Thus exploitation of provincials for private gain became a necessary incentive, tending to select those eager for it as provincial governors, while major wars and increasingly competitive ambitions for glory led to the granting of large *provinciae* with long tenure to men like L. *Licinius Lucullus (2), Pompey, Caesar and M. *Licinius Crassus (1). To stop the dangers inherent in this, Pompey, on the senate's advice, fixed an interval (perhaps of five years) between magistracy and pro-magistracy and made acceptance of provinces compulsory (52): thus men like *Cicero and M. *Calpurnius Bibulus belatedly had to accept provincial service. But the plan was nullified when civil wars supervened. It was later essentially restored by *Augustus.

2. A province was not an area under uniform administration. In Sicily, cities that joined the Romans had been declared 'free' (see FREE CITIES) when the territory was taken over from Carthage, and 'free' cities, granted various degrees of independence, remained characteristic of eastern and some western provinces. Inevitably their rights tended to be whittled down: by the early 1st cent., the free city of Utica was the seat of the governor of Africa. Many governors were less than scrupulous in respecting the rights of free cities. Tribes could also be granted various degrees of self-government, and from the late 2nd cent. colonies of citizens were founded overseas (see COLONIZATION, ROMAN). A province was therefore a mosaic of territories with different statuses, from complete subjection to nominal independence, and provincial maps were kept in Rome to show this. Most provinces were annexed after wars, and in such cases the victorious commander would organize the peace settlement (including, if appropriate, annexation) with a commission of *legati* according to a *senatus consultum*. (Pompey, characteristically, refused to accept a commission, thereby causing serious anxiety regarding his political intentions.) This settlement, later confirmed by senate or people, was called the *lex provinciae*. (See Cic. 2 *Verr.* 2. 32, 40.) It settled boundaries (though provinces facing *barbarian tribes seem to have had no fixed external frontier), local constitutions, taxation, and the administration of justice, in ways and degrees that differed considerably from one province to another. The *lex* might later be amended in detail, but remained the basis for the organization of the particular province. In the few cases where annexation did not follow upon victory, we do not know what was done, but basic rules were certainly set up (e.g. for Cyprus when it was added to *Cilicia). See LEX (1(d)).

Within the general framework, each governor issued his *edict, normally based on his predecessor's and relevant parts of those of urban magistrates. But this was never compulsory. Q. *Mucius Scaevola (2) in the 90s in Asia and Cicero, modelling himself on him in 51 in Cilicia, introduced major judicial innovations. Scaevola's reforms were made mandatory for Asia by the senate, but any extension to other provinces was haphazard. The edict was not binding on the governor, at least until 67 and perhaps after (see CORNELIUS, C.). Within the limits set by the general framework, he held absolute *imperium* over non-citizens. In fact, he was a commander and not, in the modern sense, a governor or administrator. On his departure from Rome, no matter how peaceful his province, he and his *lictors changed to military garb and his friends would escort him with prayers for his safety and success; and his return was accompanied by corresponding ceremonial. He could delegate his power to his quaestor and legates, and within limits to others. He was accompanied to his province by a large *cohors (a military term) of military and civilian attendants and friends of his and of his officers, many of them young men thus gaining their first experience of public service and rule. Among them and provincial Romans, he would choose his *consilium* (panel of advisers), to advise on, and vouch for, his judicial and other activities. Having *imperium*, he could not be challenged during his tenure, no matter how he behaved, and he could protect the actions of his officers and *cohors*, and also those of businessmen (see NEGOTIATORES) and *publicani*, by armed force and sheer terror, for immense mutual profit. The chances of having him convicted in the *repetundae* court were slim, since he was rich and well connected: nearly all cases in the late republic ended in acquittal. Even conviction might not profit the provincials (see VERRES, C.). The sum voted by the senate for the province offered further opportunities for profit: it was not expected that he would return the surplus, which was normally shared by him with his officers and *cohors*. As we have seen, these opportunities became an integral part of the system and were thus not subject to reform.

3. All indirect taxes were farmed by *publicani*. Direct taxes were originally collected by the quaestor, at greatly varying rates, though farmed at the local level. C. Gracchus arranged for the *decuma* of Asia, the wealthiest province, to be sold to *publicani* under five-year contracts. This system was apparently extended by Pompey to the provinces he organized. Asia remained a centre of exploitation and consequent resentment, due more to warfare and the actions of governors than to the *publicani*, though the latter offered easier targets for complaint. L. Lucullus tried to save it by restructuring its huge debts, and after further civil war and oppression Caesar greatly reduced its tax and restored its collection to the quaestor. There was no change in other provinces before Augustus.

4. In 27 BC, Augustus was given a large consular *provincia*, originally (it seems) Gaul, Spain, and Syria, which he governed (after 23 as proconsul) through *legati pro praetore* and which contained nearly all the legions. Its finances were administered by *procurators. The command was regularly renewed and the area changed over time. By the end of the reign the emperor's provinces were an accepted institution. The public (in fact, senatorial) provinces were governed by proconsuls, most (and within a generation all) of them without legions, but still with *imperium* and assisted by quaestors and legates. But the emperor had *imperium maius* (see IMPERIUM), which we find Augustus exercising as early as the *Cyrene edicts. He also, of course, had to approve of all proconsular appointments, especially the most prestigious ones to Asia (see ASIA, ROMAN PROVINCE) and Africa. Egypt, though 'subject to the Roman people' (RG 27), was forbidden to senators and governed for the emperor by an equestrian prefect with legionary forces (see PRAEFECTUS). Various minor provinces (e.g. *Judaea and *Noricum) were governed by prefects (later by procurators) without legions. Direct taxes were directly collected in all provinces; indirect taxes continued to be collected by *publicani*, now subject to strict regulation, but by the 3rd cent. AD were taken over by the central government.

The system established by Augustus was essentially maintained until well into the 3rd cent., although there were many changes in detail, some of them significant. *Britain was annexed by *Claudius and later extended, *Dacia and Arabia (i.e. Naba-

taea; see ARABIA; NABATAEANS) by *Trajan. (Other conquests proved ephemeral.) As expansion ceased, especially after *Trajan, frontiers were gradually marked out and defended by garrisons (see LIMES). Various *client kings were succeeded by governors and the subdivision of large provinces, begun by Augustus, was continued, especially since a constant supply of senior men was soon available. Supervision of municipal government (see CORRECTOR and CURATOR REI PUBLICAE), made necessary by AD 100 because of financial incompetence, was gradually extended and stifled civic tradition. The whole system was finally reorganized, after the strains of civil wars and invasions, by *Diocletian.

In some provinces a *concilium of local notables had developed under the republic: it could serve as a vehicle for distributing the governor's messages and would propose honours for him; it might even occasionally complain about him to the senate. These *concilia*, extended to all provinces, became the organisations in charge of the imperial cult (see RULER CULT, ROMAN), which grew out of the cult of the goddess Roma under the republic. The councils were headed by native high priests, who in due course could expect to gain citizenship; many of their descendants became *equites* or even senators. As more provincial notables gained the citizenship, the equestrian service and the senate were gradually opened up to provincials, although over a long timespan and at very varying rates for different provinces (see SENATORS, PATTERNS OF RECRUITMENT). Among the lower classes, Romanization was spread by army service (see AUXILIA), while the grant of *ius Latii* was extended among provincial communities; though the Latin language never spread to the east. By the time of *Caracalla's edict (see CONSTITUTION, ANTONINE), a unitary Roman state was *de facto* already in existence. See FINANCE, ROMAN.

Mommsen, *Röm. Staatsr.* (see index), and *The Provinces of the Roman Empire* (1909)—both still basic; A. Lintott, *Imperium Romanum* (1993); F. F. Abbott and A. C. Johnson, *Municipal Administration in the Roman Empire* (1926), with large selection of sources, chiefly documentary. See also under individual provinces and the articles referred to.

E. B.

provocatio was an appeal made to the Roman people against the action of a magistrate (see MAGISTRACY, ROMAN), whether the latter was employing summary coercion (*coercitio) on the appellant or presiding over a judicial process. The term means 'calling out' or 'calling "Out"' and referred to either the summons of the citizens who were expected to support the appeal or the summons of the magistrate concerned to a popular forum. Against the second explanation is the fact that the verb *provoco*, when it describes an appeal, is never followed by the magistrate challenged as a direct object. Roman annalists described these appeals occurring during the Conflict of the Orders (see ROME (HISTORY), § 1.2). Although they believed that *provocatio* had been given legal recognition by a *lex Valeria* of 509 BC, this law is generally now held to be a fictitious anticipation of the *lex Valeria* of 300 BC which made the disregard of *provocatio* by a magistrate a criminal offence (see LEX (2) under *Leges Valeriae*). It seems more likely that in the early republic appeals were based first on unofficial collective action by the *plebs and secondly on intervention by the tribunes. According to Cicero (*Rep.* 2. 54), the texts of the *Twelve Tables implied the existence of *provocatio* in a variety of contexts and by then (450 BC) it seems to have been recognized as a fact of Roman life. At the same time the use of plebeian assemblies as unofficial courts was probably forbidden, while capital trials before an assembly were reserved for the *comitia centuriata*. The least confrontational way now for a magistrate opposed by *provocatio* to proceed further was to take the matter to an assembly, and from 300 BC the *lex Valeria* was an additional inducement so to do. In some matters of proven guilt it seems that a simple appeal to an assembly rather than a full trial was sufficient. During the 2nd cent. the protection of citizens against summary justice was further enhanced by *leges Porciae*, apparently three in number, one of which abolished the flogging of Roman citizens and another extended *provocatio* to citizens in the military sphere (i.e. outside the city of Rome). A *lex Sempronia* of C. *Sempronius Gracchus not only reformulated one of the principles of *provocatio* by forbidding capital trials unsanctioned by the people (so helping to stimulate the growth of *quaestiones perpetuae* established by statute), but provided for assembly-trials of offenders against the law. Ultimately the grant of tribunician powers to *Augustus led to the substitution for *provocatio* of appeal to the emperor.

For Mommsen *provocatio* was the cornerstone of Roman criminal procedure, since he thought that all trials were heard by an assembly on the principle that they were appeals from the summary coercion (*coercitio*) of a magistrate. More recent scholarship has shown that *provocatio* was not a constituent part of an assembly-trial; it has also been powerfully argued that assembly-trials were not normally used for common criminals. It is in any case highly unlikely that such men would have profited from appeal to the Roman people (whose lives and goods their activities threatened), except in a highly politicized situation, where crime formed part of civil conflict.

Mommsen, *Röm. Strafr.* 167 f., 473 ff.; E. S. Staveley, *Hist.* 1955; W. Kunkel, *Untersuchungen zur Entstehung der römischen Kriminalverfahrens in vorsullanischer Zeit* (1962); P. Garnsey, *JRS* 1967; A. W. Lintott, *ANRW* 1. 2 (1972), 226–67. E. S. S.; A. W. L.

proxenos/proxeny Since Greek states did not send permanent diplomatic representatives abroad, local citizens served as *proxenoi* to look after the interests of other states in their community. By the beginning of the 5th cent. this 'proxeny' system had developed from earlier practices of hospitality under which some relied on hereditary ties with foreign families (see FRIENDSHIP, RITUALIZED) and others on the more general respect for strangers and suppliants. Survivals from this were the continued existence of private friends in foreign states (ἰδιόξενοι) and the practice of a few states of appointing *proxenoi* to look after visitors. More commonly states selected their own *proxenoi* in other states and, in return for services already rendered and expected in the future, bestowed honours and privileges upon them. Such appointments were much coveted, and many voluntarily assumed the burdens in the hope of gaining the title. The position was often hereditary. A *proxenos* was usually a citizen of the state in which he served and not of the state he represented. Later, however, when honours were bestowed more freely and had little practical significance, *proxenia* (proxeny) and honorary citizenship frequently were combined in the same grant.

M. Walbank, *Athenian Proxenies of the Fifth Century BC* (1978); C. Marek, *Die Proxenie* (1984); A. Gerolymatos, *Espionage and Treason: A Study of the Proxenia* (1986); J. K. Davies, *Democracy and Classical Greece*[2] (1993), 69 ff. J. A. O. L.; S. H.

Prudentius, Aurelius Clemens (AD 348–after 405), greatest of the Christian Latin poets, was a native of the Ebro valley in NE Spain and abandoned a distinguished administrative career for Christian poetry. His works are (*a*) lyrical: *Cathemerinon*, 'Hymns for the day' and *Peristephanon*, 'Crowns of the martyrs'; (*b*) didactic: *Apotheosis*, 'The divinity of Christ', *Hamartigenia*, 'The origin

of sin', *Psychomachia*, 'Battle of the Soul' (an allegory), and the *Dittochaeon*, four-line poems on biblical topics; (*c*) polemic: *Contra Symmachum*, 'Against Symmachus', in two books, based on the Altar of Victory controversy in 384 (see SYMMACHUS (2)). 'The Christian Virgil and Horace' (Bentley), Prudentius adapted classical poetic forms and metres to convey the Christian message, introducing into Christian poetry the literary hymn, the allegorical epic, and the Christian ballad. His work profoundly influenced medieval art and Church liturgy as well as poetry.

TEXT Ed. Bergman, *CSEL* 61; Cunningham, *CCSL* 126 (1966); with trans.: Lavarenne (1943–51, Fr.); Thomson (Loeb, 1949–53); Guillen–Rodriguez (1950). A. H.-W.; J. D. H.

Prusias (1) **I Cholus** ('the Lame', *c*.230–182 BC), son of Ziaëlas, king of *Bithynia. After war with *Byzantium (220) and a celebrated victory over invading *Celts in 216, his policy revolved about friendship with *Macedonia and enmity towards *Pergamum. He invaded Pergamene territory when *Attalus I was fighting with Rome against *Philip (3) V in Greece (208) and was included in the Peace of Phoenice (205) on Philip's side. From Philip he received the *Propontis ports of Cius and Myrlea (202), renaming them Prusias and Apamea. In 198 he took Phrygia Epictetus from Attalus, and Cierus and Tieum on the Euxine from *Heraclea (3). After receiving assurances from the Scipios (190) (See CORNELIUS SCIPIO AFRICANUS, P. and CORNELIUS SCIPIO ASIAGENES, L.) he remained neutral in Rome's war with *Antiochus (3) III, but the subsequent demand (188) that he return Phrygia to *Eumenes (2) II of Pergamum led to a war (188–183) which he lost. Prusias was required to relinquish Phrygia, and to surrender *Hannibal, a refugee at his court and his admiral during this conflict, to Rome. Hannibal chose suicide. Both Prusias and Hannibal are credited with the foundation of Prusa.

See Prusias (2) II for bibliography. P. S. D.

Prusias (2) **II Cynegus** ('the Hunter', 182–149 BC), son of *Prusias (1) I, king of Bithynia, joined *Eumenes (2) II in a war against Pharnaces of Pontus (181–179). After marrying the sister of *Perseus (2) of Macedon, he abstained from the latter's conflict with Rome; when it was over Prusias appeared before the senate (167/6) clad in the garb of a Roman *freedman and addressed his audience as 'saviour gods' (Polyb. 30. 18. 5). This won him favour at Rome (for a time) and contempt amongst Greeks (enduring). Invasion of Pergamene territory (156–154; see PERGAMUM) ended in defeat, and an indemnity was imposed by Rome. He sent his son *Nicomedes (2) II to seek release from this, but the latter, learning that death would be the penalty for failure (and fearing that Prusias would supplant him in favour of his son by a second wife), revolted. Nicomedes was encouraged by Rome and aided by Pergamum; Prusias fled to *Nicomedia, where the citizens, sharing in the hatred widespread amongst his subjects, surrendered him and were allowed to stone him to death.

RE 23. 1 (with 23. 2. 2463 ff.), 'Prusias' (1) and (2); D. C. Braund, *CQ* 1982, 353 f.; C. Habicht, *CAH* 8[2] (1989), 324 ff. See also bibliog. to NICOMEDES. P. S. D.

prytaneion, symbolic centre of the *polis, housing its communal hearth (*koinē hestia*), eternal flame, and public dining-room where civic hospitality was offered; usually in or off the *agora. A facility of ancient origin (the Athenian *prytaneion* was allegedly founded by *Theseus: Thuc. 2. 15), it probably took its name from the post-regal magistracy of the *prytaneis, with whom it sometimes remained closely linked (e.g. at *Ephesus); in *Dorian cities its functions could be housed in the offices of the *hierothytai* ('sacrificers'), as on Hellenistic *Rhodes and (after *Nabis) at Sparta. The privilege of permanent maintenance (sitēsis) in the prytaneion was highly honorific (see Cic. De or. 1. 54. 232) and, in Classical times, sparingly conceded; less honorific was the once-only invitation to a meal (deipnon, xenia). Excavated prytaneia tend to be architecturally modest, as might have been the fare, at least at democratic Athens (see Ath. 4. 137e). See HESTIA.

L. Gernet, Anthropologie de la Grèce ancienne (1978; Eng. trans. The Anthropology of Ancient Greece (1981), ch. 15; S. Miller, The Prytaneion (1978); M. Osborne, ZPE 41 (1981), 153–70.   A. J. S. S.

prytaneis (πρυτάνεις) means 'presidents', sing. prytanis (πρύτανις). In Athens the *boulē, after it was reorganized in 508/7 BC by *Cleisthenes (2), consisted of fifty men chosen by lot from each of the ten *phylai, and each group of fifty served as prytaneis for one-tenth of the year (see CALENDAR, GREEK). This period was called a prytany (πρυτανεία); owing to the vagaries of Athenian methods of reckoning a year, a prytany might be anything from 35 to 39 days. It was reduced to one-twelfth of the year when the number of phylai was increased to twelve in 307/6. To decide which phylē's group was to be prytaneis next, lots were drawn shortly before the beginning of each prytany except the last by all the groups which had not been prytaneis so far that year.

The prytaneis were on duty every day. They made arrangements for meetings of the boulē and *ekklēsia, received envoys and letters addressed to the state, and conducted other day-to-day business. Between 470 and 460 an office, called the *tholos because of its circular shape, was built for them next to the bouleutērion on the west side of the Agora. There they dined every day at public expense. Earlier they may have used the Prytaneion as their office; an alternative view is that the prytaneis did not exist before the time when the tholos was built.

Each day one of the prytaneis was picked by lot to be their foreman (epistatēs). He remained on duty in the tholos for one night and day, with one-third of the prytaneis. He had charge of the state seal and of the keys of the treasuries and archives. In the 5th cent. he was the chairman at any meeting of the boulē or ekklēsia held on his day (see SOCRATES—the most famous epistatēs, and on a famous occasion), but in the 4th cent. this duty was taken over by the *proedroi. No one could be foreman more than once, and consequently a considerable proportion (perhaps half) of the citizens held this position at some time in their lives. The whole system of the prytaneis and their foreman, based on lot and rotation, was a means of involving ordinary citizens in public administration, and thus a fundamental part of Athenian democracy.

Prytanis is also found outside Athens as the title of a state official, often with responsibility (individually or as a college) for presiding over a city council. Prytaneis are definitely attested at *Rhodes, *Alexandria (1) in Egypt, and a number of places in western *Asia Minor and the E. Aegean, in the Classical and Hellenistic periods; also more doubtfully at Archaic *Corinth.

P. J. Rhodes, The Athenian Boule (1972), 16–25; F. Gschnitzer, RE suppl. 13 (1973), 730–816, 'Prytanis'   D. M. M.; S. H.

Psammetichus I, first of the *Saites, came to the throne in 664 but initially had to contend for control of Egypt with rival kinglets, Assyrians, and Nubians (see ASSYRIA; NUBIA). With the help of Carian (see CARIA) and *Ionian *mercenaries and diplomatic skill he secured the entire country by 656. This position he consolidated by establishing permanent mercenary camps in the Delta and by developing commercial links with the Greeks, particularly through the trading post of *Naucratis. In foreign policy

his major concern was the Levant where he successfully defended Egyptian interests against Assyrians, Scythians, and Chaldaeans. He died in 610 and was buried at Sais.

CAH 3². 2, Index, under the name; W. Helck, RE 23, 1305 ff.; F. K. Kienitz, Die politische Geschichte Ägyptens vom 7. bis zum 4. Jahrhundert vor der Zeitwende (1953); K. Kitchen, The Third Intermediate Period (1973), index; Alan B. Lloyd, Herodotus Book II, 3 (1988), Index; A. Spalinger in Lexikon der Ägyptologie 4. 1164 ff.   A. B. L.

Psaon of *Plataea, historian (probably late 3rd cent. BC). He wrote a thirty-book history of Greece, continuing *Diyllus from 297/6 BC, covering partly the same period as *Phylarchus. His work perhaps extended to Ol. 140 (220–217), where *Polybius (1) began, and was continued by *Menodotus (1). *Dionysius (7) of Halicarnassus criticized the history for being dry and in the tradition of *Isocrates.

FGrH 78.   A. H. McD.; K. S. S.

Psellus, Michael (baptismal name Constantine) (AD 1018–after 1081). Byzantine man of letters. Born and educated in *Constantinople, he became an imperial secretary and probably also gave private tuition in philosophy and other subjects. Psellus belonged to a group of young intellectuals, pupils of John Mauropous, which included the future patriarchs John Xiphilinus and Constantine Leichoudes. They played a prominent role—though probably less prominent than Psellus would have us believe—in the revival of higher learning in the 11th cent., and entertained hopes of exercising real power during the enlightened reign of Constantine IX Monomachus (1042–55). Their hopes were not fulfilled, and Psellus found it politic to retire to a monastery in *Bithynia in 1054–5. Constantine IX granted him the title of hypatos tōn philosophōn ('highest of philosophers'), which seems to have been largely honorific, though it may have implied some kind of supervision of higher education and some teaching duties.

Psellus was an erudite, wide-ranging, and immensely productive writer. Many works attributed to him are still of doubtful authenticity. His authentic works include:

1. Historiography. A brief and jejune chronicle of traditional form, probably an early work. His Chronographia, a lively and colourful account of the years 976–1077, in which the causes of events are sought in the interplay of character, ambitions, emotions, and intrigues. The latter part of the Chronographia owes much to the author's personal observation, and he somewhat exaggerates his own part in the events which he recounts. Though not always entirely reliable, the work represents a new departure in medieval Greek historiography.

2. Rhetoric. Numerous panegyrics, funeral orations, and other occasional pieces, together with some 500 letters, which provide a lively picture of Byzantine life as well as of the author himself.

3. Philosophy. Commentaries on works of *Plato (1) and *Aristotle, a philosophical miscellany, De omnifaria doctrina (Διδασκαλία παντοδαπή); the remarkable and original De operatione daemonum (Περὶ ἐνεργείας δαιμόνων), and numerous minor treatises.

4. Scientific and literary. Treatises on mathematics, music, astronomy, alchemy, medicine, jurisprudence, as well as studies on Athenian judicial terminology and on the topography of Athens.

5. Miscellaneous. Homeric paraphrases, rhetorical exercises, occasional verse, didactic, satirical and epigrammatic. Psellus was a man of encyclopaedic learning and great literary gifts. At a time when scholarship was at a low ebb after the advances in

the 10th cent., he had a keen though self-conscious love of classical and patristic literature, and was passionately devoted to Plato and the Neoplatonists. His own style owed much to imitation of Plato, Aelius *Aristides, and *Gregory (2) of Nazianzus. More than any other man he laid the foundations of the Byzantine literary and philosophical renascence of the 12th cent.

Migne, *PG* 122 (1864); K. N. Sathas, Μεσαιωνική βιβλιοθήκη 4–5 (1874–69); E. Kurtz and F. Drexl, *Scripta minora* 2 vols. (1936–41); F. Boissonade, *De operatione daemonum* (1838); L. G. Westerink, *Omnifaria doctrina* (1948); *Chronographia*, ed. E. Renault, 2 vols. (1920–8); ed. S. Impellizeri, 2 vols. (1984); Eng. trans. E. R. A. Sewter (1953); *Historia syntoma*, ed. W. J. Aerts (1990); *Oratoria minora*, ed. A. R. Littlewood (1985); *Philosophica minora*, 1, ed. J. M. Duffy (1992); 2, ed. D. J. O'Meara (1989); *Theologica*, 1, ed. P. Gautier (1989); *Poemata*, ed. L. G. Westerink (1992). A. R. Dyck, *The Essays on Euripides and George of Pisidia and on Heliodorus and Achilles Tatius* (1986); J. M. Hussey, *Church and Learning in the Byzantine Empire* (1937); G. Weiss, *Oströmische Beamten im Spiegel der Schriften des Michael Psellos* (1937); Ja. N. Ljubarskij, *Mikhail Psellos. Lichnost' i tvorchestvo* (1978); P. Lemerle, *Cinq études sur le XIe siècle byzantin* (1977), 193–248.   R. B.

psephisma See LAW AND PROCEDURE, ATHENIAN.

pseudepigraphic literature Antiquity has left us a number of writings which evidence, internal or external, proves not to be the work of the authors whose names are traditionally attached to them. The causes of this seems to be chiefly: (*a*) a tendency to ascribe anonymous pieces to a well-known author of like genre. Thus, the whole *Epic Cycle and other hexameter poems were at one time or another ascribed to *Homer; in Latin several compositions more or less epic in style, as the *Culex* and *Ciris*, have become attached to the name of Virgil (see APPENDIX VERGILIANA), others, in elegiacs, to those of Tibullus and Ovid. (*b*) Works by the followers of a philosopher tended to be credited to their master; for instance, several short dialogues by members of the *Academy bear the name of *Plato (1), and, e.g., the *Problēmata*, which are Peripatetic, are preserved as by *Aristotle. (*c*) Rhetorical exercises in the form of speeches, letters, etc., supposed to be by well-known persons, and now and then were taken for their real works. Thus, no. 11 of our collection of *Demosthenes (2)'s speeches is a clever imitation of him, said by some (*Didymus (1), *In Demosth.* col. 11, 10) to come from the *Philippica* of *Anaximenes (2) of Lampsacus. The Epistles of Phalaris are the most notorious work of this kind, thanks to Bentley's exposure of them. (*d*) The existence of deliberate forgeries, made to sell (see FORGERIES, LITERARY), is vouched for by *Galen (*In Hipp. de nat. hominis* 2. 57, 12 Mewaldt). (*e*) Various mechanical accidents of copying account for a few pseudepigraphies. (*f*) But the most frequent cases are of rather late date and connected with the craze for producing evidence of the doctrine one favoured being of great age. For instance, the numerous Neopythagorean treatises (H. Thesleff, *Pythagorean Texts of the Hellenistic Period*, 1965; see NEOPYTHAGOREANISM) are regularly attached to the names of prominent early Pythagoreans, including *Pythagoras (1) himself, despite the fairly constant tradition that he wrote nothing. The Sibylline oracles (see SIBYL) are an outstanding instance of this; Phocylides is the alleged author of a long set of moralizing verses pretty certainly the work of an unknown Jew and of late date (see PHOCYLIDES (2)). Christian literature has some glaring examples of this practice, notably the Clementine Recognitions and Homilies, most certainly neither by *Clement of Rome nor any contemporary, and the works attributed to *Dionysius (4) the Areopagite, really produced some four centuries after his death. Cf. also HERMES TRISMEGISTUS.

N. Brox, *Pseudépigraphie* (1977).   H. J. R.; P. J. P.

Pseudo-Callisthenes, the so-called Alexander-Romance, falsely ascribed to *Callisthenes, survives in several versions, beginning in the 3rd cent. AD. It is popular fiction, a pseudo-historical narrative interspersed with an 'epistolary novel', bogus correspondence between *Alexander (3) 'the Great' and *Darius III. Some of the material is comparatively early; the account of Alexander's death may echo propaganda of the early Successors and the will contains a Rhodian interpolation of Hellenistic origin. There is also an Egyptian strand which introduces the last Pharaoh, Nectanebos II, as a significant actor (seducer of *Olympias) and adds curious detail about *Alexandria (1), including its foundation date. But the historical nucleus is small and unusable. What matters is the fiction which had an enormous international vogue, translated into most major languages in medieval times and transmuted into innumerable variations in Greek, Syriac and Arabic tradition.

TEXT W. Kroll, *Historia Alexandri Magni* (1926); trans. R. Stoneman, *The Greek Alexander-Romance* (1991). See also R. Merkelbach, *Die Quellen des gr. Alexanderromans*² (1977); W. Heckel, *The Last Days and Testament of Alexander the Great* (1988).   A. B. B.

psychē is the Greek term for '*soul', but modern concepts like psychology or psychiatry wrongly suggest that the Greeks viewed the soul in the modern way. In our oldest source, Homer, we still find a widespread soul system, in which *psychē* was the 'free-soul', which represented the individual personality only when the body was inactive: during swoons or at the moment of death. On the other hand, psychological functions were occupied by 'body-souls', such as *thymos* and *menos*. It is also the *psychē* that leaves for the Underworld and the dead are indeed frequently, but not exclusively, called *psychai*; on black-figure vases of *c*.500 BC we can see a homunculus, sometimes armed, hovering above the dead warrior. Towards the end of the Archaic age two important developments took place. First, *Pythagoras (1) and other philosophers introduced the notion of reincarnation. The development is still unexplained, but it certainly meant an upgrading of the soul, which we subsequently find in *Pindar called 'immortal'. However, it would only be in post-Classical times that this notion became popular. Second, *psychē* started to incorporate the *thymos* and thus became the centre of consciousness. This development culminated in the Socratic notion that man had to take care of his *psychē* (see SOCRATES). In Greek philosophy, except *Aristotle, care for and cure of the soul now became an important topic of reflection. From the Hellenistic period onwards *Eros is often pictured with a girl and it is attractive to see here a model for *Apuleius' fairy-tale-like story *Amor and Psyche*. Unfortunately, Psyche's ancestry still remains very much obscure.

N. Icard–Gianolio, *LIMC* under the name; F. Solmsen, *Kl. Schr.* 3 (1982), 464–94 (Plato); J. Bremmer, *The Early Greek Concept of the Soul* (1983); M. Maaskant–Kleibrink, in H. Hofmann (ed), *Groningen Colloquia on the Novel 3* (1990), 13–33 (Psyche in art); M. Halm–Tisserant, *Ktema* 1988 (1992), 233–44 (soul as homunculus).   J. N. B.

psychoanalysis See LITERARY THEORY AND CLASSICAL STUDIES.

Ptah, the mummiform Egyptian god primarily of *Memphis whom, as a creator-god, patron of craftsmen, the Greeks recognized as *Hephaestus. The great temple at Memphis also contained the enclosure of the *Apis bull and other sacred animals, considered as different embodiments of Ptah. It was here that the Ptolemies were crowned, at least from the reign of *Ptolemy (1) V Epiphanes.   D. J. T.

Ptoion, sanctuary of *Apollo located in the territory of *Acraephnium in *Boeotia. The ruins of the oracle on Mt. Ptoon consist of the remains of a temple, a grotto and spring, and various sacred buildings. Excavations have found rich dedications of Archaic date, especially statuary. The cult dates at least from the 8th cent. BC, and was marked by a male prophet who gave responses in a state of *ecstasy. Apollo was associated with a female goddess or heroine. *Pindar (fr. 51b; *Paian* 7. f.) and *Herodotus (1) (8. 135) constitute the earliest literary evidence for the origin of the cult. The sanctuary, but not the oracle, flourished until the third century AD.

P. Guillon, *Les Trépieds du Ptoion* (1943); J. Ducat, *Les Kouroi de Ptoion* (1971); A. Schachter, *Cults of Boiotia*, 1 (1981), and in R. Osborne and S. Hornblower (eds.), *Ritual, Finance, Politics* (1994), 291 ff.   J. Bu.

Ptolemaeus (1) of Ascalon, of uncertain date, is said by Steph. Byz. to have been a pupil of *Aristarchus (2), and in the *Suda* to have been father (or teacher) of Archibius (a grammarian at Rome under Trajan). Ptolemaeus joined the Pergamenes (see CRATES (3)) and disputed the Aristarchan texts of Homer. He also wrote Περὶ διαφορᾶς λέξεων, Περὶ ὀρθογραφίας, and Περὶ μέτρων ('on distinctions between words'; 'on orthography'; 'on metre'). (Probably not the same as no. 7 below, see bibliography there cited.)

M. Baoege, *De Pt. Ascalonita* (1882).   P. B. R. F.; N. G. W.; S. H.

Ptolemaeus (2) **Chennos** ('quail') of *Alexandria (1) (fl. *c.* AD 100) wrote the *Sphinx*, a mythologico-grammatical work, perhaps in dramatic form (ἱστορικὸν δρᾶμα, *Suda*), though this is disputed; *Authomeros*, in twenty-four rhapsodies, correcting Homer's errors; Παράδοξος (or Καινὴ) ἱστορία ('Marvellous (or 'New') History') of which *Photius gives an extract. There are no adequate grounds for identifying this Ptolemaeus with the philosopher and biographer of *Aristotle (A. Dihle, *Hermes* 1957, 314 ff.).   J. D. D.; K. J. D.

Ptolemaeus (3) **Epithetes,** grammarian so nicknamed because of his attacks on *Aristarchus (2). He was a pupil of *Hellanicus (2), but his date cannot be precisely established. He wrote among other things Περὶ τῶν παρ' Ὁμήρῳ πληγῶν ('on the thefts in Homer') and an exposition of *Zenodotus' textual choices in *Homer.

EDITION F. Montanari (1988).   N. G. W.

Ptolemaeus (4) of Mende, a priest, wrote on the Egyptian kings in three books. He wrote before Apion (first half of the 1st cent. BC), who refers to him. He attributes the Hebrew Exodus under Moses to the time of king Amosis (founder of the 18th dynasty).

FGrH 611; M. Stern, *Greek and Latin Authors on Jews and Judaism* (1976), 1. 379 f.   K. S. S.

Ptolemaeus (5) of Naucratis (2nd cent. AD), a sophist (see SECOND SOPHISTIC) taught by Herodes Atticus (see CLAUDIUS ATTICUS HERODES (2), TI.), but more influenced by the style of *Polemon (4).

Philostr. *VS* 2. 15 (595–6).   M. B. T.

Ptolemaeus (6) **Pindarion** grammarian (2nd cent. BC), pupil of *Aristarchus (2). He wrote a number of worker on *Homer, and sometimes disagreed with his master on matter of textual criticism. He also concerned himself with the concepts of συνήθεια (ordinary language) and ἀναλογία (see ANALOGY AND ANOMALY).   N. G. W.

Ptolemaeus (7) of Ascalon (early 1st cent. AD), grammarian and author of a work on *Herod (1), in which he referred to the king's Idumaean origins.

FGrH 199 and comm.; Schürer, *History*, 1. 27–8.   K. S. S.

Ptolemaïs of *Cyrene (perhaps early 1st cent. AD), antiquity's only known woman musicologist (see MUSIC), wrote an 'introductory treatise', *Pythagorean Elements of Music*, in question-and-answer form (see PYTHAGORAS (1)). Quotations in *Porphyry, *On Ptolemy's Harmonics* (see PTOLEMY (4)) concern distinctions between schools of harmonic theory (especially Pythagorean and Aristoxenian; see ARISTOXENUS), focusing on controversies about the roles of reason and perception. Her brief but intelligent reflections probably reached Ptolemy through their elaborations by *Didymus (1). She is otherwise unknown.   A. D. B.

Ptolemais (1) (Acco, Ake). A *Phoenician city, which issued coins of *Alexander (3) the Great, and received its name from *Ptolemy (1) II (P. Cairo Zen. 25004, ?259 BC). It was consistently hostile to the *Hasmoneans. *Claudius established a colony and settled veterans (see COLONIZATION, ROMAN). In AD 66, many of the local Jews were massacred by the Greeks, and *Cestius Gallus mustered his troops there; in 67 *Vespasian advanced from there against Galilee.

Schürer, *History* 2. 121–5.   T. R.

Ptolemais (2) **Hermiou** (El-Menshā), a Greek city on the W. bank of the Nile in Upper Egypt, founded by *Ptolemy (1) I, having *boulē and *ekklēsia. It served as *metropolis (c) of the Thinite nome. *Strabo classed it with *Memphis in importance. *PHib*. 28 may be part of its constitution, Mitteis, *Chr.* 369 part of the municipal law-code. It had a theatre, cults of *Zeus, *Dionysus, *Asclepius, and public games (see AGŌNES). It remained important under Rome. Few buildings survive.

Strabo 17. 1. 42. Inscriptions: OGI 47–52, 103, 703, 728, 743; *IGRom* 1153–6; *SB* 7286, 9820. Papyri: Calderini, *Dizionario dei nomi geografici dell'Egitto* 4. 210. G. Plaumann, *Ptolemais in Oberägypten* (1910). J. Scherer, *BIFAO* 1942. J. de Morgan, *MIFAO* 1889.   W. E. H. C.

Ptolemais (3) **Theron** ('of the hunts') on the W. coast of the *Red Sea probably at Aqiq (18° 12′ N; 38° 10′ E), founded by *Ptolemy (1) II in 270–264 BC for *elephant hunts; it was a staging-post to *Meroë.

E. Naville, 'Le stèle de Pithom', *ZÄS* 40 (1902), 66–75; Agatharchides 84, 105 (GGM 1. 174, 192) = 86, 107, UP3 Burstein; Strabo 2. 1. 36, 16. 4. 7; Pliny, *HN* 2. 183, 6. 171. L. Casson (ed.), *Periplus Maris Erythraei* 3, 14. J. W. Crowfoot, *GJ* 37 (1911), 523–50.   W. E. H. C.

Ptolemais / Barca See PENTAPOLIS.

Ptolemy (Ptolemaeus) (1). The name of all the Macedonian kings of Egypt.

Ptolemy I Soter ('Saviour') (367/6–282 BC), son of Lagus and Arsinoë, served *Alexander (3) the Great of Macedon as an experienced general and childhood friend. At Susa in 324 he married Artacama (also called Apame), daughter of *Artabazus, whom he later divorced. He later married the Macedonian Eurydice (6 children) and subsequently *Berenice (1) I, mother of the dynastic line. On Alexander's death (323) he hijacked the conqueror's corpse and, taking it to Memphis in Egypt, established himself as satrap in place of *Cleomenes (3). In the following year he took Cyrene and in 321 repulsed the invasion of *Perdiccas (3). In the complex struggles of Alexander's successors he was not at first particularly successful. In 295 however he recovered Cyprus, lost in 306 to *Demetrius (4) Poliorcetes, and from 291 he increasingly controlled the Aegean League of Islanders (see CYCLADES). Ptolemy took the title of King (*basileus*) in 305; this served as the first year of his reign. Responsible for initiating a Greek-speaking administration in Egypt, he consulted Egyptians (*Manetho and others), exploiting their local expertise. The cult of *Sarapis, in origin the Egyptian Osiris-Apis, was probably developed under Soter as a unifying force. There are few papyri from his reign, but hieroglyphic inscriptions from the Delta (especially the 'Satrap Stele') present him as a traditional pharaoh. In Upper Egypt he founded *Ptolemais (2) Hermiou (modern El-Mansha) as a second Greek administrative centre. Moving the capital from *Memphis to *Alexandria (1), he brought Egypt into the mainstream of the Hellenistic world.   D. J. T.

Ptolemy I as historian Ptolemy I wrote a history of the reign of *Alexander (3) 'the Great'. Much about it is obscure, notably its title, dimensions and even its date of composition. Apart from a single citation in *Strabo our knowledge of it is wholly due to *Arrian who selected it, along with *Aristobulus (1), as his principal source. The work was evidently comprehensive, covering the period from at least 335 BC to the death of Alexander, and it provided a wealth of 'factual' detail, including most of our information about the terminology and organization of the Macedonian army. The popular theory that Ptolemy based his work upon a court journal rests ultimately on his use of the *Ephemerides for Alexander's last illness. Rather the narrative, as it is reconstructed from Arrian, suggests that Ptolemy had propagandist aims (not surprisingly, given his skill at publicity). He emphasized his personal contribution to the campaign and tended to suppress or denigrate the achievements of his rivals, both important in an age when service under Alexander was a considerable political asset. There is also a tendency to eulogize Alexander (whose body he kept interred in state) and gloss over darker episodes like the 'conspiracy' of *Philotas. The king accordingly appears as a paradigm of generalship, his conquests achieved at minimum cost and maximum profit, and Ptolemy continuously figures in the action. His account is contemporary and valuable; but it is not holy writ and needs to be controlled by other evidence.

FGrH 138; L. Pearson, *Lost Histories of Alexander* (1960); P. Pédech, *Historiens compagnons d'Alexandre* (1984); Heckel, *Marshals*, 222 ff.
                                                                    A. B. B.

Ptolemy II Philadelphus ('Sister-loving') (308–246 BC), son of Ptolemy I and *Berenice (1) I, born on *Cos, first married *Lysimachus' daughter *Arsinoë I, mother to Ptolemy III, Lysimachus, and Berenice, and then his sister *Arsinoë II, who brought him her Aegean possessions. He became joint ruler with his father in 285, succeeding to the throne in 282. Externally, he expanded the Ptolemaic overseas empire in *Asia Minor and *Syria, fighting two Syrian Wars, against the *Seleucid king *Antiochus (1) I (274–271) and, with less success, against *Antiochus (2) II in 260–253; in 252 his daughter *Berenice (2) II was married to Antiochus II. The Chremonidean War (267–261; see CHREMONIDES) against Macedon in Greece and the western Aegean involved some Ptolemaic losses. *Cyrene was re-established under Ptolemaic rule (250); Red Sea trading-posts were founded. Internally, an increasing number of Greek and demotic papyri (see PAPYROLOGY, GREEK) illuminate a developing bureaucracy and control of the population through a tax-system based on a census and land-survey. Land, especially in the *Fayūm, was reclaimed and settled with military cleruchs and in gift-estates (see APOLLONIUS (3); MOERIS). It was a period of experiment and

expansion. Royal patronage benefited *Alexandria (1); the Pharos, *Museum, Library (see LIBRARIES), and other buildings graced the city, which developed as a centre of artistic and cultural life. Honouring his parents with a festival, the Ptolemaieia (279/8), Philadelphos further instituted a Greek royal cult for himself and Arsinoë II (see RULER-CULT, I, *Greek*).   D. J. T.

Ptolemy III Euergetes ('Benefactor') (b. 284 BC), son of Ptolemy II and *Arsinoë I, ruled from early 246 until his death in February 221. His wife was *Berenice (3) II of Cyrene. They had at least six children, including Ptolemy IV and the young Berenice whose death resulted in the priestly Canopus Decree (238) which details her honours as an Egyptian goddess and prescribes a calendar (not adopted) of 365 days with an extra day every four years. In the Third Syrian War against *Seleucus (2) II (246–241) Euergetes acquired important towns in Syria and Asia Minor, but this represented the limit of Ptolemaic expansion. The Alexandrian Serapeum was founded in this reign.   D. J. T.

Ptolemy IV Philopator ('Father-loving') (c.244–205 BC), son of Ptolemy III and *Berenice (3) II, succeeded in 221 and married his sister *Arsinoë III in 217. His success in the Fourth Syrian War (219–217), started when *Antiochus (3) III invaded Palestine, brought internal problems. In the battle of *Raphia (217), which restored Coele Syria to Egypt, the substantial use of native Egyptian troops was seen to mark a turning point in the internal cohesion of Egypt. From 206 *Thebes (2) was lost to central control for twenty years. In *Alexandria (1) Philopator's construction of the Sema, a tomb centre for Alexander and the Ptolemies, further strengthened the dynastic cult. Philopator was murdered in a palace coup by Sosibius and Agothocles and news of his death was kept secret for several months.   D. J. T.

Ptolemy V Epiphanes ('Made manifest') (210–180 BC), son of Ptolemy IV and *Arsinoe III, succeeded as a child following his father's murder. He married a *Seleucid, *Cleopatra I, in 193. His official succession was followed by revolts within Egypt and by the Seleucid and Macedonian kings' joint enterprise to seize Egypt's external possessions. Most Ptolemaic possessions in the Aegean and Asia Minor were lost and, following the battle of Panium in 200, also Palestine. Following the Macedonian ceremony of coming-of-age (*anakleteria*) in *Alexandria (1), in 197 Epiphanes was crowned at *Memphis in a traditional Egyptian ceremony. The priestly Rosetta Decree which followed (196; see OGI 90), marked the start of a more explicit policy in which Ptolemy and priests cooperated in both their interests. *Thebes (2) was recovered in 186.   D. J. T.

Ptolemy VI Philometor ('Mother-loving'), son of Ptolemy V and *Cleopatra I, started his reign still a child in joint rule with his mother (180 BC); on her death in 176 he married his sister *Cleopatra II. His reign was marked by struggles both at home (with his brother, Ptolemy VIII Euergetes II) and abroad. *Antiochus (4) IV invaded Egypt twice (169–168, initially with the support of Philometor), and in July 168, formally crowned as king, he only left when Rome intervened. The temporary reconciliation of the brothers, with a joint reign of Ptolemies VI and VIII and Cleopatra II from 169–164, could not discount this new influence on Egyptian affairs. Ejected in 164, Philometor visited Rome to plead for his throne. In 163 the brothers finally agreed to disagree, with Philometor restored to *Alexandria (1) and his brother ruling *Cyrene. Philometor kept his throne but died fighting *Alexander (10) Balas in *Syria in 145. Whatever his personal qualities, he had been unable to prevent an unsettled reign full of turmoil; besides dynastic troubles there were rebellion and revolts in Alexandria and throughout the country.

D. J. T.

Ptolemy VII Neos Philopator ('Young father-loving'), son of Ptolemy VI and *Cleopatra II, ruled briefly together with his father in 145 and following Philometor's death; he was speedily liquidated by his uncle Ptolemy VIII.

D. J. T.

Ptolemy VIII Euergetes II ('Benefactor') (*c*.182/1–116 BC), also called Physcon ('Potbelly') was younger brother of Ptolemy VI. He ruled jointly with Ptolemy VI and *Cleopatra II in 170–164, alone in 164–163, and in Cyrene from 163 until 145 when he succeeded his brother in Egypt. He married his brother's widow (his sister) Cleopatra II and then took her daughter (his niece) *Cleopatra III as a second wife. The ensuing civil war (132–130) brought devastation to the countryside as well as *Alexandria (1). A joint reign of Euergetes and the two Cleopatras followed from 124 until his death. Continually hostile to the Alexandrians (who had favoured Philometor in 163), he was responsible for severe destruction, persecutions and expulsions (including many of the intelligentsia). The long amnesty decree of 118 (*PTeb.* 5) represents a traditional response to trouble.

D. J. T.

Ptolemy IX Soter II ('Saviour') (142–80 BC), also known as Lathyrus ('Chickpea'), was the elder son of Ptolemy VIII and *Cleopatra III. He married two of his sisters, first Cleopatra IV, probably the mother of Berenice IV (Cleopatra Berenice), and then Cleopatra V Selene, who bore him two sons. (The mother of Ptolemy XII was probably a concubine.) On the death of his father (116), although not her favourite, his dominant mother installed him joint-ruler with her and, briefly, with *Cleopatra II, who died soon after. In 107, ejected by his mother in favour of his brother, he fled to *Cyprus and became embroiled in Palestinian affairs. Victorious against his mother and the Jews, he re-established himself in Egypt in 88 BC. With *Thebes (2) in revolt, Soter elicited aid from *Memphis, and in 86 he celebrated an Egyptian 30-year jubilee (a Sed Festival) in that city. He remained on the throne until his death.

D. J. T.

Ptolemy X Alexander I (*c*.140–88 BC), younger brother of Ptolemy IX, from 116 served as governor of *Cyprus, until recalled by his mother to Egypt in 107. A short joint reign ended in October 101 with the death of his mother (murdered by Alexander according to the more sensational accounts). Ptolemy X then married his niece, Cleopatra Berenice, daughter of his exiled brother Ptolemy IX. Their joint rule was ended when he in turn was expelled in 88. Attempts to retake Egypt from Syria and Asia Minor were unsuccessful; he died soon after at sea. Continual dynastic conflict is reflected in the bull-cults of Egypt; strongly supported by Soter II, during the rule of Alexander these suffered from neglect.

D. J. T.

Ptolemy XI Alexander II (*c*.100/99–80 BC), the younger son of Ptolemy X by an unnamed wife, left the kingdom of Egypt (including *Cyprus) to Rome. Briefly succeeding his uncle Ptolemy IX in 80, he was established by L. *Cornelius Sulla as joint ruler with and husband of his stepmother Cleopatra Berenice. He murdered her within three weeks and was in turn murdered by the Alexandrians.

D. J. T.

Ptolemy XII Neos Dionysus (*Auletes*, 'Fluteplayer'), son, by a mistress, of Ptolemy IX, succeeded Alexander II in 80 and married his sister Cleopatra Tryphaena ('the opulent one'). His cultivation of friendly relations with Rome led to his expulsion by the Alexandrians in 58. After visiting Rome, where his restoration became a mainstream political issue, and through heavy expenditure, in 55 he was restored by A. *Gabinius (2), Roman governor of Syria. Auletes was the first Ptolemy to adopt Theos ('god') in his Greek titulature. His use of Egypt's wealth in pursuit of his throne brought hardship on the country.

D. J. T.

Ptolemy XIII (63–47 BC), younger brother of *Cleopatra VII, who married and briefly ruled with him from 51. He sided with the nationalists against Cleopatra VII and *Caesar in the Alexandrian war and, on defeat, was drowned in the Nile.

D. J. T.

Ptolemy XIV (*c*.59–44 BC), the younger of Cleopatra VII's two young brothers, was appointed governor of Cyprus in 48. In 47 Caesar made him his sister's husband and consort. He was murdered on her orders.

D. J. T.

Ptolemy (RE Ptolemaios 37) *XV Caesar*, nicknamed 'Caesarion' (Little Caesar), eldest son of *Cleopatra VII, who claimed *Caesar as his father and gave him the royal names of God Philopator and Philometor ('loving his father and his mother'). Born 47 BC, he later appears as co-ruler; from 36 his years may be separately numbered. In the 'Donations of Alexandria' (34: see ANTONIUS (2), M.) he was named 'king of kings', with Cleopatra 'queen of kings'. Antonius asserted Caesar's paternity to the senate, claiming Caesar had acknowledged it, and setting up Caesar's natural son as a rival to his adopted son Octavian for the loyalty of Caesarians. It was denied by C. *Oppius (2) and by later official tradition. The facts are beyond recovery. In 30 he officially came of age and was told to escape to India via Ethiopia. But he was overtaken or betrayed by his tutor to Octavian (see AUGUSTUS), who had him executed.

H. Heinen, *Hist.* 1969, 181 ff. (chiefly on paternity); A. E. Samuel, *Ptolemaic Chronology* (1962), 159 (chronology). T. J. C.; E. B.

U. Wilcken, *RE*, 'Arsinoe', 'Berenike'; F. Stählin, *RE*, 'Kleopatra'; H. Volkmann, *RE*, 'Ptolemaios'; E. R. Bevan, *A History of Egypt under the Ptolemaic Dynasty* (1927, repr. 1968); P. M. Fraser, *Ptolemaic Alexandria* (1972). For chronology, see T. C. Skeat, *The Reigns of the Ptolemies* (1954); A. E. Samuel, *Ptolemaic Chronology* (1962); P. W. Pestman, *Chronologie égyptienne d'après les textes démotiques* (1967); W. Clarysse and G. van de Veken, *The Eponymous Priests of Ptolemaic Egypt* (1983); G. Hölbl, *Geschichte des Ptolemäerreiches* (1994). D. J. T.

Ptolemy (2) (RE 62), king of *Mauretania AD 23–40, son of *Juba II and Cleopatra Selene and grandson of Antony (M. *Antonius (2)). He shared some responsibility for government in his father's later years. For his help in the war against *Tacfarinas he was recognized as 'king, ally, and friend of the Roman people'; the sceptre and robe that the senate sent him were displayed on his coinage. In 39–40 his cousin *Gaius (1) (Caligula) summoned and executed him, perhaps because he wore a spectacular purple cloak in public (*Suetonius), perhaps for his wealth (*Cassius Dio). Other suggested reasons include friction over primacy within the *Isis cult, complicity with Cn. *Cornelius Lentulus Gaetulicus, and (perhaps most plausibly) a desire of Gaius to bring Mauretania under closer imperial control.

D. Fishwick, *Hist.* 1971, 467–73; J.-C. Faur, *Klio* 1973, 249–71.

C. B. R. P.

Ptolemy (3) of Cyrene revived the sceptical school of philosophy (see SCEPTICS) about 100 BC (Diog. Laert. 9. 115).

See Zeller, *Phil. d. Griechen* 3. 2⁴. 2. S. H.

Ptolemy (4) (RE 66) (Claudius Ptolemaeus) wrote at *Alexandria (1), between AD 146 and *c*.170, definitive works in many of the mathematical sciences (see MATHEMATICS), including *astronomy and *geography. Ptolemy's earliest work, the *Canobic Inscription*,

Ptolemy

is a (manuscript) list of astronomical constants dedicated by him in 146/7. Most of these are identical with those of the *Almagest*, but a few were corrected in the latter, which must have been published *c*.150. This, entitled μαθηματικὴ σύνταξις ('mathematical systematic treatise': the name 'Almagest' derives from the Arabic form of ἡ μεγίστη sc. σύνταξις), is a complete textbook of astronomy in thirteen books. Starting from first principles and using carefully selected observations, Ptolemy develops the theories and tables necessary for describing and computing the positions of sun, moon, the five planets and the fixed stars. The mathematical basis is the traditional epicyclic/eccentric model. In logical order, Ptolemy treats: the features of the geocentric universe and trigonometric theory and practice (book 1); spherical astronomy as related to the observer's location on earth (2); solar theory (3); lunar theory, including parallax (4 and 5); eclipses (6); the fixed stars, including a catalogue of all important stars visible from *Alexandria (1) (7 and 8); the theory of the planets in longitude (9–11); planetary stations and retrogradations (12) and planetary latitudes (13). Commentaries by *Pappus and *Theon (4) are partly preserved. The *Almagest* is a masterpiece of clear and orderly exposition, which became canonical, dominating astronomical theory for 1,300 years, in Byzantium, the Islamic world, and later medieval Europe. Its dominance caused the disappearance of all earlier works on similar topics, notably those of *Hipparchus (3) (to which Ptolemy often refers). Hence Ptolemy has been erroneously considered a mere compiler of the work of his predecessors. He should rather be regarded as a reformer, who established Greek astronomy on a valid (i.e. geometrically rigorous) basis, replacing in one sweep the confusion of models and methods which characterized practical astronomy after Hipparchus. He was an innovator in other ways, notably in introducing the 'equant' for the planets to produce remarkable agreement of theory with observation.

2. Other astronomical works are (*a*) *Planetary Hypotheses* (ὑποθέσεις τῶν πλανωμένων), in two books (only the first part of book 1 extant in Greek, the whole in Arabic), a résumé of the results of the *Almagest* and a description of the 'physical' models for use in constructing a planetarium. At the end of book 1 he proposes the system of 'nested spheres', in which each body's 'sphere' is contiguous to the next: he is thus able to compute the absolute distances of all heavenly bodies out to the fixed stars (in the *Almagest* this is done only for sun and moon). This feature was generally accepted throughout the Middle Ages, and determined the usual view of the (small) size of the universe to Dante and beyond. (*b*) *Planisphaerium* (extant in Arabic and medieval Latin translations), describing the stereographic projection of the celestial sphere on to the plane of the equator (the theoretical basis of the astrolabe). (*c*) *Analemma* (extant only in Latin translation from the Greek, except for some palimpsest fragments), an application of nomographic techniques to problems of spherical geometry encountered in the theory of sundials (see CLOCKS). (*d*) πρόχειροι κανόνες (*Handy Tables*), a revised and enlarged version of the *Almagest* tables, extant in the edition by Theon of Alexandria; Ptolemy's own rules for their use survive. (*e*) φάσεις ἀπλανῶν ἀστέρων, on the heliacal risings and settings of bright stars, and weather predictions therefrom. This was part of traditional Greek astronomy, but Ptolemy introduced rigorous trigonometrical methods. Only the second of two books survives.

3. The *Geography* (γεωγραφικὴ ὑφήγησις), in eight books, is an attempt to map the known world (see MAPS). The bulk (books 2–7) consists of lists of places with longitude and latitude, with brief descriptions of important topographical features. Although, as Ptolemy tells us, it was based in part on the work of Marinus of Tyre (otherwise unknown), it seems probable that Ptolemy was the first to employ systematically latitude and longitude as terrestrial co-ordinates. Book 1 includes instructions for drawing a world map, with two different projections (Ptolemy's chief contribution to scientific map-making). Book 8 describes the breakdown of the world map into 26 individual maps of smaller areas. The maps accompanying the existing mss. are descended from a Byzantine archetype; whether Ptolemy himself 'published' maps to accompany the text is disputed. The work is certainly intended to enable the reader to draw his own maps. Given the nature of its sources (mainly travellers' *itineraries), the factual content of the *Geography* is inevitably inaccurate. The main systematic error, the excessive elongation of the *Mediterranean in the east–west direction, was due to one of the few astronomical data utilized, the lunar eclipse of 20 September 331 BC observed simultaneously at *Carthage and Arbela (see GAUGAMELA): the faulty report from Arbela led Ptolemy to assume a time difference of three (instead of two) hours between the two places, leading to a 50 per cent error in longitude. Although the general outlines of areas within the Roman empire and immediately adjacent are moderately accurate, there are numerous individual distortions, and beyond those areas the map becomes almost unrecognizable. A notorious error is a southern land-mass connecting Africa with China (making the Indian Ocean into a lake). Nevertheless, the *Geography* was a remarkable achievement for its time, and became the standard work on the subject (revised innumerable times) until the 16th cent. See GEOGRAPHY.

4. Other surviving works. (*a*) ἀποτελεσματικά (*Astrological Influences*) or τετράβιβλος (from its four books) was the astrological complement to the *Almagest*, and although not as dominant, was influential as an attempt to provide a 'scientific' basis for astrological practice (see ASTROLOGY). καρπός (*Fruit*, Latin *Centiloquium*), a collection of 100 astrological aphorisms, is spurious. (*b*) *Optics*, in five books, is extant only in Latin translation from the Arabic, from which book 1 and the end of book 5 are missing. Book 1 dealt with the theory of vision (using the doctrine of 'visual rays'); book 2 deals with the role of light and colour in vision, books 3 and 4 with the theory of reflection in plane and spherical mirrors, book 5 with refraction. This contains some remarkable experiments, including some to determine the angles of refraction between various media (see CATOPTRICS; PHYSICS). In comparison with the earlier optical work of *Euclid, Ptolemy's treatise is greatly advanced in mathematical refinement and the representation of physical and physiological reality, but it is difficult to estimate its originality, because of the loss of such works as the *Catoptrics* of *Archimedes. It had considerable indirect influence on medieval and later optics through the work of ibn al-Haytham (Alhazen), which incorporated and greatly improved on it. See OPTICS. (*c*) A slight philosophical work, περὶ κριτηρίου καὶ ἡγεμονικοῦ (*On the Faculties of Judgement and Control*) is attributed to Ptolemy. (*d*) *Harmonics* (see below).

5. Lost works. Excerpts from a work on Euclid's 'parallel postulate' are given by *Proclus, *Comm. in Eucl.* *Simplicius (*in Ar. de caelo* 9) mentions a work περὶ διαστάσεως (*On Dimension*), in which Ptolemy 'proved' that there are only three dimensions. *Suda* (see below the title) says that he wrote μηχανικά in three books; this is probably the same as the περὶ ῥοπῶν mentioned by Simplicius (*in Ar. de caelo* 710). Simplicius also mentions a work περὶ τῶν στοιχείων (*On the Elements*) (*in Ar. de caelo* 20).

LIFE F. Boll, *Jarhb. f. Cl. Phil. Suppl.* 1894, 51 ff.

ALMAGEST ed. J. L. Heiberg, 2 vols. (Teubner, 1898, 1903); trans. G. J. Toomer, *Ptolemy's Almagest* (1984); Comm. *HAMA* 1. 21–261. On the star catalogue see G. Grasshoff, *The History of Ptolemy's Star Catalogue* (1990).

OTHER ASTRONOMICAL WORKS *Canobic Inscription*, ed. Heiberg in Ptolemy's *Opera Astronomica Minora* (Teubner, 1907). N. T. Hamilton, N. M. Swerdlow, and G. J. Toomer, in *From Ancient Omens to Statistical Mechanics* (1987), 55 ff. *Planetary Hypotheses*: text of surviving Greek, with Ger. trans. of the Arabic, in *Opera Minora*, which however omits the last part of book 1 (on the 'nested spheres'). An Eng. trans. of this (with Arabic of the whole) is supplied by B. R. Goldstein, *Trans. Am. Phil. Soc.* NS 57.4 (1967), 3–55; *HAMA* 2. 900 ff. *Planisphaerium*: the medieval Latin trans. in *Opera Minora*; the Arabic, with Eng. trans. in C. Anagnostakis, *The Arabic Version of Ptolemy's Planisphaerium*, Ph.D. Diss. Yale (1984), *HAMA* 2. 857 ff. *Analemma*: ed. in *Opera Minora*, trans. and re-ed. D. Edwards, *Ptolemy's Περὶ ἀναλήμματος*, Ph.D. Diss. Brown University (1984); *HAMA* 2. 839 ff. *Handy Tables* ed. Halma, *Tables manuelles astronomiques de Ptolémée et de Théon*, 3 vols. (1822–25); *HAMA* 2. 969 ff. *φάσεις*: ed. in *Opera Minora*; *HAMA* 2. 926 ff.

GEOGRAPHY The edns. by C. Nobbe (1843–5), the only complete modern one, and that of bks. 1–5 by C. Müller (Paris, 1883, 1901), with Latin trans., are unreliable. The trans. by E. L. Stevenson, *Claudius Ptolemy, the Geography* (1932, repr. 1991) is very faulty. For bk. 1 there is an excellent Ger. trans. and comm. by H. v. Mžik, *Des Klaudios Ptolemaios Einführung in die darstellende Erdkunde* (1938). See also *HAMA* 2. 934 ff. For reproductions of the maps see J. Fischer, *Claudii Ptolemaei Geographiae Codex Urbinas Graecus 82* (1932) and the reconstructions by R. Kiepert, *Formae Orbis Antiquae*, nos. 35 and 36 (1911).

OTHER WORKS Astrological works and περὶ κριτηρίου ed. Boll, Boer, and Lammert in Ptolemy's *Opera* (Teubner) 3. 1 and 2. For the *Tetrabiblos* see also the Loeb edn. by F. E. Robbins. Bouché-Leclercq, *L'Astrologie grecque* (1899 repr. 1963). *Optics*: ed. A. Lejeune, *L'Optique de Claude Ptolémée*[2] (1989), with Fr. trans. See also his *Euclide et Ptolémée* (Louvain, 1948). Fragments and testimonia to the lost works in *Opera Minora*, 263 ff. G. J. T.

Ptolemy's Harmonics Ptolemy's *Harmonics* is outstanding in its field, and significant in the history of scientific thought for its sophisticated blend of rationalist and empiricist methodology. While rejecting Aristoxenian empiricism (see ARISTOXENUS) outright, insisting with the Pythagoreans that musical structures must be analysed through the mathematics of ratio and shown to conform to 'rational' principles, Ptolemy criticizes the Pythagoreans for neglecting perceptual evidence: the credentials of rationally excogitated systems must ultimately be assessed by ear. He pursues this approach with meticulous attention to mathematical detail, to the minutiae of experimental procedures, and to the design and use of the special instruments they demand.

Book 1 establishes the ratios of concords and melodic intervals, and divisions of tetrachords in each genus. Here and in book 2 Ptolemy's criticisms of earlier theorists preserve important information, especially about *Archytas and *Didymus (3). Book 2 analyses complete two-octave systems. Perhaps mistakenly, it dismisses as musically insignificant the contemporary conception of τόνοι as 'keys', thirteen (or fifteen) transpositions of identical structures: on Ptolemy's view their role is to bring different species of the octave into the same central range, and there can be only seven. Three invaluable chapters (1. 16, 2. 1, 2. 16) analyse attunements actually used by contemporary performers. Experimental instruments are discussed as they become relevant throughout books 1–2, and in 3. 1–2. The rest of book 3 extends harmonic analysis to the structures of all perfect beings, especially the *soul and the heavens. Ideas from book 1, modified and abbreviated, survived into the Middle Ages through *Boethius'

paraphrase: in the Renaissance the work became a major focus of musicological controversy.

TEXT I. Düring, *Die Harmonielehre des Klaudios Ptolemaios* (1930); see also Düring's *Porphyrios Kommentar zur Harmonielehre des Ptolemaios* (1932); Ger. tr. in his *Ptolemaios und Porphyrios über die Musik* (1934); Eng. tr. in A. Barker, *Greek Musical Writings*, 2 (1989). A. D. B.

publicani Since the Roman republic had only a rudimentary 'civil service' (see *apparitores*) and primitive budgeting methods, the collection of public revenue, except for the *tributum*, was sold as a public contract to the highest bidder, who reimbursed himself with what profit he could, at the tax rate set by the state. In addition, as in other states, there were contracts for public works, supplies and services (*ultro tributa*). The purchasers of these contracts provided the logistic background to the Roman victories in the *Punic Wars and in the eastern wars of the 2nd cent. BC, and managed the building of the Roman *roads. Roman expansion also expanded their activities; thus the traditional contracts for the exploitation of *mines were extended to the vastly profitable Spanish mines (see e.g. Strabo 3. 2. 10. 147–8 C, from Polybius), and the profits of victory also financed a boom in public construction. Tax collection expanded correspondingly, as more harbours and toll stations came under Roman control and much conquered land became *ager publicus*. In Italy there seems to have been a basic shift in sources of revenue between 179 and 167, with indirect taxes (especially *portoria) collected by *publicani* taking the place of *tributum*. The increase in their opportunities led to some conflicts with the senate and the *censors, in which the latter always prevailed. (See e.g. M. *Porcius Cato (1).)

In *Sicily the main tax was collected according to the law of *Hiero (2) II, which protected the population against serious abuse. In Spain, a *stipendium*, originally to pay for the Roman troops, was collected by the quaestors. We do not know how the taxes were collected in the provinces acquired in 146 and originally in Asia, but in 123 C. *Sempronius Gracchus changed history by providing that the tithe of Asia was to be sold in Rome by the censors every five years. The sums involved were spectacular: the companies (*societates publicanorum*) had to become much larger and more complex in organization. Henceforth taxes far surpassed *ultro tributa* as sources of profit, especially when *Pompey extended the Asian system to the provinces he organized. The wealthiest of the *publicani* gained a dominant role in the *repetundae court and other *quaestiones and in the *ordo* of *equites. They became the most powerful pressure group in Rome, and they dominated finance in the provinces and allied states.

The companies, by special legislation, possessed privileges unknown in normal Roman company law. They consisted of *socii* (partners), who put up the capital and were governed by one or more *magistri*, one of them probably the *manceps who bought the contract. Provincial offices were run by a *pro magistro* (who might be an *eques*) and might have large staffs, including *familiae* of hundreds of slaves and freedmen. By the late republic they acted as bankers to the state (avoiding the shipment of large sums in coin) and their messengers (*tabellarii) would transport mail for officials and important private persons.

Complaints about their abuses were frequent. Proconsuls found it more profitable to co-operate with them in exploitation than to protect the provincials. The fate of P. *Rutilius Rufus and L. *Licinius Lucullus (2) shows the risks of opposing them; but these cases were exceptional and partly due to personal character. Cicero showed that tactful and honest governors could gain their co-operation in relieving provincials of unbearable burdens in return for secure profits. Extortion by senatorial commanders and their staffs seems to have far surpassed any due to the *publicani*. In the late republic there was a market for unregistered shares (*partes*) in the companies in Rome, enabling senators (e.g. *Caesar and M. *Licinius Crassus (1)), who were not allowed to be *socii*, to share in the profits of the companies and no doubt to be influential in running them. The largest companies now tended to form a cartel: thus the main company for *Bithynia consisted of all the other companies.

The Civil Wars brought the companies huge losses, as their provincial *fisci* were appropriated by opposing commanders. They never recovered their wealth and power. Caesar somewhat restricted their activities by depriving them of the Asian *decuma*. Under the empire, tribute came to be collected by quaestors and *procurators, though *publicani* might be used at the local level. Other revenues continued to be in their hands and we have plentiful evidence for their elaborate organization. Complaints against them continued, but they had little political influence. *Nero strictly regulated their activities, and from the second century AD their place was increasingly taken by individual *conductores*. See FINANCE, ROMAN.

Cicero's *Verrines* are the principal evidence for their organization in the late republic. Most of his other speeches also document their activities. C. Nicolet, in *Points de vue sur la fiscalité antique* (ed. H. van Effenterre, 1979), 89–95, gives a list of known republican *societates* with organizational details recorded. See further G. Ürögdi, *RE* Suppl. 11 cols. 1184 ff.; E. Badian, *Publicans and Sinners*² (1983) for the republic. A recently discovered document (*Das Zollgesetz der Provinz Asia*, ed. H. Engelmann and D. Knibbe, 1989) gives details of the collection of Asian *portoria*, recording changes in the late republic and early empire.
E. B.

Publilius (*RE* 11) **Philo, Quintus,** was consul in 339, 327, 320, and 315 BC, and the first plebeian praetor in 336. He reputedly served on a commission to organize debt relief in 352 and as dictator in 339 passed three laws: (1) one censor must always be plebeian; (2) the sanction accorded by patrician senators (*patrum auctoritas*) must now be given before the presentation of legislation to the centuriate assembly (thus limiting patrician obstruction); (3) decisions of the plebeian assembly (*plebiscita*; see PLEBISCITUM) were to be binding on the whole people. The last of these duplicates the measure of Q. *Hortensius in 287/6 BC and is probably fictitious. Publilius' dictatorship is also suspect but if he passed the first two measures (perhaps as consul), this marks a significant development in plebeian use of a curule magistracy for political reform.

In 339 Philo also triumphed (see TRIUMPH) for a victory over the Latins (see LATINI) and in his censorship (332; see CENSOR) enrolled new Latin citizens and created two new tribes (the Maecia and Scaptia). In 327–6 he besieged Naples (*Neapolis) and Palaeopolis and through his contacts with philo-Roman elements secured their surrender: the Greek interests attested by his *cognomen* Philo (see NAMES, PERSONAL, ROMAN) may have assisted here and he triumphed in 326 as the first historical proconsul (see PRO CONSULE). The victories in Campania and Apulia credited to him and L. *Papirius Cursor (1) by some sources in 320 constitute a suspect revenge for the *Caudine Forks but his reelection with Cursor for 315 testifies to his standing and reputation.

E. T. Salmon, *Samnium and the Samnites* (1967); M. W. Frederiksen, *Campania* (1984); K.-J. Hölkeskamp, *Die Entstehung der Nobilität* (1987); *CAH* 7². 2 (1989), index.
A. D.

Publilius (*RE* 28) **Syrus** (not Publius, Wölfflin *Philol.* 1865, 439) was brought to Rome (perhaps from *Antioch (1), *Pliny (1) *HN* 35. 199) as a slave in the 1st cent. BC. According to *Macrobius (*Saturn.* 2. 7. 6–10 he was freed for his wit and educated by his master and composed and performed his own *mimes throughout Italy. Invited by *Caesar to perform at the games of 46 BC (see LUDI) he challenged other mime-writers to improvise on a given scenario and was declared victor by Caesar over his chief rival *Laberius. Only two of his titles are recorded, *Putatores* (Nonius 2. 133)) and *Mumurco* ('The mutterer'?, *Priscian, *Inst.* K. 2. 532. 25), and no fragments that indicate the action or themes of his mimes. It became a commonplace (*Cassius Severus in L. *Annaeus Seneca (1) Rhetor, *Contr.* 7. 3. 8, L. *Annaeus Seneca (2), *Ep. Mor.* 8. 9–10) that his aphorisms expressed moral teaching better than serious dramatists, and a set of fourteen maxims is quoted by *Gellius (*NA* 17. 14: cf. Macrobius 2. 7. 11). (Trimalchio's 'quotation' from Publilius at Petronius *Sat.* 55 is spurious).

In the 1st cent. AD apophthegms uttered by various dramatic roles in the mimes were selected and alphabetically arranged as proverbial wisdom for schoolboys to copy or memorize. These formed a fixed syllabus with e.g. the distichs of M. *Porcius Cato (1), so that in the 4th cent. *Jerome learned in class a line which he quotes twice *aegre reprehendas quod sinas consuescere* (Hieron. *Ep.* 107. 8; 128. 4). It is difficult to distinguish original Publilian *sententiae* from accretions due to paraphrase of genuine verses, or insertions of Senecan and pseudo-Senecan ideas (see ANNAEUS SENECA (2), L.), or distortions of the original iambic senarii and trochaic septenarii that led copyists to mistake them for prose.

One would not expect a common ethical standard among maxims spoken by different characters in a mime. Some contradict others, as proverbs often do. Although many advocate selfish pragmatism, their prevailing terseness of expression gives them an undeniable attraction. See MIME, Roman.

TEXTS J. C. Orelli *Publii* (sic) *Syri Mimi et aliquorum sententiae* (1822; 791 iambics and 83 trochaics with Scaliger's Greek verse trans.), W. Meyer, *Publii* (sic) *Syri Sententiae* (1880) 733 lines), O. Friedrich, *Publilii Syri Mimi Sententiae* (1880), R. A. H. Bickford-Smith, *Pub. Syr. Sent.* (1895) 722 lines)
TRANSLATION Duff, *Minor Latin Poets* (734 lines). J. W. D.; E. F.

Publilius (*RE* 10) **Volero,** reputedly tribune of the plebs (see TRIBUNI PLEBIS) in 472–1 BC. He is credited with (1) an exemplary assertion of the right of appeal to the people (*provocatio), and plebiscites (see PLEBISCITUM) that (2) raised the number of *tribunes to five (so already Piso fr. 23P.) and (3) established the plebeian tribal assembly (see COMITIA). However, the first is probably anachronistic, there are conflicting accounts of the increases in the tribunate, and the third may be inspired by the alleged law on plebiscites of Q. *Publilius Philo.

Ogilvie, *Comm. Livy 1–5*, 373 ff.; A. W. Lintott, *ANRW* 1. 2. 229 ff.
A. D.

Pudicitia, the personification at Rome of women's *chastity and modesty, interestingly identified originally as specific to patrician women until the cult of Pudicitia Patricia in the *forum Boarium was challenged (296 BC) by one Virginia, a patrician lady married to a plebeian consul (Livy 10. 23. 6–10), who established a cult of Pudicitia Plebeia in part of her home. The cult was also exclusive of all but women who had married only once. *Livy laments the decline in moral standards of participants in the cult by his time.

J. Gagé, *Matronalia. Essai sur les dévotions et les organisations cultuelles des femmes dans l'ancienne Rome* (1963).
N. P.

pulvinar, a cushioned couch on which images (or representations, *struppi,* bundles of herbs, Festus, *Gloss. Lat.* 56, 408, 437) of gods were placed at a **lectisternium,* either inside (Livy 21. 62. 5) or in front of a temple or **altar (also loosely used to denote a podium or temple, Ps.-Acro, Hor. *Carm.* 1. 37. 3; Serv. *Georg.* 3. 532). Most but apparently not all gods had *pulvinaria* (Livy 24. 10. 13). Later *pulvinaria* figured among other tokens of divine honours voted by the **senate (Cic. *Phil.* 2. 110; Suet. *Iul.* 76; Tac. *Ann.* 15. 23. 3).

S. Weinstock, *Divus Julius* (1971).   J. L.

Punic Wars (264–146 BC) or wars between Rome and *Carthage ('Carthaginians' = Latin 'Poeni'). Down to 264, Carthage's relations with Rome and the Italian maritime peoples had been almost uniformly friendly (treaties with Rome, 509, 348, probably 306, and 279 (against *Pyrrhus). However, when Rome became the *hegemōn* (ruler) of *Magna Graecia, and in particular of *Rhegium (Reggio di Calabria), closely associated with *Messana (Messina) since the time of *Anaxilas (1), it was virtually inevitable that she would be drawn into the centuries-old conflict between the Greeks and Carthage for the control of Sicily.

The First Punic War (264–241) The war seems to have been unsought by either side; it arose from an 'incident' that was allowed to escalate. Rome offered her protection to the *Mamertines, in order to prevent Messana from falling into the hands of either Carthage or *Hieron II of Syracuse, who looked like becoming another *Dionysius I or *Agathocles (1). Hieron and Carthage joined forces against Messana, probably expecting that the Carthaginian navy could prevent the Romans from landing in Sicily, and that a serious collision could be avoided. The consul Ap. *Claudius Caudex, sent to relieve Messana, attempted to negotiate and then got his army across the straits on allied ships and raised the siege. His successor, M'. *Valerius Maximus Messalla, besieged Syracuse, forcing Hieron to accept generous terms, which left him, as the ally of Rome, in possession of much of his kingdom. This alliance, and the secession of some of her allies, alarmed Carthage for the security of her province, and in 262 she sent strong forces into Sicily. The Romans besieged *Acragas (Agrigento), Carthage's ally, defeated the Carthaginians in the field and sacked Acragas with a brutality that alienated many Sicilian communities. Inconclusive land-fighting and Carthaginian naval activity in 261 convinced the Romans that they must gain the command of the sea; and in the spring of 260 they built a fleet of 100 *quinqueremes (probably utilizing Italian expertise) and fitted them with the *corvus,* a rotatable boarding-bridge; and with these C. *Duilius won the battle of Mylae (Milazzo). Neither side made much progress during the next three years; but in 256 the Romans, after defeating the enemy in a huge sea-battle off Ecnomus (Licata), put the consul M. *Regulus Atilius ashore with his army at Clupea (on C. Bon peninsula). Regulus defeated the Carthaginians and occupied *Tunis, but the unreasonableness of his demands led to the breakdown of peace negotiations, and in 255 his army was almost annihilated by a mercenary force under *Xanthippus (2) and he himself was captured. The survivors were evacuated after a Roman victory at sea, but most of the fleet was destroyed by a gale, off Camarina. In 254 the Romans captured *Panormus (Palermo), but in 253 the consul C. Sempronius Blaesus lost most of his fleet in a storm, returning from a raid on Africa. During these and the following years, the Carthaginians' main effort was directed to the restoration of their dominion over the Libyans and Numidians (shaken by Regulus' invasion); but in 251 they reinforced their army in

Sicily; however, it was routed next year near Panormus by L. *Caecilius Metellus, and the Romans began the siege of *Lilybaeum (Marsala) (250–241). In 249 a new Roman fleet, raised with difficulty, was totally defeated at Drepana (Trapani), and a huge convoy bound for Lilybaeum was destroyed by a storm in the Bay of *Gela; but they captured *Eryx (Erice). Neither side had the resources to mount a major offensive in Sicily; but in 247 the Carthaginians replaced their successful admiral Carthalo by *Hamilcar (2) Barca, who, after raiding the Italian coast, established himself at *Heircte (probably M. Castellacio, near Palermo) and waged guerrilla war, diversified with raids on Italy, until 244, when he recaptured Eryx (Erice) and continued his guerrilla operations from there. In 243, the Romans, having been given a breathing-space from costly naval operations, raised another fleet (by contributions from the wealthy), with which C. *Lutatius Catulus besieged Drepana in 242, and in 241 defeated a Carthaginian relief fleet near the Aegates Insulae (Isole Egadi). Carthage, financially exhausted, instructed Hamilcar to make peace. The Carthaginians evacuated Sicily—which (except for Hiero's kingdom) became Rome's first overseas province (see *provincia*)—and the adjacent islands and undertook to pay an indemnity of 3,200 talents over a period of ten years. From 241 to 237 Carthage was involved in the Truceless (or Libyan) War, against its mutinous (because unpaid) mercenaries, supported by most of the Libyans and even by some cities, including Tunis and *Utica. The war was successfully concluded by the uneasy co-operation of Hamilcar and *Hanno (2), the recent conqueror of Libya. Rome, alarmed by Carthage's recovery, exploited a revolt of the Sardinians (see SARDINIA) to seize the island, so depriving Carthage of its principal granary and inducing a deep distrust of Rome in the minds of the rulers of Carthage. To compensate for the loss of Sardinia, to secure its supply of silver, and to provide a standing army for the defence of its empire, Carthage now decided to extend its control in Spain (where she had long had a foothold), entrusting this to Hamilcar, and after his death (229) to his son-in-law *Hasdrubal (1). Mainly by diplomacy Hasdrubal advanced Carthage's suzerainty towards the river Ebro, which, in 226, he gave the Romans a formal undertaking not to cross, so alleviating their fears on the eve of the Celtic invasion of Italy. In 221 *Hannibal succeeded to his family's satrapal position (cf. SATRAP), and made conquests in cis-Ebro Spain on the east coast and inland. Seeing *Saguntum (Sagunto), a Roman ally 'for many years' (Polyb. 3. 30. 1), as a threat to Carthage's hold on Spain, Hannibal took the city (219), with the approval of Carthage, thus, from personal as well as imperial motives, provoking the Second Punic War.

The Second Punic War (218–201). For details of Hannibal's Italian campaign, see HANNIBAL. His crushing victory at *Cannae (216) led to the defection of most of S. Italy, apart from the Latin colonies; but this meant that Hannibal, obliged to protect his new allies (*Capua was to be the leader of a new Italian Confederation), was himself put on the defensive; and with Rome's adoption of the Fabian policy 'always to fight him where he is not' (Gen. Moreau, apropos of Napoleon), the initiative passed to her: see FABIUS MAXIMUS VERRUCOSUS, Q. Hannibal remained invincible in the field, but he was unable either to widen effectively the area of revolt, despite the defections of *Syracuse (214) and *Tarentum/Taras (Taranto) (212), the destruction of a Roman army in Gaul (216), and a certain amount of unrest in Etruria; or to prevent the inexorable reconquest of rebel areas: a process which resulted in Hannibal's being confined, by the end of 211, to *Lucania and Bruttium (see BRUTTII), and in 207, to Bruttium. Roman control of the sea, a crucial factor in the war (see SEA POWER), meant that few supplies or reinforcements could reach Hannibal from Carthage. An alliance with *Philip (3) V of Macedon brought Hannibal no relief, thanks to the generalship and diplomatic skill of M. *Valerius Laevinus, who drove Philip out of the Adriatic and involved him in war with the *Aetolian Confederacy (for the First Macedonian War see ROME (HISTORY)). In 215, the Carthaginians diverted 13,500 men, with *elephants and ships, intended for Hannibal to Spain, and sent almost as many to Sardinia, in a disastrous attempt to recover the island. In 213 they sent 28,000 men, with elephants, to Sicily, but these failed to prevent M. *Claudius Marcellus (1) from taking Syracuse in 212, and Sicily was pacified by Laevinus in 210. In Spain, where Hannibal's brother *Hasdrubal (2) had been left in command, the brothers P. *Cornelius Scipio (1) and Cn. *Cornelius Scipio Calvus won a crushing victory near Ibera (on the Ebro) in 215, and recovered Saguntum; but in 211 they were both killed, with more than half their men, in the Tader (Segura) valley. However, P. *Cornelius Scipio Africanus (his *cognomen*, 'Africanus' (see NAMES, PERSONAL, ROMAN), was actually acquired later), son of P. Cornelius Scipio (1), above, was sent to Spain in 210 as proconsul. He captured *Carthago Nova (Cartagena) in 209, after a forced march from the Ebro, and won over many Spanish tribes. In 208 he defeated Hasdrubal at Baecula (Bailen), in the upper Baetis (Guadalquivir) valley. Hasdrubal escaped with a part of his forces to Italy, was joined by some Gauls, but in 207, while attempting to join forces with Hannibal, was defeated and killed by M. *Livius Salinator and C. *Claudius Nero at the *Metaurus in Umbria. This disaster put paid to any hopes that Hannibal might still have entertained of winning the war. Scipio completed the defeat of the Carthaginians in Spain (battle of Ilipa, north of Seville (206)) and won over the Numidian princes *Syphax (who later returned to his Carthaginian allegiance) and *Masinissa. In 205 Hannibal's brother *Mago (2) arrived from Spain in Liguria with about 14,000 men but effected nothing, and in 203 he was defeated in Cisalpine Gaul and died on his way back to Africa. In 204 Scipio (consul 205) crossed from Sicily to Africa and won a cavalry fight but failed to take Utica. In 203 he defeated the Carthaginians and Syphax in two major battles and occupied Tunis; he recognized Masinissa as king of the Numidians and concluded a short-lived treaty with Carthage. Hannibal—by now confined to an area about *Croton—was recalled to defend Carthage; but in the autumn of 202 he was completely defeated by Scipio near *Zama (Seba Bir), and advised the Carthaginians to sue for peace. Carthage was allowed to retain all the cities and territory in Africa that it held before the war (Polyb. 15. 18. 1), surrendered its fleet and elephants and all prisoners of war and deserters, undertook not to rearm or to make war without Rome's permission, to restore to Masinissa everything that had belonged to him or his ancestors, and to pay 10,000 talents in indemnity over a period of fifty years.

Hannibal and Carthage provoked the war in order to reverse the decision of the first war and, by permanently weakening Rome, to make Carthage's western Mediterranean empire safe. They lost because the Romans, with huge reserves of high-quality manpower, refused to admit defeat; central Italy and the colonies did not revolt; the Gauls, as a nation, did not join Hannibal (or Hasdrubal); Carthage failed to gain the command of the sea and dissipated its war-effort (as it had done in the first war), and to no effect; the Scipios confined Hasdrubal to Spain until 208, and

produced, in Scipio Africanus, a soldier whose genius was at least the equal of Hannibal's. 'The war was a turning-point in ancient history; it had profound effects on the political, economic, social and religious life of Italy, while thereafter for centuries no power could endanger Rome's existence' (H. H. Scullard). Carthage's rapid recovery after the war (together with Hannibal's dealings with *Antiochus (3) III) made the Romans apprehensive, and reawoke their hatred and desire for vengeance; and although Carthage offered, and gave, Rome assistance in its wars, they regularly countenanced Masinissa's endless encroachments upon Carthage's possessions. A more truculent nationalism emerged at Carthage, which led to the reiterated demand of M. *Porcius Cato (1), 'that Carthage should be wiped out'.

The Third Punic War (149–146). In 150, having paid off the war indemnity, Carthage supplied Rome with a *casus belli* (pretext for war) by rearming, crossing its borders and fighting Masinissa with over 31,000 men; and although this army was largely destroyed and Carthage humbled itself, the Romans declared the war on which the senate had already secretly decided, and sent a large expeditionary force to Libya, where Utica had already defected. After agreeing (*Appian) to make *deditio* (unconditional surrender) and to hand over hostages and all their war-material, the Carthaginians were ordered by the consul L. Marcius Censorinus to abandon their city and resettle at least ten (Roman) miles from the sea. They decided to fight, and successfully repulsed all the attempts of incompetent Roman generals either to take Carthage or to starve it into surrender. Finally, in 147 P. *Cornelius Scipio Aemilianus walled off both the city and its harbour and in 146 took Carthage by storm. The population was sold and the city utterly destroyed; its territory became the Roman province of Africa (see AFRICA, ROMAN).

CAH 7²/2 (1989), ch. 11 (Scullard), 8² (1989), chs. 2 (Scullard), 3 (Briscoe), 4 (Errington), 5 (Harris). Walbank, *HCP* (1957–79); G. De Sanctis, *Storia dei Romani*, 3, 4. 3 (1916–1964); B. M. Caven, *The Punic Wars* (1980); A. E. Astin, *Scipio Aemilianus* (1967); H. H. Scullard, *Scipio Africanus* (1970), J. F. Lazenby, *The First Punic War* (1996) and *Hannibal's War* (1978); J. H. Thiel, *A History of Roman Seapower* (1954).   B. M. C.

punishment, Greek and Roman practice According to *Cicero (*Ad Brut.* 23. 3), it was a dictum of *Solon's that a community was held together by rewards and penalties, and the ascription seems plausible, in so far as Archaic Greek law-codes already show the city asserting its authority in laying down penalties both for universally recognized crimes and for failure to perform the duties imposed by its statutes. Cicero himself argued that the instinct to take vengeance (*vindicatio*) is nature's gift to man to ensure his own and his family's survival (*Inv.* 2. 65). Both in Greece and Rome criminal law emerged as an attempt to circumscribe and replace private revenge. Accordingly, just as prosecution in many cases fell to injured persons or their relatives, so the treatment of the convicted man was often closely related to his victims, for example in early homicide law and in matters of physical injury and *theft. There are also the religious aspects of punishment, which extend beyond offences against the gods themselves—for example at Athens and Rome in relation to blood-guilt (see POLLUTION) and at Rome in relation to certain political offences.

In fixing penalties legislators were guided to some extent both by the severity of the offence and the intention of the wrongdoer. Another consideration was the *status of the convicted person. Punishment of slaves, for example, was harsher and more humiliating than that of free men (see SLAVERY). Two other factors should be borne in mind: first, limited financial resources made any great expenditure on punishment impossible in practice in the majority of communities, even if it was thinkable; secondly, the high value attached to official membership of a community through citizenship made the removal (or diminution) of this status, i.e. *exile or loss of political rights, an effective form of punishment.

The supreme penalty, execution, had a two-way relationship to exile. One might escape execution by voluntary exile, whereupon the self-imposed penalty was aggravated by a ban on return (on pain of death) and confiscation of property. Alternatively one might be condemned to exile with loss of property with the threat of a full capital penalty for illegal return. A form of inflicting dishonour less severe than exile was the removal of some citizen-privileges (*atimia at Athens, *infamia at Rome), e.g. loss of the right to speak or vote in an assembly or of membership of the senate at Rome or in a Roman municipality.

Long-term imprisonment by the community is not usually found in Greek cities or under the Roman republic (see PRISON), but a similar effect might be achieved by selling delinquents into chattel-slavery or turning them into virtual slaves to the person they had offended (the fate of condemned thieves under the Roman republic). Under the Principate we find condemnation to the *mines, public works, or gladiatorial schools (see GLADIATORS, COMBATANTS AT GAMES) not only in Italy but the provinces.

Flogging was normally thought appropriate only for the punishment of slaves under Athenian democracy, not for that of free men. Whips were associated with tyrants; thus the Thirty (see THIRTY TYRANTS) had 300 whip-carriers. However, whips were used on free men elsewhere in the Greek world, notably at the games (*agōnes). At Rome, apart from being an element in the traditional form of execution (symbolized in the *fasces, where the rods surrounded the axe), flogging was apparently inflicted on citizens at Rome as reprisal for disobedience to magistrates until the lex Porcia, probably passed by M. *Porcius Cato (1) (Censorius) in 198 or 195 BC; even after this it remained a feature of military discipline and was employed on non-Romans anywhere.

Financial penalties were both employed to recompense injured parties, as in the Roman lex de repetundis (see REPETUNDAE), and as fines paid to the community, in some instances being deliberately made so large as to entail the financial ruin of the convicted person—an early example is the ruinous fine imposed on *Miltiades in 489 BC (Hdt. 6. 136).

Punishments which seem to us barbarous and grotesque should not be assumed to be primitive. The Roman penalty for parricide (*parricidium)—drowning in a sack with a dog, cock, ape, and viper (Cic. Rosc. Am. 70; Dig. 48. 9. 9)—must have been devised after a distinction was drawn between the killing of parents and grandparents and that of other relatives. A particularly recherché punishment under the Principate was the use of criminals as entertainment, when they were condemned to fight as gladiators or beast-fighters in the arena, often being forced to act mythological characters in dramas of blood which culminated in real death (S. Bartsch, Actors in the Audience (1994), 50 ff.).

Revenge, recompense, and the assertion of civic authority are the main themes in the Greek and Roman practice of punishment. The last involved rewarding the good and punishing the bad, hence encouraging citizens to virtue and deterring them from vice. To this extent only was punishment related to moral reform. See next entry.

Du châtiment dans la cité, Coll. de l'école française à Rome 79 (1984).

A. W. L.

punishment, Greek theories about Punishment may be defined as 'suffering inflicted on an offender in return for the suffering he inflicted'. On this definition the first holder of a theory of punishment is the Homeric hero (see HOMER); for when he retaliates against an offender he can articulate his purposes: (1) to restore or enhance his own timē (wealth, status) by exacting recompense, preferably large, from the offender; (2) satisfaction of his affronted feelings, in the shape of pleasure at the sight of the offender's discomfiture occasioned by (1); (3) publicity for his own superior strength; (4) deterrence of the offender (and of others) for the future. In achieving these aims he causes the offender to suffer reciprocally, as the definition requires. (However, other views of punishment in Homer are on offer: Adkins 'assimilates' it to (1), Mackenzie desiderates an impartial 'penal authority'.)

Implicitly or explicitly, these four purposes dominated in penal contexts in all Greek life and literature. The strongly vindictive demand from injured parties for recompense in some form, even if only satisfaction of feelings, generated among other things: (a) severe penalties (confiscation of property, heavy fines, exile, and death were commonplace); (b) surrogate punishees, i.e. third parties who were themselves innocent, but somehow linked to the offender; (c) a belief in supernatural surrogate punishers, gods and *Erinyes etc., to deal with offenders who escaped human justice; (d) a certain fascination, chiefly in imaginative literature, with crime-specific punishments, i.e. those that specify the offence in some satisfyingly neat or amusing way.

Penology became a topic of public debate in Athens only to the extent that prosecutors and defendants adduced a wide variety of excuses, palliations, and aggravations, calculated to persuade juries to waive, mitigate, or increase penalties. Juries had therefore to consider the validity of general arguments in particular circumstances. But they could decide exactly as they pleased; there was no professional judiciary to ensure principled uniformity in sentencing.

The only challenges to the orthodoxy of (1)–(4) came from certain intellectuals. For instance, Diodotus, an Athenian speaker in *Thucydides (2), deprecated extreme punishments (Thuc. 3. 37–40); so did *Isocrates, who also discussed the social causes of crime and advocated prevention in preference to cure; and *Protagoras recommended ignoring the past and using the reform / deterrence of the offender as the sole determinant of penalty. *Plato (1) argued similarly, but even more radically: crime is a mistake; recompense must invariably be paid, but it is not a penal matter; the punishment proper, which may take any form (even 'gifts' for the offender) likely to be effective, must be precisely calibrated to 'cure' his mental and moral 'disease'. Plato seems to take the medical terminology literally: the *soul is something curable physically. This uncompromisingly utilitarian policy he attempts to build into his long and elaborate penal code of the Laws.

*Aristotle prescinds from a programme of reform, but discusses punishment in numerous passages, notably in his Art of Rhetoric and Nicomachean Ethics, in connection with topics such as justice, equity, and the emotions. Post-Aristotelian sources are very scattered, but note especially the Younger Seneca (L. *Annaeus Seneca (2)), On Anger; *Plutarch, On the Delays in Divine Vengeance; and *Cassius Dio 55. 14 ff. See PUNISHMENT, GREEK AND ROMAN PRACTICE; RECIPROCITY (GREECE); SIN; THEODICY.

K. Latte, Hermes, 1931; A. W. H. Adkins, BICS 1960; R. Sorabji, Necessity, Cause and Blame (1980), part 5 (Aristotle); M. M. Mackenzie, Plato on Punishment (1981); G. Courtois, Arch. Philos. du Droit, 28 (1983) (Aristotle and Seneca); T. J. Saunders, Plato's Penal Code: Tradition,

Controversy, and Reform in Greek Penology (1991), and *Studi Economico-Giuridici*, 54 (1991–2) (Plutarch).   T. J. S.

Pupius, Publius, contemporary with *Horace, who called his tragedies 'tearful poems' (*Epist.* 1. 1. 67).

Courtney, *FLP* 307.   E. C.

Pupius (*RE* 10) **Piso Frugi (Calpurnianus), Marcus,** a Calpurnius Piso adopted by an aged senator M. Pupius, was in his youth a promising orator and friend of Cicero's. Marrying the widow of L. *Cornelius Cinna (1), he became quaestor 83 BC, but deserted to *Sulla and divorced his wife. He was praetor 72 or 71 and proconsul as Q. *Caecilius Metellus Pius' successor in Spain, triumphing in 69. Giving up oratory, i.a. as too strenuous for his health (thus Cic. *Brut.* 236), he chose the military life, served *Pompey as a legate 67–62 and was rewarded by him with a consulship (61). He supported P. *Clodius Pulcher and irritated Cicero (see CALPURNIUS PISO (1), C.), who prevented him from obtaining the province of Syria. He failed to secure the ratification of Pompey's eastern arrangements and died soon after.

                                                                              E. B.

purification, Greek (καθαρμός). The concept of 'purification', like that of *pollution, was applied in very diverse ways in Greek *ritual. Many purifications were performed not in response to specific pollutions, but as preparation for particular events or actions or on a regular calendar basis. The Athenian assembly (see EKKLĒSIA), for instance, was purified at the start of meetings (by carrying the body of a sacrificed piglet around it), and temples could be treated similarly; individuals purified themselves by washing before approaching the gods. Most drastically, some whole cities of ancient Ionia, not excluding Athens, were purified annually by the expulsion of human scapegoats at the festival *Thargelia.

There were many different techniques of purification: by washing or sprinkling, by fumigation (with sulphur above all), by 'rubbing off' with mud or bran; all admitted various degrees of symbolic elaboration (the use of sea-water, or water from a special spring, or even from seven springs, for instance). *Sacrifice too, or modified forms of it, often functioned as a purification: the corpse might be carried around the place to be purified (see above), while the blood supposedly sticking to a killer was 'washed off with blood' by pouring that of the animal victim over his hands. Where actual pollutions are concerned, however, these issues of technique and symbolism are less important than the question of the circumstances in which purification was permitted and deemed effective. Even minor and inescapable pollutions such as contact with a death could not be removed immediately: the major pollution of blood-guilt required a period of exile before the killer could (if at all) be readmitted to the community after purification. (The fullest regulation of degrees of bloodguilt is *Plato (1)'s in *Laws*.) Thus the most powerful of all purifying agents was in a sense time.

Purification was related to *medicine in two distinct ways. On the one hand, seers professed to be able to cure certain *diseases, epilepsy above all, by purifications of religious type. On the other, theories about the need to 'purify' different organs of the body had considerable importance in early Greek scientific medicine. Much though 'scientific' doctors despised purifiers (see *Hippocrates (2), *On the Sacred Disease*), their theories in a sense represent a transposition of traditional religious ideas into a secular key.

Purification was given heightened significance by the otherworldly movements in Greek thought, *Orphism and Pythagoreanism (see PYTHAGORAS (1)). For them, purification signified an escape not just from particular pollutions but from man's fallen condition, his imprisonment in the body. This was a new metaphorical extension of the traditional idea; but adherents of these movements also underwent purifications and observed abstinences of a more conventional type (see FASTING), so that the new 'purification' had a considerable psychological continuity with the old.

The god who presided over purification from blood-guilt was *Zeus Catharsios, 'Of purification'; this role derived from his general concern for the reintegration into society of displaced persons (cf. Zeus 'Of suppliants' and 'Of strangers'). *Apollo by contrast was not formally called Catharsios; he could, however, be seen as a 'purifier of men's houses' (Aesch. *Eum.* 63) because his oracle at Delphi (see DELPHIC ORACLE) regularly gave advice on such matters. On a more everyday level, similar advice was available to Athenians from publicly-appointed 'exegetes' (see EXĒGĒTĒS).

J. N. Bremmer, *Harv. Stud.* 1983 (scapegoats); and see the works cited under POLLUTION.   R. C. T. P.

purification, Jewish See RELIGION, JEWISH.

purification, Roman See LUSTRATION.

purple Of the two main kinds of purple-yielding shellfish described by *Pliny (1) (*HN* 9. 125–41), *purpura* and *pelagia* (Greek πορφύρα) correspond to the Linnaean murex, *murex* and *bucinum* (κῆρυξ) to the smaller and less precious *purpura haemostoma*. In antiquity the purple of *Tyre always retained its primacy, but purple dyeing was practised also in the Greek cities of Asia, the Greek mainland and islands, S. Italy, and N. Africa. After being gathered or caught in baskets and killed suddenly to preserve the secretion, the molluscs were either opened (esp. the larger) or crushed. The mass was then left in salt for three days, extracted with water, and slowly inspissated to one-sixteenth of its original volume. Impurities were removed during this process, and the liquid was then tested with flocks of wool until the colour was right. Many shades within the violet–scarlet range, and even a bluish green, could be obtained by mixing the dyes from different species and by intercepting the photochemical reaction which gives the secretion its colour. ('Twice-dyed' (δίβαφος) Tyrian purple resulted from consecutive steeping in *pelagium* and *bucinum*.) Less expensive imitation purple dyes, for which several recipes survive, were also made. In Rome, where the use of purple garments was always a mark of rank (see TOGA), purple dyeing became a state monopoly under Alexander Severus (see AURELIUS SEVERUS ALEXANDER, M.). See DYEING; TEXTILE PRODUCTION.

M. Reinhold, *History of Purple as a Status Symbol in Antiquity* (Coll. Latomus 116) (1970); G. Steigerwald, *Byzantinische Forschungen*, 15 (1990), 219 ff.   L. A. M.

puteal, the circular stone surround of a well-head, but also the stone coping marking a place that was sacred. Thus the *puteal Libonis* or *Scribonianum* in the forum Romanum was a monument shaped like a well-head marking the spot where lightning had struck: the form of the monument is known from its representation on coins, but only the tufa foundations were excavated in 1950.

Nash, *Pict. Dict.* 2. 259–61.   G. D.

Puteoli (mod. Pozzuoli), 12 km. (7½ mi.) north of Naples

(*Neapolis). The earliest settlement was a Greek foundation, Dicaearchia (c.521 BC). Its early relations with Rome are uncertain, but it may have become an ally in 338. It was an important harbour in the Hannibalic war (see PUNIC WARS), and became a Roman colony in 194 (see COLONIZATION, ROMAN). There were also colonizations under *Augustus and *Nero (or *Vespasian), although the small size of the *ager Puteolanus* makes it unlikely that these were large (*ILS* 5317; Plut. *Sull.* 37; Tac. *Ann.* 14. 27; Plin. *HN* 3. 61). In the 2nd cent. BC, Puteoli's commercial importance grew, thanks to the development of trade between Italy and the east. It handled a large proportion of trade with the eastern empire and grain imports for Rome. It was also a fashionable resort, located between Neapolis and *Cumae, and many of the Roman élite owned *villas there. Archaeological remains include the so-called temple of Augustus (probably the *capitolium*), dating to the 2nd cent. BC, several other temples, shops and baths, amphitheatres of the 2nd cent. BC and Flavian period, a *macellum*, traces of the harbour, and numerous tombs. Greek and Latin epigraphy attests a flourishing civic life. Its *agōnes* in memory of *Hadrian, the Eusebeia, were panhellenic (see PANHELLENISM). See OSTIA; PORTUS.

A. Maiuri, *The Phlegraean Fields* (1957); J. D'Arms, *Romans on the Bay of Naples* (1970), and *Commerce and Social Standing in Ancient Rome* (1982); S. De Caro and A. Greco, *Campania* (1981); M. W. Frederiksen, *Campania* (1984).   K. L.

Pyanopsia, an Attic festival of *Apollo, celebrated at Athens on the 7th of the month Pyanopsion (i.e. roughly late October). It was probably once a widespread Ionian festival, to judge from the diffusion of the month name Pyanopsion. The attested activities are (1) carrying and dedication of the *eiresiōnē* (a branch wound with wool and hung with fruit) (2) preparation—and no doubt dedication and consumption—of a dish of boiled beans and other vegetables and cereals, from which the festival derives its name, 'Bean-boiling'. Like the Oschophoria, celebrated within a few days of it, the Pyanopsia was linked aetiologically with the homecoming of Theseus. See ATTIC CULTS AND MYTHS; IONIAN FESTIVALS.

C. Calame, *Thésée et l'imaginaire athénien* (1991), 150–3, 291–324.
                                                                R. C. T. P.

Pydna The battle of Pydna takes its name from the town on the north-east coast of Greece, where the Romans under L. *Aemilius Paullus (2) put an end to the Macedonian monarchy by defeating king *Perseus (2) (22 June 168 BC). As was the case with *Cynoscephalae, the battle seems to have been brought about by an unintentional clash, this time between light troops. The main Macedonian army deployed more quickly than the Roman, and at first the *phalanx carried all before it. But it became disrupted, possibly by the terrain over which it was advancing, and the Romans were able to infiltrate its formation by dividing into maniples. At the same time, Roman cavalry and *elephants defeated the Macedonian left wing, thus enveloping the phalanx's left flank, and the same thing probably happened on the Macedonian right. Some 20,000 Macedonians were killed, and about 11,000 taken prisoner, only the cavalry escaping in any numbers.

RE Suppl. 10; Polyb. 29. 17; Livy 44. 36–43; Plut. *Aem.* 16–23; N. G. L. Hammond, *JHS* 1984, 31 ff. and in *HM* 3 (1988), 547 ff.   J. F. La.

Pygmalion, name (perhaps *Phoenician) of two legendary E. Mediterranean kings: (1) king of *Cyprus, father-in-law (Apollod. 3. 14. 3) or grandfather (Ovid) of Cinyras, with whom he shared

a devotion to the cult of *Aphrodite-Astarte. It was originally an ivory cult-statue of the goddess for which he conceived a fetishistic passion (Philostephanus in Clem. Al. *Protr.* 4. 57. 1); but in Ovid's version (*Met.* 10. 243 ff.) the king himself carves the image of his ideal woman, who is then brought to life by Aphrodite, becomes his wife, and bears a daughter, eponym of the town of *Paphos. (2) king of *Tyre and brother of Elissa (*Dido), whose husband Sychaeus (or Acherbas, Justin *epitome* 18. 4. 5) he killed in the hope of seizing his fortune (Verg. *Aen.* 1. 343 ff.).

(1) H. Dörrie, *Pygmalion* (1974). (2) A. S. Pease, *Aeneidos Liber Quartus* (1935, repr.), 14–17.   A. H. G.

pygmies, dwarves who live in *Africa, *India, *Scythia, or *Thrace. They are usually discussed in Greek mythology in connection with their fight against the cranes. *Homer (*Il.* 3. 3–6) says that the cranes flee before the winter to the (Southern) stream of Oceanus and bring death to the Pygmies. *Hecataeus (1), who located the pygmies in southern Egypt, *Ctesias, and the writers on India (e.g. *Megasthenes) considerably elaborated the story. Pygmies disguise themselves as rams, or ride on rams and goats. They battle with the cranes to protect their fields (perhaps a reflection of the farmer's life), and conduct operations to destroy the cranes' eggs and young. Other mythographers invented explanations for the struggle, tracing the enmity to a beautiful pygmy girl transformed into a crane (Boeus in Ath. 9. 393e–f). Philostratus (*Eik.* 2.22; see PHILOSTRATI) tells of an unsuccessful pygmy attack on *Heracles after he killed *Antaeus.

The geranomachy is often shown in Greek art, first on the François vase c.570, where the pygmies are shown as midgets battling with clubs, hooked sticks, and slings, and riding goats. On later Archaic and Classical vases they become podgy and grotesquely proportioned. Some 4th-cent. vases show them with pelts and poses like giants; like them, they were earth-born (hence their defence of Antaeus). Pygmies appear on Hellenistic rhyta and, in isolated groups, on *gems. In Hellenistic and Roman art, they occur on Campanian wall-paintings as fully armed warriors with no *deformity, and in Nilotic paintings and mosaics deformed, often in humorous confontations with crocodiles or hippopotami.

RE 23², 'Pygmaioi'; *EAA* 6, 'Pigmei'; V. Dasen, *Dwarfs in Ancient Egypt and Greece* (1993); *LIMC* 7. 1 (1994), 594–601.   K. W. A.

Pylaemenes, a minor Iliadic character (see HOMER), king of the Paphlagonian Enetoi (see PAPHLAGONIA), fighting on the Trojan side (*Iliad* 2. 851–5). He is chiefly notorious for appearing alive in 13. 643–59, after he has been killed in 5. 576–9, a famous inconsistency in ancient criticism (Schol. A Hom. *Iliad* 2. 851).
                                                                E. Ke.

Pylos was the classical name of sites in *Elis, Triphylia (S. of Elis), and *Messenia, all of which claimed to be the Pylos which is *Nestor (1)'s capital in the Homeric poems (Strabo 8. 3; cf. Ar. *Eq.* 1059); but many textual references to 'sandy Pylos' better suit a region, probably that around Navarino Bay (cf. *MME* 82, 84, 93), although there was a 'Pylian plain' in Triphylia (Strabo 8. 3. 14). Strabo's preferred candidate for Nestor's capital was the Triphylian Pylos, although it was well inland (8. 3. 14), whereas references in the Odyssey (3. 4–5, 386–7, 423–4; 15. 215–6) imply a site close to the sea; but Triphylian Pylos was unknown to Pausanias, who records local tradition placing the house, tomb, and cave of Nestor and the tomb of *Thrasymedes, Nestor's son, at Messenian Pylos (4. 36. 1–2). This was the rocky peninsula, more precisely called Coryphasium (now Palaiokastro), north of

Pyramus and Thisbe

Navarino Bay and joined by a sand spit to the mainland, which was occupied by the Athenians between 425 and 409 BC. There was prehistoric and later occupation in the neighbourhood (*MME* 264, sites 7–10): 'Nestor's cave' can be identified as one on the acropolis which has produced much neolithic material as well as some later prehistoric and classical pottery, while 'the tomb of Thrasymedes' was probably the tholos tomb at Voïdhokoilia, where a hero cult was established from late Classical times (*AR* 1983–4, 28; 1984–5, 25).

But the most important prehistoric site in the western Peloponnese which was called Pylos, as its Linear B texts demonstrate, is at Epano Englianos, some 9 km. (5½ miles) north-east of Navarino Bay. This is a low flat-topped hill, steepest on the north, which seems to have been first occupied in the Middle Helladic period, like many other sites in this part of Messenia. Information on its earliest phases is very scanty, but the evidence for wealthy burials in the nearby 'grave circle' and tholos tomb IV, roughly contemporary with those of the later shaft graves at *Mycenae, testifies to the development of a centre of power here by the beginning of the Mycenaean period. See MYCENAEAN CIVILIZATION. The site probably increased in importance during the 15th and earlier 14th cent. BC, to which the remains of a gateway and likely fortification and more than one phase of substantial structures beneath the later palace belong, and became the capital of a state controlling much of Messenia after the mid-14th cent. At this time all earlier structures on the site were apparently dismantled, apart from the gateway, and it was reserved for an unfortified palace complex; the surrounding settlement extended over a very considerable area, as survey-work (1992 onwards) is demonstrating. The large quantities of Linear B tablets preserved by the burning of the palace *c.*1200 BC provide the best available picture of the workings of a Mycenaean state (see PRE-ALPHABETIC SCRIPTS (GREECE)). After this burning, the site was thought to have been abandoned, but reoccupation of part of the palace in the twelfth century has been suggested (M. R. Popham, *OJA* 10 (1991), 315 ff.), and seems increasingly likely from recent re-examination of the site and the excavation records; one nearby chamber tomb certainly continued in use until late in Late Helladic IIIC. There is also considerable evidence for habitation in the Dark Age, to which a small tholos tomb found nearby belongs. This habitation probably extended into the 8th c., but thereafter the site was abandoned until mediaeval times; its existence was clearly unknown in Classical times, so that Greek tradition seems to have preserved little more than a name in the right region.

Pylos' most famous moment in Classical Greek history was during the *Peloponnesian War, in 425 BC, when Pylos was occupied by an Athenian force. This occupation led in turn to the capture of a force of Spartans on the adjacent island of Sphacteria. This episode was very fully described by *Thucydides (2) (4. 2–41). See DEMOSTHENES (1); also CLEON; BRASIDAS. Anxiety about the return of the prisoners taken 'on the island', i.e. Sphacteria (see Thuc. 5. 15. 1), was one main Spartan motive for accepting peace in 421, the so-called Peace of *Nicias (1). The Athenians held Pylos with a garrison of Messenians (see MESSENIA) until 409 (Diod. 13. 64).

GAC, D 1; C. W. Blegen and others, *The Palace of Nestor at Pylos I–III* (1966, 1969, 1973); T. G. Palaima and C. W. Shelmerdine (eds.), *Pylos Comes Alive* (1984); on the latest investigations, C. Griebel, *AJArch.* 97 (1993). On the topographical problems of Thuc. 4. 2 ff. (the Athenian fortification of Pylos) see W. K. Pritchett, *Studies in Ancient Greek Topography*, 1 (1965), 6 ff. and *Essays in Greek History* (1994), 145 ff.; J. B. Wilson, *Pylos 425 BC* (1979); R. Bauslaugh, *JHS* 1979, 1 ff.; H. D. Westlake, *Studies* (1989), ch. 5; W. Ball, *Pylos 425* (annotated filmstrip, 1990). O. T. P. K. D., S. H.

Pyramus and Thisbe, hero and heroine of a love-story almost unknown except from Ovid, *Met.* 4. 55 ff., who says, 53, that it is not a common tale. They were next-door neighbours in *Babylon, and, as their parents would not let them marry, they talked with each other through the party-wall of the houses, which was cracked. Finally, they arranged to meet at Ninus' tomb. There Thisbe was frightened by a lion coming from its kill; she dropped her cloak as she ran and the lion mouthed it. Pyramus, finding the bloodstained cloak and supposing her dead, killed himself; she returned, found his body, and followed his example. Their blood stained a mulberry-tree, whose fruit has ever since been black when ripe, in sign of mourning for them.

LIMC 7. 1 (1994), 605–7. H. J. R.

Pyrenees (Πυρήνη, τὰ Πυρηναῖα ὄρη; *Pyrenaeus mons*), the range of mountains between *Gaul (Transalpine) and Hispania (*Spain). The name derived from a city, or port of call, frequented by traders from *Massalia. *Avienus (559) knew both the town and the mountains, the former near Portus Veneris (*Port Vendres*). All classical estimates as to length were excessive and *Pliny (1) first correctly ascribes an east–west direction for the range (4. 110). The chief highway (via Herculea, later the via Augusta) crossed the mountains near their eastern limit (Col de Perthus). Excavations here have shown that its passage was marked by *Pompey's Trophies (71 BC), a monument commemorating his defeat of Q. *Sertorius. This road was supplemented by another running from Jaca to Pau (*Itin. Ant.* 452. 6) and another from Pamplona to Dax (ibid. 453. 4). Metals were an important resource exploited in antiquity, although timber, hams, and bacon also made a contribution to the economic life of the peninsula.

A. Schulten, *Iberische Landeskunde. Geographie des antiken Spanien* (1974). J. J. van N.; S. J. K.

Pyrgi, modern Santa Severa, was the main port of *Caere, and famous as the site of a wealthy *Etruscan sanctuary sacked by *Dionysius (1) I in 384 BC (Diod. Sic. 15. 14). Excavation (1957 onwards) has revealed two Archaic temples: *B* (*c.*500) is a Graeco-Tuscan compromise, and *A* (*c.*480–470) is typically Tuscan. Both were destroyed in the 3rd cent. BC. Three inscribed gold tablets were found between the two temples in 1964: one is the only Phoenicio-Punic text known in the Italian peninsula; the other two are in Etruscan. All three concern the dedication of Temple *B* by the Etruscan ruler of Caere to the Phoenician goddess Astarte; they demonstrate the close ties that enabled Carthage to influence the internal politics of the cities of Etruria *c.*500 (cf Arist. *Pol.* 1280ᵃ 38 ff.; Polyb. 3. 22. 4–13). A line of small rooms along one wall of the sanctuary is fully contextual with Temple *B*, and has been connected with sacred prostitution rites of Phoenician type (see PROSTITUTION, SACRED); these cubicles could equally well have served as pilgrim shelters. The establishment of a Roman military colony at Pyrgi in the 3rd cent. BC reflects the same naval strategy that prompted the near-contemporary foundations of Castrum Novum (modern Santa Marinella nearby), *Cosa and *Paestum.

CAH 4² *Plates* (1988), pl. 297a–g. Definitive reports: G. Colonna and others, *Not. Scav.* 1959, 143 ff.; 1970, Suppl. 2 (1972); 1988–9, Suppl. 2 (1992). Synthesis of exegetical and other items: F. R. Serra Ridgway, in J.-P. Descoeudres (ed.), *Greek Colonists and Native Populations* (1990), 511 ff. D. W. R. R.

Pyrrha, a small *polis on the gulf of Kalloní in *Lesbos, with a prehistoric predecessor. The earliest Greek burials are Proto-Geometric; an early apsidal building may be a temple. *Mytilene reinforced Pyrrha's fortifications in 428: a wall, and probable shipsheds, have been identified. In the Ionian war the Spartans failed to detach Pyrrha from Athens. Later it joined the *Second Athenian Confederacy, and after a period of Persian rule (see PERSIA) it was taken by *Alexander (3) the Great. It may have been relocated during the Hellenistic period: *Pliny (1) the Elder says it was drowned by the sea, but like other Lesbian towns it flourished in Roman and early Christian times.

RE 24 (1963), 1403–20; N. Spencer, BSA 1995; W. Schering, Arch. Anz. 1989 (new excavations). D. G. J. S.

Pyrrhon of Elis (c.365–275 BC), the founder of Greek Scepticism (see SCEPTICS). He was a painter early in his life, but then studied with a certain Bryson (it is not clear which) and with the Demo-critean *Anaxarchus, with whom he travelled to India in the train of *Alexander (3) the Great. There he is said to have encountered the 'gymnosophists' and 'magi' who were thought to have influenced his later philosophical views. He returned to his native town and lived a quiet and modest life, honoured and respected by his fellow citizens.

Pyrrhon wrote nothing, and what we know of him goes back to the writings of his main pupil, *Timon (2) of Phlius. Later accounts of Pyrrhon's philosophy tend to be heavily influenced by the philosophers of the Pyrrhonist revival after *Aenesidemus. From a passage attributed to Timon we learn that Pyrrhon claimed that nothing can be found out about the nature of things because neither our senses nor our opinions are true or false. Hence we should be without opinions or inclinations, saying about all things that they no more are than they are not (οὐ μᾶλλον). This attitude will result first in non-assertion, then in tranquillity (ἀταραξία). The claim that things cannot be known is stated without reservations, and the emphasis lies on the alleged result of suspending judgement—tranquillity. This accords well with the rest of our evidence from Timon, who satirized all other philosophers by contrasting their empty talk and fruitless worries with the supreme calm and serenity of Pyrrhon. Later Pyrrhon-ists took care to soften the dogmatic tone of Pyrrhon's statements about the impossibility of finding the truth, and to reject the anecdotes that had grown around Pyrrhon's lifestyle, arguing that he would live in accordance with appearances (φαινόμενα) and hence have no grounds for departing from ordinary customs. We do not have an account of Pyrrhon's arguments for the claim that things are unknowable, but it is likely that he used some of the examples of conflicting appearances and opinions familiar to philosophers since the time of the *sophists and *Democritus. Those materials were later systematized in the ten Modes of inducing suspension of judgement by Aenesidemus.

Pirrone, Testimonianze, ed. F. Decleva Caizzi, 1981 (with Ital. trans. and comm.). See bibliog. under SCEPTICS. G. S.

Pyrrhus See NEOPTOLEMUS (1).

Pyrrhus of *Epirus (319–272 BC), son of Aeacides and Phthia, most famous of the Molossian kings (see MOLOSSI), chief architect of a large, powerful, and Hellenized Epirote state (see HELLENISM; EPIRUS), and builder of the great theatre at *Dodona. After reigning as a minor from 307/6 to 303/2, he was driven out and followed for a time the fortunes of *Demetrius (4) Poliorcetes. With the support of *Ptolemy (1) I, whose stepdaughter Antigone he married, and of *Agathocles (1) of Syracuse, he became joint king with Neoptolemus, whom he soon removed. Early in his reign he annexed and retained southern Illyria (see ILLYRII), probably as far as *Epidamnus. He tried to emancipate Epirus from Macedonia. By intervening in a dynastic quarrel in Macedonia Pyrrhus obtained the frontier provinces of Parauaea and Tymphaea, together with *Ambracia, Amphilochia (see AMPHILOCHI), and *Acarnania. On the death of Antigone he acquired *Corcyra and *Leucas as the dowry of his new wife, Lanassa daughter of Agathocles, and made alliances with the Dardanian chief Bardylis (see DARDANI) and the Paeonian king Audoleon, whose daughters he also married. Conflict with Demetrius (from 291), now king of Macedon, saw substantial gains in Thessaly and Macedonia, but these were largely lost later to *Lysimachus (284).

Appealed to by the Tarentines (as his uncle *Alexander (6) of Epirus and the Spartans *Archidamus III and Cleonymus before him), Pyrrhus went to assist them in their Hellenic struggle against Rome. With a force of 25,000 infantry, 3,000 horse, and 20 elephants he defeated the Romans at *Heraclea (1) (280), though not without loss, and won the support of the Samnites, Lucanians, Bruttians (see SAMNIUM; LUCANIA; BRUTTII), and Greek cities of the south. He marched towards Rome, but prolonged negotiations failed to secure peace. In 279 he defeated the Romans again, at *Ausculum, but again with heavy losses. Late in the same year he received an appeal from *Syracuse and in 278 sailed to Sicily, where he fought the Carthaginians, then allies of Rome, and *Mamertines. In 276 he abandoned the campaign (perhaps by then a lost cause) and returned to Italy, whither he was urgently summoned by his allies in the south. After more losses (including eight elephants and his camp) in battle with the Romans at Malventum (renamed thereafter *Beneventum) in 275, he returned to Epirus with less than a third of his original force. A garrison was left behind at *Tarentum, signifying perhaps future intent, but the Italian manpower at Rome's disposal had triumphed decisively. Pyrrhus himself embarked upon a new attempt at Macedonia. Initial success and a brief time as king there in 274 gave way to unpopularity after he plundered the royal tombs at *Aegae, and in 273 he marched into the Peloponnesus. Following a failed attack on Sparta he went to *Argos (2), where in 272 he died, struck on the head by a tile thrown from the roof of a house; in the same year Tarentum fell to the Romans.

RE 24, 'Pyrrhos (13)'; FGrH 229 (a work on tactics and, less certainly, memoirs); P. Wuilleumier, Tarente, des origines à la conquête romaine (1939); G. Nenci, Pirro (1953); P. Lévêque, Pyrrhos (1957); N. G. L. Hammond, Epirus (1967), and HM 3 (1988); P. R. Franke, CAH 7²/2 (1989), 456 ff. (with bibliog.). P. S. D.

Pythagoras (1), **Pythagoreanism**

1. Pythagoras Pythagoras, son of Mnesarchus, one of the most mysterious and influential figures in Greek intellectual history, was born in *Samos in the mid-6th cent. BC and migrated to *Croton in c.530 BC. There he founded the sect or society that bore his name, and that seems to have played an important role in the political life of *Magna Graecia for several generations. Pythagoras himself is said to have died as a refugee in Metapontum. Pythagorean political influence is attested well into the 4th cent., with *Archytas of Tarentum.

The name of Pythagoras is connected with two parallel traditions, one religious and one scientific. Pythagoras is said to have introduced the doctrine of transmigration of *souls into Greece, and his religious influence is reflected in the cult organization of the Pythagorean society, with periods of initiation, secret doctrines and passwords (*akousmata* and *symbola*), special dietary restrictions (see ANIMALS, ATTITUDES TO), and burial rites. Pythagoras seems to have become a legendary figure in his own lifetime and was identified by some with the *Hyperborean *Apollo. His supernatural status was confirmed by a golden thigh, the gift of bilocation, and the capacity to recall his previous incarnations. Classical authors imagine him studying in Egypt; in the later tradition he gains universal wisdom by travels in the east. Pythagoras becomes the pattern of the 'divine man': at once a sage, a seer, a teacher, and a benefactor of the human race.

The scientific tradition ascribes to Pythagoras a number of important discoveries, including the famous geometric theorem that still bears his name. Even more significant for Pythagorean thought is the discovery of the musical consonances: the ratios 2 : 1, 3 : 2, and 4 : 3 representing the length of strings corresponding to the octave and the basic harmonies (the fifth and the fourth). These ratios are displayed in the *tetractys*, an equilateral triangle composed of 10 dots; the Pythagoreans swear an oath by Pythagoras as author of the *tetractys*. The same ratios are presumably reflected in the music of the spheres, which Pythagoras alone was said to hear.

In the absence of written records before *Philolaus in the late 5th cent., it is impossible to tell how much of the Pythagorean tradition in *mathematics, *music, and *astronomy can be traced back to the founder and his early followers. Since the fundamental work of Walter Burkert, it has been generally recognized that the conception of Pythagorean philosophy preserved in later antiquity was the creation of *Plato (1) and his school, and that the only reliable pre-Platonic account of Pythagorean thought is the system of Philolaus. *Aristotle reports that for the Pythagoreans all things are numbers or imitate numbers. In Philolaus we read that it is by number and proportion that the world becomes organized and knowable. The basic principles are the Unlimited (*apeira*) and the Limiting (*perainonta*). The generation of the numbers, beginning with One in the centre, seems to coincide with the structuring of the cosmos. There must be enough cosmic bodies to correspond to the perfect number 10; the earth is a kind of heavenly body, revolving around an invisible central fire. This fact permitted Copernicus to name 'Philolaus the Pythagorean' as one of his predecessors.

Plato was deeply influenced by the Pythagorean tradition in his judgement myths, in his conception of the soul as transcending the body, and in the mathematical interpretation of nature. The *Phaedo* and the *Timaeus*, respectively, became the classical formulations for the religious and cosmological aspects of the Pythagorean world view. In the *Philebus* (16c) begins the transformation of Pythagoras into the archetype of philosophy. This view is developed by *Speusippus, who replaces Plato's Forms by Pythagorean numbers. Hence *Theophrastus can assign to Pythagoras the late Platonic 'unwritten doctrines' of the One and the Infinite Dyad, and these two principles appear in all later versions of Pythagorean philosophy.

In the 1st cent. BC, P. *Nigidius Figulus revived the Pythagorean tradition in Rome, while in *Alexandria (1) the Platonist *Eudorus (2) attributed to the Pythagoreans a supreme One, above the two older principles of One and Dyad. This monistic Platonism was developed by the Neopythagoreans: *Moderatus of Gades in the 1st cent. AD, *Nicomachus (3) of Gerasa and *Numenius of Apamea in the 2nd cent. See NEOPYTHAGOREANISM. Their innovations were absorbed into the great Neoplatonic synthesis of *Plotinus (see NEOPLATONISM), and thereafter no

distinction can be drawn between Pythagoreans and Neoplatonists. Porphyry and Iamblichus both composed lives of Pythagoras in which he is represented as the source of Platonic philosophy.

There is an important pseudonymous literature of texts ascribed to Pythagoras, Archytas, and other members of the school. This begins in the 3rd cent. BC and continues down to Byzantine times. A number of these texts have survived, thanks to the prestige of their supposed authors.

DK 14 and 44–58; Burnet, *EGP.* 80 ff., 276 ff.; Guthrie, *Hist. Gr. Phil.* 1. 146 ff.; Kirk–Raven–Schofield, 214 ff., 322 ff.; J. Barnes, *The Presocratic Philosophers*, 1 (1979), 100 ff.; W. Burkert, *Lore and Science in Ancient Pythagoreanism* (1972; Ger. orig., *Weisheit und Wissenschaft*, 1962); C. A. Huffman, *Philolaus of Croton* (1993); C. H. Kahn, in A. P. D. Mourelatos (ed.), *The Pre-Socratics* (1974, repr. 1993); H. Thesleff, *The Pythagorean Texts of the Hellenistic Period* (1965); T. A. Szlezák, *Pseudo-Archytas über die Kategorien* (1972); W. Burkert, *Philologus*, 1961, 16 ff., 226 ff.; D. J. O'Meara, *Pythagoras Revived* (1989) on the Neopythagoreans.

C. H. K.

2. Pythagoreanism (Religious Aspects) Pythagoreanism is the name given to the philosophical and religious movement(s) allegedly derived from the teachings of Pythagoras. Reliable tradition on the early form of Pythagoreanism, coming chiefly from *Aristotle and his school, presents Pythagoras and his followers as a religious and political association in S. Italy (chiefly Croton) where they gained considerable political influence, until their power was broken in a catastrophe in about 450 BC. From then on, Pythagoreanism survived in two distinct forms, a scientific, philosophical form (the so-called μαθηματικοί) which in the 4th cent. manifested itself in the thinking of *Philolaus and *Archytas of Tarentum and the Pythagoreans whom Plato knew and followed, and a religious, sectarian form (ἀκουσματικοί those following certain oral teachings (ἀκούσματα or σύμβολα), which manifested itself in the migrant Pythagoristai of Middle Comedy. After the analysis of W. Burkert, it is universally recognized that scientific Pythagoreanism is a reform of its earlier, religious way ascribed to *Hippasus of Metapontum around 450 BC.

Despite the fact that many pseudepigraphical Pythagorean writings are dated to Hellenistic times, the continuity of any form of Pythagoreanism after the Classical age is disputed. *Neopythagoreanism existed at any rate in the late Hellenistic (the Roman P. *Nigidius Figulus, founder of Neoplatonism according to Cic. *Tim.* 1) and early imperial epochs (*Apollonius (12) of Tyana); through the alleged derivation of *Pompilius Numa's teaching from that of Pythagoras, it gained popularity in Rome (see Ov. *Met.* 15. 60–496). It continued into the related Neoplatonist movement (see NEOPLATONISM); prominent Neoplatonists such as *Porphyry and his pupil *Iamblichus (2) wrote on Pythagoreanism (*De vita Pythagorica*). The hexametrical collection of life rules, under the title Golden Words (Χρυσῆ Ἔπη) ascribed to Pythagoras himself, appears at the same date.

While among the philosophical disciplines of the mathematici, arithmetic, theory of number and music are prominent and influential, the doctrines of the acusmatici laid down rules for a distinctive life style, the "Pythagorean life". The originally oral *akousmata* (collected by later authors; a list in Iamb. *V. Pyth.* 82–6) contained unrelated and often strange answers to the questions 'What exists?', 'What is the best thing?', 'What should one do?' Prominent among the rules of life is a complicated (and in our sources not consistent) vegetarianism, based on the doctrine of metempsychosis and already ascribed to Pythagoras himself during his life-time (Xenophanes, DK 21 B 7); total vegetarianism excludes participation in sacrifice and marginalizes those who profess it, at the same time all the more efficiently binding them together in their own sectarian group. Metempsychosis and, more generally, an interest in the afterlife connects Pythagoreanism with Orphism; Plato associates vegetarianism with the Orphic life-style (βίος Ὀρφικός Plat. *Laws* 6. 783 C), and authors from about 400 BC onwards name Pythagoreans as authors of certain Orphic texts.

See ANIMALS, ATTITUDES TO; ORPHIC LITERATURE; ORPHISM.

TEXTS M. Timpanaro Cardini (ed.), *Pitagorici. Testimonianze e frammenti* (1958–64); H. Thesleff (ed.), *The Pythagorean Texts of the Hellenistic Period* (1965); Golden Words: D. Young (ed.), *Theognis, Ps.-Phocylides,* etc. (1961). A magisterial survey: K. von Fritz and others, *RE* 47 (1963) 171–300, 'Pythagoras', esp. 209–68 (K. von Fritz), and 268–77 (H. Dörrie); a radically new evaluation of the tradition: W. Burkert, *Lore and Science in Ancient Pythagoreanism* (1972, Ger. orig. 1962); Hellenistic Pythagoreanism: W. Burkert, *Philologus*, 1961, 16–43, 226–40; H. Thesleff, *An Introduction to the Pythagorean Writings of the Hellenistic Period* (1961). F. G.

Pythagoras (2), Greek sculptor, active *c.*490–450 BC. A Samian (see SAMOS) who migrated to *Rhegium in Italy, probably after the *Ionian Revolt collapsed in 494. Working exclusively in bronze and a rival of *Myron (1), he made victor-statues, heroes, and gods, and pioneered the study of movement and proportion.

A. F. Stewart, *Greek Sculpture* (1990), 138 f., 254 f. A. F. S.

Pytheas (*c.*310–306 BC), Greek navigator of *Massalia, author of a lost work 'About the Ocean', object of ancient distrust. From *Strabo, *Diodorus (3), and *Pliny (1) mostly we learn that, sailing from *Gades (Cadiz) past Cape Ortegal, the Loire, northwest France, and Uxisame (Ushant), he visited Belerium (Cornwall) and the tin-depot at *Ictis (St Michael's Mount), circumnavigated *Britain, described its inhabitants and climate, reported an island *Thule (Norway or Iceland), sailed perhaps to the Vistula, and reported an estuary (Frisian Bight?) and an island (Heligoland?) abounding in *amber. Pytheas calculated closely the latitude of Massalia and laid bases for cartographic parallels through north France and Britain. See CASSITERIDES.

D. R. Dicks, *The Geographical Fragments of Hipparchus* (1960), 179 ff.; C. Hawkes, *Pytheas: Europe and the Greek Explorers* (8th J. L. Myres Memorial Lecture (1977)). E. H. W.; A. J. S. S.

Pythermus (1), poet, of *Teos, wrote drinking-songs, of which one line survives. He composed in the Ionian mode and was mentioned by *Hipponax (Ath. 14. 625c).

Page, *Poet. Mel. Gr.* 910. E. Kr.

Pythermus (2) of *Ephesus, writing after *Antiochus (1) I or (2) II but probably before the historian *Hegesander (*c.*150 BC), wrote a Hellenistic history in at least eight books. Too little survives for us to be able to draw conclusions about its contents or merits.

FGrH 80. K. S. S.

Pythia See DELPHIC ORACLE; WOMEN IN CULT.

Pythian Games Originally the Pythian festival at *Delphi took place every eight years, and there was a single contest, the singing of a hymn to *Apollo accompanied by the cithara. After the First *Sacred War the festival was reorganized under the control of the *amphictiony, and further musical and athletic contests (see AGŌNES) were added. These games were next in importance to the *Olympian Games, and were held quadrennially in late August of the third year in each *Olympiad. The Pythiads were reckoned from 582 BC. The musical contests consisted in singing to the cithara, cithara-playing, and flute-playing, and the athletic contests resembled those at Olympia. The horse races were always held below Delphi in the plain of *Crisa. The stadium lies above the sanctuary under Mount *Parnassus, and the *gymnasium and *palaestra are near the temple of *Athena Pronaia. The prize was a crown of bay leaves cut in the Valley of *Tempe.

E. N. Gardiner, *Greek Athletic Sports and Festivals* (1910); H. A. Harris, *Greek Athletes and Athletics* (1964); P. Aupert, *Fouilles de Delphes Tome II: Le Stade* (1979); J. Fontenrose, in W. J. Raschke (ed.), *The Archaeology of the Olympics* (1988), 121–40; C. Morgan, *Athletes and Oracles: The Transformation of Olympia and Delphi in the Eighth Century B.C.* (1990). N. J. R.

Pythius of *Priene (4th cent. BC), architect. He designed the *Mausoleum at Halicarnassus and the temple of Athena Polias at Priene, both in the Ionic order. He held the opinion that architects should be well versed in the arts, and objected to the use of the Doric order in sacred buildings because of the complications arising from the spacing of the triglyphs. See ORDERS, ARCHITECTURAL. His books on the temple and the Mausoleum have not survived. (Vitr. 1. 1; 4. 3; 7, *praef.*; Pliny, *HN* 36. 30–1. It should be noted that the spelling of the name in the MSS is very confused. One cannot be quite sure that the architect of the Mausoleum and the architect of Priene are one and the same man.)

M. Robertson, *History of Greek Art* (1975), 448 f., 458; S. Hornblower, *Mausolus* (1982), 227 ff., 323 ff.; J. B. Carter, *The Sculpture of the Sanctuary of Athena Polias at Priene* (1983), 25–43; S. M. Sherwin-White, *JHS* 1985, 70. H. W. R.; R. E. W.; S. H.

Python (mythical) See APOLLO; SNAKES.

Python is said by *Athenaeus (1) (2. 50f; 13. 586d, 595e–6b) to be the author of a short satyr-play (see SATYRIC DRAMA) called *Agen,* produced in the camp of *Alexander (3) 'the Great' on the Hydaspes (in the Punjab) in 324 BC. From the play he cites eighteen lines about the relations of *Harpalus (recently absconded with Alexander's treasure) with the courtesans Pythionice and Glycera.

TrGF 91; B. Snell, *Scenes from Greek Drama* (1964), chs. 5, 6.; H. Lloyd-Jones, *Gnomon* 1966, 16 f. = *Greek Epic, Lyric and Tragedy: The Academic Papers of Sir H. Lloyd-Jones* (1990), 214 ff. R. A. S. S.

Quadi, a German tribe of the *Suebic group, left the Main region (c.8 BC) and went to Moravia; they were closely connected to the *Marcomanni. Vannius established a kingdom between the March and the Waag, but was overthrown c. AD 50, his followers being settled by the Romans in *Pannonia. After a war against *Domitian the Quadi maintained peace till the great Marcomannic wars. Though defeated by Rome, in the later-3rd and 4th cents. they became increasingly less tractable and, often in company with the Marcomanni or *Sarmatae-*Iazyges, made serious raids across the central Danube: *Valentinian I died campaigning against them (375). Later some of the Quadi joined the *Vandals and *Alani and went to Spain.

L. Schmidt, *Geschichte der deutschen Stämme . . . Die Westgermanen*[2] (1938); E. A. Thompson, *The Early Germans* (1965); A. Garzetti, *From Tiberius to the Antonines* (1974), 484 ff.; M. Todd, *The Northern Barbarians* (1975).   F. A. W. S.; J. F. Dr.

Quadrivium See EDUCATION, GREEK, § (3); MARTIANUS MINNEUS FELIX CAPELLA.

quaestiones, Roman tribunals of inquiry into crimes, later standing courts. In the first three centuries of the Roman republic alleged crimes against the state, if too serious for summary action by a magistrate (or perhaps after such action had been blocked by *provocatio), were tried before the assembly. Crimes against private persons were tried by a magistrate, eventually normally a praetor (but murder was originally a matter for *quaestores parricidii*) with a personally selected *consilium* of assessors. A form of civil procedure would have been used, perhaps that involving *sacramentum. By the 2nd cent. BC some political crimes and instances of mass law-breaking with serious public implications came to be handed over to a *quaestio*, at this point an *ad hoc* commission under a magistrate, appointed by the senate or the people or both, which investigated cases laid before it without the need for formal prosecution. See e.g. Livy 9. 26. 2 (314 BC); the *Bacchanalia (Livy 39. 14 f.: 186 BC); the corruption of L. Hostilius Tubulus (Cic. *Fin.* 2. 54: 141 BC) and the murders in the Silva Sila (Cic. *Brut.* 85 f.: 138 BC). Trials of bandits or assassins (*sicarii*) and poisoners (*venefici*) were on a number of occasions subject to a *quaestio* under a praetor or his deputy before permanent courts were set up (c.100 BC).

Meanwhile, a new form of *quaestio*, a standing court (q. *perpetua*), was introduced by L. *Calpurnius Piso Frugi, tribune of the plebs (see TRIBUNI PLEBIS) 149 BC, to deal with *repetundae* cases. Like ad hoc *quaestiones* it was under the presidency and control of a praetor, and the jurors or assessors were drawn from senators, but prosecutions were conducted by the civil procedure of *sacramentum. This court was completely overhauled by C. *Sempronius Gracchus, who substituted a form of denunciation

for the civil procedure, introduced a large non-senatorial jury with full responsibility for verdict and damages, made these damages penal by doubling the amount originally taken, rewarded successful prosecutors, and formulated elaborate regulations for the conduct of the court.

In the next forty years, while *ad hoc quaestiones* continued to be set up for special offences (e.g. the *quaestio Mamilia* of 110 BC, see C. *Mamilius Limetanus), several *quaestiones perpetuae*, modelled on the *repetundae* court were created—apart from those *de veneficis* and *de sicariis*, these concerned *maiestas, *ambitus, and probably *peculatus*. The composition of the juries in the *repetundae* court was changed by Q. *Servilius Caepio (1) in 106, who mixed senators and *equites, but C. *Servilius Glaucia restored entirely equestrian juries, and this was certainly the pattern of the *maiestas* court and possibly others. After an abortive attempt by M. *Livius Drusus (2) in 91 to staff the courts from an enlarged senate, M. *Plautius Silvanus (tribune of the plebs 89) introduced juries chosen freely by the individual tribes (which allowed the selection of those neither senators nor *equites, although doubtless votes tended to be cast for better-known men). *Sulla, increasing the senate to about 600 men, followed Drusus' plan also in entrusting the courts to senators. He brought the number of *quaestiones perpetuae* to at least seven, with a praetor or, since there were not enough praetors available, a *iudex quaestionis* (normally an ex-aedile) in charge of each. When Sulla's juries had turned out to be unsatisfactory, L. *Aurelius Cotta in 70 created three jury-albums (*decuriae*), assigning one to senators (later this was 300 strong), one to *equites, and one to *tribuni aerarii. From these albums juries were chosen by lot (one third from each) for individual trials, with prosecution and defence having a limited right of rejection. The size of juries varied in the different courts. *Repetundae* and perhaps *maiestas* had juries of 75, while in the *quaestio de vi* the jury numbered 51. Procedure also varied. As far as we know, only the *repetundae* court prescribed *comperendinatio*, a trial in two parts and after conviction a separate assessment of damages (*litis aestimatio* (see LAW AND PROCEDURE, ROMAN, §§ 2. 5, 3. 9)).

There was no public prosecutor at Rome, nor were prosecutions initiated by the magistrates in charge of *quaestiones perpetuae* (as opposed to ad hoc *quaestiones*). Originally in *repetundae* cases charges were brought by the wronged individual, a member of his close famiiy, or his chosen representative. Later, as in other *quaestiones*, any private citizen could request authority from a presiding magistrate to prosecute before his court. If several men wished to bring the same accusation against a person, then (from the time of either Caepio's or Glaucia's law onwards) the relevant magistrate held a special pre-trial hearing, in which a panel of jurors, apparently not on oath, decided who should be the accuser (the latter might, however, be backed by *subscriptores*, those who would sign the indictment). This preliminary hearing was known as *divinatio* (thus Cicero's *Divinatio in Caecilium* sought to show why Cicero, rather than Q. Caecilius Niger, should be chosen as C. *Verres' accuser). The authorized prosecutor then formally denounced the defendant to the magistrate (*nomen deferre*), who accepted the charge (*nomen recipere*), interrogated the defendant and, unless the latter pleaded guilty, formally recorded the indictment (*inscriptio*) and fixed the date of the hearing. At the end of the trial the jury gave its decision by majority vote (a tie acquitted). The presiding magistrate did not vote but pronounced judgement and sentence, against which under the republic there was no appeal. Under the majority of late republican statutes the maximum capital penalty seems to have been exile. Senior magistrates and men absent on public business could not be prosecuted in a *quaestio*.

After 70, although numerous laws were passed about individual courts (especially the *quaestio de ambitu*, since electoral bribery proved uncontrollable), the system remained basically unchanged, although it gradually lost importance during the Principate. Special *quaestiones* on the old model are still found in the late Republic, e.g. that on the *Bona Dea affair in 61, and even after *Caesar's murder as a result of the *lex Pedia* about Caesar's assassins (see PEDIUS, Q.); their jury-panels were normally chosen according to the prevailing system, but some were specially constituted in order to exclude intimidation and corruption (e.g. those established by Pompey in 52). Caesar suppressed the lowest *decuria* of jurors; Mark Antony (M. *Antonius (2)) tried to bring it back in a new form, probably unsuccessfully. *Augustus not only brought back the *tribuni aerarii* into his three main panels, but added a fourth panel (of lower census, for less serious offences). *Gaius (1) added a fifth panel, while a further development seems to have been the disappearance of senators from the three chief panels. Augustus also reorganized some of the courts and added one for *adultery. He clearly intended the system of *quaestiones* to continue, and in fact it remained in use during the early Principate and only became completely obsolete in the 3rd cent. AD. However, thanks to the development of senatorial and imperial jurisdiction in major cases (which also made our sources lose interest in the *quaestiones*) and the jurisdiction of the *praefectus urbi* and, later, the *praefectus praetorio* over the lower classes, the *quaestiones* in due course became unimportant and we have little evidence for their working.

Mommsen, *Röm. Strafr.*; A. H. J. Greenidge, *Legal Procedure of Cicero's Time* (1901); W. Kunkel, *Unters. z. Entwicklung d. röm. Kriminalverfahrens in vorsullanischer Zeit* (1962), and *RE* 24 (1963), 720–801, 'quaestio'.
E. B.; A. W. L.

quaestor *Quaestores parricidii* (see PARRICIDIUM) are said to have been appointed by the kings. Under the republic there were two, who prosecuted some capital cases before the people. They fade from our record by the 2nd cent. BC.

Financial quaestors (perhaps not connected with them) were at first appointed by the consuls, one by each; after 447 BC (Tac. *Ann.* 11. 22) they were elected by the tribal assembly. Two were added when plebeians were admitted (421), to administer the *aerarium* in Rome (hence *urbani*) under the senate's direction. Four more were instituted in 267 (Tac. loc. cit.; Livy, *Per.* 15), perhaps called *classici* and stationed in various Italian towns, notably *Ostia (see FOOD SUPPLY). More (we do not know how many and when) were added as various provinces were organized (Sicily even had two), until *Sulla, finding nineteen needed for all these duties, added one for the *water-supply and raised the total to twenty. Caesar doubled this number, but Augustus— proposing to rely less on regular magistrates—returned to it.

The quaestorship was commonly held at the age of 27 to 30 (often—in the late republic normally—after a military tribunate and/or a civil minor magistracy). It was the lowest of the regular magistracies. By the late 2nd cent. BC, most ex-quaestors were enrolled in the Senate, but the size of the Senate did not permit the enrolment of all. Sulla, who doubled the size of the Senate, made quaestors' entry automatic. *Provinciae* of quaestors were normally allotted, but—in a tradition going back to the origins of the office—magistrates could choose a quaestor *extra sortem* for personal reasons. Quaestors attached to magistrates or promagistrates abroad (*militiae*) did not normally serve more than two years: C. *Sempronius Gracchus thought he had been imposed upon by having to serve three. In addition to managing the *fiscus, they had judicial and military duties. When their superior left or was disabled, they were expected to assume command *pro praetore* (see PRO CONSULE, PRO PRAETORE). Quaestors were supposed to remain bound to their commanders in *fides* for life. But their accounts were prime evidence in *repetundae* trials, and some were tempted to apply to prosecute their own commanders, to advance their own careers. They seem normally to have been rejected.

*Augustus and—after a brief restoration by *Claudius—*Nero removed the quaestors from the *aerarium*; but under the empire the *princeps*, as well as each consul, had two quaestors; the *quaestores Caesaris*, chosen by the emperor himself, were often patricians and always young men of distinction. The actual duties of the quaestors in Italy were gradually taken over by imperial officials, but in the public provinces quaestors retained some financial functions throughout the Principate.

Colonies and *municipia* (see MUNICIPIUM), and normally *collegia also had quaestors in charge of their finances. In the later empire the office of emperor's quaestor (sometimes called *quaestor sacri palatii*: quaestor of the sacred palace) grew in importance since he assumed the role of spokesman for the emperor and in particular drafted laws for the imperial consistory. The quaestorship was held by prominent lawyers such as *Antiochus (13) Chuzon and *Tribonianus, the architects of the *Theodosian Code and of *Justinian's codification respectively, but more often by men of literary talent such as *Ausonius and *Nicomachus (4) Flavianus. The quaestor did not have his own staff but could draw on expertise from the imperial offices (*scrinia*).

RE 24 (1963), 801–27, 'quaestor'; W. V. Harris, *CQ* 1976, 92 ff.; E. Badian, *AJPhil.* 1983, 156 ff.; T. Honoré, *ZRG* 1986, 139–56, 181–222; J. Harries, *JRS* 1988, 148–72.
E. B.; T. Hon.

quarries Stone was an important material in both the Greek and Roman periods, not only for building, but also for decoration, sculpture, and vases. Whatever the stone, its geology defines the quarrying methodology and its subsequent uses. The Greeks started to extract stone by quarrying from the 7th cent. BC. Blocks were isolated by trenches using a quarry hammer. Metal wedges were then used to split them from the parent rock. The natural cleaving planes of the stone were at all times exploited. Open quarrying was preferred on grounds of ease and expense. However, if the good-quality material ran out above ground, underground workings were often opened, for example in the marble quarries of *Paros and the limestone 'La Pyramide' quarries near *Glanum. The Romans continued to use the same quarrying methods, also adopting some Egyptian techniques—for example the use of wooden wedges. However, the major difference between Greek and Roman quarrying was the scale of exploitation. The building records from Athens and *Epidaurus clearly demonstrate the piecemeal nature of Greek quarrying. Roman quarrying was carried out on a more modular basis. This can be seen clearly with the exploitation of decorative stones in particular. A system of accountancy was developed in some quarries from the middle of the 1st cent. AD. Inscriptions were carved on blocks indicating the area of extraction and the personnel involved. Often objects were roughed out in the quarry before their export. In the Classical Greek period quarries probably belonged to and were administered by the nearest town. In the Roman period there was much more diversity in ownership. Some marble and granite quarries were owned by the emperor and administered by his representatives. The Egyptian quarries came under the jurisdiction of the military. Quarrying was a skilled activity, but convicts and slaves could form part of the labour-force, presumably carrying out the unskilled tasks. See CARRARA; DOCIMIUM; MARBLE; MONS CLAUDIANUS; PENTELICON.

A. Dworakowska, *Quarries in Ancient Greece* (1975); *Quarries in Roman Provinces* (1983); R. Bedon, *Les Carrières et les carriers de la Gaule romaine* (1984).   H. D.

Querolus, 'The Grumbler', anonymous comedy, also called *Aulularia* ('The Pot of Gold') because of some resemblance to *Plautus' *Aulularia*, and accepted as Plautine in the Middle Ages. Probably written in Gaul *c.*AD 400. In prose, but with many metrical clausulae and verbal echoes of Plautus and Terence, it combines features of their dramatic technique with discourses on religious and philosophical themes. See COMEDY, LATIN.

Ed. and comm. G. Ranstrand (1951); tr. G. E. Duckworth, *The Complete Roman Drama 2* (1942); Schanz–Hosius, § 791; K. Gaiser, *Menanders 'Hydria'* (1977, with a speculative reconstruction of its relationship to plays by Menander and Plautus); L. Braun, *MH* 1984. Bibliographic survey by G. Lana, *Bollettino di studi latini* 1985.   P. G. M. B.

Quietus See AVIDIUS QUIETUS, T.; LUSIUS.

Quinctilius Valerius Maximus, Sextus born in *Alexandria (7) Troas, received the *latus clavus* (senatorial stripe) from *Nerva (*ILS* 1018), and is probably identical with an Epicurean (see EPICURUS) friend of *Pliny (2) the Younger, who served as *legatus Augusti ad corrigendum statum liberarum ciuitatium* ('legate—see LEGATI—of the Augustus (i.e. the emperor, see AUGUSTUS, AUGUSTA, AS TITLES) for correcting the state of the *free cities') in *Achaia, probably not after AD 108–9 (*Ep*. 8. 24).

Syme, *Tacitus*, 84 n.; H. Halfmann, *Die Senatoren aus dem östlichen Teil des Imperium Romanum* (1979), no. 40.   A. M.

Quinctilius (*RE* 28) **Varus**, son of the following. While son-in-law of Germanicus, he declaimed under *Cestius Pius, who commented on his father's disaster (Sen. *Controv*. 1. 3. 10). He fell foul of *Domitius Afer in AD 27 (Tac. *Ann*. 4. 66).

Syme, *AA*, 327.   M. W.

Quinctilius (*RE* 20) **Varus, Publius,** of a patrician family that had been of no importance for centuries. He owed his career to the favour of *Augustus. He was consul 13 BC with the future emperor *Tiberius; like him, Varus was at the time the husband of a daughter of M. *Vipsanius Agrippa. Later he married Claudia Pulchra, the grand-niece of Augustus, and was able to acquire some political influence (his two sisters made good marriages, cf. Syme, *AA*, Table XXVI). Varus became proconsul of Africa

(?7–6 BC; see AFRICA, ROMAN), and then legate (see LEGATI) of *Syria. When *Judaea revolted after the death of *Herod (1) the Great he marched rapidly southwards and dealt firmly with the insurgents (Joseph. *BJ* 2. 39 ff., etc.). Varus is next heard of as legate of the Rhine army in AD 9. When marching back with three legions from the summer-camp near the Weser, he was treacherously attacked in difficult country by *Arminius, whom he had trusted. The Roman army was destroyed in the *Teutoburgiensis Saltus, and Varus took his own life (Dio 56. 18–22; Vell. Pat. 2. 117–20; Florus 2. 30). The defeat had a profound effect on Augustus (the regime noticeably deteriorates in the last few years). Varus was made the scapegoat for the signal failure of Augustus' whole German policy (see GERMANIA). He is alleged to have been grossly extortionate in Syria, torpid and incompetent in his German command (Vell. Pat. 2. 117. 2).   R. S.; E. B.

Quinctius (*RE* 21) **Atta, Titus** (d. 77 BC, according to Jerome), author of *fabulae togatae* (some 25 lines and twelve titles survive) and epigrams (one hexameter survives). Praised in antiquity for his character-drawing and reproduction of female speech.

Schanz–Hosius, i. 144; and see TOGATA.   P. G. M. B.

Quinctius (*RE* 24) **Capitolinus Barbatus, Titus,** was reputedly consul in 471, 468, 465, 446, 443, and 439 BC, but the last three consulships may belong to a different individual. He is attributed campaigns against the *Aequi and/or *Volsci in 471, 468, 465, and 446, but only one triumph (in 468, for the capture of Antium). As 'proconsul' in 464 he reputedly used Latin and Hernican troops (see LATINI; HERNICI) to rescue the consul Sp. Furius Medullinus Fusus, when he was trapped by the Aequi. This anachronistic narrative (further elaborated by *Valerius Antias (fr. 19P.)) duplicates L. *Quinctius Cincinnatus' exploit in 458 and theories that it reflects the workings of the Roman-Latin alliance are therefore highly speculative.

Ogilvie, *Comm. Livy 1–5*.   A. D.

Quinctius (*RE* 27) **Cincinnatus, Lucius,** a *patrician listed in the *fasti* as suffect consul in 460 BC. In 458, according to tradition, when a Roman army under the consul L. Minucius Esquilinus Augurinus was besieged by the *Aequi on Mt *Algidus, Cincinnatus was called from the plough and appointed dictator. Within fifteen days he assembled an army, defeated the Aequi, triumphed, laid down his office, and returned to his ploughing. The story was frequently cited as a moral example, illustrating the austere modesty of early Rome and its leaders. An area on the right bank of the Tiber called the 'Quinctian Meadows' (*prata Quinctia*) was regarded as the site of Cincinnatus' four-*iugera* farm (Liv. 3. 26. 8). He is said to have been appointed dictator a second time in 439 BC during the Sp. *Maelius crisis; Cicero says that it was on this occasion that he was called from the plough (*De sen*. 56). It was this detail that was firmly fixed in the Roman tradition; the historical context was less certain. The campaign of 458 recalls the rescue of C. Minucius in 217, and Cincinnatus' supposedly crushing victory is suspect, since the Aequi returned to the attack again in 457 and 455.

Ogilvie, *Comm. Livy 1–5*, 416 ff.   T. J. Co.

Quinctius (*RE* 43) **Flamininus, Lucius,** brother of following. Augur 213 BC, curule aedile 201, *praetor urbanus* 199. As his brother's legate in charge of the fleet and the Greek coastline (198–194), most of the time co-operating with the fleets of Rhodes and of Pergamum, he used superior force to secure the alliance of the *Achaean Confederacy and of *Acarnania, including

*Leucas (see *ILLRP* 321). During the war with *Nabis he occupied the coastal towns of Laconia. As consul 192 he fought in Liguria (see LIGURIANS), then served as legate under M'. *Acilius Glabrio (1) in Greece. In 184 he was expelled from the Senate by the censors (one of them M. *Porcius Cato (1)) for a moral offence committed in his consulship. He died in 170.   E. B.

Quinctius (*RE* 45) **Flamininus, Titus,** brother of preceding. Born *c.*229 BC, military tribune 208 under M. *Claudius Marcellus (1), then quaestor, probably at *Tarentum, where he held praetorian *imperium* for some years from 205. Decemvir for distributing land to P. *Cornelius Scipio Africanus' veterans 201, he concurrently became triumvir to supplement *Venusia (200). In 198, against some opposition but with the support of the veterans he had settled, he was elected consul and sent to take over the war against *Philip (3) V with a new army and a new political approach. After driving Philip from a strong position in the Aous gorge separating Macedonia from Epirus, he moved towards central Greece against stiff resistance, but with his brother's help forced the *Achaean Confederacy into alliance and now gained some further allies. Meeting Philip late in 198, he demanded the evacuation of all of Greece (unacceptable to Philip at this point), but apparently hinted to Philip that the senate might modify the terms. He instructed his friends in Rome to work for peace if he could not be continued in command and for war if he could complete it; he was prorogued, and the senate insisted on his terms. In spring 197, after gaining the alliance of most of Greece, he decisively defeated Philip by superior tactical skill at *Cynoscephalae. He now granted Philip an armistice on the same terms, which the senate confirmed as peace terms. Advancing implausible excuses, he refused to allow his Aetolian allies to annex some cities promised to them (see AETOLIAN CONFEDERACY). He thus secured a balance of power in the north, but gravely offended the Aetolians, making them eager to welcome *Antiochus (3) III. In a spectacular ceremony (see Polyb. 18. 46) he announced the unrestricted freedom of the Greeks in Europe at the *Isthmia of 196 and persuaded a reluctant senate commission that this pledge had to be carried out if Greek confidence was to be retained against Antiochus, who was about to cross into Europe. He now initiated a diplomatic effort to keep Antiochus out of Europe and deprive him of the Greek cities in Asia Minor. The final settlement of Greece involved a difficult war against *Nabis, nominally as head of an almost Panhellenic alliance. The settlement paralleled that with Philip: Nabis was left to rule Sparta, to secure a balance of power between him and Rome's Achaean allies. In 194 all Roman troops were withdrawn. Henceforth Flamininus was showered with honours (including divine honours) in Greece. He issued a commemorative gold coin with his portrait (*RRC* 548) and left for Rome to celebrate an unparalleled three-day triumph (Livy 34. 52). A bronze statue with a Greek inscription was erected to him in Rome by his Greek clients (Plut. *Titus* 1. 1).

In 193 he was entrusted with secret negotiations with Antiochus' envoys; when they refused his offer of undisturbed possession of Asia in return for withdrawal from Europe, he proclaimed to the Greek world that Rome would liberate the Greeks of Asia from Antiochus. Sent to Greece to secure the loyalty of the Greeks and of Philip, he was partly successful; but *Demetrias, afraid of being surrendered to Philip, became an Aetolian bridgehead for Antiochus. He remained diplomatically active in 191–190, both in the war and in Peloponnesian affairs, handing Messene over to the Achaeans and annexing Zacynthus for

Rome. In 189 he was censor. In 183, sent to Asia on an embassy, he unsuccessfully tried to intervene in Peloponnesian affairs on his way, then took it upon himself to demand the extradition of *Hannibal from *Prusias (1) I. (Hannibal committed suicide.) With the senate working to substitute Demetrius, Philip's pro-Roman younger son, for *Perseus (2) as designated successor, he hatched a plot to substitute Demetrius for Philip as king (see Polyb. 23. 3, cf. 7; Livy 40. 23, denying the charge). The result was Demetrius' execution (181). After this failure he disappears from public affairs until his death (174).

A typical patrician noble, he saw his world in terms of personal ambition, Roman patriotism, family loyalty, and patron–client relationships. He was the first to develop a policy of turning the Greek world—cities, leagues, and kings—into clients of Rome and of himself, nominally free or allied, but subject to interference for Rome's advantage. The Greeks, whom he had liberated, he expected to follow his instructions even without a public mandate. Aware of Greek history and traditions, he attracted many Greeks by charm and tact, but aroused antagonism by unscrupulous trickery. Midway between arrogant imperialists and the genuine philhellenes of a later period, he laid the foundations of the uneasy acceptance of Roman hegemony by the Greek world. See also PHILHELLENISM.

The chief sources are Polyb. 18–23 (with Walbank, *HCP*), Livy 32–40 (with Briscoe, *Comm.*), and Plut. *Titus*. Greek honours for him are collected in *RE*; a supplement on inscriptions by G. Klaffenbach, *Chiron* 1971, 168. Modern works: E. Badian, *Foreign Clientelae 264–70 BC* (1958), see index; 'Titus Quinctius Flamininus' (1970) in *Univ. of Cincinnati Classical Studies* 1973, 271 ff. (summary 323 ff.); *JRS* 1971, 102 ff. (family and background); E. S. Gruen, *The Hellenistic World and the Coming of Rome* (1984), see index; Hammond in *HM* f.); J.-L. Ferrary, *Philhellénisme et Impérialisme* (1988), see index; Hammond in *HM* 3, chs. 20–2.   E. B.

quindecimviri sacris faciundis, one of the four major colleges (see COLLEGIUM) of the Roman priesthood (see PRIESTS). The size of the college increased gradually, starting at two (*duoviri*), reaching ten (*decimviri*) in 367 BC, fifteen, and finally sixteen (though the name remained *quindecimviri*) in the late republic. Like the other colleges, they lost the right to select their own members through the *lex Domitia* of 104 BC, but continued to be recruited by popular election from the noblest families. Their main functions throughout their history were to guard the Sibylline books (Greek oracles, dating supposedly from the reign of King Tarquin (*Tarquinius Superbus), and consisting for the most part of ritual texts, not prophetic utterances; see SIBYL); to consult the books when asked to do so by the senate, particularly in response to prodigies (see PORTENTS) or other disasters; and to provide the appropriate religious remedies derived from them. Their recommendations led to the importation, from the 5th cent. BC onwards and especially in the 3rd, of Greek cults and rituals, over which they maintained at least some oversight. They reached particular prominence in the early empire as the responsible authorities for the *Secular Games, radically reconstructed from the republican series to suit the new regime's ideas.

Wissowa, *RK* 534–43; G. Radke, *RE* 24 (1963), 1114–48, 'Quindecimviri'; H. W. Parke, *Sibyls and Sibylline Prophecy in Classical Antiquity* (1988), 190–215; M. Beard and J. North (eds.), *Pagan Priests* (1990).
                    J. A. N.

Quinquatrus, Roman festival on 19 March which opened the army's new campaign season. Later connected with Minerva: Ov. *Fast.* 3. 809 ff. with Bömer's notes.

Inscr. Ital. 13.2.426 ff., Latte, *RR* 117, 164 n. 5.   C. R. P.

Quinquennium Neronis

Quinquennium Neronis See NERO.

quinquereme (Greek πεντήρης, Latin *quinqueremis*), was a warship rowed by oarsmen arranged in groups of five, perhaps with three banks of oars, one above the other, the top two each pulled by a pair of men, the bottom by one. The details of particular ships are unclear and other possible variations may have been developed. Its origins are uncertain, but it first appears in Athenian naval lists in 325/4 BC (*IG* 2² 1629. 811), and by the end of the 4th cent. BC it could be found in the navies of most Hellenistic states. Larger and heavier than a *trireme, it offered space for more marines, missile weapons, and the Roman boarding-bridge (Latin *corvus*, raven). The Romans adopted it as their main warship in the *Punic Wars, modelling their fleets on captured Carthaginian vessels (Polyb. 1. 20 and 59). After the battle of *Actium it was superseded by smaller vessels. See SHIPS.

L. Casson, *Ships and Seamanship in the Ancient World*² (1986). P. de S.

Quintilian (Marcus Fabius (*RE* 137; *PIR*² F 59) **Quintilianus),** Roman advocate and famous authority on rhetoric. He was born around AD 35 at Calagurris (Calahorra) in Spain. His father seems to have been an orator also (*Inst.* 9. 3. 73), but his relationship to the Quintilianus named by the Elder Seneca (L. *Annaeus Seneca (1)) (*Controv.* 10 pr. 2) is not to be known. The young Quintilian may have been taught in Rome by the grammarian *Remmius Palaemon (schol. on Juv. 6. 452); he certainly attached himself there to the orator *Domitius Afer (e.g. *Inst.* 5. 7. 7), who died in 59. At some point he returned to Spain, if *Jerome is correct in saying that he was brought to the capital by *Galba in 68. Jerome also states that he was the first rhetorician to receive a salary from the *fiscus, a practice instituted by *Vespasian (Suet. *Vesp.* 18). His school brought him unusual wealth for one of his profession (Juv. 7. 188–9). He taught for twenty years (*Inst.* 1 pr. 1), numbering the younger *Pliny (2) among his pupils, and retired with unimpaired powers (2. 12. 12), perhaps in 88, to write his masterpiece. *Domitian made him tutor to his two great-nephews and heirs (4 pr. 2), the sons of *Flavius Clemens, through whom he gained the *ornamenta consularia* (Auson. *Grat. Act.* 31). His wife died while not yet 19, leaving two little sons; the younger child died aged five, the elder aged nine, and his overwhelming grief at these losses is touchingly expressed in the preface to *Inst.* 6. The date of his own death is not known, but is generally assumed to have been in the 90s.

Works 1. *De causis corruptae eloquentiae*, 'On the causes of the corruption of eloquence', not extant (it is not, as was once thought, the *Dialogus*, now firmly attributed to *Tacitus (1)); some idea of its contents can be gained from allusions to it in the *Institutio*.

2. A (lost) speech *pro Naevio Arpiniano* (*Inst.* 7. 2. 24), whose publication Quintilian acknowledges as authentic, as opposed to other speeches circulating under his name. He also defended the Jewish queen *Berenice (4) (4. 1. 19) and a woman accused of forgery (9. 2. 73).

3. Two books on rhetoric, taken down without his permission from his lectures by over-zealous students (1 pr. 7), now lost.

4. The extant *Institutio Oratoria*, 'Training in Oratory', written and probably published before Domitian's death in 96 (note the flattery of the emperor in 10. 1. 91) and dedicated to *Victorius Marcellus; its composition took rather more than two years, after which it was put aside for some time (see the letter to the bookseller Trypho which prefaces the work). It covers the training of an orator from babyhood to the peak of his career.

Book 1 discusses the education of the child, a practical, humane, and fascinating section, and goes on to the technicalities of grammar, which Quintilian clearly found of great interest. In Book 2 the boy enters the school of rhetoric; there is a memorable chapter on the Good Schoolmaster (2. 2), and Quintilian gives a balanced account of the virtues and vices of *declamation, before going on to a discussion of *rhetorikē*, drawing on the prolegomena to Greek rhetorical handbooks. Book 3 names his authorities and goes into much detail on the *status*-lore, besides giving most of what Quintilian has to say on deliberative and epideictic oratory. Books 4–6 take us through the parts of a speech, with appendices on various topics, including the arousal of emotions and of laughter. Invention thus dealt with, Quintilian proceeds to arrangement in Book 7, with much on the different kinds of *status*, and to style in books 8 and 9, full of examples from prose and poetry. Book 10, the most accessible of all, shows how the student is to acquire a 'firm facility' by reading, writing, and imitating good exemplars. The first chapter ends with a famous critique of Greek and Latin writers; Quintilian's concern is to direct his readers towards predecessors who will be useful in the acquisition of oratorical techniques; hence what might otherwise seem strange judgements, brevities ('some prefer Propertius'), and omissions: despite this limitation, many of his dicta have become classics of ancient criticism. The Greek section is derivative; the Latin, in which Quintilian is often at pains to show how Roman writers can stand up to Greek counterparts, is more original. In Book 11 the traditional five parts of rhetoric are rounded off with discussion of memory and delivery; fascinating details of dress and *gesture are here preserved. There is also an important chapter on propriety. The final book shows the Complete Orator, *vir bonus dicendi peritus* (12. 1. 1: 'the good man skilled in speaking') in action, a man of the highest character and ideals, the consummation of all that is best in morals, training, and stylistic discernment; Quintilian's insistence on eloquence as a moral force is here at its most impressive.

Quintilian's style, never less than workmanlike, is not without its variety and power. But it was content that most concerned him. Deeply imbued in Ciceronian ideas, and reacting sharply against the trends of his own century, his great book is a storehouse of sanity, humane scholarship and good sense. Its influence in the Middle Ages was limited by gaps in the manuscripts most widely available at that period: but after Poggio's discovery of a complete text at St Gall in 1416 it grew in fame, and it was important until the end of the 18th cent.

See also LITERARY CRITICISM IN ANTIQUITY; RHETORIC, LATIN; and DECLAMATIONES PSEUDO-QUINTILIANAE.

TEXTS K. Halm (1868–9), an extraordinary achievement; L. Radermacher (1907, 1935, repr. 1959 with additions by V. Buchheit); M. Winterbottom (1970).

COMMENTARIES G. L. Spalding (1798–1816, completed by P. Buttmann after Spalding's death in 1811); supp. vol. by K. T. Zumpt (1829); the 6th vol., E. Bonnell's *Lexicon Quintilianeum* (1834, repr. 1962) is still invaluable. J. Cousin's Budé (1975–80) has useful notes. Bk. 1, F. H. Colson (1924), esp. useful on the *Fortleben*; Bk. 3, J. Adamietz (1966); Bk. 10, W. Peterson (1891); Bk. 12, R. G. Austin (1948, rev. 1954).

TRANSLATIONS J. S. Watson (1856), excellent; H. E. Butler (Loeb, 1921–2), less reliable; J. Cousin (see above).

SOURCES J. Cousin, *Études sur Quintilien* (1936).

CONCORDANCE José Javier Iso Echegoyen (1989).

GENERAL Schanz–Hosius, §§ 481–6; G. A. Kennedy, *Quintilian* (1969); (ed. T. A. Dorey) *Empire and Aftermath* (1975), chs. 4 (M. Winterbottom) and 5 (M. L. Clarke). R. G. A.; M. W.

Quintilii brothers, from the Roman colony of *Alexandria (7) Troas, Sex. Quintilius Condianus and Sex. Quintilius Valerius Maximus, whose father had been made a senator by *Nerva. Their mutual harmony became proverbial and was recalled by *Ammianus Marcellinus: they shared the consulship in AD 151, and held other posts jointly, including a special commission in *Achaia, where they came into conflict with Ti. *Claudius Atticus Herodes (2). Their sons, consuls in AD 172 and 180, held high office, but the family became victims of *Commodus (AD 183), who confiscated their villas outside Rome.

Cass. Dio 71–2; Philostr. *VS*; SHA *Comm.*; Amm. Marc. 28; *RE* 24 (1963), 984–7, 'Quintilius' nos. 22, 27.   A. R. Bi.

Quintus, Hippocratic (see HIPPOCRATES (2)), anatomist and physician of the eclectic school in Rome, in the age of *Hadrian (AD 117–38), and pupil of *Marinus. He founded an important medical school, to which the teachers of *Galen belonged. Later he was driven out of Rome and died in Pergamum. He left no written works, but his anatomical teaching had great influence, e.g. on Galen.   W. D. R.; V. N.

Quintus Smyrnaeus, i.e. of *Smyrna (probably 3rd cent. AD), wrote the 14-book *Posthomerica* (Οἱ μεθ' Ὅμηρον λόγοι), an *epic poem which fills the gap, originally treated by works in the *Epic Cycle, between the *Iliad* and the *Odyssey* of *Homer. Book 1 has no proem, but continues from the last line of the *Iliad*; episodes include the death of *Achilles, the suicide of Ajax (*Aias (1)), the arrival of *Philoctetes, the Wooden Horse and the capture of *Troy, and the wrecking of the Greek fleet. The poem echoes Homeric episodes similar to these, and its diction is modestly innovative within traditional parameters. The influence of *Virgil's *Aeneid* has been suspected but not proved. At 12. 308–13, in a clear allusion to *Hesiod and *Callimachus (3), Quintus claims to have been inspired by the Muses while pasturing his flocks near Smyrna 'on a mountain neither too high nor too low'. The latter detail is a reference to his adoption of the 'middle style', neither sublime nor pedestrian; and the fact that Smyrna was one reputed birthplace of Homer casts doubt on the literal truth of his origin there.

TEXT F. Vian (3 vols, Budé, 1963–9); Bk. 12, M. Campbell, *A Commentary on Q.S. Posthomerica XII* (1981) = *Mnemosyne Supplement* 71.
METRE M. L. West, *Greek Metre* (1982), 177–9.
CRITICISM F. Vian, *Recherches sur les Posthomerica de Quintus de Smyrne* (1959) = *Études et commentaires* 30.   N. H.

Quirinal, the northernmost hill of Rome (see SEVEN HILLS), traditionally occupied by Sabines (see SABINI), and certainly the site of an early settlement, which became one of the four regions of republican Rome. On it were many famous temples, including the age-old *Capitolium vetus* and those of *Semo Sancus (466 BC), *Salus (302 BC), *Quirinus (293 BC), *Venus Erycina (181 BC), and *Caracalla's temple of *Sarapis. Later, the hill was an important residential area; T. *Pomponius Atticus and *Martial lived here, and *Domitian built the *templum gentis Flaviae* on the site of his ancestral home. *Diocletian and *Constantine I erected large *thermae*. The north fringe of the hill was bordered by cemeteries and by the *horti Sallustiani* (gardens of Sallust).

E. Gjerstad, *Early Rome* 4 (1966), 49 ff, 182 ff; Coarelli, *Roma*, 236–9; Richardson, *Topog. Dict. Ancient Rome*, 324–6.   I. A. R.; J. R. P.

Quirinus, a god claimed as Sabine in origin by the ancients (e.g. Ov. *Fast.* 2. 475 ff.). Except that his functions resembled those of *Mars and that he had sacred arms (Festus, 238, 9 Lindsay), we know little of him; he regularly forms a third with *Jupiter and Mars (e.g. Livy 8. 9. 6); his *flamen* is the lowest of the three *flamines maiores* and the third *spolia opima* belong to him (Servius on *Aen.* 6. 859). His *flamen's* activities are known only in the service of other deities (Gell. 7. 77. 7; Ov. *Fasti* 4. 910; Tert. *De Spect.* 5). His festival is on 17 Feb.; his cult-partner is Hora (Gell. 13. 23. 2), of whom nothing is known. He may first have appeared as a local deity of a community on the *Quirinal, but the most plausible etymology is still that of Kretschmer (*Glotta* 1920, 147 ff.), that the name was originally †co-uiri-um, 'assembly of the men', hence also *Quirites*. His function is much debated. Even if he is sometimes identified as Mars, or as the god of the first furrow, a founder assimilated to *Romulus, the most satisfying solution is to see him as a sort of peaceful 'double' of Mars (Serv. on *Aen.* 1. 292), a god of the 'organized social totality' (Dumézil), with its activities both political and military. Dumézil links him with his third function. From the 3rd cent. BC on, he was assimilated to Romulus.

Wissowa, *RK* 153 ff.; Latte, *RR* 113; Dumézil, *ARR* 246 ff.; D. Porte, *ANRW* 2. 17. 1 (1981), 300 ff.; Radke, *Götter*, 276 ff., and *Entwicklung*, 138 ff.; Magdelain, *MÉFRA* 1984, 195 ff.; H. S. Versnel, *Inconsistencies in Greek and Roman Religion* 2 (1992), 332; Ziolkowski, *Temples*, 139 ff.   H. J. R.; J. Sch.

Qumran See DEAD SEA SCROLLS.

rabbis The Hebrew term 'rabbi' which means 'my master', was a term of respect among Jews which by late Hellenistic times seems to have been particularly applied to religious teachers. According to the Gospels, Jesus was called 'rabbi' by some who addressed him. The term is also found in Greek transliteration on epitaphs from the late Roman period. But after AD 70 its main use was with reference to the religious authorities whose sayings are found in the *Mishnah and *Talmuds and who came to dominate Judaism by the end of antiquity.

Later rabbinic tradition attributes the foundation of rabbinic Judaism to the efforts of Yohanan ben Zakkai and a few colleagues in their academy at Jamnia (Yavneh) in Judaea after the destruction of the Jerusalem Temple in AD 70. Rabbis taught primarily in Judaea from AD 70 to the *Bar Kokhba war (AD 132–5), and mostly in *Galilee from AD 135 to c.200. In the following centuries smaller centres of rabbinic activity were found elsewhere in Palestine, especially *Caesarea (2) and southern Judaea, but the main competition to the Galilean schools were those in Babylonia, which was under Sasanian control (see SASANIDS). Evidence for rabbis teaching in any of the Jewish diaspora communities within the Roman empire is sparse.

Rabbinic Judaism differed from earlier forms of Judaism primarily in its emphasis on study as a form of worship. The rabbis of late antiquity evolved a complex legal structure, based on the Hebrew bible and shaping both religious and secular aspects of Jewish life. Legislation evolved partly through *midrash on scriptural passages, partly through sophisticated forms of logical argument similar to those used in contemporary Greek rhetoric.

The stages of development of rabbinic law can be traced from one generation to the next only with difficulty. The evidence is complicated by occasional pseudepigraphic attributions·and by the rabbis' assumption that the law is unchanging, and that the views of each sage were therefore implicit in the sayings of his predecessors. Particular concerns of the rabbis in the late 1st and the 2nd cents. AD according to the extant evidence were the rules for sacrifices in the Jerusalem Temple (already a theoretical topic, since it had been destroyed in AD 70), the sources of pollution, and the correct tithing of agricultural produce. These interests coincide with those of the *Pharisees before AD 70 according to some sources. It is thus reasonable to assume that the rabbis may have continued some of the traditions of Pharisaism, especially since figures revered in the rabbinic sources from the family of Hillel, such as Rabban Gamaliel, are described in other sources as Pharisees. However, it is noteworthy that the rabbis never called themselves Pharisees, preferring the self-designation 'hakham' ('sage'). Whatever the precise relationship between Pharisaism and rabbinic Judaism, it is highly likely that the developed rabbinic theology found in the Talmud differed greatly from the teachings of the Pharisees three or four centuries previously.

The extent of rabbinic control over the Jews of late antiquity is debated. The rabbis assumed that they spoke for all Israel, but they themselves sometimes referred to Jews who did not follow their teachings. One important factor in the eventual supremacy of rabbinic Judaism may have been the rabbis' control of the calendar, an important matter in a religion with a strong sense of sacred time.

Another factor was the role of the patriarch (*nasi*) in Palestine. Confined almost exclusively to the wealthy descendants of the 1st-cent. AD sage Hillel, this post was accorded great prestige within rabbinic circles, although political disagreements between sages and patriarch are also recorded. Judah haNasi, patriarch at the end of the 2nd cent., was the compiler of the Mishnah. By the late 4th cent., if not before, the patriarch was recognized by the Roman state as the main representative of Jews throughout the Roman empire and granted the status of an honorary praetorian prefect. The patriarchate came to an end in AD 429. See JEWS; RELIGION, JEWISH.

E. E. Urbach, *The Sages: Their Concepts and Beliefs* (2nd Eng. edn. 1987); J. Neusner, *Judaism: The Evidence of the Mishnah* (1981); L. I. Levine, *The Rabbinic Class of Roman Palestine* (Eng. trans. 1989); H. L. Strack and G. Stemberger, *Introduction to the Talmud and Midrash* (Eng. trans. 1991; German 8th edn., Stemberger, *Einleitung* (1992)).   M. D. G.

Rabirius (1) (*RE* 5), **Gaius,** an *eques* (see EQUITES), later a back-bench senator, prominent in the action against L. *Appuleius Saturninus. After some earlier attacks on him by *populares* (see OPTIMATES), he was accused of **perduellio* in 63 BC and condemned by *duoviri* (one of them *Caesar) in a revival of an archaic process. *Cicero's speech was probably delivered on appeal from the verdict to the *comitia centuriata*, with T. *Labienus (1) as prosecutor (though the legal details are obscure). The aim was no doubt, as Cicero says, to impugn the Senate's emergency decree, the use of which Cicero foresaw against *Catiline. Having made their challenge, the prosecution preferred to leave the issue in doubt and Q. *Caecilius Metellus Celer, as praetor, no doubt by collusion, terminated the trial by lowering the flag on the Janiculum, which dissolved the *comitia*.

E. G. Hardy, *Some Problems in Roman History* (1924), 27 ff., 99 ff.; W. B. Tyrrell, *A Legal and Historical Commentary to Cicero's Oratio Pro Rabirio Perduellionis Reo* (1978).   E. B.

Rabirius (2) (*RE* 7), **Gaius,** epic poet ranked with Virgil above *Ovid and Tibullus by Velleius (2. 36. 3), and described by Ovid (*Pont.* 4. 16. 5) as 'resounding', but evaluated by *Quintilian (10. 1. 90) with *Albinovanus Pedo as second-rate. Five lines survive, one (quoted by Sen. *De ben.* 6. 31) about the fall of Antony (M. *Antonius (2)); this forms the slender basis for the highly dubious attribution to him of the *Carmen de bello Aegyptiaco.

Courtney, *FLP* 332. E. C.

Rabirius (*RE* 6) **Postumus, Gaius,** son of an *eques* (see EQUITES) C. Curtius, adopted by his uncle C. *Rabirius (1). Inheriting his father's banking business, he placed money throughout the Roman world. For *Ptolemy (1) XII Auletes he procured the vast sums needed to effect his restoration, then went to *Alexandria (1) to recover them. He was appointed the king's treasurer and collected taxes and supplies until the king finally expelled him. After the conviction of A. *Gabinius (2) in 54 BC, Rabirius was prosecuted for receiving part of his spoils, but was acquitted as a result of *Cicero's appealing to the sympathy of *equites* on the jury. He attached himself to *Caesar and by 49 was a senator and ardent Caesarian, becoming proconsul of Asia (47) and serving in the African War. In 45 Cicero reports he was considering a consular candidacy (*Att.* 12. 49. 2). After Caesar's death he attached himself to Octavian (see AUGUSTUS) and procured money for him.

Cic. *Rab. Post.*; H. Dessau, *Hermes* 1911, 613 ff.; Broughton, *MRR* 3. 181. G. E. F. C.; E. B.

race Greeks and Romans were avid observers in art and text of departures among foreigners (*allophyloi*, *alienigeni*) from their own somatic norms. But it is difficult to discern any lasting ascription of general inferiority to any ethnic group in antiquity solely on the basis of body-type. The explanation is partly conceptual: although *Aristotle realized that pigmentation was biologically transmitted (*Gen. An.* 1. 18, 722[a]; see EMBRYOLOGY), popular *anthropology understood cultural variation among humankind in terms, not of nature (i.e. heredity), but nurture, and specifically environment (thus the Hippocratic *Air, Waters, Places* 12. 17–24; see HIPPOCRATES (2)), which shaped 'customs, appearance and colour' (Polyb. 4. 21), the sunny south generating blackness, the north 'glacial whiteness' (Plin. *HN* 2. 80. 189); thus, as *Strabo implies, it was only their poor soil which debarred the Arians of E. Iran from the pleasures of civilization (25. 32). Although profoundly ethnocentric and, along the way, idealizing one somatic norm (Graeco-Roman) over others, this outlook none the less inhibited the emergence of 'white' as a privileged somatic category (with 'black' as its antithesis), as did the fact that both Greeks and Romans defined themselves in opposition to a *cultural* construct, the *barbarian, which embraced mainly peoples of similarly pale skin-tone. A variety of ancient sensory responses can be detected to the physiognomies of Mediterranean blacks (usually from Nilotic or NW Africa and, whatever their hue, classed generally as *Aethiopes*, *Aἰθίοπες*), ranging from the negative (e.g. the description of a negroid woman in the (?Virgilian) *Moretum*, ed. E. J. Kenney, 1984, ll. 31–5; see APPENDIX VERGILIANA) to the admiring (the dignified negroid head-vases of Attic Greek *pottery, or the Mauretanian with skin 'like Corinthian bronze' of a Roman epitaph, *SEG* 40. 397); more problematic is the extent to which ancient colour-symbolism linked blackness stereotypically with the ill-omened—death, demons (in Christian thought), and so on. Less often remarked on are the hints of Roman somatic distaste for northerners, in particular the paleness (*pallor*) of the men and their superior height (Caes. *BGall.* 2. 30. 4; 4. 1. 9). Racism must be distinguished from—even if somatic judgements may form an element in—*cultural* prejudice (ethnocentrism), which by contrast certainly *was* a historical motor in antiquity, shaping (e.g.) a Graeco-Roman *orientalism to an extent, and in ways, which scholars have yet to map fully. See ETHNICITY; JEWS; NATIONALISM.

A. N. Sherwin-White, *Racial Prejudice in Imperial Rome* (1967) (with no distinction, however, between racial prejudice and ethnocentrism); D. Saddington, *ANRW* 2. 3 (1975), 112 f.; J. P. D. V. Balsdon, *Romans and Aliens* (1979), esp. 214 ff.; F. Snowden, *LIMC* 1. 1 (1981), 413 ff. (*Aithiopes*), and *Before Color Prejudice* (1983); L. Thompson, *Romans and Blacks* (1989); P. Bilde and others (eds.), *Ethnicity in Hellenistic Egypt* (1992). A. J. S. S.

Raetia, a Roman Alpine province (see ALPS), including Tyrol and parts of Bavaria and Switzerland. Though small, Raetia was important because it blocked potential invasion-routes into Italy.

Immediately after the south-east Alpine tribes had been defeated by P. Silius Nerva, Drusus (see CLAUDIUS DRUSUS, NERO) and *Tiberius launched a joint campaign of conquest from the south and the west (15 BC). However, the final province was a peculiar hybrid. By stretching from Italy to the Danube, *Raetia et Vindelicia* took in two relatively undeveloped and somewhat dissimilar groups of peoples, the mixed Raeti of the central Alps and the mainly Celtic Vindelici of the *Alpenvorland*. Though an outlying region, the Vallis Poenina (modern Valais), was disconnected from Raetia after *Claudius and before M. *Aurelius, it was replaced by another very distinct area between the Danube and the German *limes, bordering the *Agri Decumates. Raetia's economic and social development was slow and fragile, and seems to have been to a large degree imposed from above (there is evidence for significant immigration from Italy and elsewhere).

The complex nature of the province, and its first-rate strategic importance, are reflected in its administrative and military history. At first managed by centurions posted as *praefecti*, Raetia was made an equestrian province by Claudius (see CENTURIO; PRAEFECTUS; EQUITES, *Imperial period*; PROVINCIA). The procuratorial governors (see PROCURATOR) resided in *Augusta Vindelicorum (mod. Augsburg) and commanded troops: 4 *alae* and 11 *cohortes* (see COHORS) in AD 107 (*CIL* 16. 55), and 3 *alae* and 13 *cohortes* in 166 (ibid. 121). The province suffered badly in the Marcomannic wars, and it was then that the newly raised Legio III Italica Concors (see LEGION) was quartered in Raetia at *Castra Regina, its commanding officer becoming the praetorian governor of the province. During the troubles of the later 3rd cent. when, now lacking the protection of the trans-Danubian *limes* and the *Agri Decumates, it faced barbarian invaders and Gallic usurpers alike, Raetia was returned to equestrian control and was frequently put in charge of battle-group commanders (e.g. *Aureolus, *Carus). Significantly, though under Diocletian its civil administration was divided—between Raetia I (capital probably Curia) and Raetia II (capital Augusta Vindelicorum)—its military command was left in the hands of the *dux Raetiarum* who resided at Augusta Vindelicorum. The lake Constance–Iller–Danube defence-line was developed to protect the now-exposed western corner of the province, but from the beginning of the 5th cent. it was gradually taken over by the *Alamanni.

F. Stähelin, *Die Schweiz in römischer Zeit*[3] (1948); J. Garbsch, *Das Donau–Iller–Rhein Limes* (1970); C. M. Wells, *The German Policy of Augustus* (1972); G. Overbeck, *Geschichte des Alpenrheintals*, 1 (1982); D. van Berchem, *Les routes et l'histoire* (1982); Bayerisches Landesamt für Denkmalpflege, *Die Römer in Schwaben* (1985); H. Wolff, *Ostbairische Grenzmarken* 1986, 152 ff. J. F. Dr.

rainbow See IRIS.

rainfall See CLIMATE.

rape See HETEROSEXUALITY; HUBRIS; SABINI; SEXUALITY; and E. M. Harris, *CQ* 1990; S. Cole, *CPhil.* 1984; S. Deacy and K. Pierce, *Rape in Antiquity* (1997).

Raphia, battle of, takes its name from a town in southern Palestine where *Ptolemy (1) IV defeated *Antiochus (3) III (23 June 217 BC). Ptolemy had 5000 cavalry and 73 African *elephants, but his infantry numbers depend on whether the 20,000 native Egyptians, recruited for the first time, were included in the 25,000-strong *phalanx also mentioned by Polybius (5. 65), or additional: in the former case he had 50,000 infantry, in the latter 70,000; Antiochus had 62,000 infantry, 6,000 cavalry, and 102 Indian elephants. The battle opened with Antiochus' 60 right-wing elephants charging the 40 on Ptolemy's left, and when the latter gave way, Antiochus followed with a successful cavalry attack, led by himself. Antiochus' left was, however, defeated, and as *Demetrius (4) had done at *Ipsus, he rode too far in pursuit, allowing Ptolemy, who had initially been carried away by the flight of his left wing, to disengage himself, and personally lead a successful counter-attack with his phalanx.

Polyb. 5. 82–6; P. Chantraine, *Rev. Phil.* 1951; M. Cary, *History of the Greek World 323 to 146 BC* (1972); B. Bar-Kochva, *The Seleucid Army* (1976), ch. 10.   J. F. La.

Ratae (mod. Leicester), a town of Roman *Britain and *civitas*-capital of the *Corieltauvi. A possible military base was constructed over part of an iron age *oppidum under *Claudius. The town developed after *c.* AD 80, with the street grid dated *c.* AD 90–100. It grew to 42 ha. within its 3rd-cent. walls, although recent excavations show that it was never densely occupied. It possessed distinguished public buildings and was possibly raised to municipal rank in the later 2nd cent. The forum is late Hadrianic; the public baths with exercise-hall (of which the surviving Jewry Wall is part) were built under *Antoninus Pius; and at the end of the 2nd cent. an additional market square with basilica was provided.

M. Todd, *The Coritani*[2] (1991).   S. S. F.; M. J. M.

Ravenna, city of the Po delta (see PADUS), in ancient times in a marshy and lagoonal setting (similar to those of modern Comacchio and Venice), but now on dry land some kilometres from the sea. The earliest excavated remains are of the 5th cent. BC, though an inscribed Etruscan figurine of slightly earlier date is known to come from the site. In the last century of the republic, Ravenna was allied with Rome; it was described by *Strabo (5. 1. 7) as the largest city of the Po marshes, built of wood and criss-crossed by watercourses.

In 49 BC Ravenna was granted full Roman status, probably as a *municipium. Augustus based here the Roman Adriatic fleet (the other main base was *Misenum; see NAVIES), and built a new port to the south of the city, linked to a branch of the Po by a canal, the Fossa Augusta. This port later formed the nucleus of the settlement of Classis (named after the fleet). The city of Ravenna gradually acquired the amenities of Roman city-life: some rich mosaiced private houses, and public buildings including a particularly lavish gateway, the Porta Aurea, built by Claudius, and an aqueduct, built by Trajan.

In 402, when the presence of the *Goths in the Po plain made the former capital Milan unsafe, the western emperor *Honorius transferred the court to Ravenna, chosen because of its secure setting behind marshes. This move transformed the fortunes of the city, which was more than tripled in size, given a new defensive wall, and embellished with the palaces of emperors and their courtiers. Little survives of this late-antique capital, except the many churches built during this period, which are eloquent testimony to the wealth and splendour of the city. Ravenna continued

as an important capital, now of a barbarian kingdom, after the deposition of the last western emperor in 476. Under the Ostrogoths (493–540), two rival church hierarchies (one Orthodox, the other Arian) existed in Ravenna, and some of the finest churches of the city were built or begun (in particular, Theodoric's Arian S. Apollinare Nuovo, and the Orthodox S. Vitale and S. Apollinare in Classe, both paid for by a local banker, Julianus). Because of the later ravages of iconoclasm in Constantinople, Ravenna now contains much the largest and finest group of late-antique church mosaics to be found anywhere in the empire.

Ravenna was captured by Justinian's forces in 540 and served as the capital of Byzantine Italy; however, because of imperial indifference to a distant and beleaguered province, it lost the wealth and importance it had enjoyed in the period 402–540.

F. W. Deichmann, *Ravenna: Hauptstadt des spätantiken Abendlandes*, 5 vols. (1969–89); *Storia di Ravenna*, 1 (ed. G. Susini) and 2. 1 (ed. A. Carile), (1990 and 1991).   B. R. W.-P.

readers, reading See ANAGNŌSTĒS; LITERACY; RECEPTION; and entries listed under WRITING.

Reate (mod. Rieti), a town in Sabine country (see SABINI), on the River Velino, and a place always prone to flooding. *Curius Dentatus brought it under Roman control (290 BC) and, obtaining full Roman *citizenship in 268 BC, it later became a *municipium. Terentius *Varro and the emperor *Vespasian were born there. It was, not, however, a large place.

Rieti e il suo territorio (1981); A. M. Reggiani, *Rieti: Rinvenimenti della città e del territorio* (1981).   E. T. S., T. W. P.

reception 'Our literature is characterized by the pitiless divorce which the literary institution maintains between the producer of the text and its user ... between its author and its reader. This reader is thereby plunged into a kind of idleness—he is intransitive' (Roland Barthes, *S/Z*). 'Reception', in the specialized sense used within literary theory, is a concept of German origin, associated primarily with the Constance school of critics led by H. R. Jauss and W. Iser, and is often now used to replace words like tradition, heritage, influence, etc., each key-word having its own implied agenda. Studies of reception-history (*Rezeptions-geschichte*) are studies of the reading, interpretation, (re)fashioning, appropriation, use, and abuse of past texts over the centuries, reception-theory the theory underpinning such studies. Jauss starts from the proposition, previously advanced within German hermeneutics, eg. in Hans-Georg Gadamer's *Truth and Method* (1960; Eng. trans. 1975), that interpretation always takes place *within history*, and is subject to the contingencies of its historical moment; there is no permanently 'correct' reading of a text, but an ever-changing 'fusion of horizons' between text and interpreter. Thus reception-theory, like other modern theories of reading (including the 'reader-response criticism' associated with the American scholar Stanley Fish, with his dictum that 'the reader's response is not *to* the meaning, it *is* the meaning'), stresses the importance of the reader, within the triangle writer–text–reader, for the construction of meaning. So Horace, as a man, as a body of texts, as an authority for different ways of living, has been diversely read in the west over the last 500 years, by scholars, poets, and 'men of letters', and our current images are shaped in response to that reception-history.

Some scholars argue that the proper meaning of a text is the meaning (meanings?) assigned by its original readers. Ancient theorists certainly stress the response of audiences; Aristotle makes the arousal of pity and fear crucial for tragic effect, while the rhetoricians expound the use of tropes and figures to control more effectively the reactions of auditors. Ancient *literary criticism is in that sense primarily *affective*, more concerned with emotional response than with interpretation. A famous anecdote describes the extraordinary impact of *Cicero's *Pro Ligario* on a reluctant *Caesar (Plut. *Cic.* 39). But we know virtually nothing in detail about contemporary responses to ancient texts, so that appeals to them become circular arguments. Much of the evidence is from late antiquity; we should remember that e.g. *Servius' commentary postdates *Virgil by several centuries (had it been written 200 years later it would doubtless be dismissed as medieval).

Reception-study is necessarily of importance to all classicists, but the nature of that importance can be differently conceived. Reception-study can be seen as a historical study in its own right, casting fresh light on the past and underlining the difference of its reading practices from those of the present (no one today would subscribe to Neoplatonic readings of *Homer (see NEOPLATONISM) or Christian allegorizations of *Ovid). But, by revealing different perspectives on classical texts, it can also change the way we look at the classical world and its productions. The changing responses to antiquity can be seen as strategies for mediating cultural change and (re)negotiating relationships with the past which are significant for the receivers (so, e.g., Virgil was used in the Renaissance to justify princely rule or in the 19th cent. to underwrite British imperialism). Our own readings too are analysable in these terms, readings which have been affected by post-classical interpretations and constructed in turn as a further link in the chain of receptions (e.g. T. S. Eliot's influential view of Virgil was partly based on his interpretation of Dante's Virgil). Reception-theory thus dissolves the distinction between texts in their initial contexts, read 'in their own terms', and the afterlife of those texts, in a way which threatens traditional positivistic attempts to reconstitute 'original' meanings as the only true meanings. To a reception-theorist this dictionary is not a compendium of timeless, unmediated, unsituated 'facts' about antiquity but another small chapter in its never-to-be-stilled reception-history. See also LITERARY THEORY AND CLASSICAL STUDIES.

S. Fish, *Is There A Text In This Class?* (1980); R. C. Holub, *Reception Theory: A Critical Introduction* (1990); H. R. Jauss, *Toward an Aesthetic of Reception* (trans. 1982); R. Lamberton, *Homer the Theologian* (1986); R. Lamberton and J. J. Keaney (eds.), *Homer's Ancient Readers* (1992); C. Martindale, *Redeeming The Text: Latin Poetry and the Hermeneutics of Reception* (1993); C. Martindale and D. Hopkins (eds.), *Horace Made New*, introduction (1993); A. Woodman and J. Powell (eds.), *Author and Audience in Latin Literature* (1992), esp. epilogue.   C. A. Ma.

reciprocity (Greece) The idea that giving goods or rendering services imposed upon the recipient a moral obligation to respond pervaded Greek thought from its earliest documented history. Linguistically, the idea is most commonly signalled by the preposition *anti*, either by itself or attached to a noun or verb.

Reciprocity was one of the central issues around which the moral existence of the Homeric heroes revolved; see HOMER. In the poems, it is consistently implied and sometimes plainly stated that a *gift or service should be repaid with a counter-gift or a counter-service. This need not be forthcoming immediately, and may not be in the same category as the original gift or service. In the long run, however, allowing for slight temporary imbalances, the gifts and services exchanged must be equal in value and bestow equal benefits upon both parties. In making this assumption the Homeric world differs significantly from that of

the Old Testament, in which God rather than the recipient is said to requite both good and bad deeds. Gain, profit, and loss belonged in Homer to the world of traders, or to that of aristocrats engaged in plunder and spoliation. Reciprocity aimed at the forging of binding relationships (see FRIENDSHIP; GREECE; FRIENDSHIP, RITUALIZED; MARRIAGE LAW) between status equals, from which a long series of unspecified mutual acts of assistance could be expected to flow.

The assumption of equivalence did not extend into the realm of hostile encounters. Here there was no taking of an eye for an eye. Instead, what Dover has called the 'head for an eye' principle prevailed: upon being provoked, offended, or injured, the hero was expected to give free rein to his passionate desire for revenge. Although the more peaceful alternative of material compensation for an insult or an injury was also available (see e.g. *Il.* 9. 634), over-retaliation was undoubtedly the norm.

A system of thought striving at equivalence of give and take faces a practical difficulty: how to assess the values of exchangeable items with any precision. It is presumably this difficulty that precipitated the invention, at some time after Homer's day, of *coinage.

The *polis* brought about a threefold change in the operation of reciprocity. Firstly, it turned communal interest into a new standard of individual morality, reinterpreting the norms inherited from the past accordingly. When *Themistocles tells *Artaxerxes (1), 'I deserve to be repaid for the help I gave you' (Thuc. 1. 137), *Thucydides (2) makes it clear that the first half of this reciprocal action gave rise to the suspicion that its other half was to be Themistocles' recruitment to the Persian court. This, in turn, posed a threat to the community to which no Athenian could be indifferent. In Homer no moral norms which compete with the unhindered exercise of reciprocity are visible. Secondly, the *polis* promoted the ideal of communal altruism: the performance of actions beneficial to the community but potentially detrimental to the individual performing them (e.g. nursing the sick during a plague or donating money as liturgies; see LITURGY, GREEK). The pre-*polis* equation dictating equivalence of give and take here breaks down in favour of individual sacrifices for the benefit of the community. (Individual benefit derived from communal benefit is of another order.) Thirdly, the *polis* in general, and Athens in particular, endorsed the ideal of self-restraint as a means of checking hostile encounters. When provoked, offended, or injured, the citizen was expected to refrain from retaliating or taking revenge, relinquishing the right to inflict punishment to the civic authorities.

W. Donlan, *CW* 1981–2, 135 ff.; K. J. Dover, *Greek Popular Morality* (1974); M. I. Finley, *The World of Odysseus*[2] (1977); J. Gould, *Give and Take in Herodotus*, Myres Memorial Lecture (1991); G. Herman, *Ritualised Friendship and the Greek City* (1987); G. Herman, *CQ* 1993, 406 ff., and in R. Osborne and S. Hornblower (eds.), *Ritual, Finance, Politics* (1994), 9 ff., and in W. Eder (ed.), *Die athenische Demokratie im 4. Jahrhundert v. Chr.* (1995), 43 ff.; I. Morris, *Man* 1986, 1 ff.   G. H.

recitatio, the public reading of a literary work by the author himself. The practice certainly originated in Greece, though details are more or less untrustworthy (*Herodotus (1) reading his history at the *Olympian Games, *Sophocles (1) dying while reciting the *Antigone*, *Antimachus being left with an audience of one, *Plato (1)). At Rome we are told that C. *Asinius Pollio 'was the first of all Romans to recite what he had written before an invited audience' (Sen. *Controv.* 4 pr. 2), probably after 38 BC. Horace's allusion to reading his poems to select groups of friends (*Sat.* 1. 4. 73) probably refers to something less formal. The readings of poetry by grammarians, said to have started in Rome after the visit of *Crates (3) in 168 BC (Suet. *Gramm.* 2), are a different matter.

Recitation became common under the empire. We hear of readings of tragedy (Tac. *Dial.* 2. 1), comedy (Plin. *Ep.* 6. 21. 2), lyric (ibid. 7. 17. 3), elegy (Juv. 1. 4) and history (Sen. *Controv.* 10 pr. 8); and the younger *Pliny (2) employed recitation as a stage between delivery of a speech and its publication (*Ep.* 5. 12. 1, 7. 17. 5). A well-to-do author would hire a hall and send out invitations: a poorer poet might make do with a public place. Hadrian's *Athenaeum eventually provided a formal venue in Rome. A recitation might be preceded by a *praefatio* or preamble (Plin. *Ep.* 1. 13. 2). The satirists make fun of the affectation of some performances (Pers. 1. 15–18). Recitation was a good way of publicizing one's work, and Maternus puts it alongside forensic oratory as a means of gaining fame (Tac. *Dial.* 11. 2). But it could be a trial to the listeners (see the end of Horace's *Ars Poetica*), and an audience might show its contempt openly (Plin. *Ep.* 1. 13. 2).

Pliny (e.g. *Ep.* 5. 12. 1–2) regarded recitation as a convenient way of soliciting criticism from educated friends (compare Quintilius' advice in Horace, *Ars Poetica* 438 ff.). But there was a risk of insincere flattery (*Ars P.* 428–31); certainly applause and extravagant compliment were habitual. And recitation, like *declamation, could encourage showy and superficial writing.

J. E. B. Mayor, *Thirteen Satires of Juvenal*[2] 1 (1877), 173–82; L. Friedländer, *Rom. Life*, 3. 38–43; A. Dalzell, *Hermathena* 1955, 20–8.

M. W.

records and record-keeping, attitudes to Greeks and Romans kept records on stone or bronze, lead, wooden tablets (waxed or whitened), papyrus (see BOOKS, GREEK AND ROMAN), *ostraca, even precious metals. The different materials often bear certain associations and reflect ancient attitudes to records: e.g. bronze documents in Athens have religious associations, as do the bronze tablets of Roman laws. Stone inscriptions promised permanence and importance, publicly visible reminders of the decree (etc.) they record: in *Athens, matters of particular concern to the gods went up on stone (e.g. the *tribute lists). Athenian inscriptions (see EPIGRAPHY, GREEK) are read and referred to, but they may also serve as memorials of the decision they record, so that their destruction signifies the end of that transaction (e.g. Dem. 16. 27); inscribed laws are often dedicated to a god. The relation of the inscribed records to those in the archives is therefore complex. Some scholars believe that archival texts are the originals, the inscriptions merely copies, and that there were always archival copies. The situation changes in the Hellenistic period, but the terminology, even then, is inconsistent and inscribed texts are treated as authoritative, indicating a less archive-oriented attitude to records. Archive organization, where we have evidence, is often primitive, and not all archive documents are preserved: in classical Athens certain documents are destroyed when the transaction is complete (e.g. records of state debtors), or for political reasons (e.g. *IG* 1³ 127, 27 ff, for *Samos), or as a *damnatio memoriae*, as in Rome. Certain information was not recorded at all. However written documentation increasingly takes over from memory and oral proof in Athens during the 4th cent., and the archives came to be used more extensively.

Romans generally attach more importance to written record than Classical Greece, and archives are more sophisticated. The public inscriptions, especially those on the *Capitol, have powerful symbolic value, however (see Suet. *Vesp.* 8. 5), as well as being fundamental records: as in Greece, their removal would annul

the transaction they record (e.g. Plut. *Cic.* 34. 1). The extent of centralization may have been exaggerated, and evidence for reforms in the *aerarium imply negligence, falsification, and loss of documents (Plut. *Cat. Min.* 16–18; Dio 54. 36. 1, 57. 16. 2). *Cicero lamented the lack of a proper guardianship and public record of the laws (*de leg.* 3. 20. 46). The extent to which the *aerarium* was really used for reference is controversial; senatorial writers consulted individuals or private records (including private collections of laws) as well as state archives. Political facts may lie behind these differing attitudes to written record. Apart from the *senatus consulta, there were no official records of senatorial business until *Caesar proposed the *acta be published (59 BC, Suet. *Div. Jul.* 20; rescinded, *Aug.* 36). Provincial cities keep their own copies of relevant documents, sometimes not reliably (cf. *Pliny (2), *Ep.* 10. 65–6, 72–3, who sends back to *Trajan for accurate versions). Even in the elaborate bureaucracy of the late Empire, it has been argued (Mommsen) that the *Theodosian Code was partly compiled not from a central imperial archive but from individuals, law schools, and provincial archives.

See also ARCHIVES.

R. Thomas, *Literacy and Orality in Ancient Greece* (1992); M. Beard, *PBSR* 1985, 114 ff.; R. MacMullen, *AJPhil.* 1982, 233 ff.; W. V. Harris, *Ancient Literacy* (1989); T. Mommsen, *ZRG* 1900, 149 ff.   R. T.

recuperatores were jurymen (usually three or five) who acted in the second stage of Roman civil proceedings in place of the single *iudex*. They may have been first established by international treaties for cases involving foreigners (Festus, '*reciperatio*'), but in historical times they were available in proceedings between citizens. An advantage of a trial before *recuperatores* seems to have been its celerity, including the fact that it could be held even on *dies nefasti*, when other judicial business could not be conducted. *Recuperatores* could evidently hear a variety of cases (Gai. *Inst.* 4. 46, 141, 185; and there were others), but no obvious common feature is discernible, save perhaps elements of urgency and public interest. There is much controversy.

B. Schmidlin, *Das Rekuperatorenverfahren* (1963); J. M. Kelly, *Studies in the Civil Judicature of the Roman Republic* (1976); D. N. Johnston, *JRS* 1987, 62 ff.   B. N.

Rediculus When *Hannibal, attempting to raise the siege of *Capua in 211 BC, made a demonstration against Rome, a shrine was erected at Rome to the unknown power which made him go back again, under the name of Rediculus, from *redere*, 'to turn back' (Festus 354. 25; 355. 6 Lindsay). It stood outside the porta Capena, and the deity may have been surnamed Tutanus (Varro, *Sat. Men.*, fr. 213 Buecheler). This connection, however, and even the association with Hannibal are denied by Latte, *RR* 53.

H. J. R.

Red Sea (*Erythra Thalassa*; *Rubrum Mare*). This name, from a legendary eponymous king of the *Persian Gulf, was extended by the ancients to cover all eastern waters, including the Indian Ocean; it specifically referred to the mod. Red Sea and Persian Gulf. The Red Sea proper was navigated by the Egyptians, Israelites, and Phoenicians, and Herodotus (2. 11) was acquainted with its shape; he had also heard about the Persian Gulf (3. 93), later explored by *Nearchus (Arrian, *Ind.*). In an attempt to circumnavigate Arabia, *Alexander (3) the Great sent ships from Suez which sailed as far as Yemen (Theophrastus, *Hist. Pl.* 9. 4. I), and from the Persian Gulf to the Oman peninsula (Arrian, *An.* 7. 20. 7–8). The Ptolemies (see PTOLEMY (1)) opened up the Red Sea completely. Under *Ptolemy I the west coast was explored; under

Ptolemy II forts and stations for elephant-hunts were founded here (see BERENICE (C–D), MYOS HORMOS, PTOLEMAIS (3) THERON). In the 1st cent. BC (74/73, *AncSoc*. 1983, 161 ff.) a *'strategos* of the Red Sea' makes his appearance. It is very likely that a Seleucid fleet used to navigate the Persian Gulf in the 3rd cent. Under the Caesars the Red Sea became an important channel for trade between the Roman Empire and the eastern seas (*India, Sri Lanka, (see TAPROBANE)).

L. Casson, *The Periplus Mari Erythraei* (1989); S. E. Sidebotham, *Erythra Thalassa* (1986); J. Rougé in *AMB* I, 59 ff.   E. H. W.; J.-F. S.

refugees See EXILE.

Regia, traditionally the home of King Numa (see POMPILIUS NUMA), was situated at the east end of the *forum Romanum, between the *via Sacra and the precinct of *Vesta. Under the Republic it was the seat of authority of the *pontifex maximus* and contained his *archives; also shrines dedicated to *Mars (which held the sacred shields carried in procession by the *Salii) and to *Ops Consiva. Excavations in the 1960s revealed that archaic huts on the site were in the late 7th cent. replaced by a stone building around a courtyard, recalling the palaces of Etruria. Rebuilt several times, the structure took on its definitive plan at the end of the 6th cent.; this was then preserved throughout antiquity, despite several reconstructions, notably in the 3rd cent. and again in 148 BC. Following a fire in 36 BC, the Regia was rebuilt in marble by Cn. *Domitius Calvinus, once again on the traditional plan.

F. E. Brown, *Rend. Pont.* 1974–5, 15–36; F. Coarelli, *Il foro romano* 1 (1983), 56–79; Richardson, *Topog. Dict. Ancient Rome*, 328–9.
                    I. A. R.; F. C.; J. R. P.

Regifugium, Roman festival falling on 24 February (Ov. *Fast.* 2. 685 ff., Plut. *Quaest. Rom.* 63 with Rose's notes) associated with the expulsion of the kings (*reges*). Of unclear origins: its calendar note Q(*uando*) R(*ex*) C(*omitiavit*) F(*as*) (when the king sacrificed in the *comitium*) was misunderstood as Q(*uod*) R(*ex*) C(*omitio*) F(*ugerit*) (that the king fled the *comitium*: Festus 310, 346 Lindsay). Of unclear day: the Fasti Antiates (*Inscr. Ital.* 13. 2. 27) place it six days before the March Kalends in the intercalary month; cf. A. K. Michels, *The Calendar of the Roman Republic* (1967), 160 ff.
                                        C. R. P.

Regillus, lake Lake Regillus, the site of an alleged heroic Roman victory (aided by the intervention of *Castor and Pollux) over the *Latini (led by Octav(i)us *Mamilius) in 499 or 496 BC, was in Tusculan territory, perhaps at Prata Porci or Pantano Secco (2 miles north of Frascati). See also POSTUMIUS TUBERTUS, A.

Ogilvie, *Comm. Livy 1–5*, 283 ff.   A. D.

regio, ancient term for the four major subdivisions of the extensive area covered by the republican city of Rome (Livy 1. 43; Varro, *Ling.* 5. 45), perhaps having some relationship to the four urban *tribus, and linked in Roman thought to the belief that Rome had been formed by the union of smaller village settlements in the regal period. *Augustus (probably in 7 BC) divided Rome into 14 *regiones* (as he divided *Italy into 11) as a basis for allotting some administrative competences, such as the fire-brigade (*vigiles). The building-blocks of the new *regiones* were the *vici* or local units of the city population (see VICUS), and the supervision of each *regio* was assigned to various senatorial magistrates (Dio 55. 8), and eventually to specific *curatores*. The regional organization was imitated in *coloniae* and later at *Constantinople. See POMERIUM.

O. Robinson, *Ancient Rome: City-Planning and Administration* (1992).
                                        N. P.

register (esp. Latin), the level of language, especially with respect to vocabulary, appropriate to a particular *genre. Studies have concentrated on poetic rather than prose texts, though there are distinctions between e.g. the speeches of *Cicero and his more colloquial prose letters.

Latin prose and poetry share a common vocabulary: even the most elevated poetic genre, *epic, contains a large proportion of everyday words. There are, however, important differences between (1) poetry and prose and (2) the various genres of poetry.
1. The language of poetry has been distinguished from that of prose by two methods. (*a*) Leumann demonstrated the existence of vocabulary and syntax with a peculiarly poetic colouring, i.e. not found in the 'standard' prose of *Caesar and Cicero. (*b*) Axelson showed that many words or classes of words (e.g. diminutives) occur rarely, if ever, in poetry; these he labelled *unpoetisch* (unpoetic).
2. In selection of vocabulary, Latin poets were influenced by the place of their genre in a hierarchy which ranged from epic at the higher end to *epigram at the lower. In general, the 'higher' the genre, the more poetic vocabulary and the fewer unpoetic words it contains. As well as generic appropriateness, subject matter may also affect vocabulary usage: e.g. the emotive/'unpoetic' *formosus* ('attractive') is common in *Ovid's epic *Metamorphoses* in erotic contexts. Furthermore, though Axelson criticized *Horace in the *Odes* for excessive use of unpoetic words, vocabulary normally avoided in the 'higher' genres is often employed for special effect, e.g. at Verg. Aen. 4. 328 the abandoned *Dido's wish for a 'parvulus Aeneas' ('darling little *Aeneas') gains special poignancy because of the rarity of the emotional/everyday diminutive 'parvulus'. All in all, Axelson's findings have been widely influential as a tool of stylistic analysis.

B. Axelson, *Unpoetische Wörter* (1945); Leumann, *MH* 1947; Wilkinson, *CQ* 1959; G. Williams, *Tradition and Originality in Roman Poetry* (1968); Watson, *CQ* 1985; R. O. A. M. Lyne, *Words and the Poet* (1989).   P. W.

Regnenses See REG(I)NI.

Reg(i)ni (also known as **Regnenses**), a *civitas* of Roman *Britain created from the kingdom of *Cogidubnus. Its capital Noviomagus (Chichester), which lay within an Iron-Age *oppidum*, also has evidence for an early military base. Romanization was early achieved on an impressive scale under Cogidubnus, as indicated by early villas (Fishbourne, Angmering) and the monuments of Chichester, but thereafter slowed down. Apart from the important iron industry of the Weald, agriculture was the basis of the economy; in the 4th cent. the Bignor villa, well-known for its mosaics, grew to great size.

B. W. Cunliffe, *The Regni* (1973); P. Drewett, D. Rudling, and M. Gardiner, *The South-east to AD 1000* (1988).   S. S. F.; M. J. M.

Regulus See AQUILIUS REGULUS, M.; ATILIUS; MEMMIUS REGULUS, P.

relativism See POLITICAL THEORY; PROTAGORAS; SOPHISTS; cf. XENOPHANES.

relegation (Lat. *relegatio*). The relationship between this and *deportatio*, within the generic category of exile (*exsilium*; see EXILE, Roman), is not altogether clear, but *relegatio* covers milder forms of exile. It might be either decreed by a magistrate (from the late republic) as a coercive measure or imposed as a penalty in a criminal trial. In the latter form it had different gradations ranging from mere temporary expulsion to *deportatio* (introduced by Tiberius). This was a perpetual banishment to a particular place (see ISLANDS), combined with confiscation of property and loss of citizenship. Banishment in all its forms was especially a punishment for the higher classes. The lower classes were punished for similar crimes with forced labour or even death. See PUNISHMENT (GREEK AND ROMAN PRACTICE).

See bibliography on EXILE, *Roman*, and Zmigryder-Konopka, *Rev. hist. de droit français* 1939. B. N.

relics, the remains (complete or partial) or property of a dead person (real or fictional) which were imbued with the power to benefit their possessor. Inevitably, the veneration of relics in ancient Greece occurs within the context of *hero cult.

There are numerous examples of relics, which fall into three main categories: first, those put into a certain place on purpose and subsequently worshipped there; second, those brought from one place to another for worship at the latter; third, those found by chance, given an identity, and venerated.

Examples of the first group are (*a*) oikists' tombs (Graham, 29–30), (*b*) the tombs of fallen warriors (e.g. the fallen at Plataea; see PLATAEA, BATTLE OF (Plut. *Arist.* 21. 3–6 (332A–C)); Glaucus at *Thasos (Grandjean, 469–70 and 483; Pouilloux, 31–42)); in the second group belong (*a*) the bones of *Orestes brought to Sparta from *Tegea (Hdt. 1. 67–8), (*b*) those of *Melanippus to Sicyon from Thebes (Hdt. 5. 67), (*c*) those of *Theseus from *Scyros to Athens (Plut. *Thes.* 36. 1–4 (17B–C), cf. Kearns, 168–9); of the third (*a*) the so-called tombs of the *Seven against Thebes at *Eleusis (first mentioned by Aeschylus, *Eleusinioi*, *TrGF* 3. 175–6; these were probably the MH tombs disturbed in the Geometric period, walled in and venerated: Mylonas, 62), (*b*) the 'sceptre of *Agamemnon' found near *Chaeronea (Paus. 9. 40. 11–12). On tomb cult in general, see Alcock. See also RHESUS, bibliog.

The practice goes back at least to the Geometric period, persisted throughout antiquity, and has survived within the Catholic and Orthodox churches (Bentley).

S. E. Alcock, *AJArch.* 1991, 447–67; J. Bentley, *Restless Bones: The Story of Relics* (1985), esp. 40–1; A. J. Graham, *Colony and Mother City in Ancient Greece* (1964); Y. Grandjean, *Études thasiennes* 12. 2 (1988); E. Kearns, *The Heroes of Attica* (1989); G. E. Mylonas, *Eleusis and the Eleusinian Mysteries* (1961); R. Pfister, *Der Reliquienkult im Altertum* (1909 and 1912); J. Pouilloux, *D'Archiloque à Plutarque* (1986). A. Sch.

religion, Aetolian See AETOLIAN CULTS AND MYTHS.

religion, Anatolian See ANATOLIAN DEITIES.

religion, Arcadian See ARCADIAN CULTS AND MYTHS.

religion, Argive See ARGOS (2), *Cults*.

religion, Athenian See ATTIC CULTS AND MYTHS, and Parker, *ARH*.

religion, Boeotian See BOEOTIA, CULTS.

religion, Celtic The three main sources for Celtic religion are Romano-Celtic epigraphy and iconography, the comments of classical authors, and insular Celtic tradition as represented by recorded Irish and Welsh literature. The problem they pose the modern observer is one of reconciling their very different *modalités* and frames of reference, and of matching insular myth to Romano-Celtic image. The iconography is largely derived from Graeco-Roman models and reflects the considerable element of religious and cultural *syncretism which obtained throughout the Romano-Celtic areas. More importantly, on mainland Europe it lacks the verbal tradition which provided its ideological context but which, being unwritten, perished along with the Celtic languages. In Ireland, however, and to a lesser

extent in Wales, a rich vernacular literature has survived in writing, much of which is concerned with mythico-heroic tradition and with socio-religious institutions and ideology. But since in the pre-Norman period the writing of the vernacular was virtually confined to the monasteries, one must reckon with the fact that the extant corpus, though in many ways deeply conservative, has nevertheless been passed through the filter of monastic, biblically-oriented, scholarship. Among the areas of pre-Christian belief and practice which seem to have best survived this process of selection and adaptation are mythico-heroic narrative in general and those traditions associated with certain key institutions such as the sacral kingship which, subject to the necessary adjustment, were accommodated under the new dispensation. One important factor in this regard was the existence of a highly organized oral learning maintained by three orders of practicians headed by the priestly fraternity of the druids and apparently replicated throughout the Celtic world. While the druids were eliminated by the Romans in Britain and displaced by Christianity in Ireland, the other two orders—the Gaulish *'vates' and bards—survived into the late Middle Ages in Ireland and Wales as privileged praise-poets maintaining the residual ideology and ritual of sacral kingship.

*Caesar (*BGall.* 6. 7) names five principal gods of the Gauls—not a complete catalogue—together with their functions; unfortunately, he follows the *interpretatio Romana* in referring to them by the names of their nearest Roman equivalents. Similarly in many of the Romano-Celtic dedications the deity is assigned a Roman name, often accompanied by a native name or epithet, and since many of the latter are either infrequent or regional in distribution, some scholars have assumed that the Celtic gods as a whole were local and tribal, not national. But there is reason to believe that in many instances the Roman name conceals a Celtic equivalent with the by-name or epithet referring to a local form of a more extended cult. What is certain is that there were gods whose cults were either pan-Celtic or enjoyed wide currency among the Celtic peoples. Caesar's Mercurius is the god †Lugus, personification of kingship and patron of the arts, whose name is commemorated in place-names throughout Europe and survives in medieval Irish and Welsh literature as Lugh and Lleu respectively, and whose festival of Lughnasa is still widely celebrated. His Minerva corresponds to the multi-functional goddess best known as the Irish Brigit and British †Brigantī/Brigantia, patron deity of the *Brigantes. The horse goddess *Epona has several insular equivalents, including Welsh Rhiannon, 'Divine Queen', and Irish Macha, eponym of Armagh, the future ecclesiastical metropolis. The divine triad of Father, Mother, and Son is attested throughout the Celtic realm, with names which are substantially equivalent. Such deities indicate a greater degree of religious homogeneity among the Celtic peoples than might appear from the wide disparity of our sources, and this is borne out by the evidence of a common fund of themes, concepts, and motifs attested by insular story, continental sculpture, and classical commentator, or indeed by language and toponymy: the remarkable prevalence of triadic grouping, for example, or the cult of the centre, whether within the tribal kingdom or the greater cultural nation. Most of the Celtic gods and many of their myths are recognizably Indo-European, as has been demonstrated by Georges Dumézil and his disciples and others less committed to his trifunctional theory; in this regard it may be noted that the functions of the Celtic gods are less clearly differentiated in the literary sources than in Caesar's succinct, schematic version. The goddesses are more closely linked to land and locality: in general, as with the *matres* in particular, they promote fertility, and as a personification of a given territory, e.g. Ireland or one of its constituent kingdoms, the goddess participates in the *hieros gamos* (see MARRIAGE, SACRED) which legitimizes each new king, a sacred union which may form part of the symbolism of the many divine couples of Romano-Celtic iconography. Some of the more popular and widespread elements of pagan Celtic belief and ritual, such as pilgrimage, healing wells, and the rich mythology of the otherworld, were easily assimilated to the Christian repertoire or survived under the protective guise of folk culture. See CELTS.

J. Zwicker, *Fontes Historiae Religionis Celticae* (1934–5); M.-L. Sjoestedt, *Gods and Heroes of the Celts*, trans. (1949); J. Vendryes, *Mana* 2. 3 (1948); Jan de Vries, *Keltische Religion* (1961); A. Ross, *Pagan Celtic Britain: Studies in Tradition and Iconography* ((1967); E. Thevenot, *Divinités et sanctuaires de la Gaule* (1968); Paul-Marie Duval, *Les dieux de la Gaule* (1976); F. Le Roux, Chr.-J. Guyonvarc'h, *Les Druides* (1986).   P. MacC.

religion, Corinthian See CORINTHIAN CULTS AND MYTHS.

religion, Cretan See CRETAN CULTS AND MYTHS.

religion, Egyptian See EGYPTIAN DEITIES.

religion, Etruscan Our information comes from archaeological evidence (reliefs, tomb paintings, statues, mirrors, altars, temples, funerary urns) and Etruscan inscriptions, especially the 'liturgical' texts such as the linen wrappings on the Zagreb (Agram) mummmy (a ritual calendar) and the Capua tile (a list of sacrifices). Aulus *Caecina, *Tarquitius Priscus (both of Etruscan origin), *Nigidius Figulus, and Fonteius Capito produced at the end of the Republic antiquarian treatises containing translations from Etruscan ritual books; in the Empire Umbricius Melior in the 1st and *Cornelius Labeo in the 3rd dealt cent. with the Etruscan discipline. The surviving fragments often show a curious mixture of Etruscan, Egyptian, and Chaldaean tenets, and of Hellenistic and Neoplatonic philosophy. Of extant authors especially important are Cicero (*Div.*; *Har. Resp.*), *Martianus Capella, and Johannes *Lydus; and there are scattered notices in *Varro, L. *Annaeus Seneca (2), the elder *Pliny (1), *Pompeius Festus, *Arnobius, *Macrobius, *Fulgentius, and the *Scholia on *Virgil.

Etruscan religion, unlike Greek and Roman, was a revealed religion. The revelation was ascribed to the semi-divine seer *Tages, and to the *nymph Vegoia (Begoe, Etr. *Vecui(a)*). Their teaching, with later accretions, formed a code of religious practices, *Etrusca disciplina*. It included *libri haruspicini*, *fulgurales*, and *rituales* (Cic. *Div.* 1. 72; 2. 49). See HARUSPICES.

The haruspical books dealt with inspecting the entrails (*exta*) of victims, especially the liver. A bronze model of a sheep's liver found near Piacenza (*Placentia) has its convex side divided into 40 sections (16 border, 24 inner), inscribed with the names of some 28 deities. The liver reflected the heavens. Its sections corresponded to the abodes of the gods in the sky (esp. the 16 border sections to the 16 regions of the celestial *templum*; Plin. *HN* 2. 143–4; Mart. Capella, 1. 41–61, whose description of the dwelling-places of the gods shows striking parallels with the regions of the liver), and thus the haruspex distinguishing the favourable and inimical part of the liver (*pars familiaris* and *hostilis*) and paying attention to the slightest irregularities was able to establish which gods were angry, which favourable or neutral, and what the future held.

The fulgural books concerned the interpretation of thunder (bolt) and lightning (*fulgur*, *fulmen*); the portentous meaning depended on the part of the sky from which they were coming. Nine gods threw thunderbolts (*manubiae*), Jupiter (*Tin*) three kinds: foretelling and warning (*praesagum* or *consiliarium*), frightening (*ostentatorium*), and destroying (*peremptorium*). The first he sent alone, the second on the advice of his counsellors (*Consentes Di*), and the third with the approval of *dei superiores et involuti*, 'the higher and veiled gods' = the Fates (Sen. *QNat.* 2. 41). There existed various other subdivisions of thunderbolts, but the 'brontoscopic calendar' indicating the significance of thunderbolts for every day of the year (preserved by Lydus, *Ost.* 27–38, and attributed to Nigidius) appears to exhibit rather Chaldaean than Etruscan wisdom.

The ritual books contained 'prescriptions concerning the founding of cities, the consecration of altars and temples, the inviolability (*sanctitas*) of ramparts, the laws relative to city gates, also how tribes (*tribus*), *curiae*, and centuries are distributed, the army constituted and ordered, and other things of this nature concerning war and peace' (Festus, *Gloss. Lat.* 386). The *libri Acheruntici* dealt with the underworld, and the *Ostentaria* were the manuals for the interpretation of portents.

The Etruscan word for 'god' is *ais* (pl. *aiser*). We know a great number of Etruscan deities, but their functions and relations often remain obscure. They mostly bear Etruscan names, but were early subjected to Greek influences. The highest was the thundergod *Tin*/*Tinia* (*Zeus/*Jupiter); there is no compelling evidence that he formed with *Uni* (*Juno) and *Men(e)rva* (*Minerva, assimilated to *Athena) a triad worshipped in tripartite temples (as on the *Capitol). *Voltumna (*Velthumna*, *Vortumnus/*Vertumnus*), perhaps = *Tin* of *Volsinii, presided over the league of twelve Etruscan cities. *Cath*/*Cavtha* and *Usil* were solar deities (cf. HELIOS; SOL), *Cel* a goddess of Earth (Ge, *Gaia Tellus) and *Thesan* of dawn (*Eos, Aurora), *Tiv* a moon god, and *Neth*/*Nethuns* (*Neptunus) a water god. *Vetis*/*Veive* corresponded to *chthonian *Vediovis*/*Veiovis*, but *Maris* (a youthful male deity) was not a counterpart of *Mars (as a war-god there appears *Lar*/*Laran*), and *Velch*/*Velchans* (originally a vegetation god?) was assimilated only late to Vulcan (*Volcanus). It was *Sethlans* who was identified with *Hephaestus, *Turms* with *Hermes, *Fufluns* with *Dionysus (who also appears as *Pacha* = Bacchus), and *Turan* (a mother goddess) with *Aphrodite. *Apollo (*Aplu*), *Artemis (*Aritimi*/*Artumes*), and *Heracles (*Hercle*) kept their Greek names, but sometimes assumed new features. In the tablets from *Pyrgi *Uni* is conflated with the Punic Astarte (perhaps corresponding to Roman Mater Matuta). Most prominent were various underworld and funerary deities: *Thanr*, *Calu*, and their attendants *Charun* (*Charon (1)) and *Tuchulcha*, and the female winged demon *Vanth*.

Etruscan religious expertise made a lasting impression upon the Romans. Livy (5. 1. 6) called the Etruscans 'a nation (*gens*) more than any other devoted to religious rites, all the more as it excelled in the art of practising them'. The Christian *Arnobius proclaimed Etruria *genetrix et mater superstitionum*, 'begetter and mother of superstitions' (*Adv. Nat.* 7. 26).

C. O. Thulin, *Die etruskische Disciplin* (1905–6, 1909, repr. 1968); S. Weinstock, *JRS* 1946, 101 ff. (Martianus Capella and the cosmic system), *PBSR* 1950, 44 ff. (*libri Tagetici*), *PBSR* 1951, 122 ff. (*libri fulgurales*); M. Pallottino, *Testimonia Linguae Etruscae*[2] (1968), *The Etruscans* (1978); A. J. Pfiffig, *Studien zu den Agramer Mumienbinden* (1963), *Religio Etrusca* (1975), *Akten des Kolloquiums 'Die Göttin von Pyrgi'* (1981); L. Bonfante (ed.), *Etruscan Life and Afterlife* (1986); I. Krauskopff, *Todesdämonen und Totengötter im vorhellenistischen Etrurien* (1987); L. B. Van der Meer, *The Bronze Liver of Piacenza* (1987); A. Valvo, *La 'Profezia di Vegoia'* (1988); E. Simon, *Die Götter der Römer* (1990).   J. H.; J. L.

religion, Greek Despite the diversity of the Greek world, which is fully reflected in its approach to things divine, the cult practices and pantheons current among different communities have enough in common to be seen as essentially one system, and were generally understood as such by the Greeks. This is not to say that the Greeks were familiar with the concept of 'a religion', a set of beliefs and practices espoused by its adherents as a matter of conscious choice, more or less to the exclusion of others; such a framework was not applied to Greek religion before late antiquity, and then under pressure from Christianity. Boundaries between Greek and non-Greek religion were far less sharp than is generally the case in comparable modern situations, but they were perceived to exist. The tone is set by *Herodotus (1) (8. 144. 2), who characterizes 'Greekness' (τὸ ἑλληνικόν) as having common temples and rituals (as well as common descent, language, and customs). Thus, despite his willingness to identify individual Persian or Egyptian deities with Greek ones (a practice followed by most Greek ethnographers), and indeed despite his attribution of most of the system of divine nomenclature to the Egyptians (2. 50–2), he still sees a body of religious thought and practice which is distinctively Greek. Many modern scholars go further and see a certain overall coherence in this body which enables us to speak of a 'system' despite the lack of formal dogma or canonical ritual.

Origins The system, then, as known to Herodotus, had clearly developed over a long period. The origins of some ritual acts may even predate the human species itself. More definitely, we can clearly trace some Greek deities to *Indo-European origins: *Zeus, like *Jupiter, has evolved from an original Sky Father, while the relation between the *Dioscuri and the Aśvins, the twin horsemen of the Vedas, is too close for coincidence. Another source of input will have been the indigenous religious forms of Greece, originating before the arrival of Greek-speakers. Sorting such elements from 'Greek' ones in the amalgam we call Minoan-Mycenaean religion is an impossible task; it is easier to trace Minoan-Mycenaean elements in the religion of later periods. See RELIGION, MINOAN AND MYCENAEAN. Most obviously, many of the names of the major Greek gods are found already in Linear B (see MYCENAEAN LANGUAGE), but recent discoveries also indicate that some elements of classical cult practice have their roots in this period. It remains true, however, that the total complex of cult presents a very different aspect.

At various periods the religion of Greece came under substantial influence from the Near East. Much in the traditions of creation and theogony represented for us in *Hesiod has very striking parallels in several West Asian sources, probably reflecting contact in the Minoan-Mycenaean period. Cult practice, however, does not seem to have been open to influence from the east much before the Geometric period, when we begin to find the construction of large temples containing cult images, a form which is likely to owe more to Near Eastern/West Semitic culture than to the Bronze Age in Greece. Elements of the classical form of sacrificial ritual can also be derived from the east. A final 'source' for later Greek religion is formed by the poems of *Homer and Hesiod, who though they did not, as Herodotus claims, give the Gods their cult titles and forms (2. 53. 2), certainly fixed in Greek consciousness a highly anthropomorphic and more or less stable picture of divine society, a pattern extremely influential throughout antiquity despite its frequent incompatibility with ritual practices and local beliefs.

General characteristics Turning to the analysis of Greek religion as it appears in the post-Geometric period, we find in common with most pre-modern societies a strong link between religion and society, to the extent that the sacred/secular dichotomy as we know it has little meaning for the Greek world. Greek religion is community-based, and to the extent that the *polis forms the most conspicuous of communities, it is therefore *polis*-based. The importance of this connection began to wane somewhat in the Hellenistic period and later, but to the end of antiquity it remains true to say that Greek religion is primarily a public religion rather than a religion of the individual. Reciprocally, religious observances contributed to the structuring of society, as kinship groups (real or fictitious), local habitations, or less obviously related groups of friends constructed their corporate identity around shared deities and cults. One major difference in the socio-religious organization of Greece from that of many other cultures concerns priestly office, not in the Greek world a special status indicating integration in a special group or caste, but rather parallel to a magistracy, even where, as often, a particular priesthood is hereditary. See PRIESTS.

Cult Specific religious practices are described more fully under separate headings (see also RITUAL); the following is a very brief résumé. Probably the central ritual act in Greek cult, certainly the most conspicuous, is animal *sacrifice, featured in the overwhelming majority of religious gatherings. Its overlapping layers of significance have been much debated, but it is clear that sacrifice relates both to human–divine relations (the celebration of and offering to a deity) and to a bonding of the human community (the shared sacrificial meal). The act might take place at most times, but on certain dates it was celebrated regularly at a particular sanctuary, usually in combination with a special and distinctive ritual complex; the word '*festival' is loosely but conveniently applied to such rites, whether panhellenic like the *Olympian Games (see PANHELLENISM) or intimate and secret like the *Arrephoria in Athens. Festivals, at least those of the more public type, articulated the calendar year and provided an opportunity for communal recreation. A more specialized type of gathering was provided by rites known as *mysteries, participation in which was usually felt to confer special benefits, often a better fate after death. Secrecy was a prominent characteristic of these rites, and the experience was often a profoundly emotional one. There were of course more basic methods of communicating with the divine. Most obviously, *prayer was an indispensable part of any public ritual, but was also used on other occasions, often by individuals. *Votive offerings were a very common individual religious act throughout the Greek world. On a day-to-day basis, individuals would greet deities whose shrines they were passing, and might also show piety by garlanding an image or making a personal, unscheduled sacrifice—often bloodless, consisting of *cakes or other vegetarian foods, or a pinch of incense. Sometimes they might experience a divine *epiphany in the form of a dream or a waking vision. Both individuals and *poleis* might make use of various types of *prophecies; methods were very various, but generally the process was understood as another form of divine–human communication.

Gods and other cult figures The pantheon certainly showed some local variations, but presented a recognizable picture throughout the Greek world. Zeus, *Demeter, *Hermes, for instance, were names to which any Greek could respond. Again, the fundamental qualities or 'personality' of a deity remained to some extent consistent across different areas of Greece, but exceptions spring readily to mind; *Persephone (Kore), typically an underworld goddess, is at *Locri Epizephyrii more concerned with human fertility and the life of women, while the normally strong connection of *Artemis with her brother *Apollo is virtually absent in her Arcadian manifestations (see ARCADIAN CULTS AND MYTHS). Looking at this another way, we might speak of a multiplicity of deities in different locations, who share their name with others of partially similar character. This analysis, although incomplete, accounts better for the existence of certain local deities who are not, or not completely, identified with the great Panhellenic gods. Thus for instance at Aegina and elsewhere we find *Damia and Auxesia, clearly goddesses very roughly of the Demeter-Kore type, but too different to be readily identified with them. Cretan *Britomartis appears both as herself and as a form of Artemis. More generally, we might ask in what sense, and to what extent, *Hera of *Samos is identical with Hera of *Argos (2), or indeed within the same city whether Apollo Pythios is 'the same' god as Apollo Agyieus. From one point of view it could be said that every sanctuary housed a 'different' god. On the other hand, the desire to schematize was clearly a strong centripetal force, as was the anthropomorphizing concept of the gods exemplified and promoted by the Homeric poems and their milieu. The boundaries of divine individuality could be drawn in quite different ways depending on context and circumstance.

An anthropomorphic view of the Gods also encouraged a concept of a divine society, probably influenced by west Asian models and very prominent in Homer. Prayer formulae locate deities in their sanctuaries or favourite place on earth, but much mythology creates a picture of a group of Gods living more or less together in (albeit rather eccentric) family relationships. Since their home was traditionally *Olympus (1), the Gods most prone to this presentation were the 'Olympians', by and large those who were most widely known and worshipped. Sometimes these deities were schematized into the 'Twelve Gods', a group whose composition varied slightly and might include such figures as *Hades/Pluto (widely known, but not situated on Olympus) and *Hestia, the hearth (Olympian, but scarcely personified), whose presence is due to their Homeric or Hesiodic status as siblings of Zeus. (The twelve on the *Parthenon frieze are *Aphrodite, Apollo, *Ares, Artemis, *Athena, Demeter, Dionysus, *Hephaestus, Hera, Hermes, *Poseidon, Zeus.) However, any local pantheon would also exhibit deities who were not so universally known or who, though the object of widespread cult, were scarcely perceived as personal mythological figures. As examples of the former we could adduce Eleusinian *Da(e)ira or Arcadian *Despoina; of the latter, such well-known divinities as *Gaia/Ge (who seems scarcely affected by her presentation in Hesiod) and *Kourotrophos. There were also 'new', 'foreign' Gods such as *Adonis or *Sabazius who were difficult to place in the pre-existing framework of divine personalities; and there were deities like the *Cabiri who had a Panhellenic reputation although their cult remained confined to a very few locations. More localized still were the 'minor' figures of cult such as *nymphs and heroes (see HERO-CULT), for here there was much less tendency to assimilate figures with others more universally known. True, local heroes were sometimes identified with characters in Panhellenic mythology, but such identifications often remained speculative and were by no means the invariable rule. Nymphs and heroes were generally thought of as residing in one specific place, and though in that place their powers were often considerable, they were usually perceived as ranking lower than gods. They were however a characteristic and indispensable part of the circle of superhuman beings.

Later developments The above sketch is based mainly on evidence from before the 3rd cent. BC. Much of the picture is applicable also to Greece in the Hellenistic and Roman periods; religious thought and practice were constantly evolving rather than undergoing sudden transformation. But during the period of *Alexander (3) the Great and his successors, the Greek world acquired a vastly greater geographical extent, and at the same time the significance of the *polis* was gradually changing. These changes inevitably had an influence on religious development. Overall, it seems that many distinctive local practices were giving way to wider trends. It is easy to exaggerate the extent to which this occurred; *Pausanias (3), writing in the 2nd cent. AD, still found a vast diversity of cult in old Greece. On the other hand, it is undeniable that the worship of certain 'new' deities was steadily gaining in popularity over the Greek world as a whole. One of the most spectacular examples is the cult of *Tyche (Chance, Fortune), while also conspicuous in the later period were Egyptian and Anatolian deities such as *Isis, *Sarapis, and *Men, whose cults showed a large admixture of Greek elements. The payment of divine honours to rulers (see RULER-CULT), originating with Alexander, soon became standard, modifying pre-existing religious forms in a new direction.

Only a small selection of general works is given here. A selective bibliography (to 1985; supplements to follow) is *Mentor: guide bibliographique de la religion grecque* (1992: Kernos suppl. 2). W. Burkert, *Greek Religion* (1985; Ger. orig. 1977); J. Rudhardt, *Notions fondamentales de la pensée religieuse et actes constitutifs du culte dans la Grèce classique²* (1992); L. Gernet and A. Boulanger, *Le génie grec dans la religion²* (1970); A. Brelich, *I greci e gli déi* (1985); J-P. Vernant, in M. Eliade (ed.), *The Encyclopaedia of Religion*, 6 (1987), 99–118; L. Bruit Zaidman and P. Schmitt Pantel, *Religion in the Ancient Greek City* (1992; Fr. orig. 1989); J. N. Bremmer, *Greek Religion* (G&R Survey, 1994). Sources: much epigraphic documentation in F. Sokolowski, *Lois sacrées de l'Asie mineure* (1955), *Lois sacrées: supplément* (1962), and *Lois sacrées des cités grecques* (1969). Translations of epigraphic and literary sources in D. G. Rice and J. E. Stambaugh, *Sources for the Study of Greek Religion* (1979). Older encyclopaedic works, still useful: L. R. Farnell, *The Cults of the Greek States* (5 vols., 1896–1909); P. Stengel, *Die griechischen Kultusaltertümer³* (1920); M. P. Nilsson, *Geschichte der griechischen Religion* (1³. 1967; 2², 1961). Others: W. Burkert, *Structure and History in Greek Mythology and Ritual* (1979); J-P. Vernant, *Mythe et pensée chez les Grecs* (1965, Eng. trans. 1983), 267–82; C. Sourvinou-Inwood, in O. Murray and S. Price (eds.), *The Greek City* (1990), 295–322; E. Kearns in A. Powell (ed.), *The Greek World* (1995), 511–29.

See also the bibliographies to MYTHOLOGY and RITUAL.   E. Ke.

religion, Greek, terms relating to The semantics of Greek and Latin in this regard are very different from those of modern European languages. In Greek, the most important word denoting the sacred was ἱερός, denoting basically something which is consecrated to a god, although its use in Homer may reflect an original meaning 'strong'. A related sense is 'connected with cult'; thus ἱερά are religious rites, or materials, especially victims, for them. Contrasting with ἱερός, both ὅσιος and εὐσεβής, with their corresponding abstract nouns, cover some of the meaning of 'religion', 'religious'. Ὅσιος seems to mean primitively 'usage', 'custom', hence 'good, commendable, pious usage' or the feelings which go with it. It tends to specialize into meaning that which is proper and lawful with regard to holy things, or to traditional morality; it is, for instance, ἀνόσιον to commit murder. Its sense of 'lawful' can, however, further develop into 'that which is permitted, as not sacred or taboo', and thus may contrast with ἱερός, coming to mean almost 'profane, secular.' Εὐσεβής, literally 'reverent', does not necessarily indicate reverence towards the gods unless a qualifying phrase is added; in this respect it is like Latin *pius* (see PIETAS). A word belonging essentially to the religious vocabulary in Classical times is θέμις, since that which it is or is not θέμις to do is respectively allowed or disallowed by religious custom; but the word is also used of traditional, non-religious custom, particularly in *Homer. Words for reverence include αἰδοῦμαι, 'to feel respect' and σέβομαι/σέβω, 'to honour'; what is honoured may be σεμνόν or (less often) ἅγιον. The latter word, though probably distinct in etymology, seems to have been felt as related to ἅγος, 'curse', in both cases, something outside normal every-day life is being described. Related too is ἅγνος, 'pure', referring generally to a particular state of remoteness from pollutions such as those of sex and death, appropriate for the gods and for dealings with them. Δεισιδαίμων varies between 'pietistic' (traditionally 'superstitious') and 'pious', but is more often pejorative (see DEISIDAIMONIA). As regards cult acts, the simple word τιμή, 'honour', is common; a worshipper is often said to 'attend on' or 'serve' the gods (θεραπεύειν and synonyms, rarely δουλεύειν). To be a regular worshipper, e.g. of the particular gods of the state, is νομίζειν θεούς, which may also mean to believe in their existence. Occasionally (as in Hdt. 2. 64. 2), θρησκεύειν has the former sense; θρησκεία is a common, though mostly late, word for worship. Λατρεία, λατρεύειν are also found (Plato, *Ap.* 23b, *Phaedr.* 244e, Eur. *Ion* 152). A τελετή or τέλος is any rite, though in Hellenistic Greek it tends to mean a mystical rite or even secret doctrine (see TELETĒ).

J. Rudhardt, *Notions fondamentales de la pensée religieuse . . .*² (1992), 21–52; Burkert, *GR* 268–75; W. R. Connor, *Anc. Soc.* 1988, 161–88; H. W. Pleket, in H. S. Versnel (ed.), *Faith Hope and Worship* (1981), 152–92.

E. Ke.

religion, Italic In a strict sense this concept refers to religions of various Indo-European tribes forming the Italic linguistic league, Umbrians, Sabello-Oscans (Sabines, Samnites, and a number of others such as Vestini, Marrucini, Paeligni, Marsi, Frentani, Campani, Lucani), and Latins (see ITALY, LANGUAGES OF). In a broader sense it may also include the cults of the Veneti in the north-east, and those of the speakers of *Messapic (cognate with the Illyrian) in the south-east (*Apulia); excluded are the religions of the Etruscans, Greeks, Ligurians, and Celts. The cults of the Indo-European settlers were first amalgamated with the autochthonous Mediterranean elements, and later exposed to Etruscan and (from the 8th cent.) Greek influences.

Roman and Italic religion belonged to the same cultural universe; hence after the Roman conquest, and the gradual extinction of the Italic languages and their replacement by Latin, the Italic cults were relatively easily assimilated to the Roman cult. Roman authors provide precious information, especially *Varro (cf. *Ling.* 5. 74, a list of deities venerated by the Sabines), *Ovid's *Fasti*, *Pompeius Festus, and the *scholia to *Virgil. Archaeological evidence (cultic statuary, temples, tomb paintings, funerary urns, votive offerings) presents a vivid picture of religious life; it has been enriched particularly by excavations in the sanctuaries of *Fortuna Primigenia in *Praeneste, *Juno in *Gabii, the precinct of Thirteen Altars in *Lavinium, Mater Matuta in *Satricum, a (Samnite) sanctuary at *Pietrabbondante, Mefitis in Rossano di Vaglio (in Lucania).

But above all we have inscriptional evidence in Italic languages (4th–1st cents. BC), with numerous dedications to various deities. The principal documents are:

1. The Umbrian *Tabulae Iguvinae*, seven bronze tables from *Iguvium describing in great detail various religious ceremonies,

lustration, sacrifices, and auspication (nothing as detailed exists either in Latin or Greek).

2. The Oscan Table from Agnone in Samnium (*c.* mid-3rd cent. BC, and thus predating all Latin literary texts), a list of seventeen deities who possessed altars in the precinct (*húrz*, cf. Lat. *hortus*, 'garden') of Ceres, and to whom sacrifices (cf. the distinction between *aasai* and *aasai purasiai*, 'altars' and 'the fire altars') were made on certain days (to some deities on the feast of Flora, *fiuusasiais*).

3. The so-called *iúvila* inscriptions, Oscan funerary stelae from *Capua (4th–3rd cents. BC), indicating the name(s) of the deceased, and recording or prescribing the dates of (annual) sacrifices, e.g. 'this is the *iúvila* of Sp(urius) Kaluvius and (his) brothers. At the feast (*fiisiais*, cf. Lat. *feriae*) of *púmperiai praimamerttiai* (i.e. taking place in the month that precedes the month of March, so circumscribed because it was devoted to the cult of the dead and its real name was regarded as inauspicious) (blood) sacrifices (*sakrasias*; *kersnasias* were bloodless) were made in the presence of (or in the year when) L(ucius) Pettius (was) the chief magistrate (*L. Pettieis meddikiai*').

4. Oscan lead imprecations, also from Capua, very similar to Greek or Latin specimens, one of them mentioning (in dat.) *Keri arent[ikai]*, Ceres the Avenger (cf. Hor. *Epod.* 17. 28, *Sabella carmina*, 'Sabinian spells').

Still our knowledge of Italic pantheon and cult is fragmentary. Common to all Italics were *Jupiter as the chief sky-god (Umbr. *Iupater, Iuve*; Osc. *Iúveis, Iuvei*) and *Mars (Osc. *Mamars*, cf. *Mamertini* or *Mamertines*, Italian mercenaries who seized Greek *Messana (Messina) in 288) as the war-god. In Iguvium together with the obscure *Vofionus* they formed a triad, all bearing the epithet *Grabovius* (perhaps 'of the oak'). Next the cult of *Hercules (*Hercle, Hercele, Herekleís*) and of the *Dioscuri (cf. the Paelignian dedication *Ioviois Pouclois*, and archaic Latin *Castorei Podlouquei qurois* from Lavinium). Very prominent were female (most often fertility) deities, Juno (esp. in Latium, in Lanuvium, Ardea, Gabii, Tibur, Tusculum), and in the *Faliscan Falerii; *Ceres (partially identified with Demeter; cf. *Damatra* frequent in Messapic dedications; *Herentas* (= *Venus; cf. Messapic *Aprodita*); *Mefitis* (also identified with Venus; cf. the Lucanian dedication *Mamartei Mefitanoi*: 'to Mars (of) Mefitis'); *Angitia* (particularly among the Marsi and Paeligni), often associated with Ceres; *Fortuna in Latin Praeneste, where she was called *Primigenia* (cf. the archaic inscription *Fortuna Diovo fileia primogenia*, 'First-born daughter of Jove'), and in Antium; *Reitia* (etymology disputed) among the Veneti, often with the epithet *sainatis*, 'healer', later identified with Juno; Umbrian *Cubrar Mater* (gen.), and in Picenum *dea Cupra* (cf. Sabinian *ci(u)prum*, 'good', and Roman *Bona Dea*); further *Diana, esp. in Latium, where her grove (*nemus*) at Aricia (Nemi) was the centre of the Latin League, and in Campania (mount Tifata near Capua).

In the Table of Agnone a striking feature is deities representing various aspects of Ceres (all forms in dat. sing. or plur.): *Ammai, Diumpais, Pernai, Fluusai, Anafríss, Maatúis*. These names are followed by the adjective *Kerrí-* = *Cerealis*, 'of Ceres', i.e. Ceres as Nurse, Nymph, *Perna* (?), *Flora* ('Bloom'), *Imbres* ('rain water') and 'Mother(s)' (cf. *Mater Matuta*). There appears also *Futrei Kerríiai* ('Daughter of Ceres'; cf. *Persepona* in a Paelignian inscription), and *Hereklúi Kerriiúí* ('Hercules of Ceres'). Next Jupiter (*Diúvei*) in his two functions, *Verehasiúí* (*Iuvenis? Frugifer?*) and *Regaturei* ('Irrigating'?). Further *Vezkei* (?); *Evklúi* (*Eukolos, Eukles*, a chthonic deity); *Anter Statai* (a goddess 'standing between'); *Liganakdíkei Entrai* (meaning disputed); *Patanaí Piístíai*

('Opening and Pounding', sc. the husks; cf. the Roman goddess *Panda*); *Deívaí Genetaí* (cf. Roman *Genita Mana*). Most of these deities (as also those in Iguvium) have no direct counterparts in Rome, but their name-forms and minute specialization recall those innumerable Roman gods who according to the pontifical doctrine presided over every stage and aspect of life. In Rome their names and functions (with the exception of four deities recorded in the acts of Arvals; see FRATRES ARVALES) have been preserved by antiquarians and church writers; in the Table of Agnone we meet them not as an antiquarian curiosity but as part of a flourishing cult.

J. Heurgon, *Recherches sur l'histoire, la religion et la civilisation de Capoue préromaine* (1942); A. J. Pfiffig, *Religio Iguvina* (1964); G. Devoto, *Gli antichi Italici*[3] (1967); E. T. Salmon, *Samnium and the Samnites* (1967); G. Radke, *Die Götter Altitaliens*[2] (1975) and *Zur Entwicklung des Gottesvorstellung in Rom* (1987); F. Coarelli, *I santuari di Lazio* (1987); A. Mastrocinque, *Santuari e divinità dei Paleoveneti* (1987); *Corpus delle stipi votive in Italia* (1986–   ).

COLLECTIONS OF WRITTEN SOURCES: R. S. Conway, *The Italic Dialects* (1897); R. S. Conway, J. Whatmough, and S. E. Johnson, *The Prae-Italic Dialects of Italy* 1–3 (1933); E. Vetter, *Handbuch der italischen Dialekte* (1953); J. W. Poultney, *The Bronze Tables of Iguvium* (1959); O. Parlangèli, *Studi Messapici* (1960); M. G. Tibiletti Bruno, *I Sabini* (1969); G. B. Pellegrini and A. L. Prosdocimi, *La lingua venetica* (1967); P. Poccetti, *Nuovi documenti Italici* (1979); A. Franchi De Bellis, *Le Iovile Capuane* (1981); C. Santoro, *Nuovi Studi Messapici* (1982).   J. L.

religion, Jewish Judaism in Graeco-Roman antiquity is better known than any other ancient religion apart from Christianity, primarily because of the survival to modern times of traditions about ancient Judaism through rabbinic and Christian literature. However, this same factor creates its own problems of bias in the selection and interpretation of evidence.

The main sources of knowledge about Judaism are the Old and New Testaments and other religious texts preserved in Greek within the Christian Church: the apocrypha and pseudepigrapha, and the writings of *Philon (4) and *Josephus. The works composed in Hebrew and *Aramaic produced by the rabbis after AD 70 stress rather different aspects. A fresh light has been shone on Judaism by the chance discovery of Jewish papyri in Elephantine and especially by the *Dead Sea Scrolls, which revealed the incompleteness of the later Jewish and Christian traditions even about the 1st cent. AD, the period for which most evidence survives. Pagan Greek and Latin writers emphasized the aspects of Judaism most surprising to outsiders but many of their comments were ignorant and prejudiced.

Many of the basic elements of Jewish worship were shared with other religions of classical antiquity. The prime form of worship was by sacrifices and other offerings in the Jerusalem Temple. In this respect the Jewish cult differed from most in the Greek and Roman world only in the exceptional scrupulousness of its observance; in the assumption of most Jews that sacrifices were only valid if performed in Jerusalem, even though this meant that the sacrificial cult was for many only known from a distance; in the role of the priestly caste, who inherited the prerogative to serve in the sanctuary under the authority of an autocratic high priest who at certain periods also operated as political leader of the nation; and in their strong sense of the special sanctity of the land of Israel and the city of *Jerusalem and its shrine.

Of the special elements of Judaism noted in antiquity, most striking to pagans was the exclusive monotheism of Jews: most Jews worshipped only their own deity and either asserted that other gods did not exist or chose to ignore them. Equally strange

was the lack of any cult image and the insistence of most Jews by the Hellenistic period that Jewish sacrificial worship was only permitted in the Jerusalem Temple, despite the existence of Jewish temples at Elephantine in Egypt in the 5th cent. BC and at Leontopolis in the Nile delta from the mid-2nd cent. BC to AD 72, and the Samaritan temple on Mt. Gerizim, which was destroyed only in the 120s BC.

Jews were in general believed by outsiders to be specially devoted to their religion, a trait interpreted sometimes negatively as superstition, sometimes positively as philosophy. The foundation of this devotion lay in the Torah, the law governing all aspects of Jewish life which Jews considered had been handed down to them through Moses on Mt. Sinai as part of the covenant between God and Israel. The Torah is enshrined in the Hebrew bible, and pre-eminently in the Pentateuch (the first five books). Jews treated the scrolls on which the Torah was recorded with exceptional reverence; if written in the correct fashion, such scrolls were holy objects in themselves. The covenant, marked by circumcision for males, involved the observance of moral and ethical laws as well as taboos about food and sacred time (especially the sabbath).

The main elements of Judaism as here presented were already in place by the 3rd and 2nd cents. BC, when the final books of the Hebrew bible were composed, but the Jewish religion was to undergo much change over the following centuries. One new development was the gradual emergence of the notion of a canon of scripture treated as more authoritative than other writings.

Agreement about the authority of particular books did not lead to uniformity, or even the notion of orthodoxy. The Hebrew bible left many opportunities for diversity of interpretation. The extent of variety, at least up to AD 70, is clear from the Dead Sea scrolls. Disagreements may have been fuelled in part by diverse reactions to the surrounding Hellenistic culture. The continuation of variety after *c.* AD 100, after which Christians ceased to preserve Jewish texts and Judaism is known almost only through the rabbinic tradition, is uncertain.

From the 2nd cent. BC self-aware philosophies began to proclaim themselves within Judaism: *Pharisees, *Sadducees, and *Essenes, and perhaps others. These groups differed on correct practice in the Jerusalem cult as well as on quite fundamental issues of theology, such as the role of fate and the existence of an afterlife. However, apart perhaps from the Dead Sea sectarians, who saw themselves as the True Israel, all these Jews believed that they belonged within a united religion: Josephus, who described the three main Jewish philosophies in detail (*BJ* 2. 119–66; *AJ* 18. 11–22) elsewhere boasted that Jews are remarkable for their unanimity on religious issues (*Ap.* 2. 181). The earliest followers of Jesus are best considered in the context of such variety within Judaism.

In the Hellenistic and early Roman periods some aspects of the biblical tradition were particularly emphasized by Jews. Ritual purity as a metaphor for holiness was stressed by Jews of all persuasions: *mikvaoth* (ritual baths) have been excavated in many Jewish sites in the land of Israel, both Pharisees and Essenes elaborated complex elucidations of the biblical purity rules, and restrictions on the use of gentile foodstuffs became more widespread.

Some Jews indulged in speculation about the end of days, which was variously envisaged as a victory of Israel over the nations under God's suzerainty or the total cessation of mundane life. In some texts a leading role was accorded to a messianic figure, but ideas about the personality and function of a messiah or messiahs varied greatly, and the extent to which messianic expectations dominated Judaism in any period is debated. Much of the extant eschatological literature is composed in the form of apocalyptic, in which a vision is said to have been vouchsafed to a holy seer. All the apocalyptic texts from the post-biblical period are either anonymous or pseudepigraphic, reflecting a general belief that the reliability of prophetic inspiration had declined since biblical times.

Religious ideas of all kinds within Judaism were generated or confirmed by study and *midrash of the biblical books. According to Josephus in his defence and summary of Judaism in *Ap.* 2. 181–220, Jews were uniquely concerned to learn their own law. The primary locus of teaching was the synagogue, where the Pentateuch was read and explained at least once a week, on sabbaths. Special buildings for such teaching, and probably for public prayer, are first attested in Egypt in the 3rd cent. BC. In the late-Roman period some *synagogue buildings were designed with monumental architecture similar to pagan temples and were treated as sacred places.

The increased ascription of sanctity to synagogues was in part a reaction to the destruction of the Jerusalem Temple by Roman forces under *Titus in AD 70 (see JEWS). The destruction, at the end of the great Jewish revolt of AD 66–70, was eventually to have important consequences for the development of Judaism, although new theologies were slow to emerge: Josephus in the nineties AD still assumed that God is best worshipped by sacrifices in Jerusalem, and about a third of the *Mishnah, redacted *c.* AD 200, is concerned with the Temple cult.

In the diaspora the Temple had in any case always dominated more as an idea than as an element in religious practice, since only occasional pilgrimage was ever possible. The synagogues at Dura *Europus and *Sardis may reveal Judaisms based on synagogue liturgy. An honorific inscription probably of the 3rd cent. AD from *Aphrodisias in Caria reveals that, in that Jewish community at least, gentile God-fearers may have participated in Jewish religious institutions.

The Judaism of the *rabbis differed from other forms of Judaism mainly in its emphasis on learning as a form of worship. Rabbinic academies, first in Yavneh (Jamnia) on the coast of Judaea immediately after AD 70, but from the mid-2nd cent. mainly in Galilee and (from the 3rd cent.) in Babylonia, specialized in the elucidation of Jewish law, producing a huge literature by the end of antiquity. Their most important products, were the Mishnah, composed in Hebrew *c.* AD 200, and the two *Talmuds, redacted (mainly in Aramaic) in Palestine in *c.* AD 400 and in Babylonia in *c.* AD 500; but they also produced a large corpus of midrashic texts commenting on the bible, and they or others in late antiquity composed the Hekhalot texts, which attest to a continued mystical tradition. See CHRISTIANITY.

G. F. Moore, *Judaism in the First Centuries of the Christian Era* (3 vols.; 1927); Schürer, *History*, 2. 237–597; S. W. Baron, *A Social and Religious History of the Jews*[2] (1952–93) (vols. 1 and 2 on ancient times); S. J. D. Cohen, *From the Maccabees to the Mishnah* (1987); L. H. Schiffman, *From Text to Tradition* (1991); E. P. Sanders, *Judaism: Practice and Belief, 63 BCE-66 CE* (1992). M. D. G.

religion, Macedonian See MACEDONIA, CULTS.

religion, Magna Graecia See SICILY AND MAGNA GRAECIA, CULTS AND MYTHOLOGY.

religion, Messenian See MESSENIAN CULTS AND MYTHS.

religion, Minoan and Mycenaean Bronze age Cretan

(Minoan) religion assumed what we may take to be its canonical form with the second palaces in the middle bronze age. From the latter half of the second millennium BC (late bronze age) the Mycenaeans appear to have been politically dominant in Crete and Greece and clearly took over some Minoan cult traditions, although as a whole their religious system seems to show as many differences as similarities. Both civilizations sprang from centralized urban theocratic societies along contemporary eastern models. The earliest evidence of communal religious activity in Crete derives from early bronze age tombs (3rd millennium BC), mainly the round *tholoi* of the Mesara, and from caves which had been used for habitation and burial since neolithic times. A probable cult complex at the EM II settlement of Myrtos consisted of a rectangular bench-type sanctuary which preserved what may be the earliest female cult idol (Lady of Myrtos). The shrine may have been associated with an open area for cult, foreshadowing the central court of the later Minoan palace with shrines leading off from it. (Even after the palaces disappeared the arrangement of open space and adjoining shrines was retained.) At *Cnossus the western side of the court opened onto a complex of sanctuaries. Pillar crypts there, and lustral basins in the Throne Room and elsewhere in the palace, perhaps recall the stalagmites and spring water basins of the natural cave shrines. The palace was one of the major foci of religious ritual, often containing several cult complexes; it seems likely that much activity there had in some way to do with cult. The other major types of cult-place, especially in the First Palace Period, were cave sanctuaries and peak sanctuaries, which are often thought to have functioned in relation to the palace or similar administrative centre. It is possible that this is reflected in topography: the cult cave at Amnisos and the mountain sanctuary on Juktas south of Cnossus looked directly at the palace, while the Kamares cave on the southern slope of Mt. Ida was also visible from, and aligned with, the palace of Phaestos. Visibility seems in general to have been an important criterion for the siting of peak sanctuaries.

Minoan gems showed sacred enclosures in the open with one or more trees as central features. Like the related pillars and baetyls (sacred stones), these are likely to have been potent religious symbols rather than objects of cult themselves. Bull horns, aptly named 'horns of consecration' by A. Evans, indicated the sacred nature of what was placed between them. Sacred buildings were generally decorated with a pair or entire row of stylized horns. A cultic role may also be implicated in the famous bull-leaping games which took place in the central court of the palace. There is no unequivocal evidence of bull-cult, however, or of a bull-god, any more than of a snake- or bird-deity. Animals did however play an important part in Minoan religion. In a ritual context they could suggest a numinous presence, or they could symbolize divine powers of regeneration, chthonic and protective forces. The most important symbol was the double axe. In votive form it appears in caves like Arkalochori, in peak shrines (Juktas), in palace sanctuaries, standing between horns of consecration but also in tombs and engraved on pillars. Its meaning has been variously interpreted, but the Minoan religious context and later tradition suggest that the axe represented the instrument of sacrifice. Going a stage further in speculation, we might guess that it was both lethal weapon and symbol of new life arising from the blood of the sacrificial victim. Certainly it could be set up in the tomb or used at the ritual in honour of the dead, as on the Ayia Triada sarcophagus. Specialized cultic vessels like the so-called snake tubes to direct libations to the dead show a deep respect for the influence of chthonic powers.

Whether the Minoan world was acquainted with permanent anthropomorphic cult images, like those of contemporary near eastern and later Greek societies, is not yet established with certainty. Even small iconic idols (e.g. the faience figurines of a goddess—or priestess?—holding *snakes from the Cnossian Temple Repositories) were relatively rare in the later palace period until the appearance in LM IIIB of what may be a new format of representing the goddess (see below). Homer (*Od.* 19. 188) and Linear B (KN Gg 705; see MYCENAEAN LANGUAGE) identify the name of the birth-goddess *Eileithyia in the Amnisos cave and the type of cult practised there. It is still debated whether Minoan religion, like the systems of the contemporary near east and of the Mycenaeans and later Greeks, was clearly polytheistic, or whether, as Evans was the first to suggest, essentially a single goddess, accompanied by a youthful male associate, was worshipped in different forms. To judge by the iconography, goddesses were more prominent than male deities. They could have been called on by an invocatory title such as Potnia ('Lady', 'Mistress'), *Ariadne ('Holy One'), *Europa ('Far Seeing'), or Pasiphae ('All Seeing'). Such names, surviving in tradition, suggest a close Homeric-type *parousia* of worshippers and divinity who was expected to appear in direct *epiphany. This is borne out by the religious scenes in frescos and on *gems. Minoan ritual shared some basic features with Greek practice in the manner of their *prayer, use of *altars, and burnt *sacrifice, in their elaborate processions with offerings of gifts, including spring flowers or even a peplos-type garment. Lively ceremonial dances celebrated the various stages of the annual cycle of nature. The seasonal renewal of crops, hope for new life from the death of the old, were primary motivating forces of Minoan religion.

Mycenaean religious life outside Crete first manifested itself in the Shaft Graves of *Mycenae in the 16th cent. BC. Depictions of rituals on finds from the graves are identical with Minoan forms. It has been argued that the meaning of symbols had changed or been lost to Mycenaean perception. However, there are further traces of Minoan religious traditions on the mainland at Asine, Mt. Kynortion, while on Crete itself, apart from Cnossus, the rural sanctuary of Kato Symi may perhaps show a fusion of traditions. Here continuity of cult suggests that 'Minoans' and 'Mycenaeans' could have worshipped side by side in a place whose holiness endured into historical times, when it was dedicated to *Hermes and *Aphrodite. Comparable in some ways is the sanctuary at Ayia Irini on *Ceos, laid out in the middle bronze age and continuing in use into Hellenistic times as a temple of *Dionysus. Bronze Age clay statues of Minoan appearance were found here, but no trace of such typical Minoan ritual objects as double axes, horns of consecration, clay tubes, etc. Conversely, Mycenae itself has yielded ritual figures of 'apotropaic' appearance which have as yet no parallel from Minoan Crete. The characteristic Minoan cave and peak sanctuary, as well as the lustral basin, had no exact parallels on the mainland. The Mycenaean palace, which succeeded its Cretan model, may have confined its worship to the megaron. Open sanctuary areas were distinctive developments at the end of the bronze age. At Mycenae such a cult centre competed with the palace, but elsewhere modest bench-type shrines on their own and as part of hypaethral (roofless) precincts replaced the palace sanctuaries. This happened in *Tiryns, for example, in the 'Unterburg', and in Crete in the *Piazzale dei Sacelli* at Ayia Triada. The format of the bench shrine proved popular until Hellenic times. Curiously in Crete cave sanctuaries enjoyed a renaissance at the end of the bronze age. They, too, went on into Roman times and became

places of Christian *pilgrimage. Modern Cretan chapels still show the birth of the infant Christ in a cave.

The Mycenaeans of the late bronze age showed a preference for anthropomorphic divine representation in apparent contrast with Minoan iconic forms. Some relatively large goddess figures survive from Mycenae, Tiryns, and Phylakopi (see MELOS), together with countless stylized figurines. A new cult assemblage at the end of the Bronze Age emphasized the growing importance of the god beside distinctive idols of the goddess with her arms upraised. He resembles the oriental Warrior God whose iconographic type spread west across the Aegean and provided the model for early Archaic sculptures of Zeus and Poseidon. The increasing prominence of male deities is reflected in Linear B, which was familiar with *Zeus, *Poseidon, Enyalius (see ARES), *Paean, Dionysus, Hermes, and probably *Ares. Other names of Olympians, beside the general *theos* and 'all the gods' (*pasi teoi*), are *Hera, *Artemis, *Athena, and perhaps *Demeter. These stand beside the invocatory titles Potnia, Wanassa ('Queen'), and Wanax ('Lord', 'King'), and beside other divine names which did not survive in later use. None can be safely identified from the iconography. But they probably reflect both Minoan and Mycenaean cult figures, although their status and function remain uncertain. The documents bear out the Homeric tradition (*Od.* 3) of Poseidon's pre-eminence at *Pylos in Nestor's time. At Cnossus Zeus has the greater prominence. His probable epithet of Dictaeus (*dikatajo diwe(?)* Fp1) reveals his link with the Minoan Divine Child who was born in the Psychro Cave on Mt. Dicte. But in Pylos he was already linked with Hera (Tn 316). Other theophoric names, as well as religious titles such as 'slave of the god' (*teojo doero*) remain obscure. But the many unknown elements in the script hint at the complexity of Aegean bronze age religion. Much of it continued into later Greece, notably features in the administration of cult, in ceremonial ritual, paraphernalia, and the characteristic festal calendar. However, given the many factors that influence the development of Greek religion, the precise ratio of old to new will never be known. See MINOAN CIVILIZATION; MYCENAEAN CIVILIZATION.

N. Marinatos, *Minoan Religion* (1993); O. Dickinson, *The Aegean Bronze Age* (1994), 257–94; W. Pötscher, *Aspekte und Probleme der minoischen Religion* (1990); B. Rutkowski, *The Cult Places of the Aegean* (1986); Burkert, GR 10–46; B. C. Dietrich. *The Origins of Greek Religion* (1974); E. Vermeule, *Götterkult* (1974); M. P. Nilsson, GGR 1³ 256–303 and *The Minoan-Mycenaean Religion and its Survival in Greek Religion*² (1950).

B. C. D.

religion, oriental See ORIENTAL CULTS AND RELIGION.

religion, Persian Two religious complexes are discernible in the first millennium BC in Iran.

1. The eastern Iranian tradition of Zarathuštra (see ZOROASTER), with the Avesta as its sacred writings. The Older Avesta consists of the Gāthās (c.1000 BC) and the *Yasna Haptaŋ hāiti*, which were transmitted orally for many centuries. The remainder of the Avestan texts are dated later (5th cent. BC at the earliest) on linguistic grounds. The texts were written down in Sasanian times (see SASANIDS) when Zoroastrianism became the state religion. This tradition cannot be provided with a historical or archaeological context.

2. The western Iranian religion of the *Achaemenids is attested in iconography, epigraphy, and in administrative texts; no sacred texts were preserved. *Ahuramazda is the only god invoked by name in the OP inscriptions (until Artaxerxes II) and is portrayed as a winged deity on reliefs and seals (although some interpret

this figure as the *khvarnah*). Sanctuaries have not yet been identi-fied in the Achaemenid residences, although *Darius I (DB 1. 63 f.) claims to have restored the sanctuaries (OP *āyadanā*) des-troyed by Gaumata. Two altar-plinths at *Pasargadae remain the only (uninformative but certain) cult structures. Evidence for cult-practices consists of tomb-reliefs where the king worships the sacred *fire. Around the residences, the picture is more diver-sified. *Persepolis administrative tablets (*PFT*) mention several Iranian gods, as well as Elamite Humban and Babylonian Adad, who receive rations for sacrifices from the royal treasuries. Mithra (see MITHRAS) occurs frequently in names such as Mithradates, but is otherwise unattested until Artaxerxes II. There is no evi-dence that the cult of Ahuramazda was imposed on subjects or even particularly favoured in Fārs.

Research has focused excessively on the question whether the Achaemenids were Zoroastrians. This presupposes thorough understanding of the contents of the older Avesta, although these texts contain many incomprehensible parts and modern transla-tions differ considerably, and insight into the relationship between the older Avesta and pre-Avestan Iranian religious devel-opments. As recently argued (Kellens 1991), it is preferable to regard both complexes of data as part of developments as yet incompletely understood.

The often-supposed Iranian influence on Presocratic Greek philosophy remains largely speculative. *Herodotus (1)'s descrip-tion of Persian cult (1. 131–2) is substantially correct, although he confuses Mithra with *Anahita. Sacrifices to fire, earth, and water (Hdt. 1. 131, Strabo 15. 3. 13, Diog. Laert. Prooem. 6) are partly confirmed by the *PFT*. Fire-worship was known from personal observation in Asia Minor (Strabo 15. 3. 14; also Phoenix fr. 1 Powell; Paus. 5. 27. 5–6). Herodotus and *Plato (1) (*Alc.* 122a) emphasize the importance of 'truth' (Av. *aša*, OP *arta*) to the Persians (although Plato mistakes Ahuramazda for Zarathuštra's father). *Aristotle (in Diog. Laert. Proem. 8) on the two opposing principles of good (Oromasdes) and evil Añgra-Mainyu (Ahriman, Ἀρειμάνιος) and Plut. (*Mor.* 369d–370c) on the cre-ation of the Aməša Spentas give valuable information on the development of Iranian religious thought. In general, Greek lit-erature contains useful information on Persian religious develop-ments, provided it is analysed with due attention to the period and place it refers to.

C. Clemen, *Fontes historiae religionis persicae* (1920); J. Kellens, 'Avesta', EncIr 3. 35–45 (with literature); J. Duchesne-Guillemin, *Beiträge zur Achämenidengeschichte*, 18 (1972) 59–82; J. Kellens, in *La Religion irani-enne à l'époque achéménide*, IrAnt Suppl. 5 (1991), 81–86; G. Widengren, *Die Religionen Irans* (1965); J. Duchesne-Guillemin, *La Religion de l'Iran ancien* (1962); M. Boyce, *A History of Zoroastrianism*, (1982–91); H. Koch, *Die religiösen Verhältnisse der Dareioszeit* (1977); A. Momigliano, *Alien Wisdom* (1975), for Iranian influence on *Presocratics.   H. S.-W.

religion, Rhodian See RHODES, CULTS AND MYTHS.

religion, Roman The history of Roman religion might be said to begin with *Varro's *Human and Divine Antiquities* (47 BC), of which the second half, 16 books on Divine Antiquities, codified for the first time Roman religious institutions: priests, temples, festivals, rites, and gods. This work, which may have had the unsettling effect of enabling people to see how imperfectly the existing system corresponded to the 'ideal', was extremely influ-ential on traditionalists, and provided ammunition for Christians such as *Augustine in the *City of God*. Nineteenth-cent. scholar-ship on Roman religion, in attempting a diachronic history down to the age of Varro, assumed an ideal phase, in which religion was

perfectly attuned to the agricultural year, from which republican religion was a sorry decline: politics increasingly obtruded on religion, and scepticism was rife. This decline model, which underlies the two standard handbooks of Wissowa and Latte, has become increasingly unpopular. In its place scholars now prefer to stress the dynamic changes of republican religion, including its position in public life, and also the continuing significance of public religion in the imperial age.

Defining 'Roman religion' is harder than it might seem. The emphasis of scholars has generally been on the public festivals and institutions, on the ground that they provided the framework within which private rituals were constructed; only those com-mitted to a protestant view of personal piety will argue that public rituals lack real religious feeling or significance. The geo-graphical focus of the phrase changes radically over time, from the regal period when Rome was an individual city-state through to Rome's acquisition of an empire stretching from Scotland to Syria. Two related themes run through that expansion: the role of specifically Roman cults outside Rome, and the religious impact of empire on Rome itself.

Our knowledge of the early phase of Roman religion is patchy, and subject, like all early Roman history, to later myth-making. For the regal period archaeology casts some light, for example on the extent of Greek influence in the area; the principal festivals of the regal calendar are all attested, in all probability, in the calendar of the late republic. For the republic, archaeological evidence, for example of temples, remains important, and the literary tradition becomes increasingly reliable, especially from the mid-4th or 3rd down to the 1st cent. BC. It becomes possible to produce a diachronic history of the changes to the public cults of the city of Rome, such as the introduction of the cult of Magna Mater (204 BC; see CYBELE; PESSINUS; PHILHELLENISM), the suppression of the *Bacchanalia (186 BC), the creation in Italy and the provinces of *coloniae* whose religious institutions were modelled on those of Rome, and the increasing divine aura assumed by dynasts of the late republic.

The Augustan 'restoration' of religion (see AUGUSTUS) was in reality more a restructuring, with the figure of the emperor incorporated at many points. Some 'ancient' cults were given a fresh impetus, while Augustus also built major new temples in the city (*Apollo; *Mars Ultor), which expressed his relationship to the divine. This Augustan system remained fundamental to the public religious life of Rome to the end of antiquity. The religious life of the city also became increasingly cosmopolitan under the empire, with a flourishing of associations focused on gods both Roman and foreign, some within individual house-holds, others drawing their membership from a wider circle. In the high empire the civic cults of Rome operated alongside associations devoted to Isis, Mithras, Jahveh, or Christ. Outside Rome, civic cults of the Greek east continued to offer a sense of identity to Greeks under Roman rule, but hardly fall under the rubric 'Roman religion'; civic cults in the Latin west, however, took on a strongly Roman cast. Pre-Roman gods were reinter-preted and local pantheons modelled on the Roman (see INTER-PRETATIO ROMANA). In the 3rd and 4th cents., there was an increasing conceptual opposition between Roman religion and Christianity (cf. CHRISTIANITY), but elements of the Roman system proved to be very enduring: in Rome the *Lupercalia were still celebrated in the late 5th cent. AD.

Wissowa, *RK*; Latte, *RR*; J. Toutain, *Les Cultes païens dans l'empire romain* (1907–25); J. Bayet, *Histoire politique et psychologique de la religion romaine* (1957); J. Beaujeu, *La Religion romaine à l'apogée de l'empire* (1955); G.

Dumézil, *Archaic Roman Religion* (1970); R. MacMullen, *Paganism in the Roman Empire* (1981); J. Scheid, *Religion et piété à Rome* (1985), and *Romulus et ses frères* (1990); R. Turcan, *Religion romaine* (1988)—iconography; M. Beard, J. North, and S. Price, *Religions of Rome* (1998).

See also: CALENDAR, ROMAN; FESTIVALS, ROMAN; ORIENTAL CULTS; RELIGION, GREEK; RULER-CULT; also individual deities, festivals, priesthoods, and the next entry. S. R. F. P.

religion, Roman, terms relating to Latin *religio* was likened by the ancients to *relegere*, 'to go over again in thought' (Cic. *Nat. D.* 2. 72) or to *religare*, 'to bind' (Lucr. 1. 931; Livy 5. 23. 10), and designates religious scrupulosity as well as the sense of bonds between gods and humans. Knowledge of these bonds incites men and women to be scrupulous in their relations with gods, notably by respecting their dignity and moral obligations towards them: the term *religio* is thus defined as 'justice rendered to the gods', *iustitia erga deos*, and is parallel to *pietas*, the justice rendered to parents (Cic. *Part. Or.* 78). But *pius, pietas*, which correspond fairly closely to Greek *eusebes* and *eusebeia*, apply equally to the religious domain: Virgil's Aeneas is *pius* because he observes right relations to all things human and divine. Generally *religio* has a good meaning, but *religiosus* designates frequently an exaggerated scrupulosity towards the gods and approaches *superstitiosus* in sense (see SUPERSTITIO). There exists no idea of 'the sacred' in Rome. In its proper sense, i.e. in Roman sacred law, *sacer* signifies 'consecrated to, property of' the gods (Cic. *Dom.* 136; Festus 318 Lindsay; Gai. *Inst.* 2. 5), in contrast to what belongs to humans (the *di *manes* (*res religiosa*). A temple is *sacer*, likewise a duly consecrated object, a sacrificial victim after *immolatio* (see SACRIFICE, ROMAN), or a man consecrated to a deity after a crime. The meanings 'entitled to veneration' or 'accursed' are secondary. *Sanctus* is that which is guaranteed by an oath—thus what is inviolable, e.g. the walls of a city (Gai. *Inst.* 2. 8; cf. Plut. *Quaest. Rom.* 27), certain laws, the tribunes of the plebs, deities. *Profanus* is an ambiguous term. It qualifies sacred objects rendered suitable for human use by a ritual (*profanare*), like the meat of a sacrificial victim consumed by the participants; in a secondary sense *profanus* and *profanare* signify that which is not consecrated (e.g. Macr. *Sat.* 3. 3. 1) or is 'made profane', i.e. unduly removed from divine ownership, and submitted to violence. But in certain texts concerning the cult of *Hercules or that of *Mercurius (*Gallia* 1993, 95 ff., no. 2) *profanare* means—without doubt more widely—'to sacrifice'. *Ritus* serves to qualify, not religious acts *tout court* (these are called *religiones, caerimoniae*, or *sacra*; and note *sacra facere*, 'to perform a religious ceremony'), but the manner of celebrating religious acts (*Romano ritu, Graeco ritu*, 'by the Roman/Greek rite'). See RELIGION, GREEK, TERMS RELATING TO.

See Wissowa, *RK*, and Latte, *RR*, under the various Latin words; R. Schilling, *Rites, cultes, dieux de Rome* (1979), 30 ff.; Y. Thomas, *L'Écrit du temps* (1986), 66 ff.; J.-L. Durand and J. Scheid, *ASSR* 1994, 23 ff.

J. Sch.

religion, Sicilian See SICILY AND MAGNA GRAECIA, CULTS AND MYTHOLOGY.

religion, Spartan See SPARTAN CULTS.

religion, Syrian See SYRIAN DEITIES.

religion, Thracian Accounts in Greek and Latin authors are an important source of information for the religion of *Thrace. *Herodotus (1) (5. 7) writes that the Thracians worshipped only *Ares, *Dionysus, and *Artemis, though their kings also had a cult of *Hermes. No doubt this is a typical case of *interpretatio Graeca*, 'Greek interpretation'. That is, the functions of these deities were meant to illustrate the nature of the Thracian gods for a Greek audience. Ares suggests the existence of a war-god, Dionysus probably stood for a deity of orgiastic character linked with fertility and vegetation, while Artemis was an embodiment of the female principle. One may assume the worship of a Great Goddess, which may have shown similarities with the Artemis cult in Asia Minor or the cult of *Cybele. This Great Goddess was introduced to Athens as the Thracian goddess *Bendis in the 5th cent. BC. Herodotus understood Hermes to be a dynastic deity, worshipped as the ancestor of royal lines. The constellation of gods in Herodotus was probably restricted to the southern parts of Thrace. Its interpretation is still much disputed. On the whole there seems to have existed a strong particularism in religious beliefs and practices. Thus *Zalmoxis is only attested for the *Getae along the lower Danube. According to Herodotus (4. 94. 1–4) he was worshipped as the only god and had extremely celestial features. According to a Hellenized i.e. Greek version (Photius, entry under Zalmoxis) Zalmoxis once upon a time did live on earth. This may reflect the idea of heroization prevalent in Thracian thought, which in pre-Roman times was restricted to members of the nobility and the royal family. *Rhesus, the mythical king of Thrace, on his death was given a cult as *anthropo-daimōn* in the *Pangaeus mountains (Philostratus, Heroicus 17. 3–6).

The existence of a cult of *Helios has been postulated on the evidence of *Sophocles (1) (*Tereus*, fr. 582) and archaeological and numismatic finds. This assumption is further supported by the myth of *Orpheus. Still, the dualism of the orgiastic Dionysus cult and the more moderate *Apollo/Helios cult of this myth seems to suggest local cult-constellations from the south of Thrace.

The second important source for Thracian religion is the archaeological monuments of pre-Roman times. Tumuli and edifices illustrate the native nobility's idea of heroization (see HERO-CULT). A clear example is the mural paintings in the grave of a prince in Sveshtari near Razgrad (early 3rd cent. BC.) The deceased is depicted as Heros Equitans, the *rider-god, attested as a hunter from the 5th cent., who plays an important part in Thracian metalwork. There are also monuments that represent a rider receiving insignia of power from a goddess or holding these insignia.

Female deities with their attributes do appear in Thracian toreutics. It is still not clear, however, whether these are representations of functionally different types of the same Great Goddess or altogether separate deities. The double depiction of a god driving a chariot adorned with feathers (silver pitcher of Vratsa) may be associated with the Apollo myth of the *Hyperboreans.

The third source is the monuments of the Roman imperial period, chiefly votive reliefs and small statues representing, in the manner of conventional Graeco-Roman iconography, *Asclepius and *Hygieia (occasionally *Telesphorus), Apollo, *Zeus, *Hera, Hermes, Artemis (sometimes on a hind), *Heracles, the *nymphs, Cybele, *Hecate, *Demeter, to name but the most important. The occasional Thracian epithet, numerous native dedicants, and rural cult places suggest that a few older features of Thracian religion survived in Greek or Roman guises. In addition there are *c*.2500 votive monuments in stone representing a rider, often hunting. Here, too, the local character is shown by Thracian *epithets mentioned in the Greek votive inscriptions. The so-called *Thracian Rider* was most frequently identified as Apollo or Asclepius. There are also connections and for some parts identifications with Dionysus, *Silvanus, *Sabazius, Pluto (see HADES), the *Dioscuri, and other deities. The iconographical formula stems in principle from the Greek hero-relief. Consequently the oldest monuments of the Thracian Rider are Hellenistic and come from the Greek *poleis* (cities) along the Aegean and western Pontic coast. This kind of votive monument flourished in the latter half of the second and the first half of the third century BC.

Other grave monuments show that the deceased, like a god, was represented as *Heros Equitans* and that furthermore the idea of heroization had reached a wider spectrum of the population. See also ROGOZEN.

> G. I. Kazarow, *RE* 6/1 (1936), 472–551; A. Fol, I. Venedikov, I. Marazov, and D. Popov, *Thracian Legends* (1976, with bibliography); A. Fol, M. Chichikova, T. Ivanov, and T. Teofilov, *The Thracian Tomb near the Village of Sveshtari* (1986); A. Fol, B. Nikolov, S. Mashov, and P. Ivanov, *The Thracian Treasure from Rogozen* (1988); V. Velkov and V. Gerasimova-Tomova, *ANRW* 2. 18. 1 (1989), 1317–61.   M. O.

Remmius (*RE* 4) **Palaemon, Quintus**, a *freedman and highly successful grammarian under *Tiberius and *Claudius, admired for his learning and verbal facility but condemned for his vicious character (Suet. *Gramm.* 23). His grammatical handbook (*ars) is the first such work in Latin whose existence and authorship are explicitly attested: only fragments survive (the *Ars Palaemonis* printed in Keil, *Gramm. Lat.* at 5. 533–47 is spurious; cf. also Fantelli, *Aevum* 1950, 434 ff.), but its influence on the later artigraphic tradition was significant (K. Barwick, *Remmius Palaemon und die römische Ars grammatica* (1922), is overstated but fundamental). See GRAMMAR, GRAMMARIANS, LATIN.

> Mazzarino, *Gramm. Rom. Frag.*, 68–102; Herzog–Schmidt, § 320.
>   R. A. K.

Remus See ROMULUS AND REMUS.

rents See LEASES, AGRICULTURAL.

repetundae (*pecuniae*), (money) to be recovered. The *quaestio de repetundis* (see QUAESTIONES) was a court established to secure compensation for the illegal acquisition of money or property by Romans in authority abroad. Before the establishment of the permanent *quaestio*, such offences were either brought before an assembly or tried by a panel of *recuperatores in a quasi-civil suit (Livy 43. 2). A civil procedure was also used originally to bring prosecutions in the *quaestio*, i.e. the *actio sacramento*, and a verdict of guilty was followed by an assessment of damages, *litis aestimatio, and simple repayment. C. *Sempronius Gracchus, finding this court corrupt and its senatorial jurors unwilling to convict fellow-senators, had a law passed (which may not be a *lex Sempronia*, but the *lex Acilia* mentioned by Cicero), of which major fragments survive on bronze (*CIL* 1². 583). It was a radical reform: those liable were now all senators, ex-magistrates, or their close relatives (but not *equites who did not fall into either of the last two categories); prosecution took place through denunciation to the *praetor, not a form of civil procedure; wronged parties or their delegates, even non-Romans, were themselves expected to prosecute; a 50-strong trial jury was drawn from an album of *equites* with no connections with the senate; the penalty was double repayment; rewards, including Roman citizenship, were offered to successful prosecutors; the whole trial procedure was set out in minute detail with emphasis on openness and accountability. What had been treated as a civil matter was now clearly

a criminal matter, and magistrates and senators might be convicted by their inferiors after being prosecuted by aliens. It is not surprising that the law caused disquiet among the Roman aristocracy.

There was a reaction which led to variations in the composition of the juries (for which see QUAESTIONES), and also reforms which in some ways strengthened the court, but also made it less accessible to non-citizen victims of Roman misgovernment. C. *Servilius Glaucia established a compulsory two-part trial (*comperendinatio*) and a consequential action to recover money from those to whom it had been passed on (*quo ea pecunia pervenerit*). He also probably was the first to introduce *infamia for those convicted, involving *inter alia* disqualification from seeking magistracies and membership of the senate. However, either through his law or the preceding reactionary law of Q. *Servilius Caepio (1), there were two more important changes. First, Romans were now allowed to undertake prosecutions on behalf of all the plaintiffs against a particular defendant, competing for the right to do so before a jury (the procedure was called *divinatio*). Secondly, the law was extended to cover bribes or presents freely given to the accused (not something which the giver could reasonably have claimed back). In consequence the law was applied to senatorial jurors who took bribes. After *Sulla's reform we hear of capital penalties in some cases, which may have applied since money was taken in the course of a graver illegality or simply because an offence against the Roman state had by now been subsumed under the *repetundae* procedure. This was certainly true of *Caesar's *lex Iulia de repetundis* of 59 BC, which included a number of provisions regulating the behaviour of magistrates in provinces, some of which had earlier formed part of other laws. This law, comprehensive and immensely elaborate, remained the basis of controlling misbehaviour of men in authority in the provinces under the emperors, and as such figures in Justinian's *Digest*; see JUSTINIAN'S CODIFICATION.

The emphasis in the law was now on punishing improper behaviour and the interests of the Roman state. The losses and sufferings of the victims were not so important in their own right as they had been in the law of C. Gracchus. It is interesting, therefore, that *Augustus in 4 BC procured the *SC Calvisianum* (*FIRA* 1, p. 609; see CYRENE, EDICTS OF), by which provincials, who only wished simple restitution for their losses, could with the senate's permission have their case investigated by five senatorial *recuperatores*. This return in effect to civil procedure, by reducing the defendant's liability, would be more likely to secure a conviction and compensation, and with less expense and inconvenience, thanks to the swift and less elaborate procedure. Conviction still apparently carried *infamia*, but intercession with the *princeps* could and did reverse this. Cases involving criminal penalties continued alongside the new procedure and many were tried in the senate, after it came to be used as a court in the latter part of Augustus' reign. But senators were reluctant to condemn their peers, and men who enjoyed the emperor's favour were hard to convict. As a result, under *Trajan, the *optimus princeps* ('best emperor'), his clemency was invoked to prevent the punishment even of known offenders. Meanwhile the law came to apply to equestrian jurors and, later, to municipal senators. In the later Empire, the emperor (or praetorian prefect) assumed jurisdiction, and the *Codes* give detailed regulations. By then governors and their staffs were no longer the most serious burden on provincials.

> Text, translation, and commentary on C. Gracchus' law preserved on bronze in A. W. Lintott, *Judicial Reform and Land Reform in the Roman*

Republic (1992). J. P. Balsdon, *PBSR* 1938; A. N. Sherwin-White, *PBSR* 1949; *JRS* 1972, 1982; P. A. Brunt, *Historia* 1961; A. W. Lintott, *ZSS* 1981; J. S. Richardson, *JRS* 1987.   E. B.; A. W. L.

Reposianus (*PLRE* 1. 764), author of a poem in 182 hexameters on the love-affair between *Mars and *Venus, in expression displaying debts to *Virgil and *Ovid. Date uncertain; conjectures range from the 2nd to the early 6th cent. AD.

Texts: *Anth. Lat.* 253 Riese, 247 Shackleton Bailey; with tr., Duff, *Minor Lat. Poets.*   J. H. D. S.

representation, representative government See DEMES; FEDERAL STATES.

reprisal See SYLĒ.

Res Gestae (of *Augustus). Augustus left four documents with the Vestal Virgins (see VESTA) to be read, after his death, in the senate (Suet. *Aug.* 101). One of these was a record of his achievements (*Index rerum a se gestarum*), in the style of the claims of the *triumphatores* of the Roman past, which was to be erected on bronze pillars at the entrance of his mausoleum in the *Campus Martius at Rome. This is known to us from a copy, updated after Augustus' death, which was piously affixed (with a Greek translation) to the *antae* of the front of the *cella* of the temple of Rome and Augustus at *Ancyra, capital of *Galatia and therefore centre of the imperial cult of the province. Small fragments of other copies have been found at *Apollonia and *Antioch (2) in Pisidia (also in the province of Galatia); it is likely but not established that copies were widely set up in the provinces.

As it stands, the document seems to have been composed immediately before Augustus' death, but it is certain that it was in existence in some form in AD 13 and likely that it existed considerably before that. It is remarkable for the claims that it makes for the legality and constitutional propriety of Augustus' position, and plays down a number of considerations, relating especially to the period before *Actium, which might be seen less favourably.

The emphases are extremely interesting: first, the bestowal of honours on Augustus by the community is stressed, consensus being a striking theme; second, the expenditures made, as a great benefactor, by Augustus, are outlined (this is announced in the opening words, which entitle the document a Record of the Achievements and Expenses of the Divine Augustus); third, the military achievements of the age, with the emphasis on *imperium* and the personal glory of Augustus, a historic and unthreatening boast in terms of Roman politics; and a final summary of the position with a justification of the superior *auctoritas* which all of this entailed, and particular notice, accordingly, of the title *pater patriae*. This is a record in the tradition of self-advertisement used by great men under the republic, and not a royal manifesto; it omits anything which might suggest an unconstitutional overall guidance of Roman decision-making, and is not a complete record of either his legislation or his administrative innovations. The document illustrates very well the speciously libertarian traditionalism which *Tacitus (1) so deftly punctures in the opening chapters of the *Annals*; but it is also a very important source for a great deal of detail not attested elsewhere.

Commentaries: Mommsen[2] (1883); E. G. Hardy (1923); P. A. Brunt and J. M. Moore, *Res Gestae Divi Augusti* (1967). See Z. Yavetz, in F. Millar, and E. Segal (eds.), *Augustus Caesar: Seven Aspects* (1984), 1 ff.   N. P.

restaurants See INNS, RESTAURANTS.

restitution 'It is by nature fair that nobody should enrich himself at the expense of another': this is, in the words of Sex. *Pomponius (*Dig.* 12. 6. 14; cf. also *Dig.* 50. 17. 206), the general proposition underlying what is usually referred to as the law of restitution (= unjust enrichment). Obligations arising from unjust enrichment are, as Gaius realized, based neither on contract nor on delict (the main classes (*summa divisio*) of the law of obligations). Justinian placed them in the category of 'quasi-contracts'. The Roman lawyers carved out certain typical situations in which they were prepared to grant a claim (the so-called *condictio*) on the basis that the defendant had no good reason to keep what he had received (*causa retinendi*). A person was granted restitution (*a*) if he had mistakenly paid or delivered what he did not owe (*condictio indebiti*); (*b*) if he had handed over something for a purpose that failed to materialize (*condictio causa data causa non secuta*); (*c*) if he had made a payment or delivery, acceptance of which offended the traditional standards of honest and moral behaviour (*condictio ob turpem vel iniustam causam*; recovery was, however, excluded, where the behaviour of the giver was also morally reprehensible: *in pari turpitudine melior est causa possidentis*); (*d*) in miscellaneous other cases of enrichment without cause (*condictio sine causa*); (*e*) if there had been an unjustified interference with his property (like theft; *condictio ex causa furtiva*). This system of *condictiones* tied in with and ingeniously supplemented the Roman contractual system and was one of the most distinctive achievements of Roman jurisprudence.

F. Schwarz, *Die Grundlage der condictio* (1952); H. Niederländer, *Bereicherungshaftung* (1953); R. Santoro, *Studi Palermo* 1971, 181 ff.; H. Honsell, *Rückabwicklung sittenwidriger und verbotener Geschäfte* (1974); D. Liebs, *Essays Honoré* (1986), 163 ff.; R. Zimmermann, *The Law of Obligations* (1990), 834 ff.   R. Z.

retrospective styles in sculpture. At various times, each of the three main Greek sculptural styles, the Archaic, the Classical, and the Hellenistic Baroque, was revived by both Greeks and Romans, for a variety of reasons and in a variety of contexts (see CLASSICISM; cf. the linguistic phenomenon of ARCHAISM IN LATIN).

1. Archaizing and archaistic sculpture. 'Mannered' or 'archaizing' traits occasionally appear in late Archaic sculpture, and 'lingering Archaic' is a persistent phenomenon of the 5th cent. BC. By *c*.400, however, both the archaizing and completely archaistic styles are fully established. Examples of the former are the Hermes Propylaeus and Hecate Epipyrgidia of *Phidias' pupil *Alcamenes, dated *c*.420. The Hermes grafts an 'Archaic' coiffure on to a classical physiognomy, and the Hecate wears 'Archaic' step-fold drapery. Both stood on the Acropolis, and use the style to convey an aura of ancient sanctity. Fully 'archaic' cult statues appear in pedimental sculpture (the Sack of Troy) at the Argive *Heraion (see ARGOS (2)) and *Epidaurus *c*.410 and 380, and on Attic document reliefs of 356 and 321. Thereafter, both archaizing and fully archaistic sculpture in the round and in relief flourished in both Greece and Rome. Important examples include the frieze of the Propylon at *Samothrace (*c*.340), the Apollo from Piombino (a fake made by Menodotus of Tyre, *c*.50), and the early imperial Artemis from *Pompeii, in Naples.

B. S. Ridgway, *The Archaic Style in Greek Sculpture* (1977), 303 ff.; A. F. Stewart, *Greek Sculpture* (1990), 45, 135, 137 ff., 165, figs. 178, 238, 256, 400, 427, 451, 825, 847, 857; M. D. Fullerton, *The Archaistic Style in Roman Statuary* (1990).

2. Classicizing sculpture. The earliest secure instance of neo-

classicism is the Eirene of *Cephisodotus (1) of *c*.370, which celebrated Athens' recovery from the defeat of 404 by reviving the drapery style of *Phidias. By the Hellenistic period, classicism's connotations of stability, rationality, and authority made it attractive to a turbulent world. Hellenistic neo-classic work ranges from quotations of classic formulae (Great Altar of *Pergamum), through new sculpture—esp. cult statues—partly or wholly in classic style (see DAMOPHON, PASITELES, POLYCLES), to copies and versions of authentically classical originals (Athena Parthenos at Pergamum; see also AGASIAS (1), APOLLONIUS (6), GLYCON (2)).

Neo-classicism particularly flourished in Athens; as the city's political importance declined, nostalgia for vanished glories was joined by a strong commitment to cultural imperialism. The 'Neo-Attic' reliefs are a special case; produced at Athens from *c*.150 BC, they copy works by Phidias and his school (see AGORACRITUS, CALLIMACHUS (2)) for a Roman clientele, often transferring them to decorative items like marble vases. *Augustus made neo-classicism the official style of his reborn Rome *c*.30 BC, and thereafter it became the touchstone for Roman imperial art through Constantine and beyond.

A. F. Stewart, *Greek Sculpture* (1990); D. E. E. Kleiner, *Roman Sculpture* (1992).

3. Neo-baroque sculpture. The Hellenistic baroque was revived in Italy during the late republic and the Augustan period (see APOLLONIUS (7), HAGESANDER), and during the Empire the school of *Aphrodisias produced numerous copies and neo-baroque works. The style's rhetorical character made it generally unsuitable for Roman official sculpture, except in special cases where extreme pathos was required: examples are the panel reliefs and column of Marcus *Aurelius in Rome, the Parthian monument of Lucius *Verus at Ephesus, and several Antonine *sarcophagi.

A. F. Stewart, *Greek Sculpture* (1990), 96 ff., 215 f., 230, figs. 732 ff., 856; D. E. E. Kleiner, *Roman Sculpture* (1992), 288 ff., figs. 257, 266 f., 269, 280, 359. A. F. S.

revenge See CURSES; ERINYES; LAW AND PROCEDURE, ROMAN, § 3. 1; LAW IN GREECE; NEMESIS; PUNISHMENT (GREEK AND ROMAN PRACTICE); RECIPROCITY (GREECE).

rex, the Latin word for king, has an Indo-European root which is found also in *Celtic and *Indo-Iranian languages. Traditionally Rome itself was ruled by kings during its earliest history, but curiously the literary sources are reticent about kingship among other Italic peoples, including the Latins. Apart from a few isolated examples such as king Acron of Caenina (see SPOLIA OPIMA), early Latin kings are rare in the sources, which tend to suggest that the Latin cities were ruled by aristocracies, even during the Roman monarchy. By contrast kings are much better attested among the Etruscans. *Rex* is however found as a priestly title at *Aricia, where the priesthood of *Diana was held by the *rex nemorensis* ('king of the wood'), a runaway slave who had killed his predecessor in single combat and held office for as long as he could defend himself against aspiring successors. At Rome too there was a priest known as the *rex sacrorum* (or *rex sacrificulus*), who in the Republic was confined to minor ritual duties connected with the calendar, but was believed once to have been the most important figure in the priestly hierarchy (Festus, p. 198 Lindsay). The traditional explanation of the *rex sacrorum* is that he was a priest created at the beginning of the Republic to carry out the religious tasks previously performed by the real king. If

this is correct the office of the *rex sacrorum* can be added to the list of relics of monarchy that survived into the Republic (e.g. the *interrex*, the *Regia).

That early Rome was ruled by kings is virtually certain, even if none of the traditional kings has yet been authenticated by direct testimony such as a contemporary inscription. There were supposedly seven kings, whose reigns spanned nearly 250 years, from the founding of the city to the expulsion of Tarquinius Superbus. This is far too long, and there are other reasons too for doubting the chronology of the regal period (see TARQUINIUS SUPERBUS, L.) and for treating the traditional list of kings as an artificial construct. Alternative traditions preserved the names of kings (see TATIUS, T.; MASTARNA), who were not included among the famous seven, and of these latter the first, *Romulus, is clearly no more than a legendary eponym. Of the others, who may be authentic, one (Tullus *Hostilius) was Latin (see LATINI), two (Numa *Pompilius, Ancus *Marcius) were Sabine (see SABINI), and two (the Tarquins) were Etruscan (see TARQUINIUS PRISCUS, L. and SUPERBUS). The origin of Servius *Tullius was disputed.

According to tradition the Roman monarchy was not hereditary but elective. Under the regular procedure the *patricians nominated the king through tenure of the office of *interrex, but their choice had to be ratified by a vote of the *comitia curiata and by favourable signs from the gods at an inauguration ceremony (Livy 1. 18. 6–10). It is noteworthy that none of the traditional kings was a patrician; most of them were in some sense outsiders, some indeed foreigners. This feature, which has many parallels in other historical monarchies, should not be dismissed as fictitious, nor should it be assumed that the accession of an Etruscan (Tarquinius Priscus) occurred because Rome had been the victim of an Etruscan conquest. The last two kings, Servius Tullius and Tarquinius Superbus, are presented in the sources as usurpers who adopted a tyrannical style of rule. This is quite possibly historical, given the close contacts between Rome and the Greek world in the 6th cent. BC: see TYRANNY

The powers of the king cannot be reconstructed in detail. The accounts of the sources presuppose that the king's power was enshrined in the concept of *imperium, which was taken over by the magistrates of the republic. It is probable enough that the trappings of power, which symbolized the absolute authority of the holder of *imperium*, go back to the time of the kings; they include the *fasces, purple robes, and the *sella curulis, which were supposedly borrowed from the Etruscans. The ceremony of the *triumph, in which the victorious general bore all the regal insignia, was probably also a relic of the monarchy (it too was of Etruscan origin). It seems likely that the king commanded in war and exercised supreme jurisdiction; on the other hand he probably had to work with an advisory council (the senate) and a popular assembly (the *comitia curiata*), both of which seem to have existed in the regal period.

The religious authority of the kings is more problematic. Even if the king, and his Republican surrogate, the *rex sacrorum*, held the highest priestly position, tradition also traces other major priesthoods, such as the pontiffs and the augurs (see PRIESTS; PONTIFEX; AUGURES), back to the regal period. This must imply that the king did not have a monopoly of priestly authority. Conflict between king and priest is clearly evident in the story of Tarquin the Elder and the augur Attus Navius (Livy 1. 36; Dion. Hal. 3. 70–1; Cic. *de div.* 1. 31–2).

On the other hand, a well-known theory maintains that the king retained his religious authority longer than his other powers, and that the *rex sacrorum* of the republic was in fact the real king who had been gradually reduced to a purely ceremonial figure by a gradual process of change during the archaic period. On this view the king's military and judicial powers were taken over by a secular magistrate, either an annual *dictator or *magister populi*, or by a supreme *praetor maximus* (cf. Livy 7. 3. 5; see PRAETOR). Only at a secondary stage, variously dated to *c.*450 or even 367 BC, did the Romans institute the collegiate office of two equal *consuls. The traditional story, however, which most scholars are inclined to accept in broad outline, is that at the end of the 6th cent. the last king was expelled by a group of aristocrats, who set up a republic under two annually elected consuls.

During the republic the Romans are supposed to have been profoundly hostile to the very idea of kingship. It is doubtful, however, if this was ever a deeply held popular view; it seems rather to have been part of the aristocratic ideology of the Republican ruling class which viewed the rise of charismatic individuals with alarm, particularly if they were backed by popular support. It is no accident that all serious charges of monarchism (*regnum*) were levelled against mavericks from the ruling élite who attempted to help the poor—Sp. *Cassius Vecellinus, Sp. *Maelius, M. *Manlius Capitolinus, the *Gracchi. When the Caesars revived the monarchy at Rome (see IULIUS CAESAR (1), C.; AUGUSTUS), they avoided the title *rex* not because it was unpopular, but because it was unacceptable to the nobility.

H. Jordan, *Die Könige im alten Italien* (1887); Mommsen, *Staatsr.* 2². 1 (1887), 4 ff.; J. G. Frazer, *Lectures on the Early History of the Kingship* (1905); A. Rosenberg, *RE* 5 A 1, 703–21, 'Rex'; S. Mazzarino, *Dalla monarchia allo stato repubblicano* (1945); U. Coli, *Regnum* (*Studia et documenta historiae et iuris*, 1951); F. De Martino, *Storia della costituzione romana* 1² (1972); J. Heurgon, *The Rise of Rome* (1973), 112 ff.; P. M. Martin, *L'Idée de royauté a Rome* 1 (1982); J. Poucet, *Les origines de Rome* (1985); G. Valditara, *Studi sul magister populi* (1989); A. Momigliano, *CAH* 7²/2 (1989), 87 ff.; E. Rawson, *Roman Culture and Society* (1991), ch. 9.   T. J. Co.

rex nemorensis, the 'king of the grove', i.e. *Diana's grove near *Aricia, in central Italy. This priest was unique among religious officials of the Roman world, in being an escaped slave who acquired office by killing his predecessor, after issuing a challenge by plucking a branch from a particular tree in the grove. See Strabo 5. 3. 12, 239; Suet. *Calig.* 35; Servius on *Aen.* 6. 36. The 'mystery' of the priest of Nemi is the starting-point of J. G. Frazer's *The Golden Bough*.

T. Blagg, in O. de Cazanove and J. Scheid (eds.), *Les Bois sacrés* (1993); J. Z. Smith, *Map is Not Territory* (1978), ch. 10.   M. B.

rex sacrorum On the expulsion of the kings from Rome (see REX; TARQUINIUS SUPERBUS, L.) their sacral functions were partially assumed by a priest called *rex sacrorum* 'the king for sacred rites' (and his wife, the *regina*, 'queen'). He sacrificed on the Kalends; on the Nones he announced the days of festivals, *feriae* (Varro, *Ling.* 6. 13, 28; Macrob. *Sat.* 1. 15. 9–12, 19); and he celebrated the rite of *regifugium*. A *patrician, born of 'confarreate' marriage (Gaius 1. 112; see MANUS), he ranked first among the priests (Festus, *Gloss. Lat.* 299), but was subordinate to the *pontifex maximus. He served for life, and might hold no other post (Livy 2. 2; 40. 42. 9; Dion. Hal. *Ant. Rom.* 4. 74. 4). See REX.

R. E. A. Palmer, *The King and the Comitium* (1969); R. Seguin, in *Hommages H. Le Bonniec* (1988), 405 ff.   J. L.

Rhadamanthys, in mythology usually the son of *Zeus and *Europa (Hom. *Il.* 14. 321–2, Hes. fr. 141. 13 M–W), although an obscure tradition gives the genealogy Cres (eponymous hero of *Crete)–*Talos (1)–*Hephaestus–Rhadamanthys (Cinaethon in

Paus. 8. 53. 5). He did not die but went to *Elysium, where the most blessed mortals live in bliss. There he is a ruler and judge (Pind. *Ol.* 2. 75 ff.). He is universally renowned for his wisdom and justice (e.g. Pind. *Pyth.* 2. 73 f.), and is one of the judges of the dead in the Underworld, along with his brother *Minos and *Aeacus (Pl. *Apol.* 41a adds *Triptolemus). In *Virgil (*Aen.* 6. 566) he presides over *Tartarus and punishes the wicked for their sins. It is sometimes said that he married *Alcmene after the death of *Amphitryon and lived in exile at Ocaleae in *Boeotia (Apollod. 2. 4. 1, Plut. *Lysander* 28).

LIMC 7. 1 (1994), 626–8.   J. R. M.

Rhamnus, a *deme of moderate size on the north-east coast of *Attica, overlooking the narrow waters to *Euboea. It was the site of an important fort, constructed in the 5th cent. BC and enlarged in the 4th, on an acropolis by the coast and including a gymnasium and theatre within its walls. A road lined with a series of monumental tombs runs inland from this acropolis to the sanctuary of *Nemesis with its two 5th-cent. temples. The late 5th-cent. temple of Nemesis is relatively well preserved, and it has been possible to reconstruct its entablature and a large part of the famous cult statue, attributed to *Agoracritus, with its base. Neolithic and late Bronze Age finds have also been made at the sanctuary site. The epigraphic record from 5th–3rd-cent. Rhamnus gives uniquely rich coverage of the interactions between garrison troops and local population.

Paus. 1. 32. 2–8; Plin. *HN* 36. 17; J. Pouilloux, *La Forteresse de Rhamnonte* (1954); *Hesperia* 1989, 133–249; R. G. Osborne, in O. Murray and S. Price (eds.), *The Greek City* (1990), 277–93.   C. W. J. E.; R. G. O.

Rhampsinitus, i.e. Ramses (III?), to whom a folk-tale (Stith Thompson, K 315. 1) is attached in *Herodotus (1) 2. 121. The builder of his treasury left a secret entrance and after his death his two sons stole therefrom. One being trapped, the other beheaded him, avoided capture himself, and at last was reconciled to the king. It has been suggested (Fehling) that Herodotus got the story from the *Telegony* (see EPIC CYCLE).

D. Fehling, *Herodotus and his 'Sources'* (1989), 199, 210 f.; W. K. Pritchett, *The Liar School of Herodotus* (1993), 23.   H. J. R.; S. H.

rhapsodes were professional reciters of poetry, particularly of *Homer but also of other poets (Ath. 14. 620 a–d, cf. Pl. *Ion* 531 a). The name, which means 'song-stitcher', is first attested in the 5th cent. (*GDI* 5786, Hdt. 5. 67, Soph. *OT* 391), but implies the formulaic compositional technique of earlier minstrels; cf. ῥάψαντες ἀοιδήν 'stitching song' 'Hes.' fr. 357 M–W, ῥαπτῶν ἐπέων ἀοιδοί 'singers of stitched words' Pind. *Nem.* 2. 1 (variously explained by schol.). Originally reciters of *epic accompanied themselves on the lyre, but later they carried a staff instead (cf. Hes. *Th.* 30 with 95). Both are shown on vases; *Plato (1) distinguishes rhapsodes from citharodes, but classes Homer's Phemius as a rhapsode (*Ion* 533 b–c). In the 5th and 4th cents. rhapsodes were a familiar sight, especially at public festivals and games, where they competed for prizes. They declaimed from a dais (ibid. 535 e), and hoped to attract a crowd by their conspicuous attire (ibid. 530 b, 535 d) and loud melodious voice (Diod. 14. 109). They would be likely to own texts of Homer (Xen. *Mem.* 4. 2. 10), but recited from memory (Xen. *Symp.* 3. 6). They were carefully trained, and preserved a traditional pronunciation of Homer down to Alexandrian times (J. Wackernagel, *Kl. Schr.* (1956), 1094 ff.), probably under the influence of the *Homeridae, who were looked up to as authorities and arbiters (cf. Pl. *Ion* 530 d). A good rhapsode might be filled with emotion while reciting, and communicate it to his audience (ibid. 535 b–e), and there was felt to be a kinship between him and the actor (ibid. 532 d, 536 a, *Resp.* 395 a; Alcid. *Soph.* 14; Arist. *Rhet.* 1403[b]22); but he is not to be confused with the 'Homerist' ('Ομηριστής), the low-class actor of Homeric scenes who was later popular (Dem. Phal. in Ath. 14. 620 b, Petron. 59, Artemid. 4. 2, Ach. Tat. 3. 20. 4, *POxy.* 519. 4, etc.). Though despised as stupid by the educated (Xen. as above) and a byword for unreliability (*Suda* iv. 286. 26, 30, 287. 6 Adler), rhapsodes continued to practise their art and compete at games at least down to the 3rd cent. AD (e.g. *SIG*[3] 711 1 30, 958. 35, 959. 9, *IG* 7. 1773. 17, 1776. 15). M. L. W.

Rhea See CRONUS; MELISSA; ROMULUS AND REMUS.

Rhegium (mod. Reggio di Calabria), a Chalcidian colony in S. Italy (see CHALCIS; COLONIZATION, GREEK), founded *c.*720 BC and reinforced by Messenians (see MESSENIA) *c.*600 BC; it dominated the Straits of Messina (see MESSANA). In the 5th cent. it was ruled by the tyrants *Anaxilas (1) and Micythus, before adopting an oligarchic constitution. External relations hinged on alliance with Messana and rivalry with Locri until the 4th cent., when *Dionysius (1) I backed *Locri Epizephyrii against Rhegium and ultimately sacked it. It was restored *c.*350 by *Dionysius (2) II, but remained under Syracusan influence. Relations with Rome were good, and Rhegium was one of the few Greek cities to ally with Rome against *Pyrrhus. It was garrisoned by Rome's Campanian allies, who turned on the Rhegines, killed their ruling élite, and took control of the city, possibly to forestall a secession to Pyrrhus. They remained in power until 275, when Rome ejected them and restored the city to the Greeks. Rhegium remained loyal during the *Punic Wars and the *Social War (3) and became a *municipium*, gaining the title Regium Iulium after 33 BC, although apparently without the foundation of a colony. It remained important as a route to Sicily, and retained some of its Greek cults and institutions until the 2nd cent. AD.

G. Vallet, *Rhégion et Zancle* (1958). K. L.

Rhenus, the Rhine (from the Celtic *Renos*). The Rhine became the Roman frontier in *Caesar's time and, despite *Augustus' attempt (12 BC–AD 9) to move beyond it and a somewhat longer (Flavians to *c.* AD 260) projection of the Upper German frontier to the *limes*, it remained so until the collapse of the western Empire. A strong military presence on the Rhine gave Roman Gaul its shape and its *raison d'être* (the shielding of Italy); once this was gone, the north-western provinces were just a burden.

As a means of communication, the river, with its important tributaries and outlets to the North Sea, was of vital military importance, as between units, between the armies of Germany and Britain, and during campaigns. From 12 BC the Romans maintained a fleet on it, with its headquarters at Cologne (see COLONIA AGRIPPINENSIS). It was also a great channel of commerce. Roman bridges existed above Basle and at Mainz, Coblenz, and Cologne; Caesar's bridges were built near Andernach.

Ancient writers regarded the Rhine as having two or three mouths, probably the Waal (Vahalis), the Old Rhine, and the Vecht. Nero *Claudius Drusus canalized the Vecht outlet, and he also raised a dike, near the delta, completed by Pompeius Paulinus in AD 55 to regulate the flow of the Rhine. Cn. *Domitius Corbulo dug a channel, the Vliet, between Rhine and Meuse. Generally, however, the Roman river was much different from its modern, canalized, successor. It was longer, wider and therefore, at times, much shallower—which, for example, made it much more subject to freezing in winter.

C. G. Starr, *Roman Imperial Navy* (1960); J. du Plat Taylor and J. Cleere (eds.), *Roman Shipping and Trade* (1978).

Another Rhenus (Reno) flowed into the Po near Bononia, and on an island here the Triumvirate (see TRIUMVIRI) was formed in 43 BC. J. F. Dr.

Rhesis See SPEECH PRESENTATION.

Rhesus, a *Thracian ally of *Priam. *Iliad* 10 (a post-Homeric addition) tells how *Odysseus and *Diomedes (2), learning of his arrival before Troy from the Trojan spy Dolon, stole into his camp, killed him and twelve of his men, and carried off his magnificent horses. Other authors told of a prophecy that, if his horses had fed or drunk at Troy, the city could not have fallen (so Verg. *Aen.* 1. 469–73), or alternatively credited him with some fighting at Troy before his death. The story is also the subject of the *Rhesus* attributed to *Euripides. While *Iliad* 10 makes Rhesus the son of Eïoneus, the play makes him the son of the river Strymon and a Muse (see MUSES). The Muse appears with his body at the end, and declares that he will live on as a demigod (970–3).

B. Fenik, *Iliad X and the Rhesos: the Myth* (*Latomus* 1964); P. Borgeaud in Borgeaud (ed.), *Orphisme et Orphée* (1991), 51 ff.; R. Parker in R. Osborne and S. Hornblower (eds.), *Ritual, Finance, Politics* (1994), 340 and n. 4 (both on the connection between the founding of *Amphipolis and the bones of Rhesus; see Polyaenus, *Strat.* 6. 53, and cf. RELICS). A. L. B.

rhetoric, Greek The art of public speaking (ῥητορική (sc. τέχνη)) was vitally important in ancient city-states, and it was generally supposed to be teachable, at least to some extent. This article surveys the development of this teaching in the Greek-speaking world, and offers a summary of the system in which it was generally organized. The concepts and terminology of rhetoric are almost entirely Greek: the Romans provided a wider field of activity for the teachers, and certain new emphases in response to practical needs.

Effective speaking of course existed long before any theory or teaching. Later rhetors wisely referred pupils to the speeches in *Homer (see Quintilian 10. 1. 46 ff.), and his descriptions of the oratory of the heroes (see LITERARY CRITICISM, § 2) were taken as evidence that 'rhetoric' was known in his day. In fact, the teaching of these skills probably began (as *Aristotle thought) under the pressure of social and political needs in the 5th-cent. democracies of Syracuse and Athens (see CORAX; TISIAS; GORGIAS (1)). Even if the first mode of teaching was primarily by example (as in the demonstration pieces of Gorgias, *Thrasymachus, and *Antiphon (1)), this presupposes some theory of the parts of a speech (prologue, narrative, argument, counter-argument, epilogue) and some discussion of probable arguments and the value of different kinds of evidence. The early teachers cannot be responsible for the brilliant achievements of Attic orators from *Lysias to *Hyperides; these are due to individual genius and political stimulus. Behind the great orators, however, stood the mass of average Athenians, dependent for their success in life, and often for their personal safety, on the exertions of speechwriters (*logographoi; Lysias and *Demosthenes (2) both wrote speeches for others) or on the teaching they could pick up themselves. The large jury-courts made forensic oratory almost as much a matter of mass appeal as deliberative speeches in the assembly, but there were naturally substantial differences between these two genres which the teachers recognized. Ceremonial speeches (like the public funeral speeches, see EPITAPHIOS) again made different demands–less argument, more emotion, more ornamentation. The *Rhetorica ad Alexandrum* (see ANAXIMENES (2)) gives an idea of the type of teaching available in the late 4th cent.:

systematic, but arid, and with no attention to basic principles. But questions about the status and value of rhetoric were already being asked; and both *Isocrates and the philosophers made important contributions. Isocrates wrote speeches for litigants, and is credited (probably wrongly) with having written a textbook. His importance is as an educator, whose 'philosophy' ($\phi\iota\lambda o\sigma o\phi\acute{\iota}\alpha$) was distinct from the *sophists' logic and rhetoric and also from the dialectic and mathematics of *Plato (1). He wished to give his pupils the right moral and political attitudes, and his method was to make them write about such things and criticize and discuss his own work (5. 17 ff., 12. 200 ff.). This was to make a claim for instruction in writing and speaking, under the name of 'philosophy', as a complete education in itself. For Plato, Isocrates' approach was hardly more valid than that of the sophists and rhetoricians of the previous age. He attacks them all (*Gorgias, Phaedrus*) as deceivers and perverters of the truth. A 'philosophical' rhetoric, he says (*Phaedrus* 271c ff.), would be based on an adequate psychology; this at least would have some value. Plato's hint was taken up by his pupil, Aristotle, who gave instruction in rhetoric as well as in philosophy, and wrote the most influential of all treatises on the subject. This work, the *Rhetoric*, the product of many years and some changes of mind, deals in its three books with three main topics: (*a*) the theory of rhetorical, as distinct from philosophical, argument—enthymeme and example; (*b*) the state of mind of the audience and the ways of appealing to their prejudices and emotions; (*c*) style, its basic virtues (clarity, appropriateness), and the use of metaphor. Much of what Aristotle left inchoate (delivery ($\dot{\upsilon}\pi\acute{o}\kappa\rho\iota\sigma\iota s$), the virtues and types of style) was developed by his pupil *Theophrastus (see LITERARY CRITICISM IN ANTIQUITY, § 5).

When forensic and political oratory became less important, under the Hellenistic monarchies and later, rhetoric still continued; outliving its original function, it became the principal educational instrument in the spread of Greek culture. Isocrates' attitudes triumphed. We know little about the technical rhetoric of Hellenistic times. *Hermagoras, with his doctrine of types of issue ($\sigma\tau\acute{\alpha}\sigma\epsilon\iota s$), is probably the most important figure. The philosophical schools, especially the Stoics (see STOICISM), were also concerned with the subject. It is the *Rhetoric* of *Philodemus that gives us our best Greek evidence for the discussion of wider questions, e.g. whether rhetoric is an art, and whether forensic and epideictic oratory can be regarded as species of the same activity. The stimulus of Rome, where significant political activity was in the hands of an aristocracy eager to learn, led to a revival of rhetoric in the 1st cent. BC (see RHETORIC, LATIN). The work of people like *Apollodorus (5), *Apollonius (9), *Theodorus (3) is only to be understood against a Roman background. With the revival of a more independent Greek literature in imperial times, Greek rhetoric (especially epideictic) took on a new lease of life; success in the schools might lead to a brilliant career as a sophist; see SECOND SOPHISTIC. The bulk of the extant works on rhetoric comes from this period, or later. The last great systematizer was *Hermogenes (2); his work and the voluminous later commentaries on it (especially those of *Syrianus) afford the best extant synthesis in Greek, though R. Volkmann (1885) was surely right to find in the more humane Roman *Quintilian the only 'Ariadne's clue' to the labyrinth of confusing terminology and theory.

Volkmann (and e.g. J. Martin (1974)) are able to set out a description of ancient rhetorical teaching which would be roughly valid for the whole Hellenistic and Roman period, because the conservatism of the educational system ensured that,

whatever refinements individual teachers or schools introduced, the main lines of instruction remained the same. The basic divisions of a speech (prologue, etc.) and the basic classification of oratory (forensic, deliberative, epideictic) go back, as we have seen, to the 4th cent. BC. They continue to fulfil a useful function in all later writers; but the method of organizing the whole subject which prevailed later derives ultimately from Aristotle's *Rhetoric*, and comprises five divisions:

1. 'Invention' ($\epsilon\ddot{\upsilon}\rho\epsilon\sigma\iota s$) is the most important, and corresponds essentially to Aristotle's 'proofs' ($\pi\acute{\iota}\sigma\tau\epsilon\iota s$). It teaches how to 'find' ($\epsilon\dot{\upsilon}\rho\acute{\iota}\sigma\kappa\epsilon\iota\nu$) things to say to meet the question at issue. The central doctrine is that of 'issue' ($\sigma\tau\acute{\alpha}\sigma\iota s$, Lat. *status*), developed by Hermagoras and refined by many later writers. Hermagoras distinguished four 'issues': 'conjecture' ($\sigma\tau o\chi\alpha\sigma\mu\acute{o}s$), e.g. 'Did X kill Y?'; 'definition' ($\ddot{o}\rho os$), e.g. 'Was it murder?'; 'quality' ($\pi o\iota\acute{o}\tau\eta s$), e.g. 'Was it honourable or expedient?'; 'transference' ($\mu\epsilon\tau\acute{\alpha}\lambda\eta\psi\iota s$), e.g. 'It was all Y's fault.' Such analyses, obviously useful to advocates and debaters and for interpreting the orators, inevitably led into great scholastic complexities, as in Hermogenes or *Sopater (2).

2. 'Disposition' ($o\dot{\iota}\kappa o\nu o\mu\acute{\iota}\alpha$) comprises prescriptions for the division of subject-matter within the 'parts' of a speech, and some common-sense advice about arrangement—e.g. 'put your weakest points in the middle'.

3. Diction ($\lambda\acute{\epsilon}\xi\iota s$, $\phi\rho\acute{\alpha}\sigma\iota s$) was the area where rhetoric comes closest to literary criticism as it was practised in ancient times. Not only types of style, but figures, tropes, word-order, rhythm, and euphony were discussed. Figures ($\sigma\chi\acute{\eta}\mu\alpha\tau\alpha$), at least in the developed systems (see CAECILIUS (1); GORGIAS (2)), were generally regarded as deviant or unnatural ($\pi\alpha\rho\grave{\alpha}$ $\phi\acute{\upsilon}\sigma\iota\nu$) forms of expression or thought; tropes ($\tau\rho\acute{o}\pi o\iota$) were similarly deviant (abnormal, non-literal) uses of words, such as occur in metaphor, metonymy, hyperbole, etc.

4. Delivery ($\dot{\upsilon}\pi\acute{o}\kappa\rho\iota\sigma\iota s$) was clearly a vital skill, and ancient taste approved of much artifice in pronunciation and gesture, so long as the orator's dignity was preserved.

5. 'Memory' ($\mu\nu\acute{\eta}\mu\eta$) was also a subject of instruction and various forms of 'arts of memory' were taught, involving memorization of visual features (e.g. columns in a colonnade) and the trick of associating these with the points to be made. It was bad form to read from a text, and speeches in court could be very long.

Naturally, the order in which these skills were taught did not follow this pattern. One cannot teach 'invention' and 'diction' quite separately. There was however a recognized course of exercises (see PROGYMNASMATA; DECLAMATION), and if we look for the influence of rhetorical teaching on literary practice, it is here that it is principally to be found.

TEXTS C. Walz, *Rhetores Graeci*, 9 vols. (1832–6) contains the fullest collection. L. Spengel, *Rhetores Graeci*, 3 vols. (1853–6; 1² rev. C. Hammer, 1894) remains the handiest selection. Some authors (e.g. 'Aristides', Hermogenes) have been critically edited in the Teubner series by H. Rabe and others. See also PROGYMNASMATA; MENANDER (4) 'RHETOR'; ANAXIMENES (2).

Pre-Aristotelian texts are collected in L. Radermacher, *Artium Scriptores* (1951). Aristotle's *Rhetoric*: comm. E. Cope (1867–77), critical text R. Kassel (1976), trans. W. Rhys Roberts (1924), G. A. Kennedy (1991), H. Lawson-Tancred (1991).

J. C. G. Ernesti, *Lexicon Technologiae Graecorum Rhetoricae* (1795, repr. 1962), has not been superseded. G. Ueding, *Historisches Wörterbuch der Rhetorik* (1992–), is a valuable reference work just beginning to appear.

Surveys of the whole field include: W. Kroll, in *RE* Suppl. 7 (1940) 1040–1138; R. Volkmann, *Die Rhetorik der Griechen und Römer*² (1885);

J. Martin, *Antike Rhetorik* (1974); B. Vickers, *In Defence of Rhetoric* (1988). G. A. Kennedy's three volumes (*The Art of Persuasion in Greece*, 1963; *The Art of Rhetoric in the Roman World*, 1972; *Greek Rhetoric under Christian Emperors*, 1983) provide a full and readable historical account. See also: C. S. Baldwin, *Ancient Rhetoric and Poetic* (1928); D. L. Clark, *Rhetoric in Greco-Roman Education* (1957); D. A. Russell, *Greek Declamation* (1983); T. Cole, *The Origin of Rhetoric in Ancient Greece* (1991); and other references under RHETORIC, LATIN.

The International Society for the History of Rhetoric, and its journal *Rhetorica*, make important contributions to the subject, which has wide ramifications in literary studies of all kinds.   D. A. R.

rhetoric, Latin Oratory at Rome was born early. Rhetoric—speaking reduced to a method—came later, an import from Greece that aroused suspicion. M. *Porcius Cato (1) (the Censor), himself a distinguished speaker, pronounced *rem tene, verba sequentur*, 'get a grip on the content: the words will follow'; and rhetoricians professing to supply the words risked expulsion (as in 161 BC). But Greek teachers trained the Gracchi; *Lucilius (1) teased T. *Albucius for the intricacy of his Graecizing mosaics in words; and *Cicero marks out M. Aemilius Lepidus Porcina (consul 137) as the first master of a smoothness and periodic structure that rivalled the Greeks. In the last quarter of the 2nd cent. prose rhythms based on contemporary Hellenistic practice appear unmistakably in the orators' fragments. In 92 BC Latin rhetoricians came under the castigation of the *censors; Cicero for one wanted to be taught by them, but was kept by his elders to the normal path of instruction in Greek exercises, doubtless declamation. The respectable orator M. *Antonius (1) wrote a *libellus* that showed knowledge of Hermagoras' *status*-lore. Soon came both the *Rhetorica ad Herennium* and Cicero's *De inventione*: the former a complete manual, the latter, closely related to it, only partial, but both evidence of the sophisticated declamation-based rhetoric taught by Greeks in Rome in the 80s.

Cicero never came nearer than this to writing a rhetorical handbook, though his *Partitiones oratoriae* and *Topica* handled aspects of the subject. In his major rhetorical work, the *De oratore* (55), dialogue form militates against technical exposition; moreover, Cicero was concerned to inculcate his idea of the philosophic orator, with the widest possible education, able to speak 'ornately and copiously' (1. 21) on any topic, and this naturally went with criticism of those who thought that one could become an orator by reading a textbook. Nevertheless, the *De oratore* contained much traditional material; as did the later *Orator* (46 BC), in which Cicero contrasted the 'perfect orator', well educated and commanding every kind of style, modelled on Demosthenes and, implicitly, on Cicero himself, with the so-called Atticists, contemporaries who had a narrower and more austere ideal of oratory (see ASIANISM AND ATTICISM). Cicero thus was here defending his own oratorical practice, especially in the matter of wordplay and rhythm; and this practice, no less than the precepts educed from his rhetorical works, was carefully studied by later rhetoricians.

The *Philippics* of Cicero, however, were the last examples of great oratory used to influence political action at Rome. Oratory of course went on under the Principate, but its practical effect was mainly in the lawcourts. Declamation continued to dominate the schools, fascinating even grown men; and it increasingly imparted a crisper style not only to public oratory but also to literature in general. As in the period after the death of *Demosthenes (2), rhetorical theory, which had always concentrated on forensic oratory, was if anything encouraged by the new political climate. The dispute of *Apollodorus (5) and

*Theodorus (3) about the rigidity with which rhetorical rules were to be observed was typical of the new mood; and C. *Valgius Rufus brought Apollodorus' precepts to Latin readers. The first half of the 1st cent. AD was marked by the contribution of *Cornelius Celsus, whose encyclopaedia went into some detail on rhetoric, and by *Rutilius Lupus' translation (of which part survives) of a Greek work on figures. A little later the elder *Pliny (1) wrote a (lost) work giving detailed instructions on the education of an orator.

The massive *Institutio* of *Quintilian takes account of this earlier work, if only to reject it; but, more important, it looks back over it to Cicero, and amidst all its detail retains Cicero's enthusiasm for a wide training and his dislike of trivial technicality. There was much in the *Institutio* that reflected contemporary conditions, especially its concern with declamation; but it maintained, in defiance of history, the ideal of the 'good man skilled in speaking' (*vir bonus dicendi peritus*: M. *Porcius Cato (1)'s phrase), whose eloquence should guide the senate and people of Rome (12. 1. 26). For a more realistic assessment of oratory under the early Empire we have to look to *Tacitus (1)'s more or less contemporary *Dialogus*. Despite all this, the *Institutio* retained interest, particularly in the Renaissance, as a handbook on style and a repository of rhetorical wisdom.

Halm's collection of *Rhetores Latini Minores* may illustrate the ossification and puerility of Latin rhetoric after the 1st cent., in the pat question-and-answer of Fortunatianus and the derivative compendium of *Iulius Victor. Oratory of this period is represented by the *Panegyrici Latini* that have come down to us (see PANEGYRIC (LATIN)); and the letters of *Fronto in the 2nd cent. reflect the new importance of eulogy. From the schoolroom we have the extravagances of the *Major Declamations*. Rhetoricians continued to flourish, and even found themselves celebrated in the poetry of *Ausonius; their pupils were in demand as barristers and imperial officials. Many of the Church fathers started out teaching the subject; and rhetoric was turned to Christian uses in the *De Doctrina Christiana* of *Augustine and *Cassiodorus' *Institutiones*.

For a summary of ancient rhetorical doctrine, which was usually Greek in origin but found some of its best surviving expositors in Latin, see RHETORIC, GREEK. See also COLOR; COMMUNES LOCI; DECLAMATION; DIVISIO; IMITATIO; INVECTIVE; NARRATIO; PROSE-RHYTHM, LATIN; TOPOS.

To the bibliography for RHETORIC, GREEK (see also those on DECLAMATION and QUINTILIAN) add M. L. Clarke, *Rhetoric at Rome* (1953); H. Lausberg, *Handbuch der literarischen Rhetorik* (1960). On rhetoric in the speeches of Cicero see C. Neumeister, *Grundsätze der forensischen Rhetorik* (1964); W. Stroh, *Taxis und Taktik* (1975); C. J. Classen, *Recht–Rhetorik–Politik* (1985).   M. W.

Rhetorica ad Herennium The treatise on rhetoric in four books addressed to an unidentified C. Herennius (perhaps written *c*.86–82 BC) is by an unknown author. Some, interpreting passages of *Quintilian, assign it to *Cornificius (1). The manuscripts' attribution to Cicero is no longer accepted, though the book seems to emerge from the same source as the contemporary *De inventione*. Rhetoric is treated under five traditional heads, Invention, Arrangement, Delivery, Memory, and Style. This last, taking up the whole of bk. 4, is especially valuable; it is rich in examples, most notably of the Grand, Middle, and Plain Styles, together with their neighbouring 'vices' (4. 11–16). The author polemicizes against Greek rhetoricians, and studiedly gives his inherited material a Roman tone. The book was exceedingly popular in the Middle Ages. See RHETORIC, LATIN.

TEXTS F. Marx (major edn. 1894, with Prolegomena and Index; minor edn. 1923, repr. 1964, with addenda by W. Trillitzsch (Teubner)); H. Caplan (Loeb, 1954), with excellent trans. and notes; G. Achard, (Budé, 1989).

COMMENTARY G. Calboli (1969).

CONCORDANCE Abbott–Oldfather–Canter (see under CICERO).

GENERAL J. Adamietz, *Ciceros De inventione und die Rhetorik ad Herennium* (1960).   H. Cn.; M. W.

Rhetra, the Great See SPARTA, § (2); TYRTAEUS.

Rhianus of *Crete, poet and scholar; born *c.*275 BC at Bene (?= Lebena) or Ceraea; began life as a slave, working as attendant at a wrestling-school, but was later educated and became a school-teacher. One of his epigrams (70 Powell) mentions *Troezen, and it has been conjectured that he moved to mainland Greece.

Works Rhianus produced an influential edition of *Homer, more conservative than *Zenodotus'. He also wrote epigrams (66–76 Powell), mostly on erotic themes, but was best known as a prolific writer of epic poetry. Only small fragments (mostly geographical names) survive of his *Heracleia* (probably in 14 books), possibly modelled on that of *Panyassis, and the ethnographical epics *Thessalica* (at least 16 books), *Achaïca* (at least 4 books), and *Eliaca* (at least 3 books). We are better informed about the *Messeniaca* (at least 6 books): two papyrus fragments (*Suppl. Hell.* 923, 946) have been plausibly attributed to it, and *Pausanias (3) used it as a source for his narrative (4. 14–24) of the 'Second Messenian War'; see MESSENIA, *Myth-history*. It recounted the uprising of the Messenians, led by *Aristomenes (1), against Spartan rule, the siege and fall of their stronghold on Mt. Hira, the adventures of the defeated insurgents, and Aristomenes' death in Rhodes. (Historians generally place these events in the early 5th cent.; but Wade-Gery argues for a dating *c.*600.) We cannot determine which elements in Pausanias can be ascribed to Rhianus, but such episodes as Aristomenes' affair with the priestess (4. 17. 1), his escape from prison (4. 18. 5–6), and the adulterous intrigue of the herdsman double-agent (4. 20. 5–10) have a poetic flavour. It is not known to which, if any, of the epics the longest fragment (1 Powell) belongs: some regard it as a complete poem; its 21 lines, on human folly, written in straightforward Homerizing style with an admixture of Hesiodic diction, are sometimes interpreted as an attack on the pretensions of Hellenistic monarchs.

Rhianus represents a type of poetry very different from that of *Callimachus (3), but the scantiness of his surviving fragments makes aesthetic judgements hazardous.

TEXTS Powell, *Coll. Alex.* 9–21; *Suppl. Hell.* 715–6, 923, 946 (? and 941–5); Jacoby, *FGrH* 265; (epigrams) Gow–Page, *HE* 1. 174–6, 2. 503–8.

GENERAL M. Kokolakis, Ῥιανὸς ὁ Κρής (1968: repr. Φιλολογικὰ Μελετήματα [1976] 129–62); K. Rigsby, *Rev. Ét. Grec.* 1986, 350–5 (on birthplace); H. T. Wade-Gery, in E. Badian (ed.), *Ancient Society and its Institutions* (1966), 289–302; R. Pfeiffer, *Hist. Class. Schol.*, 1 (1968), 122, 148–9; A. Cameron, *Callimachus and his Critics* (1995) 297 ff.   F. W.

Rhine See RHENUS.

Rhinthon, writer of phlyax-plays (see PHLYAKES). A potter's son, probably from *Tarentum (Steph. Byz. under Τάρας, Suda ρ 171), living early in the 3rd cent. BC. He was honoured with an epitaph by the poetess *Nossis of Locri (*Anth. Pal.* 7. 414 = Gow–Page, *HE*, 1. x), who calls him a *Syracusan and praises the originality of his 'tragic *phlyakes*', presumably because he gave dignity to a previously crude genre by his comic treatment of tragic themes. Of 38 pieces attributed to Rhinthon nine titles are preserved (almost all burlesques of Euripidean subjects; see EURIPIDES), but very meagre fragments (in Doric) survive. One (fr. 10) from his *Orestas* (Orestes) mentions 'the metre of *Hipponax', i.e. scazons, after a curse in that metre has apparently been inserted into the more normal iambic trimeters.

FRAGMENTS E. Völker, *Rhinthonis fragmenta* (1887); G. Kaibel, *CGF* (1899), 183–9; A. Olivieri, *Frammenti della commedia greca e del mimo nella Sicilia e nella Magna Grecia* 2² (1947), 7–24.

INTERPRETATION A. Körte in *RE* 2 A 1 (1914), 843 f., under Ῥίνθων; M. Gigante, *Rintone e il teatro in Magna Grecia* (1971); L. Sanesi Mastrocinque, *PP* 1983, 386 ff.   W. G. A.

Rhipaei montes (Ῥιπαῖα ὄρη), the 'gusty' and ever snowy mountains, imagined from *Homer onwards to exist north of the known parts of Europe. From them blew the North Wind; beyond, down to the Northern Ocean, dwelt *Hyperboreans. *Herodotus (1) ignored the Rhipaeans, and *Strabo denied their existence. Those who believed in them differed as to their location. *Aeschylus and *Pindar regarded them as the source of the Danube (*Danuvius), and *Posidonius (2) thought originally that the *Alps were meant. On the other hand, *Aristotle placed them beyond *Scythia, and Roman poets put them in the extreme north. In general, their latitude was moved northward as knowledge increased. *Ptolemy (4), who considered that they were of moderate altitude, located them in Russia (lat. 57° 30'–63° 21'), between rivers flowing into Baltic and Euxine. They remained on maps until modern times.

Ptol. *Geog.* 3. 5, 15, 22; E. Kiessling, *RE* 1 A (1920), 846–916, Ῥιπαῖα ὄρη.   E. H. W.

rhizotomy ('root-cutting') See BOTANY; MAGIC, § 4(*b*); MEDICINE § 1. 2; PHARMACOLOGY.

Rhodanus, the river Rhône, from its source in the *Alps through the lake of Geneva to its outlet in the Mediterranean (*c.*900 km). It provided a major channel for communication and trade between the Mediterranean and central Gaul; and, with its chief tributary the Arar (modern Saône), gave access to the Rhineland, to the Seine basin, and, by a short portage to the Loire, to north-west France. These routes achieved especial importance from the 6th cent. BC after the foundation of *Massalia. The river was one of the main arteries of Roman Gaul and the Germanies, and traffic on it and its tributaries, centred on the port at *Lugdunum (1), was heavy. It was controlled by associations of river-shippers (e.g. *nautae Rhodanici et Ararici*: *CIL* 13. 1688 *et al.*). In the late empire imperial warships operated on both it and the Saône (*Not. Dign.* [*occ.*] 42). Strabo (4. 189) says that the swift current caused wagons to be used for some northbound traffic, but a relief (E. Espérandieu, *Recueil général des bas-reliefs, statues et bustes de la Gaule romaine*, 9 (1925), 6699) shows the haulage of ships, at least on the Durance. Silting in the delta caused difficulties and in 104–102 BC C. *Marius (1) cut a canal (*Fossa Marianae*, now Bras Mort) from the main stream near Grand Passon to the sea west of Fos, where a port was built (now submerged); the canal was handed over to the Massaliotes, but its use contributed to the eclipse of Marseilles by Arles (see ARELATE). A scheme put forward in AD 58 to join the Saône and the Moselle by canal, thus linking the Rhône and the Rhine, came to nothing (Tac. *Ann.* 13. 53).

D. van Berchem, *Les Routes et l'histoire* (1982); A. L. F. Rivet, *Gallia Narbonensis* (1988).   A. L. F. R.; J. F. Dr.

Rhodes, largest island of the mod. Dodecanese (*c.*1400 sq. km.), lying close to the mainland of *Caria.

The earlier prehistory of Rhodes is unclear, but by the 16th cent. (LM I) the Minoans (see MINOAN CIVILIZATION) had established a settlement at Trianda on the north-west coast, presumably to facilitate trade between *Crete and the eastern Mediterranean. The Minoans were followed in the 14th cent. (LH IIIA1) by Mycenaeans, apparently from the Peloponnese, whose numerous chamber-tomb cemeteries suggest a more thorough colonization of the island. Although no Mycenaean settlements have as yet been excavated, the grave offerings, from the cemetery at *Ialysus in particular, indicate considerable prosperity.

Dark-Age Rhodes was settled by *Dorian Greeks who formed three city-states, *Lindus, *Ialysus, and *Camirus. Their development in the Archaic period was typical for the time and place: they sent out colonies (*Gela in Sicily and *Phaselis in *Lycia were Lindian foundations), they were ruled by local tyrants, they submitted to Persia in 490. In the 5th cent., they were members of the Athenian Confederacy (see DELIAN LEAGUE), and all appear in the Athenian tribute-lists. The cities revolted from Athens in 412/11, perhaps under the influence of Dorieus, an Ialysian aristocrat of the Diagoridai clan who had been exiled by Athens at the beginning of the Peloponnesian war and turned to Sparta. In 408/7 the three cities renounced their independent political status, synoecized (see SYNOECISM), and founded a *federal state, Rhodes. The reason for this decision was probably commercial rather than military. Existing alongside the new federal capital (also called Rhodes) built on the northern tip of the island in Ialysian territory, the cities retained autonomy in local civic and religious matters and continued to be inhabited, although in the course of time much of the population would naturally have moved to the capital.

Rhodes remained loyal to Sparta until 395, when the pro-Athenian faction drove out the Diagoridai. Severe internal *stasis* between rival factions continued, but the next decades saw the establishment of the democratic constitution and probably also the organization of the population into demes divided among the three old cities. Rhodes became a member of the *Second Athenian Confederacy in 378/7, but was detached from it by the intervention of the Carian satrap *Mausolus, eager to extend his influence into the Aegean. The *Social War (1) against Athens broke out in 357 and Rhodes was granted independence, only to suffer Carian domination until the arrival of *Alexander (3) the Great in 332. Relations with Alexander are obscure, but an unpopular Macedonian garrison was installed on Rhodes.

Rhodes flourished in the age of the *Diadochi. The foundation of new cities in the East meant the transfer of trade to the eastern Mediterranean, and Rhodes with its five harbours was ideally placed for this commercial traffic. The famous year-long siege of Rhodes by *Demetrius (4) I Poliorcetes in 305/4 (Diod. Sic. 20. 81–8; 91–100) arose when Demetrius tried to win the Rhodian fleet and dockyards for himself, thereby threatening a favourable Rhodian alliance with the Ptolemies (see PTOLEMY (1)). The Rhodians resisted heroically. Demetrius was forced to withdraw after wasting a year, and from the sale of his siege equipment the Rhodians financed the Colossus, a 33 m. tall statue of their patron god *Helios (see CHARES (4); SEVEN WONDERS OF THE ANCIENT WORLD). Rhodes' survival on this occasion increased its prestige and self-confidence, so that throughout the 3rd cent. it successfully avoided subservience to any of the larger powers, although close political and commercial ties with Egypt were maintained. By the second half of the century the distinguished Rhodian fleet replaced the Ptolemaic navy as the enemy of piracy on the high seas and as protector of the island communities.

Rhodes owned substantial territory on the opposite mainland or *peraea (some probably acquired by the old cities before the synoecism). The communities which were integral parts of the Rhodian state became *demes assigned to one of the three old cities and their citizens ranked equally with those of the island. This so-called 'Incorporated Peraea' is distinct from outlying territory which was controlled by Rhodes, the 'Subject Peraea', the population of which were not citizens of the Rhodian state and were governed by Rhodian officials. In time Rhodes gained control of the islands of Syme, *Carpathos, Casos, *Nisyros, Telos, Chalce, and Megiste (Castellorizo), and these were also incorporated as demes of the old cities in the Rhodian state.

Rhodes (with *Pergamum) played a role in the first major intervention of Rome in eastern affairs. It co-operated with Rome (not previously an ally) in the wars against *Philip (3) V and *Antiochus (3) III, and was rewarded after Apamea (see SELEUCIDS) with territory in Caria and Lycia. Ancient sources vividly attest the *stasis* between the pro- and anti-Roman factions in the Rhodian assembly in the complex political manœuvrings of these years. Rome punished the equivocal attitude of Rhodes in the Third Macedonian War by depriving it of this extra territory and more besides, and by proclaiming *Delos a free port (167), thereby ending Rhodian commercial supremacy as the centre of the Mediterranean transit trade. Rhodes sought safety within an unequal alliance with Rome (164), which effectively ended its political independence and role as a major Mediterranean power. It successfully withstood a siege by *Mithradates VI in 88, but was captured and pillaged by C. *Cassius Longinus in 43. Nevertheless, under Roman rule Rhodes retained her democratic constitution and social cohesiveness, and traditional civic life continued in the capital as well as in the three old cities. Rhodes remained prosperous and was known as a centre of cultural activity. The Rhodian school of Stoic philosophy (see STOICISM) boasted *Panaetius and *Posidonius (2) among its distinguished members, and *Cicero studied there. There was a flourishing school of local sculpture, and the epic poet *Apollonius (1) Rhodius was a native. *Strabo (14. 2. 5 [652]) lavishly praises the city and Rhodian civic institutions, *Dio Cocceianus (Dio Chrys. Or. 31) the pre-eminent wealth of the city, and [ps.] Aristides (25 [43]; see ARISTIDES, AELIUS) its outstanding beauty before the severe *earthquake damage of c. AD 142.

Much of the ancient city, built on a rectangular grid, lies under the medieval walled town of the Knights of St John and the modern town, but identifiable remains include stretches of the city wall, several temples, harbour installations, the acropolis, a stadium, odeum, and extensive necropolis areas which have produced rich finds.

Inscriptions in IG 12/1 1 (1895) and Supplement (1939); G. G. Porro and A. Maiuri, ASAA 1916, 103 ff.; A. Maiuri, Nuova silloge epigrafica di Rodi e Cos (1925); G. Pugliese Carratelli, ASAA 1952–4, 247 ff., 1955–6, 157 ff.; Clara Rhodos (1928–41). H. van Gelder, Geschichte der alten Rhodier (1900); RE Suppl. 5, 731 ff.; P. M. Fraser and G. E. Bean, The Rhodian Peraea and Islands (1954); H. H. Schmitt, Rom und Rhodos (1957); P. M. Fraser, Rhodian Funerary Monuments (1977); C. Mee, Rhodes in the Bronze Age (1982).   C. B. M., E. E. R.

Rhodes, cults and myths The island was sacred to *Helios who claimed it before it rose from beneath the sea. He had seven sons (Haliadae) with the *nymph Rhodos (who gave her name to the island), and three grandsons, the eponymous heroes of the chief Rhodian cities *Camirus, *Ialysus, and *Lindus (Pind. Ol. 7. 69–76). The brilliant panhellenic Halieia were celebrated quinquennially with great pomp and games. Expensive gifts to the god included *Chares (4)'s Colossus of Rhodes (Athen. 561F; *Xenophon (2), *Ephes.* 5. 11; see SEVEN WONDERS OF THE ANCIENT WORLD); and every year a *quadriga* (chariot), horses and all (with which the god circled the world), was thrown into the sea in his honour. The festival replaced the Tlapolemeia of the founding hero and son of *Heracles (Pind. *Ol.* 7. 20), whose myth records the island's *Dorian settlement. Heracles Bouthoinas had a cult at Lindus with curious rites resembling the Attic Bouphonia (Lact. *inst. div.* 1. 21. 31). The Sminthia at Lindus celebrated *Apollo 'mouse killer', well known in that function, and *Dionysus, as destroyers of mice which attacked the vines (Athen. 445A–B).

On Mt. Atabyris bronze bull votives were offered to *Zeus. The animals were said to bellow when evil befell Rhodes (schol. on Pind. *Ol.* 7. 87). The mountain cult and legend connect Zeus Atabyrius with *Crete, but *Athena Lindia's cult was older, possibly Mycenaean. In legend the Danaides (see DANAUS AND THE DANAIDS) founded her sanctuary during their flight to *Argos (2) (Hdt. 2. 182). The goddess received unburnt sacrifice, because the Haliadae forgot to bring fire when they came to pay their respects (Pind. *Ol.* 7. 42–8). In Hellenistic times Egyptian cults, notably of *Sarapis and *Isis, were imported to Rhodes and Lindus.

Nilsson, *Feste*, 307; 478; *GGR* 2² (1961), 117–18; A. B. Cook, *Zeus* 2/2 (1925), 922–4; U. Bianchi, *Epigraphica* 1957, 11; C. Blinkenberg, *Die lindische Tempelchronik* (1915), on the chronicle-inscription of Athena Lindia's temple; I. K. Papachristodoulou, *Οἱ ἀρχαῖοι ῥοδιακοὶ δῆμοι ... Ἰαλυσία* (1989), esp. p. 152.   H. J. R.; B. C. D.

Rhodiapolis See LYCIA; MYRA; OPRAMOAS.

Rhone See RHODANUS.

'Riace warriors', two masterpieces of Greek bronze-casting, from (it seems) an ancient *shipwreck; found off the toe of Italy in 1972. Standing nudes, 1.97–8 m. high, they originally held weapons; on technical grounds they are thought to come from the same workshop. A dating round the mid-5th cent. BC is gaining ground; later dates have advocates. Attempts to see in them famous lost works are, by their nature, highly speculative. See PHIDIAS; SCULPTURE, GREEK.

A. Stewart, *History of Greek Sculpture* 1 (1990), 147–8 (bibliog. at 343).   A. J. S. S.

rich, riches See WEALTH, ATTITUDES TO.

Ricimer, general and patrician. His maternal grandfather was the Gothic king Vallia (see GOTHS), but his career was entirely Roman. He came to power after the assassinations of *Aetius (1) and *Valentinian (3) III, forcing *Avitus to abdicate (AD 456) and elevating *Majorian in his place (457). He deposed and killed Majorian in 461, proclaiming instead Libius Severus (461–5). He co-operated with *Anthemius, an eastern nominee, before having him killed in 472. He had already advanced Olybrius to the throne, but himself died in 472.   P. J. H.

riddles The Greek word is γρῖφος (a plaited creel, i.e. something intricate) or αἴνιγμα, the noun of αἰνίσσομαι, derived from αἶνος = a tale or fable containing a hidden lesson for the addressee (*Homer, *Od.* 14. 508, Hes. *Op.* 202, etc.). Riddling language, in which a thing's or person's identity is concealed under obscure circumlocutions, metaphors, or puzzling predications, was a feature of some high-flown poetry, such as parts of *Hesiod (e.g. *Op.* 524 f., 742 f.), *Aeschylus, and some later tragedians and dithyrambists, culminating in the *Alexandra* of *Lycophron (2 b).

Sometimes the 'riddle' was followed by its solution, as in Aesch. *Ag.* 494 'mud's coterminous sister—thirsty dust'. The independent riddle, set as a challenge, was mostly a form of social amusement, but in myth at least it could be deadly serious. Those who cannot answer the *Sphinx's riddle die, and when *Oedipus answers it, she dies; similarly, in the Homer legend, the poet dies when he fails to solve the fisher-boys' riddle. (There are analogous stories of seers' contests of skill, cf. Hes. fr. 278.) Some *oracles, such as that in Hdt. 1. 67, were in effect riddles that the recipient had to solve in order to escape ruin.

One of the poems attributed to Hesiod described riddles propounded at Keyx's wedding feast (frs. 266–8). From the 5th cent. BC, if not before, riddles were a familiar diversion at the symposium (Simon. eleg. 25 W², Ar. *Wasps* 20 f., Antiphanes, fr. 122 KA, Pl. *Resp.* 479bc, etc.; for poems cast in riddling form cf. Theog. 257–60, 667–82, 1229–30). Prizes and penalties, such as kisses and sconces, were sometimes attached (Antiphanes, fr. 75, Clearchus, fr. 63 Wehrli, Poll. 6. 107). Besides riddles there were various other forms of intellectual game and quizzery, all discussed by the *Peripatetic *Clearchus (3) in his work on γρῖφοι (frs. 84–95). Riddles were commonly in verse (hexameters, elegiacs, or iambics), and occasionally attributed to a specific author such as Cleobulus (of the *Seven Sages), his daughter Cleobulina (who may have been an invention of *Cratinus in his comedy *Kleoboulinai*: Wilamowitz, *Kl. Schr.* 4. 60–3), and Panarces. Often the object to be guessed was made to describe itself: 'I give birth to my mother, and am born myself; sometimes I am bigger than her, sometimes smaller' (*Anth. Pal.* 14. 41: day and night). Other formats are 'There is a thing which . . .', 'What is it that . . .', 'I saw a man who . . .'. A different type consisted of reciting an apparently nonsensical verse which the other person had to make sense of by supplying a continuation: 'So they dined on beef and the horses' necks'—'They unyoked, all sweaty, having fought enough' (Ar. *Peace* 1282 f.; *Certamen Hom. et Hes.* 107 ff.).

The main collections of Greek riddles appear in Ath. 10. 448b–459b (mostly from comedy) and *Anth. Pal.* 14. 1–64, 101, 103–11. There seems to be no strong independent Roman tradition: the 'old' word for 'riddle' cited by Gell. *NA* 12. 6. 1, *scirpus*, lit. 'basketrush', seems a calque on γρῖφος, and the riddles occasionally found in Latin literature (Varro in Gell. ibid., Verg. *Ecl.* 3. 104–7, Petron. *Sat.* 58) seem to follow Greek patterns. A late collection of 100 verse riddles is preserved under the name *Symphosius (i.e. Συμπόσιος).

K. Ohlert, *Rätsel und Rätselspiele der alten Griechen*² (1912); W. Schultz, *Rätsel aus dem hellenischen Kulturkreise* (1909–12), and *RE* 1 A (1920), 62–125, 'Rätsel'; E. Cougny (ed.), *Anth. Pal.* 3 (1890), 563 ff. (examples from various sources); E. S. Forster, *G&R* 1945, 42–7.   M. L. W.

rider-gods and heroes The representation of a deity on horseback is relatively rare in the central areas of the Graeco-Roman world. The best example is provided by the *Dioscuri. Ridergods, albeit with varying regional characteristics are more frequent around the periphery, in Hellenistic-Roman Egypt, Syria, Asia Minor, and north Africa.

Rider-gods were extremely popular in the Eastern Balkans, where they often appeared as a hunter on horseback. This kind of votive monument is known as *Thracian Rider* and is not to be confused with the *Danubian Rider*—mostly votive tablets of smaller format. The latter belongs to a mystery cult with Mithraic elements found in the lower and middle Danube area in the 2nd and 3rd cents. AD. The central figure of a goddess is flanked by one or two riders. An example of the rider-god from the Rhine area is the Jupiter-rider.

Rimini

Common features are difficult to distinguish, but it seems that rider-gods frequently fulfilled the function of helper and saviour. Finally, cult-heroes, too, were represented as riders or in connection with horses. The depiction of the deceased as *Heros Equitans* was especially popular. In the Thracian area these representations were assimilated to the figures of the *Thracian Rider*. Hence they seem to suggest deification of the person thus depicted. See RELIGION, THRACIAN.

E. Will, *Le Relief culturel greco-romain* (1955), 55–124 ('Les dieux cavaliers'); LIMC 6 (1992), 1019–1081, 'Heros Equitans'. M. O.

Rimini See ARIMINUM.

rings (δακτύλιος, *anulus*) were used in Minoan and Mycenaean times (see MINOAN and MYCENAEAN CIVILIZATION) both as signets and as ornaments. They are not mentioned in *Homer and are rarely found in early iron age deposits. From the early 6th cent. BC they were in regular use as signets. The practice of wearing rings as ornaments is rare before the 4th cent. and reaches its height under the Roman Empire. Collections of rings are mentioned at this period. Rings also had special uses at Rome: the gold ring as a military decoration and as a mark of rank, originally limited to *nobiles* (see NOBILITAS) and *equites*, extended under the empire to denote *ingenuitas*; and the betrothal ring, first of iron, later of gold (apparently unknown in Greece).

Plin. *HN* 33. 8–32. F. H. Marshall, *Catalogue of the Greek, Etruscan, and Roman Finger Rings in the British Museum* (1907); F. Henkel, *Die römischen Fingerringe der Rheinlande* (1913). F. N. P.; M. V.

rites of passage is the term first used by A. van Gennep in his classic study *The Rites of Passage* (1960; 1st Fr. edn. 1909) for mainly those rituals which dramatize passages in the life-cycle and the calendar. According to Van Gennep, these rites were characterized by a separation from the old status, a liminal phase 'betwixt and between', and the incorporation into the new condition. More importantly, an analysis of these rituals shows which transitions were deemed important, which parts of these transitions, which symbols were used, and what they signify.

The main passages in the ancient life-cycle were birth, *initiation, *marriage, and death, although in Rome initiation must have been abolished at a relatively early period because only traces of these institutions have survived. It is much harder to see which parts of the transitions received attention in which periods. Whereas on Attic black-figure vases of the late Archaic period the public procession of the couple to the bridegroom's home received all attention, the red-figure vases focused on the relationship of bride and groom: a nice illustration of a shift in attention from public to private. Unfortunately, our information about the rites is usually so fragmentary that development within these (as in other) rites is often hard to document.

Important symbols in the transitions were bathing or washing, change of clothes and hairstyle, and the use of *crowns. It is important to look at the timing and the shape of the symbol: the occurrence of a particular haircut, black or white clothes, crowns of fertile or fruitless plants. It is only the combination of symbols which gives meaning, not the individual symbols: both the dead and grooms wear white clothes, but they have different crowns. And when the Greek dead wear crowns but the mourners do not, it is the contrast which supplies meaning, not the crown itself.

Regarding the calendar, the most important change was the transition from Old to New Year, which took place via one or more festivals: the break was felt to be too big to take place in

just one day as in modern times. In Athens, the New Year month was inaugurated by the Cronia, the scene of role reversals between masters and slaves, and only then came the Synoikia, the commemoration of the foundation of Athens (see SYNOECISM). The Roman first month was preceded by the sombre month of February, the month of purification (*februare* means 'to purify'); see LUSTRATION. In other words, for a right understanding of the calendar we have to analyse carefully the meaning and mood of the various festivals and not look at them in isolation.

RAC 2 (1954), 'Bestattung', 9 (1976), 'Geburt', 15 (1991), 'Hochzeit'; E. Samter, *Geburt, Hochzeit und Tod* (1911); R. Garland, *The Greek Way of Life* (1990). J. N. B.

ritual Both definition and interpretation of ritual are highly debated among social scientists. On a minimal definition (at least in the context of Greek and Roman cultures), ritual could be seen as symbolic activity in a religious context. A ritual (or ceremony) is composed of several single acts, the rites. Ritual is an activity whose imminent practical aim has become secondary, replaced by the aim of communication; this does not preclude ritual from having other, less immediate practical goals. Form and meaning of ritual are determined by tradition; they are malleable according to the needs of any present situation, as long as the performers understand them as being traditional. As to interpretation, in an era where often loosely associated Frazerian meanings dominated the field, the seminal work of A. van Gennep (1909; see the preceding entry) made it clear that rituals with seemingly widely different goals have common structures; this developed the insight, deepened by structuralism, that in ritual, structures are prior to meaning. French sociology (E. Durkheim) and British social anthropology (E. E. Evans-Pritchard) saw society as the main frame of reference for the interpretation of ritual meaning; V. Turner analysed the anti-structural aspects of Van Gennepian ritual. Insights from social anthropology have been applied to classical studies by J. E. Harrison, *Themis* (1911, 1927), and W. Burkert, *Structure and History in Greek Mythology and Ritual* (1979). See ANTHROPOLOGY AND THE CLASSICS.

The study of ritual in Greek and Roman religion, as in most religions of the past, is hampered by lack of sufficient data. Social anthropology developed its interpretative models with societies where the rituals are documented in all their details, both the ordinary and the uncommon ceremonies and rites. Ancient sources, local historians and antiquarians, as well as sacred laws, recorded only the exceptional and aberrant rituals, not the familiar and ordinary ones which were part of daily life; and because they recorded only the salient features, entire scenarios are very rare. Further, instruction in the correct performance of ritual was part of an oral tradition, from generation to generation or from priest to priest, esp. in the Greek sacerdotal families like the Eumolpidae in *Eleusis or the Iamidae in *Olympia (see EUMOLPIDAE; IAMUS), or in the collegia (see COLLEGIUM) in Rome. See PRIESTS. Elaborate ritual texts such as those known from Near Eastern, notably Hittite sources, are therefore absent in Greece and Rome. The exception, the Greek magical papyri, confirm the rule; magical rituals were transmitted in books from one practitioner to another one because these individual practices lacked any organizational form. But the magical papyri, combining different religious traditions, are of only limited value for a study of Greek and Roman ritual; see MAGIC.

Neither Greek nor Roman cultures analysed ritual as a specific category of religious activity. In Greek, the closest equivalent is τελετή (see TELETĒ), but this term tended to be used in a much narrower sense for specific rituals of an exceptional nature, like those of the mystery cults (see C. Zijderveld, *ΤΕΛΕΤΗ: Bijdrage tot de kennis der religieuze terminologie in het Grieks* (1934)); other terms, as the frequent ἱερά, 'sacred things', or (θεῶν) θεραπεία, 'service (of the gods)' (Plat. *Rep.* 427b), are much wider; a term often used in *Attic texts, τὰ νομιζόμενα, 'what is customary', underscores the importance of tradition (J. Rudhardt, *Notions fondamentales de la pensée religieuse et actes constitutifs du culte dans la Grèce classique* (1958)). In Rome, the closest equivalents are *caerimonia* and *ritus*; both, however, rather mean subjectively the 'manner of a religious (or profane) observance'. See RELIGION, GREEK, TERMS RELATING TO, and RELIGION, ROMAN, TERMS RELATING TO.

In modern discussions of ancient ritual, the dichotomy Olympian (see RELIGION, GREEK) versus *chthonian often plays an important role: rituals destined for Olympian gods would be categorically distinguished from those of chthonian gods or heroes. This dichotomy is the product of late antique scholarship, not of observation of religious usage; it might have some explicatory value in late antiquity, much less for the Archaic and Classical epochs.

The central rite of Greek and Roman religion is animal *sacrifice. Whatever the theories about its origin, Greek and Roman analysis understood it as a gift to the gods; the myth of its institution by the trickster *Prometheus (Hes. *Th.* 535–616) explained less its function as communication between man and god than the deficiency of something which should have been a nourishing gift from man to god. Beyond this indigenous interpretation, ordinary animal sacrifice with its ensuing meal repeated and reinforced the structure of society and was used to express the societal values; changes of ritual reflected changes in values. Specific significations went together with specific forms of the ritual: the change from ordinary sheep or goat sacrifice to extraordinary sacrifice of bovines expressed a heightening of expense, festivity, and social status (religious reformers exposed the fundamental lack of moral values in such a differentiation, Philostr. *VA* 1. 11); more specific animals were used for specific deities, chiefly as a function of their relationship to the central *polis values (dog sacrifice to Enyalius (see ARES), *Hecate, or *Robigus). Holocaust sacrifice, which destroyed the entire animal, was offered in marginal contexts, but not only with extraordinary animals. See ANIMALS IN CULT.

Besides animal sacrifice, there existed different kinds of bloodless sacrifice. A common gift was the cake (see CAKES), in specific forms which again were determined by the character of the divinity and its position in society (C. A. Lobeck, *Aglaophamus* (1829), 1050–1985, gives a still useful *pemmatologia sacra*). Other sacrifices comprised fruits or grains, often mixed and even cooked as a specific ritual dish (κυκεών in Eleusis, 'hot-pot' of *Pyanopsia or *Thargelia, *puls* in Rome), as a function of the specific value of the festival. *Libation was used combined with animal sacrifice, but also as a ritual of its own. Again, the use of different liquids was determined by the function of the ritual; the main opposition was between mixed wine, the ordinary libation liquid as it was the ordinary drink, and unmixed *wine, *milk, *water, oil (see OLIVE), or *honey. Already *Peripatetic cultural theory explained many of the substances as survivals from an earlier period without wine libations and animal sacrifice (see *Porphyry, *De abstinentia*).

Another important group are purificatory rituals; see PURIFICATION; LUSTRATION. Their aim is to remove *pollution, either on a regular basis, as in the ritual of the *pharmakos of the Greek Thargelia or in the festivals of the Roman month Februarius which derived its name from *februa*, a twig bundle used in purificatory rites, or in specific cases, to heal misfortune caused by pollution, as in the rites to cure epilepsy (see ps.-Hippocrates, *De morbo sacro*; cf. HIPPOCRATES (2)), or in the many rites instituted by oracles to avert a *plague. Cathartic rituals precede any new beginning; therefore, they belong to New Year cycles (Februarius precedes the new beginning of the Kalends of March) or initiatory rites. The forms of apotropaic rituals vary from ritual washing to holocaust sacrifices, and many forms used are not specific to cathartic rituals. A common idea, though, is to identify the pollution with an object and then to destroy it, by either burning it entirely (holocaust sacrifice of pigs) or expelling it (*pharmakos*; cure of epilepsy, where the *katharmata*, the unclean substances, are carried beyond the borders of the *polis*).

A further group of rituals which has attracted scholarly interest is *initiation rituals, or rather rituals which can be seen as transformation from rituals which, in a hypothetical earlier phase of Greek or Roman society, fulfilled the function tribal initiation fulfils in ethnological societies; in them, the Van Gennepian tripartite structure is particularly visible (see RITES OF PASSAGE). In historical Greece, the possible transformations were many. One group of rituals retains the function of introducing the young generation into the community; beside the rituals in the archaic Spartan and Cretan societies, the institution of the *ephēbeia* (see EPHĒBOI) belongs to this group. Other rituals concentrate upon a few elected members, like the Arrephori in the cult of the Athenian Athena (see ARREPHORIA), or the Roman *Salii where some rites preserve traces of their respective practical functions, namely to initiate women into weaving as the main female technology, or to initiate young men into armed dancing as training for *hoplite combat. A specific group of rituals whose roots, at least partly, lie in initiation, are the *mystery cults of Eleusis, *Samothrace, and the Theban and Lemnian *Cabiri (see THEBES (1); LEMNOS); here, earlier initiation into a family group or a secret society has been transformed into a panhellenic ritual (see PANHELLENISM) by emphasizing and elaborating the anti-structural aspect. See also previous entry.

The social function of ritual was used by Hellenistic kings and Roman emperors alike to legitimate and base their rule on a religious foundation; in *ruler-cult, traditional forms like sacrifice were taken up to express these new concerns; modern negative judgements of such cults misunderstand the fundamental social and political meaning of much of ancient religion, where refusal of such rites by Christians was rightly understood as refusal to recognize the political supremacy of the ruler. See RULER-CULT; CHRISTIANITY.

For a survey of the literature see T. Ahlbäck (ed.), *The Problem of Ritual* (1993), esp. Jørgen Podeman Sørensen, 'Ritualistics: A new discipline in the history of religions' (9–25).

GENERAL A. van Gennep, *Les Rites de passage* (1909; Eng. trans. 1960); E. Evans-Pritchard, *Theories of Primitive Religion* (1965); V. Turner, *The Ritual Process: Structure and Anti-structure* (1969), with the reflections by B. C. Alexander, *Victor Turner Revisited: Ritual as Social Change* (1991), and the radical discussions by Jack Goody, 'Religion and ritual: The definitional problem', *Brit. Journ. Sociol.* 1961, 142–64, and F. Staal, *Rules Without Meaning: Rituals, Mantras and the Human Sciences* (1989).

GREECE P. Stengel, *Die griechischen Kultusaltertümer*[3] (1920) is still indispensable for the facts.

ROME G. Wissowa, *Religion und Kultus der Römer*[2] (1912) still is the main source of information, while for a particular case, J. Scheid, *Romulus et ses frères: Le collège des frères arvales, modèle du culte public dans la Rome des empereurs* (1990) presents a model interpretation.

On rituals of sacrifice, purification, initiation, and ruler cult, see the bibliographies to those entries.. F. G.

ritualized friendship See FRIENDSHIP, RITUALIZED.

river-gods Rivers and seas are ultimately derived from Oceanus, the father of all rivers (Hom. *Il.* 21. 196; Hes. *Theog.* 337; see OCEANUS (MYTHOLOGICAL)). As personifications of animate powers river-gods such as *Scamander in the Trojan plain may assume human form (conversation with *Achilles) but attack as gushing waters. River-gods also assemble in the council of *Zeus. Rivers are ancestors of 'older' heroes (Inachus, father of Io), articulating a differentiation of the landscape and humanity's link with it. Rivers can function as guardians: the river Erasinus refused to abandon the citizens of *Argos (2) to the Spartan *Cleomenes (1) (Paus. 2. 20. 6). One tenth of the property of the traitors of *Amphipolis (the city 'surrounded by river') was dedicated to the river.

River-gods, such as the *Nile or the *Tiber, are quintessentially male, and are often represented as bulls (also as horses and snakes) and appear thus—or as humans with bull-attributes, sometimes swimming—on coins (especially from Sicily). Live bulls, a natural metaphor for the roaring waters, were occasionally sacrificed by throwing them into the river (horses too, sometimes). *Ritual acts and cult seem to have been ubiquitous. Before crossing a river one must, says *Hesiod, pray and wash the hands (*Op.* 737). A vision of rivers is a sign of offspring, says *Artemidorus (6) (2. 38). River shrines, such as Spercheius', were located at river-banks (*Il.* 23. 148). Scamander had a special priest; Trojan maidens are said to have entered its waters and asked the god to take their virginity as a gift. Hair was consecrated to rivers at puberty, e.g. at Phigaleia (Paus. 8. 24. 12), and their function as 'youth-nourishers' (*kourotrophoi*) is attested early (Hom. *Il.* 23. 46; Aesch. *Cho.* 6; see KOUROTROPHOS). Oaths are sworn by invoking rivers (Hom. *Il.* 3. 276). During a battle the diviners (*manteis*) would offer sacrifices to the river (Xen. *Anab.* 4. 3. 18–19).

*Acheloüs was perceived as the archetypal river; it had a shrine by the Ilissus in *Attica (with the *nymphs: Pl. *Phaedr.* 230b). A son of Oceanus and *Tethys, it wrestled with *Heracles for *Deianira; when it metamorphosed into a bull, Heracles won by breaking one of its horns. Achelous was a father of several nymphs associated with water, such as Castalia (the spring at *Delphi), or the *Sirens. In Italy, we are best informed about the Tiber, which by contrast developed little mythology. Neither did it possess a temple; prayers were addressed (see e.g. Livy 2. 10. 11 with Ogilvie's comm. for *Horatius Cocles) and offerings made directly to the river itself. Its cult was particularly concerned with purification (see LUSTRATION) and healing.

J. le Gall, *Recherches sur le culte du Tibre* (1953). I. M.

rivers See NAVIGATION; RIVER-GODS; names of particular rivers e.g. NILE; TIBER.

roads Ancient road-theory divides into two categories: the art of enhancing communications through built or dug works; and the planning and maintaining of large-scale communications networks based on such works.

Ramps, cuttings, stone pavements, zig-zags, and pull-offs are found on local roads from Archaic Greek times, and were clearly designed to facilitate wheeled traction: there are Mycenaean precursors, and parallels in many parts of the Mediterranean, such as Etruria. Improved routes for specialized purposes such

as the haulage-route to Athens from the *marble *quarries of Mt. *Pentelicon, or the *diolkos across the isthmus of Corinth, are found, and fine paved processional ways like the Athenian Sacred Way or the approaches to great *sanctuaries like *Delphi. The technological repertoire was greatly increased by the deployment of arched construction on a large scale (see ARCHES), which made *bridges and viaducts feasible; and where labour was cheap, and petrology favourable, major cuttings and tunnels could be contemplated. Such things, like the deployment of the older road technologies on any very large scale required large-scale organization, intercommunity co-operation, voluntary or enforced, and very large resources, all of which escaped the Greek world of the Archaic and Classical periods.

The *Royal Road of the Achaemenid empire did not, in all likelihood, comprise a continuous line of built structure; but what the scope of Persian power made distinctively possible along this 1,600-mile stretch was the vision of a line joining distinct regions. This second category of ancient road-theory is first and foremost a way of looking at the layout of the world and expressing the power of the state or the individual in relation to it. The manifold technologies of improving the route are deployed in the service of that aim.

In this the road-building of the Roman republic was strikingly original. Between 312 (the date of the first stretch of the *via Appia) and 147 BC (when the *via Postumia joined Adriatic to Tyrrhenian and spanned Cisalpine Gaul) Roman planners had perfected a way of turning the military journey-routes of commanders with *imperium (*itinera*) into a theoretically sophisticated network which formally linked Roman communities with Rome, and (linked as the road-building and city-foundation alike were with land-division: see CENTURIATION) spectacularly expressed Rome's power over the landscape. The system already involved using the available technological skills to make showily straight connections across natural obstacles, and that was a precedent taken up with enthusiasm in the road plans of C. *Sempronius Gracchus. Around the same time the first large-scale application of *milestones (though they are attested on Thasos in the 5th cent.), docketing and measuring the domains of Rome, and the first really ambitious roads of the provincial empire are found, notably the *via Egnatia linking the Adriatic with the Aegean and eventually the *Bosporus (1), and the *via Domitia running from the *Alps across the Rhone (see RHODANUS) and *Pyrenees into *Spain.

The origins of the idea remain obscure: locally the layout of Roman roads resembles *Etruscan practice, for instance in preferring to follow the summits of long ridges, but in the crucial scale of the geographical vision, which is already there in the via Appia, even the Royal Road does not really provide a precedent. The ancient routes of west central Italy like the *via Salaria and *via Latina, which may have an economic origin, are a possible precedent, but their date is uncertain.

The early emperors made road-building their own. *Augustus rebuilt the *via Flaminia as the highway to his *provincia* in the settlement of 27; *Claudius commemorated his triumphal journey back to Rome from *Britain by piously completing the road which his father Nero *Claudius Drusus had begun on his own military expeditions across the Alps. The imitation of their practice by governors, and of both by municipal benefactors, spread a dense capillary net of roads across the whole empire. While the routes of Augustus and Claudius were single highways (M. *Vipsanius Agrippa's great highway from *Lugdunum (1) to the Channel should also be mentioned), there is a growing sense of the application of a blueprint (developed long before in Italy), of boxing in territories with crisscross roads on a huge scale. These are the *limites* which were eventually to give their name to the frontier works of the empire (see LIMES). Strategic road-building on a scale large enough to cross provincial boundaries reaches its peak under the Flavians, Trajan and Hadrian, with the systematic reshaping of the networks of Anatolia and the whole eastern frontier, eventually down to Aqaba. Something similar happens in the Balkans at the same period.

R. Chevallier, *Roman Roads* (1976); G. Radke, *Viae Publicae Romanae* (1971). N. P.

Robigus, Roman spirit of wheat rust. His festival (Robigalia) was on 25 April (Ov. *Fast.* 4. 901 ff. with Bömer's notes), at the fifth milestone of the via Claudia; the flamen Quirinalis (see FLAMINES; QUIRINUS) offered a red dog and a sheep, praying to avert the rust. The red dog of the July moveable festival *Augurium Canarium implies a connection: Ov. *Fast.* 4. 939–40 (cf. Plin. *HN* 18. 14; Festus 39. 13 ff., 358. 27 ff. L). See RITUAL.

C. R. P.

Rogozen, Bulgarian site in ancient *Thrace (see also RELIGION, THRACIAN), at which important finds of beautiful 4th-cent. BC silver and silver-gilt vessels were made in 1986. Some carry Greek inscriptions (e.g. the name of *Cersobleptes) and depict Greek mythological scenes.

A. Fol and others, *The New Thracian Treasure from Rogozen, Bulgaria* (1986); B. F. Cook (ed.), *The Rogozen Treasure* (1987); Z. Archibald, *CAH* 6² (1994), 461–3; B. F. Sparkes in J. Boardman (ed.), *CAH Plates to Vols. V and VI* (1994), 49 f. no. 56; J. Boardman, *The Diffusion of Classical Art in Antiquity* (1995), 184 f. and 338 n. 6. S. H.

Romanization

I. In the west. This term describes the processes by which indigenous peoples incorporated into the empire acquired cultural attributes which made them appear as Romans. Since the Romans had no single unitary culture but rather absorbed traits from others, including the conquered, the process was not a one-way passing of ideas and styles from Roman to indigene but rather an exchange which led to the metropolitan mix of styles which characterized the Roman world. Styles of art and architecture, town-planning and villa-living, as well as the adoption of Latin and the worship of the Roman pantheon, are all amongst its expressions. The result of Romanization was not homogeneity, since indigenous characteristics blended to create hybrids like Romano-Celtic religion or Gallo-Roman sculpture.

Its manifestations were not uniform, and there is debate over the relative importance of directed policy and local initiative. Rome promoted aspects of her culture to integrate the provinces and facilitate government with least effort. Provincial centres like *Tarraco and *Lugdunum (1) were created to promote loyalty to the state through the worship of Roman gods, and their priesthoods became a focus for the ambitions of provincials. *Tacitus (1) (*Agr.* 21) states that Cn. *Iulius Agricola in *Britain promoted public building and education for these purposes. Roman culture was also spread less deliberately by Roman actions. Mass movements of soldiers brought goods and ideas to newly conquered areas, whilst the construction of new *roads in their wake speeded communication and facilitated further cultural exchange. *Trade both within and beyond the frontiers brought Roman culture to new peoples. Equally, conquered people themselves sought to acquire Roman goods and values to curry favour with their conquerors and confer or maintain status within their own societies. In Gaul local aristocrats were obtaining Roman *citizenship in the Julio-Claudian period, establishing for themselves a new status in relation to Rome and their own peoples. Emulation of Roman customs and styles accompanied their rise. Thus in Claudian Britain, Ti. *Claudius Cogidubnus almost certainly constructed the highly sophisticated Roman villa at Fishbourne, and presided over a client kingdom where a temple of Neptune and Minerva was built. This copying of things Roman by indigenes was probably the most important motive for these cultural changes.

T. F. C. Blagg and M. J. Millett (eds.), *The Early Roman Empire in the West* (1990); M. Wood and F. Queiroga (eds.), *Current Research on the Romanization of the Western Provinces* (1992); Brunt, *RIT.* M. J. M.

II. In the east. No ancient writer provides any general description or explanation of the impact of Roman culture and institutions on the eastern provinces of the empire. The term Romanization is best applied to specific developments which can be traced to the patterns of Roman rule.

Military The language used by the legions and most auxiliary regiments, both officially and privately, was Latin. Building inscriptions, gravestones, dedications, and casual graffiti provide evidence for a Latin-speaking culture in and around fortresses and also in towns which were accustomed to heavy military traffic on the roads to the eastern frontiers.

Administrative practices The staff of a provincial governor or of a provincial procurator was too small to have any significant effect on the culture of the communities where they resided or which they visited. Many officials, in any case, were Greek-speaking by birth or by inclination. Latin, however, seems to have been widely used for the administration of imperial estates (see DOMAINS); Latin gravestones are the rule for the freedmen and imperial slaves who ran them.

Citizenship and Law Roman *citizenship spread rapidly in the Greek east, and became almost universal with the Antonine constitution of AD 212 (see CONSTITUTION, ANTONINE). Roman citizens were notionally entitled to be tried or to conduct cases within the framework of Roman law. This will have swiftly led the Greek cities and other communities of the east to bring their own legal practices into conformity with Roman law.

Urbanization and architecture The most characteristic form of Roman town, the colony, was introduced on a large scale to the Greek east. *Caesar and *Augustus settled veterans in colonies in Macedonia, Asia Minor, and Syria. The practice of introducing new settlers became rare under their successors, but existing communities were often raised to the status of colonies, particularly from the Severan period through the 3rd cent. More important than the practice of founding colonies (see COLONIZATION, ROMAN) was the fact that Roman provincial administration could only function in regions where an infrastructure of self-governing cities existed. Since much of the area between the Aegean and the Euphrates, especially the interior of Asia Minor, was only thinly urbanized in the Hellenistic age, Roman rule led to the creation of hundreds of new cities. Although these had the constitution and institutions of Greek *poleis* (see POLIS) they owed their existence directly to Roman control (see URBANISM). Civic culture, both in colonies and cities, also underwent radical changes. Since civic independence was now a thing of the past, much more emphasis was laid on the externals of city life, above all splendid public buildings, which were the hallmark of a Roman city, especially in the 1st and 2nd cents. AD. Certain building types reflected specific Roman influence: temples and other structures associated with the Imperial cult often dominated both old and newly founded cities; not only *amphitheatres (which were relatively infrequent in the Greek east) but theatres were built to accommodate gladiatorial shows and other forms of public entertainment; above all, the *baths, *aqueducts, and spectacular fountain houses (see NYMPHAEUM), which were present everywhere and served almost as a defining characteristic of city life, were specifically Roman supplements to the existing character of a city.

Language Although no attempt was made to introduce or impose Latin as the spoken language of the population of the eastern provinces, it was the language of the army, of administration, and of the lawyers. During the 3rd and 4th cents. the attractions of a local career in a city were far outweighed by the prospect and possibilities of imperial service, as a soldier, an officer, or as a member of the imperial administrative cadre. Knowledge of Latin was effectively a precondition for anyone who wished to enter this world. The law school at *Berytus, whose students needed to master the language as well as the niceties of Roman law, provided a focal point where members of the Hellenized upper classes of the later Empire acquired these two essential elements of the new, Romanized culture.

Religion and Cult Specifically Roman cults, such as that of *Jupiter Optimus Maximus or of the Capitoline Triad (see CAPITOL) made little impact on the Greek east outside military camps. The Roman *ruler-cult, however, whose origins lay in a collaboration between the Roman authorities, especially provincial governors, and the upper classes of the eastern provinces, and which evolved a new form of politico-religious expression within the framework of imperial rule, had an enormous impact. Imperial temples and other buildings often dominated the cities; priesthoods and other offices concerned with the cult became the peak of a local political career; games and festivals in honour of the emperors dominated civic calendars. Much of the 'Romanness' of a city of the eastern provinces during the imperial period could therefore be traced directly to the institution of emperor-worship.

S. Macready and F. H. Thompson (eds.), *Roman Architecture in the Greek World* (1987); A. N. Sherwin-White, *The Roman Citizenship*[2] (1973); F. Millar, *The Roman Near East 31 BC–AD 337* (1993); G. Woolf, *PCPS* 1994, 116 ff.; Brunt, *RIT*. S. M.

Rome (history)

1. *From the Origins to 31 BC*

1. The origins of Rome

Surviving literary accounts of the beginnings of Rome are based entirely on legend. The stories provide evidence of what the Romans at various times thought about their own origins and how they liked to see themselves. The developed version of the story contained two main legends, those of *Aeneas and *Romulus, which were artificially combined at an unknown date (but certainly before 300 BC). Although both legends are very ancient, they are, as far as we can tell, quite unhistorical, although certain incidental details (e.g. the idea that Romulus founded his settlement on the *Palatine) are consistent with the archaeological facts.

The archaeological evidence now available shows that one or more villages were established on the hills of Rome (including the Palatine) from the end of the bronze age (c.1000 BC). These communities were similar to other hilltop settlements that have been identified throughout Latium Vetus, whose cemeteries

provide evidence of a distinct form of material culture known as the *cultura laziale*. In the earliest phases (10th and 9th cents. BC) the settlements were small, isolated villages consisting of a few thatched huts. During the 8th and 7th cents. they grew in size and sophistication, with the development of external trade (including contacts with the Greek world), specialized craft production, and the emergence of a wealthy aristocracy. At Rome the Palatine settlement expanded by 700 to include the Forum valley and possibly the *Quirinal, and the main cemetery moved from the Forum to the *Esquiline. Towards the end of the 7th cent. the Forum was laid out as a public meeting place (see FORUM ROMANUM), and monumental buildings made their first appearance. At this point Rome was transformed into an organized city-state.

As befits a frontier town on an important river crossing, Rome seems to have had a mixed population, including Sabines (see SABINI), Greeks and, it seems, large numbers of *Etruscans. Two of the kings were traditionally of Etruscan origin, but this does not mean that Rome was conquered by the Etruscans or that it became in any other sense an 'Etruscan city' this is a false deduction from the fact that it shared the same (Hellenizing) material culture as the cities of southern Etruria (see HELLENISM; HELLENIZATION). Although heavily influenced by contacts with the outside world (including Greece and the near east, as well as Etruria and *Campania), Rome remained fundamentally a Latin city. This is borne out by an ever-increasing body of Latin inscriptions, which also prove incidentally that Roman culture had been literate from probably about 600 BC.

What passes for the history of Rome at this early period is recorded in literary sources of the 1st cent. BC and later, which are unlikely to contain much reliable information about events hundreds of years earlier. According to the sources the city was originally ruled by kings, which is likely enough, but no confidence can be placed in the complex dynastic history or the dating of the canonical seven: Romulus, Numa *Pompilius, Tullus *Hostilius, Ancus *Marcius, *Tarquinius Priscus, Servius *Tullius, and *Tarquinius Superbus. See REX. With the exception of the eponymous Romulus these names may be those of genuine kings, but the notion that their reigns occupied the whole of the period from the 8th cent. BC to the end of the 6th is unacceptable. The conventional foundation date, fixed at 753 BC by *Varro, is the result of artificial manipulation, and does not accord with any archaeological starting point; the earliest settlement is much earlier than 753, and the formation of an urbanized city-state considerably later. It is necessary to suppose either that the regal period was much shorter than the conventional 250 years, or that there were more kings than the conventional seven. As it happens there are good reasons for doing both, since alternative traditions record the names of kings not in the canonical list (e.g. Titus *Tatius and *Mastarna).

The detailed narratives of their reigns must be regarded largely as fictitious elaboration; but it is nevertheless possible that some elements are based, however dimly, on genuine memory. For instance, accounts of the Roman conquest of the Alban hills region (traditionally attributed to Tullus Hostilius) and the lower Tiber valley (Ancus Marcius) describe an extension of Roman territory that must have occurred before the end of the 6th cent. Similarly the organization of the calendar and the major priesthoods, traditionally the work of Numa, can be dated with some confidence to the 6th cent. or even earlier. The belief that the Roman monarchy was elective rather than hereditary is unlikely to be an invention, and many institutions associated with the election process, such as the *interrex, the lex curiata de imperio (see COMITIA), and the ceremony of inauguration, were probably genuine relics of the time of the kings. The earliest institutions of the state, the three pre-Servian tribes and the thirty curiae, of which only residual traces survived in the later republic, almost certainly go back to the early monarchic period (tradition ascribes them to Romulus). The centuriate reform attributed to Servius Tullius, as it is described in the surviving narratives, belongs to the middle republic, but a simpler system dividing the citizens according to their capacity to arm themselves (see CLASSIS) may well be a genuine reform of the 6th cent.; it is also likely that the innovation of locally based tribes is of pre-republican origin.

The last two kings are presented as tyrants—illegal usurpers who adopted a flamboyant and populist style of rule similar to that of the contemporary Greek tyrants (see TYRANNY). Like the latter, they pursued an ambitious foreign policy, patronized the arts, and embarked on extensive and grandiose building projects. In view of the extent to which 6th-cent. Rome was subject to Greek influence, this need not surprise us; moreover the archaeological evidence confirms that Rome was indeed a powerful, sophisticated, and cosmopolitan city at this time—in the well-known phrase that has recently become something of a cliché: la grande Roma dei Tarquini ('the great Rome of the Tarquins'). Finally, *Tarquinius Superbus is said to have created a miniature 'empire' in Latium, a state of affairs that is also presupposed in the first Carthaginian treaty (Polyb. 3. 22); this coincidence between the annalistic tradition and an apparently contemporary document tends to confirm the authenticity of both.

2. The early republic and the 'Conflict of the Orders'

The portrayal of the later kings as tyrannical populists is consistent with the story that the last of them, Tarquinius Superbus, was expelled in an aristocratic coup, and replaced by a republic under two annually elected *consuls. These basic elements of the traditional story are more credible than an alternative modern theory that the monarchy was not overthrown in a sudden coup, but slowly faded away, the king being gradually reduced to a purely ceremonial figure (the *rex sacrorum), and replaced as ruler by a supreme magistrate (see MAGISTRACY, ROMAN), variously defined as *dictator, magister populi, or praetor maximus. The dual consulship, on this view, was a later development.

The principal objection to this ingenious theory is that it conflicts with the evidence of the *Fasti, the list of consuls preserved in a number of sources (with only minor variations) and widely regarded as authentic. The Fasti list the two consuls of each year going back to around 500 BC (the version of the Fasti Capitolini, based on the researches of *Varro, places the beginning of the list, and therefore the beginning of the republic, in 509 BC; this Varronian system of dating, though incorrect in places, is conventionally followed by modern historians). A late 6th-cent. date for the beginning of the republic is likely to be correct in general terms, and seems to be confirmed by independent Greek sources (see ARISTODEMUS (2)).

In this connection it is worth noting that the sources for the republic are in general more soundly based than for the preceding monarchic period. The accounts we can read all date from the late republic and early empire (the most important ones from the second half of the 1st cent. BC). These sources are in their turn based on earlier accounts, now lost, the earliest of which were written at the end of the 3rd cent. BC. Where the earliest Roman historians obtained their material is largely a matter for conjecture, but their sources undoubtedly included the following: accounts of Greek historians, oral memory, the traditions of the great noble families (at least partly preserved in written form), and public documents such as laws, treaties, and senatorial decrees. It is also evident that they had access to archival documents in chronicle form, above all the *annales maximi, which included the magistrates of each year together with other information about public events. Naturally the 5th-cent. notices were meagre and uncertain, and the later literary narratives introduced much secondary elaboration and perhaps even invention; but there is no reason to doubt that a basic structure of documentary material lies behind the accounts of our sources for the history of the republic.

During the early republic power rested in the hands of an aristocratic clique known as the patriciate (see PATRICIANS). Patricians were members of certain privileged clans (gentes; see GENS) which had probably obtained special status under the kings. This would seem to follow from the fact that only patricians could hold the office of interrex, an obvious relic of the monarchy. The patricians had an exclusive hold on all the chief religious offices, and it was they who gave their assent (the auctoritas patrum; see PATRUM AUCTORITAS) to decisions of the comitia before they became binding. Most consuls were patricians, but it appears from the Fasti that they did not have a monopoly of political office until the middle of the 5th cent.

The early republic appears to have been a period when Rome experienced military difficulties and economic recession. Not surprisingly it was the poorer citizens who suffered most, especially without the protection of the kings who had relied on their support. Debt, land-hunger, and food shortages are recorded as the main grievances. Some of these poorer citizens are said to have taken matters into their own hands in 494 BC, when they withdrew from the city (see SECESSIO) and formed their own alternative state. The *plebs, as they were called, formed an assembly (the concilium plebis), elected their own officers (tribunes—*tribuni plebis—and *aediles), and set up their own cult (of *Ceres, Liber, and Libera (see LIBER PATER)). For the next two centuries this remarkable plebeian organization fought to improve the lot of its members, by passing resolutions (plebiscita—see PLEBISCITUM), by backing the authority of the tribunes, whose sacrosanctity enabled them to frustrate the actions of magistrates through personal intervention, and if necessary by secession.

The principal demands of the plebs were for debt relief and a more equitable distribution of economic resources, especially land. Tradition maintained that the codification of the *Twelve Tables in 450 BC was also a product of plebeian agitation. The plebeian organization was gradually recognized, and obtained a limited right to pass plebiscites (see PLEBISCITUM) binding on the whole people (in 449, extended in 339). Its membership seems to have increased, and to have come to include growing numbers of wealthy and politically ambitious citizens. In the 4th cent. (if not earlier) these richer plebeians began to use the organization as a means to break down the exclusive privileges of the patricians. It was only at this secondary stage that the struggle became a direct conflict between patricians and plebeians.

In 367 BC the Licinio-Sextian laws (see LICINIUS STOLO, L.) made plebeians eligible for the consulship, and in 342 the rule was established that one of the two consuls must be a plebeian (see GENUCIUS, L.). A similar rule was extended to the censorship in 339, the same year as the auctoritas patrum was reduced to a formality; and in 300 the major priestly colleges were divided between the two orders (see OGULNIUS GALLUS, Q.). By these and similar measures the plebeians were gradually reintegrated into the state, a process that was completed in *c*.287 BC when plebiscites were made binding on the people and became equivalent to laws (see HORTENSIUS, Q.).

The plebeians also succeeded in obtaining relief from debt (by a series of measures in the 4th cent.), and particularly from the institution of debt-bondage (*nexum*), which was abolished by statute in 326. They also gained increased access to *ager publicus by limiting the amounts an individual could hold (a *lex Licinia Sextia* of 367 set the maximum at 500 *iugera*). But the most important factor in the emancipation of the *plebs* was the redistribution of newly conquered territory in allotments to poorer citizens. It was the programme of colonization and settlement during the late 4th cent. that did most to relieve the burdens of the poor and to end the plebeian struggle as a radical movement.

The main political result was the rise of the nobility, consisting of both patricians and plebeians, who formed a new ruling class based on tenure of office and descent from former office-holders. By the mid-4th cent. a hierarchy of magistracies had been established, resulting from the gradual creation of additional offices alongside the consulship: the quaestors (before 447), the censors (443), the praetor and curule aediles (367). Successful nobles expected to hold a succession of these offices, and a rudimentary career pattern (*cursus honorum*) was established. With the end of the plebeian struggle and the integration of its institutions, the posts of plebeian tribune and aedile became equivalent to magistracies, and were frequently held by young plebeian nobles who used them as stepping-stones to the consulship. After the *lex Ovinia* in the later 4th cent. the *senate became an independent body of permanent life-members, most of them ex-magistrates, and took an increasingly important role in the routine administration of the state and the formation of policy. This was in part an inevitable consequence of the increasing complexity of government as Rome expanded at the expense of its neighbours.

3. The Roman conquest of Italy

After the fall of the monarchy Rome was faced with a revolt of the Latins which led to the battle of Lake *Regillus and the treaty of Spurius *Cassius Vecellinus (493 BC). The result was a military alliance which enabled Rome and the Latins to resist the incursions of threatening neighbours, the Sabines, *Aequi, and *Volsci. By the second half of the 5th cent. the regular raids by these peoples gradually ceased, and the Romans (with allied support) were able to take the offensive. During the last years of the 5th cent. they were engaged in the conquest and colonization of southern Latium. They also gained the upper hand against the Etruscan city of *Veii, a long-standing rival, which they captured and destroyed in 396. Rome's advance continued in the 4th cent., despite the sack of the city by a Celtic war-band in 390 (Varronian; the true date is probably 386), which proved only a temporary setback. Rome's recovery was rapid, and in the following decades the setting of Roman military activity shifted to *Samnium and Campania in the south, and to the territory of Tarquinii and Caere in the north. Relations with the Latins also deteriorated, as the Romans' imperialist intentions became clear. The great Latin war which broke out in 341 BC was crucial, and the Roman victory and subsequent settlement (338 BC) marked a decisive stage in the process of Roman expansion (see LATINI).

The Romans followed up their victory by further conquests and a programme of colonization which led to the foundation of *Cales (334) and *Fregellae (328); the second of these colonies provoked the great conflict known to moderns as the Second Samnite War (327–304; see SAMNIUM), in which the Romans, after a major setback at the *Caudine Forks (321 BC), strengthened their hold on Campania, made alliances in northern *Apulia, Etruria, and Umbria (see UMBRIANS), and advanced into central Italy, where they overcame the *Hernici and Aequi, and made alliances with the *Marsi, *Paeligni, Marrucini, *Frentani, and *Vestini. These military alliances (see SOCII) greatly extended the warlike capacity of Rome, which by 300 was the dominant power in Italy. A few years later the Samnite leader Gellius *Egnatius succeeded in forming an anti-Roman alliance of Samnites, Gauls, Etruscans, and Umbrians, but their joint forces were destroyed at *Sentinum in 296, a battle that decided the fate of Italy. In the following decades, which are poorly documented in the surviving literature, Rome completed the conquest of peninsular Italy by forcing all its peoples to become allies, either by defeating them in war or compelling them to surrender in advance. The last to succumb were the Greek cities of the south, particularly *Tarentum, which in 280 BC summoned *Pyrrhus of Epirus to Italy to lead the war against Rome. The defeat of Pyrrhus in 275 was a turning point, not only because it was virtually the final act in the Roman conquest of Italy (Tarentum held out for a few years, but was captured in 272), but because it brought Rome to the attention of a wider world; the defeat of a powerful king with a fully trained professional army by a hitherto unknown Italian republic created a sensation in the Hellenistic east. A new world power had emerged.

The final stages of the conquest had been completed extremely quickly; barely fifty years elapsed between the outbreak of the Second Samnite War and the fall of Tarentum. And yet the Romans' hold over the Italian allies proved remarkably thorough and lasting. Their success was partly due to the policy of founding colonies throughout the peninsula (19 were established between 334 and 263), on strategic sites linked by a network of well-constructed military roads. A second factor that secured the loyalty of the allies was Rome's support for local aristocracies, who saw the oligarchic republic as their natural ally, and relied on Roman backing to keep them in power at home. Finally, the cohesiveness of the system of alliances was a result of continuous and successful warfare, in which the allies took part and from which they gained a share of the profits. The system was a remarkably effective military machine. War was its *raison d'être*, and its inevitable product. This fact bears directly on the much debated question of Roman imperialism. Roman *imperialism was the result of continuous war, and continuous war was the result of the Roman system of alliances in Italy.

4. Roman imperialism and its consequences

It was inevitable that, after completing the conquest of peninsular Italy, the Romans would embark on military adventures beyond its borders. Less than a decade after the fall of Tarentum they became involved in a major overseas war, when they challenged the Carthaginians for the control of Sicily. In spite of immense losses Rome finally emerged as the victor in this First Punic War (264–241 BC), and *Sicily became the first province. A second was added shortly afterwards, when *Sardinia was seized from an enfeebled Carthage (238). Twenty years later the Second Punic War began when the Romans declared war over the *Saguntum affair and *Hannibal invaded Italy (218). In spite of spectacular victories in the field Hannibal failed to win over Rome's Italian allies, most of whom remained loyal, and was gradually worn down; he withdrew from Italy in 204 and was finally defeated at *Zama in 202 (see PUNIC WARS).

As a result the Romans obtained further provinces from the former Carthaginian possessions in Spain, and were drawn into imperialistic ventures in the eastern Mediterranean. They also resumed the conquest of northern Italy, which had begun in 224 but had been interrupted by Hannibal's invasion (see CISALPINE GAUL). In the period to c.175 BC Roman armies overran the Po Valley, Liguria, and the Istrian peninsula. At the same time they were engaged in fierce fighting in Spain, which continued intermittently until 133 and led to the conquest of Lusitania and Celtiberia, although the north-west corner of the Iberian peninsula remained unconquered until the time of Augustus. Finally, campaigns in southern Gaul from 125 to 121 BC resulted in the conquest of Gallia Narbonensis (Provence).

During the same period Rome became increasingly involved in the affairs of the eastern Mediterranean. The first Roman venture east of the Adriatic was in Illyria during the 220s (see TEUTA). A Second Illyrian War occurred in 219 (see DEMETRIUS (7)), and was viewed with alarm by the Macedonian king, *Philip (3) V. In 215 Philip made an alliance with Hannibal, which provoked the Romans into the so-called First Macedonian War (214–205), a half-hearted affair to which they were unable or unwilling to commit large military forces. After Zama, however, they felt free to give more attention to the east, and embarked on the Second Macedonian War in 200. Roman troops invaded the Balkans and defeated Philip at *Cynoscephalae (197), but these forces were withdrawn in 194 after T. *Quinctius Flamininus had confined Philip to Macedonia and pronounced 'the freedom of the Greeks'. Roman efforts to control events in the Greek world by diplomacy and threats were eventually unsuccessful, however, and further military interventions occurred in 191–188, when the Romans invaded Asia Minor and defeated *Antiochus (3) III, and in the Third Macedonian War (171–167), when the kingdom of Macedon was destroyed by the Roman victory at *Pydna. Finally, in the 140s, Roman armies crushed revolts in *Macedonia and Greece, which were made into provinces ruled directly from Rome (see ACHAIA). The Romans emphasized their dominance by ruthlessness, the most brutal example of which was the destruction of Corinth in 146 BC. In the same year Carthage was destroyed after a Third Punic War (149–146), and its territory became the Roman province of Africa (see AFRICA, ROMAN). Further annexations occurred in Asia (133; see ASIA (ROMAN PROVINCE)), *Cilicia (101), and *Cyrene (96).

The successful pattern of overseas conquests had dramatic effects on all aspects of life in Rome and Italy. In the first place it consolidated the power of the patrician-plebeian élite, which dominated the senate and virtually monopolized the senior offices of state. The plebs were happy to acquiesce in this as long as they benefited from the proceeds of military conquest, as were the Italian allies. Secondly the growth of empire vastly increased the wealth of the upper classes, which began to adopt luxurious and increasingly sophisticated habits. The influence of Greek culture became pervasive, and wealthy Romans began to affect the leisured style of the great centres of the Hellenistic world; see HELLENISM. Architecture and the visual arts flourished, as the Romans imitated all the trappings of Greek civilization. One of the results was the development of Roman literature on the Greek model, including drama, epic poetry and, not least, historiography.

But overseas conquests also had unforeseen and sometimes damaging effects on the economy and society of Italy. The conspicuous consumption of the élite was fuelled by investment in Italian land. This led to the growth of large landed estates in Italy, worked by war captives who were imported as slaves. The slave-worked estates introduced new methods of farming, designed to provide absentee landlords with an income from the sale of cash crops (a regime described in the handbook On Agriculture by M. *Porcius Cato (1)). Large-scale grazing was also a profitable form of investment, particularly in southern Italy, where much land had been made available by the devastations and confiscations associated with the Hannibalic War. Some of the land in question was technically ager publicus, but the Roman government turned a blind eye to its expropriation by the rich, and did not enforce the legal limits on the size of holdings.

There has been much discussion about the nature of these large estates, the extent of their spread in various regions of Italy, their impact on existing agrarian structures, and their effect on the growth of urban markets. The result of modern research, involving new theoretical models and the use of archaeological evidence, has been to produce a complex picture of varying types of land-use, tenure, and labour exploitation. Nevertheless, it is probable that our sources (particularly Appian, Civil Wars I) are right to stress that one of the effects of the changes was large-scale peasant displacement. This had alarming implications for the government, because small peasant proprietors formed the backbone of the Roman army; the situation was aggravated by the fact that prolonged military service in distant theatres made it increasingly difficult for such men to maintain their farms. Roman and Italian peasant-soldiers were thus the victims of their own success, and were driven off the land to a life of penury and unemployment. Since the law laid down a property qualification for army service, the displaced and impoverished peasants were no longer available for recruitment. The result was a manpower crisis, as well as discontent and growing social tension, which came increasingly to threaten the longstanding political consensus. See AGRICULTURE, ROMAN; LATIFUNDIA.

5. The Roman revolution

The widening gulf between rich and poor eventually gave rise to social conflict and political breakdown. In 133 BC a tribune (see TRIBUNI PLEBIS), Tiberius *Sempronius Gracchus (3), introduced a land reform which proposed to enforce the ancient and long-neglected limit of 500 iugera on holdings of ager publicus, and to redistribute the reclaimed surplus in allotments to the poor (see AGRARIAN LAWS AND POLICY). Not surprisingly there was furious opposition, and Gracchus was eventually murdered in an outbreak of political violence instigated by the *optimates (conservative senators). Ten years later his brother, Gaius *Sempronius Gracchus suffered the same fate, when he attempted to bring in a series of reforms, which ranged far more widely than his brother's single law. Gaius' legislation embraced provincial administration and taxation, the urban grain supply, judicial reform, and the extension of Roman citizenship to the Italian allies. His aim was to ensure that all citizens, not just the ruling class, should benefit from the proceeds of empire, and that those who governed it should be made accountable for their actions. But his efforts were in vain; most of the measures that he succeeded in passing into law were repealed after his murder (121 BC).

In the following generation Rome faced military difficulties in every part of the empire. These included a war in Africa (see JUGURTHA), a slave revolt in Sicily (103–101 BC; an earlier revolt there had been crushed in 132), and an invasion of Italy by migrating German tribes, the *Cimbri and *Teutones. In attempting to respond to these crises the ruling oligarchy showed itself corrupt and incompetent, and they were only resolved by allowing an able and ambitious parvenu, C. *Marius (1), to hold an unprecedented succession of consulships, and to recruit a professional army from the proletariat.

Rome (history)

These measures solved the military problems, but had fatal long-term consequences, because they provided the poor with a means to redress their grievances, and ambitious nobles with the chance to gain personal power by means of armed force. Matters were brought to a head in the aftermath of the *Social War (3) (91–89 BC), the revolt of the Italian allies who had taken up arms in order to obtain the Roman citizenship, and by an invasion of the eastern provinces by *Mithradates (6) VI of Pontus, who was welcomed as a liberator by many provincial communities. These events created political chaos at Rome. L. *Cornelius Sulla, the consul of 88, was appointed by the senate to lead an expedition against Mithradates; but the plebeian assembly, at the bidding of the tribune P. Sulpicius Rufus, overturned this arrangement and gave the command instead to Marius. Sulla responded by marching on the city and imposing his will by force. Marius was driven out and Sulpicius murdered. But when Sulla and his army left for the east, Marius and his followers marched on the city in their turn, massacred their opponents and seized power (87 BC). When Sulla returned after defeating Mithradates at the end of 83, the stage was set for a full scale civil war between his army and those of Marius' successors (Marius himself had died in 86).

After a series of extremely bloody encounters, Sulla emerged victorious and set himself up as dictator in 81. He purged his opponents by means of the notorious *proscriptions and attempted to reform the constitution, in particular by strengthening the position of the senate and abolishing most of the powers of the tribunes. These efforts were ineffectual, however, since they addressed the symptoms, not the cause, of the problem, and the same lethal trends continued. A fresh series of military crises in the 70s (see AEMILIUS LEPIDUS (2), M.; SERTORIUS, Q.; SPARTACUS) brought the popular generals *Pompey and *Crassus to power. As consuls in 70 they repealed most of Sulla's laws and restored the powers of the tribunes.

These events, combined with scandals such as the trial of *Verres, left the senate with little power and even less authority, at a time when military difficulties and economic crises continued to afflict the empire. In 67 Pompey was given (by a tribunician plebiscite) an overriding command against the pirates, and in 66 was appointed, again by plebiscite and in place of L. *Licinius Lucullus (2), the senate's commander, to take charge of a war in the east against Mithradates. This he quickly brought to an end, and settled by a complete reorganization of the east, annexing territory, founding cities, and disposing kingdoms. In Italy meanwhile social unrest and discontent erupted in the conspiracy of *Catiline (63), which was ruthlessly put down by the consul *Cicero, who himself portrayed the outcome as a triumph for moderation.

In 62 Pompey returned, a conquering hero, to a magnificent triumph and what he no doubt hoped would be a life of ease and dignity as Rome's leading statesman. If so he was disappointed, since the *optimates, led by Lucullus and M. *Porcius Cato (2), frustrated his efforts to gain the land allotments he had promised as a reward for his veterans. The effect was to drive Pompey into an informal pact with Crassus and *Caesar, sometimes called (in modern books, not in the ancient sources) the First Triumvirate. This alliance proved irresistible. Pompey had overwhelming popular support, Crassus had unlimited money, and Caesar, who was even more unscrupulous than his partners, turned out to have the brains. As consul in 59 Caesar enacted all the measures his partners wanted, and rewarded himself with a special command in Gaul, which he proceeded to conquer in a brilliant (if brutal) campaign (58–51 BC).

In Rome during the 50s the senate was powerless in the face of the dynasts, but the latter had less control over the tribunes, as the activities of P. *Clodius Pulcher demonstrated. Towards the end of the decade order threatened to break down completely (see ANNIUS MILO, T.), and in 52 Pompey was appointed sole consul when riots prevented elections. By this time relations between Pompey and Caesar were becoming strained (Crassus had been killed in battle in 53). Fear of Caesar drove Pompey and the optimates closer together, as they attempted to frustrate Caesar's aim of passing directly from his Gallic command to a second consulship. Caesar refused to lay down his arms, and in 49 he invaded Italy at the head of an army and once again plunged the empire into civil war. Pompey, who presented himself as defender of the republic, had some initial successes, but was eventually beaten at *Pharsalus (48), and was murdered after fleeing to Egypt. Caesar then overcame the republicans in Africa and Spain, before returning to Italy where he became consul and dictator for life.

Caesar embarked on a series of grandiose and visionary schemes, but his monarchical tendencies went against republican tradition and offended the nobles. On 15 March, 44 BC, he was stabbed to death by a group of senators led by *Brutus and *Cassius. The conspirators were unable to restore the republic, however, because Caesar's chief aides, Mark Antony (see ANTONIUS (2), M.) and M. *Aemilius Lepidus (3), had the support of his armies; in 43 they joined together with Caesar's heir, the 19-year-old Caesar Octavian (see AUGUSTUS), to form a Triumvirate (a formally constituted board of three for the organization of the state—see TRIUMVIRS), whereupon they divided the empire between them, and purged their opponents (including Cicero) by reviving Sulla's device of proscriptions. Lepidus was soon squeezed out, and the empire was uneasily divided between Octavian and Antony until 31 BC, when the issue was finally decided in Octavian's favour at the battle of *Actium. Mark Antony and his mistress *Cleopatra VII committed suicide, leaving Octavian in complete control of the Roman empire.

GENERAL *CAH* 7²/2 (1989), 8² (1989), 9² (1994)—comprehensive and up-to-date, with full bibliographies. See also A. Momigliano and A. Schiavone (eds.), *Storia di Roma* 1–2 (1988–91). Among older works: T. Mommsen, *Römische Geschichte* (1854–6; Eng. trans., *History of Rome*, 1894); G. De Sanctis, *Storia dei Romani* 1–4 (1907–64); A. J. Toynbee, *Hannibal's Legacy* 1–2 (1965); P. A. Brunt, *Social Conflicts in the Roman Republic* (1971); H. H. Scullard, *History of the Roman World, 753–146 BC*⁴ (1980), and *From the Gracchi to Nero*⁵ (1982); M. Crawford, *The Roman Republic*² (1992). Two classic studies, which range far more widely than their titles suggest: E. Badian, *Foreign Clientelae, 264–70 BC* (1958), and P. A. Brunt, *Italian Manpower, 225 BC–AD 14* (1971).

ORIGINS AND EARLY HISTORY General accounts: Beloch, *Röm. Gesch.*; J. Heurgon, *The Rise of Rome to 264 BC* (1973; Fr. orig. 1969); R. M. Ogilvie, *Early Rome and the Etruscans* (1976); M. Pallottino, *Origini e storia primitiva di Roma* (1994); see also the important series of articles by Momigliano, *Terzo contributo*, 545 ff.; *Quarto contributo* (1969), 273 ff. On the legends G. Dumézil, *Mythe et épopée* 1–3 (1968–73); J. Poucet, *Les Origines de Rome* (1985); N. Horsfall and J. Bremmer, *Roman Myth and Mythography* (1987); A. Grandazzi, *La Fondation de Rome* (1993). Archaeological evidence: E. Gjerstad, *Early Rome* 1–4 (1953–66), with a comprehensive account of material evidence, but unsound interpretation; G. Colonna, in *Popoli e civiltà dell'Italia antica* 2 (1974), 283 ff.; *La grande Roma dei Tarquini* (exhib. cat. 1990); R. Ross Holloway, *The Archaeology of Early Rome and Latium* (1994). The later monarchy: S. Mazzarino, *Dalla monarchia allo stato repubblicano* (1945); G. Valditara, *Studi sul magister populi* (1989). On patricians and plebeians: J.-C. Richard, *Les Origines de la plèbe romaine* (1978); K. Raaflaub (ed.), *Social Struggles in Archaic Rome* (1986); R. E. Mitchell, *Patricians and Plebeians* (1992); T. Cornell, *The Beginnings of Rome* (1995).

THE REPUBLICAN CONSTITUTION AND THE NATURE OF POLITICS General: Mommsen, *Röm. Staatsr.*; F. De Martino, *Storia della costituzione romana*² 1–5 (1972–5). Institutions: G. W. Botsford, *The Roman Assemblies* (1909); L. R. Taylor, *The Voting Districts of the Roman Republic* (1960), and *Roman Voting Assemblies* (1966); C. Nicolet, *The World of the Citizen in Republican Rome* (1980; Fr. orig. 1976), and *Rome et la conquête du monde méditerranéen, 1. Les Structures de l'Italie romaine* (1977). The structure of politics: M. Gelzer, *The Roman Nobility* (1969; Ger. orig. 1912); F. Münzer, *Römische Adelsparteien und Adelsfamilien* (1921); L. R. Taylor, *Party Politics in the Age of Caesar* (1949); T. P. Wiseman, *New Men in the Roman Senate* (1971); H. H. Scullard, *Roman Politics, 220–150 BC*² (1973); P. A. Brunt, *JRS* 1982, 1 ff.; K. Hopkins (and G. P. Burton), *Death and Renewal* (1983); M. I. Finley, *Politics in the Ancient World* (1983); F. G. B. Millar, *JRS* 1984, 1 ff.; 1986, 1 ff.; K. J. Hölkeskamp, *Die Entstehung der Nobilität* (1987); W. Eder (ed.), *Staat und Staatlichkeit in der frühen römischen Republik* (1990).

ROME AND ITS NEIGHBOURS: THE CONQUEST OF ITALY A. Afzelius, *Die römische Eroberung Italiens* (1942); A. Alföldi, *Early Rome and the Latins* (1965); E. T. Salmon, *Samnium and the Samnites* (1967), and *Roman Colonization under the Republic* (1969); W. V. Harris, *Rome in Etruria and Umbria* (1971); A. N. Sherwin-White, *The Roman Citizenship*² (1972); H. Galsterer, *Herrschaft und Verwaltung im republikanischen Italien* (1976); M. Humbert, *Municipium et civitas sine suffragio* (1978); C. G. Starr, *The Beginnings of Imperial Rome* (1980); E. T. Salmon, *The Making of Roman Italy* (1982); M. W. Frederiksen, *Campania* (1984); K. Lomas, *Rome and the Italian Greeks* (1993).

THE CONQUEST OF THE MEDITERRANEAN M. Holleaux, *Rome, la Grèce et les monarchies hellénistiques* (1921); E. Badian, *Roman Imperialism in the Late Republic* (1968), and *Publicans and Sinners* (1972); J. Deininger, *Der politische Widerstand gegen Rom in Griechenland* (1971); C. Nicolet, *Rome et le conquête du monde méditerranéen, 2. Genèse d'un empire* (1978); J. F. Lazenby, *Hannibal's War* (1978); P. Garnsey and C. R. Whittaker (eds.), *Imperialism in the Ancient World* (1978); W. V. Harris, *War and Imperialism in Republican Rome* (1979); E. S. Gruen, *The Hellenistic World and the Coming of Rome* 1–2 (1984); A. N. Sherwin-White, *Roman Foreign Policy in the East* (1984); J. S. Richardson, *Hispaniae* (1986); J.-L. Ferrary, *Philhellénisme et impérialisme* (1988); A. W. Lintott, *Imperium Romanum* (1994); R. Kallet–Marx, *Hegemony to Empire* (1995).

SOCIAL AND ECONOMIC CONSEQUENCES OF EMPIRE E. Gabba, *Republican Rome: The Army and the Allies* (1976); K. Hopkins, *Conquerors and Slaves* (1978); E. Gabba, *Strutture agrarie e l'allevamento transumante nell'Italia romana* (1979); A. Carandini and S. Settis, *Schiavi e padroni nell'Etruria romana* (1979); A. Giardina and A. Schiavone (eds.), *Società romana e produzione schiavistica* 1–3 (1981); P. W. De Neeve, *Colonus* (1984), and *Peasants in Peril* (1984); K. R. Bradley, *Slavery and Rebellion in the Roman World* (1989); A. W. Lintott, *Judicial Reform and Land Reform in the Roman Republic* (1992).

THE ROMAN REVOLUTION Syme, *Rom. Rev.*; C. Meier, *Res Publica Amissa* (1966); Lintott, *Violence*; R. Seager (ed.), *The Crisis of the Roman Republic* (1969); Gruen, *LGRR*; L. Keppie, *Colonization and Veteran Settlement in Italy, 47–14 BC* (1983); M. Beard and M. Crawford, *Rome in the Late Republic* (1985); P. A. Brunt, *The Fall of the Roman Republic and Related Essays* (1988).   T. J. Co.

2. From Augustus to the Antonines (31 BC–AD 192)

1. Augustus and the foundation of imperial rule

After victory over the forces of Mark Antony (M. *Antonius (2)) and *Cleopatra VII at *Actium (31 BC) and the subsequent annexation of Egypt in the summer of 30 BC, Octavian (see AUGUSTUS) and his generals were masters of the Mediterranean world. To create a system of permanent rule they needed both to gain the acceptance of their power by the majority of the senatorial and equestrian élite, even if a majority of die-hard republicans could not be won over, and to maintain the loyalty of the soldiery. The armed forces in turn were to revert to their traditional role of war against foreign enemies. The great and successful wars of conquest initiated by Augustus and M. *Vip-

sanius Agrippa became one of the key sources of legitimacy and prestige of the new regime (see below, § 3).

Octavian and his key political allies (such as Agrippa and T. *Statilius Taurus) proceeded cautiously and by trial and error in their search for an enduring political settlement. Already in 32 BC 700 senators (out of a total of about 1,000) had sworn a personal oath of loyalty to Octavian. In 28 BC Octavian and Agrippa assumed censorial powers (see CENSOR), completed the first full census of the citizen body since 69, and revised the rolls of the *senate. One hundred and ninety 'unworthy' members were removed. Grants of special powers by senate and people, most notably in 28 and 23 BC, ensued, which formalized and legitimated Augustus' pre-eminent position. Augustus, 'revered', was a title conferred on Octavian in 27 BC. Augustus' most important right was that of directly appointing all senior army officers and the governors of key (especially military) provinces. At all times he ensured that any new powers were formally voted to him and made a great show of rejecting anything which hinted at monarchy or dictatorship. Among his fellow aristocrats he portrayed himself as 'first among equals'. The lessons of *Caesar's fate had been well learnt. In the years up to his death in 13 BC Agrippa acted as almost co-regent of the empire. He was also the recipient of grants of special powers in 23 and 18 BC. Together they took active measures to reconstruct the state's financial infrastructure. Both men spent long periods touring the provinces especially in the decade after the political settlement of 23 BC. In the long term their most important administrative innovation was the introduction of provincial censuses which were designed to map out the resources of the provinces and provide a more rational framework for the assessment and levying of direct taxation, 'the sinews of the state'. See FINANCE, ROMAN.

The senate, from whose ranks generals and most provincial governors were drawn, remained the most important political element in the state, even though its corporate powers were restricted through the *de facto* transfer of the formulation of fiscal and military policy to Augustus and his advisers. The new regime also saw the entrenchment of the equestrian order (see EQUITES, *Imperial period*) as the empire's second estate. At Rome important new positions of public authority (the prefect of the corn supply, the prefects of the praetorian guard) were created and allotted to equestrians (see PRAEFECTUS). In the provinces equestrian administrators (*procuratores*; see PROCURATOR) oversaw fiscal affairs. In the armed forces young equestrians came to form the junior officer corps as commanders of auxiliary units and as military tribunes in the legions. Augustus and his advisers thus exercised rule over the empire through the collaboration of the political élite. In turn the public careers of individual senators and equestrians were dependent on the favour of the emperor. Loyalty brought reward and success, disloyalty (real or imagined) disgrace, even execution.

The land question in general and the material demands of the veteran troops in particular had fatally undermined oligarchic rule in the late republic (see AGRARIAN LAWS AND POLICY). Augustus and his advisers took determined and decisive steps to resolve this problem. Mass demobilization immediately followed the end of the civil wars. Land in Italy and the provinces was purchased, via the vast private resources of Octavian Augustus, and distributed to these veterans. In the medium term the practice of routine distribution of land or cash to veterans was established. The creation of a special military treasury (see AERARIUM MILITARE) in AD 6, funded by a new tax on inheritances, marked the culmination of this development. The process of overseas civil and military colonization, first adumbrated by Caesar and taken to its logical conclusion by Augustus, brought about the transfer to the provinces of about 250,000 adult male Italians, roughly one fifth of the total free adult male population of Italy. In a parallel process vast resources were also expended to underpin the material interests of the free population of Rome. The regular distribution of free rations of grain, acquired by provincial taxation, became a normal feature of imperial Rome. Augustus also used his own personal fortune to make periodic distributions of cash to the inhabitants of Rome. On his own account hundreds of millions of sesterces were spent in this way between 30 BC and his death, a sum greater than the total annual revenues of the Roman state in the early 50s BC.

2. High politics, the succession, and the emperors

The resolution of the land question via overseas *colonization and the underpinning of the material livelihood of the massive population of Rome removed from the political agenda two issues which had dominated the history of the late republic. Under the emperors high politics came to centre on two interconnected issues, namely the relationship of individual emperors to the political élite, and the imperial succession. Extreme tension between sections of the political élite and the emperor, expressed most dramatically in treason-trials and executions, became the hallmark of high politics under Augustus' immediate successors, *Tiberius (AD 14–37), *Gaius (1) or Caligula (37–41), *Claudius (41–54), and *Nero (54–68), the Julio-Claudian dynasty. This tension derived structurally from the claim that the emperor was only first among his aristocratic equals, from lingering republicanism, and from the absence of any established law of succession. Consequently leading aristocrats, especially if connected by blood or marriage to the imperial family, could be regarded as threatening an individual emperor's rule. The contingent factor of the personalities and backgrounds of the Julio-Claudian emperors sharpened this structural tension. So the suspicious Tiberius had become Augustus' chosen successor only by default after the death of Augustus' two grandsons; the autocratic Caligula is said to have made senators kiss his feet; Claudius was completely without experience of public life at his accession; Nero came to power at the age of sixteen. Each turned to court-favourites to buttress their position. But the open use, especially of imperial slaves and freedmen as confidants merely served to strengthen the antagonism of the political élite.

The first imperial dynasty succumbed to insurrection and civil war in 68. Nero had both profoundly alienated the political élite by converting the imperial role into a vehicle for indulging his private interests (e.g. singing and chariot-racing) and fatally neglected to cultivate the armed forces and their commanders. When C. *Iulius Vindex, governor of Gallia Lugdunensis, revolted, support for Nero melted away. His suicide in June 68 opened the way to civil war as leading senators vied for the purple. After the brief reigns of *Galba (68–9), *Otho (69), and *Vitellius (69), order and stability were restored by *Vespasian (69–79).

The new Flavian dynasty initiated by Vespasian was short-lived. His elder son *Titus ruled for two years (79–81) and was succeeded by Vespasian's younger son *Domitian (81–96). Under Domitian, who liked to style himself 'Lord and God', tension quickly resurfaced. A serious putsch was attempted by the governor of Upper Germany in 89, and in September 96 Domitian was murdered in a palace coup. The senate nominated as his successor a leading, if elderly, senator M. Cocceius *Nerva (96–8).

The ensuing 90 years represented a high-water mark of stability. The succession problem was resolved by the chance that a series of emperors had no surviving sons. So Nerva adopted *Trajan (98–118). Trajan adopted *Hadrian (117–38), and Hadrian adopted *Antoninus Pius (138–61). All had been leading senators before their accession. The transfer of key political offices at Rome (such as those in charge of imperial correspondence and finances) from freedmen to senior equestrians further served to ameliorate relations between emperors and the élite. In 161 Marcus *Aurelius, adopted son of Pius, succeeded and immediately associated his adoptive brother Lucius *Verus (161–9) as co-emperor. Two tests of political stability now ensued. First, incursions by the Parthians in 162 and by northern tribes from 166 precipitated a period of intense and systematic military campaigning more serious than any seen since the reign of Augustus (see below, § 3). Secondly, the problem of the succession resurfaced. Marcus had a surviving son, *Commodus. Commodus was made co-emperor in 177 and succeeded in March 180. His reign reawakened political tensions reminiscent of the 1st cent. He quickly abandoned his father's senior advisers and placed his trust in confidantes of servile status. Like Nero he used the imperial role to indulge his private whims, most notably fighting as a *gladiator. The result was predictable. On New Year's Eve 192 he was assassinated in a palace coup. Official propaganda justified his murder by claiming that he intended on New Year's Day 193 to murder the incoming consuls and leading senators.

Whatever the vicissitudes of high politics the rulers of Rome in the two centuries from the accession of Augustus achieved two great objectives. Militarily they further extended the empire and protected it from external assault. Politically they maintained uninterrupted administrative control over its vast territory. Fission and secession, the normal fate of great pre-industrial empires, were conspicuous by their absence.

3. The army and military policy

The Roman imperial armed forces were a formidable institution. The state routinely mobilized an average c.350,000 men. The army was the largest element in the state's budget. It was the guarantor of the empire's security, the means for its further expansion. In the last analysis the security of any emperor depended on the loyalty of the troops and their commanders.

Augustus for the first time in Roman history had created a fully professional army with fixed terms and conditions of service. The troops swore a personal oath of loyalty to the reigning emperor (see SACRAMENTUM (MILITARY)). Above all, the loyalty of the troops was grounded in a system of material rewards (pay and donatives) which privileged them in comparison to the mass of the free inhabitants of the empire. Although no emperors could count in principle on the absolute loyalty of all their military commanders (recruited as in the republic from the senatorial and equestrian orders), a variety of devices limited the potential for revolt. All senior commanders were personally appointed by the emperor. Tenure of key positions, such as legionary commander or governor of a military province, was normally restricted to three years, while no military governor normally had above three legions under his command. That only two civil wars (68–9 and 193–7) occurred up to the end of the 2nd cent. is testimony to the success of these devices.

After twenty years of civil war Augustus put his new model army to the most traditional of Roman purposes, conquest and expansion. By the end of his reign the classic geographic contours of the empire had been set. Augustus had inherited a fundamentally Mediterranean empire; the main objectives of the campaigns fought under his auspices were conquest and expansion in continental Europe. Campaigns under Augustus and then Agrippa ensured the final subjugation, after 200 years, of Spain in 19 BC. All efforts were then directed to the north. By 14 BC all the Alpine regions were under Roman control; in the same year a series of campaigns began which led to the conquest of the Balkan peninsula up to the Danube. Roman control was also extended beyond the Rhine up to the Elbe. In AD 6 large-scale preparations were made for further expansion via the invasion of Bohemia by two army groups. These preparations were interrupted by a serious revolt in *Pannonia which took three years of hard fighting, under the command of Tiberius, to suppress. Celebration of this victory in AD 9 was cut short by the news of the loss of three complete legions in the area between the Rhine and the Elbe. Attempts at continued expansion were then abandoned and the line of the Rhine–Danube *de facto* became the empire's northern frontier.

Augustus, despite the great conquests of his reign, left to his successors the advice to keep the empire within its current territorial limits. For nearly a century they adhered, in general, to this advice. Consolidation, rather than conquest, came to epitomize Roman policy. Some new accretion of territory occurred through the assimilation as provinces of previously client territory (*Cappadocia in AD 17; the Mauretanias (see MAURETANIA) in 42. *Thrace in 46, all of *Judaea by 44, *Commagene in 72, and Nabataea (see ARABIA; NABATAEANS) in 106; see CLIENT KINGS). On the northern frontier an important development was the occupation under the Flavians of the Rhine–Danube re-entrant. The only clear exception to this process of consolidation was Claudius' invasion of *Britain in 43. Britain was never to be fully conquered. In the longer term its garrison of three legions represented an anomalous diversion of resources to a strategically unimportant area.

The reign of Trajan marked a temporary return to determined expansionism. In the north two major expeditions were mounted on the Danube in 101–2 and 105–6 which saw the annexation of *Dacia and its attendant gold-mines. In the east Trajan was the first emperor to try to destroy the military capacity of the Parthian kingdom and to annex territory east of the Euphrates. The expedition of 113–17 was at first successful, but a serious revolt in Mesopotamia in 116–17 and the death of Trajan in 117 led his successor Hadrian to abandon the attempt. No major campaigns against external enemies occurred again until the reign of Marcus Aurelius when invasion from the east and then from the north posed a classic two-pronged strategic threat. In 161 the Parthian king declared war and invaded. The counter-expedition of Lucius Verus of 162–66 was militarily successful although no attempt was made to repeat Trajan's plan of annexing Mesopotamia. In 166–7 northern tribes breached the weakened defences on the Danube, and triggered the so-called northern wars of Marcus Aurelius. By the time of Marcus' death at Vienna in 180 plans had probably been made to annex further territory north of the Danube. Commodus, however, opted for peace, and by his death the territorial extent of the empire was very much, with the exception of Britain and Dacia, as Augustus had left it in AD 14.

Given the limited number of major expansionary campaigns the prime function of the Roman armed forces became the routine defence of the empire. For the first time the territorial empire acquired clearly demarcated frontiers, especially to the north (Rhine–Danube) and the east (Euphrates). The majority of legions and auxiliary units came to be stationed on or near the frontiers in permanent fortified positions. Artificial barriers, such as Hadrian's wall (see WALL OF HADRIAN), were sometimes constructed when the frontiers were not naturally delimited. An elaborate network of roads was built up to facilitate communications and the movement of troops and supplies. The frontiers, natural or artificial, functioned as symbolic demarcation of direct Roman rule and as barriers to minor incursions rather than as major obstacles to serious attacks (see LIMES). Across time there was also a significant shift in the strategic disposition of Rome's forces. Under Tiberius there were eight legions stationed on the Rhine, six in the Balkans/Danube theatre, and only four in Syria. By the accession of Hadrian only four remained on the Rhine, twelve were now stationed in the Danube area, and six in the east. This shift of forces to the Danube–Euphrates axis represented a significant step in the process culminating in the removal of the capital of the empire from Rome to Byzantium.

4. Running an empire

The mature empire of the 2nd cent. embraced a territory of about 5 million sq. km. with a population conventionally estimated at about 55 million. Despite rudimentary technology and limited means of communication the territorial integrity of the empire was not seriously threatened in our period. The two great Jewish revolts of 66–74 and 132–5 (see JEWS) represented the only exceptions to this generalization. The principal aims of imperial rule were to maintain internal order and to extract resources, via taxation, to underpin state expenditure, especially the funding of the massive standing army. Given these limited aims, no large-scale bureaucratic apparatus was elaborated, and routine administration was predicated on the co-operation of the local élites of the provinces.

At the apex of the exercise of public authority stood the emperor. The emperor was the key source of binding rules affecting individuals, corporate groups, and the subject population as a whole; he adjudicated serious disputes and granted ideal and material privileges to both individuals and corporate groups (especially cities). His court was the supreme tribunal of the empire both at first instance and at appeal. Decision-making by the emperor was normally mediated through the mechanism of an advisory body, the *consilium principis*, whose members were drawn from the senatorial and equestrian élite. Although the senate also maintained some parallel authoritative powers they were comparatively limited in scope.

The empire was divided administratively into a series of territorial circumscriptions, of unequal size and population, called provinces (44 at the time of Trajan). In each province a governor of senatorial status exercised overall responsibility, although Egypt and some minor provinces had equestrian governors. For fiscal purposes governors were normally aided by equestrian officials called procurators. The number of élite Roman officials allotted to the provinces was very small, about 160 in the mid-2nd cent., and each had only a small administrative apparatus to help him. Consequently routine administrative activity was devolved on local cities and their magistrates and councils who formed the prime intermediary mechanism linking the state to the mass of its subjects. Each province operated administratively as an agglomeration of civic units, each unit having responsibility for the territorial hinterland and population attached to it.

In the fiscal sphere the Roman officials exercised a supervisory and adjudicatory authority. They organized the periodic censuses, made global tax-assessments for each city, and adjudicated disputes which arose in the processes of assessment and collection of taxes. In turn each city had the responsibility of collecting its own tax-assessment. The individual paid to the city, the city paid to the state. Provincial governors had supreme authority for the maintenance of order and monopolized the legitimate use of violence. Only they had the right, through both formal proceedings and summary jurisdiction, to impose capital penalties. Their tribunal operated as the prime mechanism for the resolution both of private disputes, especially those concerning Roman citizens and individuals of high social status, and of disputes between rival civic communities over their ideal and material rights. The local civic authorities underpinned the governor's role in four distinct ways. They were responsible for hunting down serious criminals (e.g. brigands, Christians, rustlers) and holding them for trial by the governor. Within their own territories they exercised a lower-level jurisdiction to resolve minor private disputes and to punish minor crimes. Administratively they supervised the internal affairs (e.g. raising and reallocating local revenues, supervising public buildings, regulating local markets) of their own cities. Finally each province had a provincial council (see CONCILIUM) whose members were recruited from individual cities' élites. The provincial councils had a double function. They were responsible for the organization of the religious ceremonies and festivals associated with the imperial cult, and members of the council acted as high-priests of the cult, a role of great prestige; diplomatically the councils could send embassies to the emperor to make representations about matters of common interest to a province or to lay accusations of misgovernment by Roman officials. This crucial intermediary role of the local élites of the provinces was recognized by privileges they came to acquire in the social order.

5. The social order

The imperial social order was deeply stratified and characterized by a marked congruence of wealth and status and by very limited opportunities for upward social mobility. At the apex of the social pyramid stood three aristocratic orders namely (in descending rank) the senatorial order, the equestrian order, and the local élites of civic councillors and magistrates. Each had differential property-qualifications for membership; each possessed distinct status symbols in terms of dress and legal privilege. Below stood the vast mass of the humble free and the slaves, the latter in strict law the chattels of their owners. Although the total number of slaves is not known, the probable proportion in Egypt of 10 per cent (inferred from census-data) is a reasonable estimate for the whole empire.

The most important social development of our period was the process by which the local élites across the empire came to acquire a common and coherent privileged status. At first the local élites were rewarded by individual grants of Roman citizenship. In the course of the 2nd cent. a series of imperial rulings granted all local councillors and magistrates a bundle of legal privileges (e.g. less severe and degrading punishments for serious crimes) which set them apart from the mass of the provincial population (see HONESTIORES). In turn new recruits into the equestrian and senatorial orders normally came from the ranks of local élites (see SENATORS, PATTERNS OF RECRUITMENT). Only two institutionalized avenues of upward social mobility, namely the army and the emancipation of slaves, existed. The economic and social status of the soldiery was enhanced by the material rewards of service and by the privileges granted to veterans. Furthermore a small minority of ranking legionaries could achieve the post of centurion and, even more spectacularly, the post of chief centurion (see PRIMIPILUS) which automatically conferred equestrian status. Private owners had the right to emanci-

pate their slaves, and a small minority of *freedmen (ex-slaves) are found entering the ranks of the local élites.

Within this stable social order dissent and desperation among the poor and immiserated expressed themselves primarily in *brigandage and piracy. No serious political ideologies of opposition existed or were developed, while the state for reasons of internal security tightly regulated freedom of association. The most important ideological developments occurred in the religious sphere notably through the dissemination of Mithraism and Christianity. But even by the late 2nd cent. the nascent world-religion had had only a limited impact. It remained primarily an urban phenomenon, and even then most widely spread in the empire's Mediterranean heartlands. Christian ideology and practices had scarcely touched the north and north-west of the empire or rural areas in general.

By the late 2nd cent. 'the immeasurable majesty of the Roman peace' (as the elder Pliny had termed it) still appeared settled and unchallenged. The political and institutional characteristics of Roman rule, even the territorial extent of the empire itself, were little different from the situation at the end of Augustus' reign. It was to be the combination of the intense civil wars that ensued on the murder of Commodus, and the advent of new and aggressive enemies to the north and east of the empire which were to put the imperial state to its first great test in the 3rd cent., to transform its political and institutional structures and to open the way for the triumph of the new world religion.

GENERAL *CAH* 10² (1996); A. Garzetti, *From Tiberius to the Antonines: A History of the Roman Empire AD 14–192* (1974); P. D. Garnsey and R. Saller, *The Roman Empire: Economy, Society and Culture* (1987); F. Jacques and J. Scheid, *Rome et l'integration de l'empire (44 BC–AD 260)*, 1 (1990) (excellent bibliography); F. Millar, *The Roman Empire and its Neighbours²* (1981); Rostovtzeff, *Roman Empire²*; J. Wacher (ed.), *The Roman World*, 2 vols. (1987); C. Wells, *The Roman Empire²* (1992).

AUGUSTUS AND HIS SUCCESSORS Detailed studies of individual reigns and their major military and political events can be found in the relevant bibliographies for each emperor. Of especial importance for our understanding of the formation and structure of the imperial regime are: J. A. Crook, *Consilium Principis* (1955); K. Hopkins, *Death and Renewal*, ch. 3 (1983); Millar, *ERW*; F. G. B. Millar and E. Segal (eds.), *Caesar Augustus: Seven Aspects* (1984); S. Price, *Rituals and Power: The Roman Imperial Cult in Asia Minor* (1984); K. A. Raaflaub and M. Toher (eds.), *Between Republic and Empire: Interpretations of Augustus and his Principate* (1990); R. Saller, *Personal Patronage under the Early Empire* (1982); Syme, *Rom. Rev.*, and *Tacitus*, 2 vols. (1958); R. Talbert, *The Senate of Imperial Rome* (1984); P. Veyne, *Le Pain et le cirque* (1978); A. von Premerstein, *Vom Werden und Wesen des Prinzipats* (1936); C. Wirszubski, *Libertas as a Political Idea at Rome* (1950); Z. Yavetz, *Plebs and Princeps* (1969).

THE ARMY AND THE FRONTIERS Important synthetic accounts are: J. B. Campbell, *The Emperor and the Roman Army, 31 BC–AD 235* (1984); B. Isaac, *The Limits of Empire²* (1991); Y. Le Bohec, *L'Armée romaine sous le Haut-Empire* (1989); E. N. Lutterworth, *The Grand Strategy of the Roman Empire* (1981); G. R. Watson, *The Roman Soldier²* (1981); G. Webster, *The Roman Imperial Army³* (1985).

RUNNING AN EMPIRE AND THE SOCIAL ORDER G. Alföldy, *The Social History of Rome* (1985); D. Braund (ed.), *The Administration of the Roman Empire* (1988); Brunt, *RIT*; J. Gagé, *Les Classes sociales dans l'Empire romain* (1964); P. D. Garnsey, *Social Status and Legal Privilege in the Roman Empire* (1970); W. V. Harris, *Ancient Literacy* (1989); O. Hirschfeld, *Die kaiserliche Verwaltungsbeamten²* (1905); A. H. M. Jones, *The Greek City from Alexander to Justinian* (1940); B. Levick, *The Government of the Roman Empire* (1985); W. Liebenam, *Stadtverwaltung im römischen Kaiserreiche* (1900); R. MacMullen, *Roman Social Relations: 50 BC–AD 284* (1974); D. Nörr, *Imperium und Polis in der hohen Prinzipatszeit* (1966); H. G. Pflaum, *Les Procurateurs équestres sous le Haut-Empire romain* (1950); A. N. Sherwin-White, *The Roman Citizenship²* (1973);

G. E. M. de Ste. Croix, *The Class Struggle in the Ancient Greek World* (1981).   G. P. B.

3. *From Septimius Severus to Constantine* (AD 193–337)

1. Political and dynastic history

The period from the Severans to Constantine the Great begins and ends with strong government, separated by a period of political instability and military stress through which shine the heroic achievements of great (but short-lived) individual emperors. *Septimius Severus (193–211) rose to power in civil wars reminiscent of those of 68–70. Proclaimed in Pannonia, he at once marched to Italy to suppress M. *Didius Severus Iulianus, after which he quickly defeated his rivals Pescennius Niger in the east and D. *Clodius Septimius Albinus in the west. After a determined and in some ways ruthless reign which did not endear him to senatorial opinion, he was succeeded at York by his son *Caracalla, who was killed in 217 during an eastern campaign by the supporters of his praetorian prefect M. *Opellius Macrinus, the first candidate of equestrian rank to achieve the imperial dignity (see PRAEFECTUS PRAETORIO). Macrinus was quickly displaced by an eastern relative of Severus' wife, the eccentric religious innovator *Elagabalus, and he in 222 by M. *Aurelius Severus Alexander, whose persistent ineffectiveness eventually alienated the army. His assassination in 235 and replacement by a tough military officer from Thrace, C. *Iulius Verus Maximinus, was an uncomfortable reminder that what the Roman empire needed was not dilettante sportsmen, exuberant child priests, or likeable youths, but disciplined officers who knew armies. The period from Maximinus to the rise of *Diocletian in 284 is traditionally known as the 'period of anarchy' of the Roman empire, and this is true if one takes as a criterion the traditional historian's task of reconstructing a narrative of events in the correct order—a task made infinitely more difficult by the deficiencies in the ancient narrative sources. In this half-century there were at least eighteen 'legitimate' emperors, and far more if one counts the numerous usurpers of the period. Nearly all met violent deaths after short reigns. What does emerge from the period, in the response of Diocletian (284–305), is a conception of the imperial office as divisible, authority in different regions being devolved to separate emperors who, instead of fighting each other for sole power, would concede each others' dignity and collaborate. This conception is at the heart of the so-called *Tetrarchy, in which Diocletian first (in 285) shared his power as Augustus with a single colleague, *Maximian, and (in 293) added to the Augusti two Caesars who would both share the burden of warfare and government and ensure an orderly succession. The first of these aims was achieved by Diocletian, but the second was not, as the planned succession was disrupted by the ambitions of rival contenders. From the complicated series of civil wars, executions, and suicides following the joint retirements of Diocletian and Maximian in 305 emerged the figures of (the newly converted) Constantine in the west, and *Licinius in the east. It was they who in 312 jointly issued the so-called 'edict of Milan' restoring peace to the church after the persecutions of Diocletian and *Galerius, and restoring to Christians their confiscated property, but Constantine's defeat of Licinius at Chrysopolis in 324 put him and his sons in sole control of the Roman empire.

2. Military policy and government

Despite political difficulties and frequent military reverses the territorial integrity of the Roman empire was maintained with surprising success. Septimius Severus had converted his early civil war against Pescennius Niger into a war of conquest in which he annexed Mesopotamia; this provided a solution to the problem of Armenia, a perennial cause of conflict between Rome and Persia. The rise of the Sasanian dynasty in Persia under Ardashir I (*c*.223–*c*.240) and especially Sapor I (*c*.240–*c*.270) posed new problems for the Roman empire in the east. See SASANIDS. The campaign against Persia of *Gordian III ended in defeat and the emperor's death, some thought by treachery of his praetorian prefect Philip (see PHILIPPUS), who succeeded him (244). In the mid 250s Sapor's invasion of the empire resulted in his penetration of Roman territories (*Antioch (1) was occupied for a time), and in 260 in the capture of the emperor *Valerian, but no territory was permanently lost, and the campaign of Galerius in the last decade of the century resulted in a settlement weighted heavily in favour of Rome. On the lower Danube the empire was confronted, also in the 250s, by invasions of *Goths, who penetrated parts of Thrace and Asia Minor (this was when the ancestors of the Gothic missionary Ulfila were taken prisoner); the death of the emperor *Decius took place in battle against this new enemy. In the 260s and 270s much was achieved in the name of Rome by the usurping regimes of *Postumus and his successors in Gaul (260–74), and in the east by the Palmyrene 'empire' of *Septimius Odaenathus and *Zenobia (see PALMYRA). Both rebellions were suppressed by *Aurelian (270–5), another of the great Illyrian emperors of the third century; but Aurelian was obliged to abandon Dacia to Gothic occupation. The only other territorial cession made in the period was the abandonment, also by Aurelian, of the *Agri Decumates, the re-entrant angle between Rhine and Danube annexed in the Flavian period.

The principle of the devolution of imperial power, referred to in § 1 above, is clearly inherent in these events. The rise of the Gallic and Palmyrene empires under Gallienus (sole ruler 260–8) secured frontiers which he could not have defended himself while also maintaining control in Italy and Illyricum. The situation that obtained under Gallienus, when the Balkans and Italy (with the addition of Africa), and separate administrations among the Gauls and in the east, were financed and governed independently of each other, clearly anticipates the regional prefectures of the fourth century. Also anticipated in the 3rd cent. is a progressive increase in the number, and reduction in the size, of provinces. After Diocletian there were more than 100 of these, compared with fewer than 50 in the time of Trajan. They were governed to an increasing extent by equestrian rather than senatorial governors. By a supposed decree of Gallienus, indeed, senators were formally excluded from military commands in order to keep them away from armies. Whether the edict is historical or not, it represents a process of change that can be traced in the developing career patterns of senators and equestrians. The army itself underwent considerable changes, the distinction between legionaries and auxiliaries disappearing as the emperors made increasing use of barbarian federates for their field armies. It was also much enlarged, a process that continued into the 4th cent. It is however far from clear that one can talk of a 'militarization' of the Roman empire, and still less so that one can assign the beginning of such a process to Septimius Severus. The legal and financial benefits offered to the army by that emperor are not out of line with their times. The right to contract legal marriages, for example, recognizes the long custom of soldiers to acquire 'common law' wives and raise children with them in stable unions.

3. The economy

The economic history of the 3rd cent., like its political history, is one of distress and recovery, the extent of both being debated by historians. The conventional picture is of a monetary decline leading to the brink of collapse, and of a transition to a largely natural economy in which the emperors secured their needs and paid their salaries by requisitions in kind rather than from the products of monetary taxation. The rampant inflation of the later part of the period can in part be attributed to the emperors' own debasement of their coin in order to meet the ever-increasing prices caused by its diminishing value as currency. But Diocletian and *Constantine I were able to restore a stable gold currency based on the *solidus* minted first at 60, then at 72 to the pound. This coin, one of the most successful ever produced, was the foundation of the late Roman and Byzantine monetary economy (see COINAGE, ROMAN). The picture is also one of urban decline, but with many variations and exceptions. Britain, largely exempt from the wars of the period, does not seem to have suffered from it, and over the longer term the prosperity of frontier regions benefited from the shift from the centre to the periphery of those resources necessary for defence. As the emperors spent more of their time in the frontier regions, their presence acted as a stimulant to the economies of these regions. And the cities which were promoted by the emperors—such as Trier, Serdica, Naissus, Thessalonica, Nicomedia, and of course Constantinople—both became great and contributed to the economic development of their hinterlands. The *constitutio Antoniniana* of 212 (see CONSTITUTION, ANTONINE), in which Caracalla extended the citizenship to all free inhabitants of the Roman empire, is presented by the historian Cassius Dio as inspired by fiscal motives; but another effect was to remove this once great privilege from the status of gift or grant to communities and individuals, and to make the city of Rome marginal to their social and legal position. Fulfilling a long development, the *civitas Romana* was now without any ambiguity citizenship of the Roman empire and not of its capital.

4. Culture

The Severan period saw the continued efflorescence of the literary culture known as the '*Second Sophistic' (the inventor of the phrase, the biographer of the sophists Philostratus (see PHILOSTRATI), published his work under Alexander Severus). Literary accomplishment was still important in the relations of cities with their rulers through embassies, and literary men were still rewarded and promoted to imperial office. Most notable is the juristic culture of the Severan Age, with great lawyers like Ulpian (*Domitius Ulpianus) and Papinian (*Aemilius Papinianus) (both of whom were killed in the dynastic upheavals of the later Severan period), but this is one of the great continuums of Roman culture. Preserving and systematizing the case law of the later first and second centuries as propounded in imperial judgements, the Classical jurists were themselves preserved for posterity by the codifications of Justinian (see JUSTINIAN'S CODIFICATION). The middle and later years of the century produced the philosopher *Plotinus and his pupil and biographer *Porphyry (see NEOPLATONISM); and the historian P. *Herennius Dexippus of Athens attests the continuing prestige of a great intellectual capital despite the physical impact of the Herulian invasion (see HERULI). Of immediate relevance to the future, the Christian church expanded considerably. At its opening *Tertullian of Carthage preached opposition to the world and secular culture, at the end of it *Eusebius of Caesarea documents the expansion of the Church and its acceptance, in the conversion of Constantine, by the empire and the world-order. See CHRISTIANITY. In the mid-3rd cent. *Cyprian, later executed in the persecution of Valerian, attests 87 bishops in North Africa, and in Rome seven deacons looked after the interests of 1,500 widows and orphans.

4. The Late Empire 1. Political and dynastic history

The three sons of Constantine who emerged from a co-ordinated killing of the more distant claimants at their father's death in 337 competed among themselves for pre-eminence; *Constantine II, who succeeded in Gaul (with Britain and Spain), was eliminated in 340 by his brother *Constans II, who had inherited Illyricum. He was in turn defeated by the usurper *Magnentius (350), and he by the surviving brother *Constantius II (353). Constantius, preoccupied in the west, appointed *Gallus Caesar to deputize in the East, and after Gallus' execution (354) tried to rule as sole emperor. Again, however, he was confronted by usurpation while he himself was committed to war with Persia, and reluctantly accepted his cousin *Julian as Caesar in Gaul. Julian's military successes and his army's growing discontent at his treatment by his senior partner led to his proclamation against Constantius, but he was spared a war which he would probably not have won by Constantius' death (361). Julian's famous attempt to restore the pagan cults of the Roman empire was cut short by his death in Persia (363), and the short reign of *Jovian was succeeded in 364 by the firm military government of the brothers *Valentinian (1) and *Valens. Valens' death at Adrianople (378) brought to the throne *Theodosius (2) I, a former general whose successes both in foreign and in civil war have tended to be overshadowed by his pro-Nicene religious policies and by his religious confrontations with St *Ambrose. The accession of Valentinian and Valens had been followed by a division of the resources of eastern and western empires, and this was repeated after Theodosius' death in 395. Theodosius' sons *Arcadius (2) (in the east) and *Honorius (in the west), and their respective successors *Theodosius (3) II and *Valentinian (3) III were, however, weak emperors, coming to power in their minority, surrounded by powerful courtiers and—especially in the west—by competing warlords and barbarian leaders who cared little for imperial authority. The ascendancy over emperors of such figures as *Stilicho, Bonifatius, Flavius *Aetius, and *Ricimer well presages the replacement of the imperial office by the kings of Italy, *Odoacer and *Theoderic (1). In the east, the death of Theodosius II was followed by a disruptive period of competition, but the competitors were on the whole vigorous, effective war leaders, and under Anastasius (491–518), Justin I (518–27), and his formidable nephew and successor *Justinian (527–65) the Byzantine empire was able to hold its own and even, under Justinian, to attempt to make good its losses by reconquest.

2. Military policy

The 4th-cent. west was threatened on the Rhine front by the Germanic federation known as the *Alamanni, and on the Danube by the *Quadi and their allies and, in particular, by the *Goths. The Alamanni succeeded in the 350s in occupying large areas of eastern Gaul, but the ground was recovered by the early campaigns of Julian (356–60) and maintained by the strenuous work of Valentinian, both in campaigning and in a building programme well attested by archaeology. In the east, traditional Roman policy, of containing Persian aggression and responding by measured counter-attacks (with tremendous sieges), was followed by Constantine (who died while setting out on a Persian campaign) and Constantius II, but broken by the invasion of Persia conducted by Julian with disastrous results; Jovian was forced after Julian's death to cede to the Persians much of what had been gained by the success of Galerius. Under Theodosius Armenia was partitioned between Rome and Persia, and thereafter relations between the two powers took on a more familiar pattern until the time of Justinian. The real crisis of the Roman empire was generated on the Danube, as the Goths, under pressure from the *Huns, negotiated or forced their way across the river, a process leading to the momentous defeat at Adrianople. Despite the treaty concluded in 382 by Theodosius, the Romans were never able fully to recover, and the ensuing fragility of their command of the Balkans is the most important strategic consideration in the division of the empire into eastern and western parts. In the 5th cent., the west was overrun by mainly Germanic invaders—Goths and then *Franks in Gaul, Goths and *Suebi in the Spanish peninsula, *Vandals in North Africa—permitting greater or lesser degrees of Roman continuity. The Gallic upper classes and church preserved much of what was important to them—including the Latin language—and the reign of Theoderic the Ostrogoth in north Italy marks something of a cultural high point. Despite pressure from the Avars and other northern peoples, the eastern empire retained its territorial integrity until the expansion of Islam in the early 7th cent. Justinian's programme of recovery of the western provinces was in the short term successful, but it is debatable whether the recovery of Gothic Italy benefited or impoverished its inhabitants, and Justinian's prolonged campaigns there were shortly followed by the invasions of the Lombards from the north.

3. Government

The military and administrative achievements of later Roman government were based on structural reforms and changes that make it look very unlike the government of the early empire. It was a strongly bureaucratized state, with large and systematically organized departments of administration staffed (often, no doubt, over-staffed) by career officials who spent their lives in a service characterized by demarcations of duties and by hierarchies of seniority within and between departments. It has been calculated that more than 30,000 men were employed in the civil branches of the service, but this figure must be set beside the vast size of the empire and the greatly increased level of governmental intervention required for its administration; since the military stresses of the second and third centuries, the 'consensual' mode of government of the early empire had been replaced by one much more authoritarian, and given the needs of empire it is hard to see that it could have been otherwise. The old aristocracies of Italy and the west, willing participants in the government of the early empire, largely stood aloof except in so far as was required to defend their essential interests; in the east they were more effectively drawn into government as its agents and allies. The foundation of *Constantinople had much to do with this different pattern in the east. The whole institution of government was glorified, from the emperor to his lowliest official, by an elaborate system of ceremonial which has its culmination in Byzantine handbooks, and is beautifully expressed in visual imagery (the *Ravenna mosaics).

There was a price to pay—the late Roman penal code was one of an unprecedented brutality, quite unmoderated by Christianity—but the success in practice of the system of government is evident. The later Roman empire enjoyed a stable currency in precious metals and limited inflation, regular taxation, good transport, and an adequate flow of supplies. Until the last decades of the 4th cent. in the west and for much longer in the east, its borders were maintained intact, trade between its regions and with the outside world flourished, and despite predictable *corruption its administrative and legal systems were stable and effective. Cities maintained their prosperity and even, in the east, increased it, and the countryside was productive and free of major disruption and banditry. Education was maintained, and

the period was marked by an efflorescence of literary and artistic culture, both Christian and pagan; it produced the Gallic panegyrists, the history of *Ammianus Marcellinus and the poetry of *Ausonius and *Claudian, the speeches of *Libanius and *Themistius, the letters of *Symmachus (2), Christian exegesis exceeding by an order of magnitude everything that had been produced before, and mountains of documentary material. In the 5th cent. *Sidonius Apollinaris and the Greek church historians are followed in the 6th by *Cassiodorus and the histories of *Procopius, not to mention those monuments to Roman juristic culture, the *Theodosian Code and the codifications of Justinian (see JUSTINIAN'S CODIFICATION).

4. The impact of Christianity

It is hard to exaggerate the importance of the conversion to Christianity of Constantine, and after him the Roman empire. Constantine's hopes that loyal bishops would deliver to him obedient tax-paying cities were disappointed by the levels of mutual disagreement (of which his historian Eusebius might have warned him) within the Christian church. The emperors of the whole period were haunted by this problem, which they tended to exacerbate by taking sides themselves. *Paganism also proved unexpectedly recalcitrant, especially in its associations with Classical culture and established patterns of life such as public games (see AGŌNES). But Christianity gave common ground in a literate culture to rulers and ruled, and provided for imperial ideologists such as Eusebius a rhetoric of power, and a model of imperial as deriving from divine authority. It gave to bishops an enhanced secular role, exemplified in their appointment as arbitrators in civil jurisdiction, an activity well-documented in the letters of bishops like *Basil of Caesarea and *Augustine of Hippo. The consequences, in an influx of Christian 'converts' using their religion to advance their personal and family interests (some Roman senatorial families were among the worst offenders), were clearly seen by some Christian writers—such as Jerome, who proposed to write a history of the church in which he would show how it had become materially richer and more powerful but poorer in virtue. At the beginning of the 4th cent. Eusebius could offer a Christian triumphalism, in which the conversion of Constantine and the participation in government of pious Christian magistrates were seen as providential and the fulfilment of Old Testament prophecy; at the beginning of the 5th, Augustine, having used the imperial power to force *Donatist schismatics into the Catholic church, developed in the City of God a theory of a mixed earthly society of the virtuous and the wicked, whom only God could separate. As a reading of Ammianus Marcellinus or the Theodosian Code will show, the conversion of Constantine to Christianity did not bring about Heaven on earth, and many a Christian sermon—such as Ambrose on usury—will cause one to doubt whether it brought earth much closer to Heaven. It could indeed be a double-edged weapon, but as an instrument of power it appealed to emperors and churchmen alike.

GENERAL E. Gibbon, Decline and Fall of the Roman Empire (ed. J. B. Bury)—because of its reliance on the Historia Augusta, less good on the third than on the fourth century; A. Piganiol, L'Empire chrétien (1947; 2nd edn. by A. Chastagnol 1972); Jones, Later Rom. Emp. (1964); C. Wells, The Roman Empire (1984); Averil Cameron, The Later Roman Empire AD 284–430 (1993), and The Mediterranean World in Late Antiquity (1993); P. Brown, The World of Late Antiquity (1971; illustrated), and The Making of Late Antiquity (1978).

SELECTED STUDIES Millar, ERW; J. B. Campbell, The Emperor and the Roman Army, 31 BC–AD 235 (1984); M. Christol, Essai sur l'évolution des carrières sénatoriales dans la 2ᵉ moitié du IIIᵉ s. ap. J.-C. (1986);

Rome (topography)

A. H. M. Jones, *The Greek City from Alexander to Justinian* (1940, repr. 1966); D. S. Potter, *Prophecy and History in the Crisis of the Roman Empire* (1990); P. J. Heather, *Goths and Romans, 332–489* (1991); J. F. Matthews, *Western Aristocracies and Imperial Court, AD 362–425* (1975, repr. 1990), and *The Roman Empire of Ammianus* (1989); Alan Cameron, *Claudian: Poetry and Propaganda at the Court of Honorius* (1970); R. Browning, *Justinian and Theodora* (1971; rev. edn. 1987); P. Brown, *Power and Persuasion in Late Antiquity* (1992); S. MacCormack, *Art and Ceremony in Late Antiquity* (1981); Bianchi Bandinelli, *Rome: the Late Empire; Roman Art AD 200–400* (1971); M. McCormick, *Eternal Victory: Triumphal Rulership in Late Antiquity, Byzantium and the Early Medieval West* (1986).
J. F. Ma.

Rome (topography) The Tiber valley at Rome is a deep trough, from 1 to 3 km wide, cut into the soft tufa floor of the river's lower basin. The edges of the trough are formed by steep weathered cliffs, seamed and even isolated by tributary streams. In this way the famous hills of Rome were formed: the Caelian (see CAELIUS MONS), Oppian, *Esquiline, *Viminal, and *Quirinal were flat-topped spurs, while the *Capitol, *Palatine and *Aventine were cut off from the main hinterland. (For the Oppian see ESQUILINE; it was not counted as one of the *seven hills of Rome.) On the valley floor itself the river meanders in an S-shaped curve, the northern twist containing the Campus Martius and skirting the Vatican plain, the southern curve skirting the Capitol, *forum Boarium, and Aventine, and enclosing *Transtiberim*, a smaller plain at the foot of the Janiculan ridge. Just below the middle of the S-curve the river runs shallow and divides at Tiber island. The ford here was the only feasible crossing-point between Rome and the sea, or for many miles upstream; so hills and spurs provided the natural strongholds suitable for defended settlement, and traffic across the heavily populated Latian plain concentrated at the Tiber ford, which was to be the key to Rome's predominance.

Archaeology has revealed the presence of bronze-age settlement on the Capitol, and Iron-Age settlements here and on many of the other hills, notably the Palatine, Esquiline, and Quirinal. Cemeteries crowded the edges of the marshy valley of the Forum Romanum; burials cease by the late 7th cent. BC, attesting the *synoecism of these different communities brought about as the area was drained by means of the *cloaca maxima* and the Forum was created as a market-place. The fortification of Servius (see WALL OF SERVIUS) on the Viminal, and cliffs elsewhere, made this unified Rome a great promontory-fortress comparable with *Veii or *Ardea; during the regal period, it grew to become one of the most substantial cities in the Mediterranean. Projects associated with the kings include the *Regia in the Forum, the temple of Jupiter Capitolinus, the temple of Diana on the Aventine, and the *pons Sublicius* which replaced the Tiber ford.

The Forum was the centre of civic life in Republican Rome; political, religious, and commercial activities took place in a square which was also surrounded by housing and shops. As the city grew, however, ceremonial activities came to play an increasingly important role there; the Palatine became a centre of aristocratic housing, and the shops moved to the periphery of the Forum, as well as the Velabrum and Forum Boarium areas, close to the Tiber port. Popular housing was concentrated in overcrowded and squalid areas such as the *Subura. As Rome's power in Italy and overseas grew, the *Campus Martius (where the *comitia centuriata* met) was increasingly characterized by competitive building, as rival aristocrats sought to impress gods and voters with temples. Similarly, the construction of *basilicas around the forum in the 2nd cent. BC provides an indication of aristocratic rivalry, while at the same time their architectural style demonstrates the Hellenization of the public spaces of the city. Meanwhile, *aqueducts were built to provide the city with an adequate water-supply, together with bridges, quays, and newly paved roads. The rise of the dynasts in the 1st cent. BC was likewise reflected in the buildings of the city; *Sulla reconstructed the *Curia to reflect the increasing authority he granted to the senate; *Pompey built Rome's first permanent stone theatre, together with an impressive portico, on the Campus Martius, while of *Caesar's grandiose schemes, including a plan to divert the Tiber, only the *forum Caesaris, Basilica Iulia, and the *Saepta remain, finished by *Augustus.

Most of the surviving monuments of ancient Rome are, however, largely the work of the emperors, whose rebuildings or additions transformed or eclipsed the older monuments. Augustus built a new *forum Augustum, decorated with statues of Roman heroes and members of the gens Iulia; his palace on the *Palatine was associated with the new temple of *Apollo, while many new monuments in the Campus, including the Mausoleum, were erected by him or M. *Vipsanius Agrippa, or by his *viri triumphales*. The combination of Saepta, *Pantheon, and Agrippa's baths rivalled Pompey's theatre and portico for scale and grandeur. The eastern end of the Forum Romanum was remodelled, with the temple of the Divine Iulius a new focal point, but ancient cult buildings were respected and in many cases restored; and the city was divided into fourteen new *regiones*. Tiberius' contributions to the urban landscape were limited, the Castra Praetoria on the outskirts of the Viminal reflecting the growing importance of the *praetorians. *Gaius (1) and *Nero, however, both sought to expand the imperial palace beyond Augustus' relatively modest habitation; Gaius linked it to the Forum by means of the temple of *Castor and Pollux. When Nero's first palace, the Domus Transitoria, was destroyed in the fire of AD 64, he built another, the lavish *Domus Aurea, on a site which extended from the Palatine to the Esquiline. The effect of these building schemes was to drive the residential quarters off the Palatine to the villas and parks of the Quirinal, Pincian, and Aventine, and to make both emperors highly unpopular with the Roman élite; the Flavians spent much energy in returning the site of the Domus Aurea to the people of Rome, by replacing it with the *Colosseum and baths of Titus, and removing many of its treasures to the new temple of Peace (see TEMPLUM PACIS). Later, the baths of Trajan were built on the site. Domitian rebuilt the Palatine palace, further extending it to overlook the Circus Maximus; two new fora were built by *Nerva and Trajan. The centrepiece of the latter was *Trajan's Column, probably of Hadrianic date; the complex also included the 'Markets of Trajan', which deliberately separated the commercial functions of the Forum from the ceremonial. Hadrian sought to establish parallels between his rule and that of Augustus (and thereby legitimate his authority) by erecting a new Mausoleum, and rebuilding the Pantheon and baths of Agrippa in the Campus; his creation of a new temple to Venus and Rome (a deity worshipped in the provinces, but not previously in the city) demonstrated that Rome had now become the capital of an empire, not Italy alone.

Then followed a pause in building activities: the Antonines could afford to live upon the prestige of their predecessors, adding only triumphal monuments and temples of the deified emperors. Later building schemes, apart from repairs, take the form of isolated monumental buildings, chiefly utilitarian in scope; typical among these are the great *thermae* (see BATHS). These tended to be on the outskirts of the city, near residential areas, *Caracalla picking the low ground outside porta Capena,

*Diocletian and *Constantine I choosing the Quirinal. Great fires offered the only chance of rebuilding in the older regions: thus, the *thermae Alexandrinae* were an enlargement of Nero's baths in the Campus, while the fire of *Carinus in 283 created space for the *basilica* of *Maxentius, the noblest experiment in vaulting in the ancient world. The city had now reached the climax of its development; soon it was to give way to Constantinople as imperial capital.

Nash, *Pict. Dict. Rome*; Richardson, *Topog. Dict. Ancient Rome*; Steinby, *Lexicon*; F. Coarelli, *Roma*⁶ (1989), *Il foro romano* 1 (1983), 2 (1985), and *Il foro Boario* (1988); D. R. Dudley, *Urbs Roma* (1967), a sourcebook of translated texts; M. Cristofani, *La grande Roma dei Tarquini* (1990). See also under the individual hills.   I. A. R.; F. C.; J. R. P.

Romulus and **Remus,** mythical founders of Rome. Their legend, though probably as old as the late 4th cent. BC in one form or another (the Ogulnii dedicated a statue of the she-wolf with the twins in 296 BC, Livy 10. 23. 12; see further C. Duliere, *Lupa Romana* (1979); F. Coarelli, *Il Foro Romano: Periodo repubblicano e augusteo* (1985) 89 ff.), cannot be very old nor contain any popular element, unless it be the almost universal one of the exposed children who rise to a great position. The name of Romulus means simply 'Roman', cf. the two forms *Sicanus* and *Siculus*; Remus (who in the Latin tradition replaces the Rhomos of most Greek authors), if not a back-formation from local place-names such as Remurinus ager, Remona (Festus, 344. 25 and 345. 10 Lindsay), is possibly formed from *Roma* by false analogy with such doublets as Κέρκυρα, Corcyra, where the o is short. The origin of the legend of Romulus and Remus has often been debated since the 19th cent. (see C. J. Classen, *Historia* 1963, 447 ff.). The discussion focuses above all on three problems: the antiquity of the myth, its meaning, and the death of Romulus. The majority opinion today is that the legend of the twins already existed by the beginning of the 3rd cent. BC (T. Cornell, *PCPS* 1975, 1 ff.), but some scholars, e.g. J. Bremmer, have no hesitation in dating its origin to the first quarter of the 6th cent., while the comparativists liken it to the Vedic Nāsataya-Ásvin (Dumézil, *ARR* 253 ff.; R. Schilling, *Rites, cultes, dieux de Rome* (1971), 103 ff.) or the creation (B. Lincoln, *HR* 1975–6, 121 ff., and *Priests, Warriors and Cattle* (1981)). Interpretations vary. While all scholars recognize that the myth narrates the foundation of Roman institutions, one version even making Romulus a Greek *ktistēs* (see FOUNDERS, CITY), historians stress variously the schemata known from *anthropology (e.g. the bands of youths: Bremmer), the Indo-European concept of twins (Dumézil, Lincoln), or the political realities of the republican period (Cornell, Wiseman, Balsdon). As to the different versions of the death of Romulus (sudden disappearance or murder followed by dismemberment), the light has yet to penetrate. The assimilation of Romulus to the god *Quirinus could go back, like the tradition about his apotheosis, to the 3rd cent. BC (von Ungern-Sternberg, 103 f.). Romulus did not receive cult.

In its normal form (Livy 1. 3. 10 ff.; Dion. Hal. *Ant. Rom.* 1. 76. 1 ff.; Plut. *Rom.* 3 ff.; more in Bremmer in *Roman Myth and Mythography* (1987), 25 ff., which article is an excellent summary of the whole matter, with relevant literature) the story runs thus. Numitor, king of *Alba Longa, had a younger brother Amulius who deposed him. To prevent the rise of avengers he made Numitor's daughter, R(h)ea Silvia, a Vestal virgin (see VESTA). But she was violated by *Mars himself, and bore twins. Amulius, who had imprisoned her, ordered the infants to be thrown into the Tiber. The river was in flood, and the receptacle in which they had been placed drifted ashore near the Ficus Ruminalis.

There was a she-wolf (Plut. *Rom.* 4 adds a woodpecker, both being sacred to Mars; see PICUS) tended and suckled them, until they were found by *Faustulus the royal herdsman. He and his wife *Acca Larentia brought them up as their own; they increased mightily in strength and boldness, and became leaders of the young men in daring exploits. In one of these Remus was captured and brought before Numitor; Romulus came to the rescue, the relationship was made known, they rose together against Amulius, killed him, and made Numitor king again. The twins then founded a city of their own on the site of Rome, beginning with a settlement on the Palatine; Romulus walled it, and he or his lieutenant Celer killed Remus for leaping over the walls. He offered asylum on the *Capitol to all fugitives, and got wives for them by stealing women from the Sabines (see SABINI), whom he invited to a festival. After a successful reign of some forty years he mysteriously vanished in a storm at Goat's Marsh and became the god Quirinus.

See also HELLENISM, bibliography (Romulus and Remus at Chios).

Bremmer in J. Bremmer and N. Horsfall (eds.), *Roman Myth and Mythography* (1987), 25 ff.; T. Cornell, *PCPS* 1975, 1 ff.; T. Wiseman, *LCM* 1991, 115 ff.; J. P. V. D. Balsdon, *JRS* 1971, 18 ff.; J. von Ungern-Sternberg in F. Graf (ed.), *Mythos in mythenloser Gesellschaft* (1993), 88 ff.; E. Gabba, *Dionysius and the History of Archaic Rome* (1991), 88 ff.; Dumézil, *ARR* 253 ff.; R. Schilling in *Rites, cultes, dieux de Rome* (1971), 103 ff.; T. P. Wiseman, *Remus* (1995).   H. J. R.; J. Sch.

Romulus Augustulus, known as the last western Roman emperor (AD 475–6), was a usurper who was not recognized in Constantinople. He owes his diminutive name to the fact that he was still a child when raised to the throne by his father Orestes. Orestes was overthrown by *Odoacer, who deposed Romulus, but spared him because of his youth and pensioned him off to Campania. One of Cassiodorus' *Variae* suggests he may have survived into the reign of *Theoderic (1).   P. J. H.

Rosalia or **Rosaria** (generally neut. plur., occasionally fem. sing., plur. rosaliae). The Romans doted on roses and regularly used them on festal occasions, at banquets both official (arval brothers: *ILS* 5039) and private (e.g. Mart. 9. 93. 5); cf. Frazer on Ov. *Fast.* 2. 539 and Bömer on 2. 538. Thus rose festivals were common, but were never fixed and public except locally. Best-known were commemorations of the dead, also called *dies rosationis*, when presumably family members met at the grave and decked it with roses. Violets were also used, hence *uiolatio, dies uiolares* or *uiolae*; cf. F. Cumont, *Lux Perpetua* (1949), 45, Hoey, below, nn. 33, 49, and A. de-Marchi, *Il Culto privato di Roma antica* (1896), 201–2. Rose festivals appear in various documents, none earlier than Domitian (*CIL* 10. 444), and extending as late as Filocalus (23 May: 'Macellus rosas sumat') and a Campanian calendar of AD 387 (*Insc. Ital.* 13. 2. 282–3), on dates from early May to mid-July, precisely when various rose species would bloom or re-bloom. These festivals did not develop from the cult of the dead; rather, these honours were a particular case of inviting them to a feast or other entertainment at which the survivors were also present, or simply a development of the custom of decking graves with flowers, cf. Nilsson, below, 313–14. Rose festivals occurred in Romanized contexts throughout the empire: *BCH* 1900, 299–323 and the *Rosaliae signorum* in the calendar of a Roman cohort at Dura-*Europus (*pridie kal. Iunias ob rosalias signorum supplicatio* (May 31)). Probably then the legionary standards received rose garlands: A. S. Hoey, *Harv. Theol. Rev.* 1937, 15–35, and R. Fink and others *YClS* 1941, 115–20.

Roscius, Sextus

M. P. Nilsson, *Opuscula Selecta* 1 (1951), 311–29; M. R. Salzman, *On Roman Time* (1990), 97–9.   C. R. P.

Roscius (*RE* 7), **Sextus,** son of a well-connected man of *Ameria. The father was killed in 81 BC, and two relatives, aided by L. *Cornelius Sulla's freedman *Chrysogonus, conspired to enter his name in the proscription lists and divide his property, finally (in 80) accusing his son of the murder. Roscius had many noble patrons, including *adfines* of Sulla; but his defence, involving an attack on Chrysogonus, might be resented by Sulla, and so they did not venture to speak for him. The main speech was entrusted—as his first major case—to young *Cicero, who made it an Optimate manifesto, powerfully contrasting the good faith and present impotence of the nobles with the irresponsible power of the freedman. Sulla, who genuinely wished to restore the traditional oligarchy, apparently realized that he must support them: Cicero won his case, and nothing further is heard of Chrysogonus.

Cic. *Rosc. Am.* E. Badian, *Foreign Clientelae* (1958), 249; T. E. Kinsey, *AC* 1980, 173 ff., and 1985, 188 ff. (hostile to Cicero); W. Buchheit, *Historia* 1975, 570 ff. (in German).   E. B.

Roscius (*RE* 16) **Gallus, Quintus,** from Solonium in the *ager Lanuvinus* (Cic. *Div.* 1. 79; cf. Cic. *Nat. D.* 179 and 82), the famous actor, was of free birth, being a knight (Macrob. *Sat.* 3. 14. 3). Handsome in person (Cic. *Arch.* 17) he had a squint (*Nat. D.* 1. 79). Time moderated his natural vivacity (ibid. 1. 254; Cic. *Leg.* 1. 11); supreme in comedy, he also played tragic parts (Cic. *De or.* 3. 102). His name became typical for a consummate actor (Cic. *Brut.* 290; *De or.* 1. 130, 258), his popularity being prodigious (*Arch.* 17). His earnings were enormous (Plin. *NH* 7. 128; Cic. *QRosc.* 23). He was on intimate terms with Q. *Lutatius Catulus (1), *Sulla (Plut. *Sulla* 36), and *Cicero, to whom he gave one of his first important briefs (*Quinct.* 77), 81 BC, and who later (in the *QRosc.*) defended him in a private suit. Cicero mentions his death as recent in 62 BC (*Arch.* 17). In post-Renaissance England his name stands for an outstanding actor, and a genre of treatises and satires on actors and acting called 'Rosciads' develops after 1750 (see C. Garton, *Personal Aspects of the Roman Theatre* (1972), 203 ff.).   G. C. R.; E. B.

Roscius (*RE* 22) **Otho, Lucius,** as tribune 67 BC opposed A. *Gabinius (2) and tried to secure the support of the *equites for the senate by restoring their right—we do not know when granted, but probably abolished by *Sulla—to occupy the first fourteen rows in the theatre. This may have been the first time it was extended to all men of equestrian census. The law was unpopular with the lower classes, and in 63 Cicero defended Roscius against their insults.   E. B.

rostra The earliest *rostra*, or speaker's platform, at Rome lay on the south side of the *comitium; it existed in 338 BC when it was adorned with the prows (*rostra*) of ships captured from Antium, later with statues and a sundial. The long, straight platform is associated with the second level of the *comitium*. When rebuilt in the mid-3rd cent. it had a curved front. *Caesar replaced the republican *rostra* with a new curved structure (the so-called hemicycle) at the west end of the forum in 44 BC. *Augustus extended the Julian rostra, adding a rectangular platform faced with marble and decorated with bronze prows. The Augustan *rostra* were called the *rostra vetera* in contrast with tribunal in front of the podium of the temple of Divus Iulius (29 BC), also treated as *rostra* (Frontin. *Aq.* 129; Dio Cass. 56. 34) with ships' prows from *Actium. A rough northward extension of the

Augustan *rostra* of about AD 470 commemorates a naval victory over the *Vandals.

F. Coarelli, *Foro romano* 1 (1983), 142 ff., and 2 (1985), 237 ff., 308 ff.; Nash, *Pict. Dict. Rome* 2, 272 ff.   I. A. R.; D. E. S.; J. D.

Roxane (d. *c*.311 BC), daughter of the Bactrian noble, Oxyartes, was captured during *Alexander (3) the Great's Sogdian campaigns of 328/7. She infatuated her conqueror, who married her (according to Macedonian custom) in the spring of 327. It was Alexander's first marriage, carefully orchestrated as the closing act in his conquest of the north-east. Resented by a large segment of the Macedonian court, she was protected by *Perdiccas (3), who pressed the claims of her unborn son (*Alexander (4) IV) at Babylon (323) and later (?322) had him proclaimed king. Thereafter her fate was linked to that of her son. Both crossed to Europe with *Antipater (1) (319) and fell into *Cassander's hands at the siege of *Pydna (spring 316). They were interned at *Amphipolis, denied regal privileges, and sordidly and secretly murdered around 311.

Berve, *Alexanderreich* 2, no. 688.   A. B. B.

Roxolani See SARMATAE.

Royal Road *Herodotus (1) describes at 5. 52–4 what he calls the Royal Road, running from *Sardis to *Susa, with its rest-houses and guard-posts. By comparing this with an *Aramaic letter of the satrap Arshama and the *Elamite tablets from *Persepolis ('Q' series—the so-called 'travel texts'), it is possible to refine and broaden analysis of the system. Although the most frequently cited journeys are those between Persepolis and Susa, it is clear from the archive that all the imperial provinces were part of a regular network linking the royal residences from the Indus to Sardis (cf. also Ctesias, *Persica* 64). Authorized travellers carried a sealed document (El. *halmi*), which gave them the right to draw on the rations held in the official storehouses. This system also explains the existence of fast couriers (El. *pirradaziš*), which so impressed the Greeks. See ROADS.

P. Briant, *Achaemenid History* 6 (1991), 67–82, and *HEA*, ch. 9; H. Koch, *AMI* 1986, 133–47, and *Achämeniden-Studien* (1993).   P. B.

Rubellius Blandus (*RE* 2), from *Tibur (Tac. *Ann.* 6. 27), the first *eques* to teach rhetoric (Sen. *Controv.* 2 pr. 5); the elder Seneca (L. *Annaeus Seneca (1)) quotes often from his declamations. He taught the philosopher *Papirius Fabianus, and may be the historian alluded to by Servius on Verg. *G.* 1. 103.

Schanz–Hosius, § 336. 9. 17.   M. W.

Rubellius (*RE* 5; Suppl. 14) **Blandus, Gaius,** grandson of C. *Rubellius Blandus, *novus homo, *suffect consul AD 18, governed Africa 35/6, *pontifex. He married Iulia, daughter of *Tiberius' son Drusus *Iulius Caesar (1), in AD 33 (Tac. *Ann.* 6. 27. 1), probably as a man unqualified for the purple. He had a son of the same name, if Juvenal is to be trusted (*Sat.* 8. 39 f.), and one named *Rubellius Plautus.

R. Syme, *AJP* 1982, 62 ff. (= *RP* 4. 177 ff.).   M. S. S.; B. M. L.

Rubellius (*RE* 8) **Plautus, ?Sergius,** son of C. *Rubellius Blandus and Iulia, granddaughter of the emperor Tiberius, was a young man of high character, an adherent of *Stoicism. His descent made him seem a plausible rival to *Nero (and in AD 55 a consort for *Iulia Agrippina, Tac. *Ann.* 13. 19. 3); in AD 60, on the emperor's advice, he withdrew to Asia (Tac. *Ann.* 14. 22). Two years later, allegedly at the instance of *Tigellinus, he was killed, though his father-in-law L. *Antistius Vetus urged him to resist (Tac. *Ann.* 14. 57–9).

> R. Syme, *AJPhil.* 1982, 62 ff. (= *RP* 4. 177 ff.).　　G. E. F. C.; B. M. L.

Rubico (commonly called **Rubicon**), reddish stream flowing into the Adriatic and marking the boundary between Italy and *Gaul (Cisalpine): possibly the modern Pisciatello. In 49 BC *Caesar, after some hesitation, precipitated civil war by crossing it.

> Plut. *Caes.* 32; Lucan 1. 213 f.; Suet. *Iul.* 31; App. *BCiv.* 2. 35.　　E. T. S.

Rudiae (mod. Rudie), Messapian settlement in S. Italy, 3 km. west of Lecce; see MESSAPII. It flourished in the 5th–3rd cents. BC, falling under Roman domination c.270, and was the birthplace of the poet *Ennius. It became a *municipium* after 89, but was eclipsed by *Lupiae.

> G. Susini, *Fonti per la storia greca e romana del Salento* (1962).　　K. L.

Rufinus (1), **Flavius** (consul AD 392), from Elusa in Gaul, *magister officiorum* (388–92), praetorian prefect of the east (392–5), left by *Theodosius (2) I as guardian of his son *Arcadius (2). He at once incurred the enmity of *Stilicho, who had him killed (November 395) in the presence of Arcadius. Although he was posthumously maligned (among others by the poet *Claudian), *Libanius praised his eastern administration.

> *PLRE* 1, 'Rufinus' 18.　　E. A. T.; A. J. S. S.

Rufinus (2) of *Aquileia, Christian writer, translator, and monastic leader, born c. AD 345 at Concordia Sagittaria of good family, boyhood friend of *Jerome, whose education he shared, baptised at Aquileia c.371, studied in Egypt for eight years under Didymus the Blind and desert hermits, presided over a monastery on the Mount of Olives, and from 393 onwards became involved in the Origenist controversy (see ORIGEN (1)), returning to Italy in 397. He there produced many translations or adaptations from the Greek, including *Eusebius' *Church History*, which he extended to 395 by adding two extra books; also Origen's *De Principiis*, commentaries on the Song of Songs and on Romans, and numerous homilies, the *Clementine Recognitions*, selected sermons of *Gregory (2) of Nazianzus and *Basil of Caesarea, and the Sentences of Sextus. He had an important influence on the development of western monasticism both personally and through his translations (Basil's *Rule*, the *Historia Monachorum*, writings of Evagrius Ponticus). His original works included the *De Adulteratione Librorum Origenis* (which he appended to a translation of Pamphilus (2), Apology for Origen), defences of his own orthodoxy to Pope Anastasius and against Jerome, and a commentary on the Apostles' Creed. He died in 411 in Sicily, whither he had fled from the Gothic invasion.

> WORKS M. Simonetti, *Tyrannii Rufini Opera*, in *CCSL* 20 (Turnhout, 1961).
>
> BIOGRAPHY, ETC. Françoise Thelamon, art. 'Rufin d'Aquilée' in *Dictionnaire de Spiritualité*, fasc. 89–90 (1988), col. 1107–17; E. A. Clark, *The Origenist Controversy* (1992).　　C. P. B.

Rufinus (3) (5th cent. AD), grammarian. His *Commentarium in metra Terentiana* and his *De compositione et de metris oratorum* are extant (ed. Keil, *Gramm. Lat.* 6. 554–78).

> Cf. Schanz–Hosius, § 1104.　　R. H. R.

Rufus of Ephesus, physician, lived in 2nd half of 1st cent. AD, studied at *Alexandria (1), visited *Caria and *Cos, and practised at *Ephesus, then a famous medical centre.

From his numerous writings, mostly on *dietetics and *pathology, are preserved tracts on anatomical nomenclature, kidney diseases, satyriasis and gonorrhoea, gout, and jaundice, and possibly some of his case notes. His *Medical questions* is a remarkable guide to bedside *diagnosis in the Hippocratic manner (see HIPPOCRATES (2)).

His Hippocratism, which earned him the respect of *Galen, was not slavish, for he was prepared to criticize and to extend the theories of Hippocrates. His pragmatism is clear in his descriptions of *anatomy, which he thought essential for good practice, and in his therapies for a variety of diseases and patients, in which he shows sympathy for often neglected groups such as slaves and the elderly. His influence was greater in the east than in the west, and many fragments of his works, e.g. *On melancholy*, survive only in Arabic intermediaries or paraphrases.

> TEXTS *Opera*, C. Daremberg and E. Ruelle (1879); *De podagra*, H. Mørland, *Symb. Osl.* 1933; *De corporis humani appellationibus*, G. Kowalski, Diss. Göttingen (1960); *Quaestiones medicinales*, H. Gärtner (*CMG* Suppl. 4, 1962; Teubner, 1970); *De renum et vesicae morbis*, A. Sideras (*CMG* 3/1, 1977); *Krankenjournale* (from Arabic), M. Ullmann (1978); *De cura icteri* (Arabic and Latin), M. Ullmann (1983); also ed. Ullmann, Arabic fragments from his dietetics in *Medizinhistorisches Journal* 1974, 23–40, from his paediatrics, *Medizinhistorisches Journal* 1975, 165–90, and from *On melancholy*, in *Islamic medicine* (1978).
>
> MODERN LITERATURE J. Ilberg, *Abh. Sächs. Akad.* 1930; H. Gossen, *RE* 1 A 1207; F. Kudlien, *Dict. Sci. Biogr.* 11 (1975), 601–3; G. E. R. Lloyd, *Science, Folklore, and Ideology* (1983); H. Thomssen, *Die Medizin des Rufus von Ephesos* (1989); A. Abou-Aly, *The Medical Writings of Rufus of Ephesus* (1992), with new Arabic material.　　L. E.; V. N.

ruler-cult

I. Greek The essential characteristic of Greek ruler-worship is the rendering, as to a god or hero, of honours to individuals deemed superior to other people because of their achievements, position, or power. The roots of this lie in Greece, though parallels are to be found in other near eastern societies.

In the aristocratic society of the Archaic age, as in the Classical *polis* of the 5th cent., no person could reach a position of such generally acknowledged pre-eminence as to cause the granting of divine honours to be thought appropriate: posthumous heroization (see HERO-CULT), rather than deification, was the honour for city-*founders. The first case of divine honours occurred in the confused period at the end of the Peloponnesian War, when *Lysander, the most powerful man in the Aegean, received divine cult on *Samos. There are some other, 4th-cent. examples.

Ruler-cult in a developed form first appears during the reign of *Alexander (3) the Great, and is directly inspired by his conquests, personality, and in particular his absolute and undisputed power. Alexander's attempt to force the Greeks and Macedonians in his entourage to adopt the Persian custom of prostration before the king (*proskynēsis*), which for the Persians did not imply worship, was an isolated and unsuccessful experiment without consequence. Much more important is his encounter with the priest of *Ammon at *Siwa in 331 BC. The priest seemingly addressed Alexander as the son of Amon-Ra, the traditional salutation due to any Pharaoh of Egypt, but the prestige which the oracle of Ammon then enjoyed throughout the Greek world had a decisive effect, not only on the Greeks, but also and in particular on the romantic imagination of the young king himself. It is probably the progressive development of these emotions which caused Alexander in 324, when he ordered the restoration of political *exiles, to apply pressure on the Greek cities to offer him divine cult; some cities certainly responded, though contemporary evidence remains thin. Alexander also secured heroic honours for his dead intimate *Hephaestion (1), as official recognition of his outstanding achievements.

The cults of Alexander's successors are found in various different contexts. The principal context was that of the Greek cities dependent on particular kings, both ancient cities and those founded by the king himself. The cities acknowledged benefactions received from a king by the establishment of a cult, with temple or altar, priest, sacrifices, and games, modelled on that granted to the Olympian gods (*isotheoi timai*). Rulers were also honoured by having their statues placed in an already existing temple. The king was thought to share the temple with the god (as *sunnaos theos*, 'temple-sharing god'), and thus to partake in the honours rendered to the deity and, on occasion, in the deity's qualities.

The other main context was that of the court itself. The Greek monarchies of the east in time created their own official cults. The dynastic cult of the Ptolemies (see PTOLEMY (1)) at *Alexandria (1) (a cult founded by 285/4) in its developed form by the end of the 3rd cent. BC consisted of priests of Alexander, of each pair of deceased rulers, and of the reigning king and queen. In 280 *Antiochus (1) I deified his dead father *Seleucus (1) I and dedicated to him a temple and precinct at *Seleuceia (2) in Pieria; *Antiochus (3) III extended a court cult throughout his newly reconquered Seleucid empire, with high priests of the living king and his divine ancestors in each province of the empire. In the later dynastic cult of the Attalids (see PERGAMUM) the kings were deified only after death.

Cults are also found outside strictly Greek contexts. In *Commagene a complex cult, organized by Antiochus I (1st cent. BC; see under ANTIOCHUS (9); ARSAMEIA; NEMRUT DAG) round different cult centres, was a blend of Greek and Persian traditions. In Egyptian temples cult of the Ptolemies continued on the model of Pharaonic practice. Incorporation of Greek practice might, however, be controversial: the erection of a statue of the Seleucid *Antiochus (4) IV in the Temple at Jerusalem stimulated the writing of the Book of Daniel, with its attack on Nebuchadnezzar's demand for worship, and was one factor that provoked the Maccabean Revolt (see MACCABEES).

Even within Greek contexts, at the outset there were debates about the propriety of divine honours for human beings, though the cults gradually became an accepted practice. That it became accepted does not prove it was essentially a political and not a religious phenomenon: to press the distinction is to deny significance to the creation of a symbolic system calqued on the cult of the gods. Those responsible for the cults, whether at court or in cities, were attempting to articulate an understanding of the power of the king.

E. J. Bikerman, *Institutions des Séleucides* (1938); A. D. Nock, *Harv. Stud.* 1930 = *Essays* (1972), 1; C. Habicht, *Gottmenschentum und griechische Städte*[2] (1970); P. M. Fraser, *Ptol. Alex.*; E. Badian, in *Ancient Macedonian Studies . . . C. F. Edson* (1981); S. R. F. Price, *Rituals and Power* (1984); F. W. Walbank, *CAH* 7[2]/1 (1984), ch. 3; D. J. Thompson, *Memphis under the Ptolemies* (1988).   C. F. E.; S. R. F. P.

II. Roman The offering of divine honours to humans was not indigenous to Italy. The Romans had long sacrificed to the ghosts of the dead (*Manes*) and conceived of a semi-independent spirit (*genius*) attached to living people. But the myth of a deified founder, *Romulus, was invented only in or after the 4th cent. BC, under Greek influence, and developed in the new political circumstances of the late Republic. From the time of M. *Claudius Marcellus (1)'s conquest of *Syracuse in 212 BC, Roman officials received divine honours in Greek cities; a notable instance is the 'liberator' of Greece, T. *Quinctius Flamininus (c.191 BC),

whose cult survived into the imperial period. At Rome such honours are met only from the late 2nd cent. BC, and then exceptionally, e.g. those offered privately to C. *Marius (1) (101 BC) and popularly to the demagogue *Marius Gratidianus (86 BC). Under Stoic influence (see STOICISM) the idea that worthy individuals might become divine after death appeared in *Cicero's *Somnium Scipionis* (c.51 BC) and in the shrine he planned for his daughter *Tullia (2) (d. 45 BC). Though the evidence is controversial, *Caesar as dictator in 45–44 BC probably received divine honours, based on Roman models (cults of *Alexander (3) the Great and Hellenistic kings took different forms). After his assassination the triumvirs, supported by popular agitation, secured from the senate his formal deification in 42 BC as Divus Iulius.

Worship of emperors and members of their families has two aspects, the worship of the living, including identification with the gods, and the apotheosis of the dead. It took different forms in different contexts: Rome; provincial assemblies (see CONCILIUM); towns; and in private. At Rome *Augustus and later 'good' emperors avoided official deification in their lifetimes; *Gaius (1) Caligula and *Commodus were exceptional in seeking to emphasize their own divinity. Augustus was *divi filius* (son of the deified one), and enjoyed a mediating role with the divine, as implied by his name, and as a result of becoming *pontifex maximus* in 12 BC. He also in 7 BC reorganized the cults of the 265 wards (*vici*; see VICUS) of the city: henceforth the officials of the wards, mainly *freedmen, worshipped the Augustan Lares and the Genius of Augustus. The worship appropriate for a household was now performed throughout the city. Poets played with the association of Augustus with the gods, and assumed that he would be deified posthumously. In AD 14 Augustus' funeral managed both to evoke, on a grand scale, traditional aristocratic funerals and to permit his formal deification by the senate; it was the precedent for all subsequent emperors up to *Constantine. After *Livia Drusilla in AD 41, imperial relatives, male and female, could also be deified posthumously. After Constantine's avowal of *Christianity, it became increasingly difficult for traditional practices to continue: Christ alone had combined human and divine, and the prevalent doctrine, formulated by *Eusebius, was that the emperor ruled by divine favour.

In the Greek east provincial assemblies (*koina*) were permitted to establish cults of Roma and Augustus: the precedent was set in Asia (see ASIA, ROMAN PROVINCE) at *Pergamum and in *Bithynia at *Nicomedia in 29 BC. In 'civilised' western provinces provincial assemblies (*concilia*) followed the Roman model, on the precedent of Hispania *Tarraconensis which was granted permission to establish a temple and *flamen* (see FLAMINES) to Divus Augustus at *Tarraco in AD 15. Assemblies in more recently conquered western provinces had cults of the living Augustus and Roma (Three Gauls at *Lugdunum (1), 12 BC; Germany near Cologne (*Colonia Agrippinensis), 8–7 BC?); these centred on *altars, not temples, and had *sacerdotes* not *flamines* (the title indicating that they were not Roman priesthoods).

Below the provincial level different forms of cult are found, depending in part on local traditions. In the (non-Greek) Egyptian temples Augustus and other emperors were accorded the position of high priest, like the Ptolemies and the Pharaohs before them. In Greek contexts, in Egypt and the rest of the Greek east, emperors were generally accommodated within the context of the ordinary cult of the *Olympian gods. In cities throughout the east living emperors were granted temples and cult statues, priests and processions, sacrifices and games. At first the cult focused specifically on Augustus, and then often became a general cult of the emperors. Though some cults of Hellenistic kings did survive through to Roman times, the imperial cult was more varied and more dynamic than Hellenistic cults had been. Towns in Italy and the west also established cults of the living Augustus (not his *genius*) and his successors; some, especially *coloniae*, chose to follow the Roman model.

Private households in Rome and elsewhere included associations of worshippers of Augustus (Tac. *Ann.* 1. 73), who will mainly have been the slaves and freedmen of the house. *Ovid in exile makes great play of his piety in praying at dawn each day before his household shrine with images of Augustus, Livia, *Tiberius, Germanicus *Iulius Caesar, and Drusus *Iulius Caesar (1) (*Pont.* 4. 9). In Italy and the west there were also the *Augustales, a high-ranking status for Roman freedmen, whose officials are sometimes associated with the imperial cult.

The significance of the imperial cult has been much debated. Was it a form of *Graeca adulatio* (Tac. *Ann.* 6. 18: divine honours to a human as Greek adulation), a system that was really political and not religious? On the other side it has been argued that to impose a distinction between religion and politics is anachronistic and Christianizing, and that it is illegitimate to undercut the implicit meanings of the rituals by claims about insincerity and flattery. The way forward is to investigate the different ritual systems that honoured the emperor in their different social and cultural contexts. As the cult was in general not imposed from above, it is essential to examine the contexts from which it sprang and which gave it meaning. There is a profound difference between a Greek city with its stable Olympian pantheon within which the emperor was accommodated and a town in Gaul whose pre-Roman pantheon was restructured on Roman models before the emperor found a place in it. Focus on actual divinization of the emperor is also too narrow. There was a whole range of religious honours, only some of which placed the emperor unambiguously among the gods. In some sense there was no such thing as 'the imperial cult'. See CHRISTIANITY.

ROME G. Herzog-Hauser, *RE* Suppl. 4. 814–53; L. R. Taylor, *The Divinity of the Roman Emperor* (1931); K. Scott, *The Imperial Cult under the Flavians* (1936); F. Taeger, *Charisma* 1960; S. Weinstock, *Divus Julius* (1971); W. den Boer (ed.), *Le Culte des souverains dans l'empire romain* (1973); *ANRW* 2. 16. 2 (1978); H. Hänlein-Schäfer, *Veneratio Augusti* (1985); T. Pekáry, *Das römische Kaiserbildnisse . . .* (1985); D. N. Cannadine and S. R. F. Price (eds.), *Rituals of Royalty* (1987); J. R. Fears, *RAC* 1988, 1047–93; M. Beard, J. A. North and S. R. F. Price, *Religions of Rome* (1998).

PROVINCES R. Etienne, *Le Culte impériale dans la péninsule ibérique d'Auguste à Dioclétien* (1958); R. Mellor, *Thea Rhome* (1975); C. Fayer, *Il culto della dea Roma* (1976); F. Dunand, in *Das römisch-byzantinische Ägypten* (1983); S. R. F. Price, *Rituals and Power* (1984); D. Fishwick, *The Imperial Cult in the Latin West* (EPRO 108, 1987–). M. H.; S. R. F. P.

Rullus See SERVILIUS.

Rumina, an obscure Roman goddess, whose significance depends on her name's etymology. Wissowa, *RK* 242, following Varro, *Rust.* 2. 11. 5, connects her with *ruma* (breast) and hence suckling. This is appropriate for her shrine and sacred fig-tree (*ficus Ruminalis*) near the Lupercal (see LUPERCALIA), where milk, not wine, was offered; cf. Ogilvie on Livy 1. 4. 5. Latte, *RR* 111, following G. Herbig, *Phil. Wochenschr.* 1916, 1440 ff., accepts an *Etruscan connection, thus relating her to Roma, the city's deity.

R. E. A. Palmer, *Roman Religion & Roman Empire* (1974), 17 ff. C. R. P.

rumour See PHĒMĒ.

Rupilius (*RE* 5), **Publius,** of an eminent Praenestine family of

*publicani (see PRAENESTE), as a friend of P. *Cornelius Scipio Aemilianus reached the consulship (132 BC), in which, for a time, he participated in the action of P. *Popillius Laenas against the adherents of Ti. *Sempronius Gracchus (3); but he soon went to Sicily, where he put an end to the slave revolt, capturing *Eunus. With a senatorial commission he imposed a severe settlement on the province. He died soon after his return, it was said of grief over his brother's failure in a consular election. E. B.

Rusellae (mod. Roselle), an *Etruscan city, stood on a two-crowned hill to the east of the bay that is now the Grosseto plain. Its walls, of polygonal limestone blocks overlaying a 7th cent. defence wall of sun-dried bricks, are dated to the early 6th cent. and are thus the oldest-known Etruscan stone fortifications. The area within them was inhabited from late Villanovan to late imperial times, with particularly flourishing periods between the 6th and 4th centuries, characterized by imported Attic pottery, and in Hellenistic times, when the city attained its maximum expansion. On the south-east hill, a portion of the Etruscan city of Hellenistic date has been revealed, superimposed on remains of the 5th–4th centuries: this area has produced a well-stratified sequence of bucchero and of local Campana A and B wares. Rusellae was captured by Rome in 294 BC.

Excavation reports and studies in *Stud. Etr.* 1959 onwards; *Roselle: gli scavi e la mostra* (exhib. cat., Florence 1975); A. Mazzolai, *Il museo archeologico della Maremma* (1977). D. W. R. R.

Rutilius Claudius Namatianus (*PLRE* 2. 770 f.), the author of an elaborate poetical itinerary in elegiacs conventionally referred to as the *De reditu suo* (the original title is lost), was a member of an aristocratic Gallo-Roman family, possibly from Toulouse (*Tolosa). He held the offices of *magister officiorum* (c. AD 412) and *praefectus urbi* (414). His poem has come down to us in an incomplete state. The beginning of the first book is lost, and 644 lines survive; of the second book two portions are extant, the first 68 lines and a further fragment of 39 half-lines first published in 1973. The poem recounts the voyage undertaken by the author in 417 (though the date has been disputed) from Rome to Gaul, where his estates had suffered from barbarian inroads; his party has reached Luna on the bay of La Spezia when the main part of the text breaks off. The account of the journey and the descriptions of the places visited or passed are interwoven with personal and historical reflections of the poet. The poem is most notable, however, for its intensely pro-Roman, classical outlook. In its existing form it opens with a long eulogy of Rome, most of it presented as an address to the city by the poet on the point of departure. This attitude, combined with other features of the work, such as the *invective against the Jews, the monks of Capraria, and *Stilicho, who had burned the Sibylline books, strongly suggests that Namatianus was an adherent of the old paganism; but he need not have been an extreme opponent of Christianity. At all events, his poetic stance is located solidly in the classical tradition, as is his style. He is an elegant poet, schooled in the best verse of the classical period, but possessing originality and flair, and capable of rising to impressive heights. The rhetorical tone of parts of his work is typical of his time.

TEXTS J. Vessereau and F. Préchac² (1961); P. van de Woestijne (1936); with comm., C. H. Keene (1907; Eng. verse trans.), R. Helm (1933), E. Castorina (1967), E. Doblhofer (1972–7); with trans., Duff, *Minor Lat. Poets.* New fragment: M. Ferrari, *Italia medioevale e umanistica* 1973, 15–30.

STUDIES J. Carcopino, *Rev. Ét. Lat.* 1928, 180–200; I. Lana, *Rutilio*

Rutilius Gallicus, Gaius

Namaziano (1961); A. Cameron, *JRS* 1967, 31–9; F. Corsaro, *Studi rutiliani* (1981).   J. H. D. S.

Rutilius (*RE* 19) **Gallicus, Gaius,** (*suffect consul AD 71 or 72; consul for the 2nd time probably 85; from *Augusta Taurinorum (Turin), whose career is celebrated in a poem of Statius (*Silv.* 1. 4; cf. *ILS* 9499), was legate of *Galatia for about six years under *Corbulo, governor of Galatia-Cappadocia. In 73/4 he conducted a census in Africa, and as governor of Lower Germany *c.*76–9 defeated the *Bructeri, capturing the priestess Veleda, who had helped to inspire the rebellion of C. *Iulius Civilis (*Silv.* 1. 4. 89–90). Soon after 81 he was proconsul of Asia (*Silv.* 1. 4. 80–1); by 89 he had been appointed prefect of the city, but died in 91 or 92.

R. Syme, *Act. Phil. Fenn.* 1984, 149 = *RP* 5 (1988), 514.   J. B. C.

Rutilius (*RE* 28) **Lupus, Publius** (early 1st cent. AD) produced a Latin abbreviation of a work on rhetorical figures by *Gorgias (2). Only two books survive, on figures of speech, though the whole was available to *Quintilian (esp. *Inst.* 9. 2. 102); they preserve valuable extracts from lost Hellenistic writers.

Ed. E. Brooks (1970), not replacing Halm, *Rhet. Lat. Min.* 3–21; Schanz–Hosius, § 480.   M. W.

Rutilius (*RE* 34) **Rufus, Publius,** born 160 BC or soon after, studied philosophy under *Panaetius (becoming a firm Stoic), law under P. *Mucius Scaevola (becoming an expert jurisconsult), and oratory under Ser. *Sulpicius Galba (1) (without becoming an effective speaker), then served as military tribune under P. *Cornelius Scipio Aemilianus at *Numantia. His wife was a Livia, probably a sister of M. *Livius Drusus (1), and his sister married a Cotta, to whom she bore C., L., and M. *Aurelius Cotta. Despite his connections, he was defeated for the consulship of 115 by M. *Aemilius Scaurus (1), prosecuted him, and was in turn prosecuted by him (both unsuccessfully) for *ambitus*. In 109–108 he and C. *Marius (1) served with distinction as *legati* under Q. *Caecilius Metellus Numidicus in Numidia, where they became bitter enemies. As consul 105 he restored Roman morale after the disaster of *Arausio and introduced military reforms (among them arms drill), on which Marius later built his own army reforms and his German victories. As legate (see LEGATI) of Q. *Mucius Scaevola (2) he was left in charge of Asia when Scaevola returned to Rome, and he offended the *publicani* by strictly controlling their activities. (The date should be in and after Scaevola's consulship, since no ex-consul is ever recorded as serving under a praetor.) In 92 he was prosecuted for *repetundae* (the prosecution was encouraged by Marius), took *Socrates as his model in his defence, and was convicted by the court manned by *equites. He went into exile at Smyrna and there wrote a largely autobiographical and highly personal history of his time, much used by later historians of the period. His conviction marked the bankruptcy of the equestrian courts first instituted by C. *Sempronius Gracchus and led to the attempted reform by his nephew M. *Livius Drusus (2).

Sallust, *Iug.*, is the source for the Jugurthine War. The trial is widely reported and is put in its chronological and political context: thus frequently by Cicero (and cf. Asconius, p. 21 Clark) and by various later historians.

M. C. Alexander, *Trials in the Late Roman Republic* (1990) 49 f., with all sources and some bibliography; E. Badian, *Studies in Greek and Roman History* (1964), see index, and *Publicans and Sinners* (rev. edn. 1983), 169 ff. with notes; R. Kallet-Marx, *Phoenix* 1990, 122 ff. (against the evidence of the sources, trying to date the trial *c.*94 and to deny its connection with Drusus' reforms); Marshall, *Asconius Comm.* 134 f. And see under Q. Mucius Scaevola (2)..   E. B.

Rutupiae (mod. Richborough (Kent)), town in *Britain situated originally on a mainland peninsula of the now silted Thanet channel; a pair of ditches were very probably the defences of a Claudian landing-party (AD 43) and the site was used as a stores base for the conquest. About AD 80–90 a 25 m.-high, marble-clad, monumental, *quadrifrons*, *arch was built, probably as a symbolic gateway to Britain, celebrating Rome's conquest. Rutupiae was the principal landing-place from the continent, so that in authors 'Rutupinus' = British. A civil settlement and *mansio* were built, but before AD 250 the ruined trophy was surrounded by three ditches, which were soon replaced by the stone *Saxon Shore fort of *c.*2.4 ha. built in *c.*275. Coinage demonstrates that the site continued in importance into the 5th cent. The fort is surrounded by a substantial settlement with an amphitheatre. An early Christian church has been excavated in the north-west corner of the fort.

B. Cunliffe (ed.), *Fifth Report on the Excavations at Richborough, Kent* (1968); T. F. C. Blagg, in V. A. Maxfield, *The Saxon Shore* (1989).   C. E. S.; M. J. M.

Saalburg, near Bad Homburg, a strong point on the Upper German *limes*, controlling traffic across the Taunus. Roman troops first occupied the position during the Chattian campaigns of AD 83–5 (see DOMITIAN; CHATTI); they built a fortlet here, just behind the *limes* proper, c.90. A timber fort for an auxiliary cohort was built between 125 and 128 and given a composite wall of dry stone and timber before 139. This was later reconstructed entirely in stone, probably 200–13. There was further work in the 230s, but the fort was evacuated following invasion and civil war c.260. The forts and extensive *vicus* have been excavated, and the walls and principal buildings of the cohort fort were reconstructed 1898–1907 to create an unusual and important museum.

H. Schönberger, *JRS* 1969, 144 ff.; J. von Elbe, *Roman Germany: A Guide to Sites*² (1973); D. Baatz, *Der römische Limes*² (1975); D. Baatz and F. R. Herrman (eds.), *Die Römer in Hessen* (1982).　　　J. F. Dr.

Saba, St, a Gothic martyr (see GOTHS) killed on 12 April 372 during the Gothic persecution of Christians which followed the peace of 369. His remains were secured by Junius Soranus, *dux Scythiae*, and sent to his native Cappadocia; the *Passion* is the accompanying letter. Saba's example was exploited by *Basil of Caesarea (*Epp.* 164–5), who was facing the emperor *Valens' anti-Nicene church policies, to launch a paean on the early church, persecuted but united, as opposed to the contemporary church riven with heresy and dissension.

Knopf-Kruger, *Ausgewählte Martyrerakten* (4th. edn., 1965), trans. P. J. Heather and J. F. Matthews, *The Goths in the Fourth Century* (1991), 111–17.　　　P. J. H.

Sabazius (Σαβάζιος—but numerous other spellings occur), a god first attested in several slighting allusions in *Aristophanes (1); there are also 4th-cent. references to his unofficial cult in *Attica. Aristophanes treats him as a Phrygian (see PHRYGIA); the bulk of the surviving dedications derive from Anatolia, particularly from Phrygia; *Attalus III in 135/4 BC claimed to be incorporating 'Zeus Sabazios' (cf. ZEUS) into the state cult of *Pergamum (a rare instance of official recognition for Sabazius) as an 'ancestral god' of his mother, Stratonice of *Cappadocia (*OGIS* 331). Later, Sabazius also appears as an 'ancestral god' of Thrace (see RELIGION, THRACIAN). Except in Attica, the cult is little attested until the late Hellenistic period; it eventually penetrated almost every corner of the Roman empire, normally at the level of private associations. From Rome itself, according to a puzzling report in *Valerius Maximus (1. 3. 2), the *praetor peregrinus* had already in 139 BC expelled 'the Jews who had tried to contaminate Roman traditions through the worship of Jupiter Sabazius' (cf. JUPITER). Specific rites and beliefs are hard to identify, since reports are few and hostile. It is not certain that the disreputable initiations and purifications lampooned by *Demosthenes (2) (18.

259–60) are Sabazian; *Diodorus (3) tells of rites celebrated at night because of their shameful character (4. 4); Christian polemicists speak of snake-handling. The murals and inscriptions of the tomb of Vincentius in the catacomb of Praetextatus at Rome (Dessau, *ILS* 3961) show that in the late 3rd or early 4th cent. AD a devotee of Sabazius could nourish hopes for the afterlife. In art, Sabazius appears either in Phrygian costume or with the attributes of Zeus/Jupiter, with whom he was, from the time of Attalus III, regularly identified. A typical form of Sabazian monument is the votive hand, making the so-called *benedictio Latina* and adorned with numerous cult symbols.

M. J. Vermaseren and E. N. Lane, *Corpus Cultus Iovis Sabazii*, 3 vols. (1983–9); R. Turcan, *Les Cultes orientaux dans le monde romain* (Paris, 1989).　　　R. C. T. P.

Sabelli is not synonymous with *Sabini. It is the Roman name for speakers of *Oscan. They called themselves *Safineis* and their chief official *meddix. They expanded from their original habitat (reputedly Sabine Amiternum) by proclaiming sacred springs (see VER SACRUM) and settling in fresh lands where they usually imposed their language and coalesced with the pre-Sabellian populations. Thus originated Samnites, Frentani, Campani, Lucani, Apuli, Bruttii, and Mamertini. (Paeligni, Vestini, Marrucini, Marsi, and Aequi(?), who spoke Oscan-type dialects, presumably had a similar origin.) These migrations were still continuing in the 5th cent. BC and later: Sabelli conquered *Campania c.450–420, *Lucania c.420–390; *Bruttii appeared c.356. But the Sabelli were more expansive than cohesive. The Samnites (see SAMNIUM), the most typical Sabelli, had no feeling of political unity with their ancestors the Sabines, nor the *Frentani with theirs, the Samnites.

Old Sabellic is the description inaccurately applied to some untranslated inscriptions from *Picenum, including the oldest non-Etruscan inscriptions from Italy. See ITALY, LANGUAGES OF.

E. T. Salmon, *Samnium and the Samnites* (1967); M. Pallottino, *Storia della prima Italia* (1984), 183 f.　　　E. T. S., T. W. P.

Sabina Augusta (*RE* Suppl. 15, Vibius 72b), daughter of *Matidia, *Trajan's niece, and, probably, of L. Vibius Sabinus, married *Hadrian in AD 100, thus strengthening his claims to succeed his childless kinsman. Nothing is heard of her before Hadrian's accession, but she accompanied him on several journeys; an obscure imbroglio in Britain (AD 122) led to the dismissal of the praetorian prefect (*praefectus praetorio) and *ab epistulis* (Suetonius) for showing her 'insufficient respect'. Hadrian said he 'would have divorced her for her disagreeable character' had he been a private citizen; she is said to have ensured that she remained childless since any offspring of Hadrian's would have been a monster. However, she received the title *Augusta* at latest in 128, when she began to appear on the coinage, and was present with Hadrian in Egypt in 130, when her friend *Iulia Balbilla paid tribute to her beauty with a poem carved on the statue of Memnon. Her death (in 136 or 137) was ascribed to poisoning by Hadrian, but she was declared *Diva* by him.

M. T. Raepsaet-Charlier, *Prosopographie des femmes de l'ordre sénatorial* (1987), no. 802. A. R. Bi.

Sabini, people of ancient Italy. The Sabines occupied an area to the north-east of Rome along the eastern side of the *Tiber valley and extending to the *Apennine uplands. Their main centres in the Tiber valley were Cures, Eretum, and Trebula Mutuesca, and in the central Apennines *Reate, Amiternum, and Nursia. Tradition maintained that the Sabines were the ancestors of all the 'Sabellian' peoples (see SABELLI), including the Picentines and Samnites, who migrated from the Sabine heartland in a series of sacred springs (see VER SACRUM). They also play an important part in the legends of early Rome. The rape of the Sabine women, and the subsequent war and reconciliation, leading to the integration of the Sabines into the community under the joint rule of *Romulus and Titus *Tatius are central elements in the story of how the city of Rome was formed.

The legends have been variously interpreted. For Dumézil they represent a historicized version of an *Indo-European myth, in which a complete society of gods is formed from the fusion of two opposing but incomplete groups, one possessing magical strength and bravery, the other wealth and fecundity, as in the Icelandic myth of the Aesir and the Vanir, who correspond in the Roman story to the Romans and Sabines respectively. Others have suggested that the story is a projection back into the prehistoric past of events that occurred centuries later, namely the incursions of Sabines into *Latium in the 5th cent. BC and their incorporation in the Roman state in 290. But the majority of scholars are prepared to accept that the legends reflect a historical fact, namely the presence of a significant Sabine element in the Roman population from the earliest times. The peaceful infiltration of Sabines in the 6th cent., e.g. the migration of the Claudii (Livy 2. 16), may have been going on for a long time; other clans, such as the Valerii, claimed a Sabine origin, and two of the kings, Numa *Pompilius and Ancus *Marcius, were Sabine—or three if one counts Titus *Tatius.

Archaeological evidence is so far meagre, but recent excavations in the Tiber valley, at Cures, Poggio Sommavilla, Colli del Forno (Eretum?), and Magliana Sabina, have revealed a high level of material culture during the iron age similar to that of Latium (but note that this makes it difficult to distinguish Sabines in Rome by archaeological means).

During the 5th cent. the sources record numerous warlike incursions into Latium by the Sabines, but they were defeated in 449 and disppear from the record until 290, when they were conquered by M'. *Curius Dentatus and incorporated as Roman citizens without suffrage. They received full citizenship in 268.

E. T. Salmon, *The Making of Roman Italy* (1982), 23 ff.; J. Poucet, *Recherches sur la légende Sabine* (1967), and *Origines de Rome* (1985); G. Dumézil, *Archaic Roman Religion* (1970; Fr. orig. 1966); A. Momigliano, *JRS* 1963, 95–121 = *Terzo Contributo*, 545–98. Archaeological evidence: *Civiltà arcaica dei Sabini* 1–3 (1973–7); and see annual reports of archaeology in Sabina in the periodical *Archeologia Laziale*. T. J. Co.

Sabinus, lawyer See MASURIUS SABINUS.

Sabinus, friend of *Ovid, who composed replies from heroes to Ovid's letters from heroines (*Heroides*) and modelled a work on

the *Fasti* (Ov. *Am.* 2. 18. 27–34, *Pont.* 4. 16. 13–16); perhaps identical with a Tullius Sabinus, author of two surviving Greek epigrams (Gow–Page, GP 2. 404). E. C.

Sabratha (neo-Punic *Sbrt'n*). A settlement with a small natural harbour east of the Lesser *Syrtis, probably founded by *Phoenicians (Sil. *Pun.* 3. 256), although the archaeological evidence to date is no earlier than the 5th cent. BC. Some remains of the 4th / 3rd-cent. city, when the urban street-grid in the central sector was first established, have been identified, as well as the Hellenistic necropolis. One 23 m. high Punico-Hellenistic mausoleum in the latter, of the 2nd cent. BC, bearing sculptured decoration, has been re-erected. Shadrapha, worshipped in Roman times as *Liber Pater, and Melqart-*Hercules, were the principal city deities, commemorated on the local coinage. Sabratha's prosperity in the early Empire was interrupted only temporarily by a mid-1st cent. earthquake. The *elephant in the mosaic floor of the office of the *Sabratenses* at *Ostia, of c. AD 100, indicates an export trade in those animals to Italy; the fruits of trans-Saharan trade were another source of revenue. The 2nd cent., when a new quarter was laid out east of the central sector, saw the zenith of Sabratha's prosperity; it was then that the city won colonial status. Extensively damaged in the earthquake of AD 365, after which outlying quarters of the city were abandoned, Sabratha saw to the repair of some of its public buildings; but the city decayed further in the 5th cent. under the *Vandals, and revival under the Byzantines, who constructed a new defensive circuit, was brief and spasmodic. Large areas of the city have been excavated. Public buildings include the forum, the curia, the basilica where *Apuleius must have been brought to trial (*Apol.* 73), baths, the theatre, and an extramural amphitheatre. Five temples have been excavated in and around the forum, and others to Hercules and *Isis in the eastern quarter; four churches are known, of which one, Justinianic (Procop. *Aed.* 6. 4. 13), possessed outstanding *mosaics now in the site museum.

PECS 779–80; D. E. L. Haynes, *Antiquities of Tripolitania* (1956), 107–34; P. Ward, *Sabratha: A Guide for Visitors* (1970); P. M. Kenrick, *Excavations at Sabratha 1948–1951* (1986); J. Dore and N. Keay, *Excavations at Sabratha 1948–1951, 2: The Finds, Part 1* (1989). Individual monuments: G. Pesce, *Il tempio d'Iside in Sabratha*, Monografie di archeologia libica 4 (1953); G. Caputo, *Il teatro di Sabratha*, ibid. 6 (1959); E. Joly and F. Tomasello, *Il tempio a divinità ignota di Sabratha*, ibid. 18 (1984); G. Caputo and F. Ghedini, *Il tempio di Ercole di Sabratha*, ibid. 19 (1984). O. B.; R. J. A. W.

Sacadas (Σακάδας), 7th / 6th cent. BC, musician and poet, of *Argos (2) (Paus. 9. 30. 2), connected with the second phase of musical organization in *Sparta (i.e. the Gymnopaedia, ps.-Plut. *De mus.* 8). He won three successive Pythian victories (see PYTHIAN GAMES) with the flute, and his Pythian *nomos (2) representing *Apollo's fight against the serpent became a traditional set-piece. He also composed tunes and elegiac poems set to music (ibid. 8). Nothing of his work survives. See MUSIC. C. M. B.; E. Kr.

Sacaea (Σάκαια), a name used by several ancient writers to describe, in a confused and contradictory way, an event which seems originally to have been an annual Babylonian festival (see BABYLON), whose most striking feature was a ritual of social inversion. It is possible that in the Persian period the festival blended with the period of official *anomia* declared on the death of the king; it is also possible that it relates to a partial assimilation to the Babylonian ritual of the 'substitute king'.

P. Briant, in J. Kellens (ed.), *La Religion iranienne à l'époque achéménide*, *Ir Ant* Suppl. 5 (1991), 3–4.   P. B.

Sacerdos, Marius Plotius (*RE* 17; *PLRE* 1. 795), late 3rd-cent. AD?, Roman grammarian, wrote the first large-scale Latin *ars* to survive in (roughly) its original form (Keil, *Gramm. Lat.* 6. 427–546). Book 1, surveying the parts, 'flaws', and 'virtues' of speech, and Book 2, reviewing nominal and verbal endings and (briefly) prose rhythm, are preserved together in a defective Naples codex; a virtually identical version of Book 2 circulated as the *Catholica* falsely attributed to *Valerius Probus (Keil, ibid. 4. 3–43). Book 3, on metre, is transmitted separately, with Sacerdos' preface describing the dedication of the three books to various men of senatorial rank. See GRAMMAR, GRAMMARIANS, LATIN.

Herzog–Schmidt, § 522. 3.   R. A. K.

sacramentum **(legal)** *Sacramentum* signified in the oldest Roman civil proceeding (*legis actio sacramento*) the sum of money deposited as a stake by both litigants in the stage before the magistrate (*in iure*). The opposite assertions of the parties as to the plaintiff's claim formed a kind of wager, and it was presumably the wager which was, in form, the issue to be decided by the judge. Although *sacramentum* has this meaning as early as the *Twelve Tables, the word literally means an oath. Since *Cicero (*Caec.* 97) speaks of the judge as deciding which *sacramentum* was *iustum* and we are told that originally the money was paid to the pontiffs and spent on public sacrifices (Varro, *Ling.* 5. 180; Festus, under *sacramentum*), it is a reasonable conjecture that in the beginning each party called on heaven to witness to the justice of his claim and the loser's stake paid for sacrifices in expiation of his perjury. In later times the money was not deposited, but guaranteed by sureties (*praedes*).   B. N.

sacramentum **(military)**, the oath of allegiance, sworn on attestation by a Roman recruit; the most strictly observed of all Roman oaths according to Dion. Hal. *Ant. Rom.* 11. 43. Its content stressed obedience to the consuls or commanding officers and good discipline (Dion. Hal. *Ant. Rom.* 10. 18); in the mid-2nd cent. BC the tribunes administered it (Polyb. 6. 21. 2). After the reforms of C. *Marius (1) soldiers swore the oath to their general, and it took on a personal hue (e.g. Plut. *Sull.* 27. 3), thus encouraging the personal armies of the late Republic. From *Augustus loyalty was sworn to the emperor, before the standards (Tac. *Ann.* 15. 29); the oath was renewed annually on New Year's Day or the anniversary of the emperor's accession (Tac. *Hist.* 1. 55; Plin. *Ep.* 10. 60). In the Christian empire soldiers swore much the same oath but by God, Christ, and the Holy Ghost (Vegetius 2. 5). See OATHS.

E. de Backer, *Sacramentum* (1911); D. Michaelides, *Sacramentum* (1970); R. Smith, *Service in the Post-Marian Army* (1958), 29 ff.; J. B. Campbell, *Emperor and Roman Army* (1984), 19 ff.   G. R. W.; A. J. S. S.

Sacred Band, élite infantry unit formed by Gorgidas after the liberation of *Thebes (1) from Spartan occupation (379/8 BC), perhaps as a symbolic counterpart to élite Spartan units, and comprising 150 pairs of lovers maintained at state expense. The original plan was to use them as a unit only in limited operations requiring rapid deployment while distributing them through the front infantry ranks in formal battle, but *Pelopidas' victory at *Tegyra (375) led to their deployment together on all occasions. This made for a crucial role at *Leuctra (details are controversial)—and complete annihilation at *Chaeronea. Their burial *en masse* beneath the Lion Monument is disputed, but the unit certainly never reformed. Military sources for 378–338

mention the Band very rarely, and its real importance is hard to assess.

J. de Voto, *Ancient World* 1992; J. Buckler, *Theban Hegemony* (1980).   C. J. T.

Sacred Wars Four wars declared by the Delphic *amphictiony (see DELPHI) against states allegedly guilty of sacrilege against *Apollo.

The *First* involved *Solon and resulted in *Cirrha's destruction as a punishment for 'brigandage' and impious treatment of pilgrims and dedications (early 6th cent.). Claims that this is a pseudo-historical event, invented in the 340s, are dubitable given *Isocrates' reference in *Plataicus* (14.31: 373/2).

The *Second* arose when Athens placed the sanctuary under Phocian control (see PHOCIS). *Sparta intervened to restore Delphian authority and *Athens countered by restoring Phocis (*c*.448). The Phocians lost control again after 446. The affair is obscure (*Thucydides (2)'s treatment is inadequate); Sparta's intervention in *Doris in 458 is probably part of the background.

The *Third*. Phocian intentions were suspect in 363, but it was a Delphian denunciation (357) for cultivation of the Crisaean plain (between Delphi and the coast) which precipitated war. Phocis ignored a large amphictionic fine and, with financial and moral support from Athens and Sparta, *Philomelus seized the sanctuary (summer 356). Within the year the amphictiony declared a war which re-energized post-*Leuctra politico-military divisions but eventually helped transform the political scene, when a Theban invitation permitted *Philip (1) II to win Hellenic status by championing Apollo's cause and destroying Phocis (346). The conflict (disfigured by atrocities on both sides) has three periods corresponding to the generalships of (*a*) Philomelus, (*b*) *Onomarchus, and (*c*) *Phayllus (2) and *Phalaecus, and was largely fought in the Cephissus Valley (355, 351–348; see CEPHISSUS, Boeotian section) and western Boeotia (354–347). (Phocis was theoretically vulnerable from all directions. But western Locris and *Doris were neutralized immediately and the northern approaches controlled by conquests in eastern Locris (354, 351); *Thessaly was anyway distracted by civil war.) It was prolonged by Theban and Macedonian failure to exploit victories at Neon (355) and Crocus Field (353/2). Liberation of Delphi was not a consistent absolute priority (Thebes also pursued Peloponnesian interests, for example), and people only slowly appreciated the implications of Phocian pillaging of Delphian treasuries (over 10,000 talents, the majority under Phayllus): this permitted unprecedented large-scale state-employment of *mercenaries (general and army actually came to supersede the state's authority), and following satrapal disbandment of forces in the 350s there were many professionals available to fill dead men's shoes, especially at rates 50–100 per cent above normal. (Thebes, by contrast, was financially strained and diverted troops to Anatolia in 355/4 to raise money.)

The *Fourth*. When *Amphissa proposed that Athens be fined for rededicating Persian Wars booty taken from the Thebans (340), *Aeschines (1) denounced Amphissa's cultivation of Cirrhaean land. Official inspectors destroyed some buildings, but were physically attacked, whereupon an extraordinary amphictiony meeting (winter 340/339) declared war. Military attack led to a fine, removal of the guilty parties, and restoration of exiles, but when Amphissa failed to pay and reversed the other arrangements *Philip (1) II was invoked as hegemon (autumn 339). The upshot was occupation of Elatea and the campaign which ended at *Chaeronea (338). How far the whole war had been provoked to provide Philip an *entrée* to central Greece is disputed.

H. W. Parke and D. E. Wormell, *Delphic Oracle* (1956). *First war*: W. G. Forrest, *BCH* 1956; J. Davies, in S. Hornblower (ed.), *Greek Historiography* (1994), ch. 7. *Second war*: S. Hornblower, *Harv. Stud.* 1992, 169 ff. and *Comm. on Thuc.* 1, n. on 1. 112. 5. *Third war*: J. Buckler *Third Sacred War* (1989); J. R. Ellis, *Philip II* (1976). *Fourth war*: Ellis, as above and in *CAH* 6² (1994), 778 ff.   C. J. T.

sacrifice, Greek Sacrifice was the most important form of action in Greek religion (see RELIGION, GREEK), but we should note at once that there is no single Greek equivalent to the English word 'sacrifice'. The practices we bring together under this heading were described by a series of overlapping terms conveying ideas such as 'killing', 'destroying', 'burning', 'cutting', 'consecrating', 'performing sacred acts', 'giving', 'presenting', but not at all the idea present in 'it was a great sacrifice for him'. As occasions for sacrifice *Theophrastus distinguished 'honour, gratitude, and need' (in *Porphyry, *Abst.* 2. 24), but his categories do not correspond to fixed types, and in fact the rite could be performed on almost any occasion.

Vegetable products, savoury *cakes above all, were occasionally 'sacrificed' (the same vocabulary is used as for animal sacrifice) in lieu of animals or, much more commonly, in addition to them. But animal sacrifice was the standard type. The main species used were sheep, goats, pigs, and cattle. In a few cults fish and fowl were offered, wild animals still more rarely; dogs and horses appear in a few sacrifices of special type that were not followed by a feast. Human sacrifice occurred only in myth and scandalous story. The choice between the main species was largely a matter of cost and scale, a piglet costing about 3 drachmae, a sheep or goat 12, a pig 20 or more, a cow up to 80. Within the species symbolic factors were sometimes also relevant: the virgins *Athena and *Artemis might require unbroken cattle, fertile Earth a pregnant sow. See ANIMALS IN CULT.

The most important step-by-step accounts of a standard sacrifice are a series of Homeric scenes, of which the fullest is *Od.* 3. 430–63; Eur. *El.* 774–843; and Ar. *Birds* 938 ff. Attic practice differs or may have done from Homeric in several significant details, but the basic articulations of the rite are the same in all sources. Vase-paintings and votive reliefs provide extremely important supplementary evidence, though by their nature they very rarely depict the full succession of actions as a sequence. Three main stages can be distinguished:

1. Preparatory. An animal was led to the altar, usually in *procession. The participants assembled in a circle, rinsed their hands in lustral water, and took a handful of barley grain from a basket. Water was sprinkled on the victim to force it to 'nod' agreement to its own sacrifice. The main sacrificer (not necessarily a priest) then cut hair from the victim, put it on the *altar fire, and uttered a *prayer which defined the return that was desired (e.g. 'health and safety') for the offering. The other participants threw forwards their barley grains.

2. The kill. The victim's throat was cut with a knife; larger victims had been stunned with a blow from an axe first. Women participants raised the cry known as *ololygē*. In Attic practice it was important to 'bloody the altar'; small animals were held over it to be killed, the blood from larger ones was caught in a bowl and poured out over it.

3. Treatment of the meat, which itself had three stages. First the god's portion, typically the thigh bones wrapped in fat with (in Homer) small portions of meat cut 'from all the limbs' set on top, was burnt on the altar fire. *Wine was poured on as it burnt.

(Further portions for the gods were sometimes put on a table or even on the knees or in the hands of their statues; in practice, these became priests' perquisites.) Then the entrails were roasted on skewers and shared among all the participants. Finally the rest of the meat was boiled and distributed (normally in equal portions); in contrast to the entrails, this boiled meat was occasionally taken away for consumption at home, though a communal feast on the spot was the norm (see DINING-ROOMS). Omens were often taken both from the burning of the god's portion and from the condition of the entrails.

A distinction is drawn in Herodotus (2. 44) between sacrifice to the gods, θύειν, and to heroes, ἐναγίζειν (see HERO-CULT). It used to be common to draw a contrast between the normal Olympian sacrifice outlined and a 'chthonian' type which supposedly diverged from the other systematically: the victim would be dark, not light; it would be killed with its head pressed down into a low pit or hearth, not drawn back over a high altar; the accompanying libations would be 'wineless'; and, above all, the animal's flesh would not be eaten. But it is now clear that these divergences from the standard type more often occurred individually than as a group, and also that they might be present in 'Olympian' sacrifice, absent (largely or wholly) from sacrifice to chthonian gods or heroes. See CHTHONIAN GODS; OLYMPIAN GODS.

There were also certain 'quasi-sacrifices' which contained several of the actions listed above and could be described by some, though not all, of the group of words that denote sacrifice. The killing of animals to ratify an oath, for instance, followed many of the stages mentioned under 1 and 2 above; stage 3, however, was omitted entirely, the carcass being carried away or thrown in the sea (cf. Hom. *Il.* 3. 245–313, 19. 250–68). See OATHS. And similar quasi-sacrificial ritual killings occurred in certain *purifications and before battle.

Explicit early reflection on sacrifice is sparse. (But see too ANIMALS, ATTITUDES TO.) The division whereby men received most of the meat was explained by a trick played on *Zeus by the man-loving god *Prometheus at the time of the first sacrifice (Hes. *Theog.* 535–61). The rite of *Bouphonia (part of the Attic festival Dipolieia; see ATTIC CULTS AND MYTHS) raised the issue of the institution's moral legitimacy: an ox sacrifice was followed by a 'trial' at which guilt for the killing was eventually fixed on the sacrificial axe or knife. *Plato (1)'s Euthyphro no doubt echoes popular usage in describing sacrifice as a form of 'gift' to the gods (*Euthyphro* 14c).

Recent interpretations are largely divided between those which see sacrifice (perhaps with reference to its hypothetical origins among prehistoric hunters) as a dramatization of killing, violence, and the associated guilt, and those for which by contrast it is a way of legitimizing meat-eating by treating the taking of life that necessarily precedes it as a ritual, i.e. a licensed act: the former approach stresses that rituals such as the Bouphonia raise the issue of sacrificial guilt, the latter that they resolve it. Sacrifice is normally killing followed by eating, but where does the emphasis lie? In the vast majority of cases, clearly, on the eating; but all the uneaten sacrifices and quasi-sacrifices have to be set aside if the institution is to be understood by reference to the communal feast alone.

GENERAL P. Stengel, *Opferbräuche der Griechen* (1910); K. Meuli, 'Griechische Opferbräuche', in *Phyllobolia. Festschrift P. von der Mühll* (1946), 185–288 = Meuli, *Gesammelte Schriften* 2 (1975), 907–1021; J. Rudhardt, *Notions fondamentales de la pensée religieuse et actes constitutifs du culte dans la Grèce classique* (1958), ch. 5; J. Casabona, *Recherches sur le vocabulaire des sacrifices en grec* (1966); M. Detienne and J. P. Vernant (eds.), *La cuisine du sacrifice en pays grec* (1979); *Le Sacrifice dans l'anti-quité*, Entretiens Hardt 27 (1981); W. Burkert, *Homo Necans* (trans. P. Bing, 1983); G. Berthiaume, *Les Rôles du mágeiros* (1982); J. L. Durand, *Sacrifice et labour en Grèce ancienne* (1986); D. D. Hughes, *Human Sacrifice in Ancient Greece* (1991).

THEORY For contrasting views see esp. Burkert and Vernant, in *Le Sacrifice dans l'antiquité* (above).

SPECIAL ASPECTS The god's portion, and omens from it: F. van Straten, in R. Hägg and others (eds.), *Early Greek Cult Practice* (1988), 51–68; M. H. Jameson, in *Greek Tragedy and its Legacy: Essays presented to D. J. Conacher* (1986), 59–66. Table offerings: D. Gill, *Harv. Theol. Rev.* 1974, 117–37; F. Graf, *Nordionische Kulte* (1985), 251–2. Choice and cost of animals: F. van Straten, in T. Linders and G. Nordquist (eds.), *Gifts t° the Gods* (1987), 159–70; M. H. Jameson, in C. R. Whittaker (ed.), *Pastoral Economies in Classical Antiquity* (1988), 87–119. Archaeological aspects: R. Étienne and M.-T. Le Dinahet (eds.), *L'Espace sacrificiel* (1991). Military sacrifices: W. K. Pritchett, *The Greek State at War*, 3 (1979), 83–90; M. H. Jameson, in V. D. Hanson (ed.), *Hoplites* (1991), 197 ff.   R. C. T. P.

sacrifice, Roman Roman sacrificial practices were not func-tionally different from Greek, although there are no sources for them earlier than the 2nd cent. BC, and the *modalités* of Roman sacrifice were complex, since several rites existed (Roman, Greek, and Etruscan). In any case, as in the Greek world, sacrifice was a central act of religion. The expression *rem divinam facere*, 'to make a thing sacred', often abridged to *facere* ('to sacrifice'), and the etymology of the words designating sacrificial activity, *sacrificare*, *sacrificium* (*sacrum facere*, 'to perform a religious ceremony'), show the importance of these acts and signal that sacrifice was an act of transfer of ownership. On its own or part of larger celebrations, the typical sacrifice embraced four phases: the *prae-fatio*, the *immolatio*, the slaughtering, and the banquet.

1. After the purification (see LUSTRATION) of the participants and of the victims (always domestic animals) chosen in accord-ance with the divinity's function and the context, a procession led them to the *altar of the divinity. There the presiding figure celebrated the *praefatio* ('preface') on a portable hearth (*focus*, *foculus*) set up beside the sacrificial altar (*ara*). This rite consisted of offering *incense and *wine, and, according to the ancient commentators, was the equivalent of a solemn salutation affirming the superiority of the gods. At the same time this rite opened a ritual space and announced what was to follow.

2. The second stage of the sacrifice was the *immolatio*. The presiding figure poured wine on the victim's brow, sprinkled its back with salted flour (*mola salsa*, whence *immolare*), doubtless prepared by the *Vestals, and finally passed a sacrificial knife over the victim's spine. According to ancient commentators and the *prayer spoken during this rite, immolation transferred the victim from human possession into the divine.

3. Once this transfer was effected, the sacrificers (*popae*, *vic-timarii*; cf. Gr. *mageiroi*) felled the victim, butchered it, and opened the corpse, now on its back. The presiding figure then performed the *extispicina*, the inspection of the *exta* (vital organs: the periton-eum, liver, gall bladder, lungs, and, from the beginning of the 3rd cent. BC (Plin. *HN* 11. 186), the heart), to decide if they were in the good shape which would signal the deity's acceptance (*litatio*) of the sacrifice. If the victim was unacceptable, the sacrifice had to begin again.

4. The banquet comprised two phases. Once acceptance was obtained, the sacrificers beheaded the victim, set aside the *exta*, and prepared them for offering: the *exta* of bovines were boiled in cooking pots (*ollae extares*), those of ovines and the pig-family

were grilled on spits. This cooking done, the *exta* were offered to the divinity (*porricere*; *pollucere* for Hercules), i.e. burnt, basted with *mola salsa* and wine, sometimes along with pieces of meat designated on the victim in advance (*magmentum*). This was done on the altar if celestial divinities were in question; offerings to aquatic deities were thrown into the water, those for epichthonic or chthonic divinities were placed on the ground or in ditches. Offerings for the di *manes were made on a pyre itself resting on the ground (*ILS* 139, 16 ff.; *CIL* 11. 5047). When the offering to the deity had been consumed, the rest of the victim was seized (*profanare*), no doubt by imposition of the hand, and thus rendered fit for human consumption. In principle all sacrifices, except those addressed to divinities of the under-world, were followed by a sacrificial banquet (*cena*, *visceratio*). But the procedures at these banquets are ill-understood, because of both the complexity of communal banquets in Rome's strongly hierarchical society, and the enormous numbers having the right to take part (e.g. the citizens). Sometimes the banquet was celebrated (doubtless on behalf of all) by just the immediate participants and their helpers, along with those possessing privil-eges in a particular sanctuary (e.g. the flute-players at the temple of Jupiter); sometimes the banquet united the chief sections of society (e.g. the Roman élite for the *epulum Jovis*); sometimes the meat was sold in butchers' shops (i.e. it was accessible to all); sometimes, finally, it was eaten at great communal banquets, ultimately financed by benefactors. At the *ara maxima* of Hercu-les, sacrificial meat had to be eaten or burnt before nightfall, a requirement giving rise to a very generous form of sacrificial banquet even if the cult's foundation-myth barred one of the families in charge of the cult, the Pinarii, from taking part.

In public sacrifices conducted in accordance with Greek ritual (*Graeco ritu*), the details of which are very poorly known, the conduct of the presiding figure was different. While in the Roman rite he wore the *toga praetexta, draped in such a way as to allow a flap of cloth to cover the head, in the Greek ritual he sometimes removed the praetexta before proceeding with the *immolatio*, and for the rest of the proceedings; he certainly sacrificed with head uncovered, sometimes wearing a laurel-wreath. The commen-tators on the *Secular Games show that sacrifice according to the Greek rite was no different functionally from the Roman rite. Only the *immolatio* differed, since the presiding figure burnt hairs cut from the animal's brow and offered crowns, and in addition the *exta* were called *splanchna* (G. Pighi, *De ludis saecularibus* (1965), 154 f.); but it is not known whether the rules for the division of the victims differed from the 'Roman' ones. At any rate, Roman sacrifices according to the 'Greek ritual' were much more complicated than has been thought, although the state of the sources prevents a full understanding of them. Of sacrifices according to Etruscan ritual we know even less, save that the inspection of the *exta* (*haruspicatio*) permitted *divination. Even if they had no special name, the sacrificial rituals of certain cults of the imperial age differed from traditional sacrifices, at least to judge from the evidence of imagery. If we are to believe the sources, the *taurobolium* (or *criobolium*) in some way reproduced the myth of *Attis, by creating a central role for blood and for the setting aside of the testicles of the sacrificial victim. Of Mithraic sacrifice, represented on numerous altars of *Mithras, too little is known for comparison with traditional Roman sacrifice. All that can be said is that Mithraic imagery emphasizes violence where representations of traditional sacrifice underline calm.

Communal sacrifices were celebrated by those who exercised power in the community in question: the *paterfamilias, magistrates and *priests, and the presidents (*magistri*) of *clubs. In spite of a few exceptions, women could not sacrifice on behalf of the whole community. Many sacrifices were part of much larger celebrations, and in certain cases the sacrifices themselves were celebrated in more spectacular fashion (e.g. at the *lectisternium). Occasions for sacrifice were innumerable, from regular acts of homage shaped by sacred calendars and the ritual obligations of the city and its constituent associations to thanks-offerings or contractual sacrifices (*vota*, vows). Faults and involuntary oversights committed in the celebration of the cult, or the involuntary deterioration of the patrimony of the gods, were expiated by *piacula*, sacrifices the purpose of which was to present excuses for past or imminent action (e.g. maintenance works in a sanctuary).

By way of a global view of what traditional Roman sacrifice articulated and realized, it can be understood as establishing—with the help of a solemn sharing of food—a hierarchy between three partners: gods, humans, and animals (see ANIMALS IN CULT). To the gods was assured absolute priority in the course of a symbolic feast, during which they shared with humans an animal victim or a vegetable-offering. The different Roman myths which commented on sacrificial practices—those concerning the *instauratio of the cult of the Ara Maxima, the two groups of Luperci (see LUPERCALIA), and the *Vinalia, as well as those revealing the origin of sacrifice (Ov. *Met.* 15. 60 ff.; *Fast.* 1. 335 ff.)—all insist on the fact that, by the privilege of priority, essential in Roman society, and the quality of the offerings (the *exta*, seat of the animal's vitality, the incense and the pure wine, all reserved for the immortals), sacrifice fixed the superiority and immortality of the gods, along with the mortal condition and the pious submission of their human partners, at the expense of the animal victims. At the same time the sacrificial rite was capable of expressing, by the right to take part in the banquet and by the privilege of priority, the hierarchy among mortals.

Latte, *RR* 375 ff.; R. Schilling, *Dictionnaire des mythologies et des religions* 2 (1981), 398 ff.; J. Scheid, in C. Grottanelli and N. Parisi (eds.), *Sacrificio e società nel mondo antico* (1988), 267 ff., and *Romulus et ses frères* (1990), 357 ff.; P. Veyne, *Metis* (1990), 17 ff.; R. Turcan, in *L'Espace sacrificiel* (1991), 217 ff. For the imagery see M. Torelli, *Typology and Structure of Roman Historical Reliefs* (1982); R. Turcan, *Religion romaine* (1988); J. Elsner, *JRS* 1991, 50 ff. For modern theories about sacrifice see SACRIFICE, GREEK.   J. Sch.

Sadducees, a religious group within Judaism attested in Judaea from the 2nd cent. BC to the 1st cent. AD. The Sadducees are described by *Josephus and are mentioned in the New Testament and in rabbinic texts, usually as opponents of the *Pharisees in matters concerning law or theology. According to the generally unfavourable picture given by Josephus, their distinctive tenets consisted in a refusal to accept the unwritten religious traditions championed by the Pharisees, an unwillingness to ascribe human fortunes to the operations of fate, and unwillingness to accept the notion of life after death. Josephus also accused them of harshness in judgement and claimed that they had little influence over the people.

Josephus stated that most Sadducees came from the rich and powerful part of Judaean society. This assertion, together with the evidence of Acts 5: 17 and the probable derivation of the name 'Sadducees' from Zadok, the ancestor of the high priests in earlier times, has led many scholars to identify the Sadducees with the ruling priests in Jerusalem. Some overlap between these groups is certain, but some influential priests (including high priests) were not Sadducees, and there is no reason to doubt that some Sadducees were not priests.

Some of the legal views ascribed to Sadducees in early rabbinic texts have been paralleled in sectarian writings found among the *Dead Sea Scrolls, but the view that the Qumran sectarians should be classified as a type of Sadducee is debated. See RELIGION, JEWISH.

Joseph. *BJ* 2. 164–6; *Ant.* 13. 173; 18. 16–17. J. Le Moyne, *Les Sadducéens* (1972); E. P. Sanders, *Judaism: Practice and Belief, 63 BCE–66 CE* (1992), 317–40.   M. D. G.

Saepinum (mod. Altilia), originally a Samnite mountain town (at Torrevecchia), destroyed by the Romans in 293 BC; see SAMNIUM. The new town was placed athwart a sheep-*transhumance route, the subject of disputes. The well-preserved walls and gates date to *c*. AD 4, and there are many other significant remains, currently under excavation and restoration.

M. Matteini Chiari, *Saepinum* (1982); M. Corbier, *JRS* 1983, 126 f.; M. Gaggiotti, in *Samnium* (1991), 243 f.   E. T. S.; T. W. P.

Saepta Iulia, the voting enclosure for the *comitia tributa*, between the Pantheon and the temple of Isis in the *Campus Martius; it was planned and possibly begun by C. *Iulius Caesar (1) (Cic. *Att.* 4. 16. 14) and completed by M. *Vipsanius Agrippa in 26 BC. The long rectangular voting area (*c*.300 × 95 m.), orientated due north and south, was flanked by colonnades, the porticus of Meleager on the east and the porticus of the Argonauts on the west; the Diribitorium, where the votes were counted, closed its southern end. Parts of the building appear on the Severan *Forma Urbis, and some walls of the porticus Argonautarum and Diribitorium survive, dating from a reconstruction after the fire of AD 80.

When the building lost its original purpose, it was used for gladiatorial contests and other forms of entertainment, and served as a luxury bazaar (Mart. 9. 59).

G. Gatti, *L'Urbe* 1937, fasc. 9, 8 ff.; G. Carettoni, *Forma Urbis Romae* (1960), 97 ff.; Nash, *Pict. Dict. Rome*, 2. 291 ff.; L. R. Taylor, *Roman Voting Assemblies* (1966), 47 ff.   D. E. S.; J. D.

Saguntum (*Arse* on coins, now Sagunto), a city of the Edetani about 16 miles north of *Valentia in Spain. Traces of its Iberian wall and some houses survive on the side of the citadel. It was an ally of Rome, and its subsequent siege by *Hannibal (219 BC) was a catalyst in the outbreak of the Second *Punic War. The elder Scipios (see CORNELIUS SCIPIO CALVUS, CN., and CORNELIUS SCIPIO, PUBLIUS) had recaptured it by 212 BC. Q. *Sertorius occupied it, but was driven out by Q. *Caecilius Metellus Pius and *Pompey in 75. It remained an allied town until at least 56 BC. By the Augustan age Saguntum had become a *municipium* and the forum was built on the citadel. The theatre was built under *Tiberius; a circus is known. The town was overshadowed by *Valentia under the Empire, although its port (*Grau Vell*) shows that it was active until the mid-5th cent. AD.

J. Richardson, *Hispaniae* (1986), 20 f.; M. J. Peña, *Estudios de la antigüedad* (1984), 1. 72; C. Aranegui, *JRA* 1992, 56 ff.   S. J. K.

Saites, the Egyptian 26th dynasty (664–525 BC), comprised six pharaohs: *Psammetichus I (664–610), Necho II (610–595), Psammetichus II (595–589), *Apries (589–570), *Amasis (570–526), and Psammetichus III (526–525). Internally they faced the challenge of the native Egyptian warrior class (*machimoi*) and the Theban priesthood of Amon-re´ (see THEBES (2)). The first was countered by basing Carian and Ionian troops permanently in the country. An anti-Greek rebellion under Amasis, who defeated and expelled

Apries in 570, brought only a brief reversal of this policy. Theban power, on the other hand, was neutralized by diplomatic means. Economically, close links were maintained with the Greeks, particularly through *Naucratis. Abroad, the Saites dealt effectively with *Assyria, *Nubia, and Chaldaea, but finally succumbed to the Persians in 525. Culturally, the period was a brilliant success with particular emphasis on the resuscitation of past glories. Archaism, therefore, became a major feature of cultural expression.

F. K. Kienitz, *Die politische Geschichte Ägyptens vom 7. bis zum 4. Jahrhundert vor der Zeitwende* (1953); E. Drioton and J. Vandier, *L'Égypte*⁴ (1962); T. G. H. James, *CAH* 3²/2 (1991), ch. 35; K. A. Kitchen, *The Third Intermediate Period in Egypt* (1973); *Lexikon der Ägyptologie*, 5. 357; B. Trigger and others, *Ancient Egypt: A Social History* (1992).   A. B. L.

Salaminioi See GENOS; OSCHOPHORIA; SALAMIS (1); SUNIUM.

Salamis (1), an island in the Saronic Gulf between the western coast of *Attica and the eastern coast of the Megarid (the territory of *Megara), closes the bay of *Eleusis on the south. In the strait formed by the slopes of Mt. Aegaleus, the island of Psyttaleia, and the promontory of Cynosura on the south, and the small island of St. George on the west, the Persian fleet was crushingly defeated (September 480 BC). See PERSIAN WARS; SALAMIS, BATTLE OF. There is an important early iron age cemetery. Though probably colonized by, and originally belonging to, *Aegina, and temporarily occupied by Megara (c.600 BC), Salamis became an Athenian possession (thanks in part to propagandist use of the Ajax (see AIAS) connection) in the age of *Solon and *Pisistratus. There is epigraphic evidence for a *genos of the Salaminioi, who are however connected with Sunium as well as with Salamis; see OSCHOPHORIA; SUNIUM. Declared a *cleruchy soon after *Cleisthenes (2)'s reforms (ML 14), Salamis was consequently exploited. In 318 it was conquered by Macedonia. *Aratus (1) restored it to Athens (c.230), but the city lost it again (early 1st cent. AD), before a rich Syrian bought it back for Athens (Dio Chrys. 31. 116 with C. Habicht, *ZPE* 111 (1996) 79 ff.).

P–K, *GL* 1. 3. 5 (b); C. F. Styrenius, *Op. Arch.* 1946; W. K. Pritchett, *AJArch.* 1959, 251 ff. and *Studies in Ancient Greek Topography* 1 (1965), 94 ff.; N. G. L. Hammond, *Studies* (1973), ch. 8 (the battle); J. F. Lazenby, *The Defence of Greece* (1993), ch. 7. Ajax link, Salaminioi: W. S. Ferguson, *Hesperia* 1938, 1 ff. esp. 15 f.; E. Kearns, *The Heroes of Attica* (1989), 141; R. Osborne, in S. Alcock and R. Osborne (eds.), *Placing the Gods* (1994), 155 ff.; Parker, *ARH* 57 ff., 308 ff.   P. T.; S. H.

Salamis (2), largest city of *Cyprus (2 km. from north to south and 1 km. from east to west), was traditionally founded by *Teucer (2). It stands on the east coast at the Pediaeos mouth, where in the 11th cent. BC it replaced the major bronze age town at Enkomi, 5 km. inland to the south-west. Though few pre-Hellenistic remains survive, the monumental 'royal' tombs in the west necropolis establish its 8th–7th-cent. importance and its strong links with Greece and the Levant. The coin-series introduced c.538 by Euelthon records many kings' names. Its rulers' ambivalence during the Greek–Persian struggle for the eastern Mediterranean is epitomized by the Gorgus who commanded ships for the Persians at Greek Salamis in 480 (see next entry), having survived expulsion by his pro-Greek brother Onesilus in the *Ionian Revolt and returned after the latter's death in 498 in the land-battle before Salamis. Most famous was the pro-Greek *Evagoras I; archaeology has yet to corroborate his reputation as a builder. The wars of the *Diadochi were fatal to the Teucrid kings, the last of whom, Nicocreon, was forced into suicide by *Ptolemy (1) I, 311/10; it may be he and his family who perished in a self-inflicted holocaust commemorated by a unique cenotaph in the west cemetery. Salamis yielded its primacy to *Paphos c.200 BC, only regaining it in the 4th cent. AD when refounded by *Constantius II as Constantia. Among its excavated monuments are a major Hellenistic-Roman temple complex of Zeus, a Roman gymnasium and theatre, and the huge early Christian basilicas of Ayios Epiphanios and Campanopetra.

Excavations: J. A. R. Munro and H. A. Tubbs, *JHS* 1891, 59 ff.; V. Karageorghis, *Salamis in Cyprus* (1969), and *Excavations in the Nekropolis of Salamis* 1–4 (1967, 1970, 1973, 1978); M. Yon, in *Kinyras: l'archéologie française à Chypre* (1993), 139 ff.   H. W. C.

Salamis, battle of (480 BC). The Persians, tempted, perhaps, by a message from *Themistocles, moved into the channel between the island and the mainland, almost certainly at night, to confront the Greek fleet, based on the island. Their intention was to surprise the Greeks at their anchorage, and prevent their escape by flanking their lines of retreat, but the Greeks were warned in time by a deserting Tenian ship (see TENOS). When battle was joined in the morning, the two fleets were almost certainly aligned east–west, with the Persians along the shore of Attica, and in the initial stages the Phoenicians and other squadrons on the Persian right may have been isolated and outnumbered. But what actually happened is obscure. All we know is that the Persian fleet was defeated, and soon afterwards withdrew to Asia Minor.

RE 1 A 2 (1920), 1830–1, 'Salamis' 1, 1. 2; Aesch., *Pers.* 353–432; Hdt. 8. 70–95; Diod. Sic. 11. 16–19; Plut., *Them.* 12–15. C. Hignett, *Xerxes' Invasion of Greece* (1963); J. F. Lazenby, *The Defence of Greece* (1993).
        J. F. La.

Salapia (mod. Salpi), in Italy, an important *Daunian settlement on the gulf of Manfredonia, occupied from the 10th–1st cents. BC. It defected during the *Punic Wars and was *Hannibal's base from 214 until its recapture in 210. It was sacked during the *Social War (3) and the original site abandoned in favour of a less marshy and malarial location 6km. inland (Vitr. *De Arch.* 1. 4. 12). This refoundation became a *municipium and has remains of Roman and medieval building. The original site is now submerged, due to changes in the coastline, but aerial photography has identified the line of the walls.

M. D. Marin, 'L'attività archeologica in Puglia', *ACMG* 8 (1969). K. L.

salarium is a term used in the imperial period to denote regular payments to officials. *Augustus instituted the making of regular payments to senatorial and equestrian officials in the provinces (Cass. Dio. 53. 15). The word *salarium* was used (Tac. *Agr.* 42) for the pay of a proconsul which was 1,000,000 sesterces p.a. It is not specifically attested for the different sums paid to *procuratores. Fronto, for example, writes of *stipendia* (*Ad Ant. P.* 10). It is also used, for example, of the payment by the emperor to his *quaestor Augusti* (ILS 8973), payments by an emperor or governor to his *comites* (Suet. *Tib.* 46; *Dig.* 1. 22. 4; 50. 13. 1. 8), and the payment by the *fiscus to regular *advocati fisci*. A few inscriptions are known in which soldiers, mostly *evocati* of the praetorian cohorts, describe themselves as *salarii*.

*Vespasian instituted the payment of salaries to public teachers of Greek and Latin rhetoric at Rome, a practice extended to teachers of philosophy and rhetoric at Athens by Marcus *Aurelius. Local communities could also pay salaries to doctors and teachers of rhetoric (*Dig.* 50. 9. 4. 2).

The rule of classical Roman law that the hire of services could not be the object of *locatio conductio was waived in the case of such local teachers and, by analogy, of *comites (*Dig.* 50. 13) who were thus able to bring actions for the payment of *salaria* by extraordinary proceedings.

Millar, *ERW*, chs. 6, 8. F. G. B. M.; G. P. B.

Salassi, a Gallic tribe occupying the Val d'Aosta and controlling the Great and Little St Bernard passes (see ALPS) and the mining industry of the valley (gold, iron, and probably other metals). The gold-mines were acquired by Rome in 143 BC, and the route into the Po valley was controlled from 100 BC by the colony planted at *Eporedia. The tribe was conquered in 25 BC by A. *Terentius Varro Murena, and the colony of *Augusta Praetoria founded in the following year.

Strabo 4. 206 (4. 6. 7); Cass. Dio, 53. 25. G. E. F. Chilver, *Cisalpine Gaul* (1941); L. J. F. Keppie, *Colonisation and Veteran Settlement in Italy* (1983), 206 ff.; D. Vitali, in *The Celts* (1991), 220 f. P. S.; T. W. P.

sale (*emptio, venditio*) was by far the most important of the Roman consensual *contracts. The parties merely had to agree on the object to be sold and on a price. The handing over of an *arrha* (earnest) was not required to create contractual liability. Only specific objects could be sold; generic sales (sales by description) were not recognized. Generally, the object of the sale had to exist at the time the contract was concluded. Future objects (*res futurae*) could, however, be sold conditionally (*emptio rei speratae*) or as a speculation (*emptio spei*). According to prevailing opinion, the price had to be in money (i.e. exchange transactions did not amount to sale); also, it had to be real and certain but not necessarily fair (*Dig.* 19. 2. 22. 3). Justinian, however, (see JUSTINIAN'S CODIFICATION) recognized an exception: the vendor could rescind the contract, if he had sold land for less than half its true value (*Cod.* 4. 44. 2: *laesio enormis*). The contract of sale (in classical law a purely executory transaction) gave rise to two actions based on good faith (*bonae fidei iudicia*). The vendor could claim payment of purchase price (*actio venditi*), the purchaser could request to receive, and to be maintained in, free and unimpeded possession (*actio empti*). Sale did not therefore imply warranty of title; only if the purchaser was evicted (and not just because he lacked title) could he sue the vendor. The risk of accidental loss or destruction normally passed to the purchaser when the sale was concluded (*emptione perfecta periculum est emptoris*). The vendor, however, was still liable for safe keeping (*custodia*). If the object of the sale suffered from a latent defect, the purchaser could originally only sue if the vendor had either given an express warranty or had failed to disclose the defect. But the curule *aediles imposed an additional 'objective' liability (i.e. independent of fault or warranty) on vendors of slaves and cattle by introducing actions for the return of the thing sold (*actio redhibitoria*) or a reduction in its price (*actio quanti minoris*). These remedies were later generalized; they allowed the purchaser to ask for rescission or reduction of the purchase price.

F. de Zulueta, *Roman Law of Sale* (1945); *Studies in Memory of F. de Zulueta* (1959); V. Arangio-Ruíz, *Compravendita* (1961), 2 (1954); R. Zimmermann, *The Law of Obligation* (1990), 230 ff. R. Z.

Saleius Bassus, a respected but impoverished epic poet who died young; *Vespasian assisted him financially (Quin. *Inst.* 10. 1. 90, Juv. 7. 80. Tac. *Dial.* 5. 2, 9. 2–5). E. C.

Salernum (mod. Salerno), a Roman colony founded 194 BC (Livy 32. 29) to the south of the bay of Naples (*Neapolis). A nearby cemetery with Campanian and Etruscan material shows flourishing earlier settlement in the area. Salernum became an important city, from which much epigraphy but little other archaeological evidence survives.

V. Bracco, *Salerno Romana* (1980). K. L.

Salii (from *salire*, 'to dance'), an ancient ritual *sodalitas* (see SODALES) found in many towns of central Italy, usually in association with the war-god. Outside Rome, they are heard of at *Lavinium, *Tusculum, *Aricia, *Anagnia, and especially at *Tibur where they were attached to *Hercules (Servius, on *Aen.* 8. 285). Their attachment at Rome was to *Mars, though it is a possibility that one of the two companies of twelve (Palatini and Collini) belonged originally to *Quirinus. Salii had to be of *patrician birth and to have both father and mother living. They wore the dress of an archaic Italian foot-soldier: *tunica picta* (painted tunic), with breastplate covered by the short military cloak (*trabea*), and the *apex (a conical felt cap; see Dion. Hal. 2. 70). They also wore a sword and, on the left arm, carried one of the *ancilia*; the original *ancile* fell from heaven as a gift from *Jupiter to Numa *Pompilius (Ov. *Fast.* 3. 365–92), but many copies were made to conceal which was the original; in the right hand they carried a spear or staff (Dion. Hal., as above). The Salii played a prominent part in the *Quinquatrus of 19 March: it is much more doubtful whether they also did so at the *Armilustrium of 19 October. During March and October the Calendars note that the *ancilia* were moved, presumably involving *processions by the Salii. When they processed they halted at certain spots and performed elaborate ritual dances (*tripudium*, cf. Plut. *Numa* 13), beating their shields with staves and singing the *Carmen Saliare, of which fragments are preserved. The idea that their activities marked the opening and closing of a symbolic campaigning season is modern theorizing, open to question. See also RITUAL.

K. Latte, *RR* (1960), 115; J. Rupke, *Domi Militiae: die religiöse Konstruktion des Krieges in Rom* (1990), 22–8. C. B.; J. A. N.

Sallust (Gaius Sallustius (*RE* 10) Crispus), Roman historian,

probably 86–35 BC. A Sabine (see SABINI) from Amiternum, he probably derived from the municipal aristocracy. The earliest certain information of his career concerns his tribunate in 52 (see TRIBUNI PLEBIS), when he acted against *Cicero and T. *Annius Milo (Asc. *Mil.* 37, 45, 49, 51 C). He was expelled from the senate in 50; *Inv. in Sall.* 16 alleges immorality, but the real grounds were probably his actions in 52. He now joined *Caesar, commanding a legion in 49. As praetor in 46 he took part in the African campaign, and was appointed the first governor of Africa Nova. On his return to Rome he was charged with malpractice, allegedly escaping only on Caesar's intervention (Cass. Dio 43. 9. 2, *Inv. in Sall.* 19). With no immediate prospect of advancement, Sallust withdrew from public life—the proems of both *Cat.* and *Iug.* defend that decision—and turned to historiography.

In his first two works he avoided the usual annalistic presentation, preferring the monograph form introduced to Rome by *Coelius Antipater. The first, the *Bellum Catilinae* (c.42/1 BC), treats the conspiracy of Catiline (see SERGIUS CATILINA, L.), 'especially memorable for the unprecedented quality of the crime and the danger' (*Cat.* 4. 4). This is set against, and illustrates, the political and moral decline of Rome, begun after the fall of *Carthage, quickening after *Sulla's dictatorship, and spreading from the dissolute nobility to infect all Roman politics (*Cat.* 6–14, 36–9). There are no doubts about the guilt of the 'conspirators', and Sallust so far accepts the assessment of Cicero, who must have been one of his principal sources (supplemented by oral testimony, *Cat.* 48. 9). But Cicero himself is less prominent than might be expected; the heroes are Caesar and M. *Porcius Cato (2), the two examples of *virtus* ('excellence') which stand out from the moral gloom of their day (53–4), and their speeches in the final debate are presented at a length which risks unbalancing the whole (51–2). Sallust's even-handedness between the two men would have struck contemporaries familiar with the fiercely polarized propaganda since Cato's death (see ANTICATO).

The second monograph, the more ambitious and assured *Bellum Iugurthinum* (*c*.41–40 BC), again emphasizes moral decline. The Jugurthan War (see JUGURTHA) is chosen 'both because it was great, bloody, and of shifting fortunes, and because it represented the first challenge to the arrogance of the nobility' (*Iug.* 5. 1): a strange judgement, but one which reflects the work's interest in the interrelation of domestic strife and external warfare. The military narrative is patchy and selective. Politics are presented simply but vigorously, with decline again spreading from the venal nobility. This decline is presented more dynamically than in *Cat.*, as several individuals fail to live up to promising beginnings: Jugurtha himself, C. *Marius (1), *Sulla, and even Q. *Caecilius Metellus Numidicus, who comes closest to being a hero. Speeches and especially digressions divide the work into distinct panels, and implied comparisons—C. *Memmius (1) and Marius, Metellus and Marius, Marius and Sulla—further plot the changes in political and military style. For sources Sallust perhaps used a general history and the autobiographies of M. *Aemilius Scaurus (1), P. *Rutilius Rufus, and Sulla; some geographical notions, but not much more, may derive from *Posidonius (2). Little seems owed to the 'Punic books' mentioned at 17. 7.

Sallust's last work, the *Histories*, was annalistic (see ANNALS, ANNALISTS). It covered events from 78, perhaps continuing *Sisenna, though it included a retrospect of earlier events. The last datable fragment, from book 5, concerns the year 67, hardly his chosen terminus. Speeches and letters survive entire, though the other fragments are scrappy. He again emphasized the decline of the state after Sulla, and was not generous to Pompey.

The 'Invective against Cicero' ascribed to Sallust in the manuscripts and cited as genuine by *Quintilian (4. 1. 68, 9. 3. 89) is not appropriate to Sallust in 54 (its ostensible date); its author was probably an Augustan rhetorician. The authenticity question is more difficult with the two 'Letters to the elderly Caesar', purportedly of 46 (or 48) and *c*.50 BC, but they too are most likely later works, probably *suasoriae* (see DECLAMATION) of the early empire.

As a historian Sallust has weaknesses. His leading theme is decline, but this is presented schematically and unsubtly; his characters have vigour, but seldom convince. The interpretation of Roman politics is often crude; but if the *nobiles* (see NOBILITAS) come in for most criticism, this is because they set the pattern; their more popular opponents were no better. Still, the choice of the monograph form was enterprising, and he avoids the danger of drifting into biography; the use of particular episodes to illuminate a general theme is deft; he shows an increasing grasp of structure; the rhetoric, especially in speeches and letters, has concentration and verve; and the man has style. The influence of *Thucydides (2) is pervasive, though he cannot match his model's intellectual depth. Many stylistic features are also owed to the Roman tradition, particularly the elder Cato (M. *Porcius Cato (1)). The characteristics are noted by ancient writers (*testimonia* in Kurfess edn., pp. xxvi ff.): archaisms, 'truncated epigrams, words coming before expected, obscure brevity' (Sen. *Ep.* 114. 17), recherché vocabulary, rapidity. He won many admirers in later antiquity and was the greatest single influence on *Tacitus (1).

TEXTS *Cat.*, *Iug.*, select fragments of the *Hist.*, *Letters*, *Invective*: L. D. Reynolds (OCT, 1991). *Cat.*, *Iug.*, and longer fragments from *Hist.*: A. Kurfess³ (Teubner, 1957). *Hist.* (with comm.): B. Maurenbrecher (1891–2). *Letters*, *Invective*: A. Kurfess (6th, 4th edns., Teubner, 1962).

TRANSLATIONS J. C. Rolfe (Loeb); A. Ernout (Budé); S. A. Handford (1963). *Hist.*: P. McGushin, with comm. (1992–4).

COMMENTARIES *Cat.*: K. Vretska, 2 vols. (1976), P. McGushin (1977). *Iug.*: E. Koestermann (1971), G. M. Paul (1984). *Letters*, *Invective*: K. Vretska, 2 vols. (1961).

SPECIAL STUDIES A. D. Leeman, *A Systematical Bibliography of Sallust (1879–1964)* (1965). Also W. Steidle, *Sallusts historische Monographien* (1958); K. Büchner, *Sallust* (1960); D. C. Earl, *The Political Thought of Sallust* (1961); R. Syme, *Sallust* (1964); A. La Penna, *Sallustio e la 'rivoluzione' romana* (1968); V. Pöschl (ed.), *Sallust*, Wege der Forschung 94 (1970); T. F. Scanlon, *The Influence of Thucydides on Sallust* (1980); D. S. Levene on *Iug.*, *JRS* 1992, 53–70.   C. B. R. P.

Sallustius (*PLRE* 1, 'Sallustius' 1), author of a brief manual of Neoplatonic piety known as *On the gods and the world*; see NEOPLATONISM. He is probably to be identified with the emperor *Julian's friend, Flavius Sallustius, consul 363 (*PLRE* 1, 'Sallustius' 5). His book echoes the language and ideas of *Iamblichus (2) and Julian, and seems to have been written under Julian (AD 361–3) to support the pagan reaction against Christianity.

Ed. A. D. Nock with Eng. trans. and valuable prolegomena (1926); G. Rochefort (Budé, 1960). Trans. and discussed by G. Murray, *Five Stages of Greek Religion* (1951).   E. R. D.

Sallustius (*RE* 11) **Crispus, Gaius,** great-nephew and adopted son of the historian *Sallust, became the counsellor of *Augustus and *Tiberius, remaining an *eques* like *Maecenas. He was privy to the killing of Agrippa Postumus (Agrippa *Iulius Caesar) in AD 14 and in 16 arrested the slave who impersonated him. He owned copper mines in the Graian Alps (cf. Hor. *Carm.* 2. 2. 1 ff., an ode addressed to him). He died in 20, no longer in favour (Tac. *Ann.* 3. 30), and leaving his wealth to an adoptive son, C. Sallustius Crispus Passienus—a noted orator, suffect consul 27; consul *ordinarius* (see CONSUL) 44—who married Nero's aunt Domitia and subsequently his mother *Iulia Agrippina; the name of his daughter Sallustia Calvina, wife of the prefect of Egypt P. *Ostorius Scapula, shows a marriage connection with the Domitii Calvini.

Syme, *Rom. Rev.*, and *Tacitus*, indexes; H. W. Benario, *CJ* 1961/2, 321 f.   A. M.; T. J. C.; B. M. L.

Salluvii (or Salyes), a people dwelling north of *Massalia from at least the 6th cent. BC. Though earlier writers called them *Ligurian, *Strabo preferred 'Celtoligurian'; and a Celtic element is suggested by their religion, which centred on the cult of the *tête coupée*. The chief shrines were at Roquepertuse (re-erected in Musée Borély, Marseilles) and Entremont (north of Aix). This hill-fort was apparently their capital and displays Greek influence in its sculpture, its defences (with bastions), and the layout of its streets. The Salluvii constantly opposed the Massaliotes and later the Romans until C. *Sextius Calvinus destroyed their capital (123 BC). Revolts were crushed in 90 and 83 BC.

F. Benoit, *Recherches sur l'hellénisation du midi de la Gaule* (1965); G. Barruol, *Les Peuples préromains du sud-est de la Gaule* (1969); C. Ebel, *Transalpine Gaul* (1976); F. Benoit, *Entremont*, 1981; M. Bats and H. Tréziny, *Études massaliètes* 1 (1986); A. L. F. Rivet, *Gallia Narbonensis* (1988).   A. L. F. R.; J. F. Dr.

Salmoneus, a son of *Aeolus (1). *Homer calls Salmoneus 'blameless' (*Od.* 11. 235 f.), but post-Homeric tradition pictures him as the eponymous king of Salmone in *Elis, who in a case of *hubris pretended to be *Zeus, flinging torches for lightning and making a noise like thunder with his chariot; Zeus killed him with a real thunderbolt. *Sophocles (1) wrote a *Salmoneus Satyricus*.

O. Weinreich, *Religionsgeschichtliche Studien* (1968), 390–3 (= *Tübinger Beiträge z. Altertumsw.* 18, 1933, 86–9). H. J. R.; J. N. B.

Salonae (later **Salona**) was a city of *Dalmatia near Split in Croatia. In 118–117 BC it served as a base for L. *Caecilius Delmaticus Metellus but had to be recaptured by C. Cosconius in 78–76 BC. The *conventus civium Romanorum* (see CONVENTUS (1)) established there defeated the Pompeian admiral M. Octavius in 48 BC (Caes. *BCiv.* 3. 9). Caesar's legate A. *Gabinius (2) died there (47 BC). Soon afterwards a *colonia* was established there (*Martia Iulia Salona*, *CIL* 3. 1933; see COLONIZATION, ROMAN) and after AD 9 it became the provincial capital of Dalmatia. As the focal point of the newly established road system (*CIL* 3. 3198–3201 and *add.*) it grew very rapidly and prospered. During the Marcomannic wars in AD 170 (see MARCOMANNI) its walls were repaired by detachments drawn from newly raised legions II Pia and III Concordia (later II and III Italica) (*CIL* 3. 1980); see LEGION. On his retirement in AD 305 *Diocletian, who was born in the vicinity of Salonae, lived in the villa which he built on the coast a few miles away. When much later Salonae was threatened by *Avaro-Slav invasions the population retreated within the walls of Diocletian's palace, which became the nucleus of the medieval town (*Spalato*).

On the *colonia*: J. J. Wilkes, *Dalmatia* (1969), 220 ff. Remains of the city: C. W. Clairmont, *Excavations at Salona, Yugoslavia (1969–1972)* (1975). Diocletian's Palace: J. J. Wilkes, *Diocletian's Palace, Split*[2] (1993). J. J. W.

Salpensa, See MALACA; TABULA IRNITANA.

Salus, a deified 'virtue', the safety and welfare of the state (akin to, and perhaps influenced by, the Greek *Soteria), with a temple on the Quirinal vowed in the Samnite War in 311 and dedicated in 302 BC (Livy 10. 1. 9). Her feast (*natalis*, 'birthday') was on 5 August (Cic. *Att.* 42. 4; *Sest.* 131; and the calendars). There may have existed an earlier cult of *Salus* (Varro, *Ling.* 5. 52); her association with *Semonia* (related to the *Semunes* of the archaic *Carmen Arvale) suggests *Salus* as protectress of the sowing (Macrob. *Sat.* 1. 16. 8; Festus, *Gloss. Lat.* 406; *ILS* 3090; on some imperial coins she holds corn-ears). From the 2nd cent. BC she became identified with the Greek *Hygieia, 'Health'. *Salus Augusta* or *Augusti*, the 'Health' and 'Saving Power' of the emperor, frequently appears on inscriptions and coins (enthroned, holding sceptre and dish, often feeding the snake). Public and private vows for the *salus* of the emperor (often associated with the *Salus Publica*, esp. in the records of the Arvals; see FRATRES ARVALES), and the oaths by his *salus*, became ubiquitous events. Particularly numerous are dedications to *Salus* in Spain, and by the *equites singulares*. With the *augurium salutis* the goddess *Salus* does not appear to be connected.

J. R. Fears, *ANRW* 2. 17. 2 (1981), 827 ff.; M. A. Marwood, *The Roman Cult of Salus* (1988); L. Winkler, *Salus* (1995). J. L.

salutatio, a formal greeting; especially at the *levée* (*admissio*) of an eminent Roman. Etiquette required a *client to attend in formal dress (*togatus*) at his patron's house at dawn, to greet him (*salutare*) and escort him to work (*deducere*), both for protection and for prestige. Friends of equal or nearly equal standing might also attend, out of special respect or flattery (cf. Cic. *Fam.* 9. 20. 3). A great man—like a Hellenistic king—would admit his visitors in groups, according to class, a practice started by the aristocratic tribune C. *Sempronius Gracchus, then copied by his imitator

M. *Livius Drusus (2); and his standing to some extent depended on the number and class of those attending him. Under the early empire lower-class clients degenerated into a parasitical claque, and the invitation to a meal or gift of money or food that they had traditionally received was generally converted to a standard payment of 25 asses, with special gifts at the *Saturnalia, and perhaps occasional invitations to dinner. Members of the upper classes continued to be assiduous in *salutatio*, and according to the satirists would also take their 25 asses. See PATRONAGE (NON-LITERARY); PATRONUS.

Dar.–Sag. 'Salutatio'; L. Friedländer, *Roman Life and Manners under the Early Empire* 4 (1928), 77 ff. E. B.

Salvianus, of Marseilles (*Massalia), was born *c.* AD 400 somewhere in the Rhineland; he had relatives at Cologne and in 418 witnessed the Frankish attack (see FRANKS) upon Trier (*Augusta Treverorum). In 425, with his wife Palladia's consent, he joined Honoratus' monastery at Lérins and *c.*439 became presbyter at Marseilles until his death (after 470). The German invaders he interpreted in his best-known work, *De Gubernatione Dei*, as an instrument of divine wrath against the decadent Roman empire, contrasting Christian laxity with the high morality of the barbarians who erred 'in good faith'. Faced by misery and pauperism he urged that all estates be bequeathed for the poor and denounced inherited wealth. Extant, apart from the eight books *De Gubernatione Dei*, are nine letters and a tract '*ad Ecclesiam*' against avarice.

Ed. F. Pauly (*CSEL* 8). P. Courcelle, *Histoire littéraire des grandes invasions germaniques* (1948), 119 ff.; *ODCC*[2] 948. J. F. Ma.

Salvidienus Rufus, Quintus Salvius (*RE* 4; the precise form of his name is uncertain), Roman commander, remarkable for his rapid advance and his abrupt fall. Of humble origin, perhaps from the country of the Vestini, he was one of Octavian's associates in 44 BC (see AUGUSTUS) and swiftly became one of his principal generals. In 42 he was worsted by Sextus *Pompeius in a naval battle off Rhegium and in 41 sent to Spain with six legions, but the Antonian generals (see ANTONIUS (2), M.) blocked his way in North Italy. He was presently recalled for the impending war of *Perusia, in which he played a prominent part. In 40 he was appointed governor of Gaul and designated consul, though still an *eques* (see EQUITES). After the Pact of *Brundisium, Octavian summoned him to Rome and denounced him in the senate: he had been plotting with Antony earlier in the year, as Antony had now admitted—or so Octavian claimed. The senate declared Salvidienus a public enemy, and he either committed suicide or was executed.

R. Syme, *Rom. Rev.*, see index; T. P. Wiseman, *CQ* 1964, 130; D. R. Shackleton Bailey, *Two Studies in Roman Nomenclature* (1976), 64. C. B. R. P.

Samaria was from the early *Seleucid period the name of an administrative district in Palestine, alongside *Judaea and, later, *Galilee, and lying between the two. The inhabitants were mainly of mixed race, the product of intermarriage between the Israelites and their neighbours. Their religion was essentially Jewish, but they temporarily accepted from *Antiochus (4) IV a pagan cult on their sacred mountain, Gerizim, and they became increasingly detached from Jewry. The city of Samaria was resettled by *Alexander (3) the Great with Macedonian colonists, while nearby Shechem remained in the hands of native Samaritans. John Hyrcanus destroyed Samaria (see HASMONEANS); A. *Gabinius (2) detached it again from Jewish territory (see JEWS); and *Herod (1) rebuilt it as a major city, Sebaste. His loyal Sebastene cohorts played an important role in the control of the Jews until the first Revolt.   T. R.

Samian Ware See POTTERY, ROMAN.

Samnium, an Oscan-speaking district in the central southern *Apennines. A warlike people, the Samnites were divided into four tribal states (Caraceni, Caudini, Hirpini, Pentri), each administered by a *meddix, but were linked together in a confederation which had a federal diet and possibly an assembly. A generalissimo led the confederation in wartime. (*Frentani and other *Sabelli, although ethnic Samnites, were not members of it.) After their treaty with Rome (354 BC) the *Liris evidently became their boundary with *Latium. Shortly thereafter their neighbours sought Roman protection. By granting it the Romans precipitated the Samnite Wars. The First (343–341), often unconvincingly reckoned apocryphal, resulted in Roman control of northern *Campania; the Second (327–321, 316–304), despite the Samnite success at the *Caudine Forks, prevented Samnite control of *Apulia, *Lucania, and southern Campania; the Third (298–290) involved and decided the destiny of all peninsular Italy. Samnium, still unbowed, then supported *Pyrrhus, but the Romans defeated him and split Samnium apart with Latin colonies at *Beneventum (268 BC) and *Aesernia (263). Samnium helped *Hannibal and lost both population and territory when the Second *Punic War was over. Samnites also fought implacably in the *Social War (3) (Aesernia was for a time headquarters of the rebels), and in the Civil War, against *Sulla. Romanization was slow, although wealth was channelled into the *oppidum at Monte Vairano and into rural sanctuaries such as that at *Pietrabbondante. Under *Augustus, however, municipalization of the region (see MUNICIPIUM) greatly advanced (e.g. *Saepinum), and from the late 1st cent. AD, men of Samnite stock were increasingly to be found in the *senate. Even so, large parts of Samnium remained very rural.

> E. T. Salmon, *Samnium and the Samnites* (1967); A. La Regina and others, *Sannio: Pentri e Frentani dal VI al I sec. a.c.* (1980), and *Sannio* (1984), esp. A. La Regina, 'Aspetti istituzionali nel mondo sannitico', 17 ff.; J. R. Patterson, *PBSR* 1987, 115 ff., and *Samnites, Ligurians and Romans* (1988).   E. T. S.; T. W. P.

Samos, an important *polis on the large Aegean island of the same name (476 sq. km.), only 1.8 km. from Asia Minor. Though western Samos is dominated by Mt. Kerkis (1, 433 m.; ancient Cerceteus) and the centre by Mt. Karvounis (1, 153 m.)—whose ancient name (Ampelus) implies viticulture—Samos has arable slopes and coastal plains, and was considered fertile. Wheat was grown in the *peraea (mainland territory) in Asia Minor, possibly by a serf population. Exports included olive oil and Samian Earth (a clay used in fulling); Samian transport *amphorae are a distinct type.

The city was in the south-eastern lowlands, at modern Pythagorio (or Tigani); 8 km. to the west along a sacred road, at the site of a bronze age cult, lay the *Heraion or sanctuary of Hera, the city's patron goddess. Both sites have Mycenaean remains. Samos was reputedly Carian (see CARIA) before *Ionians arrived, perhaps in the 10th cent.; classical Samians spoke a local version of Ionic Greek. The first Hera temple (early 8th cent.) was one of the earliest stone temples in Greece, receiving lavish dedications as an emerging élite developed overseas contacts. Samians colonized *Cilicia, the *Propontis, and the Black (*Euxine) Sea, helped found *Cyrene, and built a temple at *Naucratis (see COLONIZATION, GREEK).

Detailed history is lacking before the tyranny of *Polycrates (1) (c.550–522). His warships dominated nearby islands and towns, and his court was frequented by artists and poets (including *Ibycus and *Anacreon). Refugees from the tyranny included the philosopher *Pythagoras (1), who settled in Italy; others founded Dicaearchia (*Puteoli). Polycrates probably commissioned the three constructions mentioned by *Herodotus (1) (3. 60), all of them still extant: a long harbour mole, the resplendent fortification walls, and a tunnel over 1 km. long, driven through the acropolis by Eupalinus of Megara to bring piped water into the city (see AQUEDUCTS). A new Hera temple begun earlier by the artist Rhoecus had proved unstable: its replacement, by *Theodorus (1), probably dates to Polycrates' reign (like the colossal *kouros recently found there). Though never finished, it was the largest Greek temple known to Herodotus.

The Persians killed Polycrates and installed tyrants friendly to themselves. Many Samian captains deserted the Ionians at Lade. Prominent in the *Delian League, Samos contributed ships until its revolt in 440, which took *Pericles (1) eight months to suppress. Cleruchs (see CLERUCHY) were installed, and the ruling élite remained pro-Athenian in the *Peloponnesian War. For a time Samians shared Athens' radical democracy: in 405 they even received Athenian citizenship. After the war *Lysander installed a decarchy and received divine honours. After the fall of his regime Samos was generally pro-Athenian until *Mausolus renewed Persian domination. In 365 the Athenians again cleruchized the island, allegedly expelling the entire population. Liberated by *Alexander (3) the Great's 'Exiles' Decree' (see EXILE, Greek), Samos was disputed between the Successors (see DIADOCHI); the historian *Duris became tyrant of his own city. From 281 it was a Ptolemaic base; after being attacked by *Philip (3) V it came under Rhodian hegemony (see RHODES), confirmed by Rome in 188.

In the period after Alexander, power once more lay with a landed élite. They redesigned the town and built fine houses; the Heraion saw its first major additions since Polycrates. Samos suffered occasional wheat shortages, but continued to exploit the *peraia as well as Corsiae (the nearby Phoúrnoi islets), *Icaros (1), and *Amorgos. Exports to *Alexandria (1), documented on papyri, were perhaps aimed at Greeks: Samian émigrés there were numerous and included intellectuals such as *Aristarchus (1), *Asclepiades (2), and *Conon (2) the mathematician.

In 129 Samos became part of the Roman province of Asia (see ASIA, ROMAN PROVINCE); élite contacts with Rome were cultivated. The Heraion suffered at *Verres' hands; his prosecutor *Cicero was later honoured in Samos. Octavian turned down a request for tribute remission, but as *Augustus he declared Samos free (see FREE CITIES). Though *Vespasian reduced the island's privileges, its prosperity increased in Roman times, to judge by the new public buildings (including a bath complex, gymnasium, and basilicas) and the expansion of rural settlement into the west.

> G. Shipley, *A History of Samos 800–188 BC* (1987); excavation reports in *AΔ* and in the *Samos* volumes of the Deutsches Archäologisches Institut; J. P. Barron, *The Silver Coins of Samos* (1966); *RE* 1 A 2 (1920), 2161–2218; [British Admiralty] Naval Intelligence Division, *Greece* 3 (1945), 532–46. On the 4th.-cent. cleruchy see C. Habicht and K. Hallof, *MDAI(A)* forthcoming (new epigraphic evidence).   D. G. J. S.

Samosata (mod. Samsât), a fortified city on the right bank of the *Euphrates; the residence of the kings of *Commagene. Like *Zeugma, it guarded an important crossing of the river on one of the main caravan routes from east to west, and it was consequently of considerable strategic and commercial importance.

Samothrace

Its formidable defences twice withstood a Roman siege, but in AD 72, when the client-kingdom of Commagene was annexed, it was forced to surrender, and it was then garrisoned by a Roman legion. The city was captured by *Sapor I (256) and had a chequered history during the frontier wars against the *Sasanid Persians until in 637 it was finally captured by the Arabs. The partly excavated remains include the walls mentioned by *Lucian (*Hist. conscr.* 24), the city's most famous son.

PECS 803 f.; F. Millar, *The Roman Near East 31 B.C.–A.D. 337* (1993), index.   M. S. D.; E. W. G.; A. J. S. S.

Samothrace, a mountainous island in the northern Aegean. Inhabited from Neolithic times, it was settled *c.*700 BC by Greeks who intermingled with the local Thracian population. A member of both Athenian maritime alliances, Samothrace gained its fame as a cult centre which was heavily patronized by the Macedonian royal house and their successors. Control of the island passed among several Hellenistic dynasts, and under the Romans it became a *free city. The popular cult of twin gods, the *Cabiri, was centred in a major sanctuary near the northern coast. The sanctuary was open to all visitors, and initiates sought protection, moral improvement, and the promise of immortality. During the Hellenistic era the sanctuary was lavishly endowed by royal patrons, who constructed several grand buildings. The site has been well excavated since the 1930s by the American archaeologists, K. and P. Lehmann and J. McCredie, who have published extensive reports.

Samothrace: Excavations Conducted by the Institute of Fine Arts, New York University (1958–90, in progress); K. Lehmann, *Samothrace: A Guide to the Excavations and the Museum*[5] (1983); W. Burkert, in N. Marinatos and R. Hägg, *Greek Sanctuaries* (1993), 178 ff.   E. N. B.

Sanchuniathon is cited by *Philon (5) of Byblos as a pre-Trojan War authority for his *Phoenician History* (preserved in Eusebius). Sanchuniathon himself is impossible to date (*c.*700–500 BC?), but the name is known in Phoenician and Philon is apparently reporting genuine traditions, as is now confirmed in general terms by the Ugaritic texts (see UGARIT).

FGrH 790; H. W. Attridge and R. Oden, *Philō of Byblos: The Phoenician History* (1981); O. Eissfeldt, *Sanchunjaton von Berut und Ilumilku von Ugarit* (1952).   J. F. H.

sanctuaries, Greek Sanctuaries in the Greek world (see also TEMENOS) were areas set aside for religious purposes and separate from the normal secular world. The boundary (*peribolos*) might be an actual wall, but more often would be indicated by boundary markers. Traditional Greek and Roman worship was not restricted to initiates (except for the *mysteries at *Eleusis and elsewhere) who had to be accommodated in closeable buildings suitable for private ritual: the open space of the sanctuary was where the worshippers congregated to observe and participate in the ritual which was enacted on their behalf; for this, the main requisite was sufficient space.

The *festivals which were the occasion for such worship were normally annual, though sanctuaries would be accessible for individual acts of worship and the performance of vows. Within the sanctuary space were the buildings and other structures dedicated to the use of the god, especially the *altar at which the burnt *sacrifice, essential to the religious functioning of the sanctuary, was made. Other buildings responded to various religious needs, and are not always found. There is normally a *temple to house the image which was the god, which watched and so received the sacrifice. The temple was itself both an offering to

the god, and a store room for *votive offerings. The open area of the sanctuary round the *altar was the place where, at the god's festival, worshippers would witness the sacrifices. The meat from these was then divided amongst them, and normally consumed within the sanctuary: some sanctuaries had laws which stipulated that the meat had to be consumed within their boundaries. Most worshippers seem to have feasted al fresco, but certain sanctuaries contained special *dining rooms (*hestiatoria*) for at least a privileged section of the worshippers. Other religious functions accommodated include contests of song and dance, as well as athletic ones (see AGŌNES). Specialized structures (see THEATRE; ODEUM; STADIUM) eventually developed for these.

The size and arrangement of a sanctuary depended on the importance and nature of the cult. In large sanctuaries it is often possible to distinguish between an innermost sacred area round the altar as place of sacrifice and the temple as the abode of the god, and an outer area given over to human activity, the feasting and contests. As a result theatres and stadia are often on the periphery. In healing sanctuaries, such as the Asclepieion at *Epidaurus, or the sanctuary of *Amphiaraus at *Oropus, buildings where those seeking the god's cure might spend the night in the sanctuary (see INCUBATION) were normally adjacent to the temple itself. In some sanctuaries the distinction between the two areas is clearly marked: at Olympia a wall was eventually built round the innermost sanctuary, leaving outside gymnasia, stadium, and the course for the chariot races. Here and at Epidaurus a vaulted passage leads from the inner area into the stadium. In other sanctuaries the distinction is not so clear cut. At the sanctuary of *Poseidon at *Isthmia the original running track has been found very close to the temple; later it was removed to a nearby valley which perhaps afforded a better locality for the spectators.

Though undoubtedly there were shrines and religious places in the Greek settlements of the *Mycenaean civilization, the sanctuaries of the Classical period develop at the earliest in the 8th cent. BC, as far as can be judged from the archaeological evidence. Reasons for the choice of a sanctuary site are quite unclear. Some are based on places of late bronze age occupation, though it is not known whether this in any way denotes continuity of cult or rather a sense of awe inspired by the visible remains of an earlier age. Natural features such as *springs may be the attraction; *water is an important element in the performance of cult. A spring in the sanctuary, or its vicinity, was often embellished with a fountain house. Water may have to be provided artificially, as at *Perachora, or by the construction of wells. It was needed for ritual *purification, but also, when feasting buildings were provided, for more normal cleaning purposes. Sometimes the reason for the location of a sanctuary may be nothing more than an awareness of some unusual character of a place. Shrines in Minoan *Crete, in the palaces and elsewhere, were often aligned with 'peak sanctuaries' on a prominent visible mountain top; the idea that similar alignments may explain classical sanctuaries has been promoted, but is unconvincing (see RELIGION, MINOAN AND MYCENAEAN). Some sanctuaries are developed for particular communities, and each *polis would possess one of major significance to it, dedicated to its protecting deity. Others belong to less important gods, or serve only limited sections of the community, classes in society, or villages outside the urban centre of the state. Within the *polis*-context, the location of major extra-urban sanctuaries (see HERAION) could serve to demarcate a community's territory in the face of competing claims by neighbours (as argued by de Polignac and others). Other sanctuaries develop to serve more than one community, up to the 'international' sanctuary such as *Delphi or *Olympia which attract support and worshippers from all over Greece.

The earliest stages of the sanctuaries, where known, are often small and simple. Increasing popularity, larger numbers of worshippers, and the acquisition of greater wealth lead to discernible expansion. Control over the sanctuary, and responsibility for its development, rests extensively with the community at large (see POLIS), through its political bodies, supervising finance, approving and supporting building programmes, and passing all necessary legislation for the conduct of its affairs. Immediate direction is often vested in groups of officials (who have a religious function but are not *priests; see HIEROMNĒMONES): in democratic Athens, and elsewhere, the accounts were scrutinized and published as inscriptions. Smaller sanctuaries were of lower, or minimal, public concern. Many major sanctuaries were not limited to single cults. The acropolis of Athens within the surrounding walls and the gateway, the *Propylaea, was a sacred area, the pivot of which was the altar to *Athena. *Pausanias (3) lists a whole succession of cult-places within the sacred area, including, for example, a precinct of Brauronian Artemis (see ARTEMIS, and cf. BRAURON). See ATHENS, TOPOGRAPHY. Asclepius at Epidaurus shared his sanctuary with his father, Apollo (probably the original owner), as well as Hera.

The sanctuary would contain 'sacred property'. This might include the utensils and other paraphernalia of sacrifice and feasting, recorded on inscriptions. These both belonged to the god and were used by the god, or his worshippers. They include, at times, valuable *plate, in gold or silver, which in itself constitutes a special offering, but is still essentially a possession to be used. Other offerings are often described as votives, strictly gifts made in response to the successful outcome of a vow, but even with these there may be a related purpose. A statue may well constitute an offering (see STATUES (CULT OF)), but is also a commemoration, of service by priests or priestesses (especially those whose office was temporary), of successful achievement whether by the community in war or the individual in athletic contest. In 'international' sanctuaries, individual cities might dedicate 'thesauroi'; the term means treasury, but this is a misleading translation, since they are not mere storehouses but offerings in their own right, often dedicated to the god to commemorate a victory in war. Some sanctuaries are oracular and thus needed to provide for the appropriate consultation process; these might require modification of the temple plan (as at Delphi) with perhaps, in addition, special office-type buildings, as at *Didyma.

The sanctuaries of the Roman period represent an essential continuation of these concepts. An important right, confirmed by the Roman authorities in a limited number of cases, is that of asylum (see ASYLIA), though strictly all sanctuaries, being sacred places, offered potential refuge. In the early 5th cent. BC the regent *Pausanias (1), condemned by his fellow Spartiates, sought refuge in the sanctuary of Athena Chalcioecus, where he could not be put to death, or even allowed to die when he was starved out. In form, Roman sanctuaries are often more regularly planned, a characteristic inherited from Hellenistic architectural concepts, typified by the sanctuary of Artemis at *Magnesia ad Maeandrum in its redeveloped, 2nd-cent. BC form. Such sanctuaries are normally a strict rectangle in plan, surrounded by porticos round the boundaries, and with formal gateway buildings which can be closed. The temple, with its altar directly in front, is placed within the resulting courtyard, and often situated to the back of it. The Severan marble plan (see FORMA URBIS) of the city of Rome shows several such sanctuaries for which other archaeological evidence is inadequate; but this form also characterizes the so-called imperial fora, such as those of Caesar, Augustus, and Trajan, which are essentially courtyard sanctuaries. See FORUM, various entries; ROME (TOPOGRAPHY). This concept, of the chief temple in its precinct, which continues over a road and frequently a barrier to form the civic *forum, is typical of towns in the western Roman provinces.

In Roman *Syria these precincts assume a complex form: large rectangles with formal entrances on all four sides, the principal 'Golden Gate' to the east and the whole structure embellished with towers. The formalism of such sanctuaries may owe something to local cult needs, and the political significance of the priests who control them, but the underlying concepts are general to the entire classical world. See ALTARS; BOOTY; DINING ROOMS; MARKETS AND FAIRS; PAINTING; PRIESTS; SCULPTURE; TEMPLUM; THOLOS.

B. Bergquist, *The Archaic Greek Temenos* (1967); R. A. Tomlinson *Greek Sanctuaries* (1976); F. de Polignac, *La Naissance de la cité grecque* (1984), Eng. trans. *Cults, Territory and the Origins of the Greek City-State* (1995); C. Morgan, *Athletes and Oracles* (1990); L. B. Zaidman and P. Schmitt Pantel, *Religion in the Ancient Greek City* (1992, Fr. orig. 1989), part II and app. I–II; N. Marinatos and R. Hägg (eds.), *Greek Sanctuaries* (1993); A. Schachter (ed.), *Le sanctuaire grec.* Entretiens Hardt 37 (1992); S. Alcock and R. Osborne (eds.), *Placing the Gods* (1994).   R. A. T.

sanctuaries, Italian See ALBANUS MONS; ARDEA; ARICIA; AVENTINE; FREGELLAE; GABII; LATINI; LAVINIUM; LOCRI EPIZEPHYRII; PIETTRABONDANTE; PYRGI; see also previous entry, and T. Cornell, *The Beginnings of Rome* (1995) 27, 108–12.

sanctuary (in medieval and modern sense) See ASYLIA.

Sandas (Σάνδας and variants), an indigenous god of *Tarsus, whose symbols (club, bow) and fire-ritual probably account for his Hellenization (i.e. his Greek form) as *Heracles. The cult recurs in *Lydia (where he was the consort of *Cybele), *Cappadocia, and other nearby regions.

Roscher, *Lex.* 'Sandas'; H. Goldmann, *Hesperia* suppl. 7 (1949) 164 ff.   F. R. W.

Sandracottus, the Greek form of the Sanskrit name Chandragupta, said to be of humble origin and founder of the *Mauryan empire. In c.324/21 BC, with the help of Chanakya, sometimes known as Kautilya, an experienced *brahmana* statesman to whom is ascribed a comprehensive book on political economy and statecraft, the *Arthashastra*, he overthrew the Nanda king of Magadha (part of the modern Bihar State). The power and wealth of the Nandas were such that his renown may have been a factor in the refusal of *Alexander (3) the Great's army to advance beyond the river Beas (Hyphasis). According to a Sanskrit drama of a later period, the *Mudrarakshasa*, a prince named Parvataka (who is perhaps *Porus) helped Chandragupta. By 305, before the encounter of *Seleucus (1) I with Chandragupta, the latter appears to have been already in possession of almost the whole of the Indo-Pakistan sub-continent north of the Vindhya mountains. The encounter possibly took place in *Gandhara, west of the Indus (although Seleucus is said to have crossed the river). Seleucus did not succeed in his designs and he ceded to Chandragupta the satrapies of Gandhara, Gedrosia, Paropamisadae, and at least eastern Arachosia. A matrimonial alliance is referred to, perhaps between the two royal families. Chandragupta made a present of 500 *elephants, and Seleucus sent a resident, *Megasthenes, to the Mauryan court. Chandragupta is also credited (although the evidence for this is slight), with conquests in south India up to Karnataka, where he is referred to in local inscriptions of the 12th cent. The Jaina tradition maintains that he adopted the Jaina religion, abdicated the throne, and migrated to the south with his *guru* Bhadrabahu, where he eventually died in the orthodox Jaina manner through slow starvation. His administration was an attempt at central control and careful supervision. He ruled his empire from Pataliputra (see PALIBOTHRA). Chandragupta is said to have reigned for about 24 years up to 300/297 BC.

K. A. Nilakantha Sastri (ed.), *The Age of the Nandas and Mauryas* (1952) and *A Comprehensive History of India* 2/1. (1957). A. K. N.; R. Th.

Sangarius (mod. Sakarya), important river of north-west *Asia Minor already known to *Hesiod and *Homer. Rising in *Phrygia near *Pessinus (Strabo 12. 3. 7; coins, Head, *Hist. Num.*[2] 748) on Mt. Adoreus (Livy 38. 18), it flowed in a winding course through Phrygia Epictetus (south of Bithynia) and *Bithynia to enter the Black (*Euxine) Sea west of the territory of Heraclea Pontica. The Bithynian section was navigable and rich in fish (Strabo and Livy, as above). Its valley provides a line of access from the coast to the plateau, but for part of its course its gorge is a barrier to movements west and east. E. W. G.

San Giovenale takes its name from the medieval castle on the plateau overlooking the river Vesca north of the Tolfa Hills, 25 km. east of *Tarquinii. The plateau was inhabited from the bronze age, represented by *Apennine-culture pottery associated with houses and a fortification wall of large blocks. An extensive iron-age village of oval huts dates mainly from the 8th to the late 6th cents., and an Etruscan settlement lasted until the beginning of the 5th. Tomb-types in the area range from *pozzi* to *Etruscan chamber tombs; a late (3rd-cent. BC) tomb was reused in Hadrianic times. Occupation at Luni, 6 km. west of San Giovenale, also extends from the bronze age to the middle ages: the Apennine levels produced five Mycenaean sherds.

The definitive report on the San Giovenale excavations by the Swedish Institute, Rome, appears in the fascicules of its *Skrifter/Acta*, 4th series, 26 (1967 onwards). D. Ridgway, *Erasmus* 1979, 491 ff., and *CR* 1983, 364 ff.; *Architettura etrusca nel Viterbese* (exhib. cat., Viterbo 1986). D. W. R. R.

sanitation

Greek Developed arrangements in Greek towns for sanitation are a relatively late phenomenon, coming in with the planned cities in the 4th cent. BC. Scenes of the *symposium on Greek vases depict the use of the chamber-pot, whose contents would be thrown out of the house, probably into open channels along the road surfaces. No recognizable system of drainage exists in Athens, other than the canalized stream which flows through the area of houses west of the Areopagus. The houses of *Olynthus provide evidence for bathrooms and tubs, with terracotta drainpipes leading the waste away from the house and along the streets. What appears to be a fixed latrine was found in house A vii 9; it had an extended spout passing through the wall of the house, to empty directly onto the street. A similar example has been found in the Xenon at *Nemea. The streets of *Pella have substantial covered sewers into which all waste from the adjacent houses drained. Such arrangements also existed at *Priene, in conjunction with a piped water-supply, though only four actual latrines were found in the houses. The fullest evidence comes from the houses at *Delos; by the later Hellenistic period houses generally have a recognizable built-in latrine, linked to covered drains running along the streets. The

latrines empty into narrow channels, and are flushed by water used to wash down the floors. *Antioch (1) had a sewage system, emptying into the river *Orontes (Polyb. 5. 58), while excavations at *Alexandria (1) have produced evidence for drainage systems in the streets. R. A. T.

Roman Despite Roman proficiency in hydraulic engineering, sanitation through the provision of a clean water-supply and the hygienic removal of human and other waste was a low priority. The role of impure *water and ordure in causing *disease was little understood, and sewage was abhorred rather because it was noisome and made 'taint' other substances.

Private water-supplies were usually obtained from wells, and also from cisterns in dry climates. Only the wealthy could afford to tap the public *aqueducts. Domestic sanitation was provided by the cesspit (which might be near the well). Multi-storey buildings (*insulae*) could be linked by gravity-fed pipes to a main cesspit. Night-soil was taken out to be spread on the fields. Chamber-pots, empty *amphorae, and the public gutters were also commonly used.

City aqueducts afforded a supply of drinkable water to street fountains. Covered sewers and drains were usually multi-purpose, combining sanitation with land- and rainfall-drainage, as in the *Cloaca Maxima (Great Drain) of Rome. Excess aqueduct water was used to flush these sewers. Open sewers and gutters ran down the centre or sides of streets. Bath-houses commonly contained latrines, using their water-supply. The latrines consisted of benches with holes over drains. Water for users' cleanliness was supplied in basins or channels. At Rome large urinal pots stood at street corners, the contents being used by the fullers (see TEXTILE PRODUCTION). When these were taxed by *Vespasian the pots were nicknamed after him.

The army understood the value of hygiene in maintaining military effectiveness. Some temporary camps had cesspits, permanent forts had a clean water-supply and latrines which flushed outside the defences.

GREEK D. M. Robinson, *Excavations at Olynthus* 8 (1938), 205; J. Chamonard, *Exploration archéologique de Délos* 8 (1922), 181–90; T. Wiegand and H. Schrader, *Priene* (1904), 294 f. (drainage, 74 f.).

ROMAN A. Trevor Hodge, *Roman Aqueducts and Water Supply* (1992); R. Jackson, *Doctors and Diseases in the Roman Empire* (1988); R. Neudecker, *Die Pracht der Latrine* (1994); A. Scobie, *Klio* (1986). A. S. E. C.

Sannyrion, Athenian comic poet, produced *Danae* after Eur. *Or.* (408 BC), to which fr. 8 refers. We have titles and a dozen citations. Fr. 1 ('we gods . . . you mortals . . .') shows that in *Laughter* at least one deity was a character.

Kassel–Austin, *PCG* 7. 585 ff. (*CAF* 1. 793 ff.). K. J. D.

Santorini See THERA.

Santra, Roman tragic poet and scholar (1st cent. BC), wrote lives of literary figures and a work *On the Antiquity of Words.*

G. Funaioli, *Gramm. Rom. Frag.* 384–9. Mazzacane, *Studi Noniani* 1982, 192–222. R. A. K.

Sapor (*Shabuhr*), name of kings of the Iranian *Sasanid dynasty, of which the most famous was Sapor I (reigned AD 240–72), son of *Artaxerxes (6) I (*Ardashir*) and co-regent with him 240/1 (?). He continued, with spectacular success, his father's policy of aggression against Rome, taking full advantage of the internal crisis in the Roman empire. After *Hatra and the Roman outposts in *Mesopotamia fell to the Sasanians in the late 230s and early 240s, *Gordian III started a counter-offensive, but was beaten and died in the battle of Misiche (244). The subsequent peace treaty between Sapor and Philip (see IULIUS PHILIPPUS, M.) forced the Romans to pay a great amount of ransom. A further attack by Sapor led to the occupation of *Armenia, the devastation of *Syria, and the first conquest of *Antioch (1) (252/3). The third campaign of the Sasanid 'King of Kings, King of Iran and Non-Iran' saw the capture of *Valerian (260) and Persian raids into Syria, Cilicia, and Cappadocia. It was left to *Septimius Odaenathus, dynast of *Palmyra, to play the major role in forcing Sapor to withdraw from Roman territory (262–6). In addition to his military achievements (listed in his great inscription at *Naqš-i Rustam, the *Res Gestae Divi Saporis*, and depicted in his famous rock-reliefs), Sapor was famed for his grandiose building operations (he used the labour of Roman captives) and for his relations with the religious leader Mani (see MANICHAEISM), who began his preaching in the Persian empire at the time of Sapor's investiture.

E. Kettenhofen, *Die römisch-persischen Kriege des 3. Jahrhunderts n. Chr.* (1982); M. H. Dodgeon and S. N. C. Lieu (eds.), *The Roman Eastern Frontier and the Persian Wars AD 226–363* (1991); S. N. C. Lieu, *Manichaeism in the Later Roman Empire*² (1992), 71 ff.   J. Wi.

Sappho, lyric poet. Born on *Lesbos in the second half of the 7th cent. BC, she was hailed in antiquity as 'the tenth Muse' (*Anth. Pal.* 9. 506), and her poetry was collected into nine books (arranged according to metre) in the canonical Alexandrian edition. Only one complete poem and some substantial fragments survive, culled from quotations in other writers or from papyrus finds.

Most of her poems were for solo performance, and many refer to love between women or girls. Other subjects include *hymns to deities and apparently personal concerns such as her brother's safety (fr. 5). Wedding songs, and snatches from a lament for *Adonis (fr. 140) are clearly for several singers. Fr. 44, describing the marriage of *Hector and *Andromache, is unusual in its narrative length and proximity to *epic.

Little about her life is certain: biographies (*POxy.* 1800, *Suda*, 'Sappho') are late and sometimes contradictory. She may have had some involvement in the aristocratic power struggles of Lesbos (fr. 71), leading to a period of exile in Sicily (*Marm. Par.* 36). She was probably married, though only a brother and (probably) a daughter, Cleis, figure in the poems. The story of her suicide for love of *Phaon is almost certainly fictional.

Her sexual inclinations have occasioned much speculation from antiquity to the present. From Attic comedy onwards she was credited with an implausible selection of male lovers. She is described as a lover of women only in post-Classical times, and in later European tradition was often regarded as heterosexual. See HOMOSEXUALITY.

Her own poetry remains the major source for the controversial question of how she related to the companions (fr. 160) who formed her audience. An important parallel is *Alcman's *partheneia* (maiden-songs) written for girls' choruses, in which the singers praise each other in erotic terms. Sappho's term for her companions is *parthenos* (girl). This, and the frequent references to partings and absence in her poems, suggest that most of her circle shared their lives for only a limited period before marriage. Homoeroticism was probably institutionalized at this stage of life, as it was elsewhere for young men. The group's preoccupations—love, beauty, poetry—are indicated by the divinities most often invoked in Sappho: *Aphrodite, the Graces (see CHARITES), and the *Muses.

But despite the likely educational and religious function of her group, Sappho herself emerges from the poems as far from the chaste headmistress figure constructed by 19th- and early 20th-cent. German philology. In fr. 1, the poet names herself in a prayer enlisting *Aphrodite's help in winning the love of an unresponsive girl. In fr. 16 the singer links her own love for the absent Anactoria with that of *Helen for *Paris, and fr. 31 famously charts the singer's despair as she watches a beloved girl sitting next to a man. Sappho's love poetry differs from that of male writers in the almost complete absence of a sharp distinction between lover and beloved.

Poems such as these reveal an accomplished poet who can achieve effects of great subtlety beneath an apparently simple surface; other, less complex poems (frs. 102, 114) seem influenced by folk-song. Like her contemporary *Alcaeus (1) she writes in a literary Aeolic dialect (see GREEK LANGUAGE, §4). Her work was admired in antiquity for its euphony (Dion. Hal. *Comp.* 23) and she was credited with musical invention; the Sapphic stanza was used by later poets such as *Horace. Notable imitations include *Catullus (1) 51, 61, and 62, while *Ovid's imaginary epistle from Sappho to Phaon (*Her.* 15) was the progenitor of many subsequent fictions about her.

TEXT E. M. Voigt, *Sappho et Alcaeus* (1971); E. Lobel and D. L. Page, *Poetarum Lesbiorum Fragmenta* (1955); D. Campbell, *Greek Lyric* 1 (1982) (with Eng. trans.).
CRITICISM D. L. Page, *Sappho and Alcaeus* (1955); A. P. Burnett, *Three Archaic Poets* (1983); A. Lardinois, in J. Bremmer, *From Sappho to de Sade* (1989); *RE* suppl. 11. 1222 ff; M. Williamson, *Sappho's Immortal Daughters* (1995).   M. Wil.

Sarapis (in Latin, *Serapis*), the Hellenized (Greek) form of Egypt. *wsir ḥp*, *Osiris-*Apis (Osorapis, Oser-), the hypostasis of Osiris and of Apis-bulls entombed at Saqqara (Plut. *De Is. et Os.* 29, 362cd). The cult was performed in the temple complex rebuilt by Nectanebo I and II (380–343 BC) above the 'great chambers', later called the *Memphis Serapeum. This rebuilding was probably in recognition of the crowds of pilgrims, including many foreigners, who sought healing by incubation, oracles, and *dream-interpretation. Recent excavation has shown that officials, priests, and poor alike were buried around the Serapeum way. The cult's importance was immediately grasped by the Macedonian occupiers left by *Alexander (3) the Great (*JEg. Arch.* 1974, 239). *Ptolemy (1) I made an extra loan of 50 talents for the burial of the Apis-bull (Diod. Sic. 1. 84. 8) and rebuilt the temple *dromos*.

To provide themselves with a divine Graeco-Egyptian patron, the early Ptolemies (I, II, and III are all cited in the sources: the archaeological evidence suggests all three had a hand) founded a Serapeum on the hill of Rhacotis at *Alexandria (1). The account of Ptolemy's dream and discovery of a statue of ?Pluto at 'Sinope' (Tac. *Hist.* 4. 83 f.; Plut. *De Is. et Os.* 28, 361f–62a, etc.) is a pious fraud based on Osorapis' regular mode of communication; there were quite different traditions, one of which made *Sesostris' responsible. The discordant interpretations by Hellenistic writers, equating Sarapis with Osiris, *Dionysus, Pluto (*Hades), *Zeus, *Asclepius, etc. (cf. Diod. Sic. 1. 25), suggest something of the creative fusion or melting of categories that Sarapis evoked in Alexandria and beyond: the cult-statue, whose attribution to the sculptor Bryaxis has been needlessly disputed, combined the traits of a benign Pluto with an Osirian deviation, the *kalathos* with ears of grain on his head. In *Memphis, Sarapis remained essentially Osorapis, lord of the underworld, demiurge 'from the grave' (Clem. Al. *Protr.* 4. 48. 6), providing oracles and cures through dreams. But in Alexandria, or Canopus (Strab. 17. 1. 17), he was free to be reinterpreted according to political, local, or individual requirement (Ael. Arist. 40. 18–20, comm. A. Höfler,

sarcophagi

1935). Certainly Alexandrian Sarapis was at first a god with close connections at court, only later acquiring a following among the Hellenized inhabitants of the *chora*.

At Memphis, and elsewhere in Egypt, Sarapis 'detained' individuals as *katochoi* in the Serapeum. The fullest subjective account of this status derives from the archive of Ptolemaeus (172–152 BC). This confinement had a religious grain, even if individuals' motives for surrendering their freedom of movement varied. Outside Egypt, analogous self-dedication in the temple is also found (*IG* 5. 2. 472; Apul. *Met*. 11. 19); but devotion to Sarapis generally took a different form, membership of a *thiasos* which met for worship and feasting (*sarapiastai*). It was the cult of Sarapis which often inspired the initial Hellenistic expansion of Egyptian cults into the Aegean (Apollonius on *Delos sang daily paeans in honour of his miracles: *IG* 11. 4. 1299. 48 f.; Powell. *Coll. Alex*. 68–71). A gradual decline of dedications (2nd cent. BC–2nd cent. AD) is associated with the growing predominance of Isis, who appears in the royal oath of *Ptolemy (1) III Euergetes (246–222 BC) as the secondary element of the pair, but in the Maroneia eulogy of *Isis (*c*.100 BC) as the active partner, selecting Sarapis as her consort. Plutarch, *De Is. et Os*. hardly mentions Sarapis, presumably because he was so closely aligned with Osiris and had no separate myth. The cult of Sarapis is also secondary in Italy, and much of the western empire, where he appears mainly as a transcendent god, as Zeus, *megas, dominus, conservator, invictus*. This emphasis descends directly from the Ptolemaic cult associating the ruling sovereign with Sarapis as guarantor of royal power, which was transferred to the Roman emperors after 31 BC (cf. *Vespasian as 'new Sarapis': *PFouad*. 8, and the repeated evocation of Sarapis in relation to *Hadrian in AD 130). The dominance of the theme in the west, and the revival of an old link with *Helios (2nd–3rd cents. AD), seems to coincide with an erosion of Sarapis' association with the underworld. This also gave him some value in imperial iconography, especially in the coinage of *Commodus and *Caracalla, though its significance has been exaggerated.

Origins: Fraser, *Ptol. Alex*. 1. 246–59; J. E. Stambaugh, *Sarapis under the early Ptolemies* (1972); J. D. Ray, in P. J. Ucko and others (eds.), *Man, Settlement and Urbanism* (1972), 699–704; C. Préaux, *Le Monde hellénistique* (1978) 649–55; R. Merkelbach, *Isis-regina, Zeus Sarapis* (1996). Ptolemaeus archive: D. J. Thompson, *Memphis under the Ptolemies* (1988), 212–65. Iconography: W. Hornbostel, *Sarapis* (1973); G. J. F. Kater-Sibbes, *Preliminary Catalogue of Sarapis Monuments* (1973) (bare catalogue); *LIMC* 7.1 (1994), 666–92. For Sarapis outside Egypt, see EGYPTIAN DEITIES.   R. L. G.

sarcophagi A sarcophagus is a coffin for inhumation which in ancient times was often richly decorated. In Minoan Crete and Mycenaean Greece (see MINOAN and MYCENAEAN CIVILIZATION) two standard shapes of terracotta coffin—the bath-tub and the chest on four legs with a gable roof—were in use especially from the 14th to the 12th cents. BC, and some, including the famous Haghia Triada sarcophagus, were richly painted. In the late Archaic period sarcophagi of painted clay and rectangular or trapezoidal form were made at or near *Clazomenae in western Asia Minor. Sculptured stone sarcophagi appear first in the 5th cent. BC: the finest anthropoid and casket sarcophagi with sculptured reliefs were made by Greek craftsmen for the kings of *Sidon from the 5th cent. to about 300 BC; anthropoid sarcophagi are also known from other sites on the Mediterranean and Black (*Euxine) Sea coasts. A distinctive type of sarcophagus with ogival roof was made in *Lycia. Some Hellenistic wooden sarcophagi with painted decoration have survived in southern Ukraine.

The *Etruscans used sculptured sarcophagi of clay and stone from the 6th cent. BC; the two commonest forms are the casket with gabled lid and the type with a reclining effigy of the dead. A few families of republican Rome buried their dead in sarcophagi: that of L. *Cornelius Scipio Barbatus (consul 298 BC) imitates the form of a contemporary altar. The prevailing rite of cremation in Rome gave way to inhumation in the early 2nd cent. AD, and the rich series of Roman sculptured marble sarcophagi begins about the time of Trajan. These were made all over the Roman world; two of the best-known centres were in Athens and *Docimium (Phrygia), where large sarcophagi were made with figures set between columns. At Rome, especially in the 3rd cent. AD, roughly cut chests were imported from the Greek island quarries of *Thasos and Proconnesus (see PROPONTIS) to be decorated to the taste of local clients. In some areas with no local supply of stone decorated lead coffins were made, notably in Syria-Palestine and in Britain, where they were often set inside plain stone chests.

See DEAD, DISPOSAL OF; ART, FUNERARY, ROMAN.

R. M. Cook, *Clazomenian Sarcophagi* (1981); V. von Graeve, *Der Alexander-Sarkophag und seine Werkstatt* (1970); P. Demargne, *Fouilles de Xanthos, 5. Tombes maisons, tombes rupestres et Sarcophages* (1974); G. Koch, *Sarkophage der römischen Kaiserzeit* (1993). C. Robert and others, *Die antiken Sarkophagreliefs* (1890–).   D. E. S.; S. E. C. W.

Sardinia, (Σαρδώ), a large central Mediterranean island, with a mountainous interior, but with rich deposits of *iron, copper, *lead, and *silver. From the early 2nd millennium BC, there was a relatively advanced civilization, based around massive stone-built towers called *nuraghi*, some 8000 of which are known. There were close contacts with Cypriots (see CYPRUS) in the later 2nd millennium (who were perhaps searching for iron); metalworking in particular flourished. *Phoenicians settled there from the 9th cent. BC or before, although no Greek colonies are known; and the Carthaginians (see CARTHAGE) annexed the island *c*.500 BC. Rome took Sardinia in 238 BC and in 227 organized it as a province with *Corsica (which in imperial times became separate). The Romans despised the Sardinians (e.g. Festus 428 Lindsay), and the island was treated as conquered land, with no free city in republican times. There were constant revolts, ceasing only in 114 BC, although *brigandage continued into the empire (Tac. *Ann*. 2. 85). But cities such as Karalis (*Cagliari*), Turris Libisonis (*Porto Torres*), Olbia, Nora, and Tharros flourished, the mineral wealth of the island was extensively exploited, and it became an important granary for Rome (e.g. Strabo 5. 2. 7). Romanization was however, uneven, especially in the mountains, and many *nuraghi* continued to be frequented. Eventually it fell successively to *Vandals, *Goths, Byzantine emperors, and Saracens. See also SEMPRONIUS GRACCHUS, TI.

Ancient writers seldom mention Sardinia. The important references are: Strabo 5. 223 f.; Plin. *HN* 3. 83 f.; Paus. 10. 17. 2 f.; Diod. Sic. 4. 29 f., 5. 15; Justin, bks. 18 and 19; Cic. *Scaur*. Livy, bks. 21–30. Modern literature includes: P. Meloni, *La Sardegna romana* (1975); G. Lilliu, *La civiltà nuragica* (1982); M. S. Balmuth and R. J. Rowland, Jr. (eds.), *Studies in Sardinian Archaeology* 1 (1984); M. S. Balmuth (ed.), *Studies in Sardinian Archaeology* 2 (1986); F. Barecco, *La civiltà fenicio-punica in Sardegna* (1986); S. Moscati (ed.), *The Phoenicians* (1988); R. J. Rowlands, Jr., *ANRW* 2. 2. 1 (1988), 740–875; G. S. Webster, *A Prehistory of Sardinia* (1996); R. J. A. Wilson, *CAH* 10² (1996), ch. 13b.

E. T. S.; T. W. P.

Sardis, the chief city of *Lydia, lying under a fortified, precipitous hill in the Hermus valley, near the junction of roads from

*Ephesus, *Smyrna, *Pergamum, and inner Anatolia. As the capital of the Lydian kingdom, especially under *Croesus, and later as the headquarters of the principal Persian satrapy (see PERSIA; SATRAP), it was the political centre of the Lydian dynasty and of *Achaemenid Asia Minor. Thus the town of Sardis was captured and burned by Ionians in 498 BC, and *Xerxes mustered his troops there before he crossed the Hellespont. After *Alexander (3) the Great, it was controlled first by *Antigonus (1), and then, from 282, by the Seleucid kingdom. Its geopolitical importance and the Achaemenid heritage led the *Seleucids to make Sardis one of the 'royal capitals' of their realm.

The archaeological record from the American excavations has shown the impact of Greek (and other) material cultures from the Archaic period, long before the conquest of Anatolia by Alexander. But Lydian was still used for public documents in the 4th cent. BC, as were Lydian 'laws' (Arrian, *Anab.* 1. 17. 3) (see ANATOLIAN LANGUAGES; LYDIAN LANGUAGE).

It was during Seleucid rule in the 3rd cent. that Sardis became formally Hellenized in acquiring the status and socio-political institutions of a Greek *polis*, as recent publication of a series of public Greek inscriptions, documenting the relations of Sardis with *Antiochus (3) III (from 213), attests; *Zeuxis (4) features prominently. This is after Antiochus' siege and capture of Sardis (Polyb. 7. 15–17), from the rebel *Achaeus (3). The excavations have established that the new, huge, temple of *Artemis dates to the early 3rd cent., i.e. in the period of Seleucid rule, and the Greek theatre is similarly dated. The excavations also revealed that the town was rebuilt on the so-called Hippodamian scheme of Greek city planning (see HIPPODAMUS), after the destruction caused by Antiochus III's siege of Sardis. The gymnasium, theatre, and hippodrome predate this change. It seems very likely, especially in view of the Seleucids' choice of Sardis as a capital, and the evidence of their financial support for Sardis, that it was under Seleucid influence that Sardis became a Greek *polis*, as one of their 'royal capitals.'

After the Peace of Apamea (188 BC; see ANTIOCHUS (3); SELEUCIDS), Sardis came under the control of the Attalids (see EUMENES (2) II). In 133 it passed to the Romans, who made it the capital of a *conventus* in the province of Asia (see ASIA, ROMAN PROVINCE). It later became the capital of the new province of Lydia created by Diocletian, and therefore also a metropolitan bishopric; as a centre of administration the city seems to have flourished until the Persian attacks of the early 7th cent.

G. M. A. Hanfmann (assisted by W. E. Mierse), *Sardis from Prehistoric to Roman Times* (1983); P. Gauthier, *Nouvelles inscriptions de Sardes 2* (1989); S. M. Sherwin-White and A. Kuhrt, *From Samarkhand to Sardis: A New Approach to the Seleucid Empire* (1993), 180 f.; S. Mitchell, *Arch. Rep.* 1989/90, 95–7; C. Foss, *Byzantine and Turkish Sardis* (1976).
W. M. C.; J. M. C.; S. S.-W.; C. M. R.

Sarepta, *Phoenician city on the coast of Lebanon, 16 km. (10 mi.) south of *Sidon (mod. Sarafand). An important industrial centre revealed by archaeological excavations, it belonged to Sidon or *Tyre in turn throughout its history and had a famous sanctuary of Asclepius/Eshmun.

DCPP, 'Sarepta'; J. B. Pritchard, BMB 1971, 39 ff., and *Sarepta* (1978).
J.-F. S.

Sarmatae (Σαρμάται, Σαυρομάται), nomadic tribe of Iranian origin, closely related to the Scythians (see SCYTHIA), and speaking a similar *Indo-European language, but showing some points of difference in material culture. Their women had a freer position, and, in the days of *Herodotus (1) at least, hunted and fought alongside the men (4. 116–17). Their fighters were all mounted, but while the rank and file were archers, the chieftains and their retainers wore armour and used heavy lances. Until c.250 BC the Sarmatae dwelt east of the river *Tanais. During the next 300 years they moved slowly westwards, displacing the Scythians. Of their two main branches, the Roxolani advanced to the Danube estuary, the *Iazyges crossed the Carpathians and occupied the plain between the middle Danube and the Theiss. The Roxolani, checked by the generals of Augustus (Florus, *Epit.* 2. 28) and Nero (ILS 986), became clients of Rome; and the Iazyges entered into similar relations, serving as a buffer between the Dacians and the province of *Pannonia. In the 2nd and 3rd cents. the Sarmatae were again set moving by the pressure of German tribes. The Iazyges allied with the *Marcomanni against M. *Aurelius, and the Roxolani shared the Gothic raids into *Moesia. Eventually large numbers of them were settled within Roman territory by *Constantine I; the rest were partly absorbed by their German neighbours, partly driven back into the Caucasus.

T. Sulimirski, *The Sarmatians* (1970).
M. C.; J. J. W.

Sarpedon, in *Homer's *Iliad* the son of *Zeus and Laodamia, the daughter of *Bellerophon; he was commander of the Lycian contingent of *Priam's allies (2. 876; see LYCIA). He is one of the strongest warriors on the Trojan side and takes a prominent part in the fighting, killing *Heracles' son *Tlepolemus (5. 628–62), leading an assaulting group of the allies on to the Greek wall (12. 101 ff.), and making the first breach (290 ff.). The story of his death at the hands of *Patroclus is narrated in detail (16. 419–683): Zeus, knowing that he is fated to die, wishes to save his beloved son, but, rebuked by *Hera, allows his death and marks it by causing bloody rain to fall. There is a great fight over Sarpedon's corpse, until *Apollo rescues it on Zeus' instructions; it is then carried back home to Lycia by Sleep and Death (*Hypnos and *Thanatos; subject of a famous late-Archaic Attic vase by Euphronius: New York, MMA 1972. 11. 10) and given honourable burial.

Post-Homeric accounts make Sarpedon one of the sons of Zeus and *Europa, explaining the chronological discrepancy by supposing that Zeus allowed him to live for three generations (Apollod. 3. 1. 2), or by making the Cretan Sarpedon, driven out from Crete to southern Asia Minor by his brother *Minos, grandfather of the Iliadic hero (Diod. Sic. 5. 79. 3). Ancient critics had already noticed that the Cretan connection was secondary (schol. *Il.* 6. 199, which makes the difference of time six generations). There was a *hero-cult of Sarpedon in Lycia of great antiquity (his hero-shrine is mentioned, for instance, by schol. *Il.* 16. 673, and a Sarpedonium is attested at 1st-cent. BC *Xanthus), with which the Homeric story of his burial is presumably to be connected.

LIMC 7.1 (1994), 696–700.
J. R. M.

Sasanids, kings of Iran AD 224–651. The dynasty derived its name from Sasan, the supposed grandfather of *Artaxerxes (6) I in later Arab-Persian tradition. Though very often labelled heirs to the *Achaemenids, they actually owed much more to the Parthians (see PARTHIA). Their empire at its greatest extent stretched from Syria to India and from Iberia to the *Persian Gulf. The Sasanids constantly sought to alter the military *status quo* in the Mesopotamian, Armenian, and Syrian areas; and the forts of the *Euphrates *limes* were fortified against attacks from them. Major campaigns were undertaken against them by various Roman emperors. *Valerian was defeated and captured by *Sapor I, *Diocletian and *Galerius defeated Narses in 297, *Jovian had to make large concessions to Sapor II after the death of *Julian in Mesopotamia (363), Kavadh was defeated by *Belisarius; Khosroes II conquered Asia Minor, Palestine, and Egypt, and even threatened *Constantinople, but was driven back by Heraclius. On their north-eastern boundary the Sasanids were menaced by the Hephthalites ('White Huns') and Turks. Their empire came to an end when the *Arabs conquered Mesopotamia and Iran.

Though Zoroastrianism (see ZOROASTER) was the most important cult in Sasanid Iran, and although most kings tried to present themselves as devout Mazda-worshippers and a priestly hierarchy developed in the course of time, religious minorities like the Christians, the Manichaeans (see MANICHAEISM), and the *Jews were allowed to practise their faith. Persecutions of these groups were not so much a sign of religious intolerance by the kings, but the result of specific foreign and domestic crises. A characteristic of Sasanid ideology was the development of the idea of 'Iran' as a concept of 'national' political and cultural identity.

SOURCES Inscriptions: M. Back, *Die sassanidischen Staatsinschriften* (1978). Reliefs: *Iranische Denkmäler; reliefs and other archaeological remains (bullae, seals, palaces, fire-temples e.a.)*: D. Huff, *Enc. Ir.* 2 (1987), 302 ff. Coins: R. Göbl, *Sasanian Numismatics* (1971); M. Alram, *Nomina Propria in Nummis* (1986), 186 ff. Classical texts: Cassius Dio, Herodian, Ammianus Marc., Procopius, Agathias. 'Oriental' texts: Armenian: Agathangelus, Faustus Byz. Christian: Chronicles (of Arbela, Se'ert) and Acts of Martyrs (S. Brock, *Syriac Perspectives on Late Antiquity* (1984)). Manichaean: W. Sundermann, *Altorientalische Forschungen* 1986/7. Middle-Persian: M. Boyce, *Handbuch der Orientalistik* 1. 4. 2. 1 (1968), 31 ff. New Persian and Arabic: E. Yarshater, *Cambridge History of Iran* 3. 1 (1983), 359 ff.

MODERN WORKS A. Christensen, *L'Iran sous les Sassanides*[2] (1944); P. Gignoux, in *Prolegomena to the Sources on the History of Pre-Islamic Central Asia* (1979), 137 ff.; K. Schippmann, *Grundzüge der Geschichte des sasanidischen Reiches* (1990); *Cambridge History of Iran* 3. 1–2 (1983); R. Gyselen, *La Géographie administrative de l'empire sassanide* (1989). See *Enc. Ir.* for articles on individual kings, places, and subjects.   J. Wi.

Saserna, name of the father and son whose lost work (early 1st cent. BC) on agriculture *Varro criticized for irrelevance. Saserna may be a non-Latin *nomen* (cf. the *Etruscan *Perperna (1)) or a *cognomen*, as with the Hostilii Sasernae, Caesarian senators and possible kinsmen (cf. NAMES, PERSONAL, ROMAN).

RE 8 (1913), 2512–13, 'Hostilius' (22 ff.); E. Rawson, *Intellectual Life in the Late Roman Republic* (1985), esp. 136.   A. J. S. S.

Sassanids See SASANIDS.

satire (*satura*) was first classified as a literary form in Rome. 'Satire, at any rate, is all our own,' boasted *Quintilian (10. 1. 93) of the genre that depicted Rome in the least flattering light. Originally simply a hotch-potch (in verse, or in prose and verse mixed), satire soon acquired its specific character as a humorous or malicious exposé of hypocrisy and pretension; however, it continued to be a hold-all for mismatched subjects, written in an uneven style and overlapping with other genres. The author himself figured prominently in a variety of shifting roles: civic watchdog, sneering cynic, mocking or indignant observer, and social outcast.

Name   *Satura* is the feminine of *satur*, 'full', and was transferred to literary miscellanies from *lanx satura*, a dish crammed with first fruits, or from *satura*, a mixed stuffing or sausage. *Juvenal, for example, claims (1. 86) to be filling his writing tablets with a *farrago* (mixed mash) of urban vice. Mixture and variety remained constant features of satire: many satirical techniques—*parody,

exaggeration, deflation, caricature—depend on incongruous juxtapositions, and satirists were self-conscious about the uneven qualities of their writing. Shared elements of irreverence and burlesque gave rise to an alternative, though false, derivation, from *satyri*, 'satyrs': hence *Horace's pose as *Priapus (*Sat.* 1. 8) and the punning title of *Petronius Arbiter's satirical novel *Satyrica*, 'Adventures of Satyrs'. *Livy's assertion (7. 2) that variety shows called *saturae* were an early form of Roman drama looks like a spurious attempt to link Roman satire with Greek satyr-plays. In the 2nd cent. BC, while the first satires were being written, the name *lex per saturam* was given to any suspiciously mixed political bill, which increased the reputation of satire as a dubious concoction. Both Horace (*Sat.* 2. 1. 1–2) and Juvenal (6. 635) speak of transgressing a 'law' of satire, partly as a pun on these bills, partly as a joke, as satire was a law unto itself, and partly in earnest, as satire was genuinely constrained by external laws. Finally, a bogus link was drawn with the similar-sounding festival of the Saturnalia (see SATURNUS), the Romans' temporary season for free abuse, which satire often adopted as a dramatic context (Hor. *Sat.* 2. 3, 2. 7; Petr. *Sat.* 44, 58, 69).

Influences Greece
The idea of the satirist as a vindictive member of society originated with the iambics of *Archilochus and *Hipponax. Athenian Old Comedy, especially that of *Aristophanes (1), was often cited as a model for outspoken abuse of other citizens (e.g. Hor. *Sat.* 1. 4. 1–5; see COMEDY (GREEK), OLD). However, both iambics and comedy also inspired defensive apologies with which Roman satirists deflected charges of spite on to their critics.

The Hellenistic *diatribe, a lecture which popularized moral philosophy with jokes, parody, fables, and split dialogue, was also a strong influence (Horace acknowledges a specific debt to the itinerant philosopher *Bion (1) of Borysthenes, *Ep.* 2. 2. 60). Its conscious mixture of serious and humorous elements (also known as *spoudogeloion*) lies behind Horace's laughing candour (*ridentem dicere verum* 'to tell the truth smiling' *Sat.* 1. 1. 24) as well as the bitterer invective of *Persius and Juvenal. The *Cynic philosopher *Menippus (1) of Gadara was associated with so-called *Menippean satire, a mixture of prose and verse which inspired experiments by *Varro, Petronius, and L. *Annaeus Seneca (2); he also presides over several of the satirical dialogues of *Lucian.

Rome
Satire, for the Romans, enshrined a national characteristic, blunt free speech, and was later a reminder of the republican past. They were proud of traditional social outlets for satirical feeling—the Saturnalia, *Fescennini, lampoons, pillorying of army commanders after a triumph. Yet in practice literary satire only pays lip-service to these. It was dangerous to write undiluted satire in all periods of Roman history, right from the *Twelve Tables' ban on malicious imprecations (*mala carmina*); and libel usually carried severe penalties (see INIURIA AND DEFAMATION). That is why satire is more of a discussion of the limits imposed on aggression, and why satirists tend to equivocate rather than take risks. Roman satire's bark was always worse than its bite.

Development   *Ennius wrote the first *saturae*, up to six books in various metres, of which only 31 lines survive. A sideline from his monumental *Annales*, they were miscellanies of Hellenistic culture which, though not noticeably acerbic, contained many ingredients of later satire in embryo: animal fables, moral censure, ethical dialogue, and the self-conscious presence of the author himself.

*Lucilius (1), according to ancient tradition, was the true father of satire: he specialized in outspoken criticism of contemporaries, and fixed the hexameter as the conventional satirical metre. His prolific writings (30 books, of which about 1300 lines survive) reveal a strong autobiographical element and an earthy, conversational style which is less spontaneous than it seems. Already the satirical personality is split between moral censor (e.g. in the mock 'trials' of Lentulus Lupus and Mucius Scaevola and the exposure of urban dinner-parties) and rollicking adventurer. Horace thought Lucilius prolix, but admired him for stripping the skin off a corrupt society. He was unanimously held up as a symbol of Republican liberty, especially during the civil wars, but in reality he owed his freedom of expression to his patrons, P. *Cornelius Scipio Aemilianus and C. *Laelius (2).

Varro added a new dimension to the principle of variety with his 150 books of Menippean satires, in verse and prose mixed, also now in fragments. Their titles—e.g. 'False Aeneas', 'Split Varro', 'Socratic Hercules'—give a clue to their hybrid contents—'a dash of philosophy, with a pinch of dialogue and humour thrown in' (Cic. *Acad.* 1. 8).

At the end of the republic, satire became yet more constrained. Horace's *Satires* (or *Sermones*, 'Conversations') are a sensitive gauge of the political changes through which he lived. Book 1, ten satires written during the transition from civil war to new civic order, is a tight blend of ingredients based on principles of moderation, finesse, and inoffensiveness, in direct contrast with Lucilius. Although Horace rejects the venom of traditional satire ('black squid-ink' and 'Italian vinegar', *Sat.* 1. 4. 100, 1. 7. 32), and claims to be satisfied with his humble status, the odd trace of nostalgia for republican free speech remains below the surface. In Book 2, eight satires written in the more restricted environment of the Augustan regime, Horace symbolically hands over Saturnalian opportunities for free speech to pundits on various controversial themes: gastronomy, legacy-hunting, Stoic philosophy (see STOICISM). The book ends on an unsatisfying note with an unfinished feast.

In imperial Rome, satirists risked reprisals from their capricious rulers. The tyranny of *Nero, surprisingly, was a fruitful period. However, Persius switches his focus from political to philosophical freedom, and confines his secrets to a hole in the ground or a darkened study. His six poems are puzzlingly disjointed Stoic diatribes, where satirical language reaches a new pitch of concentration. Two Menippean satires date from the same time. The courtier Petronius' picaresque novel, *Satyrica*, is a loosely Epicurean mock-epic (see EPICURUS), where the narrator appears to be pursued by a wrathful Priapus; but it is hard to find any strong moral basis when Encolpius himself is a victim of the decay he observes in society. The longest extended fragment, the 'Cena Trimalchionis', dissects a tasteless Saturnalian dinner hosted by an ex-slave. L. Annaeus Seneca (2)'s *Apocolocyntosis* ('Pumpkinification') is an inverted apotheosis-myth, depicting the emperor *Claudius as a carnival king, prematurely senile, with filthy habits and a penchant for dicing. It is significant that it was probably written for the first Saturnalia of Nero's reign, not during the lifetime of its subject. Two lines survive from the Flavian satirist *Turnus (2), exposing one of Nero's own crimes, the murder of *Britannicus, after the event.

With Juvenal, imperial satire seems to have been stretched to its full potential. His sixteen satires, spanning the reigns of *Domitian, *Nerva, *Trajan, and *Hadrian, take in not only a bloated metropolis but also the ends of the earth. The satirist now adopts a posture of savage indignation: only hyperbole is

adequate for describing the depravity of modern Rome, where vice has reached mythic proportions. Despite his sense of outrage, Juvenal's moral standpoint is strangely unstable: his language swells into tragic bombast, then plunges just as dramatically into bathos. These extremes of indignation are best seen in Satire 3, on the tottering city of Rome, the monstrous Satire 6, on women, and Satire 10, on ambition, with its striking images, such as that of the statue of L. *Aelius Seianus melted down into chamber-pots. However, Juvenal's claim to be returning to Lucilius is another rhetorical posture: most of his victims are either stereotypical ones—women, homosexuals, foreigners—or ghosts from the reign of Domitian.

*Lucian gave a satirical flavour to Greek dialogue, which he claims to have corrupted under the influence of iambics, Old Comedy, and the Cynicism of Menippus ('a dog who laughs when he bites'). Although he specialized in fantastical, timeless perspectives on terrestrial folly (seen from above and below in *Icaromenippus* and *Menippus*), his own viewpoint as a subject-Greek inspired some pointed satires on Roman culture (e.g. *Nigrinus*, *De Mercede Conductis*).

The history of Roman satire reached an apt conclusion two centuries later with the last classical Menippean satire, *Julian's *Caesars*, a character-assessment of his dead predecessors written (in Greek) by the emperor himself.

See FABLE; IAMBIC POETRY (LATIN).

J. Adamietz (ed.), *Die römische Satire* (1986); W. S. Anderson, *Essays on Roman Satire* (1982); S. H. Braund, *G&R* New Surveys in the Classics 23: *Roman Verse Satire* (1992); M. Coffey, *Roman Satire*[2] (1989); R. C. LaFleur, *ANRW* 2. 31. 3 (1981), 1790–1826; U. Knoche, *Die römische Satire*[3] (1971), trans. E. Ramage (1975) as *Roman Satire*; N. Rudd, *Themes in Roman Satire* (1986); J. P. Sullivan (ed.), *Critical Essays on Roman Literature: Satire* (1963); C. A. Van Rooy, *Studies in Classical Satire and Related Literary Theory* (1966); J. C. Relihan *Ancient Menippean Satire* (1993); and the bibliog. by W. S. Anderson in *CW* 1956–7, 1963–4, 1969–70.
E. J. G.

satrap (OP *xšaçapāvā*); etymological meaning 'protector of power [kingdom]'. The Persian title (see PERSIA) appears first in the *Bisitun inscription to describe two of *Darius I's representatives in charge of maintaining order in *Bactria and Arachosia. It is found, in transliterated form, in all the languages of the Achaemenid empire (Gr. *satrapēs*; Bab. *aḫšadrapānu*; El. *šakšabama*, etc.). The current understanding of the term is that it designates the governor of a formal territorial subdivision known as a satrapy. However, the chief of a provincial government can also have the more general title of 'governor' (Gr. *hyparchos*; Bab. *piḫātu*); conversely, the term satrap does not always designate a precise function, but reflects instead a title linked to royal favour and social status (e.g. Strabo 15. 3. 18; Polyaenus 7. 10).

R. Schmitt, *Studies L. R. Palmer* (1976), 379–90; T. Petit, *Satrapes et satrapies dans l'empire achéménide* (1990).
P. B.

Satraps' Revolt (Revolt of the Satraps). Revolts by Persian *satraps against central authority are not rare, esp. in the 4th cent. BC, but the term 'Satraps' Revolt' usually refers to the major episode described by *Diodorus (3) (15. 90 ff.), our main source, under 362/1 (but the trouble started earlier). Its scale and historicity have been doubted, and it is true that Persia could and did contain this sort of insurrection; but Diodorus' source surely did not invent the basic fact.

S. Hornblower, *Mausolus* (1982), 170 ff., and *CAH* 6[2] (1994), 84 ff.; M. Weiskopf, *The So-Called "Great Satraps' Revolt" 366–360 BC* (1989).
S. H.

Satricum

Satricum (1), mod. Conca in *Latium. A Volscian centre (see VOLSCI), originating in the 10th cent. BC. From the late 7th cent. it became an important cult and commercial centre, in which Rome took a close interest. Successive temples (of *c*.550 and 480 BC) of Mater *Matuta have been excavated. The city was destroyed by Rome (346 BC) and, the sanctuary apart, diminished into insignificance.

> M. Maaskant Kleibrink, *Settlement Excavations at Borgo Le Ferriere 'Satricum'* (1987); B. Heldring, C. M. Stibbe, *Arch. Laz.* 1990.

(2) Like-named town in the *Liris valley (mod. Monte San Giovanni?), severely punished by Rome for revolting after the *Caudine Forks disaster (320 BC) (Livy 9. 12–16; Cic. *QFr.* 3. 1. 4). E. T. S.; T. W. P.

Saturnia, minor *Etruscan hill town in the Albegna valley. It received a Roman *colonia* in 183 BC but is otherwise unrecorded in antiquity. Its surviving polygonal walls and interesting necropolis, however, attest its early importance.

> A. Minto, *Mon. Ant.* 1925, 585 ff.; F. Coarelli (ed.), *Etruscan Cities* (1973; Eng. trans. 1975) 132 f. E. T. S.

Saturnian verse, a form of verse employed in the 3rd and 2nd cents. BC for epitaphs and triumphal commemorations. According to *Ennius, the utterances of prophetic mediums had once been cast in it. A politician of the late 3rd cent. underlined a threat with its rhythm: *malum dabunt Metelli Naevio poetae*, 'the Metelli will give the poet Naevius a thrashing'. *Livius Andronicus set in it a translation of *Homer's *Odyssey*, and Cn. *Naevius a narrative account of the First *Punic War. The poets of the Augustan period talked of its shaggy and unclean rhythm (Hor. *Epist.* 2. 1. 156–9). Some theoreticians thought that the form had originated in Italy—the name was linked to the story of *Cronus/*Saturnus' enforced sojourn in *Latium—and had never had metrical regularity imposed upon it. (cf. Servius, Verg. *Georg.* 2. 385). Others detected analogues in Ionian iambic and Athenian dramatic verse. Heavily influential on all later discussion has been *Caesius Bassus' analysis of *malum dabunt Metelli Naevio poetae* as a combination of a short iambic with a short trochaic length. Theodor Korsch won many adherents to a theory of a fourfold division of the verse (1868).

Study of early Germanic and Celtic forms of verse led to the proposal of a theory that the Saturnian was a pattern of accented and unaccented syllables rather than one of longs and shorts. This view was formulated by O. Keller (1883–6) and R. Thurneysen (1885) in Germany and publicized in the USA and Great Britain by W. M. Lindsay (1893). It proved attractive to students of Romance versification. F. Leo re-established the conventional view (1905) by pointing out both the general unlikelihood of two different systems of versification cohabiting and the particular similarities which obtained between the 'cola' of the Saturnian verse and those of the '*cantica' of early Roman drama, but he left unclear the historical process which brought the quantitative verse-form to Latium. Two pupils of Leo, G. Pasquali and E. Fraenkel, tried to remedy this defect. According to the former a Latin-speaker around the end of the 6th cent. amalgamated two metrical lengths, which he had heard in the cult songs of some Greek city of south Italy, to serve as a vehicle for narrative poetry in his own language. The latter maintained on the other hand that the verse came as a whole straight from a Greek cult song. Objections are easy to formulate. One wants to know why Livius and Naevius chose such a form for extremely lengthy narratives,

and it serves no purpose to postulate a wholly unevidenced tradition of three centuries. The kind of correspondences between the 'cola' observable in Greek *lyric poetry and explicable in the context of large strophic correspondences accompanied by music are harder to accept in a series of brief stichic verses recited without any accompaniment. A large number of peculiarly Latin liberties, the irrational long syllable or the double short in the breve, the short syllable in the longum formed by word-end, hiatus between final and initial vowels, and perhaps even '*brevis brevians', have to be assumed in addition to the Greek liberties. Leo and his pupils may have set up a theory which saves the phenomena, but they failed to establish what a poet putting five words together as a Saturnian verse had to avoid. See METRE, LATIN.

> F. Leo, *Der saturnische Vers* (1905); A. W. De Groot, *Rev. Ét. Lat.* 1934, 284 ff.; G. Pasquali, *Preistoria della poesia romana* (1936); E. Fraenkel, *JRS* 1937, 262 ff., and *Eranos* 1957, 170 f.; E. Grassi, *Atena e Roma* 1961, 160 f.; B. Luiselli, *Il verso saturnio* (1967); M. L. West, *Glotta* 1973, 175 ff.; S. Timpanaro, introducing a reprint of Pasquali's book (1981). H. D. J.

Saturnus, Saturnalia Saturnus is one of the most puzzling gods in Roman cult. His festival (below) was part of the 'Calendar of Numa' (see POMPILIUS, NUMA), and its position, 17 December, midway between *Consualia* and *Opalia*, is intelligible if we suppose, as has commonly been done (e.g. by Wissowa, *RK* 204) that his name (*Sāturnus*, also *Saeturnus*) is to be connected with *sătus* and taken as that of a god of sowing, or of seed-corn. Other historians derive the god from the Etruscan Satre. But neither of these explanations resolves the difficulties raised by the cult of Saturn. The god, whose temple was sited by the NW corner of the *forum Romanum, is now considered as an Italo-Roman deity (his name is mentioned in the *Carmen saliare) who underwent a Hellenizing i.e. Greek *interpretatio* (see INTERPRETATIO ROMANA) from the end of the 3rd cent. BC. The difficulty arises from the fact that the cult was celebrated according to the Greek rite, i.e. with the head uncovered (Festus 432. 1 Lindsay; see SACRIFICE, ROMAN). To account for these facts, along with the other rites of the Saturnalia of 17 December, notably the fact that the statue of Saturnus, bound for the rest of the year, was freed for this day, as well as other inversion-rituals, the god's function has been defined as that of liberation, one which the obscure Lua Saturni might amplify.

Of the early history of his festival nothing is known: Livy (2. 21) speaks as if it originated in 496 BC, which is obviously not so. At most, some modification of the ritual in the direct of Hellenization took place then. In *Cicero's day, at any rate, the festival lasted for seven days. *Augustus reduced it to three, but from the reigns of *Gaius (1) and *Claudius it attained five days, quite apart from the fact that everyone continued to celebrate for seven days. The Saturnalia were celebrated down to the Christian age and beyond (under the name of *Brumalia*). In the Chronographer of AD 354 the vignette characterizing the month of December represents a person celebrating the Saturnalia, and it is in this context that the famous work of *Macrobius entitled *Saturnalia* must be placed. The Saturnalia were the merriest festival of the year, 'the best of days' (Catull. 14. 15). Slaves were allowed temporary liberty to do as they liked, presents were exchanged, particularly wax candles and *sigillaria (Macrob. *Sat.* 1. 7. 18 ff.; see Versnel, *Inconsistencies* 2. 148 for more refs.). There was also a sort of mock king, *Saturnalicius princeps*, 'leader of the Saturnalia', who presided over the feasts and amusements (Sen.

Apocol. 8. 2; Epict. *Diss.* 1. 25. 8; Lucian, *Saturnalia* 2 and 4). As a general rule, Romans at this time adopted a comportment inverting their normal conduct. Slaves dined before their masters and could allow themselves a certain insolence, leisure-wear (*synthesis*) was worn instead of the *toga, as well as the felt bonnet proper to slaves (*pilleus*), and the time was spent eating, drinking, and playing. There is a debate about the claims of Christian writers that *gladiators were linked to Saturn and that they were a form of human sacrifice (Wissowa, *RK* 207; Versnel, 210 ff.).

H. Versnel, *Inconsistencies in Greek and Roman Religion, 2. Transition and Reversal in Myth and Ritual* (1992), 136 ff.; M. Nilsson, *RE* entry under Saturnalia (1921); P. Pensabene, *Tempio di Saturno* (1984); M. Meslin, *Collection Latomus* (1970) (on the 4th–5th cents. AD).　　　　J. Sch.

satyric drama In the Classical period it was normal for a satyr-play to be written by each tragedian for performance after his set of three tragedies at the Athenian City *Dionysia. The chorus is composed of satyrs (see next entry), and is closely associated with their father Silenus. One complete satyr-play 709 lines long (*Euripides' *Cyclops*), survives, together with numerous fragments, notably about half of *Sophocles (1)'s *Ichneutae* ('Trackers') preserved on papyrus, and numerous vase-paintings inspired by satyr-plays, notably the Pronomos vase (Beazley, *ARV*² 1336. 1), which displays the entire cast of a victorious play. The themes were taken from myth (sometimes connected with the theme of the trilogy), and the earthy preoccupations of the satyrs may have had the effect of reducing the dignity of various heroes, as happens to *Odysseus in the *Cyclops*. Odysseus' speech is, metrically and stylistically, virtually indistinguishable from tragic speech, and even that of the satyrs and Silenus, though lower in tone, remains much closer to tragedy than to comedy. Horace describes tragedy as like a matron who does not descend to uttering trivial verses as she consorts modestly with the impudent satyrs at a festival (*Ars P.* 231–3).

There is a set of typical motifs, notably the captivity (explaining their presence in various myths) and eventual liberation of the satyrs, marvellous inventions and creations (of wine, the lyre, fire, etc.), *riddles, emergence from the underworld, the care of divine or heroic infants, and athletics. Some of them may reflect the activities of the satyrs in cult (notably initiation into the Dionysiac *thiasos* (see DIONYSUS; THIASOS)). *Aristotle reports that tragedy developed from the σατυρικόν (satyr-play-like); see TRAGEDY, GREEK, § I.1. And it seems that satyric drama was thereafter formally instituted in the festival to preserve what was being lost from tragedy as it turned to non-Dionysiac stories (the first satyric dramatist was said to be *Pratinas of Phlius). Certainly it is too simple to see the function of satyric drama as merely to alleviate the effect of the seriousness of tragedy with comic relief, which could after all have been provided by comedy. Less universal in its appeal than tragedy and comedy, satyric drama had by the mid-4th cent. become detached from the tragic contest. But we hear of a production as late as the 2nd cent. AD, and there is good evidence for its performance in Rome.

F. Brommer, *Satyrspiele* (1959); D. F. Sutton, *The Greek Satyr Play* (1980); R. Seaford, introduction to *Euripides' Cyclops* (1984); T. P. Wiseman, *JRS* 1988, 1–13; B. Seidensticker (ed.), *Satyrspiel* (1989).　　R. A. S. S.

satyrs and **silens** are imaginary male inhabitants of the wild, comparable to the 'wild men' of the European folk tradition, with some animal features, unrestrained in their desire for sex and wine, and generally represented naked. The first mention in literature of 'silens' is as making love to *nymphs in caves (*Hymn. Hom. Ven.* 262–3); of 'satyrs' it is as 'worthless and mischievous'

(Hes. fr. 123). On the Attic François vase (*c.*570 BC) the horse–human hybrids accompanying *Hephaestus (with *Dionysus) back to *Olympus (1) are labelled as silens. It seems that in the course of the 6th cent. BC the (Attic-Ionic) silens were amalgamated with the (Peloponnesian) satyrs (so that the names were used interchangeably) to form, along with nymphs or maenads, the sacred band (*thiasos*) of Dionysus. It is a *thiasos* of young satyrs that, in the 5th cent., forms the chorus of *satyric drama, with Silenus (in keeping with the ancient belief in individual silens) as father of the satyrs. In vase-painting satyrs are at first present in a limited number of myths (the Return of Hephaestus, the Gigantomachy (see GIANTS), etc.), but in the 5th cent. this number grows considerably, at least partly under the influence of satyric drama.

People dressed up as satyrs, e.g. at the Athenian *Anthesteria, where their frolics are depicted on the 'Choes' vases. Also at the Anthesteria was the procession in which Dionysus arrived in a ship-cart accompanied by satyrs, who are prominent also in great *processions at *Alexandria (1) (Ath. 196a–203b; see CALLIXEINUS) and Rome (Dion. Hal. 7. 72). In contrast to this public presence, satyrs also conducted mystic *initiation (e.g. Pl. *Leg.* 815c, and the paintings at the Villa of the Mysteries at *Pompeii; see MYSTERIES). To be initiated might be to join a satyric *thiasos*, a community of this world and the next. Hence the occurrence of satyrs in funerary art throughout most of antiquity.

Analogous to this contrast is the ambiguity of the satyrs as grotesque hedonists and yet the immortal companions of a god, cruder than men and yet somehow wiser, combining mischief with wisdom, lewdness with skill in music, animality with divinity. In satyric drama they are the first to sample the creation of culture out of nature in the invention of *wine, of the lyre, of the pipe, and so on. Silenus is the educator of Dionysus. King *Midas (1) extracted from a silen, whom he had trapped in his garden, the wisdom that for men it is best never to have been born, second best to die as soon as possible (Hdt. 8. 138; Aristot. fr. 44). And Virgil's shepherds extract from Silenus a song of great beauty and wisdom (*Ecl.* 6). This ambiguity is exploited in *Alcibiades' famous comparison of *Socrates to the musical satyr Marsyas (Pl. *Symp.* 215).

At first somewhat equine, the satyrs become progressively more human in appearance (though from the Hellenistic period more caprine than equine, perhaps through association with *Pan), and may decorate a pastoral landscape or embody, for the visual artist, the charm of a not quite human body, as in the sculpted sleeping satyr known as the 'Barberini Faun'. Popular belief in the presence of satyrs in the wild no doubt persisted throughout antiquity (e.g. Plut. *Sull.* 27), as did the practice of imitating them in urban festivals, which was banned in Constantinople in AD 692.

F. Buschor, *Satyroi* (1937); T. H. Carpenter, *Dionysian Imagery in Archaic Greek Art* (1984), ch. 5; F. Lissarrague, in J. Winkler and F. Zeitlin (eds.), *Nothing to do with Dionysos* (1990), 228 ff.　　R. A. S. S.

Satyrus (1) (*RE* 16) (fl. probably 3rd cent. BC), *Peripatetic littérateur from Callatis (Mangalia, Romania). Works: (1) *Bioi* (*Lives*) of kings, statesmen, orators, philosophers, and poets, known chiefly from citations by *Athenaeus (1) and *Diogenes (6) Laertius. *POxy.* 1176 preserves a substantial fragment on *Euripides from book 6, which also covered *Aeschylus and *Sophocles (1). Satyrus evidently used a *dialogue form; though the style is agreeable, the approach is unscholarly, material being drawn from comedy and anecdote, and from passages in Euripides'

Satyrus

plays uncritically treated as autobiographical. (2) *Peri characteron* (*On characters*); the one fragment, a passage quoted by Athenaeus (4. 168e), exhibits the moralistic propensity observable in the fragments of the *Lives*. (Other authors of the same name should be credited with works On the **Demes* of **Alexandria* (1) (*FGrH* 631, cf. *POxy.* 2465 (*RE* 18), on myths (*RE* 19; see next entry), and on gems (*RE* 20).)

> TEXT *FHG* 3. 159–66; A. S. Hunt, *POxy.* 9 (1912), 1176 (with trans.); G. Arrighetti, *Satiro: Vita di Euripide* (1964) (with It. trans.). See also K. F. Kumaniecki, *De Satyro Peripatetico* (1929); M. R. Lefkowitz, *The Lives of the Greek Poets* (1981). **S. R. W.**

Satyrus (2) (2nd cent. BC) nicknamed *Zeta*, pupil of *Aristarchus (2), was perhaps the author of a collection of ancient myths (*FGrH* 20). On the (?) different writers called Satyrus (a hopeless muddle) see Fraser, *Ptol. Alex.* 2. 656–7, n. 57.

Satyrus (3) (fl. *c.*150 BC), physician, pupil of *Quintus of Rome, and teacher of *Galen at *Pergamum. He was a faithful follower of Quintus in the exegesis of *Hippocrates (2) and in the teaching of *anatomy and *pharmacology.

Saxon Shore (*Litus Saxonicum*), name given to the coasts of south-east *Britain and north-west Gaul either because they were attacked by *Saxons or were settled by them. Defended by a series of forts which eventually came under the command of a *comes litoris Saxonici*, 'count of the Saxon Shore' (Not. Dign. 27). Ten forts are known in Britain, the earliest—Brancaster and Reculver—dating to the early 3rd cent. AD. The latest, Pevensey, post-dates AD 330. The forts were located at strategic points along the coast. They may have served (at least in the early stages) to monitor shipping as well as to counter raids from across the North Sea. A unified defence system may have been established under *Carausius in the late 3rd cent., but there is little reason to suppose that the post of *comes litoris Saxonici* existed before the early 4th cent. The construction of Pevensey, and the coin evidence from other forts, suggests a new initiative in the 330s. Most of the forts were occupied into the 5th cent., while there is evidence for medieval activity at Portchester.

> J. S. Johnson, *The Roman Forts of the Saxon Shore* (1976); papers in D. E. Johnston (ed.), *The Saxon Shore* (1977); P. Salway, *Roman Britain* (1981); V. Maxfield (ed.), *The Saxon Shore: A Handbook* (1989). **J. F. Mo.**

Saxons, a Germanic tribe (see GERMANY) referred to in many classical sources as raiders on the empire. The forts of the *Saxon Shore may have been constructed as protection against such raids. In AD 364 *Britain was harassed by Picts, Saxons, Scots, and Attacotti (Amm. Marc. 26. 4. 5), and in AD 367 Saxons attacked Gaul (Amm. Marc. 27. 8. 5). However, they are best known—along with the Angles and Jutes—as one of the 'three most formidable races of Germany' who were invited to defend Britain in AD 449 by Vortigern (Bede, *HE* 1. 15). They are subsequently said to have revolted and invited their compatriots across the North Sea to settle. However, the Gallic Chronicle tells us that in 441 Britain came under the control of the Saxons, and recent historical research has dated the *adventus Saxonum* (the coming of the Saxons) to *c.*430. The early settlements in eastern England would seem to have been on a small scale, and may be represented archaeologically by brooches and pottery similar to that found in the continental homelands of north-west Germany. In the course of the 5th and 6th cents. Germanic material culture became prevalent across southern and eastern England, but the scale of further immigration is difficult to assess since it is possible that 'native' Britons had become acculturated to Ger-

manic ways. By this time the use of Germanic objects was no real indicator of ethnic origins.

> N. Higham, *Rome, Britain and the Anglo-Saxons* (1992) presents an up-to-date account. J. N. L. Myres, *The English Settlements* (1986) is already somewhat dated. **J. F. Mo.**

Scamander, a river of the *Troas (now called *Menderes su*), rising in Mt. Ida and flowing into the *Hellespont after a course of *c.*60 miles. Despite *Pliny (1)'s phrase 'amnis navigabilis' (*HN* 5. 124), it can never have been open to shipping. Lechevalier's view that the perennial stream flowing from the springs at Bunarbashi (Kirk Göz) was *Homer's Scamander is now abandoned.

> J. M. Cook, *The Troad* (1973), esp. 140 ff., 293, and in L. Foxhall and J. K. Davies (eds.), *The Trojan War* (1984), 163 ff.; N. J. Richardson, *Comm. on Iliad 21–24* (1993), 123 f.; B. Rubens and O. Taplin, *Odyssey round Odysseus* (1989), 93 ff. **J. M. C.; S. H.**

Scamandrius See ASTYANAX.

scapegoat See PHARMAKOS.

Scepsis, a city of the *Troas, reputed to be a foundation of Scamandrius (see ASTYANAX) and *Ascanius, whose descendants ruled there. It seems to have been an Aeolic settlement but reinforced by Milesians (see MILETUS). Released by *Lysimachus from incorporation in *Alexandria (7) Troas (301 BC), Scepsis enjoyed a vigorous cultural life into Roman times; *Aristotle's library was kept there for two centuries. The site is on Kurşunlu Tepe in the upper Scamander valley; there is little to be seen since the surviving remains were carted off by the Muteselim of Bayramiç about 1800.

> W. Leaf, *Strabo on the Troad* (1923), 269–84; J. M. Cook, *The Troad* (1973), 345 ff. **J. M. C.; S. H.**

Sceptics, philosophers who hold no doctrine and suspend judgement on everything. The label σκεπτικός ('inquirer', but used with the implicit understanding that the inquiry does not end) was introduced in the 1st cent. BC, probably by the younger Pyrrhonists; before then, these philosophers would be known as Pyrrhonists or Academics, respectively.

Early Pyrrhonism. According to the ancient tradition, the founder of scepticism was *Pyrrhon of Elis (*c.*365–275 BC). He held that it was not possible to determine whether things are one way rather than another, and that one should therefore refrain from asserting anything. Arguments to the effect that conflicts of appearances and opinions cannot be decided had been around since the time of *Protagoras and *Democritus, but Pyrrhon was probably the first to adopt the attitude of non-assertion and promote it as the foundation of peace of mind or tranquillity. Pyrrhon's school does not seem to have had any immediate followers after the time of his main pupil, *Timon (2) of Phlius.

Scepticism in the *Academy. The second version of scepticism was developed in the Academy from *Arcesilaus in the 3rd cent. BC to *Philon (3) of Larissa in the first. The Academic sceptics saw themselves as followers of *Socrates. They practised his dialectical method by arguing for and against any given thesis and refuting the doctrines of other philosophers. Arcesilaus' criticism of Stoic epistemology (see STOICISM) started a lively debate between the two schools that went on for two centuries and covered all parts of philosophy, including theology and ethics. Both sides were forced to revise and refine their arguments in the process. While the Academics would argue that, given Stoic assumptions, knowledge was impossible, the Stoics would defend their conception of knowledge and force the Academics to elaborate a sophisticated defence of the claim that it is possible to lead a normal life while suspending judgement on everything. The most detailed reply to the 'inactivity' argument, *Carneades' theory of the 'plausible impression', eventually became the basis of a return to philosophical doctrine in the Academy under the scholarchate of Philon of Larissa, in the form of the cautious fallibilism presented in *Cicero's *Academici libri*.

The Pyrrhonist Revival. In the 1st cent. BC, when Academic scepticism had lost its vigour, Pyrrhonism was revived by *Aenesidemus as a more radical form of scepticism. This new version of Pyrrhonism was clearly influenced by the preceding debate between Academics and Stoics. But Aenesidemus also picked up the older arguments from conflicting appearances, systematizing them in his list of ten 'Modes' for inducing suspension of judgement, and he revived the claim that scepticism can serve as a way to tranquillity. Unlike Pyrrhon, the later Pyrrhonists would avoid any dogmatic assertions about the impossibility of knowledge, presenting their views instead as an expression of what appeared to them to be the case. They also worked out a reply to the charge that scepticism makes life impossible, by saying that they would be guided in their everyday activities by simple appearances without strong assent.

Aenesidemus' main source of information about Pyrrhon was probably Timon, but it is very likely that he was also influenced by the epistemological and methodological debates that had been going on between the different schools of medicine (see MEDICINE, § 5.3). The list of Aenesidemus' followers contains the names of several prominent doctors, and the final and most sophisticated version of Pyrrhonism is preserved for us in the writings of the Empiricist physician *Sextus Empiricus (fl. *c.* AD 200). After Sextus, we do not hear of any important representatives of the school, and scepticism as a philosophical movement seems to have come to an end.

V. Brochard, *Les Sceptiques grecs* (1887, 1923²), repr. 1981); L. Robin, *Pyrrhon et le scepticisme grec* (1944); M. Dal Pra, *Lo scetticismo greco* (1950, 1975²); C. L. Stough, *Greek Skepticism* (1969); M. Burnyeat (ed.), *The Skeptical Tradition* (1983); A. A. Long and D. N. Sedley, *The Hellenistic Philosophers* (1987), chs. 1–3, 68–72; R. J. Hankinson, *The Sceptics* (1995).   G. S.

Scerdilaidas, an Illyrian chieftain, probably son of King Pleuratus and brother of King Agron. When Agron was succeeded in 230 BC by his widow *Teuta (as regent for her stepson Pinnes), Scerdilaidas led her forces against *Epirus. After Teuta's defeat by Rome (229/8) and during most of the subsequent hegemony of *Demetrius (7) of Pharos, Scerdilaidas' position is obscure. Then in 220 he sailed past Lissus with Demetrius, allied himself with the Aetolians, and, breaking with them, joined the Hellenic symmachy (see ALLIANCE (GREEK)) of *Philip (3) V. After the defeat of Demetrius by the Romans (219) Scerdilaidas became king in Illyria (before 211), perhaps after a time as regent for Pinnes. In winter 217/16 he informed the Romans of Philip's shipbuilding activity, and an appeal brought him help in the form of ten Roman ships (216). With his son Pleuratus he joined the Roman-Aetolian alliance (211). His death fell not long after that: in the Peace of Phoenice (205) Pleuratus appears on the Roman side without Scerdilaidas.

RE Supp. 5, 'Skerdilaïdas'; S. Le Bohec, in P. Cabanes (ed.), *L'Illyrie méridionale et l'Épire dans l'Antiquité* (1987), 203 ff.; A. Coppola, *Demetrio di Faro* (1993).   P. S. D.

Scheria (Σχερία, epic Σχερίη), the land of the Phaeacians, at which *Odysseus arrives after his shipwreck (*Od.* 5. 451 ff., cf.

34). It is a fertile country, apparently an island (6. 204), having an excellent, almost land-locked harbour (263 ff.), by which its city stands, at least one river (5. 451), and a mild climate (cf. 7. 117 ff.; fruits grow all the year round). The population are enterprising and very skilful seafarers, great gossips, boastful, and rather impudent, not very warlike or athletic, fond of pleasure, but kindly and willing to escort strangers in their wonderful ships. Various real places have been suggested as the original of Scheria, the most popular in ancient and modern times being *Corcyra (Corfu); but as that is within some 80 miles of *Ithaca, whereas Scheria is distant a night's voyage for one of the magical Phaeacian ships (*Od.* 13. 81 ff.), the identification is unlikely. See J. B. Hainsworth, *Comm. on Odyssey,* 6. 8 (and add a ref. to Thuc. 3. 70, the *temenos* of *Alcinous (1) at Corcyra). That details of real places have been used for the picture is likely.   H. J. R.; S. H.

scholarship, ancient

Greek In one sense of the term scholarship began when literature became a central element of education and the prescribed texts had to be explained and interpreted to pupils in a class. An early reflex of this activity is the reported invention by *Theagenes (2) of Rhegium (late 6th cent. BC) of the allegorical method of interpretation, which could be used to deny the literal meaning of supposedly objectionable passages of *Homer. But scholarship, like literary criticism, was slow to develop in the Classical period. In the Peripatos (see PERIPATETIC SCHOOL) *Aristotle and his disciples were not primarily concerned with literature or history, but their discussions of Homer and concern with the chronology of Athenian dramatic festivals was a step forward. Recognizably scholarly work, including the composition of books or pamphlets about literary texts, began early in the 3rd cent. BC in *Alexandria (1) under the patronage of the Ptolemies (see PTOLEMY (1)); to what extent the ideals of the Peripatos were influential, possibly through the influence of *Demetrius (3) of Phalerum, is a disputed question. The *Museum, where scholars enjoyed good working conditions, became a centre where literary topics were discussed regularly; according to one report a record was kept of the discussions. The Library (see LIBRARIES) acquired a virtually complete collection of books written in Greek, to which *Callimachus (3) wrote an enormous bibliographical guide, and it looks as if copies of the classics, such as Homer, which reflected the results of work done in the Museum, came to be regarded as standard. Between *c.*285 and 145 BC a series of Alexandrian scholars, who variously combined one or more of the professions of poet, tutor to the children of the royal family, and librarian of the Museum, brought scholarship to a high level. They edited texts by comparing different exemplars, commented on them by writing either notes on difficult passages or extended running commentaries, and composed innumerable treatises on individual problems, some of them historical and antiquarian rather than literary. Questions of authenticity also had to be addressed. The leading figures in this process were *Zenodotus, *Callimachus (3), *Eratosthenes, *Aristophanes (2) of Byzantium, and *Aristarchus (2). Not all their decisions about puzzles in Homer win the approval of a modern reader, and they seem to have been too prone to reject lines as being unworthy of Homer or inconsistent with the context; but luckily they did not remove such lines from the texts in circulation. Good copies of leading authors were often equipped with a kind of *apparatus criticus* in the margin; this consisted of signs indicating e.g. the dubious status of a line of verse, or some point of general interest in the text, on which the reader could expect to find guidance in a note in a separate book containing a commentary. During part of the Hellenistic period there was also a rival school in Pergamum (see CRATES (3)), but very little is known in detail about it, and it does not seem to have achieved the prestige of the Museum.

Much ancient scholarship can be seen as the response to the difficulties created by the handwritten book (see BOOKS). Different copies of the same text diverged. Although this was most notable in the case of Homer, it was true of all texts in some degree, and even by Hellenistic times a number of passages in other classical authors had become obscure or unintelligible. Scribal error was recognized as a factor to be reckoned with; the term γραφικὸν ἁμάρτημα (lit. 'mistake in writing') is found e.g. in *Harpocration, and the Homer scholia discuss variant readings, while from time to time we find that scholars ventured upon emendation in passages they believed to be meaningless. The best critics, however, did not content themselves with the removal of obvious corruptions. They devised principles of interpretation, a famous case being the maxim traditionally but perhaps wrongly attributed to Aristarchus, that one should interpret an author by reference to his own usage elsewhere (Ὅμηρον ἐξ Ὁμήρου σαφηνίζειν (lit. 'clarify Homer through Homer')). Another good rule was that a unique word should not be deleted from a poetic text just because it was unique. They also attempted aesthetic appreciation: the scholia on Homer contain many remarks of this kind which a modern reader will agree with and respect. These notes employ such concepts as poetic licence, the scale, structure, unity, and variety in the composition of the epic, the characterization and the stylistic level. Since none of the works of the greatest scholars survive, and there is very little left even of what their lesser contemporaries and successors wrote, it is hard to write a convincing account of the development of scholarship; to concentrate on the relatively few known facts about the leading figures risks neglect of all the achievements that cannot be safely attributed to an individual. Our main source of information is the material known as *scholia, i.e. notes written in the margins of ancient and medieval copies of our texts.

From late Hellenistic and Roman times there is less to report about literary scholarship. As specimens of what scholars wrote we have the Technē grammatikē of *Dionysius (15) Thrax (though many authorities now believe it to be a product of late antiquity), the short essay on *allegory in Homer by Heraclitus, and a substantial papyrus fragment of a work by *Didymus (1) on *Demosthenes (2), which does not cast a flattering light on his standards of scholarship. In the Roman empire literary life altered under the influence of the new fashion of Atticism (see ASIANISM AND ATTICISM), and much effort was spent on compiling manuals that would ensure accurate imitation of the classics, such as the extant lexicographical guides of *Pollux, *Phrynichus (3), and *Moeris. The grammatical writings of *Herodian (1) and *Apollonius (13) Dyscolus, especially the latter's long book on syntax, were also a serious contribution to their subject. The Christians soon learned to adopt the techniques that had served the pagans well, and we find in *Origen (1) much that is reminiscent of Alexandrian philology, both in the handling of details—he needed to establish the text of the *Septuagint—and in the use of the allegorical method. The later rival school of *Antioch (1) was if anything even closer in its adherence to Alexandrian methods.

Early in the 3rd cent. AD we find the first important representative of another group of scholars whose work is extant in substantial quantities, the commentators on *Plato (1) and Aristotle.

From *Alexander (14) of Aphrodisias, who began lecturing on Aristotle c. AD 198, to the middle of the 6th cent. the philosophical schools in Athens and Alexandria (the latter had no connection with the Museum, by now defunct) were highly productive. There are two other developments dating from late antiquity which deserve mention. One is the invention, perhaps to be credited to Procopius of Gaza (c.500), of the catena, which is made up of short excerpts from two or more existing commentaries on a given book of the Bible, with the name of each author normally prefixed to each excerpt. This type of compilation is akin to, though it was not necessarily the model for, the scholia. The formation of the extant corpora of scholia probably took place in late antiquity, and the process may have been continued in the early centuries of Byzantium. Original works of Hellenistic and later scholarship were the raw material for this process, and once a compilation had been made from them they were discarded. Unfortunately the scholia do not often name the authorities responsible for the views or information presented, nor do they give what look like verbatim quotations. This is the main reason why, given the loss of the original texts, it is still so difficult to reconstruct the history of scholarship from material that does in large part ultimately derive from such texts.

For a short account see L. D. Reynolds and N. G. Wilson, Scribes and Scholars³ (1991). The only longer account which is reasonably up-to-date is R. Pfeiffer, History of Classical Scholarship: From the Beginnings to the End of the Hellenistic Age (1968), reviewed by N. G. Wilson, CR 1969, 366–72. On literary criticism in the Homeric scholia see N. J. Richardson in CQ 1980, 265–87; on scholia more generally N. G. Wilson, 'Scoliasti e commentatori', in Studi classici e orientali 1983, 83–112. For late antiquity see N. G. Wilson, Scholars of Byzantium (1983).
N. G. W.

Latin The origins of scholarship at Rome are lost to view, along with much of Rome's earliest scholarly writing. *Suetonius' attempt (Gramm. 2) to trace Rome's first experience of Hellenistic scholarship to the visit of *Crates (3) of Mallos around 167 BC is more colourful than reliable; it no doubt captures, however, the kind of contact that was influential in the course of the 2nd cent., when a 'great flock' of learned men came to Rome from Greece (Polyb. 31. 24. 6 f.). By the end of the 2nd cent. and the start of the 1st not only was there substantial learning displayed in the Didascalica of *Accius and the satires of *Lucilius (1), but L. *Aelius had developed what would be the three main foci of Roman scholarship: 'antiquities', treating the institutions and beliefs of Rome and her neighbours; literary studies, including questions of authenticity and literary history (but little that we would recognize as 'literary criticism'); and the more or less systematic study of language, especially (in this early period) *etymology and semantics. Aelius, Rome's first true scholar, in turn influenced M. Terentius *Varro, Rome's greatest scholar, whose antiquarian research (Antiquitates rerum humanarum et divinarum), study of Latinity (De lingua Latina), and investigations of literary history (De poetis) provided a model and a resource for all other scholars (e.g. *Cornelius Nepos, *Verrius Flaccus) and some authors of imaginative literature (e.g. *Ovid).

Varro and Aelius, who were not professional teachers, established a tradition of 'amateur' scholarship that continued throughout later antiquity and included (to note only authors of works still extant) the elder *Pliny (1), who extended the methods of antiquarian scholarship to the investigation of the natural world (Historia Naturalis); Aulus *Gellius, whose Attic Nights gathered edifying or beguiling excerpts from his varied reading; *Censorinus, who wrote on the reckoning of human life and time (*De die natali*) in the 3rd cent.; *Nonius Marcellus (4th cent. AD?), whose encyclopedic dictionary (*De compendiosa doctrina*) embraces both linguistic oddments and *Realien*; and two 5th-cent. authors, *Macrobius (*Saturnalia*) and *Martianus Minneus Felix Capella (*De nuptiis Philologiae et Mercurii*), whose learned compilations are cast (respectively) as an elaborate *dialogue and an *allegory. Though arising from different motives in different milieux, all such works are alike in suggesting which elements of their culture the authors thought it worthwhile to explain and preserve for their posterity.

The transmission of culture was also central to the second main stream of Latin scholarship, which arose from the schools of *grammaticē* and rhetoric that began to proliferate in the 1st cent. BC. Here commentaries on literary texts and handbooks (see ARS) surveying grammatical and rhetorical doctrine were the chief staple. Precepts on Latin rhetoric were being compiled as early as the 80s BC, when the anonymous *Rhetorica ad Herennium* was written; the main surviving example of the genre is *Quintilian's great survey of the education suitable for an orator (*c.* AD 95). Quintilian's older contemporary *Remmius Palaemon wins the credit for writing the first *ars grammatica* of which we are specifically informed, though examples of the type almost certainly existed by the mid-1st cent. BC. Commentaries on literary texts, especially those read in schools, are also attested for the 1st cent. BC, though it is not until *Pomponius Porphyrio's commentary on Horace (3rd cent. AD) that we have an example surviving in something resembling its original form. In later antiquity the teachers Aelius *Donatus (1) (mid–4th cent. AD), *Servius (late 4th–early 5th cent.), and *Priscian (late 5th–early 6th cent.) are the emblematic figures: the first as author of commentaries on *Terence and *Virgil and of two highly influential grammars (the *Ars minor* and the *Ars maior*), the second as author of extant commentaries on Virgil and Donatus' *artes*, the third as author of the greatest compilation of Latin linguistic knowledge to survive from antiquity.

See also LITERARY CRITICISM IN ANTIQUITY; GRAMMAR, GRAMMAR-IANS, LATIN; AEMILIUS ASPER; ASCONIUS PEDIANUS, Q.; ATEIUS PHILO-LOGUS, L.; AURELIUS OPILLUS; CAESIUS BASSUS; CHARISIUS, FLAVIUS SOSIPATER; DIOMEDES (3); FENESTELLA; HELENIUS ACRO; HYGINUS (1); IULIUS ROMANUS; JULIUS SOLINUS; NIGIDIUS FIGULUS, P.; SACERDOS, MARIUS PLOTIUS; SUETONIUS; TERENTIANUS MAURUS; TERENTIUS SCAURUS, Q.; VALERIUS CATO, P.; VALERIUS PROBUS, M.; VICTORINUS, MARIUS.

J. E. G. Zetzel, *Latin Textual Criticism in Antiquity* (1984); E. Rawson, *Intellectual Life in the Later Roman Republic* (1985); R. A. Kaster, *Guardians of Language* (1988); L. D. Reynolds and N. G. Wilson, *Scribes and Scholars*[3] (1991), chs. 4–10.   R. A. K.

scholarship, classical, history of

scholarship, classical, history of (from the Renaissance) Classical texts formed the core of the arts curriculum in medieval schools and universities and were central to two of the three higher faculties, law and medicine, as well. But modern classical scholarship—the systematic effort to collect and study the written and material remains of the ancient world as a whole— came into being in 14th-cent. northern Italy. Here teachers of rhetoric began to teach from *Cicero rather than the 'modern'— i.e. medieval—texts they had previously used. Formal imitation of the classics became systematic. Scholars began to see classical Latin texts as distinctively better than later ones: they copied, read, and studied a wide range of literary and historical texts that had generally not been read in the Middle Ages. Access to new material created new questions: problems of attribution and

dating that had not interested medieval scholars cropped up and new techniques were devised to solve them. Before 1320 Giovanni de Matociis of Verona had established in a formal essay that the Pliny who wrote the *Natural History* could not have written the *Letters* as well (see PLINY (1–2)). He also wrote a history of the Roman emperors in which he drew on the evidence of coins as well as that of the ancient historians.

The poet and philosopher Petrarch (Francesco Petrarca, 1304–74) knitted these technical threads together into the programme for a new scholarship. Convinced that 'all history but the praise of Rome' and that he himself lived in an inferior, 'dark' age, he dedicated his life to the study and imitation of the ancients—by which, as a list of his favourite books that he drew up reveals, he meant Romans like *Livy and *Virgil and Saint *Augustine. Thanks to his connections with the papal curia, which spent much of the 14th cent. in Avignon, and with influential Italian clerics and statesmen, he gained access to the treasures of both Italian and northern libraries. Petrarca assembled a remarkable library of his own: his copy of Livy, for example, brought together from diverse sources three decades, the bulk of the text that survives today, and though he never learned Greek, he had manuscripts of *Plato (1) and *Homer. He studied and annotated his books with care and intelligence, hunted for other texts that they mentioned, and explored the ruins of Rome as well as its literary canon. His own works—which included an epic, bucolics, philosophical dialogues, historical compilations, and lively letters modelled on those of Cicero—represented a dramatic effort to revive the main genres of Latin literature. He insisted that the literature, history, and moral philosophy of the classical world could form a more solid and satisfactory basis for education and a better model for modern writers than the technical philosophy of Aristotle and his medieval commentators, which dominated the universities of northern Europe and were also becoming fashionable in Italian universities. He thus provided both a model for classical studies and a new justification for them: both proved vastly influential.

For the next century, Italian humanists followed the lines Petrarca had laid down. They hunted little-known classical texts all over Europe, copying what they discovered and stealing what they had no chance to copy; gradually they assembled what remains the basic canon of Latin texts. They established schools, both in republican Florence and Venice and at the courts of Ferrara, Mantua, and Milan, where young men could master the grammar and literature of classical Latin and learn the lessons of ancient history and moral philosophy. The correction of textual errors became a fashion and gave rise to sharp debates. Before the middle of the 15th cent. Lorenzo Valla wrote the first modern manual of classical Latin usage; unmasked a medieval legal text, the *Donation of Constantine*, as written in a non-classical Latin and therefore forged; and brilliantly corrected the text (and the content) of Livy. Meanwhile specialist antiquaries like Cyriacus of Ancona explored ancient sites and filled notebooks with drawings of ruins and texts of inscriptions (see EPIGRAPHY, GREEK). The study of Greek revived as well, first of all in Florence, where Emanuel Chrysoloras taught for three years from 1397. He also produced a practical Greek grammar. Unsystematic but energetic efforts at translation brought Plato and *Lucian, Homer and *Aristophanes (1) into Latin, and a modest command of Greek became part of the normal scholar's arsenal.

From the middle of the 15th cent. new public libraries like that of the Vatican gave the new canon of classical texts permanent homes. The support of patrons like Cosimo de' Medici and Pope

Nicholas V made possible the translation of the major works of Greek prose: Plato and *Plotinus were translated for the Medici by Marsilio Ficino, *Thucydides (2) and *Herodotus (1) for Nicholas V by Valla. The invention of printing ensured the survival, first of the major Latin works and, from the 1480s, of the Greek classics as well. Meanwhile commentators tried, at increasing length, to remedy the corruptions, explain the difficulties, and emphasize the beauties of the classical texts. Much of the scholarly work of this period was done too rapidly. Angelo Poliziano, who devised before his early death in 1494 the basic principles of textual criticism, insisting that before trying to correct a given text one must examine all the manuscripts and eliminate from consideration those copied from other extant ones, argued this thesis so forcefully precisely because he held that the editions of his time were based on randomly chosen manuscripts, silently emended and wilfully explained. With few exceptions, he was right.

None the less, by the end of the 15th cent. many central techniques of classical scholarship had been formulated and applied. Poliziano's *Miscellanea* of 1489, Ermolao Barbaro's *Castigationes Plinianae* of 1492–3, and many less ambitious works deployed a vast range of Greek and Latin sources to correct and explicate texts and solve problems in every field of ancient culture. Poliziano showed how to compare Latin writers systematically with their Greek sources. More generally, he and others insisted that only the philologist could correct and explicate classical texts—even the technical classics of law, medicine, and philosophy, which had long been the province of professional practitioners of those disciplines. A new critical and historical method had come into being. At the same time, however, classical scholarship revived old myths and created new ones. Ficino, Pico, and others developed from their reading of Neo-Platonic texts like the *Hermetic Corpus* what became the popular theory that the Greek philosophers had derived their central ideas from the Egyptians and Chaldeans. And the papal theologian Annius of Viterbo, who published what he described as the fragments of the lost histories of *Berosus, *Manetho, and others in 1498, embedded in a huge commentary, foisted actual forgeries on a Europe-wide public. Spanish and English readers delighted in his meticulously argued demonstration that their nations were directly descended from exiled Trojans.

The later 15th and 16th cents. saw all of these new methods and interests spread to northern Europe. Some northern scholars—like Beatus Rhenanus—continued the technical efforts of Poliziano and others, working with librarians and printers to produce clean editions of texts based on the best sources. Others continued the more contentious effort to show that humanistic methods could be applied to all ancient texts. Guillaume Budé wrote the first full humanistic commentary on the *Digest*, founding what became a French speciality. Biblical scholarship developed even more rapidly. Valla had already argued that the text of the New Testament needed the same sort of critical treatment as the classics. The great Dutch scholar Erasmus, who printed Valla's New Testament commentary, produced and printed a full new Latin translation of the New Testament, with a Greek text to support it. He also argued that the historical and philological methods of the humanists could yield the best understanding of the biblical text. The Reformation and Counter-Reformation, though Erasmus and others initially saw them as a threat to the humanities, ultimately reinforced their enterprise. Catholics and Protestants alike accepted the need to study the Bible in its original languages, while Protestant academies and

Jesuit colleges both adopted and systematized the humanist curriculum.

In the second half of the 16th cent. scholarship in several technical disciplines reached maturity. Textual criticism, of Greek as well as Latin, found many original practitioners, like Jean Dorat, and a few theorists, like Francesco Robortello, who wrote the first manual of the art. Denys Lambin and others drew up spectacularly detailed commentaries on the central Latin texts and their Greek literary background. Students of Roman history and Greek poetry and philosophy compiled the first collections of fragments of authors whose works had been wholly or partially lost. Antiquarians and Roman lawyers like Antonio Agustin, Carlo Sigonio, and Jacques Cujas traced the development of the Roman constitution and legal system over the centuries, from the *Twelve Tables to the *Corpus Iuris*, which received critical editions and elaborate commentary (see JUSTINIAN'S CODIFICATION). Antiquaries also collected, organized, and published the first corpora of inscriptions and wrote systematic treatises on virtually every aspect of ancient social and cultural life. Justus Lipsius, for example, reconstructed the military and organizational practices of the Roman army. Systematic descriptions made the main ancient ruins and artworks of Rome and other cities widely known: especially important were the Roman consular *Fasti* and *Triumphs*, discovered and reassembled in the 1540s, which inspired Sigonio and others to rework the chronology of Roman history. Joseph Scaliger and other chronologers extended this enterprise, establishing what remains the chronological framework of ancient history, Greek and Near Eastern as well as Roman. They also reconstructed the central ancient calendars and their development. See CALENDAR, GREEK and ROMAN; ECLIPSES; TIME-RECKONING.

By the end of the 16th cent. most of the classical texts now known had been printed, an enormous technical literature had been produced, and central problems of ancient political and literary history—like that of the origins of Rome—had begun to be studied in a critical, open-minded way that owed little to ancient precedent. The Dutch universities—above all Leiden, where Lipsius taught and Scaliger enjoyed the first full-time research post created in the modern world—became centres of classical research, with remarkable libraries and publishing facilities. At the same time, however, the historical texts forged by Annius of Viterbo still outsold Herodotus. Jean Bodin, who wrote the first manual on how to read and assess the sources of ancient and modern history, took central theses from them. The myth of a glamorous Egyptian *prisca philosophia* found adherents across Europe. Though a few scholars, like Isaac Casaubon, saw that the *Hermetic Corpus* was neither Egyptian nor ancient, most continued to treat it as the source from which Plato drew his central theses. See HERMES TRISMEGISTUS.

The 17th and 18th cents. saw the gains of the Renaissance consolidated, especially in the Netherlands. Huge collections of historical and antiquarian treatises enabled readers to follow the growth of debate over Athenian festivals or the Roman constitution, and variorum editions collected the results of textual criticism and explanatory comments, text by text. Some new texts, like the *Cena Trimalchionis* (see PETRONIUS ARBITER), were discovered: textual critics like Gronovius and Heinsius continued to explore manuscript traditions and propose brilliant conjectural emendations; and a vast range of late Greek texts, like those of many Church Fathers and Byzantine historians, saw print for the first time. The good money of the genuine ancient historians gradually drove Annius' bad money off the market. Much attention was also paid to relics that did not come from classical Greece or Rome—like the Egyptian obelisks, sometimes adorned with hieroglyphic inscriptions, found in Rome, in which many scholars thought they could see the relics of the *prisca philosophia*, or the Roman catacombs, in which ecclesiastical historians found the visual remains of an ancient world very different from that presented in the literary canon. Enormous effort went into assembling and interpreting the sources of the history of ancient philosophy, but debate still raged over the extent of the Greek thinkers' debt to the ancient near east.

Despite this intense continued activity, the significance of classical learning was challenged more profoundly than ever before. Bacon, Galileo, and Descartes insisted, in different ways, that knowledge of nature had more to offer than knowledge of texts, and that a modern philosophy and curriculum could not rest on the study of books written in what had actually been a more primitive time. The rise of modern languages and literatures challenged the pre-eminence of the classics. A reading public grew up which felt less at ease with Greek and Latin than with French, English, or Italian. And the undeniable fact that many issues in ancient literature, history, and philosophy had remained the objects of endless debate for centuries called the intellectual validity of classical studies into question. The scholarly response to this challenge took varied forms. Some antiquaries and archaeologists claimed—not without exaggeration—that their first-hand study of material remains rested on the same methods of exact measurement as the experiments of the scientists. The late 17th and 18th cents. certainly witnessed an intensive effort to explore and record Greek as well as Roman ruins, as well as the vastly important excavation of *Herculaneum and *Pompeii. *Textual criticism benefited from the systematic efforts of Mabillon, Montfaucon, and Maffei to date manuscripts systematically, on the basis of their materials and script.

But the most profound changes took place in what had traditionally been seen as the central areas of classical studies. Historians like Giambattista Vico and Jacobus Perizonius and philologists like Jean Leclerc and Richard Bentley worked in radically different contexts and from radically different assumptions. All of them agreed, however, that the study of the ancient world must become as modern as the New Philosophy. The scholar must read the classics in a critical spirit; must eliminate or alter any passage in a text, however familiar, if the evidence of the manuscripts and of 'reason' did not support its presence; must abandon the traditional narrative of Roman history or the traditional view that Homer had written elaborate works of high literature, if the sources, rationally considered, did not justify them. It became clear that every text—even those of the Old and New Testaments—had changed over time, thanks to human action and intervention: also that the ancients themselves had not fully understood the development of their languages, literatures, and societies. The modern Dutch or English scholar knew his ancient texts too well to believe that they encompassed all knowledge—or even all the tools needed to analyse them. Homer himself, long seen as the first and greatest of classics, was re-imagined as a primitive poet, more like a modern Bedouin than a modern Englishman.

This approach, with its stress on the otherness of the Greek and Roman past, might seem to undermine the value of classical studies. In later 18th-cent. Germany, however, it became the core of the intellectual programme that restored classical scholarship to a central position in higher education. The art historian Winckelmann, the Göttingen professor Heyne, and his brilliant, rebelli-

ous pupil Friedrich August Wolf admitted that the ancient world was very different from their own. Only by dropping all familiar assumptions and undertaking a comprehensive study of every aspect of antiquity, from literature to history to archaeology and religion, they held, could a scholar hope to interpret a given text or solve a given problem. But they also insisted that this exercise had a unique intellectual value. By working his way into every nook and cranny of ancient life, by coming to understand the Greek spirit as a whole, the scholar—and the student—would develop his own sensibility and intellect in a uniquely rich and rewarding way, for which the study of the natural world offered no parallel. The value of this new approach was dramatized by a series of brilliant, iconoclastic publications, including Winckelmann's *History of Art in Antiquity*, Wolf's *Prolegomena to Homer*, and Barthold Georg Niebuhr's *History of Rome*. It won the support of the reformer of Prussian education, Wilhelm von Humboldt, and found institutional homes in the Prussian universities and Gymnasien. And it led to the creation of new methods and new literatures in every field: to the production of vast new series of publications, from corpora of Roman and Greek inscriptions and the Teubner texts to classical journals in which specialized results could be presented and debated; to the rise of a newly rigorous textual criticism; to the effort, never wholly successful, to create histories of Greece and Rome that integrated the traditional historian's effort to provide a narrative account of central events with what had been the antiquarian tradition of systematic analysis of laws, institutions, and rituals.

The German classicists were not, in fact, so original as they claimed. Their approach to textual criticism was modelled on that of 18th-cent. biblical scholars, and their efforts to write a new history of the ancient world came after the pioneering models established by two English amateurs, Edward Gibbon and George Grote. England, France, and Italy continued to foster partly or wholly independent scholarly methods and enterprises. In the course of the 19th and 20th centuries, however, the comprehensive programme known as *Altertumswissenschaft* gradually put its stamp on classical studies throughout the western world. Even the sharpest critics of particular German scholars—like A. E. Housman—generally learned their trade by mastering what they saw as the core of the German tradition. Even Hitler's expulsion of the Jews, which did incalculable harm to German scholarship, paradoxically conveyed its methods and results to universities and scholarly communities in France, England, the United States, and elsewhere.

The new scholarship proved as fertile a ground for debates and polemics as the old. Schools developed, whose members proved incapable of seeing outsiders' points of view, and both substantive and methodological questions proved capable of serving as the occasions of philological warfare. The increasing specialization and technicality of the new scholarship also provoked criticism—most notably and influentially from Friedrich Nietzsche, himself a product of it. Meanwhile the competition of modern forms of secondary education chipped away, slowly but inevitably, at the central position of classical studies in the university. None the less, classical scholarship finished the 20th cent. in a condition that would have been recognizable two hundred years before: as an interdisciplinary, rigorous, and creative enterprise.

E. J. Kenney, *The Classical Text* (1974); A. Momigliano, *Studies in Historiography* (1966); L. D. Reynolds and N. G. Wilson, *Scribes and Scholars*[3] (1991); S. Timpanaro, *La genesi del metodo del Lachmann* (1985); A. T. Grafton, *Joseph Scaliger* (1983–93).   A. T. G.

scholia—from the Greek σχόλιον, first attested when *Cicero quotes it back at T. *Pomponius Atticus (*Att.* 16. 7. 3)—are notes on a text, anything from a continuous commentary to one-word jottings; but normally the term refers to substantial sets of exegetical and critical notes written in the margin or between the lines of manuscripts. As many of these go back to ancient commentaries, it carries historical implications absent from 'gloss', which suggests paraphrase or humdrum explanation.

In antiquity commentaries filled volumes of their own, and some survive in that form, such as *Hipparchus (3) on *Aratus (1) or *Asconius on Cicero's speeches. Text and commentary alternate in *PLille* 76d of *Callimachus (3) (3rd cent. BC) and *POxy.* 2221 of *Nicander (1st cent. AD); notes occupy the margins of some papyri, such as *POxy.* 841 of *Pindar (2nd cent. AD); but even after the adoption of the codex no Latin scribes before the Carolingian revival surround the text with commentary, and products like *POxy.* 2258 of the 6th or 7th cent., a copy of Callimachus with an old commentary in the margin, are too rare to have ended debate over whether Greek scribes made the innovation before Latin. Some commentaries were reduced to marginal notes and later reassembled; *Donatus (1) on *Terence suffered this fate, only for one scribe to put it back in the margin of his Terence (British Library Add. 11906).

Written round the text, then, and usually in a smaller or less formal script, scholia result from excerption, abbreviation, and conflation, brought about partly by readers' needs and partly by lack of space. A frequent casualty was the lemma, the brief quotation by which a commentator keyed a note to the text. Lemmata may preserve ancient readings that improve the medieval text or shed light on its ancestry; but when notes migrated to margins, the lemmata might be dropped or adjusted. Transitions like ἄλλως or *sive*, 'alternatively', often betray conflation of different commentaries; illogical connections betray either conflation or abbreviation.

These processes have left the history of most collections quite obscure. References to late authorities may be accretions, and the conservative language of scholarly comment seldom yields secure dates. In Latin, clausulae (see PROSE RHYTHM, LATIN) guarantee antiquity, but in both Greek and Latin the commonest guarantee is the presence of credible material not preserved elsewhere. Many Greek scholia rest on work done as far back as the 3rd cent. BC, often, it seems, filtered through two scholars of roughly Augustan date, namely *Didymus (1) whose commentary on *Demosthenes (2) is represented on papyrus, and *Theon (1), who specialized in Alexandrian poets. Similarly, Latin commentators of the 4th or 5th cents. cited scholars as old as the Republic. No less than any other text, scholia may emerge late: one that transforms the interpretation of *Juvenal, *Satire* 4 by quoting from *Statius' *Bellum Germanicum* survives only in a printed edition of 1486. See SCHOLARSHIP, ANCIENT, *Greek*.

Like their modern successors, ancient commentators sometimes guessed or talked nonsense, but at their best scholia are a mine of information, though less in Latin than in Greek. *Aristophanes (1) benefits most, because explanation of topical or literary references and allusions began at *Alexandria (1) in the heyday of the Library. The scholia in the codex Venetus A of the *Iliad* (Marc. Gr. 454, 10th cent.) give a detailed picture of Alexandrian editing, not least the critical notation employed. Scholia on other authors too preserve ancient readings, whether cited explicitly or implied by the argument. Those on tragedy, for instance, sometimes allege interpolation by actors; less polemically, one on Pindar, *Nemean* 10. 62, cites the attempts of

*Aristarchus (2) and Didymus at reconciling Pindar with the *Cypria* (see EPIC CYCLE). Variants from scholia often entered the text; manuscripts of the *Aeneid* that include the *Ille ego* lines (which precede 1.1 in some editions) or the Helen episode (2. 567–88) doubtless drew on *Servius.

Though transmission has largely effaced the cultural context of the original commentaries, scholia often reveal interesting attitudes either moral or literary. A commentator for once given a name, *Ulpianus, compares Demosthenes' *First Olynthiac* to speeches in *Thucydides (2) and *Homer. Commentators' interpretations might influence the young at school or poets when they read earlier poets.

Printed editions at first retained the layout of manuscripts and framed the text in scholia. Not until the 18th cent. did scholia begin to be analysed in earnest and edited in their own right. No recent editor has caused the same sensation as Villoison in 1788 when he published the scholia from the Venetus A and spurred Wolf to his *Prolegomena* of 1795, the bible of the Homeric question. Editing scholia is an important task. Their instability, however, tends to make reconstruction arbitrary; and while bringing different versions together creates awkward problems of presentation, publishing them singly tries the patience of readers.

G. Zuntz, *Die Aristophanes-Scholien der Papyri* (1938–9, 1975); J. Irigoin, N. G. Wilson, and L. Holtz, in *Il libro e il testo*, ed. C. Questa and R. Raffaelli (1984); H. Erbse, *Beiträge zur Überlieferung der Iliasscholien* (1960); J. E. G. Zetzel, *Latin Textual Criticism in Antiquity* (1981); H. D. Jocelyn, 'The annotations of M. Valerius Probus', *CQ* 1984, 1985; A. La Penna, *Scholia in P. Ovidi Nasonis Ibin* (1959), pp. v–xxxviii; M. Schmidt, *Die Erklärungen zum Weltbild Homers und zur Kultur der Heroenzeit in den bT-Scholien zur Ilias* (1976); R. Meijering, *Literary and Rhetorical Theories in Greek Scholia* (1987); R. R. Schlunk, *The Homeric Scholia and the Aeneid* (1974); for editions see under *Scholia* in TLG: *Canon of Greek authors and works* (1990); *TLL: Index* (1990). For a concise review of typical problems, P. Wessner, *RE* 12 (1925), 356–61, 'Lactantius Placidus'.
M. D. R.

science See particular sciences e.g. ANATOMY; ASTRONOMY; BOTANY; CATOPTRICS, etc.; and see EXPERIMENT.

Sciathos, a small Aegean island (48 sq. km.), hilly and wooded, between the Magnesian mainland and the wealthier island of *Peparethos. An allegedly Carian and Thessalian population was superseded by Chalcidians (see CHALCIS) who founded the town in the south-east; some pre-Greeks perhaps survived, though references to 'Palaiskiathioi' may imply only a resiting of the town. Remains include 4th-cent. fortification walls, coastal watchtowers, and Roman burials.

The islanders joined the *Delian League (paying 1,000 drachmas) and *Second Athenian Confederacy, but rarely determined their own fate: Sciathos was a valuable base for the Greeks in 480, for Athens habitually, and later for Macedonia, Rome, and *Mithradates VI. Freed by Rome in 197, it was returned to Athens by Antony (M. *Antonius (2)) but freed again under the principate.

ML 90; *RE* 3 A 1 (1929), 520–1; C. Fredrich and A. J. B. Wace, *MDAI(A)* 1906; *Arch. Rep.* 1992–3; [British Admiralty] Naval Intelligence Division, *Greece* 3 (1945), 395–7.
D. G. J. S.

Scione, city in north Greece, near the tip of the western (Pallene) peninsula of *Chalcidice, south-east of modern Nea Skioni. Chance finds include coins and walls. *Thucydides (2) (4. 120) says it was a settlement of Peloponnesians from Pellene in *Achaea, but there was also a tradition that *Protesilaus was the founder. Scione normally paid 6 talents tribute to Athens in the time of the *Delian League. Its most famous hour was its enthusiastic but unwise reception of the Spartan *Brasidas in 423 BC (Thuc. 4. 121. 1); this led to harsh Athenian reprisals instigated by *Cleon (Thuc. 4. 122. 6; 5. 32, the site given to exiles from *Plataea). Athenian treatment of Scione was a standard 4th-cent. reproach: Isoc. 4. 100, where Scione is bracketed with *Melos. In truth, Sparta's betrayal of Scione was no less of a disgrace. After the *Peloponnesian War, *Lysander restored the Scionaeans (Plut. *Lys.* 14; this must mean there were after all survivors of the Athenian punitive action) and Scione revived modestly.

Hdt. 7. 123, 8. 128; B. Meritt, *AJArch.* 1923, 450 f.; E. Oberhummer, *RE* 3 A (1927), 529; M. Zahrnt, *Olynth und die Chalkidier* (1971), 234–6 and in *Lexikon der historischen Stätten* 623–4; Meiggs, *AE* 528; M. McAllister, *PECS* 845; Hornblower, *Comm. on Thuc.* 2 on 4. 120 ff.   S. H.

Scipio Aemilianus See CORNELIUS SCIPIO AEMILIANUS AFRICANUS (NUMANTINUS), P.

Scipio Africanus See CORNELIUS SCIPIO AFRICANUS, P.

Scipionic Circle is a term used to describe P. *Cornelius Scipio Aemilianus and his friends, who were considered to be a group sharing the same cultural and even political outlook. The concept emerged during the 19th cent. and had become a commonplace of scholarship by the early 20th, although today it is regarded with suspicion. It is heavily dependent on *Cicero's *Rep.* and *Amic.* (esp. 69), the former gathering together Scipio and his 'friends' for a discussion on government, the latter listing his friends; but the fictitious nature of these dialogues means that they should be treated very cautiously. The 'circle' was held to include prominent Romans such as C. *Laelius (2) and L. *Furius Philus, younger men such as P. *Rutilius Rufus, writers such as *Terence and *Lucilius (1), and the Greeks *Polybius (1) and *Panaetius. Together they were the main advocates of Greek culture within Rome (see PHILHELLENISM), in sharp contrast to the traditionalists whose cause was embodied by M. *Porcius Cato (1); some scholars have even given the division a wider political significance. This polarization into philhellenists and traditionalists seems to underestimate the complexity of the Roman reaction to Greece as well as creating an unwarranted Scipionic monopoly of Greek culture. The concept of the 'Scipionic Circle' gives Scipio's friends a unity which is not supported by the evidence. Recent scholarship has tended to focus on the relationship between Panaetius and the more philosophically-inclined members of the 'circle'.

R. M. Brown, *A Study of the Scipionic Circle* (1934); A. E. Astin, *Scipio Aemilianus* (1967); H. Strasburger, *Hermes* 1966; J.-L. Ferrary, *Philhellénisme et impérialisme* (1988).   A. W. E.

Sciras, writer of phlyax-plays (see PHLYAKES), like *Rhinthon, also from *Tarentum, probably 3rd cent. BC. One title (*Meleager*) survives, with one fragment that parodies *Euripides, *Hipp.* 75; see PARODY, GREEK.

FRAGMENT G. Kaibel, *CGF* (1899), 190; A. Olivieri, *Frammenti della commedia greca e del mimo nella Sicilia e nella Magna Grecia* 2² (1947), 24–6.
INTERPRETATION A. Körte in *RE* 3 A 1 (1927), 535, under *Skiras* 3.   W. G. A.

Sciron or **Sciros,** names of several related heroic figures connected with *Attica, *Salamis (1), and *Megara. The name suggests a possible connection with *Athena Sciras and the *Scirophoria, and this is borne out by the cult-places: at Sciron on the Sacred Way, the destination of the Scirophoria procession (Paus. 1. 36. 4), and at *Phaleron near the sanctuary of Athena

Sciras (ibid. with Philochorus, *FGrH* 328 F 111; cf. Ferguson, *Hesp.* 1938, 28, where the pair receive *sacrifice at the same altar). From a later period, presumably, comes the integration into Attic mythology, largely through the figure of *Theseus. The Thesean saga distinguishes two figures. Sciron of Megara was one of the many brigands killed by Theseus on his journey to claim his Athenian inheritance; he presumably derives from a Megarian hero, since *Plutarch (*Thes.* 10. 3) reports the Megarian tradition making him a just man. Sciros king of Salamis helped Theseus by giving him skilled navigators for the voyage to Crete. Another mythical Sciros, identified by *Pausanias (3) with the hero buried at Sciron, fought with the Eleusinians against *Erechtheus; see ELEUSIS.

C. Calame, *Thésée et l'imaginaire athénien* (1990), 339–55.   E. Ke.

Scirophoria or **Scira,** an Athenian religious festival celebrated on 12 Scirophorion (June), primarily by women. It featured a procession, including the priestess of *Athena, the priest of *Poseidon-*Erechtheus, and perhaps that of *Helios, from the Acropolis to a sanctuary of Athena Sciras at Sciron on the road to *Eleusis near the crossing of the *Cephissus. The ceremony involved the 'carrying of the *skira*' which may have been a large sunshade (σκίρον) or an image of Athena made of gypsum (σκίρα). At Sciron there was a sanctuary of *Demeter, Kore (see PERSEPHONE), Athena, and Poseidon (Paus. 1. 37. 2), quite likely the site of the festival. Some think that there the women performed rites preliminary to Demeter's later *Thesmophoria, but the evidence (schol. to Lucian 275. 23) is garbled and inconclusive. In any case the deities and location of the festival suggest an amalgamation of Eleusinian and Athenian cults.

Burkert, *HN* 143–9; Parke, *Festivals of the Athenians* (1977), 156–62; Jacoby on *FGrH* 328 F 14–16.   J. D. M.

scolia, drinking-songs, especially Attic (see ATTICA). *Athenaeus (1) (15. 693 f.) preserves a collection from the late 6th and early 5th cents. They were sung in the *prytaneion; a singer held a myrtle-branch and, when he had finished, passed the branch to another and called on him for a song. The process is illustrated in Ar. *Vesp.* 1216 ff., cf. schol. Pl. *Grg.* 451e, Plut. *Quaest. conv.* 1. 1. 5. There were also choral *scolia*, possibly of a later date, like two pieces in a papyrus at Berlin (*Scol. Anon.* 30).

Page, *PMG* 472–8. R. Reitzenstein, *Epigramm und Skolion* (1893), 3 ff.; C. M. Bowra, *Greek Lyric Poetry*² (1962), 373 ff.   C. M. B.

Scopadae See CRANNON; SIMONIDES.

Scopas, Parian sculptor and architect, active *c.*370–330 BC. Specializing in younger divinities, he was reckoned among the three principal Greek 'sculptors of gods' (ἀγαλματοποιοί) and 'sculptors of men' (ἀνδριαντοποιοί) (*Laterculi Alexandrini* 7. 3 ff.; *POxy.* 10. 1241. 1. 3 ff.); he was also famous for his architectural sculpture. He worked mostly in marble; his only recorded bronze was an Aphrodite Pandemos for *Elis. He made an *Aphrodite and Pothos (longing) for *Samothrace and an Eros, Himeros (desire), and Pothos for *Megara (exhibited with statues by *Praxiteles around the ancient image of Aphrodite Praxis); an Aphrodite which Pliny (*HN* 36. 26) preferred to Praxiteles' Cnidia; an Apollo at *Rhamnus and another for the Smintheion (*Troas); an *Ares; an *Artemis and *Athena in *Thebes (1); an Athena and *Dionysus in *Cnidus; an *Asclepius and *Hygieia in *Gortyn and *Tegea; a *Hecate in *Argos (2); a *Hermes; a *Hestia; a *Leto and Ortygia in *Ephesus; two Furies (*Erinyes) in Athens; a *Heracles in *Sicyon; a *maenad; and a basket-bearer. Several of these were later taken to Rome. The Pothos, maenad, Rhamnuntine Apollo, and Heracles have been recognized in copy.

His architectural sculpture included a column-drum for the Artemisium at Ephesus and the east side of the *Mausoleum at Halicarnassus; a group of Poseidon, Thetis, Achilles, Nereids, Tritons, and various sea-monsters, later in Rome, was perhaps also architectural. Of these, little survives: the fragments from Ephesus are eclectic, and nothing was found *in situ* on the east side of the Mausoleum; a Triton in Berlin may come from the marine group. *Pausanias (3) (8. 45) says that he designed the great Doric temple of Athena Alea at Tegea, which replaced one burnt in 395. His design was highly original. He unified the interior spatially by engaging the colonnade in the cella walls; unusually, the lower order was Corinthian, the upper, Ionic (see ORDERS, ARCHITECTURAL). The pediments (the Calydonian boar-hunt (see MELEAGER (1)) and the battle between *Telephus (1) and *Achilles by the Caicus), are equally innovative—craggy and strongly expressive—prompting their ascription to Scopas. With the Pothos and maenad, they certify him as a master of pathos, inaugurating many trends later fully developed in Hellenistic sculpture. Attributions (all copies) include the Lansdowne Heracles in Malibu, a Meleager, and a Nereid in Ostia.

C. Dugas and others, *Le Sanctuaire d'Aléa Athéna à Tégée* (1924); A. F. Stewart, *Skopas of Paros* (1977), and *Greek Sculpture* (1990), 182 ff., 284 ff., figs. 540 ff.; N. Norman, *AJArch.* 88 (1984), 169 ff.; B. S. Ridgway, *Hellenistic Sculpture* 1 (1991), 82 ff., pls. 44 ff.   A. F. S.

Scopelianus of *Clazomenae (1st–2nd cent. AD), sophist and teacher of *Herodes Atticus; he wrote an epic *Gigantia*.

Philostr. *VS* 1. 21 (514–21).   M. B. T.

Scordisci were a Celtic tribe, later much intermingled with *Illyrii and Thracians (see THRACE), who invaded Greece in the early 3rd cent. BC and then settled around the confluence of the Savus and the Danube to the east of *Sirmium and southwards to the upper Margus (Just. 32. 3). In the later 2nd and early 1st cent. BC many Roman governors of Macedonia undertook campaigns against them. As late as 16 BC they were still raiding Macedonia but had been conquered or won over by 12 BC, when they co-operated with Tiberius in attacks on the Pannonian Breuci (Cass. Dio 54. 30. 3; 31. 2–4). A *civitas Scordiscorum* in Pannonia governed by native *principes* and *praefecti* (see PRAEFECTUS) is attested in inscriptions of the late 1st cent. AD (A. Mócsy, *Hist.* 1957, 488 f.).

J. Wilkes, *The Illyrians* (1992), 201 ff.   J. J. W.

scribae See APPARITORES.

Scribonia (*RE* 32), sister of L. *Scribonius Libo, was married at least three times. Her first two husbands, both of whom allegedly held the consulship, are hard to identify; by one of them (a Scipio) she was the mother of Cornelia, wife of Paullus *Aemilius Lepidus. The third was Octavian (see AUGUSTUS), who married her in 40 BC in order to conciliate Sextus *Pompeius, Libo's son-in-law, but in 39, on the birth of their daughter *Iulia (3), divorced her. She accompanied Iulia into exile in 2 BC, remaining with her until her death in AD 14. She herself was still alive in 16.

Syme, *AA* 247 ff. table XX.   T. J. C.; R. J. S.

Scribonius (*RE* 6) **Aphrodisius,** freedman of *Augustus' second wife, *Scribonia, and formerly slave of *Horace's teacher *Orbilius Pupillus, wrote on Latin orthography, attacking the

work and character of his contemporary *Verrius Flaccus (Suet. *Gramm.* 19).   R. A. K.

Scribonius (*RE* 10) **Curio** (1), **Gaius,** after early forensic activity was tribune 90 BC, served under *Sulla in the east, and later enriched himself in the proscriptions. Consul 76, he opposed Cn. *Sicinius, then fought in Macedonia and triumphed (73). He supported *Verres and though a poor orator, was henceforth active in the courts and in politics and became censor 61 with L. *Iulius Caesar (2). By assisting P. *Clodius Pulcher (61), he irritated *Cicero, who wrote a pamphlet against him and later, needing his help when in exile, wanted to deny authorship. He consistently opposed *Caesar until his death in 53 (Cic. *Fam.* 2. 2).   E. B.

Scribonius (*RE* 11) **Curio** (2), **Gaius,** son of (1), was a friend of P. *Clodius Pulcher whose widow *Fulvia he later married, and had a relationship with M. *Antonius (2). Yet in the 50s he joined his father (who disapproved of his personal life) in supporting the *optimates. He helped to expose L. *Vettius and was quaestor 54. Elected tribune 50 as an enemy of *Caesar, he was bribed by Caesar with a vast sum, perhaps when his own ambitious legislation was rejected by the senate. He tried to halt the drift towards civil war, proposing to disarm both Caesar and *Pompey. This was finally carried in the senate by 370 votes to 22 (App. *BCiv.* 2. 30. 119), but the consul C. *Claudius Marcellus (1) refused to accept the vote. In 49 Curio served under Caesar in Italy (incidentally trying to win over *Cicero), then was sent *pro praetore* to Sicily, which he occupied, and to Africa. There, after initial successes, he was trapped and killed by *Juba (1) I.

Gruen, *LGRR*, see index; M. H. Dettenhofer, *Perdita Iuventus* (1992), 34 ff., 146 ff.   E. B.

Scribonius Largus, Roman physician c. AD 1–50, studied at Rome in the time of *Tiberius. In 43 he accompanied *Claudius on his British campaign, probably on the recommendation of his patron C. *Iulius Callistus, secretary to Claudius, who also procured the Emperor's patronage for Scribonius' writings. In gratitude Scribonius dedicated to Callistus his only work to come down to us, the *Compositiones* (prescriptions). The contents of this show him to be an empiricist in method, closely akin to *Celsus. His work was largely used by (among other writers) Marcellus Empiricus. See also PHARMACOLOGY.

Ed. G. Helmreich (1887); S. Sconocchia (1983); K. Deichgräber, *Professio Medici. Zum Vorwort des S. Largus* (1950). B. Baldwin, *Rh. Mus.* 1992, 74 ff.   W. D. R.; V. N.

Scribonius (*RE* 20) **Libo, Lucius,** born c.90 BC (moneyer 62), of praetorian family, father-in-law of Sextus *Pompeius, probably as plebeian tribune supported *Pompey's pretensions to an Egyptian command in 56 BC and later was in charge of part of his fleet in the Adriatic (49–48). By the end of 46 he was reconciled with *Caesar, but must have been proscribed in 43: in 40, as one of Sextus' adherents, he was sent to Mark Antony (M. *Antonius (2)) to arrange an alliance against Octavian (see AUGUSTUS). However, he agreed to Octavian's marriage with his sister *Scribonia and in 39 left Sicily to prepare the ground for the Pact of Misenum. In 36 he accompanied Sextus to Asia, but abandoned him for Antony in 35. He was consul in 34, and perhaps still alive (as an Arval brother; see FRATRES ARVALES) in 21. He left two sons, and M. *Scribonius Libo Drusus was his grandson.

Syme, *Rom. Rev.* and *AA*, indexes.   T. J. C.; B. M. L.

Scribonius (*RE* 23) **Libo Drusus, Marcus,** great-grandson of

*Pompey, pontifex and praetor or praetor designate, in AD 16 underwent the first great political trial of *Tiberius' Principate. For *Tacitus (1) (*Ann.* 2. 27 ff.) an innocent, if foolish, victim of conspiracy, officially (*Fasti Amiternini,* Sept. 13) he planned to assassinate Tiberius, his sons, and other leading citizens. He committed suicide during the trial.

Syme, *Tacitus,* 399 f., and *AA*; B. Levick, *Tiberius the Politician* (1976), indexes.   J. P. D.; B. M. L.

scripts, pre-alphabetic See PRE-ALPHABETIC SCRIPTS.

sculpture, Greek

Origins (c.1000–c.600 BC) Of Dark-Age sculpture, only small bronzes and terracottas survive; unpretentious at first, by the 8th cent. they tend to favour the rigorously analytical forms of contemporary vase-painting. Some wooden cult images certainly existed, though most were perhaps aniconic or semi-iconic. Yet *Homer describes an *Athena at *Troy that was probably lifesize and fully human in form (*Il.* 6. 297 ff.); and a half-lifesize *Apollo, a *Leto, and an *Artemis, bronze-plated over a wooden core, survive from Cretan Drerus (see CRETE) as confirmation (*c.*750). This *sphyrelaton* technique is near-eastern in origin. On close inspection the works reveal a careful attention to proportions, a command of volume and mass, and a strong sense of articulation (based on the natural jointing of the core). Converting the flux of appearance into a regular, harmonious, yet visually credible form, this unknown artist is a true pioneer.

The Cretan *poleis* (see POLIS) were socially and politically precocious, and their eastern trade, in which *Corinth soon joined, set off a new cycle of experimentation *c.*700. In sculpture, the most popular of these *orientalizing styles is usually called 'Daedalic' after the mythical founder of Greek sculpture (see DAEDALUS). Diffused through terracotta plaques and popular in a wide variety of media and scales, Daedalic is characterized by a strict frontality and an equally strict adherence to stylized, angular forms; coiffures are elaborately layered in the Syrian manner. When employed on temples (*Gortyn, Prinias), it often follows near-eastern precedent in both placement and iconography.

Meanwhile, Cycladic sculptors were looking to Egypt, receptive to foreigners from 664. After *c.*650 the walking, kilted Egyptian males were adapted to form the *kouros* type, nude and free-standing—supposedly a 'discovery' of *Daedalus (Diod. Sic. 1. 97. 5, etc.). *Marble was the preferred medium, and adherence to the quarried block tended to make the finished work look like a four-sided relief. The type soon spread to east Greece and the mainland. In the earliest *kouroi,* as in their draped female counterparts, the *korai,* the Daedalic style predominated, but by *c.*600 its rigid stylization was breaking down as sculptors sought new ways of communicating male and female beauty, to delight the gods or to commemorate the dead.

Archaic sculpture (c.600–c.480 BC) Archaic sculpture seeks exemplary patterns for reality, somewhat akin to the formulae of Homeric and archaic poetry. The aim was still to make sense of the phenomenal world, to generalize from experience, but in a more flexible and direct way. Each local school developed its own preferences in ideal male beauty. Naxians liked a sinuous contour and clear-cut, elegantly stylized anatomy; Samians massively rounded forms and powerfully articulated joints; Boeotians a craggy masculinity; and so on. Only in Athens did a thoroughgoing naturalism evolve, as a by-product of a desire to understand the tectonics of the perfect human body in their entirety. By

*c.*500 Athenian *kouroi* were fully developed human beings, their anatomy closely observed, clearly articulated, and skilfully integrated with the underlying physical and geometric structure of the body.

Korai offered fewer opportunities for detailed physical observation, but just as many for displays of beauty appropriate to their subjects' station in life and value to a male-dominated world. Their sculptors concentrated upon refining the facial features, creating a truly feminine proportional canon, and indicating the curves of the body beneath the drapery. The mainland tunic or *peplos* offered little here, but from *c.*560 the possibilities of the more complex Ionian chiton and himation began to fascinate the eastern Greeks. Soon, refugees fleeing from the Persians helped the fashion to catch on elsewhere, particularly in Attica. Yet by *c.*500, serious interest in the behaviour of cloth had given way to a passion for novelty: sculptors now pursued a decorative brilliance enhanced by a lavish application of colour.

Both types could be adapted for cult statues (see STATUES (CULT OF)), and the sources recount much work in this genre (see ARCHERMUS; THEODORUS (1)), often associated with the new stone *temples that now served as focal points of *polis* religion. Gold and ivory (*chryselephantine*) statues also begin to appear; several have been found at Delphi. From *c.*600, temple exteriors were often embellished with architectural sculpture, first in limestone, then in marble; treasuries for votives were soon enhanced in the same way. Mythological narratives first supplemented, then supplanted primitive power-symbols like gorgons and lions (Corfu (*Corcyra), 'Hekatompedon', and Hydra pediments at Athens). Sculptors soon adapted their subjects to their frames, whether triangular (see above), rectangular (Ionic friezes at *Ephesus, *Samos, and *Delphi), or square (metopes of the Sicyonian treasury at Delphi and temples at *Paestum and *Selinus); to carve pediments in higher relief and even in the round ('Old temple' pediments at Athens; Apollo temple at Delphi); and to dramatize the story by judicious timing, lively postures and gestures, and compelling rendering of detail.

By *c.*500 the drive to narrate convincingly had permeated virtually all sculptural genres, from gravestones to statue-bases. Hollow-cast *bronze also began to replace marble (see ANTENOR (2)), at least in free-standing sculpture. Its greater tensile strength now removed any technical restraint in the handling of narrative action poses. Only the *kouroi* and *korai* remained aloof—and look increasingly old-fashioned in consequence. A revolution was brewing, and could not be long delayed.

Classical sculpture (c.480–c.330 BC) 'The dynamic of the subject-matter'—the living body, unencumbered by arcane symbolism or religious inhibitions—had always played an important part in modifying the formulaic style, and surely contributed signally to its abandonment, but other factors also helped. Three stand out: a strong commitment to credible narration, prompting sculptors to think of the body as an integrated organism, not a mechanism assembled from discrete parts; a feeling that naturalism was a mixed blessing, requiring corrective measures to preserve the statue's monumentality; and a new quest for interiority, for exploring man's inner self. Around 480 even the automaton-like *kouros* gave way to more subtly mobile, narrative-oriented figures, monumental in physique and grave of countenance, pausing as if to think, like the '*Critius' boy, or resolute in action, like the Tyrannicides (see CRITIUS).

This more flexible, holistic, and contextual view of man was abetted by a simultaneous repudiation of late Archaic 'excess' in decorative patterning in favour of a rigorously applied doctrine of formal restraint. The new style strongly recalls the *sōphrosynē* or 'wise moderation' urged by the poets. This was an ethic much in vogue after the replacement of aristocracies at Athens and elsewhere by limited democracies, and particularly after the spectacular defeat of the hybristic and excessive Persians in 490 and 480. This early Classical phase is often (appropriately) called 'Severe'.

Sōphrosynē is best exemplified in the sculptures of the temple of *Zeus at *Olympia, carved between 470 and 457 (Paus. 5. 10). Their themes bespeak *hubris* overcome by divinely-inspired wisdom, and the participants act out their characters like participants in a tragedy. The expansive rendering brings power to the narrative, while a self-imposed economy of means allows bold distinctions in characterization, unhampered by distracting clutter. The same is true of bronzes like the Zeus from *Artemisium and *Riace Warrior A, whose carefully calculated postures are eloquent, respectively, of divine might and heroic potency; and of works known only in copy like the Discobolos of *Myron (1), whose swinging curves capture the essence of athletic endeavour.

Throughout, the aim is to find forms or modes that express the general or typical, yet are open to some variation for individuality's sake: witness the differences between the two Riace warriors. Further progress was the work of two geniuses, *Polyclitus of Argos and *Phidias of Athens (active *c*.470–420). In his bronze *Doryphoros* or 'Spearbearer', Polyclitus created a new standard or *canon (also written up as a treatise) for the youthful nude male. Powerfully muscled, proportioned with meticulous exactitude, composed around carefully-calibrated cross-relationships among the limbs, and finished with painstaking precision, it was a paradigm of measured humanity. The Mean personified, it was restrained yet limber, self-controlled yet ever-ready for action. Polyclitus produced many variations on this theme and future generations were to follow it 'like a law' (Plin. *HN* 34. 55).

Polyclitus was remembered as supreme in the rendering of mortals, Phidias as the unsurpassed interpreter of the divine, master of chryselephantine, and propagandist for Periclean Athens (Quint. 12. 10. 9; cf. PERICLES (1)). In his Athena Parthenos and Zeus at Olympia he sought to convey the majesty of the gods by subtle manipulation of the rendering, and by surrounding them with mythological sagas to demonstrate their power. On the *Parthenon (447–432) he extended this technique to the exterior sculpture. Athena's power and reach are proclaimed by a closely co-ordinated programme of narratives, and her chosen people, the Athenians, are exalted by a rendering unsurpassed in Greek sculpture for its fluency, grace, harmony of body and clothing, and perfection of formal design. In this way the typical became the citizen ideal.

Phidias' followers, active during the *Peloponnesian War (431–404) both pressed his style to its limits and turned it to other ends (see AGORACRITUS; ALCAMENES; CALLIMACHUS (2); PAEONIUS). Paeonius' *Nike and the parapet of the Nike Temple on the Athenian Acropolis manipulate drapery to create a surface brilliance that seduces the spectator into believing that what he sees is truth: victory scintillates before his eyes. Hitherto a more-or-less objective analysis of reality, here sculpture becomes a vehicle for the subjective and rhetorical, initiating yet another phase of restless experiment. The pendulum was to swing back somewhat with the 4th-cent. masters, but henceforth, as the ancient critics realized (Quint. 12. 10. 9), it is the phenomena that tend to coerce the sculptor, not vice versa. The war was not wholly to blame: the *sophists had done their work well, particularly in Athens.

Whereas in the Peloponnese the war only benefited the conservative pupils of Polyclitus, in postwar Athens, demand for sculpture was virtually restricted to gravestones, revived around 430 (see ART, FUNERARY, GREEK). Not until *c*.370 could the Athenians celebrate recovery by commissioning a bronze Eirene and Plutus (Peace and Wealth) from *Cephisodotus (1), a work that exudes Phidian majesty and harmony (see also retrospective styles). Also seeking new ways to the divine, Cephisodotus' son *Praxiteles created his revolutionary Aphrodite of Cnidus, proclaiming the power of the love goddess through total nudity and a beguiling radiance of feature and surface. Meanwhile, his contemporary *Scopas sought to perfect an acceptable formula for conveying the passions of gods and men.

Scopas was a leading sculptor in the team engaged by *Mausolus of Caria for his gigantic tomb, the *Mausoleum. Its unparalleled magnificence announced the advent of the Hellenistic world; a pointer, too, was the hiring away of the best artistic talent by a '*barbarian' patron. The real revolutionary, though, was *Lysippus (2) of Sicyon (active *c*.370–310), who radically transformed Greek sculpture's central genre, the male nude. His Apoxyomenos or 'Body-scraper' not only rocks back and forth before our eyes and extends an arm into our space, but was planned according to a new canon which sought slimness, elegance, and the appearance of greater height (Plin. *HN*. 34. 65). This and his minute attention to details made him popular as a portraitist, particularly with *Alexander (3) the Great (reigned 336–323), from whose features he created a new ideal that was firmly rooted in reality. Greek portraiture, which had hitherto veered between slight modifications to standard types and a sometimes trenchant realism, was transformed at a stroke (see PORTRAITURE, GREEK).

Hellenistic sculpture (c.330–c.30) The phenomenal expansion of the Greek world under Alexander created a bonanza of opportunity for sculptors. Lysippus' pupils and others were hired to create commemorative, votive, and cult statues for the new kingdoms (see EUTYCHIDES; LYSIPPUS, SCHOOL OF). Portraitists were particularly in demand to render and where necessary improve the features of Successor kings (see DIADOCHI), generals, and dignitaries.

Yet the political chaos after Alexander's death, together with the transformations being undergone by the independent *polis in old Greece, sculpture's homeland, undermined the art's social and religious foundations. Furthermore, Lysippus' commitment to the subjective had severely compromised whatever shared artistic values still existed; together with a feeling that little now remained to be discovered, this often tended to promote either eclectic blends of Scopaic, Praxitelean, and Lysippic (in portraiture) or a cautious neo-classicism.

Lysippus' school dominated the Peloponnese and was popular with the Successors, while more conservative patrons could choose the Athenians. As Athens declined, her sculptors increasingly sought permanent employment abroad: *Alexandria (1), *Rhodes, and the Asian cities were the main beneficiaries. In Alexandria (1), Attic-style gravestones were popular for a while, and the comfortably-off soon became avid consumers of grotesques; meanwhile, Ptolemaic royal portraits (see PTOLEMY (1)) exude an aura of suprahuman calm. In *Pergamum, a liking for the vigorous realism of the local sculptor *Epigonus, in monuments celebrating the defeats of the *Celts and *Seleucids (237 and after), did not preclude the hiring of the Athenian *Phyromachus to create cult-images, portraits, and battle-groups in a turbulent 'baroque' style derived from late 4th-cent. art. Style was now a matter of choice, and form could follow function—or not, as the patron wished.

The devastating wars of the years around 200 mark a watershed in Hellenistic sculpture. Following Pergamene precedent, the victorious Romans looted hundreds of statues and began to entice Greek sculptors west to work directly for them; realistic portraiture and Athenian neo-Classical cult-images were most in demand (see POLYCLES). As the Roman market grew, Greek workshops also began to respond with decorative copies and reworkings of Classical masterpieces for direct shipment to Italy (see AGASIAS (1); APOLLONIUS (6) AND (7); COSSUTII).

Meanwhile the main beneficiaries of Rome's intervention, Pergamum and Achaea, celebrated in style. *Eumenes II of Pergamum built the Great Altar, probably after Macedon's final defeat in 168, embellishing it with a 'baroque' Gigantomachy (see GIANTS) and a quasi-pictorial inner frieze narrating the life of the city's mythical founder, *Telephus (1). He also installed a copy of the Athena Parthenos in the Pergamene library to advertise his claim to rule the 'Athens of the east'. Neo-classical sculpture was also favoured in the Achaean cities, where *Damophon of Messene sought to update the style of Phidias. Athens preferred an even more rigid classicism, while on *Delos from 166 to *Mithradates VI's sack of 88 the Italian business community erected hard-boiled portraits of each other and bought dainty statuettes for their homes.

Attalus III of Pergamum willed his domains to Rome in 133, bringing its sculptural tradition to a close, but the most crushing blow was dealt by the Mithradatic Wars (88–66), which left Greece and Asia devastated and impoverished. Though some striking work was still produced, largely in portraiture, sculptors now moved to Italy in large numbers (see HAGESANDER; MENELAUS (2); PASITELES), creating the last of the great Hellenistic schools, but now on foreign soil and pledged to foreign masters. When the *Carrara quarries opened c.50 and *Augustus officially endorsed imperial classicism after *Cleopatra VII's defeat in 31, the west at last reigned supreme.

See IMAGERY; SCULPTURE, ROMAN.

J. J. Pollitt, *The Art of Ancient Greece: Sources and Documents* (1990); M. Robertson, *Greek Art* (1975); J. Boardman, *Greek Sculpture: The Archaic Period* (1978), and *The Classical Period* (1985); R. R. R. Smith, *Hellenistic Sculpture* (1991); B. S. Ridgway, *The Archaic Style in Greek Sculpture* (1977), *The Severe Style in Greek Sculpture* (1970), *Fifth-Century Styles in Greek Sculpture* (1981), and *Hellenistic Sculpture 1* (1991); A. F. Stewart, *Greek Sculpture* (1990). A. F. S.

sculpture, Roman Roman sculpture was produced in a variety of materials (bronze, marble, other stones, precious metals, terracotta) but it is *marble that is seen as typically Roman because so much that survives is in this medium. Sculpture was used for commemorative purposes (for display in public and in private contexts, especially the tomb), for state *propaganda, in religious settings, and for decorative purposes, and various different forms were developed: statues and busts, relief friezes and panels, and architectural embellishments.

Early sculpture in Rome (e.g. the bronze she-wolf of c.500 BC) was heavily influenced by *Etruscan work, and Etruscan sculptors would appear to have worked in Rome in the regal period and the early Republic. Rome's contacts with the Greek world, at first with the colonies of southern Italy and later through wars of conquest in Greece and Asia Minor, resulted in a knowledge of and growing taste for Greek sculpture: at first

statues arrived as war *booty, but growing demand created a flourishing trade in new work. The taste for sculpture in the Classical Greek style was fostered by the Augustan regime (see AUGUSTUS), and had periodic revivals, most notably in the reign of *Hadrian, but from the late republic onwards there were developments in subject matter and style that are distinctly Roman, though owing much to Greek precursors. This is seen for example in the development of portraiture in late Republican Rome (see PORTRAITURE, ROMAN).

Perhaps the most original Roman developments occurred in the series of historical reliefs used to decorate major state monuments and to express current ideologies. The taste for the representation of contemporary events first appears in the late republic (e.g. the relief from the so-called 'altar of Domitius Ahenobarbus' in the Louvre, with its scene of a sacrifice at the closure of the census): such a documentary approach continues under the Empire, and can be seen at its most developed on the columns of *Trajan and Marcus *Aurelius, where the stories of Rome's wars with the barbarians are represented on a long relief spiralling round the column. These use 'continuous narrative': the episodes run into one another without obvious breaks between scenes, and those on *Trajan's column in particular show great attention to the factual recording of details. However, a more allegorical approach also developed alongside this realism, and some reliefs show a love of drama derived from the art of Hellenistic Greece (e.g. the Great Trajanic Frieze). Realism and allegory appear side by side on one of the most complex and subtle Roman propaganda monuments, the *Ara Pacis Augustae, where 'realistic' procession scenes are placed next to mythological, allegorical, and decorative panels to express the ideals of the Augustan regime. Later state reliefs might combine the two approaches, as in the panels inside the arch of *Titus representing the Judaean *triumph (see JEWS): the carrying of the spoils of *Jerusalem is represented in a realistic (if dramatic) way, whereas the emperor in his triumphal chariot is accompanied by deities and allegorical figures. The deep, many-layered relief of these scenes was further developed in the 2nd cent. AD, with experiments in the representation of perspective, overlapping crowds, and the pictorial effects of light and shade. Towards the end of the century (Severan period) repetition and frontality of poses began to be used as a means of clarifying the narrative and isolating and emphasizing the emperor. This tendency is more marked by the time of the tetrarchs (see TETRARCHY) and *Constantine I, and is a hallmark of late antique sculpture. The origins of frontality have been variously ascribed to a 'popular' or 'plebeian' style of art in Rome and to the influence of the east, but its adoption certainly accorded with late antique imperial ideology.

Sculptured relief was also produced for private patrons, especially for the tomb: relief panels decorated the exterior walls, and ash-chests, grave *altars and *sarcophagi were placed inside. A rich repertoire of motifs was used, including mythological (and later, Christian) themes, battles, hunts, genre scenes, and portraits, drawing on classical and Hellenistic Greek art and contemporary state reliefs as sources of inspiration. Sculpture was also widely used to decorate public buildings, temples, and private homes and *gardens.

In the provinces local styles and schools of sculpture developed. The sculptors of the eastern provinces, especially Greece and Asia Minor, continued and developed the Classical and Hellenistic styles: they travelled widely around the empire, working on major monuments such as the 'Sebasteion' at

*Aphrodisias or the forum of *Septimius Severus at *Lepcis Magna: they also created the large series of eastern sarcophagi exported to Rome and elsewhere. In the northern and western provinces Celtic traditions fused with Roman to produce interesting hybrids, such as the pediment of the temple of Sulis Minerva at Bath (*Aquae Sulis). On the frontiers the lively but unsophisticated sculpture produced by and for the military (e.g. the Tropaeum Traiani at *Adamklissi in Romania) form an instructive contrast to the polished monuments in the Classical style at Rome and in the eastern provinces. See ART, ANCIENT ATTITUDES TO; ART, FUNERARY, ROMAN; IMAGERY; PAINTING, ROMAN; RETROSPECTIVE STYLES.

> D. E. E. Kleiner, *Roman Sculpture* (1992); D. E. Strong, *Roman Imperial Sculpture* (1961) and *Roman Art* (1976); R. Bianchi Bandinelli, *Rome, the Centre of Power* (1970) and *Rome, the Late Empire* (1971); M. Torelli, *Typology and Structure of Roman Historical Reliefs* (1982); R. Brilliant, *Visual Narratives: Storytelling in Etruscan and Roman Art* (1984); N. Hannestad, *Roman Art and Imperial Policy* (1986); K. Erim, *Aphrodisias: City of Venus Aphrodite* (1986); J. M. C. Toynbee, *Art in Britain under the Romans* (1964).   G. D.

Scylacium (mod. Squillace), in S. Italy, a Greek colony (probably Crotoniate) of the 6th cent., 60 km. south of *Croton. Initially a Crotoniate dependency, it passed into Locrian, then Bruttian, control in the 4th cent (see LOCRI EPIZEPHYRII; BRUTTII). In 122 BC the Gracchan colony of Minervia was founded (see SEMPRONIUS GRACCHUS, C.), with a second colony added by *Nerva (see COLONIZATION, ROMAN). It was the home of *Cassiodorus, but was abandoned in the 6th cent.   K. L.

Scylax of Caryanda, by order of *Darius I, is said to have sailed down the Indus to its mouth, and thence to have reached the isthmus of Suez (Hdt. 4. 44). Though the voyage has been doubted, the book that he wrote is quoted by *Hecataeus (1) (cf. F. 295, 296), as well as by later authors like *Aristotle, *Strabo, and *Avienus. No manuscript has survived; the periplus (see PERIPLOI) that bears his name was written in the 4th cent. BC and may well be a compilation of various accounts of explorations.

> GGM 1 pp. xxxiii–li, 15–96 (text of Periplus); FGrH 709. RE 3 A 1, cols. 620–46; J.-F. Salles, AMB I, 79–81; C. Tuplin, in H. Sancisi-Weerdenburg and A. Kuhrt (eds.), *Achaemenid History* 6 (1991), 75 ff.
>   E. H. W.; J.-F. S.

Scylla (Σκύλλη) (1), fantastic monster with twelve feet and six heads who lurked in a cave situated high up on the cliff opposite Charybdis, darting her necks out like a kind of multiple moray eel to seize dolphins, sharks, or passing sailors: Hom. *Od*. 12. 85 ff. (*Circe's warning), 245 ff. (the encounter, in which *Odysseus loses six of his best crewmen). Her voice is the yelp of a new-born pup (86, etymologizing on σκύλαξ), and she has other canine elements: three rows of teeth, like a shark (κύων), and a mother who in the *Odyssey* is called Crataïïs but whom *Hesiod and *Acusilaus (schol. Ap. Rh. 4. 829) identify as *Hecate, the underworld goddess associated with a pack of savage hounds; *Od*. 11. 597 shows that *Apollonius (1) was right to identify the two. In art (e.g. coin of *Acragas, late 5th cent.) and later literature (Lucr. 5. 892 f., etc.) the dog-heads are transposed to her waist, an iconography also attested for Hecate in the 5th cent. (Vermeule, p. 109), thus freeing her upper body to become an alluring woman, while her lower body becomes fishy. Later authors elaborate, equipping her with an earlier human existence (which leads to a frequent conflation with *Scylla (2), the daughter of *Nisus (1), as at Verg. *Ecl*. 6. 74–7) from which she had been metamorphosed by a jealous love-rival—Circe, according

to Ovid (*Met*. 13. 730 ff., 14. 1 ff.). *Lycophron (2(b)) knows a story that she was killed by *Heracles (651 ff.) but restored to life by her father *Phorcys, who scorched her corpse with torches (47 f.; another Hecate motif).

> E. Vermeule, *Aspects of Death in Early Greek Art and Poetry* (1979), ch. 6.
>   A. H. G.

Scylla (2) See NISUS (1).

Scymnus of Chios, author in the second quarter of the 2nd cent. BC of a geographical treatise (*periegesis*), whose name has been used to refer to a surviving fragment of a *periegesis* dedicated to King Nicomedes of Bithynia (about 90 BC), following the Mediterranean coasts from Spain eastwards in the style of *periploi*. This fragment preserves useful historical material on Greek settlements, but only the coasts of Spain, Italy, Sicily, Dalmatia, the Euxine, and Asia survive.

> GGM 1, pp. lxxiv f., 196 f. A. Diller, *The Tradition of the Minor Greek Geographers* (1952), 165–76.   N. P.

Scyros, an Aegean island (209 sq. km.) in the Sporades; the town of the same name lay in a fertile plain on the east coast. Here, according to legend, *Achilles (disguised as a girl) was hidden by *Thetis, and *Theseus was murdered.

There are important stone- and bronze-age sites, including Palamári. Burials from early geometric times have been found, for example at Chórapha near the town, but the island seems not to have been wealthy in archaic or classical times. Around 475 *Cimon seized it for Athens, enslaving the inhabitants, installing *cleruchs, and bringing home to Athens the 'bones of Theseus' (see RELICS). Inscriptions show the settlers maintaining an Athenian-style political and legal framework. Apart from interludes of Macedonian rule Scyros remained Athenian until Roman imperial times, valued for its strategic position on the Black Sea route. Marble was quarried and exported. Though Classical temples have been found in the town and elsewhere, and new cults were adopted in the Hellenistic period, the Roman and early Christian remains (bath complex, churches, cemeteries, etc.) are among the most substantial.

> RE² 3 A 1 (1929), 690–1; *Admiralty Handbook to Greece* iii. 403–6; C. Fredrich, *MDAI(A)* 1906; *Arch. Rep.* 1977–8; 1991–2, etc.   D. G. J. S.

scytale See SKYTALE.

Scythia The broad term used by Greeks and Romans to characterize the lands to their north and east, roughly from the Danube to the Don, Caucasus, and Volga. Typically, classical writers present Scythia as a chill wilderness, an 'otherness' of savages and uncivilized practices (from blinding, scalping, and flaying through tattooing to the drinking of wine unmixed with water). Scythians and Scythian customs were a favourite literary theme from *Herodotus (1) and Pseudo-Hippocrates (see HIPPOCRATES (2)) onwards. The historicity of such accounts remains the subject of scholarly debate, but their ideological function has been established beyond doubt. Classical writers were particularly interested in Scythian *nomadism, uncivilized but attractive in its primitive simplicity (see BARBARIAN; NOMADS). Accordingly, Scythia might be imagined as a source of ignorance: for example, the uncivilized Scythian archer-police-slaves of 5th-cent. Athens as mocked by *Aristophanes (1). But it can also be a source of wisdom, as personified by the legendary figure of the wise Scythian prince *Anacharsis.

The history of Scythia resists construction. Archaeology has revealed myriad burial-mounds (*kurgans*) and also settlements.

Persian iconography is suggestive, notably at *Bisitun and *Persepolis. However, attempts to bring the material record together with the tribal terminology and group-identities presented in classical written sources founder upon the imprecision and value-laden perspectives of the latter, which have themselves set much of the agenda for the archaeology which purports to inform them. Hypotheses on Scythian origins proliferate, varying in the degree of their assertions of Scythian easternness or autochthony. However, there is a very broad consensus on the course of Scythian history from the early 7th cent. when, as Herodotus would have it, Scythians forced the *Cimmerians southwards across the Black (*Euxine) Sea and themselves campaigned deep through the near east.

From c.600 BC the arrival of Greek settlers and traders on the north coast of the Black Sea brought Scythians into close contact with a new cultural influence. About 400 BC, the first fortified city appeared in Scythia on the steppes of the lower Dnieper (Kamenskoye Gorodishche): it has been seen as the political and economic centre of a Scythian kingdom. Through the 4th cent. BC Scythia was at the height of its prosperity, particularly under King Atheas, who established his authority as far as the Danube, only to be killed by *Philip (1) II. In 331 BC the Scythians were still strong enough to defeat the large army of Alexander (3) the Great's general Zopyrion. But, disunited, the Scythians were conquered in turn by a new force from the east across the Don, the Sauromates (see SARMATAE). The Scythians proper seem to have been restricted to the Crimea (see CHERSONESUS (2)), where they enjoyed a settled existence around their new city of Neapolis (near mod. Simferopol).

Scythian history as usually conceived comes to an end in the 3rd cent. AD, when Neapolis was abandoned. Thereafter, a range of peoples were located in Scythia (*Huns, *Alans, *Goths): they are often given the characteristics of their Scythian predecessors and are themselves regularly termed 'Scythian'.

K. Marchenko and Y. Vinogradov, *Antiquity* 1989, 803–13; F. Hartog, *The Mirror of Herodotus* (Eng. trans. 1988); J. Matthews, *The Roman Empire of Ammianus Marcellinus* (1989), 304–82; R. Rolle, *The World of the Scythians* (Eng. trans. 1989). D. C. B.

Scythinus of Teos, contemporary of *Plato (1), wrote *Iambics* which expressed *Heraclitus' doctrine in verse, and also a prose work Περὶ φύσεως ('on nature') and a Ἱστορία (history, inquiry) which was a novelistic account of *Heracles' deeds as benefactor of the human race.

West, *IE²*, pp. 97–8. W. D. R.; J. S. R.

Scythopolis (now Beth-Shean), a Canaanite, then Israelite, city on the right bank of the Jordan, its Greek name of unclear origin. It was conquered by *Antiochus (3) III from the Ptolemies (see PTOLEMY (1)); an inscribed dossier reveals his intervention to protect illegal billeting in nearby villages (*SEG* 41 (1991), 1574; Eng. trans. in S. Sherwin-White and A. Kuhrt (eds.), *From Samarkhand to Sardis* (1993), 49 f.). Passing to the *Hasmoneans in 107 BC, it was rebuilt by A. *Gabinius (2) (Joseph. *AJ* 14. 88); in the 2nd cent. AD it was a predominantly Greek garrison-town in Roman *Judaea. Excavations have revealed extensive Roman and Byzantine remains with a colonnaded street laid out as late as AD 522.

PECS 815 f.; B. Lifshitz, *ANRW* 2. 8 (1978), 262 ff.; F. Millar, *The Roman Near East* (1993), index. A. J. S. S.

sea See ADRIATIC; AEGEAN; ARCHAEOLOGY, UNDERWATER; BOSPORUS (1); CASPIAN; EUXINE; FISHING; HARBOURS; HELLESPONT; ISLANDS; LIGHTHOUSES; MEDITERRANEAN; NAVIES; NAVIGATION; NEPTUNUS; OCEANUS (both entries); PERIPLOI; PERSIAN GULF; PIRACY; PONTUS (second entry); POSEIDON; PROPONTIS; QUINQUEREME; RED SEA; SEA POWER; SHIPS; TRADE, GREEK and ROMAN; TRAVEL; TRIREME.

sea power, Greek and Roman The Greek for sea power is θαλασσοκρατία, thalassocracy. In a simple sense sea power has been exercised for as long as human beings have used ships for military purposes. But Greeks started thinking about thalassocracy seriously in the fifth cent. BC, when Athens maintained its empire by naval power, Thuc. 2. 13. 2. The idea of Athens the great sea-power was balanced by that of Sparta the great land-power, Thuc. 1. 18. 2. *Thucydides (2) can however make *Pericles (1) speak in an adventurous moment of Athens' potential control of both elements, 2. 62. 2. This combination, 'land and sea', γῆ καὶ θάλασσα, *terra marique*, was emotive for Greeks and Romans, a way of describing indefinite empire. It is found in the *Old Oligarch (2. 2), like Thucydides' *History*, a product of the *Peloponnesian War (this writer stresses the advantages of being an *island). Fifth-cent. Greeks regarded *Minos as the first great 'thalassocrat', Hdt. 3. 122, echoed by Thuc. 1. 4, from the so-called *Archaeology* (Thuc. 1–20). Part of Thucydides' purpose in the *Archaeology* is to stress and trace the importance of sea power, hence his early and programmatic stress on *Delos, the actual and symbolic centre of the Aegean (1. 8, cf. 1. 96). Thus from Minos he passes to *Agamemnon and to historical wielders of sea power like *Polycrates (1) of Samos; *Herodotus (1) 3. 122 (cf. above) calls Polycrates the first *historical* thalassocrat. In this serial approach to sea power Thucydides (and perhaps also Herodotus) may have been drawing on or influenced by so-called 'thalassocracy lists', as preserved in Diod. Sic. 7. 11.

After the end of the Athenian empire, when Sparta displaced Athens as leader of Greece, Sparta displaced Athens symbolically and emphatically at Delos too (see Tod 99, in assertive Laconian script). But a combination of Athenian leadership and Persian money produced a fleet which defeated Sparta at *Cnidus in 394: Persian sea power tended to be exercised vicariously through *Phoenicians, Egyptians, and other subject peoples; this usually meant building a fleet from scratch over periods of up to three years. The *Second Athenian Confederacy gave Athens Delos again, and a further spell of sea power. *Thebes (1) in the 360s briefly challenged this, and tried to rule 'by land and sea' (Isoc. 5. 53, cf. Aeschin. 2. 105 and Tod 160 for this policy as both replacement and imitation of Athens). *Alexander (3) the Great famously 'conquered the Persian fleet by land' i.e. by capturing Persian naval bases. No great sea victories mark his reign, or that of his father *Philip (1) II before him.

Alexander's successors recognized once again the importance of Delos, and the Nesiotic League or League of Islanders had its centre there (see CYCLADES; and cf. TENOS). This league was an instrument, at various times, of Ptolemaic and Macedonian aspirations to sea power. Some of the greatest sea-battles of the ancient world, such as Cos and Andros, were fought between these powers; but meanwhile *Rhodes established itself as a major sea power, and Rhodian sea law passed to the Middle Ages. In the Hellenistic period, though hardly as early as his alleged date in the early 3rd cent., *Lycophron (2(b)) (*Alexandra* 1229) prophesied Roman 'sceptre and monarchy over land and sea'. *Duumviri navales (naval duumvirs) at Rome go back to the late 4th cent., and at about the same period *Theophrastus (*Hist. Pl.* 5. 8. 1) tells a strange story implying Roman interest in *Corsica for its ship-building *timber; but it was not until the *Punic Wars

seals

that Rome became a real sea power. (Rhodian influence has been detected in matters of organization.) The contribution of the naval arm to Rome's success in the Hannibalic Wars was largely negative and defensive (preventing Carthaginian supplies and reinforcements from reaching Hannibal), but nevertheless crucial. Rome had trouble with pirates until surprisingly late dates: this was due less to feebleness than lack of will (complete elimination of pirates would remove a source of slaves); but otherwise Rome controlled the Mediterranean from the 2nd cent. BC onwards. See also NAVIES; PIRACY; SHIPS; TRIREME.

A. Momigliano, *Secondo Contributo* (1962), 431 ff.; P. Hardie, *Virgil's Aeneid: Cosmos and Imperium* (1986), 302 ff.; S. Hornblower, *Comm. on Thuc.* 1, on the passages cited; C. Starr, *The Influence of Sea Power in Ancient History* (1989); H. T. Wallinga, *Ships and Sea-Power before the Great Persian War* (1993); L. Kallet-Marx, *Money, Expense and Naval Power in Thucydides' History 1–5.24* (1993); J. H. Thiel, *Studies on the History of Roman Sea-Power in Republican Times* (1946) and *Roman Sea-Power before the Second Punic War* (1954). S. H.

seals (σφραγίς, *signum*, *sigillum*) played an important part in ancient life, taking the place of the modern signature on documents and, to some extent, of *keys and locks. The materials for sealings were *lead and wax for documents; in commerce a lump of clay was commonly pressed down over the cordage. In Roman times small seal-cases were frequently employed to protect the impression from damage. The seals themselves were generally of stone or metal, sometimes of *ivory, *glass, and other materials; some early seals, pierced by string holes, were worn round the neck or wrist, but ancient seals were frequently worn as signet *rings.

The use of seals began in neolithic times in Greece and they were in common use in EH. Seals of ivory, hard stones, and precious metals were made in Crete where they appear in EM II; the two main types were the stamp and the cylinder seal; the finest Minoan and Mycenaean seals were cut in hard stone and precious metal. The techniques of cutting stone seals were revived in the later geometric period, the most notable series being the so-called Island Gems; hard stones—chalcedony, cornelian, rock crystal, and others—were used again from the middle of the 6th cent. The scarab form which had been popular in Egypt from the ninth dynasty was adopted in Archaic Greece and the scaraboid was the commonest form in the 5th cent. Gold signet rings were also popular.

The principal device on ancient seals was usually pictorial—a favourite deity, a mythical hero, animals, and later, portraits. The seal devices of several prominent men of Roman times are known; *Augustus first used a *sphinx and later a portrait of *Alexander (3) the Great.

Greek cities possessed civic seals, for public documents or public property; the Romans utilized a magistrate's personal seal. See ARCHIVES; SPHRAGIS (for literary signatures).

P. Zazoff, *Die Antiken Gemmen* (1983); J. Boardman, *Greek Gems and Finger Rings* (1970); V. Chapot, Dar.–Sag., under 'signum'. F. N. P.; D. E. S.; M. V.

seasons See CLIMATE, ANCIENT; HORAE.

secessio ('secession') is the term used in Latin sources to describe the withdrawal of the Roman *plebs to a hill outside the sacred boundary (*pomerium) of the city. It implies detachment from public life as well as emigration from Rome, and was an extreme form of civil disobedience, particularly as it entailed refusal of military service. The fact that the state was not immediately brought to its knees proves that the plebs did not form a majority

of the population, still less of the army. The first secession is said to have occurred in 494 BC, when the plebeians, oppressed by debt and arbitrary treatment, seceded to the Sacred Mount (*Mons Sacer), a hill to the north-east of Rome (though some sources say the *Aventine). The crisis, which was resolved by Agrippa *Menenius Lanatus, produced the plebeian organization. See ROME (HISTORY), §1.2. The second secession, to the *Aventine, brought down the decemvirs (449 BC; see DECEMVIRATES). The last secession, to the *Janiculum, was provoked by a debt crisis in c.287, and was resolved by the dictator Q. *Hortensius. It is uncertain whether tradition knew of any other instances. Only the unreliable *Florus (1) (1. 25) mentions a secession in 445 BC, and one of the few certain things about the obscure military revolt of 342 (Livy 7. 38–42), sometimes called 'the fourth secession' in modern books, is that it was nothing of the kind. The act of secession had an important place in the historical tradition of the plebs, and it is possible that, when in 121 BC C. *Sempronius Gracchus and his followers withdrew to the Aventine, they were attempting to revive the ancient practice of secession.

Ed. Meyer, *Kl. Schr.* 1² (1924), 373 ff.; Ogilvie, *Comm. Livy 1–5*, 309 ff.; J.-C. Richard, *Les Origines de la plèbe romaine* (1978), 541 ff.; A. Drummond, *CAH* 7²/2 (1989), 212 ff., 227 ff. P. T.; T. J. Co.

Second Athenian Confederacy A maritime defensive alliance-system open to cities and dynasts outside Anatolia, whose original motive—obsolete once *Thebes (1) replaced *Sparta as principal adversary (c.371 BC)—was to ensure that Sparta respected the *freedom and *autonomy guaranteed by the *King's Peace. Its foundation (379/8) involved converting several existing bilateral alliances into a system which eventually (early 377) offered special rights, viz. a deliberative assembly (*synhedrion*), no internal political interference, tribute, governors, or garrisons, and no *cleruchy or private Athenian property-ownership within allied states. Starting with six members, the confederacy burgeoned in 378–373, as *Chabrias and *Timotheus (2) voyaged in Aegean and north-western waters urging Athens' goodwill and demonstrating it by e.g. protecting *Abdera from marauding Triballians. Spartan naval challenges were crushed at *Naxos (1) (376) and Alyzeia (375). In 375/4 Sparta conceded that the confederacy did not infringe autonomy, while the Peace of Athens (371/70) treated confederacy decisions as defining it. But the membership-list was neglected after 373, and few, if any, further states were accorded the protection of confederate alliance. Defections or disturbances occurred intermittently from 373/2 on, and the rebellion of *Byzantium, *Chios, and *Rhodes in 357–355 (see SOCIAL WAR (1)) remained unsuppressed thanks to military failure (particularly Embata) and Persian threats (about *Chares (1)).

Some doubt that this Social War proves that Athens was felt to have turned confederacy into empire. But, though external interference (*Epaminondas, *Mausolus) and Chares' malefactions certainly fuelled disaffection and anti-imperialist rhetoric, manifesto principles did not apply strictly or constrain Athens' general foreign policy. Tribute remained—annually assessed *syntaxis* (invented by *Callistratus (2))—and governors, garrisons, and political/judicial interference appear in confederate states: there may have been 'good' reasons, but the slippage towards 5th-cent. behaviour is unmistakable. The *synhedrion* theoretically gave allies an important voice in confederate activities. But evidence about procedure is partial and confusing; and who defined confederate activities? The sources' consistent failure to address this question suggests that allies were generally manipulated

1376

or sidelined; and in crises (e.g. peace negotiations in 346) the *synhedrion* view ultimately lacked practical authority. Repossession of *Amphipolis and the *Chersonese (1) became leading Athenian objectives from 368, and cleruchies were established, notably in *Samos (366/5): the Athenians' (not just Chares') inclination to *polypragmosyne* (meddling interference) was unabated, and this must affect global assessment of the confederacy period. The system was dismantled after the creation of the Corinthian League (see CORINTH, LEAGUE OF).

Tod 123 = Harding 35; Diod. Sic. 15. 25 ff.; J. Cargill, *Second Athenian League* (1981); G. L. Cawkwell, *JHS* 1981, 40 ff.; S. Hornblower, *Mausolus* (1982), ch. 7; R. Seager, *CAH* 6² (1994), ch. 6; E. Badian in W. Eder (ed.), *Die athenische Demokratie im 4. Jahrhundert v. Chr.* (1995), 79 ff.; M. Dreher, *Hegemon und Symmachie* (1995). C. J. T.

Second Sophistic is the term regularly applied in modern scholarship to the period *c.* AD 60–230 when *declamation became the most prestigious literary activity in the Greek world. Philostratus (see PHILOSTRATI (no. 2)) coined the term in his *Lives of the Sophists*, claiming a link between the Classical *sophists and the movement whose first member he identified as Nicetes of Smyrna in the reign of *Nero (*Lives* 1. 19). The term sophist (σοφιστής; verb σοφιστεύειν) seems restricted to rhetors (public speakers, see RHETORIC, GREEK) who entered upon a career of public displays, though usage even in the *Digest* is erratic, and Philostratus' Dionysius of Miletus (*Lives* 1. 22) is simply *rhetor* on his sarcophagus at Ephesus (*Inschriften von Ephesos* 426).

On the evidence of Philostratus, whose 40 lives of imperial sophists include several Severan contemporaries, and of other literary and epigraphic texts, it is clear that for these 170 years declamation was not simply an exercise for teachers of rhetoric and their pupils but a major art form in its own right. It flourished especially in Athens and the great cities of western Asia Minor, above all *Pergamum, *Smyrna, and *Ephesus. Rhetors (ῥήτορες), whether resident teachers of rhetoric or touring eminences, would draw aficionados in large numbers to private or imperial mansions, lecture halls in libraries, *bouleuteria*, *odeia*, and even theatres. After a less formal discourse (διάλεξις, λαλιά) which acted as a prelude (προλαλιά), their formal speech (μελέτη) was more usually deliberative (Latin *suasoria*; see RHETORIC, LATIN) recreating a historical situation, invariably from before 323 BC (e.g. Artabanus urges *Xerxes not to invade Greece, *Lives* 2. 5, cf. Hdt. 7. 10), than forensic (*controversia*—e.g. should a man who both started and then halted civil war be rewarded or punished? *Lives* 1. 26), often involving tyrants, pirates, or rape. Rhetors also had opportunities to deliver diverse epideictic speeches: e.g. *Polemon (4)'s speech commemorating the dedication of the Athenian *Olympieum in AD 131/2, or Aelius *Aristides' praise of Rome (26 Keil) and lament (μονῳδία) for Smyrna devastated by an earthquake (18 Keil). Aristides also claimed to innovate in composing prose hymns to gods. Although many of *Dio Cocceianus' over 70 surviving speeches are sophistic, of Philostratus' sophists only Aristides has a substantial surviving corpus (over 40 speeches, the longest running to 230 modern pages) which demonstrates the range covered by sophistic speeches: otherwise we have only a pair of Polemon's declamations ('Who was the best fighter at *Marathon?'), a few by *Lucian, and perhaps one each from *Herodes Atticus and *Adrianus of Tyre.

Many sophists, especially of those written up by Philostratus, were influential in their cities and even provinces, intervening to check civic disorder or inter-city rivalry (e.g. Aristides 23K), or dispatched as envoys to congratulate emperors on their accession or to win or secure privileges for their cities (and often themselves). We know of some omitted by Philostratus who, like his sophists, held city offices or were honoured with statues.

But for the majority teaching must have taken more time and energy than declamation, and it was to encourage education that *Vespasian gave rhetors, like *grammatici* and doctors, immunities from city offices, judicial service, and priesthoods whether city or provincial, immunities confirmed by his successors and extended to philosophers by *Nerva or *Trajan (see IMMUNITAS; LITURGY). *Antoninus Pius limited holders to between three and five according to the city's size (and excluded philosophers), though those deemed of special excellence (ἄγαν ἐπιστήμονες) were supernumerary and, unlike the others, immune even when teaching outside their city. Emperors also established salaried chairs of rhetoric: Vespasian of both Greek and Latin at Rome, Pius allegedly throughout the empire (SHA *Pius* 11. 3). To the civic chair of Greek rhetoric then founded at Athens with a salary of a talent (*Lives* 2. 20, 600), Marcus *Aurelius added *c.* AD 170 an imperial chair salaried at 10,000 drachmae. From no later than *Hadrian the equestrian post (see EQUITES, *Imperial period*) ab epistulis Graecis or secretary for Greek correspondence was, appropriately, often held by a distinguished rhetor, and this led to a procuratorial career (see PROCURATOR) and further rewards. Some posts, however, and the elevation of sophists to the senate, like their authority within city or province, may be as much attributable to their birth into their cities' governing élites as to their skill in manipulating enthusiastic audiences.

Competition for such distinctions encouraged professional quarrels in a breed already competitive. Such rivalry added spice to performances and tempted fans to trap their hero's rival, as when Herodes' pupils spoiled a supposedly extempore performance of Philagrus by reading out the speech, which had already been published (*Lives* 2. 8, 579).

Many rhetors' intellectual activities extended beyond declamation. Some composed poetry, whether shorter pieces, where extempore composition was similarly esteemed, or epic and tragedy. Others, classified apart by Philostratus (*Lives* 1. 1–8), also lectured or wrote on philosophical issues, whether throughout their career, like the Hellenized eunuch from Arles, *Favorinus, or after a 'conversion' from sophistic, as claimed by his teacher Dio Cocceianus. Herodes Atticus not only combined teaching and declamation with unusual wealth and power, exercised in an Athenian and a Roman senatorial career (consul 143), but argued knowledgeably with philosophers and grammarians in the circle of A. *Gellius. Others wrote history, like Antiochus of Aegeae (*Lives* 2. 4, 570).

Such literary products need not have been strongly influenced by rhetorical training or the declamatory milieu. Others were: for instance, the exercise of *ekphrasis (set-piece description) found in rhetorical handbooks spawned a whole genre, the descriptions of imaginary paintings, exemplified by the *Imagines* of the two *Philostrati, and influenced *Aelian's *Varia historia*, *History of Animals*, and (imaginary) *Letters*. *Ekphrasis* is also prominent in novelists, two of whom (*Longus and *Achilles Tatius (1)) are described as sophists by their manuscripts, and in Philostratus' novelistic work on *Apollonius (12) of Tyana. Lucian not only exploits *ekphrasis* in some προλαλιαί but developed the διάλεξις into a humorous art-form: its use for lighter entertainment is already discernible in Dio, but only from Lucian (who claimed to have started as a rhetor) do we have a wide range of entertaining works of which it is often hard to know whether they were delivered to an audience, circulated as letters or pamphlets, or both. There are other writers, not attested as sophists, whose works' manner and style would surely have been different had they not lived in the Second Sophistic—the perieg-ete *Pausanias (3), the historian *Herodian (2).

It is clear, however, that the prominence of declamatory rhet-oric was not limited to Philostratus' favoured period. It continued as a major cultural phenomenon, little abated by the 3rd-cent. crisis, into the 4th and 5th cents., whose properly sophistic texts are more voluminous than those surviving from AD 60–230. We also already find rhetors active in Greek city politics by the late 1st cent. BC, and the declaimers of Augustan and Tiberian Rome (see AUGUSTUS; TIBERIUS) are documented by the elder Seneca (L. *Annaeus Seneca (2)). The change about the time of *Nero may not have been so much one of the rhetors' role as of the theatre in which they played. The Greek world was recovering from Roman expansion and civil wars, Nero's short-lived gift of 'freedom' to *Achaia stirred consciousness, and Philostratus' period saw an economic, cultural, and even (in limited terms) political recovery in the Greek world that has fairly been termed a renaissance and is even (loosely) called the Second Sophistic. What was uttered and done by rhetors in this period breathed more confidence and had a wider impact than what went before, and they themselves were prominent among the many elements of Greek culture that found a high place in Roman esteem and society.

G. Anderson, *The Second Sophistic* (1993); D. A. Russell, *Greek Declama-tion* (1983) and (ed.), *Antonine Literature* (1990); Christ–Schmid–Stählin 2/2⁶, 688–828; A. Lesky, *A History of Greek Literature* (1966), 829–57; G. W. Bowersock, *Greek Sophists in the Roman Empire* (1969) and with E. L. Bowie, *CHCL* 1 (1985), 655–83 (= paperback 1. 4 (1989), 95–123); E. L. Bowie, *P & P* 1970 and *YClS* 1982; B. P. Reardon, *Courants littéraires grecs des IIe et IIIe siècles après J.-C.* (1971); G. Kennedy, *The Art of Rhetoric in the Roman World* (1972); A. Dihle, *Die griechische und lateinische Literatur der Kaiserzeit* (1989); P. A. Brunt, *BICS* 1994; S. Swain, *Hellenism and Empire* (1996).   E. L. B.

Secular Games,

Secular Games, theatrical games (*ludi scaenici*; see LUDI) and sacrifices (see SACRIFICE, ROMAN) performed by the Roman state to commemorate the end of one *saeculum* and the beginning of a new one. The *saeculum*, defined as the longest span of human life, was fixed in the republic as an era of 100 years. The ceremony took place in the *Campus Martius*, near the Tiber. The aetiol-ogical myth was that one Valesius, who wished to save his children from the plague, inadvertently fulfilled an oracle by giving them water to drink from an altar of Dis Pater and *Persephone, at a spot which was known as Tarentum or Terentum; in thanks for their cure he established here three nights of sacrifices and games. Republican celebrations of the Secular Games are not well attested. Those ascribed to the consulship of Valerius Corvus, 348 BC, who belonged to the same *gens* as the mythical Valesius, may be mythical; the Secular Games of 249 BC, are probably the first authentic ones. The celebration, resulting from consultation of the Sibylline Books (see QUINDECIMVIRI; SYBIL), was under the direction of the *decemviri* (later *quindecimviri*) *sacris faciundis*. Many scholars believe that the ceremony was actually introduced in 249 from *Tarentum, though the connection of the games with the south Italian city is by no means certain. The next celebration took place in 146 BC (a date attested by contemporary writers, and therefore more trustworthy than Livy's date of 149). A century later there was concern about the ending of the *saecu-lum* and games may have been planned. None were held, but the messianic expectations of *Virgil's *Fourth Eclogue* arose from speculations about *Caesar's relation to the *saeculum*.

*Augustus' plans to celebrate the *saeculum* were known in the 20s BC, and were referred to by Virgil in the *Aeneid* ('aurea condet saecula': 6. 792–3; cf. 6. 65–70). At Augustus' request, the *quindec-imviri* consulted the Sibylline Books and discovered a prophecy sanctioning Secular Games with many novel features. The *ludi* of 17 BC are fully recorded in an inscription, set up at the Tarentum (above). The *saeculum* was now fixed at 110 years. The *ludi* retained three nights of sacrifices and games, but Dis Pater and Persephone were replaced by the Moerae (Fates), the Eileithyiae (Goddesses of Childbirth, see EILEITHYIA), and Terra Mater (Mother Earth), and three daytime celebrations were added, to *Jupiter, *Juno, and *Apollo and *Diana. The Augustan games marked not the passing of an era, but the birth of a new age. Other novelties include the addition of seven supplementary days of more modern entertainment in theatre and circus, and *sellisternia held by 110 matrons for Juno and Diana. After the offerings on the third day, 27 boys and 27 girls (cf. *camillus) sang *Horace's *Secular Hymn*, first at the temple of Apollo and then on the *Capitol. In the hymn Horace brings into great prominence Augustus' patron god Apollo in his new *Palatine temple.

The antiquarian emperor *Claudius next celebrated games, in AD 47, on a new cycle, the eight-hundredth birthday of Rome. Taking their lead from Claudius, games were also held the follow-ing two centuries, in AD 148 and 248, but these were not counted in the official numbered sequence of games. The next games on (or nearly on) the Augustan cycle were celebrated by *Domitian in AD 88 (six years early) and *Septimius Severus in 204 (back on the Augustan cycle). Another inscription from the Tarentum records this celebration (which included a new secular hymn). It was to be the last celebration, as games were not held in AD 314 by *Constantine I, newly converted to *Christianity.

Livy, *Per.* 49; Hor. *Carm. saec.* and the scholia; Val. Max. 2. 4. 5; Zosimus 2. 1–7; CIL 6. 32323–36; *Not. Scav.* 1931, 313–45. Full collection of sources in G. B. Pighi, *De Ludis Saecularibus*² (1965), with L. Moretti, *RPAA* 1982–4, 361–79. M. P. Nilsson, *RE* 1 A (1920), 1696–1720; J. Gagé, *Rev. Ét. Lat.* 1932, 1933, and *Mélanges F. Cumont* (1936), 1; S. Weinstock, *Divus Julius* (1971), 191–7; speculations on topography in E. La Rocca, *La riva e mezzaluna* (1984).   L. R. T.; S. R. F. P.

Securitas, often with epithets like 'publica', 'Augusta' or 'temporum' (of the times), associated with the emperor or the state as a 'virtue' or 'desirable state'. Securitas was invoked when some imminent danger had been averted or on an occasion like 10 January AD 69, when the Arval Brothers (*fratres arvales) sacrificed to her among other gods on *Galba's adoption of L. *Calpurnius Piso Frugi Licinianus. On coins her characteristic attribute is the column on which she leans.

Wissowa, *RK*, 335.   H. M.; S. R. F. P.

security in Roman law was given to the creditor in the form either of rights over the property of the debtor (real security, mortgage) or of a surety (personal security). By the earliest real security, *fiducia*, the debtor conveyed the ownership of an object to the creditor by *mancipatio or in iure cessio, subject to an agreement for its reconveyance after payment of the debt. The agreement would also usually regulate the creditor's right of sale, etc. *Pignus* (pledge), on the other hand, only gave the creditor a limited real right (*ius in re aliena*) over the pledged object. *Pignus* required agreement and delivery; by it the creditor obtained a possession protected by interdict. However, because of the inconvenience of the debtor's losing possession, the praetor also protected non-possessory pledges (usually referred to as *hypotheca*)—at first probably in the case of pledges by agricultural tenants to their landlords of slaves, cattle, agricultural implements, etc. The debtor could mortgage the same object successively to several creditors, but the earlier mortgagee enjoyed priority (*prior tempore, potior iure*). Some mortgages, as for taxes due to the *fiscus* or (by a reform of *Justinian) for the dowry of a woman, were implied by law and privileged (i.e. given overriding priority).

Personal security (which was generally preferred) usually required a stipulation (*stipulatio*) between creditor and surety. As a result of restrictive legislation, two early forms of suretyship-stipulations (called *sponsio* and *fidepromissio*, from the verbs used) had become unattractive by the end of the Republic and were superseded by the more modern *fideiussio*. In contrast to *sponsio* and *fidepromissio*, *fideiussio* was available whether the principal debt arose from a stipulation or in any other way. The surety promised to discharge the same obligation (*idem*) as the principal debtor. His obligation was 'accessory', i.e. it depended, as far as extent and existence were concerned, upon that of the principal debtor. As with *sponsio* and *fidepromissio*, the legislator gradually improved the position of the surety. *Hadrian effectively limited the liability of co-sureties to their *per capita* share (*beneficium divisionis*); Justinian made the liability of sureties subsidiary (i.e. the creditor first had to try to obtain satisfaction from the principal debtor (*beneficium excussionis vel ordinis*)); and, also according to Justinian, the surety could, before paying, demand cession of the creditor's actions against the principal debtor and other sureties (*beneficium cedendarum actionum*). By the *senatus consultum Vellaeanum* of between 41 and 65 AD women were prohibited from 'interceding', that is, from incurring liability for the benefit of others.

D. Medicus, *Senatus Consultum Velleianum* (1957); P. Frezza, *Garanzie delle obbligazioni* (1, 1962; 2, 1963); H. Wagner, *Legalhypotheken* (1974); M. Kaser, *Studien zum römischen Pfandrecht* (1982); R. Zimmermann, *The Law of Obligations* (1990), 114 ff.   R. Z.

Sedulius (fl. AD 435). His *Paschale Carmen*, five books of hexameters (with prose paraphrase) on Christ's life and miracles, is mainly a Christologically didactic adaptation of the Gospels. Thick with Virgilian echoes (see VIRGIL), and perhaps intended to rival the *Aeneid*, it long proved popular. Two hymns also survive.

Ed. J. Huemer, *CSEL* 10 (1885); Eng. tr. G. Sigerson (1922). C. P. E. Springer, *Gospel as Epic in Late Antiquity* (1988); M. Roberts, *Biblical Epic and Paraphrase in Late Antiquity* (1985).   S. J. B. B.

seers See AUGURES; DIVINATION; IAMUS; LAMPON; MELAMPUS (1); MOPSUS; PROPHECIES; TIRESIAS.

Segesta (Greek Ἔγεστα, 'Egesta', the Greeks apparently not appreciating the indigenous initial sibilant), principal city of the Elymi in north-west *Sicily, on Monte Barbaro, 3 km. north-west of mod. Calatafimi. By the 6th cent. BC it was already considerably Hellenized, Greek pottery arriving from c.630 onwards, mainly from *Selinus. The Segestans wrote their Elymian language in Greek characters, of which graffiti on Greek pottery are our best testimony. They developed a traditional hostility with Selinus, in pursuit of which they allied themselves with Athens (*IG* 1³. 11, traditionally put 458/7 but see *SEG* 39.1 for a controversial re-dating to 418/17) and with *Carthage (410). There was war between Segesta and Selinus in 580–76 (Diod. Sic. 5. 9) and again in 454 (if Diod. Sic. 11. 86 is to be so interpreted) as well as in 416, when Athenian intervention was successfully encouraged with a false display of wealth (Thuc. 6. 6–8 and 46). In 409

Carthage achieved what Athens had not: Selinus was sacked, but Segesta passed into the Carthaginian sphere of domination. *Agathocles (1) of Syracuse seized it in 307, treating the population with exceptional barbarity and changing its name to Dicaeopolis; it also came briefly into *Pyrrhus' control (276).

In the First *Punic War Segesta immediately surrendered to and was generously treated by the Romans, who like the Segestans claimed Trojan descent (see TROY; KINSHIP). It became a *civitas libera et immunis* (see FREE CITIES) but declined after the Second Slave War (104–100). Granted the *ius Latii by Augustus (Pliny, *HN* 3. 91), it controlled a large *territorium* which included the sanctuary on *Eryx (cf. Tac. *Ann.* 4. 43); but, although *Vespasian settled veterans in its territory (*Liber Coloniarum* 1. 211), Segesta itself had been abandoned by the end of the 2nd cent. AD (apart from early medieval reoccupation), in favour of a spa settlement in the valley 5 km. to the north-east, Aquae Segestanae (mod. Terme Segestane).

The principal monuments are: an Archaic extramural sanctuary, with 6th-cent. Doric temple; a sophisticated 5th-cent. temple, but unfinished, also Doric and also extramural; two walled circuits, both undated; and a theatre, probably c.170 BC. The agora and several houses are currently (1995) under excavation. See also ACESTES.

PECS 817–18; Gabba–Vallet, *Sicilia antica* 1. 723–9; V. Tusa, *Segesta* (1991). Early imports and Hellenization: J. de la Genière, *Kokalos* 1976–7, 680–8, *MÉFRA* 1978, 33–48, and *ASNP* 1988, 287–316. Temple: D. Mertens, *Der Tempel von Segesta und die dorische Tempelbaukunst des griechischen Westens in klassischer Zeit* (1984). See: H. P. Isler, *Numismatica e antichità classiche* 1981, 154–64, but for its date, W. von Sydow, *MDAI(R)* 1984, 263–5 and 350. Recent work: G. Nenci, V. and S. Tusa (eds.), *Gli Elimi e l'area elima* [= *Archivio Storico Siciliano*⁴ 14–15] (1990), 259–76; L. Biondi and others, *Giornate internazionali di studi sull'area elima: Atti* (1992), 63–127, 139–50, 617–45.   A. G. W.; R. J. A. W.

Segesta in Pannonia. See SISCIA.

seisachtheia See SOLON.

seismology See EARTHQUAKES.

Sejanus See AELIUS SEIANUS, L.

Selene, Greek moon-goddess, was according to *Hesiod (*Theog.* 371) daughter of the Titans (see TITAN) *Hyperion and Theia, sister of *Helios and *Eos; she later became Helios' daughter, in recognition apparently of the idea that the moon shines by borrowed light (see D. J. Mastronarde's note on Eur. *Phoen.* 175; for other genealogies see *RE*, entry under 'Selene', 1137). Selene drives the moon chariot, drawn by a pair of horses or oxen, or she rides on a horse or mule or ox.

In myth, she is best known for her love for *Endymion, which caused Zeus to cast him into an eternal sleep in a cave on M. Latmus (see HERACLEA (2)), where Selene visits him (first in Sappho fr. 199); similar stories attach to Eos, the Dawn. In another myth she was lured into the woods by amorous *Pan (Verg. *G.* 3. 391–3, from *Nicander). Actual worship of Selene, as of Helios, is treated by *Aristophanes (1) as characteristic of *barbarians in opposition to Greeks (*Pax* 406). Like Helios, if in lesser degree, she seems to have infiltrated cult from the late Hellenistic period onwards. A more important way in which the moon had a place in religious life was through the identification with it (but not necessarily via the mythological Selene) of major goddesses such as *Artemis (first in Aesch. fr. 170) or *Hecate (Soph. fr. 535); see also MEN.

W. H. Roscher, *Über Selene und Verwandtes* (1890); F. Schwenn, *RE* 1136–

44 'Selene'; Nilsson, *GGR* 2, see index. Iconography: F. Brommer, *Arch. Anz.* 1963, 680–9; C. Préaux, *La Lune dans la pensée grecque* (1973); *LIMC* 7. 1 (1994), 706–15.   R. C. T. P.

Seleuceia (1) **on Tigris** was founded by *Seleucus (1) I as king at Tell Umar, on the left bank of the *Tigris (below Baghdad), *c.*305, as the 'royal capital' of his expanding empire in the middle-east. Seleuceia-Tigris probably replaced ancient Opis, a small settlement on the opposite side of the Tigris, as the city dominating the terminus of the important Khorasan route up to *Ecbatana and *Media, and the river crossing. It was connected with the *Euphrates river by a royal canal and had great strategic importance for communications west to Anatolia via Babylonia, Mesopotamia, and Syria and east to Iran.

The civic institutions included the specifically Macedonian 'council of elders' (*peliganes*), possibly reflecting the 'strength' of a Macedonian colonial presence (Polyb. 5. 52 f.). The Seleucid levels of the huge site have barely been excavated beyond the so-called 'administrative block', perhaps a palace, and a later building (? a herōon) of the 2nd cent. The great size and scale of Seleuceia-Tigris by comparison with other Seleucid Greek city foundations, such as *Antioch (1) and *Seleuceia (2) in Pieria, needs stressing. If another complex of buildings is of Seleucid (and not earlier) date, its probable identification as a sanctuary of Mesopotamian character (perhaps a ziggurat) is significant, situated as it is in the middle of a Seleucid royal capital. It would then fit with other evidence (*Ai-Khanoum, Dura-*Europus) for the use of non-Greek architectural elements in Seleucid building programmes, just as the archaeological finds (*bullae*, terracottas, statues) reflect the non-Greek influences of the mixed population of Seleuceia.

Seleuceia-Tigris (initially seized in 141) was conquered by the great Parthian king Mithradates I and brought under Parthian control. The Parthians allowed the Greek/Macedonian institutions of Seleuceia to continue, keeping their troops and administrative officials at *Ctesiphon on the opposite river bank. In the Parthian period Seleuceia was still a great commercial centre, in spite of the rivalry of Vologesocerta. But it became the seat of violent factions and dynastic quarrels; after a seven-year revolt (AD 35–42, Tac. *Ann.* 11. 9. 6) it was heavily punished. Excavations show that the city gradually became 'Parthianized'; burnt down by *Trajan, it was rebuilt in Parthian style. It was destroyed by *Avidius Cassius in AD 164. See PARTHIA, PARTHIAN EMPIRE.

L. Waterman, *Preliminary Report upon the Excavations at Tell Umar* (1931) and *Second Preliminary Report upon the Excavations at Tell Umar, Iraq* (1933); R. H. McDowell, *Stamped and Inscribed Objects from Seleucia on the Tigris* (1935); A. Invernizzi, in *Mesopotamia* 1968, 69 f. and in *Sumer* 1976, 166 f.; M. Colledge, *Parthian Art* (1976); S. Downey, *Mesopotamian Temple Architecture: Alexander through the Parthians* (1988); S. Sherwin-White and A. Kuhrt, *From Samarkhand to Sardis* (1993).   M. S. D.; S. S.-W.

Seleuceia (2) **in Pieria** was founded *c.*300 by *Seleucus (1) I, after his victory at the battle of *Ipsus (301) secured him north Syria. Seleuceia was built at the mouth of the river *Orontes, providing the Seleucids with a naval base of strategic and economic importance, linked by the Orontes to *Antioch (1). Seleucus I was buried here by his son *Antiochus (1) I, who 'built a temple over him and surrounded it with a sanctuary and called the sanctuary Nikatoreion' (belonging to the Nicator (Conqueror) i.e. Seleucus I; Appian, *Syr.* 63), housing a cult of uncertain character for the dead king. *Polybius (1) (5. 59–61) importantly describes a well-fortified city, built on the foothills of

Mt. Coryphaeum with its suburbs, business quarter, fine temples, and civic buildings. Most of the archaeological remains are of Roman date, including the theatre. The civic institutions of the Hellenistic *polis*, including magistrates, priests, and governor, are revealed by Seleucid period inscriptions and by the Gurob papyrus, which attests the ceremonial welcome given to *Ptolemy (1) III as capturer of the city in 246 (*FGrH* 160). Seleuceia, whose offensive and defensive value to the Seleucids was emphasized by Polybius, was regained by *Antiochus (3) III (219). It then had 6000 'free men.' The comparative size of the male population in this period is uncertain, since whether these figures represent male citizens only, or the total of free male inhabitants, remains obscure. In 108 Seleuceia received its freedom, which was confirmed by *Pompey (64) in reward for its resistance to *Tigranes (1). It was the station of an imperial fleet; *Vespasian improved the harbour, whence St *Paul had sailed on his first mission *c.* AD 46.

H. Seyrig, *Syria* 1970, 290–311; F. Millar, in A. Kuhrt and S. Sherwin-White (eds.), *Hellenism in the East* (1987) 110 f.; J. D. Grainger, *The Cities of Seleucid Syria* (1989); S. Sherwin-White and A. Kuhrt, *From Samarkhand to Sardis* (1993).   A. H. M. J.; H. S.; S. S.-W.

Seleucids, rulers of the empire founded by *Seleucus (1) I, governing a vast realm, stretching from Anatolia, via Syria and Babylonia to Iran and thence to central Asia. The Seleucids from the start continued (and adapted) *Achaemenid institutions in the army (use of local peoples), in administration (e.g. taxation and satrapal organization; see SATRAP), colonizing policies, the use of plural 'royal capitals' (*Seleucia (1) on Tigris, *Antioch (1), *Sardis), the use of local languages (and people) in local bureaucracy; also, from the beginning, *Babylon, *Babylonia, and the Babylonian kingship were central, in Seleucid planning, to an empire, the pivotal point of which, joining east and west, was the Fertile Crescent.

By the peace of Apamea (188), negotiated between *Antiochus (3) III and Rome, the Seleucids gave up possessions north of the Taurus mountains in Anatolia, retaining *Pamphylia, *Cilicia in southern Turkey, plus their large empire in the east. It was the complex interaction of dynastic strife, from the later 2nd cent., the advance of the Parthians, under Mithradates I of *Parthia, who had conquered Babylonia by the 120s, and the interference of Rome, that gradually destroyed the Seleucid empire. Pompey annexed Syria in 64 BC, ending just over two and a half centuries of Seleucid rule.

Rulers: Seleucus I Nicator, 305–281 BC; *Antiochus (1) I Soter, 281–261; *Antiochus (2) II Theos, 261–246; *Seleucus (2) II Callinicus, 246–225; *Seleucus (3) III Soter, 225–223; *Antiochus (3) III the Great, 223–187; *Seleucus (4) IV Philopator, 187–175; *Antiochus (4) IV Epiphanes, 175–164; *Antiochus (5) V Eupator, 164–162; *Demetrius (10) I Soter, 162–150; *Alexander (10) Balas, 150–145; *Demetrius (11) II Nicator, 145–141; *Antiochus (6) VI Epiphanes, 145–142; *Antiochus (7) VII Sidetes, 138–129; Demetrius II Nicator, 129–125; Cleopatra Thea, 126; Cleopatra Thea and *Antiochus (8) VIII Grypus, 125–121; Seleucus V, 125; Antiochus VIII Grypus, 121–96; Antiochus IX Cyzicenus, 115–95; Seleucus VI, Antiochus X, *c.*95; Antiochus XI, *c.*95; Demetrius III, *c.*95–88; Philip I, *c.*95–84/3; Antiochus XII, 87; the final turbulent phase included Philip II and Antiochus XIII Asiaticus, who was deposed in 64 BC by *Pompey.

E. R. Bevan, *The House of Seleucus: A History of the Hellenistic Near East under the Seleucid Dynasty,* 2 vols. (1902); E. Bikerman, *Institutions des Séleucides* (1938); M. Rostovtzeff, *The Social and Economic History of the*

Hellenistic World[2] (1951); R. A. Parker and W. Dubberstein, *Babylonian Chronology 626 B.C.–A.D. 75* (1958); T. Fischer, *Untersuchungen zum Partherkrieg Antiochos' VII* (1970); E. Will, *Histoire politique du monde hellénistique 1–2*[2] (1979–82); *CAH* 7[2]/1 (1984), chs. 6 (D. Musti) and 11 (H. Heinen), and 8[2] (1989), ch. 10 (C. Habicht; date chart at 517); A. Kuhrt and S. Sherwin-White (eds.), *Hellenism in the East* (1987); S. Sherwin-White and A. Kuhrt, *From Samarkhand to Sardis* (1993).   S. S.-W.

Seleucus (1) **I** (**Nicator:** Conqueror) (*c*.358–281 BC), son of Antiochus (unknown), fought with *Alexander (3) the Great in the latter's campaigns from *Asia Minor to *Persia, *Bactria, Sogdiana and, 'India', as a general. Subsequently he was to replay this 'conquest' as he, and his son, *Antiochus (1) I, brought the eastern 'Upper Satrapies' (see SATRAP) of the former *Achaemenid empire gradually under Seleucid control and colonization, wisely negotiating after invasion (*c*.306) of the Indus region a settlement with *Sandracottus, founder of the empire of the *Mauryas. The detailed interpretation of the terms of this peace is uncertain, but Seleucus ceded the Indus valley, desert Gedrosia, *Gandhara, the Swat valley tribes of the Parapamisadae, and east (i.e. desert) Arachosia.

After Alexander's death, Seleucus gained the satrapy of *Babylonia (321), which was to form the core of his later kingdom. There he initially supported *Antigonus (1), but was ousted by him (316) and fled to Egypt. He regained Babylonia (312) with a small task force in a spectacular exploit and thence took *Media, Susiana, and perhaps Persis too; as a Babylonian chronicle shows, fighting against Antigonus continued until a battle (308) left Seleucus in control of Babylonia. Seleucus then embarked on further campaigns to the 'Upper (i.e. eastern) Satrapies', to Bactria-Sogdiana, and the Indus region (above). He founded *Seleuceia (1) on Tigris (*c*.305) as a royal capital, returning westwards to join the coalition of 'separatist' generals against Antigonus.

The victory of Ipsus (301) gave Seleucus north Syria and access to the Mediterranean through Syria and Cilicia. He built *Antioch (1) (300) as another of his royal capitals to serve the then limits of his kingdom. Campaigns and colonization by Seleucus, Antiochus, and their officers, continued in the Upper Satrapies (e.g. Media, Sogdiana-Bactria, the Arab-*Persian Gulf). See COLONIZATION, HELLENISTIC. Seleucus finally won Asia Minor with the victory of Corupedium over *Lysimachus (281). A new Babylonian chronicle fragment reveals Seleucus' military objectives after Corupedium as 'Macedon, his land,' apparently aiming at the reconstitution of Alexander's unified empire of Macedon and Asia. He launched a campaign, but was assassinated by Ptolemy Ceraunus, who wanted Macedonia for himself.

Seleucus was married to the Bactrian princess *Apame, mother of his successor and eldest son, the half-Iranian *Antiochus (1) I, a prototype of the dynastic-marriage alliances with non-Greek dynasties that the Seleucids pursued as a continuing policy in their relations with non-Greek peoples in and beyond their realms. Seleucus had prepared Antiochus for the throne since he acted as crown prince (*mār šarri*) in Babylonia before he was appointed co-regent (292/1–281/0), a mechanism that facilitated the Seleucid succession and continued to be utilized. Seleucus' second marriage to *Stratonice, daughter of *Demetrius (4) Poliorcetes (290s), seems mainly to have been directed by politics, i.e. a (temporary) pact with Demetrius. It is uncertain if Apame was still alive. However, Stratonice was passed to Antiochus as queen and wife, and Antiochus was dispatched to the eastern satrapies as king with full royal authority (and armies). This is probably to be understood as a recognition of the need to consolidate in the Upper Satrapies and for royal authority to do it, leaving Seleucus free to deal with problems in Syria and Anatolia.

Seleucus was certainly one of the ablest of the Successors ('the greatest king of those who succeeded Alexander': Arr. *Anab*. 7. 22. 5). Apart from his military victories, he took great care to 'respect' and utilize local traditions (e.g. the Babylonian kingship and Babylonian traditions) and to proffer patronage to non-Greek communities and their sanctuaries as well as Greek ones.

ANCIENT SOURCES Appian, *Syr.*; Diod. Sic. 18–20; A. K. Grayson, *Assyrian and Babylonian Chronicles* (1975), 115 f.; see also S. Sherwin-White and A. Kuhrt, *From Samarkhand to Sardis* (1993).

MODERN LITERATURE E. R. Bevan, *The House of Seleucus* (1902); E. Bikerman, *Institutions des Séleucides* (1938); Rostovtzeff, *Hellenistic World*[2] (1951); E. Will, *Histoire politique du monde hellénistique* 1 (1967); A. Mehl, *Seleukos Nikator und sein Reich* 1 (1986); J. D. Grainger, *Seleukos Nikator* (1990); S. Sherwin-White, in A. Kuhrt and S. Sherwin-White (eds.), *Hellenism and the East* (1987), and in S. Sherwin-White and A. Kuhrt (eds.), *From Samarkhand to Sardis* (1993).   G. T. G.; S. S.-W.

Seleucus (2) **II** (**Callinicus:** Gloriously Victorious) (*c*.265–225 BC) was the eldest son of *Antiochus (1) II and *Laodice (2). In his reign (beginning in 246), a separate kingdom of *Bactria, led by a Greek usurper, *Diodotus (1), claimed independence from the Seleucids, at least by the early 230s. Seleucus also faced trouble in *Parthia, where the nomadic Parthians had infiltrated and were slowly carving out an emerging realm from the Seleucid satrapy. Seleucus campaigned against them, claiming victories the reality and extent of which are difficult to assess. A recently published Babylonian astronomical diary also reveals that between 238 and 235 some kind of serious military revolt was taking place, one of the centres being Babylon. Seleucus was further hampered throughout his reign by dynastic troubles; first the ambitions of his step-brother which produced the invasion of *Ptolemy (1) III with its spectacular (though ephemeral) successes ('Third Syrian War,' 246–241) and, later, those of his younger brother *Antiochus (8) Hierax in Asia Minor. Seleucus spent his reign on campaign, but it remained for his son *Antiochus (3) III ('The Great') to restore the kingdom. However, the Seleucid policy of patronizing Greek and non-Greek places continued—notably e.g. *Babylon, whence comes a Babylonian chronicle fragment referring to a letter from the king to the chief administrator of the great sanctuary of Esagil, attesting the king's support for Babylonian religious rites and his close relations with the Babylonian administrator. Seleucus II, like other contemporary monarchs, also provided massive material relief and aid (plus 10 warships) to *Rhodes after a devastating earthquake (Polyb. 5. 83. 8–9).

E. Will, *Histoire politique du monde hellénistique* 1 (1967); S. Sherwin-White and A. Kuhrt, *From Samarkhand to Sardis* (1993).   G. T. G.; S. S.-W.

Seleucus (3) **III** (**Ceraunus:** Thunderbolt) (*c*.243–223 BC), eldest son of *Seleucus (2) II, reigned three years only. He was assassinated, within the army, while on a campaign against *Attalus I of Pergamum which aimed to regain Seleucid possessions in Asia Minor. Since he had no heirs, his younger brother, *Antiochus (3) (III), was 'recalled by the army' to be king.

                                                                   S. S.-W.

Seleucus (4) **IV** (**Philopator:** Father-lover) (*c*.218–175 BC), second son of *Antiochus (3) III, in whose lifetime he already held important commands, was made co-regent after the battle of Magnesia (189; see MAGNESIA, BATTLE OF). In his reign (commencing 187), he maintained careful relations with Rome and observed the harsh terms of the peace of Apamea (188), which forbade the Seleucid navy to sail west of the river Caly-cadnus and the promontory of Sarpedon on offensive missions, and rendered such missions difficult because of the severe indemnity imposed upon the Seleucids. However, Seleucus toyed with the notion of intervening in aid of *Pharnaces (1) I, king of Pontus, against Pergamum (Diod. Sic. 29. 24). The implication is that beyond the river *Halys the policy of the Seleucid king was not limited by consideration of Roman interests, any more than it was in the existing Seleucid empire from *Syria eastwards. Seleucus was assassinated in 175 by Heliodorus, one of his ministers, for reasons which remain obscure.

E. Will, *Histoire politique du monde hellénistique* 2 (1967); A. N. Sherwin-White, *Roman Foreign Policy in the East* (1984). G. T. G.; S. S.-W.

Seleucus (5) (*RE* 38 cf. Suppl. 5), of Seleuceia on the Red Sea, astronomer (*c*.150 BC), is described by *Strabo (16. 1. 6) as a Chaldaean (i.e. an adept of Babylonian *astrology). He supported the heliocentric theory of *Aristarchus (1), connecting it with his own explanation of the tides, which from his observations on the *Red Sea he perceived to be governed in part by the moon; he criticized the tidal theory of *Crates (3).

HAMA 2. 610–11, 697. On Seleucus' city (*not* *Seleuceia (1) on Tigris) see Cumont, *Syria* 1927, 83 ff. G. J. T.

Seleucus (6) **Homericus** of *Alexandria (1) was perhaps at the court of the emperor *Tiberius (Suet. *Tib.* 56). He is said to have written commentaries in Greek on practically every Greek poet. Besides works on Greek language and style and on Alexandrian proverbs, he wrote a criticism of the critical signs used by *Aristarchus (2), a biographical work probably on literary figures, a theological treatise, a paradoxographical study (see PARADOXOGRAPHERS), a miscellany, and a commentary on the axones of *Solon. It is doubtful whether the Περὶ φιλοσοφίας ('on philosophy') mentioned by *Diogenes (6) Laertius is by this Seleucus.

FHG 3. 500; *FGrH* 341; M. Müller, *De Seleuco Homerico* (1891); R. Reitzenstein, *Geschichte der griechischen Etymologika* (1897), 157 ff. J. F. L.; R. B.; N. G. W.

Selinus (Σελινοῦς, mod. Selinunte), founded by *Megara Hyblaea on the south-west coast of *Sicily, lies on two low eminences (the acropolis and the Manuzza hill), commanding an extensive, fertile plain. *Diodorus (3)'s early date for its foundation (13. 59. 4: 651 BC) finds some support in Corinthian pottery (middle and late proto-corinthian; see POTTERY, GREEK) found in the Manuzza necropolis, but there was no occupation on the acropolis before the last quarter of the 7th cent., and for the main colonial foundation *Thucydides (2)'s date (6. 4. 2: 628 BC) is to be preferred. Prospering quickly, it embarked in the first half of the 6th cent. on an ambitious street layout which embraced not only the acropolis and Manuzza hills but the flanking valleys on either side as well: Selinus was conceived as a megalopolis on the truly grand scale, reflected also in its massive temple-building spree in the 6th and 5th cents. (ten of that date are known), some adorned with sculptured metopes among the earliest in the west. The shattered remains of the temples on the acropolis and on the extramural eastern hill make a striking sight. So too do the imposing defences, which belong to at least four phases.

As the westernmost Greek city it was in uncomfortable proximity to both *Phoenicians and Elymians, and a pro-Punic policy, followed by tyrants in the early period, aligned Selinus with *Carthage in 480 (Diod. Sic. 13. 55). Long-standing enmity with

*Segesta brought Athenian intervention in Sicily (415) and the Carthaginian invasion of 409, when Hannibal sacked Selinus. Refounded soon after by refugees, the city took on a distinctly Punic flavour, and remained firmly within Carthaginian control until the site was abandoned in 250 BC. Its site then became, as it still is, deserted: Pliny's reference (*HN* 3. 91) to Selinunti(ni) was probably meant to indicate the inhabitants of Thermae Selinuntinae (modern Sciacca), 24 km. to the east.

PECS 823–5: Gabba–Vallet, *Sicilia antica* 1. 637–53; Dunbabin, *Western Greeks*, passim. R. Martin, *CR Acad. Inscr.* 1977, 46–63. Street grid: J. de la Genière, *Rend. Linc.* 1979, 35 ff, 1981, 211–17, and 1985, 289–97. Defences: D. Mertens, *MDAI(R)* 1989, 87–154. Temples: G. Pugliese Carratelli (ed.), *Sikanie* (1985), 422 ff. (but with controversial dating); their sculpture: L. Giuliani, *Die archaischen Metopen von Selinunt* (1979); V. Tusa, *La scultura in pietra di Selinunte* (1984). Quarries for temples: A. Peschlow-Bindokat, *Die Steinbrüche von Selinunt* (1990); M. H. Jameson and others, *A 'lex sacra' from Selinous* (1993). A. G. W.; R. J. A. W.

sella curulis ('curule chair') was an ivory folding seat, without back or arms, used by the higher Roman magistrates (hence the title 'curule' magistrates; see MAGISTRACY, ROMAN). The sources maintain that it was a simplified version of the throne used by the old kings, and that it was among the trappings of royal authority that Rome borrowed from the *Etruscans. Examples have been found in Etruscan tombs, and from the 6th cent. BC onwards the *sella curulis* is represented in paintings and reliefs found at Etruscan sites (but also at Rome and other Latin towns such as *Velitrae). The name was derived (Gell. 3. 18. 3 ff.) from the chariot (Latin *currus*) in which the magistrate was conveyed to the place of judgement, and originally the *sella curulis* served as the seat of justice.

Mommsen, *Röm. Staatsr.* 1³ 399 ff.; R. Lambrechts, *Essai sur les magistratures des républiques étrusques* (1959). P. T.; T. J. Co.

sellisternium (Festus, *Gloss. Lat.* 398), a religious banquet at which the goddesses sat on chairs (*sellae*; Val. Max. 2. 1. 2: *Juno and *Minerva at the *epulum Iovis*, 'the banquet for *Jupiter'), whereas at the *lectisternium they reclined (at least originally, Livy 5. 13. 5; 22. 10. 9) together with the gods on couches. *Sellisternia* were commonly offered by women (for Juno, Tac. *Ann.* 15. 44, and at the *Secular Games for Juno and *Diana, *CIL* 6. 32323). Also in the cult of *Hercules at the Ara Maxima ('The Greatest Altar') only chairs were used at banquets (Macrob. *Sat.* 3. 6. 16). J. L.

Semele, a daughter of *Cadmus of *Thebes (1), seduced by *Zeus, who visited her unseen, and by whom she conceived a child. At the urging of *Hera, she persuaded Zeus to show himself to her: he appeared in the form of a thunderbolt, which killed her. Zeus removed the embryo from the corpse, sewed it into his own thigh, and eventually gave birth to *Dionysus, whom *Hermes handed over to Semele's sister Ino, to rear. The story is summarized by *Apollodorus (6) 3. 4. 3 (see too Frazer's note). *Homer's version (*Il.* 14. 323–5), although brief, implies that the birth was normal (325: 'Semele gave birth to Dionysus'); so does Hesiod, *Theog.* 940–2 (and see West's note on 942).

As a cult figure, Semele possessed a *sēkos*—an open-air enclosure, formerly her bridal chamber—on the Cadmeia at Thebes, which was the focal point of the sanctuary of Dionysus Cadmeus (Schachter 1. 187–8 and cf. 2. 62, for the *sēkos* of *Ino at *Chaeronea).

There is no agreement about Semele's origins: divine or human, Greek or non-Greek; Thraco-Phrygian, Semitic, and

Egyptian etymologies compete, but without conviction (see Bernal, 69–70, Burkert, 163, Dodds, 63 and n. 3).

Apollodorus, *The Library* (trans. J. G. Frazer) (1921); M. Bernal, *Black Athena* 2 (1991); W. Burkert, *Greek Religion* (1985); Euripides, *Bacchae*, ed. E. R. Dodds (1960); J. Gasparri, *LIMC* 3 / 1 (1986), 478–9 (nos. 664–8); Hesiod, *Theogony*, ed. M. L. West (1966); A. Schachter, *Cults of Boiotia* 1 (1981), 2 (1986); A. Veneri, *LIMC* 3 / 1 (1986) 416–17.   A. Sch.

Semiramis in history was Sammu-ramat, wife of Shamshi-Adad V of *Assyria, mother of Adad-nirari III, with whom she campaigned against *Commagene in 805 BC. Her inscribed stela stood with stelae of kings and high officials in Aššur. In Greek legend, she was the daughter of the Syrian goddess Derceto at Ascalon, wife of Onnes (probably the first Sumerian sage Oannes) and then of Ninos, eponymous king of *Nineveh; she conquered '*Bactria' and built '*Babylon' (*Berossus denied this). In Armenian legend, she conquered *Armenia (ancient *Urartu), built a palace and waterworks, and left inscriptions.

W. Schramm, *Historia* 1972, 513–21; F. W. König, *Die Persika des Ktesias von Knidos, Archiv für Orientforschung* Beiheft 18 (1972), 37–40; V. Donbaz, *Annual Review of the Royal Inscriptions of Mesopotamia Project* (1990), 5–10; Moses Khorenats'i, *History of the Armenians*, ed. R. W. Thomson (1978), 93–104.   S. M. D.

Semitic, a term derived from the Old Testament personal name Shem, refers to a middle eastern language group. Principal ancient constituents are *Akkadian, Ugaritic (see UGARIT), Phoenician, *Aramaic, Biblical Hebrew, Sabaic, and Ethiopic (Ge'ez). Modern languages include Arabic, Amharic, and Israeli Hebrew. These languages display common features (e.g. the predominance of tri-consonantal roots and, originally, a system of case-endings). Comparative Semitic philology is largely concerned with a hypothetical Proto-Semitic.

G. Bergsträsser, *Introduction to the Semitic Languages* (trans. P. T. Daniels, 1977; Ger. orig. 1928); S. Moscati and others, *An Introduction to the Comparative Grammar of the Semitic Languages* (1964).   J. F. H.

semitism (pagan), anti- The anti-Jewish movements of Graeco-Roman antiquity have led to scholarly debate over (*a*) their causes and (*b*) their relationship to 'anti-semitism'—i.e. the modern phenomenon of ideologically driven prejudice against *Jews and the Jewish religion (see RELIGION, JEWISH). The episodes most discussed are the measures of *Antiochus (4) IV and his successors in *Judaea, the *stasis between *metic Jews and 'Greek' citizens in the eastern Roman provinces (above all Syria and *Alexandria (1), and the series of expulsions of Jews from Rome). As to (*a*), scholarly argument focuses on how far, if at all, ancient anti-Jewishness in essence was a response to the religious and cultural alterity (see BARBARIAN) of Jews, described with varied reactions (sympathy included) by classical writers from *Hecataeus (2) on (the 'substantialist' model); or whether (the 'functionalist' model) it was grounded in concrete, localized conflicts (at Alexandria, Jewish aspirations to Greek citizenship; Greek resentment of Roman protection of the Jews). As to (*b*), many scholars see 'anti-semitism' as a modern concept unsuited for retrojection to antiquity; others claim to recognize a unique type of ancient antipathy directed at the Jews alone, prefiguring the (in some ways related) phenomenon of Roman hostility to and persecution of early *Christianity.

M. Stern, *Greek and Latin Authors on Jews and Judaism*, 3 vols. (1974–84) (transl. texts with comm.); S. Cohen in D. Berger (ed.), *History and Hate* (1986); G. Langmuir, *Towards a Definition of Antisemitism* (1990); P. Schäfer, *Judeophobia* (1997); Z. Yavetz, *Journal of Jewish Studies* 1993, 1 ff.   A. J. S. S.

Semo Sancus Dius Fidius (for the full name see Dion. Hal. *Ant. Rom.* 4. 58. 4; *CIL* 6. 30994), a deity of puzzling origin, nature, and name, said to be Sabine, see SABINI (e.g. Prop. 4. 9. 74; he is here identified with *Hercules, apparently from the interpretation of Dius Fidius as *Iovis filius*, 'son of *Jupiter'). The name of the god is thought to be Sancus (sometimes Sanctus, not necessarily from a copyist's error: see *CIL* 6. 568 and 30994), from *sancire*, 'sanction'. Against Latte (*RR* 128), Radke (*Entwicklung*, 116 ff.) accepts the affirmation of *Lydus (*Mens.* 4. 90 p. 138. 1 ff. Wünsch) that *sancus* is the Sabine word for 'sky'. Semo has no clear meaning. Wissowa proposed to see a generic name like *genius, but the view today is that a seed-god is in question, although his relation with Sancus is unexplained. In any case Dius Fidius, whose name locates him in Jupiter's ambit (the *Oscan and Umbrian *Fisius Sancios* makes this explicit), in the historical period is firmly united with Sermo Sancus (against Latte, *RR* 126 ff.), and is worshipped with him in the temple on the *Quirinal and on the *Tiber island. In everyday speech Sancus was the name used (*porta Sanqualis*), in the language of the calendars Dius Fidius (5 June). In historical times SSDF is connected with oaths and treaties, hence the common oath *medius fidius* and the deposition of the treaty with *Gabii in the Quirinal temple. Hence he has some connection with thunder. Christians believed that dedications 'to Semo Deus Sanctus' (*Semoni deo Sancto*) referred to the deification of Simon the mage (e.g. Tertull. *Apol.* 13. 9).

Linke, *RE* 1 A 2 (1921), under the name; Radke, *Entwicklung* 115 ff.; Richardson, *Topogr. Dict. Anc. Rome*, 347.   J. Sch.

Semonides (Σημωνίδης, in MSS usually Σιμ-) of *Amorgos, Greek iambic poet (see IAMBIC POETRY, GREEK), said to be one of those who led the Samian colonists to Amorgos (see SAMOS; COLONIZATION, GREEK), which would put him in the mid 7th cent. BC and agree with the ancient opinion that he was contemporary with *Archilochus (Eus. *Chron.*, Ol. 28; cf. E. Rohde, *Kl. Schr.* 1. 149 ff.). The longest fragment (7 W., 118 lines, almost a complete poem) expounds the thesis that different types of women were created from different animals and have their qualities. Some fragments (1–4) contain pessimistic moralizing, others (e.g. 13–14, 16–18) suggest entertaining and obscene narratives. Two books of *iamboi* are cited. Statements that Semonides also composed elegy and a work on Samian antiquity (*Suda*) are suspect; the elegiac fragment in Stob. 4. 34. 28 that has sometimes been ascribed to Semonides (fr. 29 Diehl) is now known to be a conflation of two excerpts from *Simonides of Ceos. See also ANIMALS, KNOWLEDGE ABOUT.

TEXT West, *IE*² 2 (1992).

COMMENTARY D. A. Campbell, *Greek Lyric Poetry* (1967); H. Lloyd-Jones, *Females of the Species* (1975).

TRANSLATION West, *GLP*. See also N. Loraux, *Les Enfants d'Athéna* (1981), ch. 2.   M. L. W.

Semos of *Delos (*c.*200 BC), Greek antiquarian, was a careful, scholarly compiler, whose geographical and antiquarian works include: *Delias*, an 8-book survey of the geography, antiquities, institutions, and products of Delos, from which *Athenaeus (1) quotes extensively; *Nesias*, a work on *islands; *On Paros*; *On Pergamum*; and a *Periodoi*. From his *On *Paeans*, a valuable fragment survives (Athen. 14. 622 a–d) describing the masks, dress, and performance of αὐτοκάβδαλοι (improvisers), ἰθύφαλλοι (erect phalli), and φαλλοφόροι (phallus-bearers).

FGrH 396.   J. F. L.; K. S. S.

Sempronius Asellio

Sempronius Asellio (*RE* 16), Roman historian, military tribune at *Numantia in 134–3 BC. He wrote a history (*res gestae*) of his own time. In the proem he distinguished his work from annals: he would not just list events, but explain motives and reasons (this surely reflects the influence of *Polybius (1)): that was the way to inspire virtue and patriotism. His work perhaps began in 146 (possibly continuing Polybius); it covered the year 137 in bk. 4, Ti. *Sempronius Gracchus (3)'s death in bk. 5, and M. *Livius Drusus (2)'s death (91 BC) in bk 14. *Cicero thought it artistically retrograde (*de Leg.* 1. 6).

> Frs. in H. Peter, *HR Rel.* 1², pp. ccxlii–ccxlv, 179–84. G. Morelli, *Studi Urbinati* 1975, 81–94; B. Gentili and G. Cerri, *History and Biography in Ancient Thought* (1988; It. orig. 1983), 52–9.   C. B. R. P.

Sempronius (*RE* 47) **Gracchus, Gaius,** younger brother of Ti. *Sempronius Gracchus (3), served under his cousin and brother-in-law P. *Cornelius Scipio Aemilianus at *Numantia. A member of his brother's land commission, he supported the plans of M. *Fulvius Flaccus in 126 BC, then went to Sardinia as quaestor. Returning before his commander in 124, he was accused before the censors but acquitted, and elected tribune for 123 and again for 122, when he was joined by Flaccus, by then *consularis* and *triumphalis*. After laws meant to avenge his brother and secure himself against a similar fate, he embarked on a programme of reform, aided by friendly colleagues. The most important measures were: (1) a *lex frumentaria* assuring citizens of wheat, normally at a subsidized price; (2) laws providing for the resumption of land distribution and the foundation of colonies, including one on the ritually cursed site of *Carthage, which Gracchus himself, as commissioner, helped to establish; (3) laws regulating army service and providing for public works—all these to gain the support of the plebs and relieve poverty and exploitation; (4) a law to have the *decuma* of the new province of Asia sold by the censors in Rome; (5) laws (probably two) regulating *repetundae* trials, the second (passed by M'. *Acilius Glabrio (2)) introducing elements of criminal procedure and taking juries from the *equites*—these to protect provincials from magistrates' rapacity, to secure the treasury's major revenue against peculation, and to set up members of the non-political class to control politicians; (6) a law to make the senate's designation of consular provinces immune to tribunician veto and to have it before the elections—this to remove the most important administrative decision of the year from personal prejudice. This law shows how far he was from being a 'democrat'.

Finally, in 122, he proposed to offer citizenship to Latins and Latin status (see IUS LATII) to Italian allies, both to protect them from the excesses of Roman magistrates and to make them subject to his brother's agrarian law. The law was opposed by C. *Fannius, whom he had supported for the consulship, and by M. *Livius Drusus (1), who outbid him with an unrealistic colonial programme. It was defeated, and Gracchus was not re-elected. In 121, with his legislation under attack, Gracchus, supported by Flaccus, resorted to armed insurrection. It was suppressed after the first use of the so-called *senatus consultum ultimum*; they and many of their supporters were killed, others executed after arrest.

C. Gracchus had more ambitious plans than his brother, whose memory he revered. He saw the need for major administrative reforms. A proud aristocrat, he wanted to leave the Senate in charge of directing policy and the magistrates in charge of its execution, subject to constitutional checks and removed from financial temptation, with the people sharing in the profits of empire without excessive exploitation of the subjects. The ultimate result of his legislation was to set up the *publicani* as a new exploiting class, not restrained by a tradition of service or by accountability at law. But this did not become clear for a generation, and he cannot be blamed for not foreseeing it.

> The Gracchi, Tiberius and Gaius, are usually treated together. For separate treatments of Tiberius see below. There are none of Gaius. Our chief sources are Plutarch's *Tiberius and Gaius Gracchus* and Appian, *BCiv.* 1. Gracchus was a great orator (see Cic. *Brut.* 125 f.) and many fragments of his speeches survive: see *ORF*⁴, pp. 174–98. Cicero provides many detailed comments. For details of the tribunates see Broughton, *MRR* 1 (and cf. 3. 88). There is no major modern synthesis, although many works discuss aspects of the legislation, and older treatments use misleading models. D. Stockton, *The Gracchi* (1979), gives a useful insight into Oxford interpretations.   E. B.

Sempronius (*RE* 51) **Gracchus (1), Tiberius,** son of a consul of 238 BC, as curule aedile (216) was made *magister equitum* after *Cannae and at once consul (215). With an army including slaves he relieved *Cumae and captured *Philip (3) V's envoys to *Hannibal. As proconsul (214) he prevented Hanno from joining Hannibal, whereupon the slaves were freed and he was elected consul for the second time (213). As proconsul (212) he died in an ambush, no one ever knew how.

> Livy, bks. 22–5.   E. B.

Sempronius (*RE* 53) **Gracchus (2), Tiberius,** nephew of (1), served under L. *Cornelius Scipio Asiagenes in 190 BC, and as tribune 187 or 184 supported Scipio in his trial. (The details are submerged in legend.) After serving on an embassy to Greece and on a board founding a colony he was aedile 182 and demanded such heavy contributions from subjects and clients that the senate limited future aediles' expenditure. As praetor and proconsul in Spain (180–178) he decisively defeated the *Celtiberians, imposed a settlement they regarded as bearable and founded a city (Gracchuris) for them. He was rewarded with a *triumph and the consulate of 177. He took *Sardinia from its commanders and in two ruthless campaigns subdued the Sardi, celebrating another triumph and recording his deeds in a temple on the *forum Boarium. As censor 169, he and his colleague C. *Claudius Pulcher supported the levies for the Macedonian War and dealt harshly with *equites and *publicani. Prosecuted by a tribune, they were acquitted. Gracchus restricted freedmen's votes and built the basilica Sempronia. As consul for the second time (163) he again went to Sardinia, from where he remembered, as augur, that his successors had been illegally elected, forcing them to resign. He headed two embassies to the east, establishing useful personal connections. He married *Cornelia, daughter of P. *Cornelius Scipio Africanus, who bore him twelve children, only three of whom (Ti. *Sempronius Gracchus (3), C. *Sempronius Gracchus, and a daughter) survived.

> Livy, bks. 37–45, and Polyb. bks. 25 and 30–3 are the main sources. Cf. next entry.   E. B.

Sempronius (*RE* 54) **Gracchus (3), Tiberius,** son of (2) and of *Cornelia, served at Carthage under his cousin P. *Cornelius Scipio Aemilianus, who married his sister. As quaestor in Spain (137 BC), he used his father's connections to save the army of C. *Hostilius Mancinus by a treaty later disowned by the senate on Scipio's motion. Thus attacked in his *fides*, he joined a group hostile to Scipio: his father-in-law Ap. *Claudius (1) Pulcher, *princeps senatus* and augur; the consul for 133 P. *Mucius Scaevola and his brother P. *Licinius Crassus Dives Mucianus, both eminent lawyers and *pontifices* (see PONTIFEX). As tribune 133, in

Scipio's absence, he proposed, with their aid and advice, a law designed to solve Rome's interlocking problems: departure or expulsion of small landowners from their properties, leading to insuperable difficulties in recruiting armies; danger from increasing numbers of slaves; and lack of an assured food supply for the capital. The law reaffirmed the long-ignored limit of 500 *iugera* of arable public land per person and instituted a commission (to which he, his brother Gaius (see above) and his father-in-law were ultimately elected) to find and confiscate surplus land and distribute it in small lots to poor citizens. A compromise offering 250 additional *iugera* for each child was withdrawn when it failed to secure his opponents' acceptance of the law. Following good precedent and with his eminent supporters' approval, he submitted the law to the *plebs* without previous discussion in the senate. It was vetoed by M. *Octavius, taken to the senate for adjudication, and rejected. Gracchus none the less resubmitted it, and Octavius persisted in his veto, both contrary to *mos maiorum*. To end the unprecedented impasse Gracchus had Octavius removed from office—again an unprecedented step, but without objection by the other tribunes, who did not veto it. When Pergamene envoys brought news of *Attalus III's death and will, leaving his estate to Rome, Gracchus (with whom they probably stayed owing to his father's *hospitium* with the dynasty) proposed to prejudge the issue of acceptance, ignoring the senate's traditional right to guide foreign affairs, and to distribute Attalus' property to Roman citizens, perhaps as equipment grants for his new allotment-holders.

He next sought re-election, to escape certain conviction on *perduellio* charges. This last unprecedented step alienated earlier supporters and increased fear of tyranny among opponents. When the consul Scaevola refused to stop him by force, the *pontifex maximus* P. *Cornelius Scipio Nasica Serapio led a mob of senators and their clients 'to save the Republic'. Gracchus and many of his supporters were killed on the Capitol, others were later punished by a commission under P. *Popillius Laenas, consul 132. The land commission, however, continued unimpeded until 129 (see CORNELIUS SCIPIO AEMILIANUS AFRICANUS, P.).

His tribunate marks the beginning of 'the Roman Revolution': the introduction of murder into politics and the breakdown of *concordia* (the tradition of not pushing legal powers to extremes) on which the republic is based. See also AGRARIAN LAWS AND POLICY.

D. C. Earl, *Tiberius Gracchus* (1963), refreshingly realistic; E. Badian, 'Tiberius Gracchus and the Beginning of the Roman Revolution', *ANRW* 1 (1972), 668–731; A. H. Bernstein, *Tiberius Sempronius Gracchus* (1978), balanced and well documented (ch. 1 gives a useful survey of Ti. Gracchus (2)). See further on Gaius Gracchus (above).　　E. B.

Sempronius (*RE* 92) **Tuditanus, Gaius,** consul 129 BC, when the senate, on the motion of P. *Cornelius Scipio Aemilianus, transferred the judicial powers of the agrarian commission established by Ti. *Sempronius Gracchus (3) to him. Refusing to exercise them, and thus paralysing the commission, he went to Illyria, where with the help of his legate D. *Iunius Brutus Callaicus he defeated various tribes and earned a triumph. To immortalize his achievements, he set up a statue of a river god near Duino (Plin. *NH* 129; *ILLRP* 334) and a commemorative inscription in *Saturnian verse at *Aquileia (*ILLRP* 335). He wrote a work on Roman magistrates and perhaps a historical work. Only small fragments remain.

M. G. Morgan, *Athenaeum*, 1971, 271 ff.; *Philologus*, 1973, 29 ff., with an alternative text of *ILLRP* 335 (p. 48). Peter, *HRRel.* 1², pp. cci ff., 143 ff. (discussion and fragments of his works).　　E. B.

Sempronius (*RE* 96) **Tuditanus, Publius,** served as military tribune at *Cannae in 216 BC, and was curule aedile in 214. He was praetor 213, commanding in northern Italy until 211, and censor 209. In 206 or 205 he was appointed to succeed P. *Sulpicius Galba as commander in the First Macedonian War, which he brought to an end by negotiating the Peace of Phoenice. Consul 204, he suffered a reverse in Bruttium at the hands of *Hannibal, but he and a P. Licinius Crassus then joined forces and won a victory; he recaptured a number of towns, including *Consentia. He was one of three ambassadors sent to the east in 201–200 before the Second Macedonian War.

J. W. Rich, *PCPS* 1984, esp. 136–51.　　J. Br.

senate

Regal and republican Age **Composition**

In the time of the *Gracchi (*c*.133–121 BC) the senate was a body of around 300 wealthy men of aristocratic birth, most of them ex-magistrates. Although the sources tend to assume that this state of affairs had always existed, in fact it was the product of historical development and change. Since in the early republic there were very few magistrates, and iteration of office was common, it follows that there was a time when either the majority of senators had never held a magistracy, or their number was considerably less than 300. Probably both conclusions are true for the 5th cent. This must cast doubt on the notion that the number 300 is connected with the three tribes and thirty *curiae* (see CURIA (1)); in fact there is no basis for this theory in the ancient sources, and tradition itself implicitly denies it in maintaining that *Romulus, who founded the tribes (see TRIBUS) and *curiae*, chose 100 men to form the first senate.

Very little is actually known about the origins and early history of the senate. Traditionally it was the council of the kings, then of the consuls. There is no reason to think that it was ever an exclusively patrician body. Collectively the senators were addressed as *patres et conscripti*; since the *patres* were *patricians, it would seem to follow that the *conscripti* were not. The distinction was certainly very ancient, and it may go back to the monarchy. Senators were chosen first by the kings, then by the consuls. Festus (p. 290 Lindsay) tells us that they had a free choice, and that before the *lex Ovinia* it was not considered disgraceful to be omitted from the senate. This can only mean that membership was not fixed, but depended on the whim of the magistrates in office; it clearly implies that before the *lex Ovinia* the senate was little more than an *ad hoc* advisory council. Festus may or may not be right; but his statement is the only evidence we have.

The date of the *lex Ovinia* is unknown, but it was probably after 339 and certainly before 318 BC. It laid down that the censors were to choose the senate according to fixed criteria; only men guilty of serious misconduct could be omitted from the list. As a result membership became effectively lifelong, and expulsion from the senate meant disgrace. The criteria of selection are unfortunately not recorded, but it was probably as a consequence of this reform that ex-magistrates were chosen automatically. By the later 3rd cent. ex-magistrates were permitted to take part in sessions before being formally enrolled at the *census. The *censors nevertheless retained the right to make up numbers by choosing additional senators, and to exclude persons considered guilty of immoral behaviour or following disreputable professions. *Freedmen and sons of freedmen were usually not admitted. It is also evident that senators had to be qualified for membership of the equestrian order, which meant ownership of landed property worth 400,000 sesterces. *Sulla increased the size of the senate by adding 300 new members and making entry dependent on tenure of the quaestorship; the number of *quaestors was raised to twenty to maintain numbers thenceforth. *Caesar rewarded his supporters by admitting them to the senate, which in 45 BC had 900 members; under the triumvirate the figure rose to over a thousand, but was reduced to around 600 by *Augustus.

Senators wore the *latus* *clavus* and special shoes. They had reserved seats at religious ceremonies and games. They were not allowed to leave Italy without the senate's permission. Being excluded from state contracts and ownership of large ships (see CLAUDIUS, Q.), they were predominantly a landowning class. Although heredity was a strong recommendation for magisterial office, the senate was far from being an exclusively hereditary body; it seems always to have contained numbers of 'new men' (i.e. first-generation senators; see NOVUS HOMO), particularly among the lower ranks (though for a new man to rise to high office was naturally unusual).

Procedure

The senate was summoned by the presiding magistrates, either holders of *imperium* or, later, tribunes, according to an order of precedence. Sessions were held between dawn and sunset, but were forbidden by a *lex Pupia* (2nd or 1st cent. BC) during the *comitia*. Meetings had to take place in Rome (see CURIA (2)) or within a mile of the city boundary, in a place both public and consecrated. The first sitting of the year was in the temple of Jupiter Capitolinus.

Sittings were held in private, but with open doors, the tribunes of the *plebs* (see TRIBUNI PLEBIS) sitting in the vestibule in the period before their admission to sessions (4th cent. BC?). A session opened with a statement by the chairman or another magistrate, outlining the matter for discussion. Each senator then gave his opinion (*sententia*) in order of rank—beginning with ex-censors (*censorii*), followed by *consulares*, *praetorii*, and so on. The senior patrician ex-censor, who gave his opinion first, was known as the *princeps senatus*. After Sulla the magistrate gave precedence to the consuls designate or, in their absence, to a senator of consular rank, and *princeps senatus* became a purely social title open to plebeians. Each senator spoke from his seat. Freedom of speech was unlimited in the republic, but Augustus imposed a time-limit. After the debate a vote was taken; the decree resulting from a positive vote was known as a *senatus consultum*. Sometimes a vote was taken directly after the opening statement with no intervening debate; and on some issues a quorum was required. A *senatus consultum* could be vetoed by the tribunes. Records of proceedings were kept by the urban quaestors in the *aerarium*, and in 59 BC Caesar ordered them to be published (Suet. *Caes.* 20).

Functions

The senate's formal role was to advise the magistrates. Its advice covered all matters of domestic and foreign policy, finance, and religion. In the 3rd and 2nd cents. it was customary, but not obligatory, for magistrates (and tribunes) to submit legislative proposals to the senate for discussion, and to obtain a *senatus consultum* before presenting a bill to the *comitia*. The senate could also invalidate laws already passed by pointing out technical flaws in procedure.

Since the senate included ex-magistrates who were effectively (after the *lex Ovinia*) members for life, its decisions inevitably came to bind those of its members who happened to be holding senior magistracies at any given time. And by the start of the 3rd cent. the growth of the Roman state and the increasing complexity of its affairs gave the senate an ever greater control of government business. It was the only permanent body with the necessary knowledge and experience to supervise policy in a wide range of fields. It controlled the state's finances, the levying and disposal of military forces, the allocation of magisterial tasks ('provinces'; see PROVINCIA), relations with foreign powers, and the maintenance of law and order in Rome and Italy. It was the senate that decided whether to extend the period of a magistrate's command (*prorogatio imperii*; see PRO CONSULE, PRO PRAETORE), and although the people in the *comitia centuriata* had the final say on declarations of war and the ratification of treaties, it is clear that, by the end of the 3rd cent. at least, they merely gave formal assent to decisions taken in advance by the senate. The senate supervised the religious life of the community, and the major priestly colleges consisted largely of senators. The senate received reports of prodigies and decided on the appropriate action; and it was the senate that ordered the performance of special religious ceremonies and decided on the introduction of new cults.

In the late republic the senate claimed the right to wield absolute power in certain circumstances. It could order dispensation from the observance of law, and during the Gracchan period it asserted the right to declare a state of emergency by passing its 'ultimate decree' (*senatus consultum ultimum*), which gave the magistrates unfettered power to act as they saw fit. But these developments occurred at a time when the senate's authority was being challenged by the *populares* (see OPTIMATES), and in the succeeding decades it was completely undermined by armed force. The collapse of the senate's authority marked the end of the republic.

GENERAL P. Willems, *Le Sénat de la république romaine*[2] (1885); Mommsen, *Röm. Staatsr.* 3/2; A. O'Brien Moore, *RE* suppl. 6, 660; E. Meyer, *Röm. Staat u. Staatsgedanke*[2] (1961); J. Gaudemet, *Institutions de l'antiquité* (1967); C. Nicolet, *Rome et le conquête du monde méditerranéen*[2] (1979), 1, 357 ff.; M. Bonnefond-Coudry, *Le Sénat de la république romaine* (1989). On the social composition of the senate in the republic: T. P. Wiseman, *New Men in the Roman Senate* (1971); G. P. Burton and K. Hopkins, in K. Hopkins, *Death and Renewal* (1983), 31 ff.; I. Shatzman, *Senatorial Wealth in Roman Politics* (1975); C. Nicolet, *JRS* 1976, 20–38 (on the census qualification of senators).   A. M.; T. J. Co.

The Imperial Age Under *Augustus and his successors far-reaching modifications of the social origins and the corporate and individual functions of senators occurred. Despite those changes the senatorial *ordo* remained the most important political and social body in the empire, its first estate.

The *ordo* and its recruitment

By the end of the civil wars the ranks of senators had increased to about 1,000. Augustus initiated a series of revisions of the senate of which the most important occurred in 28 BC and 18 BC. After the latter the size of the senate was fixed at 600, which remained its normal figure through the first two and a half centuries of the Principate. A new property qualification of one million sesterces was introduced, which served to differentiate more clearly the senatorial from the equestrian order (see EQUITES). Sons of senators gained the automatic right to assume the *latus* *clavus* at 17 years of age and to stand, later, for membership of the senate. Sons of senators normally served for one year as a military tribune, then held a post in the vigintivirate (see VIGINTISEXVIRI) before standing for election to the senate (through the quaestorship; see QUAESTOR) at 25. Twenty quaestors were elected each year; from the beginning of *Tiberius' reign the election of junior magistrates (most notably the quaestors and praetors) was transferred to the senate.

The main thrust of Augustus' reforms was to introduce *de iure* a strong hereditary element into the senate. However throughout the Principate some senatorial families were impoverished by over-expenditure, others fell into political disfavour or were eliminated; still other senatorial families had no surviving sons. In addition some sons of senators probably (though this issue is disputed) chose not to try to follow in their fathers' footsteps. Consequently in each generation opportunities arose for new families, through the patronage of the emperors, to enter the senate. Emperors promoted new men into the senate either through the grant of the *latus clavus*, which gave individuals the right to stand for the quaestorship, or through direct *adlection. By these means imperial *patronage continuously transformed the social origins of senators.

The influx of new families recruited from the élites of the provinces transformed the geographic composition of the order. Under Augustus the senate remained primarily Italian in origin. Under the Julio-Claudian emperors provincial senators, especially from *Baetica and Gallia Narbonensis (see GAUL (TRANS-ALPINE))), emerged. In the course of the later 1st and 2nd cents. new families emerged from the north African and eastern provinces, though very few senators ever came from the northern and Danubian provinces. By the time of the Severan emperors over 50 per cent of senators were of non-Italian origin. In the long term the social and geographic transformation of the senate allowed the socio-political élite of the conquered to be gradually fused with the élite of the conquerors. See next entry.

Functions and roles

Although financial policy, diplomacy, and military policy became the preserve of the emperors, the senate still exercised certain important corporate functions. It acted as a source of binding rule-making, as *senatus consulta* acquired the full force of law (see SENATUS CONSULTUM); surviving legislation predominantly concerns the rules of status and of inheritance and the maintenance of public order. As a court it tried its own members, chiefly on charges of extortion. Most importantly it formally conferred powers on new emperors (and members of their families), and the acknowledgement of the senate was, therefore, the condition of legitimacy of any emperor. It also claimed the right to declare them public enemies, condemn their memory (*damnatio memoriae*) and rescind their acts.

Senatorial membership, as in the republic, continued to be a precondition for exercising key individual political and administrative roles. For example the civil and military administration of the majority of the provinces lay in the hands of individual senators in their role as provincial governors (proconsuls—see PRO CONSULE, PRO PRAETORE, and *legati Augusti*—see LEGATI). Even in AD 200 29 out of 33 legions were still commanded by senators. The civil and military posts, in Rome and the provinces, allocated to senators were ranked in a clear hierarchy; some were reserved for ex-praetors, others for ex-consuls. The most successful senators politically were those who governed the senior provinces reserved for ex-consuls. Senators also exercised direct influence on the administration, jurisdiction, and military policy of the emperors through their membership of the *consilium principis*. In short imperial rule was predicated on the active participation of the empire's political élite formed by the senate. Indeed in the 1st and 2nd cents. emperors, when they had no male heir, adopted a senator as their successor (so *Nerva adopted *Trajan who, in turn, adopted *Hadrian). When political legitimacy at Rome broke down and civil war occurred (as in 68–9 and 193–7), it was senior senators who vied for the purple.

The third-century crisis and the later empire

The crisis of the 3rd cent. and major reforms by *Diocletian and *Constantine I modified profoundly the political role and social characteristics of the senatorial order. During the crisis many political and military offices were transferred on an *ad hoc* basis to equestrians. This process was first codified by *Gallienus and then carried further by Diocletian. By the end of his reign only a few civilian posts, such as proconsul of Africa or Asia and prefect of the city of Rome (see PRAEFECTUS URBI), remained open to senators.

Further substantial and complex reforms were introduced through the 4th cent. Under Constantine a general fusion of the senatorial and equestrian orders occurred whereby high-ranking equestrians were enrolled in the senate and senior equestrian officers were converted into senatorial ones. In turn it became normal practice to confer senatorial status on the holders of key military (e.g. *duces*, *magistri militum* (see DUX; MAGISTER MILITUM) and fiscal (e.g. *comites* of the *sacrae largitiones* and *res privata*) offices. In consequence the number of senators increased to about 2,000 in the 4th cent. In a parallel development Constantine created a second senate at the newly founded capital of *Constantinople whose membership also quickly rose to about 2,000. A new socio-political hierarchy evolved within the senatorial order. By a law of *Valentinian I of 372 three grades were codified, namely, in descending status, the *illustres*, the *spectabiles*, and the *clarissimi*.

The senate of the later empire exhibits strong contrasts to its predecessors. Politically, as a corporate body, it ceased to be an effective council of state. Power lay with the emperor, his court, the *consistorium, and the *comitatus*. The residence of emperors at sites such as *Ravenna and Milan (*Mediolanum) of itself diminished the importance of Rome and its senate. Socially, the enlarged order was far more heterogeneous. Traditional aristocratic families co-existed with *parvenu* military men of humble origin. Although a senator's son was by right a senator (at the level of a *clarissimus*), the higher grades of the order were achieved by the tenure of the appropriate office. Status had become a reward for, rather than a precondition of, high office.

THE SENATE OF THE PRINCIPATE Syme, *Rom. Rev.*; J. Crook, *Consilium Principis* (1955); M. Hammond, *JRS* 1957, 74 ff.; Syme, *Tacitus*; W. Eck, *Senatoren von Vespasian bis Hadrian* (1970); Millar, *ERW*; G. Alföldy, *Konsulat und Senatorenstand unter den Antoninen* (1977); R. P. Saller, *Personal Patronage under the Early Empire* (1982); K. Hopkins, *Death and Renewal* (1983); G. Alföldy, *The Social History of Rome* (1985); R. Talbert, *The Senate of Imperial Rome* (1984); F. Jacques, *Annales ESC* 1988, 1287 ff.; P. M. M. Leunissen, *Konsuln und Konsulare in der Zeit von Commodus bis Severus Alexander (183–235 n. Chr.)* (1989).

THIRD-CENTURY CRISIS AND LATER EMPIRE G. Barbieri, *L'albo senatorio da Settimio Severo a Carino* (1952); P. Petit, *Ant. Class.* 1957, 347 ff.; A. Chastagnol, *La Préfecture urbaine à Rome sous le bas-empire* (1960); Jones, *Later Rom. Emp.*, ch. 15; A. Chastagnol, *Le Sénat sous le règne d'Odoacre* (1966), and *Revue historique* 1970, 305 ff.; H. G. Pflaum, *Historia* 1976, 109 ff.; A. Demandt, *Chiron* 1980, 609 ff.; G. Alföldy, *The Social History of Rome* (1985); J. Matthews, *Western Aristocracies and Imperial Court AD 364–425*[2] (1990). G. P. B.

senators, patterns of recruitment The emperor *Claudius pointed out in AD 48 (*ILS* 212, trans. D. Braund, *Augustus to Nero*, no. 570) that newcomers had reigned in the regal period; the senate was never a closed body. Claudius' *patrician ancestors were immigrants into Rome of the monarchy (Ogilvie on Livy 2. 16. 4; see SABINI). Before the *Social War (3) (91–88 BC) 'new men' (see NOVUS HOMO) entered from regions already enjoying citizenship (Wiseman, *New Men*, 184–7): M. *Porcius Cato (1)

senatus consultum

(184 BC) from *Tusculum, C. *Marius (1) (consul for the first time 107) from *Arpinum. The enfranchisement due to the war and *Sulla's enlargement of the senate to *c*.600, with membership through election to the quaestorship (now twenty *per annum*; see QUAESTOR), widened the recruiting area, although 'new men' met prejudice, especially when trying for consulships. *Caesar's supremacy left a senate swollen to 900 (Cass. Dio 43. 47. 3) by the admission of partisans. A few came from Spain and Gaul; for all the mockery (ibid. 76. 3; 80. 2) they were probably descended from Italian emigrants. Political expediency likewise raised numbers during the triumviral period (see TRIUMVIRI) to more than 1,000, which *Augustus reduced to the Sullan level. One survivor, P. Paquius Scaeva from Histonium (Wiseman's no. 308), conforms to Claudius' claim that Augustus and *Tiberius decided to admit men from the whole of Italy; certainly Augustus was cautious in admitting men from the provinces, though prepared to make an exception for a noble Greek with imperial connections (Pompeius Macer of Mytilene, relative of *Theophanes, and Wiseman's no. 330). Claudius, seeking to admit Gauls from Comata, still had to face resistance, though a number of individuals from *Baetica, Narbonensis (see GAUL (TRANSALPINE)), and even *Pamphylia, men from local dynasties or Roman settler families, are attested under Tiberius. The widening of the catchment area was irresistible, though Cisalpine Gaul (see GAUL (CISALPINE)) did not make full impact until the reign of Nero. Otho exaggerates when in 69 he calls the senate the glory of all the provinces (Tac. *Hist.* 1. 84), but the crisis of 68–9 and the accession of Vespasian accelerated change, favouring the east, especially Asia, and including royalty (C. *Iulius Antiochus Epiphanes Philopappus, *suffect consul 109). The reigns of *Domitian and *Trajan have been seen as the real turning point for easterners; by the reign of Marcus *Aurelius they formed the majority of the provincials in the senate; Italians came to be outnumbered overall under the Severi.

Whatever the place of origin, connections helped (cf. Plin. *Ep.* 10. 4), and Claudius' criteria—wealth (Augustus had set the property qualification at one million sesterces) and respectability (including good birth and a correct attitude towards the *princeps*)—remained applicable: the scandal of freedmen admitted under *Caesar and the Triumvirs had been remedied by Augustus' purges (Suet. *Div. Aug.* 35. 1). The wealth of the newcomers, however, was also seen as a threat (Tac. *Ann.* 11. 23. 5 f.); Trajan made it a condition of entry for one-third of their money to be invested in Italian land (Plin. *Ep.* 6. 19). See NEGOTIATORES.

K. Hopkins and G. Burton, 'Political succession in the late Republic (249–50 BC)', in K. Hopkins, *Death and Renewal* (1983), 31 ff.; T. P. Wiseman, *New Men in the Roman Senate 139 B.C.–14 A.D.* (1971); M. Hammond, *JRS* 1957, 74 ff. (composition 68–235); W. Eck, *Senatoren von Vespasian bis Hadrian* (1970); R. Syme, *Colonial Élites* (1958); H. Halfmann, *Die Senatoren aus dem östlichen Teil des Imperium Romanum bis zum Ende des 2. Jh. n. Chr.* (1979); *Epigrafia e ordine senatorio* (Tituli 4–5), 2 vols. (1982).

B. M. L.

senatus consultum was the advice of the senate (see SENATUS) to the magistrates, and was expressed in the form of a resolution or decree. In Republican times it had no legal force, but in practice it was always obeyed and, except when vetoed, it acquired the force of law when implemented. During the empire *senatus consulta* were at first implemented by a clause in the praetor's edict; after Hadrian certain *senatus consulta* had immediate legal force. The *senatus consultum* was drafted after the session of the senate in the presence of the presiding magistrate and some witnesses, usually including the proposer. If necessary, it was translated into Greek. Many *senatus consulta* are preserved in Greek translations.

A *senatus consultum* (commonly abbreviated SC, plural SCC) usually contained: (1) the name of the presiding magistrate; (2) a statement by the proposing magistrate, ending with the formula *d(e) e(a) r(e) i(ta) c(ensuerunt)* ('concerning the matter in hand they [i.e. the senators present] decreed as follows'); (3) the decree itself, often expressed in the form of advice to the magistrates: *s(i) e(is) v(idebitur)* ('if it shall seem right to them'); (4) the mark of approval, indicated by the letter C (*censuerunt*, 'they decreed'). In the imperial age *senatus consulta* also recorded the number of senators present.

The texts of *senatus consulta* were deposited in the *aerarium, and from an early date (traditionally 449 BC) the plebeian *aediles were allowed to keep copies in the temple of Ceres. The documents were classified, but not sufficiently to prevent losses and falsifications. The jurists often named them after one of the consuls of the year (*SC Orfitianum*, AD 178), or more rarely after the emperor who proposed them (*SC Claudianum*) or after the occasion of the SC (*SC Macedonianum*).

Many *senatus consulta* are collected in Bruns, *Fontes*[7] (1909), and in Riccobono, *FIRA* 1. For Greek texts see R. K. Sherk, *Roman Documents from the Greek East* (1969), with an important account of senatorial procedure, pp. 4–19. On procedure see esp. R. J. A. Talbert, *The Senate of Imperial Rome* (1984), with lists of SCC on pp. 435 ff.

A. M.; T. J. Co.

senatus consultum ultimum, 'the ultimate decree of the *senate', a modern term, deriving from Caes. *BCiv.* 1. 5, for what was in fact a declaration of emergency.

This decree urged magistrates, usually the consul or consuls, to take measures to defend the *respublica* and see that it came to no harm (Cic. *Phil.* 5. 34; Sall. *Cat.* 29). It was interpreted as authorizing the magistrates to employ physical repression against (unspecified) public enemies without being bound by strict legality. Inevitably it was a matter of political controversy, since questions arose whether the circumstances merited this decree and what level of force and illegality was appropriate after it.

The decree was first both passed and accepted by the consul in 121 BC, against C. *Sempronius Gracchus and M. *Fulvius Flaccus. It was later used against L. *Appuleius Saturninus and C. *Servilius Glaucia (100), M. *Aemilius Lepidus (2) (77), the Catilinarians (see SERGIUS CATILINA, L.) (63), Q. *Caecilius Metellus Nepos and C. *Iulius Caesar (1) (62), the supporters of P. *Clodius Pulcher and T. *Annius Milo (52), *Caesar (49), M. *Caelius Rufus (48), P. *Cornelius Dolabella (1) (47), M. *Antonius (2) (Mark Antony), and later *Octavian (43), *Q. Salvidienus Rufus (40). It was originally passed after disturbances in Rome itself, but it came to be used when the primary threat came from outside Rome, as with Lepidus and the Catilinarians, and later was employed against an alleged external enemy, when there was no threat of violence in Rome at all (so Caesar complained in 49, and this was certainly true in 43 and 40).

When this decree had led to deaths, especially those of eminent men, there was bitter reaction after the event against magistrates responsible—L. *Opimius, *Cicero—and, in the long-deferred case of C. *Rabirius (1) (prosecuted in 63 for what he did in 100), a man under C. *Marius (1)'s command. The usual ground of complaint was that citizens had been killed without proper trial—which was in fact true: the question was whether this illegality could be justified.

G. Plaumann, *Klio* 1913, 321 ff.; H. M. Last, *JRS* 1943, 94 ff.; A. W.

Lintott, *Violence in Rep. Rome*, ch. 11; J. Ungern-Sternberg, *Untersuch. z. spätrepublikan. Notstandrecht* (1970); M. I. Finley, *Politics in the Ancient World* (1983), 3 ff.; W. Nippel, *JRS* 1984, 25 f. and *Public Order in Ancient Rome* (1995), 63 ff.   A. M.; A. W. L.

Seneca (the Elder) See ANNAEUS SENECA (1), L.

Seneca (the Younger) See ANNAEUS SENECA (2), L.

Senones, a Gallic tribe from a parent stock that in *Caesar's time inhabited the Seine basin (Caes. *BGall.* 2. 2 etc.). The tradition (Livy 5. 34. 5) that they were the last Gauls to settle in Italy is to be resisted on archaeological grounds. Here they ousted the *Umbrians on the Adriatic coast between *Ariminum and *Ancona, the *ager Gallicus* of historical times. They are said to have led the Gallic band that captured Rome in 390 BC. Thereafter Senones remained a constant menace for 100 years until Rome subjugated them in 283 (Polyb. 2. 17 f.; Diod. Sic. 14. 113 f.; Livy 5. 35). They then disappeared from Italy, being either expelled or massacred. Their territory was used partly for colonies (Sena, Ariminum), partly for the allotments which C. *Flaminius assigned to individual Roman citizens in 232.

D. G. Lollini, in P-M. Duval and V. Kruta (eds.), *Les Mouvements celtiques du Vᵉ au Iᵉʳ siècle avant notre ère* (1976), 55 ff.; D. Vitali, in *The Celts* (1991), 233 ff.   E. T. S.; T. W. P.

sententia, whose basic meaning is 'way of thinking', came to have specialized senses, such as an opinion expressed in the senate, the judgement of a judge, and the spirit (as opposed to the letter) of the law. In literary criticism, it came to connote a brief saying embodying a striking thought. Such sayings could be gnomic (see GNŌMĒ) and moralizing (so Cic. *Nat. D.* 1. 85 of *Epicurus' *Kyriai Doxai*); a collection attributed to *Publilius Syrus survives. But they were often specially coined for a particular context. They probably played a part in 'Asianic' rhetoric and *declamation (see ASIANISM AND ATTICISM); but Latin, with its terseness and love of antithesis and word play, took to them with especial enthusiasm. Even the florid *Cicero was thought not to lack them (Quint. 12. 10. 48), and the declamation school gave them a natural home; the elder Seneca's collection (see ANNAEUS SENECA (1), L.) makes *sententiae* a main rubric. At their worst, they descend to puerile punning; at their best they are pointed, allusive, witty. They are typical of Silver Latin from Sallust onwards. Where declaimers might use them merely for pleasurable effect, orators (Quint., as above) and philosophers (Sen. *Ep.* 94. 43) found they could be persuasive too, because they stuck in the mind; and they were perfectly designed to give emphatic *closure to speech or section. Tacitus used them masterfully (*Agr.* 30 *ubi solitudinem faciunt, pacem appellant,* 'they make a desert and call it peace'). So too in verse of different kinds: Seneca's drama, *Lucan's epic (1. 128 *victrix causa deis placuit, sed victa Catoni,* 'if the victor had the gods on his side, the vanquished had Cato' (Duff), typically hard to translate), *Juvenal's satire (1. 74 *probitas laudatur et alget,* 'rectitude is praised—and left out in the cold'), and *Martial's epigram rely heavily on them.

Quint. 8. 5 is the *locus classicus* (see J. Cousin's notes); W. C. Summers, *Select Letters of Seneca* (1910), pp. xv–xli, is still valuable on the pointed style: S. F. Bonner, *Roman Declamation* (1949), 54–5 and ch. 8; P. Morillon, *Sentire, sensus, sententia* (1974).   W. S. W.; M. W.

Sentinum near mod. Sassoferrato, in Umbria. Here the Romans defeated Samnites (see SAMNIUM), Gauls, *Etruscans, and *Umbrians in the decisive battle for the supremacy of Italy (295 BC). Sentinum became a *municipium* with walls of Augustan date, and was occupied into the 5th cent. AD.

P. Sommela, *Antichi campi di battaglia in Italia* (1967), 35 ff.
                                    E. T. S.; T. W. P.

Sentius Augurinus, a young friend praised by *Pliny (2) (*Ep.* 4. 27; 9. 8) for writing 'Poems in Little' (*poematia*) marked by charm and tenderness, but sometimes by satire. Pliny quotes eight hendecasyllabics by him in the manner of *Catullus and *C. Licinius Calvus. Probably identical with Q. Gellius Sentius Augurinus, proconsul under *Hadrian (*PIR*² G 135).

A. Sherwin-White, *Letters of Pliny* (1966), 306.
                                    J. W. D.; G. B. A. F.; A. J. S. S.

Sentius (*RE* 9) **Saturninus, Gaius** (consul 19 BC), of a reputable family from Atina (C. Sentius was praetor 94 BC). Further, he was related to that *Scribonia who married *Octavian in 40 (*ILS* 8892). Consul without colleague for the greater part of the year, he dealt firmly with electoral disorders, refusing to recognize the candidature of M. *Egnatius Rufus and thwarting his 'conspiracy'. Proconsul of *Africa (*c.*14 BC); legate (see LEGATI) of *Syria (*c.*9–6 BC), Sentius next appears as legate under *Tiberius in Germany (AD 4–5); in AD 6 he led the Rhine army east for the campaign against *Maroboduus, winning *ornamenta triumphalia. *Velleius praises this useful public servant and friend of Tiberius as a man of manifold merits, energetic, quick, foresighted, etc. (2. 105. 1); he produced sons, consuls in AD 4.

R. Syme, *Hist.* 1964, 156 ff. (= *RP* 2. 605 ff.).   R. S.; B. M. L.

septemviri epulones, the latest addition to the four major colleges of Roman *priests. They were instituted by law in 196 BC (Livy 33. 42) and were then three in number (*tresviri*), all apparently plebeians and including C. Licinius Lucullus, the tribune who had proposed the bill. Their first responsibility, from which they take their name, was the organization of the *epulum Iovis*, a great feast at the games (see LUDI), attended by the senate and people and presided over by the images of the Capitoline deities (see CAPITOL). The number of priests increased from three to seven and later ten, though the seven remained their title.

Wissowa, *RK* 518; Latte, *RRG* 398–9.   H. J. R.; J. A. N.

Septimius, Publius, a republican writer on architecture mentioned by Vitruvius (7. *praef.* 14).

Septimius Geta (1), Publius, brother of the emperor L. *Septimius Severus, had a long senatorial career known from an inscription at *Lepcis Magna (*Inscriptions of Roman Tripolitania* 541). He was governor of Lower *Moesia when *Septimius Severus seized power and was then appointed legate (see LEGATI) of *Dacia (where he is attested in AD 195). He became consul for the 2nd time in AD 203 and, shortly before his death the next year, warned Severus about L. *Fulvius Plautianus, whom he hated.

Dio Cass. 76; SHA *Sev.*; A. R. Birley, *The African Emperor Septimius Severus*² (1988), 218, no. 21.   A. R. Bi.

Septimius (*RE* 32) **Geta (2), Publius,** younger son of L. *Septimius Severus and *Iulia Domna, born 7 March 189, was made 'most noble Caesar' on 28 January 198, when his brother M. *Aurelius Antoninus (1) (Caracalla) became Augustus (see AUGUSTUS, AUGUSTA AS TITLES) and co-emperor. Geta (whose praenomen is given on many inscriptions as L. instead of P.) and Caracalla hated one another: Severus was claimed to have launched the British expedition partly to discipline them. Geta was given duties within the province, while Caracalla campaigned in Scotland with Severus. He at last became Augustus in 210 and co-emperor

Septimius Nestor, Lucius

on Severus' death in February 211; but was murdered by Caracalla on 26 December and subjected to *damnatio memoriae*.

Dio Cass. 76–7; Herodian 3–4; SHA *Sev.*; *Carac.*; *Geta* (largely fiction); B.M. *Coins, Rom. Emp.* 5; A. R. Birley, *The African Emperor Septimius Severus*[2] (1988), esp. 218 (dates of birth, promotion to Augustus, and death). A. R. Bi.

Septimius Nestor, Lucius, of Laranda in *Lycaonia, lived in the reign of *Septimius Severus (AD 193–211), and wrote, among other works, an Ἰλιὰς λειπογράμματος ('Missing-letter *Iliad*'), in each of the 24 books of which one letter of the alphabet did not appear; and Μεταμορφώσεις or 'Transformations' (*Anth. Pal.* 9. 129, 364). He set up marble tablets at *Ostia commemorating *oracles given him there by the *Dioscuri; they assure him of his talents and future fame, and tell him to set up his statue in the temple. He may well have composed these oracular responses himself: poets like Nestor must have been in demand at oracular shrines. Inscriptions show his relations with members of the Roman aristocracy. His son was the epic poet *Pisander (3) of Laranda.

R. Meriç and others, *Die Inschriften von Ephesos* 7/1 (1981), no. 3607 (with bibliog.); P. M. Fraser, *Report of Dept. of Antiq., Cyprus*, 1984, 278 f.; R. Lane Fox, *Pagans and Christians* (1986), 189.
J. D. D.; S. H.; A. J. S. S.

Septimius (*RE* Suppl. 11, 2; *PLRE* 1. 638 f.) **Odaenathus,** a Palmyrene noble (see PALMYRA) who from *c.* AD 250 cleverly exploited the weaknesses of Rome and Persia (see SASANIDS) to establish his city, with himself as its king, as a major power in the east. Already a valued ally under *Valerian, *Gallienus rewarded him with the titles *dux* and *corrector totius Orientis* 'of the whole east' for his help against *Sapor I and Quietus (see FULVIUS IUNIUS MACRIANUS, T.), and thereby entrusted him with the protection of the eastern empire. Though Odaenathus enjoyed further significant successes against Persia, he always carefully acknowledged the suzerainty of Rome, and thus justified Gallienus' policy of *laissez faire*, following the death of Valerian. However, Palmyra's irregular position caused increasing stress on both sides, creating a problem that could not long go unresolved. Killed in a family quarrel in 267, Odaenathus was effectively succeeded by his widow, *Zenobia.

E. Kettenhofen, *Die römisch-persischen Kriege des 3. Jhdts n. Chr.* (1982); J. F. Drinkwater, *RSA* 1989, 123 ff.; D. Potter, *History and Prophecy . . .* (1990), 381 ff. J. F. D.

Septimius Serenus seems to have flourished in the mid-third cent. AD. He wrote at least two books of *Opuscula Ruralia* in a wide variety of often recherché metres, some introduced by himself; the influence of *Laevius is apparent in metre and diction. This work was widely read and popular; it survived until the 10th cent., when a Bobbio library catalogue lists it united with the translation of *Dictys of Crete by L. Septimius with whom he may be identical. See SERENUS SAMMONICUS.

See A. D. E. Cameron *Harv. Stud.* 1980, 172; E. T. Champlin, ibid. 1981, 207 (dubious conclusions); S. Mattiacci, *I frammenti dei 'Poetae Novelli'* (1982), 105; Courtney, *FLP* 406. E. C.

Septimius Severus, Lucius (*RE* Severus 13), emperor AD 193–211. The Septimii were of Punic origin, his mother's family (Fulvii) of Italian descent. His equestrian grandfather, probably identical with the poet *Statius' friend Septimius Severus, was the leading figure at *Lepcis Magna under *Trajan; his father held no office, but two Septimii were already senators when Severus was born (145). One of them secured senatorial rank for

him from M. Aurelius; he and his brother P. *Septimius Geta (1) had normal careers under Marcus and Commodus. Consul in 190, by now with a second wife, *Iulia Domna, and two young sons, he became governor of Pannonia Superior in 191 through the praetorian prefect Q. *Aemilius Laetus, a fellow-African. Twelve days after P. *Helvius Pertinax's murder (28 March 193) he was proclaimed emperor at Carnuntum (9 April) as avenger of Pertinax, whose name he assumed. Backed by all sixteen Rhine and Danube legions he marched on Rome, securing the support of *Clodius Septimius Albinus, governor of Britain, by granting him the title *Caesar*. By 1 June, 60 miles north of Rome, Severus was recognized by the senate; Pertinax's successor *Didius Severus Julianus was murdered, and Severus entered Rome without opposition on 9 June 193. The *praetorians were dismissed and a new guard, twice as large, was formed from the Danubian legions; three new legions (I–III Parthicae) were raised, one of which (II Parthica) was to be based at Alba, near Rome. See LEGION. This, together with increases in the *vigiles*, urban cohorts (see COHORTES URBANAE), and other units, radically enlarged the capital's garrison. Army pay was raised (for the first time since AD 84) and the men gained new privileges, e.g. the right to marry (see CONTUBERNIUM). Then Severus moved against *Pescennius Niger, proclaimed emperor in Syria in April 193. Advance forces under L. *Fabius Cilo halted Niger at Perinthus; his base at Byzantium was besieged by *Marius Maximus with troops from Moesia. By the end of 193 Severan generals defeated Niger at Cyzicus and Nicaea; Egypt had recognized Severus by February 194. The final encounter (spring 194), near Issus, was followed by Niger's death. Syria was divided into two provinces, Coele and Phoenice, *Antioch (1) and other cities that had supported Niger being punished. Severus now launched a campaign against the Parthian vassals who had backed Niger. Most of *Osroëne was annexed, perhaps other parts of N. Mesopotamia too. Severus became *Parthicus Arabicus* and *Parthicus Adiabenicus* in 195. In the same year he proclaimed himself son of the deified Marcus and brother of the deified Commodus, renamed his elder son (Caracalla) M. *Aurelius Antoninus (1) and made him Caesar, and gave his wife the title 'mother of the camp'. This clearly dynastic move led his ally Albinus Caesar to rebel and cross to Gaul with the British army. Severus hurried back west for this final civil war, won at the battle of *Lugdunum (1) (19 February 197).

In a purge of Albinus' supporters 29 senators, and numerous others in Gaul, Spain, and Africa were executed. Severus left for the east in summer 197 for his Second Parthian War, invading in winter and capturing *Ctesiphon, on 28 January 198. On this day, the centenary of Trajan's accession, he became *Parthicus Maximus*, raised Caracalla to the rank of Augustus, and made P. *Septimius Geta (2) Caesar. The new province of Mesopotamia was garrisoned by two of the new legions (I and III Parthicae), with an equestrian prefect as governor. Two attempts to capture *Hatra failed. After a lengthy stay in Syria, the imperial party entered Egypt before the end of 199, remaining for about twelve months: the province was reorganized, notably by the grant of a city council to *Alexandria (1). At the end of 200 Severus returned to Syria for another year; he was consul for the 3rd time at Antioch, with Caracalla as colleague, on 1 January 202.

Back at Rome in early summer 202 he celebrated *decennalia* with lavish victory games (declining a triumph, although the arch in the Forum had already been voted by the senate), followed by Caracalla's marriage to *Fulvia Plautilla, daughter of the seemingly all-powerful praetorian prefect C. *Fulvius Plautianus. In the autumn the imperial family sailed for Africa: their native Lepcis, *Carthage and *Utica received *ius Italicum, while Severus crushed the desert tribes beyond Tripolitania. From 203 to 208 he remained in Italy, holding *Secular Games in 204. Early in 205 Plautianus was killed and replaced by Papinian (*Aemilius Papinianus), who, with his fellow-jurists Ulpian and Paulus (*Domitius Ulpianus, *Iulius Paulus), made the Severan era a golden age of Roman jurisprudence. In 208 minor hostilities in Britain gave an excuse for another war, which Severus supposedly thought would benefit his quarrelling sons. The entire family, with Papinian, elements of the guard and other troops, crossed to Britain that year and took up residence at *Eburacum (York). Severus and Caracalla led two campaigns in northern Scotland, with the professed intention of conquering the whole of Britain; a new advance base was built at Carpow on the Tay, and victory was claimed in 210 with the title Britannicus for Severus and his sons, the younger becoming Augustus at last to ensure a joint succession. Long a victim of gout, Severus died at York on 4 February 211, leaving his sons the advice 'not to disagree, give money to the soldiers, and ignore the rest'. See BRITAIN, ROMAN.

Cass. Dio 72–6; Herodian 2–3; SHA Sev.; RIC 4. 1. A. M. McCann, The Portraits of Septimius Severus (1968); A. R. Birley, The African Emperor Septimius Severus[2] (1988).   A. R. Bi.

Septimius (PLRE 1. 122) **Vaballathus,** the son of *Septimius Odaenathus by *Zenobia, was a child when his father was killed but was made his successor, under the guardianship of his mother. He was given the titles of king of kings and corrector totius Orientis, and then, late in AD 270, of consul, dux Romanorum, and imperator. In 272, following *Aurelian's attack, he was proclaimed Augustus, as Lucius Iulius Aurelius Septimius Vaballathus Athenodorus, after which he disappears from view. He had a brother.

ILS 8924. See also under SEPTIMIUS ODAENATHUS and ZENOBIA. J. F. Dr.

Septizodium (or **Septizonium),** a free-standing ornamental façade and nymphaeum dedicated by *Septimius Severus in AD 203 (CIL 6. 31229), closing the vista of the *via Appia and screening the south-east corner of the *Palatine hill at Rome. It was designed like the scaenae frons of a theatre, with a series of large semi-circular niches, framed by three storeys of Corinthian columns and decorated with statuary. Although part of the building appears on the *Forma Urbis and the east end survived into the 16th cent., the exact reconstruction is debated. Earlier examples of septizodia occur in Rome (Suet. Titus 2, schol. cod. Berolin. fol. 337) and *Lambaesis (CIL 8. 2657). The adjective *ἑπτάζωνος (seven-statued) was applied to the seven planets which governed the days of the week, but it is not clear what if any astronomical or astrological significance was attached to these structures.

T. Dombart, Das Septizonium zu Rom (1922); G. P. Sartorio, Arch. Laz. (1987), 57 ff.; G. Carretoni, Forma Urbis Romae (1960), 66 f.; Nash, Pict. Dict. Rome 2. 302 ff.   I. A. R.; J. D.

Septuagint (in abbreviation, LXX), the collection of Jewish writings which became the Old Testament of the Greek-speaking Christians. They are mainly translated from the Hebrew (or *Aramaic) scriptures but include also some other pieces composed by Jews in the Hellenistic period, some in Greek and others translated from lost Semitic originals.

The name is derived from a story preserved in Greek, the Letter of Aristeas (probably of the mid-2nd cent. BC; see ARISTEAS, LETTER

OF), relating that Ptolemy II Philadelphus (see PTOLEMY (1)), the contemporary king of Egypt, asked for a translation of the Jewish Law (the Torah, i.e. the Pentateuch), and was sent from Jerusalem 72 learned Jews who on the island of Pharos near *Alexandria (1) made a Greek translation of it for the royal library. (The number 70 became a popular alternative to 72 probably because of the widespread use of this number elsewhere in Jewish tradition.) The story which at first had some verisimilitude was embellished by later writers with legendary elements and was extended to include beside the Pentateuch the other translated books. The LXX was authoritative for *Philon (4), who claimed that the translators had been divinely inspired.

The translation was evidently done by different hands at different times between the 3rd cent. BC and the beginning of the Christian era. It was intended primarily for those Jews who having migrated into Egypt and other Greek-speaking lands became more at home with the Greek language than with the Hebrew. The Septuagint early became the Bible of the Christian movement and is quoted in the New Testament and in later Christian writers as well as by the Jews Philon and Josephus, although even before the Christian era some Jews had begun to revise it in the light of the Hebrew text. Apart from Jews and Christians few ancient writers show any knowledge of it. Greek and Roman references to things Jewish are not derived directly from it. The citation of Genesis in the anonymous treatise On the Sublime 9. 9 (see 'LONGINUS') is a single exception that proves the rule. The influence of the LXX is probably first manifest in less literary circles, as in the Corpus Hermeticum (see HERMES TRISMEGISTUS) and in the magical papyri. Translations of the Old Testament into Latin and some other languages were chiefly based upon the Greek, so that *Jerome's decision to use the Hebrew in preparing the Latin Vulgate was revolutionary.

The Greek translations of the several books or parts of them vary in style and in degree of literalness. When not influenced by the original Semitic idiom, their Greek, as in the New Testament, and in non-literary documents of the period, represents the vernacular Hellenistic (koinē); see GREEK LANGUAGE.

Since the Hebrew from which the LXX was translated is older than the major Hebrew MSS known to us and than the standardized (Masoretic) text of the Old Testament, its apparent differences reflect some variation in the underlying Hebrew. The discovery of the *Dead Sea Scrolls shows that such differences existed before AD 70. These early MSS sometimes agree with the Septuagint against the Masoretic text, sometimes vice versa, and (in the Pentateuch) sometimes with the Samaritan Hebrew. Sometimes they contain a text different from all other known texts. Just what is the history of such variant texts is still under debate.

In like manner the Greek MSS show variation, suggesting that they were corrupted in copying or were deliberately edited or revised. This variation also is the object of continuing study. Again, limited finds near the Dead Sea or elsewhere of fragmentary early Greek MSS of parts of the Old Testament have provided fresh grounds for conjecture in this field, particularly from the evidence of Theodotion-type readings in the Greek Minor Prophets scroll from Nahal Hever. Each form of text, whether Hebrew or Greek, had its own associations and history to the extent that it may be misleading to refer to the LXX as if a single original text had once existed.

Perhaps just because the Christians used the LXX, later Jews, if they wished a Greek translation at all, made new ones or revived earlier ones. Three of these are attached to the names of Theodotion, Aquila, and Symmachus, and were copied in columns parallel to the Hebrew and the Septuagint in the famous *Hexapla* of *Origen (1) in the 3rd cent. of the Christian era. They are no longer extensively preserved. See JEWISH-GREEK LITERATURE.

LETTER TO ARISTEAS Text: Teubner (Wendland, 1900), Swete (Introduction, see below). Translation: Thackeray (1917), R. J. H. Shutt in J. H. Charlesworth, ed., *The Old Testament Pseudepigrapha* 2 (1985), 7–34.

COMMENTARY H. O. Meecham (1935), M. Hadas (1951), A. Pelletier (1962).

HANDY EDITIONS OF THE LXX TEXT WITH MINIMAL APPARATUS H. B. Swete, 3 vols. (1887–94) and later editions; A. Rahlfs, 2 vols. (*c*.1935). Text with critical apparatus: A. E. Brooks, N. McLean and others (1906–40) (incomplete); A. Rahlfs, J. Ziegler and others (1931–), in progress. E. Tov (ed.), *The Greek Minor Prophets Scroll from Nahal Hever* (1990).

INTRODUCTION H. B. Swete, rev. R. R. Ottley (1914); S. Jellicoe, *The Septuagint and Modern Study* (1968); M. K. H. Peters, *Anchor Bible Dictionary*, under 'Septuagint'. Handbooks: R. R. Ottley (1920); M. Harl, G. Dorival, and O. Munnich, *La Bible grecque des septante* (1988).

GRAMMAR R. Helbing (1907); H. St. J. Thackeray (1909).

CONCORDANCE E. Hatch and H. A. Redpath, 2 vols. and supplement (1897–1906). LEXICON J. F. Schleusner², 3 vols. (1822). INFLUENCE A. Deissmann, *[Neue] Jahrb.* (1903); H. St. J. Thackeray, *The Septuagint and Jewish Worship²* (1923); C. H. Dodd, *The Bible and the Greeks* (1934).

SUMMARIES OF RECENT RESEARCH H. M. Orlinsky, *Journal of American Oriental Society* 1941, 81 ff.; J. W. Wevers, *Theologische Rundschau* 1954, 85 ff., 171 ff.; 1968, 18 ff.; S. P. Brock, C. T. Fritsch, and S. Jellicoe (eds.), *A Classified Bibliography of the Septuagint* (1973); N. Fernández-Marcos, *La septuaginta en la investigación contemporanea* (1985); bibliographies in *Bulletin of the International Organization for Septuagint and Cognate Studies* (BIOSCS).

ON THE HEXAPLA F. Field, *Origenis Hexaplorum quae supersunt*, 2 vols. (1867–74). H. J. C.; M. D. G.

Sequani See VESONTIO.

Serapion (1) **(or Sarapion)** of *Alexandria (1) (fl. late-3rd cent. BC?), succeeded *Philinus of Cos as the leading Empiricist physician (see MEDICINE, § 5.3). He claimed that experience is the sole viable foundation of medicine. Whether he 'merely used' analogical reasoning (ὁμοίου μετάβασις) or, like some Empiricists, also regarded it as a constitutive part of medicine, was a controversial issue already in antiquity. His extant drug prescriptions may belong to his best attested work, *Therapeutics*.

Ed., comm.: K. Deichgräber, *Die griechische Empirikerschule* (1930, ²1965). H. v. S.

Serapion (2) (*RE* 4), of *Antioch (1) (fl. 1st cent. BC), wrote on geography (Cic. *ad Att.* 2. 6. 1) and astrology, and said that the sun was 18 times the size of the earth. The Serapion who commented on *Ptolemy (4)'s *Handy Tables* is much later.

Extracts from the astrological work: *CCAG* 8. 4. 225 ff. On the identification: A. Tihon, *Le 'Grand Commentaire' de Théon* 1 (1985), 294 ff. G. J. T.

Serapis See SARAPIS.

Serenus (*RE* 10), of Antinoeia in Egypt (4th cent. AD or later), wrote *Section of a Cylinder* and *Section of a Cone*, containing trivial propositions on conics. His commentary on the *Conics* of *Apollonius (2) is lost, but fragments of his mathematical *Lemmas* survive in Greek (ed. Heiberg 18–19) and Arabic.

περὶ κυλίνδρου τομῆς and περὶ κώνου τομῆς ed. Heiberg (Teubner, 1896), with Latin trans.; French trans. by P. Ver Eecke (1929). Heath, *Hist. of Greek Maths.* 2. 519 ff. For the Arabic sources: F. Sezgin, *Geschichte des arabischen Schrifttums* 5 (1974), 186. G. J. T.

Serenus (or Serenius), Quintus (or Quinctius), author of a medical textbook in verse, *Liber medicinalis*, which may be dated between the end of the 2nd and 4th cents. It depends in the main on *Cornelius Celsus, the *Medicina Plinii*, and *Pliny (1)'s *Natural History*. The author may have been the poet Serenus Sammonicus (son of the other *Serenus Sammonicus), who was a friend of *Gordian I (b. *c.* AD 159) and the teacher of Gordian II (b. *c*.192), and died before 235.

Ed. F. Vollmer, *CML* ii. 3; R. Pépin (1950); I. F. Shuts'tsa (1961). W. D. R.; V. N.

Serenus (*RE* 6) **Sammonicus,** prolific scholar who wrote an antiquarian work, *Res reconditae* (at least 5 books), addressed to *Septimius Severus and (probably) to *Caracalla, on whose orders he was murdered early in 212. He is possibly to be identified with the poet *Septimius Serenus.

E. Champlin, *Harv. Stud.* 1981, 189–212; Herzog–Schmidt, § 484. R. A. K.

Seres, the name 'silk-people', is little more than a conventional label for the most remote inhabitants of Asia, source of the finest silk (as opposed to the various other insect-derived textiles known in various parts of the Old World: see SILK) and of celebrated iron and hides. The details are idealized and fantastic, and have very little to do with the reality of China; and the origin of silk was in any case attributed, not untypically, to various peoples along the routes by which it reached the west, including probably the inhabitants of the Tibetan plateau and the central Asian oases: silk was, in any case, produced in *India too by the Hellenistic period. While the nebulous and adjustable idea of the Seres had a long life in the high geographical / literary tradition, actual commercial contacts were providing a different picture, reflected for us first in the *Periplus Maris Erythraei* (1st cent. AD; see PERIPLOI), naming 'Thin' for the first time and then in *Ptolemy (4) (6. 16; 7. 3; 1. 11), whose knowledge of Sinae was based on the journey of one Alexander (? in the late 1st cent. AD): he also used the reports provided to an entrepreneur of *Damascus called 'Maes, also known as Titianus' of the overland routes. The availability of silk on the routes of Asia seems to have been derived not from a production for export as such, but from its value as a symbol of status and culture among the peoples of the Chinese periphery and especially the Hsiung-nu empire (from the 3rd cent. BC), which received enormous quantities in the form of gifts and tribute. It is tempting to attribute the beginnings of ancient consciousness of Han China to the consolidation of contacts westwards into central Asia which followed diplomatic and military initiatives of the Chinese state against the Hsiung-nu. After AD 73 these efforts were largely successful, and it is then that Chinese sources document Kan Ying's embassy to the Romans to at least the head of the *Persian Gulf. Roman missions in the other direction are attested in 166 and 284. Much of the western trade went south from the central Asian states through the powerful Kushan kingdom to the ports of NW India and thence by sea; the collapse of the Kushan state at the hands of the White Huns in the 4th cent. must have impeded this relationship, while war between Rome and *Sasanid Persia blocked the northern branch of the Silk Route. Demand had become a major political issue by the time of *Justinian (Procopius 1. 20. 9; 6. 25. 12–22), but there is no reason to exaggerate the price or rarity of silk in the earlier period. Silk-moth eggs reached *Constantinople clandestinely in *c*.550, but it is noteworthy that earlier Chinese accounts of Ta-ts'in (the

Roman empire) list silk-production as one of its resources. Highly finished luxury items like *glass and rare commodities like coral had their place in the eastbound trade, but at no point is it necessary to model Asian exchange-networks as parts of a mercantile economy. Contacts were opportunistic, and political and social factors far outweighed economic ones in determining the modalities of exchange.

X. Liu, *Ancient India and Ancient China: Trade and Religious Exchanges A.D. 1–600* (1988); A. Dihle, *Antike und Orient: Gesammelte Aufsätze*, ed. V. Pöschl and H. Petersmann (1984), 201–15; J.-M. Poinsotte, *MÉFRA* 91 (1979), 431–79; M. G. Raschke, *ANRW* 2. 9. 2 (1978), 604–1361.

N. P.

'Sergius', name under which are transmitted the *Explanationes in Donatum* (*GL* 4. 486–565, cf. *Anecdota Helvetica* 143–58, and U. Schindel, *Die lateinischen Figurenlehren* [1975]) and several other minor treatises (Keil, *Gramm. Lat.* 4. 475–85, 6. 240–42, 7. 537–39). The name 'Sergius' is often confused in manuscripts with '*Servius*'.

Cf. Herzog–Schmidt, § 612.

R. A. K.

Sergius (*RE* 23) **Catilina, Lucius,** of *patrician, but not recently distinguished, family, served with *Pompey and *Cicero under Cn. *Pompeius Strabo in the *Social War (3). He next appears as a lieutenant of *Sulla both in the *bellum Sullanum* after Sulla's invasion of Italy and in the *proscriptions when, incited by Q. *Lutatius Catulus (2), he killed his brother-in-law M. *Marius Gratidianus. There is no further record of him until his praetorship (68 BC), after which he governed Africa for two years. Prosecuted *repetundarum* on his return, he was prevented from standing for the consulship for 65 and 64, but was finally acquitted with the help of his prosecutor P. *Clodius Pulcher. In 66/5 he was said to be involved in a plot with P. *Autronius and P. *Cornelius Sulla; the details are obscured by gossip and propaganda, and his involvement is doubtful. Frustrated ambition now became his driving force. In the elections for 63 he made a compact with C. *Antonius 'Hybrida' and gained the support of *Caesar and M. *Licinius Crassus, but was defeated by Cicero. He then began to champion the cause of the poor and dispossessed: dissolute aristocrats, bankrupt Sullan veterans, and those whom they had driven from their lands. Again defeated for 62, he organized a widespread conspiracy with ramifications throughout Italy. Cicero, kept informed by his spies, could not take decisive action owing to lack of sufficient support, for Catiline—an old Sullan, a patrician, and now a demagogue—was both popular and well connected. In November Cicero succeeded in frightening Catiline into leaving Rome to join a force of destitute veterans in Etruria. Soon afterwards, some Allobrogan envoys, carelessly given letters by conspirators in Rome (see CORNELIUS LENTULUS SURA, P.), provided Cicero with the written evidence he needed (see FABIUS SANGA, Q.). The leaders of the conspiracy in Rome were arrested and, after a long debate and a vote in the senate, executed. The consul Antonius marched out against Catiline, who was caught between two armies and was defeated and killed by M. *Petreius near Pistoria (early January 62). Cicero was hailed as saviour of Rome, but was open to the charge of having executed citizens without trial.

The chief sources are Cicero, *Cat.*, and Sallust, *BC*. Modern discussions are numerous. C. John, *Die Entstehungsgeschichte der catilinarischen Verschwörung* (1876) is a classic. See also E. G. Hardy, *The Catilinarian Conspiracy* (1924); Z. Yavetz, *Historia* 1963, 485 ff.; Gruen, *LGRR*, esp. 416 ff.; T. P. Wiseman, *CAH* 9² (1994), ch. 9; and biographies of Cicero. On Sallust, *BC* see R. Syme, *Sallust* (1964), 60 ff., and P. McGushin, *C.*

Sallustius Crispus, Bellum Catilinae: A Commentary (1977). See also N. Criniti, *Bibliografia catilinaria* (1971), a full list of titles without comments.

E. B.

sermo has a variety of meanings in Latin. They include (1) conversation and the style of conversation (contrasted with *contentio*, in effect 'oratory', by Cic. *Off.* 1. 132); (2) verse in a conversational manner (esp. of Horace's *Satires* and *Epistles*: see *Epist.* 1. 4. 1); (3) language or dialect (thus Cic. *De Or.* 3. 42, *in Latino sermone*, 'in the Latin tongue'); and, technically, a short introduction often prefacing the *Minor Declamations* attributed to *Quintilian.

J. W. D.; M. W.

Serranus, an epic poet who, like *Saleius Bassus (with whom he is linked by Quint. 10. 1. 89–90 and Juv. 7. 80), died prematurely.

E. C.

Sertorius (*RE* 3), **Quintus** (c.126–73 BC), an *eques* (see EQUITES) from Sabine Nursia (Norcia), distinguished himself in the Cimbrian Wars under Q. *Servilius Caepio (1) and C. *Marius (1), and under T. *Didius in Spain. Quaestor in 91, then a senior officer in the *Social War (3), he was thwarted by *Sulla in his candidacy for a tribunate (89 or 88) and joined *Cinna. He shared responsibility for the capture of Rome (87) and subsequent executions, but ended the indiscriminate terror of Marius' slave-bands. He became praetor (probably) in 85; kept in Italy by Sulla's impending return, he criticized, unsuccessfully, the Cinno-Marian leaders for their conduct of the civil war and finally took command of Spain (winter 83/2). Proscribed and driven out (81), he went to *Mauretania as a *condottiere*. Invited by the Lusitanians and anti-Sullan Roman exiles, he returned to Spain (80) and soon gained widespread support among the natives, owing to his bravery, justice, and skill in exploiting their religious beliefs. (His white doe was regarded as a sign of divine inspiration.) Through crafty employment of guerrilla methods (and, for naval support, 'Cilician' pirates) he was successful against many Roman commanders, notably Q. *Caecilius Metellus Pius in Farther Spain, and by 77 he held most of Roman Spain. He tried to Romanize Hispanian leaders and acted throughout as a Roman proconsul, relying heavily on Roman and Italian exiles in the province; creating a 'counter-senate' from among them, he made Spain the focal point of resistance against the post-Sullan regime in Rome. When approached by *Mithradates VI he concluded an alliance, yet refused to surrender Asia to him (76/5). The arrival of M. *Perperna Veiento with substantial remnants of the army of M. *Aemilius Lepidus (2) enabled him to take the offensive against *Pompey—now commanding in Further Spain—whom he defeated at Lauro (77). But costly failures, of his own and his lieutenants, in several pitched battles (76) soon forced him to revert to guerrilla warfare, with waning success after 75. Losing the confidence of his Roman and Hispanian followers alike and embittered by failure, he became increasingly despotic and was assassinated by Perperna.

A. Schulten, *Sertorius* (1926); E. Gabba, *Athenaeum* 1954, 293 = *Esercito e società* (1973), 193; P. O. Spann, *Quintus Sertorius and the Legacy of Sulla* (1987); on the chief source, C. F. Konrad, *Plutarch's Sertorius: A Historical Commentary* (1994).

C. F. K.

Servasius, Sulpicius Lupercus, Junior (his name is uncertain: 'Serbastus', MS Leiden Voss. Lat. F 111; 'Sebastus', Schryver, Baehrens; 'Servastus', Wernsdorf; 'Servasius', Riese; ?'Sebastius', Smolak), author of a poem in three Sapphic stanzas on the effects of time, and of another, in 42 elegiac lines, on greed. Date unknown (4th cent. AD or later?).

Servilia

TEXTS *Anth. Lat.* 648–9 Riese; with trans., Duff, *Minor Lat. Poets*.

J. H. D. S.

Servilia (*RE* 'Servilius' 101), daughter of Q. *Servilius Caepio (2) and Livia, daughter of M. *Livius Drusus (1), who was the mother of M. *Porcius Cato (2). Born *c*.100 BC, she married first M. *Iunius Brutus (1), to whom she bore M. *Iunius Brutus (2), then D. *Iunius Silanus (1); her daughters by Silanus married, respectively, P. *Servilius Isauricus, M. *Aemilius Lepidus (3), and C. *Cassius Longinus (1), the tyrannicide. *Caesar was her lover for many years and remained on good terms with her after: it was rumoured (implausibly) that Brutus, for whom he showed particular favour, was his son, and she profited in his sale of the Pompeians' confiscated estates (Cic. *Att.* 14. 21. 3). She may have been discreetly involved in high politics before the Civil War, and after Caesar's death Cicero's letters show her playing a leading part in the tyrannicides' deliberations, always protecting her son's interests. (She prided herself on descent from C. *Servilius Ahala.) After her son's death at *Philippi she fell from power (cf. Nep. *Att.* 11. 4) and we hear no more about her. But for a short time, at least, she was the most powerful woman of her generation.

Syme, *RR* (see index); Bauman, *WPAR* 73 ff.   T. J. C.; E. B.

Servilius (*RE* 32) **Ahala, Gaius,** was celebrated in Roman tradition as a hero who freed his country from the threat of tyranny by killing Sp. *Maelius (439 BC) with a dagger he had hidden under his arm—whence the surname Ahala (= 'armpit'). The story was embellished in later times, and there was much dispute, e.g. about whether Servilius had acted as a private citizen or as Master of the Horse (see MAGISTER EQUITUM) to the dictator *Cincinnatus. Many details of the story are doubtful, but the episode was recorded in early sources including *Cincius Alimentus, L. *Ennius and L. *Calpurnius Piso Frugi, and may be based on fact.

Mommsen, *Röm. Forsch.* 2. 199 ff.; A. W. Lintott, *Historia* 1970, 13–18; T. J. Cornell, in K. Raaflaub (ed.), *Social Struggles in Archaic Rome* (1986), 59 f.   T. J. Co.

Servilius (*RE* 49) **Caepio (1), Quintus,** served under M'. *Aquillius (1) in Asia. As praetor 109 BC he went to Hispania Ulterior and returned to triumph (107). Made consul 106, partly in reaction against C. *Marius' (1) failure to finish the war against *Jugurtha, he passed a law, strongly supported by L. *Licinius Crassus, giving senators a share on criminal juries, thus abolishing the monopoly by *equites introduced by C. *Sempronius Gracchus (see QUAESTIONES). Sent to fight against the Tectosages in southern France, he took *Tolosa and captured a large treasure identified with that seized by the Gauls at Delphi in 279 and thus under a curse. The gold disappeared on the road to *Massalia, and Caepio was suspected of having appropriated it. As proconsul 105 he refused to co-operate with the consul Cn. Mallius Maximus, sent against the *Cimbri and their allies. This led to the disaster of *Arausio and indirectly to Marius' series of consulships. Caepio had his *imperium* abrogated, was expelled from the senate, and finally prosecuted by C. *Norbanus (1) for stealing the Tolosa treasure. He went into exile at *Smyrna and died there.

See under the following.   E. B.

Servilius (*RE* 50) **Caepio (2), Quintus,** relative of (1), brother-in-law and friend of M. *Livius Drusus (2). As quaestor 103 BC (or possibly 100: see APPULEIUS SATURNINUS, L.), he opposed Saturninus' grain law and used force in trying to prevent its

passage. After it passed, he and a colleague L. Calpurnius Piso issued coins 'For the purchase of wheat by decree of the senate' (*RRC* 330), implying senate sponsorship of the law. Probably *c*.95 he was accused of *maiestas for his actions as quaestor, defended (half-heartedly) by L. *Licinius Crassus and acquitted. Quarrelling with Drusus for private reasons, he drew closer to the enemies of the senate. In 92 he engaged in a duel of unsuccessful prosecutions with M. *Aemilius Scaurus (1) and in 91 was a leading opponent of Drusus, who threatened to throw him from the *Tarpeian Rock. At some time in the late 90s he was praetor. Early in 90 he prosecuted Scaurus under the *lex Varia* (see LEX (2) and VARIUS SEVERUS 'HYBRIDA', Q.), but had to leave for service as a *legatus* in the *Social War (3). He fought against the *Marsi and was killed by Q. *Poppaedius Silo in an ambush.

J. D. Morgan, forthcoming.   E. B.

Servilius Casca (*RE* 52 and 53). Two brothers so named joined the conspiracy against *Caesar in 44 BC. One, Publius Longus, took a leading part and was the first to strike on the Ides (15th) of March. In 43 he was tribune, but when *Octavian marched on Rome he fled and joined *Brutus. He struck coins for him, one issue with Brutus' portrait (*RRC* 502). The brothers killed themselves after Philippi (*Anth. Lat.* 457).

A third Casca, with the *praenomen* Gaius, apparently from a *gens* other than the Servilia, was tribune in 44; alarmed at the fate of C. *Helvius Cinna, he put out a statement asserting that he had nothing but the *cognomen* Casca in common with the conspirators.   T. J. C.; E. B.

Servilius (*RE* 67) **Isauricus, Publius,** son of P. *Servilius Vatia Isauricus, as praetor 54 BC supported M. *Porcius Cato (2), but became a Caesarian and *Caesar's colleague as consul 48. After suppressing the disturbances of M. *Caelius Rufus he governed Asia, and from there corresponded with Cicero in 46. After Caesar's murder Cicero affected to regard him as an ally, but knew him for a man of straw or worse (cf. *ad Brut.* 2. 2. 3 if genuine) and in 43 Servilius betrothed his daughter to Octavian (see AUGUSTUS) and became reconciled to *M. Antonius (2) (Mark Antony). Octavian jilted Servilia, but compensated her father with the consulate of 41, in which he showed his usual caution during the Perusine War (see PERUSIA).

Syme, *RR* (see index).   G. E. F. C.; E. B.

Servilius (*RE* 65) **Glaucia, Gaius,** probably of remote noble descent (*PBSR* 52 1984, 62 f.), demagogue and clever and witty orator (Cic. *Brut.* 224), quaestor before 107 BC. In 102 Q. *Caecilius Metellus Numidicus, as censor, unsuccessfully tried to expel him from the senate. As tribune 101 and praetor 100 he co-operated with L. *Appuleius Saturninus and in one of those years passed a *repetundae law restoring the court to the *equites and checking procedural delays. He hoped to become consul 99, with Saturninus again tribune, but his candidature was disallowed and he died with Saturninus, probably trying to reinstate it.

J. P. V. D. Balsdon, *PBSR* 14 1938, 98 ff.; E. Badian, *Chiron* 1984, 106 ff.   E. B.

Servilius (*RE* 69; and suppl. 6) **Nonianus, Marcus** (born *c*.2 BC, son of the consul of AD 3, consul 35, proconsul of Africa *c*.47, died 59), famous for his *recitationes*, the applause on one occasion attracting *Claudius, later emperor, into the audience (Plin. *Ep.* 1. 13. 3). His history (from AD 14?) was probably a source of *Tacitus (1)'s *Annals*; Tacitus gives a favourable obituary. For his style see Quint. *Inst.* 10. 1. 102; Tac. *Dial.* 23. 4; Peter, *HR Rel.* 2. 98, cxxviii.

R. Syme, *Hermes* 1964, 408 ff. (= *Ten Studies in Tacitus* (1970), 91 ff.); *RP*, indexes.　　　　　　　　　　　　　　　　　　　　B. M. L.

Servilius (*RE* 80) **Rullus, Publius,** as tribune (63 BC) introduced a major agrarian bill, establishing a commission with extravagant powers to redistribute *ager publicus* in Rome and the provinces. It was probably inspired by *Crassus and was supported by *Caesar. Perhaps both the commission and the land were meant as a bargaining counter to hold against *Pompey, whose return with a large army was expected. Cicero, presenting himself as a *popularis* (see OPTIMATES) and as defending Pompey's interests, secured the withdrawal of the bill by his (largely extant) speeches *De lege agraria*.

Cic. *De leg. agr.* Gruen, *LGRR* (see index); G. V. Sumner, *TAPA* 1966, 569 ff. (a different interpretation). For his family see E. Badian, *PBSR* 1984, 63–5.　　　　　　　　　　　　　　　　　　　　　　　　E. B.

Servilius (*RE* 93) **Vatia Isauricus, Publius,** grandson of Q. *Caecilius Metellus Macedonicus, praetor and propraetor (perhaps in Sardinia), he was given a *triumph in 88 BC by *Sulla and intended for the consulate of 87, but was defeated by L. *Cornelius Cinna (1) owing to Sulla's unpopularity. Serving with distinction in the *bellum Sullanum* (83–81), he became consul (79) and, as proconsul in Cilicia, fought successfully against pirates (see PIRACY) and mountain tribes, capturing Isaura Vetus (where a votive inscription has been found) and first establishing a solid territorial base for the province. He assumed the name 'Isauricus' as a reward. Triumphing again (74), he became an influential politician, reaching the censorship in 55 (with M. *Valerius Messalla 'Niger'—they regulated the Tiber). He failed to become pontifex maximus in 63 (see CAESAR). During the 60s and 50s he generally shared Cicero's views. He died in 44, aged 90.

For his campaigns see H. A. Ormerod, *JRS* 1922, 35 ff.; Magie, *Rom. Rule Asia Min.* 1. 287 ff. (with notes in vol. 2).; E. Badian, *PBSR* 1984, 54 f., 59 ff. (descent); A. S. Hall, *VI. Internat. Kongress für griech. u. lat. Epigraphik* (1973), 568 ff. (the Isaura inscription—often misrepresented as an *evocatio*).　　　　　　　　　　　　　　　　　　E. B.

servitudes Until late classical Roman law, the term *servitutes* (servitudes) was applied to restrictions on the ownership of land in favour of neighbouring land (e.g. a right of way from one plot over another to the highway, or a right that nothing be built on one plot so as to obstruct the light to a building on the other). The term expresses the idea that one plot serves the other. An owner would usually pay a price or give some other consideration to acquire such a right over the neighbouring land. In this way various amenities were arranged among neighbouring properties. Unlike a contractual right which could bind and entitle only the parties to the contract, once established servitudes bound and entitled whoever were the owners for the time being of the land in question. A distinction was made between rustic servitudes and urban servitudes according as they served a predominantly agricultural purpose or not (e.g. a right of way, as opposed to a right of light), though urban servitudes could be attached to land in the country. Rustic servitudes developed earlier and were *res mancipi* (see MANCIPATIO). In Classical law all servitudes could be created by a fictitious lawsuit (*in iure cessio*) and rustic servitudes by *mancipatio*. An owner asserted or denied a right to a servitude by actions to establish their existence (*actio*

confessoria) or non-existence (*actio negatoria*). It is questionable if these names are classical.

Justinian, apparently following the late classical jurist *Aelius Marcianus, included under the term *servitutes* another class of restrictions on ownership. See JUSTINIAN'S CODIFICATION. These comprise usufruct or the right to use and take the fruits of another's property (*ususfructus*); the right simply to use another's property (*usus*); and the right to use another's house (*habitatio*) or slaves (*operae servorum*), which were modifications of the right of use. These personal servitudes (*servitutes personarum*) are like servitudes over land in that they bind whoever is the owner of a thing for the time being, but are unlike them in that they entitle a particular person, irrespective of his ownership of anything. They are personal to him and inalienable, and can be created only for his life or some shorter period. Personal servitudes effect (to some extent) a division in time of a single ownership. Thus, usufruct was a method by which a Roman could give a life interest to another (e.g. bequeathing a house to a child, subject to a life-time usufruct for the testator's widow). Usufructs were indeed usually created by legacy, but other methods such as *in iure cessio* were available in classical law. The usufructuary had an action (*vindicatio*; see OWNERSHIP) to assert his usufruct over any property if the owner contested it, while an owner who denied that his property was subject to a usufruct could bring an action asserting that it was free from any burden.

R. Elvers, *Die römische Servitutenlehre* (1856); G. Grosso, *Le servitù prediali nel diritto romano* (1969); A. Watson, *The Law of Property in the Later Roman Republic* (1968); A. Rodger, *Owners and Neighbours in Roman Law* (1972); L. Capogrossi Colognesi, *La struttura della proprietà e la formazione dei 'iura praediorum' nell'età repubblicana* 2 (1976); G. Grosso, *Usufrutto e figure affine nel diritto romano*² (1958); M. Bretone, *La nozione romana di usufrutto* (1962, 1967).　　　　　　　　B. N.; A. F. R.

Servius (Roman king). See TULLIUS, SERVIUS.

Servius (*PLRE* 1. 827) (4th cent. AD), grammarian and commentator (called Marius or Maurus Servius Honoratus in manuscripts from the 9th cent. onwards), author of a celebrated commentary on *Virgil, based on an earlier work (now lost) of Aelius *Donatus (1). Servius is one of the participants in *Macrobius' dialogue the *Saturnalia* (dramatic date 383–4: cf. P. V. Davies, *Macrobius, The Saturnalia* (1969), 9), where he is depicted as a young man. The Virgil commentary exists in two forms: the longer, known as *Servius Auctus, Servius Danielis, DServius,* or *DS,* was first published in 1600 by Pierre Daniel, and is thought to be a 7th–8th cent. AD expansion of the shorter form on the basis of earlier material from Donatus' commentary not used by Servius himself. Both versions, but especially *DServius,* contain important information about Latinity, Roman customs and institutions (especially in relation to religion), and intertextuality with works now lost to us, though neither are completely reliable in matters such as statements of usage in earlier writers. But Servius' own poetics merit investigation and appreciation (cf. J. E. G. Zetzel, *CPhil.* 1984, 139–42, and *Latin Textual Criticism* (below), 81–147, and esp. C. Lazzarini, *MD* 1984, 117–44, and *Stud. Ital.* 1989, 56–109, 241–260). As well as the commentary, he wrote an *Explanatio in artem Donati, De finalibus, De centum metris,* and *De metris Horatii:* the *Glossae Servii grammatici* are an apocryphal compilation.

MSS P. K. Marshall in *Texts and Transmission,* 385–8.

EDITIONS Virgil comm.: G. Thilo and H. Hagen (1881–1902); 'Harvard Servius' (vol. 2, *Aen.* 1–2 (1946), vol. 3, *Aen.* 3–5 (1965); *Explanatio* etc.: Keil, *Gramm. Lat.* 4. 405–72; *Glossae* etc.: G. Goetz, *Corp. Gloss. Lat.* 2. 507–33.

LIFE P. Wessner, *RE* 2 A, 1834–48, 'Servius' 8; H. Georgii, *Philologus* 1912, 518–28.

INDEX TO COMMENTARY J. F. Mountford and J. T. Schultz (1930).

STUDIES E. Thomas, *Essai sur Servius et son commentaire sur Virgile* (1880); A. F. Stocker, *Vergilius* 1963, 9–15; E. Fraenkel, *Kl. Beitr.* (1964), 339 ff., G. P. Goold, *Harv. Stud.* 1970, 101–18; J. E. G. Zetzel, *Latin Textual Criticism in Antiquity* (1981), 81–147; L. Holz, *Donat et la tradition de l'enseignement grammatical* (1981), 223–30 and index (on the *Explanatio* and other minor works); R. A. Kaster, *Guardians of Language* (1989), 169–97.
J. F. M.; P. G. F., D. P. F.

Sesostris (Hdt. 2. 102–10) was a legendary Egyptian king to whom were ascribed great conquests in Africa and Asia. Though based on several rulers of the Twelfth Dynasty called Senwosret, he ultimately became an embodiment of the ideal of Egyptian kingship much used in nationalist propaganda. The lengthy discussions of *Herodotus (1) and *Diodorus (3) are evidence of two stages in the development of that tradition but should not be taken seriously as history.

C. Froidefond, *Le Mirage égyptien* (1971), index; K. Lange, *Sesostris* (1954); A. B. Lloyd, *Herodotus Book II*, 3 (1988), 16 ff.
A. B. L.

Sestius (*RE* 6), **Publius,** one of very few senators from the humble Collina *tribus,* served under C. *Antonius Hybrida as quaestor 63 BC against *Catiline and as proquaestor 62 in Macedonia. As tribune designate and tribune (58–57) he worked hard for Cicero's restoration from exile and, with T. *Annius Milo, opposed P. *Clodius Pulcher, suffering injuries in street fighting. Prosecuted for *vis (56), he was defended by M. *Licinius Crassus, Q. *Hortensius Hortalus, and Cicero and acquitted. (Cicero's speech, as published, is an *optimate manifesto.) Praetor by 54, he was prosecuted for *ambitus and again defended by Cicero and acquitted. Appointed by the Senate to Cilicia in 49, he joined *Caesar after *Pharsalus and continued to serve under him. His second wife was a daughter or granddaughter of L. *Cornelius Scipio Asiagenus, the exiled enemy of *Sulla. His son (see following article) became consul suffect 23. He himself was not prominent after Caesar's death, and is attested as a senator until 35. Cicero, who remained in touch with him down to his own death, remained loyal to him and recognized Sestius' loyalty, but thought his temperament morose (*QFr.* 2. 4. 1) and his style deplorable (*Att.* 7. 17. 2), a judgement confirmed by Catullus (44).

Cic. *Pro Sestio* is the main source on his early life. For his activity in the senate during the Triumvirate, see J. M. Reynolds, *Aphrodisias and Rome* (1982), 69 ff.
E. B.

Sestius (*RE* 3) **Quirinalis Albinianus, Lucius,** son of the preceding, born *c.*73 BC, joined the *tyrannicides in 44 and coined as *pro quaestore* for M. *Iunius Brutus (2) (*RRC* 502). Proscribed, then pardoned, he was chosen by *Augustus to be consul *suffect in 23, when Augustus gave up his consulship held since 31, to symbolize the return of the republic. He governed Further Spain after this and erected the *arae Sestianae* (Plin. *HN* 4. 111) to mark the completion of its conquest in 19. Horace published *Odes* 1–3 in his consulship and dedicated 1. 4 to him. Augustus did not disapprove of his continuing to display the portrait of Brutus (App. *BCiv.* 4. 51. 223: 'Publius').

Syme, *RR* 334 f., *RP* 2. 735 f.; R. G. M. Nisbet and M. Hubbard, *A Commentary on Horace Odes Book I* (1970), p. xxxvi.
E. B.

Sestus, a city of the Thracian *Chersonesus (1), located on an elevated plateau overlooking a bay favoured by wind and current. Sestus commanded the main crossing of the *Hellespont (Dardanelles), lying just opposite *Abydos on the Asian side. Originally a Thracian settlement (see THRACE), its Greek population were colonists from *Lesbos (see COLONIZATION, GREEK), but its importance began with the advent of Athenian interest in the time of the elder Miltiades' settlements (see MILTIADES) in the Chersonesus. It was at Sestus that *Xerxes first set foot in Europe, crossing the strait on a bridge of boats. See PERSIAN WARS. The city was among the first freed from Persian rule by the Athenian fleet (479–478 BC). Well-situated by reason of its excellent harbour to control ship traffic through the narrows of the Hellespont, Sestus was one of Athens' most important naval stations and tributary states in the 5th cent *Delian League. After a brief occupation by Sparta at the end of the *Peloponnesian War, the city returned to Athenian rule. Sestus experienced several changes of overlords during the Hellenistic era, and eventually became a free city under Roman rule. Although it lost its importance as the principal crossing-point between Europe and Asia, it retained its value as a port, and was refortified by the emperor *Justinian. The precise location of the city has not been determined, as the Chersonesus has not been explored much archaeologically.

S. Casson, *Macedonia, Thrace and Illyria* (1926); B. Isaac, *The Greek Settlements in Thrace until the Macedonian Conquest* (1986).
E. N. B.

Set (called Typhon by the Greeks) was a god of Upper Egypt. He appears in the myth of *Osiris as the wicked brother who murders the great god of the underworld and wounds his son *Horus. The role of Set in this myth was well known to the Greeks, hence he is the wicked Typhon in *Plutarch's essay concerning *Isis and Osiris (13 ff.). The Greek *Typhon was a wicked son of *Gaea and *Tartarus who was overcome by *Zeus, just as Horus finally overcame Set.

G. Roeder, art. 'Set' in Roscher's *Lexikon*; J. G. Griffiths, *The Conflict of Horus and Seth* (1960).
T. A. B.

Settefinestre, a Roman *villa near *Cosa in Tuscany. Built in the later 1st cent. BC, it may exemplify the rural residence and working farm of a senatorial aristocrat (possibly the family of the Sestii), laid out on lines recommended by Varro and Columella. Fronted by a miniature 'town wall' with turrets, there was elegant accommodation, as well as three wine presses, one oil press, a granary, a walled orchard, quarters for slaves and three gardens. A piggery, new baths, and extended slave quarters were added in the early 2nd cent. AD, but the villa was abandoned in the Antonine period. See AGRICULTURE, ROMAN.

A. Carandini (ed.), *Settefinestre: Una villa schiavistica nell'Etruria romana* (1985); N. Purcell, *JRS* 1988, 194 ff.
T. W. P.

settlement patterns See ARCHAEOLOGY, CLASSICAL; SYNOECISM; and entries listed under MIGRATION.

Seven against Thebes, myth, and play by *Aeschylus. *Oedipus' curse upon his sons *Eteocles ('True Glory') and Polynices ('Much Strife') results in their dispute over the throne of Thebes and in Polynices calling upon his father-in-law *Adrastus (1), King of *Argos (2), and five other heroes (in the epic, *Tydeus, Capaneus, *Parthenopaeus, Mecisteus, and the seer *Amphiaraus). These seven heroes fight at, and match, the mythical seven gates of *Thebes (1) (details in e.g. Apollod. *Bibl.* 3. 6). In particular, Zeus strikes Capaneus with a lightning-bolt, the two brothers slaughter each other, the seer Amphiaraus (who joins the expedition through the treachery of his wife Eriphyle) is swallowed up by the earth, and Tydeus is denied immortality when Athene finds him devouring the brains of *Melanippus.

This failed expedition was recounted in three epic *Thebaids* (1) around 700 / 600 BC, in *c.*7,000 lines, (2) by *Antimachus, so long-winded that it took 24 books to reach Thebes, (3) by *Statius. See EPIC CYCLE. *Corinna too wrote a lyric *Seven against Thebes* (Page, *PMG* 659). Capaneus, Tydeus, Amphiaraus and Adrastus provided material for various lesser tragedians. In the case of *Sophocles (1) we only know of an *Amphiaraus*. *Euripides' *Phoenician Women* is set in Thebes during the conflict, *Hypsipyle* drew on an episode at Nemea as the Argive army advanced towards Thebes and the *Suppliant Women* presents Adrastus and the mothers of the fallen, unburied, Argive heroes appealing to *Theseus and Athenian civilized values.

Aeschylus' *Seven against Thebes* (Latin title: *Septem contra Thebas*) was the last play of his Theban trilogy (467 BC), following the *Laius* and *Oedipus*. It focuses on Eteocles' acceptance of the task of fighting his own brother and the impact of their deaths on the family—a catastrophic end to the House of Laius. It was an esteemed play, whose text appears to have been rehandled, particularly to allow a final view of *Antigone in the light of Sophocles' *Antigone*. Its rich thematic interest has been explored in recent studies. See also EPIGONI.

W. Burkert, *Die orientalisierende Epoche* (1984), ch. 3. 4; G. O. Hutchinson, *Aeschylus, Septem contra Thebas* (1985); W. G. Thalman, *Dramatic Art in Aeschylus's Seven Against Thebes* (1978); F. I. Zeitlin, *Under the Sign of the Shield: Semiotics and Aeschylus' Seven against Thebes* (1982).
K. D.

Seven hills of Rome See CAPITOL; PALATINE; AVENTINE; QUIRINAL; VIMINAL; ESQUILINE; CAELIUS MONS. Also ROME (TOPOGRAPHY).

Seven Liberal Arts See EDUCATION, GREEK, § (4); MARTIANUS MINNEUS FELIX CAPELLA.

Seven Sages *Sophia*, which may cover the domains of wisdom, cleverness, and poetic skill, had always been admired in Greek society, as the character of *Odysseus demonstrates; and with the rise of the agonistic spirit ($\zeta\tilde{\eta}\lambda o\varsigma$), fostered by the panhellenic games (see AGŌNES; PANHELLENISM) and displayed in such stories as that of Agariste's suitors (Hdt. 6. 126–30; see CLEISTHENES 1 and 2), there developed the idea that in wisdom too the Greek *poleis* should put up competing rivals. The original *sophoi* belong to the early decades of the 6th cent., and the usual list comprises four members from the eastern cities (*Thales of Miletus, Bias of Priene, Cleobulus from Lindus on Rhodes, and *Pittacus of Mytilene) and three from the homeland (*Solon from Athens, *Chilon from Sparta, and *Periander the Corinthian tyrant). The way *Simonides vigorously sets out to refute the maxims of both Pittacus (fr. 542) and Cleobulus (fr. 581)—and claim a place for himself?—suggests that the *canon was forming, if not formed, by the beginning of the 5th cent.; though the first explicit attestation of a Group of Seven is in *Plato (1) (*Prot.* 343a). Their thoughtful wisdom was often expressed in pithy or 'Delphic' mottoes; but they were men involved with the problems of contemporary statecraft, not hermits. Herodotus gives many examples of their political and practical acuity, e.g. bk. 1, ch. 27 (Bias, or Pittacus), 29 (Solon), 59 (Chilon), 74 f. (Thales), 170 (Thales, Bias).

Later generations felt it inappropriate that a tyrant with a brutal reputation like Periander should be included, and substitutes like 'Myson of Chēn' (Plato, *Prot.* 343a—famous for his very obscurity), or *Anacharsis, were proposed. Traditions

about other 6th-cent. figures like *Heraclitus, Cyrus (1), or the pharaoh *Amasis (Hdt. 2. 172 ff.) show that their images, too, were brought into conformity with the developing standard profile.

Elaborations of the theme include the 'Banquet of the Seven Sages' at which all were supposedly present (see Plutarch's fine dialogue, depending on a tradition probably going back to the 5th cent.) and the legend of the gold cup bequeathed by the dying Arcadian Bathycles 'to The Wisest', which all modestly declined in turn (Callim. *Ia*. 1).

B. Snell, *Leben und Meinungen der Sieben Weisen*[4] (1971); A. R. Burn, *The Lyric Age of Greece* (1960), 207–9; D. Fehling, *Die Sieben Weisen und die frühgr. Chronologie* (1985).
A. H. G.

Seven Wonders of the ancient world, *canon of seven 'sights' ($\theta\epsilon\acute{\alpha}\mu\alpha\tau\alpha$) of art and architecture. First attested in the 2nd cent. BC in the *Laterculi Alexandrini* (*PBerol*. 13044[v], col. 8–9) and in *Antipater (3) of Sidon (*Anth. Pal.* 9. 58), the *canon comprises the pyramids of Egypt, the city walls of *Babylon, the hanging gardens of *Semiramis there, the temple of Artemis at *Ephesus, the statue of Zeus at *Olympia, the *Mausoleum of *Halicarnassus, and the colossus of *Rhodes (see CHARES (4)). The concept was developed in individual references to a single wonder and especially in complete lists of seven, sometimes drawn up to celebrate an 'eighth' wonder (like the *Colosseum in Rome in Martial, *Spect.* 1, or Saint Basil's hospital in *Gregory (2) of Nazianzus, *Or*. 43. 63 = *PG* 36. 577).

Later lists keep the number, but not always the identity of the wonders. While a late antique rhetorical treatise purporting to be a guidebook to the seven wonders for the armchair traveller and attributed to the engineer *Philon (2) of Byzantium still refers to the seven of the old canon, other wonders like the Pharus of *Alexandria (1), the *labyrinth, Egyptian *Thebes (2), and the temple of Zeus at *Cyzicus first feature in Pliny's list (*HN* 36. 75 ff.), the altar of horns at *Delos first in Martial (as above), the *Ecbatana palace of *Cyrus (1) first in Ampelius (*Liber memorialis* 8), the Asclepieum of *Pergamum and the *Capitol of Rome first in *Anth. Pal.* 9. 656.

Christian authors replace pagan sanctuaries with Noah's ark and Solomon's temple (Gregory of Tours, *De cursu stellarum* 1 ff.) or add the Hagia Sophia church in *Constantinople (Cosmas of Jerusalem, *PG* 38. 547), eventually listing up to sixteen to accommodate both traditional and new wonders.

P. A. Clayton and M. J. Price (eds.), *The Seven Wonders of the Ancient World* (1988); K. Brodersen, *Reiseführer zu den Sieben Weltwundern* (1992; collects the Greek and Latin wonder lists).
K. B.

Severan emperors and period See ROME (HISTORY), § 3.1.

Severus (emperor) See SEPTIMIUS SEVERUS, L.

Severus Alexander (emperor) See AURELIUS SEVERUS ALEXANDER, M.

Severus (*RE* 15), **Flavius Valerius,** an Illyrian military commander of humble birth, and friend of *Galerius, at whose wish *Maximian on abdicating (1 May, AD 305) proclaimed him at Milan as Caesar, with charge of Italy and Africa. When Constantius I died (306) Galerius made him Augustus but accepted Constantine as Caesar. His attempt to register the *plebs* of Rome provoked *Maxentius' rebellion. Sent from Milan to suppress this, he advanced close to Rome (spring 307), but was forced to retreat by desertions in his army. He fled to Ravenna, where Maximian compelled him to abdicate, leaving his dominions in

Severus, Sulpicius

Maxentius' control. Galerius then invaded Italy; Maxentius had Severus taken to Rome and either executed him or forced him to suicide. R. P. D.

Severus, Sulpicius (*PLRE* 2, 'Severus' 20), Latin historian who was born in Aquitania *c.* AD 360. A member of a prominent family, he studied law in Bordeaux and became a convert to Christianity *c.*389 together with his friend *Paulinus of Nola. After the death of his aristocratic wife, he organized under the influence of Bishop Martin of Tours a sort of monastic life on his own estates for himself and his friends. In old age he seems to have passed through a period of Pelagianism (see PELAGIUS). He died *c.* AD 420. Gennadius wrote a brief biography of him (*Vir. ill.* 19), and we have also thirteen letters to him by Paulinus. His extant works are: (1) a life of (Saint) Martin of Tours which is an apology for *asceticism and is supplemented by three letters on Martin's miracles and death and by a dialogue which compares Martin's feats with those of the Egyptian hermits; (2) a universal chronicle to AD 400 which is an important source for the history of 4th-cent. events, esp. the heresy of the *Priscillianists (Severus disapproved of the execution of Priscillianus). The whole book is an interesting attempt to present a 'breviarium' of history from the Christian point of view: it uses Christian chronographers, especially St *Jerome, but also pagan writers. J. Bernays suggested that for the destruction of Jerusalem in AD 70 Sulpicius followed the lost account of *Tacitus (1). *Sallust and Tacitus are his models in the matter of style.

Best edn. C. Halm (1866). Life of Martin: ed. and trans. J. Fontaine (133–5, 1967–9). For the Chronicle also A. Lavertujon (1896–9), with J. Fontaine's important comm. (1968).; J. Bernays, *Ges. Abhandl.* 2. 1885, 81 ff.; Schanz–Hosius iv. 2, 472 ff.; H. Delehaye, *Anal. Boll.* 1920, 5 ff.; P. Hylten, *Studien zu Sulpicius Severus* (1940), on style and text; S. Prete, *I Chronica di S. S.* (1955); H. Montefiore, *Hist.* 1962, 156 ff.; C. Saumagne, *Rev. Hist.* 1964, 67 ff.; J. Fontaine, *Mél. Chr. Mohrmann* (1964), 84 ff.; C. Stancliffe, *St. Martin and His Hagiographer: History and Miracle in Sulpicius Severus* (1983). A. M.; A. J. S. S.

Seville See HISPALIS.

Sevius (*RE* 2) **Nicanor, Marcus** (late 2nd–early 1st cent. BC), a *freedman and the first Roman grammarian to win fame by teaching, wrote *commentarii* (said to be largely plagiarized) and a *satura* (Suet. *Gramm.* 5; see SATIRE).

J. Christes, *Sklaven und Freigelassene als Grammatiker und Philologen* etc. (1979), 15 ff. R. A. K.

sewers See CLOACA MAXIMA; SANITATION.

Sexi, a *Phoenician settlement at Almuñécar on the coast of southern Spain in *Baetica, founded in the 8th cent. BC; it issued bronze coins depicting tunny fish during the republic. As *Sexi Firmum Iulium* it was a *municipium in the early empire, and a vaulted monument, aqueduct, and *columbaria* have been found. Fish-sauce was manufactured here until the 4th cent. AD.

F. Molina (ed.), *Almuñécar: Arqueología y historia*, 3 vols. (1983–6); L. Villaronga, *Numismática antigua de Hispania* (1979), 161 ff. S. J. K.

Sextilius Ena, a Spaniard from Corduba reported by L. *Annaeus Seneca (1) (*Suas.* 6. 27) as reciting a poem on the *proscriptions of 43 BC in the house of M. *Valerius Messalla Corvinus. E. C.

Sextius (*RE* 10), **Quintus,** philosopher of the Augustan period, refused a political career and founded a significant but short-lived philosophical movement. Though influenced by *Stoicism and *Neopythagoreanism, his school had a Roman character, which

made it of interest to Seneca the Younger (L. *Annaeus Seneca (2)). He emphasized vegetarianism (see ANIMALS, ATTITUDES TO), transmigration, the incorporeality of the *soul, and an asceticism akin to that of the *Cynics. Sextians included *Sotion (1) of Alexandria, *Cornelius Celsus, Lucius Crassicius, and *Papirius Fabianus. His son and successor was probably the botanical and medical writer Sextius Niger, whose work Περὶ ὕλης ἰατρικῆς (on *materia medica*) was used by *Pliny (1) the Elder and *Dioscorides (2). B. I.

Sextius (*RE* 13), **Titus,** Roman military man. Of obscure family, perhaps from *Ostia, he held commands under *Caesar in Gaul (53–50 BC?) and perhaps in the Civil War. In 44 he became governor of Africa Nova (Numidia), and supported Antony (M. *Antonius (2)). After *Mutina he was ordered by the senate to send two of his legions back to Italy for the defence of the state and to transfer the third to Q. *Cornificius, governor of Africa Vetus. Later he attacked Cornificius on behalf of the triumvirs (Antony, Octavian (see AUGUSTUS), and M. *Aemilius Lepidus (3)), defeated and killed him (42), and ruled both provinces till 41, when on request from L. *Antonius (Pietas) he handed them over to Octavian's lieutenant C. Fuficius Fango. He remained in Africa and regained the provinces for Antony during the Perusine War (see PERUSIA), then surrendered them to Lepidus in 40. His descendants, some of whom assumed the surname Africanus, held several consulships.

T. P. Wiseman, *CQ* 1964, 130–1; P. Romanelli, *Storia delle province romane dell' Africa* (1959), 142–7; C. R. Whittaker, *CAH* 10² (1996), 590. C. B. R. P.

Sextius (*RE* 20) **Calvinus, Gaius,** as consul in 124 BC and proconsul fought successfully in Transalpine Gaul, triumphing (see TRIUMPH) over Ligurians, Vocontians, and Salluvians *c.*122. He founded *Aquae Sextiae as a Roman garrison post. E. B.

Sextus (1) (*RE* 2) of *Chaeronea, nephew of *Plutarch, professional (Platonist) philosopher, teacher and mentor of Marcus *Aurelius, who still attended his lectures in Rome as emperor. He also taught L. Aurelius *Verus. A. J. S. S.

Sextus (2), originator of a collection of maxims, mentioned by *Origen (1) and translated into Latin by *Rufinus (2) under the title *Anulus*. The Syriac translation bears the title *Dicta Selecta Sancti Xysti Episcopi Romani*, but *Jerome denies the attribution to Xystus (AD 256–8), calling the author Sextus Pythagoreus. The popularity of these sayings in Christian circles is attested by the discovery of a defective Coptic version at Nag Hammadi, Egypt, in 1945. The original collection was probably non-Christian, made in the 2nd cent. AD, and, while Christian additions were gradually made, definite allusions to Christ were avoided.

Ed. A. Elter (1891–2); H. Chadwick, *The Sayings of Sextus* (1959). Coptic edn. P.-H. Poirier (1983), C. Hedrick, *Nag Hammadi Codices* 11, 12, and 13 (1991). W. D. R.; M. J. E.

Sextus Empiricus, Pyrrhonist Sceptic (see PYRRHON; SCEPTICS) and medical doctor. Nothing is known about his life, but the name 'Empiricus' shows that he was a member of the Empiricist school of medicine (see MEDICINE, § 5.3; PHILINUS (1); SERAPION (1)). *Diogenes (6) Laertius (9. 116) tells us that his teacher was Herodotus, also a doctor. Most scholars now agree that Sextus' works were written towards the end of the 2nd cent. AD.

Sextus' extant works are traditionally cited under two titles: 1. Πυρρώνειοι ὑποτυπώσεις (*Outlines of Pyrrhonism*, abbrev. *PH*), in three books; the first offers a general outline of Pyrrhonist scepticism, including the Modes of *Aenesidemus and *Agrippa, and a discussion of the differences between Pyrrhonism and other schools or philosophers alleged to have held similar views; the second and third books contain refutations of dogmatic philosophies, divided by subject-matter: epistemology and logic, philosophy of nature, ethics.

2. *Adversus Mathematicos* (*Against the professors*, abbrev. *M*), in eleven books, originally no doubt two different works. *M* 7–11, also entitled Πρὸς δογματικούς (*Against the dogmatists*), is a critique of dogmatic philosophies parallel to but more detailed than *PH* 2–3; *M* 1–6 (Πρὸς μαθηματικούς, *Against the professors*) criticizes other disciplines, as follows: grammar (1), rhetoric (2), geometry (3), arithmetic (4), astrology (5), music (6). Sextus' books on medicine and on the *soul are lost.

Sextus is the only Pyrrhonist philosopher whose work has survived. The first book of *PH* offers a detailed and subtle defence of scepticism, its aims, and methods. Though Sextus obviously draws upon his predecessors and doxographical works, he is an intelligent compiler who writes clearly and concentrates on argument rather than on anecdotes. His discussions of the doctrines of other schools have preserved a wealth of information, in particular about Stoic logic (see STOICISM) and Hellenistic epistemology. Much work still needs to be done to explore the various strands of Pyrrhonism between Aenesidemus and Sextus that seem to lie behind his exposition, as well as the connections between Pyrrhonism and the ancient schools of medicine.

GREEK TEXTS Ed. H. Mutschmann and J. Mau (Teubner: vol. 1, 1958²; vol. 2, 1914, repr. 1984; vol. 3, 1961², vol. 4—Indexes, coll. K. Janacek, 1962); Greek with Eng. trans., ed. J. B. Bury (Loeb, 4 vols., 1933–49). Modern discussions: K. Janacek, *Prolegomena to Sextus Empiricus*, 1948; J. Annas and J. Barnes, *The Modes of Scepticism*, 1985 (trans. of *PH* 1. 40–163 and parallel passages, with introd. and comm.); J. Allen, 'Medical Empiricism and Pyrrhonian Scepticism', *ANRW* 2. 37. 1 (1993). G. S.

Sextus Pompeius See POMPEIUS MAGNUS (PIUS), SEXTUS.

sexuality In the ancient Mediterranean, as elsewhere, sexuality recapitulates power relations within individual cultures. Greeks, Romans, and their neighbours have left definitions of sexual norms, obscenity, and sexual practice and identity; their systems have usefully been compared with anthropological accounts of modern Mediterranean and other patriarchal cultures, although recent debate has contested the degree to which modern sexual categories existed in antiquity (see HOMOSEXUALITY).

Both Greeks and Romans divided sexual behaviour into active/passive as well as (some say, and not) homosexual/heterosexual. The normative role for adult males was penetrative ('active'); penetrated ('passive') partners were normally women, and boys aged 12 to 17. Texts generally convey the experience of penetrators, and evaluate passivity negatively, at worst (oral) as contaminating; the experience of the passive has to be reconstructed.

Philosophers debated the merits of intercourse—different for men and women—and regulated sexual desire along with other bodily needs. Medical writers catalogued the human body, comprehending *cosmetics, *gynaecology, embryology, and obstetrics, as well as male physiology. Greek scientists, notably Aristotle, defined the female body as physiologically inferior to the male, even repellent, and sometimes justified gender hierarchy thereby. Intercourse and *childbirth conveyed *pollution; Roman menstrual revulsion seems likely to have had Greek parallels (see MENSTRUATION). Sexual categories in *astrology, *physiognomy, and dream-interpretation tally with their social valences (see DREAMS).

Sex with men for free women was defined in terms of marriage; girls married, often soon after puberty, and commonly remarried after divorce or widowhood. Virtue for women meant fidelity, though texts stereotype women as promiscuous. Their access to extramarital sex was always more or less controlled, adultery being defined as sex with a married woman; she or her lover might be killed (or, after Augustus, prosecuted), while the lover might be beaten or raped. Yet the elegist *Sulpicia (1) voices her desire. Free men married later, and extramarital sex between male and (subordinate) female is again widely attested. Rape of woman or boy dishonoured the victim and was punished by law. Historians of the family have clarified the circumstances of sexuality within marriage, exploring such issues as *contraception, affection between husband and wife, fertility, pregnancy and childbirth.

Class greatly affected sexual realities: slaves were by definition penetrable, and at Rome freed slaves bore a concomitant stigma. Non-marital alliances were available to non-élite classes. *Prostitution flourished, and many prostitutes were slaves; free Roman prostitutes were *infames* (see INFAMIA), along with pimps and theatre performers. Slaves' access to procreation was closely controlled; male slaves might be infibulated, or castrated, though this practice was sometimes outlawed (see EUNUCHS). Graffiti suggest that slaves' own sexual norms matched those of free people; inscriptions commemorate freed slave marriages and families.

*Ethnicity (though not colour: see RACE) figures in hegemonic sexual discourse. Asia Minor was frequently associated in ancient texts with sexual luxury and effeminacy, and Roman texts express a preference for boys from Asia. Although some early and many late sources are available for Egypt and the Near East, the sexual experience of indigenous peoples, especially in northern Europe and Africa, is largely lost to us.

Study of ancient Hebrew cultures has covered both the sexual symbolism of sacred texts and the realities of law and life. Christian *asceticism, like some contemporary pagan and Jewish versions, both devalued and focused on the sexual body; in some gnostic and Montanist circles, the feminine had a relatively high value (see GNOSTICISM; MONTANISM). In late antique Christianity, sexuality became associated with the idea of *sin, perhaps a watershed in the history of western sexuality.

See HETEROSEXUALITY; LOVE AND FRIENDSHIP; PORNOGRAPHY; WOMEN.

J. Henderson, *The Maculate Muse* (1975 [1991]); K. Dover, *Greek Homosexuality* (1978); M. Foucault, *History of Sexuality*, 3 vols. (1978–86; Fr. orig. 1976–84); C. Johns, *Sex or Symbol?* (1982); A. Richlin, *Garden of Priapus* (1983 [1992]); E. Keuls, *Reign of the Phallus* (1985); P. Brown, *Body and Society* (1988); P. du Bois, *Sowing the Body* (1988); K. King (ed.), *Images of the Feminine in Gnosticism* (1988); J. Hallett, *Yale Journal of Criticism* 1989, 209 ff.; D. Halperin, *One Hundred Years of Homosexuality* (1990); D. Halperin and others (eds.), *Before Sexuality* (1990); J. Winkler, *Constraints of Desire* (1990); D. Cohen, *Law, Sexuality, and Society* (1991); S. Treggiari, *Roman Marriage* (1991); A. Richlin (ed.), *Pornography and Representation in Greece and Rome* (1992); D. Boyarin, *Carnal Israel* (1993); L. Dean-Jones, *Women's Bodies in Classical Greek Science* (1993); C. Edwards, *Politics of Immorality in Ancient Rome* (1993); G. Robins, *Women in Ancient Egypt* (1993); T. McGinn, *Prostitution, Sexuality and the Law in Ancient Rome* (1995). A. R.

shamans See ABARIS; ARISTEAS; EMPEDOCLES; EPIMENIDES; PYTHAGORAS (1); ZALMOXIS; and cf. E. R. Dodds, *The Greeks and the Irrational* (1951), ch. 5.

shame See HUBRIS; NEMESIS; PUDICITIA; SUICIDE; also D. L. Cairns, *Aidos* (1993) and B. Williams, *Shame and Necessity* (1993).

sheep See PASTORALISM.

ships The earliest seagoing vessels in the ancient world were probably very small rafts and boats, made from skins, bundles of reeds, or carved out of tree-trunks. Even in such tiny craft it was possible to make quite lengthy journeys, but the need for greater capacity and security encouraged the development of larger, more stable vessels. The first ships were probably paddled, but oars appear to have been used from the 3rd millennium BC. The oldest representations of ships with sails are from Egypt and date to around 3100 BC. By the end of the 2nd millennium ships equipped with oars and a square sail were found all over the eastern Mediterranean.

From the Archaic period onwards the peoples of the eastern Mediterranean developed specialized types of ships which gradually came to be used throughout the ancient world. For war they used long ships, rowed by 50 or more oarsmen, on up to three levels, with masts and sails for long journeys. (The *pentecontor* or fifty-oared ship was largely superseded from perhaps the 6th cent. BC by the *trireme.) For *trade they commonly used ships of a more rounded appearance and deeper draft, which often required ballast to keep them afloat. They usually relied on sails for propulsion, which allowed more space for the storage of cargo, but also meant that they were at the mercy of the weather.

The typical sailing rig of ancient ships consisted of one square sail, hung from a yard attached to a mast, which was fixed approximately in the centre of the ship. Sails were normally trimmed using brails, which gave great flexibility. In addition to the square sail, triangular or lateen sails might be used, as well as spritsails and lugsails. Large ships often had more than one mast and carried triangular topsails. Mediterranean ships generally used sails made of *linen, which could be dyed and decorated. The sailcloth was often strengthened using leather patches in the corners and light lines stitched horizontally and vertically. Leather sails were used in north-western Europe, as were sails strengthened with battens.

Construction materials and methods for ships varied, but the predominant one for wooden ships in the Mediterranean was the 'shell first' technique, with planking being attached directly to the keel, and inner frames added afterwards for strength (e.g. Hom. *Od.* 5. 244–61).

The rudder was not used in antiquity. Ships were steered using one or two steering oars in the stern, usually fitted with transverse handles to make their handling easier. Steering was a skilled job and the helmsman (Greek *kybernētēs*, Latin *gubernator*) was one of the most important members of the crew.

The size of ancient ships varied greatly. Among the largest ancient *shipwrecks yet discovered were vessels that could carry cargoes weighing 250 tons or more. These ships mostly date to the period 100 BC to AD 200, when the conditions of the Roman empire encouraged maritime trade on a large scale.

See NAVIES; QUINQUEREME; SEA POWER; TIMBER; TRIREME.

L. Casson, *Ships and Seamanship in the Ancient World*, 2nd edn. (1986), and *Ships and Seafaring in Ancient Times* (1994); J. S. Morrison and R. T. Williams, *Greek Oared Ships 900–322 B.C.* (1968); A. J. Parker, *Ancient Shipwrecks of the Mediterranean and the Roman Provinces* (1992).

P. de S.

shipwrecks, ancient Over 1,000 ancient shipwreck sites are known from the Mediterranean, and many more no doubt remain to be found. The earliest vessel found is, however, an Egyptian river-boat, the ship of Cheops (mid-3rd millennium); this craft would probably not have been able to undertake seago-

ing voyages. Some elements of its relatively weak construction appear still to be incorporated in the earliest ship to be found in the open sea, the wreck of Ulu Burun (*Lycia, 14th cent. BC); this was a floating treasury of metals, minerals, and exotic products. Archaic wrecks, such as that at Pointe Lequin (late 6th cent. BC), likewise tend to produce rare items, but more mundane, 'commercial' cargoes come to dominate the Aegean and then the rest of the Mediterranean from the 4th cent. BC onwards. The greatest frequency of wrecks is in the 1st cent. BC and 1st cent. AD, and reported sites are most dense in the western Mediterranean, especially along the French coast, where they reflect above all the export of Italian *wine to Gaul during the late republic (e.g. the wreck of La Madrague de Giens, *c.*70–50 BC). Such cargoes may have weighed as much as 500 tons, though many ancient ships carried much less, and were rather small; the Kyrenia wreck (Cyprus, *c.*300 BC), which has been particularly well studied, was less than 14 m. long overall, and had perhaps as little as 20 tons of cargo on board when she sank. Many details of ship construction, of cargoes and of life on board have come from excavated wrecks: published examples are Valle Ponti and Le Grand Ribaud D (both late 1st cent. BC) and the Byzantine wreck of Yassı Ada (Bodrum, Turkey, 7th cent. AD). During the Roman Empire period variations in ship construction reflect special cargoes such as marble or roof-tiles, and greater economy of labour and materials was practised from the late 3rd cent. onwards, resulting eventually in skeleton-based structures such as that of the Serçe Limanı wreck (11th cent. AD). Wreck discoveries have not included much evidence for certain periods, or for certain types of ship, such as oared warships, though much has been learnt from the bronze ram found near Atlit.

See ARCHAEOLOGY, UNDERWATER; SHIPS; TRADE; WINE.

A. J. Parker, *Ancient Shipwrecks of the Mediterranean and the Roman Provinces* (1992); L. Casson, *Ships and Seafaring in Ancient Times* (1994); P. A. Gianfrotta and P. Pomey, *Archeologia Subacquea* (1981); P. Throckmorton, (ed.), *History from the Sea: Shipwrecks and Archaeology* (1987).

A. J. P.

shorthand See TACHYGRAPHY.

Sibyl The word *Sibylla*, of uncertain etymology, appears first in Heraclitus (DK 22 B 92) and was used as a proper name by the 5th cent. BC (e.g. Ar. *Pax* 1095, 1116). Specific oracles relating to events in the 4th cent. appear to have been attributed to the Sibyl by *Ephorus. Originally the Sibyl seems to have been a single prophetic woman, but by the time of *Heraclides (1) Ponticus (fr. 130–41 Wehrli) a number of places claimed to be the birthplace of Sibylla, traditions concerning a number of different Sibyls began to circulate, and the word came to be a generic term rather than a name. There are a number of Sibylline catalogues, of which the most important was that compiled by *Varro for his *Res Divinae*. It lists ten: (1) Persian; (2) Libyan; (3) Delphic; (4) Cimmerian (in Italy); (5) Erythraean (named Herophile); (6) Samian; (7) Cumaean; (8) Hellespontine; (9) Phrygian; (10) Tiburtine. Other sources mention Egyptian, Sardian, Hebrew, and Thessalian Sibyls (Rzach, *RE*). The most important discussion of different traditions, which emphasizes the local connections of Sibyls, is given by *Pausanias (3) (10. 12). Inscriptions from *Erythrae record sacrifices to the Sibyl and a sacred grove theoretically marking Herophile's birthplace (*I. Eryth. u. Klaz.* 207; 224). There are coins commemorating local Sibyls from Erythrae, *Cumae, and Gergis.

The nature of Sibylline inspiration is diversely reported. *Virgil offers a famous description of the Cumaean Sibyl uttering ecstatic prophecy under the inspiration of *Apollo, but texts from Erythrae or recorded in various ways by *Phlegon of Tralles, *Plutarch, and Pausanias clearly state that the Sibyl spoke under her own inspiration. The evidence for Sibylline inspiration provided by the extant corpus of Sibylline oracles is inconsistent (Potter, 181). Until the 4th cent. AD, the format is consistent: all but one of the extant texts are in Greek hexameter verse. Latin translations of Greek texts, and, possibly, some original Latin compositions date from the 4th cent. or later, as does the Greek archetype of the prose oracle of the Tiburtine Sibyl (subsequently much adapted in Latin, Arabic, and Old French down to the 12th cent.).

Widespread interest in Sibyls throughout the Mediterranean world probably stems from the connection between the Sibyl and Rome that dates to, at the very latest, the early 5th cent. BC (Dion. Hal. *Ant. Rom.* 6. 17). Legend has it that the collection first came to Rome in the reign of *Tarquinius Priscus, who is said to have bought three books from the Cumaean Sibyl and placed them in the care of a priestly college (see QUINDECIMVIRI SACRIS FACIUNDIS), to be consulted only at the command of the senate; the senate could also vote to add new books to the state's collection after inspection by the college. This collection was housed in the temple of Capitoline Jupiter (see CAPITOL), where it was destroyed in the burning of the Capitol in 83 BC. After this the senate commissioned a board of three to make a collection from various places. Augustus subsequently moved this collection to the temple of *Palatine Apollo. The last known consultation of these books (to which additions had been made from time to time) was in AD 363 (Amm. Marc. 23. 1. 7); they were destroyed in the time of *Stilicho (Rut. Namat. 2. 52). The books were consulted by order of the senate in times of crisis, and the one extant example, preserved by Phlegon of Tralles, suggests that the oracles contained a statement of the problem, followed by various remedies (*FGrH* 257). Sibylline texts in Latin, of quite different style, in the hands of members of the Roman aristocracy, were consulted in AD 536/7 (Procop. *Goth.* 1. 24).

The Sibyl's intimate connection with Rome made her a natural choice for Christians who sought evidence from pagan sources for the truth of their beliefs. Her earliest appearance is in the vision of *The Shepherd of Hermas*; with the development of the apologetic tradition, she begins to appear with more frequency (Parke, 152–73). Belief that Virgil's *Fourth Eclogue* (modelled on sibylline prophecy) was in fact inspired by the Cumaean Sibyl combined with this interest to elevate the Sibyl to a position of remarkable importance in Christian literature and art.

Two collections of Sibylline oracles survive from late antiquity, one dating to the end of the 5th cent. AD, the other to the period just after the Arab conquest of Egypt in the 7th cent. One contains texts numbered 1–8, the other includes oracles numbered 11–14. The material in these collections is extremely diverse. Some is manifestly Christian, other passages are almost certainly Jewish, and yet other material is pagan. The subject matter ranges from Christian doctrine and predictions of woe for cities and peoples to Roman history and sibylline biography.

Ed. J. Geffcken (1902); H. W. Parke, *Sibyls and Sibylline Prophecy* (1989); D. S. Potter, *Prophets and Emperors* (1994); A. Momigliano, *Ottavo Contributo* (1987), 349 ff. (in English). A. S. P.; D. S. P.

Sicans See SICILY.

Sicca Veneria, mod. Le Kef, a Roman town in Tunisia 170 km. south-west of *Carthage. Originally a Libyan community under Carthaginian control, it became a Numidian town, probably after

201, and was the scene of an incident between *Jugurtha and C. *Marius (1) (Sall. *Jug.* 56). It became a *colonia* before 27 BC (Colonia Iulia Veneria Cirta Nova Sicca: *ILS* 6783). It was the centre of a cult of *Venus, said to have been introduced from *Eryx in Sicily (Solinus 27. 8); at both sacred prostitution was practised (see PROSTITUTION, SACRED). The town was the birthplace of *Arnobius, and received substantial fortifications in the Byzantine period.

N. Ferchiou, *MDAI(R)* 1982, 441–5; N. Beschaouch, *CRAcad. Inscr.* 1981, 105–22. B. H. W.; R. J. A. W.

Siccius (*RE* 3) **Dentatus, Lucius** A tradition which perhaps derives from *Varro celebrates the numerous military campaigns, exploits, wounds, and honours of this legendary 'Roman *Achilles' (Gell. *NA* 2. 11. 1; etc.). Roman historians made him a mid-5th cent. plebeian hero whose death was plotted unsuccessfully in 455 BC by the consul T. Romilius (whom Siccius prosecuted as tribune in 454) and implemented by the Second *Decemvirate in 450/449. These stories are obvious duplicates and neither probably historical.

S. P. Oakley, *CQ* 1985, 409 f. A. D.

Sicels (Siculi) 'Sicel' appears to be a generic term applied by Greeks to the indigenous peoples they encountered when founding their colonies on the east coast of *Sicily towards the end of the 8th cent. BC; they were supposed to have arrived comparatively recently from the Italian mainland (Hellanicus, *FGrH* 4 F 79b; Dion. Hal. 1. 22; Thuc. 6. 2. 5), where their presence is traditionally attested in the south and perhaps linguistically also in *Latium. It is, however, more than usually difficult in Sicily to correlate the complex origins and vicissitudes of semi-legendary ethnic groups with the testimony of the spade: a purely archaeological distinction between, say, '*Ausonian' and 'Sicel' sites simply cannot be drawn. In 1892, P. Orsi achieved his seminal and long-lasting division of Sicilian prehistory into four post-neolithic 'Siculan' periods, and christened as 'Sicels' all the peoples of eastern Sicily throughout the early bronze age Castelluccio and middle bronze age Thapsos cultures: both are considerably earlier than the period suggested by the ancient sources for the Sicel incursion.

L. Bernabò Brea, *Sicily before the Greeks*[2] (1966); E. Gabba and G. Vallet (eds.), *La Sicilia antica* 1/1 (1980); R. Ross Holloway, *The Archaeology of Ancient Sicily* (1991). D. W. R. R.

Sicilian Expedition See PELOPONNESIAN WAR; SICILY, § 4; SYRACUSE; THUCYDIDES (2).

Sicily

1. *Prehistory* Ancient writers distinguished three indigenous peoples—Sicani in central, *Sicels in eastern, and Elymi in western Sicily. *Thucydides (2) (6. 2) attributes an Iberian origin to the Sicans, an Italic to the Sicels, and a Trojan to the Elymi. Archaeologically there is no differentiation of culture between east and west corresponding to the Sicel–Sican distinction, but the Italian origin of immigrants to Sicily in the late bronze age is confirmed by evidence from the Aeolian islands (see AEOLIAE INSULAE) and north-eastern Sicily, showing phases of the *Apennine culture known as *Ausonian. Surviving Sicel linguistic elements argue in the same direction. In south-east Sicily the pre-Greek culture does not show the same clear Italic affinities.

2. *The Greek Settlement* Despite Thucydides' account, the *Phoenicians did not apparently settle in Sicily before the Greeks, and their colonization was limited to *Motya, *Panormus, and

Soloeis. The Elymi, whose principal centres were *Segesta, *Eryx, and Entella, became traditional allies of the Carthaginians. From c.735 BC (Thucydides' date-indications in 6. 3–5 form the chronological basis) there followed a prolonged period of Greek *colonization. The indigenes were sometimes ejected from the colonized sites or reduced to dependent status; occasionally (as at *Leontini) there was peaceful co-existence. Once established, the Greeks and their civilization gradually penetrated and transformed the indigenous area; in many places the process was quite rapid. By the Hellenistic period the island was a Siculo-Greek amalgam. The Greeks exploited the island's economic potential, and Corinthian, East Greek, and (later) Laconian and especially Attic imported pottery (see POTTERY, GREEK) illustrates the considerable trade with Greece. Markets in Africa, south Italy, and (after c.500) Rome were also available. Temple-building and rapid urbanization attest the wealth and culture of the Archaic period, and the first Sicilian coinage (see COINAGE, GREEK) belongs to the second half of the 6th cent. The Phoenicians acquiesced in the Greek settlement, but defended their enclave against Pentathlus (c.580) and *Dorieus (c.510).

3. Early tyrannies As in Greece, *tyranny emerged, but the aristocracies were tenacious, while the threat, potential or actual, of *Carthage and the Sicels affected internal politics; this in turn produced greater social instability. Early tyrannies in *Acragas and elsewhere foreshadowed the despotism of *Hippocrates (1) of *Gela, who was the first of the great tyrants in Sicily. His successor *Gelon transferred his capital to *Syracuse. A Carthaginian attempt, at the instigation of some still independent Greek cities, to check Gelon and his ally *Theron of Acragas, met with disaster at *Himera (480). Under Gelon and *Hieron (1) Siceliot-Greek culture reached its classical zenith. It penetrated the Phoenician colonies, and the cities of the interior became increasingly Hellenized. After the deaths of Theron and Hieron the tyrannies soon came to an end. The attempt of the Sicel leader *Ducetius to organize a national movement proved abortive.

4. The age of Dionysius In the latter part of the 5th cent. the cities maintained their mutual independence and were democratically governed. But *democracy did not strike such deep roots in Sicily as in Greece, and external dangers demanded a more authoritarian organization. The Athenians twice intervened in the island (427–424 and 415–413) on the basis of alliances with Leontini and Segesta, with hopes of ultimately controlling it; the first intervention did not succeed, and the second ('Great') expedition ended in utter failure. Carthage now profited by the exhaustion of Syracuse to attempt the complete conquest of Sicily (409). *Selinus and Himera fell in 409, Acragas and Gela in 406/5. In the days of crisis *Dionysius (1) I succeeded in establishing himself as tyrant of Syracuse; the Carthaginians were repulsed, and Syracuse, which came to control all Sicily outside Carthage's *epikrateia* ('dominion') in the far west, prospered; but the cost was tyranny and the loss of political freedom. (Settlement patterns were altered by all this turmoil; from a remarkable dossier of inscriptions published in 1980, see bibliog., we know that some troops from *Campania who settled forcibly at Entella in 404, Diod. Sic. 14. 9. 9, cf. FGrH 70 Ephorus F 68, were still there in perhaps the 280s. Their names are partly *Oscan but their language is Greek and their constitutional forms look Greek too.) Dionysius' death (367) was followed, after a decade, by civil war; petty tyrants established themselves in the various cities, and the Carthaginians again intervened.

5. The Hellenistic period At this low ebb in their fortunes the

Syracusans sent for the Corinthian *Timoleon, who defeated the Carthaginians at the river Crimisus (probably in 341) and re-established settled government. His arrangements did not long survive his retirement (c.336), and oligarchy prevailed. In 317 *Agathocles (1) seized the Syracusan tyranny and subjugated most of the island. When he died (289) fresh anarchy ensued; there were more local tyrants, Carthage again threatened, and the tyrant's ex-mercenaries (*Mamertines) carved out a dominion for themselves in *Messana. City-state Sicily was in fact in dissolution. *Pyrrhus of Epirus was called in, but despite quick successes produced no lasting effect. *Hieron (2) II of Syracuse to some extent halted the decline, but his defeat of the Mamertini brought on a Carthaginian occupation of Messana and was the occasion for Roman interference and the First *Punic War (264–41), after which most of the island became a Roman province (see PROVINCIA). Hieron's kingdom remained autonomous and prosperous until his death in 215, when Syracuse went over to Carthage. After the Roman capture of Syracuse (211), all Sicily was unified as a Roman province.

6. The Roman republican period The province was under the control of a governor (praetor) with a quaestor in Syracuse and another in *Lilybaeum, but the cities continued to enjoy a large measure of independence with their own self-government. A provincial Sicilian council (*concilium) had no real power. Messana, *Tauromenium, and Netum, which had voluntarily accepted Rome's alliance, were distinguished as *civitates foederatae*; and five other communities were *free cities (Centuripae, Halaesa, Halicyae, Panormus, and Segesta). Of the remainder some paid a tithe (*civitates decumanae*; see DECUMA) on a system established by Hieron II; the land of others became *ager publicus, for which they paid rent in addition to the tithe (*civitates censoriae*). Local autonomy was infringed by governors such as C. *Verres (73–1) but generally respected; many cities issued small-denomination coinage until the early empire. Under the Republic wheat-growing, vital to Rome's *food supply, was fostered; large *latifundia* grew up, as a result of big Roman (and Sicilian) purchases of landed estates. These were worked by slaves whose conditions provoked the serious rebellions of 137–133 and 104–101 BC. Some of the urban centres were attacked and damaged, but despite these setbacks a majority of the Sicilian towns flourished in the 2nd and 1st cents. BC. The north-east of the island also suffered in 36 when Octavian (see AUGUSTUS) expelled Sex. *Pompeius, in whose occupation of Sicily (from 42) he and Antony had acquiesced in 39.

7. The Imperial Period The island continued to prosper under the Empire, governed by a proconsul (later a *corrector, then a *consularis*), and Latin and Greek culture long co-existed. *Caesar granted the Sicilians Latin rights (see IUS LATII), and Antony (M. *Antonius (2)) claimed that Caesar intended to make them full citizens (see CITIZENSHIP, ROMAN), but Octavian was less generous. As Augustus he founded veteran colonies at *Catana, Panormus, Syracuse, Tauromenium, Thermae, and Tyndaris (see COLONIZATION, ROMAN), and he gave Latin rights to a handful of others. It is possible that a later emperor extended this to all Sicilian communities, but the evidence is fragile. A fixed levy replaced the tithe. *Latifundia*, among them large imperial estates (see DOMAINS), remained an important feature of the agricultural pattern. Yet village life and smallholdings evidently flourished also, and the population in general was more dispersed in the countryside than hitherto, especially with the decline and abandonment of many of the old hill-towns of the interior. The coastal cities by contrast flourished, at least until the late empire, and the prosperity of the countryside in the 4th cent. is witnessed by luxury villas such as those of *Piazza Armerina, Patti Marina, and Tellaro. Grain continued to be the most significant export, although Sicily was now less important to Rome's food supply than Africa and Egypt; other exports included *wine, *timber, *wool, and sulphur.

GENERAL A. Holm, *Geschichte Siziliens in Alterthum* (1870–8); It. trans., *Storia della Sicilia nell'antichità* (1896–1906); L. Bernabò Brea, *Musei e monumenti della Sicilia* (1959); L. von Matt and P. Griffo, *Ancient Sicily* (1960); M. I. Finley, *Ancient Sicily*² (1979); E. Gabba and G. Vallet (eds.), *La Sicilia antica*, 2 vols. in 5 (1980); R. R. Holloway, *The Archaeology of Ancient Sicily* (1991). Guides: M. Guido, *Sicily, an Archaeological Guide*, rev. edn. (1977); F. Coarelli and M. Torelli, *Sicilia* (1984).

PREHISTORY L. Bernabò Brea, *Sicily before the Greeks*² (1967); S. Tusa, *La Sicilia nella preistoria* (1983).

SOURCES E. Manni, *Geografia fisica e politica della Sicilia antica* (1981); M. Sordi, *La Sicilia dal 368/7 al 337/6 B.C.* (1983); R. Marino, *La Sicilia dal 241 al 210 a.C.* (1988).

GREEK PERIOD E. A. Freeman, *History of Sicily*, 4 vols. (1890–4); B. Pace, *Arte e civiltà della Sicilia antica*, 4 vols. (1935–49; 2nd edn. of vol. 1, 1958); W. G. Dunbabin, *The Western Greeks* (1948); R. van Compernolle, *Étude de chronologie et d'histoire siciliotes* (1959); A. G. Woodhead, *Greeks in the West* (1962); A. Schenk, Graf von Stauffenberg, *Trinakria* (1963); E. Langlotz and M. Hirmer, *Art of Magna Graecia* (1965); M. Miller, *Sicilian Colony Dates* (1970); E. Sjøqvist, *Sicily and the Greeks* (1973); G. Nenci and G. Vallet, *Bibliografia topografica della colonizzazione greca in Italia e nelle isole tirreniche* 1– (1977–); J. Boardman, *The Greeks Overseas*³ (1980); L.-M. Hans, *Karthago und Sizilien* (1983); G. Pugliese Carratelli (ed.), *Sikanie: storia e civiltà della Sicilia greca* (1985); A. J. Domínguez, *La colonización griega en Sicilia* (1989); *CAH* 3²/3 (1982), chs. 37.3 and 38 (A. J. Graham); 4² (1988), ch. 16 (D. Asheri); 5² (1992), chs. 7 (D. Asheri) and 10 (A. Andrewes); 6² (1994), chs. 5 (D. M. Lewis) and 13 (H. D. Westlake); 7²/1 (1984), ch. 10 (K. Meister).

ROMAN PERIOD R. J. A. Wilson, *Sicily under the Roman Empire* (1990); G. Salmeri, *La Sicilia romana: aspetti e problemi* (1992); R. J. A. Wilson, *CAH* 10² (1996), ch. 13*b*.

INSCRIPTIONS *IG* 14 with supplementary material in *SEG*; *CIL* 10/2, with supplementary material in *AE*; R. Arena (ed.), *Iscrizioni greche arcaiche di Sicilia e Magna Grecia: Iscrizioni di Sicilia* 1 (1989); L. Dubois, *Inscriptions grecques dialectales de Sicile* (1989); M. del Amor López Jiménez, *Las tabellae defixiones de la Sicilia griega* (1991). Museum catalogues: M. T. Manni Piraino, *Iscrizioni greche lapidarie del Museo di Palermo* (1973); L. Bivona, *Iscrizioni latine lapidarie del Museo di Palermo* (1970). For the Entella material, *SEG* 30, 1117 ff.; 32, 914; 35,999; see also D. M. Lewis, *CAH* 6² (1994), 153.

COINAGE G. F. Hill, *Coins of Ancient Sicily* (1903); G. E. Rizzo, *Monete greche della Sicilia* (1946); E. Gabrici, *La monetazione del bronzo nella Sicilia antica* (1927); C. M. Kraay, *Archaic and Classical Greek Coins* (1976), 204–38; K. Jenkins, *Coins of Greek Sicily*² (1976); A. Mini, *Monete di bronzo della Sicilia antica* (1977).   A. M.; A. G. W.; R. J. A. W.

Sicily and Magna Graecia, cults and mythology

Greek settlers in *Sicily and *Magna Graecia brought with them the principal cults of old Greece. Those of *Demeter and *Persephone are particularly widespread and conspicuous in the archaeological evidence, reflecting perhaps the urgency of ensuring fertility and survival in a new environment. Rural and extraurban shrines helped to mark the claims of the communities to the land. The degree of interaction with the cults of indigenous peoples is questionable, but note the association of Demeter and Persephone with the Sicel centre of Enna.

The geographical position of the western Greeks accounts in part for the importance of *Zeus Olympios (e.g. at *Syracuse and *Locri Epizephyrii); his great sanctuary at *Olympia in the north-western Peloponnese more than any shrine in Italy or

Sicily served them as a common cult centre. More complex are the reasons for the popularity of *Hera (notably at *Croton and Poseidonia/*Paestum), though both with her and Persephone (especially at Locri, which produced a rich repertoire of terracotta plaques) female rites of passage seem to have been important.

While common Greek cults naturally predominate in the new cities of mixed origin there are exceptions. The Megarian cult (see MEGARA) of (Demeter) Malophoros was established outside the town soon after the foundation of *Selinus. But alongside her sanctuary was that of Zeus Meilichios, a figure associated with familial and personal welfare, worshipped widely (though not in the west) and sometimes, as here, for the most part aniconically. At *Metapontum a comparable cult, of Apollo Lykeios, is plausibly associated with male rites of passage.

There are various indications of an interest in Orphic and Dionysiac eschatology beginning in the Classical period, but Pythagorean doctrines, known from literary sources, have yet to appear in the epigraphic or artistic evidence (see ORPHISM; DIONYSUS; PYTHAGORAS (1)). A scarcity of inscriptions and the absence of a *Pausanias (3) leave some of the great temples insecurely identified. For myth as well as cult, *Heracles is important in the west (cf. his adventures in capturing the cattle of Geryon, recounted by *Stesichorus: Davies, *PMGF* S17, S19). Less is known about other heroes. Leucaspis, perhaps originally Sicel, seems to have been brought to Attica. The heroization of city *founders was common (see HERO-CULT). From Taras (*Tarentum) there are many representations of an anonymous reclining hero. In general, the spate of archaeological evidence has outstripped all attempts at synthesis. See also PALICI; SIRENS.

B. Pace, *Arte e civiltà della Sicilia antica* 3 (1945), 453–686; G. Zuntz, *Persephone* (1971); C. Sourvinou-Inwood, 'Persephone and Aphrodite at Locri', *JHS* 1978, 101–21; D. Musti (ed.), *Le Tavole di Locri* (1979); F. Graf, 'Culti e credenze religiose della Magna Grecia', in *Megale Hellas, nome e immagine* (1982), 157–85; C. Parisi Presicce, 'L'importanza di Hera nelle spedizioni coloniali', *Archeologia Classica* 1985, 44–83; E. Østby, 'Twenty-five years of research on Greek sanctuaries: a bibliography', in N. Marinatos and R. Hägg (eds.), *Greek Sanctuaries: New Approaches* (1993), 223–7.   M. H. J.

Sicinius (*RE* 9), **Gnaeus**, a witty orator (Cic. *Brut.* 216 f.), as tribune 76 BC was prevented by the consuls (one of them C. *Scribonius Curio (1)) from reversing some of *Sulla's legislation against the tribunate. Curio brought about his death, we do not know how.   E. B.

Siculus Flaccus (uncertain date), writer on surveying, discussed types of land tenure in Italy and the provinces, and boundary designation. See GROMATICI.   J. B. C.

Sicyon, city west of *Corinth: they shared a proverbially rich coastal plain. The original site remains unknown: it was captured in 303 BC by *Demetrius (4) Poliorcetes and moved to an acropolis above the plain. The tyrant dynasty (see TYRANNY) of the Orthagorids began c.650 BC and lasted for a century; it was the longest known to *Aristotle. *Cleisthenes (1) (c.600–570) gave insulting names to the Dorian tribes (see DORIANS) as much for enmity to *Argos (2) as to enhance the standing of his own non-Dorian tribe. He destroyed Cirrha in the First *Sacred War. He held a magnificent contest for the hand of his daughter Agariste, and through her became grandfather of *Cleisthenes (2) of Athens. Sparta ejected the last tyrant and Sicyon became an ally. It played some part in the First Peloponnesian War; Athenians twice landed and won battles in the territory. Sparta intervened in 417 to make an already existing oligarchy narrower. Euphron established a democracy in the 360s; after frequent changes of side he was murdered at Thebes. His enemies referred to him as a tyrant; but the *dēmos* buried him in the agora and honoured him as founder of the city. Demetrius named Sicyon Demetrias, but the name did not last. A succession of tyrants ruled before *Aratus (2) returned from exile, captured Sicyon in 251 and took it into the *Achaean Confederacy. Archaic and Classical Sicyonian art, especially sculpture and painting, enjoyed a high reputation. Although the city retained its autonomy in the Principate, it was overshadowed in every way by the neighbouring *colonia* at Corinth.

RE 2 A 2 (1923) and Suppl. 9 (1962), 'Sikyon' (1); A. Griffin, *Sikyon* (1982).   J. B. S.

Side, city with a good harbour on the coast of *Pamphylia. Founded according to *Eusebius in 1405 BC, it remained a *barbarian city until resettled by colonists from Aeolian *Cyme in the 7th or 6th cent. *Arrian says, quoting the Sidetans themselves, that the colonists at once forgot their Greek and began to speak an unknown barbaric tongue (*Anab.* 1. 26. 4). The story is illustrated by the peculiar script used on coins and inscriptions, and apparently to add glosses to a Greek handbook used in the local medical school (see ANATOLIAN LANGUAGES). The city's situation and its *harbours enabled it to function as the hub of sea connections which linked it with Syria, Egypt, and Cyprus in the east as well as with Rhodes and the Aegean in the west. It was a centre of the Anatolian slave trade and served as a naval base in the Hellenistic period and under the Roman empire. Side submitted quietly to *Alexander (3) the Great, and in 190 BC was the scene of an indecisive naval battle between *Antiochus (3) III and the Rhodians (see RHODES), who were supporting Rome. In the 2nd and 1st cents. BC it was deeply implicated in Cilician *piracy (see CILICIA), affording the pirates both a dockyard and a market for their prisoners. In the Republican period Side was the farthest city of the province of Asia and linked to the Aegean by the Roman road built by M'. *Aquillius (1) between 129 and 126 BC. Under the Roman empire the city became rich and was locked in rivalry with *Perge. In the 3rd cent. AD it served as a harbour from which provisions were transported to Roman troops in Syria and in the 4th as a campaigning base against Isaurian insurrections (see ISAURIA) in the *Taurus mountains. The ruins are extensive and have been excavated and partly restored by Turkish archaeologists.

J. Nollé, *Die Inschriften von Side* 1 (1993) (including testimonia). A. M. Mansel, *Die Ruinen von Side* (1964); G. E. Bean, *PECS* 835–6.
G. E. B.; S. H.

Sidicini, *Oscan-speaking neighbours of the *Aurunci immediately north of Campania. By threatening their chief town, *Teanum Sidicinum, the Samnites (see SAMNIUM) precipitated the First Samnite War (343 BC). The Sidicini came under Roman domination, probably during the Second Samnite War, but remained technically independent until the *Social War (3). They were rapidly Romanized thereafter.

P. Arthur, *Romans in Northern Campania* (1991).   E. T. S.; T. W. P.

Sidon, a *Phoenician metropolis on the coast of mod. Lebanon. The Sidonians are often synonymous with the *Phoenicians in classical texts (e.g. *Homer), and the development of the city is closely bound up with the history of Phoenicia (e.g. King Luli) and *Cyprus. In *Achaemenid times it was ruled by a native dynasty which had close commercial relations with Athens and was strongly Hellenized: this is shown by the sarcophagi of its

kings and the nearby temple of Eshmun / Asclepius at Bostan esh-Shaikh. The dynasty was confirmed by *Alexander (3) the Great but suppressed in the early 3rd cent. (the last known king was the Ptolemaic admiral Philocles; see EGYPT, *Ptolemaic*), and Sidon became a republic, ruled by *suffetes*. From *Antiochus (4) IV's reign it issued a municipal coinage, mostly inscribed in Phoenician. In 111 BC it gained its freedom, which was recognized by *Pompey. It received from Augustus a large accession of territory up to Mount Hermon (see ITUREA). Under *Elagabalus it became a Roman colony. Sidon was a great commercial city and also possessed two industries, *purple-dyeing and glass-blowing.

DCPP 'Sidon'; R. A. Stucky, *Tribune d'Echmoun* (1984); J. Elayi, *Sidon* (1989).   A. H. M. J.; J-F. S.

Sidonius Apollinaris (Gaius Sollius Modestus Apollinaris Sidonius) was a leading political and literary figure in 5th-cent. Gaul, whose career and writings are central to the period. Born at Lyons (*Lugdunum (1)) *c.*430, he was educated with fellow-nobles at Lyons and Arles (*Arelate). Through his marriage with Papianilla (*c.*450), he entered the family of Eparchius *Avitus (Augustus 455–6), in whose honour he composed his first published panegyric (*Carm.* 7), delivered at Rome on 1 January, 456. He held offices at the courts of Avitus and *Majorian, but returned to Gaul after Majorian's fall in 461. His participation in a Gallic embassy to *Anthemius in 467 led to a renewal of contacts with eminent Roman senators, his panegyric in honour of Anthemius, and his prefecture of Rome in 468. However, his support for the traitor Arvandus, whose illicit contacts with the *Goths at Toulouse were uncomfortably close to Sidonius' own dealings, led to Sidonius' final withdrawal to Gaul, where he was consecrated bishop of Clermont in 470. Baptism by Faustus of Riez and participation in the Christian philosophical seminars at Vienne of Claudianus Mamertus in the 460s had prepared the Christian aristocrat for his new role, which he performed with diligence and compassion, concentrating on preaching and patronage, but avoiding theological controversy. His first five years were dominated by the Gothic siege of Clermont, resistance to which was led by Sidonius and his brother-in-law, Ecdicius. After the surrender of the city by the emperor's negotiators in 475, described by Sidonius as 'enslavement', the bishop was confined at Liviana, near Carcassonne, but was later released and allowed to return as bishop to Clermont, under Gothic supervision.

Works (1) *Carmina*, issued as a collection in 469, consisting of (*a*) *panegyrics of Anthemius, Majorian, and Avitus, with prefaces, in reverse chronological order, and (*b*) occasional poems on both serious and trivial themes; (2) *Epistulae* in nine books, the first seven collected *c.*477, the last two issued separately and concluding after 481; (3) *Missae*, now lost but known to Gregory of Tours.

His excessive fondness for literary conceits may irritate, but Sidonius' originality was greater than his detractors allow, given the constraints of the literary conventions within which he operated. While the panegyrics were modelled on *Claudian, and his more literary letters on *Pliny (2), Sidonius' later writings increasingly incorporated Christian themes, often allusively, into the classical tradition and his collected correspondence was to form a bridge between the classical productions of Pliny, M. *Cornelius Fronto, and *Symmachus (2) and the episcopal collections of the 6th cent. Moreover, with their strong focus on aristocratic social behaviour and ambitions and the expanding role of the Germanic courts, Sidonius' writings mirror the conflict of traditional values with new realities and the effects on Gallic society of the Germanic presence and the declining power of Rome.

> TEXT Ed. J. Savaron (1609); J. Sirmond (1652); Luetjohann (1887); Mohr (1895); W. B. Anderson, with trans. and notes (1936 and 1965); A. Loyen (1960 and 1970).
> BOOKS (WITH BIBLIOG.) C. E. Stevens, *Sidonius Apollinaris and his Age* (1933); J. Harries, *Sidonius Apollinaris and the Fall of Rome* (forthcoming). J. D. H.

siegecraft, Greek The Greek national epics focused on the siege of a city, but it took ten years to capture *Troy, even if, in the end, the 'wooden horse' was some kind of sophisticated siege device. The inability to take walled towns other than by treachery or blockade persisted into the historical period, despite a growing awareness of such techniques as the Persian siege-mound (cf. Hdt. 1. 162. 2) and undermining (Hdt. 5. 115. 2). *Pericles (1) is said to have been the first to use 'siege-engines' (*mēchanai*) at *Samos in 440/39 BC—they included 'rams' and 'tortoises' (i.e. sheds to protect undermining parties: Diod. Sic. 12. 28. 2–3). But despite the Athenian reputation for siegecraft (cf. Thuc. 1. 102. 2), they took three years to capture *Potidaea (432–429), and mainly relied on blockade, though in 430 they made some use of 'siege-engines', perhaps towers (Thuc. 2. 58. 1). Similarly, though the Spartans and their allies used a mound, battering-rams and even fire against *Plataea (Thuc. 2. 75 ff.), this little town, too, stood a two-year siege (429–427 BC), and only surrendered through lack of food. The Athenian, *Nicias (1), also used ship-borne 'siege-engines' to capture two towers on Minoa near *Megara in 427 (Thuc. 3. 51. 3), but against *Syracuse seems never to have tried anything but circumvallation (414–413 BC).

Part of the reason for the poor showing of Classical Greeks in siege techniques may have been that their strength lay in hoplites, who were ill-suited to siege operations, and that there were too few archers and slingers to provide proper covering fire. It may be significant that when the *Boeotians, for example, attacked the temple precinct at *Delion which the Athenians had fortified, in 424 BC, they sent for javelineers and slingers from Malis, though they eventually took the place by means of a primitive flame-thrower (Thuc. 4. 100).

The first Greeks reliably attested to have used siege-towers were the Sicilians under *Dionysius (1) I, at the siege of *Motya (Diod. Sic. 14. 49 ff.), and they perhaps learned about them from the Carthaginians, who allegedly used them against *Selinus in 409 (Diod. Sic. 13. 54. 7); at Motya Dionysius also used arrow-firing catapults. Such weapons were known in Greece by about 375 BC and are mentioned once by *Aeneas Tacticus (32. 8), as are towers on wheels (32. 1 and 8), 'masts' (32. 1)—perhaps pivoting beams holding leather or wicker cradles capable of carrying men—rams and 'drills' (32. 5–6), 'tortoises' (*chelōnai*: 32. 11 and 33. 1), scaling-ladders (36. 1), and tunnelling (37. 1 ff.).

It was perhaps under *Philip (1) II that siegecraft really began to develop in mainland Greece, though he still only had arrow-firing catapults—the 75 mm. (3-inch), three-barbed, bronze arrow-heads, inscribed with the king's name, found at *Olynthus, possibly came from these. But even Olynthus fell in the end through treachery, and Philip's 80-cubit towers and catapults failed to take *Perinthus in 340 BC (Diod. 16. 74 f.). By this time, too, catapults were also being used in the defence of towns, and it was probably a bolt from one of these which put out Philip's eye at the siege of Methone.

Nevertheless, Philip clearly bequeathed both siege expertise and siege experts to his son, *Alexander (3) the Great, and it was under the latter that Greek siegecraft finally came into its own,

playing a vital part in the conquest of Persia, particularly in the early years. With more powerful, torsion catapults, capable of throwing stones, it was now possible to smash battlements and even help to batter down walls. Alexander's sieges of *Miletus, *Halicarnassus, *Tyre, and *Gaza display fully-developed siege-techniques.

Some of the 'Successors', too, were notable besiegers, especially *Demetrius (4) son of *Antigonus (1) Monophthalmos, who was nick-named 'Poliorcetes' ('The Besieger'). *Diodorus (3) Siculus' accounts of Demetrius' sieges of *Salamis (2) on *Cyprus and, above all, *Rhodes (20. 85–8, 93–7), are a rich source of evidence for Hellenistic siegecraft. Devices included mining, timbered galleries (*stoas*), artillery, giant siege-towers (*helepoleis*) carrying catapults and drawbridges (*epibathrai*), mechanical scaling-ladders (*sambukai*), various mobile-sheds (*chelōnai*) for ditch-filling (*chostrides*), digging saps (*oruktrides*) and carrying rams (*kriophoroi*). By the end of the 3rd cent. besiegers generally held the whip hand, though a wealthy city, such as Syracuse, was still capable of withstanding a lengthy siege. See ARTILLERY; FORTIFICATIONS.

> E. W. Marsden, *Greek and Roman Artillery* (1969); Y. Garlan, *Recherches de poliorcétique grecque* (1974); A. W. Lawrence, *Greek Aims in Fortification* (1979); D. Whitehead, *Aineias the Tactician: How to Survive under Siege* (1990). J. F. La.

siegecraft, Roman Early Roman besiegers employed blockade (*obsidio*) with methodical circumvallation, exploited surprise, and sometimes, especially after weakening the besiegers by *obsidio*, clinched matters by assault (*oppugnatio*), using ladders (*scalae*) and possibly ramps (*aggeres*) and rams (*arietes*). *Veii, blockaded 405–396 BC, apparently fell to assault by mine (*cuniculus*).

From the 3rd cent. BC, the Romans assimilated and improved the machinery and techniques of Hellenistic siegecraft, and continued to use elaborate fieldworks. Accounts of the sieges of *Syracuse by M. *Claudius Marcellus (1), of *Piraeus by *Sulla, and those of the Gallic, Jewish, Sasanid, and Gothic wars are instructive, as are the surviving technical treatises. Equipment included bolt-shooting and stone-throwing *artillery, mobile towers, mechanical ladders, movable siege-sheds and rams, protective galleries, mobile screens, wall-borers, and hooks and crowbars for dislodging masonry (cf. *Vitruvius, *Vegetius). The design of equipment for going under, through, or over *fortifications was ingenious, but its quantity depended on the initiative of individual commanders.

During the Principate, Roman siege technology developed principally in the eastern theatre; wars with Parthians and Sasanids were dominated by heavily fortified cities. In Roman literature the Sasanids are distinguished from their predecessors by their ability in siege-warfare, which they learned specifically from the Romans. Thus, Roman eastern fortresses were also on the defensive, using artillery and other equipment accordingly.

Republican sieges in the west are reflected archaeologically by camps, contravallations, circumvallations, and missile artefacts (*Numantia, *Pompeii, *Perusia, *Gergovia, *Alesia). Imperial practice-siegeworks may be seen at Woden Law and Burnswark in Scotland. Jewish-War sites have fieldworks and projectiles (Gamala, Herodium, Jerusalem, Machaerus, Battir, *Masada). Third-cent. AD sieges, both Roman and Sasanid (Cremna, Dura-*Europos, *Hatra), are represented by fieldworks, ramps, mines, artefacts, and even artillery components.

> J. Kromayer and G. Veith, *Heerwesen und Kriegführung der Griechen und der Römer* (1928), 373–6, 442–9, 600–1; E. W. Marsden, *Greek and Roman*

Artillery: Historical Development (1969); O. Lendle, *Schildkröten: Antike Kriegsmaschinen in poliorketischen Texten* (1975); P. Connolly, *Greece and Rome at War* (1981), 290–303; O. Lendle, *Texte und Untersuchungen zum technischen Bereich der antiken Poliorketik* (1983); D. Kennedy and D. Riley, *Rome's Desert Frontier* (1990), 95–110. J. C. N. C.

Sigeum, important site in the *Troas (NW *Asia Minor), acquired by Athens—the first overseas Athenian possession—in the late 7th cent. BC, after *arbitration by *Periander between Athens and *Mytilene (see also ALCAEUS (1)), but then lost by Athens to Mytilene, until reconquered by *Pisistratus, who made his son Hegesistratus ruler (Hdt. 5. 94 f.); cf. the inscribed vase *LSAG*[2], 366 and below, Phanodicus). *Hippias (1), Pisistratus' son, retired there after his eviction from Athens, and struck a remarkable coin with an Athenian owl and the letters 'HIP(pias)': *Historia Numorum*[2], 377. In the *Delian League Sigeum was notably loyal (*IG* 1[3]. 17); it usually paid 1000 drachmas from about the mid-5th cent., but six times that (1 talent) in 418/17: ML 75. In the 4th cent., it was controlled by *Chares (1) (355 to 332), then garrisoned by *Lysimachus (302). An interesting inscription honouring a benefactor (see EUERGETISM) may attest a period of independence thereafter (*SEG* 15. 751); it is curious that one of the earliest (mid-6th cent.) epigraphic texts thanking a benefactor also relates to Sigeum (Dittenberg., *SIG* 2, *LSAG*[2] 72, 366 f., M. Guarducci, in G. Richter, *Archaic Gravestones of Attica* (1961), 165 ff.). It honours Phanodicus of Proconnesus who gave the Sigeans a mixing-bowl and strainer). Sigeum was destroyed by *Ilium (*Troy), ? mid-3rd cent. BC: Strabo 13. 600.

D. L. Page, *Sappho and Alcaeus* (1956) 152 f.; *ATL* 1. 547 f.; Meiggs, *AE* 117; J. M. Cook, *The Troad* (1973), 178 ff. S. H.

Sigillaria, the fair on the last of the seven days of the Saturnalia (see SATURNUS), when pottery figurines (*sigilla*) were given as gifts; as well as these, other trifling wares were sold (Auson. *Cent. Nupt.* 206. 7 Peiper). It was usual to give dependants money for this fair (e.g. Suet. *Claud.* 5). The origin of the custom is not known. H. J. R.; A. J. S. S.

signa militaria, Roman military standards. The earliest standard (Latin *signum*) of the Roman army was that of the maniple (see MANIPULUS). When the *cohort superseded the maniple as the tactical unit, the standard of the leading maniple became the chief standard of the cohort. The century had no separate standard. The basic form of a Roman standard was a hand on the top of a pole, frequently a spear, decorated with *phalerae* (metal discs), crescents, laurel wreaths, mural crowns, and other emblems representing the battle honours won by the unit.

In the pre-Marian army (see MARIUS (1), c.) there were also five legionary standards (see LEGION), which were placed for safety in battle between the first two lines. Marius replaced these by giving each legion an eagle (*aquila*) of silver or gold, with wreaths as its sole decoration. The eagle embodied the spirit of the legion and was the object of religious veneration. Its loss was the worst form of disgrace, and sometimes entailed the disbandment of the legion. Under the Principate the legion retained its eagle and standards, and to these were added *imagines*, standards bearing the portraits of the reigning and deified emperors.

The cavalry standard was known as a *vexillum*. *Vexilla* were also employed in the legion to mark detachments (*vexillationes*), and, in the 1st cent. AD, the corps of veterans *sub vexillo*. In cohorts of *auxilia the infantry had *signa*, the mounted men *vexilla*: in the *alae there was a regimental standard carried by the *vexillarius alae*, and the *turmae* had *signa* in addition. *Imagines* came to be carried by all units, including the *numeri*, except the *praetorians, who had only *signa* and *vexilla*.

In the late empire the traditional standards were retained (but not the *imagines*), and two new ones added, the *draco* ('dragon') and the *labarum* (a military standard whose features included a cross, a crown, and the first two letters of the name Jesus Christ). The former was probably of Dacian origin (see DACIA), while the latter was not so much a military standard as a symbol of triumphant *Christianity.

A. von Domaszewski, *Die Fahnen im römischen Heere* (1885); Parker, *Roman Legions*[2] (1971), 36 ff.; M. Marin y Pena, *Instituciones militares romanas* (1958), 375 ff.; V. Maxfield, *The Military Decorations of the Roman Army* (1981), 218 ff.; G. Webster, *The Roman Imperial Army*[3] (1985), 133 ff. H. M. D. P.; G. R. W.; T. J. Co.

Signia, modern Segni, strongly placed at the north-east angle of the Volscian mountains in Latium. A Latin colony here (495 BC; see COLONIZATION, ROMAN) helped contain the *Volsci. *Sulla defeated the Marians near by (battle of Sacriportus, 82 BC; see MARIUS (2), c.). Ancient ruins include spectacular polygonal walls, corbelled gate (*porta Saracena*), temple in squared masonry, large open-air reservoir.

Segni: Quad. Dip. Sc. Ant. Un. Salerno, Archeologia 1. 1990.
E. T. S.; T. W. P.

Sila, the mountainous and heavily forested Aspromonte massif in *Calabria. Originally Bruttian territory (see BRUTTII), it was confiscated by Rome *c.*270 BC and its timber exploited for pitch and shipbuilding. K. L.

Silanion, Athenian sculptor, active *c.*360–320 BC. He specialized in heroes and portraits in bronze, and was the first portraitist to write on proportion. His *Plato (1) and *Corinna have been recognized in copy, and a bronze boxer from Olympia has been connected with his Satyrus (victor in 332 and 328). The Plato apparently provided the prototype for many ancient philosopher-statues: seated, unpretentiously dressed, and contemplative. Attributions include the Ince *Theseus and the Ludovisi *Ares (*Achilles?), both copies.

A. F. Stewart, *Greek Sculpture* (1990), 179 f., 288 f., figs. 513 f. A. F. S.

silence Narrators, dramatists, and orators know that there are times when silence is far more effective than the most powerful speech. Only a brief selection can be attempted. The chief motives for silence in Greek epic and drama are intense grief (compare Job 2: 10–3: 1), deep anger, or some other form of emotional distress (including passionate love). Examples are *Homer, *Il.* 1. 511 ff. (*Zeus), *Od.* 11. 563 ff. (*Ajax), the latter imitated by Verg. *Aen.* 6. 469 ff. (*Dido); Aesch. *Agam.* 1035 ff. (the role of *Cassandra), paralleled in the lost Niobe and Myrmidons and parodied by Ar. *Frogs* 833 ff., cf. 907–26; Soph. *OC* 1252 ff. (Oedipus); Eur. *Hipp.* 310 and elsewhere (on the theme of speech and silence in that play see Knox). *Herodotus (1) uses the same technique (e.g. 1. 86. 3–4). In a slightly different category comes Pylades in Aesch. *Cho.* 900–2, who dramatically breaks silence for one momentous speech, when we have supposed him to be a mute actor. Tragic consequences also often follow from oaths of silence (Barrett on *Hipp.* 710–12). In rhetoric, play is often made with the idea of crimes or disasters being too great for words (Cic. *Rosc. Am.* 124); related are both the *praeteritio* (i.e. ostentatiously 'passing over' a subject) and the 'inexpressibility-topos' (e.g. Cic. *Marcell.* 4, Woodman on Velleius 2. 104. 4). Ancient criticism recognized the effect of silence: cf. schol. *Od.*

11. 536, *Il.* 17. 695, and esp. [Longinus] 9. 2, who declares the silence of Ajax more sublime than any words could have been.

O. Taplin, *Harv. Stud.* 1972, 57–97; B. Knox, *Word and Action* (1979), 205–30. On aposiopesis see [Cic.] *ad Herenn.* 4. 30 and 37 with Caplan's note.　　　　　　　　　　　　　　　　　　　　　　　　R. B. R.

Silenus, probably of Caleacte in Sicily, wrote a history of Sicily. With *Sosylus, he accompanied *Hannibal's expedition as an official historian and wrote a history of it, which *Coelius Antipater and *Polybius (1) later used. Hence he is one of the ultimate sources for *Livy's third decade. We have too few fragments to judge the work, but the description of two dreams shows Hellenistic ornamentation and probably reminiscence of *Herodotus (1).

FGrHist 175 with Jacoby's comm.　　　　　　　　　　F. W. W.; E. B.

silens, Silenus See SATYRS AND SILENS.

Silius (*RE* 4), **Gaius,** grandson of P. Silius Nerva (consul 20 BC), consul-designate for AD 48 and 'fairest of the Roman youth' (Tac. *Ann.* 11. 12), attracted *Valeria Messallina; their liaison involved a scheme either to displace *Claudius, or (better) to make him abandon *freedmen advisers for senators and knights (see EQUITES). The lovers celebrated a 'marriage' while the emperor was at Ostia (48), and the freedmen made Claudius act: Silius and Messallina were killed.

B. Levick, *Claudius* (1990), 64 ff.　　　　　　　　　R. S.; B. M. L.

Silius (*RE* 17) **Italicus, Tiberius Catius Asconius** (*c.* AD 26–102), Roman politician and poet, author of the *Punica*, an *epic of 17 books on the Second *Punic War, at over 12,000 lines the longest poem in Latin. Before turning to the composition of poetry in retirement Silius had an outstanding public career (the evidence for his life comes from *Martial's epigrams and a distinctly tepid death-notice in *Pliny (2), *Ep.* 3. 7). Zealous in prosecution under *Nero, he was the last consul appointed by the emperor in AD 68, at an early age for a *novus homo*. In the turmoil of the next year he was engaged in tense high-level negotiations between A. *Vitellius and *Vespasian's brother (Tac. *Hist.* 3. 65); his support for Vitellius did not harm him, for he reached the peak of a senator's career under Vespasian, as proconsul of Asia (*c.*77). One of his sons followed him to the consulate, and there were hopes for the second son, disappointed by death (Mart. 8. 66, 9. 86). He retired to *Campania, where he owned many *villas, and spent his last years as an artistic connoisseur, attracting adverse comment for conspicuous consumption. He owned one of *Cicero's villas and the tomb of *Virgil, whose memory he revered (Mart. 11. 48). Many assume that he began his poem in the late 80s on the rather shaky grounds that only then does Martial start referring to his poetic activity (4. 14); the praise of the Flavian dynasty at 3. 593–629 suggests that the poem was either published before Domitian's death (September 96) or, more probably, still not fully revised at the poet's death some years later. Afflicted by an incurable ailment, Silius starved himself to death at the age of 76, perhaps as late as 103. The *Stoicism often attributed to him is based on no external evidence other than a hostile story told by *Epictetus about one Italicus, whom there is no need to identify with the poet (Arr. *Epict. Diss.* 3. 8. 7).

With *Livy's third decade as the principal historical source, and Virgil's *Aeneid* as the principal poetic model, the *Punica* traverses the entire Second Punic War, casting itself as the fulfilment of the curse with which *Dido conjures eternal enmity between her people and *Aeneas' (*Aen.* 4. 622–9). A mythological dimension is immediately present, therefore: Hannibal is not just a formidable human antagonist but the hellish tool of Juno's unassuaged hate, and the gods participate throughout. Silius' decision not to follow *Lucan's removal of the gods as characters has attracted the censure of modern critics, but it is symptomatic of his forswearing of Lucan's nihilism in favour of a more traditional view of divine sanction for imperial destiny (debts to Lucan are ubiquitous, however, especially in the Caesarian portrayal of Hannibal). The poem celebrates Roman fortitude by displaying such mighty heroes as M. *Atilius Regulus, Q. *Fabius Maximus Verrucosus, M. *Claudius Marcellus (1), and P. *Cornelius Scipio Africanus, and by organizing the mass of 15 years' history to centre on the catastrophic defeat at *Cannae in 216 BC (bks. 8–10, with seven books before and after): nostalgia for a simpler and nobler past is shot through with the apprehension that Rome's victory over Carthage held the seeds of contemporary decline.

Discovered only in 1417, the *Punica* had some esteem as a paradigm of courtly virtue until the end of the 16th cent., but for centuries its reputation has been in steep decline, and it is now scarcely read. Recent attempts at rehabilitation have concentrated on Silius' thematic concerns, structural skill, and professional engagement with his tradition. Further systematic and detailed study, especially of his language, is needed before Silius' achievement and stature can be convincingly reassessed.

TEXT J. Delz (1987).
COMMENTARIES G. A. Ruperti (1795–8); F. Spaltenstein (1986).
CONCORDANCE M. Wacht (1989).
TRANSLATION J. D. Duff (Loeb, 1934).
STUDIES M. von Albrecht, *Silius Italicus* (1964); R. Häussler, *Studien zum historischen Epos der Antike* 2 (1978); P. Hardie, *The Epic Successors of Virgil* (1993).　　　　　　　　　　　　　　　　　　D. C. F.

silk (τὸ σηρικόν, *serica vestis*), a fine light-reflecting filament extruded by silkworms, especially the domesticated mulberry silkworm of China (*Bombyx mori*), to build cocoons. The earliest extant silk fabrics in the classical world come from a high-status grave in the *Ceramicus cemetery, Athens, dated to *c.*430–400 BC. They show the hallmarks of western, not eastern, weaving. *Aristotle (HA 5. 97. 6 (551b)) describes briefly the lifecycle of a wild silkmoth associated with *Cos in the eastern Aegean. Coan silks (*Coae vestes*), a byword for hedonism, are frequently mentioned by the Augustan poets—but no later. Pliny (*HN* 11. 76) extends Aristotle's account to an Assyrian wild silkmoth; this and the Coan moth are arguably the *Pachypasa otus*. On present evidence it seems unlikely that Bombyx silk reached the Mediterranean from China (see SERES) before Han expansion into central Asia in the 2nd cent. BC. The *Periplus Maris Erythraei* (*c.* AD 50; see PERIPLOI) records the importation of silk (floss, yarn, and cloth) through India to Egypt; that silk cloth was unravelled in the west to provide yarn, as once believed, is unlikely. Han Chinese woven fabrics have been found in graves in the Crimea (1st cent. AD) and Palmyra (3rd cent. AD). Roman weavers were creating tapestry-woven decorative silks and, from the 3rd cent. AD, complex damask and compound weaves. The Edict of *Diocletian (AD 301) lists prices for raw silk (μέταξα) and various silk garments; but Roman writers were curiously ignorant of how silk was obtained. Only in the mid-6th cent. was sericulture with *Bombyx mori* eggs and the white mulberry introduced into the Mediterranean region.

ANRW 2. 9. 2 (1978); R. J. Forbes, *Stud. Anc. Technol.* 4². 50 ff.　　J. P. W.

silphium See CYRENE; PHARMACOLOGY.

Silures, a tribe in south-west Wales. Under *Caratacus, they gave trouble to the Roman armies, and a base of the Legio XX Valeria (see LEGION) was established at Usk in c.58. They were finally subdued by Sex. *Iulius Frontinus (AD 74–8), who planted a fortress of Legio II Augusta at Isca (Caerleon). A Roman town in the plain (*Venta Silurum, Caerwent) became their *civitas*-capital. There are few *villas and little evidence of Romanization outside Caerwent.

S. S. Frere, *Britannia*³ (1987).　　　　C. E. S.; M. J. M.

silva (plural *silvae*), properly woodland, undergrowth, uncultivated land, or a wooded hill-slope (used in Italy for pasture, hence symbolic of *pastoral poetry), metaphorically denotes profuse variety or (like its Greek counterpart ὕλη) raw material, including a rough draft (Quint. *Inst.* 10. 3. 17) or a collection of notes (Suet. *Gram.* 24. 5; *Ateius Philologus used the Greek word, ibid. 10. 5). The title *Silvae*, reported among those of learned miscellanies (Gell. *NA* pr. 6), was bestowed by *Statius (apparently following M. *Annaeus Lucanus, and followed in turn by Renaissance poets) on his books of shorter poems, varied in subject and form.

K. M. Coleman, *Statius: Silvae IV* (1988), pp. xxii–xxiv.　　L. A. H.-S.

Silvanus, Roman god of the countryside. Apparently of ancient origin, he is rarely attested before the Augustan period, but during the empire was one of the most popular deities in the western and Danubian provinces, where he appears in over 1,100 inscriptions. He was associated primarily with forests (as reflected in his name) and agriculture, to a lesser extent with hunting and herding. Although in ancient literature he is sometimes linked or confused with *Faunus and *Pan, he lacks their prophetic abilities and wild personalities. Instead, he generally appears in inscriptions and monuments as a benign anthropomorphic deity, accompanied at times by female deities named Silvanae or Nymphae. In some areas (e.g. southern France) he was regularly identified with local gods, while in others (e. g. Romania) he apparently retained his purely Roman character. Silvanus never received any public cult either in Rome or in the provinces, although a number of *collegia* were organized in his name. Most of the dedications to the god were erected by individuals, of whom fewer than 10 per cent seem to have been members of the élite. His cult was thus essentially popular in character.

P. F. Dorcey, *The Cult of Silvanus* (1992); *LIMC* 7.1 (1994), 763 ff.
　　　　　　　　　　　　　　　　　　　　J. B. R.

silver While *gold could be easily obtained from alluvial deposits by washing, silver had to be extracted by regular mining processes. The *Phoenicians are said to have been the first to bring silver into general use; several of the silver objects mentioned in *Homer have Sidonian associations (see SIDON). The main sources for classical Greece were Mt. *Pangaeus in *Thrace, *Lydia, *Colchis, *Bactria, Siphnos, and *Laurium which provided abundant supplies for *Athens. In the western Mediterranean *Spain was the most prolific source of supply, with *Sardinia, Gaul, and Britain as minor sources. The conquests of Spain and Asia made silver plentiful at Rome, where it had previously been rare.

Silver was worked with a hammer into plates which were soldered or riveted together and then decorated with repoussé work (ἐμπαιστική), stamping, chasing, or engraving. Vases might be hammered or cast from a mould and were often adorned with reliefs (*emblemata*) let into the body of the vessel or *crustae* soldered upon the surface. For coins molten dumps were struck

between dies (see COINAGE, GREEK). To provide colour contrast silver objects were often gilded with gold leaf (whence figure-decorated pottery at Athens and in Southern Italy?). In the Roman period, this was achieved with the help of a mercury amalgam. Niello, a black metallic sulphide used as inlay, was employed in the bronze age, and from the Hellenistic period on.

Silver was extensively used for statuettes (but rarely for larger sculpture), for temple offerings, and for the domestic *plate of wealthy Greeks and Romans. A few Greek vessels have survived in Thracian and Scythian tombs (see also ROGOZEN); many more Roman services (*ministeria*) have been preserved, examples being the Treasures of *Hildesheim in Berlin, and of *Boscoreale in Paris, both of the early empire; and the Esquiline and Mildenhall Treasures in London, of the late Empire. They include flat dishes for eating (*lances*), flat or hemispherical bowls for drinking (*calices, scyphi*), jugs (*urceoli*), saucepans (*trulli*), buckets for fruit (*situlae*), spoons (*cochlearia*), pepper-castors (*piperatoria*), etc. Cups were the special subjects of artisans of whom *Pliny (1) gives a list dating from the 4th and 3rd cents. BC; he remarks that while no names of goldsmiths have been preserved, the silversmiths (*argentarii*) are numerous. See METALLURGY; MINES.

Plin. *HN* 33. R. J. Forbes, *Studies in Ancient Technology* 8 (1971), 196–266; D. E. Strong, *Greek and Roman Gold and Silver Plate* (1966); A. Oliver Jr, *Silver for the Gods: 800 Years of Greek and Roman Silver* (1977); F. Baratte and K. Painter, *Trésors d'orfèvrerie gallo-romains* (1989); M. Vickers and D. Gill, *Artful Crafts: Ancient Greek Silverware and Pottery* (1994).　　　　　F. N. P.; J. B.; M. V.

Silvius, son of *Aeneas and Lavinia, father of Silvius Aeneas and ancestor of the Alban royal house of Silvii (Verg. *Aen.* 6. 760–7; Livy 1. 3). A legend due to the name, but unknown to Virgil, told that Lavinia, fearing the jealousy of *Ascanius, fled to the woods and there gave birth to her son (Dion. Hal. 1. 70).　　　　C. B.

Simitthus (mod. Chemtou in north-western Tunisia) lies in the fertile Bagradas valley at the crossroads of the major routes from Carthage to *Hippo Regius and from Thabraca (on the north coast) to *Sicca Veneria; but its importance derived largely from the quarries of yellow fine-grained *marble known as *giallo antico*, the *marmor Numidicum* of antiquity (Plin. *HN* 5. 2). First exploited by the Numidians (see NUMIDIA) in the 2nd cent. BC, who built a temple (possibly in memory of *Masinissa) of this material on top of one of three hills which dominate the site, Simitthus marble was first imported into Rome in 78 BC (Plin. *HN* 36. 49), and then on a greatly increased scale from Augustus onwards, who used it in his own forum (*forum Augusti) and for the colonnade of *Caesar's forum (*forum Caesaris) (Suet. *Div. Iul.* 85). It was later employed as a construction marble in scattered locations all over the empire, especially in prestige projects associated with the emperor (such as *Hadrian's gymnasium at Athens: Paus. 1. 18. 9); its smaller-scale use in marble pavements and as wall veneer was commonplace. Of the Numidian settlement at Simitthus most is known of its necropolis, with stone-built monumental tombs, including circular mausoleums, underlying the later forum. *Augustus founded a *colonia* at the site, and it continued to flourish into the 3rd cent. at least; under the Severans the forum was remodelled with a new monumental arch and basilica, and a large bath-house was added. A unique discovery near the quarries is a 2nd cent. *ergastulum* for the quarry workers, converted in the 3rd cent. into a workshop for fashioning plates, basins, and statuettes of *giallo antico* for the export market. Under the Romans the Numidian temple was replaced by one to *Saturnus; the slopes of the hill below it are carved with nearly 200 miniature votive reliefs in honour of the god. Other visible Roman monuments include an aqueduct, a theatre, an impressive bridge over the Bagradas (probably a replacement for a Trajanic one upstream of AD 112; *CIL* 8. 10117), and a well-preserved example alongside it of a flour mill, operated by water power when the river was in spate.

PECS 841; H. G. Horn, in H. G. Horn and C. B. Rüger (eds.), *Die Numider* (1979), 173–80; F. Rakob, in A. Schiavone (ed.), *Storia di Roma* 3/2 (1993), 363–6, and (ed.), *Simitthus* 1 (1993).   R. J. A. W.

Simmias (1) (or Simias) of *Thebes (1), a main character in *Plato (1)'s *Phaedo* (and in *Plutarch's *De genio Socratis*, which contains many echoes of the *Phaedo*), was evidently a veteran member of Socrates' circle. Although, with *Cebes, he was 'together with' (συγγίγνεσθαι) Philolaus in Thebes (*Phaedo* 61d–e), his Pythagorean credentials (see PYTHAGORAS (1)) are poor; Plato represents him putting forward an un-Pythagorean theory of soul (as a 'kind of harmony' of bodily constituents), and generally as a sound (Socratic) philosopher, and instigator of arguments (*Phaedrus* 242b). *Diogenes (6) Laertius gives him 23 (named) *dialogues, which, if they existed, are lost.   C. J. R.

Simmias (2) (or **Simias**) of Rhodes, scholar-poet of the early 3rd cent. BC, author of three books of lexicographical studies (*glossai*, see GLOSSA, GLOSSARY; some quotations survive in *Athenaeus (1)) and four of poetry. Remains of the latter include fragments of hexameter poems called *Apollo*, *Gorgo*, and Μῆνες (months), as well as lyric pieces and epigrams; but he is best known for his three pattern-poems (*technopaignia*), the *Wings*, the *Axe* (both in choriambic rhythm), and the *Egg*.

TEXTS Powell, *Coll. Alex.* 109–20; cf. *Suppl. Hell.* 411 f., R. Merkelbach, *Aegyptus* 1951, 257–60. For the *technopaignia*, Gow, *Bucolici Graeci* 172–7.

EDITION WITH COMM. H. Fränkel, *De Simia Rhodio* (1915).
          A. H. G.

Simon of Athens, a shoemaker, was according to a late tradition a friend of *Socrates, who used to visit him in his workshop and discuss philosophical questions with him. He plays a considerable part in the (late) *Socratic letters* (*Ep. Graec.* 609 ff.), and *Diogenes (6) Laertius (2. 122) says he was the first to write reminiscences of Socrates in *dialogue form. He is never mentioned by *Plato (1) or *Xenophon (1), but his existence has now been confirmed by the discovery of a black-glazed cup on which is scratched ΣΙΜΩΝΟΣ ('Simon's'), together with hobnails and bone rings for laced boots, on a site just outside the *agora* (see ATHENS, TOPOGRAPHY)—evidently Simon's cobbler shop.

R. F. Hock, *GRBS* 1976, 41 ff.; M. Lang, *Socrates in the Agora* (Agora picture book 17) (1978); J. M. Camp, *The Athenian Agora*, (1986), 145 ff.
          W. D. R.; S. H.

Simonides (RE 2), Greek poet, from Iulis on *Ceos; son of Leoprepes, grandson or descendant of Hylichus (Callim. frr. 64. 8; 222), uncle of *Bacchylides (Strab. 10. 5. 6). If he worked at the court of *Hipparchus (1) ([Pl.], *Hipparch.* 228c; Arist., *Ath. Pol.* 18. 1), his career began before 514 BC; his praises of Eualcidas of Eretria (fr. 518) date before 498, his *Battle of Plataea* (frr. 10–17 W²; see PLATAEA, BATTLE OF) in or after 479; he finished at the court of *Hieron (1), and his tomb was shown at *Acragas (Callim. fr. 64. 4). Tradition made him live to be 90; most sources set his birth *c.*556 (others *c.*532).

No poem of Simonides survives intact, except the epigrams attributed to him; even the *Suda*'s list of works (which should preserve the outlines of the Alexandrian edition) is garbled. But the fragments make it clear that Simonides commanded a wide variety of genres. In choral lyric, he composed *epinicians, of which he and perhaps *Ibycus are the first known practitioners; *dithyrambs, with which according to a (Hellenistic) epigram (xxvii Page) he won at least 57 competitions; *thrēnoi* (laments: see DIRGE); *paeans; encomia; Partheneia and the like (cf. Ar. *Av.* 919). His elegies, which occupied at least one book, included some sympotic pieces (see SYMPOSIUM LITERATURE), and some historical (on the battles of Artemisium (see ARTEMISIUM, BATTLE OF) and Plataea). Many *epigrams, especially epigrams relating to the *Persian Wars, were collected under Simonides' name; the epitaph for the seer Megistias (vi Page) may be genuine (cf. Hdt. 7. 228. 4). Simonides' clients included cities, individual athletes like Eualcidas and Astylus of *Croton (fr. 506), tyrants like *Anaxilas of Rhegium (fr. 515), and various Thessalian dynasts, e.g. the *Aleuadae and the Scopadae, for whom see CRANNON (Theoc. 16. 42–7). Xenocrates of *Acragas (fr. 513) and the Corinthian Oligaethidae (fr. 519A, 21+22; see CORINTH) commissioned poems from him, and also from *Pindar (*Isthm.* 2, *Pyth.* 6; *Ol.* 13). Tradition connected him with *Themistocles and *Pausanias (1); poetic enemies included *Timocreon (fr. 10 W; Arist. fr. 75).

For the next generation, Simonides belonged to the classic (old-fashioned) poets (Ar. *Nub.* 1355; Eup. fr. 148 KA). He had the reputation of a money-grubber (Xenoph. fr. 21 W; Ar. *Pax* 698 f.), and at some stage *Pindar's attack on the 'Muse for hire' was applied to him (*Isthm.* 2. 6, Callim. fr. 222). He acquired also the reputation of a sage, like Bias and *Pittacus (Pl. *Resp.* 335e; see SEVEN SAGES); various apophthegms were ascribed to him, mostly cynical; the saying 'painting is silent poetry and poetry painting that speaks' (Plut., *Mor.* 346f) forms the starting point of Lessing's *Laokoon*. He was credited further with discovering the third note of the lyre; the long and double letters; and the art of memory (Callim. fr. 64; *Suda*).

What little remains of Simonides shows a professional poet of great scope and range, much in demand over his long life, spanning the tyrants and the new democracy (see DEMOCRACY, ATHENIAN). Ancient critics admired him for simple pathos (Quint. *Inst.* 10. 1. 64), and that appears in noble verses for the dead of Thermopylae (fr. 531; see THERMOPYLAE, BATTLE OF). But the tragic threnody of Danaë (fr. 543), and the devious gnomic textures of *To Scopas* (fr. 542), show other talents; in the elegies, lush eroticism (frr. 21–2 W²) contrasts with the pocket epic *Plataea*, whose form (a hymn to *Achilles introducing a narrative of the campaign) enforces the parallel between the Trojan and *Persian Wars, and between *Homer and Simonides.

Testimonia and fragments: D. A. Campbell, *Greek Lyric* 3 (Loeb, 1991); elegies: M. L. West, *IE* 2² (1992); epigrams: D. L. Page, *Further Greek Epigrams* (1981); J. H. Molyneux, *Simonides* (1992); P. J. Parsons, *Ox. Pap.* 59 (1992), 4 ff.; M. L. West, *ZPE* 98 (1993), 1 ff.   P. J. P.

Simplicius, 6th-cent. AD Neoplatonist (see NEOPLATONISM) and one of seven philosophers who left Athens for *Ctesiphon after *Justinian closed the Athenian Neoplatonist school in 529. He probably wrote all his commentaries after 532, when it was safe for the philosophers to leave Ctesiphon. Recent evidence suggests that he may have settled at Ḥarrân (ancient *Carrhae) in present-day Turkey from where Platonism was brought back in the 9th cent. to Baghdad. Simplicius was taught by *Ammonius (2) in Alexandria and by Damascius, head of the Athenian school. He wrote commentaries, all extant, on *Aristotle's *De caelo*, *Physics*, and *Categories* (in that order), and on Epictetus' *Manual*, among other works. A commentary on Aristotle's *De anima* is of disputed authorship. His are the fullest of all Aristotle comment-aries, recording debates on Aristotle from the preceding 850 years, and embedding many fragments from the entire millen-nium. At the same time, Simplicius gave his own views on many topics, including place, time, and matter. His commentaries express the revulsion of a devout Neoplatonist for Christianity and for its arch philosophical defender, *Philoponus.

Commentaria in Aristotelem Graeca 7–11 (1882–1907), partly trans. in R. Sorabji (ed.), *The Ancient Commentators on Aristotle*, (1987–); *In Ench. Epict.*, ed. Dübner (1840), trans. G. Stanhope (1694). I. Hadot (ed.), *Simplicius, sa vie, son œuvre, sa survie* (1987); M. Tardieu, *Coutumes mésopotamiennes* (1991); *RE* 3 A 1 (1927).　　　　　　R. R. K. S.

Simylus (1) author of (? Hellenistic) didactic iambics (*Suppl. Hell.* 726–8). Probably to be distinguished from (2), a comic poet competing in 284 BC (Kassel–Austin, *PCG* 7. 591–2). (3) Author of a Greek elegy (presumably no earlier than 2nd cent. BC) claim-ing that it was to the Gauls, not the Sabines (*Sabini) that *Tarpeia betrayed the *Capitol for love (Plut. *Rom* 17; *Suppl. Hell.* 724).

E. Diehl, *RE* 3 A 216–7; A. Momigliano, *Quarto contributo* (1969), 482–3.　　　　　　A. D. E. C.

sin The modern term has no equivalent in either Greek or Latin. The Christian concept of sin accommodates two basic and coherent senses: offence against moral codes, and action against the laws or the will of God. It presupposes conscious voluntari-ness, while remorse may be associated with its consequences, interpreted as an expression of estrangement from God. Although some of these characteristics can be found in the archaic and classical religions of Greece and Rome, as a whole this complex is not clearly represented. Various aspects are denoted by different terms such as Greek *adikia* (wrongdoing, injustice), *anomia* (lawless conduct), *hamartia, hamartēma* (failure, fault, error), or Latin *vitium* (fault, blemish), *scelus* (evil deed, crime), *peccatum* (fault, error), etc. The term *syneidēsis* (Lat. *conscientia*), originally 'awareness, consciousness', developed the sense 'consciousness of right and wrong, conscience' (adopted by early Christianity) only in the Hellenistic and more especially imperial period. The Greek term *hamartia* approximates most closely (but cannot be identified with) our concept 'sin' and was adopted in the *Septuagint and early Christian scriptures for rendering and developing the biblical concept of sin (cf. Lat. *peccare, peccatum*, etc.).

Three of the most remarkable ancient characteristics as opposed to modern ones, are:

1. In the earlier period voluntary and involuntary offences against moral or divine laws were both equally reprehensible and hence liable to divine vengeance. Evil intention is not necessarily implied in the ancient definition of wrongdoing. The Greek concept of *atē* (delusion, infatuation, through which 'the evil appears good' Soph. *Ant.* 622), which in the early period was often held responsible for human error, was either understood as divinely inspired—thus providing an escape from the problem of human responsibility, though *not* from divine punishment—or as rooted in personal (and condemnable) rashness, being a corollary of *hubris.

2. Closely related is the ancient belief that as far as effects are concerned no clear distinction can be drawn between offences against ethical, legal, and social prescriptions on the one hand and violation of ritual rules on the other.

3. Accordingly, it is often impossible to draw a sharp line between the state of impurity (see PURIFICATION) as result of a ritual fault and the state of moral blemish. Murder is a case in point. The

earliest phases of (Greek and Roman) civilization did privilege an emphasis on the ritual aspects, and through the ages a gradual development can be perceived toward a more personally felt ethical experience of guilt. That said, even in our earliest source, Homer, there are unmistakable traces of ethical codes warranted by the gods.

Greece In Homer it was especially *Zeus who had the domain of guarding the laws of hospitality in the house and the court and of protecting strangers and suppliants. What happened on the other side of the boundary did not affect him, except in cases of either ritual offence or personal acts of *hubris* defying his honour. *Dikē (man's duty to his fellows) is not synonymous with *themis* (man's duty according to divine institution). But the two may coincide, e.g. in the sin of *hubris* or disregard of the right of others (both mortals and gods). However, Hesiod pictures *dikē* as Zeus's central responsibility, even making Dikē the daughter of Zeus. He also presents an interesting mixture of ethical and ritual aspects. In his view, divine vengeance will equally follow both transgression of a certain branch of moral offences, such as ill-treatment of orphans or one's own parents (*Op.* 330 ff.), and purely ritual offences such as omitting to wash one's hands before pouring libation (*Op.* 724). In fact the core of his poem is an appeal to the justice of Zeus: whoever offends human or divine laws will encounter divine anger.

Divine punishment
Early Greece made impressive attempts to bracket together two eternal problems: that of the cause of illness and disaster and that of *theodicy, the question of the justice of the gods. In the expression 'By day and night diseases of themselves come upon man, and do him harm silently, for cunning Zeus took out their voice' (Hes. *Op.* 102–4), Zeus can be seen as a designation of blind fate or fortune, making man a plaything of an arbitrary and unfathomable divine power. Otherwise illness is a penalty for evil acts, sent by Zeus in his quality of divine judge. Both options were eagerly exploited, the first being a typical expression of so-called 'archaic pessimism', so characteristic of much *lyric poetry (Greek), the latter providing an explanation that permits control, in cases of sudden unaccountable illness, more especially of epi-demics (see DISEASE). These disasters were often seen as caused by the sin of one person (Hes. *Op.* 238 ff., 260 f.), even by a sin unwittingly committed: 'Not willingly am I detained, but I must have sinned (*alitesthai*: the Homeric term for offending a god) against the deathless gods', says *Odysseus (Hom. *Od.* 4. 377 f.). An oracle then might be consulted as to the nature of the unknown sin and the manner of its expiation.

The interpretation of illness as the punishment of sin cannot but raise another question of theodicy: what if patent sinners do *not* fall ill? 'How, O son of Cronus, does your mind manage to award the same portion to evil-doers and just men?' (Hes. *Theog.* 373–8, cf. 1110–11). By way of solution, Archaic literature offers three variations on the theme of temporary postponement: evil-doers will be punished but not always immediately (*Op.* 218 ff., 333; *Theog.* 201 ff.), or the penalty will strike a later generation (*Op.* 284 f.; Solon, fr. 36. 3 West). Combinations occur (Hom. *Il.* 4. 160 ff.; *Theog.* 203 ff.). Although these solutions share the belief that the sinner literally must 'pay' ($\alpha\pi o)\tau\iota\nu\omega$ (the common word for being punished), it is obvious that no uniform and consistent doctrine can be vindicated for archaic and classical Greece. Various options concerning sin and retaliation coexisted, some-times in the mind of one person. This is particularly marked in the third variant: the idea of retaliation in the afterlife and the netherworld.

Punishment in the hereafter

As early as in Homer three different conceptions are faintly discernible: (1) the netherworld as a cheerless and gloomy place where all souls assemble, without any connotation of retaliation or reward; (2) the *Islands of the Blessed, reserved for the (heroic) happy few, likewise without clear references to any ordeal; and (3) a place where the divine judges *Aeacus, *Minos, and *Rhadamanthys judge the dead. However, with one exception (Hom. *Il.* 3. 278 ff.: general punishment of perjury in the netherworld), the only condemned persons mentioned, *Orion, *Tityus, *Tantalus, and *Sisyphus (Hom. *Od.* 11. 576–600, perhaps a later interpolation) are sentenced not for 'normal' moral offences, but as a result of their defying the gods. Their offence is an act of *hubris* against the honour of the Homeric gods.

Remarkably enough the early doctrine of the Eleusinian mysteries (see ELEUSIS), as represented in the *Homeric Hymn to Demeter* (*c*.700 BC), though promising the initiated a blissful stay in the underworld, did not require any proof of good behaviour; from a later period we learn that in this respect there was only one requirement: not to have impure hands tainted with blood. On the other hand, we hear that the Samothracian mysteries (see CABIRI) required a confession of sins as a preliminary to the initiation: nothing more was apparently needed, the confession being an expiation of the state of sinfulness and impurity.

Most probably it was the Orphic movement (see ORPHISM) that helped two different solutions to develop: the first was the construction of something that can be called 'hell', with penalties through eternal suffering in mud, etc. Basically different, and no doubt inspired by influences from Pythagoreanism (see PYTHAGORAS (1)), was the idea that evil is a corollary of bodily existence, the body being the prison for the *soul, which is thus punished for sins in previous lives. If these sins are not expiated during one incarnation, the soul transmigrates to another body (see TRANSMIGRATION). Thus, this doctrine of reincarnation provided an elegant solution to the dilemma of divine justice and human suffering. Moreover, it opened an avenue to personal responsibility and an escape from the ritualist group solidarity which involved vicarious suffering for another's fault. Overall, however, the idea of punishment in the afterlife never attained the refinement and popularity that it later enjoyed in Christianity.

Classical developments

The 5th and 4th cents. BC reflected and expanded on earlier archaic initiatives. We can only indicate superficially the most important tendencies. Fifth-cent. Greek *tragedy problematized all existing ideas on sin, retaliation, and theodicy. *Aeschylus (esp. in his *Oresteia*), fascinated by the idea of hereditary curses, tested ways in which a descendant from a doomed house could escape his fate. *Sophocles (1) explored both the question of guiltless guilt (*OT*) and the tensions between human and divine law (*Ant.*). *Euripides added a theological critique: gods who make unfair demands cannot be gods. Like other thinkers under the influence of the ideas of the *sophists, he demonstrated that gods and ethics are often very difficult to reconcile. In the late 5th cent. this could (but in only a few scattered instances actually did) lead to atheistic expressions (*Diagoras). In this same period the debate about the distinction between the laws of man and those of the gods begins (for instance Xen. *Mem.* 4. 4). It is argued that the unwritten laws are in the hands of the gods and carry their own unavoidable punishment, whereas penalties resulting from violation of human law are avoidable. Others argued that the

gods were the invention of a clever politician in order to bind people to laws which could not otherwise be enforced (most emphatically in the satyr play *Sisyphos* (see SATYRIC DRAMA) by Euripides or *Critias; also in Arist. *Metaph.* 1074^{b}1–8; Isoc. *Bus.* 25).

From the 4th cent. onwards the major philosophical schools inherited from *Plato (1)'s *Socrates the basic conviction that 'no one sins willingly', wrongdoing being regarded as an error of judgement. *Stoicism especially puts the emphasis on individual autonomy within a human communion whose cement is the divine principle of Reason (*logos*) which permeates the whole. Here universal laws are identical with divine laws, human life being a divine service. Sin is error, the violation of cosmic laws.

Confession of sins

A wrongdoer was either punished by the law or by the gods (or not at all), but (public) confession of sins was not in vogue in Greek culture. The earliest hints of something of this kind (apart from recognition of *hamartia* in tragedy) can be found in the 4th-cent. *iamata* of *Epidaurus: cure-inscriptions detailing the healing miracles of *Asclepius (see MEDICINE, § (2); INCUBATION). In the same period curse tablets (see CURSES) develop a special variant: the prayer to the gods for (judicial) help in cases of theft, black magic, slander, etc., where sometimes the wish is added that the culprit should publicly confess his misdeed. The same idea takes pride of place in the so-called confession inscriptions from Maeonia (Lydia and the bordering area of Phrygia, 2nd and 3rd cents. AD), where we read accounts of private offences resulting in punishment by the god, redressal of the crime or a sacrifice of atonement, and public confession, followed by praise of the power of the god. The influence, either of indigenous Anatolian traditions or of *oriental cults is probable, as the sin- and guilt-culture of, for instance, the cult of *Atargatis, including sackcloth and ashes, seems to be related.

Rome For early Rome a similar state of things can be detected to that of early Greece. Legends abound about the grave consequences resulting from wholly accidental *vitia* in ritual matters. In the Roman *ius divinum* ('divine law'), as in the secular law, a casual slip in a ceremonial action or utterance might entail dire consequences comparable to those assigned to arrogant neglect of the deity. One of the earliest attestations of a movement towards more enlightened views can be found in the *Twelve Tables: they make provision for lenient treatment of a merely accidental homicide (Cicero, *Top.* 64). In Rome no independent reflection on the nature and origin of evil or disaster developed; but from the 2nd cent. BC onwards *Stoicism (see above) deeply influenced Roman thought in the field of (social) ethics. See also CHRISTIANITY; PUNISHMENT, GREEK THEORIES ABOUT.

K. Latte, *ARW* 1920/21, 254 ff. = *Kleine Schriften* (1968), 3–35; K. Latte, *Heiliges Recht: Untersuchungen zur Geschichte der sakralen Rechtsformen in Griechenland* (1920); R. Pettazzoni, *La confessione dei peccati*, part 2, vol. 3 (1936); E. R. Dodds, *The Greeks and the Irrational* (1951); A. E. Wilhelm-Hooijberg, *Peccatum: Sin and Guilt in Ancient Rome* (1954); E. R. Dodds, *Pagan and Christian in an Age of Anxiety* (1965); P. W. Schönlein, *Rh. Mus.* 1969, 289–305; H. Lloyd-Jones, *The Justice of Zeus* (1971); K. J. Dover, *Greek Popular Morality in the Time of Plato and Aristotle* (1974); F. Graf, *Eleusis und die orphische Dichtung Athens in vorhellenistischer Zeit* (1974); H. Chadwick, *RAC* 10 (1978), 1025–1107; W. Speyer, *RAC* 11 (1981), 996–1043; R. C. T. Parker, *Miasma: Pollution and Purification in Early Greek Religion* (1983); K. van der Toorn, *Sin and Sanction in Israel and Mesopotamia: A Comparative Study* (1985); H. S. Versnel, in C. Faraone and D. Obbink (eds.), *Magika Hiera: Ancient Greek Magic and Religion* (1991), 60–106; G. Thome, *Ant. Class.* 1992, 73–98, and *Vorstellungen vom Bösen in der lateinischen Literatur* (1993). H. S. V.

Sindus

Sindus archaeologically important (late Archaic and Classical) cemetery site near Thessaloniki (ancient *Thessalonica) in north Greece. The settlement was basically Thracian (see THRACE) but there is also Greek and Persian influence. The finds are in Thessaloniki Museum.

> Hdt. 7. 123. J. Boardman, *The Diffusion of Classical Art in Antiquity* (1995), 184, giving refs. at 338 n. 3.   S. H.

Singara, a city in northern Mesopotamia situated on the southern slope of the range of the same name (mod. Jebel Sinjar). Captured by *Trajan in AD 114 and again in *Verus' campaign, it became part of the Roman eastern *limes defences and was an important military base in the frontier province created by *Septimius Severus (garrison of the Legio I Parthica; see LEGION). Under M. *Aurelius Severus Alexander it became a *colonia, but it was captured by the *Sasanid king Sapor II in 360 and in 363 was ceded to the Persians by *Jovian. The Romans made skilful use of the Singara hills in the organization of their Mesopotamian *limes. Singara's importance in this was due to its position on the central Mesopotamian trade route that came into being in the Parthian period (see HATRA).

> M. P. Speidel and J. Reynolds, *Epigraphica Anatolica* 1985, 31 ff.; M. H. Dodgeon and S. N. C. Lieu (eds.), *The Roman Eastern Frontier and the Persian Wars AD 226–363* (1991); J.-M. Fiey, *Nisibe* (1977), 269 ff.
>   E. W. G.; J. Wi.

Sinis, a son of *Poseidon who waylaid travellers at the Isthmus of *Corinth and was killed by *Theseus on his way from *Troezen to Athens (Bacchyl. 18. 19–22 and many later writers). He was called Pityocamptes (pine-bender), either because he made his victims hold down a bent pine tree which sprang back and flung them through the air or because he tied them between two bent pine trees which tore them apart.   A. L. B.

Sinnius (*RE* 2) **Capito,** a younger contemporary of *Varro whose scholarly writings—a treatise on syllables, *Epistulae* (with grammatical discussions), and antiquarian works—were used by *Verrius Flaccus, *Gellius, and others.

> Funaioli, *Gramm. Rom. Frag.* 457–66. Herzog–Schmidt, § 283.
>   R. A. K.

Sinon, character in literature and mythology, a Greek who claimed falsely to have deserted from the Greek forces at *Troy and who inveigled the Trojans into taking the Trojan Horse inside the walls of Troy; he then later released the Greek heroes from the Horse and joined them in sacking the city. This story is related by *Virgil in the *Aeneid* (2. 57–194), but was treated earlier in the cyclic *Parva Ilias* and *Iliu Persis* (Ar. Rh. 1459^b7, Proclus, *Chrest.*; see EPIC CYCLE) and in the *Sinon* of *Sophocles (1) (frs. 542–4 Radt); it is found in a number of later texts.

> C. Deroux, *Enc. Virg.*, 'Sinone'; *LIMC* 7.1 (1994), 777–8.   S. J. Ha.

Sinope, a town situated almost at the midpoint of the south shore of the *Euxine on an easily defended peninsula with two good harbours about its base, and near the place where the crossing to the Crimea (see CHERSONESUS (2)) is shortest. The promontory is well watered and fertile (*Strabo speaks of market-gardens), the tunny catch was famous, and the mountains noted for their *timber woods. Founded by *Miletus probably in the late-7th cent. (traditionally founded before 756 BC, destroyed by the *Cimmerians and refounded before 600), it early commanded the maritime trade of much of both coasts of the Pontic region (see PONTUS) and established many colonies along the coast, some of which were tributary to it in *Xenophon (1)'s

time. In spite of mountain barriers it drew trade from the interior, notably in Sinopic earth (cinnabar). About 437 it was freed from a tyrant by *Pericles (1) and received Athenian settlers (Plut. *Per.* 20). It was attacked and occupied briefly by the Persian satrap *Datames (*c.*375). The town probably maintained its freedom under *Alexander (3) the Great and his immediate successors, and with the assistance of *Rhodes repulsed Mithradates III of Pontus in 220, but was finally occupied by *Pharnaces (1) I in 183 and soon became the Pontic capital. In the Third Mithradatic War (see MITHRADATES VI) it was captured and constituted a free town by L. *Licinius Lucullus (2). It was occupied and suffered severely at the hands of *Pharnaces (1) II, but *Caesar repaired its losses by settling a Roman colony (see COLONIZATION, ROMAN) with the title of Colonia Iulia Felix Sinope. In the 3rd cent. AD it possessed *ius Italicum. An abundant coinage attests its prosperity both in the early and the imperial periods, and the appearance of men of Sinope all about the Euxine, at Athens, and at Rhodes, as well as widely distributed *amphora stamps, attests the commercial connections of the city. Its vigorous *Hellenism is shown by the names of *Diogenes (2) the Cynic, *Diphilus the comic poet, and other men of letters. Strabo describes it as a city with fine buildings, market-place, porticoes, *gymnasium, and fortifications.

> Strabo 12. 545. D. M. Robinson, *Ancient Sinope* (1906); C. Roebuck, *Ionian Trade and Colonization* (1959), 117 ff., and index; Magie, *Rom. Rule Asia Min.* 183 ff., and index; E. Akurgal, *PECS* 842 (archaeology); *CAH* 6^2 (1994), 221 (S. Hornblower); 489–500 (J. Hind).
>   T. R. S. B.; S. M.

Sinuri, sanctuary of, in *Caria, south of *Mylasa, patronized by the 4th-cent. BC Hecatomnid satraps *Hecatomnus, *Idrieus, and *Ada. Sinuri was an indigenous god, who gave his name to the sanctuary, but the many inscriptions are in Greek. Most, apart from the Hecatomnid material, are of the 2nd or 1st cent. BC, but no. 12 mentions the *Seleucid Antiochus (III? see J. and L. Robert, *Fouilles d'Amyzon* (1983), 187).

> *Le Sanctuaire de Sinuri près de Mylasa*, vol. 1 (inscriptions) by L. Robert (1945); vol. 2 (architecture and pottery) by P. Devambez and E. Haspels (1959); S. Hornblower, *Mausolus* (1982), see index.   S. H.

Siphnos, a mountainous island (74 km.^2) in the south-western *Cyclades, noted for its mineral resources. *Silver and *lead were mined at Agios Sostis in the early bronze age. At the end of the late bronze age a fortified acropolis existed at Agios Andreas, reoccupied *c.*900 BC when Siphnos was settled by *Ionians. By *c.*700 BC the ancient city (modern Kastro) on the east coast had become the prime settlement. During the 6th cent. Siphnos prospered from its silver and gold *mines, the proceeds being distributed among the citizen-body and used to construct public buildings of Parian *marble (see PAROS) and the famous treasury at *Delphi (*c.*535 BC) from the tithe paid to *Apollo. Samian exiles plundered the island and seized 100 talents of silver *c.*525 BC. Siphnos contributed one *pentecontor* (see SHIPS) to the Greek fleet in the *Persian Wars. Under the Athenian empire (see DELIAN LEAGUE) its tribute was three talents, a relatively high sum. From the 4th cent. Siphnos became synonymous with small-state insignificance. Exhaustion of the richest seams probably led to its decline, which *Pausanias (3) mistakenly attributed to flooding of the mines. Towers (55 known) occur throughout the island, built between the 6th cent. and the Hellenistic period, the earlier to defend the mines, the later to protect rural property.

> *RE* 3 A (1929), 263–8, 'Siphnos' 1–2; *PECS* 842; *IG* 12 (5); *BSA* 1949, 1 ff.; *ΠΑΕ* 1975–80; G. A. Wagner and G. Weisgerber, *Silber, Blei und Gold*

auf *Sifnos* (1985); G. Daux and E. Hansen, *Le Trésor de Siphnos* (1987); N. G. Ashton, *Siphnos: Ancient Towers B.C.* (1991). R. W. V. C.

Sipontum (mod. Siponto), in Italy, the port of *Arpi. Its legendary founder was *Diomedes (2) (Strabo 6. 3. 9), but its origins were *Daunian, not Greek. Its strategic position made it a magnet for the Greek condottieri employed by *Tarentum in the 4th cent. BC, and it was occupied by the Molossian *Alexander (6) I in 338. It became a Roman colony in 194, with a second deduction (instalment of colonists) in 186/5. The city walls date to this period. Little is known of its later history, but it may have retained its commercial importance until the 13th cent., when bradyseism and malaria caused its abandonment.

M. Marin, *Topografia storica del Daunia antica* (1970). K. L.

Sippar, (mod. Abu Habba), *c*.28 km. south-west of Baghdad, source of thousands of *cuneiform tablets dating *c*.2000–1600 BC and from the 7th to the early 5th cents. BC. The temple (Ebabbar) of the sun-god (Shamash) was partially explored by H. Rassam (1881–2); Belgian excavations (1970s) show that Sippar was inhabited until the 2nd cent. AD; late Parthian/Sasanian graves (see PARTHIA; SASANIDS) were found at nearby Tell ed-Der. In the 1980s, the Iraqis uncovered a large library of literary texts dating into the first millennium BC. Sippar's identity with *Pliny (1) the Elder's 'Hipparenum' (*HN* 6. 123) is disputed.

EXCAVATION H. Rassam, *Asshur and the Land of Nimrod* (1897); L. de Meyer (ed.), *Tell ed-Der* 2 (1978), 109–19, *Tell ed-Der* 3 (1980), 37–52, 53–79, 93–114; *Iraq* 1987, 248–9.

TEXTS E. Leichty and others, *Catalogue of the Babylonian Tablets in the British Museum*, vols. 7–8: *Tablets from Sippar* 1–3 (1986–8).

HELLENISTIC PERIOD J. Oelsner, *Materialien zur babylonischen Gesellschaft und Kultur in hellenistischer Zeit* (1986), 129–131; R. J. van der Spek, in M. de Jong Ellis and others (eds.), *Nippur at the Centennial* (1992), 235–60. A. T. L. K.

Sirens, enchantresses who live on an island near *Scylla and *Charybdis in *Homer's *Odyssey* (12. 39–54, 158–200). Sailors charmed by their song land and perish; their meadow is full of mouldering corpses. They attempt to lure *Odysseus by claiming omniscience, but on *Circe's advice he has himself bound to the mast and stops his comrades' ears with wax. Likewise *Orpheus saves the *Argonauts by overpowering their song with his lyre (Ap. Rhod. *Argon.* 4. 891–919). In some versions they die or commit suicide if a mortal can resist them (Lycophron, *Alex.* 712 ff., Hyg. *Fab.* 141). The escape of Odysseus or of Orpheus leads to their death, as does their defeat in a singing contest with the *Muses. They also have power to calm the winds (*Od.* 12. 168 f.; Hes. fr. 28 M–W).

In Homer there are two Sirens (*Od.* 12. 52, 167), later often three, whose names vary. They are the daughters of *Phorcys (S. fr. 861 Radt), of Earth, *Gaia (E. *Hel.* 168), of *Acheloüs and Sterope (Apollod. 1. 7. 10, etc.), or of one of the Muses (Ap. Rhod. *Argon.* 4. 895 f.; *Lycophron (2(*b*)), *Alex.* 713; Apollod. 1. 3. 4, etc.). They are often associated with death in both literature and art. They are companions of *Persephone at her rape, and in their search for her are turned to birds with girls' faces (Ap. Rhod. *Argon.* 4. 896–8, Ov. *Met.* 5. 552–63), or are punished with bird form for their failure to guard her (Hyg. *Fab.* 141). *Alcman equates Muse with Siren (*PMG* 30), and *Plato (1) has eight celestial Sirens producing the harmony of the spheres (*Rep.* 617b), a Pythagorean idea (Iamblichus, *Vita Pythagorae* 82 = DK 58C4; see PYTHAGORAS (1)). They were located or received cults in various parts of Sicily or southern Italy, especially Naples (*Neapolis), *Surrentum, and Tereina in Bruttium (see BRUTTII).

In art they are usually represented as birds with women's heads, though some of the earliest examples are bearded. They are often shown crowning tombs, and also with musical instruments or in musical contexts. A frequent type from the 8th cent. BC onwards is the Siren as attachment to a bronze cauldron. They are common on vases from 600 BC, especially in scenes with Odysseus, and their suicide is already implied on some 6th-cent. BC examples. They also appear with *Dionysus and the *satyrs. Early Sirens have claws like vultures or eagles, but in Classical and Hellenistic art they become beautiful, melancholy creatures, representative of music almost as much as the Muses.

The Sirens were allegorized by both classical and Christian writers as representing the lusts of the flesh, the insatiable desire for knowledge, the dangers of flattery, or as celestial music drawing souls upwards to heaven. Odysseus bound to the mast even came to be seen as an allegory of Christ on the cross.

GENERAL Zwicker, *RE* 3 A, 288–308; E. Buschor, *Die Musen des Jenseits* (1944); J. R. T. Pollard, *CR* 1952, 60–3, and *Seers, Shrines and Sirens* (1965), 137–45; G. K. Gresseth, *TAPA* 1970, 203–18.

ART G. Weicker in Roscher, *Lex.* 4. 601–39; E. Kunze, *MDAI(A)* 1932, 124–41; *LIMC* 6.1 (1992), 962 ff.

ALLEGORY F. Buffière, *Les Mythes d'Homère et la pensée grecque* (1956), 236 f., 380–6, 418, 467–81; H. Rahner, *Greek Myths and Christian Mystery* (1963), 328–86 (= *Griechische Mythen in christlicher Deutung*³ (1966, 281–328); E. Kaiser, *MH* 1964, 109–36. N. J. R.

Siris (mod. Nova Siri), in S. Italy, 7th-cent. colony (Achaean or Ionian), on the river Sinni. It controlled good agricultural land, attaining great wealth, but was destroyed by *Sybaris, *Croton, and *Metapontum, *c*.550–530 BC. Coins issued *c*.530 with the legend 'Sirinos' may refer to an unknown city, not to Siris. The site is partly occupied by the later colony of *Heraclea (1), but there are extensive remains of Siris.

D. Adamesteanu (ed.), *Siris-Poleion* (1986). K. L.

Sirmium, a strategically located city on the Sava in *Pannonia (Inferior), was probably originally the *oppidum of the Amantini (Plin. *HN* 3. 148). It was occupied by the Romans probably during the Pannonian War of 12–9 BC, and became an important Roman military base in the 1st cent. AD (Cass. Dio 55. 29). A colony was established there under *Vespasian. In the later empire it was often the residence of emperors and high officials, due largely to its importance as a road-junction in the Danube area. It possessed an imperial arms factory (Not. Dign. [occ.] 9. 18), was a fleet station (ibid. 32, 50), and the site of an imperial mint which flourished 320–6, 351–65 (gold, silver, and copper) and 379 and possibly 394–6 (gold only). Large numbers of laws were issued at Sirmium from *Diocletian onwards.

V. Popović (ed.), *Sirmium* 1 (1971). On the coinage cf. Mattingly–Sydenham, *RIC* 7. 462; 9. 156 f.; R. A. G. Carson and others, *Late Roman Bronze Coinage, 324–498* (1960), 76. J. J. W.

Sirtica, semi-arid coastal area along the shore of the Greater Syrtis (Gulf of Sidra), home of Gaetuli, Marmaridae, and the Nasamones who were 'forbidden to exist' by the emperor *Domitian (Cass. Dio, 67. 4. 6), raiders of the Roman provinces of Africa and Cyrenaica (see AFRICA, ROMAN; PENTAPOLIS); crossed by tracks leading southwards, which perhaps, as in medieval times, carried central African goods. It was divided at Arae Philaenorum (Ras el Aali), originally the boundary of Carthaginian and Cyrenean zones of influence, then of the Roman provinces of Africa (later *Tripolitania) and Cyrenaica. Ancient accounts stress its dangers (cf. the monster *Lamia; modern archaeological surveys reveal some cultivation, mainly in the wadis, at least under the Romans and up to the mid-3rd cent. AD. Greek mariners' guides (see PERIPLOI) and Roman itineraries record coastal settlements, some with immigrant populations, e.g. Jewish. After the Gaetulian and Marmaric wars in *Augustus' reign, a line of small Roman forts protected the approaches to Cyrenaica, while army patrols and, from the Severan period, a fort at Bu Ngem, guarded Tripolitania; both systems broke down in later antiquity. See CYRENE; LIMES; NOMADS.

RE 4 A (1932), 1796 f.; R. G. Goodchild, *Tabula Imperii Romani*, sheets H. 1. 33 Lepcis Magna, and H. 1. 34 Cyrene (1954), and *Libyan Studies* (his selected papers, ed. J. Reynolds, 1976), 133–209; J. Desanges, *Catalogue des tribus africaines de l'antiquité classique* (1962), and in *Mélanges Renard* (1969), 197–213; R. Rebuffat, *Libya Antiqua* 1969–70, 181–7, and *Studi Magrebini* 3 1990, 1–20; M. Reddé, *Prospections des vallées du nord de la Libye (1979–80): la région de Syrte à l'époque romaine* (1988); G. W. W. Barker and G. D. B. Jones, Unesco Libyan Valleys Survey 6, in *Libyan Studies* 1984, 1 f.; A. Laronde, *Cyrène et la Libye hellénistique* (1987), ch. 9. J. M. R.

Siscia, called also **Segesta** (from the island between the rivers Savus and Colapis in which it stood, Plin. *HN* 3. 148, cf. App. *Ill.* 10. 22 f.), was a city in *Pannonia (Superior). Probably taken by Roman commanders in 119 BC (App. *Ill.* 10), it was captured by Octavian (see AUGUSTUS) in 35 BC and a garrison established there. During the early 1st cent. AD it may have been the station of Legio IX Hispana (see LEGION). Under *Vespasian a colony was settled there with fleet *veterans, which later acquired the title Septimia from *Septimius Severus. Siscia functioned as an imperial mint (c. AD 260–385). Its natural strength was increased by the construction of a canal across the confluence of the rivers under *Tiberius (Cass. Dio 49. 37. 3), and it served both as a fleet station (Not. Dign. [occ.] 32. 56) and probably a customs post (*CIL* 3. 10821, 13408).

J. Šašel, *RE* Suppl. 14 (1974), 'Siscia'. J. J. W.

Sisenna See CORNELIUS SISENNA, L.

Sisyphus, son of *Aeolus (1), and king and founder of *Corinth, of legendary cunning, a trickster who cheated death, and one of the sinners punished in *Hades in Hom. *Od.* 11. 593–600: he is pushing a large boulder up a hill, and it keeps rolling back, and he has to start again. One way he cheated death was by persuading the underworld deities to let him return to the upper world for some reason and then not returning below. In one version (cf. esp. Pherecydes, *FGrH* 3 F 119) *Zeus sent *Thanatos to him as punishment for revealing to Asopus that Zeus had abducted his daughter, but Sisyphus bound up Thanatos so that no one could die, until *Ares freed Thanatos and handed Sisyphus over to him. But before he died he instructed his wife not to give him the proper funerary rites and then persuaded Hades to allow him to return to complain; when in the upper world he refused to return and died in old age. (Cf. also esp. Alc. fr. 38a. 5 ff.; Theog. 1. 701–12; Schol. *Od.* 11. 593; Apollod. 1. 9. 3; Paus. 2. 5. 1; Schol. Pind. *Ol.* 1. 97.)

In one version, he founded the *Isthmian Games in honour of Palaemon/*Melicertes (cf. e.g. Pind. fr. 5; Paus. 2. 1. 3). In some post-Homeric versions he is *Odysseus' real father (cf. e.g. Soph. *Phil.* 417 and schol.). He stopped *Autolycus (1) from stealing his cattle by attaching to their hooves lead tablets on which was inscribed 'Autolycus stole them', and thus tracking them (Polyaenus, *Strat.* 6. 52).

A. C. Pearson, *The Fragments of Sophocles* (1917), 2. 184–5; P. Zancani Montuoro, *AttiSocMGr* 1964, 60–70; E. Simon, *JDAI* 1967, 275–9; C. Sourvinou-Inwood, *BICS* 1986, 37–58; E. Pellizer, *La pripezia dell'eletto*

(1991), 124–43; E. R. Gebhard, in W. Coulson and H. Kyrieleis (eds.), *Proceedings of an International Symposium on the Olympic Games* (1992), 73–5; *LIMC* 7.1 (1994) 781–7. C. S.-I.

Sitalces, son of Teres, king of the Odrysae of *Thrace. Sitalces continued the policy of his father, and under him the Odrysian kingdom took shape, until it covered a larger area than the whole of central Greece, extending from the Danube on the north to the Aegean on the south, and the Euxine on the east, a kingdom more powerful and better equipped than the Macedonian. In 431 BC through the agency of Nymphodorus of Abdera, Athenian *proxenos in Thrace, whose sister was married to Sitalces, the Athenians approached Sitalces to obtain his help in controlling *Perdiccas (2) of Macedon and the towns of Thrace (Thuc. 2. 29). In the following year (430) the Spartans tried in vain (Thuc. 2. 67) to persuade Sitalces to abandon his alliance with Athens and to send an army to relieve *Potidaea, which was being besieged by the Athenians. In 429 BC Sitalces marched against Perdiccas and the Chalcidians, taking with him Amyntas, son of Philip, brother of Perdiccas, whom he intended to put on the throne of Macedonia. Sitalces overran *Chalcidice and Bottiaea, but, after a campaign of thirty days, he returned to his own country having achieved nothing. In taking this action he seems to have acted on the advice of his nephew, Seuthes, who later married Perdiccas' daughter, Stratonice. In 424 Sitalces organized an expedition against the Triballi, which ended in disaster and his death (Thuc. 4. 101).

Thuc. 2. 29, 95–101 with Hornblower, *Comm. on Thuc.* 1. A. Hoeck, 'Das Odrysenreich in Thrakien', *Hermes*, 1891, 76 ff.; S. Casson, *Macedonia, Thrace and Illyria* (1926); B. Isaac, *The Greek Settlements in Thrace* (1986), 99 ff.; E. Badian, *From Plataea to Potidaea* (1993), ch. 6; Z. Archibald, *CAH* 6² (1994), ch. 9e; Parker, *ARH* 173 f. J. M. R. C.; S. H.

sitophylakes (σιτοφύλακες) were Athenian officials appointed annually by lot to supervise the sale of grain, barley-meal, and bread, and prevent overcharging. There were originally five for the town of Athens and five for *Piraeus, but later the numbers were increased to twenty and fifteen respectively.

Rhodes, *CAAP*, on 51. 3. D. M. M.

Sittius (*RE* 3), **Publius,** of *Nuceria, a wealthy *eques* (see EQUITES) and a friend of *Sulla and of Cicero (see Cic. *Fam.* 5. 17), had extensive business interests in Spain and Mauretania. While in Spain, he was suspected of involvement with *Catiline. (Cicero, *Sull.* 56 ff., vigorously denies it.) He preferred to sell up his Italian estates and go to Mauretania, where he collected a mercenary force and entered the service of *Bocchus (2). In 46 BC they attacked the Pompeians' ally *Juba (1) and after Thapsus Sittius annihilated most of the Pompeian remnants, capturing and executing L. *Afranius (2) and Faustus *Cornelius Sulla and surrounding the ship of Q. *Caecilius Metellus Pius Scipio, forcing him to commit suicide (*BAfr* 95 f.). Caesar rewarded him with a principality based on *Cirta, where he settled his mercenaries as colonists. In 44 he was assassinated by a native chieftain, but his principality, as *colonia Cirta Sittianorum*, long retained a distinct identity. E. B.

Siwa, large and fertile *oasis in Egypt's western desert, c.540 km. (335 mi.) south-west of *Alexandria (1), home in antiquity to a populous community of farmers (the Ammonioi) ruled by local chiefs (e.g. Hdt. 2. 31–2), nominally subject to Egypt's rulers. The well-preserved remains of the famous oracular temple of *Ammon, built in the Egyptian style under (probably) *Amasis, are at modern Aghurmi, with the ruins of a second sanctuary of Ammon near by. Excavations at the site of El-Maraki have revealed a Graeco-Egyptian sanctuary with a small Doric temple (also known from early travellers) and a (Greek) inscription recording building work by local landowners under Trajan. Siwa remained a bastion of paganism until at least the 6th cent. AD (Procop. *Aed.* 6. 2. 16–18).

Diod. Sic. 17. 49 ff.; Curt. 4. 7. 16 ff.; Paus. 9. 16. 1; A. Fakhry, *Siwa Oasis* (1944), and *Siwa Oasis* (1973; repr. 1993). El-Maraki finds (announced in 1995): A. Spawforth, *Ad Familiares* 11 (1996).   A. J. S. S.

skolia See SCOLIA.

skytalē is a word found in Spartan contexts, apparently to describe a message written on leather wrapped round a stick. The view that it was used for *secret* messages is found in late writers (Plut. *Lys.* 19; Aul. Gell. 17. 9) but not in e.g. *Thucydides (2) on the one occasion that he uses the word (1. 131. 1), or in *Xenophon (1), and has been shown to be highly unlikely.

D. Kelly, in J. W. Eadie and J. Ober (eds.), *The Craft of the Ancient Historian* (1985), 141–69.   S. H.

slavery

Greek From *Homer's claim that a man loses half his selfhood when 'the day of slavery' comes upon him (*Il.* 6. 463) to *Aristotle's doctrine of 'natural slavery' (*Pol.* bk. 1), Greek life and thought were inextricably bound up with the ideology and practice of human servitude. Eventually, and incompletely, the notion became established that it was not right for Greeks to enslave their fellow-Greeks, and the correlative idea prevailed that non-Greek 'barbarians' were fitted for servitude by their very nature (not just social or political organization). See BARBARIAN. But that did not prevent the continuing enslavement of Greeks by Greeks, and the language of slavery in the Greek New Testament was by no means a dead metaphor.

'Slavery', however, covered a multitude of sins and life-chances. The ideal type of the slave is the socially dead chattel, ripped forcibly from organic ties of kin and community, transported to an alien environment there to be treated as merely a piece of property or as a factor of production to be used and abused at will, an animate tool or beast of burden with no sense of self other than that allowed by the slaveowner and no legal, let alone civic, personality whatsoever. Societies with large numbers of such slaves, let alone societies based on them, have been very few. The city of Athens and central Roman Italy for periods in antiquity, and in modern times the slave states of the American Old South, the Caribbean, and Brazil, are the only known instances. But even in Athens there were gradations of status and degrees of exploitation regardless of uniformity of legal status.

At the top of the heap were the few hundreds of publicly owned slaves (*dēmosioi*), who served as a token *police force or as other sorts of public functionary such as official coin-tester (*dokimastēs*) in the Agora or clerk to a jury-court. Below them were the privately owned, skilled slaves who 'lived apart' (*khōris oikountes*) in craft workshops established with start-up capital by their owners to whom they remitted a share of their profits, or who were hired out for specific tasks such as harvesting (*sōmata misthophorounta*). Then there were household slaves (*oiketai*), male and female, of whom the males of a smaller household might also work in the fields. Harder was the lot of the agricultural slaves of a rich citizen householder. But worst of all was that of the mine-slaves who were either directly employed by or hired out to work the state-owned silver mines of *Laurium: for

them an early death might be considered a happy release. Reliable statistics of numbers are not available, but a reasonable guess would be that between 450 and 320 BC about 80,000–100,000 slaves of all kinds were active in Attica at any one time (out of a total population of perhaps a quarter of a million).

The Athenian model of chattel slavery became widely diffused in the Greek world, although the size and complexity of the original were never emulated or even approached. The prevalence of inter-Greek warfare ensured that Greek slavedealers (*andrapodistai, andrapodokapeloi*) had plenty of custom, even if it was rare for a Greek to be removed from his or her native community into permanent servitude elsewhere in the Greek or non-Greek world. On the other hand, the flow of non-Greek slaves into the Greek world continued unabated, giving rise to the popular identification (and Aristotle's flawed justification thereof) of 'barbarians' as 'natural' slaves.

Despite the impression created by imprecision of terminology, or inadequate use of such relatively precise terms as did exist, by no means all those broadly labelled *douloi* ('unfree') in Greece were chattel-slave *douloi*. The two largest classes of these other unfree persons were respectively those enslaved for *debt and the communally enslaved *helot-type populations. Debt-bondsmen technically forfeited their liberty only temporarily, pending repayment of their debt; in practice, the condition might be permanent and hereditary, and on occasion prompted violent political upheaval, as at Athens in about 600 BC. *Solon's response to that crisis was remarkable in several ways, not least in that he outlawed debt-bondage for citizens altogether. Elsewhere in the Greek world the practice continued and constituted a principal source of exploited labour-power for Greek propertied classes in default of or as a complement to slave *labour.

There were apparently some chattel slaves in Sparta, but the overwhelming majority of its servile labour force was constituted by the native helot class (see HELOTS). The fact that they were Greek and enjoyed some signal privileges, above all a family life, suggested to one ancient commentator that they ought to be classified as somewhere between outright chattel slaves and completely free people. But this picture of relative privilege is darkened by the knowledge that at any time their masters might legally kill them with impunity. More important for classificatory purposes is that the helots were enslaved collectively as a community, a feature they shared with several other Greek and native servile populations ranging from *Heraclea (3) on the Black Sea to *Syracuse in Sicily by way of *Thessaly and *Crete. There may still be room for argument whether Greek civilization as a whole was 'based' on 'slavery', but the ubiquitousness and centrality of servitude in the Greek imagination as in Greek everyday reality are beyond question.   P. A. C.

Roman Slavery in the strict sense of chattel-slavery, whereby the slaveowner enjoyed complete mastery (*dominium*) over the slave's physical being (*Dig.* 1. 5. 4. 1), the power of life and death included (Gai. *Inst.* 1. 52), was evident throughout the central era of Roman history, and in Roman no less than Greek thought was regarded as both the necessary antithesis of civic freedom and the guarantee of their civic superiority to those who enjoyed it. From this structural point of view Roman society, like Greek, was a genuine slave-society.

Although for no period of antiquity is it possible to determine accurately the size of the slave population, the necessary statistical information being simply unavailable, modern estimates of 2,000,000 slaves in Italy at the close of the republic conform to a slave : free ratio of roughly 1 : 3 in evidence from the major slave-societies of the New World. Slave-ownership was a prerogative of the wealthy, although the scale of ownership was larger in the Roman world than the Greek, and the élite could possess hundreds of slaves. *Pompey's son Cn. *Pompeius Magnus (2) recruited 800 of his personal slaves and shepherds for the war against *Caesar (Caes. BCiv. 3. 4. 4), and the city prefect L. Pedanius Secundus maintained under *Nero some 400 slaves in his urban residence alone (Tac. Ann. 14. 42. 45). Slave-owning, however, was not confined to the very rich. There is evidence to suggest that artisans in Roman Egypt regularly kept two or three slaves. The Roman naval veteran C. Longinus Castor identified just three slaves in his possession in his will in AD 194 (FIRA 3, no. 50). Slave-owning was a mark of status to be sought for its own sake, and even slaves and ex-slaves became slave-owners, especially those at Rome who belonged to the *familia Caesaris* and prospered from their favoured status (and see Plin. HN 33. 134 for the Augustan freedman C. Caecilius Isidorus, said to have owned 4,116 slaves at his death). While the evidence on slave numbers is obviously no more than anecdotal, it suffices to show that there was no social limit on the desire to exercise absolute power over others.

Slaves were procured chiefly as captives in war (see BOOTY), as the victims of organized *piracy and *brigandage, through natural reproduction, and through *trade. The growth of the Roman empire in the 2nd and 1st cents. BC produced vast numbers of prisoners who were transported as slaves to the Italian heartland. Romans, like Greeks, tended to shun enslavement of co-nationals, assimilating slavery to the 'barbarian' character of other peoples; consequently Syrians and Jews were peoples born for enslavement (although, unlike New World slavery, classical slavery was never in itself racially grounded). Piracy is best illustrated from the activities of the Cilician bandits of the late republic, notorious for discharging great quantities of enslaved victims in the port of *Delos, where traders swiftly redistributed them, particularly to the west (Strabo 14. 5. 2). But a recently discovered letter of St *Augustine (Ep. 10) indicates how piracy and brigandage were still rampant in late antiquity, and also how demand for slaves had in no way diminished. Children born to a slave mother (vernae) were typically themselves slaves (the status of the father was immaterial); so natural reproduction constantly contributed to the slave supply. To judge from random remarks like those of *Columella (Rust. 1. 8. 19; cf. Varro, Rust. 2. 10. 6), slave-owners were sometimes prepared to sanction, if not encourage, reproduction among their slaves when it suited them, and they might allow slaves to enter into informal unions of marriage as a prelude. But the degree of conscious slave-breeding, a highly charged term, is impossible to ascertain in Graeco-Roman society. Slave-traders like A. Kapreilius Timotheus (AE 1946, 229) operated throughout the Mediterranean, in war and peace, as distributors of captives and home-born slaves alike, at times combining their interests in slaves with trade in other commodities (cf. Petron. Sat. 76. 6). At no time are complaints heard of slaves being in short supply, even in late antiquity.

Slaves can be observed in almost every area of human activity, the holding of public office apart, and in a world where capitalist ideas were unknown, there was no concept of competition between slave and free labour; in fact it was conventional in certain contexts (e.g. manufacturing) for slave and free to work side by side. In late republican Italy the extensive development of slave-run *latifundia consequent on the growth of the empire

(cf. App. BCiv. 1. 7) meant that the rural slave presence was very high (although the survival of independent smallholders is now well attested from archaeological survey), and, to judge from Columella's handbook on farming, which gives more attention to slave management than the earlier treatises of M. *Porcius Cato (1) and *Varro, it was still high, in some regions of Italy at least, under the Principate (see AGRICULTURE, ROMAN). Domestic labour and the dangerous and heavily exploitative work in the *mines were something of a slave preserve; the gold and silver mines in Roman Spain consumed human labour at a prodigious rate.

The slave-owner's prerogative of setting the slave free was frequently exercised in classical antiquity, and at Rome, contrary to Greek practice, the slave could even be admitted to citizenship (see FREEDMEN), although a high frequency should not be equated with a high incidence of manumission, and most slaves were probably not set free; many who were paid their owners a price for their freedom from savings (see PECULIUM).

Practically all knowledge of classical slavery derives from sources representing the attitudes and ideology of slave-owners. It is impossible therefore to understand fully the nature of life in slavery in Graeco-Roman society. Given the patterns of behaviour observable in New World slave societies, it is likely that ancient slaves were at all times obliged to come to terms with the oppression they constantly endured by adopting strategies of accommodation and resistance in their daily lives. Many slaves must have responded with conscious obedience to the rewards for good behaviour—time off from work, superior rations of food and clothing, freedom—that owners offered them as incentives (Varro, Rust. 1. 17. 5–7; Col. Rust. 1. 8. 15–20; cp. Xen. Oec. 13. 9–12; Arist. [Oec.] 1. 5. 3–6), knowing that physical coercion was always predictable if acquiescence were not forthcoming. The element of calculation this required, however, suggests that obedience was not altogether synonymous with passivity, thus offsetting the dominant stereotype. As for resistance, it is most easily recognized in the occasional episodes of open revolt, notably the movement led by *Spartacus in Italy in the late seventies BC. Their object was not to eradicate slavery but to extricate the disaffected from its rigours. Revolt was a dangerous form of resistance, however, jeopardizing prospects of emancipation and the family relationships slaves constructed. Slaves therefore tended to display resistance more commonly by running away, playing truant, working inefficiently, pilfering or sabotaging property—annoying and frustrating tactics for owners, but less personally threatening for the perpetrators (e.g. Col. Rust. 1. 7. 6–7). Running away was endemic (e.g. *Cicero's slave Dionysius: Cic. Fam. 13. 77. 3; cf. the mass flight of 20,000 slaves to *Decelea in 413 BC: Thuc. 7. 27. 5), and slave-owners had to advertise rewards for the return of their runaways, engage professional slave-catchers (fugitivarii) to track them down, or do the job themselves.

At no time was there any serious questioning of the structural role of slavery in Graeco-Roman society. At Rome *Stoicism is said to have mitigated attitudes towards slaves and to have inspired humane legislation rendering slavery more tolerable, especially under the Principate. In reality Stoic moralists (cf. Sen. Ep. 47) were more concerned with the effects of slaveholding on the moral health of the slave-owners than with the conditions under which slaves lived, while Roman legislation, although showing an increasing interest in the public regulation of slavery, was primarily driven by the aim of perpetuating the slavery system as it was and did little to effect permanent improvement. *Christianity likewise displayed no interest in social change from which slaves might benefit, and the result of the Christian attitude symbolized by the repeated injunction that slaves should obey their masters 'with fear and trembling' (e.g. Eph. 6: 5; *Didache* 4: 11)—a vigorous reaffirmation that slavery was an institution based essentially on violence—was to make slavery even harsher in late antiquity than in earlier eras. See also MARXISM AND CLASSICAL ANTIQUITY.

Access to bibliography on classical slavery is provided by N. Brockmeyer, *Antike Sklaverei* (1979) and by J. Vogt and H. Bellen (eds.), *Bibliographie zur antiken Sklaverei*, revised by E. Herrmann and N. Brockmeyer (1983). Annual surveys of new scholarship appear in the journal *Slavery & Abolition.*

GENERAL D. B. Davis, *The Problem of Slavery in Western Culture* (1966); M. I. Finley, *Slavery in Classical Antiquity*[2] (1968), and *Ancient Slavery and Modern Ideology* (1980); T. Wiedemann, *Greek and Roman Slavery* (1981, sources in Eng. trans.); G. E. M. de Ste Croix, *The Class Struggle in the Ancient Greek World* (1981); O. Patterson, *Slavery and Social Death* (1982); M. I. Finley (ed.), *Classical Slavery* (1987).

GREECE M. H. Jameson, 'Agriculture and Slavery in Classical Athens', *CJ* 1977, 122–45; M. I. Finley, *Economy and Society in Ancient Greece* (1981); P. A. Cartledge, 'Rebels & Sambos in Classical Greece: A Comparative View', in P. A. Cartledge and F. D. Harvey (eds.), *Crux: Essays Presented to G. E. M. de Ste Croix* (1985), 16–46; P. Vidal-Naquet, *The Black Hunter* (1986), chs. 7–10; Y. Garlan, *Slavery in Ancient Greece* (1988, Fr. orig. 1982); E. M. Wood, *Peasant-Citizen and Slave* (1988); W. Pritchett, *The Greek State at War* 5 (1992), 68 ff. ('Booty'); P. A. Brunt, *Studies in Greek History and Thought* (1993), ch. 11; A. Burford, *Land and Labour in the Greek World* (1993), ch. 5; P. A. Cartledge, *The Greeks* (1993), ch. 6; N. R. E. Fisher, *Slavery in Classical Greece* (1993).

EGYPT I. M. Biezunska-Malowist, *L'Esclavage dans l'Égypte gréco-romaine*, 1. *Période ptolemaïque* (1974), 2. *Période romaine* (1977); J. A. Straus, 'L'Esclavage dans l'Égypte romaine', *ANRW* 2. 10. 1 (1988), 841–911; R. Scholl, *Corpus der Ptolemäischen Sklaventexte*, 3 vols. (1990).

ROME W. W. Buckland, *The Roman Law of Slavery* (1908); P. A. Brunt, *Italian Manpower* (1971); P. R. C. Weaver, *Familia Caesaris* (1972); K. Hopkins, *Conquerors and Slaves* (1978); K. R. Bradley, *Slaves and Masters in the Roman Empire* (1987); A. Watson, *Roman Slave Law* (1987); J.-C. Dumont, *Servus: Rome et l'esclavage sous la République* (1987); K. R. Bradley, *Slavery and Rebellion in the Roman World* (1989); S. R. Joshel, *Work, Identity, and Legal Status at Rome* (1992); K. Hopkins, 'Novel Evidence for Roman Slavery', *P&P* 1993, 3–27; W. Eck and J. Heinrichs (eds.), *Sklaven und Freigelassene in der Gesellschaft der römischen Kaiserzeit* (1993, sources with Ger. trans.); K. R. Bradley, *Slavery and Society at Rome* (1994). K. R. B.

Slavs See AVARO-SLAV INVASIONS.

sleep See DREAMS; HYPNOS; INCUBATION; MEDICINE, § 2; MORPHEUS; PALINURUS; STATIUS.

slingers The sling is possibly depicted on the silver 'Siege Rhyton' from Shaft Grave IV at *Mycenae, and sling-bullets were found at *Knossos; the earliest literary reference may be in the *Iliad* (13. 716). Thereafter there is a long gap until we meet them in *Thucydides (2)'s account of the *Peloponnesian War: even *Xerxes' army contained no slingers, if we are to believe Herodotus. Thucydides mentions the Acarnanians (see ACARNANIA) as expert slingers in 429 BC (2. 81. 8–9), and in 424 the Boeotians (see BOEOTIA) sent for slingers from Malis before their assault on the Athenian fort at *Delion (4. 100. 1). By 415, at latest, the Rhodians (see RHODES) were known as expert slingers, and the Athenians took 700 of them to *Sicily (Thuc. 6. 43. 2); even Rhodians who had not originally enlisted as slingers proved expert with the weapon during the retreat of the 10,000 (Xen. *An.* 3. 3. 16). *Xenophon (1) also mentions 'at least 400'

slingers from the border-districts of *Elis as taking part in the battle of the *Nemea (*Hell.* 4. 2. 16). *Philip (1) II of Macedonia certainly used slingers at *Olynthus in 348, for many of their sling-bullets have been found, and some of *Alexander (3) the Great's Agrianes served as slingers. In the western Mediterranean Balearic slingers (see BALEARES ET PITHYUSAE INSULAE) took the place of Rhodians, and were used, for example, by *Hannibal (Polyb. 3. 83. 3, 113. 6), and, later, by the Romans.

Xenophon tells us that the Rhodian slingers among the 10,000 were able to improvise slings and lead bullets, and were even able to outrange most enemy archers; the maximum range of the sling was possibly as much as 350 metres (380 yards). Bullets could be either stone, clay, or lead. The lead bullets used by the Macedonians at Olynthus averaged about 30 grams, those of the defenders about 20, but examples above and below these weights are known, and *Diodorus (3) Siculus alleges that the Balearic slingers used stones weighing a *mina* (c.350g.). Bullets from Olynthus are often inscribed, some with the names of Philip or his officers, but some with slogans like 'take that' or 'a nasty present'. See FULVIA, bibliog.

RE 3 A 2 (1929), 1695–1700, σφενδονῆται; M. Korfmann, *Scientific American* 1973; A. M. Snodgrass, *Arms and Armour of the Greeks* (1967); W. K. Pritchett, *The Greek State at War* 5 (1991). J. F. La.

Smyrna (mod. Izmir), a city on the west coast of Asia Minor at the head of the Hermaic Gulf, the natural outlet of the trade of the *Hermus valley and within easy reach of the *Maeander valley. Old Smyrna lay at the NE corner of the gulf. Occupied by Greeks c.1000 BC, the site is important archaeologically, with excavations revealing a Dark Age Greek settlement, its village-like layout replaced in the 7th cent. by a handsome fortified city with regular streets. Captured by *Alyattes c.600 BC, the city was thereafter inhabited 'village-fashion' (Strab. 14. 1. 37). It was refounded on its present site around Mt. Pagus by *Alexander (3) or his successors *Antigonus (1) and *Lysimachus; its Augustan appearance is recorded by Strabo (ibid.). Throughout the Roman period it was famous for its wealth, fine buildings and devotion to science and medicine. A major centre of the *Second Sophistic, it was home to Aelius *Aristides, who persuaded Marcus *Aurelius to restore it after earthquakes in AD 178 and 180. Its prosperity in late antiquity is implied by verse dedications of new buildings (including a public lavatory) recorded in the *Greek Anthology.* *Homer was reputed to be a Smyrnaean by birth.

PECS 847 f.; C. Foss, *AJArch.* 1977, 469 ff., 481 f. = C. Foss, *History and Archaeology of Byzantine Asia Minor* (1990), 2; G. Petzl, *Inschriften von Smyrna* 1–2 (1982–90); E. Akurgal, *Alt-Smyrna* (1983); D. Klose, *Die Münzprägung von Smyrna in der römischen Kaiserzeit* (1987). W. M. C.; J. M. C.; A. J. S. S.; C. R.

snakes were regarded in Greek and Roman religion mostly as guardians, e.g. of houses, tombs, springs, and altars. Snakes appear as attributes of bell-shaped idols in Minoan houses and small sanctuaries; coiled terracotta snakes were found in Mycenaean palaces, perhaps indicating their later, attested function as domestic guardians. See RELIGION, MINOAN AND MYCENAEAN. Probably evoking their hidden, secretive natural habitat of crevices and the world of 'under' in general, snakes were associated with *chthonian powers. They were linked either with what emerges from the earth, such as trees or springs, or what is placed inside it, such as foundations of houses and altars, or graves.

Snakes guard sacred places (the garden of the Golden Apples of the *Hesperides) or objects (the Golden Fleece; see JASON (1)).

social legislation

*Apollo killed the Python which guarded *Delphi for its patron goddess, Earth (Ge, *Gaia); the sacred snake of Athena is said to have abandoned the Acropolis when the Athenians left for *Salamis (1) (Hdt. 8. 41). In art and ritual snakes often appear coiled around sacred trees, at the foot of altars, on tombstones, and as guardians of caves facing dedicants who present them with sacred *cakes (the *oracle of *Trophonius). In fantastic compositions we find men-snakes (*Cecrops, *Erichthonius), or metamorphoses: *Thetis took on the form of a snake to escape *Peleus; Cychreus, king of Salamis, was worshipped by the Athenians as a snake. As an attribute of gods, snakes were close to *Demeter with her serpent-chariot, used also by *Athena (and *Medea). As healing powers, they were associated with *Asclepius, especially in Hellenistic and Roman religion.

Feared for their deadly venom, perhaps striking archetypical psychological chords of terror, the frightening aspect of snakes finds expression more in myth and art than in cult. Snakes (or 'dragons') were born of the earth or of the drops of Titans' blood (see TITAN); they are entwined in the Gorgon's hair (see GORGO), coiled around the body of *Cerberus, accompany the Furies (see ERINYES), and sent by *Hera to kill baby *Heracles and his twin. To strike terror they were depicted on hoplites' shields or, as an expression of victory, on commemorative monuments (the Serpent Monument, dedicated at *Delphi as a thank-offering after the *Persian Wars: ML 27).

At Sparta snakes were the holy animals of the *Dioscuri, perhaps originally house-gods. Real house-snakes may have been regarded as the Divine Twins attending a *theoxenia, the participation of gods in a meal reception. See also ALEXANDER (13); NAASSENES.

E. Küster, *Die Schlange in der griech. Kunst und religion*, RVV 13. 2 (1913); M. P. Nilsson, *Greek Folk Religion* (1940), 67–72; J. A. Oliver, *Snakes in Fact and Fiction* (1959); E. Mitropoulou, *Deities and Heroes in the Form of Snakes* (1977).   I. M.

social legislation See AUGUSTUS; DEDITICII; FREEDMEN; FREEDWOMEN; LEX (2), *Lex Aelia Sentia, Lex Papia Poppaea*; MARRIAGE LAW, ROMAN; PATERFAMILIAS; SLAVERY; and articles listed under SUMPTUARY LEGISLATION.

social status See STATUS, LEGAL AND SOCIAL.

Social Wars (πόλεμος συμμαχικός, *bellum sociale*) is the name given to a conflict collectively involving allies (σύμμαχοι, *socii*).

(1) ὁ συμμαχικὸς πόλεμος, the revolt of the allies of *Athens (357–355 BC), led by *Rhodes, *Cos, and *Chios, with the support of *Byzantium and *Mausolus of Caria, caused by discontent at Athenian supremacy and the exactions imposed by Athenian generals and mercenaries. The defeat of Athens at sea at Embata (356) and the threat of Persian intervention (355) led to negotiations and peace. See SECOND ATHENIAN CONFEDERACY.

S. Hornblower, *Mausolus* (1982), 206 ff.

(2) The conflict (220–217 BC) in which *Philip (3) V of Macedon and his Hellenic League fought against the Aetolians (see AETOLIAN CONFEDERACY), Sparta, and *Elis. It began with Aetolian aggression and ended with the Peace of Naupactus, when concerted attempts at mediation (by *Ptolemy (1) IV, *Chios, *Rhodes, *Byzantium) coincided with Philip's desire to take advantage of *Hannibal's success against Rome and extend his influence into the Adriatic. Philip's gains were the greater, but nothing was resolved, and the hostilities were resuscitated when the Romans allied themselves with the Aetolians against Philip in 211.

Polyb. 4. 5. Walbank, *Philip V, HCP* 1, and *CAH* 7²/1 (1984), 473 ff.; *HM* 3 (1988), 370 ff.

(3) The Social, Marsic, or Italic War (91–87 BC; the main fighting being in 90–89), waged by Rome's Italian allies (*socii*, among whom the *Marsi were prominent) against her predominance. Rome gained the victory largely through the political concession of granting her citizenship to the enemy. Thereafter Italy, south of the Po (see PADUS), was united by the common bond of citizenship (see CITIZENSHIP, ROMAN).

E. Gabba *CAH* 9² (1994), ch. 4.   H. H. S.; P. S. D.

socii were allies of Rome. The Roman conquest of Italy resulted in a system of military alliances by which native communities remained theoretically independent but were in practice reduced to subjects. This relationship was enshrined in treaties of alliance (see FOEDUS) which the Italian peoples made with Rome, on terms that were more or less favourable, depending on whether they joined Rome voluntarily or were defeated in war. By the time of the *Punic Wars more than 150 separate treaties had been concluded, and all the peoples of non-Roman Italy had become *socii*. Although the more equal treaties stipulated military partnership, in practice all the allies were obliged to assist the Romans by sending contingents of troops to fight alongside the legions. These obligations were set out in a document called the *formula togatorum* ('the list of those who wear the toga'), about which little is known, but which seems to have defined the number of troops each allied community could be called upon to contribute. Some such assessment probably lies behind *Polybius (1)'s account of the manpower available to Rome in 225 BC (Polyb. 2. 24 with *HCP*). During the 3rd and 2nd cents. BC Roman armies (see ARMIES, ROMAN) always contained a large proportion, varying between half and two thirds, of allied troops. In exchange for their contribution the allies received security and a share of the profits of conquest, particularly the right to take part in land assignations and colonies. This doubtless explains the remarkable loyalty of the allies, even when tested to the limit in the Hannibalic War (see HANNIBAL; PUNIC WARS). During the 2nd cent., however, the relationship changed, as colonization ceased and the profits of empire, in the form of regular provincial taxation, were monopolized by Rome. By the time of C. *Marius (1) the system had become exploitative, and in 91 BC allied discontent gave rise to the *Social War (3) (i.e. the war against the *socii*). This bloody conflict ended when the allies were given Roman *citizenship and incorporated in the Roman state.

From early times Rome also had allies outside Italy, notably *Carthage and Massilia (see MASSALIA), and their number increased rapidly after 200 BC as kings, city-states, and confederations made treaties with Rome on nominally equal terms. Unlike the Italian allies, they did not contribute troops on a regular basis, although they were expected to undertake military action on Rome's behalf when local circumstances demanded it. With the growth of the empire these allied states gradually lost their independence and became merely the most privileged class of provincial communities; their number also declined during the period of the civil wars, when many revolted or joined the wrong side, and lost their privileged status in consequence. The few that survived into the Principate were known as *civitates foederatae*, while the term *socii* came increasingly to be used indiscriminately for all Rome's free provincial subjects.

J. Beloch, *Der italische Bund* (1880), and *Römische Geschichte* (1926); E. Täubler, *Imperium Romanum* (1913); A. N. Sherwin-White, *The Roman Citizenship*² (1974); E. Gabba, *Republican Rome: The Army and the Allies*

(1975), 70 ff., *CAH* 8² (1989), 207 ff., and *CAH* 9² (1994) 104 ff.; E. Badian, *Foreign Clientelae* (1958); A. J. Toynbee, *Hannibal's Legacy* (1965) 1, chs. 3, 5; 2, ch. 4; W. V. Harris, *Rome in Etruria and Umbria* (1971); P. A. Brunt, *Italian Manpower* (1971), and *The Fall of the Roman Republic* (1988), 93 ff.; V. Ilari, *Gli italici nelle strutture militari romane* (1974); H. Galsterer, *Herrschaft und Verwaltung im republikanischen Italien* (1976); T. Hantos, *Das römische Bundesgenossensystem in Italien* (1983); T. J. Cornell, *CAH* 7²/2 (1989), 381 ff.; M. Crawford, *The Roman Republic*² (1992). A. N. S.-W.; T. J. Co.

sociology of Roman law See LAW, ROMAN, SOCIOLOGY OF.

Socrates (469–399 BC), Athenian public figure and central participant in the intellectual debates so common in the city in the middle and late 5th cent. His influence has been enormous, although he himself wrote nothing.

Socrates' philosophy and personality reached a broad ancient audience mainly through the dialogues a number of his associates wrote with him as protagonist. These were numerous and popular enough for *Aristotle to classify them in the *Poetics* as a species of fiction in their own right. But apart from the works of *Plato (1), only a few fragments survive of the dialogues of *Antisthenes, *Aeschines (2) of Sphettus, and *Phaedon of Elis, and nothing of the *dialogues of *Aristippus (1), *Cebes of Thebes, and many others. In addition to Plato, most of our own information about Socrates comes from *Aristophanes (1) and *Xenophon (1), both of whom also knew him personally, and from Aristotle, who did not.

Socrates was the son of Sophroniscus and Phaenarete, of the *deme of Alopece. Though Plato and Xenophon depict him as a poor man, he must at some time have owned sufficient property to qualify for service as a *hoplite in the battles of *Potidaea, *Amphipolis, and *Delium, through which he acquired a reputation for courage. He was married to Xanthippe and was the father of three sons.

As a citizen, Socrates seems to have avoided active participation in politics. He was, however, one of the Presidents (see PRYTANEIS) of the assembly (*ekklēsia) when the generals at the sea-battle at *Arginusae were put on trial for abandoning the bodies of the Athenian dead there. Socrates (who was foreman of the *prytaneis* on the crucial day, Xen. *Mem.* 1. 1. 18, 4. 4. 2, Pl. *Grg.* 473e, but see Dodds' n.; cp. Xen. *Hell.* 1. 7, 15, Pl. *Ap.* 32b) alone voted against the illegal motion to try the generals as a single group, and they were executed. After the defeat of Athens in the *Peloponnesian War, he openly ignored an order by the *Thirty Tyrants to arrest an innocent citizen (Pl. *Ap.* 32c–d).

Socrates' circle included a number of figures who turned against democracy in Athens, including *Critias, *Charmides, and *Alcibiades. (See OLIGARCHY; FOUR HUNDRED, THE; DEMOCRACY, ATHENIAN.) This may well have been the underlying reason why he himself was tried and put to death by drinking hemlock in 399 BC. He was charged with impiety, specifically with introducing new gods and corrupting young men (see ATHEISM). This charge may have masked the political motives of his accusers, since the *amnesty of 403 BC prohibited prosecution for most offences committed before that date.

Socrates' execution prompted Plato and Xenophon to create portraits intended to refute the formal charge under which he was tried and to counter his popular image, which may have been inspired by Aristophanes' *Clouds*. Aristophanes had depicted Socrates engaged in natural philosophy and willing to teach his students how 'to make the weaker argument stronger'—a commonplace charge against the *sophists. Both Plato and Xenophon were intent on distinguishing Socrates as radically as possible from other members of the sophistic movement, with whom he may actually have had some affinities. But their strategies differ. In both authors, Socrates devotes himself, like the sophists, to dialectical argument and the drawing of distinctions. In both, he refuses, unlike the sophists, to receive payment. In Xenophon, however, he uses argument to support, in contrast to the sophists, a traditional and conventional understanding of the virtues. In Plato, on the other hand, it is a serious question whether he holds any views of his own, and his main difference from the sophists is that, unlike them, he never presents himself as a teacher of any subject.

Plato's and Xenophon's portraits, inconsistent as they are with Aristophanes', are also inconsistent with each other. This is the root of 'the Socratic problem', the question whether we can ever capture the personality and philosophy of the historical Socrates or whether we must limit ourselves to the interpretation of one or another of his literary representations. For various reasons, in the mid-19th cent. Plato replaced Xenophon as the most reliable witness for the historical Socrates, even though it is accepted that our knowledge of the latter can be at best a matter of speculation. And, though recent attempts to rehabilitate Xenophon are not lacking, most contemporary scholars turn to Plato for information on Socrates' ideas and character.

That character is cool, distant, reticent and ironic, in contrast to Xenophon's more conventional, straightforward, almost avuncular figure. Plato's Socrates refrains from expounding complicated positive views of his own, preferring instead to question those who claim to have such views themselves. In Plato's early or 'Socratic' dialogues his questions mainly concern the nature and teachability of *aretē* ('virtue', 'excellence', or perhaps 'success') and what produces it, both in one's person and in one's activities, and its species—courage, wisdom, piety, self-control, and justice. By means of the procedure of question and answer which came to be known as the *elenchus* (see DIALECTIC), Socrates refutes all those who claim to know what *aretē* is by showing their views to be internally inconsistent.

The Platonic Socrates is utterly serious about *aretē* and the nature of the good and happy life. His commitment to do what is, by his best lights, the right thing to do in all cases is unwavering. This commitment ultimately cost him his life: according to Plato's *Apology*, he antagonized his jury by insisting that his life had been as good as any human being's and that far from having committed any wrongs he had brought the greatest benefits to Athens.

Socrates seems to have been convinced that wisdom and virtue were ultimately the same—that if one knows what the good is, one will always do it. His argument was that the good, or *aretē*, either leads to or is itself part of the happy life. Since everyone wants to be happy above everything else, no one who knows what the good is will not choose to do it. This 'intellectualist' approach to ethics implies that there is no such thing as 'weakness of the will'. It is impossible to know the better and choose the worse: the only reason people choose a worse course of action is that they are ignorant of what is better. This is one of the 'Socratic paradoxes', which contradict everyday experience but have proved surprisingly intransigent to analysis and refutation.

Plato's Socrates consistently denied that he had the knowledge of *aretē* that he considered necessary for the good and happy life. He sometimes referred to this knowledge as 'divine', in opposition to the 'human' knowledge he himself possessed and which consisted in his awareness of his own ignorance. This, he claimed, made him wiser than others, who were both ignorant of *arete* and ignorant of their very ignorance. In the *Apology*, he claimed that this was the meaning of the Delphic oracle saying that no one in Athens was wiser that he was.

Socrates often, in both Plato and Xenophon, referred to a 'divine sign', a *daimonion*, which prevented him from taking certain courses of action—he attributes his reluctance to participate in active politics to this sign's intervention. His religious views, even though they sometimes overlapped with those of tradition (he acknowledged the authority of *Apollo, for example, when he received the *Delphic oracle), must have been quite novel, since he appears to have thought that the gods could never cause evil or misery to each other or to human beings. He also seems, as we see in Plato's *Euthyphro*, to claim that the gods' approval or disapproval does not render actions right or wrong. On the contrary, rightness and wrongness are established independently, and the gods, knowing what these are, both engage in the former and shun the latter and approve of human beings for acting likewise.

Socrates' moral seriousness is counterbalanced by a worldly personality who enjoys good food and company—goods which he is also willing to forgo without complaint if they are not available or if they conflict with the much more important pursuit of *arete*. He had an uncanny ability, as we see in both Plato and Xenophon, not to do anything wrong, and his relation to positive philosophical views was fundamentally ambiguous. These features, along with the vividness with which Plato portrays his complex personality, are doubtless responsible for the fact that so many ancient philosophical schools, from the Academic *Sceptics and the *Cyrenaics to the Stoics (see STOICISM) and the *Cynics, considered him as the person most closely approximating their respective ideal.

With the renewed study of Greek texts in the Renaissance, Socrates became an influence on modern philosophy as well. He provides the first model of a philosopher primarily devoted to the pursuit of ethical issues. His pursuit is systematic, and his emphasis on the necessity of knowing the definitions of the virtues if we are to decide securely what does and what does not fall under them provided an impetus for the development of logic. In addition, he still constitutes the paradigmatic figure in whom philosophy, even in its most abstract manifestations, is never severed from the concerns of life. He lived and—most importantly—he died in accordance with his philosophical principles. Plato's lively portrait makes it believable that such a life is possible. But since his principles are not always clear and we cannot be certain whether he himself knew exactly what they were, Socrates continues to constitute a mystery with which anyone interested in philosophy or in the writings of the Greeks must contend.

PRIMARY ANCIENT SOURCES Aristophanes, *Nub.*; Plato; Xenophon, *Mem., Ap., Symp., Oec.*; Aeschines of Sphettus (fragments, ed. Dittmar); Antisthenes and others (fragments, ed. Giannantoni, *Socratis et Socraticorum reliquiae*, 1990); Aristotle, *Met., Eth. Nic., Mag. Mor.*

MODERN AUTHORS G. Grote, *Plato and the Other Companions of Sokrates* (1875); E. Zeller, *Sokrates und die Sokratiker* (1889); A. E. Taylor, *Varia Socratica* (1911); H. Maier, *Sokrates* (1913); W. D. Ross, *Aristotle's Metaphysics*, introd. 2 (1924); G. C. Field, *Plato and his Contemporaries* (1920); O. Gigon, *Sokrates* (1947); A.-H. Chroust, *Socrates: Man or Myth* (1947); R. Robinson, *Plato's Earlier Dialectic*[2] (1953); W. K. C. Guthrie, *A History of Greek Philosophy* 3 (1969); T. H. Irwin, *Plato's Moral Theory* (1977); G. Vlastos, *Socrates: Ironist and Moral Philosopher* (1991), and *Socratic Studies* (1994); Parker, *ARH* 199 ff.   A. N.

Socrates Scholasticus, a lawyer in *Constantinople, con-

tinued the *Historia Ecclesiastica* of *Eusebius from AD 305 to 439, basing his account on documentary and first-hand testimony, as Eusebius had done. Books 1–2, at first dependent on the history of *Rufinus (2) of Aquileia, were revised in the light of *Athanasius' writings; Socrates' sources for the eastern Church (he knew little of the west) included documentary collections such as the conciliar *Acta* assembled by bishop Sabinus of Heraclea in 375, now lost. As a layman, he was relatively indifferent to doctrinal minutiae and had little time for episcopal squabbling. Writing, unlike the early Eusebius, under a Christian empire, Socrates, like *Sozomen, perceived a need to redefine the genre of church history invented by Eusebius by analysing the relationship of ecclesiastical to secular events. His history was the main source for Sozomen and *Theodoret, and the three histories were later edited to form the Latin *Historia Tripartita*.

TEXT Ed. W. Bright (1883).   J. D. H.

sodales are either 'companions, mates', or else 'members of a single college or fraternity'. Examples of the latter sense are the secondary religious groups of Rome: these include the **fetiales*, who made treaties and declared war; and three *sodalitates* that were concerned with performing specific annual rites—the *Salii, active in March and perhaps October; the Luperci, whose festival was the *Lupercalia of February; and the best-recorded of them all, the *fratres arvales, whose cult of *Dea Dia was originally agrarian and concerned with boundaries, later with the celebration of the imperial house.

Some of these were formed of one (Sodales Titii) or more (Luperci Faviani and Luperci Quintiliani) of the ancient clans (*gentes*; see GENS). It is not, however, clear that *sodalitates* were always based on gentile links. New ones were formed when a new cult was brought to Rome, for instance those of the Great Mother (Magna Mater, *Cybele) when the cult was introduced from the east in 204 BC (see PESSINUS; PHILHELLENISM); or those of the new Divi under the Empire, the Sodales Augustales after the death of *Augustus, the Sodales Flaviales, Hadrianales, and Antoniniani under later dynasties.

The discovery of an archaic dedication to *Mars at *Satricum by the *suodales* of Poplios Valesios (P. Valerius) has raised new questions about the origins of the institution: one possibility is that this was a religious fraternity like the Roman ones already discussed; another that these sodales were the clients of a *gens (see CLIENS), like the Fabian clients who fought at the battle of the *Cremera (Livy 2. 49), led by a war-leader (whether or not Valerius himself was a Roman). There is evidence both from Italy and elsewhere of groups of comrades, sometimes bound by oath, supporting leaders in peace and war. It is clear that there were different types of *sodalitates*; less clear how far the types overlapped.

H. S. Versnel, 'Historical Implications', in C. M. Stibbe and others (eds.), *Lapis Satricanus* (1980), 108–27; J. Scheid, *Romulus et ses frères* (1990), 252–60.   J. A. N.

Sogdiana See BACTRIA; MARAKANDA.

Sol The name of the Sun is given to two utterly different deities in Rome. The older is Sol Indiges, of whom we know that he had a sacrifice on 9 August (Augustan calendars for that date: *Soli Indigiti in colle Quirinale*), while calendars for 11 December, especially the Fasti Antiates, give AG(onium) IND(igetis). Nothing more is known with any certainty; the indication for 11 December is supplemented by Lydus (*Mens* 4. 155, 172. 22 Wuensch), who says that the festival was in honour of Helios.

See Koch, *Gestirnverehrung im alten Italien* (1933), 63 ff., against Wissowa, *RK* 317; but some of Koch's combinations are very hazardous. This cult was native, apparently, and is connected by Latte (*RR* 44) with the agricultural calendar. There existed at the Circus Maximus a temple of Sol and *Luna (*Fast. Filoc.* on 28 August), which may date from the 3rd cent. BC (cf. Ziolkowski, *Temples*, 150 ff.). A *lucus Solis indigetis* is attested at *Lavinium (Plin. *HN* 3. 56). Much later and certainly foreign (Syrian) was the worship of *deus Sol Invictus (the invincible Sun-god), to give him his most characteristic title. Eastern sun-gods had been making their way in the west, helped no doubt by the current identification of *Apollo with *Helios (e.g. Hor. *Carm. Saec.* 9), for some time; but the first attempt to make the Sun's the chief worship was that of *Elagabalus (AD 218–22) (SHA *Heliogab.* 6. 7 and 17. 8), who introduced the god of *Emesa, whose priest and, apparently, incarnation he was, El Gabal. Elagabalus' excesses and consequent unpopularity and assassination checked the cult, but *Aurelian (270–5) reintroduced a similar worship, also oriental; he was himself the cult of a priestess of the Sun (see SHA *Aurel.* 5. 5 and 35. 3). This remained the chief imperial and official worship till *Christianity displaced it, although the cult of the older gods, especially *Jupiter, did not cease, but rather the new one was in some sort parallel to it, the Sun's clergy being called *pontifices Solis* (cf. PONTIFEX), a significant name which was part of a policy of Romanizing the oriental god. Sol had a magnificent temple on the campus Agrippae, see Richardson, *Topogr. Dict. Anc. Rome*, 363 ff. Its dedication day (*natalis*) was 25 December.

Wissowa, *RK* 365 ff.; Latte, *RR* 231 ff.; Radke, *Götter*, 290; R. Schilling, *Rev. Ét. Lat.* 1979, 177 ff.; LIMC 4/1 (1988), 592 ff.   H. J. R.; J. Sch.

Solarium or **Horologium Augusti** in the northern *Campus Martius at Rome, a great double-axe shaped sundial which acted as calendar as well as timepiece. It was laid out on travertine paving with bronze strips, using an obelisk from Heliopolis as the gnomon (pointer). It was dedicated by *Augustus as a victory monument over Egypt (*CIL* 6. 702), possibly on the same occasion as the nearby *Ara Pacis which lay at the end of one of its meridians. Excavations in 1979/80 uncovered a section of the sundial belonging to a Domitianic restoration.

E. Buchner, *Die Sonnenuhr des Augustus* (1982).   J. D.

Solinus See IULIUS SOLINUS, C.

Solon, Athenian politician and poet, was of noble descent but, whether or not the tradition that he was of moderate means is correct, came to sympathize with the poor. He was prominent in the war against *Megara for the possession of *Salamis (1), urging the Athenians to renewed effort when they despaired of success (*c.*600 BC). In 594/3 he was archon (see ARCHONTES), and the link between his archonship and his reforms is probably to be accepted, though some have wanted to put the reforms 20 years later. He is said to have spent the 10 years after his reforms in overseas travel, during which his measures were not to be altered: if he continued to travel after that, he may have met *Amasis of Egypt and Philocyprus of Cyprus, but if he died *c.*560/59 he is unlikely to have met *Croesus of Lydia (though that tradition is as old as Hdt. 1. 29–33). It may be true that he was in Athens at the time of the troubles in which *Pisistratus first seized power, and tried to warn the Athenians against Pisistratus.

For *Herodotus (1) Solon was a sage, a lawgiver, and a poet; *Thucydides (2) does not mention him. It was at the end of the 5th cent. that the democrats began to think of him as their founding hero: if 4th-cent. writers had access not only to his poems but also to the *axones (revolving pillars) on which the laws were inscribed, they will have had a firm basis for their accounts of him, even though they were capable of anachronistic misinterpretation, and though the orators tended to ascribe to him all the laws current in the 4th cent.

Solon's *seisachtheia* ('shaking-off of burdens') is represented as a cancellation of all *debts, but should probably be seen as the liberation of the *hektēmoroi ('sixth-parters'), men in a state of servitude who had to give a sixth of their produce to an overlord: their obligation was abolished and they became the absolute owners of their land; men who had been enslaved for debt (many of them, perhaps, *hektēmoroi* who had defaulted on their obligation) were freed, and for the future enslavement for debt was banned. Grants of *citizenship to immigrant craftsmen, and a ban on the export of agricultural products other than olive oil, encouraging the growth of *olives, will have helped to move Athens from a largely self-contained towards a trading economy (see TRADE). Behind an alleged series of changes in Athens' measures, weights, and *coinage we should perhaps see legislation for the use of standard measures and weights (not necessarily different from those already in use in Attica); but even the earliest coins are almost certainly later than the time of Solon.

Solon organized the Athenian citizens in four property classes (*pentakosiomedimnoi, *hippeis, *zeugitai, *thētes), and made these the basis of all political rights, to break the monopoly of the noble families: the major offices were reserved for the two highest classes; the *zeugitai* were eligible for the minor offices; the *thētes* could not hold office but could attend the assembly (*ekklēsia) and *ēliaia. He may have included an element of allotment in the appointment of the archons, to improve the chances of candidates who were rich but not noble. He probably created a new council of 400 to prepare business for the assembly, and provided for regular meetings of the assembly.

He compiled a new code of laws, superseding the more severe laws of *Draco except in the area of homicide, and probably extending written laws into areas not touched by Draco. He created a category of public lawsuits, in which any citizen might prosecute, in contrast to the private lawsuits in which only the injured party or his family could prosecute; and he provided for appeals against the verdicts of magistrates to the *ēliaia* (possibly a judicial meeting of the assembly).

Solon shows in his poems that he was trying to achieve a compromise between the demands of the rich and privileged and of the poor and unprivileged, and that he satisfied neither: the *hektēmoroi* were not given the total redistribution of land which some had wanted, but their liberation angered the deprived overlords; the nobles were reluctant to share political power with the non-nobles, and there was trouble over appointments to the archonship in the years that followed; tension continued until the three seizures of power by Pisistratus, between *c.*561/0 and *c.*546/5. Nevertheless, in the creation of a free peasantry, the weakening of the *aristocracy and the strengthening of the assembly and the judicial system, Solon laid the foundations for the successful and stable society of Classical Athens.

See also DEMOCRACY, ATHENIAN; PATRIOS POLITEIA.

PA 12806; *APF* 322–4, 334–5. *Ath. Pol.* 2–13, Plut. *Sol.*; fragments of poems: West, *IE* 2² (1992), 139–65 of laws: E. Ruschenbusch, *Σόλωνος νόμοι* (*Hist.* Einzelschriften 9, 1966). I. M. Linforth, *Solon the Athenian* (1919). *Axones*: R. S. Stroud, *The axones and kyrbeis of Drakon and Solon* (U. Calif. Pub. Cl. Stud. 19, 1979). Archonship and reforms: R. W. Wallace, *AJAH* 1983, 81–95. *Hektēmoroi*: P. B. Manville, *The Origins of*

Citizenship in Ancient Athens (1990), ch. 5. Measures and weights: M. H. Crawford, *Eirene* 1972, 5–8; P. J. Rhodes, *Num. Chron.*[7] 1975, 1–11. *Heliaia*: M. H. Hansen, *C&M* 1982, 9–47 = *The Athenian Ecclesia* 2 (1989), 219–61; R. Thomas in R. Osborne and S. Hornblower (eds.), *Ritual, Finance, Politics* (1994), 119 ff. A. W. G.; T. J. Ca.; P. J. R.

Somnus (Roman god of sleep) See PALINURUS; and cf. HYPNOS.

Sopater (1) of *Paphos, Greek parodist and writer of *phlyakes*. He flourished from the time of *Alexander (3) the Great to that of *Ptolemy (1) II. Fr. 19 mentions *Thibron (2), who put *Harpalus to death in 324 BC. It may be inferred from frs. 1 and 24 that Sopater lived in *Alexandria (1). Fourteen titles of plays survive: three (*Bacchis, Bacchis' Suitors, Bacchis' Marriage*) seem to form a triad, unless merely varied names for the same piece; *Ghosts Called Up* (Νέκυια), *Hippolytus* and *Orestes* must be burlesques of myth or tragedy (cf. COMEDY (GREEK), MIDDLE). Fr. 6 (12 vv.: the longest extant phlyax fragment) from *The Gauls* contains raillery of the Stoics (see STOICISM); this passage, far removed from the buffoonery of the original *phlyakes*, approaches the spirit and language of Attic comedy.

FRAGMENTS *CGF* 192–7; A. Olivieri, *Frammenti della commedia greca e del mimo nella Sicilia e nella Magna Grecia* 2[2] (1947), 27–42.
INTERPRETATION A. Körte in *RE* 3 A 1 (1927), 1001 f., 'Sopatros' 9; T. B. L. Webster, *Hellenistic Poetry and Art* (1964), 126 f.; M. Gigante, *Annali dell' Istituto Italiano per gli studi storici* 1967/8, 56 ff. W. G. A.

Sopater (Σώπατρος) (2), Greek rhetor working in Athens in the 4th cent. AD, probably a pupil of *Himerius; the most significant work attributed to him is *Diairesis Zētēmatōn*, 'Division of Questions', a collection of 81 declamation themes, with instructions on how to treat them, and partial 'fair copies': it gives the best insight we have into how rhetors and their pupils actually worked in school. It is uncertain whether the commentary on *Hermogenes (2) and the *progymnasmata* also attributed to Sopatros are by the same person. The philosopher Sopatros of Apamea (a pupil of Iamblichus) is earlier.

TEXTS *Diairesis* in Walz 8 (and see D. C. Innes and M. Winterbottom, *BICS* Bulletin Supplement 48, 1988); comm. on Hermogenes in Walz, 5. See also G. A. Kennedy, *Greek Rhetoric under Christian Emperors* (1983), 104–8. D. A. R.

Sophaenetus of *Stymphalus. One of *Cyrus (2)'s mercenary generals, he helped lead the Greeks back to the Black Sea (see PONTUS) (401/400), though he was fined 10 *minae* at Cotyora for neglecting duties. The lost *Anabasis* ascribed to him by *Stephanus of Byzantium may be the source which ultimately accounts for non-Xenophontic elements in Diodorus' account (presumably *via* the Oxyrhynchus historian), though some regard it as a post-Plutarchan forgery. (See XENOPHON (1); DIODORUS (3); OXYRHYNCHUS, THE HISTORIAN FROM).

RE 3 A (1929), 1008–13, 'Sophainetos'. *FGrH* 109. H. D. Westlake, *Studies in Thucydides and Greek Historiography* (1989), 267 ff. C. J. T.

Sophilus, comic poet, τῆς μέσης κωμῳδίας 'of the middle comedy' (see COMEDY (GREEK), MIDDLE), and 'Sicyonian or Theban' (*Suda*), but he certainly wrote for the *Attic theatre (Ath. 123 d, 228 b). We have nine titles; it is conceivable that his *Androcles* refers to the man mentioned in *Menander (1), *Sam.* 606 f.

Kassel–Austin, *PCG* 7. 594 ff. (*CAF* 2. 444 ff.). K. J. D.

Sophistic, Second See SECOND SOPHISTIC.

sophists Itinerant professors of higher education. From its original senses of 'sage' and 'expert' the word came to be applied in the 5th. cent. BC in the technical sense given above to a number of individuals who travelled widely through the Greek world, giving popular lectures and specialized instruction in a wide range of topics. They were not a school, nor even a single movement, having neither a common set of doctrines nor any shared organization.

Their activities included the popularization of Ionian natural philosophy, *mathematics and the 'social sciences' of history, *geography, and speculative *anthropology; *Hippias (2) was active in all and *Protagoras in at least some of these fields. They pioneered the systematic study of techniques of persuasion and argument, which embraced various forms of the study of language, including grammar, literary criticism, and semantics. Protagoras was reputedly the first person to write a treatise on techniques of argument, and was notorious for his claim to 'make the weaker argument the stronger'.

The sophists aroused strong reactions, both positive and negative. On the positive side, the highly successful careers of the most celebrated testify to a considerable demand for their services, especially in providing rhetorical training for aspiring politicians. On the negative, they were regarded, especially by those of conservative views, as subversive of morality and tradition, in view both of their naturalistic outlook on morality and religion, and of their teaching (especially to the young) of techniques of argument.

Various sophists did indeed subject morality to critical scrutiny. Protagoras maintained (apparently inconsistently with his universal subjectivism) a form of moral relativism, in which moral beliefs are true for those communities in which they are maintained. *Plato (1) represents more radical critics of morality in the persons of the sophist *Thrasymachus and of *Callicles, a pupil of *Gorgias (1). It is, however, oversimplified to regard the sophists as a group as having shared a generally sceptical or radical outlook on morality. *Xenophon (1) reports Hippias as maintaining the traditional doctrine that there exist certain natural laws common to all societies, while Plato reports Protagoras as holding that the sophist complements, rather than subverts, the traditional educational institutions of the community in their task of imparting the basic social virtues.

As the writings of the sophists are lost, we depend for our information on others, principally Plato, who is a hostile witness. He believed, very probably truly, that the suspicion which certain sophists had attracted had contributed to the unpopularity and ultimately to the condemnation of *Socrates, and therefore depicts the sophists predominantly as charlatans, in contrast to Socrates, the paradigm of the true philosopher. See EDUCATION, GREEK, § (3).

Testimonia and fragments in DK, 2. 252–416, English tr. in R. K. Sprague (ed.), *The Older Sophists* (1972); W. K. C. Guthrie, *A History of Greek Philosophy* 3 (1969); C. J. Classen (ed.), *Sophistik* (1976); G. B. Kerferd, *The Sophistic Movement* (1981), and (ed.), *The Sophists and Their Legacy* (Hermes Einzelschriften 44, 1981); R. Bett, 'The Sophists and Relativism', *Phronesis* 1989; J. de Romilly, *The Great Sophists in Periclean Athens* (1992; Fr. orig. 1988); M. Ostwald, *CAH* 5[2] (1992), 341 ff. C. C. W. T.

Sophocles (1), Athenian tragic playwright.

Career Sophocles' career in the theatre was a remarkably long one. He first competed against *Aeschylus in 468 BC (*FGrH* 239 *Marm. Par.* A 56; see MARMOR PARIUM; Plut. *Cim.* 8. 7: also his first victory in the competition) more than a decade before Aeschylus' death; he lived to compete for the last time at the *Dionysia of 406 BC, dressing his chorus and actors in mourning, we are told, to mark the death of *Euripides, news of which had just reached Athens (*Life of Eur.* 3. 11 ff., ed. E. Schwartz, *Scholia in Euripidem*, 1 (1887)). He died a few months later (Ar. *Frogs* 82; hyp. 2 (second *hypothesis (1)) to the *Oedipus at Colonos*); he was born in the 490s BC (probably 496 or 495: *Marm. Par.* A 56).

He wrote more than 120 plays (*Suda*) and won at least 20 victories, 18 at the City Dionysia (*IG* 2². 2325): he was thus markedly the most successful of the three great 5th-cent. playwrights. He was second often and never third (i.e. last). He is said to have given up acting in his own plays early in his career (because he did not have a sufficiently powerful voice) and to have written frequently for a particular actor, Tlepolemus, so as to draw on his strengths as a performer (Schol. Ar. *Clouds* 1267). He also figures in the public life of Athens when already in his fifties: he was one of the Treasurers of the Greeks (see HELLENOTAMIAE) in 443–442 BC and a general (see STRATĒGOI), with *Pericles (1), probably in 441/0 (*FGrH* 324 Androtion F 38), during the revolt of *Samos. In the political crisis that followed the defeat of the Athenian armada at Syracuse in 413 he is said to have been one of the ten 'advisers' (*probouloi*) appointed to deal with the state of emergency (Arist. *Rhet.* 1419ª25). There are a number of stories of his friendships with other leading figures of the day, e.g. with the younger tragic playwright, *Ion (2) of Chios, who wrote a memoir of his conversations with him (Athen. 13. 603 ff.: cf. the scene in *Plato (1) in which Cephalus, the father of the orator *Lysias, reports having been present at a conversation which included the aged Sophocles (Pl. *Resp.* 1. 329a–c)). He was apparently a priest of the hero Halon (Life; see HERO-CULT) and welcomed the new cult of the healing god *Asclepius and the snake which symbolized him into his own house while a sanctuary was built (Plut. *Num.* 3: probably in 420–19). After his death he was given the honours of a hero cult himself, with the new name Dexion (*Etym. Magn.*). We must be wary of ancient 'biographical' data (many of which are cautionary fictions: M. Lefkowitz, *Lives of the Greek Poets*, 1981) but with Sophocles there seems to be just enough reliable material to construct a public persona.

Plays Paradoxically facts are scarcer when it comes to Sophocles' theatrical output. We have dates for only two of the seven surviving plays (the last two): a victory with *Philoctetes* in 409 (hyp.) and another with *Oedipus at Colonos* in 401 (a posthumous victory, the play being produced by his grandson, *Sophocles (2): hyp. 2). We know of victories in 447 (*IG* 2². 2318: plays unknown) and 438 (over Euripides: hyp. Eur. *Alc.*: plays again unknown); and with *Antigone* at a date unknown; also of defeats in 459 (*POxy*. 2256, fr. 3; by Aeschylus with the *Supplices* trilogy; Sophocles' plays of this year are uncertain); in 431 (hyp. Eur. *Med.*; by *Euphorion (1), Aeschylus' son: Euripides was third) and in the year of *Oedipus Tyrannus* (by *Philocles, Aeschylus' nephew; date unknown). We have no evidence at all for the dates of *Ajax*, *Oedipus Tyrannus*, *Electra*, and *Trachiniae* and only unreliable and unconvincing anecdotal evidence for *Antigone*.

Theatricality Readings of Sophocles in the earlier part of this century tended to be determined by the influence of *Aristophanes (1)'s passing remark about him, only months after his death, as 'easy-going' or 'relaxed' (*Frogs* 82) and by the judgement of later ancient critics of style which identified Sophocles' with the 'middle, well-blended' style, neither grand and austere (like Aeschylus and *Thucydides (2)) nor smooth and pedestrian (like *Isocrates and Euripides: Dion. Hall., *Comp.* 21–4; cf. Dio Chrys. *Or.* 52. 15, for a reading of *Philoctetes* which sets Sophocles 'midway between' Aeschylus and Euripides). Sophocles thus emerged as 'middling'—stable, harmonious, and at ease with

experience. Such readings ignored the frequently discomforting nature of much Sophoclean theatre (esp. in *Antigone*, *Oedipus Tyrannus*, and *Trachiniae*, for example) and largely denied his insistent theatricality. Sophocles is the master of the enacted metaphor—metaphors of blindness in the two *Oedipus plays and *Antigone*, of bestiality in *Trachiniae*—which is momentarily 'realized' in the text as it is performed. The theatricality of such pervasive dramatic metaphors emerges in moments such as the messenger speech of *Oedipus Tyrannus* and the immediately following scene with the entry of the now blinded but 'seeing' Oedipus (*OT* 1223–1415), and in the first stasimon of the chorus in *Trachiniae* (497–530), where *Deianira herself is imagined as an 'abandoned calf' helplessly watching two beast-men fighting in a 'game' (like a *wrestling match at *Olympia) for the right to take her. Such moments are moments of stunning theatrical power, and 'middling' is not a word to apply to them. Sophocles can produce equally powerful effects of the eerie and uncanny: e.g. in the opening scene of *Ajax*, where the unseen *Athena manipulates a puppet-like Ajax (see AIAS (1)) and is resisted by the matching subtlety of *Odysseus (1–133: the scene becomes even eerier in retrospect when Tecmessa reports it as if Ajax had been speaking to a vacancy, 301–6).

Much of Sophoclean theatricality resides in his dramatic use of significant objects and significant actions, especially exits and entrances. *Electra*, for example, is a play of thwarted recognition and its centrepiece enacts a sinister game of illusion, of disguises and deceptions. The game involves not only a brilliantly theatrical messenger speech evoking and narrating, in the bravura style of such speeches, distant events which culminate in the violent death of *Orestes and which we know have not occurred (680–763), but also the bringing of Orestes' 'ashes', carried in an urn by the unrecognized Orestes himself. The urn is taken by *Electra (3) whose grief for her dead brother and lament for the irreparable loss of her own hoped-for future are directed to it, focused on the 'little weight' which is his tomb and which she now holds in her hands (1126–69). She begs to be allowed to join him in it, 'nothing with nothing', and even when Orestes struggles to disclose himself and to be recognized, she will not let go of it. The urn is 'what is closest' to her (1205–8). The fusing of game-playing, irony, and intensity of tragic emotion is mediated through the simple 'prop'. Other such powerfully meaningful props are the sword in *Ajax* and the bow in *Philoctetes*. Sophocles' dramatic imagination is before all else physical and concrete. It reveals much about him that in *Philoctetes* the isolation and the loss of identity of the hero (see PHILOCTETES) is figured in physical terms by the deserted, uninhabited island with its cave and sea, its springs, rocks, and wild animals, whereas in the Philoctetes plays of Aeschylus and Euripides *Lemnos remains the inhabited island of ordinary experience. See ISLANDS.

Entrances and exits were always, given the layout of the theatre space, of more importance in Greek tragedy than in later forms of built theatre. Sophocles' use of them is, however, markedly his own. The entrance of the self-blinded Oedipus in *Oedipus Tyrannus*, immediately after one of Sophocles' most powerful messenger speeches, has already been mentioned (*OT* 1287 ff.). The final entrance of *Creon (1), carrying the body of his son, in *Antigone* (1257 ff.) is another *coup-de-théâtre*: it follows almost without pause on the exit of his wife, turning away in silence from the messenger's narrative of her son's death. As Creon enters, he is instantly met by the same messenger emerging from the palace to announce his wife's death and by the 'rolling out' of the theatrical device called the *ekkyklēma*, carrying a tableau of his wife's body and the sword with which she has this moment killed herself. Entering and carrying one body, he confronts another.

Sophocles' last two plays offer a unique sense of space and 'place where', in relation to which alone the action has meaning. The deserted island of Lemnos in *Philoctetes* and the grove of the Semnai (see ERINYES) at *Colonos in *Oedipus at Colonos* are heavily loaded with meaning as places to be left or reached. In both plays entrances and exits are thus equally full of significance. In *Oedipus at Colonos* the act of entering unknowingly upon sacred ground and above all that of leaving it are given dramatic weight by the slow measured extension of the blind Oedipus' movements (153–202). Later in the play the entry of Ismene is similarly extended, this time from the moment the figures on stage first catch sight of her (in the approach to the acting area) until she is within range of speech and touch (310–29). These are adagio movements; in *Philoctetes*, it is the suddenness, for example, of Odysseus' entries at 974 (in mid-line) and 1293 that gives them their theatrical quality. But in *Philoctetes* it is above all the thwarted exit that defines the theatricality of the play. The play's action requires that Philoctetes leave Lemnos for Troy. That exit is four times launched, delayed, and then thwarted (645–750; 877–926; 982–1056; 1362–1410: the final exit, at *Heracles' urging, at 1449–71). Each thwarted exit is different in its implications from each of the others and the last, completed exit is itself ambiguous in its meaning.

Language, form and structure The language that Sophocles deploys in his plays has, arguably, a greater range than that of either Aeschylus or Euripides, from the baroque sonorities of Ajax' great 'deception speech' (*Ajax* 646–92) or the messenger's opening proclamation of his news in *Oedipus Tyrannus* (1223–31) to the rambling, self-defensive preambles of the guard in *Antigone* (223–47; 388–405). It is a language which is often difficult, even inscrutable (especially in its syntax and particularly in the songs of the chorus); it is never less than formal and it does not yield its sense easily. But it has a flexibility that is very much Sophocles'. It is a mark of Sophoclean writing that it operates within highly formalized structures but uses those structures with masterly tact and subtlety. Sophocles uses the iambic trimeter of tragic dialogue (see METRE, GREEK, § 4(a)) for the most part in its severe form (without, that is, the fluid resolutions that Euripides increasingly used to free the verse) but he treats such formal boundaries as line-end, for example, with a relaxed ease; clauses, even prepositional phrases, may run over into the next line; occasionally a final vowel at the end of one line may be elided (i.e. run into) the opening vowel of the next. The pulse of the verse is kept steady but the rhythmical structure of the whole speech is given a new fluidity by Sophocles' informal treatment of metrical pause. So too with dialogue: like the other tragedians, Sophocles only divides a line between speakers as a sign of greatly heightened emotional tension but the length of the speeches that are exchanged is left much more fluid than those of Euripides, for example.

The fusion of formal symmetries with a more 'naturalistic' use of speech is well illustrated by the pivotal scene of *Oedipus Tyrannus* which embraces the quarrel between Oedipus and Creon, the entry and intervention of Jocasta, and the following dialogue between Oedipus and Jocasta (512–833). With the entry first of Creon and then of Oedipus the quarrel develops from Oedipus' opening speech of denunciation into a rapid, heated exchange of short speeches which keeps drifting into and out of the formal severities of *stichomythia* (the tightly controlled

exchange of single lines); it culminates in Creon's long speech of reasoned self-defence and Oedipus' curt proclamation of death, not exile, as Creon's punishment. This in turn leads at once into a vicious exchange of tense, broken lines, a choral intervention in spoken iambics and Jocasta's entry. The three characters now present (most of our sources attribute to Sophocles the innovation of using three actors: Arist. *Poetics* 1449ª15) engage in dialogue with a marked tendency towards symmetry. The formal severity of the scene is suddenly tightened still more when the chorus break in again, this time in song, and confront, first Oedipus, then Jocasta in a mixture of sung and spoken dialogue; the two confrontations, which respond with precise symmetry, are separated by the final, spoken exchanges between Oedipus and Creon, ending in another broken verse and Creon's exit. The chorus in song briefly assure Oedipus of their absolute loyalty, and Jocasta then begins a new scene of spoken, loosely structured dialogue in which it gradually emerges, with a high degree of psychologically persuasive 'naturalness', that it may be Oedipus himself who killed his own predecessor as king, Jocasta's first husband, Laius.

The idea of flexibility in the deployment of a tightly controlled formal structure applies also to resonances and responsions between plays. Sophocles turned three times to the cycle of traditional stories associated with *Thebes (1), not to produce a continuous 'trilogy' in the manner of Aeschylus but to explore certain recurring themes (the plays are sometimes called the 'Theban plays' or even the 'Theban trilogy'; both titles mislead, the second grossly: if the traditional chronology has any basis in fact the plays were written in the order: *Antigone*, *Oedipus Tyrannus*, *Oedipus at Colonos* and may well have been separated by decades). *Antigone* is often taken to be a broken-backed and structureless play (who is its 'hero'—Antigone, who disappears barely two-thirds of the way through the play, at l. 943 and never re-appears, or Creon, who is alienated from us almost from the first by the brutal autocracy of his language? Similar questions have been raised over *Trachiniae*); *Oedipus Tyrannus*, ever since Aristotle (*Poetics* 1452ª17–32), has been read as the paradigm of a well-structured play. But in important ways Sophocles uses these two differently structured theatrical experiences to explore closely related themes. *Oedipus Tyrannus* has a smoothly pivotal structure in which, with no appearance of discontinuity, we turn from one issue (the salvation of Thebes from plague brought on by *pollution) to another (is Oedipus guilty both of parricide and incest?). *Antigone* seems very different: it is more like a revolving stage on which, from Antigone's exit under sentence of death at 582, one character is replaced by another (*Antigone (1)–*Haemon (3)–Antigone–*Tiresias–Messenger–Eurydice–Creon) until in the closing scene of the play all but Tiresias and the dead Antigone are assembled together in final confrontation with death and, for Creon, tragic recognition. But the two plays are tightly bound together by common themes (*pollution through violent death; human blindness to truth; the impenetrability of the divine and the opaqueness of the riddling language of divinity); in both plays humans are left for carrion to devour, and boundaries between the two worlds of gods and men are thereby crossed with deadly results; in both the bonds of kinship have been distorted into horrific travesties of family. *Antigone* ends in inescapable bleakness; *Oedipus Tyrannus*, more positively, with Oedipus re-confronting the world in his blindness.

Tragedy and 'recognition' *Aristotle in the *Poetics* makes much use of the idea of 'recognition' (*anagnōrisis*) in his analysis of the tragic effect. The idea is not of much help in reading Aeschylus and of intermittent usefulness in Euripides. But in Sophocles (as arguably in *Homer's *Iliad*) it is an illuminating critical tool. In play after play, one or more characters is brought to a realization that he or she has misperceived the nature of reality and the realization is almost always associated with pain, suffering, and death. The idea of recognition is more often than not also associated with relationships between man and divinity. Between the two worlds of gods and men there is communication, in the imagined world of Sophoclean theatre: it comes in the form of dreams, oracles, and the reading of signs by seers such as Tiresias. Men and women try to guide their decisions by their understanding of such communications. But such understanding is almost always false: the language and the signs used by divinity are everywhere ambiguous, however simple in appearance, and they are systematically and readily misunderstandable, even if they are to hand. In *Ajax*, at a crucial moment, men learn too late of the seer's reading of Athena's intentions and Ajax dies; in *Trachiniae* both Deianira and Heracles only perceive the true meaning of a series of oracles and non-human communications when it is too late and the recognition cannot save them from the consequences of catastrophically mistaken action. In *Antigone*, both Antigone and Creon believe that they are acting as the gods require of them: Antigone dies with that belief shaken and perhaps foundering (919–27) and Creon confronts his misreading of the requirements of divinity only when not just Antigone but his son and wife also are already dead (1257–76). In *Philoctetes* the oracle is never brought sharply into focus but none the less haunts the play; in *Oedipus Tyrannus* the simplicities of the oracle's language become utterly opaque when read through the lens of Oedipus' 'knowledge' of the truth about himself. The recurring pattern of Sophoclean tragedy is that all falls into place and coheres only in retrospect: recognition comes after the event.

Reception Successful in his lifetime, Sophocles continued to be a powerful presence in the Greek tragic theatre in the following century. His plays seem to have been frequently revived, and the leading parts in them were taken by great actors of the period, such as Polus and Theodorus (Dem. *De fals. leg.* 246–7; Epictetus *Diss.* fr. 11 Schenkl; Gell. *NA* 6. 5). For Aristotle, the *Oedipus Tyrannus* is a paradigm of how to maximize the tragic effect, even in reading (*Poetics* 1453[b]2). Indeed Sophocles seems to have been read and performed through much of European history. *Oedipus Tyrannus* was the first drama to be performed in Palladio's Teatro Olimpico at Vicenza in the 17th cent. *Antigone* has haunted the European imagination for centuries (George Steiner, *Antigones* (1984)) and in the last century and subsequently Freud's reading of *Oedipus Tyrannus* as the enactment of a universal male fantasy has been widely influential (though not among classical scholars: for a rebuttal of Freudian readings of the play, see J.-P. Vernant, 'Oedipus without the complex', in *Myth and Tragedy*, 85 ff.). In this century, *Electra* caught the imagination of Hugo von Hofmannsthal and of Richard Strauss, *Trachiniae* that of Ezra Pound. The readings that such continuous interest in Sophocles has led to have been extremely various: they attest the richness, as well as the inscrutability, of his text. See also TRAGEDY, GREEK.

GREEK TEXT H. Lloyd-Jones and N. G. Wilson (OCT, 1990, corrected repr. 1992); R. Dawe (Teubner[2], 1984); with Fr. trans., A. Dain and P. Mazon (Budé, 1955–8); fragments: A. C. Pearson (1917); S. Radt (Göttingen, 1977).

COMMENTARIES R. C. Jebb's comm. (1883–96) is still the most valuable; that by J. C. Kamerbeek (1959–84) is sometimes useful; see also *Ajax*, by W. B. Stanford (1963); *Trachiniae*, by P. E. Easterling (1982)

and M. Davies (1992); *Philoctetes* by T. B. L. Webster (1970); *Oedipus Tyrannus* by R. D. Dawe (1982); *Electra* by J. H. Kells (1974).

TRANSLATION R. Lattimore and D. Grene[2] (1992); also *Trachiniae*, by E. Pound (1969).

LEXICON F. Ellendt (2nd edn., by H. Genthe, 1872).

SCHOLIA Papageorgiou (Teubner, 1888). *Ajax*: G. A. Christodoulou (1977); *OC*: V. de Marco (1952).

CRITICISM T. von Wilamowitz, *Die dramatische Technik des Sophokles* (1917); K. Reinhardt, *Sophocles* (Eng. trans. 1979); C. M. Bowra, *Sophoclean Tragedy* (1944); A. J. A. Waldock, *Sophocles the Dramatist* (1951); R. F. Goheen, *The Imagery of Sophocles' Antigone* (1951); A. Lesky, *Tragische Dichtung der Hellenen*[3] (1972; Eng. trans. 1983); B. M. W. Knox, *Oedipus at Thebes* (1957), *The Heroic Temper* (1964), *Word and Action* (1979); R. Lattimore, *The Poetry of Greek Tragedy* (1957); J. Jones, *On Aristotle and Greek Tragedy* (1962); G. Gellie, *Sophocles: a Reading* (1972); E. R. Dodds, *The Ancient Concept of Progress* (1973); O. Taplin, *Greek Tragedy in Action* (1978); R. P. Winnington-Ingram, *Sophocles: An Interpretation* (1980); R. W. B. Burton, *The Chorus in Sophocles' Tragedies* (1980); C. Segal, *Tragedy and Civilization* (1981), *Interpreting Greek Tragedy* (1986); R. G. A. Buxton, *Sophocles* (Greece and Rome, New Surveys 16, 1984: with further bibliography), *Persuasion in Greek Tragedy* (1982); J.-P. Vernant and P. Vidal-Naquet, *Mythe et Tragédie* (2 vols. 1972 and 1986; Eng. trans. *Myth and Tragedy in Ancient Greece* (1988)); R. W. Bushnell, *Prophesying Tragedy* (1988); M. W. Blundell, *Helping Friends and Harming Enemies* (1989); A. C. Moorhouse, *The Syntax of Sophocles* (1982); H. Lloyd-Jones and N. G. Wilson, *Sophoclea* (1990).   J. P. A. G.

Sophocles (2), son of Ariston and grandson of *Sophocles (1), produced his grandfather's *Oedipus at Colonos* in 401 BC and plays of his own from 396 to at least 375. The numbers of his plays and victories are variously given.

TrGF 1[2] 208.   A. L. B.

Sophonisba (*Sophoniba* Livy; Σοφωνίβα Appian; the correct name is Saphanba ʿal), Numidian queen (see NUMIDIA), daughter of *Hasdrubal (3) and wife of *Syphax, king of the Masaesylii, whom she thus won over to the Carthaginian cause. When *Masinissa and C. *Laelius (1) overthrew Syphax (203 BC) Sophonisba took poison which according to the romantic story (Livy 30. 12–15) was sent to her by Masinissa, now enamoured of her and unable by any other means to save her from captivity at Rome. Details of her story (e.g. that before her marriage to Syphax she had been betrothed to Masinissa) may be false, but the outline need not be questioned.   H. H. S.

Sophron (Σώφρων) (5th cent. BC), Syracusan writer of *mimes. His mimes were divided according to subject-matter into ἀνδρεῖοι and γυναικεῖοι (to do with men/women). We have one important papyrus fragment and some 170 short citations, mostly preserved to illustrate the Doric dialect. He wrote in prose (*Suda*) but, according to schol. Greg. Naz. 120, it was rather a kind of poetry which employed a variety of cola without regard for rhythmical homogeneity or responsion. That description is in part (but not throughout) applicable to the extant fragment of ταὶ γυναῖκες αἴ φαντι τὰν θεὸν ἐξελᾶν, 'The women who claim that they will expel the goddess (i.e. *Hecate)'. Sophron was admired by *Plato (1) (*Duris (2) of Samos, *FGrH* 76 F 72), though the implication of Arist. *Poet.* 1447[b]10 f. is that they were poles apart in subject (as indeed they were). *Herodas was probably influenced by Sophron, and *Theocritus certainly was, particularly in his poems 2 and 15 (cf. the scholia on both ad init.).

Kaibel, *CGF* 152 ff.; Olivieri, *Frammenti ecc.* 2; Page, *Select Literary Papyri* 328 ff.   K. J. D.

Sophronius, *c*. AD 560–638, 'the Sophist', patriarch of Jerusalem (from 634) at the time of the Arab conquest of 637. He wrote a theological manifesto against the doctrine that although Christ had two natures he had only one will, panegyrics on Egyptian saints (Cyrus and John, John the Almsgiver, Maria the penitent prostitute), sermons for Christmas and other feasts, and 23 anacreontic odes of esoteric difficulty.

Ed. Migne, *PG* 87 (3), 3147 ff.; *Odes*, ed. M. Gigante (1957). H. G. Beck, *Kirche und theologische Literatur im byzantinischen Reich* (1959), 434 ff.; *ODCC*², 1291. J. F. Ma.

Sora, south-east of Rome, at the big bend of the river *Liris. Rome took Sora from the *Volsci in 345 BC, but Samnites (see SAMNIUM) disputed control of it until a Latin colony was established there (303 BC; see COLONIZATION, ROMAN). It has always been an important town with an acropolis girdled by polygonal fortifications.

E. M. Beranger, *La cinta muraria di Sora* (1981). E. T. S.; T. W. P.

Soracte, mod. Soratte, the isolated mountain 691 m. (2,267 ft.) high to the north of Rome, from which it is sometimes visible. Celebrated by *Horace (*Odes* 1. 9), there were priests here called Hirpi, resembling Roman Luperci (cf. LUPERCALIA). They worshipped *Apollo Soranus by walking over hot coals (Plin. *HN* 7. 19); the pestiferous cave alluded to by *Servius in describing the origin of the Hirpi (*Aen.* 11. 787) has been located.

G. D. B. Jones, *PBSR* 1963, 125 ff. E. T. S.; T. W. P.

Soranus of Ephesus, physician under *Trajan and *Hadrian (AD 98–138), studied at *Alexandria (1) and practised at Rome.

He wrote around twenty books, their subjects including a wide range of medical topics (e.g. *On Hygiene, On Acute and Chronic Diseases*), medical biography, commentaries and discussions of grammar and etymology. Those surviving in Greek are sections and fragments of *On Signs of Fractures* and *On Bandages*—these may both belong to the same lost work, *On the Art of Surgery*—and *Gynaecology*. The latter gives valuable information on *gynaecology and obstetrics in the Roman empire, and is divided into (1) the midwife, female anatomy and conception; (2) *childbirth and the care of the newborn; (3) *pathology and diet; (4) *surgery and drugs (see PHARMACOLOGY).

Soranus shared the theoretical standpoint of the Methodists (see MEDICINE, § 5.3), but his version of Methodism was less schematic in its classification of diseases, giving more space for individual variation between patients. He preserved many fragments of lost works, his practice being to summarize previous theories and therapies before defending his own.

Although *Galen was the more influential writer for gynaecology in the Latin west in late antiquity and the Middle Ages, sections of Soranus were translated into Latin and adapted for different audiences. In the Greek east, Soranus' gynaecology survived in the work of the encyclopaedists. Particularly influential was his image of the ideal midwife: literate, sober, discreet, free from superstition, and equally well acquainted with both theory and practice (see MIDWIVES).

TEXT J. Ilberg, *CMG* 4 (1927); P. Burguière and others, *Soranos d'Éphèse: Maladies des femmes* (1988–); cf. also M. and I. Drabkin, *Bull. Hist. Medicine*, Suppl. 13 (1951); Transl. of *Gynaecology*: O. Temkin, *Soranus' Gynaecology* (1956).
LITERATURE surveys, *RE* 3 A 1113–30; M. Michler, *Dict. Sc. Biogr.* 12 (1975), 538–42; G. E. R. Lloyd, *Science, Folklore and Ideology* (1983); P. Manuli, *Memoria* 1982, 39–49; history of text and place of Soranus in ancient medical tradition covered by introd. chs. to P. Burguière and others (above). H. K.

sortition (*klērōsis*), election by lot, a method of appointing officials in Greek city-states, especially in democracies (see DEMOCRACY, both entries). It was based on the idea of equality and reduced outside influence. Little is known of its use except at Athens. It remains uncertain when sortition was introduced there, perhaps as early as *Solon. From 487/6 BC the archons (see ARCHONTES) were appointed by lot out of nominated candidates (*prokritoi*, the process being *prokrisis*, and the whole two-stage process being *klērōsis ek prokritōn*); later, this became a double sortition. From the time when the archons began to be elected by lot, they lost political leadership. But all ordinary magistrates, a few excepted, were thus appointed; also the *boulē (a prytany of fifty from each *phylē*; see PHYLAI; PRYTANEIS) and the juries (by a very complicated procedure; see LAW AND PROCEDURE, ATHENIAN, § 2). Lot decided very many questions in political and social life. Politically, sortition, combined with the prohibition or at least severe restriction of re-election, enabled rotation in office, and electoral contests were avoided by its use; moreover, the power of magistrates was reduced, and thus the sovereignty of the popular assembly guaranteed. Sortition was practicable, as almost every citizen had a minimum of political experience, and nobody could be elected without having presented himself. Certain precautions were always taken (see DOKIMASIA), and military and some technical (especially financial) officials were appointed by vote. Except by a few critics like *Socrates, the principle of sortition was never discussed. It was, indeed, a necessary and fundamental element of the democratic *polis. See EKKLĒSIA; ELECTIONS AND VOTING, Greek.

Ath. Pol. with Rhodes, *CAAP*. T. W. Headlam, *Election by Lot at Athens* (1891, 2nd edn. 1933); V. Ehrenberg, *RE* 13 (1927), 1451–1503, 'Losung'; V. Abel, *Prokrisis* (1983), with M. H. Hansen, *CPhil.* 1986, 223 ff.; Hansen, *The Athenian Democracy in the Age of Demosthenes* (1991), 36 f.; 50 f.; 197 ff.; 235 ff.; 247 ff. V. E.; S. H.

Sosibius of Sparta, antiquarian writer of uncertain date, probably mid-3rd cent. BC. He went to Egypt and became closely associated with the *Alexandrian school. His works included studies on chronology and Spartan literature and institutions. It is doubtful whether he should be identified with the grammarian Sosibius ὁ λυτικός ('the solver'), so called because of his ability to deal with Homeric problems.

FGrH 595. G. L. B.; N. G. W.

Sosicrates, historian and biographer, perhaps from *Rhodes (Diog. Laert. 2. 84). He probably flourished mid-2nd cent. BC as a contemporary of *Apollodorus (6). His φιλοσόφων διάδοχή ('succession of philosophers') is a series of biographies of philosophers, following the teacher–pupil relationship. Its sources included *Hermippus (2) and perhaps *Satyrus (1) (see BIOGRAPHY, GREEK); whether he used Apollodorus is disputed: a common source in *Eratosthenes may explain similarities. *Diogenes (6) Laertius and *Athenaeus (1) draw on it. He also wrote a history of *Crete, which contains traditions similar to Apollodorus' commentary on *Homer's Ship Catalogue in *Iliad* 2; the relationship between the works remains uncertain.

FHG 4. 500–3; *FGrH* 461. F. W. W.; K. S. S.

Sosigenes (1) (*RE* 6), astronomer, advised Caesar in his reform of the Roman calendar (47 BC), and possibly composed the astronomical calendar associated with it. See CALENDAR, ROMAN.

HAMA 2. 575, 612. G. J. T.

Sosigenes (2) (*RE* 7), *Peripatetic philosopher, teacher of *Alexander (14) of Aphrodisias, is dated to AD 164 by his observation of an annular eclipse. He wrote, besides works on *logic and *optics, on astronomy, criticizing the theory of homocentric spheres (see ASTRONOMY) and constructing an enormous period for the return of the heavenly bodies, called τέλειος ἐνιαυτός (*Perfect Year*).

HAMA 1. 104, 2. 606, 684.   G. J. T.

Sosipater, New Comedy poet (see COMEDY (GREEK), NEW) of the 3rd cent. BC. In fr. 1 a cook boasts about his profession.

PCG 7 (1989), 604–7. Meineke, FCG 1. 477; A. Körte, in RE 3 A 1 (1927), 1167, 'Sosipatros' 2; A. Giannini, Acme 1960, 166 f.; H. Dohm, Mageiros (1964), 190 ff.   W. G. A.

Sosiphanes of *Syracuse, a tragic poet credited by the *Suda* with 73 tragedies and seven victories. There is confusion over his dates, and there may have been two poets of this name, one active in the 4th cent. BC and one in the 3rd (the latter being included in some lists of the *Pleiad).

TrGF 1². 261–3, 280.   A. R. Bi.

Sositheus from *Alexandria (7) Troas, one of the tragic *Pleiad at (Egyptian) *Alexandria (1) under *Ptolemy (1) II Philadelphus. The major surviving fragment is 21 verses from the satyric *Daphnis or Lityerses*. An epigram of *Dioscorides (1) (*Anth. Pal.* 7. 707 = 23 Gow–Page) praises him as the restorer of true *satyric drama.

TrGF 99; Latte, Kleine Schriften, 890–4.   R. L. Hu.

Sosius (RE 2), **Gaius,** Roman politician and general. He served Antony (M. *Antonius (2)) as quaestor c.39 BC, was appointed by him governor of Syria and Cilicia in 38, captured Jerusalem and installed *Herod (1) as king in 37, and celebrated a triumph in September 34. In 32 he and Cn. *Domitius Ahenobarbus (4) were consuls. Early in the year Sosius launched a public attack on Octavian (see AUGUSTUS), who responded vigorously, and the consuls and many senators fled to Antony. Sosius fought in the *Actium campaign, commanding the left wing of the fleet in the battle, and was subsequently pardoned by Octavian at the instance of L. *Arruntius (1). He restored the temple of *Apollo in the Circus Maximus, and attended the *Secular Games of 17 BC as *quindecimuir sacris faciundis*.

Syme, Rom. Rev. and AA, see indexes; Platner–Ashby, 15–16; P. Zanker, The Power of Images in the Age of Augustus (1988, Ger. orig. 1987), index under 'Temple of Apollo in Circo'.   C. B. R. P.

Sosius (RE 11) **Senecio, Quintus** (consul AD 99 and 107) was a significant public figure in the time of *Trajan, although attempts to reconstruct his career are largely speculative and depend partly on the disputed attribution to him of an acephalous inscription also ascribed to L. *Licinius Sura (*ILS* 1022). Married to the daughter of the distinguished Sex. *Iulius Frontinus, he was one of the first two ordinary consuls of the reign (for *consules ordinarii* see CONSUL), and the date of his second consulship held with Sura, and the honorary statue granted to him by the emperor (Dio Cass. 68. 16), suggest that he held a command in the second Dacian war (105–6; see DACIA). On one hypothesis he had already held a governorship, perhaps in Upper *Moesia (cf. Plin. *Ep.* 4. 4).

Senecio was a cultured man, interested in poetry and philosophy, a friend of *Pliny the Younger, whose literary interests he shared, and of *Plutarch, who dedicated several works to him, including the *Parallel Lives* and *Table Talk*, and refers to many congenial conversations over dinner; Senecio also enjoyed the friendship of *Hadrian (SHA *Hadr.* 4. 2). Although he had no son,

his daughter, Sosia Polla, married Q. *Pompeius Falco (*suffect consul 108), establishing a family that remained in the forefront of the senatorial aristocracy throughout the 2nd cent. Senecio's great-great-grandson, Q. Sosius Falco (consul 193), was considered by the rebellious praetorians as a suitable candidate for the purple in 193.

C. P. Jones, JRS 1970, 98.   J. B. C.

Sostratus (of Aegina). See AEGINA; TRADE, GREEK.

Sostratus, leading surgeon and zoologist, probably practised in *Alexandria (1) after 30 BC. His medical works dealt chiefly with *gynaecology. In zoology (see ANIMALS, KNOWLEDGE ABOUT) he perhaps ranks next after *Aristotle among the Greeks.

Works Περὶ ζῴων ('On animals') or Περὶ φύσεως ζῴων ('On the nature of animals'); Περὶ βλητῶν καὶ δακέτων ('On animals which strike and ones which bite'). *Aelian and the *scholia to *Nicander preserve much information about his zoological works.   W. D. R.

Sosylus of Sparta, Greek historian of the late 3rd to early 2nd cent. BC. He accompanied *Hannibal and wrote a history of his campaigns in seven books. *Polybius (1) criticized him severely on one occasion (3. 20. 5) but used him extensively. A fragment of bk. 4 is preserved on papyrus, containing a very competent account of a naval engagement early in the war.

F. Jacoby, RE 3 A (1929), 1204–6, 'Sosylos'; FGrH no. 176; R. A. Pack, The Greek and Latin Literary Texts from Greco-Roman Egypt² (1965), 87, no. 1484 (bibliography); K. Meister, Historische Kritik bei Polybios (1975), 167 ff.   P. S. D.

Sotades (1), Athenian comic poet, τῆς μέσης κωμῳδίας ('of the middle comedy', see COMEDY (GREEK), MIDDLE) according to the *Suda*, and (fr. 3, cf. schol. Aeschin. 1. 64) a contemporary of *Demosthenes (2). We have three titles and three citations; fr. 1 is a long description of the cooking of fish.

Kassel–Austin, PCG 7. 609 ff. (CAF 2. 447 ff.).   K. J. D.

Sotades (2) of Maroneia, poet of the first half of the 3rd cent. BC. The *prōtos heuretēs* i.e. inventor (Strabo 14. 1. 41) of *cinaedic poetry and probably the first literary writer of the 'sotadean', a stichic ionic verse (--∪∪--∪∪--∪∪--) in which -∪-× may replace --∪∪ and which allows great freedom of resolution and substitution. Sotades was notorious for riddling verses making fun of great men (Ath. 14. 620f–621b, Plut. *Mor.* 11a), including *Ptolemy (1) II Philadelphus, whose marriage to his sister *Arsinoe II the poet commemorated with his most famous verse, 'you are pushing the prick into an unholy hole' (fr. 1). His abuse of Ptolemy is variously said to have led to his death or a long spell in prison. Other poems included a sotadean version of *Homer's *Iliad* (frs. 4a–c) and a *Katabasis (Descent)* to *Hades. Moralizing verses ascribed to Sotades by *Stobaeus are almost certainly not his.

FRAGMENTS Powell, Coll. Alex. 238–45.
STUDIES L. Escher, De Sotadis Maronitae Reliquiis (1913); I. H. M. Hendriks, P. J. Parsons and K. A. Worp, ZPE 41 (1981), 76–8; M. Bettini, Materiali e discussioni 1982, 59–105; R. Pretagostini, Ricerche sulla poesia alessandrina (1984), 139–47; Alan Cameron, Callimachus and his Critics (1995), 18 ff.   R. L. Hu.

Soter, fem. **Soteira,** a title of several deities (e.g. *Zeus Soter, *Artemis Soteira), expressing their power to save people from danger. It has no Latin equivalent (Cic. *Verr.* 2. 2. 154), except perhaps for Juno Sospita. Christian ideas of the Saviour must not be projected onto pre-Christian usage. 'Soter' comments on function, and does not imply divine status. But from early times the word was used by analogy of humans who performed extraordinary deeds worthy of divine cult (Aesch. *Supp.* 980–2; cf. Thuc. 5. 11. 1). In the Hellenistic period it was often used of kings: *Antigonus (3) Doson was called Euergetes (Benefactor) in his lifetime, Soter after his death (Polyb. 5. 9. 10); *Ptolemy (1) I Soter is perhaps the most famous holder of the title. It became a commonplace of honours to Roman officials in the east (including Verres, Cic. ibid.). See RULER-CULT.

A. D. Nock, *Essays* (1972), 1. 78–84, 2. 720–35.   H. J. R.; S. R. F. P.

Soteria The term was applied to a sacrifice or festival celebrating deliverance from danger, on behalf of individuals or a community. The gods in general (e.g. Xen. *Anab.* 3. 2. 9) or a particular god could be the recipient of the sacrifice. *Soter, 'the Deliverer', was especially an epithet of *Zeus, as appropriately at the seaport of *Piraeus. Recently heroized men regarded as deliverers, such as *Aratus (2) at *Sicyon and *Philopoemen at *Megalopolis, could be associated with Zeus Soter and his Soteria. See HERO-CULT. In the Hellenistic period a number of regular annual or quadrennial festivals with this name were instituted (see AGŌNES). Of the sixteen known, the most famous was that established at *Delphi shortly after the gods were said to have appeared and turned back the *Celts under the command of *Brennus (2) in 279/8 BC. These Soteria are known from Delphic inscriptions and from the inscribed acceptances to Delphic invitations to participate by a number of Greek cities. They were reorganized by the *Aetolian Confederacy c.246 BC. In addition to athletic events musical competitions were conspicuous. See also SALUS.

F. Pfister, *RE* 3 A (1927), 'Soteria'; G. Nachtergael, *Les Galates en Grèce* (1977), 209–495.   M. H. J.

Soterichus (c. AD 300), epic poet from Libya; the *Suda* lists epics on various mythical and historical subjects and an *Encomium of *Diocletian.   R. L. Hu.

Sotion (1) (*RE* 1) of *Alexandria (1), *Peripatetic, wrote (? between 200 and 170 BC) *Succession of the Philosophers* in thirteen books, and a book on *Timon (1)'s *Silloi*. The former work, treating each philosopher as the definite successor of another, was a main though not a direct source for *Diogenes (6) Laertius, and for the doxographic summaries in patristic writers such as *Eusebius and *Theodoret; it apparently introduced the division of philosophical successions into Ionian and Italian.

TEXTS F. Wehrli, *Die Schule des Aristoteles*, suppl. vol. 2 (1978).
STUDIES F. Wehrli, in Ueberweg–Flashar, 584–7; Diels, *Dox. Graec.* 147–9.   R. W. S.

Sotion (2) (*RE* 2) Peripatetic, not earlier than AD 14. Works: *Cornucopia*; *Strange Stories about rivers, springs, and pools* (formerly identified with the surviving *Paradoxographus Florentinus*); *Dioclean Disputations* (against *Epicurus); commentary on the *Topics*.

A. Giannini, *Acme* 1964, 128, 135–6, and *Paradoxographorum Graecorum Reliquiae* (1966), 167 f. P. Moraux, *Der Aristotelismus* 2 (1984), 212–14.   W. D. R.; R. W. S.

soul The term in Greek nearest to English 'soul', ψυχή (*psyche*, Latin *anima*), has a long history and a wide variety of senses in both philosophical and non-philosophical contexts. In *Homer, the psyche is what leaves the *body on death (i.e. life, or breath?), but also an insubstantial image of the dead person, existing in *Hades and emphatically not something alive. But some vague idea of psyche as the essence of the individual, capable of surviv-

ing the body (and perhaps entering another) is well-established by the 5th cent. (e.g. *IG* 1³. 1179. 6; Pindar, *Ol.* 2. 56–80), though without necessarily displacing the older idea and even being combined with it (Pindar, fr. 131 *b* Snell/Maehler). Simultaneously, in medical contexts and elsewhere, psyche begins to be found regularly in contrast with σῶμα (*sōma*), suggesting something like the modern contrast between 'mind' and body.

All of these ideas are found, separately or in combination, in the philosophers. *Democritus stresses the interconnectedness of psyche ('mind') and body, while *Socrates regards the psyche primarily as our essence *qua* moral beings. Socrates was probably agnostic about whether it was something capable of surviving death; Plato, by contrast, offers repeated arguments for the immortality of the psyche, which he combines with the (originally Pythagorean) idea that it transmigrates, after the death of the person, into another body, human or animal. See PYTHAGORAS (1); TRANSMIGRATION. Sometimes he represents the psyche as something purely (or ultimately) rational, sometimes as irrevocably including irrational elements. At the same time his myths include many aspects of Homeric eschatology, which may have retained an important place in popular belief. *Aristotle is at the furthest remove from non-philosophical attitudes, adopting a largely biological approach which says that the psyche is the 'form' of the living creature, i.e. the combination of powers or capacities to do the things which are characteristic of its species.

In philosophical contexts, the primary connotations of psyche are probably life, consciousness, and 'self-caused' movement. Psyche, or an aspect of it, is typically made the ultimate cause of all or most movement, whether in the shape of a world soul, as in Platonism (see PLATO (1)), or of god, as in Aristotle and *Stoicism. The chief exception is Epicureanism (see EPICURUS), which makes the movements of atoms themselves primary. It was also the Epicureans, among the philosophers, who most resolutely opposed the idea of an immortal psyche (even Aristotle allowed that the highest aspect of reason might be immortal and divine). Outside philosophy, until the Christian era, the idea, or notions more or less vaguely resembling it, are found chiefly in the context of mystery or ecstatic religion (see ECSTASY; MYSTERIES), and in literature reflecting influence from such sources.

J. Bremmer, *The Early Greek Concept of the Soul* (1983); S. Everson (ed.), *Psychology* (Companions to Ancient Thought 2, 1991).   C. J. R.

sovereignty See AUTONOMY; DEMOCRACY; KINGSHIP; OLIGARCHY; PLEBISCITUM; POLIS; POLITICAL THEORY; SENATE.

Sozomen (Salamanes Hermeias Sozomenus), an advocate in *Constantinople in the 5th cent. AD, wrote a compendium of history from the Ascension to 324 in two books (now lost) and a continuation of *Eusebius' *Historia Ecclesiastica* to 439 (although the conclusion is missing). Born into a family near Gaza recently converted to Christianity, he was ambitious for imperial notice, dedicating his History to *Theodosius (3) II. Perceiving, like *Socrates Scholasticus before him, the need to redefine ecclesiastical history under a Christian empire, Sozomen stressed the propriety of including secular material, with special reference to laws, perhaps inspired by the recent publication of the *Theodosian Code (438). More stylish than Socrates, he includes additional material on monasticism and his last book depends heavily on the pagan Olympiodorus' account of western events (published in 425). His History was edited along with those of Socrates and *Theodoret to form the Latin manual, the *Historia Tripartita*.

TEXT Ed. J. Bidez and G. C. Hansen (1960).   J. D. H.

Spain

Prehistory The geographical diversity of the Iberian peninsula enforced cultural heterogeneity. Native peoples drew upon abundant metal resources and rich agricultural areas to achieve a cultural balance between tradition and foreign influence. This was the basis for the emergence of the bronze age Argaric culture (2nd millennium BC) of the south-east, the Atlantic bronze age complex (early 1st millennium BC), and the arrival of the Urnfields (see CELTS) in the north-east (early 1st millennium BC). Contact with the *Phoenicians and Greeks gave rise to the *Tartessus and eventually the urbanized Iberian peoples (5th cent. BC onwards) of the Mediterranean coast. The culture and later urbanization of central (including the *Celtiberians), western, northern, and some parts of southern Iberia were conditioned by the movement of Celtic peoples or cultural types from *c*.500 BC onwards.

Phoenicians, Greeks, Carthaginians Traditionally Phoenicians from *Tyre founded *Gades *c*.1100 BC, although archaeologists have lowered the date to the 8th cent. BC. Nine further colonies were later established along the coast of southern Spain between Abdera and the river Guadalhorce, and at Ebusus (Ibiza). These traded with *Tartessus until the 6th cent. BC, when waning Phoenician power was replaced by that of *Carthage. In the mid-6th cent. BC Greeks from Phocaea founded colonies in Iberia, notably at *Emporion, Rhode (Roses) and Maenace (near Málaga), the latter perhaps an attempt to profit from the Phoenician decline. Carthaginian power in Iberia was enhanced with the conquests in the south by *Hamilcar (2) Barca and *Hannibal from 237 BC. These culminated in the foundation of *Carthago Nova, as Carthage mobilized Iberian manpower and metal resources for the attack on Rome. The Second *Punic War, starting from Hannibal's siege of Rome's ally *Saguntum and his approach to the Ebro, continued in the Iberian theatre until Carthage was driven out by P. *Cornelius Scipio Africanus in 206 BC.

The Roman Provinces Roman territory was formally constituted as two separate provinces, Hispania Citerior (the eastern coastal strip) and Hispania Ulterior (the south-east coast and the Guadalquivir valley) in 197 BC. Both provinces were gradually extended inland in rapacious and reactive campaigns against native peoples and tribes bordering the provinces, culminating in the Lusitanian (155–139 BC) and Celtiberian (155–133 BC) wars. This left the greater part of Iberia in Roman hands. Further conquest was halted and further operations—sorties by triumph-hunting generals, and *Caesar's civil war against the Pompeians (49–45 BC; see POMPEIUS MAGNUS (2), CN.; POMPEIUS MAGNUS, SEXTUS)—were not attempts at expansion. Systematic exploitation of the provinces appears not to have begun before the 170s BC. Tribute eventually comprised a fixed money payment and one-twentieth of the grain crop, and prompted the silver and bronze issues minted by native communities in northern Citerior and Ulterior (bronze only) at Rome's behest. Cases of misgovernment led in 171 to the institution of trials *de repetundis* (see REPETUNDAE), but the picture of oppression was exaggerated by unreliable sources. *Mines (those of Carthago Nova yielded 2,500 *drachmae* daily) were rented out, for a fixed payment related to production, to Italian businessmen (see NEGOTIATORES), who settled in moderate numbers in centres like Carthago Nova, *Corduba, and *Tarraco. There were also substantial bodies of Roman settlers at *Italica (206) and *Valentia (138), half-Iberian *libertini* (*freedman) at *Carteia (171), and *hybridae* (half-Spanish settlers) and natives at Palma and Pollentia (122/121), and possibly in other centres. Elsewhere Rome fostered new native towns (e.g. Gracchuris,

founded in 179 by Ti. *Sempronius Gracchus (2). In general terms, however, there is little evidence that Rome either systematically urbanized the provinces or attempted to enhance native agriculture before the mid-1st cent. BC.

The conquest of Iberia was completed by *Augustus in the Cantabrian Wars (26–19 BC). This resulted in a largely new province of *Lusitania and a great new extension of Citerior (renamed *Tarraconensis) to the north and west ocean. These provinces were assigned to the emperor; most of Ulterior (renamed *Baetica) was returned to the senate in 27 BC. The new Augustan conquest required three legions in north-west Tarraconensis; by the time of *Vespasian they had been reduced to VII Gemina only (see LEGION). Twenty-two colonies were founded (see COLONIZATION, ROMAN), and a large number of *municipia* created, under Caesar and Augustus, forming the basis for a Roman urban network within juridical *conventus* (2) in each province. Following the development of a municipal imperial cult at Tarraco (AD 15), there soon followed the establishment of a conventual (Tarraconensis) and provincial imperial cult (under the Flavians). See RULER-CULT.

The density and sophistication of Hispano-Roman towns varied greatly from region to region. However, a substantial number of the 1st-cent. provincial senators at Rome came from the colonies of the Hispaniae (see SENATORS, PATTERNS OF RECRUITMENT). In literature they produced the Senecas (see ANNAEUS SENECA (1) AND (2), L.) and Lucan (ANNAEUS LUCANUS, M.; *Columella, *Quintilian, and *Martial were of native stock. The emperors *Trajan, *Hadrian, and Marcus *Aurelius had Spanish ancestry. However, despite *Vespasian's grant of Latin rights (see IUS LATII) to all Spanish communities, many retained native cultural traits. The systematic and large-scale exploitation of gold in north-west Tarraconensis, as well as silver (especially near *Castulo) and other metals (as at Río Tinto), provided important revenue for Rome and was underwritten by an extensive road network (notably the via Augusta, the Asturica to *Emerita Augusta road). Wine (from Tarraconensis) and fish-sauce were widely distributed, while the state monitored the production of Baetican olive oil for Rome and the frontiers (see AMPHORAE, ROMAN).

The mid-3rd cent. Frankish invasions were of little consequence for the long-term development of the provinces. However, this century saw the diminution of Spanish exports and accelerating municipal decline. *Diocletian divided Hispania Tarraconensis into three and added Tingitana: the Balearics were added in 395. The rewalling and continued decline of many towns in the 4th cent. was matched by the flourishing of large residential country villas and the emergence of powerful country-based aristocracies, like the family of emperor *Theodosius (2) I. A powerful church by the early 4th cent. is evident from the council of Elvira (Illiberis, mod. Granada), and its position was enhanced by Hosius (Ossius), bishop of Corduba; it also produced *Prudentius and *Orosius. The barbarian invasions of 409 rapidly led to the loss of Roman control in all provinces, except the Balearics (by 455; see BALEARES ET PITHYUSAE INSULAE) and Tarraconensis (by 475). Unified Visigothic control (see GOTHS) was established by 586, although parts of southern Spain were held by the Byzantines between 552 and 624.

CLASSICAL SOURCES *Fontes Hispaniae Antiquae* 1–8 (1922–1950), ed. A. Schulten, P. Bosch Gimpera, L. Pericot; Strabo, bk. 3; Plin. *HN* 3 and 4. 20–3; Ptolemy, 2. 3–5. Inscriptions: *CIL* 2 and Suppl.; A. Tovar, *Iberische Landeskunde* 1 (1974), 2 (1976), 3 (1989). Coins: L. Villaronga, *Numismática Antigua de Hispania* (1979); A. Guadán, *La Moneda Ibérica*

Spain, pre-Roman scripts and languages

(1980); A. Burnett and others, *Roman Provincial Coinage* 1 (1992). Monuments: S. Keay, *Roman Spain* (1988); W. Trillmich and P. Zanker (eds.), *Städtbild und Ideologie* (1990); J. G. Gorges, *Les Villas Hispano-Romaines* (1979).

MODERN WORKS Early Spain: H. Savory, *Spain and Portugal* (1968); F. Jordá Cerdá and others, *Historia de España*, 1. *Prehistoria* (1986); M. E. Aubet, *Tiro y Las Colonias Fenicias De Occidente* (1987); A. García y Bellido, *Hispania Graeca* (1948); A. Ruíz and M. Molinos (eds.), *Iberos* (1987); R. Menéndez Pidal (ed.), *Historia de España* 1 (1954), 5 ff. Early Roman Spain: J. Richardson, *Hispaniae* (1986); N. Mackie, *Local Administration in Roman Spain AD 14–212* (1983); R. Menéndez Pidal (ed.), *Historia de España* 1 (1981), 2 (1982); P. Le Roux, *L'Armée romaine et l'organisation des provinces ibériques d'Auguste à l'invasion de 409* (1982); R. Étienne, *Le Culte impérial dans la péninsule ibérique d'Auguste à Dioclétien* (1958); C. Domergue, *Les Mines de la péninsule ibérique dans l'antiquité romaine* (1990); *Producción y comercio del aceite en la Antigüedad: Primer* (1981) and *Segundo* (1983) *congreso internacional*; G. Alföldy, *CAH* 10² (1996), ch. 13c. Late Roman Spain: J. Arce, *El último siglo de la España romana* (1982); R. Collins, *Early Medieval Spain* (1983). S. J. K.

Spain, pre-Roman scripts and languages There are two scripts, narrowly delimited in time and place, that were taken over directly from outside the peninsula: a variant of the Libyan alphabet appears on coins in southern Andalucia; an early Ionian-Greek alphabet was used about 400 BC for writing the Iberian language in the area of the modern provinces of Alicante and Murcia, the most notable find-place being Alcoy (prov. Alicante), the most important text being preserved on a lead plaque, inscribed on both sides, found at that site.

Much more widespread are the three variants of the ancient Hispanic script: the Tartessian, the Southern Iberian, and the Northeastern Iberian. They derive from a combination, created in the peninsula itself, of Greek and *Phoenician elements, and differ from all other scripts of the ancient Mediterranean area in their system. Vowels and sonants are represented by one letter each. Stops can only be represented in connection with a vowel, i.e. as syllabic signs (*ba*, *be*, *bi*, *bo*, *bu*, etc.). We do not know exactly when and where the script was created: probably about 600 BC in the south-western part of the peninsula. The Northeastern Iberian alphabet is now completely legible, thanks to its decipherment in 1920 by the Spanish scholar M. Gómez-Moreno. With some delay—due to the much poorer attestation—the values of most signs of the Southern Iberian and the Tartessian script (cf. TARTESSUS) have now been established. The present state of interpretation is shown in Fig. 1.

The Tartessian variant, attested perhaps as early as the 6th cent. BC, is particularly well represented in southern Portugal. Most of the 65 documents are stone funeral stelae. The language has not yet been identified—it does not seem to conform to any other ancient language of the peninsula.

The Southern Iberian, very similar to the Tartessian script, is found in an area between Andalucia and the Cabo de la Nao. All the documents (mostly graffiti on ceramics and silver vessels and a few lead plaques) are—like the inscriptions in Greek script from the same area—in the language conventionally called 'Iberian', which, although not yet understood, can be recognized by specific morphological elements, by frequently recurring words, and, above all, by personal names. It seems certain that Iberian does not belong to the *Indo-European family.

The best attested script is the Northeastern Iberian: it dominates the coast between Valencia in Spain and Béziers in southern

Ancient Hispanic Scripts			
	north-east →	southern ←	tartessian ←
a	P R	Λ	Λ
e	Ⴑ Ⴒ	o	o
i	⋈	⋈	⋈
o	H	⊤ ‡	‡
u	↑	Ч	u
l	Γ Λ	⌐	⌐
r	⊲ ◁	q	q
ŕ	Φ Φ	⋊	⋊
n	Ⴁ	⋎	⋎
m	Ⴗ (ⴸⴸ)		M ?
s	⊰ ⊱	‡	‡
ś	M	M	M
ka	Λ Λ	Λ	Λ
ke	⊰ ⊱	⊁	⊁
ki	⋏	⋏	?
ko	⧖	⋈	⋈
ku	◇ ⊙		⊟ ?
ta	⤬	+ ⤬	⤬
te	◇ ⊘ ⊗	Φ ?	⊟ ?
ti	Ψ Ψ	Φ Φ	Φ
to	Ш	?	Λ
tu	Δ	Δ	Δ
ba	⟨ ⟨	⌐	⟨
be	⊗ ⊗ ⊍	⋜ ?	⊖
bi	⌐	↑	?
bo	✳	⋈	☐
bu	☐	?	⋈

France and the north-eastern Spanish inland regions to the upper Douro, the upper and middle Ebro, reaching into the Catalonian Pyrenees. It is used for two completely different languages: in the area between the Ebro, the Cantabrian mountains, and the upper part of the Tagus, there is an Old Celtic dialect, called 'Celtiberian', attested by about 60 documents dating from the 2nd and 1st cents. BC, mostly coins, but also including small bronze objects with *tesserae hospitales* (friendship certificates) and two extensive texts on bronze tablets, both discovered at Contrebia Belaisca near the present-day site of Botorrita (prov. Zaragoza).

All other inscriptions in the Northeastern Iberian script—

about 1,500 altogether (many very short)—are in the Iberian language already mentioned. They are preserved on coins, lead plaques, gravestones, pottery, and many other ornamental objects and domestic implements. The most important find-places are Liria (prov. Valencia), Sagunto, Azaila (prov. Zaragoza), Tarragona, Ullastret (prov. Gerona), Ampurias (*Emporion*), and Ensérune near Béziers in southern France. The oldest texts are dated to the 5th cent. BC, the latest to about 50 BC.

The indigenous language of *Lusitania, the present-day Portugal, appears only very late, in the 1st cent. BC, in a small number of inscriptions in Latin script. This too is probably to be ascribed to the Celtic language group, and will therefore be closely related to, though not identical with, Celtiberian.

Proper names provide a less direct source for the languages. It is only after the Latinization of the peninsula that we find them everywhere, but they are survivals from the pre-Roman period and so provide further information about the nature and distribution of the pre-Roman languages. Personal names (predominantly in Latin inscriptions of the imperial period) and place names (known principally from the writings of *Pliny (1) and *Ptolemy (4)) are available for the whole of Hispania; for the centre, and particularly for the north-west, there are also very characteristic divine names. These sources confirm in all essential points the picture presented by the pre-Roman inscriptions: there are two main language areas—the Iberian and the Celtiberian, of which the Iberian, especially in northern Aragon, clearly extends beyond the range of the inscriptions, while the Celtiberian proves to be part of a great Celtic-speaking Hispania, comprising Lusitania, Galicia, Asturia, Cantabria, and the whole of the inland areas between Gudiana and the Ebro.

J. A. Correa, 'El signario de Espanca (Castro Verde) y la escritura tartesia', in *Actas del V Coloquio sobre lenguas y culturas prerromanas de la Península Ibérica (Köln 1989)* (1993), 499–541; J. de Hoz, 'Origine ed evoluzione delle scritture ispaniche', AION 1983, 27–61, and 'Las lenguas y la epigrafia prerromanas de la Península Ibérica', in *Actas del VI Congreso Español de Estudios Clásicos, Madrid* (1983), 351–96; C. M. de Mello Beirão, *Une civilisation protohistorique du sud de Portugal (1er age du fer)* (1986); J. Untermann, *Monumenta Linguarum Hispanicarum* 1–3 (1975–90); D. E. Evans, 'The identification of Continental Celtic with special reference to Hispano-Celtic', in *Actas del V Coloquio sobre lenguas y culturas prerromanas de la Península Ibérica (Köln 1989)* (1993), 563–608; F. Villar, 'Indo-Européen et Pré-Indo-Européen dans la Péninsule Ibérique', in T. L. Markey, J. A. C. Greppin (eds.), *When Worlds Collide* (Bellagio Conference, 1990), 363–94.   J. U.

Sparta

1. Prehistory Sparta ('the sown land'?) lies *c*.56 km. (35 miles) south of *Tegea, and 48 km. (30 mi.) north of Gytheum, at the heart of the fertile alluvial valley of the Eurotas. See LACONIA. Very few prehistoric remains are known from the site of historical Sparta, but there was a substantial neolithic community not far south, and a major late bronze age settlement about 3 km. northeast (the '*Menelaion' site at Therapne). The circumstances of the settlement of Sparta town are enveloped in the fog of myth and legend: the 'Return of the Heraclids', as the ancients put it, and the 'Dorian Invasion', in modern parlance (see DORIANS; HERACLIDAE). Archaeology as currently understood suggests a cultural break with the bronze age and a humble new beginning somewhere in the darkness of the 10th cent.; the initial relationship between Sparta and *Amyclae, which by 700 had been incorporated on equal terms with the other four villages comprising Sparta town, is no less obscure.

2. Archaic and Classical In a long war, usually placed in the later 8th cent., much of neighbouring Messenia was annexed and its population helotized (see HELOTS). The conquest transformed Sparta into a leading Greek state, culturally as well as militarily, as attested by the wealth of dedications at the sanctuary of *Artemis Orthia and numerous visits by foreign poets. But it also prompted the (poorly understood) dispute surrounding the Partheniai, who departed to found Taras (*Tarentum, mod. Taranto) *c*.700; and it saddled Sparta with lasting problems of security, both internal and external. During the 7th cent. Sparta was confronted with a major Messenian revolt (the 'Second Messenian War'; see MESSENIA, *Myth-history*), internal discontent from poor citizens, and probably military defeat by *Argos (2) at Hysiae in 669. During the 6th cent. the external problem was solved by several successful wars—especially against Argos *c*.545 and, after a serious defeat, against *Tegea—followed by a new policy that created a system of unequal alliances which developed into the *'Peloponnesian League'. The League, which underpinned Sparta's dominance until the mid-4th cent., provided external co-operation against the helots in return for support for broadly-based oligarchies. An alliance with *Croesus of Lydia and an expedition against *Polycrates (1) of Samos *c*.525 are signs of Sparta's prominence among Greek states.

Sparta's internal problems were tackled by extending her control over the whole of Messenia and through a thoroughgoing reorganization of Spartan institutions and way of life which embodied a social compromise between rich and poor citizens. The exact chronology of this reorganization is uncertain. Later Spartans attributed it to a single, early lawgiver, *Lycurgus (2). Most current opinion, while agreeing that the fundamental changes were consciously planned following a common logic, views them as being implemented in a continuing process of adaptation between the 7th and 5th cents. There were three essential elements of the 'remodelled' Spartan society. First, an economic system, according to which *citizenship was extended to a body of several thousand men who, as full-time hoplites supported by produce delivered by helots who worked their private estates, were debarred from agricultural labour, business activity, and a range of expenditures for consumption and display. Secondly, a political system initiated by the 7th-cent. 'Great Rhetra' (Plut. *Lyc.* 6) which combined a limited right of veto for the citizen assembly with the strong executive powers of the *ephors, the extra-constitutional influence of the two kings, and the formidable, conservative authority of the *gerousia (council of elders). Thirdly, a social and ritual system, as part of which every Spartiate or full citizen (except the two kings and their immediate heirs) underwent an austere public upbringing (the *agōgē) followed by a common lifestyle of participation in the messes (*syssitia) and in military training and service in the army.

The result was the creation of the famous *eunomia* ('good order'), admired by both contemporaries and later generations for its long-term stability. Few of its specific institutions were in themselves unique; many were transformations of earlier institutions or were paralleled elsewhere in Greece. What was distinctive was their combination into a coherent structure which attempted to produce a unified citizen body of *homoioi* ('Peers' rather than 'Equals') whose subservience to collective interests and military training would ensure effective policing of the helots. The reorganization had its limits. The cultural impact was gradual: Olympic athletic victories continued until *c*.550 (see OLYMPIAN GAMES), and Laconian painted pottery and bronze vessel production until a generation later. Several spheres of Spartiate society were only partially affected, especially the strength of family allegiances and more independent role of citizen women. Although this is controversial, land tenure probably remained essentially private and its distribution very unequal.

During the reign of *Cleomenes (1) I (c.520–490) Sparta ousted the tyrants from Athens (see HIPPIAS (1)), but failed to control the subsequent democracy and declined various external appeals for assistance, especially against Persia. Sparta commanded the Greek resistance to *Xerxes' invasion (480/79; see PERSIAN WARS); but afterwards its leadership of the Greek alliance and campaigns against medizing states in northern Greece foundered amidst the disgrace of the regent *Pausanias (1) and King *Leotychidas II. The 470s and 460s were decades of crisis marked by conflict with her Arcadian allies and a long helot revolt following losses in the severe earthquake of c.465. The remainder of the 5th cent. was dominated by wars with Athens (the so-called 'First' *Peloponnesian war c.460–446 being conventionally distinguished from that of 431–404). Their controversial origins were, on Sparta's side, connected with her fear that Athenian imperialism would destabilize the Peloponnesian League. Sparta's traditional strategy of invading Attic territory failed; but Athens was ultimately starved into surrender after *Lysander, with Persian financial help, destroyed her fleet at Aegospotami (405). Sparta's subsequent imperialist activities in Asia Minor, central and northern Greece, and even in *Sicily and (possibly) Egypt, led to the *Corinthian War (394–387) against a hostile Graeco-Persian coalition. In the *King's Peace (387/6) Sparta traded her overseas empire for domination in mainland Greece, which was pursued vigorously against *Thebes (1) by King *Agesilaus II; but her supremacy was destroyed by defeat at *Leuctra (371). Ensuing Theban invasions brought the liberation of Messenia (370/69), the foundation of *Megalopolis (368) in south-western *Arcadia, and the demise of the Peloponnesian League (366), thereby reducing her to a second-rate power.

The roots of Sparta's international decline lay in internal difficulties. Inequalities in landholding developed during the 5th cent. as the employment of wealth for élite activities such as chariot racing became increasingly significant as a determinant of status. Many poorer Spartiates became unable to provide their contributions to the common messes which were a necessary condition of citizenship. The homoioi, 8,000 strong in 480, dwindled to c.1500 by 371. The sources' claim that Sparta was ruined by the influx of imperial wealth may be merely moralizing commonplace; but the development of independent foreign commands and of competing internal factions during the period of empire did mean enlarged opportunities for economic patronage. Unwilling to address the problems of poor Spartiates, the authorities' increasing reliance on non-Spartiate troops left Sparta unable to resist her enemies' dismantling of her power.

3. Hellenistic and Roman Down to the early 2nd cent. BC Sparta intermittently—and unsuccessfully—launched attempts to regain her old hegemony by challenging successively the domination of the Peloponnese by *Macedonia and the *Achaean Confederacy; in the same period the Spartan polity and way of life lost much of its distinctiveness (in the mid-3rd cent. the *agōgē* lapsed; and *Areus refashioned the royal dyarchy into a Hellenistic-style kingship). *Cleomenes (2) III sought a root-and-branch internal reform in a (failed) attempt to revitalize Sparta's military machine; in doing so he claimed to be recreating the laws of Lycurgus, many of which, as recorded by *Plutarch and other later writers, were probably invented at this time (see PATRONOMOS). The reign of

*Nabis marks the last glow of Spartan independence; his assassination, and Sparta's subsequent forced inclusion in the Achaean Confederacy (195 BC) marks its final extinction; in 147 BC, in response to Spartan complaints, Rome allowed the city to leave the confederacy, a development prompting the Achaean War and *Greece's partial provincialization. After 146 Sparta remained on good terms with the Romans, admirers of Classical Sparta, and counted among *Achaia's *free cities. Under Augustus his partisan C. *Iulius Eurycles founded a Spartan client-dynasty lasting (with breaks) until Nero. Roman Sparta, its 'Lycurgan customs' now an object of cultural *tourism, is a particularly well-documented example of the archaism marking Greek civic life in the age of the *Panhellenion and the *Second Sophistic. There are extensive remains of the Roman city, which survived, spatially much reduced, a sack by *Alaric (AD 396).

KING-LIST. Before c.800 BC the list is very hypothetical. Until 491/90, the Spartans claimed, son had succeeded father; though it is difficult to believe, there is no evidence to refute the claim. Thereafter relationship is indicated in brackets, the reference being to the preceding king. On the problems of the king-lists in their early reaches (Hdt. 7. 204 and 8. 131) see Cartledge, *Sparta and Lakonia* app. 3 and *Agesilaos* 22 f. 102 f., and fig. 7 (for these works see bibliog. below).

*AGIADS	*EURYPONTIDS
Agis, 930–900.	Eurypon, 890–860.
Echestratus, 900–870.	Prytanis, 860–830.
Leobotes, 870–840.	Polydectes, 830–800.
Dorussus, 840–820.	Eunomus, 800–780.
Agesilaus I, 820–790.	Charillus, c.780–750.
Archelaus, c.790–760.	Nicandrus, c.750–720.
Teleclus, c.760–740.	*Theopompus (1), c.720–675.
Alcamenes, c.740–700.	Anaxandridas, c.675–665.
Polydorus, c.700–665.	Archidamus I, c.665–645.
Eurycrates, c.665–640.	Anaxilas, c.645–625.
Anaxandrus, c.640–615.	Leotychidas I, c.625–600.
Eurycratidas, c.615–590.	Hippocratidas, c.600–575.
Leon, c.590–560.	Agasicles, c.575–550.
Anaxandridas, c.560–520.	Ariston, c.550–515.
*Cleomenes (1) I, c.520–490.	*Demaratus (2), c.515–491.
*Leonidas (1) I (brother), 490–480.	*Leotychidas II (cousin—great-grandson of Hippocratidas), 491–469.
Pleistarchus (son), 480–459.	
Pleistoanax (son), 459–409.	*Archidamus II (grandson), 469–427.
*Pausanias (2) (son), 409–395.	*Agis II (son), 427–400.
Agesipolis I (son), 395–380.	*Agesilaus II (brother), 400–360.
Cleombrotus I (brother), 380–371.	*Archidamus III (son), 360–338.
Agesipolis II (son), 371–370.	*Agis III (son), 338–330.
Cleomenes II (brother), 370–309.	Eudamidas I (brother), 330–c.305.
*Areus I (grandson), 309–265.	Archidamus IV (son), c.305–275.
Acrotatus (son), 265–262.	Eudamidas II (son), c.275–244.
Areus II (son), 262–254.	*Agis IV (son), c.244–241.
Leonidas II (grandson of Cleomenes (2) II), 254–235.	Eudamidas III (son), 241–c.228.
*Cleomenes III (son), 235–222.	Archidamus V (uncle), 228–227.
Agesipolis III (grandson of Cleombrotus II), 219–215.	Eucleidas (Agiad—brother of Cleomenes III), 227–222.
	(See also NABIS)

EXCAVATIONS AND ANTIQUITIES P. Cartledge, *PECS* entries 'Amyclae' and 'Sparta'; Greek rescue-excavations are reported in *AΔ*, British work in *BSA*, esp. vols. 12 (1905–6)–15 (1908–9), 26 (1923–5)–30 (1928–30), and 88 (1994). R. Dawkins (ed.), *Artemis Orthia* (1929), with J. Boardman, *BSA* 1963, 1 ff.; M. Tod and A. Wace, *Catalogue of the Sparta Museum* (1906); Cartledge and Spawforth (below), app. 1 (Roman-period monuments).

ANCIENT SOURCES Documents: *IG* 5. 1. 1 ff.; thereafter new finds in *BE* and *SEG* (esp. vol. 11); W. T. Loomis, *The Spartan War Fund* (1992); ML 67 (67 bis in 1988 repr.), 95; Tod 99; *BSA* 1994, 433 ff.
Coins: S. Grunauer-von Hoerschelmann, *Die Münzpräger der Lakedaimonier* (1978).
Poets: see Alcman and Tyrtaeus; Homer, esp. *Od.* 4. Prose: Hdt. 1. 65 ff., bks. 5–6 *passim* (Cleomenes), bks. 7–9 (Persian Wars); Thuc. 1. 10, 18, 89 ff., 101–3, 128 ff. (Pausanias), bks. 2–8 *passim* (Peloponnesian War); *Hell. Oxy. passim*; Xen. *Hell. passim* (empire and decline), *Anab.* bks. 1, 6–7, *Ages.*, *Lac.*; Arist. *Pol.* 2. 9, 5. 7, and *passim*; Diod. bks. 7–15 *passim*; Plut. *Lyc.*, *Lys.*, *Ages.*, *Agis* (IV), *Cleomenes* (III), *Apophthegmata Lac.* For topography: Strabo 8. 4–6 (Laconia); Pausanias 3. 11–20 (Sparta).
MODERN WORKS The article 'Sparta' in *RE* 3 A 2 (1929) is still valuable. More recent works include P. Cartledge, *Sparta and Lakonia: A Regional History, 1300–362 BC*, 2nd edn. (2002), and *Agesilaos and the Crisis of Sparta* (1987); P. Cartledge and A. Spawforth, *Hellenistic and Roman Sparta*, 2nd edn. (2002); W. G. Forrest, *A History of Sparta, 950–192 BC* (repr. 1980); L. F. Fitzhardinge, *The Spartans* (repr. 1985) (on Laconian art); M. I. Finley, 'Sparta', in *The Use and Abuse of History* (corr. repr. 1990), ch. 10; N. Kennell, *The Gymnasium of Virtue* (1995, on the *agōgē*); A. Powell (ed.), *Classical Sparta* (1989); A. Powell and S. Hodkinson (eds.), *The Shadow of Sparta* (1994); D. M. MacDowell, *Spartan Law* (1986); E. N. Tigerstedt, *The Legend of Sparta in Classical Antiquity*, 3 vols. (1965–78); M. Clauss, *Sparta* (1983), with a detailed bibliography; J. Sanders (ed.), *ΦΙΛΟΛΑΚΩΝ: Lakonian Studies in honour of Hector Catling* (1992) (chs. by Cartledge and P. Calligas deal with the 'Dark Age').
TOPOGRAPHY C. Stibbe, *BaBesch*. 1989, 61 ff.
P. A. C.; S. J. Ho.; A. J. S. S.

Sparta (site) The settlement developed at the northern end of the central plain of *Laconia on land sloping eastwards to the marshy banks (hence 'Limnae': see below) of the river Eurotas and punctuated with low hills, one the so-called acropolis. Relating the extensive site (just under 209 ha. within the Hellenistic city-wall) to the description of *Pausanias (3) is bedevilled by failure so far to locate the *agora. The only major public buildings of the Classical 'city' identified to date are the sanctuaries of *Artemis Orthia ('Limnaeum', 'Artemisium') on the west bank of the river, and of *Athena Chalcioecus ('Bronze House') on the acropolis, both by their modesty (e.g. small, non-peripteral *temples) supporting the claim of *Thucydides (2) (1. 10. 2) that Sparta in its heyday lacked architecture commensurate with its power (although the Persian Stoa, begun with *Persian Wars *booty, impressed later generations: Paus. 3. 11. 3). The Classical city was also notable because (1) Spartan military self-confidence allowed it to remain without *fortifications (first attested as a defence against *Cassander, with a continuous circuit-wall, in mudbrick, completed only under *Nabis); and (2) its inhabitants lived in villages (four of them: Pitana, Mesoa, Limnae, and Cynosura), an old-fashioned pattern persisting into Augustan times. Archaeology has yet to illuminate the 'typical' Spartan house (hardly 'home') of Classical times. Routine forms of Graeco-Roman *urbanism appear in Sparta only with the final decay of its distinctive socio-political structure after the death of Nabis: e.g. comfortable private houses (attested from the late 2nd cent. BC to the 4th AD) and, under the Principate, *baths, a theatre, etc. An inner city-wall of disputed date, enclosing the acropolis only and built from demolished Classical buildings, may be as late as the early 5th cent. See also AMYCLAE; MENELAION.

See bibliog. under SPARTA; also G. Waywell, *BKS* 43 (1999). A. J. S. S.

Spartacus, a Thracian *gladiator (see THRACE) and former Roman auxiliary soldier (see AUXILIA), who led a revolt which began in the gladiatorial schools (see GLADIATORS) at *Capua in 73 BC. He was first supported by fighters of Thracian and Celtic extraction (see CELTS), but later acquired adherents from slaves and even the free proletariat in the countryside of southern Italy (many of these would have been working the large estates or *latifundia devoted to stockraising in that area). Ultimately his army was estimated at figures ranging from 70,000 to 120,000. In 73 he defeated two Roman commanders and ranged over southern Italy. In 72, although his Celtic lieutenant Crixus was defeated, he himself overcame both consuls and reached *Cisalpine Gaul, whence, it is said, he hoped his followers would disperse to their homes. They, however, preferred to continue to ravage Italy. Spartacus, accordingly, returned south and after at least one major victory, devastated Lucania and would have invaded Sicily, if he had succeeded in obtaining transport from the pirates. In 71 *Crassus, after trying to cut off Spartacus in Bruttium (see BRUTTII), caught and destroyed his army in *Lucania, subsequently crucifying any survivors he captured. Spartacus himself was killed, though his body was never found. *Pompey on his return from Spain annihilated others who had escaped. This rebellion was outstanding for its scale and temporary success. It was quite unlike the other small outbreaks by gladiators of which we have evidence and resembled more the major slave-revolts in Sicily of 137–3 and 104–1 BC, inasmuch as it drew in a depressed rural population. Spartacus quickly became a legend: he was competent, brave, physically powerful, and humane with those he led. See SLAVERY.

T. Rice Holmes, *The Roman Republic* 1. 156 f., 386 ff.; J. Vogt, *Ancient Slavery and the Ideal of Man* (1974), ch. 3; Rubensohn, *RFIC* 1971; R. Seager, *CAH* 9² (1994), 221–3. E. T. S.; A. W. L.

Spartan cults The three greatest Spartan festivals, the ones that attracted visitors, all honoured *Apollo: the *Carnea, the Gymnopaedia (at which choirs competed for long hours in baking heat), and the Hyacinthia. This last comprised choral performances (again), spectacle, and feasting, spread over several days only some of which were tinged with melancholy; it honoured Apollo of Amyclae and his dead lover *Hyacinthus. The importance of Artemis Orthia is clear from the 100,000 or so small dedications found at her shrine; hers was a celebrated festival at which youths undergoing the Spartan military training (see AGŌGĒ) sought to steal cheese from the altar and were whipped if caught, and it may have been ephebes again who wore the various masks found in her precinct. Other prominent cults honoured *Menelaus (1) and *Helen, who were revered 'like gods' at the *Menelaion a couple of miles to the south-east of the city; the daughters of Leucippus, Phoebe and Hilaeira (see LEUCIPPIDES), who like Helen were probably closely linked with the choral training that constituted education for young Spartan girls; the *Dioscuri, glamorous local heroes many dedications to whom have been found; Athena of the Bronze House, whose bronze-plated temple occupied the lowly Spartan acropolis; and *Poseidon of *Taenarum (1), who in wrath at a violation of sanctuary supposedly caused the great earthquake of the 460s. *Lycurgus (2) too, the *founder of the Spartan system, was worshipped 'as a god', though we do not know on what scale. And there were many Spartan *hero-cults, as we learn both from literary sources and from a distinctive type of hero-relief found throughout *Laconia; *Agamemnon, *Orestes, *Talthybius, and the ephor *Chilon were among those so honoured. See RELICS. Many further archaic-sounding cults have some prominence in post-classical sources, but one must beware of the 'invention of tradition' in prosperous Roman Sparta.

Spartocids

S. Wide, *Lakonische Kulte* (1893); L. Ziehen, *RE* under 'Sparta (Kulte)'; C. Calame, *Les Chœurs de jeunes filles en Grèce archaïque* (1977); R. Parker, in A. Powell, *Classical Sparta* (1989); A. Hupfloher, *Kulte im Kaiserzeitlichen Sparta* (2000); M. Pettersson, *Cults of Apollo at Sparta* (1992).

R. C. T. P.

Spartocids The ruling dynasty of the Bosporan kingdom in the eastern Crimea and Taman' peninsula (see BOSPORUS (2); CHERSONESUS (2)). It was founded by a Thracian mercenary, Spartocus, who ruled from 438/7 to 433/2 BC, following the dynasty of the Archeanactidae (480–438). The Spartocids remained in power until about 110 BC, when they were replaced by *Mithradates VI Eupator. The last of the dynasty, Paerisades V, seems to have called for the assistance of Mithradates. However, Paerisades was killed in an uprising led by one Saumacus. The Bosporan kingdom was taken over by Mithradates, to whom it had possibly been bequeathed by Paerisades.

The earlier members of the dynasty did not use royal titles, but styled themselves archons (lit. 'rulers'). Spartocus III (ruled 304–284 BC) seems to have been the first of the Spartocids to call himself king. They engaged in energetic diplomacy with the Aegean world, especially the city of Athens. Their ability to control substantial grain-supplies and other resources was a fundamental part of that diplomacy. See FOOD SUPPLY, and Tod 115, 163, 167, 171.

The Spartocid dynasty comprised (all dates are BC): Spartocus I (438/7–433/2), Satyrus I (433/2–389/8), Leucon I (389/8–349/8), Spartocus II (349/8–344/3), Paerisades I (344/4–311/10), Satyrus II (311/10–310/309), Prytanis (310/309), Eumelus (310/309–304/303), Spartocus III (304/303–284/3), Paerisades II (284/3–*c*.245), Spartocus IV (*c*.245–*c*.240), Leucon II (*c*.240–*c*.220), Hygiaenon (*c*.220–*c*.200), Spartocus V (*c*.200–*c*.180), Paerisades III (*c*.180–*c*.150), Paerisades IV (*c*.150–*c*.125), Paerisades V (*c*.125–*c*.110).

V. F. Gajdukevich, *Das Bosporanische Reich* (revd. transl. 1971); J. F. Hind, *CAH* 6² (1994), 490 ff.

D. C. B.

Spartoi, see CADMUS. Their descendants had a birth-mark in the shape of a spearhead, Arist. *Poet.* 1454^b22 (from *Euripides' *Antigone*?), by which they could be known.

speech presentation The *rhēsis* (a formally constructed monologue in direct discourse) is the most frequent way of presenting the speech of characters in Greek and Roman literature. *Rhēseis* are prevalent in *narrative *genres as well as in drama. Although the rapid exchange between characters of a few words of direct discourse is also common in drama and can be found in *dialogue, prose fiction and satire, it is relatively rare in the major narrative genres. Various forms of indirect discourse are also used by narrators in ancient texts. However, for most authors, direct discourse is the preferred medium for the presentation of characters' speech. Roman historiography offers a significant exception to this general practice: speeches are most often presented in indirect discourse or free indirect style. See HISTORIOGRAPHY, all three entries.

The importance of *rhetoric and oratory in the Graeco-Roman world in part explains the continuing trend in ancient literature for presenting characters' discourse in *rhēseis*. But that trend goes back to *Homer—it may also be explained by the extent to which narrative literature might have been designed for public recitation rather than private reading.

*Plato (1) *Republic* 392c6–394d9 is the most useful (if controversial) ancient discussion of speech presentation. *Socrates equates deceptive poetic imitation (*mimēsis*; see IMITATIO) with the direct discourse poets use to pretend their characters are speaking. Socrates offers an example of 'pure' narrative without *mimēsis*: a re-telling of the opening of the *Iliad* in which he renders Homer's first *rhēsis* in indirect discourse. It is then suggested that literary genres can be distinguished according to the amount of direct discourse they employ. That suggestion was echoed by *Aristotle (*Poetics* 1448^a19–28), and later by *Servius (*Eclogues* 3. 1 ad loc.). The grammarian *Diomedes (3) followed this division of genres according to speech presentation, ensuring it had an extensive influence in the medieval period.

In general, see G. Genette, *Narrative Discourse* (1980), 169 ff. (Fr. orig. 1972); Genette, *Narrative Discourse Revisited* (1988), 50 ff. (Fr. orig. 1983), and *The Architext, an introduction* (1992, orig. 1979) have further discussion and bibliography. M. J. Toolan, *Narrative; A Critical Linguistic Introduction* (1988), 119–38, is helpful on work in English. V. N. Voloshinov, in *Marxism and the Philosophy of Language* (1973), 109–60 (Russian orig. 1929) (speech presentation from a sociological perspective). A. Ernout and F. Thomas, *Syntaxe latine* (1951), 421–36 (indirect discourse in Latin). M. Fantuzzi, *Ricerche su Apollonio Rhodio* (1988), 47–87 (relation between speech and narrative in Greek poetic theory and practice). Treatments of particular ancient authors include: I. De Jong, *Narrative in Drama: The Art of the Euripidean Messenger Speech* (1991); G. Highet, *The Speeches in Virgil's Aeneid* (1972); S. Hornblower, *Thucydides* (1987), 45–72; R. Ullmann, *La Technique des discours dans Salluste, Tite-Live et Tacite* (1927).

A. J. W. L.

Spelunca (mod. Sperlonga), a natural grotto on the Tyrrhenian coast of Italy, where the emperor *Tiberius had a villa. *Aelius Seianus rescued him from a cave-in there. The grotto has yielded impressive sculptural groups by the authors of the Laocoon (see HAGESANDER).

G. Iacopi, *L'Antro di Tiberio a Sperlonga* (1963); *PECS* 856; A. F. Stewart, *JRS* 1977, 76 ff.

A. F. S.

Spes, the personification of hope (with particular reference to the safety of the younger generation) worshipped at Rome by the 5th cent. BC (Livy 2. 51. 2) and given a temple in the forum Holitorium (remains survive, built into the church of S. Nicola in Carcere) by A. *Atilius Calatinus (consul 258 BC). Destroyed by arson in 31 BC, the temple was restored by *Germanicus (Tac. *Ann.* 2. 49), appropriately, since the cult of Spes (Augusta) was now concerned principally with the imperial succession.

J. R. Fears, *ANRW* 2. 17. 2. 861–3.

N. P.

Speusippus (*c*.407–339 BC), Athenian philosopher, son of Eurymedon and of *Plato (1)'s sister Potone. He accompanied Plato on his last visit to Sicily (361) and succeeded him as head of the *Academy from 347 to 339. Of his voluminous writings (Diog. Laert. 4. 4) only fragments and later reports remain, but Aristotle treats him with respect and it is clear that he continued and helped to shape some major philosophical interests which the Academy had acquired under Plato.

(a) Definition Speusippus argued that, since a definition is designed to identify its subject and differentiate it from everything else, it can only be established by knowing everything there is. This can hardly have been intended, as some ancient critics thought, to refute all attempts at defining. More probably it was this view of definition which prompted Speusippus in his ten books of *Homoia* ('Similar Things') to set about collecting the observable resemblances between different sorts of plant and animal, for he may have thought (as *Aristotle sometimes did, *An. Post.* B 13) that a species can be defined by discovering a set of characteristics which it shares with various other species, taken collectively, but not with any one other species.

The Academy's interest in definition had led to the recognition that some expressions have more than one meaning. Speusippus marked this by drawing distinctions comparable to, but fuller than, those familiar from Aristotle's *logic. Where a single word is in question, it may have one sense or more than one (*synōnyma, homōnyma*); where more than one word is in question, they may stand for one thing or for quite different things, or one may derive its sense from the other (*polyōnyma, heterōnyma, parōnyma*). This in itself would give Speusippus his place at the birth of logic in the Academy.

(b) Philosophy and Exact Science Speusippus wrote on Pythagorean mathematics (see PYTHAGORAS (1)), endorsing the search for the elements of numbers which Plato had taken over from the Pythagoreans (see the newly discovered fragment of Speusippus, *Plato Latinus* 3. 40 1–5). But he refused to equate numbers with Platonic Ideas, which like others in the Academy he rejected; and he further denied the claim, which Aristotle ascribes to the Pythagoreans and Plato, that the elements of number are the elements of everything else. Other sorts and levels of reality, he argued, need other sorts of element. Hence Aristotle accuses him of making the universe 'episodic', disconnected; but it is Speusippus' theory that underlies Aristotle's attempt in *Metaph. A* to show that it is not strictly true, but only true 'by analogy', that all things have the same elements.

(c) Ethics In the Academic debate which can be heard behind Plato's *Philebus* and the ethical writings of Aristotle Speusippus makes two appearances. He holds, first, that pleasure is neither good nor evil in itself, and second, that goodness is to be found only in the final stages of development and not in the origins.

Under all these heads it is likely that the best of his work has been digested in that of Aristotle and his successors, and in particular that his biological observations in the *Homoia* were largely absorbed in the treatises of the Lyceum.

Testimonia and fragments in P. Lang, *De Speusippi Academici Scriptis* (1911). Zeller, 2. 1⁴. 982–1010; E. Hambruch, *Logische Regeln der plat. Schule in der aristotel. Topik* (1904); J. Stenzel, in *RE* 3 A 1636 ff.; H. Cherniss, *Aristotle's Criticism of Plato and the Acad.* 1 (1944), esp. ch. 1; P. Merlan, *From Platonism to Neoplatonism*² (1961); M. Ostwald and J. P. Lynch, *CAH* 6² (1994), 610 ff.   G. E. L. O.; S. H.

Sphacteria See PYLOS.

Sphaerus of Borysthenes (b. *c.*285 or 265, lived at least to 221 BC), Stoic (see STOICISM), pupil of *Zeno (2) and *Cleanthes; adviser of the Spartan reforming king *Cleomenes (2) III, he also attended the court of *Ptolemy (1) II. His numerous writings dealt with all branches of philosophy and with *Heraclitus; he is linked by anecdote to epistemological dispute. His definitions were highly esteemed by the Stoics.

Testimonia in H. von Arnim, *SVF* 1. 139–42.   J. A.

sphinx, a hybrid creature, like the *Chimaera and the griffin. Illustrations can be traced back to Egypt and Mesopotamia in the mid-3rd millenium BC (impossible to accord priority, although the Egyptian version is known to be a late-comer to local iconography). Basically the Sphinx possessed the body of an animal (usually a lion) and a human head (male or female). Variations include wings (common) and horns.

The Egyptian and Mesopotamian sphinx is depicted in religious and/or heraldic contexts, from the monumental (i.e. the Sphinx at Giza) to the minute. The Egyptian is held to embody the king as *Horus supplicating the sun god Re. Both are some-

times shown slaying humans, presumably enemies of the king (the foregoing based on Demisch).

Sphinxes appear in Minoan and Mycenaean art (see MINOAN AND MYCENAEAN CIVILIZATION), in *Crete and the mainland, the ultimate inspiration probably Egypt (Immerwahr, 35). The sphinx later becomes a popular figure in Greek art—monumental and funerary—of the archaic and later periods (Donadoni; Vermeule, 171–5). This is an extension of her role as guardian spirit.

The only literary references are to the Greek sphinx, whence the name, which came from a monster of Theban legend (see THEBES (1)), (S)phix, that inhabited a mountain at the western edge of Theban territory, waylaid passers-by, and wrought havoc on the Cadmeans (see CADMUS; the story is referred to by Hesiod, *Theogony* 326, where she is daughter of *Echidna and Orthos, and sister of the Nemean lion). Popular Greek etymologizing derived the name from the verb *sphingein* ('bind/hold fast'), perhaps influenced by the story (see West on *Theog.* 326 and Chantraine, 1077).

Her hostility to the Thebans may be connected with the traditional war between *Minyan *Orchomenus (1) and Cadmean Thebes, which was begun and ended near Mt. Phicion, at Onchestus and the Teneric plain respectively. She would have been performing her accustomed role as guardian, this time of Minyan territory (it is to be remarked that as one approaches the mountain from the west—that is, from the direction of Orchomenus—it resembles in outline a crouching beast: this might have caused the connection to be made). Eventually she met her match in *Oedipus, who either answered her *riddle, causing her to commit suicide (e.g. Apollod. 3. 5. 8), or actually killed her (Corinna, fr. 672 PMG). The attachment of the sphinx to the Oedipus legend is regarded as secondary (Edmunds), and may have been grafted on to it from its original place in the story of the war.

Apollodorus, *The Library* (trans. J. G. Frazer) (1921). P. Chantraine, *Dictionnaire étymologique de la langue Grecque* 4 (1977); H. Demisch, *Die Sphinx* (1977); S. Donadoni, in *EAA* 7 (1966), 230–2; L. Edmunds, *The Sphinx in the Oedipus Legend* (1981); S. A. Immerwahr, *Aegean Painting in the Bronze Age* (1990); E. T. Vermeule, *Aspects of Death in Early Greek Art and Poetry* (1979).   A. Sch.

sphragis, literally seal or signet, a motif in which an author names or otherwise identifies himself or herself, especially at the beginning or end of a poem or collection of poems. This modern critical usage of the term looks back to two possibly related metaphorical uses in antiquity, both incompletely understood: *Theognis (1) (19–23) speaks of setting his seal (*sphrēgis*) on his verses, to protect them from tampering (see PLAGIARISM), and the *sphragis* that was one of the concluding sections of the nome (see NOMOS (2); Pollux 4. 66) may on the evidence of *Timotheus (1)'s *Persians* have named the author. Such self-identification, sometimes programmatic, is to be found as early as *Hesiod's *Theogony*; its initial function may in part have been to identify a work or body of work with its author in a period of poetic fluidity. But the use of the *sphragis*, especially to end a collection of poems, continues into Hellenistic and Roman literature; see e.g. *Nicander, *Theriaca* 957–8, *Virgil, *Georgics* 4. 563–6, *Horace, *Odes* 3. 30, *Ovid, *Amores* 3. 15.

W. Kranz, 'Sphragis', in *Studien zur Antiken Literatur und ihrem Fortwirken* (1967), 27–78 [*Rh.Mus.* 1961, 3–46, 97–124]; R. G. M. Nisbet and M. Hubbard, *A Commentary on Horace: Odes Book II* (1978), on 2. 20.   D. H. R.

spices, from Lat. *species*, signifying a commodity of special value, commonly a flavoured and aromatic vegetal substance used as a condiment, most often of Asian origin. Spices were classified by *Theophrastus (*Od.*) as hot, pungent, biting, bitter, or astringent. They were used to add fragrance to perfumes and to enrich the flavour of *wine, as well as in the preparation of medicines and in cooking. It is apparent that, with the opening up of direct sea trade between Egypt and *India in about the time of Augustus and Tiberius (see MONSOON), much more scope existed than previously for the importation of a wide variety of spices into the eastern Mediterranean. Miller lists no fewer than 142 spices attested in classical sources. Some, like cassia, cloves, ginger, nutmeg, and mace, came from as far away as China (see SERES), south-east *Asia, and Indonesia (generally re-exported from India), while many originated in India (e.g. turmeric, cardamom, cinnamon, and pepper), and still others came from east Africa, Arabia, and Iran. North Africa, Asia Minor, Syria, Greece, and parts of Europe, however, also provided more common varieties such as basil, bay, chive, dill, fennel, mustard, rosemary, sage, and thyme. The *Peripl. M. Rubr.* § 10 (see PERIPLOI) mentions the large size of the spice-carrying ships at the Egyptian port of Mosullon, and, speaking of Bacare and Nelcynda in India, says (§ 56), 'They send large ships to these market-towns on account of the great quantity and bulk of pepper and malabathrum [cinnamon leaf]'. The popularity of pepper at Rome is reflected in the fact that, in AD 92, *Domitian constructed the *horrea piperataria*, pepper warehouses, in the spice quarter of the imperial capital. Information on prices is available from several sources. Pliny (*HN* 12) provides details on the spices available in his day, on a regional basis, as well as their prices. *Diocletian's price edict of AD 301 fixed prices on, inter alia, spices, and Justinian's *Digest* (see JUSTINIAN'S CODIFICATION) contains a list of goods subject to import duty upon arrival at *Alexandria (1), naming 23 individual spices.

J. I. Miller, *The Spice Trade of the Roman Empire* (1969); M. G. Raschke, *ANRW* 2. 9. 2 (1978). D. T. P.

Spina, in N. Italy, situated on what was the mouth of the southern branch of the Po (*Padus), seems to have been established *c.*520–510 BC by *Etruscans to compete with the Aeginetan foundation (see AEGINA) at nearby *Atria. Like the latter, it supplied *Felsina and Etruria Padana (the Etruscans in the Po region)—and ultimately Europe north of the Alps—with fine Etruscan bronzes and with the products of the rich 5th-cent. Greek commerce. A great quantity of Attic red-figure and other Greek pottery has been recovered from the Valle Trebba and Valle Pega cemeteries; it is now in the museum at Ferrara. Spina exercised considerable naval influence in the Adriatic and maintained a 'treasury' (see SANCTUARIES) at *Delphi.

S. Aurigemma, *Scavi di Spina* (1960 onwards); L. Massei, *Askoi a figure rosse nei corredi funerari delle necropoli di Spina* (1978); N. Alfieri, *Spina: Il Museo Archeologico Nazionale di Ferrara* 1: *Ceramica* (1979); F. Berti, *Il Museo Archeologico Nazionale di Ferrara* (1983); E. Hostetter, *Bronzes from Spina* 1 (1986); L. Paoli and A. Parrini, *Corredi di età ellenistica dalle necropoli di Spina* (1988). D. W. R. R.

spinning. See TEXTILE PRODUCTION.

Spoletium (mod. Spoleto), in central Italy, a major iron-age settlement (with walls in polygonal masonry), which became a Latin colony (241 BC; see COLONIZATION, ROMAN), and rendered valuable service against *Hannibal. Served by the eastern branch of the *via Flaminia, it became a flourishing *municipium*. It had a noteworthy history in late antiquity, and from AD 570 was an important Lombard duchy. There are significant remains of walls, temples, theatre and an arch of Drusus *Iulius Caesar (1) (AD 23).

L. di Marco, *Spoletium: Topografia e urbanistica* (1975).

E. T. S.; T. W. P.

spolia opima were spoils offered by a Roman general who had slain an enemy leader in single combat. The practice was traditionally instituted by *Romulus, who fought a victorious duel against King Acron of Caenina, stripped him of his armour, and dedicated it in the newly built temple of Jupiter Feretrius (Liv. 1. 10; Plut. *Rom.* 16). The only other recorded instances were in 437 BC, when the military tribune (see TRIBUNI MILITUM) A. *Cornelius Cossus killed Lars Tolumnius of *Veii, and in 222, when M. *Claudius Marcellus (1) overcame the Celtic chieftain Viridomarus. Interest in the *spolia opima* revived in 29 BC when M. *Licinius Crassus (2) killed Deldo, king of the *Bastarnae, and claimed the right to dedicate the spoils. Octavian (see AUGUSTUS) rejected the claim on the (probably spurious) grounds that only the commander of the army was entitled to the *spolia opima*, and backed his argument by the 'discovery' that Cossus had been consul when he slew Tolumnius. *Livy, who gives us this information (4. 20. 5 ff.), also makes it clear that Octavian's view was contradicted by that of all earlier historians.

J. Marquardt, *Röm. Staatsverw.* 2. 560 f.; Ogilvie, *Comm. Livy 1–5*, 71 ff.; 563 f. P. T.; T. J. Co.

spondai See LIBATIONS.

sponsio See SECURITY.

springs, sacred Contrary to common belief, not every *sanctuary had access to running *water (e.g. *Aphaea, on *Aegina did not), nor, in all likelihood, was *every* spring sacred. A thing, place, or person became 'sacred' (*hieros*) by being placed under the tutelage and control of a deity. It was a matter of function or utility, rather than ontology. Thus, Cassotis at *Delphi was a sacred spring because it was held to convey mantic power (i.e. power of divination) from the god to the person who drank of it. Similar examples abound of springs performing similar functions, some oracular (see ORACLES), others merely inspirational (such as Acidalia, Hippocrene on Mt. *Helicon, Aganippe), artists being held themselves to be human vessels transmitting divine messages.

At sanctuaries where cleanliness (e.g. *Asclepius and other medical gods) and purity (*mystery sanctuaries, as at *Eleusis and the Theban Cabirium; see THEBES (1); CABIRI) were important, water—from springs and elsewhere—was an essential element, and in this sense the springs concerned would have been regarded as sacred.

The waters of springs served as means of *purification at the critical points of life: birth, *initiation, marriage, and death, but this function was shared by rivers, that is, by any source of fresh, running water. In the Mediterranean world, where this resource is often at a premium, its availability is singularly important. It does not of course follow that the source itself is sacred for its own sake in the sense given above. On the other hand, the strategic location of a spring, as for example at a settlement site or a caravanserai, might be sufficient to imbue it with divine power (the sacred spring at *Corinth and the Boeotian spring Tilphossa *en route* to Delphi are examples of each).

Sacred springs were a feature of the Roman landscape, urban and rural. For example, inscriptions refer to a god Fontanus (*CIL* 2. 150, 10. 6071) and goddess Fontana (2. 6277): the deified Fons had an altar on the Janiculum; outside the Porta Capena was a grove with a spring of the Casmenae to which the Vestal virgins (see VESTA) resorted daily; and on 13 October the Romans celebrated Fontinalia, a rite to honour natural springs (Dumézil; Horace's *Ode* to the spring Bandusia (3. 13. 3) has been linked with the Fontinalia). Another important complex of springs and sanctuaries was to be found in Umbria at *Clitumnus (Schoder; elegantly described by *Pliny (2) the Younger, *Ep.* 8. 8).

In general sacred springs were presided over by female spirits—*nymphs—but it is not certain that every such spring had its attendant nymph.

G. Dumézil, *ARR* 1 (1970), 387–9; M. Ninck, *Die Bedeutung des Wassers im Kult und Leben der Alten* (1921); R. V. Schoder, *PECS* 227.   A. Sch.

Sri Lanka See TAPROBANE.

Staberius Eros, a scholar, originally a slave, who taught the children of those proscribed by *Sulla free. M. *Iunius Brutus (2) and C. *Cassius Longinus (1) were his pupils.

Plin. *HN* 35. 199; Suet. *Gram.* 13.

Stabiae, with *Pompeii and *Nuceria an important pre-Roman settlement of the Sarno plain in south *Campania, destroyed by Sulla in the *Social War (3). The fashionable resort which succeeded was buried in the eruption of AD 79 (in which the elder *Pliny (1) died here): excavations since the 18th cent. have revealed a series of very lavish luxury estates, scenically located at Varano above Castellammare, of which the S. Marco and Arianna sites are most important archaeologically.

D. Camardo and A. Ferrara, *Stabia: le ville* (1989); P. Miniero Forte, *Stabiae: pitture e stucchi delle ville romane* (1989).   N. P.

stade See MEASURES; STADIUM.

stadium (Greek στάδιον), running track, about 200 m. long (the term also signifies a comparable unit of linear measurement i.e. a 'stade'; see MEASURES). Athletic activity often antedates the surviving stadia (e.g. at *Nemea); presumably any area of flat ground was used. One of the earliest definable stadia, that in the sanctuary of *Poseidon at *Isthmia, consists simply of a starting gate on the relatively level ground of the sanctuary, with a bank raised artificially to one side for spectators. The architectural development of stadia can be seen by the 4th cent. BC with the running track and seats to one or, preferably, either side. Early examples may have both ends straight or near straight (*Olympia, *Epidaurus). Later the end is semicircular. Double races (the diaulos) and other long-distance races, however, started at a straight starting line at this closed end. This definitive form is still used in structures of the Roman period. One of the first examples is that at Nemea (*c.*325 BC). A vaulted passage under the seating area gives convenient access to the running tracks; similar passages, Hellenistic in date, are at Epidaurus and Olympia.

Whether the seating rests on natural hill slopes, artificial terraces, or built vaulted substructures (the stadium of the Roman period at *Perge) they served as natural catchment areas for rainwater, and required drainage. This often takes the form of a channel at the edge of the running track, perhaps punctuated with water basins at intervals. These probably facilitated cleaning of the channels rather than the provision of water for either spectators or athletes.

See ATHLETICS; SANCTUARIES.

E. N. Gardiner, *Athletics of the Ancient World* (1930), 128 ff.; O. Broneer, *Isthmia* 2 (1973), 47; A. Mallwitz, *Olympia und seine Bauten* (1972), 180;

R. A. Tomlinson, *Epidauros* (1983); S. Miller, *Hesperia* 1979, 93 ff.; 1981, 65 ff.   R. A. T.

Stagira or **Stagirus,** town in *Chalcidice and the birthplace of *Aristotle; but the modern inland town of Stagira, with its statue of him, is not the ancient site, which is just off the road at modern Olympias, on the coast to the north of the Akte prong of Chalcidice and about half-way between *Acanthus and Argilos. There are good fortifications and a 5th-cent. BC *stoa in the *agora. It was a colony of *Andros (Thuc. 4. 88), a member of Athens' *Delian League in the 5th cent. BC when it paid a normal tribute of only 1,000 drachmas; it went over to the Spartan *Brasidas in 424 along with Acanthus. *Cleon tried to recapture it in 422 but failed (Thuc. 5. 6. 1). In the Peace of *Nicias (1) it was 'autonomous but tribute-paying' i.e. to Athens. In the 4th cent. it was probably a member of the Chalcidic League for a time (see CHALCIDICE). It was destroyed by *Philip (1) II of Macedon in 349, but at Aristotle's plea he or *Alexander (3) the Great restored it (Plut. *Alex.* 7. 3).

Thuc. 4. 84–8; M. Zahrnt, *Olynth und die Chalkidier* (1971), 238–43 and in *Lexikon der historischen Stätten* 636; *Arch. Rep.* 1994–5, 43.   S. H.

Staius (*RE* 2) **Murcus, Lucius,** perhaps from *Sulmo (*ILLRP* 444), was a legate of *Caesar in Gaul and Africa (48–46 BC) and probably praetor 45. Approving of Caesar's murder, he was sent to Syria as proconsul by the senate (44), where, with Q. Marcius Crispus, he besieged Q. *Caecilius Bassus at Apamea. When *Cassius arrived in 43, all three armies joined him and Staius was appointed prefect of a fleet. After winning several victories he was joined by Cn. *Domitius Ahenobarbus (4) and between them they controlled the seas between Italy and Greece, defeating Cn. *Domitius Calvinus (42). Staius issued coins with the head of *Neptunus (*RRC* 510). Quarrelling with Domitius, he joined Sextus *Pompeius, but Sextus soon came to distrust him and had him killed (40/39).   H. H. S.; E. B.

standards, cult of Every permanent station of a Roman military unit, especially legionary, and every camp regularly constructed contained a chapel, which, at least in imperial times (Vegetius, *De re mil.* 2. 6), was under the charge of the first cohort, or headquarters company. This cohort kept both the statues of gods worshipped by the troops and of the emperors and also the standards (*signa militaria*) of the unit and its component parts; all received divine or quasi-divine honours. Scholarship has wrongly attributed this to C. *Marius (1)'s legionary reforms by conflating two notices in Pliny: *HN* 10. 16 credits Marius with assigning eagles to legions, while at 13. 23 Pliny clearly states that the originator of standard-worship is unknown. They were anointed and otherwise tended on feast-days (Pliny, ibid.). A suppliant might take refuge at them (Tac. *Ann.* 1. 39); an altar was on occasion dedicated at least partly to them or at least to the most important, the eagle of the legion (*CIL* 3. 7591; no. 14 v. Domaszewski); the *natalis* of the eagle, presumably the anniversary of the day when the unit was first commissioned, was celebrated (*CIL* 2. 6183; no. 3 v. Domaszewski); sacrifice was made to them particularly after a victory (Joseph. *BJ* 6. 316). Tertullian even says, rhetorically exaggerating, that the soldiers venerated them beyond all gods (*Apol.* 16). They are not precisely gods, but are associated with *genius and *uirtus* (*CIL* 3. 7591, above), and are *propria legionum numina* ('the legions' particular spirits': Tac. *Ann.* 2. 17. 2). *Numina* demonstrates their association with religious forces, although ongoing controversy over the precise scope of the term (see NUMEN) hinders analysis; cf. H. Wagenvoort, *Roman Dynamism* (1947), 73–103; Dumézil, *ARR* (1970), 28–30.

A. von Domaszewski, *Die Religion des römischen Heeres* (1895), 9–45; J. Rüpke, *Domi militiae* (1990), 184–8.   C. R. P.

Staphylus (1), personification of the grape-cluster, σταφυλή. He is vaguely attached to *Dionysus, as his son by *Ariadne (Plut. *Thes.* 20); his favourite (schol. Ar. *Plut.* 1021); an Assyrian king who welcomes him during his Indian campaign (Nonnus, *Dion.* 18. 5 ff.). Or he discovered the vine and informed *Oeneus ('Probus' on Verg. *G.* 1. 9).   H. J. R.

Staphylus (2) of *Naucratis (before 150 BC), an Alexandrian (see ALEXANDRIA (1)), who wrote on Athens, Aeolia (precise scope doubtful), *Arcadia, and *Thessaly. All of the few surviving fragments concern the prehistoric period. His work is cited among those of prominent historians.

FGrH 269.   K. S. S.

stars See ASTROLOGY; ASTRONOMY; CONSTELLATIONS AND NAMED STARS.

Staseas of Naples, the first *Peripatetic philosopher known to have settled in Rome. M. *Pupius Piso Frugi became his pupil *c.*92 BC. He is frequently mentioned by *Cicero. He seems to have occupied himself particularly with the problem of the normal length of human life.

E. Rawson, *Intellectual Life in the Late Roman Republic* (1985), 6.   W. D. R.; A. J. S. S.

Stasinus of *Cyprus, poet sometimes named as author of the *Cypria* (see EPIC CYCLE). *Pindar (fr. 265 S.-M.) already knew the story that *Homer gave Stasinus the poem as a dowry. The tale served to reconcile alternative ascriptions.   M. L. W.

stasis (lit. 'standing'), a Greek word commonly used for a group of men who take a stand in a political dispute, i.e. a party or faction, and by extension for the dispute itself, especially when the prosecution of the dispute goes beyond normal political activity to plotting and violence. The grounds for political dispute could be various, in the Greek world as in the modern, but from the 5th cent. BC onwards there was a tendency for disputants to represent themselves, and for the sources to represent them, as champions of the rich or the poor, or of the oligarchs or the democrats, or of one outside power or another. *Herodotus (1) writes of the rise of *Pisistratus in 6th-cent. *Athens in terms of three *staseis* with regional bases (1. 59. 3); later sources retain the regional bases for the *staseis* but give them ideological stances also (e.g. *Ath. Pol.* 13. 4–5). Despite the value placed on independence in the Greek states, political leaders would often prefer to be on the winning side with the support of one of the greater states rather than on the losing side in an independent state, and the leading states were glad to extend their influence in this way. Thus disputes which had a local origin often acquired an inter-state dimension; but in the 5th and 4th cents. *Sparta and Athens were able to give the states under their influence a measure of enforced stability by keeping their own supporters in power. The violence and the outside involvement to which *stasis* could lead had a damaging effect on the states: the worsening of this as attitudes were polarized in the *Peloponnesian War is analysed in Thuc. 3. 82–4 (but ch. 84 is probably not by *Thucydides (2)). See CLASS STRUGGLE.

A. W. Lintott, *Violence, Civil Strife and Revolution in the Classical City, 750–330 BC* (1982); H.-J. Gehrke, *Stasis* (1985).   P. J. R.

state, states See BUREAUCRACY; DECISION-MAKING; DEMOCRACY (both entries); FEDERAL STATES; GOVERNMENT; POLIS; POLITICAL THEORY.

statics, or 'barycentric theory' (in the phrase of *Pappus), is the branch of *mechanics dealing with the relations of weights in static equilibrium. The classic formulation of the principles is from *Archimedes (*Plane Equilibria*, bk. 1) in which he proves that the centre of gravity of two weights is the point dividing the line between their respective centres of gravity into segments inversely proportional to the weights (props. 6–7). This is apparently a reformulation in statical terms of the analogous principle of the lever, conceived dynamically in the Peripatetic *Mechanica*. Archimedes' definition of centre of gravity is not transmitted in his extant mechanical writings, but can be inferred from accounts by *Heron, Pappus, and Eutocius. In a lost work *On balances* (*Peri zygōn*) Archimedes appears to have applied a version of the equilibrium principle toward the analysis of uneven-armed balances of the bismar type. In the *Plane Equilibria* he determines the barycentres of the parallelogram, triangle, trapezium, and parabolic segment. In a lost work, the *Equilibria*, he appears to have made analogous determinations for solids: the pyramid, the cone, and segments of the sphere and conoids of revolution. Heuristic versions of the latter results are set out in the extant *Method*.

E. J. Dijksterhuis, *Archimedes* (1956; corr. edn. 1987), chs. 9–12; A. G. Drachmann, *Centaurus* 1963, 91–146; W. R. Knorr, *Mathematical Intelligencer* 1978, 102–8, and *Ancient Sources of the Medieval Tradition of Mechanics* (1982).   W. R. K.

Statilia (*RE* 45) **Messal(l)ina**, third wife of *Nero (AD 66), who put to death her fourth husband Iulius Vestinus Atticus, was great-great-granddaughter of *Augustus' partisan T. *Statilius Taurus and probably daughter of T. Statilius Taurus (consul AD 44). She accompanied Nero on his artistic tour in Greece, where she was honoured (*ILS* 8794). After Nero's death she maintained a brilliant position, and is said to have been noted for her eloquence and literary culture as well as for her beauty. *Otho contemplated marriage with her.

Suet. *Nero* 35. 1; *Otho* 10. 2; scholiast on Juvenal 6. 434.   A. M.; M. T. G.

Statilius Crito (Κρίτων), **Titus,** of Carian Heraclea-Salbace, doctor (*archiatros*) to Trajan, who designated him an *amicus Augusti*, took him on one of his Dacian campaigns, the basis for his *Getic History* (*FGH* 2. 3. 200), and made him an imperial procurator. Through Galen considerable fragments survive of his works *Cosmetics* and *On the composition of drugs*.

Mart. 11. 60. 6; Gal. 12. 455. J. Scarborough in J. W. Eadie and J. Ober (eds.), *The Craft of the Ancient Historian* (1985), 387 ff.; V. Nutton, *From Democedes to Harvey* (1988), 22 (inscriptions).   A. J. S. S.

Statilius (*RE* 34) **Taurus, Titus** (suffect consul 37 BC, 2nd consulship 26 BC), the greatest Augustan marshal after *Agrippa. Of uncertain origin (perhaps Lucanian), by military talent and loyalty he attained wealth and honours; he was thrice acclaimed *imperator* by the legions and held several priesthoods (*ILS* 893; 893a). His earliest recorded service was as admiral in the *Bellum Siculum* (36). He then crossed to Africa and secured it, holding a triumph in 34 (the amphitheatre erected in commemoration on the *Campus Martius was completed in 30). He also fought in *Illyricum (34–33), commanded the land army in the campaign of *Actium (31), perhaps became *Octavian's first governor of Macedonia, and operated in Spain (29). After 26 the only record is of his post in charge of Rome (*praefectus urbi*) in 16 when Augustus left for the western provinces (Cass. Dio 54. 19. 6; Tac. *Ann.* 6. 11). He probably died not long after. Of his descendants the last and brightest was *Statilia Messallina, Nero's third wife.

R. Syme, *Rom. Rev.*; *AA*, indexes.   R. S.; B. M. L.

Statius, Publius Papinius (*RE* 8), Roman poet. Born between AD 45 and the early 50s in the distinctively Greek city of Naples (*Neapolis), Statius was the son of a man who had a glittering career first as a professional poet on the Greek festival circuit (see AGŌNES), and then as a teacher in Naples and in Rome, where the family moved when Statius was in his teens (*Silv.* 5. 3). Although Statius did not follow either of these careers, his debt to his father's inheritance is manifest particularly in the *Silvae*, where the often impromptu praise-displays of the Greek festivals blend with the Roman tradition of friendship poetry to produce something new in Latin literature. Popular from a young age as a poet in Rome, he may have composed a *pantomime libretto for Paris, *Domitian's favourite (executed AD 83: Juv. 7. 82–7). He was victorious in the poetry competition at Domitian's annual Alban games (prob. March 90), but suffered a mortifying failure in the much more prestigious Capitoline Games, almost certainly later in the same year (*Silv.* 3. 5. 31–3). By now he had married Claudia, widow of another poet, who brought him a step-daughter (he had no children of his own). The poem to Claudia (*Silv.* 3. 5), persuading her to leave Rome and follow him to Naples, speaks of her devoted support, and her nursing of Statius in illness. His epic, the *Thebaid*, was published in 91/2, after many partial recitations and many years of work (one for each of the twelve books he says, with suspicious symmetry, *Theb.* 12. 811–12). There followed the occasional poems of the *Silvae*. Books 1–3 were published together in 93 or 94; Book 4 was published in 95, by which time he had left Rome for Naples; and Book 5 (together with his unfinished second epic, the *Achilleid*) was published after his death, which is conventionally dated before the assassination of Domitian (Sept. 96).

Works **Lost Works**
The pantomime libretto *Agave* has not survived (if it was ever written); nor have his poems for the Neapolitan, Alban, or Capitoline games, although we may have a fragment of the Alban piece in four hexameter lines from a Statian poem on Domitian's German wars quoted by Valla on Juvenal 4. 94 (cf. *Silv.* 4. 2. 65–7); see SCHOLIA.

Thebaid
The only surviving Roman *epic which can securely be said to have been published as a completed work by its author, the *Thebaid* recounts the war between the sons of *Oedipus over the kingship of *Thebes ((1); cf. SEVEN AGAINST THEBES). Statius may well have begun the poem before he turned 30; it is an acutely self-conscious masterpiece, which has only recently begun to emerge from the neglect that overtook it after its prolonged popularity in the Middle Ages and Renaissance. The poem extravagantly explores human violence and madness. Its cosmic framework draws upon *Ovid's *Metamorphoses* to chart the essential boundaries of human possibilities, and its political framework draws upon *Virgil and *Lucan (Statius' near-contemporary) to probe the imperial themes of absolutism and civil war. Seneca's tragedies (see ANNAEUS SENECA (2), L.) are the principal source for the atmosphere of doomed familial insanity. The diverse problems of succession and authority which face the brothers, the audience, and the poet reflect upon one other throughout, and this self-awareness renders nugatory the trad-

itional criticism of Statius as derivative. In the divine action above all Statius shows himself to be a bold critic and innovator, undermining his inherited epic apparatus and experimenting with allegorical modes in ways which were to be profoundly influential in the Middle Ages. The verse is superbly accomplished, the style too aestheticized for many. In both respects Statius is rather nearer to Ovid, and further from Virgil, than his contemporaries *Valerius Flaccus and *Silius Italicus.

Silvae
Thirty-two poems, of which twenty-six are in hexameters, the standard metre for post-classical Greek encomiastic poetry. The only popular poem in the collection has been the exceptional poem to Sleep (5. 4). The poems evince a not very intimate acquaintance with a not very large or eminent group, marking noteworthy moments such as marriage, official advancement, or bereavement, and celebrating the taste shown in artistic acquisition or architectural construction. In the service of these quasi-professional relationships Statius marshals the panoply of Greek praise-poetry inherited from his father, boasting self-deprecatingly of the impromptu production of the requisite verses (*Silv.* 1 *Pr.*). Generally knowing and light in touch, rather than ponderous, the poems none the less usually avoid banter and ease. Domitian, an intimidating and distant personality, receives six poems which modern taste has found repellent for sycophancy, though a more charitable reading might focus on the anxiety behind them: 4. 2, thanking the emperor for an invitation to dinner in 94, betrays relief after four long years since the last sign of favour at Alba. See SILVA.

Achilleid
The plan was to tell the whole life of *Achilles, but the poet died before even getting his hero to Troy, and the epic breaks off some 160 lines into the second book. The charming, almost novelistic fragment represents a striking departure from the more elevated and passionate *Thebaid*.

> TEXTS *Silvae*: E. Courtney (1990). *Thebaid*: A. Klotz (1908; rev. T. C. Klinnert, 1973); D. E. Hill (1983). *Achilleid*: O. A. W. Dilke (1954); A. Marastoni (1974).
>
> COMMENTARIES *Silvae*: F. Vollmer (1898); 2, H.-J. van Dam (1984); 4, K. Coleman (1988). *Thebaid*: 1, H. Heuvel (1932) and F. Caviglia (1973); 2, H. M. Mulder (1954); 3, H. Snijder (1968); 6. 1–295, H. W. Fortgens (1934); 7. 1–451, J. J. L. Smolenaars (1983); 9, M. Dewar (1991), with section on Nachleben; 10, R. D. Williams (1972); 11, P. Venini (1970). *Achilleid*: O. A. W. Dilke (1954).
>
> CONCORDANCE J. Klecka (1983).
>
> TRANSLATIONS J. H. Mozley (Loeb, 1928). *Thebaid*: J. B. Poynton (1971–5); A. D. Melville (1992).
>
> STUDIES A. Hardie, *Statius and the Silvae* (1983); W. Schetter, *Untersuchungen zur epischen Kunst des Statius* (1960); D. W. T. C. Vessey, *Statius and the Thebaid* (1973); P. Hardie, *The Epic Successors of Virgil* (1993).
>   D. C. F.

statues (cult of)

Prehistory There is no unequivocal evidence for the worship of statues in prehistory. Neolithic marble figurines and figures from the *Cyclades, with their stylized and exaggerated female attributes, are funerary and votive in character, rather than embodying the essential nature of any cult (as previously thought). Large wheel-made, hollow-bodied figures from late bronze age shrines at Phylakopi (*Melos), *Mycenae, and elsewhere are religious in character, although whether they represent deities is unclear, since their raised arms may rather indicate a votary. See RELIGION, MINOAN AND MYCENAEAN.

Greece There is no certain evidence for the cult of statues in the dark ages. *Pausanias (3) knew of an aniconic period, and in his day stones sacred to individual deities could be seen in Greece, although their date is guesswork (Paus. 7. 22. 4; 4. 22. 1). The veneration of images of deities was well-established by the 7th cent. BC, when monumental temples to house a cult's principal statue became common (for possibly the earliest such 'cult-statues' extant, from Drerus on *Crete, *c.*700 BC, see J. Boardman, *Greek Sculpture: The Archaic Period* (1978) fig. 16); in the manufacture of colossal cult-statues in precious metals from the 5th cent. BC sculptors like *Phidias may have sought to visualize the divine attributes of brightness and abnormal height. *Prayer was offered to statues of deities, including cult-statues as such (e.g. Hdt. 6. 61), which probably were more accessible to worshippers than traditionally thought (Corbett). Hand-held images were a feature of some cults (e.g. *SEG* 23. 220); borne by priests or acolytes, they presided over ritual (Paus. 3. 16. 10–11). Divine effigies could even be vehicles for political protest, as when one at Athens spat blood at *Augustus (Cass. Dio 54. 7. 1–4).

From the later 6th cent. BC on there are critiques of the use of statues. Those dealt with cultural relativism (*Xenophanes, DK 21 B 15–16), involved larger philosophical agenda (*Heraclitus, DK 22 B 5, Strabo 16. 2. 35, *Zeno (2) in Origen, *c. Cels.* 1. 5, *SVF* 1, fr. 265; B. de Borries, *Quid veteres philosophi de idolatria senserint* (diss. Göttingen, 1918) or focused on *barbarians' lack of images (Hdt. 4. 62; Amm. Marc. 31. 2. 23).

Rome According to *Varro (*ARD* 18 Cardauns = August. *De civ. Dei* 4. 31. 21–9; cf. Plut. *Numa* 8. 7–8, Servius on *Aen.* 1. 505) the earliest Romans lacked cult images. While archaeological evidence such as figurines of the *Di penates* (see PENATES DI) contradicts this, an archaic de-emphasis is plausible because of the amorphous quality of *numen, a spiritual force common at all periods in Roman religion. Aniconic worship continued in the cases of the *manalis lapis* (Festus, 115 Lindsay, Serv. on *Aen.* 3. 175, Latte, *RR* 78 n. 4, Roscher, *Lex.* 2. 2308–9), and Jupiter Elicius (*RE* 10. 1128, Ogilvie on Livy 1. 20. 7, Latte, *RR* 78–9; cf. L. Fiedler, *Antike Wetterzauber* (1931), 65–8).

Statues had special uses too. Élite Roman families kept wax images of their ancestors (*imagines) which they displayed in funeral processions (*Kleine Pauly* 2. 1371–3). Some thought movement and appearance of statues constituted significant divine communication (Cic. *Div.* 1. 20, with Pease's notes; Verg. *Aen.* 2. 171–82); in the myth of *Pygmalion the statue came to life (Ovid, *Met.* 10. 243–97, with Bömer's notes). In the later empire appears literary (Eunap. *VS* 475) and papyrological (*PMG* 12. 318–24, 4. 1830–4, 2360–72) evidence of theurgic methods of animating statues of divinities to facilitate communication; cf. E. R. Dodds, *JRS* 1947, 62–5, Faraone (below). Such animation should not be considered 'magical' but, rather, religious; cf. *ANET*, p. 5. See THEURGY.

Judaeo-Christian Worship of graven images was religiously forbidden in Judaism (Exod. 20: 4, 34: 17, Deut. 27: 15, Jer. 10: 3–5; see RELIGION, JEWISH) and continued in the more secularized context of *Mishnah Abodah Zarah* 3. 6–7, 4. 4–7 with W. Elmslie, *The Mishna on Idolatry* (1911) ad loc. The continued denunciation bespeaks early Judaism's tendency towards such worship: Gen. 12: 6, 13: 18 with M. Noth, *The History of Israel*[2] (Ger. orig. 1960), 121–2; cf. 1 Kings 12: 28–30, Hosea 3: 4. This bemused pagans: Juv. 6. 542–7, 14. 96–7, with Courtney's notes, Tac. *Hist.* 5. 5. Christianity appropriated the Jewish view (1 Cor. 8: 4, 12: 2; Tert. *De Idolatr.*). Further, worship of statues not only became part of anti-pagan polemic (Justin Mart. *Apol.* 1. 9, 20) but also theurgic

animation could be charged against a heresiarch such as Simon Magus (ps.-Clem. *Rom. Hom.* 2. 32); idolatry could be charged against rival sects: W. Frend, *The Donatist Church* (1952), 189.

RE Suppl. 5. 472–511; G. Wissowa, *Ges. Abh.* (1904), 280 ff. (Roman); M. de Wisser, *Die nicht menschengestaltigen Götter der Griechen* (1903); G. Wissowa, *Ges. Abh.* (1904), 280 ff. (Roman); J. Geffcken, *ARW* 1916–19, 286 ff.; P. E. Corbett, *BICS* 1970, 149 ff. (access to temples); W. Burkert, *Greek Religion* (1977, Eng. trans. 1985), 88 ff.; R. L. Gordon, *Art History* 1979, 5–34; C. H. Funke, *RAC* 11 (1981), 659 ff. (general); C. Faraone, *Talismans and Trojan Horses* (1992); *Encyclopedia of Religion* 7. 73–82 (idolatry); D. Steiner, *Images in Mind* (2001). C. R. P.

status, legal and social

Greek Greek social and legal status terminology was rich, complex, and confused. There was a multiplicity of Greek communities, often very different in character, which although typically small in scale were yet complex in organization. The consequent confusion was not clarified by the Greek equivalent of Roman jurisprudents and jurisconsults, since such persons did not exist. In all Greek societies at all periods the fundamental status division was between the free and the unfree. But whereas the former could be divided fairly simply into citizen and non-citizen, men and women, adults and children, the Greeks devised no fewer than a dozen words for various types and degrees of unfree people.

Everywhere in the Greek world the normative type of the high status person was the citizen (*politēs*), free, adult, and male (see CITIZENSHIP, GREEK). Qualifications for citizenship (*politeia*) varied from community to community, but in all birth—membership of a corporate descent-group—was assumed to be primary. Only in Sparta was this coupled with a test of achievement, successful passage through the compulsory state educational curriculum and consequent election to a common mess. Further distinctions between active and passive, or first-class and second-class, citizenship might be drawn on grounds of age, gender, or wealth. Democratic Athens thus pioneered the idea that to be a full active citizen it was enough for a man to be of legitimate Athenian birth and duly registered with the appropriate authorities to qualify for the exercise of full public and private citizen prerogatives (the most extensive then available anywhere). But even Athens insisted (after 451 BC) on double descent, from a citizen-status mother as well as father. Elsewhere the exercise of citizenship typically remained conditional upon property-ownership in various ways.

No Greek city permitted women the political rights of citizenship, but Athens may have been unusual in the rigour with which physically mature, married citizen women were nevertheless treated virtually as minors at law throughout their lives. Yet, paradoxically, one of the most important public religious functionaries at Athens, the priestess of the city's chief divinity Athena Polias, was by ascribed prerogative a woman from a specified noble lineage. Even in democratic Athens distinctions of birth continued to count for something, as they did more obviously in Sparta, another ideologically egalitarian peer-group society. Indeed, in Sparta there were not only noble families but also two hereditary royal houses (see AGIADS and EURYPONTIDS).

Between the citizen and the free but non-resident foreigner came the free resident alien or *metic (metoikos). This status is attested in some seventy communities but most extensively at Athens, where it can be seen not to have been especially privileged. Metics were required to pay a poll tax and to be represented at law by a citizen patron; metic status, moreover, was that assigned to privately manumitted slaves, most of whom were non-Greek. It was exceedingly rare for an ex-slave such as *Pasion, father of *Apollodorus (2), to crash the barrier of full citizen status.

Of the dozen or so current Greek words for the unfree, *doulos* was the most general and the most common. Yet the term could be applied with liberal abandon both to the chattel-slaves of Athens, for example, and to the quite different helot bondsmen of Sparta (see SLAVERY, Greek; HELOTS). The chattel-slave was a socially dead being, categorizable as 'an animate tool'; but even chattel-slaves were granted some legal protection, if only in virtue of their master's rights of property. Besides the helots, there were some other local collective groups of unfree persons each defined by a distinctive name, of which the best attested if ill understood are those of *Crete. The classification of all such groups as 'between free people and *douloi*' perfectly illustrates both the complexity of Greek societies and the inadequacy of Greek social terminology. See FREEDMEN.

C. B. Patterson, *Pericles' Citizenship Law, 451–450 B.C.* (1981); J. Bordes, *Politeia dans la pensée grecque d'Homère à Aristote* (1982); N. F. Jones, *Public Organization in Ancient Greece* (1987); A. Molho, K. Raaflaub, and J. Emlen (eds.), *City-States in Classical Antiquity and Medieval Italy: Athens and Rome; Florence and Venice* (1991); M. I. Finley *Economy and Society in Ancient Greece* (1981), part 2; D. Whitehead *The Ideology of the Athenian Metic* (PCPhS Supp. 2, 1977); J. C. Trevett, *Apollodoros of Athens* (1992); Y. Garlan, *Slavery in Ancient Greece* (1988).   P. A. C.

Roman In Roman law, *status* describes the 'legal position' of an individual with respect to both that person's household (*familia*) and the broader civic community of Rome. The concept of *status* is linked to *caput* or *persona*, an individual's legal 'personality'. Personality roughly defines the limits of what an individual is legally able to do: marry, make contracts, commit crimes or delicts, bring lawsuits, and so on. In modern law, such issues are treated as aspects of legal capacity; but the Roman jurists lack this more sophisticated concept.

The most systematic exposition of *status* comes in Roman sources discussing change of status, what *Cicero (*Top.* 18, 29) and the jurists (esp. Gaius, *Inst.* 1. 158–63; *Dig.* 4. 5) call *capitis deminutio*. Three issues are paramount, and they are arranged hierarchically: freedom, citizenship, and membership in a household. The most fundamental division is between free persons and slaves (Gaius, 1. 9; see SLAVERY, Roman); then, among free persons, between Roman citizens and others; and finally, especially among Roman citizens, between those who head households (the *sui iuris*) and those subject to the power of a head (the *alieni iuris*).

The complex rules of *capitis deminutio* determine what happens when an individual's legal status changes; the consequences may concern not only the individual but others as well. For example, under the *senatusconsultum Claudianum* of AD 52, a woman who despite warning cohabits with another's slave can herself become that person's slave, thereby simultaneously losing her freedom, citizenship, and position as a household member; but legal questions may then arise about the enslaved woman's property, her former family relationships, and so on. The jurists decide such questions pragmatically (e.g., Gaius, *Inst.* 1. 91, 160).

Legal status is central to Roman private law and much more significant than in modern law. Other areas of Roman law, such as property, contracts, and testamentary succession, often appear remarkably liberal by modern standards; but all are subject to limitations that status imposes on legal capacity to act. For instance, although in principle Roman jurists permit owners to deal in virtually unrestricted fashion with their property, only sane *sui iuris* persons have completely effective legal ownership of property. When resolution of a lawsuit hinges in part on a question of status (*quaestio status*), especially whether an individual is free or a slave, this issue is always tried first (*Dig.* 40. 12).

Granted the importance of status, the Romans were surprisingly casual in providing means to prove it. Beginning with *Augustus, children of a legitimate marriage were registered soon after birth; from Marcus *Aurelius, illegitimate children were also registered. But these evidently incomplete or inaccurate records did not have conclusive legal force. Marriages, upon the legitimacy of which the civil status of children depended, were not registered at all.

Proving one's freedom or citizenship could be challenging, as is shown by a remarkable set of trial documents preserved from Herculaneum. The jurist *Iulius Paulus drily observes that 'distinguishing a free person from a slave can be difficult' (*Dig.* 18. 1. 5); just how difficult is demonstrated by many legal sources dealing with a free person 'serving in good faith' (*bona fide serviens*), held as a slave by an 'owner' unaware of the person's true status. Free persons held as slaves could not assert their own freedom and had to find an outsider willing to take up the burden of proof.

As a result, civil status, though a cornerstone of Roman law, was always potentially at risk; at any moment it might be challenged, and it could disappear overnight. None the less, Roman citizens clung tenaciously to the belief that their civil status protected them from harm; as Cicero puts it, the cry 'I am a Roman citizen' brought safety the world over (2 *Verr.* 5. 147, 165; cf. Acts 22: 25–9).

In the modern social sciences, status has a more than purely legal meaning: it refers to social position, particularly as determined by birth, wealth, and external markers like honour, place of residence, or badges of distinction. The Roman empire's small social élite was highly stratified by status: the 'orders' (*ordines*) of senators (see SENATE), *equites, and municipal councillors (*decuriones*). All three orders had minimum wealth requirements, but were also to a large extent hereditary. The rest of the free population was less formally stratified, though quasi-status groups often formed around a common occupation, residence, or civil status; of special note is the order of *freedmen (*ordo libertinorum*), attested from the late republic on.

Such status groups played a significant social, political, and economic role, but were at first not clearly recognized by law; in theory, Roman citizens were equal before the law. However, during the early empire, through a process still not entirely understood, civic equality began to erode, especially in criminal law; criminal procedure and punishment distinguished the 'more upright' (*honestiores*) from the 'more base' (*humiliores*). By the early 2nd cent. AD, this distinction was hardening into law; the *honestiores*, generally defined as the three uppermost social orders, received better legal treatment and milder penalties. In private law, prohibitions on intermarriage and status-based penalties for anti-social behavior also furthered the bifurcation of society.

The society of the high and late empire was not simply bifurcated, however. Particularly the late imperial bureaucracy saw a profusion of titles and distinctions of rank, all deriving ultimately from the emperor and his court.

B. Albanese, *Le persone nel diritto privato Romano* (1979); C. Nicolet (ed.), *Des Ordres à Rome* (1984); P. W. Duff, *Personality in Roman Private*

stele

Law (1938); P. Garnsey, *Social Status and Legal Privilege in the Roman Empire* (1970); Jones, *Later Rom. Emp.*; M. Kaser, *Das römische Privatrecht* 1 (1971), esp. 270–89; R. MacMullen, *Roman Social Relations, 50 B.C. to A.D. 284* (1974); C. Nicolet, *The World of the Citizen in Republican Rome* (trans. P. S. Falla, 1980). B. W. F.

stele, stone slab, in particular one bearing figured decoration or an inscribed text. Grave markers are found occasionally in bronze age Greece, the most notable being those with relief decoration above the Shaft Graves at *Mycenae. In Geometric and early Archaic Greece such stelai are rare, but in Athens about 600 BC there begins a distinguished series with relief decoration on the shaft, topped first by a *sphinx, then by a palmette finial. The latter type originated in east Greece, and it persisted after 500 in the islands, after the Athenian series had already ended. A new type of stele in Athens appears after the mid-5th cent. It is broader, with pilasters at the side and a pediment above, and carries relief representations of the dead or scenes of parting. This ever more monumental series was stopped by a decree of *Demetrius (3) of Phaleron in c.317–16, and later Attic grave markers are simple short cylindrical blocks. Stelai were also regularly used in many parts of the Greek world from the later 7th cent. onwards for the publication of decrees and other texts, and also as *horoi* marking the limits of property. See ART, FUNERARY, GREEK; EPIGRAPHY, GREEK.

G. M. A. Richter, *The Archaic Gravestones of Attica* (1961); K. F. Johansen, *The Attic Grave Reliefs* (1951); L. H. Jeffery, *BSA* 1962, 115 ff.; J. Kirchner, *Imagines inscriptionum atticarum* (1948). J. B.; A. W. J.

Stentor, a man who became proverbial from *Homer's statement that he had a 'brazen voice' equal to that of fifty other men (*Il.* 5. 785–6). He died after his defeat by *Hermes in a shouting contest. J. R. M.

Stephanus of Byzantium was a Greek grammarian, probably a contemporary of Justinian, and a publicly appointed teacher in Constantinople. Nothing is known in detail of his life except that he was a Christian. He is the author of *Ethnica*, in sixty books, an alphabetical list of place-names together with the adjectives derived from them. The original work, which contained information on foundation-legends, etymologies, changes of name, oracles, historical anecdotes, proverbs, etc., is lost. The surviving *epitome, consisting mainly of jejune entries, was compiled some time between the 6th and 10th cents. AD. It may be the work of one Hermolaus, mentioned in the *Suda*, but some scholars believe that it is actually a conflation of at least two *epitomes, made on slightly different principles. There are fragments of the original extensive text embedded in the *De Administrando Imperio* and *De Thematibus* of Constantine Porphyrogenitus.

Stephanus was neither a geographer—he makes no direct use of *Ptolemy (4)—nor a historian—he puts down side by side information dating from different epochs—but a grammarian. His prime interest is the correct formation of ethnic adjectives, for which he has two criteria, morphological regularity and regional usage. His direct sources, which he sometimes mentions, include *Herodian (1), Oros of Miletus, *Philo (5) of Byblos Περὶ πόλεων ('On Cities'), *Dionysius (9) Periegetes, *Strabo, historians from *Hecataeus (1) to *Polybius (1), and lost grammarians and antiquarians. He is not entirely uncritical in his handling of his sources, but his main value is as a compilation of material from writers whose works are lost. The surviving epitome was used by the *Etymologicum Magnum, *Eustathius, and probably the *Suda. The last writer to use the original version was Constantine Porphyrogenitus. The *Ethnica* are preserved in a large number of manuscripts, mainly dating from the Renaissance. There is no satisfactory critical edition.

Ed. A. Meineke (1849, repr. 1958 and 1992); H. Diller, *TAPA* 1938, 333–48; H. Erbse, *Beiträge zur Überlieferung der Iliasscholien* (Zetemata 24, 1960), 251–69; D. Whitehead, *Hist.* Einzelschrift 87 (1994), 99 ff. R. B.

Sterope or **Asterope,** (1) one of the Pleiads (see PLEIAD), wife of *Oenomaus (Paus. 5. 10. 6); (2) daughter of Cepheus king of Tegea (Apollod. 2. 144). *Heracles gave her (in Paus. 8. 47. 5, Athena gave Cepheus) some of the hair of Medusa (see GORGO), bidding her lift it three times above the city wall, to put attackers to flight. H. J. R.

LIMC 7. 1 (1994), 809–20.

Stertinius, a Stoic writer (see STOICISM), alleged source in Hor. *Sat.* 2. 3 (see l. 296) said by [Helenius Acro] (on Hor. *Epist.* 1. 12. 20) to have written 220 books; the implication that these were in verse is not credible. E. C.

Stesichorus (*RE* 1), Greek lyric poet, active c.600–550 BC. Greek tradition made him later than *Alcman, and contemporary with *Sappho and *Alcaeus (1) (*Suda*); Simonides (fr. 564) referred back to him and to *Homer. He was connected with Mataurus in Bruttium (Steph. Byz., *Suda*; see BRUTTII), and with *Himera in Sicily (already Pl., *Phdr.* 244a); Arist. *Rh.* 1393[b] tells an anecdote of him and Phalaris. His tomb was shown at Himera (Poll. 9. 100) or *Catana (Antip. Thess., *Anth. Pal.* 7. 75, etc.). Some said that his real name was Teisias (*Suda*).

Stesichorus' works were collected in 26 books (*Suda*); nothing now survives but quotations and some fragmentary papyri. The poems are cited by title, not by book-number. That suggests substantial pieces, and what detail we know confirms it. *Geryoneis* apparently reached at least 1300 lines; *Oresteia*, and perhaps *Helen*, occupied two books. The titles cover a whole range of major myths: *Helen*, *Wooden Horse*, *Sack of Troy*, *Homecomings*, *Oresteia* belong to the Trojan cycle, *Geryoneis*, *Cycnus*, and *Cerberus* to the adventures of *Heracles, *Eriphyle*, *Europia*, and the untitled fragment about *Eteocles and Polynices to the Theban story (see SEVEN AGAINST THEBES); *Boar-hunters* was concerned with *Meleager (1), *Funeral Games for Pelias* with the *Argonauts.

These poems represent a kind of lyric epic. Their metre, 'Doric' dialect, and triadic form seem to attach them to the 'choral lyric' tradition represented by Alcman and *Pindar. But their large scale and narrative sweep recall the traditional epic; their language is often Homeric, their metres dactylic (fr. 222A even has some quasi-hexameters); it has been argued that such long pieces must have been performed, like epic, by a solo poet or reciter, not by a chorus. See METRE, GREEK, §§ 3 and 4. The prehistory of this form is obscure (see XANTHUS (1)), and Stesichorus seems to have no successors: perhaps this was a unique attempt to transfuse epic material into a new medium. Not only is his diction 'Homeric' in general; he seems to know at least individual passages of the *Iliad* and *Odyssey* as we have them. Thus fr. 209 reworks the departure of *Telemachus from Sparta (*Od.* 15. 164 ff.); Geryones borrows rhetoric from *Sarpedon (S11; *Il.* 12. 322 ff.) and dies like Gorgythion (S14; *Il.* 8. 306–8), his mother speaks as *Hecuba (S13; *Il.* 22. 83). Ancient critics duly called Stesichorus 'Homeric'; *Quintilian (*Inst.* 10. 1. 62) praises his dignity but criticizes his diffuseness. Certainly the few continuous pieces suggest a narrative well spaced with direct speech. In the 'Thebaid' (fr. 222A) *Oedipus' widow proposes a compromise between her warring sons, the sons agree, *Tiresias predicts disaster if the bargain is broken, Polynices leaves, and travels towards *Argos (2): this takes 100 lines, of which the speeches occupy 70. In *Geryoneis* Heracles crosses Ocean in the cup of the Sun, kills the triple Geryones, and drives away his cattle: there is time for a heroic speech by Geryones, and a lament by his mother, before Heracles destroys his heads one by one. Stesichorus came from the fringes of the Greek world: that may explain the idiosyncratic form, and the idiosyncratic versions of myth which the tragedians later borrowed (see frs. 193, 217). His influence has been suspected in the metopes of the *Heraion at Foce del Sele (see PAESTUM), and in Attic vase-painting of the later 6th cent.; one of the Tabulae Iliacae (a Roman monument of the 1st cent. AD found near *Bovillae, for which see N. Horsfall, *JHS* 1979, 26 ff.) claims to represent his *Sack of Troy*.

TESTIMONIA AND TEXT Davies, *PMGF* 1 (1991). P. Brise, *Die Geryoneis des Stesichoros und die frühe griechische Kunst* (1980); P. J. Parsons, *ZPE* 26 (1977), 7–36; W. Burkert, in C. M. Robertson and others, *Papers on the Amasis Painter and his World* (1987), 43 ff.; A. Burnett, *Class. Ant.* 1988, 107 ff. P. J. P.

Stesimbrotus (fl. late 5th cent. BC), biographer (see BIOGRAPHY, GREEK) from *Thasos, who taught at Athens.

Works (*FGrH* 107) (1) Homeric studies; (2) *On *teletē*, on the Samothracian mysteries; (3) Περὶ Θεμιστοκλέους καὶ Θουκυδίδου καὶ Περικλέους ('On Themistocles, Thucydides, and Pericles'; frs. in Plut.). Stesimbrotus gives full biographical details, but criticizes *Themistocles and *Pericles (1) and lauds *Cimon; no preserved fragments concern *Thucydides (1) (son of Melesias).

K. Meister, *Historia* 1978, 274 ff. and *Die griechische Geschichtsschreibung* (1990), 43; F. J. Frost, *Plutarch's Themistocles Commentary* (1980), 16 f., 86 f.; P. A. Stadter, *Comm. Plut. Pericles* (1989), pp. lxii f.; H. Strasburger, *Studien zur alten Geschichte* 3 (1990), 341–51. F. W. W.; S. H.

Sthenelus, a 5th-cent. tragic poet mentioned by *Aristotle (*Poet.* 22) as an example of flat style resulting from the use of commonplace words. *Aristophanes (1) calls him insipid at fr. 158, and the point of *Wasps* 1313 may be that he relied on stage properties rather than poetic merits.

TrGF 1² 150–1. A. L. B.

Sthenidas of *Locri Epizephyrii, nominal author of a Neopythagorean work *On Kingship* (variously dated between the 3rd cent. BC and the 2nd cent. AD) which calls for the king to imitate the universal rule of the highest god. See KINGSHIP; NEOPYTHAGOREANISM.

Ed. H. Thesleff, *The Pythagorean Texts of the Hellenistic Period* (1965), 187–8. See ECPHANTUS. D. O'M.

stichometry, the modern name for an ancient system of numbering lines in literary texts. In Greek papyri, this numbering takes two forms. (1) Marginal: each hundredth line marked with a letter of the alphabet (A = 100 up to Ω = 2400, then again from A). (2) Final: the sum total of lines in the work (roll) stated at the end, often introduced by ἀριθμός, 'number', and most often in acrophonic numerals (see NUMBERS, GREEK). Any individual copy may exhibit both, one, or neither; a few copies show lines checked off in fives, tens, or twenties. In verse, the 'line' defines itself. In prose, the numbering assumes a notional or standard line (the actual lines would differ in length from copy to copy): apparently 15–16 syllables (cf. Galen, *De placit. Hipp. et Plat.* 8. 1. 23, p. 486. 2–3 de Lacy), equivalent to an average hexameter (the terminology uses ἔπος, 'epic verse' as synonymous with στίχος, 'line'). The earliest surviving examples date from the later 3rd cent. BC: for

example, the Sorbonne papyrus of *Menander (1)'s *Sicyonius*. But prose-writers of the 4th cent. BC were already counting their ἔπη (Theopompus, *FGrH* 115 F 25); and the use of acrophonic numerals, which became obsolete outside Attica from the 3rd cent. BC, may also suggest that the practice began in classical Athens. Final stichometry, and occasionally marginal stichometry, survive here and there in medieval manuscripts, for example those of *Demosthenes (2). In Latin, the practice was certainly known (the 'Cheltenham Catalogue' of *c.* AD 360 reckons up the books of the Bible and St Cyprian according to the *versus Vergilianus* of 16 syllables), but is rarely if ever noted in manuscripts. Stichometry (it can be guessed) served (1) to estimate the payment of the scribe and the cost to the purchaser; (2) to guarantee the completeness of the text (*Callimachus (3) included stichometric totals in his *Pinakes*, fr. 434); (3) to pinpoint a reference. This last (our normal use) is extremely rare: first attested in *Diogenes (6) Laertius (7. 33, 187–8), where critics of *Zeno (2) and *Chrysippus cite their texts in round hundreds. By contrast, *Asconius keys his commentaries to *Cicero's text on a primitive count which shows that the roll before him was not professionally numbered.

K. Ohly, *Stichometrische Untersuchungen* (1928); C. Wendel, *Die griechisch-römische Buchbeschreibung* (1949), 34–44; G. Cavallo, *Libri scritture scribi a Ercolano* (1983), 20–2; E. G. Turner, *Greek Manuscripts of the Ancient World*² (1987), 16. P. J. P.

stichomythia is a form of dramatic dialogue in which each utterance by each speaker consists of a single line of verse. Under the same general heading come forms in which each utterance consists of two lines (sometimes called distichomythia) or half a line (sometimes called hemistichomythia). Stichomythia is the form usually employed for rapid exchanges in Greek tragedy. Thus it is the usual alternative, in dialogue scenes, to extended speeches (*rhēseis*; see SPEECH PRESENTATION), although freer, more naturalistic forms of exchange also occur, especially in *Sophocles (1). It can extend for long stretches, especially in *Euripides (e.g. *Ion* 255–368, 113 lines including a brief two-line section), despite the danger of monotony (to modern taste) and the occasional need for padding.

Common uses of the form are where one party questions and the other answers (e.g. Aesch. *Pers.* 231–45, Eur. *IT* 492–569); where one persuades and the other resists (e.g. Aesch. *Cho.* 908–30, Eur. *Med.* 324–39); and where the two exchange insults (e.g. Soph. *Ant.* 726–57, and often when tempers rise following the set speeches of an *agon* or verbal contest).

Sustained stichomythia is much less common in Greek comedy (e.g. Ar. *Ach.* 1097–1142, *Lys.* 212–36, both for special effect; Men. *Pk.* 779–809, with interruptions) and Latin tragedy (e.g. Sen. *Ag.* 145–57), and barely occurs in Latin comedy.

B. Seidensticker, 'Die Stichomythie', in W. Jens, *Die Bauformen der griechischen Tragödie* (1971), 183–220. A. L. B.

Stilicho, adviser of *Theodosius (2) I, became regent for his son *Honorius and ruler of the west AD 395–408. He sought to unify east and west, particularly up to *c.*400. Two attempts to quell *Alaric (395 and 397) and move on to *Constantinople were, however, ineffective. He successfully parried Alaric's first invasion of Italy in 402, but was unable to maintain his control of the west in the face of a series of crises. First Radagaisus invaded Italy in 405–6, then came the Rhine crossing of 31 December 406 and the associated usurpation of *Constantine III, and, in the mean time, a previously arranged alliance with Alaric (perhaps part of another attempt on the east) caused the latter to make heavy financial demands. These military and political disasters allowed rivals to win Honorius over; Stilicho fell in a *coup d'état* in 408.

A. M. Cameron, *Claudian* (1970); J. F. Matthews, *Western Aristocracies and Imperial Court 364–425* (1975). P. J. H.

Stilo Praeconinus See AELIUS, L.

Stilpon of Megara (died early 3rd cent. BC), third and perhaps last head of the *Megarian school. He was a familiar and popular figure in Athens. His numerous pupils included *Zeno (2) the founder of Stoicism, *Menedemus (1) the founder of the *Eretrian school, and the orator Alcimus. He is reported to have written at least twenty dialogues.

His teaching was largely ethical—Socratic in inspiration, with some Cynic colouring (see CYNICS). Renowned for overcoming his own innate moral weaknesses (Cicero, *Fat.* 10), he taught the autonomy of human good: moral and intellectual attainments, he maintained, were inalienable. In metaphysics, he argued against Platonic Forms, and rejected the copula as incoherent, dismissing all 'x is y' statements as false identity-statements.

G. Giannantoni, *Socratis et Socraticorum Reliquiae* (1990); K. Döring, *Die Megariker* (1972); E. Zeller, *Socrates and the Socratic Schools* (Eng. trans. 1868). D. N. S.

stipendium denoted a cash payment and later a permanent tax; it also meant the regular cash payment received by soldiers at the end of the campaigning season, and consequently came to mean a period of military service, originally a season, but subsequently a year. In the imperial period *stipendium* designated military pay, specifically one of the three annual instalments by which the troops were paid, or one year of service.

Pay Around 400 BC during the war with *Veii a payment was first made to Roman soldiers while on long campaigns to assist with their living expenses. In the 2nd cent. BC according to *Polybius (1) (6. 39) the legionary was receiving two obols a day, which, if this represented five *asses*, would be 180 *denarii* in a year of 360 days. After the revaluation of the coinage in the time of the *Gracchi this will have amounted to 112½ *denarii*, which accords with Suetonius' statement that *Caesar doubled legionary pay, since legionaries received 225 *denarii* under *Augustus and there is no indication that he made an increase. There were fixed deductions to meet the cost of food, clothing, and the repair or replacement of weapons; although C. *Sempronius Gracchus had provided that soldiers should receive an issue of clothing at the state's expense, it is possible that this law did not long survive his downfall. Deductions seem to have continued throughout the imperial period. *Domitian was the first emperor to increase military pay, by adding another instalment of 75 *denarii*, then *Septimius Severus increased it, probably to 600, and *Caracalla to 900 *denarii*. *Praetorians received higher rates, more than three times legionary pay by AD 14 (750 *denarii*), and this differential was maintained. The salary of the soldiers of the Urban Cohorts was 375 *denarii*. The pay of the *vigiles and the fleets cannot be discovered, though the latter may be equated with the auxiliaries; on the evidence of military pay records an auxiliary infantryman probably received 5/6 of a legionary's pay, with higher rates for cavalrymen (see AUXILIA).

Principales were paid at a rate one and a half times or twice the normal scale, while centurions and *primipili* received very substantial salaries (perhaps 13,500 *denarii* for a chief centurion in the early first century). By the end of the 3rd cent. inflation

had so reduced the value of military salaries that a system of payment in kind had been adopted.

Length of service In the republic a man between the age of 17 and 46 was expected to be available for up to 16 years service as an infantryman (10 years as a cavalryman), although in the 2nd cent. he would not normally serve more than six years continuously on active service. In 13 BC Augustus established or confirmed conditions of service for his troops—16 years for the legionaries (plus a further four years as a reservist), 12 years for the praetorians. However, it proved impossible to maintain this system, through shortage of recruits and the expense of discharge payments, and in AD 5 service was increased to 20 years (with probably five as a reservist) for legionaries, and 16 for praetorians. But the mutineers in AD 14 claimed that men were kept on long after their time, for 30 or 40 years. Sailors in the fleets served for 26 years, auxiliary soldiers for 25, and by the mid-1st cent. the service time had been set at 25 years for legionaries.

Pay scales from Domitian to Septimius Severus (in *denarii*):

praetorians	1000	Auxiliary *alae*	350
urban cohorts	500	part-mounted cohorts	300
legionaries	300	infantry cohorts	250

See ARMIES, ROMAN.

P. A. Brunt, *PBSR* 1950, 50; G. R. Watson, *The Roman Soldier* (1969), 89; D. Breeze, *JRS* 1971, 130; M. P. Speidel, *JRS* 1973, 141; J. Jahn, *ZPE* 53 (1983), 217; M. A. Speidel, *JRS* 1992, 87. J. B. C.

stipulatio (stipulation) was a formal *contract concluded orally in the form of question (made by the future creditor, *stipulator*: 'Do you pledge that 100 will be given?' (*centum dari spondes?*)), and answer (by the future debtor, *promissor*: 'I pledge' (*spondeo*)). Question and answer had to correspond (same verb!) and had to follow each other immediately (*unitas actus*). *Stipulatio* already existed at the time of the *Twelve Tables and it soon became the cornerstone of the Roman system of contractual obligations. Any agreement could be given legal effect by using this simple oral form. Use of the verb *spondere* (hence the term *sponsio*) was confined to Roman citizens; in classical law, other verbs (like *promittere*; cf. Gai. *Inst.* 3. 92) were permissible and were also open to foreigners.

The scope of the contract of stipulation was immense. For a whole variety of purposes the Romans regularly, or even exclusively, used stipulations: in order to strengthen a loan and to promise interest; to stand surety; to replace an already existing obligation with a new one (*novatio*); to promise a dowry, a gift, or payment of a penalty; or to give specific guarantees (these are the manifold *cautiones* that we find both in private law and in the law of procedure).

Stipulatio underwent a 'degeneration', the pace, extent and character of which are disputed. On the one hand, the strictness of the formal oral requirements was increasingly relaxed, until, by an obscure constitution of *Leo (2) I dated AD 472 (C. 8. 37. 10; cf. also Justinian, *Inst.* 3. 15. 1; see JUSTINIAN'S CODIFICATION) the need for 'sollemnia verba' was removed altogether. On the other hand, the emphasis shifted from the oral act to the written evidence of it. For since witnesses were unnecessary, it became usual to draw up a written memorandum; already in the time of Cicero (*Top.* 26. 96) *stipulatio* could thus be classed as a written act. It is probable that well before Justinian the document (with a 'stipulatory clause' normally attached to it) had in practice replaced the oral form. Justinian ruled that even a document made between parties who were not present together (*inter* *absentes*) should be valid unless the parties could be proved to have been in different places for the whole day in question (C. 8. 37. 14. 2). See OBLIGATION.

B. Nicholas, *Law Quart. Review* 1953, 63 ff., 233 ff., and *An Introduction to Roman Law* (1962); S. Riccobono, ZRG 1914, 214 ff.; 1922, 262 ff. (Eng. trans. with supplements and notes by B. Beinart, *Stipulation and the Theory of Contract* (1957)); D. Simon, *Stipulationsklausel* (1964); M. Kaser, *Römisches Privatrecht* 1² (1971), 168 ff., 538 ff.; 2² (1975), 373 ff.; G. MacCormack, *Studies Thomas* (1983), 96 ff.; M. Dobbertin, *Auslegung der Stipulation* (1987); R. Zimmermann, *The Law of Obligation* (1990), 68 ff.; A. Watson, *The Law of Obligations in the Later Roman Republic* (1965); H. F. Jolowicz and B. Nicholas, *Historical Introduction to the Study of Roman Law* (3rd edn., 1972). R. Z.

stoa The name stoa is applied to various types of building, comprising essentially an open colonnade, generally in the Doric order (see ORDERS, ARCHITECTURAL), and a roof over the space to a rear wall.

There are many possible elaborations of this simplest type. An interior colonnade may be added, often of Ionic columns rather than the outer Doric, supporting the ridge of the roof. This gives more usable space (the Ionic columns being at double the exterior interval to minimize obstruction). Rooms may be added, behind the wall.

In plan, they may be elaborated by construction of additional wings, to give ⌐ and ⌐ shaped structures, or completely surrounding a courtyard. Most are single storey. The first stoa to have an additional storey is that constructed about 300 BC at *Perachora, where ground space is severely limited; the upper colonnade is Ionic, a distinction which becomes normal in two-storey stoas. Pergamene architects constructed stoas to an even greater height, by building them against terraces, facing inward over the terrace and outward in the form of basements utilized for storage and shops. See PERGAMUM.

In their simplest form they provide shade and shelter, whether for people watching religious activities in a sanctuary (the stoa at the Samian *Heraion, of the 7th cent. BC; see SAMOS) or engaged in the various activities of the *agora; these can be political, judicial, or social, whether philosophical discussions (see STOA POECILE) or feasting (the south stoa of the Athenian agora has a series of rooms behind its double-aisled facade clearly arranged to accommodate dining couches).

Rooms behind the north stoa of the agora at *Priene were covered with official inscriptions, suggesting they served as a record office; varied but indefinable office functions can be attributed to rooms behind other stoas, such as the Stoa of Attalus at Athens. See ATHENS, TOPOGRAPHY.

In *sanctuaries, stoas are inevitably ancillary to the main religious structures. As architecture, their main impact is on the agora, which they help to define by being placed on the boundary. In the agoras of planned cities this can lead to their being nothing more than linked lines of columns defining a regular shape. In the irregular agoras of unplanned cities, more variety is possible. Thus the agora at Athens, already by the end of the 5th cent., had acquired several stoas of differing forms and functions.

Construction is generally inferior in quality to temples. Stone work is limestone, not marble, columns are more spaced; the cheaper Doric is preferred to Ionic even in east Greece. Floors are often of beaten earth, walls may be mudbrick. Quality improves in the Hellenistic period, especially in stoas like that of Attalus II at Athens, a royal gift to the city.

See BASILICA; PORTICO.

R. Martin, *Recherches sur l'Agora grecque* (1951), 440 ff.; R. E. Wycherley, *How the Greeks Built Cities*² (1962), 110 ff.; J. J. Coulton, *The Architectural Development of the Greek Stoa* (1976). R. A. T.

Stoa Poecile ('painted'). Known from over 50 literary testimonia, and excavated from 1981, it lies in the NW part of the Athenian Agora; see ATHENS, TOPOGRAPHY. It measures 12.5 by *c*.36 m., made of various limestones, with Doric exterior columns, and Ionic interior columns with marble capitals (see ORDERS, ARCHITECTURAL), and is finely jointed. It dates from *c*.475–450, part of the Cimonian improvement of the area; see CIMON. The name 'Poecile' (first attested in the 4th cent.), derived from the panel paintings it housed. Pausanias (1. 15. 1–4) gives the fullest account, mentioning scenes of the Athenians arrayed against the Spartans at Oenoe near *Argos (2) (perhaps an error for one of the *Attic *demes called Oenoe and preparations for Marathon; see MARATHON, BATTLE OF), the Amazonomachy, Greeks at Troy, and the battle of *Marathon. Sources name the painters as *Micon, *Polygnotus, and *Panaenus.

The Poecile had no single function, being used for proclaiming the Eleusinian *mysteries (see ELEUSIS), and occasional legal matters; shields from Sphacteria were displayed (see PYLOS). The philosopher *Zeno (2) frequented it so much that his followers became known as 'Stoics'; see STOICISM.

J. Camp, *The Athenian Agora* (1986); *Agora* 3 (1957), 31–45; E. D. Francis and M. Vickers, BSA 1985, 99–113. K. W. A.

Stobaeus (Ἰωάννης Στοβαῖος, 'John of *Stobi'), author of an anthology of excerpts from poets and prose-writers, intended in the first instance for the instruction of his son Septimius. The work was probably composed in the early 5th cent. AD; it consisted originally of four books, which came to be grouped later under the titles *Eklogai* ('Selections') and *Anthologion* ('Anthology'), though subject-matter and treatment are essentially homogeneous. It deals with a variety of topics, from metaphysics to household economy; from bk. 2 onwards it is concerned chiefly with ethical questions. The illustrative extracts, which Stobaeus probably owed in large measure to earlier collectors, are arranged under successive headings, being grouped generally in the same order, beginning with the poets. Stobaeus cites a multitude of authors, from *Homer to *Themistius; the writers of the *Second Sophistic are scarcely represented, but there are many excerpts from the Neoplatonists (see NEOPLATONISM); the absence of excerpts from Christian authors suggests that he was a pagan. *Photius (9th cent.) commends the work for its usefulness, especially to writers and speakers. Its value for us consists in the large number of citations from earlier literature, which not only supplement our knowledge of classical authors, but often throw light upon difficulties in the regular manuscript tradition.

Suda (under Ἰωάννης); Photius, *Bibl.*, cod. 167.
EDITION C. Wachsmuth and O. Hense (1884–1923).
CRITICISM A. Elter, *De Ioh. St. cod. Phot.* (1880) and id. *De gnom. graec. hist. et orig.* (1893–6); O. Hense, RE 20. 2549 ff.; K. Wachsmuth, *Studien zu den griechischen Florilegien* (1882); S. Luria, 'Entstellungen des klassischen Textes bei Stobaeus', *Rh. Mus.* 1929, 81–104.
W. M. E.; R. B.

Stobi, a strategically located settlement of Paeonia (see MACEDONIA) at the confluence of the Axius (Vardar) and Erigon (Crna Reka), was a Macedonian stronghold by the 2nd cent. BC and in the Roman period flourished as a *municipium; it was later promoted to *colonia* (see COLONIZATION, ROMAN) and enjoyed the status of *ius Italicum* (*Dig.* 50. 15. 8. 8). In the later Roman empire it was capital of *Macedonia Secunda* or *Salutaris* and was captured

Stoicism

by the Ostrogoths (see GOTHS) under *Theoderic (1) in 479. The many visible remains date mostly from the 4th–6th cents.

J. Wiseman, *Stobi: A Guide to the Excavations* (1973), and (ed.), *Studies in the Antiquities of Stobi 1–* (1973–). J. J. W.

Stoicism, philosophical movement, founded by *Zeno (2) of Citium, who came to Athens in 313 BC, and, after studying with various philosophers, taught in his own right in the *Stoa Poecile (Painted Porch). Zeno developed a distinctive philosophical position divided into three parts, logic, physics, and ethics. We know little of the institutional organization of the school, except that at Zeno's death one of his pupils, *Cleanthes, took over the 'headship' of the school. He was not, however, the most famous of Zeno's pupils, and the original position got developed in different directions. *Ariston (1) of Chios stressed ethics to the exclusion of physics and logic; *Herillus emphasized knowledge at the expense of moral action. Cleanthes stressed a religious view of the world, interpreting Stoic ideas in works like his *Hymn to Zeus*. Stoicism was in danger of dissolving into a number of different positions, but was rescued by Cleanthes' pupil *Chrysippus of Soli. He restated and recast Zeno's position in his voluminous writings, defending it with powerful arguments. It was correctly thought later that 'if there had been no Chrysippus there would have been no Stoa'; the work of Zeno's earlier pupils came to be seen as unorthodox, and Chrysippus' works became the standard formulation of Stoicism. Although Chrysippus claimed to adhere to Zeno's ideas, modern scholars have often held that there are divergences between them; but this is hazardous given the fragmentary state of our sources. Chrysippus' own innovations were mainly in the technical area of logic.

The methodology of Stoicism is holistic: there is no foundational part which supports the others. Different Stoics disagreed radically both over the correct structure of their position and the correct order of teaching it. Thus the theory can be fully understood only as a whole, one of the respects in which it is markedly 'ideal' and makes high demands on the student. However, logic, physics, and ethics are distinguishable at a preliminary stage, and in fact the Stoics developed them with great sophistication. *Logic includes logic in the technical sense, in which the Stoics made great advances in what is now called the logic of propositions. It also includes philosophy of language, including grammar and rhetoric, and epistemology. The Stoics are radically empiricist; they give an account of knowledge which traces it from the impact made on the human mind by 'appearances' from the outside world. Some of these appearances, they claim, are such that they could not be wrong; this gave rise to a debate with the Academic *Sceptics. Knowledge proper, however, requires understanding of the principles which define the area in question.

Stoic *physics gives an account of the world which is strongly materialist. It is also determinist; the world as a whole is made up of material objects and their interactions, which occur according to exceptionless laws, which are called 'fate'. However, their account is also strongly teleological; everything happens according to providence, which is identified with fate. Further, they are compatibilists; human action is free and morally responsible despite fate. The Stoics defended this problematic set of ideas with sophistication and power. The details of their physical account are more naïve: they take *fire to be the basic substrate from which things are produced, though Chrysippus, possibly influenced by contemporary medicine, used the mechanism of differing degrees of tension of *pneuma or 'breath'.

Stoic ethics is marked by a set of uncompromising theses: virtue is sufficient for happiness; nothing except virtue is good; emotions are always bad. Easily ridiculed in isolation, these theses can be defended when seen as contributing to an overall theory in which what is most important is the difference in kind between the value of virtue and other, 'non-moral' value, virtue being conceived of as the skill of putting other things to correct use. The Stoics give the most demanding account of virtue in ancient ethics, and put the most strain on their account of the happiness which is the virtuous person's aim.

In all areas of philosophy there is appeal to the notions of nature and of reason, which have two roles, in the world as a whole and in us humans. Humans should live in accordance with human nature, which is, for them, to live in accordance with human reason, humans being rational animals. Properly used, human reason will enable us to understand the role of reason in the world, and thus of the world's nature. Nature and reason are in Stoicism objective notions: for us to think rationally is for us to think in ways which converge with other rational thinkers and reach the truth. Those who use their reason form a kind of community of reason, which is sometimes characterized as the only true community, transcending mere earthly bonds.

Early Stoicism remained essentially unmodified in form until *Diogenes (3) of Babylon, who, as is increasingly clear from the *Herculaneum papyri, began changes of detail and presentation usually associated with his pupil *Panaetius, and by *Posidonius (2) and *Hecaton. The so-called 'Middle Stoa' attempted to make the position more accessible to educated Romans (successfully in the case of Panaetius) and was more hospitable to ideas from other philosophers, particularly *Plato (1) and *Aristotle. Posidonius had much independent interest in science and causality, and Panaetius and Hecaton develop more interest in 'applied ethics' than their predecessors.

In the later period Stoicism survived in its standard form, as we can see from a textbook like *Hierocles, and continued to be an object of philosophical discussion; some of the Church Fathers, such as *Tertullian, were influenced by it. We also find writers less interested in philosophical argument than in presenting Stoicism as an attitude or way of life. The letters and essays of L. *Annaeus Seneca (2), the essays of *Musonius Rufus, the reported lectures of *Epictetus and the meditations of Marcus *Aurelius are examples of this. They tend to edifying and moralizing discussion and give little indication of the philosophical structure of their positions.

SVF. J. Rist, *Stoic Philosophy* (1969); M. Frede, *Die stoische Logik* (1974); S. Samburský, *Physics of the Stoics* (1959); D. Hahm, *The Origins of Stoic Cosmology* (1977); B. Inwood, *Ethics and Human Action in Early Stoicism* (1985). J. A.

stones, sacred There are two kinds of sacred stone: stones embedded in the earth, and free-standing stones. The first kind is found in mystery sanctuaries: the Mirthless Stone of *Eleusis, the 'Felsengruppe' of the Theban Cabirion (see THEBES (1); CABIRI), one or more of the 'rock altars' at *Samothrace (Schachter, 74). These are natural rock formations, whose function in cult was to provide a visible and tangible link between the upper and nether worlds. Far better known is the free-standing variety, which ranges from the Delphic Omphalos (see DELPHI) to various unworked lumps of rock set up in sanctuaries. Between the two extremes are rocks or heaps of rocks placed at doorways of houses and at crossroads, to act as talismans, guides, or averters of evil. Some of these were said to have fallen from the skies, and some were worshipped as cult objects.

The ancient Hebrews regarded stone worship as an evil to be eradicated (Exod. 23: 24, but cf. Gen. 28: 18–19 and 35: 14, for Jacob's Pillow), while Greeks acknowledged it with embarrassment as a sign of superstition (Theophr. *Char.* 16), or even madness (Xen. *Mem.* 1. 1. 14). The Romans, on the other hand, took it very seriously indeed, particularly in their worship of the boundary stone as the god *Terminus (Merbach). There are other indications that stone worship was an important feature of early religious sentiment (see e.g. the roughly shaped *stele from *Metapontum, 6th-cent. BC, inscribed 'I am [the stone, or image?] of *Apollo Lyk[ios], [property] of Theages [and] Byros [?]', as interpreted by Jeffery, 255).

The Roman tendency to worship stones may explain the relatively high concentration of sacred stones of one sort or another noticed by *Pausanias (3) in *Boeotia (Latte, 2298; de Visser, 56, 97, 99, 100): this was a part of Greece heavily settled by people of Italian stock (Kahrstedt, 76–115, esp. 93–4, 112).

On the whole, therefore, it is best to be sceptical about the evidence for stone worship in Greece and resist the temptation to see it as a survival from high antiquity as a form of fetishism (a point made by Hermann, 25–30).

H. V. Hermann, *Omphalos* (1959); Jeffery, *LSAG*; U. Kahrstedt, *Das wirtschaftliche Gesicht Griechenlands in der Kaiserzeit* (1954); K. Latte, *RE* 3 A (1929); E. Merbach, *RE* 5 A (1934), 781–4; A. Schachter, *Cults of Boiotia* 2 (1986); M. W. de Visser, *Die Nichtmenschengestaltigen Götter der Griechen* (1903). A. Sch.

Strabo of *Amaseia (*Pontus), author of a *Geographia* in 17 books, by far the most important source for ancient *geography, a priceless document of the Augustan age, and a compendium of important material derived from lost authors.

The family was prominent in the politics of Pontus since before the time of *Mithradates VI. Born about 64 BC, he studied grammar under Aristodemus of Nysa, and later at Rome under *Tyrannio (1) of Amisus, and philosophy under Xenarchus of Seleuceia (his teachers were *Peripatetic; his views align him with the Stoics; see STOICISM). He knew *Posidonius (2), whose work he used, and from whom he may have drawn his idea of a conjoint interest in history (with its ethical implications) and geography (historical notes (*hypomnēmata*) in 47 books, 43 after the conclusion of *Polybius (1), were his first work). The empires of Romans and Parthians allowed him to do for the Augustan empire what *Eratosthenes had been able to do in the aftermath of *Alexander (3) the Great (1. 2. 1 [14]).

In the debate over how to do geography, however, he is very critical of Eratosthenes (and many other experts), though, compared with them, he is inclined to be amateurish about mathematics and cosmology, in general preferring the practical to the theoretical and the particular to the general, which locates him in the *periēgēsis* tradition (see HECATAEUS (1)), and leads him to call his work 'chorography'. He therefore lays little stress on geographical wonders, and in searching for detailed information retails long passages of by then out-of-date description, which can make the interpretation of his evidence very hazardous. He travelled extensively, but does not bother to make very frequent boasts about autopsy (but see 2. 5. 11 [117]); a long stay in Egypt in the 20s when his patron *Aelius Gallus was prefect (see PRAEFECTUS), and several visits to Rome, are noteworthy; he has been thought to have returned to Amaseia and remained there until his death (after AD 21). Parts at least of the *Geographia* were composed under Tiberius.

This experience of the patronage of Roman leaders and education among the foremost intellectuals (many Greeks of Asia like himself) made Strabo (almost certainly a Roman citizen, with a Latin *cognomen*) an eloquent witness of the ways in which the Augustan settlement related to, depended on, and forever changed the plurifarious Mediterranean world of the late republic. Accommodation to Rome was part of the training of all his contemporaries, and he inherited the tradition of Panaetius, Polybius and Posidonius. Beside *Nicolaus of Damascus and *Dionysius (7) of Halicarnassus and in the same circles of patronage as the latter (Aelius Gallus, Q. *Aelius Tubero, the circle of L. *Aelius Seianus and *Tiberius) he made his job the interpretation of Greek and Roman to each other in a way that looks forward to *Plutarch and *Cassius Dio, and at the same time uses the geographical necessities of Roman power to justify and explain the patriarchal hegemony of Augustus. It is no coincidence that this turning-point in Roman imperial power produced the *chef d'œuvre* of ancient geography.

Strabo emphasizes the usefulness of geography for statesmen and generals, those 'who bring together' cities and peoples into a single empire and political management' (1. 1. 16 [9]). He speaks from knowledge of the central concerns of Roman government and is a precious witness to them (as on the lack of profit to be had from lands on the fringes of the inhabited world such as *Britain, 2. 5. 8 [115–16]). It is now clear (against the once influential view of Ettore Pais, which relegated him to an Anatolian milieu) that he is speaking from and about the centre of imperial power. The work is an extraordinary achievement—he likens it himself, apologetically (1. 1. 23 [13–14], *kolossourgia*), to a colossal statue whose detailing is less significant than the overall effect— and justifies his more ambitous claim to have fused the disciplines to produce out of a historical and chorographical framework a philosophy of geography. See also GEOGRAPHY.

Edns.: H. L. Jones (Loeb), W. Aly (Teubner). F. Lasserre, *ANRW* 2. 30. 1 (1983), 867–96; C. Nicolet, *Space, Geography and Politics in the Early Roman Empire* (1991; Fr. orig. 1988), esp. 18, 93–5, 253–5; G. W. Bowersock, *Augustus and the Greek World* (1965), 126–34; G. Aujac, *Strabon et la science de son temps* (1966); A. M. Biraschi and others, *Strabone, Saggio di Bibliografia 1469–1978* (1981); R. Syme (ed. A. Birley), *Anatolica* (1995). N. P.

stratēgoi (στρατηγοί) was the ordinary term for military commanders in Greece, but in Athens in the 5th cent. BC *stratēgoi* had political as well as military importance. Little is known of the number and method of appointment of Athenian *stratēgoi* in the 6th cent., but in 501/0 a new arrangement was introduced by which ten *stratēgoi* were elected annually, one from each *phylē* (see PHYLAI). The ten were of equal status: at Marathon in 490 (according to Hdt. 6. 109–10; see MARATHON, BATTLE OF) they decided strategy by majority vote, and each held the presidency in daily rotation. At this date the *polemarchos* had a casting vote, and one view is that he was the commander-in-chief; but from 487/6 onwards the polemarch, like the other *archontes* was appointed by lot. Good leaders, whether military or political, obviously could not be regularly selected by lot; so now, if not before, the polemarch ceased to command the army, and the *stratēgoi*, who continued to be elected, not only were the chief military commanders, but in some cases became political leaders too.

*Themistocles, *Aristides (1), and *Cimon were early examples of *stratēgoi* who were politicians as well as generals. *Pericles (1) was a *stratēgos* very often throughout his career; from 443 he held the office almost continuously until his death in 429. *Cleon, *Nicias, and *Alcibiades were all *stratēgoi*. But at the end of the 5th cent., with the collapse of the military and naval power of Athens, and later because of an increasing tendency to specialization, military office ceased to be a means of acquiring political influence.

The annual election of *stratēgoi* was held in the spring, and their term of office coincided with the ordinary Athenian year, from midsummer to midsummer. If a *stratēgos* died or was dismissed from office, a by-election might be held to replace him for the remainder of the year. The original rule that one *stratēgos* was elected from each *phylē* underwent some modification: in several years one *phylē* is known to have supplied two *stratēgoi* simultaneously. The earliest known instance is puzzling: a fragment of *Androtion (*FGrH* 324 F 38) purports to list the ten *stratēgoi* sent to *Samos in 441/0 and gives eleven names, including two (Pericles (1) and Glaucon) from Acamantis and one from each of the other *phylai*. Various explanations have been proposed. The most widely accepted is that one name has been included in error, and that there were always only ten *stratēgoi*, but that it was possible for two to be elected from the same *phylē* leaving another *phylē* unrepresented; the difficulty with this explanation is to see how and why one *phylē* could have been chosen for non-representation. Another view is that there were eleven *stratēgoi*, at least in some years, a distinguished man such as Pericles being additional to the ten representatives of the *phylai*. A third view is that representation of *phylai* had already been abandoned by this date. Certainly it was abandoned in the 4th cent., when ten *stratēgoi* were elected annually from all Athenians.

Stratēgoi commanded both by land and by sea. A particular military or naval expedition might have one or several *stratēgoi* in command; only occasionally did all ten go together. A *stratēgos* might be given special powers to take decisions in the field without reference back to Athens (*stratēgos autokratōr*). At home the *stratēgoi* were responsible for calling up citizens and metics for military and naval service, and for organizing the maintenance and command of ships by the system of trierarchies. When a legal case arose from any of these matters, such as a prosecution for desertion or evasion of military service, or a dispute over the duty to perform a trierarchy, the *stratēgoi* were the magistrates responsible for bringing the case to court and presiding over the trial. Probably in the 4th cent. (although some scholars believe the arrangement began in the 5th) a systematic division of duties was made: one *stratēgos* led the *hoplites, one was in charge of the defence of *Attica, two were in charge of the defence of *Piraeus, and one supervised the trierarchies (see TRIERARCHY), leaving five available for other duties.

The Athenian people kept a close watch on their *stratēgoi*. Like other magistrates, at the end of their term of office they were subject to *euthyna, and in addition there was a vote in the *ekklēsia* every prytany on the question whether they were performing their duties well; if the vote went against anyone, he was deposed from office and as a rule tried by a jury. Pericles himself in 430 was removed from office as *stratēgos* and fined, and in 406 the eight *stratēgoi* who commanded the fleet at *Arginusae were all removed from office and condemned to death. These arrangements illustrate one of the most striking features of Athenian democracy (see DEMOCRACY, ATHENIAN): reluctance to give power to individuals and fear that it might be abused.

In the Hellenistic age, *stratēgos* was the title of officials with wide powers political as well as military, in the *Aetolian Confederacy and in the *Achaean Confederacy. It was also used for the governor of a district in Ptolemaic Egypt (see NOMOS (1)) and elsewhere in the Hellenistic empires, and it became the regular Greek word for the Roman *praetor.

ATHENS C. W. Fornara, *The Athenian Board of Generals* (1971); N. G. L. Hammond, *Studies in Greek History* (1973), 346–94; W. K. Pritchett, *The Greek State at War* 2 (1974); M. Piérart, 'À propos de l'élection des stratèges athéniens', *BCH* 1974, 125–46.
HELLENISTIC AGE Bengtson, *Strategie*.
ROMAN EGYPT *ANRW* 2. 10. 1 (1988), 598–611.　　　　D. M. M.

Stratocles, son of Euthydemus, Athenian from the *deme of Diomeia (*c*.355 to after 292 BC). He was the official prosecutor of *Harpalus (Din. 1. 1. 20) (324/3). After *Demetrius (4)'s democratic restoration in 307, Stratocles distinguished himself by unscrupulous demagogy and excessive praise of Demetrius and his entourage, whose agent in Athens he became. Inscriptions confirm *Plutarch's unsavoury picture of him (*Demetr*. 11 ff.). His influence disappeared with Demetrius' defeat at Ipsus (301), but his recovery of Athens in 294 brought Stratocles back to the fore: his honorary decree for *Lysimachus' friend, the poet *Philippides, in April 292 is preserved (*IG* 2². 649).

Davies, *APF*, no. 12938; *RE* 4 A 1, 'Stratokles' 5.　　　　R. M. E.

Straton (1) of *Lampsacus, philosopher, head of the *Peripatetic school after *Theophrastus until his death (*c*.287–269 BC). The preserved list of his books (Diog. Laert. 5. 59–60) includes ethics, cosmology, zoology, psychology, physics, and logic; his work on physics and cosmology earned him the name 'The Natural Philosopher.' Fragments (but only fragments) of several of his books survive; a substantial portion of his doctrine about the void may be preserved in the introduction to *Heron's *Pneumatica* (see Gottschalk, *Strato*).

He rejected *Aristotle's theory of place and contradicted him in asserting the existence of void in the cosmos. This has been taken as a concession to the atomists (see ATOMISM), but it seems unlikely; Straton argued only for 'disseminate void'—i.e. void interstices of small dimensions separating particles of matter. His reasoning was drawn chiefly from the penetration of apparently solid objects by 'physical powers' such as heat and light. The origin of the theory is Theophrastus' theory of 'pores', rather than anything in the atomists.

Straton argued that the processes of nature were to be explained by natural causes, not by the action of any god. This is mainly an attack on the Stoics, but it also dispenses, apparently, with the very limited part played by Aristotle's divine unmoved movers of the heavens. Straton rejected the universal teleology of the Stoics (see STOICISM); the evidence is not sufficient to decide to what extent he denied that kind of teleology which is the characteristic thesis of Aristotelian biology.

He was an orthodox Aristotelian in his view of the cosmos as unique, uncreated, and geocentric. Like the Stoics, he modified the Aristotelian theory of the natural motions of the primary bodies to give to fire and air not absolute lightness but simply less weight than the other two *elements; and he dispensed with the fifth body (aether) with its natural circular motion.

He was the last head of the Peripatetic school to do important original work. His theory about the void, his most famous contribution, was important in the history of physiology through its adoption by *Erasistratus, and in technology through its adoption by Heron.

F. Wehrli, *Die Schule des Aristoteles* 5 (1950; 2nd edn. 1969; text of fragments with German comm.); H. B. Gottschalk, *Strato of Lampsacus: Some Texts* (Proceedings of the Leeds Philosophical and Literary Society, Lit. and Hist. Section, 11.6, 1965); H. Diels, 'Über das physicalischen System des Strato' (*S.-Ber. Akad. Berlin*, 1893); W. Capelle, *RE* 4 A (1931), 'Straton der Physiker'; M. Gatzemeier, *Die Naturphilosophie des Straton von Lampsakos* (1979); L. Repici, *La natura dell' anima: saggi su Straton* (1988); D. J. Furley, 'Strato's theory of the void,' in *Cosmic Problems: Essays on Greek and Roman Philosophy of Nature* (1989).

D. J. F.

Straton (2), New Comedy poet (see COMEDY (GREEK), NEW). The only extant fragment is a skit upon glossomania, with the speaker describing a conversation with a cook in which the latter's fondness for obsolete (and especially Homeric) words and phrases leads the other to call him 'slave of some kind of rhapsode' (vv. 48 f.). The play from which the fragment derives is dated *c.*300 BC by a reference (v. 43) to the work of *Philitas of Cos.

Kassel–Austin, *PCG* 7 (1989), 617–22.; Meineke, *FCG* 1. 426 ff.; A. Körte, in *RE* 4 A 1 (1931), 275 f., 'Straton' 11; A. Giannini, *Acme* 1960, 164 f.; H. Dohm, *Mageiros* (1964), 198 ff.; T. B. L. Webster, *Studies in Later Greek Comedy*² (1970), 145; R. Kassel, *ZPE* 14 (1974), 121 ff.   W. G. A.

Straton (3) of Sardis, who lived in the time of *Hadrian, specialized in pederastic epigrams; about 100 of his poems are to be found in bks. 11 and 12 of the Greek *Anthology. He follows contemporary fashion in striving for point and originality of expression, though many of his themes are traditional. Some of his poems are more sexually explicit than is usual in Greek *epigrams.

N. H.

Stratonice, daughter of *Demetrius (4) Poliorcetes and of Phila (daughter of *Antipater (1)). *Seleucus I's second marriage to her (290s BC), after his first to *Apame, which produced a child, may have been a potential threat to his elder son, *Antiochus (1) I and to Apame, if still alive, but was mainly dictated by the politics of a (temporary) pact with Demetrius. But Antiochus was given the title and status of king, and Stratonice was passed on to him by Seleucus as his queen and wife, so strengthening the succession. Antiochus and Stratonice were then sent to the eastern satrapies for Antiochus to govern (Appian, *Syr.* 61) as co-regent. Hellenistic authors built from this a court drama, modelled on *Euripides' *Hippolytus*, of Antiochus pining to death with secret love for Stratonice, and being saved by the diagnosis of the court doctor (*Erasistratus) of his 'love sickness'; in this story he then managed to get Seleucus' agreement for the resolution described above. Stratonice gave Antiochus two sons, *Antiochus (2) II and Seleucus, plus a daughter, Apame, married to Magas of Cyrene.

A. Kuhrt and S. Sherwin-White, *JHS* 1991, 83–5; S. Sherwin-White and A. Kuhrt, *From Samarkhand to Sardis* (1993), index.   S. S.-W.

Stratonicea (mod. Eskihisar), *Seleucid foundation in the interior of *Caria, called after *Stratonice, wife and queen of *Antiochus (1) I, and probably founded by him, had a Macedonian colony and was established as part of the Seleucids' efforts to extend control in Caria. The city was presented to *Rhodes by 'Antiochus and Seleucus' (Polyb. 30. 31. 6), a problematic pairing, see *HCP*. Perhaps the likeliest view is that *Seleucus (2) II and *Antiochus (3) III are meant. Lost by Rhodes, probably to *Philip (3) V, it was recovered in 197 BC. Rhodian possession was confirmed by the Romans at Apamea (188), but revoked in 167 during Rome's split with Rhodes. Like *Mylasa, Stratonicea gained favour with Rome by resisting Q. *Labienus in 40, and was one of the *free cities under the empire.

Stratonicea possessed two important sanctuaries: the famous temple of *Hecate at Lagina, and that of *Zeus Chrysaoreus near the city. The latter served as the religious and political centre of a Chrysaoric League common to all Carians, to which the Stratoniceans were admitted (Strabo, 660). Under the early empire Stratonicea, perhaps surprisingly in view of its origin,

claimed the title of 'autochthonous' (*SEG* 4. 263; cf. AUTOCHTHONS); one possible explanation is that the city was founded on the site of an earlier Carian town (Steph. Byz. mentions a Carian city of Idrias 'formerly called Chrysaoris', otherwise unknown); also the Seleucid foundation is likely to have included a Carian element.

The sites at Eskihisar have been excavated by Turkish archaeologists since 1979 and important buildings and structures of the city uncovered and identified; these include fortifications and a gate, a *bouleutērion*, previously identified as a temple of Serapis, an exedra (dated towards the end of the 2nd cent. BC and restored under Vespasian) and a Corinthian building of the same period, probably part of a gymnasium complex. From the theatre came several new finds, including part of a Doric frieze from the stage building.

P. M. Fraser and G. E. Bean, *The Rhodian Peraea*, (1954), chs. 2, 4; S. Mitchell, *Arch Rep.* 1990, 110; J. and L. Robert in L. Robert, *OMS* 5 (1989), 449 ff.   G. E. B.; S. S.-W.

Stratonicus (*c.*410–360 BC), of Athens, famous citharist (see MUSIC, § 3.1 (*a*)), remembered especially for his witticisms which are mainly preserved by *Athenaeus (1). According to *Phaenias (at Ath. 352c) he introduced multiplicity of notes (*polychordia*) into unaccompanied cithara-playing, i.e. he used an instrument with up to eleven strings.

RE 4 A 1, 326 f. (Maas); M. L. West, *Greek Music* (1992), 367 f.   B. Z.

Strattis, Athenian comic poet, produced *Anthroporestes* after Eur. *Or.* (408) and *Atalanta* 'long after' (schol. Ar. *Ran.* 146) Ar. *Ran.* (405). We have 19 titles and 70 citations; many titles suggest tragic parody (blended with mythological burlesque; see PARODY, GREEK), e.g. *Medea*, *Philoctetes*, *Phoenissae*. A traditional figure, the gluttonous *Heracles, was a character (fr. 12) in *Callippides*.

Kassel–Austin, *PCG* 7 623 ff. (*CAF* 1. 711 ff.).   K. J. D.

strenae, originally the luck-bringing (mostly laurel) twigs (from the grove of the goddess Strenia), also figs, honey-cakes, and dates, later any gifts, lamps, coins, and even gold, exchanged by the Romans (and accompanied by good wishes) on New Year's Day. In the case of the houses of the *rex sacrorum* and the major *flamines, the temple of Vesta, and the *curiae* (see CURIA (1)), the laurel branches were placed there on 1 March, the old New Year (Fest. *Gloss. Lat.* 408; Ov. *Fast.* 1. 175–226; 3. 137–42; Suet. *Aug.* 57; *Tib.* 34; Mart. 8. 33; 13. 27; Macrob. *Sat.* 1. 12. 6; Symmachus, *Relat.* 7, 15; Lydus, *Mens.* 4. 4; *ILS* 7214). Hence the meaning of *strena* as 'good omen' (already in Plautus). The custom was (unsuccessfully) combated by the Church (cf. August. *Serm.* 198. 2).

B. Curran and F. Williams, *LCM* 1981, 209 ff.; D. Baudy, *Rh. Mus.* 1987, 1 ff.   J. L.

strife See ERIS; STASIS.

structuralism See LINGUISTICS; LITERARY THEORY AND CLASSICAL STUDIES.

Stymphalus, *polis of NE *Arcadia, situated in a long, narrow, enclosed upland basin. The basin, with no outward surface drainage, floods and produces a lake of varying size, famous in antiquity as the home of the man-eating Stymphalian birds killed by *Heracles. An older settlement (not securely located) was replaced in the 4th cent. BC by a fortified, orthogonally planned, town on the north shore of the lake. Stymphalus' limited resources gave it only modest political influence. By the 2nd cent.

AD Stymphalus, like neighbouring Alea, was linked to the Argolid (see ARGOS (2)) rather than Arcadia.

RE 4 A 436–53; M. Jost, *Sanctuaires et cultes d'Arcadie* (1985), 99–106; H. Williams, *EMC* 1983, 194–205; 1984, 169–86; 1985, 215–24; (on lake and birds) W. R. P. Bourne and J. J. Hall, *JHS* 1982, 234–6.   J. R.

Styx, eldest of the daughters of Ocean (see OCEANUS) and *Tethys, located at the bottom of *Tartarus (Hes. *Theog.* 775–806). Having helped *Zeus against the Titans (see TITAN), she became the 'great oath of the gods' (ibid. 400). In later writers, the Styx is the river of the Underworld (see HADES). *Herodotus (1) places the Styx in *Arcadia (6. 74), as do *Strabo (8. 8. 4), *Pliny (1) (*HN* 2. 231), and *Pausanias (3) (8. 17. 6: near Nonacris, not far from Pheneos). The Arcadians took *oaths by the waters of the Styx, which was believed to have harmful properties. Since the 19th cent., the Styx has been identified with the falls of Mavronero, which flow down the length of a rocky slope near the village of Solos, at the foot of the highest peak of Mount Chelmos. The myth's origins must lie in geography.

R. Baladié, *Le Péloponnèse de Strabon* (1980), 79–82.   M. J.

sublime (ὕψος, *sublimitas*), that quality of genius in great literary works which irresistibly delights, inspires, and overwhelms the reader.

Although ancient rhetoric, in its theory of the three *genera dicendi* (e.g. Cicero, *Orat.* 21. 69; Quintilian, *Inst.* 12. 10. 58), distinguished a grandiloquent style, for arousing the listeners' passions (ἁδρόν, *grande, vehemens, sublime*), from a dry one, for demonstrating by arguments (ἰσχνόν, *subtile, tenue, gracile*), and a moderate or ornate one, for providing pleasure (γλαφυρόν, *medium, mediocre, floridum*), the isolation and glorification of the sublime as a central aesthetic category is largely the achievement of the anonymous author of the treatise Περὶ ὕψους, 'On the sublime' (1st cent. AD), long attributed to *Cassius Longinus (see 'LONGINUS'). Applying Platonic views on poetic inspiration to the needs of the rhetorical schools, ps.-Longinus emphasizes the imaginative power of the canonical poets and prose authors of earlier periods (*Homer, *Demosthenes (2), but also Genesis and *Cicero), which enthrals, enhances, yet also annihilates the reader. The quality of the sublime usually (but cf. 35. 3–4) attaches to works of literature rather than to natural phenomena and (much like Matthew Arnold's 'touchstones') less to whole works than to individual passages. It results from a superhuman natural capacity, not just study; yet specifiable rules and techniques produced it once and can produce it even today—or, if violated, can obstruct it, resulting in such faults as pomposity or frigidity. Hence, though the present age is mediocre in comparison with the greatness of the past, the sublime provides a channel whereby the ancients' *enthousiasmos* can lift us above our quotidian banalities and put us in touch with finer minds, and, above all, with more unobstructed emotions.

'Longinus' ' treatise, less impressive for systematic rigour than for its own enthusiasm and its lively appreciation of the classical authors, seems to have had no impact upon ancient rhetorical theory and reached the Middle Ages only in a single, incomplete manuscript; even after its rediscovery in the Renaissance it was only in the late 17th cent. that it entered French Neoclassical literary discussion, largely via Boileau's paraphrase. Thereafter the sublime became a central category of 18th- and 19th-cent. literary criticism and philosophy (Burke, Kant, Hegel) and of Romantic poetry (Wordsworth, Hölderlin, Leopardi). Whether nature could be sublime and which arts, authors, works, etc.

were most sublime were hotly debated questions. By the mid-19th cent. the concept's popularity as an object for serious aesthetic speculation had crested, though the word has remained alive in ordinary vocabulary to express unreserved, unspecific approval—thereby returning to something like ps.-Longinus' own usage.

Ed. D. A. Russell (1964). D. C. Innes, *CQ* 1979, 165 ff. (connection with natural philosophy); A. Michel, *Rev. Ét. Lat.* 1976, 278 ff.; E. Burke, *A Philosophical Enquiry into the Origins of the Sublime and Beautiful*, ed. J. T. Boulton (1958); S. H. Monk, *The Sublime*[2] (1960), T. E. B. Wood, *The Word "Sublime" and its Context, 1650–1760* (1972).   G. W. M.; G. B. C.

subscriptions in ancient texts, usually retained after each book of a work copied from rolls into a codex, were the forerunners of titles. Detached from the text and therefore distinct from 'seals' (see SPHRAGIS) like those of *Thucydides (2) in bks. 2–4 or *Virgil in the *Georgics*, they might give author, work, book number, length in lines, or anything else that a scribe, corrector, or owner, wished to record. A *Herculaneum papyrus of *Epicurus, *On nature* 28, appends the date of composition; after *Esther* in the Codex Sinaiticus a corrector reports the subscription of a predecessor, Pamphilus (f 309); and a subscription in V of *Aristophanes (1) names the authorities for the colometry (see METRE, GREEK, § 2 on *cōla*) and the scholia. Latin manuscripts yield far more, though apparently only one in a secular text before the late 4th cent., and correctors heavily outnumber scribes. A restrained example, on Livy 5: *Nicomachus Dexter v.c. emendavi ad exemplum parentis mei Clementiani* ('corrected by me, Nicomachus Dexter of senatorial rank, against my father Clementianus' copy').

Some traditions descend entirely from the subscriber's copy, such as those of *Cicero's first speech *De lege agraria*, corrected by Statilius Maximus in the 2nd cent. from six copies; of *Apuleius, corrected at Rome in 395 and at Constantinople in 397 by *Sallustius, who perhaps made the selection of *Florida*; and of *Pomponius Mela, corrected at Ravenna by Rusticius. Similarly, bks. 21–5 of *Livy have come down only through an extant copy of 21–30 corrected at Avellino, and the work done on *Martial by Gennadius lies behind one manuscript family. Often, however, the subscriber's copy, like the *Juvenal that Nicaeus corrected in *Servius' school, has no clear place in the stemma.

While some correctors worked without another copy, others name and even disparage their sources. One Caecilius records variants in an extant Fronto (see CORNELIUS FRONTO, M.), and variants and notes added by Victorianus and later by *Nicomachus (4) Flavianus still betray themselves in manuscripts of Livy 1–10. Good wishes like *Quirine floreas* were presumably added to manuscripts given as presents, when correction beforehand would convey respect (cf. *Symmachus (2), *Ep.* 1. 24, 9. 13); and the donor of a *Cornelius Nepos to *Theodosius (3) II, himself the scribe of a Solinus (see IULIUS SOLINUS, C.), appended an *epigram.

Sabinus in AD 402, on service in the upper ranks, corrected *Persius at Barcelona and something unidentified at Toulouse, and other correctors of similar date also belonged to the governing classes. Some have seen their attention to the secular heritage as defiance of Christianity, others as stabilization in the new form of the codex. Whatever the truth (and did prestigious subscriptions more often survive?), examples continue well into the 6th cent., many in recent authors like *Martianus Minneus Felix Capella. Asterius, consul in 494, corrected the *Eclogues* of *Virgil and edited *Sedulius' *Carmen paschale*; *Mavortius corrected Horace's *Epodes* after 527 and signed an extant Prudentius.

Whether legal subscriptions (see below) influenced literary is disputed, but some scribes, especially in Christian texts, adjure their successors to make a faithful copy and check it against the exemplar. Subscriptions themselves, sometimes attested as late as the 15th cent., have suffered displacement and corruption. One poor sinner, at the end of Livy 8, even mistook *Hennam* for *Ierusalem*.

For a legal meaning see CONSTITUTIONS.

V. Gardthausen, *Griechische Paläographie*² 2 (1913), 424–40; E. G. Turner, *Greek Manuscripts of the Ancient World* (1971, 1987); B. Bischoff, *Paläographie* (1979, 1986, trans. 1990); Bénédictins du Bouveret, *Colophons* (1965–82); L. D. Reynolds and N. G. Wilson, *Scribes and Scholars* (1968, 1991), ch. 1 § 10, with bibliog.   M. D. R.

Subura, the valley between the *Viminal and *Esquiline hills of Rome, was connected to the *forum Romanum by way of the Argiletum and Forum Transitorium (see FORUM NERVAE). The district was notorious for its bustle, noise, and dirt, and for *prostitution. It was a well-known centre of trade and manufacture (*CIL* 6 (1953), 9284, 9399, 9491, 33862). Here lay a Jewish *synagogue (*CIJ* 2. 380). Distinguished residents included *Caesar, prior to his election as *pontifex maximus* (Suet. *Iul.* 46).

Juv. 11. 51, 141; Mart. 2. 17; 5. 22. 5–9; 6. 66. 1–3; 7. 31; 10. 94. 5–6; 12. 18. 2; Pers. 5. 32.   I. A. R.; J. R. P.

Suda (ἡ' Σοῦδα) or **Suidas** is the name of a lexicon, not an author: the word is a Latin loanword, and means *Fortress* or *Stronghold*: see F. Dölger, *Der Titel der Suda* (1936), who instances other fanciful names for reference works, e.g. Pamphilus' Λειμών (*Meadow*). The lexicon, which is a historical encyclopaedia rather than a mere word-list, was compiled about the end of the 10th cent. AD. Texts (with *scholia) of *Homer, *Sophocles (1), *Aristophanes (1), the *Anth. Pal.* (see ANTHOLOGY), and the Bible were directly consulted; otherwise work is mainly based on abridgements or selections made by later scholars, e.g. the *Synagōgē* (see LEXICA SEGUERIANA), *Harpocration, and *Diogenianus (2). The historians are quoted from the *Excerpts* of Constantine Porphyrogenitus; biography comes mainly from Hesychius of Miletus. It is a compilation of compilations, and like most works of its kind has suffered from interpolation. Nevertheless, in spite of its contradictions and other ineptitudes, it is of the highest importance, since it preserves (however imperfectly) much that is ultimately derived from the earliest or best authorities in ancient scholarship, and includes material from many departments of Greek learning and civilization.

EDITION A. Adler (Teubner's *Lexicog. Gr.* 1, 5 vols.), 1928–38. Sources etc.: A. Adler, *RE* 7 A, 675 ff.; P. Lemerle, *Le premier humanisme byzantin* (1970), 287–91 (Eng. trans. *Byzantine Humanism* (1986), 343–5; A. Steiner in E. Trapp and others, *Studien zur byzantinischen Lexikographie* (1988), 149–81; N. G. Wilson, *Scholars of Byzantium* (1983), 145–7.   R. B.

Suebi, an elusive term, applied by *Tacitus (1) in his *Germania* to an extensive group of German peoples living east of the Elbe and including the Hermunduri, *Marcomanni, *Quadi, Semnones, and others, but used rather more narrowly by other Roman writers, beginning with *Caesar. Tacitus himself in his later works limits the name to the Marcomanni and the Quadi. The central tribe of the Suebi was that of the Semnones living in Brandenburg, who controlled a shrine respected by all other Suebi and the scene of human sacrifices. We do not know the relationship between the Suebi of whom Tacitus speaks and the Suebi who crossed the Rhine in AD 406 and entered Spain in 409.

Rübekeil proposes that the Suebic grouping was forged on the upper Rhine c.60 BC, and was the first manifestation of German self-awareness and co-operation. See GERMANS.

L. Rübekeil, *Suebica* (1992).   J. F. Dr.

Sueius, a poet probably contemporary with *Lucretius, wrote a pedantic *Moretum* showing some resemblances to the pseudo-Vergilian poem of that name (see APPENDIX VERGILIANA), and other poems of uncertain content.

See E. J. Kenney, *The Ploughman's Lunch* (1984), p. xxviii; Courtney, *FLP* 112.   E. C.

Suessa Aurunca (mod. Sessa), in central Italy, a Latin colony (see COLONIZATION, ROMAN), founded 313 BC in the *Liris valley. There is no trace of significant pre-Roman occupation. The area was ravaged by *Hannibal in 211. It became a *municipium* c.89 BC and supported *Sulla. Remains include parts of the theatre and amphitheatre, a cryptoporticus, and rural sanctuaries.

P. Arthur, *Romans in Northern Campania* (1991).   K. L.

Suessula (mod. Cancello), a Campanian city (see CAMPANIA), mid-way between *Capua and *Nola, and a member of the Capuan league. It received *civitas sine suffragio* (see CITIZENSHIP, ROMAN) in 338 BC, and was a Roman base during the Hannibalic war (see PUNIC WARS). It is otherwise unknown from literary sources, but inscriptions indicate a flourishing city throughout antiquity.

S. De Caro and A. Greco, *Campania* (1981).   K. L.

Suetonius (Gaius Suetonius (*RE* 4) Tranquillus) (b. *c.* AD 70), Roman biographer. Suetonius was the son of the equestrian (see EQUITES, *Imperial period*) Suetonius Laetus, tribune (see TRIBUNI MILITUM) of Legio XIII (see LEGION) at *Bedriacum in AD 69, and originated perhaps from Pisaurum in Umbria or (see UMBRIANS), more likely, *Hippo Regius (mod. Bône) in Numidia. From the correspondence of the younger *Pliny (2), he appears already to have attracted attention in Rome as an author and scholar by *c.* AD 97, and also to have gained experience in advocacy. Perhaps intending to pursue the equestrian *cursus*, he secured through Pliny's patronage a military tribunate in Britain *c.*102, which in the event he declined to hold; *c.* AD 110, however, he probably travelled with Pliny to *Bithynia as a member of the provincial governor's retinue, gaining soon after, again through Pliny's intercession, the *ius trium liberorum* (see IUS LIBERORUM). In the late years of *Trajan's reign and under *Hadrian, Suetonius held three important posts in the imperial administration, the secretaryships *a studiis*, *a bibliothecis*, and *ab epistulis*, as a fragmentary inscription found in 1952 at Hippo Regius records (*AE* 1953. 73). As *ab epistulis* he is likely to have accompanied Hadrian to Gaul, Germany and Britain in AD 121–2, but then for unknown reasons was dismissed from office when Hadrian simultaneously deposed as praetorian prefect (see PRAEFECTUS PRAETORIO) C. Septicius Clarus, the dedicant of Suetonius' collection of imperial biographies, the *Caesares*. He presumably continued to write until his death, perhaps *c.* AD 130, but if a public career continued nothing is known of it.

Works 1. *De viris illustribus*, a now incomplete set of biographies of Roman men of letters arranged in categories—grammarians and rhetoricians, poets, orators, historians, philosophers—probably written before the *Caesares* (below). The segment *De grammaticis et rhetoribus* is preserved independently, and a few other lives, variously abbreviated or corrupt, are known from manuscripts of other authors' works: thus *Terence*, *Horace*, *Lucan*, and the Donatus *Virgil* are generally regarded as deriving from the

Suetonius Paulinus, Gaius

section on poets. *Jerome drew on the work in his *Chronicle*, naming from it 32 poets, from *Ennius to *Lucan, fifteen orators, from *Cicero to Cn. *Domitius Afer, and six historians, from *Sallust to the elder *Pliny (1). The full collection, however, may have contained as many as a hundred lives. A particular interest in the age of Cicero and *Augustus and, to a lesser extent, in the Julio-Claudian era has been discerned in the work, while the relationship between authors and the public world in which they lived may have been its principal theme.

2. *De vita Caesarum* (the *Caesares*), a set of twelve imperial biographies from *Caesar to *Domitian, composed in the early 2nd cent. and complete except for the first few chapters of Caesar (lost between the 6th and 9th cents.).

3. Lost works, in Greek as well as Latin, some known from a list in the *Suda* (under 'Trankullos'), others from random citations in later authors. They included other apparently biographical works, on kings and famous courtesans; works on such institutions as Greek games, the Roman year, Roman customs, spectacles, and public offices; and works perhaps of a lexicographical sort, on the names and types of clothes, on physical defects, on weather-signs, on the names of seas and rivers, and on the names of winds. There was too a work on Cicero's *Republic*. Several of these may have comprised the *Pratum* or *Prata* (*Meadows*), a miscellany probably also known as *De variis rebus* (*On Various Subjects*).

Suetonius was a scholar of wide-ranging antiquarian interests. But it is as an imperial biographer that he must be principally judged. Little that is safe can be said of the literary tradition, or traditions, in which he worked, since apart from *Cornelius Nepos he is the first Latin biographer whose work has survived. Consequently the *Caesares* have to be evaluated largely in their own historical context, with Suetonius' exposure to the heart of imperial government during his years of administrative service very much in the forefront of consideration.

A striking feature of the biographies is their thematic, rather than strictly chronological, arrangement: after an introductory section on ancestry and a second on the subject's early life and pre-accession career, a sequence of recurring rubrics follows, in which Suetonius details the emperor's accomplishments and his personal characteristics, often providing anecdotes to illustrate general statements. The lives conclude with an account of the subject's death, sometimes accompanied by a description of his physical appearance and personal idiosyncrasies. Though the framework of presentation varies from life to life, the principle of organization is consistent throughout.

The repetition from life to life of common topics, especially those such as the building operations or the public entertainments for which a particular emperor was responsible, suggests that the topics themselves had special significance for Suetonius and his contemporaries; and through comparison with other sources such as the *Res Gestae of Augustus and the *Panegyric* of Pliny (2), where an ideal standard of imperial comportment is clearly perceptible, it emerges that Suetonius used the topics to judge his subjects against a set of popular expectations of imperial behaviour that had taken shape by the time the *Caesares* were composed. *Tiberius, for example, is repeatedly criticized for having failed to live up to expectation, whereas even *Nero and Domitian, rulers on whom Suetonius' final judgement is damning, can nevertheless be commended for having successfully met some of their imperial responsibilities. Suetonius' concern with such aspects of private behaviour as the subject's sexual and religious tastes has been taken also to reflect

the increasing Hellenization of upper-class Roman society (see HELLENISM).

In modern times, simplicity has been seen as the main characteristic of Suetonius' writing, in the absence of any obvious literary artistry. He is notable for citing earlier writers verbatim and quotes liberally from various documents—the letters of Augustus for instance—in Greek as well as Latin. (Suetonius may have exploited his period of administrative service under Trajan and Hadrian to seek out archival material for his biographies.) The Flavian lives are much shorter than those of the Julio-Claudians, and they in turn are less substantial than those of Caesar and Augustus. This again suggests that Suetonius' main historical preoccupation was the period from which the Principate ultimately appeared as a new form of government.

Suetonius, however, was not in the first instance a historian, and he should not therefore be compared with Sallust, Livy, or Tacitus. His principal concern was to collect and present material pertinent to the biographical goal of realistically illustrating imperial performance and personality, and in this he stands apart from the historians; for while fully capable of detailed analysis and sustained narrative composition if he wished, he had no interest in the moralistic or didactic as they did. As one author later expressed it, while the historians wrote *diserte* ('eloquently'), Suetonius wrote *vere* ('truthfully') (SHA *Prob.* 2. 7). Suetonius was followed as an imperial biographer by *Marius Maximus, who wrote a sequence of imperial biographies, no longer extant, from Trajan to *Commodus, and by the author, or authors, of the 4th-cent. *Historia Augusta. He served also as the model for Einhard's *Life of Charlemagne* in the 9th cent., and lost his position in Europe as the classic biographer only when Plutarch's lives were translated into the vernacular languages. See BIOGRAPHY, ROMAN.

BIBLIOGRAPHY P. Galand-Hallyn, *ANRW* 2. 33. 5 (1991), 3576–3622; D. T. Benediktson, *CW* 1993, 377–447.

TEXTS *Praeter Caesarum libros reliquiae*, ed. A. Reifferscheid (1860); *De vita Caesarum*, ed. M. Ihm (1907 ed. maior, 1908 ed. minor); *De grammaticis et rhetoribus*, ed. G. Brugnoli³ (1972).

COMMENTARIES *Caesar*, G. B. Townend (1982); *Augustus*, J. M. Carter (1982); *Tiberius*, M. J. duFour (1941), J. R. Rietra (1928) (repr. in one 1979); *Caligula*, D. W. Hurley (1993); *Claudius*, J. Mottershead (1986); *Nero*, B. H. Warmington (1977), K. R. Bradley (1978); *Galba, Otho, Vitellius*, P. C. Venini (1977); *Titus*, H. C. Martinet (1981); *Vespasian*, A. W. Braithwaite (1927); *Domitian*, P. E. Arias (1945); *De Poetis*, A. Rostagni (1944); *Peri blasphemion, Peri paidion*, J. Taillardat (1967); *De Grammaticis*, R. A. Kaster (1995).

STUDIES W. Steidle, *Sueton und die antike Biographie*² (1963); B. Baldwin, *Suetonius* (1983); A. Wallace-Hadrill, *Suetonius: The Scholar and his Caesars* (1983); J. Gascou, *Suétone historien* (1984). K. R. B.

Suetonius Paulinus, Gaius, as ex-praetor in AD 41, commanded against the Mauretanians (see MAURETANIA) and was the first Roman to cross the *Atlas mountains, of which he wrote a description (Plin. *HN* 5. 14). He was *suffect consul in the forties. In 58 he was appointed governor of *Britain and at once began a forward movement reaching the Irish Sea and subduing *Mona (Anglesey), a stronghold of druidism (see RELIGION, CELTIC). During the campaign he learnt of *Boudicca's revolt (60) and swiftly returned with his advance-guard, but, unable to concentrate an adequate force, was compelled to abandon *Londinium and *Verulamium to be sacked. Retreating (along Watling Street) to his main force, he routed Boudicca's attack. His severity towards the rebels led to discords with the *procurator *Iulius Classicianus and his own recall (61). In 69 he supported *Otho, and took a leading part in the campaign of *Bedriacum, after which he came to terms with A. *Vitellius.

A. Birley, *The Fasti of Roman Britain* (1981), 54 ff. C. E. S.

Sufetula (mod. Sbeitla), a town of the High Plateaux in central Tunisia, stands at a major cross-roads, especially of the *Theveste–Thenae and Thelepte–*Hadrumetum highways. A Flavian *municipium* founded on a virgin site probably *c.* AD 75, Sufetula has a very regular urban layout (445 m. by 425 m.) covering 19 hectares, which invites comparison with *Thamugadi. The 2nd-cent. forum at its heart, with entrance gateway (AD 139) and three imposing temples side by side, is one of the best-preserved examples of its type. Later, as at Thamugadi, Sufetula expanded beyond the regular nucleus, with a theatre, 3rd-cent. baths, and a Severan arch (AD 209/11) to the east and south-east, and an amphitheatre to the north-west. Promoted to the rank of *colonia'* (see COLONIZATION, ROMAN) sometime before AD 235, Sufetula in the 4th cent. covered *c.*50 hectares, its prosperity derived from cereals and above all intensive olive cultivation in its surrounding territory. Seven churches of the 4th/6th cents. are known, but the town had declined by late Byzantine times into a scattered village, with fortified blockhouses, and an olive press built across a major street. The decisive confrontation between Arab and Byzantine armies which took place near here in 647 marked the final collapse of Byzantine rule in Africa.

PECS 865–6; N. Duval and F. Baratte, *Les Ruines de Sufetula-Sbeitla* (1973); N. Duval, *Recherches archéologiques à Sbeitla* 1: *Les Églises de Sbeitla à deux sanctuaires opposés* (1971), and ANRW 2. 10. 2 (1982), 596–632.

R. J. A. W.

suffect, suffectio *suffectio* was the procedure by which a substitute or suffect (*suffectus*) was appointed whenever a Roman magistrate (see MAGISTRACY, ROMAN) resigned or died in office. It was employed to fill vacancies even of very short duration: in 45 BC C. *Caninius Rebilus was consul only for a few hours. Under the empire consuls ceased to hold office for a full year; those appointed after the original ('ordinary') pair were *suffecti*. They did not give their names to the year, unlike 'ordinary' ones, although they had the appropriate rank and title of *consularis*.

Mommsen, *Röm. Staatsr.* 1³. 592; R. Talbert, *The Senate of Imperial Rome* (1984), index. P. T.; B. M. L.

suffragium See CITIZENSHIP, ROMAN; MUNICIPIUM.

suicide The Latin word *suicidium*, from which the English derives, is not classical Latin: pronouns were not used as prefixes in compounds, and the word could only have meant 'the killing of a pig'. The first uses of *suicidium* found so far are by Gauthier de Saint-Victor in 1177/8 and, in English, by Sir Thomas Browne in *Religio Medici* published in 1643, who probably invented it afresh. The nearest to a technical term in antiquity was *mors voluntaria* (voluntary death) and the Greek equivalent, verbal phrases being used for the most part. Some ancient terminology reveals that suicide was often subsumed in categories regarded as more fundamental: thus a βιαιοθάνατος (Latin *biothanatos*) was any victim of premature, violent death, and an αὐτόχειρ was someone who kills his kin.

The limited and unsystematic nature of our evidence for Greek and Roman suicide does not allow for quantitative studies. Reliant as we are for the most part on literary accounts (some fictional, even mythical, all artistically shaped), we can only draw conclusions about attitudes and values. If a sociological approach is difficult, so is a psychiatric one, for in antiquity suicide was described on the assumption that it was a conscious intentional act: mental imbalance, though occasionally given as a cause of suicide, was not the central case it has become in the modern world. The ancients, including hard-headed Roman jurists who needed to distinguish suicides motivated by fear of condemnation from others that brought exemption from confiscation, felt confident that they could distinguish individual motives. They were not troubled by notions of unconscious motivation. This fact, in combination with the lack of reversible methods, may explain why the suicide attempts reported in the ancient sources are relatively few when compared with the modern ratio of attempted to accomplished suicides.

Some of the chief motives mentioned are shame (typically, for men, because of defeat; for women, loss of chastity); severe pain, incurable illness, or old age; self-sacrifice for country or friend. Suicide was neither wholly approved nor wholly condemned: everything depended on the motive, the manner, and the method. When arising from shame and dishonour, suicide was regarded as appropriate; self-sacrifice was admired; impulsive suicide was less esteemed than a calculated, rational act; death by jumping from a height (including drowning) or by hanging was despised and regarded as fit only for women, slaves, or the lower classes, apparently because it was disfiguring; death by weapons was regarded as more respectable, even heroic.

The concern of philosophers with minimizing the fear of death by the application of reason led them to discuss suicide, and to consider, alongside obvious cases, compulsory suicide at one extreme and martyrdom at the other (a combination also covered by Durkheim's definition, 'any death which is the direct or indirect result of a positive or negative act accomplished by the victim himself, which he knows should produce this result', though he wished to exclude the criterion of intention). The *locus classicus* for philosophical discussions of suicide was the death of *Socrates (which exemplifies both extremes), as described by *Plato (1) in the *Phaedo*. Although suicide, except under necessity, is there condemned, Socrates was adopted as a model, not only by L. *Annaeus Seneca (2) who was ordered to kill himself, but by M. *Porcius Cato (2), who chose to refuse *Caesar's pardon. These were adherents of the Stoa, which advocated the rational exit from life, provided certain conditions were fulfilled (see STOICISM). Plato and *Aristotle had been more negative, though Plato in *The Laws* admitted inevitable misfortune and intolerable shame as justifications and Aristotle allowed self-sacrifice for country or friends, while otherwise rejecting suicide as an injustice to society. The Epicureans (see EPICURUS) reluctantly permitted suicide when the balance of pleasure over pain could not be maintained. A calm demeanour and the giving of reasons to friends and relatives were the hallmark of the philosophically justified suicide: they could be histrionic, not only in literature but in life, for the jurists recognized 'showing off' as a motive for suicide characteristic of philosophers (*Dig.* 28. 3. 6. 7).

At all levels of society then, there seems to have been no blanket approval or condemnation of suicide, even though it was occasionally compared to murder (Elder Seneca (L. *Annaeus Seneca (1)), *Controv.* 8. 4; Quint. 7. 3. 7). It was left to 4th-cent. *Christianity, confronting the incentive to suicide presented by the heavenly rewards of martyrdom, to throw its authority behind the Platonic belief that man must not pre-empt God's decision.

R. Hirzel, ARW 1908, 75–104, 243–84, 417–76; Y. Grisé, *Le Suicide dans la Rome antique* (1982); A. J. L. van Hooff, *From Autothanasia to Suicide* (1990); M. Griffin, *G&R* 1986, 64 ff., 192 ff. M. T. G.

Suillius Rufus, Publius

Suillius (*RE* 4) **Rufus, Publius,** married Vistilia—mother by other husbands of Cn. *Domitius Corbulo and of Caesonia wife of *Gaius (1) (Caligula)—then *Ovid's step-daughter. Quaestor of *Germanicus (AD 15?), probably praetor in 23, he was banished in 24 and recalled by Gaius; under *Claudius he was consul (43 or 45), proconsul of Asia, and a notorious prosecutor. L. *Annaeus Seneca (2) secured his banishment, in extreme age, in AD 58.

R. Syme, *JRS* 1970, 27 ff. (= *RP* 2. 806 ff.).   J. P. B.; B. M. L.

Sulla See CORNELIUS SULLA FELIX, L.

Sulmo, mod. Sulmona, in Italy, a town of the *Paeligni in the Abruzzi. It resisted *Hannibal (211 BC), and supported *Caesar (49 BC), but is famed chiefly as *Ovid's birthplace (43 BC). It was a *municipium, and had an important terraced sanctuary of *Hercules Curinus, mainly of Republican date, outside the town.

F. van Wonterghem, *Superaequum, Corfinium, Sulmo* (Forma Italiae 4, 1 (1984).   E. T. S.; T. W. P.

Sulpicia (1) (*RE* under Sulpicius 114), daughter of Servius *Sulpicius Rufus, niece and ward of M. *Valerius Messalla Corvinus. Her six short elegies, 3. 13–18 (= 4. 7–12) in the Tibullan collection (see TIBULLUS, ALBIUS), are the only extant poems by a woman in the Classical era. They record her love affair with a young man of her own class whom she calls, in accordance with the elegiac tradition, by the Greek pseudonym Cerinthus. Whether or not the affair was a prelude to marriage, the public display of sexual independence on the part of an unmarried female aristocrat runs counter to conventional morality. Syntactical idiosyncrasies have caused the poems to be branded as amateurish, but behind the apparent spontaneity and sincerity lies a self-conscious artistry and originality of thought and expression.

Text/trans. in edns. of Tibullus; comm. in Smith and Tränkle, *Appendix Tibulliana* (1990); E. Bréguet, *Le Roman de Sulpicia* (1946); M. S. Santirocco, *CJ* 1979; H. Mac L. Currie, ANRW 2. 30. 3, 1751–64; H. Hinds, *Hermathena* 1987; N. J. Lowe, *CQ* 1988.   P. W.

Sulpicia (2) (*RE* under Sulpicius 115), poet of the age of *Domitian. *Martial 10. 38, which must have been written on her death (lines 12–14) after 15 years of happy marriage, is to be dated between AD 94 and 98. She wrote love poems addressed to her husband Calenus, expressing, according to Martial (10. 35, 38), both total fidelity and bold sensuality, a feature confirmed by her one surviving fragment, which is a rare example in Latin poetry of married eroticism. She is mentioned on several occasions in later literature (Auson. p. 218. 10 P., Sidon. *Carm.* 9. 261, Fulgent. *Myth.* 1. 4) and a poem in 70 hexameters, the *Sulpiciae conquestio* (*Epigrammata Bobiensia* 70), is written in her name. In it she is made to abandon minor verse (in hendecasyllables, iambic trimeters, and scazons) and to denounce the degradation of the empire under Domitian, in relation to a suppression of philosophers; the victims of this suppression supposedly include Calenus. The style, prosody, and implausibility of the piece point to its being a late text, probably from the same date as the Bobbio collection itself (end of 4th or beginning of 5th cent. AD).

Courtney, *FLP*; *Epigrammata Bobiensia*, ed. F. Munari (1955), W. Speyer (1963); *Sulpiciae Conquestio*, ed. A. Giordano Rampioni (1982). W. Kroll, *RE* 4 A (1931); S. Mariotti, *RE* Suppl. 9 (1962), 'Epigrammata Bobiensia'.   M. Ci.

Sulpicia, Servius, author of erotic poems (Ov. *Tr.* 2. 441, Plin. *Ep.* 3. 5. 3).   E. C.

Sulpicius (*RE* 22) **Apollinaris, Gaius** (2nd cent. AD), scholar; taught Aulus *Gellius and the emperor *Pertinax. He published discussions of learned questions in letter-form (now lost) and wrote metrical summaries (*periochae) of the plays of *Terence (included in editions of Ter.), but not the verse summaries of the *Aeneid* attributed to him (Baehrens, *PLM* 4. 169).

Schanz–Hosius § 597; L. Holford-Strevens, *Aulus Gellius* (1988), 61–3.   P. G. M. B.

Sulpicius Blitho (1st cent. BC), one of *Cornelius Nepos' sources (*Hannibal* 13. 1), otherwise unknown, as is the name of his work.   A. J. S. S.

Sulpicius Camerinus wrote a sequel to *Homer's *Iliad* (Ovid, *Pont.* 4. 16. 19); if identical with the consul of AD 9 he was Quintus.   E. C.

Sulpicius (*RE* 51) **Galba** (1), **Gaius,** son of Servius *Sulpicius Galba (1), in 143 BC married Licinia, the elder daughter of P. *Licinius Crassus Dives Mucianus, father-in-law of C. *Sempronius Gracchus. He probably served on a land-commission in Africa *c.*121–119 (see Degrassi, *ILLRP* 475). Though an augur, he was condemned by the Mamilian commission (109, see MAMILIUS LIMETANUS, c.) for malpractices in the Jugurthine War (see JUGURTHA); the peroration (*Epilogus*) of his defence was a choice specimen of oratory to be committed to memory in *Cicero's boyhood (*Brut.* 127).   H. H. S.; E. B.

Sulpicius (*RE* 52) **Galba** (2), **Gaius,** son of Servius *Sulpicius Galba (2) and grandfather of the emperor *Galba, wrote an historical work cited by *Juba (2).

Peter, *HR Rel.* ii. 421; *FGrH* 92.   R. J. S.

Sulpicius (*RE* 58) **Galba** (1), **Servius,** served as a military tribune under L. *Aemilius Paullus (2) at the battle of *Pydna in 168 BC; in 167 he unsuccessfully opposed the granting of a triumph to Paullus. Praetor 151, he won a victory over the Lusitani (see LUSITANIA), but suffered losses in the subsequent pursuit; in 150 he treacherously killed or sold into slavery 8,000 Lusitani who had surrendered. In 149 a tribune proposed the establishment of a special court to try him. Galba secured the bill's rejection despite the fact that it was supported by M. *Porcius Cato (1), in the last speech of his life. He was consul 144, but his desire for another Spanish proconsulate was thwarted by P. *Cornelius Scipio Aemilianus. In 138 he successfully defended the *publicani before the consuls in the *cause célèbre* of the murders in the *Silva Sila* (in the mountains of Bruttium; see BRUTTII). He was one of the leading orators of his time, but by *Cicero's day his speeches were no longer read.

Fragments: *ORF*[4] 109–15. Cicero, *Brutus* 82, 85–90; A. E. Astin, *Cato the Censor* (1978), 111–13.   J. Br.

Sulpicius (*RE* 61) **Galba** (2), **Servius,** probably grandson of C. *Sulpicius Galba (1), was a *legatus* (see LEGATI) in Gaul under C. Pomptinus (62–60 BC) and *Caesar (58–56), and praetor 54 when he secured a triumph for Pomptinus. In 50 he stood unsuccessfully for the consulship. In the Civil War he took Caesar's side (Cic. *Att.* 9. 9. 3; Tac. *Hist.* 1. 15?) and assisted him as an augur, but in 44 joined in his assassination. In 43 he fought against M. *Antonius (2) (Mark Antony) in the battle of Forum Gallorum, which he described in a letter to *Cicero (*Fam.* 10. 30). He was condemned for Caesar's murder under a law of Q. *Pedius.   T. J. C.; E. B.

Sulpicius (*RE* 64) **Galba Maximus, Publius,** was elected consul for 211 BC, having held no previous curule office; he defended Rome against *Philip (3) V in the First Macedonian

War (see ROME (HISTORY), § 1. 4). Though little was achieved, the view that the war was conducted half-heartedly and that Sulpicius was insensitive to Greek opinion may be exaggerated. He was dictator 203, nominally to conduct the elections, but in fact with wider responsibilities in Italy. Consul for the second time in 200, he was the first commander in the Second Macedonian War. He did not arrive in Greece until October and spent the winter at *Apollonia. In 199 he attempted to invade Macedonia from the west. He defeated Philip and forced the pass into Macedonia, but ran short of supplies and was forced to retreat to the coast. The campaign, however, persuaded the *Aetolian Confederacy, to whom Sulpicius had sent an envoy the previous winter, to rejoin Rome. Sulpicius served as a legate under T. *Quinctius Flamininus in 197, and was one of the ten commissioners appointed to advise on the settlement of Greece in 196. He negotiated with the representatives of *Antiochus (3) III at Rome in 193, and later that year was the spokesman for the three ambassadors sent to continue negotiations in Asia.

F. W. Walbank, *Philip V* (1940), 88–102, 138–44; N. G. L. Hammond, *JRS* 1966, 42–5 (topography); J. Briscoe, *Comm. 31–33*, 115–46; J. W. Rich, *PCPS* 1984, 126–80, esp. 131–6, 143–7.   J. Br.

Sulpicius (*RE* 66) **Gallus, Gaius,** perhaps served under L. *Aemilius Paullus (2) in Spain (191–190 BC), then in Liguria (see LIGURIANS) in 182–1. In 171 he was one of the patrons chosen by the peoples of Spain to present their complaints against Roman governors. He was urban *praetor 169 and a military tribune (see TRIBUNI MILITUM) or legate (see LEGATI) under Paullus in 168, when he explained, though he probably did not predict, the eclipse of the moon which took place before the battle of *Pydna. In 167 he was rebuked by Paullus for guarding *Perseus (2) carelessly and for indulging his own soldiers. Consul 166, he celebrated a *triumph over the *Ligurians. On a diplomatic mission to Greece and Asia Minor in 164, he tried to engineer revolts in the *Achaean Confederacy and invited complaints against *Eumenes (2) II of Pergamum. *Polybius (1) (31. 6) in this context describes him as 'out of his mind'. He wrote a book on *eclipses (Plin. *HN* 2. 53).

J. Briscoe, *Historia* 1969, 65–6.   J. Br.

Sulpicius (*RE* 90) **Quirinius, Publius,** consul 12 BC, a *novus homo* from *Lanuvium (on his career cf. Tac. *Ann.* 3. 48). Quirinius defeated the Marmaridae (Florus 2. 31), perhaps as proconsul of *Crete and *Cyrene (*c.*15 BC). Between 12 BC and AD 2 he subjugated the Homanadenses, 'Cilician' brigands (see BRIGANDAGE) on Lake Trogitis (Strabo 569). The precise date of this war and the command held by Quirinius are disputed. It has been argued that he must have been legate of *Syria at the time; but the war could have been conducted only from the side of *Galatia, which province, though normally governed by imperial legates (see LEGATI) of praetorian rank, might easily have been placed under a consular (cf. L. *Calpurnius Piso (2), *c.*13 BC, and M. *Plautius Silvanus in AD 6). Quirinius prudently paid court to *Tiberius on Rhodes, succeeded M. *Lollius as guide and supervisor of C. *Iulius Caesar (2) in the east (AD 2), and shortly after married Aemilia Lepida, a descendant of *Sulla and *Pompey. Legate of Syria in AD 6, he supervised the assessment of *Judaea when that territory was annexed after the deposition of *Archelaus (5) (Joseph. *AJ* 17. 1 ff., cf. *ILS* 2683 = EJ 231 (tr. D. Braund, *From Augustus to Nero*, no. 446); also Acts 5: 37, which mentions the insurrection of Judas the Galilaean 'in the days of the taxing'). In order to reconcile and explain Luke 2: 1 and

establish a date for the Nativity before the death of *Herod (1) the Great (i.e. before 4 BC), various attempts have been made to discover an earlier governorship of Syria by Quirinius, and, by implication, an earlier census in Judaea. The acephalous (= top missing) elogium from Tibur (*ILS* 918 = EJ 199; tr. D. Braund, no. 362) sometimes attributed to Quirinius more probably honours Piso (above), and in any case could not prove two governorships of Syria. Quirinius lived to a wealthy and unpopular old age. In 21 he died and was granted a public funeral on the motion of Tiberius, who recounted his meritorious services (Tac., above).

L. R. Taylor, *AJPhil.* 1933, 120 ff.; R. Syme, *Klio* 1934, 122 ff., and *Rom. Rev.*, index; A. N. Sherwin-White, *Roman Society and Roman Law in the New Testament* (1963), 162 ff.; B. Levick, *Roman Colonies in Southern Asia Minor* (1967), 203 ff.; R. Syme, *Akten des VI. Int. Kongr. f. gr. u. lat. Epigr.* (1972), 585 ff. (= *RP* 3. 869 ff.).   R. S.; B. M. L.

Sulpicius (*RE* 92) **Rufus, Publius,** was a member (with M. *Livius Drusus (2), and L. *Aurelius Cotta) of a circle of brilliant and ambitious young nobles taught by L. *Licinius Crassus. In 95 BC he prosecuted C. *Norbanus and as tribune in 88 tried to carry on Drusus' ideas by securing the fair distribution of the enfranchised Italians in the tribes. Opposed by the *optimates (including his friend, the consul Q. *Pompeius Rufus), he began to stress the *populares* (see OPTIMATES) aspects of his programme and turned for support to C. *Marius (1), with whom he had found himself collaborating in opposition to the consular candidature of C. *Iulius Caesar Strabo. In return for transferring the command against *Mithradates VI from *Sulla to Marius, he was able to pass his laws (with some violence), but, when Sulla reacted by marching on Rome, had to flee. He was captured and executed and his laws were annulled.

E. Badian, *Foreign Clientelae* (1958), 230, and *Hist.* 1969, 481 ff.; H. B. Mattingly, *Athenaeum* 1975, 264 ff. (rejects Val. Max. 6. 5. 7—stating that Sulpicius was descended from the *patrician Sulpicii—and the cognomen Rufus); A. Keaveney, *Eirene* 1983, 53 ff.   E. B.

Sulpicius (*RE* 95) **Rufus, Servius,** Roman lawyer. He prosecuted L. *Licinius Murena when defeated by him in the consular elections for 62 BC; in his speech *Pro Murena* *Cicero makes fun of Sulpicius' legal expertise. He was eventually consul in 51. After hesitation he half-heartedly joined *Pompey in 49; Caesar pardoned him, and in 46 he governed *Achaia. He died on an embassy to Antony (M. *Antonius (2)) in January 43, and was honoured with a public funeral. The *Ninth Philippic* is Cicero's eulogy. Known to lawyers as Servius, he was, next to Q. *Mucius Scaevola (2), the leading lawyer of the Roman republic and the first after Mucius to attain the consulship. The story that he left up to 180 books (*libri*) on legal subjects is not credible, but his views are recorded in nearly a hundred texts, mainly from Justinian's (see JUSTINIAN'S CODIFICATION) *Digest*. A student of philosophy, he extended Scaevola's efforts at classification, for instance distinguishing four types of *theft. Cicero (*Brutus* 41. 151–5) later attributed to him more 'art' (technical skill?) than to his admired teacher Scaevola. He had many pupils, including P. *Alfenus Varus. He wrote Cicero two celebrated letters (*Fam.* 4. 5 and 12), and *Quintilian knew of three speeches.

ORF, 376–9; Lenel, *Pal.* 2. 322–34; P. Meloni, *Ann. Fac. Cagliari* 1946, 67–245; F. Schulz, *History of Roman Legal Science* (1946); A. Watson, *Law-Making in the Later Roman Republic* (1974); E. Rawson, *Intellectual Life in the Late Roman Republic* (1985), see indexes; Wieacker, *RRG* 1 (1988), 602–7.   E. B.; C. B. R. P.; T. H.

Sulpicius Severus See SEVERUS, SULPICIUS.

sum–, sun–

sum–, sun– See SYM–, SYN–.

Sumerian is the earliest known language of ancient *Mesopotamia, written on clay and stone in *cuneiform script. Unrelated to other known languages, it is agglutinative and ergative. Largely superseded by (semitic) *Akkadian, it was used for some religious and literary purposes into the Seleucid period.

M.-L. Thomsen, *The Sumerian Language* (1984). S. M. D.

Summanus, god who sends nocturnal thunderbolts (Festus 254. 3 Lindsay). Latte (*RR* 208) derives the cult from an omen during the war with *Pyrrhus when a temple was founded (?276 BC), located 'at the Circus Maximus' (Ziolkowski, *Temples* 154). Wheel-shaped *cakes called *summonalia* were offered to him (Festus 471. 17 Lindsay). Late authors identified him with Dis Pater (Arn. 5. 37. 6. 8; 6. 3. 44; Martianus Capella 2. 161). In AD 224 Summanus Pater received black victims (see SACRIFICE, ROMAN) in an expiation of nocturnal thunderbolts (*CIL* 6. 2107a. 11).

Wissowa, *RK* 135. J. Sch.

sumptuary legislation See DEMETRIUS (3) OF PHALERON; LEX (2), *leges sumptuariae*; PERIANDER.

sun See ASTROLOGY; ASTRONOMY; HELIOS; HYPERION; MEDEA; SOL.

sundials See CLOCKS.

Sunium, the name of the southernmost part of *Attica including the bold promontory with its temples to *Poseidon and *Athena and its fort. There are Early Helladic finds from the promontory, but the sanctuary seems to date from the 7th cent., at the end of which several *kouroi* (see SCULPTURE, GREEK) were dedicated, one of them colossal. The early 5th-cent. Ionic temple to Athena was of unusual asymmetrical design; the well-preserved Doric temple to Poseidon was architecturally closely related to the temple of *Nemesis at *Rhamnus. See ORDERS, ARCHITECTURAL. In 413 the Athenians fortified the promontory (Thuc. 8. 4), and this fort was rebuilt in the 3rd cent. incorporating ship-sheds. The *deme of Sunium seems to have been centred to the north, in the Agrilesa valley (see LAURIUM), which is rich in marble quarries and silver mining remains (see MINES AND MINING), where a deme decree concerning a new *agora was found (*IG* 2². 1180). In the Hellenistic period there seems to have been a substantial coastal development at Pasa Limani, where another agora has been excavated. Interesting but problematic epigraphic evidence connects the *genos* of the *Salaminioi with Sunium (see also SALAMIS (1).)

AΔ 1977, 182–217; H. Lauter, *Marburger Winckelmann-Programm* 1988, 11–33; J. Travlos, *Bildlexikon zur Topographie des antiken Attika* (1988), 404–29. For the Salaminioi see W. S. Ferguson, *Hesp.* 1938, 1 ff., R. G. Osborne in S. Alcock and R. G. Osborne (eds.), *Placing the Gods* (1994), 154 ff., and Parker, *ARH* 57 ff., 308 ff. C. W. J. E.; R. G. O.

suovetaurilia (*suovi*-), a purificatory sacrifice at the conclusion of *lustratio of three (generic) victims: pig, sheep, bull (*sus, ovis, taurus*). *Suovetaurilia lactentia* ('suckling') consisted of *porcus, agnus, vitulus*, male pig, lamb, calf (Cato, *Agr.* 141), and were employed at the *lustration of private fields. At public lustrations (at the census, of the army) the *suovetaurilia maiora* ('greater') were used consisting of full-grown victims, *verres, aries, taurus*, boar, ram, bull (Varro, *Rust.* 2. 1. 10; Livy 1. 44. 2; *Acta fr. Arv.* p. 143 Henzen). The term *solitaurilia* Quintilian (*Inst.* 1. 5. 67) regarded as a corruption of *suovetaurilia*; others (in antiquity

and recently) have proposed various etymologies, none fully convincing.

I. S. Ryberg, *Rites of the State Religion in Roman Art* (1955); U. W. Scholz, *Philol.* 1973, 3 ff.; S. Tortorella, *Ostraka* 1992, 81 ff. J. L.

superstitio designated for the Romans a negative attitude. At first positive, the term *superstitio* became pejorative from the end of the 1st cent. BC. Superstition meant a free citizen's forgetting his dignity by throwing himself into the servitude of deities conceived as tyrants. The civic ideal of piety (see PIETAS) envisaged above all honouring the gods while preserving one's freedom—that is, with restraint and measure. Thus the superstitious were supposed to submit themselves to exaggerated *rituals, to adhere in credulous fashion to *prophecies, and to allow themselves to be abused by charlatans. The reproach was addressed to women (Juv. *Sat.* 6) as well as to the members of the social and intellectual élite portrayed by *Cicero in his *On the Nature of the Gods* and *On Divination*. This conception corresponded to that conveyed by the Greek *deisidaimonia*, as it is discussed by *Plutarch in the *On Deisidaemonia*. As a general rule the Romans considered strangers, and especially *barbarians, as superstitious, either because they celebrated monstrous cults, like the Gauls, or because they were terrified by every exceptional happening and attributed it to divine wrath. But one could equally be considered superstitious, like the Jews, in submitting without flinching to the prophecies of sacred books (Tac. *Hist.* 5. 13. 2; see JEWS; RELIGION, JEWISH). With the coming of *Christianity, two new forms of superstitious aberration appeared, which both could be described (following Lactant. *Div. Inst.* 4. 28. 11) as 'the cult of the wrong gods'. One was the retention, despite all the strong disapproval of the doctors of the Church, of purely pagan beliefs. The other was the use of Christian names, holy books, etc. in *magic. See RELIGION, ROMAN, TERMS RELATING TO.

W. Belardi, *Superstitio* (1976); D. Grodzinski, *Rev. Ét. Anc.* 1974, 36 ff.; J. Scheid, *Religion et piété* (1985), 133. J. Sc.

supplication, Greek (*hiketeia*) See J. Gould, *JHS* 1973, 74 ff.

supplication, Roman (*supplicationes*). When calamity struck (pestilence, defeat) or danger threatened, the senate, advised by priests, often decreed adoration by all the people, or part of it, especially women (Livy 25. 12. 15) of all or certain gods (often placed on *pulvinaria* (see PULVINAR), with the temples open) to expiate transgressions (*obsecratio*) or to ensure future support. *Supplicationes* were also decreed to render thanks (*gratulatio*) for a signal victory. This double character of the rite favours the etymological connection with *placo*, 'give satisfaction', rather than with *plico*, 'to bend' (one's knees). Originally lasting one day, they reached 12 days for *Pompey, 50 for *Caesar, and 55 supplications with the total of 890 days for *Augustus (*RG* 4. 2; on the supplications under the Empire, see the *Feriale Cumanum*, *ILS* 108). Apparently it was an old Roman rite, but it fell under Greek influence: more than half of expiatory supplications were held at the suggestion of decemvirs (and the Sibylline books; see QUINDECIMVIRI; SIBYL); they were occasionally associated with a *lectisternium (Livy 22. 10. 8–9), and the participants frequently wore wreaths (*coronati*).

L. Halkin, *La Supplication d'action des grâces chez les Romains* (1953); G. Freyburger, *Latomus* 1977, 283 ff.; 1988, 501 ff.; *ANRW* 2. 16. 2 (1978), 1462 ff. J. L.

Surenas or **Sūrēn,** name of one of the seven great Parthian families (see PARTHIA). They ruled Seistan as vassals of the *Arsacids, and held certain hereditary rights and functions, especially those of crowning the king at the coronation ceremony and of military command in the field: thus 'the Suren' may designate the king's hereditary commander. The best-known Suren formed or took over a highly trained professional army of 10,000 heavy-armed cavalry and horse-archers, with a baggage-train of 1,000 Arabian *camels carrying a huge reserve of arrows. With this force he overthrew Mithradates III and secured *Orodes his throne (55/4 BC), and then defeated *Crassus' invasion (53). His successes stirred jealousy among the Parthian nobles and nervousness in Orodes, who put him to death. Another 'Surena' in AD 36 crowned the pretender *Tiridates (3) king of Parthia (Tac. *Ann.* 6. 42). The Surens played an important role in later wars between their *Sasanid overlords and Rome and Byzantium.

A. D. H. Bivar, *Cambridge History of Iran* 3/1 (1983), 48–55; A. N. Sherwin-White, *Roman Foreign Policy in the East* (1984), 279–90.
C. B. R. P.

surface survey See ARCHAEOLOGY, CLASSICAL.

surgery

1. Before 300 BC In the Homeric poems (see HOMER) references to surgery are found mainly in the *Iliad* and concerned with the treatment of wounds. The wound is cleaned; blood squeezed or sucked out; edges united by bandaging; and an analgesic of dried herbs rubbed in and applied as an air-tight pad. Treatments resemble those recorded in early Egyptian medicine, although it is disputed whether this indicates a direct borrowing from Egyptian healers, whose reputation for surgery certainly had reached Asia Minor by 1000 BC. They were also known at the Persian court, where a Greek physician and surgeon, *Democedes of Croton, made a spectacular cure of King *Darius I.

Surgery occupies an ambiguous place in the Hippocratic Corpus (see HIPPOCRATES (2); MEDICINE, § 4 (c)). Not every medical practitioner wished to perform surgery, and some expressly left it to experts in military medicine, bone-setting, or cutting for the stone. Yet few ancient cities were large enough for such specializations to flourish, and most healers will have had of necessity to practise at least basic surgery. *Galen expected his average practitioner to be able to carry out at least some basic operations, and to know how to reduce the pain and post-operative complications of surgery. Swabbing with wine would have helped to reduce wound infection, although the recommended opiates and analgesics would not have diminished the actual pain and shock of surgery or cauterizing.

The surgical part of the Hippocratic collection is in confusion. *Fractures, Dislocations* (i.e. ἄρθρων, of joints), and *Wounds of the head* are of about 400 BC, the two former being parts of a larger work. *The nature of bones* is of about 350 BC. *On surgery and Mochlicon* (= *Instruments of reduction*) are later abbreviations of earlier works, but the introductory chapter of *Mochlicon* is the displaced first part of *The nature of bones*. Treatises covering the whole medical field were, Galen indicates, commonly called 'Concerning the things of surgery'. Some idea of such a work is gained by reading the above works in the following order: *On surgery*, being a greatly abbreviated introduction to the whole; introductory chapter of *Mochlicon*, being descriptions of the bones; *The nature of bones*, a sketch of theoretical anatomy for the surgeon, omitting bones (despite title); *Fractures*; *Dislocations*; remaining chapters of *Mochlicon*; *Wounds of the head*. It must be remembered that the parts differ greatly in age and state and that there is repetition and overlapping.

Startlingly modern are the minute directions for preparation of the operating room, and such points as the management of light—both artificial and natural—scrupulous cleanliness of hands, care and use of instruments with special precautions for those of iron, decencies of the operating chamber, modes of dressing wounds, use of splints, and need for tidiness, cleanliness, aftercare, and nursing. The directions for bandaging and for diagnosis and treatment of dislocations and fractures, especially of depressed fractures of the skull, are very impressive. In *Fractures* and *Dislocations* certain procedures for reduction are identical with those now in use, but other passages are incompatible with the facts of anatomy. *Wounds of the head* has a special place in the history of surgery. It is a practical work by a highly skilled craftsman, and every sentence suggests experience. Although its treatment of depressed fractures has been criticized from an early date, the book was in current use until the middle of the 18th cent. It introduces technical terms, two of which, *bregma* and *diploe*, survive in modern usage.

Among instruments described is the 'bench of Hippocrates', a bed for reducing dislocations, especially of the hip. The form is so ancient as to antedate the screw as a mechanical power. Lever, crank, windlass, and pulley are employed. With minor changes it was in continuous use for at least 2,000 years. There is no reason to associate it with Hippocrates; it may well be more ancient than he, but the name is late.

*2. *Alexandria (1) and the Roman empire* Alexandrian surgeons had a reputation for excellence that lasted from the 3rd cent. BC until the 4th cent. AD, if not beyond. Building on the anatomical discoveries of *Herophilus and *Erasistratus, they invented new methods of repairing shoulder- and hip-joints, as well as of bandaging and repairing anal fistulae. Their work survives only in fragments, except for the commentary of *Apollonius (8) of Citium on *On joints*, an orthopaedic text that was from the start illustrated with drawings.

Greek surgeons were active in Rome by the end of the 3rd cent. BC, even if the failure of Archagathus of Laconia in 219 earned him the soubriquet of 'Butcher'. By AD 100 *Heliodorus (3) had given the first account of ligation and torsion of blood-vessels, treated stricture by internal section, performed radical cures for hernias, and was skilled in skull operations. *Archigenes of Apamaea also wrote much on amputation. *Antyllus treated cataracts surgically and removed aneurysms by applying two ligatures and cutting down between them—an operation still occasionally called by his name.

Much surgical information is contained in bk. 7 of *De medicina* by A. *Cornelius Celsus, some certainly obtained from earlier Greek sources, some equally certainly showing evidence of experience of operations. Celsus gives details of some very dangerous operations to extirpate a goitre and to remove tonsils, as well as a very simple and practical method of cutting for bladder stone. He also describes the removal of polyps from the face and mouth, and of unsightly blemishes. His account of *dentistry includes the wiring of loose teeth and the use of a dental mirror.

Although he made his early reputation as a surgeon and reports such complicated operations as removing a suppurating breastbone and sewing back an omentum after a sword wound, Galen never wrote a specific book on surgery, although he reveals much about the treatment of ulcers, fistulae, and dislocations. In *On examining a physician* he lists essential surgical knowledge, which includes, above all, how to treat surgical conditions without having recourse to the knife. The complexity and sophistication of contemporary surgery are revealed in the ps.-Galenic

Introduction, which gives remarkably modern-sounding advice on wounds and on internal surgery. Later encyclopaedists preserve many fragments of earlier surgery, and *Paul of Aegina in particular gives the best surviving account of ancient military surgery in bk. 6, and records over 120 different operations.

Literary evidence is complemented by that of illustrations, on Attic vases and Roman gravestones, as well as those in manuscripts. The so-called Nicetas codex of *Soranus and Apollonius of Citium (see above) contains striking illustrations of bandaging and of orthopaedics around AD 900, but clearly depending on much earlier models. Continuing finds of surgical instruments reveal the complexity of ancient surgery, both in large instruments, like the trivalve vaginal speculum, and in small, with specially adapted and finished knives, scalpels, and probes. Their ubiquity, not least at *Pompeii, where one smith manufactured instruments, confirms Galen's belief in the general acceptance of some operations as part of normal medical practice.

Writers on *veterinary medicine also include valuable information about veterinary surgery, although this usually forms only a small part of their books.

TEXTS The surgical texts in the Hippocratic Corpus are most easily found in vol. 3 of the Loeb *Hippocrates*, trans. E. T. Withington (1927). J. E. Petrequin, *Chirurgie d'Hippocrate* (1877–8), is still valuable. For Apollonius, see the *CMG* edn. of F. Kudlien and J. Kollesch (1965), which includes the illustrations from the Nicetas codex. For Celsus, see the Loeb edn. of W. G. Spencer (1936–8), which reprints the *CML* text of F. Marx (1915). The ps.-Galenic *Introduction* is printed in vol. 14 of Kühn's edition of Galen (1827). Galen's comments on the average surgeon's ability are found in *On Examining a Physician, CMG Suppl. Or.* 4 (1988). The Eng. trans. of Paul by F. Adams, *The Seven Books of Paulus Aegineta* (1844–7), is unsurpassed, and its notes are informative about the problems of surgery before antiseptics and anaesthetics. Veterinary surgery is contained e.g. in Vegetius, *Mulomedicina* (1919), and the Teubner *Hippiatrica Graeca* (1924–7).

LITERATURE General: F. J. Gurlt, *Geschichte der Chirurgie* (1898); O. H. and S. D. Wangensteen, *The Rise of Surgery* (1975); G. Majno, *The Healing Hand: Man and Wound in the Ancient World* (1975). Homeric surgery: S. Laser, *Medizin u. Körperpflege* (1983). Hippocratic surgery is less studied; V. Di Benedetto, *Il medico e la malattia* (1986) gives the most recent survey of the problems. For Hellenistic surgery, M. Michler, *Die hellenistische Chirurgie* (1968), is standard. Much information is given in H. von Staden, *Herophilus* (1989), esp. in Part 2, and in Fraser, *Ptol. Alex.* Later surgery is poorly covered, except for R. Jackson, *Doctors and Diseases in the Roman Empire* (1988), ch. 5; L. Toledo-Pereyra, *Journ. Hist. Med.* 1973, 357–73, on Galen and ps.-Galen, and for Byzantine surgery, L. Bliquez, *DOP* 1984, 187–204. Veterinary surgery is discussed by F. Smith, *Early History of Veterinary Literature* (1919); and A. M. Doyen-Huguet, *DOP* 1984, 111–20. For instruments, see J. S. Milne, *Surgical Instruments in Greek and Roman Times* (1907); E. Künzl, *Medizinische Instrumente aus Sepulkralfunden der römischen Kaiserzeit* (1983).

C. S.; V. N.

Surrentum (mod. Sorrento), in Italy, possibly a Greek colony (see COLONIZATION, GREEK) but dominated by *Etruscans in the 5th cent. BC and under *Oscan rule, as part of the Nucerian League, from 420. It revolted during the *Social War (3) and was colonized by *Sulla and *Augustus (see COLONIZATION, ROMAN). Many rich Romans owned villas there from the 1st cent. BC.

P. Mingazzini and F. Pfister, *Forma Italiae: Surrentum* (1946). K. L.

survey archaeology See ARCHAEOLOGY, CLASSICAL.

Susa, the 'city of lilies', was the capital of Elam, and afterwards the Achaemenid winter capital, where *Darius I built a palace with a large audience hall (*Apadana) and a monumental gateway. The surviving sculpture includes a large statue of Darius

on a base inscribed with the names of subject peoples, as well as glazed brick reliefs of guardsmen. Under *Seleucids and Parthians (see PARTHIA) its name was Seleuceia-on-the-Eulaeus; Susa was a *polis by the time of *Antiochus (3) III. In AD 21 it was still a fully Greek city, with a council, assembly, and elected magistrates whose qualifications were scrutinized; it could send embassies and though subject to Parthia, it had more than local autonomy. Beside Greeks, other peoples can be traced—Persians, Syrians, Jews, Anatolians, Babylonians, Elymaeans; its city-goddess was the Elamite Nanaia, renamed Artemis. Four Greek poems are known, one a lyric ode (1st cent. BC) addressed to Apollo by a Syrian title, Mara (Lord); they and the forms of decrees and manumissions show that Susa was well within the Greek culture-sphere.

E. Porada, *Cambridge History of Iran* 2 (1985), 806–12, 816–19, 923; W. W. Tarn, *The Greeks in Bactria and India* (1938), 27, 39, 68; G. le Rider, *Suse sous les Séleucides et les Parthes* (1965); P. Harper, J. Aruz, and F. Tallon (eds.), *The Royal City of Susa* (1992). W. W. T.; M. V.

Susarion is first mentioned in the Parian Marble (see MARMOR PARIUM), under some year between 581 and 560, as having originated Comedy in the Attic *deme Icaria. A later tradition makes him a *Megarian, as he calls himself υἱὸς Φιλίνου Μεγαρόθεν Τριποδίσκιος ('son of Philinus of Megara, from Tripodiscus') in the only putative citation from his work. This citation is in normal Attic, and its authenticity is highly improbable; Susarion may indeed be a fictitious person. See COMEDY (GREEK), ORIGINS OF, B 4.

Kassel–Austin, *PCG* 7. 661 ff.; Pickard-Cambridge–Webster, *Dithyramb*[2], 183 ff. K. J. D.

Sutorius (*RE* 21) **Macro, Quintus Naevius Cordus,** of *Alba Fucens. Prefect (see PRAEFECTUS) of the *vigiles in AD 31, he was *Tiberius' agent in the overthrow of L. *Aelius Seianus, whom he succeeded as commander of the Praetorian Guard (see PRAEFECTUS PRAETORIO); he may have been an instigator of the move against him. Macro predominated in politics while Tiberius lived and was influential in securing *Gaius (1)'s succession, but, appointed Prefect of Egypt in 38, he was forced to suicide with his wife Ennia before taking up office. His will, leaving his native city money for an amphitheatre, remained valid.

Smallwood, *Docs. . . . Gaius*, 254 (bibl.), trans. D. Braund, *Augustus to Nero: A sourcebook of Roman History 31 B.C.–A.D. 68* (1985), 458; F. De Visscher, *Rend. Linc.* 1957, 39 ff.; *Mélanges A. Piganiol* (1966), 761 ff. J. P. B.; B. M. L.

Sutrium (mod. Sutri), in Italy, a small but strategically important *Etruscan town, 45 km. (28 miles) north-west of Rome and 10 km. (6 miles) west of *Nepete. Founded perhaps as late as the 5th cent. BC to control the important road (later the *via Cassia) through the Ciminian forest, it played an important part in the fighting that followed the destruction of *Veii in 396 BC (Livy 6. 9. 3), very soon after which date it became a Latin colony (see COLONIZATION, ROMAN). Its subsequent history was mainly uneventful until the early Middle Ages, when its position made it once more an important defensive outpost of Rome. It became a *municipium after the *Social War (3) and received a fresh group of colonists soon after the death of *Caesar, under the name of Colonia Coniuncta Iulia Sutrina.

CIL 11. 489. G. Duncan, *PBSR* 1958, 63 ff. J. B. W.-P.; D. W. R. R.

Sybaris (mod. Sibari) in S. Italy, an Achaean / Troezenian colony (founded *c*.720 BC) near the mouth of the river Crati. See ACHAEA; COLONIZATION, GREEK; TROEZEN. It expanded rapidly, founding

*Laos, Poseidonia (*Paestum), and Scidrus, and exploited its agrarian resources and its trading connections with the *Etruscans. The wealth and luxury of the city became a *topos in ancient literature. It was one of the coalition of cities which destroyed *Siris, but was itself destroyed in 510 BC. Exiled Sybarites sought assistance from *Croton, which defeated Sybaris, and razed the city. The population fled to Laos and Paestum, but attempted to refound the city. Some joined the Athenian-led initiative to found a colony at *Thurii, but were soon ejected and founded a new city, also called Sybaris, on the river Traente. The site is obscured by later buildings, but archaic remains have been found at Parco Cavallo and Casa Bianca.

Sibari e Thurii (suppl. ASMG 1974); *Not. Scav.* Suppls. 1969, 1970, 1972, 1973.   K. L.

sycophants (συκοφάνται), habitual prosecutors. In Athens there were, for most offences, no public prosecutors, but anyone (for some offences, any citizen) who wished was allowed to prosecute in a public action. Some individuals made a habit of bringing prosecutions, either to gain the financial rewards given to successful prosecutors in certain actions (notably *phasis* and *apographē*; see LAW AND PROCEDURE, ATHENIAN), or to gain money by blackmailing a man who was willing to pay to avoid prosecution, or to earn payment from someone who had reasons for wanting a man to be prosecuted, or to make a political or oratorical reputation. Such persons came to be called sycophants (lit. 'fig-revealers'; the origin of the usage is obscure). The word is often used as a term of disparagement or abuse in the Attic orators and in *Aristophanes (1), who shows sycophants in action in *Acharnians*.

The Athenians wished to check sycophants, who prosecuted without good reason, but not to discourage public-spirited prosecutors. Therefore the rewards for successful prosecution were not abolished, but penalties were introduced in most public actions for a prosecutor who dropped a case after starting it, or whose case was so weak that he failed to obtain one-fifth of the jury's votes. In addition sycophancy was an offence for which a man could be prosecuted. *Graphē*, *probolē*, *eisangelia*, *apagogē*, and *endeixis* are all said to have been possible methods of accusing sycophants (see LAW AND PROCEDURE, ATHENIAN), but it is not known how the offence was defined; perhaps there was no legal definition.

Nobody has yet come up with a good explanation of how the word got its modern sense of 'flatterers'.

R. J. Bonner and G. Smith, *The Administration of Justice from Homer to Aristotle* 2 (1938), 39–74; D. M. MacDowell, *The Law in Classical Athens* (1978), 62–6; R. Osborne and D. Harvey, in P. Cartledge, P. Millett, and S. Todd (eds.), *Nomos* (1990), 83–121.   D. M. M.

Syene (mod. Aswân), town in Upper Egypt on the east bank of the *Nile below the first cataract. A customs-post on the Nubian frontier, it had important banks under the Ptolemies and military garrisons under Rome. Because it was near the Tropic of Cancer, *Eratosthenes used the well, which cast no shadow at the solstice, to calculate the earth's diameter. Its *quarries supplied red granite.

Strabo 17. 1. 48; *PLondon* 5 (1917); *PMonac.* 1 (1914). A. Calderini, *Dizionario dei nomi geografici dell'Egitto* 4 (1986), 316–17; U. Wilcken, *Griechische Ostraka aus Aegypten* (1899). Inscriptions: *OGI* 122; 168; *IGRom.* 1292.   W. E. H. C.

sylē (η᾽ σύλη) and its cognate verb (συλᾶν) denoted the act of stripping an outsider or an enemy of his possessions by force, nominally in reprisal for previous hurt or outstanding *debt (cf. Hom. *Il.* 11. 670–761). In archaic, classical, and Hellenistic Greek contexts where redress by legal process could not be enforced outside the citizen body or its territory, *sylē* was at once a means of direct or indirect redress and a pretext for predatory violence, especially against merchant ships and their cargoes. Bilateral treaties allowing direct access by one state's nationals to the courts of the other (*symbola*, see SYMBOLON), or formal recognition by one community of the inviolability (*asylia) of an individual, a sanctuary, or a territory, gradually reduced the scope of *sylē*, but Aetolians and Cretans (see AETOLIA; CRETE) exploited the custom through the 3rd cent. BC and beyond. See PIRACY.

P. Gauthier, *Symbola* (1972), 209–19; *SEG* 1980, 1825, summarizing B. Bravo, *ASNP* 1980, 675–987 and others; J. K. Davies, *CAH* 7²/1 (1984), 287 ff.   J. K. D.

symbolon, originally a physical object, intended as a material indication of identification or agreement. What may have begun as a private practice as a reminder of *xenia* or ritualized friendship (see FRIENDSHIP, RITUALIZED; matching 'tallies' between individuals: Pl. *Symp.* 191d) came to have wider ramifications. A gold cup served as a *symbolon* between the Persian king and a 5th-cent. Athenian (Lys. 19. 25); in this case, the *symbolon* was transferable, giving its possessor command over goods and money all over *Asia Minor (or so it was claimed). At an inter-state level, *symbola* are mentioned in a mid-4th-cent. treaty between Athens and Strato, king of *Sidon (*IG* 2². 141 (Tod 139), line 19). Whereas the cognate term *symbolaion* came to mean an agreement or contract (e.g. over a loan), *symbola* typically referred to inter-state agreements, dealing with legal relations between individuals of different states, or between a state and an individual. To those travelling abroad, *symbola* offered protection from *sylē* (summary seizure of property) and other forms of harassment (as exemplified by the terms of the treaty between Oeanthea and Chaleion from c.450 BC: Tod 34). States agreed that, in any dispute, their respective citizens would have access to the legal process *via* judicial reciprocity. *Dikai apo symbolōn* were lawsuits conducted according to the terms of these treaties (ML 31). Surviving evidence suggests that the actual cases may have involved issues of crime as often as contract. In the 4th cent. ([Dem.] 7. 12 f.) the normal practice was apparently for *symbola* to provide for cases to be settled in the courts of the state of the defendant. Whether this convention was ignored by the 5th-cent. Athenians in dealings with their subjects depends on a disputed passage in *Thucydides (2) (1. 77. 1). In 4th-cent. Athens, *emporikai dikai* (explicitly 'commercial suits') apparently took over some of the functions of *symbola*.

G. Herman, *Ritualised Friendship and the Greek City* (1987); J. Vélissaropoulos, *Panteios* 1980, 93 ff.; J. W. Jones, *The Law and Legal Theory of the Greeks* (1956); A. R. W. Harrison, *The Law of Athens* 2 (1971); D. M. MacDowell, *The Law in Classical Athens* (1978); G. E. M. de Ste. Croix, *CQ* 1961, 94 ff.; 1962, 268 ff.; *HCT* and Hornblower, *Comm. on Thuc.*, both on 1. 77. 1; P. Gauthier, *Symbola: Les étrangers et la justice dans les cités grecques* (1972); P. Gauthier, *Revue historique de droit français et étranger* 1982, 553 ff.; B. Bravo, *ASNP* 1980, 675 ff.; E. E. Cohen, *Ancient Athenian Maritime Courts* (1973).   R. J. H.; P. C. M.

symmachia See ALLIANCE, GREEK.

Symmachus (1) (fl. *c.* AD 100) wrote a commentary with ὑποθέσεις (see HYPOTHESIS, LITERARY (*Greek*) § (1)) on *Aristophanes (1) which owed much to *Didymus (1) and was one of the main sources of the oldest *scholia to Aristophanes.

G. Zuntz, *Die Aristophanes-Scholien der Papyri* (1975).   N. G. W.

Symmachus, Quintus Aurelius

Symmachus (2), **Quintus Aurelius** (*c.* AD 340–402), Roman senator, orator, and epistolographer (cf. LETTERS, LATIN), and leading proponent of the pagan religious cause against the Christian emperors, was educated by a Gallic teacher and enjoyed a highly successful political career. After visiting the court of *Valentinian (1) I in 369–70, where he delivered the three panegyrics of which fragments survive and made the lasting acquaintance of *Ausonius, he was proconsul of Africa (373) and prefect of Rome (383–4). Despite his support in a lost panegyric for the usurper *Magnus Maximus, he was made consul in 391. In the last decade of his life, through his extensive correspondence and personal contacts he tirelessly promoted the interests of his family and friends; the letters in which he arranged the praetorian games of his son are of special interest. He died in 402, shortly after leading an embassy to the imperial court at *Ravenna during the first occupation of north Italy by *Alaric. The letters of Symmachus were edited by his son Q. Fabius Memmius Symmachus, who arranged them after the manner of the younger *Pliny (2), in nine books of private letters, the tenth being composed of letters addressed to the emperor. These include the 49 *relationes* addressed to *Valentinian (2) II during Symmachus' tenure of the urban prefecture (see PRAEFECTUS URBI), the most famous being *Relatio 3*, in which he argued for the restoration of the Altar of Victory to the senate-house (see CURIA (2)). Symmachus failed to win over Valentinian against the influence of *Ambrose of Milan, whose own two letters on the subject are also extant. Symmachus' religious attitudes seem to focus upon the maintenance of the public cults of Rome and their priesthoods. In this he would contrast—though this may be a misleading impression—with the more varied religious tastes of *Praetextatus, and he did not follow his intimate friend *Nicomachus (4) Flavianus into armed opposition to *Theodosius (2) I in 393/4. Nevertheless, Symmachus' public career is marked by a high level of integrity and courage, in which he was not afraid to speak directly in criticism to emperors. His correspondence, for long dismissed as artificial and highly formal without much substantial content, is a fine monument to the character of senatorial influence and the literary culture of senators, though it reveals much less than one would wish of Symmachus' private tastes. Among his 130 known correspondents (others are anonymous), Symmachus included many of the most important political figures of his day, from cultivated court officials to barbarian generals. Symmachus' son, the editor of the letters, married a grand-daughter of Nicomachus Flavianus, and his daughter married Flavianus *iunior*. The names of the two families are preserved on the two leaves of an ivory diptych, respectively in the Victoria and Albert, and Cluny, Museums.

PLRE 1, pp. 865–70 ('Symmachus' 4). Editions: O. Seeck (1883, repr. 1961). Translations and Commentaries: *Letters*, J.-P. Callu (bks. 1–5; Budé, 2 vols. 1972, 1982); A. Marcone (bks. 4, 6; 1987, 1983); S. Roda (bk. 9; 1981); *Relationes*, R. H. Barrow (1973); D. Vera (1981). Studies: S. Dill, *Roman Society in the Last Century of the Western Empire* (1905); J. A. MacGeachy, *Quintus Aurelius Symmachus and the Senatorial Aristocracy of the West* (1942); H. Bloch, in A. Momigliano (ed.), *The Conflict between Paganism and Christianity in the Fourth Century* (1963), ch. 8; J. F. Matthews, *Western Aristocracies and Imperial Court, AD 364–425* (1975), also in J. W. Binns (ed.), *Latin Literature of the Fourth Century* (1974), ch. 3, and *JRS* 1973, 175 ff.; F. Paschoud (ed.), *Colloque Genevois sur Symmaque* (1986); P. Bruggisser, *Symmaque, ou le rituel epistolaire de l'amitié littéraire* (1993).

J. F. Ma.

symmoria ('partnership'), in Athens a group of men liable for payment of the tax called *eisphora* or for the *liturgy of the *trierarchy. In 378/7 BC all payers of *eisphora* were organized in 100 *symmoriai*, for administrative convenience: each member continued to be taxed on his own property, but from a later date the three richest members of each *symmoria* could be made to advance the sum due from the whole *symmoria* as a *proeisphora*. In 357/6 a law of Periander extended this system to the trierarchy: the 1,200 richest citizens were grouped in 20 *symmoriai* (probably independent of the *symmoriai* for *eisphora*, but this has been doubted), and through the *symmoriai* the total cost of the trierarchy each year was divided equally among all of the 1,200 except those who could claim exemption. Reforms in the trierarchic symmories were proposed by *Demosthenes (2) in 354 and made by him in 340; further changes were made later. In the 330s or 320s one of the generals (*stratēgoi*) was placed 'in charge of the *symmoriai*', to supervise the working of the trierarchic system. *Symmoriai* are found in Hellenistic *Teos and in Roman Nysa (in *Caria) as units of the citizen body smaller than a tribe.

Athens: R. Thomsen, *Eisphora* (1964); E. Ruschenbusch, *ZPE* 31 (1978), 275–84; P. J. Rhodes, *AJAH* 1982, 1–19. Teos and Nysa: N. F. Jones, *Public Organization in Ancient Greece* (1987), 306–10, 358–9.

F. M. H., P. J. R.

Symphosius (*PLRE* 2, 'Symphosius'; perhaps 4th–5th cent. AD), the reputed author of a series of a hundred Latin riddles, each consisting of three hexameters, claimed in the preface to have been composed *ex tempore* during the Saturnalia (see SATURNUS). The work was regarded as a model for the poetic riddle and had an important influence on medieval books of riddles, e.g. Aldhelm's. See also RIDDLES.

TEXTS *PLM* 4; *Anth. Lat.* 1²; with trans. and comm. R. T. Ohl (1928).

A. H.-W.

Symplegades, the 'Clashing Rocks' which, according to legend, guarded the entrance at the *Bosporus (1) to the Black Sea (see EUXINE); they are also regularly called 'Dark (*Kyaneai*) Rocks' (first at Hdt. 4. 85. 1 and Soph. *Ant.* 966). They ceased clashing together when *Jason (1)'s ship, the *Argo* (see ARGONAUTS) succeeded in passing between them. The name 'Symplegades' occurs first in *Euripides; *Pindar speaks of 'rocks that run together' (*Pyth.* 4. 208–9). They were presumably originally identified with the Planktai, 'Wandering Rocks', which the Homeric *Circe (see HOMER) says were safely navigated by the *Argo* with *Hera's help (*Od.* 12. 59–72), but these were later sited in the western Mediterranean (usually in the Aeolian islands near Sicily; see AEOLIAE INSULAE) and distinguished from the Symplegades. *Apollonius (1) of Rhodes has a marvellous description of the *Argo*'s passage through the Symplegades (*Arg.* 2. 549–606).

A. Heubeck, *Comm. on Homer's Odyssey* (1989), on 12. 55–72.

R. L. Hu.

sympoliteia ('joint citizenship'). The verb *sympoliteuein* is used from the late 5th cent. BC onwards to denote the merging of separate communities in a single state, similar to *synoecism (Thuc. 6. 4. 1, Xen. *Hell.* 5. 2. 12). In inscriptions the verb and the noun are used of the merging of two or more communities in one, especially when a greater state politically absorbs but does not physically obliterate a lesser state (e.g. *IG* 9. 1. 32 = *SIG*³ 647); modern scholars use *sympoliteia* as a technical term in this sense; but inscriptions sometimes use other terms (e.g. *synoikia*, *IG* 5. 2. 343; *homopoliteia*, *Staatsverträge* 545), and *sympoliteia* is used also of the right of citizenship conferred on an individual (*IG* 4². 1. 59), and of the admission of a particular city to the *sympoliteia* of the Lycian nation (*SEG* 18. 570, 58–61; see LYCIA); in one remarkable text *Pharsalus gives *politeia* to a community which already has *sympoliteia* with it (*IG* 9. 2. 234). Similarly, *Polybius (1) uses both the verb and the noun to refer to membership of the *Achaean and *Aetolian Confederacies, by states which retained their own identity, including the attachment of distant states to the Aetolian Confederacy which was made by a treaty of *isopoliteia* ('equal citizenship') with the Confederacy or with one of its cities (e.g. 4. 3. 6), and he also uses the term on other occasions when we might expect *isopoliteia* (e.g. 28. 14. 3).

G. Busolt, *Griechische Staatskunde*[3] 1 (1920), 156; L. Robert, *Villes d'Asie mineure*[2] (1962), 54–69; J. A. O. Larsen, *Greek Federal States* (1968), 202–7; A. Giovannini, *Untersuchungen über die Natur und die Anfänge der bundesstaatlichen Sympolitien in Griechenland* (1971), 20–4; F. W. Walbank, *Scripta Classica Israelica* 1976/7, 32–5; G.-J.-M.-J. te Riele, *BCH* 1987, 167–90.　　　　　　　　　　　　J. A. O. L.; P. J. R.

symposium Commensality in Greece was focused both on the public civic or sacrificial meal and on the activities of smaller exclusive groups. The warrior feast was already central to the Homeric image of society (see HOMER); under the influence of the near east in the period 750–650 BC more complex rituals of pleasure arose. The time of 'drinking together' (*symposion*) was separated from the meal before it (*deipnon*) and became the main focus of attention. The male participants wore garlands (see CROWNS AND WREATHS), and libations and prayers began and ended the proceedings. The Greeks adopted the practice of reclining on the left elbow (one or two to a couch); from this evolved a characteristic shape of room, and a standard size for the drinking group of between fourteen and thirty: the *andrōn* or men's room was square, arranged with a door off centre to fit usually seven or fifteen couches; larger sizes (though known) tended to destroy the unity of sympotic space. Many such rooms have been recognized archaeologically, but the best representation is the painted Tomb of the Diver at *Paestum. They were supplied with low tables, cushions, decorated couches, and wall-hangings (see DINING-ROOMS). By the late 6th cent. a repertoire of vessels had been elaborated, including different cup shapes, jugs, wine coolers, and mixing-vessels: the decoration of these vases offers a set of self-conscious images related to the activities of the drinking group (see POTTERY, GREEK). Water was mixed with the *wine in a central crater to a strength determined by the president (usually three or four to one, or about the strength of modern beer); it was served by slave boys. Equality and order in distribution were maintained: each crater measured a stage in the progress towards drunkenness. At the end of the session a procession (*komos*) in the streets would demonstrate the cohesion and power of the group.

The symposium was a male and aristocratic activity, originally based on the warrior group; its earliest poetry was the *elegiac poetry of war, and the Spartan reclining *syssition remained the basis of its military organization. Citizen women were excluded. It was a centre for the transmission of traditional values (*Theognis) and for the *homosexual bonding of young males; it could provide the organization for political action in the aristocratic *hetaireia* (see HETAIREIAI). But it was also a place of pleasure; *kottabos* (see GAMES) was a favourite pastime; professional entertainers were hired. *Dionysus was accompanied by *Aphrodite and the *Muses, in the form of female slave companions (*hetairai*) and monodic lyric poetry, which was composed for performance at symposia—at first by gifted amateurs, later by skilled professional poets. In the Archaic age the symposium was the focus for an artistic patronage (see PATRONAGE, LITERARY,

Greek) which reached its heights under the tyrants (see TYRANNY); together with wine, 'drinking in the Greek style' was exported throughout the Mediterranean in a process of acculturation that profoundly affected Etruscans, Romans, and many other peoples.

The artistic and cultural importance of the symposium declined during the Classical age, but it remained important in social life well into the Hellenistic period. Later it fused with Roman customs. The reclining symposium survives today in the ritual of the Seder or Passover Meal. See also CONVIVIUM; SYMPOSIUM LITERATURE.

M. Napoli, *La tomba del tuffatore* (1970); O. Murray (ed.), *Sympotica* (1990), and *In Vino Veritas* (1994); F. Lissarrague, *The Aesthetics of the Greek Banquet* (1991); W. J. Slater (ed.), *Dining in a Classical Context* (1991); P. Schmitt-Pantel, *La Cité au banquet* (1992).　　　O. Mu.

symposium literature Three overlapping types may be distinguished: 1. Poetry produced for the *symposium: this includes most or all Archaic monodic lyric poetry and at least some choral lyric, and much of elegiac and iambic poetry. There is a strong metasympotic element in this poetry, a tendency to relate content to context of performance; there is also a strong element of the normative: many elegiac and other poems offer rules for the conduct of symposia (*Xenophanes, *Panyassis, *Critias). Certain themes and forms like the epigram, the *skolion* (see SCOLIA), riddles, and chain poems are characteristic. From the real context of the symposium a literary context developed: much Hellenistic and Roman poetry purports to be composed for the symposium; obvious examples are the *Anacreontea* and the lyric poetry of *Horace.

2. *Plato (1) established the prose genre of the *Symposium*, an imagined dialogue of set speeches or discussions usually on themes appropriate to the occasion. Plato wrote on ideal love; *Xenophon (1)'s *Symposium* is more realistic and less serious; *Aristotle wrote on drunkenness, *Epicurus on the physical effects of wine and sex, *Heraclides (4) of Tarentum on the medical effects of food and drink (Ath. 64a). *Maecenas wrote a literary *Symposium* which contained a discussion of wine and in which *Virgil and *Horace appeared (Serv. on *Aen.* 8. 310). The *Symposia* of *Menippus (1) and *Lucian parodied the serious philosophic symposium. Banquets and symposia are a common setting in Roman satire, notably Hor. *Sat.* 2. 8 and the *Cena Trimalchionis* of *Petronius Arbiter. The only Christian *Symposium*, by *Methodius of Olympus (died AD 311), is modelled on Plato, but the cast is entirely female, the setting is an apple orchard, and the theme is praise of virginity.

3. Antiquarian works. These literary or learned discussions were probably originally modelled on the reality of Ptolemaic court symposia. They could serve to display collections of philosophical wisdom (*Plutarch's *Symposium of the Seven Wise Men*) or literary questions, or to structure information appropriate to the form, as in Plutarch's *Sympotic Questions*. The most systematic example is *Athenaeus (1)'s *Deipnosophistae*, an encyclopaedia of information on all aspects of the symposium, in which the topics are arranged for ease of reference as a discussion which takes place in the course of a meal and subsequent symposium. *Macrobius' *Saturnalia* purports to follow Plato, but uses the similar device of a succession of feast days to organize information centred on Virgil.

R. Reitzenstein, *Epigramm und Skolion* (1893); G. Giangrande, in *L'Epigramme grecque* (1968), 91–177; J. Martin, *Symposion* (1931).　　O. Mu.

synagogue (Gk. συναγωγή), the name used by Greek-speaking *Jews to describe both their communities in the diaspora and their meeting places for regular public recital and teaching of the Torah (the Law of Moses, as embodied especially in the Pentateuch).

The belief of Jews that they have a duty to hear the law being read at least on occasion can be found already in Nehemiah 8: 1–8, composed probably in the 4th cent. BC, but the first evidence of Jews dedicating buildings to this or a similar institution is found in Ptolemaic Egypt (see EGYPT, *Ptolemaic*), where Jewish inscriptions recording the erection of prayer-houses (*proseuchai*) have been found, dated to the 3rd cent. BC and after. *Josephus' use of the term *proseuchē* to describe the building in *Tiberias in *Galilee where sabbath meetings were held during the revolt against Rome in AD 67 (*Vita* 277) confirms the identity of the *proseuchē* with the *synagogē*. The New Testament and *Philon (4) take synagogue meetings for granted as part of Jewish life in the 1st cent. AD both in Galilee and in the east Mediterranean diaspora. A 1st-cent. AD inscription records the erection of a synagogue in *Jerusalem by a certain Theodotus (*CIJ* 1404). Rather more tentative should be the identification as synagogues of public buildings dated before AD 70 at Gamla (on the Golan), *Masada and Herodium (in Judaea), and at *Delos.

The term *proseuchē* ('prayer') found in the Egyptian evidence suggests that public prayer may have been part of the function of synagogues, alongside the reading and teaching of the law, at least in the diaspora. However, there is no evidence of a formal public liturgy in synagogues in the land of Israel until the late Roman period. Rabbinic texts of the 2nd cent. AD are silent about any such liturgy, and according to the Gospels (Matt. 6: 5) it was a sign of hypocrisy to pray publicly in the synagogues in order to be admired. Literary references to prayer suggest that it was a private business. It is possible that proximity to the Jerusalem Temple, where formal liturgy accompanied sacrifices, discouraged the use of synagogues for similar purposes in the land of Israel, but the evidence is inconclusive.

By contrast, distance from the Jerusalem Temple may have encouraged treatment of diaspora synagogues as sacred places as far back as the Hellenistic period. Thus the synagogue in *Antioch (1) in Syria was described by Josephus as a temple (*hieron*) (*BJ* 7. 41). Synagogues in Palestine were described on inscriptions as sacred places only in late Roman and Byzantine times, when Jews began to erect numerous synagogues in *Judaea, Galilee, and the Golan in monumental style and often with elaborate mosaics. Synagogue architecture was very varied even within Palestine, and in the diaspora the wall frescoes of the Dura-*Europus synagogue, and the huge basilica found at *Sardis, have no parallel.

In Babylonia and the land of Israel the teaching function of synagogues was fulfilled by weekly recitation of the Pentateuch in a regular (eventually annual) cycle. Explanation took the form of translation into *Aramaic (*targum*) and elucidation and elaboration (*midrash*). In the western diaspora, the law was often read in Greek, either in the *Septuagint or in one of the later versions.

Among diaspora Jews the synagogue often functioned as a community centre as well as a place for worship. The *archisynagōgos* ('ruler of the synagogue') was often the senior magistrate of the community. He and other synagogue officials enforced discipline and adjudicated between members in cases of dispute. See RELIGION, JEWISH.

Schürer, *History* 2 (1979), 423–63; L. I. Levine (ed.), *Ancient Synagogues Revealed* (1981), and (ed.), *The Synagogue in Late Antiquity* (1987).

M. D. G.

syncretism, originally a (negative) term for the eirenic theologies of Grotius (1583–1645) and Calixtus (1586–1656), was turned into a metaphor in the 1830s, apparently by J. H. Newman. Extended by C. W. King to the *Alexandrian Gnostics (1860s; see GNOSTICISM), its new meaning was summarized by Andrew Lang in relation to Egypt (1887): the word denotes the process whereby 'various god-names and god-natures are mingled so as to unite the creeds of different nomes (see NOMOS (1)) and provinces'. But the obscurity of the processes at work has meant that the term's real value lies in its imprecision. Two basic types are to be distinguished in the ancient world, 'internal' and 'contact'. Internal syncretism is typical of ancient Egyptian (and Vedic) religion, as much the result of popular piety as of temple theology. Each god appears in a variety of forms and functions. Forms, names, and epithets diversify and intermingle with boundless energy. Gods, often in triads, co-exist or cohabit within one another, remaining separate at the level of cult.

Contact syncretism itself occurs in several modes, three of which may be highlighted:

1. The construction of the 'traditional' Greek and Italo-Roman pantheons took the form of variable fusion in the proto-historic period between the incomers' deities and the religions of the indigenous populations. Consciousness of this fusion had in the historical period mostly faded, but a version of it ('*Pelasgians', etc.) was used to note local idiosyncrasy. A parallel process on a small scale appears in the course of Archaic Greek colonization (see COLONIZATION, GREEK).

2. The identification or interpretation of others' gods in Greek or Roman terms, i.e. the assertion of significant similarity in one or more respects. From the Graeco-Roman point of view, this may be a simple familiarizing device, as generally in *Herodotus (1) or *Strabo, but the religious statement may also be linked to political claims, e.g. to common origins, the possibility of cultural symbiosis, *evocatio, the subjection of inferiors, the stripping of unacceptable elements of cult. Both in the Hellenistic world and the Roman empire native divinities quite rapidly acquired Greek or Roman identities. From the point of view of the conquered élites, acceptance of the new name was one index of their loyalty; moreover, the translation valorized local divinities, in Syria, Anatolia, Africa, Gaul or along the Danube, by aligning them with the gods of the imperial power. The counterpart of *interpretatio graeca* or *romana* (the tendency to identify foreign gods with known Greek or Roman ones; see INTERPRETATIO ROMANA; RELIGION, THRACIAN) was thus the 'spontaneous' restructuring of indigenous religious systems.

3. Graeco-Roman polytheism was always marked by integrating devices (political control; poetic interpretation; shared iconography; *oracles; historical writing) to counteract its inherent fissility. Such fragmentation is particularly marked in the Hellenistic world and the Principate. Several new integrating devices were developed (e.g. cumulative assimilation, listing devices, *di Augusti*). But themes from highly-developed non-Graeco-Roman religious traditions were also used, esp. the promotion of a god, in a particular context, to universal status, by combining the name with other divine names (polyonomy), or by the locution 'One ...', 'εἷς θεός ...'. The first is typical of *Isis, but extends to other gods; the second derives from near-eastern hymn- and acclamation-formulae. The practice is pushed furthest in mystic or philosophical religion, e.g. theosophical oracles from *Claros, the magical papyri, the orations of *Julian. But it is never exclusive, remaining primarily an invocatory device.

P. Lévêque, in *Les Syncrétismes dans les religions grecques et romaines*

(1973), 179–87; F. Dunand, in F. Dunand and P. Lévêque (eds.), *Les Syncrétismes dans les religions de l'antiquité* (1975), 152–85; M. LeGlay, ibid. 123–51; P. A. Fevrier, *DHA* 1976, 305–36; M. Simon, *Perennitas, Studi A. Brelich* (1980), 503–17. R. L. G.

Synesius of Cyrene, *c.* AD 370–413, Christian Neoplatonist (see NEOPLATONISM) and bishop of Ptolemais (see PENTAPOLIS) 410–13. A pupil of *Hypatia at Alexandria, he tended towards oratory and poetry. Nine hymns, 156 letters, and a series of discourses are extant. Of the latter, the *Dion* is a powerful attack on the contemporary decline of humane culture, whether in the form of exaggerated Christian *asceticism or superstitious pagan *theurgy. He shared Neoplatonic interest in the occult (e.g. the Chaldaean oracles) and wrote on *divination by *dreams (see ALCHEMY). His wife and brother were Christians; he himself was probably a catechumen as early as 399. He spent three years in *Constantinople (probably 397/8–400) as ambassador of his city requesting tax reductions, during which he became greatly involved in imperial politics. Much recent scholarship has focused on his *De Regno* and *De Providentia*, two works written at this time which both reveal Synesius' involvement with contemporary politics and shed much light on the issues and personalities concerned. Partly because of his ability to deal with government authorities, he was elected bishop of Ptolemais (Libya: see PENTAPOLIS) in 410. He accepted after six months' hesitation, prompted amongst other things by the intellectual difficulties he found in accepting the literal truth of doctrines such as the resurrection.

Opuscula and hymns: ed. Terzaghi (1939–44); letters: ed. Hercher, *Epist. Gr.* (1873). General: C. Lacombrade, *Synesios de Cyrène, hellène et chrétien* (1951); J. Bregman, *Synesius of Cyrene* (1983). Imperial politics: T. D. Barnes, *GRBS* 1986; P. J. Heather, *Phoenix* 1988; A. Cameron, *Barbarians and Politics at the Court of Arcadius* (1993). P. J. H.

syngeneia See KINSHIP.

synhedrion See CORINTH, LEAGUE OF; SECOND ATHENIAN CONFEDERACY.

Synnada (mod. Şuhut), was an assize centre (see CONVENTUS (2)) in the province of Asia (see ASIA, ROMAN PROVINCE) and one of the most important cities of *Phrygia. In the 160s BC it played a role in the wars of *Eumenes (2) II against the Galatians (see GALATIA (1)), and was one of the minting centres of the silver cistophoric coinage (see COINAGE, GREEK, 7), after 133 BC. It lay on the route from Asia followed by *Cicero in 51 BC and briefly belonged to the province of *Cilicia. Later inscriptions show that it was the administrative centre not only for large imperial estates (see DOMAINS) but also for the *marble quarries of *Docimium, whose products were often known as Synnadic marble. Its inhabitants claimed descent from both Athenian and Spartan founders. S. M.

synoecism, (*synoikismos*), in the Greek world, the combination of several smaller communities to form a single larger community. Sometimes the union was purely political and did not affect the pattern of settlement or the physical existence of the separate communities: this is what the Athenians supposed to have happened when they attributed a synoecism to *Theseus (Thuc. 2. 15), commemorated by a festival in Classical times (the Synoecia) On other occasions it involved the migration of citizens to the new city, as in the case of *Megalopolis in *Arcadia *c.*370 BC. Sometimes a union might be undone (*dioikismos*) by an enemy which resented the power of the united state: *Mantinea was

formed out of five villages, perhaps *c.*470, in what appears from the archaeological evidence to have been a purely political union; in 385 *Sparta used the Peace of Antalcidas (see KING'S PEACE) as a pretext for splitting it into separate villages once more; in 370, when Sparta was no longer strong enough to interfere, the single *polis* was recreated.

For the unions of the Hellenistic period, often made at the demand of a king, we tend to encounter the term *sympoliteia* rather than synoecism.

M. Moggi, *I sinecismi interstatali greci, 1. Dalle origini al 338 a.C.* (1976); for Athens, see Parker, *ARH*, 10 ff. V. E.; P. J. R.

Syphax (Σόφαξ in *Polybius (1)), chief of a Numidian tribe (see NUMIDIA), the Masaesylii, in north Africa, with capitals at Siga and *Cirta. He revolted from Carthage *c.*214 BC, and made an alliance with P. *Cornelius Scipio (1) and Cn. *Cornelius Scipio Calvus in Spain. He overran part of the territory of his neighbour *Masinissa and tried to retain the friendship of both Rome and Carthage, but was won over to the latter by *Sophonisba. He fought against the Roman expeditionary forces led by *Scipio Africanus, who burnt his camp. Defeated at the Great Plains (see PUNIC WARS), he fled to his kingdom where he was beaten in battle and captured. He died in imprisonment at *Tibur in Italy in 201.

J. Briscoe, *CAH* 8² (1989), 62–3; Walbank, *HCP* 2. 306; Mazard, 17 ff. (coins). See also VERMINA. H. H. S.; J. Br.

Syracuse (Συράκουσαι, mod. Siracusa), on the east coast of *Sicily, was founded by the Corinthians (see CORINTH; COLONIZATION, GREEK), led by Archias, *c.*734 BC. The original foundation lay on the island of *Ortygia, with an abundant spring and flanked by two fine natural harbours, but almost immediately, as demonstrated by the distribution of 8th-cent. pottery, the settlement spread up to a kilometre inland on the adjacent mainland (Achradina), the two were joined by an artificial causeway. Its early government was aristocratic, the *gamoroi* forming an élite whose lands were worked by underprivileged natives (*killyrioi*). Prosperity in the Archaic period is attested by colonies at Helorus, *Acrae, and *Camarina, and at Casmenae (Monte Casale), as well as by architectural remains: temples of *Apollo, Olympian *Zeus, and *Athena, and an Ionic temple (see ORDERS, ARCHITECTURAL) of unknown dedication, all belong to the 6th cent. Defeated by *Hippocrates (1), the *gamoroi* were expelled in a democratic revolution. *Gelon espoused their cause, making himself tyrant of the city, of whose empire he thus became the founder. His brother *Hieron (1) confirmed Syracusan primacy and added a cultural splendour: *Aeschylus, *Simonides, and *Pindar all spent time at his court. After the battle of *Himera (480) he rebuilt the temple of Athena, the shell of which still stands, remarkably, within the cathedral of Syracuse. The city expanded northwards from Achradina and took in areas known as Tyche and Temenites, the latter also referred to as Neapolis.

Soon after Hieron's death Syracuse regained democratic freedom but lost her empire. The democracy operated through an assembly and council (*boulē*); annual *stratēgoi* ('generals'), whose number varied, formed the chief executive. For a short time a device resembling *ostracism, called *petalismos*, sought to check abuses of power. In 412, after Athens' defeat, the democracy became more complete by the reforms of *Diocles (1), but *Dionysius (1) I soon established his tyranny, preserving nevertheless the accepted organs of the constitution.

The new democracy after 466 had difficulties with the tyrants' ex-soldiers and new citizens, and faced wars with *Acragas and with the *Sicels under *Ducetius. But these were overcome, as later were the wars with Athens (427–424 and 415–413), in which the statesmanship of *Hermocrates was influential. After 406 *Carthage was the chief enemy. Dionysius I fought four Carthaginian wars, and more than once the Syracusans were in great difficulties. But the early 4th cent. was a period of great prosperity, and it was now that the enormous girdle of *fortifications, an astonishing 27 km. (17 mi.) long, were built to include the plateau of Epipolae (to the north of the city) within the defended area. Rigorously but astutely guided by its tyrant, Syracuse now controlled the greater part of Sicily and much of southern Italy. *Dionysius (2) II enjoyed ten peaceful years before *Dion challenged his rule (356); thereafter Syracusan affairs became increasingly anarchic, and the city's power and population declined. *Timoleon restored the situation, introducing a moderately oligarchic government on the Corinthian model, but after twenty years this was overthrown by *Agathocles (1), who made himself first tyrant (317) and later king (305/4).

At Agathocles' death (289) a further period of instability ensued. A new tyrant *Hicetas (288–78) was defeated by Carthage; *Pyrrhus remedied the situation but was unable to revive the empire of Dionysius and Agathocles. After his withdrawal from the scene, conflict with the *Mamertini in Messana produced a new leader, who as *Hieron (2) II led Syracuse into a prosperous Indian summer, when the city became a significant intellectual and artistic centre. The economy prospered, with commercial contacts in both the eastern and western Mediterranean as well as with Carthage; and ambitious building projects included the great theatre (238/215 BC), one of the largest in the Greek world (diameter 138 m. (127 yards)), a grandiose Π-shaped stoa with sides 100 m. (92 yards) long above the theatre, and a gigantic altar to Zeus Eleutherius, 200 m. (184 yards) long. By now, however, Syracusan independence existed by courtesy of the Romans, and when in 215 Hieronymus, Hieron's successor, preferred Carthage to Rome, its end was at hand. After a long siege (213–211), in which *Archimedes played a substantial part, M. *Claudius Marcellus (1) sacked the city.

Under the Roman republic Syracuse became a *civitas decumana* (city liable to pay a tithe; see DECUMA) and the centre of provincial government, retaining both its beauty and a certain importance. It suffered at *Verres' hands, and in 21 BC received an Augustan *colonia*: a new public square near Hieron's altar, a monumental arch, and the amphitheatre belong to this period. Although the topography of Roman Syracuse is poorly known (a 2nd-cent. theatre-temple complex being the only other major surviving public monument), there is little doubt that Syracusan prosperity continued beyond the Frankish raid of AD 278 to its capture by the Arabs in 878. Extensive *catacombs attest its populousness in the early Christian period (3rd–7th cents.).

PECS 871–4; Gabba–Vallet, *Sicilia antica* 1. 655–93; Dunbabin, *Western Greeks, passim*; A. G. Woodhead, *Greeks in the West* (1962); M. P. Loicq-Berger, *Syracuse* (1967); H. P. Drögemüller, *Syrakus* (1969); B. D. Wescoat (ed.), *Syracuse, the Fairest Greek City* (1989). Constitution: W. Hüttl, *Verfassungsgeschichte von Syrakus* (1929). Theatre: L. Bernabò Brea, *Palladio* 1967, 97–154; L. Polacco, *Il teatro antico di Siracusa*, 2 vols. (1981, 1990); L. Polacco and others, *Il santuario di Cere e Libera ad summam Neapolim di Siracusa* (1989). Roman period: R. J. A. Wilson, *ANRW* 2. 11. 1 (1988), 111–23, and *Sicily under the Roman Empire* (1990), *passim*.
A. G. W.; R. J. A. W.

Syria

Pre-Roman This region was a satrapy ('Beyond the River', i.e.

the *Euphrates) of the Persian empire (see PERSIA) until it was conquered by *Alexander (3) the Great in 332 BC. On his death (323) it was assigned to the Macedonian Laomedon, who was in 319–18 ejected by *Ptolemy (1) I. Thereafter it was disputed between Ptolemy and *Antigonus (1). After the battle of *Ipsus (301), *Seleucus (1) I gained north Syria (from the Amanus mountains in the north to the river Eleutherus in the south), which he kept, as well as 'on paper' Coele ('Hollow') Syria (the country behind the Lebanese coastal plain) and the Phoenician cities. However, Ptolemy I was already in occupation, and claimed control, of these last two areas; Seleucus I chose to drop his rights to Coele Syria and Phoenicia, with the southern border dividing off Ptolemaic possessions set at the river Eleutherus. The whole region suffered from repeated wars between the Ptolemies (see PTOLEMY (1)) and the *Seleucids in the 3rd cent. until *Antiochus (3) III won (in campaigns, 202–198 BC) the strategically and economically important sectors of Coele Syria and the Phoenician cities, along with *Judaea and Transjordania, bringing the southern borders of Seleucid rule in this area for the first time to the Sinai desert. *Pompey annexed Seleucid Syria in 64 BC, and it became a Roman province.

The Seleucids, especially Seleucus I, as part of the physical occupation of this region and a policy of gaining control over major strategic routes, founded many colonies and cities in north Syria, including the tetrapolis of *Seleuceia (2), *Antioch (1) (one of the Seleucid royal capitals), *Apamea in the middle Orontes valley, and Laodicea-Mare (mod. Latakiye), which like Seleuceia was developed as a naval base, as well as e.g. Beroea (Aleppo), Cyrrhus, and *Zeugma.

This region had been open to Greek trade and to Greek (and other) cultural influences for centuries before Alexander. It is a moot point whether the lack of archaeological evidence from the Hellenistic period is accidental, the result mainly of the fact that the great Roman sites of north Syria obliterated almost completely the remains of the earlier Hellenistic cities; at any rate, the impact of 'Hellenism' on local cultures, under Seleucid rule, is hard to assess, quite apart from the fact that there is no reason to assume any longer that 'Hellenization' was a particular aim of the Seleucid kings (see HELLENISM, HELLENIZATION).

Roman The Roman province comprised besides the cities, a few of which were free, the client kingdoms of *Commagene and *Arabia, the ethnarchy of the Jews (*Judaea), the tetrarchy of the Ituraeans (*Ituraea), and many minor tetrarchies in the north. Antony (M. *Antonius (2)) gave to Cleopatra the Ituraean tetrarchy, the coast up to the Eleutherus (except *Tyre and *Sidon), *Damascus and Coele Syria, and parts of the Jewish and *Nabataean kingdoms.

Syria (which probably included *Cilicia Pedias from c.44 BC to AD 72) was under the Principate an important military command; its legate (see LEGATI), a consular, had down to AD 70 normally four *legions at his disposal. The client kingdoms were gradually annexed. *Commagene was finally incorporated in the province in AD 72, Ituraea partly in 24 BC, partly (*Iulius Agrippa (2) II's kingdom) c. AD 93. Judaea, at first governed by *procurators, became in AD 70 a regular province ruled by a praetorian legate, who commanded a legion withdrawn from Syria; under *Hadrian the province, henceforth usually known as Syria Palaestina, became consular, a second legion being added. The Nabataean kingdom (see NABATAEANS) became in AD 105 the province of *Arabia, ruled by a praetorian legate with one legion. *Septimius Severus divided Syria into a northern province with two legions (Syria Coele) and a southern with one legion (Syria Phoenice). Urbanization made little progress under the empire. Commagene and Arabia were on annexation partitioned into city-territories, but much of Ituraea was added to the territories of *Berytus, *Sidon, and Damascus, and in the rest the villages became the units of government. In Judaea the centralized bureaucracy established by the Ptolemies and maintained by the Seleucids, *Maccabees, and Herodians survived in some areas throughout the Principate; in others cities were founded by Vespasian, Hadrian, and the Severan emperors. Of the minor principalities some, such as Chalcis ad Belum, *Emesa, and Arca, became cities, but most seem to have been incorporated in the territories of existing towns. In late antiquity, Syria was split into four with Antioch, Apamea, Tyre, and Damascus as provincial capitals. Large and well-built villages developed up to the desert edge. Impressive remains survive. Cities, of which Apamea is best known through excavations, flourished up to the mid-6th cent. (see also SCYTHOPOLIS). Then earthquakes, plague, and Persian invasions greatly weakened the province, which easily fell to the Arabs after the battle of the Yarmuk in 636. The leading classes in city and country were Hellenized, and Greek-speaking or bilingual, but *Aramaic was widely spoken in the countryside. In the 3rd cent. in eastern Syria and Mesopotamia Aramaic developed into a literary language (Syriac), producing a literature, including translations from the Greek, but also much, mainly religious, original writing. Aramaic became the language in numerous monophysite monasteries.

Olives were produced for export in many parts, also wine. Other agricultural products were nuts, plums of Damascus, the dates of Jericho, and Ascalonite onions. The principal industries were linen-weaving (at Laodicea and in several Phoenician and north Palestinian towns), wool-weaving (at Damascus), purple-dyeing (on the Phoenician and Palestinian coast), and glass-blowing (at Sidon). The transit trade from Babylonia, Arabia Felix, and the far east passed by caravan over the Arabian desert, via such *emporia* as *Palmyra, Damascus, *Bostra or *Petra, to the coastal ports.

PRE-ROMAN H. Seyrig, *Syria* 1970, 290 f.; J. Teixidor, *The Pagan God: Popular Religion in the Ancient Near East* (1977); F. Millar, in A. Kuhrt and S. Sherwin-White (eds.), *Hellenism in the East* (1987), ch. 5; J. D. Grainger, *The Cities of Seleukid Syria* (1989); S. Sherwin-White and A. Kuhrt, *From Samarkhand to Sardis* (1993); J. M. Dentzer and W. Orthmann (eds.), *Archéologie de la Syrie* 2 (1989) (*Achaemenids to Islam).

ROMAN R. Dussaud, *Topographie historique de la Syrie antique et médiévale* (1927); F. M. Heichelheim, *An Economic Survey of Ancient Rome* 4 (1938), 120 ff.; J. Lassus, *Sanctuaires chrétiennes de la Syrie* (1944); G. B. Tchalenko, *Villages antiques de la Syrie du Nord* (1953–8), and *La Pénétration des Arabes en Syrie avant l'Islam*, 2nd edn. (1955); G. W. Bowersock, *JRS* 1973, 133 ff.; H. Kennedy, *Byz. Forsch.* 1985, 141–83; Jones, *Cities E. Rom. Prov.*[2] 227 ff.; B. Isaac, *The Limits of Empire* (1990); F. Millar, *The Roman Near East 31 B.C.–A.D. 337* (1993).

A. H. M. J.; H. S.; S. S.-W.; W. L.

Syrian deities Almost all the deities worshipped in Greek and Roman *Syria were Semitic. In spite of regional differences, a few main types of cult can be distinguished. One group comprises the cults of high places, of waters and springs, of trees and of stones, especially meteorites. Secondly, the close associations between some animals and certain anthropomorphic deities—particularly the bull, lion, horse, camel, snake, dove, and fish—may imply earlier identifications. The largest group consists of deities in human form. These are often divinities of agriculture and fertility, of the sky and thunder; they may be protectors, or bringers of military and commercial success; they may represent the sun, moon, or stars. Annual death and resurrection occur in some cults. Most characteristic of Syrian religion were the 'Lord' and 'Lady', the Ba'al and his consort the Ba'alat (or El and Elat), pairs of deities who could take many of the above-mentioned forms. Each pair originally protected a Semitic tribe; when the tribe settled, the divine pair were regarded as owning the tribal territory, and sometimes their influence spread beyond it.

Ancient Mesopotamian deities (such as Bel and Nebo) often constituted a part of the syncretistic mixture and certain religious developments reveal the continuing influence of the Babylonian astrologers, the 'Chaldaeans'. Deities were frequently grouped into triads (god, goddess, son; Bel, sun, moon, etc.). Furthermore, when the cyclical nature of the movement of the heavenly bodies was recognized, deities of the skies and stars (e.g. Ba'alshamin) became omnipotent masters of the universe and eternity, and so of the whole of human life and the after-life. Finally, in the Roman period, the Syrian deities were welded into one eternal and omnipotent power, manifest in the Sun. This trend may be regarded as 'solar henotheism'.

Worship included ritual banquets, *processions in which symbols or statues of the deity were carried, dancing, *libations, and *sacrifices, *divination, sacred prostitution (see PROSTITUTION, SACRED), and *mysteries. Imposing temples in the traditions of Syrian Hellenistic architecture still stand at *Palmyra, Baalbek, etc.; others, at Hierapolis-Bambyce, *Edessa, etc., have now disappeared.

The deities of human form are usually depicted in Hellenistic or Roman guise, although many symbols from the ancient near eastern iconographic tradition (e.g. astral signs) and occasional items of costume survive. At the same time there remain in some areas traces of an older austere aniconic theology (Nabataean and, of course, Jewish), though western influence could not be totally resisted.

Many Semitic deities received approximate Greek or Roman identifications: Bel–*Zeus, Allat–*Athena, Nergal–*Heracles, etc. The local Ba'al was often romanized as *Jupiter (Dolichenus, Heliopolitanus, Damascenus; Ba'alshamin as Jupiter Caelestis). Syrian cults were carried west especially during the Severan period, usually by soldiers, slaves, and merchants. The emperor *Elagabalus and *Aurelian attempted to establish Syrian solar cults as supreme in Rome. See ATARGATIS; ELAGABALUS (the deity); ORIENTAL CULTS AND RELIGION.

Lucian, *De dea Syria*; Philon of Byblos; Apuleius; *Corpus Inscriptionum Semiticarum*. F. Cumont, *Les Religions orientales dans le paganisme romain* (1929[4], Eng. 1911), ch. 5; M. J. Vermaseren (ed.), *Die orientalischen Religionen im Römerreich* (1981); J. Teixidor, *The Pagan God: Popular religion in the Greco-Roman Near East* (1977); J. T. Milik, *Dédicaces faites par des dieux (Palmyre, Hatra, Tyr) et des thiases sémitiques à l'époque romaine* (1972).

J. F. H.

Syrian Goddess, the See ATARGATIS.

Syrian Wars See LAODICE (2); PTOLEMY (1), various entries.

Syrianus, rhetorician and Neoplatonist philosopher (see NEOPLATONISM), who succeeded Plutarch of Athens as head of the *Academy in AD 431/2. His own pupil and successor was *Proclus, who owed much to him. Extant works are a commentary on Aristotle's *Metaphysics*, and commentaries on *Hermogenes (2)'s *Peri ideōn* (*On Types of Style*) and *Peri staseōn* (*On Issues*).

TEXTS Aristotle commentary, ed. W. Kroll, 1902; commentaries on Hermogenes, ed. H. Rabe, 1892–3. See also K. Praechter, *RE* 4 A 1728–75; R. T. Wallis, *Neoplatonism* (1972), 138 ff.; A. C. Lloyd, in A. H.

Syrinx

Armstrong (ed.), *Cambridge History of Later Greek and Early Mediaeval Philosophy* (1967), 302 ff.; G. A. Kennedy, *Greek Rhetoric under Christian Emperors* (1983), 109–12; A. D. R. Sheppard, *Studies in the 5th and 6th Essays of Proclus' Commentary on the Republic* (1980), ch. 2.   D. A. R.

Syrinx (Σῦριγξ), a nymph loved by *Pan. She ran away from him and begged the earth, or the river nymphs, to help her; she became a reed-bed, from which Pan made his pipe (σῦριγξ). See also HERMES.

Ov. *Met.* 1. 689 ff.; Longus 2. 34. Servius on Verg. *Ecl.* 2. 31.

Syros See CYCLADES.

Syrtes, the notoriously dangerous shoals and shallows (the tidal range is greater than normal in the Mediterranean) of the Libyan continental shelf of north Africa from Cyrenaica (see PENTAPOLIS) through *Tripolitania to Tunisia: the Greater Syrtis to the south-east and the Lesser off Gabés to the south-west (the myth of the *lotus-eaters was localized here on the island Meninx, Djerba). The dangers to the coasting voyage (which the difficult conditions of the land journey exacerbated) did not prevent the maritime prosperity of the Three Cities of *Sabratha, *Lepcis Magna, and *Oea, which also functioned as outlets for the semi-arid hinterland and trans-Saharan trade; and the ports of south Tunisia, such as Tacape, were of some importance.

Plin. *HN* 5. 26–41, with comm. of J. Desanges (1980).   N. P.

syssitia, the generic name for mess-companies of citizens, mentioned by the sources in various Greek cities, but especially in *Sparta and *Crete. Some scholars view them as successors of the common messes of archaic warrior clubs or 'men's houses';

others as resulting from the transformation of voluntary *symposia into compulsory public associations.

In Classical Sparta the messes (called *sysskania* or *pheiditia*), each some 15 strong, were located in separate structures by the Hyacinthian Way. Membership of a mess, obtainable only by unanimous vote of its members, was a requirement of citizenship. Each member had to supply a fixed monthly amount of produce on pain of disfranchisement; from the later 5th cent. many poor citizens defaulted, thus becoming Inferiors (*Hypomeiones*). Prestigious additional donations came from hunting or from wealthier messmates; but the prohibition of excessive drinking and eating, and the range of ages within each mess, inhibited the violent behaviour attendant upon *symposia* elsewhere. Different messes probably combined into the basic army unit, the *enōmotia*. Spartan boys had separate messes, but sometimes attended the adults' messes. A public mess housed both kings, who received double rations for sharing with honoured guests. Less austere in the early Hellenistic period, the *syssitia* were reformed into 15 messes some 200/400 strong in the late 3rd cent. BC, but abolished by *Philopoemen in 188.

The literary sources write, somewhat implausibly, of a single Cretan mess system; they may be generalizing from the system at Lyctus, the only city specifically mentioned (although messes probably also existed elsewhere). The messes described met in a single building (*andreion*) and were publicly funded from a tithe of agricultural produce and a serf poll tax. Operating under a leader who received a quadruple portion, they formed the basis of army organization. Young boys attended with their fathers, later joining the messes of their lovers.

N. R. E. Fisher, in A. Powell (ed.), *Classical Sparta* (1989), ch. 2; R. F. Willetts, *Aristocratic Society in Ancient Crete* (1955), 18–27; P. Perlman, *CPhil.* 1992, 193–205, esp. 199–201.   S. J. Ho.

tabellarii, *freedmen or slaves employed as couriers by the Roman state and by companies and private citizens of importance. To reduce costs, friends might share their services; and under the republic the couriers of the state and of the *publicani would carry private mail for important men. An eminent Roman, when abroad, would put someone in Rome in charge of forwarding (as *Caesar did when in Gaul). But for reasons of security—especially in times of trouble—it was essential to have one's own trusted letter-carriers for confidential messages. A good messenger, in the best conditions, could apparently cover 60 Roman miles or more in a day. In the Principate, the *cursus publicus* (see POSTAL SERVICE) used highly organized imperial *tabellarii*, but did not carry private mail. These *tabellarii* were of slave status and of 'sub-clerical rank' (Weaver). They had no prospect of promotion except, in rare cases, to supervisor (*optio*—indicating military organization), which went with emancipation. The imperial *tabellarii* disappear by the 3rd cent. AD, as the 'postal service' becomes militarized.

P. R. Weaver, *Familia Caesaris* (1972), 227 ff. for imperial *tabellarii*.
E. B.

tabula Bantina, fragments of a bronze tablet deriving from near *Bantia in *Lucania. One large group of fragments was discovered in the 18th cent. and a third piece in 1967. They are engraved on both sides, having on one side the Latin text of a Roman criminal statute, on the other an *Oscan text (though in Latin and written left to right) relating to a local constitution. The recently discovered fragment contains the end of both documents. A nail-hole underneath the Latin text but with the Oscan text written round it shows that the Oscan is the later of the two. See LEX (2), under Lex Osca and Lex Latina.

Lex Latina Tabulae Bantinae, the Roman criminal statute on the obverse of the tabula Bantina: it is earlier than its Oscan counterpart but from its content cannot antedate the late 2nd cent. BC. Identification is difficult as only the enforcement clauses and the oath prescribed at the end of the law are preserved. It is most commonly thought to be the *lex Appuleia maiestatis* (see APPULEIUS SATURNINUS, L.; MAIESTAS), but other attributions are possible.

Lex Osca Tabulae Bantinae, the local statute on the reverse of the tabula Bantina: the surviving chapters deal with trial before the assembly, the census and penalties for non-registration, procedures *in iure*, the *cursus honorum*, and, lastly, procedure for the imposition of fines, probably as part of an enforcement clause. It is virtually certain that the statute antedates the incorporation of Bantia into the Roman *res publica* at the end of the *Social War (3) and it may well reflect the constitution of the neighbouring Latin colony (see COLONIZATION, ROMAN) of *Venusia.
A. W. L.

tabula Hebana, a bronze tablet found (1947) in the Tiber valley near the site of ancient Heba (mod. Magliano). It bears part of the text of a *rogatio* (bill) conferring honours upon the dead *Germanicus (cf. Tac. *Ann.* 2. 73; 83; 3. 1–6). The earlier part of the same text (they overlap) was found (1982) on fragments of a bronze tablet from Siarum, near Seville, the *tabula Siarensis: both were copies of a document that authorities throughout the empire were encouraged to display. The *rogatio* takes the form of a senatorial decree incorporating an earlier decree passed on 16 December, AD 19; publication in this form suggests that its conversion into a *lex (Valeria Aurelia) by the incoming consuls was a formality. The text throws light on: the methods used to commemorate members of the imperial house; Germanicus' activities in Gaul and Germany and in the east; the role of the people in the mourning; the educational purpose of commemorations; the new electoral procedure introduced in AD 5 to honour C. *Iulius Caesar (2) and L. *Iulius Caesar (4) (*lex Valeria Cornelia*; see DESTINATIO) and now modified; the structure and functions of the equestrian order (see EQUITES); and the reliability of *Tacitus (1)'s *Annals*. Similar honours were conferred on Drusus *Iulius Caesar (1) in 23 (Tac. *Ann.* 4. 9. 2 f.).

EJ 94a (bibliog.), 94b (Drusus); J. González, *ZPE* 55 (1984), 55 ff. (Siarensis); Sherk, *Hadrian*, 36 (trans. of both).   E. S. S.; B. M. L.

tabula Irnitana, the most recently discovered and the completest copy of the Flavian *lex* for the new *municipia* (see MUNICIPIUM) of *Baetica created after the wars of AD 68–9; of ten tablets, we have 3, 5, 7–10, together with three small fragments; part of what was on 6 is preserved on one of the two substantial copies previously known, the *lex Malacitana* (the other is the *lex Salpensana*; see MALACA). The definition of the citizen body and the regulation of its religious affairs are missing, but we have much of the material on magistrates, decurions, and elections and all of that on general administration and jurisdiction.

The best text, with English trans. and comm., is J. González, *JRS* 1986, 147–243; the three small fragments are in F. Fernández Gómez and M. del Amo y de la Hera, *La Lex Irnitana y su contexto arqueologico* (1990); see also F. Lamberti, *Tabulae Irnitanae: municipalità e ius Romanorum* (1993).   M. H. C.

tabula pontificum See ANNALES MAXIMI.

tabula Siarensis Bronze tablet found in Spain in 1982; it contains part of a text conferring honours on *Germanicus. See TABULA HEBANA.

tabulae Iguvinae At Gubbio (*Iguvium; see UMBRIANS), there were discovered in 1444 seven bronze tablets of varying sizes (the largest measure 86 by 56.5 cm. (33 by 22 inches), the smallest 40 by 28 cm. (16 by 12 inches)), engraved on one or both sides with

tabulae Iliacae

Umbrian texts, partly in the native, partly in the Latin alphabet. These are the famous Iguvine Tables. They range in date probably from *c*.200 BC to the early 1st cent. BC and are the main source of our knowledge of Umbrian (see OSCAN AND UMBRIAN).

The texts contain the proceedings and liturgy of a brotherhood of priests, the *frater atiieřiur* 'Atiedian Brethren', not unlike the Roman arval brethren (see FRATRES ARVALES). The name is clearly to be linked with *atiieřiate* (dative sing.), the name of one of the family groupings (*fameřias*) within Iguvine society; it had two subdivisions, which may correspond to two *gentes* mentioned in rituals as having sacrifices performed on their behalf (*petruniaper natine, vuçiiaper natine*).

The ceremonies include the purification of the Fisian Mount (the city of Iguvium), in which sacrifice is offered to the triad Jupiter Grabovius, Mars Grabovius, and Vofionus Grabovius (cf. the Roman triad *Jupiter, *Mars, *Quirinus) before the three gates of the city to Treba Jovia/Trebus Jovius, Fisus Sancius (cf. Lat. *Dius Fidius, Sancus*), and Tefer Jovius (perhaps a god of the hearth) behind the three gates of the city; the lustration of the *poplo* of Iguvium (the military levies, the original meaning of Lat. *populus*), in which sacrifice is offered to the triad Çerfus Martius (Çerfus being etymologically connected with Lat. *Ceres*), Prestota Çerfia of Çerfus Martius, and Torsa Çerfia of Çerfus Martius (these and other double names probably mark functional or ideological connections rather than genealogical relationships), and a threefold circuit of the assembled *poplo* is made (cf. the Roman *lustratio* in which sacrifice was offered to Mars); sacrifices in the event of unfavourable auspices offered to Dicamnus Jovius, Ahtus Jupiter, and Ahtus Mars (Jupiter and Mars as oracles; cf. Lat. *Aius*); a private sacrifice of a dog on behalf of the *gens Petronia* to Hondus (cf. Greek χθόνιος, and see CHTHONIAN GODS) Jovius; sacrifices at the festival of *Semo on behalf of the *fameřias* of the Iguvine people offered to Jupiter Sancius; a procession through the fields to a grove where sacrifice is made to Jupiter, to Pomonus Poplicus, and to Vesona of Pomonus Poplicus. In scope, content, and antiquity the Iguvine Tables surpass all other documents for the study of Italic religion (see RELIGION, ITALIC) even though the interpretation of several passages remains uncertain. In many details they show resemblance to Roman ritual and cult but such analogies must be used with extreme caution, particularly since the Tables record a relatively developed stage of Iguvine religion. See LUSTRATION.

G. Devoto, *Tabulae Iguvinae*[3] (1962); J. W. Poultney, *The Bronze Tables of Iguvium* (1959); A. Prosdocimi, *Le Tavole Iguvine* 1 (1984).

J. W.; R. M. O.; J. H. W. P.

tabulae Iliacae See STESICHORUS.

tabularium (1) The record-office at Rome (see ARCHIVES (Roman)), possibly serving the adjacent *aerarium* (treasury) of Saturn and built according to *CIL* 1². 737 by Q. *Lutatius Catulus (1) in 78 BC, but not mentioned in literary sources. It is traditionally associated with the trapezoidal building lying between the two summits of the *Capitol with its main front towards the Campus Martius. On the opposite side, closing the west end of the *forum Romanum, the elevation consisted of a massive substructure of ashlar masonry with an arcade of eleven arches flanked by Doric half-columns above it. A second storey of Corinthian columns, now disappeared, was probably added in Flavian times. A stairway from the Forum climbed through the ground floor of the substructure to the front hall of the building. The first floor contained a service corridor, leading from the top of the *porticus Deorum Consentium* to two floors of eastern strong-

rooms. The arcade with shops or offices masks two inaccessible vaulted undercrofts suggestive of two large asymmetrical halls, now vanished, at the level of the upper storey.

R. Delbrueck, *Hellenistische Bauten in Latium* 1 (1907), 23 ff.; Nash, *Pict. Dict. Rome* 2. 402 ff.; Richardson, *Topog. Dict. Ancient Rome* 376 f.

(2) Other *tabularia* in Rome were the Aventine *templum Cereris*, for plebiscites and decrees of the senate; *Atrium Libertatis*, the censors' registry of punishments and citizen-rolls; *Aedes Nympharum*, the censors' tax-registry; *tabularium Caesaris*, for cadastral records; *tabularium castrense*, for the imperial household; and taxation sub-offices (*CIL* 6. 8431).

(3) Outside Rome there were: *tabularium Caesaris* in provinces for imperial rescripts, etc. (*CIL* 10. 7852); *tabularium Caesaris* in provincial capitals for tax-returns, census, imperial domain-land, birth-registration (SHA *Marc.* 6); military *tabularia* in legionary fortresses and frontier forts (*CIL* 8. 2852); *tabularia civitatum* for municipal or cantonal records and local taxation.

O. Hirschfeld, *Die kaiserlichen Verwaltungsbeamten* (1963); J. Marquardt, *Römische Staatsverwaltung*[2] 1, 2 (1881–5); Mommsen, *Ges. Schr.* (1905–13), 5. 329.

J. D.

Tacfarinas, a Numidian (see NUMIDIA), formerly an auxiliary trooper, took to brigandage and stirred up insurrection in Africa (AD 17; see AFRICA, ROMAN). Despite the victories of successive proconsuls, Furius Camillus, L. *Apronius, and Q. *Iunius Blaesus (the last of whom his troops acclaimed *imperator*), he prosecuted his depredations until trapped and killed at Auzia by P. *Cornelius Dolabella (2) (24). Dolabella's dedication to *Victoria Augusta* has been found at *Lepcis (*AE* 1960, 107).

R. Syme, *Studies in Rom. Econ. and Soc. Hist. in Honour of A. D. Johnson* (1951), 113 ff. (= *RP* 1. 218 ff.); M. Rachet, *Rome et les Berbères* (1970), index; M. Bénabou, *La Résistance africaine à la romanisation* (1975), 75 ff.

R. S.; B. M. L.

tachygraphy There is no clear evidence for the existence and use of a Greek system of shorthand before the Roman period. Two inscriptions, one from the Athenian Acropolis (*IG* 2/3². 2783; 4th cent. BC) and one in *Delphi (J. Bousquet, *BCH* 1956, 20–32; 3rd cent. BC), which have been thought to represent shorthand, are to be interpreted as experimental proposals for a system of abbreviations rather than as the kind of shorthand that would have enabled a secretary to take down a speech verbatim.

The first speech which, according to *Plutarch (*Cat. min.* 23. 3), was recorded in this way was the one delivered by M. *Porcius Cato (2) on 5 December 63 BC in which he demanded the death penalty for the Catilinarians (see SERGIUS CATILINA, L.). Plutarch adds that *Cicero had scribes specially trained for this purpose, because at that time professional shorthand scribes (σημειογράφοι) did not yet exist, as the new technique was only just beginning to develop. Its invention is ascribed to Cicero's freedman and secretary, M. *Tullius Tiro, who seems to have devised a system of signs (*notae*, σημεῖα) for prepositions and other short words. The next step was the invention of signs for endings (*declinationes*). These *notae Tironianae*, widely used in the imperial administration and later by the Church, were later, from the 3rd or 4th cent. onwards, modified into a system of syllabic shorthand. *Martial mentions both the shorthand scribe (*notarius*, 14. 208) and the shorthand teacher (10. 62. 4).

Evidence for Greek shorthand comes from papyri and wax tablets found in Egypt. *POxy.* 4. 724 (AD 155) is an apprenticeship contract with a shorthand teacher. From the 2nd cent. AD onwards, specimens of Greek shorthand and portions of manuals survive in large numbers. These show a fully organized system, composed of a syllabary and a (so-called) Commentary

($\kappa o\mu\epsilon\nu\tau\acute{a}\rho\iota o\nu$), consisting of groups of words, arranged in fours or occasionally eights, with a sign attached to each, which had to be memorized. The tetrads include some element of association (e.g. one sign represents $\Gamma\alpha\nu\upsilon\mu\acute{\eta}\delta\eta s$, $o\emph{i}\nu o\chi o\epsilon\emph{i}$; $\nu\acute{\epsilon}\kappa\tau\alpha\rho$, $\mu\iota\xi o\beta\acute{a}\rho\beta\alpha\rho o s$: Ganymede, pours, nectar, the half-barbarian), but more often it is not discernible. In the ancient systems of shorthand, as in the modern, one sign may have several interpretations, and in order to interpret shorthand records it is necessary to have a clue to the subject, and (often) to remember something of what was said. Thus stock phrases such as $\mathring{\omega}$ $\overset{\prime}{a}\nu\delta\rho\epsilon s$ $A\theta\eta\nu a\hat{\iota}o\iota$ or $\tau\acute{\iota}$ $\delta\epsilon\iota\tilde{\ }$ $\mu\alpha\kappa\rho o\lambda o\gamma\epsilon\hat{\iota}\nu$ ('O men of Athens'; 'Why should I use many words?') were represented by single signs. Greek shorthand texts from Egypt are listed in R. A. Pack, *The Greek and Latin Literary Texts from Greco-Roman Egypt*[2] (1965), nos. 2753–79, and in the introd. to *PYale* 2. 129; *PColon.* 7. 294–6.

H. J. M. Milne, *Greek Shorthand Manuals* (1934); A. Mentz, *Arch. Pap.* 1926, 34–59; H. Boge, *Griechische Tachygraphie und Tironische Noten: Ein Handbuch der antiken und mittelalterlichen Schnellschrift* (1973, with bibliog.). H. Ma.

Tacitus (1), Roman historian.

1. P.(?) Cornelius Tacitus was born *c.* AD 56, probably in Narbonese or Cisalpine Gaul (see GAUL (TRANSALPINE) and GAUL (CISALPINE)). He was in Rome at latest by 75, where an uninterrupted career under *Vespasian, *Titus, and *Domitian (*Hist.* 1. 1. 3) brought him to the praetorship in 88, by which time he was also a member of the prestigious priesthood, the college of the *Quindecimviri sacris faciundis. During 89–93 he was absent from Rome (*Agr.* 45. 5), presumably holding government posts. In 97 he was suffect consul and pronounced the funeral oration upon L. *Verginius Rufus. We know of no other office held by Tacitus, till seniority brought him the proconsulship of Asia (see ASIA, ROMAN PROVINCE; PRO CONSULE) for 112–13 (*IMylasa* 365, with W. Eck, *ZPE* 45 (1982), 139–53). The date of his death is unknown, but can scarcely have been before 118 (see below).

2. Early in 98 Tacitus published his first work, the *Agricola* (*De vita Iulii Agricolae*), a biography of his father-in-law Cn. *Iulius Agricola, governor of *Britain for seven years from 77 (or 78). That governorship, culminating in the decisive victory of mons Graupius, forms the work's central core (chs. 18–38). But the work is more than a panegyric of a dead man. The opening chapters, without naming Domitian, declare that recent times were hostile both to the performance and to the chronicling of great deeds. The final chapters develop that theme: a fierce *invective against Domitian is followed by a moving *consolatio* (see CONSOLATION) for the dead Agricola; and the final words, again linking subject and biographer, affirm that Agricola will live on through Tacitus' biography.

Later in the same year came the *Germania* (*De origine et situ Germanorum*). In its first half (to 27. 1), after arguing briefly that the *Germans are indigenous and racially pure, Tacitus describes their public and private life. Comparisons, implicit and explicit, between Germans and contemporary Roman society abound, not always to the advantage of the latter. However, the *Germania* is not to be seen as a mirror of morals (or, as some have argued, a historical excursus): its second half, devoted entirely to describing individual tribes, confirms that it is an ethnographical monograph, in which (naturally enough) a foreign people is viewed through Roman eyes.

The third of Tacitus' *opera minora*, the *Dialogus* (*Dialogus de oratoribus*), was perhaps written *c.*101/2; the belief that its neo-Ciceronian style (see TULLIUS CICERO (1), M.) indicates an early,

pre-Domitianic, date has now been discarded. It is an urbane and good-natured discussion about the causes of the contemporary decline in oratory; following the fiction of Cicero's *De oratore*, Tacitus affects to recall a discussion he heard as a young man in 75. Of its three speakers Marcus *Aper champions modern oratory, while *Vipstanus Messalla affirms that the decline can be remedied by a return to old-fashioned morals and education. *Curiatius Maternus, in whose house the discussion takes place, ascribes the decline to political changes: in the late republic oratory had flourished amid virtual anarchy; now, under a benevolent and all-wise ruler, great oratory was no longer needed. While that may come closest to Tacitus' own view, it is simplistic to equate Maternus with Tacitus. Ambivalences attach to the opinions of all three speakers, and Tacitus characteristically leaves readers to elicit their own answers.

3. By about 105–6 Tacitus was collecting material for a historical work, almost certainly the *Histories* (Plin. *Ep.* 6. 16 and 20); the date of its completion is unknown, but may be *c.*109–10. When complete it comprised twelve or fourteen books, covering the years 69–96; only the first four and a quarter books survive, bringing the narrative to 70.

The subject-matter of bks. 1–3, dealing with the civil wars between *Galba, *Otho, A. *Vitellius, and Vespasian, is predominantly military, and it is for his handling of this material that Mommsen called Tacitus 'most unmilitary of writers'. It is true that the reader is repeatedly puzzled or irritated by the absence of information on chronology, topography, strategy, and logistics. But Tacitus did not write according to the canons of modern historiography. His aim is to provide a narrative that will hold the reader's attention. By that standard chs. 12–49 of bk. 1 (perhaps matched by the graphic description of the night battle of Cremona and the storming and sacking of the city in 3. 19–34) present a sustained narrative of unsurpassed pace and brilliance. From the moment when a handful of soldiers proclaim Otho emperor (27. 2) till Tacitus delivers his obituary over the murdered Galba (49. 4 'omnium consensu capax imperii, nisi imperasset': 'by universal consent fitted to rule—had he not ruled') the ebb and flow of fortune and emotion are portrayed with masterly skill.

The loss of the later books is particularly frustrating, since they deal with a time when Tacitus was himself close to the centre of political activity. From what survives we can surmise that he was no less hostile to Domitian than he had been in the *Agricola*, and that the senate, despite loud professions of independence, was quick to back down when faced by imperial opposition (4. 44. 1). And though Vespasian alone of emperors is said to have changed for the better (1. 50. 4), it is unlikely that Tacitus thought his reign without blemish.

4. At the beginning of the *Histories* (1. 1. 4) Tacitus had spoken of going on to write of *Nerva and *Trajan. In the event he chose to go back to the Julio-Claudian dynasty from the accession of *Tiberius. The *Annals* (more exactly *Ab excessu divi Augusti*; the titles *Historiae* and *Annales* date only from the 16th cent.) originally consisted of eighteen (or sixteen) books—six for Tiberius, six for Gaius and Claudius, six (or four) for Nero. Of these there are lost most of 5, all of 7–10, the first half of 11, and everything after the middle of 16. Whether Tacitus completed the *Annals* is not known; nor do we know the date of composition, though two passages (2. 56. 1 and 4. 5. 2) seem datable to 114 and 115 respectively. That would suggest that the last books can scarcely have been written before the early years of *Hadrian's reign, perhaps *c.*120.

Tacitus

The six books of Tiberius' reign are structured as two triads. The dichotomy, marked by the striking opening of bk. 4, emphasizes that the reign took a decisive turn for the worse in AD 23 with the rise to power of the ambitious L. *Aelius Seianus. But even the excellence of the earlier years is attributed to Tiberius' concealment (*dissimulatio*) of his true character. Whether that explanation, which does not originate with Tacitus, is consistent with Tacitus' claim to write impartially (*Ann.* 1. 1. 3 'sine ira et studio') is open to question; but it is skilfully used to probe the ambiguities of Tiberius' behaviour, as the emperor sought to combine a *de facto* autocracy with a show of constitutional republicanism.

For *Claudius, Tacitus accepted the traditional picture of an emperor dominated by his wives and freedmen and gave great (perhaps excessive) prominence to the sexual scandals of *Valeria Messallina and the dynastic scheming of *Iulia Agrippina. But in much of his dealings with the senate Claudius emerges as a pedantically thoughtful personality, e.g. 11. 13 and 24 (in the latter case uniquely we can compare Tacitus' version with the speech that Claudius actually delivered (*ILS* 212)).

*Nero's portrait also is simple: an initial quinquennium of mostly good government ends with the murder of Agrippina in 59, which frees Nero to follow his own desires (14. 13. 2). His extravagance, sexual depravity, and un-Roman innovations are depicted with verve and disapproval. Tacitus also pillories the servility of a senate that congratulates Nero when his mother is murdered (14. 12; cf. 59. 4 and 16. 16), while *Thrasea Paetus' attempts to uphold senatorial independence (13. 49; 14. 12, 48–9; 15. 20 and 23) lead only to his condemnation.

If political debate is less sharp in the Neronian books, foreign affairs and Nero's flamboyant behaviour fully extend Tacitus' descriptive powers. Their impact is strengthened by the organization of incidents into larger continuous units, a structural feature first observable in the Claudian books (so Messalina's final excesses in 11. 26–38 and the account of British affairs, covering several years, in 12. 31–40); similarly, in the Neronian books: British affairs in 14. 29–39 and the annual accounts of Cn. *Domitius Corbulo's eastern campaigns, and (at home) Agrippina's murder (14. 1–13), the Great Fire of Rome and its aftermath (15. 38–45), and the Pisonian conspiracy (15. 48–74); see CALPURNIUS PISO (2), C.

5. Though none of the sources used by Tacitus has survived, many scholars from Mommsen onwards have held that for continuous sections of his narrative Tacitus followed an unnamed single source; *Cluvius Rufus, *Pliny (1) the Elder, *Aufidius Bassus, and *Fabius Rusticus are among the names that have been suggested. Close and sustained similarities between Tacitus and *Plutarch for the reigns of Galba and Otho make the theory plausible for the period of the civil war, but it is unlikely that Tacitus restricted himself to a single source thereafter, since already at *Hist.* 2. 101 he expresses scepticism of pro-Flavian accounts. For the *Annals*, especially from bk. 6, similarities between Tacitus, *Suetonius, and *Cassius Dio suggest frequent, though not continuous, use of a common source (see also Tacitus' own statement at 13. 20. 2). However, it is probable that Tacitus proceeded differently with different types of material. For senatorial business the *acta senatus* (see ACTA) would provide a starting-point, but no more; their bureaucratic language and official version of events would be repugnant to Tacitus. For the private life of the emperor and his family the more lurid and sensational items could be published only after his death, when different versions would multiply (see *Ann.* 14. 2. 1–2 for Agrip-

pina, and *Hist.* 1. 13 and *Ann.* 13. 45 for *Poppaea Sabina). For military matters formal reports in the *acta senatus* could be supplemented from elsewhere (e.g. the Elder Pliny's twenty volumes on wars in Germany or Cn. Domitius Corbulo's memoirs of his eastern campaigns). But convention also allowed the ancient historian licence to elaborate or invent incidents to make his narrative more colourful and exciting (cf. *Ann.* 4. 46–51 with Caesar, *BGall.* 7. 69 ff. and Sallust, *H.* 2. 87). Yet, whatever the source, the resulting narrative is, by selection, arrangement, and interpretation, wholly Tacitean.

6. Though regret for the lost freedoms of the republic is evident throughout Tacitus, he accepted the necessity of the rule of one man (*Hist.* 1. 1. 1; *Ann.* 4. 33. 2) and praised those few who served the state honourably but without servility (*Ann.* 4. 20. 3; cf. *Agr.* 42. 4). Yet pessimism and hints of a darker underlying reality are ever-present: motives are rarely simple; innuendo often suggests that the less creditable explanation is the more probable; and an awareness of the gulf in political life between what was professed and what was practised informs all his writing and finds fitting expression in a unique prose style.

7. Tacitus' style is marked by a fastidious and continuous avoidance of the trite and hackneyed. Elevation is lent to his language by archaic and poetic words and an admixture of neologisms, while his extensive use of *metaphor more closely resembles poetic than prose usage. In much of this he follows *Sallust, at times even echoing whole passages: so at *Ann.* 4. 1. 3 his portrait of Sejanus recalls (but modifies) Sallust's picture of Catiline at *Cat.* 5 (see SERGIUS CATILINA, L.). But to Sallust's renowned brevity Tacitus adds a greater compression of thought. The sinewy strength of his language is reinforced by a deliberate rejection of balance (*concinnitas*) in favour of syntactical disruption (*variatio*), a device he uses with special effectiveness to underline alternative motives. The same aim is served by a peculiarly Tacitean type of sentence construction in which the main syntactical statement stands at or near the beginning, and then has appended to it (by various syntactical means, of which the ablative absolute is one of the most common) comments that suggest motives or record men's reactions (for extended examples cf. *Ann.* 3. 3. 1 and 14. 49. 3). This type of sentence allows Tacitus to concentrate, often with sardonic comment, on the underlying psychology of men's actions and is tellingly employed in his portrait of Tiberius.

8. The surviving texts of Tacitus' works reached the age of printing by three tenuous threads. A Carolingian manuscript of the minor works came from Hersfeld in Germany to Rome *c.*1455, but disappeared after numerous 15th-cent. copies had been made; whether the 9th-cent. quire of the *Agricola* that survived till the 1940s was part of that manuscript is uncertain. *Annals* 1–6 depend on a single manuscript, the first Medicean, written in Germany (possibly Fulda) *c.*850, and now in the Laurentian Library in Florence. *Annals* 11–16 and *Histories* 1–5 (numbered consecutively as bks. 11–21) also depend on a single manuscript, the second Medicean, written in a Beneventan script in the 11th cent.; modern attempts to show that any 15th-cent. manuscript is independent of the second Medicean seem unfounded.

GENERAL R. Syme, *Tacitus*, 2 vols. (1958), *Ten Studies in Tacitus* (1970), *Roman Papers* (see indexes, 'Tacitus'), 7 vols. (1979–91); E. Paratore, *Tacito*² (1962); S. Borzsák, *RE* Suppl. 11 (1968), 395, 'Cornelius'; T. A. Dorey (ed.), *Tacitus* (1968); M. Fuhrmann, *Kl. Pauly* (1975), 'Tacitus'; F. R. D. Goodyear, *Tacitus, G&R* New Surveys 4 (1979²); R. (H.) Martin, *Tacitus*² (1989); R. Mellor, *Tacitus* (1993); R. Häussler,

Tacitus und das historische Bewusstsein (1965); D. Flach, *Tacitus in der Tradition der antiken Geschichtsschreibung* (1973); G. Wille, *Der Aufbau der Werke des Tacitus* (1983); T. J. Luce and A. J. Woodman (eds.), *Tacitus and the Tacitean Tradition* (1993); C. Questa, *Studi sulle fonti degli Annales*[2] (1963); B. Walker, *The Annals of Tacitus*[3] (1968); J. Ginsburg, *Tradition and Theme in the Annals of Tacitus* (1981); H. Jankuhn and D. Timpe (eds.), *Beiträge zum Verständnis der Germania des Tacitus* (1989); ANRW vols. 2. 33. 2, 33. 3, 33. 4 (1990–1).

TEXTS *Agr., Germ., Dial.* Winterbottom and Ogilvie (OCT, 1975); Delz, Önnerfors, Heubner, 3 vols. (Teubner, 1983). *Hist.* Fisher (OCT, 1911); Giarratano (Rome, 1939); Heubner (Teubner (Stuttgart), 1975); Wellesley (Teubner (Leipzig) 1989). *Ann.* Fisher (OCT, 1906); Heubner (Teubner (Stuttgart), 1983); Borzsák (bks. 1–6: Teubner (Leipzig), 1992); Wellesley (bks. 11–16: Teubner (Leipzig), 1986).

COMMENTARIES (* = no Latin text). *Agr.* Ogilvie and Richmond (1967). *Germ.* Anderson (1938); Much–Jankuhn–Lange[3] (1967); Lund (1988). *Dial.* Gudeman[2] (1914); Güngerich* (1980). *Hist.* Heubner*, 5 vols. (1963–82); Chilver* (bks. 1–2, 1979); Wellesley (bk. 3, 1972); Chilver–Townend* (bks. 4–5, 1985). *Ann.* Furneaux (bks. 1–6, 1896; bks. 11–16, rev. Fisher, 1907); Koestermann*, 4 vols. (1963–8); Goodyear (bks. 1–2, 1972, 1981); Woodman and Martin (bk. 3, 1996); Martin and Woodman (bk. 4, 1989).

TRANSLATIONS Church and Brodribb, 3 vols. (numerous reprints from 1864); *Agr., Germ., Dial.* Hutton and Peterson (rev. Ogilvie, Warmington, Winterbottom, Loeb, 1970). *Hist.* and *Ann.* Moore, Jackson, 4 vols. (Loeb, 1931–7). *Hist.* Ramsay (1915); Wellesley[2] (Penguin, 1975). *Ann.* Ramsay (1904); Grant[2] (Penguin, 1971); Wuilleumier, 4 vols. (Budé, 1974–8).

STYLE N. Eriksson, *Studien zu den Annalen des Tacitus* (1934); G. Sörbom, *Variatio sermonis Taciti ...* (1935); F. Kuntz, *Die Sprache des Tacitus ...* (1962); F. R. D. Goodyear, 'Development of Language and Style in the *Annals* of Tacitus', JRS 1968; J. N. Adams, 'The Language of the Later Books of Tacitus' *Annals*', CQ 1972, and 'The Vocabulary of the Speeches ...', BICS 1973.

LEXICA Gerber–Greef, *Lexicon Taciteum* (1877–90); Blackman–Betts, *Concordantia Tacitea* (1986).

BIBLIOGRAPHICAL SURVEYS ANRW 2. 33. 2 (Suerbaum, esp. 1049; Benario, esp. 1478); 2. 33. 3 (Murison, esp. 1688 n. 4). There are ongoing surveys in AAHG (latest, Römer 1984 and 1985) and CW (Benario, latest 1995).

MANUSCRIPTS Tarrant (*Ann.* and *Hist.*) and Winterbottom (minor works) in *Texts and Transmission*, ed. L. D. Reynolds (1983); F. Römer in ANRW 2. 33. 3 (1991).   R. H. M.

Tacitus (2) (*RE* 361) **Marcus Claudius,** an elderly senator, chosen to succeed *Aurelian late in AD 275. He soon moved east, and defeated the *Goths who had invaded *Pontus, but in mid-276 he was killed by his own troops at Tyana.

Tacitus made no attempt to restore senatorial authority in the face of the military: he may have been a veteran himself. The initial confusion of his reign, its brevity and its violent end, indicate continuing instability in the Roman empire, even after the reforms of Aurelian. (*PLRE* 1. 873.)

R. Syme, *Emperors and Biography* (1971), 237 ff.   J. F. Dr.

Taenarum (Ταίναρον, more rarely Ταίναρος) (1) The central peninsula of the south *Peloponnesus (mod. Mani) and its terminal cape, near which stood a temple of *Poseidon of which scanty traces remain, recently restudied. Through a cave nearby, *Heracles traditionally dragged up *Cerberus from *Hades. The sanctuary enjoyed a right of asylum (cf. Thuc. 1. 133; see ASYLIA), and private slaves were manumitted there (IG 5. 1. 1228 ff.). In the later 4th cent. the district was an important headquarters for *mercenaries. It contained *quarries of red (*rosso antico*) and black ('Taenarian') *marble; and iron was mined near the cape.

R. Baladié, *Le Péloponnèse de Strabon* (1980), 207–9, 247–8. L. and T. Moschou, *Peloponnesiaka* 1978–9, 72–114 (sanctuary).

(2) A city on the west coast of the above peninsula, later a member of the Eleutherolaconian League (see LACONIA), alternatively known as Caenepolis. Roman and Byzantine remains survive.   A. M. W.; W. G. F.; A. J. S. S.

Tages, a figure of *Etruscan mythology, an example of *puer senex*, 'aged child', childlike in appearance but of divine wisdom. He sprang out during ploughing from a furrow near *Tarquinii, and revealed (to *Tarchon or to the twelve *lucumones*—Etruscan priests) the art of Etruscan *disciplina*, i.e. *divination, especially haruspicy (the books of Tages, *libri Tagetici*), and immediately died. See HARUSPICES; RELIGION, ETRUSCAN; TARQUITIUS PRISCUS (all on Etruscan *disciplina*).

A. S. Pease on Cic. *Div.* 2. 50; S. Weinstock, *PBSR* 1950, 44 ff.; E. Zwierlein-Diehl, in *Tainia R. Hampe* (1978), 421 ff.; J. R. Wood, *Latomus* 1980, 325 ff.   J. L.

tagos (ταγός), considered the official title of the supreme civil and military magistrate of the Thessalians (see THESSALY) since E. Meyer, who tried to establish a list of these alleged leaders in the 6th and 5th cents. BC. But this sense is attested once only, in *Xenophon (1), for *Jason (2) of Pherae when he mobilized the Thessalians in order to extend his domination of the region and prop up his foreign policy. All other texts present these chiefs as ἀρχός, ἄρχων, or τέτραρχος (archos, archōn, or tetrarchos); as distinct from the title *basileus*, used by the aristocratic families, e.g. the *Aleuadae. Contrary to the traditional view, two inscriptions from the late 6th and the 5th cents. BC set the tagoi among other civic magistrates: here they are not eponymous, and their duties concern mobilization and the military function of the citizens; their activities belong to wartime. Etymology suggests that the tagoi were responsible for the taxeis, 'companies', the smaller units within the *phalanx. As such they were always in charge of mobilized citizens.

The evolution of the art of *war and the opening up of office to the mass of citizens enhanced the role of the tagoi in the Thessalian federal army (*Jason (2) assumed this title on reforming the army and increasing its efficacy) and in the cities. The tagoi, becoming (probably from c.300 BC) the chief civic magistrates, lasted as long as the cities—to the close of the imperial period.

E. Meyer, *Theopomps Hellenika* (1909); M. Sordi, *La lega tessala* (1958); B. Helly, *L'état thessalien, Aleuas le Roux, les tétrades et les tagoi* (1995).   B. H.

talents See WEIGHTS.

Talmud The greatest achievement of rabbinic Judaism in late antiquity, the Talmuds are compendia of legal opinions, sayings, and stories by and about the *rabbis of the first five centuries of the Christian era. Two quite separate Talmuds are extant: the Palestinian (or Jerusalem) Talmud, redacted in Palestine in *c.* AD 400, and the Babylonian Talmud, redacted in Mesopotamia in *c.* AD 500. Both Talmuds are organized as commentaries on the *Mishnah, tractate by tractate; for some tractates a commentary is found only in the Babylonian Talmud. The commentary (termed *gemarah*, lit. 'completion') attempts harmonization of conflicting views expressed in the Mishnah, and elucidation of obscure passages, in order to produce a complete, unified account of Jewish law. In the process the editors included much extra material of only tangential relevance to the Mishnaic passage under discussion. This extra material consists partly in homiletic narratives about rabbis, partly in independent literary units containing disputes over legal interpretation, partly (but less frequently) in *midrash of biblical texts.

Talos

The Mishnaic text quoted within each Talmud is in Hebrew, as are some sayings (*beraitot*) composed, or purporting to have been composed, by rabbis before the compilation of the Mishnah (i.e. in the 1st and 2nd cents. AD). The rest of both Talmuds is in *Aramaic, expressed in a style so elliptic and formulaic that the meaning of many passages is only apparent with the help of the medieval commentaries traditionally used by Jews engaged in study of the Talmud. The obscurantism of Talmudic discourse appears to be deliberate, reflecting the origin of the text in scholarly discussions within rabbinic academies, where both the main premisses of the subject debated, and the types of argument permitted on either side, were taken for granted.

The Talmuds deal with civil, criminal, and matrimonial law as well as more strictly religious matters. They have less discussion about the sacrificial rites in the *Jerusalem Temple than does the Mishnah; conversely, they contain more information about the operation of rabbinic academies. The Babylonian Talmud quotes the views of many Palestinian scholars, and vice versa, but the two compilations do in general reflect differences in outlook between the two centres of rabbinic learning. It is also sometimes possible to discern the distinct views of particular rabbinic schools or groups.

The rabbis quoted in the *gemarah* date from the 3rd to 4th cent. (Palestinian Talmud) or the 3rd to 5th cent. (Babylonian Talmud), but the extent to which their sayings are correctly reported is debated. Medieval traditions ascribing the editing of the Talmuds to particular rabbis are worth little, but some scholars have perceived evidence of a strong editorial hand in the statements transmitted anonymously as a commentary on the discussions recorded (the *stam*) and in the shaping of individual tractates. It is certain that some sayings were wrongly attributed to particular rabbis on the principle that, in the light of his other views as recorded elsewhere, this is what that rabbi would have said if he had given an opinion.

The prolonged interest by Jews in the Babylonian Talmud as an authoritative legal source has ensured that this huge document from late antiquity survives more or less intact, but there are numerous references by medieval commentators to textual variants no longer attested in the extant manuscripts, and the argumentative style of the Talmud, with the preservation of divergent views on many topics and a tendency to pseudepigraphy, makes its use as a source for the history of *Jews and Judaism complex. See RELIGION, JEWISH.

> PALESTINIAN TALMUD Text: Venice edn. (1523–4); Krotoschin edn. (1866; the version most often cited); Zhitomir edn. (1860–7); Romm Wilna (1922). Eng. trans.: J. Neusner, *The Talmud of the Land of Israel* (1982–). Concordance: M. Kosovsky (1979–).
>
> BABYLONIAN TALMUD Text: Bomberg edn. (1520–3); Vilna edn. (1880–6); Steinsalz edn. (1967–) (vocalized). Eng. trans.: I. Epstein (ed.), *The Babylonian Talmud* (1935–52); J. Neusner (ed.), *The Talmud of Babylonia: An American Translation* (1984–). Concordance: H. J. and B. Kassovsky, *Thesaurus Talmudis* (1954–82).
>
> DISCUSSIONS H. L. Strack and G. Stemberger, *Introduction to the Talmud and Midrash* (Eng. trans., 1991), 182–244 (with bibliog.); German 8th edn., Stemberger, *Einleitung* (1992), 167–223.   M. D. G.

Talos (*Τάλως*) (1) An animated bronze man, in the usual account made by *Hephaestus to guard *Europa; later the guardian of *Crete. There are several variant accounts of his origin and function. He kept strangers off by throwing stones (Ap. Rhod. 4. 1638–88), or burned them (Simonides, in Page, *PMG* 568), or heated himself red-hot and clasped them in his arms (Eust. *Od.* 20. 302). His vital fluid was kept in a magic membrane in his foot; *Medea cast him into a magic sleep and cut the membrane, thus killing him.

(2) Nephew of *Daedalus, sometimes called Kalos or Perdix (the latter is also given as his mother's name). Daedalus was jealous of his inventive talent and so killed him. According to *Apollodorus (6) (3. 15. 8), his invention was to make a saw from a snake's jaw-bone.

> M. Delcourt, *Hephaistos ou la légende du magicien* (1957), 159–62; M. Dickie, *Papers of the Leeds International Latin Seminar* (1990), 267 ff.; *LIMC* 7. 1 (1994), 834–7.   E. Ke.

Talthybius, *Agamemnon's herald (*Il.* 1. 320). For some reason his name remains familiar in later writings, while his comrade Eurybates is forgotten. He was the *eponym of a herald-clan at *Sparta, the Talthybiadae (see Hdt. 7. 134. 1). See SPARTAN CULTS.
                                                    S. H.

tamiai (*ταμίαι*) means 'treasurers'. In Athens the most important officials with this title were the treasurers of Athena. They were ten in number, appointed annually by lot, one from each of the ten *phylai. According to a law attributed to *Solon only *pentakosiomedimnoi* were eligible, but by the 4th cent. BC this rule was no longer enforced. They had charge of the money and treasures of Athena on the Acropolis. They kept the money in a building called *opisthodomos* (the location of which is doubtful), and they received and made payments in accordance with the decisions of the people. They paid out money not only for religious purposes but also for military use, especially during the *Peloponnesian War, and to defray other secular expenses. Many of their records are preserved on stone and are an important source of information about Athenian finance.

In 434 a similar board of ten treasurers of 'the other gods' was instituted to take charge of money and treasures belonging to other Attic shrines, which were now brought together into a single fund. It also was kept in the *opisthodomos*, but separately from the money of Athena. In 406 the two boards were replaced by a single board of ten treasurers of Athena and the other gods. The two separate boards were re-established in 385, but by 341 they were again replaced by a single board.

After the abolition of the *kōlakretai and the *Hellenotamiai other treasurers were instituted to take charge of various funds: the treasurer of the people (*ταμίας τοῦ δήμου*), the treasurer of military funds (*ταμίας στρατιωτικῶν*), and so on.

> W. S. Ferguson, *The Treasurers of Athena* (1932).   D. M. M.

Tanagra, in *Boeotia, city dominating the eastern part of the Asopus plain, *Homer's *Graia* by the sea. *Herodotus (1) (5. 55–61) states that the earliest inhabitants were the *Gephyraioi*, who entered Boeotia from *Eretria. He equated them with the Phoenician followers of *Cadmus, whom the Boeotians later expelled. The Tanagrans refused to join the expedition to Troy. The most famous literary figure from Tanagra was the poetess *Corinna, who legend avers had won a victory over *Pindar at *Thebes (1). The scanty remains of Tanagra include the circuit-wall and foundations of a few buildings within it. In art it is best known for its numerous, beautiful *terracotta figurines.

In 457 BC Tanagra was the scene of a major Spartan and Boeotian victory over Athens. Months later Athens defeated the Boeotians at nearby Oenophyta, and overran Boeotia and Locris. After Tolmides' defeat at *Coronea in 447 BC, Tanagra rejoined the new Boeotian Confederacy, in which it held one vote (see FEDERAL STATES). It participated in the defeat of Athens at *Delion in 424, but suffered from the depredations of *Agesilaus in 378 and 377. None the less, it flourished during the Hellenistic and Roman periods.

P. W. Wallace, *Strabo's Description of Greece* (1979); D. Roller, *Boeotia Antiqua* 1 (1989), 129 ff. J. Bu.

Tanaïs, the river Don and a city at its estuary, at the modern village of Nedvigovka. The river was usually taken to be the boundary between Europe and Asia (but see PHASIS). The river offered access deep into the hinterland towards the Volga basin, though the Graeco-Roman world seems to have had only the most imprecise notion of its geography.

Tanaïs was established *c.*300 BC, apparently taking over from the earlier Greek presence (from *c.*500 BC) in the Don delta at Elizavetovskoye. *Strabo describes lively trade at Tanaïs, confirmed archaeologically from the 3rd cent. BC onwards, Rhodian *amphorae (see RHODES) being particularly commonplace. The lack of coin-finds before the 1st cent. BC may indicate that barter was the norm there. Archaeology also shows agriculture, herding, fishing, and fish-salting at Tanais, not simply trade.

Epigraphy shows its population divided between Greeks and Tanaites by the early centuries AD, which may explain the division of the city into two sectors, divided by substantial walls, in the Hellenistic period, destroyed in the sack of *Polemon (1) I. Thereafter, it was controlled by the Bosporan kings (see BOSPORUS (2)) until its end by AD 450.

D. B. Shelov, *Tanais i Nizhniy Don v III–I vv. do n.e.* (1972); Y. Garlan, *DHA* 1982, 145–52; G. A. Koshelenko, I. T. Kruglikova, V. S. Dolgorukov (eds.), *Antichnye gosudarstva Severnovo Prichernomor'ya* (1984), 93–5. D. C. B.

Tanaquil was wife of *Tarquinius Priscus. In Livy (1. 34) she fosters Priscus' ambition, encourages his emigration to Rome, and interprets an eagle omen as portending his future kingship. She subsequently similarly explains a fire portent concerning Servius *Tullius (and in other accounts the previous appearance of a *phallus that led to Servius' birth) and engineers Servius' succession after Priscus' assassination. Tanaquil's role in the Tarquin dynasty and her prophetic powers probably belong to the earliest Roman literary accounts (cf. Q. *Fabius Pictor fr. 11b Peter; Enn. *Ann.* 145–6 Skutsch), but only *Livy develops her as a masterful political figure; other traditions apparently stressed her domestic rectitude (cf. Enn. *Ann.* 147 Skutsch; Plin. *HN* 8. 194; Paul. *Fest.* 85 Lindsay). That she originated as a human double of *Fortuna is unsubstantiated speculation, and though her name is *Etruscan, her portrayal probably reflects Greek literary models and Roman male preoccupations rather than an enhanced role for women in Etruscan society.

Ogilvie, *Comm. Livy 1–5,* 140 ff.; P. M. Martin, *Latomus* 1985, 5 ff.; F. Coarelli, *Il foro boario* (1988), 313 ff. A. D.

Tantalus, legendary king of Sipylus on the borders of *Phrygia and *Lydia, son of *Zeus and father of *Pelops and *Niobe; like other Asian rulers (*Midas (1), *Croesus) he was proverbial for his wealth, as the phrase τὰ Ταντάλου τάλαντα ('the talents of Tantalus') (Anac. fr. 355) shows. Along with *Lycaon (3), *Tityus, *Ixion, and *Sisyphus he belongs to the group of archetypal violators of the laws laid down by Zeus for the conduct of human society, criminals whose exemplary punishment stands as a moral landmark for posterity. His offence was to abuse the great privilege he enjoyed, as one of the first generation of mortals, in being allowed to dine with the gods. Either he blabbed about the divine policy discussions he had overheard; or he stole and distributed to mortals the nectar and *ambrosia served at the feast (Pind. *Ol.*

1); or, most commonly, he tested the gods by killing and cooking his son Pelops to see whether they would detect the forbidden food. Only *Demeter, distracted by sorrow for her missing daughter, ate a piece of shoulder from the stew; this meant that when the child was reconstituted and brought back to life an ivory prosthesis was necessary. Tantalus suffers eternal and condign punishment, 'tantalized' by having to stand in a pool which drains away when he tries to drink, with fruit dangling before his eyes which are whisked away as soon as he reaches for them (*Od.* 11. 583 ff.); other authors, including Pindar (*Ol.* 1), describe a rock teetering overhead, adding terror to the pains of hunger.

E. Simon, *JDAI* 1967, 275–95; C. Sourvinou-Inwood, *BICS* 1986, 37–58; *LIMC* 7. 1 (1994), 839–43. A. H. G.

Tanusius (*RE* 2) **Geminus,** anti-Caesarian historian (and senator?) of the late republic, used by *Plutarch (*Caes.* 22. 3) and by L. *Suetonius (*Iul.* 9. 2). L. *Annaeus Seneca (2) speaks of his Annals as 'heavy-going' (*Ep.* 93. 11). Probably of *Etruscan origin.

Fragments: Peter, *HR Rel.* 2. 49.; E. Rawson, *Intellectual Life in the Late Roman Republic* (1985), 221 and *Roman Culture and Society* (1991), 322. C. J. F.; A. J. S. S.

Taprobane (also Palaesimundu, Salice), ancient names for Sri Lanka (Ceylon). Mentioned by *Onesicritus, *Megasthenes, *Eratosthenes, *Hipparchus (3), and *Ptolemy (4), as a large island south of *India, twenty days' sail from the mouth of the Indus and projecting west almost to Africa. Mantai, perhaps Ptolemy's *Moduttu *emporion, was the main port from the mid-1st millennium BC. Trade with the Mediterranean in pearls, tortoiseshell, precious stones, and muslin was well established by the 1st cent. BC (*Peripl. M. Rubr.* 61. 20) and Indo-Roman Rouletted Ware is known from many sites including Mantai, Kantarodai, and Anuradhapura. *Pliny (1) refers to Ceylonese envoys in Rome and coins of Nero have been found, but after the 1st cent. AD trade with the west declined, to be revived by the Axumites (see AXUMIS) in the 4th–6th cents., when many late Roman coins are known.

L. Casson, *The Periplus Maris Erythraei* (1989); Y. Begley and R. D. De Puma (eds.), *Rome and India: The Ancient Sea Trade* (1991). I. C. G.

Tarchon, companion, son or brother of Tyrrhenus, founder of *Tarquinii, also of Pisa and Mantua (Cato, *Orig.* fr. 45 Peter; Strabo, 5. 219; *Serv. Dan. Aen.* 10. 198). The scene on a bronze mirror from Tuscania does not refer to him, but rather to his son, Avl(e) Tarchunus: with his cap of a haruspex (see HARUSPICES) thrown onto his back, he watches the youthful Pava Tarchies (not to be identified with Tages) examining a liver for omens.

J. R. Wood, *Latomus* 1980, 325 ff.; M. Cristofani, *Prospettiva* 1985, 4 ff.; M. Torelli, *Studia Tarquiniensia* (1988), 109 ff.; D. Briquel, *L'Origine lydienne des Étrusques* (1991). J. L.

Tarentum (Taras; mod. Taranto), in S. Italy, an 8th-cent. Spartan colony (see COLONIZATION, GREEK; SPARTA) dominating the best harbour on the gulf of Tarentum. The literary tradition dates it to 706 BC and names Phalanthus as founder. The colonists were said to be the offspring of *helots and Spartan women. Mycenaean finds close to Taranto (see MYCENAEAN CIVILIZATION) suggest a long-standing Greek connection with the area. Initially, Tarentum seems to have been overshadowed by its more powerful Greek neighbours, but victories over the Messapians and Peucetians *c.*490 and 460 BC, which were commemorated at *Delphi, mark the beginning of Tarentine expansion (see MESSAPII for refs.). In *c.*475, however, it suffered a heavy defeat by the Messapians which destroyed much of the army and was a catalyst for the overthrow of the ruling élite and establishment of a democracy. Towards the end of the 5th cent. it recovered and began to expand into the power vacuum left by the decline of *Croton. *Heraclea (1), founded in 433, was a Tarentine counter-weight to the new colony of *Thurii (cf. ML 57 for hostility between Thurii and Tarentum), and also the headquarters of the Italiote League. The date at which it became so, marking Tarentine assumption of leadership, is uncertain, but must fall between 433 and the Syracusan invasion of Italy in 390 (see SYRACUSE; DIONYSIUS (1)). The extent of Tarentine economic and political power is marked by the wide distribution of Tarentine *coinage along the Adriatic coast and in southern Italy, and by the wide distribution of artefacts made in, or influenced by, Tarentum. The early 4th cent. is marked by the ascendancy of *Archytas, a Pythagorean (see PYTHAGORAS (1)), who dominated Tarentine politics and successfully expanded Tarentine influence, probably in alliance with Syracuse. After his death c.350 BC, Tarentum adopted a policy of employing mercenary generals, mainly Spartans and Epirotes (see EPIRUS; ALEXANDER (6); ARCHIDAMUS III), to control increasing pressure from the Lucanians (see LUCANIA) and Messapians, but with very limited success. The last of the *condottieri*, *Pyrrhus, was involved in a full-scale war with Rome. After several inconclusive battles, he was forced to withdraw and Tarentum fell to Rome, becoming an ally in 270. In 213 a faction of Tarentine aristocrats seized power and revolted from Rome. After a period of stalemate, during which *Hannibal held the city and Rome held the acropolis, Tarentum was recaptured, with heavy losses (209). For a time, it was directly governed by a Roman praetor, but probably regained allied status in the 180s. The foundation of *Brundisium and extension of the *via Appia undercut Tarentine trade and part of the territory was confiscated after 209. A Gracchan colony (Neptunia; see SEMPRONIUS GRACCHUS, C.) was founded in 122, but was ultimately absorbed into the city in 89 BC. A second colony was founded in AD 60. (See COLONIZATION, ROMAN.) Despite assertions of decline in later authors, epigraphy indicates considerable civic activity, and there are numerous references to the importance of its wool, textiles, purple dye, and agricultural produce. There were numerous villas in the territory of Tarentum, some of them imperial, and a high density of rural population. *Strabo (6. 1. 2) asserts that Tarentum was still linguistically and culturally Greek in his day. There is less epigraphic support for this than is the case at *Rhegium and *Neapolis, but it is not entirely impossible. See also ARISTOXENUS; PHLYAKES; RHINTHON.

P. Wuilleumier, *Tarente* (1939); C. Belli, *Il tesoro di Taras* (1970); G. Brauer, *Taras: Its History and Coinage* (1986); *Taranto nell'civiltà della Magna Grecia*, Atti 10 Convegno (1971); L. Gasperini, in *Terza misc. greca e romana* (1971); N. Purcell, *CAH* 6² (1994), ch. 9 (b); I. Malkin, *Myth and Territory in the Spartan Mediterranean* (1994), ch. 4.　　K. L.

Tarius (*RE* 3) **Rufus, Lucius,** Roman military man of humble origin. He served Octavian (see AUGUSTUS) as an officer in the *Actium campaign, as proconsul of Cyprus, and (*c.*27 BC) as a commander in the Balkans. Augustus rewarded him with the suffect consulship (16) and with gifts totalling ten million sesterces which he invested in land in *Picenum. He was merciful to his only son, who tried to murder him. The *curator aquarum* (see AQUEDUCTS) of AD 23–4 is unlikely to be the same man.

Syme, *Rom. Rev.* and *AA*; see indexes.　　C. B. R. P.

Tarpeia (*RE* 6) in the war between *Romulus and Titus *Tatius supposedly betrayed the *Capitol to the Sabines (see SABINI) for what they wore on their left arms, but instead of being rewarded with the gold bracelets she expected, was crushed to death by their shields. This cautionary tale of female treachery (and, remarkably, Sabine luxury) goes back to *Fabius Pictor (fr. 8 Peter) and borrowed Hellenistic motifs to provide an aetiology of the *Tarpeian Rock. L. *Calpurnius Piso Frugi (fr. 5 Peter), however, inferred from the public sacrifice made at the supposed tomb of Tarpeia that she was a national heroine, attempting to disarm the Sabines by trickery.

Ogilvie, *Comm. Livy 1–5*, 74 f.; N. M. Horsfall, in J. N. Bremmer and N. M. Horsfall, *Roman Myth and Mythography* (1987), 68 ff.　　A. D.

Tarpeian Rock A precipitous cliff on the *Capitol from which murderers and traitors were thrown (see TARPEIA). Some ancient sources (e.g. Varro, *Ling.* 5. 41) place it close to the temple of *Jupiter Capitolinus; Dion. Hal. (7. 35. 4; 8. 78. 5); however, locates it at the south-east corner of the hill above the Roman Forum. The latter seems more likely, given the proximity of the Carcer and Scalae Gemoniae, which were also traditional places of execution.

T. P. Wiseman, *Historia* 1979, 41–5; Richardson, *Topog. Dict. Ancient Rome*, 377–8.　　I. A. R.; J. R. P.

Tarquinii (Etr. *Tarχ(u)na-*; mod. Tarquinia, formerly Corneto), the chief of the twelve cities of Etruria, stood on a high plateau about 90 km. (56 mi.) from Rome and 6 km. (3½ mi.) inland; it was the reputed refuge after 657 of the Corinthian merchant *Demaratus (1). The greatest glory of Tarquinii is the series, much augmented by modern geophysical prospecting (Lerici), of painted chamber-tombs dating from the mid-6th cent. onwards. The wealth of material found in Tarquinia's vast cemeteries has made them basic to the study of *Villanovan chronology and Etruscan arts and crafts; traces of an extensive Villanovan settlement have been revealed beneath the Etruscan tumuli in the Monterozzi cemetery. The chief surviving monument of the later city is a 4th-cent. temple, the so-called Ara della Regina on the Pian di Città; there too, excavation (1982 onwards) has unexpectedly revealed an isolated 9th-cent. child burial that was clearly the object of prolonged subsequent veneration (*CAH* 4² (1988), plate 295: *Tages?). The late (Latin) inscriptions known as the *Elogia Tarquiniensia* commemorate the careers and exploits of earlier famous citizens and thus reflect local Etruscan history. At Gravisca, the port of Tarquinia, a prosperous sanctuary was founded c.600 by Greek residents within the Etruscan community. See ETRUSCANS.

M. Pallottino, *Tarquinia, Mon. Ant.* (1937); C. M. Lerici, *Una grande avventura dell'archeologia moderna* (1965); H. Hencken, *Tarquinia, Villanovans and Early Etruscans* (1968); M. Torelli, *Elogia Tarquiniensia* (1975), and *PP* 1977, 398 ff. (Gravisca); S. Steingräber, *Etruscan painting* (1986), nos. 38–173; *Gli Etruschi di Tarquinia* (exhib. cat. Milan, 1986); M. Bonghi Jovino and C. Chiaramonte Treré (eds.), *Tarquinia: Ricerche scavi e prospettive* (1988); L. Cavagnaro Vanoni and F. R. Serra Ridgway, *Vasi etruschi a figure rosse . . . a Tarquinia* (1989).　　D. W. R. R.

Tarquinius Collatinus, Lucius, great-nephew of *Tarquinius Priscus, husband of *Lucretia, and one of the founders of the Roman republic. After his wife's suicide he and L. *Iunius Brutus conspired to overthrow *Tarquinius Superbus, and became the first consuls (509 BC: see CONSUL). But Collatinus was compelled to resign and go into exile when the people, instigated by Brutus, voted that all members of the Tarquinian *gens* should be banished from Rome (Livy 2. 2. 11). The sources present him as an innocent and high-minded victim of circumstances, but cannot hide the fact that the story of his election and subsequent retirement is incoherent and hardly credible as it stands. It is possible that in fact the overthrow of Tarquinius Superbus was a palace revolution followed by a struggle for the succession among his close relatives, such as Collatinus and Brutus, who was himself a nephew of the tyrant; but any such reconstruction must remain speculative in the present state of knowledge.

Ogilvie, *Comm. Livy 1–5*, 232, 238 ff.; T. N. Gantz, *Historia* 1975, 539–54. T. J. Co.

Tarquinius Priscus, Lucius, the fifth king of Rome (traditionally 616–579 BC), was believed to be the son of *Demaratus (1) of *Corinth, who fled to *Tarquinii to escape the *tyranny of *Cypselus. Tarquin himself migrated to Rome with his entourage, including his wife *Tanaquil, and became the right-hand man of Ancus *Marcius. When Marcius died, Tarquin was chosen, by the regular procedure, as his successor. The story provides interesting examples of the horizontal mobility that characterized élite society in the Archaic period, when high-ranking individuals and groups could move freely from one community to another without loss of social position. This phenomenon, which is documented in the *Etruscan cities by contemporary inscriptions, is consistent with the Demaratus story, which is in any case made plausible by archaeological evidence of cultural and trade relations between Etruria and Greece (especially Corinth). It also makes the traditional account of Tarquin's accession at Rome far more likely than the alternative modern theory of an Etruscan conquest of Rome, for which there is no supporting evidence. On the other hand, the connection between Demaratus and Tarquin may be artificial; it cannot be historical if the two Tarquins who ruled at Rome were father and son, as the oldest tradition maintained (Q. *Fabius Pictor fr. 11 Peter). As king, Tarquin is said to have increased the size of the senate and raised the number of cavalry centuries from three to six; and he conducted successful wars against the Latins (see LATINI), Sabines (see SABINI), and Etruscans. *Dionysius (7) of Halicarnassus makes him conquer the Etruscans, but this version, which is not found in *Livy, is doubtless exaggerated. He is also said to have started the construction of the temple of Jupiter Capitolinus, a task completed by his son; but this is probably a compromise designed to overcome the fact that the same building was attributed by different versions of the tradition to both Tarquins. This process of duplication is evident elsewhere, for instance in the case of the drainage works they are both said to have carried out (Cassius Hemina fr. 15 Peter; Plin. *HN* 36. 107). Tarquin was assassinated by the sons of Ancus Marcius, but their bid for the throne was thwarted by Tanaquil, who secured it for her favourite Servius *Tullius. This bizarre story is made all the more odd by the fact that Tarquin himself is credited with two sons, Lucius (*Tarquinius Superbus) and *Arruns. Of his two daughters, one married Servius Tullius, the other M. Brutus and thus became the mother of L. *Iunius Brutus, the founder of the republic.

F. Schachermeyr, *RE* 4 A 2 (1932), 2348 ff., 'Tarquinius'; A. Blakeway, *JRS* 1935, 129 ff.; Ogilvie, *Comm. Livy 1–5*, 145 ff.; T. N. Gantz, *Historia* 1975, 539–54; C. Ampolo, *Dial. di Arch.* 1976–7, 333–45; L. Bessone, *RFIC* 1982, 394–415; O. Cazenove, *MÉFRA* 1988, 615–48. T. J. Co.

Tarquinius Superbus, Lucius, traditionally the last king of Rome (534–510 BC). According to the oldest sources (Q. *Fabius Pictor fr. 11 Peter) he was the son of *Tarquinius Priscus, although on the traditional chronology that is impossible (Dion. Hal. 4. 6–7). It follows either that Superbus was in fact the grandson of Priscus (thus Piso fr. 15 P. = Dion. Hal. 4. 6–7), or, more probably, that the traditional chronology of the regal period is unsound. Tarquin is said to have pursued an aggressive foreign policy; he captured several Latin towns and reorganized the Latin League (see LATINI) into a regular military alliance under Roman leadership (Livy 1. 52), a state of affairs that is reflected in the first treaty between Rome and Carthage (Polyb. 3. 22: 509 BC). The text of the treaty he made with *Gabii is supposed to have survived until the time of *Augustus. He is also famous for having completed the temple of Capitoline Jupiter (see CAPITOL), and notorious for his tyrannical rule which eventually led to his downfall. Terracottas from the temple site at Sant'Omobono may belong to the reign of Superbus; in any event they confirm that the later Roman kings were flamboyant rulers who modelled themselves on contemporary Greek tyrants (see TYRANNY). This proves that Superbus' reputation as a tyrant is not (or not entirely) the result of secondary elaboration in the annalistic tradition in an artificial attempt to assimilate Rome and Greece.

For the story of his accession see TULLIA (1), for that of his fall see LUCRETIA, IUNIUS BRUTUS, L., and TARQUINIUS COLLATINUS, L. After his expulsion from Rome Tarquin fled to *Caere, and persuaded *Veii and *Tarquinii to attack Rome. After their defeat at Silva Arsia, he appealed to Lars *Porsenna, whose assault on Rome is said to have been aimed at restoring Tarquin to power; but this cannot have been so if Porsenna succeeded in taking the city, and it is hard to reconcile with the story that Tarquin then turned to his son-in-law Octavius *Mamilius, *dictator of the Latins (see LATINI), since the Latins had vanquished Porsenna. After the defeat of Mamilius at Lake Regillus (see REGILLUS, LAKE), Tarquin took refuge with *Aristodemus (2) of *Cumae, where he died in 495 BC.

A. Alföldi, *Early Rome and the Latins* (1965); Ogilvie, *Comm. Livy 1–5*, 194 ff.; T. J. Cornell, *CAH* 7²/2 (1989), 257 ff.; M. Cristofani (ed.), *La Grande Roman dei Tarquini* (1990); M. Pallottino, *Origini e storia primitiva di Roma* (1993). T. J. Co.

Tarquitius (*RE* 7) **Priscus,** an authority on 'Etruscan lore', *Etrusca disciplina* (see RELIGION, ETRUSCAN). He appears to have lived at the end of the republic. *Macrobius (*Sat.* 3. 7. 2; 20. 3) quotes a passage from his book, translated (*transcriptus*) from *Ostentarium Tuscum* ('Etruscan Prognostications'), on the felicitous omen of the ram with reddish or golden hue (*purpureo aureove colore*), and another from *Ostentarium arborarium* ('Prognostication from Trees'), concerning unfruitful and unlucky trees (*arbores infelices*). *Pliny (1) (*HN* 1) lists him among his sources for books 2 and 11, and *Ammianus Marcellinus (25. 2. 7) mentions the 'books of Tarquitius' (*Tarquitiani libri*). He is possibly mentioned by Varro, *Rust.* 1. 2. 27 and [Verg.], *Catal.* 5. 3; that he was the subject of a mutilated inscription from *Tarquinii (*ILS* 2924) is now disputed.

J. Heurgon, in *Mélanges J. Collart* (1978), 101 ff.; M. Torelli, *Elogia Tarquiniensia* (1975); W. Fauth, *Latomus* 1976, 469 ff.; E. Rawson, *JRS* 1978, 132 ff. = *Roman Culture and Society* (1991), 289 ff., also *Intellectual Life in the Late Roman Republic* (1985). J. L.

Tarracina (mod. Terracina), the former Volscian stronghold (see VOLSCI) of Anxur. A citizen colony from 329 BC, it was the southern terminus of the *Pomptine Marshes canal, and an important station on the via Appia (re-routed by Trajan). There was a major sanctuary to Jupiter Anxur (1st cent. BC). The town greatly expanded in the 2nd and 3rd cents., and was of considerable significance in late antiquity, with 5th-cent. defences.

A. Bianchi, *Storia di Terracina* (1977); R. Malizia and P. C. Innico, *Terracina romana* (1986); A. R. Mari and others, *La Via Appia a Terracina* (1988); N. Christie and A. Rushforth, *JRA* 1988, 73 ff.

E. T. S.; T. W. P.

Tarraco

Tarraco (mod. Tarragona), on the north-east coast of *Spain, was placed on or near Iberian Cese (Κίσσα, Cissis), city of the Cessetani people. In 218 BC it was the base of P. *Cornelius Scipio and Cn. *Cornelius Scipio Calvus, whose fortifications still enclose part of the citadel. It was important as a Roman strategic centre during the Celtiberian wars (155–133 BC) and issued coins until the reign of *Tiberius. Under *Caesar it became the *Colonia Iulia Urbs Triumphalis*. Under *Augustus Tarraco became capital of Hispania *Tarraconensis. It also erected an altar to Augustus and a posthumous temple to him in the lower town. Other monuments include a theatre and amphitheatre. Later in the 1st cent. AD a terraced complex of temple-precinct for the provincial cult, forum for the provincial *concilium*, and a circus was built in the citadel. Tarraco survived the Frankish sack (AD 264). The 4th and early 5th cent. saw a gradual decline and loss of prestige, although its early Christian cemetery suggests a substantial population. It was the residence of the usurper Maximus Tyrannus (410–11) and a centre of Roman power until AD 476. As a metropolitan bishopric it was still an important spiritual centre and mint throughout the Visigothic period (see GOTHS).

G. Alfoldy, *RE* 14 (1978); X. Aquilue and others, *Tarraco: Guía Arqueologica* (1991).   S. J. K.

Tarraconensis was the largest of Rome's Spanish provinces under the early empire. Its initial nucleus had been formed by the province originally (197 BC) called Hispania Citerior (Hither Spain), which had important *silver *mines at *Carthago Nova. This grew in size as Rome advanced westwards in the 2nd cent. BC and only reached its full extent at the end of the Cantabrian wars (19 BC). Under *Augustus (27 BC) it came to be administered as an imperial province which comprised all of Iberia except for *Baetica and *Lusitania: after 9 BC it gained Callaecia from Lusitania and the eastern edge of Baetica. The province was subdivided into seven *conventus* centred at *Tarraco (the capital), Carthago Nova, *Caesaraugusta, *Clunia, Asturica (see ASTURES), Bracara, and Lucus. By the reign of *Vespasian the military garrison comprised one legion (VII Gemina; see LEGION) stationed at Legio (mod. León), which helped administer the major gold-mines in the territory of the Astures. This was the most culturally varied of the Spanish provinces. Its urban development was uneven, despite the creation of colonies (see COLONIZATION, ROMAN) and *municipia* (see MUNICIPIUM) by *Caesar and Augustus and the extension of the *ius Latii* by Vespasian. Tarraconensis was known for its fine-quality wine and fish sauce. In the Diocletianic reforms (see DIOCLETIAN) it was reduced in size by the creation of the provinces of Carthaginensis and Gallaecia. It remained under Roman control until *c*. AD 475, when it was seized by the Visigoths (see GOTHS).

A. Tovar, *Iberische Landeskunde 3: Tarraconensis* (1989), 5 ff.   S. J. K.

Tarsus, a native Cilician (see CILICIA) town with a long prehistoric past, which later claimed *Triptolemus, *Perseus (1), and above all *Heracles as its founder. It was capital of the Cilician kings and of the Persian satraps of the region (see PERSIA; SATRAP), but it issued coins in its own name with Greek and *Aramaic legends and with predominantly Persian types during the 5th and 4th cents. BC. It was renamed Antioch on the Cydnus and issued coins in this name under *Antiochus (4) IV between 175 and 164; the old name prevailed later and is still used today. Annexed to Cilicia by *Pompey it was granted freedom and immunity (see FREE CITIES; IMMUNITAS) by Antony (M. *Antonius (2)) and was capital of the province of Cilicia from *c*. AD 72. The

city's prosperity owed much to the linen industry and it was a notable centre of commerce. During the 1st cent. BC it was the centre of a famous philosophical school and was the birthplace of St *Paul. Under the empire its inhabitants earned a reputation for insubordination and were reproached in two speeches by *Dio Cocceianus (Dio Chrys. *Or.* 33 and 34). The city's link with Heracles attracted the attention of Commodus, who held the chief magistracy (*dēmiourgos*). Temples for the provincial imperial cult were built under Hadrian and under Commodus; foundations for the latter, originally an enormous structure of Proconnesian marble (see PROPONTIS), have been identified. Tarsus served as a base for *Caracalla's Parthian war in AD 216 (see PARTHIA), and the tribulations which this brought to the city were offset by various privileges granted by the emperor. During the 3rd cent. its history was dominated by rivalry with its local rival Anazarbus.

W. Ruge, *RE* 4 A (1932), 2413–39; C. P. Jones, *The Roman World of Dio Chrysostom* (1978), 71–82; M. Gough, *PECS* 883–4; *Arch. Rep.* 1989/90, 131 (temple); R. Ziegler, *Städtisches Prestige und Kaiserliche Politik* (1985) (the 3rd cent.).   A. H. M. J.; S. M.

Tartarus, son of *Gaia (Earth) and *Aither (Sky; cf. NYX); and father of *Typhon by (again) Gaia, his own mother (Hes. *Theog.* 822). Tartarus was also the name for the deepest region of the underworld, lower even than *Hades (Hom. *Il.* 8. 13 ff. with Kirk's n., and Hes. *Theog.* 119 with West's n.); a place of punishment. There is an alternative neuter plural form Tartara, because 'in form the word is an adjective' (West). See also DEATH, ATTITUDES TO; STYX; TITAN.

LIMC 7. 1 (1994), 848.   S. H.

Tartessus, a cultural grouping in south Spain between the lower Guadalquivir valley and the Guadiana which is often identified with biblical Tarshish. Tartessus developed from strong native roots from *c*.750 BC by exploiting the rich metal resources in the hinterland of Onoba (mod. Huelva). These were traded with *Gades (Gadir) and the *Phoenician *emporia* (see EMPORION (first entry)) along the south coast in exchange for exotic metalwork, jewellery, ivory, and ceramics, which were then traded within Iberia and further afield. Contact with the Phoenicians and Phocaean Greeks generated a unique Tartessian *orientalizing culture, reflected in sculpture, jewellery, and architecture, along with the introduction of iron-technology, the potter's wheel, and indigenous scripts. The reason for the collapse of Tartessus *c*.550 BC is unknown, but has been linked to historically documented external conflicts or an internal crisis. It precipitated the fragmentation of the region into the peoples of the Turdetani, Bastetani, etc.

M. E. Aubet (ed.), *Tartessos: Arqueología Protohistórica del Bajo Guadalquivir* (1989).

S. J. K.

Taruttienus Paternus, Publius, praetorian prefect (see PRAEFECTUS PRAETORIO) of Marcus *Aurelius and *Commodus, and a jurist. First mentioned as *ab epistulis Latinis* (in charge of imperial correspondence in Latin) during the Marcomannic War, when he negotiated with the Transdanubian Cotini, Paternus was praetorian prefect in the late 170s, winning a victory in AD 179. He remained prefect after M. Aurelius' death, but in 182 was removed from office by his colleague *Tigidius Perennis and then executed for alleged conspiracy.

Dio Cass. 71–2; SHA *Comm.*; *Dig.*; *AE* 1971, 534; A. R. Birley, *Marcus Aurelius*, 2nd edn. (1987).   A. R. Bi.

Tasciovanus, king of the British *Catuvellauni (*c*.20 BC–AD 5) and father of *Cunobel(l)inus, was perhaps the grandson of *Cassivellaunus. He minted coins bearing the place-name VERLAMIO(N) (= *Verulamium) and the *oppidum there was presumably his capital. Some of his coins were among the earliest in Britain to imitate classical designs, though his policy was not philo-Roman.

S. S. Frere, *Britannia*, 3rd edn. (1987). S. S. F.; M. J. M.

Tatian, Greek-speaking Christian philosopher from Mesopotamia, pupil of *Justin Martyr in Rome. After Justin's death he split from the Roman community (*c.* AD 172) and returned to the east where he lived as an ascetic (see ASCETICISM). He is the author of the *Oration to the Greeks* (an attack on pagan philosophy and culture and in praise of the 'barbarian philosophy' of the Christians) and of the *Diatessaron*, an edition of the Gospels in a single narrative.

EDITIONS *Tatian—Oratio ad Graecos* and Fragments, ed. and trans. M. Whittaker (OECT, 1982); A. S. Marmardji, *Diatessaron de Tatien* (1935).
ENG. TRANS. J. H. Hill, *The Earliest Life of Christ ever Compiled from the Gospels: Being the* Diatessaron *of Tatian* (1910). F. Bolgiani, *EEC* 2 (1992), 815. W. K.

Tatius, Titus, king of the Sabines (see SABINI), who led an attack on Rome after the rape of the Sabine women and captured the *Capitol (see TARPEIA). After the women had reconciled them, the Romans and Sabines formed a single community under the joint rule of Titus Tatius and *Romulus. Tatius was assassinated while sacrificing at Lavinium, in suspicious circumstances (some sources hint at Romulus' involvement). The legend of their joint rule has been variously interpreted, most famously (by Mommsen) as prefiguring the collegiate magistracy of the republic.

Mommsen, *Hermes* 1886, 570–84 = *Ges. Schr.* 4 (1906), 22–35; J. Poucet, *Recherches sur la légende sabine* (1967). T. J. Co.

Taucheira See PENTAPOLIS.

Tauriscus (1), an anomalist grammarian, pupil of *Crates (3) of Mallus, first used τρόπος (trope) as contrasted with κυριολεξία (use of literal expressions): cf. Sext. Emp. *Math.* 1. 248 f. See ANALOGY AND ANOMALY.

H. J. Matte, *Parateresis* (1952), 56 ff. J. S. R.

Tauriscus (2) (1st cent. BC), sculptor, son of Artemidorus, of Tralles. Works (owned by C. *Asinius Pollio): 1. Hermerotes, probably a pair of *herms with bodies and heads of Erotes (see EROS). 2 (with his brother, Apollonius). Marble group from Rhodes of Zethus, *Amphion, *Dirke, and the bull, inspired by a painting and by earlier sculpture. The Farnese Bull Group from the baths of Caracalla (Winter, *KB* 357. 1) is a copy with the added figure of *Antiope, etc.

Bieber, *Sculpt. Hellenist. Age*, 133 ff. T. B. L. W.

Tauromenium (Ταυρομένιον; mod. Taormina), in eastern Sicily above *Naxos (2), was established in 396/5 BC by the Carthaginian *Himilco (2), who planted there on the site of a small existing settlement (already Hellenized (see HELLENISM) in the Archaic period, as painted architectural terracottas show) the *Sicels to whom *Dionysius (1) I had given the site of Naxos. Dionysius captured it and refounded it as a Greek city (392). In 358 Andromachus, father of the historian *Timaeus (2), gathered the Naxian refugees there and became tyrant. The Tauromenitans promptly gave support to *Timoleon and *Pyrrhus in 344 and 278. About 316 Tauromenium passed under the control of *Aga-

thocles (1) of Syracuse and about 285 under that of a local tyrant Tyndarion, but under *Hieron (2) II it again formed part of the Syracusan dominions. On his death it submitted to Rome, becoming a *civitas foederata* (see SOCII; FOEDUS): its chief magistrates then were *stratēgoi*. Seized by the rebels in the First Slave War, it was recaptured with difficulty by Rutilius Lupus (132). In 36 BC Sex. *Pompeius Magnus inflicted a near-fatal reverse on Octavian there. Becoming an Augustan *colonia* (see AUGUSTUS; COLONIZATION, ROMAN), it has yielded the only example of a Roman calendar (*fasti*) from a provincial city. Tauromenium flourished during the early and middle empire, to which period most of its numerous surviving monuments belong—several house-tombs and reservoirs, a house, an aqueduct, a bath-house, an odeum, and a strikingly situated theatre. Its later history is obscure (there are few late-Roman inscriptions), but the city was one of the early Sicilian centres of Christianity and was a bishopric by the 6th cent. (and probably already in the 4th).

PECS 886–7; P. Rizzo, *Tauromenion* (1928); M. Santangelo, *Taormina e dintorni* (1950); R. J. A. Wilson, *ANRW* 2. 11. 1 (1988), 101–11, and *Sicily under the Roman Empire* (1990), *passim*. Fasti: G. Manganaro, *Arch. Class.* 1963, 13–19, *CronASA* 1964, 38–41; G. M. Bacci, *Kokalos* 1984–5, 724–5. A. G. W.; R. J. A. W.

Taurus mountain range, properly the mostly well-wooded heights (average 2,100 m./7,000 ft.) beginning in SW Asia Minor, and continuing along the coast of *Lycia and through *Pisidia and *Isauria to the borders of *Cilicia and *Lycaonia. It then divides into: (1) Antitaurus, apparently the heights going northeast through *Cappadocia (mons Argaeus) and *Armenia (mons Capotes) towards the *Caucasus; (2) Abus or Macis (Massis), through Armenia towards the *Caspian Sea, keeping the name Taurus and sending southwards Mt. *Amanus and (beyond the *Euphrates) Mt. Masius. There were subsidiary ranges south of the Euphrates, and Mt. Zagrus separating *Media from *Assyria and *Babylonia. The name Taurus was extended to include not only the heights of north Iran, but also the Paropamisus (Hindu Kush) and Emodus or Imaus (Himalayas); and was continued by hearsay to the eastern Ocean at 'Tamus Headland'. The whole range was regarded as the backbone of *Asia, and along it *Dicaearchus (*c.*300 BC) fixed for geographers a parallel or median in cartography, dividing the land mass into the cool and warm regions. E. H. W.

taxation See CENSORS; DECUMA; EISPHORA; FINANCE, GREEK AND HELLENISTIC, and ROMAN; GOVERNMENT; LITURGY; PŌLĒTAI; PORTORIA; PROCURATOR; PROVINCIA; PUBLICANI; VECTIGAL.

Taxiles, eponymous ruler of the territory between the Indus and Jhelum dominated by the city of Taxila (Takshashila). He made overtures to *Alexander (3) the Great while the king was engaged in Sogdiana, and was confirmed in his realm when Alexander crossed the Indus (spring 326). He came immediately under the control of a Macedonian satrap (Philippus) and was eclipsed in Alexander's favour by his former enemy, *Porus. By Alexander's death he had won some independence, but his realm was soon swallowed by the expanding empire of Chandragupta (*Sandracottus).

Berve, *Alexanderreich* 2, no. 739. A. B. B.

Taygetus See LACONIA.

Teanum Apulum (mod. S. Paolo), in central Italy, a *Daunian city, originally called Teate. It was on the borders between Daunian and Frentanian territory and shows signs of Oscanization (see OSCANS) by the 4th cent. BC, notably in issues of coins with *Oscan legends. It fought against Rome in the Second Samnite War (see SAMNIUM), but became an ally in 318 BC and remained loyal thereafter. The Daunian city was fortified with an 11-km. (7-mi.) earth rampart and is similar to *Arpi in size and structure. A Roman aqueduct and temple have been discovered.

A. Russi, *Teanum Apulum* (1976). K. L.

Teanum Sidicinum (mod. Teano), in Italy, the second city of *Campania after *Neapolis (Naples), located on the *via Latina south-east of Roccamonfina. Inhabited from the 7th cent. BC, it grew rapidly in the 4th. Archaeological evidence includes an Archaic sanctuary, Hellenistic and Roman cemeteries, baths, an amphitheatre, and a sanctuary and theatre similar to *Pietrabbondante. There are numerous villas in the area, and traces of mining. K. L.

technology Modern definitions of technology merely stress the systematic application of knowledge, and underline the difficulty of addressing ancient technology with concepts relevant to antiquity. Lynn White Jr. observed that 'no Greek or Roman ever told us, either in words or in iconography, what he or his society wanted from technology, or why they wanted it', and Moses Finley criticized 'an artificial insistence on isolating technology as an autonomous subject'. The problem of definition is exacerbated by relative judgements made about the success, or failure, of ancient technology. Whatever the practical significance of ancient philosophical concepts of progress may have been, there has been general agreement amongst historians of technology that the modest number of items that can be claimed as Greek or Roman inventions were not exploited, and that this failure was attributable to social factors. A potent assertion maintained by many commentators on supposed advances in medieval technology is that not until Rome was converted to *Christianity could liberation from animism be achieved, and value consequently placed upon *labour and production. However, this kind of 'Darwinian' concept of ancient technology, which assumes that technical progress was a natural path of development towards the Industrial Revolution, seems inappropriate on empirical, as well as theoretical, grounds. If we *must* judge ancient technology, should success be measured by showing that inventions known from documentary sources actually existed, or should we demand that they were widely and productively employed? Whose needs should we consider—the state, the army, a social élite, or the multitude?

Most elements of Graeco-Roman technology were either inherited from prehistoric times, or adopted from '*barbarian' peoples. Some significant inventions were made, such as hydraulic concrete, the geared 'Vitruvian' water-mill (see MILLS), blown *glass, the screw-press, and a remarkable harvesting machine, the *vallus*. Inventions that were applied included items for use in essential activities such as draining mines, and, above all, in processing the products of the single most important industry—agriculture. The study of their date and application is complicated by the survival of a mere handful of detailed works by technical writers such as *Heron or *Vitruvius, and the comparative inattention to technical matters by others, such as *Pliny (1). Archaeological evidence plays a growing role in establishing the date and diffusion of applied technology, and it also provides examples of devices that do not appear in the written sources, which (for example) give an incomplete view of the range of pumps. Interpretation is complicated by a tendency amongst

classical scholars to approach Roman technology in the light of its Greek background, without adjusting the context from city-state to empire. A persistent stereotype contrasts Greek theory and invention with Roman practical application, and overlooks the fact that much of the engineering associated with 'Greek science' was Roman in date, and developed in *Alexandria (1).

Technology remained stable (which does not mean stagnant) in most areas of *metallurgy, stoneworking, ceramics, engineering, *architecture, *agriculture, and transport. Extraction and processing of silver at the Athenian mines at *Laurium varied in scale, not technique, from Classical Greek to Byzantine times. Finds from Egypt, Spain, and Wales show that the same techniques were applied across the entire empire in the Roman period. The Roman army evidently acted as an important agent of technology-transfer by spreading *literacy and skills to frontier regions. Thus, intensification rather than innovation characterized Roman technology, assisted by the geographical expansion of Rome and the reliance of its administration on secure and effective transport of men, foodstuffs, and both raw materials and finished goods. It is no accident that Roman engineers are remembered primarily because of the number of *roads, *bridges, and *harbours that survive; archaeological evidence shows that these facilities were used by a comprehensive range of vehicles and *ships whose size and technical complexity was matched to varying requirements. A similar flexibility—and availability—of *building materials and construction skills was able to create farms, workshops, and accommodation in rural and urban environments to house producers and consumers alike.

Greece and Rome constructed marble buildings on an unprecedented scale, and minted millions of gold, silver, and bronze coins. Thousands of ordinary farmers and urban craft-workers possessed more iron tools, architectural stonework, and fine tableware than ever before, to an extent that would not be matched again until the post-medieval period. A combination of effective transport and appropriate coin denominations helped to sustain trade in these materials, far beyond the requirements of the state and the army alone. None of this caused, or resulted from, an Industrial Revolution; the significant growth factor was proliferation and intensification as a result of expanding conquest and trade. Evidence for extensive industries and widespread application of technology in the ancient world can be accepted without having to explain why they did not cause economic 'take-off'. See ECONOMY; INDUSTRY; MECHANICS; TRADE.

K. D. White, *Greek and Roman Technology* (1984); J. P. Oleson, *Bronze Age, Greek and Roman Technology: A Select, Annotated Bibliography* (1986); A. G. Drachmann, *The Mechanical Technology of Greek and Roman Antiquity: A Study of the Literary Sources* (1963); K. Greene, *OJA* 1990, 209 ff., *JRA* 1994, and *CAH* 11 (forthcoming). K. T. G.

technopaignia ('games of skill'), poems whose varying verse-lengths produce a pattern mimicking the shape of an object. No doubt the idea stems from real dedicatory inscriptions, but in the Hellenistic period it became a literary conceit, generating poems in complex metres and sometimes riddling language. Examples are the *Wings*, *Axe*, and *Egg* of *Simmias (2), the *Altar* of *Dosiadas, and the *Pan-pipe* ascribed to *Theocritus; *Laevius produced one in Latin.

TEXTS Gow (ed.), *Bucolici Graeci*, 172–85; Morel, *FPL*, 60 (Laevius fr. 22).
CRITICISM C. Lenz, 'Carmina figurata', *RAC* 2. 910–12. A. H. G.

Tegea, a *polis* of SE *Arcadia situated in a high upland basin crossed by important routes to *Argos (2), Sparta, and SW and E. Arcadia. The *polis* was formed from nine local communities, but when an urban centre was created (before the later 5th cent. BC) is unknown. Few traces of the town survive. Outside it there was, however, an important cult of *Athena Alea; its site has yielded finds from Mycenaean times onwards (see MYCENAEAN CIVILIZATION), and there was a cult centre at least from the 8th cent.; current excavation has found a Geometric temple; and the later Classical temple, burnt down in 395, was magnificently replaced by *Scopas. Around 550 Tegea was compelled by its southern neighbour Sparta to become an ally, and remained so, despite occasional reaction against Sparta, till *Leuctra. Tegea none the less provided asylum for several prominent Spartan exiles. It was also a bitter rival of its northern neighbour *Mantinea. In 370–369 Tegea and Mantinea co-operated to produce the *Arcadian League, but soon quarrelled. Thereafter Tegea played a lively part in the complex Peloponnesian politics of the 4th to 2nd cents. The community survived, though with reduced importance, into late antiquity.

RE 5 A 107–18; C. Callmer, *Studien zur Geschichte Arkadiens* (1943); M. Moggi, *I sinecismi interstatali greci* (1976); M. Jost, *Sanctuaires et cultes d'Arcadie* (1985), 142–65; *Arch. Rep.* 1991–2, 17–18; 1992–3, 20–1.   J. R.

Tegianum (mod. Teggiano), in S. Italy, a Hellenized Lucanian (see HELLENISM; LUCANIA) settlement in the Valle di Diano. There was Gracchan colonization (see SEMPRONIUS GRACCHUS, C.) in the 2nd cent. BC, and a larger colonization programme under *Nero (Plin. *HN.* 3. 98). See COLONIZATION, ROMAN.

E. Greco, *Magna Grecia* (1981).   K. L.

Tegyra north of *Orchomenus (1) and close to Lake *Copais in *Boeotia, site of an oracular sanctuary of *Apollo (Plut. *Pelop.* 16; see LETO and ORACLES) and of a battle in 375 BC when the Theban *Pelopidas inflicted a defeat on the Spartans (Diod. Sic. 15. 37, *FGrHist* 124 Callisthenes F 11 and 18, and Plut. *Pelop.* 16–17). This Spartan reverse is notoriously not mentioned by *Xenophon (1) (though see *Hell.* 6. 4. 10) but is important as anticipating the battle of *Leuctra in 371.

M. Sordi in H. Beister and J. Buckler (eds.), *Boiotika* (1989), 123–30; R. Seager, *CAH* 6² (1994), 173–4; R. J. Buck, *Boiotia and the Boiotian League 423–371 BC* (1994), 99.   S. H.

Teiresias See TIRESIAS.

Telamon (1), in mythology son of *Aeacus and Endeis, and brother of *Peleus. He and Peleus were banished for killing their bastard half-brother, *Phocus; and Telamon settled in *Salamis (1), where he became king (Apollod. 3. 12). He was one of the *Argonauts, and a participator in the Calydonian boarhunt (see MELEAGER (1)). By his wife, Eriboea or Periboea, he fathered the great *Aias (1). By his slave-concubine, *Hesione, the daughter of King *Laomedon of *Troy and given him by *Heracles for his help in taking Troy, he fathered *Teucer (2). When Teucer returned home from the Trojan War without Aias, Telamon banished him (Eur. *Hel.* 91 ff.). For Telamon's *hero-cult, see e.g. Hdt. 8. 64. 2.

LIMC 7. 1 (1994), 852–4.   J. R. M.

Telamon (2), modern Talamone on the coast of Etruria (midway between Rome and Pisa; see PISAE), was already inhabited in *Etruscan times. Here the Romans annihilated the *Celts of Cisalpine Gaul (see GAUL (CISALPINE)) in 225 BC (Polyb. 2. 27–31). Here too C. *Marius (1) landed in 87 BC (Plut. *Mar.* 41. 2). Otherwise the village played little part in recorded history.

P. Sommella, *Antichi campi di battaglia in Italia* (1967); O. W. von Vacano, *Gli Etruschi a Talamone* (1985).   E. T. S.; D. W. R. R.

Telchines (*Τελχῖνες*), an ancient race of Nibelung-like godlings, inventors of the craft of metalwork (see CULTURE-BRINGERS); associated chiefly with the islands of *Rhodes, *Cyprus, *Ceos, and *Crete, but traces of their folklore are also found in *Boeotia ('*Athena Telchinia', Paus. 9. 19. 1), *Sicyon, and elsewhere on the mainland. Their 'magical' skill brought with it allegations of wizardry, the blighting of crops with their sulphur and foul water (Strabo 14. 654), and the evil eye. Hence their reputation as spiteful, jealous gnomes whom *Zeus attempted to drown (Ovid, *Met.* 7. 365 ff.) or scatter; hence too, most famously, *Callimachus (3)'s pillorying of his literary enemies under their name (*Aetia* fr. 1, cf. frs. 75, 64, ed. C. Trypanis (Loeb)).

H. Herter, *RE* 5 A 1, 197 ff.   A. H. G.

Teleclides, Athenian comic poet (see COMEDY (GREEK), OLD), won three victories at the City *Dionysia, the first *c.*445 BC (*IG* 2². 2325. 54), and five at the *Lenaea, the first *c.*440 (ibid. 119). We have eight titles (including *Eumenides* and *Hesiodoi* (cf. CRATINUS)) and seventy citations. The largest, fr. 1 (*Amphictions*), describes the *golden age in extravagant terms; frs. 41 and 42 associate *Socrates with *Euripides, and frs. 45 and 47 attack *Pericles (1).

PCG 2. 667 ff. (*CAF* 1. 209 ff.).   K. J. D.

Telemachus, the son of *Odysseus and *Penelope in *Homer's *Odyssey*, where he plays a prominent part, with the narrative showing his development from a timid and unenterprising youth, quite unable to restrain the unruly suitors, to a self-reliant and resourceful young man who helps his father to kill them. In books 1–4, inspired by *Athena, he sails from *Ithaca to the mainland to inquire after his father at the courts of *Nestor (1) at Pylos and *Menelaus (1) and *Helen at Sparta. He sails home by a different route, thus avoiding an ambush laid for him by the suitors. After reaching Ithaca once more, he is reunited with his father in the hut of *Eumaeus the swineherd (16. 4–219), and father and son together plot the suitors' destruction. Telemachus fights valiantly beside Odysseus in the final battle where all the suitors are killed (22. 91 ff.).

According to *Hyginus (3 (*a*)) (*Fab.* 95. 2), *Palamedes put the baby Telemachus in front of his father's ploughshare, or, according to *Apollodorus (6) (*Epit.* 3. 7), threatened him with a sword, so as to expose Odysseus' pretended madness. Odysseus saved his son and thus gave himself away. According to the *Telegonia* (see EPIC CYCLE), after Odysseus' death Telemachus married *Circe and was made immortal by her.

LIMC 7. 1 (1994), 855–7.   J. R. M.

Telemus (*Τήλεμος*), in mythology, a prophet who foretold to Polyphemus the *Cyclops that *Odysseus would one day blind him; *Od.* 9. 507 ff.   S. H.

Telephus (1) (*Τήλεφος*), an Arcadian hero. He was son of *Heracles and of Auge, daughter of Aleus king of *Tegea and priestess of *Athena Alea. The baby was hidden by his mother in Athena's sanctuary, and in consequence the land became barren. To get rid of his daughter and her son, Aleus decided to set them adrift at sea (Euripides, quoted in Strabo 13. 1. 69), but they reached King Teuthras in Mysia. In some versions deriving from Arcadian tradition (Apollod. 2. 146) Auge alone was exiled to Mysia, while Telephus was exposed on Mt. Parthenion, where he was suckled by a hind (his name contains ἔλαφος 'deer' or 'hind') and rescued by shepherds. Fourth-cent. coins of Tegea show Telephus with the hind, and there was a precinct sacred to him on Mt. Parthenion. When he grew up, Telephus consulted the *Delphic oracle and was reunited with his mother; Teuthras made him his heir. Later, when the Greeks stopped in Mysia on their way to Troy, Telephus killed many of them, but as he fled from *Achilles in the Caïcus plain he caught his foot in a vine placed there by Dionysus and was wounded by him. The episode is depicted on the west pediment of the temple of Tegea. Eight years later, following an oracle, Telephus was healed by Achilles' spear, and led the Greeks to Troy. The story of Telephus was taken up by the Attalids, and represented on the small frieze of the altar of *Pergamum (see SCULPTURE, GREEK).

C. Bauchhenns-Thüriedl, *Der Mythos von Telephos in der antiken Bildkunst* (1971); *LIMC* 7. 1 (1994), 856–7. M. J.

Telephus (2) of Pergamum (2nd cent. AD), a Stoic grammarian (see STOICISM), teacher of the emperor Lucius *Verus, wrote on *Homer, on the history of literature and of scholarship, on bibliography and antiquities, and on *Attic Syntax* (five books); he compiled an alphabetical lexicon of things in common use, and an *Okytokion* (in ten books) of adjectives for the aid of writers and orators. His works are lost.

C. Wendel, *RE* 9 A 369 ff. P. B. R. F.

Teles (*Τέλης*) (fl. *c.*235 BC), *Cynic philosopher, probably of *Megara, is the oldest of the many authors of Cynic or Stoic (see STOICISM) *diatribes (short ethical discussions), fragments of whose works have been preserved (in his case, in the pages of Stobaeus). His diatribes have no claim to philosophical distinction; they simply commend the Cynic way of life in popular language; but he is interesting because of his references to earlier writers like *Bion (1) of Borysthenes, *Stilpon, and *Crates (2) the Cynic.

Ed. O. Hense² (1909); text and trans. in E. O'Neil, *Teles* (1977).
W. D. R.

Telesilla, Argive poet (see ARGOS (2)) of the 5th cent. BC. Later tradition (probably of Argive origin, since her statue at *Argos (2) showed her putting on a helmet: Paus. 2. 20. 7) credited her with arming the women of Argos after its defeat by *Cleomenes (1) I (Paus. 2. 20. 8; Plut. *Mor.* 245c–f). *Herodotus (1) 6. 76 ff. does not mention her, and it has been suggested that the incident is a fabrication based on the oracle cited there. Nine fragments survive, possibly from *hymns. Her songs, written in the choral lyric dialect, were composed for choirs of girls (*PMG* fr. 717); *Artemis and *Apollo are prominent in the meagre remains; mythic narrative was present, with a strong local colour. The Telesilleion, or acephalous glyconic, is called after her (see METRE, GREEK, § 4 (*h*), cf. 4 (*d*)).

TEXT Page, *PMG* 372–4; D. Campbell, *Greek Lyric* (Loeb) 4 (1992), 70–83.
CRITICISM J. M. Snyder, *The Woman and the Lyre* (1989), 59 ff.
C. C.

Telesphorus, a healing deity associated with *Asclepius, with a speaking name (*τελεσφόρος* 'bringing fulfilment'), son of Asclepius in an Athenian hymn (*IG* 2². 2127, after AD 250). He is always represented as a boy in a hooded cloak.

Telesphorus must have originated around AD 100 in *Pergamum, where he had been introduced by an oracle, as a personification of the hopes for healing, equivalent to the Epidaurian daughter of Asclepius, *Akesis*, 'Healing' (Paus. 2. 11. 7; see EPIDAURUS). His first known statue was dedicated in AD 98/102 by a treasurer of the emperor *Trajan (*Altertümer von Pergamon*

8. 3. 135); under *Hadrian (reigned 117–38) his image appears first on Pergamene, then on other Anatolian coins; P. Aelius *Aristides, permanent invalid in Pergamum after AD 145, often acknowledges his help. His popularity rose rapidly during the 2nd cent. when first *Epidaurus, and later other places, adopted his cult (see the Athenian hymn). Representations, especially small statuettes and coins of the boyish Telesphorus are frequent in Anatolia and the Danube provinces.

E. Ohlemutz, *Die Kulte und Heiligtümer der Götter in Pergamon* (1940); W. Deonna, *De Télesphore au moine 'bourru'* (1955); B. M. Felletti Maj, *EAA* 7 (1966), 674 f., 'Telesforo'; *LIMC* 7. 1 (1994), 870–8. F. G.

Telestes, *dithyrambic poet of *Selinus (Ath. 616 f., Diod. Sic. 46. 6), won victory at Athens 402/1 BC (*Marm. Par.* 79). Titles of his dithyrambs are *Argo, Asclepius,* and *Hymenaeus,* of which in all four fragments survive. The comedian *Theopompus (2) referred to him (Ath. 501 f.). In style and music he resembled *Timotheus (1) and *Philoxenus (1) (Dion. Hal. *Comp.* 132). *Alexander (3) the Great read him (Plut. *Alex.* 8), and the tyrant Aristratus of Sicyon put up a statue to him (Plin. *HN* 35. 109).

Page, *PMG* 419–22. C. M. B.

teletē (*τελετή*). Being related to *τελεῖν* (accomplish, finish), this word properly means no more than 'accomplishment', 'performance'. However, already at its earliest occurrence (*Pindar), it had a special meaning: the accomplishment of a ceremony with a religious nature or connotation. So Pindar uses it of the *Olympian Games and of Athenian festivals including athletic contests. In *Euripides *τελετή* often means a rite, in particular a more or less eccentric or orgiastic rite. *Aristophanes (1) uses it for religious celebrations of any kind (cf. *Pax* 418–20). But from the 5th cent. (Hdt.; Andoc. 1. 111) onwards it tends to be used especially for *mysteries and mystic cults, sometimes, as for example in *Plato (1), with special reference to the initiatory parts of mysteries or to *initiation in general. From the Hellenistic period onwards the word also acquires a more general meaning as a rite containing some hidden philosophic or gnostic meaning. It can also signify a magical or supernatural action or even force. This finally develops, especially in *Philon (4) of Alexandria, into the sense of 'inner meaning', or even 'allegorical interpretation'.

C. Zijderveld, *ΤΕΛΕΤΗ. Bijdragen tot de kennis der religieuse terminologie in het Grieksch* (1934); A. D. Nock, *Essays on Religion and the Ancient World* 2 (1972), 797–801; *Kl. Pauly,* 'Telete'. H. S. V.

Tellus, the Roman earth-goddess, probably very old, though her temple on the Esquiline dates only from 268 BC. (Ziolkowski, *Temples* 155 ff.). She should not be confused with *Ceres. According to Ovid (*Fast.* 1. 671 ff.), Tellus was patroness of the place of cultivation, Ceres of cultivation's origins; and while Terra describes the element 'earth', Tellus is the name of its protecting deity (Serv. on *Aeneid,* 1. 171; 12. 778). Terra mater, 'Mother Earth', is only attested from the 2nd cent. BC (Pacuvius fr. 93 Ribbeck). For the question of Greek influence on her ritual see F. Altheim, *Terra Mater* (1931); S. Weinstock in *RE* 'Terra Mater'; H. Le Bonniec, *Le Culte de Cérès* (1958), 111 ff. She is associated in cult with Tellumo (Varro in August. *De civ. D.* 7. 23); with Altor ('Feeder') and Rusor ('Ploughman'?), ibid.; perhaps with the doubtful Tellurus (Mart. Cap. 1. 49). No festival is named after her and she has no flamen (see FLAMINES); but she is the deity concerned in the *feriae sementivae* (see FESTIVALS, ROMAN) (Ovid, *Fasti* 1. 657 ff.; see J. Bayet, *Croyances et rites dans la Rome antique* (1971), 177 ff.); the *Fordicidia of 15 April (Ovid, *Fasti* 4. 629 ff.; the offering, a cow in calf, is typical for powers of fertility); and the sacrifice of the *porca praecidanea* (Varro in Nonius, 163 M., Gell. *NA* 4. 6. 8, who adds Ceres), a sin-offering for neglect of rites, especially those of the dead. See further Weinstock (see above), Dumézil, *ARR* 375 ff.

LIMC 7. 1 (1994), 879–89.   H. J. R.; J. Sch.

Telmessus See PERICLES (2).

temenos, a demarcated sacred land, subject to rules of purity, reserved as a sanctuary (*hieron*) and containing an altar (*bōmos*; see ALTARS) and optional edifices, such as temples, treasuries, and priests' houses. *Temenos* kept its original meaning of an estate, the result of the community 'cutting off' (*temnein*) and allocating choice lands to prominent men: the Lawagetas and Wanax in Mycenaean Greek (*te-me-no*; see MYCENAEAN LANGUAGE), Homeric kings and heroes, and exceptional kings in the Classical period (the Battiads at *Cyrene). In *Homer, the verb of possession, *nemein*, preserves the sense of allocation. Beginning with Homer we also find the ritual '*temenos* and fragrant altar', giving the impression of rather small sites compared with the revenue-bearing estate-*temenē*.

What was indispensable for Greek cult was the altar alone, constituting a 'sacred spot'. All the physical landscape could be perceived by Greeks as imbued with the presence of gods and punctuated with landmarks of sacred sites (and altars). With no need for demarcation, many did not constitute *temenē*. The Homeric *alsos*, sacred grove, need not have implied an artificially demarcated spatial perception. The public sacrifice to *Poseidon at *Pylos (*Od.* 3. 1–68) took place on the beach, not in a precinct. The transition to the sacred 'space', the precinct with its clearly demarcated boundaries (cf. the terms *herkos, sēkos, anaktoron*), delimited against other private and public lands, developed in the context of the rise of the 8th-cent. political community, the *ethnos* (see ETHNICITY) or the **polis*. In ritual terms people set up (*hidruein*) altars (to *Apollo *Archegetes at *Naxos (2), a sacred spot in a new land: Thuc. 6. 3. 1); depending on the context, they also marked around it (*horizein*) the *temenos* (Hdt. 3. 142. 2). The larger precinct allowed the community to gather inside it, in contrast, for example, to the tiny early temples of Dreros and Prinias in *Crete. It implied a relation of the sovereign community with the gods, less dependent on royal or aristocratic mediation. The *temenos* became indispensable for small communities (not colonies) living among foreigners, as at *Naucratis (Egypt) and Gravisca (Etruria; see TARQUINII). The addition of the spatial dimension to that of the 'sacred spot' also emphasized the new value attached to land-ownership as an expression of citizenship and participation in the *polis*: gods too had become sharers in the city, possessing plots of land. In 8th-cent. colonies land was initially parcelled and plots (*klēroi*) allocated to settlers and to the gods (*temenē*). In the context of the *polis*, the *temenos* was probably linked to the emergence of the **agora*, a public, differentiated, 'political' (and to a degree also sacred) space.

Urban *temenē* were usually smaller than extra-urban ones, which sometimes served as revenue-bearing estates for the finances of cult (the exception, lands whose tilling was forbidden as at *Eleusis or *Delphi, illustrates the rule). In the synoecized city (see SYNOECISM) *temenē* tended to converge towards the centre (Athens, *Corinth); by contrast, in the colonies (*Syracuse, *Thasos) more sub- and extra-urban sanctuaries were created. It has been claimed (with the clearest examples from colonies) that extra-urban *temenē*, located near boundaries, were created to proclaim territorial sovereignty and to constitute the 'foundation'

of the *polis*. However, since such *temenē* were in fact created later than the foundation, since colonies had no boundaries but open-ended frontiers, and since safer lands (nearest the settlement) were needed for the settlers, it seems rather that extra-urban sanctuaries were initially reserved (*exairein*) as (potential) revenue-bearing estates; in religious terms the division of the 'whole' land was analogous to the division of sacrificial meat: a whole divided between humans and gods, the humans receiving edible meat—the gods the fat and fragrance. It also seems probable that sometimes (the Argive *Heraion? *Perachora?) peripheral locations enhanced a function of social mediation between various communities.

The distinction between public *temenē* and public lands (*chōria*), first made explicit by *Solon (frs. 4, 12, West), makes it clear that the two were not synonyms. *Aristotle speaks of selling and leasing *temenē dēmosia* (public *temenē*) at *Byzantium, mentioning also *temenē thiasiōtika* (serving cults of particular groups) and *temenē patriōtika* (perhaps of ancestral, or heroic cults). The *temenos*, then, acquired its sacred character gradually, when particular sacred functions (a communal sacrifice or a source of sacred revenues), or monuments (an altar or temple containing a cult image), were attached to it. Mostly it expressed the intimate links of the gods with the soil, simultaneously separating sacred and profane and making the Greek community a unity of both gods and men. See SANCTUARIES, GREEK.

B. Bergquist, *The Archaic Greek Temenos: A Study of Structure and Function* (1967); W. Burkert in M. V. Fox (ed.), *Temple in Society* (1988), 27–48; M. Casevitz in Roux (1984), 81–95; P. E. Corbett, *BICS* 1970, 149–58; H. Drerup, *Griechische Baukunst in Geometrischer Zeit: Archaeologia Homerica* 2. O (1969); I. E. M. Edlund, *The Gods and the Place: Location and Function of Sanctuaries in the Countryside of Etruria and Magna Graecia (700–400 BC)* (1987); E. Greco in M. Vegetti (ed.), *L'esperienza religiosa antica: Introduzione alle culture antiche* (1992), 55–66; R. Hägg (ed.), *The Greek Renaissance of the Eighth Century BC: Tradition and Innovation*, (1983); G. P. Lavas, *Altgriechische Temenos* (1974); *Le Sanctuaire grec*, Fondation Hardt 37 (1992); I. Malkin, *Religion and Colonization in Ancient Greece* (1987), ch. 4; N. Marinatos and R. Hägg (eds.), *Greek Sanctuaries: New Approaches* (1993); R. Martin in *Architecture et société: de l'archaïsme grec à la fin de la république romaine* (1983), 9–41; F. de Polignac, *La naissance de la cité grecque* (1984), Eng. trans. *Cults, Territory, and the Origins of the Greek City-State* (1995); G. Roux (ed.), *Temples et sanctuaires*, Travaux de la maison de l'Orient 7 (1984); M. Sordi (ed.), *Santuari e politica nel mondo antico*, Contributi dell'Istituto di storia antica 9 (1983); P. Stengel, *Griechische Kultusaltertümer* (1920), 10–31; R. A. Tomlinson, *Greek Sanctuaries* (1976); Parker, *ARH* 145.   I. M.

Temenus of Argos, a Heraclid (see HERACLIDAE, son of Aristomachus, ancestor of the Macedonian royal house (Ephorus *FGrH* 70 F 115; Theopompus *FGrH* 115 F 393; Nicolaus of Damascus *FGrH* 90 F 30; Apollod. 2. 8. 2–5; Paus. 2. 19. 1–2). He was a leader of the successful Heraclid/*Dorian invasion of the *Peloponnesus, at the conclusion of which he received *Argos (2) as his portion. *Pheidon, who was believed to be Temenus' descendant, presented his expansionist policies in the guise of claiming the heritage of Temenus.

Temenus' sons arranged his murder because he had favoured their sister *Hyrnetho and her husband *Deiphontes over them. A descendant of Temenus called Perdiccas (Hdt. 8. 137–8) or his son Archelaus (cf. Euripides, *Archelaus*) founded the royal house of *Macedonia. Temenus received hero cult at his grave at Temenion (Paus. 2. 38. 1; Strabo 8. 6. 2).

RE 5 A 438–42; A. Andrewes, *CQ* 1951, 39–42; L. H. Jeffery, *Archaic Greece* (1976), 13–15, 143 n. 2; A. Harder, *Euripides' Kresphontes and Archelaos* (1985), 125–290.   C. S.-I.

Temesa

Temesa, in S. Italy, a 6th-cent. BC Aetolian colony (see AETOLIA; COLONIZATION, GREEK) noted for its copper (Strabo 6. 1. 5), whose site is not identified. It fell under Bruttian control in the 4th cent., but was devastated and abandoned during the *Punic Wars. The Roman colony of Tempsa was founded there in 194 BC (Livy 34. 45. 3–5). See EUTHYMUS.

G. Maddoli, *Temesa e il suo territorio* (1982). K. L.

Tempe, defile about 8 km. (5 mi.) long in NE *Thessaly by which the river Peneus reaches the sea. The common word *tempē* described all defiles, *thessalika tempea* all the passes giving access to Thessaly or linking its two plains; the Tempe of the Peneus, between Mts. *Olympus (1) and *Ossa, is the most famous. In antiquity seen as the work of *earthquakes, the gorge was formed by fluvial erosion and tectonic movement. It formed the easiest route between Thessaly and *Macedonia, but could be blocked by a small force; it could be turned by various mountain routes. In 480 BC the Greeks occupied Tempe with Thessalian cavalry; but *Xerxes opted for a mountain route, a scenario repeated in later antiquity. See PERSIAN WARS.

H. E. Schneider, *Zur quartärgeologischen Entwicklungsgeschichte Thessaliens* (1968), 60 ff.; W. K. Pritchett, *AJArch.* 1961, 369 ff. B. H.

temple The Greek temple was the house of the god, whose image it contained, usually placed so that at the annual festival it could watch through the open door the burning of the sacrifice at the altar which stood outside (see STATUES, CULT OF). It was not a congregational building, the worshippers instead gathering round the altar in the open air, where they would be given the meat of the victims to consume (see SACRIFICE, GREEK). *Orientation was generally towards the east, and often towards that point on the skyline where (allowing for the vagaries of ancient Greek calendars) the sun rose on the day of the festival. The temple also served as a repository for the property of the god, especially the more valuable possessions of gold and silver *plate (see VOTIVE OFFERINGS).

The core of the temple is the cella, a rectangular room whose side walls are prolonged beyond one end to form a porch, either with columns between them (in antis) or in a row across the front (prostyle). More prestigious temples surround this with an external colonnade (and are described as peripteral). They generally duplicate the porch with a corresponding prolongation of the walls at the rear of the cella, *without*, however, making another doorway into the cella (the opisthodomus, or false porch). Some temples, such as the *Parthenon, have a double cella with a western as well as an eastern room, in which case the porch has a door in it.

The origins of this are uncertain. No provable temples exist (excluding the very different shrine buildings of the late bronze age) before the 8th cent. BC.

By the end of the 7th cent. the rectangular form is normal. Cut stone replaces the earlier mudbrick structures, and important temples are peripteral 'hundred footers' (*hekatompeda*); the 6th cent. sees a handful of exceptionally large 85 metres (300-ft.) examples, such as *Artemis at *Ephesus and the Samian *Heraion. From the 6th cent. stone-built temples are normal; *marble begins to be utilized where readily available. Doric temples (see ORDERS, ARCHITECTURAL) generally stand on a base (*crēpis*) with three steps, though the enlarged dimensions of the building make these excessively high for human use; they have to be doubled at the east-end approach, or replaced there by a ramp; Ionic temples often have more steps. Roofs are generally

now of terracotta tiles; gutters occur infrequently in Doric temples, regularly in Ionic. Marble tiles (introduced first in Ionic) are used in the Parthenon. The roof is supported on beams and rafters. Wider buildings require internal supports within the cella; these may also be added as decoration, even when the span is too small to require their support. Some of the very large Ionic temples do not seem to have had internal supports in their cellas, which must therefore have been unroofed or 'hypaethral', though the surrounding colonnades were roofed up to the cella wall.

There are recognizable regional variations, even within the broad distinctions of Doric and Ionic. Approach ramps at the east end are regular in Peloponnesian temples, which often restrict carved decoration in the Doric metopes to those of the inner entablatures over the porch. Sicilian Doric temples may have four rather than three steps, and frequently have narrower cellas, without any internal supports.

Only exceptional buildings, such as the Parthenon, have full pedimental sculpture, let alone carved figures on every metope of the external entablature, while the frieze which replaces the metope frieze over the prostyle porches, and is continued along both sides of the cella, is a unique additional embellishment.

Roman temples derive from Etruscan prototypes, themselves possibly influenced by the simple Greek temples of the 8th and 7th cents. BC. They stand on high *podia*, with stepped approaches only at the front (temples of the Roman period in the Greek part of the empire often continue the tradition of the lower Greek stepped *crēpis*). Roofs are steeper (reflecting perhaps the wetter climate of Etruria); more lavish carved decoration may derive from western Greek taste. The Corinthian order, used for some Hellenistic temples, became the preferred form. Marble is common in the Augustan period, white, with fluted columns; later polished smooth shafts of variegated marbles, granites, etc. are preferred. Regional variations continue to be important. The western provinces generally follow the example of Rome. See PAINTING; SANCTUARIES, GREEK; SCULPTURE; TEMENOS.

D. S. Robertson, *A Handbook of Greek and Roman Architecture*[2] (1943); A. W. Lawrence, *Greek Architecture*[4] (ed. R. A. Tomlinson) (1983); W. B. Dinsmoor, *Architecture of Ancient Greece*[3] (1950); A. Boethius, *Etruscan and Roman Republican Architecture* (1984); J. B. Ward-Perkins, *Roman Imperial Architecture*[2] (1981). R. A. T.

temple officials Greek and Roman temples served as the houses of gods and goddesses, but also as centres of religious activity, meeting-places, storehouses for dedications, and secure locations for the keeping of valuables. They do not seem in general to have played as great a role in the social and economic life of the cities as did the great temples of Egypt and the near east, but all the same they must have required regular control, care, and funding in fulfilling their tasks and maintaining their fabric.

In Greece we have a picture of how the temples operated. There were normally *priests or priestesses in charge of each; in any large temple they would be assisted by minor officials. *Aristotle (*Pol.* 6. 1322[b]) distinguishes three types of these: first, there were cult officials who assisted in the sacrifices and rituals (*hieropoioi*), who would have received their share of the sacrificial meat and other perquisites; secondly, there were wardens or caretakers (*neōkoroi, naophylakes*) who controlled access to the sanctuary, carried out purifications of those entering, and cleaned the sanctuary; thirdly, there were treasurers (*hierotamiae*), who assisted with financial administration, took care of treasures and votives, and oversaw the raising of revenue. The detail of all this varies greatly from sanctuary to sanctuary and from city to city; there was much overlapping in the functions of the officials and many more titles occur in the rich record of the inscriptions (cantors, musicians, sacred heralds, libation-pourers, etc.).

For Rome and central Italy it is far less clear how temple administration would have worked. In Rome, at least, priests were not normally attached to temples or responsible for them; exceptions occur when foreign cults were introduced, as with the Greek priestesses of the Greek *Ceres or the priestly personnel who accompanied the cult of the Magna Mater (see CYBELE). The only temple official we hear of is the *aedituus; many other religious officials are known—*victimarii (sacrificers), tibicines (flute-players), pullarii (keepers of sacred chickens)—some of whom would have had functions similar to the Greek hieropoioi, but these are not directly attached to temples, work with magistrates as well as with priests, and form groups or colleges of their own. The work corresponding to that of the Greek temple officials must have been done by the slaves and freedmen of the aeditui, but nothing of their work is recorded.

K. Latte, *Römische Religionsgeschichte* (1960), 408–10; P. Stengel, *Griechische Kultusaltertümer* (1920), 48 ff.; G. Berthiaume, *Les rôles du mageiros* (1982).   J. A. N.

templum, an augural term denoting (a) the field of vision defined by a ritual formula (*templum in aere*) to observe the (impetrative) auspices (see AUSPICIUM) from the flight of birds; lightning was observed in the semicircular celestial *templum*; (b) the quadrangular area delimited and inaugurated by the *augures. Many official state functions had to take place in a *templum* (especially the senatorial meetings and observations of the impetrative auspices); most shrines (*aedes sacrae*) were *templa* (but not that of *Vesta), also the *Curia (2) and the *Rostra (Varro in Gell. *NA* 14. 7. 7; *Ling.* 6. 91, 7. 6–13).

P. Catalano, *ANRW* 2. 16. 1 (1978), 440 ff.; J. Linderski, *ANRW* 2. 16. 3 (1986), 2256 ff.   J. L.

templum Pacis, later called forum Pacis or Vespasiani, was the precinct of the temple of Peace at Rome, dedicated by *Vespasian in AD 75. The area (145 × 100 m.) was surrounded by marble porticoes within an enclosure wall of peperino and laid out as a garden. The temple, a rectangular hall in the centre of the east side set flush with the portico, housed the spoils from *Jerusalem. It was flanked by a library, the bibliotheca Pacis, and various other halls. One of these carried the *Forma Urbis and may have housed the office of the urban prefect. After the fire of *Commodus the complex was restored by *Septimius Severus.

J. Anderson, *The Historical Topography of the Imperial Fora* (1984), 101 ff.; Nash, *Pict. Dict. Rome* 1. 439 ff.   J. D.

Tenedos (island off *Troas, mod. Bozcaada; see Tod 175 for anc. refs.) See TENES (i.e. next entry below).

Tenes or **Tennes,** eponymous hero (see EPONYMOI; HERO-CULT) of *Tenedos and owner of a *sanctuary there. Son of *Apollo or of Cycnus, king of Colonae in the Troad (see TROAS), he was falsely accused of rape by his stepmother, and Cycnus set him and his sister *Hemithea adrift in a chest which landed at Tenedos. Later, Cycnus discovered the truth and attempted a reconciliation, but Tenes with an axe cut the moorings of his boat when Cycnus visited Tenedos, hence the proverb 'Tenedian axe' for a refusal to be addressed. Tenes was finally killed by *Achilles while defending Hemithea; this was the mythological explanation for the taboo on the name Achilles at the *hērōon* of Tenes, just as flute-players were forbidden entry because a flute-

player had denounced Tenes to Cycnus. Both types of taboo can be paralleled elsewhere.

Plutarch, *Quaest. Graec.* 28 (*Mor.* 297d–f); W. R. Halliday, *CQ* 1927, 37–44; *LIMC* 7. 1 (1994), 892.   E. Ke.

Tenos, a large island (195 sq. km.) in the northern *Cyclades. A Mycenaean tholos-tomb (see MYCENAEAN CIVILIZATION) is the only noteworthy relic from prehistory. Settled by *Ionians *c.*950 BC, it had connections with the Thessalo-Euboean region (see THESSALY; EUBOEA) in the Geometric period. The city was initially at Xobourgo, a massive granite outcrop overlooking the fertile central plateau. Having submitted to *Persia its *trireme deserted to the Greek fleet before Salamis (see SALAMIS, BATTLE OF). Under the Athenian empire its tribute was reduced from three to two talents *c.*446 BC. The city was relocated in the later 4th cent. to the south coast. Simultaneously a sanctuary of *Poseidon and Amphitrite was founded near by, an important cult centre in the Hellenistic period. In the early 2nd cent. BC Tenos became the centre of the revived Island League (see DELOS; SEA POWER). Recovery from the upheavals of the 1st cent. BC was modest; city and sanctuary were deserted by the 4th cent. AD.

RE 5 A 507 ff.; *PECS* 923–4; *IG* 12 (5); ΠΑΕ 1949–50, 1952–3, 1955, 1958; R. Étienne and others, *Ténos* 1–2 (1986–90); G. Reger, *CQ* 1992, 365 ff.   R. W. V. C.

Teos (*Τέως*), one of the twelve cities of the Ionian League (see IONIANS; PANIONIUM), on the coast north of *Ephesus. Tradition said that it was founded first by *Minyans from *Orchomenus (1), then by Ionians and Athenians under the sons of *Codrus. After the Persian occupation of Ionia the Teians sailed in a body to *Thrace, where they founded *Abdera; many soon returned and took part in the battle of Lade in 494 BC. In the *Delian League Teos was assessed at six talents, on a par with *Ephesus. Antigonus (1) proposed to synoecize Teos and Lebedus (see SYNOECISM), but this was never carried out. About 200 BC Teos was chosen as the seat of the artists of Dionysus (see DIONYSUS, ARTISTS OF), but these soon made themselves unpopular and were moved elsewhere. The ruins at Sığacık are only moderately well preserved; they include a theatre, an odeum, and the famous temple of *Dionysus by *Hermogenes (1). The city's two harbours, mentioned by Livy 37. 27–8, are identifiable on the north and south sides of the isthmus.

G. E. Bean, *Aegean Turkey*[2] (1980), 136 ff.; *SEG* 31 (1981), 985; ML 30 (public *curses at Teos); D. M. Lewis, *ZPE* 47 (1982), 71 f. (population); G. Huxley in *Studies . . . Sterling Dow* (1984), 149 ff. (*Pindar's second Paean, written for Teos); A. J. Graham, *JHS* 1992, 44 ff. (relation to Abdera).   G. E. B.; S. H.

Terence (*RE* 36) **(Publius Terentius Afer),** the Roman playwright, author of *fabulae palliatae* in the 160s BC. The *Life* by *Suetonius records that he was born at Carthage, came to Rome as a slave in the household of a senator called Terentius Lucanus, was soon freed, but died still young on a visit to Greece in 159. As usual, we have no way to check this information; his Carthaginian birth (see CARTHAGE) may have been an incorrect deduction from his *cognomen* (*Afer,* 'the African'; see NAMES, PERSONAL, ROMAN). He was patronized by prominent Romans, and his last play, *Adelphoe,* was commissioned by P. *Cornelius Scipio Aemilianus and his brother for performance at the funeral games for their father L. *Aemilius Paullus (2) in 160. The previous year, his *Eunuchus* had been an outstanding success, marked by a repeat performance and an unprecedentedly large financial reward. His one known failure was *Hecyra,* which twice had to be abandoned in the face of competition from rival attractions (first a tightrope walker and boxers, then a gladiatorial show); Terence's account of these misfortunes in his prologue for the third production is exceptional evidence for conditions of performance at the time.

All his six plays survive. Their dates are given by the *didascaliae*, which are generally accepted as reliable in spite of some difficulties: *Andria* ('The Girl from Andros', Megalesian Games 166; cf. LUDI); *Hecyra* ('The Mother-in-Law', Megalesian Games 165, revived in 160 at Aemilius Paullus' funeral games and again later that year); *Heautontimorumenos* ('The Self-Tormentor', Megalesian Games 163); *Eunuchus* ('The Eunuch', Megalesian Games 161); *Phormio* (Roman Games 161); and *Adelphoe* ('The Brothers', Aemilius Paullus' funeral games in 160). *Hecyra* and *Phormio* were based on originals by *Apollodorus (3) of Carystus, the other four on plays by *Menander (1); Terence preserved the Greek titles of all but *Phormio* (named after the main character; Apollodorus' title was *Epidikazomenos*, 'The Claimant at Law'). All the plays were produced by *Ambivius Turpio, with music by one Flaccus, slave of Claudius.

In adapting *Andria*, Terence added material from Menander's *Perinthia* ('The Girl from Perinthos'); for his *Eunuchus* he added the characters of the parasite and the soldier from Menander's *Kolax* ('The Toady'); and in *Adelphoe* he added a scene from *Diphilus' *Synapothnēskontes* ('Comrades in Death'). We learn this from the prologues to these plays, where he defends himself against charges of 'spoiling' the Greek plays and of 'theft' from earlier Latin plays (see CONTAMINATIO; LUSCIUS LANUVINUS). But he made more radical changes than these. The commentary by *Donatus (1) provides some further information, e.g. that the first 20 lines of *Andria* are an entirely original creation, and that Terence has converted monologue to dialogue in the central scene of *Eunuchus* (539–614). The extent and implications of these and other changes are much disputed; it is a mark of Terence's skill that we cannot be sure of the boundaries of inserted material even when he tells us that it has been added. It is widely believed that he made significant changes to the endings of several plays (particularly *Eun.* and *Ad.*), but the meagre fragments that survive of his Greek originals force us to rely heavily on intuition about what Menander and Apollodorus are likely to have done.

One clear innovation was Terence's use of a prologue to conduct feuds with his critics; he never used one to tell the spectators about the background to the plot (see ARGUMENTUM). It has been suggested that he preferred to exploit effects of surprise rather than irony and to involve his audience more directly in the emotions of the characters (most notably in *Hecyra*, where it is laid bare how women are misunderstood, maligned, and mistreated by men). But the scope for ironic effect varies from play to play; in some cases he includes essential background information in the mouths of the characters at an early stage. It seems more likely that he dispensed with expository prologues because he regarded them as an unrealistic device. Consistent with this is his avoidance of direct audience address in his plays, though he does include some 'metatheatrical' remarks at *An.* 474–94 and *Hec.* 865–8.

There is a world of difference between Terence and *Plautus. In general, Terence seems to have preserved the ethos of his originals more faithfully, with well-constructed plots, consistent characterization, and very few overtly Roman intrusions into the Greek setting. Like Plautus, he increased the proportion of lines with musical accompaniment; but he hardly ever used lyric metres, and he was more sparing in his use of set-piece *cantica. His plays repay thoughtful study and give a sympathetic portrayal of human relationships (*Haut.* and *Ad.* both deal with questions of openness and tolerance between fathers and adolescent sons). On the other hand, he added stock characters and boisterous scenes to *Eun.* and *Ad.*, and he appealed to the precedent of Plautus and others when accused of *contaminatio*; he was not faithful enough to the Greek originals for some of his contemporaries. He deserves his reputation for *humanitas*, a humane sympathy for the predicaments of human beings, but his plays are also lively and entertaining situation comedies.

Terence's greatest contribution to the development of literary Latin was the creation of a naturalistic style far closer to the language of everyday conversation than that of Plautus or the other authors of *palliatae*, with much exclamation, aposiopesis, and ellipsis; many of its features are paralleled in *Cicero's letters and *Catullus (1)'s shorter poems. But he did also sometimes use a more ornate and repetitive style, both in the plays themselves and above all in the prologues, which are highly elaborate rhetorical pieces with much antithesis, alliteration, etc. He does not reproduce the fantastic verbal exuberance of Plautus.

Terence was widely read for many centuries after his death, above all for his style and moral sentiments. Over 650 manuscripts of his plays survive, including a number with famous miniature illustrations. In the 10th cent. the nun Hrothswitha of Gandersheim wrote six Christian comedies in imitation of Terence, and he was both imitated and revived in the Renaissance (see PALLIATA). He held a central place in the European school curriculum until the 19th cent.

TEXT R. Kauer and W. M. Lindsay (OCT); J. Sargeaunt (Loeb, with Eng. trans.); J. Marouzeau (Budé, with Fr. trans.). On the manuscripts, G. Jachmann, *Die Geschichte des Terenztextes im Altertum* (1924); L. W. Jones and C. R. Morey, *The Miniatures of the Manuscripts of Terence prior to the Thirteenth Century* (1931); M. D. Reeve in L. D. Reynolds (ed.), *Texts and Transmission* (1983); J. N. Grant, *Studies in the Textual Tradition of Terence* (1986).

COMMENTARIES Ancient commentaries by Donatus and Eugraphius. All the plays: S. G. Ashmore (1908). *Andria*: G. P. Shipp (1960²). *Haut.*: A. J. Brothers (1988). *Eunuchus*: P. Fabia (French, 1895). *Phormio*: K. Dziatzko and E. Hauler (German, 1913⁴); R. H. Martin (1959). *Hecyra*: S. Ireland (1990). *Adelphoe*: K. Dziatzko and R. Kauer (German, 1903²); R. H. Martin (1976); A. S. Gratwick (1987). Companion to the Penguin trans. of *Eun.*, *Phorm.*, and *Ad.* by J. Barsby (1991).

TRANSLATIONS B. Radice (Penguin, 1976²); F. O. Copley (1967); P. Bovie, C. Carrier, and D. Parker (1974).

BIBLIOGRAPHIC SURVEYS H. Marti, *Lustrum* (1961, 1963); S. M. Goldberg, *CW* 1981; G. Cupaiuolo, *Bibliografia Terenziana 1470–1983* (1984, with suppl. in *Bollettino di Studi Latini* 1992).

LEXICON P. McGlynn, *Lexicon Terentianum* (1963, 1967).

STUDIES K. Büchner, *Das Theater des Terenz* (1974); S. M. Goldberg, *Understanding Terence* (1986); H. Haffter, *Terenz und seine künstlerische Eigenart* (1967, from *MH* 1953; It. trans. by D. Nardo, 1969); F. Leo, *Gesch. der römischen Literatur* (1913), 232 ff.; W. Ludwig, *GRBS* 1968; G. Norwood, *The Art of Terence* (1923), *Plautus and Terence* (1932); and see COMEDY, LATIN. P. G. M. B.

Terentia (*RE* 'Terentius' 95), first wife of *Cicero (see TULLIUS CICERO (1), M.), wealthy and probably noble (a Fabia was her half-sister), bore him M. *Tullius Cicero (2) and *Tullia (2) and is said to have had great influence over him, inciting him (e.g.) to severity against the followers of *Catiline and (through dislike of *Clodia) against P. *Clodius Pulcher. During his exile she worked in his interest and they were still on good terms in 49 BC. During 48 he began to suspect her of financial dishonesty (the details are obscure) and soon divorced her, although he found it hard to repay her dowry. She is said to have later married *Sallust and M. *Valerius Messalla Corvinus and lived to be 103.

Cic. *Fam.* 14 and *Att.* (*passim*); Plut. *Cic.* (see esp. ch. 41).　　E. B.

Terentianus (*RE* 1) **Maurus** (late 2nd–early 3rd cent. AD), authority on phonology, prosody, and metre who composed his works entirely in verse (Keil, *Gramm. Lat.* 6. 325–413: 2,981 lines, lacking the end). He relied heavily on *Caesius Bassus and in turn was much used by later scholars.

Herzog–Schmidt, § 493.　　R. A. K.

Terentius (*RE* 43) **Culleo, Quintus,** a senator when captured by the Carthaginians during the war against *Hannibal, was freed in 201 BC, and showed his gratitude by marching in P. *Cornelius Scipio Africanus' triumphal procession wearing a freedman's cap. As tribune in 189 he passed a law compelling the censors to register sons of *freedmen in all 35 tribes. *Praetor peregrinus* (see PRAETOR (REPUBLIC)) in 187, he compelled 12,000 Latins to return from Rome to their native towns (Livy 39. 3. 4 ff.). He is said by Livy, following *Valerius (5) Antias, to have been appointed to preside over the court set up to try L. *Cornelius Scipio Asiagenes, but this belongs to a false account of the procedure then adopted. He served on a diplomatic mission to Africa in 195 and 171.

Briscoe, *ANRW* (1982) 2. 30. 2. 1102.　　J. Br.

Terentius (*RE* 70) **Scaurus, Quintus,** noted grammarian under Hadrian. His commentary on *Horace (in at least ten books) and polemics against *Caesellius Vindex are lost; a version of his writings on orthography survives (Keil, *Gramm. Lat.* 7. 11–33). His large-scale *Ars grammatica* (more than one book), used by later writers, is lost, but a version simplified for school use may be preserved in a 9th-cent. manuscript now in Munich (V. Law, *Rh. Mus.* 1987, 67–89: an edition is promised).

Herzog–Schmidt, § 433 (cf. § 522. 1–2).　　R. A. K.

Terentius (*RE* 83) **Varro, Gaius,** was praetor 218 BC, and consul 216, when he and L. *Aemilius Paullus (1) led the Roman army that met with disaster at *Cannae. In Livy, perhaps deriving from Q. *Fabius Pictor, Varro is a butcher's son and a radical demagogue. In fact he may have been elected with the support of the Scipios and their allies. The decision to face *Hannibal in open battle again was taken by the *senate as a whole and the hostile picture of Varro is belied by the senate and people's vote of thanks to him after the battle (Livy 22. 61. 14) and the fact that he was subsequently employed in a number of responsible positions—he was proconsul in *Picenum 215–213, propraetor in Etruria 208–7, served on diplomatic missions to Greece (203) and Africa (200), and was a commissioner to supplement the colony of *Venusia in 200.

Briscoe, *CAH* 8² (1989), 51–2, 69, 79–80.　　J. Br.

Terentius (*RE* 88) **Varro Atacinus, Publius,** a poet born in the Atax (Aude) valley in Gallia Narbonensis or at *Narbo itself in 82 BC. Nothing is known of his life except that he learned Greek at the age of 35 (Jerome, *Chronicle*). The first of his poems was no doubt his *Bellum Sequanicum*, a historical epic on *Caesar's campaign of 58 BC. After he learned Greek he translated *Apollonius (1) Rhodius under the title *Argonautae*, wrote amatory verse addressed to a 'Leucadia' (Prop. 2. 34. 85; Ov. *Tr.* 2. 439), a name chosen, like 'Lesbia', to recall *Sappho (if this was in elegiacs it was his only work not in hexameters), and composed two didactic works, *Chorographia* (which seems to show knowledge of Alexander of Ephesus) and *Ephemeris* (the title is an emendation), a poem on weather-forecasting in which he used *Aratus (1) (his version influenced *Virgil's treatment of the same topic in G. 1.

375–97). He also wrote unsuccessful satires (Hor. *Sat.* 1. 10. 46).

See Courtney, in Buechner, *FLP* 235.　　E. C.

Terentius (*RE* 'Licinius' 109) **Varro Lucullus, Marcus,** younger brother of L. *Licinius Lucullus (2), adopted by a Varro. Born 116 BC, he served under *Sulla in the east and with distinction in the *bellum Sullanum* and with his brother held a splendid aedileship (79). As peregrine praetor 76 (see PRAETOR, *Republic*) he established a *iudicium* on violence by gangs. As consul 73, with his colleague C. Cassius Longinus, he passed a *lex frumentaria* providing for the supply of wheat to the city *plebs*. Proconsul in Macedonia, he extended Roman control up to the Danube and the Black Sea and triumphed in 71. With his brother, he was harassed in the 60s. He supported *Cicero in 63 and especially over his recall from exile (57) and, as senior *pontifex, over the restitution of his property. He died soon after his brother.

　　E. B.

Terentius (*RE* 92) **Varro Murena, Aulus,** to be distinguished from the consul designate of 23 BC. The name derives from the adoption, in the previous generation, of a Licinius Murena by a Terentius Varro. Brother-in-law of C. *Maecenas, but not the recipient of *Horace, *Odes* 2. 10, he may or may not be the Terentius Varro who conquered the Salassi in 26 or 25. In 23 or (more probably) 22 he defended M. Primus, ex-governor of Macedonia, on a charge of *maiestas and then joined *Fannius Caepio and others in a conspiracy and was condemned and executed.

Syme, *AA* 387 ff.; E. Badian, in G. Wirth and others (eds.), *Romanitas, Christianitas* (1982), 18 ff., 28 ff.　　T. J. C.; R. J. S.; E. B.

Tereus See PHILOMELA.

Tergeste (mod. Trieste), in north Italy, probably in origin a settlement of the *Veneti (2), was a Roman colony (see COLONIZATION, ROMAN), whose foundation date is disputed. *Augustus provided the walls and towers, and the city, as a hub in the road-network and a port, flourished in imperial times. Monuments included a gate (?Augustan) and a Trajanic *basilica and theatre. There are also important early Christian remains.

V. Scrinari, *Tergeste* (1951); E. Godoli, *Trieste* (1989); L. J. F. Keppie, *Colonisation and Veteran Settlement in Italy* (1983), 201 ff.; F. Maselli Scotti, in *La città nell'Italia settentrionale in età romana* (1990), 617 ff.　　H. H. S.; T. W. P.

Termessus See LEX (2), lex Antonia de Termessibus; PISIDIA. For 'Termessus Minor' see OENOANDA.

Terminus, a boundary-marker; in Roman religion, the god who protected these markers, which were set up with ceremony, sacrifices being made and blood and other offerings, with the ashes of the fire, put into the hole which was to contain the *terminus* (Siculus Flaccus in F. Blume, K. Lachmann, A. Rudorff, *Die Schriften der römischen Feldmesser* (1848) 141. 4 ff.). Enunciation of the function of both god and markers was repeated by means of a yearly sacrifice and feast (Ov. *Fast.* 2. 638 ff.) by the neighbours, on 23 February (Terminalia). On the same day a public sacrifice, celebrated on the sixth milestone of the via Laurentina, affirmed the symbolic limit of the *ager Romanus antiquus*, the earliest territory of Rome. According to myth, the Terminus on the *Capitol had been there before the temple of *Jupiter Optimus Maximus was built, and refused to move; he therefore was left inside the temple, with an opening in the roof above, as he had to be under the open sky (Ov. *Fast.* 669 ff.); but this is just an interpretation of elements linked with the cult of *Jupiter (see Latte, *RR* 80 n. 3, and Jupiter Terminus in *CIL* 11. 351).

Latte, *RR* 64; G. Piccaluga, *Terminus* (1974); G. Dumézil, *ARR* 200 ff., and *Dieux souverains des Indo-européens* (1977), 168 ff.; A. Magdelain, *Ius imperium auctoritas* (1990), 279 ff.
H. J. R.; J. Sch.

Terpander (*Τέρπανδρος*) of *Antissa in *Lesbos, outstanding musician and poet of the early 7th cent. BC, head of the guild of citharodes in Antissa; yet his main activity was focused in *Sparta (Arist. fr. 551 Gigon = T 60 c Gostoli), where he instituted and won the first citharodic competition at the *Carnea (676/3 BC; Ath. 635e; ps.-Plut. *De mus. 9 = Mor.* 1134b). He also won four successive victories at the Pythian festival (see PYTHIAN GAMES) (ibid. 4). He is considered the creator of the canon of the seven citharodic nomes (see MUSIC) which he used for the setting to music of his own compositions and the verses of *Homer (ibid. 3). He composed citharodic prooemia (preludes) and *scolia (i.e. drinking songs, ibid. 28), invented the seven-stringed cithara or lyre, introduced the Mixolydian tune, and prevented a civil war in Sparta either by singing with his cithara or by playing the pipes. It is doubtful whether the fragments ascribed to him are genuine; they include such subjects as 'the new song', 'the Muses', 'Zeus, the beginning of the universe'. The existence of an Alexandrian edition seems unlikely. See also MUSIC.

A. Gostoli, *Terpandro: Introduzione, testimonianze, testo critico, traduzione e commento* (1990); D. Campbell, *Greek Lyric* (Loeb) 2 (1988), 294 ff.
C. M. B.; E. Kr.

terra sigillata See POTTERY, ROMAN.

terracottas The term properly includes all objects made of fired clay; commonly, pots and household vessels are treated separately. Fabricants (*κοροπλάθοι, κοροπλάσται*) were originally potters; later they were specialists who occasionally inscribed workshop or personal names. Earlier terracottas were modelled free-hand; after the 6th cent. BC they were usually made in moulds. Decoration at first resembled that of pots; from the 6th cent. figurative work was covered with a white slip (perhaps to evoke ivory?) and details painted. The relative status of terracotta was low; cf. *Apollonius (12) of Tyana who preferred 'to find an image of gold and ivory in a small shrine, than a big shrine with nothing but a rubbishy terracotta thing in it' (Philostr. *VA* 5. 2).

Architectural Terracotta was used for: *sarcophagi (*Crete, *Clazomenae, Etruria; see ETRUSCANS), ash-urns (Etruria), *altars (*arulae*), incense burners (*thymiatēria*), and roofing. Revetment adorned all buildings in Archaic times; metal and stone have usually been robbed, but clay being intrinsically valueless has often survived. Roof tiles (*κεραμίδες, tegulae*) were commonly of terracotta, constructed on two systems: Laconian (curvilinear), Corinthian (rectilinear). Western colonies copied the system of mother cities. Ornamental elements, simas, metopes, antefixes, acroteria, etc., were decorated with geometric and floral designs. In Italy and Sicily especially, architectural sculpture was made in terracotta. Large tiles were employed in Roman *heating systems (see BATHS) to support the floor and to permit hot air to circulate through walls (*t. mammatae*). Large moulded relief plaques survive from Roman houses.

Figurative Representational terracottas of large size were sometimes made in Greece as votives (Olympia); in Etruria they were common. *Corinth in Greece, and *Veii in Etruria seem to have been especially productive. The Etruscan repertory was largely religious, but also included sarcophagi with life-size figures reclining on the lid. In Sicily large busts of the Eleusinian deities were favoured. Small scale representational terracottas—*masks, reliefs, and figurines—were made as votives for sanctuaries, graves, and house-shrines. Crude human figures appear in Greece in neolithic times, steatopygous females, a few males, and animals. Rare in the early bronze age, female figures, numerous horses, and riders characterize the terracottas of the late iron age. In the 7th cent. *orientalizing types (first with moulded heads), masks, and horses were made in *Cyprus, *Rhodes, and *Crete, and subsequently all over the classical world. Archaic local production centres developed, particularly in Asia Minor, *Boeotia, Corinth, *Laconia, *Argos (2), Magna Graecia, and Etruria. Relatively few and chiefly hieratic types were made in the 5th cent. BC. Votive plaques (Locrian, Melian) were popular. In the 4th cent. the craft flourished, especially in Athens and Boeotia (*Tanagra). The repertory contained few religious types (Aphrodite and Eros), and many of theatrical genre (actors and comic figures). Cemeteries near Tanagra supplied so many charming figures in the 1870s that Greek figurines became a craze in Europe under the name 'Tanagras'. During the 3rd cent. these types spread everywhere. Accomplished local workshops developed in *Alexandria (1), Sicily, south Italy (*Tarentum). Later Hellenistic types were varied, including new religious themes, imaginative genre, and echoes of sculpture. The most active centres were in Asia Minor: *Amisus, *Ilium, *Pergamum, *Priene, Myrina, *Smyrna, *Tarsus. Roman workshops continued the Hellenistic repertory with local additions. Prolific centres were established in the Rhône and Rhine valleys during the first two Christian centuries. Figurines were also produced in the rest of the empire, often adapting Mediterranean types to local cults, until *c*. AD 200. Thereafter they died out in the north, continuing in the south for another two centuries, particularly in Athens, Corinth, the *Fayūm, Jordan, *Mesopotamia. With the establishment of Christianity, the craft ended completely in the 5th cent. AD.

Miscellaneous Many minor objects were made in terracotta, often as substitutes for more expensive materials. These include ornaments applied to wooden *furniture and sarcophagi. Relief decoration was used for vases imitating metalwork. It consisted of moulded figures affixed to the body or modelled vases in the form of animals or figures (plaquette ware, plastic vases). Cheap votives include miniatures of all sorts; jewellery, wreaths and flowers, furniture, implements, armour, vehicles, theatrical masks. *Toys are numerous, particularly rattles and dolls. Categories that have been well classified are: *lamps, loom-weights, spindle-whorls, stamps, sealings, tokens, metal impressions, moulds. Excavators find these useful for dating stratification. See VOTIVE OFFERINGS.

ARCHITECTURAL *RE* 5 A, 'tegula'; Å. Åkerström, *Die Architektonischen terrakotten Kleinasiens* (1966); R. R. Knoop, *Antefixa Satricana* (1987); N. Winter, *Greek Architectural Terracottas from the Prehistoric to the End of the Archaic Period* (1994).

FIGURATIVE Technical: R. V. Nicholls, *BSA* 1952; B. Neutsch, *Studien zur vortanagräisch-attischen Koroplastik* (1952). General: F. Winter, *Die Typen der figürlichen Terrakotten* (1903); S. Mollard-Besques, *Les Terres cuites grecques* (1963); R. A. Higgins, *Greek Terracottas* (1968), and *Tanagra and the Figurines* (1987). Museum Catalogues: R. A. Higgins, British Museum (1954–); S. Mollard-Besques, Louvre (1954–); P. Pensabene and M. R. Sanzi do Mino, Museo Nazionale Romano (1983–); P. G. Leyenaar-Plaisier, Leiden (1979).

MISCELLANEOUS Excavation publications, esp. of Alexandria, the Athenian Agora, *Capua, *Delos, Corinth, *Olynthus, *Perachora, Priene, Pergamum, Samos, *Thebes.
D. B. T.; M. V.

terramara derives from the Emilian dialect expression ('terra marna') for the fertile black soil that first brought a distinctive type of settlement site to the notice of early archaeologists. It has given its name to an important culture of the Italian middle and late bronze age, concentrated in the modern provinces of Modena, Reggio Emilia, Parma, and Piacenza; some sites in Lombardy and the southern Veneto are also thought to be related. Detailed assessment of the culture is hampered by the lack of stratigraphical observation in the 19th cent.

The *terramara* settlements consisted of hut villages, often enclosed by a bank and ditch. Although some of them were clearly raised deliberately above the flood level of the surrounding plain, modern excavation at Monte Leoni (Parma) suggests that the *terramara* sites were not restricted to low-lying areas.

The economy of the *terremare* seems to have been based on hunting (bear, boar, deer), cattle-raising (cows, goats, pigs, sheep), and agriculture. A highly developed bronze industry, no doubt controlled by specialist smiths, suggests transalpine and transadriatic contacts, with supplies of metal presumably being drawn from the Austrian Alps. The stylistic affinities of *terramara* pottery and bronzes must in fact be sought in the repertoire of the Hungarian early and middle bronze age, notable for its population movements and the consequent spread of cremation as a burial rite: an offshoot could very well have been dispatched to northern Italy, where the presence of the horse in the Terramara culture may be inferred from the presence of a Hungarian type of horn cheek-piece. These affinities, and the fact that the best *terramara* pottery is also the earliest, confirm one aspect of the 'Pigorini theory': the *terramaricoli* appeared with their culture already fully formed. The extension of this theory—i.e. that the *terramaricoli* were the prehistoric ancestors of the Romans, and went south in the 12th cent. BC—is wholly unacceptable.

Contact between the Terramara culture and the peninsular *Apennine culture (known until 1931 as the *cultura extra-terramaricola*) heralded the opening of the Italian late bronze age and was far-reaching in its shaping of the Italian iron age. The *terramara* impact on the south was made possible above all by metallurgy, in which Apennine Italy was notoriously backward. *Terramara* products could now travel south as objects of trade: the many parallels between the bronzes from the *terremare* and those from Scoglio del Tonno illustrate the role of the Tarentino in particular as an area specializing in east Mediterranean trade, the nature of which is confirmed by the discovery of a mould for casting a *terramara* axe among the burnt debris of the LH IIIB House of the Oil Merchant at *Mycenae.

G. Säflund, *Le Terremare* (1939), discussed by C. F. C. Hawkes and E. Stiassny, *JRS* 1940, 89 ff.; L. Barfield, *Northern Italy before Rome* (1971), 90 ff.; A. Ammerman, *Preistoria alpina* 1975, 1 ff. (Monte Leoni); J. M. Coles and A. F. Harding, *The Bronze Age in Europe* (1979), 167 f.

D. W. R. R.

Tertullian (Quintus Septimius Florens Tertullianus) (AD *c*.160–*c*.240), born in or near *Carthage, the son of a centurion (see CENTURIO). The tradition that he was a lawyer rests chiefly on the questionable authority of *Jerome (see appendix to this entry). None the less, he uses brilliant gifts of advocacy, rhetoric, and irony in favour of the rigorist party among the Carthaginian Christians. From the first he was steeped in the spirit of the martyrs. His *Ad martyres*, *Ad nationes*, and *Apologeticus* (all written *c*.197) defended Christianity against pagan charges of atheism, black magic, and sedition, while maintaining that only in martyrdom could the Christian be assured of his salvation. Next (198–

205) he devoted himself largely to Christian ethical problems. His *De oratione*, *Ad uxorem*, *De paenitentia*, and *De baptismo* all make high demands on the Christian life.

Tertullian's sole authority, apart from his verbal and intellectual acumen, was the Bible. Where, as in the *De anima*, he cites Stoics with approval, it is as the confirmation, not the source, of his beliefs. His *De testimonio animae* is a classic exposition of the view that all men have innate knowledge of God; yet heresy is found, in his *De praescriptione haereticorum*, to result from the illegitimate substitution of philosophy for the 'rule of faith' (*regula fidei*). This was followed by works against the followers of the Platonizing Christian Valentinus, and (between 207 and 211) five books against the arch-heretic Marcion. Against Marcion's belittlement of the Old Testament and violent emendation of the New, he argues for the integrity of scripture and a unity of purpose between the 'just' Father and the 'good' Son.

At some time he joined the Montanists (see MONTANISM), disciples of a new era of the Spirit, from whom they claimed to be receiving immediate direction. His action may have been precipitated by disgust with Catholic laxity, and perhaps by a dispute with the clergy at Rome. Yet, to judge by his subsequent reputation, there was never a formal schism. The transition seems to have taken place by 207. Believing that it was time for man to regain his unfallen image, he wrote his *Ad Scapulam* (212) to a local pagan governor in defence of religious freedom; his *De fuga in persecutione* and *De corona militis* against Christians who complied with the authorities; and his *De ieiunio* and *De monogamia* to enjoin a rigour in discipline that went beyond scriptural teaching. See FASTING.

His important doctrinal writings of this period are the *De carne Christi*, *De resurrectione carnis*, *De anima*, and *Adversus Praxean*, all notable for their hostility to dualistic thought. Body and soul are one, God himself is a body (though its matter is Spirit), and the body of Christ that died on the cross is identical with the risen one. His last surviving work, *De pudicitia*, was probably directed against measures by Callistus, bishop of Rome (217–22), to relax the Christian penitential system. The work is fundamental for its theology of a gathered Church and the study of the western doctrine of the Holy Spirit.

Tertullian seems to have lived to a ripe old age, and finally to have broken with the Montanists to found his own sect of Tertullianists, more rigorous than they. With the possible exception of *Minucius Felix, he is the first Latin churchman, and, as a favourite of both *Cyprian and *Augustine, exercised a great and abiding influence upon Christian theology in the west. He shares with his contemporary *Hippolytus (2) a hatred of Callistus, an aversion to all philosophy, a rebellious spirit harnessed to a strong ecclesiology, and a belief in the importance of distinguishing the persons of the Godhead (see *Adv. Praxean*). The affinity illustrates the close relations between north Africa and the capital in this period; he is, however, unparalleled in both the originality and the difficulty of his Latin style.

EDITIONS *Apologeticus*: T. R. Glover (Loeb, with *De spectaculis*); C. Becker (1961). *De anima*: J. H. Waszink (1947). *De baptismo*, *Adv. Praxean*, *De carne Christi*, *De resurrectione*: E. Evans (1947–64). *Adversus Marcionem*: E. Evans (1972). Other works: A. Reifferscheid, E. Kroymann, and V. Buhlart, *CSEL* 20, 70, 76.

MODERN WORKS A. d'Ales, *La Théologie de Tertullien* (1905); K. Adam, *Der Kirchenbegriff Tertullians* (1907); P. de Labriolle, *La Crise Montaniste* (1913); J. Berton, *Tertullien le schismatique* (1928); E. Allo Isichei, *Political Thinking and Social Experience: Some Christian Interpreta-*

tions of the Roman Empire from Tertullian to Salvian (1964); T. D. Barnes, Tertullian (1971; rev. 1985); J.-C. Frédouille, Tertullien et la conversion de la culture antique (1972); J. Daniélou, Les Origines du christianisme latin (Eng. trans. London 1977). W. H. C. F.; M. J. E.

Appendix: Tertullian as lawyer? Whether the church father and the legal writer, author of eight books of Quaestiones ('Problems') and a monograph De castrensi peculio ('On Soldiers' Property'), who was active between the time of Sextus *Pomponius and Ulpian (*Domitius Ulpianus), are the same has been disputed. The dates do not rule out their identity, and the churchman's knowledge of the law is exceptional. The five passages from Tertullian's work excerpted by Justinian's compilers (see JUSTINIAN'S CODIFICATION) show him to have been an incisive lawyer.

Lenel, Pal. 2. 341–4; PIR¹ S 324; HLL 4 (forthcoming), § 417. 2; T. D. Barnes, Tertullian² (1985), 22–9; R. Martini, Studia et documenta historiae et iuris 1975, 79–124. T. Hon.

tessera, a die or gaming piece; also a ticket or token, used in the Roman world for a great variety of purposes. Surviving examples include stamped, mostly round, pieces of lead, bronze, or terracotta, sometimes with a brief legend, and inscribed, mostly rectangular, pieces of bone, ivory, or wood. In the late republic and the Julio-Claudian period, tesserae of bone or ivory, called tesserae nummulariae by modern scholars, were attached to bags of silver coins by bankers to indicate that they had tested their genuineness (see NUMMULARIUS). Wooden tesserae were used in the Roman army as an adjunct to passwords. In the empire tesserae frumentariae, whose exact form is a matter of controversy, were issued to the privileged citizens entitled to free wheat rations at Rome, *Oxyrhynchus, and perhaps other cities (see FOOD SUPPLY). Coin-like tesserae, often bearing the head of the emperor, and marked balls exchangeable for cash or various presents from the imperial treasury and warehouses were thrown to the crowd by the emperor at some festivals in Rome. Similar tesserae were issued by private patrons entitling their clients to free meals, gifts, admission to games and public shows, and so on (most of the surviving tesserae are probably of this type), while tesserae hospitales established the claim of the bearer to hospitality when travelling.

M. Rostovtzeff, Klio 1905; J. Andreau, La Vie financière dans le monde romain (1987), 486–506; G. Rickman, The Corn Supply of Ancient Rome (1980), app. 8; C. Virlouvet, Tessera frumentaria (1995). H. M.; D. W. R.

Testamentum Porcelli, the purported will (4th cent. AD) of a piglet before slaughter at the Saturnalia, parodying the informal military will; beloved of schoolboys and deplored by Jerome, it combines simple humour with social satire.

Texts and commentaries: F. Bücheler (edn. of Petronius); Á. d'Ors (1953); N. A. Bott (1972); B. Mocci (1981). Trans.: D. Daube, Roman Law (1969), 77–81. Discussion: E. Champlin, Phoenix 1987, 174–83. L. A. H.-S.

Tethys (Τηθύς), in mythology, daughter of Earth (*Gaia) and Heaven, sister of Ocean (Hes. Theog. 136; see OCEANUS (MYTHOLOGICAL)); becomes the consort of Ocean and bears the Rivers, also the three thousand Oceanids (see NYMPHS), whose work it is to aid the rivers and *Apollo to bring young men to their prime, and *Styx, chief of them all (ibid. 337 ff.). See also MEDITERRANEAN. H. J. R.

tetrarchy (tetrarchia, i.e. the fourth part of an archē, 'dominion') was first used to denote one of the four political divisions of *Thessaly ('tetrad' being a purely geographical term). The term

found its way to the Hellenistic east and was applied to the four divisions into which each of the three Celtic tribes of *Galatia was subdivided (Strab. 12. 5. 1, 567 C). In Roman times many Hellenized *client kings in Syria and Palestine were styled 'tetrarch', but the number of tetrarchies in any political organization ceased to be necessarily four, denoting merely the realm of a subordinate dynast. Modern scholars conventionally describe as a 'tetrarchy' the system of collegiate government (two senior Augusti, two junior Caesars) instituted by *Diocletian (AD 293); the usage has no ancient authority.

W. Schwahn, RE 5 A 1 (1934), 1089–97; F. Gschnitzer, Hermes 1954, 451 ff.; B. Helly, L'état Thessalien (1995). H. D. W.; A. J. S. S.

Tetricus, Gaius Pius Esuvius, became emperor in Gaul in AD 271. In the literary tradition he appears weaker than *Postumus and *Victorinus, finally betraying his own army to *Aurelian at Châlons-sur-Marne (274). However, his coins (which show the late elevation of his son, Tetricus II, as Caesar) suggest a more resolute regime. Having led Tetricus in triumph, Aurelian gave him a senatorial appointment in Italy (PLRE 1. 885).

I. König, Die gallischen Usurpatoren (1981); J. F. Drinkwater, The Gallic Empire (1987). J. F. Dr.

Teucer (Τεῦκρος) (1) In mythology son of the river *Scamander and a nymph Idaea, and ancestor of the Trojan kings. He married his daughter Bateia (or Arisbe) to *Dardanus, and from this marriage was born Erichthonius, father of Tros (Apollod. 3. 12, which also gives the later genealogy).

(2) Son of *Telamon (1) by *Hesione. Throughout *Homer's Iliad he is a valiant archer, and faithful comrade of his half-brother, the greater Ajax (*Aias (1)). His character is similarly depicted in later works, e.g. the Ajax of *Sophocles (1). He was absent at the time of Ajax's suicide (Ajax 342–3), but returned (974) in time to take a leading part in the struggle to secure him honourable burial. After his banishment (see TELAMON (1)) he founded *Salamis (2) in Cyprus (Horace, Odes 1. 7. 27 ff. and often). H. J. R.; J. R. M.

Teucer (3) of *Cyzicus (probably mid-1st cent. BC) wrote several books about the contemporary near east, including coverage of *Pompey's settlement in 63–62. His Περὶ χρυσοφόρου γῆς ('On the Gold-Producing Land') does not necessarily identify him with *Teucer (4) of Babylon.

FGrH 274 and 314. A. H. McD.; K. S. S.

Teucer (4) of Babylon (probably the Babylon in Egypt), astrologer, is conjectured to belong to the 1st cent. AD. He expounded the traditional astrology of Egypt and united with it oriental and Greek elements. He had a great influence on Arabian and medieval *astrology, through his description of the *constellations. Fragments of his works have been preserved.

Ed. F. Boll, Sphaera (1903), 16, 31; CCAG 7. 194 ff., 8. 196 ff., 9. 2. 180 ff.; RE 5 A 1132 f. W. D. R.

Teuta, queen of the Illyrian Ardiaei (see ILLYRII) and regent for Pinnes after the death of his father, King Agron (231 BC). Teuta maintained Agron's policy of expansion in the Adriatic, but Rome's notice had already been attracted; as she continued the siege of Issa (230), the embassy of the brothers Gaius and Lucius *Coruncanius was being dispatched. Whether the embassy reached Teuta or not is disputed, but the death of one of the Roman envoys at the hands of Illyrian pirates (see PIRACY) gave Rome the occasion to declare war against her (229). Teuta was betrayed by *Demetrius (7) of Pharos, who offered *Corcyra and his services to the Romans, and after the war (229–228) she saw her realm confined to an area north of Lissus.

See bibliog. to CORUNCANIUS, GAIUS and LUCIUS, and add RE 5 A 'Teuta'; H. J. Dell, Historia 1967, 344 ff.; N. G. L. Hammond, JRS 1968, 1 ff.; A. Coppola, Demetrio di Faro (1993).   P. S. D.

Teutoburgiensis, saltus, the district where, in AD 9, the army of P. *Quinctilius Varus was destroyed on the march from summer to winter quarters. Its location was until very recently the subject of much speculation: the Teutoburger Wald of modern maps was no indication, being an archaizing name given in the 17th cent. However, striking archaeological discoveries (especially, of coins, legionary weaponry, and the usual impedimenta of a full Roman army on the march—including artillery and surgical equipment) now appear to confirm Mommsen's suggestion that the battle took place near modern Kalkriese, 16 km. (10 mi.) north of Osnabrück. Study of the remains of barricades reveals the skill of the German commanders in harassing, frustrating, and exhausting the Roman troops as they marched through a depression between a hillside and a moor. The Hermannsdenkmal (Hermann monument i.e. monument to *Arminius) at Detmold lies over 70 km. (44 mi.) to the southeast.

W. Schlüter, Germania 1992, 307 ff.   J. F. Dr.

Teutones, a Germanic tribe, known chiefly from their migration with the *Cimbri, whose neighbours they had been in Jutland, to southern France, where C. *Marius (1) annihilated them in the battle of Aquae Sextiae in 102 BC. The Aduatuci whom *Caesar (BGall. 2. 29) defeated in Gaul claimed to be descended from the Cimbri and Teutones. From a boundary-marker (ILS 9377) it has been inferred, perhaps hazardously, that a remnant of them survived at Miltenburg on the Main. Curiously, *Tacitus (1) does not mention them or the Ambrones, who marched with them and the Cimbri, were immediately demonized by the Romans as archetypal northern savages. 'Teuton' as a synonym for German was used by Latin poets long after the Teutones became extinct. See GERMANS.
          E. A. T.; J. F. D.

textile production 1. *Social Significance* Spinning and weaving held considerable symbolic and economic importance for women. In the *Gortyn law code (3. 17) a woman who was widowed or divorced could keep half of what she had woven in the marriage. Women took pride in men's praise of their skills (e.g. Hom. *Od.* 2. 104–5, 117; 19. 241–2; Pl. *Resp.* 455c) and to 'keep the house and work in wool' was also a typical way of praising a woman after her death (epitaph of Claudia, 2nd cent. BC Rome, CIL 6. 15346). Weaving also carries the suggestion of deception; in Athenian tragedy, *Deianira and *Medea trap men with fatal robes. The association with women is so strong that to accuse a man of weaving is to suggest that he is effeminate (e.g. Cleisthenes (Ar. *Av.* 831), Egilius (Cic. *De or.* 2. 277)).

In the empire, the strong gender connotations of spinning and weaving weakened; most weaving was done by men, although women were still clothes-makers and menders.   H. K.

2. *Production* Once the raw textile fibres had been removed from the parent body and prepared (see COTTON, LINEN, SILK, WOOL) they were ready for spinning. (Wool was dyed before spinning, flax afterwards; see DYEING.) Wool was sometimes converted first into rovings, loose rolls of fibre half-way to yarn. In a Classical Greek context that was achieved by rolling the fibres out on an *epinetron* (ἐπίνητρον), a terracotta sheath that fitted

over the knee. The principal spinning implement was the spindle (ἄτρακτος, *fusus*), a tapered rod of wood or bone about 20 cm. (8 inches) long with a swelling towards one end on which the whorl (σφόνδυλος, *turbo*) was jammed. The latter, a circle with central hole cut from a potsherd or shaped from bone, jet, or terracotta, gave the required momentum to the rotation of the spindle: north of the Mediterranean it was mounted at the bottom; to the south and east, at the top of the shaft. The unspun fibre was loaded on a distaff (ἠλακάτη (probably), *colus*), a short carrying staff made at its simplest from a (forked) stick and at its most refined from jet or *amber segments. Holding the distaff in her left hand the spinner drew out unspun fibres, a few at a time, fastened them to the tip of the spindle and set the latter rotating. The spindle, hanging free and spinning round, imparted twist and hence strength to the yarn. Spinning—seated, standing, or walking—was a chore for all women from materfamilias to slave girl as their tombstones and epitaphs attest, and their level of competence demonstrated by surviving textiles is remarkable. The direction of rotation, clockwise or anticlockwise, was a matter of long-standing convention: yarns spun clockwise, for example, are found everywhere, but in northern and western Europe they were used for warp, while in the eastern Mediterranean they might appear as weft or in a tapestry band. Yarns were sometimes plied for strength, usually in the opposite direction from the spin. A fine gold or silver ribbon could be wound round a textile fibre core to make metal thread for fancy textiles, like the gold and purple coverlet from a Macedonian royal tomb at Vergina (see AEGAE).

Graeco-Roman weaving technology changed radically in the centuries between Homer and Justinian; in the Roman empire particularly there was considerable regional diversity reflecting varied climatic factors and cultural influences. The underlying trend was to develop and enhance the pattern-making capacity of even the simplest looms: the ultimate achievements are the late Roman silks with their breathtakingly complex polychrome decorative schemes. From Archaic Greece to the early Roman empire the basic loom was vertical and warp-weighted, consisting of two upright timbers (perhaps 2m. (6½ ft.) long) (ἱστόποδες) joined across the top by a horizontal cloth-beam. It did not stand vertically, but was made to lean against a roof strut or wall at a slight angle. The warp-threads were secured to the cloth-beam by a specially pre-woven starting-border or starting-cord. Half of the warp (all the even-numbered or odd-numbered threads) was fastened to loomweights and hung straight down behind the loom. The rest of the warp was tied to a front row of weights and passed over a fixed horizontal shed-rod that linked the uprights at about knee height: these warp-threads remained therefore in the same plane as the tilted uprights. The 'natural shed', the angle between the two sheets of warp in this position, was changed by means of heddles, loops of string that fastened each individual rear warp-thread to a heddle-rod which rested on brackets projecting from the uprights at the front of the loom. When the heddle-rod was lifted forward, it brought the rear warp between, and to a position in advance of, the front warp, creating the second, 'artificial', shed. The process of weaving then consisted of the weaver introducing a ball or spool of weft thread from the side into and through the first shed, changing to the 'artificial' shed and passing the weft back through that. By repeating the process 1/1 tabby weave, the simplest and commonest weave structure, was achieved. Freshly inserted weft was beaten hard against the web of cloth already woven by means of a weaving sword thrust into the shed: the bare warp was kept in order by running a pin-beater (κερκίς, *radius*), a small pointed implement, lightly across it, making it 'sing' (Soph. *Fr.* 890). Loomweights (ἀγνῦθες, *pondera*), usually of *terracotta, are found in lenticular, conical, or pyramidal shapes, with a hole for suspension: the form varies with time and place.

By the end of the 2nd cent. AD the warp-weighted loom (at which the weaver stood and pushed the weft upwards) had been largely replaced by the two-beam vertical loom at which the weaver sat and beat the weft downwards with a short-toothed wooden comb. The two-beam loom was ideal for tapestry weaving whereby a 'mosaic' is built by hand from yarns of contrasting colours. As time passed, ever more advanced devices for the mechanical shedding of patterns were introduced. Simple geometric damasks in wool had appeared by AD 100 (later than that in silk), together with compound weaves in which the pattern weft could be selectively drawn to the surface or concealed within its structure. Compound twill, in production by the 5th cent. AD, came to dominate the silk industry of late antiquity. At some point during this development sequence the loom became horizontal. On a smaller scale bands could be woven without a loom-frame using three- or four-hole tablets (like a pack of cards which twisted the warp into parallel cords) or the rigid heddle on which the warp passed alternately through holes in slats or between slats. The warp-interlace technique of *sprang* carried out on a small frame was employed, as finds show, for hairnets. An ever-lengthening list of textile-finds demonstrates the ancient weaver's skill and range. Garments were regularly woven to shape on the loom with integral ornament where relevant: the role of the tailor was minimal. In the west twill weaves in wool were pre-eminent: decoration was in subtle checks or occasionally tapestry-woven bands. The Greek-speaking east was much more diverse, exploiting to the full the properties of both dyed wool and natural linen. At Phrygian *Gordium in the 8th cent. BC there were decorative bands in warp pick-up weave and tapestry-woven fabrics. An aristocratic grave of *c.*1000 BC at *Lefkandi on Euboea contained a tunic decorated with looped pile. The beginnings of fancy damask and compound weaving belong to the late Hellenistic or early Roman period. Embroidery was rare. In the west most weaving was on a domestic scale, with occasional production for profit, but in the east there were professional weavers and specialized workshops.

Wool cloth was taken direct from the loom to the fuller (κναφεύς, *fullo*) for cleaning and shrinking. He also acted as laundryman. Fullers' workshops uncovered in *Pompeii and *Ostia show how he operated. Clothing was trodden underfoot in wooden or terracotta tubs in a mixture of water, stale urine, and fuller's earth to disperse the grease and dirt, then rinsed in tanks. The nap on a woollen garment could be raised with a spiked board (*aena*) and trimmed with cropping shears to give a soft finish (*vestis pexa*). Cloth could be bleached over sulphur for enhanced whiteness. Finally, garments were carefully folded and pressed in a screw-press to make the neat creases which fashion demanded. See also BYSSUS; DRESS.

R. J. Forbes, *Stud. Anc. Technol.* 4². 149 ff.; E. J. W. Barber, *Prehistoric Textiles* (1991), 39 ff.; J. P. Wild, *Textile Manufacture in the Northern Roman Provinces* (1970); R. Pfister, *Textiles de Palmyre* (1940), 3; M. Flury-Lemberg, *Textile Conservation and Research* (1988), 234–9, 358–429.

J. P. W.

textual criticism sets out to establish what a text originally said or meant to say. Anyone who checks a garbled message with the sender has given a faultless demonstration of it. Classical texts, which have mostly come down through a succession of copies, present stiffer challenges. Even some inscriptions (see EPIGRAPHY) are corrupt.

Politian (Poliziano; see SCHOLARSHIP, CLASSICAL, HISTORY OF) in 1489 first refined ancient methods by showing that for historical reconstruction authorities were less to be counted than weighed and derivative ones ignored. He made such arresting discoveries as that all copies of *Cicero's *Ad familiares* in circulation derived from one misbound ancestor. For 300 years these insights were seldom exploited even by critics good at picking out valuable witnesses, like Heinsius and Bentley; and when genealogical classification finally took hold, among editors of the Bible in the later 18th cent. and of classical texts in the 1820s, it was not until 1872 that the historical linguist Johannes Schmidt framed the cardinal principle, still often flouted, that in a family only shared innovations indicate a closer relationship. Usually called stemmatic method, genealogical classification received its tautest exposition in 1927 from Maas. Bédier objected that the method led suspiciously often to stemmata with two branches, Pasquali that Maas disregarded the rich diversity of actual traditions; and both objections are much discussed. A sketch of the method and its snags now follows.

Copies must first be sought out and collated, tasks often skimped. Before collation, valuable witnesses may stand out by origin: a German manuscript of the *Panegyrici* (see PANEGYRIC (LATIN)) balances the Italian tradition. Age can mislead: the oldest witness must be independent, but a manuscript of *Querolus written in 1660 balances the rest, which start in the 9th cent. If the material is too bulky to collate in full, checking a list of readings in each copy may suffice for assigning it to a group, but relationships within groups will emerge only from collation of continuous passages.

Analysis rests on four assumptions: that every scribe aims at faithful transcription, that none uses more than one exemplar, that no two commit the same error, and that some errors are detectable. If copies share the same error, therefore, it first occurred either in one of them or in a common ancestor. If one of them has no further errors, then the rest derive from it, or might as well, and can be ignored. Copies that cannot be ignored are traced through a succession of common ancestors to the nearest common ancestor of all copies, known as the archetype. The stemma once established, variants anywhere can be plotted against it, and errors of single copies, extant or reconstructed, will fall away by simple logic as one approaches the archetype.

The fourth assumption has been attacked as circular: if I am inquiring what the author wrote, I cannot yet declare this or that an error. Really? Sense, syntax, idiom, sources, analogues, metre, clausulae, all tell me with a high degree of probability what he did not write, and so do scribal habits in general or the stages that a particular text must have passed through (a copy with no word-division, or in Visigothic script (see PALAEOGRAPHY, *Latin*), or annotated, or full of abbreviations). A broad principle helps: *utrum in alterum abiturum erat?* ('which was going to finish up as the other?'). At Manilius 1. 423 (see MANILIUS, M.) was *esurcione*, not Latin and unmetrical, going to finish up as *dubitavit*, or the reverse?

Stemmatists do recognize that none of the four assumptions need hold. Above all, scribes often resort to interpolation, namely rewriting, or contamination, namely switching exemplars or borrowing variants from elsewhere; and some manuscripts serve as exemplars both before and after correction or damage. Interpolation for the sake of restoring the original text may create the illusion of common errors in the other witnesses, and interpolation for the sake of improving it may go so far, especially in works designed for practical use, that editors lose hope of reconstructing any text that ever existed. Contamination has vexed many editors and more theorists. While some decry the very method that has revealed it, others look to historical evidence or computers: the environment where a manuscript was produced affects the likelihood of contamination or interpolation, and amid shifting alliances computers make shorter work than people of finding what they are told to look for, such as the witnesses that least agree. Historical evidence has shed light on many traditions, and they on history; but what editors should tell computers to look for is controversial, and no computer has yet delivered impressive results.

Indirect evidence may supervene. A joke in *Plutarch was funnier if a 4th-cent. performance of *Sophocles (1)'s *Electra* began with line 2. The manuscripts of *Tibullus, none older than the 1370s, read *magna* at 1. 1. 2, but an ancient grammarian and two medieval anthologies quote the couplet with *multa*. Sometimes, however, indirect witnesses distort quotations for reasons of their own.

After this sifting of evidence, often called recension, comes selecting the best of the readings that have survived it. If many passages exhibit very different but equally acceptable readings, perhaps the author issued different versions. Where no reading meets all requirements, another must be thought up. People usually expect it to account for the transmitted readings. Better a satisfactory conjecture that does not, though, than an improbable one that does. Better too, if the text is suspect, an unsatisfactory conjecture at the foot of the page than nothing at all: it may provoke a conclusive solution.

Textual criticism has its fashions: Heath added γε, Cobet atticized, Jachmann deleted, Housman flayed other textual critics, geese hiss at Housman. Through and beyond such fashions runs a more or less friendly tussle between conservative and sceptical critics. The former twit the latter with rewriting the author, point out that most conjectures have convinced no one but the proposer, and print transmitted readings as long as they seem possible; the latter twit the former with worshipping scribes, point out that many conjectures have been confirmed by new evidence, and print what seems the most probable reading whether transmitted or not. Only the latter have a patron saint: whoever first saw that errors may pass because nothing looks wrong.

GENERAL J. P. Postgate in *Enc. Brit.*, 11th edn. (1911); L. D. Reynolds and N. G. Wilson, *Scribes and Scholars* (1968, 1991), ch. 6; R. Renehan, *Greek Textual Criticism* (1969); J. Willis, *Latin Textual Criticism* (1972); M. L. West, *Textual Criticism and Editorial Technique* (1973).

HISTORY A. T. Grafton, *Defenders of the Text* (1991), ch. 2; S. Timpanaro, *La genesi del metodo del Lachmann* (1963, 1985); E. J. Kenney, *The Classical Text* (1975); P. L. Schmidt, in A. C. Dionisotti and others (eds.), *The Uses of Greek and Latin* (1988).

STEMMATIC THEORY P. Maas, *Textkritik* (1927, trans. 1958); J. Bédier, *La Tradition manuscrite du 'Lai de l'Ombre'* (1929); G. Pasquali, *Storia della tradizione e critica del testo* (1934); M.D.R. in P. Ganz (ed.), *The Role of the Book in Medieval Culture* (1986); H. M. Hoenigswald and L. F. Wiener (eds.), *Biological Metaphor and Cladistic Classification: An Interdisciplinary Perspective* (1987); on physical evidence of descent, M.D.R. in J. N. Grant (ed.), *Editing Greek and Latin Texts* (1989).

PRACTICE On lazy editing, A. Severyns, *Texte et apparat* (1962); for tractable contamination, M.D.R. on Florus, *CQ* 1991; for stemmatics as cultural history, G. Billanovich on Petrarch and Livy, *JWI* 1951, A. C. Dionisotti on Polybius in E. Gabba (ed.), *Tria corda* (1983); on computational methods, M. P. Weitzman, *Studies in Bibliography* 1985;

for a model of recension, S. Rizzo on *Pro Cluentio* (monograph 1979, catalogue 1983, edn. 1991).

INDIRECT TRADITION R. Tosi, *Studi sulla tradizione indiretta dei classici greci* (1988).

JUDGEMENT J. F. Gronovius, *Observationes* (1639–62); R. Bentley, *Epistola ad Ioannem Millium* (1691, 1962); A. E. Housman's Manilius (1903–30), Juvenal (1905, 1931), Lucan (1926, 1927), and 'The Application of Thought to Textual Criticism', in *Selected Prose* (1961); G. P. Goold, *Harv. Stud.* 1965; R. G. M. Nisbet, 'How textual conjectures are made?' *MD* 1991.   M. D. R.

thalassocracy See SEA POWER.

Thales of Miletus, the most scientific member of the *Seven Sages, was credited in antiquity with the prediction of a solar *eclipse (Hdt. 1. 74. 2) that modern scholars have dated in 585 BC. He was reported to have advised the *Ionians to form a political union (Hdt. 1. 170. 3). Thales acquired legendary status as engineer, geometer, and astronomer; in *Aristotle's view he was the first natural philosopher and cosmologist. Since Thales left no written work (with the dubious exception of a navigational handbook, a *Nautical Astronomy* in hexameter verse), it is impossible to know how much historical basis there is for the achievements attributed to him in the ancient tradition. These include various geometrical discoveries and feats of mensuration (e.g. calculating the height of the pyramids by the length of their shadow), the study of solstices and measurement of the astronomical seasons, and several physical theses: that the earth floats on water, that a magnetic stone has a *psychē* since it makes things move, that all things are full of gods, and that *water is the *archē*, the beginning or first principle of all things (Arist. *Metaph.* A 3, 983^{b}20 ff.). The primeval importance of water can be paralleled in Egyptian and Babylonian myths, as in the first verses of Genesis. The figure of Thales remained in popular memory as a marker of the moment when oriental science and myth were being transformed into the beginnings of Greek geometry, *astronomy, and cosmology.

DK 11; Burnet, *EGP* 40 ff.; Guthrie, *Hist. Gk. Phil.* 1. 45 ff.; Kirk–Raven–Schofield, *Presocratic Philosophers*, 76 ff.; J. Barnes, *The Presocratic Philosophers* 1 (1979), 5 ff.   C. H. K.

Thaletas, of Gortyn in *Crete (Paus. 1. 14. 4), worked at Sparta in the 7th cent. BC, where he founded the Gymnopaedia (ps.-Plut. *De mus.* 9) and cured the plague or prevented a civil war with his songs. He wrote poems which urged obedience to the laws (Plut. *Lyc.* 4), and also composed *paeans and hyporchemata (songs accompanied by dance). He introduced the paeonic and cretic (see METRE, GREEK § 4 (*d*)) rhythms (Ephorus, *FGrH* 70 F 149; ps.-Plut. *De mus.* 10, cf. 42). Only a few very dubious fragments of his work survive.

D. Campbell, *Greek Lyric* 2 (1988), 314 ff.; Page, *PMG* 362–3.
                                                        C. M. B.; E. Kr.

Thallus, Greek chronographer of imperial date, published a work in three books, from the Trojan War to Ol. 167 (112–109 BC) according to *Eusebius; but on the evidence of the fragments, from the Assyrian king Belus to at least the death of Christ. If Eusebius is right, Thallus' work must have been later extended. Euhemeristic in character (see EUHEMERUS), it was used by the Christian *apologists. He may, perhaps, be the Samaritan Thallus, *Augustus' secretary or *Tiberius' *freedman.

FGrH 256; A. E. Mosshammer, *The Chronicle of Eusebius and Greek Chronographic Tradition* (1979), 148 ff.   A. H. McD.; A. J. S. S.

Thamugadi (mod. Timgad), a settlement in *Numidia 32 km. (20 mi.) east of *Lambaesis, one of the few totally excavated towns in the Roman empire. Founded in AD 100 by Trajan as a veteran colony (*ILS* 6841), the original town was designed on a very regular orthogonal street grid; *cardo* and *decumanus* intersect at right angles, *curia*, basilica, and forum were placed at this intersection, and smaller streets run parallel to the two main roads. Thamugadi had fourteen public baths and a theatre; public-spirited citizens gave it a market and (in the 4th cent.) a library. When it outgrew the original walled square (which measured 200 Roman feet each side, making it a 12.5 hectare settlement), an enormous Capitoline temple was built in the second half of the 2nd cent. outside the walls (which were largely dismantled as the city grew). African cults, however, with thinly Romanizing veneer, flourished: especially numerous are stelai (see STELE) to Baal-Saturn, worshipped in another extramural temple. Among the numerous private houses, the larger ones with central peristyles nearly all had a piped water-supply.

The fertile countryside brought great prosperity under the Septimian dynasty (see SEPTIMIUS SEVERUS; ROME (HISTORY), § 3.1), when a great sanctuary was built in 213 around a spring south of the town, the aqua Septimiana Felix (*AE* 1948, 111 and 113). Most of the mosaics, with exuberant and distinctive floral and geometric patterns, belong to the 3rd and early 4th cent., when the city was still growing. In the 4th cent. Thamugadi was a centre of the *Donatists, and what are claimed as the remains of separate Donatist and Catholic 'cathedrals', along with six other churches and three chapels, have been identified. In the Vandal period Berber raiders sacked it. The Byzantines in 539/40 built a protective fort to the south of the town, among the best preserved of its type in north Africa, but there is little sign of Byzantine urban regeneration. See URBANISM.

PECS 899–902; A. Ballu, *Les Ruines de Timgad*² (1904), and *Les Ruines de Timgad: Sept années de découvertes (1903–1910)* (1911); C. Courtois, *Timgad, antique Thamugadi* (1951); S. Germain, *Les Mosaiques de Timgad* (1969); J. Lassus, *Visite à Timgad* (1969); E. W. B. Fentress, *Numidia and the Roman Army* (1979), 126–32; H. Lohmann, *Wohnung im Altertum* (1979), 167–87. Churches: I. Gui, N. Duval, and J.-P. Caillet, *Basiliques chrétiennes d'Afrique du Nord* 1 (1992), 263–86. Byzantine fort: J. Lassus, *La Forteresse byzantine de Thamugadi* 1 (1981). W. N. W.; R. J. A. W.

Thamyris (Θάμυρις) or **Thamyras** (Θαμύρας), a Thracian bard, who boasted that he would win a contest even if the *Muses opposed him, whereat they maimed or blinded him and made him forget his skill (*Il.* 2. 594 ff.). Later authors attribute musical inventions to him.

Höfer in Roscher's *Lexikon*; LIMC 7. 1 (1994), 902–4. H. J. R.

Thanatos, mythological figure personifying death, the son of *Nyx or Night (Hes. *Th.* 211–12). In *Homer he is not an agent of death. He and his twin *Hypnos carried *Sarpedon's corpse to *Lycia for burial (*Il.* 16. 671–5), an incident represented in art which also inspired the creation of images on white-ground lecythi in which the two carry the corpse of ordinary people, representing the notion 'good death'. Thanatos is winged and usually has an ordinary regular face, but sometimes he has an ugly rough one. In post-Homeric times he is the agent of death, most notably in Eur. *Alc.*, where he has a prominent role (and where (5. 262) he is also metaphorically described as *pterōtos Haidas*, 'winged *Hades'); also, in one version of *Sisyphus' myth (Pherecydes FGrH 3 F 119) Sisyphus bound up Thanatos when the latter came to collect him so that no one could die, until *Ares freed Thanatos—and handed Sisyphus over to him.

E. Vermeule, *Aspects of Death in Early Greek Art and Poetry* (1979), 145–51; R. Garland, *The Greek Way of Death* (1985), 56–9; E. Peifer, *Eidola*

und andere mit dem Sterben verbundene Flügelwesen in der attischen Vasenmalerei in spätarchaischer und klassischer Zeit (1989), 212–66 passim; Jean-Pierre Vernant, *Mortals and Immortals: Collected Essays*, ed. F. I. Zeitlin, (1991), 95–7; 101; C. Sourvinou-Inwood, *'Reading' Greek Death* (1995), ch. 5; LIMC 7. 1 (1994), 904–8; G. Wöhrle, *Hypnos der Allbezwinger* (1995). C. S.-I.

Thargelia, a festival of *Apollo and held in Athens (7th of Thargelion, late May), some *Ionian cities, and their colonies; it belongs to the pre-colonial calendar (see COLONIZATION, GREEK; CALENDAR, GREEK). Scholars in antiquity explained its name from a *first-fruits sacrifice, a pot with the first cereals which was offered in Athens; the festival marks the beginning of the harvest season. At the same time, it had a manifestly cathartic character (cf. PURIFICATION), which explains the presence of Apollo: on the previous day in Athens, in the course of the festival in the Ionian towns, the citizens expelled the *pharmakos*, the 'scapegoat'. The rite is well attested with only minor local variations: the city fed a marginal person, often a criminal, for a certain time; during the festival he was decked out, led around the town, and driven out or even thrown from a cliff. At a crucial junction of the year, the expulsion of a member of society cleanses the town and prepares for the new harvest.

Nilsson, *Feste*; L. Deubner, *Attische Feste* (1932); J. N. Bremmer, *Harv. Stud.* 1983, 299–320. F. G.

Thasos, a large wooded island of the north *Aegean, colonized from *Paros (see COLONIZATION, GREEK) in the early 7th cent. BC. It was rich in *timber and precious metals. Thasos sent colonists to the nearby Thracian mainland to develop gold mines in the region of Mt. *Pangaeus. In the 6th cent. a mining outpost was established at Crenides, which was seized by *Philip (1) II of Macedon in 356 BC, and refounded as *Philippi. Various commercial and mining interests produced a revenue of 200–300 talents (if Hdt. 6. 46. 2 is to be trusted), making Thasos the most prosperous state in the region. It was part of the *Delian League but seceded *c*.465 in a dispute with the Athenians over mining and trading rights on the mainland. It took the Athenians more than two years to subdue the island, and the Thasians were deprived of their *peraea* or mainland possessions (Thuc. 1. 100–1). It is a matter of dispute whether they were recovered shortly thereafter. In the 4th cent. Thasos joined the *Second Athenian Confederacy, but it was taken by Philip II *c*.340. It remained a Macedonian dependency until freed by the Romans in 196. Thasos enjoyed many of its traditional liberties and mainland privileges well into the Roman period. Its declining revenues from mining were partially compensated by an increase in the production and export of its fine wines (see WINE), as evidenced by the large number and wide distribution of Thasian wine-*amphorae bearing the official stamp of the city. Thasian coinage, minted to a high standard, also circulated widely in the Balkans.

Thasos had a flourishing school of sculpture in the early period, and it was home to the painter *Polygnotus. Archaeologists from the French School at Athens have revealed a large, prosperous city on the north coast, with an excellent harbour and impressive walls and buildings from the Classical period.

École française, *Guide de Thasos* (1967); *Études Thasiennes* (1944–). E. N. B.

Theaetetus (*c*.415–369 BC) of Athens, geometer, initiated the special definitions and theory of irrational lines fundamental for book 10 of *Euclid's *Elements* (cf. Eudemus, cited by Pappus, ed. Junge and Thomson, 63–4); one infers that he formulated a proportion theory based on the Euclidean division (*anthyphairesis*) and perhaps also set out the associated number theory of *Elements*, book 7. He also worked out constructions of the regular solids as in Euclid's book 13 (cf. scholium no. 1 to book 13, ed. Heiberg). He is intimately portrayed by *Plato (1) in the *Theaetetus*.

W. R. Knorr, *Evolution of the Euclidean Elements* (1975), and *Bulletin of the American Mathematical Society* 1983, 41–69; D. H. Fowler, *Mathematics in Plato's Academy* (1987).　　　　W. R. K.

Theagenes (1) of *Megara slaughtered the flocks and herds of the wealthy, secured a bodyguard, and made himself tyrant (see TYRANNY). He married his daughter to *Cylon of Athens, and supported Cylon's unsuccessful attempt to make himself tyrant; he may have been the first to attach *Salamis (1) to Megara. He constructed a famous fountain-house in Megara, now rediscovered (Gruben, *AΔ* 1964, 37 ff.). He was later banished. The date of his tyranny hangs on that of Cylon (attempted coup before *Draco; *Olympic victor in 640, thus somewhere between 640 and 620 BC).

Thuc. 1. 126; Arist. *Pol.* 1305ᵃ, *Rh.* 1357ᵇ; Paus. 1. 40, 41; Plut. *Quaest. Graec.* 18. L. Jeffery, *Archaic Greece: The City-States c.700–500 B.C.* (1976); R. P. Legon, *Megara: The Political History of a Greek City State to 336 B.C.* (1981).　　　　R. T.

Theagenes (2) of *Rhegium (fl. *c*.525 BC), grammarian and Homeric critic (see HOMER). Ancient sources claim him as the first both to raise questions of style ('Ελληνισμός, 'Hellenism'; see GREEK LANGUAGE, § 1.3) and to defend Homer's account of the strife of the gods (*Il.* 20) as an *allegory of the 'strife' of the natural elements.

DK⁶ 8 (1. 51–2).　　　　M. B. T.

Theagenes (or Theogenes) (3) of *Thasos, 5th.-cent. BC victor in the *Olympian Games, given cult at Thasos. See J. Pouilloux, *BCH* 1994, 199 ff.　　　　S. H.

Theages, pupil of *Socrates (1). *Plato (1) refers in the *Republic* (496b) to 'the bridle of Theages', the bad health which kept him out of politics and saved him for philosophy. On the basis of this reference an imitator of Plato wrote a *Theages* dealing with the relation between philosophy and politics, and this is included in the corpus of Plato's works.　　　　W. D. R.

Theano was probably the wife of *Pythagoras (1), possibly a daughter or disciple. She is said to have written a few things (Diog. Laert. 8. 43). Letters attributed to her and a fragment *On Piety* are of uncertain, though later, date. Texts in H. Thesleff, *The Pythagorean Texts of the Hellenistic Period* (1965). F. V. Fritz, *RE* 5 A (1934), 1379–81, 'Theano'. See WOMEN IN PHILOSOPHY.
　　　　V. L. H.

theatre staging, Greek The visual element in Greek theatre is demonstrably strong from the time of the earliest formal drama; the importance accorded to stage production may be judged from *Aristophanes (1)'s *parodies of tragic performances in his comedies, or indeed from the whole development of theatre as a genre in the 5th and 4th cents.; if confirmation were needed, it would come from the reservations *Aristotle expresses about production as opposed to composition in his lectures on composition in the *Poetics* (1450ᵇ17–20; 1453ᵇ1 ff.).

Theatres in antiquity were constantly modified and rebuilt, and the surviving remains give few clear clues to the nature of the theatrical space available to the Classical dramatists of the 5th cent. In the Theatre of Dionysus at Athens, the wall of conglomerate stone (H, with its projection T), which was trad-

itionally taken as belonging to the stage building of the later 5th cent., is now thought by some to date to the mid-4th. (See next entry but one.) Certainly there is no physical evidence for a circular orchestra earlier than that of the great theatre at *Epidaurus about 330 BC. For 5th-cent. Athens, one might think of a metropolitan version of the deme-theatres (see DEMES) at *Thoricus and Trachones in Attica where the audience was seated much closer to the stage in a rectilinear arrangement. The stage and most probably the stage building were wooden at this period. Vases with scenes from Attic comedy from the late 5th and early 4th cents. suggest that by this time the stage was about a metre high with a flight of steps in the centre communicating with the orchestra. The stage was entered from either side (and some plays exploit the contrast), and from a central door in the stage building, representing palace, temple (and sometimes pavilion, tomb, or cave) in tragedy; for comedy, three doors are certain for the 4th cent., and were probably available in the 5th. The central door also housed the *ekkyklēma*, a wheeled platform perhaps measuring *c*.2.5 × 1.5 m. and in any case large enough to display set-pieces of events that had taken place inside, like Ajax's torture and slaughtering of the animals in his tent in *Sophocles (1)'s play *Ajax*. Towards the right (western) end of the stage area a crane (*mēchanē, machina*) could be manipulated from behind the stage building to bring gods or heroes through the air onto the stage, or to have them fly up from it, like Bellerophon on Pegasos in a scene of *Euripides which Aristophanes parodies in *Peace*. The roof of the stage building was also accessible: it was used for the watchman on the roof in *Aeschylus' *Agamemnon*, but in later tragedy mostly for the appearance of gods. The contrast between the hidden interior of the stage building and the daylight outside, between the gods on high and the actors on stage, and between these and the chorus, half-way to the audience and virtually within its territory, are all physical facts which the playwrights exploited. It is possible that the stage building had wings already in the later 5th cent. but the evidence is uncertain. In the 4th cent. the most important development was the so-called Lycurgan theatre (see LYCURGUS (3)) with its stone stage building faced with semi-columns.

It is difficult to say much of the appearance of tragedy in the Classical period since depictions in vase-paintings translate the stage action into the further reality of the myth intended by the performance. *Masks probably had conventionalized, but not exaggerated features, with costumes rich and formal, as is suggested by the actors' costumes on the Pronomos vase of the end of the 5th cent.: that is presumably why Aristophanes could make jokes against Euripides when he abandoned some of its magnificence for his royal heroes in distress, like *Telephus (1) king of Mysia as an exile and a beggar. Comedy is better represented in the material remains. From the mid-6th cent. onwards comic choruses are shown in careful and colourful detail, and to identify a comedy by its chorus remained an artistic convention until the middle of the 4th cent. From the time of Aristophanes onwards we also find representations of actors, both in clay figurines and in vase-paintings, where they are often shown in stage action. Best known among the latter are those made in the Greek colonies of Taras (*Tarentum), *Metapontum, *Syracuse, and *Paestum, on which the scenes demonstrably show the actors wearing costume and mask of Athenian derivation; in a number of cases the plays can be shown to be Athenian too (as with the bell-crater in Würzburg with a scene from Aristophanes' *Thesmophoriazusae*).

The basic costume of Old and Middle Comedy (see COMEDY

(GREEK), OLD and MIDDLE) consisted of tights which terminated at ankle and wrist and which held heavy padding on the rump and belly; there was also a prominent leather *phallus. The costume appropriate to the role (male or female) was placed over this. Certainly from the later part of the 5th cent. the masks were developed as standard types, recognizable once the characters came on stage, and the clothing was normally standardized to the part also, as the short tunic fastened at one shoulder (*exōmis*) for the slave, the cloak and conical fur or felt hat (*pilos*) for the traveller, and so on.

The award of prizes to actors from the middle of the 5th cent. is symptomatic of the growing importance given them as interpreters of roles. They were not yet, however, professionals. In depictions like that on the Pronomos vase (see above) the actor still has a full beard, whereas on the Würzburg fragment of the middle of the 4th cent. with a tragic actor holding his mask, he trims his beard short because he regularly wears a mask. Actors had become professional in the meantime and they had been given increased public standing. It was the growing popularity of theatre across the Greek world which prompted the construction of huge theatres like that at Epidaurus, with their audiences arranged round a circular orchestra and the stage raised higher to give the actors better visibility. These conditions may have prompted the development of the *onkos* or crown of raised hair above the brow of tragic masks, a feature which appeared first in the later part of the 4th cent.; so too the platform soles for their boots (*kothornoi*).

The so-called New Comedy (see COMEDY (GREEK), NEW) of *Menander (1) and his contemporaries in the later 4th cent., however, was perceived as naturalistic not only in style and handling of plot but in presentation on stage. The grotesque padding and the artificial phallus worn by actors of Old and Middle Comedy were abandoned and clothing was given a more naturalistic length and appearance. The range of mask-types was multiplied, especially for the younger men and women, so as to allow a greater subtlety in their differentiation, paralleling the finer delineations of character found in the text.

During the Hellenistic period theatre continued as the major form of public entertainment and Menander's comedies became if anything more popular. But in later years, as his plays steadily came to be regarded as classics remote from the realities of the contemporary world, so the costume and performance style became more conventionalized. Many of the depictions of masks and comic scenes from Pompeii are copies of the cultural heritage of the 2nd cent. BC. Under the Roman empire it is harder to point to concrete evidence of performance of traditional theatre, but the continuing development of mask- and costume-design demonstrates that it continued not uncommonly until perhaps the 3rd cent. AD, though in the Greek rather than the Latin world, and less frequently (perhaps in recitals of famous passages and in private gatherings) until the beginning of the 6th cent., roughly as long as papyrus texts of Menander's plays continued to be copied.

M. Bieber, *The History of the Greek and Roman Theater*, 2nd edn. (1961); P. Ghiron-Bistagne, *Recherches sur les acteurs dans la Grèce antique* (1976); J. R. Green, 'On Seeing and Depicting the Theatre in Classical Athens', *GRBS* 1991, 15–50, and *Theatre and Greek Society* (1994); J. R. Green and E. W. Handley, *Images of Greek Theatre* (1994); A. D. Trendall, *Phlyax Vases*, 3rd edn. (forthcoming); A. D. Trendall and T. B. L. Webster, *Illustrations of Greek Drama* (1970); A. W. Pickard-Cambridge, *The Theatre of Dionysos in Athens* (1946), *Dithyramb, Tragedy and Comedy*, 2nd edn. rev. by T. B. L. Webster (1962), and *The Dramatic Festivals of Athens*, 2nd edn. by J. Gould and D. M. Lewis (1968; reissued with suppl. and corrections, 1988); L. Polacco, *Il teatro di Dioniso Eleutereo ad Atene* (1990); T. B. L. Webster, *Monuments Illustrating Tragedy and Satyr Play*, 2nd edn., *BICS* Suppl. 20 (1967), *Greek Theatre Production*, 2nd edn. (1970), *Monuments Illustrating Old and Middle Comedy*, 3rd edn. rev. and enl. by J. R. Green, *BICS* Suppl. 39 (1978), and *Monuments Illustrating New Comedy*, 3rd edn. rev. and enlarged by J. R. Green and A. Seeberg, *BICS* Suppl. 50 (1994); J. Gould, *CHCL* 1 (1985), 268–81; O. Taplin, *Comic Angels* (1993); K. Mitens, *Teatri greci e teatri ispirati all'architettura greca in Sicilia e nell'Italia meridionale* (1988); R. Rehm, *Greek Tragic Theatre* (1992). J. R. G.

theatre staging, Roman The staging of the plays of *Plautus and *Terence has to be worked out almost entirely from the texts themselves; the theatres in which they were performed have not survived. (The first Roman theatre to last for any length of time was built by *Pompey in 55 BC, with a seating capacity estimated at 10,000. Later theatres in the Roman world were increasingly elaborate: see THEATRES (GREEK AND ROMAN), STRUCTURE.) Plays put on at the Megalesian Games (see LUDI) were performed outside the temple of *Cybele on the *Palatine, others probably outside other temples or in the *forum Romanum, normally on wooden stages erected for the occasion. As in Greece, plays were performed in daytime in the open air, and the action was supposed to take place out of doors.

The stage generally represents a street, fronted by at most three houses, and with side-exits/-entrances to left and right; the street is normally called *platea*, rarely *angiportum* (more commonly used to refer to a back street not visible to the spectators). There has been much discussion of whether each side-exit was supposed by convention (perhaps adapted from Greek practice) to lead in a particular direction (e.g. right to the centre of town, left to the harbour or the country), but different plays conjure up different off-stage locations, and the alleged convention seems pointless. Nor need there have been any attempt to assimilate the stage setting to the location of the theatre within Rome; there are very occasional references to Roman topography, but the plays are set in the Greek world (not always in a city).

On the stage stood an altar. Further details of the setting (e.g. of the rocky landscape in Plautus' *Rudens*) may well have been left to the audience's imagination, and there was perhaps no painted scenery. The structure representing the houses had to be strong enough to withstand repeated opening and shutting of the doors (and knocking on them, if this was performed realistically), and at *Amphitruo* 1008 ff. Mercury appears on the roof. There was no drop-curtain between the stage and the audience, although at a later date we hear of a curtain lowered at the start of the performance and raised at the end. A passage of *Cicero (*Pro Murena* 26) suggests that in dramatic performances in his lifetime the pipe-player in sections with musical accompaniment was seen to pass on the stage from one performer to another.

It is generally assumed that the actors in these comedies were male and wore *masks. They performed in Greek dress; Plautus' *Rudens* 429 and *Casina* 875, 932 are unusual in suggesting an erect *phallus as part of the costume. Many of the conventions (such as asides and overheard monologues) were inherited from (Greek) New *Comedy, but many scenes differ from the surviving Greek remains in requiring four or more speaking actors.

G. E. Duckworth, *The Nature of Roman Comedy* (1952), 79 ff.; M. Bieber, *The History of the Greek and Roman Theater*[2] (1961); W. Beare, *The Roman Stage*[3] (1964), 159 ff. and apps.; D. Bain, *Actors and Audience* (1977), 154 ff. P. G. M. B.

theatres (Greek and Roman), structure The Greek theatre consisted essentially of the orchestra, the flat dancing-place for the choral song and dance out of which grew tragedy and comedy; and the auditorium (the *theatron* proper, Latin *cavea*), normally a convenient slope on which spectators could sit or stand. In early theatres wooden seating was constructed, though it is not clear how this was done. Seats were sometimes cut in the rock; by the time theatres reached a more definitive form, in the 4th cent. BC, seats consisted of stone benches of simple form, rising in tiers. These were curved, reflecting the normal circular shape of the orchestra. A rectangular orchestra survives at the well-preserved theatre at *Thoricus, partly faced by seats in a straight line, curving only at the ends. The orchestra consisted of hard earth—paving was not introduced till Roman times. The *skēnē* (tent or hut) was in origin a simple structure for the convenience of the performers, which could also form a background for the plays. In the course of the 5th cent. it became a more solid building, ultimately acquiring a handsome architectural form sometimes with projecting wings. The fully developed auditorium was wherever possible rather more than a semicircle in plan, opening out a little at the outer ends, where the line of seats was drawn on a slightly greater radius. The outer sectors required embankments and solid retaining walls, while the inner was hollowed out of the hillside; there were no elaborate substructures as in Roman theatres. The auditorium did not link up with the *skēnē*, except perhaps by means of light gateways, and the intervening passages on either side were called *parodoi*. Stairways radiated from the orchestra, dividing the seating into 'wedges', and in large theatres there were horizontal passages too (*diazōma*). The front tiers were sometimes provided with more elaborate and comfortable seating for priests and officials (so-called *proedria*).

In the 5th cent., since archaeological evidence is lacking, the level at which the action took place is not certain: probably at orchestra level, with at most a low wooden platform, easily accessible by steps, in front of the *skēnē*, which provided the door openings necessary for the action of all classical drama. Later, the *proskēnion* was introduced, a row of columns in front of the *skēnē* supporting a high platform (seen to good advantage at *Oropus, where it has been reconstructed). This came to be used as a raised stage, a feature appropriate to New Comedy (see COMEDY (GREEK), NEW), which would have been out of place in the theatre of *Sophocles (1) or *Aristophanes (1). *Proskēnia* were usual in Hellenistic theatres, and were added to old theatres at Athens and elsewhere. At Athens itself tradition speaks of an early theatre in the Agora. The theatre attached to the shrine of *Dionysus Eleuthereus on the south slope of the Acropolis developed from crude beginnings in the latter part of the 6th cent. BC; its peculiar and complicated history is the subject of much dispute. Architecturally it was still simple and undeveloped in the time of the great 5th-cent. dramatists. The theatre at the shrine of Asclepius near *Epidaurus shows the perfection of design achieved in the 4th cent. Even then the theatre was by no means standardized and there are many local variations.

Roman theatres conformed to a type which made a complete building, though, in larger examples, the auditorium—a semicircle—was not roofed; instead, awnings (*vela*) could be drawn on ropes over the auditorium as necessary. The stage, certainly roofed and close to the semicircular orchestra, was a wide and fairly deep raised platform, backed by a wall (*scaenae frons*) as high as the top of the *cavea*, treated as an elaborate front towards the stage, with columns, niches, and the requisite doors. Sub-

structures of *cavea* and stage often consisted of vaulted passages, etc., with staircases, and the outer walls enclosing the back of the *cavea*, sometimes squared, were of arched construction in tiers, with order-treatments, though where the auditorium could rest directly on the hillside, this could be used for part of the auditorium. Simple theatres in the western provinces might have auditoria resting on terraces of earth fill supported by walls. The best preserved Roman theatres are at *Aspendus and *Perge in Pamphylia (eastern type, with flat *scaenae frons*) and at *Arausio (western type, with indented *scaenae frons*). See ODEUM.

A. W. Pickard-Cambridge, *The Theatre of Dionysus in Athens* (1946); M. Bieber, *The History of the Greek and Roman Theater*² (1961) (bibliog. 325 ff.); A. von Gerkan and W. Müller-Wiener, *Das Theater von Epidauros* (1961); D. de Bernardi Ferrero, *Teatri classici in Asia Minore* (1966–74); P. C. Rossetto and G. P. Sartori (eds.), *Teatri greci e romani*, 3 vols. (1994). See bibliogs. to ARCHITECTURE   R. A. T.

Thebes (1) (Θῆβαι)

Prehistoric Thebes, on the south edge of the eastern plain of *Boeotia, has been one of the major settlements of Greece since the early bronze age, but its prehistoric phases remain relatively poorly known. The oval plateau of the Cadmea (the acropolis or citadel of Thebes) was already extensively occupied in early Helladic II, to which period belong the remains of a 'corridor house', an associated fortification wall, and other substantial structures in the centre, and of an elaborate, originally rich mud-brick and stone tomb on the Ampheion hill to the north. Its middle Helladic and early Mycenaean history (see MYCENAEAN CIVILIZATION) are obscure, although it evidently remained a large settlement, and some well-provided tombs indicate the growth of wealth at the beginning of the Mycenaean period. By the mid-14th cent. BC Thebes was one of the great centres of the Mycenaean world, covering some 30 hectares and containing a substantial palace, some of whose administrative rooms, store-rooms, and workshops have been uncovered. Other finds include a fortification wall and a very extensive chamber-tomb cemetery, including one exceptionally large, frescoed, potentially 'royal' tomb. To judge from references in the Linear B material (see MYCENAEAN LANGUAGE), Thebes may have ruled a state extending to southern *Euboea; but claims of special links with the near east have no basis other than the much-discussed near eastern cylinder seals, which were probably acquired for their material, lapis lazuli. The palace may have suffered damage in the late 14th cent. BC and been rebuilt on a different orientation, but a much more widespread and damaging destruction horizon on the Cadmea belongs around 1250 BC. Tombs indicate continued occupation into and through the Dark Age, but evidence is scanty.

GAC, G 23; K. Demakopoulou, *BCH* Suppl. 20 (1990), 307 ff.
O. T. P. K. D.

Historic Thebes was the birthplace of *Heracles, who, as its champion, threw off the tribute imposed upon it by the king of *Orchomenus (1). The legend of Heracles reflects the essence of Boeotian politics, which were moulded by rivalry between Thebes and Orchomenus. *Herodotus (1) (5. 57–61) erroneously attributes to Thebes the introduction of the alphabet to Greece (though he is right to speak in this connection of *Phoenicians; see ALPHABET, GREEK; and for the allegedly Phoenician origins of the Thebans, see CADMUS). *Aristotle (*Pol.* 2. 9. 7, 1274ᵃ 31) claims that the Bacchiad Philolaus of *Corinth became a lawgiver to Thebes in familial matters and rights of property. By the late 6th cent. BC Thebes had organized an alliance or rudimentary confederacy consisting of its neighbours, with Orchomenus conspicuously absent. Thereafter, it vied for the hegemony of all Boeotia. It maintained friendly relations with the Pisistratids (see ATHENS *History*; HIPPIAS (1); HIPPARCHUS (1); PISISTRATUS), but hostility to Athens arose over *Plataea, which joined Athens in either 519 or 509 BC. One group of Thebans stood with the other Greeks at Thermopylae, while other Thebans medized (see MEDISM; THERMOPYLAE, BATTLE OF; PERSIAN WARS). The Greek victory at Plataea in 479 BC led to the temporary eclipse of Theban power. Thebes allied itself with Sparta in 457 BC, but was overwhelmed by Athenian counter-attack at Oenophyta later that year. After a period of Athenian domination, the Boeotians rose against Athens, and defeated Tolmides at the battle of *Coronea in 447 BC. Thebes and other major Boeotian cities thereupon formed the Boeotian Confederacy described in the Oxyrhynchus historian (see FEDERAL STATES; OXYRHYNCHUS, HISTORIAN FROM). Thebes at the outset possessed two of the eleven units of the federal government. It was instrumental in igniting the *Peloponnesian War by attacking Plataea in time of peace. Upon its surrender Thebes occupied its territory and assumed its two units within the confederacy. Using the war to further its ambitions, Thebes destroyed the walls of *Thespiae after the battle of *Delion in 424 BC, and sometime later reduced the power of Orchomenus. It had thereby gained a position of ascendancy within the confederacy. After the defeat of Athens, Thebes became estranged from Sparta, and offered sanctuary to Athenian exiles hostile to the *Thirty Tyrants. Thebes and the confederacy joined Athens, Corinth, and *Argos (2) to oppose Sparta in the *Corinthian War, but defeat entailed the dissolution of the confederacy and the loss of Theban power. In 382 BC Sparta seized it in time of peace, only to lose it to a popular uprising in 379 BC. Thebes thence re-established the confederacy, brought it fully under Theban control, and used its resources to defeat Sparta at the battle of *Leuctra in 371 BC. The victory led to an ephemeral Theban hegemony of Greece under *Epaminondas and *Pelopidas, which ended with the former's death at the battle of Mantinea in 362 BC (see MANTINEA, BATTLES OF). The fortunes of Thebes declined owing to losses during the Third *Sacred War, and its opposition to *Philip (1) II at the battle of Chaeronea led to its downfall (see CHAERONEA, BATTLES OF). Although Philip spared the city, its revolt against *Alexander (3) the Great resulted in its destruction. *Cassander rebuilt the Cadmea in 316 BC (see above, *Prehistoric* section), but Thebes played a minor role in Hellenistic politics. None the less, Thebans and other Greeks defended *Delphi (2) against *Brennus (2) in 279 BC. Yet Thebes suffered further damage at the hands of Q. *Caecilius Metellus Macedonicus in 146 BC and again under *Sulla in 86 BC, who confiscated half its territory. Thereafter eclipsed by Lebadea (see TROPHONIUS) and *Thespiae until the 3rd cent. AD, Roman Thebes none the less became a comfortable city, restricted to the Cadmea and some suburbs, known for its gardens, ample waters and panhellenic *agōnes (see PANHELLENISM) for *Heracles. *Hadrian honoured it with a visit in AD 125. It withstood the Gothic attack of AD 395 (see GOTHS), after which *Justinian refortified it.

P. Cloché, *Thèbes de Béotie* (1952); J. Buckler, *The Theban Hegemony* (1980); S. Symeonoglou, *The Topography of Thebes* (1985). J. Bu.

Thebes (2) (anc. Egyptian name Waset, mod. Luxor), sometime capital of pharaonic *Egypt, visited by *Herodotus (1) (2. 143), and still an important city at the Macedonian conquest, whereafter it declined into the 'village-style' settlement seen by *Strabo (17. 1. 46, 815–16 C), having suffered through serving twice (207/6 and 88 BC) as a base for indigenous revolts against the

Ptolemies; and in 30 or 29 BC C. *Cornelius Gallus sacked the city following anti-Roman unrest. Even so, Ptolemaic patronage of Egyptian religion extended to the Theban temples. Sporadic building continued under the Principate at least as late as *c.* AD 150; but the Egyptian cult in the temple of Amon (Karnak) had been abandoned before the late 3rd cent., when the complex became a Roman fortress and pharaonic statuary was carefully buried. Long before, the Theban monuments had become a centre for Roman *tourism, above all the colossi of *Memnon and the pharaonic tombs. *Constantius II presented a Theban obelisk to Rome in 357.

J. Bingen, *Chron. d'É.* 1986, 330 ff.; G. Fowden, *JHS* 1987, 51 ff. (obelisk); *Egyptian Archaeology* 1992, 8 f. (statuary). J. G. M.; A. J. S. S.

theft (*furtum*), as its probable etymology suggests, was originally confined to cases involving a carrying away (*ferre*). But in the course of the republic, the notion was extended very considerably until it covered almost any species of dishonesty. However, as a result of the introduction and extension of other delictual remedies, a tendency to retrench gained ground. More particularly, handling (*contrectatio*) and the intention of making an unlawful gain (*animus lucri faciendi causa*) emerged as the two distinctive elements normally to be found in cases of theft. They also form the cornerstones of the famous definition contained in Justinian's *Digest* (47. 2. 1. 3); see JUSTINIAN'S CODIFICATION. However, the notion of theft remained fairly broad: no intention permanently to deprive the owner was required (borrowing without consent (*furtum usus*), therefore, was covered by the definition); the owner himself could be liable for theft (e.g. by taking his property from a pledgee: *furtum possessionis*); embezzlement was included; and even certain cases of fraud were taken to constitute theft. A person could also be liable for theft, if he had merely rendered physical assistance (*ops*) or participated in the delict by way of instigation or advice (*consilium*). But the suggestion that land could be stolen was widely rejected.

A thief was normally liable for double the value of the object stolen (*actio furti nec manifesti*). If, however, he had been caught in the act, the *actio furti manifesti* was available against him for four times the value (in mitigation of the much harsher regime still prevailing at the time of the *Twelve Tables, when, for instance, a thief who came by night or who used a weapon, could be killed out of hand). The right to sue vested in the owner or any other person who had an interest in the security of the thing stolen (*cuius interest rem salvam esse*; Gai. *Inst.* 3. 203), such as a usufructuary or a pledgee (disputed). The purely penal actions on theft were preserved by Justinian, although it is probable that by the 3rd cent. AD criminal prosecution was the normal procedure. The owner also had an action to reclaim the thing stolen (*rei vindicatio*) or compensation if it no longer existed (*condictio ex causa furtiva*).

H. F. Jolowicz, *Digest 47. 2 De Furtis* (1940); W. Pika, *Ex causa furtiva condicere* (1988); R. Zimmermann, *The Law of Obligations* (1990), 922 ff. R. Z.

Themis, daughter of *Gaia and *Ouranos (Hes. *Theog.* 135). She is associated with Gaia in the myth of previous owners of the *Delphic oracle. Her identification with Gaia in Aesch. *PV* 211 ff. (where Themis is Prometheus' mother and utters prophecies) is a theological statement, not a reflection of cult. In Pind. *Isthm.* 8. 31–6 she gave a prophecy to *Zeus and *Poseidon. On the cup Berlin 2538 (*ARV* 1269. 5; *Para* 471; *Add* 356) she is represented in the role of the Delphic Pythia, delivering prophecies while sitting on a tripod holding a laurel-branch. She is a primordial goddess, but she is closely associated with Zeus' order, and with justice, with right, law, ordinances. In Hes. *Theog.* 901–6 she is Zeus' second wife and she bore him the Hours (*Horae), Good Order (*Eunomia), Justice (*Dike) and Peace (*Eirene), and the Fates (see FATE). In *Ephorus (*FGrH* 70 F 31b) *Apollo and Themis founded the oracle together, to guide and civilize humanity. The conceptual association between the two is also expressed in the Homeric *Hymn to Apollo 124–5, where Themis fed the newborn Apollo nectar and *ambrosia.

H. Vos, *Themis* (1956), 39–78; F. W. Hamdorf, *Griechische Kultpersonifikationen der vorhellenistischen Zeit* (1964), 50–1, 108–10; Burkert, *GR* 185–6; Nilsson, *GGR* 1³ (1967), 171–2; W. Pötscher, *Wien. Stud.* 1960, 31–5.   C. S.-I.

Themison (*RE* 7) of *Laodicea (probably Lycus), a pupil of *Asclepiades (3) of Bithynia, probably lived towards the end of the 1st cent. BC and spent at least part of his working life in Rome. None of his writings survives, and attempts to associate certain anonymous collections of medical texts with his name have been largely unsuccessful. Some sources insist he was the founder of Methodism (see MEDICINE, § 5.3), but *Thessalus (2) of Tralles may have a stronger claim. Galen frequently underlines similarities between Themison's and Thessalus' medical theory and practice, but later Methodist doctors, especially Caelius Aurelianus, are at pains to distance Themison from the early history of their sect, claiming that his ideas about theory and practice were much closer to those of Asclepiades. It seems unlikely that he went as far as Thessalus in claiming that the diseased body presented to the doctor two phenomenally evident common states from which the indication for treatment followed directly. No surviving Methodist source has much praise for Themison, generally on account of his attitude to the role of theory, but he is credited with the authorship of the first work on chronic diseases, a form particularly favoured by some Methodist physicians.

Text: There is no edition of the fragments, but see R. Fuchs, *Rh. Mus.* 1903, 67–114 for the disputed texts. Literature: K. Deichgräber, *RE* Suppl. 5 A 1632, 'Themison'; L. Edelstein, *RE* Suppl. 6. 358, 'Methodiker'; J. T. Vallance, *The Lost Theory of Asclepiades of Bithynia* (1990), 141–2.   J. T. V.

Themistius, Greek philosopher and rhetorician, was born in *Paphlagonia *c.* AD 317 of a cultured family of pagan landowners, and studied in the eastern provinces and in *Constantinople, where he opened a school (*c.*345). Attracting the attention of the imperial government, he was soon appointed to an official chair and became a member of the Constantinopolitan senate. His eloquent and often constructive exposition of the ideology of monarchy in a succession of panegyrics and other speeches won and retained for him the favour of every emperor from *Constantius II to *Theodosius (2) I, who appointed him prefect of the city (383–4) and entrusted him with the education of his son, the future emperor *Arcadius (2). He travelled widely in the empire, in attendance on the imperial court and on official missions, such as that to the Roman senate in 357. He died in Constantinople about 388.

In spite of his professed admiration for *Plato (1), Themistius found the pragmatic and realistic approach of *Aristotle more congenial, and he was little influenced by contemporary *Neoplatonism, with its other-worldly overtones. In his early years as a teacher he wrote explanatory paraphrases of many of Aristotle's works, setting a pattern of exegesis which continued to be followed throughout the Middle Ages. A convinced but unfanatical pagan, he yet refrained from overt attacks on Christianity except

in an address to *Julian, now lost, which evoked from the emperor the celebrated letter (253–67 Spanheim) setting out the principles of his proposed restoration of paganism.

Of his numerous works there survive: 34 speeches, mainly official addresses to emperors, but including an interesting funeral oration on his father (*Or.* 20); and paraphrases of Aristotle's *Posterior Analytics*, *Physics*, *De anima* (in the Greek original), *De caelo* and *Metaphysics XII* (in a medieval Hebrew translation made from an Arabic version). Themistius was neither a great philosopher nor a great statesman, yet his speeches are valuable as sources for the history of his time and as specimens of pagan political ideology in the Christian empire, and his Aristotelian paraphrases embody material from lost commentaries.

H. Schenkl, G. Downey, A. F. Norman (eds.), *Themistii orationes*, 3 vols. (1965–74); M. Wallies and others, *Paraphrases*, *Commentaria in Aristotelem Graeca* 5 (1899–1900); C. Prato and A. Fornaro, *Giuliano imperatore: Epistola a Temistio* (1984); G. Dagron, *Travaux et Mémoires* 1968, 1–142, and *Naissance d'une capitale: Constantinople et ses institutions de 330 à 451* (1974) *passim*; G. A. Kennedy, *Greek Rhetoric under Christian Emperors* (1983), 32–5; *PLRE* 1 (1970), 889–94.   R. B.

Themisto, name of several heroines, the only one of importance being the daughter of Hypseus (Nonnus, *Dion.* 9. 305 f.), wife of *Athamas. Herodorus, in schol. Ap. Rhod. 2. 1144, makes his first wife and mother of several children, including Phrixus and Helle.

See Höfer in Roscher, 'Themisto'.   H. J. R.

Themistocles (*c.*524–459 BC), Athenian politician, was a member of the ancient Lycomid family but by a non-Athenian mother. *Herodotus (1)'s informants accused him of corruption and said that in 480 he had 'recently come to the fore', though he was archon in 493/2; but *Thucydides (2) admired him for his far-sightedness and considered him one of the greatest men of his generation.

As archon, Themistocles began the development of the *Piraeus as Athens' harbour; it may be that *Phrynichus (1)'s *Capture of Miletus* and subsequent trial, and *Miltiades' return to Athens from the *Chersonesus (1) and his subsequent trial, belong to 493/2 and that Themistocles was involved in these episodes. In the *ostracisms of the 480s he regularly attracted votes but was not himself ostracized (altogether, 2,264 ostraca against him are known, including a set of 190 prepared by fourteen hands): the expulsion of *Xanthippus (1) in 484 and *Aristides (1) in 482 may represent a three-cornered battle in which Themistocles was the winner. Attempts to connect him with a change from direct election to partial *sortition in the appointment of the *archontes, in 487/6, have no foundation in the sources; but he was behind the decision in 483/2 to spend a surplus from the silver mines (see LAURIUM) on enlarging Athens' navy from 70 to 200 ships—allegedly for use against *Aegina, but these ships played a crucial part in the defeat of the Persian navy in 480 (see PERSIAN WARS).

In 480 he was the general who commanded Athens' contingents in the Greek forces against the invading Persians: on land in *Thessaly, and then on sea at Artemisium and at Salamis (see ARTEMISIUM, BATTLE OF; SALAMIS, BATTLE OF); he interpreted an oracle to predict victory at Salamis, argued for staying at Salamis rather than retiring beyond the isthmus of Corinth, and tricked the Persians into throwing away their advantage by entering the straits. The Decree of Themistocles inscribed at Troezen in the 3rd cent. probably contains authentic material but has at least undergone substantial editing. In the winter of 480/79 he received unprecedented honours at Sparta, but in 479 we hear nothing of him and Athens' forces were commanded by Aristides and Xanthippus.

After the Persian War there are various stories of his coming into conflict with Sparta (in the best attested he took delaying action at Sparta while the Athenians rebuilt their city walls), while the *Delian League was built up by the pro-Spartan *Cimon. In the main tradition the cunning, democratic Themistocles is opposed to the upright, aristocratic Aristides, but there are indications that Aristides was now a supporter rather than an opponent of Themistocles. About the end of the 470s Themistocles was ostracized (see OSTRACISM), went to live at *Argos (2), and 'visited other places in the Peloponnese' (Thuc. 1. 135. 3), where an anti-Spartan alliance was growing. When Sparta became alarmed, and claimed to have evidence that he was involved with *Pausanias (1) in intrigues with Persia, he fled, first westwards to *Corcyra and *Epirus but then via *Macedonia and the *Aegean Sea to *Asia Minor. The Athenians condemned him to death in his absence; after 465 the new king, *Artaxerxes I, made him governor of *Magnesia (1) on the Maeander, where coins bearing his name and portrait were issued. He probably died a natural death, though there was a legend that he committed suicide; after his death, his family returned to Athens. Democracy did not become an issue while he was in Athens (see DEMOCRACY, ATHENIAN), but there are links between him and the democratic, anti-Spartan politicians who came to power at the end of the 460s.

PA 6669; APF 211–18; Hdt. 7–8; Thuc. 1. 74, 93, 135–8; Ath. Pol. 22; Plut. Them.; ML 23 = Fornara 55 (Decree of Themistocles). A. J. Podlecki, The Life of Themistocles (1975); R. J. Lenardon, The Saga of Themistocles (1978). Archonship: D. M. Lewis and W. W. Dickie, Hist. 1973, 757–9. Ostraca: O. Broneer, Hesp. 1938, 228–43; D. M. Lewis, ZPE 14 (1974), 1–4, Athenian Agora 1990, 142–61. Peloponnese: W. G. Forrest, CQ 1960, 221–41. Coins: H. A. Cahn and D. Gerin, Num. Chron. 1988, 13–20. A. R. B.; P. J. R.

Themistogenes of *Syracuse, pseudonym under which *Xenophon (1) published the Anabasis (Hell. 3. 1, 2), in order to create the impression of greater objectivity (Plut. Mor. 345). The *Suda accepts Themistogenes' historicity; but it is unlikely that a third author should have written on the march of the 10,000 in addition to *Sophaenetus (FGrH 109) and Xenophon.

FGrH 108; H. R. Breitenbach, RE 9 A (1967), 1644 ff.; K. Meister, Die griechische Geschichtsschreibung (1990), 72; O. Lendle, Einführung in die griechische Geschichtsschreibung (1992), 114, 119. K. M.

Theocritus, poet from *Syracuse, early 3rd cent. BC (working at the *Alexandrian court in the 270s); creator of the bucolic genre, but a writer who drew inspiration from many earlier literary forms, cleverly blending them into a new amalgam which nevertheless displays constant invention and seeks variety rather than homogeneity. Thirty poems and a few fragments, together with twenty-four epigrams, are ascribed to him, several (e.g. 19, 20, 21, 23) clearly spurious and others (e.g. 25, 26) of doubtful authenticity. A scholar called Artemidorus boasts in an epigram transmitted along with the ancient scholia (which are very full and learned) that he has rounded up 'the Pastoral Muses' so that 'scattered once, all are now a single fold and flock'; his edition no doubt included a good deal of anonymous material in the most distinctive of the various Theocritean styles (rural sketches written in the Doric dialect; see GREEK LANGUAGE, § 4) alongside the master's work, and authorship is sometimes hard to determine.

A near-contemporary of the great innovator *Callimachus (3),

Theocritus too was a remaker of the Greek poetic tradition, though his own method of propagating the gospel of tightly organized, perfectly finished writing on a miniature scale was to demonstrate by implicit example rather than engage in neurotic combat against real or imaginary enemies. The closest he comes to a manifesto, and a text that is central for understanding his art, is poem 7 in the collection, which bears the title Thalysia, 'The Harvest Home'. Cast in elusively autobiographical form, it describes a journey undertaken by a conveniently assumed persona, 'Simichidas', during his younger days on the island of *Cos. On the road he meets a Cretan called Lycidas, 'a goatherd— nor could anyone have mistaken him for anything else, since he looked so very like a goatherd'. The two engage in a song contest, preceded by a discussion of the current state of poetry; *Philitas and 'Sicelidas of Samos' (a near-anagram for Asclepiades; see ASCLEPIADES (2)) are mentioned, and Lycidas praises his young companion for his refusal to write Homeric pastiche (see HOMER). The result of the 'competition' is a foregone conclusion, for Simichidas is promised his prize in advance; just as well, since his clumsy party-piece is no match for the smiling Lycidas' sophisticated song. And no wonder: for as F. Williams showed, focusing earlier partial insights into a conclusive picture, Lycidas is *Apollo, the god of poetry himself, and his *epiphany in the poem marks it out as an account of the 'poet's consecration' (Dichterweihe) of the kind *Hesiod and *Archilochus had received from the Muses (CQ 1971, 137–45).

Other poems in the bucolic main sequence (1–7) also contain passages with programmatic implications—in particular the meticulous description of the wonderfully carved cup in poem 1, whose scenes (especially the culminating picture of the boy concentrating on weaving a tiny cage for a singing cricket, oblivious to all else) seem intended as a visual correlative of Theocritus' poetic agenda. There are also pieces which refer more directly to the problems of the writer in the Hellenistic world. Poem 16 imaginatively reworks themes from *Simonides in appealing for patronage (see PATRONAGE, LITERARY, Greek) to *Hieron (2) II of Syracuse, and 17 is a similar request to *Ptolemy (1) II Philadelphus, less inspired overall but with a splendidly impish portrayal of the afterlife which the king's father is fancied to be enjoying on *Olympus (1) with *Alexander (3) the Great and *Heracles as his heavenly drinking-companions (16–33). Life in contemporary *Alexandria (1), and praise of its enlightened ruler, is again the theme of 14, an exploratory transposition of a scene of New Comedy (see COMEDY (GREEK), NEW) into hexameter form; while 15, one of the two 'urban *mimes' in the collection which develop the form invented by *Sophron in the 5th cent., gives us a glimpse of the annual *Adonis festival in Ptolemy's palace. We watch the celebration, and hear the hymn (T. is fond of encapsulated song) through the eyes and ears of a pair of suburban housewives, Gorgo and Praxinoa, who have spent the first part of the poem (he is no less fond of diptychal composition) stunning the reader by the banality of their conversation.

The other mime (2) is also a dipytch, this time cast as a monologue. A young Alexandrian woman, Simaetha, instructs her servant Thestylis in the performance of a *magic ritual designed to charm back a wandering lover—or else destroy him; then, after the slave's departure with the drug, she recalls the occasion of her first sight of the youth, and her seduction. Both the incantations and the first part of the solo scene are punctuated with refrains appropriate to the situation, a hypnotic feature that recurs in the song on the death of *Daphnis in 1. The poem is an excellent example of Theocritus' originality in expanding the catchment area of material to be considered 'fit for poetry'; the effect was permanent, and echoes of the double perspective here (the ironic yet fundamentally humane vision of the author laid over the distressed naïveté of the girl; cf. 11) can still be traced in *Tiresias' description of the similarly squalid seduction in Eliot's *The Waste Land*. Though (like all of Theocritus' work) the piece is primarily designed for an audience of sophisticated readers, there is an emotional power here that makes it performable.

But Theocritus was also interested in staking a claim on more 'mainstream' territory, as his choice of the hexameter (see METRE, GREEK, § 4 (*b*)) as his regular vehicle suggests (the only exceptions to this rule are three rather contrived experiments in Aeolic lyric, 28–30 cf. GREEK LANGUAGE, § 4; METRE, GREEK, § 4 (*h*)). *Epic remained the ultimate challenge. Two poems (13, on *Hylas; and 22, the second part of which narrates the fight between Polydeuces (see DIOSCURI) and *Amycus) take up Argonautic subjects (see ARGONAUTS), and must relate somehow to the contemporary long poem by *Apollonius (1) of Rhodes—perhaps Theocritus is showing his less radical rival how to do it properly. *Pindar (*Nem.* 1) is recast into epic and updated in the treatment of Heracles' cradle-confrontation with the snakes in 24; only as babies or lovers (cf. *Menelaus in the Spartan epithalamium, 18) can the traditional heroes retain their tenuous grasp on the Hellenistic imagination. The rhetorical sequence at 16. 48–57 makes all clear: two lines for Homer's *Iliad* (and even here the emphasis is given to the losers, and to the *handsomest* Greek fighter at Troy, Cycnus, never even mentioned in Homer's poem) are followed by six for the *Odyssey*, with the peasants given pride of place over the eponymous hero.

New, yet in some ways older, characters are brought forward to supplant the epic warrior: Daphnis (1), Hylas (13), and Adonis (15), each of whom swoons in erotic death, and Polyphemus (6, 11; see CYCLOPES), who joins Simaetha and the goatherd in 3 as a failed lover and displaces *Odysseus from centre-stage. Instead of the bloody duels of epic, the new model of competition is the agonistic singing of the goatherds (for which see PASTORAL POETRY, GREEK). Old false ideals and fantasies are pared away, and the new ones that Theocritus puts in their place are justified, paradoxically, by their very self-conscious artificiality. In an age of uncertainty and unbelief, Theocritus offers three beacons by which life may be orientated: love (which must ultimately fail, through rejection or death), personal determination, and art. Each of these is symbolically figured in turn on the cup, the αἰπολικὸν θάημα ('marvel for goatherds'), at 1. 27–55.

At some point in the ancient tradition Theocritus' poems acquired the generic title εἰδύλλια, 'vignettes'; in so far as the transliteration 'idylls' may conjure up a misleading image of rustic languor and passivity it is perhaps best avoided as a label for the poems of this energetic, engaged, and acutely intelligent writer.

Text: A. S. F. Gow (ed.), *Bucolici Graeci* (1952). Trans.: Gow, *The Greek Bucolic Poets* (1953). Comm.: Gow, *Theocritus* (1952), with trans.; K. J. Dover (1971; select poems). Studies: Ph.-É. Legrand, *Étude sur Théocrite* (1898); G. Lawall, *Theocritus' Coan Pastorals* (1967); T. G. Rosenmeyer, *The Green Cabinet: Theocritus and the European Pastoral Lyric* (1969); C. Segal, *Poetry and Myth in Ancient Pastoral* (1981); K. J. Gutzwiller, *Theocritus' Pastoral Analogies: The Formation of a Genre* (1991); S. Goldhill, *The Poet's Voice* (1991), ch. 4; R. Hunter, *Theocritus and the Archaeology of Greek Poetry* (1996). A. H. G.

Theodectes, a tragic poet, orator, writer on rhetoric, and composer of *riddles in verse, was born at *Phaselis in Lycia but probably lived mainly at Athens. The *Suda and other sources

claim that he was a pupil of *Plato (1), *Isocrates, and *Aristotle (but in fact he was clearly older than Aristotle and influenced him), produced 50 plays at thirteen competitions, and won eight victories. An inscription (which calls him 'Theodektas', perhaps more correctly) attests seven victories at the Great *Dionysia, the first shortly after 372 BC. Titles included *Aias, Alcmaeon, Helen, Lynceus* (Aristotle, *Poet.* 11, commends its *peripeteia*, plot-reversal), *Mausolus* (concerning *Mausolus, the satrap of Caria, or a mythical ancestor of his), *Oedipus, Orestes, Philoctetes,* and *Tydeus.* The fragments consist mainly of elegantly expressed commonplaces in the Euripidean manner (see EURIPIDES).

As an orator he competed with *Theopompus (3), Naucrates of Erythrae, and perhaps Isocrates (or another Isocrates, of Apollonia) at the dedication of the *Mausoleum, when Mausolus' widow *Artemisia (2) had offered a prize for the best encomium of her husband. The winner was probably Theopompus, but Theodectes is said to have enjoyed more success with his tragedy *Mausolus* (Aulus Gellius 10. 18. 5). *Cicero, *Orat.* 172, praises his polished prose style. His work on rhetorical theory, which included analysis of the parts of a speech and their objects and virtues, was considered important, notably by Aristotle, whose *Theodectea* apparently summarized his views. After his death *Alexander (3) the Great is said to have honoured a statue of him at Phaselis, having known him when studying with Aristotle (Plut. *Alex.* 17. 9).

V. Rose, *Aristotelis Fragmenta* (1886), 114–18; TrGF 1². 227–37; *Musa Tragica* 168–79, 291–2; G. Xanthakis-Karamanos, *Studies in Fourth-Century Tragedy* (1981), 53–70; S. Hornblower, *Mausolus* (1982), 333–6. A. L. B.

Theoderic (1), Gothic king of Italy (AD 493–526; see GOTHS), spent ten years (aged 8–18) as hostage in *Constantinople. Made a sub-king on his return to *Pannonia in *c.*471, he and his father Thiudimer invaded the Roman Balkans in *c.*473. Becoming king on his father's death in *c.*474, he had by 483/4 united most of *Theoderic (2)'s following to his own, continuing the process by which his uncle (Valamer) and father had progressively united disparate Gothic groups as the Hunnic empire collapsed (see HUNS). Theoderic's new force—the so-called Ostrogoths—was too powerful for emperor Zeno to tolerate so close to Constantinople, and a series of conflicts followed; sending the Goths to Italy in 488/9 broke the impasse. By 493 Theoderic had murdered *Odoacer to establish an essentially independent rule, although he acknowledged certain prerogatives claimed by Constantinople. He retained Roman-style administration, carefully presented his rule as the 'Roman empire continued', and, although an Arian (see ARIANISM), cultivated excellent relations with the papacy. In foreign affairs his propaganda claimed hegemony over other western successor kingdoms; this partly reflected reality, especially after 511 when he united both Gothic kingdoms to encompass Italy, southern Gaul, and Spain. His declining years were darkened by tension with Constantinople, the death of his chosen heir, and the execution of *Boethius. He died in 526.

H. Wolfram, *History of the Goths* (1988), pt. 3; P. J. Heather, *Goths and Romans 332–489* (1991), pt. 3; J. Moorhead, *Theoderic in Italy* (1992). P. J. H.

Theoderic (2), known as Strabo or the son of Triarius, led one of two Gothic groups (see GOTHS) which united to create the Ostrogoths. By AD 471 Strabo's Goths had close relations with Constantinople, but the murder of their patron Aspar prompted a revolt during which Strabo established his pre-eminence. From

473 to 481, when he died in an accident, he used a mixture of strategies to compete for Roman favour with the Goths of *Theoderic (1).

P. J. Heather, *Goths and Romans 332–489* (1991).　　　P. J. H.

theodicy is the effort to explain (*a*) phenomena appearing to demonstrate a divinity's hostility to virtuous people or to people whose actions suggest that they should expect to be recipients of divine favour, or (*b*), more generally, reasons for divine anger with humanity. Theodical explanations are well attested in Egyptian and Mesopotamian literature, and they form the basis for significant portions of the Hebrew Bible. Theodicy is particularly important in societies that view divine forces as guarantors of good.

*Hesiod is the most important early source for Greek theodicies. The story of *Pandora, which explains the existence of evil in the world as a response to *Prometheus' deceit, is one such, another the story that *Zeus decided to destroy the human race as a result of its *hubris (Hes. *Op.* 47–105; *Eoiae* fr. 204 M–W). Early Greek elegy contains other examples in, for instance, *Solon's poem on the subject of *Dikē (fr. 13 West). The notion that a good person can be punished for the evil of an ancestor or ancestors is brought out perhaps most clearly in the Delphic explanation (see DELPHIC ORACLE) of the fall of *Croesus, who is told explicitly that his misfortune is the consequence of the crime of *Gyges (Hdt. 1. 91). *Aeschylus' *Oresteia* and *Sophocles (1)'s *Oedipus Tyrannus* are powerful explorations of the theme.

The fundamental concern with divine punishment in Greek religion is most plainly evident in the Greek preoccupation with ritual purity and impurity (see PURIFICATION, GREEK; POLLUTION). A society that does not take care to ensure the punishment or purification of individuals who had incurred *miasma* (pollution) invites divine punishment for the society as a whole. The prosecution of individuals for *asebeia* (impiety) is another illustration of this problem, raising the question of a society's responsibility for thoughts that the gods might consider offensive as well as for actions (Parker, 144–90). See INTOLERANCE, INTELLECTUAL AND RELIGIOUS.

In republican Rome, theodicy is intimately connected with conceptions of impiety or *impietas* (cf. Pietas) and *vitium* (error). Both concepts provided powerful explanations for disasters affecting society as a whole. If *vitium* went undetected in the taking of the *auspices or at a sacrifice, it could be taken as a sufficient explanation for military disaster, and the senate would take charge of the examination of ritual actions during a magistrate's term in office to determine the point at which *vitium* had occurred. Favourable signs observed after *vitium* had occurred would be taken as a sign of a divinity's determination to punish the previous error by leading a magistrate into a fatal situation. In such cases blame for disaster could be diffused quite widely through Roman society. Cases of open *impietas*, the wilful flouting of divine authority (the story that P. *Claudius Pulcher threw sacred chickens into the sea before the battle of Drepanum) are less common, though in such cases blame for disaster could be fixed upon an individual (Scheid, 17–57).

Theodical explanations for social disorder are common in the literature of the late republic and early empire. *Horace, *Carm.* 1. 2, for instance offers a theodicy based upon the story of Rhea Silvia's execution (cf. ROMULUS), the preface to Lucan's *Pharsalia* (see ANNAEUS LUCANUS, M.) suggests that the civil wars were the result of the general immorality of the Roman people, and Jupiter's explanation of the Hannibalic War (see PUNIC WARS) as a necessary event for the regeneration of the Roman people in *Silius Italicus' *Punica* is overtly theodical (*Pun.* 3. 153–5, 573–5). *Tacitus (1) describes various disasters connected with the civil war of AD 69 as manifestations of the anger of the gods against the human race, and *Ammianus Marcellinus presents the disaster at Adrianople as divine revenge upon *Valens for his crimes (Tac. *Hist.* 1. 3; Amm. Marc. 29. 2. 20, 31. 1. 3).

Theodical ideas were not restricted to the realm of magistrates and intellectuals. Thus there appears to have been considerable unrest in the reign of *Nero, resulting from his matricide, which could be taken as an explanation for the Great Fire of 64 (Cassius Dio 62. 18). Various natural disasters resulted in the persecution of Christians, whose presence in a community could be thought to attract divine anger (see e.g. Tert. *Apol.* 40. 2), and the sack of Rome in 410 was widely interpreted (by polytheists) as a manifestation of divine anger at a society that had fallen away from its proper religious customs (August. *De civ. D.* 1. 1).

Some fascinating examples of direct divine intervention in the lives of the common people of *Phrygia have survived in two series of 'confession steles', one from the sanctuary of *Apollo Lairbenos in Phrygian Hierapolis, another from north-east *Lydia. These texts were carved at the expense of people who had been shown by a god (often regarded as the ruler of the community) to have committed a crime. It is impossible to know if these confession texts reflect attitudes towards divine judgement outside the immediate area where they were discovered, since the procedure is not attested elsewhere (Mitchell, 191–5).

In Christian society, concern with divine judgement is widely attested. In the first three centuries, its most important direct application was probably as an explanation of persecution (see e.g. Cyprian, *De lapsis*, 11). After the conversion of *Constantine I, the most important and wide-ranging exposition of a theodical explanation for good and evil in the world appears in *Augustine's *City of God* (*De civ. D.* 11. 16–18; 12. 1–9). See SIN.

D. N. Freedman, *Anchor Bible Dictionary*, 'Theodicy' (near eastern and biblical instances with bibliography); S. Mitchell, *Anatolia* 1 (1993); R. Parker, *Miasma* (1983); J. Scheid, *Religion et piété à Rome* (1985).
　　　D. S. P.

Theodora See JUSTINIAN.

Theodoret, *c.* AD 393–466. After a good education he became a monk and from 423 bishop of Cyrrhus in Syria. From 428 he supported his friend Nestorius in the Christological controversy against *Cyril of Alexandria, of whom he became a leading critic. Deposed by the monophysite council of Ephesus, he was rehabilitated at Chalcedon despite strenuous protests (451), but his attacks on Cyril were condemned under Justinian at the council of Constantinople (553). His elegant letters are informative about both secular and ecclesiastical matters. His *Graecarum Affectionum Curatio* supplies unique testimonia on the lives and teachings of pagan philosophers. His *Church History* from *Constantine I to 428 includes many invaluable documents; the *Religious History* contains biographies of ascetics. His *Eranistes* is notable for its marginal indications of speakers' names, and his Pauline commentaries (see PAUL, ST) for their notion of *psychagōgia* (winning of souls).

Migne, *PG* 80–4. *Graec. Aff. Cur.* ed. J. Raeder (Teubner, 1904); *Hist. Eccl.* ed. L. Parmentier (1911); *Letters*, ed. Y. Azema, 3 vols. (1955–65); *Eranistes*, ed. G. H. Ettlinger (1975). J. Schulte, *Theodoret von Cyrus als Apologet* (1904); R. V. Sellers, *The Council of Chalcedon* (1961); N. G. Wilson, *CQ* 1970; F. M. Young, *From Nicea to Chalcedon* (1983).
　　　H. C.; M. J. E.

Theodoridas of *Syracuse (second half of 3rd cent. BC), a versatile poet of whom *dithyrambic and hexameter fragments
survive, as well as nineteen largely funerary and dedicatory *epigrams. Metrically noteworthy are VI Gow–Page ('archilochians')
and XV Gow–Page on Mnasalces (iambic trimeter followed by
ithyphallic); XIV Gow–Page concerns *Euphorion (2).

Suppl. Hell. 739–47; Gow–Page, HE 2. 537–51; W. Seelbach, Die Epigramme des Mnasalkes von Sikyon und des Theodoridas von Syrakus (1964).
R. L. Hu.

Theodorus (1), Samian architect (see SAMOS), sculptor, and met-
alworker, active c.550–520 BC. He made two massive silver craters
dedicated by *Croesus at *Delphi, *Polycrates (1)'s famous ring,
and a golden vine eventually owned by *Darius I (Hdt. 1. 51, 3.
41, 7. 27). He also built the 'Scias' at Sparta (apparently an
assembly-hall), and assisted in the construction of the *Heraion
at Samos (upon which he wrote a book) and the Ephesian Artemision (Vitr. 7 pref. 12; Plin. HN 36. 95; see EPHESUS). He reportedly invented the line, rule, lathe, and lever, and made advances
in bronze-casting (Plin. HN 7. 198; 35. 152; 36. 90; Paus. 10. 38.
6 f.). His bronze self-portrait was renowned for its realism, and
showed him holding a file and a tiny chariot-and-four; the latter
was exhibited at *Praeneste in *Pliny (1)'s time (HN 34. 183).
*Diodorus (3) (2. 98) describes his collaboration with Telecles on
a statue of Pythian *Apollo (i.e. Apollo of Delphi) for Samos,
which was proportioned in the Egyptian fashion.

J. J. Coulton, Ancient Greek Architects at Work (1977), 24; A. W. Lawrence,
Greek Architecture² (1983), 162 f.; A. F. Stewart, Greek Sculpture (1990),
37, 39, 68, 125, 244 ff. A. F. S.

Theodorus (2) (fl. late 5th cent. BC) of *Cyrene, geometer,
portrayed in *Plato (1)'s Theaetetus as a former disciple of *Protagoras, an associate of *Socrates, and a teacher of *Theaetetus.
Plato describes him as showing the irrationality of √3, √5, etc.
up to √17 (Tht. 147d–148b). Many reconstructions of the passage
have been proposed, but its historicity has also been questioned
and no other attributions of explicit achievements are made to
him in extant ancient sources.

W. R. Knorr, Evolution of the Euclidean Elements (1975); M. Burnyeat,
Isis 1978, 489–513. W. R. K.

Theodorus (3) of Gadara, a celebrated rhetor, was a teacher of
the future emperor *Tiberius (Suet. Tib. 57), and later settled
in *Rhodes. He is said to have allowed more freedom in the
arrangement and composition of speeches than did *Apollodorus (5) of Pergamum, and evidently had an interest in stylistic
faults and virtues ('Longinus' 3. 5). He is frequently cited by
*Quintilian.

G. A. Kennedy, Art of Rhetoric in the Roman World (1972), 340–2.
D. A. R.

Theodosian Code (Codex Theodosianus), a collection of some
2,500 imperial laws collected and published between AD 429 and
438 on the authority of *Theodosius (3) II. By about 400 it had
become clear that a new collection was needed to supplement
the Codex Gregorianus and Hermogenianus of a century earlier (see
CODEX). The law in the western and eastern parts of the empire
had to be harmonized, its bulk reduced, forgeries eliminated,
and a decision reached on which imperial laws were general, and
so entitled to prevail over corrupt or improvident concessions
to petitioners (rescripta, adnotationes). Given the disorder of the
western empire, the eastern government took the initiative. In
March 429 Theodosius II in Constantinople set up a commission,
consisting of eight officials or ex-officials and a practising advocate, to collect all the general laws they could find from Constantine onwards, arrange them in chronological order under subject-
headings, and shorten them so that only the operative part
remained (CTh. 1. 1. 5). They were not to harmonize conflicting
laws, but it was envisaged that ultimately the new Codex, together
with the Gregorianus, the Hermogenianus and the writings of
lawyers of authority would be fused in a harmonious whole.

By December 435 the available laws had been collected from
various sources, eastern and western. CTh. 1. 1. 6 of that date
shows that Theodosius then reconstituted his commission as a
body of sixteen charged with proceeding to the next stage, that
of editing the projected codex; but some scholars have supposed
that Theodosius abandoned the original project as a failure and
began again. The laws were to be edited so as to make them clear
and elegant. By the end of 437 the commission had completed
the Codex in sixteen books (libri) divided into subject-headings.
In February 438 Theodosius promulgated it in a law addressed
to the senate of Constantinople (NTh. 1), in which he thanked
the eight commissioners who had seen the project through to
the end, chief among them its guiding spirit *Antiochus (13)
Chuzon, a lawyer from Antioch. The Codex was then presented
to the senate of Rome, which acclaimed it for the increased
certainty and security it brought.

The Theodosian Code could not by itself arrest the decline of
the western empire, but in its own terms it was a success. It set
out the text of all general laws in force since Constantine, thus
resolving doubts about what was general, and hampering falsification. The texts were dated so that conflicts between them
could be settled on the basis that the later prevails over the earlier.
The Code provided for mutual recognition of future laws by
west and east, though the system for ensuring this broke down.
Theodosius did not go on to the ambitious project, adumbrated
in 429, of a harmonious restatement of the whole law; but even
a hundred years later Justinian was able to achieve this only in
part (see JUSTINIAN'S CODIFICATION). Justinian included much of
the Theodosian Code in his own Codex, but repealed the rest.
Outside his sphere of authority Alaric II embodied about a
quarter of it in his Lex Romana Visigothorum (Roman Law according to the Visigoths) of 506 and it helped to mould the law in the
other kingdoms that replaced the western Roman empire.

T. Mommsen and P. M. Meyer, Theodosiani libri XVI (1905), trans.
with notes by C. Pharr, The Theodosian Code and Novels (1952); O.
Gradenwitz, Heidelberger Index zum Theodosianus (1925, 1929); G. G.
Archi, Teodosio II e la sua codificazione (1976); E. Volterra, Bullettino
dell'Istituto di diritto romano 1984 (1981), 85–124; T. Honoré, ZRG 1986,
133–222; W. Turpin RIDA 1988, 285–307; J. Harries (ed.), Essays on the
Theodosian Code (forthcoming). T. Hon.

Theodosius (1) (RE 9), **Flavius,** count (see COMITES), wealthy
landowner of Cauca (mod. Coca) in Gallaecia, was a general of
*Valentinian I and father of the emperor *Theodosius (2) I. In AD
367 he recovered *Britain, which had been overrun by *Saxons,
Picts, and Scots (the so-called 'barbarian conspiracy'); the
invaders had reached the vicinity of London. In 369–73 he was
Valentinian's magister equitum (see MAGISTER MILITUM) against the
*Alamanni and *Alans, and in 373–5, in campaigns described in
detail by *Ammianus Marcellinus he was active in Mauretanian
Africa, where he suppressed the revolt of the local chieftain
Firmus. He was put to death for unknown reasons at Carthage
in 376.

PLRE 1. 902–4 (Theodosius 3). J. F. Ma.

Theodosius (2) **I,** 'the Great' (RE 10; Suppl. 13. 837–961), the

son of count *Theodosius (1), was born *c*. AD 346. He was promoted early, serving as *dux* of *Moesia Superior in 374. On his
father's sudden disgrace and execution in 376 he retired to the
family properties at Cauca but in 378, after the defeat and death
of *Valens at Adrianople, *Gratian appointed him *magister
militum* to fight the *Goths, and shortly afterwards (19 January
379) proclaimed him Augustus of the eastern parts, including
the dioceses of *Dacia and *Macedonia. For the next few years
Theodosius conducted campaigns against the Goths, basing
himself at first at Thessalonica (379–80), then at Constantinople.
Failing to eject the Goths from the empire, on 3 October 382 he
signed a treaty with them, recognizing them as federates and
assigning them lands in *Thrace and Lower *Moesia. In 386 he
signed a treaty with Persia, whereby the long-disputed kingdom
of Armenia was partitioned between the two empires. Both these
treaties are shown on the base of the obelisk of Theodosius,
erected in the hippodrome at Constantinople in 390, as triumphs
of Roman arms. When the usurper *Magnus Maximus killed
Gratian in 383 and occupied the Gauls, Theodosius for a time
recognized him, but when in 387 Maximus expelled *Valentinian
II from Italy, he marched west, defeated Maximus at Siscia and
Poetovio, and put him to death at Aquileia. Theodosius stayed
in the west for three years, and made a state visit to Rome in 389,
the occasion of the delivery to him of the panegyric of the Gallic
rhetorician Pacatus, and of cordial relations between the emperor
and even pagan members of the senatorial aristocracy; *Symmachus (2), who had praised Maximus in a panegyric, was made
consul for 391. At this time Valentinian II was established in
Gaul, while Theodosius' elder son *Arcadius (2), whom he had
proclaimed Augustus in 383, had been left in nominal control of
the east. Theodosius returned to Constantinople in 391, but
again had to march west in 394 to subdue the usurper *Eugenius,
who had displaced Valentinian. He again left Arcadius in the east
and took with him to the west his younger son *Honorius,
proclaimed Augustus in 393. He defeated Eugenius at the river
Frigidus on 6 September 394 but died at Milan on 17 January 395,
to be succeeded by his sons Arcadius and Honorius in east and
west respectively.

Theodosius was a pious Christian and, unlike his predecessor
Valens, an adherent of the Nicene creed, an allegiance which he
owed to his origin and upbringing in the west. He was also
surrounded by westerners, relatives and others, to whom he gave
advancement, many of them individuals of intense personal piety.
He was baptized very early in his reign, during a serious illness
at Thessalonica. On 27 February 380 (before he had come to
Constantinople) he issued a constitution declaring that the faith
professed by Pope *Damasus and by Peter, bishop of Alexandria,
was the true Catholic faith. He deposed Demophilus, the Arian
bishop of Constantinople (see ARIANISM), and recognized as
bishop the Nicene protagonist, *Gregory (2) of Nazianzus. On
10 January 381 he ordered that all churches be surrendered to
the Catholic bishops as defined by himself. He then called a
council of about 150 bishops at Constantinople, which ratified
Theodosius' action but refused to accept Gregory of Nazianzus.
Theodosius asked them to produce a short list and chose Nec-
tarius, a former senator of Constantinople, as bishop.

Theodosius was very severe against heretics, issuing eighteen
constitutions against them; he even ordained the death penalty
for some extremist sects. Towards the pagans his policy was at
first ambivalent. He did not forbid sacrifice, but was so severe
against *divination as to prevent it. He did not close the
temples, but allowed fanatical Christians, including his own prae-

torian prefect Cynegius, to destroy them, or granted them to
petitioners. In a law issued at Milan in 391 he abruptly closed all
temples and banned all forms of pagan cult. This step was probably taken under the influence of *Ambrose, bishop of Milan,
who had obtained great ascendancy over him since his arrival in
the west. Late in 388 Ambrose forced him to leave unpunished
the bishop of Callinicum, who had burned down a synagogue,
and in 390, when Theodosius ordered retributive killings at Thessalonica to avenge the death in a riot of the general Butheric, he
refused him communion until he had done penance.

Theodosius' death was followed by what is often seen as the
formal division of the Roman empire into eastern and western
parts. His settlement with the Goths had long-term effects, as
under their leaders the Goths installed themselves ever more
intimately into the political structure and society of the Roman
empire. His religious policies mark a significant step in the developing alliance between Church and State, and were greeted with
delight by Christian writers like *Orosius and *Augustine, and
with dismay by Eunapius. But he was brought to the throne at a
time of major crisis, overcame it to the benefit of the empire, and
imposed his personality on Roman history.

E. Stein, *Histoire du Bas-Empire* 1 (1959), 191 ff.; Jones, *Later Rom. Emp.*
156 ff.; W. Ensslin, *Die Religionspolitik des Kaisers Theodosius des Gr.*,
Sber. der Bayerischen Akad. (1953); A. Lippold, *Theodosius der Grosse
und seine Zeit* (1968); J. F. Matthews, *Western Aristocracies and Imperial
Court, AD 364–425* (1975); P. J. Heather, *Goths and Romans, 332–489*
(1991); N. McLynn, *Ambrose of Milan: Church and Court in a Christian
Capital* (1994).   J. F. Ma.

Theodosius (3) **II,** son of *Arcadius (2), born in AD 401, was
proclaimed Augustus in 402. He succeeded his father in 408 and
reigned rather than ruled the empire until his death in 450. He
was very piously educated by his elder sister, Pulcheria, who
exercised a strong influence over him until the early 440s. For a
time he was also much influenced by his wife Eudocia, whom
he married in 421. During the earlier part of his reign the empire
was in fact governed by *Anthemius, praetorian prefect of the
east (see PRAEFECTUS PRAETORIO) from 405 to 414, and then probably by Helion, master of the offices from 414 to 427. From
the early 440s the emperor was controlled by Chrysaphius, an
imperial *eunuch, and Nomus, master of the offices.

The chief military events of the reign were two successful
Persian wars (421–2 and 441; see SASANIDS), the defeat of the
usurper John in the west, and the installation of *Valentinian
III at Rome (425), an unsuccessful naval expedition against the
*Vandals (441), and a series of wars and negotiations with Rua and
*Attila, kings of the *Huns. The Roman armies proved helpless
against the Huns, and peace was obtained only by paying ever
increasing subsidies (350 lb. gold per annum from 422, 700 lb.
from 434, 2,100 lb. from 443).

The chief ecclesiastical events were the condemnation of Nestorius, bishop of Constantinople, by the council of Ephesus in
431, and of Flavian, bishop of Constantinople, by the second
council of Ephesus in 449; Cyril and Dioscurus, bishops of Alexandria, were moving spirits in these two councils; see CYRIL OF
ALEXANDRIA.

In 429 a commission was appointed under Antiochus, praetorian prefect and former quaestor, to codify all laws issued since
312. This attempt to reform the law failed, but in 435 a second
commission under the same *Antiochus (13) Chuzon carried out
the task and in 438 the *Theodosian Code was promulgated in
both parts of the empire.

J. B. Bury, *A History of the Later Roman Empire* (1923); E. Stein, *Histoire* du Bas-Empire 1 (1959); RE Suppl. 13 (1973), 961–1043; K. Holum, Theodosian Empresses (1982).   A. H. M. J.; W. L.

Theodosius (4) (RE 5) of Bithynia, astronomer and mathematician (fl. c.100 BC), wrote three treatises on elementary 'spherics': Σφαιρικά, in three books, dealing with great and small circles on the sphere; Περὶ οἰκήσεων ('On Habitations'), on the variations in celestial phenomena at different terrestrial latitudes; and Περὶ ἡμερῶν καὶ νυκτῶν ('On Days and Nights'), in two books, on the variations in the length of day and night resulting from the sun's travel through the zodiac. Among lost works was a commentary on the Method of *Archimedes.

> Editions and trans.: Sphaerica, ed. Heiberg (1927), with Lat. trans. De Habitationibus and De Diebus et Noctibus, ed. R. Fecht (1927), with Lat. trans. Fr. trans. by P. Ver Eecke (1927). Comment: Neugebauer, HAMA 2. 749 ff.   G. J. T.

Theognetus, one of the later poets of New Comedy (see COMEDY (GREEK), NEW). Fr. 1 ridicules excessive preoccupation with philosophy, fr. 2 describes the juggler Pantaleon.

> FRAGMENTS Kassel–Austin, PCG 7 (1989), 696–8.
> INTERPRETATION Meineke, FCG 1. 487; A. Körte in RE 5 A 2 (1934), 1971 f., 'Theognetos' 3.   W. G. A.

Theogenes See THEAGENES (3).

Theognis (1), elegiac poet, of *Megara. Chronographers dated him c.550–540 BC, making him synchronous with Phocylides (see PHOCYLIDES (1)) (with whom he was often coupled as a moralist); historical allusions have been held to point to a much higher dating (c.640–600). A corpus of some 1,400 verses survives in manuscript tradition, labelled as Theognis' work. A few scholars have tried to defend the unity of the collection, but everything points to its being a composite from two or three ancient (Hellenistic) anthologies of elegiac excerpts, Theognis being only one of many poets represented. Crucial points are: (1) Theognis habitually addresses a friend Cyrnus, also called Polypaides (see 19–26). In some parts of the collection (19–254, 319–72, 539–54, 805–22, 1171–84b) nearly every item contains this address, whereas elsewhere it is absent for long stretches. (2) Several pieces are identifiable from other sources as the work of *Tyrtaeus, *Mimnermus, *Solon, and perhaps *Euenus. (3) Some pieces clearly date from as late as the *Persian Wars (757–64, 773–82; 903–30 is also surely 5th-cent.). (4) Many items are duplicated, with or without the textual divergences typical of anthologies. The corpus divides into five clear sections. 1–18: addresses to gods, gathered at the beginning. 19–254: nearly all Cyrnus-poems, serious in tone, with the first and last excerpts chosen to serve as prologue and epilogue. 255–1022: a much more heterogeneous and disorderly collection, with a few Cyrnus-blocks here and there. 1023–1220: similar in character, but with a high proportion of couplets duplicated elsewhere. (1221–30: added by editors from other sources.) 1231–1389: amatory poems, mostly addressed to boys. This section survives only in the 10th-cent. MS A (where it is designated 'book 2') and was unknown until Bekker's edition of 1815.

The addresses to Cyrnus, plus a few pre-Hellenistic citations naming the author, allow us to identify some 308 verses as Theognis'. Some of the rest may be his, but it is prudent to treat the greater part as anonymous and to call the corpus 'the Theognidea', not 'Theognis'. Theognis addresses Cyrnus in three roles: adviser, lover, and confederate. He makes many allusions to political turbulence. He appears as a 'squirearch', a man of standing in Megara, but subject to criticism and hostility, eventually betrayed by those he trusted, dispossessed of his estates in a civic upheaval, and forced into exile, where he dreams of revenge. He expects his verses to circulate at banquets everywhere, far into the future (237 ff.). Many of the anonymous Theognidea too were clearly composed for convivial gatherings (see SYMPOSIUM; SYMPOSIUM LITERATURE). Drinking and merry-making are frequent themes. Other pieces are reflective or philosophic. The love poems of 'book 2' are often banal, but sometimes touching. The collection as a whole contains many delightful things. It may be taken as a representative cross-section of the elegiac poetry circulating in social settings between the late 7th and early 5th cent., and it is our best source for the ordinary man's ideas about life, friendship, fate, death, and other matters. See ELEGIAC POETRY, GREEK.

> TEXT M. L. West, Iambi et Elegi² 1 (1989).
> TRANSLATION M. L. West, Greek Lyric Poetry (1993).
> COMMENTARY T. Hudson-Williams (1910); B. A. van Groningen (1966, bk. 1 only); M. Vetta (1980, bk. 2 only); M. L. West, Theognidis et Phocylidis Fragmenta (1978, Theognis only).
> GENERAL A. R. Burn, The Lyric Age of Greece (1960), 247–64; M. L. West, Studies in Greek Elegy and Iambus (1974), 40–71; H. Fränkel, Early Greek Poetry and Philosophy (1975), 401–25 (Ger. orig. 1962); T. J. Figueira and G. Nagy (eds.), Theognis of Megara: Poetry and the Polis (1985).   M. L. W.

Theognis (2), a tragic poet derided by *Aristophanes (1) (Ach. 11–12, 139–40; Thesm. 170) for his 'coldness'—i.e. dullness, lack of talent. A scholiast identifies him with the Theognis who was one of the *Thirty Tyrants.

> TrGF 1². 146–7.   A. L. B.

theoi patrooi See PATRŌOI THEOI.

Theologumena arithmeticae This work is anonymous in the manuscripts, but has been attributed to *Iamblichus (2), on the ground of his promise at the end of his On Nicomachus' Arithmetical Introduction (In Nic.) to write about the properties of the numbers within the decad. However, this is certainly not that work, but is a compilation of material, perhaps by a student, based on works of Anatolius and *Nicomachus (3). Nevertheless, it is a useful repository of Neopythagorean arithmological lore.

> Ed. V. de Falco (1922); trans. with notes, R. Waterfield, The Theology of Arithmetic (1988).   J. M. D.

Theon (1) of *Alexandria (1) (1st cent. BC), son of *Artemidorus (1) of Tarsus, and head of the school at Alexandria. He wrote on *Homer and other classical authors, and compiled a lexicon of words used in Comedy and Tragedy. His main claim to fame, however, lies in his commentaries on the chief Alexandrian poets.

> C. Wendel, RE 10 A 2054 ff.; C. Guhl, Die Fragmente des alexandrinischen Grammatikers Theon (1969).   N. G. W.

Theon (2) of *Smyrna (fl. c. AD 115–40), Platonist (cf. PLATO (1)), author of an extant work, Aspects of Mathematics Useful for the Reading of Plato (Expos.), and of a lost commentary on the Republic. His treatise on the order of study of Plato's writings has recently been discovered in an Arabic translation. Aspects of Mathematics is an elementary work on arithmetic (especially on the types of numbers), the theory of musical harmony, and astronomy.

> Ed. E. Hiller (Teubner, 1878).   J. M. D.

Theon (3) (RE 5), **Aelius**, of Alexandria, a rhetor of the 1st cent. AD, said to have written works on *Xenophon (1), *Isocrates, and *Demosthenes (2), as well as an Art of Rhetoric (Τέχνη), a treatise on figures, and a set of *progymnasmata. This last is extant (though in a somewhat mangled form), and is the earliest specimen of the genre we possess.

Spengel, *Rhetores Graeci* 2. 59 ff.; *The Progymnasmata of Theon*, ed. J. R. Butts (1987); W. Stegemann, *RE* 5. 2. 2038 ff.   D. A. R.

Theon (4) (*RE* 15), of *Alexandria (1) (fl. AD 364), mathematical commentator. Extant works are (1) a commentary on *Ptolemy (4)'s *Almagest* (the sections on bk. 11 and parts of other books are lost); (2) a large commentary on the *Handy Tables* of Ptolemy; (3) a small introduction to the *Handy Tables*. He also produced 'editions' (i.e. trivial reworkings) of (*a*) *Euclid (*Elements, Data,* and *Optics*); (*b*) Ptolemy's *Handy Tables*, which exist only in Theon's version. Theon was competent in mathematics, but completely unoriginal; his importance lies in his role in the preservation and transmission of older works. It was in his version that Ptolemy's astronomical tables were known to Islamic science, whence they passed to medieval Europe.

EDITIONS *Comm. on Almagest*: bks. 1–4 ed. A. Rome, *Studi e Testi* 72 and 106 (1936, 1943); the remainder only in the 1538 Basel edn. *Handy Tables*, ed. Halma, 3 vols. (1822, 1823, 1825), with Fr. trans. 'Large commentary' ed. with Fr. trans., *Le 'Grand Commentaire' de Théon*, bk. 1, by J. Mogenet and A. Tihon, *Studi e Testi* 315 (1985); bks. 2 and 3, by Tihon, *Studi e Testi* 340 (1991); rest unpublished. 'Small introduction' ed. with Fr. trans. by Tihon, *Le 'Petit Commentaire' de Théon*, *Studi e Testi* 282 (1978).

COMMENT On Theon's 'edition' of Euclid: Heiberg, *Litterargesch. Studien über Euklid* (1882). General: G. J. Toomer, *Dict. Sci. Biogr.* 13 (1976), 321 ff.; Heath, *Hist. of Greek Maths.* 1. 58 ff.; 2. 526 ff.   G. J. T.

Theophanes (Gnaeus Pompeius Theophanes), leading citizen and magistrate of *Mytilene, friend and historian of Cn. *Pompeius Magnus (1), whom he accompanied in the Third Mithradatic War, receiving Roman citizenship from him, and later serving in the civil war (49/8 BC) as his *praefectus fabrum.* A *Callisthenes to Pompey's *Alexander (3) the Great, he appears to have written up only Pompey's campaigns; he may also have helped Pompey in his reorganization of the east. Mytilene posthumously deified him as 'Zeus Eleutherius Theophanes'.

FGrH 188; V. Anastasiadis and G. Souris, *Chiron* 1992, 377 ff.
A. H. McD.; A. J. S. S.

Theophilus (1), Athenian comic poet; he won a victory in 329 BC. Eight titles and twelve citations survive (frs. 6 and 12 are gnomic).

PCG 7. 700 ff. (*CAF* 2. 473 ff.).   K. J. D.

Theophilus (2), bishop of *Antioch (1), author of the three books *To Autolycus* (written shortly after AD 180), which include a defence of basic Christian doctrines (see APOLOGISTS, CHRISTIAN) and an attack on paganism, in particular Greek poetry and philosophy. In addition, the second book contains an exegetical treatment of the early chapters of Genesis. Theophilus' numerous other writings are known by their titles only.

Edn. and Eng. trans. in Theophilus of Antioch, *Ad Autolycum*, by R. M. Grant (1970). P. Nautin, *EEC* 2 (1992), 831 f.   W. K.

Theophilus (3) of *Alexandria (1), patriarch AD 385–412, was no thinker but a zealous pastor who vigorously suppressed Egyptian paganism (he was instrumental in destroying the great temple of *Sarapis at Alexandria in 391: see SERAPION (1)) and advanced the power of his see by opposing John Chrysostom of Constantinople. He is presented in hostile spirit in the writings of *Jerome but in a kind light in *Synesius' letters.

Migne, *PG* 65. 33 ff.; N. H. Baynes, *Byzantine Studies* 97 ff.; *ODCC*² 1364.
J. F. Ma.

theophoric names See NAMES, PERSONAL, GREEK.

Theophrastus (*RE* 3) (372/1 or 371/70–288/7 or 287/6 BC) of *Eresus in Lesbos, associate and successor of *Aristotle. In spite of a tradition that he had been a pupil of *Plato (1), it is probable that he first joined Aristotle when the latter was at *Assos. He became head of the Lyceum (see ARISTOTLE, § 5) when Aristotle withdrew from Athens on the death of *Alexander (3) the Great. His most famous pupil was *Demetrius (3) of Phalerum, through whose influence he, though a *metic, was allowed to own property. He was also on friendly terms with *Cassander and *Ptolemy (1) I. He was succeeded as head of the school by *Straton (1).

Theophrastus shared in, continued, and extended Aristotle's activity in every subject. His surviving works cover only a small part of the range of interests indicated by the lists of book-titles preserved in the biography by *Diogenes (6) Laertius (5. 36–57) and by numerous reports in later authors. The extent to which he consciously diverged from Aristotle on major issues is a subject of debate; it is likely that he saw himself as continuing and developing Aristotle's work of discussion and observation. Much of his writing seems, like the extant *Metaphysics*, to have raised questions rather than categorically asserting a position.

Together with *Eudemus, Theophrastus made important modifications to Aristotle's modal logic. His research in propositional logic anticipated and probably influenced the Stoic *Chrysippus; but it was Chrysippus rather than Theophrastus who made this the foundation of a new logical system (see LOGIC). Theophrastus certainly rejected Aristotle's Unmoved Mover, and argued—though not necessarily against Aristotle—that teleological explanation could not be applied to every aspect of the natural world. He retained a belief in the divinity of the heavens and the eternity of the universe; the evidence for his rejecting the fifth, heavenly element (the *aithēr*) and regarding fire as fundamentally different in kind from the other sublunary elements is uncertain. He raised objections to Aristotle's definition of place; *Simplicius was able to interpret him as anticipating Damascius' explanation of place in terms of position in the universe as an organic whole, but again it is unclear how far Theophrastus saw himself as introducing a new theory of place to supplant Aristotle's. He differed from Aristotle in involving material effluences in his explanation of the sense of smell. His collection of information about earlier philosophers (of which the extant treatise *On the Senses* formed part), undertaken in the context of his own philosophical concerns, was fundamental for later doxographers. His work on *meteorology was exploited by *Epicurus and thence by *Lucretius.

In *botany, the only area in which most of Theophrastus' work survives intact, he so far surpassed his predecessors that the history of the subject in the west can be said effectively to begin with him. In zoology (see ANIMALS, KNOWLEDGE ABOUT) he was apparently more concerned with the behaviour and habitat of living creatures, and with physiological processes, than with anatomical description. His interest in human behaviour is shown by his best-known surviving work, the *Characters*—a series of sketches of thirty more or less undesirable types of personality; its connections with systematic ethics, with rhetorical portrayal, or with the writing of comedy are still debated. (The preface and some of the contents are Byzantine interpolations.) His work on friendship was used by *Cicero, who elsewhere portrays him as laying more emphasis on the importance of fortune and external goods for happiness than did Aristotle; rhetorical exaggeration may, however, be suspected here. He was best known in the Middle Ages for an attack on marriage preserved by St Jerome (included in the compilation which angered Chaucer's Wife of Bath); this may have been one side of a debate rather than a statement of Theophrastus' own views. The same may also apply to arguments for vegetarianism based on the affinity between men and animals, asserting that justice is relevant to relations between men and animals where Aristotle had denied this (see ANIMALS, ATTITUDES TO). These arguments have led some to see Theophrastus as the source of the Stoic ethical theory of 'appropriation' (οἰκείωσις), but the connection is doubtful. Theophrastus developed Aristotle's theory of the virtues of rhetorical style, wrote on rhetorical delivery, which Aristotle had neglected, and supplemented his political studies by the collection of laws and customs and the analysis of action in times of crisis.

TEXTS, TRANSLATIONS, AND COMMENTARIES Surviving works: *Research on Plants*, Hort (Loeb, 1916–26; the botanical identifications are unreliable; also includes *On Odours* and the spurious *On Weather-Signs*); S. Amigues (Budé, 4 vols., 1988–). *Plant Explanations*, Einarson and Link (Loeb, 3 vols., 1976–90). *Metaphysics*, W. D. Ross and F. H. Fobes (1929); A. Laks and G. Most (Budé, forthcoming). *On the Senses*, H. Diels, *Doxographi Graeci* (1879), 497–527; G. M. Stratton, *Theophrastus and the Greek Physiological Psychology before Aristotle* (1917). *On Fire*, V. Coutant (1971). *On Stones*, E. R. Caley and J. C. Richards (1956); D. E. Eichholz (1965). *On Winds*, V. Coutant and V. Eichenlaub (1975). *Meteorology* (preserved only in Syriac and Arabic), H. Daiber in *Rutgers Studies* 1992. *Characters*, R. G. Ussher (1960); P. Steinmetz (1960–2). For other surviving minor works (*On Perspiration, On Tiredness, On Giddiness*) reference must still be made to the 3rd vol. of F. Wimmer's Teubner edn. (1854–62) or his Didot edn. (1866, repr. 1964). Fragments and testimonia: W. W. Fortenbaugh, P. M. Huby, R. W. Sharples (Gk. and Lat.) and D. Gutas (Arabic) (eds.), *Theophrastus of Eresus* (text and trans. 2 vols., 1992; commentaries forthcoming). On particular topics: logic: A. Graeser (1973), L. Repici (1977); physical doxography: Diels, *Dox. Graec.* 473–95; intellect: E. Barbotin (1957); ethics: W. W. Fortenbaugh (1984); *On Piety*, W. Pötscher (1964); *Laws*, A. Szegedy-Maszak (1981).
STUDIES Fundamental is O. Regenbogen in *RE* Suppl. 7 (1940), 1354–1562. Also W. Burnikel, *Textgeschichtliche Untersuchungen zu neun Opuscula Theophrasts* (1974); F. Wehrli, in Überweg–Flashar, 474–522. Logic: I. M. Bochénski, *La Logique de Théophraste* (1947). Physics: P. Steinmetz, *Die Physik des Theophrast* (1964). Doxography: J. B. McDiarmid, *Harv. Stud.* 1953. Botany: G. Wöhrle, *Theophrasts Methode in seinen botanischen Schriften* (1985), and P. M. Fraser, in S. Hornblower (ed.), *Greek Historiography* (1994), ch. 6. Ethics: C. O. Brink, *Phronesis* 1956. Numerous papers on various aspects of Theophrastus' work in W. W. Fortenbaugh and others (eds.), *Rutgers University Studies in Classical Humanities* 2 (1985), 3 (1988), 5 (1992), and 7 (forthcoming). R. W. S.

Theopompus (1), *Eurypontid king of Sparta (reigned ?720–675 BC), was associated by name in the near-contemporary poetry of *Tyrtaeus with two momentous developments: the first conquest of *Messenia (c.710), and the constitutional reform embodied in the 'Great Rhetra' otherwise attributed to *Lycurgus (2) (see SPARTA, § 2). His alleged creation of the ephorate (see EPHORS) is a later tradition, or invention.

Tyrtaeus fr. 4 West. *Kl. Pauly*, 'Theopompos (2)'; P. Cartledge, *Sparta and Lakonia* (1979). P. A. C.

Theopompus (2), Athenian comic poet, was active from c.410 BC (probably not earlier) to c.370. We have twenty titles (including *Odysseus, Penelope*, and *Sirens*) and over 100 citations (many of them only glosses).

PCG 7. 708 ff. (*CAF* 1. 733 ff.). K. J. D.

Theopompus (3) of *Chios, important Greek historian of the

4th cent. BC, the main exponent of rhetorical historiography alongside *Ephorus (see HISTORIOGRAPHY, GREEK). According to a short *vita* (life) by *Photius (*Bibl.* 176 = T 2) he was born in 378/7, and was still young when he and his father Damasistratus were exiled from Chios for *lakōnismos* (sympathizing with Sparta). At the instigation of *Alexander (3) the Great he was allowed to return in 333/2 when he was 45 years old. After Alexander's death he was exiled a second time; 'driven out from everywhere' he eventually reached the court of *Ptolemy I, who wished to have the 'trouble-maker' done away with. Theopompus was saved by the intervention of some friends and died probably shortly after 320. According to ancient tradition (cf. T 1, 5 a) he was a pupil of *Isocrates and worked for a long time as an orator (fr. 25). Extant titles of epideictic speeches are (T 48): *To Euagoras, Panathenaicus, Laconicus, Olympicus*; in addition he wrote political pamphlets (T 48): *Letters from Chios, Panegyric on *Philip (1) II, Advice for Alexander*; and also an *Invective against *Plato (1) and his School* (T 7. 48; fr. 259).

Historical works (1) *Epitome of *Herodotus (1)* in two books (T 1, fr. 1–4), the first demonstrable *epitome of an earlier work in antiquity; (2) *Hellenica* in twelve books: a continuation of *Thucydides (2) from 411 to 394, namely the sea battle of *Cnidus, which marked the end of Sparta's short-lived hegemony (T 13 and 14). With this work Th. entered into competition with *Xenophon (1), *Hellenica* (1–4. 2), but he wrote in far greater detail than Xenophon. Only nineteen partly trivial fragments are extant (frs. 5–23), hence it is impossible to draw any definite conclusions as to contents, arrangement, bias, style, and quality. The *Hellenica* of the Oxyrhynchus Historian (see OXYRHYNCHUS, THE HISTORIAN FROM), frequently ascribed to Theopompus by modern scholars, is certainly not identical with this work; (3) *Philippica* or rather *Philippikai historiai* ('The History of Philip') in 58 books, Theopompus' main work, published late, after 324 (fr. 330); numerous fragments (frs. 24–396) and c.500 lines of verbal quotations are extant. It was not merely a history of Philip of Macedon, but a universal history including 'the deeds of Greeks and barbarians' (fr. 25) centring on Philip II: when *Philip (3) V later had only the accounts of Philip II's exploits excerpted, the number of books was reduced to fifteen (T 31).

Characteristics (1) Theopompus had a universal conception of history; he focused not only on political and military events but showed an interest in ethnography, geography, cultural history, history of religion, day-to-day life, memorabilia, *thaumasia* (marvels), even myth (fr. 381). (2) He was fond of extensive digressions of all kinds: especially noteworthy are the digressions on *thaumasia* (bk. 8 and part of 9; fr. 64–84); 'On the Athenian *demagogues' (bk. 10; frs. 85–100); and the three books on Sicilian history, covering the tyranny of *Dionysius (1) I and (2) II, 406/5–344/3 (cf. frs. 184, 183–205). (3) The rhetorical character of Theopompus' historical writing was very marked. He goes in for meticulous and skilful stylization, including numerous Gorgianic (see GORGIAS (1)) figures of speech (cf. e.g. 34, frs. 225, 263). (4) There is much moralizing in Theopompus. He incessantly denounced the moral depravity of leading politicians. (5) Political tendencies: Theopompus' attitude was that of a conservative aristocrat with Spartan sympathies. Philip II's patriarchal monarchy came closest to a realization of his ideal political and social system. Theopompus venerated him: 'Europe had never before produced such a man as Philip son of Amyntas' (fr. 27).

Sources The accounts of contemporary history are frequently

theōrika

based on autopsy, personal research and experiences (test. 20a): Theopompus spent some considerable time at Philip's court (T 7) and travelled throughout Greece (fr. 25); for the earlier periods he used historical and literary material such as speeches, comedies, and pamphlets. He was one of the most widely read and influential Greek historians in Graeco-Roman times. *Dionysius (7) of Halicarnassus (*Pomp.* 6 = T 20) praises him for veracity, erudition, meticulous research, versatility, and his personal enthusiasm as well as for the purity, magnificence, and grandeur of his style. He does, however, find fault with Theopompus' invectives and excessive digressions. *Pompeius Trogus, in Augustan times, called his own history *Historiae Philippicae* in imitation of Theopompus.

FGrH 115. K. von Fritz, *A&A* 1954, 45 ff.; W. R. Connor, *Theopompus and Fifth-Century Athens* (1968); G. Bonamente, *Annali dell'Istituto italiano per gli studi storici* 1973/5, 1 ff.; K. Reed, 'Theopompos of Chios: History and Oratory in the Fourth Century' (Diss. Univ. of California, 1976); R. Lane Fox in J. Boardman and C. Vaphopoulou-Richardson (eds.), *Chios* (1986), 105 ff.; P. Pédech, *Trois historiens méconnus: Theopompe, Duris, Phylarque* (1989); K. Meister, *Die griechische Geschichtsschreibung* (1990), 90 ff.; G. S. Shrimpton, *Theopompus the Historian* (1991), extensive bibliog.; O. Lendle, *Einführung in die griechische Geschichtsschreibung* (1992), 129 ff.; M. Christ, *CQ* 1993, 47 ff. (the Herodotus epitome); M. Ostwald and J. P. Lynch, *CAH* 6² (1994), 601 f.; M. A. Flower, *Theopompus of Chios* (1994). K. M.

theōrika, 'spectacle' grants, paid by the state to the citizens of Athens to enable them to attend the theatre at the major festivals. Attributions of these grants to *Pericles (1) (who introduced payment for jurors) and to *Agyrrhius (who introduced payment for attending the assembly) are both undermined by the silence of *Aristophanes (1) on the subject, and the likeliest attribution is to *Eubulus (1) and Diophantus after the *Social War (1) of the 350s BC (schol. Aeschin. 3. 24). In peace time the fund received not only a regular allocation (*merismos*) but also any surplus revenue, and became rich enough to pay for a variety of projects; this, together with the fact that the treasurer of the fund was elected and could be re-elected, and shared with the council the oversight of the old financial committees, made the fund and its treasurer very powerful. A law of the 330s weakened the treasurer, perhaps by substituting a board of ten for the single official and limiting tenure, but a similarly powerful position in Athenian finance was occupied in the 330s and 320s by *Lycurgus (3).

The term is found also in Roman Egypt, where it seems to denote funds for local religious festivals, which had to be supplied by taxation.

J. J. Buchanan, *Theorika* (1962); P. J. Rhodes, *The Athenian Boule* (1972), 235–40. F. M. H.; P. J. R.

theōroi (θεωροί), 'observers', a word originally applied to sightseeing travellers (see TOURISM) and to those attending festivals in distant cities. It became an official title given to a city's representatives at another city's festival. The great panhellenic festivals (see AGŌNES; PANHELLENISM) were attended by theoric delegations (θεωρίαι) from every Greek state. Cities to which theōroi regularly came assigned the duty of receiving them to official theōrodokoi (θεωροδόκοι). At the festivals the theōroi offered sacrifices in the name of their cities, and so the title was likewise given to the envoys that a city sent to a distant shrine to offer sacrifice in its name and to the envoys that it sent to consult a distant oracle. The envoys that were sent round to announce the coming celebration of a festival and, after the creation of new panhellenic agonistic festivals in the 3rd cent. BC and later, to announce the new games to all the Greek states were also called theōroi. It thus

became the accepted title of all sacred envoys. The religious functions of theōroi eventually obscured the original purpose of their office; although Greek cities continued to dispatch festival-embassies into the 3rd cent. AD (e.g. *SEG* 11. 500–1), under the Principate another term, *synthutēs* ('co-sacrificer'), usually described their personnel (L. Robert, *CRAcad. Inscr.* 1970, 6 = *OMS* 5 (1989), 647).

P. Boesch, Θεωρός (1908); A. Boethius, *Die Pythais* (1918); P. Charneux, *BCH* 1966, 156 ff.; P. J. Perlman, *The Theorodokia in the Peloponnese* (Berkeley diss., 1988). J. E. F.; A. J. S. S.

theos (θεός) is the common word denoting a god, especially one of the great gods (see OLYMPIAN GODS). Although often referring to an individual deity in his anthropomorphical representation, the term is rarely used to address a god: no vocative exists. The term is often used instead of the proper name of a god, e.g. when the god's name is under certain restrictions or reserved for direct dealings with the deity, as in the mysteries: τὼ θεώ is the normal expression there for *Demeter and Kore (*Persephone), ὁ θεός and ἡ θεά are Pluto (*Hades) and Persephone. It is also employed when identification of an individual god is precarious, for instance in the case of an *epiphany or vision, or as a comprehensive reference to any inarticulate, anonymous divine operator (θεός τις, θεοί: 'some god', 'the gods'); it alternates in Homer with δαίμων (*daimōn) to denote some unidentifiable divine operator. Later τὸ θεῖον ('the divine power') becomes an equivalent, which, from Herodotus onwards, refers to occurrences that cannot be explained by natural causes. Accordingly, the term is often used in a predicative way to denote events or behaviour which are beyond human understanding: 'recognition of your own kin is θεός'. No plausible etymology of the word has been proposed.

H. J. Rose and others, *La Notion du divin* (1952); W. Pötscher, *Theos* (Diss. Vienna, 1953); G. François, *Le Polythéisme et l'emploi au singulier des mots THEOS, DAIMON* (1957); S. R. F. Price, *JHS* 1984, 79–95. H. S. V.

theoxenia ('theoxeny'), in myth and cult the entertaining of a god or gods by humans, usually at a meal. The thought pattern is old, and reaches beyond the Graeco-Roman world. In Homer, the gods are said to 'meet' or be present at a sacrifice; more specifically, at *Od.* 17. 485–8 they roam the earth in disguise, testing the moral qualities of mortals. This is the germ of the typical theoxeny myth, in which a deity is given—or refused—hospitality, and after an *epiphany effects a reward or punishment. 'Failed' theoxenies are exemplified by the story of *Pentheus, while successful ones form an aetiology for very many cults, especially of *Demeter and *Dionysus. In this pattern the host is often worshipped as a hero (see HERO-CULT), having been instructed by the deity and thus become the cult's first priest or the introducer of a new technique such as viticulture (see CULTURE-BRINGERS). The reception of Demeter at *Eleusis, narrated in the Homeric *Hymn to Demeter, has elements of both success and failure. But perhaps the best-known literary version, probably deriving ultimately from local Anatolian sources, is the story of *Baucis and Philemon (Ovid, *Met.* 8. 618–724).

In ancient usage, the term *theoxenia* is confined to cult, whereas as a festival name it indicates a specific type of worship in which a table is spread and a banqueting couch laid out for the divine guest or guests. The meal is commonly shared by the worshippers, thus contrasting with normal sacrifice, which distinguishes human from divine portions. One of the best-known examples was the Theoxenia of Delphi, which attracted delegates from all over Greece as well as numerous gods, among whom Apollo was predominant. The rite seems to be particularly characteristic of the cult of the *Dioscuri, for whom Theoxenia are celebrated not only in the Peloponnese and in Dorian-speaking areas, but also, for instance, in Attica and on Paros. A parallel ritual, partly influenced by Greek custom, is the Roman *lectisternium.

F. Deneken, *De theoxeniis* (1881); D. Flückinger-Guggenheim, *Göttliche Gäste* (1984); O. Walter, *MDAI(A)* 1937, 41–51 ('Herakles'); A. P. Burnett, *CPhil.* 1970, 15–29 (Pentheus); D. Gill, *Harv. Theol. Rev.* 1974, 117–37 (table-offerings); A. S. Hollis (ed.), *Callimachus Hecale* (1990), app. 3; E. Kearns, *CQ* 1982, 2 ff.; L. Bruit, *Rev. Hist. Rel.* 1984, 358–67 (Delphi). M. Jameson in R. Hägg (ed.), *Ancient Greek Cult Practice from the Epigraphical Evidence* (1994), 35–57.   E. Ke.

Thera (mod. Santorini, 76 km.²), the southernmost of the *Cyclades. It and Therasia are the remnants of a volcanic island destroyed in a cataclysmic eruption *c.*1650–1500 BC, burying the prehistoric landscape under volcanic ash. The absolute date of the eruption and its impact on *Minoan civilization are disputed (see ATLANTIS). Viticulture thrives in its arid climate and light soils.

At Akroteri a bronze age town, deserted before the final eruption, has been uncovered, providing unique insights into the life of a community *c.*1600 BC. Buildings survive up to two storeys and preserve a splendid series of frescos depicting scenes of nature, daily life, and cult. Most remarkable is a frieze in miniature style showing ships, towns, and landscapes. Of neolithic origins, Akroteri flourished between *c.*2000 and 1600 BC, when it had close connections with Crete. Local art combines Minoan influences with a vigorous naturalistic style (see MINOAN CIVILIZATION). Subsequently Thera remained uninhabited until *c.*1200 BC when Mycenaeans settled briefly at Monolithos (see MYCENAEAN CIVILIZATION). Recolonized by *Dorians from *Laconia *c.*850 BC, the ancient city occupied a naturally defensible, wind-swept ridge in the south-east with harbours on either side. Its rich Geometric to Classical cemeteries signal its prosperity. Following a prolonged drought, *c.*630 BC a colony was dispatched to *Cyrene. Thera avoided involvement in the *Persian Wars and remained independent of Athens until the *Peloponnesian War. Payment of tribute of three talents and an indemnity began in 430 BC. In the 3rd and early 2nd cents. BC it was a Ptolemaic possession, serving as a naval base. The city's remains belong chiefly to the Hellenistic and Roman periods.

P. Wilski and F. Hiller von Gaertringen, *RE* 5 A 2260 ff.; *PECS* 908–9; *IG* 12 (3); H. von Gaertringen and others, *Thera* 1–3 (1899–1904); *MDAI(A)* 1903, 1 ff.; J. W. Sperling, *Thera and Therasia* (1973); *Thera and the Aegean World* (1978–80, 1990); C. G. Doumas, *Thera* (1983), and *The Wall-Paintings of Thera* (1992); *ΠΑΕ* 1961, 1963, 1965–   ; I. Malkin, *Myth and Territory in the Spartan Mediterranean* (1994), ch. 3.
                    R. W. V. C.

Theramenes (d. 404/3 BC), Athenian politician, son of Hagnon (cf. AMPHIPOLIS). He played an active part in establishing the *Four Hundred in 411, but four months later he was active in overthrowing them and establishing the Five Thousand, a more moderate but still not fully democratic regime which succeeded the Four Hundred briefly. When full democracy was restored in 410 he was in the *Hellespont, assisting in the recovery of Athens' naval supremacy. At *Arginusae (406) he commanded only a single ship, but was one of those instructed to rescue survivors and corpses after the battle. Failure to achieve that was probably due only to bad weather, but later the blame was disputed between Theramenes and the generals (*stratēgoi), and after a largely illegal trial six generals were put to death. *Xenophon (1) blames Theramenes for orchestrating this miscarriage of justice;

but in *Diodorus (3) Siculus' account his role is less sinister, and *Aristophanes (1) in the *Frogs* next spring treated him lightly, as an adroit politician. In 404 he was sent to negotiate with *Lysander, and afterwards brought back the final terms of peace from Sparta. He was involved in setting up the *oligarchy of the *Thirty Tyrants, and was himself one of the Thirty, but he soon quarrelled with the extremists, especially Critias, who had him executed.

His frequent changes of side were criticized both by democrats like *Lysias and by oligarchs like *Critias, but in the 4th cent. he could be defended as a moderate seeking a genuine political mean. The 'Theramenes papyrus' is probably part of a defence of him, written early in the 4th cent. by a man who knew Lys. 12 and 13 (but other interpretations have been proposed). If he was sincere, he was at least guilty of misjudgement, and must bear a share of the blame for the internal troubles which weakened Athens in the last years of the *Peloponnesian War.

See also PATRIOS POLITEIA.

PA 7234; *APF* 228–9. P. E. Harding, *Phoenix* 1974, 101–11; A. Andrewes, *Phoen.* 1974, 112–22 and *CAH* 5² (1992), ch. 11. Theramenes papyrus: PMich. 5982, published R. Merkelbach and H. C. Youtie, *ZPE* 2 (1968), 161–9; interpreted A. Henrichs, *ZPE* 3 (1969), 101–8, A. Andrewes, *ZPE* 6 (1970), 35–8. See also D. M. Lewis, *CAH* 6² (1994), 32 ff.
                    A. A.; P. J. R.

Therapne See MENELAION.

Thermopylae ('Hot Gates', from its hot sulphur springs) or just the 'Gates' (Πύλαι), strategic pass between Mt. Callidromus and the Euripus channel carrying the main land-route in antiquity from north to central and southern Greece (since when the coastline has receded); also site of the sanctuary of *Demeter at Pylaea (Πυλαία), one of the twin cult-centres of the Delphic–Pylaean Amphictiony (see DELPHI; AMPHICTIONY), of which traces survive (see Plut. *Mor.* 409a for its Roman-period refurbishment). As a defence position, where the road defiled between fierce cliffs and the sea, its weakness was that there is easy ground above, 'along the spine of the mountain' (Hdt. 7. 216), could an invader but find his way to it; and thus the pass was outflanked repeatedly, by 6th-cent. Thessalians, by the Persians, by the Gauls in 279 (Paus. 10. 22), and by Cato in 191 (Plut. *Cato Mai.* 13; see next entry). See PERSIAN WARS.

G. Daux, *Rev. Arch.* 1938, 3 ff. (Pylaea); A. R. Burn, *Persia and the Greeks* (1962), 407 ff.; W. Pritchett, *Studies in Ancient Greek Topography* 1 (1965), 71 ff.; P. MacKay, *AJArch.* 1963, 241 ff.   A. R. B.; A. J. S. S.

Thermopylae, battle of In the pass between the mountains and the sea (see preceding entry) 6,000–7,000 Greeks, led by *Leonidas (1) king of Sparta, attempted to hold the invading Persians, probably in August 480 BC. See PERSIAN WARS. The small size of the army may have been due to religious reasons, or to Peloponnesian reluctance to send troops so far north. The Greeks held their position for two days, but then a local Greek betrayed the existence of an alternative route. The Phocians (see PHOCIS) guarding this route withdrew to the nearest hill, leaving the way open, and when the rest of the Greeks learned of the enemy's approach, most retreated, either in panic, or because Leonidas told them to go. He, with the remnants of the Spartans, Thespians, Thebans, and, possibly, Mycenaeans (see THESPIAE; THEBES (1); MYCENAE), perhaps acting as a rearguard, fought to the last, except possibly the Thebans, who are said to have surrendered. There was a second battle of Thermopylae in 191 BC, when *Antiochus (3) III was defeated by the Romans (see B. Bar-

Kochva, *The Seleucid Army* (1976), ch. 13). See preceding entry.

RE (2nd ser.) 5 A 2, 'Thermopylae'; Hdt. 7. 201–33; Diod. Sic. 11. 5. 4 ff.; C. Hignett, *Xerxes' Invasion of Greece* (1963); J. F. Lazenby, *The Defence of Greece* (1993).   J. F. La.

Thermum, religious and political centre of *Aetolia. Situated north-east of Lake Trichonis on a natural rock-castle, it commanded the central plains of Aetolia and formed the meeting-place for the *Aetolian Confederacy. Extensive excavation has revealed its occupation from the bronze age and its importance as a cult centre for the worship of *Apollo Thermios, Apollo Lykeios, and Artemis; oval houses, a horseshoe-shaped building surrounded by wooden posts (Megaron B, probably of Geometric date), and three Archaic temples are the most important discoveries.

Terracotta metopes from one of these temples date to about 625 BC, and are either Corinthian or made under direct Corinthian influence (see PAINTING, GREEK). Antefixes in the form of heads also reveal Corinthian influence. Thermum's historical importance derives from its status as the administrative centre of the Aetolian Confederacy, though it was never a city. It was sacked in 218 BC by *Philip (3) V of Macedon.

B. Bommelje, P. Doorn, and others (eds.), *Studia Aetolica* 1 (1987), with full refs.   R. A. T.

Theron (*RE* 1), tyrant of *Acragas (Agrigento) in Sicily, *c.*489–473 BC; see TYRANNY. Probably *Gelon's ally (his daughter, Damarete, became Gelon's wife) in a war with the Phoenicians of western Sicily (before 485). His seizure of *Himera (483), expelling Terillus, *guest-friend of *Hamilcar (1), led to Hamilcar's invasion of Sicily (480), and his defeat at Himera by Gelon and Theron. After Gelon's death (478/7), Theron fell out with *Hieron (1)—family matters and a dispute over Himera—but actual hostilities were narrowly averted, and Hieron married Theron's niece; Theron largely repeopled Himera. Theron beautified and enriched Acragas (public buildings and an enlightened agricultural policy), using Carthaginian spoils. A just and undespotic ruler and a patron of literature and the arts, he was honoured by the Acragantines as a hero after his death.

D. Asheri, *CAH* 4² (1988), ch. 16; H. Berve, *Die Tyrannis bei den Griechen*, 132–6.   B. M. C.

Thersander, name of five mythological characters; the one of most importance in terms of *genealogy is son of Polynices and Argela, from whom *Theron of Acragas claimed descent (Pind. *Ol.* 2. 43 ff.). He was one of the *Epigoni.

LIMC 7. 1 (1994), 920–1.   H. J. R.

Thersites, according to Homer the ugliest man at Troy, lame, bow-legged, round-shouldered, almost bald, who abuses Agamemnon until beaten into silence by *Odysseus (*Il.* 2. 212 ff.). Here, evidently, he is of low birth; but in post-Homeric tradition (schol. *Il.* 2. 212) he is of good family, son of Agrius brother of *Oeneus, and therefore related to *Diomedes (2). So, when he is killed by *Achilles for jeering at him because of his supposed love for the dead *Penthesilea (*Aethiopis*—see EPIC CYCLE), a dispute arises and Achilles sails to *Lesbos to be purified (see PURIFICATION).   J. R. M.

Theseus, a legendary king of Athens, who came to embody many of the qualities Athenians thought important about their city. Apparently originating without special Attic connections, he may perhaps have merged with a local hero of northern *Attica, where several of his myths are situated, and his prominence in Athenian tradition seems not to pre-date the 6th cent. BC, deriving at least in part from an epic or epics; the developed

tradition of his life indicates a very different figure from older Athenian heroes such as *Cecrops or *Erechtheus. Detailed accounts of his life are given in Apollod. 3. 16. 1 continued by Epit. 1. 24 and *Plutarch's *Life of Theseus.*

Theseus' claim to membership of the Athenian royal line is somewhat shaky, since his father king *Aegeus was probably a late addition to the stemma, made precisely to accommodate Theseus. The alternative version, that his real father was *Poseidon, scarcely helps. In either case, his mother was *Aethra, daughter of *Pittheus of *Troezen. With her, Aegeus left instructions that if on reaching manhood his son was able to lift a certain rock under which Aegeus had placed sandals and a sword, he was to take the tokens and travel to Athens. This Theseus did, choosing the dangerous land-route, on which he encountered and defeated many dangerous brigands and monsters, such as *Procrustes, *Sciron, and the wild sow of Crommyon. On arrival in Athens, Theseus faced more dangers from *Medea, his father's new wife, and from his cousins the Pallantidae, but escaped their respective attempts at poisoning and ambush. He next defeated the troublesome Marathonian bull (cf. MARATHON); it was on this expedition that he was given hospitality by *Hecale. But the major exploit of this part of his life was the journey to Crete and killing of the Minotaur (see CRETAN CULTS AND MYTHS). In revenge for the death of his son *Androgeus, *Minos had laid upon Athens an annual tribute of seven youths and seven maidens to be given to the Minotaur (for which see MINOS); Theseus now travelled to Crete as one of the youths and killed the beast, escaping from the *labyrinth in which it was kept, with the help of a thread given him by Minos' daughter *Ariadne. He then fled Crete with Ariadne, but for reasons variously given abandoned her on *Naxos (1). On his return to Athens with his companions, he was unwittingly responsible for his father's death, by forgetting to hoist the white sails indicating his survival; Aegeus, thinking his son was dead, hurled himself off the Acropolis or into the sea.

Theseus thus became king. His greatest achievement as such was the *synoecism of Attica—the conversion of numerous small towns into one political unit centred on Athens. This was accomplished by persuasion, but other exploits, not all respectable, relied on force. Like (sometimes with) *Heracles, he undertook an expedition against the *Amazons, winning Antiope or Hippolyte for himself, but provoking an Amazon invasion of *Attica, which was finally defeated. His friendship with the Lapith *Pirithous led him to join the fight against the *Centaurs, and later to attempt to carry off *Persephone from the underworld (rationalizing alternative in Plut. *Thes.* 31). In the usual version, after their failure and imprisonment, Theseus was rescued by Heracles, but Pirithous remained below. Theseus also kidnapped the child *Helen and kept her in the care of his mother until she should mature—though *Iphigenia was said by *Stesichorus (Page, *PMG* fr. 191) and others to be the child of this union. In either case, he was forced to hand her back to her brothers the *Dioscuri when they invaded Attica. This gave Theseus' enemies, headed by *Menestheus, their chance, and in the ensuing political confusion Theseus sent his sons *Acamas and *Demophon to Euboea and himself fled to *Scyros, where he was treacherously killed by King Lycomedes.

The formation of this tradition has clearly been influenced at several points by the figure of Heracles, notably in the monster-killing episodes at the beginning of his career (which, according to Plutarch, ch. 9, he undertook in emulation of his great contemporary). Evidently the developed Theseus saga was built up from pre-existing snippets to satisfy Athenian desire for a home-grown and clearly non-*Dorian hero of Heraclean type, a process which should be dated to roughly the last quarter, even the last decade, of the 6th cent., when there is a dramatic increase in the popularity of Theseus in the visual arts (see below). It is quite possible that the interest of *Pisistratus and/or his sons (see HIPPIAS (1); HIPPARCHUS (1)) may have been a factor contributing to this growth, but it seems very likely that the political significance of the 'new' hero soon became linked with *Cleisthenes (2), whose regional reforms could be seen as similar in spirit to the synoecism. Later, it seems we can trace a connection with the family of *Miltiades and *Cimon, culminating in the latter's transferral of the hero's bones from Scyros to Athens (see RELICS). But by the time of the tragedies of the last 30 or so years of the 5th cent., far from being the property of any one party Theseus is clearly a universally respected figure, the heroic representative of his city's greatness. True, *Euripides' *Hippolytus* presents him as incautious and mistaken (and outside drama, the distinctly negative traditions of the rape of Helen and the attempt on Persephone survived) but the usual picture of him in tragedy is of a strong, fair-minded, and compassionate man presiding with perfect confidence over a proto-democracy (see DEMOCRACY, ATHENIAN), the antithesis of the tragic tyrant.

Coming to prominence relatively late, Theseus had few major sanctuaries in Attica. This was explained by the view that the living Theseus had handed over all, or almost all, of his lands (*temenē*; see TEMENOS) to Heracles (Eur. *HF* 1328–33; Philochorus *FGrH* 328 F 18), whose cult is in fact clearly older in Attica. On the other hand, Theseus became deeply embedded in the festival cycle. As well as having his own festival, the Theseia, on 8th Pyanopsion, he was honoured to a lesser extent on the eighth day of every month (the day also sacred to Poseidon). Moreover, his journey to and return from Crete came to be associated with several cult-complexes and *rituals. Among these were the *Oschophoria, where ritual *transvestism was explained by the story that two of the 'girls' sent to Crete had been young men in disguise, and the juxtaposed cries of joy and grief by the coincidence of Theseus' return with Aegeus' death; and the *Pyanopsia, an Apolline festival (see APOLLO) said to derive from Theseus' *sacrifice in payment of a vow. It is possible to see Theseus here and elsewhere as the heroic prototype of the young men whose transition to adulthood seems to be one concern of the rites. Outside Athens, Theseus was said on his return from Crete to have established various sacrifices and the 'crane-dance' on *Delos, a tradition helpful to the Athenians in their claim to Ionian primacy (see IONIANS; PROPAGANDA). See also HIPPOLYTUS (1).

F. Brommer, *Theseus* (1982); H. Herter, *Rh. Mus.* 1936, 177–239; 1939, 289–36; and *RE* Suppl. 13. 1045–1238; C. Calame, *Thésée et l'imaginaire athénien* (1990); C. Sourvinou-Inwood, *Theseus as Son and Stepson* (1979); J. Boardman, in D. Kurtz and B. Sparkes (eds.), *The Eye of Greece* (1982); R. A. Garland, *Introducing New Gods* (1992), 82–98; Kearns, *Heroes of Attica* (1989), 120–4; J. Neils, *The Youthful Deeds of Theseus* (1987); H. A. Shapiro, *Art and Cult under the Tyrants in Athens* (1989), 143–9.   E. Ke.

Theseus in art The fight with the Minotaur, the only Theseus story regularly shown in Archaic art, is among the most popular of all scenes, continuing to imperial times in many media. The Minotaur is shown with bull's head (early, with human head), being killed; on the Amyclaean throne (mid-6th cent.), it was merely captured (Paus. 3. 18. 11; cf. AMYCLAE). Roman paintings often show the aftermath rather than the fight.

From the late 6th cent. a cycle of Theseus' adventures on the road from Troezen appears, perhaps derived from poetry, or the adoption of Theseus as hero of the new democracy, resulting in

the creation of a complementary series of 'Labours' to those of the Pisistratid hero, Heracles. Such cycles appear on the metopes of the late Archaic Athenian treasury at Delphi, the Hephaesteion in Athens c.450 (see ATHENS, TOPOGRAPHY), and the frieze of Gjölbaschi-Trysa (*Lycia), c.370. Several vases depict cycles, but the scenes generally appear in groups or individually, mostly c.520–420. Theseus may be naked or wear a short cloak, and his weapons vary; his opponent is bearded and naked. Frequently, rocks and trees suggest Theseus' travels.

The lifting of the rock appears also on imperial Campana reliefs (also *Sinis, *Sciron, the Marathonian bull) and *gems. On Classical vases, Theseus attacks a woman who may be Medea (rather than Aethra), and Medea may be identified watching Theseus and the Marathonian bull on a series of late Classical vases; her attempt to poison Theseus is shown on Classical vases and Roman copies of Classical reliefs.

Theseus in the Underworld was painted in the Cnidian Lesche or club-house for the people of *Cnidus at Delphi (Paus. 10. 29. 9–10; see POLYGNOTUS); in the Stoa of Zeus with Democracy and the *Demos (1. 3. 3); in the *Stoa Poecile fighting the Amazons (also on the temple of Apollo at *Eretria, the Zeus at *Olympia, Athena Parthenos, Trysa, and some Classical vases), and rising from the plain of Marathon; and in the Theseion (see MICON). The visit to the sea in the latter appears on Classical vases (see TRITON). *Euphranor and *Parrhasius painted Theseus. *Pausanias (3) notes sculptures of Sciron (1. 3. 1), the Minotaur (1. 24. 1), the Marathonian bull (1. 27. 9–10), and Theseus in the Calydonian boarhunt (8. 45. 6; see MELEAGER (1)).

Bibliog. as above; also: J. Neils with S. Woodford, *LIMC* 7. 1 (1994), 922–51.   K. W. A.

Thesmophoria, a women's festival in honour of *Demeter, common to all Greeks, celebrated in the autumn (on 13th Pyanopsion in Athens), before the time of sowing. Men were excluded and the women camped out, sometimes at a little distance from the town, for three days. At Athens the first day was the *anodos*, 'way up', the second *nēsteia*, 'fasting', the third *kalligeneia*, referring to a goddess of 'Fair Birth'. Pigs were thrown into pits or caves, such as have been found at some Demeter shrines. The putrified remains brought up by 'Balers', *antlētriai*, and placed on altars of Demeter and Kore (see PERSEPHONE), ensured a good harvest when mixed with the seed corn. (It is uncertain when the pigs were cast down. The suggestion of the festival of *Scirophoria, in summer after harvest, is far from certain.) The festival included obscenity and a sacrifice. Otherwise, the secrets of the Thesmophoria have been well kept, as *Aristophanes (1)'s uninformative play, *Thesmophoriazousae*, shows.

Nilsson, *Feste*; L. Deubner, *Attische Feste* (1932); A. Brumfield, *The Attic Festivals of Demeter* (1985), 70–103; Burkert, *GR*.   M. P. N.; M. H. J.

thesmothetai (θεσμοθέται) in Athens were the six junior of the nine *archontes, appointed annually. They were instituted in the 7th cent. BC. *Thesmos* is an early word for 'law' or 'rule', but it is unlikely that the *thesmothetai* ever made laws; their original function must have been 'laying down the law' in the sense of pronouncing verdicts on accusations and disputes.

After the establishment of juries, the main function of the *thesmothetai* was to receive charges in various legal actions and arrange for a trial by jury, at which one *thesmothetēs* was the chairman. Their trials were held in the building known as the *Eliaia. The public actions for which they were responsible included *eisangelia for treason, *probolē* (see LAW AND PROCEDURE, ATHENIAN), and *graphē for many offences, including *graphē par-

anomōn. They took trials arising from **dokimasia*, and they also took some private actions, including mercantile cases held under the monthly procedure after the middle of the 4th cent. They could authorize the execution without trial of persons exiled for homicide who were afterwards found in Attica. In the 4th cent., after magistrates ceased to sit regularly in the same courts, it was the *thesmothetai* who arranged the dates for trials and allotted courts to magistrates each day.

Rhodes, *CAAP*, comm. on 3. 4 and 59.   D. M. M.

Thespiae, city in south-central **Boeotia, commanding a small region of rich river valleys overlooked by low hills, with access to the Corinthian Gulf at Creusis. The few surviving remains include a *polyandreion*, thought to have contained the remains of Thespians who fell in the battle of **Delion (424 BC); the city-site and the surrounding country have been intensively surveyed by British archaeologists, permitting a detailed reconstruction of regional settlement-history. Thespians fought at Thermopylae (see THERM-OPYLAE, BATTLE OF); and after the battle of **Coronea in 447 BC, together with **Thisbe and Eutresis, held two votes in the new Boeotian Confederacy (see FEDERAL STATES). The losses suffered at Delion afforded **Thebes (1) the opportunity to dismantle Thespiae's walls. Resulting political unrest continued until 415 BC, when Thebes crushed pro-Athenian elements within the city. Autonomous after the **King's Peace, Thespiae was again subdued by Thebes in 373 BC, but **Epaminondas allowed the Thespian contingent to withdraw before the battle of **Leuctra in 371 BC. Thespiae joined forces with **Alexander (3) the Great and others in the destruction of Thebes in 335 BC. Having suffered the ravages of war during the Hellenistic period, it supported Rome against **Mithradates VI, its reward to become a '*free city'. It hosted an important community of Roman **negotiatores* until the refoundation of **Corinth (44 BC) diminished its commercial role; but its festivals of **Eros and the **Muses (providing the setting for Plut. *Amat.*) remained panhellenic (see PANHELLENISM) into the 3rd cent. AD, when it produced a Roman consul. The site is prolific in inscriptions, notably the nine stelai (see STELE) listing the Thespian war-dead at Delion (*IG* 7. 1888), a long text giving details of political and administrative life in the 3rd cent. BC (Roesch 1965, 3 ff.), and a decree recording a Thespian levy for the German wars of M. **Aurelius (*Nouveau choix d'inscriptions grecques* (1971), no. 15).

P. Roesch, *Thespies et la confédération béotienne* (1965), and *Études béoti-ennes* (1982); C. P. Jones, *Harv. Stud.* 1970, 223 ff.; J. Fossey, *Topography and Population of Ancient Boiotia* (1988), 135 ff.; J. Bintliff and A. Snod-grass, *Antiquity* (1988), 57 ff.; R. Osborne in *La Béotie antique* (1985), 317 ff.; M. Kajava, *ZPE* 79 (1989), 139 ff.   J. Bu.; A. J. S. S.

Thespis was believed in antiquity to have invented tragedy. **Horace (*Ars P.* 275–7) has him taking his plays around on wagons, with the players' faces smeared with wine-lees. The **Suda* says that he invented the mask. And in **Plutarch he consorts with **Solon (*Sol.* 29). But none of these details is reliable. Nor are any of the few surviving fragments and titles likely to be authentic. And there were other nominations for the inventor of tragedy (**Epigenes (1) of Sicyon, **Arion (2) of Methymna). The Parian Marble (43) (see MARMOR PARIUM) dates his first activity to somewhere between 538 and 528 BC. But the statement in the *Suda*, on which is based the modern view that he first produced tragedy at the Dionysia in one of the years 535–533, is in fact unreliable (Connor). Worthy of respect, however, is the remark attributed to Aristotle that Thespis added prologue and speech to what had been a choral performance (Themistios 26. 316d). See TRAGEDY, GREEK, §I. 2.

TrGF 1; A. Lesky, *Greek Tragic Poetry* (1983; Ger. orig. 1972), ch. 2; M. L. West, *CQ* 1989, 251–4; W. R. Connor in *Aspects of Athenian Democracy* (Cl. et Med. Dissertationes 11, 1990), 7 ff.   R. A. S. S.

Thesproti, a people mentioned in **Homer's *Odyssey* with a king of **Ephyra in the Acheron valley (in this region a tholos-tomb and Mycenaean weapons have been found; see MYCENAEAN CIVILIZATION) and probably extending over **Epirus in the late bronze age. Later confined to south-west Epirus, their territory included for a time **Dodona and always the *Nekyomanteion* or Oracle of the Dead. The Thesproti formed a tribal state (*koinon*), which entered the Epirote Alliance and the Epirote Confederacy, sided with Rome in 170 BC, and survived under the Roman settlement.

N. G. L. Hammond, *Epirus* (1967); S. I. Dakaris, *Thesprotia* (1972, in Greek), and *The Acheron Necromanteion* (n.d.).   N. G. L. H.

Thessaliotis, one of the four *tetrades* (districts) of **Thessaly, organized by Aleuas the Red in the 6th cent. BC (see ALEUADAE), and located in the southern half of the west Thessalian plain (region of mod. Karditsa) on the fertile terraces stretching between the foothills of Mt. Pindus and the river Peneus. The local population of pastoralists and peasant-farmers gradually acquired a distinctive identity marked by Greek culture and a 'mixed' language, Proto-Aeolian (see GREEK LANGUAGE). The emergence of this population of self-styled *Thessaloi* occurred *c.*1000 BC. Myth gives as the oldest settlement of Thessaliotis Arne, later Cierium; archaeology has revealed, a few km. to the south, the site of the sanctuary of the Thessalian *ethnos*, the Itonium, with its temple of Athena Itonia.

Thessaliotis in origin (as with the other tetrads) comprised four cities: Cierium and Thetonium were certainly among these; the other two were probably Methylium and Limnaeum. Demographic and political development led to the emergence of other cities: Ortha and Callithera under the south Pindus, Phacium near the north Pindus.

F. Gschnitzer, *Hermes* 1954, 451 ff.; J.-C. Decourt, *La Vallée de l'Enipeus*, *BCH* Suppl. 21 (1991), 147 ff; B. Helly, *L'état Thessalien* (1995).   B. H.

Thessalonica, a city of **Macedonia, founded by **Cassander, who synoecized the small towns at the head of the Thermaic Gulf (see SYNOECISM); perhaps on the site of Therme (Strabo 7 fr. 24). It was named after Cassander's wife. It stood at the junction of the Morava–Axius route from the Danube basin with the route from the Adriatic to Byzantium (the later **via Egnatia). An open roadstead sheltered by **Chalcidice, Thessalonica became the chief Macedonian port, displacing **Pella when its harbour was silted up. Strongly fortified, it withstood a Roman siege but surrendered after the battle of **Pydna. It became the capital of the Roman province of Macedonia (see PROVINCIA), and it served as **Pompey's base in the Civil War. As a '*free city' and as the main station on the **via Egnatia, it enjoyed great prosperity, to which its prolific **coinage bears witness. It was made a Roman colony by **Decius *c.*250 AD (see COLONIZATION, ROMAN). The population included a large Roman element and many Jewish settlers, who were visited by the apostle **Paul. One of his disciples, Aristarchus, became the first bishop of Thessalonica. In the Byzantine empire Thessalonica was second only to Constantinople. Its strong walls and its early Byzantine churches belong to that period. It was sacked by Saracens in 904.   N. G. L. H.

Thessalus (1) (*RE* 5), of **Cos (fl. late 5th cent. BC), according to some a 'son of Hippocrates' (see HIPPOCRATES (2)). Next to nothing is known of him, yet attempts were made in later antiquity by *Galen and others to attribute certain Hippocratic works to him, including parts of the *Epidemics*, *On Nutriment*, and *In the Surgery*.   J. T. V.

Thessalus (2) (*RE* 6), a doctor from *Tralles. He worked in Rome and was probably dead by AD 79. None of his writings survive, but he is often mentioned by other medical writers. *Galen (10. 7 Kühn) claims that he wrote to *Nero boasting of founding 'a new sect, and the only true one'. *Pliny (1) (*HN* 29. 9) says that he described himself as the 'conqueror of physicians'. The new sect was 'Methodism' (see MEDICINE, § 5. 3); it is a matter of some doubt whether he actually founded it or not and his own debt to *Themison of Laodicea is unclear. (Although some later Methodists certainly saw him as some kind of forerunner, if not founder.) The method of Methodism was a treatment which involved rectifying one of two phenomenally evident abnormal states in the affected body, stricture or flux (or in some cases a combination of the two). Methodists like *Soranus of Ephesus stressed the importance of independence from theory, and one important Methodist source, Caelius Aurelianus, attacks Thessalus for being too theoretical in his account of the background to the method. This could be a reflection of the sect's lack of internal coherence, or simply a sign of the level of dissent that was tolerated in all the medical sects.

Text: Fragments not collected. Literature: L. Edelstein, *RE* Suppl. 6, 'Methodiker'; M. Frede, in J. Barnes and others (eds.), *Science and Speculation* (1982). R. J. Hankinson, *Galen on the Therapeutic Method, Books I & II* (1991).   J. T. V.

Thessaly, region of N. Greece, divided into the four *tetrades* (districts) of *Thessaliotis, *Hestiaeotis, *Pelasgiotis, and *Phthiotis, along with the so-called perioecic regions (see PERIOIKOI) of Perrhaebia (see PERRHAEBI), Magnesia, Achaea Phthiotis, and Dolopia. Comprising two vast plains divided by the modern Revenia hills, Thessaly is enclosed by mountains (notably *Olympus (1), *Ossa, *Pelion, Othrys, and Pindus) which, far from forming obstacles to communication with neighbours, are pierced by valleys and passes with the generic ancient name of *tempē* (cf. TEMPE), by which, in all periods, travellers, merchants, and armies have reached the Thessalian plains. Thessaly has access to the sea only by the gulf of *Pagasae, with its two neighbouring ports, the one in the bay of Volos, in antiquity successively Iolcus, Pagasai, and *Demetrias, the other in the bay of Halmyrus (Pyrasus, or Demetrieum, absorbed *c*.300 BC into the city of Thebes in Achaea Phthiotis); a third port, Phalara near Lamia, was accessible to the Thessalians of the Spercheios valley. Thessaly has a continental climate, far more marked than in the coastal plains further south, with extremely fertile soils; it was rich in grain, horses, and other livestock, although its relative coolness precluded (with exceptions) cultivation of the vine and olive.

Over the last 30 years archaeology has greatly improved our knowledge of ancient Thessaly. Human activity is now attested from the end of the palaeolithic age, and the eastern plain was densely settled in the neolithic, with more than 400 sites so far known (see GREECE, *stone age*); in late Helladic times Mycenaean culture spread via *Iolcus into the two plains and the peripheral mountains.

In the southern half of the eastern plain a population of pastoralists and peasant-farmers calling themselves *Thessaloi* (probably coming from the Balkans) gradually emerged with a distinctive identity based on Greek culture and a 'mixed' language, proto-Aeolian (see GREEK LANGUAGE). From *c*.1000 BC these Thessalians progressively took over more and more land, eventually coming to dominate (over the passage of almost a thousand years) the two plains and also the surrounding mountains. The Thessalian *ethnos* early on formed itself into an organized state, with cities led by aristocratic families and grouped into a federation under the authority of a chief called *archos* or *archōn* (not *tagos*, as used to be thought).

Their military power first gave the Thessalians access to the Peneus basin and part of the eastern plain, as well as the southern regions of the Othrys range, the Spercheios valley, and the coasts of the Maliac Gulf; then central Greece. Winning control of the *amphictiony formed by the population of these districts and based first at Anthela, then at *Delphi (see SACRED WARS), the Thessalians were for a while a dominant power in central Greece. But from *c*.600 BC they were forced to fall back on Thessaly proper. In the second half of the 6th cent. BC the Thessalian state was reorganized by Aleuas the Red (see ALEUADAE), who created the four tetrads, each of four cities; the federal chief now received the title of tetrarch (see TETRARCHY). Aleuas adapted the territories of each city for military mobilization by creating land-allotments (*klēroi*) controlled by the *tagoi*, officials charged with organizing the state's military units, and thus created an effective army. See also CRANNON (for the Scopadae, rivals of the Aleuadae).

In the 5th cent. BC the Thessalians strengthened their hold on Thessaly as a whole; of the population of the two plains a part was now integrated into the cities (which increased in number), the rest expelled to the mountains. Federal ties weakened following the rise to political and economic dominance over their neighbours of the cities of *Larissa, *Pherae, and *Pharsalus. Urbanization progressed and wealth accumulated; aristocratic families engaged in their rivalries, but also were forced to cede to political pressure from ordinary citizens seeking a say in local government, which became progressively more democratic.

Inter-city rivalries worsened *c*.400 BC. The Aleuadae of Larissa directly opposed the tyrant *Lycophron (1) of Pherae with the help of the kings of Macedon, to whom they thereby gave the means of intervening in Thessaly. Lycophron's successor, *Jason (2), sought to become master of all Thessaly, using the federal army; after initiating an important military reform (whence his title of *tagos*) he attempted to reassert federal power. After his assassination and the coming to power of *Alexander (5) in Pherae, internal wrangling brought Thessalian politics to a new low and facilitated the intervention of *Philip (1) II of Macedon, who assumed control of the federation. Philip delegated his authority to his own appointees, four tetradarchs, through whom the submission of the Thessalians was assured. The Thessalian cavalry fought with distinction in Asia under *Alexander (3) the Great, but in the *Lamian War the Thessalians actively sided with the Greeks. In the 3rd cent. BC Thessaly was effectively partitioned, with some areas in Macedonian hands and others controlled by the *Aetolian Confederacy; it now became a theatre for the military engagements of other powers, including, from the end of the century, the Romans.

The declaration of Greek freedom by T. *Quinctius Flamininus in 196 BC ostensibly liberated the Thessalian cities, but Rome kept control of them. Enlarged after 146 BC and again under *Augustus to include the perioecic regions, the Thessalian federation survived as a Roman administrative tool until the end of the 4th cent. AD. See also MAGIC (Thessalian witches); ORPHIC LITERATURE; ORPHISM (Orphic gold tablet from Thessaly).

H. D. Westlake, *Thessaly in the Fourth Century* BC (1935); E. Kirsten, in A. Philippson, *Griechische Landschaften*[2] 1 (1953), 259 ff.; M. Sordi, *La*

Thestius

lega tessala fino ad Alessandro Magno (1958); B. Helly, L'état Thessalien (1995).

B. H.

Thestius, in mythology, king of Pleuron, father of Lynceus and Idas (*Argonauts and hunters of the Calydonian boar (see MELEAGER)) and of Althaea, wife of *Oeneus (Ov. *Met.* 8. 304, 446, and elsewhere).

Thestor (Θέστωρ). Of the five persons so called (Höfer in Roscher, *Lex.*), the least obscure is the father of *Calchas (*Il.* 1. 69). He has no legend, the tale in Hyginus, *Fab.* 190, being manifestly late romance.

thētes, hired labourers, the lowest class of free men in a Greek state. At Athens, after *Solon, the lowest of the four property classes, comprising men who did not own land yielding as much as 200 *medimnoi* of corn or the equivalent in other produce. (The others classes were *pentakosiomedimnoi, *zeugitai, *hippeis). Solon admitted them to the assembly (*ekklēsia) and *ēliaia (indeed, probably they had never been formally excluded from the assembly), but not to magistracies (see MAGISTRACY, GREEK) or, presumably, the council (*boulē) (Arist. *Ath. Pol.* 7. 3–8. 1). This limitation was never formally abolished, but by the second half of the 4th cent. it was being ignored in practice. Because they could not afford the armour, *thētes* did not fight as *hoplites, but when Athens became mainly a naval power they acquired an important role as oarsmen in the fleet; they may also have served in such bodies as the archers. Whether they were included among the *ephēboi ('cadets') as reorganized in the 330s is disputed.

A. W. G.; T. J. C.; P. J. R.

Thetis, a sea-*nymph, daughter of *Nereus, wife of *Peleus, and mother of *Achilles. The *Cypria* (fr. 2 Davies; see EPIC CYCLE) accounted for her marriage to Peleus by saying that she refused the advances of *Zeus to avoid offending *Hera and that Zeus, in anger, swore that she must marry a mortal. According to *Pindar, however (*Isthm.* 8. 26–57), she was desired by both Zeus and *Poseidon, but *Themis revealed that Thetis was fated to bear a son stronger than his father, and for this reason she was married off to Peleus. This version was exploited in the *Prometheus* plays attributed to *Aeschylus, where *Prometheus knew of the prophecy about Thetis and used the knowledge as a bargaining counter (*PV* 757–70, 907–27).

Before marrying Thetis, Peleus had to capture her while she assumed different forms to escape him (e.g. Ovid, *Met.* 11. 221–65). The wedding was attended by the gods, who brought gifts (e.g. Catullus 64). Both the capture and the wedding are very popular subjects in Greek art.

Most sources say that Thetis abandoned Peleus after her unsuccessful attempt to make the infant Achilles immortal; but *Homer sometimes implies that she stayed with him. She plays a crucial role in the *Iliad* as intermediary between Achilles and the gods, interceding with Zeus on his behalf at 1. 348–430, 493–533, commissioning new armour for him in books 18–19, and bringing him the gods' command to release *Hector's body at 24. 77–142.

J. R. March, *The Creative Poet*, *BICS* Suppl. 49 (1987), 1–26; L. M. Slatkin, *The Power of Thetis* (1991).

A. L. B.

theurgy was a form of pagan religious *magic associated with the *Chaldaean Oracles* and taken up by the later Neoplatonists. It covered a range of magical practices, from rain-making and cures to animating statues of the gods. Like other forms of *magic, theurgy was based on a theory of cosmic sympathy

but in theurgy, as in Neoplatonist metaphysics, sympathy was thought to extend beyond the material world and to unite it with a higher, divine world. Theurgy was accordingly believed to promote the union of the human soul with the divine. Plotinus shows no interest in theurgy but in the next generation it became the focus of a dispute between *Porphyry and *Iamblichus (2). Iamblichus' *On the Mysteries* argues, against Porphyry, that the human soul cannot attain union with the divine purely by its own efforts of philosophical contemplation; such union requires the assistance of the gods, which can be brought about by theurgy. Most of the later Neoplatonists accepted Iamblichus' position, although they varied in the emphasis they placed on theurgy. *Eunapius records that the pupils of Iamblichus' pupil *Aedesius differed on this point: Eusebius of Myndus apparently disapproved of theurgy while Chrysanthius and *Maximus (3) were enthusiastic practitioners. *Proclus and his school at Athens followed Iamblichus. It has often been thought that the 5th- and 6th-cent. Neoplatonists of *Alexandria (1) were less committed to theurgy than their Athenian contemporaries. In fact, of the pagan Neoplatonists at Alexandria, Ammonius son of Hermeias is notably silent about both theurgy and the *Chaldaean Oracles* but the rest share the views of the Athenian school. Theurgy continued to attract the interest of the Byzantine Neoplatonists, particularly Michael *Psellus. See NEOPLATONISM.

E. R. Dodds, *The Greeks and the Irrational* (1951); A. Smith, *Porphyry's Place in the Neoplatonic Tradition* (1974); G. Shaw, *Traditio* 1985, 1 ff.

A. D. S.

Theveste (mod. Tébessa), an old Berber town commanding the upper Ampsaga, at the east end of the High Plateaux in eastern Algeria, 38 km. (25 mi.) south-west of *Ammaedara. It is probably to be identified with the Hecatompylos of *Polybius (1) (1. 73. 1) and *Diodorus (3) (4. 18. 1 and 24. 10. 2); the earliest occupation archaeologically attested is of the 4th/3rd cent. BC. *Hanno (2) conquered it for *Carthage c.247 BC. From the early Flavian period (c. AD 75) to late in *Trajan's reign (c.115/17), when it was moved to *Lambaesis, the Legio III Augusta (see LEGION) was stationed at Theveste on the evidence of tombstones and other military inscriptions, but no archaeological trace of the fortress has ever been found. The town that replaced it soon became a *colonia*, possibly already under Trajan, and certainly no later than 180/2 (*ILAlg.* 1. 3032); it early embraced *Christianity, and was a bishopric at least by 256. Connected with Carthage by one of the main roads of north Africa, it served as the economic and administrative centre of an extensive area covering parts of south-eastern Algeria and south-western Tunisia. *Olive cultivation was widespread in the region (the olive farm with six presses at Brisgane, 35 km. (22 mi.) south of Theveste, is one of the best preserved examples of its type), and that it continued into the late 5th cent. is witnessed by the remarkable wooden tablets inscribed in ink from 100 km. (63 mi.) south of Theveste, datable to AD 493/6, which provide a unique glimpse of estate administration under the *Vandals. Substantial monuments of Theveste survive: the amphitheatre, a tetrapylon of Caracalla (214), a perfectly preserved temple ('of Minerva'), a large church and ancillary Christian buildings of the late 4th and 5th cents., and a complete circuit of Byzantine fortifications.

PECS 913–14; R. Cagnat, *Carthage, Timgad, Tébessa*[2] (1909); E. S. de Roch, *Tébessa, antique Theveste* (1952); R. Lequément, *Fouilles à l'amphithéâtre de Tébessa* (1965–8, 1979); J. Christern, *Das frühchristliche Pilgerheiligtum von Tebessa* (1976). Brisgane (also called Bir Sgaoun): S. Gsell, *Les Monuments antiques de l'Algérie* 2 (1901), 30–1. Vandal tablets:

C. Courtois and others, *Tablettes Albertini: Actes privés de l'époque vandale (fin du Vᵉ siècle)* (1952).　　　　　B. H. W.; R. J. A. W.

thiasos (θίασος), a group of worshippers of a god. Permanent *thiasoi* are attested epigraphically from the Hellenistic period in much of the Greek world: they are associations centred, at least in theory, on the worship of a particular god or hero, and are not clearly distinguishable from other Hellenistic forms of religious or pseudo-religious club. Earlier, *thiasoi* appear in literary sources in connection with *Dionysus and with other (cf. Dem. 18. 260) ecstatic cults (see ECSTASY). How these earlier *thiasoi* were organized is unknown; possibly they were brought together for no longer than the duration of a particular rite. However that may be, the members were united by a strong sense of undergoing an experience in common: *Euripides speaks, untranslatably, of θιασεύεσθαι ψυχάν (*Bacchae* 75), 'entering the *thiasos* in soul'.

Some and possibly all Attic *phratries were also subdivided into *thiasoi* by the early 4th cent. (A. Andrewes, *JHS* 1961, 9–12). It is not known whether these phratry *thiasoi* had the religious function that the name seems to suggest; possibly the hereditary 'thiasoi of *Heracles' that are mentioned (Isaeus 9. 30), without further details, are instances of such phratry segments. A 'law of *Solon' (*Digest* 47. 22. 4) guaranteed the right of association to groups of *thiasōtai* (of what type?). See CLUBS, GREEK.

F. Poland, *Geschichte des griechischen Vereinswesens* (1909); W. S. Ferguson, *Harv. Theol. Rev.* 1944; *L'association dionysiaque dans les sociétés anciennes: Colloque 1984* (1986); H. S. Versnel, *Ter Unus* (1990).
　　　　　R. C. T. P.

Thibron (1) (d. 391 BC), Spartan general. He was sent to Ionia in 400 BC to protect the Asian Greek cities from *Tissaphernes. Deficient in siege-equipment and cavalry, he captured Magnesia but failed at *Tralles and avoided confrontations on level ground until he recruited the survivors of *Cyrus (2)'s Greek mercenaries in spring 399. He won over Pergamus (the later *Pergamum) and some minor cities of Aeolis, took others by storm, but failed again at 'Egyptian' Larissa. Ordered to attack *Caria, he was soon replaced by *Dercylidas and exiled for allowing his troops to plunder Sparta's allies. Apparently subsequently recalled, he was sent again in 391 to Asia Minor to operate against the anti-Spartan Persian *satrap Strouthas. He was surprised and killed, however, in an enemy cavalry attack on his ill-organized raiding party. He may be the Thibron mentioned by *Aristotle (*Pol.* 1333ᵇ) as author of a work which praised *Lycurgus (2) for having trained men to face dangers and so come to rule over many, hence seemingly supporting Sparta's imperialist policies.

RE 6 A 273–5 'Thibron 1'; PB nos. 374–5.　　　　　S. J. Ho.

Thibron (2) (d. 322 BC), Spartan mercenary commander, served under *Harpalus, whom he murdered and supplanted (late 324). He intervened with devastating effect in Cyrenaica and became briefly master of the *Pentapolis, driving the oligarchic exiles into the arms of *Ptolemy (1) I, whose general (*Ophellas) captured Thibron and annexed the territory (322).　　　　　A. B. B.

Thirty Tyrants Upon Athens' defeat in the *Peloponnesian War (April 404 BC) Spartan support gave Athenian oligarchs the upper hand (see OLIGARCHY). Under the peace terms imposed by *Lysander thirty men were chosen to run the government and write new laws following the 'ancestral constitution' (*patrios politeia). These Thirty, with *Critias leading the extremists and *Theramenes the moderates, appointed sympathetic members to the new *boulē*, created a board of Ten to rule *Piraeus, abolished the popular juries, and began to remove their democratic

opponents and certain *sycophants (malicious prosecutors). The purge soon broadened to include respectable citizens and *metics. When Theramenes tried to broaden the franchise beyond the 3,000 citizens initially approved, Critias had him condemned and executed. 1,500 are said to have been executed in all; many others left Athens. In January 403 *Thrasybulus and a few democrats outside the city took up arms against the Thirty, who responded by stationing a Spartan garrison on the Acropolis thereby further alienating the Athenian people. Thrasybulus and his band grew larger and moved to Piraeus, where they defeated the forces of the Thirty in a battle in which Critias was killed (May 403). The Thirty were now replaced by a more moderate board of Ten; the same policies continued in effect, but the Ten began negotiations with Thrasybulus' forces. Reconciliation was facilitated by the new Spartan commander, *Pausanias (2), and democracy was restored in September 403. *Amnesty was extended to all but the Thirty and a few others, who had fled to *Eleusis; most of these were killed two or three years later. They were first called the Thirty Tyrants, as far as we can see, by *Diodorus (3) Siculus (14. 3. 7), unless this reflects the language of his source (?*Ephorus).

Lysias 12, 13; Xen. *Hell.* 2. 3–4; *Ath. Pol.* 34–40 (less trustworthy than Xenophon); Diod. Sic. 14. 3–6, 32–3. Cf. P. Krentz, *The Thirty at Athens* (1982); M. Ostwald, *Popular Sovereignty* (1986), 460–96.　　　　　M. Ga.

'thirty tyrants', the name given in the *Historia Augusta* (Pollio) to the pretenders who arose in the provinces in the mid-3rd cent. AD. The author's original plan was to write on twenty, but the number was raised to that of the 'thirty tyrants' of Athens by admitted padding; 32 names appear in the collection, including two women. The object was to denigrate *Gallienus, in whose reign most of the pretenders are said to have lived; in fact only nine are authenticated for his reign. Of the others, some were children of pretenders, some certainly never wore the purple, others are almost certainly fictions, and a few occurred in other reigns. The whole collection is worthless as a historical source. In the list which follows (not in the order of the *Historia*) italicized names are known from coins or other sources.

In Gaul: *Postumus = M. Cassianius Latinius Postumus Aug., 259–68; Postumus Junior, said to be Caesar, and son of Postumus; *Lollianus* = C. Ulpius Cornelius Laelianus Aug., 268, rebelled against Postumus; *Marius* = M. Aurelius Marius Aug., 268; *Victorinus* = M. Piavonius Victorinus Aug., 268–70; Victorinus Junior, said to be son of Victorinus, existence doubtful; *Tetricus* = C. Pius Esuvius Tetricus Aug., 270–4; *Tetricus Junior*, Caesar, son of Tetricus.

In Illyricum: Ingenuus, full name unknown, c.259; *Regalianus* = P. C. . . . Regalianus Aug., c.260; *Aureolus, full name unknown, 268.

In Greece: Piso, 261, an invention; *Valens*, 261.

In Isauria: Trebellianus: highly dubious.

In Syria: *Cyriades* = Mareades, c.258, never emperor; *Macrianus* = (Fulvius) Macrianus, 260, never emperor; *Macrianus Junior* = T. Fulvius Macrianus Aug., 260–1; *Ballista, 260–1, never emperor; *Quietus* = T. Fulvius Iunius Quietus Aug., 260–1; *Odaenathus* = *Septimius Odaenathus, 260–7, never emperor; Herodes, Herennianus, and Timolaus, c.268 ff., said to be sons of Odaenathus, never emperors; Maeonius, c.268, a relative of Odaenathus, never emperor.

In Egypt: *Aemilianus* = L. Mussius Aemilianus, c.261.

Others: Celsus and Saturninus, both fictions; *Victoria*, mother of Victorinus; *Zenobia, wife of Odaenathus; *Valens Superior*, at

Rome in 250; *Titus*, probably = Quartinus, 238; Censorinus, a fiction.

R. Syme, *Ammianus and the Historia Augusta* (1968). B. H. W.

Thirty Years Peace, agreement between Sparta and Athens in 446, which ended the First *Peloponnesian War after *c*.15 years. Its exact terms are unknown but by it Athens (after a recent defeat in *Boeotia, see CORONEA, BATTLE OF) abandoned its recent land acquisitions (Nisaea, Pegae, *Troezen, *Achaea), including and especially Boeotia, effectively in return for a free hand on revolted *Euboea (Thuc. 1. 115. 1). Armed attacks were renounced if the other side was prepared to go to *arbitration (Thuc. 1. 78. 4, 140. 2, 144. 2, 145; 7. 18). There was possibly a general clause stipulating *autonomy; at least, the Aeginetans (see AEGINA) complain (Thuc. 1. 67) that theirs has been infringed, though this may be a reference to a special guarantee to Aegina. *Argos (2) and other cities not included in the treaty could join whichever side they liked (Thuc. 1. 35; Paus. 5. 23. 4 for Argos). NB there was *no* general clause of 446 recognizing possessions as they then stood, i.e. acknowledging the existence of the Athenian empire: Thuc. 1. 140. 2 ('having what they hold') merely refers to interim arrangements pending arbitration. Much of our evidence for the Peace comes from the late 430s, in the run-up to the main Peloponnesian War, when the question arose whether Athens had broken the Peace.

SvT 2², no. 156; G.E.M. de Ste. Croix, *The Origins of the Peloponnesian War* (1972), app. 1; E. Badian, *From Plataea to Potidaea* (1993), ch. 4.
S. H.

Thisbe, city in SW *Boeotia, described in *Homer's *Iliad* (2. 502) as rich in doves. Situated at the eastern defile of Mt. *Helicon, it commanded a small plain near the Corinthian Gulf. Together with *Thespiae and Eutresis it contributed two units to the Boeotian Confederacy (see FEDERAL STATES). Cleombrotus of Sparta chose it as the point of invasion before the battle of *Leuctra. In the Third Macedonian War Thisbe took the side of Macedonian King *Perseus (2) against Rome, and was subsequently punished. Its walls were rebuilt during the Roman empire, and it flourished during the Byzantine period.

F. G. Maier, *MDAI(A)* 73 (1958); P. W. Wallace, *Strabo's Description of Boiotia* (1979). J. Bu.

tholos In classical architecture a tholos is a circular building. Examples include that on the west side of the Athenian Agora (otherwise referred to as the *Skias*, or parasol, from the shape of its roof; see ATHENS, TOPOGRAPHY). Built about 470 BC, it consisted of a circular drum with a conical roof supported by internal wooden posts on an elliptical plan. It was used as a dining hall for the *prytaneis. The tholos in the sanctuary of Athena Pronaea at *Delphi, dating to *c*.375 BC, had a peristyle of twenty Doric columns (see ORDERS, ARCHITECTURAL). Its function is uncertain. The later tholos (properly called the Thymele) at *Epidaurus, with a peristyle of twenty-six Doric columns, may have been the cenotaph of *Asclepius—while the Ionic Philippeum at *Olympia, erected by *Alexander (3) the Great, was a memorial to his father (see PHILIP (1) II). A general link between tholoi and *dining-rooms is suggested, but the evidence for this is slender.

F. Seiler *Die griechische Tholos* (1986); F. Cooper and S. Morris, in O. Murray (ed.), *Sympotica* (1990). R. A. T.

Thomas Magister (*Theodulos* in religion) of *Thessalonica was the secretary of the Byzantine emperor Andronicus II (AD 1282–

1328), but withdrew to a monastery, where he devoted himself to scholarship.

Works 1. *Ecloga Vocum Atticarum* (Ἐκλογὴ ὀνομάτων καὶ ῥημάτων Ἀττικῶν, 'Selection of *Attic nouns and verbs'), based especially on *Phrynichus (3), *Ammonius (1), *Herodian (1), and *Moeris, but with much added material that is less valuable, drawn from his own reading, e.g. in *Herodotus (1), *Thucydides (2), Aelius *Aristides, and *Synesius.

2. Texts, with *scholia, of *Aeschylus; *Sophocles (1), *Aj.*, *El.*, *OT*; *Euripides, *Hec.*, *Or.*, *Phoen.*; *Aristophanes (1), *Plut.*, *Nub.*, *Ran.*; and *Pindar. These give an insight into the oral instruction provided by a late Byzantine teacher. Thomas is well informed on *realien*, tolerably knowledgeable on rare words, and totally ignorant of metre. Lives of these poets appear under his name in some manuscripts.

3. Declamations on set themes in the manner of the ancient orators, e.g. *De Regis Officiis* (Περὶ βασιλείας, 'on *kingship'); panegyrics on famous personalities of earlier date, e.g. *Gregory (2) of Nazianzus; eulogistic addresses to contemporaries; deliberative discourses on questions of the moment.

4. Letters.

Ecloga, F. Ritschl (1832); J. P. Migne, *PG* 145; F. W. Lenz, *Fünf Reden Th. M.'s* (1963); T. Hopfner, *Sitz. Wien. Akad.* 1912; A. Turyn, *The Manuscript Tradition of the Tragedies of Aeschylus* (1943), 67 ff., and *Studies in the Manuscript Tradition of the Tragedies of Sophocles* (1952), 31 ff.; J. Irigoin, *Histoire du texte de Pindare* (1952), 180 ff.; A. Turyn, *The Byzantine Manuscript Tradition of the Tragedies of Euripides* (1957), 165 ff.; N. G. Wilson, *Scholars of Byzantium* (1987), 247–9; R. Skalistes, *Thomas Magistros: Ho bios kai to ergo tou* (1984). J. F. L.; R. B.

Thoricus, coastal *deme of SE *Attica, now a bare twin-peaked hill north of modern Laurion. In legend, one of King *Cecrops' twelve Attic townships, home of the hunter king *Cephalus, and landing-place of *Demeter, travelling from *Crete to *Eleusis. An important centre of the Classical silver-mine industry, it became a ghost-town by the 1st cent. AD. Excavated remains include, on the higher slopes, five Helladic tombs, Geometric graves and houses, and, lower down, extensive remains of the Archaic–Classical town: a theatre of unusual plan (see THEATRES (GREEK AND ROMAN), STRUCTURE; THEATRE STAGING, GREEK), adjacent temple-foundations, tombs, houses, ore-washeries (one restored) and a large mine-gallery (with early bronze to later Roman sherds), and an 'industrial quarter' of streets, houses and washeries, an outlying tower, and a silted-over temple, perhaps Demeter's. A remarkable inscription (*SEG* 33. 147) gives the calendar (see CALENDAR, GREEK) for *sacrifices to be made by the deme. Also noteworthy are a peninsular fort, an ore-smeltery, and more mining installations on the fringes of the coastal plain. See LAURIUM; MINES AND MINING.

H. F. Mussche, *Thorikos: A Guide to the Excavations* (1974); J. Travlos, *Bildlexikon zur Topographie des antiken Attika* (1988), 430 ff. J. E. J.

Thrace The boundaries of Thrace varied at different times; in the 5th cent. BC the kingdom of the Odrysae, the leading tribe of Thrace, extended over present-day Bulgaria, Turkish Thrace (east of the Hebrus), and Greece between the Hebrus and Strymon, except for the coastal strip with its Greek cities, i.e. from the Danube on the north to the *Hellespont and the Greek fringe on the south, and from *Byzantium to the sources of the Strymon in south-west Bulgaria; whereas the Roman province (see PROVINCIA) of Thrace was bounded on the north by the Haemus, on the east by the *Euxine, on the south by the

*Propontis, Hellespont, and Aegean, and on the west by the Nestus.

By ancient writers the Thracians (who were of *Indo-European stock) were considered a primitive people, consisting of the warlike and ferocious tribes dwelling in the mountains of Haemus and Rhodope, and the peaceable dwellers in the plain, who came into contact with the Greek colonies on the Aegean and the Propontis. Until Classical times the Thracians lived in open villages; only in Roman times was urban civilization developed. *Herodotus (1) remarks (5. 3) that, if they could have been united under a single king, they would have been invincible, a view corroborated by *Thucydides (2) (2. 95–101); in fact, unlike the Macedonians, the Thracians never achieved a national history. From the 8th cent. BC the coast of Thrace was colonized by Greeks at *Abdera, Maroneia, Aenus, *Perinthus, *Byzantium, Apollonia, and Mesambria, but the Thracians resisted Greek influence.

We have very little historical information about the Thracians, except when they were brought into contact with the Greeks. Many burial tumuli in Thrace contain large quantities of gold and silver objects, most imported from classical lands (see ROGOZEN). The Thracians were subdued by the Persians c.516 BC, and some of them fought against the Greeks under *Xerxes I in 480 BC. Shortly afterwards the first king of the Odrysae, Teres, attempted to carve an empire out of the territory occupied by the Thracian tribes (Thuc. 2. 29), and his sovereignty extended as far as the Euxine and the Hellespont. His son *Sitalces enlarged his kingdom, subjugating the tribes of Rhodope as far as the Strymon, and the *Getae, north of the Haemus. Thenceforward the king of the Odrysae called himself king of the Thracians. Sitalces allied himself with the Athenians against the Macedonians, but his invasion of Macedonia in 429 BC achieved nothing. Sitalces was succeeded by Seuthes, his nephew, who married Stratonice, sister of *Perdiccas (2) II. In 382 BC Cotys succeeded to the monarchy and made war on Athens, assisted by his son-in-law *Iphicrates, the Athenian. After Cotys' death in 358 BC three princes claimed the succession, *Cersobleptes, his son, Berisades, and Amadocus.

On the collapse of the Odrysian power in the mid-4th cent., *Philip (1) II of Macedon invaded Thrace and made its princes tributary; he founded *Philippopolis in his own honour. After the death of *Alexander (3) the Great, who had left Thrace under his generals, Thrace fell to *Lysimachus, who founded Lysimacheia in 308 BC, and thereafter it was a protectorate of the successive rulers of Macedonia. After the Roman victory at Pydna in 168 BC, Thrace west of the Hebrus was incorporated in Macedonia, and in 129 BC the coastal cities were included.

For the religion of the Thracians, see RELIGION, THRACIAN; RIDER-GODS AND HEROES; MACEDONIA, CULTS.

S. Casson, *Macedonia, Thrace and Illyria* (1926); Head, *Hist. Num.*² 246 ff.; G. Mihailov (ed.), *Inscriptiones Graecae in Bulgaria Repertae*, 1²– (1970–); A. Fol, *Thrace and the Thracians* (1977); R. F. Hoddinott, *The Thracians* (1987); B. Isaac, *The Greek Settlements in Thrace until the Macedonian Conquest* (1986). J. M. R. C.

Thrace and Rome The Romans were slow to realize that the destruction of the Macedonian monarchy would involve them with the Thracians, but when *Andriscus revolted (149 BC) he drew most of his support from Thrace (Florus 1. 30) and the subsequent annexation of Macedon made Rome responsible for the eastern border of Macedon with Thrace. Later, raids by Thracian tribes into Macedonia and punitive campaigns by Roman proconsuls of Macedonia are regularly attested. Some

peoples in Thrace, however, made alliances with Rome. The Dentheletae had long been faithful allies when wantonly attacked by L. *Calpurnius Piso Caesoninus, and *Cicero calls Rabocentus, chief of the Bessi, a faithful ally, although hitherto they had been troublesome (Cic. *Pis.* 84). Later Thrace was consolidated into a kingdom ruled by a dynasty from the Sapaei, who lived in the south close to Macedonia. The first-known ruler was Rhascuporis (or Rhescuporis), son of Cotys, who helped *Pompey against *Caesar and later *Brutus against Antony (M. *Antonius (2)) and Octavian (see AUGUSTUS), while his brother Rhascus supported the latter. He was succeeded as king by his son Cotys (IG 3. 552, 553), who strengthened the dynasty by a marriage-alliance with the Astae, whose capital was at Bizye in eastern Thrace. A Cotys of this family had sent his son Sadalas to help Pompey; later Sadalas' widow Polemocratia entrusted her infant son Cotys to Brutus, who seized the royal treasure and sent the boy to Cyzicus. This Cotys, who was restored to his kingdom apparently while still a boy, married the daughter of Cotys the Sapaean. The latter acted as regent for his son-in-law and he was followed by his son Rhoemetalces, who acted as regent for his nephews, the sons of Cotys, when the latter died. When the Bessi, already subdued by M. *Lollius (19– 18 BC), broke away from the Astae (c.11 BC) and killed Rhascuporis, the only surviving son of Cotys, the Romans awarded the kingdom to Rhoemetalces, Rhascuporis' uncle and guardian, who later ruled the whole of Thrace. When Rhoemetalces died (AD 12) Augustus partitioned the kingdom between his son Cotys, who received the urbanized coastal area, and his brother Rhascuporis, who received the non-urbanized interior with only the title of dynast (Tac. *Ann.* 2. 64). In AD 19 Rhascuporis killed Cotys and *Tiberius deposed him, dividing the kingdom between Rhoemetalces, son of Rhascuporis, as dynast, and the sons of Cotys under a Roman guardian, Trebellenus Rufus. One of these sons, Rhoemetalces, was made king of his father's portion by *Gaius (1) in AD 38. Later the kingdom was reunited, since in AD 46 a certain Rhoemetalces was murdered by his wife and his kingdom became the Roman province of Thracia.

The province was governed by procurators (see PROCURATOR) until the reign of *Trajan, when they were superseded by praetorian legates (see LEGATI), assisted by procurators, both of whom were based at Perinthus. Although defence was in the hands of the legate in *Moesia, some troops were maintained; late in Nero's reign there were 2,000 (Joseph. *BJ* 2. 16. 4.). With very few cities, Thrace was administered on a centralized system, the province being divided into *strategiai*, each under a *strategos* (or military commander, cf. STRATEGOI) appointed by a governor. Colonies (see COLONIZATION, ROMAN) were founded at Aprus (*Colonia Claudia Aprensis*) by *Claudius or *Nero, and at Deultum (*Colonia Flavia Pacensis Deultum*) under *Vespasian. Reorganization under Trajan produced at least seven new cities, based mostly on older settlements, although the mass of the population continued to live in villages. Under *Diocletian Thrace was split into a number of small provinces, and more cities were founded. From the 3rd cent. AD onwards Thrace was periodically ravaged by barbarian invaders. After the reconstruction of the defences under *Justinian there were 100 forts in the Thracian provinces (Procop. *Aed.* 4. 11).

Jones, *Cities* 1 ff.; R. F. Hoddinott, *Bulgaria in Antiquity* (1975); R. D. Sullivan, *ANRW* 2. 7. 2 (1979), 186 ff.; B. Gerov, *Landownership in Roman Thracia and Moesia* (1st–3rd cent.) (1988). J. J. W.

Thrasea Paetus See CLODIUS THRASEA PAETUS, P.

Thrasybulus

Thrasybulus, tyrant of Miletus See MILETUS.

Thrasybulus (d. 388 BC), son of Lycus, Athenian general and statesman. (Xenophon, *Hell*. 4. 8. 25 calls him Thrasybulus of (the *deme of) Steiria to distinguish him from Thrasybulus of Collytus, *Hell*. 5. 1. 26, and modern books often do the same.) In 411 he was a leader of the democratic state formed by the navy at *Samos in opposition to the *Four Hundred. He was responsible for the recall of *Alcibiades and contributed largely to the naval success of the following years.

He was banished by the *Thirty Tyrants and fled to *Thebes (1), where he organized a band of 70 exiles and occupied *Phyle (late autumn, 404). When his followers had increased to a thousand, he seized the *Piraeus and defeated the troops of the Thirty. Thanks to an *amnesty proclaimed at the instance of Sparta, he led his men to Athens, and the democracy was restored. During the *Corinthian War he played a prominent part in reviving Athenian imperialism, and in 389/8 he commanded a fleet which gained many allies but suffered from lack of financial support. At *Aspendus his troops plundered the natives, who murdered him in his tent.

Thrasybulus showed ability and gallantry as a military leader. He was a staunch champion of democracy but was wise enough to make concessions in order to restore Athenian unity. In his last years he failed to appreciate that the imperialistic policy to which he gave his support was far beyond the material resources of Athens at that time.

> *Ath. Pol.* (with Rhodes, *CAAP* 417 ff.; 450 ff.; 474 ff.); Lys. 28; Thuc. bk. 8; Xen. *Hell*. bks. 1–4; Diod. bks. 13–14; Tod 100 + *SEG* 12. 84; Tod 114. R. Seager, *JHS* 1967, 95 ff. and *CAH* 6² (1994), ch. 4; G. L. Cawkwell, *CQ* 1976, 270 ff.; A. Andrewes, *CAH* 5² (1992), ch. 11.   H. D. W.; S. H.

Thrasyllus, 5th-cent. BC Athenian democratic politician and soldier. At the time of the Athenian oligarchic coup of 411 BC, he organized democratic support in the fleet at *Samos, where he was elected general (see STRATĒGOI) for 411/10 by the fleet (Thuc. 8. 76. 2) in the unusual circumstances of the moment; see FOUR HUNDRED; ATHENS (*History*). He helped *Thrasybulus win at the battle of Cynossema (411 BC), repelled an attack by the Spartan king *Agis II (410), and in 409 fought in mainland Ionia (see IONIANS), campaigning described by *Xenophon (1) and new fragments of the Oxyrhynchus Historian (see OXYRHYNCHUS, THE HISTORIAN FROM). ('In sending Thrasyllus to Ionia rather than the Hellespont the democrats may have hoped for a success there that would balance the glamour of Cyzicus': Andrewes, *CAH* 5². 486; Cyzicus was a victory won by *Alcibiades in 410.) Thrasyllus was elected general for 406/5 after Alcibiades' fall from favour, but was executed in the notorious aftermath of *Arginusae for not picking up the survivors (or the dead) after the sea-battle.

> Thuc. 8; Xen. *Hell*. 1; Diod. 13; *Oxyrhynchus Historian* (Cairo frs., ed. Bartoletti and Chambers (1993) and ed. McKechnie and Kern (1988), 30 ff.); A. Andrewes, *JHS* 1953, 1 ff., and in *HCT* 5 (1981) and *CAH* 5² (1992), see indexes; W. McKoy, *AJPhil*. 1977, 264 ff.; D. Kagan, *The Fall of the Athenian Empire* (1987), see index; *AO* under 411/10, 410, 409, 408, 406; P. Krentz, *CJ* 1988, 206 ff.   S. H.

Thrasyllus (*Tiberius' astrologer) See CLAUDIUS THRASYLLUS, TI.

Thrasymachus of Chalcedon (fl. *c*.430–400 BC), *sophist and rhetorician, is best known for his defence, in *Plato (1)'s *Republic*, of the thesis that justice is the interest of the stronger. He played an important part in the development of Greek oratory, by his elaboration of the appeal to the emotions by means of elocution and 'action' (delivery), and in the development of prose style by

his attention to rhythm and to the building up of periods (see PROSE-RHYTHM, GREEK). A surviving part of a work 'on the constitution' has, near the end, an interesting reference to *patrios politeia*.

> DK 85; G. Kennedy, *The Art of Persuasion in Greece* (1963), see index; M. Ostwald, *CAH* 5² (1992), 348.   W. D. R.; S. H.

Thrasymedes, a son of *Nestor with a minor part in *Homer's *Iliad* (10. 255, 16. 321 ff., and elsewhere). He was one of the Greeks in the Wooden Horse (Quint. Smyrn. 12. 319); and later with his father he welcomed *Telemachus at *Pylos (*Od*. 3. 39).
>
>   J. R. M.

Thubursicum Numidarum (near mod. Khamissa), a market town on a hilly site in eastern Algeria, on the road from *Hippo Regius to *Theveste. Lying in the rich Bagradas valley, it first became a prosperous agricultural centre under *Masinissa (although little is known of this phase), and played a part in *Tacfarinas' revolt (AD 17–24), if *Tacitus (1)'s Thubuscum (*Ann*. 4. 24. 1) is a corruption of Thubursicum, as seems probable. Under Roman rule it remained the centre of one of the tribes called Numidae, as its name reflects, and was jointly administered by native chieftains and military prefects. The separate existence of the native community was acknowledged even after the town achieved the status of *municipium c.* AD 100/13 (*ILAlg*. 1. 1240), since a 'chief of the tribe of the Numidae' (*princeps gentis Numidarum*) is still attested in the mid-2nd cent. (*ILAlg*. 1. 1297). It was raised to colonial status sometime in the 3rd cent. before 270 (*CIL* 8. 4876). Its extensive ruins include a forum terraced in the hillside, with accompanying basilica and temples; a theatre; and a sanctuary around a spring regarded in antiquity to have been the source of the Bagradas (mod. Medjerda). Thubursicum was still flourishing in the 4th cent. when the forum was repaved (323/33), and a second forum (360/70) and fresh baths were added in a new quarter at the foot of the hill. Decline had set in by the 6th cent., when the Byzantines converted these baths into a fort. See NUMIDIA.

> *PECS* 917; S. Gsell and C. A. Joly, *Khamissa, Mdaourouch, Announa* (1922).   W. N. W.; B. H. W.; R. J. A. W.

Thucydides (1), son of Melesias, Athenian politician (born *c*.500 BC). He was an aristocrat, connected by marriage with *Cimon. After the death of Cimon he succeeded him as the leading conservative opponent of *Pericles (1): he is said to have objected particularly to the building programme, and to have organized his supporters in a block in the assembly. Possibly he had been involved in the refoundation of *Sybaris in 446/5 and was prosecuted afterwards; his clash with Pericles led to his *ostracism *c*.443; he presumably returned to Athens after the statutory ten years, and he was prosecuted in old age by one Cephisodemus (Ar. *Ach*. 676–718). *Thucydides (2) the historian was probably a member of the same family: possibly his mother was a daughter of Thucydides son of Melesias.

> *PA* 7268; Davies, *APF* 230–7; *LGPN* 2 (1994), Thucydides no. 7. A. Andrewes, *JHS* 1978, 1–8.   A. W. G., T. J. Ca., P. J. R.

Thucydides (2), author of the (incomplete) History of the War (*Peloponnesian War) between Athens and Sparta, 431–404 BC, in eight books.

Life He was born probably between 460 and 455 BC: he was general (see STRATĒGOI) in 424 (4. 104) and must then have been at least 30 years old; while his claim in 5. 26. 5 that he was of years of discretion from beginning to end of the war perhaps suggests that he was not much more than grown up in 431. He probably died about 400. He shows no knowledge of 4th-cent. events. The revival of Athenian sea power under *Conon (1) and *Thrasybulus, from 394 on, made the decision of Aegospotami (405: see ATHENS, *History*) less decisive than it seemed to Thucydides (compare e.g. 5. 26. 1 with Xen. *Hell*. 5. 1. 35). Of the three writers who undertook to complete his History, only *Xenophon (1) took his view that the story ended in 404 (or 401). *Theopompus (3) took it down to 394, and so probably did *Cratippus (Plut. *Mor*. 345d). If, as seems likely, the very respectable author Oxyrhynchus Historian is Cratippus (see OXYRHYNCHUS, THE HISTORIAN FROM), then both his work and Theopompus' are on a very much larger scale than Xenophon's, a scale like Thucydides' own. This fact, as well as considerations of language and outlook, makes it likely that Xenophon wrote his continuation (*Hell*. books 1–2) earlier than the others, and indeed, before the battle of *Coronea in 394. But if this be so, then Thucydides cannot have lived more than a year or so into the 4th cent. *Marcellinus (2), in his Life, ch. 34, says that Thucydides was 'over 50' when he died. If he was born about 455 and died about 400, this will be true. The figure may be from Cratippus, who evidently gave some biographical data: Marcellinus quotes him just before (33) for the view that Thucydides died in *Thrace.

Thucydides, then, was part of that ardent youth whose abundance on both sides seemed to him to distinguish the war he wrote of. Something of his ardour may be felt in 2. 31: his pride in the soldier's profession and his devotion to the great commander, *Pericles (1).

He caught the *plague, some time between 430 and 427, but recovered, and in 424 failed in the task of saving *Amphipolis from *Brasidas. Not to have been a match for Brasidas does not prove him a bad soldier: from his history one receives the impression of a first-rate regimental officer, ashore or afloat, who saw war as a matter of style; perhaps his defence of the generals before *Megara in 4. 73. 4 (cf. 108. 5) says worse of his judgement of problems of high command than his failure against Brasidas. He was exiled for this (424 winter) and returned twenty years later, after the war was over, and died within a few years.

He had property and influence in the mining district of Thrace (4. 105. 1). His father's name was Olorus (4. 104. 4), the name of *Cimon's Thracian grandfather; his tomb was in Cimon's family vault. It is almost certain he was related by blood to Cimon, and probably to *Thucydides (1) the statesman (*JHS* 1932, 210); born in the anti-Pericles opposition, he followed Pericles with a convert's zeal.

Parts of the History The incomplete history falls into five parts: A, an introduction (book 1); B, the ten years war (2. 1–5. 24); C, the precarious peace (5. 25–end); D, the Sicilian War (6 and 7); E, fragment of the Decelean War (8). It is convenient to take first B and D, the two complete wars.

B is enclosed between two statements that 'the continuous war has herein been described'. It was therefore provisionally finished (if these are Thucydides' words). It contains one allusion to the fall of Athens (2. 65. 12) and several allusions to events late in the twenty-seven years: these are no doubt additions made to an already existing narrative, since one passage certainly (2. 23. 3) was not written as late as the last decade of the century. The narrative gets rather more summary after Thucydides' exile (424): e.g. after the futile embassy to *Artaxerxes (1) I of *Persia (4. 50) nothing is said of the important negotiations with *Darius II.

D is the most finished portion. As it stands it is adapted to a history of the whole war (6. 7. 4, 6. 93. 4, 7. 18. 4, cf. 7. 9 etc., also 7. 44. 1, 7. 87. 5), and twice at least refers to events of 404 or later (7. 57. 2, 6. 15. 3–4). But these may be revisions and it has been suggested that Thucydides published it separately; and this opinion, though little held now, is not disproved. B and D are connected by C, sequel to B and introduction to D, and provided accordingly with a second preface. For symptoms of incompleteness, see below. C covers five and a half years, very unequally. Its two outstanding features are the description of the Mantinea campaign, and the Melian Dialogue (see MANTINEA, BATTLES OF; MELOS). The former should perhaps be regarded, with B and D, as a third completed episode. The latter foreshadows the dramatic style of D; but if we read 5. 111 with 8. 27 we shall draw no facile moral (see 8. 27. 5).

E has the same symptoms of incompleteness as C and, moreover, stops abruptly in the middle of a narrative. It is very full, covering barely two years in its 109 chapters.

A consists of (1) 1. 1–23, a long preface, illustrating the importance of Thucydides' subject by comparison with earlier history (the so-called 'archaeology') and stating his historical principles; (2) the causes of the war—that is, for the most part, an account of the political manœuvres of 433–432; he adds important digressions, especially 1. 89–117, a history of the years 479/8–440/39 (see PENTEKONTAETIA), partly to illustrate his view that the war was an inevitable result of Athens' power, partly to make his history follow without interval on that of *Herodotus (1) (1. 97. 2). The second motive perhaps explains the length of another digression (1. 128–38) on the fate of *Pausanias (1) and *Themistocles.

Incompleteness E stops in mid-narrative, in winter 411: Thucydides intended to go down to 404 (5. 26. 1). It shares with (roughly) C two peculiarities, absence of speeches and presence of documents, which are thought to show incompleteness; for these see below. The plan to make of BCDE a continuous history of the twenty-seven years is only superficially achieved, even to 411: e.g. there is nothing of Atheno–Persian relations between 424 and 412, vital though these were (2. 65. 12). We shall see below that Thucydides kept his work by him and revised continually; so he left double treatments of the same theme, one of which he meant no doubt to suppress—e.g. the *tyrannicides (1. 20, 6. 54–59); possibly 1. 23. 1–3 is a short early variant of 1. 1–19; 3. 84 of part of 82–3 (Schwartz 286 f.). It may be even suspected that 8. 82. 2 is a less accurately informed version of 86. 4–5 and the two have been merely harmonized by 85. 4. If this last suspicion were just, it would be good evidence that Thucydides' remains were put into shape by an editor, whose hand may be further suspected in the misplacement of 3. 17, in 1. 56–7 (whose author—as it stands—surely misconceived the course of events), perhaps even in 1. 118. 2 (where the last sentence seems to leap from the 450s to 432); an editorial hand has, indeed, been suspected wholesale. Though no single case is quite decisive, it is unlikely Thucydides left his unfinished work in need of no editing. If we look for an editor, one thinks naturally of Xenophon, who wrote the continuation (it seems) immediately after Thucydides' death; the suggestion was made in antiquity (Diog. Laert. 2. 57). His soldierly (if not his intellectual) qualities might commend him to Thucydides, but if it was indeed he, he worked with extreme piety, and his hand is very little apparent. Xenophon's limits and virtues alike disqualify him for the authorship of 1. 56–7.

Speeches and Documents Ancient craftsmen, and Thucydides

Thucydides

notably, aimed at exactness; but in his speeches, Thucydides admits (1. 22. 1) that exactness was beyond his powers of memory. Here, then, as in reconstructing the far past (1. 20–1), he had to trust to his historical imagination, whose use generally he planned to avoid (ὡς ἂν ἐδόκουν ἐμοὶ εἰπεῖν, 'what I think they would have said': this meant applying to the speeches the sort of rationalizing schematism that, e.g., *Hecataeus (1) applied to *geography); and even here, he promises he will control its use as rigorously as he can by the tenor of the actual words. It is much debated whether he made this profession early or late; and it has been much explained away. But it is unreasonable to doubt that from the start Thucydides took notes himself, or sought for hearers' notes, of the speeches he considered important. But since he used speeches dramatically, to reveal the workings of men's minds and the impact of circumstance, it is clear that verbatim reports would not have served even if he could have managed to get them, and he was bound to compromise (unconsciously) between dramatic and literal truth. It is likely that, as his technique developed, dramatic truth would tend to prevail; it is tempting to put his profession of method early, a young man's intention. Even so, while we cannot suppose that, at a moment when morale was vital, Pericles used the words in 2. 64. 3; while it is unlikely that the Athenian debater at Melos developed exactly the same vein of thought as Phrynichus before Miletus (5. 111–8. 27); while Pericles' first speech (1. 140 ff.) is perhaps composite, and hard to assign to a single occasion; it is yet dangerous to treat the speeches as free fiction: their dramatic truth was combined with the greatest degree of literal truth of which Thucydides was capable. He tried to recreate real occasions.

There are no speeches in E, and (except the Melian Dialogue) none in C: Cratippus (a younger contemporary) says Thucydides had decided to drop their use. Modern critics treat their absence as a symptom of incompleteness; they would have been added had he lived. But it is possible that these parts without speeches are experiments in new techniques. Thucydides may have felt, as many readers do, that the narrative of the ten years is a compromise between the methods of tragedy and of a laboratory notebook, so that between the profoundest issues and the particular detail, the middle ranges (e.g. an intelligible account of strategy) are neglected. In the later narrative the methods are more separated. The Sicilian War was capable of almost purely dramatic treatment; C and E evidently not. And in consequence in E at least a new technique is developed, less like either drama or chronicle, more of an organized narrative, with more of the writer's own judgements of values and interpretations of events. It is questionable if E would be improved by speeches, that is, could be profitably (or at all?) transformed into the style of B or D: was Cratippus perhaps right about Thucydides' intention?

This would not prevent some of the speeches in books 1–4 being composed (or revised) very late. The new experiment would not entail eliminating the dramatic from those books; Thucydides experimented to the end and never solved his problem. It is commonly thought that the Funeral Speech (2. 35 ff.; see EPITAPHIOS) was written or rewritten after Athens' fall; and 2. 64. 3 surely was. The *Corcyra debate (1. 31–44), on the contrary, has good chances of being an actual report, written up soon after delivery. Though some speeches aim at dramatic characterization (Gorgiastic (see GORGIAS (1)), 4. 61. 7: Laconic i.e. Spartan, 1. 86), all are in Thucydides' idiom. But the personalness of this idiom is often overestimated (Finley, *Thucydides*[2]).

It is noteworthy that those portions which lack speeches have (instead?) transcriptions of documents: that is, E and (roughly speaking) C.[1] If, then, we take C and E as experiments in a new method, the experiment begins in the latter part of B. These documents are usually thought (like the absence of speeches) a sign of incompleteness, since they offend against a 'law of style' which forbids the verbatim use of foreign matter in serious prose. We need not debate the general validity of this law: with so inventive a writer as Thucydides, his laws of style are to be deduced from his practice, and 5. 24. 2 (cf. 2. 1) suggests that the end of B is provisionally finished. Are they part of the experiment? One may be surprised (though grateful) that Thucydides thought the full text of the Armistice (4. 118–19) worth its room. One of the documents (5. 47) is extant in fragments (IG 1³. 83) and confirms the substantial accuracy of the copies. One conflicts gravely with the narrative (5. 23, 5. 39. 3): it would seem the narrative was written in ignorance of the exact terms, and has not been revised.

'Early' and 'Late' Thucydides says (1. 1. 1) he began to write his history as soon as war started; and it is at least arguable that much of the existing narrative, in all five parts of the work, was written, substantially as we have it, very soon after the events. But he worked slowly, and, as he says at 1. 22. 3, laboriously; correcting in the light of better information (we only detect this process where it is incomplete; e.g. 5. 39. 3 was due for correction in the light of 5. 23) or of later events (1. 97. 2; 4. 48. 5, where the qualification ὅσα γε may have been put merely *ex abundanti cautela*, from excess of caution, but more likely when the troubles started again in 410). If his point of view, or his method, changed materially during this process, it becomes of importance to know from which point of view this or that portion is written. More than a century ago, Ullrich called attention to this, believing that an important change of approach came with his discovery (announced in the second preface, 5. 26) that the war had not ended in 421.

Two criteria have been used to determine earliness or lateness: (a) reference to, or ignorance of, datable events or conditions; (b) the stage in Thucydides' own development which a passage reveals.

(a) References to late events cannot be written early, but they may be inserted in early contexts: e.g. those who think D early regard 6. 15. 3–4 and 7. 57. 2 as additions. Ignorance of late events is very much harder to establish: those same who think D early may suspect in 6. 41. 3 ignorance of *Dionysius (1) I's tyranny, or even (a very slippery question) in 6. 54. 1 ignorance of Herodotus' history—but cannot prove their suspicions; yet where such ignorance is certain (see below), we may be sure that the narrative (or line of thought) which warrants them was conceived early. The results of this method are modest: e.g. (1) 1. 10. 2 was not written after the catastrophe of 404: therefore the war against which earlier wars are being measured is not the completed twenty-seven years, and the 'end of war' mentioned in 1. 13. 3–4, 1. 18. 1, is presumably 421; (2) 2. 23. 3 was not written after the loss of *Oropus in 411: therefore some of the narrative of B was written much as we have it before 411; (3) 2. 65. 12 refers to the fall of Athens: therefore B received additions down to 404 at least.

(b) More has been hoped from the second method. Thucydides

---

[1] Not exactly C: C ends with the Melian Dialogue (which in colour belongs to D?) and B has documents instead of speeches in its latter part, i.e. after the occasion of Thucydides' exile.

worked from his twenties to his fifties, his material growing under his eyes: there must surely be some intellectual or spiritual growth, some change of outlook. The best exponent of this method is Schwartz, who gives (*Das Geschichtswerk des Thukydides*, 217–42) an eloquent account of Thucydides' growth. The danger of this method is evident: in the ablest hands it yields quite different results (Meyer, Schwartz), and its first postulate may be doubted, namely, that Thucydides' opinion on the 'true cause' of the war (1. 23. 6) was not formed till after the fall of Athens. No doubt that was his view after 404; no doubt 1. 23. 6 and 1. 88 were written (inserted?) pretty late. But much the same view is expressed by the Corcyran envoy in 1. 33. 3 (cf. 42. 2); and whether the envoy said it or not it was surely Pericles' view. Pericles believed that if Athens used her opportunity in 433 she was bound to provoke in Sparta an enmity that must be faced; all his career, against Cimon and his successors, he had fought for his conviction that Athens and Sparta were natural enemies and Greece not large enough for both. His admirers held that this clear principle (1. 140. 1) was obscured in debate by the irrelevant particulars (1. 140. 4–141. 1). We have not to consider whether Pericles was right: rather, the effect on Thucydides. The devout disciple saw the story unfold in the terms his master had foreseen (2. 65). How far such a 'Pericles-fixation' may have warped Thucydides' judgement, see below.

If this first postulate go, the second will follow it, namely that only after 404 was Pericles given the importance he now has in books 1–2, since after 404 Thucydides started to rewrite his History as a 'defence of Pericles' (Schwartz 239). It hardly needs to be said that many hold to these postulates and the present writer's disbelief is as subjective as their belief. If these are untrue, truer postulates may be found: the attempt to recreate Thucydides' experience should (and will) never be dropped.

Truthfulness Perhaps no good historian is impartial; Thucydides certainly not, though singularly candid. His tastes are clear: he liked Pericles and disliked *Cleon. He had for Pericles a regard comparable to Plato's for *Socrates and an equal regard for Pericles' Athens. These things were personal: but in principle, concentrations of energy (like Athens or *Alcibiades) were to his taste. Their impact on a less dynamic world was likely to be disastrous—but whose fault was that? The world's, he says, consistently (1. 99; 1. 23. 6 etc.; 6. 15; 6. 28; cf. 2. 64. 3–5): and though this consistency may surprise us, we need not quarrel with it. Such judgements are rare, since Thucydides conceives his task as like medical research (see below, and cf. 3. 82. 2) where blame is irrelevant; the disconcerting simplicity of 2. 64. 3 (power and energy are absolute goods) is the more striking.

We need not here investigate Thucydides' possible mistakes. The present writer believes that Pericles (having planned an offensive war) lost its striking power, first because *Potidaea revolted, next because of the plague. Forced to the defensive, he left that as his testament. Thucydides was reluctant to face the fact of this failure, and accepted the testament, siding with the defeatist officer class against the revived offensive of Cleon (4. 27. 5, 28. 5, 65. 4, 73. 4; cf. 5. 7. 2). This is why Pericles' huge effort against *Epidaurus (6. 31. 2; motive, cf. 5. 53) is recorded as a minor futility (2. 56. 4); why *Phormion (1)'s first campaign in *Acarnania (2. 68. 7–9; of 432?) is left timeless; why we hear nothing of the purpose of the Megara decree; why, when that nearly bore fruit at last, Thucydides suggests that the capture of Megara was of no great moment (4. 73. 4; but cf. 72. 1).

Such criticisms hardly detract much from his singular truthfulness. Readers of all opinions will probably agree that he saw more truly, inquired more responsibly, and reported more faithfully than any other ancient historian. That is a symptom of his greatness, but not its core. Another symptom is his style: it is innocent of those clichés of which *Isocrates hoped to make the norm of Attic style; in its 'old-fashioned wilful beauty' (*Dionysius (7)) every word tells. Like English prose before Dryden and Addison, it uses a language largely moulded by poets: its precision is a poet's precision, a union of passion and candour. After Thucydides history mostly practised the corrupting art of persuasion (cf. Isoc. 4. 8): his scientific tradition survived in the antiquarians, of whom he is the pioneer (1. 8. 1, 2. 15. 2, 3. 104. 4–6, 6. 55. 1), but the instinctive exactness of early Greek observation was lost. To combine his predecessors' candour of vision with his successors' apparatus of scholarship was a necessity laid on him by his sense of the greatness of his subject: he could no more distort or compromise with what he wished to convey than Shakespeare or Michelangelo could.

Thucydides would no doubt prefer to substitute, for these great names, the practice of any honest doctor. He was not modest, but in his statement of his principles he is singularly unaware of his unique equipment, and claims rather that he has spared no pains. The proper context for this statement (1. 20–2) is, first, his very similar statement about his own account of the plague (2. 48. 3), and then the physician *Hippocrates (2)'s maxim, 'ars longa vita brevis'. The 'art' which outlasts individual lives is the scientific study of man: the physician studied his clinical, Thucydides his political, behaviour. To know either so well that you can control it (and civilization is largely made up of such controls) is a task for many generations: a piece of that task well done is something gained for ever (1. 22. 4).

H. T. W.-G.

Style In a famous sentence (*Thuc.* 24) *Dionysius (7) gives as the four 'tools' in Thucydides' workshop τὸ ποιητικὸν τῶν ὀνομάτων, τὸ πολυειδὲς τῶν σχημάτων, τὸ τραχὺ τῆς ἁρμονίας, τὸ τάχος τῶν σημασιῶν, 'poetical vocabulary, great variety of figures, harshness of word-order, swiftness in saying what he has to say'. The first, third, and fourth of these criticisms are undoubtedly true. Thucydides' style has a poetical and archaistic flavour (it is often difficult to distinguish clearly between the two), as a reader sees at once when he turns from Thucydides to *Andocides and *Lysias. His consistent use of αἰεί for ἀεί, ξύν for σύν, and σσ for ττ is one of the signs of this tendency. 'Roughness' is to be seen in his bold changes of construction and his violent hyperbata, in which he wrests an emphatic word from its natural place in the sentence to give it more prominence (1. 19 κατ' ὀλιγαρχίαν, 1. 93. 4 τῆς θαλάσσης). 'Speed' is perhaps the most striking of all his characteristics. He achieves an extreme concision, hardly to be paralleled in Greek prose except in the gnomic utterances of *Democritus (cf. GNOME). A sentence like δοκεῖ . . . καταστροφή (2. 42. 2) is gone in a flash, and no orator, composing for the ear, could have risked such brevity. At 2. 37. 1 (μέτεστι . . . προτιμᾶται) two antitheses are telescoped into one. τὸ πολυειδὲς τῶν σχημάτων is much more open to question, especially as Dionysius has just before credited Thucydides with the use of the θεατρικὰ σχήματα (parisosis (balance of clauses), paronomasia (play on words), and antithesis) affected by *Gorgias (1) and other writers of the sophistic school (see SOPHISTS). Thucydides' thought is, it is true, markedly antithetical in cast (e.g. 1. 70. 6), and antithesis is sometimes strained (e.g. 2. 43. 3). But, unlike the Gorgianists, he has no affection for merely external antithesis,

Thucydides

and he often deliberately avoids formal balance (e.g. 4. 59. 2). He eschews almost entirely certain other common adornments of style. He is too austere to use metaphor at all freely, or asyndeton (more suited to the spoken word). He does employ certain devices of assonance, neither, like Gorgias, as ἡδύσματα, nor, like Demosthenes, for emphasis pure and simple, but for the emphasizing of a contrast (3. 82. 8 εὐσεβεία ... εὐπρεπεία, 6. 76. 2 κατοικίσαι ... ἐξοικίσαι, 76. 4 ἀξυνετωτέρου ... κακοξυνετωτέρου). He has a strong leaning, as Dionysius observed (*Amm.* 2. 5), towards abstract expression (e.g. 3. 82–3), sometimes carried to the length of personification (πόλεμος 1. 122. 1, ἐλπίς 5. 103. 1). He probably coined abstracts (especially in -σις) freely, as *Euripides did, according to the fashion of the late 5th cent., and sometimes used them out of season (7. 70. 6 ἀποστέρησιν, and the odd-looking negatived abstracts, 1. 137. 4 οὐ διάλυσιν, etc.). Like *Antiphon (1), he experimented freely with the use of neuter adjective, or even participle (1. 142. 8 ἐν τῷ μὴ μελετῶντι), to convey an abstract idea. His periods are usually loosely constructed (e.g. 3. 38. 4–7), of clauses longer in actual words, and far richer in content, than those of other Greek prose-writers (e.g. 2. 43. 2–6).

TEXTS H. Stuart-Jones (OCT, 1898–1902; repr. 1942 with app. crit. rev. J. E. Powell); C. Hude (Teubner, ed. maior 1913–25, ed. minor 1920–8 with scholia; new edn. by O. Luschnat, bks. 1–2, 1954); G. Alberti (bks. 1–2, 1972; bks. 3–5, 1992; bks. 6–8, 2000).

TRANSLATIONS R. Crawley (1910) repr. 1993 with introd. by W. R. Connor; Jowett's trans., abridged, is used by P. A. Brunt, *Thucydides* (in Trevor-Roper's ser.), *The Great Histories*, 1963 and revised S. Hornblower, World's Classics forthcoming).

COMMENTARIES A. W. Gomme, A. Andrewes, and K. J. Dover, *HCT* (bk. 1, 1945; bks. 2–5. 24, 1956; bks. 5. 25–7, 1970; bk. 8, 1981); in Ger. J. Classen (rev. J. Steup, 1892–1922); in Lat. E. F. Poppo (rev. J. M. Stahl, 1886); S. Hornblower, bks. 1–3 (1991); bks. 4–5. 24 (1996).

CRITICISM Ancient: Cratippus, *FGrH* 64: Dion. Hal. *Thuc.* [cf. *ad Amm. de T. idiom.*, *ad Pomp.*] (= *opuscula*, ed. Usener–Radermacher, 1. 325 ff. [421 ff., 221 ff.]); Marcellinus, *Life of T.*, prefixed to most texts of T.

Modern: F. E. Adcock, *T. and his History* (1963); C. N. Cochrane, *T. and the Science of History* (1929; relation to Hippocratics); J. H. Finley, *Thucydides*[2] (1947); A. W. Gomme, *Essays in Gk. Hist. and Lit.* (1937, nos. 6–9); G. B. Grundy, *T. and the History of his Age*[2] (1948); W. Jaeger, *Paideia* (Eng. tr. 1938, 1, 382 ff.); O. Luschnat, *Die Feldherrnreden im Gesch. des T.* (1942, *Philologus* Suppl. 34/2); E. Meyer, *Forschungen* 2 (1899, no. v); H. Patzer, *Das Problem der Geschichtsschreibung des T.* (1937); J. de Romilly, *Histoire et Raison chez T.* (1956, 2nd edn. 1967), and *T. and Athenian Imperialism* (Eng. trans. 1963); W. Schadewaldt, *Die Geschichtsschreibung des T.* 1929; esp. bks. 6–7); E. Schwartz, *Das Geschichtswerk des T.* (1919; *Stilgesetz*, 28 ff.); F. W. Ullrich, *Beiträge zur Erklärung des T.* (1846–52); K. Weidauer, *T. und die Hippokratischen Schriften* (1954); R. Zahn, *Die erste Periklesrede* (1934; diss. with notes by Jacoby); H. D. Westlake, *Individuals in T.* (1968), and *Essays on Greek Historians* (1969); A. G. Woodhead, *T. on the Nature of Power* (1970).

INDEX M. H. N. von Essen, *Index Thucydideus* (1887).

LEXICON E.-A. Bétant (1843, reprinted 1969).   J. D. D.

[The above entry by Wade-Gery and Denniston, which goes back essentially to 1949, is an established classic and it seems an impertinence to attempt to replace it. But merely to reprint it would be unhelpful when Thucydides has been so intensively worked on. What follows is therefore a sketch of work on Thucydides in the quarter-century since the 2nd edition.]

The most noticeable feature of Thucydidean scholarship since 1970 is the move away from preoccupation with the 'composition question' (the identification of layers of the History, with attempts to date them) to study of Thucydides' text as a complete literary whole. There is a parallel here with the move in Homeric scholarship (see HOMER) over the same period away from 'analytical' approaches and towards a 'unitarian' interest in the architecture of the two great poems. Of the 1970 Thucydides bibliography, here deliberately reprinted with minimal change, it is striking how many items addressed themselves to questions of composition, a topic to which Wade-Gery's *OCD* article was itself an influential contribution. One discussion which appeared just too late for the 2nd edn. was the relevant section of O. Luschnat's 1970 *RE* survey. The related question, whether Thucydides' work was finished, has continued to attract study, notably in Andrewes's contribution to the final (1981) volume of Gomme, Andrewes, and Dover, *HCT*, with Erbse's reply, 1989. (See also ch. 5 of Dover 1973, an admirable general survey of Thucydides.) And Rawlings (1981) has speculated about the possible content of the unwritten books 9 and 10. But even this was part of a wider attempt to detect patterning within the larger existing structure.

It would be absurd, in view of F. M. Cornford 1907, to claim that the present generation is the first to repudiate 'positivism' and treat Thucydides as a literary text to which methods used on tragedy and epic could be applied; but Cornford was missing from the bibliography in both the 1949 and 1970 editions of this dictionary. Perhaps the trouble was that he also gave hospitality to an anachronistically modernizing thesis about the causes of the Peloponnesian War. A notable absentee from the 1970 edition, which carried items as late as 1970 itself, was Stahl 1966, a book which allotted as much space to narrative as to speeches. And Strasburger's studies of the 1950s (collected now in Strasburger 1982) deserved inclusion in 1970 for their insistence on Thucydides' Homeric aspect, as did Kitto 1966 for its examination of Thucydides' tragic effects. Moving on to the post-1970 era proper, V. Hunter in 1973 set the tone for two decades by her title 'the artful reporter'; Herodotus had for centuries found himself periodically in the pillory for alleged distortion and invention, but Thucydides' authoritative and apparently scientific manner had usually been respected. Now it was suggested that Thucydides might simply have made things up, particularly his imputations of motive. This approach was also pursued by Schneider 1974. (Cf. below on the narratological problem of 'restricted access'.) Historical as well as historiographic issues are affected: thus whereas de Ste. Croix 1972 had sought to justify Thucydides (and threw in an excellent introductory section on Thucydidean methodology), Badian 1993, a collection of essays going back to the 1980s, is in complete contrast, an acute demonstration by a historian of the consequences of distrusting Thucydides.

Now the lid was off. One way of going further was to challenge the premiss that ancient historiography had pretensions to being an exact or any sort of science: perhaps (Woodman 1988) it was merely a branch of rhetoric with a different aim from factual description; perhaps, indeed, the 'facts' are nothing of the sort. (This is not just an 'ancient' problem; cf. the writings of Hayden White; but enough documentary evidence exists to control Thucydides and reassure us that there was indeed a Peloponnesian War.)

Another more acceptable approach has been to disregard the signs of incompleteness in Thucydides and insist in postmodern fashion (Connor 1977) on the autonomy of the text: whatever the authorial intention, we have a long speech-punctuated narrative of Greek prose containing patterns, significant repetitions, ring-composition, etc. See Connor 1984, but cf. also Hornblower 1987 for an attempt to combine literary criteria with recognition of the composition problem.

The detailed work of Colin Macleod (collected 1983) deserves a special word; there has been no finer treatment of the rhetoric of the Thucydidean speeches. On rhetorical issues note also Pritchett's excellent 1975 edition of Dionysius of Halicarnassus on Thucydides.

More recently still narratology has been tried on Thucydides. Narratology is nothing more frightening than the study of a branch of rhetoric, specifically of the principles underlying narrative texts. First used on modern, then on ancient, novels, it was applied in 1987 to Homer by I. de Jong (see HOMER; LITERARY THEORY AND CLASSICAL STUDIES; NARRATIVE), who demonstrated how narratology can help us see how Homer achieves his famously objective manner. The technique has been most fully applied to Thucydides by Rood 1998, but see already the short essay by Connor 1985, using, however, the term 'narrative discourse' not narratology. Some narratological terms and insights are familiar to Thucydideans under other names; e.g. 'restricted access' means the difficulty encountered by a non-omniscient narrator interested in an agent's motives. The usual response, e.g. in messenger speeches in tragedy (and in Thucydides?) is for the narrator silently to assume an omniscient pose. But the greatest narratological weapon has been focalization, i.e. the point of view or perspective from which an event is described. Choice of Homeric (and Thucydidean?) vocabulary can sometimes be explained by the wish to present events or express emotions from a certain standpoint, which may or may not be that of the author rather than that of the imagined or historical agent. (Dover 1988, 74 ff. has ingeniously pointed to one purely linguistic way of determining whether a motive reflects Thucydides' own view or that of an agent.) Again, all this is not quite new: in the 18th cent. Adam Smith in lectures on rhetoric distinguished between 'direct' and 'indirect' narration. And Westlake 1989, ch. 14 shows that problems of 'personal motives in Thucydides' can be usefully studied in very plain language. There is much work still to be done, but provided it is recognized that there was a relation between what Thucydides says and a real world which existed in the 5th cent. BC, only good can come of the recognition that his text is susceptible to literary 'close reading'.

The broad trends indicated above do not at all exhaust recent Thucydidean work. There have been commentaries on book 2 by Rusten (markedly linguistic) and books 2–5.24 by Rhodes (markedly historical) which illuminate by exact methods traditionally applied, as does the outstanding monograph of Maurer. On the 4th-cent. and Hellenistic reception of Thucydides, Luschnat 1970 is less good than Strebel 1935: see Hornblower 1995. Otherwise monographs and articles have explored Thucydides' treatment or non-treatment of particular themes such as chance and intelligence (Edmunds 1975), *ANAΓKH* (Ostwald 1988), religion esp. Delphi (Hornblower, *Harv. Stud.* 1992), money (Kallet-Marx 1993 and Kallet 2001), the tradition of funeral orations (Ziolkowski 1981, Loraux 1986), and his indebtedness to Herodotus (Pelling 1991; Hornblower, *Thucydides Commentary*, vol. 2 (1996) 19–38, 122–45). This survey may end with the suggestion that two areas needing more work are Thucydides' detailed intertextual relation to Homer and to Herodotus.

E. Badian, *From Plataea to Potidaea* (1993); W. R. Connor, *CJ* 1977, *Thucydides* (1984), and in M. Jameson (ed.), *The Greek Historians*

(Raubitschek Festschrift) (1985); F. M. Cornford, *Thucydides Mythistoricus* (1907); K. J. Dover, *G&R New Survey* (1973), and *The Greeks and their Legacy* 2 (1988); L. Edmunds, *Chance and Intelligence in Thucydides* (1975); H. Erbse, *Thukydides-Interpretationen* (1989); S. Hornblower, *Thucydides* (1987), *Harv. Stud.* 1992, in S. Hornblower (ed.), *Greek Historiography* (1994), ch. 5, and *JHS* 1995; V. Hunter, *Thucydides the Artful Reporter* (1973); L. Kallet, *Money and the Corrosion of Power in Thucydides* (2001); L. Kallet-Marx, *Money, Expense and Naval Power in Thucydides' History 1–5. 24* (1993); H. D. F. Kitto, *Poiesis* (1966); N. Loraux, *The Invention of Athens* (1986); O. Luschnat, *RE* Suppl. 12 (1970), 1147 ff.; C. Macleod, *Collected Essays* (1983); K. Maurer, *Interpolation in Thucydides* (1995); J. L. Moles, *JACT Bulletin*, autumn 1993, 14 ff.; M. Ostwald, *ANAΓKH in Thucydides* (1988); C. Pelling in Flower and Toher (eds.), *Georgica* (1991); W. K. Pritchett, *Dionysius of Halicarnassus on Thucydides* (1975) and *Thucydides' Pentekontaetia and Other Essays* (1995); H. R. Rawlings III, *The Structure of Thucydides's History* (1981); T. Rood, *Thucydides: Narrative and Explanation* (1998); R. B. Rutherford in R. Osborne and S. Hornblower (eds.), *Ritual, Finance, Politics* (1994), 53 ff. (important essay on how Thucydides intended his history to be useful); C. Schneider, *Information und Absicht bei Thukydides* (1974); H.-P. Stahl, *Thucydides: Man's Place in History* (2002); G. E. M. de Ste. Croix, *The Origins of the Peloponnesian War* (1972); H. Strasburger, *Studien zur alten Geschichte* (1982); H. Strebel, *Wirtung und Wertung des Thukydideischen Geschichtswerkes* (1935); R. Stroud, *Chiron* 1994; Syme, *RP* 6. 72 ff.; H. D. Westlake, *Studies in Thucydides and Greek History* (1989); A. J. Woodman, *Rhetoric in Classical Historiography* (1988); J. Ziolkowski, *Thucydides and the Tradition of the Funeral Oration at Athens* (1981).   S. H.

Thugga (mod. Dougga), a hill-town of Africa Proconsularis west of the road from *Carthage to *Theveste. Already a settlement of considerable size in the 4th cent. BC, when *Agathocles of Syracuse took it (Diod. Sic. 20. 57. 4: *Tōkai*), Thugga was the seat of a Numidian chieftain (see NUMIDIA) under *Masinissa and his successors, when it was much influenced by Carthaginian civilization: a mausoleum of the 2nd cent. BC survives, built for an unknown prince by the Numidian master-craftsman Atban (a less likely interpretation of the bilingual Numidian and Punic inscription makes Atban the tomb's occupant). Marian colonists were settled in the vicinity and in the 1st cent. members of the *colonia* of Carthage had lands near by. An unusual double community of native *civitas* (governed by *suffetes*) and Roman *pagus* (at first dependent on Carthage) existed until they were united by Septimius Severus (205), when Thugga became a *municipium*. Finally, between 253 and 260, it became Colonia *Licinia Septimia Aurelia Alexandriana Thuggensis*. The remains are among the finest in Roman north Africa, and include a Capitoline temple (166/7), temples of *Caelestis (222/35) and Saturn (195), a theatre (168/9), two sets of baths, and a small Byzantine fort enclosing the former forum. There are numerous private houses.

PECS 917–19; C. Poinssot, *Les Ruines de Dougga* (1958). Mausoleum: H. G. Horn and C. B. Rüger (eds.), *Die Numider* (1979), 157–8, cf. 90 and 576–7.   B. H. W.; R. J. A. W.

Thule (Θούλη), a northern land first heard of and described by *Pytheas. It was said to lie six days' sail to the north of *Britain. At midsummer the sun's and the Bear's paths, as seen at Thule, coincided, and neither set. The inhabitants ate berries, 'millet' (oats?) threshed in barns because of the dampness and the lack of sun, herbs, fruits, roots, and honey. Round Thule everything was held in an impalpable mass (perhaps thick freezing fog?) which Pytheas himself saw. It is uncertain whether Thule was Iceland or Norway and in many sources from *Virgil onwards it became a proverbial expression for the furthest place on earth.

Thurea

*Eratosthenes drew a parallel through Thule at 66° (Arctic Circle) which remained for long on maps. *Ptolemy (4) gave Thule a north–south extension of 88 km. (55 mi.) and located it at Mainland (Shetland), though he retained the belief in its midsummer midnight sun. The land of Thule which Cn. *Iulius Agricola's fleet claimed to have seen (Tac. *Agr.* 10) was no doubt a Shetland island, but not necessarily Foula, the name of which is Norse 'Fowl-island', not derived from Thule.

It may be that *Procopius was right in a wrong way when he called 'Thule' the Scandinavian 'island', old home of the *Goths, ten times as large as Britain and far north of it, most being desolate, but the rest containing the Gauti and twelve other large tribes. Other writers also seem to mean Scandinavia by 'Thule'. For earlier knowledge of Scandinavia, see Mela 3. 3. 31–2; Plin. *HN* 4. 96; Tac. *Germ.* 44; Ptol. *Geog.* 7. 5. 2.

> Plin. *HN* 2. 187, 4. 104; Diod. Sic. 5. 26; Cleomedes, *Kyklikē theōris* 1. 7. 37–8, etc.; Geminus, *Introduction to Astronomy* 6; Ptol. *Geog.* 2. 3. 14, 2. 6. 22, 8. 3. 3.; Procop. *Goth.* 2. 15. 4 ff.; A. L. F. Rivet and C. Smith, *The Place-Names of Roman Britain* (1979). E. H. W.; M. J. M.

Thurea, Thureatis See CYNURIA.

Thuria (in Messenia) See ATARGATIS; MESSENIAN CULTS AND MYTHS.

Thurii (mod. Sibari), a Greek colony in S. Italy, founded in 444/3 BC on the site of *Sybaris. It was a panhellenic foundation (see PANHELLENISM), but the main impetus was Athenian. *Herodotus (1) and *Lysias were reputedly colonists, and it was planned by *Hippodamus of Miletus. There was initial *stasis* between the surviving Sybarites and the other colonists, but the city flourished. In 390 BC, it was defeated by the Lucanians, and was under pressure from Bruttian raids for most of the 4th cent (see LUCANIA; BRUTTII). In the 330s it was the headquarters of the Italiote League for a short time (Strab. 6. 3. 4). A rift with *Tarentum occurred in 282, when Thurii appealed for Roman help against the Lucanians and a Roman garrison was installed. The Tarentines ejected it and the incident contributed to the outbreak of the Pyrrhic War (see PYRRHUS). In 212 BC, Thurii revolted from Rome and joined *Hannibal (see PUNIC WARS). A Latin colony (Copia) was founded there in 193 (see COLONIZATION, ROMAN), and continued to exist into late antiquity.

> ML 57; E. Greco, *Magna Grecia* (1981). K. L.

Thyestes See AEROPE; ATREUS.

Thyrea, Thyreatis See CYNURIA.

Thyia (Θυία), apparently the same word as θυιάς, a Bacchante (see DIONYSUS; MAENADS). There being a spot so named at *Delphi (Hdt. 7. 178. 2), she is occasionally heard of (in Herodotus) as the *nymph of the place.

Thysdrus (mod. El Djem), a market-town in eastern Tunisia lying inland, midway between *Hadrumetum (mod. Sousse) and Tacapae (mod. Sfax). Its origins are obscure, but it was probably an indigenous rather than a Punic settlement since only a single neo-Punic inscription has been found. First mentioned as a source of grain in 46 BC (Caes. *BAfr.* 36. 2), it remained an insignificant *oppidum liberum* ('free *oppidum') for much of the 1st cent. AD, but its prosperity, based on its position at the centre of a huge olive-growing area, grew rapidly during the 2nd cent. Surprisingly, however, it became a *municipium* only in *Septimius Severus' reign (*ILS* 1911) and did not achieve colonial rank until after 244. The Roman city at its greatest extent was very large, covering between 150 and 200 hectares, but excavation is ham-

pered by the presence of the modern town. The impressively preserved amphitheatre, a spectacular witness to Thysdrus' prosperity, is the best-known public monument: measuring 148 m. by 122 m. and capable of holding at least 25,000 spectators, it was built, probably in the early 3rd cent., to replace an earlier (?Flavian) and smaller amphitheatre to the south. Baths and the sites of the circus and forum are also known. Over a dozen private houses, many very spacious and nearly all with 2nd- and 3rd-cent. figured and ornamental mosaics, are a further testimony to Thysdrus' wealth. Pottery manufacture and lead- and bone-working are attested in an artisans' quarter. The elder *Gordian I was proclaimed emperor at Thysdrus in AD 238.

> PECS 919–20; L. Foucher, *La Maison de la procession dionysiaque à El Djem* (1963); H. Slim, *Dossiers d'Archéologie* 1983, 52–73; *Bulletin archéologique du Comité des Travaux*, NS 1983, 63–83, and *CR Acad. Inscr.* 1986, 440–69. R. J. A. W.

Tiber rises as a creek in the *Apennines near *Arretium, develops into central Italy's greatest river, meanders south to *Narnia (confluence with the Nar), then south-west past Rome (where it divides about the insula Tiberina), and enters the Tyrrhenian sea at *Ostia. The silt it carries down with it on its 250-mile journey accounts for its tawny colour ('Tiber-yellow', *flavus Tiberis*); it accumulates at its mouth to choke the harbour works (*Portus) built by *Trajan and others (*Claudius even excavated a separate, artificial mouth), and constantly advances the coastline at Ostia. Its tributaries are the Tinia-*Clitumnus, Clanis, Nar, *Anio, *Allia, and numerous brooks (*Pliny (1)'s 42 is actually an underestimate). *Navigation, although possible as far as Narnia, was hazardous owing to the swift current. Inundations are first recorded in 241 BC (Oros. 4. 11), but were frequent in all periods, even after Augustus instituted 'curatores riparum et alvei Tiberis' (i.e. officials responsible for the banks and channels of the Tiber: Suet. *Aug.* 37; see CURA(TIO), CURATOR). The salt deposits at its mouth were worked in very early times, although the settlement at Ostia which traditionally dates from Ancus *Marcius' period is not demonstrably older than the 4th cent. BC. The Tiber formed the eastern border of Etruria (and hence is frequently called *Tyrrhenus* or *Lydius*) and the northern boundary of *Latium. In imperial times opulent *villas studded the banks of its lower course.

See also RIVER-GODS.

> Strab. 5. 218; 232 f.; Plin. *HN* 3. 53 f.; Dion. Hal. 3. 44. S. A. Smith, *Tiber and its Tributaries* (1877); J. le Gall, *Le Tibre* (1953). E. T. S.

Tiberianus, poet of late 3rd or early 4th cent. AD, precise identity in doubt. Most notable among his surviving compositions are a philosophical hymn to the Supreme Being, and the *Amnis ibat*, whose feeling for nature prompted Baehrens's suggestion (recently restated by Alan Cameron) that Tiberianus also composed the *Pervigilium Veneris*. (*PLRE* 1. 911.)

> Texts: *Anth. Lat.* 490, 719b, 809–10 Riese; with comm., S. Mattiacci (1990), Courtney, *FLP*; with trans., Duff, *Minor Lat. Poets*. J. H. D. S.

Tiberias, on the west side of Lake Galilee, was founded by *Herod (2) Antipas. Despite its Greek constitution, it was a primarily Jewish city. It was generally treated as capital of *Galilee until *Nero gave Galilee to M. *Iulius Agrippa (2) II. In the Jewish revolt, the people were anti-Roman, but the upper classes loyal; according to *Josephus' *Life*, the city repeatedly changed sides, then surrendered to *Vespasian. Under *Hadrian, Tiberias developed a pagan aspect; but in the 3rd and 4th cents. it also became a rabbinical centre. The nearby resort, Hammath Tiberias, had a large, decorated synagogue.

Schürer, *History* 2. 178–83.   A. H. M. J.; T. R.

Tiberius, the emperor (Tiberius Iulius (*RE* 154) Caesar Augustus), was the son of Ti. *Claudius Nero and *Livia Drusilla, born 16 November 42 BC. Livia was divorced and married *Octavian in 38 shortly before the birth of Tiberius' brother Nero *Claudius Drusus. After public service in Spain with *Augustus (Suet. *Tib.* 8), Tiberius was quaestor in 23 BC, five years earlier than normal. From 20 BC, when he crowned the Roman nominee *Tigranes (2) in Armenia, until AD 12, when he returned to Rome after retrieving the situation on the Rhine after the Varian disaster (AD 9; see QUINCTILIUS VARUS, P.), Tiberius' military career was uniformly successful. In 15 and 14 BC he completed with Drusus the conquest of the *Alps; from M. *Vipsanius Agrippa's death in 12 until 9 BC he was reducing *Pannonia; from Drusus' death to 7 BC and again from AD 4 to 6 he campaigned in Germany. Between AD 6 and 9 he was engaged in suppressing the revolts of Pannonia and *Illyricum.

After Agrippa's death Tiberius divorced *Vipsania Agrippina (1) to marry Augustus' daughter *Iulia (3); their son died in infancy. After his second consulship (7 BC), Tiberius was granted tribunician power and *imperium in the east for five years for a diplomatic mission, the restoration of Roman authority in *Armenia, but the attempt to advance Augustus' grandson and adopted son C. *Iulius Caesar (2) to a premature consulship, made with or without the emperor's approval, helped provoke Tiberius' withdrawal to *Rhodes. He returned to Rome, still out of favour, in AD 2. By spring AD 4 both Augustus' adopted sons were dead and he adopted Tiberius, together with Agrippa *Iulius Caesar (Agrippa Postumus), while Tiberius adopted his nephew Germanicus *Iulius Caesar. Tiberius received tribunician power (see TRIBUNI PLEBIS) for ten years, renewed in AD 13 for a further ten; concurrently he held proconsular *imperium* (see PRO CONSULE), in 13 made equal to that of Augustus.

When Augustus died in AD 14 Tiberius was thus in full power. The nature of the embarrassing 'accession debate' (Tac. *Ann.* 1. 10–13) of 17 September remains unclear: a fresh conferment of power, or a political discussion of the (less autocratic) form to be taken by the new Principate. Certainly, he abolished Augustus' advisory council (see CONSILIUM PRINCIPIS), which in his last months had made authoritative decisions; matters came directly to the senate. Abroad, Tiberius' dislike of extravagant honours (Tac. *Ann.* 4. 37 f.) was tempered by precedent and a need to conciliate his subjects which could prevent him making his wishes clear, as to Gytheum in *Laconia in AD 15 (EJ 102 (trans. D. Braund, *Augustus to Nero, 31 B.C.–A.D. 68* (1985), 127)).

Tiberius respected Augustus and exploited his memory when taking unpopular steps (Tac. *Ann.* 1. 14. 6–15. 1). In dealing with the *Germans he followed the policy of containing the empire that Augustus laid down in his political testament (Tiberius may have helped to draft it). This conflicted with the views of Germanicus, who was recalled in AD 16. Augustus' methods of coping with *Britain and Armenia were also followed: on his mission to the east (AD 17–19) Germanicus established another Roman nominee in Armenia, who survived successfully until 35; further negotiations, backed up by the threat of force, were conducted by L. *Vitellius. Tiberius did not shrink from annexing dependent monarchies: Germanicus took over *Commagene and *Cappadocia, which made it possible to halve the Roman sales tax.

Two innovations in provincial administration are credited to Tiberius: prorogations of governors, and governorships in absence. Both were due to a shortage of satisfactory candidates, deplored by Tiberius (Tac. *Ann.* 6. 27). The second was clearly deleterious and the first kept some poor governors in office (e.g. *Pontius Pilatus (Pilate) in *Judaea).

The most notorious feature of Tiberius' principate was the incidence of trials before the senate (introduced by Augustus), some *extra ordinem* (M. *Scribonius Libo Drusus in 16; L. *Aelius Seianus (Sejanus) in 31), most for diminishing the majesty (*maiestas*) of the Roman people, the emperor, his family, or other notables, by whatever means, however trivial; at first some were discouraged by the emperor (e.g. Tac. *Ann.* 1. 73 f.). That of Cn. *Calpurnius Piso (3), also accused in AD 20 of extortion and of poisoning Germanicus, is documented not only in Tac. *Ann.* 3. 8–19, but in the decree embodying the senate's decisions and approved by the emperor (W. Eck and others, *SC de Cn. Pisone patre* (1996)), which affords an unappetizing insight into the atmosphere of the reign.

Tiberius' reign opened with army mutinies, soon suppressed; the revolt in Gaul (AD 21; see GAUL (TRANSALPINE)) was minor. Two factors undermined his principate. Tiberius inherited a poor military and economic situation: the German war was unprofitable; politicians were short of cash and were resorting to prosecutions to obtain it (cf. Tac. *Ann.* 2. 34), there was unrest at Rome due to grain shortages, and provincials were chafing under tax burdens (cf. the revolt of 21). Tiberius' answers (gifts to individuals, treasury disbursements when senators became unable to pay their debts in 33 (Tac. *Ann.* 6, 16 f.), and public economy), were inadequate, and his marked frugality (though personally generous, he built little, and gave donations and games sparingly) increased his unpopularity.

Second, there had been family jealousy since 7 BC, and the people and many senators favoured his stepsons. Rivalry after AD 4 led to the downfall of Agrippa Postumus and his adherents. Feared by former opponents, Tiberius could not make politicians trust his *moderatio* and *clementia*. They looked forward to the succession of Germanicus (Tiberius was 55 in AD 14). On his death in AD 19 and that of Tiberius' son Drusus *Iulius Caesar (1) in 23 the succession question opened up again, with the sons of Germanicus pitted against Sejanus, who seems to have supported Drusus' surviving son Tiberius *Iulius Caesar Nero Gemellus. Instead of confronting the problem, Tiberius, encouraged by Sejanus, retired to *Campania and then to *Capreae (AD 27), never to enter Rome again. While he was at the mercy of Sejanus and his freedmen, the struggle went on at Rome, until Nero *Iulius Caesar and Drusus *Iulius Caesar (2) and their mother *Vipsania Agrippina (2) were disgraced (AD 29–30) and Tiberius was given evidence that Sejanus was attempting the downfall of Germanicus' youngest son *Gaius (1) (31; Suet. *Tib.* 61), who then became the only likely successor. A purge of Sejanus' followers (and of supporters of Gemellus and rivals of Gaius' chief aide *Macro) continued until Tiberius' death on 16 March 37, which was greeted with rejoicing.

Tacitus delivers a favourable verdict on Tiberius' principate down to Sejanus' ascendancy; the five 'ages' ending with a death are another device for moving from promising beginning to disastrous end, like the hypocrisy (*dissimulatio*) also imputed to him.

Tiberius was a forceful orator, a poet (neoteric), a connoisseur, and perhaps a Sceptic (he was careless of religious ritual; see SCEPTICS)); he kept his intellect and relish for irony (Philon, *Leg.* 142; Tac. *Ann.* 6. 6). Stories of vice on Capreae (and *Rhodes) may be discounted; real defects, a cultivated sense of superiority, relentlessness and lack of affability, meditated ambiguity of language, remained.

ANCIENT SOURCES Vell. Pat. 2. 94–131; Philon, *Leg.*; Tac. *Ann.* 1–6; Suet. *Tib.*; Dio Cass. bks. 57 f. (see R. Syme, *Tacitus* (1958) and M. Baar, *Das Bild des Kaisers Tiberius bei Tacitus, Sueton und Cassius Dio* (1990)).

MODERN LITERATURE F. B. Marsh, *The Reign of Tiberius* (1931); R. Seager, *Tiberius* (1972); B. Levick, *Tiberius the Politician* (1976) (bibliog.); W. Orth, *Die Provinzialpolitik des Tiberius* (1970); R. S. Rogers, *Criminal Trials and Criminal Legislation under Tiberius* (1935); and *Studies in the Reign of Tiberius* (1943); R. F. Newbold, *AJPhil.* 1974, 110 ff.; L. Polacco, *Il Volto di Tiberio* (1955).   J. P. B.; B. M. L.

Tibullus, Albius (*RE* 12), born between 55 and 48 BC. An anonymous and corrupt Life, possibly derived from *Suetonius, tells us that he was good-looking (confirmed by Hor. *Epist.* 1. 4. 6) and something of a dandy; also that he was of equestrian rank (see EQUITES) and won *dona militaria* (military awards). The Life is preceded by an epigram of *Domitius Marsus, which fixes the date of Tibullus' death in 19 BC (cf. also the lament in Ov. *Am.* 3. 9).

Tibullus implies that his patrimony was diminished, presumably by Octavian's confiscations of 41–40 BC (1. 1. 41 f.; see AUGUSTUS; PROSCRIPTION); cf. Propertius. But his claims to poverty, *paupertas*, should not be taken too seriously. He no more than *Propertius seems to have been reduced to economic dependence. *Horace indeed suggests that he was well-off, and possessed a *villa at Pedum between *Tibur and *Praeneste (*Epist.* 1. 4; he is also probably the addressee of *Odes* 1. 33). Tibullus refused, or did not attract, the patronage of *Maecenas, and instead addresses himself to M. *Valerius Messalla Corvinus. He set out to the east in Messalla's entourage, but fell ill at Corcyra and returned to Italy (1. 3); it is uncertain whether he served under him in Gaul (1. 7. 9 and Life).

Tibullus' MSS contain three books, of which the third was divided into two by Italian scholars of the 15th cent.; these are commonly called the *Corpus Tibullianum* and only the first two belong to Tibullus himself. The dates of publication are uncertain: book 1 refers to Messalla's triumph (25 September 27 BC), book 2 to the installation of his son as one of the *quindecimviri sacris faciundis* (perhaps not long before Tibullus' death). It seems likely that Tibullus' first book appeared after Propertius' first, but before the completion of Propertius' second. Propertius 2. 5. 25 ff. seems a retort to Tibullus 1. 10. 61 ff. (on the question of the acceptability of violence in love-affairs).

Tibullus' first book deals with his love for a mistress, Delia (1, 2, 3, 5, 6); surprisingly and provocatively it professes comparable devotion to a boy, Marathus, too (4, 8, 9). *Apuleius tells us that Delia existed and that her name was Plania (*Apol.* 10). We need not doubt this, though her attributes (and those of Marathus, for that matter) seem pretty conventional. Book 2 celebrates a different mistress, whom the poet calls Nemesis (3, 4, 6). Nothing certain can be said about the social status of any of these lovers (but for Delia cf. 1. 6. 68, which suggests that she is not a *matrona*).

Tibullus, like Propertius, expresses the belief that love must be his life's occupation (e.g. 1. 1. 45 ff.), and, like Propertius, he claims love to be his *militia* (1. 1. 75 f.), in spite of his actual forays into the world of action; like Propertius too he presents himself as the slave of his lovers (1. 5. 5 f., 1. 9. 21 f.). In his use both of military and servile figures Tibullus is more specific than Propertius. For example his servile declarations express willingness to undergo servile punishments, and some scholars detect an intended, almost Ovidian humour (cf. OVID) in his use of both figures.

Unlike Propertius, Tibullus makes virtually no use of mythology. Propertius' romantic, impossible dream had been that Cynthia would be like heroines of myth. Tibullus' impossible dream is that Delia will join him in his country estate to enjoy a rural idyll (esp. 1. 5. 21 ff.). Tibullus' aspirations to live the country life, expressed in more than one poem, separate him from the urban *Catullus (1) and Propertius.

Apart from the love poems, books 1 and 2 contain poems in honour of Messalla (1. 7, 2. 5), an elegy on the blessings of peace (1. 10), and a charming representation of a rustic festival and the poet's song at it (2. 1). Book 2 is only just over 400 lines long, and may be either defective or posthumous.

The third book is a collection of poems from the circle of Messalla. It begins with six elegies by *Lygdamus, and also contains the *Panegyricus Messallae*, five poems on the love of Sulpicia for Cerinthus (known as the Garland of Sulpicia), and six short poems by *Sulpicia (1) herself. The poems on Sulpicia are conceivably by Tibullus. The book concludes with an elegy of quality purportedly by Tibullus, and an anonymous epigram.

In *Quintilian's view, Tibullus was the most 'refined and elegant' of the Roman elegists (10. 1. 93). The judgement is justified by the smooth finish of his poems; no other Roman poet writes with such refined plainness. Yet his simplicity is sometimes deceptive: the transitions by which he glides from one scene or subject to another often baffle analysis.

The almost total loss of *Cornelius Gallus makes it difficult to estimate Tibullus' originality, but it was probably considerable. Certainly his plainness, his eschewal of myth, and his rural emphasis contrast strongly with Catullus and Propertius.

EDITIONS J. P. Postgate (1915); M. Ponchont (1924); F. W. Lenz (1937; edn. 3 with G. K. Galinsky, 1970); G. Luck (1988); G. Lee (1982).

COMMENTARIES K. F. Smith (1913); E. Cesareo (1938); M. C. J. Putnam (1973); Lee (1982); of bk. 1, P. Murgatroyd (1980). Selections: Postgate (1928). Non-Tibullan poems in the *Corpus Tibullianum*: H. Tränkle (1990).

TRANSLATIONS (verse) Lee (1982); (prose) Postgate (1912).

STUDIES A. Cartault, *A propos du Corpus Tibullianum* (1906); *Le Distique élégiaque chez Tib. Sulp. Lygd.* (1911); M. Ponchont, *Étude sur le texte de T.* (1923); M. Schuster, *Tibull-Studien* (1968); F. Cairns, *Tibullus: A Hellenistic Poet at Rome* (1979); R. O. A. M. Lyne, *The Latin Love Poets from Catullus to Horace* (1980), 62–81, 149–89.   R. O. A. M. L.

Tibur (mod. Tivoli) occupies a commanding site controlling the route up the Aniene valley (see ANIO) east into the central *Apennines. Traditionally founded before Rome, it was certainly a major settlement by the end of the 7th cent. BC. An important member of the Latin League (Plin. *HN* 16. 237), in the 4th cent. BC it frequently fought Rome until deprived of its territory in 338 BC (Livy 7–8. 14). Tibur, however, remained independent, acquiring Roman citizenship (see CITIZENSHIP, ROMAN) only in 90 BC. The monuments of the Roman town are conspicuous, and include the forum; a sanctuary to Hercules Victor (?of Sullan date) and other temples; an amphitheatre and a rotunda (?4th cent. AD). The airy foothills of the Apennines around Tibur were fashionable locations for villas (e.g. those of *Catullus (1) and *Augustus). The most extraordinary was that of *Hadrian, begun *c*. AD 118 on the site of a republican–Augustan villa. The largest ever built, it incorporates many exotic buildings which reflect those that Hadrian had seen in the east Mediterranean, such as the Canopus-Serapeum, lined with statuary including *caryatids like those on the *Erechtheum in Athens. Among other important and luxurious buildings were the Poecile, the island villa, the 'Piazza d'Oro', the baths, and a temple of Venus resembling that at *Cnidus.

G. C. Giuliani, *Tibur* 1 (1970); G. de Palma, in *Enea* (1981), 38 ff.; S. Aurigemma, *La Villa Adriana presso Tivoli* (1961); M. De Franceschini, *Villa Adriana* (1991).   E. T. S.; T. W. P.

Ticida, Lucius, a Roman *eques* (see EQUITES) and partisan of *Caesar executed in 46 BC (*BAfr.* 44. 1, 46. 3), wrote poems like those of *Licinius Calvus and *Catullus (1) in style and content, including erotic poems to 'Perilla', i.e. Metella (Apul. *Apol.* 10), probably the daughter of *Clodia and Q. *Caecilius Metellus Celer.

See F. Münzer, *RE* 6 A 844; Courtney, *FLP* 228.   E. C.

Ticinum, in northern Italy near the confluence of the Ticinus and *Padus (Po). *Hannibal defeated the Romans here (218 BC), but Ticinum itself is unrecorded until imperial times. In the late empire it was an important fortress which *Attila sacked, *Theoderic (1) strengthened, and the *Lombards made their capital, calling it Papia (mod. Pavia).

D. A. Bullough, *PBSR* 1966, 82 ff.   E. T. S.; T. W. P.

Tifata, mountain overlooking *Capua and *Campania. The name allegedly meant 'oak-grove' (Festus 503 Lindsay). The basilica of Sant'Angelo in Formis has occupied the site of its famous sanctuary to *Diana (*ILS* 6306; Vell. Pat. 2. 25. 4) since the 10th cent.

A. Maiuri, *Passeggiate campana* (1957), 159 ff.; D. Mustilli, *Enciclopedia italiana* (1950), 'Tifata'; J. Heurgon, *Capoue préromaine* (1942), 299 ff.; M. Frederiksen, *Campania* (1984), see index.   E. T. S.; S. H.

Tigellinus See OFONIUS TIGELLINUS, C.

Tigidius Perennis, Sextus, praetorian prefect (see PRAEFECTUS PRAETORIO) under *Commodus. Perennis was already holding high office in AD 177, being named on the *tabula Banasitana* (*AE* 1971, 534) immediately after *Taruttienus Paternus, whose colleague he soon became. After engineering the fall of Commodus' favourite Saoterus and Paternus' removal (AD 182), Perennis was the effective ruler of the empire for three years. His policy of replacing senatorial legionary commanders by equestrians made him unpopular, and he was alleged to have planned to make his own son emperor. Commodus sacrificed him to a group of mutinous soldiers in AD 185.

Dio Cass. 72; Herod. 1; SHA, *Comm.*; *RE* 6 A 'Tigidius Perennis'.   A. R. Bi.

Tigranes (1) **II** (*RE* 1) **'the Great',** son of Tigranes I (App. *Syr.* 48) (or of Artavasdes I). Shortly after 100 BC he was set on the throne of *Armenia by the Parthians (with whom he had been a hostage for some years; see PARTHIA) in return for the cession of 'seventy valleys' (Strabo 532). He rapidly consolidated his power, forming an alliance with *Mithradates VI of Pontus, whose daughter, Cleopatra, he married. The interference of the two kings in *Cappadocia led to Roman intervention and a *démarche* by *Sulla. Tigranes turned his attention to expansion at the expense of Parthia, temporarily weakened by invasions on its eastern frontier. He ravaged *Media as far as *Ecbatana and Assyria as far as *Media Atropatene, and *Osroëne. In 83 he occupied *Syria, *Phoenicia, and *Cilicia, ejecting warring *Seleucid rivals. Greek cities that sided with him were given autonomy and coinage rights, but others, e.g. Soli in Cilicia and

Cappadocian Mazaca, were destroyed and their inhabitants transferred to his new southern metropolis *Tigranocerta. The empire of Tigranes, 'King of Kings', proved to be ephemeral. In 69 his alliance with Mithradates involved him in war with Rome. L. *Licinius Lucullus (2) captured Tigranocerta, but the issue remained undecided until *Pompey in 66 succeeded in separating the Armenian and Pontic kings. Tigranes' son rebelled and fled to Pompey; together they marched on *Artaxata and Tigranes finally surrendered (66). He lost all his territories except Armenia proper, though he later recovered Sophene and Pompey recognized his claim to *Gordyene and the seventy valleys. Henceforward, though engaging in frontier disputes with Parthia, he remained a peaceful vassal of Rome until his death in *c*.56.

H. Seyrig, *Syria* (1950); A. N. Sherwin-White, *Roman Foreign Policy in the East 168 B.C.–A.D. 1* (1984); R. D. Sullivan, *Near Eastern Royalty and Rome 100–30 BC* (1990), indexes; *B. M. Cat. Seleucid Kings of Syria*, 103 ff.; see also ARMENIA; L. LICINIUS LUCULLUS (2); POMPEY.

E. W. G.; B. M. L.

Tigranes (2) **III** (*RE* 3) (ruled 20 BC–*c*.6 BC), son of King *Artavasdes (1) II of *Armenia, grandson of *Tigranes (1) II. Captured and sent to Egypt by Antony (M. *Antonius (2)), he lived for many years in Rome. His brother Artaxias was murdered and the Armenians sent a request to Augustus that he be sent to reign (Tac. *Ann.* 2. 3; *Res Gestae* 27). *Tiberius accompanied him with an army, and Tigranes was crowned without opposition. Armenia was thus restored to the ostensible control of Rome, although Tigranes' coins bear Parthian titles.

E. T. Newell, *Numismatic Notes and Monographs*, 1926, 13 ff.; A. N. Sherwin-White, *Roman Foreign Policy in the East 168 B.C.–A.D. 1* (1984), 323 ff.   M. S. D.; E. W. G.; B. M. L.

Tigranes (3) **IV** (*RE* 4) (ruled *c*.6 BC–AD 1), son of *Tigranes (2) III. On his father's death he was crowned by the pro-Parthian party (see PARTHIA) in *Armenia, to reign jointly with his sister-consort Erato. He was expelled by the Romans, but returned after the murder of the Roman nominee a few years later. Attacked by *Augustus' adoptive son C. *Iulius Caesar (2) (AD 1), he made overtures for peace, which Augustus received favourably, but soon died fighting on his eastern frontier.

RE 6, 'Erato' 9; A. N. Sherwin-White, *Roman Foreign Policy in the East 168 BC–AD 1* (1984), 325 f.   M. S. D.; B. M. L.

Tigranes (4) **V** (*RE* 6), great-grandson of *Archelaus (5) of Cappadocia and of *Herod (1) the Great. In AD 60 he was sent from Rome to replace *Tiridates (4) on the throne of Armenia. When he proceeded to lay *Adiabene, a Parthian vassal kingdom (see PARTHIA), waste, the Arsacid king *Vologeses I sent his general Monaeses to invade Armenia, and Tigranes was shut up in *Tigranocerta; but the siege was raised after negotiations. He was withdrawn by the Romans and disappeared from history.

M.-L. Chaumont, *ANRW* 2. 9. 1 (1976), 107 ff.   J. Wi.

Tigranocerta (mod. Silvan), city in *Armenia, in Arzanene; later rechristened Martyropolis. It was founded by *Tigranes (1) II (App. *Mith.* 67) as a city in the Hellenistic style which he was building to be the centre of his new empire. Its precise position within the mons Masius is still disputed, but its general location intended it to maintain communications between Armenia and Tigranes' southern possessions. He swelled its citizen body by netting the cities of conquered *Cappadocia, *Adiabene, and *Gordyene (Plut. *Luc.* 25 f.; Strabo 12. 2. 27). Its fortifications were incomplete when L. *Licinius Lucullus (2) defeated Tigranes in 69 and easily secured its capitulation. The captured exiles were sent home, but Tigranocerta was still an important fortified city in AD 50, for example, when the Roman general Cn. *Domitius Corbulo occupied it. In the wars of the *Sasanid king, Sapor II, against Rome and Armenia in the 4th cent. AD, it was destroyed by the Sassanians, but it emerges again in the 5th cent. as Martyropolis, site of a famous church of the Martyrs.

L. Dilleman, *Haute Mésopotamie orientale* (1962), 88 f.

E. W. G.; S. S.-W.

Tigris, the more easterly of the two rivers of *Mesopotamia and, together with the *Euphrates, of decisive importance for the geological, cultural, and historical development of Mesopotamia. Rising in the outward eastern *Taurus, it flows south-east through *Assyria (2) (touching *Nineveh (1) and Assur) and *Babylonia. At *Seleuceia (1) it is only *c.*18 miles from the Euphrates and later joins this river to become the Shatt Al Arab (in the former kingdom of *Mesene / Characene). In antiquity a system of canals and arms connected the lower reaches of the Tigris with the Euphrates and guaranteed the agricultural wealth of Babylonia. Because of its torrential current here and there shipping downstream was possible.

For bibliography, see that under EUPHRATES.

J. Wi.

Timachidas of Rhodian *Lindus (late 2nd–early 1st cent. BC) composed the surviving record of dedications in the temple of *Athena, the so-called Lindian Chronicle (*FGrH* 532). He also wrote on classical authors (including *Aristophanes (1), *Euripides, and *Menander (1)), compiled an influential *Glossai* (see GLOSSA, GLOSSARY), and composed an *epic *Deipnon* (*Dinner*) in at least eleven books (Ath. 1. 5a).

K. Ziegler, *RE* 6 A 1052–60; *Suppl. Hell.* 769–73.

R. L. Hu.

Timaeus (1) of *Locri Epizephyrii in Italy, Pythagorean (see PYTHAGORAS (1)), the chief speaker in *Plato (1)'s *Timaeus*. We have no knowledge of him independent of this, and he may have been a fictitious character. The work in ps.-Doric dialect (see GREEK LANGUAGE, § 4) on the *soul, which passes under the name of Timaeus Locrus, is a late (probably 1st-cent. AD) paraphrase of the *Timaeus*: ed. (with Plato's *Timaeus*) C. F. Herman (Leipzig, 1852).

DK 49; *RE* 6 A 1203.

W. D. R.

Timaeus (2) of *Tauromenium (mod. Taormina) in *Sicily, *c.*350–260 BC, the most important western Greek historian; son of Andromachus, the dynast who refounded Tauromenium in 358. Andromachus gave *Timoleon a warm welcome in 345 and lent him his support (T 3). Timaeus was exiled in *c.*315 probably on account of his hostility towards *Agathocles (1) after the tyrant had captured Tauromenium (fr. 124d) and spent at least fifty years of his exile at Athens (fr. 34), where he studied under *Philiscus (1) of Miletus, a pupil of *Isocrates (T 1), and wrote his great work of history. It is conceivable that he returned to Sicily in *c.*265 but not certain. Timaeus died, allegedly at the age of 96 (T 5), shortly after 264 (see below).

Works 1. *Olympionikai*: a synchronic list of Olympian victors (see OLYMPIAN GAMES), Spartan kings and *ephors, the Athenian *archontes*, and the priestesses of *Hera in *Argos (2) (Polyb. 12. 11. 1 = T 11, frs. 125–8). Thereafter it became standard practice to date historical events by the years of the Olympian Games; see OLYMPIADS; TIME-RECKONING. 2. (*Sikelikai*) *Historiai* = *Sicilian History* in 38 books from mythical times to the death of Agathocles 289 / 8 (T 6–8). He also wrote a 'separate account' on the '(Roman) Wars against *Pyrrhus' and the events until the epochal

year 264 (T 9), where *Polybius (1)'s history starts, 'a fine Timaei' (from where Timaeus left off) (cf. Polyb. 1. 5. 1; 39. 8. 4 = T 6).

The arrangement is known only in outline: the five books of the introduction (*prokataskeuē*) dealt with the *geography and ethnography of the west and accounts of 'colonies, the foundation of cities, and their relations' (T 7). Books 6–15 contained the earlier history of Sicily until *Dionysius (1) I's accession to power in 406/5; books 16–33 treated the tyranny of Dionysius I and II (406/5–344/3) and events down to Agathocles. The last five books 34–8 were devoted to the history of Agathocles (T 8). The work is known through 164 fragments, the extensive use made of it by *Diodorus (3) (4–21 for the Sicilian passages), and Polybius' criticism in book 12.

Characteristics 1. *Subject-matter*: Timaeus did not restrict his treatment to Sicily but dealt with the whole west including Carthage. Most importantly he was the first Greek historian to give a comprehensive if summary account of Roman history until 264 (T 9b). Hence Aulus *Gellius (*NA* 2. 1. 1 = T 9c) even talks of 'historical works which Timaeus wrote in Greek on the history of the Roman people'. 2. *Conception of history*: Timaeus took an extremely broad view of history, including myth, geography, ethnography, political and military events, culture, religion, marvels, and *paradoxa* (see PARADOXOGRAPHERS). 3. *Sicilian patriotism*: Timaeus frequently distorted events in favour of the Siceliots (fr. 94) and conversely wrote less favourably about the Athenians and Carthaginians (on the Sicilian expedition, cf. Meister, *Gymnasium* 1970, 508 ff.); he always emphasized the contribution of the western Greeks to Greek intellectual life (e.g. *Pythagoras (1), frs. 12 ff., 131 f.; *Empedocles, frs. 14, 134; *Gorgias (1), fr. 137). 4. *Hatred of tyrants*: Timaeus, a conservative aristocrat, distorted not only the historical picture of Agathocles, who had exiled him (fr. 124), but also of other tyrants, e.g. *Hieron (1) I and Dionysius I (frs. 29, 105). 5. *Historical classification of his work*: Timaeus' work displays rhetorical, tragic, and 'pragmatic' (frs. 7, 151) features (cf. Polyb. 12. 25; frs. 22, 31) in equal proportion, hence it is an excellent example of the early blend of different kinds of historiography. 6. *Historical criticism*: Timaeus was the first Greek historian critically to appraise almost all of his predecessors, historians and other writers alike. He frequently went too far, which earned him the nickname *Epitimaeus* ('slanderer'); he was first so called by *Ister (T 1, 11, 16). He was especially vehement in the attacks on his immediate predecessor *Philistus (fr. 38, T 18, fr. 154).

Timaeus in turn was criticized by Polybius (book 12) for factual errors, his harsh criticism, and his historical methods (mere book-learning, want of autopsy, lack of political and military experience).

Timaeus was 'the most important historian between *Ephorus and Polybius' and became 'the standard authority on the history of the Greek West for nearly five centuries' (Pearson). Of Greek authors he was used by e.g. *Callimachus (3), *Lycophron (2), *Eratosthenes, *Agatharchides, Polybius, *Posidonius (2), *Diodorus (3), *Strabo, and *Plutarch; of Roman writers by Q. *Fabius Pictor, M. *Porcius Cato (1), *Cicero, Cornelius *Nepos, *Ovid, and Gellius. The writings of *Ister (T 10), *Polemon (3) of Ilium (T 26) in reaction to his work as well as Polybius, book 12, bear witness to Timaeus' great impact on historiography.

FGrH 566. T. S. Brown, *Timaeus of Tauromenium* (1958); K. Meister, *Die sizilische Geschichte bei Diodor* (Diss. Munich, 1967), and *Historische Kritik bei Polybios* (1975); F. W. Walbank, *Kokalos* 1968 / 9, 476 ff.; L. Pearson, *The Greek Historians of the West: Timaeus and his Predecessors*

(1987); K. Meister, *Die griechische Geschichtsschreibung* (1990), 131 ff.; R. Vattuone, *Sapienza d'occidente: Il pensiero storico di Timeo di Tauromenio* (1991); O. Lendle, *Einführung in die griechische Geschichtsschreibung* (1992), 211 ff.   K. M.

Timaeus (3) (between the 2nd and 5th cent. AD) compiled an extant brief lexicon of difficult words in *Plato (1).

Ed. C. Hermann, *Platonis dialogi* 6. 397 ff. K. von Fritz, *RE* 2 / 11. 1226 ff.; A. Dyck, *Harv. Stud.* 1985, 75 ff.; H. Dörrie, M. Baltes, *Der Platonismus in der Antike* 3 (1993), 58 ff., 231 ff.   D. O'M.

Timagenes of *Alexandria (1), Greek rhetor and historian, came to Rome as a captive in 55 BC with A. *Gabinius (2), was ransomed and subsequently set free by *Sulla's son Faustus *Cornelius Sulla (T 1). He lived and worked in Rome, and is mentioned alongside *Caecilius (1) of Caleacte and Craton as a distinguished rhetor (T 1 and 2). Initially a favourite of *Augustus, he later incurred the *princeps'* displeasure by his frankness and went to live at the house of C. *Asinius Pollio (T 2 and 3). 'He wrote many books' (T 1). All that is extant is the title *On Kings* (*peri basileōn*), an attempt at writing a universal history from the earliest times to *Caesar. It is hostile to Rome—*felicitati urbis inimicus*, (test. 8)—and at the same time 'hellenocentric and barbarophile' (Sordi).

FGrH 88. R. Laqueur, *RE* 6 A (1936), 1063 ff.; G. W. Bowersock, *Augustus and the Greek World* (1965), 109 f.; Fraser, *Ptol. Alex.* 1. 518 f., 2. 746 n. 202; M. Sordi, *ANRW* 2. 30. 1 (1982), 775 ff.; J. Malitz, *Die Historien des Poseidonios* (1983), 52 f.; K. Meister, *Die griechische Geschichtsschreibung* (1990), 171.   K. M.

Timanthes (late 5th cent. BC), painter, of Cythnus, later of Sicyon, contemporary of *Zeuxis (1); famed for his *ingenium* ('inventive ingenuity'). In his 'sacrifice of Iphigenia' he showed degrees of grief culminating in the veiled Agamemnon (reflections on late reliefs, Pfuhl, figs. 638–9). See PAINTING, GREEK.

Overbeck, 1734–44; M. Robertson, *History of Greek Art* 1 (1975), 412 ff.   T. B. L. W.

timber was a valuable economic product in Greece and Rome. Many Mediterranean lands were forested in ancient times, but these timber stands were drastically reduced by human exploitation and by the grazing of animals, especially goats. The Mediterranean climate is capable of sustaining forests so long as they are intact, but once the trees are cut, the combination of marginal rainfall and grazing animals makes forest regeneration difficult, if not impossible. In general, the history of timber supplies is one of gradual depletion, with little effort in antiquity to replant harvested lands. Only in those areas of continental rainfall conditions which lie at some distance from dense human settlement (e.g. the mountains of *Macedonia) have forests survived into modern times. Thus lacking much apparent physical correlation between modern scrubland and ancient forests we are dependent upon references in the ancient authors (e.g. *Theophrastus and the elder *Pliny (1)) for a description of the location and abundance of ancient timberland. Moreover, recent advances in palaeobotany as an archaeological tool have assisted in locating and describing some ancient forests not otherwise known to us. For example, *Cyprus was quite heavily forested from the central Troodos mountains down to its shorelines. Cypriot cedars of Lebanon and tall pines were much in demand for heavy construction and shipbuilding. The clearing of forest land for a variety of common uses (see below) was compounded in Cyprus by the extensive use of wood as fuel for the island's renowned smelting of copper. The result was the virtually complete stripping of the island of its famous forest cover. Much of the timberland in Cyprus today is the result of modern reforestation.

With the growth and spread of the human population throughout the Mediterranean in antiquity, there were commensurate pressures on forest lands. They were cleared for conversion to agriculture, wood was harvested for fuel—either to be burned directly or to be converted into charcoal—and used for *furniture, tools, and other domestic needs. Coniferous tall timbers—which were light and strong—were used for the construction of private and public buildings and *ships. With the disappearance of nearby forests by late prehistoric times, the timber-starved cities of the Mediterranean turned further afield for their supplies. Beginning in the Classical period, the main sources were Macedonia and *Thrace (especially for the pines and oaks necessary for shipbuilding, oars, and pitch), *Achaea, parts of *Crete and Cyprus, the south coast of the Black Sea (see EUXINE), *Cilicia, the mountains of the Levant, southern *Italy, and *Sicily.

As tall timbers became scarcer, the competition among Greek city-states for remaining supplies increased. For example, when the forest products of Achaea were denied to Athens because of depletion and politics, the Athenians turned increasingly to Macedonia, as several surviving inscriptions inform us. The Spartan general *Brasidas's prolonged campaigns in Macedonia during the *Peloponnesian War can be seen in part as a Spartan attempt to prevent Athenian access to the timberlands necessary to maintain the Athenian fleet (see NAVIES; SEA POWER). Other inscriptions tell of the importation of heavy construction timbers into Greece during the Hellenistic era. While there is no doubt, however, about the economic, military, and diplomatic importance of timber resources, we are rather poorly informed about the details of forest management, the harvesting of wood, and its transport by land and sea. Inscriptions inform us that the kings of Macedon exercised a royal monopoly over forest resources, and let contracts for the harvest and export of timber. Many Hellenistic dynasts in the eastern Mediterranean exercised similar prerogatives over the timberland under their control.

The timber shortage was never so acute for the Roman republic as for the Greek cities, due to the ample forest resources of lowland Italy, Sicily, and the accessible lower slopes of the Apennine and Alpine ranges. As wealth increased and tastes became more exotic, the Roman timber trade (like the trade in decorative building stone) went further afield to satisfy the demand for more exquisite and rare woods. See LANDSCAPES (ANCIENT GREEK).

E. C. Semple, *Geography of the Mediterranean Region* (1932); R. Meiggs, *Trees and Timber in the Ancient Mediterranean World* (1982).   E. N. B.

timē (honour) See PHILOTIMIA.

time See AION.

time-reckoning Ancient culture knew a range of expedients for dividing the twenty-four hours of the day, for marking the succession of days in the month or year, and for dating important historical events. *Hesiod already used the rising of particular *constellations to mark the changing seasons, and ascribed propitious and unpropitious qualities to the days of the month that corresponded to the phases of the moon. By the 5th cent. BC, Athenian astronomers—like their Babylonian colleagues—knew that the lunar month is approximately $29\frac{1}{2}$ and the tropical year approximately $365\frac{1}{4}$ days long, and could divide the day and night up into twelve 'seasonal' hours that varied with the length of daylight. Astronomers (see ASTRONOMY) from *Meton to *Hipparchus (3) and *Ptolemy (4) developed increasingly accurate luni-solar cycles and learned to explain and predict solar and lunar *eclipses. They also created *parapēgmata*, or public calendars, which traced the risings and settings of stars and predicted weather throughout the year. Civil practices, however, were never guided solely by astronomical expertise. Most people continued to divide the day and night into rough sections rather than precise hours. The Athenian calendar's failure to correspond with the actual movements of the moon was notorious, while the Roman months, before *Caesar reformed the calendar, deviated by a quarter of a year and more from what should have been their place in the seasons. Intercalation was often practised for political rather than calendrical ends. Only in the 1st cent. BC and after, when the spread of *astrology made it urgent to know the year, day, and hour of an individual's birth, did an interest in precise calendar dates become widespread outside scientific circles. The chief motive for interest in the calendar lay, normally, in its days of ritual or ominous import rather than in its technical basis.

Historical events were at first normally dated, by both Greeks and Romans, by the year of a given priest or magistrate into which they fell: rough lengths for a single generation were used to date past dynasties of rulers. *Thucydides (2) protested (5. 20) against the first of these methods, but he himself (esp. in his introductory *Archaeology*) seems to have used the second, generation-count, method; and the temptation, to compute dates by means of assumptions about the length of human life, was persistent. Thus even in the 2nd cent. BC, *Apollodorus (6) used an 'acme' system to date famous but poorly attested individuals like philosophers and historians; that is, he assumed that an individual reached his acme (conventionally put at age 40) at the date of some well-known external event which had occurred in the life of that individual (see F. Jacoby, *Apollodors Chronik* (1902)). From the end of the 4th cent. BC, however, when the *Seleucid era of 312/11 BC came into widespread use, more precise eras and methods gradually came into use. Scholars like *Eratosthenes and *Timaeus (2) tried to co-ordinate historical dates from different societies by measuring their distance from some single, common era, like that of the first *Olympian Games in 776 BC (see OLYMPIADS) or the founding of Rome in 753/2 BC. Other eras sometimes used included that of the Trojan War (normally given as 1183/2 BC) and the astronomers' era of Nabonassar, 26 January 747 BC. See also CALENDAR, GREEK and ROMAN; CLOCKS.

E. Bickerman, *Chronology of the Ancient World* (1968; rev. 1980); A. E. Mosshammer, *The Chronicle of Eusebius and Greek Chronographic Tradition* (1979); O. Wenskus, *Astronomische Zeitangaben von Homer bis Theophrast* (1990); A. T. Grafton, *Joseph Scaliger, A Study in the History of Classical Scholarship*, vol. 2, *Historical Chronology* (1993).　　A. T. G.

Timgad See THAMUGADI.

Timocharis (RE 1), astronomer at *Alexandria (1), made observations between 295 and 272 BC reported by *Ptolemy (4). These record positions of the moon and Venus with respect to fixed stars. He also recorded star declinations, used later by *Hipparchus (3) and Ptolemy (*Almagest* 7. 3); some are attributed to Aristyllus (RE 3), who seems to have been his associate. These are the earliest known *systematic* Greek astronomical observations.

For details of the observations see O. Pedersen, *Survey of the Almagest* (1974), 410–11, and G. J. Toomer, *Ptolemy's Almagest* (1984), index, 'Timocharis'.　　G. J. T.

Timocles, Middle Comedy poet, (see COMEDY (GREEK), MIDDLE) late in the period but much given to personal satire in the manner of earlier comedy; almost half the extant citations refer to individuals (e.g. fr. 12, on *Demosthenes (2), who 'has never yet uttered an antithesis'). He won first prize once at the Lenaea between 330 and 320 (*IG* 2². 2325. 158); the latest datable reference (fr. 34. 3) in his work is mention of the *gynaikonomoi* ('supervisors of women') instituted (317–307 BC) by *Demetrius (3) of Phaleron. Of twenty-seven known titles four indicate mythological burlesques, and one play, *Orestautokleides*, portrayed Autoclides as suffering the fate of *Orestes—beset, not by Furies, but by old whores.

PCG 7. 754 ff. (*CAF* 2. 451 ff.).　　K. J. D.

Timocreon (late 6th/early 5th cent. BC), lyric and elegiac poet, of *Ialysus on *Rhodes. He was sufficiently famous for *Aristophanes (1) to parody (*Ach.* 533 f.; *Vesp.* 1060 f.), but was remembered later chiefly for his feud with *Themistocles. Timocreon had medized (fr. 729; see MEDISM), and may have joined the court of the king of *Persia (Ath. 10. 415 f.). He attacks Themistocles for breaking his agreement to restore him to Rhodes, and mocks him for his failure to obtain the prize for excellence after *Plataea (fr. 727). The attacks continued after Themistocles' exile (fr. 729). His feud with *Simonides was equally famous (*Suda*, *Anth. Pal.* 13. 30–1; Ath. 10. 415 f.). The fragments show vigour, range of register, and a gift for *parody (*Anth. Pal.* 13. 31, fr. 727, which uses the metres of encomiastic poetry for abuse). He was also renowned as a pentathlete (see PENTATHLON) and a glutton (Ath. 10. 415 f.).

Page, *PMG* 375–8; D. A. Campbell, *Greek Lyric 4* (Loeb) (1992), 84 ff.　　C. C.

Timoleon, Corinthian who expelled *Dionysius (2) II from *Syracuse, put down other tyrants in *Sicily (see TYRANNY), and defeated *Carthage: the truth about him is not easy to discern behind our adulatory sources. In the mid-360s BC he assassinated his brother Timophanes, who exercised a brief tyranny of uncertain character at Corinth. Nothing more is known of him until two decades later, when Syracusan exiles asked Corinth for help against Dionysius II. Corinth chose Timoleon, and gave him seven ships—without crews; they were joined by two from *Corcyra and one from *Leucas. Some of the 700 mercenaries he recruited were remnants from the Third *Sacred War. He landed at *Tauromenium in 344, defeated Hicetas, tyrant of *Leontini, at Adranum, and made for Syracuse. Corinth and states of north-west Greece sent large reinforcements; Syracuse was taken, and Dionysius sent into exile at Corinth. A large Carthaginian army invaded Sicily, and Timoleon led a smaller force to victory over it at the river Crimisus. Some of the booty was sent to Corinth: part of the inscription recording its dedication is preserved (*SEG* 11. 126 A). Carthage gave assistance to tyrants of other Sicilian cities against him, but he agreed terms with the Carthaginians which limited them to the west of the island, probably to the same area as under Dionysius I, and most of the remaining tyrants were killed or expelled. He established a new Syracusan constitution. It is described as democratic, but that is unlikely: he himself had wide powers, probably as *stratēgos autokratōr*, and he secured help from two Corinthians in devising it: Corinthians had no experience of democracy. He invited settlers from mainland Greece to assist in the repopulation not only of Syracuse, but of other Sicilian cities: a figure of 60,000 is credibly reported; after the serious decline of the first half of the century Greek Sicily enjoyed a resurgence which can be traced in the archaeological record well after Timoleon himself. A further consequence was numismatic: coins of Corinthian type (*pegasi*), minted both at Corinth and in north-west Greece, seem first to have reached Sicily in quantity with Timoleon's forces; they became the standard coins of the island, and continued to arrive and circulate in huge numbers until the reign of *Agathocles (1). Timoleon resigned his office, allegedly because of blindness, died in the mid- to late 330s, and was buried in the Syracusan agora.

RE 6 A, 'Timoleon'; R. J. A. Talbert, *Timoleon and the Revival of Greek Sicily* (1974); H. D. Westlake, *Timoleon and his Relations with Tyrants* (1952), and *CAH* 6² (1994), ch. 13.   J. B. S.

Timon (*Τίμων*) (1) of Athens, the famous misanthrope, a semi-legendary character. He seems to have lived in the time of *Pericles (1). *Aristophanes (1) is the first to allude to him. He became known to Shakespeare through *Plutarch (*Ant.* 70) and *Lucian's dialogue.

PA 13845; C. Pelling, *Plutarch, Life of Antony* (1988), 291 ff.   V. E.

Timon (2) of Phlius (*c.*320–230 BC), *Sceptic, follower of *Pyrrhon. After a period of poverty in his youth, when he earned a living as a dancer, he studied in *Megara with *Stilpon and then in *Elis with Pyrrhon, and later worked as a *sophist in Chalcedon. When he had enough money, he went to Athens, where he lived until his death. Only fragments of his numerous works survive. Of his tragedies, satyr-plays (see SATYRIC DRAMA), and 'kinaidoi' (see CINAEDIC POETRY), not even the titles are given. Most fragments come from the *Silloi* (lampoons), in hexameters, a work in three books in which he ridiculed all philosophers, past and present, by contrast with Pyrrhon. Timon's *invectives against the conceit (*τῦφος*) of other philosophers, as well as his parodies (see PARODY, GREEK) of Homeric lines and scenes (see HOMER), have much in common with *Cynic writings and may have inspired *Lucian. In the *Python*, a dialogue, he recounted a conversation between himself and Pyrrhon on the way to *Delphi, in which Pyrrhon revealed to him the secret of his admirable equanimity. Timon's prose works, less popular than the *Σίλλοι*, may have contained a more philosophical exposition of sceptical arguments. In view of the connection between Pyrrhonism and Empiricist medicine (see MEDICINE, § 5. 3), it is perhaps significant that Timon had his eldest son, Xanthus, trained as a doctor.

Texts: *Suppl. Hell.* 368–95 (only verse frs.); *PPF* 173–206. Modern discussions: A. A. Long, *PCPS* 1978; M. di Marco, *Timone di Fliunte Silli* (1989).   G. S.

Timostratus, one of the latest comic poets in Athens whose fragments survive. A man of good Athenian family, he came fifth with *Λυτ*[ρούμενος] ('Man Ransoming' or 'Being Ransomed') in 188 BC, and third with *Φιλοίκειος* ('Loving the Family') in 183 (*IG* 2². 2323. 141, 155 = III B 3 col. 3a. 1, 3b. 9 Mette). His son Ariston, grandson Poses, and great-grandson Ariston seem also to have been comic poets.

Fragments: *PCG* 7 (1989), 783–6. Interpretation: Meineke, *FCG* 1. 499 f.; E. Preuner, *Rh. Mus.* 1894, 365 f.; A. Körte, *RE* 6 A 2 (1937), 1323, 'Timostratos' 2.   W. G. A.

Timotheus (1) (*c.*450–360 BC), of Miletus, famous *citharode (lyre player and singer) and dithyrambic poet (see DITHYRAMB). *Pherecrates criticizes him as the most effective musical innovator of the late 5th cent. BC (fr. 155. 19 ff. Kassel–Austin). Around 420 he won a victory as citharode over the famous Phrynis (fr. 802). In a papyrus of the 4th cent. BC large portions of his *Persians*, a citharodic nomos (see NOMOS (2)), are preserved, for which *Euripides wrote the prologue (Satyr. *Vita Eur.* fr. 39, col. 22), probably performed between 410 and 407 BC. It is an account of

the battle of Salamis mainly from a Persian point of view (see SALAMIS, BATTLE OF). The passages in which a shipwrecked Persian struggles for his life or the Persians invoke their homeland or beseech the victors in broken Greek give an especially lively picture of the events and are a sign of the mimetic character of the music. In the final lines Timotheus proclaims the newness of his art (cf. also fr. 796). The *Persians* is astrophic (see DITHYRAMB) and polymetrical, constructed mainly on iambic–trochaic and aeolic cola (see METRE, GREEK, § 4 (a and h)). The music and language of Timotheus is said to have influenced *Euripides (cf. the solo of the Phrygian slave in Eur. *Or.* 1365 ff.).

Text: Page, *PMG* 399 ff.; D. F. Sutton, *Dithyrambographi Graeci* (1989), 61 ff. Lit. and comm.: Wilamowitz, *Timotheos* (1903); Janssen, *Timotheus* (1984). Lit.: P. Maas, *RE* 6 A 2 (1937), 1331–7; M. L. West, *Greek Music* (1992), 361 ff.; E. Hall, in E. Khan (ed.), *The Birth of the European Identity*, Nottingham Class. Lit. Studies 2 (1993), 44 ff.   B. Z.

Timotheus (2), son of *Conon (1) (cf. Tod 128), Athenian general. He was a wealthy associate of *Plato (1) and *Isocrates and friend of *Jason (2), notable for modest physique, imaginative military financing (Isocrates praises him as an 'economical' general), restraint towards defeated opponents, and élitist disdain (making his eventual *rapprochement* with the assertively 'common' Iphicrates remarkable). He played a major role in establishing the *Second Athenian Confederacy (378–373)—Sparta's defeat at Alyzeia made possible the crucial Peace of 375/4 ('a new cohabitation of Victory and *Dēmos*' according to a dedication at *Delphi adorned with Praxitelean statuary; see PRAXITELES)—but unusual financial disarray in 373 led to prosecution by *Iphicrates and *Callistratus (2) and he entered service with *Artaxerxes (2) II in 372. Restored to solvency and favour, he captured *Samos (366/5) and had many successes in Hellespont, western *Thrace, and *Macedonia (365–362 or later), gaining a reputation for luck (it was said cities fell into his hands while he slept). *Amphipolis eluded him, but *Apollodorus (2)'s consequent prosecution was less successful than an earlier suit for payment of debts. In 357 his rhetoric inspired a successful lightning campaign to restore Athenian influence in *Euboea, but *Chares (1)'s denunciation, after a disagreement amongst *stratēgoi* led to defeat at Embata (356/5), finished him (see SOCIAL WAR (1)); he died in exile in *Chalcis shortly afterwards.

Isoc. 15. 101–39. *RE* 6 A, 'Timotheos' 3; Davies, *APF* 13700; *CAH* 6² (1994), chs. 6 (Seager) and 7 (Roy).   C. J. T.

Timotheus (3), Greek sculptor, active during the first half and middle of the 4th cent. BC. He took part in two important monuments of which sculptural remains survive—the temple of *Asclepius at *Epidaurus and the *Mausoleum at Halicarnassus. His share in the sculptures at Epidaurus is attested by the building inscription in which his name appears as having contracted to furnish *typoi* (reliefs?) and acroteria. *Pliny (1) (*HN* 36. 80) mentions Timotheus along with *Scopas, Bryaxis, and *Leochares as having produced the friezes of the Mausoleum. It has not been possible, however, to attribute to him any specific slabs of these friezes with any confidence, though attempts have been made. See SCULPTURE, GREEK.

B. Schlörb, *Timotheos* (1965), *JDAI* Ergänzungsheft 22; A. Stewart, *Greek Sculpture* 1 (1990), esp. 273 f.   G. M. A. R.

tin combined with copper is used to make the alloy of *bronze. Its addition to copper reduces the melting-point of the alloy, and also gives a product stronger than copper. A 4th-cent. BC inscription from *Eleusis gives the alloy composition as 8.33%

tin. Tin was also used to make pewter; five parts with two parts of lead. The principal sources available to the classical world were the Erzgebirge (cf. Scymnus 493) and western Europe. Small quantities were mined in Etruria (see ETRUSCANS) in pre-Roman times, and tin was worked at *Cirrha near *Delphi. The *Phoenicians probably controlled the Spanish tin through their settlements in the western Mediterranean. The colony of *Massalia gave the Greeks access to supplies in northern Europe and possibly Cornwall via the Rhône valley. The mythical source of tin was the *Cassiterides. There is ample evidence for the Roman pursuit of tin, including the expedition recalled by *Strabo (3. 5. 11, 176 C) of P. *Licinius Crassus (2): this either relates to an expedition between 96 and 93 BC off Spain, or in 57 BC by one of *Caesar's legates (see LEGATI) prior to the invasion of Britain.

Metallic tin must have been known to alloy in exact proportions with copper; little has survived, mainly owing to oxidization, but also because it was not of great use unalloyed. Classical writers confuse tin and *lead, because they had no clear idea of the atomic difference of metals. Mining was largely in placers; in Cornwall vein-mining was not started before late medieval times. See METALLURGY; MINES AND MINING.

See esp. Strabo 3. 175–6, Polyb. 34. 10. W. C. Borlase, *Tin-Mining in Spain Past and Present* (1897); O. Davies, *Roman Mines in Europe* (1935); *Proc. Belfast Natural History Society* 1931/2, 41; Forbes, *Stud. Anc. Technol.* 9. 124 ff.; F. Villard, *La Céramique grecque de Marseille* (1960), 137 ff.; S. Mitchell, in C. Deroux, *Studies in Latin Literature and Roman History* 3 (Coll. Latomus 180, 1983), 80 ff. (for Cornish evidence); J. D. Muhly, *AJArch.* 1985, 275 ff.; C. C. Mattusch, *Greek Bronze Statuary* (1988), 12–15 (for alloys). O. D.; D. W. J. G.

Tincommius, son of *Commius, and king of the British *Atrebates (2), *c.*25 BC–AD 1. His coinage suggests that he came under Roman influence, and he may have been supported by *Augustus to counterbalance growing Catuvellaunian power north of the Thames; see CATUVELLAUNI. Before AD 7 he had been driven into exile by his brother Eppillus and he is mentioned in the *Res Gestae of Augustus (32).

S. S. Frere, *Britannia*, 3rd edn. (1987). S. S. F.; M. J. M.

Tingis (mod. Tangier), a seaport facing Gibraltar across the Straits. It was a *Phoenician settlement, probably as early as the late 8th/early 7th cents., when Phoenician goods are attested in rural necropoleis in the hinterland; legend had it that it was founded by *Antaeus (Pomponius Mela 1. 5; Plin. *HN* 5. 2). First mentioned (as Thymiaterion) by *Hecataeus (1) of Miletus (Hanno, *Periplus* 2), it received Roman citizenship from Octavian in 38 BC (Dio Cass. 48. 45; see AUGUSTUS; CITIZENSHIP, ROMAN) as a reward for supporting him in the civil war rather than the pro-Antonian *Bogud (cf. ANTONIUS (2), M.); it was thenceforth detached from the *client kings of *Mauretania. When Mauretania became a province (see PROVINCIA) under *Claudius, Tingis became a full *colonia* and the capital of the governor (*procurator) of Mauretania Tingitana. It was cut off from Rusadir (mod. Melilla) by the Riff mountains, but was connected with *Volubilis and Sala by military roads. Its importance as a naval base lasted until the Arab conquest. Little is known archaeologically of Tingis.

PECS 923; M. Ponsich, ANRW 2. 10. 2 (1982), 787–816, and *Recherches archéologiques à Tanger et sa région* (1970).

W. N. W.; B. H. W.; R. J. A. W.

Tipasa, a Roman town in *Mauretania on the Algerian coast between Icosium (mod. Algiers) and *Caesarea (3). A Carthaginian settlement (see CARTHAGE), at least from the 6th cent. BC, it

was given Latin rights (see IUS LATII) by *Claudius when Mauretania was annexed to the Roman empire in 46 (Plin. *HN* 5. 2. 20). The town was originally situated round the harbour, but by the 2nd cent. had expanded enormously: the city walls of that date were 2.3 km. (1¼ mi.) long. It became a *colonia* (see COLONIZATION, ROMAN) before AD 200. Pagan monuments include forum, *basilica, theatre, amphitheatre, and temples; there are also numerous and important early Christian monuments, including churches, chapels, and cemeteries.

PECS 925–6; J. Baradez, *Tipasa*² (1957); S. Lancel, *Tipasa de Maurétanie*² (1971), and ANRW 2. 10. 2 (1982), 739–86; P. Aupert, *Le Nymphée de Tipasa* (1974). B. H. W.; R. J. A. W.

Tiresias, legendary seer, whose ghost was consulted by *Odysseus (*Od.* 10. 490–5, 11. 90–9). He was the resident *mantis* (seer) of the Cadmeans of *Thebes (1), surviving from the time of *Cadmus (when he was, according to *Euripides, *Bacchae*, already old) to that of the *Epigoni, that is, seven full generations. He was a pivotal figure in the Theban plays of *Sophocles (1) and Euripides, and is presented by *Pindar as an outstanding interpreter of the will of *Zeus (*Nem.* 1. 60–1).

A tradition which goes back at least to *Pherecydes (2) links Tiresias closely to the Theban legendary aristocracy, making him a descendant of Udaeus, one of the *Spartoi (*FGrH* 3 F 92). This same source tells how he was blinded because he caught sight of *Athena bathing: his mother Chariclo was a favourite of the goddess, and he was with her at the time. At her entreaty, Athena granted Tiresias the gift of prophecy (see DIVINATION, Greek) in compensation. This is the version elaborated by *Callimachus (3), *Hymn* 5.

According to the pseudo-Hesiodic *Melampodia* (see HESIOD, § 5), the blinding and the gift of prophecy came from *Hera and Zeus respectively: the goddess was displeased because Tiresias said that women enjoyed sexual intercourse more than men. The gods had asked his opinion, as he was in an excellent position to give an accurate assessment, having been both man and woman: Tiresias had wounded copulating snakes on Mt. Cyllene in *Arcadia and been turned into a woman; later, he saw them in action again and was turned back into a man (Hesiod, fr. 275 M–W; Apollod. 3. 6. 7).

Callimachus locates the blinding of Tiresias on Mt. *Helicon, and it is at the base of the Helicon massif, at the spring Tilphossa, that Tiresias met his death. He was leading the Cadmeans from Thebes after its capture by the *Epigoni, and died from drinking the water of the spring. He was buried near by (Aristophanes of Boeotia, *FGrH* 379 F 4, with Jacoby's note, and perhaps add *Pindar fr. 198b). The location of his tomb there, as well as the tradition of an *oracle of Tiresias at *Orchomenus (1), suggest that Tiresias had connections with the region at an early date, and was not exclusively a Theban figure, even to begin with.

Callimachus, *The Fifth Hymn*, ed. A. W. Bulloch (1985); G. Ugolini, *Untersuchungen zur Figur des Sehers Teiresias* (1995). A. Sch.

Tiridates (1) (*RE* 3), the supposed brother, partner in revolt, and successor in rule of Arsaces I, founder of the Parthian empire (see PARTHIA), is apocryphal.

J. Wolski, *Hist.* 1959, 222 ff. E. W. G.; B. M. L.

Tiridates (2) (*RE* 4), a pretender to the Parthian throne (see PARTHIA) in revolt against *Phraates (1) IV shortly before 31 BC and temporarily successful in dislodging him. On Phraates' recovery both contestants sought the support of Octavian (see AUGUSTUS). In 30/29 BC Octavian let Tiridates stay as a refugee in *Syria, retaining for himself as a hostage a son of Phraates kidnapped by Tiridates, but making no open offer to assist the latter. In 26 and 25 BC Tiridates carried out spring offensives as far as *Babylonia with at least the connivance of Augustus; but Augustus had no further use for Tiridates after his final ejection by Phraates (by May 25 BC), when he made an appeal for help to Augustus in Spain. The failure to eject Phraates through the instrumentality of Tiridates is ignored in Augustus' *Res gestae.

N. C. Debevoise, *A Political History of Parthia* (1958), 135 ff.

E. W. G.; B. M. L.

Tiridates (3) (*RE* 5), grandson of *Phraates (1) IV, was sent by *Tiberius to contest the Parthian throne, with the military support of L. *Vitellius, governor of *Syria (Tac. *Ann.* 6. 32). Expelling *Artabanus II, he was welcomed by the pro-Roman faction in the cities of Mesopotamia, and was crowned at Ctesiphon (AD 36); he was subsequently driven out again by Artabanus.

M. S. D.; B. M. L.

Tiridates (4) (*RE* 6), brother of *Vologeses I of Parthia, who set him on the throne of *Armenia (AD 54). He fled before the Romans and was temporarily displaced by *Tigranes (4) V, but was reinstated by Vologeses. By a compromise with Cn. *Domitius Corbulo, Tiridates agreed to journey to Rome and receive the crown of Armenia ceremonially from *Nero (AD 66). In c. AD 72 nomad Alani (see ALANS) overran his kingdom.

Tac. *Ann.* 12 ff.; Joseph. *BJ* 7. 244–51.

M. S. D.; B. M. L.

Tiryns centres on a low rocky hill in the Argive plain (see ARGOS (2)), about 4 km. (2½ mi.) north of Nauplia and 1.5 km. (1 mi.) from the sea. Inhabited intermittently from the middle neolithic phase, it became an extensive and important early Helladic II settlement, with connections extending to the *Cyclades; a remarkable feature is the tiled and two-storeyed 'round house' (*Rundbau*), 28 m. in diameter, on the upper citadel, whose function remains disputed. After an apparently universal destruction by fire at the end of early Helladic II the settlement area shrank, although still substantial. Fresco-fragments are reported from later middle Helladic and early Mycenaean contexts (see MYCENAEAN CIVILIZATION), but no impressive structures or tombs have been identified. However, the earliest parts of the preserved palace plan and fortifications date from the early 14th cent. BC, and are therefore among the first examples of the characteristically Mycenaean 'megaron' palace plan and 'Cyclopean' style of walling. The fortifications were progressively expanded to encompass the whole hill, and in later Mycenaean times the settlement again expanded around the acropolis; one building to the west has produced several Linear B texts (see MYCENAEAN LANGUAGE), and the Prophitis Ilias hill to the east was a cemetery region, where at least two tholos-tombs and many chamber-tombs have been found. The palace plan is well preserved, and the final approach to it was extremely impressive, passing through a series of propyla and courts to face the main 'megaron'; but very little was found in it apart from remains of frescos. In general, despite its impressive palace and fortifications, Tiryns is better interpreted as the second most important site in the *Mycenae state than as an independent centre; it may well have functioned as Mycenae's main port, and has produced Cretan, Cypriot, and Syro-Palestinian material. An increasing concern with defence in the late 13th cent. BC may be detected in the construction of two stone-vaulted underground tunnels from the lower citadel to natural water sources, and of vaulted galleries (to house stores or as refuges?) on the south and east. The whole site was des-

troyed by fire around 1200 BC (the excavators have attributed this to earthquake), but was reoccupied in the 12th cent. on an even larger scale, reported to cover 24 hectares, three times its previous size, reputedly on a regular, townlike plan; a smaller and narrower 'megaron' over the ruins of the great 'megaron' is dated to this time, as are the remains of an important shrine-complex in the lower citadel. It was now probably the leading settlement of the Argolid, but by the end of the bronze age had declined into a group of small villages surrounding the acropolis; a sub-Mycenaean warrior burial is nevertheless well supplied with weapons and bronze plating from a helmet, the last bronze armour before the 8th cent. BC. Tiryns was increasingly subordinated to *Argos (2) during the Dark Age (cf. T. Whitelaw and C. Morgan, *AJArch.* 1991, 79 ff.); it briefly regained enough independence (probably for the same reason as Mycenae) to send troops to the Persian War in 480–479, but was destroyed by Argos *c*.470. The surviving population went to *Halieis (Porto Cheli).

GAC, A 7; *LH Citadels*, 3 ff.; *Tiryns Forschungen und Berichte I–XI*; U. Jantzen, *Führer durch Tiryns* (1975); E. Zangger, *The Geoarchaeology of the Argolid* (1993) (ancient coastline).

O. T. P. K. D.

Tisamenus See ORESTES.

Tisamenus of Elis. See IAMUS.

Tisias of Syracuse (5th cent. BC), teacher of rhetoric, pupil of *Corax. *Plato (1) (*Phaedrus* 267a ff.) is the earliest evidence for Tisias' having taught the importance of probability (εἰκός) and the power of speech to revalue things. As with Corax, there are reasonable doubts about the form and content of his teaching.

See under CORAX for references.

D. A. R.

Tissaphernes, son of Hydarnes. Having suppressed Pissuthnes' revolt, he became *satrap of *Sardis (*c*.413 BC), receiving overall authority in western Anatolia. Instructed to collect tribute from the Greek cities, he interfered in the *Peloponnesian War, but, despite treaty-negotiations, active co-operation with Sparta soon dwindled (some blamed *Alcibiades' influence). *Cyrus (2)'s arrival in 407 sidelined Tissaphernes—and the war prospered. He took revenge by accusing Cyrus of plotting against *Artaxerxes (2) II (404), disputing control of Asiatic Greek cities after Cyrus cleared himself and resumed office, and denouncing Cyrus' insurrectionary plans in 401. Prominent at *Cunaxa and in the ensuing weeks (he negotiated with Cyrus' Greek generals and then murdered them at a meeting summoned to clarify and resolve mutual suspicions), he became Cyrus' effective successor in Anatolia. A demand for tribute from Ionia prompted Spartan intervention (400/399). His evasive military response and habit of diverting the Spartans against *Pharnabazus finally undermined his previously considerable credit with the king, perhaps even before *Agesilaus defeated his forces at Sardis (395). Invited to *Phrygia by Ariaeus, he was arrested in his bath at Colossae and executed at Celaenae. A controversial figure, his behaviour after 399 is probably that of a deceiver whose bluff has been called rather than of a would-be rebel.

RE Suppl. 7, 'Tissaphernes'; D. M. Lewis, *Sparta and Persia* (1977); H. D. Westlake, *Studies in Thucydides and Greek History* (1989); *CAH* 5² (1992), ch. 11 (Andrewes) and 6² (1994), ch. 3 (Hornblower).

C. J. T.

Titan, name inherited by *Hesiod for gods of the generation preceding the Olympians (see OLYMPIAN GODS). There is no plausible etymology unless once it meant 'king' (Hesychius interprets a word *titēnai* as 'queens'). Apart from *Cronus, there is practically no cult. Hesiod seems to have padded them out into a set of twelve (West 36): *Oceanus, Coeus, Crius, *Hyperion, *Iapetus, Theia, Rhea, *Themis, Mnemosyne, *Phoebe, *Tethys, *Cronus. (For other Titan names, see *RE* 6 A 1506–8.)

Mythologically, it is no less important to have former gods (Titans) than to have former people (*Pelasgians) so that the current order may be defined (Dowden, 135–6), hence the battle between the two sides, the 'Titanomachy'. Hittite mythology too had its 'former gods' and the imprisonment of the Titans in *Tartarus by *Zeus has its parallel (at least) in Marduk's treatment of the children of Tiamat in the Babylonian creation-epic, Enūma Eliš (cf. West on *Theogony* 133).

In 'Orphic' theology (see ORPHISM), as known to *Plato (1) and even more to Neoplatonic commentators (see NEOPLATONISM), the Titans destroyed the child *Dionysus as he played with toys and were blasted by Zeus' thunderbolt. We are, however, partly made out of their soot and as a result have a compulsive tendency to crime, to destroying the Dionysus within us, re-enacting the crimes of the Titans.

In Roman poets, Titan and Titanis are Hyperion and Phoebe, Sun and Moon. Our modern word 'titanic' derives from the monstrous power and size of the creatures preceding the rule of Zeus.

M. L. West, *Hesiod: Theogony* (1966); E. Wüst, *RE* 6 A (1937), 1491–1508; K. Dowden, *Uses of Greek Mythology* (1992).   K. D.

tithe, dekatē, the tenth part of a revenue offered as thank-offering to a god; the sense is often the same as that of *votive offering, *aparchē. For example, a certain Aeschines offered a statue to Athena as dekatē (*IG* 1³. 631). Best known are the tithes which the Athenians brought to the Eleusinian goddesses (see DEMETER; ELEUSIS; PERSEPHONE) and in a decree exhorted all Greeks to bring (*IG* 1³. 78; ML 73). See also DECUMA.   M. P. N.

Tithonus See EOS.

Titinius (*RE* 1), author of *fabulae togatae* (see FABULA; TOGATA), probably first half of 2nd cent. BC, praised for his character-drawing. Some 180 lines and 15 titles survive, showing a lively style.

H. Bardon, *La Littérature latine inconnue* (1952), 1. 39–43; and see TOGATA.   P. G. M. B.

Titius (*RE* 7), **Gaius** (2nd cent. BC), Roman *eques* (see EQUITES). *Cicero comments (*Brut.* 167) on his adroit language in both oratory and tragedy. A striking fragment of a speech survives (Macrob. *Sat.* 3. 16. 15–16).

Schanz–Hosius, § 51.   M. W.

Titius (*RE* 18), **Marcus,** Roman politician and general. He was apparently proscribed with his father Lucius in 43 BC. The father made his way to Sextus *Pompeius Magnus; the son raised a private fleet. In 40 he was captured by *Menodorus, but spared by Sextus for his father's sake; in 39 he was restored under the terms of the Pact of Misenum. He joined Mark Antony (M. *Antonius (2)), and served as his quaestor in the Parthian expedition; in 35, sent to Asia to deal with Sextus, he put him to death at Miletus, perhaps on Antony's instructions. Subsequently he became proconsul of Asia (35/4?). In 32 he and his uncle L. *Munatius Plancus deserted Antony for *Octavian, allegedly informing him of the scandalous will which Antony had deposited with the Vestals (see VESTA). In 31 he was suffect consul, and fought in the Actium campaign. Later he governed Syria (*c*.10 BC). He married into the Fabii; the origins of his own family are unknown.

T. Corbishley, *JRS* 1934, 43–9; Syme, *Rom. Rev.* and *AA*, see indexes; G. W. Bowersock, *Augustus and the Greek World* (1965), 21–2.   C. B. R. P.

Titius (*RE* 27a) **Aristo,** a Roman lawyer of high repute but possibly low birth, alive in AD 105. He learned from C. *Cassius Longinus (2), was expert in public and private law, and was admired by *Pliny (2) the Younger (*Ep.* 1. 22, 8. 14). Active as legal consultant and advocate, he perhaps acted as adviser to *Trajan. He collected decisions known as *decreta Frontiana*, perhaps rulings of the senate presided over by a consul named Fronto. Sextus *Pomponius collected various writings of Aristo under the title *Digesta* ('Ordered Abstracts'); but his work survives only in citation.

Lenel, *Pal.* 1. 59–70; Bremer, 2/2. 359–94; *RE* Suppl. 8 (1956), 857–9; 9 (1962), 1395–7; *PIR*¹ T 197; *HLL* 3 (forthcoming), § 396. 2; Kunkel 1967, 141–4; A. Longo, *Antologia Giuridica* 2. 2 (1888), 295–359.   T. Hon.

Titus (Titus Flavius (*RE* 207) **Vespasianus),** Roman emperor, AD 79–81. Born on 30 December 39, he was the elder son of *Vespasian and was brought up at court along with *Britannicus, *Claudius' son. He had considerable physical and intellectual gifts, especially in music and singing so that at one stage some viewed him as potentially a second *Nero. He married Arrecina Tertulla, daughter of the praetorian prefect of *Gaius (1) (Caligula); and she bore him a daughter, Iulia. After her death he married Marcia Furnilla, whom he later divorced. He spent his early career as a military tribune (see TRIBUNI MILITUM) in Germany and Britain, and it was probably in Lower Germany that he established his friendship with the elder *Pliny (1), who subsequently dedicated the *Natural History* to him. Although only of quaestorian rank, he joined his father in 67 in his mission to suppress the Jewish revolt, taking command of legio XV Apollinaris (see LEGION) and displaying great personal bravery. He was dispatched to convey Vespasian's congratulations to Galba, but turned back on hearing of the turmoil in Rome, pausing to consult the *oracle of Venus at *Paphos, whose allegedly encouraging response he brought to his father. He was closely involved in preparations for the Flavian bid for power which culminated on 1 July 69 when Vespasian was first acclaimed emperor by the troops in Egypt. Titus, however, remained in Judaea to take charge of the military operations and after the Flavian victory was created consul in his absence and given proconsular *imperium*. In 70 he captured *Jerusalem and was hailed as *imperator* by his troops. His exploits on campaign were recorded by the Jewish historian *Josephus, who had been befriended by the Flavians.

Hostile observers thought that Titus might use the affection of his troops to seize power for himself, since the soldiers in the east were demanding that he take them all back with him, but there is no sign of any disloyalty to his father. Once back in Rome he celebrated a *triumph with Vespasian and was elevated to share his position, receiving the tribunician power (dated from 1 July 71), holding seven consulships with him, and sharing the office of censor; he also became leader of the young men (*princeps iuventutis*) along with his brother, *Domitian. He was appointed praetorian prefect (see PRAEFECTUS PRAETORIO), a post normally held by equestrians, and incurred hostility because of his ruthless suppression of the alleged conspiracy of A. *Caecina Alienus and *Eprius Marcellus. He was also disliked for his liaison with Berenice (4), whom he had met in Judaea and who came to Rome in 75, where she probably remained until 79.

Titus succeeded smoothly after Vespasian's death on 23 June 79, and belied the fears of some by the quality of his administration. He ended, however unwillingly, his affair with Berenice, banished informers, and refused to accept treason charges. He declined to put any senator to death or confiscate property, and had a courteous relationship with the senate. Titus once memorably remarked, on observing that he had benefited no one all day, 'Friends, I have lost a day' (Suet. *Tit.* 8). He dedicated the *Colosseum begun by Vespasian, built baths, and provided lavish public spectacles. He reacted energetically to alleviate the natural disasters which occurred during his reign, the eruption of *Vesuvius in 79 and a serious fire and plague in Rome in 80. There were rumours that Titus' relationship with his brother Domitian was sometimes strained and even that he was poisoned, but his death on 13 September 81 is likely to have been from natural causes. He was remembered with affection as the 'delight and darling of the human race' (Suet. *Tit.* 1), though *Cassius Dio shrewdly commented that had he lived longer his regime might not have been judged so successful.

Sources: Suetonius, *Titus*; Cass. Dio 66. 17–26; Josephus, *Jewish War*; Modern discussions: M. Fortina, *L'Imperatore Tito* (1955); H. Castritius, *Hist.* 1969, 492; B. W. Jones, *The Emperor Titus* (1984).   J. B. C.

Tityus, a son of Earth (*Gaia), whom *Odysseus saw in *Hades, covering nine acres of ground, while two vultures tore at his liver, as a punishment for assaulting *Leto (*Od.* 11. 576–81). The seat of desire is appropriately punished. He was killed by *Zeus (Hyg. *Fab.* 55), *Apollo (Ap. Rhod. 1. 759 ff.), *Artemis (Pind. *Pyth.* 4. 90; in Euphorion, fr. 105 Powell, she was defending herself, not her mother), or Apollo and Artemis (Apollod. 1. 23). For variants in his story, which are numerous, see Waser in Roscher, 'Tityus'.   H. J. R.

Tivoli See TIBUR.

Tlepolemus, son of *Heracles (by Astyoche or Astydamia) and founder of the Rhodian cities (see RHODES). On reaching maturity he killed his father's uncle *Licymnius (1), either accidentally or in a quarrel, and fled to Rhodes (*Il.* 2.661 ff.; by oracular instruction, Pind. *Ol.* 7. 31 ff.). He led troops to *Troy, and was killed by *Sarpedon, though wounding him severely (*Il.* 5. 628 ff.).

A. Bresson, in *Les Grandes Figures religieuses*, Centre de recherche d'histoire ancienne, Besançon, 68 (1986), 411–21.   H. J. R.; E. Ke.

Tmolus (*Τμῶλος*), the deity of the Lydian mountain so named (see LYDIA). He appears, with *Midas (1), as judge of the contest between *Apollo and *Pan (Ov. *Met.* 11. 156 ff.), and as a coin-figure.

toga The toga was the principal garment of the free-born Roman male. It was also worn by *Etruscan men and originally also by women. It was usually made of undyed light wool, but for mourning was of dark wool, the *toga pulla*, and, for boys of high birth and the holders of certain offices, it had a *purple *praetexta* border along its upper edge. A decorated version worn by victorious commanders in triumphal processions, the *toga picta* or *trabea triumphalis*, was made of purple wool and gold thread.

In shape the toga was a very large semicircle, a single piece of cloth which in the 1st cent. AD measured up to 5.5 × 2.75 m. (19½ × 10 ft.) It was worn without a fastening and the wearer had to keep his left arm crooked to support its voluminous drapery. It was put on thus: one corner was placed before the feet and the straight edge was taken up and over the left shoulder, across the back and under or over the right arm, across the chest, and over the left shoulder again, the second corner hanging behind the knees; the curved edge became the garment's hem. By the imperial period, two features had developed which helped

to accommodate the garment's increased size: an *umbo* or 'navel' at the waist, resulting from the upper part of the under layer being pulled over the second layer, and a *sinus* or 'lap', created by folding down the straight edge where it passed under the right arm. In the 3rd cent. AD the *umbo* was generally folded into a band lying across the wearer's chest, and in the 4th cent. the *sinus* was usually long enough to be thrown over the left forearm.

As a result of Roman conquests the toga spread to some extent into the Roman western provinces, but in the east it never replaced the Greek rectangular mantle, the *himation* or *pallium*. Its increased size and cost caused it to decline among ordinary Romans, but portrait statues record its use by wealthier citizens at least until the end of the 4th cent. AD. A late version, smaller and decorated, is familiar from the ivory diptychs of the consuls. In the long term the toga developed into the sash-like *loros*, a vestment exclusive to the Byzantine emperor. See DRESS.

Quint. *Inst.* 2. 3. 137–42; Tertullian, *De pallio* 5. L. M. Wilson, *The Roman Toga* (1924).   H. G.-T.

togata (sc. *fabula*, 'drama in a toga'—though not all the characters are likely to have worn a *toga), a type of comedy written at Rome in the 2nd cent. BC, also apparently known as *tabernaria* ('private-house drama'). Three principal authors are known, all surviving in fragments only: *Titinius (perhaps earlier than Terence), L. *Afranius (1), and T. *Quinctius Atta (died 77 BC). The plays (in verse—and played in *masks?) showed Italian characters of all classes in Italian or Roman settings; Roman names occur in the fragments, and some interesting differences from the *palliata are reported: Donatus on Ter. *Eun.* 57 'In the palliata comic playwrights are allowed to portray slaves as wiser than their masters, which is generally not permitted in the togata' (but deceptions by slaves seem to have been found); and *Quintilian 10. 1. 100 remarks on the pederastic themes in Afranius (themes more or less excluded from New Comedy (see COMEDY (GREEK), NEW) and *palliata*). But the dramatic motifs and plots seem often to be those of (Greek) New Comedy, with love and family relationships central, and *parasites, prostitutes, and slaves among the cast. In the same tradition, Afranius used gods and goddesses or abstract concepts (such as Wisdom) to introduce the plays, and he also followed *Terence in using a prologue to reply to his critics; in his prologue to *Compitalia* ('The Crossroads Festival') he declared his debt to *Menander (1) and praised Terence. The fragments include some lines in lyric metres as well as iambics and trochaics. We know of occasional revivals in the following two centuries, and *Juvenal 1. 3 speaks of *togatae* written for recitation in his day. See COMEDY, LATIN; METRE, LATIN, § 2 (*b*).

Fragments: Ribbeck, *CRF*; A. Daviault (1981)—but see reviews in *CR* 1982 and *Gnomon* 1982; Titinius and Atta ed. T. Guardi (1984). F. Leo, *Geschichte der römischen Literatur* (1913), 374 ff.; W. Beare, *Hermathena* 1940, 35 ff., and *The Roman Stage*³ (1964), 128 ff.; E. Rawson, *PBSR* 1985, 106 ff.; T. Guardi, *Dioniso* 1991.   P. G. M. B.

toilet See COSMETICS.

tolerance See INTOLERANCE, INTELLECTUAL AND RELIGIOUS.

Tolmides, 5th cent. BC Athenian *stratēgos* See ORCHOMENUS (1); TANAGRA; THEBES (1). Also CORONEA, BATTLE OF (where he was defeated and killed).

Tolosa (mod. Toulouse), developed at an important pre-Roman road and river junction, and under *Augustus completely superseded other Hallstatt–La Tène sites (St-Roch, Butte de Cluzel, Vieille-Toulouse) to its south. In 106 BC Tolosa was wantonly sacked by the consul Q. *Servilius Caepio (1), who carried off a huge spoil. Under the empire Tolosa possessed *ius Latii and perhaps the title of colony (Ptol. 2. 10. 6). Always renowned for its literary culture, its most famous son was, however, the warrior *Antonius Primus. From 418 it was the capital of the Visigothic kingdom (regnum Tolosanum). Its ancient remains are scanty.

M. Labrousse, Toulouse antique (1968); A. L. F. Rivet, Gallia Narbonensis (1988); H. Wolfram, History of the Goths (1988). C. E. S.; J. F. Dr.

Tomis (Tomi; mod. Constantsa). Literary sources describe Tomis as a colony of the Milesians (e.g. Ps.-Scymnus, 765–6; Ov. Tr. 1. 10, 3. 9; see MILETUS; COLONIZATION, GREEK), but give no date for its foundation, which the majority of archaeologists place in the 6th cent. BC. The earliest Greek material evidence dates from c.550 BC: before the arrival of Greeks there seems to have been a local settlement on the site, which lies on a narrow elevated promontory. However, excavation is obstructed by the modern city. Tomis was the place of *Ovid's exile as set out in his Tristia and Ex Ponto.

L. Stoian, Inscriptiones Scythiae minoris, II: Tomis (1986); D. Kacharava and G. Kvirkvelia, Goroda i poseleniya Prichernomor'ya antichnoy epokhi (1991), 275–80. D. C. B.

topos, a standard form of rhetorical argumentation or a variably expressible literary commonplace.

In classical rhetoric, inventio aids the orator to find elements of persuasion: τόποι or loci are both the places where such elements (especially plausible argumentative patterns) lurk, and those patterns themselves (e.g. Arist. Rh. 2. 22–3; Quint. Inst. 5. 10); if universally applicable (in various senses) they can be called κοινοὶ τόποι or loci communes. They are the habitual tools of ordinary thought but can also be studied and technically applied. No two rhetoricians provide the same catalogue, but some of the more familiar τόποι include arguments ad hominem or a fortiori, from homonymy or *etymology, from antecedents or effects.

Although in this sense the ancient discussions remain important for contemporary analyses of everyday argumentation, the general decline of rhetoric in modern culture has led topoi, like other rhetorical concepts, to seek refuge in literary studies. The recent critical topos of applying the term also, and especially, to commonly but variably expressed literary contents (clichéd metaphors and commonplace thoughts) ultimately derives from E. R. Curtius, who sought in his European Literature and the Latin Middle Ages to refound the cultural unity of Europe upon the heritage of Latin rhetoric. Correspondingly, many of Curtius's own examples—'brevitas-formula', the composition of a poem as a nautical voyage, 'emphasis on inability to do justice to the topic', 'I bring things never said before', 'praise of forebears and their deeds', etc.—remain closely linked to traditional rhetorical structures. But his extension of the concept from rhetorical forms to literary contents paved the way for the banalizing inclusion of unformalized commonplaces (already Curtius, who sometimes linked topoi with unconscious 'archetypes', included 'all must die', 'ape as metaphor', *locus amoenus, 'perpetual spring', puer senex, 'the world upside-down'). To be sure, communication both ordinary and literary depends upon shared premisses, and novelty, like familiarity, can only be perceived against the background of what is already known. Ancient authors, perhaps because their audience was more restricted and shared with them a more limited cultural background, seem to have been fonder of such commonplaces than modern ones and to have drawn upon a smaller stock (sometimes doubtless supplied by appropriate rhetorical manuals). But they can use them for very different purposes (e.g. to create complicity with the audience, to advertise generic affiliations, to vary surprisingly in detail or context, to provide reassurance by not varying) and may often have believed in their truth. See COMMUNES LOCI; PROGYMNASMATA.

E. R. Curtius, European Literature and the Latin Middle Ages² (1990; Ger. orig. 1948); L. Hunter, Toward a Definition of Topos (1991).

G. W. M., G. B. C.

torch-race (lampadedromia), a spectacular ritual race, normally a relay, in which fire was taken from one altar to another. Most of the evidence comes from Athens, where lexicographers say three torch-races were held, at the *Panathenaea, the Hephaestea, and the Promethea (see PROMETHEUS); three more are in fact attested before the end of the 4th cent., for *Pan, for *Bendis (on horseback—a great novelty), and for *Nemesis of *Rhamnus, and several others emerge in the Hellenistic period. It was the form of ritual activity most distinctively associated with the *ephēboi (Xen. Poroi 4. 52; BCH 1877, 11), a matchless competitive display of dexterity and speed.

J. Jüthner, RE 12, λαμπαδηδρομία; D. S. Kyle, Athletics in Ancient Athens (1987); N. V. Sekunda, ZPE 83 (1990). R. C. T. P.

Torone, important north Greek city near the end of the middle prong (Sithonia) of *Chalcidice, on the south-western side, and 'one of the largest and richest cities of Chalcidice' (Cambitoglou and Papadopoulos 1988, 186) at least until 432 BC and the rise of *Olynthus as centre of the new Chalcidic league or state, for which see CHALCIDICE. (There is some evidence for tension between Torone and Olynthus, see e.g. Thuc. 4. 110. 2; in the 5th cent. at least, Torone remained separate from the league, partly through relative geographical remoteness.) The usual view that Torone was colonized from *Euboea is not altogether borne out by recent Greek/Australian excavations, to which, together with *Thucydides (2)'s rich and detailed account at 4. 110–16, we owe most of our knowledge of Torone's topography. There was a well-fortified acropolis (partly excavated), ending in the 'Lekythos' ('oil-bottle') promontory, on which stood a temple of Athena (a potsherd inscribed ΑΘΗ- has been found, SEG 37 no. 589) and the fort mentioned by Thucydides (4. 113); in addition there were three other promontories. The cemeteries of Torone have yielded finds of great interest. Torone controlled both a useful harbour immediately below the city site and an excellent, deep, sheltered harbour away to the south, the Kophos limen or 'still harbour' (modern Porto Koupho); and it possessed extensive territory. Torone began coining in the early 5th cent. BC. There are indications that it was already regionally pre-eminent in the *Persian Wars (Hdt. 8. 127); it belonged to the *Delian League in the 5th cent., paid 6 talents tribute to Athens (this was doubled in 430/29, making a notably high total), did not join the Olynthian/Chalcidian revolt from Athens in 432, and generally stood apart from the rest of Chalcidice until 424/3. In that year the Spartan *Brasidas took Torone thanks to oligarchic sympathizers, force, and what Brasidas chose to regard as an *epiphany by Athena. *Cleon won it back for Athens in 422. In the 4th cent. it was captured by the Spartan king Agesipolis (380), at which time it did belong to the Chalcidic league. Then, after Sparta's temporary dissolution of the League, Torone was independent until the Athenian *Timotheus (2) captured it in the 360s (Isoc. 15. 113, bracketing Torone and *Potidaea as places with excellent positions); it succumbed to *Philip (1) II of Macedon in 349 and shrank in size after *Cassander's *synoecism of Cassandreia (former Potidaea) in 316. Finds from excavations on the site can be seen in the museums at Polygiros and Thessalonike.

Thuc. 4. 116–20 and 5. 2–3; Xen. *Hell.* 5. 3. 18; *CAH* 6² (1994), index; B. Meritt, *AJA* 1923, 447 ff.; M. Zahrnt, *Olynth und die Chalkidier* (1971), 247–51 and in *Lexikon der historischen Stätten* 689; Hornblower, *Comm. on Thuc.*; A. Cambitoglou and J. Papadopoulos, *Torone 1* (forthcoming, and meanwhile see their reports on work since 1975 in *Mediterranean Archaeology* 1988, 180–217; 1990, 93–142; 1991, 147–71; 1994, 141 ff.); J. Papadopoulos, *OJA* 1996; S. Hornblower, *OJA* 1997. S. H.

torture at Athens and under the Roman republic was normally thought inappropriate for citizens. It might be used on slaves (see SLAVERY) and perhaps on foreigners, for example prisoners of war. Slaves might be tortured in order to extract confessions of their own guilt or evidence against other persons (the unreliability of this second kind of evidence seems to have been recognized in practice at Athens). At Rome the investigation by torture was called *quaestio*; the evidence of the tortured was not *testimonium*. Evidence under torture by slaves was not accepted against their own masters, except in matters such as treason and sacrilege, as with the Catilinarian conspirators (see SERGIUS CATILINA, L.) (Cic. *Part. Or.* 118). Augustus extended these exceptions to include *adultery in certain situations (*Dig.* 48. 5. 28 pref.) but preserved the letter of the principle by having the slaves sold to a representative of the public (Cass. Dio 55. 5; the change is wrongly ascribed to *Tiberius by Tac. *Ann.* 2. 30, cf. 3. 67). A master might prefer to liberate slaves liable to torture and it is perhaps for this reason that we first hear of the torture of free men of humble status under the Principate (Cass. Dio 57. 19; *Dig.* 48. 18. 1. 13). But we also find occasionally the torture of men of status suspected of conspiracy (Tac. *Ann.* 11. 22; 15. 56)—a practice with a long history: see, for the reign of *Alexander (3) the Great, PHILOTAS. In general we find emperors during the Principate urging that the use of torture be confined to serious cases and arguing that evidence taken under torture was fragile (*Dig.* 48. 18. 1 *pass.*); the general line taken is that torture should not be resorted to unless there is other evidence of guilt. However, we can draw no secure inference from this about what happened in practice. In the late empire torture of humbler citizens seems to have become accepted and was even extended to civil proceedings, though there was never much use of torture in civil suits (*Cod. Theod.* 2. 27. 1. 2a; *Cod. Just.* 9. 41. 15). A. W. L.

tourism (see TRAVEL). Well-known Greek tourists include *Solon, said (Hdt. 1. 30) to have visited Egypt and Lydia 'for the sake of seeing' (*theōria*), and *Herodotus (1) himself. Sea-borne *trade and sightseeing were surely companions from an early date, as they still were in the 4th cent. (Isoc. *Trapeziticus* 17. 4). A genre of Greek periegetic ('travel') literature arose by the 3rd cent., from which date fragments survive of a descriptive work, *On the Cities in Greece*, by Heraclides Criticus (ed. F. Pfister (1951); for partial trans. see Austin 83); the only fully preserved work of this type is *Pausanias (3) (see POLEMON (3)). Under Rome ancient sightseeing came into its own. A papyrus (*PTeb.* 1. 33 = Bagnall and Derow 58) of 112 BC gives instructions to prepare for a Roman senator's visit to the *Fayūm, including titbits for the crocodiles; the colossi of *Memnon and other pharaonic monuments are encrusted with Greek and Latin graffiti. Greece too was a firm favourite (for the itinerary see Livy 45. 27–8). Roman tourists were wealthy, their numbers restrained (cf. the 18th cent. Grand Tour in Europe); they might combine sightseeing (artworks, monuments, natural phenomena) with overseas study (as with *Cicero), thermal cures, and visits to *sanctuaries. See PILGRIMAGE (CHRISTIAN).

L. Casson, *Travel in the Ancient World* (1974). J.-M. André and M.-F.

Baslez (eds.), *Voyager dans l'antiquité* (1993), esp. ch. 9. A. J. S. S.

towns See URBANISM.

Toxaris, one of the two speakers in *Lucian's fictional essay of the same name, representing him as a Scythian visitor to Athens, given heroic honours there after his death in gratitude for good medical advice sent by him in a dream in time of plague.

C. Jones, *Culture and Society in Lucian* (1986), 56 ff. A. J. S. S.

toys (παίγνια, *ioculi*). Specimens from children's tombs, and representations on Greek pottery vases provide our knowledge of ancient toys, which did not differ essentially from modern ones. For the infant there were clappers and rattles (πλαταγή, *crepitaculum*), hinged surfaces of wood or revolving circles with bells or rings of metal, or in animal form with loose pebbles inside. *Crepundia* (γνωρίσματα) were miniature objects and charms hung around the infant's neck; in literature these often served to identify abandoned or kidnapped children. Bells (κώδων, *tintinnabulum*) served the double purpose of amusement and averting the evil eye. For a more advanced age the doll of rag, bone, wood, or clay was the customary plaything; the limbs were often movable (νευρόσπαστα). Doll's house furniture, chairs, couches, toilet and kitchen utensils, were used as toys as well as for *votive offerings; it was customary for girls on marriage and boys on arrival at puberty to dedicate their playthings to deities. Animals, chariots and horses in wood or clay, go-karts, and whipping-tops are represented in museums, while the use of toy wind-assisted chariots, the ball (σφαῖρα, *pila*), and hoop (τροχός, *trochus*) is illustrated on painted pottery, as are the swing and see-saw. Regular games were played with knucklebones (ἀστράγαλος, *talus*), dice (κύβος, *tessara*), and other pieces.

R. Schmidt, *Die Darstellung von Kinderspielzeug und Kinderspiel in der griechischen Kunst* (1977); A. E. Klein, *Child Life in Greek Art* (1932); H. Rühfel, *Kinderleben im klassischen Athen* (1984); British Museum, *Guide to ... Greek and Roman Life*³ (1929), 'Toys'. F. N. P.; M. V.

Trabea (*RE* 2), author of *fabulae palliatae* (two fragments in Ribbeck, *CRF*), perhaps earlier than Caecilius; he could stir the emotions, according to Varro. See PALLIATA.

J. Wright, *Dancing in Chains* (1974). P. G. M. B.

trade, Greek Exchange in some form has probably existed since the emergence of the first properly human social groups. Trade, whether local, regional, or international, is a much later development. It is a certain inference from the extant documentary records in Linear B script that the world of Mycenaean age palace-economy knew all three main forms of commerce (see MYCENAEAN CIVILIZATION; MYCENAEAN LANGUAGE), and a reasonable guess that a considerable portion of the long-distance carrying trade was in the hands of specialized professional traders. But whether that trade was 'administered' or 'free-enterprise' is impossible to say. It is one sign among many of the economic recession experienced by the Greek world generally between about 1200 and 800 BC that in these dark centuries regional and international trade dwindled to vanishing-point; the few known professional traders were typically men of non-Greek, especially *Phoenician, origin.

In book 8 of *Homer's *Odyssey* the sea-battered hero finds his way at last to the comparative calm and safety of Phaeacia, a never-never land set somewhere in the golden west (see SCHERIA), only to be roundly abused by a Phaeacian aristocrat for looking like a sordidly mercenary merchant skipper rather than a gentleman amateur sportsman. *Hesiod, composing perhaps about the same time (*c*.700 BC) in inland, rural *Boeotia, was prepared to concede that a moderately prosperous peasant farmer might load the surplus of the grain-crop produced by himself and his small workforce into his own modest boat and dispose of it down the nearby coast during the dead season of the agricultural year immediately after the grain-harvest. But to be a full-time trader was no more acceptable to Hesiod than to Homer's Phaeacian aristocrat. Each in his way was waging an ideological polemic against the development of professional trading (*emporia*) and traders (*emporoi*).

This prejudice issued from a world ruled and dominated by landed aristocrats. It was perfectly all right for a Greek aristocrat to visit his peers in other communities, then just acquiring the newfangled constitutional form of the **polis*, bearing gifts of richly woven garments or finely wrought metalwork, and to come home laden with comparable or even more lavish prestations. It was quite another matter to spend most of the recognized sailing season (late March to late September) plying the Mediterranean with a mixed cargo of, say, perfume flasks from *Corinth, hides from *Euboea, salt fish from the Black Sea (SEE EUXINE), and wine-amphorae from *Chios, making only a humble living and precluded from participating in the military and political activities that defined the status of an élite leader of his *polis*. Such trading was considered an occupation suitable only for the lower orders of Greek society, the dependants (possibly unfree) of a great landlord.

Yet the significance of traders in the early *polis* era of Homer and Hesiod must not be confused with the significance of trade, especially long-distance sea-borne commerce. Without the latter there would have been no opening from the Aegean to both east (for example, the multinational *emporion* at *Al Mina on the Orontes) and west (notably Ischia-*Pithecusae (Pithekoussai)), beginning in the half-century from 825 to 775, no movement of colonization to southern Italy, Sicily, and the Black Sea (see COLONIZATION, GREEK), no comparative knowledge of other, non-Greek cultures and thus no alphabet (see ALPHABET, GREEK)—and so, maybe, no Homer and Hesiod. By 600 BC the economic position and social status of traders may have improved, with the development of purpose-built sail-driven, round-hulled merchantmen (see SHIPS), the creation of institutions and techniques designed to facilitate multinational commerce, and the establishment of permanent *emporia* in Egypt and Etruria (see EMPORION, first entry).

*Naucratis in the Nile delta was founded in about 630 by Greek traders from western Asia Minor, the adjacent Greek islands, and *Aegina, under the auspices of the Egyptian pharaoh *Psammetichus (Psamtik). In return for Greek oil, wine, and luxury goods the Greek traders of Naucratis received Egyptian grain, metals, and slaves, from which exchange the Egyptian treasury derived extra value in taxes. Permanent transnational market-centres and ports of trade were thus established under official governmental direction, linking economies of dissimilar type. Soon Naucratis had an Italian counterpart at Gravisca (see TARQUINII) in Etruria, the happy hunting-ground of one Sostratus of Aegina.

This Sostratus, who may be identical with the Sostratus of *Herodotus (1) (4. 152), specialized in the run between Etruria and the Aegean by way of the haulway (*diolkos*) built across the isthmus of Corinth in about 600. He was a free citizen, literate (in addition to his dedication to *Apollo at Gravisca he used personalized merchant-marks on the pots he carried), and an independent entrepreneur who presumably owned his own merchant ship (or ships). Perhaps he knew some Etruscan, as the

Phocaean and Samian merchants who traded further westwards to the south of France and Spain knew the local Celtic languages and, as surviving business letters on lead attest, employed locals in their import–export businesses. A similar lead letter of the 6th cent. has survived from the other, eastern end of the world of Archaic Greek commerce, at Berezan (Olbia) in the Black Sea. But this tells an apparently darker and possibly more typical tale of (allegedly) illicit detention and confiscation; and one of the traders involved seems to have been a dependent agent-trader not a free trader working on his own behalf.

By the middle of the 5th cent. the place of Al Mina, Naucratis, and Gravisca had been taken by Athens' newly developed port city of *Piraeus. It was the Athenians' famous victory at *Salamis that enabled the development of Piraeus into a commercial as well as military harbour facility. A century later, *Isocrates hailed its creation: 'for Athens established the Piraeus as a market in the centre of Hellas—a market of such abundance that the articles which it is difficult to obtain, one here, one there, from the rest of the world, all these it is easy to produce from Athens' (*Panegyricus* 42). This testimony is corroborated by archaeology and echoed by writers as diverse as *Thucydides (2), the *Old Oligarch, and Athenian comic playwrights. As early as 421, we learn from Eupolis' *Marikas*, the characteristic institution of the maritime or bottomry loan (see MARITIME LOANS) had been developed to finance long-distance trade, above all in the staple necessity, grain, on the regular large-scale importation of which Athens had come to depend both economically and (since it was the poor majority of citizens who mainly benefited) politically.

During the currency of her 5th-cent. empire Athens, thanks to her permanently commissioned fleet of *trireme warships, was able to suppress *piracy, one of the major threats to peaceful commerce throughout antiquity, as well as to direct trade towards the Piraeus on economically favourable terms. Loss of empire was among other things bad for Aegean Greek trade generally, and bad for Athens' access to staple grain and the raising of taxes and dues on shipping and goods in particular. Over the course of the 4th cent. a whole series of legal measures was enacted by Athens to compensate for loss of military power (several mentioned in *Athenaion politeia). A combination of the stick (penalties for residents who contracted loans on cargoes of grain bound elsewhere than to Piraeus, or for not offloading a certain minimum percentage of a cargo there, and so on) and the carrot (establishment for the benefit of Athens-based traders of new specialized maritime courts; granting permission to foreign traders to set up on Attic soil sanctuaries for their native gods—*Isis and Astarte) was employed to good effect.

One measure practised by trading communities in other periods was significantly conspicuous by its absence: the Athenians never discriminated in favour of their own citizen merchants. This was partly no doubt because they constituted a small minority of the trading and commercial population, but it was also because the barriers between citizen status and the status of the majority (*metics, slaves) involved were high and sturdy—as the exceptional breach in the case of *Pasion amply proves. (See CITIZENSHIP, GREEK; SLAVERY; STATUS, LEGAL AND SOCIAL, *Greek.*) See also MARKETS AND FAIRS; SYMBOLON; TRADERS.

J. Chadwick, *The Mycenaean World* (1976); J. D. Muhly, 'Homer and the Phoenicians: The Relations between Greece and the Near East in the Late Bronze and Early Iron Ages', *Berytus* 1970, 19–64; J. Boardman, *The Greeks Overseas: Their Early Colonies and Trade* (1980); L. Casson, *The Ancient Mariners*, 2nd edn. (1992); J. B. Salmon, *Wealthy Corinth: A History of the City to 338 BC* (1984); F. Meijer and O. van Nijf, *Trade,*

Transport and Society in the Ancient World: A Sourcebook (1992); R. J. Hopper, *Trade and Industry in Classical Greece* (1979); R. Garland, *The Piraeus* (1987); P. Garnsey, *Famine and Food Supply in the Graeco-Roman World* (1988); R. Sallares, *The Ecology of the Ancient Greek World* (1991); P. J. Rhodes, *A Commentary on the Aristotelian Athenaion Politeia* (1981); Y. Garlan, 'Les Pirates', in *Guerre et économie en Grèce ancienne* (1989), 173–201; J. Hasebroek, *Trade and Politics in Ancient Greece* (Ger. orig. 1928; Eng. trans. 1933); P. Garnsey, C. R. Whittaker, and K. Hopkins (eds.), *Trade in the Ancient Economy* (1983).   P. A. C.

trade, Roman The central issue for historians has long been, and remains, how to characterize properly the scale and importance of trade and commerce in the overall economy of the Roman empire. Some seek to emphasize how different, and essentially backward, the Roman *economy was in comparison to the modern. They point to the Roman élite's apparent snobbish contempt for commerce (Cic. *Off.* 1. 150–1). The primacy of *agriculture cannot be denied, and it is noteworthy that the Roman *agricultural writers, with the large landowner in mind, betray both very little interest in markets and an aversion to risk which did not inspire entrepreneurial experiments. Factories in the modern sense did not exist in the ancient world (see INDUSTRY). Cities did not grow up as centres of manufacturing; far from it, they can be represented merely as centres of consumption (see URBANISM). The cost and difficulty of transport, particularly over land, are claimed to have made it uneconomic to trade over long distances anything other than luxury products. Of course, basic goods, such as *wine, *olive oil, and grain, also *pottery of all kinds, can be demonstrated to have been carried in large quantities over long distances. But, it is argued, something other than the free-market mechanism is at work here. First, there was the considerable circulation of goods within the extensive households of the rich, from their estates to their town houses, to their retinues and clients. Further, staples could be exchanged in large quantities as gifts between members of the élite. Examples can be identified at all periods and it has been demonstrated plausibly that such a mechanism was particularly important in the later Roman empire. The circulation of goods within the household of the emperor is the same phenomenon writ large. Secondly, and more importantly, it is claimed that the movement of staples was primarily an act of redistribution, organized by the central government, and on a smaller scale by local communities, to ensure the supply of essentials to the large cities, such as Rome, and to maintain the Roman armies, precisely because the private sector was not up to meeting needs on such a scale (see FOOD SUPPLY).

A different model has been proposed. While it is true that the Roman aristocracy on the whole maintained a distance from direct involvement in trade, even they can, and did, benefit from its profits through intermediaries (see e.g. Plut. *Cat. Mai.* 21). Besides, beyond Rome, it is much less clear that local élites shared the same distaste for trade, with investments, frequently managed by their *freedmen, in potteries, *mines, *textile production, and the like. The landowners needed markets for their products, but were able to affect a lack of interest in trade, because the whole process, often starting with a contract to gather the crop, lay in the hands of *negotiatores. The landowner was provided with a certain return, while the *negotiator* had to organize the trade and to take the risks (for an example of miscalculation of those risks see Plin. *Ep.* 8. 2). The number of *shipwrecks in the Mediterranean recorded for the period 100 BC to AD 300 is much larger than for either the preceding period or the Dark Ages; this suggests a level of operation which was not

to be reached again until the high Renaissance. The greatest spur to the development of this trade was the creation of a fully monetarized economy throughout the empire (see MONEY). Barter, exchanges in kind, of course, continued to exist; but it is quite clear from Egyptian papyri that the use of money in transactions was the norm. Strabo (7. 5. 5), in the early empire, could go out of his way to note the lack of use of coin among the Dalmatians, as a characteristic of barbarian peoples. The availability of coin could, and did, vary from place to place and time to time. This made the existence of bankers (see BANKS) who could provide *credit to facilitate deals essential. It is true that the empire did not see the growth of large international banks; but at the local level money-lenders were the key to exchanges both large and small. There are those historians who see in the spread of the use of money the creation of a Roman unified 'world economy'. This is a clear exaggeration. The empire consisted of a range of regional economies at different stages of development, which linked up with each other in ways which changed with time.

At the regional level regular markets (*nundinae*) were vital. They are found throughout the empire and were as important, perhaps more so, to the peasant as to the large landowner. The existence of these markets was strictly regulated. The senate had to be petitioned for permission to hold markets; many such requests came from large landowners who wished to hold markets on their estates. The reason for the control was probably to limit competition with well-established markets in the local towns (Plin. *Ep.* 5. 4, 5. 13). This suggests that at this local level the volume of trade in the countryside was somewhat limited. There are signs that some products circulated largely on a regional basis (the distribution of Roman *lamps, which were traded over surprising distances, nevertheless reveals several broad regional patterns of trade) (see MARKETS AND FAIRS).

At the other end of the scale came the huge cities, such as Rome. These constituted enormous markets. Much is made of the state-sponsored system for supplying Rome with corn. However, state grain met no more than a portion of the city's annual grain needs. The rest had to be supplied by the free market. Furthermore, the importation of the state grain depended upon private traders, who in times of crisis had to be offered considerable incentives to involve themselves in the trade (Suet. *Claud.* 18). *Monte Testaccio, the dump of Spanish oil amphorae, behind the port on the Tiber in Rome, is testimony to the enormous trade in oil (estimated at some 23 million kgs. per year). The annual consumption of wine in the city has been put at between 1 and 1.8 million hectolitres. For much of the empire all this was provided by the free market. Only later did oil and wine become part of the *annona* (see FOOD SUPPLY). The city of Rome was an enormous stimulus to trade.

The expansion of the empire itself could open up major new markets to be exploited. The most researched example is the large market among the Gauls for Italian wine, particularly from the west coast of Italy. However, it is all too easy to exaggerate the effect of these new markets on the agrarian economy of Italy. There were transformations, but they were confined largely to coastal regions within easy reach of ports, and they were limited in time. By the 1st cent. AD these regions were having to compete with expanding trade in wine from Spain and south Gaul. See AMPHORAE AND AMPHORAE STAMPS, ROMAN.

Because pottery survives on archaeological sites, its importance in trade can be exaggerated. However, it is clear that the industrial scale of production of *terra sigillata* in Gaul presupposes something more than a local market. Pottery on the whole was not often the primary cargo of ships, but it was frequently a part-cargo and could be an important commodity for the return leg of voyages, whose primary concern was the transport of more valuable goods. See POTTERY, ROMAN.

Trade was carried on beyond the limits of the Roman empire. Most notable was the trade in luxuries, *spices, ivories (see ELE-PHANTS; IVORY), etc. beyond the *Red Sea with the East Coast of *Africa and *India. A Greek papyrus in Vienna (*PVindob*. G40822) records one such transaction, involving nard, ivory, and textiles to a value of over 130 talents. When it is realized that some of the large ships on the eastern run could carry up to 150 such cargoes, the potential profitability of the trade is amply demonstrated. However, the handbook from the 1st cent. AD, the *Periplus Maris Erythraei* ('The Voyages round the Red Sea': see PERIPLOI), shows that although the primary interest was in these very valuable goods, shippers were also on the look-out for more mundane staples to fill their holds.

Large-scale trade continued right through the late empire. In some ways traders became less independent, more tied into work for the imperial government or for the great aristocratic houses. The patterns changed somewhat, with more regional trade and less international. This, however, should not be taken as a sign of a major decline in the system which constituted such an important part of the overall economy of the Roman empire.

J. H. D'Arms, *Commerce and Social Standing in Ancient Rome* (1981); P. Garnsey and others, *Trade in the Ancient Economy* (1983); J. M. Frayn, *Markets and Fairs in Roman Italy* (1993); J. H. D'Arms and E. C. Kopff (eds.), *The Seaborne Commerce of Ancient Rome: Studies in Archaeology and History* (1980); K. Greene, *The Archaeology of the Roman Economy* (1986); R. Duncan-Jones, *Structure and Scale in the Roman Economy* (1990); W. V. Harris (ed.), *The Inscribed Economy*, JRA suppl. ser. 6 (1993); G. Rickman, *The Corn Supply of Ancient Rome* (1980); P. Garnsey, *Famine and Food Supply in the Graeco-Roman World* (1988); D. P. S. Peacock and D. F. Williams, *Amphorae and the Roman Economy* (1986); A. Tchernia, *Le Vin de l'Italie romaine* (1986); *Producción y comercio del aceite en la antiguedad 1st International Congress* (1980), and *2nd International Congress* (1983); J. Remesal Rodríguez, *La annona militaris y la exportación de aceite bético a Germania* (1986); L. Casson, *Ancient Trade and Society* (1984), and *The Periplus Maris Erythraei* (1989). J. J. P.

traders in the ancient Mediterranean relied heavily on sea transport, reflecting terrain and the location of communities. *Plato (1) describes the Greeks as huddled around the sea 'like ants and frogs around a pond' (*Phd.* 109b); his likening of traders to migrating summer birds (*Leg.* 952d) reminds us of the realities of the Mediterranean *climate and limitations of contemporary shipping, closing the seas for between six and ten months (*Cod. Theod.* 13. 9. 3. 3; Hes. *Op.* 663 ff.; cf. Acts 27: 9). Although in the Roman west extensive use was made of river and eventually even road transport, the primacy of sea trade was never challenged. In terms of status, traders were liable to be marginalized as 'not belonging'. Homer's traders (predominantly *Phoenicians) were viewed with suspicion by the Greek élite (*Od.* 8. 14 ff.). Even after Greeks replaced Phoenicians, no formal bond existed between a *polis and those carrying on its trade: traders transporting goods to and from Athens were not necessarily Athenian citizens. Evidence for wealthy traders is slight: only two individuals from the whole of classical Greece are explicitly known to have owned more than one ship (Dem. 22. 211; 45. 6). The norm seems to have been 'tramp trading': independent shipowners sailing wherever cargoes were to be bought and sold (Xen. *Oec.* 20. 27). Though traders might be of low status, maritime trade was crucially important: not necessarily in crude quantitative terms

(as an engine of economic growth) but by way of redistributing essential raw materials (metals), alleviating temporary shortages of grain, and disseminating luxury goods. In addition, Classical Athens exceptionally depended on grain imports on an annual basis, made possible by a combination of control of the seas and imperial tribute (with corresponding problems in the 4th cent.). The city of Rome was similarly exceptional, drawing as of right on the resources of empire to feed a massive urban population. Although the status of those actually involved in trade was relatively low (senators were forbidden by law from owning an ocean-going ship: Livy 21. 63), there was probable élite involvement through agents. As provision of grain became more of a political preoccupation, and emperors eventually shouldered the burden of feeding the urban *plebs*, so traders came increasingly under state control. The *praefectus annonae* (prefect over the grain supply) regulated *collegia* of *navicularii* (associations of shipowners), via the award of civic privileges. The increase during the later empire of 'tied trade' (exchange channelled through agents away from the market by emperor, Church, and landowning élite) established a pattern carried over into the Merovingian period. See FOOD SUPPLY; SHIPS; TRADE.

L. Casson, *Ships and Seamanship in the Ancient World* (1971); J. Hasebroek, *Trade and Politics in Ancient Greece* (1933); P. McKechnie, *Outsiders in the Greek Cities in the Fourth Century BC* (1989); P. Garnsey, in P. Cartledge and F. D. Harvey (eds.), *CRUX*; P. Garnsey, K. Hopkins, and C. R. Whittaker (eds.), *Trade in the Ancient Economy* (1983); P. Garnsey, *Famine and Food Supply in the Graeco-Roman World* (1988); P. Garnsey and C. R. Whittaker (eds.), *Trade and Famine in Classical Antiquity* (1983); J. H. D'Arms and E. C. Kopff (eds.), *The Seaborne Commerce of Ancient Rome* (1980); J. H. D'Arms, *Commerce and Social Standing in Ancient Rome* (1981); G. Rickman, *The Corn Supply of Ancient Rome* (1980); J. Rougé, *Recherches sur l'organisation du commerce maritime en Méditerranée sous l'empire romain* (1966); Jones, *Later Rom. Emp.*
P. C. M.

tragedy, Greek Tragedy, one of the most influential literary forms that originated in Greece, is particularly associated with Athens in the 5th cent. BC, the period that saw its most distinctive development. All but one of the surviving plays date from the 5th cent. (the exception, *Rhesus*, attributed to *Euripides, is probably 4th cent.), but these represent only a tiny sample of the vast body of material produced from the late 6th cent. onwards; new plays were still being composed as late as the 2nd cent. AD. The popularity of the dramatic festivals at Athens attracted interest in other cities, with the result that performances of tragedy rapidly became common elsewhere, and what began as a medium reflecting the life of a particular community acquired universal appeal in the Greek-speaking world. By the end of the 3rd cent. BC, Roman translations and adaptations began to extend the range of its influence still further.

The material that follows is divided into two sections.

I Tragedy at Athens in the 5th cent. and earlier
  1. Origins
  2. Early history
  3. Dramatic festivals
  4. Form and performance
  5. Subject-matter and interpretation
II Tragedy in the Greek-speaking world and beyond
  1. The formation of a repertoire
  2. Actors and festivals
  3. Tragedy in adaptation and translation

I. 1. Origins Much the most valuable information about how Athenian tragedy came into being is preserved in the fourth chapter of *Aristotle's *Poetics*. In particular, he states that (*a*) tragedy came into being from an improvisatory origin, from the leaders (*exarchontes*) of the *dithyramb; (*b*) *Aeschylus increased the number of actors from one to two, reduced the choral part, and made the (spoken) word 'protagonist'; (*c*) *Sophocles (1) introduced the third actor and scene-painting; (*d*) because tragedy developed from the satyr-play-like (*ek saturikou*: see SATYRIC DRAMA), it was slow to become serious, abandoning its small plots and ridiculous diction; (*e*) because of the satyric and more dance-like nature of the poetry, the first metre to be used was the trochaic tetrameter, which was then replaced by the iambic trimeter.

Although it has been maintained that this account is mere hypothesis, there are good reasons for lending it some credence. One is that Aristotle was in a position to know much more than we do about the matter. And indeed in the next chapter he says that the changes that occurred in tragedy are, unlike the case of comedy, known. Moreover, the development of serious drama from boisterous performance (for this there are non-Greek parallels) is unlikely to be Aristotle's hypothesis, partly because it does in fact contradict the theoretical framework he sets out earlier in the same chapter, in which there is an early historical division between serious and trivial poetry. Some have seen an inconsistency in the development of tragedy both from the dithyramb and from the *saturikon*. But in fact the early processional dithyramb in honour of *Dionysus would naturally be performed by *satyrs, and there is evidence that satyrs did indeed perform the dithyramb. In any case *saturikon* means 'satyr-play-like', i.e. not necessarily a performance by the satyrs themselves. The word *tragōidia* probably originally meant the song sung by singers at the sacrifice of a goat (in which the goat also may have been a prize), and has no inherent connection with the satyrs, who anyway were at this period more like horses than goats.

There are several advantages to Aristotle's view that he does not mention. An origin of tragedy in the dithyramb, which was a Dionysiac hymn, coheres with the fact that tragedy was performed (along with dithyramb) in the cult of Dionysus. The cult is marked by the participants' change of identity, a change that may be achieved by the use of *masks (notably satyr-masks), and this makes it a likely context for the genesis of drama. Further, Aristotle's account coheres well both with the formal structure of extant tragedy (see § 2) and with the practice of performing a satyr-play, written by the tragedian, after each tragic trilogy (thereby forming a tetralogy). According to an ancient tradition, satyric drama was instituted so as to preserve the Dionysiac element that had been lost from tragedy (Chamaeleon fr. 38; etc.). Such a development may well have occurred, and is not inconsistent with the *Alexandrian view, to be found in *Horace's *Ars Poetica* (220–1), that satyric drama was a later addition to tragedy. But the possibility remains nevertheless that it was invented to complement the Aristotelian theory.

Another ancient tradition locates the origin of tragedy in the northern *Peloponnesus. *Herodotus (1) (1. 23) tells us that the first known composition of dithyrambs was in *Corinth, by *Arion (2) of Methymna (*c*.600 BC). A late notice (*Suda*, *Ἀρίων*) says both that Arion invented the *tragikos tropos* (i.e. probably the style or mode of music which afterwards belonged to tragedy) and that he was the first to name what was sung by the dithyrambic chorus and to bring on satyrs speaking verse (these may or may not be meant to refer to separate kinds of performance). Another late notice attributes to *Solon's elegies the statement that Arion composed the first *drāma tēs tragōidias* (fr. 30a West).

Further, Herodotus (5. 67) records that at *Sicyon the tyrant *Cleisthenes (1) transferred *tragikoi choroi* honouring the sufferings of the hero *Adrastus (1) to the cult of Dionysus, and the rest of the sacrifice to another hero, *Melanippus. (The implication of this, that a crucial stage in the genesis of tragedy was the coalescence of *hero-cult with the cult of Dionysus, is for various reasons an attractive one.) Sicyon was also the birthplace of *Epigenes (1), whom *Suda* (*Θέσπις*) calls the first tragic poet. Support for an origin in the northern Peloponnese is provided by an apparently Doric feature of tragic language, the use of long α for η, especially in the lyric portions.

I. 2. Early history Little is known about Athenian tragedy before Aeschylus. We have four names (*Thespis, *Choerilus (1), *Pratinas, and *Phrynichus (1)), to whom are attributed a few extant fragments, at least some of which are spurious. Especially suspect are the traditions about the Attic Thespis as the inventor of tragedy. Here the general unreliability of traditions about 'first inventors' is compounded by the suspicion that with Thespis the Athenians attempted to reclaim the invention of tragedy from the *Dorians. Even the view often stated in modern handbooks that Thespis first produced tragedy at the City *Dionysia in one of the years 535–533 BC has recently been shown to be suspect. It is equally possible that tragedy was instituted at the City Dionysia by the new democratic regime at the very end of the 6th cent. If anything in the tradition about Thespis deserves any credence, it is the remark attributed to Aristotle that he added prologue and speech to what had been a choral performance (Themistius 26. 316d). Although Aeschylus introduced the second actor (see above), his dialogue is (in contrast to Sophocles and Euripides) still mostly between an actor and chorus leader—even in the *Oresteia*, in which he employed the third actor recently introduced by Sophocles. All this, taken together with the fact that in Aeschylus the lyric portions generally form a greater proportion of the drama than they do in Sophocles and Euripides, suggests that the early development of tragedy was the gradual transformation of a choral performance into the structure of choral odes alternating with spoken scenes familiar from extant tragedy. This is supported also by the word for actor, *hupokritēs*, which almost certainly meant 'interpreter' (although it has been claimed that it meant 'answerer'). Perhaps the 'leader' of the dithyrambic performance also interpreted it. Scholars also used to argue (from the fact that there are 50 *Danaids in Aeschylus' *Suppliants*, taken together with Pollux 4. 110) that the number of the chorus members in early tragedy was 50, and so considerably larger than the twelve or fifteen of later tragedy. But this view has fallen out of favour, not least because of the discovery of a papyrus (*POxy.* 2256 fr. 3) showing the relatively late dating of Aesch. *Supp.* A respect in which Aeschylus is undoubtedly distinct from Sophocles and Euripides is his tendency to devote the whole trilogy to a single story (e.g. the *Oresteia*).

I. 3. The dramatic festivals in the fifth century The production of tragedy was not confined to Attica, but it was in Attica that tragedy acquired its definitive form, and it is from Attica that we have almost everything that we know about it. From the end of the 6th cent. BC, if not before, tragedies were performed in the Athenian spring festival of Dionysus Eleuthereus, the City Dionysia. This remained the main context for tragic performances, although they occurred also at the Rural Dionysia, and (probably in the 430s) a competition for two tragedians each with two tragedies was introduced into the *Lenaea. In all these festivals the tragic performances were one feature of a programme of events which, at the City Dionysia, included processions, sacrifice in the theatre, libations, the parade of war orphans, performances of dithyramb and comedy, and a final assembly to review the conduct of the festival.

At the City Dionysia three tragedians generally competed each with three tragedies and a satyr-play. In charge of the festival was a leading state official, the eponymous archon (see ARCHONTES), who chose the three tragedians (perhaps after hearing them read their plays, Pl. *Leg*. 817d). He also appointed the three wealthy *chorēgoi* who bore the expenses of training and equipping the choruses (see CHORĒGIA). Originally the tragedian acted in his own play, but later we find tragedians employing actors, as well as the appointment of protagonists by the state. This last method may have been instituted when prizes were introduced for actors in 449 BC. In a preliminary ceremony called the **proagōn* it seems that each tragedian appeared with his actors on a platform to announce the themes of his plays. Ten judges were chosen, one from each of the tribes (see PHYLAI), in a complex process involving an element of chance. The victorious poet was crowned with ivy in the theatre.   R. A. S. S.

I. 4. Form and performance Some features of the tragic performances are best understood if set in the context of Greek festival practice. The notion of performers in sports and the arts competing in honour of the gods was familiar throughout the Greek world (see AGŌNES). Individuals entered for athletic events like running or *boxing or for musical contests as solo instrumentalists, and groups participated in many forms of song and dance or in team activities such as relay races. In the case of the City Dionysia the emphasis was on competition by choruses, whether for dithyramb, tragedy and satyr-play, or comedy; thus despite the novelty of dramatic representation there was a strong element of continuity with established practice, and the competition for the best leading actor (*prōtagōnistēs*), introduced in the mid-5th cent., can be compared with competitions among solo musicians or *rhapsodes.

The importance of the choral element is shown by the fact that the main responsibility of each of the financial sponsors (*chorēgoi*: see CHORĒGIA) was the recruiting and maintenance, costuming and training of the chorus, while the city paid the leading actors and the poets. Given the competitive nature of the events it was important to have rules governing (e.g.) the choice of playwrights, the allocation of leading actors, and the procedures for judging; the apparent limitation on the number of speaking actors (often called the 'three-actor rule') may have been less a matter of strict regulation than a practical consequence of using *masks. In masked drama it is natural to confine the speaking in any one scene to a limited number of parts so that the audience can tell where each voice is coming from, and since the masks (with wigs attached) completely covered the actors' heads one performer could easily play several different roles. All the surviving plays were evidently composed to be performed (with minor, mainly musical, exceptions) by not more than three speakers at a time, and the doubling of roles was certainly standard. Dramatists may well have exploited the effects to be gained from giving two related leading parts to the same actor (e.g. *Deianira and *Heracles in Soph. *Trach*. or *Pentheus and Agave in Eur. *Bacch*.). Non-speaking roles for attendants, bodyguards, trains of captives, etc. were a different matter—powerful visual effects could be achieved by bringing groups on stage—and occasional extra solo singers (e.g. the child at Eur. *Andr*. 504–36) or supplementary choruses (e.g. the hunts-

men at Eur. *Hipp*. 61–71) might also be used. See also THEATRE STAGING, GREEK.

The metrical patterns of the surviving plays show that the typical 5th-cent. tragedy was formally much more complex than most modern drama. There was a strong musical element which bears some comparison with modern opera, most noticeably the sequences of song (and dance) performed by a chorus on its own which mark a break of some kind in the action and cover any necessary (usually short) lapse of time. Audiences could expect to see about five such performances within a single play, with the chorus in the orchestra as the centre of attention. Then there were the sung exchanges, or exchanges of alternating speech and recitative or song (*amoibaia*), between the chorus and one or more of the actors: these belonged to the same time-frame as the spoken dialogue and were used to intensify emotion or give a scene a ritual dimension, as in a shared lament or song of celebration. Singing by individual actors became more and more important as time went on; Euripides was famous for his monodies (cf. e.g. *Aristophanes (1), *Frogs* 1329–63), but there were striking examples from earlier tragedy, like the solo by the mad Io at Aesch. (?) *Prometheus Bound* 561–88. The musical accompaniment was provided by a player on a double pipe (*aulos*), who often appears in vase-paintings of dramatic scenes.

Virtuoso performance was not only musical: the speeches and dialogues in iambic trimeters intended for spoken delivery were carefully designed to have an emotive impact, whether in the narrating of shocking off-stage events, the presentation of sharply conflicting points of view in formal debate (*agōn*) scenes, or the cut and thrust of symmetrically alternating lines or pairs of lines (*stichomythia). All the surviving plays are designed to give the leading actor a series of 'big speeches', in which to show off his talent as an interpreter of character and feeling.

The physical circumstances of Greek theatres—open-air auditoria with a more or less central dancing-space for the chorus—had important consequences for acting style and dramatic design (see THEATRES (GREEK AND ROMAN), STRUCTURE). The sense of the watching community must have been strong in open-air daylight performances in front of large crowds, and the constant presence of a choral group as witnesses to the action contributed to the public character of the events portrayed. This was not drama on an intimate scale, although it could deal with intimate subject-matter: it depended on large effects of gesture and movement that could be 'read' by very diverse audiences, and all the evidence suggests that it was considered to have popular, not élitist, appeal. The comic poets would certainly not have spent so much time parodying tragedy if tragedy had not been a familiar medium that meant something important to their audiences.

I. 5. Subject-matter and interpretation All but one of the plots of the surviving sample of tragedies are drawn from heroic myth, familiar to 5th-cent. audiences from epic poetry. Aeschylus' *Persians* (472 BC) deals with the events of 480 (see PERSIAN WARS), but these are refracted through a Persian setting, and no Greeks are named. Other examples are known of plays on contemporary subjects; at the other extreme Aristotle (*Poet*. 1451[b]) cites *Agathon's *Antheus* as an example of a play with entirely fictitious characters and plot. But the normal choice of material was from the heroic past, handled without any sign of antiquarian interest; it must have come naturally to tragedians to use the habits familiar to the lyric poets and to contemporary vase-painters and sculptors. Epic story-telling by rhapsodes must have been a shared experience, and many of the heroes continued to be deeply implicated in Greek life through their worship in cult. It is no accident that Athenian tragedy often deals with heroes who were the object of cult in Attica: *Theseus, *Heracles, *Aias (1), *Erechtheus and his family, *Iphigenia, *Oedipus.

*Plato (1) called *Homer 'first of the tragic poets' (Rep. 607a), and it is true that his poetry, particularly the Iliad, offered tragic interpretations of events as well as the raw material for dramatic plots, but the plays that have survived all have a strongly contemporary application to the problems of the Athenian *polis. Stories of intra-familial conflict like that of Oedipus could be re-cast to lay stress on the tensions between family and city, or the *Argonautic tale of *Jason (1) and *Medea could be shaped in such a way as to make an Athenian audience look closely at the problematic categories of citizen and foreigner, male and female, civilized and barbarian as defined in their society.

Recent criticism has emphasized the ideological content and didactic function of 5th-cent. tragedy, linking it as a form of public discourse with debates and decision-making in the assembly (*ekklēsia) and with the speeches aimed at popular juries in the law courts (see DEMOCRACY, ATHENIAN). The importance of *rhetoric is obvious in all these contexts; the tragedies themselves contain much self-conscious reference to rhetorical techniques and to their own strategies of persuasion. Drama in all its forms could function as a powerful medium for the communication of ideas; the tragedians of the 5th cent. seem to have aimed at a balance between displacement (through the choice of a time and place different from the here and now) and the explicit linking of the play with the audience's world, as in the use of aetiology (e.g. the foundation of the *Areopagus in Aesch. Eum. or the prophecy of Athenian and *Ionian prosperity at the end of Eur. Ion) and in appeals through *ritual to their sense of community (e.g. the burial procession at the end of Soph. Aj.). There is often a similar tension of opposites in the way in which noble characters who speak in ornate and elevated language are set in plots entailing transgressive desires and actions such as kin-killing, *incest, civil conflict, treachery, or irrational violence. Comparison between early and late plays based on the same stories can help critics to trace changing patterns of attitude and perception reflected in subtle changes of language.

The study of ritual practice and of ritual patterns in drama has helped to redefine the questions that it is appropriate to ask about the gods in Greek tragedy. As in Homeric epic, the gods are everywhere, but the plays are not about theology, and critics are less ready than they used to be to identify the religious beliefs of the individual dramatists. Even a more than usually god-focused play like Eur. Heracles asks questions rather than finding answers, combining sceptical challenges to divine morality with aetiological reminders of Attic *hero-cult. But it would be wrong to underestimate the religious intensity of plays like Aesch. Ag., Soph. OC, or Eur. Bacch.; as always, it is through the use of language that the plays achieve their deepest effects. Existential issues like time and mortality, and questions that apply to individuals as well as to communities (such as 'Who am I?' and 'How should I behave?') are strongly represented in tragedy alongside questions relating to contemporary society. This must have been an important factor in the spread of the medium beyond Attica and even outside the Greek-speaking world.

II. 1. The formation of a repertoire Interest in Attic drama outside Athens can be traced to an early stage in its history: Aeschylus was invited to Sicily to compose a drama celebrating the foundation of the city of Aetna in 476/5 and returned to Sicily late

in his life. Euripides had links with *Macedonia, particularly reflected in his lost play Archelaus; so too did *Agathon, and Eur. Andr., with its references to the history of the Molossian royal family, offers a further hint that patrons from elsewhere might take an interest in commissioning plays. But the most extensive range of evidence comes from the end of the 5th cent. onwards and is seen (e.g.) in theatre-building in different parts of the Greek world and in the production in southern Italy and Sicily of large quantities of painted pottery showing tragic scenes. This evidence needs to be combined with what is known from Attica about revivals of plays at the Rural Dionysia (beginning in the 5th cent.: evidence in DFA³ 42–56; Whitehead, The Demes of Attica 212–22) and eventually in the city as well. (The first recorded instance at the City Dionysia was in 386 BC, when an old tragedy was put on by the tragōidoi (tragic actors; IG 2². 2320), but revivals of Aeschylus' plays had exceptionally been allowed in the city since his death; Life of Aesch. 12.) The fact that revivals became popular does not have to mean that tragedy was in decline: it is hard to imagine an acting profession developing without a repertoire, and the wider the demand from different communities, whether local audiences in the Attic *demes or cities outside Attica eager to build a theatrical tradition, the greater must have been the incentive to re-perform successful plays.

There seems to have been no shortage of new writing, however, and the competition for new plays continued for centuries (evidence in TGF I). Many names are known of tragic poets from other cities who came to Athens to compete, e.g. *Theodectes from Phaselis in Asia Minor, one of the most admired of the 4th-cent. dramatists. From the 5th cent. Aeschylus, Sophocles, and Euripides held pride of place as 'classic' writers and were honoured with statues in *Lycurgus (3)'s remodelled theatre of Dionysus at Athens. The fact that Lycurgus found it necessary to decree that official copies of the texts of their plays were to be preserved as a protection against interpolation by actors (Plut. Mor. 841f) is further evidence of their popularity. But they were not the only ones to survive: others of their contemporaries, e.g. *Ion (2) of Chios and *Achaeus (2), had a lasting reputation (see CANON), and some of the new plays themselves acquired classic status. Aristotle's familiar references to such plays as *Astydamas' Alcmeon (Poet. 1453ᵇ) or Theodectes' Lynceus (Poet. 1452ᵃ, 1455ᵇ) show how well known they were in his time, and papyrus fragments make clear that some went on being read and re-copied by later generations. The fact that only a very small proportion of the most celebrated tragedies has survived may have more to do with the constraints of the school curriculum in late antiquity and the early Byzantine period than with the intrinsic quality of some of the lost material.

None the less, as tragedy became an 'international' medium changes were certainly taking place, and some of them may have contributed to the eventual decline in its ideological importance. Some developments noted by Aristotle were the increasing influence and prestige of actors at the expense of dramatists (Rh. 1403ᵇ), the habit of some tragedians of writing plays for reading rather than performance (Rh. 1413ᵇ), and the growing tendency to use choral songs unconnected with the action of a particular play (embolima, Poet. 1456ᵃ). This last may not be evidence for a decline in the musical element in tragedy, even if the chorus was indeed tending to be less fully integrated in the action, but it may suggest a trend towards the development of a more adaptable and independent repertoire of song and dance. This should perhaps be associated with the growth of professional troupes, who might on some occasions take the place of specially recruited chorusmen. Aristotle also noted (*Rh.* 1404[b]) that Euripides had 'shown the way' to more natural diction in tragedy, which he evidently felt to be a desirable modern feature.

In the Hellenistic period the very thorough scholarly work done by the Alexandrian critics on what they could locate of earlier tragedy was ultimately more important than the output of new plays, although there were many tragedians still active, enough of them winning distinction at Alexandria to constitute a '*Pleiad' (*TGF* I CAT A 5). The most remarkable surviving text from the period is the *Exagōgē* of *Ezechiel, a product of the union of Greek and Hebrew traditions.

II. 2. Actors and festivals Growing professionalism must have been an important factor as the influence of tragedy began to spread, and it may have been helped at an early stage by the fact that the crafts of play-writing and producing, and of acting, often ran in families. It was actors who had the best opportunities of becoming well known in the Greek cities; as star performers they could command large fees for performances, and it was they who evidently took the initiative in putting on revivals. The organization of actors from the 3rd cent. onwards into powerful regionally defined guilds (the artists of Dionysus; see DIONYSUS, ARTISTS OF) gave them protection, immunities, and privileges as well as better access to the patronage of rulers and cities (evidence in *DFA*[3] 279–321). This is the decisive development for the history of performance in Hellenistic and Roman times, and it linked tragic performers with comic actors, rhapsodes, and musicians of all kinds. Along with the growth in the power and influence of performers went the development of *festivals. Dramatic performances were regularly put on not only at festivals of Dionysus, now very common in the Greek-speaking world, but also at many other events: special occasions such as the 'Olympian festival' held by *Philip (1) II of Macedon after he took *Olynthus in 348, a pattern followed by many other victorious generals, and regular festivals in honour of other deities, such as the Mouseia at *Thespiae, the Naia at *Dodona, the *Soteria at Delphi, and others in Asia Minor, the Aegean islands, and Egypt. Over time it probably became common to act selected scenes or speeches, 'highlights' from famous plays; inscriptions often do not make clear what the *tragōidoi* performed, but they confirm the impression given by other sources that there was a vigorous theatrical life in the Greek-speaking cities of the Roman empire long after tragedy had ceased to have any importance as a major literary genre.

II. 3. Tragedy in adaptation and translation Greek tragedy first reached Roman audiences through the plays of *Ennius, *Accius, and *Pacuvius; in the 1st cent. AD L. *Annaeus Seneca (2)'s tragedies offered a new reading of the same models, and it was through Seneca that the playwrights of the Renaissance made their first contact with the Greeks. The surviving Greek plays have had a profound influence on subsequent literature and culture, and the detailed story of their reception and influence is still waiting to be told. This task grows more complex as performance of the plays becomes more important in the modern media. In the 20th cent. influential experiments in performance in Britain, France, Germany, Greece, Italy, Japan, and north America have begun to change perceptions of the ancient material.

I. 1–3: A. W. Pickard-Cambridge, *DTC*[2] (1962), and *DFA*[3] (1968/88); E. Csapo and W. J. Slater, *The Context of Ancient Drama* (1995); W. Burkert, *GRBS* 1966, 87–121; A. Lesky, *Die tragische Dichtung der Hellenen*[3] (1972); G. Thomson, *Aeschylus and Athens*[4] (1973); H. J. Mette, *Urkunden dramatischer Aufführungen in Griechenland* (1977); B. Snell and R. Kannicht, *Tragicorum Graecorum Fragmenta* (*TGF*), 1[2] (1986). I. 4: C. J. Herington, *Poetry into Drama* (1985); W. Jens (ed.), *Die Bauformen der griechischen Tragödie* (1971); R. Rehm, *Greek Tragic Theatre* (1992). I. 5: J.-P. Vernant and P. Vidal-Naquet, *Mythe et tragédie en Grèce Ancienne*, 2 vols. (1972, 1986; Eng. tr. 1988); R. G. A. Buxton, *Persuasion in Greek Tragedy* (1982); S. D. Goldhill, *Reading Greek Tragedy* (1986); E. M. Hall, *Inventing the Barbarian* (1989); B. Williams, *Shame and Necessity* (1993). II. 1: T. B. L. Webster, *Hermes* 1954, 294–308; G. Xanthakis-Karamanos, *Studies in Fourth-century Tragedy* (1980); D. Whitehead, *The Demes of Attica* (1986); O. Taplin, *Comic Angels* (1993); G. Sifakis, *Studies in the History of Hellenistic Drama* (1967). II. 2: P. Ghiron-Bistagne, *Recherches sur les acteurs dans la Grèce antique* (1976); I. E. Stephanis, Διονυσιακοὶ Τεχνῖται (1988); C. M. Roueché, *Performers and Partisans at Aphrodisias* (1993). II. 3: G. Steiner, *Antigones* (1984); *CHCL* 1 (1985), 258–354; H. Flashar, *Inszenierung der Antike: Das griechische Drama auf der Bühne der Neuzeit* (1991); W. R. Connor in *Aspects of Athenian Democracy*, Cl. et Med. Dissertationes 11 (1990), 7 ff.; C. Sourvinou-Inwood, in R. Osborne and S. Hornblower (eds.), *Ritual, Finance, Politics: Athenian Democratic Accounts presented to David Lewis* (1994), ch. 16; R. Seaford *Reciprocity and Ritual* (1994). Collections of essays: J. J. Winkler and F. I. Zeitlin (eds.), *Nothing to do with Dionysos?* (1990); A. H. Sommerstein and others, *Tragedy, Comedy and the Polis* (1993); R. Scodel, *Theater and Society in the Classical World* (1993). P. E. E.

tragedy, Latin *Varro and T. *Pomponius Atticus put the first performance of a Latin tragedy in the year 240 BC at *Jupiter's September festival. Performances continued at this and other public festivals down to the end of the 1st cent. BC and perhaps into the 1st cent. AD. Celebrations of temple dedications and funerals of men of the aristocracy also provided occasions of performance. In 240 new plays were still being staged at the Athenian festivals of *Dionysus (see DIONYSIA; LENAEA), but the practice had grown up of reviving each year a number of old ones. Travelling companies of 'artists of Dionysus' (see DIONYSUS, ARTISTS OF) performed tragedy as well as comedy at festivals in other Greek cities and perhaps also in private houses. Three 5th-cent. poets, *Aeschylus, *Sophocles (1), and *Euripides, enjoyed the greatest continuing prestige both in the theatre and in the syllabus of the grammatical schools. There is no sign that the seven tragic poets of the court of *Ptolemy (1) II Philadelphus (285–246) won any widespread fame outside *Alexandria (1). At Rome adaptations of the better-known Attic works were offered at first under the names of the original authors. The makers of the adaptations sometimes took part in the performance of their own works.

Roman theatres probably never had much space in front of the stage platform for elaborate choral dancing. Little is known about those who performed at the pre-240 festivals (the *histriones*), or the character of their performances. The surviving scripts of Euripides' *Hecuba*, *Iphigenia in Aulis*, and *Medea* and the remnants of *Ennius' adaptations permit, however, a number of deductions about how the early Latin tragedians went about their business. The Greek choral odes did not disappear, but the volume of singing and dancing assigned to the subordinate group of bystanders was sharply reduced. The speeches of the heroic personages on the other hand were given much more musical accompaniment. The metrical structure of the Latin script was usually more varied and complex than that of its Attic model and obeyed in detail conventions long established among local theatrical performers (see METRE, LATIN).

Themes from Roman legend and history were taken up as early as the 3rd cent. and developed within the dramatic structure which had arisen from the fusion of Attic script and local theatrical tradition. *Accius presented Tarquin (see TARQUINIUS SUPERBUS, L.) talking with his councillors (Cicero, *Div.* 1. 44–5) much as Aeschylus had dramatized the dialogue between Atossa and the chorus in the *Persae* (vv. 159–225).

Despite continuing popularity at the public festivals the 3rd- and 2nd-cent. plays ran into considerable academic condemnation as a result of close comparison with their Attic originals and of acceptance of the generic schemes established in Hellenistic criticism. The apparent licentiousness of early Latin metrical practice aroused particular complaint. The *Thyestes* composed by L. *Varius Rufus for performance at the festival celebrating Octavian's victory at *Actium (see AUGUSTUS) pleased the young, and *Ovid won praise for a *Medea* written in the new style.

Composing for the public festivals continued in the 1st cent. AD (see Tacitus, *Ann.* 11. 13). Some men preferred, however, to compose poems they called tragedies for recitation to small groups in private. The pieces transmitted under the name of L. *Annaeus Seneca (2) are each divided into five units separated by choral odes, and show a metrical practice obedient to the demands made in the Augustan period. Argument rages as to what kind of audience their authors sought. Tragedy was not among the poetic genres attempted in late antiquity.

O. Ribbeck, *Die römische Tragödie im Zeitalter der Republik* (1875); K. Ziegler, *RE* 6 A (1937), 1981 ff.; H. D. Jocelyn, *The Tragedies of Ennius* (1967), 3 ff.; O. Zwierlein, *Die Rezitationsdramen Senecas* (1966).

H. D. J.

tragicocomoedia (τραγικοκωμῳδία), a play blending tragic and comic elements (Plaut. *Amph.* 50–63).

Trajan (Marcus Ulpius Traianus), Roman emperor AD 98–117, was born probably in 53 at *Italica in Spain, the son of M. *Ulpius Traianus, a distinguished consular under the Flavians. His unusually long period of service as a military tribune (though hardly ten years as *Pliny (2) the Younger alleges) included a time in *Syria during the governorship of his father *c*.75 (see TRIBUNI MILITUM). While legionary legate (see LEGATI) in Spain he marched against L. *Antonius Saturninus, governor of Upper Germany (see GERMANIA), who revolted against Domitian in 89. He was consul in 91, and then having been appointed by *Nerva in 97 as governor of Upper Germany, was adopted by that emperor, who faced growing discontent among the praetorians, as his son and co-ruler, and became *consul ordinarius* (see CONSUL) for the second time in 98. After Nerva's death Trajan first inspected the armies in *Pannonia and *Moesia, and on his arrival in Rome re-established strict discipline by disposing of the praetorian mutineers against Nerva.

As emperor his personal conduct was restrained and unassuming, qualities also exhibited by his wife *Plotina, who from about 105 had the title *Augusta* (see AUGUSTUS, AUGUSTA AS TITLES). He was courteous and friendly with individual senators, and treated the senate with respect, avoiding confiscations of property and executions. Pliny's speech (*Panegyric*) delivered in 100, the year of Trajan's third consulship, gives a senatorial appreciation of his excellent qualities. Trajan intervened to help children who had been maltreated by their fathers, and free-born children exposed at birth, and made further exemptions from the inheritance tax. He required that candidates for public office in Rome should have at least one third of their capital invested in Italian land, and he perpetuated the alimentary scheme (see ALIMENTA), probably instituted by Nerva, through which sustenance was provided for poor children in Italian communities. Trajan undertook many utilitarian and celebratory building projects, including baths, a canal to prevent the river *Tiber from flooding, a new harbour at *Ostia, the via Traiana which extended the via Appia from

*Beneventum to *Brundisium, a forum and basilica in Rome dedicated in 112 (see FORUM TRAIANI), and a column depicting the Dacian Wars (see DACIA; and next entry). He was generous to the Roman people, extending the corn doles, paying out enormous largesse partly financed by the booty of the Dacian Wars and the treasure of *Decebalus, and providing lavish spectacles; to celebrate the Dacian victory he gave games on one hundred and twenty-three days in which ten thousand gladiators fought.

The correspondence between Trajan and Pliny, who had been specially appointed to resolve administrative and financial problems in the communities in *Bithynia, shows the kind of attitude towards provincial administration that the emperor had inspired in his officials, even if the emperor's replies were not directly composed by Trajan himself. They exhibit justice, fairness, and personal probity: 'You know very well that it is my established rule not to obtain respect for my name either from people's fears and anxieties or from charges of treason' (Plin. *Ep.* 10. 82). The letters about the treatment of Christians (10. 96–7; see CHRISTIANITY) illustrate the fair-minded attitude of the emperor and his governor.

Experienced in military command, Trajan took a personal interest in the troops, whom he described as 'my excellent and most loyal fellow-soldiers', in instructions issued to governors about the soldiers' testatory privileges (*Digest* 29. 1). Two new *legions were formed, both named after himself—II Traianic Brave and XXX Ulpian Victorious, and on campaign the emperor took personal charge, marching on foot at the head of his men. Trajan's reign was marked by two great wars of conquest, in Dacia and *Parthia. His invasion in 101 of Decebalus' Dacian kingdom beyond the Danube could be justified on the grounds that the accommodation with the Dacians reached by Domitian was unsatisfactory to long-term Roman interests, and that Decebalus' power was increasing. However his principal motive may have been to win military glory. Trajan crossed the Danube at Lederata and marched north-east to Tibiscum and Tapae; there is insufficient evidence to demonstrate the presence of a second invasion column. The Dacians resisted with great determination and courage and inflicted heavy losses on the Romans in a pitched battle. In 102 Trajan resumed campaigning and by threatening Decebalus' capital at Sarmizegethusa forced the king to accept a peace by which he surrendered some territory and became a vassal of the Romans (Cass. Dio, 68. 9). Leaving garrisons behind, Trajan returned to Rome where he celebrated a triumph, accepted the title *Dacicus*, and issued coins depicting the defeat of Dacia. In 105 the emperor renewed the war, ostensibly because Decebalus was contravening the treaty, and crossed the Danube on a bridge built by Apollodorus at Drobeta (mod. Turnu-Severin). After Sarmizegethusa had fallen to the Romans, Decebalus committed suicide and his treasure was captured. Coins now proclaimed 'the capture of Dacia', and the area was turned into a Roman province with a consular governor and two legions (IV Flavia Felix and XIII Gemina). On the site of a legionary fortress about 30 km. (18 mi.) to the west of the Dacian fortress of Sarmizegethusa a new colony was established, which served as the capital of the province. At *Adamklissi a community called *Municipium Tropaeum Traiani* was set up, and a trophy containing a dedication to *Mars the Avenger made by Trajan in 107/8. In Rome, Trajan's column celebrated the emperor's prowess and the glorious achievement of the Roman army; his ashes were to be deposited in its base.

Expansion continued with the annexation of *Arabia in 106 by A. *Cornelius Palma Frontonianus, the governor of Syria.

Trajan's Column

Elsewhere in the east, contacts between Rome and Parthia, the only sophisticated empire on the periphery of Roman territory, had been characterized by diplomatic rapport and avoidance of serious warfare during the previous 150 years. The kingdom of *Armenia, between the two empires on the upper *Euphrates, though sometimes prey to Parthian influence and intervention, was generally ruled by a Roman nominee. Trajan took exception to the attempts of King Osroes of Parthia to establish control of Armenia, and refusing all diplomatic advances arrived in *Antioch (1) early in 114. Without major opposition he incorporated Armenia into the empire and then launched an attack on Parthia through *Mesopotamia while the Parthian king was beset with civil strife. In the campaigns of 115–16, the Romans crossed the *Tigris into *Adiabene and then advanced down the Euphrates, capturing the Parthian capital, *Ctesiphon. Trajan was acclaimed *imperator*, and accepted the title *Parthicus*. At least one new province (Mesopotamia) was created, and possibly another (Assyria); coins celebrated the 'capture of Parthia', and 'Armenia and Mesopotamia brought into the power of the Roman People'. The emperor advanced to the Persian Gulf, but his success proved transitory as serious uprisings occurred in the captured territory to the army's rear, and a major insurrection of the *Jews in the eastern provinces spread to Mesopotamia in 116. Trajan tried to contain the military situation, and *Lusius Quietus had some success in northern Mesopotamia while a vassal king, Parthamaspates, was imposed on the Parthians. However, as the situation remained precarious, Trajan decided to retreat. Parthamaspates proved short-lived, despite grandiloquent Roman coins proclaiming a 'king granted to the Parthians', and with his health declining Trajan decided to return to Italy; but in early August he died suddenly at Selinus. *Cassius Dio explained Trajan's aggrandisement in the east as a desire to win glory and this remains the most likely explanation for a man who had already achieved great military success. The policy was a disastrous failure but criticism was muted because he was generally popular with senators. By 114 the appellation 'Best' (*Optimus*), which had appeared early in the reign, had become one of his official titles, and is recalled in the ritual acclamation of the senate—'May you be even luckier than Augustus and even better than Trajan'.

ANCIENT SOURCES Literary: Cass. Dio, 68; Plin. *Pan.*; *Ep.*; Aur. Vict. Inscriptions: Smallwood, *Docs . . . Nerva*. Coins: *BM Coins, Rom. Emp.* 3 (ed. H. Mattingly, 1936); P. V. Hill, *Num. Chron.* 1970, 57.

MODERN DISCUSSIONS General: R. Paribeni, *Optimus Princeps*, 2 vols. (1926–7); R. Hanslick, *RE* Suppl. 10 (1965), 1035; R. Syme, *Tacitus* (1958), see index; A. Garzetti, *From Tiberius to the Antonines* (1974; Ital. orig. 1960); K. H. Waters, in J. A. S. Evans (ed.), *Polis and Imperium* (1974), 233.

Special: (*a*) Administration and finance: R. Syme, *JRS* 1930, 55 = *RP* 1 (1979), 1; C. H. V. Sutherland, *JRS* 1935, 150; G. Biraghi, *PP* 1951, 271; J. Carcopino in *Les Étapes de l'impérialisme romain* (1961), 106; alimentary scheme: R. Duncan-Jones, *PBSR* 1964, 124; P. Garnsey, *Hist.* 1968, 367; praetorian prefects: R. Syme, *JRS* 1980, 64 = *RP* 3 (1984), 1276. (*b*) Trajan's arch at *Beneventum: F. J. Hassel, *Der Trajansbogen in Benevent* (1966); I. A. Richmond, *Roman Archaeology and Art* (ed. P. Salway, 1969), 229; F. Lepper, *JRS* 1969, 250. (*c*) Public buildings, war memorials, and art: R. Brilliant, *Gesture and Rank in Roman Art* (1963); F. B. Florescu, *Das Siegesdenkmal von Adamklissi* (1965); *Die Trajanssäule* (1969); L. Rossi, *Trajan's Column and the Dacian Wars* (1971); F. Coarelli, *Guida archeologica Laterza: Roma* (1981); C. M. Amici, *Basilica Ulpia e bibliotheche* (1982); J. C. Anderson, Collection Latomus 182 (1984), 141; F. Lepper and S. Frere, *Trajan's Column* (1988); S. Settis (ed.), *La colonna Traiana* (1988); P. Pensabene and others, *Arch. Class.* 1989, 27; J. Packer, *AJArch.* 1992, 151. (*d*) Wars: (i) Dacian: I. A. Richmond, *PBSR* 1935, 1

(repr., including material on Adamklissi, 1982); M. Speidel, *JRS* 1970, 142; L. Rossi, *Trajan's Column and the Dacian Wars* (1971); R. Syme, *JRS* 1959, 26 = *Danubian Papers* (1971), 122; J. Šašel, *JRS* 1973, 80; K. Strobel, *Untersuchungen zu den Dakerkriegen Trajans* (1984); F. Lepper and S. Frere, *Trajan's Column* (1988). (ii) Parthia and the east: J. Guey, *Essai sur la guerre parthique de Trajan* (1937); F. Lepper, *Trajan's Parthian War* (1948); G. W. Bowersock, *JRS* 1971, 219; M. G. Angeli Bertinelli, *ANRW* 2. 9. 1 (1976), 3; C. S. Lightfoot, *JRS* 1990, 115.   J. B. C.

Trajan's Column (see TRAJAN). Honorific column dedicated in AD 113 as part of the *forum Traiani in Rome. It consists of a 28.9 m. (95 ft.)-tall column standing on a 6.2 m. (20 ft.)-high pedestal. An internal spiral staircase, illuminated by 40 slit-windows, connects a door in the south-east side of the base with a balcony at the top. Trajanic coin motifs represented the monument topped by an imperial statue. The pedestal has sculptured reliefs of barbarian military equipment on its four sides, and an inscription (*CIL* 6. 960). The shaft bears a helical band, 200 m. long and c.0.85–1.45 m. high (656 × 2¾–4¾ ft.), carved into its outer face with reliefs depicting Trajan's Dacian Wars (AD 101–2, 105–6; see DACIA).

Many details of the pedestal reliefs may be paralleled in the archaeological record. The helical frieze depicts the Dacian Wars separated by a Victory and trophies, and divided up into internal campaigns consisting of linked scenes. Beyond this, planning of content and 'narrative' was minimal. Some historical events were depicted and Trajan's own *commentarii* most likely contributed, but most of the scenes follow the unspecific formulae of imperial propaganda-art. However, some key compositions are arranged on vertical axes which cut across the helix to aid the viewer's comprehension (Coulston).

The sculptors worked up the spiral without laying out the composition ahead of them; they did not follow detailed cartoons and they had a wide degree of compositional freedom. Human figure-types were defined with artificial uniformity to indicate the status and ethnic identities of participants. Some expert advice on castrametation was used in garbled form, but most military material was provided through empirical observation in Rome. Thus, the reliefs are important for their propaganda function and as a sculptural *tour de force*, but the spiral frieze cannot be employed as a historical document or as a primary source for military studies. The pedestal was employed as Trajan's mausoleum after AD 117.

C. Cichorius, *Die Traianssäule* (1896, 1900); K. Lehmann-Hartleben, *Die Trajanssäule* (1926); W. Gauer, *Untersuchungen zur Trajanssäule* (1977); F. Lepper and S. Frere, *Trajan's Column* (1988); S. Settis (ed.), *La colonna Traiana* (1988); J. C. N. Coulston, *JRA* 1990, 290–309; A. Claridge, *JRA* 1993, 5–22; M. Wilson-Jones, *JRA* 1993, 23–38.   J. C. N. C.

Tralles, a city sometimes attributed to *Lydia, sometimes to *Caria, on a strong position on the north side of the richest section of the *Maeander valley; its wealth and commercial advantages are inherited by the modern Aydın. First mentioned by *Xenophon (1) (*Hell.* 3. 2. 19), it belonged to *Mausolus in the mid-4th cent., and was an important city in the Hellenistic period, called Seleuceia while controlled by the *Seleucids (before 188 BC); it was restored by Augustus after an earthquake and given the name Caesarea. Tralles seems to have flourished in late antiquity, with several new buildings; in the 6th cent. it was an important centre of Monophysite activity and missionary work among local pagans.

Strabo 14. 1. 42; *PECS* 931; C. Foss, *AJArch.* 1977, 469 ff., 483 = Foss, *History and Archaeology of Byzantine Asia Minor* (1990), vol. 2;

S. Hornblower, *Mausolus* (1982); F. Poljakov, *Die Inschriften von Tralleis und Nysa* 1 (1989–).
W. M. C.; J. M. C.; C. R.

Transalpine Gaul See GAUL (TRANSALPINE).

transhumance, a form of semi-nomadism in which pastoralists move their flocks over long distances between summer and winter pastures. Well-attested in the Mediterranean more recently, it is rarely mentioned in ancient Greek writers (Soph. *OT* 1132 ff. being one exception) and its importance is debated for *pastoralism in ancient Greece, where city-state boundaries were potential obstacles to the seasonal movements of shepherds and generated disputes between neighbours over rights to summer pasture, as between the Phocians and Locrians in 395 BC (*Hell. Oxy.* 21 Chambers). In Roman Italy, where the high Apennines favour transhumance, the practice is well attested from the late republic on, *Varro (*Rust.* 2) providing the best evidence, and was presumably facilitated by the peninsula's political unification, although its scale and the extent of the Roman state's involvement (beyond extracting pasture-dues from shepherds using the *calles* or drove-roads) are problematic. See NOMADS.

S. Georgoudi, *Rev. Ét. Grec.* 1974, 155–85; R. Osborne, *Classical Landscape with Figures* (1987), 47–52; J. Frayn, *Sheep-Rearing and the Wool Trade in Italy* (1984), ch. 3.
A. J. S. S.

translation 'Translation is so far removed from the sterile equation of two dead languages that of all literary forms it is the one charged with the special mission of watching over the maturing process of the original language and the birth pangs of its own' (Walter Benjamin, 'The Task of the Translator', trans. H. Zohn). In just this way the developing literature and culture of Rome can be seen as a series of acts of translation from Greek sources. Translation mediated the relationship between Greece and Rome and, thereafter, Rome and the European vernaculars; *Isidorus (2) of Seville (10. 123) etymologizes *interpres*, 'translator', as one standing *inter partes* 'between the two sides'. Members of the Roman élite learned, read, and spoke Greek, competing with each other in the cultural fruits of Hellenization (see HELLENISM): M. *Porcius Cato (1) ostentatiously addressed a Greek audience in Latin, using a translator, but could easily have spoken in Greek (Plutarch, *Cato Maior* 12. 4). Latin literature may be said to begin with *Livius Andronicus' versions of Greek plays and of *Homer's *Odyssey* in native *Saturnian verse. The republican dramatists closely adapted Greek comedy and tragedy for the Roman people. In the view of Aulus *Gellius, *Virgil 'translated' *Theocritus, *Hesiod, and Homer (the boundary between translation and imitation is, in practice, impossible to police). Knowledge of the Greek language aided the expansion of Roman power; e.g. *Cicero, himself an experienced translator (he produced, *inter alia*, a version of *Aratus (1)'s influential *Phaenomena*), sought a unified Graeco-Roman culture as the basis of an ordered polity, while standardization of Latin *grammar on the model of Greek helped to cement a language for empire. Public documents were translated into Greek, often with adjustment to the different conceptual worlds (so Augustus' *Res Gestae, and cf. the famous trilingual inscription set up by *Cornelius Gallus in Egypt). A number of prominent Roman authors came from non-Latin-speaking municipalities, while *Ennius famously spoke three languages: Latin, Greek, and *Oscan. Translation also encouraged Roman self-consciousness about Latin and its limitations, fuelling a sense of both inferiority and

competition; so *Lucretius (1. 139) complains of the poverty of the language, *egestas linguae*.

The Greeks of the Classical and Hellenistic eras, by contrast, seem to have been primarily monoglot (with obvious exceptions like *Polybius (1) or *Philodemus)—foreigners were *barbaroi* (see BARBARIAN), i.e. people who did not speak Greek (in this respect at least the Romans emerge as more urbane and civilized). Colonization (see COLONIZATION, GREEK and HELLENISTIC) and contact with the empires of Asia Minor must have created a need for translation, but e.g. *Herodotus (1) appears to have been dependent on native interpreters for his knowledge of matters Persian, Egyptian, etc. Initially most Greeks showed scant interest in reading the great Roman authors (though some claimed that Latin was a dialect form of Greek). It was not until the 3rd cent. AD, apparently, that Greeks in the eastern part of the empire, seeking employment in the Roman administration and needing Latin for competence in law, started to study Latin literary texts on any scale; a writer like *Claudian would have studied the same syllabus in Egypt as someone educated in Italy (and there are practical bilingual textbooks from this period known as *hermeneumata*). See BILINGUALISM.

It was the Romans, not the Greeks, who conceptualized the process of translation, establishing the framework and norms of western translation practice until the end of the 18th cent.; words used include *vertere, mutare, transferre, Latine exprimere*. The younger *Pliny (2) (*Ep.* 7. 9. 1) recommends practice in translating between Latin and Greek for promoting verbal fluency and critical discernment. The canonical case against undue 'literalism' is put by *Horace (*Ars P.* 133–4) and by *Cicero, who describes translating speeches by *Demosthenes (2) and *Aeschines (1) not word for word (*non verbum pro verbo*), but so as to retain style and impact (*De optimo genere oratorum*, 14); St *Jerome (letter 57. 5) gave the classic formulation: 'not word for word but sense for sense' (*non verbum e verbo, sed sensum exprimere de sensu*).

Translation must be a matter of concern to all students of antiquity. It is often thought of as the substitution for a foreign word of a word of the same or similar meaning, on the model of a dictionary: *amor* 'means' love. Indeed translatability, the idea that alien cultural and linguistic systems can be made intelligible to us, lies at the root of humanistic inquiry (often in conflict with a counter-claim that certain terms, e.g. *pietas or arete*, are untranslatable). However, the semantic field of a word in one language is never identical with that of a word in another (*amor*, it can be argued, has different connotations and affiliations from *love*); and words are constantly changing their significations according to shifting context and use. So it may be better to think in terms of semantic 'equivalence' rather than identity; translation involves simultaneous sameness *and* difference, and can be seen as the process of appropriating the Other. Indeed, any theory of translation obviously implies, is dependent upon, a theory of language, and is thus a philosophical or even metaphysical matter.

Translation has often been marginalized as a second-order activity, lacking in originality (though translations can become classics in their own right). The first extended study in English is Alexander Tytler's *Essay on the Principles of Translation* (1790). Before that the best discussions are to be found in prefatory remarks by practising translators; in the *Preface to Ovid's Epistles* (1680) Dryden gives his famous threefold model—metaphrase (word for word), paraphrase (retaining the sense), and imitation (modernization and adaptation). Translation studies have enhanced the subject's academic standing, producing an

1545

armoury of terms of art (source and target language, formal and dynamic equivalence, etc.), and seeking more objective, 'scientific' accounts, but translation remains obstinately immired in history and usage. For Steiner it is the best model for interpretation and human communication in general. We can say, with Kelly, that 'Western Europe owes its civilization to its translators'. See also SEPTUAGINT.

S. Bassnett-McGuire, *Translation Studies* (1980; rev. edn. 1991); L. G. Kelly, *The True Interpreter: A History of Translation Theory and Practice in the West* (1979); C. Martindale, *Redeeming the Text: Latin Poetry and the Hermeneutics of Reception* (1993), ch. 4; G. Steiner, *After Babel: Aspects of Language and Translation* (1970); A. Momigliano, *Alien Wisdom* (1975).
C. A. Ma.

transmigration The belief that on death, some aspect of us—usually identified with the '*soul' (ψυχή; see PSYCHE)—survives to enter another body, is connected with the idea of immortality, supplying one possible destination for the disembodied soul. It is particularly associated with Pythagoreans (see PYTHAGORAS (1)), and later (?) with 'Orphics' (see ORPHISM); in the 5th cent. it is attested in *Pindar (*Ol.* 2. 56–80), *Empedocles (DK 31 B115), and *Herodotus (1) (2. 123, which claims, probably wrongly, that Greeks borrowed it from Egypt). For Pythagoreans, the transmigrating entity retains its individual identity (DK 21 B7), but *Plato (1), who inherited the general idea from the Pythagoreans, specifies that souls do not remember previous bodily existences. 'Transmigration', or (in late sources) 'metempsychosis' (μετεμψύχωσις or μετενσωμάτωσις), is different from παλιγγενεσία (palingenesia), which strictly refers to the periodic recurrence of events in *Stoicism. *Caesar reports that the Gallic druids (see RELIGION, CELTIC) believe that 'souls (*animae*) do not perish, but after death pass from (their original owners) to others' (*BGall.* 6. 14. 5; *Diodorus (3) Siculus, 5. 28. 6, directly connects Gaulish with Pythagorean beliefs).

Burkert, *GR* 296–301.
C. J. R.

Transpadana, that part of Cisalpine Gaul (see GAUL (CISALPINE)) which lies beyond (from the Roman point of view) the river Po (see PADUS), as opposed to Cispadana, the area 'this side' of the Po.

See POMPEIUS STRABO, CN., and CRASSUS.

Syme, *RP* 5, 431 ff.

transport, wheeled (see also NAVIGATION; SHIPS; TRAVEL). The wheel played a prominent role in traction in the ancient Mediterranean lands (contrast its absence in pre-Columbian societies of the Americas). It is more difficult to gauge its economic and social efficacy.

The role of chariots in the poems of *Homer (an echo of the late 2nd-millennium fashion for this form of warfare, also apparent in Indian epic), established an élite function for light wheeled vehicles: this was reinforced by their use for a variety of ritual movements of cult-personnel or objects. Such vehicles were essentially for use over short distances, whether in war or religion. The war-chariot continued to be of social and military significance in the La Tène cultures (cf. that of the *Vix burial, *c*.500 BC; see also CELTS), which may have had some influence on Italic and Roman practice, in which the *tensa* for religious images, and *carpentum* or *pilentum* for privileged participants (such as *matronae* from 395 BC, Livy 5. 25. 9), were important. The light cart (*zeugos*, a yoke) for relatively rapid movement of people was a luxury but quite widespread where the terrain was suitable.

Roman practice adapted from the Celtic chariot the *essedum* and *cisium* for light rapid transit (a 90-km. (56-mile) journey in 10 hours at night with a relay of *cisia*, Cic. *Rosc. Am.* 19).

2. Carts and wagons (*hamaxa*, *plaustrum*) for the movement of heavy materials, particularly bulk foodstuffs, are attested in the cultures of the Fertile Crescent, and in Danubian Europe, from an early period, and remained in constant use in the Greek and Roman countryside, as well as for transporting goods for state-purposes as at war. The heavy *raeda* (up to 1,000 lb. (xxix) burden in late-antique legislation) was an important example: note also the *angaria* or heavy wagons of the *cursus publicus* (see POSTAL SERVICE).

3. Much of the Roman vocabulary for wheeled vehicles was of Celtic origin, but it remains unclear when, to what extent, and for what purpose which Celtic-speaking peoples disseminated the designs and their names. Nor is it clear whether the origin is to be sought more in the nomadic social forms of La Tène Europe (cf. Caesar, *BGall.* 1, 3, on the *Helvetii) or in the needs of temperate agricultural production and marketing.

Three factors govern the history of wheeled traction: vehicle design, source of traction energy, and environmental modification. For the first two we are very heavily dependent on the often inadequate representations of ancient stone reliefs: archaeological finds are beginning to correct the pessimistic picture derived from these. The technology of load-bearing wheels and axles, like so many practical deployments of *technology in antiquity, seems to have been discontinuous and unsystematic, but occasionally sophisticated: suspension was less often disregarded than was once thought. Harnessing techniques were primarily orientated towards the ox (large ox-teams were the principal traction for very heavy loads like *building materials), but they were less ill-adapted towards horses and mules than was once thought. Road-building (see ROADS) was not primarily designed to aid long-distance wheeled transport, and the extent to which even the Roman road-network at its greatest extent and pitch of maintenance did so is disputed.

Other sources of traction therefore remained important: human porterage (of individuals in sedan-chair, *diphros*/*sella* or litter, *phoreion*/*lectica*; or of goods, particularly over short distances in cities); trains of beasts of burden, horses, donkeys, mules, and increasingly in the east, *camels (as a means of carrying humans *horses retained a certain cachet, and wheeled transport was sometimes considered unmasculine or soft). Both of these were relatively efficient, but for certain very heavy loads (such as ships on the Corinthian *diolkos*) there was no alternative to dragging, which was not. River-transport (see NAVIGATION) and coastal trans-shipment were naturally preferred. Descriptions such as *Strabo's of the Alpine passes under *Augustus (see ALPS) suggest that waggons would be used on stretches of road between trans-shipment points and the steepest sections where baggage animals or porters must have taken over (e.g. 4. 6. 10–11).

In moneyed circles vehicles became very elaborate. They were a regular feature of urban existence, as can be deduced from the rutted pavements of urban roads: civic regulations governed the hours of access and regulated the type of user. But the élite came to disregard the former disapproval of the litter (which had also been subject to attempted control by legislation from time to time) and *lecticarii* (of whom eight might be required for an ornate litter) were a normal part of very rich households (cf. Quint. *Inst.* 1. 2. 7). The emperors in particular expressed their standing through the opulence of their travelling-equipment.

S. Piggott, *The Earliest Wheeled Transport from the Atlantic Coast to the Caspian Sea* (1983); K. Greene, *The Archaeology of the Roman Economy* (1986), 36–43; G. Raepsaet, *Ant. Class.* 1979, 171–6; L. Casson, *Travel in the Ancient World* (1974), 176–96; R. Chevallier, *Roman Roads* (1976), 178–81. N. P.

transvestism, ritual, the wearing of a dress of the opposite gender during *ritual. Ritual transvestism belongs to rituals of reversal where the values of ordinary life are temporarily abandoned; it is often combined with functionally similar rites, as in Dionysiac rituals (see DIONYSUS). It is a special case of ritual change of dress; a structural equivalent is the taking up of freedmen's dress by Roman citizens during the Saturnalia (see SATURNUS). In Greece it occurs in many rituals, among them those which were understood as transformations from initiatory rituals (e.g. *Oschophoria; see INITIATION) where a temporary role reversal was characteristic for marginality. Persons who perpetually live on the margins of society might perpetually wear transvestite attire, as did the eunuch priests of *Cybele (see EUNUCHS, *Religious*).

M. Delcourt, *Hermaphrodite: Mythe et rites de la bisexualité dans l'antiquité classique* (1958); C. Gallini, *SMSR* 1963, 211–28; F. Frontisi-Ducroux and F. Lissarague, in D. M. Halperin and others, *Before Sexuality* (1990), 211 ff. F. G.

Trapezus, a colony of *Sinope (see COLONIZATION, GREEK), traditionally founded in 756 BC as a trading-post in the south-east corner of the Black (*Euxine) Sea with access to the mineral wealth of eastern *Pontus and *Colchis and to the native, east Anatolian kingdom of *Urartu. Its mediocre harbour and inhospitable neighbours retarded its development and in 399 it was still only a small town tributary to Sinope. It formed part of the kingdoms of *Mithradates VI, *Deiotarus, and *Polemon (1), before it was annexed to the Roman empire in AD 64 as part of Pontus Polemoniacus, and was given the status of a free city. Thereafter its importance grew as it was the nearest port to the upper *Euphrates frontier and the harbour works were improved by *Hadrian. It was sacked by the *Goths in the late 250s but remained a garrison town of importance and was to become an important centre in the Byzantine age.

F. Cumont, *Studia Pontica* 2 (1906), 362 ff. T. B. Mitford, *ANRW* 2. 7. 2 (1980), 1187. T. R. S. B.; S. M.

Trasimene, Lake, battle of (21 June 217 BC). An ambush on a huge scale, Trasimene was the second of *Hannibal's victories. The consul, C. *Flaminius (1), with probably some 25,000 men, followed Hannibal, with perhaps some 60,000, into the narrow passage along the north shore of the lake, and found his path blocked by Spaniards and Africans, while slingers and pikemen attacked his right, Celts his left, and cavalry his rear. The consul himself fell, with 15,000 of his soldiers, and all but a handful of the rest were taken prisoner. There is some doubt about where exactly the battle took place. *Polybius (1)'s account fits the area between Passignano and Magione, and is probably to be preferred, although it has been claimed that archaeological evidence—which may not be relevant—supports *Livy's apparent location between Pieve Confini and Passignano.

RE 6 A 2, 'Trasimenischer See'; Polyb. 3. 80 ff.; Livy, 22. 4–6; J. F. Lazenby, *Hannibal's War* (1978); J. Seibert, *Hannibal* (1993). J. F. La.

travel Levels of personal mobility varied greatly in the ancient Mediterranean. Certain categories of individual were regarded as mobile throughout: the *emporos* (*trader) was a recognizable figure already in the Homeric poems, and normally rootless wanderers of the archaic period include many types of technical expert (see DĒMIOURGOI), such as healers, seers, scribes, practitioners of the visual and performance arts, and (following a practice established since the bronze age) workers in special materials such as metallurgists or glassworkers. Traders remain a standard figure of mobility, from the great wanderers in *Herodotus (1), such as Colaeus, or Sostratus (for whom see AEGINA; TRADE, GREEK), to **negotiatores* attested on Roman tomb-inscriptions.

Two forms of human service were required in sufficient quantities to generate a more substantial displacement of people: the general *labour provided by the slave, and the fighting skills of the soldier. The Archaic period saw the development of structures for the recruitment of *mercenaries, through which large numbers of fighting men moved from Greece and Anatolia to Egypt, the Levant, and the Fertile Crescent; and the distribution of demographically significant numbers of humans by the nascent slave trade (as attested in *Solon's poems).

These circumstances combined to make the Mediterranean sea-ways a world of opportunity and danger in which legality was tenuous and violence normal: the prevalence of plunder, *piracy, and razzia reflects this (see SYLĒ). Early community action exploited the opportunities too, and the movements of colonists (*apoikoi*) interested in agricultural produce, exchange-opportunities, and exploitable labour must be added to the picture (see COLONIZATION, GREEK). Women were involved in slave-mobility (witness the regulations on Hellenistic Greek islands keeping women indoors to protect them from being snatched by pirates) and in some resettlement schemes: making both much more significant demographically.

Many of these tendencies survived the regulation of international relations and the increasing orderliness of contacts and communications over the Classical period. Leaving home to be a soldier, and perhaps settling far away, remained a standard experience through the early decades of the successor kingdoms, and rising standards of urban living created an ever-growing demand for slaves, and an increasing economic interdependence which involved more people in the business of trade. The Roman dominion was also predicated on a high level of mobility, and to the other processes added the development from Hellenistic kingdoms' practice of movements which could be regarded as in some sense administrative, managing supplies and exactions and serving in the entourages of officials. As all of these processes developed, the opportunities for parasitizing them did so too, and piracy and rapine (see BRIGANDAGE) increased until the Roman state in the age of *Pompey and *Augustus had no alternative but to extirpate it in a thoroughgoing way. The regime of mobility under the Roman empire was thus more secure (the risks from robbers and brigands remained real, even in Italy), if still vulnerable to weather conditions and the multiple discomforts of ancient transportation technology. Its scale is witnessed by onomastics, epitaphs, papyrus letters, literary anecdote, cultural uniformity, economic cohesion, administrative efficacy, the existence of social and cultural diasporas and (from the Antonine age) the first instances of pandemic *disease. Soldiers, traders, officials, and slaves retained a particular role in promoting it.

The development, for reasons essentially of economic or social necessity, of widespread background mobility and its infrastructure made more or less voluntary travel and its culture possible. The result was that some provision of support in the form of *inns and eating-places came to be common, though the élite always preferred to rely on reciprocal hospitality (see FRIENDSHIP,

RITUALIZED). Journeying to the increasingly popular Panhellenic sanctuaries seems to have become socially diffused at least by the 4th cent. Élite journeys took on something of the character of *tourism, fuelled by the descriptive and geographical literature that also increased in parallel with mobility in general. Certain destinations in the Aegean and in Egypt (Athens, Sparta, *Memphis and the *Fayūm, *Thebes (2) and the Valley of the Kings) were particularly favoured. Travelling to acquire an education became common for the rich with the multiplication of centres of intellectual prestige from the 4th cent., and the cultural gradient between Greek and Roman made formative travel particularly to *Athens and the cities of Asia important to the conquering élite, who could well afford to do it in style. Touring became a pastime of the emperors, never more than in the imperial journeys of *Hadrian, whose monument was his eclectic villa near *Tibur.

On a larger scale, the related phenomena of the pursuits of religious and medical cures took more people from their homes, and late antiquity carried this on in the beginnings of *pilgrimage. At the same time there seems to have been considerable opportunistic movement towards cities, especially the very largest ones, and Rome above all, which maintained the populations of those communities against the demographic challenges of high mortality. Declining populations, increasing insecurity, and more limited mobility in the 5th and 6th cents. were thus closely interlinked phenomena.

See also NAVIGATION, ROADS, TRANSPORT, WHEELED.

L. Casson, *Travel in the Ancient World* (1974), 176–96; R. Chevallier, *Roman Roads* (1976), 178–81; G. Camassa and S. Fasce (eds.), *Idea e realtà del viaggio: Il viaggio nel mondo antico* (1991); J.-M. André and M.-F. Baslez, *Voyager dans l'antiquité* (1993). N. P.

treason See EISANGELIA; MAIESTAS; PERDUELLIO.

treasuries (in sanctuaries) See SANCTUARIES; (in Roman public finance) see AERARIUM.

treaties See ALLIANCE; FOEDUS; LAW, INTERNATIONAL; LIBATIONS; OATHS.

Trebatius (*RE* 7) **Testa, Gaius,** an equestrian (see EQUITES) Roman lawyer to whom *Cicero, a close friend, dedicated his *Topica* ('Topics'). Cicero having recommended him to *Caesar as legal adviser, he enjoyed the latter's favour and later that of *Augustus (see also Hor. *Serm.* 2. 1. 4 f.). An ingenious casuist whose extensive writings do not survive, he persuaded Augustus that informal codicils could properly be recognized as valid (Justinian, *Inst.* 2. 25). M. *Antistius Labeo was his pupil.

Lenel, *Pal.* 2. 343–52; Bremer 1. 376–424; Wieacker, *RRG* 1. 612–14; Kunkel 1974, 28; Watson 1974. T. Hon.

Trebia (now Trebbia), a river flowing north into the Po (see PADUS) near *Placentia (mod. Piacenza), and the scene of *Hannibal's first victory in Italy (December 218 BC). By sending his Numidians to harass his camp (see NUMIDIA), Hannibal induced the Roman commander, Ti. Sempronius Longus, to lead his 36,000 infantry and 4,000 cavalry across to the left bank of the river and to deploy with it at his back; Hannibal had about 29,000 infantry and 11,000 cavalry. His cavalry routed the inferior Roman cavalry, exposing their infantry's flanks to attack from cavalry, light troops, and elephants, and their rear was attacked by 2,000 picked troops, led by his brother, *Mago (2), who had been hidden somewhere to one side of the Roman line of approach. The Roman wings disintegrated and were annihilated

against the river, but the Roman centre managed to break through and make its way to Placentia.

J. F. Lazenby, *Hannibal's War* (1978); J. Seibert, *Hannibal* (1993). J. F. L.

Trebius Niger (*RE* 5) (date doubtful: perhaps 1st cent. AD) is several times quoted on points in natural history by *Pliny (1) (e.g. *HN* 9. 80, 89, 93; 10. 40; 32. 15).

Trebonianus Gallus See VIBIUS TREBONIANUS GALLUS, C.

Trebonius (*RE* 6), **Gaius,** quaestor *c.*60 BC, tribune of the *plebs* (see TRIBUNI PLEBIS) 55, when he carried the *lex Trebonia* conferring five-year commands on *Pompey and *Crassus. Pompey received the two Spanish provinces and Crassus Syria. As *legatus* (see LEGATI) he did good service in Gaul (55–50) and in 49 conducted the siege of *Massalia. Praetor in 48, he was sent next year to Spain, but failed against the Pompeians. Though appointed *suffect consul by *Caesar in 45, he is said to have plotted against him in that year, and he took part in the actual assassination in 44, detaining M. *Antonius (2) (Mark Antony) outside. Proconsul of Asia 43, he was treacherously murdered by P. *Cornelius Dolabella (1) at Smyrna. He published a collection of Cicero's witticisms. C. E. S.; E. B.

trees See ARBORICULTURE; TIMBER; TREES, SACRED.

trees, sacred Trees have been involved in cult in the Aegean world since the bronze age (see RELIGION, MINOAN AND MYCENAEAN). They perhaps symbolized the renewal of life, appearing as central features in a sanctuary or associated with anthropomorphic deities. The (probably genuine) ring of Nestor shows a Tree of Life (for which notion see G. Zuntz, *Persephone* (1971), 386 ff.). Sometimes single boughs stand inside the horns of consecration (e.g. Psychro plaque). The tree continued in Classical cult: *Dionysus stands before a Minoan-type tree sanctuary on a red-figure vase from *Gela. He received cult as *Dendritēs*, *Endendros* (both names derived from the Greek for 'tree') throughout Greece (Plut. *Quaest. conv.* 675), although he specialized in the cultivation of the vine. At Symi in Crete *Hermes Kedrites emerged from bronze age cult: he is shown sitting in a tree which represented the tree of life and vegetation. The same significance may in part lie behind the curious myths of *Helen *dendritēs*, who was hanged from a tree in *Rhodes (Paus. 3. 19. 10), and *Artemis *apanchōmenē* (hanged Artemis) in Arcadian Caphyae (Paus. 8. 23. 6).

Some trees were associated with particular divinities for special reasons, like the mantic (oracular) oak of *Zeus at *Dodona, Athena's *olive, which symbolized the source of Athens' prosperity, or the laurel of Apollo with its apotropaic and purifying properties. The palm was sacred to *Leto on *Delos; in Laconian Boeae (see LACONIA), Artemis Soteira was worshipped in the form of a myrtle (Paus. 3. 22. 12), and she had a cult as Kedreatis in Arcadian *Orchomenus (2). In popular belief trees housed some kind of 'soul'; spirits of the woods and mountains lived in them. Some were revered for their age (cf. Quint. *Inst.* 10. 1. 88 on Ennius). The *nymphs haunted sacred groves, which were the first natural sanctuaries of the gods (Hom. *Il.* 20. 8; *Od.* 10. 350; *Hymn. Hom. Ven.* 264–8). *Poseidon had a sacred grove at Onchestus in *Boeotia (Hom. *Il.* 2. 506), Athena on Phaeacia (*Od.* 6. 321; see SCHERIA). At *Curium on Cyprus the sanctuary of Apollo Hylates arose from a sacred grove.

A sacred fig-tree stood in the Roman Forum near the sanctuary of Rumina the goddess of nurture or nursing (Plut. *Rom.* 4; G.

Radke, *Götter Altitaliens* (1965), 274; cf. the cornel-tree which grew from *Romulus' javelin on the *Palatine).

Evans, *JHS* 1901, 99–204; Nilsson, *MMR*[2] (1950); N. Marinatos in *Fragen und Probleme der bronzezeitlichen ägäischen Glyptik*, Corpus der minoischen und mykenischen Siegel, Beiheft 3 (1989), 127–43 (trees in bronze age sanctuaries); Nilsson, *GGR*[3] (1967) 1, pl. 35, 1 (Gela vase), 209–12; W. Mannhardt, *Antike Wald- und Feldkulte*[2] (1904); *BCH* 1976, 211–13; *Arch. Rep.* 1974/5, 28, fig. 53 (Hermes Kedrites).
S. E.; J. H. C.; B. C. D.

Tremelius (*RE*, Tremellius 5) **Scrofa, Gnaeus,** praetor, then proconsul in Transalpine Gaul, where he led an expedition towards the Rhine, before 67 BC, perhaps as the immediate successor of M. *Fonteius. He was *Varro's colleague on *Caesar's agrarian commission in 59 and was introduced by Varro into his *De re rustica* as one of the speakers, both because of his *cognomen* (= Sow) and because he had written a treatise on agriculture, later praised by *Columella for its elegance.

P. A. Brunt, *CR* 1972, 309 ff.; G. Perl, *AJAH* 1980, 97 ff. (The *RE* article is confused.). E. B.

Treveri, a Celtic people in the Moselle basin. The ancient claim that they possessed Germanic blood is unsubstantiated by other sources. They helped *Caesar in 57 BC, but subsequently proved difficult. They caused more trouble in 29 BC, AD 21, and 70, and suffered accordingly. However, they received a new capital, *Augusta Treverorum (Trier), under Augustus; and the opportunities of the Roman peace tempted them to loyalty. During the 2nd and early 3rd cents. they appear as enterprising and prosperous farmers and traders (cf. the reliefs on the Igel column, near Trier). The invasions of the 3rd cent. damaged this culture, but the land recovered somewhat with the establishment of the imperial court at Trier. Though subject to Frankish attack from the early 5th cent., Treveran territory was perhaps still a Roman enclave *c.*500.

J. Krier, *Die Treverer ausserhalb ihrer Civitas* (1981); E. M. Wightman, *Gallia Belgica* (1985). J. F. Dr.

tria nomina See NAMES, PERSONAL, ROMAN.

tribes (subdivisions of citizen-body) See PHYLAI; TRIBUS; for *ethnē* see ETHNICITY.

Tribonianus (*RE* 1), the main architect of *Justinian's codification of Roman law in the 6th cent. AD, was a lawyer from *Side in Pamphylia who practised as an advocate and rose to be **magister officiorum** (master of offices) and in September 529 quaestor (minister of justice). He was a member of the commission to prepare Justinian's *Codex* of imperial laws (AD 528–9), and in 530 Justinian put him in charge of the preparation of the *Digesta* of legal writings (530–3), which he supervised throughout. He seems also to have played a full part (though this is disputed) in the detailed work of excerpting and editing the texts of earlier lawyers, of which he had a large personal collection and a deep knowledge. In 533 he headed a commission of three to prepare an up-to-date version of *Gaius (2)'s *Institutes*, and in 534 produced a second edition of the *Codex*. Accused of corruption and innovation, he was removed from office in January 532 as a sop to the public at the time of the Nika riots, but continued to work on the codification and by 535 had resumed the office of quaestor, which he held until his death in 541 or 542, continuing to draft new laws (*Novellae*). An erudite and self-confident man and a writer in the grand style in both Latin and Greek, Tribonianus, who is said to have been anti-Christian, was steeped in Neopla-

tonic philosophy of an Aristotelian type (see NEOPLATONISM; ARISTOTLE). In the Renaissance he was accused of ruining Roman law by introducing changes (see INTERPOLATION) into the classical legal texts, originally written 250 to 500 years earlier, when they were incorporated in Justinian's *Digesta*. On a balanced view, however, the changes he made, apart from shortening and eliminating what was obsolete, were limited; they consisted largely in developing ideas found in the earlier writers, with whom Tribonianus considered himself to be on a par. See JUSTINIAN'S CODIFICATION.

T. Honoré, *Tribonian* (1978); W. Waldstein *ZRG* 1980, 232–55; G. Lanata, *Legislazione e natura nelle Novelle Giustinianee* (1984); E. Stein, *Bull. de l'Acad. roy. Belg. cl. lett.* 1937, 365. T. Hon.

tribuni aerarii, originally treasury officials concerned with the collection of *tributum and its disbursement as military *stipendium. The office disappeared, but the title may have been preserved. It reappears in 70 BC, for the third of the classes of jurors (after senators and *equites) under the *lex Aurelia* (see AURELIUS COTTA, L.). These men had the same census qualification as the *equites* and are often subsumed under that description. It has been argued that they were men of equestrian census not enrolled by the censors in the equestrian centuries, but there is no real evidence on their definition. *Caesar removed them from the juries and the title then disappeared.

Mommsen, *Röm. Staatsr. 3*[2]. 189 ff., 532 f.; C. Nicolet, *OE* 598 ff. (all the evidence), and *Tributum* (1976), 46 ff. (evidence and speculation); T. P. Wiseman, *Roman Studies* 1987, 61 ff., 69 ff. E. B.

tribuni militum commanded the tribal contingents in the army of the early Roman state. Subsequently six were appointed as the most senior officers within a *legion, and at least five years' previous military experience was expected. They were equestrians (see EQUITES), though some were the sons of senators, and occasionally senior men took the post. The tribunes of the first four legions recruited each year were elected by the people, while those for additional legions were chosen by the commander. Two tribunes acting in rotation commanded a legion for two months, but they had no specific tactical responsibilities and their duties encompassed the general welfare and discipline of the troops and supervision of the camp. Under *Caesar, as *legati were used more extensively, tribunes declined in importance.

In the imperial period one of the six legionary tribunes was normally a senator (*tribunus laticlavius*), a young man early in his career, probably holding the post for one year. The other five tribunes were equestrians (*tribuni angusticlavii*) who were often more experienced in army life. By the mid-1st cent. AD a pattern had emerged in which many equestrians held at least three military posts—prefect of a cohort, *tribunus militum*, prefect of an *ala*. Tribunes also commanded individual cohorts in the urban troops, and sometimes larger milliary cohorts or cohorts of Roman citizens, while by the late empire the term was employed to describe officers of the imperial guards, the legions, *vexillationes* and *auxilia* of the field army, and also the cohorts of the *limitanei*. See CURSUS HONORUM.

J. Suolahti, *The Junior Officers of the Roman Army in the Republican Period* (1955), 35; A. R. Birley, *The Fasti of Roman Britain* (1981), 8. J. B. C.

tribuni plebis (or **plebi**), 'tribunes', were the officers of the *plebs first created in 500–450 BC (traditionally in 494, the date of the first *secession of the *plebs* and their corporate recognition). The word is evidently connected with *tribus, but it is uncertain whether the tribunes were at first chiefs of the tribes who later became officers of the *plebs* (they are sometimes φύλαρχοι in Greek, but δήμαρχοι is standard), or whether the title imitated that of the *tribuni militum* already existing. The original number of the tribunes is variously given as two, four, or five; by 449 it had certainly risen to ten. The tribunes were charged with the defence of the persons and property of the plebeians (*ius auxilii*). Their power derived not from statute (initially, at least) but from the oath sworn by the plebeians to guarantee their *sacrosanctitas*, or inviolability. Elected by the plebeian assembly (*concilium plebis*, more usually called *comitia plebis tributa*) and exercising their power within the precincts of the city, the tribunes could summon the *plebs* to assembly (*ius agendi*) and elicit resolutions (*plebiscita*; see PLEBISCITUM). They asserted a right of enforcing the decrees of the *plebs* and their own rights (*coercitio*); connected with *coercitio* was a measure of jurisdiction, including, probably, capital. They possessed, moreover, though perhaps not from the very first, a right of veto (*intercessio*) against any act performed by a magistrate (or by another tribune), against elections, laws, *senatus consulta*. From this veto only the *dictator (until *c.*300 BC) and, perhaps, the *interrex were exempt.

This revolutionary power was gradually recognized by the state. The tribunes became indistinguishable from magistrates of the state, although without *imperium or insignia. The full acknowledgement of their power came with the recognition of *plebiscita* as laws binding upon the whole *populus* and not just the *plebs* (by the *lex Hortensia* of 287). Tribunes were first admitted to listen to senatorial debates; at least from the 3rd cent. BC they had the right to convoke the senate; in the 2nd cent. the tribunate became sufficient qualification for membership of the senate (probably by a *lex Atinia* of 149). From the 4th and 3rd cents. the tribunate became in part an instrument by which the senate could control magistrates through the veto and the right to summon the senate. But the revolutionary potential and popular origins of the office did not disappear. In the first surviving contemporary discussion of the tribunes, from about the middle of the 2nd cent., *Polybius (1) (6. 16) states that 'they are bound to do what the people resolve and chiefly to focus upon their wishes'. Succeeding years saw the tribunate active in the pursuit of the people's interest and the principles of popular sovereignty and public accountability, as evidenced by the beginning of the practice of addressing the people in the forum directly (145), the introduction of the secret ballot in assemblies (139 and 137), concern with the corn supply (138), the agrarian legislation of Ti. *Sempronius Gracchus (3) (133), and above all by the legislation and speeches, for which contemporary evidence survives, of C. *Sempronius Gracchus (123–122). This movement continued sporadically into the tribunates of L. *Appuleius Saturninus at the end of the 2nd cent. but did not long survive the domestic chaos of 100 and the convulsion of the *Social War (3) and consequent enfranchisement of peninsular Italy. Active tribunes came increasingly to be associated with the particular interests and grievances of the urban *plebs* (and frequently with those of one or another of the emergent dynasts); the effective popular instrument was now the army. From the 130s on attempts were made to limit the legislative potential of the tribunate as well as the use of the veto. *Sulla excluded tribunes from the magistracies of the Roman People and abolished, or severely curtailed, their power to legislate, their judicial powers, and their veto. In 75 the bar from magistracies was removed, and in 70 the full *tribunicia potestas* was restored to the tribunes. This tribunician power, divorced from the office but retaining its associations, was valued by the architects of the imperial state in the construc-

tion of their personal power. *Caesar assumed at least the tribunician *sacrosanctitas*, and *Augustus, probably in three steps (36, 30, 23 BC), gained a permanent *tribunicia potestas*. Reft of its power and all independence, the tribunate itself remained as a step in the senatorial career for plebeians alternatively with the aedileship until the 3rd cent. AD, and there is still evidence for the title in the 5th.

Mommsen, *Röm. Staatsr.* 2. 272 ff.; A. H. J. Greenidge, *Roman Public Life* (1901), 93 ff.; G. Niccolini, *Il tribunato della plebe* (1932), and *I fasti dei tribuni della plebe* (1934); Lily Ross Taylor, *JRS* 1962, 19 ff.; E. Meyer, *Römische Staat und Staatsgedanke*[3] (1964); J. Bleicken, *Das Volkstribunat der klassischen Republik*[2] (1968); P. A. Brunt, *Social Conflicts in the Roman Republic* (1971); H. F. Jolowicz and B. Nicholas, *Historical Introduction to the Study of Roman Law*[3] (1972); F. Millar, *JRS* 1986, 1 ff.; L. Thommen, *Das Volkstribunat der späten römischen Republik* (1989); A. Drummond, *CAH* 7[2]/2 (1989), 212 ff. (with bibliog.); Broughton, *MRR*.   P. S. D.

***tribunicia potestas*, tribunician power** See TRIBUNI PLEBIS (final section).

tribus, division of the Roman people. In early times the Roman people were supposedly divided into three tribes (the word *tribus* may be connected with Latin *tres* = three) called Ramnes, Tities, and Luceres. There is no known parallel for this structure elsewhere in Italy. The suggestion that *Virgil (*Aen.* 10. 202, with Servius' comm.) refers to a tribal division at *Mantua is doubtful, while in the Iguvine tables (see TABULAE IGUVINAE) *trifu* (= *tribus*?) means the whole community. Everything about the three original Roman tribes is obscure. The modern theory that they represent different ethnic groups (e.g. Latins, Sabines (see SABINI), and *Etruscans) is unfounded and improbable. The three tribes were subdivided into *curiae* (see CURIA (1)) and were supposedly the basis of the earliest military organization of the state. A vestige of this system survived in the Roman cavalry; the six oldest centuries of cavalry comprised two each of Ramnes, Tities, and Luceres.

In republican times these original tribes had been replaced by a system of local tribes, to which Roman citizens belonged by virtue of residence. Tradition ascribes the local tribes to Servius *Tullius, who divided the city into four tribes, and the countryside into a number of 'rustic' tribes. By 495 BC there were seventeen rustic tribes. As Rome expanded during the 4th and 3rd cents., further tribes were created to incorporate newly won territory in which Roman citizens were settled or citizenship was conferred on the native inhabitants. By 241 BC the number of tribes had reached 35 (4 urban, 31 rustic). After that it was decided not to create any further tribes, but to include all additional territory in the existing 35. As a result the tribes ceased to be confined to single districts, and came to include separate territories in different parts of Italy.

This process became more marked when Roman citizenship was extended to all of peninsular Italy after the *Social War (3). An attempt to restrict the new citizens to a small number of tribes (in order to diminish their voting power in the *comitia) was thwarted, and they were distributed among the existing 31 rustic tribes.

The distribution of citizens among the tribes was always a sensitive political issue. In 312 BC the censor Ap. *Claudius Caecus caused a storm when he registered lower-class citizens (probably including *freedmen) in the rustic tribes. This act, the precise significance of which is not certain, was reversed in 304, and in general during the republic freedmen were confined to the urban tribes, which came to be regarded as socially inferior and politically disadvantaged. The punishment of 'removal from a tribe' (*tribu movere*), which the censors could inflict, in effect meant relegation to an urban tribe.

Every citizen had to belong to a tribe, a rule which continued in imperial times even for provincials who attained the Roman citizenship. It is not known how or why particular tribes were chosen in such cases, and no consistent rule was followed, although certain tribes tended to be favoured in certain provinces. Thus citizens from Gallia Narbonensis (see GAUL (TRANSALPINE)) were enrolled by preference in the tribus Voltinia, and those from the eastern provinces in the Collina and Quirina. From the Ciceronian age it was normal for a Roman citizen to include his tribe (written in abbreviated form) as part of his formal nomenclature; see NAMES, PERSONAL, ROMAN.

The tribes were used as constituent voting units in political assemblies, and as the basis of army recruitment, the census, and taxation. During the early republic officials called *tribuni aerarii* had charge of the financial obligations of the tribe. Officers called *curatores tribuum* are also attested, but their role is uncertain (as is their relation to the *tribuni aerarii*).

Mommsen, *Röm. Staatsr.* 3³. 161 ff.; W. Kubitschek, *De Romanorum tribuum origine ac propagatione* (1882), and *Imperium Romanum tributim descriptum* (1889); E. Meyer, *Kl. Schr.* 1² (1924), 333 ff.; G. Niccolini, *Studi Bonfante* 2 (1930), 235 ff.; P. Fraccaro, *Athenaeum* 1933, 142 ff. (= *Opuscula* 2. 149 ff.); L. R. Taylor, *Voting Districts of the Roman Republic* (1960); C. Nicolet, *The World of the Citizen in Republican Rome* (1980); R. Thomsen, *King Servius Tullius* (1980), 115 ff.; C. Ampolo, in A. Momigliano, A. Schiavone (eds.), *Storia di Roma* 1 (1988), 169 ff., 229 ff.
A. M.; T. J. Co.

tribute lists (Athenian), records of the *aparchai* (first-fruits; pl. of *aparchē*) of one-sixtieth given as an offering to *Athena from the tribute paid by the members of the *Delian League after the treasury was moved from *Delos to Athens, very probably in 454/3 BC. (It is likely that previously an offering had been given to Delian *Apollo.) From 453 the offerings were calculated not simply on the total but separately on each member's tribute, and numbered lists of these offerings were inscribed in Athens: for the first fifteen years (453–439) on a single large block of marble, for the next eight (438–431) on another large block, and thereafter on a separate stele for each year. It is possible that no tribute was collected in 448, when war against Persia had come to an end and the future of the League was uncertain (whether one year is unrepresented in the sequence on the first block continues to be disputed); in 413 a 5% duty on all goods transported by sea was substituted for the tribute (Thuc. 7. 28. 3–4), but the tribute was probably reintroduced in 410/409. From the beginning there was a tendency to list neighbouring states together; in 442 the practice began of organizing the lists in five regional panels (Ionian, Hellespontine, Thracian, Carian, Island); in 437 some inland Carian states were abandoned and what remained of the Carian panel was combined with the Ionian. Assessments of tribute (ranging from 300 drachmas to the 30 talents of *Aegina and *Thasos) were normally revised every four years: the general level remained constant before the *Peloponnesian War, and in 430, but serious increases were needed in 428 (probably) and 425. In addition to the lists of *aparchai*, we have substantial parts of the assessment list of 425 and smaller fragments of the assessment lists of 422 and 410. In so far as they are preserved or can be reconstructed, the lists give us a valuable indication of which states paid tribute, and how much they paid, from one year to another.

The standard work on the tribute records is B. D. Meritt, H. T. Wade-Gery, and M. F. McGregor, *The Athenian Tribute Lists*, 4 vols. (1939–53); for the most recent edition of the texts see *IG* 1³. 259–90 (*aparchai*), 71, 77, 100 (assessments). M. F. M.; P. J. R.

tributum was a direct tax paid by individuals to the Roman state. Until 167 BC citizens of Rome were liable to pay a *tributum* which was in principle an extraordinary (in contrast to the regular *vectigalia*) levy on their property and might be repaid. The total size of the levy was decided by the senate and varied from year to year. In some years, e.g. 347–345, no *tributum* was levied. After its suspension in 167 BC this form of *tributum* was only again levied in the exigencies of the civil wars after *Caesar's murder. Under the emperors Rome and Roman Italy were exempt from direct taxation. After 167 BC *tributum* came to denote the direct taxes raised in the provinces, either in the form of a land-tax (*tributum soli*) or poll-tax (*tributum capitis*). These were paid by all inhabitants of the provinces, whether Roman citizens or not, except by citizens of *coloniae* (see COLONIZATION, ROMAN) which normally possessed the *ius Italicum* and were consequently exempt, usually from both taxes (*Dig.* 50. 15. 1 and 8), by citizens of cities which had been granted immunity (*immunitas*) by special dispensation, or by persons specifically exempted by a *lex, senatus consultum*, or imperial decree (*SEG* 9. 8. 3).

The *tributum soli*, under the republic, was normally either a fixed sum (*stipendium*) as in Spain and Africa, or a tithe (*decuma*) paid in kind and leased by the censors in Rome to *publicani, as in Asia (see ASIA, ROMAN PROVINCE) of 123 BC (App. *BCiv.* 5. 4. 17–20). Under the emperors the system of leasing of direct taxes to *publicani* was abandoned. *Augustus instituted periodic provincial censuses which formed the basis of assessment. Each provincial city normally received a bloc assessment. The individual provincial was liable to his city, the city to the Roman government. Local magistrates were responsible for collection in their city and its territory. The tax was levied in cash or kind according to custom and regional circumstances.

The *tributum capitis* seems first to have been imposed, along with *tributum soli*, in Africa in 146 BC (App. *Pun.* 135; see AFRICA, ROMAN); otherwise it is not attested before the period of the civil wars. Under the emperors details of its character and incidence are exiguous, although it was almost certainly universal in the provinces. In *Syria we happen to know (*Dig.* 50. 15. 3) that inhabitants were liable from age 14 for men and 12 for women to 65.

In *Egypt the Romans raised a complex pattern of taxes in cash and kind (especially in grain) on the land and its produce, and also imposed a poll-tax (*laographia*) paid by native Egyptian males from 14 to 60, by the inhabitants of the *metropoleis* at reduced rates, but not by the citizens of the Greek cities.

C. Nicolet, *Tributum* (1986); L. Neesen, *Untersuchungen zu den direkten Staatsabgaben des römischen Kaiserzeit* (1980); Brunt, *RIT* ch. 15.
G. P. B.

triclinium See CONVIVIUM; DINING-ROOMS; HOUSES, ITALIAN.

Triclinius, Demetrius (early 14th cent.), one of the most important scholars of his day, lived probably at Thessalonica. He prepared editions of numerous classical poets, using his knowledge of metre to improve the text, and in some cases he also revised the accompanying corpus of *scholia. A number of his emendations are generally accepted; but though he was a better metrician than his contemporaries many of his alterations to the text are violent and unnecessary (see TEXTUAL CRITICISM). He is known to have worked on *Aeschylus, *Sophocles (1), *Euripides, *Aristophanes (1), *Pindar, *Hesiod, *Theocritus, and *Babrius. Several autograph manuscripts survive. His scientific interests are demonstrated by a recently published treatise on lunar theory.

N. G. Wilson, *Scholars of Byzantium* (1983), 249–56.   N. G. W.

Trier See AUGUSTA TREVERORUM.

trierarchy The word *trierarchos* means '*trireme-commander', but at Athens in the 5th and 4th cents. BC the trierarchy was a *liturgy, which the richest citizens could be called on to perform for a year. The state provided the ship and its basic equipment, and normally paid for the crew, but the trierarch had not only to command the ship but also to bear the costs of maintenance and repair, which could amount to as much as one talent. After 411 it became common for two men to share responsibility for a ship, and contractors could be found who would relieve the trierarchs of their personal involvement; reforms in 357 and later involved the organization of those liable in *symmoriai* ('partnerships'). The liturgy was abolished by *Demetrius (3) of Phalerum in 317–307.

The institution is found in some other states (*Rhodes, Arist. *Pol.* 5. 1304[b]; *Teos and Lebedus, *SIG*[3] 344, 66; *Priene, *SIG*[3] 1003, 29), but elsewhere *trierarchos* denotes simply the captain of a warship, and that is perhaps the meaning of the word in *Herodotus (1) (e.g. 6. 14. 2).

V. Gabrielsen, *Financing the Athenian Fleet* (1994). Evidence is to be found particularly in *Orations* 14, 47, 50, and 51 of the Demosthenic corpus (see DEMOSTHENES (2) and APOLLODORUS (2)) and in the Athenian naval records, *IG* 2². 1604–32.   C. G. S., P. J. R.

trigonometry There is no ancient term for trigonometry, since it was not counted as a branch of *mathematics, but ancillary to *astronomy, and even there does not pre-date *Hipparchus (3): when *Aristarchus (1) and *Archimedes (e.g. *Sand-Reckoner* 1. 21) address problems which we would solve by trigonometry, they employ a lemma enabling them to find upper and lower bounds, but no trigonometrical function. Such a function was introduced by Hipparchus, to solve the problem of computing specific positions from geometric models, in the form of a chord table. This was probably computed for a circle with radius 3438' (i.e. $\frac{360°}{2\pi}$, compare the modern radian), and hence is the ancestor of a sine table found in ancient Indian astronomical works. Although no sine function has yet been found in Greek, this too was probably derived by the Indians from lost Hellenistic astronomical works. With his chord table alone Hipparchus could solve all problems of plane trigonometry. Spherical trigonometry was founded by *Menelaus (3) (for the basic theorem see *Sphaerica* 3. 1). Because it lacked a tangent function ancient spherical trigonometry was based not on the spherical triangle but on the four-sided 'Menelaus configuration'. *Ptolemy (4) gives a complete exposition of the basis of plane and spherical trigonometry (*Almagest* 1. 10–13), and his accurate chord table, based on a radius of 60 units, became the norm. No further advances in trigonometry were made in antiquity.

G. J. Toomer, *Centaurus* 1973, 6–28 (for earlier literature).   G. J. T.

Trinovantes, a British tribe in Essex, probably of Belgic origin (see BRITAIN; BELGAE). Mandubracius, their prince, fled to *Caesar from *Cassivellaunus' aggression; the tribe later surrendered (54 BC) and brought over other tribes, making a turning-point in

Caesar's British war. The Trinovantes were protected in Caesar's peace-terms; they maintained an independent monarchy under Addedomarus and Dubnovellaunus down to *Cunobelinus' accession, *c.* AD 5. In 43 they were freed from Catuvellaunian rule (see CATUVELLAUNI), but in 49 suffered deprivation of territory on the foundation of the *colonia* (see COLONIZATION, ROMAN) at *Camulodunum. Aggrieved by the subsequent behaviour of the colonists, in 60 they joined *Boudicca's rebellion, and the colony was destroyed. After its refoundation, the primacy of Camulodunum as an emporium and provincial capital became eclipsed by London, but the provincial centre of the imperial cult remained there (see RULER-CULT). The tribal capital of the Trinovantes probably lay at Caesaromagus (mod. Chelmsford). The *civitas* was mainly agricultural with important timber and pottery industries, and salt-boiling and oyster-fisheries along the coast, which from the late 3rd cent. was defended by the *Saxon Shore fort of Othona (mod. Bradwell).

R. Dunnett, *The Trinovantes* (1975).   S. S. F.

trinundinum (or trinum nundinum) was the interval between three *nundinae* (market days, held every eight days), required between moving and voting a resolution, or between candidates' declaration of their intention to stand for office (*professio*) and the polling, or between the promulgation and execution of a sentence, etc. Formerly supposed to be a fixed period of twenty-four or twenty-five days, it is best interpreted as a variable interval that includes three *nundinae*. The legal force of this measure of publicity was confirmed by the *lex Caecilia Didia* (98 BC).

Mommsen, *Röm. Staatsr.* 3³. 1229 ff.; R. Ogilvie, *Comm. Livy 1–5*, 459 f.; A. Lintott, *CQ* 1965, 281 ff.; A. K. Michels, *Calendar of the Roman Republic* (1967), 191 ff.   P. T.; B. M. L.

Triopas, a *Dorian culture-hero, usually the son of *Helios, but sometimes of *Poseidon, and associated with *Cnidus. 'Concerning the genealogy of Triopas many historians and poets disagree' (Diod. Sic. 5. 61. 3), which is certainly true. Strong links with *Thessaly perhaps reflect the pre-Dorian population of the islands. According to *Diodorus (3), he fled to Cnidus after cutting down a grove of *Demeter at Dotium in *Thessaly and there founded the Triopion, a temple of *Apollo and site of an important Dorian festival (cf. HALICARNASSUS). Better known is the version in which his son, *Erysichthon, committed this outrage against Demeter and was punished with unquenchable hunger.

Wilamowitz, *Hell. Dicht.* 2. 35–40; Wüst, *RE* 7 A 168–74.   R. L. Hu.

Triphiodorus (3rd or early 4th cent. AD), epic poet, native of Egypt. He wrote *Marathoniaca*, *The Story of Hippodamea*, an Ὀδυσσεία λειπογράμματος ('Odyssey' with certain letters avoided', see SEPTIMIUS NESTOR, L.), a paraphrase of Homer's similes, and *The Capture of Troy*. Only the last, in 691 verses, survives, showing a style midway between that described under *Nonnus and the more Homeric manner (cf. HOMER) adopted by *Quintus Smyrnaeus.

Text: B. Gerlaud (Budé, 1982); E. Livrea (Teubner, 1982). With trans. and brief notes: A. W. Mair (Loeb, with Oppian and Colluthus, 1928). General: L. Ferrari, *Sulla Presa di Ilio di Trifiodoro* (1962).   M. L. W.

Tripolis, Phoenician city, a joint foundation of *Tyre, *Sidon, and *Aradus. Between 104 and 95 BC it obtained its freedom from Antiochus IX (see SELEUCIDS), but later fell under a tyrant, who was executed by *Pompey; its autonomy was then restored. Its territory produced a noted wine.

J. Elayi, *Transeuphratène*, vol. 2 (1990). A. H. M. J.; H. S.; J.-F. S.

Tripolitania, name given to an area of western *Libya containing the three cities of *Sabratha, *Oea, and *Lepcis ('Tripolis'), and their hinterlands. Founded as *Phoenician or at least Punic *emporia* (see EMPORION, first entry), they provided sheltered harbours on an otherwise inhospitable shore, but owed their importance largely to trans-Saharan trade and the considerable *olive-oil production of their hinterlands. For long dependencies of *Carthage, they were annexed by *Masinissa and remained in theory subject to the Numidian kings until the Jugurthine War (see NUMIDIA; JUGURTHA). Under Augustus they became part of Africa Proconsularis (see AFRICA, ROMAN), which extended eastwards as far as the Arae Philaenorum on the Greater Syrtis. Their southern frontier zone was administered by the legate of Numidia from early in the 1st cent. AD. The Tripolis had bishops by the mid-3rd cent.

The Tripolitanian pre-desert has been extensively surveyed, especially *c.*100 km. (63 mi.) south of *Lepcis Magna (Sofeggin and Zem-Zem wadi basins), where a complex range of Roman settlement included hilltop villages, open farms, and 'fortified' farms with stout perimeter walls, the last reflecting the need for greater security from the 3rd cent. Barley, wheat, and especially olive cultivation were made possible by efficient rainwater collection and conservation. The village of Ghirza (180 km. (113 mi.) south of Lepcis Magna), with 38 buildings and some spectacular Romano-Libyan mausolea, is particularly well preserved. Further east, in the wadi Kebir, settled agriculture was less well established, and was abandoned entirely in the mid-3rd cent.

A separate province of Tripolitania, governed from Lepcis, was established for the first time only by *Diocletian. It fell to the *Vandals in 455 and was recovered by the Byzantines in 533, when Lepcis became the seat of the *dux limitis Tripolitanae provinciae* (*dux of the *limes of the Tripolitane province). Berber revolts in the mid-6th cent. were suppressed by John Troglita. After the Arab invasions (643–4) Sabratha disappeared; Oea (mod. Tripoli), as well as Tacapae (mod. Gabes) on Tripolitania's western border, survived.

A. Merighi, *La Tripolitania antica* (1940); J. M. Reynolds and J. B. Ward-Perkins, *Inscriptions of Roman Tripolitania* (1952); D. E. L. Haynes, *The Antiquities of Tripolitania* (1956); D. J. Buck and D. J. Mattingly (eds.), *Town and Country in Roman Tripolitania* (1985); I. Sjöström, *Tripolitania in Transition: Late Roman to Early Islamic Settlement* (1993); D. Mattingly, *Tripolitania* (1995). Cults: V. Brouquier-Reddé, *Temples et cultes de Tripolitaine* (1992). Countryside: G. B. D. Jones, in Buck and Mattingly, *Town and Country*, 263–306; M. Reddé, *Prospections des vallées du nord de la Libye (1979–80): La région de Syrte à l'époque romaine* (1988); O. Brogan and D. J. Smith, *Ghirza: A Libyan Settlement in the Roman Period* (1984). Limes: P. Trousset, *Recherches sur le limes Tripolitanus* (1974).

O. B.; R. J. A. W.

Triptolemus, one of the princes of *Eleusis in the Homeric *Hymn to Demeter* (153, 474), to whom the goddess teaches her *mysteries. Athens claimed that he was given corn and the arts of agriculture by *Demeter, and then taught these to other nations. He is frequently portrayed in Attic art from the mid-6th cent. BC onwards receiving Demeter's gifts and setting out on his travels on a wheeled car, which is sometimes winged. *Sophocles' (1) *Triptolemus* (frs. 596–617 Radt) perhaps contributed to his popularity. He was worshipped at Eleusis, was regarded as a lawgiver (Xenocrates fr. 98 Heinze), and became one of the judges in the underworld (Pl. *Ap.* 41a).

F. Schwenn, *RE* 7 A 213–30; N. J. Richardson, *The Homeric Hymn to Demeter* (1974; 1979), 194–6; G. Schwartz, *Triptolemus: Ikonographie einer Agrarien- und Mysteriengottheit* (1987); Clinton, *Iconography* 38–59, 100–2, 112–13. N. J. R.

trireme The trireme (Gk. τριήρης, Lat. *triremis*) was the standard warship of the classical world for much of the time from the 5th cent. BC to the 4th cent. AD. A long rowing-ship, its principal weapon was a bronze ram, fixed on the prow at the water-line. It was rowed by oarsmen arranged in groups of three, sitting one above the other and each oarsman pulling a single oar of equal length. The topmost level of men were called in Greek *thranitai*, the middle ones *zygioi*, and the lowest ones *thalamioi*. On an Athenian trireme of the Classical period there were 170 oarsmen, ten marines, four archers, and sixteen sailors, including the helmsman, making a total of 200. Trials of a modern reconstruction of an Athenian trireme have shown that speeds in excess of 9 knots are possible. Triremes could be rowed with only some of the oars manned, but this reduced speed considerably. For long sailing passages sails were used, but masts were usually removed and left on the shore before battle.

The origins of the trireme are uncertain. There is no reliable evidence as to where the ship was first developed, although modern scholars tend to favour either Phoenicia (see PHOENICIANS) or Egypt as its birthplace, and to date its invention to the second half of the 6th cent. BC. The heyday of the trireme was the 5th cent. BC, when the finest practitioners of trireme warfare were the Athenians, who perfected the art of manœuvring at speed to ram and disable enemy ships (see DIEKPLOUS).

From the mid-4th cent. BC larger warships with oarsmen arranged in groups of four, five, six, or more were developed. These ships relied far less on ramming and high speed manœuvring, and more on boarding and missile weapons. Thus the trireme became less important in Mediterranean fleets until the creation of the Roman imperial navy, which used triremes extensively until the 4th cent. AD. See NAVIES; SHIPS.

J. S. Morrison and J. F. Coates, *The Athenian Trireme: The History and Reconstruction of an Ancient Greek Warship* (1986); H. T. Wallinga, *Ships and Sea Power before the Great Persian War: The Ancestry of the Ancient Trireme* (1993). P. de S.

Triton The meaning of the name is unknown. Tritons sometimes play a subordinate part in a legend: a triton in human form appears to the *Argonauts at Lake Tritonis and gives them a clod of earth which is the pledge of future possession of *Cyrene; *Virgil (*Aen.* 6. 171–4) tells of a triton who, furious at the presumption of the human trumpeter Misenus (see MISENUM) in daring to challenge him to a contest playing the conch, drowns him. *Pausanias (3) (9. 20. 4, 21. 1) had seen what were represented as bodies of tritons.

In art, the fish-tailed Triton wrestles with *Heracles, assuming the iconography of *Nereus around the mid-6th cent. BC; the scene is rare after *c.*510. J. Boardman (*Rev. Arch.* 1972) suggests that the story, unknown in literature, alludes to Athenian maritime success under the Pisistratids (see IMAGERY; PISISTRATUS). Triton is probably shown on two Archaic pediments on the Athenian Acropolis (see ATHENS, TOPOGRAPHY). On three 5th-cent. vases, he supports *Theseus on his visit to the Ocean. He and Nereus watch *Peleus wrestling *Thetis. Later, Triton is often shown blowing a conch.

R. Glynn, *AJArch.* 1981, 121–32. K. W. A.

tritopatores, tritopatreis The spirits of the collective ancestors of a gentilitial group (such as a *genos, 'clan') or of a community, they were concerned with its propagation and continuation. Known from *Attica, *Delos, *Troezen, *Selinus, and *Cyrene, they corresponded to the unnamed body of ancestors elsewhere. The most important source is the Attic historian *Phanodemus, FGrH 325 F 6, with Jacoby's commentary (cf. *Demon, FGrH 327 fr. 2, and *Philochorus, FGrH 328 fr. 12). Their generative force is indicated by Athenian sacrifice and prayers to them at marriage and by Philochorus' description of them as the 'parents of mankind'. Demon identified them with the impregnating winds. In the Orphic Physikos (fr. 318 Kern; see ORPHIC LITERATURE, bibliog.) they are given names and called guardians of the winds.

M. Jameson, D. Jordan, and R. Kotansky, *A lex sacra from Selinous* (1994).
M. H. J.

trittyes ('thirds'), divisions both of the four old and of the ten new tribes at Athens. Little is known of the old *trittyes*; an ancient guess that they were identical with the *phratries seems to be mistaken; that each contained four of the *naukrariai is possible but far from certain. In *Cleisthenes (2)'s new locally based organization each of the ten tribes (*phylai) was divided into *trittyes*, and it is disputed whether each *trittys* was located entirely in one of his three regions, as stated by *Ath. Pol.* 21. 4, or the regional principle was modified to produce *trittyes* of approximately equal size. Each *trittys* consisted of one or more *demes, commonly but not invariably a block of neighbouring demes. The *trittyes* did not become active corporations to the same extent as the tribes and the demes, but they played some part in the organization of the navy, and possibly of the army, and in appointment to some of the larger boards.

J. S. Traill, *The Political Organization of Attica, Hesp.* Suppl. 14 (1975), *Demos and Trittys* (1986); P. Siewert, *Die Trittyen Attikas und die Heeresreform des Kleisthenes* (1982), with D. M. Lewis, *Gnomon* 1983, 431–6; M. H. Hansen, *C & M* 1990, 51–4.   A. W. G.; T. J. C.; P. J. R.

triumph, the procession of a Roman general who had won a major victory to the temple of *Jupiter on the *Capitol. The word came to the Romans from Greek (*thriambos*) via *Etruscan and appears in Etruscan form (*triumpe*) in the *Carmen arvale. The origin of the triumph cannot be recovered. In Roman tradition, all the kings except for the peaceful *Pompilius Numa celebrated triumphs, followed by the founding consul, P. *Valerius Poplicola, but in its developed form it owed much to Etruscan influence, and Etruscan paintings show similar rituals which we cannot fully interpret. In classical times, the procession entered Rome through the *porta triumphalis* ('triumphal gate') through which no one else might enter. (It may have been part of the porta Carmentalis: see CARMENTIS OR CARMENTA.) It made its way to the Capitol by a long route including open spaces where large numbers could see it. It comprised, essentially, the *triumphator* (dressed in the costume said to have been the kings' and close to Jupiter's) on a four-horse chariot, with any sons of suitable age as outriders; eminent captives (normally destined for execution) and freed Roman prisoners of war dressed as the *triumphator's* freedmen; the major spoils captured; his army; and animals for sacrifice. The whole senate and all the magistrates were supposed to escort it. Increasingly costly and elaborate details were added from *c.*200 BC, including banners, paintings of sieges and battles, musicians, and torch-bearers. The *triumphator* was preceded by his *lictors, and a slave rode with him, holding a laurel wreath over his head and reminding him that he was mortal. The soldiers chanted insulting verses, no doubt to avert the gods' displeasure. (See FESCENNINI.) The right to triumph depended on a special

vote of the people allowing him to retain his military *imperium in the city, and so in fact on the senate's decision to ask for this vote.

In classical times the prerequisites for expecting such a decision were a victory in a declared war over a foreign enemy, with at least 5,000 of them killed and the termination of the war; the *triumphator* must have fought under his own *auspicia* (see AUSPICIUM) in his own *provincia and as a magistrate (or, later, as a promagistrate (see PRO CONSULE, PRO PRAETORE)). In the late republic *acclamation as *imperator was the first step, holding out hope of a triumph. Interpretation of entitlement was elastic and subject to intrigue, and the senate might even be bypassed (see Ap. *Claudius Pulcher (1)). From the 3rd cent. BC, some generals refused a triumph celebrated one at their own expense in a procession to Jupiter Latiaris on the Alban Mount, probably after the supposed precedent of such ceremonies in the days of the Latin League (see LATINI). If the entitlement was judged defective, the general might be awarded a 'lesser triumph' (Plin. *HN* 15. 19) called *ovatio. This has been claimed to be an old pre-Etruscan form of triumph, but in Roman tradition it was a lesser substitute, first celebrated in 503 BC (Plin. *HN* 15. 125). All forms of triumph could be equally counted in the record of a man's career, but the Capitoline triumph was the summit of a Roman aristocrat's ambition.

In the late republic interpretation of the rules came to be dominated by power and influence. Thus *Pompey celebrated two triumphs without having been a magistrate, and Caesar allowed two of his *legati* to triumph. Under the empire, triumphs soon became a monopoly of the emperor and (with his permission) his family, while the actual commander would be granted 'triumphal ornaments' (see ORNAMENTA). But as early as the 1st cent. AD these were deliberately cheapened and gradually lost their connection with military exploits.

H. S. Versnel, *Triumphus* (1970), with the important review by L. Bonfante Warren in *Gnomon* 1974, 574 ff.; T. C. Brennan in E. M. Harris and R. W. Wallace (eds.), *Transitions to Empire* (1996).   E. B.

triumphal arch, the term generally used to denote the honorific arch (*fornix, arcus*; ἁψίς, πύλη), one of the most characteristically Roman of classical buildings. Though regularly erected to commemorate military victories (cf. TRIUMPH), such arches often had religious or topographical associations that reflect the complex origins of the type, e.g. the posthumous arch of *Titus on the *via Sacra, with its representations both of his Jewish triumph and of his apotheosis; or the frequent use of such arches on *bridges or to mark provincial or city boundaries. The earliest recorded examples were built in the first years of the 2nd cent. BC in Rome itself, and the principal development took place in Rome and Italy (over 100 known arches, many of early imperial date), Gaul (36), and Africa (118); but examples are recorded from every province of the empire. The earliest surviving arches, of Augustan date, are generally simple rectangular masses of masonry, with a single archway framed between a pair of half-columns or pilasters and a trabeated entablature (*Ariminum, 27 BC; Susa, 7–6 BC), surmounted by an attic serving as the base for the statuary (frequently a chariot group) which was an integral and essential feature of the monument. The subsequent architectural development was towards a steadily greater elaboration of the decorative framework. Triple arches are known from the later 2nd cent. BC at *Cosa and become a relatively common variant from the early empire; important examples include the arches of *Septimius Severus, AD 203, and of *Constantine I,

AD 312, in Rome. A specialized form, the tetrapylon, with two carriageways intersecting at right angles, though represented in Rome (arch in the *forum Boarium), was especially common in Africa (e.g. *Lepcis Magna, Tripoli, Tebessa). See ARCHES.

RE 7 A 1 (1939), 'Triumphbogen'; *EAA*, 'Arco onorario'; S. De Maria, *Gli archi onorari di Roma e dell'Italia romana* (1988); F. S. Kleiner, *JRA* 1989, 195 ff.   J. D.

triumviri (or **tresviri**) were a board of three in Roman public life, of many different kinds, usually elected by the people. For the annual *tresviri monetales* and *capitales*/*nocturni* see VIGINTISEXVIRI. Apart from these, under the republic the most common *triumviri* were agrarian, whether for founding a colony (*coloniae deducendae*; see COLONIZATION, ROMAN) or assigning land (*agris dandis adsignandis*—*iudicandis* is added or substituted, where assignment involved judicial power). The religious college of *epulones* were originally three. We also find three *mensarii* (financial officials) appointed in 216 (Livy, 23. 21. 6). *Augustus established boards of three for maintaining the rolls of the senate and the squadrons of upper-class cavalry (*legendi senatus* and *recognoscendi turmas equitum*—Suet. *Aug.* 37; Cass. Dio 55. 13. 3). The most famous triumvirate was that consisting of Mark Antony (M. *Antonius (2)), M. *Aemilius Lepidus (3), and Octavian (see AUGUSTUS), created in 43 BC by the *lex Titia*. This was originally to last until 1 January 37 BC, but the triumvirs did not resign then and it was renewed the following summer for another five years, probably until 1 January 32. Their title was appropriate to a political crisis—*rei publicae constituendae*—but of the three only Octavian was to take a significant interest in Rome and Italy and even he undertook no major reforms as triumvir. Although republican institutions continued to function and their *imperium* was only consular, the triumvirs assumed a supreme authority, appropriate to an emergency, both at Rome and abroad, one that overarched consuls, provincial governors (it is not clear whether their *imperium* was actually defined as *maius*), and, where necessary, the law. In particular they suspended normal judicial process in decreeing the proscriptions. Lepidus was forced into retirement in 36; Antony used the title until his death in 30; Octavian seems to have dropped the title at the end of 33 but only formally abolished the triumviral emergency in 28.

The coalition formed between *Caesar, *Pompey, and *Crassus in 60 BC was wholly unofficial and never described at the time as a triumvirate, although other, insulting, names were found. 'First' and 'Second Triumvirate' are modern and misleading terms.

Mommsen, *Röm. Staatsr.* 2³. 594 ff., 624 ff., 702 ff.; Syme, *Rom. Rev.*; Millar, *JRS* 1973; J. Bleicken, *Zwischen Republik und Prinzipat* (1990); J. Reynolds, *Aphrodisias and Rome* (1982) (for triumviral documents).
T. J. C.; A. W. L.

Trivia, Latin translation of *Trioditis*, title of *Hecate as goddess of cross-roads. Since the identification of Hecate with *Artemis and *Selene was popular in Hellenistic times and *Diana was identified with Artemis, the epithet is often used of Diana, as Lucr. 1. 84; Catull. 34. 15; Verg. *Aen.* 6. 35 (Hecate and Diana).
H. J. R.

trivium See MARTIANUS MINNEUS FELIX CAPELLA.

Troas, or **Troad,** the mountainous north-west corner of Asia Minor forming a geographical unit dominated by the Ida massif and washed on three sides by the sea. Its name derives from the belief that all this area was once under Trojan rule (see TROY). The interior is inaccessible, and the more important cities were situated on the coast. The historical significance of the Troas derives from its strategic position flanking the *Hellespont (a factor which may already have weighed with the Achaeans in their attack on Troy). From the 6th cent. Athens became increasingly interested in holding the straits (see CHERSONESUS (1); SIGEUM), but after Aegospotami (see ATHENS, *History*) Persia nominally controlled the Troas. It became the battlefield in the struggle between east and west when *Alexander (3) the Great routed the Persian first line of resistance at the *Granicus. Later the Troas was ruled by *Antigonus (1), who founded Antigoneia—afterwards *Alexandria (7) Troas—and from him the country passed successively under the power of *Lysimachus, the *Seleucids, and *Attalus I of Pergamum. The Attalids bequeathed it to Rome, and the Troas suffered severely in the wars of the republic. Under the empire it enjoyed a long period of tranquillity and relative obscurity.

W. Leaf, *Strabo on the Troad* (1923); J. M. Cook, *The Troad* (1973).
D. E. W. W.; S. M.

Troezen, a city-state at the eastern end of the Argolic peninsula (see ARGOS (2)). The town (Geometric to early Byzantine) lay inland from the large anchorage, Pogon, where the Greek fleet assembled in 480 BC (see SALAMIS, BATTLE OF). Though Doric in dialect (see DIALECTS, GREEK), it had links through myth and cult with Athens (see THESEUS) and gave refuge to Athenians during *Xerxes' invasion (see PERSIAN WARS). Athens attacked and at times occupied Troezen in the First and Second *Peloponnesian Wars. Thereafter it was in the Spartan alliance and, later, the *Achaean Confederacy. Extramural sanctuaries have been excavated.

E. Meyer, *RE* 7 A (1939), 'Troezen'; G. Welter, *Troizen und Kalaureia* (1941); M. H. Jameson and others, *A Greek Countryside* (1994), esp. 72–84.   M. H. J.

Trogodytae (τρωγοδύται) were a people of '*Ethiopia', in particular the Eastern Desert of southern Egypt and north Sudan. In MSS of classical authors we frequently find a reading which, by inclusion of the letter 'l', gives, or implies, the name Troglodytae, 'cave-enterers', 'cave-dwellers'. This latter name may be applied rightly to people with that name placed by classical writers on the northern side of the *Caucasus, where 'Troglodytes' lived in caves because of the cold; to a people in north-western Africa; to a people in the interior of northern Africa; and possibly to peoples on the eastern coast of the *Red Sea. But when the people concerned are located in Egypt and to the south of it, the name Troglodytae must be taken as false, reflecting no doubt a common confusion, the true name, as various MSS and papyri show, being Trogodytae with no reference to caves. Trogodytica included the whole coastline from Suez to the straits of Bab-el-Mandeb. There were and are no natural caves in the eastern deserts of Africa; and it is probable that the Trogodytes lived in huts of wickerwork as the Beja do now. Their lands on the Red Sea coast were explored by agents of *Ptolemy (1) II and III. *PMilan.* 40 of the late 1st cent. AD records Roman conflict with Trogodytes and Ethiopians. The Trogodytes may be the same as the Blemmyes and, perhaps, the modern Beja. Their economy was probably that of cattle-herders. Archaeological work has only recently begun in this region of the Eastern Desert, but many ancient remains have been noted which could be associated with the Trogodytes. See AFRICA.

OGI 1. 70–1.   R. G. M.

Trogus, historian. See POMPEIUS TROGUS.

Troilus

Troilus (Τρωΐλος), in mythology son of *Priam and *Hecuba, though sometimes said to be son of *Apollo (Apollod. 3. 12. 5). In *Homer's *Iliad* he is mentioned only as being dead (24. 257). Later accounts, however, starting with the *Cypria* (see EPIC CYCLE; PROCLUS), specify that he was killed by *Achilles. This was clearly a popular story, for Achilles' ambush of Troilus (accompanied by *Polyxena) at the fountain, the pursuit, the slaughter of the boy on the altar of Apollo, and the battle over the mutilated body, are favourite subjects in Archaic art from the early 6th cent. and found occasionally later (see A. Kossatz-Deissmann in *LIMC* I / 1. 72–95). From Homer on, Troilus tends to be associated with horses: Homer gives him the epithet ἱππιοχάρμης, 'fighting from a chariot'; in art he is often shown fleeing on horseback from Achilles pursuing on foot; in *Sophocles (1)'s lost *Troilus* he was exercising his horses when Achilles ambushed him (*TrGF* 4 Radt, 453); in *Virgil (*Aen.* 1. 474–8) he has a chariot, but his horses bolt and he is dragged along in the dust behind, still holding the reins. A late mythographer records a prophecy that Troy would never be taken if only Troilus lived to the age of 20 (cf. Plaut. *Bacch.* 954), so this may have been Achilles' motive for killing him.

'Troilus and Cressida' (i.e. *Chryseis) is a purely medieval fiction and has no connection with antiquity (the line runs from the *Roman de Troie* to Boccaccio, *Filostrato*, to Chaucer, *Troilus and Criseyde*, to Shakespeare's *Troilus and Cressida*).   J. R. M.

Trojan War See HOMER; TROY.

trophies (τρόπαια, Lat. *trophaea*, from τροπή, a turning i.e. rout of the enemy). The act of dedicating on the field of battle a suit of enemy armour set upon a stake is a specifically Greek practice. Originally intended as a miraculous image of the *theos tropaios* who had brought about the defeat of the enemy, a trophy marked the spot where the enemy had been routed. Trophies were also dedicated in the sanctuary of the deity to whom victory was ascribed. They appear in art at the end of the 6th cent. BC and were certainly in use during the *Persian Wars.

The trophies of the 4th cent. became permanent monuments. The battle of *Leuctra (371 BC) was commemorated by a tower surmounted by a trophy of arms, and from this period onwards the name was applied to various kinds of towers and buildings commemorating military and naval victories. Trophies became a common motif of art; sculptured trophies accompanied by statues of captives and victors decorated the buildings of Hellenistic kings and took an important place in Roman triumphal art from the 1st cent. BC. The word trophy is also applied, though not with strict accuracy, to the masses of arms on sculptured monuments which appear first at *Pergamum and later on a number of Roman commemorative monuments. The best-known Roman trophy monuments are those of Augustus at La Turbie and of Trajan at *Adamklissi.

> G. C. Picard, *Les Trophées romains* (1957); W. K. Pritchett, *The Greek State at War*, pt. 3 (1979), ch. 7.   D. E. S.

Trophonius, son of Erginus, was with his brother Agamedes a renowned master-builder whose work included the lower courses of *Apollo's first temple at Delphi (*Homeric Hymn to Apollo* 295–7), the treasury of Augeas (*Telegonia Argumentum* 1 fr. 2 Bernabé, p. 72 Davies), and the treasury of Hyrieus (Paus. 9. 37. 5–7). The last, a variation of the story of *Rhampsinitus told by *Herodotus (1) (2. 121), provides the connection with Trophonius as cult figure and son of Apollo (Hesiod, see M. L. West, *ZPE* 61 (1985), 6, cf. Schachter 72 n. 3; Paus. 9. 37. 5). While

building the treasury, the brothers left a stone loose, so that they could make off with the treasure bit by bit. Hyrieus set a trap, which caught Agamedes. Trophonius cut off his brother's head, and ran off with it, pursued by Hyrieus. At Lebadea, the ground opened up and swallowed Trophonius. He lived on underground as an oracular god (a fate similar to that of *Amphiaraus: in both cases an underground oracular god—the ritual of consultation is basically identical—is identified with a figure of heroic tradition; see ORACLES).

The oracle must have been functioning by the 6th cent. BC. It was at Lebadea in western *Boeotia, separated from the town by the river Hercyna, whose eponymous nymph was said to have been Trophonius' daughter (this probably is derived from the group carved by *Praxiteles in which the pair resembled *Asclepius and *Hygieia). The cult complex—oracular male and spring *nymph at the foot of a hill or mountain—is repeated in several other sanctuaries dotted around lake *Copais.

Early consultations by *Croesus (Hdt. 1. 46) and Mys (8. 134) may be apocryphal, but the oracle was certainly well known to Athenians by the second half of the 5th cent. (e.g. Euripides, *Ion* 300–2, 404–9; passing references in *Aristophanes (1), several comedies about Trophonius). What caught the imagination was the bizarre means of consultation: there was no medium; instead the consultant, after suitable and lengthy preliminaries, descended underground and confronted the god himself (a consultation of Trophonius was called *katabasis*: 'descent'). The experience was spectacular, frightening, notorious, and expensive.

Towards the end of the 3rd cent. BC, the town of Lebadea, as part of a huge rebuilding programme, moved the oracular cave from the grove by the gorge of Hercyna to the top of the hill on which they began to build a large temple of *Zeus Basileus. The temple project foundered, but the oracle prospered at its new site (both Paus. 9. 39. 9 and Philostr. *VA* 8. 19, explicitly locate the oracle on the mountain above and beyond the grove).

*Pausanias (3) (9. 39. 2–14) gives a detailed description of the site and its monuments, and a graphic account of consultation in his day (he wrote from personal experience). The oracle functioned at least until the 3rd cent. AD.

> A. Schachter, *Cults of Boiotia* 3 (1994), 66 ff.   A. Sch.

Troy (mod. Hisarlık) lies in NW *Asia Minor, about 6½ km. (4 mi.) from the Aegean coast and rather less from the *Hellespont. The site consists of a small citadel mound with *c*.25 m. of gradually accumulated debris from human habitation, and a lower town at least 1 km. square. It was first identified as Troy by Charles Maclaren in 1820. After initial soundings by Frank Calvert in 1863 and 1865, much of the mound was excavated by H. Schliemann between 1870 and 1890. After his death digging by W. Dörpfeld in 1893 and 1894 and by the University of Cincinnati from 1932 to 1938 greatly supplemented what had previously been learned; and further illumination is expected from new excavations by an international team under M. Korfmann, begun in 1988. The site was occupied from *c*.3000 BC to *c*. AD 1200, perhaps with some intervals, and has revealed well over 46 building phases. These are conventionally grouped in nine bands, sometimes misleadingly called 'cities'.

Layers I to III, counting from the bottom, belong to the early bronze age; Layers IV and V probably belong to the middle bronze age; Layer VI, thought by Blegen to have begun in the middle bronze age, is now more probably assigned to the late bronze age to the last portion of which Layers VIIa and VIIb also belong. Layers VIII and IX are of Hellenistic, Roman, and Byzantine date.

Founded on a limestone spur projecting into a marine bay, since silted up, the citadel was fortified from an early stage. In Troy I three successive stone walls supported battlements of mudbrick; an entrance gate was flanked by projecting towers. Within was a system of parallel long-houses with party walls and flat roofs; these were built of mudbrick on stone footings. Pottery was all handmade. Copper, stone, and bone were used for tools and weapons. The bay was exploited for fish and seafood. Culturally Troy I belongs to a north-west Anatolian variant within a Thracian–Anatolian continuum. The culture of Troy I developed without a break but with increasing grandeur into Troy II. Three or more successive fortification walls were erected, each surpassing its predecessor, and each with gates and towers of stone and mudbrick. Inside the citadel a palatial hall or 'megaron' and other buildings were approached across a colonnaded courtyard. But after a devastating fire the citadel was filled in the final phases of Troy II with densely built village houses, a style of architecture which continued throughout Troy III. From Troy II Schliemann recovered weapons of bronze and precious stone, vessels of gold, silver, bronze, and copper, and, like Blegen, gold jewellery. The potter's wheel appears early in Troy II but makes little impact before the middle and late phases. During Troy II–III there was increasing contact with other parts of Anatolia, the Aegean, and north Syria. The early bronze age at Troy ended c.2000 BC.

Troy IV and V are little known, but the continuing expansion of the citadel and rebuildings of the fortifications suggest a continuing increase of importance and prosperity. Architecture, pottery, and comparative stratigraphy indicate a probable date for IV–V in the Anatolian middle bronze age, ending c.1700 BC.

Troy VI introduced sudden changes: monumental architecture, grey pottery, use of the horse. Blegen saw in these the advent of *Indo-European invaders, but the new pottery could have local origins. Three successive citadel walls of increasing strength and magnificence survive. There were at least four gateways, two protected by towers. Inside the citadel the ground rose in concentric terraces: the royal palace no doubt stood at the summit, but no remains are left since much of the top of the hill was sliced away in Hellenistic or Roman times to create a platform for the temple of Athena. Spacious free-standing houses occupied the lower terraces, many equipped with stone bases for interior wooden columns. Outside the citadel walls is evidence for a meaner lower town and, further south, for a cremation cemetery. Fallen masonry and traces of fire show that about 1270 BC Troy VI was violently destroyed.

Survivors maintaining the same culture patched the defensive walls and built modest new houses inside the fortress. This was Troy VIIa which lasted until perhaps c.1190 BC when it too was destroyed as, once again, fallen masonry and traces of fire—and this time remnants of human bones in houses and streets—show.

Once more the citadel was rebuilt and reoccupied in Troy VIIb until perhaps c.1050 BC; but alongside continuation of earlier Troy VI traditions the pottery now introduced fabrics and styles related to widespread Thracian and east European types. There may be evidence for continued occupation of the citadel on a very modest scale until it was resettled by early Greek colonists c.700 BC or earlier. The succeeding Hellenistic and Roman Troy IX gained importance as a sacred site of the classical world (see ILIUM), but declined after c. AD 550. There are traces of later occupation until c. AD 1200.

Hisarlık's identification with the Troy of *Priam has never been proved, but a ruined castle would have been visible in *Homer's day and its situation agrees with that of Troy in most classical tradition, *Strabo excepted. It is generally assumed that some residue of historical truth persists in the legends concerning the Trojan War, although how much and where is uncertain. Mycenaean Greeks (see MYCENAEAN CIVILIZATION) could plausibly have destroyed Troy VI, VIIa, or VIIb. Of these Troy VI would fit best as dating to the peak of power at both *Mycenae and Troy. An earthquake held by Blegen to have destroyed Troy VI is perhaps to be dated to VIIa instead.

H. Schliemann, *Troy and its Remains* (1875), *Ilios* (1880), *Troja* (1884), *Bericht . . . 1890* (1891); W. Dörpfeld, *Troja und Ilion* (1902); C. W. Blegen and others, *Troy 1–4* (1950–8); C. W. Blegen, *Troy and the Trojans* (1963); J. M. Cook, *The Troad* (1973); L. Foxhall and J. K. Davies (eds.), *The Trojan War: Its Historicity and Context* (1984); D. F. Easton, 'Has the Trojan War been found?', *Antiquity* 1985, 188–96; M. Séfériadès, *Troie I* (1985); M. J. Mellink (ed.), *Troy and the Trojan War* (1986); preliminary reports on M. Korfmann's excavations in *Studia Troica* 1 (1991) onwards.
C. W. B.; D. F. E.

truce See LIBATIONS.

Tryphon (1), 'royal' name (after a Seleucid king) adopted by a Sicilian slave called Salvius, who led a slave revolt near *Morgantina (104 BC). Collecting a large army, he seized a strong fortress and defeated a Roman army. On his death (102) the revolt was carried on by Athenion, who had earlier accepted a position as his subordinate.

Diod. 36. 4 ff. is the only source. E. B.

Tryphon (2), son of Ammonius, an important Greek grammarian from *Alexandria (1) (late 1st cent. BC). His works, which were used by his contemporary *Didymus (1), by *Apollonius (13) Dyscolus, and very freely by *Herodian (1), included treatises on parts of speech, pronunciation, accents, orthography, and dialect forms. His works are almost entirely lost, though some brief treatises transmitted under his name may contain elements from the original texts.

A. von Velsen, *Tryphonis grammatici Alexandrini fragmenta* (1859); C. Wendel, *RE* 7 A 25, 'Tryphon'; M. L. West, *CQ* 1965, 236–48.
P. B. R. F.; N. G. W.

Tubilustrium, Roman festival on 23 March and 23 May, whose 'trumpet purification' readied the army for war (*fasti Praenestini*; Festus 480, 481 Lindsay). Calendars added Q(uando) R(ex) C(omitiavit) F(as): the *rex sacrorum made a *nefastus* day into *fastus* (see FASTI). Celebrated in the atrium Sutorium: Platner–Ashby 57, Ov. *Fast.* 3. 849 ff. with Bömer's notes. See LUSTRATION.

Inscr. Ital. 13/2. 429 ff.; Latte, *RR* 118 ff.; *RE* 7 A 755 ff. C. R. P.

Tuder (mod. Todi), in Umbria (see UMBRIANS). An important pre-Roman settlement from at least the 6th cent. BC, Todi has produced a famous bronze statue (c. early 4th cent. BC) of *Mars (cf. Sil. 4. 222, 8. 462). Brought early under Roman domination (c. 3rd cent. BC), it was made a *colonia* c.30 BC (Plin. *HN* 3. 113); an enlarged wall circuit was added under *Augustus, and a theatre.

G. Becatti, *Tuder-Carsulae* (1938); M. T. Falconi Amorelli, *Todi pre-romana* (1977); M. Tascio, *Todi* (1989). E. T. S.; T. W. P.

Tullia (1), younger daughter of Servius *Tullius, supposedly impelled her brother-in-law *Tarquinius Superbus to murder his husband and sister, marry her, and seize power by killing her father. The narrative probably goes back to Q. *Fabius Pictor and forms part of a depiction of the last three Roman kings in Greek

Tullia

'tragic' style, as a political dynasty that ultimately wreaks its own self-destruction. Its detailed development incorporates a series of topographical aetiologies, linked particularly to *Diana and Virbius (= *Hippolytus (1)) and the traditions of the slave *rex nemorensis at Aricia. These are based on Servius' supposed slave origins and his creation of the federal Latin cult of Diana on the *Aventine.

R. Thomsen, *King Servius Tullius: A Historical Synthesis* (1980), 279 ff.

A. D.

Tullia (2) (*RE* 'Tullius' 60), *Cicero's daughter, born *c.*79 BC. By 63 she was married to C. Calpurnius Piso Frugi (quaestor 58), who worked for Cicero's return from exile, but died early in 57. In 56 she married Furius Crassipes (quaestor 51), who divorced her *c.*51, we do not know why. During Cicero's absence in *Cilicia, and with his lukewarm approval, she married P. *Cornelius Dolabella (1). She lived with him only for a few months in 50–49 and in 46 and bore him two sons, both of whom died in infancy. The marriage ended late 46 and Tullia died in February 45. Cicero, though sincerely attached to her, had taken little account of her happiness, but was overwhelmed by her death. He proposed to build a shrine for her, ultimately had to abandon the project, and turned to philosophy for consolation.

Cicero's *Letters* and Plutarch's *Cicero* are the main sources. E. B.

Tullianum, the underground execution cell of the *prison at Rome, flanking the *comitium*, and traditionally associated with Servius *Tullius (Varro, *Ling.* 5. 151; Festus 356). The derivation from *tullus*, a spring, is more attractive, for a spring still rises in the present floor, higher than the original. The existing chamber, once circular (diam. *c.*7 m.), is built in peperino ashlar not earlier than the 4th cent. BC. The room above it has a travertine front, orientated like the *comitium* by cardinal points, and repaired between AD 39 and 42 (*CIL* 6. 31674; cf. *ILS* 3. 342). Here were executed most state prisoners, including *Jugurtha, the Catilinarian (see SERGIUS CATILINA, L.) conspirators, and *Vercingetorix.

Steinby, *Lexicon* 236 ff.; Nash, *Pict. Dict. Rome* 1. 206 ff. I. A. R.; J. D.

Tullius (*RE* 18), **Servius,** the sixth king of Rome (conventionally 578–535 BC), murdered by *Tarquinius Superbus at the instigation of his daughter *Tullia (1). *Claudius identified him with the Etruscan adventurer *Mastarna but Roman sources, deriving Servius from *servus* ('slave'), made him the son of a Latin captive Ocrisia and brought up in the household of *Tarquinius Priscus. Because of his supposed slave ancestry he was credited with the enfranchisement of freedmen, the creation of the Compitalia, a close association with *Fortuna (cf. Degrassi, *ILLRP* 1070 (3rd cent.?)), and perhaps the establishment of the (certainly archaic) federal Latin sanctuary of *Diana on the *Aventine (whose dedication date coincided with a slave festival). As the penultimate king he was credited (probably by the time of *Timaeus (2)) with political and military institutions that were deemed fundamental to the republic but believed to antedate it: the centuriate organization (see CENTURIA), the first territorial tribes (see TRIBUS), and the *census. Although their initial phases may well date from the 6th cent., the form in which our sources present these innovations is anachronistic, as is the associated ascription to Servius of the first Roman *coinage, direct taxation (*tributum*), and army pay. The 'Servian wall' of Rome (see WALL OF SERVIUS) dates from the early 4th cent. (earlier 6th-cent. defences have not been securely identified) but two phases of the Sant'Omobono sanctuary (with which Servius was associated) do belong to the 6th cent. (see MATUTA MATER). *Accius already celebrated Servius as establishing 'liberty' for the citizens, but later writers offer varying interpretations of his reforms: as concentrating political power in the hands of the wealthy (Cic. *Rep.* 2. 37 ff.), as creating a timocratic socio-political hierarchy (Livy 1. 42 ff.), or simply as the work of a skilful pragmatic populist (Dion. Hal. *Ant. Rom.* 4. 1 ff.). Recent speculation has seen him as (in part) attempting to combat the power of the nascent patriciate.

J.-C. Richard, *Les Origines de la plèbe romaine* (1978), 348 ff.; R. Thomsen, *King Servius Tullius: A Historical Synthesis* (1980); F. Coarelli, *Il foro boario* (1988), 205 ff. A. D.

Tullius (*RE* 29) **Cicero** (1), **Marcus,** the famous orator **Cicero.**

Life The first of two sons of a rich and well-connected *eques* (see EQUITES, *origins and republic*) of *Arpinum, he was born on 3 January 106 BC, the year following the first consulship of C. *Marius (1), with whose family (also from Arpinum) his grandmother Gratidia had marriage connections. His intelligent and ambitious father (who was to die in the year of Cicero's canvass for the consulship), advised perhaps by L. *Licinius Crassus, gave his two sons an excellent education in philosophy and rhetoric in Rome and later in Greece, with their two first-cousins as their fellow students. Cicero did military service in 90/89 under Pompey's father, Cn. *Pompeius Strabo, and attended legal consultations of the two great Scaevolae (Q. *Mucius Scaevola (1) and (2)). He conducted his first case in 81 (*Pro Quinctio*) and made an immediate reputation through his successful defence of Sex. *Roscius of Ameria on a charge of parricide in 80, a case which reflected discreditably on the contemporary administration of the dictator *Sulla. Cicero was then from 79 to 77 a student of philosophy and oratory both in Athens and in *Rhodes, where he heard *Posidonius (2); he visited P. *Rutilius Rufus at *Smyrna.

He returned to Rome, his health greatly improved, to pursue a public career, and was elected quaestor for 75, when he served for a year in western Sicily, and praetor for 66, in each case at the earliest age at which he could legally become a candidate. By securing the condemnation of C. *Verres for extortion in Sicily in 70 he scored a resounding success against Q. *Hortensius Hortalus, eight years his senior, whom he was to replace as the leading figure at the Roman bar. In a cleverly disarming speech delivered during his praetorship (*De imperio Cn. Pompei*) he supported, against strong *optimate opposition, the tribune C. *Manilius' proposal to transfer the command in the war against *Mithradates to *Pompey; this was the first public expression of his admiration for Pompey who was, with occasional short interruptions, henceforward to be the focus of his political allegiance. He was elected consul for 63—the first *novus homo with no political background whatever since 94—because, in a poor field (including Catiline (see SERGIUS CATILINA, L.), who had tried for the office twice before), his reputation as an orator and his cultivation of aristocrats, *equites, and prominent Italians paid off. Hampered by a weak and indeed suspect colleague, C. *Antonius 'Hybrida', Cicero did very well to secure evidence which convinced the senate of the seriousness of Catiline's conspiracy. After the 'last decree' (*senatus consultum ultimum*) was passed, and Catiline left Rome for his army in Etruria, five conspirators prominent in Roman society and politics, including a praetor, P. *Cornelius Lentulus Sura, were arrested and executed on 5 December (the Nones). Although, after debate, the senate, influenced by M. *Porcius Cato (2), had recommended their execution, the act itself, a violation of the citizen's right to a trial, could be justified only by the passing of the last decree and was Cicero's personal responsibility. Though approved in the first moment of panic by all classes of society in Rome, its legality was strictly questionable, and Cicero was unwise to boast as loudly of it as he did (even in a long and indiscreet letter to Pompey in the east, *Pro Sulla* 67, *Pro Planc.* 85, cf. *Fam.* 5. 7). He published his speeches of 63, including those against Catiline, in 60, wrote of his action in prose and verse, in Greek and Latin, and invited others, including Posidonius, to do the same; and to the end of his life he never wavered in his belief that he had acted rightly and had saved Rome from catastrophe.

Though it was unlikely that he would escape prosecution, Cicero refused overtures from *Caesar, which might have saved him at the price of his political independence. In 58 P. *Clodius Pulcher, whom he had antagonized in 61 when Clodius was charged with incest, moved a bill as tribune (see TRIBUNI PLEBIS) re-enacting the law that anyone who had executed a citizen without trial should be banished. Without awaiting prosecution Cicero fled the country, to Macedonia, and Clodius passed a second bill, which Cicero regarded as unconstitutional declaring him an exile. His house on the Palatine was destroyed by Clodius' gangsters, part of its site to be made a shrine of Liberty, and his villa at *Tusculum was also badly damaged. With Pompey's belated support and with the support of the tribune T. *Annius Milo, who employed violence as irresponsibly as Clodius had done in the previous year, Cicero was recalled by a law of the people on 4 August 57 and was warmly welcomed on his return both in Italy and in Rome, which he reached on 4 September.

He returned to a busy winter, fighting to secure adequate public compensation for the damage to his property and, in the senate and in the courts, supporting those chiefly responsible for his recall. Hopes of dissociating Pompey from his close political connection with Caesar, attempts which Clodius was employed by Caesar to interrupt, were at an end when Caesar, Pompey, and *Crassus revived their political union at *Luca in April 56, and Cicero was sharply brought to heel (*Att.* 4. 5, on his 'palinode' or recantation; cf. *Fam.* 1. 9 for his later account of his conversion). He at once spoke warmly in the senate (e.g. in *De provinciis consularibus*) and on the public platform in favour of Caesar, as of a long-standing political friend. He claimed that it was the act of a realist, a *sapiens*, to accept the indisputable predominance of the Three ('temporibus adsentiendum', *Fam.* 1. 9. 21) and only revealed in conversation and in letters to such close friends as T. *Pomponius Atticus the deep wound which his pride—his *dignitas*—had suffered. He took no more part in the collapsing world of republican politics, devoting himself to writing, which he never regarded as anything but a poor substitute for active political life (the *De oratore* was published in 55, and the *De republica* finished in 51); and he was humiliated by briefs which, under pressure from Pompey and Caesar, he was forced to accept. He defended P. *Vatinius successfully and A. *Gabinius (2) unsuccessfully in 54. He was humiliated too by his failure, in a court packed with troops, to defend Milo adequately when, with the case already prejudiced, Milo was impeached for the murder of Clodius early in 52. The period brought him one consolation, when he was elected augur in 53 or 52 in the place of his earlier protégé, young P. *Licinius Crassus (2), who had been killed at *Carrhae.

Cicero was out of Rome during the eighteen months preceding the outbreak of the Civil War, being selected under regulations following Pompey's *lex de provinciis* of 52 to govern Cilicia as proconsul from summer 51 to summer 50. He was a just, if not a strong, governor, but he regarded his appointment with horror as a second relegation from Rome. However, his dis-

patches recording the successful encounter of his troops with brigands on mons Amanus earned a *supplicatio* at Rome and he returned, the *fasces* of his lictors (see LICTORES) wreathed in fading laurels, hoping that he might celebrate a triumph. Instead he was swept into the vortex of the Civil War.

Appointed district commissioner at *Capua by the government, he did not at first follow Pompey and the consuls overseas. Caesar saw him at *Formiae on 28 March 49, and invited him to join the rump of the senate in Rome on terms which with great resolution Cicero refused to accept (*Att.* 9. 11 a, to Caesar; 9. 18). His long indecision up to this point which was anything but discreditable was now at an end, and he joined the republicans in Greece, irritating their leaders by his caustic criticism, himself dismayed by the absence of any idealistic loyalty on their part to the cause of republicanism. After *Pharsalus, in which he took no part, he refused Cato's invitation to assume command of the surviving republican forces and, pardoned by Caesar, he returned to Italy. But political life was at an end, and he was utterly out of sympathy with Caesar's domination. All that he could do was to return to his writing, his only important speech being that delivered in the senate in 46 (the year in which the *Brutus* was written) in praise of Caesar's pardon of M. *Claudius Marcellus (4) (consul 51), who had done so much to precipitate the outbreak of the Civil War.

That Cicero was not invited to participate in the conspiracy to kill Caesar in 44 is not insignificant. He hailed the news of the murder on 15 March with intemperate delight (e.g. *Fam.* 6. 15). Political life began again, and Cicero had all the prestige (*auctoritas*) of a senior consular. Within three months he was saying openly that Mark Antony (M. *Antonius (2)) should have been killed too (*Att.* 15. 11. 2). He accepted the overtures of the young Caesar (Octavian; see AUGUSTUS), uncritical of the lawlessness of many of his acts, misled by his youth into a mistaken underassessment of his political acumen, and he closed his eyes to the fact that Octavian could never be reconciled to *Brutus and *Cassius. He struggled in speech after speech (the *Philippics*, the first delivered on 2 September 44, the last on 21 April 43) to induce the senate to declare Antony a public enemy. After Antony's defeat in Cisalpine Gaul in April 43, Octavian fooled Cicero for a time, perhaps with the suggestion that they might both be consuls together. But Octavian's intentions were different. After his march on Rome to secure the consulship for himself and his uncle Q. *Pedius, and the formation of the Triumvirate (see TRIUMVIRI), he did not oppose Antony's nomination of Cicero as a victim of the proscriptions which were the inauguration of the new regime (see PROSCRIPTION). The soldiers caught Cicero in a not very resolute attempt to escape by sea. His slaves did not desert him, and he died with courage on 7 December 43.

In politics he hated Clodius, with good reason, and he hated M. Crassus and, at the end of his life, Antony. For the character of Cato, eleven years his junior, he had unqualified respect, and he published a panegyric of Cato in 45, after his death; but in politics, especially in the years following Pompey's return from the east in 62, he thought Cato's uncompromising rigidity (his *constantia*) impolitic, and Cato never concealed his distaste for Cicero's policy of temporizing expediency, both at this period and when he capitulated to the Three in 56. With Pompey Cicero never established the intimacy to which, particularly after Pompey's return in 62, he aspired, suggesting that he might play a second Laelius to Pompey's Scipio (see LAELIUS (2), C. and CORNELIUS SCIPIO AEMILIANUS, P.). Few of his contemporaries, perhaps, held him in higher esteem than did his constant opponent Caesar who, though often with an imperiousness which Cicero could not tolerate, was always friendly in his approach. Cicero was not a discriminating judge of the political intentions of others, being far too susceptible to, and uncritical of, flattery; and he was inevitably condemned to a certain political isolation. Loyally and not very critically devoted to the existing republican constitution, and fascinated by the mirage of a 'concordia ordinum', he was never a liberal reformer (*popularis*); yet he was never completely acceptable to the established *optimates*, the worst of whom despised his social origin, while the rest mistrusted his personality as much as he mistrusted theirs. For both *populares* and *optimates* see OPTIMATES. And, not having the *clientela* of the noble or of the successful general, he lacked *auctoritas*. It was this political isolation which (cf. *Att.* 1. 17; 1. 18. 1, of 61/60 BC) enhanced the importance for him of his close association with the knight T. Pomponius Atticus, a man of the highest culture in both languages, his banker, financial adviser, publisher, and most generous and tolerant friend.

His marriage to *Terentia had issue: *Tullia (2), to whom he was devoted, whose death in 45 was the hardest of the blows which afflicted his private life, and M. *Tullius Cicero (2). His marriage survived the storms and stress of thirty years, until he grew irritated with Terentia and divorced her in winter 47/6, to marry the young Publilia, from whom in turn he was almost immediately divorced. Cicero was a good master to his slaves and, with the rest of his family, was devoted to Tiro (M. *Tullius Tiro), to whom twenty-one of his letters in *Fam.* 16 are addressed. He gave him his freedom in 53, 'to be our friend instead of our slave', as Q. *Tullius Cicero (1) wrote (*Fam.* 16. 16. 1).

Cicero, who was never a really rich man, had eight country residences, in Campania, at Arpinum, at Formiae, and, his suburban villa, at Tusculum; in Rome he was extremely proud of his house on the *Palatine, which he bought in 62 for $3\frac{1}{2}$ million sesterces (*Fam.* 5. 6. 2).

Apart from the surviving histories of the late republic and, in particular, Plutarch's Lives of Cicero and of his outstanding contemporaries, the bulk of our knowledge of him derives from his own writings, in particular from his letters, only a minority of which was written with any thought of publication. His reputation has therefore suffered from the fact that we have intimate knowledge of the most private part of his personal life; in this respect he has been his own worst enemy, and his critics have given undue prominence to his extremes of exaltation and depression and to the frequent expression of his evident vanity. (See J. P. V. D. Balsdon, 'Cicero the Man', in Dorey (ed.), *Cicero*.)

G. Boissier, *C. and his Friends* (1897); J. L. Strachan-Davidson, *C. and the Fall of the Roman Republic* (1894); E. G. Sihler, *C. of Arpinum* (1914); E. Ciaceri, *Cicerone e i suoi tempi*[2] (1939–41); H. Strasburger, *Concordia Ordinum* (1931); G. C. Richards, *C., a Study* (1935); H. J. Haskell, *This was Cicero* (1942); H. Willrich, *C. und Caesar* (1944); H. Frisch, *C.'s Fight for the Republic* (1946); F. R. Cowell, *C. and the Roman Republic* (1948); J. Carcopino, *C., the Secrets of his Correspondence* (1951, reviewed, *JRS* 1950, 134; *CR* 1952, 178); F. Lossmann, *C. und Caesar im Jahre 54* (1962); K. Büchner, *Cicero* (1964); T. A. Dorey (ed.), *Cicero* (1965); R. E. Smith, *C. the Statesman* (1966); M. Gelzer, *Cicero* (1969); E. Rawson, *Cicero, a Portrait* (1975); T. N. Mitchell, *Cicero: The Ascending Years* (1979) and *Cicero the Senior Statesman* (1991).   J. P. B.; M. T. G.

Works Speeches

Fifty-eight speeches of Cicero survive in whole or part; numerous others were unpublished or lost (88 are recorded by Crawford).

Cicero's normal practice, if he decided to publish a speech, was to 'write up' (*conficere*) a version after the event. In one case

we know that he delivered a speech from a script (*Post reditum in senatu*); otherwise it seems that only a few important passages, chiefly the exordium and peroration, were written out *in extenso* beforehand. The published versions of court speeches in many instances certainly represent a shortened version of the actual proceedings, as shown by Humbert; the examination of witnesses is largely omitted, and some sections of argumentation are represented only by headings. The extent to which Cicero changed the content or emphasis of his speeches when preparing them for publication is disputed. It has been thought that the speeches were regularly altered to suit the political circumstances of the time of publication, rather than the time of delivery. On the other hand, it has been pointed out that Cicero's overt reason for publication was to provide examples of successful oratory for posterity to imitate and admire, and this would naturally place limits on the degree of alteration that could reasonably be made, as would the presence among his readership of a substantial number of those who had been present at the delivery of the speech.

In certain cases there is firm evidence that our text does not represent a speech that was actually delivered. The five speeches of the *Actio secunda in Verrem* were prepared for use in court but were never actually delivered, since *Verres withdrew into exile after the *Actio prima*. The second *Philippic* was not delivered as a speech, but circulated as a pamphlet, although it observes the conventions of a senatorial speech. But these are exceptions. The *Pro Milone* is an exception in another way, being a rare example of an unsuccessful speech that was nevertheless published; our sources claim or imply that they had access to a transcript (complete with interruptions) of the actual speech, which differed from Cicero's published version, although it is not proved that the difference in content was much greater than in the case of most of Cicero's other speeches (J. N. Settle, *TAPA* 1963, 268–80).

Cicero's reputation as an orator depended on consistent practical success, although his detractors in antiquity made as much capital out of his relatively rare failures as their modern equivalents have done. In these successes a large part must have been played by his manner of delivery, of which virtually no impression can be given by a written speech; yet it is possible to see in the published versions something of the powers of advocacy that made Cicero the leading courtroom orator of his time (this has been brought out particularly clearly by Stroh). The political speeches are perhaps more difficult for a modern reader to appreciate: Cicero's self-glorifications and his unbridled *invectives tend to repel those brought up in a modern western society, while adverse judgement of his political position can hinder appreciation of his oratory. It is easy to be cynical about what *Juvenal called the 'divine Philippic' (the Second) without coming to terms with the historical circumstances that produced this and other speeches, and the oratorical qualities that made them into objects of near-universal admiration.

The style of Cicero's speeches did not remain entirely uniform. As he himself observed, in his youth he had a tendency to exuberance (so-called *Asianism), best exemplified in the *Pro Roscio Amerino* (cf. F. Solmsen, *TAPA* 1938, 542–56); this was later tempered by increasing maturity and by a change in oratorical fashion. The style also depended to some extent on the occasion; there are variations in manner between Cicero's addresses to senate and people, to a full jury, and to a single arbitrator, and Cicero himself talks of the different styles appropriate for the different sections of a speech (plain for narration, grand for the final appeal to the emotions, etc.). However, Cicero's speeches throughout his life are consistent in their rhythmical regularity, their smooth and balanced sentence-construction, and their careful choice of vocabulary and idiom (on the style of the speeches, see Laurand). Cicero's style was criticized by some of his contemporaries for lacking vigour (Tac., *Dial.* 18) and by later rhetoricians for longwindedness and lack of quotability (ibid. 22).

Cicero made good use of the theories of rhetoric current in his time, and, still more, of the great classical models of Athenian oratory. Most of the ancient structural conventions, figures of speech, and standard modes of argument can be exemplified from his writings, and some of the speeches were consistently taken as copy-book examples by later rhetoricians such as *Quintilian; but Cicero never merely followed the rules for their own sake, and examples can be found of highly effective departures from the recommended practice of the rhetoricians.

Of the extant speeches, three belong to the period before Cicero's Sicilian quaestorship (*Pro Roscio Amerino*, from Cicero's first major public trial in 80 BC, together with *Pro Quinctio* and *Pro Roscio Comoedo*). Then follows the series of speeches from the trial of Verres in 70: *Divinatio in Caecilium*, the *Actio prima in Verrem*, and the five speeches of the *Actio secunda* generally referred to as the Verrines. The *Pro Tullio*, *Pro Fonteio*, and *Pro Caecina* date from 69. Two of the extant speeches belong to Cicero's praetorship, the *Pro lege Manilia* (alias *De imperio Cn. Pompei*) and the *Pro Cluentio*. Of the 'consular' orations which Cicero himself published (a collection of twelve according to *Att.* 2. 1. 3; but see W. C. McDermott, *Philologus* 1972, 277–84), we have the three speeches *De lege agraria contra Rullum*, the *Pro Rabirio perduellionis reo*, and the four Catilinarians; the *Pro Murena* also dates from this year. From the years succeeding the consulship the *Pro Sulla*, *Pro Archia* (both 62), and *Pro Flacco* (59) survive. Another group is formed by the speeches made on returning from exile in 57 and in the following year: *Post reditum in senatu*, *Post reditum ad Quirites*, *De domo sua*, *De haruspicum responsis*, *Pro Sestio*, *In Vatinium interrogatio*. To the year 56 also belong the senatorial speech *De provinciis consularibus* and the defences of *Caelius Rufus and L. *Cornelius Balbus (1); the invective *In Pisonem* was published in 55. From 54 we have the *Pro Plancio* and the *Pro Rabirio Postumo*. In 52, Cicero defended T. *Annius Milo without success, publishing a version of the speech before departing to govern Cilicia. In 46–45, Cicero addressed the victorious Caesar on behalf of M. *Claudius Marcellus (4), *Ligarius and King *Deiotarus of Galatia. Otherwise Caesar's dictatorship offered no opportunity for Cicero to exercise his forensic gifts, and he devoted himself to the writing of treatises on rhetoric and philosophy. During his brief return to public life in 44–43, Cicero delivered the series of speeches known (at his own joking suggestion: *Ad Brut.* 2. 3. 4) as the *Philippics*, which directly or indirectly expressed his opposition to M. *Antonius (2); cf. DEMOSTHENES (2). Fourteen of these survive; at least three more have been lost.

Editions: Oxford Classical Texts, Budé, and Teubner carry full series; individual editions of the speeches are too numerous to mention here; J. Humbert, *Les Plaidoyers écrits et les plaidoiries réelles de Cicéron* (n.d.); J. Crawford, *M. Tullius Cicero: The Lost and Unpublished Orations* (1984); W. Stroh, *Taxis und Taktik: Die advokatische Dispositionskunst in Ciceros Gerichtsreden* (1975); C. Neumeister, *Grundsätze der forensischen Rhetorik, gezeigt an Gerichtsreden Ciceros* (1964); C. W. Wooten, *Cicero's Philippics and their Demosthenic Model* (1983); J. M. May, *Trials of Character* (1988); G. Kennedy, *The Art of Rhetoric in the Roman world* (1972); L. Laurand, *Étude sur le style des discours de Cicéron*, 3 vols., 2nd edn. (1925–7).

Works on Rhetoric

(*a*) *De inventione*, written in Cicero's youth, is a treatise on some techniques of rhetorical argument, which has a close resemblance to parts of the anonymous *Rhetorica ad Herennium* (once falsely attributed to Cicero).

(*b*) *De oratore* (55 BC), *Brutus*, and *Orator* (46) represent Cicero's major contribution to the theory of (Latin) *rhetoric, and he himself grouped them with his philosophical works. They present an idealized picture of the orator as a liberally educated master of his art, a picture in which the technical aspects of Greek rhetorical theory still have their place, but are supplemented by knowledge of literature, philosophy, and general culture, and by the qualities of character required of the ideal Roman aristocrat. This was endorsed by later Roman authors such as *Quintilian, and it was one of the formative influences on Renaissance ideals of character and education. The *De oratore* was closely linked with the more ambitious *De republica* which followed it, and the ideal orator depicted in the former is little different from the ideal statesman in the latter. The *Brutus* is devoted largely to a history of Roman oratory, while the *Orator* deals with more technical points of style. These last two works were written against a background of controversy regarding the desirable style or styles in oratory, in the course of which Cicero had been criticized for persisting (as it seemed) in the 'Asian' fashions of his younger days, and a plain 'Attic' style had been held up as an ideal. Cicero reacts to this by attempting to demonstrate that different styles are effective for different purposes, that there was more variety in actual Athenian oratory than the 'Atticists' allowed, and that the ideal orator should be master of several styles, including (where appropriate) the Ciceronian grand manner itself, for which *Demosthenes (2), rather than the Asian rhetoricians, is claimed as a precedent. Although this controversy was in some senses an ephemeral one, these works contain much of interest concerning the way Roman orators regarded their art, and the *Brutus* is a mine of prosopographical information as well as of Roman rhetorical criticism (see ASIANISM).

(*c*) Cicero's minor works on the subject comprise: *Partitiones oratoriae*, a 'dialogue in which Cicero instructs his son in the elements of the art; the date is uncertain, but it must belong to a time at which Cicero's son was approaching maturity; *Topica*, written in 44 BC and dedicated to C. *Trebatius Testa, an exposition of the content of *Aristotle's work of the same title; and *De optimo genere oratorum*, of disputed authenticity, an introduction to translations (which may or may not have existed) of *Aeschines (1)'s *In Ctesiphontem* and Demosthenes' *De corona*.

Editions: *De Inventione*: E. Stroebel (Teubner, 1915). *De oratore*: A. S. Wilkins (1892); K. Kumaniecki (Teubner, 1969); comm. A. Leeman and H. Pinkster (1981–). *Brutus*: A. E. Douglas (1966). *Orator*: J. Sandys (1885); R. Westman (Teubner, 1980). Minor works: A. S. Wilkins (OCT, 1903). A. Michel, *Rhétorique et philosophie chez Cicéron* (1960); A. D. Leeman, *Orationis Ratio* (1963); G. V. Sumner, *Orators in Cicero's Brutus* (1973); G. M. A. Grube, *Phoenix* 1962, 234–57 repr. in *The Greek and Roman Critics* (1965); A. E. Douglas, ANRW (1973), 1. 3. 95–137.

Poems

Cicero early acquired a reputation as a bad poet on the basis of two lines from his autobiographical compositions, 'o fortunatam natam me consule Romam' ('O happy Rome, born in my consulship') and 'cedant arma togae, concedat laurea laudi' ('yield arms to the toga, the bay to achievement') (the variant *linguae* 'to the tongue', was probably satirical). The only obvious faults of these lines are a naïve self-esteem and a somewhat old-fashioned taste for *assonance; in general, Cicero was a competent enough versifier, and despite his admiration for the older poets, his verse technique is more modern than that of his contemporary *Lucretius. He appears at times to have had serious poetic ambitions and to have regarded verse-writing as more than an amateur's accomplishment. It is perhaps less surprising in an ancient than it would be in a modern context that he chose to make verse a vehicle for personal propaganda, in the *Consulatus suus* (of which a substantial passage is quoted by Cicero himself in *Div.* 1. 17) and *De temporibus suis*. Apart from these, Cicero composed an original (probably fairly short) epic poem on his fellow-Arpinate C. *Marius (1); this must have been in circulation in the 50s BC (he refers to it at the beginning of the *De legibus*). The only part of his poetry to survive in a manuscript tradition is the so-called *Aratea*, 469 lines from a verse translation of *Aratus (1)'s *Phaenomena*; this is of interest as part of the tradition of adapting Hellenistic *didactic poetry and as a precursor of *Virgil's *Georgics*. There are some other scattered fragments of lost poems, and Cicero translated a number of passages of Greek poetry *ad hoc* for quotation in his philosophical works (in preference to the original Greek).

Editions: W. W. Ewbank, *The Poems of Cicero* (1933); A. Traglia, *Ciceronis Poetica fragmenta* (1963); *Aratea*, ed. J. Soubiran (Budé, 1972). Courtney, *FLP.* G. B. Townend, in T. A. Dorey (ed.), *Cicero* (1965).

Letters

Cicero's surviving correspondence is an invaluable collection of evidence for his biography, for the history of the time, and for Roman social life. The sixteen books *Ad familiares* were published after Cicero's death by his freedman M. *Tullius Tiro. Cicero's letters to T. *Pomponius Atticus were preserved (without the replies) by the latter and seen by *Cornelius Nepos (Nep. *Att.* 16. 2–4, referring to a collection in 11 books). They were in circulation in the reign of Nero and later, but the silence of *Asconius suggests that they were not available to him. Our present collection *Ad Atticum* consists of sixteen books, probably an augmented version of the collection known to Nepos. We also have the smaller collections *Ad Quintum fratrem* (including the *Commentariolum petitionis*) and *Ad Brutum*. Further collections of Cicero's letters apparently existed in antiquity. The *Ad familiares* collection contains, in addition to Cicero's own, letters from a variety of correspondents to him.

The letters were not in any sense written for publication; as far as is known, it was not until 44 BC that Cicero thought of publishing a selection of them (*Att.* 16. 5. 5; cf. *Fam.* 16. 17. 1), and it is not clear that this idea was ever put into practice in that form. They vary greatly in their level of formality. At the one extreme they include official dispatches and letters of a semi-public nature on matters of political importance, whose style is similar to that of the public speeches; at the other may be found casual notes to members of the family and informal exchanges with Atticus, often highly allusive and colloquial. See LETTERS, LATIN.

Edition: D. R. Shackleton Bailey, *Cicero's Letters to Atticus* (1965–70); *Ad Familiares* (1977); *Ad Quintum fratrem* and *Ad Brutum* (1980). J. G. F. P.

Philosophica

Apart from the treatises on rhetoric, an important part of the Hellenistic philosophical curriculum (though see below), these fall into two parts: (*a*) the writings on political philosophy and statecraft of the years immediately preceding Cicero's governorship of Cilicia, and (*b*) the works on epistemology, ethics,

and theology (standing in the place of physics) which were produced in the incredibly short period between February 45 and November 44. Cicero gives a list and account of his own philosophical writings at *Div.* 2. 1.

In the *De republica*, a dialogue between P. *Cornelius Scipio Aemilianus, C. *Laelius (2), and others, of which we have only parts of the six books (including the *Somnium Scipionis*, preserved as a whole by *Macrobius), Cicero discusses the ideal state, always with an eye on the history of the Roman republic, and favours a constitution combining elements of all three main forms, monarchy, oligarchy, and democracy. His discussion reflects the political conditions of the time and looks to a wise counsellor (for which part Cicero may at one time have cast *Pompey) as a remedy for Rome's political sickness. But its chief attraction for posterity lay in its assertion of human rights and of man's participation in humanity and the cosmos, a notion which eclectic developments in *Stoicism and Cicero's own predilections helped to foster. Cicero probably worked on the *De legibus* immediately after the *De republica* (cf. *Leg.* 1. 15), but did not publish it. (It does not appear in the list in *Div.* 2. 1 ff., and is not specifically mentioned in the letters.) In the three extant books (Macrobius quotes from a fifth book, and the reference to *iudicia* in 3. 47 has generally been taken to point to the subject of the fourth book) Cicero expounds the Stoic conception of divinely sanctioned Law, based on reason, and discusses legal enactments connected with religion and magistracies, drawing heavily on the 2nd-cent. BC Stoic *Diogenes (3) of Babylon.

Politically inactive under Caesar's dictatorship, the death of his daughter Tullia finally led Cicero to seek consolation in writing about philosophical subjects which had always interested him, from the early days of his studies under the Epicureans *Phaedrus (3) and *Zeno (5) (cf. EPICURUS), the Academics *Philon (3) of Larissa, *Antiochus (11) of Ascalon, at Athens and on *Rhodes the Stoic *Posidonius (2), through the years of his association with *Diodotus (3) the Stoic (who lived and died in his own home), to the time immediately after the Civil War, when C. *Matius urged him to write on philosophy in troubled times (*Fam.* 11. 27. 5). What had formerly been for Cicero a useful exercise (cf. *Tusc.* 2. 9, and his claim at *Orat.* 12 to be a product of the *Academy rather than of the rhetoricians' workshops) and a source of oratorical material (cf. *De or.* 1. 5 and *Orat.* 113 ff.; the *Paradoxa Stoicorum*, published, it seems, as late as the beginning of 46, may be an exercise in the preparation of such material) became now a haven of refuge (*Fam.* 7. 30. 2), a *doloris medicina* (*Acad. post.* 1. 11). Cicero needed to reassure himself, and hoped as well to make a name for himself as a philosophical writer (at *Off.* 1. 2 ff. he admits his inferior philosophical knowledge, but contraposes his virtues as a stylist). But Cicero was well prepared for the task, having learnt Stoic dialectic from Diodotus, rhetoric and arguing both sides of a question from the *Peripatetics, while the Academics had taught him to refute any argument. In addition Cicero had heard, and listened carefully, to the most charismatic philosophers of his time, the showmen of the day. He had a profound admiration and respect for *Plato (1) (*deus ille noster*—'our divine Plato': *Att.* 4. 16. 3) and *Aristotle. His claim to look to *Socrates (*Acad.* 1. 3) belies his sceptical method of inquiry and emphasis on ethics. He aimed above all at giving the Romans a philosophical literature and terminology, which would take the place of the Greek philosophers, on whom the Romans had been hitherto intellectually dependent. The surviving work of the Hellenistic philosophers suggests that Cicero would not be alone in following his Greek sources closely in order to engage them polemically. But some scholars have understood Cicero's words: 'ἀπόγραφα sunt, minore labore fiunt; verba tantum adfero quibus abundo' ('They are copies. They're no trouble. I just bring the words, and I've plenty of them': *Att.* 12. 52. 3) too seriously (i.e. without a hint of false modesty), and Shackleton Bailey has suggested that they do not even pertain to the *philosophica*. More trustworthy are Cicero's claims (*Off.* 1. 6) to follow the Stoics (in that work) not as a mere translator but drawing from Stoic sources as he thinks fit, and (*Fin.* 1. 6) to add his own criticism (*iudicium*) and arrangement (*scribendi ordo*) to the chosen authority.

Several lost works probably came first: a *De gloria* (a eulogy of M. *Porcius Cato (2)); the *Consolatio*, an attempt to console himself for the loss of *Tullia (2) (and unique in being addressed to himself); and the *Hortensius*, a plea for the study of philosophy, which profoundly affected St *Augustine (it turned him to God: *Conf.* 3. 4. 7). The list in *Div.* 2. 1 shows that Cicero swiftly proceeded with the construction of what is by his own description an encyclopaedia of Hellenistic philosophy: the protreptic *Hortensius* is followed by the *Academica*, on epistemology or theory of knowledge (especially concerned with the criterion of truth), originally in two books, entitled *Catulus* and *Lucullus*, of which only the second survives, but later recast in four books, of which we possess part of the first (*Academica posteriora*). It treats of the views of the New Academy after *Arcesilaus (1), and in particular of *Carneades on the impossibility of attaining certain knowledge, but conceding some *realia* as more compelling or probable than others. The recommendation (*Div.* 2. 150) to give unprejudiced consideration to different theories before approving *simillima veri* appealed to Cicero, who sometimes portrayed himself as belonging to this philosophical school (*Tusc.* 2. 5, 4. 47). In fact Cicero remained generally true to Philon's early teaching, rejecting the possibility of certain knowledge, but retaining and asserting the right to adopt whatever position seemed most compelling on each occasion.

Thus in questions of ethics Cicero often inclined toward Stoic doctrine as he recoiled from the Epicurean, as is evident in the *De finibus bonorum et malorum*, where he compiles and answers in turn the theories on the *summum bonum* ('highest good') propounded by the Epicureans and Stoics, before giving the views of Antiochus' so-called 'Old Academy' in book 5. From this encyclopaedic survey of the various schools' positions on ethics, Cicero turned in the *Tusculan Disputations* to the problems of the psychology of the happy life: death, grief, pain, fear, passion, and other mental disorders, and of what is essential for happiness, including (according to the Stoics) virtue. Concerned largely to allay his own doubts, and impressed by Stoic teaching on these subjects, he writes here with a passionate intensity and lyrical beauty.

As in the case of the contemporary Epicurean *Philodemus, theological speculation stands for Cicero in the place of a full account of natural philosophy and physical causes (such as is found, for example, in *Lucretius, Epicurus, or *Chrysippus, though *Tusc.* 1 also treats materialism in its concern for the material composition of the soul and a rational chain of causation). Thus Cicero next composes *De natura deorum* in three books, each devoted to the view of a different school (Epicurean, Stoic, Academic) on the nature of the gods and the existence of the divine, its role in human culture and the state. Having allowed Cotta to present the sceptical Academic view in book 3, after Velleius' presentation of the Epicurean in book 1, and Balbus' of the Stoic in book 2, Cicero rounds off the debate with a typically

Academic expression of his own opinion: that the Stoic's argument is more likely to be right (*ad veritatis similitudinem . . . propensior* 3. 95). In a later work, Stoic beliefs concerning Fate and the possibility of prediction are examined, with more use of anecdote and quotation perhaps indicative of a popular exposition, in the two books of the *De divinatione*, published just after Caesar's murder (*Div.* 2. 4). In this case Cicero displays no sympathy with the views of the Stoics, whose commitment to the validity of *divination was based on complex principles of logic and cosmic sympathy. Cicero's pious reaffirmation (2. 148) of his belief in the existence of a divine being, maintaining that it is prudent to keep traditional rites and ceremonies, belies his concerns in matters of theology and religion for the state above all else. Finally, the fragmentary *De fato* discusses the more specialized problem of volition and decides against Stoic determinism.

Equally specialized are the two genial and polished essays *Cato Maior de senectute* (written probably just before Caesar's murder and included in *Div.* list) and the *Laelius de amicitia*, which show once again Cicero's anxiety to reassure or occupy himself in times of stress and danger, and his last work on moral philosophy *De officiis* (finished November 44) aims at giving advice, based on Stoic precepts and in particular (for books 1 and 2) on the teachings of *Panaetius, on a variety of problems of conduct (ostensibly to Cicero's son).

These three works, along with the *Tusc.* and the *Somnium Scipionis*, were the most popular among readers in the Middle Ages, when the work of Cicero the politician and orator was almost forgotten, to be rediscovered in the Renaissance. Cicero's influence on European thought and literature ensured that what he found interesting and important in Greek philosophy became the philosophical curriculum of the Renaissance and Enlightenment. His achievement stands out as the creator of philosophical vocabulary in Latin, and as a philosophical stylist.

EDITIONS Eng. trans. of Cicero's philosophical works are available in the Loeb Classical Library series. More detailed editions, with notes: *Rep.* H. Last, G. H. Poyser (1948); G. H. Sabine, S. B. Smith, *On the Commonwealth*, introd. and trans. (1929). *Leg.* bk. 1, N. Rudd and T. Wiedemann (1987). C. Meissner, G. Landgraf (Ger.), *Somnium Scipionis* (1915). *Acad.* (45 BC), J. S. Reid (1885). *Paradoxa Stoicorum* (46 BC), A. G. Lee (1953). *Fin.* (45 BC), J. S. Reid (1925); R. Rubrichi (Ital.) (1938); bk. 3 with *Paradoxa Stoicorum*, M. R. Wright (1990). *Tusc.* (45 BC), M. Pohlenz and O. Heine, 4th edn. (1957); O. Gigon, 2nd edn. (1970); M. Giusta (1984); bks. 1, 2, and 5 A. E. Douglas (1985, 1990). *Nat. D.* (45 BC), A. S. Pease (1955). *Div.* A. S. Pease, vol. 1 (1920); vol. 2 (1923). *Fat.* (44 BC), O. Yon, 3rd edn. (1950); R. W. Sharples (1989). *Laelius de amicitia* (44 BC), J. S. Reid (1887); with *Somnium Scipionis*, J. G. F. Powell (1990). *Cato Maior de senect.* (44 BC), F. G. Moore (1903); M. Ruch (1972). *Off.*, H. A. Holden, 3rd edn. (1899); J. Higginbotham, *Cicero, On Moral Obligation*, introd. and notes (1967); M. T. Griffin and E. M. Atkins (1991).

GENERAL LITERATURE R. Philippson, 'Cicero: Philosophische Schriften', *RE* 7 (1939), 1104–92, who also treats the rhetorical works as products of Cicero's philosophic endeavour; still useful is R. Hirzel, *Untersuchungen zu Ciceros philosophischen Schriften*, 3 vols. (1877–83); A. E. Douglas, 'Cicero the Philosopher', in T. A. Dorey, *Cicero* (1965); A. E. Douglas, *Cicero*, *G&R* 2 (1968, with addenda 1978). Useful summaries of each of the works with notes in P. MacKendrick, *The Philosophical Books of Cicero* (1989). Intellectual context: E. Rawson, *Intellectual Life in the Late Roman Republic* (1985); A. A. Long and D. N. Sedley, *The Hellenistic Philosophers*, 2 vols. (1987); J. Annas, *Hellenistic Philosophy of Mind* (1993); and the essays and bibliog. in M. Schofield and G. Striker, *The Norms of Nature* (1985) and M. Griffin and J. Barnes, *Philosophia Togata* (1989). On Cicero's adherence to a particular school of philosophy: J. Glucker, in J. Dillon and A. A. Long (eds.), *The Question of 'Ecclecticism': Studies in Later Greek Philosophy* (1988), and more broadly, *Antiochus and the Later Academy* (1978). Theology as a special topic: M. van den Bruwaene, *La Théologie de Cicéron* (1939). On philosophical language: Merguet's Lexicon (1873–4); M. O. Lişcu, *L'Expression des idées philosophiques chéz Cicéron* (1937); and for Cicero as imitator and translator: P. Poncelet, *Cicéron traducteur de Platon* (1957); A. E. Douglas, *G&R* 1962, 41–51. For the influence of Cicero's philosophical works on subsequent ages: T. Zielinski's standard work, *Cicero im Wandel der Jahrhunderte* (1912), may be supplemented by M. L. Clarke and A. E. Douglas in T. A. Dorey (ed.), *Cicero* (1965).

J. H. S.; D. O.

Tullius (*RE* 30) **Cicero** (2), **Marcus**, b. 65 BC, son of *Cicero and *Terentia and thirteen years younger than his sister *Tullia (2). He was educated under his father's supervision and taken out to *Cilicia by him in 51. He was an obedient boy and a good soldier but he lacked his father's intellectual gifts. He was a successful cavalry officer in the republican army in 49/8 (*Off.* 2. 45). Pardoned after *Pharsalus, he held office in the family's home town of *Arpinum. He would have liked to serve under *Caesar in Spain (*Att.* 12. 7. 1), but instead was sent to Athens in 45 to study under the *Peripatetic Cratippus. Cicero's *De officiis* was written in the form of a letter to his son in 44, and Marcus was serving under *Brutus, who praised him highly (*Brut.* 3 (2. 3) 6), when his father was killed in the proscriptions. After *Philippi he joined Sextus *Pompeius Magnus, but took advantage of the amnesty of 39. He was elected to a priesthood (the augurate?) and was colleague to *Octavian (from 13 September to 1 November; see AUGUSTUS) as consul in 30; afterwards he governed Syria and was proconsul of Asia. There is no evidence to support the hypothesis (J. Carcopino, *Cicero, the Secrets of his Correspondence* (1951), 489 ff.) that his father's letters were published in 34/3 partly to blacken his father's memory, at the instigation of Octavian and with his co-operation. Though he was, by his own admission, idle in his student days (*Fam.* 16. 21) and drank too much (Pliny, *HN* 14. 147) and though his distinguished public career may have been partly due to Octavian's repentance for his father's murder (cf. Sen. *Ben.* 4. 30), he cannot have been without considerable administrative ability.

M. Testard, *Bulletin de l'association Guillaume Budé* 1962. 2, 198–213; M. Testard, *Cicéron Les Devoirs* (1965), vol. 1, introd.; M. Griffin and E. M. Atkins, *Cicero On Duties* (1991), xvi–xviii. J. P. B.; M. T. G.

Tullius (*RE* 31) **Cicero** (1), **Quintus** (*c*.102–43 BC), younger brother of *Cicero (see TULLIUS CICERO (1), M.) and similarly educated (they were both in Athens in 79 BC), had none of his brother's genius. He was irascible and often tactlessly outspoken; yet he was a good soldier and an able administrator. Plebeian aedile in 65 and praetor in 62 (helped, no doubt, by the fact that his brother Marcus was praetor and consul respectively when he was elected), he governed Asia (see ASIA, ROMAN PROVINCE) from 61 to 58, receiving two long letters of advice and criticism from his brother in Rome (*QFr.* 1. 1–2). He spent winter 57/6 in *Sardinia as a legate (see LEGATI) of *Pompey, when Pompey received his corn commission, and was evidently a hostage for Marcus' good behaviour in politics after his recall from exile (*Fam.* 1. 9. 9). He was legate on *Caesar's staff in Gaul from 54 to early 51, taking part in the invasion of *Britain in 54 and winning deserved praise for his courage in holding out against the *Nervii when the Gauls attacked the winter camps in 54 (*BGall.* 5. 40–52); though unwell, he drove himself so hard that his troops forced him to take some sleep at night (ibid. 40. 7). At Atuatuca a year later he took risks, probably with more excuse than Caesar allows, and was criticized (ibid. 6. 36–42). He was a valuable legate on Marcus' staff in *Cilicia in 51/50, supplying

(with C. Pomptinus) the military experience which Marcus lacked. He joined Pompey in the Civil War, was pardoned after *Pharsalus and then, with his son, behaved badly in maligning his brother to Caesar (*Att.* 11. 9 f.). He returned to Rome in 47 by Caesar's permission. Victims of the proscriptions in 43, he and his son were betrayed by their slaves.

The twenty-seven surviving letters of Marcus to Quintus were written between 60 and 54, mostly when Quintus was serving abroad. Of the four short surviving letters of Quintus, one (*Fam.* 16. 16: 53 BC) congratulated Marcus on enfranchising M. *Tullius Tiro and three (*Fam.* 16. 8: 49 BC; 16. 26 f.: 44 BC) were to Tiro. Quintus was a literary dilettante, writing four tragedies in sixteen days when in Gaul (*QFr.* 3. 5. 7). Though certainty is not possible (Balsdon, *CQ* 1963, 242 ff.), a strong case can be made for believing that neither Quintus nor, indeed, a contemporary wrote the *Commentariolum petitionis*, a long letter on Marcus' canvass for the consulship of 63. It none the less preserves some valuable information.

Like his brother, Quintus owned property near *Arpinum. His marriage to Pomponia, who was older than he and the sister of Marcus' friend T. *Pomponius Atticus, lasted from 69 to 44 and was never a happy one. It produced one son, a gifted boy whom his father indulged (see next entry).

D. R. Shackleton Bailey, *Cicero* (1971); *Epistulae ad Quintum Fratrem et M. Brutum* (1980), introd.; A. W. Lintott, *JRS* 1966, 108.

J. P. B.; M. T. G.

Tullius (*RE* 32) **Cicero** (2), **Quintus** (66–43 BC), unstable son of Q. *Tullius Cicero (1), was harmed from childhood by the disputes of his parents, each of whom canvassed his sympathy against the other. His education was supervised during his father's absences on duty abroad by his mother's brother T. *Pomponius Atticus to 54 and then by his uncle *Cicero. With his cousin M. *Tullius Cicero (2) he was taken out to Cilicia in 51–50, when his father was legate on his uncle's staff. The boys stayed for a time with King *Deiotarus of Galatia (*Att.* 5. 17. 3). On the republican side at *Pharsalus and afterwards pardoned by *Caesar, he then went to Asia with his father and sought to prejudice Caesar against his uncle (*Att.* 11. 10. 1). In 46 he was aedile at *Arpinum (*Fam.* 13. 11. 3) and became Lupercus at Rome (*Att.* 12. 5. 1) and was perhaps active as such in the *Lupercalia of 44, when Caesar was offered a crown. He may have held the quaestorship in 43 (*Att.* 16. 14. 4). He was killed with his father in the proscriptions, in December 43. J. P. B.; M. T. G.

Tullius Laurea, one of *Cicero's *freedmen, wrote an epigram on a hot spring at a villa of Cicero (Plin. *HN* 31. 7–8) and some Greek epigrams.

See Courtney, *FLP* 182; Gow–Page, *GP* 2. 461. E. C.

Tullius (*RE* 52) **Tiro, Marcus,** *Cicero's confidential secretary and literary adviser, freed by him 53 BC, perhaps on his fiftieth birthday (if, as reported, he died 4 BC in his hundredth year). From 51 he suffered from malaria, which caused Cicero great concern. After Cicero's death he published some of his speeches and letters and perhaps a collection of his jokes, and wrote a biography of him. He also wrote on grammar and on miscellaneous questions (Gell. *NA* 13. 9. 1). For his system of shorthand (the original *notae Tironianae*) see TACHYGRAPHY.

See esp. Cic. *Fam.* 16. E. B.

tumultus was a state of emergency decreed by the Roman state when threatened by hostile attack. *Cicero (*Phil.* 8. 3) states that the ancients had distinguished two types, the *tumultus Italicus*, a war in Italy (which to Cicero and his contemporaries meant a civil war), and the *tumultus Gallicus*, a Gallic attack (Gaul being the only province bordering Italy). When a *tumultus* was pronounced there was a suspension of normal state business (**iustitium*), military leave was cancelled, and all the citizens, wearing the military dress called the *sagum*, were levied (Cic. *Phil.* 5. 31). The procedure probably goes back at least as far as the Gallic raid of 390 BC (Diod. Sic. 14. 114. 1), and is recorded in accounts of the 4th cent. (e.g. Livy, 7. 9. 6, 361 BC). An emergency levy (*tumultuarius dilectus*) was the only time that **proletarii* (citizens who fell below the military census qualification for military service) could be enrolled (Gell. 16. 10. 11–13), and on a famous occasion, probably the invasion of **Pyrrhus in 281 BC, they were for the first time armed at public expense (Enn. *Ann.* 170–2 Skutsch; Cassius Hemina fr. 21 Peter). In the 2nd cent. the *dilectus tumultuarius* was used as a device for raising troops in a hurry and perhaps also for admitting volunteers to the ranks (see e.g. Livy, 31. 2. 5–6; 32. 26. 12; etc.).

E. Gabba, *Athenaeum* 1949, 189 = *Republican Rome* (1976), 8; P. A. Brunt, *Italian Manpower* (1971), 629 ff.   P. T.; T. J. Co.

Tunis (or **Tunes**), a Libyan town on the site of modern Tunis. It is frequently mentioned in connection with fighting in the vicinity of **Carthage in the campaigns of **Agathocles (1), M. **Atilius Regulus, and P. **Cornelius Scipio Africanus. Although overshadowed by Carthage, situated only a few miles away, it remained a separate community to the end of the Roman period.

M. Leglay, *Kleine Pauly* 5, 1004.   B. H. W.

Turia See 'LAUDATIO TURIAE'.

Turnus (1), Italian hero, in **Virgil son of Daunus and the **nymph Venilia and brother of the nymph Juturna; the Greek tradition calls him 'Tyrrhenus', suggesting an **Etruscan link (Dion. Hal. 1. 64. 2). His role as **Aeneas' rival in Italy is well established before Virgil (Cato frs. 9, 11 Peter; Dion. Hal. 1. 64. 2; Livy, 1. 2. 1–5). In the *Aeneid* he is king of **Ardea and the Rutulians and favoured suitor, not fiancé, of **Latinus' daughter Lavinia; rejected in favour of Aeneas and maddened by **Juno's intervention, he rouses the Latins (see LATINI) against the Trojans (*Aen.* 7). In the war (*Aen.* 9–12) he fights bravely as the Latin commander and can elicit sympathy, but is sometimes rash; his high-handed appropriation of the sword-belt of the dead **Pallas (2) leads tragically at the very end of the poem to his own death at the hands of Aeneas.

P. Schenk, *Die Gestalt des Turnus in Vergils Aeneis* (1984); A. Traina, *Enc. Virg.*, 'Turno'.   S. J. Ha.

Turnus (2), satirist of the time of **Domitian, popular in his own time (Mart. 7. 97. 8) and frequently mentioned later (Rut. Namat. 1. 603–4; Sid. Apoll. *Carm.* 9. 266; Lydus, *Mag.* 1. 41). The brother of the tragedian Scaevus **Memor (Mart. 11. 10), according to a scholion (see SCHOLIA) by **Valerius Probus, quoted by George Valla in his 1486 commentary on **Juvenal 1. 204, he was of **freedman birth but attained great fame at court. **Martial praises his vigour. A fragment on **Locusta, a notorious poisoner at the court of **Nero, suggests he dealt with social reality, perhaps in accordance with Flavian propaganda against the Neronian period. A fragment of pastoral poetry is an elegant imitation of **Virgil.

Courtney, *FLP*; V. Tandoi, in G. d'Anna and others, *Studi ... Traglia* (1979).   M. Ci.

Turpilius (*RE* 7) (died old, 103 BC, according to Jerome), author of *fabulae palliatae*. Thirteen titles and some 200 lines survive; the titles are all Greek (several from **Menander (1)), and there are no Roman allusions in the fragments, but in several other respects he is closer to **Plautus than **Terence. See PALLIATA.

Fragments: Ribbeck, *CRF*; Rychlewska (1962). J. Wright, *Dancing in Chains* (1974).   P. G. M. B.

Turranius Gracilis (*RE* 7) (of uncertain date), an authority on Spain, used by the elder **Pliny (1) (*HN*, bks. 3, 9, and 18, *index auctorum*).

Tusculum, a city near modern Frascati, 24 km. (15 mi.) southeast of Rome. Its extensive remains occupy a strong, bracing site 668 m. (2,198 ft.) above sea-level. Myths shroud its origin, but Tusculum was certainly powerful in early **Latium. Its **dictator Octavius **Mamilius allegedly supported his son-in-law **Tarquinius Superbus (508 BC); but traditions associating Tusculum with Etruscans may be mere aetiological fictions to explain its name. More credibly, Tusculum reputedly led the Latins (see LATINI) at Lake **Regillus *c*.496, when Mamilius himself fell. Thereafter, however, being exposed to Aequian attacks (see AEQUI) via **Algidus, it became Rome's ally and staunchly resisted Aequi, **Volsci, and Gauls. Tusculum, the first Latin city to obtain Roman citizenship (381; see CITIZENSHIP, ROMAN), supplied Rome with several illustrious families (Mamilii, Fulvii, Fonteii, Iuventii, Porcii). Some Tusculans joined the Latin revolt in 340 BC but usually Tusculum remained loyal (e.g. against **Hannibal; see PUNIC WARS). A **municipium under late republic and early empire, Tusculum was a fashionable resort where wealthy Romans sojourned: L. **Licinius Lucullus (2), **Maecenas, and especially M. **Tullius Cicero (1), who composed several philosophical treatises in his Tusculan villa (at mod. Poggio Tulliano?). Subsequently Tusculum is seldom mentioned, but was still an important stronghold when destroyed in medieval times. M. **Porcius Cato (1) was born there.

Strabo 5. 239; Livy 1. 49, 2. 15 f., 3. 7 f., 4. 33 f., 6. 21, 8. 7 f., 26. 9; Dion. Hal. bk. 10 *passim*. G. McCracken, *A Short History of Ancient Tusculum* (1939).   E. T. S.; T. W. P.

Tūticānus, a boyhood friend of **Ovid, who cannot fit his name into verse without the playful scansions of *Pont.* 4. 12. 10–11; cf. 4. 14. He seems to have translated the Phaeacia episode (see SCHERIA) of **Homer's *Odyssey* into Latin (ibid. 4.16. 27; cf. 12. 27).   E. C.

Tuticius Proculus, Latin grammarian from **Sicca Veneria and teacher of Marcus **Aurelius, who honoured him with a proconsulate (SHA *M. Ant.* 2. 3, 5; on the *nomen*, not 'Eutychius', Birley, *Bonner Historia-Augusta-Colloquium 1966/67* 39 f.).

Herzog–Schmidt, § 432.   R. A. K.

Twelve gods See OLYMPIAN GODS.

Twelve Tables According to Roman tradition, popular pressure led to the appointment for 451 BC of ten men with consular *imperium*, for writing down statutes, *legibus scribundis*, in order to put an end to the patrician and priestly monopoly of the law (see DECEMVIRATES, FIRST AND SECOND). They compiled ten tables, were reappointed for 450 BC, and compiled two more, including the ban on intermarriage between patricians and plebeians, which was rapidly abrogated by the *lex Canuleia* of 445 BC. An attempt to remain in office for 449 BC also failed. The fundamental consequence was that customary law was now enacted by statute

Tyche

and given legislative basis; and the Twelve Tables were seen as the starting-point of the development of Roman law.

We have no way of verifying this tradition; and it may be that the impetus came rather from a desire for self-regulation within the élite. But the legal, antiquarian, oratorical, and historical tradition preserves a remarkably consistent view of the content of the Twelve Tables, even if the language has been modernized. And it is reasonably certain both that they underlay the colonial charters of the late 4th cent. BC onwards and that legislation to revise them began in the early 3rd cent. BC.

Three points remain controversial: there is little evidence for the order of the different provisions and modern editions largely classify them perforce according to the later divisions of the law; it is uncertain how complete is the record preserved by our sources; and it is disputed how far they contained what was later regarded as public law. Our knowledge of the order depends on the fragments of the commentary by *Gaius (2) quoted in the *Digest* and on the occasional attribution of particular provisions to particular tables; but it is at least certain that the provision conventionally printed as Tabula I, 1, *is* the first. As far as the second point is concerned, there seem to be few areas of the private law of the late republic where a provision of the Twelve Tables is not at some point invoked and it is unlikely that whole fields covered by the Twelve Tables have disappeared without trace. And if one thinks in less rigid terms about the third problem, a consistent view of our tradition must lead to the conclusion that even if the Twelve Tables mostly concerned themselves with relations between individuals, they also at times concerned themselves with relations between individuals and the community.

The Twelve Tables were presumably not much systematized and perhaps put together largely from material which was readily to hand and which the ten men supposed to be actually or potentially useful, not unlike the later praetor's edict. It would be exaggerated to describe the Twelve Tables as a code. They attracted commentary from the middle republic onwards, but gradually became more and more obsolete as the praetor's edict developed, becoming progressively the province of antiquarians.

M. H. Crawford (ed.), *Roman Statutes* (1996), no. 40.　　　　M. H. C.

Tyche, fate, fortune both good and bad. The connection with τυγχάνειν always remains evident, reinforcing the sense of sudden change and fortuitous happenings in the individual's life. Like Moira (see FATE), Tyche gives everything to mortals from birth (Archil. fr. 16; Eur. *IA* 1136; Philemon, in Stob. 1. 6. 11). The mightiest of the Moirai in *Pindar (Hymn to Tyche in Paus. 7. 26. 8), she is the child of *Zeus Eleutherius (Pind. *Ol.* 12. 1 f.). A splendid lyric fragment praises noble Tyche who dispenses more good than evil from her scales: grace shines about her golden wing, and she lights up the darkness (lyric fr. 473 Page, *Lyrica Graeca Selecta*; Stob. 1. 16. 13). Though ambivalent by nature, she tends to be favourable (Aesch. *Ag.* 664, saviour and guide of the Achaeans; cf. Hesychius τύχη, εὐτυχία, comparable with the *agathos daimōn* (Ath. 15. 692 f.; 693e). *Oedipus is the child of beneficent Tyche (Soph. *OT* 1080 f.; cf. Eur. fr. 1017 TGrF Suppl. (1964), Snell: 'the man with fair *tychē* is wise'). She is divine spirit, mind, forethought and the only god who governs human affairs (Men. fr. 417 Körte); *Chaeremon (1) (TrGF 71 fr. 2). Tyche looks upon the deeds of gods and men and grants each his rightful share (*Trag. Adesp.* fr. 505 TGrF Suppl. (1964), Snell). Similar sentiments were expressed by the orators (Dem. 2. 23; Aeschin. 2. 131); but the idea of Chance as ruling principle found less favour in

philosophy, least of all with the Stoics (see STOICISM) for whom *heimarmenē* was the cause of all things. *Plato (1) set *tychē* beside *theos* (god), *kairos* (opportunity), and *technē* (skill) (*Leg.* 4, 709a–b; cf. *tychē*, *physis* (nature), *nomos* (law, convention), and *technē* in the Pythagorean *Diotogenes, Stob. 1. 7. 10; see PYTHAGORAS (1)). Tyche's personified identity remains vague, however. In tragedy she rarely rises above the basic concept of change, unexpected happening mostly sent by the gods (Eur. *Ion* 1512–14; *Alc.* 785; *Andr.* fr. 153 TGrF Suppl. (1964), Snell; cf. *Fortuna* in Hor. *Carm.* 1. 34. 13–16). Occasionally she becomes a *daimōn* herself, especially in *Euripides (*Cyc.* 606 f.; *IA* 1136).

Tyche was unknown to *Homer. She had no myth to speak of. According to *Pausanias (3) (4. 30. 4), her name occurred first in Hom. *Hymn Dem.* (420) as one of the Oceanids (see NYMPHS) and companions of *Persephone. The list derived from *Hesiod (*Theog.* 349–642): she is daughter of *Tethys and Oceanus (see OCEANUS (mythological)), sister of *Peitho and Eudore (cf. Peitho and *Eunomia and mother Promatheia (Forethought), in Alcman: fr. 64 Page, *PMG*). Tyche assumed a higher profile with the decline of the traditional gods. The momentous events of the 4th cent., the rise of Macedonian power leading to rapid change in the world order in east and west, fostered a belief in the random and irrational working of Fate. Tyche became synonymous with a general *automaton* i.e. accidental, spontaneous (Menander, in Stob. 1. 6. 14a, b; cf. Philemon fr. 137), although *Aristotle distinguished between a comprehensive *automaton* and *tychē* which applied to human affairs only (in Stob. 1. 6. 17a).

The popular view of a capricious, malignant Tyche emerges from New Comedy (see COMEDY (GREEK), NEW): she was dangerous, senseless, blind, wretched, etc. (Men. frs. 295, 348, 463, 464, 623, 630, 632, 788 Körte). In romances she figures large as a convenient plot device (E. Rohde, *Griech. Roman*[4] (1960), 296–304, who sees a deeper purpose behind Tyche; B. Reardon, *Courants litt. grecs* (1971), 309–403). Negative in *Thucydides (2) as blows of Fate (τύχαι), or an inscrutable element that confuses human affairs (6. 11. 6), she plays a larger role in *Polybius (1). Cunning Tyche is sudden (30. 10. 1), changeable (15. 6. 8), jealous (39. 8. 2). Nevertheless the historian contrasts this popular image of all-powerful Chance with what can be expected as reasonable (εἰκότως) historical development, like Rome's rise to power (1. 63. 9).

Tyche's cults spread widely from the 4th cent. (collected in *RE* 7 A 1677 ff.) at *Thebes (1), Athens, Lebadea (see TROPHONIUS), *Megara (image by *Praxiteles, Paus. 1. 43. 6), *Sicyon (Tyche Akraia on acropolis, Paus. 2. 7. 5), and her latest sanctuary at Hermione (Paus. 2. 35. 3). An altar—appropriately to Good Luck—stood in the Altis, *Olympia (Paus. 5. 15. 6). She was represented with a rudder, carrying child *Plutus or a cornucopia, and standing on a sphere. Tyche functioned as City Goddess (*Turrigera*: 'turret-crowned') similar to the old Polias in Greece (τύχη τῆς πόλεως, Athens IG 2². 3198—3rd cent.), the islands, and most frequently in the east, where she successfully competed with her Semitic counterpart Gad and with *Isis. The common phrase 'good luck' (ἀγαθῆ τύχη) endured through the ages (Ar. *Birds* 675; *Thesm.* 283) and survives in the modern Greek prayer (*kalē tychē*) for a young girl to find a good match.

See also FATE; FORTUNA / FORS.

G. Herzog-Hauser, *RE* 7A 2 (1943), 1643–89; Nilsson, *GGR* (1950), 2². 196, 200–10.　　　　N. R.; B. C. D.

Tydeus (Τυδεύς), son of *Oeneus, legendary warrior of the generation before the Trojan War. Leaving his homeland in

*Aetolia he came to *Argos (2), where *Adrastus (1) gave him his daughter Deipyle in marriage; she bore him *Diomedes (2), who is always conscious at Troy of the need to match his father's exploits. Enrolled as one of the *Seven against Thebes, he first—according to *Homer's *Iliad*, drawing and no doubt embroidering upon earlier *Thebaid* traditions, see EPIC CYCLE—took part in an embassy to the city, triumphed over the locals in a series of games, then killed all but one of a fifty-strong band sent to ambush him on his return (4. 372 ff.). In the war itself, he proved himself a fierce fighter in spite of his stocky build (5. 801); his thirst for slaughter, vividly described at Aesch. *Sept.* 377 ff., drove him to put the Theban princess Ismene ruthlessly to the sword (Mimnermus fr. 21 W), a scene shown on a Corinthian crater in the Louvre, and even in his own death-throes to try to eat out the brains of the wounded *Melanippus—an act that cost him the immortality which Athene had arranged.

R. Hampe, 'Tydeus und Ismene', *AK* 1975, 10–16. A. H. G.

Tylos, the Greek name (cf. *Tyros* (Strab. 16. 3. 4) Lat. *Tyrus* (Plin. *HN* 12. 21. 38)) given to the largest of the Bahrain islands in the *Persian Gulf, probably from Akkadian *Tilmun* via Aramaic †*Tylwos*, cf. Syriac. TLWN (attested in a letter written by the Nestorian *catholicos* Ishoyahb I in 584/5). *Androsthenes' visit in 324 BC effected the collection of detailed botanical data on Tylos, treated by *Theophrastus (*Hist. Pl.* 4. 7. 7–8; 5. 4. 7–8; *Caus. Pl.* 2. 5. 5). *Juba (2) (Pliny, *HN* 6. 28. 147) had precise information on the island's location. Tylos was famed for its pearls (Plin. *HN* 6. 28. 147). Tylos minor (Pliny, *HN* 12. 22. 39) is the neighbouring island of Muharraq, also called Arados (Strab. 16. 3. 4). The prehistory of Tylos extends back to at least the beginning of the 4th millennium BC, when it was inhabited by a population subsisting on herding, shellfish gathering, and fishing. Proto-cuneiform and Sumerian sources mentioning Sumerian *Dilmun*, and Old Babylonian letters from Ur mentioning Akkadian *Tilmun* attest to the island's early role as a trans-shipment point for copper, timber, and other goods originating further to the east (e.g. in Oman and the Indian subcontinent). From the late 8th to the mid-7th cent. BC Tilmun was tributary to the Assyrian empire. In pre-Hellenistic times the island's chief god was Inzak, called 'Nabu of Dilmun' in a neo-Assyrian god-list. The goddess Ninsikila, perhaps equivalent to the deity Meskilak mentioned in two letters sent from Tilmun to Nippur in the 14th cent. BC, appears in charge of Dilmun in the Sumerian myth 'Enki and the World Order'.

G. W. Bowersock, in H. A. A. Khalifa and M. Rice (eds.), *Bahrain through the Ages: The Archaeology* (1986), 399–406; D. T. Potts, *The Arabian Gulf in Antiquity* 1 (1990), 193–231, 287–290; 2 (1990), 125–49; O. Stein, *RE* 7 A (1948), 1732–3. D. T. P.

Tyndareos (Τυνδάρεως or -ος), in mythology husband of *Leda and father, real or putative, of *Helen, *Clytemnestra, the *Dioscuri, Timandra, and Philonoe. His brothers were said to be Leucippus, Aphareus, and Icarius (Apollod. 3. 10. 3), and sometimes *Hippocoön (ibid. 3. 10. 4). Hippocoön drove him from Sparta, but he returned and succeeded to the throne after *Heracles had invaded the land and killed Hippocoön and his twelve sons (ibid. 3. 10. 5). When suitors came, wishing to marry Helen, Tyndareos made them take an oath to protect the marriage-rights of the chosen bridegroom (ibid. 3. 10. 9), which led in due course to the Trojan War (see HOMER; TROY) when the Greek leaders marshalled troops to fetch back Helen after she deserted *Menelaus (1) for *Paris. *Hesiod (fr. 176 M–W) says that when sacrificing to the gods Tyndareos forgot *Aphrodite, so the goddess

in anger made his daughters unfaithful, Helen with Paris, Clytemnestra with *Aegisthus, and Timandra, who had married Echemus, with Phyleus. Tyndareos in due course bequeathed his kingdom to Menelaus (Apollod. *Epit.* 2. 16). *Euripides has him live long enough to bring the charge of matricide against *Orestes (*Or.*; cf. Apollod. *Epit.* 6. 25). J. R. M.

Tynnichus (early 5th cent.?), poet of *Chalcis, whose reputation rested on a *paean, of which one line was admired by *Aeschylus (test. 114 Radt = Porphyrius 2. 18, p. 148 Nauck) and by *Plato (1) (*Ion* 534d5–e1).

L. Käppel, *Paian* (1992), 359. A. Blumenthal, *RE* 18 A 2355 f. B. Z.

Typhon, monster and adversary of *Zeus. *Hesiod's Typhoeus (*Theog.* 823–35) has 100 snake-heads, eyes blazing fire, and voices that cover the gamut of gods and animals. The final child (by *Tartarus) of Earth (*Gaia), he is blasted down to the place Tartarus by Zeus' thunderbolt, but remains the source of hurricanes ('typhoon' merges Chinese *ta fēng*, 'big wind', with Greek myth). *Homer knows that Typhoeus lies amongst the Arimi (in Cilicia; *Il.* 2. 783, garbled by Verg. *Aen.* 9. 715–16). In Apollod. 1. 6. 3, the gods flee to Egypt in panic, turning themselves into animals (referring to Egyptian theriomorphism); Zeus with thunderbolts and an adamantine sickle wounds Typhon at Mt. Casius in *Syria, but is overpowered, his sinews cut out and both he and his sinews put in 'the Corycian cave' in Cilicia. *Hermes and Aegipan ('Goat-*Pan') steal the sinews and refit Zeus (in *Nonnus' *Dionysiaca* *Cadmus tricks the sinews from Typhon). The geography of the story includes Syria and *Cilicia and its motifs link it to *Hittite myths of Illuyankas ('Dragon'). See also SET.

W. Burkert, *Structure and History in Greek Mythology and Ritual* (1979), 7–9; R. Mondi in L. Edmunds, *Approaches to Greek Myth* (1990), ch. 3; P. Walcot, *Hesiod and the Near East* (1966), ch. 1. K. D.

tyrannicides, killers of tyrants (see TYRANNY) generally (see e.g. SERVILIUS AHALA, C.) but specially used of (*a*) the killers of *Hipparchus (1) of Athens (see ARISTOGITON; also CRITIUS for a famous statue group) and (*b*) the killers of *Caesar (see esp. CASSIUS LONGINUS (1), C.; IUNIUS BRUTUS (2), M.).

Tyrannio (1) the Elder (early 1st cent. BC). Theophrastus, son of Epicratides, of *Amisus (where his teacher nicknamed him Tyrannio), afterwards a pupil of *Dionysius (15) Thrax, was brought by L. *Licinius Lucullus (2) as prisoner to Rome, where he was freed and enjoyed the patronage of *Pompey, being the first Aristarchan (cf. ARISTARCHUS (2)) to teach in the city. He was a friend of *Cicero, *Caesar, and T. *Pomponius Atticus, and interested in the *Latin language, which he regarded as derived from an Aeolic Greek dialect (see DIALECTS, GREEK (PREHISTORY)). He was among those who examined the manuscripts of *Aristotle and *Theophrastus brought by *Sulla from Athens, 86 BC. His works, on metre (a comparatively rare topic), on Homeric and other criticism and exegesis (cf. HOMER), and on grammar (which, under Atticist influence (see ASIANISM AND ATTICISM), he defined as θεωρία μιμήσεως, a 'theory of imitation'), have perished. See also STRABO, who was his most famous pupil (Strabo 548).

C. Wendel, *RE* 7 A 1811 ff.; edition of the fragments: W. Haas (1977). P. B. R. F.; R. B.; N. G. W.

Tyrannio (2) the Younger, son of Artemidorus, a *Phoenician, originally named Diocles, was brought as a prisoner to Rome and freed by *Terentia, the widow of *Cicero. He was a pupil of

*Tyrannio (1) the Elder, and became an eminent grammarian at Rome. He wrote on accents and other grammatical topics, but his works have been confused with those of the elder Tyrannio, the fate of which they have shared.

See the works cited in the preceding entry.　　　P. B. R. F.; N. G. W.

tyranny (*tyrannos*, 'tyrant', was perhaps a Lydian word) is the name given to the form of monarchy set up by usurpers in many Greek states in the 7th and 6th cents. BC. The earliest occurrence of the term is in *Archilochus (*tyrannis*, fr. 19. 3 West). Tyranny was not a special form of constitution, or necessarily a reign of terror; the tyrant might either rule directly or retain the existing political institutions but exercise a preponderant influence over their working, and his rule might be benevolent or malevolent. Tyranny was given a bad sense especially by *Plato (1) and *Aristotle, for whom it was the worst possible form of constitution.

Among the best known of the early tyrants were *Pheidon of Argos, *Cypselus and *Periander of Corinth, *Cleisthenes (1) of Sicyon, *Pisistratus and his sons *Hippias (1) and *Hipparchus (1) in Athens, and *Polycrates (1) of Samos. Archaic tyranny seems to have been a response to the development of the city-states: typically a fringe member of the ruling *aristocracy would seize power with the support of discontented members of the community; but after a time the rule of the tyrant in turn became a cause of discontent, and tyranny hardly ever lasted more than two generations. These tyrants ruled in a period of growing confidence and prosperity: by encouraging national cults, by sponsoring public works, and by acting as patrons to writers and artists, they glorified both their cities and themselves. See PATRONAGE, LITERARY. Later tyrants were military dictators, among them Gelon and *Hieron (1) of Syracuse and *Theron of Acragas at the beginning of the 5th cent. and *Dionysius I and *Dionysius II of Syracuse in the late 5th and 4th cents.

A. Andrewes, *The Greek Tyrants* (1956); H. Berve, *Die Tyrannis bei den Griechen* (1967); M. M. Austin, *CQ* 1990, 289 ff.　　　V. E.; P. J. R.

Tyre, a major city in southern Phoenicia (see PHOENICIANS) with a large territory, built on an island but extending ashore, and equipped with two harbours. It is famed as the main founder of Phoenician colonies to the west (*Cyprus, *Carthage, etc.), and its international trade from Spain to the *Persian Gulf is evoked in Ezekiel's prophecies (Ezek. 26–8). The Tyrian navy is often mentioned as an ally of the Persians (see NAVIES; PERSIA). In 332 BC it offered an obstinate resistance to *Alexander (3) the Great and was captured only after a famous siege. It made a rapid recovery and became a Ptolemaic possession (see EGYPT, *Ptolemaic*) ruled by *suffetes*. Conquered by the *Seleucids in 200 BC, it became free in 126. It early struck a *foedus* with Rome. It was made a colony (see COLONIZATION, ROMAN) by *Septimius Severus and the capital of Syria Phoenice. It was a great commercial city, maintaining a *statio* (office) at *Puteoli and at Rome during the Principate, and was the seat of famous *purple-dyeing and *glass industries; its wealth is demonstrated by the beautiful *sarcophagi of its Roman necropolis.

DCPP; A. Poidebard, *Un grand port disparu* (1939); H. J. Katzenstein, *History of Tyre* (1973).　　　A. H. M. J.; H. S.; J.-F. S.

Tyro, in mythology, daughter of *Salmoneus and mother (by Cretheus) of *Jason (1)'s father Aeson and (by *Poseidon) of the twins *Pelias and *Neleus. Tyro loved the river *Enipeus, but Poseidon tricked her by assuming that river's form and lay with her (Hom. *Od.* 11. 235–59). According to a later tradition dramatized by *Sophocles (1), Tyro exposed the twins who, however,

survived to be reunited with their mother and punish their stepmother, Sidero, who had maltreated Tyro (cf. Men. *Epit.* 325–33). Her name is often connected with τυρός, 'cheese', because of her soft whiteness.

Preisendanz, in Roscher's *Lexikon* 5; Pearson, *Fragments of Sophocles* 2. 270–4.　　　R. L. Hu.

Tyrrhenus (Τυρρηνός), eponym of the Tyrrhenians (i.e. *Etruscans, though see West on Hes. *Theog.* 1016), Dion. Hal. *Ant. Rom.* 1. 27. 1, where he is son of King Atys and comes from Maeonia (Lydia); in schol. Pl. *Ti.* 25b, he is Atys' grandson; son of *Heracles, Dion. Hal. 1. 28. 1, or of *Telephus (1), ibid.; apparently god of the Tyrrhenian sea (Valerius Flaccus 4. 715). He invented trumpets (Hyg. *Fab.* 274. 20).　　　H. J. R.

Tyrtaeus, Spartan elegiac poet of the mid-7th cent. BC. His works are said to have filled five books; some 250 lines or parts of lines survive in quotations and papyri. They are of great historical interest in relation to two crises affecting Sparta at the time. One was civic unrest that threatened the authority of the kings and elders. In a poem that later came to be entitled *Eunomia* ('Law and Order') (frs. 1–4 W), Tyrtaeus reminded the citizens of the divine right by which the kings ruled, and of the oracle which had laid down the constitutional roles of kings, council, and demos; fr. 4. 3–9 quotes the four-line hexameter oracle, padded out with pentameters, and corresponding to part of the Rhetra in Plut. *Lyc.* 6. The other crisis was the Second Messenian War (see MESSENIA, *Myth-history*; SPARTA, § 2). Here too Tyrtaeus functioned as a sort of state poet, exhorting the Spartans to fight to the death for their city (frs. 10–14, 18–24). *Callinus was making similar use of elegy at the same period on the other side of the Aegean. Tyrtaeus addresses the fighting men as if they were already on the battlefield, and it is not impossible that this was the case. Certainly in the 4th cent. BC, when Tyrtaeus was an established classic, Spartan armies on campaign were made to listen to recitations of his poetry (Lycurg. *Leoc.* 107, cf. Philochorus *FGrH* 328 F 216).

Besides elegies, the *Suda* credits Tyrtaeus with 'martial songs'. This probably refers to the anapaestic and iambic chants which accompanied armed dances and processions at certain Spartan festivals (in the Hellenistic age, at any rate; fragments in Page, *PMG* nos. 856–7, 870). See METRE, GREEK, § 4 (c). These were apparently sometimes attributed to Tyrtaeus (Dio Chrys. *Or.* 2. 29 and schol. 2. 59; Ath. 630f; Poll. 4. 107); but their language does not look archaic.

Text: B. Gentili and C. Prato, *Poetae Elegiaci*, 1 (1979); West, *IE*² 2 (1992). Translation: West, *GLP.* Commentary: T. Hudson-Williams, *Early Greek Elegy* (1926); C. Prato, *Tyrtaeus* (1968).　　　M. L. W.

Tzetzes, Johannes (12th cent. AD), a copious, careless, quarrelsome Byzantine polymath. In his youth he wrote (AD 1143) a commentary on *Homer's *Iliad* of which the greater part is still unpublished, followed by *Allegories* on *Iliad* and *Odyssey* (in 10,000 verses), and other verse works on *Antehomerica, Homerica,* and *Posthomerica.* His other writings included scholia on *Hesiod, *Aristophanes, *Lycophron (2(b)), and others, and a poem on prosody. His chief work, Βίβλος Ἱστορική, *Histories,* by its first editor named Chiliades, is a review (in 12,674 verses) of Greek literature and learning, with quotations from over 400 authors. In regard to his poverty and slighted merits Tzetzes displays an engaging lack of reticence. He was not always without taste or discretion; e.g. once, when reduced to selling the rest of his library he retained his *Plutarch; nor is felicity of expression lacking in (for example) his objurgation of *Thucydides (2)'s cross-word style (λοξοσυστρόφοις λόγοις). Generally, however, his manner is dull, and he is extremely inaccurate (perhaps owing to his frequent separation from his books). His uncorroborated evidence is accordingly viewed with much suspicion. Nevertheless, he preserves a few fragments of ancient poetry and offers an engaging glimpse of the life of a Byzantine scholar in a period of intense interest in ancient Greek literature.

Editions: *Letters*: P. A. M. Leone (1972); *Chiliades*: P. A. M. Leone (1968); *Allegories*: *Iliad*: Boissonade (1851); *Odyssey*: H. Hunger, *Byz. Zeitschr.* 1955; (scholia) Cramer, *Anecd. Ox.* 3 (1836). *On Iliad*: Hermann (1812–14); Bachmann (in schol. *Iliad*) (1835–8); *Homerica, AnteH., PostH.*: Jacobs (1793); Bekker (1816; repr., Lehrs, 1868); *On Theogony*: Bekker (1842), Matranga, *Anecdota Graeca* 2 (1850); *Schol. on W. D. and Shield*: Gaisford, *Poetae Minores Graeci* 3. *Schol. on Aristophanes*: Koster and others (1960–4); *Schol. on Lycophron*: Scheer (1908). *Allegories ἐκ τῆς χρονικῆς*, etc.: Morellus (1616); Studemund, *Anecd. Gr. varia* (1886); *Schol. on Oppian*: Bussemaker (Didot) (1849); *Περὶ διαφορᾶς ποιητῶν*, etc.: W. J. W. Koster, *Prolegomena de comoedia* (1975). *On Death of Emperor Manuel* (1180): Matranga, *Anecd. Gr.* 2 (1850); C. Wendel, *RE* 7 A 1959 ff.; N. G. Wilson, *Scholars of Byzantium* (1983), 190–6.

P. B. R. F.; R. B.; N. G. W.

U

Ubii, a German tribe just east of the Rhine, which sought *Caesar's help against the *Suebi in 55 BC. In 38 BC, under renewed Suebic pressure, they persuaded *Agrippa to settle them west of the river, on land formerly belonging to the Eburones (a *German tribe). The Ubii furnished recruits to the Roman army; they joined C. *Iulius Civilis in AD 70 only under duress and returned to their allegiance to Rome at the earliest possible moment.

> M. Gechter, in T. Blagg and M. Millett (eds.), *The Early Roman Empire* (1990), 97 ff. O. B.; J. F. Dr.

Ugarit, an important kingdom of N. Syria in the late bronze age, known from the excavations at Ras Shamra (16 km. (10 mi.) north of Lattakie) and the hundreds of texts in Ugaritic (alphabetic)/*cuneiform script found on the site. The city was destroyed in the early 12th cent. BC. In the Persian period, the site was partly reoccupied by a local population, and connections with Greece are shown by finds of Attic pottery and a coin hoard. The harbour (Leukos Limen; mod. Minet el Beida) was equipped with entrepôts and protected by a city wall. Archaeological remains of the Hellenistic period were found at Ras Ibn Hani, in the vicinity of Ras Shamra, where scant traces of Roman times were uncovered.

> G. Saadé, *Ougarit* (1979); R. Stucky, *Ras Shamra* (1983). J.-F. S.

Ulfila, 'little wolf', Gothic bishop (see GOTHS), fl. c. AD 340–82, was born in Gothia of the stock of Roman prisoners from Cappadocia. Famous for translating the Gothic Bible, of which the surviving Gospels closely reflect his work. Closely involved in Gotho-Roman diplomatic relations, he worked in Gothia for only seven years before being expelled (c.348); his precise role in the formal conversion of the Goths as they crossed the Danube in 376 is unclear. He also played a major role in eastern Church affairs as a leader of the anti-Nicene coalition dominant in the mid-4th cent.

> P. J. Heather and J. F. Matthews, *The Goths in the Fourth Century* (1991); G. W. S. Friedrichsen, *The Gothic Version of the Gospels* (1926). P. J. H.

Ulpia Marciana Augusta, sister of the emperor *Trajan, wife of C. Salonius Matidius Patruinus, a senator from Vicetia, and mother of *Matidia. She received the title Augusta (see AUGUSTUS, AUGUSTA, AS TITLES) some time before AD 105 and was deified on her death in 112.

> *RE* Suppl. 15, 'Ulpius' 56a; M.-T. Raepsaet-Charlier, *Prosopographie des femmes de l'ordre sénatorial* (1987), no. 824. A. R. Bi.

Ulpian, lawyer. See DOMITIUS ULPIANUS.

Ulpianus of Ascalon taught rhetoric at *Emesa and *Antioch (1) in the reign of Constantine (AD 324–37) and wrote a number of declamations and rhetorical works (no longer extant). He is the reputed author of *scholia to eighteen speeches of *Demosthenes (2); they are of little independent value. He was a teacher of *Libanius and *Proaeresius. N. G. W.

Ulpius (*RE* 4) **Marcellus,** a lawyer of the mid-2nd cent. AD, whose family, probably from *Asia Minor, had become Roman citizens under Trajan, and was himself of equestrian rank (see EQUITES). He taught and practised law in Rome and advised *Antoninus Pius and Marcus *Aurelius as a member of their respective councils (see CONSILIUM PRINCIPIS). He wrote at least five books (*libri*): *De officio consulis* ('On the Judicial Duties of the Consul'), a book of *Responsa* ('Consultative Opinions'), and 31 of *Digesta* ('Ordered Abstracts'), his most important work, which belongs to the 160s AD. It constitutes a refined analysis of material from various sources. Q. *Cervidius Scaevola and *Ulpian annotated it. A writer of independent mind, he published notes on *Julianus' *Digesta* criticizing some of Julianus' free-wheeling innovations. Justinian's compilers excerpted over 120 passages from his work (see JUSTINIAN'S CODIFICATION).

> Lenel, *Pal.* 1. 589–640; *PIR*[1] U 556; *HLL* 4 (forthcoming), § 415. 4; Kunkel 1967, 213–14; Honoré 1962, 164–6. T. Hon.

Ulpius Traianus, Marcus, father of the emperor *Trajan, came from *Italica in *Baetica (southern Spain), where he was proconsul before commanding legio X Fretensis (see LEGION) under *Vespasian during the Jewish War. He remained in post until AD 69, when he was involved in constructing a road from *Caesarea (2) to *Scythopolis. Vespasian as emperor demonstrated his favour by granting a consulship (probably in 70) and patrician rank. Traianus is attested as governor of *Syria from 73/74 to 76/77, perhaps remaining until 78. In 75 he built a road to Sura on the upper *Euphrates, linking the city of *Palmyra to the river. His governorship helped consolidate Roman interests west of the Euphrates and he was awarded triumphal ornaments (see ORNAMENTA) for a minor, possibly diplomatic, success against the Parthians (Plin. *Pan.* 16. 1; *ILS* 8970, revised in T. Wiegand, *Milet* 1/5 (1919), 53; see PARTHIA). On a plausible reconstruction of this fragmentary inscription, Traianus was perhaps governor of the newly created province of *Cappadocia–*Galatia before moving to Syria. His career culminated with the proconsulship of Asia (79/80). During Trajan's reign his father was consecrated and celebrated on coins as 'Divine father Traianus'.

> G. Bowersock, *JRS* 1973, 133; B. Isaac and I. Roll, *JRS* 1976, 15. J. B. C.

Ulysses See ODYSSEUS.

Umbrians The word 'Umbrian' has been used by ancient and modern authors to denote a variety of ethnic, linguistic, cultural, and geographical entities. *Pliny (1) (*HN* 3. 14. 112) refers to the Umbrians as the *gens antiquissima Italiae* ('oldest of the peoples of Italy'), and derives their Greek name of Ombrikoi from their having survived the flood. Attempts to equate the Umbrians of the ancient sources with a range of archaeological terms extending from the so-called 'Villanovans' (but see VILLANOVAN CULTURE) to the Germanic Ambrones have brought little save confusion or a clarity that is at best illusory. Evidence for the *Indo-European Italic dialect known as Umbrian is found in that part of central Italy where the urnfield and inhumation rite overlapped; it is closely related to Oscan, from southern Italy (outside the urnfield area, see CELTS), and is written in a script derived via Etruscan from the western Greek alphabet. The longest documents are the ritual texts known as the *tabulae Iguvinae*.

Umbria, together with Ager Gallicus, formed the sixth *regio of Italy under *Augustus (see ITALY). As such, it included territory bounded by the Adriatic, the Crustumium, and the Aesis on the east, and by Sabine territory and the Tiber to south and west. Important towns included *Iguvium, *Camerinum, *Asisium, *Tuder, *Sentinum, *Spoletium, *Carsulae, *Ameria, *Interamna Nahars, *Narnia, *Ocriculum, and Hispellum, and in Ager Gallicus Pisaurum and Sena Gallica. See ITALY, LANGUAGES OF.

J. H. W. Penney, *CAH* 4² (1988), 720 ff. (language); *Antichità dell'Umbria* (exhib. cats.: Vatican, 1988; Budapest–Cracow, 1989; Leningrad, 1990; New York, 1991); M. Pallottino, *A History of Earliest Italy* (1991; It. orig. 1984). D. W. R. R.

unconstitutional proposals, law against (in Athens). See GRAPHĒ PARANOMŌN.

Uranius See IULIUS AURELIUS URANIUS ANTONINUS, L.

Uranus (Greek Ouranos), the divine personification of the sky in Greece. Scarcely known in cult, his best-known appearance is in *Hesiod's *Theogony* (126 ff.). He is produced by *Gaia (Earth), then becoming her consort, but hating their children, he causes them to remain confined within her. At the instigation of Gaia, he is castrated by their son *Cronus; the severed genitals are cast into the sea and engender *Aphrodite.

M. L. West, *Hesiod: Theogony* (1966), 211–13; G. S. Kirk, *Myth* (1970), 213–20. E. Ke.

Urartu, iron age kingdom (= Hebrew *Ararat*) in the territory of later *Armenia. The unified kingdom is known from its archaeology and monumental *cuneiform inscriptions under a dynasty c.830–640 BC. Its largely hostile relations with *Assyria (1) are documented by Assyrian sources. The language Urartian is considered to belong to a Caucasian group.

R. D. Barnett, *CAH* 3²/1 (1982), 8.; P. R. S. Moorey, plates to *CAH* 3² (1984), ch. 4. J. D. Ha.

urban cohorts See COHORTES URBANAE.

urbanism

I. Greek and Hellenistic Urban units are to be distinguished not simply by the size of the community, but by its topographical organization, occupational pattern, and cultural sophistication. The formation of towns is not therefore simply a matter of the agglomeration of communities, but of the forging of a community of distinct character. Archaeologists have sometimes been too willing to call early bronze age settlements towns as a result of overestimating the size of the community involved, but both the archaeological remains and the evidence of the Linear B tablets (see MYCENAEAN LANGUAGE) show that late bronze age palace centres of the *Minoan and *Mycenaean civilizations were essentially urban units in their size, occupational diversity, and culture. Particularly important seems to be the role of the palaces as centres for the storage and redistribution of agricultural produce: it may not be coincidental that both the bronze age palaces and the earliest towns develop in areas marginal for agriculture and where accumulation and storage of produce is vital if a stable community of any size is to be maintained and is a source of political power.

No Dark Age community deserves to be called a town, and the growth of towns in the 8th and 7th cents. seems in many cases to be a result of separate village communities coalescing for political and economic reasons (*synoecism). At *Corinth, for example, the creation of a single town, with a specific area devoted to burial of the dead, and the creation of a separate potters' quarter go closely together, and are followed within half a century by temple-building and by *tyranny. Corinthian pottery already follows an independent tradition before the grouping of potting activity into the potters' quarter. The impetus to urbanism in Corinth may in fact have come in part from the sending out of colonizing expeditions, which probably formed communities recognizably urban in their organization of civic space from the beginning, to judge from the way in which areas were reserved from the beginning for 'civic' activities at the Megarian colony of *Megara Hyblaea. The members of a new community, formed from scratch, must have given thought in the abstract to the requirements and organization of communal life. This may in turn have led to changes at home as well as in the daughter-community. Unification for defence seems to play little part in the urbanization of this period, and many early towns seem to have been without walls; but it is significant that colonizing and urbanism are at this stage phenomena of agriculturally marginal southern Greece, as also is that characteristic political unit, the *polis.

Greek political thought did not recognize the existence of urban communities which were not also politically independent: *Aristotle in *Politics* 1 sees the *polis* as the natural evolutionary product of the growth of the village. Urbanism and political independence should therefore be seen as going closely together. One mark of both is the focusing of the community's religious life upon certain particular *sanctuaries, both central sanctuaries and those at the margins of a city's territory which stake out claims to territorial control as well as providing a proving ground for future citizens and citizen wives (see RITES OF PASSAGE). The development of functionally specific sanctuaries, including these out-of-town sanctuaries, is part of the occupational diversity characteristic of urban life and can be observed both in southern Greece and in Greek colonies from the later 8th cent. onwards.

The assumption that urban units should also enjoy political independence had consequences for urban development across a single political territory. The main settlement tends to be very much the largest settlement in a political territory, and even when there are other populous centres they tend not to develop the full range of characteristically urban services—theatres, palaestras, diverse sanctuaries, dedicated community meeting-places. This is seen particularly clearly in the case of Athens, where some of the *demes were very much larger than *poleis elsewhere in Greece (*Acharnae may have had a population of 8,000–10,000), but where none of them seems to have developed the topographical organization, service facilities, or occupational pattern of a town.

It is characteristic of classical towns that further attention is devoted to the space within which non-religious civic activities take place and that there are buildings specifically designed for such activities. The development of the *stoa, from the mid-6th cent. onwards, had an important part to play in this: the stoa originated as a place of shelter in sanctuaries, but came to be used as a flexible meeting-place suitable both for official gatherings, such as lawcourts, and for unofficial civic activities. Flanking the *agora with stoas became a popular way of marking out the civic centre.

During the 5th, 4th, and 3rd cents. urban forms spread to mainland northern Greece, both to the seaboard under the direct influence of southern cities, and inland in Macedonia, Thessaly, and even Epirus, in association with the greater political unification of those territories. Archaeological remains from *Pella, for example, show it to have been culturally sophisticated in the 4th and 3rd cent. These new towns were all marked by regular *land division such as had marked most new developments since the 6th cent. and which had by this time become one of the hallmarks of a Greek city (see HIPPODAMUS). It is such regular planning, as well as specific Greek building types, that is exported to the near east with *Alexander (3) the Great and embodied in such Hellenistic cities as Dura-*Europus on the Euphrates.

The degree to which Greek urban types were bound up with Greek political arrangements emerges clearly in the very different sort of town which the Attalids created at *Pergamum as their capital city. Here it is not the terrain alone that precludes a regular grid plan, but the political requirement that the city focus upon its autocratic rulers. The irregularities of the landscape are exploited to produce a monumental architecture where some elements are clearly subordinated to others, and each element is visually dependent upon those around it, regardless of their functional relations. Familiar architectural forms are here combined in an entirely new way.

See ARCHITECTURE, *Greek*; COLONIZATION; ECONOMY, GREEK and HELLENISTIC; HOUSES; MARKETS AND FAIRS; SANITATION; WATER SUPPLY.

C. Roebuck, *Hesperia* 1972; F. de Polignac, *La Naissance de la cité grecque* (1984), Eng. trans. *Cults, Territory, and the Origins of the Greek City-State* (1995); R. Martin, *L'Urbanisme dans la Grèce antique*, 2nd edn. (1974).

R. G. O.

II. Roman The Romans, 'the most city-proud people known', in *Procopius' late description (*Goth*. 8. 22. 7), founded their city-policy and urban ideology principally on their own city. Already in the 6th cent. extensive in surface-area, imposing in its public buildings and private houses, and complex in its management of space, Rome both resembled the cities of the *Etruscans and Latins (*Latini) in many respects, and functioned as a show-case and pioneer of urban form.

In the 4th cent. Rome's urban functions were transformed, through the economic and prestige gains of military success, the organization of a huge territory with the expanding tribal system, and new types of relations with neighbouring cities which foreshadowed the incorporative and co-operative citizenship strategies on which a large urban population ultimately depended: the future megalopolis was conceived.

It is only from the perspective of the super-city that the long-lasting tradition of Roman urban policy can be understood. Other ancient cities produced offshoot communities which were essentially new cities. Rome alone deployed its population

resources, citizen or Latin, in planned locations, maintaining a superior position in terms of status, and a continuing political and governmental relationship which went far beyond any Greek or Carthaginian *mētropolis–*apoikia tie (cf. CARTHAGE).

The successes of the Roman élite from the Latin War to the Pyrrhic transformed Rome, under the physical influence of the developing urban tradition of Greek south Italy and Sicily (to which the Romans attributed their prison and provision-market; we may add the circular *comitium and porticoed *forum Romanum of the end of the 4th cent.). The new foundations (*Cosa, 273, or *Alba Fucens, 303, are well-preserved examples of the early stages of the process) adopted from the centre a repertoire of institutional architecture—forum, *porticoes, comitium, *temples, streets, sewers (see SANITATION, Roman), monuments—which expanded as the city grew in grandeur through the 2nd cent. BC. In mainly military installations, such as the *coloniae maritimae* or maritime colonies (the surviving walls of *Pyrgi are an example), we are reminded of the *fortifications which many Italic peoples were building in the 4th and 3rd cents. on the model of Hellenic military engineering (see COLONIZATION, ROMAN).

In these cities a citizen egalitarianism (also found in the division of the territory: see CENTURIATION) was derived from Roman constitutional theory and (therefore) linked to military needs. It was particularly apparent in the regularity and uniformity of the plan, which have become the most famous features of Roman cities, and which share a theoretical parentage with the socio-aesthetic ideas of *Hippodamus of Miletus; but is also reflected in the legal and political institutions and their architecture (comitium and *basilica, for instance), and increasingly by the late republic, the provision of the latest in the people's perks or *commoda*, such as *baths and places for spectacles.

By the age of *Cicero, the local élites of many Italian towns, even places as insignificant as *Aletrium, enriched by a century of imperial success, had embellished their communities with the latest in Hellenistic taste, in a way that was still intermittent at Rome. Swollen by centuries of opportunistic influx and impossible to plan (Livy also blamed haphazard redevelopment after the Gallic sack), the metropolis was less beautiful than its old enemy *Capua. *Sulla, *Pompey, and *Caesar made strenuous efforts to remedy this, and *Augustus completed the process of making Rome a worthy model for the founding and embellishing of cities everywhere.

The legacy of rectilinear planning and subdivision of space apart, Roman urbanism and its apparent uniformity in the early imperial period are the product of the imitation in local communities of canons of monumentality made fashionable by people further up the chain of patronage. Cities in the provinces came to have an ideological role, as exemplars of the values of Hellenic/Roman culture and a symbol of conversion from barbarism. Fortified settlements were moved from impregnable heights to the plain (like the creation of *Virunum below the Magdalensberg in Noricum, or the replacement of Wheathampstead with *Verulamium), gaining the easy communications and plain-land investment agriculture which were also signs of what the *pax Romana* offered local élites. Roman institutional statuses (see CIVITAS; MUNICIPIUM) helped the process, and the bases of the army and the veteran *coloniae* which resembled them in function and planning, provided further examples, as at Aosta (see AUGUSTA PRAETORIA), *Arelate (Arles), Merida (see EMERITA AUGUSTA), Timgad (see THAMUGADI) (but the 'chequerboard' plan should be seen as a legacy of republican thinking rather than as something distinctively military). Meanwhile Rome itself came to resemble the other cities more. Fires and expansion into the periphery made possible the development of large areas of the city on a more regular plan. The great baths and prestige projects like the *Colosseum or *Pantheon were imitated in favoured centres; in projects like the *forum Traiani, however, or the great temples of the reigns from Hadrian to Aurelian, it is the grandiose architecture of the provinces that was being recreated on a grander scale in the centre.

Cities in more civilized places had always been the organs of communication, and the respecting (or not) of privileges, age, beauty, and so on became an important part of Roman government. Thus the destruction of cities (*Carthage, *Corinth, *Jerusalem) must be considered part of Roman urban policy, throwing into relief the more desirable role of the Roman leader as *pater urbium*. Posing as the first or new founder of a city was a potent image that came to be frequently used. New imitations of the centre were made on an ambitious scale, and certain cities were singled out to enjoy the full benefit of imperial favour (*Lepcis, *Italica, *Augusta Treverorum). The whole question of the standing of cities and their claims to favour, based on the past and present attainments of their citizens, became a central feature of life under the empire. The rhetoric in which the cities competed, and which is so apparent in Antonine literature, is a part of Roman urbanism, and relevant to its extension even into remote provinces. The aspirations of communities for a higher place in the formal hierarchy of city status is a real feature of this state of affairs, and the spreading of municipal status (see MUNICIPIUM), the upgrading of villages to cities, *municipia* to *coloniae* (see COLONIZATION, ROMAN), and the increase in city institutions in places like *Egypt and *Syria where they had been less widespread, owes more to this competition than it does to imperial vision. The city was usually the focus of administration and the base for supervision, a role which it bequeathed, despite diminished populations, to late antiquity, and through the episcopate, to the Christian Middle Ages.

In general, then, we should not credit Rome with planning the efflorescence of cities or their cultural uniformity, let alone with a set of social and economic goals to be achieved through urbanization. The symbolic importance of the city often in fact concealed situations of small structural change in the organization of the productive environment. Many cities probably had quite small permanent populations, and their demise in late antiquity, where this happened, may often have been the collapse of a façade rather than the catastrophe of a structure.

P. Grimal, *Les Villes romains* (1954; trans. as *Roman Cities*, with additions, G. M. Woloch, 1983); J. B. Ward-Perkins, *Cities of Ancient Greece and Italy: Planning in Classical Antiquity* (1974); W. L. MacDonald, *The Architecture of the Roman Empire, 2: An Urban Appraisal* (1986); J. E. Stambaugh, *The Ancient Roman City* (1988).   N. P.

III. Late Roman The traditional picture of overall decline is being modified by excavations and surveys which show wide variations in place and time, and by partly semantic disputes: are we confronting the death of civic life, or transformations that show its resilience? Is the city an Aristotelian *polis (see section I above), an agency of central government, or simply a large settlement?

Imperial supervision of the cities increased greatly from the 3rd cent. The hereditary councils of local gentry that ran them (see DECURIONES), and collected and underwrote imperial taxes, were more closely watched by governors of now smaller provinces; their task was complicated by taxes now demanded in kind, though probably little heavier (see FINANCE, ROMAN). New provincial capitals might prosper (often at others' expense), but the immunities of the growing imperial bureaucracies and clergy tempted away many of the curial class; a handful of rich councillors (*principales*) dominated and exploited their remaining colleagues. Civic *gymnasia* (see GYMNASIUM) gave way to rhetorical schools, orientated to imperial careers. Curial wealth and authority in town and country was challenged by soldiers and officials, active or retired, by bishops, monasteries, and hermits; these deployed new sources of wealth, or offered new types of patronage. Many councils, none the less, proved durable; tax-collecting was often profitable; and their numerous complaints in the law-codes reflect their political influence. Their slow decline, moreover, does not imply urban disintegration: new structures of government evolved. Bishops and retired imperial officials (*honorati*) shared increasingly in civic administration, furnishing and electing new officials: the *defensor, the corn-buyer, the Father of the City. Even tax-collecting devolved onto great aristocratic houses in 5th–6th-cent. Egypt, and perhaps elsewhere in the east. Bishops used their own and imperial resources to maintain civic food-supplies, and negotiated for their cities with emperors or invaders, inheriting the rhetor's role. Although new ruling élites, like the old, often provided festivals and buildings, their interests and loyalties also belonged to Church or court. The values of the *polis* were alien to Christianity, although many bishops, like *Basil of Cappadocian Caesarea, still imbibed them with their classical education. Christian charities both inherited and challenged the tradition of civic *euergetism, being directed to the poor, rather than fellow citizens.

Urban building reflects these changes. In the 3rd cent. this declined markedly, except for walls. A glut of existing monuments was one reason; also economic or military problems; but the more stable and prosperous 4th cent. also saw imperial confiscation of civic lands and taxes. Governors and senators tended to feature as benefactors, while local noblemen merely built lavish town-houses. From the late 4th cent., however, cities regained some control over their revenue; in the east, the Father of the City deployed it for new building. Thus, *Corinth replanned and rebuilt its forum after Visigothic sack. Moreover, as in 4th-cent. *Africa, or 6th-cent. *Arabia, local benefactors may have been partly responsible for buildings for which senators, governors, or emperors took epigraphic credit. Bishops and laity who built *churches, hospices, and *martyria* (mainly during the 5th and 6th cents.) thereby increased or replaced urban monuments, but radically altered civic plans and character: declining cities might show islands of settlement around major churches or even shift site to ecclesiastical centres outside the walls. Where possible, though, bishops would occupy and redevelop town centres. Although some cities, like *Gaza, long remained obstinately pagan, an important relic, or simply an episcopal establishment, might confer a new communal identity and means of survival.

Public entertainments are another reflection. Imperial taxes increasingly sustained them, while local funds were often diverted by governors, or usurped by private persons. In the 5th cent. the organization of all public spectacles (except Christian festivals) was put under the Blue and Green chariot factions, which also had important roles in imperial ceremonial, communication between governors and subjects, and local defence; typically civic activities were thus integrated with the imperial system. Factions might also absorb the loyalties of traditional civic subgroups (thus, *Jews were often Blues), increasing tensions and violence (see AGŌNES).

Urbanus

Changes in civic economies and population are hard to estimate. With exceptions, decline was earlier and deeper northward and westward. Many cities developed fields and gardens within their walls; but some eastern cities in the 5th and 6th cents. (e.g. Palestinian *Caesarea (2)) were more populated and prosperous than in the early empire. A reduced wall circuit need not imply reduced numbers; some cities, like Corinth and *Burdigala, had large extramural settlements. Decline in one urban quarter might mean growth in another, as at *Ephesus. The 6th–7th-cent. transformation of colonnades into souks in some eastern cities indicates lively commerce, though also loss of the classical urban ideal. Some cities (at least in *Egypt) were major producers, especially of textiles, but most were probably consumers, dependent on rents, taxes, immigrants, and through-trade from the countryside. Bishops might extend the city's rural influence, but rural monasteries could challenge their dominance; in the north and west, the rich resided increasingly on their estates; and, in *Syria and elsewhere, villages grew in size and independence. When plague, war, or earthquake decimated a city, it might be hard to replace the population from the peasantry. (Bubonic plague and 6th-cent. urban decline are plausibly linked.) Imperial salaries and largess might enhance cities that combined an official presence with agricultural and commercial resources; thus, Anastasius restored the harbour of Palestinian *Caesarea (2), a provincial capital. But cities existing largely for official needs might become or remain fortified 'administrative villages', dependent for survival on the state. Justiniana Prima, Illyria (founded 535), praised by *Procopius for its large population and traditional buildings, housed only officials and clergy; it was abandoned in the 7th cent. This trend appears in the generally new and fragile cities of Britain, north Gaul, and the north Balkans from the 3rd cent., but was affecting even pre-Roman eastern cities by the early 7th.

While many cities (even western; e.g. Marseille and Córdoba) survived the empire with some prosperity, and many subsequently revived, their character, c.650, would have been unrecognizable to Aristotle, Plutarch, or even *Libanius.

A. Cameron, *The Mediterranean World in Late Antiquity* (1993); D. Claude, *Die byzantinische Stadt im 6. Jahrhundert* (1969); A. H. M. Jones, *The Greek City from Alexander to Justinian* (1940); J. Rich (ed.), *The City in Late Antiquity* (1992). Many studies of individual regions, cities, and aspects of urban life also exist; Rich's book is both general and regional.
S. J. B. B.

Urbanus, Virgilian scholar (see VIRGIL) frequently cited by *Servius in his Vergilian commentary. He wrote between the 2nd and late 4th cent. AD; his work on the *Aeneid*, probably a commentary, showed interest in legal and historical matters as well as textual criticism.

M. Geymonat, *Enc. Virg,* 'Urbano'.
S. J. Ha.

Urgulania (*RE* Suppl. 9), of Etruscan descent, mother of M. *Plautius Silvanus (2) and grandmother of Plautia Urgulanilla, the first wife of the future emperor *Claudius, powerful as a close friend of *Livia Drusilla. In AD 16, taken to court by L. *Calpurnius Piso (2), she drove to the palace and refused to appear. Tiberius agreed to represent her, but Livia met Piso's claim. She once refused to appear to testify before the senate, which sent a praetor to take her deposition. In 24, when her grandson, while praetor, was suspected of murdering his wife, she sent him a dagger and he committed suicide.

Tac. *Ann.* 2. 34, 4. 21–2 (Syme, *AA,* see index).
B. M. L.

Uricon, Uriconium See VIROCONIUM.

Urso (mod. Osuna), a native settlement in Spain some 96 km. (60 mi.) east of Seville (see HISPALIS). A centre of Pompeian resistance in 45 BC (see POMPEIUS MAGNUS (2), CN.; POMPEIUS MAGNUS (PIUS), SEX.), it was stormed by *Caesar, who later established a *colonia* (see COLONIZATION, ROMAN) drawing on Rome's urban *plebs*. Bronze tablets survive containing part of the colonial charter (*lex Coloniae Genetivae Iuliae*)—an administrative regulation (*lex data*), based on a legislative act (*lex rogata*), issued by M. *Antonius (2) on behalf of Caesar. The theatre, water cisterns, and a rock-cut cemetery survive, and distinctive military sculptures from a native funerary monument have been found.

Dessau, *ILS* 6087; trans. and comm. in E. G. Hardy, *Roman Laws and Charters* (1913); J. González, *Estudios sobre Urso: La Colonia Iulia Genetiva* (1989).
J. J. van N.; M. I. H.; S. J. K.

Uruk (mod. Warka; Gk. Ὀρχόη), c.170 km. (106 mi.) south of *Babylon. It was a substantial city from c.4000 BC to the Sasanian period (see SASANIDS) and the source of hundreds of *cuneiform texts dating between the 7th and 2nd cents. BC. German excavations (since 1912) have uncovered a walled town dominated by a sanctuary of the goddess of war and sex, *Ishtar (Eanna), replaced in importance by a temple of Anu (sky-god) and his consort (Bit Resh) in the late 5th cent. BC, and a third temple, Irigal. Architectural and textual finds of the Seleucid period are very rich. The Parthian period (see PARTHIA) is well attested by pottery, small finds, and graves. Uruk was one of the most important Babylonian cities of the neo-Babylonian (see BABYLONIA) and Seleucid periods. A *Seleucid colony 'Antioch-on-the-Ishtar-canal', is attested near Uruk in 270 BC.

Excavation reports: *Vorläufige Berichte über die Ausgrabungen in Uruk-Warka* (1930–); for overview of 1st–15th campaigns, cf. R. North, *Oriens* 1957, 185–226. Finds (including texts) are published in the series: *Ausgrabungen der Deutschen Forschungsgemeinschaft in Uruk-Warka* (1936–), and *Ausgrabungen in Uruk-Warka, Endberichte* (1987–); cf. also V. Finkbeiner, *MDAI(B)* 1982, 155 ff.; T. Leisten, *MDAI(B)* 1986, 309 ff. For Hellenistic period see: A. Falkenstein, *Topographie von Uruk, 1: Uruk zur Seleukidenzeit* (1941); J. Oelsner, *Materialien zur babylonischen Gesellschaft und Kultur in hellenistischer Zeit* (1986), 77–97; T. L. Doty, *Cuneiform Archives from Hellenistic Uruk* (Yale diss. 1977); G. J. P. McEwan, *Priest and Temple in Hellenistic Babylonia* (1981); R. J. van der Spek, in A. Kuhrt and S. Sherwin-White (eds.), *Hellenism in the East* (1987), 57–74; R. Wallenfels, *Sealed Cuneiform Tablets from Hellenistic Uruk* (Yale diss. 1990).
A. T. L. K.

usury See CREDIT; INTEREST, RATES OF.

Uthina (mod. Oudna), a Roman city in the fertile plain of the Meliana valley, 32 km. (20 mi.) south-west of *Carthage. Originally an indigenous *civitas* governed by Punic magistrates called *suffetes* (and possibly the Adys of Polyb. 1. 30. 5, a fortified city besieged by M. *Atilius Regulus in 256/5 BC), it was chosen as a *colonia* by Augustus for veterans of Legio XIII (see LEGION). Also favoured by *Hadrian (*ILS* 6784), who may have given citizenship to *peregrini in its territory, it rapidly grew to be a city of great size and prosperity, as witnessed both by the scale of its public buildings and by the luxury of its private houses from the mid-2nd cent. onwards: 67 figured *mosaics from the latter were transported to the Bardo Museum in Tunis in the 19th cent. Its 2nd-cent. *amphitheatre is one of the biggest in Africa (112 m. by 89 m. (367 × 291 ft.)); also known are the theatre (diameter 85 m. (279 ft.)), huge public *baths of symmetrical, axial type, a capitolium (see CAPITOL), and the site of the forum. Bishops are known from 256 to the early 6th cent.

PECS 949; P. Gauckler, *Monuments et mémoires Fondation Piot* 2 (1896), 177–229; P. Quonian, *Mélanges d'arch.* 1948, 35–54; H. Ben Hassan, *Archéologia* 1994, 22–9.   R. J. A. W.

Utica (mod. Utique), by tradition the oldest Phoenician settlement on the north African coast, in Tunisia, 33 km. (21 mi.) north-east of *Tunis. The traditional foundation date of 1101 BC (Plin. *HN* 16. 216; Vell. Pat. 1. 2. 4; Sil. 3. 241) is not borne out by the archaeological evidence: Utica's earliest remains are of the 8th cent. BC. Although it now lies 11 km. (7 mi.) inland because of coastline changes as a result of silting, Utica was in antiquity an important port at the mouth of the river Bagradas. Within the empire of *Carthage it always retained a position of importance (Polyb. 3. 24. 2; 7. 9. 5). Utica was conquered by *Agathocles (1) of Syracuse in 308 (Diod. Sic. 20. 54) and besieged by P. *Cornelius Scipio Africanus in 204 (Livy 30. 10. 3). A supporter of *Masinissa against Carthage in 149, Utica was rewarded by Rome with lands of the fallen city, and was made a *civitas libera* (see FREE CITIES) and the capital of the new Roman province of *Africa in 146. Italian financiers and merchants soon settled in the city, and *Pompey made the port his base for the swift campaign which won Africa from the Marians (81; see MARIUS (2), C.). Later Utica remained loyal to the Pompeian cause (cf. POMPEIUS MAGNUS (2), CN.; POMPEIUS MAGNUS (PIUS), SEX.) against the forces of C. *Scribonius Curio (2) and Caesar, and was the scene of M. *Porcius Cato (2)'s suicide. Heavily fined for its senatorial sym-pathies, Utica lost influence at the expense of the growth of *Carthage as a Roman city, but it received Latin rights (see IUS LATII) under *Augustus and became a *colonia* (*CIL* 8. 1181 (see COLONIZATION, ROMAN)) under *Hadrian. Part of a residential sector of the Roman town has been excavated; identified public buildings, now very ruinous, include baths, a theatre, and the circus.

PECS 949–50; A. Lézine, *Carthage, Utique* (1968), *Utique* (1970), and *Ant. af.* 1971, 87–93.   W. N. W.; B. H. W.; R. J. A. W.

utopias See EUHEMERUS; FANTASTIC LITERATURE; IAMBULUS; ISLANDS; POLIS.

Uxellodunum, an *oppidum* of the Cadurci, in 51 BC the scene of the last Gallic resistance to *Caesar, who took it by diverting its spring. The precise location of the place remains a little problematic. It is now generally identified with Puy d'Issolu (Lot, near Vayrac) where in 1862 Cessac discovered diversionary works at a spring on the west side of the hill-fort. However, other details are inconsistent and alternatives, e.g. Capdenac-le-Haut (Lot, south-east of Figeac), l'Impernal (Lot, Luzech), and Murcens (Lot, north-east of Cahors), remain possible.

Grenier, *Manuel* 1. 201 ff.; M. A. Cotton, in R. E. M. Wheeler and K. M. Richardson (eds.), *Hill Forts of Northern France* (1957), 159 ff.; M. Labrousse, in *Mélanges J. Carcopino* (1966), 563 ff.; J. Collis, *Oppida* (1984).   J. F. Dr.

Vaballathus See SEPTIMIUS VABALLATHUS.

Vagellius, Lucius, *suffect consul between AD 44 and 46; some of his verses are quoted by his friend L. *Annaeus Seneca (2). He may be the stupid orator of Juv. 13. 119 and 16. 23.

See Courtney, *FLP* 347.   E. C.

Valens, Roman emperor (AD 364–78), the younger brother of *Valentinian I, who proclaimed him emperor of the eastern empire. He lacked his brother's military ability and forceful personality, but was an obedient colleague. His principal achievement was to reduce taxation by careful economy. Unlike his brother, he was a baptized Arian (see ARIANISM) and half-heartedly persecuted the eastern Catholics. After surviving a rebellion led by *Julian's kinsman Procopius (365–6), he was able to impose terms upon the *Goths (369) and to intervene successfully in *Armenia (from 371), thanks to the competent generals he had inherited. However, when the Goths sought refuge from the *Huns in 376, they were allowed to cross the Danube and settle under Roman supervision. This policy led to disaster, for when the Goths rebelled, Valens' attempts to coerce them ended in the battle of Adrianople (9 August 378), in which he and two-thirds of his army were killed. His body was never recovered.

R. S. O. T.

Valentia (mod. Valencia) on the south-east coast of Hispania Citerior (Hither *Spain), probably founded by D. *Iunius Brutus Callaicus (138 BC) for soldiers who had fought under him against *Viriatus. The inhabitants supported *Sertorius' cause even after his death. It was a mint, and had become a Latin colony by 60 BC (see COLONIZATION, ROMAN). Excavations have revealed the topography of the town (forum, walls, houses), as well as evidence for its survival into the Visigothic period (late Roman cemetery and basilica; see GOTHS).

M. J. Peña, *Estudios de la antigüedad* (1984), 64 ff.; A. Ribera, *La arqueologia romana de Valentia* (1983).   S. J. K.

Valentinian I, Roman emperor (AD 364–75), born in 321 at Cibalae in *Pannonia. In February 364 when *Jovian died, he was commanding a guards regiment, and at Nicaea the generals and civil dignitaries elected him emperor. At Constantinople in March he proclaimed his brother *Valens, and took the west for himself. Here he concentrated on frontier defence. The *Alamanni who invaded Gaul were destroyed, and their homeland was devastated; fortifications on the Rhine and Danube were reconstructed for the last time. In Britain and Africa order was brutally restored by his general *Theodosius (1). In 375 Valentinian left Gaul because Pannonia had been invaded, and while

berating a delegation of those responsible, he suffered a stroke and died at *Brigetio (17 November).

This fit of rage was characteristic, but Valentinian was a conscientious administrator who tried to control abuses and overtaxation, failing notably in *Illyricum where Petronius Probus (see PROBUS (2), SEXTUS CLAUDIUS PETRONIUS) was praetorian prefect (see PRAEFECTUS PRAETORIO). Valentinian was unusual in being a Catholic tolerant of pagans and most heretics; he intervened in Church politics only to maintain public order. Relations with the senatorial aristocracy were strained: he promoted professional soldiers and bureaucrats, and senators at Rome were executed by his ministers for sexual misdemeanours or magic.

R. S. O. T.

Valentinian II (*RE* 3), Roman emperor (AD 375–92), was the son of *Valentinian I. Born in 371, he was upon his father's death elevated by the troops at *Aquincum, but without the consent of *Valens and *Gratian. Technically ruler of Italy, Africa, and Illyricum, he seems to have been kept well under the control of Gratian, upon whose death at the hands of the usurper *Magnus Maximus in 383, he succeeded as legitimate western emperor. Expelled from Italy by Maximus in 387, he was in the following year restored by *Theodosius (2) I. He was found dead, whether by suicide or murder, at Vienne in 392 and was succeeded in the west by the usurper *Eugenius.   J. F. Ma.

Valentinian III, western Roman emperor (AD 425–55), born in 419, was the son of *Constantius III and Galla *Placidia. Expelled by a usurper, he was restored in 425 by his cousin, the eastern emperor *Theodosius (3) II, whose daughter, Eudoxia, he married in 437. Unmilitary and ineffectual, his reign was dominated first by Placidia and, after 433, by the general Flavius *Aetius, who campaigned vigorously in Gaul, supported by Hunnic auxiliaries. Without a navy, Valentinian's Italy came under Vandal attack from the sea and the emperor could do no more than urge local militias to defend themselves (*Novella* 9). His 36 surviving laws (*novellae*) cover matters ranging from murder and tomb violation to property, taxes, the status of tenants, episcopal courts, and the supremacy of the bishop of Rome. In 454 Valentinian murdered Aetius with his own hand but was himself killed by two followers of Aetius in 455.   J. D. H.

Valeria (*RE* 403) **Messal(l)ina,** great-granddaughter of *Augustus' sister *Octavia (2) on her father's and mother's sides, was born before AD 20. In AD 39 or 40 she married her second cousin *Claudius, then *c*.50 years old, and bore him two children, *Claudia Octavia and *Britannicus. Claudius alone was blind to her sexual profligacy (which *Juvenal travestied in Satires 6 and 10), even to her eventual participation in the formalities of a marriage service with the consul-designate C. *Silius in AD 48. The freedman *Narcissus (2) turned against her and, while Claudius was in a state of stunned incredulity, ensured that an executioner was sent. Encouraged by her mother Domitia Lepida, she committed suicide.　　　　　J. P. B.; M. T. G.

Valerian See LICINIUS VALERIANUS, P.

Valerius (*RE* 95) **Aedituus,** author of two erotic epigrams quoted by *Gellius 19. 9 alongside others by *Lutatius Catulus (1) and *Porcius Licinius, with whom he must have been contemporary (end of the 2nd cent. BC?). The three poets are also linked in Apul. *Apol.* 9, and they may have been collected in an anthology which was Gellius' source for the quotations. Valerius imitates *Sappho 31 LP (the poem later translated by *Catullus (2) in poem 51) and Hellenistic poetry, but the abundant use of alliteration and the metrical technique show the persistent influence of archaic Latin style.

　　Courtney, *FLP* 72 ff.; D. O. Ross, *Style and Tradition in Catullus* (1969).
　　　　　　　　　　　　　　　　　　　　　　　　　　M. Ci.

Valerius (*RE* 98) **Antias,** Roman historian of the 1st cent. BC. His work, known only through quotations and allusions in later authors, covered the history of Rome from the origins down to 91 BC at least. The reign of *Pompilius Numa was treated in book 2, and the *Hostilius Mancinus affair (136 BC) in book 22. Since the whole occupied at least 75 books, the scale of the narrative must have increased as it reached the author's own times. For earlier periods Antias' treatment was far less expansive than that of *Livy or *Dionysius (7). Livy mentions him frequently, but usually to disagree with him on points of detail and to criticize his tendency to exaggerate numbers (e.g. of battle casualties). He may nevertheless have been one of Livy's main sources, although the evidence for this is not conclusive. In general the character of his work is hard to judge, and he remains a little-known figure. His first name is not recorded, and scholars disagree on the date at which he was writing. Most experts place him in the age of *Sulla (following Velleius 2. 9. 6), but others date him to the 40s BC on the grounds that he is nowhere mentioned by *Cicero—not necessarily a strong argument. Most modern attempts to characterize Antias and his work are founded on a priori conjectures and inferences from passages of Livy that are assumed to be based on him. The resulting theories, about his social standing, his rhetorical aims, his glorification of the Valerian clan (see GENS; VALERIUS, various entries), his chauvinism, and his conservative political bias, are all based on circular reasoning and have no secure foundation in the evidence.

　　Peter, *HRRel.* 1². cccv; 238; F. Münzer, *De Gente Valeria* (1891); M. L. W. Laistner, *The Greater Roman Historians* (1947); P. G. Walsh, *Livy* (1961); E. Badian, in T. A. Dorey (ed.), *Latin Historians* (1966), 18 ff.; Ogilvie, *Comm. Livy 1–5*, 12 ff.; T. J. Luce, *Livy: The Composition of his History* (1977); T. P. Wiseman, *Clio's Cosmetics* (1979); T. J. Cornell, in I. S. Moxon and others (eds.), *Past Perspectives* (1986), 67–86.　T. J. Co.

Valerius Asiaticus, Decimus (?) (suffect consul AD 35; *consul ordinarius* (see CONSUL) for the second time AD 46), magnate and *novus homo* from Allobrogian *Vienna (see ALLOBROGES), almost certainly the first Gallic consul. Brother-in-law (through *Lollia Paulina) of *Gaius (1), whose adultery with his wife allegedly caused him to join the plot to murder the emperor. At first enjoying the favour of *Claudius, whom he accompanied to Britain, he fell victim to *Valeria Messallina's plotting, was charged with treason, and committed suicide. His prestige in

Gaul may have helped sway Claudius, who attacked his memory in the senate (*ILS* 212. 2. 14–17 = Sherk, *Hadrian* 55). His son and grandson both reached the consulship.

　　B. Levick, *Claudius* (1990), 61 ff.　　　　　T. J. C.; A. J. S. S.

Valerius (*RE* 117) **Cato, Publius,** *grammaticus* and poet, born in (Cisalpine?) Gaul probably *c*.90 BC (see GAUL (CISALPINE)). Almost all of our knowledge of him comes from Suetonius (*Gram.* 11) and nothing has survived from his writings. They included, besides works of scholarship (in which a special interest in *Lucilius (1) appeared), an *Indignatio*, in which he complained of the loss of his patrimony under Sulla, and two poems, *Lydia* (not the *Lydia* in the Virgilian appendix, cf. APPENDIX VERGILIANA), probably amatory, and *Diana* (*Dictynna*?), a narrative poem, probably drawn on by the author of the *Ciris, on the Hellenistic story of *Britomartis. He was an outstanding interpreter and nurturer of poets; compliments are paid to him by *Helvius Cinna, *Ticida, and *Furius Bibaculus, he may be mentioned in the *Cornelius Gallus fragment (line 9), and he is probably the Cato to whom *Catullus (1) (56), another Valerius from Cisalpine Gaul with a related *cognomen* (see NAMES, PERSONAL, ROMAN), imparts a naughty episode. However, there is no evidence that any of these was his pupil, and they were probably too old to have been such. He lived in poverty to old age.

　　R. P. Robinson, *TAPA* 1923, 98; R. O. A. M. Lyne, *Ciris* (1978), 223; Courtney, *FLP* 189.　　　　　　　　　　　　　　E. C.

Valerius Comazon, Publius, served as a common soldier in *Thrace in the reign of *Commodus but rose to high equestrian rank (see EQUITES, *Imperial period*). In the east in AD 218, perhaps as prefect (*praefectus*) of the *legion II Parthica, he joined the rebellion of Elagabalus (M. *Aurelius Antoninus (2)), and became praetorian prefect (see PRAEFECTUS PRAETORIO), then a senator, *consul ordinarius* (see CONSUL) in 220, and city prefect on three separate occasions, the third after Elagabalus' downfall. Because of his *cognomen* (see NAMES, PERSONAL, ROMAN) he has been confused with another supporter of Elagabalus in AD 218, the former dancer Eutychianus.

　　Dio Cass. 79–80; Herodian 5; SHA *Heliogab.*; E. Kettenhofen, *Die syrischen Augustae in der historischen Überlieferung* (1979), 29 ff.　A. R. Bi.

Valerius Festus, Gaius Calpetanus (*RE* 2) **Rantius Quirinalis,** a new man (*novus homo*) from *Arretium, *suffect consul AD 71, was legate (see LEGATI) of the African *legion in 69. He arranged the murder of the proconsul L. *Calpurnius Piso (3): allegedly (as a marriage connection of the defeated *Vitellius) to demonstrate his loyalty to *Vespasian. He then campaigned against the Garamantes (see AFRICA (LIBYA), EXPLORATION), and was given *ornamenta triumphalia*. After his consulship he became pontifex, curator of the *Tiber, legate (see LEGATI) of *Pannonia (73), and of *Tarraconensis (78–81?). He died, still an *amicus of the emperor, early in *Domitian's reign (Mart. 1. 78).

　　Syme, *RP*, indexes.　　　　　　　　　　　　G. E. F. C.; B. M. L.

Valerius (*RE* 173) **Flaccus (1), Lucius,** was the patron of M. *Porcius Cato (1) at the beginning of Cato's career, and held both consulship and censorship with him. He was curule *aedile 201 BC and praetor 199 (in Sicily) and became consul 195, fighting in northern Italy. He became a *pontifex 196. He served with Cato in the Thermopylae campaign (191; see THERMOPYLAE and THERMOPYLAE, BATTLE OF) as a military tribune or legate (see TRIBUNI MILITUM; LEGATI). In 190 and 189 he was one of three commissioners appointed to supplement colonies at *Placentia and *Cremona, and to found one at *Bononia (see COLONIZATION, ROMAN). In 189 he and Cato stood unsuccessfully for the censorship (see CENSOR), but they reached the office on a common programme in 184, carried out their severe measures in total harmony, and Valerius was made *princeps senatus*. He died in 180.

A. E. Astin, *Cato the Censor* (1978), see index.   J. Br.

Valerius (*RE* 176) **Flaccus** (2), **Lucius,** *flamen Martialis* (priest of *Mars; see FLAMINES); as consul 100 BC with C. *Marius (1), he was, according to P. *Rutilius Rufus, 'more his slave than his colleague'. As censor (97) with M. *Antonius (1), he apparently helped to enrol Italians generously as citizens. Made *princeps senatus* by the censors of 86, L. *Marcius Philippus (1) and M. *Perperna (2), he worked for accommodation with *Sulla. Joining him in time, he secured him, as *interrex*, a vote of indemnity and appointment to the dictatorship, becoming his *magister equitum*. He seems to have died soon after, as he is not mentioned again.   E. B.

Valerius (*RE* 178) **Flaccus** (3), **Lucius,** was unsuccessfully prosecuted after his aedileship (98 BC) by C. *Appuleius Decianus; he governed Asia after his praetorship and was prosecuted *repetundarum* (Cic. *Div. Caec.* 63: see Sumner, *Orators* 79 ff.; see REPETUNDAE). As *suffect consul succeeding C. *Marius (1), he was given the command against *Mithradates VI, passed a law cancelling three-quarters of all debts, and left for Asia (86), which he reached without clashing with *Sulla. He was murdered in a mutiny instigated by C. *Flavius Fimbria, who assumed his *imperium* (85).   E. B.

Valerius (*RE* 179) **Flaccus** (4), **Lucius,** son of (3), served under his father and on the latter's death fled to his uncle C. Flaccus in Gaul. He was military tribune under P. *Servilius Vatia Isauricus in Cilicia, quaestor in Spain under M. *Pupius Piso, legate of Q. *Caecilius Metellus (Creticus) in Crete, then under *Pompey in Asia. As urban praetor (63 BC), he assisted *Cicero against *Catiline and, after governing Asia (62–61), was successfully defended by him *repetundarum* in a largely extant speech (59). He was legate (see LEGATI) of L. *Calpurnius Piso Caesoninus in Macedonia and died *c.*54.   E. B.

Valerius (*RE* 170) **Flaccus Setinus Balbus, Gaius,** the Roman poet **Valerius Flaccus,** author of the *Argonautica,* an epic poem on the voyage of *Jason (1) and the *Argonauts to *Colchis in search of the Golden Fleece. There is no external evidence for his biography apart from *Quintilian's remark (*c.* AD 95) that 'we have recently suffered a great loss in Valerius Flaccus' (10. 1. 90); since Quintilian can use 'recent' of *Caesius Bassus' death in AD 79 (10. 1. 96), the conventional dating of Valerius' death to the early 90s is without foundation. The evidence of the poem itself is controversial. The conventional claim that Valerius was a *quindecimvir sacris faciundis* is based on lines in the proem which by no means dictate such a conclusion (1. 5–7). The one certainty is the reference in a simile to the eruption of *Vesuvius, which occurred on 24 August 79 (4. 507–9; cf. 3. 208–9). The date of the composition of the proem, which alludes to *Vespasian, *Titus, and *Domitian, is keenly contested, with advocates for a date under each of the three. The most that can be securely stated is that the *Argonautica* is a Flavian epic (a fact of more than chronological importance).

Indebted to the *Argonautica* of *Apollonius (1) Rhodius (and perhaps of P. *Terentius Varro Atacinus), but moulded above all by *Virgil, Valerius' poem follows the Argonauts' expedition through many famous adventures to the point where Jason absconds from Colchis with *Medea. The poem breaks off at 8. 467 as Medea is persuading Jason not to hand her back to her brother Absyrtus. The conventional view is that the poet died before finishing his work, although the latest editor believes that the poem was completed in eight books, with the second half of the last book lost in transmission.

The poem owes much to Apollonius' *Argonautica* as a quest with a strong interest in the problems of epic heroism. Valerius, though, departs radically from Apollonius when he concentrates on Argo as the first ship, harbinger of human civilization (1. 1–4), placing his poem in a long and energetic Roman tradition of appropriation of the *golden age and iron age myths. A cosmic frame is provided by Jupiter's concern for the expedition, which will reproduce on earth the patterns of order and dominance guaranteed universally by his own recent victory in the Gigantomachy. The cycles set in train by Argo's voyage will carry on down to the contemporary world of the Flavian empire (1. 537–60), where the Flavian house likewise rules after the chaos of civil war. Hyperbolically inflating Apollonius' interest in aetiology, Valerius recounts the origin of warfare and imperial institutions, so that the poem is studded with overt references to contemporary Roman practices (in marked contrast with *Statius' *Thebaid*). Valerius exploits Virgil's *Georgics* and L. *Annaeus Seneca (2)'s *Medea* to stress the ambivalence of iron age achievement, for navigation is a violation of natural boundaries, and hence either magnificent or impious in its audacity. In cunning and ironic counterpoint to these grand themes is the love story which overtakes the narrative in book 5. Valerius rises to the daunting challenge of going where Apollonius, Virgil, and Ovid had gone before, exploiting his great goddesses to present a sombre and frightening image of Medea's passion.

Valerius has unjustly suffered from being viewed as a doggedly earnest imitator of mightier models; his self-awareness and wry humour have gone largely unnoticed, although he has been commended for the poise of his versification and the acuity of his observation.

Text: E. Courtney (1970); W.-W. Ehlers (1980). Comm.: P. Langen (1896–7; repr. 1964); 2, H. M. Poortvliet (1991); 4. 1–343, M. Korn (1989). Concordance: M. Korn and W. Slaby (1988). Trans.: J. H. Mozley (Loeb, rev. edn. 1936). Studies: W. C. Summers, *A Study of the Argonautica* (1894); F. Mehmel, *Valerius Flaccus* (1934); J. Adamietz, *Zur Komposition der Argonautica des Valerius Flaccus* (1976).   D. C. F.

Valerius (*RE* 211) **Laevinus, Marcus,** was praetor 227 BC and elected consul for 220, but did not take up office, presumably because the election was declared faulty. Praetor again 215, he was appointed Roman commander against *Philip (3) V in the First Macedonian War. In 212–211 he secured the support of the *Aetolian Confederacy, with whom he made a treaty, and of *Attalus I of Pergamum. Elected consul 210, he succeeded M. *Claudius Marcellus (1) in Sicily. He recaptured Agrigentum (*Acragas) and remained in Sicily as proconsul in 209 and 208. He helped to re-establish Sicilian cereal farming, and in 208 raided Africa and defeated a Carthaginian fleet. In 205 he headed the embassy that brought the sacred stone of the Magna Mater (*Cybele) to Rome; see PESSINUS; PHILHELLENISM. He was probably sent to Greece again in 200. He died later that year.

Briscoe, *Comm.* 31–33, 60–1.   J. Br.

Valerius Licinianus, Lucius, a senator of praetorian rank exiled by *Domitian for misconduct with a Vestal (see VESTA), but permitted by *Nerva to settle in Sicily, where he professed oratory (Plin. *Ep.* 4. 11). Lucius Licinianus from Bilbilis (Mart. 1. 61. 11; 4. 55. 1) was a senatorial advocate whom *Martial considered a Spanish *Cicero. It is uncertain if they are to be identified.

A. N. Sherwin-White, *The Letters of Pliny* (1966), 280 ff.   B. M. L.

Valerius Maximianus, Marcus, son of a local magistrate in the Pannonian colony of *Poetovio, served as an equestrian officer in the early 160s AD. Recalled to a special command during the Marcomannic invasions (see MARCOMANNI), he was rapidly promoted and *c.* AD 175 made a senator, holding five successive legionary commands in the Danubian provinces. As legate of II Adiutrix (see LEGATI; LEGION) he wintered at Leugaricio (mod. Trenčin), 120 km. (75 mi.) north of the Danube (AD 179–80). He later became legate of *Numidia, and while there was consul *suffect (*c.* AD 185). He was a Mithraist (the first known senatorial initiate; see MITHRAS).

H.-G. Pflaum, *Les Carrières procuratoriennes équestres* (1960–1), no. 181 bis; P. M. M. Leunissen, *Konsuln und Konsulare in der Zeit von Commodus bis Severus Alexander* (1989).   A. R. Bi.

Valerius (*RE* 239) **Maximus,** in *Tiberius' reign composed a handbook of illustrative examples of 'memorable deeds and sayings', *Factorum ac dictorum memorabilium libri IX.* He was a friend of a Sextus Pompeius whom, if he is correctly identified with the Sextus Pompeius who was consul in AD 14, he accompanied to his governorship in Asia (Val. Max. 2. 6. 8: AD 24/5?), composing his book after their return. It is dedicated to Tiberius, to whom constant flattery is addressed; and the violent denunciation of a conspirator usually identified with L. *Aelius Seianus (9. 10. *Externa* 4) suggests, if this identification is correct, that it was published soon after his downfall in 31. The subject-matter has no clearly defined plan, but is divided under headings mostly moral or philosophical in character (e.g. Omens, Moderation, Gratitude, Chastity, Cruelty), usually illustrated by Roman (*domestica*) and foreign (*externa*) examples. The latter, chiefly Greek, are admittedly less important, and in keeping with the strongly national spirit of the compilation are outnumbered by the *domestica* by two to one. Valerius' chief sources seem to have been *Livy and *Cicero, but there are indications of many others, such as *Varro, *Coelius Antipater, *Pompeius Trogus, and several Greek writers. His use of this material is almost entirely non-critical, and varies greatly in extent and accuracy. The work has been condemned as shallow, sententious, and bombastic, full of the boldest metaphor and rhetorical artifices of the Silver Age, especially forced antitheses and far-fetched epigrams, only occasionally relieved by touches of poetic fancy or neat passages of narrative or dialogue; but its sources and alignment have begun to attract attention. The variety and convenience of the compilation ensured some measure of success in antiquity, and considerably more in the Middle Ages. It is referred to by *Pliny (1) the Elder, *Plutarch, and others. Most significant, however, is the existence of two later epitomes. The first is by Iulius Paris (4th cent.?) and has attached to it a summary on Roman names, *De praenominibus,* ascribed to a certain C. Titius Probus and elsewhere erroneously included in MSS as book 10 of Valerius' own work. The second, by *Ianuarius Nepotianus (5th cent.?), breaks off early in book 3.

EDITIONS A. Torrenius (1726; notes and index); C. Kempf (1854; Teubner 1888); P. Constant (1935; Fr. trans.).

STUDIES C. Bosch, *Die Quellen des Val. Max.* (1929); A. Klotz, 'Studien', *Sitz. Wien* 1942. 5; D. M. Schullian, in *Studies in Honor of*

Ullman (1960); R. Syme, *History in Ovid* (1978), 162 f.; G. Maslakov, *ANRW* 2. 32. 1 (1984), 437 ff.; W. Bloomer, *Val. Maximus and the Rhetoric of the New Nobility* (1993).   G. C. W.; B. M. L.

Valerius (*RE* 137) **(Maximus?) Corvus, Marcus,** was consul in 348, 346, 343, and 335 BC, and reputedly in 300 and 299 (suffect), but the last two consulships and (if historical) his dictatorship of 302/1 (see DICTATOR) probably belong to M. Valerius Maximus (Corvinus), consul 312, 289 (R. Rilinger, *Chiron* 1978, 295 f.). Corvus is credited with *triumphs for the capture of *Satricum (1) (346), for victories at mons Gauros and Suessula in the First Samnite War (343; see SAMNIUM), and for the capture of *Cales (335), although the historicity and course of the First Samnite War are controversial (M. W. Frederiksen, *Campania* (1984), 181 ff.) and Valerius' colleague in 335, M. Atilius Regulus Calenus, may have taken Cales. His equitable settlement of a mutiny as dictator in 342 (attributed to the consuls in some sources) is probably a fiction, exemplifying the conventional devotion of the Valerii to political harmony. Valerius' *cognomen* (see NAMES, PERSONAL, ROMAN) reputedly derived from the raven (*corvus*) which attacked a Gaul whom he fought in a duel (usually dated to 349). If this aetiology is historical, the bird may in reality have been an emblem on his opponent's helmet (S. P. Oakley, *CQ* 1985, 394; cf. T. Köves-Zulauf, *A&A* 1985, 353 ff.). See also PROVOCATIO.   A. D.

Valerius (*RE* 247) **Maximus Messal(l)a, Manius,** consul 263, censor 252 BC. In 263, alone or with his colleague M'. Otacilius Crassus, he secured the surrender of several communities in eastern Sicily and compelled *Hieron (2) II of Syracuse to make peace. He triumphed (see TRIUMPH) for his successes against the Carthaginians (see PUNIC WARS) and Hieron. These ensured the security of *Messana and he took the name Messal(l)a in commemoration. He was the first to set up in public at Rome a painting of his military engagement(s) and (in *Varro's version) a (Greek) sundial (see CLOCKS).

CAH 7²/2 (1989), 545 ff.   A. D.

Valerius (*RE* 266) **Messalla, Marcus,** called 'Niger' to distinguish him from 'Rufus' (below), was *pontifex (perhaps appointed by *Sulla) and quaestor before 70 BC, when it seems the censors expelled him from the senate (Val. Max. 2. 9. 9). Urban praetor 64 and assiduous as defence counsel (Cic. *Brut.* 246), he became consul 61, the first of his family since an ancestor in 161, then served on *Caesar's agrarian commission (59). As censor 55/4, with his colleague P. *Servilius Vatia Isauricus, he regulated the *Tiber after a flood in 54 (ILLRP 476). He was *interrex* three times in the troubled later 50s and died soon after.

ILS 46 (his *elogium*).   E. B.

Valerius (*RE* 268) **Messalla, Marcus,** called 'Rufus' to distinguish him from 'Niger' (above), also descended from the consul of 161, was made augur by *Sulla (81 BC), who married his sister. Probably praetor 62 or 61, he failed to reach the consulship in the early 50s and, as a candidate in 54, was involved in an unprecedented bribery scandal with the consuls, which delayed the elections until mid-53. Elected for the rest of 53, he was twice prosecuted in 51 and convicted. He joined *Caesar in the Civil War and served with distinction in Africa and Spain. Although not prominent after this, he was still active in the senate in 39 (*MRR* 3. 214). His books on augural matters (see AUGURES) and on noble families were a major source for later writers, but have not survived.   E. B.

1579

Valerius Messalla Corvinus, Marcus

Valerius (*RE* 261) **Messalla Corvinus, Marcus** (64 BC–AD 8), Roman public figure. He first distinguished himself in the *Philippi campaign (43–42 BC), following his hero *Cassius. Declining command of the republican army after this defeat, he transferred his allegiance first to Antony (M. *Antonius (2)), then at an uncertain date to Octavian (see AUGUSTUS). He fought against Sextus *Pompeius (36) and in Illyricum (35–34), subdued the Alpine *Salassi (?34–33), wrote pamphlets against Antony, and as consul with Octavian (31) took part in the battle of *Actium. After a command in *Syria (?30–29) he governed Gaul (?28–27), where he conquered the Aquitani (see AQUITANIA), celebrating a *triumph in September 27. In 26 or 25 he was made *praefectus urbi* but resigned after a few days, claiming that he was uncertain how to operate (Tac. *Ann.* 6. 11. 4) or, more bluntly, that the power was unsuitable for a citizen amongst citizens (Jerome, *Chron.* 164H). Thereafter he enjoyed less public prominence, but there was no public breach with *Augustus. Already an augur and by 20 BC an arval brother (see FRATRES ARVALES), he became the first permanent *curator aquarum* (commissioner for the water-supply) in 11, and it was he who proposed the title of 'father of his country' for Augustus (2 BC): that record of independence perhaps contributed to his selection. He reconstructed part of the *via Latina and several public buildings; he gained fame as an orator, though some found him lacking in concision and bite; he wrote his memoirs, dabbled in bucolic poetry, philosophy, and grammar, and was patron of an impressive literary circle—*Tibullus, *Lygdamus, the young *Ovid, and his own niece *Sulpicia (1). One of his protégés fêted him in the extant *Panegyricus Messallae*.

> Historical fragments in Peter, *HR Rel.* 2. lxxviii–lxxxiii and 65–7; grammatical, Funaioli, *Gramm. Rom. Frag.* 1. 503–7; rhetorical, Malcovati, *ORF*[4] no. 176.
> STUDIES J. Hammer, *Prolegomena to an Edition of the Panegyricus Messallae* (1925); C. Davies, *G & R* 1973, 25–35; A. Valvo, *ANRW* 2. 30. 3 (1983), 1663–80; Syme, *AA* 200–26.   C. B. R. P.

Valerius (*RE* 264) **Messalla Messallinus, Marcus** (consul 3 BC), son of M. *Valerius Messalla Corvinus, and a person of distinction and oratorical talent, though not comparable with his parent. Legate (see LEGATI) of *Illyricum in AD 6, he was sent back by *Tiberius from the campaign against *Maroboduus to deal with the rebellious Pannonians and Dalmatians (see PANNONIA; DALMATIA) and reached *Siscia after fighting a battle; he received *ornamenta triumphalia*. Sycophantic proposals are ascribed to him in the senate under Tiberius. His election as one of the *quindecimviri* in charge of the Sibylline books (*c.*21 BC; see SIBYL) is celebrated in the longest poem (2.5) of *Tibullus, who enjoyed the patronage of Messallinus' father; he also received three poems from the exiled *Ovid (*Tr.* 4. 1; *Pont.* 1. 7; 2. 2).

> R. Syme, *History in Ovid* (1978), index; *AA*, index and table 9.
> R. S.; B. M. L.

Valerius (*RE* 302) **Poplicola, Publius,** reputedly consul in 509, 508, 507, 504 BC. His alleged role in the overthrow of *Tarquinius Superbus and *suffect consulship in 509 are certainly secondary fictions. Misinterpretation of his *cognomen* (see NAMES, PERSONAL, ROMAN) as 'courting the people' and the attribution of fundamental features of liberty to the first year of the republic resulted in crediting him (and/or his fellow consul(s) of 509) with the first law of appeal (*provocatio), the alternation of the *fasces, and other popular measures. His dealings with *Porsenna (508/7) and successes against Etruscans (509, 504) and Sabines (504) are also probably invented. A (late 6th-cent.?) dedication to *Matuta

Mater at *Satricum (1) by comrades of a P. Valerius has suggested that Valerius was a powerful semi-autonomous figure (prompting later stories that he was suspected of harbouring monarchical ambitions), but although M. *Valerius (Maximus?) Corvus reputedly spared the Satrican shrine in 346, any link with Poplicola is entirely conjectural.

> Ogilvie, *Comm. Livy 1–5*, 250 ff.; M. Guarducci, *Rend. Linc.* 1980, 479 ff.; F. Coarelli, *Il foro romano: Periodo arcaico*[2] (1986), 79 ff.   A. D.

Valerius (*RE* 304) **Poplicola Potitus, Lucius,** and M. Horatius Barbatus (*RE* 8) were consuls in 449 BC, immediately after the Second *Decemvirate. Livy (3. 55. 3 ff.) ascribes to them three laws: (1) measures passed by the *plebs* in a tribal assembly were to be binding on the entire people (cf. Dion. Hal. *Ant. Rom.* 11. 45. 1 ff. and see PLEBISCITUM); (2) no magistrate was to be elected who was not subject to appeal (*provocatio) (cf. Cic. *Rep.* 2. 54); (3) severe penalties were to be inflicted on those harming the tribunes or other plebeian officers. *Diodorus (3) (12. 26. 1) says nothing of these measures and their historicity is controversial. The first is also ascribed to Q. *Publilius Philo (339) and Q. *Hortensius (287/6), though some suppose that the *lex Valeria Horatia* established either the legislative powers of the *comitia tributa* or the validity of plebiscites that received patrician or senatorial sanction. The measure on *provocatio* (also ascribed to a tribune (C. Duillius)) depends on the fictions of the tyrannous Second Decemvirate (supposedly not subject to *provocatio) and the creation of the right of *provocatio* in 509. The third law may reflect a tradition which ascribed the creation of the tribunate to the Second Secession (see SECESSIO). Cumulatively, all three laws replicate for the aftermath of the Decemvirate the same creation or reinforcement of key popular rights that supposedly followed the overthrow of the monarchy in 509 (when a Valerius and Horatius were also reputedly consuls). The role of Valerius and Horatius in negotiating the end of the Second Secession and Second Decemvirate will certainly be annalistic fiction, as also the story that the people, not the senate, granted them triumphs for victories over the *Aequi and *Volsci (Valerius) and Sabines (Horatius).

> Ogilvie, *Comm. Livy 1–5*, 497 ff.; *CAH* 7²/2 (1989), 227 ff.; 733 ff.; 742 ff. (bibliog.); M. Humbert, *Mélanges d'arch.* 1988, 468 ff.   A. D.

Valerius (*RE* 315) **Probus, Marcus,** grammarian from *Berytus (mod. Beirut) who flourished under the Flavians, devoting himself especially to the study of republican authors (Suet. *Gram.* 24): sources indicate his interest in (e.g.) *Plautus, *Terence, *Sallust, and *Virgil. He collected many texts, which he punctuated, 'corrected', and marked with critical signs (*notae*); these were probably resources for his own scholarship, not 'editions' with full commentaries for public consumption. He published a very few minor works and communicated his learning in conversations with small circles of followers; but he left substantial notes on 'old' Latin usage (Suet. *Gram.*), and these probably circulated after his death. He is cited respectfully by Aulus *Gellius, who claims to have known both his writings and several of his disciples; and by later commentators on Terence and Virgil (the origin of these citations is controversial). His fame caused some certainly spurious works to be attributed to him: these include several technical treatises (*Catholica*, Keil, *Gramm. Lat.* 4. 3–43; *Instituta artium*, ibid. 47–192; *Appendix*, ibid. 193–204; *De nomine*, ibid. 207–16 and ed. Passalacqua (1984); *De ultimis syllabis*, *GL* 4. 219–64), a commentary on Virgil's *Eclogues* and *Georgics* (3. 2. 323–87 Thilo-Hagen (see SERVIUS), cf. M. Gioseffi, *Studi sul* *commento a Virgilio dello Pseudo-Probo* (1991)), and a life of *Persius Flaccus (ed. Clausen, pp. 37–9). See SCHOLARSHIP, ANCIENT, *Latin*.

Fragments: Aistermann, *De M. Valerio Probo Berytio* (1910). Bibliography: Herzog–Schmidt, § 393.   R. A. K.

Valerius (*RE* 345) **Soranus, Quintus,** scholar and poet, and probably the *tribunus plebis* (82 BC? see TRIBUNI PLEBIS) put to death for speaking the secret name of Rome (*MRR* 2. 68, cf. 3. 214). His younger contemporary *Cicero refers to him (*Brut.* 169, *De or.* 3. 43), and *Varro quotes both his verses on *Jupiter (Buechner, *FPL* 53) and his views on linguistic matters (Funaioli, *Gramm. Rom. Frag.* 78 f.). His books of *Epoptides*, of uncertain content, are mentioned by *Pliny (1) (*HN* pref. 33).

Herzog–Schmidt, § 145.   R. A. K.

Valerius (*RE* 363) **Triarius, Gaius,** defeated M. *Aemilius Lepidus (2) in Sardinia (77 BC). He successfully served as legate of L. *Licinius Lucullus (2) against Mithradates, taking several cities and winning a naval victory at Tenedos, but in 67 suffered a disastrous defeat at *Zela.   E. B.

Valgius (*RE* 7) **Rufus,** *suffect consul 12 BC, was respected as a literary judge by *Horace (*Sat.* 1. 10. 82), who wrote *Carm.* 2. 9 to console him for the loss of his *puer delicatus* Mystes; Valgius himself had lamented his loss probably in elegiacs. He also wrote a variety of short poems and perhaps some more substantial work, since *Panegyricus Messallae* 179 suggests him as a panegyrist. In prose he wrote on rhetoric (he was a pupil and translator of Octavian's teacher *Apollodorus (5) (cf. AUGUSTUS); Quint. 3. 1. 18, 1. 5. 17), grammar, and herbal medicines.

See H. Dahlmann, *AAWM* 11 (1982), 34; Courtney, *FLP* 287.   E. C.

Vallius Syriacus, declaimer. He was taught by the easygoing *Theodorus (3) (Sen. *Controv.* 2. 1. 36). Tiberius put him to death in AD 30 as a friend of *Asinius Gallus (Cass. Dio 58. 3. 7).

RE 8 A 2. 2391. Schanz–Hosius, § 337; *RE* 8 A 2. 2391.   M. W.

Vandals, a Germanic people or confederation of peoples (see GERMANS) met with in *Pliny (1) and *Tacitus (1) as the Vandili, an overall designation which seems to have included later independent groups such as *Goths and *Burgundians. The extent of the confederation may possibly be identified with the Przeworsk culture dating from the early centuries AD found on the territory of modern Poland. By *c.* AD 200 some Vandals had moved south to lands north-east of the Tisza, a movement associated with the Marcomannic wars (see MARCOMANNI). At this date, they were already divided into at least two groups: Hasdings and Silings. Vandals seem to have played no major role in the 3rd-cent. invasions, although contact with the Roman empire was plentiful. On 31 December 406, however, they crossed the Rhine near Mainz along with *Alans and *Suebi. After three years of widespread devastation in Gaul, they moved over the Pyrenees, and in 411 the invaders divided the Spanish provinces between them. The Silings occupied *Baetica, the Alans *Lusitania, and the Hasdings and Suebi Gallaecia. Probably from *c.*416, a combined Roman–Gothic force destroyed the Silings and so hit the Alans that the survivors attached themselves to the Hasdings, whose leaders were henceforth officially titled 'kings of the Vandals and Alans'. Under Gunderic (d. 428) the new combined force moved to southern Spain, and, under his successor *Gaiseric, to north Africa in 429. An initial series of campaigns led to their establishment in *Numidia and *Mauretania by treaty in 436. In 439 they broke the treaty and captured *Carthage to establish a kingdom further east in the richer Roman provinces: Byzacena and Pro-

consularis (see AFRICA, ROMAN). The west Romans recognized the conquests by treaty in 442, but the east Romans not until 472. The Unesco excavations at Carthage have produced much new archaeological evidence for the social and economic history of the kingdom, which was eventually destroyed by *Belisarius in 533.

C. Courtois, *Les Vandales et l'Afrique* (1955); *Excavations at Carthage* (1976–82).   P. J. H.

Vargunteius (*RE* 5), **Quintus,** gave recitations of *Ennius' *Annals* to large crowds. Like *Octavius Lampadio, he allegedly was influenced by *Crates (3) of Mallus, in the second half of the 2nd cent. BC (Suet. *Gram.* 2).   R. A. K.

Vari in *Attica (anc. *deme of Anagyrous) See FARM BUILDINGS, *Greek*; NYMPHS; PAN.

Varius Marcellus, Sextus, father of the emperor Elagabalus (M. *Aurelius Antoninus (2)). An equestrian (see EQUITES, *Imperial period*) from *Apamea in Syria, Marcellus was married to *Iulia Soaemias Bassiana. He began a procuratorial career (see PROCURATOR) after *Septimius Severus, husband of his wife's aunt (*Iulia Domna), became emperor. He was procurator of *Britain at the time of Severus' expedition there (AD 208–11). After P. *Septimius Geta (2)'s murder (at the end of 211), *Caracalla made Marcellus acting praetorian and city prefect. He was then adlected to the senate and served as prefect of the *aerarium militare* and governor of *Numidia, where he evidently died, without ever reaching the consulship.

ILS 478; H. Halfmann, *Chiron* 1982, 217 ff.; A. R. Birley, *The African Emperor Septimius Severus* (1988), 224, no. 50.   A. R. Bi.

Varius (*RE* 21) **Rufus,** an Augustan poet, friend of *Virgil (*Catal.* 7, *Ecl.* 9. 35) and member with him, P. *Quinctilius Varus, and *Plotius Tucca of an Epicurean group (Probus, *Vit. Verg.*) referred to by *Philodemus. He was also a friend of *Maecenas, to whom he and Virgil introduced *Horace (*Sat.* 1. 5. 40, 6. 55, 10. 81). He wrote a hexameter poem *De morte*, probably intended on Epicurean lines (cf. EPICURUS) to free men from the fear of death. It was apparently written *c.*43 BC and contained uncomplimentary allusions to M. *Antonius (2); these and other passages were imitated by Virgil. Horace speaks of him as pre-eminent in *epic (*Sat.* 1. 10. 43) and suggests him as a panegyrist of M. *Vipsanius Agrippa (*Carm.* 1. 6), but no work of this type by him is known. His tragedy *Thyestes*, which was greatly admired, was commissioned by Augustus for his games of 29 BC in celebration of Actium and lavishly rewarded by him. An alleged *Panegyricus Augusti* (scholia on Hor. *Epist.* 1. 16. 27) is very doubtful. After Virgil's death he (and Tucca?) prepared the *Aeneid* for publication.

A. S. Hollis, *CQ* 1977, 187; M. Gigante, *Stud. Ital.* 1989, 3; P. V. Cova, *Il poeta Vario* (1989); Klotz, in Ribbeck, *TRF* 309; Courtney, *FLP* 271.   E. C.

Varius (*RE* 7) **Severus** (?) **'Hybrida', Quintus,** of Sucro (near *Valentia), called by *Cicero a good orator but an evil man. As tribune 90 BC he unsuccessfully attacked M. *Aemilius Scaurus (1) and, when the courts had been suspended owing to the *Social War (3), irregularly passed a law setting up a special court with equestrian jurors (see EQUITES, *Origins and republic*), to try those who had aided or incited the Italians. The trials were political and several prominent men were convicted. In 89, after the jury reform of M. *Plautius Silvanus (1), he was convicted under his own law and died in exile.

1581

Varro (Marcus Terentius Varro)

E. Badian, *Historia* 1969, 447 ff. On the trials see M. C. Alexander, *Trials in the Late Roman Republic 149 BC to 50 BC* (1990), nos. 100–6, 108–10.

E. B.

Varro (Marcus Terentius (*RE* 84, Suppl. 6) **Varro)** (116–27 BC), was born at *Reate, in the Sabine territory (see SABINI) north-east of Rome. After studying at Rome with L. *Aelius, the first true scholar of Latin literature and antiquities, and at Athens with the Academic philosopher *Antiochus (11) of Ascalon, Varro began a public career that brought him to the praetorship and, ultimately, to service on the Pompeian side (see POMPEIUS MAGNUS (1), C.) in the Civil War. Having received *Caesar's clemency after *Pharsalus, he was asked to plan and organize the first public library (see LIBRARIES) at Rome. But this project went unrealized, and after Caesar's assassination he was proscribed by Mark Antony (M. *Antonius (2)): his library at *Casinum was plundered, but he escaped to live the rest of his life in scholarly retirement. He had completed 490 books by the start of his 78th year (Gell. 3. 10. 17): 55 titles are known in all, and his *œuvre* has been estimated to include nearly 75 different works totalling *c.*620 books (Ritschl, *Opuscula* 3. 485 ff.).

Works Varro's combination of methodical analysis, vast range, and original learning made him Rome's greatest scholar. His writings covered nearly every branch of inquiry: history (*De vita populi Romani*, on Roman 'social history'; *De gente populi Romani*, placing Rome's remote past in a Greek context), geography, rhetoric, law (*De iure civili lib. XV*), philosophy, music, medicine, architecture, literary history (*De poetis, De comoediis Plautinis*), religion, agriculture, and language (at least 10 works on this last alone). The achievements of the Augustans and of later authors, in both poetry and prose, are scarcely conceivable without the groundwork that he laid. See also SCHOLARSHIP, ANCIENT, *Latin*.

Only two of his works survive substantially:

1. *De lingua Latina*, in 25 books, of which books 5–10 are partly extant (5 and 6 entirely). Book 1 provided an introduction; 2–7 dealt with *etymology, and the connection between words and the entities they represent; 8–13, with inflectional morphology and the conflict (which Varro probably exaggerated) between 'anomalists' and 'analogists' (see ANALOGY AND ANOMALY; CRATES (3)); 14–25, with syntax and the proper formation of 'proposi-tions' (*proloquia*, a topic derived from Stoic *dialectic; see STOICISM). Varro dedicated books 2–4 to his quaestor, the subsequent books to Cicero; the work was published before *Cicero's death, probably in 43. See also GRAMMAR, GRAMMARIANS, LATIN.

2. *De re rustica* (3 books: 37 BC), a treatise on farming in dialogue form, intended as an agreeable entertainment for men of Varro's own class. It deals with agriculture in general (book 1), cattle- and sheep-breeding (book 2), and smaller farm-animals (birds, bees, etc.: book 3). The work, which survives entirely and shows some amusing strokes of characterization, reveals very strikingly Varro's fondness for analysing his subjects into their parts, and those parts into their sub-parts: though this analysis is sometimes carried to unhelpful lengths, it also represents a new stage in the logical organization of prose at Rome. See AGRICULTURE, ROMAN; AGRICULTURAL WRITERS.

Among Varro's lost works the following are especially note-worthy:

1. *Saturae Menippeae* (150 books: prob. 81–67 BC), humorous essays on topics of contemporary vice and folly, mingling verse with prose; Varro professed to imitate the 3rd-cent. Cynic philo-sopher *Menippus (1) of Gadara. Ninety titles and 600 fragments survive. See MENIPPEAN SATIRE.

2. *Antiquitates rerum humanarum et divinarum* (41 books: 47 BC). Of the first 25 books, on human (i.e. Roman) antiquities, little is known: the introductory book was followed by four segments of (probably) six books each, on persons (*de hominibus*: the inhabit-ants of Italy), places (*de locis*), times (*de temporibus*), and things (*de rebus*). The remaining sixteen books, dedicated to *Caesar as *pontifex maximus, took up the human construction of the divine: another book of general introduction, then five triads, on priesthoods (27–9), holy places (30–2), holy times (33–5), rites (36–8), and kinds of gods (39–41). Among the lost works of republican prose, the *Antiquitates* is perhaps the one we most sorely miss.

3. *Logistorici* (76 books: 44 BC?), a series of dialogues on various subjects, each taking its name from a noted person: e.g. *Marius de fortuna, Tubero de origine humana, Curio de cultu*.

4. *Hebdomades vel de imaginibus* (15 books: 39 BC), a collection of 700 portraits of celebrated Greeks and Romans, in which each portrait was accompanied by an epigram; the number 7 played an important (if now obscure) role in the work's organization (cf. Gell. 3. 10. 1).

5. *Disciplinae* (9 books), a late work surveying the essential terms and principles of the learned 'disciplines' that a free man should command: these *artes liberales* included 'grammar', rhet-oric, dialectic, arithmetic, geometry, astronomy, music, medi-cine, and architecture (cf. MARTIANUS MINNEUS FELIX CAPELLA; SEVEN LIBERAL ARTS).

LIFE AND WORKS G. Boissier, *Étude sur la vie et les ouvrages de Varron* (1861); H. Dahlmann, *RE* Suppl. 6 (1935), 1172–1277; E. Rawson, *Intellectual Life in the Late Roman Republic* (1985), *passim*.

TEXTS F. Semi, *Terentius Varro: quae extant* (1965–6: earlier editions collected in 8 vols.). *Ling. Lat.*: G. Goetz and F. Schoell (1910), R. G. Kent (Loeb, 1951); grammatical fragments also in Funaioli, *Gramm. Rom. Frag.* (1907). *Res rust.*: G. Goetz (1929²), W. D. Hooper and H. B. Ash (Loeb, 1935). *Sat. Men.*: R. Astbury (1985). *Antiq.*: P. Mirsch, *Leipziger Studien* 1882, 1–144 (*res humanae* only), B. Cardauns (1976: *res divinae* only). *Logist.*: E. Bolisani (1937). *Discip.*: F. Ritschl, *Opuscula* 3. 352–402. *Hist.*: *De vita pop. Rom.*, B. Riposati (1939); *De gente pop. Rom.*, P. Fraccaro (1907); Peter, *HRRel.* 2. 9–25, xxxii–xxxx.

COMMENTARIES *Ling. Lat.*: bk. 5, J. Collart (1954); bk. 6, E. Riganti (1978), P. Flobert (1985); bk. 8, H. Dahlmann (1940); bk. 10, A. Traglia (1956). *Res rust.*: J. G. Schneider, *Scriptorum rei rusticae* 1 (1794); H. Keil, 3 vols. (1884–1902); bk. 1, J. Heurgon (1978); bk. 2, C. Guiraud (1985). *Sat. Men.*: J.-P. Cèbe, 9 vols. to date, to fr. 383 (1972–).

STYLE G. Heidrich, *Der Stil des Varro* (1892); E. Norden, *Antike Kunstprosa* 1 (1909), 194–200; E. Laughton, *CQ* 1960, 1–28.

SPECIAL STUDIES *Ling. Lat.*: J. Collart, *Varron: grammairien latin* (1954); D. Fehling, *Glotta* 1956, 214–70; 1957, 48–100; H. Dahlmann, *Varro und die hellenistische Sprachtheorie*² (1964); D. J. Taylor, *Declinatio: A Study of the Linguistic Theory of Marcus Terentius Varro* (1974); W. Pfaffel, *Quartus gradus etymologiae: Untersuchungen zur Etymologie Varros in De lingua Latina* (1981). *Res rust.*: J. E. Skydsgaard, *Varro the Scholar: Studies in the First Book of Varro's 'De Re Rustica'* (1968); K. D. White, *ANRW* 1. 4 (1973), 463–94. *Sat. Men.*: C. Cichorius, *Römische Studien* 1922, 207–26; L. Riccomagno, *Studio sulle Satire Menippee di Marco Terenzio Varrone Reatino* (1931); E. Woytek, *Sprachliche Studien zur Satura Menippea Varros* (1970). *Antiq.*: H. D. Jocelyn, *Bull. Rylands Libr.* 1982, 148–205. *Logist.*: H. Dahlmann, *Varronische Studien I–II*, Abh. Akad. Wiss. Mainz 4 (1957) and 11 (1959); B. Zucchelli, *Varro logistoricus* (1981).

BIBLIOGRAPHY H. Dahlmann, *ANRW* 1. 3 (1973), 3–18. *Atti del Congresso internazionale di studi varroniani*, 2 vols. (1976). B. Cardauns, *Stand und Aufgabe der Varroforschung*, Abh. Akad. Wiss. Mainz 4 (1982). Herzog–Schmidt, § 284.   R. A. K.

vase-painting See PAINTING, GREEK; POTTERY, GREEK.

vates, 'prophet', 'seer', used by *Ennius as an insulting term for his predecessors (*Ann.* fr. 207 Skutsch) became by the Augustan period a central term for the inspired poet with an assumed social role as 'master of truth' (first in Verg. *Ecl.* 7. 28, and esp. 9. 34) and generated a constant interplay between the roles of poet and prophet.

> H. Dahlmann, *Philol.* 1948, 337–53; E. Bickel, *Rh. Mus.* 1951, 256–314; J. K. Newman, *The Concept of Vates in Augustan Poetry* (1967); Nisbet–Hubbard on Hor. *Carm.* 1. 1. 35; Skutsch on Ennius, *Ann.* 207; M. Massenzio in *Enc. Virg.*; D. O'Higgins, *Cl.Ant.* 1988, 208–26.
> P. G. F.; D. P. F.

Vatican, an extramural area of the city of Rome, on the right bank of the *Tiber around the mons Vaticanus. In the early empire the Vatican was the site of an imperial park (the horti Agrippinae); and of entertainment structures, the *Naumachiae* (see NAUMACHIA), where mock sea-battles were exhibited, and the Vatican *circus, where *Gaius (1) set up a great obelisk from Heliopolis and which was traditionally the site of the martyrdom of St Peter. There was also an important shrine of *Cybele (or the Magna Mater) attested in inscriptions; and along the two roads that crossed the area, the via Cornelia and the via Triumphalis, were cemeteries. A group of mausolea on the footslopes of the mons Vaticanus were excavated under St Peter's in the 1940s, and within this cemetery (directly under the high altar of St Peter's) was found a small 2nd-cent. shrine, marking the probable burial-site of Peter, apostle and first bishop of Rome.

With *Constantine I's conversion, and capture of Rome in 312, the importance and appearance of the Vatican area were transformed by the building of a huge five-aisled *basilica in honour of St Peter, some 250 m. (820 ft.) long including its atrium and preceding steps. The high altar of this church was sited directly over the shrine and probable body of the saint, which required closing a functioning cemetery and a tremendous task of levelling to create a flat platform for the new building. The importance of this church gradually attracted other new buildings around it. Mausolea, including that of the Honorian dynasty, were built immediately to the south, and the church was linked to the main part of the city by a new porticoed street leading to the pons Aelius. This street clearly became a Christian via sacra (sacred way), culminating in St Peter's, since it was here, rather than in the forum, that two new imperial triumphal arches were erected in the years around AD 400.

> J. Toynbee and J. Ward-Perkins, *The Shrine of St. Peter* (1956), which also discusses the classical topography; L. Reekmans, in *Mélanges ... Jacques Lavallege* (1970), 197–235.
> B. R. W.-P.

Vatinius (*RE* 3), **Publius,** tribune 59 BC (see TRIBUNI PLEBIS), sponsored the bills granting *Caesar Cisalpine Gaul (see GAUL (CISALPINE)) and *Illyricum, and the right to send Roman colonists to *Comum (see COLONIZATION, ROMAN), and confirming the eastern settlement of *Pompey. He also features prominently in attacks on M. *Calpurnius Bibulus and in the affair of L. *Vettius. In 56 he was a witness against P. *Sestius, and *Cicero, defending Sestius, delivered the invective *in P. Vatinium testem interrogatio*. But the forensic relationship was soon reversed: Vatinius was praetor 55, and in 54, obedient to Caesar, Pompey, and *Crassus, Cicero successfully defended Vatinius on a bribery charge arising from his election to the praetorship. After serving with Caesar in Gaul, Vatinius won a victory in the Adriatic in 47, and in December received the consulate, an office he had always boasted

he would hold. As proconsul in Illyricum (45) he won a *supplicatio and, although he had surrendered to *Brutus in 43, was allowed an Illyrian triumph (42). Vatinius was an easy butt because of his personal disabilities, weak legs, and scrofulous swellings; but he took raillery well, and in later life was genuinely reconciled with Cicero, to whom in later life he wrote *Fam.* 5. 10 (cf. Catull. 14. 3 and 52–3).

> L. G. Pocock, *A Commentary on Cicero In Vatinium* (1926).
> G. E. F. C.; E. B.

vectigal meant primarily revenue derived from public land, mines, saltworks, etc., and in general, rents derived from state property. Such sources provided the basic revenues of the early republic, and remained the most important form of income for the *municipia* and *civitates* of the empire (see MUNICIPIUM; CIVITAS). The term was also extended to cover indirect taxes of which only the *portoria and the *vicesima libertatis*, a tax of 5 per cent on the value of manumitted slaves, existed in the republic. In the Principate the number of *vectigalia* was increased, and they provided a considerable part of the state revenues. The inhabitants of Italy, who were exempt from *tributum, only paid *vectigalia*. The most important of the *vectigalia* were the *portoria*. A new document from Ephesus (*AE* 1989, 681) of AD 62 on the *portoria* of Asia indicates the elaborate character of the regulations which in this case stretched back to 75 BC and concerned (e.g.) the standard rate (2.5 per cent), exemptions, the sites of customs posts, and the procedures for letting contracts.

*Augustus, in order to raise revenues for the provision of discharge-donations to veterans, founded the *aerarium militare into which was paid the yield of two new taxes. The *centesima rerum venalium*, a tax of 1 per cent on sales by auction, was reduced to half per cent by *Tiberius and abolished, in Italy, by *Gaius (1). The *vicesima hereditatum* was a charge of 5 per cent, only paid by citizens, on significant sums bequeathed to persons other than near relatives (see Plin. *Pan.* 37–40). The spread of citizenship increased its yield, and this was claimed to be the motive behind *Caracalla's universal grant of citizenship (Cass. Dio, 78. 9; see CONSTITUTION, ANTONINE). Augustus also established in AD 7 the *quinta et vicesima venalium mancipiorum*, a 4 per cent tax on sale of slaves, to provide the pay of the *vigiles. A number of minor *vectigalia* were also established by *Gaius (1) (Suet. *Calig.* 40). The collection of *vectigalia* in the republic and Principate was let out to companies of *publicani. In the Principate *procuratores (whether the provincial procurator or procurators specifically designated to a tax for a defined area) became responsible for supervising the process of collection. See also FINANCE, ROMAN.

> G. P. B.

Vectis (also Victis or Ictis), the classical name of the Isle of Wight. The separate identification of Ictis with St Michael's Mount is not favoured, given the confusion surrounding its mention in relation to the mythical *Cassiterides. The Isle of Wight was well settled and an important navigation point.

> A. L. F. Rivet and C. Smith, *The Place-Names of Roman Britain* (1979); D. J. Tomalin, *Roman Wight* (1987).
> M. J. M.

Ve(d)iovis, Roman god, a form of *Jupiter, with a festival on 21 May, and temples on the *Tiber island and between the two summits of the Capitoline hill (see CAPITOL). Important remains of the latter, including the marble cult-statue, have been explored under the Palazzo Senatorio, revealing several rebuildings. The cult had important links with the *gens Iulia* (an ancient altar at suburban *Bovillae dedicated by its members, *ILLRP* 270; see GENS; IULIUS, various entries), and was the object of considerable antiquarian speculation in antiquity. Associations with both youth and the underworld appear to be present.

S. Weinstock, *Divus Iulius* (1971), 8–12; H. Scullard, *Festivals and Ceremonies of the Roman Republic* (1981), 56–8. N. P.

Vedius (*RE* 8) **Pollio, Publius,** a *freedman's son and friend and assistant of *Augustus, perhaps from *Beneventum, attained equestrian rank (SEE EQUITES). He appears to have been active in Asia both in an official capacity, after *Actium or perhaps after the earthquake of 27 BC, and as a private benefactor. Rich and cruel, he allegedly would punish slaves by throwing them alive to his moray eels. He died in 15 BC, leaving Augustus much of his property, including his villa *Pausilypon and his mansion on the *Esquiline, which Augustus pulled down, building the porticus Liviae on the site.

K. Scott, *AJPhil.* 1939, 459 f.; R. Syme, *JRS* 1961, 23 ff. (= *RP* 2. 518 ff.); Smallwood, *Docs. Gaius* . . . 380 (trans. D. Braund, *Augustus to Nero: A Sourcebook of Roman History 31 B.C.–A.D. 68* (1985), 586); K. M. T. Atkinson, *RIDA* 1962, 261 ff.; Platner–Ashby, 197, 423; *Cat. of the Coins of the Rom. Emp. in the Ashmolean Museum* 1 (1975), Tralles 1363 n. (portrait). A. M.; T. J. C.; B. M. L.

vegetarianism See ANIMALS, ATTITUDES TO.

Vegetius Renatus, Flavius, wrote an *Epitoma rei militaris* in four books, which is the only account of Roman military practice to have survived intact. The work was written after AD 383 but before 450, when Eutropius undertook a critical revision at *Constantinople, and the single emperor who is its addressee may be *Theodosius (2) the Great (383–95), the occasion perhaps being his visit to Italy from August 388 to June 391.

Book 1 discusses the recruit, book 2 army organization, book 3 tactics and strategy, book 4 fortifications and naval warfare. Vegetius examines important themes—the maintenance of discipline and morale, vigilant preparations in enemy territory, establishing a camp, campaign planning, tactical adaptability in battle, conducting a retreat, and the use of stratagems. He also quotes some general maxims which 'tested by different ages and proved by constant experience, have been passed down by distinguished writers' (3. 26). Vegetius is convinced of the relevance of this approach. The emperor had instructed him to abridge ancient authors, and sought instruction from past exploits despite his own achievements.

Vegetius was not himself a soldier or historian, but served in the imperial administration, perhaps as *comes sacrarum largitionum* (see FINANCE, ROMAN). He took an antiquarian interest in the army, ignoring the detailed changes accomplished by *Diocletian and *Constantine I, and for his manual collected material from many sources and chronological periods without adequate differentiation and classification. This impairs his value as a source for the organization and practices of the Roman army. He mentions some of his sources: M. *Porcius Cato (1), Sex. *Iulius Frontinus, *Taruttienus Paternus (praetorian prefect of Marcus *Aurelius; see PRAEFECTUS PRAETORIO), and the ordinances of *Augustus, *Trajan, and *Hadrian. But there is no reason to assume that he always consulted these at first hand or that they were his only sources. The 'old legion' (*antiqua legio*) to which Vegetius refers (2. 4–14), and which is clearly not from his own day, should probably be dated to the late 3rd cent.

An interesting feature of Vegetius' treatise is the significant influence which it had upon the military thinking of the Middle Ages and the Renaissance. See also ARMIES; VETERINARY MEDICINE.

TEXT C. Lang[2] (1885). Trans.: J. Clarke (1767), in T. R. Phillips (ed.), *Roots of Strategy* (1943); N. P. Milner, trans. with notes and introd. (1993).

STUDIES D. Schenk, *Klio*, Suppl. 22 (1930; repr. 1963), H. M. D. Parker, *CQ* 1932, 137; A. R. Neumann, *RE* Suppl. 10 (1965), 992; G. R. Watson, *The Roman Soldier* (1969); T. D. Barnes, *Phoenix* 1979, 254.
J. B. C.

Vegoia See RELIGION, ETRUSCAN.

Veii (mod. Isola Farnese), 16 km. (10 mi.) north of Rome, was the most southerly of the great Etruscan cities. Extensive excavation (and in one case prompt publication) of its vast *Villanovan cemeteries, well supplied with imported Greek Geometric pottery, has provided a firm basis for the relative and absolute chronology of the local Villanovan iron age. Later, the inexorable expansion of Rome led to rivalry; after a long siege the city was destroyed in 396 BC (Livy, 5. 1–22; Plut. *Cam.* 2–6) and its territory annexed. A small urban nucleus survived and shortly before 2 BC became the modest *municipium Augustum Veiens* (Prop. 4. 10. 27 ff.). The *Etruscan city, of which little is known, was provided with imposing defences in the late 5th cent. It was famous for its statuary: *Pliny (1) (*HN* 35. 157) records the name of Vulca, commissioned to furnish statues for *Jupiter's temple on the Roman *Capitol. His school was probably responsible for the terracotta statues of Apollo and other divinities found in the extra-urban sanctuary of Portonaccio.

J. B. Ward-Perkins, *PBSR* 1965 (historical topography); A. Kahane, *PBSR* 1968 (Ager Veientanus); L. Vagnetti, *Il deposito votivo di Campetti a Veio* (1971); F. Delpino, *Cronache veientane* 1 (1985); P. Liverani, *Municipium Augustum Veiens* (1987). Villanovan: *Not. Scav.* 1961–75 (Quattro Fontanili); G. Bartoloni and F. Delpino, *Veio I* (*Mon. Ant.* 1979); J. Toms, *Annali dell'Istituto Universitario Orientale di Napoli: archeologia e storia antica* 1986, 41 ff. J. B. W.-P.; D. W. R. R.

Velabrum was an area of low ground between the Capitol and Palatine in Rome. Originally a swamp open to Tiber floods, it was drained by the *Cloaca Maxima, and eventually became one of the busiest commercial centres of the city; the vicus Tuscus and vicus Iugarius, which carried traffic between the *forum Romanum and the Tiber, passed through it.

Richardson, *Topog. Dict. Ancient Rome*, 406–7. I. A. R.; J. R. P.

Veleia See ALIMENTA.

Velia, a hill located between the *Palatine and Oppian hills of Rome, overlooking the *forum Romanum; traditionally King Tullus *Hostilius lived here, and P. *Valerius Poplicola (consul 509 BC) (Cic. *Rep.* 2. 53; Livy, 2. 7. 6–12). The appearance of the area under the republic is now difficult to reconstruct due to the effect of major imperial building projects (the vestibule of *Nero's *Domus Aurea, *Hadrian's temple of Venus and Rome, and the *basilica of *Maxentius) and the destruction caused by the building of the via dell'Impero (now via dei Fori Imperiali) in 1933. See PENATES, DI.

N. Terrenato, in E. Herring, R. Whitehouse, and J. Wilkins (eds.), *Papers of the Fourth Conference of Italian Archaeology* (1992), 31–47.
I. A. R.; J. R. P.

Velia See ELEA; ELEATIC SCHOOL.

velites, lightly armed soldiers with little defensive armour, were introduced perhaps in 211 BC (Livy, 26. 4), replacing the light-armed troops called *rorarii* of the middle republic, a development possibly associated with a reduction in the property qualification for military service, *c*.214, and were subsequently recruited from the youngest and poorest men. There were 1,200 *velites* in each *legion and, armed with swords, light javelins, and small circular shields, they served as skirmishers in front of the three main legionary lines. The *velites* threw their spears and then retreated through the ranks. They are last mentioned in 109–108 BC during the war against *Jugurtha (Sall. *Iug.* 46, 105), and with the emergence of the *cohort were probably subsumed into the centuries of the legion (see CENTURIA). See also ARMIES, ROMAN.

M. J. V. Bell, *Hist.* 1965, 419.   J. B. C.

Velitrae (mod. Velletri): Volscian town (see VOLSCI) on the southern rim of the Alban hills (see ALBANUS MONS) in *Latium. It frequently fought early Rome, until annexed by the latter (338 BC). It still spoke Volscian then, but was soon completely Latinized. *Augustus originated from Velitrae. *Claudius made it a *colonia* (see COLONIZATION, ROMAN).

H. Solin, R. Volpe, *Velitrae*, Supplementa Italica NS 2 (1983), 11–94.
          E. T. S.; T. W. P.

Velius (*RE* 10) **Longus** (early 2nd cent. AD) wrote a treatise on the language of republican authors, a commentary on the *Aeneid*, and an extant handbook on orthography (Keil, *Gramm. Lat.* 7. 48–81, cf. 154 f.). He cites *Varro and *Verrius Flaccus and is cited by (e.g.) *Gellius, *Iulius Romanus, and the scholiasts (see SCHOLIA) of *Virgil.

Herzog–Schmidt, § 435.   R. A. K.

Velleius (*RE* 5) **Paterculus**, Roman historical writer, provides details of himself in his work. Among his maternal ancestors were Minatus Magius of Aeclanum and Decius Magius of Capua (2. 16. 2–3); his paternal grandfather was C. Velleius, *praefectus fabrum* (see PRAEFECTUS) to *Pompey, *Brutus, and Ti. *Claudius Nero, father of the emperor *Tiberius (2. 76. 1); the senator Capito, who helped to prosecute the Caesaricide *Cassius in 43 BC, was a paternal uncle (2. 69. 5). Velleius himself was born in (probably) 20 or 19 BC. Having begun his career as military tribune around the turn of the millennium (2. 101. 3); he joined the staff of C. *Iulius Caesar (2) in the east (2. 101–102. 1); later he became *praefectus equitum* (see PRAEFECTUS), as his father had been, and spent AD 4–12 serving under the future emperor Tiberius in Germany (twice; see GERMANIA), *Pannonia, and *Dalmatia (2. 104. 3, 111. 3, 114. 2, 115. 5). In AD 6, having completed his service as an equestrian officer (see EQUITES, *Imperial period*), he returned briefly to Rome and was elected quaestor for AD 7 (2. 111. 4); in AD 12 he and his brother Magius Celer Velleianus, who had also served in Dalmatia (2. 115. 1), took part in Tiberius' Illyrian *triumph (2. 121. 3; see ILLYRICUM); and, when *Augustus died in AD 14, both were already designated 'candidates of Caesar' (*candidati Caesaris*) for the praetorship of AD 15 (2. 124. 4). Nothing further is certainly known of him, apart from the fact that he dedicated his work to M. *Vinicius, the consul of AD 30, the presumed year of its publication. There is no evidence for the suggestion that he was executed in the aftermath of L. *Aelius Seianus' fall in AD 31; the *suffect consuls of AD 60 and 61 are thought to be two sons.

Velleius' work begins with Greek mythology and ends in AD 29, a span of time which he encompassed in only two volumes. 'I hardly know any historical work of which the scale is so small, and the subject so extensive', said Macaulay. Like *Cornelius Nepos and *Florus (1) he is thus a writer of summary history, something to which he draws frequent attention (1. 16. 1, 2. 29. 2, 38. 1, 41. 1, 52. 3, 55. 1, 66. 3, 86. 1, 89. 1, 96. 3, 99. 4, 108. 2,

124. 1). Almost all of book 1 is now lost: not only do we lack the preface and very beginning of the narrative but a vast lacuna has deprived us of his history of Rome between the time of *Romulus (1. 8. 4–6) and the battle of *Pydna in 168 BC (1. 9), although a stray fragment on *Cimon (1. 8. 6) shows that he continued to refer to Greek history at least as late as the 5th cent. BC. Book 1 is separated from book 2 by two excursuses, which would be notable even in a full-length history (1. 14–15 on Roman colonization, see COLONIZATION, ROMAN; 1. 16–18 on Greek and Latin literature); and book 2 begins, as the narrative part of book 1 had ended (12–13), with the destruction of *Carthage in 146 BC, which Velleius, like *Sallust, saw as a turning-point in Roman history. Although the following years to 59 BC are dispatched in a mere 40 chapters, which notably include three further excursuses of varying length (2. 9 and 36. 2–3 on Roman authors, 2. 38–9 on Roman provincialization), Velleius devotes increasing amounts of space to *Caesar (2. 41–59), Augustus (2. 59–93), and especially Tiberius (2. 94–131), whose career forms the climax of his work. Whether he intended seriously to write his own full-length history, as he often promises (2. 48. 5, 89. 1, 96. 3, 99. 3, 103. 4, 114. 4, 119. 1), is uncertain.

Though Velleius constantly imitates the phraseology of both Sallust and *Cicero, it is the fullness and balance (*concinnitas*) of the latter's style that he aimed generally to reproduce. His sentences, replete with antithesis and point, are often long and involved; and he has a gift for pithy characterization. Yet readers have been dismayed by the successive rhetorical questions (e.g. 2. 122) and exclamations (e.g. 2. 129–30) in his account of Tiberius, which in general, like his treatment of Seianus (2. 127–8), has been regarded as mere panegyric. On such grounds Sir Ronald Syme and most other 20th-cent. scholars have dismissed with contempt his work as a whole.

Yet in imperial times the traditional patriotism of Roman historians was inevitably focused on the emperor of the day, who in Velleius' case was also his former commander; and his account of Tiberius is valuable in presenting the establishment view of events for which Tacitus, from the safer perspective of the 2nd cent. AD, supplies an opposition view. Even so the prayer, which forms the unconventional conclusion to his work (2. 131), is arguably a recognition of the political crisis of AD 29, while the treatment of Seianus, which is not a panegyric of the man but a defence of his elevation by Tiberius, betrays some of the very unease which it seems designed to dispel.

Velleius, like *Polybius (1), travelled widely (cf. 2. 101. 3); he was a senator, like Sallust and *Tacitus (1), and held magisterial office; like *Thucydides (2) he witnessed and took part in a significant number of the events he describes (2. 104. 3, 106. 1, 113. 3, 118. 1). He thus enjoyed many of the advantages conventionally associated with the ideal historian. He regularly provides information on topics about which we would otherwise be ignorant; and he is the only Latin historian of Roman affairs to have survived from the period between *Livy and Tacitus. These seem reasons enough to justify his more favourable assessment in recent years.

Velleius' text depends upon a single codex, designated M, discovered by Beatus Rhenanus at Murbach in 1515 but now lost. From a lost copy of the codex derive both Amerbach's apograph (1516) and Rhenanus' first edition (dated 1520, Basel), the latter containing Burer's collation of the edition with M. The relative merits of apograph and first edition are disputed.

TEXTS F. W. Shipley (with Eng. trans., Loeb, 1924); J. Hellegouarc'h (with Fr. trans., 2 vols., Budé, 1982); W. S. Watt (Teubner, 1988).

COMMENTARY (on 2. 41–131) A. J. Woodman (1977, 1983).

CONCORDANCE M. Elefante (1992).

GENERAL A. Dihle, *RE* 8 A 1 (1955), 637–59; J. Hellegouarc'h, *ANRW* 2. 32. 1 (1984), 404–36 (bibliographical essay); C. Kuntze, *Zur Darstellung des Kaisers Tiberius und seiner Zeit bei V. P.* (1985); I. Lana, *V. P. o della propaganda* (1952); G. V. Sumner, *Harv. Stud.* 1970 (ancestry, career, historical value); Syme, *RP 3* (1984), 1090–1104 ('mendacity'), and *AA* 421–38 (*nobiles* in V. P.); A. J. Woodman, in T. A. Dorey (ed.), *Empire and Aftermath: Silver Latin II* (1975), 1–25 (literary appraisal), and *CQ* 1975 (date of composition, genre). A. J. W.

Venafrum (mod. Venafro), a Samnite (Pentrian; see SAMNIUM) city on the borders of *Latium and *Campania. It came under Roman control *c.*290 BC. In the *Social War (3), it was captured and the Roman garrison slaughtered. A colony was founded there, possibly Augustan (*CIL* 10. 4875, 4894), which coincided with a major phase of public building. It continued to flourish and was famous for its agriculture, particularly olives.

F. Valente, *Venafro, origine e crescita di una città* (1979). K. L.

Venantius Honorius Clementianus Fortunatus (*c.* AD 540–*c.*600), Christian Latin poet, born near Treviso in northern Italy and educated at Ravenna, he left Italy in 565 and later lived at Poitiers, where he knew St Radegunda and ultimately became bishop. He is best known for his numerous poems on secular and especially religious themes, including the great Passion hymns, *Pange lingua* and *Vexilla regis*, and is arguably both the last classical and the first medieval Latin poet.

TEXT F. Leo (poems) and B. Krusch (prose), *MGH AA* 4. J. George, *Venantius Fortunatus* (1992). J. D. H.

venationes 'Hunts', involving the slaughter of *animals, especially fierce ones, by other animals or human *bestiarii* (fighters of wild beasts)—and sometimes of criminals by animals, see below—were a major spectacle at Rome from 186 BC. They displayed the ingenuity and generosity of the sponsoring politician, and the reach of Rome, and its power over nature, in procuring exotic species (lions, panthers, bears, bulls, crocodiles, hippopotamuses, rhinoceroses, elephants): they admitted a privileged city-audience to the glories of traditional aristocratic hunting. Along with gladiatorial fights, they were a principal reason for building *amphitheatres. The emperors gave especially sumptuous displays: 5,000 wild and 4,000 tame animals died at the inauguration of *Titus' *Colosseum in 80, and 11,000 at *Trajan's Dacian *triumph (see DACIA). Especially in the later 1st cent. AD, criminals might be forced to re-enact gruesome myths (e.g. the killing of *Orpheus by a bear). See GLADIATORS; HUNTING.

J.-C. Golvin, *L'Amphithéâtre romain: Essai sur la théorisation de sa forme et ses fonctions* (1988); L. Robert, *Les Gladiateurs dans l'Orient grec* (1940), ch. 5; K. Coleman, *JRS* 1990, 44 ff. N. P.

Veneti (1), a Gallic seafaring people occupying modern Morbihan. Though their strongly 'Atlantic' culture was but lightly touched by Celticism in the La Tène period (see CELTS), they themselves strongly influenced south-west British culture (see BRITAIN) by their trade, which stimulated their resistance to *Caesar. They were defeated by D. *Iunius Brutus Albinus in a naval battle (56 BC). Under the empire their commerce declined, but a prosperous agricultural life has been indicated by widespread villa-finds. Their *civitas*-capital was Darioritum (Vannes). The region was occupied by emigrant Britons from the 5th cent.

M. Merlat, *Les Venètes d'Amorique*, (1982); P. Galliou, *L'Armorique romaine* (1983); B. Cunliffe, *Greeks, Romans and Barbarians* (1988). J. F. Dr.

Veneti (2) inhabited fertile country about the head of the Adriatic. Chief cities: *Ateste in prehistoric times, *Patavium in historic (see ANTENOR (1)). They may be of Illyrian extraction (cf. Hdt. 1. 196), although their surviving inscriptions (5th–1st cent. BC) are not in an *Illyrian language. Archaeological evidence reveals that they immigrated into north Italy *c.*950; here they preceded and later successfully resisted *Etruscans and Gauls. They were highly civilized, preferred horse-breeding and commerce to war, and early organized the Baltic *amber trade. They particularly worshipped a goddess of healing, Rehtia (or Reitia: see RELIGION, ITALIC). Always friendly to the Romans, the Veneti aided them against Gauls (390 BC) and *Hannibal (see PUNIC WARS). Later from allies they became subjects, though retaining local autonomy. Presumably they obtained Latin rights (see IUS LATII) in 89, full citizenship in 49 BC (see CITIZENSHIP, ROMAN). Their *Romanization ensued. See next entry.

Strab. 5. 212; Polyb. 2. 17 f.; Livy, 1. 1, 5. 33, 10. 2. R. S. Conway, *Prae-Italic Dialects* 1 (1933), 230; J. Whatmough, *Foundations of Roman Italy* (1937), 171 (with bibliog.); M. S. Beeler, *The Venetic Language* (1949). For their alleged Paphlagonian origin see Serv. on *Aen.* 1. 242; Hom. *Il.* 2. 852; Strab. 12. 543. E. T. S.; T. W. P.

Venetic language The *Veneti (2) learnt to write from the *Etruscans during the 6th cent. BC and some 250 to 300 inscriptions survive, mostly votive or funerary, all quite short (none has more than a dozen words); these texts range from the last quarter of the 6th to the last quarter of the 2nd cent. BC. With the onset of Romanization, some texts were written in the native language but in the Latin alphabet. The Venetic script has two noteworthy features: different signs for *t* and *d* in each Venetic city; on the other hand, generalization to all regions, from the 5th cent. BC onwards, of a system of syllabic punctuation that involved bracketing with dots any syllable-initial vowel and any consonant that closed a syllable (e.g. . *e . g o, don a . s . t o*).

Examples of texts (with punctuation omitted): *mego doto vhugsiia votna . . . reitiai op voltiio leno* ('Fuxia, wife of Voto, gave me to . . . [the goddess] Reitia by act of spontaneous will'); *osts katusiaiios donasto, atra es termonios deivos* ('Osts, son of Katusios, offered [this precinct], entrance [allowed only] up to the Boundary Gods'); *enoni ontei appioi sselboisselboi andeticobos ecupetaris* ('grave of Ennonios for Onts, for Appios and for himself, [all three] sons of Andetios'); *kellos pittamnikos toler trumusijatei donom* ('Kellos son of Pittamnos brought a gift to [the goddess] Trumusiatis').

Once believed to be an '*Illyrian' language, Venetic has now, in the light of improved readings and greater knowledge, turned out to be definitely Italic, and furthermore closer to Latin than any other Italic dialect. Venetic words similar to Latin include: *deivos* 'gods', *donon* 'gift', *ekvon* 'horse', *vhagsto* 'made', *murtuvoi ~ vivoi* 'dead ~ alive', *kve* 'and', etc. There are some similarities with Germanic, but they are quite rare: *ego ~ mego* 'I ~ me', *sselbo-* 'self'.

The Venetic system of personal names differs from the gentilitial system of Etruscan, *Latin, *Oscan, and *Umbrian: there are no family names. Men and women bear individual names, such as masc. *Akuts, Iuvants, Moldo, Voltiomnos*, etc. or fem. *Fougonta, Frema, Kanta, Nerka*, etc. As an optional addition, for both men and women, there may appear a patronymic adjective (derived from the individual name of the father, with the suffix *-io-*/*-ia* or *-ko-*/*-ka*), and for married women, a gamonymic adjective (derived from the individual name of the husband, with the suffix *-na*). For instance, the wife of *Lemetor* may have *Lemetorna* as an additional name, and his children may have *Lemetorios* (masc.) or *Lemetoria* (fem.). It is only during the 1st cent. BC, under Roman influence (see NAMES, PERSONAL, ROMAN), that the gentilitial system spreads throughout the Venetic region. See also ITALY, LANGUAGES OF.

G. B. Pellegrini and A. L. Prosdocimi, *La lingua venetica*, 2 vols. (1967); M. Lejeune, *Manuel de la langue vénète* (1974); M. Lejeune, *Ateste à l'heure de la romanisation* (1978); G. Fogolari and A. L. Prosdocimi, *I Veneti antichi* (1988). M. Lej.

vengeance See CURSES; ERINYES; LAW AND PROCEDURE, ROMAN, § 3.1; LAW IN GREECE; NEMESIS; PUNISHMENT (*Greek and Roman practice*); RECIPROCITY.

Vennonius, an early Roman author, now lost, whose history *Cicero greatly regrets not to have at hand (*Att.* 12. 3. 1; cf. *Leg.* 1. 6). He is cited by *Dionysius (7) of Halicarnassus, 4. 15.

Peter, *HR Rel.* 1. 142.

Venta Silurum, a town of Roman *Britain in South Wales (mod. Caerwent) the *civitas*-capital of the *Silures. A dedication to Ti. Claudius Paulinus, former commander of Legio II Augusta (*RIB.* 311; see LEGION), forms important evidence for the character of local government in Britain. Although it was founded in the late 1st cent. AD, there is little evidence for development until into the 2nd cent. Recent excavations in the *forum-*basilica suggest mid-2nd-cent. construction. The town was defended by earthworks in the late 2nd cent. and a town wall was added after AD 330; this was supplemented with external towers dated to after AD 348–9. These defences enclosed only 18 hectares, which were extensively explored between 1899 and 1913. More recent work has examined a temple, the forum-basilica, and private housing.

R. Brewer, in B. C. Burnham and J. L. Davies (eds.), *Conquest of Co-existence and Change* (1990). S. S. F.; M. J. M.

Ventidius (*RE* 5), **Publius,** Roman military man, famous for his rise from humble origins. He was born in *Picenum, probably of respectable municipal family, and in infancy walked in the triumph of Cn. *Pompeius Strabo (89 BC). Said to earn his living as a 'muleteer', he was probably an army-contractor. He served in Gaul with *Caesar, who brought him into the senate in 47. Praetor in 43, he made a rapid march to link with the army of Antony (M. *Antonius (2)) soon after *Mutina, and was rewarded with the consulship for the last weeks of the year. In 42 he probably governed one of the Gallic provinces; in 41 he moved with an army into Italy, but avoided any serious involvement in the Perusine War. After the Pact of *Brundisium he was sent to drive the Parthians out of Asia and Syria (see PARTHIA), and he won brilliant victories at the Cilician Gates and Mt. Amanus (39) and at Gindarus (38), then besieged *Antiochus (9) I of Commagene in Samosata. Superseded by Antony, he returned to Rome, celebrated his Parthian *triumph (November 38), and died soon after. He was honoured with a public funeral.

Syme, *Rom. Rev.*, see index, and *Latomus* 1958, 73–80 (= *RP* 1 (1979), 393–9); C. Nicolet, *L'Ordre équestre* (1974). 2. 1066–7. C. B. R. P.

Venus The debate over the original nature of this goddess, who does not belong to Rome's oldest pantheon but is attested fairly early at *Lavinium, has been partly resolved (Schilling 1954). It is now accepted that the neuter †*venus*, 'charm', cannot be separated from the terms *venia*, *venerari*, *venenum* ('gracefulness', 'to exercise a persuasive charm', 'poison', against Radke, *Götter* 311 ff.)). How this neuter was transformed into a feminine, a process attested for the Osco-Umbrian goddess Herentas (cf. OSCANS; UMBRIANS), is ill-understood in the absence of evidence.

Schilling thinks that it took place at the federal sanctuary of Lavinium, a city with old and well-attested links with the Greek world and the legend of *Troy. Whatever the case, from the 3rd cent. BC, Venus was the patron of all persuasive seductions, between gods and mortals, and between men and women (Venus Verticordia). Because of her links with the extraordinary power of *wine, Venus is presented in the rites and myth of the *Vinalia as a powerful mediatrix between *Jupiter and the Romans. The first known temple is that of Venus Obsequens ('Propitious'), vowed in 295 BC and built some years later. During the *Punic Wars, the tutelary and diplomatic role of Venus grew continually, in proportion to the process of her assimilation to Greek *Aphrodite. In the 1st cent. BC she even acquired a political value. She was claimed by *Sulla as his protectress (his *agnomen* Epaphroditus means 'favoured by Venus'), as by *Pompey (Venus Victrix) and *Caesar (Venus Genetrix), while *Aphrodisias in Caria benefited progressively from important privileges. Under the empire Venus became one of the major divinities of the official pantheon.

Schilling, *La Religion romaine de Vénus* (1954; repr. 1982), and *Rites, cultes, dieux de Rome* (1979), 290 ff. For the temples of Venus see Richardson, *Topog. Dict. Ancient Rome*, 408 ff.; Ziolkowski, *Temples*, 167 ff. (Venus Obsequens); Schilling, *Rites* 94 ff. (Venus Erucina on the Capitol, built in 215 BC); Venus Victrix, dedicated in 55 BC (F. Coarelli, *Rend. Pont.* (1971–2), 99 ff.); Venus and Roma, consecrated in AD 121, completed after 137, rebuilt by Maxentius in 307 (M. Boatwright, *Hadrian and the City of Rome* (1987), 120 ff.). J. Sch.

Venusia (mod. Venosa), in south Italy, a Peucetian city (see MESSAPII) on the *via Appia, 82 km. (51 mi.) north of Potenza (see POTENTIA). There was a pre-Roman settlement, but there is little evidence for it. It came into contact with Rome in 317 BC, and it may by this date have been Oscanized (see OSCANS). A large Latin colony was founded there in 291 (Dion. Hal. *Ant. Rom.* 17–18), after which it became increasingly important. It remained loyal to Rome until 90 BC, when it revolted, and was not recaptured until 88. It became a *municipium* but regained colonial status (see COLONIZATION, ROMAN) in the 1st cent. AD; continuing to be noted as one of the most important cities of *Apulia, it was the birthplace of *Horace (*Sat.* 2. 1. 34). Recent surveys of its territory have revealed clusters of farms and smallholdings, probably pertaining to various colonial settlements.

N. Jacobone, *Venusia* (1909); A. Small in G. Barker and J. Lloyd, *Roman Landscapes* (1991). K. L.

Vercellae (mod. Vercelli) originated as an *oppidum of the Celtic Libici, near the gold-mines of north-western Cisalpine Gaul (see GAUL (CISALPINE)). A garrison-town and a *municipium under the early empire, it became an important Christian centre in the 4th and 5th cents. AD.

V. Viale, *Vercelli e il Vercellese nell'antichità* (1971). E. T. S.; T. W. P.

Vercingetorix, son of a powerful and ambitious Arvernian nobleman (see ARVERNI), Celtillus, raised the revolt against *Caesar in 52 BC and was acclaimed king of his people and general of the confederates. Defeated at Noviodunum Biturigum, he turned to depriving Caesar of supplies while tempting him either to attack or ingloriously decline to attack an impregnable foe. The policy succeeded admirably near Avaricum, where Caesar did not attack, and at *Gergovia, where he did. Vercingetorix then risked another attack on Caesar in the field, which was badly defeated, so that he retreated to another prepared fortress, Alesia. Caesar had an unexpected weapon, the circumvallation, with which he beat off not only Vercingetorix but also additional Gallic forces summoned to relieve *Alesia. Vercingetorix surrendered and was put to death after Caesar's *triumph (46 BC).

Vercingetorix's career shows how dangerous the developed Gallic nations were to Rome, yet how profoundly, once defeated, they succumbed to foreign rule: he was never apparently venerated as a national hero. See GALLIC WARS.

J. Harmand, *Vercingétorix* (1984). J. F. Dr.

Vergil See VIRGIL.

Vergiliomastix, 'the scourge of *Virgil', a work or critic attacking Virgil cited twice by *Servius' commentary (on *Ecl.* 2. 23 and *Aen.* 5. 521), and therefore pre-dating it (before late 4th cent. AD). Such detractors of Virgil were common (Donatus, *Vit. Verg.* 43–6); the name 'Vergiliomastix' may be linked with the similar 'Aeneidomastix' of one of these, Curvilius Pictor (*Vit. Verg.* 44; cf. the 'Ciceromastix' of *Larcius Licinus, Gell. 17. 1. 1).

S. J. Ha.

Vergilius Romanus, Latin author, contemporary with the younger *Pliny (2), who devotes *Ep.* 6. 21 to praise of him (otherwise unknown); he wrote *mimiambi* (for *mimiambi* cf. IAMBIC POETRY, GREEK), *palliatae* (rated by Pliny the equal of these of *Plautus and *Terence), and—most unusually—a comedy modelled on (Greek) Old Comedy (see COMEDY (GREEK), OLD). No doubt his works were written for recitation only. See PALLIATA.

P. G. M. B.

Vergina See AEGAE.

Verginia was traditionally killed by her own father to save her from the lust of the decemvir Appius *Claudius Crassus Inregillensis Sabinus. This event prompted a secession of the *plebs to the *Aventine and ultimately led to the overthrow of the decemvirs (449 BC); see DECEMVIRATES. Verginia herself resembles *Lucretia, and her name seems too good to be true; but it does not follow that the story is a late invention. The poetic details, clearly evident in Livy's magnificent narrative (3. 44–8), led Macaulay and De Sanctis to postulate a traditional ballad. In *Diodorus (3), whose account (12. 24. 2–4) may represent an early version of the story, the protagonists are not named, but referred to simply as 'a maiden' and 'one of the decemvirs'. The notion that in the original version Verginia was a patrician is based on a mistranslation of Diodorus' text.

Macaulay, *Lays of Ancient Rome*; De Sanctis, *Stor. Rom.* 2². 44 ff.; J. Bayet, *Tite-Live, Histoire romaine 3* (1942), 134; Ogilvie, *Comm. Livy 1–5*, 476 ff.; T. P. Wiseman, *Clio's Cosmetics* (1979). P. T.; T. J. Co.

Verginius (*RE* 29) **Flavus**, rhetor and teacher of *Persius Flaccus. He wrote an *ars rhetorica* valued by *Quintilian (7. 4. 40). His popularity led to his exile by *Nero in AD 65 (Tac. *Ann.* 15. 71).

Schanz–Hosius, § 480.1. M. W.

Verginius (*RE* 27) **Rufus, Lucius**, from Mediolanum (Milan), consul AD 63, became governor of Upper Germany (see GERMANIA) in 67. He apparently held discussions with the rebel C. *Iulius Vindex and may have been forced into battle at Vesontio by the precipitate action of his troops (Cass. Dio, 63. 24; Plut. *Galb.* 6). Rejecting his army's attempts to declare him emperor, he was nevertheless slow to support *Galba, remitting the choice to the senate. Removed from office by the suspicious Galba, Verginius became *suffect consul for the second time under *Otho, and after his murder again refused the purple. Thereafter he lived quietly, becoming consul for the third time with *Nerva

in 97. When he died soon after, his funeral oration was delivered by *Tacitus (1). He was *Pliny (2) the Younger's guardian.

His epitaph reads (ambiguously): 'Here lies Rufus, who, after Vindex had been defeated, liberated the imperial power, not for himself, but for his country' (Plin. *Ep.* 9. 19).

D. C. A. Shotter, *CQ* 1967, 370; B. Levick, *Rh. Mus.* 1985, 319.

J. B. C.

Vermina was the son of *Syphax. After Syphax's capture in 203 BC, Vermina remained in control of most of Syphax's kingdom, and fought on the Carthaginian side at *Zama (see PUNIC WARS). After Rome's peace with Carthage, he asked the senate for recognition as king and as friend of Rome (200). The senate replied that he must first make peace on Rome's terms. Vermina agreed, and was left in possession of part of Syphax's former kingdom.

Habel, *RE* 4 A 1477, 'Syphax'; Briscoe, *Comm. 31–33*, 84, 108. J. BR.

Verona, a town of the *Veneti (2) on the river Adige, perhaps also occupied by the *Cenomani (Plin. *HN* 3. 130; Livy, 5. 35). Little is known of this period in its history, but the oldest inscription is a milestone from the *via Postumia of 148 BC. *Catullus (1) was born here, and *Martial (14. 195. 1) and *Strabo (5. 1. 6) call Roman Verona a large and important city. By AD 69 it was a *colonia* (Tac. *Hist.* 3. 8; see COLONIZATION, ROMAN). There are many monuments including the magnificent 1st-cent. amphitheatre; a theatre; and walls of *Gallienus. The *gens Gavia were generous patrons. It retained its importance in late antiquity, and was occupied by *Constantine I (312), *Theoderic (1) (499), and the *Lombards (568). Excavation suggests that occupation continued unbroken into the Middle Ages, although in an impoverished way.

Verona e il suo territorio (1960); C. La Rocca Hudson, *Archeologia medievale* 1986, 31 ff.; G. Cavalieri Manasse, in *La città nell'Italia settentrionale in età romana* (1990), 579 f. E. T. S.; T. W. P.

Verres (*RE* 1), **Gaius**, perhaps the son of one of *Sulla's new senators who, as an ex-*divisor* (see CANDIDATUS), had considerable influence. He may be the moneyer VER (*RRC* 350, dated 86 BC), an issue usually (but implausibly) assigned to an ex-tribune. Quaestor in 84, he deserted Cn. *Papirius Carbo for Sulla, appropriating his *fiscus*. As legate (eventually *pro quaestore*) of Cn. *Cornelius Dolabella (2) in Cilicia (see LEGATI), he helped him plunder his province and Asia, but on their return helped to secure his conviction. As *praetor urbanus* (74), he is charged by *Cicero with having flagrantly sold justice. Assigned Sicily as proconsul (73–71), he exploited and oppressed the province (except for *Messana, in league with him) and even Roman citizens living or trading there by all means at his disposal. Unwisely offending some senators and ill-treating clients of *Pompey, he yet evaded the effect of a senate decree censuring him, passed on the motion of the consuls of 72, and was again prorogued. On his return, he used his great wealth (much of it acquired in Sicily) and his connections, and exploited the hostility of leading nobles (especially most of the Metelli) to Pompey, to gain strong and eminent support. Q. *Hortensius Hortalus, consul designate for 69 with a friendly Metellus (Q. *Caecilius Metellus Creticus), defended him against a prosecution launched in the *quaestio repetundarum* (see QUAESTIONES; REPETUNDAE) by Cicero (70) and tried to drag the case on into his year of office. Outwitted by Cicero's speed and forensic tactics, and despite the efforts of a Metellus as Verres' successor in Sicily, he found the case caught up in the popular agitation for jury reform (see AURELIUS COTTA, L.) and succumbed to Pompey's influence exerted against Verres.

On his advice, Verres fled into exile at *Massalia. Cicero nevertheless published the second *actio* (oration) he had prepared, to drive home Verres' guilt and demonstrate his own skill and efforts. The evidence in fact seems overwhelming. But after his victory Cicero conciliated Verres' many noble supporters by agreeing to a low assessment of damages (Plut. *Cic.* 8. 1).

His *Verrines* give us our best insight into provincial administration and its abuses in the late republic. After Verres' proconsulship Sicily ceased to be Rome's main granary (see FOOD SUPPLY, ROMAN). Verres died at Massalia, allegedly proscribed (see PROSCRIPTION) for his stolen art treasures by M. *Antonius (2).

Cic. *Verrines.* Gruen, *LGRR*, see index; E. Badian, *Publicans and Sinners* (1978), *passim*; Alexander, *Trials* 88 ff.   E. B.

Verrius (*RE* 2) **Flaccus, Marcus** (*c*.55 BC?–*c*. AD 20?), a *freedman and innovative teacher who became tutor of *Augustus' grandsons (see IULIUS CAESAR (2), C. and IULIUS CAESAR (4), L.). He was, after *Varro, the most distinguished scholar of Rome, cultivating the joint study of language and antiquities characteristic of Latin scholarship since L. *Aelius. His (lost) minor works ranged from orthography and the language of M. *Porcius Cato (1) (*De obscuris Catonis*), to *res Etruscae* (*Etruscan matters) and the Saturnalia (*Saturnus*; see SATURNUS, SATURNALIA), to 'things worth remembering' (*res memoria dignae*, a miscellany much used by the elder *Plin. (1)); he also compiled the *Fasti Praenestini* (*Inscr. Ital.* 13. 2: 107 ff.). The breadth of learning that marked such writings made his major work, *De verborum significatu*, the richest and most influential achievement of ancient Latin lexicography. Arranged alphabetically, with several books for each letter, the work treated rare and obsolete words, incorporating extracts from early authors and much other antiquarian material; it is known from the partially preserved epitome of Sex. *Pompeius Festus and from the abridgment of Festus made by Paulus Diaconus (8th cent.).

Herzog–Schmidt, § 318.   R. A. K.

ver sacrum, 'the sacred spring', a ritual practised in Italy, particularly by the Sabellic (*Oscan) tribes; see SABELLI. In times of distress all produce of the spring (or the whole year) was consecrated to a deity, primarily *Mars. The animals were sacrificed; the humans, when of age, were sent away. This controlled overpopulation; led by a god or totemic animal the *sacrani* ('devoted') founded new communities: so originated the Picentes (from *picus*, 'woodpecker'; see PICENUM), Samnites (see SAMNIUM), *Mamertines (Men of Mars). In Rome the only recorded *ver sacrum* was vowed (to *Jupiter) in 217 BC; human offspring were not included (Strabo, 5. 4. 12; Dion. Hal. *Ant. Rom.* 1. 16; Festus, *Gloss. Lat.* 276, 414, 467; Livy, 22. 10; 33. 44; 34. 44).

J. Heurgon, *Trois études sur le 'Ver sacrum'* (1957); P. M. Martin, *Latomus* 1973, 32 ff.   J. L.

Vertumnus (Vortumnus), supposedly an *Etruscan god: so Varro, *Ling.* 5. 46 and Prop. 4. 2. 4, who says he came from *Volsinii; but nothing proves this view (Radke, *Götter* 317 ff.; Dumézil, *ARR* 339 f.), which may just be speculation based on the resemblance of his name to that of *Voltumna and the fact that his temple on the *Aventine (its anniversary 13 August) displayed a painting of M. Fulvius Flaccus, conqueror of Volsinii in 264 BC. His statue stood in the vicus Tuscus in Rome, and *Propertius (4. 2. 13 ff.) indicates that the shopkeepers there made frequent offerings to him. Nothing is known of his functions, since all ancient interpretations played with the various meanings of the verb *vertere*, from which they derived the god's

name (e.g. Prop. 4. 2. 21 ff.; Ov. *Met.* 14. 642 ff.). The hypothesis that his name can be connected with the Etruscan family *ultimni*, Latinized Veldumnius, is not acceptable. More interesting, but lacking decisive proof, are the theories of G. Radke, who proposes to see here an 'introducing god' akin to Roman *Janus, who would be of *Umbrian origin. See also RELIGION, ETRUSCAN.

Wissowa in Roscher, *Lex.*; Latte, *RR* 191 f.; Radke, *Götter* 317 ff.
H. J. R.; J. Sch.

Verulamium, a town in *Britain near modern St Albans (Herts.). The town was built on part of the iron age *oppidum* (Verlamio(n)), capital of *Tasciovanus, on which had been placed a short-lived Roman fort. The settlement was probably accorded the status of *municipium* by *Claudius (Tac. *Ann.* 14. 33). The earliest shops were half-timbered multiple buildings used for commercial purposes. After the sack by *Boudicca (AD 60/61) rebuilding was delayed, but by AD 79 a new masonry forum of Gallic design was dedicated, under Cn. *Iulius Agricola, as the inscription (*JRS* 1956, 147) shows. The earliest defensive earthwork (perhaps pre-Flavian) enclosed 48 ha.; it became obsolete early in the 2nd cent. and the town expanded over it. Stone public buildings of the late 1st and early 2nd cents. include two temples of non-classical type and a market hall; but domestic building was still in half-timber. About AD 155 much of the town, including the forum, was burnt down; in the restoration a theatre and palatial town houses in masonry were built. Around AD 140–55 a new earthwork defence was begun, but was replaced before 250 by a town wall on a different line enclosing 81 ha. Two monumental arches in the main street now marked the vanished original boundary, and a third was added near the theatre *c*. AD 300. There was much building activity early in the 4th cent., continuing here and there to the town's end and beyond. At least one large house was built after *c*. AD 370 and structural activity on its site can be traced to perhaps *c*. AD 450. Here Alban was martyred (perhaps under *Septimius Severus); in AD 429 Germanus visited his shrine (*Script. rer. Meroving.* 7. 262), which probably lies beneath the medieval abbey and modern cathedral. The site became deserted in the late 5th or 6th cent. and the ruins were much pillaged for the monastic buildings of St Albans in the early Middle Ages.

S. S. Frere, *Verulamium Excavations* 1 (1972), 2 (1983), 3 (1984); M. J. Millett, *The Romanization of Britain* (1990).   S. S. F.; M. J. M.

Verus, Lucius, Roman emperor AD 161–9, was born in 130 and named L. Ceionius (*RE* 8) Commodus, son of L. *Aelius Caesar. On Aelius' death, *Hadrian required his second choice as heir, *Antoninus Pius, to adopt Lucius along with his own nephew *Marcus Aurelius; he now had the names Lucius (Aelius) Aurelius Commodus, but unlike Marcus did not become Caesar. He became consul in 154 and was consul again in 161 with Marcus, who, following the death of Antoninus, at once made him co-emperor. He dropped the name Commodus, taking his adoptive brother's name Verus instead. He was thus the first joint Augustus, equal in all respects except for the position of pontifex maximus. When the Parthians invaded the empire (see PARTHIA), he took nominal command of the ensuing Parthian War (162–6), in fact waged by his generals. In 164 he went to Ephesus to marry Marcus' daughter *Annia Aurelia Galeria Lucilla, by whom he had several children. For his victories he assumed the titles Armeniacus, Parthicus, and Medicus, and held a *triumph jointly with Marcus in October 166. He reluctantly accompanied Marcus to the Danubian provinces in 168, to prepare for an offensive against the threatening German tribes, but, alarmed by the spread of plague in winter-quarters at Aquileia, persuaded Marcus to set out for Rome in January 169; on the journey he suffered a stroke at Altinum and died a few days later. He was deified as *divus Verus*.

Fronto, *Ep.*; Cass. Dio 71; SHA *Marc.*; SHA *Verus*; BM *Coins, Rom. Emp.* 4; A. R. Birley, *Marcus Aurelius*, 2nd edn. (1987). A. R. Bi.

Vesontio (mod. Besançon), capital of the Sequani, an advanced central Gallic people (cf. *Aedui, *Allobroges, *Arverni). Strategically important for its command of the Belfort gap, it was occupied by *Caesar in 58 BC and in AD 68 saw the conflict between C. *Iulius Vindex and *Verginius Rufus. Included in Gallia Belgica (see GAUL (TRANSALPINE)) by *Augustus, the Sequani were transferred under the Flavians to *Germania Superior, and in the late empire Vesontio became the provincial capital of Maxima Sequanorum. The Roman city directly succeeded the Celtic *oppidum sited, as Caesar accurately described, in a bend of the river Dubis (now Doubs). The most important surviving monument is the Porte Noire, but the forum and amphitheatre are also known.

Caes. *BGall.* 1. 38–9; Grenier, *Manuel* 1. 560 ff., 3. 353 ff., 692 ff.; F. Passard and J.-P. Urlacher, *Archéologia* 1983, 32 ff. A. L. F. R.; J. F. Dr.

Vespae iudicium coci et pistoris iudice Volcano, poem in 99 hexameters by Vespa, an itinerant rhetorician, in which baker and cook argue their respective merits before Vulcan. Metrical and other considerations suggest a late 3rd- or 4th-cent. date. Full of mythological learning, the poem, which parodies bucolic competition, is most notable for its humour, particularly its puns.

TEXTS *Anth. Lat.* 199 Riese, 190 Shackleton Bailey; with comm., F. Pini (1958); with trans., Shackleton Bailey, *Harv. Stud.* 1980, 210–17.

J. H. D. S.

Vespasian (Titus Flavius (*RE* 206) **Vespasianus)**, emperor AD 69–79, was born on 9 November, AD 9, at Sabine *Reate. His father, Flavius Sabinus (for his elder brother of the same name see FLAVIUS SABINUS), was a tax-gatherer; his mother also was of equestrian family, but her brother entered the senate, reaching the praetorship. Vespasian was military tribune (see TRIBUNI MILITUM) in 27, serving in Thrace, quaestor in Crete in the mid-30s, aedile (at the second attempt) in 38, and praetor in 40. Claudius' freedman *Narcissus (2) now advanced his undistinguished career, and he became legate of legio II Augusta (see LEGION) at *Argentorate, commanding it in the invasion of *Britain in 43 and subduing the south-west as far as Exeter (43–7); for this he won triumphal ornaments (see ORNAMENTA) and two priesthoods (see PRIESTS (GREEK AND ROMAN)). He was *suffect consul in November–December 51 and is next heard of as an unpopular proconsul of Africa (c.62 (see PRO CONSULE; AFRICA, ROMAN)); any unemployment may be due to the deaths of Narcissus and L. *Vitellius and the eclipse of other supporters during the ascendancy of *Iulia Agrippina. In 66 he accompanied Nero to Greece and allegedly offended him by falling asleep at one of his recitals, but at the end of the year he was entrusted with suppressing the rebellion in *Judaea. By mid-68 he had largely subdued Judaea apart from Jerusalem itself but conducted no further large-scale campaigns.

Vespasian now settled his differences with the governor of Syria, C. *Licinius Mucianus. They successively recognized *Galba, *Otho, and A. *Vitellius, but the idea of using the eastern legions to attain power became a plan in the spring of 69. On 1 July the two Egyptian legions under Ti. *Iulius Alexander

proclaimed Vespasian; those in Judaea did so on 3 July, and the Syrian legions a little later. Mucianus set out with a task-force against Italy while Vespasian was to hold up the grain ships at *Alexandria (1) and probably *Carthage. However, the Danubian legions declared for Vespasian, and the legionary legate M. *Antonius Primus invaded Italy. After his crushing victory at *Cremona the city was brutally sacked. Primus fell from favour in 70 and took the blame. It was alleged that Primus' invasion was against orders (certainly Mucianus would have opposed his action), but victory could never have been bloodless. Primus pressed on, entering Rome on 21 December, the day after Vitellius' death. The senate immediately conferred all the usual powers on Vespasian, though he dated his tribunician years from 1 July, negating the acts of senate and people and treating his legions as an electoral college.

A fragment of an enabling law has survived (*ILS* 244 = EJ 364, trans. D. Braund, *Augustus to Nero* no. 293) conferring powers, privileges, and exemptions, most with Julio-Claudian precedents. It is disputed whether this was part of the original tralatician grant of powers, surviving only in Vespasian's case, or of a supplementary grant, due to difficulties with the senate, conferring by law the right to perform acts never questioned in a Julio-Claudian but which from Vespasian might be challenged. It sanctioned all he had done up to the passing of the law and empowered him to act in whatever way he deemed advantageous to the Roman people. Vespasian's standing was lower than that of any of his predecessors and the law took the place of the *auctoritas* (prestige, influence) he lacked. Vespasian was careful to publicize a number of divine omens which portended his accession; he frequently took the consulship, however briefly, and accumulated imperatorial salutations. Vespasian insisted that the succession would devolve on his son (Suet. *Div. Vesp.* 25; sons, Dio Cass. 65. 12). Controversy over the dynastic principle, part of a wider controversy over the role of the senate in government, may have caused his quarrel with doctrinaire senators like *Helvidius Priscus, who was exiled and later executed.

Vespasian returned to Italy in the late summer of 70. While at Alexandria he had been concerned with raising money, and his sales of imperial estates and new taxes caused discontent there. He claimed that forty thousand million sesterces (so Suet. *Div. Vesp.* 16. 3) were needed to support the state. He increased, sometimes doubled, provincial taxation and revoked imperial immunities (see IMMUNITAS). Such measures were essential after the costs incurred by Nero and the devastation of the civil wars; contemporaries inevitably charged Vespasian with 'avarice'. He was able to restore the *Capitol, burnt in December 69, to build his forum and temple of Peace, and to begin the *Colosseum. An attempt by senators in 70 to diminish expenditure by the state treasury (*aerarium), so promoting senatorial independence, was promptly vetoed.

It may have been in part for financial reasons that in 73–4 he held the censorship (see CENSOR) with *Titus. But both as censor and previously, he recruited many new members, Italian and provincial, to the senate, and conferred rights on communities abroad, notably a grant of Latin rights (see IUS LATII) to all native communities in Spain.

Vespasian restored discipline to the armies after the events of 68–9. Before his return Mucianus had reduced the praetorian guard, enlarged by Vitellius, to approximately its old size, and they were entrusted to Titus on his return (see PRAETORIANS). The legions were regrouped so that Vitellian troops would not occupy dangerous positions. In the east Vespasian by the end of his reign had substituted three armies (six legions) in Syria, Cappadocia, and Judaea for the single army (until Nero's time only four legions) in Syria. After the Jewish and Rhineland rebellions (see TITUS; IULIUS CIVILIS, C.) had been suppressed, Vespasian continued imperial expansion with the annexation of northern England, the pacification of Wales, and an advance into Scotland (see IULIUS AGRICOLA, CN.), as well as in south-west Germany between Rhine and Danube.

On his death on 23 June 79 he was accorded deification, though Titus did not act at once (he had been Vespasian's colleague since 71 and the ceremony, last held on Claudius' death in 54, may have seemed discredited). Unassuming behaviour had partially conciliated the aristocracy, although some of his friends were informers or otherwise disreputable (see EPRIUS MARCELLUS, T. CLODIUS; VIBIUS CRISPUS, Q.); Tacitus, *Hist.* 1. 50, claims that he was the first man to improve after becoming emperor, and the reign seems to have been tranquil after conflicts with the senate had been won. The years after 75 were marred (as far as is known) only by Titus' execution of A. *Caecina Alienus and his forcing Marcellus to suicide.

Vespasian was industrious, and his simple life a model for contemporaries. Matching his rugged features he cultivated a bluff manner, parading humble origins and ridiculing a man who corrected his accent. His initial appointments (see CAESENNIUS PAETUS, L.; PETILLIUS CERIALIS CAESIUS RUFUS, Q.) show astuteness in building a powerful party of which the core was his own family. To have ended the wars was an achievement, and *Pax was a principal motif on his coinage. His proclaimed purposes were the restoration and enhancement of the state, and he made no great break with tradition. In style of government, however, and in the composition of the governing class, the reign paved the way for the 2nd cent.

Nothing is known of Vespasian's education (he was no orator, but could quote *Homer), but his sons were cultivated, and he attended to the needs of Rome and the empire by founding chairs of rhetoric and philosophy and by granting fiscal privileges to teachers and doctors.

Vespasian's wife Flavia Domitilla was alleged to be only of Latin status until her father Liberalis proved her Roman citizenship. Besides his two sons she bore a daughter also named Flavia Domitilla; wife and daughter died before Vespasian's accession. He then lived with an earlier mistress, Caenis, a freedwoman of *Antonia (3).

Suet. *Div. Vesp.*; Tac. *Hist.* 2–5; Cass. Dio bks. 65 f. (Epitome); M. McCrum and A. G. Woodhead, *Docs. of the Principates of the Flavian Emperors 68–96* (1961). L. Homo, *Vespasien, l'Empereur du bon sens (69–79 ap. J.-C.)* (1949); R. Syme, *Tacitus* (1958), index; J. Nicols, *Vespasian and the partes Flavianiae*, (1978); B. Levick, *The Emperor Vespasian* (1993) (bibliog.). G. E. F. C.; B. M. L.

Vesta, Vestals Vesta was the Roman goddess of (the hearth-) fire, *custos flammae* (Ov. *Fast.* 6. 258, comm. F. Bömer), one of the twelve *di *consentes*. The cult is also known from *Pompeii and *Latium: it was believed to have been introduced into Rome by *Pompilius Numa—or *Romulus—from *Alba Longa (Dion. Hal. *Ant. Rom.* 2. 64. 5 ff.; Serv. on *Aen.* 1. 273). An ancient etymology linked Vesta to Greek *Hestia (Cic. *Nat. D.* 2. 67): her cult expressed and guaranteed Rome's permanence. Vesta's main public shrine, never inaugurated *certis verbis* and so never a true *templum*, was a circular building just south-east of Augustus' arch in the *forum Romanum (the original 7th-cent. BC shape is unknown). In the late republic its form was taken to be that of a primitive house, intimating a connection between public and private cults of the hearth. In the historical period, the state cult (Vestalia, 9 June) effectively displaced private cults. There was no statue of Vesta within the shrine (Ov. *Fast.* 295–8): it contained only the fire and, in the *penus* (inner sanctum), the 'sacred things that may not be divulged'—esp. the *Palladium (Livy, 26. 27. 14), and the *fascinum*, the erect *phallus that averted evil. On being elected *pontifex maximus in 12 BC, Augustus created another shrine for Vesta on the *Palatine.

Though she bore the title *mater*, Vesta was thought of as virgin, by contrast with her sisters *Juno and *Ceres. She was 'the same as the earth', which also contains *fire, and was sacrificed to on low altars; she protected all altar-fires. Her character gains contour from a contrast with *Volcanus. The sacral status of the six *sacerdotes Vestales*, the Vestal Virgins (the sole female priesthood in Rome), was manifested in many ways. Though they were required to maintain strict sexual purity during their minimum of 30 years' service, their dress (*stola, vittae*) alluded to matrons' wear, their hair-style probably to a bride's. They were excised from their own family (freed from their father's *potestas*, ineligible to inherit under the rules of intestacy) without acceding to another. It was a capital offence to pass beneath their litter in the street.

There were several restrictions upon eligibility (Gell. 1. 12. 1–7); most known Vestals are of senatorial family. Though they had many ceremonial roles, their main ritual tasks were the preparation of the grain mixed with salt (*mola salsa*) for public sacrifices (Serv. *Ecl.* 8. 82) and the tending of Vesta's 'undying fire' (*ignis inextinctus*). The extinction of the fire provided the prima-facie evidence that a Vestal was impure: impurity spelled danger to Rome. The last known case of living entombment in the Campus Sceleratus (near Colline gate) occurred under *Domitian in AD ?89 (Plin. *Ep.* 4. 11; cf. Plut. *Num.* 10. 4–7). The last known chief vestal (*vestalis maxima*) is Coelia Concordia (AD 380); the cult was finally abandoned in 394.

C. Koch, in *RE* 8 A (1958), 1717–76; H. Hommel, in *ANRW* 1. 2 (1972), 397–420; Dumézil, *ARR* Eng. trans. 311–26; W. Pötscher, in *Satura F. Rodríguez Adrados* (1987), 2. 743–62; iconogr.: T. Fischer-Hansen, *LIMC* 5 (1990), 412–20. Vestals: F. Guizzi, *Aspetti giuridici del sacerdozio romano: il sacerdozio di Vesta* (1968); M. Beard, *JRS* 1980, 12–27; social origins: M. Raepset-Charlier, *Μνήμη G. A. Petropoulos* (1984), 253–70.
R. L. G.

Vestini, a central Italian tribe living near the Gran Sasso, highest peak of the Apennines. They spoke an *Oscan-type dialect. Chief towns: Pinna, Aternum. They became allies of Rome before 300 BC but joined their close associates, the *Marsi, *Marrucini, and *Paeligni in the *Social War (3) rebellion against her. Their *Romanization quickly ensued.

A. La Regina, *Mem. dei Lincei* 1968, 361 ff. E. T. S.; T. W. P.

Vestricius (*RE*, entry under Vestricius) **Spurinna, Titus** Born *c.* AD 25, operating under Annius Gallus, Othonian commander in northern Italy (69; see OTHO), secured *Placentia against the Vitellians (see VITELLIUS, A.) and disciplined his turbulent troops. *Suffect consul under *Vespasian, he was voted a triumphal statue by the senate for establishing a king of the *Bructeri (Plin. *Ep.* 2. 7), presumably while governing Lower Germany (see GERMANIA); he perhaps held this post briefly in 97, although he was about 73 years old, rather than under *Domitian. Spurinna was consul for the second time in 98. A friend of *Pliny (2) the Younger and possibly an oral source for *Tacitus (1)'s *Histories*, he remained vigorous, liking country walks and ball games, and writing poems in Latin and Greek.

Vesuvius

R. Syme, *Tacitus* (1958), app. 6; *ZPE* 1985, 275 = *RP* 5 (1988), 510.

J. B. C.

Vesuvius, the famous volcano on the bay of Naples, rises isolated out of the surrounding plain of *Campania. Its base is some 48 km. (30 mi.) in circumference, its central cone over 1,216 m. (4,000 ft.) high, and its general appearance picturesque since the mountain-sides have been largely blown away. Vesuvius is mentioned only twice during the Roman republic: in the Latin War of 340, where the allusion (Livy, 8. 8. 19) seems erroneous, and in the revolt of *Spartacus, who used its crater as a stronghold in 73. It appeared extinct (Diod. 4. 21. 5), and its fertile slopes were extensively cultivated, with vineyards mostly (Strabo 5. 4. 8, 247). On 5 February AD 63 a damaging earthquake presaged the first recorded eruption, the severe one of 24 August 79 that buried *Pompeii in sand, stones, and mud, *Herculaneum in liquid tufa, and *Stabiae in ashes, asphyxiated *Pliny (1) the Elder, and is described by *Pliny (2) the Younger, an eyewitness, in letters to *Tacitus (1) (*Ep.* 6. 16, 20). Antiquity witnessed three subsequent eruptions (in 202, 472, and 512), and violent activity still periodically recurs.

M. Frederiksen, *Campania* (1984), see index.　　　E. T. S.; N. P.

Vetera, near Birten, a major Augustan military base on the Rhine, and then a permanent station for two legions. After its destruction by C. *Iulius Civilis in 70, a one-legion fortress was erected on a new site. This appears to have been occupied to the late 3rd/early 4th cent., and may have been refortified by Julian. A walled colony (*Colonia Ulpia Traiana*) was founded (between 98 and 107) nearby at Xanten; see COLONIZATION, ROMAN. By the late empire, occupation had moved to the extramural shrine of Ad Sanctos.

C. M. Wells, *The German Policy of Augustus* (1972), 123 ff.; H. Hinz, *ANRW* 2. 4 (1975), 825 ff., and *Xanten der Römerzeit* (1976); H. Schönberger, *BRGK* 1985, 321 ff.; U. Heimberg, *BJ* 1987, 411 ff.　　J. F. Dr.

veterans Legionaries in the late republic, though frequently serving for long periods, had no recognized right to discharge bounties. Such rewards, often plots of land since most soldiers came from a rural background, were organized through the initiative of individual commanders, and this fostered a close personal loyalty among their troops which could then be exploited in politics. *Augustus, wishing to be sole benefactor of his army, but needing to avoid the land confiscations and disruption which frequently accompanied veteran settlements, between 30 and 2 BC spent 1,260 million sesterces in buying land and providing cash payments for veterans. In AD 5 he finally established a discharge bounty of 20,000 sesterces for praetorian veterans and 12,000 for legionary veterans; auxiliaries were apparently excluded, at least in the early empire, but received benefits of citizenship. Augustus funded superannuation from his own pocket, but in AD 6 he at last made the state responsible by establishing the military treasury (*aerarium militare*) with a personal grant of 170 million sesterces, to be supported in perpetuity by taxes on inheritance and auctions.

Land allocations to some veterans, either individually or in colonies, continued in the provinces until the 2nd cent. (in Italy until Flavian times), and in some areas colonies became an important source of recruits, although the practice of colonial settlement was neither systematic nor coherent. Veteran colonies often brought benefits to the vicinity: increased security, urban development, an influx of Roman citizens, and imperial benevolence. Many prospered, e.g. *Thamugadi (Timgad), established

(AD 100) in Africa for veterans of legio III Augusta (see LEGION), on a plan reminiscent of a military camp, which became a highly developed community with extensive civic amenities. However, the founding of veteran colonies ended in the reign of Hadrian, because land was becoming more difficult and expensive to obtain, and, as local recruitment became more common, veterans increasingly preferred to settle close to the permanent camp where they had served rather than to be moved to a colony elsewhere.

Veterans were a privileged group, having exemption from certain taxes, compulsory public services, municipal duties, and degrading punishments. Some acquired status in their local communities and held public office, though evidence for this is limited.

L. Keppie, *Colonisation and Veteran Settlement in Italy 47–14 BC* (1983); J. C. Mann, *Legionary Recruitment and Veteran Settlement during the Principate* (1983); S. Link, *Konzepte der Privilegierung römischer Veteranen* (1989).　　J. B. C.

veterinary medicine deals with treatments, cures, and all the other means by which the health of livestock may be preserved or restored. It is rooted in the early management of stock breeding, when rearers had to initiate medical care for their herds. As a recognized profession, veterinarians are mentioned in the early second millennium BC in Mesopotamia (Code of Hammurabi, reign: 1792–1750 BC) as well as in ancient Egypt (papyrus of Kahun, 12th dynasty: *c.*1850 BC). The earliest Greek evidence so far discovered for veterinarians called *hippiatroi* (horse doctors) is an honorific inscription of *c.*130 BC. In Rome, an *equarius medicus* (horse doctor) is attested by the end of the 1st cent. BC. Afterwards, terms such as *mulomedicus* (mule doctor), *medicus veterinarius*, *medicus iumentarius*, or *medicus pecuarius* (livestock doctor) are attested in the late-Roman empire, albeit rarely. The usual names for veterinarians in both Greek and Latin focus primarily on the treatment of horses and equids. These animals, together with oxen, were essential to the general economy, civilian and military transportation, wars, etc., and therefore the most carefully looked after (see TRANSPORT, WHEELED). But there is enough evidence to assume that medical care was extended to all domestic animals (see Varro, *Rust.* 2. 7. 16) long before our earliest information on veterinarians. Agronomists indicate that, besides professional practitioners, breeders and herders themselves were responsible for treating ordinary illnesses and injuries while herds were grazing in remote areas (see e.g. Varro, *Rust.* 2. 1. 21). Whether applied by the *magister pecoris* (head shepherd; ibid. 2. 2. 20) or by the *medicus pecorum* (livestock doctor; ibid. 2. 7. 16), veterinary medicine was and remained throughout classical antiquity primarily a matter of empirical practice, never reaching any level comparable to that of Aristotelian zoology or human medicine of the Hippocratic school. Prejudices against the activities and status of ancient veterinarians stemmed from this lack of theoretical development and such other factors as that they dealt with animals (Vegetius, *Mulomedicina*, prol. 1 and 13).

Greek sources We know of a lost treatise on horsemanship by the Athenian Simon (5th cent. BC). Our first two extant authors were not themselves veterinarians, though both contributed to the field: *Xenophon (1) and *Aristotle. In the treatise *On Hunting* and, to a greater extent, in those *On the Art of Horsemanship* (aimed at the private owner) and *The Cavalry Commander* (a military treatise), Xenophon relies upon his own experience to explain how to breed, select, and train horses and hounds. In these chapters he focuses on zootechnics rather than on veterinary medicine. But the medical background is obviously understood in such matters as how to deal with pregnant mares or bitches before and after giving birth, look after foals and puppies, start training young animals, etc. Conforming to the criteria of ancient zoology, Aristotle includes domestic animals in his survey of the whole animal kingdom (*Historia animalium*). He discusses some of their illnesses and injuries and includes remarks and treatments of veterinary interest. However, the main Greek work on veterinary medicine is the collection known as the *Corpus Hippiatricorum Graecorum (CHG)*. It consists of both textual and non-textual excerpts borrowed from lost writings on the medical treatment of horses and other equids. Its contents are either anonymous or attributed to otherwise unknown or little-known authors of the 4th cent. AD: Apsyrtus, Eumelus, Hierocles, etc. First thought to have been composed in the 9th cent. AD, the *CHG* is now recognized as a collection anonymously compiled in early Byzantine times and revised for the emperor Constantine VII Porphyrogenitus (905–959). Long neglected by classicists, *CHG* raises many difficult questions to do with manuscripts, textual criticism, technical content, etc. Closely related to the *CHG* as regards their sources and composition, books 16 (on horses, donkeys, and camels) and 17 (on cattle) of the *Geoponica* complete and enlarge the extensive surviving Greek tradition on veterinary medicine.

Latin sources Veterinary medicine in the Latin tradition is documented by two different, but complementary, kinds of writings. First, all the *agricultural writers contain some medical information, even if most are mainly orientated towards zootechnics and management rather than veterinary medicine as such: M. *Porcius Cato (1), *De Agricultura* (with the least developed account of animal health); Varro, *De re rustica* (bks. 2–3); *Virgil, *Georgics* (bk. 3 on large and small animals; bk. 4 on apiculture; see BEE-KEEPING); *Columella, *De re rustica* (bks. 6–9, the largest extant Latin account of medical care, not discounting magical recipes, for large (bk. 6) and small (bk. 7) animals; *Gargilius Martialis, *Curae boum* (excerpts only); and *Palladius (1), *De veterinaria medicina* (bk. 14 of his *Opus agriculturae* or calendar of farm work). The elder *Pliny (1)'s chapters on domestic animals in his *Historia naturalis* complete our agronomic sources.

The other group of Latin sources consists of three veterinarian treatises written by authors who are all seasoned compilers rather than practitioners. Indeed they were interested in and well informed about everything to do with the health of horses and other equids (secondarily of oxen and other farm animals). The so-called *Mulomedicina Chironis* (10 bks.), the commentaries on veterinary medicine of Pelagonius (the original title is lost), and the *Mulomedicina* (4 bks.) of *Vegetius were all written within the same century or so, most probably between AD 330 and 450. Each raises many questions about authorship, sources, transmission, vocabulary, contents, etc. Although recent research shows promise, much more is needed before the main philological and technical issues are satisfactorily resolved. But Roman veterinary medicine remains significant to modern practitioners. Ancient veterinarians showed great interest in semiotics and aetiology and excelled in the careful observation and analysis of visible causes. For therapy, they used pharmacological prescriptions. They also practised surgery to an extent still to be evaluated. As for plagues, they developed a more thoroughly grounded and more efficient approach than that generally prevalent in ancient human medicine. In all cases, they were guided by constant attention to animal welfare and they expressed a genuine sympathy for these mute creatures under their care. Such conceptions

and feelings played a role in their approach, a fact which should not be underestimated or minimized if one wants to understand fully the specific and lasting quality of ancient veterinary medicine. See also ANIMALS, KNOWLEDGE ABOUT; ANIMALS, ATTITUDES TO.

SOURCES Cato the Elder, *De agricultura*, A. Mazzarino (Teubner, 1962); Columella, *Opera quae exstant. Fasciculus quartus*, W. Lundström (1940), *Fasciculus quintus*, V. Lundström and A. Josephson (1945). *Corpus Hippiatricorum Graecorum*, E. Oder and C. Hoppe (Teubner, 1924). Gargilius Martialis, *Curae boum*: see below, under Vegetius. *Geoponica*, H. Beckh (Teubner, 1895). *Mulomedicina Chironis*, E. Oder (Teubner, 1905). Palladius, *Opus agriculturae. De veterinaria medicina. De insitione*, R. H. Rodgers (Teubner, 1975). Pelagonius, *Ars veterinaria*, K.-D. Fischer (Teubner, 1980). Varro, *De re rustica*, G. Goetz (Teubner, 1929, 2nd edn.). Vegetius, *Digestorum artis mulomedicinae libri*, E. Lommatzsch (Teubner, 1903).

MODERN LITERATURE L. Bodson, 'The Welfare of Livestock and Work Animals in Ancient Greece and Rome', in *Medical Heritage* 1986, 244–249; K.-D. Fischer, 'Ancient Veterinary Medicine: A Survey of Greek and Latin Sources and Some Recent Scholarship', in *Medizinhistorisches Journal* 1988, 191–209 (the bibliog. includes trans. and comm. on the *Geoponica*, *Corpus Hippiatricorum Medicorum*, and *Mulomedicina Chironis* presented as Ph.D. theses in the research programme of the Institut für Palaeoanatomie, Domestikationsforschung und Geschichte der Tiermedizin der Universtät Munchen; and full reference to the Ph.D. of A.-M. Doyen on *CHG* (Louvain-la-Neuve, 1983), still unpublished, and related papers; S. Georgoudi, *Des chevaux et des bœufs dans le monde grec* (1991); D. Karasszon, *A Concise History of Veterinary Medicine* (1988); A. von den Driesch, *Geschichte der Tiermedizin: 5000 Jahre Tierheilkunde* (1989); R. E. Walker, *Roman Veterinary Medicine*, = appendix to J. M. C. Toynbee, *Animals in Roman Life and Art* (1973), 303–43 (Ger. trans. 1983). L. B.

veto See INTERCESSIO; TRIBUNI PLEBIS.

Vettius (*RE* 6), **Lucius,** an *eques* (see EQUITES, *Origins and republic*) from *Picenum, served under Cn. *Pompeius Strabo and *Sulla and became a friend of L. *Sergius Catilina. Involved in his conspiracy (63 BC), he turned informer and gave *Cicero useful help, but came to grief trying to denounce *Caesar. In 59—perhaps now Caesar's agent—he denounced an *optimate 'plot' against *Pompey, involving many prominent men, including the Curiones (see SCRIBONIUS CURIO, C. (1) and (2)) and L. *Licinius Lucullus (2). Disbelieved, he was gaoled and mysteriously killed. The facts remain obscure.

C. Meier, *Hist.* 1961, 88 (with bibliog.); Gruen, *LGRR* 95 f., 286. E. B.

Vettius (*RE* 25) **Bolanus, Marcus,** commanded a legion under *Corbulo in Armenia (AD 62), was *suffect consul about 66, and was sent by A. *Vitellius as legate (see LEGATI) of *Britain in 69. With his army depleted by the Civil Wars, he was of necessity relatively inactive (Tac. *Agr.* 16. 5); but before his recall in 71 he had probably conducted important operations in Brigantia (Tac. *Hist.* 3. 45; see BRIGANTES). He was proconsul of Asia, and raised to the patriciate, perhaps by *Vespasian. *Status addressed a poem (*Silv.* 5. 2) celebrating his achievements to his son Crispinus.

E. Birley, *Roman Britain and the Roman Army* (1953), 10 ff.; 46; A. Birley, *The* Fasti *of Roman Britain* (1981), 62–5. G. E. F. C.; M. T. G.

Vettius (*RE* 13) **Philocomus,** a friend of *Lucilius (1) and probably a *freedman, with whom the poet and grammarian *Valerius Cato read Lucilius' satires (Suet. *Gram.* 2). R. A. K.

Vettius (*RE* 6) **Scato, Publius,** Marsic 'praetor' i.e. commander in the *Social War (3); see MARSI. In summer 90 BC he won several victories, finally killing the consul P. Rutilius Lupus. Driven back by Lupus' legate C. *Marius (1), he marched south and, after defeating the other consul L. *Iulius Caesar (1), captured *Aesernia. In 89 he vainly negotiated with the consul Cn. *Pompeius Strabo through Pompeius' brother, who was his guest-friend; see FRIENDSHIP, RITUALIZED. (Cicero, serving under Pompeius, witnessed this: *Phil.* 12. 27.) Defeated by Pompeius, he was surrendered by his own army and was killed by a loyal slave to prevent his falling into the victor's hands (Sen. *Ben.* 3. 23. 5).   E. B.

Vettius Valens, Greek astrologer from *Antioch (1), wrote (between AD 152 and 162) the *Anthologies*, an extant nine-book treatise on *astrology, preserving the only major collection of Greek horoscopes (*c.*130) outside the papyri; it was heavily used in the Middle Ages.

Ed. D. Pingree (Teubner, 1986); see also T. Barton, *Ancient Astrology* (1994).   A. J. S. S.

Vetulonia (Etr. Vetluna), in the hills to the west of the bay that is now the Grosseto plain, was one of the twelve cities of Etruria (see ETRUSCANS). Excavation has been mainly confined to the extensive cemeteries. The earliest material is Protovillanovan (see VILLANOVAN CULTURE); the most notable comes from a series of wealthy orientalizing 'circle tombs', consisting of trenches surrounded by stones and covered by a tumulus. The Circolo dei Lebeti contained bronze cauldrons with siren heads and griffin protomes that have Greek and oriental parallels respectively. The Pietrera tumulus contained a single chamber in which a central pillar supports a corbelled dome: here as elsewhere in northern Etruria, the suggestion of affinities with Sardinian building techniques gains credit from the presence of nuragic imports in a number of other graves (see SARDINIA). According to *Silius Italicus (8. 484–8) the Romans assumed the Etruscan royal insignia of *fasces*, *sella curulis*, etc. from Vetulonia: an axe bound with iron rods was found in an early tomb there.

I. Falchi, *Vetulonia e la sua necropoli antichissima* (1891); G. Camporeale, *La Tomba del Duce* (1967), and *I commerci di Vetulonia in età orientalizzante* (1968); C. Curri, *Vetulonia I* (1978).   D. W. R. R.

vexillum, a military standard consisting of a square-shaped piece of cloth attached to a crossbar, borne on a pole. In the republic this served as the standard of the legionary cavalry, and in imperial times usually was carried by cavalry units, notably by *alae*, under the charge of the senior standard-bearer (*vexillarius*). It also represented a detached unit (*vexillatio*) and so came to mean the unit itself. Veterans who still served as reservists had a special *vexillum*. In general, a *vexillum* was a commander's flag used for signalling. Miniature representations of *vexilla* were issued as military decorations. See SIGNA MILITARIA.   J. B. C.

via Aemilia, named after its builder, M. *Aemilius Lepidus (1), consul 187 BC (Livy, 39. 2), and subsequently repaired by *Augustus and *Trajan, ran from *Ariminum 281 km. (176 mi.) north-west to *Placentia (with later extensions to *Augusta Praetoria (Aosta), to Segusio, to *Aquileia, all somewhat inaccurately called via Aemilia). The Aemilia helped to Romanize Cisalpine Gaul rapidly (see ROMANIZATION; GAUL (CISALPINE)): with its extensions it touched every important city of the district (still called Emilia) except *Ravenna.

It is to be distinguished from the via Aemilia Scauri.

Strabo 5. 217. N. Lamboglia, *Athenaeum* 1937; T. P. Wiseman, *PBSR* 1970, 126 f.   E. T. S.; T. W. P.

via Aemilia Scauri, highway built by M. *Aemilius Scaurus (1), *censor 109 BC, linking the *via Aurelia and *via Postumia. It ran from Vada Volaterrana through *Pisae, *Genua, and Vada Sabatia and thence inland to Dertona. From Vada Sabatia the via Iulia Augusta (built by *Augustus) continued along the coast to beyond Albintimilium (mod. Ventimiglia).

E. Fentress, *PBSR* 1984, 72 ff.   E. T. S.; T. W. P.

via Annia (1) Highway built in northern Italy, perhaps by T. Annius Luscus, consul 153 BC. It probably linked *Bononia with *Aquileia via *Patavium, *Altinum, and Concordia.

(2) The extension of the via Appia, which ran from *Capua through *Nola, *Nuceria (1), *Consentia, and Vibo (see HIPPONIUM) to *Rhegium, may also have been a via Annia (not via Popillia, as usually stated), built perhaps by T. Annius Rufus, propraetor 131 BC.

(3) Road near Falerii (see FALISCANS) in Etruria.

T. P. Wiseman, *PBSR* 1964, 211 ff.; 1969, 82 ff.; and 1970, 128 ff.
                                                        E. T. S.; T. W. P.

via Appia, the Romans' principal route to south Italy and beyond (Strabo, 6. 283). Ap. *Claudius Caecus, *censor 312 BC, built and named the 211-km. (132-mi.) section from Rome to *Capua (Livy, 9. 29). It had probably been extended by 244 through *Beneventum, *Venusia, and *Tarentum to *Brundisium (374 km., 234 mi.). Paving of the Appia commenced in 295 and apparently was complete by *Gracchan times (Livy, 10. 23; Plut. *C. Gracch.* 7; reject Diod. Sic. 20. 36). In imperial times a praetorian *curator* (see CURA(TIO), CURATOR; PRAETOR, *Caesar and imperial period*) kept the road in order. Its exact line can be traced most of the way to Beneventum, but less securely beyond, since the shorter route to Brundisium via *Canusium and *Barium, which the via Traiana later used, led to neglect of the Appia. Between Rome and Beneventum, however, one can still see roadside tombs (e.g. the Scipios', Caecilia Metella's), the ancient pavement, a rock-cutting (at *Tarracina), embankments (e.g. at *Aricia and Itri), *bridges (three between Caudium and Beneventum), and milestones. One of these proves that, even though travellers preferred the 30-km.-long (19 mi.) ship canal, the Appia from its earliest days crossed the *Pomptine Marshes. Various branches, e.g. the one to Rhegium (see VIA ANNIA (2)), were also somewhat inaccurately called via Appia.

T. P. Wiseman, *PBSR* 1970, 130 f.; S. Quilici Gigli (ed.), *La Via Appia* (1990).   E. T. S.; T. W. P.

via Aurelia, an important highway up the western coast of Italy. Possibly first laid out as far as Cosa by C. Aurelius Cotta, *censor in 241 BC, it was later rebuilt on a different line, and extended by M. *Aemilius Scaurus (1) in 109 BC to Dertona and thence to *Arelate, in the newly acquired Gallia Narbonensis (see NARBO; GAUL (TRANSALPINE)). Later the longer route by the *via Flaminia and *via Aemilia was preferred, perhaps because of malarial conditions along the Aurelia (for malaria see DISEASE).

L. Quilici, *Quad. Ist. Top. Roma* 1968, 13 ff.; T. P. Wiseman, *PBSR* 1970, 133; E. Fentress, *PBSR* 1984, 72 ff.   E. T. S.; T. W. P.

via Cassia, a road running north from Rome through *Sutrium, *Volsinii to *Arretium. Here it joined with a road which led across the *Apennines to *Bononia and then *Aquileia. The Cassia proper was almost certainly the work of C. Cassius Longinus, *censor in 154 BC, and is notable for the way that it bypassed old *Etruscan cities such as *Veii.

W. V. Harris, *Rome in Etruria and Umbria* (1971), 114; T. P. Wiseman, *PBSR* 1970, 136 f.   E. T. S.; T. W. P.

via Clodia, a road running north from Rome, through south-western Etruria (see ETRUSCANS) via the west side of Lake Bracciano and Etruscan towns such as Blera, Norchia, and Tuscania as far as *Saturnia. Incorporating many stretches of older Etruscan roads, it was probably laid out as a middle-distance route in the first half of the 3rd cent. BC.

J. B. Ward-Perkins, *JRS* 1957, 139 ff., *PBSR* 1955, 44 ff., and 1957, 67 ff.; P. Hemphill, *PBSR* 1975, 149 ff.; W. V. Harris, *Rome in Etruria and Umbria* (1971), 166–7.   E. T. S.; T. W. P.

via Domitia, a road which probably ran from *Narbo through *Nemausus to *Arelate on the Rhône. It was built by the conqueror of Narbonensis (see GAUL (TRANSALPINE)), Cn. *Domitius Ahenobarbus (2) (121 BC); a milestone of Domitius survives (Degrassi, *ILLRP* 460a). It was repaired by M. *Fonteius (c.75 BC), and under the empire by *Tiberius (AD 31–2), *Claudius (41), *Antoninus Pius (145), Maximinus (see IULIUS VERUS MAXIMINUS, C.) (235–8), and *Diocletian (284–305).

T. P. Wiseman, *PBSR* 1970, 139 f.; A. L. F. Rivet, *Gallia Narbonensis* (1988), 43 f.   C. E. S.; T. W. P.

via Domitiana, highway built by *Domitian (AD 95), running from Sinuessa on the *via Appia through Volturnum, *Liternum, and *Cumae to *Puteoli, where it joined a road to *Neapolis.

Stat. *Silv.* 4. 3.   E. T. S.; T. W. P.

via Egnatia, Roman road built c.130 BC from the *Adriatic coast to *Byzantium; named after the proconsul in Macedonia Cn. *Egnatius (*AE* 1973, 492), the via Egnatia was the main route from Rome to the east. Two branches of the road, starting respectively from *Dyrrhachium and *Apollonia, united in the Skumbi valley, crossed the Balkan range by Lake Lychnidus (now Ochrida), and descended to *Thessalonica by way of Heraclea, Eordaea, *Aegae, and *Pella, whence it followed the Thracian coast to Byzantium. It followed the line of a trade-route through the Balkan range which Corinth had exploited.

N. G. L. Hammond, *A History of Macedonia* 1 (1972), 19–58, and *JRS* 1974, 185 ff.; F. W. Walbank, *Selected Papers* (1985), 193 ff., and in *Ancient Macedonia* 4 (1986), 673 ff.   N. G. L. H.

via Flaminia, the great northern highway of Italy, built 220 BC by C. *Flaminius (1), when censor (Livy, *Epit.* 20; reject Strabo 5. 217). It was 334 km. (209 mi.) long from Rome by way of *Narnia, Mevania, *Nuceria (2), and Helvillum to *Fanum Fortunae, where it turned north-west and followed the Adriatic coastline via Pisaurum to *Ariminum. After AD 69 the section between Narnia and Nuceria was provided with an alternative, 9-km. (5½-mi.) longer route through *Interamna Nahars, *Spoletium, and Fulginium. From its earliest days the Flaminia was much frequented; its importance was, if anything, enhanced in late imperial times when the imperial court was at Milan (*Mediolanum) or *Ravenna. Large towns grew up along its tomb-lined course. The road was often repaired: by C. *Sempronius Gracchus, *Augustus (parts of whose bridge at Narnia and whose honorific arch at Ariminum survive), Vespasian (whose tunnel through the Intercisa Pass still exists near Calles), *Trajan, *Hadrian. Various branches, e.g. from Nuceria to *Ancona, were also inaccurately called via Flaminia.

T. Ashby and R. A. L. Fell, *JRS* 1921, 125 f.; M. Luni (ed.), *Nuovi documenti sulla Flaminia* (1989).   E. T. S.; T. W. P.

via Labicana, highway running south-east from Rome to Labici

and the country of the *Hernici. Avoiding the Alban hills (see ALBANUS MONS), it joined the *via Latina near *Anagnia.
                                                     E. T. S.; T. W. P.

via Latina had both an 'old' and a 'new' route, as curators' inscriptions make clear (*ILS* 1159, 1174, 8980). The older ran south-west from Rome, through the country of the Latins (see LATINI) and down the Sacco and *Liris valleys into *Campania; it may have been established during Etruscan expansion in the 6th cent. BC. The later road followed the Trerus valley through the Hernici country where the via Labicana joined it near *Anagnia. It crossed the Liris at *Fregellae, then proceeded via Aquinium, *Casinum, *Venafrum, *Teanum Sidicinum, and *Cales across the *Volturnus to *Casilinum, where it merged with the Appia (see VIA APPIA). It may have been built by the consul L. Cornelius Cinna in 127 BC (*ILLRP* 457). The Latina was much frequented (Strabo 5. 237), and was used by both *Pyrrhus and *Hannibal, presumably because it followed an easier line than the via Appia.

T. P. Wiseman, *PBSR* 1970, 139.   E. T. S.; T. W. P.

via Popillia, highway in northern Italy, linking *Ariminum, *Atria, and *Altinum with *Aquileia, built by P. *Popillius Laenas, consul 132 BC (Dessau, *ILS* 5807). The road from *Capua to *Rhegium in southern Italy is also often attributed to him, but incorrectly: see VIA ANNIA (2).

T. P. Wiseman, *PBSR* 1970, 128 ff.   E. T. S.; T. W. P.

via Postumia, north Italian highway centring on *Cremona, whence it ran in one direction through Placentia and Dertona to *Genua, and in the other through *Bedriacum, *Verona, Vicetia, and Opitergium to *Aquileia. Built by Sp. *Postumius Albinus (consul 148 BC), it consolidated the conquest of the Transpadane region (see TRANSPADANA). The *itineraries regard its western section as part of the *via Aurelia. Ancient authors virtually ignore it.

Dessau, *ILS* 5806, 5946; Tac. *Hist.* 3. 21.   E. T. S.; T. W. P.

via Sacra, the 'sacred way', street connecting the *forum Romanum with the *Velia, affording access to the *Palatine. According to *Varro and *Pompeius Festus, the stretch of road popularly known as via Sacra lay between the *Regia and the house of the *rex sacrorum*, which was at a point known as Summa Sacra Via; as properly defined, however, the road led from the Sacellum Streniae (cf. STRENAE) on the Carinae to the Arx (Varro, *Ling.* 5. 47; Festus, 372 Lindsay). The location of Summa Sacra Via is, however, disputed by modern scholars, being identified either with the area adjacent to the so-called 'Tempio di Romolo', or near the arch of *Titus. In AD 64, *Nero planned the street anew as a noble colonnaded avenue, leading from the forum to the entrance to the *Domus Aurea, which was flanked by shops for jewellers, and other luxury-traders.

F. Coarelli, *Il Foro Romano* (1983), 11–118; F. Castagnoli, *Quad. Ist. Top. Roma* 1988, 99–114; Richardson, *Topog. Dict. Ancient Rome*, 338–40.
                                                     I. A. R.; J. R. P.

via Salaria, an old-established route which facilitated the salt trade from the *Tiber mouth. It ran north-east from Rome to *Reate in the Sabine country. Later extensions, (1) through Amiternum and (2) through *Asculum Picenum, carried it to the *Adriatic.   E. T. S.; T. W. P.

via Sebaste, the Roman key to the control and pacification of *Pisidia, in the southern part of the Augustan province of *Galatia. It ran from the coast of *Pamphylia (probably *Perge),

via Traiana

through the Döşeme pass (known to Polybius as the Climax) into the Pisidian highlands, past the Roman colonies or colonial settlements of Comama and Apollonia, until it reached the *caput viae*, Pisidian *Antioch (2). A further extension continued east to the colonies of Iconium and Lystra. According to *milestones it was completed in 6 BC by the governor of Galatia, Cornutus Arruntius Aquila. Archaeological remains show that it was a highway between 6 and 8 m. (20–6 ft.) broad, which could carry wheeled traffic along its entire length. Its significance may be compared with that of the *via Domitia in Gallia Narbonensis, of the *via Egnatia in Macedonia, and of the road built from Pergamum to Pamphylia at the creation of the Asian province by M'. *Aquillius (1).   S. M.

via Traiana, highway built (AD 109) by *Trajan, which replaced the *via Appia as the usual route between *Beneventum and *Brundisium. It touched Aequum Tuticum, *Aecae, *Herdonia, *Canusium, *Barium, and *Gnathia. Its identification with the republican via Minucia mentioned by *Cicero (*Att.* 9. 6. 1) and others is very dubious.

> T. Ashby and R. Gardner, *PBSR* 1914, 104 f.   E. T. S.; T. W. P.

via Valeria, an important road that ran eastwards from Rome to its colony of *Alba Fucens (founded 303 BC), and later to Aternum on the *Adriatic. Of great antiquity, it may have originated as a *transhumance track, used by shepherds taking their flocks into the *Apennines to graze on the summer pastures. The first 28 km. (18 mi.) comprised the via Tiburtina. The extension of the road to Alba Fucens may have been the work of the censor M. Valerius Maximus in 307 BC (Livy, 9. 43. 25). This later became a paved highway, perhaps in the censorship of M. Valerius Messalla (154 BC) and was the via Valeria proper (cf. Strabo, 5. 238). Finally, the emperor *Claudius continued the road as the via Claudia Valeria from Cerfennia to the Adriatic.

> T. Ashby, *PBSR* 1906, 84 ff. (via Tiburtina); C. van Essen, *PBSR* 1957, 22 ff. (centre); R. Gardner, *PBSR* 1920, 75 ff. (via Claudia Valeria).
>   E. T. S.; T. W. P.

viatores were attendants on magistrates (see MAGISTRACY, ROMAN), one of whose main functions was to summon persons to the magistrate's presence. Thus they might be used, for example, to call senators to a meeting from their country homes. However, they also had a function more akin to that of a bailiff, acting in the presence of a magistrate to seize a criminal or his property or indeed a recalcitrant political opponent. This last function was especially useful to a tribune (see TRIBUNI PLEBIS), who, unlike a consul or praetor, had not the help of *lictors. So *Caesar had M. *Porcius (2) Cato dragged from the senate, and Ti. *Sempronius Gracchus (3) removed his fellow-tribune M. *Octavius from the tribunal. By the late republic they formed a corporation divided into several *decuriae* according to the rank of the magistrates (the first was therefore the *decuria consularis*). They are also found on the staffs of local magistrates and of Roman magistrates in the provinces. Although many were in origin freedmen or of low birth, the posts seem to have carried considerable prestige for those who held them.

> Mommsen, *Röm. Staatsr.* 1³. 360 ff.; A. H. M. Jones, *Studies in Roman Government and Law* (1960), 154 ff.; N. Purcell, *PBSR* 1983.
>   P. T.; A. W. L.

Vibenna, Caelius (or Caeles), an *Etruscan adventurer who, according to Roman tradition, came to help *Tarquinius Priscus (Tac. *Ann.* 4. 65; *Romulus according to *Varro, *Ling.* 5. 46; Paul.–Fest. 38 L) and settled with his followers on the hill which later

bore his name (the *Caelius mons). He and his brother, Aulus, were also well-known figures in Etruscan tradition. They are represented on funerary urns from Chiusi (Brunn–Körte, *Urne etrusche* 2. 254 ff.) and a bronze mirror from Bolsena (BMC Bronzes, no. 633), but most famously in the François tomb-painting from *Vulci (late 4th cent. BC) which shows Caeles Vibenna being released by his friend *Mastarna, while Aulus Vibenna and other companions dispatch their adversaries, who include a Cn. Tarquinius from Rome. The name *Aules V(i)pinas* appears on a 5th-cent. Etruscan red-figure cup of unknown provenance (CVA France, no. 16), and may be evidence of a hero-cult; on the other hand, a votive bucchero vase from Veii inscribed *Avile Vipiiennas* (Villa Giulia inv. VTP 519) dates from the mid-6th cent., and is therefore contemporary with Aulus Vibenna, who may indeed have dedicated it in person.

> A. Momigliano, *Claudius²*, 10 ff.; A. Alföldi, *Early Rome and the Latins* (1965), 212 ff.; R. Thomsen, *King Servius Tullius* (1980), 96 ff.; F. Coarelli, *Dialoghi di archeologia* 1983, 43–69; F. Buranelli (ed.), *La Tomba François di Vulci* (1987); C. Ampolo, in Momigliano and Schiavone (eds.), *Storia di Roma* 1 (1988), 205 ff.   H. H. S.; T. J. Co.

Vibius (*RE* 28) **Crispus, Lucius Iunius Quintus,** from *Vercellae (mod. Vercelli) in Transpadane Italy (see TRANSPADANA), was *suffect consul AD ?61, 74, and early 83. He was *curator aquarum* 68–71 (see CURA(TIO), CURATOR), probably proconsul (see PRO CONSULE) of Africa in 71/2, and legate (see LEGATI) of *Tarraconensis in 73/4. He is a sinister figure in *Tacitus (1) (*Hist.* 2. 10, 4. 41–2), responsible for the fall of the Scribonii brothers; his protégés probably included L. *Verginius Rufus and the elder and younger *Pliny (1–2). His wit and pleasing oratory, praised by *Quintilian (see also Suet. *Dom.* 3; Dio Cass. 65. 2. 3), were probably one source of his influence with *Vespasian, who cherished him (Tac. *Dial.* 8, 13); pliability (Juv. 4. 81 ff.) enabled him to survive until 80 where others, like T. Clodius *Eprius Marcellus, came to grief.

> R. Syme, *Rev. Ét. Anc.* 1956, 236 ff.; *RP*, indexes.   G. E. F. C.; B. M. L.

Vibius (*RE* 39) **Marsus, Gaius,** suffect consul AD 17, was a legate (see LEGATI) of *Germanicus in the east and after his death in 19 conducted *Vipsania Agrippina (2) back to Rome; his daughter married into the Plautii. From 26/27 to 29/30 he was proconsul (see PRO CONSULE) of Africa. In 37, accused of treason and adultery, he was saved by the death of *Tiberius. *Claudius returned him to *Syria as governor (*c.*42–5). There he was hostile to M. *Iulius Agrippa (1) and checked the designs on *Armenia of Vardanes, king of *Parthia.

> U. Vogel-Weidemann, *Die Statthalter von Africa und Asia in den Jahren 14–68 n. Chr.* (1982), 92 f.; Syme, *RP*, indexes.   T. J. C.; B. M. L.

Vibius (*RE* 40) **Maximus, Gaius,** attested as prefect (see PRAEFECTUS) of Egypt from August AD 103 to March 107, condemned for maladministration (May 109 onwards). He may be a friend of *Martial (11. 106) or of *Statius; the close of *Silvae* 4. 7 suggests that its honorand produced a handbook of world history with an *epitome of *Sallust and *Livy; if so, he was a native of *Verona and had been prefect of a cavalry squadron in *Syria, *procurator of *Dalmatia (AD 95), *praefectus vigilum*, and *praefectus annonae* (101).

> H. A. Musurillo, *The Acts of the Pagan Martyrs* (1954), 150 ff.; R. Syme, *Hist.* 1957, 480 ff. (= *RP* 1. 353 ff.); cf. P. White, *Hist.* 1973, 275 ff.
>   J. W. D.; G. B. A. F.; B. M. L.

Vibius (*RE* 16) **Pansa Caetronianus, Gaius,** Roman general and politician. He served with *Caesar in Gaul, defended his interests as tribune in 51 BC (see TRIBUNI PLEBIS), governed *Bithynia in 47–6 and Cisalpine Gaul (see GAUL (CISALPINE)) in 45, and was designated by Caesar consul for 43. In March 43 he led four legions of recruits to join A. *Hirtius against Antony (M. *Antonius (2)). He was wounded in a preliminary engagement at Forum Gallorum near *Mutina, and after the battle of Mutina he died. Gossip alleged that Octavian (see AUGUSTUS) had poisoned him.

Cic. *Phil.* trans. D. R. Shackleton Bailey (1986); Syme, *Rom. Rev.* (1939), index.
C. B. R. P.

Vibius (*RE* 48) **Rufus, Gaius,** declaimer (perhaps C. Vibius Rufus Rufinus, *suffect consul AD 16). L. *Annaeus Seneca (1), who quotes him frequently, records that he spoke 'in the old way' (*Controv.* 9. 2. 25).

Schanz–Hosius, § 336. 9. 22; Syme, *AA* 71, 225.
M. W.

Vibius (*RE* 58) **Trebonianus Gallus, Gaius,** the emperor **Trebonianus Gallus,** ruled AD 251–3. A successful senatorial governor of *Moesia, he was acclaimed by the army immediately after *Decius' death. He made an unfavourable peace with the *Goths, then returned to Rome, where he adopted Decius' young son. Perhaps distracted by the effects of a severe plague, he appeared to ignore renewed *Sasanid aggression (including the capture of *Antioch (1)) and failed even to return to the Danube to avenge his predecessor (whose end he was suspected of having contrived). When the Danubian troops forced *Aemilianus' usurpation in 253 (early summer), Gallus sent *Valerian to gather reinforcements, but was killed at *Interamna Nahars by his own men before these could arrive (late summer).

M. Christol, *RN* 1980, 63 ff.
J. F. Dr.

Vibo Valentia See HIPPONIUM.

vicarius During the first two cents. AD, *vicarius* meant a substitute for an absent or deceased provincial governor. In the 3rd cent. *vicarii* were the equestrian *procurators of provinces who were specially appointed by the emperor to take the place of the regular senatorial governors. When *Diocletian grouped the provinces into twelve dioceses, each diocese (see DIOECESIS) was entrusted to a *vicarius*, so called because he was officially the deputy of the praetorian prefects (*vices agens praefectorum praetorio*). He supervised the provincial governors and heard appeals from their courts, but in practice he was often bypassed when the emperor wrote to provincial governors or they to him.

Jones, *Later Rom. Emp.* 47, 373–5.
R. S. O. T.

vicomagistri, officials of a *vicus, which was a miniature body politic, and was entitled to possess property, administer common funds, and appoint officials. These *magistri* or *vicomagistri*, who were allowed to wear the *toga praetexta, had a role in representing their community in the *res publica*. In the late republic the *vici* offered a chance of finding a sense of community in the chaotic life of the city, and so they and their leaders, like the leaders of the *collegia* (see COLLEGIUM, played an important part in the organization of mass politics.

Augustus reorganized the *vici* at the same time as the *regiones* (see REGIO). Their centre was a *compitum* or cross-roads, at which a cult of the *Lares or guardian deities of that locality was maintained, involving in particular a festival of the *compitum* called *ludi compitalicii* (see LUDI), which had often been a focus for disturbances in the late republic. The cult now came to include Augustan Lares and the *genius of the emperor. The *magistri*, who are now usually *freedmen (now four per *vicus), become more prominent in dedicating elaborate compital sanctuaries,

and from 7 BC counted a sequence of five-year periods or *lustra* in a sort of era to date their activities in relation to the Augustan reform. A role in the politically sensitive control of fires passed to the *vigiles in AD 6.

O. Robinson, *Ancient Rome: City-Planning and Administration* (1992); M. Flambard, *Ktema* 1981, 143–66.
N. P.

victimarius, sacrificial slaughterer; see SACRIFICE, ROMAN. The magistrate in charge of a sacrifice did not perform the act of killing himself; he performed symbolic acts and pronounced the prayers, but a *victimarius* took over the killing and butchering from him. In imperial times, we know that they formed a college of their own.

Latte, *RR* (1960), 383.
H. J. R.; J. A. N.

Victoria, the Roman equivalent of *Nike. There is no evidence that she is anything more, mentions of an early cult of Victory being referable to Vacuna or Vica Pota (Dion. Hal. *Ant. Rom.* 1. 15. 1; Asc. *Pis.*, p. 13. 15 Clark). She is associated in cult with *Jupiter (Victor), as in the *acta arvalium* (p. cxcviii Henzen), oftener with Mars (as ibid., p. clxv), also with other deities. She was worshipped by the army, as was natural (Domaszewski, *Rel. des röm. Heeres* (Westd. Zeit. 1895), 4 ff.), and hence is given surnames associating her with particular legions and more commonly still with emperors (list in Roscher, 6. 299; cf. J. Gagé, *Rev. Arch.* 1930, 1 ff., *Rev. Hist.* 1933, 1 ff.). Her temple on the clivus Victoriae leading up to the *Palatine dates from 294 BC (see Richardson, *Topogr. Dict. Anc. Rome* 420); from 204 BC it housed temporarily the sacred stone of her future neighbour, the Magna Mater (see CYBELE; PESSINUS; PHILHELLENISM). In 193 BC M. *Porcius Cato (1) added a shrine (*aedicula*) to her temple; in the early Principate both sanctuaries celebrated their anniversary on 1 August, no doubt because of Octavian's victory in *Alexandria (1) in 30 BC; see AUGUSTUS. Her most famous monument was perhaps her altar in the senate-house, put there by Augustus in 29 BC, removed under *Constantius II, replaced by the pagan party in Rome, removed again by *Gratian in 382, replaced for a short time by *Eugenius and perhaps once more by *Stilicho, and finally vanishing with the other vestiges of pagan cult (Ambrosius, *Epp.* 17, 18, 57. 6; cf. Paulinus, *Vit. Ambros.* 26; Symmachus, *Relat.* 3; Claudian, 28. 597).

Latte, in Roscher, *Lex.* and *RR*, see index; S. Weinstock, *Harv. Theol. Rev.* 1957, 211 ff.; T. Hölscher, *Victoria Romana* (1967); J. R. Fears, *Princeps a diis electus: The Divine Election of the Emperor as a Political Concept at Rome* (1977), 90 ff., and *ANRW* 2. 17. 1 (1981), 3 ff.
H. J. R.; J. Sch.

Victorinus, Marcus Piavvonius, praetorian prefect (see PRAEFECTUS PRAETORIO) of the Gallic usurper, *Postumus, whom he succeeded in AD 269 after the ephemeral reign of Marius. Though he abandoned *Spain and lost eastern Narbonensis (see GAUL (TRANSALPINE)) to *Claudius II Gothicus, he successfully resisted other efforts to undermine his regime and suppressed a major revolt at Autun (*Augustodunum). He was killed in a court-intrigue at Cologne (*Colonia Agrippinensis) in 271. He may have been of Gallic aristocratic origin. Upon his death, his mother, Victoria, acted as king-maker, and had *Tetricus chosen as his successor. (*PLRE* 1. 965.)

I. König, *Die gallischen Usurpatoren* (1981); J. F. Drinkwater, *The Gallic Empire* (1987).
J. F. Dr.

Victorinus, Marius (4th cent. AD; full name Gaius Marius Victorinus) was the author of philosophical (Neoplatonic), rhetorical, and grammatical works. His reputation was such that a statue in his honour was set up in the *forum Traiani. After becoming a Christian, he wrote theological treatises. Most of his *Ars grammatica* (ed. Keil, *Gramm. Lat.* 6. 3–184) has been ousted in our manuscripts by the *De metris* of *Aphthonius. His translations of *Plato (1), *Aristotle, and *Porphyry are lost, as is his commentary on the *Topics* of Cicero (see TULLIUS CICERO (1), M.); but his *explanationes* (a commentary) of the *De Inventione* of Cicero are preserved (ed. Halm, *Rhet. Lat. Min.* 155–304). His Christian writings (in Migne, *PL* 8) included commentaries on some Pauline epistles (see PAUL, ST.), *De trinitate contra Arium* ('On the Trinity against Arius' see ARIANISM), *De ὁμοουσίῳ recipiendo* (a treatise on 'Homoeanism', for which see again ARIANISM), and possibly a work against the Manichaeans (see MANICHAEISM). See also NEOPLATONISM.

Schanz–Hosius, sections 828–31a.; P. Hadot, *Marius Victorinus. Recherches sur sa vie et ses œuvres* (1971); J. F. Matthews, *Western Aristocracies and Imperial Court AD 364–425* (1975) 217; R. MacMullen, *Christianizing the Roman Empire AD 100–400* (1984) 69 and 149 n. 7.   J. F. Ma.; S. H.

Victorinus, Maximus See 'MAXIMUS VICTORINUS'.

Victorius (*RE* 2) **Marcellus, Marcus,** *suffect consul AD 105, from Teate Marrucinorum (mod. Chieti), dedicatee both of *Quintilian's *Institutio* (intended as a manual for his son Geta and a son of Quintilian's own) and of *Statius' *Silvae* book 4 (see esp. the fourth poem, which reveals that he was a practising orator and alludes to his post as *curator viae Latinae*, official in charge of the *via Latina; see CURA(TIO), CURATOR).

RE Suppl. 9. 1744; *ZPE* 37 (1980), 5 f.; K. M. Coleman, *Statius Silvae iv* (1988), 135–8.   M. W.

vicus, 'village', one of a series of Roman terms for settlements of lower status than towns (such as *pagus). In administrative law the term was used for places with recognizably independent institutions in the territory of a city or on a private estate. Like *pagi*, these communities and their magistrates were relatively important in the less urbanized parts of the Italian countryside in the late republic, and are quite well represented in the epigraphic record. The term was also used of local subdivisions of the city, cf. Greek *amphoda*, named after a street, local cult, or other landmark, and are found notably at Rome (though they are also attested in other cities). *Pliny (1) gives the number of vici at Rome as 265 (*HN* 3. 5. 66); they too had an independent institutional existence, and appointed officials known as *vicomagistri.

M. W. Frederiksen in P. Zanker (ed.), *Hellenismus in Mittelitalien* (1976), 341–55.   N. P.

Vienna (mod. Vienne), a town in Gallia Narbonensis (see GAUL (TRANSALPINE)), *civitas-capital of the *Allobroges. Perhaps created a *colonia Latina* by *Caesar, it was made a full colony by *Gaius (1) (as *Colonia Iulia Augusta Florentia Vienna*; see COLONIZATION, ROMAN). It subsequently flourished, even though, in 69, it narrowly escaped destruction from A. *Vitellius' army—encouraged by its jealous neighbour, *Lugdunum (1). In the later empire Vienne completely eclipsed Lugdunum, and rivalled *Arelate, becoming capital of the diocese of Viennensis, and seat of an important bishopric.

There exist very significant remains of this large straggling town, which spread beyond its Augustan *enceinte*. Most notable is the forum-temple of Rome and Augustus (originally Julio-Claudian, later altered and rededicated).

A. Pelletier, *Vienne antique* (1982); A. L. F. Rivet, *Gallia Narbonensis* (1988).   J. F. Dr.

vigiles Ancient cities made various arrangements for maintaining security at night; bands of night-wardens (*nuktophulakes*) were more often aimed at the prevention of sedition than the protection of property from theft, but fire, accidental or deliberate, was always the main preoccupation. Order in republican Rome was the responsibility of junior magistrates called *tresviri capitales* (see VIGINTISEXVIRI) who were replaced at night by *quinqueviri cis Tiberim* (a team of five men with duties 'this side of *Tiber') because senators could not be expected to be on duty at unseasonable hours.

The political importance of fire-protection at Rome had been recognized by M. *Licinius Crassus (1) and was exploited by M. *Egnatius Rufus. Augustus gave the *aediles a force of 600 slaves to deal with the problem after a fire in 23 BC (Cass. Dio 54. 2); in 7 the city was reorganized into *regiones* and *vici* (see REGIO; VICUS) and the officials of the latter made responsible for fire-prevention (Cass. Dio 55. 8); in AD 6 he created a very substantial force from the freedman population: 'one of the biggest fire-brigades in relation to its ground area, of all time' (Rainbird). By the 3rd cent. some 7,000 *vigiles* were distributed in one cohort of 1,000 men for each pair of *regiones*, housed in purpose-built barracks (*excubitoria*); only fragments of these have been explored at Rome, but a well-preserved example survives at *Ostia, where a detachment of *vigiles* on the Roman model was set up in the later 1st cent. The earlier strength may have been little more than half this figure, but was still designed to cope with fires by the rapid deployment of manpower to demolish buildings rather than by extinguishing the flames directly (which was beyond the available technology).

Their commander was an equestrian *praefectus (see EQUITES, Imperial period) who became also a judge in petty criminal cases (*Dig.* 1. 15. 3); the post was one of the more senior in the equestrian *cursus* (i.e. career path, cf. CURSUS HONORUM). See also POLICE.

O. Robinson, *Ancient Rome: City-Planning and Administration* (1992), 105–10; J. Rainbird, *PBSR* 1986, 147–69; P. K. Baillie Reynolds, *The Vigiles of Imperial Rome* (1926).   N. P.

vigintisexviri, vigintiviri Six boards of minor magistrates at Rome were known by the collective designation *vigintisexviri* (the Twenty-Six) in the late republic: membership was a precursor to the quaestorship and the beginning of a senatorial career (Cic. *Leg.* 3. 3. 6; the collective title is attested in inscriptions); see CURSUS HONORUM. The label may be late, even post-Sullan (i.e. after about 80 BC, see CORNELIUS SULLA FELIX, L.), but the administrative theory involved is probably of the 3rd cent., the date attributed to the creation of all the boards by Sex. *Pomponius (*Digest* 1. 2. 2. 31). The most important board, the judicial *decemviri stlitibus iudicandis*, may have much earlier origins (Livy, 3. 55 suggests the existence of a ten-man panel of *iudices* in the 5th cent.), and the practice of sending *praefecti* (see PRAEFECTUS) to *Campania, if not the developed institution of the four *praefecti Capuam Cumas*, may have begun in 318 BC (Livy, 9. 20; major changes followed the Hannibalic War; see PUNIC WARS). The *tresviri capitales* or *nocturni* had a police-function in Rome (see POLICE; TRIUMVIRI); the *tresviri monetales* or *aere argento auro flando feriundo* were in charge of minting coin (for the *monetales* or moneyers see COINAGE, ROMAN); the *quattuorviri viis in urbe purgandis* and *duoviri viis extra urbem purgandis* (boards of four and two respectively) oversaw the maintenance of streets in Rome and its immediate environs respectively. The last, with the *praefecti Capuam Cumas*, were abolished by *Augustus (in 13 BC according to Cass. Dio 54. 26. 7), leaving the whole collectivity as *vigintiviri* (the Twenty). All four remaining boards continued to function, though with changed responsibilities, in the senatorial *cursus* until the 3rd cent.

Mommsen, *Röm. Staatsr.* 2. 592–610; O. Robinson, *Ancient Rome: City-Planning and Administration* (1992).   N. P.

villa was the Latin word for a rural dwelling associated with an estate, and ranging in character from functional farms to the luxurious country seats of the élite (Varro, *Rust.* 1. 11. 1–12. 4; 3. 2. 1–2. 18). Most of the literary evidence relates to Italy and primarily described farms run for the benefit of urban-based proprietors (Vitr. *De arch.* 6. 6. 1), though the most opulent seaside villas of the Roman aristocracy were sometimes built solely for pleasure. Aristocratic enjoyment of rural retreats and pride in creating architectural splendours there are well attested (Pliny, *Ep.* 2. 17). However, the classic Italian villa, comprising a luxurious dwelling for the use of the owner on visits to the estate (*pars urbana*), the working *farm buildings (*pars rustica*), and the storage buildings and barns (*pars fructuaria*), is perfectly illustrated by the excavations at *Settefinestre, with its aristocratic *domus* (mansion), baths, slave quarters, wine and olive presses, piggery, substantial granary, and formal gardens (Carandini and others, 1985; cf. Columella, *Rust.* 1. 4. 6–6. 24). The development of villas in different regions of Italy from the 2nd cent. BC is generally equated with the rise of large slave-run estates (see LATIFUNDIA), though these regions commonly exhibit divergent patterns of rural settlement and varied types of villa (from simple farmhouses to 'palaces'). Similarly the relative success and longevity of villas differed from one part of Italy to another: certain coastal areas famous for viticulture in the late republic had declined markedly by the 2nd cent. AD, whereas villas in some inland areas survived into late antiquity.

Provincial villa studies suffer from a geographical imbalance, with far more excavated and published sites in north-western Europe than from the Mediterranean countries. In peripheral territories such as *Britain, where it can be exceedingly difficult to decide whether a particular structure would have been considered a villa by the Romans themselves, different criteria have commonly been used to define villas, encompassing aspects of Romanized construction or lifestyle (characterized by mosaics, painted plaster, hypocausts, baths, use of dressed stone and tile, etc.). Mediterranean-style peristyle houses are uncommon in Britain and Belgica (see GAUL (TRANSALPINE)), where winged corridor and aisled buildings tend to predominate, and other regions reveal their own characteristic styles. Important new approaches to villas in Britain look beyond their main Romanized buildings, to explore subsidiary farm buildings, field systems, pre-Roman and sub-Roman phases, and palaeoeconomic evidence for crops and livestock. See AGRICULTURE, ROMAN.

J. Percival, *The Roman Villa* (1976); A. G. McKay, *Houses, Villas and Palaces in the Roman World* (1975); H. Mielsch, *La villa romana* (It. trans. 1990); A. Carandini and others, *Settefinestre: Una villa schiavistica nell'Etruria romana* (1985); R. C. Carrington, *JRS* 1931, 110 ff.; M. Cotton, *The Late Republican Villa at Posto, Francolise* (1979); M. Cotton and G. Metraux, *The San Rocco Villa at Francolise* (1985); J. D'Arms, *Romans on the Bay of Naples* (1970); A. L. F. Rivet, *The Roman Villa in Britain* (1969); M. Todd, *Studies in the Romano-British Villa* (1978); K. Branigan and D. Miles, *The Economies of Romano-British Villas* (1988); D. Neal and others, *Excavation of the Iron Age, Roman and Medieval Settlement of Gorhambury, St Albans* (1990); J. G. Gorges, *Les Villas hispano-romaines: Inventaire et problématique archéologiques* (1979); E. M. Wightman, *ANRW* 2. 1. 584 ff.; J. Rossiter, *JRA* 1989, 101 ff.; S. Alcock, *Graecia Capta* (1993), index (for Roman Greece).   D. J. Ma.

Villanovan culture takes its name from the Bolognese estate owned by G. Gozzadini, who in 1853 excavated near by the first of many iron age cemeteries in the modern provinces of Bologna, Faenza, Forli, and Ravenna. The term is applied not only to these cemeteries of the 9th cent. BC onwards, but also to their contemporaries south of the Apennines, around the previously uninhabited iron age centres destined for continuing greatness as *Etruscan cities. Further south still, the Villanovan phenomenon is represented at *Capua, *Pontecagnano, and Sala Consilina in Campania; and there is also an isolated Villanovan cemetery at Fermo in the Marche.

Both north and south of the *Apennines, the Villanovan culture is characterized in its original form by cremation burials in biconical ossuaries with incised decoration. There were no such people as 'the Villanovans', in spite of the fact that this unjustified ethnic extrapolation from the modern toponym of an archaeological site has often been used in juxtaposition with the historical Etruscans to imply the substitution, or even invasion, of the former by the latter. In fact, the indigenous possessors of the Villanovan culture of the 9th and 8th cents. in Etruria may confidently be defined as *Etruscans at the iron age stage of their ethnic formation and already in receipt of the influences that reached the Tyrrhenian seaboard from the outside world. These began to arrive in the first half of the 8th cent., with the Greek and other entrepreneurs who, prior to the establishment of the Euboean *emporion at *Pithecusae (see EUBOEA), were keen to exploit the resources of the metal-rich region of north-west Etruria. Their impact is most clearly reflected by evidence from Villanovan contexts in southern Etruria for an increased awareness of the industrial possibilities of bronze and iron, accompanied by imported Greek Geometric pottery and competent local versions of it—some at least of which are likely to have been made by immigrant Euboean potters (based most probably at *Veii). The presence of imported material of known date in numerous Villanovan graves in southern Etruria and *Campania (even if opinions vary as to the precise dates involved) has made it possible to convert a number of local sequences into more or less reliably dated phases. In southern Etruria, the transition from Villanovan to *orientalizing, and so to Etruscan, was complete by the beginning of the 7th cent. By then, too, there is a not inconsiderable body of evidence for commercial and cultural contact and exchange across the Apennines, particularly between Veii and Bologna (*Bononia). The sheer density of the Villanovan concentration around the latter site must surely mean that it was playing an important part in commercial expansion to the north long before the foundation of *Felsina in the 6th cent.

Unfortunately, knowledge of the Villanovan culture is derived to a large extent from funerary evidence. From such settlements as have been investigated (e.g. at *San Giovenale), it seems safe to conclude that Villanovan economy was based on agriculture, stock-raising, and hunting; an extensive use of the horse is indicated by the numerous horse-bits found in graves. By at least the middle of the 8th cent., the fine quality both of pottery and of cast and sheet bronze indicates that their production had passed into the hands of professional craftsmen. This early degree of craft specialization accords well with the signs of the growing complexity and proto-urban nature of Villanovan society that emerge from the analysis of the grave goods associated with the predominantly single depositions made—in their thousands—in the Villanovan cemeteries. The dimensions and temporal range of many of these speak volumes for an unprecedented degree of stability in settlement. Late 8th-cent. graves that have yielded particularly rich selections of the sophisticated artefacts required for the exercise of the martial arts, personal adornment, feasting and drinking may reasonably be assigned to members of the nascent élite that finds its fullest archaeological expression in the 'princely' graves of the succeeding orientalizing period in Etruria and Campania.

H. Müller-Karpe, *Beiträge zur Chronologie der Urnenfelderzeit nördlich und südlich der Alpen* (1959), discussed by M. Pallottino, *Stud. Etr.* 1960, 11 ff.; B. d'Agostino, in *PCIA* 2 (1974), 11 ff.; M. Zuffa, in *PCIA* 5 (1976), 199 ff.; W. Johannowsky, *Materiali di età arcaica della Campania* (1983); M. A. Fugazzola Delpino, *La cultura villanoviana* (1984: Villa Giulia museum, Rome); D. Ridgway, in *CAH* 4² (1988), 640 ff., and *The First Western Greeks* (1992), 121 ff.; G. Bartoloni, *La cultura villanoviana* (1989); R. Peroni, in *PCIA* 9 (1989), 395 ff.; C. Belardelli and others, *L'Europa a sud e a nord delle Alpi alle soglie della svolta protourbana* (1990). D. W. R. R.

Villius (*RE* 5) **(Annalis), Lucius,** tribune of the *plebs* in 180 BC (see TRIBUNI PLEBIS), passed the first law to stipulate minimum ages for tenure of each (curule) magistracy (42 for the consulship); see MAGISTRACY, ROMAN. It was possibly this law which required an interval of two years between curule magistracies. Villius' measure probably aimed to regulate the number of men campaigning for higher office in any one year: Livy implies that his law was built upon the *lex Baebia* of 181 (see BAEBIUS TAMPHILUS, M.), which contained an anti-electoral bribery provision (see AMBITUS) as well as a (short-lived) requirement that four and six praetors respectively be elected in alternate years (thereby reducing competition for the consulship). The provisions of the *lex Villia annalis* remained largely unchanged until the Principate, when the minimum ages were lowered.

Livy, 40. 44. 1–2; cf. 19. 11. See A. Astin, *The Lex Annalis before Sulla* (1958); R. J. Evans and M. Kleijwegt, *ZPE* 92 (1992), 181–95. T. C. B.

Viminacium (mod. Kostolac), on the Danube east of Belgrade, was a Celtic settlement (see CELTS) which became a legionary fortress and city in *Moesia Superior. Its permanent garrison (probably from AD 56/7) was Legio VII Claudia (see LEGION); for a period under *Trajan it was also occupied by Legio IV Flavia. The civil settlement became a *municipium (Aelium) under *Hadrian and a *colonia under *Gordian III.

Inscriptions de la Mésie Superieure 2, ed. M. Mirković (1986). J. J. W.

Viminal, one of the *Seven hills of Rome. It lay between the *Esquiline and the *Quirinal.

Vinalia, Roman wine festivals on 23 April (*Priora*), 19 August (*Rustica*). The *Priora* probably offered *Jupiter new wine at the time of sale (Plin. *HN* 18. 287, *fasti Praenestini*); Ov. *Fast.* 4. 863 ff. with Bömer's notes, Plutarch, *Quaest. Rom.* 45 with Rose's notes. Varro, *Rust.* 1. 1. 6 substitutes *Venus (cf. *Ling.* 6. 16), chronologically difficult since her first temple (Venus Obsequens) was dedicated 295 BC (Livy, 10. 31. 9), understandable from its 19 August dedication. The *Rustica* propitiated the weather; Plin. *HN.* 18. 284: *tria namque tempora fructibus metuebant* ('they feared three times of year for the crops').

Inscr. Ital. 13. 2. 446 ff., 497 ff.; F. Bömer, *Rh. Mus.* 1941, 30 ff.; G. Dumézil, *Fêtes romaines d'été et d'automne* (1975), 87 ff.; R. Schilling, *La Religion romaine de Vénus* (1954), 91 ff. C. R. P.

Vindelici, a people of mainly Celtic origin (see CELTS) but including Illyrian (see ILLYRII) and other elements, inhabited the Schwabian–Bavarian plateau and reached from the southern slopes of the *Alps up to the Danube. Conquered by *Tiberius and Nero *Claudius Drusus in 15 BC, they later occupied the eastern part of the province of *Raetia (Vindelicia). Though their name was commemorated in the city of *Augusta Vindelicorum (mod. Augsburg) their general *Romanization appears fragile. See RAETIA.

G. Gottlieb (ed.), *Raumordnung im römischen Reich* (1989), 75 ff.
J. J. W.; J. F. Dr.

Vindex See IULIUS VINDEX, C.

vindicatio See OWNERSHIP.

Vindobona (mod. Vienna) on the Danube, lay in the territory of the *Boii, a Celtic people (see CELTS) included within *Pannonia (Superior). In the 1st cent. AD it was garrisoned by the *Ala Flavia Domitiana Augusta Britannica milliaria civium Romanorum* (under *Domitian: *CIL* 3. 15197; see ALAE). At the beginning of *Trajan's reign, probably on the occasion of his visit in 98, Legio XIII Gemina (see LEGION) was moved there from *Poetovio and began the construction of a legionary fortress before it departed for the Dacian Wars (*CIL* 3. 14359 no. 32). In its place came Legio XIV Gemina Martia Victrix, which remained until the end of Trajan's reign when it moved to *Carnuntum, while Legio X Gemina was moved from *Aquincum to become the permanent garrison at Vindobona.

At some date in the 3rd cent. a civil settlement became a *municipium (*CIL* 3. 4557) while Vindobona was also a *statio* (base) of the *classis Histrica* or Danube fleet (*Not. Dign.* [*occ.*] 34. 28). Though not in administrative terms the equal of Carnuntum, Vindobona was an important fortress, especially in the Marcomannic Wars (see MARCOMANNI), during which it was apparently destroyed, though rebuilt almost immediately. Marcus *Aurelius died there. Later (perhaps from *c.*406) Vindobona was lost to the empire to be controlled in the 6th cent. by Langobardi (*Lombards) and subsequently by Avars (see AVARO-SLAV INVASIONS).

A. Neumann, *Vindobona: Die römische Vergangenheit Wiens* (1980).
J. J. W.

Vindolanda tablets During the 1970s and 1980s several hundred wooden writing-tablets were discovered at the Roman fort of Vindolanda near Hadrian's Wall (see WALL OF HADRIAN); a further 400 turned up in 1993. Of the earlier finds, some were of the well-known stylus type, but the vast majority were made of thin, wooden leaves, written in ink with a pen. Only a handful of tablets of this type was previously known, and the concentration of such numbers at one site is unique. They date between *c.* AD 90 and 120, when the fort was occupied first by Cohors I Tungrorum and later by Cohors IX Batavorum (see COHORS).

The Vindolanda material includes the largest group of Latin letters ever discovered (see LETTERS, LATIN). There are also literary fragments, shorthand texts, military reports, applications for leave, and accounts. The letters often bear on the official and private concerns of the officers, their families, and slaves, while the military documents tell us much about the way the Romans organized a newly acquired frontier area. In addition the tablets provide valuable information on *palaeography and the *Latin language.

A. K. Bowman, J. D. Thomas, *The Vindolanda Writing-Tablets (Tabulae Vindolandenses II)* (1994); J. N. Adams, *JRS* 1995, 86 ff. J. D. T.

Vindonissa (mod. Windisch, Switzerland), a prehistoric site on the lower Aar, occupied *c.* AD 17 by Legio XIII, which was replaced in 45–6 by Legio XXI Rapax (see LEGION), whose violent behaviour to the *Helvetii induced *Vespasian to send it elsewhere. Legio XI Claudia Pia Fidelis then held Vindonissa to *c.*100, when it was realized that the site was too far from any theatre of war. A considerable civil population remained, at least until the troubles of the mid-3rd cent. In the late empire a small fort was built near by. The fortress and the forum of the *canabae* have been partially excavated.

R. Fellman, *Hist.* 1955, 209 ff.; R. Laur-Belart, *Führer durch . . . Vindonissa*[4] (1969). C. E. S.; J. F. Dr.

Vinicius (*RE* 5), **Lucius** (*suffect consul 5 BC), a relation of P. and M. *Vinicius (see next two entries). *Augustus commented on his extempore pleading (Sen. *Controv.* 2. 5. 20) and his association with *Iulia (2) at *Baiae (Suet. *Aug.* 64).

Schanz–Hosius, § 336. 9. 23; R. Syme, *History in Ovid* (1978), 92. M. W.

Vinicius (*RE* 6), **Marcus** (*suffect consul 19 BC), a *novus homo* from *Cales in *Campania, is first mentioned as legate (see LEGATI) of *Augustus in Gaul (25 BC). In *Illyricum (13 BC, perhaps as proconsul; see PRO CONSULE) he and M. *Vipsanius Agrippa began the *bellum Pannonicum* (war in *Pannonia) terminated by *Tiberius (12–9). Vinicius is next (and last) heard of in AD 1 or 2 as commander of the Rhine army. The acephalous (= top missing) elogium from *Tusculum, recording operations against Transdanubian peoples (*ILS* 8965 = EJ 43a) is now generally attributed to Vinicius, but the dating and details of that campaign are uncertain (14–13, 10, and *c.*1 BC have been suggested). The historian *Velleius Paterculus enjoyed the patronage of the Vinicii, dedicating his work to the grandson, M. Vinicius.

R. Syme, *CQ* 1933, 142 ff. (= *Danubian Pap.* (1971), 26 ff.); *Hist.* 1962, 148 (= *RP* 2. 532); A. v. Premerstein, *JÖAI* 1934, 60 ff. R. S.; B. M. L.

Vinicius (*RE* 8), **Publius** (consul AD 2), declaimer and orator, son of M. *Vinicius (above). An admirer of *Ovid, he was praised for his preciseness (Sen. *Controv.* 7. 5. 11, 10. 4. 25). He was proconsul (see PRO CONSULE) of Asia, and emerges under *Tiberius (Tac. *Ann.* 3. 11). See also MOESIA.

Schanz–Hosius § 336. 9. 24; R. Syme, *History in Ovid* (1978), 68, 92. M. W.

Vinius (*RE* 5), **Titus,** influential associate of *Galba and his colleague as consul in AD 69, had been imprisoned while military tribune (see TRIBUNI MILITUM) in Germany in 39 on the charge of adultery with his commanding officer's wife. Released by *Claudius he served as legionary legate but incurred further disgrace for allegedly stealing a gold cup at the emperor's banquet. Nevertheless his subsequent governorship of Gallia Narbonensis (see GAUL (TRANSALPINE)) was creditable. He was in Spain when Galba rebelled, possibly commanding legio VI Victrix (see LEGION). Unscrupulous and cunning, he urged the adoption of *Otho, but was nevertheless murdered along with Galba by Otho's troops. *Tacitus (1) is probably mistaken in giving his age as 57 (*Hist.* 1. 48), which would mean that he was unusually old (28) during his military tribunate. J. B. C.

violence For *Greece* see HUBRIS; RECIPROCITY (GREECE); also A. W. Lintott, *Violence, Civil Strife and Revolution in the Classical City* (1982); G. Herman, *CQ* 1993, 406 ff., and in R. Osborne and S. Hornblower (eds.), *Ritual, Finance, Politics* (1994), 9 ff., and in W. Eder (ed.), *Die athenische Demokratie im 4. Jahrhundert v. Chr.* (1995), 43 ff. For *Rome* see VIS.

Vipsania Agrippina (1) (d. AD 20) was daughter of M. *Vipsanius Agrippa and granddaughter of T. *Pomponius Atticus.

Married to *Tiberius, she bore him a son, Nero *Claudius Drusus, but he was forced by Augustus, against his will, to divorce her and marry Julia (see IULIA (3)) in 12 BC. She then married C. *Asinius Gallus and bore him at least five sons.

J. P. B.; A. J. S. S.

Vipsania Agrippina (2), 'the Elder Agrippina' (*c.*14 BC–AD 33), the daughter of M. *Vipsanius Agrippa and of *Iulia ((3), daughter of *Augustus). She married *Germanicus (probably in AD 5), to whom she bore nine children. She was with Germanicus on the Rhine from 14 to 16 and in the east from 18 until his death in the following year. From 19 to 29 she lived in Rome, the rallying point of a party of senators who opposed the growing power of Sejanus (see AELIUS SEIANUS, L.). With *Tiberius, whom she suspected (without evidence) of causing her husband's death, her relations were consistently bad, and he refused her request in 26 for leave to marry again. She was arrested in 29 on the instruction of Tiberius and banished by the senate to Pandateria (cf. ISLANDS), where she starved to death in 33. She was survived by one son, the future emperor *Gaius (1), and three daughters, *Iulia Agrippina, *Iulia Drusilla, and *Iulia (5).

A. Barrett, *Caligula* (1989), 4 ff. Portraits: Fittschen and Zanker, 3, no. 4 with refs. J. P. B.; A. J. S. S.

Vipsanius (*RE* 2) **Agrippa, Marcus,** the lifelong friend and supporter of *Augustus, was born in 64, 63, or even 62 BC of obscure but probably well-to-do family (he neglected his undistinguished family name). He accompanied Octavius (the future Octavian and Augustus) to Rome from *Apollonia after *Caesar's murder, helped him to raise a private army, prosecuted *Cassius in the court set up by Q. *Pedius in 43, and was prominent in the war against L. *Antonius (Pietas). After holding the tribunate of the *plebs* (see TRIBUNI PLEBIS) in 43 or a little later, and so entering the *senate, he was urban praetor in 40. As governor of Gaul in 38 he suppressed a rebellion in *Aquitania, led a punitive expedition across the Rhine, and either now or in 20 settled the *Ubii on the left bank. As consul (37) he fitted out and trained a new fleet for Octavian's war against Sextus *Pompeius, converting the lacus *Avernus near *Cumae into a harbour (portus Iulius) for the purpose, and in 36 won two decisive naval engagements at Mylae and Naulochus, where his improved grapnel was highly effective. In 35–34 he took part in the Illyrian War. Although an ex-consul he held the aedileship in 33, contributing greatly to Octavian's popularity. In 31 his vigorous naval operations were the primary cause of Mark Antony's defeat (see ANTONIUS (2), M.); at *Actium he commanded the left wing. He next (31–29), with *Maecenas, managed affairs in Italy in Octavian's absence. On Octavian's return he helped carry out a purge of the senate and a *census (29–8) and held second and third consulships in the crucial years 28 and 27. In 23 Augustus, ill and embroiled in political controversy, handed him his signet-ring, conferring an unofficial status (most importantly in the eyes of the armies) that would have meant his supremacy if Augustus had died. He was entrusted with a mission in the eastern half of the empire, probably with proconsular power (see PRO CONSULE), which he carried out from *Mytilene. The claim that rivalry with Augustus' nephew M. *Claudius Marcellus (5) had sent him into virtual exile cannot be substantiated. More likely it was a constitutional crisis, with Agrippa put in easy reach of the armies of the Balkans and Syria if Augustus' position were undermined or his life threatened. He was recalled in 21 to represent Augustus in Rome; in 20 he proceeded to Gaul and in 19 to Spain where he quelled the *Cantabri. In 18 he was given tribunician power (see TRIBUNI

PLEBIS, end of entry) for five years, a power held otherwise only by Augustus, and his *imperium was renewed for the same period. In 13 his tribunician power was renewed for five more years, and his *imperium apparently made superior to that of all other holders, like that of Augustus (the extent and development of Agrippa's powers, outlined in the fragmentary papyrus (*Kölner Pap.* 1 (1976), 10 = EJ 366) that contains part of Augustus' funerary elogium on him, remains controversial). As a *quindecimvir sacris faciundis (from before 37) he assisted in the celebration of the *Secular Games in 17. His second mission to the east (17 / 16–13) is notable for the establishment of *Polemon (1) of Pontus in the Bosporan kingdom, the settlement of veterans at *Berytus and *Heliopolis, and his friendship with *Herod (1) and benevolent treatment of the *Jews. Early in 12 he went to *Pannonia where there was a danger of revolt, but fell ill on his return and died about the end of March. After a public funeral he was buried in the mausoleum of Augustus.

Agrippa's wealth was spent freely in the service of the Roman people and the empire, winning him lasting popularity. He restored the sewers of Rome and reorganized the water supply, constructing two new *aqueducts (Iulia, 33 BC, and Virgo, 19 BC), and a network of distribution installations. Virgo fed Rome's first public *baths, close to his *Pantheon, and the expanded *Saepta Iulia (26 BC), all in a huge recreational area. He also built a granary (horrea Agrippiana) behind the Forum (*forum Romanum) and a new bridge over the *Tiber. Constructions in the provinces included buildings at *Nemausus and a road system radiating from *Lugdunum (1). By his will Augustus received the greater part of his property, including the Thracian Chersonese (see CHERSONESUS (1)); he also made generous bequests to the people of Rome.

He wrote an autobiography (now lost) and a geographical commentary (also lost, but used by *Strabo and *Pliny (1)) from which a map of the empire was constructed, to be displayed after his death on the porticus Vipsania (see MAPS).

Agrippa was married three times: in 37 to *Caecilia Attica, in 28 to Augustus' niece the elder Marcella, whom he divorced in 21 to marry Augustus' daughter *Iulia (3). The first two wives produced daughters, Attica's including *Vipsania Agrippina (1), the first wife of the later emperor *Tiberius, Marcella's the Vipsania who married P. *Quinctilius Varus. Iulia had three sons, Gaius *Iulius Caesar (2) and Lucius *Iulius Caesar (4), who were adopted by Augustus in 17, and Agrippa *Iulius Caesar (Agrippa Postumus); and two daughters, *Iulia (4) and *Agrippina (2); through her he was grandfather and great-grandfather respectively of the emperors *Gaius (1) and *Nero.

Agrippa, portrayed as upright, simple, and modest, a man who subordinated his ambitions to those of Augustus, was by 12 BC a partner nearly equal in power. Refusing three *triumphs (19 BC onwards) and failing even to report his Spanish successes inhibited private men from applying and contributed to the end of such triumphs. Like his advocacy of public display of works of art (he was a noted collector), it went against the interests of the ruling class, who boycotted his funeral games. To Augustus he may sometimes have been an embarrassment.

M. Reinhold, *Marcus Agrippa* (1933); R. Daniel, *M. Vipsanius Agrippa* (1933); J.-M. Roddaz, *Marcus Agrippa*, Bibl. Éc. fr. d'Ath. et de Rome 253 (1983); Syme, *Rom. Rev.*, and *AA*; L. Koenen, *ZPE* 5 (1970), 217 ff.; E. W. Gray, *ZPE* 6 (1970), 227 ff.; E. Badian, *CJ* 1980, 97 ff. (elogium); F. W. Shipley, *Agrippa's Building Activities in Rome* (1933); Schanz–Hosius, 2. 329 ff.; P. Zanker, *The Power of Images in the Age of Augustus* (1988); A. Klotz, *Klio* 1931, 35 ff.; 386 ff. (geography); J. J. Tierney, *Proc.* Royal Irish Acad. 1963, 151 ff. (map); F. Poulsen, *Röm. Privatporträts und Prinzenbildnisse* (1939), 11 ff.; *CAH* 10² (1996), see index.

G. W. R.; T. J. C.; B. M. L.

Vipstanus (*RE* 6) **Messalla,** great-grandson of M. *Valerius Messalla Messallinus, military tribune in AD 69 (see TRIBUNI MILITUM), took temporary command of Legio VII Claudia (see LEGION) at the battle of *Cremona. He was perhaps a source for the account of the campaign in *Tacitus (1), who names him twice (*Hist.* 3. 25, 28). In Tacitus' *Dialogus*, he is a defender of classical orators against more recent fashions. Messalla spoke for his half-brother M. *Aquilius Regulus when he was attacked in 70 (Tac. *Hist.* 4. 42). He probably died young, but his son was consul in 115.

H. H. S.; B. M. L.

Virgil (Publius Vergilius Maro) (70–19 BC), Roman poet. The contemporary spelling of Virgil's name was with an *e*: the first occurrence with an *i* is on an honorific inscription to *Claudian in Greek (*CIL* 6. 1710 = *ILS* 1. 2949). Virgil is traditional in English, but the slightly historicizing Vergil is preferred by some modern critics. Virgil and his friends in any case punned on *virgo*, a virgin (*G.* 4. 564, perhaps 1. 430, *Donatus (1)'s 'Life' of Virgil 11). *Varius Rufus is said to have written on Virgil (Quint. 10. 3. 8) and there were other accounts by friends and acquaintances (cf. Gell. *NA* 17. 10. 2): the extant lives go back in part to *Suetonius, *De poetis*. Much (but not all) of the information in them derives from interpretation of the poems (including the spurious ones in the *Appendix Vergiliana*), and few details, however circumstantial, can be regarded as certain.

Nevertheless, Virgil is said to have been born on 15 October 70 BC in Andes, a village near *Mantua. *Macrobius (*Sat.* 5. 2. 1) says that he was 'born in the Veneto of country parents and brought up amongst the woods and shrubs', and his father is variously described as a potter and a courier who married the boss's daughter (*Vit. Don.* 1), but the real status of the family is uncertain. His mother was a Magia: both the *gentes* (see GENS) covered a spectrum of social levels. Virgil is said to have been educated in *Cremona and Milan (*Mediolanum) before coming to Rome (*Vit. Don.* 7) and the family would clearly have had to be sufficiently well-off for such an education to be feasible. At some stage Virgil was associated with the Epicurean (see EPICURUS) community in Naples (*Neapolis; see M. Gigante, *Stud. Ital.* 1989, 3–6: his name appears in a papyrus from *Herculaneum with *Plotius Tucca, Varius Rufus, and P. *Quinctilius Varus); *Catalepton* 5 and 8, if either genuine or based on a sound biographical tradition, have him fleeing from the normal rhetorical education of a Roman to Epicurean retirement (cf. *G.* 4. 563–4, where he is again (?) enjoying *otium*, leisure, in Naples).

After the defeat of the *tyrannicides in 42 BC, Octavian (see AUGUSTUS) attempted to settle members of his army on confiscated land (see PROSCRIPTION), a controversial move which led to the Perusine War (see PERUSIA): full-scale war between Antony (M. *Antonius (2)) and Octavian was only narrowly (and temporarily) avoided by the treaty of *Brundisium in 40 BC. Virgil's first collection of poems, the *Eclogues*, probably appeared around 39–38 BC (controversial: see R. J. Tarrant and G. W. Bowersock in *Harv. Stud.* 1978, 197–202) in the midst of the turmoil: the confiscations are a central topic in *Eclogues* 1 and 9. In the first poem, a slave Tityrus says that he has to thank a young man for freedom and security (1. 42): in the context of the times, this can only be Octavian. Other poems mention a Varus (6. 7, 9. 27), presumably the jurist P. *Alfenus Varus, suffect consul 39 BC, C. *Asinius Pollio (4. 12, and probably the addressee of 8—for the controversy, see Tarrant and Bowersock), consul 40 BC, one of Antony's most important supporters and an architect of the Peace of Brundisium, and the important *eques* and poet C. *Cornelius Gallus (6. 64–73, 10 *passim*). These three men are said to have been involved in the distribution of land, though the arrangements are uncertain and the Virgilian commentators our only source (cf. *MRR* 2. 377–8). The biographical tradition says that Virgil's father's land was amongst the land confiscated, and some personal experience of loss is suggested by *Ecl.* 9. 27–9 'Mantua, all too near to unhappy Cremona' and *G.* 2. 198 'the land unfortunate Mantua lost', but it is impossible to know how many of the details derive from allegorical reading of the poems.

At some time after the publication of the *Eclogues*, Virgil entered the circle of *Maecenas, and thus of the future Augustus. He is mentioned several times in the first book of *Horace's *Satires*, published at the end of the decade; in 1. 6. 55 he is said to have introduced Horace to Maecenas, and in 1. 5 (40, 48) he is described as joining the 'journey to Brundisium'. The dramatic date of the latter poem is 38 or 37, depending on which of the two possible diplomatic missions it is associated with (cf. I. M. Le M. DuQuesnay, in T. Woodman and D. West, *Poetry and Politics in the Age of Augustus* (1984), 39–43). In the concluding satire of the book (1. 10. 45, cf. 81) Virgil is one of the poets whose achievements Horace contrasts with his own: 'to Virgil the Muses who delight in the countryside have granted tenderness and charm' (*molle atque facetum*, trans. P. M. Brown). The sixteenth of Horace's *Epodes* (*Iambi*), also published at the end of the 30s, parodies *Ecl.* 4 in a context which highlights the violent alternation of hope and despair which characterized the decade.

The publication of Virgil's second major work, the *Georgics*, is usually dated to 29 BC; the battle of *Actium (31 BC) is referred to in *Georgics* 3. 28–9 and according to the Donatus life, Virgil read the poem to Octavian 'after his return from the victory at Actium' (*Vit. Don.* 27): Octavian reached Italy in the summer of 29 BC, and celebrated a great 'triple triumph' in August of that year, though the description of his achievements as depicted on the metaphorical temple at the opening of *Georgic* 3 (26–39) can plausibly be dated before or after this triumph. There was a story that the work had originally ended with praise of Cornelius Gallus, which was removed after his fall and suicide in 26 BC (Servius on *Ecl.* 10. 1; *G.* 4. 1) but this is unlikely to be true (J. Griffin, *Latin Poets and Roman Life* (1985), 180–2).

Like the *Eclogues*, the *Georgics* are a constant presence in the poetry of the 20s BC, but by the time that the final poem of *Propertius' second (?) book of elegies is published some time after Gallus' death (2. 34. 91–2), 'something greater than the *Iliad* is being brought to birth' (2. 34. 66), that is, the *Aeneid*. Macrobius quotes a letter from Virgil to Augustus declining to send any samples as more work is needed; this may be a reply to the letter of Augustus quoted at *Vit. Don.* 31 asking for a sketch or fragment, and to be dated to 27–25 BC since Augustus is described as away from Rome in Spain. It is possible, however, that more scepticism as to the genuineness of these letters is in order. Horace, *Odes* 1. 3 addresses a ship carrying a Vergilius to Greece; if this is taken to be Virgil, the bold enterprise of the ship's journey may also be read metapoetically of the vast undertaking of the *Aeneid*. The tradition claims that books 2 (or 3), 4, and 6 were recited to Augustus, the reference to the young M. *Claudius Marcellus (5) in 6 causing *Octavia (2) to faint (*Vit. Don.* 32; Servius on *Aen.* 4. 323, 6. 861); this episode, whether true or not, must be set after the death of Marcellus in 23 BC. Virgil himself, however, died in 19 BC, with the poem apparently felt to be unfinished: 'in the 42nd year of his life, intending to finish the *Aeneid*, he decided to go off to Greece and Asia Minor, and to spend three straight years simply in correcting the poem, to leave the rest of his life free for philosophy. But when he had set out on his trip, he met Augustus in Athens returning to Rome from the east, and decided not to go off, and even to return with Augustus. He visited a small town near *Megara in very hot sun and caught a fever; this was made worse by his continued journey, to the extent that he was somewhat sicker when he put into Brundisium, where he died on 20 September' (*Vit. Don.* 35). He was buried at Naples 'within the second milestone on the road to *Puteoli' (*Vit. Don.* 36: this does not fit the tomb known to tradition), and is said to have composed his own epitaph on his death-bed:

> Mantua me genuit, Calabri rapuere, tenet nunc
> Parthenope; cecini pascua rura duces.
>
> Mantua bore me, Calabria snatched me away, now
> Naples holds me; I sang of pastures, fields, and kings.

Varius Rufus and *Plotius Tucca were said to have 'emended' the *Aeneid* after Virgil's death, but without making any additions. The tradition also preserves the famous story that Virgil wished to burn the *Aeneid* on his death-bed: like everything else in the tradition, this may or may not be true.

Propertius' prophecy came to pass on the publication of the *Aeneid*: Virgil became the Roman *Homer, the *Aeneid* in particular serving as the great Roman classic against which later epic poets and in a sense all Latin poets had to situate themselves (cf. P. Hardie, *The Epic Successors of Vergil* (1993), cf. e.g. Pliny, *Ep.* 3. 7. 8 on Silius' veneration). Schoolboys studied it, even in Roman Egypt (R. Cavenaile, *Corpus Papyrorum Latinorum* (1958), 7–70), and its opening words became a common graffito on the walls of *Pompeii (R. P. Hoogma, *Der Einfluss Vergils auf die Carmina Latina Epigraphica* (1952)). Already in his lifetime Virgil is said to have been famous (Tac. *Dial.* 13. 3) and his friendship with the great brought him considerable wealth: according to *Valerius Probus' life (15–16) he was given ten million sesterces by Augustus (cf. Hor. *Epist.* 2. 1. 245–7 with *Helenius Acro's comm.). As with Homer, all human learning came to be seen as condensed in the *Aeneid*, a view which finds full expression in Macrobius' *Saturnalia*: the ancient biographical tradition already shows a tendency to see Virgil as a *theios anēr*, a divine genius, and this became pronounced in the Middle Ages, with the legends of Virgil the Magician (D. Comparetti, *Virgilio nel Medievo*[2], ed. G. Pasquali (1937–41; 1st edn. trans. E. F. Benecke 1895); cf. also C. G. Leland, *The Unpublished Legends of Virgil* (1879); J. W. Spargo, *Virgil the Necromancer* (1934); V. Zabughin, *Virgilio nel rinascimento italiano* (1921–3)). The text of the *Aeneid* was consulted as an *oracle in the *sortes Vergilianae* (cf. SHA *Hadr.* 2. 8).

A number of portraits of Virgil are known (*Enc. Virg.* V** 103–4; see below, bibliography after *Enc. Virg.*): there is no reason to believe that any are based on a genuine likeness, but the tradition describes him as a valetudinarian who never married and preferred sex with boys (variously identified amongst the characters of the poems). All of this, naturally, tells us more about Roman constructions of gender and culture than about 'the man Virgil'.

The Literary Works   The Eclogues

If any of the poems in the *Appendix Vergiliana* are genuine (which is unlikely), they may have been juvenilia, but essentially Virgil enters world literature with his first collection, the *Eclogues*, published probably around 39–38 BC (see above): ten short hexameter poems (the longest is 111 lines long) in the pastoral genre. The original title was *Bucolica*, 'cowherd songs' (*Eclogae*, N. Horsfall, *BICS* 1981, 108); *eclogae* means 'selections (from a larger corpus)' and it is unfortunate that a version of this later title has become usual in English. *Bucolica* as a title signals a clear allusion to pastoral (in Greek *ta bukolika*) and to *Theocritus in particular (cf. the refrain 'begin the bucolic song' in *Idyll* 1; in *Moschus 3. 11 the pastoral poet Bion is called a cowherd, *boukolos*), and the collection makes constant reference to Theocritus' *Idylls*: commentators note four separate echoes in the first line. But the intertextuality with earlier Roman poetry is as dense: the opening lines are also significantly Lucretian (cf. G. Castelli, *RSC* 1966, 313–42; 1967, 14–39; see LUCRETIUS) and the 'Song of Silenus' in the sixth poem seems to interact with a broad selection of contemporary poetry, hints of only some of which are we able to pick up (cf. D. O. Ross, *Backgrounds to Augustan Poetry* (1975), 25; P. E. Knox, *Ovid's Metamorphoses and the Tradition of Augustan Poetry* (1986), 11–26).

This combination of the Greek and the Roman, the ancient and the contemporary, and the rustic and the sophisticated is typical of the collection as a whole. Although we do not know exactly in what form the poems of Theocritus and the other bucolic poets circulated in Rome (cf. A. F. S. Gow, *Theocritus* (1952), 1. lix–lxii, lxvi–lxxii), it is likely that any edition included both the strictly pastoral poems like the first idyll, urban mimes like 15, and the encomiastic poems 16 and 17. In one sense, Virgil carries this mixture further: just as Theocritus addresses his friend Nicias in the frame of *Idyll* 11, Virgil addresses Varus in 6 (though there Virgil is called 'Tityrus' himself by Apollo) and Pollio (?) in 8, but his contemporaries also make an appearance *within* the bucolic setting (3. 84–91, 6. 64–73, 9. 47, 10 *passim*). *Idyll* 7, the nearest equivalent in Theocritus, is much less explicit. In another sense, however, Virgil is more consistently pastoral: the encomiastic birth poem 4, explicitly *paulo maiora*, 'a little greater (in theme)', is still more consistently pastoral than Theocritus 16 or 17 (cf. *Ecl.* 4. 3, 21–2, 42–5, 55–9).

The ten poems are intricately arranged around the central poem 5; the first and ninth poems deal with the subject of the land confiscations, 2 and 8 contain long laments by star-crossed lovers, 3 and 7 are both '*amoebean*' with exchanges of song, and 4 and 6 are the most obviously 'elevated' of the collection. Poem 5, another amoebean exchange, describes the apotheosis of Daphnis; 10 concludes the collection with Cornelius Gallus taking on the role of dying lover played by *Daphnis in Theocritus, *Idyll* 1. Some supplement this patterning with numerological correspondences, of varying suggestiveness (cf. J. Van Sickle, *The Design of Virgil's Bucolics* (1978)); certainly *Eclogue* 4, which is 63 (9 × 7) lines long, is structured around the magical number seven, but this has special point in relation to its oracular tone and subject-matter. The collection equally responds, however, to a serial reading. There is a clear movement from the first poem, where Tityrus describes how his land was saved, to the ninth, where Moeris says that he was not so fortunate: 'our poems, Lycidas, have as much power amongst the weapons of *Mars as they say the Chaonian doves have when the eagle comes' (9. 11–13, with a pun on the 'eagle' of the legionary standard; for the doves see DODONA and cf. CHAONES). Poem 6 opens with a 'proem in the middle' (cf. G. B. Conte, *YClS* 1992, 147–59) which echoes the opening of *Callimachus (3)'s *Aetia* and establishes the pastoral *deductum carmen*, 'fine-spun song', as the equivalent to Callimachus' 'slender muse' (*Ecl.* 6. 5, cf. 6. 8). At the end of the collection, Gallus gives in to love (10. 69), the poet rises from

his pastoral ease in the shade (75–6), and the goats are told to go home, now fed to satiety (77).

As this suggests, the *Eclogues* are highly 'artificial' and metaliterary, and the relation of the world of song to the world outside is a central concern. Virgil toys with a variety of partial identifications in the poems: in 5. 86–7 Menalcas claims to have written *Eclogues* 2 and 3 and in 9. 10 Lycidas says that the same character 'saved all with his poems' but *Apollo calls the narrator Tityrus in 6. 4 and it is not hard to see him in the idle singer of an empty day in the first poem (cf. *G.* 565–6); in a broader sense he is also the helpless Corydon of 2 and the magical Silenus (see SATYRS AND SILENS) of 6. Interwoven with and inseparable from the literary texture are the celebrated descriptive passages that so appealed to Romantic enthusiasts like Samuel Palmer, the buzzing bees and cool springs of the pastoral world (cf. e.g. 1. 51–8). The union of the two was an inheritance from Theocritus which Virgil passed on to the west, particularly through Renaissance imitators like Mantuan and especially Sannazaro; although 'Arcadia' is mentioned only rarely in the poems (7. 4, 26, 10. 31, 33, cf. 4. 58–9, 10. 26) and its significance is disputed (B. Snell, *The Discovery of the Mind*, trans. T. G. Rosenmeyer, ch. 13; D. Kennedy, *Hermathena* 1984, 47–59; R. Jenkyns, *JRS* 1989, 26–39), the *Eclogues* came to signify Arcady as a place where poetry and love meet with or avoid the worlds of politics, cities, and empires.

One of the *Eclogues* came to have particular significance for later readers: *Eclogue* 4, with its description of the birth of a child whose lifetime will see a return of the world to the *golden age. There were several possible candidates for the identification of the child even for contemporary readers (cf. E. Coleiro, *An Introduction to Vergil's Bucolics with an Edition of the Text* (1979), 222–32: the modern favourite is an anticipated son of M. *Antonius (2) and Octavia, a hope already dashed by the time of the *Eclogues'* publication), but the poem can equally be read as a broader allegory of renewal; Christian readers naturally saw reference to the birth of Jesus (cf. Coleiro, 232–3; Constantine, *Oratio ad sanctum coetum* 19–21, *PL* 8. 454–66). The influence of Jewish messianic writing on the poem is nowhere a required hypothesis, but is not in itself unlikely (cf. R. G. M. Nisbet, *BICS* 1978, 59–78). See PASTORAL POETRY, GREEK and LATIN.

The Georgics

Virgil's call to himself to 'rise' at the end of the *Eclogues* (10. 75 *surgamus*) was answered by a rise in generic level with his next work, the *Georgics*, a didactic poem in four books on farming (book 1: crops, book 2: trees and shrubs, book 3: livestock, book 4: bees). Again there are Hellenistic Greek models: little can be said of the lost *Georgica* of *Nicander (fragments in A. F. S. Gow and A. F. Scholfield, *Nicander* (1953), 145–61), but it is clear even from the fragments that we have of Callimachus' *Aetia* that that was an important model (four-book structure, and especially the links between the proem to the third and conclusion to the fourth book of each work: R. F. Thomas, *CQ* 1983, 92–113) and *Aratus (1)'s *Phaenomena* was both a central Hellenistic text (translated by *Cicero and P. *Terentius Varro Atacinus) and of particular relevance to the discussion of weather in book 1 (cf. also the translation of a passage from *Eratosthenes at *G.* 1. 233–51). But there was also now an important archaic model in *Hesiod's *Works and Days* (cf. 2. 176 *Ascraeum . . . carmen*, 'Hesiodic song'), and the relationship to Lucretius' *De rerum natura* is so central that the *Georgics* may be seen as an *anti-Lucretius* (cf. P. R. Hardie, *Virgil's Aeneid: Cosmos and Imperium* (1986), 157–67, and in general J. Farrell, *Vergil's Georgics and the Traditions of Ancient Epic* (1991)). Lucretius' confident exposition of the power of reason is 'remythologized' into a more sceptical and yet more accepting attitude towards the natural world and its traditional divinities (2. 490–4).

Just as Aratus' *Phaenomena* had been based on a prose treatise of *Eudoxus (1) and the *De rerum natura* on Epicurean texts, especially the *Letter to Herodotus*, so the *Georgics* also have important prose models, though none is as central as in those texts. Virgil's sources for the agricultural lore were various (L. A. Jermyn, *G&R* 1949, 50) but the most significant was *Varro's *Res rusticae*, published in 37 BC and influential especially in books 3 and 4 (but note also *Rust*. 1. 1. 4–7 with the opening invocation of the gods in G. 1. 8–23, and *Rust*. 1. 69. 2–3 with the end of the first book). The didactic narrator is portrayed as a saviour-sage, taking pity on 'the farmers . . . ignorant of the path' (1. 41, with Lucretian overtones: cf. Hardie, 158) but the practical advice avoids technical precision (in contrast to the fragments of Nicander) and the addressee is the extremely unrustic Maecenas (1. 2, 2. 41, 3. 41, 5. 2; cf. also L. P. Wilkinson, *The Georgics of Virgil* (1969), 52–5; S. Spurr, *G&R* 1986, 171–5). As with the *De rerum natura*, the central concern is rather the place in the world of human beings and their possibilities of happiness.

In the established manner of *didactic poetry, passages of direct instruction are interspersed with 'digressions', descriptive or reflective passages with a more figured relationship to the main theme, such as *Jupiter's paternal disruption of the golden age (1. 121–59) or the 'praises of Italy' (2. 136–77). In particular, on the Lucretian model, the concluding section of each book stands out: the troubles of Italy in 1 (464–514), the virtues of the country life in 2 (475–540), the Noric plague in 3 (478–566, imitating the end of the *De rerum natura*: for book 3 as a microcosm of that work, cf. M. Gale, *CQ* 1991, 414–26), and especially the '*epyllion*' of *Aristaeus and *Orpheus that ends book 4 (315–58). This last section dramatizes (but also in part deconstructs) the opposition between the successful conquest of nature through hard work (Aristaeus) and the pathos of loss and failure (Orpheus) which can be traced throughout the *Georgics* and which has led to a debate over the 'optimism' or 'pessimism' of the work which parallels similar disputes over the *Aeneid* (cf. D. O. Ross, *Virgil's Elements* (1987); C. Perkell, *The Poet's Truth* (1989); T. Habinek, in M. Griffith and D. J. Mastronarde (eds.), *Cabinet of the Muses* (1990), 209–23; and R. F. Thomas, *CPhil*. 1991, 211–18). The contemporary relevance of this is reinforced by a constant comparison between the bee society of book 4 and Rome (cf. J. Griffin, *Latin Poets* (1985), 163–82).

The poem concludes with an epilogue (modelled in part on the conclusion to Callimachus' *Aetia*) in which Virgil contrasts Augustus' 'thundering' on the *Euphrates (cf. R. F. Thomas and R. Scodel, *AJPhil*. 1984, 339; J. Clauss, *AJPhil*. 1988, 309–20) with his own easeful retirement in Naples (4. 559–64) and looks back to the *Eclogues*, depicted as the playful work of his youth (565–6). At the opening of *Georgics* 3 he had promised to write a political epic (3. 46–8), a familiar enough turn in the *recusatio* (refusal to handle a topic), but just as Callimachus at the end of the *Aetia* prophesies a move 'down' to the *Iambi* (fr. 112), so at the end of the *Georgics* we are left feeling that for Virgil the next move would be 'up' in the hierarchy of genres (cf. Farrell, *Vergil's Georgics*).

Aeneid

Virgil's final work was the *Aeneid* (in Latin *Aeneis*), an account in twelve books of hexameter verse of the flight of *Aeneas from *Troy and his battles in Italy against *Turnus (1) to found a new home, the origin of Rome. As an *epic, the *Aeneid* occupies the summit of ancient generic classification. Epic was the sustained

narration of great events ('kings and heroes' according to Callimachus fr. 1) by an inspired, omniscient, but distanced narrator (see VATES); it was also the genre in which the anxiety of influence was greatest, since any epic was inevitably read against Homer's *Iliad* and *Odyssey*, by common consent the greatest poems of antiquity. Intertextuality with both poems is intense: the standard study takes 60 pages just to list the most obvious parallels (G. N. Knauer, *Die Aeneis und Homer* (1964), 371–431). The basic armature is that of the *Odyssey* (note also the focus on the hero in the title, though that has other implications: cf. *Aristotle, *Poetics* 1451ᵃ 20): the first half of each epic describes the wanderings of the hero, the second his fight for victory in his home (cf. also the 'overlap' in the book-structure in the middle of each: *Od*. 13. 1–91 with *Aen*. 7. 1–36, and contrast *Apollonius (1) Rhodius, 3. 1), and Aeneas is harried by *Juno as *Odysseus is by *Poseidon, but the anger of Juno (cf. 1. 4, 11) also corresponds to the anger of *Achilles (and Apollo) in the *Iliad*, and the end of the poem is more like the battle between Achilles and *Hector in *Iliad* 22 than the killing of the suitors in *Odyssey* 22 (*contra* F. Cairns, *Virgil's Augustan Epic* (1989), 177–214). One may also contrast the first six books as 'Odyssean' with the second half as 'Iliadic' (cf. K. W. Gransden, *Virgil's Second Iliad* (1984): for a different version of this opposition, cf. D. Quint, *Epic and Empire* (1993)). But the correspondences with both epics go much further and much deeper (cf. Knauer, *Aeneis*; *ANRW* 2. 31. 2 (1981), 870–918; A. Barchiesi, *La traccia del modello* (1985); R. R. Schlunk, *The Homeric Scholia and the Aeneid* (1974)). The relationship is signalled in the famous opening words of the poem, *arma virumque cano*, 'arms and the man I sing', where 'arms' points to the *Iliad*, 'man' to the *Odyssey* (and 'I sing' perhaps to 'Cyclic' epic, cf. *Ilias parva* fr. 1).

Two other epics are also of importance: the *Argonautica* of Apollonius Rhodius (cf. D. P. Nelis, *The Aeneid and the Argonautica of Apollonius Rhodius* (1997)) and *Ennius' *Annales* (E. Norden (ed.), *Aen*. 6 (1926), 365–75; M. Wigodsky, *Vergil and Early Latin Poetry* (1972), 40–79). The relationship with Ennius is of great ideological significance (cf. G. B. Conte, *The Rhetoric of Imitation* (1986), 141–84). But the range of material whose traces may be interpreted in the *Aeneid* is vast: other earlier epics like Greek 'cyclic' epic (E. Christian Kopff, *ANRW* 2. 31. 2 (1981), 919–47; see EPIC CYCLE) and *Naevius' *Punica* (M. Barchiesi, *Nevio Epico* (1962), 50–1 and *passim*), Greek and Roman tragedy (Wigodsky, 80–97; A. König, *Die Aeneis und die griechische Tragödie* (1970); P. Hardie, *PVS* 1991, 29–45), Hellenistic poetry (W. Clausen, *Virgil's Aeneid and the Tradition of Hellenistic Poetry* (1987)), lyric and elegy (F. Cairns, 129–76), and many other *genres (cf. N. Horsfall, *G&R* 1991, 203–11). The *Aeneid* thus both preserves the narrower generic norms of epic and expands the genre towards the variety that critics like M. Bakhtin have reserved for the modern novel, a process taken further by *Ovid (J. B. Solodow, *The World of Ovid's Metamorphoses* (1988), 25). The included genres maintain, however, their separate ideological implications.

Although the particular version of the Aeneas legend presented in the *Aeneid* has become canonical, the versions of the myth in the preceding tradition were many and varied (N. M. Horsfall, in J. N. Bremmer and N. M. Horsfall, *Roman Myth and Mythography*, *BICS* Suppl. 52 (1987), 12–24), and the reconstruction of the matrix of possibilities against which the *Aeneid* situates itself has always been a standard critical procedure (cf. esp. R. Heinze, *Virgil's Epic Technique*, trans. H. and D. Harvey and F. Robertson (1993); N. Horsfall, *Virgilio: l'epopea in alambicco* (1991)). It is clear that many of the details offered by Virgil were by no means the standard ones in his day, that his 'sources'

Virgil (Publius Vergilius Maro)

were multiple, and that there was no compunction against free invention. The *Aeneid* is not therefore a 'safe' text to use for the investigation of early Latin history and cult. The story as told by Virgil takes the reader, as in the *Odyssey*, *in medias res*. Aeneas on his way to Italy is blown off course to North Africa by a storm instigated by Juno (book 1). There he meets *Dido, and tells her the story of the fall of Troy (book 2) and his subsequent wanderings (book 3). He and Dido become lovers, and he forgets his mission; Mercury is sent to remind him, and his departure leads to Dido's tragic suicide (book 4). In book 5, the threat of another storm forces Aeneas to put into Sicily, where funeral games are celebrated for his dead father *Anchises; after Juno instigates the Trojan women to burn the ships, part of the group are left behind in Sicily and Anchises appears in a dream to urge Aeneas to visit the *Sibyl of *Cumae (near Naples). The first half of the epic concludes with the consultation of the Sibyl and their visit to the Underworld, where Aeneas meets his father and receives a vision of the future of Rome (book 6).

The events of the second half are described by Virgil as a 'greater work' (7. 44, *maius opus*). Landing in Latium, Aeneas sends a successful embassy of peace to the Latin king *Latinus; but Juno uses the Fury Allecto (see ERINYES) to stir up the young Rutulian king Turnus and Latinus' wife Amata to encourage war. Aeneas' son Iulus kills a pet stag while hunting, and from that small spark a full-blown war develops. Before battle commences we are given a catalogue of Italian forces (book 7). In book 8 Aeneas, advised by the god of the river *Tiber in a dream, visits the Arcadian king *Evander, who is living on the future site of Rome; Evander's young son Pallas (see PALLAS (2)) joins the Trojan forces, and Aeneas receives a gift of armour from his mother Venus, including a shield which again depicts future events in the history of Rome, most notably the battle of Actium (book 8). In the succeeding books of fighting, emphasis falls on the terrible cost of the war, as the young lovers *Nisus (2) and Euryalus die in a night expedition (book 9), Turnus kills Pallas, and Aeneas kills both the equally tragic youth Lausus and his father the evil *Mezentius (book 10), and Turnus' ally the female warrior *Camilla is killed by an arrow to her breast (book 11). Finally in book 12 Aeneas and Turnus meet in single combat, despite Juno's attempts to delay the duel; Aeneas is victorious, and hesitates over sparing Turnus until he sees the sword-belt that Turnus had taken from the dead Pallas. In a paroxysm of love and anger, he slaughters Turnus.

Throughout the *Aeneid*, as this summary suggests, there is a strong narrative teleology, reaching beyond the events of the story to the future Rome. 'Fate' is a central concept; it coincides with the will of Jupiter, though the exact relationship is kept vague (C. Bailey, *Religion in Vergil* (1935), 204–40). Juno, pained and angry at past events (1. 25–8), attempts always to retard the progress of the story, as a sort of 'counter-fate' (7. 294, 313–16). She is always doomed to failure; at the end of the epic she is reconciled to the fate of Aeneas (12. 808–28) but we know that this is only temporary (10. 11–15: D. Feeney, in *Oxford Readings in Virgil's Aeneid* (1992), 339–62). Onto the opposition between the king and queen (1. 9) of heaven may be projected many other oppositions in the poem: heaven and hell, order and disorder, reason and emotion, success and failure, future and past, epic and tragedy. The treatment of these oppositions has been the central issue in the criticism of the *Aeneid*. It is clear that although many of them coincide, the contrast is never absolute: if Juno naturally turns to Allecto and the underworld (7. 312), Jupiter god of the bright sky (1. 253) also uses the infernal Dirae (see

ERINYES) as the instruments of his wrath (12. 849–52); if Aeneas like *Hercules (cf. 8. 299, contrast 2. 314) represents reason and self-control, he also concludes the epic with an act of passion (12. 946–7). It is possible to see these inconsistencies as 'energising contradictions' (C. Martindale, *Redeeming the Text* (1993), 51) which forge a successful viewpoint on the world; or to see them as undermining or subverting the claims to dominance of Roman order, as in the 'two-voices' school of criticism that came to prominence in Harvard in the 1960s (cf. A. Parry, *Arion* 1963, 66–80; W. Clausen, *Harv. Stud.* 1964, 139–47; M. C. J. Putnam, *The Poetry of the Aeneid* (1965); R. O. A. M. Lyne, *Further Voices in Vergil's Aeneid* (1987)); or more generally to see the oppositions (like all oppositions) as inherently unstable and liable to deconstruction. Naturally, simple appeal to the text or its historical setting cannot settle which of these approaches is adopted.

Three particular aspects of the debate may, however, be mentioned. First, the opposition between Jupiter and Juno is a gendered one, and many of the other contrasts drawn relate to ancient (and modern) conceptions of typically male or female characteristics, such as reason and emotion. Women in the *Aeneid* feature predominantly as suffering victims opposed to the progress of history (Juno, Dido, Amata, Camilla, Juturna), and this may be read either as an affront to the values of martial epic or as reinforcing them. At any rate, Virgil's treatment of gender is distinctive and central to the interpretation of the poem, though it is idle to use it to speculate about his own sexuality.

Second, the political aspects of the oppositions are more than implicit. The hero of the epic is *pius* Aeneas (1. 378; see PIETAS; RELIGION, ROMAN, TERMS RELATING TO), a man marked out by attachment to communal values who at the fall of Troy turns away from individual heroism to save his father and in *Carthage rejects personal happiness for the sake of his son's future and the destiny of Rome (4. 267–76). This subordination of the individual to the collective is often seen as a prime component of Roman ideology, and its embodiment in Aeneas a central feature of the epic. At the same time, as in Virgil's earlier work (J. Griffin, *Latin Poets* (1985), 163–82), the pain and loss suffered by individuals are at least equally as prominent in the poem. The question of the relationship between individual and community is raised in a different form by the question of the poem's relationship to the new autocratic rule of Augustus. The purpose of the *Aeneid* was commonly seen in antiquity as to praise Augustus (Servius, *Aen.* pref.), who receives explicit eulogy from Jupiter (1. 286–96, though *Caesar* in 286 is ambiguous), Anchises (6. 791–805), and the primary narrator in the description of Aeneas' divine shield (8. 671–728). Much of the imagery of the *Aeneid* can be related to Augustan symbolic discourse (P. Hardie, *Virgil's Aeneid: Cosmos and Imperium*; P. Zanker, *The Power of Images in the Age of Augustus* (1988)) and there are many typological links between Augustus and Aeneas and other figures such as Hercules (cf. G. Binder, *Aeneas und Augustus* (1971); K. W. Gransden, *PVS* 1973–4, 14–27; J. Griffin, *Latin Poets* (1985), 183–97). On the other hand, many have again seen the poem's tragic elements as incompatible with a celebration of power. It is impossible to separate the question of the *Aeneid*'s political tendency—in its crudest form, whether we make it pro- or anti-Augustan—from the wider ideological issues mentioned above, and again the debate cannot be resolved by an appeal to text or history (cf. D. Kennedy, in A. Powell (ed.), *Roman Poetry and Propaganda in the Age of Augustus* (1992), 26–58). See PROPAGANDA.

Finally, these same issues have also surfaced in relation to the philosophical aspects of the *Aeneid*. Just as the *Georgics* may be read as a reply to the *De rerum natura*, so the *Aeneid* may be seen as again 'remythologizing' Lucretian rationalism (P. Hardie, *Virgil's Aeneid: Cosmos and Imperium, passim*); as Aeneas rejects retirement in Carthage or Sicily for his fate in Italy, so the *Aeneid* turns from 'ignoble ease' to harsh commitment (cf. 6. 851 with *De rerum natura* 5. 1130, though there is more than one way of reading the intertextuality). Several passages of the *Aeneid* are explicitly philosophical in their language, most notably Anchises' account of the *soul in 6. 724–51; this contains both Stoic and Platonic elements (see STOICISM; PLATO (1)), and such eclecticism is typical and unsurprising in a period where the two schools pulled closer with figures such as *Antiochus (11) and *Posidonius (2). But the debates over the philosophy of the *Aeneid* have concentrated on ethics and the theory of the passions, especially anger. Is the *Aeneid* essentially a Stoic text, which deprecates emotion? Or is it rather *Peripatetic, and thereby endorsing a right measure of anger (A. Thornton, *The Living Universe* (1976), esp. 159–63)? Others have looked to Cynicism (F. Cairns, *Virgil's Augustan Epic* (1989), 33–8) or the Epicurean theory of anger as presented in *Philodemus' *De ira* (cf. G. K. Galinsky *AJPhil.* 1988, 321–48; M. Erler, *GB* (1991)). Any decision on these matters involves a consideration of the poem's imagery, as well as explicit statement by characters and the narrator; and once again the evaluation of these images is not a simple one. A similar ambivalence attends the depiction of the gods: although they may at times function as metaphors for psychological activity on the human plane (G. W. Williams, *Technique and Ideas in the Aeneid* (1983)), they cannot simply be reduced to allegory (D. Feeney, *The Gods in Epic* (1991), 129–87).

The classic status of the *Aeneid* is at once apparent from the *parody of its opening line (and 7. 41) as the epitome of epic openings in the first of Ovid's *Amores* (date uncertain, but perhaps before 7 BC: cf. Mckeown on *Am.* 1. 1. 1–2). Intertextuality with the *Aeneid* is the central way in which Ovid's *Metamorphoses*, Lucan's *De bello civili* (see ANNAEUS LUCANUS, M.), and especially the works of the Flavian epicists generate meaning: the *Aeneid* is figured as the official voice of the empire, to be subverted or recuperated (cf. P. Hardie, *The Epic Successors of Virgil*). But just as all Greek literature everywhere of necessity situates itself against Homer, so traces of the *Aeneid* can be seen in every genre of verse and prose, Christian as well as pagan (cf. W. Suerbaum, *ANRW* 2. 31. 1 (1986), 308–37; W. F. Jackson Knight, *Roman Virgil* (1966), 362–98). Inevitably, this role as a machine for generating meaning in others, a stable backdrop for new dramas, may lead to a simplification of the possibilities of the original text, but equally the links between parts of the *Aeneid* established by imitations often offer the possibility of new critical insights into the *Aeneid* itself (cf. P. Hardie, in A. J. Boyle (ed.), *The Imperial Muse: Flavian Epicist to Claudian* (1990), 3–20).

Fortuna

Virgil's works, but especially the *Aeneid*, retained their classic status throughout the Middle Ages and Renaissance as prime examples of pastoral (cf. A. M. Patterson, *Pastoral and Ideology* (1988); S. Chaudhuri, *Renaissance Pastoral and its English Developments* (1989)), didactic (cf. J. Calker, *The English Georgic* (1969)), and most obviously epic, from Dante to Milton (cf. T. M. Green, *The Light in Troy* (1982); D. Quint, *Epic and Empire* (1993)). Many aspects of this *reception in the various vernaculars were studied in the publications connected with the bimillenary celebrations of 1981–2 (lists in A. Wlosok, *Gnomon* 1985, 127–34 and *Enc. Virg.* V** (1991), 114–18: cf. C. Martindale, *Virgil and his Influence* (1984) and *Redeeming the Text* (1993)). Although in English literature the Augustan period is most obviously an *aetas Vergiliana*, he has

played a surprisingly important role in the modern period, from Eliot to Hermann Broch (T. Ziolkowski, *Virgil and the Moderns* (1991)); if no major work stands in relation to the *Aeneid* as Joyce's *Ulysses* does to the *Odyssey*, the tactics that novel adopts towards its model are entirely Virgilian. For Eliot as for Milton and Dryden Virgil was *the* classic; if this centrality has given way first before vernacular heroes (Shakespeare, Dante) and then before a more general scepticism towards the canon, Virgil continues to possess the alternative canonic virtue of continual reinterpretation and cultural reuse (cf. W. Suerbaum, *Vergils Aeneis, Beiträge zu ihrer Rezeption in Gegenwart und Geschichte* (1981)).

TEXTS R. A. B. Mynors (1972); M. Geymonat (1973).

TRANSLATIONS C. Day Lewis (*Eclogues & Georgics*, 1983, *Aeneid*, 1986, with introd. by R. O. A. M. Lyne & J. Griffin respectively); G. Lee (*Eclogues*, 1980); D. West (*Aeneid*, 1990); H. R. Fairclough (Loeb, 1934–5).

COMMENTARIES *Complete*: C. G. Heyne and G. P. E. Wagner, 4th edn. (1830–41, Lat.); T. Ladewig (1876–86, Ger.); J. Conington and H. Nettleship, 3rd edn. (1881–93); T. E. Page (1894–1900); R. D. Williams (1972–9); *Eclogues*: C. Hosius (1915, Lat.); R. Coleman (1977); E. Coleiro (1979); W. V. Clausen (1994); *Georgics*: R. F. Thomas (1988); R. A. B. Mynors (1990). *Aeneid*: bks. 1, 2, 4, 6, R. G. Austin (1971, 1966, 1955, 1977); bks. 3 and 5, R. D. Williams (1962, 1960); bk. 4, A. S. Pease (1935); bk. 6, E. Norden, 3rd edn. (1926, Ger.); bks. 7 and 8, C. J. Fordyce (1977); bk. 8, P. T. Eden (1975); K. W. Gransden (1976); bk. 10, S. J. Harrison (1992); bk. 11, K. W. Gransden (1991). See also APPENDIX VERGILIANA for the spurious works attributed to Virgil.

BIBLIOGRAPHIES W. Suerbaum, ANRW 31. 1 (1980, *Aeneid*), 31. 2 (1981, *Georgics*); W. W. Briggs, ANRW 31. 2 (1981), 1265–1357 (*Eclogues*); M. T. Morano Rando, *Bibliografia Virgiliana* (1987).

COMPANION *Enciclopedia Virgiliana* (1984–91): the last volume (V**) includes texts, It. trans., biographical material, etc.

STUDIES *General*: J. Griffin, *Virgil* (1986); W. F. Jackson Knight, *Roman Vergil*, 2nd edn. (1966); B. Otis, *Virgil: A Study in Civilized Poetry* (1964); K. Büchner, *RE*, 'P. Vergilius Maro' (also published separately, 1955, Ger.); F. Klingner, *Virgil* (1967, Ger.). *Collections of essays*: S. Commager (1966); T. A. Dorey (1969); F. Robertson (1988); I. McAuslan and P. Walcot (1990). *Eclogues*: H. J. Rose, *The Eclogues of Vergil* (1942); M. C. J. Putnam, *Vergil's Pastoral Art* (1970); E. W. Leach, *Vergil's Eclogues: Landscapes of Experience* (1974); J. Van Sickle, *The Design of Virgil's Bucolics* (1978); P. J. Alpers, *The Singer of the Eclogues* (1979). *Georgics*: L. P. Wilkinson, *The Georgics of Virgil* (1969); M. C. J. Putnam, *Virgil's Poem of the Earth* (1979); G. B. Miles, *Virgil's Georgics: A New Interpretation* (1980); P. A. Johnston, *Vergil's Agricultural Golden Age* (1980); D. O. Ross, *Virgil's Elements* (1987); C. Perkell, *The Poet's Truth* (1989); J. Farrell, *Vergil's Georgics and the Traditions of Ancient Epic* (1991). *Aeneid*: *introductory*: W. A. Camps, *Introduction to Virgil's Aeneid* (1969); R. D. Williams, *The Aeneid* (1987); K. W. Gransden, *Virgil: The Aeneid* (1990); *collection of essays*: S. J. Harrison (1990); *major studies*: R. Heinze, *Virgil's Epic Technique* (trans. H. and D. Harvey and F. Robertson 1993; orig. edn. 3, 1915); V. Pöschl, *The Art of Virgil* (trans. G. Seligson 1962; later edn. 3, of Ger. orig., *Die Dichtkunst Virgils: Bild und Symbol in der Aeneis* (1977)); F. J. Worstbrock, *Elemente einer Poetik der Aeneis* (1963); V. Buchheit, *Vergil über die Sendung Roms* (1963); M. C. J. Putnam, *The Poetry of the Aeneid* (1965); K. Quinn, *Virgil's Aeneid: A Critical Introduction* (1968); W. R. Johnson, *Darkness Visible* (1976); G. Williams, *Techniques and Ideas in the Aeneid* (1983); P. R. Hardie, *Virgil's Aeneid: Cosmos and Imperium* (1986); R. O. A. M. Lyne, *Further Voices in Vergil's Aeneid* (1987), and *Words and the Poet* (1989); F. Cairns, *Virgil's Augustan Epic* (1990).
D. P. F., P. G. F.

virginity See CHASTITY; VESTA, VESTALS.

Viriatus (*c*.180–139 BC), a Lusitanian shepherd (see LUSITANIA), escaped from the massacre of Ser. *Sulpicius Galba (1) (150), rallied his people, and became their war-leader (by 147). Exploiting Roman commitments in Africa and Greece (until 145), he strove to preserve Lusitanian independence from Roman rule.

Viroconium

With small guerrilla forces and skilful use of terrain and ambush, he defeated a series of Roman commanders—in both Further and Hither Spain—and won the co-operation (143) of Celtiberian tribes (out of which arose the Numantine War; see NUMANTIA). After defeating Q. Fabius Maximus Servilianus he refrained from destroying his army, securing instead a favourable peace (ratified by the Roman people) and recognition as an ally (140). But Fabius' successor, Cn. Servilius Caepio, persuaded the senate to authorize the resumption of hostilities, and through bribery contrived Viriatus' assassination; the Lusitanians soon surrendered (138). Viriatus remains a national hero in Portugal.

> The chief source is Appian, *Iberica* (60–75), based on Polybius. H. Simon, *Roms Kriege in Spanien* (1962); Z. W. Rubinsohn, *RSA* 1981, 161.
> E. B.; C. F. K.

Viroconium (also **Uri(o)conium** or **Viriconium**), a town in Roman *Britain (mod. Wroxeter, in Shropshire). The site, which controlled the route via the Severn valley into Wales, was the focus of considerable military activity during the conquest and afterwards. Numerous forts have been found hereabouts. A fortress of Legio XIV Gemina (see LEGION) was established at Wroxeter *c.* AD 55. This legion was replaced by Legio XX Valeria in AD 65/66, which remained in occupation until *c.* AD 83. After this the fortress site was developed as the *civitas* capital of the *Cornovii. Late 1st-cent. baths, perhaps intended for the legion, were left incomplete, to be swept away by *Hadrian, in whose reign a normal forum-basilica replaced them. The forum is dated by a dedication to Hadrian of AD 120–30 by the *civitas Cornoviorum* (*RIB* 288). Big new public baths, architecturally combined with a shopping precinct and large public latrine (see SANITATION), were built shortly after AD 150; they were provided with a great open-air swimming bath and a covered exercise hall. About AD 165 the centre of the town was damaged by fire, but was soon rebuilt. Air photographs have revealed much of the plan of the town and an aqueduct. An earth rampart was provided towards the end of the 2nd cent., enclosing *c.*77 ha., and a town wall was inserted in its front sometime later. A significant part of the enclosed area was not certainly built up. Before AD 300 the forum was destroyed by fire and not rebuilt, but the town apparently prospered until late in the 4th cent. The demolition of the baths-basilica in the later 4th cent. was followed by the construction of a substantial timber palace which appears to have continued in occupation into the 5th cent.

> G. Webster, *The Cornovii*, 2nd edn. (1991), and in G. Webster (ed.), *Fortress into City* (1988); G. Barker, *Wroxeter Roman City: Excavations 1966–80* (1981). S. S. F.; M. J. M.

Virtus See HONOS AND VIRTUS.

Virunum, a city in southern *Noricum near the river Glan at modern Zollfeld. It lay in the territory of the Celtic Norici, whose centre was on the Magdalensberg 1,058 metres (half a mile) south-east of Klagenfurt. At first the site of a Celtic *oppidum, terraces on the hillside were occupied by more than three square kilometres of buildings, including a forum, a temple, and a centre for the imperial cult constructed by the Norican peoples under *Augustus. Most of the buildings are in the classical style and date from the late 1st cent. BC to the reign of *Claudius. From here the Norici were administered by a Roman *conventus organization and the place was also the centre of the *concilium provinciae. Under Claudius a *municipium was established at Virunum (*CIL* 3. 11555: *municipium Claudium Virunum*), enrolled in the voting-tribe Claudia. Until the establishment of the legion-

ary fortress at *Lauriacum under Marcus *Aurelius, Virunum was the residence of the governing procurator. Gradually the buildings on the Magdalensberg fell out of use as the centre of administration was transferred to Virunum. The forum, *capitolium* (see CAPITOL), baths, amphitheatre, and private dwellings of Virunum have been discovered while its street-grid occupied over one kilometre square. Destroyed by fire (the city appears never to have acquired a defensive wall) during the Marcomannic invasions (169–75; see MARCOMANNI), the city was later rebuilt. In the provincial reorganization of *Diocletian it was the capital of *Noricum Mediterranea*.

> R. Egger, *Die Stadt auf dem Magdalensberg, ein Grosshandelsplatz* (1961); G. Alföldy, *Noricum* (1974), 70 ff. (Magdalensberg); 87 ff. (*municipium*).
> J. J. W.

vis Latin word, means neutrally 'force' and pejoratively 'violence'. It is the latter sense that is treated here. For Greece see under VIOLENCE.

(*a*) Political Violence. Apart from the major non-violent secessions, 'the Conflict of the Orders' in the early republic (see ROME (HISTORY), § 1.2) seems to have involved small-scale violence between the plebeians, defending each other and their tribunes, and the patricians supported by their clients (see CLIENS; PATRICIANS; PLEBS; SECESSIO; TRIBUNI PLEBIS). However, in the last century of the republic violence became an ever increasing factor, not as a mass revolutionary movement, but as a political weapon largely exploited by magistrates for limited ends. The notion of a police authority was alien to republican thought and, if violence became serious, often the only counter was a state of emergency (see SENATUS CONSULTUM ULTIMUM). From 78 BC *vis* was an offence under the *leges* Lutatia and Plautia. After the *lex* Caecilia Didia of 98 (see LEX (2)), laws passed by violence were sometimes annulled by the senate. Comprehensive legislation against all political violence was provided by a *lex Iulia de vi publica* of *Augustus; practical security was provided for by Augustus' creation of the urban cohorts (see COHORTES URBANAE) and the *vigiles. See also POLICE.

(*b*) Private Violence. For the ordinary citizen both Rome and the Italian countryside were frequently violent places where it was necessary to defend oneself with the assistance of family, friends, patrons, or clients. Self-help was also originally recognized in the procedures of private law from the time of the *Twelve Tables onwards, most obviously as a means of bringing a reluctant opponent to court. In the later republic we find a particular interest in the restriction of violence in property disputes, as shown in the interdicts concerning *possession and *vis* (known by 161 and 111 BC respectively). After *Sulla an interdict was instituted specifically against the use of armed gangs, also actions for the recovery of property taken by armed gangs and extorted by force or menaces. In addition to these measures providing restitution and compensation, a *lex Iulia de vi privata* (perhaps linked with that *de vi publica* in a single law) established penalties. If the avoidance of violence was by then a legal norm, it is far from clear whether it actually declined under the emperors.

> A. W. Lintott, *Violence in Republican Rome* (1968); Z. Yavetz, *Plebs and Princeps* (1969); R. MacMullen, *Roman Social Relations* (1974); W. Nippel, *JRS* 1984 and *Public Order in Ancient Rome* (1995). A. W. L.

Visigoths See GOTHS.

Vitellius (*RE* Suppl. 9, 7b), **Aulus** (AD 15–69), Roman emperor in 69, son of Lucius *Vitellius, an influential figure under the Julio-Claudians, was friendly with *Gaius (1), *Claudius, and

*Nero. Consul in 48, he became proconsul of Africa (see PRO CONSULE; AFRICA, ROMAN), then served as legate (see LEGATI) to his brother in the same post. *Galba appointed him governor of Lower Germany (see GERMANIA) in November 68, perhaps thinking that his reputed indolence made him less of a political threat. Vitellius won over the disaffected soldiers in the province by an ostentatious display of generosity. On 2 January 69 Vitellius was proclaimed emperor by his troops, and quickly won the support of the legions of Upper Germany, which had refused allegiance to Galba on 1 January. His main supporters were the legionary legates *Fabius Valens and A. *Caecina Alienus, and soon most of the western provinces and Africa were on his side. Galba had been replaced by *Otho, who committed suicide on 16 April after his army had been defeated at *Bedriacum by the Vitellian forces. After an undisciplined march Vitellius entered Rome in July; he made offerings to Nero, and had himself created consul in perpetuity. Hostile sources emphasize Vitellius' gluttony, indolence, and incompetence, though he displayed restraint in dealing with Otho's supporters. He replaced the existing praetorian guard (see PRAETORIANS) with sixteen *cohorts recruited from his German *legions. But he did nothing to placate troops who had been defeated or betrayed at Bedriacum, and detachments of the three Moesian legions (see MOESIA) summoned by Otho returned to their bases having agitated against Vitellius at *Aquileia.

At the beginning of July *Vespasian was saluted emperor and soon all the troops in the east supported him. The legions in *Pannonia, *Dalmatia, and Moesia rapidly deserted Vitellius, and under the leadership of M. *Antonius Primus, invaded Italy. Vitellius failed to block the Alpine passes, leaving the defence of Italy to Valens, who was ill, and Caecina, who occupied *Cremona and Hostilia with an army including four legions and legionary detachments; he aimed to defend the line of the river Po, but collaborated with the Flavians. Although the Ravenna fleet defected, Caecina's army refused to follow his lead and arrested him. Junior officers led the army back to Cremona, near which in a hard-fought battle (October 69) the Vitellian forces were defeated. Valens was captured while trying to escape to Gaul. As the Flavians advanced on Rome there were steady desertions from Vitellius' cause, though his praetorians remained loyal. Vespasian's brother, *Flavius Sabinus, prefect of the city (see PRAEFECTUS URBI), persuaded Vitellius to abdicate, but the agreement was frustrated by the mob in Rome, and some of the emperor's soldiers who forced Sabinus and his supporters to take refuge on the *Capitol, where the temple of *Jupiter was burnt down. The Flavian army now attacked the city and overcame Vitellian resistance in fierce street fighting. On 20 December Vitellius was dragged through the streets, humiliated, tortured, and killed.

Ancient sources: Suet. *Vit.*; Tac. *Hist.* 2–3. Modern discussion: K. Wellesley, *The Long Year, AD 69* (1975). J. B. C.

Vitellius (*RE* Suppl. 9), **Lucius** (consul AD 34, consul for the second time in 43, and for the third in 47), son of P. Vitellius (a Roman knight from *Luceria (*not* Nuceria: *RE* Suppl. 9. 1741), *procurator of *Augustus), father of the emperor *Vitellius (see previous entry), was a friend of the emperor *Claudius and the most successful politician of the age: he received a public funeral and a statue in the Forum commemorating 'unswerving devotion to the Princeps' (Suet. *Vit.* 3): it was indeed to the source of patronage and power that he attached himself, linking the history of three reigns; his position was strengthened by a nexus between

Vitellii, Plautii, and Petronii. He was a vigorous legate (see LEGATI) of *Syria (AD 35–7), inducing the Parthian *Artabanus II to pay homage and conciliating the Jews: 'he acted with the integrity of ancient times' (Tac. *Ann.* 6. 32). At Rome, however, he earned a different reputation—'he is held by later generations to be an example of the ignominy that goes with sycophancy' (ibid.). Claudius left him in charge of Rome during the invasion of Britain in 43 and chose him for colleague in the censorship (47). Vitellius contributed largely to the ruin of D. *Valerius Asiaticus; and, adopting the cause of *Iulia Agrippina, he acted as a mouthpiece of a loyal senate in advocating her marriage to Claudius. An attempt to prosecute him in 51 failed; he probably died soon after.

Syme, *RP*, see indexes; B. Levick, *Claudius* (1990), indexes.
R. S.; B. M. L.

viticulture See WINE.

Vitruvius (Pol(l)io) (see MAMURRA), a Roman architect and military engineer, in which capacity he served *Caesar. He built a basilica at *Fanum Fortunae; but his fame rests chiefly on a treatise, *De architectura*, on architecture and engineering, compiled partly from his own experience, partly from work by *Hermogenes (1) (to whom he is heavily indebted) and other Greek authors to which his own experiences have been added, sometimes in a disjointed fashion. It is hardly a handbook for *architects: rather a book for people who need to understand architecture. Perhaps its main function was place-seeking from Octavian (see AUGUSTUS), to whom it is addressed. His outlook is essentially Hellenistic, and there is a marked absence of reference to important buildings of *Augustus' reign, though he knows of Roman technical developments, such as concrete construction (which he mistrusts). *De architectura*, the only work of its kind which has survived, is divided into ten books. Book 1 treats of town-planning, architecture in general, and of the qualifications proper in an architect; 2 of building-materials; 3 and 4 of temples and of the 'orders' (see ORDERS, ARCHITECTURAL); 5 of other civic buildings; 6 of domestic buildings; 7 of pavements and decorative plaster-work; 8 of water-supplies; 9 of geometry, mensuration, *astronomy, etc.; 10 of machines, civil and military. The information on materials and methods of construction in 2 and 7, and on rules of proportion in 3 and 4, is of great value.

Vitruvius' importance as an architect is very nearly matched by his significance as a historian of many different departments of ancient science and philosophy, ranging from mathematics to astronomy, to meteorology and medicine. Just as the Hippocratic doctors appreciated the importance of environment to good health, Vitruvius appreciated that in its general and most humane form, architecture included everything which touches on the physical and intellectual life of man and his surroundings.

Often, his encyclopaedic concern with covering a subject thoroughly seems odd to us. In book 2. 1–2 of the *On Architecture* he suggests that the architect who uses bricks needs to be familiar with pre-Socratic theories of matter if he is to understand how his materials can be expected to behave. The doxographies are combed for suitable information. In book 9, the highly abstract geometry of Plato is put to the use of the surveyor—something of which Plato himself might hardly have approved. Similar practical use is made of the mathematics of *Archytas, *Eratosthenes, *Democritus, and *Archimedes, and Vitruvius remains an important source for our knowledge of a great many early Greek scientists. (It was Vitruvius who preserved the famous story of

vivisection

Archimedes' discovery in his bathtub of a way of detecting the adulteration of *Hieron (2) II of Syracuse's golden crown (9, Pref. 9–12).) And so Vitruvius goes on, often employing the theories of the most anti-banausic Greek thinkers to elucidate his very practical subject. Astronomy is necessary for an understanding of the use of *sundials, and surveying instruments; astrology for the insights it offers into the organization of human life; machines and their principles (book 10) because of their utility in the manipulation of materials. As he notes at 10. 1. 4, all machines are created by nature, and the revolutions of the universe ultimately set them in motion. For a man with interests practical and theoretical in equal measure, understanding the nature of nature was central to all.

> TEXT F. Krohn (Teubner, 1912); with Fr. trans. and comm. A. Choisy (1909); with Eng. trans. F. Granger (Loeb, 1931–4), with Ger. trans. and notes C. Fensterbusch (1964); trans. only: M. H. Morgan (1914; new edn. 1960).   R. A. T.; J. T. V.

vivisection Squeamishness about the dissection (let alone vivisection) of animals is a mark of much ancient medicine and zoology, and there is no firm evidence for vivisection in those Hippocratic works (see HIPPOCRATES (2)) which are generally dated to the 5th or 4th cent. BC. (The passage in the Hippocratic treatise *On the Heart* describing the vivisection of a pig (9. 80 Littré) is generally dated to the 3rd cent. BC.) Physicians and zoologists from *Aristotle onwards do, however, seem to have vivisected animals and in some cases even humans. Practitioners themselves rarely show signs of concern with the morality of causing animals suffering in the name of knowledge, although such concern was voiced in other quarters (see ANIMALS, ATTITUDES TO and KNOWLEDGE ABOUT).

Two ancient physicians are notoriously connected with the practice of human vivisection. A. *Cornelius Celsus reports that the Alexandrian anatomists *Herophilus and *Erasistratus vivisected criminals provided for them by the king (see ANATOMY AND PHYSIOLOGY, § IV). Erasistratus at least seems to have been motivated by the belief that the bodies of the living and the dead differ in important physical respects, and that conclusions drawn from the study of a cadaver will not necessarily hold for a living man. Celsus remarks (*De medicina* 1, Proem 26) that the practice had its supporters, who argued that agony for a few is justified by the widespread benefits that accrue from increased understanding of the body's vital functions, but Celsus himself regards it with distaste. The other major ancient witness, *Tertullian (*De anima* 10), manifests his Christian horror at the practice. The truth of these reports has been fiercely disputed in modern times. Some feel that it is difficult to *prove* that human subjects were ever used—and they add that there is very little evidence that the practice was subsequently used in antiquity. Moreover, Galen himself based much of his own human anatomy on his dissections and vivisections of the Barbary ape and the Rhesus monkey, creatures which he thought most closely resembled humans. The implication is that, for Galen at least, humans were not possible subjects. The balance of modern opinion, however, seems to be in favour of accepting the veracity of Celsus' and Tertullian's reports.

> LITERATURE The evidence for Herophilus and Erasistratus is collected and discussed, with a general summary of earlier work, in H. von Staden, *Herophilus: The Art of Medicine in Early Alexandria* (1989), ch. vi; G. E. R. Lloyd, in *Methods and Problems in Greek Science* (1991).   J. T. V.

Vix, a Hallstatt (late 6th-cent. BC) sepulchral mound by Mont Lassois (Côte-d'Or). Its rich grave goods, including a massive bronze Greek mixing-bowl, suggest the growing influence of the cities of the Mediterranean littoral (principally *Massalia) on the tribes of the Celtic hinterland.

> J. Collis, *The European Iron Age* (1984).   J. F. Dr.

Voconius (*RE* 6) **Romanus, Gaius Licinius Marinus,** Spanish literary friend and correspondent of the Younger *Pliny (2), who said his letters read as if the Muses were speaking in Latin (*Ep.* 2. 13), and tried to advance his career. His family came from *Saguntum, and he rose to high office in his province. (*PIR*² L210.)   M. W.

Vocontii, a Celtic people of Gallia Narbonensis (see CELTS; GAUL (TRANSALPINE)) who, from at least the 3rd cent. BC (Livy, 21. 31) occupied the western foothills of the Alps south of the *Allobroges. Under Roman control they remained a *civitas foederata* (see FOEDUS) with the unusual arrangement of two capitals (Plin. *HN* 3. 37), each enjoying *ius Latii*. These were Vasio (mod. Vaison-la-Romaine) and Lucus Augusti (mod. Luc-en-Diois), while Die became *Colonia Dea Augusta Vocontiorum* (*CIL* 12. 690). Vaison, extensively—though not always well—excavated, appears to have originated in a hill-fort south of the Ouvèze, but the Roman town lay mainly north of the river (crossed by a Roman bridge) and the many fine structures uncovered include a theatre, the so-called portico of Pompey, and two groups of houses. Prominent citizens of Vasio were *Afranius Burrus, *Pompeius Trogus, and perhaps *Tacitus (1). Vocontian cavalry fought for *Pompey in Spain and later contributed *alae to the imperial *auxilia.

> R. Syme, *Tacitus* (1958), 613 ff.; C. Goudineau, *Les Fouilles de la Maison du Dauphin à Vaison* (1979); C. Goudineau and Y. de Kisch, *Vaison la Romaine* (1984); A. L. F. Rivet, *Gallia Narbonensis* (1988), 286 ff.   A. L. F. R.; J. F. Dr.

Volaterrae (Etr. Velaθri; mod. Volterra), one of the twelve cities of Etruria (see ETRUSCANS) and capital of the mineral-rich zone of central Tuscany, was established in Villanovan times on a hill dominating the Cecina valley. It is notable for its 4th-cent. walls with arched gates. Volaterrae produced distinctive Archaic and Hellenistic votive bronzes, early stone funerary steles, (late) red-figured and black-glazed pottery, and carved alabaster ash urns: 109 of the latter were found in a circular chamber-tomb, ranging in date from the late 4th to the 1st cent. BC. The city withstood a two-year (82–80 BC) siege by *Sulla's army, and subsequently became a colony for his veterans; *Cicero defended a native of Volaterrae against the loss of his rights of citizenship (Cic. *Caecin.*).

> M. Montagna Pasquinucci, *Kelebai volterrane* (1968), and *Mélanges d'arch.* 1972, 269 ff.; E. Fiumi, *Volterra etrusca e romana* (1976); G. Cateni and F. Fiaschi, *Le urne di Volterra* (1984); G. Cateni, *Volterra: The Etruscan Museum* (1989).   D. W. R. R.

Volcacius (*RE* Suppl. 9, 14) **Moschus,** declaimer from *Pergamum and pupil of *Apollodorus (5). L. *Annaeus Seneca (1), who criticizes him for excessive use of figures (*Controv.* 10 pref. 10), records (ibid. 2. 5. 13) that, after being convicted for poisoning in Rome, he taught at *Massalia (Marseille). He left his money in gratitude to that city (Tac. *Ann.* 4. 43).

> Schanz–Hosius, § 334.   C. J. F.; M. W.

Volcacius Sedigitus (*RE* Volcatius 6), early 1st cent. BC, author of a work *De poetis* ('On Poets') in iambic senarii, of which the largest surviving fragment (quoted by Gell. NA 15. 24) ranks ten authors of *fabulae palliatae* in order of merit: *Caecilius Statius,

*Plautus, *Naevius, *Licinius Imbrex, *Atilius, *Terence, *Turpilius, *Trabea, *Luscius, *Ennius. Further fragments are quoted in *Suetonius' *Life of Terence*, and he discussed the authenticity of plays attributed to Plautus. See PALLIATA.

Courtney, *FLP*; Schanz–Hosius, 1. 165–6.   P. G. M. B.

Volcanus (Volkanus, Vulcanus), an ancient Roman god of destructive, devouring *fire, in both the human environment and in nature: e.g. in volcanoes (see Strabo 5. 246 for his worship at the *Solfatare* of *Puteoli, and Plin. *HN* 2. 240 for fire coming out of the ground near *Mutina), which explains why his temple should always stand outside a city (Vitr. 1. 7. 1), on the authority of the *Etruscan *haruspices. He was associated with *Maia (2) (Gell. *NA* 13. 23. 2 'Maiam Volcani'), the goddess of the irrepressible development of the fire, and was worshipped at Rome from the earliest-known times, having a flamen (see FLAMINES) and a festival, the Volcanalia, on 23 August (calendars). His shrine, the Volcanal, stood in the Area Volcani in the *forum Romanum at the foot of the *Capitol; it may therefore go back to a time when the Forum was still outside the city (see F. Coarelli, *Il Foro Romano, 1: Periodo arcaico* (1983), 164 ff.). A newer temple (before 214 BC) stood in the *Campus Martius. His name is certainly not Latin, the nearest to it in sound being the Cretan Ϝελχανός (for whom see Cook, *Zeus* 2. 946 ff.), who, however, seems to have no resemblance to him in functions. For Etruscan names suggesting Volcanus see F. Altheim, *Griechische Götter* (1930), 172. It is thus possible, but unproved, that he came in from the eastern Mediterranean, through Etruria. He seems to have been worshipped principally to avert fires, hence his by-name Mulciber ('qui ignem mulcet', 'he who mitigates fire'), his title Quietus, and his association with Stata Mater (Dessau, *ILS* 3295, 3306), apparently the goddess who makes fires stand still. On the Volcanalia, when sacrifice (see SACRIFICE, ROMAN) was also made to Juturna, the *Nymphs, *Ops Opifera, and *Quirinus, he was given a curious and (at least for Rome) unexampled sacrifice, live fish from the *Tiber being flung into a fire (see calendars and Varro, *Ling.* 6. 20, Festus, 274. 35 ff. Lindsay). This also can be readily explained as an offering of creatures usually safe from him to induce him to spare those things which at so hot a time of year are particularly liable to be burned. He had a considerable cult at *Ostia, where he seems to have been the chief god (R. Meiggs, *Roman Ostia* (1960), 337 ff.). In classical times he is fully identified with *Hephaestus.

Wissowa, in Roscher, *Lex.* Latte, *RR* 130; Radke, *Götter*, 343 ff. and *Entwicklung*, 92 ff.; Dumézil, *ARR* 320 f.; G. Camassa, *Rivista storica Italiana* 1984, 811 ff.; G. Capdeville, *Volcanus* (1995).   H. J. R.; J. Sch.

Volcei (mod. Buccino), in south Italy, Lucanian city (see LUCANIA) near the Valle di Diano. It was inhabited from the bronze age, and prominent under Roman rule. It entered alliance with Rome *c*.327/6 BC, but revolted during the Hannibalic War (see PUNIC WARS). By resuming alliance with Rome voluntarily in 209, it escaped punishment, and later became a *municipium*, absorbing several neighbouring settlements (Plin. *HN* 3. 98). There are several *villas near the city.

V. Bracco, *Volcei: Forma Italiae 3* (1978); S. L. Dyson, *The Roman Villas of Buccino* (1983).   K. L.

Vologeses I, king of *Parthia, AD 51/2–79/80. His family belonged to *Media Atropatene. Much of his reign was spent in wars with Rome and on his eastern frontier. In 54 Vologeses set his brother *Tiridates (3) on the throne of *Armenia (Tac. *Ann.*

12. 50). Cn. *Domitius Corbulo, sent to re-establish Roman influence, was at first successful, Vologeses being occupied on his eastern frontier with a rebellion. Tiridates fled, and a Roman nominee *Tigranes (4) was crowned as king of Armenia. But Vologeses returned to the war, and at one time gained an advantageous treaty from L. *Caesennius Paetus, after the latter's capitulation at Rhandeia. Finally, peace was made and Tiridates agreed (63) to go to Rome and pay homage to *Nero for his throne: this he did in 66. Vologeses' later relations with Rome were friendlier: he sought *Vespasian's help against the invading Alani (Suet. *Dom.* 2. 2; see ALANS). In his reign Zoroastrianism (see ZOROASTER) made great advances, and the books of the Avesta were collected. In his reign too began a strong reaction against Hellenic influences: Pahlavi first appears along with Greek on his coins. He founded Vologesia near *Seleuceia (1) as a commercial rival. For Vologeses II–V, see ARSACIDS.

N. C. Debevoise, *Political History of Parthia* (1938), 174 ff. (bibliog. on wars with Corbulo n. 101); E. Dąbrowa, *L'Asie Mineure sous les Flaviens* (1980), 18 ff.   M. S. D.; E. W. G.; B. M. L.

Volsci, people of ancient Italy. The Volsci first become prominent in ancient historical narratives of the early 5th cent., when they overran southern *Latium and occupied the Monti Lepini, most of the Pomptine plain, and the coastal region from *Antium to *Tarracina. That the Volscian presence in this area was a new phenomenon is suggested by the traditional accounts of Roman hegemony in southern Latium in the late 6th cent., itself confirmed by the text of the first treaty between Rome and *Carthage (Polyb. 3. 22, 509 BC). The story of *Marcius Coriolanus also points to a vigorous Volscian offensive at this time, and recent excavations at *Satricum (1) (Lat. Pometia), indicate changes in the early 5th cent. which can be explained by the arrival of new people. Satricum became one of the chief Volscian centres; others were Ecetra, Antium, *Velitrae, *Circeii, and Tarracina (which they renamed Anxur).

The Volsci are generally considered to have been an Italic people who migrated to southern Latium from the central *Apennines; this is partly confirmed by the presence of another branch of the Volscians in the middle *Liris valley, around *Sora, *Arpinum, and *Atina (Livy, 10. 1). It is also consistent with linguistic evidence provided by the tiny handful of surviving Volscian inscriptions, especially a bronze tablet from Velitrae known as the *tabula Veliterna* (Vetter, no. 222), dating from the 3rd cent. BC and written in a language similar to *Umbrian (see ITALY, LANGUAGES OF).

During the 5th cent. the Volsci frequently attacked the territory of Rome and its Latin allies, often in concert with the *Aequi. Both peoples were heavily defeated in 431, however, after which their raids virtually ceased. At the end of the 5th cent. and the first decades of the 4th the Romans took the initiative, and gradually conquered the Volsci, founding Latin colonies (see COLONIZATION, ROMAN) at Circeii (393), Satricum (385), and Setia (382), and annexing the Pomptine plain (the territory of the tribe Pomptina) in 358. The Volsci opposed Rome in the Latin War, but were defeated by C. *Maenius in 338. The Volsci of the Liris valley were conquered during the Second Samnite War (see ROME (HISTORY; SAMNIUM), and Sora became a Latin colony in 304. After that they were rapidly and thoroughly Romanized. C. *Marius (1) and *Cicero (both from Arpinum) seem Roman enough.

G. Radke, *RE* 9 A 1, 'Volsci', 773–827; E. Vetter, *Handbuch der italische Dialekte* (1953), 1. 156; E. T. Salmon, *The Making of Roman Italy* (1982), 9 ff.; T. J. Cornell, *CAH* 7²/2 (1989), 281 ff.; F. Coarelli, in *Crise et*

1611

transformation des sociétés archaïques, CEFR 137 (1990), 117–33; M. Cristofani and others, *I Volsci*, in *Arch. Laz.* 11/1 (1992).   T. J. Co.

Volsinii (Etr. Velzna-). Volsinii Veteres, one of the twelve cities of Etruria (see ETRUSCANS), may safely be equated with medieval and modern Orvieto and its temples (notably Belvedere, of *Vitruvius' Tuscan type), painted tombs, and 6th-/5th-cent. Cannicella and Crocefisso del Tufo cemeteries. The latter are laid out in well-planned 'streets' of built chambers; epigraphy attests 90 prosperous families at Crocefisso del Tufo between 550 and 500 BC, among them Italic foreigners and at least one Celt. The survivors of the Volsinian rebellion of 294 BC were resettled by Rome at Volsinii Novi (Zonar. 8. 7. 8), identified with the late republican centre excavated (1946 onwards) near Bolsena by the École Française. The original Volsinii was traditionally associated with the federal sanctuary of the twelve Etruscan cities known as the Fanum Voltumnae (Livy, 4. 60. 9–5. 1): see VOLTUMNA; this continues to elude archaeological definition.

B. Klakowicz, *Topografia e storia delle ricerche archeologiche in Orvieto e suo contado* (5 vols.; 1972–8); *Annali Museo Claudio Faina*, 1980 onwards (conference proceedings); A. E. Feruglio (ed.), *Pittura etrusca a Orvieto* (1982); M. Garofoli, *Orvieto, Crocefisso del Tufo* (1983); *Bolsena 1946–1986* (exhib. cat. Rome, 1987: École Française excavations). Epigraphy: M. Pallottino, *Stud. Etr.* 1950–1, 229 ff. and 1952–3, 179 ff.; C. De Simone, *PP* 1978, 370 ff. (Celtic Katacina).   D. W. R. R.

Voltacilius (?) Pilutus (so the MSS) is said by *Suetonius (*Gramm. Rhet.* 27 Brugnoli, citing *Cornelius Nepos) to have been the first freedman to write history at Rome, and to have recorded the deeds of *Pompey and Pompey's father (see POMPEIUS STRABO, CN.). *Jerome, who calls him Vultacilius Plotus, says he opened a school in Rome in 81 BC. He may be the same as 'M. Votacilius Pitholaus' (Macrob. *Sat.* 2. 2. 13), the poet Pitholaus of Suet. *Iul.* 75, and even the Pitholeon from Rhodes of Hor. *Sat.* 1. 10. 22.

Schanz–Hosius, § 115.   M. W.

Voltumna, an Etruscan goddess, at whose shrine the Etruscan federal council met (Livy, 4. 23. 5; 25. 7; 61. 2; 5. 17. 6; 6. 2. 2; cf. *CIL* 11. 5265 and J. Gascou, *Mélanges d'arch.* 1967, for the survival of these meetings.). Nothing more is known of her and the site of the shrine is uncertain (see VOLSINII). Some connection with *Vertumnus etymologically is likely.

L. R. Taylor, *Local Cults of Etruria* (1923), 230 ff.; W. Eisenhut, *RE* 9 A 850 ff.   J. Sch.

Volturnus, the principal river of *Campania, a considerable stream often mentioned in ancient accounts of Samnite and Hannibalic Wars (see SAMNIUM; PUNIC WARS). It rises in Samnium and flows southward past *Aesernia, *Venafrum, and *Allifae until joined by its tributary, the Calor, whereupon it turns abruptly westward to enter the Tyrrhenian sea about 32 km. (20 mi.) below *Casilinum.   E. T. S.

Volubilis (mod. Oubili), a town in the Djebel Zerhoun plain in Morocco, 20 km. (12 mi.) north of Meknes. Already in existence in the 4th or early 3rd cent. BC, it soon became thoroughly Punicized, with *suffetes* as chief magistrates (see CARTHAGE). The 2nd- and 1st-cent. BC town already covered some 15 ha. and had a regular street grid. It particularly flourished as the western capital of *Juba II; two temples under the later forum, and a monumental altar under the capitolium (see CAPITOL), belong to this phase. It was rewarded by *Claudius with the rank of *municipium* for supporting Rome against Aedmon's rebellion. Thereafter expansion was rapid. The forum is probably Neronian

(i.e. AD 54–68, see NERO), the two sets of baths are both Flavian in origin, and two street grids with different orientations in the north and north-eastern quarters are both now known to date from before the end of the 1st cent. The city walls (2.35 km. (1.5 mi.) long, with eight gates), enclosing an area of c.40 hectares, were added in the 160s. The forum was remodelled in the 3rd cent. and the capitolium completed; a monumental arch was added under *Caracalla. The north-east quarter was also substantially rebuilt in Severan times and later, when many of its peristyle houses received figured *mosaics. Field survey in the Sebou valley north of Volubilis has shown that the countryside was also extensively settled with farms in the 1st cent. AD and reached its greatest prosperity in the 2nd cent. The farming economy was based in part on the *olive, the importance of which in Volubilis itself is demonstrated by the discovery of 55 oil-presses in the town. Both Volubilis and surrounding farms were abandoned c.285 as a result of the Diocletianic reorganization (see DIOCLETIAN) of *Mauretania Tingitanis.

PECS, entry under 'Volubilis'; R. Thouvenot, *Volubilis* (1949); R. Étienne, *Le Quartier nord-est de Volubilis* (1960); R. Rebuffat, *Volubilis* (1972); H. Morestin, *Le Temple B de Volubilis* (1980); A. Jodin, *Volubilis Regia Iubae* (1987). Oileries: A. Akerraz and E. Lenoir, *Bulletin d'Archéologie Marocaine* 1981–2, 69–101. Territory: A. Akerraz and E. Lenoir, in *L'Afrique dans l'occident romain* (1990), 213–29.   B. H. W.; R. J. A. W.

Volumnius (*RE* 8), **Publius,** a philosopher who accompanied *Brutus in his campaign against the triumvirs (see TRIUMVIRI). He recorded, perhaps in a biography, prodigies (see PORTENTS) which preceded Brutus' last battle (Plut. *Brut.* 48).   M. T. G.

Volusius (*RE* 7) **Maecianus, Lucius,** a lawyer of the mid-2nd cent. AD, probably came from *Ostia, where inscriptions recording his career have been found. He became *a libellis* (secretary for petitions) to *Antoninus Pius in *Hadrian's reign, and about AD 150 returned as *a libellis* to Pius, now sole emperor, then became *praefectus annonae* (prefect of the corn supply) and in 160–2 governor of Egypt. He taught Marcus *Aurelius, even writing a book on fractions and measurements for him, but failed to impress the future emperor. He seems to have written in Greek on the Rhodian sea law; and his fourteen books (*libri*) on *Iudicia publica* ('Serious Crimes') broke new ground on a scale never later reached, as did his sixteen books on *Fideicommissa* (somewhat resembling trusts). (*PIR*[2] 5. 657.)

Lenel, *Pal.* 1. 575–88; *HLL* 4 (forthcoming), § 419. 2; Kunkel (1967), 174–6; L. Fanizza, *Giuristi crimini leggi nell'età degli Antonini* (1982); Honoré (1962), 162–3.   T. Hon.

Votienus (*RE*, entry under 'Votienus') **Montanus,** orator from *Narbo. Although L. *Annaeus Seneca (1), *Controv.* 9, pref., assigns him a long speech explaining why he never took part in *declamations, numerous extracts, chiefly from the same book, show him taking an active part in *controversiae*. Mam. *Aemilius Scaurus called him the *Ovid of orators, because he would never let well alone. In AD 25 he was sentenced to exile in a senate trial embarrassing to *Tiberius and probably engineered by L. *Aelius (Tac. *Ann.* 4. 42). He died in exile a few years later.   E. B.

voting See ELECTIONS AND VOTING, *Greek and Roman*; also (for *suffragium*) CITIZENSHIP, ROMAN; MUNICIPIUM.

votive offerings are voluntary dedications to the gods, resulting not from prescribed ritual or sacred calendars but from *ad hoc* vows of individuals or communities in circumstances usually of anxiety, transition, or achievement. Votives display a considerable number of constant features in both Greek and Roman religions. Dedications consisted in renunciation and long-term symbolic investment in the divine, in expectation of good things to come. Unlike *sacrifice, where one 'destroys', by depositing a perceptible object in a sanctuary one both loses it and makes it eternal. One of the primary functions of *temples was to house expensive dedications; the temple itself was a communal dedication, *anathēma*, to the god (cf. Plut. *Per.* 12, 14).

On a personal level, just like prayers, votive offerings emphasize the individual's 'if–then' relations with the gods. The gift to the sanctuary both mediates and serves as testimony to the occasion of the vow. 'If my ship arrives safely, if I recover from illness, if my crop succeeds, etc. ... I shall dedicate a statue, a *tithe, a temple', and so on. One of the earliest Greek inscriptions (*c.*700 BC, on a bronze statuette) says: 'Mantiklos, has dedicated me to the Striker from Afar with the Silver Bow [*Apollo] ... grant in exchange, Phoebus, an agreeable reward' (*LSAG* 94, no. 1).

Votive offerings punctuate life's passages: emerging from puberty, boys and girls dedicate toys or locks of their hair (girls: also girdles to *Artemis), thus 'letting go' (*aphienai*) of a part of their changing body to the god. Retiring craftsmen may 'give up' tools of their trade: what sustained one's passing life is now renounced to become 'sacred' and permanent at a sanctuary. Personal victory at competitions could be followed by an offering of the prize: *Hesiod, for example, dedicated the tripod he won at the competition in *Chalcis to the *Muses at *Helicon, where they first taught him 'the way of clear song' (*Works and Days* 659). Such dedications could become compulsory: the victors in the Triopia (see TRIOPAS) were compelled to leave their tripods as dedications to Apollo (Hdt. 1. 144). War served as occasion for both individual and collective offerings. *Hector swears to hang the arms of his foe in the temple of Apollo (*Il.* 7. 83). After simultaneous victories over the Persians (see PERSIAN WARS) and *Carthage in 480 BC, *Themistocles (Plut. *Them.* 22) and *Gelon (Diod. Sic. 11. 26. 7) dedicated temples. Similarly, in 296 Ap. *Claudius Caecus vowed a temple to *Bellona Victrix (Livy, 9. 43. 25), in 195 M. *Porcius Cato (1) fulfilled his vow to *Victoria Virgo, and so on. Collective dedications in the form of a tithe (*dekatē*) or the 'top' of the piles of booty (*akrothinia*), a percentage from the sales of prisoners, and so on, became common from the Archaic period. Treasuries in the Panhellenic sanctuaries contained dedicated memorials of victories won over centuries, serving as reminders of fluctuating fortunes and animosities.

The vow as well as the act of giving was made publicly, accompanied by *euchē*, a word signifying both cry, *prayer, and vow (the Latin formula *ex voto* was so common as to become a noun). The dedicated object, such as a mask or a figurine, would be deposited at the shrine. Sometimes paintings or sculptural reliefs portray (vowed?) acts of sacrifice (which leave no traces). The perpetuation of the gift could be enhanced by an inscription: 'Mnasithales dedicated me [= the vase] to Antiphamos' (the hero-*founder of *Gela in Sicily), reads the text on a 5th-cent. cup (*LSAG* 278, no. 53). The variety of dedicated objects could be enormous, depending on occasion and function of the deity. Representations of limbs (e.g. hands, legs, penises) were deposited at healing sanctuaries; cakes, garments, masks, arms, and especially figurines were common (e.g. about 100,000 excavated at the sanctuary of *Artemis Orthia at Sparta). Most prominent and well known for their artistic value were the statues (not cult-images) 'set up' (*anathēmata*) in sanctuaries, advertising the donors and evoking the god. See next entry; also SANCTUARIES, GREEK.

W. H. D. Rouse, *Greek Votive Offerings: An Essay in the History of Greek Religion* (1902; repr. 1976); F. T. van Straten, in H. S. Versnel (ed.), *Faith, Hope and Worship* (1981), 65–151; T. Linders and G. Nordquist (eds.), *Gifts to the Gods: Proceedings of the Uppsala Symposium 1985* (1987); B. Alroth, *Greek Gods and Figurines: Aspects of the Anthropomorphic Dedications* (1989).
I. M.

votum, a vow. Both Greeks and Romans habitually made promises to gods, in order to persuade them to grant a favour stipulated in advance. If the gods fulfilled their part, the vow-maker fell under the obligation to do as he had promised. Although the practice was no less popular in Greece, the vow developed an institutional form especially in Rome, due to the practical and juridical nature of Roman religion. Expressions such as *v(otum) s(oluit) l(ibens) m(erito)* ('NN has paid his vow with pleasure and deservedly'), mainly in private votive gifts, and *voti reus, voti damnatus* ('obliged to fulfil his vow'), mainly in public vows, belong to the fixed formulas. In the private sphere *prayers for recovery and good health, crops, childbirth, safe return from an expedition, etc. were, in case of fulfilment, answered by a great variety of *votive offerings. In public votive religion it was the magistrate who in the name of the state undertook to offer to a god or gods sacrifices, games, the building of a temple or an altar etc., if the god on his side would give his assistance in such basic collective crises as war, epidemics, and drought. Formulas had to be pronounced in public and were very strict: mistakes required the repetition of the whole ceremony. In addition to these extraordinary vows there were also regular *vota*, pronounced for a definite period: e.g. the annually renewed *vota* of the magistrates for the welfare of the state on 1 January before the first regular sitting of the senate, and the *vota* at the termination of the *lustrum* (see LUSTRATION). Such vows found their direct continuation under the empire in the *vota pro salute imperatoris* (for the health or safety of emperor and his family) and became periodical: *vota quinquennalia, decennalia* (for five, ten years). Extraordinary vows (for the safe return of the emperor from an expedition, for the recovery of the empress in cases of sudden illness) continued to exist into late antiquity. The text of the *votum* was officially fixed in the presence of the pontifices (see PONTIFEX), and the document went into the archives.

W. Eisenhut, *RE* Suppl. 14 (1974), 964–73, 'Votum'; J. Scheid, *Romulus et ses frères* (1990).
H. S. V.

vows See PRAYER; VOTIVE OFFERINGS; VOTUM.

Vulcan See VOLCANUS.

Vulci (Etr. *Velχ-*), 20 km. (12½ mi.) north-west of *Tarquinii in central Italy, situated on a plateau overlooking the river Fiora and with a commanding view of Monte Argentario and Cosa, was one of the twelve cities of Etruria (see ETRUSCANS). It was an important centre by the late 8th cent. BC, rich in painted pottery and bronze; its *orientalizing period has much in common with that of *Vetulonia. From the late 7th cent., Vulci was the centre of schools of stone-carving, vase-painting, and of the manufacture of bronze utensils that were widely exported. Official and clandestine attention has been mainly concentrated on the tombs, dating from the Villanovan period onwards (see VILLANO-VAN CULTURE), several thousands of which had been emptied by the mid-19th cent.: Vulci was the principal importer to Etruria of Attic black- and red-figure vases (see POTTERY, GREEK).

S. Gsell, *Fouilles dans la nécropole de Vulci* (1891); *Atti X Convegno Studi Etruschi 1975* (1977); G. Riccioni, in *IBR* 241 ff.; N. J. Spivey, *The Micali Painter and his Followers* (1987); F. Buranelli, *Gli scavi a Vulci della Società*

Vulgate

Vincenzo Campanari—Governo Pontificio (1835–1837) (1991).

D. W. R. R.

Vulgate, Latin version of the Bible. The first Latin translations of scripture (*Vetus Latina*, Old Latin) appeared in the 2nd cent. AD. But by a variety of processes the texts in use began to diverge more and more, and by the 4th cent. the situation was chaotic. An attempt to impose order was made in the early 380s by Pope *Damasus, who commissioned *Jerome to revise the Latin text of the Gospels, and perhaps of the whole of the Bible, in the light of the Greek. The gospel revision was completed in 384, and during his early years in the Holy Land (386–*c.*390) Jerome went on to produce versions of the Psalter (the 'Gallican Psalter') and of other books of the OT (Old Testament) on the basis of the LXX (see SEPTUAGINT). But around 390 Jerome became convinced that a translation of a translation would not do, particularly when arguing points of scripture with Jews, and during the next fifteen years or thereabouts he produced a completely new translation of the Hebrew books of the OT on the basis of the original, and with the aid of the Greek versions of Aquila and Symmachus. At the request of friends, and with the aid of an interpreter, he also translated from the *Aramaic the books of Tobit and Judith, which he did not recognize as part of the canon.

Jerome's revision of the Gospels was essentially conservative; in his preface he maintained that he had altered the Old Latin text only when it seemed absolutely necessary, retaining in other cases what had become familiar phraseology. This principle, though by no means rigorously observed throughout, explains inconsistencies in practice (e.g. 'high priest' is usually translated in Matthew and Luke by *princeps sacerdotum*, in Mark by *summus sacerdos*, and in John by *pontifex*). His own new translations from the Hebrew also display apparent contradictions: at times they are slavishly literal, at others extremely free. At no point, however, did Jerome attempt to render Scripture in a stylish, classicizing Latin: what mattered was not the literary packaging but the content, and the word of God should be written in language ordinary people could understand and appreciate.

Though it took centuries to win complete acceptance by the Church, Jerome's translation of the Hebrew OT, together with his revision of the Gospels, came to form the backbone of the Vulgate, which coalesced around the 8th cent. and became the standard Latin text of the Bible. The Vulgate also included the Gallican Psalter (preferred to the version from the Hebrew), Jerome's translations of Tobit and Judith, and the remaining books of the Apocrypha and NT in non-Jeromian versions; the revision from the Old Latin of *Acts, Epistles, and Revelation may be attributable to Jerome's follower, Rufinus the Syrian.

TEXTS *Biblia Sacra iuxta Latinam Vulgatam Versionem* (Benedictine edn.), Genesis– (1926–); R. Weber (3rd edn., 1983).
CONCORDANCE B. Fischer (1977).
STUDIES H. J. Vogels, *Vulgatastudien* (1928); H. F. D. Sparks, in *The Cambridge History of the Bible*, 1 (1970), 510–26; B. Fischer, in K. Aland, *Die alten Übersetzungen des Neuen Testaments* (1972), 1–92; B. M. Metzger, *The Early Versions of the New Testament* (1977), 330 ff.; P.-M. Bogaert, *Revue théologique de Louvain* 1988, 137–59, 276–314.
J. H. D. S.

Vulgate tradition, about Alexander the Great. See ALEXANDER (3) THE GREAT (bibliog.); CLEITARCHUS.

wager, judicial See LAW AND PROCEDURE, ROMAN, § 3.2; SACRA-MENTUM.

wages, payment in cash or kind in return for labour services, are attested as early as the *thētes* (landless labourers) of the *Iliad* and *Odyssey.* Homeric references point to the depressed status of the *thēs*: uncertain of receiving promised pay (*Il.* 21. 441 ff.) and, lacking protection of the *oikos* (household), they ranked even lower than slaves (*Od.* 11. 489 ff.). With significant exceptions, precariousness remained the characteristic of the wage-labourer through antiquity, dependent on availability of casual employment (e.g. at harvest time, on public building projects, in service as a *mercenary). The divisions between different types of *labour were fluid, with *peasants, *artisans, and slaves (see SLAVERY) potentially doubling up as wage-labourers. In late 5th-cent. Athens, the *metic Simias hired himself out along with his four slaves to work on the *Erechtheum. Roman law made special provision for the hiring out of slaves. In Athens, those looking for work gathered each day on a hill overlooking the *agora. From the mid-5th cent., Athens was exceptional among Greek states in offering an increasing range of payment for public service (jurors, council members, minor officials, and, eventually, those attending the assembly). The relationship between Athens as *emmisthos polis* ('a *polis in receipt of pay') and exploitation of the 5th-cent. empire is disputed. Although there is room for doubting the literal truth of *Aristotle's claim that 'more than twenty thousand men' were supported from internal and external sources (*Ath. Pol.* 24. 3), public pay buttressed democracy (see DEMOCRACY, ATHENIAN) by enhancing participation and reducing dependence of the poor on the wealthy. Throughout the ancient world, wage rates were fixed more by custom than by demand and supply and were slow to change. Figures have little meaning without detailed knowledge of circumstances and overall cost of living. The skilled workers on the Erechtheum earning one drachma per day would not always have found employment; likewise the jurors, receiving two obols (three after *c.*425) for each day in court. For the city of Rome, a combination of dependence on patrons and receipt of the corn dole (see FOOD SUPPLY) distorts any overall assessment of rates of pay. *Cicero's rhetorical claim (*QRosc.* 28) that a feeble slave could earn three sesterces per day in Rome forms a fragile basis for generalization. *Diocletian's 'Price Edict' of AD 296, has as its lowest maximum wage that of the farm labourer at 25 denarii per day, with an unspecified payment in kind. Comparisons of annual pay of legionaries (1,200 sesterces in 2nd cent. AD; 1,800 under Diocletian) are similarly complicated by payments in kind, donatives, and deductions for equipment.

M. I. Finley, *The World of Odysseus* (1977); A. Fuks, *Social Conflict in Greece* (1984), 303 ff.; J. H. Randall, *AJArch.* 1953, 199 ff.; P. A. Brunt, *JRS* 1980, 81 ff.; P. Garnsey (ed.), *Non-Slave Labour in the Greco-Roman World* (1980); G. E. M. de Ste. Croix, *The Class Struggle in the Ancient Greek World* (1981), and *CQ* 1975, 48 ff.; M. I. Finley, *The Ancient Economy* (1973; repr. 1985), and *Economy and Society in Ancient Greece* (1981), 41 ff.; M. M. Markle, in P. Cartledge and F. D. Harvey (eds.), *CRUX* (1985), 265 ff.; D. M. Halperin, *One Hundred Years of Homosexuality* (1990), 107 ff.; R. Duncan-Jones, *The Economy of the Roman Empire* (1974), and *Structure and Scale in the Roman Economy* (1990), 105 ff.; S. Lauffer, *Diokletians Preisedikt* (1971).   P. C. M.

wall of Antoninus, a Roman frontier-wall 59 km. (37 mi.) long, running from Bridgeness on the Forth to Old Kilpatrick on the Clyde, built for *Antoninus Pius (SHA *Ant. Pius* 5. 4) in AD 139–42 by Q. *Lollius Urbicus. The wall was of turf, standing upon a cobbled foundation 4.5–5 m. (*c.*15–16 ft.) wide and systematically built in long sectors by Legions II, VI, and XX (see LEGION), who marked their work by inscribed slabs (*RIB* 2139, 2173, 2184–6, 2193–4, 2196–200, 2203–6, 2208). Seven metres (23 ft.) or more in front of the wall lay a ditch, approaching 12 m. (39 ft.) wide and not less than 3.6 m. (11½ ft.) deep. Forts occur at Carriden (1.6 ha.), Inveravon, Mumrills (2.6 ha.), Falkirk, Rough Castle (0.4 ha.), Castlecary (1.4 ha.), Westerwood (0.8 ha.), Croy Hill (0.6 ha.), Bar Hill (1.3 ha.), Auchendavy (1.1 ha.), Kirkintilloch, Cadder (1.1 ha.), Balmuildy (1.6 ha.), Bearsden (0.9 ha.), Castlehill (1 ha.), Duntocher (0.2 ha.), Old Kilpatrick (1.7 ha.). Minor structures are signalling platforms, occurring at high points, and fortlets (0.04 ha.), one of them at the passage of the northward road at Watling Lodge, near Falkirk. Thus, the Antonine wall is structurally an advance upon Hadrian's turf wall (see WALL OF HADRIAN) in its economy of material and rubble foundation, allowing better drainage, while its garrison was distributed in small close-spaced forts instead of large forts and milecastles. Beyond the wall outposts/forts of the north road were held as far as Strathearn on the east, while on the west a road led towards Dumbarton, to a fortified port as yet unknown. Posts on the flank are also known.

Excavation of the forts reveals two principal periods of occupation, a suspected third being probably no more than traces of levelling and tidying-up on evacuation. Period I (*c.*139/42–154/8) witnessed a change in the building plan with an increase in the number of forts over those originally planned. The initial plan resembled that of the last constructional phase of Hadrian's Wall. Period I ended with demolition when the troops were withdrawn south. The short-lived reoccupation of Period II was begun before the death of Antoninus Pius, perhaps under the governor Iulius Verus *c.*158, and ended in *c.*164. There was no subsequent activity at the wall forts, although others in southern Scotland were retained as outposts for Hadrian's Wall.

wall of Aurelian

W. Hanson and G. Maxwell, *Rome's North-West Frontier: The Antonine Wall* (1983).   I. A. R.; S. S. F.; M. J. M.

wall of Aurelian, the city wall of Rome, constructed by *Aurelian in AD 271–5 in anticipation of a sudden barbarian inroad (SHA *Aurel.* 21. 9, 39. 2; Aurel. Vict. *Caes.* 35; Malalas, *Chron.* 12. 299), and completed by Probus (Zos. 1. 49). The original wall, about 6.5 m. (21 ft.) high to the battlements, extended for 18.8 km. (11½ mi.) with 381 projecting rectangular towers at intervals of 100 Roman ft. (29.6 m.; 32.4 yds.), except along the river. The wall was usually solid but in places had an internal gallery or was treated as a revetment. It frequently incorporated earlier structures, such as the terrace wall of the horti Aciliani (*muro torto*), the Castra Praetoria, the Amphitheatrum Castrense, private houses and tenements, and the tomb of *Cestius Epulo. It enclosed most of the fourteen regions (see REGIO) but only a relatively small part of Trastevere. The gates, mostly named from the principal roads, were portae *Flaminia*, Pinciana, Salaria, Nomentana, 'Chiusa', Tiburtina, Praenestina-Labicana, Asinaria, Metrobia, Latina, *Appia*, Ardeatina, *Ostiensis*, *Portuensis*, Aurelia-Pancraziana, Septimiana, Aurelia-Sancti Petri. All were flanked by simple semicircular towers, those italicized originally having two openings. There were also at least six postern gates. The wall was thus designed to repel a raid rather than stand siege. *Maxentius (AD 306–12) made repairs and began a ditch; the doubling in height of the wall by adding a gallery and the remodelling of the gates usually associated with this have now been attributed to *Stilicho in 401–3 (*CIL* 6. 1188–90; Claud. *VI cons. Hon.* 529). Later repairs occurred under *Valentinian III, probably after the earthquake of 442, and under *Theoderic (1) in 507–11. *Belisarius, in preparation for the siege of 536, refurbished the wall and dug a large ditch in front of it.

I. A. Richmond, *The City Wall of Imperial Rome* (1930); M. Todd, *The Walls of Rome* (1978); L. Cozza, *Analecta Romana Instituti Danici* (1987), 25 ff.; Nash, *Pict. Dict. Rome* 2. 86 ff.   I. A. R.; J. D.

wall of Hadrian, a frontier-wall (see LIMES) of Roman *Britain, running for 80 Roman miles (118 km.; 73 mi.) from Wallsend-on-Tyne to Bowness-on-Solway. Erected under the governor A. *Platorius Nepos in *c.* AD 122–6, it was first designed to start at Pons Aelius, Newcastle upon Tyne, the eastern 67 km. (42 mi.) being in stone (3 m. (10 ft.) thick and perhaps 4.2 m. (13½ ft.) high) and the western 46 km. (31 mi.) in turf (6 m. (19½ ft.) broad at the base and some 4.2 m. (13½ ft.) high). Six metres (19½ ft.) in front of the wall ran a V-shaped ditch (generally 8.2 m. (26½ ft.) wide and 3 m. (10 ft.) deep). Fortified gateways (milecastles), with towered gates to the north, occurred every Roman mile (1,481 m.; 1,620 yds.) and there were intermediate turrets (observation towers) every third of a mile (494 m.; 540 yds.). Milecastles and turrets continued to the west down the Cumbrian coast to St Bees Head. Similar provisions may have existed on the south bank of the Tyne from Newcastle to the South Shields fort. North of the barrier were three outpost forts at Bewcastle, Netherby, and Birrens. As construction progressed, changes came. The stone wall was reduced to 2.5 m. (7½ ft.) in width, and extended 6 km. (4 mi.) eastwards to Wallsend, and 6 km. westward (replacing the Turf Wall).

As planned, garrison forts remained behind the barrier on the Stanegate, the Trajanic road from Corbridge to Carlisle. At an early stage in construction the decision was taken to build a series of twelve forts astride the wall. These were at Wallsend (1.6 ha.), Benwell (2.2 ha.), Rudchester (1.8 ha.), Halton Chesters (1.7 ha.), Chesters (2.3 ha.), Housesteads (2.0 ha.), Great Chesters (1.35 ha.), Birdoswald (2.15 ha.), Castlesteads (1.5 ha.), Stanwix (3.7 ha.), Burgh-by-Sands (2 ha.) and Bowness-on-Solway (2.8 ha.). On the Cumbrian coast Beckford (1.0 ha.) and Moresby (1.4 ha.) were also added on either side of the existing fort at Maryport. After the decision to move forts onto the line of the frontier the so-called vallum was added to the south of the Wall. The vallum was a flat-bottomed ditch 6 m. (19½ ft.) wide and 3 m. (10 ft.) deep with the upcast disposed in two turf-curbed mounds, one on either side, set back 9 m. (29½ ft.) from the lip of the ditch. This provided a continuous cleared area behind the forts along the full length of the frontier, presumably designed to ensure security. Crossings were limited to causeways at the forts. Lateral communication was first supplied by branches from the Stanegate; only later did the Military Way, between vallum and wall, connect forts and milecastles. Before the end of the reign of *Hadrian further forts were added to the system at Carrawburgh (1.6 ha.), Carvoran (1.4 ha.), and Drumburgh (0.8 ha.), bringing the garrison to *c.*9,090 men (excluding the Cumbrian coast) in auxiliary units.

After the accession of *Antoninus Pius the frontier was advanced to the *wall of Antoninus on the Forth–Clyde line. Hadrian's wall was rendered open to traffic by removing the gates from milecastles and slighting the vallum. In the 160s the wall was brought back into full use with the abandonment of the Antonine wall. There was extensive rebuilding and repair, but forts were reoccupied by units of similar size and type to those previously present. Decreasing emphasis was placed on turrets and milecastles, with those on the Cumbrian coast apparently abandoned. The pattern so established endured for almost two hundred years with only gradual modification, piecemeal rebuilding, and a slow decline in the effective size of the garrisons. The lack of evidence for the late Roman field army suggests that the wall remained effective. There is no sound evidence for any violent destruction or wholesale removal of the garrison in the late 4th or early 5th cent.

D. J. Breeze and B. Dobson, *Hadrian's Wall*, 3rd edn. (1987); J. C. Bruce, *Handbook to the Roman Wall*, 13th edn., ed. C. M. Daniels (1978).   I. A. R.; S. S. F.; M. J. M.

wall of Servius, the city-wall of republican Rome, traditionally assigned to King Servius *Tullius, actually belongs to 378 BC. It is of Grotta Oscura tufa, built in headers and stretchers, 4.5 m. (15 ft.) thick and at least 8.5 m. (28 ft.) high, retaining an earth bank or terrace, and is comparable to the contemporary wall of *Pompeii II. The masons' marks, with Hellenistic affinities, suggest Greek contractors. The wall was some 11 km. (7 mi.) long and its course, dictated by contours, enclosed an irregular area, estimated at 426 ha. (Beloch, *Röm. Gesch.* 208), and embracing the *Quirinal, *Viminal, Oppian, Caelian (see CAELIUS MONS), *Aventine, and fortified Capitoline hills (see CAPITOL). There is dispute about the course between the last two points (Coarelli, 13 ff.), and about the relation of the wall to the *Palatine fortification. The names of the gates are well known, but the location of some is debated and their structure is uncertain. In the 2nd cent. BC the wall was heightened to some 16 m. (52 ft.), and was also supplied with casemates for *ballistae* (see ARTILLERY), covering approaches to the gates. During the 1st cent. BC neglect and encroachment made the course hard to find in places even by *Augustus' time, though elsewhere it remained visible, and one or two substantial sections are still standing, most notably on the south side of the Aventine and in the Piazza dei Cinquecento outside the Termini station.

The nature of Rome's defences before 378 BC is problematic. That the republican wall was preceded by an earlier fortification along the same line is unlikely; the events of the Gallic sack of 390 BC clearly imply that Rome had no effective all-round defences. Servius Tullius is said to have established the sacred boundary of the city (the *pomerium*), but this had a different course and was probably not accompanied by fortifications. The most detailed sources (esp. Strab. 5. 3. 7, p. 234 C) tell us that Servius' contribution to Rome's defences was to fortify the vulnerable section between the Viminal and the Esquiline with a large earthwork. This is a clear reference to the so-called *agger*, which may well date back to the 6th cent. BC (the find of a small sherd of Attic red-figure pottery of *c*.480 BC, is insufficient to provide a firm *terminus post quem*, as Gjerstad thought—*Early Rome 3*. 27 ff.). The *agger* is a typical promontory defence, as at *Ardea. *Varro speaks of an earth wall (*murus terreus*) at the Carinae (*Ling*. 5. 48), which may have been an inner line of defence; the rest of the fortification, as at Ardea, would depend on scarped cliffs in the individual hills.

G. Säflund, *Le mura di Roma repubblicana* (1932); *Roma Medio-Repubblicana*, exhib. cat. (1973), 7–31; R. Thomsen, *King Servius Tullius* (1980), 218–35; F. Coarelli, *Il foro Boario* (1988), 13 ff.; 35 ff.; Richardson, *Topog. Dict. Ancient Rome*, 262–3; R. Ross Holloway, *The Archaeology of Early Rome and Latium* (1994), 91–102. Ardea: C. Morselli, E. Tortorici, *Ardea* (1982).   I. A. R.; T. J. Co.

war, art of, Greek Before the second half of the 5th cent. BC, when some of the *sophists are said to have studied the art of war, the Greeks seem to have made no attempt to systematize military theory. The only such works to have survived are *Xenophon (1)'s essay on the duties of a cavalry officer, his fictional account of Cyrus' organization of his army in the *Cyropaedia*, and the treatise on siege-craft by *Aeneas Tacticus. We are thus largely left to deduce the Greek art of war from the warfare itself.

Early wars, *Thucydides (2) says (1. 15. 3–5), were between neighbours, and even the exception he mentions—the 8th-cent. BC Lelantine War—seems just to have been a series of such conflicts; see GREECE (PREHISTORY AND HISTORY), *Archaic age*. They were also clearly fought for territory, involving a relatively straightforward strategy, and this remained true even when the object was no longer territorial aggrandizement but hegemony, for ravaging could usually compel confrontation, and, if the invaders won, the acceptance of a more or less subordinate relationship.

As for tactics, it is difficult to discern what, if any, were employed. The *Iliad* (see HOMER) is the earliest surviving account of warfare, but it is uncertain how far it reflects reality in giving prominence to a few heroes and their exploits. If it does, there was really no place for tactics, and even when, about a century later, *Tyrtaeus begins to emphasize the necessity of maintaining cohesion, and missile-armed troops like Homer's spear-throwing heroes have become quite unimportant, we still learn nothing about how a battle was won, other than by an exemplary display of courage.

The first time the Greeks had to think in more complex strategic terms was probably during the *Persian Wars, but even then the Athenians probably never thought of anything else but of confronting the invader at Marathon (see MARATHON, BATTLE OF), and in 480, though confrontation in the open was evidently to be avoided, the Greeks initially seem to have decided just to try to hold the invader as far north as possible; in 479, when they took the offensive, they also simply moved to confront the enemy at Plataea (see PLATAEA, BATTLE OF). Tactics, too, seem still to have been primitive, with the possible exception of those employed at

Marathon. At Thermopylae, according to Herodotus, the Spartans made use of feigned retreats (see THERMOPYLAE, BATTLE OF), but Plataea was again a matter of head-on collision.

The development of Athenian sea power added a new dimension to warfare, and during the *Peloponnesian War, the Spartans were initially baffled by the Athenian strategy of taking refuge in the fortified Athens–*Piraeus complex and relying on sea-borne supplies. But this was a recipe for survival rather than victory, and raids on the Peloponnese and even the establishment of permanent bases on and off its coast, could not defeat Sparta. The nearest Athens came to victory was when, as *Alcibiades is said to have claimed, the Spartans had to fight for their all at Mantinea (Thuc. 6. 16. 6; see MANTINEA, BATTLES OF), and it was the Spartans who eventually turned the tables by using *sea power to cut off Athens' sea-borne supplies.

The first battle of Mantinea was also the first battle which can be said to have been won by tactics. The Spartan victory on the right may have been normal in a *hoplite battle (cf. Thuc. 4. 134 and 5. 71. 1), but the way in which they then took their opponents' right in its shieldless flank as it attempted to retreat across the battlefield, was not. These tactics were repeated even more deliberately at the Nemea (see NEMEA, BATTLE OF THE).

The drawback was that they involved sacrificing the left, and it was the Theban, *Epaminondas (see THEBES (1)), who both perfected hoplite tactics at *Leuctra and ushered in a new era at the second battle of Mantinea. At the former he attacked with his best troops on the left, while refusing his right, at the latter with a combination of cavalry, hoplites, and infantry specially trained to co-operate with cavalry, which foreshadows the tactics of *Alexander (3) the Great.

Unfortunately the evidence is too scanty to enable us to be certain of *Philip (1) II's place in the development of the art of war. In his first battle—against the *Illyrii—he seems to have used his newly created 'foot companions' (cf. HETAIROI) to pin the enemy, while his cavalry attacked their flanks and rear, and at Chaeronea (see CHAERONEA, BATTLES OF) he may have feigned retreat with his right to stretch the enemy line and provide a gap for his cavalry (see HIPPEIS) to exploit. But strategically, Philip was a master of diplomacy, including the use of bribery, and of avoidance of confrontation wherever possible. The way in which he bypassed *Thermopylae in 339 and the manœuvres which led to Chaeronea show that he was also a master of campaign-strategy.

Alexander, too, made the best possible use of the various elements in his forces, usually relying on cavalry to make the crucial breakthrough, but adding—at *Gaugamela—the holding back of part of his army as a reserve, and the pressing of pursuit to prevent any recovery. As a strategist, however, he seems to have lacked his father's ability to look ahead and to know when to stop. After him, warfare became even more complex, with *elephants and heavy-armed cavalry being added to the arms available, but there were few innovations in tactics, and when Hellenistic armies were confronted by a new kind of war-machine, the Roman army, they were decisively defeated. See ARMIES, GREEK AND HELLENISTIC; and general entries listed at end of next entry.

F. E. Adcock, *The Greek and Macedonian Art of War* (1957); J. K. Anderson, *Military Theory and Practice in the Age of Xenophon* (1970); W. K. Pritchett, *The Greek State at War*, 5 vols. (1971–91); V. D. Hanson, *The Western Way of War* (1988); and see bibliog. to WARFARE, ATTITUDES TO. J. F. La.

war, art of, Roman The earliest Roman battle-order was probably the spear-armed *hoplite *phalanx, a single, close-order infantry formation. In the 4th cent. BC this was replaced by the more flexible manipular organization (see MANIPULUS) whereby the *legion was drawn up in three lines of maniples behind a screen of light infantry (*velites) and with cavalry on the wings. Each line was supported by, and could fall back upon, the line behind. All were spear-armed initially, but by the 2nd cent. BC the first two (hastati, principes) had javelins (pila).

From the late 3rd cent. three maniples were grouped into a *cohort by taking one maniple from each line. First a tactical expedient, by the 1st cent. BC this became a permanent organization, coinciding with the equipping of all legionaries with pila. Roman close-order infantry men evolved from being primarily spearmen to swordsmen with javelins. The manipular organization proved flexible and resilient enough to defeat Celtic, Carthaginian, and Hellenistic infantry (see ROME (HISTORY), § 1.3–4). The cohorts were sizeable tactical units with uniform equipment, reflecting the move away from socio-economic differentiation within the ranks. Shortages of light infantry and cavalry (especially against Hannibal; see PUNIC WARS) were serious weaknesses only partially remedied during the republic.

Throughout the Principate legionaries remained armoured swordsmen, although fencing styles evolved from short- to longsword. Differently armed soldiers acted as integral *archers and javelin-men, whilst the pilum also gave way to javelins and spears.

Imperial commanders now had at their disposal the regular support troops (*auxilia). The legions continued as the main-line troops, drawn up in the centre between wings and behind screens of auxiliaries. The tactical problems posed by mounted enemies in the Danubian and eastern theatres necessitated deepened legionary formations and increased effectiveness of missiles (cf. *Arrian, *Vegetius). Specialists were also transferred around the empire to best tactical advantage, e.g. oriental archers used against Germans, infantry bowmen and Moorish cavalry against Sarmatians, western cavalry against eastern horse-archers. An increasing emphasis was placed on cavalry of all types, especially in late antiquity, but not until the 5th cent. did mounted troops under Hunnic influence (see HUNS) take over from close-order infantry as the main battle-line (cf. *Ammianus Marcellinus, *Procopius, Mauricius).

Military treatises and accounts of campaigns demonstrate the care with which the imperial army's orders-of-march were formulated. Scouts (exploratores), interpreters, and guides were institutionalized to ease passage and avoid ambushes of an advancing army. *Itineraries were used on known routes; pictorial *maps were not employed before the modern period. Emphasis was placed on fortified camp-sites for protection overnight and as fallback positions.

The adoption and development of Hellenistic military technology gave Roman armies the option of 'scientific' siege operations. During the Principate military installations were lightly defended and Roman armies hoped to operate offensively beyond the frontiers. However, Roman units tended to be strung out along frontier lines and already in the 2nd cent. AD troops were becoming attached to their bases (see LIMES). To form campaigning armies increased resort was made to drawing away detachments (vexillationes; see VEXILLUM) for service in other theatres. Many never returned to parent units, and the late-Roman army consisted of large numbers of small formations (500–1,500 strong?), lower status ones on the frontiers, senior ones in the 'field armies' (*comitatenses). The 3rd-cent. crisis brought new emphasis on strong fortification of fortresses and towns, both supporting Roman forces in the field.

Technical expertise for battle order, command/control, siegework, and castrametation (see CAMPS; GROMATICI) resided within the legions, especially at centurial level, where a continuous tradition of skills was developed and passed on (see CENTURIO). A militarized aristocracy exercised higher command during the republic and the Principate (see CAREERS, Roman), but from the later 2nd cent. a military élite developed within the army, providing professional commanders and emperors who preserved the empire. See ARMIES, ROMAN; ARTILLERY; BOOTY; FORTIFICATIONS; MERCENARIES; SIEGECRAFT, ROMAN.

J. Kromayer and G. Veith, *Heerwesen und Kriegführung der Griechen und Römer* (1928); P. Connolly, *Greece and Rome at War* (1981); L. Keppie, *The Making of the Roman Army* (1984); J. C. Coulston, in P. Freeman and D. Kennedy, *The Defence of the Roman and Byzantine East* (1986), 59–75.
J. C. N. C.

war, rules of These, like much other international law (see LAW, INTERNATIONAL), depended on custom and showed a constant conflict between the higher standards of optimistic theory and the harsher measures permitted by actual usage, while passion and expediency frequently caused the most fundamental rules to be violated. Thus, the temptation to profit from a surprise at times led to the opening of hostilities without a declaration of war. Probably the law most generally observed was that of the sanctity of *heralds, for heralds were essential to communications between belligerents. Nor did Greeks frequently refuse a defeated army a truce for burying its dead, for the request of such a truce meant an admission of defeat and was usually followed by retreat. Beyond this there were few restraints except humanitarian considerations and the universal condemnation of excessive harshness. Plundering and the destruction of crops and property were legitimate, and were carried on both by regular armies and fleets, and by informal raiding-parties and privateers, and even the sanctity of temples was not always respected. Prisoners, if not protected by special terms of surrender, were at the mercy of their captors, who could execute them or sell them into *slavery (see BOOTY). The warfare of the Hellenistic age was somewhat more humane, though with the actions of the Achaean general *Aratus (2) against 'tyrants' and still more with the wars of Rome and *Philip (3) V deterioration began once more. Roman warfare at its worst was extremely cruel and sometimes went to the length of killing all living things, even animals, in cities taken by storm, but it was often tempered by mercy. Though surrender (deditio) gave full power to the captors, it was unusual to use extreme measures against a city that surrendered and appealed to the fides of (i.e. entrusted themselves to) Rome. The protection of the rules of war was not extended to pirates (see PIRACY) and not always to *barbarians.

The sources are ancient accounts of wars, especially those of *Thucydides (1), *Polybius (1), and *Livy. C. Phillipson, *The International Law and Custom of Ancient Greece and Rome* (1911), chs. 22–8; Rostovtzeff, *Hellenistic World*, 140 ff., 192 ff., 603 ff., 1258 f. Piganiol, *RIDA* 1950; A. Aymard, *Études d'histoire ancienne* (1967), 499 ff.; J. de Romilly, in J.-P. Vernant (ed.), *Problèmes de la guerre* (1968); P. Ducrey, *Le Traitement des prisonniers de guerre dans la Grèce antique* (1968); D. J. Mosley, *RIDA* 1973, 161 ff.; Y. Garlan, *War in the Ancient World* (1975), 57 ff.; W. R. Connor, *Past and Present* 1988, 3 ff., esp. 19 ff. (stressing ritual aspects).
J. A. O. L.; S. H.

warfare, attitudes to (Greek and Hellenistic) *Homer's *Iliad*, a poem about war, does not glorify war: it celebrates martial prowess but also portrays the sufferings caused by war, and *Ares, god of war, is rebuked by Zeus as the most hateful of all the gods, to whom strife, wars, and slaughter are forever dear (*Il.* 5. 890 f.). The same ambivalence pervades Greek attitudes to warfare. War in Greece was a recurring phenomenon, and conflicts multiplied in numbers and scale as larger power blocks emerged. Greek history divides according to major conflicts: the *Persian Wars, the *Peloponnesian War and its sequels, the rise of *Macedonia, *Alexander (3) the Great's conquest of Asia and the wars of the successor kingdoms (see DIADOCHI; PTOLEMY (1); SELEUCIDS). These provide the subject-matter of much of Greek historical writing. There were also innumerable local wars, less prominent in the record. 'War is the father of all things' (Heraclitus, DK 22 B 53). It shaped the institutions, society, and economy of the Greek world. Military function and social and political *status were closely related (Arist. *Pol.* 4. 1297^{b}10–24; cf. already *Il.* 12. 309–28), hence the predominance in the classical period of the male citizen-warrior, the exclusion of *women from the political sphere, and the constant celebration in literature of military valour. Success in war was ascribed to divine favour and ostentatiously commemorated in *sanctuaries through dedications and offerings from enemy spoils, including captured weapons. In Classical Athens the war-dead received burial every year in a public ceremony, and the funeral oration (see EPITAPHIOS) linked the fallen warriors with the collective achievements of the *polis. On the other hand, the destructive aspects of war receive constant emphasis in literature. 'No one is so foolish as to prefer war to peace: in peace children bury their fathers, while in war fathers bury their children' (Hdt. 1. 87. 4). Tragedy and comedy exploited the theme in many ways (Aesch. *Ag.*; Eur. *Tro.* and *Hec.*; Ar. *Ach.*, *Pax*, and *Lys.*). For *Thucydides (2) war was 'a violent teacher' (3. 82. 2). Later historians often used the sacking of cities and the fate of the defeated for pathos and sensational effect (cf. the critique of *Polybius (1) 2. 56–63). But attempts to limit war were few and ineffective, and it is doubtful whether there was any successful move towards humanizing warfare, even between Greeks. With the Persian Wars and the emergence of the antithesis between Greek and *barbarian, the view gained ground that Greeks should not fight wars against other Greeks or enslave Greek war captives (cf. Pl. *Resp.* 5. 469b–470c). After the failure of Athens in 355 in the *Social War (1) voices were raised in condemnation of Athenian imperialism and in favour of peace (Xen. *Vect.*; Isoc. *De Pace* and *Areopagiticus*). But the legitimacy of war itself was not challenged: the same writers preached a profitable war of aggression against the Persian empire as an alternative to wars among Greeks (Xen. *An.* 3. 2. 4–6; Isoc. *Paneg.* and *Philip*; cf. already Hdt. 5. 49). In short, throughout Greek history 'war was a part of the fabric of society, on a par with earthquakes, droughts, destructive storms, and slavery' (W. K. Pritchett). See also BOOTY; IMPERIALISM, *Greek and Hellenistic*; TROPHIES; WAR, ART OF, GREEK; WAR, RULES OF.

Y. Garlan, *War in the Ancient World: A Social History* (1982); W. K. Pritchett, *The Greek State at War*, 5 vols. (1971–91); J. W. Rich and G. Shipley (eds.), *War and Society in the Greek World* (1993); J.-P. Vernant (ed.), *Problèmes de la guerre en Grèce ancienne* (1968); Momigliano, 'Some Observations on the Causes of War in Ancient Historiography', in *Secondo contributo* 13–27; J. Cobet, 'Herodotus and Thucydides on War', in I. S. Moxon, J. D. Smart, and A. J. Woodman (eds.), *Past Perspectives: Studies in Greek and Roman Historical Writing* (1986), 1–18; M. M. Austin, *CQ* 1986, 450 ff. (Hellenistic attitudes); bibliographical survey of Greek warfare down to the classical period in R. Lonis, *Rev. Ét. Grec.* 1985, 321–79. M. M. A.

water (ὕδωρ, *aqua*) in the mostly arid Mediterranean climate by its local availability shaped patterns of settlement and, as erratic rainfall, determined harvest-fluctuations and food-shortages (see FAMINE; FOOD SUPPLY). In *agriculture, although dry-farming was the norm in ancient Greece and Italy, *irrigation was by no means unknown (e.g. at Hellenistic Sparta: *SEG* 40. 348. For the Persian empire see AI KHANOUM). The use of hydraulic technology to increase the *water supply was an early concern of the *polis; some of the most spectacular installations (e.g. on *Samos) were the work of the Archaic tyrants (see also TYRANNY; THEAGENES (1) for *Megara); Rome pioneered raised *aqueducts. Communal fountains were a social focus (e.g. Eur. *Med.* 68–9, about *Corinth's Pirene); in Roman times they were civic status-symbols liable to lavish architectural embellishment (see NYMPHAEUM). Apart from drinking and *sanitation, ancient cities needed water for reasons of personal health (directions about baths figure in the Hippocratic *On Regimen and Health* 6. 72 ff. Littré; see HIPPOCRATES (2)) as well as hygiene. In Greece domestic baths were increasingly common by the 4th cent. BC (terracotta bath-tubs or special bathrooms were found in one-third of the houses at *Olynthus). Public (including hot) *baths were common by the mid-5th cent. BC; baths were among the standard amenities of the Greek *gymnasium; in Roman cities they were a central social and cultural institution and, when based on therapeutic springs, the *raison d'être* of spa-towns (see AEDEPSUS; AQUAE MATTIACAE, etc.). The play of water was an integral part of ancient, especially Roman, gardens and of the Roman idea of the *locus amoenus. In mythology spring-water had sacred power; in real life springs often prompted cult (see NYMPHS; SPRINGS, SACRED). Together with *fire, water was widely used in cult for *purification (including bathing), in libations, and in *sacrifice; extra-urban *sanctuaries were as concerned as cities to secure a good supply. Purificatory water was also used in rites of birth, marriage, and death, the dead being considered 'thirsty'. In the so-called 'Orphic' texts on gold plates (see ORPHISM), the soul is 'parched with thirst' and wants to drink the water of Memory; in the eschatological myths of *Plato (1) and *Virgil (*Aen.* 6. 714, 749), the *souls drink the water of Oblivion. Finally, water was a primal *element in cosmogonic thought; this applies equally to philosophy (see THALES) and to the early mythical cosmogonies (on which see Kirk–Raven–Schofield, *Presocratic Philosophers* ch. 1; and for *Oceanus as the source of all, 11 ff.). See also HYDROSTATICS; NEPTUNUS; OASIS.

M. Ninck, 'Die Bedeutung des Wassers im Kult und Leben der Alten', *Philol.* Suppl. 14/2 (1921); R. Buxton, *Imaginary Greece* (1994), 109 ff.; M. Wörrle, *Wasser in antiken Hellas* (1981); D. P. Crouch, *Water Management in Ancient Greek Cities* (1993). J. H. C.; A. J. S. S.

water supply

1. Greece The preferred source of water in Classical Greece is a natural perennial spring. Failing this, rainwater has to be conserved in cisterns, or raised from wells.

Improvement of natural water supplies leads to the construction of fountain houses where water is fed through spouts (normally decorated in the form of a lion's head) into drawbasins; such constructions are usually placed behind architectural façades with a roof to shade (and keep cool) the drawbasins. These already existed in the 6th cent. BC (Enneakrounos at Athens, built by *Pisistratus). Pirene at Corinth was successively improved from Archaic to Roman times. The use of terracotta pipes and built or rock-cut conduits to lead water from a spring to a locality where it was needed develops from the Archaic period (see AQUEDUCT).

Cisterns may be rock-cut, but generally have to be lined with cement to retain water. They may be fed from rainwater trapped on roofs, or on the ground surface, led into settling tanks for cleaning before storage. Cisterns under the courtyards of houses in *Delos are reached by well heads, hollowed cylinders of marble, usually decorated (see PUTEAL). Wells leading to underground water-bearing levels are usually circular in section.

The sanctuary at *Perachora has a representative variety of waterwork systems: (1) a possible original spring supplemented by surface-trapped rainwater led through a stone-built conduit via a diversion point to a settling tank and into a built long cistern with apsidal ends, originally roofed; (2) a large circular catchment tank with a cement floor to hold rain falling on it; and (3) (c.300 BC) deep rectangular shafts tapping underground water 35 m. (115 ft.) deep, lifted by machinery and fed via a built conduit into storage tanks behind a fountain house façade. See NYMPHAEUM.

T. Wiegand and H. Schrader, *Priene* (1904), 68; F. Glaser, *Antike Brunenbauten in Griechenland* (1983); also bibliog. for WATER.   R. A. T.

2. Rome See AQUEDUCTS and NYMPHAEUM.

wealth, attitudes to Classical societies developed a range of responses to the universal ambition of individuals to amass property and possessions. One extreme response, characteristic of societies where the wealthy had retained or regained preponderant influence in public affairs, was to impose little or no restriction on accumulation: early Hellenistic Sparta and late republican Rome were examples. Conversely, Greek colonies were often founded on an 'equal and like' basis, and Roman colonial foundations regularly assigned the same land-area to each colonist. However, few colonies remained egalitarian for long (Diod. Sic. 5. 9. 4–5 for an exception, Lipara; see AEOLIAE INSULAE). See COLONIZATION, GREEK and ROMAN.

More normally, attitudes oscillated unsystematically within such extremes. Amassing wealth, possessing it, and spending it aroused differing responses, and varied also with the nature and the status of the gainful activity (Cato, *Agr.* pref.; Cic. *Off.* 1. 150 ff. and 2. 52 ff.). Greeks saw the rich as potentially hubristic, extravagant, profiteering, and soft, probably dishonest if newly wealthy and lucky rather than worthy if of longer standing, but also as prudent and as potentially generous and magnanimous benefactors (cf. Arist. *Pol.* 1. 8–9). Romans likewise might profess contempt for *usury while legally requiring guardians to use their wards' spare capital profitably (*Dig.* 26. 7 passim); might be represented as vaunting their wealth, as *Petronius Arbiter's Trimalchio did or as the shippers of Trier (see AUGUSTA TREVERORUM) did on their grave-monuments, or as hoarding it Scrooge-fashion (Hor. *Sat.* 1); or might combine positive and negative attitudes in the same treatise, as L. *Annaeus Seneca (2) did repeatedly. Behind some such inconsistencies lay the influence of Greek philosophies. *Cynics preferred poverty and refused possessions, a pattern later followed by some wealthy Christians (see ASCETICISM; CHRISTIANITY), while some exponents of Stoicism associated joy with the use of wealth. Mainstream *Stoicism counted wealth among the 'useful indifferents', and Aristotelian tradition (see ARISTOTLE; PERIPATETIC SCHOOL) saw at least a comfortable independence as essential to the virtuous life. Other attitudes were less coherent. The idea that poverty had made Rome great, while wealth and luxury would ruin her, was a cliché of late republican ideology, explicit in *Sallust, *Horace, and *Livy, just when the wealthy of Rome and Italy were energetically exploiting every opportunity for investment and accumulation.

Some public policies, expressed in law or custom, attempted

to restrain such behaviour. Partible inheritance ensured that an eldest son had no economic advantage, and the revocability of dowries checked some accumulation strategies, though the later freedoms of bequest and adoption largely eroded such restraints. The military need for citizen soldiers long kept the number of free smallholders high, but was overtaken by army professionalization for centuries until the barbarian settlements reinstated the practice. Sumptuary laws, or officials such as the *gynaikonomoi* ('women's wardens'), attempted to restrict extravagant display, especially at funerals or festivals. Most effective of all was the expectation that the wealthy would use at least some of their wealth for public benefit. The idea came closest to enforceable obligation in the institution of *liturgies at Athens and elsewhere, but normally emphasized the voluntariness of such benefaction and the goodwill thereby accruing to the benefactor (see EUERGETISM). In Greek contexts the objectives might be contributions to corn-buying or building funds, educational or cult foundations, help in manumission costs, or the ransoming of captives. In Roman contexts expenditure on games, public spectacles, and food hand-outs tended to predominate, along with expenditure on *alimenta-schemes, temple building, the patronage of *collegia* (see COLLEGIUM), and later the endowment of churches and monasteries.

M. I. Finley, *The Ancient Economy* (1973); K. J. Dover, *Greek Popular Morality* (1974), 109–12 and 170–80; I. Shatzman, *Senatorial Wealth and Roman Politics* (1975); M. I. Finley (ed.), *Studies in Roman Property* (1976); M. T. Griffin, *Seneca: A Philosopher in Politics* (1976), ch. 9; P. Veyne, *Bread and Circuses* (Eng. trans. 1990).   J. K. D.

weaving See TEXTILE PRODUCTION.

weighing instruments The balance ($\sigma\tau\alpha\theta\mu\acute{o}s$, *libra*, *bilanx*) of two pans at equal distance from the point of suspension is an invention of the earliest times; in Mycenaean tablets (see MYCENAEAN LANGUAGE) it is the symbol for the largest unit of weight, and Homer is familiar with its use, which persisted through antiquity. The steelyard, in which the rod is unequally divided, the object to be weighed being suspended from the short arm against a sliding counterweight on the longer, does not appear before Roman times (*statera*: originally *statera campana*, from an alleged Campanian origin; see CAMPANIA); but from its greater convenience it became the most popular form of balance. There may be alternative positions for the fulcrum, and two different scales can be marked on the bar. Inscriptions can guarantee the standard. *Trutina* is a pan-balance for large masses; *momentana* and *moneta* are for small objects, or coins. Weighing instruments were only as accurate as the weights used, and it seems that some error was created by using worn items. See WEIGHTS.

E. Michon, in Dar.–Sag., 'Libra'; J. Ward-Perkins and A. Claridge, *Pompeii AD 79* (1976), nos. 248–9; M. Vickers, in *Boreas* 1992, 68.
          F. N. P.; M. L.; D. W. J. G.

weights Weights of the Greek bronze age are usually flattened cylinders of stone or metal, incised circles on the upper surface indicating the unit of measurement. Other forms are the duck and the bull's head. An octopus weight from Minoan Cnossus weighs 29 kg. (64 lb.) and the average weight of nineteen copper ingots from Agia Triada is 29.132 kg. (64 lb. 4½ oz.) Several standards appear to have been current, extant Minoan weights (see MINOAN CIVILIZATION) having been related to the Egyptian, Babylonian, and Phoenician systems. Mycenaean texts from *Cnossus, *Pylos, and *Mycenae (see MYCENAEAN LANGUAGE) allow an approximate table of values to be created:

Unit 1	c.30 kg.	
Unit 2	c.1 kg.	
Unit 3	c.250 g.	
Unit 4	c.20.8 g.	
Unit 5	c.3.4 g. or less.	

The typical weight of historic Greece is a square plaque of lead with a badge, and sometimes the denomination, the name of the issuing city, or other official guarantees on the top in relief. The principal types on the most widespread series of Attic weights are the astragalos (stater), dolphin (mina), amphora (one-third stater with half-amphora as one-sixth), tortoise (one-fourth stater with half-tortoise as one-eighth). There were many other forms, as caprice or local custom dictated. Roman weights show less variety, the common form being a spheroid of stone or metal, with flattened top and bottom; the denomination is generally expressed in punctured characters on the top.

Several weight standards were used in the eastern Mediterranean; the principal ones were the Aeginetic (cf. AEGINA), traditionally associated with *Pheidon of Argos, and the Euboic (cf. EUBOEA), said to have been introduced by *Solon into Attica. This latter standard tended to oust the Aeginetic. The historical origin of these standards is disputed; the Greeks held that they were based on natural units, e.g. in the Attic-Euboic system on the barley-corn, of which twelve went to the obol. Extant weights often show considerable variations from the norm, which creates difficulties in defining the actual weight of any single unit. A theoretical Greek table is:

	Attic-Euboic standard	Aeginetic standard
The *obol*, or metal spit	0.72 g.	1.05 g.
The *drachma*, bundle of six spits	4.31 g.	6.30 g.
The *mina*, 100 drachmae	431.00 g.	630.00 g.
The *talent*, 60 minae	25.86 kg.	37.80 kg.

Analysis of temple inventories in Greece, and especially at Athens, has shown the presence of gold and silver items apparently made to a *Persian unit of measurement. Some of the gold objects from the *Parthenon inventories, although weighed in Attic drachmae, seem to have been made to a round number of darics. Likewise silver items can be read in round numbers of sigloi. This is not to say that the objects are necessarily Persian, but rather that these units of measurement were used outside their immediate geographical areas. Key Persian weights are:

siglos	c.5.20–5.49 g.
	c.5.40–5.67 g. (later standard)
daric	8.25–8.46 g.
karsha	83.3 g.

Silver *plate from *Thrace seems to have been made to another local standard.

The Roman system was based upon the pound, *libra*, of 327.45 grammes = 0.721 of the pound avoirdupois, which was divided into 12 ounces, *unciae*. The names of, and the symbols applied to the subdivisions, are:

libra or *as*	1 pound	I
deunx	11 oz.	S = = −
dextans	10 oz.	S = =
dodrans	9 oz.	S = −
bes	8 oz.	S =
septunx	7 oz.	S −
semis	6 oz.	S
quincunx	5 oz.	= = −
triens	4 oz.	= =
quadrans	3 oz.	= −
sextans	2 oz.	=
sescuncia	1½ oz.	⟨ −
uncia	1 oz.	−
semuncia	½ oz.	⟨
sicilicus	¼ oz.	⟩
sextula	⅙ oz.	Ϛ
semisextula	1/12 oz.	S
scriptulum	1/24 oz.	Ɜ

A. J. Evans, 'Minoan Weights', in *Corolla Numismatica* (1906), 336 ff.; E. Michon, in Dar.–Sag., 'Libra', 'Pondus'; O. Viedebandt, *Antike Gewichtsnormen* (1923); W. Ridgeway, *The Origin of Metallic Currency and Weight Standards* (1892); J. Chadwick, *Documents in Mycenaean Greek*, 2nd edn. (1973); M. Lang and M. Crosby, *Weights, Measures and Tokens*, *Athenian Agora* 10 (1964); F. Hultsch, *Reliquiae Scriptorum Metrologicorum* ([1774–5] 1864 and 1866); M. Vickers, *AJArch.* 1990, 613 ff.; M. Vickers, in B. F. Cook, *The Rogozen Treasure* (1989), 101 ff.

F. N. P.; M. L.; D. W. J. G.

werewolves See LYCANTHROPY.

West, Western Greeks modern expressions for the Greeks of Italy and Sicily, cf. MAGNA GRAECIA. (But 'western Greece' can mean the western part of Greece proper.)

widows in Classical Athens were expected to live under the protection of a male relative and to remarry if possible. There was often an age-gap between husband and wife, and young widows were thought to be at risk of ill-health and sexual temptation. Older widows caused less anxiety and had more freedom of movement. The widow's dowry reverted to the man who took responsibility for her, but in practice some widows (including *Demosthenes (2)'s mother) kept control. Some men, including *Aristotle, made provision by will for their widow's remarriage to a trusted friend. The archon had special responsibility for widows who might give birth to a posthumous heir.

Romans admired the *univira*, the woman who married only once; some Roman rituals were reserved for *univirae* and in some noble families (according to *Jerome, *Ep.* 54) the women had a tradition of not remarrying. But remarriage was not discouraged, except during the period of mourning which traditionally lasted ten months. Greeks and Romans both acknowledged that a second marriage could disadvantage the children of the first. Roman widows were sometimes given a life interest in their husband's property, provided they did not remarry. They could also be rich and influential on their own account. Some (including *Cornelia (1), mother of the Gracchi) were famous examples of motherhood. *Augustus restricted the inheritance rights (except from near relatives) of childless widows under 50 who did not remarry.

Many Christians opposed the remarriage of widows, on the grounds that death does not end a marriage and that celibacy is better anyway. A distinction was made, following 1 Tim. 5: 3–16, between young widows who should remarry to avoid scandal and temptation, and 'real' widows, preferably aged 60 or above, devoted to prayer and good works. Poor widows were traditional objects of charity, and churches supported widows who had no family backing. Until the 3rd cent. AD there seems to have been a distinct order of widows within the Church; after this, female communities were their natural home. Christian discussions reveal that widowhood could be difficult for women who were trying to manage property and needed support in legal and financial matters, but also that some widows greatly enjoyed their freedom of action.

R. Just, *Women in Athenian Law and Life* (1989); J. Gardner, *Women in Roman Law and Society* (1986), 51–6; G. Clark, *Women in Late Antiquity* (1993); M. Lightman and W. Zeisel, *Church History* 1977, 19–32.

E. G. C.

wind-gods are attested as the object of anxious cultic attention as early as the Mycenaean period, when a priestess of the winds (*anemōn iereia*) is recorded on the *Cnossus tablets (see MYCENAEAN CIVILIZATION and MYCENAEAN LANGUAGE); *Hesychius provides the names *Anemokoitai* 'Windbedders' and *Heudanemoi* 'Windlullers' for specialized *priests at *Corinth and Athens respectively. Most *rituals (for which hilltops were the favoured site) aimed at pre-emptive placation of these powerful forces, though the conjuring of beneficent winds also had its place (priests on *Ceos who summon the Etesian winds, Callim. *Aet.* fr. 75, 36 f.; *Achilles' prayer to *Boreas and *Zephyrus to blow on *Patroclus' pyre, *Il.* 23. 194 ff.). At *Methana, the *sacrifice of a white cock sought to protect the budding vines from the onslaught of the *Lips*, the SW gale (Paus. 2. 34. 2 f.), while a black lamb is a suitable victim to appease 'Typhos' at *Aristophanes (1), *Frogs* 847 f. Persian *magi* (see MAGUS) are described by *Herodotus (1) as quelling the devastating storm off Sepias in 480 BC by casting spells and sacrificing to *Thetis and the Nereids (7. 191; see NEREUS). As violent aerial daimons, the female wind-spirits called *Aellai* or *Thyellai* are close to the Harpies or *Harpyiae (one of whom, Podarge, bore Achilles' wind-swift horses to Zephyrus, *Il.* 16. 150 ff.), and may bring sudden death to women by snatching them up—a fate for which *Penelope longs at *Od.* 20. 61 f., Helen at *Il.* 6. 345 ff. More kindly breezes waft the souls of heroes from their pyre, whence no doubt their appearance as a motif on Roman *sarcophagi. Male winds like Boreas have the power of impregnating mares (*Il.* 20. 222 ff.), and are themselves thought of as winged stallions. The precise naming of winds from various quarters of the compass led naturally to personification: at *Od.* 5. 295 Homer adds Eurus, the East wind, to the triad of Zephyrus (W), Boreas (N), and Notus (S) catalogued by *Hesiod at *Th.* 378–80. But epic may conceive of them, as convenient, either as minor gods who feast in their own palaces (*Il.* 23. 200 ff.) or as unruly elemental forces who are controlled by *Aeolus (1) from his floating prison-island and can be confined in a leather bag (*Od.* 10. 1 ff.). For some evidence of Roman cult, see Frazer on Ovid, *Fasti* 6. 193. See BOREAS; ZEPHYRUS.

W. Burkert, *Greek Religion* (Eng. trans. 1985), 175; E. Vermeule, *Aspects of Death in Early Greek Art and Poetry* (1979), 168 f.; J. Travlos, *Pictorial Dictionary of Ancient Athens* (1971), 'Horologion of Andronikos' (the Tower of the Winds).

A. H. G.

wine (Greek and Roman) The grape vine, which grows naturally in the highlands between the 10° C and 20° C annual isotherms (approximately between 30° and 50° north), had appeared in a cultivated form (*vitis vinifera sativa*) in the *Caucasus at least by the neolithic period. Viticulture had become fully established in the Greek world by Mycenaean times, as it had even earlier in its near eastern neighbours. By the earliest historical period wine had already become a fundamental component of classical culture. This is not simply the result of ecological determinism; viticulture represented an important cultural and social choice. Contemporaries were aware that the considerable geographical expansion of vine-growing which happened throughout classical history (in the Black Sea region (see EUXINE) in the Hellenistic period and, most notably, in southern

Spain and France after the Roman conquest) was closely associated with the dissemination of classical culture. So the Phocaean settlers of *Massalia (Marseilles; see PHOCAEA; COLONIZATION, GREEK) are represented by Justin (43. 4) as teaching the Gauls not just the pleasures of urban life and constitutional government, but also viticulture.

The evidence, particularly the literary sources, for viticulture in Classical Greece is inadequate; not even *Theophrastus offers much detail. On the other hand, the techniques of wine-production figure prominently in the Roman *agricultural writers and *Pliny (1) (*HN* 14 and 17), whose information is derived not just from personal experience, but also the numerous handbooks produced in the Hellenistic period. Yet, even in Classical Greece it was already acknowledged that the particular character of a wine depended primarily on a combination of the type of vine, the soil, and the climate. Most of the modern methods of training and pruning vines were already known, from the free-standing bush, propped vines, to trellising, and most notably the growing of vines up trees. This last was such a distinctive feature of some of the most prized vineyards of Roman Italy (e.g. Caecuban and Falernian) that Pliny (*HN* 17. 199) could claim that 'classic wines can only be produced from vines grown on trees'. Cited yields varied enormously; but these depended on grape type and the density of planting. The choices here depended on which market the producer was aiming at: young wines for mass consumption or fine wines for the élite.

The descriptive lists of wines which can be found in authors, such as Pliny and *Athenaeus (1), must be used with caution, because many of them are not the judgements of connoisseurs, but are derived from the accounts of medical writers, who assessed wines for their effects as remedies. Athenaeus (1. 27d) has the most useful account of Greek wines with a wide selection of citations from ancient authors. Among the most noted Greek wines were those of *Cos, *Chios, *Thasos, *Lesbos, and *Rhodes. A distinctive feature of several of these wines, particularly Coan, was the practice of cutting the must with quantities of sea water 'to enliven a wine's smoothness' (Plin. *HN* 14. 120) (presumably to increase its acidity). So many of Greece's most prominent wines and the ones which were exported on a large scale down to the Roman imperial period came from the islands. Viticulture probably played a greater role in their economy than that of mainland areas such as *Attica. Two fragmentary inscriptions from 5th-cent. Thasos, an important producer and exporter, contain elaborate regulations about the sale of wine. Sometimes interpreted as trade protection, they are more likely a cumbersome attempt to assure the consumer of the genuineness and quality of their purchase.

In Roman Italy there was a close link between prestige vineyards and the favoured locations of the Roman élite's country estates, most particularly the Alban hills or *Albanus mons (Alban, Velletri, Setian wine), further south in Latium (Caecuban), the northern borders of Campania (Massic, Falernian), and round the bay of Naples (Gauranum, Surrentinum). In the reign of *Augustus there was a great interest in the wines of NE Italy. Most of the prized wines were sweet whites. Characteristically they were aged for a considerable number of years, with a resultant darkening of colour as a result of madderization. This process of ageing was often accelerated by exposing the wine to heat by storing it in lofts above hearths. While it was accepted that wine ideally should be unadulterated, the long lists of additives in Pliny and *Columella suggest that producers were frequently forced to disguise a deteriorating product.

The widespread finds of Italian *amphorae are testimony to the success of Italian wines in the growing markets of the city of Rome itself, in Spain and Gaul, and even in the Greek east. But Italian dominance of this trade lasted for only a fairly short time, from the late 2nd cent. BC to the mid-1st cent. AD. By then the wines of south Spain and southern Gaul were competing successfully in these markets, so much so that Columella (*Rust.* 3. 3) was forced to produce a detailed argument for the continued profitability of viticulture to counter growing scepticism in Italy.

Wine was the everyday drink of all classes in Greece and Rome. It was also a key component of one of the central social institutions of the élite, the dinner and drinking party (see CONVIVIUM; SYMPOSIUM). On such occasions large quantities of wine were drunk, but it was invariably heavily diluted with water. It was considered a mark of uncivilized peoples, untouched by classical culture, that they drank wine neat with supposed disastrous effects on their mental and physical health (Ammianus Marcellinus, 15. 12). See AGRICULTURE; ALCOHOLISM; DIONYSUS.

For the Thasian wine laws: J. Pouilloux, *Recherches sur l'histoire et les cultes de Thasos* 1 (1954); R. Billiard, *La Vigne dans l'antiquité* (1913); R. Dion, *Histoire de la vigne et du vin en France des origines aux XIXe siècle* (1959); W. Younger, *Gods, Men and Wine* (1966); M. Lambert-Gocs, *The Wines of Greece* (1990); A. Tchernia, *Le Vin de l'Italie romaine* (1986); D. Rathbone, *Economic Rationalism and Rural Society in Third-Century A.D. Egypt* (1991); P. Scarpi (ed.), *Storie del vino* (1991).   J. J. P.

wisdom See SEVEN SAGES.

wolf, wolves See APOLLO; LUPERCALIA; LYCANTHROPY; LYCUS (1); OGULNIUS, GALLUS Q.; ROMULUS AND REMUS.

witchcraft, witches See AMULETS; CURSES; MAGIC.

women Almost all information about women in antiquity comes to us from male sources. Some women could read and write (see LITERACY), at least to the level needed for their role as guardians of the *household stores (e.g. Xen. *Oec.* 7. 5 and 9. 10; see HOUSEWORK) but, although there are many references to literary works by women, very few texts survive. The 'exceptions' to male authorship include women poets (e.g. *Sappho, *Corinna, *Erinna, *Nossis, *Sulpicia (1 and 2)), early philosophers (some Hellenistic pamphlets are attributed to Pythagorean women; see WOMEN IN PHILOSOPHY), personal letters from women, and the 5th-cent. AD travel diary of Egeria (*Itinerarium Egeriae*). Many attributions to women are problematic. Were women's letters written by scribes? Is a text ascribed to a woman simply in order to attack a man (e.g. *Aspasia's alleged authorship of *Pericles (1)'s speeches)?

The central source problems, and the strategies developed to overcome them, underpin the large amount of work on ancient women produced in the last twenty years. First, every type of evidence has had to be re-examined in order to discover what it can contribute. This has led many scholars to concentrate on very small areas of specialism, leaving the work of synthesis to the reader of the collections of essays in which much recent work has been published. Secondly, the indirect nature of much of the evidence has made necessary a theoretically sophisticated approach, open to methods developed in cognate disciplines.

The source problems used to be solved by dividing material up according to its 'level'; for example, seeing drama as fantasy, legal materials as nearer to the reality of daily life. In considering ancient women under the heading 'women, position of', the 2nd, 1970, edn. of the *OCD* reflected the dominant questions of the age; first, whether 5th-cent. Athenian women were kept in

'oriental seclusion' or allowed 'freedom', and secondly, whether this meant that they were 'despised' or 'honoured'. Whereas literature and the visual arts were thought to assign women a prominent role, legal and historical material suggested that, in practice, women were seen as perpetual minors. A comparable approach divides the statements of the ideal situation from the incidental, apparently naïve, remarks about women's lives which are thought to reveal the reality.

The problem in both cases is how to weight different types of source material. For example, *Creon (1) orders *Antigone (1) and Ismene to 'be women' and stay 'inside' (Soph. *Ant.* 578 ff.). Is this evidence that women's domain was normally the home? The 'norm' is only stated because of the perception that it is being breached, so how would we know about a norm which remained unbreached and was therefore unstated? Other sources (drama, philosophy, lawcourt speeches) suggest that Athenian women left the *oikos* to visit relatives, work in the fields, fetch water, and attend weddings and religious festivals. So is this not a norm, but an ideal practised by a very few wealthy households? Or should we argue that what was said did not match what was done?

There is currently an increased awareness that all types of source material were produced by the same society, and that none gives direct access to reality. For example, funerary inscriptions may seem less value-laden than plays, but they operate by their own rules; a woman is praised for her appearance and her personal qualities, a man for what he has done. Fourth-cent. Greek lawcourt speeches are not transparent, but are public discourses designed to win a case by appealing to a shared social ideal of female nature and behaviour. From the late republic onwards, Roman sources praise maternal *breast-feeding, yet discuss the use of a wet-nurse.

Much recent work on women in antiquity looks not at 'the position of women' but at the creation of the concept 'woman'. Woman is deeply ambiguous, a 'beautiful evil' who is both wild and tamed, essential to the continuation of the human race while herself being a member of the separate 'race of women' (Hes. *Theog.* 585–90). Her dual role is reflected in medical and philosophical texts which focus on the reproductive function while seeing women as physically and mentally falling short of the ideal which is the adult male citizen. It is also increasingly recognized that 'women' are not a unified group. For example, rituals may divide women by social status or sexual availability; at the *Matuta Mater festival, restricted to women married only once, Roman matrons bring a slave woman into the enclosure and then drive her out with blows and slaps (Plut. *Mor.* 267d, *Cam.* 5).

In certain areas of life the similarities between the position and the experience of Greek and Roman women in all historical periods outweigh the differences, so that a number of generalizations may be made. For all women, their main role was as bearers of legitimate children; even when Spartan women, seen as radically 'different' by the Athenian and Roman men who wrote about them, engaged in physical training it was to strengthen their bodies for *childbirth (e.g. Xen. *Spartan Constitution* 1. 49). Concern with ensuring legitimacy of heirs led both to tight control of women's sexuality—including early marriage, at or before puberty—and fear of the power of that sexuality. Women must be tamed, instructed, and watched.

Ancient women lacked political rights; they could not attend, speak at, or vote in political assemblies, nor could they hold office. However, they could exert influence through men. In the Roman empire it has been argued that their political exclusion meant less after the decline in the roles of senate and assemblies, while the importance of the imperial family gave increased influence to its women. By the 2nd cent. AD the status of imperial women declined in a reaction against the roles of *Livia Drusilla and *Iulia Agrippina. When women are represented in Roman sources as taking a public role, this tends to be accompanied by allusions to female spite, treachery, or lack of self-control. References to women's political action are intended to discredit the men associated with them (e.g. *Clodia, in Cic. *Cael.*).

Because they were thought to be easily deceived and thus unable to make sensible judgements (Gai. *Inst.* 144, 190–1), women were supposed to have a guardian; in the absence of a father or husband, a *kyrios* or *tutor* acted for them in economic transactions. In the Roman world the exceptions were the Vestals (see VESTA) and, after Augustus, free-born women who had given birth to three children (see IUS LIBERORUM), and freedwomen with four, who were not under the tutelage of a father or husband. However, the system could be used purely as a matter of form, to give the appearance of male control over property; on the death of their husbands, *widows would take over their businesses, while in the eastern provinces women made contracts and used their wealth as benefactors of their communities from the Hellenistic period onwards (see EUERGETISM). By imperial times, male guardianship of Roman women had become a formality.

Although lower-class women in the ancient world often worked outside the home, in agriculture, as market-traders, and as craftswomen (see ARTISANS AND CRAFTSMEN), as well as in more obviously 'female' roles such as *midwives and wet-nurses, women were traditionally praised for silence and invisibility. Their appearances in lawcourts were restricted to displays of grief in support of male relatives; in Athens, their evidence was only used when a free woman swore an oath on the heads of her children. In Classical Greece a woman's name was not given in public unless she was dead, or of ill repute, and glory for a woman was defined in *Thucydides (2)'s Funeral Speech of Pericles as 'not to be spoken of, whether in praise or blame' (2. 45; see EPITAPHIOS). In Roman society, naming reflected this invisibility; women took the name of their father, but in time they acquired a *cognomen*, so that sisters were differentiated as (e.g.) Iulia Agrippina and Iulia Drusilla. See NAMES, PERSONAL, ROMAN, § 7; and entries under the names.

In both the Greek and Roman worlds, discrepancies seem to have existed between norms and practice, with 'real' women— if it is possible to separate these out from the multiple images of the sources—apparently acting in ways which were contrary to the stated ideals.

Current work concerns non-élite women, working women, slave-women and the relationship between status and gender. Some attempts are also being made to discover how ancient women saw their world, rather than stopping at how men saw women. The ancient sources suggest that women simply reproduced the values of their culture. *Plutarch's *Sayings of Spartan Women* consist of statements on the traditional role of women as mothers and affirmations of Spartan values ('Come home with your shield or on it'). Roman women were represented as the guardians of Roman culture and traditional morality; for example, *Lucretia, the model of chastity, and *Marcius Coriolanus' mother Veturia.

Now, however, there is interest in seeing women as agents with their own culture. One example of this work is Winkler's analysis of the Greek festivals of *Aphrodite and *Demeter (the Adonia, Stenia, *Haloa, and *Thesmophoria) which included

rituals restricted to women and which involved sexual humour (cf. the Roman Consualia). Where Detienne saw these as emphasizing women's approved social role in reproducing the city, Winkler proposes that women's own understanding of them could have been far more subversive. Doubting whether women would celebrate their alleged inferiority, he instead argues that women were laughing at the limitations of male sexuality. In a comparable study, Dean-Jones suggests that women saw the opposition between men who fight and may die for the city, and women who give birth and may die for the city, differently from men. For women, their bodies were superior, men's expendable, and even seclusion could thus be seen as a way of expressing their value. Finally, Osborne investigates how women would have responded to sculpted images of mortal women and goddesses. He argues that, while Classical statues spoke only to the male viewer, late Archaic images of *korai* (see SCULPTURE, GREEK) made female viewers see themselves as tokens of exchange in male systems. This role could give women power, as agents, because the system could not continue without them as tokens linking male households in marriage. See GYNAECOLOGY; HETEROSEXUALITY; HOMOSEXUALITY; MARRIAGE CEREMONIES; MARRIAGE LAW; MOTHERHOOD; PROSTITUTION; SEXUALITY.

SOURCEBOOKS E. Fantham and others, *Women in the Classical World* (1994); M. R. Lefkowitz and M. B. Fant, *Women's Life in Greece and Rome* (1982). Survey: G. Clark, *Women in the Ancient World*, *G&R* New Survey 21 (1989). Bibliographies: S. B. Pomeroy, in Peradotto and Sullivan (below); P. Culham, *Helios* 1986, 9–30.

COLLECTIONS L. Archer, S. Fischler, and M. Wyke (eds.), *Women in Ancient Societies: An Illusion of the Night* (1994); S. Blundell, *Women in Ancient Greece* (1995); A. Cameron and A. Kuhrt (eds.), *Images of Women in Antiquity* (1983); H. Foley (ed.), *Reflections of Women in Antiquity* (1981); 'Studies on Roman Women' 1 and 2, *Helios* 1989; *Pallas* 32 (1985); J. Peradotto and J. P. Sullivan (eds.), *Women in the Ancient World: The Arethusa Papers* (1984); N. S. Rabinowitz and A. Richlin (eds.), *Feminist Theory and the Classics* (1993); P. Schmitt-Pantel, *A History of Women in the West* 1: *From Ancient Goddesses to Christian Saints* (1992; It. orig. 1990); M. B. Skinner, *Rescuing Creusa: New Methodological Approaches to Women in Antiquity* (1987); A. M. Vérilhac (ed.), *La Femme dans le monde méditerranéen* 1: *Antiquité* (1985).

OTHERS R. A. Bauman, *Women and Politics in Ancient Rome* (1992); M. Boatwright, *AJPhil.* 1991, 513–40; G. Clark, *Women in Late Antiquity* (1993); D. Cohen, *Law, Sexuality and Society* (1991); L. Dean-Jones, *Women's Bodies in Classical Greek Science* (1992); M. Detienne, *The Gardens of Adonis* (1977; Fr. orig. 1972); S. Dixon, *The Roman Mother* (1988); J. F. Gardner, *Women in Roman Law and Society* (1987); J. P. Hallett, *Fathers and Daughters in Roman Society* (1984); P. Herfst, *Le Travail de la femme dans la Grèce ancienne* (1922); K. G. Holum, *Theodosian Empresses* (1982); R. Just, *Women in Athenian Law and Life* (1989); R. Osborne, in I. Morris (ed.), *Classical Greece: Ancient Histories and Modern Archaeologies* (1994), 81–96; S. B. Pomeroy, *Goddesses, Wives, Whores and Slaves* (1975), and *Women in Hellenistic Egypt* (1984); A. Richlin, *The Garden of Priapus* (1983; rev. edn. 1992), and *Helios* 1991, 160–80; D. M. Schaps, *Economic Rights of Women in Ancient Greece* (1979); J. Snyder, *The Woman and the Lyre* (1989); H. Versnel, in J. Blok and P. Mason (eds.), *Sexual Asymmetry: Studies in Ancient Society* (1987); J. Winkler, *The Constraints of Desire* (1992). H. K.

women in cult Women played a prominent part in the public religious life of the Greek cities, their roles being in many respects different from those of men. Most, though not all, cults of a female deity were served by a female rather than a male priest, each local sanctuary following its own tradition here. A few cults of male deities, as for instance frequently those of *Dionysus, were also served by priestesses (ἱέρειαι). Some cults stipulated that the priestess must be virgin (thus a little girl), a few (e.g. Paus. 8. 5. 12) that she have 'finished association with men', but the majority made no such provision; thus Lysimache was priestess of *Athena Polias in Athens for 64 years in the 5th cent. The role of a priestess was exactly parallel to that of a priest (see PRIESTS). Both sexes mediated between worshippers and worshipped, principally by presiding over sacrifices. A woman would not normally deal the fatal blow to the sacrificial victim, but except in the case of very small cults, neither did a male priest; that act was the preserve of a special official. Women other than the priestess also normally had a special role in the act of sacrifice: the basket containing the sacrificial knife was carried in the procession by an unmarried girl (*kanephoros), while the moment of the victim's death was marked by ululation (ololygmos) from all women present. A few local cults, however, banned the presence of women altogether.

Some women who were not priestesses as such had also special religious roles to play, the best-known example perhaps being that of the Pythia at *Delphi, an elderly woman who, probably in a trance-like state, became the medium for *Apollo's prophecy; see DELPHIC ORACLE. In Athens the wife of the basileus (see ARCHONTES) performed various sacred functions, including becoming in some way the bride of Dionysus at the *Anthesteria (see MARRIAGE, SACRED). Far less exclusive were the 'women's festivals', annual celebrations known all over the Greek world, from which men were rigorously excluded. Some of these, like the *Arrhephoria and the Braunonian bear-ritual (see BRAURON) in Attica, involved unmarried girls and almost certainly developed from *initiation ceremonies in which the girls in ritual seclusion were symbolically prepared for marriage and motherhood. Others, of which the very widespread *Thesmophoria may be seen as typical, were largely the concern of married women and seem to have been particularly concerned with fertility—vegetable, animal, and human. Such festivals also gave symbolic expression to the ambiguous position of women in relation to the polis. Other types of celebration, such as some of the wilder forms of Dionysiac ritual (see DIONYSUS; MAENADS), or the 'unofficial' Adonia (see ADONIS) which became popular in Athens at the end of the 5th cent., seem to have involved women in a more overtly emotional, perhaps sometimes ecstatic, form of religious experience. Women's participation in cults open to both sexes is also amply attested by *votive offerings and literary references.

Despite some Greek influence from Sicily and southern Italy, the Roman state presented a radically different form of religious organization, and the place of women was correspondingly different. Most of the major priesthoods, even of female deities, were held by men. In contrast to normal Greek custom (the priestly couples of some cults in Asia Minor are closer) the wives of some of these priests held a quasi-sacerdotal office by virtue of their marriage; notable is the wife of the flamen dialis, known as flaminica, whose assistance was necessary at certain public rituals and whose death compelled her husband to relinquish office (see FLAMINES). An even more clearly priestly role was taken by the Vestals, unmarried women who served the cult of *Vesta for thirty years from before puberty, whose peculiar status gave them elements akin to both married women (matronae) and to men (cf. Beard). Their presence was required at many public religious rites, at some of which they undertook parts of the sacrificial process which normally seem to have been barred to women. Like the Greek cities, however, Rome had its women's festivals, although it is argued that such celebrations were marginal to the city's religious life (Scheid). One among several known to us was the festival of the *Bona Dea, celebrated with great secrecy in the house of the highest magistrate present in

Rome, which attained notoriety when P. *Clodius Pulcher gained entry to *Caesar's house on this occasion (prompting the latter's remark that his wife must be above suspicion). Women were often more conspicuous in cults with a 'foreign' tinge, ranging from the city cult of *Ceres (originating from south Italy) which was served by a priestess, to the prominence of female devotees of *Isis (although until the imperial period all Isiac priests were apparently male, in conformity with Egyptian usage). Mithraic initiation (see MITHRAS) was confined to men (although dedications by women have been found in mithraea), but there is ample testimony also of the interest many Graeco-Roman women took in Judaism (see RELIGION, JEWISH) and *Christianity. The epistles of *Paul, among other sources, demonstrate the difficulties faced by the new religion in assigning an agreed role to women.

R. S. Kraemer, Her Share of the Blessings (1992), with review by R. Hawley, CR 1993, 314–16. Greece: C. Calame, Les Chœurs des jeunes filles en Grèce archaïque (1977); E. S. Holderman, The Study of the Greek Priestess (1913 diss.; It. trans. in G. Arrigoni (ed.), Le donne in Grecia (1985)); P. Brulé, La Fille d'Athènes (1987); C. Sourvinou-Inwood, Studies in Girls' Transitions (1988); F. Zeitlin, Arethusa 1982, 1299–57. Rome: J. Scheid, in P. Schmitt-Pantel (ed.), A History of Women in the West 1 (1992; It. orig. 1990), 377–408; O. de Cazenove, Phoenix 1987, 159–73; M. Beard, JRS 1980, 12–27; S. K. Heyob, The Cult of Isis among Women in the Graeco-Roman World (1975; modified by F. Mora, Prosopographia isiaca, 1990). E. Ke.

women in philosophy are recorded in antiquity, though extant writings are few, and there is controversy over dating and authorship of texts. Most of the women whom ancient sources identify as philosophers are associated with schools or societies that admitted women, or are related to philosophers who made education available to them. Women are reported as writing philosophical and mathematical works, and teaching in positions of authority in established schools.

Pythagoreanism seems to have been hospitable to women from the start (see PYTHAGORAS (1)). This philosophical tradition, which held a doctrine of the *transmigration of *souls, began as a religious society at *Croton in the late 6th cent. BC. Pythagoras taught women as well as men, and many are associated with the society. *Iamblichus (2) names sixteen (Life of Pythagoras 267), and other sources such as *Hermesianax (in Athenaeus 13), *Clement of Alexandria (Strom. 4. 19), *Diogenes (6) Laertius (8. 42–3), *Porphyry (Life of Pythagoras 4), and the *Suda also cite Pythagorean women by name. Among them are *Theano, who is probably Pythagoras' wife, though possibly a daughter or disciple, and *Myia and Arignote, daughters. These names are also notable because writings are attributed to them, including some extant writings of uncertain, though later, date. These need not be forgeries in a modern sense (cf. FORGERIES, LITERACY, Greek). It was a convention for later Pythagoreans to attribute their work to earlier ones ('genuine pseudepigrapha'); alternatively, more than one person in antiquity can have the same name. Nor need one assume these texts must be written by men using women's names as a literary conceit. Extant are letters (see LETTERS, GREEK) attributed to Theano, Myia, and Melissa, and fragments attributed to Theano (On Piety), Phintys (On Moderation of Women), Perictione (On Harmony of Women and On Wisdom), and, possibly, Aesara (On Human Nature). Dates and places of origin are very controversial.

In other schools, Axiothea (who dressed like a man) and Lastheneia are cited as students of *Plato (1) and *Speusippus (Diog. Laert. 3. 46, 4. 2); *Epicurus admitted women to the

Garden, including Leontion, who is chided in *Cicero for writing against *Theophrastus (*Nat. D.* 1. 93); Hipparchia, who married *Crates (2), is noted for her cynic way of life (Diog. Laert. 6. 96–8). Arete is cited among the *Cyrenaics: the daughter of Aristippus, her son of the same name is described as 'mother-taught'. *Strabo (17. 3. 22) says Arete became head of the school; probably a confusion. The Roman empress *Iulia Domna (AD 170–217) is noted for her lively circle of philosophers and sophists (see SECOND SOPHISTIC). Philostratus (*VS*; see PHILOSTRATI) calls her 'the philosopher Iulia'.

Perhaps the best-known woman in ancient philosophy lived in late antiquity. *Hypatia, daughter of the mathematician Theon, became head of the Neoplatonic school (see NEOPLATONISM) in *Alexandria (1). She taught philosophy and wrote the *Astronomical Canon* and commentaries on *Diophantus and *Apollonius (2), traces of which may survive. A contemporary account of her tragic death in AD 415 is given by the ecclesiastical historian *Socrates Scholasticus (*Hist. Eccl.* 7. 15). There are also letters to her from her student *Synesius.

> H. Thesleff (ed.), *The Pythagorean Texts of the Hellenistic Period* (1965); Eng. trans. in M. Waithe, *A History of Women Philosophers*, 1 (1987). See also H. Thesleff, *An Introduction to the Pythagorean Texts of the Hellenistic Period* (1961), and individual entries in *RE*: Arete 3 *RE* 2, Arignote *RE* 2, Hypatia *RE* 9, Leontion 1 *RE* 12, Melissa 4 *RE* 15, Myia 2 *RE* 16/1, Periktione 2 *RE* 19/1, Phintys *RE* 20/1, Theano 5 *RE* 5 A 1.   V. L. H.

wool (ἔριον, *lana*), the principal textile fibre of the Mediterranean region, was taken from the coat of the European domestic sheep, descendant of the wild *mouflon* of western Asia. (Goat- and camel-hair, used by ancient weavers, are excluded from the definition.) The structure of wool makes it warm, water-resistant and easy to spin; throughout antiquity fleece character was enhanced by selective breeding. The best wool was technically 'generalized medium' or 'fine'; pigmented (brown) fibres gave way to un-pigmented (white), but fleece-weights rarely exceeded 1 kg. (unwashed). The beginnings of a Greek woollen industry may be seen in the flock records of Minoan *Cnossus (*c.*1380 BC), which reveal an advanced management-regime. Sheep were a core component of Greek upland agriculture. The highest accolades for wool quality went to *Miletus, and true 'fine-wool' has been identified in extant fabrics from Nymphaeum (mod. Geroevka) in the Crimea (5th cent. BC; see CHERSONESUS (2)). Enterprising estate-owners, including the Ptolemies (see PTOLEMY (1); EGYPT, *Ptolemaic*), improved their flocks by importing breeding stock; the fleeces of their fine-woolled sheep were often protected with skin jackets (Diog. Laert. 6. 41; Colum. 6. 4. 1). The Greek colonies in Italy, notably *Tarentum, set high standards for Roman wool producers to emulate. Wool from farms in the Po valley (see PADUS) and several regions of *Spain was particularly prized, and marketed by weight. *Laodicea-Lycus succeeded Miletus as the leading eastern provincial source. Shearing with sprung-iron shears never completely replaced the older practice of plucking the fleece (πόκος, *vellus*); there were professional shearers (ἐριοκάρται, *tonsores*). Inscriptions mention woolcombers who separated long from short staples with flat iron combs. Some raw wool was converted directly into felt, but most was spun for the manufacture of all manner of clothing and furnishings; since wool takes dyes easily, they were often in bright colours. See DYEING; PASTORALISM; TEXTILE PRODUCTION.

> *RE* 12. 594–617; Forbes, *Stud. Anc. Technol.* 4². 2 ff.; M. L. Ryder, *Sheep and Man* (1983); J. M. Frayn, *Sheep-Rearing and the Wool Trade in Italy during the Roman Period* (1984); E. J. W. Barber, *Prehistoric Textiles* (1991).   J. P. W.

work See LABOUR.

worship, household The domestic cult of a Greek family concerned the protection and prosperity of the house and its occupants, with daily small offerings and prayers to *Zeus Ctesius (protector of the stores), Zeus Herceus (protector of the wall or fence surrounding the house), and *Apollo Agyieus (of the streets) whose image stood at the house's street entrance. The hearth, as Hestia, was sacred, and at mealtimes a bit of food was placed there as a *first-fruits offering (Plut. *Mor.* 703d; Theophr. in Porph. *Abst.* 2. 20). Similarly, before drinking wine, libations were poured on the floor to *Hestia (*h. Hom.* 29. 4–6) or at formal banquets to Zeus and the heroes, to the *Agathos Daimon, or to other deities (Ath. 15. 692f–693f; Arist. fr. 55 Rose). In these family cults the rituals seem of primary importance and hence were widespread while the deities honoured varied from place to place. The father served as priest for the family, however, and that may partially explain the regular appearance of Zeus, father of the gods. The admission of new members to the family (brides, babies, and slaves) was marked by initiation rites, often involving the hearth and featuring fertility symbols. Death brought to the household a pollution which was effaced only by the passage of a set period of time.

The Roman domestic cult was similar, centred on the hearth (*Vesta), with somewhat more elaborate table ritual, and with *Janus watching the door, the Di Penates (see PENATES DI) guarding the stores, and the Lar Familiaris (see LARES), of obscure origin, offering more general protection (e.g. Plaut. *Aul.* 1–27, *Merc.* 830–7; Hor. *Carm.* 3. 23). Like their Greek counterparts these deities remained numinous, without distinct personality or mythology. The functions of the Lares and Di Penates overlapped to the degree that they were regularly confused or generalized. They were housed, along with the *genius* of the *paterfamilias* and other particularly favoured deities, in the *lararium*, many examples of which are known from Pompeii (G. K. Boyce, *MAAR* 14 (1937)).

> Nilsson, *GGR* 1³. 337–8, 402–6, and *Opuscula Romana* 1 (1954), 77–85; H. J. Rose, *Religion in Greece and Rome* (1959), 29–35, 175–83.   J. D. M.

wreaths See CROWNS AND WREATHS.

wrestling This was a popular exercise among the Greeks. They used a wide variety of holds and throws, many of which are illustrated in vase-paintings and statuettes of wrestlers. The object was to throw an opponent to the ground, and generally three throws were required for victory. In the major *agōnes* wrestling was both a separate event and the last of the events of the *pentathlon; though weight was an advantage, general athletic ability was required too. Wrestling was also practised extensively to acquire general physical fitness (cf. Plato, *Symp.* 217c), and was considered particularly valuable, together with boxing, as a part of military training. See ATHLETICS.

> ANCIENT SOURCES *IP*. 23. 700–39; Paus. 6. 14. 5–8 (on Milo).
> MODERN LITERATURE M. Poliakoff, *Combat Sports in the Ancient World* (1987), 23–53.   R. L. H.; S. J. I.

writing See ALPHABET, GREEK; ALPHABETS OF ITALY; ARCHIVES; BELLEROPHON; BOOKS, GREEK AND ROMAN; BUREAUCRACY (GREEK); EPIGRAPHY, GREEK and LATIN; LETTERS, GREEK and LATIN; LIBRARIES; LITERACY; OSTRACA; PALAEOGRAPHY; PAPYROLOGY, GREEK and LATIN; POTTERY (GREEK), INSCRIPTIONS ON; RECORDS AND RECORD-KEEPING, ATTITUDES TO; TABULA (various entries); TACHYGRAPHY; VINDOLANDA TABLETS.

Xanthippus (1), husband of *Cleisthenes (2)'s niece Agariste and father of *Pericles (1). He prosecuted *Miltiades after his unsuccessful attack on *Paros in 490–489 BC; he was ostracized (see OSTRACISM) in 484, perhaps in a three-cornered rivalry involving *Themistocles and *Aristides (1), but was recalled with the other victims of ostracism before *Xerxes' invasion. As a general in 479 (see PERSIAN WARS) he commanded the Athenian contingent at Mycale; after the Spartans had returned home, he led some of the Greeks in an attack on *Sestus, which was captured from the Persians after a winter siege. He was presumably dead by 472, when Pericles acted as *chorēgos* (see CHORĒGIA) for *Aeschylus.

PA 11169; APF 455–7; for the 'Xanthippos *ostrakon*' see ML 42.
P. T.; P. J. R.

Xanthippus (2) (*RE* 9) was a Spartan mercenary commander who fought for *Carthage against M. *Atilius Regulus in 255 BC (see PUNIC WARS). He reorganized the Carthaginian army and annihilated the Roman expeditionary force, making brilliant use of the Carthaginian *elephants and cavalry to outflank and mow down the Romans. After his victory he left Carthage. He may be identical with the Xanthippus whom *Ptolemy (1) III appointed to govern the lands he claimed to control across the river *Euphrates.

Walbank, HCP 1 91–4.
J. Br.

Xanthus was called the largest city in *Lycia by *Strabo (14. 3. 6, 666), a claim borne out by its extensive remains; prosperity was based on the fertile plain of the river Xanthus, with access to the sea at *Patara. The city was known to Homer, and *Herodotus (1) describes its capitulation to Persia in the famous siege of 545 BC (1. 176); in the 5th cent. it was ruled by a line of Persian client-dynasts (the self-styled '*genos* of Karika'). There are impressive and highly distinctive tombs of the 5th and early 4th cents., notably that of the dynast Gergis, with a trilingual (Greek and two types of Lycian) inscription detailing Xanthian involvement in the *Peloponnesian War (ML 93; *c*.410 BC), and the famous Nereid Monument (see ART, FUNERARY, GREEK (4)), thought to be the heroon of the dynast Arbinas (*c*.390: cp. *SEG* 39. 1414). In the territory was a major sanctuary of *Leto, later the cult-centre of the Lycian League, where the finds include a trilingual inscription (Greek, Lycian, *Aramaic) relating to the foundation of a cult of 'King Caunius' during a period of Hecatomnid control (*SEG* 27. 942, of 337 BC; see PIXODARUS). Falling to *Alexander (3) the Great in 333 BC, the city became a Ptolemaic dependency (see EGYPT, *Ptolemaic*); an interesting 108-line inscription from the Letoon (208 BC) records the diplomatic niceties of a (failed) request for financial assistance from *Cytin-

ium (*SEG* 38. 1476). The siege by *Brutus (42 BC) prompted mass self-immolation by the citizens according to App. *BCiv.* 4. 76. But the city prospered under the Roman empire. Cf. PERICLES (2) (rival of Xanthus).

H. Metzger and others, *Fouilles de Xanthos* 1– (1958–); *Arch. Rep.* 1978/9, 83–5; 1984/5, 101; 1989/90, for recent work, esp. at the Letoon. A. Keen, *Anat. Stud.* 42 (1992) (dynasts).   S. M., A. J. S. S.

Xanthus (1) (*RE* 26), poet, mentioned by *Stesichorus, who adapted many works from him, including the *Oresteia*; he presented *Heracles in his Homeric guise, and said that Laodice (cf. *Il.* 9. 145) was renamed Electra because unmarried (ἄλεκτρος). This information can be traced back no further than the Homeric scholar Megaclides (later 4th cent. BC?).

Page, *Poet. Mel. Gr.* 699–700; D. Campbell, *Greek Lyric* (Loeb) 3 (1991), 26–7.
P. J. P.

Xanthus (2) Hellenized Lydian from *Sardis, older contemporary of *Herodotus (1). Author of *Lydiaca* in 4 books on the origin and history of the Lydian people, maybe down to the capture of Sardis by *Cyrus (1) the Great in 547/6. According to *Ephorus (*FGrH* 70 F 180 = Xanthus T 5) he was used by Herodotus, but the fragments do not admit of definite conclusions. Xanthus lived to the time of *Thucydides (2) (Dion. Hal. *De Thuc.* 5 = T 4). The fragments show a desire to support partly mythical native traditions with geological, linguistic (F 16), rationalistic and scientific (F12, 13) arguments: this is Xanthus' chief contribution to historical methodology. It is certain that he was used by *Nicolaus of Damascus, but in what way and to what extent has been much discussed, resulting in various reconstructions of the *Lydiaca*: cf. Herter on one side, von Fritz on the other. There are conspicuous correspondences with regard to some details of the early history of Lydia and the royal genealogy—cf. e.g. Nicolaus *FGrH* 90 F 15, 16, 22 and Xanthus F 16–18. But in other parts one finds unmistakable differences—cf. e.g. Nicolaus F 71 and Xanthus F 15. The 'melodramatic and fantastic tales' (von Fritz) about Ardys, *Gyges, and *Croesus in Nicolaus F 44, 47, 68, which historians usually trace back to Xanthus, display such significant differences in style and mode from the genuine and partially very early attested fragments of Xanthus that an immediate influence can be ruled out. One may assume the existence of a Hellenistic adaptation as the source for Nicolaus. *On Empedocles* (Diog. Laert. 8. 63) and *Magica* (Clem. Alex. *Strom.* 3. 11. 1) are not very well attested and consequently their historicity is in doubt.

FGrH 765. H. Herter, *RE* 9 A (1967), 1354 ff.; H. Diller, in *Navicula Chilonensis, Festschrift F. Jacoby* (1956); K. von Fritz, *Die griechische Geschichtsschreibung*, 2 vols. (1967); R. Drews, *The Greek Accounts of Eastern History* (1973), 100 ff.; O. Lendle, *Einführung in die griechische Geschichtsschreibung* (1992).
K. M.

Xenagoras

Xenagoras (2nd cent. BC), a Greek, wrote Χρόνοι (*Chronologies*) of the Greek world, with special interest in *Sicily and the west, and Περὶ νήσων (*On the islands*). See also ISLANDS.

FGrH 240.

K. S. S.

Xenarchus (1), Sicilian mime-writer (see MIME) of the late 5th cent. BC, son of *Sophron.

Arist. *Poet.* 1447ᵇ 3; Kaibel, *CGF*, 182.

S. H.

Xenarchus (2), a frank and lively Middle Comedy poet (see COMEDY (GREEK), MIDDLE). Eight titles survive, mainly from daily life. Fr. 1; a parody of tragic style; 4: young men's sexual preference for married women over prostitutes; 7: illegal watering of fish; 14: happy cicadas, whose wives have no voice.

FRAGMENTS Kassel–Austin, *PCG* 7 (1989), 791–801.
INTERPRETATION Meineke, *FCG* 1. 434; A. Körte in *RE* 9 A 2 (1967), 1421 f., 'Xenarchos 2'.

W. G. A.

xenia See FRIENDSHIP, RITUALIZED.

Xenocles, son of the elder *Carcinus (1), was a tragic poet who defeated *Euripides in 415 with his *Oedipus, Lycaon, Bacchae* and *Athamas* (satyric). His *Licymnius* is parodied by *Aristophanes (1) (*Clouds* 1264 f.), and there are contemptuous references to him at Ar. *Thesm.* 169, 440–2, *Frogs* 86. He seems to have been noted for a fondness for mechanical devices.

TrGF 1². 151–3; Davies, *APF* 283–5.

A. L. B.

Xenocrates (1) of Chalcedon, son of Agathenor, disciple of *Plato (1) and head of the *Academy from 339 to 314 BC. He is presented to us as a man of impressive personality, with a combination of austere dignity and kindliness which exercised a great influence on all who came in contact with him. He was generally respected in Athens and was employed by the citizens as ambassador to *Antipater (1) in 322 BC.

His philosophical contributions, so far as we can reconstruct them from the scanty evidence, were less impressive. He seems, in general, to have attempted to reproduce Plato's thought in a stereotyped and formalized system, though on one or two points he probably preserved the correct tradition of interpretation as against Aristotle. He also interested himself in giving a systematic account of the nature of the gods and daemons and their relations to the heavenly bodies, in a way which foreshadowed the constructs of later *Neoplatonism. From the titles of his works we may conjecture that his chief interest lay in moral questions, but rather in the direction of teaching a practical morality than of ethical analysis, a line which his immediate successors in the Academy appear to have followed. His only known excursion into mathematics issued in a defence of 'indivisible lines', which Aristotle thereupon proved indefensible.

R. Heinze, *Xenocrates* (1892); S. Pines, 'A New Fragment of Xenocrates', *TAPA* 1961; M. Ostwald and J. P. Lynch, *CAH* 6² (1994), 611 f.

G. C. F.; S. H.

Xenocrates (2) of *Aphrodisias, physician of the time of *Nero and the Flavians (AD 54–96).

Works Περὶ τῆς ἀπὸ τοῦ ἀνθρώπου καὶ τῶν ζώων ὠφελείας ('On the uses of human beings and animals'), full of superstitious means of treatment, borrowed largely from previous works such as Ps.-Democritus' *Lithognomon*, a lexicon of *gems (frs. ed. M. Wellmann in *Quellen u. Studien zur Geschichte der Naturwissenschaften u. der Medizin*, 1935); Περὶ τῆς τῶν ἐνύδρων τροφῆς ('On the mode of nutrition of water creatures'); *On the healing properties of plants*; *On the names of plants*; *On the meaning of the flight of birds*.

Frs. ed. J. L. Ideler in *Physici et Medici Graeci Minores* (1841), 1. 121.

W. D. R.

Xenophanes of Colophon, poet, theologian, and natural philosopher, left Ionia (see IONIANS) at the age of 25, probably after the Persian Conquest in 545 BC, and led a wandering life for 67 years, as he tells us himself in a preserved passage from an elegiac poem (DK 21 B 8). He lived in several cities in Sicily, and is reported to have composed an epic on the colonization of *Elea (see COLONIZATION, GREEK), but the tradition that he was the teacher of *Parmenides is doubtful. He is credited with being the first author of satirical verses (*Silloi*). The extant fragments, in various metres and genres, include two long elegiac passages on how to conduct a civilized *symposium and on the civic importance of his own work and wisdom (*sophiē*).

A skilful poet in the tradition of *Tyrtaeus and *Solon, Xenophanes carried the Ionian intellectual enlightenment to *Magna Graecia. His natural philosophy is a somewhat simplified version of the new Milesian cosmology, supplemented by interesting inferences from observed fossils. The origin of things is from earth and water; meteorological and celestial phenomena (including sun, moon, and stars) are explained by clouds formed from the sea. In theology and epistemology he was an original and influential thinker. He attacks *Homer and *Hesiod for portraying the gods as behaving in ways that are blameworthy for mortals. He mocks anthropomorphic conceptions of deity, and undermines the supernatural interpretation of natural phenomena. In place of the Homeric pantheon he offers the vision of a supreme god, 'greatest among gods and men, like unto mortals neither in body nor in mind' (fr. 23), who without effort sways the universe with his thought. Moderns have imagined him a monotheist, but he seems rather to have preached a harmonious polytheism, without conflict among the gods. In our ignorance of Milesian speculation about the gods, Xenophanes appears as the first thinker systematically to formulate the conception of a cosmic god, and thus to found the tradition of natural theology followed by *Plato (1), *Aristotle, and the Stoics (see STOICISM). Pursuing a theme of archaic poetry, Xenophanes is the first to reflect systematically on the distinction between human opinion or guesswork (*dokos*) and certain knowledge.

DK 21; Diehl, *Anth. Lyr. Graec.* 1.³ 63 ff. W. Jaeger, *The Theology of the Early Greek Philosophers* (1947), 38 ff.; Guthrie, *Hist. Gk. Phil.* 1. 360 ff.; Kirk–Raven–Schofield, 163 ff.; J. H. Lesher, *Xenophanes of Colophon* (1992); J. Barnes, *The Presocratic Philosophers* 1 (1979), 82 ff. C. H. K.

Xenophon (1)

Life Xenophon, son of Gryllus, from the Athenian *deme of Erchia, was born into a wealthy but politically inactive family around 430 BC. He presumably served in the cavalry (see HIPPEIS (2) and (4)) and certainly (like other affluent young men) associated with *Socrates. This background did not encourage enthusiasm for democracy (see DEMOCRACY, ATHENIAN). He apparently stayed in Athens under the *Thirty Tyrants and fought the democratic insurgents in the civil war (404–403). The political *amnesty of 403/2 theoretically protected him, and material in *Hellenica* and *Memorabilia* shows that (like *Plato (1)) he was critical of the Thirty, but insecurity was surely one reason why he accepted the suggestion of a Boeotian friend, Proxenus, to enrol as a *mercenary with *Cyrus (2). He was thus among the 10,000 Greeks involved in Cyrus' rebellion and defeat at *Cunaxa (401). When *Tissaphernes liquidated the Greek generals, Xenophon emerged as a replacement and led the survivors through Mesopotamia, Armenia, and northern Anatolia to *Byzantium and then into service with the Thracian Seuthes. He alleges a wish to go home at this stage but for various reasons neither did so nor availed himself of Seuthes' offers of land and marriage-alliance. Consequently, when the Spartans under *Thibron (1) arrived in Anatolia for a war of 'liberation' (399) and took over the Cyreans (i.e. Cyrus' veterans), he became a Spartan mercenary. Nothing is known of his role in ensuing campaigns except that he self-defensively endorsed criticisms which led to Thibron's dismissal. Subsequent Spartan commanders, *Dercylidas and *Agesilaus, were more to his taste and he forged close associations with them. In 394 Agesilaus returned home to confront rebellion amongst Sparta's allies and Xenophon fought for the Spartan cause at *Coronea against, among others, his fellow-Athenians. Exiled as a result of this (if not, as some think, earlier, as part of an Athenian attempt to win Persian goodwill) he was settled by the Spartans at Scillus, near *Olympia. (His estate and the sanctuary funded by booty from his Asiatic adventures are described idyllically in Anab. 5. 3. 5 ff.). As a Spartan protégé (he was their *proxenos at Olympia and his children were allegedly educated in Sparta) he became vulnerable during the disturbances which followed *Leuctra, was expelled, and spent the rest of his life in *Corinth. There was, however, a reconciliation with Athens. Works such as Cavalry Commander and Ways and Means disclose a sympathetic interest in the city; and in 362 his son Gryllus was killed fighting in the Athenian cavalry (see HIPPEIS) at *Mantinea. The posthumous eulogies this earned were in part a tribute to his father.

Works Most famous in antiquity as a 'philosopher' or mercenary-leader (ostensibly regarded as a perfect model for the young by *Dio Cocceianus of Prusa, and systematically 'imitated' by *Arrian), Xenophon produced a large output, all known parts of which survive. The chronology is only vaguely established. Most works fall into three categories: long (quasi-) historical narratives, Socratic texts (surely Athenocentric works, not mere by-products of contact with supposed Socratic 'cells' in *Elis or Phlius), and technical treatises. There are also monographs (encomium; non-Socratic political *dialogue; politico-economic pamphlet; institutional analysis), though their secondary relation to the major categories is obvious. Many are the earliest (or earliest surviving) examples of particular *genres. The clearest common features are (1) intimate relationship with Xenophon's personal experiences and (2) taste for didactic discourse. Xenophon's moral system is conventional, underpinned by belief in the gods and the importance of omen and ritual: divine power (often anonymous and not infrequently singular) is everywhere in Xenophon's writings, though not absolutely stultifyingly—when consulting the oracle at Delphi (see DELPHIC ORACLE) about going to Asia he famously framed the question so as to get the 'right' answer; and at the climactic moment in Anabasis where the Greeks reach the sea they are too excited to think of sacrificing to the gods. But it is not these things in their own right so much as issues of leadership (by states as well as individuals) or military skill which engage his didactic muse. That even purely practical pursuits have a moral component because they have social implications is a characteristic Xenophontic perception; and the would-be leader must, whatever else, earn his right to lead by superior wisdom and a capacity to match or outdo his subordinates in all the tasks which he demands of them.

In antiquity his style was judged to be simple, sweet, persuasive, graceful, poetic, and a model of *Attic purity. This is understandable, though there are deviations from standard Attic and

some would call the style jejune; both rhetoric (e.g. Hell. 7. 5. 1–27) and narrative can sometimes be awkward. The range of stylistic figures employed is modest (simile is quite common, with a penchant for animal comparisons). The overall effect (style *and* content) can seem naïve. A (perhaps the) central question, which divides modern readers into two camps, is how far style and content are really *faux-naif* and informed by humour and irony. One should perhaps reflect that (a) Xenophon's emergence as a leader in N. Mesopotamia in late summer 401 must disclose special qualities and (b) 4th-cent. Greece was full of men of 'upper-class' origin and of (ex-)mercenaries, and possibly not short of men who were both, but only one of them produced five (modern) volumes of varied, sometimes innovatory, writing. We should give Xenophon the benefit of the doubt, and conclude that there was more, not less, to him than there appears.

Hellenica. A seven-book history of Greek affairs, in two linguistically distinguishable parts, perhaps created at widely differing times, the first possibly as early as the 380s, the second in the mid-350s. (a) 1. 1. 1–2. 3. 10 covers the *Peloponnesian War from 411 to the destruction of Athens' walls, the overthrow of democracy and the surrender of *Samos (404). The opening narrative links imperfectly with Thuc. 8. 109, but the intention can only be to 'complete' the Thucydidean account (see THUCYDIDES (2)), though this is achieved with little reproduction of Thucydides' historiographical characteristics. (b) 2. 3. 11–7. 5. 27 continues the story, covering the Thirty Tyrants (404–403), Sparta's Asiatic campaigns (399–394), the *Corinthian War and *King's Peace (395–387/6), Spartan imperialism in Greece (386–379), the rise of Thebes (379–371) and the Peloponnesian consequences of *Leuctra (371–362). The text ends at Mantinea (362; see MANTINEA, BATTLES OF), with Greece in an unabated state of uncertainty and confusion. The account is centred on Sparta and characterized by surprising omissions (e.g. the name of *Epaminondas the architect of Leuctra is not given at all in book 6 where the battle is described; the liberation of *Messenia; Athens' Aegean policies in 378–362), a tendency to expose the shortcomings of all states, including Sparta, and recurrent hostility to imperial aspirations. A curious amalgam of straight history and political pamphlet, it was relatively little read in antiquity, and its modern status has declined in recent years. But it remains an indispensable source, and the tendency to regard the presumed qualities of Hellenica Oxyrhynchia (see OXYRHYNCHUS, THE HISTORIAN FROM) as a reason for simply preferring alternative historical traditions should be questioned.

Anabasis. An account (date uncertain)—perhaps initially circulated under the name *Themistogenes (cf. Hell. 3. 1. 2)—of Cyrus' rebellion and the fate of his Greek mercenaries, dominated in 3–7 by Xenophon's personal role in rescuing the army. The work's motive is not overtly stated. Apologia and self-advertisement are evident (there were other, and different, accounts in circulation); there is implicit endorsement of the panhellenist thesis (see PANHELLENISM) that Persia was vulnerable to concerted attack and of a more general view about Greek superiority over *barbarians (the army is an emblematic *polis on the move); and a didactic interest in leadership and military stratagem is obvious (though the account of Cunaxa is strangely flawed). Equally striking is the care taken to construct a varied and genuinely arresting narrative. The work's modern reputation has suffered from traditional use in language learning (cf. *Caesar's Gallic War).

Cyropaedia. A pseudo-historical account of the life of *Cyrus (1) I the Great, often invoked in accounts of the background of the Greek *novel. (There is even a significant, though sketchily narrated, 'love interest' in the story of Panthea and Abradatas.) The institutional framework preserves useful *Achaemenid (see PERSIA) information (though the oriental decor is not as pronounced as it might be; need for compromise with Greek suspicion of the orient makes difficulties here; see ORIENTALISM), but the story-line as it stands flagrantly contradicts other source material (e.g. Cyrus acquires *Media by inheritance not conquest, and he dies in bed not battle); suggestions that it may sometimes represent alternative historical tradition (not mere invention) are optimistic. The chief concern (cf. 1. 1. 1) is with techniques of military and political leadership, which are exposed both paradigmatically and through passages of explicit instruction (often involving dialogue). There is also some suggestion that even Cyrus can be corrupted by the acquisition of empire, and a final chapter (post-362) excoriates contemporary Persian vices. Very popular in antiquity (and sometimes thought important enough to have prompted a response from Plato in parts of *Laws*), Cyropaedia has been found dull in modern times. But a revival of interest is under way, and it is arguably a litmus-test for true appreciation of Xenophon in general.

Apology. A brief (perhaps very early) work with a purported extract from the court-room defence of Socrates against charges of religious deviance and corruption of the young sandwiched between a preliminary dialogue with Hermogenes and various carefree observations made after the trial was over. The stated purpose is to explain the *megalēgoria* ('big-talking') which previous writers agreed was a feature of Socrates' reaction to prosecution and show why he did not fear death. (Opportunity is also found to note the prosecutor *Anytus' son's history of alcohol abuse).

Symposium. 'In writing of great men it is proper to record not only their serious activities but their diversions' (1. 1), and entertainment at *Callias (4)'s party is a mixture of cabaret (music, song, and dance, a sexually titillating tableau of *Dionysus and *Ariadne) and more-or-less serious conversation about the guests' account of their most prized assets (e.g. beauty, wealth, poverty, making people better, recitation, joke-telling, skill at procuring). There is much explicit or implicit reference to personal relationships (doubtless a feature of real sympotic conversation), so Socrates' eventual discourse on common and celestial love is an unsurprising development, though the Platonic model is probably relevant. See SYMPOSIUM LITERATURE.

Socratic Memoirs. A collection of conversations, probably not planned as a coherent whole. 1. 1–2 explicitly address charges advanced at Socrates' trial, but the whole work presents him as respecting the gods and helping (not corrupting) his fellow-men. Broad thematic patterns are visible—1 dwells on religion and moderate life-style, 2 on friendship and family, and 3 on Socrates' help to 'those ambitious of good things', while 4 is more disparate (education; the existence of god; temperance; justice) and pretentious—but the pleasure of the work is in its individual vignettes and convincing (not necessarily authentic) picture of a down-to-earth Socrates equally happy debating with sophists, courtesans, and victims of the collapse of Athenian imperialism, and concerned with practicalities as well as philosophy. (As with Plato, drawing the line between genuine Socratic conversational subjects and Xenophontic ones is not easy.)

Oeconomicus. A conversation with Critobulus (1–6) establishes the importance of *agriculture. Socrates then reports a conversation with Ischomachus—itself containing a conversation between Ischomachus and his wife (7–10)—covering household

organization, the daily pursuits of a rich Athenian, the role of bailiffs, and technical details of cereal and fruit cultivation. Much of it is effectively about leadership—a harder skill than agriculture, as Ischomachus remarks. The work is an important (though, given Socratic—and Xenophontic—unconventionality, slippery) source for social history. Particularly notable is Ischomachus' wife, married young so she will be a *tabula rasa* on which her husband can write what he will, but accorded a significant—if sex-stereotyped—role in the running of the household (see HOUSEWORK; WOMEN).

Cavalry Commander deals with the management and improvement of the Athenian cavalry force (which ought—9. 3—to include foreign mercenaries); see HIPPEIS. After comments on recruitment (1. 2, 9–13), securing good horses (1. 3–4, 14–16), general horsemanship (1. 5–6, 17–21), armament (1. 7, 22–3), discipline (1. 7, 24), the need for good phylarchs (brigade-commanders; cf. PHYLAI) and political allies (1. 8, 25–6) and tactical formations (2. 1–9) Xenophon formally turns to the cavalry-commander's duties (3. 1 ff.). There follow sections on festival performances (3), conduct of marches and intelligence-gathering (4), deception (5), inducing respect of subordinates by knowledge and example (6), the defence of *Attica and more general tactical/strategic points (7, 8. 17–25), horsemanship (8. 1–8), questions of numerical advantage (8. 9–16). Treatment of topics is inexhaustive, unsystematic and inclined to repetition (e.g. numerical issues appear in 5. 1 f., 7. 5 f., 8. 9 f.). Characteristically Xenophon begins and ends with the gods, asserts that no art should be practised more than warfare (8. 7)—gymnastics are frivolous—and stresses the importance of leadership qualities. See WAR, ART OF, GREEK.

On Horsemanship. 'Instruction and exercises' for the private and apparently rather ignorant individual (the specific addressees are 'younger friends': 1. 1). It is the earliest surviving such work (one by Simon is an acknowledged predecessor) and covers purchase, housing and grooming (1–6), mounting, riding, galloping and jumping (7–8), correction of vivacity and sluggishness (9), dressage and manipulation of appearance (10–11), and equestrian armour and weaponry (12). Its precepts are well regarded by modern experts. See HORSES.

On Hunting. A technical treatise dealing with nets (2), *dogs and their training (3, 4. 11, 7) and the timing and conduct of the hunt (5–6, 8). The hunter is on foot, the normal prey a hare (an animal of notably good organic design: 5. 29), though Xenophon also mentions deer, boar and the wild cats of *Macedonia, Mysia and *Syria (9–11). He disapproves of the hunting of foxes (6. 3). The activity is non-utilitarian (quick capture shows perseverance, but is not real hunting: 6. 8), intensely pleasurable—the sight of a hare running is so charming that to see one tracked, found, pursued, and caught is enough to make a man forget all other passions (5. 33)—and a divine invention which promotes military, intellectual, and moral excellence (1, 12). A contrast is drawn with the corrupt verbal wisdom of '*sophists' (a group not treated elsewhere in Xenophon as a coherent evil), and the hunter beats the politician in point of ethical standing and social value (13). Suspicions about the work's authenticity are unfounded. See HUNTING.

Agesilaus. Posthumous encomium of 'a perfectly good man' (1. 1). An uneven chronological account (long stretches in close verbal parallel to passages of *Hellenica*) is followed by a survey (with some anecdotal examples) of principal virtues (piety, justice, continence, courage, wisdom, patriotism, charm, dignity, austerity). Little solid information is offered which is not in

Hellenica, but a new gloss (sometimes panhellenic, occasionally critical) is put on already familiar facts. The work (like *Isocrates' *Evagoras*; see EVAGORAS) is normally regarded as an important contribution to the development of biography. See AGESILAUS; BIOGRAPHY, GREEK.

Hieron. A dialogue version of the 'wise man meets autocrat' scenario (cf. *Herodotus (1) on *Solon and *Croesus, see Hdt. 1. 29 ff.) in which, contrary to expectation, *Hieron (1) refutes Simonides' claim that it is pleasant to be a *tyrant, while Simonides supplies suggestions for improving the situation, not least by manipulation of public opinion. The original readers will inevitably have thought of 4th-cent. Syracusan tyranny (*Dionysius (1) I and (2) II), but this may not be a specifically intended subtext.

Ways and Means. Politicians claim that poverty compels Athens to treat other cities unjustly. So Xenophon advises alleviation of that poverty through innocent means, particularly (*a*) attracting revenue-creating foreign residents and (*b*) using state-owned slaves in the *Laurium silver *mines (*b*) to increase income and generate a dole (*trophē*) for citizens. The economic plan (a curious mixture of the apparently familiar and completely alien) has been much criticized; but the primary imperative is political—to devise a new imperialism based on peace and consensual hegemony.

Constitution of the Spartans. An account of the Spartan system (attributed to a single lawgiver, *Lycurgus (2)) which demonstrates the rationality of its consistent contradiction of normal Greek practices. The tone is laudatory except in a final chapter (misplaced in the manuscripts) which notes the decline from Lycurgan values associated with 4th-cent. imperialism.

(The non-Xenophontic *Constitution of the Athenians*, conceding that democracy, though repellent, was rational in Athenian circumstances, was allowed into the corpus by a later editor as a companion piece. The treatise is often called the 'Old Oligarch' (see separate entry OLD OLIGARCH).)

GENERAL Diog. Laert. 2. 48–50; Dio Chrys. *Or.* 18. J. Luccioni, *Les Idées sociales et politiques de Xénophon* (1947); H. Breitenbach, *Historische Anschauungsformen Xenophons* (1950) and *RE* 9 A, cols 1567–2052; E. Delebecque, *Essai sur la vie de Xénophon* (1957); J. K. Anderson, *Xenophon* (1974); W. E. Higgins, *Xenophon the Athenian* (1977); S. Hirsch, *The Friendship of the Barbarians* (1985); G. Proietti, *Xenophon's Sparta: An Introduction* (1987); L. Gautier, *La Langue de Xénophon* (1911); K. Münscher, *Xenophon in der gr.-röm. Literatur* (1920).

TEXTS OCT (Marchant). Teubner (Gemoll, Hude, etc.).

COMMENTARIES *Hell.*: G. E. Underhill (1906); P. Krentz (1989: 1–2. 3. 10 and 1995: 2. 3. 11–4. 2. 8). *An.*: W. Vollbrecht (1907–12); O. Lendle (1995). *Cyr.*: Holden (1890). *Lac.*: F. Ollier (1934). *Vect.*: G. Bodei Giglioni (1970); P. Gauthier (1976). *De Re Eq.*: E. Delebecque (1950). *Symp.*: G. J. Woldinga (1938/9). *Mem.*: O. Gigon (1953, 1956: 1, 2 only); A. Delatte (1933: 3 only). *Socratic Works* (all): R. Laurenti (1961). *Oec.*: S. Pomeroy (1994).

TRANSLATIONS H. G. Dakyns (1890 etc.). R. Warner, *Anabasis²* (1972), *Hellenica²* (1977). C. J. Tuplin, *Anabasis, Hellenica* (in preparation). H. Tredennick, *Memoirs of Socrates & Symposium*, with text: Loeb and Budé series.

PARTICULAR WORKS *Hell.*: W. P. Henry, *Greek Historical Writing* (1966); G. Cawkwell, introd. to Warner's trans.; V. Gray, *The Character of Xenophon's Hellenica* (1989); C. J. Tuplin, *The Failings of Empire* (1993); J. Dillery, *Xenophon and the History of his Times* (1995). *Cyr.*: P. Carlier, *Ktema* 1978, 133–63; J. Tatum, *Xenophon's Imperial Fiction* (1989); B. Due, *The Cyropaedia* (1989); D. Gera, *Xenophon's Cyropaedia* (1994); C. Mueller-Goldingen, *Untersuchungen zu Xenophons Kyrupädie* (1995). *An.*: G. Cawkwell, intro. to Warner's trans.; G. Nussbaum, *The Ten Thousand* (1967); V. Manfredi, *La Strada dei Diecimila* (1986); P. Briant (ed.), *Dans les pas des Dix-Mille* (1996). *Lac.*: K. Chrimes (1948). *Mem., Ap.,*

Symp.: L. Strauss, *Xenophon's Socrates* (1972). *Oec.*: L. Strauss, *Xenophon's Socratic Discourse* (1970); S. Pomeroy (ed., trans., comm., 1994). *Hiero.*: L. Strauss, *On Tyranny* (1968); M. Sordi, *Athen.* 1980, 3–13; V. Gray, *CQ* 1981, 321–34; *De Re Eq.*: J. K. Anderson, *Ancient Greek Horsemanship* (1961). *Cyn.*: V. Gray, *Hermes*, 1985, 156–71. *Ag.*: G. Seyffert (1909); K. Bringmann, *Gymnasium* 1971, 224–41. *Symp.*: V. Gray, *Hermes*, 1992, 58 ff.
C. J. T.

Xenophon (2), Greek novelist (see NOVEL, GREEK), author of *The Ephesian story of Anthia and Habrocomes* (Τὰ κατὰ Ἀνθίαν καὶ Ἀβροκόμην Ἐφεσιακά). Mention (2. 13. 3) of an eirenarch, an office not attested before *Trajan, together with the early place in the genre's development suggested by Xenophon's unambitious treatment of his story, indicates a date between AD 100 and 150: so far no papyri have been published. The *Suda calls him a historian and alleges other works, specifying only one, *On the city of Ephesus*, and gives *Ephesus as his origin, though the novel's knowledge of Ephesus has been argued to be second-hand. Xenophon tells, as omniscient narrator, how the young lovers from Ephesus were sent abroad by their parents soon after marriage in response to an oracle, became separated whilst on a voyage, and were conveyed round much of the Mediterranean world (even Italy), surviving all sorts of trials (shipwrecks, attacks by pirates and brigands, enslavement, advances by powerful suitors) and remaining faithful to each other. Reunited at last in *Rhodes they returned to Ephesus, to live happily ever after.

Occasional incoherence in a generically typical plot has been explained by the hypothesis that our text is an abridgement (the *Suda* reports ten books) or by Xenophon's clumsiness. His characterization is indeed unimpressive, and abridgement hardly explains some weaknesses in plot (e.g. the parents' decision to dispatch the couple on a journey that an oracle predicts as disastrous). His language, although often drawing on the vocabulary of the Athenian *Xenophon (1), has too many later features to be seen as Atticizing (see ASIANISM AND ATTICISM).

EDITIO PRINCEPS A. Cocchia (1726).

STANDARD EDITIONS G. Dalmeyda (Budé, 1926) (introd. still useful); A. D. Papanikolaou (Teubner 1973) (with index verborum).

COMMENTARY A. E. Locella (1796).

TRANSLATIONS M. Hadas, *Three Greek Romances* (1953). G. Anderson in B. P. Reardon (ed.), *Collected Ancient Greek Novels* (1989).

CRITICISM G. L. Schmeling, *Xenophon of Ephesus* (1980); Rohde, *Griech. Roman*, 409 ff.; Christ–Schmid–Stählin 2. 2⁶. 810 ff.; A. Lesky, *A History of Greek Literature* (1966), 863–4; H. Gärtner, *RE* 9 A 2 (1967), 2055–89; E. L. Bowie, *CHCL* 1 (1985), 690–2 (= paperback 1.4 (1989), 130–2); G. Anderson, *Eros sophistes* (1982), 62–3 and *Ancient Fiction* (1984), 144–8; E. Mann, *Über den Sprachgebrauch des Xenophon Ephesius* (Progr. Kaiserslautern 1895–6); K. Bürger, *Hermes* 1892, 36–67; O. Schissel von Fleschenberg, *Die Rahmenerzählung in den Ephesischen Geschichten des Xen. Ephes.* (1909); B. Lavagnini, *Studi sul romanzo greco* (1950), 145 ff.; T. Hägg, *Classica et Medievalia* 1966, 118–61, and *Narrative Technique in Ancient Greek Romances* (1971); J. O'Sullivan, *Xenophon of Ephesus* (1995).
E. L. B.

Xerxes I (OP Khšāyaršā), son of *Darius (1) and Atossa, king of *Persia 486–465 BC, chosen by his father as successor (XPf ll. 31 ff.; Hdt. 7. 2–3). At the beginning of his reign he crushed a revolt in Egypt (Hdt. 7. 3) and later two rebellions in *Babylon. Plans for an expedition against Greece were inherited from Darius: for the course of events see PERSIAN WARS. No Persian document mentions the expedition.

The more important palaces on the terrace of *Persepolis were built in Xerxes' reign, including the *Apadana with its impressive reliefs, illustrating the structure and the extent of the empire: king, court, and subject populations with their ethnographic characteristics. In the Daiva-inscription (XPh ll. 28–41) rebellion is equated with the neglect of *Ahuramazda and the worship of *daiva*'s ('bad gods'). Xerxes' destruction of the *daiva*-sanctuary marks no breach with his ancestors' presumed religious tolerance, as is often thought, since DB 5 already contains similar phraseology. Xerxes' reputation as a weakling and a womanizer depends on certain recognizably novelistic passages in Herodotus (7. 2–3, 9. 108–13) and on the reading of royal inscriptions as personal messages by the kings, rather than as formulaic royal statements. Seen from the heartland, his reign forms a period of consolidation, not of incipient decay. Xerxes was murdered in 465.

R. G. Kent, *Old Persian* (1953); for abbreviations of old Persian inscriptions, see Kent, pp. 107–15; W. Hinz, *Altiranische Funde und Forschungen* (1969) for the inscriptions; M. C. Root, *King and Kingship in Achaemenid Art* (1979) for the reliefs; J. M. Cook, *The Persian Empire* (1983); A. Kuhrt and S. Sherwin-White, *Achaemenid History 2: The Greek Sources*

(1987), 69–78; P. Briant, *Les Grandes figures religieuses. Fonctionnement pratique et symbolique dans l'Antiquité* (1986), 425–43, and *De Cyrus à Alexandre* (1995), ch. 13; A. Kuhrt, *The Ancient Near East* (1995), ch. 13.
H. S.-W.

Xiphilinus See CASSIUS DIO; ZONARAS, JOHANNES.

Xuthus, a mythological figure connected with the perceived racial divisions among the Greeks. According to *Hesiod (fr. 9 M–W) he was son of *Hellen and brother of Dorus and *Aeolus (2), the eponyms of the *Dorians and Aeolians; his sons by the Athenian Kreousa, *Ion (1) and Achaeus (fr. 10a 20–3), are also eponymous. This version reflects Athenian claims to Ionian primacy (see IONIANS), but originally Xuthus may have been Euboean (see EUBOEA). The variant making Ion son of *Apollo and Creusa is later and may even be Euripidean innovation (see EURIPIDES); here, Xuthus' true sons are Dorus and *Achaeus (1) (Eur. *Ion* 1589–94).

M. L. West, *The Hesiodic Catalogue of Women* (1985) 57–8.　　E. Ke.

Zacynthus, the southernmost of the western Greek islands, located in the *Ionian Sea south of *Cephallenia, 16 km. (10 mi.) west of *Elis. Prehistoric remains (paleolithic to Mycenaean; see MYCENAEAN CIVILIZATION) attest to the early habitation of Zacynthus which bears the distinctive '-nthus' form of pre-Greek names. A part of *Odysseus' realm in *Homer's *Catalogue of Ships* (*Il.* 2. 634), in historical times the island was settled either by the Achaeans (Thuc. 2. 66) or the Arcadians (Paus. 8. 24. 3; see ACHAEA; ARCADIA) and may have served as a staging point for Greek colonization to the west (see COLONIZATION, GREEK). During the *Peloponnesian War, Zacynthus was a fleet station for Athens, and after the war, allied to Sparta. The island participated in the panhellenic alliance with *Philip (1) II and *Alexander (3) the Great, was conquered by the Romans in 211 and granted the status of a 'free state' in 189. During the Roman empire, Zacynthus prospered and served as a place of mild banishment (Apul. *Met.* 7. 6; see ISLANDS). The main city of the island was also called Zacynthus and is located at the modern town of the same name.

Kl. *Pauly* 5 (1975), 1452–3; *Lexikon der historischen Stätten*, 716–18.
W. M. M.

Zaleucus, lawgiver of Italian *Locri Epizephyrii, and probably the earliest lawgiver in Greece, perhaps *c.*650 BC. The traditions about him are poor, later accounts (e.g. Diod. Sic. 12. 19–21) largely legendary and influenced by Pythagoreanism (see PYTHAGORAS (1); cf. *FGrH* 566, F 130 with Jacoby's comments), and he is best seen in conjunction with other early lawgivers. He prescribed exact penalties for crimes (in the earlier, more reliable tradition), and is attributed with the use of the lex talionis ('eye for eye': Dem. 24. 140). His legislation was notorious for its severity, and was intended to remain unchanged (Dem. 24. 139, Polyb. 12. 16). Like other lawgivers, he was probably a conciliator of social unrest, though a conservative one (Locri remained aristocratic). There are signs of at least later (5th cent.) influence of his laws in Italian and Sicilian cities.

Arist. *Pol.* 1274ª, fr. 548 Rose; T. J. Dunbabin, *The Western Greeks* (1948), 68 ff.; M. Gagarin, *Early Greek Law* (1986); S. Link, *Klio* 1992, 11 ff.
R. T.

Zalmoxis (Ζάλμοξις, Σάλμοξις). According to *Herodotus (1) (4. 94–6), a god of the *Getae in Thrace ('also called Gebeleizis') who promised immortality to his devotees; the tribe communicated with him by despatching a messenger-victim every four years. Also offered is an alternative, euhemeristic version (cf. EUHEMERUS) in which Zalmoxis was a charlatan who imported ideas picked up from *Pythagoras (1), whose slave he had been, and faked a 'resurrection' by reappearing from a hidden underground chamber after three years. Later, *Plato (1) presents him

as a divinized king to whom, like *Abaris, healing spells were ascribed (*Chrm.* 156d–158b).
A. H. G.

Zama was the name of more than one locality in present-day Tunisia. It is best known as the alleged site of *Hannibal's defeat by P. *Cornelius Scipio Africanus (see PUNIC WARS; and next entry) in 202 BC (so Nep. *Hann.* 6. 3); but Hannibal only camped at Zama (Polyb. 15. 5. 3), before moving to another camp (15. 6. 2) immediately before the battle. Livy says explicitly that Scipio camped at Naraggara before the battle (the Margarion of Polyb. 15. 5. 14 is probably a corruption of Naraggara), and this is modern Sakiet Sidi Youssef on the Tunisio-Algerian border 32 km. (20 mi.) west of Sicca; the battlefield of 'Zama' must lie nearby. The town of Zama where Hannibal camped is likely to have been Zama Regia, besieged unsuccessfully by Q. *Caecilius Metellus Numidicus in 109 BC (Sall. *Iug.* 56. 1), and Juba I's capital (hence *Regia*) until its capture by T. Sextius in 41 BC. It became a *colonia* under *Hadrian (see COLONIZATION, ROMAN): it is named *Colonia Aelia Hadriana Augusta Zama Regia* on an inscription from Rome (*CIL* 6. 1686). It is probably identical with the Zama Maior implied by *Ptolemy (4) (4. 3. 8: Μείζων); a Zama Minor is therefore also postulated. Locations are disputed. One Zama was surely at modern Jama (or Gama), 30 km. (19 mi.) north of Mactar, not only because of toponymical similarity, but also because an inscription found there reads ?*colonia] Augusta Zama M[* (*CIL* 8. 16442). That this is Zama M[inor] rather than M[aior] is likely for two reasons: modern Jama occupies a strong hilltop position whereas Sallust's Zama lay on a plain with no natural defences (*Iug.* 56. 1); and Zama Regia is placed by the *Peutinger Table on the road between Assuras (Zannfour) and Usappa (El Ksour), at 10 (Roman) miles (*c.*15 km.) from the former, which modern Jama is not (it lies *c.*28 km. (18 mi.) from Zannfour as the crow flies). Zama Regia may therefore underlie the modern settlement of Sebaa Biar, even though no ancient remains are attested there. Another candidate for identification as Zama Regia, the site at Ksar Toual Zouamel near the impressive Numidian temple of Kbor Klib, can now be shown to have been the *vicus Maracitanus* in the territory of Zama; another view, that a Zama lay at Sidi Abd el Djeddidi, 50 km. (31 mi.) north-west of Kairouan, is now discounted.

PECS 997–8; C. Saumagne, *CRAcad. Inscr.* 1941, 445–53; L. Déroche, *MÉFRA* 60 (1948), 55–104; Walbank, *HCP* 2 (1967), 446–9.

KBOR KLIB H. G. Horn and C. B. Rüger (eds.), *Die Numider* (1979), 129–32; N. Ferchiou, *QAL* 1991, 45–97.
R. J. A. W.

Zama, battle of Zama is the name given to the final battle of the Second *Punic War, though it was not actually fought near any of the places so-called (see preceding entry). *Hannibal had perhaps 36,000 infantry, 4,000 cavalry and 80 *elephants, P. *Cornelius Scipio Africanus perhaps 29,000 infantry and 6,000 cavalry. The elephants, opening the battle, were either ushered down corridors Scipio had left in his formation or driven out to the flanks where they collided with Hannibal's cavalry, which was then routed by the Roman cavalry. When the infantry lines closed, the Roman first line may have defeated both Hannibal's first and second lines, though the remnants may have reformed on the wings of his third line, composed of his veterans from Italy. Scipio, too, reformed his lines at this point, and a titanic struggle developed until the Roman cavalry, returning from the pursuit, charged into Hannibal's rear, whereupon his army disintegrated.

Polyb. 15. 9–16 and Walbank in *HCP*; Livy 30. 29–35. H. H. Scullard, *Scipio Africanus: Soldier and Politician* (1970); F. M. Russell, *Archaeology* 1970, 120 ff.; J. F. Lazenby, *Hannibal's War* (1978); J. Seibert, *Hannibal* (1993).
J. F. La.

Zancle See MESSANA.

Zealots, a Jewish political group in the 1st cent. AD. According to *Josephus the Zealots were one of the three factions who controlled *Jerusalem in the last years of the Jewish revolt against Rome (AD 66–70). In 68 the Zealots attacked the existing leaders of the rebel Jewish state, seized control of the Temple and, despite reverses at the hands of other Jewish factions, maintained an independent role until the capture of Jerusalem by *Titus in AD 70.

Josephus' depiction of the excesses of the Zealots when in power in Jerusalem is deeply hostile (*BJ* 4. 128 ff.), but he none the less described their leaders as priests of distinguished lineage (*BJ* 5. 6). Their supporters included country people from northern Judaea. They signalled a break from the previous leadership in Jerusalem by execution of political opponents and by appointing a high priest from a non-traditional family. The name *zēlōtēs* was apparently a self-designation (*BJ* 4. 160–1).

The relationship between the Zealots and other movements in 1st-cent. Jewish society as described by Josephus, especially the *sicarii* ('dagger-men') and the Fourth Philosophy (see JEWS), is debated. Members of all these movements at times sought religious justification for a strongly anti-Roman stance. Josephus sometimes suggested a connection between them and condemned them all equally, but at other times he was at pains to distinguish each group as separate.

M. Smith, *Harv. Theol. Rev.* 1971, 1–19; M. Stern, *Enc. Judaica Year Book* (1973), 135–52; R. A. Horsley and J. S. Hanson, *Bandits, Prophets and Messiahs* (1985); M. Hengel, *The Zealots* (Eng. trans. 1989).
M. D. G.

Zela (mod. Zile), an ancient temple-state of *Pontus with a large and fertile territory and a considerable population of sacred slaves (*hierodouloi*) attached to the land and to the service of Anaitis (*Anahita) and 'the Persian deities'. Here *Mithradates VI defeated C. *Valerius Triarius in 67 and *Caesar *Pharnaces II in 47 BC, the occasion of his famous remark 'veni, vidi, vici', 'I came, I saw, I conquered'. Originally ruled by priests, it became one of *Pompey's Pontic cities. It was handed over to dynasts by Antony (M. *Antonius (2)) but was reannexed with the rest of the kingdom of *Polemon (1) in AD 64.

Strabo 11. 512, 12. 559; F. Cumont, *Studia Pontica* 2 (1906), 188 ff., 3 (1910), 233 ff.; D. R. Wilson, *PECS* 999.
T. R. S. B.; S. M.

Zeno (1) of *Elea is portrayed by *Plato (1) (*Prm.* 127b) as the pupil and friend of *Parmenides, and junior to him by 25 years. Their fictional meeting with a 'very young' *Socrates (ibid.) gives little basis for firm chronology. We may conclude only that Zeno

was active in the early part of the 5th cent. BC. Whether the work from which Plato makes him read was his only book is uncertain.

The most famous of Zeno's arguments are the four paradoxes about motion paraphrased by *Aristotle (*Ph.* 6. 9), which have intrigued thinkers down to Bertrand Russell in our era. The Achilles paradox proposes that a quicker can never overtake a slower runner who starts ahead of him, since he must always first reach the place the slower has already occupied. His task is in truth an infinite sequence of tasks, and can therefore never be completed. The Arrow paradox argues that in the present a body in motion occupies a place just its own size, and is therefore at rest. But since it is in the present throughout its movement, it is always at rest. The Dichotomy raises the same issues about infinite divisibility as the Achilles; the Arrow and the Stadium (an obscure puzzle about the relative motion of bodies) are perhaps directed against the implicit assumption of indivisible minima.

According to Plato Zeno's method was to attack an assumption by deriving contradictory consequences from it (*Prm.* 127d–e). *Simplicius quotes fragments in which Zeno adopts precisely this strategy against the hypothesis of plurality (*In Phys.* 139–41). Thus fr. 3 proves that if there are many things their number is both limited and unlimited. Frs. 1 and 2 evidently formed parts of a more elaborate argument from the same hypothesis. Each member of a plurality must be self-identical and one and therefore (grounds for this inference are not preserved) so small as to be without magnitude. Anything with magnitude, by contrast, has an infinite number of parts, each possessing magnitude, and must accordingly itself be so large as to be infinite. No other examples survive, although it is conceivable that the paradoxes of motion originally took the form of antinomies (cf. D. L. 9. 72) about plurality.

Plato's assessment of the purpose of Zeno's book is now usually accepted. He reads the antinomies as assaults on common sense; more specifically as an indirect defence of Parmenidean monism against outraged common sense (*Prm.* 128a–e). But perhaps Zeno intended not so much to shake belief in the existence of plurality and motion as to question the coherence of our understanding of these phenomena. On either interpretation Aristotle was right to see in Zeno the founder of *dialectic (Diog. Laert. 8. 57).

TEXTS DK 29.

DISCUSSION/TRANSLATION J. Barnes, *The Presocratic Philosophers* (2nd edn. 1982).

ALSO W. D. Ross, *Aristotle's Physics* (1936), esp. 71 ff.; H. D. P. Lee, *Zeno of Elea* (1936); W. C. Salmon (ed.), *Zeno's Paradoxes* (1970); R. E. Allen and D. J. Furley (eds.), *Studies in Presocratic Philosophy,* 2 (1975).
M. Sch.

Zeno (2) of Citium (*Cyprus), (335–263 BC), founder of *Stoicism. He came to Athens in 313 and is said to have studied with or been influenced by various philosophers, notably *Crates (2) the Cynic, *Antisthenes (1) the Socratic, and the Academics *Xenocrates (1) and particularly *Polemon (2), who seems to have stressed the notion of nature. Zeno taught in the *Stoa Poecile ('Painted Colonnade') which gave its name to Stoicism. He was well respected at Athens, and in old age was invited by *Antigonus (2) Gonatas to go to his court, but sent two students instead.

Zeno's writings established Stoicism as a set of ideas articulated into three parts: *logic (and theory of knowledge), *physics (and metaphysics), and ethics. Later Stoics developed some of his ideas in differing ways until an orthodoxy on fundamentals was established by the writings of *Chrysippus. Stoicism is holistic in method: logic, say, or ethics can be developed in relative independence, but are ultimately to be seen to fit into the set of Stoic ideas as a whole, while no part serves as foundation for the others. Stoicism is materialist, regarding everything as part of a universal natural system subject to deterministic laws; however, it is also teleological and compatibilist. In method and epistemology it is uncompromisingly empiricist, but again shows no reductive tendencies, laying great stress on reason and its capacities; Stoic logic is one of its most distinctive and original contributions. Stoic ethics lays great stress on the difference of kind in value between virtue and other kinds of advantage such as health and wealth, although these are natural for us to pursue. This difference is such that virtue even without these is sufficient for happiness; thus stress on the importance of virtue leads to radical redefinition of happiness, our final end. The Stoics stressed the role of rules and principles in moral reasoning; early writings of Zeno stressed that even basic moral rules could have justified exceptions, but later Stoics downplayed this, and distanced themselves from Zeno's *Republic*, in which an ideal community, radically rejecting convention, was developed.

Testimonia in H. von Arnim, *SVF* 1. 3–72; Diog. Laert. 7. 1–160.   J. A.

Zeno (3) of *Tarsus, Stoic (see STOICISM), *Chrysippus' successor as head of the Stoa in 204 BC. He had many followers, but wrote little; he had doubts about *ekpyrōsis* (conversion into *fire).

Testimonia in H. von Arnim, *SVF* 3. 209.   J. A.

Zeno (4) of *Rhodes (early 2nd cent. BC) was a politician who wrote a history of Rhodes from the beginnings to his own times. *Polybius (1) used it (along with the work of *Antisthenes (2)), although he criticized its patriotic exaggeration (Polyb. 16. 14); Zeno's tradition may also appear in *Diodorus (3).

FGrH 523; P. Köln 246; G. A. Lehmann, *ZPE* 72, 1988, 1–17.   K. S. S.

Zeno (5) (RE 5) of *Sidon (b. *c.*150 BC), Epicurean (see EPICURUS), pupil of the Epicurean Apollodorus and probably head of the school between him and *Phaedrus (3). *Cicero heard him lecture in Athens in 79–78, and found him querulous and irascible in manner and style: not only did he heap abuse on contemporaries, but he called *Socrates the *scurra Atticus* (the Attic equivalent of a Roman festive buffoon), and never referred to *Chrysippus except in the feminine gender (*Nat. D.* 1. 93). No writings by Zeno have been found among the Epicurean library excavated at *Herculaneum, but *Philodemus, whose writings were found there in abundance, studied with him at Athens, and boasts that he was a devoted ἐραστής (admirer) of Zeno while he lived, and an indefatigable ὑμνητής, 'laudator' i.e. 'eulogist' of him after his death. Philodemus' *On Speaking Frankly* (Περὶ παρρησίας) is a selection from Zeno's teachings, and Philodemus' *On Signs* (Περὶ σημείων) reiterates lectures by Zeno and his disputes with adversaries of his own day.

Fragments collected by A. Angeli and M. Colaizzo, *Cron. Erc.* 9 (1979), 47–133. Discussion in A. Angeli, *Filodemo. Agli amici di scuola* (PHerc. 1005), La scuola di Epicuro 7 (1988), introd.; D. Sedley, in M. Griffin and J. Barnes (eds.), *Philosophia Togata* (1989), 97–119. On Zeno's dates see T. Dorandi, *Ricerche sulla cronologia dei filosofi ellenistici*, Beiträge zur Altertumskunde 19 (1991).   W. D. R.; D. O.

Zeno (6) of *Sidon, Stoic (see STOICISM), pupil of *Diodorus (2) Cronus and of *Zeno (2).

Zeller, *Phil. d. Gr.* 3. 1, 40.   J. A.

Zeno (7) (2nd cent. BC), a physician of the 'school' of *Herophilus, participated in the Herophilean traditions of innovative pulse

theory, *pharmacology, and Hippocratic lexicography (see HIPPOCRATES (2)). He achieved more lasting prominence, however, by 'decoding' (and attributing to Hippocrates himself) certain letter symbols (χαρακτῆρες), such as ΠΔΕΗΘ or ΠΣΖΘ, found in clusters of four or five at the conclusion of individual case histories in some *Alexandrian manuscripts of the Hippocratic work *Epidemics* 3. Members of the Empiricist school of medicine (see MEDICINE, § 5.3), including *Heraclides (4) of Tarentum, fiercely attacked Zeno's views about the provenance and meaning of the symbols. Some Empiricists, attributing the invention of the symbols to Mnemon of Side, charged Zeno with altering the marks whenever he could not find a plausible interpretation; another Empiricist, Apollonius Byblas, questioned the authenticity of the symbols, claiming that Zeno's version of the symbols in *Epidemics* 3, case-history 8, could not be found in any of three copies of the Hippocratic treatise that he had examined.

Ed., trans., comm., H. von Staden, *From Andreas to Demosthenes Philalethes* (1995), ch. 5, and *Herophilus* (1989), 501–5; E. Wenkebach, *Sitz. Berlin* (1920), 241–53.   H. v. S.

Zeno archive See APOLLONIUS (3).

Zenobia (Septimia), or in *Aramaic *Bath Zabbai*, one of the great women of classical antiquity (*PLRE* 1. 990 f.). The second wife of *Septimius Odaenathus of *Palmyra, on his death in AD 267, in suspicious circumstances, she secured power for herself in the name of her young son, *Septimius Vaballathus. As long as Zenobia kept the east secure, *Gallienus and *Claudius (II) Gothicus were prepared to accept her regime, including its bestowal upon Vaballathus of his father's Roman titles, and hence of the claim to be more than just king of Palmyra. However, in 270 Zenobia exploited the political instability that followed the death of Claudius to expand beyond Syria by taking over Egypt and much of Asia Minor, and further to enhance Vaballathus' Roman titles, while continuing to recognize *Aurelian as emperor. When Aurelian finally moved against her in 272, her forces failed to stop him at *Antioch (1) and *Emesa, and—now calling her son *Augustus* and herself *Augusta*—she was besieged in Palmyra. She was captured while attempting to escape, shortly before the fall of the city. She was spared. Many tales were told of her subsequent life; little is certain, though it is likely that she was paraded in Aurelian's triumph.

F. G. B. Millar, *JRS* 1971, 1 ff.; A. Baldini, *ZPE* 30, 1978, 145 ff.; D. Rathbone, *ZPE* 62, 1986, 121 ff.; E. Schneider, *Septimia Zenobia Sebaste* (1993).   J. F. Dr.

Zenobius See PAROEMIOGRAPHERS.

Zenodorus (RE 3), mathematician (fl. 200 BC) wrote Περὶ ἰσοπερίμετρων σχημάτων (*On figures of equal boundary*), parts of which are preserved by *Theon (4) and *Pappus.

T. L. Heath, *History of Greek Maths* (2 vols., 1921), 2. 207–13; W. Müller, *Sudhoffs Archiv*, 1953, 39–71. On the date and identification of Zenodorus see G. J. Toomer, *GRBS* 1972, 177–92.   G. J. T.

Zenodotus of Ephesus (b. *c.*325 BC), pupil of *Philitas, became the first head of the Library at *Alexandria (*c.*284) and undertook the classification of the Greek epic and lyric poets, some of whom he edited.

Works (1) Lexicography: *Homeric Glossary* (Γλῶσσαι), which was in alphabetical order. There was also a collection of words used in Greek dialects. (2) Editions (διορθώσεις). His recension of

Zenon archive

*Homer's *Iliad* and *Odyssey*, in which the poems may have been divided into twenty-four books for the first time, represented the first scientific attempt to get back to the original Homeric text by the collation of several manuscripts. He marked lines of the genuineness of which he felt doubt with a newly-invented sign, the *obelus*. Some modern critics have accused him of altering the text drastically; more recent research suggests that this picture of an arbitrary and subjective manipulator of the text is unfair. (3) He produced also recensions of *Hesiod, *Theog.*, *Anacreon, *Pindar (*POxy.* 5. 841). (4) He may also have written treatises about Homer, or a commentary on some parts of the text.

H. Düntzer, *De Zenodoti studiis Homericis* (1848); K. Lehrs, *De Aristarchi studiis Homericis*[3] (1882); A. Römer, *Über die Homerrezension des Zenodot* (1886); R. Pfeiffer, *History of Classical Scholarship: From the Beginnings to the End of the Hellenistic Age* (1968), 105–19; K. Nickau, *Untersuchungen zur textkritischen Methode des Zenodotos von Ephesos* (1977); H. van Thiel, *ZPE* 90, 1992, 4–14.   J. F. L.; R. B.; N. G. W.

Zenon archive See APOLLONIUS (3).

Zephyrus (W), Boreas (N), and Notus (S) winds catalogued by *Hesiod at *Theog.* 378–80. But epic may conceive of them, as convenient, either as minor gods who feast in their own palaces (*Il.* 23. 200 ff.) or as unruly elemental forces who are controlled by *Aeolus (1) from his floating prison-island and can be confined in a leather bag (*Od.* 10. 1 ff.). For some evidence of Roman cult, see Frazer on Ovid, *Fast.* 6. 193. See WIND-GODS.

Burkert, *GR* 175; E. Vermeule, *Aspects of Death in Early Greek Art and Poetry* (1979), 168 f.; J. Travlos, *Pictorial Dictionary of Ancient Athens* (1971), 'Horologion of Andronikos' (the 'Tower of the Winds').
                    A. H. G.

Zetes See CALAIS.

Zethus See AMPHION.

zeugitai (from *zeugos*, 'yoke'), at Athens, *Solon's third property class, comprising men whose land yielded between 200 and 300 *medimnoi* of corn or the equivalent in other produce (the other three classes were *pentakosiomedimnoi, *hippeis, *thētes). The name identifies them as those who served in the army in close ranks (cf. Plut. *Pel.* 23), i.e. as *hoplites, or, less probably, as those rich enough to own a yoke of oxen. Many of the farmers and craftsmen of *Attica fell into this class, and it provided the bulk of the city's hoplite army. Under Solon's constitution the *zeugitai* enjoyed full citizen rights except that they were not admitted to the highest magistracies (see MAGISTRACY, GREEK). The archonships (see ARCHONTES) were opened to them from 457/6.

D. Whitehead, *CQ* 1981, 282–6.   A. W. G.; T. J. C.; P. J. R.

Zeugitana The name, of unknown origin, sometimes applied to the northern part of the province of Africa (see AFRICA, ROMAN), centred on *Carthage. It is used by *Pliny (1) (*HN* 5. 23), but then seems to have gone out of use, to reappear in the 4th cent. when it was occasionally used of Africa (Proconsularis), now much smaller in area after the division of the old province of Africa by *Diocletian.   B. H. W.

Zeugma (mod. Bâlkîs, opposite Bîrecik), in *Syria on the right bank of the *Euphrates at its chief crossing, about 112 km. (70 miles) below *Samosata. Twin colonies Seleuceia (right bank) and Apamea (left bank) were founded by *Seleucus (1) I (Plin. *HN* 5. 86), which came to be known by the generic name Zeugma ('junction'), and gave Seleucus control of the lower river crossings

of the Euphrates. It is possible that Apamea was merely a suburb of Seleuceia. It was here (in 221) that *Antiochus (3) III met his own bride, *Laodice (3), daughter of *Mithradates II of *Pontus, on her journey from Pontus and celebrated the royal wedding (Polyb. 5. 43. 1–4).

J. D. Grainger, *The Cities of Seleucid Syria*, (1989); S. Sherwin-White and A. Kuhrt, *From Samarkhand to Sardis*, (1993), 15.
                    M. S. D.; E. W. G.; S. S.-W.

Zeus, the main divinity of the Greek pantheon (see OLYMPIAN GODS; RELIGION, GREEK) and the only major Greek god whose *Indo-European origin is undisputed. His name is connected with Latin *Iu-p-piter*, Rigveda *Dyaus pitar*, derived from the root †*diéu-*, 'day (as opposed to night)' (Lat. *dies*), '(clear) sky'; as the Rigveda and Latin parallels suggest, his role as father, not in a theogonical or anthropogonical sense, but as having the power of a father in a patriarchal system, is Indo-European too. Thus in *Homer, Zeus is both πατήρ, 'father', and ἄναξ, 'king' or 'lord'. His cult is attested in bronze-age Greece (see RELIGION, MINOAN AND MYCENAEAN); the Linear B texts (see MYCENAEAN LANGUAGE) attest several sanctuaries (*Pylos, Chania) and, at Minoan Cnossus, a month name or a festival, if in fact the Mycenaean names of months derive from festivals (KN Fp 5, 1). Another Cnossian text attests the epiclesis Dictaeus, Zeus of Mt. Dicte (KN Fp 1, 2), which remained an important place of cult in the first millennium. A text from Chania gives a common cult of Zeus and *Dionysus, a Pylos text (PY Tn 316, 8–10) one of Zeus, *Hera, and (a figure later unknown) Drimios son of Zeus, which suggests Hera as the consort of Zeus, as in later mythology.

Zeus, the Indo-European god of the bright sky, is transformed in Greece into Zeus the weather god, whose paramount and specific place of worship is a mountain top (Hdt. 1. 131. 1). Among his mountains (list: Cook 2. 868–987), the most important is Mt. *Olympus (1), a real mountain which was already a mythical place before Homer. Many mountain cults are reflected only in an epiclesis, which does not necessarily imply the existence of a peak sanctuary. Few such sanctuaries are excavated (e.g. on Mt. *Hymettus in Attica); those attested in literature are mostly connected with rain rituals (Zeus Hyetios or Ombrios); the sanctuary on the Arcadian Mt. Lycaeum had an initiatory function as well (see ARCADIAN CULTS AND MYTHS). As νεφεληγερέτα, 'the gatherer of clouds' (a common Homeric epithet), he was generally believed to cause rain (comic parody: Aristoph. *Nub.* 373). With the god of clouds comes the god of thunder (ὑψιβρεμέτης) and of lightning (τερπικέραυνος); a spot struck by lightning is inviolable (ἄβατον) and often sacred to Zeus Καταιβάτης, 'He who comes down'. As the master of tempest, he is supposed to give signs through thunder and lightning and to strike evildoers, as at the beginning of his reign he struck the *Giants and the monstrous *Typhon.

But already for the early archaic Greeks (as, presumably, for the Mycenaeans), Zeus had much more fundamental functions. According to the succession myth in Hes. *Theog.* (whose main elements are also known to Homer), Zeus deposed his father *Cronus, who had deposed and castrated his father *Uranus; after his accession to power, Zeus fought the Giants and the monster Typhon who challenged his reign, and drew up the present world-order by attributing to each divinity his or her respective sphere: to his brothers *Poseidon and *Hades-Pluton, he allotted two thirds of the cosmos, to the one the sea, to the other the nether-world, to his sisters Hera (also his wife) and *Demeter, and to his many divine children their respective domains in the human world; mankind had existed before Zeus' reign. Thus, Zeus became the ruler over both the other gods and the human world; the order of things as it is now is Zeus' work.

Closely related succession myths are attested from *Hittite Anatolia (see ANATOLIAN DEITIES) and from Mesopotamia. In Hittite mythology, the succession passes through Anu, 'Sky', who is deposed and castrated by Kumarbi, finally to Teshub, the Storm God, who would correspond to Zeus; other myths narrate the attacks of Kumarbi and his followers on Teshub's reign. Myths from Mesopotamia present a similar, though more varied structure; the Babylonian Enūma Elish moves from a primeval pair, Apsu and Tiamat, to the reign of Marduk, the city god of Babylon and in many respects comparable to Ba'al and Zeus; a later version of the Typhon myth (Apollod. Bibl. 1. 6. 3) locates part of it on Syrian Mt. Kasion, seat of a peak cult of Ba'al Zaphon (Zeus *Kasios). The conception of Zeus as the kingly ruler of the present world is unthinkable without oriental influence. In a similar way, the shift from Indo-European god of the bright sky to the Greek master of sky and storms is inconceivable without the influence of the weather gods of Anatolia and Syria-Palestine with whom he was later identified (Zeus Βεελσάμημ, Philo in Eus. PE 1. 10. 7).

Zeus is a king, not a tyrant. One of his main domains is right and justice: any transgression of his cosmic order is injustice; if necessary, Zeus punishes transgressors. Human kings are under his special protection, but they have to endorse his justice (Hes. Theog. 80 ff.). Zeus himself protects those outside ordinary social bonds—strangers, suppliants (Hom. Od. 9. 296 ff.) and beggars (Od. 6. 207 f.; 14. 57 ff.); cult attests Zeus Ξένιος and Zeus Ἱκέσιος. To preserve his order, he is himself subject to it: he is committed to Fate.

In many instances (e.g. the Trojan War), human affairs follow the plan of Zeus despite apparent setbacks. He might hasten perfection, if asked in prayer to do so (Zeus Τέλειος, Aesch. Ag. 973), and he might signal his will, either asked for or unasked, in dreams, augural signs, thunder and lightning (Hom. Il. 2. 353, 3. 242), but also by provoking ominous human utterances (thunder and utterance, φήμη, in Hom. Od. 20. 95 ff.). In cult, this function is expressed in rare epicleses like Φαντήρ, 'he who signals', Τεράστιος 'he of the omens', Φήμιος or Κληδόνιος, 'who gives oracular sayings'.

In these cases, the prophetic power of Zeus is occasional and accessory. It becomes central in the only Greek *oracle of Zeus, *Dodona in Epirus, reputed to be the oldest Greek oracle, known already to Homer (Il. 16. 233 ff.; Od. 14. 327 f.). It was active until late-hellenistic times; though consulted by cities too, its main clients were private individuals from north-western Greece. Zeus is here paired with *Dione, mother of *Aphrodite in ordinary Greek myth. Homer mentions the Selloi as prophets, 'barefoot, sleeping on the earth' (Il. 16. 234 f.). They disappear without a trace; Hdt. 2. 53 knows only of priestesses; later authors add that they prophesy in *ecstasy (Aristid. Or. 45. 11). Zeus manifested himself in the sounds of the holy oak-tree (Od. 14. 27 f., 19. 296 f.) and in doves, whose call from the holy oak-tree or whose flight are used as divine signs (Hdt. 2. 55–8); other sources know also *divination by lots (cleromancy), water vessels (hydromancy), and by the sounds of a gong.

Zeus has only a few major *polis *festivals; and though he often is called Πολιεύς, he has no major temple on an acropolis, unlike the Roman *Jupiter Capitolinus. A few month names attest early festivals: the bronze-age month Diwos (Cnossus) to

which corresponds the Macedonian, Aetolian, and Thessalian Δῖος, the Attic Maimakterion which pertains to the festival of a shadowy Zeus Μαιμάκτης, and the Cretan (V)elchanios which derives from the Cretan (Zeus) Velchanos. Of some importance for the poleis in question were the sacrifice of a bull of Zeus Polieus on *Cos and the festival of Zeus Sosipolis at *Magnesia (1) ad Maeandrum, both attested in Hellenistic sacred laws. Athenian festivals of Zeus are less self-asserting. The Diisoteria featured a sacrifice and a procession for Zeus Soter and Athena Soteira—it was a festival to honour Zeus 'Saviour of the City'. As to date and place, however, it was more marginal than the Coan festival: it was celebrated outside the city in *Piraeus, although with the participation of the city. Closer to the centre were the Dipolieia (see ATTIC CULTS AND MYTHS; BOUPHONIA) and *Diasia. The Dipolieia featured the strange and guilt-ridden sacrifice of an ox on the altar of Zeus Polieus on the acropolis, the *Bouphonia; they belong among the rituals around New Year. *Aristophanes (1) thought it rather old-fashioned (Nub. 984): the ritual killing of the ox, the myth which makes all participants guilty, with the ensuing prosecution of the killer with the formal condemnation of axe and knife, enacts a crisis, not a bright festival.

The Diasia, 'the greatest Athenian festival of Zeus' (Thuc. 1. 126. 6), had an even less auspicious character. The festival took place in honour of Zeus *Meilichios who appears in reliefs in the shape of a huge snake. His cult took place outside the town, with animal sacrifice or bloodless cakes; the sacrificial animals were burnt whole. This meant no common meal to release the tension of the sacrifice; instead, there were banquets in small family circles and gifts to the children: the polis community passes through a phase of disintegration, characteristic of the entire month, Anthesterion, whose festival, the *Anthesteria, had an even more marked character of uncanny disintegration.

This apparent paucity of polis festivals is not out of tune with the general image of Zeus. The polis has to be under the protection of a specific patron deity, *Athena or *Apollo, while Zeus is the overall protector and cannot confine himself to one polis only; his protection adds itself to that of the specific polis deities. From early on, he is prominent as a panhellenic deity. The founding hero of Dodona, *Deucalion, father of Hellen, discloses the oracle's panhellenic aspirations. But Zeus' main Greek festival is the penteteric *Olympian Games with the splendid sacrifice to Zeus Olympios and the ensuing panhellenic agōn (see AGŌNES). Their introduction in 776 BC, according to tradition, marked the end of the isolation of the Dark-Age communities; the common festival took place at a spot outside an individual polis and under the protection of a superior god. Analysis of the sacrifices points to an origin in *initiation rituals of young warriors which had been widened and generalized in an epoch not too distant from the Homeric poems, with their own universalist conception of Zeus.

In the polis at large, Zeus' own province is the *agora, where he presides, as Zeus Ἀγοραῖος, over both the political and the commercial life of the community; thus, he can be counted among the main divinities of a city, like *Hestia Prytaneia and Athena Poliouchos or Polias. Among the smaller social units, he is one of the patrons of *phratries and clans (Zeus Φράτριος or Πατρῷος/Πάτριος, sometimes together with Athena Phratria or Patr(o)ia, Plat. Euthyd. 302d; for clans see GENOS). He also protects individual households: as Zeus Ἑρκεῖος, he receives sacrifices on an altar in the courtyard (Hom. Il. 11. 772 ff.; Od. 22. 334 ff.; every Athenian family had to have one, Arist. Ath. Pol.

55), as Zeus Ἐφέστιος, on the hearth of a house. See WORSHIP, HOUSEHOLD.

There are functions of Zeus at the level of the family which are easily extended both to individuals and to the *polis*. Since property is indispensable for the constitution of a household, Zeus is also protector of property (Κτήσιος); as such, he receives cults from families (*Thasos: Zeus Ktesios Patroios), from cities (Athens: a sacrifice by the *prytaneis in 174/3 BC) and from individuals (*Stratonicea: to Zeus Ktesios and *Tyche). In many places Zeus Ktesios has the appearance of a snake (Athens, *Thespiae): property is bound to the ground, at least in the still agrarian mentality of ancient Greece, and its protectors belong to the earth. The same holds true for Zeus Μειλίχιος. For the individual, Xenophon attests his efficiency in providing funds (*Anab.* 7. 8. 1 ff.), while in many communities Zeus Meilichios protects families or clans; in Athens, he receives the *polis* festival of the Diasia; here also and elsewhere, he has the form of a snake. And finally, one might add Zeus Φίλιος, protector of friendship between individuals and also between entire communities.

As the most powerful god, Zeus has a very general function which cuts across all groups and gains in importance in the course of time: he is Σωτήρ, the 'Saviour' par excellence (see SOTER). As such, he receives prayers and dedications from individuals, groups, and entire towns. These dedications reflect different possible situations of crisis, from very private ones (where Zeus competes with *Asclepius Soter, see e.g. Zeus Soter Asclepius in *Pergamum, *Altertümer von Pergamon* 8. 3 no. 63) to political troubles (Athens: *SEG* 26 no. 106, 7), natural catastrophes (earthquake: *BCH* 102, 1978, 399) or military attacks (*Delphi, Soteria after the attack by the Gauls; see GALATIA).

The Zeus cults of *Crete fit only partially into this picture (see Verbruggen). Myth places both his birth and his grave in Crete: according to *Hesiod, in order to save him from Cronus, Rhea gave birth to Zeus and entrusted the baby to *Gaia, who hid it in a cave near Lyctus, on Mt. Aegaeum (Hes. *Theog.* 468 ff.). Later authors replace Gaea by the *Curetes, armed demons, whose noisy dance kept Cronus away, and name other mountains, usually Mt. Ida or Mt. Dicte. This complex of myths reflects cult in caves, which partly go back to Minoan times, and armed dances by young Cretan warriors like those attested in the famous hymn to Zeus from Palaikastro (sanctuary of Zeus Δικταῖος), which belong to the context of initiatory rituals of young warriors; in the actual oaths of Cretan *epheboi, Zeus plays an important role. In this function, Zeus (exceptionally) can be young—the Palaikastro hymn calls him κοῦρος, 'youngster'; the statue in the sanctuary of Zeus Dictaeus was beardless, and coins from Cnossus show a beardless (Zeus) Welchanos. There certainly are Minoan (and presumably Mycenaean) elements present in the complex, but it would be wrong to separate Cretan Zeus too radically from the rest of the Greek evidence; both the cults of Mt. Lycaeum and of Olympia contain initiatory features. See CRETAN CULTS AND MYTHS.

Already in Homer (much more than in actual cult), Zeus had reached a very dominant position. During the Classical and Hellenistic age, religious thinkers developed this into a sort of 'Zeus monotheism'. To *Aeschylus, Zeus had begun to move away from the object of simple human knowledge ('Zeus, whoever you are . . .', *Ag.* 160 ff.) to a nearly universal function ('Zeus is ether, Zeus is earth, Zeus is sky, Zeus is everything and more than that', fr. 105); *Sophocles (1) sees Zeus' hand in all human affairs ('Nothing of this is not Zeus', *Trach.* 1278). The main document of this monotheism, however, is the hymn to

Zeus by the Stoic philosopher *Cleanthes (*SVF* I 121 no. 537); Zeus, mythical image of the Stoic logos (see STOICISM; LOGOS), becomes the commander of the entire cosmos and its 'universal law', and at the same time the guarantor of goodness and benign protector of man. This marks the high point of a development— other gods, though briefly mentioned, become insignificant besides this Zeus.

Neoplatonist speculation marks something of a regression: in the elaborate chains of divine beings, Zeus is never set at the very top; the Neoplatonists allegorize the succession from Uranus through Cronus to Zeus and consequently assign him to a lower level. See NEOPLATONISM.

K. Arafat, *Classical Zeus: A Study in Art and Literature* (1990); U. Bianchi, *Dios Aisa. Destino, nomi e divinità nell'epos, nelle teogonie e nel culto dei Greci* (1953). Cook, *Zeus.* P. Faure, *Fonctions des cavernes crétoises* (1964). K. Kerényi, *Zeus and Hera: Archetypal Image of Father, Husband and Wife* (1975). H. Lloyd-Jones, *The Justice of Zeus* (1971, 1983). H. W. Parke, *The Oracles of Zeus* (1967); H. Schwabl, Zeus 1 (Epiklesen), *RE* 10 A (1972), 253–376; 2, *RE* Suppl. 15 (1978), 993–1411; 3 (E. Simon: Archäologische Zeugnisse. Nachträge), *RE* Suppl. 15 (1978), 1411–81. E. Simon, *Die Götter der Griechen*³ (1985). H. Verbruggen, *Le Zeus crétois* (1981).
F. G.

Zeus in art Although 8th-cent. figurines may represent Zeus, he does not assume a type until early Archaic, when he strides with thunderbolt and, rarely, eagle. In the Classical period, Zeus is quieter, often seated and with a sceptre: the prime example is *Phidias' cult statue at *Olympia, familiar from literature (esp. Paus. 5. 11), coins, gems, and echoes on vases. The type continues in the Hellenistic period.

Zeus participates in many scenes. The east pediments of Olympia and the *Parthenon centred on him. He fights in the Gigantomachy (see GIANTS) from Attic and S. Italian Archaic and Classical vases to the Hellenistic Pergamum altar frieze. On Classical vases and sculpture, his pursuits include Aegina (the eponymous heroine of *Aegina, see EPONYMOI) and *Ganymede. His transformations occur, particularly in depictions of his seduction of Europa from early Archaic, and *Leda from late Classical. He is common on coins. Zeus was favoured by *Alexander (3) the Great and some Roman emperors, especially *Hadrian (see OLYMPIEUM).

RE Suppl. 15. 3, 'Zeus'; Cook, *Zeus*; K. W. Arafat, *Classical Zeus* (1990).
K. W. A.

Zeuxis (1), painter, of *Heraclea (1) in Lucania, pupil of Neseus of Thasos or Damophilus of Himera. *Pliny (1) dates him 397 BC, rejecting 424. *Quintilian dates both him and *Parrhasius to the *Peloponnesian War. In *Plato (1)'s *Protagoras* (dramatic date about 430) he is young and a newcomer to Athens. His rose-wreathed *Eros is mentioned in Ar. *Ach.* 991–2 (425). He painted Alcmena for Acragas before 406, and *Archelaus (2)'s palace between 413 and 399. He 'entered the door opened by Apollodorus and stole his art'; he added the use of highlights to shading, and *Lucian praises in the *Centaur family (an instance of the unusual subjects which Zeuxis preferred) the subtle gradation of colour from the human to the animal body of the female Centaur; his paintings of grapes were said to have deceived birds; he said that if he had painted the boy carrying the grapes better, the birds would have been frightened off. His figures lacked the *ethos* (character) of *Polygnotus, although his Penelope was morality itself, and his Helen (for Croton or Acragas) an ideal picture compiled from several models; *pathos* (emotion) rather than *ethos* distinguished the Autoboreas with *Titan look and wild hair, and the *Menelaus (1) drenched in tears. He also painted monochromes on white. He was wealthy and arrogant, giving away his paintings since no price was sufficient for them. See PAINTING, GREEK. K. W. A.

Zeuxis (2), a physician of the Empiricist school (see MEDICINE, § 5.3; probably 2nd cent. BC), wrote commentaries on all the 'authentic' works of *Hippocrates (2) (according to *Galen), often taking issue with other interpreters, including Herophileans (see HEROPHILUS) and fellow-Empiricists (e.g. Glaucias). His commentaries offered variants, emendations, glosses, and historical but partisan accounts of critical controversies, such as the one triggered by the Herophilean *Zeno (7)'s interpretation of the mysterious symbols in some copies of the Hippocratic *Epidemics*. Galen still had access to some of Zeuxis' commentaries.

Ed. and comm. K. Deichgräber, *Die griechische Empirikerschule* (1930; 2nd edn. 1965). H. v. S.

Zeuxis (3) Philalethes (the 'Truth-lover'), physician, founder of the Asian branch of the 'school' of *Herophilus. A contemporary of Strabo (*Geography* 12. 8. 20, 580c), he established the 'school' (διδασκαλεῖον) at the temple of *Men Karou between Laodicea and Carura. Bronze coins from Laodicea, bearing the head of Augustus on the obverse, commemorate Zeuxis on the reverse. Other ancient sources often leave unclear whether Zeuxis Philalethes or *Zeuxis (2) the Empiricist is meant.

Ed., trans., and comm. H. von Staden, *From Andreas to Demosthenes Philalethes* (1995), ch. 11. See also his *Herophilus* (1989), 529–31; J. Benedum, *Gesnerus* 1974, 221–36. H. v. S.

Zeuxis (4), important *Seleucid viceroy of the time of *Antiochus (3) III: Polyb. 5. 45. 4 and 16. 1. 8 with Walbank, *HCP*. Cf. *SEG* 36. 973 for his title. See AMYZON; SARDIS. S. H.

Zodiac, twelve signs of the See CONSTELLATIONS AND NAMED STARS.

Zoïlus (Ζωΐλος) of *Amphipolis (4th cent. BC), the *cynic philosopher, pupil of *Polycrates (2) and teacher of *Anaximenes (2) of Lampsacus; is described by the *Suda* as ῥήτωρ καὶ φιλόσοφος (rhetorician and philosopher), by Aelian, *VH* 11. 10, as κύων ῥητορικός and ψογερός, a 'cynic rhetorician' and 'censorious'. He was notorious for the bitterness of his attacks on *Isocrates, *Plato (1), and especially *Homer. He probably visited *Alexandria (1) when the Library and *Museum were being established.

Works (1) *Against Isocrates*. (2) *Against Plato*, favourably mentioned by Dion. Hal. *Pomp.* 1. (3) *Against Homer* (Καθ' Ὁμήρου or Κατὰ τῆς Ὁμήρου ποιήσεως 'Against Homer's poetry' or perhaps Ὁμηρομάστιξ 'scourge of Homer', which became the author's nickname). This work was chiefly devoted to severe, though often captious, criticism of the poet's invention, of the credibility of incidents (e.g. *Il.* 23. 100), and of the characters (e.g. *Il.* 1. 50). *Aristotle's lost Ἀπορήματα Ὁμηρικά ('Homeric puzzles') was a reply to Zoïlus and his followers. (4) *Censure of Homer* (Ψόγος Ὁμήρου), probably a declamation. (5) *Panegyric on the People of Tenedos*. (6) *On Figures*, a technical rhetorical treatise; his definition σχῆμά ἐστιν ἕτερον μὲν προσποιεῖσθαι ἕτερον δὲ λέγειν ('A figure is to pretend one thing and say another') is criticized by *Quintilian (9. 1. 14). He was the first to use σχῆμα, 'figure', in this technical sense. (7) *On Amphipolis*. (8) A history of Greece from the Theogony to the death of *Philip (1) II of Macedon.

FGrH 71; U. Friedländer, *De Zoilo aliisque Homeri obtrectatoribus* (1895). J. F. L.; R. B.

Zonaras, Johannes, Byzantine historian and canonist of the 12th cent. A commander of the body-guard and imperial secretary, he was probably forced to retire into monastic life after the failure of the conspiracy to make Anna Comnena empress in AD 1118. Living in exile on an island far from the capital he devoted himself to writing. He composed an authoritative commentary to Byzantine canon law, commentaries on the poems of *Gregory (2) of Nazianzus and on the terminology of religious poetry. Various other exegetic books and lives of saints go under his name; he is also the author of at least one religious poem. As a historian he wrote a universal history from the creation to AD 1118. Zonaras never claimed to be more than a compiler. For Greek history he mainly used *Herodotus (1), *Xenophon (1), *Plutarch, and *Arrian. For Roman history to the destruction of *Carthage he excerpted Plutarch and the first twenty-one books of *Cassius Dio, for which he is our only important source. He was compelled to omit the history of the late Roman republic because he did not have the relevant books of Dio (he only gives some excerpts from Plutarch's *Pompey* and *Caesar*), but was able to use Dio's books 44–68 and is, together with Xiphilinus, our main source for the reconstruction of Dio's books 61–8. For the period after *Domitian he followed Xiphilinus instead of the original Dio. He added information from other sources (e.g. *Eusebius). Petrus Patricius was his chief source for the period between M. *Aurelius Severus Alexander and *Constantine I. The rest derives from various chronicles, not all of which have been identified. Zonaras is especially important as a source for the period AD 450–550. His excerpts are faithful in content, but stylistically independent. See CASSIUS DIO.

Zonaras is not the author of the lexicon that usually goes under his name, a compilation probably made between 1204 and 1253, and much used by the Byzantines.

His works collected in Migne, *PG* 38, 134–7.
CRITICAL EDITIONS M. Pinder–Th. Büttner-Wobst (1841–97); L. Dindorf (1868–75).
ON SOURCES Th. Büttner-Wobst, *Commentationes Fleckeisenianae* (1890), 123 ff.; V. Ph. Boissevain, *Hermes* 1891, 440 ff.; F. Millar, *A Study of Cassius Dio* (1964), 2 ff., 195 ff.
GENERAL WORKS K. Ziegler and K. Alpers in *RE*, 'Zonaras'; H. G. Beck, *Kirche und theologische Literatur in Byzanz* (1959), 656–7. A. M.

Zonas of *Sardis, author of nine *epigrams in the Greek *Anthology from the *Garland* of Philip. If the Diodorus Zonas of Strabo 627–8, then he lived about 80 BC (see Page in *GLP* 2. 263–4). He writes on humble folk and rural themes, 'among the most attractive of the imitators of *Leonidas, far superior to their model' (*GLP* 413). A. D. E. C.

zoology See ANIMALS, KNOWLEDGE ABOUT.

Zopyrus, writer on *physiognomy, known from his judgement on *Socrates' appearance.

See Förster, *Scriptores Physiognomonici* 1, prol. vii ff.

Zoroaster, Ζωροάστρης, is the Greek form of Iranian Zarathuštra. It is not clear whether Zarathuštra was a reformer or the creator of a new religion, a prophet. In the oldest part of the Avesta, the 17 Gāthās, ascribed to Zoroaster himself, he is called a *manthrān*, 'he who possesses the sacred formulas'. The Gāthās portray a dualistic system in which *aša* (truth, rightness) is opposed to *druj* (lie, deceit) with *Ahuramazda as the supreme deity. It is occasionally doubted whether he was a historical figure. Of the various dates for Zoroaster, that of the 6th cent. BC

1639

Zosimus

is based on a late Zoroastrian tradition, that of c.1000 BC is arrived at by linguistic arguments and therefore preferable. The Greeks had heard of Zoroaster as early as the 5th cent. BC (*Xanthus (2) of Lydia in Diog. Laert. pr. 2). By the time of Plato and Aristotle they had some notion of the contents of his teaching. He is often called a *magus and regarded as a sage (sophos). Legendary details of all sorts accumulated about him. He was (incorrectly) credited with the authorship of numerous works on theology, natural science, astrology, and magic. See RELIGION, PERSIAN.

J. Bidez and F. Cumont, Les Mages hellénisés (1938); H. Humbach, Die Gathas des Zarathustra (1959); J. Kellens, Qui était Zarathustra?² (1993); J. Duchesne-Guillemin, The Western Response to Zoroaster (1958); B. Schlerath (ed.), Zarathustra (Wege der Forschung 169, 1970).

H. S.-W.

Zosimus, Greek historian. Little is known of his life except that he had been advocatus fisci (see FISCUS) and obtained the dignity of comes (see COMITES). His identification with either the sophist Zosimus of Ascalon or the sophist Zosimus of Gaza is very unlikely (see SECOND SOPHISTIC). He wrote a history (Historia nova) of the Roman empire from *Augustus reaching as far as AD 410, where his extant text terminates just before the sack of Rome by *Alaric. He completed his work after 498, if indeed he refers to the abolition of the auri lustralis collatio (2. 38; see COLLATIO LUSTRALIS), and c.518, since the work is quoted in the chronicle of Eustathius of Epiphania, written apparently in the early years of Justin II. Book 1 summarizes the history of the first three centuries of the empire (the section of *Diocletian is lost); in books 2–4 he gives a more precise account of the 4th cent. and in books 5–6 a narrative of the years 395–410 for which he is our most important historical source. His excursus on the secular games (2. 1–6) derives from *Phlegon of Tralles, and for the fourth and early fifth centuries he used extensively and uncritically the histories of *Eunapius and *Olympiodorus (3), enabling the reconstruction of the texts and attitudes of these writers. His view of events is determined, even at the late date at which he wrote, by his paganism. He sees the decadence of the empire as a consequence of the rejection of paganism. He is naturally hostile to *Constantine I and *Theodosius (2) I and favourable to *Julian, reproducing in these attitudes those of Eunapius. As he reached 407 he changed his source from Eunapius to Olympiodorus, and his view of *Stilicho changed correspondingly from one of hostility to one of favour. The same moment is marked by a change in emphasis from eastern to western events, and by the appearance, from then to the end of his surviving text, of Latin transcriptions and quoted phrases.

EDITIONS L. Mendelssohn (1887); with comm., F. Paschoud (Budé, 1971–89). S. Mazzarino, The End of the Ancient World (1966; It. orig. 1959), chs. 4, 6; A. Cameron, Philologus 1969, 110 ff.; J. F. Matthews, JRS 1970, 79 ff.

J. F. Ma.